AMERICAN ART DIRECTORY®

2019

73rd EDITION

NRP Direct, a division of Treasured Works, LLC

New Providence, New Jersey

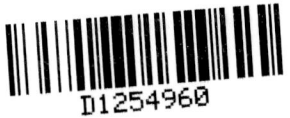

American Art Directory®, 73rd Edition

President	R. Brett Grayson
Publisher	Robert Docherty

Editorial

Managing Editor	Eileen Fanning
Content Manager	Ian Sidney O'Blenis
Content Editor	Linda Hummer

Marketing

Creative Services Manager	Kathleen F. Stein

Sales

Wholesale Account Representative	April Tann

Published by NRP Direct, a division of Treasured Works, LLC.

Printed and bound in the United States of America.
International Standard Book Number: 978-0-87217-074-2
International Standard Serial Number: 0065-6968
Library of Congress Catalog Number: 99-1016

Contents

Preface v

I ART ORGANIZATIONS

Arrangement and Abbreviations viii
National and Regional Organizations in the U.S. 1
Museums, Libraries and Associations in the U.S. 11
National and Regional Organizations in Canada 439
Museums, Libraries and Associations in Canada 441

II ART SCHOOLS

Art Schools in the U.S 477
Art Schools in Canada 623

III ART INFORMATION

Museums Abroad 631
Art Schools Abroad 709
State Arts Councils 719
State Directors and Supervisors of Art Education 724
Art Magazines 728

IV INDEXES

Subject 733
Personnel 857
Organizational 1075

Preface

The American Art Directory®, first published in 1898 as the American Art Annual, continues in its tradition of excellence with the 73rd edition. The directory is a standard in the field of art, and an indispensable reference to art museums, libraries, organizations, schools and corporate art holdings.

CONTENT AND COVERAGE

The information for the directory is collected by means of direct communication whenever possible. Forms are sent to all entrants for corroboration and updating, and information submitted by entrants is included as completely as possible within the boundaries of editorial and space restrictions. Information for new entrants is in response to questionnaires or the result of research. Alphabetizing in the directory is strictly letter-by-letter. Those museums, libraries, associations and organizations which bear an individual's name are alphabetized by the last name of that individual. Colleges and universities are alphabetized by the first word of their name, whether or not it is named for an individual.

CONTENT AND COVERAGE

Section 1 lists The National and Regional Organizations, which are arranged alphabetically and contain over 100 organizations which administer and coordinate the arts within the United States and Canada. Included here are libraries affiliated with these organizations. The Museums, Libraries and Associations listings are arranged geographically, and contain listings for more than 2,700 main museums, 280 main libraries, 110 area associations, and 71 corporations with art holdings within the United States and Canada. There are more than 1,700 additional listings for galleries, museums and libraries affiliated with main entries.

A classification key is printed to the left of each entry to designate the type:

A—Association
C—Corporate Art
L—Library
M—Museum
O—Organization

The key "M" is assigned to organizations whose primary function is gathering and preserving the visual arts. The "O" designation is given to national and regional organizations supporting the arts through sponsorship of art activities. The "A" code is given to those supporting the arts on more local levels.

Section II lists detailed information on more than 1,680 art schools, and college and university departments of art, art history, and architecture in the United States and Canada.

Section III provides reference to more than 1,060 art museums and 140 schools abroad, state arts councils, directors and supervisors of art education, art magazines, newspapers and their art critics.

Section IV is composed of three alphabetical indexes; organizational, personnel, and subject. The subject index includes general art subjects and specific collections, along with the name and location of the holding organization.

Please address any suggestions, comments or questions to The Editors, *American Art Directory*, NRP Direct, 430 Mountain Avenue, Suite 403, New Providence, New Jersey 07974.

I ART ORGANIZATIONS

Arrangement and Abbreviations
Key to Art Organizations

ARRANGEMENT OF DATA

Name and Address of institution; telephone number, including area code.
Names and titles of key personnel.
Hours open; admission fees; date established and purpose; average annual attendance; membership.
Annual figures on income and purchases.
Collections with enlarging collections indicated.
Exhibitions.
Activities sponsored, including classes for adults and children, dramatic programs and docent training; lectures, concerts, gallery talks and tours; competitions, awards, scholarships and fellowships; lending programs; museum or sales shops.
Libraries also list number of book volumes, periodical subscriptions, and audiovisual and micro holdings; subject covered by name of special collections.

ABBREVIATIONS AND SYMBOLS

Acad—Academic
Admin—Administration, Administrative
Adminr—Administrator
Admis—Admission
A-tapes—Audio-tapes
Adv—Advisory
AM—Morning
Ann—Annual
Approx—Approximate, Approximately
Asn—Association
Assoc—Associate
Asst—Assistant
AV—Audiovisual
Ave—Avenue
Bldg—Building
Blvd—Boulevard
Bro—Brother
C—circa
Cert—Certificate
Chap—Chapter
Chmn—Chairman
Circ—Circulation
Cl—Closed
Col— College
Coll—Collection
Comt—Committee
Coordr—Coordinator
Corresp—Corresponding
Cr—Credit
Cur—Curator
D—Day
Den—Denominational
Dept—Department
Develop—Development
Dipl—Diploma
Dir—Director
Dist—District
Div—Division
Dorm—Dormitory
Dr—Doctor, Drive
E—East, Evening
Ed—Editor
Educ—Education
Elec Mail—Electronic Mail
Enrol—Enrollment
Ent—Entrance
Ent Req—Entrance Requirements
Est, Estab—Established
Exec—Executive
Exhib—Exhibition
Exten—Extension
Fel(s)—Fellowships
Fri—Friday
Fs—Filmstrips
Ft—Feet
FT—Full Time Instructor
GC—Graduate Course
Gen—General
Grad—Graduate
Hon—Honorary
Hr—Hour
HS—High School
Hwy—Highway
Inc—Incorporated
Incl—Including
Jr—Junior
Lect—Lecture(s)
Lectr—Lecturer
Librn—Librarian
M—Men
Maj—Major in Art
Mem—Membership
Mgr—Manager
Mon—Monday
Mss—Manuscripts
Mus—Museums
N—North
Nat—National
Nonres—Nonresident
Per subs—Periodical subscriptions
PM—Afternoon
Pres—President
Prin—Principal
Prof—Professor
Prog—Program
PT—Part Time Instructor
Pts—Points
Pub—Public
Publ—Publication
Publr—Publisher
Pvt—Private
Qtr—Quarter
Rd—Road
Rec—Records
Reg—Registration
Req—Requirements
Res—Residence, Resident
S—South
Sat—Saturday
Schol—Scholarship
Secy—Secretary
Sem—Semeseter
Soc—Society
Sq—Square
Sr—Senior, Sister
St—Street
Ste—Suite
Sun—Sunday
Supt—Superintendent
Supv—Supervisor
Thurs—Thursday
Treas—Treasurer
Tues—Tuesday
Tui—Tuition
TV—Television
Undergrad—Undergraduate
Univ—University
Vis—Visiting
Vol—Volunteer
Vols—Volumes
VPres—Vice President
V-tapes—Videotapes
Vols—Volumes
W—West, Women
Wed—Wednesday
Wk—Week
Yr—Year(s)

A Association
C Corporate Art Holding
L Library
M Museum
O Organization

National & Regional Organizations in the U.S.

O **ALLIED ARTISTS OF AMERICA, INC,** 10 Harvale Dr, Florham Park, NJ 07932. Web: alliedartistsofamerica.org; *Pres* Mitzura Salgian; *VPres* Gabrielle Dellosso; *Treas* Christina Debarry; *Corresp Secy & Nominations Chmn* RhodaYanow; *Corresp Secy* Robert Palevitz; *Rec Secy* Annie Patt
Estab 1914, incorporated 1922, as a self-supporting exhibition cooperative, with juries elected each yr by the mem, to promote work by American artists; Mem: 3601; dues $40 & up; 3 annual meetings - Apr, Sept & Dec
Income: Financed by members' fees
Exhibitions: Members' Regional AAA exhibitions; annual exhibition in the winter; Annual held at National Arts Club; numerous awards & medals
Activities: Lects open to pub, 1-3 vis lectrs per yr; gallery talks; competitions with awards

O **AMERICAN ABSTRACT ARTISTS,** 194 Powers St, Brooklyn, NY 11211-4922. Email amabartcom@gmail.com; Web: www.americanabstractartists.org; *Pres* Daniel G Hill; *VPres* Emily Berger; *Secy* Jim Osman; *Asst Secy* Don Voisine; *Treas* James Juszczyk; *Asst Treas* Gail Gregg
Estab 1936, active 1937, to promote American abstract art; develop & educate through exhibitions & publications; to provide forums for the exchange of ideas among artists; Mem: 94; dues $75; 5 meetings per yr
Income: Financed by mem
Publications: Portfolio of prints, journal
Activities: Lects open to pub; 1 vis lectr per yr; individual and original objects of art lent to responsible galleries, museums and universities; organize traveling exhibs to univ galleries, non-profit spaces; originate traveling exhibs

O **AMERICAN ACADEMY OF ARTS & LETTERS,** 633 W 155th St, New York, NY 10032-7501. Tel 212-368-5900; Fax 212-491-4615; Email academy@artsandletters.org; Web: www.artsandletters.org; *Pres* Yehudi Wyner; *VPres Art* Henry N Cobb; *VPres Literature* Kwame Anthony Appiah; *VPres Music* Tobias Picker; *Secy* Calvin Trillin; *Treas* Charles Wuorinen; *Exec Dir* Cody Upton
Open Mon - Fri 9:30 AM - 5 PM (office); galleries open during exhibs only: Thurs - Sun 1 - 4 PM; No admis fee; Estab 1898 as an honorary mem organization of artists, writers & composers whose function it is to foster, assist & sustain an interest in literature, music & the fine arts; Maintains reference library of books & papers of members; Average Annual Attendance: 6,000; Mem: 250; mem is by election; no dues; annual meeting in May
Income: $1,400,000 (financed by endowment)
Purchases: $80,000-$90,000 Hassam Speicher Purchase Program
Collections: Works by members
Exhibitions: Exhibition of Candidates for Art Awards; Exhibition of Paintings Eligible for Hassam Fund Purchase; Newly Elected Members & Recipients of Honors & Awards Exhibitions, art, scores & manuscripts; Richard Rodgers Awards in Musical Theater (competition); Special Exhibitions
Publications: Proceedings, annual; exhibition catalogs
Activities: Awards given (nominations come from members)

O **AMERICAN ALLIANCE OF MUSEUMS,** (American Association of Museums), 2451 Crystal Dr, Ste 1005 Arlington, VA 22202-4804. Tel 202-289-1818; Fax 202-289-6578; Email membership@aam-us.org; Web: www.aam-us.org; *Pres & CEO* Laura L. Lott; *Exec VPres & CPO* Robert J Stein; *VPres Strategic Foresight* Elizabeth Merritt; *VPres Devel* Arthur Affleck; *VPres Govt Rels & Communs* Gail Ravnitzky Silberglied; *VPres Memberships & Programs* Janet Vaughan
Estab 1906 to provide advocacy, professional education, networking opportunities news & information and standards & best practices for museum professionals & museums; Mem: 30,000; dues $50 & up

O **AMERICAN ANTIQUARIAN SOCIETY,** 185 Salisbury St, Worcester, MA 01609-1634. Tel 508-755-5221; Fax 508-753-3311; Email library@mwa.org; Web: www.americanantiquarian.org; *Pres* Ellen S Dunlap; *Finance Dir* Susan Forgit; *Marcus A McCorison Librn & Cur Manuscripts* Thomas G Knoles; *VPres Prog & Outreach* James David Moran; *Exec VPres External Affairs* Matthew Shakespeare; *Head Bldgs & Grounds* Andrew Cariglia; *Dir Information Technology* Nick Conti; *Head Cataloging Svcs* Alan N Degutis; *Chief Conservator* Babette Gehnrich; *Cur Newspapers & Periodicals* Vincent L Golden; *Andrew W Mellon Cur Graphic Arts* Lauren B Hewes; *Colls Mgr* Marie E Lamoureux; *Head Acquisitions* Peg Lesinski; *Sr Cataloger Rare Books* Doris N O'Keefe; *Cur Books* Elizabeth Watts Pope; *Head Readers' Serv* Kimberly Toney; *Cur Children's Literature* Laura E Wasowicz
Open Mon - Tues & Thurs - Fri 9 AM - 5 PM, Wed 10 AM - 8 PM, cl legal holidays; No admis fee; Estab 1812 to collect, preserve & encourage serious study of the materials of American history & life through 1876; Maintains reference library; Mem: 775 honorary; meetings third Fri in Apr & Oct
Income: Financed by endowment, gifts & grants
Purchases: $273,900
Library Holdings: Auction Catalogs, Book Volumes, CD-ROMs, Exhibition Catalogs, Manuscripts, Maps, Original Art Works, Original Documents, Pamphlets, Periodical Subscriptions, Photographs, Prints, Reproductions, Sculpture
Special Subjects: Bookplates & Bindings, Cartoons, Etchings & Engravings, Graphics, Maps, Painting-American, Prints, Woodcuts
Collections: Early American Portraits, Staffordshire Pottery, bookplates, prints, lithographs, cartoons, engravings, Colonial furniture, photographs
Publications: Monographs; newsletters; Commonplace; Online Journal
Activities: Undergraduate seminar in American Studies; docent training; lects open to public 4-6 per yr; scholarships & fels offered; sales shop sells books & postcards

O **AMERICAN ARTISTS PROFESSIONAL LEAGUE, INC,** 47 Fifth Ave, New York, NY 10003. Tel 212-645-1345; Fax 212-792-2275; Email office@aaplinc.org; Web: www.americanartistsprofessionalleague.org; *Pres* Peter Rossi; *VPres* Lou Spina; *Rec Secy* Susie Gach Peelle; *Counsel* Michael J Hughes Esq; *Dir* Don L Huber
Estab 1928 to advance the cause of fine arts in America, through the promotion of high standards of beauty, integrity & craftsmanship in painting, sculpture & the graphic arts; to emphasize the importance of order & coherent commun as prime requisites of works of art through exhibitions & publications; Mem: 1000; election by jury of professional artists National Board of Dir; dues $75; annual meeting in Nov;
Income: Financed by mem
Exhibitions: Annual Grand National Exhibition
Publications: AAPL News Bulletin, semi-annually
Activities: Competitions with awards; scholarships & fels offered

O **AMERICAN ASSOCIATION OF UNIVERSITY WOMEN,** 1310 L St NW, Ste 1000 Washington, DC 20005. Tel 202-785-7700; Fax 202-872-1425; Email connect@aauw.org; Web: www.aauw.org; *Bd Chair* Julia Brown; *Bd Vice Chair* Peggy Ryan Williams; *Bd Finance Vice Chair* Janet Bunger; *Bd Secy* Cherly Sorokin; *CEO* Kimberly Churches
Open to AAUW members only Mon - Fri 8 AM - 4 PM; No admis fee; Estab 1881 to unite alumnae of different institutions for practical educational work; to further the advancement of women, lifelong learning, & responsibility to soc expressed through action, advocacy, research & enlightened leadership; Mem: 150,000; dues $49 - $980; holds biennial conventions
Library Holdings: Audio Tapes, Clipping Files, Fiche, Memorabilia, Original Art Works, Original Documents, Periodical Subscriptions, Photographs, Prints, Reels, Sculpture, Slides, Video Tapes
Special Subjects: Painting-American, Historical Material
Publications: Action Alert, biweekly; AAUW Outlook, quarterly; Leader in Action, quarterly; brochures; booklets; research studies; study guides
Activities: Assn local branches develop & maintain progs in the arts. AAUW Foundation funds first professional degree in architecture, doctoral/post doctoral candidates in the arts

O **AMERICAN COLOR PRINT SOCIETY,** 205 Woodside Ave, Narberth, PA 19072. Email membership@americancolorprintsociety.org; Web: www.americancolorprintsociety.org; *Pres* Carole J Meyers; *VPres & Treas* Elizabeth H MacDonald; *Pub Chmn* Sy Hakim; *Bd Mem* Alan J Klawans; *Bd Mem* Libby Calamia; *Bd Mem* Art Brener; *Bd Mem* Thelma Grobes; *Bd Mem* Marlene Adler; *Bd Mem* Reena Brooks; *Ed Color Proof* Patricia Shaw Lima
Estab 1939 to exhibit color prints; exhibits the work of original prints; Mem: 75; dues $40; professional printmaker's work is juried by board mems
Income: Financed by mem; non-profit 501C
Collections: The Philadelphia Museum of Art, Philadelphia, PA, Central Philadelphia Free Library print coll, Villanova Univ, Villanova, PA
Publications: The Color Proof-Semi Annual
Activities: Lect & symposium; sponsors annual national members exhibition of all media color prints; 7 annual prizes, Stella Draken Memorial Awards; Hutton Prize; Michael Lasuchin Memorial Award; Grever Award; Stanley Cluck Memorial Award; scholarships offered; originates traveling exhibs for mems

O **AMERICAN CRAFT COUNCIL,** 1224 Marshall St NE, #200 Minneapolis, MN 55413-1036. Tel 612-206-3100; Fax 612-355-2330; Email council@craftcouncil.org; Web: www.craftcouncil.org; *Bd Chair* Stuart Kestenbaum; *Vice Chair* Chuck Duddingston; *Treas* Kevin Buchi; *Secy* Libba Evans; *Interim Dir Develop* Paul Johnson; *Dir Finance & Admin* Greg Allen; *Show Dir* Melanie Little; *Dir Mktg & Communs* Pamela Diamond; *Editor in Chief American Craft Mag* Monica Moses; *Dir Educ* Michael Radyk
Open Mon - Thus 10 AM - 5 PM, Fri 9 AM - 4 PM; Estab 1943 to promote understanding and appreciation of American craft; Mem: 32,000; dues $40
Income: Financed by mem, private donations & government grants
Exhibitions: Ten shows & markets per yr
Publications: American Craft Magazine (formerly Craft Horizons), bimonthly
Activities: Competition with awards

L **Library,** 1224 Marshall St NE #200, Minneapolis, MN 55413-1036. Tel 612-206-3118; Fax 612-355-2330; Email library@craftcouncil.org; Web: www.craftcouncil.org; *Librn* Jessica Shaykett; *Libr Asst* Dulcey Heller

Open Mon - Fri 10 AM - 5 PM; Estab 1950s to serve as the repository for information on contemporary American craft; For reference only
Library Holdings: Auction Catalogs, Audio Tapes, Book Volumes 6000, Cassettes, Clipping Files, DVDs, Exhibition Catalogs 8000, Filmstrips, Motion Pictures, Original Documents, Other Holdings Journals 110, Pamphlets, Periodical Subscriptions 200, Photographs, Slides 40,000, Video Tapes 100
Special Subjects: Ceramics, Crafts, Decorative Arts, Embroidery, Enamels, Folk Art, Furniture, Glass, Goldsmithing, Handicrafts, Jewelry, Leather, Metalwork, Mixed Media, Porcelain, Pottery, Sculpture, Silversmithing, Stained Glass, Tapestries, Textiles, Woodcarvings
Collections: ACC Fellows, American Craft Museum Slide Kits, Archives of the American Council & American Craft Museum (until 1990), Award Winners & Artists featured in American Craft Magazine, newsletters & catalogs of craft organizations & educational programs, 20th & 21st-century Fine Craft, with emphasis on post WW II Period (1945)
Activities: Lectrs open to pub

O **THE AMERICAN FEDERATION OF ARTS,** 305 E 47th St, Fl 10 New York, NY 10017-2312. Tel 212-988-7700; Fax 212-861-2487; Email info@amfedarts.org; Web: www.afaweb.org; *Dir* Pauline Willis; *Sr Accnt* Victoria Proios; *Assoc Dir Finance & Opers* Caroline Chin; *HR Resources & Office Mgr* Misti Wills; *Mgr Special Events* Kristin Sarli; *Cur* Suzanne Ramljak; *Cur* Margery King; *Head Registrar* Elizabeth Abbarno; *Assoc Dir Develop* Brian Keliher; *Mgr Publs* Audrey Walen
Estab 1909 by an act of Congress, initiates & organizes a national and international prog of art exhibs, publ & educational activities to benefit the mus community and enrich the public's experience and understanding of art and culture; Mem: 200 museum mem dues $250 - $675, 150 individual mem dues $100 - $3,000
Income: Financed by government agencies, corporations, foundations & mem
Publications: Exhibition catalogues
Activities: Educ components are developed to accompany exhibitions; lects open to pub; 2-3 vis lectrs per yr; gallery talks; tours; originates and tours exhibs of fine arts; originates Cur Forum and Dir Forum (annual events) to national & international mus

O **AMERICAN INSTITUTE FOR CONSERVATION OF HISTORIC & ARTISTIC WORKS,** 727 15th St NW, Ste 500 Washington, DC 20005. Tel 202-452-9545; Fax 202-452-9328; Email info@conservation-us.org; Web: www.conservation-us.org; *Exec Dir* Eryl Wentworth; *Finance Mgr* Linda Budhinata; *Membership & Mktg Assoc* Katelin Lee; *Commun & Membership Dir* Bonnie Naugle; *Institutional Advancement Dir* Eric Pourchot; *Meetings Dir* Ruth Seyler
Open Mon - Fri 9 AM - 5 PM, cl national holidays; Estab 1972 as a national organization supporting conservation professionals in preserving cultural heritage by establishing and upholding professional standards, promoting research & publications, providing educational opportunities and fostering exchange of knowledge among conservators, allied professionals and the public; Mem: 3500; dues $71-$149; ann meeting
Income: Financed by private grants, member dues
Publications: Update newsletter

O **AMERICAN INSTITUTE OF ARCHITECTS,** The Octagon Museum, 1735 New York Ave NW, Washington, DC 20006-5292. Tel 202-626-7300; Fax 202-626-7547; Email infocentral@aia.org; Web: www.aia.org; *Pres* Carl Elefante; *Secy* Bruce W Sekanick; *Exec VP & CEO* Robert A Ivy
Open Mon - Fri 8:30 AM - 5 PM; Estab 1857 to organize & unite the architects of the United States & to promote the aesthetic, scientific & practical efficiency of the profession
Income: Financed by members
Library Holdings: Book Volumes 40,000, CD-ROMs 50, Motion Pictures, Periodical Subscriptions 200, Slides 100,000, Video Tapes 200
Publications: AIArchitect (online newsletter) monthly
Activities: Continuing educ prog; awards given, Gold Medal, Kemper Award, Architectural Firm Award, R S Reynolds Memorial Award & Reynolds Aluminum Prize Citation of Honor, AIA Honor Awards, Institute Honors; sales shop sells books

O **AMERICAN INSTITUTE OF GRAPHIC ARTS,** National Design Center, 233 Broadway, Fl 17 New York, NY 10010-1802. Tel 212-807-1990; Email general@aiga.org; Web: www.aiga.org; *Pres* Dana Arnett; *Treas* Andrew Twigg; *Exec Dir* Julie Anixter; *COO & CFO* Hezron Gurley; *Chief of Staff* Amy Chapman; *Controller* Kathleen Cox
Open Mon, Thurs & Fri 11 AM - 5 PM by appointment; No admis fee; Estab 1914 as a national nonprofit educational organization devoted to raising standards in all branches of the graphic arts; Art gallery showcases AIGA design competition, exhib, and exhib organized by visiting designers and cur; maintains library & slide archives; Mem: 17,000; dues contributing mem $50, supporting mem $160, sustaining mem $250, leader mem $500; trustee mem $2,500
Income: Financed by mem
Exhibitions: Rotating exhibits
Publications: hardbound annual, AIGA Graphic Design USA; quarterly, AIGA Journal of Graphic Design
Activities: Awards AIGA Medal for distinguished contributions to the graphic arts; originate traveling exhibs

O **AMERICAN NUMISMATIC ASSOCIATION,** Edward C. Rochette Money Museum, 818 N Cascade Ave, Colorado Springs, CO 80903-3279. Tel 719-482-9828; Fax 719-634-4085; Email ana@money.org; Web: www.money.org; *Pres* Gary Adkins; *VPres* Donald Kagin; *Treas* Larry Baber; *Exec Dir* Kim Kiick; *Secy* Sandy Pearl; *Museum Dir & Cur* Douglas Mudd
Open Tues - Fri 9 AM - 5 PM, Sat 10 AM - 5 PM, Sun Noon - 5 PM, cl Mon; No admis fee; Estab 1891 as an international organization to promote numismatics as a means of recording history; Maintains a mus & library; galleries display numismatic material from paper money through coins & art medals; Average Annual Attendance: 30,000; Mem: 34,000; to qualify for mem, one should be interested in coin collecting; dues $36; annual meeting held at National Conventions in Mar & Aug
Income: Financed by mem, endowment, donations & miscellaneous sources
Library Holdings: Auction Catalogs, Audio Tapes, Book Volumes, CD-ROMs, Cards, Cassettes, Compact Disks, Exhibition Catalogs, Fiche, Filmstrips, Kodachrome Transparencies, Manuscripts, Memorabilia, Original Documents, Pamphlets, Periodical Subscriptions, Photographs, Slides, Video Tapes
Special Subjects: Antiquities-Egyptian, Antiquities-Oriental, Coins & Medals, Gold, Historical Material
Collections: Aubrey & Adeline Bebee Collection of US Paper Money, Robert T Herdegen Memorial Collection of Coins of the World, Norman H Liebman Collection of Abraham Lincoln on Paper Money, Elliott Markoff Collection of Presidential Memorabilia, general and specialized collections from all other fields of numismatics
Exhibitions: Changing galleries exhibiting coins of the American Colonial period, the United States 1792 to date and Modern Medallic Art from contemporary medals; Global Ideas in Medallic Sculpture; An Exploration of Cromwell's England
Publications: Numismatist, monthly
Activities: Classes for adults & children; annual seminar on campus of Colorado College, Colorado Springs; lects open to pub, 50+ vis lectrs per yr; tours; sponsorship of National Coin Week third week in Apr (when members throughout the United States promote their avocations through exhibs in local areas); presentation of awards; scholarships offered; mus shop sells books, magazines, slides, medals & souvenir jewelry

L **Library,** 818 N Cascade Ave, Colorado Springs, CO 80903. Tel 719-632-2646; Fax 719-632-5208; Email library@money.org; Web: www.money.org/resourcecenter.html; *Interim Librn* Nancy W Green; *Asst Librn* Jane Colvard
Open Tues - Fri 9 AM - 5 PM, Sat 10 AM - 5 PM; No admis fee; Estab 1891 to provide research materials to the members of the Assn & the general pub; Circ 4500; Open to the pub for reference; lending restricted to members; Mem: 30,000; dues $33 first year, $26 to renew mem; meetings twice a year
Income: Financed by assn & mem, endowments, donations
Library Holdings: Auction Catalogs, Audio Tapes, Book Volumes 35,000, CD-ROMs, Cards, Cassettes, Compact Disks, Exhibition Catalogs, Fiche, Filmstrips, Kodachrome Transparencies, Manuscripts, Memorabilia, Original Documents, Other Holdings Auction catalogs 20,000; Microfilm, Pamphlets, Periodical Subscriptions 110, Photographs, Slides, Video Tapes
Special Subjects: Coins & Medals
Collections: books, auction catalogs & periodicals, all on numismatics, Arthur Braddan Coole Library on Oriental Numismatics
Exhibitions: Annual Summer Conference
Activities: Classes for adults & children

O **AMERICAN NUMISMATIC SOCIETY,** 75 Varick St, 11th Fl New York, NY 10013-1917. Tel 212-571-4470; Fax 212-571-4479; Email membership@numismatics.org; Web: numismatics.org; *Pres* Sydney F Martin; *Treas & Asst Secy* Kenneth L Edlow; *Exec Dir & Secy* Ute Wartenberg Kagan; *Mus Admin* Joanne Isaac; *Assoc Cur* Gilles Bransbourg; *Assoc Cur* David Hendin; *Cur* Peter van Alfen
Open (collection) Mon - Fri 9:30 AM - 4:30 PM; (office) Mon - Fri 9 AM - 5 PM; $10 - 20 admin fee; Estab 1858 as an international organization for the advancement of numismatic knowledge; Maintains mus & library; one exhibition hall, devoted to the World of Coins; Average Annual Attendance: 18,000; Mem: 2279; dues assoc $60 - $10,000; annual meeting second Sat in Oct
Income: Financed by endowment
Collections: Universal numismatics
Publications: American Journal of Numismatics, annual; Numismatic Literature, semi-annual
Activities: Lect open to public, 2 vis lectrs per year; scholarships offered

L **Library,** 75 Varick St, 11th Fl New York, NY 10013-1917. Tel 212-571-4470, ext 170; Fax 212-571-4479; Email library@numismatics.org; Web: www.numismatics.org/Library/Library; *Librn* Elizabeth Hahn
Open Mon - Fri 9:30 AM - 4:30 PM; No admis fee; Estab 1858; For reference only
Library Holdings: Auction Catalogs, Book Volumes 100,000, Exhibition Catalogs, Filmstrips, Manuscripts, Other Holdings Auction catalogs, Pamphlets, Periodical Subscriptions 246, Reels 200, Slides
Special Subjects: Coins & Medals
Collections: Auction catalogs
Activities: Grad student summer seminar; mus shop sells books, magazines

O **AMERICAN SOCIETY FOR AESTHETICS,** 1550 Larimer St, #644 Denver, CO 80202. Tel 562-331-4424; Email secretary-treasurer@aesthetics-online.org; Web: aesthetics-online.org; *Pres* Kathleen Higgins; *VPres* Susan L Feagin; *Secy & Treas* Julie Van Camp
Estab 1942 for the advancement of philosophical & scientific study of the arts & related fields; Mem: 800; dues $80
Income: Financed by mem, dues, subscriptions
Publications: Journal of Aesthetics & Art Criticism, quarterly; ASA Newsletter, 3 times per year; ASAGE (grad e-journal)
Activities: Ann conferences; Selma Jeanne Cohen Price in Dance Aesthetics; divisional meetings; monograph prize; Ted Cohen Prize

O **AMERICAN SOCIETY OF ARTISTS, INC,** PO Box 1326, Palatine, IL 60078-1326. Tel 312-751-2500, 847-991-4748; Email asoaartists@aol.com; Web: www.americansocietyofartists.org; *VPres* Helen DelValle; *Dir Promotional Svcs* Arnold Jackson; *American Artisans Dir* Judy A Edborg; *Dir Lect & Demonstration Serv* Charles J Gruner; *Spec Arts Services Dir* Patricia E Nolan; *Midwest Representative* Alajos Acs; *Chicago Representative* Donald Metcoff; *Southern Illinois Representative* Ann Childers; *Pres* Nancy J Fregin
Estab 1972, mem organization of professional artists; Mem: Over 10,000; qualifications for mem, must have work juried & pass jury to be accepted; dues $55, plus one initiation fee of $20; patron-ship, associateship & international mem also available
Income: Financed by mem
Library Holdings: Audio Tapes, Book Volumes, Clipping Files, Lantern Slides, Periodical Subscriptions, Photographs, Slides
Collections: Photographs & slides of members works
Exhibitions: Approx 25 indoor & outdoor juried shows per yr

Publications: Art Lovers' Art and Craft Fair Bulletin, quarterly; ASA Artisan, quarterly
Activities: Lect & demonstration service; assists members with various problems

L **Library Organization**, PO Box 1326, Palatine, IL 60078. Tel 312-751-2500, 847-991-4748; Email asoa@netzero.com; Asoaartists@aol.com; Web: americansocietyofartists.org; *Librn* Donald Metcoff
Open for mem use only; Estab 1978 to provide reference material for member artists only
Income: Financed by dues & fees
Library Holdings: Audio Tapes, Book Volumes, Clipping Files, Lantern Slides, Periodical Subscriptions 8, Photographs, Slides
Special Subjects: Art Education
Publications: Publication for Members
Activities: Lect & demonstration service

O **AMERICAN SOCIETY OF BOOKPLATE COLLECTORS & DESIGNERS,** PO Box 14964, Tucson, AZ 85732-4964. Tel 626-570-9404; Email info@bookplate.org; Web: www.bookplate.org; *Dir* James P Keenan
Estab 1922 as an international organization to foster an interest in the art of the bookplate through the publication of a yearbook & to encourage friendship & a greater knowledge of bookplates among members by an exchange membership list; Mem: 200 who are interested in bookplates as either a collector or artist, or just have an interest in bookplates & graphic arts; dues $85 which includes yearbook & quarterly newsletter
Income: Financed by members
Exhibitions: Bookplates, Prints in Miniature
Publications: Bookplates in the News, quarterly newsletter; YearBook, annually
Activities: Lects given upon request; contributes bookplates to the Prints & Photographs Division of the Library of Congress & furnishes them with copies of quarterly & Year Book; originate traveling exhibs

O **AMERICAN SOCIETY OF CONTEMPORARY ARTISTS (ASCA),** 3600 Curry St, c/o Barbara Schiller Yorktown Heights, NY 10598-2206. Tel 914-245-3776; Email bobbybschiller@gmail.com; Web: ascartists.org; *Pres* Barbara Schiller; *Chmn New Mem* Raymond Weinstein; *Pres Emerita* Harriet FeBland; *VPres* Raymond Shanfeld
Estab 1917 as the Brooklyn Society of Artists. Adopted its current name in 1963; Mem: 100 elected on basis of high level of professional distinction; professional artists juried by mems in Mar & Oct; dues $65; annual meeting Jan
Income: Financed by members
Library Holdings: Book Volumes
Exhibitions: Notto Gallery, Chelsea (in Dec); 2 or 3 other exhibs per yr at various institutions, galleries, museums, etc
Publications: Quarterly Newsletter
Activities: Educ dept; demonstrations in graphics, painting & sculpture; lects open to pub; lects given by mems & visiting artists; lects at cols; 10 two hundred dollar annual cash awards with certs for col students; jurors' awards; various awards given by mems honoring others & Friends of ASCA; originates occasional traveling exhibs to college & other galleries

O **AMERICAN WATERCOLOR SOCIETY, INC,** 47 Fifth Ave, New York, NY 10003. Tel 212-206-8986; Fax 212-206-1960; Email info@americanwatercolorsociety.org; Web: www.americanwatercolorsociety.org; *Pres* Antonio Masi; *VPres* Carole McDermott; *VPres* Joel Popadics; *Treas* Michele L Izzo; *Corresp Secy* Nessa Grainger
Open Tues - Sat 10 AM - 5 PM, Sun 11 AM - 5 PM, cl Mon; Admis special exhibs (includes permanent coll): adults $15, seniors (60+) & students with ID $12, youth (13-18) $10, child (12 & under) no charge; permanent coll: adults $10, seniors (60 +) & students with ID $8, youth (13-18) $6, child (12 & under) no charge; Estab 1866 as a national organization to foster the advancement of the art of watercolor painting & to further the interests of painters in watercolor throughout the United States; occupies the galleries of the Salmagundi Club, 47 Fifth Ave, New York City for four weeks each yr for annual international exhibition usually in Apr; Average Annual Attendance: 4,000-5,000; Mem: 500 signature; to qualify for mem, an artist must exhibit in two annuals then submit application to mem chmn; dues $50; annual meeting in Apr
Income: Financed by mem & donations
Library Holdings: Exhibition Catalogs
Exhibitions: One annual international exhib each Spring; Travel Show
Publications: AWS Newsletter, semi-annually; full color annual exhibition catalog; CD of complete exhibitions
Activities: Lects open to pub; demonstrations & presentations by Signature Members during annual exhibitions; evening demonstrations; awards given at annual exhibs, 26 per yr; schols offered; originates traveling exhibs, 8 per year, recipients vary

O **AMERICANS FOR THE ARTS,** 1000 Vermont Ave NW, 6th Fl, Washington, DC 20005. Tel 202-371-2830; Fax 202-371-0424; Email info@artsusa.org; Web: www.americansforthearts.org; *Pres & CEO* Robert L Lynch
Open Mon - Fri 9 AM - 5:30 PM; Estab 1960 to support the arts & culture through pub & private resource develop, leadership develop, pub policy develop, information services, pub awareness & educ; Mem: 5,000; annual meeting June; membership not limited; mktg & fundraising conference in Nov
Income: Financed by mem, foundations, corporations & government
Publications: Periodic journals; quarterly newsletter
Activities: Annual convention; regional workshops; technical assistance; annual conventions; lects open to pub; mus shop online

O **AMERICANS FOR THE ARTS,** 1 E 53rd St, Fl 2 New York, NY 10022-4242. Tel 212-223-2787; Fax 212-980-4857; Email rlynch@aartusa.org; Web: www.americansforthearts.org; *Pres & CEO* Robert L Lynch; *COO* Mara Walker; *VPres Develop* Kate Gibney; *VPres Finance* R Brent Stanley; *VPres Mktg & Communs* Graham Dunstan
Open by appointment; No admis fee; Estab 1960; Mem: 2500; dues organizations $75-$1,250, individual $30-$250
Income: Financed by mem
Publications: ACA Update, monthly newsletter of legislative & advocacy information available to members; books on arts policy, management, education & information for artists

L **Library**, One E 53rd St, New York, NY 10022-4210. Tel 212-223-2787, Ext 224; Fax 212-223-4857; Email bdavidson@artsusa.org; Web: www.artsusa.org; *Dir* Ben Davidson
Open for research on an appointment only basis for a fee; information/referral service by phone, FAX & mail; No admis fee; Estab 1994; For reference only
Library Holdings: Book Volumes 7000, Other Holdings Vertical files, Periodical Subscriptions 300
Special Subjects: Art Education

O **APERTURE FOUNDATION,** 547 W 27th St, 4th Fl, New York, NY 10001-5511. Tel 212-505-5555; Fax 212-598-4015; Email customerservice@aperture.org; Web: www.aperture.org; *Exec Dir* Chris Boot; *Book Publisher* Lesley A Martin; *Chmn* Cathy M Kaplan; *Dir Exhibitions* Annette Booth; *Magazine Ed* Michael Famighetti; *Treas* Michael Hoeh; *Secy* Anne Stark Locher
Open Mon - Sat 10 AM - 5:30 PM; No admis fee; Estab 1952 dedicated to advancing fine photography; Foundation for fine art photography; 3,000 sq ft gallery space presenting exhibitions dedicated to contemporary & classic photography; Mem: 20, dues $50 - $450
Income: Financed by mem, book & magazine publisher
Collections: Paul Strand Archive
Exhibitions: Lisette Model and Her Successors
Publications: Books on fine photography; 22 books per year
Activities: Lects open to the pub, 3 vis lectrs per year; Aperture Prize; Annual Aperture West Book Prize, annual book prize to an artist living west of the Mississippi; originate 13 traveling exhibitions per year; mus shop sells books, magazines & prints

O **ARCHAEOLOGICAL INSTITUTE OF AMERICA,** 44 Beacon St, Boston, MA 02108. Tel 857-305-9350; Fax 857-233-4270; Email website@archaeological.org; Web: www.archaeological.org; *Exec Dir* Ann Benbow; *Dir Devel* Bruce Keeler; *Dir Programs* Ben Thomas
Open 9:30 AM - 5 PM; Estab 1879 as an international organization concerned with two major areas of responsibility: facilitating archaeological research & disseminating the results to the pub; Mem: 11,000 consisting of professionals & laypersons interested in archaeology; $70-175 for annual meeting in Dec
Income: Financed by endowment, mem & earned income from publications
Publications: Archaeology Magazine, bimonthly; Archaeological Fieldwork Opportunities Bulletin, annual; American Journal of Archaeology, quarterly; Colloquia Conference Paper Series
Activities: Classes for children; lect open to pub, 250 vis lectrs per yr; lect for members only; tours & awards given; one or more fellowships awarded for an acad yr

O **ART DEALERS ASSOCIATION OF AMERICA, INC,** 205 Lexington Ave, Ste 901 New York, NY 10016-6022. Tel 212-488-5550; Fax 646-688-6809; Email lmitchem@artdealers.org; Web: www.artdealers.org; *Pres* Adam Sheffer; *VPres* Anthony Meier; *VPres* Frances Beatty; *Admin VPres & Counsel* Gilbert S Edelson; *Treas* Susan Dunne; *Exec Dir* Linda Blumberg; *Dir Admin* Grace Boyd-Pollack; *Appraisal Dept Coord* Nicole Castaldo
Estab 1962 as a national organization to improve the stature & status of the art-dealing profession; Mem: 175; mem by invitation
Income: Financed by mem & services
Exhibitions: The Art Show, annual fair ADAA members
Publications: Activities & Membership Roster; ADAA Collector's Guide
Activities: Lects open to pub, 4 vis lectrs per yr - Collector's Forum Series; appraisal service for donors contributing works of art to nonprofit institutions; estate tax appraisals; collectors forums

O **ART SERVICES INTERNATIONAL,** 119 Duke St, Alexandria, VA 22314-3803. Tel 703-548-4554; Fax 703-548-3305; Email info@asiexhibitions.org; Web: www.asiexhibitions.org; *Dir & CEO* Lynn K Rogerson; *Deputy Dir Exhibs* Doug Shawn; *Registrar* Heather S Greenleaf; *Mgr Finance & Admin* Marek Wrega; *Gen Counsel* Michael F McAllister Esq; *Exec Asst* Kathy Turner
Nonprofit, educational institution which organizes & circulates fine arts exhibitions to museums & galleries in the US & abroad
Publications: Catalogs

O **ARTISTS' FELLOWSHIP, INC,** 47 Fifth Ave, New York, NY 10003. Tel 212-255-7740 ext 216; Email info@artistsfellowship.org; Web: artistsfellowship.org; *Pres* Charles Yoder; *VPres* Sharon Sprung; *Treas* Pamela Singleton; *Corresp Secy* Joyce Zeller; *Historian* Jonathan Harding
Estab 1859, reorganized 1889 as Artists' Aid Society, then incorporated 1925 as Artists' Fellowship; to aid professional fine artists & their families in emergency situations including illness, disability & bereavement; Mem: 400; dues $40 - $275, annual meeting in Dec
Income: From mems
Publications: Quarterly newsletter
Activities: Awards the Gari Melchers Gold Medal for distinguished service to the arts, and Benjamin West Clinedinst Memorial Medal for outstanding achievement in the arts

O **ARTS EXTENSION SERVICE,** 221 Hampshire House, 131 County Cir, UMass Amherst Amherst, MA 01003. Tel 413-545-2360; Fax 413-545-2361; Email aes@acad.umass.edu; Web: www.artsextensionservice.org; *Dir* Dee Boyle-Clapp; *Prog Coordr* Todd Trebour; *Admin Asst* Priya Nadkarni
Open Mon - Fri 9 AM - 5 PM; No admis fee; Estab 1973 as a National Arts Service Organization facilitating the educ of artists, arts managers & community leaders. AES works for better access to the arts & integration of the arts in communities. AES is a program of the University of Massachusetts Amherst
Collections: National Arts Policy Archive & Library
Publications: Arts Management Bibliography & Publishers; Community Cultural Planning Work Kit; Education Collaborations; Fundamentals of Arts Management; Intersections, Community Arts & Education Collaborations; Partners in Creative Economy: Planning Workbook

Activities: Classes for adults; professional level arts management & arts entrepreneurship workshops; consulting; AES serves civic sectors, community arts organizations, artists, state & local arts agency staff

O **ASSOCIATION OF AFRICAN AMERICAN MUSEUMS,** PO Box 23698, Washington, DC 20026. Tel 202-633-2869; Email blackmuseums@gmail.com; Web: www.blackmuseums.org; *Pres* Brian J Carter; *VPres* Auntaneshia Staveloz; *Treas* Tsitsi Jones; *Secy* LaNesha DeBardelaben
Open Mon - Fri 9 AM - 5 PM; Estab 1978 to represent black museums around the country. Offers consulting & networking services. Sponsors annual conferences; Mem: 496; dues trustee/bd mem & scholar $75, individual $55, student $25
Publications: Profile of Black Museums - A Survey; biannual directory; quarterly newsletter for mem only

O **ASSOCIATION OF ART MUSEUM DIRECTORS,** 120 E 56th St, Ste 520 New York, NY 10022. Tel 212-754-8084; Fax 212-754-8087; Email aamd@amn.org; Web: www.aamd.org; *Pres* Lori Fogarty; *VPres & Secy* Madeleine Grynsztejn; *Treas* Jeff Fleming
Estab 1916; focuses on instilling engagement, leadership, and collaboration in museum directors and their field; Mem: 242; chief staff officers of major art museums
Income: Financed by mem dues
Publications: Annual Salary Survey; Model Museum Directors Employment Contract; Professional Practices in Art Museums

O **ASSOCIATION OF COLLEGIATE SCHOOLS OF ARCHITECTURE,** 1735 New York Ave NW, Washington, DC 20006-5209. Tel 202-785-2324; Fax 202-628-0448; Email info@acsa-arch.org; Web: www.acsa-arch.org; *Exec Dir* Michael J Monti, PhD; *Dir Operations & Prog* Eric Ellis; *Prog Mgr* Allison Smith; *Dir Mem & Mktg* Danielle V Dent; *Commun Mgr* Amanda Gann
Open Mon - Fri 8:30 AM - 5:30 PM; No admis fee; Estab 1912 as a non-profit, mem organization furthering the advancement of architectural educ; Mem: 3500 architecture faculty members; mem open to schools & their faculty as well as individuals; mem rates vary; annual meeting in Mar
Income: $1.4 million (financed by endowment, mem, state appropriation & grants)
Publications: ACSA News, 9 times per year; Journal of Architectural Education, quarterly; Annual Meeting Proceedings; Guide to Architecture Schools in North America, biannually
Activities: Educ seminars; institutes; publications; services to membership; sponsor student design competitions with awards

O **ASSOCIATION OF INDEPENDENT COLLEGES OF ART & DESIGN,** 236 Hope St, Providence, RI 02906. Tel 401-270-5991; Fax 401-270-5993; Email deborah@aicad.org; Web: www.aicad.org; *Chmn* Jay Coogan; *Vice Chmn* Denise Mullen; *Secy* Sammy Hoi; *Treas* Dianne Taylor-Gearing; *Pres & Exec Dir* Deborah Obalil; *Prog & Operations Mgr* Lee Ann Adams; *Asst Dir Research* Joanne Kersh
Open by appointment only; Estab 1991 to improve quality of mem cols & provide information on art educ; Mem: 35; must be independent art college, fully accredited & grant BFA; dues $5500-$8000 depending on size; annual meeting in Oct
Income: $500,000 (financed by mem & occasional grants)
Publications: Internal newsletter

O **ASSOCIATION OF MEDICAL ILLUSTRATORS,** 201 E Main St, Ste 1405 Lexington, KY 40507-2003. Tel 866-393-4264; Fax 859-514-9166; Email info@ami.org; Web: www.ami.org; *Pres* Kathleen Jung; *Sec* Joan Tycko; *Treas* Scott Weldon; *Exec Dir* Melanie J Bowzer
Estab 1945 as an international organization to encourage the advancement of medical illustration & allied fields of visual educ; to promote understanding & cooperation with the medical & related professions; Mem: 800; dues active $315; student $115; annual meeting in July
Income: Financed by mem
Exhibitions: Annual salon exhibition at national meeting
Publications: Journal of Biocommunications, 4 times per year; Medical Illustration, brochure; Newsletter, 4 times per year

O **ATLATL,** PO Box 34090, Phoenix, AZ 85067-4090. Tel 602-277-3711; Fax 602-277-3690; Email atlatl@atlatl.org; Email fnahwooksy@atlatl.org; *Exec Dir* Lorenzo J Begay; *Proj Dir* Mark A Little; *Chmn* Aurolyn Stwyer
Open Mon - Fri 9 AM - 5 PM; No admis fee; Estab 1981 as a national service organization for Native American Art. Atlatl creates an informational network between Native American artists & art organizations as well as between mainstream institutions & emerging organizations. Maintains a National Registry of Native American Artists which currently includes more than 2500 artists; Mem: 300; dues vary; mem open to all
Income: Financed by federal grants
Collections: Native American Artists files
Exhibitions: Annual Beyond Beads & Performing Arts Series; Hiapsi Wami Seewam: Flowers of Life; Native Women of Hope
Publications: Quarterly newsletter
Activities: Lects open to pub, 5 or more vis lectrs per yr; concerts; competitions; artmobile; circulates av materials such as slides sets & videotapes by Native American artists; book traveling exhibs 2-5 per yr; originate exhibs of Native American art to a variety of institutions including tribal museums, community & university galleries & fine art museums

O **COLLEGE ART ASSOCIATION,** 50 Broadway 21st Fl, New York, NY 10004-1680. Tel 212-691-1051; Fax 212-627-2381; Email nyoffice@collegeart.org; Web: www.collegeart.org; *Pres* Suzanne Preston Blier; *Pres* Anne Collins Goodyear; *Exec Dir* Hunter O'Hanian; *CFO* Teresa Lopez; *Dir Information Technology* Michael Goodman
Open Mon - Fri 9 AM - 5 PM; Estab 1911 as a national organization to further scholarship & excellence in the teaching & practice of art & art history; Mem: 16,000, open to all individuals & institutions interested in the purposes of the Assoc; dues life $5000, institution $680, individual $60-$195 (scaled to salary), student $50-$60; annual meeting in Feb
Income: Financed by mem
Publications: The Art Bulletin, quarterly; Art Journal, quarterly; CAA Newsletter, weekly; Careers, bimonthly
Activities: Awards: Distinguished Teaching of Art History Award; Distinguished Teaching of Art Award; Charles Rufus Morey Book Award; Frank Jewett Mather Award for Distinction in Art & Architectural Criticism; Arthur Kingsley Porter Prize for Best Article by Younger Scholar in The Art Bulletin; Alfred H Barr, Jr Award for Museum Scholarship; Distinguished Artist Award for Lifetime Achievement; Award for a Distinguished Body of Work, Exhibition, Presentation or Performance; Annual Conference; Prof develop fels; Meiss book grants; schols offered

O **COLOR ASSOCIATION OF THE UNITED STATES,** 33 Whitehall St Ste M3, New York, NY 10004-2112; 23 Roosevelt Ave, Old Greenwich, CT 06870. Tel 212-947-7774; Fax 212-594-6987; Email info@colorassociation.com; Web: www.colorassociation.com; *Exec Dir* Leslie Harrington; *Dir Data & Educ* Anat Lechner, PhD
Open Mon - Fri 9 AM - 5 PM; Estab 1915 for the purpose of forecasting fashion colors & standards in the United States; Mem: 1000; dues $750-$1500
Income: Financed by mem
Collections: Colored Swatch Archives date back to 1915
Publications: CAUS Newsletter, 6 times per year; The Color Compendium; Living Colors; The Standard Color Reference of America
Activities: Workshops; classes for adults; lect, 12 vis lectrs per year

O **FEDERATION OF MODERN PAINTERS & SCULPTORS,** 113 Greene St, New York, NY 10012-3823. Tel 212-966-4864; Email info@fedart.org; Web: www.fedart.org; *Pres* Anneli Arms; *VPres & Sec* Vincent Pinto; *Treas* Jon Rettich
Estab 1940 as a national organization to promote the cultural interests of free progressive artists working in the United States; Mem: 60; selected by mem comt; working artist (painter, sculptor); dues $35; meeting every 2 months
Income: Financed by mem
Library Holdings: Exhibition Catalogs
Exhibitions: Exhibition at Art Students League; A Decade for Renewal, at Lever House, NYC; Fordham Univ; Broome St Gallery, NYC; Westbeth Gallery, NYC; Sylvia Wald & Po Kim Gallery, NYC
Publications: Exhibit catalog
Activities: Lects open to public, 1-2 vis lectrs per yr; symposium; originate traveling exhibs

O **GUILD OF BOOK WORKERS,** 521 5th Ave, Fl 17 New York, NY 10175-0003. Tel 212-292-4444; Email communications@guildofbookworkers.org; Web: www.guildofbookworkers.org; *Pres* Bexx Caswell; *VPres* Brien Beidler; *Sec* Katy Baum; *Treas* Laura Bedford; *Commun Chmn* Marianna Brotherton
Call for hours; No admis fee; Estab 1906 as a national organization to establish & maintain a feeling of kinship & mutual interest among workers in the several hand book crafts; Mem: 900; mem open to all interested persons; dues national; $85, chap (New York, New England, Midwest, Lone Star, Delaware Valley, Potomac, Rocky Mountain, California, Southeast, Northwest) $10 for each chap; annual meeting in Oct; Canadian mem additional $10; overseas mems additional $15; students $30 (allowed for 3 yrs w/ ID)
Income: Financed by mem
Publications: Guild of Book Workers Journal, 1 time per year; newsletter, 6 times per yr
Activities: Classes for adults; lects open to members only; tours; workshops; annual seminar on Standards of Excellence in Hand Bookbinding; awards given for mems, 2 per yr as necessary; chaps have exhibs

L **Library,** 100 Main Library, Univ of Iowa Conservation Dept Iowa City, IA 52242-1420. Tel 319-335-5908; Fax 319-335-5900; Email anna-embree@uiowa.edu; Web: palimpsest.stanford.edu/byorg/gbw/library.shtml; *Guild Librn* Anna Embree
Open by appointment; Open to Guild members for lending & reference
Income: Financed by mem
Library Holdings: Book Volumes 700

O **INDUSTRIAL DESIGNERS SOCIETY OF AMERICA,** 555 Grove St, Ste 200 Herndon, VA 20170-4728. Tel 703-707-6000; Fax 703-787-8501; Email idsa@idsa.org; Web: www.idsa.org; *Chmn* Megan Neese; *Secy & Treas* David Wynne; *Exec Dir* Daniel Martinage
Open daily 9 AM - 5 PM; No admis fee; Estab & inc 1965 as a nonprofit national organization representing the profession of industrial design; Mem: 3300; dues full, affiliate & international $285, assoc $140
Publications: Innovation, quarterly; IDSA Newsletter, monthly; Membership Directory; other surveys & studies
Activities: IDSA Student Chap; IDSA Student Merit Awards; lect; competitions; scholarships offered

O **INTER-SOCIETY COLOR COUNCIL,** 7820B Wormans Mill Rd, Ste 115 Frederick, MD 21701. Tel 866-876-4816; Email isccoffice@iscc.org; Web: www.iscc.org; *Pres* Jerald Dimas; *Pres Elect* Dr Renzo Shamey; *Secy* Ann C Laidlaw; *Treas* Dr C Cameron Miller
Estab 1931 as a national organization to stimulate & coordinate the study of color in science, art & industry; federation of 29 national societies & individuals interested in colors; Mem: 900; members must show an interest in color & in the aims & purposes of the Council; dues individual $50; annual meeting usually Apr
Income: Financed by mem
Publications: Inter-Society Color Council Newsletter, bimonthly
Activities: Lects open to public; lects at meetings; gives Macbeth Award and Godlove Award

O **INTERMUSEUM CONSERVATION ASSOCIATION,** 2915 Detroit Ave, Cleveland, OH 44113-2709. Tel 216-658-8700; Fax 216-658-8709; Email ica@ica-artconservation.org; Web: www.ica-artconservation.org; *Exec Dir* Aaron Marcovy; *Art Transport Mgr & Preparator* Charles Eiben; *Sr Paintings Conservator* Andrea Chevalier; *Opers Mgr* Christopher Pelrine
Estab 1952 as a nonprofit conservation laboratory to aid in the maintenance of the collections of its member museums; Maintains a technical conservation library;

Mem: 28; must be nonprofit cultural institution; dues $100-$600; meetings biannually
Income: Financed by membership, private & public grants
Activities: Lect open to public; 3-6 vis lectrs per year; seminars twice a year; scholarships for advanced training of conservators

O **INTERNATIONAL FOUNDATION FOR ART RESEARCH, INC (IFAR),** 500 Fifth Ave, Ste 935, New York, NY 10110. Tel 212-391-6234; Fax 212-391-8794; Email kferg@infar.org; Web: www.ifar.org; *Exec Dir, Ed in Chief* Dr Sharon Flescher; *Asst to Dir* Kathleen Ferguson; *Chmn* Anthony Williams; *Dir Art Research* Dr Lisa Duffy-Zeballos
Open Mon - Fri 9:30 AM - 5:30 PM; Estab 1968, IFAR is a nonprofit educational and research organization dedicated to integrity in the visual arts. It focuses on issues relating to art authenticity & ownership, art ethics, law, & connoisseurship. IFAR operates at the intersection of the scholarly, legal & commercial art worlds. Created to adjudicate questions concerning attribution & authenticity of major works of art; expanded in 1975 to include issues of art theft and art law & ethics. IFAR organizes pub prog & pub a quarterly journal, offers provenance & authentication research services, & provides several research tools on its website including the Catalogue Raisonne database & the Art Law Cultural Property database; Mem: Mem/supporter $250 and up
Income: Financed by donations, mem & fees
Publications: IFAR Journal, quarterly; Reference Material
Activities: Lect open to pub & symposia are conducted throughout the year on subjects relating to connoisseurship, authenticity, provenance research, art law & art theft & fraud; tours
—**Authentication Service**, 500 Fifth Ave, Ste 1234, New York, NY 10110. Tel 212-391-6234; Fax 212-391-8794; *Dir* Dr Sharon Flescher
Through this service, the resources of leading institutional experts, both scholarly & scientific, are made available to the pub in order to answer questions relating to authenticity & proper attribution of works of art

O **INTERNATIONAL SOCIETY OF COPIER ARTISTS (ISCA),** 759 President St, Apt 2H, Brooklyn, NY 11215-1362. Tel 718-638-3264; Email isca4art2b@aol.com; *Dir* Louise Neaderland
Open by appt; No admis fee; Estab 1981 to promote use of copier as a creative tool; Circ 125 (ltd edition); Mem: 150; dues international subscriber $110, domestic $90 and $30, $40 annual dues; mem open to artists using the copier for printmaking & bookmaking; contributing artist membership outside US $40, domestic $30 (slides or samples of work)
Income: $10,000 (financed by mem & subscriptions to Quarterly)
Collections: Slide Archive of Xerographic Prints & Books
Exhibitions: ISCA GRAPHICS; Using the Copier as a Creative Tool; The Artists Book
Publications: Quarterly of Xerographic Prints & Artists Books
Activities: Gallery talks; tours; 1 book traveling exhib per yr; originate traveling exhibs to universities, art schools & libraries

O **KAPPA PI INTERNATIONAL HONORARY ART FRATERNITY,** 307 S Fifth Ave, Cleveland, MS 38732-3745. Tel 712-420-0866; Email info@kappapiart.com; Web: www.kappapiart.com; *Pres* Michael Stanley; *VPres* Dr Jeff Brown; *Treas* Ky Johnston; *Secy* Amy Cannestra; *Historian* Cliff Tresner
Mon - Fri 9 AM - 5 PM; Estab 1911 as an international honorary art fraternity for men & women in cols, universities & art schools; Mem: 185 chap; dues $10 & up
Income: Financed by mem
Publications: Sketch Pad Newsletter, annually in the fall; Sketch Book, annual spring magazine
Activities: Sponsors competition in art; annual scholarships available to active members

O **LANNAN FOUNDATION,** 313 Read St, Santa Fe, NM 81501-2628. Tel 505-986-8160; Fax 505-986-8195; Email info@lannan.org; Web: www.lannan.org; *Prog Dir* Christie Davis; *Program Asst* AnaMaria Moreno; *Admin* Susie Bousson; *Accounting Mgr* Linda Carey; *Pres* Patrick Lannan
Open by appointment; Estab 1960 for the support of work by contemporary artists; Installations of new & old work from Lannan Collection
Library Holdings: Book Volumes, Exhibition Catalogs, Video Tapes
Special Subjects: Painting-American, Painting-European, Photography, Sculpture
Collections: Small collection of modern & contemporary art
Activities: Lect open to public; 15 vis lectrs per yr; grants offered; individual paintings & original objects of art lent

O **MID-AMERICA ARTS ALLIANCE & EXHIBITS USA,** 2018 Baltimore Ave, Kansas City, MO 64108-1914. Tel 816-421-1388; Fax 816-421-3918; Email info@maaa.org; Web: www.maaa.org; *CEO* Todd Stein; *Dir Art & Humanities Programming* Kathy Dowell, PhD; *Dir Mktg & Communs* Margaret A Keough
Estab 1972, a national division of Mid-America Arts Alliance created to organize & tour art exhibits throughout the United States & beyond
Income: $1,000,000 (financed by federal & state grants, private contributions & exhibition fees)
Exhibitions: Various Exhibs
Publications: Exhibition catalogs & brochures
Activities: Educ guides; Book traveling exhibs; originate traveling exhibs to various museums, historical societies, libraries, art centers & galleries

O **MIDWEST ART HISTORY SOCIETY,** One Bear Pl #97263 Dept of Art, Baylor Univ Waco, TX 76798. Email info@mahsonline.org; Web: www.mahsonline.org; *Pres* Heidi Hornik; *Secy* Paula Wisotzki; *Treas* Valerie Hedquist
Estab 1973 to further art history in the Midwest as a discipline & a profession; Average Annual Attendance: 150 at meetings; Mem: 600; mem is open to institutions, students & acad & mus art historians in the Midwest; dues institution $150, individuall $60, student $30; annual meeting in Mar or early Apr
Income: $3,500 (financed by mem)
Publications: Midwest Art History Society Newsletter, Oct & Apr
Activities: Lect provided; small travel grants for grad student travel to ann conference; award for best conference paper by a grad student

O **THE NAMES PROJECT FOUNDATION AIDS MEMORIAL QUILT,** 204 14th St NW, Atlanta, GA 30318-5304. Tel 415-882-5500; 404-688-5500; Fax 404-688-5552; Email info@aidsquilt.org; Web: www.aidsquilt.org; *Chap Prog Coord* Brad Gammell; *Warehouse Opers Mgr* Kevin Crane; *Quilt Opers Mgr* Brian Holman; *Quilt Production Mgr* Gert McMullin; *Pres & CEO* Julie Rhoad; *Dir Opers* Roddy Williams
Estab June 1987; Average Annual Attendance: 13,800,000
Collections: AIDS Memorial Quilt, over 40,000 individual memorial panels commemorating people lost to AIDS
Publications: On Display, newsletter
Activities: Sales shop sells prints, buttons, magnets, clothing, cards

O **NATIONAL ACADEMY MUSEUM & SCHOOL,** 1083 5th Ave, New York, NY 10128-0114. Tel 212-369-4880; Fax 212-426-1711; Email info@nationalacademy.org; Web: www.nationalacademy.org; *Exec Dir* Maura Reilly; *Pres* Bruce Fowle, NA; *Co-Chair* Walter Chatham, NA; *Co-Chair* Tim Walch; *Dean* Maurizio Pellegrin; *Dir Collections & Cur* Diana Thompson
Open Wed - Sun 11 AM - 6 PM, cl Mon, Tues, New Year's, Thanksgiving & Christmas; Estab 1825, honorary arts organization for American artists & architects; Average Annual Attendance: 30,000; Mem: 3000; Nat Academy elected by peers
Income: Financed by mem, endowment & grants
Special Subjects: Architecture, Drawings, Landscapes, Painting-American, Photography, Prints, Watercolors, Sculpture
Collections: Permanent collection consists of 5000 watercolors, drawings & graphics, 2000 paintings, 250 sculptures, mostly the gifts of the artist & architectural members of the Academy from 1825 to present, American art from mid-nineteenth century to the present
Exhibitions: exhibition of contemporary art; exhibitions of permanent collection & loan exhibitions
Publications: Annual exhibition catalogue; catalogues of exhibitions of permanent collection; catalogues of spec loan exhibitions
Activities: Classes for adults & children; docent training; lects open to pub; 10 vis lectrs per yr; gallery talks; tours by appointment; Awards - Henry Legrand Cannon Prize, Andrew Carnegie Prize, Alex Ettl Award for Sculpture, Malvina Hoffman Artists Fund Prize, Leo Meissner Prize, Edwin Palmer Memorial Prize, William A Paton Prize, Henry Ward Ranger Purchase Award; schols & fellowships offered; individual paintings & original objects of art lent to other mus; originates traveling exhibs to other mus; mus shop sells books, posters, catalogues & postcards; original art; prints

L **Archives**, 1083 5th Ave, New York, NY 10128. Tel 212-369-4880; Fax 212-360-6795; Web: www.nationalacademy.org; *Sr Cur Nineteenth Century Art* Bruce Weber, PhD; *Asst Cur Contemporary Art* Marshall Price; *Dir Operations* Charles Biada; *School Dir* Nancy Little; *Dir Artist Mem* Nancy Malloy; *Chief Conservator* Lucie Kinsolving; *Dir* Carmine Branagan; *Dir Finance & Human Resources* Michael McKay; *Dir Communs* Mary Fichter; *Cur Educ* Sandy Martiny; *Registrar* Athena LaTocha
Open Wed - Thurs Noon - 5 PM, Fri - Sun 11 AM - 6 PM; Admis general $10, students & seniors $5; Estab 1825 to promote American art through exhib and educ; For reference; Average Annual Attendance: 35,000; Mem: mem artists are invited and elected by current artist mem
Library Holdings: Clipping Files, Exhibition Catalogs, Manuscripts, Memorabilia, Original Art Works, Other Holdings Biographical Member Files; National Academy of Design Records, Pamphlets, Photographs, Prints, Sculpture
Special Subjects: American Western Art
Collections: Dipl works of artists elected to membership
Activities: Classes for adults & children; docent training; lects open to pub; 10 vis lectrs per yr; gallery talks; tours; awards, Henry Legrand Cannon Prize, Andrew Carnegie Prize, Alex Ettl Award for Sculpture, Malvina Hoffman Artists Fund Prize, Leo Meissner Prize, Edwin Palmer Memorial Prize, William A Paton Prize Henry Ward Ranger Purchase Award; schols & fels offered; originates traveling exhibs to various US mus; mus shop sells books and original art

O **NATIONAL ALLIANCE FOR MEDIA ARTS & CULTURE,** 145 9th St, Ste 230 San Francisco, CA 94103-2641. Tel 415-431-1391; Fax 415-431-1392; Email namac@namac.org; Web: www.namac.org; *Exec Dir* Wendy Levy; *Pres* Kasandra VerBrugghen; *Mem & Communs* Megan A Zebrowski
Estab 1980 for the purpose of furthering diversity & participation in all forms of the media arts, including film, video, audio & multimedia production; Mem: 350; dues $60 - $450; support media arts field
Income: $200,000 (financed by grants & mem dues)
Publications: Field Guide; Main newsletter, bimonthly; NAMAC Member Directory, online; The National Media Education Directory; Digital Directions: Convergence Planning for the Media Arts; A Closer Look: Media Arts 2000; BULLETin, biweekly electronic newsletter
Activities: Online salons; 2 vis lectrs per yr; lectrs for mems only; William Kirby Award in Media Arts

O **NATIONAL ANTIQUE & ART DEALERS ASSOCIATION OF AMERICA, INC,** 220 E 57th St, New York, NY 10022-2805. Tel 212-826-9707; Email naadaa.antiques@gmail.com; Web: www.naadaa.org; *Pres* James R McConnaughy; *1st VPres* Mark Jacoby; *Secy* Arlie Sulka; *Treas* Steven J Chait
Estab 1954 to promote the best interests of the antique & art trade; to collect & circulate reports, statistics & other information pertaining to art; to sponsor & organize antique & art exhibitions; to promote just, honorable & ethical trade practices
Income: Financed by member dues
Exhibitions: International Fine Art & Antique Dealers Show
Publications: NAADA Directory, biannual
Activities: Lect

O **NATIONAL ARCHITECTURAL ACCREDITING BOARD, INC,** 1101 Connecticut Ave NW, Ste 410 Washington, DC 20036-4351. Tel 202-783-2007; Fax 202-783-2822; Email info@naab.org; Web: www.naab.org; Pres Judith A Kinnard; *Treas* Celeste Allen Novak; *Secy* Thomas R Wood; *Interim Exec Dir* Helene Combs Dreiling; *Assoc Dir* Ellen Cathey
Open Mon - Fri 8 AM - 5 PM; Estab 1940 to produce & maintain a current list of accredited programs in architecture in the United States & its jurisdictions, with the

general objective that a well-integrated program of architectural educ be developed which will be national in scope; Mem: 115
Income: Financed by contributions
Publications: Criteria and Procedures, pamphlet; List of Accredited Programs in Architecture, annually

O **NATIONAL ART EDUCATION ASSOCIATION,** 901 Prince St, Alexandria, VA 22314-3008. Tel 703-860-8000; Fax 703-860-2960; Email info@arteducators.org; Web: www.arteducators.org; *Exec Dir* Deborah B Reeve, EdD; *COO* Melanie Dixon; *Convention & Progs Coordr* Kathy Duse; *Publications Mgr* Lynn Ezell; *Web & eCommuns Mgr* Linda Scott; *Mem Svcs Mgr & Database Opers Mgr* Christie Castillo
Open Mon - Fri 8:15 AM - 4:30 PM; Estab 1947 through the affiliation of four regional groups, Eastern, Western, Pacific & Southeastern Arts Assn. The NAEA is a national organization devoted to the advancement of the professional interests & competence of teachers of art at all educational levels. Promotes the study of the problems of teaching art; encourages research & experimentation; facilitates the professional & personal cooperation of its members; holds public discussions & progs; publishes desirable articles, reports & surveys; integrates efforts of others with similar purposes; Mem: 29,000 art teachers, administrators, supervisors & students; fee institutional comprehensive $150, active $50
Income: Programs financed through mem, sales of publications & annual convention
Publications: Art Education, 6 issues per year; NAEA Advisory, 4 issues per year; NAEA News, 6 issues per year; Studies in Art Education, 4 times per year; spec publs

O **NATIONAL ASSEMBLY OF STATE ARTS AGENCIES,** 1200 18th St NW, Ste 1100 Washington, DC 20036-2561. Tel 202-347-6352; Fax 202-737-0526; Email nasaa@nasaa-arts.org; Web: www.nasaa-arts.org; *CEO* Pam Breaux; *COO* Sylvia Prickett; *Chief Prog & Planning Officer* Kelly J Barsdate; *Chief Advancement Officer* Laura S Smith; *Commun Mgr* Sue Struve; *Pres* Gary Gibbs
Open by appointment only; Estab 1975 to enhance the growth & develop of the arts through an informed & skilled mem; to provide forums for the review & develop of national arts policy; Mem: 56; members are the fifty-six state & jurisdictional arts agencies, affiliate memberships are open to public; annual meeting in the fall
Income: Financed by mem & federal grants
Publications: Annual survey of state appropriations to arts councils; NASAA Notes, monthly
Activities: Co-manages The Arts Educ Partnership (www.aep-arts.org)

O **NATIONAL ASSOCIATION OF SCHOOLS OF ART & DESIGN,** 11250 Roger Bacon Dr, Ste 21, Reston, VA 20190. Tel 703-437-0700; Fax 703-437-6312; Email info@arts-accredit.org; Web: www.arts-accredit.org; *Pres* Denise Mullen
Formerly the National Conference of Schools of Design, holding its first conference in 1944. Changed name in 1948, at which time its constitution & by-laws were adopted. Changed its name again in 1960 from National Assn of Schools of Design to National Assn of Schools of Art. Name changed again in 1981 to National Assn of Schools of Art & Design. NASAD is the national accrediting agency for art & design institutions & progs in higher education; Mem: 315 institutions; to qualify for mem, institutions must meet accreditation standards; annual meeting in Oct
Publications: Online Directory of Member Institutions, annually; Handbook of Accreditation Standards, ann
Activities: Awards given

O **NATIONAL ASSOCIATION OF WOMEN ARTISTS, INC,** NAWA Gallery, 315 W 39th St, Ste 508 New York, NY 10018; 315 W 39th St, Rm 1201 New York, NY 10018-3975. Tel 212-675-1616; Fax 212-675-8257; Email office@thenawa.org; Web: www.thenawa.org; *Pres* Jill Cliffer Baratta; *VPres* Sonia Stark; *Secy* Mark Altschul; *Treas* Carol Brady; *Exec Dir* Susan G Hammond
Open Tues - Fri 10 AM - 5 PM, cl Sat & Sun; No admis fee; Estab 1889 as a national organization to encourage & promote the creative output of women artists; fosters awareness of the contributions of women artists to the ongoing history of American art; Maintains reference library & solo & group exhibs; Average Annual Attendance: 2,000; Mem: 800; member work is juried prior to selection; dues $150; meetings in Nov & May
Income: Financed by mem
Collections: Permanent collection at Jane Vorhees Zimmerli Museum, Rutgers Univ
Exhibitions: Annual members' exhibition in spring or fall with awards; annual traveling exhibitions of oils, acrylics, works on paper, printmaking; annual New York City shows of oils, acrylics, works on paper, printmaking & sculpture; MA Chapter shows; FL Chapter shows; NAWA gallery shows; library shows; numerous outside shows
Publications: The Annual Members' Exhibition Catalog; One Hundred Years-A Centennial Celebration of the National Assn of Women Artists; A View of One's Own, brochure; pamphlets
Activities: Classes for adults; lects & panels coordinated with exhib; workshop presentations & panel discussions; lects open to pub, 2 vis lectrs per yr; gallery talks; sponsoring of competitions; $10,000 in awards given annually; $5,000 biennial Hammerschlag Direct Carving Competition; organizes book traveling exhibs to mus & univ; originate traveling exhibs to mus, univ galleries, art ctrs

O **NATIONAL CARTOONISTS SOCIETY,** PO Box 592927, Orlando, FL 32859-2927. Tel 407-994-6703; Fax 407-629-2502; Email info@reuben.org; Web: www.reuben.org; *Pres* Bill Morrison
Estab 1946 to advance the ideals & standards of the profession of cartooning; to stimulate interest in the art of cartooning by cooperating with estab schools; to encourage talented students; to assist governmental & charitable institutes; Mem: 480; annual Reuben Awards Dinner in Apr
Collections: Milt Gross Fund, National Cartoonists Society Collection
Publications: The Cartoonist, bimonthly
Activities: Educ dept to supply material & information to students; individual cartoonists to lect, chalk talks can be arranged; cartoon auctions; proceeds from traveling exhibitions & auctions support Milt Gross Fund assisting needy cartoonists, widows & children; gives Reuben Award to Outstanding Cartoonist of the Year, Silver Plaque Awards to best cartoonists in individual categories of cartooning; original cartoons lent to schools, libraries & galleries; originate traveling exhibs

O **NATIONAL COUNCIL ON EDUCATION FOR THE CERAMIC ARTS (NCECA),** 4845 Pearl East Cir, Ste 101 Boulder, CO 80301. Tel 866-266-2322, 303-828-2811; Fax 303-828-0911; Email info@nceca.net; Web: www.nceca.net; *Exec Dir* Joshua Green; *Conf Mgr* Dori Nielsen; *Projects Mgr* Kate Vorhaus; *Office Mgr* Jacqueline Hardy; *Pres* Chris Staley; *Website/Communs* Candice Finn
Open Mon - Fri 8 AM - 5 PM; Estab 1966 as a nonprofit organization to promote & improve ceramic art, design, craft & educ through the exchange of information among artists, teachers & individuals in the ceramic art community; Average Annual Attendance: 4,500; Mem: 4,000; dues $25 - $500
Income: Financed by annual conferences & mem
Library Holdings: CD-ROMs, DVDs, Exhibition Catalogs, Original Art Works, Periodical Subscriptions, Photographs
Exhibitions: Annual Conference Exhibitions; Open regional & nat exhibs (see website)
Publications: Journal, annual; Information Annual Conference, spring; Monthly electronic print newsletter available to mems; newsletters by request
Activities: Educ progs; conferences & symposia; organize traveling exhibs

O **NATIONAL ENDOWMENT FOR THE ARTS,** 400 7th St SW, Washington, DC 20506-0001. Tel 202-682-5400; Email webmgr@arts.endow.gov; Web: arts.gov; *Chmn* Jane Chu; *Dir Mus, Visual Arts & Indemnity* Wendy Clark; *Arts Educ Dir* Ayanna N Hudson
Open 9 AM - 5:30 PM; No admis fee; The NEA is a public agency dedicated to supporting excellence in the arts, both new & established; bringing the arts to all Americans; & providing leadership in arts educ. Estab 1965 by Congress as an independent agency of the federal govt, the NEW is the nation's largest annual national funder of the arts, bringing great art to all 50 states, incl rural areas, inner cities & military bases
Income: Financed by federal appropriation
Publications: Annual Report; Guide to the National Endowment for the Arts; Research Publications
Activities: Funding opportunities can be found at www.arts.gov/grants

O **NATIONAL LEAGUE OF AMERICAN PEN WOMEN,** 1300 17th St NW, Washington, DC 20036-1973. Tel 202-785-1997; Fax 202-452-6868; Email contact@nlapw.org; Web: nlapw.org; *National Pres* Virginia Franklin Campbell; *First VPres* Lorna Jean Hagstrom; *Second VPres* Sheila M Byrnes; *Recording Secy* Mary Pat Canes; *Treas* Evelyn B Wofford
Estab 1897 to support women in the arts; Maintains member reference library; Mem: 1500; 79 local branches; dues $60
Income: Financed by mem dues & legacies
Library Holdings: Manuscripts, Memorabilia, Original Art Works, Original Documents, Periodical Subscriptions, Photographs, Sculpture
Collections: Purchase award
Exhibitions: NLAPW Biennial Arts Show at national Biennial Convention
Publications: The Pen Women, bi-monthly magazine (4 times per year)
Activities: Lect open to public; concerts; competitions with awards; scholarships offered

O **NATIONAL OIL & ACRYLIC PAINTERS SOCIETY,** PO Box 468, Houston, TX 77269. Tel 847-361-5124; Email membership@noaps.org; Web: www.noaps.org; *Pres* Michelle Murray; *Dir of Publicity* Hebe Brooks; *Secy* Karolyn Farrell; *Dir* Linda Lucas Hardy
Open 10 AM - 5 PM; No admis fee; Estab 1990 to promote the work of exceptional living artists working in oil & acrylic paint & to expand the pub awareness, knowledge & appreciation of fine art, particularly in these two mediums; Main Hall, Columbia College; Average Annual Attendance: 5,000; Mem: Dues $50
Income: Not-for-profit 401C3
Exhibitions: Annual exhibit
Publications: Annual catalog; semiannual newsletter
Activities: Gallery talks; tours; originates traveling exhibs to Missouri galleries

O **NATIONAL SCULPTURE SOCIETY,** 75 Varick St, c/o ANS Fl 11 New York, NY 10013-1917. Tel 212-764-5645; Fax 212-764-5651; Email media@nationalsculpture.org; Web: www.nationalsculpture.org; *Pres* Michel Langlais; *1st VPres* Amy Kann; *Treas* Hiram Ball; *Secy* Greg Wyatt; *Exec Dir* Gwen P Pier; *Exhibitions Coord* Patricia Delahanty; *Prog & Circulation Dir* Elizabeth Helm
Open by appt only; No admis fee; Estab 1893 as a national organization to spread the knowledge of good sculpture; Mem: 2,500; work juried for sculptor mem; vote of Board of Dir for allied professional & patron mem; dues $75-$350; meetings in May & Oct
Income: Financed by endowment, mem & donations
Library Holdings: Book Volumes, Clipping Files, Exhibition Catalogs, Photographs, Slides, Video Tapes
Exhibitions: 2-3 exhibitions annually on a rotating basis; open to all United States citizens and residents
Publications: Sculpture Review Magazine, quarterly; NSS; Sculpture News, electronic bimonthly
Activities: Educ progs; lects open to pub; tours; competitions with prizes; sculpture celebration conference hosted annually; schols & fels offered; Alex J Ettl Grant, schol; Henry Hering Award; originate traveling exhibs 1 per yr

O **NATIONAL SOCIETY OF MURAL PAINTERS, INC,** 450 W 31st St, 7th Fl New York, NY 10001-4608. Tel 212-244-2800; Email info@nationalsocietyofmuralpainters.com; Email info@evergreene.com; Web: nationalsocietyofmuralpainters.com; *Pres* Carly Bartlett; *Vice Pres* Bill Mensching
Estab and incorporated 1895 to encourage and advance the standards of mural painting in America; to formulate a code for decorative competitions and by-laws to regulate professional practice; Mem: 100; dues $25-$45
Income: Financed by dues & tax deductible contributions
Exhibitions: The Freedom Murals

Publications: Biographies and articles pertinent to the mural painting profession; Press Sheets of photographs and articles of the executed work of the members of society
Activities: Lects available to members only & their guests, 4 vis lectrs per yr; individual paintings & original objects of art lent to galleries, museums & special charitable events; lending collection contains original art works & slides; book traveling exhibs; originate traveling exhibs

O **NATIONAL SOCIETY OF PAINTERS IN CASEIN & ACRYLIC, INC,** 969 Catasauqua Rd, Whitehall, PA 18052-5501. Tel 610-264-7472; Email doug602ku@aol.com; Web: www.nationalsocietyofpaintersincaseinandacrylic.com; *VPres* Robert Dunn; *Pres* Douglas Wiltrout
Open in June during exhibition; Estab 1952 as a national organization for a showcase for artists in casein & acrylic; Galleries rented from Salmagundi Club; Average Annual Attendance: 800 during exhibition; Mem: 120; mem by invitation, work must pass three juries; dues $25; annual meeting in May
Income: $3000 (financed by mem)
Exhibitions: Annual Exhibition
Publications: Exhibition Catalog, annually
Activities: Demonstrations; medals & $3500 in prizes given at annual exhib; originate traveling exhibs

O **NATIONAL WATERCOLOR SOCIETY,** 915 S Pacific Ave, San Pedro, CA 97031-3201. Tel 310-831-1099; Web: nationalwatercolorsociety.org; *Pres* Ken Goldman; *1st VPres* Denise Willing-Booher; *3rd VPres* Carol Newsom; *4th VPres* Beatrice Trautman; *Recording Secy* Stephanie Goldman; *Treas* Alice Kayuha; *Mem/Communs* N C Swan; *Historian* Lowri Sprung; *Newsletter Editor* Matthew Bird
Gallery hours Thurs - Fri 10 AM - 2 PM. Open by appointment Sat - Sun 12 PM - 4 PM. For calendar, directions, maps, check web page; No admis fee; Estab 1921 to sponsor art exhibits for the cultural & educational benefit of the pub; Circ 20,000; Mem: 2300; dues $40 associates, $45 signature mems beginning each yr in Mar (must be juried into signature mem); annual meeting in Jan; Assoc mem open to all; signature mem juried
Income: Financed by members
Purchases: One purchase award painting for permanent coll
Library Holdings: Compact Disks, Exhibition Catalogs, Original Art Works, Slides
Collections: Award-winning paintings from 1954 to present
Exhibitions: Spring Membership Exhibition; International Annual Exhibition (Fall)
Publications: Society's quarterly newsletter; color annual exhib catalog
Activities: Lects open to pub; sponsor yearly grant to children's art program of LA Southwest Museum; NWS award - $4000 - plus 30 awards totaling $30,000; demonstrations; lectrs; organize travel exhibs to art museums, art centers & libraries; originate traveling exhibs to art centers, college galleries, libr

O **NATIONAL YOUNGARTS FOUNDATION,** (National Foundation for Advancement in the Arts), 2100 Biscayne Blvd, Miami, FL 33137-5014. Tel 305-377-1140; Fax 305-377-1149; Email info@youngarts.org; Web: www.youngarts.org; *Pres & CEO* Carolina Garcia Sayaram; *COO* Jewel Malone; *Alumni Community Coord* Kelley Kessell; *Dir Productions* Roberta Behrendt Fliss; *Progs Mgr* Joseph Nesmith; *Progs Coordr* Neidra Ward
Open Mon - Fri 9 AM - 5:30 PM (office); gallery open Tues - Fri 10 AM - 4 PM; weekends by appt only; cl Mon; Estab 1981 to identify & reward young artists at critical stages in their develop
Income: Financed by private funding
Activities: Dramatic progs; master classes for prog participants; lects open to pub; concerts; gallery talks; tours

O **NEW ENGLAND WATERCOLOR SOCIETY,** PO Box 170140, Boston, MA 02117. Tel 617-536-7660; Web: www.newenglandwatercolorsociety.org; *Pres* Wendy Hale; *VPres* Julie Blanchard; *Recording Secy* Dawn Evans Scaltreto; *Corresp Secy* Anne Belson; *Treas* Chris Hale
Open Mon - Fri 9 AM - 5 PM; Estab 1886 to advance the fine art of aqua media; Mem: 200, assoc mem 80; annual meeting in Mar
Income: Financed by mem
Exhibitions: Annual winter membership exhibit; Biennial-North America National Show-Juried Exhibit; 2-3 exhibits per year
Activities: Demonstrations, lects & gallery works open to pub during exhibitions

O **THE ONE CLUB FOR CREATIVITY,** 260 Fifth Ave, Fl 2 New York, NY 10001-5301. Tel 212-979-1900; Fax 212-979-5006; Email info@oneclub.org; Web: www.oneclub.org; *CEO, The One Club* Kevin Swanepoel; *VPres Content & Mktg* Yash Egami; *Visual Content Mgr* Alison Bourdon; *Dir Events & Membership* Lucila Lopez Travez; *Dir Awards & Design* Gabriela Mirensky; *Exec Dir, ADC* Michael O'Rourke; *Creative Mgr* Brett McKenzie
Open Mon - Fri 10 AM - 6 PM; No admis fee; Estab 2016 umbrella organization of The One Club and the Art Directors Club to celebrate the legacy of creative advertising & design and to use that legacy to inspire future generations; Owns gallery; Mem: Dues $95-$200, ann show, awards & creative week
Income: Financed by mem
Library Holdings: Book Volumes, Exhibition Catalogs
Exhibitions: The One Club producer of the prestigious One Show, ADC Annual Awards & Creative Week, Young Guns, Young Ones, One Screen & Hall of Fame celebrating the intersection of advertising and the arts
Publications: bimonthly newsletter
Activities: Job fair; portfolio review programs; speaker events; seminars; lects open to pub, vis lectrs; competitions with awards; creative week; hall of fame; scholarships offered; originate traveling exhibs

O **PASTEL SOCIETY OF AMERICA,** National Arts Club, Grand Gallery, 15 Gramercy Park S, New York, NY 10003-1705. Tel 212-533-6931; Fax 212-353-8140; Email psaoffice@pastelsocietyofamerican.org; Web: pastelsocietyofamerica.org; *Founder & Hon Chair* Flora B Giffuni, MFA; *Pres* Jimmy Wright, PSA; *1st VPres* Dianne B Berhard, PSA; *2nd VPres* Duane Wakeham, PSA; *Treas* JoAnn Giffuni Wellner, PSA; *Recording Secy* Arlene Richman, PSA; *Corresp Secy* Wende Caporale, PSA
Open Mon - Thurs 10 AM - 3:30 PM, Fri 10 AM - 2 PM (office); Estab 1972 to promote & encourage pastel painting/artists; Mem: 925; dues $25-$100 ; mem open to professional artists
Income: donations
Library Holdings: Audio Tapes, CD-ROMs, Clipping Files, Exhibition Catalogs, Original Art Works, Slides, Video Tapes
Collections: Raymond Kintsler, Robert Phillip, Constance F Pratt & other master pastellists
Exhibitions: For Pastels Only-Annual
Publications: Pastelagram, bi-annual
Activities: Classes for adults; lects open to pub; gallery talks; sponsoring of competitions; Art Spirit Foundation, Dianne B Bernhard Gold Medal Award, Great American Artworks Award, Herman Margulies Award for Excellence, Andrew Giffuni Memorial Award, Joseph V. Giffuni Memorial Award; scholarships offered; exten dept serves lending collection of paintings; book traveling exhibs; originate traveling exhibs to galleries & museums

O **PASTEL SOCIETY OF OREGON,** PO Box 105, Roseburg, OR 97470-0016. Tel 541-440-0567; Email block.lora@gmail.com; Web: www.pastelsocietyoforegon.com; *Pres* Lora Block
Estab 1987 to promote pastel as an art medium & to educate the pub on pastel; Mem: 80; dues $35 per yr; mem open to artists working in pastels; monthly working meetings
Income: $2000 (financed by mem & shows)
Publications: Pastel Newsletter, bi-monthly
Activities: Classes for adults; hands on exhibitions for schools

O **PASTEL SOCIETY OF THE WEST COAST,** Sacramento Fine Arts Center, 2003 No Van Ness Blvd, Fresno, CA 93704. Tel 559-392-6775; Email info@pswc.ws; Web: www.pswc.ws; *Pres & Exhibits Chair* Susan Goodmundson; *VPres* Tina Moore; *Treas* LaVone Sterling; *Recording Secy* Marie Gonzales; *Mem Chair* GinnyBurdick
Call for hours; Estab 1984 to promote soft pastel medium & exhibitions, workshops; Mem: 427; dues $35-50; quarterly meetings in Jan, Apr, July & Oct 3rd Wed
Income: Financed by mem & donations
Library Holdings: Video Tapes
Exhibitions: Three exhibitions per yr
Publications: PSWC newsletter, quarterly; exhibit catalogs
Activities: Classes for adults; lect open to public, 3-4 vis lectrs per year; competitions with awards; scholarships offered

O **PORTRAIT SOCIETY OF AMERICA,** PO Box 11272, Tallahassee, FL 32302. Tel 877-772-4321; Fax 334-270-0150; Email info@portraitsociety.com; Web: www.portraitsociety.com; WATS 850-222-7890; *Chmn* Edward Jonas; *VChmn* Dawn Whitelaw; *Sec* Sam Adoquei; *Treas* Michael Shane Neal; *Exec Dir* Christine Egnoski
Estab 1998 to further the traditions of fine art portraiture & figurative art; Mem: dues $70; national annual conference
Activities: Lect open to public; competitions with awards

O **THE PRINT CENTER,** 1614 Latimer St, Philadelphia, PA 19103-6308. Tel 215-735-6090; Email info@printcenter.org; Web: www.printcenter.org; *Pres* Hester Stinnett; *Chmn* Frances G Gerson; *Exec Dir* Elizabeth F Spungen; *Cur* John Caperton; *Dir Asst* Mikaela Hawk; *Sls & Prog Mgr* Evan Laudenslager; *Communs & Special Events Mgr* Michele Bregande
Open Tues - Sat 11 AM - 6 PM, cl major holidays; No admis fee; Estab 1915 to encourage the growth and understanding of photography & printmaking as vital contemporary arts through exhibitions, publications & educational programs; Contemporary prints, photographs & printed images; Average Annual Attendance: 8,000; Mem: dues $30-$10,000
Income: $530,000 (financed by individual donors, government grants, private foundation, fundraising events, art sales, competition fees & membership)
Special Subjects: Etchings & Engravings, Photography, Prints, Woodcuts
Collections: The Print Center Permanent Collection (prints & photograph collection held at the Philadelphia Museum of Art), The Print Center Archives (documents, books & catalogues held at the Historical Society of Pennsylvania)
Exhibitions: Temporary exhibitions of prints & photographs; Annual International Competition
Publications: Edna Andrade - Color Motion; Isaac Tin Wel Lin - One of Us; Emma Wilcox - Where It Falls; Will Brown & Thomas Devaney - The Picture That Remains; Demetrius Oliver - Canicular
Activities: Educational progs for adults; Artists-in-Schools prog; lect open to public; concerts; gallery talks; tours; competitions & awards; The Print Center Gallery Store sells original prints, photographs & printed objects

O **PRINT COUNCIL OF AMERICA,** 111 S Michigan Ave, c/o Art Institute of Chicago Dept of Prints & Drawings Chicago, IL 60603-6110. Email slangdale@philamuseum.org; Web: www.printcouncil.org; *IPCR Proj Coordr* Stephen Goddard; *Pres* Shelley R Langdale
Estab 1956 as a nonprofit organization fostering the study & appreciation of fine prints, new & old; Mem: 240 museum & university professionals interested in prints; quals for mem incl specialization in works on paper, nomination & second by current mem; annual meeting in Apr or May
Income: Financed by dues & publication royalties
Publications: Occasional publications on old & modern prints; The Print Council Index to Oeuvre-Catalogues of Prints by European & American Artists; see website

O **SALMAGUNDI CLUB,** 47 Fifth Ave, New York, NY 10003. Tel 212-255-7740; Email info@salmagundi.org; Web: www.salmagundi.org; *Pres* Robert Pillsbury; *Bd Chmn* Tim Newton; *1st VPres* Elizabeth Spencer; *2nd VPres* Janet Bauman; *Treas* John Morehouse; *Recording Secy* Griff Seymour
Open Mon - Fri 1 PM - 6 PM, Sat & Sun 1 - 5 PM; No admis fee; Estab 1871, incorporated 1880, to enhance the advancement of art appreciation, building purchased 1917; Clubhouse restaurant & bar, 3 galleries, Billiard room, library & board room. Maintains art reference library; Average Annual Attendance: 10,000;

Mem: 815; dues resident artist & patron $720, non-resident artist & patron $266, scholarship graduated to scale
Income: Financed by dues, donations, bequests
Special Subjects: American Western Art, Etchings & Engravings, Graphics, Landscapes, Marine Painting, Painting-American, Period Rooms, Photography, Portraits, Posters, Sculpture, Watercolors, Woodcuts
Collections: Club coll of past & present members, antique poster coll, coll of painters palettes
Exhibitions: 12 per year by artist members with cash awards; two per year by non-members (artists, photographers, sculptors) with cash awards; Annual Junior/ Scholarship exhibition in January
Publications: Centennial Roster published in 1972; Salmagundi Membership Roster, every three years (www.salmagundi.org)
Activities: Classes for adults; demonstrations; lect, 10-12 vis lectrs per year; gallery talks; tours; concerts; competitions with awards; scholarships & fels offered; individual paintings & original objects of art lent to various museums & special exhibitions; lending collection contains over 50 original art works, over 50 paintings, 10 sculptures; mus shop sells books, magazines, patches, ties & tie tacks

L **Library**, 47 Fifth Ave, New York, NY 10003. Tel 212-255-7740; Web: www.salmagundi.org; *Librn* Kenneth W Fitch
Open Tues 10:30 AM - 5 PM; For reference only
Library Holdings: Book Volumes 10,000, Exhibition Catalogs, Original Art Works, Other Holdings Steinway Player piano with 100 rolls, Periodical Subscriptions 10, Photographs, Sculpture
Special Subjects: Architecture, Art History, Drawings, Folk Art, Graphic Arts, Historical Material, History of Art & Archaeology, Illustration, Landscapes, Painting-American, Photography, Posters, Sculpture, Watercolors, Woodcuts

O **SCULPTORS GUILD, INC,** 526 LaGuardia Pl, Fl 2 Brooklyn, NY 11201-1073. Tel 718-422-0555; Fax 718-422-0555; Email sculptorsguild@gmail.com; Web: www.sculptorsguild.org; *Pres* Elaine Lorenz; *VPres* Ginger Andro; *Treas* Eric David Laxman; *Secy* Sarah Haviland
Open Tues & Thurs 12 PM - 5 PM (office); No admis fee; Estab 1937 to promote sculpture & show members' work in an annual show & throughout the country; Contemporary sculpture; Average Annual Attendance: 1,500; Mem: 120; qualifications for mem, quality of work & professionalism; dues $300; annual meeting in May
Income: Financed by mem dues, donations, & commissions on sales
Exhibitions: Various exhibitions of small works are held in the Sculptors Guild Gallery; Ann exhibs at Governors Island, Saks Fifth Ave Windows, Housatonic Mus
Publications: Brochure 1985; exhibit catalogs, every other year for annual exhibitions; 50th Anniversary Catalog 1937-1938; The Guild Reporter, Vol. 1, No. 1, 1986, annually
Activities: Speakers bureau; lect open to public; original objects of art lent to patrons & for movie & TV productions; lending collection contains cassettes & 50 sculptures; book traveling exhibs; originate traveling exhibs; sales shop sells original art

O **SOCIETY OF AMERICAN GRAPHIC ARTISTS,** 32 Union Sq, Ste 1214 New York, NY 10003. Tel 212-260-5706; Email sagaprints@verizon.net; Web: www.sagaprints.com; *VPres* Michael Arike; *VPres* Masaaki Noda; *Treas* Joseph Essig; *Pres* Linda Adato
Estab 1915 as a society of printmakers, now a society of graphic artists; Mem: 250 voted in by merit; dues $60; annual meeting May; juried by membership comt
Income: Financed by mem & assoc mem
Exhibitions: Semi-annual Open Competition National Print Exhibition; Semi-annual Closed Members Exhibit;
Publications: Exhibition Catalog, annually; Presentation Prints for Assoc Membership
Activities: Lects open to pub, 1 vis lectr per yr; sponsors competitive & members' exhibits with awards; original objects of art lent, lending coll contains original prints; originate traveling exhibs

O **SOCIETY OF AMERICAN HISTORICAL ARTISTS,** 146 Dartmouth Dr, Oyster Bay, NY 11801-3423. Tel 516-681-8820; Fax 516-822-2253; *VPres* William Muller; *Pres* John Duillo
Estab 1980 for furthering American Historical Art, especially authenticity; Mem: 16; dues $150; meetings 3-4 per yr
Activities: Awards for excellence

O **SOCIETY OF ARCHITECTURAL HISTORIANS,** 1365 N Astor St, Chicago, IL 60610-2144. Tel 312-573-1365; Fax 312-573-1141; Email info@sah.org; Web: www.sah.org; *Pres* Ken Tadashi Oshima; *First VPres* Sandy Isenstadt; *Second VPres* Victoria Young; *Secy* Kathryn O'Rourke; *Treas* Michael J Gibson; *Exec Dir* Pauline Saliga; *Dir Progs* Christopher Kirbabas; *Dir Mem* Anne Bird
Open Wed for tours noon, Sat 10 AM & 1 PM; Admis $10 on Sat, free on Wed; Estab 1940 to provide an international forum for those interested in architecture & its related arts, to encourage scholarly research in the field & to promote the preservation of significant architectural monuments throughout the world; House Mus; Mem: 3500; show an interest in architecture, past, present & future; dues $145-$155; annual meeting Apr
Income: Financed by mem
Library Holdings: Book Volumes, Exhibition Catalogs, Other Holdings
Publications: Journal, quarterly; Newsletter, quarterly; Preservation Forum, ann
Activities: Docent training; sponsors competitions; Antoinette Forrester Downing Award; Founder's Award; Alice Davis Hitchcock Book Award; Philip Johnson Award; Elizabeth MacDougall Award; Spiro Kostof Award; field study progs; fellowships offered; sales shop sells architectural guides & booklets & also back issues of the Journal, reproductions, prints, postcards

O **SOCIETY OF ILLUSTRATORS,** 128 E 63rd St, New York, NY 10065-7392. Tel 212-838-2560; Fax 212-838-2561; Email info@societyillustrators.org; Web: www.societyillustrators.org; *Pres* Tim O'Brien; *Exec VPres* Victor Juhasz; *VPres* Karen Green; *Secy* Leslie Cober Gentry; *Treas* David Reuss
Open Tues & Thurs 10 AM - 8 PM, Wed & Fri 10 AM - 5 PM, Sat 11 AM - 5PM, cl most holidays; No admis fee; Estab 1901 as a national organization of professional illustrators and art dir; Gallery has group, theme, one-man & juried shows, approx every four wks; Average Annual Attendance: 40,000; Mem: 850; professional illustrators 33 & up; resident dues $500, non-resident dues $300
Publications: Illustrators Annual
Activities: Lects open to pub; 7 vis lectrs per yr; sponsoring of competitions; holds annual national juried exhibition of best illustrations of the yr; awards scholarships to college level art students; originate traveling exhibs to college galleries; sales shop sells books

O **SOCIETY OF NORTH AMERICAN GOLDSMITHS,** 541 Willamette St, Ste 209 Eugene, OR 97401; PO Box 1355, Eugene, OR 97440-1355. Tel 541-345-5689; Fax 541-345-1123; Email info@snagmetalsmith.org; Web: www.snagmetalsmith.org; *Pres* Brigitte Martin; *Secy* Becky McDonah; *Treas* Anne Havel; *Exec Dir* Gwynne Rukenbrod Smith; *Conf & Prog Mgr* Alaina Clarke; *Opers Mgr* Tara Decklin
Open Mon - Fri 8:30 AM - 5 PM; No admis fee; Estab 1969; international mem org for jewelers, designers & metalsmiths; Maintains rental library; Average Annual Attendance: 800; Mem: 3,300; dues $85; annual meeting in late spring or early summer
Income: $600,000 (financed by mem)
Exhibitions: Distinguished Members of SNAG; Jewelry USA
Publications: Metalsmith magazine, 5 per year; bi-monthly newsletter; SNAG news
Activities: Lect open to members only; 3 vis lectrs per yr; competitions; ann conference; seminars; scholarships; originate traveling exhibs

O **SPECIAL LIBRARIES ASSOCIATION,** 7918 Jones Branch Dr, Ste 300 Mc Lean, VA 22102-3345. Tel 703-647-4900; Fax 703-506-3266; Email sla@sla.org; Web: www.sla.org; *Pres* Roberto Sarmiento; *Treas* Nicholas Collison; *Exec Dir* Amy Lestition Burke; *CFO* Kristen Hewlett
Estab 1909 to provide an information forum & exchange for librarians in the specialized fields of museums, arts & humanities; Mem: 14,000; dues $50-$750; annual meeting in early June
Publications: Museums, Arts & Humanities Division Bulletin, semi-annual

O **THE STAINED GLASS ASSOCIATION OF AMERICA,** 9313 E 63rd St, Raytown, MO 64133-4901. Tel 816-737-2090; Fax 816-737-2801; Email headquarters@sgaaonline.com; Web: www.stainedglass.org; *Pres* Kathy Barnard; *1st VPres* David Judson; *2nd VPres* Al Priest; *Financial Secy* Bill Klopsch; *Treas* Sue Shea; *Recording Secy* James Piercey
Estab 1903 as an international organization to promote the develop & advancement of the stained glass craft; Mem: 600; dues accredited $350, active $150, affiliate $75, student $50 (various criteria apply to each mem)
Income: Financed by mem dues
Library Holdings: Slides, Video Tapes
Special Subjects: Stained Glass
Publications: Stained Glass magazine, quarterly
Activities: Educ dept with two & three week courses

O **UNITED STATES DEPARTMENT OF THE INTERIOR,** Indian Arts & Crafts Board, 1849 C St NW, MS 2528-MIB, Washington, DC 20240. Tel 202-208-3773; 888-ART-FAKE; Fax 202-208-5196; Email iacb@ios.doi.gov; Web: www.doi.gov/iacb; *Dir* Meridith Z Stanton; *Prog Specialist* Lars Krutak; *Program Specialist* Ken Van Wey; *Admin Officer* Michele Hill; *Chmn* Harvey Pratt; *Commissioner* Ruth Blalock Jones; *Commissioner* Rose Fosdick; *Commissioner* Charles Harwood; *Sec* Ferdousi Khanam; *Commissioner* Vic Colombe
Open Mon - Fri 8 AM - 5 PM; No admis fee; Estab 1935 to promote contemporary arts by Indians & Alaska Natives of the United States; Board administers the Southern Plains Indian Museum, Anadarko, OK; Museum of the Plains Indian, Browning, MT; Sioux Indian Museum, Rapid City, SD; Average Annual Attendance: 150,000
Income: Financed by federal appropriation
Special Subjects: American Indian Art, Eskimo Art, Painting-Dutch
Collections: Contemporary American Indian & Alaska Native Arts
Exhibitions: Twelve special exhibitions among the three museums
Publications: Source Directory of American Indian & Alaska Native owned & operated arts & crafts bus
Activities: Information & advice on matters pertaining to contemporary Indian, Eskimo & Aleut arts & crafts

O **UNITED STATES GENERAL SERVICES ADMINISTRATION,** Art in Architecture and Fine Arts, 1800 F St NW (PCAC), Washington, DC 20405-0002. Tel 202-501-0930; Email jennifer.gibson@gsa.gov; Web: www.gsa.gov/fa; *Dir* Jennifer Gibson; *Proj Mgr* Nicole Avila; *Proj Mgr* William Caine; *Project Mgr* Kim Baker; *Colls Mgr* Mary Margaret Carr; *Colls Mgr* Julie Redwine
Open to public by appointment: 9 AM to 5 PM; No Admis Fees; GSA's Art in Architecture Program commissions artists, working in close consultation with project design teams, to create artwork that is appropriate to the diverse uses and architectural vocabularies of new federal buildings. These permanent installations of contemporary art within the nation's civic buildings afford unique opportunities for exploring the integration of art and architecture, and facilitate a meaningful cultural dialogue between the American people and their government. A panel that includes the project architect, art professionals, the federal client, and representatives of the community advises GSA in selecting the most suitable artist for each Art in Architecture commission, Artwork is funded by 0.5% of each building's construction budget. GSA&s Fine Arts Prog is responsible for the stewardship of the Fine Arts coll & all policies & procedures concerning its preservation, legal compliance accessibility & interpretation. The coll includes works from the 1850s to the present day.
Library Holdings: Book Volumes, CD-ROMs, Clipping Files, Compact Disks, DVDs, Exhibition Catalogs, Original Documents, Pamphlets, Photographs, Records, Slides, Video Tapes
Collections: Fine Arts Collection includes permanently installed & moveable mural paintings, sculpture, architectural or environmental works of art, works on paper located in Federal buildings, courthouses & land ports of entry across the US, Art in Architecture Marquettes, Design excellence architectural models, New Deal artworks allocated or on loan to institutions around the country

O **UNITED STATES NATIONAL COMMITTEE OF THE INTERNATIONAL COUNCIL OF MUSEUMS,** 1000 Potomac St NW, Ste 108, Washington, DC 20007-3599. Tel 202-452-1200; Fax 202-833-3636; Email icomus@icom.museum; Web: www.icomus.org; *Co-Chair* Lonnie G Bunch III; *Co-Chair* Kate Quinn; *Dir & CEO* Thomas J Loughman, PhD
Open 9 AM - 5 PM; No admis fee; Estab 1947; represents international museum interests within the United States & US museum interests abroad through the ICOM-US office which disseminates information on international conferences, publications, travel & study grants & training programs; Mem: 1100; members must be museum professionals or institutions; dues vary according to member category; members meet annually at the AAM annual meeting every spring and once every 3 yrs at the ICOM triennial conference
Income: Financed by mem dues
Publications: International Column in Aviso, monthly; ICOM News, quarterly (from ICOM Secretariat in Paris); occasional articles in Museum News, AAM's bi-monthly magazine
Activities: Specialty committees; annual meeting; international meetings; professional exchanges; publications catalogue available; International Service Citation

O **VAN ALEN INSTITUTE,** 30 W 22nd St, 6th Fl New York, NY 10010-5816. Tel 212-924-7000; Fax 212-366-5836; Email vai@vanalen.org; Web: www.vanalen.org; *Chair* Jared Della Valle; *Vice Chair* Jessica Healy; *Treas* Raymond Quinn; *Exec Dir* David van der Leer
Open Mon - Fri 10 AM - 6 PM; No admis fee; Inc 1894 as Society of Beaux-Arts Architects, which was dissolved Dec 1941; Beaux-Arts Institute of Design estab 1916, name changed 1956 to present name; Average Annual Attendance: 2,500; Mem: 600; dues $50 & up; annual meeting end of Oct
Income: mems, grants, corporate, found, gov grants
Exhibitions: Prize-winning drawings of competitions held during year; Rotating exhibits
Publications: Yearbook, annually in October
Activities: Lects open to pub, 4-5 vis lectrs per yr; competitions with awards; trustee for the Lloyd Warren Fellowship (Paris Prize in Architecture) for study & travel abroad; William Van Allen Architect Memorial Award (international competition) annual scholarship for further study or research project of some architectural nature; & other trust funds for prize awards for study & travel abroad & educational activities in the United States; individual paintings & original objects of art lent; lending collection contains 200 original prints; book traveling exhibs 3-4 per yr; originate traveling exhibs

O **VIRGINIA CENTER FOR THE CREATIVE ARTS,** 154 San Angelo Dr, Amherst, VA 25421-3257. Tel 434-946-7236; Fax 434-946-7239; Email vcca@vcca.com; Web: www.vcca.com; *Pres* Margaret B Ingraham; *Secy* Thomas Y Hiner; *Treas* Kenneth H Jones; *Exec Dir* Joy Peterson Heyrman; *Deputy Dir & Dir Artists' Servs* Sheila Gully Pleasants; *Asst Dir Artists' Servs* Dana Jones; *Develop & Grants Asst* Kmberley Stiffler; *Dir Individual Giving* Emily Joseph
Open Mon - Fri 9 AM - 5 PM; Estab 1971 as a residential retreat for writers, composers & visual artists; Facilities include 25 studios, y, a darkroom, a printing press, a library, private bedrooms in a modern residence. Breakfast & dinner served in dining room, lunch is delivered to Studio Barn. Access to Sweet Briar College facilities; Average Annual Attendance: 400 professional writers, composers & visual artists
Income: individual contributions, residency contributions
Collections: Books & artwork by Fellows
Exhibitions: exhibitions are in the summers, no proposals accepted
Publications: Annual newsletter; Notes From Mt San Angelo
Activities: Lect & readings open to public, 2-3 vis lectrs per year; concerts; tours; individual paintings & original objects of art lent through a leasing program to bus & individuals

O **VISUAL ARTISTS & GALLERIES ASSOCIATION (VAGA),** 111 Broadway, New York, NY 10006. Tel 212-736-6666; Fax 212-736-6767; Email info@vagarights.com; Web: vagarights.com; *Exec Dir* Robert Panzer
Estab 1976 to help artists control the reproduction of their works, from sculptures to photographs in textbooks; to act as a clearinghouse for licensing reproduction rights & setting up a directory of artists & other owners of reproduction rights for international use; Mem: European 3000, American 500; dues gallery & assoc $300, estates $75, artist $50
Income: Financed by mem & royalties
Publications: Newsletter

O **WASHINGTON SCULPTORS GROUP,** PO Box 42534, Washington, DC 20015-0534. Tel 202-686-8696; Fax 202-364-1053; Email exhibits@washingtonsculptors.org; Web: www.washingtonsculptors.org; *Pres* Artemis Herber; *VPres* Elsabé Dixon; *Treas* Zoie Lafis; *Sec* Cat Lukins
Estab 1983 to promote sculpture; Use art & corporate space for exhibitions; members' juried exhibitions available for exchange shows; Average Annual Attendance: 1,500; Mem: 400 mem; dues $35
Income: $10,000 (financed by mem & occasional grants)
Exhibitions: 3-5 juried exhibitions per year with various locales
Publications: Exhibition brochures & catalogs; newsletters, 3 per year; website
Activities: Lects open to pub, 6-8 vis lectrs per yr; image bank; gallery talks; tours; Mayor's Art Award, Washington, DC; originate traveling exhibs circulating to art spaces, galleries & museums

O **WOMEN'S CAUCUS FOR ART,** PO Box 1498, Canal St Sta New York, NY 10013. Tel 212-634-0007; Email president@nationalwca.org; Web: www.nationalwca.org; *Pres* Susan M King; *Treas & Secy* Janice Nesser-Chu; *VPres* Danielle Eubank; *Dir Opers* Karin Luner
Estab 1972 as a nonprofit women's professional & service organization for visual arts; Average Annual Attendance: 200; Mem: 1,600; annual meeting in Feb
Income: $55,000 (financed by mem)
Library Holdings: Exhibition Catalogs, Original Documents, Other Holdings, Periodical Subscriptions, Photographs
Exhibitions: (2016) Trending - Contemporary Art Now!
Publications: Honors Catalogue (annual); Art Lines (3 times per yr)
Activities: Lects open to pub; lects for mems only, vis lectrs 100 per yr; gallery talks; tours, sponsoring of competitions; scholarships; Lifetime Achievement awards; awards stipend to Feb conference student; schols awarded; originates traveling exhibs to university galleries

U.S. Museums, Libraries & Associations

ALABAMA

ANNISTON

M **ANNISTON MUSEUM OF NATURAL HISTORY,** 800 Museum Dr, Anniston, AL 36206-2813; PO Box 1587, Anniston, AL 36202-1587. Tel 256-237-6766; Fax 256-237-6776; Email cbragg@annistonmuseum.org; Web: www.annistonmuseum.org; *Dir* Cheryl Bragg; *Dir Develop* Lindie K Brown; *Dir Mktg* Margie Conner; *Tour Coordr* Donna Kopet; *Mus Store Mgr* Gina Cooper; *Chm (V)* Paula Watkins; *Facilities Mgr* Scott Williamon; *Cur Collections* Daniel Spaulding; *Dir Prog & Educ* Gina Morey
Open Tues - Sat 10 AM - 5 PM, Sun 1 - 5 PM, summer open Mon; Admis adults $4.50, children 4-17 $3.50, 3 & under free; Estab 1930, nationally accredited mus with the purpose of enhancing pub knowledge, understanding & appreciation of living things & their environments; Permanent exhibit halls interpret many aspects of natural history and the Environment; changing exhibit gallery features exhibitions focusing on interrelationships between nature & art; Average Annual Attendance: 70,000; Mem: 1600; dues family $35, individual $25; annual meeting in Sept
Income: Financed by mem, earned income, donations & city appropriations
Collections: Archaeology, Ethnology, Natural Science, Wildlife Art
Exhibitions: 4-6 rotating per yr
Activities: Classes for adults & children; docent progs; lects open to pub, 2-6 vis lectrs per yr; concerts; book traveling exhibs 2-4 per yr; retail store sells books, original art & reproductions

M **BERMAN MUSEUM,** 840 Museum Dr, Anniston, AL 36206; PO Box 2245, Anniston, AL 36202-2245. Tel 256-237-6261; Fax 256-238-9055; Email dford@bermanmuseum.org; Web: www.bermanmuseum.org
Open June - Aug Mon - Sat 10 AM - 5 PM, Sun 1 - 5 PM; Sept - May Tues - Sat. 10 AM - 5 PM,Sun. 1 - 5 PM; cl New Year's Day, Thanksgiving, Christmas Eve & Day; Admis adults $3.50, seniors $3, children 4 - 17 $2.50, discount to AAA mems & active military, children 3 & under no admis fee; Mus houses 3,000 objects related to world history in five galleries. The coll was that of Farley L & Germaine K Berman, both who served in counterintelligence during WWII. They met in North Africa & traveled the world collecting rare & unusual artifacts for more than seventy years; Mem: Dues Benefactor $500 & up; Patron $250; Sustainer $100; Contributor $50; Family $25; Indiv $20; Student (FT) $10
Special Subjects: Sculpture, Bronzes, American Western Art, American Indian Art, Antiquities-Oriental, Ceramics, Gold, Archaeology, Flasks & Bottles, Religious Art, Painting-American, Painting-European
Collections: Spy coll including a silver flute, various ink pens, walking canes, box of antacids, & WWII German cigarette lighter, all of which were designed to conceal a firing mechanism, coll of bronzes including figural & animal subject matter, created & cast by European, Asian, and American artists and foundries, religious & ordinary objects created by Asian artisans over a span of nine centuries, traveling pistols of Jefferson Davis, Pres of the Confederacy, dressing set of Napoleon Bonaparte, royal Persian scimitar encrusted with 1,295 rose-cut diamonds and rubies, single 40-carat emerald, all set in three pounds of gold, coll of weapons & bronze sculptures from the American West
Activities: Art Camp and Etiquette For Children; History Festival; rotating exhibs

AUBURN

M **AUBURN UNIVERSITY,** Jule Collins Smith Museum of Fine Art, 901 S College St, Auburn, AL 36849-5109. Tel 334-844-1484; Fax 334-844-1463; Email crh0035@auburn.edu; Web: www.jcsm.auburn.edu; *Financial Admin* Janice Allen; *Interim Museum Dir* Andy Tennant; *Perparator* Christopher L Carr; *Registrar* Danielle Mohr Funderburk; *Cur of Collections & Exhibitions* Dennis Harper; *Cur Asst* Jessica Hughes; *Cur of Education* Scott Bishop; *Devel Coord* Joshlyn Bess; *Devel Officer* Catherine Thompson; *Membership Officer* Cindy Cox; *Comm & Mktg Specialist* Charlotte R Hendrix; *Comm & Mktg Specialist* Connor Lowry; *Museum Shop Mgr.* Renée Maurer; *Special Events Specialist* Rachel SoloRio; *IT Specialist* Mike Cortez
Open Tues - Wed & Fri - Sat 10 AM - 4:30 PM, Thurs 10 AM - 8 PM, Sun 1 - 4 PM, cl Mon; No admis fee (suggested donation $5); Estab 2003 as an art mus; Mus is home to Auburn Univ's coll of American & European art. nearly 40,000 sq ft bldg; 130-seat auditorium; Average Annual Attendance: 30,000; Mem: Dues Patron $500; Benefactor $250; Sustaining $125; Family or Dual $90; Indiv $50; AI Student free online mem
Income: University funding & private donations
Special Subjects: Bronzes, Painting-American, Painting-European, Prints, Sculpture
Collections: Advancing American Art Collection, The Louise Hauss & David Brent Miller Audubon Coll, American & European 19th & 20th century art including paintings, sculpture & prints, The Bill L Harbert Collection of European Art, monumental mural Alma Mater by William Baggett, The Nelson and Joan Cousins Hartman Collection of Tibetan Bronzes, E Kelund & Thornton Collection of 20th century Mexican Art imprinting the South Collection of southern works on paper
Activities: Classes for adults & children; gallery talks; walking paths with botanical gardens; docent training; lects open to pub; lects for mems only; concerts; gallery talks; tours; sponsoring of competitions; traveling & rotating exhibs; mus related items for sale

BIRMINGHAM

M **BIRMINGHAM MUSEUM OF ART,** 2000 Reverend Abraham Woods Jr Blvd, Birmingham, AL 35203-2205. Tel 205-254-2565; Fax 205-731-9425; Email museum@artsbma.org; Web: www.artsbma.org; *Dir* Graham C Boettcher; *CFO* Johnny McIntosh; *Chief Registrar* Rose Wood; *Creative Dir* James Williams; *Chief Cur & Cur Decorative Arts* Anne Forschler-Tarrasch PhD; *Mgr Vis & Vol Servs* Lindsey Hamnel; *Chief Security* J R Feagins; *Exhibs Designer* Terry Beckham; *Business Office Mgr* Jennifer Powell; *Cur European Art* Robert Schindler; *Sr Cur & Cur Arts of Africa & Americas* Emily G Hanna; *William Cary Hulsey Cur American Art* Katelyn Crawford; *Cur Educ* Rachel White; *Dir Mktg & Commun* Cate McCusker Boehm; *Dir Develop* Kate Tully Delgreco; *Exhibs Officer* Kristi Taft; *Cur Support Group Mgr* Bethany McClellan; *Museum Store Mgr* Kristie Allen
Open Tues - Sat 10 AM - 5 PM, Sun Noon - 5 PM, 1st Fri 10 AM - 9 PM, cl major holidays; No admis fee; Estab 1951 as a general art mus with collections from earliest manifestation of man's creativity to contemporary work. Its goal is to illustrate the highest level of man's artistic work in an art historical context; The 36 galleries are climate controlled; lighting system is modern & controlled to latest safety standards; visit artsbma.org for exhib info; Mem: dues $50 & up
Income: $7,000,000 (financed by mem, city appropriation & annual donations)
Purchases: $650,000
Library Holdings: Auction Catalogs, Book Volumes, Clipping Files, DVDs, Exhibition Catalogs, Original Documents, Pamphlets, Periodical Subscriptions, Records
Special Subjects: African Art, Afro-American Art, American Indian Art, American Western Art, Asian Art, Baroque Art, Ceramics, Costumes, Decorative Arts, Drawings, Enamels, Etchings & Engravings, Folk Art, Furniture, Glass, Jade, Landscapes, Pre-Columbian Art, Oriental Art, Painting-American, Painting-British, Painting-Dutch, Painting-European, Painting-French, Painting-Italian, Painting-Japanese, Photography, Porcelain, Portraits, Pottery, Primitive art, Prints, Religious Art, Renaissance Art, Sculpture, Silver, Textiles
Collections: English ceramics & silver, American painting & sculpture, American decorative arts 19th-20th centuries, Ethnographic Collection, African, American Indian, Pre-Columbian works, Oriental Collection, Indian, Korean, Chinese & Southeast Asian works, Oriental Rug Collection, European paintings, Wedgwood collection, photography, prints and drawings, 18th-19th centuries, American Decorative Arts, 19th-20th Centuries, Renaissance 20th Century Art
Publications: Quarterly newsletter; catalogues of spec exhibs & permanent collections; self-guided tour brochures; teacher packets
Activities: Classes for adults & children; docent training; lects open to pub, lects for mems only, 6 vis lectrs per yr; concerts; gallery talks; tours; fells; competitions; individual paintings lent to other mus; artmobile; book traveling exhibs; originates & circulates traveling exhibs; mus shop sells books, reproductions, prints and gifts

L **Clarence B Hanson Jr Library**, 2000 Rev Abraham Woods Jr Blvd, Birmingham, AL 35203. Tel 205-297-8065; Fax 205-254-2714; Email library@artsBMA.org; Web: www.ArtsBMA.org; *Mus Dir* Graham C Boettcher PhD
Open by appt only; No admis fee; Estab 1951; Reference only
Income: Financed by city & private funding
Library Holdings: Auction Catalogs, Book Volumes 25,000, CD-ROMs, Clipping Files, Compact Disks, DVDs, Exhibition Catalogs, Manuscripts, Memorabilia, Original Documents, Other Holdings, Pamphlets, Periodical Subscriptions 110, Records, Slides, Video Tapes
Special Subjects: Drawings, American Western Art, Art History, Asian Art, Ceramics, Decorative Arts, Painting-American, Painting-European, Porcelain, Pre-Columbian Art, Primitive art, Afro-American Art, Film, Folk Art, Glass, Jade, Landscapes
Collections: Kress Collection of Italian Renaissance Art, Beeson Wedgewood Collection, Lamprecht Collection of Cast Iron Art, Hitt Collection of 19th Century French Furniture, Ireland Sculpture Garden, Oliver Collection of English Porcelain, Collins Collection of English Ceramics, Cooper Collection of Rugs, Simon Collection of Art of the American West, Cargo Collection of American Quilts
Activities: Classes for adults & children; dramatic progs; docent training; lects open to pub, 30 vis lectrs per yr; concerts; gallery talks; tours; sponsoring of competitions; Vol of Yr award; Youth Art Month Juried Competition; scholarships; exten prog to Jefferson and Shelby counties; approx 6 traveling exhibs per yr; originates traveling exhibs to pub mus and galleries; mus shop sells publications, books, jewelry, toys, fine art, decorative arts, handicrafts & stationery

L **BIRMINGHAM PUBLIC LIBRARY,** Arts, Literature & Sports Department, 2100 Park Pl, Birmingham, AL 35203-2794. Tel 205-226-3600; Email hm@bham.lib.al.us; Web: www.bham-lib.al.us; *Exec Dir* Floyd Council
Open Mon - Tues 9 AM - 8 PM, Wes - Sat 9 AM - 6 PM, Sun 2 - 6 PM; Estab 1886 to serve the Jefferson County area
Income: Financed by city & state appropriations, pub & pvt grants
Library Holdings: Audio Tapes, Book Volumes 40,000, Cassettes, Compact Disks, DVDs, Fiche, Framed Reproductions 200, Periodical Subscriptions 155, Prints, Records, Video Tapes
Special Subjects: Architecture, Art History, Asian Art, Decorative Arts, Folk Art, Graphic Design, History of Art & Archaeology, Islamic Art, Mixed Media, Pewter, Porcelain, Portraits, Pottery, Pre-Columbian Art, Sculpture

M **BIRMINGHAM SOUTHERN COLLEGE,** Doris Wainwright Kennedy Art Center, 900 Arkadelphia Rd, Birmingham, AL 35254-0002; PO Box 549021, Birmingham, AL 35254. Tel 205-226-4928; Email kspies@bsc.edu; Web: www.bsc.edu; *Prof* Jim Neel; *Prof* Pamela Venz; *Prof* Steve Cole; *Prof* Kevin Shook; *Prof* Timothy Smith; *Prof* Kathleen Spies
Open Mon - Fri 8:30 AM - 4:45 PM; No admis fee
Income: Financed by the college
Exhibitions: Steve Cole faculty exhib

M **SLOSS FURNACES NATIONAL HISTORIC LANDMARK,** 20 32nd St N, Birmingham, AL 35222-1236. Tel 205-254-2025; Email marshall@slossfurnaces.com; Web: www.slossfurnaces.com; *Exec Dir* John W Nixon Jr; *Admin Svcs Mgr* Niki Frazier; *Cur & Historian* Karen Utz; *Educ* Ty Malugani; *Metal Arts* Marshall Christie
Open Tues - Sat 10 AM - 4 PM, Sun Noon - 4 PM; No admis fee; Estab 1983 as mus of industrial history, former blast furnace plant; temporary exhibitions, especially in metal arts
Income: Financed by City of Birmingham
Library Holdings: Audio Tapes, Book Volumes, CD-ROMs, Cassettes, Clipping Files, DVDs, Manuscripts, Maps, Memorabilia, Original Art Works, Original Documents, Pamphlets, Photographs, Prints, Records, Reels, Sculpture, Slides, Video Tapes
Special Subjects: Metalwork, Historical Material
Activities: Classes for adults & children; festivals; events; kids club; dramatic progs; docent training; lects open to pub; concerts; tours; gallery talks; mus shop sells books, magazines, original art, prints, original art, metal art

M **SPACE ONE ELEVEN, INC,** 2409 2nd Ave N, Birmingham, AL 35203-3809. Tel 205-328-0553; Web: www.spaceoneeleven.org; *Co-Founder & CEO* Peter Prinz; *Dir Progs* Cheryl Lewis; *Arts Educ Coordr* Janna Phillips
Open Tues - Fri 10 AM - 5 PM and by appt; No admis fee; Estab 1986 to explore, communicate & develop experimental ideas, issues & new work; 10,000 sq ft; twin 100-year old warehouses, 1200 sq ft of galleries, windows exhibition space, artist projects & education studios, rental facilities
Activities: Classes for children; lects open to pub; gallery talks; financial assistance to children in city center arts program; book traveling exhibitions; originate traveling exhibitions; sales shop sells ceramics & art goods

M **UNIVERSITY OF ALABAMA AT BIRMINGHAM,** Abroms-Engel Institute for the Visual Arts, 1221 10th Ave S, Birmingham, AL 35205. Tel 205-975-6436; Email aeiva@uab.edu; Web: uab.edu/cas/aeiva; *Cur* John Fields; *Colls Mgr & Coordr Exhibs & Progs* Christina McClellan; *Events, Membership & Vis Svcs Coordr* Samantha Roberts
Open Mon - Fri 10 AM - 6 PM, Sat noon - 6 PM; No admis fee; Mem: dues $15 - $1,000
Income: Financed by university & private donations
Special Subjects: African Art, Afro-American Art, American Indian Art, Architecture, Asian Art, Ceramics, Collages, Decorative Arts, Drawings, Eskimo Art, Etchings & Engravings, Furniture, Graphics, Historical Material, Jade, Landscapes, Oriental Art, Painting-American, Photography, Portraits, Prints, Silver, Woodcuts
Collections: Contemporary art, Student & faculty works since 1950, Works on paper since 1750
Exhibitions: Excavating the Seventies Parts 1 & 2
Publications: Exhibit catalogs
Activities: Lect open to pub, 2 vis lectrs per year; gallery talks; tours; competitions; awards; scholarships offered; individual and original objects of art lent to qualified mus & galleries; book traveling exhibitions; mus shop sells gallery publications & posters

DAPHNE

M **AMERICAN SPORT ART MUSEUM AND ARCHIVES,** One Academy Dr, Daphne, AL 36526-7055. Tel 251-626-3303; Fax 251-621-8829; Email asama@ussa.edu; Web: www.asama.org; *CEO* Dr T J Rosandich
Open Mon - Fri 9 AM - 4 PM; No admis fee; Estab 1984; dedicated to the preservation of sports history, art & literature; over 1,800 pieces of fine sport art in all mediums; Average Annual Attendance: 5,000
Special Subjects: Afro-American Art, American Indian Art, Bronzes, Calligraphy, Collages, Marine Painting, Painting-American, Painting-Australian, Painting-European, Painting-Spanish, Photography, Posters, Pottery, Prints, Sculpture
Collections: bronze sculptures, paintings, murals, lithographs, photography, prints, posters
Exhibitions: Wyland-Sport Art for the Green Olympics original artwork on display-ongoing
Publications: The Academy; The Sport Journal-www.thesportjournal.org; The Sport Digest-www.thesportdigest.com
Activities: Guided tours; competitions; Academy's Sport Artist of the Year-see www.asama.org; originates traveling exhibitions to universities; shop sells books, original art, reproductions, prints, clothing & more

DECATUR

M **JOHN C CALHOUN STATE COMMUNITY COLLEGE,** Art Gallery, 6250 Hwy 31 Decatur, AL 35609; PO Box 2216, Decatur, AL 35609-2216. Tel 256-306-2500, 306-2695; Fax 256-306-2925; *Pres* Dr Richard Carpenter; *Dept Chair* John Colagross; *Art Instr* Katherine Vaughn
Open weekdays 9AM-5PM, special weekend openings; No admis fee; Estab 1965 to provide temporary exhibits of fine art during the school year for the benefit of the surrounding three county area & for the students & faculty of the col; Located in a fine arts building completed June 1979, the gallery has 105 linear ft of carpeted wall space with adjustable incandescent track lighting & fluorescent general lights in a controlled & well-secured environment; Average Annual Attendance: 20,000
Special Subjects: Graphics
Collections: Permanent collection consists of graphics collection as well as selected student & faculty works
Exhibitions: Student Art Exhibit; Student Photographs; Faculty Exhibit
Publications: Announcements; exhibition catalogs
Activities: Classes for adults; lect open to public, 3 vis lectrs per yr; gallery talks; tours; competitions with awards; scholarships and fels offered; individual paintings & original objects of art lent to museums, galleries & college art departments; lending collection contains 40 original art works & 85 original prints; book traveling exhibitions, biannually

DOTHAN

M **WIREGRASS MUSEUM OF ART,** 126 Museum Ave, Dothan, AL 36303-4802; PO Box 1624, Dothan, AL 36302. Tel 334-794-3871; Fax 334-792-9035; Email delemmer@wiregrassmuseum.org; Web: www.wiregrassmuseum.org; *Exec Dir* Susan Robertson; *Pres* Harry Hall; *Dir Community Rels* Deidre Frith; *Spec Events Mng* Holly Roberts; *Assoc Cur* Alison Beeson
Open Tues - Sat 10 AM - 5 PM, cl Mon & Sun; No Admis fee; Estab 1988 to provide exhibits & educational programs; Seven galleries & children's hands-on gallery; Average Annual Attendance: 25,000; Mem: 850; dues $25 - $3000
Income: $250,000 (financed by mem, city appropriation, special events & fees)
Special Subjects: Afro-American Art, Ceramics, Collages, Costumes, Decorative Arts, Drawings, Etchings & Engravings, Folk Art, Glass, Glass, Graphics, Jewelry, Juvenile Art, Landscapes, Latin American Art, Mosaics, Painting-American, Painting-American, Photography, Porcelain, Portraits, Pottery, Prints, Prints, Reproductions, Sculpture, Silver, Stained Glass, Watercolors, Woodcarvings, Woodcuts
Collections: 19th & 20th century works on paper, decorative arts, paintings & sculpture
Publications: Sketches, bi-monthly newsletter
Activities: Classes for adults & children; docent training; lect open to public, gallery talks, tours; mus shop sells books, original art, reproductions & prints

FAIRHOPE

A **EASTERN SHORE ART ASSOCIATION, INC,** Eastern Shore Art Center, 401 Oak St, Fairhope, AL 36532. Tel 334-928-2228; Fax 334-928-5188; Email brayant@esartcenter.org; Web: esartcenter.org; *Registrar* Sheri Vanche; *Pub Rels Coordr* Charlene Patterson; *Spec Events* Jane Bostrom; *ABC Project Dir* Nancy Raia; *Develop Dir* Marty Albritton
Open Mon - Fri 10 AM - 4 PM, Sat 10 AM - 2 PM, cl Sun, New Year's Day, Thanksgiving & Christmas; No admis fee; Estab 1954 to increase enjoyment of participation in arts; Four galleries change monthly, a fifth gallery is for members only. Maintains library; Average Annual Attendance: 12,000; Mem: 1760
Income: Fundraising, classes, workshops & two outdoor shows
Library Holdings: Book Volumes 700, Clipping Files, Exhibition Catalogs, Memorabilia, Original Art Works, Pamphlets
Collections: Herman Bischoff, drawings, oils & watercolors, Maria Martinez, pottery, Emily Woodward Collection, contemporary American paintings from Gulf coast area, primarily southern artist
Exhibitions: Rotating exhibits monthly
Publications: Monthly newsletter; Yearbook
Activities: Educ prog; classes for adults & children; lects open to pub; concerts quarterly; gallery talks; tours; competitions with awards; schols; outreach educational prog arranges gallery tours, slide progs & portable exhibits; original art lent to local bus; mus shop sells original art & prints

FAYETTE

M **CITY OF FAYETTE, ALABAMA,** Fayette Art Museum, 530 N Temple Ave, Fayette, AL 35555. Tel 205-932-8727; Fax 205-932-8727; Email fayetteartmuseum@yahoo.com; Web: fayetteartmuseum.vpweb.com; *Bd Chmn & Cur* Jack Black; *Asst Cur* Kathy Stoner
Open Mon - Fri 9AM-noon & 1PM-4PM; No admis fee; Estab 1969 to offer on continuous basis exhibits of visual arts free to the pub; All facilities are at Fayette Civic Center: six multi-purpose galleries, seven folk art galleries plus lobby & corridors; 1200 running ft of exhibition space; Average Annual Attendance: 38,000
Income: Financed by city appropriation & Annual Art Festival
Purchases: Very limited purchases of paintings & sculpture
Library Holdings: Auction Catalogs, Audio Tapes, Book Volumes, Cassettes, Memorabilia
Special Subjects: African Art, Afro-American Art, Drawings, Folk Art, Graphics, Landscapes, Metalwork, Miniatures, Painting-American, Painting-Australian, Painting-Canadian, Portraits, Primitive art, Sculpture, Textiles, Watercolors, Woodcarvings, Woodcuts
Collections: 3,700 paintings, 2,600 by Lois Wilson, a former resident, others by local folk artists Jimmy Lee Sudduth, Benjamin Perkins, Fred Webster, Sybil Gibson, Margarette Guinther & Braxton Ponder
Exhibitions: Permanent gallery for Jimmy Lee Sudduth (folk art); Rev Benjamin Perkins (folk art); Fred Webster & Sybil Gibson

Publications: Souls Grown Deep
Activities: Educ prog varies; lects open to pub; gallery talks; tours; individual paintings & original objects of art lent to museums & galleries; originate traveling exhibs to qualified museums

GADSDEN

M **GADSDEN MUSEUM OF ART,** 515 Broad St, Gadsden, AL 35901-3719. Tel 256-546-7365; Fax 256-549-4748; Email museum@cityofgadsden.com; Web: www.gadsdenmuseum.com; *Cur* Ray Wetzel; *Education Coordr* Nicole Papa-Tudor
Open Mon - Sat 10 AM - 4 PM, also open first Fri of month 4 - 8 PM; No admis fee; Estab 1965 to promote, foster, & preserve the collection of paintings, sculpture, artifacts & antiques; 8,000 sq ft; Average Annual Attendance: 8,000; Mem: 75; dues individual $25, family $50
Income: Financed by mem, city & local government & grants
Library Holdings: Book Volumes, Clipping Files, Framed Reproductions, Maps, Memorabilia, Original Art Works, Original Documents, Photographs, Prints, Records, Reproductions, Sculpture
Special Subjects: Folk Art, Furniture, Glass, Graphics, Historical Material, Landscapes, Maps, Photography, Porcelain, Portraits, Pottery, Prints, Sculpture, Silver, Watercolors, Woodcarvings, Woodcuts
Collections: Snelgrove Historical Collection, Fowler Collection (paintings, sculpture & porcelain)
Exhibitions: Quilt exhibit; antique radios; annual juried art show; Alabama's Finest
Activities: Classes for adults & children; workshops; lect open to public, 500 vis lectrs per year; competitions with awards; mus shop sells books, original art, reproductions & prints

HANCEVILLE

M **WALLACE STATE COMMUNITY COLLEGE,** Evelyn Burrow Museum, 801 Main St NW, Hanceville, AL 35077-5462; PO Box 2000, Hanceville, AL 35077-2000. Tel 256-352-8457; Fax 256-352-8314; Email donny.wilson@wallacestate.edu; Web: www.burrowmuseum.org; *Dir* Donny Wilson
Open Tues - Fri 9 AM - 5 PM, Sat 10 AM - 2 PM; No admis fee; Decorative arts from Victorian era to modern times
Special Subjects: Ceramics, Decorative Arts, Furniture, Glass, Porcelain, Portraits, Pottery, Religious Art, Sculpture, Bronzes
Collections: porcelain; pottery; period furnishings; fine art; bronzes; cut glass
Activities: Lect open to pub; gallery talks; tours

HUNTSVILLE

A **HUNTSVILLE ART LEAGUE,** Lowe Mill Arts & Entertainment, 2211 Seminole Dr, Studio 2013 Huntsville, AL 35805. Tel 256-534-3860; Email marciafreeland@lowemill.net; Web: www.lowemill.net; *Pres* Walt Schumacher; *1st VPres* Sandra Lasater; *2nd VPres* Paul Fulda; *Treas* Harriet Dobbins; *Secy* S Renee Prasil
Open Mon - Fri 10 AM - 6 PM, Sat noon - 4 PM; No admis fee; Estab 1957. The League is a nonprofit organization dedicated to promoting & stimulating the appreciation of the visual arts; Circ 200; 70 local artists exhibiting, all mediums, special exhibitions; Average Annual Attendance: 6,000; Mem: 295; dues vary (art or educ interest); meetings held every 2nd Tues of each month
Income: Financed by mem, commissions, grants
Library Holdings: Auction Catalogs, Book Volumes, Clipping Files, Memorabilia, Periodical Subscriptions
Exhibitions: Unique Views (Sept); Annual juried show; rotate art exhibits every month; workshops
Publications: Newsletter on activities & exhibition opportunities in the Southeast, monthly; mem books
Activities: Classes for adults & children; docent training; workshops; gallery talks; tours; sponsoring of competitions; schols; lect open to public, 12 vis lectrs per year; competitions; tours; talks, demos & classes for various at-risk or underserved population; individual paintings & original objects of art leased to banks, restaurants, theaters; lending collection contains original art works, original prints, paintings, photographs, sculpture; organize traveling exhibs to various areas locally; sales shop sells original art, reproductions, prints, jewelry, pottery, fiber arts, small handmade art objects

M **HUNTSVILLE MUSEUM OF ART,** 300 Church St S, Huntsville, AL 35801-4910. Tel 256-535-4350; Fax 256-532-1743; Email info@hsvmuseum.org; Web: www.hsvmuseum.org; *Dir Cur Affairs* Peter J Baldaia; *Cur Colls & Exhibs* David Reyes; *CFO* Debbie Higdon; *Pres & CEO* Clayton Bass; *Deputy Dir* Carolyn Faraci; *Mus Academy Dir* Laura Smith; *Communs Mgr* Jenny Lane; *Security Supvr* Linda Berry
Open Tues - Sat 11 AM - 4 PM, Thurs until 8 PM, Sun 1-4 PM; Admis adults $8, military, seniors 60+, students w/ID, military & educators $7, children 6-11 $4, mems & children under 6 free; group rates available; Estab 1970; 7 galleries & a reception area; Average Annual Attendance: 63,000; Mem: 1200; dues student $20, individual $35, family $60, friend $150, sponsor $300, patron $600, benefactor $1,200, president's circle $2,500
Income: $1,000,000 (financed by mem, city appropriation, grants & support groups)
Purchases: $25,000
Special Subjects: Painting-American, Photography, Prints, Sculpture, Watercolors
Collections: American art, 1700-present, including paintings & works on paper, local & regional art, African art, Oriental art
Exhibitions: Annual Youth Art Month & Holiday Celebrations Exhibitions
Publications: Brochures; catalogs, occasionally; Museum Calendar, quarterly
Activities: Classes for adults & children; internships; docent training; Partnership in Art Educ prog; lects open to pub, 3-4 vis lectrs per yr; concerts; gallery talks; tours; competitions with awards; schols offered; collection loan prog; book traveling exhibs 8-10 per yr; originate traveling exhibs

L **Reference Library,** 300 Church St SW, Huntsville, AL 35801-4910. Tel 256-535-4350; Fax 256-532-1743; Email info@hsvmuseum.org; Web: www.hsvmuseum.org; *Curatorial Affairs Dir* Peter J Baldaia; *Dir* Christopher Madkour; *Dir Educ* Laura E Smith
Open Tue, Wed & Fri - Sat 11 AM - 5 PM, Thurs 11 AM - 8 PM, Sun noon - 5 PM, closed on Monday; Admis adults $10, children 6-11 $5, free to members & children under 6, discount to seniors over 60, military, students with proper ID & people in groups of 10 or more; Estab 1970 to bring art & people together; 22,000 sq ft of gallery space in 13 galleries; Average Annual Attendance: 100,000; Mem: 3200; dues family $75
Income: Memberships, corporate underwriting, city funding, grants
Library Holdings: Book Volumes 3800, CD-ROMs 5-10, Clipping Files, Exhibition Catalogs 2000, Pamphlets, Periodical Subscriptions 20, Slides, Video Tapes 25
Special Subjects: Antiquities-Greek, Architecture, Bronzes, Ceramics, Crafts, Decorative Arts, Etchings & Engravings, Glass, Graphic Arts, Metalwork, Miniatures, Oriental Art, Photography, Pottery, Sculpture
Collections: 19th & 20th century American art with an emphasis on the region of the South; Asian art, African art, postwar graphics, Sellars Collection of Art by American Women
Exhibitions: Biennial Red Clay Survey Exhibition, southern contemporary art; Encounters solo exhibitions of contemporary southern art; Permanent collection exhibitions; travelling exhibitions
Publications: Family Gallery Guides, exhib catalogues
Activities: Classes for adults & children; docent training; outreach into classroom; lects open to pub, lects for members only; 2 vis lectrs per yr; concerts; gallery talks; tours; competitions with awards; schols offered; 4 book traveling exhibs per yr; originate traveling exhibs regionally & nationally; mus shop sells books, original art, reproductions, prints

M **UNIVERSITY OF ALABAMA AT HUNTSVILLE,** Union Grove Gallery & University Center Gallery, Roberts Hall, Room 313, Huntsville, AL 35899. Tel 256-890-6114; Fax 256-824-6438; Email art@uah.edu; *Gallery Adminr* Kristy From; *Staff Asst* Marylyn Coffey
Open Mon - Fri 12:30 - 4:30 PM; No admis fee; Estab 1975; An intimate & small renovated chapel with a reserved section for exhibits located in the University Center; Average Annual Attendance: 1,800
Income: Financed by admin
Special Subjects: Drawings, Painting-American, Photography, Prints, Sculpture
Exhibitions: Contemporary artwork (US & international); Annual Juried Exhibition
Activities: Lects open to pub, 7-10 vis lectrs per yr; gallery talks; competitions with awards; individual paintings & original objects of art lent; book traveling exhibs 3 per yr; originate traveling exhibs

MADISON

M **CLAY HOUSE MUSEUM,** 16 Main St, Madison, AL 35758. Tel 256-325-1018; Facebook
Open by appointment

MOBILE

M **HISTORY MUSEUM OF MOBILE,** 111 S Royal St, Mobile, AL 36602-3101; PO Box 2068, Mobile, 36652-2068. Tel 251-208-7569; Fax 251-208-7686; Email museum@cityofmobile.org; Web: www.museumofmobile.com; *Dir* Ron Jamro; *Cur Educ* Jennifer Theeck; *Cur Colls* Nick Beeson; *Asst Cur* Scott Corcoran; *Researcher* Charles Torrey
Open Mon - Sat 9 AM - 5 PM, Sun 1 - 5 PM, cl some city holidays; Admis adults $10, youth 13-17 $7.50, children 6-12 $5, children 5 & under free; Estab 1964 to interpret Mobile's history; A 21st Century state of the history museum; five exhibit experiences offer people of all ages the chance to learn about more than 300 yrs of Mobile history; permanent exhibit presents survey of history of Mobile area; Average Annual Attendance: 66,000; Mem: 400; dues $15 - $10,000
Income: Financed by city appropriation
Library Holdings: Book Volumes, Clipping Files, Framed Reproductions, Manuscripts, Maps, Memorabilia, Original Art Works, Original Documents, Other Holdings, Pamphlets, Periodical Subscriptions, Photographs, Prints, Records, Sculpture, Slides, Video Tapes
Special Subjects: Archaeology, Ceramics, Coins & Medals, Decorative Arts, Historical Material, Manuscripts, Maps, Silver
Collections: CSS Hunley, Queens of Mobile Mardi Gras, Admiral Raphael Semmes Collection: incl Confederate presentation sword, along with a presentation cased revolver & accessories, books, paintings, documents, personal papers & ship models, Mardi Gras Gallery, 80,000 items reflecting the entire span of the history of Mobile
Exhibitions: Eudora Welty (traveling exhibit from in-house)
Publications: Exhibition & collection catalogs
Activities: Pub progs for adults & children; docent training; teacher training; lects open to pub; 11-16 lectrs per yr; galley talks; tours; concerts; sponsored competitions; Volunteer Mobile Inc Heart of Gold 2001 award; Main St Mobile's Leadership Achievement award; Herstory award; original objects of art lent to other mus; originate book traveling exhibs 1-4 per yr; organize traveling exhibs to Eudora Welty & to various venues; mus shop sells books, gifts, jewelry, toys, clothing, magnets, original art, reproductions, prints, Mobile mementoes & unique gifts; evening spec event rentals, birthday parties, daytime event space; Ft Conde & Phoenix Fire Mus

L **Reference Library,** 111 S Royal St, Mobile, AL 36602-3101; PO Box 2068, Mobile, AL 36652-2068. Tel 334-208-7569; Fax 334-208-7686; Web: www.museumofmobile.com; *Research Historian* Charles Torrey
Estab 1964; For reference only
Library Holdings: Book Volumes 3000, Clipping Files, Memorabilia, Original Art Works, Periodical Subscriptions 12, Photographs, Prints, Sculpture, Slides

M **Carlen House,** 54 S Carlen St, Mobile, AL 36606; PO Box 2068, Mobile, AL 36652-2068. Tel 251-208-7569; Web: www.museumofmobile.com

Temporarily closed; Estab 1970 to preserve an authentic representation of Southern architecture; The Carlen House is an important representation of Mobile's unique contribution to American regional architecture. It is a fine example of the Creole Cottage as it evolved from the French Colonial form & was adapted for early American use. The house was erected in 1842; furnishings are from the collections of the Museum of the City of Mobile & are typical of a house of that period; Average Annual Attendance: 30,000
Income: Financed by city appropriation
Activities: Lects open to pub; group tours are conducted by guides in period costumes who emphasize aspects of everyday life in Mobile in the mid-nineteenth century. The making of material is demonstrated by the guide who cards wool, spins fibers & weaves cloth; individual paintings & original objects of art lent to other mus; sales shop sells books, slides & souvenirs

M **MOBILE MUSEUM OF ART,** 4850 Museum Dr, Mobile, AL 36608-1917. Tel 251-208-5200; Fax 251-208-5201; Email marylee.montgomery@mobilemuseumofart.com; Web: www.mobilemuseumofart.com; Cable FAMOS; *Dir* Deborah Velders; *Dir Fin* Lianne Kenney; *Cur Exhibs* Donan Klooz; *Mgr Curatorial Affairs* Kurtis Thomas; *Cur Adult Educ* Angie King; *Cur Educ* Kim Wood; *Spec Events Mgr* Meredith Ivy; *Vol Coordr* Theresa Orrell; *Cur Progs* Elizabet Elliot; *Mgr External Affairs* Stan Hackney; *Media Mktg Specialist* Mary Beth Lursen; *Mgr Pub Rels* Glenn Robertson
Open Tues - Wed & Fri - Sun 10 AM - 5 PM, Thurs 10 AM - 9 PM, cl Mon; Admis adults $12, seniors $10, students $8, children under 6 free; Estab 1964 to foster the appreciation of art & provide art educ programs for the community; Circ Reference non-circulating art libraries; Primarily American 19th & 20th Century, contemporary crafts; Average Annual Attendance: 37,500; Mem: Patron $1,000, supporting $500, assoc $250, friend $150, family $75, individual $45
Income: Financed by mem, city appropriation & state grants, county & foundations
Library Holdings: Auction Catalogs, Book Volumes, Exhibition Catalogs, Periodical Subscriptions, Slides
Special Subjects: African Art, Afro-American Art, American Indian Art, American Western Art, Antiquities-Byzantine, Antiquities-Roman, Asian Art, Bronzes, Ceramics, Collages, Crafts, Decorative Arts, Drawings, Enamels, Eskimo Art, Etchings & Engravings, Folk Art, Furniture, Glass, Graphics, Islamic Art, Jewelry, Landscapes, Marine Painting, Metalwork, Oriental Art, Painting-American, Painting-Australian, Painting-British, Painting-Canadian, Painting-Dutch, Painting-European, Painting-French, Painting-Italian, Photography, Porcelain, Portraits, Posters, Pottery, Prints, Religious Art, Sculpture, Silver, Textiles, Watercolors, Woodcarvings, Woodcuts
Collections: American Crafts, 19th & 20th century American & European paintings, sculpture, prints, & decorative arts, Chinese ceramics, European paintings & sculpture, 17th to 20th century, Southern furniture, 1930s - 1940s paintings & graphics, International Contemporary Glass Collection, Wellington Collection of Wood Engravings
Publications: MMoA Mem Bulletin, 4 per year; Richard Jolley & Tommie Rush: A Life in Glass
Activities: Classes for adults & children; docent training; lects open to pub, gallery talks, tours, competitions with awards; scholarships offered; individual paintings & objects of art lent; books traveling exhibs; mus shop sells books, original art, jewelry & gifts

L **Library**, 4850 Museum Dr, Mobile, AL 36608-1917. Tel 251-208-5200; Fax 251-208-5201; Email prichelson@mobilemuseumofart.com; Web: www.MobileMuseumofArt.com; *Dir* Deborah Velders; *Cur Educ* Kim Wood; *Mgr Curatorial Affairs* Kurtis Thomas; *Cur Exhibs* Donan Klooz
Open Mon - Sat 10 AM - 5 PM, Sun 1 PM - 5 PM; Admis $10 general plus additional for special exhibitions; Estab 1963; For reference only; Average Annual Attendance: 90,000; Mem: 3000
Income: City of Mobile; pvt 501(c)3
Purchases: American Art, craft, Berbizan
Library Holdings: Auction Catalogs, Book Volumes 1800, Clipping Files, DVDs, Exhibition Catalogs, Framed Reproductions, Pamphlets, Periodical Subscriptions 20, Photographs, Prints, Reproductions, Slides
Special Subjects: Asian Art, Crafts, Decorative Arts, Painting-American, Painting-European
Publications: Numerous
Activities: Classes for adults and children; dramatic progs; docent training; film; lects open to public; lects for mems only; 3 vis lectrs per yr; gallery talks; tours; sponsoring of competitions; 5 book traveling exhibs per yr; originates traveling exhibs to Southern art museums; mus shop sells books

L **UNIVERSITY OF SOUTH ALABAMA,** Ethnic American Slide Library, 307 N University Blvd, Dept Arts & Art History Mobile, AL 36608-3074. Tel 251-460-6101; Fax 334-414-8294
Open daily 8 AM - 5 PM; No admis fee; Estab for the acquisition of slides of works produced by Afro-American, Mexican-American & Native American artists & the distribution of duplicate slides of these works to educational institutions & individuals engaged in research
Library Holdings: Slides
Collections: 19th & 20th centuries ethnic American art works in ceramics, drawing, painting, photography, printmaking, sculpture
Publications: Slide Catalog

MONTEVALLO

M **UNIVERSITY OF MONTEVALLO,** The Gallery, Sta 6400, Art Dept Montevallo, AL 35115. Tel 205-665-6400; Fax 205-665-6383; Email terrell@montevallo.edu; Web: www.montevallo.edu/art; *Gallery Dir* Mr Lee Somers
Open Mon - Fri 10 AM - 4 PM; No admis fee; Estab Sept 1977 to supply students & pub with high quality contemporary art; The gallery is 27 x 54 ft with track lighting; no windows; Average Annual Attendance: 3,000
Income: Financed by state appropriation & regular dept budget
Collections: WPA Prints
Exhibitions: Rotating exhibits
Publications: High quality catalogs & posters
Activities: Management classes; lects open to pub, 4-5 vis lectrs per yr; gallery talks; originate traveling exhibs

MONTGOMERY

M **ALABAMA DEPARTMENT OF ARCHIVES & HISTORY,** Museum of Alabama, 624 Washington Ave, Montgomery, AL 36130-3003. Tel 334-242-4435; Fax 334-240-3433; Email maryjo.scott@archives.alabama.gov; Web: www.museum.albama.gov; *Asst Dir Government Records* Tracey Berezansky; *Asst Dir Pub Svcs* Debbie Pendleton; *Dir* Steve Murray; *Cur Colls* Bob Bradley; *Mus Shop Mgr* Allison Gore; *Asst Dir Admin* Steve Wheat
Open Mon - Sat 8:30 AM - 4:30 PM; No admis fee; Estab 1901; Reference only; Average Annual Attendance: 35,000
Income: Financed by state appropriation
Special Subjects: American Indian Art, Archaeology, Decorative Arts, Dioramas, Furniture, Historical Material, Manuscripts, Maps, Military Art, Miniatures, Painting-American, Period Rooms, Photography, Portraits, Sculpture, Silver, Textiles
Collections: Hands On Gallery & Grandma's Attic (for children of all ages)
Exhibitions: Alabama Voices; First Alabamians; Alabama Treasury
Activities: Classes for adults; docent training; lects open to pub, 15 vis lectrs per yr; gallery talks; tours; sales shop sells books, Civil War & Civil Rights related materials, reproduced arrowheads, jewelry & posters

M **MONTGOMERY MUSEUM OF FINE ARTS,** One Museum Dr, Montgomery, AL 36117; PO Box 230819, Montgomery, AL 36123-0819. Tel 334-240-4333; Fax 334-240-4384; Email museuminfo@mmfa.org; Web: www.mmfa.org; *Dir* Mark M Johnson; *Asst Dir Opers* Steve Shuemake; *Develop Officer* Jill Barry; *Dir Mktg & Pub Rels* Cynthia Milledge; *Sr Cur Art* Margaret Lynne Ausfeld; *Cur Art* Michael Panhorst; *Registrar* Pamela Bransford; *Asst Cur Educ* Donna Pickens; *Librn* Amy Johnson; *Develop Asst* Jennifer Eitzmann; *Spec Events Coordr* Blake Rosen; *Museum Shop Mgr* Ward Chesser; *Vol Coordr* Brenda Daly; *Preparator & Designer* Jeff Dutton; *Bd Pres* Roger Spain; *Cur Art* Jennifer Jankauskas
Open Tues - Sat 10 AM - 5 PM, Thurs evening until 9 PM, Sun Noon - 5 PM; No admis fee; Estab 1930 to generally promote the cultural artistic & higher educ life of the city of Montgomery by all methods that may be properly pursued by a mus or art gallery; Mus housed in 73,000 sq ft facility located on 35 acres in landscaped park, adjacent to the Alabama Shakespeare festival. Galleries occupy lower & upper levels of two story neo-palladian structure. An educ wing includes Artworks a 4,400 sq ft hands-on, interactive gallery & studios. The Weil Graphics Arts Study Center provides an environment for small specialized exhibitions & educational programs emphasizing works of art on paper. It is designed as a conference space with av & computer resources to serve advanced school groups & seminar participants. 240 seat auditorium; Average Annual Attendance: 160,000; Mem: 1700; dues dir circle $1,200-$5,000, patron $150-$1,199, general $45-$149; ann meeting in Oct
Income: Financed by mem, city & county appropriations & grants
Purchases: Max Weber (American 1881-1961) View of Roslyn, NY; 1922-1925 oil on canvas; Thomas Hart Benton (American 1889-1974; Ozark Autumn. 1949 gifts of the Ida Bell Young Art Acquisition Fund; Harvey Littleton (American 1922-2013); Orange Triple Movement 1983, Decorative Arts Fund
Library Holdings: Auction Catalogs, Book Volumes, Clipping Files, Exhibition Catalogs, Pamphlets, Periodical Subscriptions, Photographs, Slides, Video Tapes
Special Subjects: Decorative Arts, Drawings, Etchings & Engravings, Folk Art, Glass, Graphics, Juvenile Art, Landscapes, Painting-American, Photography, Porcelain, Portraits, Prints, Sculpture, Watercolors, Woodcuts
Collections: American paintings, sculpture & works on paper from the 18th century to contemporary, European old master prints, First period Worcester porcelain & Chinese export porcelain, American historical glass & studio art glass of the 20th & 21st centuries, American self-taught art, specifically artists from Alabama & the American south, African Art
Publications: Annual Report; On Exhibit quarterly magazine; exhibitions catalogs for selected shows
Activities: Classes for adults & children; docent training; lects open to pub, 20 vis lectrs per yr; films; concerts; gallery talks; tours; schols & fels offered; individual paintings & original objects of art lent to galleries which meet AAM standards for security & preservation; book traveling exhibs 12 per yr; originate traveling exhibs, national & international; mus shop sells books, original art, reproductions, prints & gift items

L **Library**, One Museum Dr, Montgomery, AL 36117; PO Box 230819, Montgomery, AL 36123-0819. Tel 334-240-4333; Fax 334-240-4384; Web: www.mmfa.org; *Dir* Mark M Johnson; *Librn* Amy Johnson; *Colls Information Specialist* Sarah Puckitt; *Cur Art* Jennifer Jankauskas; *Cur Art* Dr Michael Panhorst; *Sr Cur Art* Margaret Lynne Ausfeld; *Deputy Dir Develop* Jill Barry; *Asst Dir Opers* Steve Shuemake; *Dirk Mktg & Pub Relations* Cynthia Milledge; *Cur Educ* Tim Brown; *Asst Cur Educ* Donna Pickens; *Asst Cur Educ* Alice Novak; *Dir Servs* Tisha Rhodes; *Registrar* Pam Bransford; *Accountant* Jaret Carroll
Open Tues - Sat 10 AM - 5 PM, Thurs 10 AM - 9 PM, Sun noon - 5 PM; No admis fee; Estab 1975 to assist the staff & community with reliable art research material; Circ Non-circ; For reference; Average Annual Attendance: 139,942
Income: Financed by City of Montgomery & Mus Assoc
Purchases: 19th & 20th century American paintings, studio glass
Library Holdings: Auction Catalogs, Book Volumes 5000, Clipping Files, Exhibition Catalogs, Pamphlets, Periodical Subscriptions 25, Photographs, Prints, Slides, Video Tapes
Special Subjects: Afro-American Art, American Indian Art, American Western Art, Architecture, Art Education, Art History, Asian Art, Bronzes, Ceramics, Collages, Commercial Art, Conceptual Art, Crafts, Decorative Arts, Drawings, Embroidery, Enamels, Eskimo Art, Etchings & Engravings, Ethnology, Folk Art, Furniture, Glass, Graphic Arts, Graphic Design, History of Art & Archaeology, Illustration, Industrial Design, Islamic Art, Ivory, Landscape Architecture, Landscapes, Latin American Art, Manuscripts, Metalwork, Mexican Art, Mixed Media, Oriental Art, Painting-American, Photography, Porcelain, Portraits, Posters, Pottery, Pre-Columbian Art, Primitive art, Printmaking, Prints, Religious Art, Restoration & Conservation, Sculpture, Silver, Southwestern Art, Stained Glass, Tapestries, Textiles, Video, Watercolors, Woodcuts

Collections: 19th & 20th century American paintings, studio glass, sculptures, old master prints, southern regional art, decorative arts, African art
Publications: Material Transformations
Activities: Classes for adults & children; docent training; dramatic progs; lects open to pub; 68 vis lectrs per yr; gallery talks; tours; concerts; sponsoring of competitions; awards, Docent Prog & Vol Recognition; schols; extension prog, Montgomery City school students; 4-6 book traveling exhibs per yr; organize traveling exhibs to other regional & nat mus; mus shop sells books, original art, reproductions, prints & children's items; Art Works

PORTRAIT SOCIETY OF AMERICA
For further information, see National and Regional Organizations

M **TUSKEGEE INSTITUTE NATIONAL HISTORIC SITE,** George Washington Carver & The Oaks, 1212 W Montgomery Rd Montgomery, AL 36083. Tel 334-727-3200; Fax 334-727-1448; Web: www.nps.gov.tuin; *Supt* Sandra L Taylor
Open 9 AM - 4:30 PM, cl New Year's, Thanksgiving & Christmas; No admis fee; Original mus estab 1941 & National Park in 1976 to interpret life & work of George Washington Carver & the history of Tuskegee Institute; Maintains small reference library; Average Annual Attendance: 50,000
Income: Financed by federal funds
Collections: Artifacts interpreting life & work of George Washington Carver & history of Tuskegee Institute, life & contributions of Booker T Washington
Exhibitions: Exhibitions of local artwork 6-8 time per yr
Activities: Lects open to pub; gallery talks; guided tours; sponsor competitions with awards; individual & original objects of art lent to other parks & museums; lending limited to photos, films, slides & reproductions; book traveling exhibs; originate traveling exhibs; sales shop sells books, reproductions, prints & slides

NORTHPORT

M **KENTUCK MUSEUM ASSOCIATION, INC,** Kentuck Art Center & Festival of the Arts, 503 Main Ave, Northport, AL 35476-4483. Tel 205-758-1257; Fax 205-758-1258; Email kentuck@kentuck.org; Web: www.kentuck.org; *Exec Dir* Shweta Gamble; *Asst Dir* Emily Leigh; *Prog Mgr* Michaela Lewellyn; *Opers Mgr* Anden Houben
Open Tues - Fri 9 AM - 5 PM, Sat 10 AM - 4:30 PM, cl Sun; No admis fee; Estab 1971 to perpetuate the arts, empower artists & engage the community; Exhibs open ea month in the Main Avenue Gallery & the Clarke Gallery; total 24+ ea yr; Average Annual Attendance: 12,000 festival; 6,000 art ctr; Mem: 350; dues $30-$1,000
Income: $399,950 (financed by mem, city & state appropriations, rental of studios, workshops, shop sales, festival ticket sales & booth rentals & other proceeds, corporate sponsorships)
Exhibitions: Exhibits change monthly
Activities: Classes for adults & children; lect open to public, 6 vis lectrs per year; competitions & awards; sales shop sells books, original art, crafts

SELMA

M **STURDIVANT MUSEUM ASSOCIATION,** Sturdivant Museum, 713 Mabry St, Selma, AL 36701-5521; PO Box 1205, Selma, AL 36702-1205. Tel 334-872-5626; Fax 334-872-5626; Email info@sturdivanthall.com; Web: www.sturdivanthall.com; *Cur* Manera S Searcy; *Cur* Nancy Gantt; *Pres* Anne Knight; *VPres* Carolyn Cox; *Mus Shop Mgr* Patty Debardeleben
Open Tues - Sat 10AM-4PM; Admis adults $5, student $2, children under 6 free; group rates available; Estab 1957 as a mus with emphasis on the historical South. Period furniture of the 1850s in a magnificent architectural edifice built 1852-53; Average Annual Attendance: 10,000; Mem: 350; dues $30 - $1000; annual meeting in Sept
Income: Financed by mem, city & county appropriations, events
Library Holdings: Clipping Files, Manuscripts, Original Art Works, Original Documents, Prints
Special Subjects: Architecture, Dolls, Embroidery, Etchings & Engravings, Flasks & Bottles, Furniture, Historical Material, Painting-American, Period Rooms, Porcelain, Portraits, Silver, Drawings, Manuscripts
Collections: Objects of art, period furniture, textiles, dolls, porcelain, Clara Weaver Parish Collection
Publications: Brochure
Activities: Lects open to pub; tours; mus shop sells books, reproductions, prints, lamps, silver, linens & gift items

THEODORE

M **BELLINGRATH GARDENS & HOME,** 12401 Bellingrath Gardens Rd, Theodore, AL 36582-8496. Tel 251-973-2217; Fax 251-973-0540; Email bellingrath@bellingrath.org; Web: www.bellingrath.org; *Dir Mus* Thomas C McGehee; *Exec Dir* Dr William E Barrick; *Vol Coordr* William Darr
Open daily 8 AM - 5 PM; Admis home & garden $21, children 5-12 $13 garden only $13, children under 5 free admis to home & to garden; children 5-12 $7.50; Estab 1932 to perpetuate an appreciation of nature & display man-made objects d'art; The gallery houses the world's largest public display of Boehm porcelain & the Bellingrath Home contains priceless antiques; Average Annual Attendance: 150,000
Income: Financed by Foundation & admissions
Special Subjects: Porcelain
Collections: Early-mid 19th Century American antique furnishings from South, silver & crystal, separate Boehm Gallery from Bellingrath Home: porcelains by Meissen, Dresden, Copeland, Capo di Monte, Sevres, Boehm Collection
Activities: Classes for children; tours; lending collection contains kodachromes, motion pictures, slides; sales shop sells books, magazines, prints, reproductions & slides

TOWN CREEK

M **WATERCOLOR SOCIETY OF ALABAMA,** 1571 County Rd 414, Town Creek, AL 35672. Tel 256-810-9240; Email jaeshep@aol.com; Web: watercolorsocietyofal.org; Facebook; *Pres* Tora Johnson; *Pres Elect* Walt J Costilow; *1st VPres & Exhib Dir* Jaceena Shepard; *2nd VPres* Heike Covell; *3rd VPres* Lyn Gill; *Treas* Charlotte McDavid
Call for hours; Admis free; Estab 1940 to promote watercolor painting; Average Annual Attendance: 120; Mem: 408; open to persons 18 & over; dues $40; annual meeting in spring
Income: financed by mem, exhib competitions, award donations
Publications: Newsletters, quarterly; national catalog
Activities: Classes for adults; art workshops; lect open to public, 2 vis lectrs per year; gallery talks; competitions with prizes, approx $9,000 for national level competition & $1,500 for Alabama competitions

TROY

M **TROY-PIKE CULTURAL ARTS CENTER,** 300 E. Walnut St., Troy, AL 36081. Tel 334-670-2287; Fax 334-808-4025; Email vicki@johnsoncenterarts.org; Web: www.johnsoncenterarts.org; *Exec Dir* Vicki Gaines Pritchett; *Develop Coord* Wiley White; *Exhib Coordr* Jordan Owen Williams
Open Wed - Fri 10 AM - 5 PM & Sat 10 AM - 3 PM; No admis fee; Estab 2000 to promote the arts & educate citizens of Troy; Preserved 1910 post office; Mem: dues $50 & up
Income: Financed by contributions & sponsorships
Special Subjects: Photography
Collections: Paintings & photographs by regional, national & international artists
Exhibitions: Temporary exhibits
Activities: Educ progs; Tours; art events

TUSCALOOSA

A **ARTS & HUMANITIES COUNCIL OF TUSCALOOSA,** Junior League Gallery, Dinah Washington Cultural Arts Center Galleries, 620 Greensboro Ave, Tuscaloosa, AL 35401; PO Box 1117, Tuscaloosa, AL 35403-1117. Tel 205-758-5195; Fax 205-345-2787; Email director@tuscarts.org; Web: www.tuscarts.org; *Exec Dir* Sandra Wolfe; *Gallery Coordr* Sharron Rudowski
Open Mon - Fri 9 AM - 4 PM; No admis fee; Estab 1970 for the develop, promotion & coordination of educational, cultural & artistic activities of the city & county of Tuscaloosa; Offices adjoin historic Bama Theatre; Average Annual Attendance: 3,000; Mem: 500 individual, 40 organization; dues organization $75, individual $50; annual meeting in Oct, meetings quarterly
Income: Financed by mem, city, state & county appropriation
Exhibitions: Jan & Feb: Double Exposure Photography Competition; Feb & March: Visual Art Achievement Award; Nov & Dec: West AL Juried Show
Publications: Arts calendar, monthly newsletter; semi-annual arts magazine, Jubilation
Activities: Dramatic progs; Bama Fanfare (professional performances for students K - 12); Bama Art House movie series; sponsor of educ program called SPECTRA (Special Teaching Resources in the Arts); lects open to pub; concert series, gallery talks; tours; competition sponsorship

M **UNIVERSITY OF ALABAMA,** Sarah Moody Gallery of Art, 103 Garland Hall, Tuscaloosa, AL 35487-0270; UA Box 870270, Tuscaloosa, AL 35487-0270. Tel 205-348-5967 (Art Dept); 205-348-1891; Fax 205-348-0287; Email wtdooley@bama.ua.edu; Web: http://art.ua.edu/gallery/smga/; *Dir* William Dooley; *Exhib Coordr* Vicki Rial
Open Mon - Fri 9 AM - 4:30 PM, Thurs until 8PM; No admis fee; Estab 1946; Exhibitions of national, regional contemporary art; Average Annual Attendance: 1,500-2,000
Income: Financed by the college
Collections: Small collection of paintings, prints, photography, drawings, primarily contemporary
Exhibitions: Exhibits rotate once a month
Publications: Exhibit catalogs
Activities: Lects open to public; 3 vis lectrs per yr; gallery talks; originate traveling exhibs

TUSCUMBIA

A **TENNESSEE VALLEY ART ASSOCIATION,** 511 N Water St, Tuscumbia, AL 35674-1931; PO Box 474, Tuscumbia, AL 35674-0474. Tel 256-383-0533; Fax 256-383-0535; Email tvaa@comcast.net; Web: www.tvaa.net; *Exhibit Coordr* Lucie Ayers; *Exec Dir* Mary Settle-Cooney; *Pub Rels & Mem* Mary Jo Parker; *Tech Dir Ritz Theater* Jake Barrow
Open Mon - Fri 9 AM - 5 PM, Sun 1-3PM; Admis varies, call for details; Incorp 1964 to promote the arts in the Tennessee Valley. Building completed 1972; Main Gallery 60 x 40 ft; West Gallery for small exhibits, meetings and arts and crafts classes. Located one block from the birthplace of Helen Keller in Tuscumbia. During the Helen Keller Festival, TVAC sponsors the Arts and Crafts Festival; Average Annual Attendance: 10,000; Mem: Dues patron $500, benefactor $100, family $50, sustaining $30, student $10, individual $20
Income: $300,000 (financed by appropriations, donations, grants & mem)
Collections: Reynolds Collection of Paintings, TVAA Crafts Collection
Exhibitions: Exhibition South (paintings, sculpture, prints), annual fall juried art show for mid-south states; Spring Photo Show, annual juried; exhibits feature work by national artists, members & students; handicraft exhibits
Activities: Classes for adults and children; dramatic progs; docent training; class instruction in a variety of arts and crafts; workshops & performances in drama; lects open to pub; concerts; competitions with awards; individual paintings lent; book traveling exhibs; mus shop sells books, reproductions, prints, puppets, jewelry, & stationary

ALASKA

ANCHORAGE

M **ALASKA HERITAGE MUSEUM AT WELLS FARGO,** 301 W Northern Lights Blvd, Anchorage, AK 99503-2655. Tel 907-265-2834; Web: www.wellsfargohistory.com/museums/anchorage/
Open Mon - Fri 12 - 4 PM; No admis fee; Average Annual Attendance: 5,000
Special Subjects: American Indian Art, Anthropology, Archaeology, Coins & Medals, Conceptual Art, Dolls, Drawings, Eskimo Art, Ethnology, Gold, Historical Material, Ivory, Jade, Manuscripts, Maps, Painting-American, Photography, Primitive art, Prints, Scrimshaw, Sculpture, Watercolors, Woodcuts
Collections: Alaskan Native cultures, fine art by Alaskan artists
Activities: Educ prog for children; guided tours

M **ALASKA MUSEUM OF SCIENCE & NATURE,** 201 N Bragaw, Anchorage, AK 99508. Tel 907-274-2400; Email akscl@gmx.com; Web: www.alaskamuseum.org; *Dir* Gordon Harper; *Dir* Anne Pasch
Open Thurs - Sat 10 AM - 4 PM, Mon - Weds by appt; Admis adults $8, seniors & military with ID $7, youth 3 - 18 & college student with ID $6, mems & toddlers under 3 free; Mission is to study & exhibit natural history materials relating to Alaska's natural history & to promote and develop educational progs which benefit students & enrich the curricula of schools & univs in Alaska. Nonprofit org; Mem: dues Life $1,000; Gift or Reg Mem $30
Special Subjects: Archaeology, Historical Material
Collections: History on the Alaskan Gold Rush, Alaskan rocks, minerals & fossils, Alaska's oldest known dinosaur, Native American cultural artifacts, 11,100 year-old Northern Paleoindian Hunting Camp
Exhibitions: The Dinosaurs of Darkness
Publications: Nunatak, quarterly newsletter
Activities: Group tours; summer camps for children; volunteer activities; lects; mus related items for sale

A **ALASKA WATERCOLOR SOCIETY,** PO Box 90714, Anchorage, AK 99509-0714. Web: www.akws.org; *Pres* Chris Zafren
No admis fee; Estab 1977; Circ 200; Maintains library; Mem: dues $5 - $25; monthly meeting Sept-Jun 2nd Wed of month
Income: Financed by mem
Exhibitions: Bi-annual juried watercolor exhibit at the Anchorage Museum of History & Art
Activities: Workshops; scholarships offered; originate traveling exhibs

M **ANCHORAGE MUSEUM AT RASMUSON CENTER,** 625 C St, Anchorage, AK 99501. Tel 907-929-9200; Fax 907-929-9290; Email museumdirector@anchoragemuseum.org; Web: www.anchoragemuseum.org; *Dir & CEO* Julie Decker; *Assoc Dir Media & Tech* Craig Suchland; *CFO* Kirsten Newby; *Chief HR Officer* Ann Kjera; *Chief Digital Officer* Doug Adams; *Deputy Dir Facilities & Opers* Brian Steele; *Dir Colls & Chief Conservator* Monica Shah; *Deputy Dir & Chief Cur* Kirsten Anderson; *Chief Devel Officer* Ann Hale; *Dir Exhibs* Ryan Kenny; *Dir Design* Jonny Hayes; *Dir Community Partnerships & Outreach* Adam Baldwin; *Dir Learning & Engagement* Hollis Mickey; *Mktg & Pub Rels Dir* Janet Asaro; *Dir Vis Svcs* Krystal Juba; *Arctic Studies Center Dir* Aron Crowell
Open May to Sept see website for hours, Oct - April Tues-Sat 10 AM - 6 PM, Sun noon - 6 PM; Admis adults $18, AK residents $15, seniors, students, military with ID $12, children 3-12 $9, children 2 & under free; Estab 1968 to collect & display Alaskan art & artifacts of all periods; to present changing exhibs of art, history & science
Library Holdings: Auction Catalogs, Book Volumes, CD-ROMs, Cards, Clipping Files, Compact Disks, DVDs, Exhibition Catalogs, Fiche, Framed Reproductions, Manuscripts, Maps, Memorabilia, Original Documents, Other Holdings, Pamphlets, Periodical Subscriptions, Photographs, Prints, Slides, Video Tapes
Special Subjects: American Indian Art, Anthropology, Archaeology, Carpets & Rugs, Costumes, Crafts, Dolls, Drawings, Eskimo Art, Etchings & Engravings, Ethnology, Historical Material, Ivory, Landscapes, Maps, Painting-American, Photography, Pre-Columbian Art, Primitive art, Prints, Religious Art, Sculpture, Textiles, Watercolors
Exhibitions: Exploration in the North Pacific 1750-1850 Travels; Arctic Transformations: The Jewelry of Denise and Samuel Wallace
Publications: Agayuliyararput: Our Way of Making Prayer: The living tradition of Yupik masks (with University of Washington Press); Painting in the North: Alaskan art in the Anchorage Museum of History & Art; exhibition catalogs; monthly newsletters; occasional papers; A Northern Adventure: The Art of Fred Machetanz; Eskimo Drawings; John Hoover: Art and Life; Sydney Laurence, Painter of the North; Spirit of the North: The Art of Eustace Paul Ziegler; True North: Contemporary Art of the Circumpolar North
Activities: Classes for adults & children; dramatic progs; docent training; lect open to pub; vis lectrs 24-40 per yr; concerts; gallery talks; tours; competitions; awards; individual paintings & original objects of art lent to AAM accredited museums; lending coll contains original art works, original prints, paintings, photographs, sculpture & slides; book traveling exhibs 10 per yr; originate traveling exhibs 2 per yr to 51 AK mus; mus shop sells books, magazines, original art, reproductions, prints, slides, Alaskan Native art, & jewelry

L **Atwood Alaska Resource Center,** 625 C St, Anchorage, AK 99501. Tel 907-929-9235; Email twilliams@anchoragemuseum.org; Web: www.anchoragemuseum.org; *Resource Ctr Mgr/Librn* Teressa Williams; *Archivist* Sara Piasecki
Open Tues - Fri 10 AM - 2 PM, Sat by appointment only; No admis fee; Estab 1968 to maintain archives of Alaska materials, particularly the Cook Inlet area; A non-circulating library for reference use only
Library Holdings: Auction Catalogs, Book Volumes 15,000, Clipping Files, DVDs, Exhibition Catalogs, Fiche, Kodachrome Transparencies, Lantern Slides, Maps 800, Memorabilia, Other Holdings Original documents, Pamphlets, Periodical Subscriptions 48, Photographs 600,000, Reels, Slides, Video Tapes
Special Subjects: American Indian Art, Anthropology, Eskimo Art, Historical Material, Scrimshaw, Art Education, Art History, Dolls, Etchings & Engravings, Ethnology, Ivory, Maps, Photography, Religious Art, Restoration & Conservation
Collections: Alaska Railroad Collection: 19,000 historical photos, Reeve Collection: historical maps, Ward Wells Anchorage Photo Collection 1950-80: 125,000 items, Lu Liston Photo Collection 1920-1950, 6,000 photos, Steve McCutcheon Photo Collection, 150,000, J N Wyman (Upper Koyukon) 1989: 500 glass plates, Vern Brickley Photograph Collection (WWII to 1970) 30,000
Activities: Classes for adults & children; docent training; lects open to pub; gallery talks; mus shop sells books & original art

FAIRBANKS

M **ALASKA HOUSE ART GALLERY,** 1003 Cushman St, Fairbanks, AK 99701. Tel 907-456-6449; Email info@thealaskahouse.com; Web: www.thealaskahouse.com; *Owner* Yolande Fejes; *Owner* Ron Veliz
Open Tues - Sat 11 AM - 6 PM; No admis fee; Estab 1964; to promote & preserve Alaskan art; Contemporary & historical Alaskan art
Collections: Works of Claire Fejes & other Alaskan artists; paintings; drawings; prints; sculpture; carvings; masks; fabric art.
Activities: Poetry readings; special events; lects open to the pub; concerts; gallery talks

A **FAIRBANKS ARTS ASSOCIATION,** Bear Gallery, 2300 Airport Way, Pioneer Park Fairbanks, AK 99707-4014; PO Box 72786, Fairbanks, AK 99707-2786. Tel 907-456-6485; Email info@fairbanksarts.org; Web: www.fairbanksarts.org; *Exec Dir* Jess Pena; *Opers Mgr & Educ Coordr* Angela Bingley; *Bookkeeper* David McDowell; *Visual Arts & Literary Arts Prog Coordr* Alyssa Enriquez
Open winter: Tues - Sat Noon - 6 PM; summer: daily noon - 8 PM; No admis fee; Estab 1965 to promote contemporary & traditional art in the interior of Alaska; 4000 sq ft contemporary art gallery
Income: Financed by city & state appropriations, national grants, contributions
Activities: Classes for adults & children; performing arts progs; docent training; professional workshops; lects open to pub, 10 vis lectrs per yr; gallery talks; tours; competitions with awards; scholarships & fels offered; book traveling exhibs semi-annually; originate traveling exhibs; mus shop sells books, magazines, original art, reproductions & prints

M **UNIVERSITY OF ALASKA,** Museum of the North, 1962 Yukon Dr, Fairbanks, AK 99775; PO Box 756960, Fairbanks, AK 99775-6960. Tel 907-474-7505; Fax 907-474-5469; Email ajonaitis@alaska.edu; Web: www.uaf.edu/museum; *Dir* Pat Druckenmiller; *Devel Coord* Aelin Allegood; *Educ & Public Programs Mgr* Jennifer Arseneau; *Dir of Exhibits* Roger Topp; *Cur* Leonard Kamerling
Open summer (June - Aug) daily 9 AM - 7 PM, winter (Sept - May) Mon - Sat 9 AM - 5 PM, cl Sun; Admis adults $14, youth 5-14 $8; Estab 1929 to collect, preserve & interpret the natural & cultural history of Alaska; Gallery contains 10,000 sq ft of exhibition space divided into 5 ecological & cultural regions; Average Annual Attendance: 120,000; Mem: Individual $40; Dual $75; Family $85; Family Plus $165
Income: Financed by state appropriation, pub & private donations, grants & contracts
Special Subjects: American Indian Art, Archaeology, Eskimo Art, Ethnology, Ivory, Painting-American, Photography, Scrimshaw
Collections: contemporary Alaska photography, ethnographic coll, paintings & lithographs of Alaska subjects, native artifacts & art
Exhibitions: Temporary exhibits rotate every two to three months; summer free explainer program with talks on bears, wolves, Alaskan art & culture; presentation & explanation on Northern Lights
Activities: Classes for adults & children; lects open to pub; docent tours for grades K-6; mus shop sells books, original art, reproductions, prints, slides

L **Elmer E Rasmuson Library,** 1732 Tanana Loop, Fairbanks, AK 99775; PO Box 756800, Fairbanks, AK 99775-6800. Tel 907-474-7224; Fax 907-474-6841; Web: www.uaf.edu/library; *Develop & Pub Info Officer* Suznne Bishop; *Interim Dean Libraries* Suzan Hahn
See website for hours; Estab 1922 to support research & curriculum of the university; Circ 147,000
Income: Financed by state appropriation
Library Holdings: Book Volumes 2,260,000, Compact Disks, Manuscripts, Other Holdings Audio tapes; Film; Government documents, Photographs, Slides, Video Tapes
Collections: Lithographs of Fred Machetanz, paintings by Alaskan artists, C Rusty Heurlin, photographs of Early Alaskan bush pilots, print reference photograph coll on Alaska & the Polar Regions

HAINES

M **SHELDON MUSEUM & CULTURAL CENTER, INC,** Sheldon Museum & Cultural Center, 11 Main St, Haines, AK 99827; PO Box 269, Haines, AK 99827-0269. Tel 907-766-2366; Fax 907-766-2368; Web: www.sheldonmuseum.org; *Dir* Helen Alten; *Mus Asst, Colls* Aly Zeiger; *Educ Coordr* Jacqueline St. Claire; *Acctg* Briana Wright
Open Mon - Fri 1 PM -5PM, Sat - Sun 1 PM - 4 PM; Admis adults $7, Haines residents & children under 12 free; Estab 1924, under operation of Chilkat Valley Historical Society 1975 - 1991, incorporated Haines Borough facility, 1991; Art, history, culture & maintains reference library; Average Annual Attendance: 14,000
Income: Admis, mus store, Haines Borough appropriations, federal & state grants
Library Holdings: Audio Tapes, Book Volumes, Cassettes, Clipping Files, DVDs, Fiche, Framed Reproductions, Kodachrome Transparencies, Lantern Slides, Manuscripts, Maps, Memorabilia, Motion Pictures, Original Art Works, Original Documents, Pamphlets, Periodical Subscriptions, Photographs, Prints, Records, Slides, Video Tapes
Special Subjects: American Indian Art, Eskimo Art, Ethnology, Ivory, Metalwork, Photography, Scrimshaw, Woodcarvings

Collections: Chilkat blankets, Tlingit Indian artifacts, ivory, silver, wood carvings, native baskets, pioneer artifacts, photos, maps, oral histories, archival, Eldred Rock Lighthouse Lens, local art
Exhibitions: Solo & group art exhibs by local artists Apr-Sep
Publications: Haines - The First Century; A Personal Look at the Sheldon Museum & Cultural Center; Journey to the Tlingits; More Than Gold-Nuggets of Haines History
Activities: Classes for adults & children; Tlingit language class; docent training; lects open to pub; number of vis lectrs per yr varies; competitions; Friday brown bag lunches with historical programs; original objects of art lent to other mus; book traveling exhibs; mus store sells books, original art, prints, slides, jewelry, wood crafts

HOMER

M **BUNNELL STREET ARTS CENTER,** 106 W Bunnel, Ste A, Homer, AK 99603. Tel 907-235-2662; Email info@bunnellarts.org; Web: www.bunnellarts.org; *Asst Dir* Adele Person; *Develop Coordr* Brianna Allen
Open winter: Mon - Sat 11 AM - 6 PM, Sun Noon - 4 PM; call for summer hours; No admis fee; Estab 1994 for art exhibitions & educ; Historic landmark building displaying innovative contemporary art; Mem: dues $25 - $1,000
Income: $250,000 (financed by mem, city & state appropriation, fund raising, Alaska State Council on the Arts, City of Homer Grant Prog through the Homer Foundation & NEA, Rasmuson, PGA Foundation)
Exhibitions: Decolonizing Alaska 2016-2018 (national tour)
Publications: Newsletter, quarterly
Activities: Classes for adults & children; docent training; dramatic progs; internships; music; artist in schools; lects open to public, 15 vis lectrs per year; concerts; gallery talks; tours; poetry readings; piano concerts; slide lect by artist; art workshops various media; schols; awards, Alex Combs Award, Governor's Award, ArtPlace America; scholarship offered; sales shop sells original art

M **FIREWEED GALLERY,** 475 E Pioneer Ave, Homer, AK 99603. Tel 907-235-3411; Email art@fireweedgallery.com; Web: www.fireweedgallery.com; *Owner* Irene Randolph
Open Mon - Sat 11 AM - 5:30 PM, cl Sun; Estab 1996
Special Subjects: Ceramics, Sculpture, Jewelry, Photography, Metalwork, Glass, Eskimo Art
Collections: Contemporary works by Alaskan artists including paintings, sculpture, ceramics, jewelry, photography, metal, glass & indigenous works
Exhibitions: Temporary exhibits
Activities: Mus shop sells dolls, clothing & accessories

JUNEAU

L **ALASKA STATE LIBRARY,** Alaska Historical Collections, 395 Whittier St, State Office Bldg Juneau, AK 99801; PO Box 110571, Juneau, AK 99811-0571. Tel 907-465-2925; Fax 907-465-2151; Email asl.historical@alaska.gov; Web: library.alaska.gov; *Librn, Head Historical Coll* Jim Simard
Open Tues - Fri 10 AM - 4 PM; No admis fee; Estab 1900; Part of library
Income: State appropriation
Library Holdings: Book Volumes 34,000, Periodical Subscriptions 75, Photographs 110,000
Special Subjects: American Indian Art, Anthropology, Eskimo Art, Ethnology, Historical Material, Manuscripts, Maps, Photography
Collections: Winter & Pond, Wickersham Historical Site Collection, Skinner Foundation Collection, Grainger Post Card Collection
Publications: Books about Alaska, annual; Inventories for Individual Collections

M **ALASKA STATE MUSEUM,** 395 Whittier St, Juneau, AK 99801-1746. Tel 907-465-2901; Fax 907-465-2151; Web: museums.alaska.gov; *Chief Cur* Addison Field; *Cur Coll* Steve Henrikson; *Cur Mus Svcs* Scott Carrlee; *Registrar* Andrew Washburn; *Cur Exhibs* Jackie Manning; *Mus Protection & Vis Svcs Coordr* Mary Irvine; *Exhibits Designer* Aaron Elmore; *Conservator* Ellen Carrlee
Open Winter Tues - Sat 10 Am - noon & 1 PM - 4 PM; see website for summer hours; Admis adults $5, seniors 65 & over $4, youth 18 & under free; Estab 1900 to collect, preserve, exhibit & interpret objects of special significance or value in order to promote pub appreciation of Alaska's cultural heritage, history, art & natural environment; Gallery occupies one floor of the newly build APK building, housing permanent & temporary exhibits on over 24,000 sq ft
Income: Financed by state appropriation & grants
Library Holdings: Book Volumes, Fiche, Filmstrips, Framed Reproductions, Manuscripts, Maps, Memorabilia, Motion Pictures, Original Art Works, Original Documents, Other Holdings, Photographs, Prints, Records, Reels, Reproductions, Sculpture, Slides, Video Tapes
Special Subjects: American Indian Art, Anthropology, Archaeology, Cartoons, Ceramics, Coins & Medals, Collages, Costumes, Crafts, Decorative Arts, Dolls, Drawings, Embroidery, Eskimo Art, Etchings & Engravings, Ethnology, Flasks & Bottles, Folk Art, Furniture, Glass, Graphics, Historical Material, Landscapes, Maps, Photography, Portraits, Posters, Pottery, Prints, Sculpture, Silver, Stained Glass, Tapestries, Textiles, Watercolors
Collections: Alaskan ethnographic material including Eskimo, Aleut, Athabaskan, Tlingit, Haida & Tsimshian artifacts, Gold Rush & early Alaskan industrial & historical material, historical & contemporary Alaskan art, Natural History
Exhibitions: Dale DeArmand: The Nandalton Legends; Kayaks of Alaska and Sibera; Lockwood DeForest: Alaska Oil Sketches; Case & Draper Photographs 1898 - 1920
Publications: Eight Stars of Gold: The Story of Alaska's Flag (with CD)
Activities: Classes for adults & children; docent training; lects open to pub, 12 vis lectrs per yr; gallery talks, tours & demonstrations; paintings & objects lent to other museums & Alaskan schols; 2 book traveling exhibs per yr; originate traveling exhibs to AK mus; Mus shop sells books, magazines, reproductions, prints, Alaskan Native arts & crafts, outreach services to other mus

KETCHIKAN

M **CITY OF KETCHIKAN MUSEUM DEPARTMENT,** Totem Heritage Center, 601 Deermount St, Ketchikan, AK 99901. Tel 907-225-5900; Email anitam@ktn-ak.us; Web: www.ktn-ak.us/totem-heritage-center; *Acting Dir & Sr Cur Progs* Anita Maxwell; *Sr Cur Colls* Hayley Chambers; *Registrar* Erika Brown; *Prog Coordr* Ann Froeschle; *Cur Exhibs* Steven Villano
Open May - Sept: daily 8 AM - 5 PM; Oct - April: Mon - Fri 1 PM - 5 PM; Admis $5, local residents & children under 12 free; Estab 1976 to preserve & teach traditional Northwest Coast Indian Arts; Average Annual Attendance: 60,000
Income: $360,000
Special Subjects: Historical Material, Sculpture
Collections: Native American arts, original totem poles, monumental sculpture
Activities: Classes for adults & children; docent training; workshops; lects open to pub, 20 vis lectrs per yr; gallery talks; tours; arts & crafts festival; schols & work-study awards offered; mus shop sells books, magazines, original art, reproductions, prints, slides & native art

M **CITY OF KETCHIKAN MUSEUM DEPARTMENT,** Tongass Historical Museum, 629 Dock St, Ketchikan, AK 99901-6529. Tel 907-225-5600; Email anitam@ktn-ak.us; Web: www.ktn-ak-us/tongass-historical-museum/; *Acting Dir & Sr Cur Progs* Anita Maxwell; *Sr Cur Colls* Hayley Chambers
Open May - Sept: daily 8 AM - 5 PM; see website for winter hours; Admis adults $3, local residents & children 12 & under free; Estab 1967 to collect, preserve & exhibit area articles & collect area photographs
Collections: North West Indian Collection, ethnographic & develop history, local artists contemporary artwork, local area history artifacts, works from local & Alaskan artists, photographs, manuscripts & newspaper archives
Publications: Art class listings; Calendar; Newsletter
Activities: Classes for adults; docent training; lects open to public, 5 vis lectrs per year; book traveling exhibitions

NOME

M **CITY OF NOME ALASKA MEMORIAL MUSEUM,** Carrie M McLain Memorial Museum, 100 W 7th Ave, Nome, AK 99762; PO Box 53, Nome, AK 99762-0053. Tel 907-443-6630; Fax 907-443-7955; Email museum@nomealaska.org; Web: www.nomealaska.org; *Dir* Amy Chan
Open Mon - Thurs noon - 7 PM, Fri - Sat noon - 6 PM; Admis adults $7, youth & elder $6, mems & 1st Fri free; Estab 1967 to show the history of Nome, Nome Gold Rush, Bering Strait Eskimo, Aviation, Dog mushing
Income: Financed by City of Nome & supplemental grant projects & donations
Special Subjects: Archaeology, Dolls, Drawings, Eskimo Art, Ethnology, Flasks & Bottles, Gold, Historical Material, Ivory, Jewelry, Landscapes, Manuscripts, Maps, Photography, Restorations, Scrimshaw, Woodcarvings
Collections: permanent coll includes examples of art from 1890-1998, including basketry, carved ivory, ink, oil, skin drawings, stone carving, woodworking, extensive photography coll on database, gold rush & dog sledding memorabilia, Bering Strait Eskimo, Coons Collection, McLain Collection, Mielke Collection
Activities: lects open to pub; vis lectrs 4 per yr; gallery talks; tours; individual paintings & original objects of art lent

SITKA

M **ALASKA DEPARTMENT OF EDUCATION, DIVISION OF LIBRARIES, ARCHIVES & MUSEUMS,** Sheldon Jackson Museum, 104 College Dr, Sitka, AK 99835-7657. Tel 907-747-8981; Fax 907-465-2151; Email jacqueline.fernandez@alaska.gov; Web: museums.alaska.gov; *Cur Colls* Jackie Hamberg
Open Winter Tues - Sat 10 AM - noon & 1 PM - 4 PM; see website for summer hours; Admis adults $5, seniors 65 & over $4, youth 18 & under free; Estab 1888, the first permanent mus in Alaska, for the purpose of collecting & preserving the cultural heritage of Alaskan Natives in the form of artifacts; The mus, one of two Alaska State Museums, occupies a concrete, octagonal structure from 1895 with permanent displays concerning Tlingit, Tsimshian, Haida, Aleut, Athabaskan & Eskimo Inupiat and Yup'ik cultures; Average Annual Attendance: 20,000; Mem: 200
Income: $30,000 (financed by admis fee, sales, donation, State of Alaska)
Library Holdings: Book Volumes In-house reference only
Special Subjects: American Indian Art, Anthropology, Ethnology, Ivory, Scrimshaw, Woodcarvings, Eskimo Art, Costumes
Collections: Ethnographic material from Tlingit, Haida, Tsimshian, Aleut, Athabaskan & Eskimo people, Alaskan ethnology produced through 1930
Publications: Brochures; catalogs of Ethnological Collection
Activities: Classes for adults & children K-12; gallery interpreters & demonstrations; workshops; lects open to pub, 4 vis lectrs per yr; gallery talks; exten dept serves Alaska educators; lending of original art to museums, Alaska teachers; hands on ed coll; mus shop sells books, original art

M **SITKA HISTORICAL SOCIETY,** Sitka History Museum, 330 Harbor Dr, Sitka, AK 99835-7553. Tel 907-747-6455; Fax 907-747-6588; Email halspackman@sitkahistory.org; Web: www.sitkahistory.org; *Exec Dir* Hal Spackman; *Cur* Kristy Griffin
See website for hours; No admis fee; Estab 1971 to preserve the history of Sitka, its people & industries; Average Annual Attendance: 70,000; Mem: 225; dues $15-$100; annual meeting in Oct
Income: Financed by grants, mem, donations & gift shop sales
Library Holdings: Audio Tapes, Cards, Cassettes, Clipping Files, DVDs, Kodachrome Transparencies, Original Art Works, Other Holdings, Pamphlets, Periodical Subscriptions, Photographs, Prints, Slides, Video Tapes
Special Subjects: Historical Material
Collections: Copy of warrant that purchased Alaska, 2000 documents, Russian artifacts, library paintings of Alaska scenes, 10000 photographs, carved ivory, items for post-Russia Sitka through 1950

Exhibitions: Alaska Purchase; Diorama of Sitka in 1867 (Year of the Transfer); Forest Products Exhibit (past & present); Russian-American era Tlingit Culture; Last Qtr 19th Century Victorian Parlor & US Military Presence; First Flight Around the World; WWII in Sitka
Activities: Classes for adults & children; lects open to pub, 4 vis lectrs per yr; tours; awards given; sales shop sells books, magazines, original art, reproductions of artifacts, prints & slides

SKAGWAY

M **SKAGWAY CITY MUSEUM & ARCHIVES,** 700 Spring St, Skagway, AK 99840. Tel 907-983-2420; Email j.munns@skagway.org; *Dir* Judith Munns
Open Summer Mon - Fri 9 AM - 5 PM, Sat 10 AM - 5 PM, Sun 10 AM - 4 PM, call for winter hours; Estab 1961 to preserve & display items relating to the Klondike Gold Rush & Skagway history
Income: Financed by admis
Collections: Gold Rush Era artifacts, Tlingit; traveling war canoe, duck neck quilt
Publications: Brochures
Activities: Sales shop sells, books, reproductions of old newspapers & postcards

ARIZONA

BISBEE

L **BISBEE ARTS & HUMANITIES COUNCIL,** Lemuel Shattuck Memorial Library, 5 Copper Queen Plaza, Bisbee, AZ 85603. Tel 520-432-7071; Email admin@bisbeemuseum.org; Web: www.bisbeemuseum.org; *Dir* Carrie Gustavson; *Cur Educ & Colls* Amanda Hetro
Open daily 10 AM - 4 PM; Admis adults $8, seniors 60 and over $7, children under 16 $3; Estab 1971 to provide research facilities on copper mining & social history of Bisbee, Arizona, Cochise County & Northern Sonora, Mexico; For reference only; Average Annual Attendance: 18,336; Mem: dues $30 - $500
Library Holdings: Book Volumes 1,600, Cassettes 300, Clipping Files, Manuscripts, Periodical Subscriptions 3, Photographs 23,000, Reels 200
Special Subjects: Historical Material, Manuscripts, Maps, Photography, Costume Design & Constr, Dolls, Drawings, Furniture, Posters, Textiles, Painting-American
Collections: 25 original works of art, 15,000 photographs, extensive textile coll
Activities: Classes for adults & children; lects open to pub, 3 vis lectrs per yr; sales shop sells book

DOUGLAS

L **COCHISE COLLEGE,** Charles Di Peso Library, 4190 W Hwy 80, Art Dept Douglas, AZ 85607-6100. Tel 520-417-4082; Web: www.cochise.edu/library; *Libr Dir* Karly Scarbrough
Open Mon - Thurs 8 AM - 8 PM, Fri 8 AM - 4 PM; No admis fee; Estab 1965
Income: Financed by state & local funds & the college
Library Holdings: Book Volumes 61,000, Exhibition Catalogs, Framed Reproductions, Memorabilia, Original Art Works, Periodical Subscriptions 300, Photographs, Prints, Reproductions, Sculpture
Special Subjects: Oriental Art
Collections: Oriental originals (ceramics & paintings), 19th century American & European Impressionists

M **DOUGLAS ART ASSOCIATION,** The Gallery and Gift Shop, 625 Tenth St, Douglas, AZ 85607. Tel 520-364-6410
Open Mon - Sat 10:00 AM - 4 PM; No admis fee; Estab 1960 as a nonprofit tax exempt organization dedicated to promoting the visual arts & general cultural awareness in the Douglas, Arizona & Agua Prieta, Sonora area; The Gallery is operated in a city owned building with city cooperation; Average Annual Attendance: 2,000; Mem: 100; dues $15, $25 & $50
Income: Financed by mem & fundraising events, some lottery funds
Special Subjects: Southwestern Art
Exhibitions: Shows change about every six weeks
Publications: Monthly newsletter
Activities: Classes for adults & children; workshops in painting & various art activities; lect open to pub; gallery talks; competitions with cash awards; sales shop sells books, original art, prints, hand-made arts and crafts

DRAGOON

A **AMERIND FOUNDATION, INC,** Amerind Museum, Fulton-Hayden Memorial Art Gallery, 2100 N Amerind Rd, Dragoon, AZ 85609; PO Box 400, Dragoon, AZ 85609-0400. Tel 520-586-3666; Fax 520-586-4679; Email amerind@amerind.org; Web: www.amerind.org; *Exec Dir* Christine Szuter; *Chief Cur* Eric Kaldahl; *Mus Store Mgr* Tammy Stansberry
Open Tues-Sun 10 AM - 4 PM, cl major holidays; Admis adults $10, sr citizens & college students with ID $9, youth 10 - 17 $8, children under 10 free; Estab 1937 as a private, nonprofit archeological research facility & mus focusing on the native people of the Americas; Works on western & southwestern themes, paintings & sculptures by 19th & 20th century Anglo & Native American artists; Mem: dues $40 & up
Income: Financed by endowment income, grants, gifts
Special Subjects: American Indian Art, American Western Art, Archaeology, Eskimo Art, Ethnology, Painting-American, Pottery, Scrimshaw, Sculpture, Southwestern Art, Textiles, Watercolors, Mexican Art
Collections: Archaeological & ethnological materials from the Americas, antique furniture, archives on film, ivory & scrimshaw, oil paintings, research & technical reports, sculpture
Exhibitions: Images in Time; Traditions in Clay; The Prehistoric Southwest; recent acquisitions
Publications: Amerind Foundation Publication Series; Amerind New World Studies Series
Activities: Docent training; seminars; sch prog, day visits; lects open to pub, 6 vis lectrs per yr; gallery talks; tours for school groups; mus shop sells books, prints, original art, Native American Arts & Crafts

L **Fulton-Hayden Memorial Library & Art Gallery**, 2100 N Amerind Rd, Dragoon, AZ 85609; PO Box 400, Dragoon, AZ 85609-0400. Tel 520-586-3666; Fax 520-586-4679; Email libros@amerind.org; Web: www.amerind.org; *Librn* Sally Newland; *Exec Dir* Christine Szuter, PhD; *Chief Cur* Eric Kaldahl PhD, RPA
Open by appointment only; Estab 1962 as archaeological research library for scholars; American oils, sculpture, drawings, Native American Art; Mem: Museum mem 1,000
Income: Financed by endowment income, grants, gifts
Purchases: Miscellaneous ethnographic material from the American Southwest & Northern Mexico
Library Holdings: Audio Tapes, Book Volumes 22,000, CD-ROMs, Cards, Cassettes, Clipping Files, Compact Disks, Exhibition Catalogs, Fiche, Filmstrips, Kodachrome Transparencies, Lantern Slides, Manuscripts, Maps, Memorabilia, Micro Print, Motion Pictures, Original Art Works, Original Documents, Pamphlets, Periodical Subscriptions 60, Photographs, Reels, Reproductions, Sculpture, Slides, Video Tapes
Special Subjects: American Indian Art, American Western Art, Anthropology, Archaeology, Architecture, Art History, Ceramics, Costume Design & Constr, Decorative Arts, Drawings, Eskimo Art, Etchings & Engravings, Furniture, Historical Material, History of Art & Archaeology, Jewelry, Latin American Art, Manuscripts, Maps, Mexican Art, Painting-American, Pottery, Pre-Columbian Art, Religious Art, Scrimshaw, Sculpture, Silver, Silversmithing, Southwestern Art, Textiles, Watercolors, Prints
Collections: American Oils, sculpture, works on paper, Navajo & Hopi watercolors
Publications: Amerind Foundation Publications; Amerind Studies in Archaeology
Activities: Classes for adults & children; docent training; lects open to pub; lects for mems only; vis lectrs 6 per yr; gallery talks; tours; museum shop sells books, prints, Native American jewelry & crafts

FLAGSTAFF

M **MUSEUM OF NORTHERN ARIZONA,** 3101 N Fort Valley Rd, Flagstaff, AZ 86001-8348. Tel 928-774-5213; Email info@musnaz.org; Web: www.musnaz.org; *Danson Cur Anthropology* Kelley Hays-Gilpin, PhD; *Dir Colls* Elaine Hughes, PhD; *Cur Geology* David D Gillette, PhD
Open Mon - Sat 10 AM - 5 PM, Sun noon - 5 PM, cl New Year's Day, Thanksgiving & Christmas; Admis adults $12, sr citizens (65+) $10, youth, students with ID, Native Americans with tribal affiliation $8, children under 10 free; Estab 1928 to collect, study, interpret and preserve the art, cultural, natural history of the Colorado Plateau; Maintains reference library; Mem: dues $25 - $5,000
Special Subjects: American Indian Art, American Western Art, Anthropology, Archaeology, Carpets & Rugs, Ceramics, Crafts, Ethnology, Folk Art, Hispanic Art, Historical Material, Jewelry, Juvenile Art, Landscapes, Painting-American, Painting-American, Photography, Pottery, Pottery, Sculpture, Silver, Southwestern Art, Textiles, Woodcarvings
Collections: Works of Southwestern Native American artists, non-Indian art depicting Colorado Plateau subjects, archaeological, ethnographic artifacts, natural history specimens of the Colorado Plateau
Exhibitions: Geology, archaeology, ethnology, Native cultures, additional changing exhibits of fine art & natural sciences
Publications: Plateau Magazine; semiannual; museum notes; semiannual
Activities: Adventurous outdoor experiences; group tours; Discovery prog for youths of all ages; docent training; lects open to pub, gallery talks; individual paintings & original objects of art lent to various institutions; lending coll contains 2200 original art works; mus shop sells books, magazines, original art, reproductions, prints, & mus quality Native arts by master and emerging artists of the Colorado Plateau

M **NORTHERN ARIZONA UNIVERSITY,** Art Museum & Galleries, 620 S Knoles Dr, Bldg #10, Rm #M205 Flagstaff, AZ 86011; PO Box 6021, Flagstaff, AZ 86011-6021. Tel 928-523-3471; Fax 928-523-1424; Email artmuseum@nau.edu; Web: www.nau.edu/art_museum; *Dir* George Speer; *Sr Curatorial Specialist* Ty Miller
Open Tues-Sat noon - 5 PM; No admis fee; Estab 1968 for the continuing educ & service to the students & the Flagstaff community in all aspects of fine arts & to national & international fine arts communities; Gallery is a nonprofit educational institution
Special Subjects: Coins & Medals, Southwestern Art
Collections: Contemporary ceramics, Master prints of the 20th c & American painting of the Southwest, Weiss Collection: Early 20th c Antiques, Sculptures & Paintings
Activities: Educ prog includes outreach to local schools; lects open to pub, 3 vis lectrs per yr; national & international workshops & conferences; concerts; tours; competitions with awards; gallery talks; scholarships; originate traveling exhibs; mus shop sells books, original art works, prints & posters, reproductions, Hopi jewelry & other gift items; Beasley Student & Faculty Gallery Bldg 37 Flagstaff

GANADO

M **NATIONAL PARK SERVICE,** Hubbell Trading Post National Historic Site, PO Box 150, Ganado, AZ 86505-0150. Tel 928-755-3475; Email hubbell@wnpa.org; Web: www.nps.gov/hutr; *Cur* Nancy Mahaney; *Mus Tech* Kathy Tabaha; *Educ Dir & Chief Interpreter* Ailema Benally; *Park Supt* Lloyd Masayamptewa
Open May - Sept 8 AM - 6 PM, Oct - Apr 8 AM - 5 PM; Admis $2 Hubbell family home tour, Trading Post free; Estab 1967 to set aside Hubbell Trading Post as a historic site as the best example in Southwest of an Indian Trading Post; Historic home & trading post
Income: Financed by federal appropriation

Special Subjects: American Indian Art, American Western Art, Anthropology, Archaeology, Painting-American, Photography, Southwestern Art, Period Rooms
Collections: Western artists, ethnohistoric arts & crafts, furnishings, photographs
Exhibitions: Fully furnished 19th & 20th Century Trading Post & family home; Historic Overview of the Site (located in Vis Center)
Activities: Educ dept; lect open to public; tours; presentations; competitions; individual paintings & art objects are lent to cert museums; sales shop sells books, Indian arts & crafts, magazines, original art, prints & slides; semi annual Native American art auctions (May & Sep)

KINGMAN

M **MOHAVE MUSEUM OF HISTORY & ARTS,** 400 W Beale St, Kingman, AZ 86401. Tel 928-753-3195; Fax 928-753-3195; Email museum@mohavemuseum.org; Web: www.mohavemuseum.org; *Dir* Shannon Rossiter
Open Mon - Fri 9 AM - 5 PM, Sat 1 - 5 PM; Admis adults $4, seniors $3, children free; Estab 1960 to preserve & present to the pub the art & history of Northwest Arizona; Mem: dues $30-$500
Income: Financed by endowment, mem, sales & donations
Special Subjects: American Indian Art, Anthropology, Archaeology, Ethnology, Historical Material, Manuscripts, Restorations
Collections: American Indian Art, art & history of Northwest Arizona
Exhibitions: Quilt Show (Oct)
Activities: Classes for children; docent progs; lects open to pub; mus shop sells books, prints, original art, craft items, reproductions

MESA

M **I.D.E.A. MUSEUM,** 150 W Pepper Pl, Mesa, AZ 85201. Tel 480-644-2468; Fax 480-644-2466; Email ideamuseum@mesaaz.gov; Web: ideamuseum.org; *Exec Dir* Sunnee D O'Rork; *Cur* Jeffory Morris; *Cur Educ* Dena Milliron; *Mktg Dir* Yvette Armendariz; *Develop Mgr* Lindsay Hochhalter; *Acctg Specialist* Tarjani Patel; *Exhibs Designer* Rex Witte; *Exhib Technician* Brian Asdell
Open Tues - Thurs & Sat 10 AM - 4 PM, Fri 9 AM - 6 PM, Sun noon - 4 PM, cl Mon; Admis $9, mems & children under 1 free; Estab 1978 as fine art museum for children. Specially curated exhibits installed with original hands-on activities to involve children & families in the appreciation & making of art; Mem: dues $55 - $190
Special Subjects: Archaeology, Ceramics, Collages, Costumes, Crafts, Decorative Arts, Drawings, Etchings & Engravings, Graphics, Painting-American, Photography, Prints, Sculpture, Southwestern Art, Textiles, Watercolors, Woodcarvings, Woodcuts
Exhibitions: 3 changing exhibs per yr, see website
Publications: Member e-newsletter; pre-visit & follow-up brochures for teachers
Activities: Classes for children; docent training; tours; gallery talks; book traveling exhibs, 2-3 per yr; mus shop sells books & items for children as related to specific exhibit themes

M **MESA ARTS CENTER,** Mesa Contemporary Arts Museum, 1 E Main St, Mesa, AZ 85201; PO Box 1466, Mesa, AZ 85211-1466. Tel 480-644-6560; Email artscenterinfo@mesaartscenter.com; Web: www.mesaartscenter.com; *Exec Dir* Cindy Ornstein; *Asst Dir Educ & Visual Arts* Robert Schultz; *Asst Dir Theaters & Opers* Randall Vogel; *Arts & Culture Fin Dir* Teri Siggins; *Dir Community Engaged Practice* Mandy Tripoli; *Dir Ticketing* Andrew Douglas; *Pub Rels Dir* Casey Blake; *Events Svcs Dir* Kim Forbes; *Educ Dir, Studio Progs* Billy Jones; *Devel Dir* Renee Lopata; *Vol & Festivals Dir* Shawn Lawson; *Mesa Contemp Arts Chief Cur* Pattty Haberman; *Cur Exhibs* Tiffany Fairall
Open Tues, Wed, Fri & Sat 10 AM - 5 PM, Thurs 10 AM - 8 PM, Sun noon - 5 PM; No admis fee; Estab 1981 to exhibit the artwork of contemporary artists nationally; 5 galleries, 5,500 sq ft exhibition space; Average Annual Attendance: 34,000
Income: Financed by city appropriation
Special Subjects: Ceramics, Collages, Crafts, Drawings, Enamels, Etchings & Engravings, Furniture, Glass, Hispanic Art, Jewelry, Landscapes, Latin American Art, Metalwork, Mosaics, Painting-American, Photography, Pottery, Prints, Sculpture, Southwestern Art, Textiles, Watercolors, Woodcuts
Collections: Permanent collection of contemporary arts & crafts, prints, crafts & traditional media
Exhibitions: 16 exhibs ann
Activities: Classes & workshops for adults & children; docent training; awards $2,000 per juried exhibs; lects open to public, 2 vis lectrs per yr; gallery talks; tours; competitions with awards; book traveling exhibs annually; originate traveling exhibs artist coop; mus shop sells original art

MIAMI

M **BULLION PLAZA CULTURAL CENTER & MUSEUM,** 150 N Plaza Cir, Miami, AZ 85539. Tel 928-473-3700; Web: bullionplazamuseum.org; *Exec Dir* Thomas Foster
Open Thurs - Sat 11 AM - 3 PM, Sun Noon - 3 PM & by appt; Estab to conserve Arizona's cultural history & examine its natural environment
Special Subjects: American Indian Art, Photography, Military Art, Video, Ceramics
Collections: Mining Heritage Collection
Exhibitions: Permanent exhibs include minerals & geology, McKusick tile works, ranching, military, dignitary exhibs & Mexican, Slavic & Native American cultural exhibs
Activities: Educ progs; coll educ; concerts; tours; art programming; outreach progs; cultural events; Mus shop sells books, jewelry, gemstones & gifts

NOGALES

A **PIMERIA ALTA HISTORICAL SOCIETY,** 136 N Grand Ave, Nogales, AZ 85621-3211. Tel 520-287-4621; Email pimerlaaltamuseum@gmail.com; Web: www.pimeriaaltamuseum.org; *Pres* Jose Ramon Garcia
Open Tues-Sat 11 AM - 4 PM; No admis fee; Estab 1948 to preserve the unique heritage of northern Sonora Mexico & southern Arizona from 1000 AD to present; art is incorporated into interpretive exhibits; Also maintains a photo gallery - archival photographic library restoration of Salvador Corona murals; Mem: dues $5 - $1,000
Library Holdings: Audio Tapes, Book Volumes, CD-ROMs, Cards, Cassettes, Clipping Files, Compact Disks, DVDs, Exhibition Catalogs, Framed Reproductions, Kodachrome Transparencies, Manuscripts, Maps, Memorabilia, Micro Print, Motion Pictures, Original Art Works, Original Documents, Other Holdings, Pamphlets, Photographs, Prints, Records, Reels, Slides, Video Tapes
Collections: Art & artifacts of Hohokam & Piman Indians, Spanish mission era & Mexican ranchers, Anglo pioneer settlement, early territorial maps, women costumes, natural & southwest borderland studies materials
Exhibitions: Railroad mining; firefighter - pharmacy - Hoho Kan; David Swing murals; Salvador Corona murals; Pimeria Post
Publications: Centennial Book of Nogales; newsletter, 10 per year; annual calendar on historic subjects; Open Range & Hidden Silver
Activities: Classes for adults & children; docent training; lects open to pub, 5 vis lectrs per yr; gallery talks; tours; competitions; traveling exhibs to outreach school related & senior projects; originate traveling exhibs; sales shop sells books, reproductions, prints, maps & pins; entire mus is fully interactive - bicultural & bilingual

L **Library,** 136 N Grand Ave, Nogales, AZ 85621-3211. Tel 520-287-4621; Email pimeriaaltalmuseum@gmail.com; Web: www.pimeriaaltamuseum.org; *President* Jose Ramon Garcia
Tues - Sat 11 AM - 4 PM; No admis fee; Collects books & archival material on Pimeria Alta, Northern Sonora & Southern Arizona
Income: Membership Dues, Donations & Fundraisers
Library Holdings: Book Volumes 1,000, Cassettes, Clipping Files, Manuscripts, Memorabilia, Other Holdings Historical Photos & Maps 5,000, Pamphlets, Periodical Subscriptions 3
Special Subjects: Historical Material
Collections: The Jack Kemmer Memorial Collection, books on the cattle industry of Texas, New Mexico, Arizona and California
Publications: Primeria Post - Quarterly Newsletter
Activities: Classes for children; Shop sells books

PHOENIX

A **ARIZONA ARTISTS GUILD,** 18411 N 7th St, Phoenix, AZ 85023; PO Box 41534, Phoenix, AZ 85080. Tel 602-944-9713; Email info@arizonaartistsguild.org; Web: arizonaartistsguild.net; *Pres* Tess Mosko Scheren
Estab 1928 to foster guild spirit, to assist in raising standards of art in the community & to assume civic responsibility in matters relating to art; Average Annual Attendance: 450
Income: Financed by endowment & mem
Exhibitions: Horizons (annually in spring, members only); fall exhibition for members only; juried exhibition
Publications: AAG news, monthly
Activities: Classes for adults; lects sometimes open to public, 12 or more vis lectrs per year; gallery talks; competitions with awards; workshops by vis professionals offered; paint-outs; sketch groups; demonstrations; schols offered

A **ARIZONA COMMISSION ON THE ARTS,** 417 W Roosevelt St, Phoenix, AZ 85003-1326. Tel 602-771-6501; Fax 602-256-0282; Email info@azarts.gov; Web: www.azarts.gov; *Exec Dir* Jaime Dempsey; *Deputy Dir* Alex Nelson; *Fiscal Office Mgr* Kim McCreary; *Communs Dir* Steve Wilcox; *Grants & Research Dir* Ben Watters; *Artist Progs Mgr* Gabriela Munoz; *Organizational Grants & Svcs Mgr* Kristen Pierce
Open 8 AM - 5 PM; No admis fee; Estab 1966 to promote & encourage the arts in the State of Arizona; Maintains reference library; Mem: Meetings, quarterly
Publications: Artists' Guide to Programs; monthly bulletin guide to programs
Activities: Workshops; conferences; artists-in-education grants prog; scholarships & fels offered; originate traveling exhibs 20-30 per yr

L **Reference Library,** 417 W Roosevelt, Phoenix, AZ 85003. Tel 602-771-6501; Fax 602-256-0282; Email info@azarts.gov; Web: www.azarts.gov; *Exec Dir* Jaime Dempsey
Open 8 AM to 5 PM; Topics related to the bus of the arts. For reference only
Library Holdings: Book Volumes 900, Pamphlets, Periodical Subscriptions 25, Slides
Special Subjects: Art Education

M **ARIZONA STATE UNIVERSITY,** (Deer Valley Rock Art Center) Deer Valley Petroglyph Preserve, 3711 W Deer Valley Rd Phoenix, AZ 85308. Tel 623-582-8007; Email dvrac@asu.edu; Web: shesc.asu.edu/dvpp; *Dir* Richard Toon
Open Tues - Sat 9 AM - 4:30 PM; Admis adults $7, seniors 62 & up, military & students $4, children 6-12 $3, ASU students, mems & children 5 & under free; Estab to preserve & provide pub access to the Hedgpeth Hills petroglyph site, to interpret the cultural expressions & be a center for rock art research; Average Annual Attendance: 15,000
Library Holdings: Original Documents, Prints, Slides
Special Subjects: American Indian Art, Anthropology, Archaeology, Southwestern Art
Collections: Over 1500 petroglyphs, artifacts, library & archives
Exhibitions: permanent exhib ongoing
Activities: Classes for adults & children; docent training; summer camps; festivals; storytelling prog; monthly lects; concerts; gallery talks; tours; mus shop sells books, magazines, original art, jewelry, clothing

A **ARIZONA WATERCOLOR ASSOCIATION,** 18411 N 7th Ave, Phoenix, AZ 85023; PO Box 30693, Phoenix, AZ 85046. Tel 602-228-1217; Email

awapresident@azwatercolor.com; Web: www.azwatercolor.com; *Pres* Ruth Philliben; *1st VPres* Sally Golzalez; *2nd VPres* Jane Underhill
Estab 1960 to further activity & interest in the watermedia, promote growth of individuals & group & maintain high quality of professional exhibits; Two membership shows each yr, location varies; Mem: 320; qualifications for juried mem must be accepted in three different approved juried shows; all members who pay dues are considered members; dues $40
Income: Financed by dues & donations $14,000 per yr
Exhibitions: Two exhibitions yearly: Membership Show
Publications: AWA Newsletter, monthly; Directory, annual
Activities: Workshops; lect for members only; paint outs; competitions with 10 awards per exhib

ATLATL
For further information, see National and Regional Organizations

M **HEARD MUSEUM,** 2301 N Central Ave, Phoenix, AZ 85004-1323. Tel 602-252-8840; Fax 602-252-9757; Email contact@heard.org; Web: heard.org; *Dir & CEO* David Roche; *Dir Educ* Sharah Nieto; *COO & Deputy Dir* John R Bulla; *Dir Strategic Devel & Programming* Dan Hagerty; *Dir Community Engagement* Marcus Monenerkit; *Dir Library & Archives* Mario Nick Klimiades
Open Mon - Sat 9:30 AM - 5 PM, Sun 11 AM - 5 PM, cl Easter, July 4, Thanksgiving Day & Christmas; Admis general $18, seniors $15, students w/ID & children 6-17 $7.50, children under 6, mems & Native Americans with proof of tribal heritage free; Estab 1929 to collect, preserve & exhibit Native American art & artifacts, offering an expansive view of the Southwest as it was thousands of years ago & is today & to increase general awareness about Native American cultures, traditions & art; Average Annual Attendance: 200,000; Mem: 5000; dues varies
Library Holdings: Auction Catalogs, Audio Tapes, Book Volumes 52,000, CD-ROMs, Cassettes, Clipping Files, Compact Disks, DVDs, Exhibition Catalogs, Fiche, Filmstrips, Kodachrome Transparencies, Lantern Slides, Manuscripts, Maps, Micro Print, Motion Pictures, Original Documents, Pamphlets 88, Periodical Subscriptions 350, Photographs, Prints, Records, Reels, Reproductions, Slides, Video Tapes 450
Special Subjects: African Art, American Indian Art, American Western Art, Archaeology, Bronzes, Ceramics, Decorative Arts, Dolls, Drawings, Glass, Hispanic Art, Historical Material, Jewelry, Mexican Art, Painting-American, Photography, Pottery, Primitive art, Prints, Religious Art, Restorations, Sculpture, Silver, Southwestern Art, Tapestries, Textiles, Watercolors, Woodcarvings, Asian Art
Collections: Barry M Goldwater Photograph Collection, C G Wallace Collection, Fred Harvey Fine Arts Collection
Exhibitions: Home: Native People in the Southwest (ongoing); Remembering Our Indian School Days (ongoing)
Publications: Earth Song Calendar, quarterly; exhibition catalogs
Activities: Classes for adults & children; dramatic progs; docent training; outreach progs; music & dance performances; movie screenings; book signings; festivals; lects open to pub, 6-8 vis lectrs per yr; concerts; gallery talks; tours; competitions with awards, World Championship Hoop Dance Contest, Spirit of the Heard Award; scholarships & fels offered; exten dept serves southwest, county, state & regional; individual paintings & original objects of art lent to other art institutions & mus for exhibs internationally; one book traveling exhib per yr; originate traveling exhibs to other art institutions, mus & schools; mus shop sells books, magazines, original art work & Native American art

L **Billie Jane Baguley Library and Archives**, 2301 N Central Ave, Phoenix, AZ 85004-1323. Tel 602-252-8840; Fax 602-252-9757; Email mario@heard.org; Web: www.heard.org; *Library Archives Dir* Mario Nick Klimiades; *Librn* Betty Murphy; *Library & Archives Liaison* Donita Beckham; *Dir* David Roche; *Creative Dir* Caesar Chaves; *Dir Institutional Advancement Opers* James Weaver
Open Mon - Fri 10 AM - 4:45 PM to American Indians, mus visitors & mus members; open to public by appointment only; No admis fee; For reference only
Income: $11,000 (financed by mem & mus budget)
Library Holdings: Auction Catalogs, Audio Tapes 1,300, Book Volumes 37,300, Cassettes, Clipping Files, Exhibition Catalogs, Fiche, Filmstrips, Kodachrome Transparencies, Lantern Slides, Manuscripts, Maps, Memorabilia, Micro Print, Motion Pictures, Pamphlets 133 linear ft, Periodical Subscriptions 260, Photographs 300,000, Prints, Records 500 linear ft, Reels, Reproductions, Slides, Video Tapes 1,200
Special Subjects: American Indian Art, Anthropology, Archaeology, Crafts, Eskimo Art, Ethnology, Folk Art, Mexican Art, Painting-American, Pre-Columbian Art, Primitive art, Southwestern Art
Collections: Native American Artists Resource Collection, Fred Harvey Company Research Collection

M **MONORCHID GALLERY,** 214 E Roosevelt St, Phoenix, AZ 85004. Tel 602-253-0339; Email info@monorchid.com; Web: www.monorchid.com; *Production* Christopher Oshana
Open Mon - Fri 6:30 AM - 8 PM, Sat 6:30 AM - 3:30 PM, Sun 7:30 AM - 8 PM; Estab 1999 to promote the arts by focusing on aesthetic clarity and fostering artistic dialogue; Convertible, open-floor gallery housed in a 14,000 sq ft warehouse
Collections: 21st century art
Exhibitions: Temporary exhibits
Activities: Events; dance & theatre performances

M **PHOENIX ART MUSEUM,** 1625 N Central Ave, Phoenix, AZ 85004-1685. Tel 602-257-1880; Fax 602-253-8662; Email info@phxart.org; Web: www.phxart.org; *Cur American Art* Betsy Fahlman; *Dir* Amanda Cruz; *Chief Cur* Gilbert Vicario; *Cur Photog* Becky Senf; *Cur Latin American Art* Vanessa Davidson; *Cur Asian Art* Janet Baker; *Cur Fashion Design* Dennita Sewell
Open Tues & Thurs - Sat 10 AM - 5 PM, Wed 10 AM - 9 PM, Sun noon - 5 PM; First Fri 10 AM - 10 PM; Admis $18 adults, seniors 65+ $15, students (with ID) $13, children (6-17) $9, mem & children under 6, Wed evenings 3 - 9 PM and first Fri of the month 6 - 10 PM Free; Estab 1925, mus constructed 1959; Average Annual Attendance: 250,000; Mem: 9,000; dues $80 & up; annual meeting in Sep
Income: $8,000,000 (financed by pub & private funds)
Library Holdings: Auction Catalogs, Clipping Files, Exhibition Catalogs, Fiche, Pamphlets, Periodical Subscriptions, Slides
Special Subjects: Asian Art, Baroque Art, Calligraphy, Costumes, Decorative Arts, Hispanic Art, Latin American Art, Mexican Art, Miniatures, Painting-American, Painting-British, Painting-Dutch, Painting-European, Painting-Flemish, Painting-Polish, Photography, Portraits, Prints, Renaissance Art, Sculpture, Silver, Textiles, Watercolors, Woodcuts
Collections: Asian art, decorative arts, fashion design, 14th-20th century European & American art, Latin American art, Spanish Colonial art, Thorne Miniature Rooms, Western American art, Renaissance, Western American art, Medieval art, contemporary art
Publications: Annual report; exhibition catalogs; quarterly newsletter
Activities: Classes for adults & children; docent training; lects open to pub, 12 vis lectrs per yr; lects for mems only; concerts; gallery talks; tours; competitions; book travelling exhibs, 5 per yr; originates traveling exhibs, 2 per yr; mus shop sells books, magazines, reproductions, prints, jewelry, slides & gifts from around the world

L **Lemon Art Research Library**, 1625 N Central Ave, Phoenix, AZ 85004-1685. Tel 602-257-2136; Fax 602-253-8662; Email library@phxart.org; Web: www.phxart.org; *Librn* Abigail Nersesian
Open Wed - Fri 10 AM - 4 PM; Estab 1959 to serve reference needs of the mus staff, docents, mem, students & pub; For reference only
Income: Financed by Museum operating funds
Library Holdings: Auction Catalogs, Book Volumes 50,000, Clipping Files, DVDs 100, Exhibition Catalogs, Memorabilia, Other Holdings Auction Records; Ephemera, Pamphlets, Periodical Subscriptions 60, Reproductions, Slides
Special Subjects: Art Education, Art History, Asian Art, Ceramics, Conceptual Art, Decorative Arts, Drawings, Embroidery, Etchings & Engravings, Folk Art, Furniture, Glass, Graphic Arts, Illustration, Ivory, Jade, Jewelry, Latin American Art, Manuscripts, Marine Painting, Metalwork, Mexican Art, Miniatures, Mixed Media, Oriental Art, Painting-American, Painting-British, Painting-Dutch, Painting-European, Painting-Flemish, Painting-French, Painting-German, Painting-Israeli, Painting-Italian, Painting-Japanese, Painting-Polish, Painting-Russian, Painting-Scandinavian, Painting-Spanish, Photography, Porcelain, Portraits, Pottery, Pre-Columbian Art, Printmaking, Prints, Sculpture, Southwestern Art, Textiles, Watercolors, Woodcarvings, Woodcuts
Collections: Arizona Artist Files, auction catalogs, museum archives, Astaire Library of Costumes & Fashion, special collections, periodicals

M **PHOENIX CENTER FOR THE ARTS,** 1202 N 3rd St, Phoenix, AZ 85004-1812. Tel 602-254-3100; Email info@phoenixcenterforthearts.org; Web: phoenixcenterforthearts.org; *Dir* Joseph Benesh; *Deputy Dir* Lauren Henschen
Open Mon - Fri 9 AM - 9 PM, Sat 9 AM - 4 PM, Sun 9 AM - 1 PM
Activities: Classes for adults & children

C **WELLS FARGO,** Wells Fargo History Museum, 145 W Adams St, Phoenix, AZ 85003. Tel 602-378-1852; Web: www.wellsfargohistory.com
Open Mon - Fri 9 AM - 5 PM, cl bank holidays; No admis fee; Estab Oct 3 2003 History Museum with art gallery
Collections: Western scenes, Remington Bronzes, NC Wyeth, F Schnoover, M Dixon, Solon Borglum Bronzes, Charles Russell Bronzes
Activities: Tours

A **XICO INC,** 1008 E Buckeye Rd, # 220, Box A West-2 Phoenix, AZ 85034. Tel 480-833-5875; Fax 480-890-2327; Email info@xicoinc.com; Web: www.xicoinc.com; *Exec Dir* Laura Wilde; *Educ & Engagement Mgr* Diana Calderon
Open Wed - Fri 10 AM - 5 PM, Sat 11 AM - 3 PM (call to confirm); No admis fee; Estab 1977 as a nonprofit organization of Native American & Xicanindio artist to promote cross cultural understanding, preserve tradition & develop grass roots educational programs
Income: financed by endowment, city & state appropriation
Publications: Papel Picado (paper cut-out techniques)
Activities: Lects open to pub, 1 vis lectrs per yr

PRESCOTT

M **GEORGE PHIPPEN MEMORIAL FOUNDATION,** Phippen Museum - Art of the American West, 4701 Hwy 89 N, Prescott, AZ 86301. Tel 928-778-1385; Email phippen@phippenartmuseum.org; Web: www.phippenartmuseum.org; *Dir* Kim Villalpando; *Mtkg & Communs Mgr* Edd Kellerman; *Cur, Colls Mgr & Museum Store* Lynette Tritel; *Gallery Manager* Brenda Smith; *Education Coordinator* Neal McEwen
Open Tues - Sat 10 AM - 4 PM, Sun 1 PM - 4 PM; cl Mon; Admis adults $7, AAA mems $6, students $5, mems & children 12 & under free; Estab 1974 to exhibit art of the American West, collect & educ; Circ Reference only; Gallery has 17,000 sq ft; maintains reference library; Average Annual Attendance: 13,000; Mem: dues $40 & up
Library Holdings: Auction Catalogs, Book Volumes, Clipping Files, DVDs, Exhibition Catalogs, Original Documents, Periodical Subscriptions, Prints, Reproductions, Video Tapes
Special Subjects: American Indian Art, American Western Art, Art Education, Art History, Bronzes, Drawings, Historical Material, Landscapes, Leather, Military Art, Miniatures, Painting-American, Pewter, Photography, Portraits, Pottery, Prints, Reproductions, Southwestern Art, Textiles, Watercolors, Woodcarvings, Sculpture
Collections: Permanent collection contains fine art depicting art of the American West
Exhibitions: Phippen Memorial Day Art Show; Annual Art Show, juried with 140 artists; Miniature Masterpiece Show & Sale; Hold Your Horses
Publications: Canvas, Phippen Museum members newsletter
Activities: Classes for adults & children; docent training; educ prog; lects open to pub, 24 vis lectrs per yr; concerts; gallery talks; tours; competitions & awards; individual paintings & original objects of art lent to various mus in the country; lending collection contains original art works, paintings & sculpture; book traveling exhibs; originate traveling exhibs; mus shop sells books, original art, reproductions, prints & gifts

A **PRESCOTT FINE ARTS ASSOCIATION,** Gallery, 208 N Marina St, Prescott, AZ 86301-3106. Tel 928-445-3286; Fax 928-778-7888; Email director@pca-az.net; Web: www.pca-az.net; *Exec Dir* Robyn Allen; *Fin Dir* Nancy Dunham; *Tech Dir* Stan Reed
Open Mon 11 AM - 3 PM, Tues - Sat 10 AM - 3 PM, Sun Noon - 4 PM; No admis fee, donations accepted; Estab 1968 as a nonprofit gallery & theatre to promote arts within the county & local community; Art Gallery is one large room below theater section in what was previously a Catholic Church; Mem: dues $50 - $500
Collections: 10 each yr-constantly changing
Publications: Newsletter
Activities: Classes for adults & children; docent training; lect open to pub, 2-3 vis lectrs per yr; concerts; scholarship; competitions with awards; gallery talks; scholarships offered; sales shop sells original art, prints, pottery, jewelry, glass & woven items

SCOTTSDALE

M **CONGREGATION BETH ISRAEL'S PLOTKIN JUDAICA MUSEUM,** 10460 N 56th St, Scottsdale, AZ 85253-1133. Tel 480-951-0323; Fax 480-951-7150; Email info@cbiaz.org; Web: www.cbiaz.org; *Dir* Carol Reynolds
Call for hours; No admis fee; Estab 1970 to promote educ of Judaism; Tunisian Synagogue Gallery. Maintains library
Income: (financed by endowment, mem & gifts)
Special Subjects: Judaica, Period Rooms, Photography, Religious Art, Sculpture, Silver, Tapestries, Textiles
Collections: Contemporary art reflecting the Jewish experience, Holiday Judaica, Jewish Life Cycles, Synagogue Period Room, Tunisian, AZ Jewish Experience
Publications: HA-OR, three times a year
Activities: Classes for adults & children; docent progs; lects open to pub, 3 vis lectrs per yr; concerts; tours; films; individual paintings & original objects of art are lent to other mus; lending collection contains 15,000 books & 200 videos; book traveling exhibs 3 per yr; originate traveling exhibs 1 per yr; mus shop sells original art

L **FRANK LLOYD WRIGHT SCHOOL,** William Wesley Peters Library, 12621 N Frank Lloyd Wright Blvd, PO Box 4430 Scottsdale, AZ 85261-4430. Tel 480-860-2700; Fax 480-860-8472; Email wwplib@taliesin.edu; *Dir of Library* Elizabeth Dawsari
Open by appointment; Estab 1983
Library Holdings: Audio Tapes 19,000, Book Volumes 16,000, Cassettes, Clipping Files, Exhibition Catalogs, Pamphlets, Photographs, Reproductions, Slides, Video Tapes
Collections: 25,000 Collateral files & material; 100,000 drawings

A **SCOTTSDALE ARTISTS' LEAGUE,** P.O. Box 1071, Scottsdale, AZ 85252. Tel 480-998-8782; Email info@scottsdaleartistsleague.org; Web: www.scottsdaleartistsleague.org; *Pres* Freddie Lieberman; *1st VPres Progs* Patrick Serie; *2nd VPres Shows* Marsha Klinger
No admis fee; donation suggested; Estab 1961 to encourage the practice of art & to support & encourage the study & application of art as an avocation, to promote ethical principles & practice, to advance the interest & appreciation of art in all its forms & to increase the usefulness of art to the public at large; Average Annual Attendance: 4,800; Mem: dues $42-75; $42 suggested mem donations, monthly meetings every first Tues
Exhibitions: Yearly juried exhibition for members only; yearly juried exhibition for all Arizona artists (open shows); Desert Botanical Garden Paintout every March
Publications: Art Beat, monthly
Activities: Classes for adults; lect open to public, 11 vis lectrs per yr; gallery talks; tours; scholarships offered to art students

M **SCOTTSDALE CULTURAL COUNCIL,** Scottsdale Museum of Contemporary Art, 7374 E Second St, Scottsdale, AZ 85251; 7380 E Second St, Scottsdale, AZ 85251. Tel 480-874-4666; Fax 480-874-4655; Email smoca@sccarts.org; Web: www.smoca.org; *Dir* Tim Rodgers; *Asst Cur* Claire Carter; *Assoc Cur* Cassandra Coblentz; *Cur Educ* Carolyn Robbins; *Registrar* Pat Evans
Open Tues. Wed & Sun noon - 5 PM, Thurs noon - 8 PM, Fri & Sat noon - 10 PM (free admis 5PM - 10PM), cl Mon; Admis $7 adults; $5 students; free for members & children under 15 & Thurs; Opened in 1999; presents exhibitions of modern & contemporary art, architecture & design; Designed by Will Bruder, SMOCA features five galleries and an outdoor sculpture garden with one of James Turrell's "Skyspaces"; Average Annual Attendance: 40,000; Mem: 2,900; dues $30 - $5,000
Income: Financed by mem, city appropriation & corporate sponsorship
Library Holdings: Book Volumes, Exhibition Catalogs
Special Subjects: Architecture, Drawings, Furniture, Glass, Photography, Prints, Sculpture, Ceramics
Collections: Paintings, prints, sculptures, photographs, drawings, James Turrell "Skyspace"
Exhibitions: Rotating exhibits
Publications: Exhibition catalogs
Activities: Classes for adults & children; docent training; gallery talks; tours; lects open to public, 10 vis lectrs per year; exten dept serves local schools; book traveling exhibs 5-6 per yr; originates traveling exhibs to other museums; sales shop sells books, magazines, reproductions, prints, craft items & jewelry; Junior mus: Young @ Art Gallery, 7380 E Second St, Scottsdale, AZ 85251

SECOND MESA

M **HOPI CULTURAL CENTER MUSEUM,** Rte 264, Second Mesa, AZ 86043; PO Box 67, Second Mesa, AZ 86043-0067. Tel 928-734-2401; Fax 520-734-6650; Email hopi3@psv.com; *Dir* Anna Silas
Open Mon - Fri 8 AM - 5 PM, Sat - Sun 8 AM - 3 PM
Collections: Hopi arts & crafts, pre-historic & historic pottery, weavings, wood carvings, silver

TEMPE

M **ARIZONA STATE UNIVERSITY,** ASU Art Museum, Mill Ave & 10th St, 51 E 10th St Tempe, AZ 85281; PO Box 872911, Tempe, AZ 85287-2911. Tel 480-965-2787; Fax 480-965-5254; Email asuartmuseum@asu.edu; Web: asuartmuseum.asu.edu; *Dir* Miki GarciaMiki.Garcia@asu.edu; *Lead Registrar* Elisa Beavidez HayesElisa.Benavidez@asu.edu; *Cur of Education* Andrea FellerAndrea.Feller@asu.edu; *Cur Coord* Brittany CorralesBrittany.Corrales@asu.edu; *Devel Coord* Lizabeth DionLizabeth.Dion@asu.edu
Open academic yr Tues - Wed & Fri - Sat 11 AM - 5 PM, Thurs 11 AM - 8 PM, cl Sun, Mon & university holidays; No admis fee; Estab 1950 to provide esthetic & educational service for students & the citizens of the state; Permanent installations, changing galleries & various changing area; 48 shows annually; Average Annual Attendance: 55,000; Mem: Individual $50; Active $100; Supporting $250; Contributing $500; Patron $1,000; Leadership $2,500; Director's Council $5,000; Season Sponsor $10,000
Income: $250,000 (financed by state appropriations, donations & earnings)
Library Holdings: Exhibition Catalogs, Prints
Special Subjects: Ceramics, Crafts, Glass, Hispanic Art, Latin American Art, Manuscripts, Mexican Art, Painting-American, Painting-Australian, Painting-Canadian, Painting-French, Painting-Japanese, Painting-Spanish, Photography, Portraits, Prints, Sculpture, Watercolors, Calligraphy
Collections: American crafts, especially ceramics & glass, American painting & sculpture, 18th Century to present, Contemporary art, print coll, 15th Century to present, Latin American Art, Folk Art, 20th century ceramics
Publications: Too Late for Goya: Works by Francesc Torres; Art Under Duress: El Salvador 1980-Present; Bill Biola: Buried Secrets; Art of the Edge of Fashion
Activities: Educ dept; docent training; student docent prog; special events; lects open to pub, 12 vis lectrs per yr; gallery talks; tours; competitions; originate traveling exhibs; mus shop sells books, reproductions, original art & crafts, jewelry, cards

L **ASU Library**, PO Box 871006, Tempe, AZ 85287-1006. Tel 480-965-6164; Web: www.asu.edulib; *Art Specialist* Dennis Brunning; *Architecture Librn* Deborah Koshinsky; *Univ Librn* Sherrie Schmidt
Open Mon-Thurs 7AM-Midnight, Fri 7AM-7PM, Sat 9AM-5PM, Sun 10AM-Midnight
Income: Financed by state & other investors
Library Holdings: Book Volumes 2,826,679, Cards, Cassettes, Exhibition Catalogs, Fiche, Maps, Periodical Subscriptions 31,694, Reels, Video Tapes
Special Subjects: American Indian Art, American Western Art, Anthropology, Archaeology, Architecture, Art Education, Art History, Coins & Medals, History of Art & Archaeology, Interior Design

M **Memorial Union Gallery**, PO Box 870901, Tempe, AZ 85287-0901. Tel 480-965-6649; Fax 480-727-6212; Web: eoss.asu.edu/mu; *Prog Coordr* Joy Klein
Open Mon - Fri 9 AM - 5 PM; No admis fee; Estab to exhibit work that has strong individual qualities from the United States, also some Arizona work that has not been shown on campus; Gallery is contained in two rooms with 1,400 sq ft space; fireplace; one wall is glass; 20 ft ceiling; 26 4 x 8 partitions; track lighting; one entrance and exit; located in area with maximum traffic; Average Annual Attendance: 30,000
Income: Financed by admin appropriation
Purchases: $3,000
Collections: Painting, print & sculpture, primarily Altma, Gorman, Mahaffey, Schoulder & Slater
Exhibitions: Rotating exhibits
Activities: Internships; lects open to pub, 4 vis lectrs per yr; gallery talks; competitions; originate traveling exhibs

L **Architecture & Environmental Design Library**, PO Box 871006, Tempe, AZ 85287-1006. Tel 480-965-6400; Fax 480-727-6965; Web: lib.asu.edu/design; *Adminr & Asc Librn* Deborah Koshinsky
Open acad yr Mon - Thurs 8 AM - 10 PM, Fri 8 AM - 5 PM, Sat Noon - 4 PM, Sun 2 - 10 PM; Estab 1959 to serve the College of Architecture & Environmental Design & the university community with reference & research material in the subjects of architecture, planning, landscape architecture, industrial design & interior design; Circ 35,000
Income: Financed by state appropriation
Library Holdings: Audio Tapes, Book Volumes 30,000, Cassettes, Fiche, Manuscripts, Memorabilia, Micro Print, Other Holdings Architectural models, Periodical Subscriptions 130, Photographs, Prints, Reels, Slides, Video Tapes
Special Subjects: Architecture, Furniture, Industrial Design, Interior Design, Landscape Architecture
Collections: Paolo Soleri & Frank Lloyd Wright Special Research Collections, Victor Olgyzy, Paul Schweikher, Litchfield Park, Will Bruder, Albert Chase MacArthur, other drawings & documents

TUBAC

M **TUBAC CENTER OF THE ARTS,** Santa Cruz Valley Art Association, 9 Plaza Rd, Tubac, AZ 85646; PO Box 1911, Tubac, AZ 85646-1911. Tel 520-398-2371; Fax 520-398-9511; Email contactus@tubacarts.org; Web: www.tubacarts.org; *Co-Dir* Karin Topping; *Co-Dir* Susannah Castro; *Pres* Jan Schoeben; *Gift Shop Mgr* Bonme Jaus; *Educ Coordr* Jo Edmondson; *Weekend Supv* Karon Leigh
Open Mon - Sat 10 AM - 4:30 PM, Sun noon - 4:30 PM; No admis fee; Estab 1963 to promote interest in arts and art education; Three galleries, in a Spanish Colonial Building, 300 running ft of exhibit space; Average Annual Attendance: 40,000; Mem: 800; dues $45-$2500; annual meeting in Oct
Income: State arts council, grants, membership & contributions
Special Subjects: American Indian Art, American Western Art, Ceramics, Crafts, Decorative Arts, Historical Material, Landscapes, Painting-American, Portraits, Sculpture, Textiles, Watercolors
Exhibitions: Invitationals; members & non-members shows
Activities: Classes for adults & children; dramatic prog; docent training; lects open to pub 10 per yr; competitions with awards; concerts; gallery talks; tours; sales shop sells books, original art, reproductions, prints, jewelry, ceramics, fine crafts & art

L **Library**, 9 Plaza Rd, Tubac, AZ 85646; PO Box 1911, Tubac, AZ 85646. Tel 520-398-2371; Fax 520-398-9511; Email jdefalla@tabacarts.org; Web: www.tubacarts.org; *Dir* Annette Brink
Open Tues - Sat 10 AM - 4:30 PM; No admis fee; Estab 1964, 501(c)3 arts center; Brick territorial style bldg, 5,000 sq ft with patio; Average Annual Attendance: 50,000; Mem: 850, $45 annual dues
Income: Financed by grants, gifts & contributions
Library Holdings: Book Volumes 850, Cards, Exhibition Catalogs, Slides
Special Subjects: Art History
Activities: Classes for adults & children; dramatic progs, docent training; lects open to pub; concerts; gallery talks; tours; cash & non-cash exhib awards; mus shop sells books, original art, reproductions, prints, jewelry, pottery & wearable art

TUCSON

AMERICAN SOCIETY OF BOOKPLATE COLLECTORS & DESIGNERS
For further information, see National and Regional Organizations

A **NATIONAL NATIVE AMERICAN CO-OPERATIVE,** North American Indian Information & Trade Center, PO Box 27626, Tucson, AZ 85726-7626. Tel 520-248-5849; Email fredusaindian@aol.com; Web: www.usaindianinfo.com; *Dir & Consultant* Fred Synder
Call for hours, hours change for different events; Admis free; scholarship donations appreciated; Estab 1969 to provide incentive to 2700 American Indian artists representing over 410 tribes for the preservation of their contemporary & traditional crafts, culture & educ through involvement in Indian cultural programs, including dances, traditional food, fashion shows & performances. Also sponsors various Indian events; Authentic hand-made American Indian crafts; art from over 140 tribal nations; Average Annual Attendance: 50,000-60,000; Mem: 2,700; meetings in Nov & Jan; American Indian Artists only; no dues; qualification for mem: quality craftsmanship
Income: Financed through sales of Native American Directory: Alaska, Canada & US
Purchases: Quality authentic crafts
Library Holdings: Book Volumes, Cassettes, Compact Disks, DVDs, Original Art Works, Pamphlets, Periodical Subscriptions, Photographs
Special Subjects: American Indian Art, Crafts, Eskimo Art, Gold, Jewelry, Miniatures, Scrimshaw, Sculpture, Silver, Southwestern Art, Woodcarvings, Handicrafts, Historical Material, Ivory, Pottery
Collections: Native American arts & crafts, including jewelry, basketry, wood & stone carving, weaving, pottery, beadwork, quill-work, rug-making, tanning & leatherwork, dance & cookery; books; 30+ year turquoise collection - 50,000 stones;
Exhibitions: Dance/Craft Competition (2 events yearly); American Indian Exposition, last Sun in Jan - 2nd Sun in Feb; Native American Heritage Month Social & Craft Market (always Thanksgiving weekend (Fri-Sun)
Publications: Native American Directory: Alaska, Canada, United States; Native American Reference Book (1996-2012); Pow-Wow on the Red Road; American Indian Events: AZ, NM, CO, UT, NV (2017-2019)
Activities: Classes for adults; volunteer; lects open to pub, 5-10 vis lectrs per yr; concerts; competitions with prizes; 2 schols offered every Oct (1 acad & 1 cultural); artmobile; book traveling exhibs 40-50 per yr; originate traveling exhibs among American Indian events: conferences, pow-wows; sales shop sells books & original art

M **TOHONO CHUL PARK,** 7366 N Paseo del Norte, Tucson, AZ 85704-4415. Tel 520-742-6455; Fax 520-797-1213; Email marmstrong@tohonochul.org; Web: www.tohonochulpark.org; *Cur Exhibis* James Schaub; *Asst Cur Exhbs & Colls Mgr* Karen Hayes; *Dir Educ & Visitor Servs* Jo Falls; *Exec Dir* Dr Christine Conte; *Retail Mgr* Linda Wolfe
Open daily 9 AM - 5 PM; Admis $13, seniors, students & military $10, children (5-12) $3, children under 5 free; Estab 1985 for people to experience the wonders of the Sonoran Desert & gain knowledge of natural & cultural heritage of the region; Changing exhibits featuring regional arts & artists; Average Annual Attendance: 130,000; Mem: 6,000; dues $20-$5000
Income: $2,400,000 (financed by mem, grants, donations & earned income)
Special Subjects: American Indian Art, Carpets & Rugs, Ceramics, Collages, Crafts, Decorative Arts, Dioramas, Dolls, Drawings, Embroidery, Etchings & Engravings, Ethnology, Flasks & Bottles, Folk Art, Furniture, Hispanic Art, Jewelry, Juvenile Art, Laces, Landscapes, Mexican Art, Miniatures, Mosaics, Photography, Porcelain, Sculpture, Silver, Southwestern Art, Watercolors, Woodcarvings, Woodcuts, Primitive art, Prints, Religious Art
Collections: Modern & contemporary Native American crafts of the Southwest
Exhibitions: 12 - 14 changing exhibits per year
Publications: Desert Corner Journal newsletter, 5 times per yr
Activities: Classes for children & adults; docent training; concerts; tours; field trips; lects open to pub, 12 - 15 vis lectrs per yr; gallery talks; competitions; Lumie Award, 2009; mus store sells books, original art, reproductions, prints

M **TUCSON MUSEUM OF ART AND HISTORIC BLOCK,** 140 N Main Ave, Tucson, AZ 85701-8290. Tel 520-624-2333; Fax 520-624-7202; Email info@tucsonmuseumofart.org; Web: www.tucsonmuseumofart.org; *CEO* Jeremy Mikolajczak; *Cur Educ & Community Partnerships* Morgan Wells; *Chief Develop Officer* Alba Rojas-Sukkar; *CFO* Christopher Gordon; *Marketing & Digital Content Coordr* Jordan Bohannon; *Chief Cur & Cur Modern & Contemporary Art* Dr Julie Sasse; *Preparator* David Longwell; *Chief Bldg, Grounds & Security* Dave Hopkins Jr; *Coll Mgr & Registrar* Rachel Adler; *Grants Mgr* Nancy Weant; *Retail Mgr* Justin Germain; *Dir Accounting & HR* Andra Allen; *Cur Community Engagement* Marianna Pegno; *Colls Mgr & Registrar* Rachel Adler; *Glasser Cur Art American West* Christine Brindza
Open Tues - Sat 10 AM - 5 PM, Sun Noon - 5 PM, cl Mon, New Year's Day, Independence Day, Thanksgiving & Christmas Day; Admis adults $12, sr citizens (65+) $10, youth (13-17) & students with col ID $7, children (12 & under) veterans with ID, mus mems & first Thurs of month 5 - 8 PM free, 1st Sun of month half price; Estab 1924 to operate a private nonprofit civic art gallery to promote art educ, to hold art exhibitions & to further art appreciation for the pub; Galleries display permanent collections & changing exhibitions; Average Annual Attendance: 237,035; Mem: 3,500; AAM accredited; dues Dir Circle $1000, President's Circle $500, patron $250, sustaining $120, family $60, individual $50; student $35; annual meeting in Sept
Income: $3,000,000 (financed by grants, endowment, mem, city & state appropriations, contributions & generated income)
Library Holdings: Auction Catalogs, Book Volumes, CD-ROMs, Compact Disks, DVDs, Exhibition Catalogs, Maps, Original Documents, Pamphlets, Periodical Subscriptions, Photographs, Slides, Video Tapes
Special Subjects: Landscapes, Latin American Art, Mexican Art, Oriental Art, Painting-American, Painting-American, Painting-European, Period Rooms, Photography, Portraits, Pottery, Pre-Columbian Art, Sculpture, Prints, Sculpture, Southwestern Art, Textiles, Watercolors
Collections: Contemporary & decorative arts, contemporary Southwest, folk, Mexican, Pre-Columbian, Spanish Colonial, Western American & 20th century art, modern
Publications: Exhibition catalogs; digital collections catalogs
Activities: Classes for adults & children; docent training; start organization for emerging artists & young professionals; lect open to public; concerts; gallery talks; tours; sponsored competitions; scholarships offered; mus shop sells books, magazines, original art, reproductions, prints, crafts, jewelry & ceramics

L **Library**, 140 N Main Ave, Tucson, AZ 85701-8290. Tel 520-624-2333, Ext 122; Fax 520-624-7202; Email jprovan@tucsonarts.com; Web: www.tucsonarts.com; *Librn* Jill E Provan; *Grant Proj Dir* Jan Willkom
Open Tues - Thurs 10 AM - 3 PM; No admis fee; Estab 1974 for bibliographic & research needs of Mus staff, faculty, students & docents; Circ 1,200; Open to public for research & study; Average Annual Attendance: 1,800; Mem: 2,000 - open for circulation to all museum members
Income: Financed by gifts & fund allocations
Purchases: 360 titles per yr
Library Holdings: Book Volumes 11,000, Cards, Clipping Files, Exhibition Catalogs 500, Fiche, Kodachrome Transparencies, Manuscripts, Other Holdings Indexes; Museum archives, Pamphlets 5,000, Periodical Subscriptions 35, Photographs, Prints, Slides 24,000, Video Tapes 100
Special Subjects: Afro-American Art, American Indian Art, American Western Art, Art Education, Asian Art, Carpets & Rugs, Ceramics, Costume Design & Constr, Crafts, Decorative Arts, Drawings, Enamels, Eskimo Art, Etchings & Engravings, Folk Art, Furniture, Glass, Handicrafts, Historical Material, History of Art & Archaeology, Jade, Jewelry, Landscapes, Latin American Art, Marine Painting, Metalwork, Mexican Art, Mixed Media, Mosaics, Oriental Art, Painting-American, Painting-British, Painting-Dutch, Painting-European, Painting-Flemish, Painting-French, Painting-German, Painting-Italian, Painting-Japanese, Painting-Spanish, Photography, Porcelain, Pre-Columbian Art, Printmaking, Prints, Religious Art, Scrimshaw, Sculpture, Silversmithing, Southwestern Art, Stained Glass, Tapestries, Textiles, Watercolors, Woodcarvings, Woodcuts
Collections: Biographic material documenting Arizona artists, Pre-Columbian, Spanish colonial, Latin American art TMA museum, Catalogs, historic block archives
Activities: Classes for adults & children; docent training; annual book sale fundraiser; book discussion groups; lects open to public; 10 vis lectrs per yr; annual book talk at local book store; gallery talks; tours; sponsored competitions; sells books & original art

M **UNIVERSITY OF ARIZONA,** Museum of Art & Archive of Visual Arts, 1031 N Olive Rd, Tucson, AZ 85721-0002; PO Box 210002, Tucson, AZ 85721-0002. Tel 520-621-7567; Fax 520-621-8770; Email artmuseum@email.arizona.edu; Web: artmuseum.arizona.edu; *Interim Dir* Jill McCleary; *Cur Exhibs & Educ* Olivia Miller; *Registrar* Kristen Schmidt; *Sr Exhib Specialist* Nathan Saxton
Open Tues - Fri 9 AM - 4 PM, Sat 9 AM - 5 PM, Sun Noon - 5 PM, cl Mon & university holidays; Admis adults $8, mem, seniors $6.50, children, students with ID & active military free; Estab 1955 to share with the Tucson community, visitors & the university students the treasures of three remarkable permanent collections: the C Leonard Pfeiffer Collection, the Samuel H Kress Collection & the Edward J Gallagher Jr Collection; Special exhibitions are maintained on the first floor of the mus; the permanent collections are housed on the second floor. AAM Accredited; Average Annual Attendance: 23,000
Income: Financed by state appropriation & endowments
Library Holdings: Book Volumes, Exhibition Catalogs, Original Documents
Special Subjects: Afro-American Art, Baroque Art, Collages, Drawings, Etchings & Engravings, Hispanic Art, Landscapes, Latin American Art, Marine Painting, Mexican Art, Painting-American, Painting-British, Painting-Dutch, Painting-European, Painting-Flemish, Painting-French, Painting-German, Painting-Italian, Painting-Japanese, Painting-Polish, Painting-Russian, Painting-Spanish, Portraits, Prints
Collections: Edward J Gallagher Collection of over a hundred paintings of national & international artists, Samuel H Kress Collection of 26 Renaissance works & 26 paintings of the 15th century Spanish Retablo by Fernando Gallego, C Leonard Pfeiffer Collection of American Artists of the 30s, 40s & 50s, Jacques Lipchitz Collection of 70 plaster models
Publications: Fully illustrated catalogs on all spec exhibs
Activities: Docent training; lects open to public, 10 vis lectrs per yr; concerts; gallery talks; tours; sales shop sells books, cards & poster reproductions

L **UA Museum of Art**, Speedway & Olive, Tucson, AZ 85721; PO Box 210002, Tucson, AZ 85721-0002. Tel 520-621-7567; Fax 520-621-8770; Email artmuseum@email.arizona.edu; Web: www.artmuseum.arizona.edu
Open Tues - Fri 9 AM - 4 PM, Sat 9 AM - 5 PM, Sun noon - 5 PM; Admis adults $8, seniors $6.50, students, children & mem free; 1956; UAMA is a forum for teaching, research & services related to the history & meaning of the visual arts; Not open to pub; telephone requests for information answered; Mem: 350; dues vary
Special Subjects: Art History, Painting-American, Painting-European, Sculpture, Watercolors, Woodcuts
Collections: Seven centuries of art - one museum, 15th century Spanish Altarpiece, American, Modern & contemporary art
Activities: Lects & exhibs throughout the year; mus shop sells books & art related merchandize

M **Center for Creative Photography**, 1030 N Olive Rd, Tucson, AZ 85721. Tel 520-621-7968; Fax 520-621-9444; Email info@ccp.arizona.edu; Web: www.creativephotography.org; *Registrar* Megan Clancy; *Archivist* Leslie Squyres; *Chief Cur* Rebecca Senf
Open Tues - Fri 9 AM - 4 PM, Sat 1 - 4 PM, cl Sun - Mon; No admis fee; Estab 1975 to house & organize the archives of numerous major photographers & to act as a research center in 20th century photography; Gallery exhibs changing approx 3 times per yr; Average Annual Attendance: 30,000+
Income: Financed by state, federal, private & corporate sources
Special Subjects: Photography
Collections: Archives of Ansel Adams, Wynn Bullock, Harry Callahan, Aaron Siskind, W Eugene Smith, Frederick Sommer, Paul Strand, Edward Weston, Richard Aredon & others
Exhibitions: Various rotating exhibits, call for details
Activities: Lects open to pub; gallery talks; research fel; original objects of art lent to qualified museums; originate traveling exhibitions worldwide

L **Library**, PO Box 210002, Tucson, AZ 85721. Tel 520-621-6442; Fax 520-621-9444; Email library@arizona.edu; Web: new.library.arizona.edu; *Librn* Stephen Bosch
Main library open 24 hrs; Circ Non-circulating; Open to the pub for print viewing & research
Library Holdings: Audio Tapes, Book Volumes 15,000, Cassettes, Clipping Files, Exhibition Catalogs, Fiche, Manuscripts, Memorabilia, Original Art Works, Pamphlets, Periodical Subscriptions 95, Photographs, Reels, Slides, Video Tapes
Collections: Limited edition books, hand-made books, books illustrated with original photographs, artists' books

L **Architecture Collection**, PO Box 210075, Tucson, AZ 85721-0075. Tel 520-621-6384
Open daily 7:30 AM - 1 AM; Estab 1965; The bulk of the collection is located at the Science-Engineering Library, Fl 5 with a small portion remaining at the Fine Arts Library, on the 2nd fl of the Music Bldg; slides relocated to the Visual Resources Ctr
Library Holdings: Book Volumes 20,000, Periodical Subscriptions 120, Video Tapes
Special Subjects: Architecture, Drafting, Landscape Architecture

M **WOMANKRAFT ART CENTER,** 388 S Stone Ave, Tucson, AZ 85701-2318. Tel 520-629-9976; Web: www.womankraft.org; *Exec Dir* Grace Rhyne; *Dir Exhibs* Zoe Rhyne; *Dir School of Arts* Gayle Swanbeck
Open Wed - Sat 1 PM - 5PM, 1st Sat of month 7PM - 10 PM, cl Jan & Aug; No admis fee; Estab 1974 to claim & validate women artists; Craft area, topic gallery, performance space, School of the Arts; Average Annual Attendance: 5,000; Mem: 100; dues $30
Collections: Members art collection
Activities: Classes for adults & children; dramatic progs; workshops & workshop series-poetry readings & performance; lects open to pub; concerts

WICKENBURG

M **MARICOPA COUNTY HISTORICAL SOCIETY,** Desert Caballeros Western Museum, 21 N Frontier St, Wickenburg, AZ 85390-3431. Tel 928-684-2272; Fax 928-684-5794; Email info@westernmuseum.org; Web: www.westernmuseum.org; *Exec Dir* W James Burns, PhD; *Cur* Mary Ann Igna; *Store Mgr* Marilu Rix
Open Mon - Sat 10 AM - 5 PM, Sun 12 - 4 PM; cl Mon Memorial Day - Labor Day; Admis general $9, sr citizens $7, children 16 and under free; Estab 1960 to educate & enhance the appreciation & understanding of the art, history, cultural legacy & wonder of the American West; The museum houses western art gallery, mineral room, American Indian Artifacts room, period rooms & gold mining equipment; Average Annual Attendance: 64,000; Mem: 600; dues $25-$75; annual meeting in Jan
Income: $200,000 (financed by mem, private donations, endowments); non-profit 501c3 org
Special Subjects: American Indian Art, American Western Art, Bronzes, Carpets & Rugs, Costumes, Decorative Arts, Dioramas, Dolls, Drawings, Folk Art, Furniture, Glass, Historical Material, Jewelry, Landscapes, Manuscripts, Painting-American, Period Rooms, Photography, Sculpture, Southwestern Art, Textiles, Watercolors
Collections: George Phippen Memorial Western Bronze Collection, Joe Beeler, Charles Russell, Frederick Remington
Exhibitions: Hays Spirit of the West
Publications: A History of Wickenburg to 1875 by Helen B Hawkins; The Right Side Up Town on the Upside Down River; Museum Highlights, newsletter bimonthly; Crossroads: The Museum at 50
Activities: Classes for adults & children; docent training; lects open to pub, 12 vis lectrs per yr; gallery talks; tours; individual paintings & original objects of art lent to mus; book traveling exhibs two per yr; mus shop sells books, magazines, original art, reproductions, prints & slides

L **Eleanor Blossom Memorial Library**, 21 N Frontier St, Wickenburg, AZ 85358-3431. Tel 520-684-2272; Fax 520-684-5794; Email dcwm@aol.com; Web: www.westernmuseum.org; *Dir* Michael Ettema
Open Mon - Sat 10 AM - 5 PM by appointment; Open to members for reference only
Library Holdings: Book Volumes 2000, Periodical Subscriptions 25
Special Subjects: American Western Art, History of Art & Archaeology, Manuscripts

WINDOW ROCK

M **NAVAJO NATION,** Navajo Nation Museum, PO Box 1840, Window Rock, AZ 86515-1840. Tel 928-871-7941; Fax 928-871-7942; Email info@navajonationmuseum.org; Web: www.navajonationmuseum.org; *Dir* Geoffrey I Brown; *Cur* Clarenda Begay; *Archivist* Eunice Kahn; *Educ Cur* Norman Bahe
Open Mon 8 AM - 5 PM, Tues - Fri 8 AM - 8 PM, Sat 9 AM - 5 PM, cl Sun, Federal and tribal holidays; No admis fee; Estab 1961 to collect & preserve items depicting Navajo history & culture art & natural history of region; Exhibit area approx 13,000 sq ft; Average Annual Attendance: 35,000
Income: Financed by tribal appropriation & donations
Special Subjects: American Indian Art, Anthropology, Drawings, Historical Material, Jewelry, Miniatures, Pottery, Sculpture, Silver, Textiles, Watercolors
Collections: Works in all media by Navajo Indian artists, & non-Navajo artists who depict Navajo subject matter, Navajo textiles, jewelry & historical objects
Publications: Artist's directory & biographical file, exhibition publs
Activities: Educ prog; classes for adults & children; school presentations; tours; conference/meeting/performance facilities for events; lects open to pub; 4-6 vis lectrs per yr; concerts; gallery talks; tours; individual paintings & original works of art; lending collection contains 300 original works of art & 50,000 photographs; mus shop sells books, magazines, original art, reproductions, prints, video tapes, DVDs, t-shirts, arts & crafts

L **NAVAJO NATION LIBRARY SYSTEM,** PO Box 9040, Window Rock, AZ 86515-9040. Tel 520-871-6376; Fax 520-871-7304; Email irvingnelson@navajo.org; Web: www.nnib.org; *Librn* Irving Nelson
Open Mon 8 AM-5 PM, Tues - Fri 8 AM - 8 PM, Sat 9 AM - 5 PM, cl Sun; No admis fee; Estab 1949
Income: through the Navajo Nation
Library Holdings: Book Volumes 21,000, Periodical Subscriptions 50

YUMA

M **ARIZONA HISTORICAL SOCIETY-YUMA,** Sanguinetti House Museum & Garden, 240 Madison Ave, Yuma, AZ 85364. Tel 928-782-1841; Fax 928-783-0680; Email ahsyuma@azhs.gov; Web: www.arizonahistoricalsociety.org; *Cur* Carol Brooks
Open Tues - Sat 10 AM - 4 PM; Admis adults $3, seniors & students $2, members & children under 12 free; Estab 1963 to collect, preserve & interpret the history of the lower Colorado River Regions; Average Annual Attendance: 2,500; Mem: 200; dues $50 individual, $65 household; annual meeting in Apr
Income: Financed by mem, state appropriation & donations
Library Holdings: Book Volumes, Clipping Files, Manuscripts, Maps, Original Art Works, Original Documents, Other Holdings Oral History Tapes, Photographs
Special Subjects: Costumes, Dolls, Drawings, Embroidery, Ethnology, Flasks & Bottles, Folk Art, Furniture, Glass, Historical Material, Manuscripts, Maps, Military Art, Period Rooms, Photography, Porcelain, Portraits, Pottery, Tapestries, Textiles
Collections: Clothing, Furniture & Household Items, Archives; 12,400 Photos; Maps; Trade & Bus Items, Books, Artifacts, Album-Scrapbooks
Exhibitions: Lower Colorado River Region from 1540-1940; History Exhibits; Period Rooms
Publications: Newsletter; Quarterly Journal
Activities: Lects open to pub; 10 vis lectrs per yr; non-circulating library; mus shop sells books, reproductions, prints & turn of the century style gifts

M **YUMA FINE ARTS ASSOCIATION,** Yuma Art Center, 254 S Main St, Yuma, AZ 85364-1425. Tel 928-329-6607; Fax 928-329-6616; Email director@yumafinearts.org; Web: www.yumafinearts.org; *Dir* David Woodward; *Bd Pres* Renee Smith; *Gift Shop Mgr* Catherine Rone
Open Tues, Wed, Thurs 10 AM - 6 PM, Fri 10 AM - 7 PM, Sat 10 AM - 5 PM; No admis fee; Estab 1962 to promote the arts in the Yuma area & to provide exhib space for contemporary art & art of the Southwest; 4 galleries in the Yuma Art Center; Average Annual Attendance: 50,000; Mem: 350; dues $60, $100, $300, $5000
Income: Financed by endowment, mem & city contract, grants & fundraising events
Special Subjects: American Indian Art, American Western Art, Bronzes, Ceramics, Collages, Drawings, Etchings & Engravings, Glass, Graphics, Hispanic Art, Jewelry, Landscapes, Latin American Art, Marine Painting, Metalwork, Mexican Art, Military Art, Painting-American, Painting-Canadian, Photography, Pottery, Prints, Sculpture, Southwestern Art, Woodcarvings, Woodcuts, Watercolors
Collections: Contemporary Art, Art of the Southwest
Exhibitions: Approx 17 exhibs presented annually
Publications: Art Notes Southwest, quarterly
Activities: Classes for adults & children; lects open to pub, 10 vis lectrs per yr; concerts; gallery talks; tours; competitions; $3000 awards annually; individual paintings & original objects of art lent to other mus for specific exhibs; book traveling exhibs 6-10 times per yr; originate traveling exhibs; sales shop sells original art, reproductions, prints, jewelry, pottery, wood, sculptures

ARKANSAS

BATESVILLE

M **LYON COLLEGE KRESGE GALLERY,** Highland & 22nd Sts, Batesville, AR 72503. Tel 870-307-7242; Email ian.campbell@lyon.edu; @KresgeGalleryLyonCollege; *Asst Prof Art* Ian Campbell
Open Mon - Fri 9 AM - 7 PM, cl Sat - Sun; Estab as a gift from the Kresge Foundation; Gallery located in the Alphin Humanities Building across classrooms & studios
Special Subjects: Photography, Sculpture
Collections: paintings; photographs; sculpture
Exhibitions: Temporary exhibs include travelling colls, professional artists & student artwork
Activities: Events

BENTONVILLE

M **CRYSTAL BRIDGES MUSEUM OF AMERICAN ART,** 600 Museum Way, Bentonville, AR 72712. Tel 479-418-5700; Fax 479-418-5701; Email info@crystalbridges.org; Web: www.crystalbridges.org; *Exec Dir* Rod Bigelow;

Deputy Dir Sandra Keiser Edwards; *Dir Curatorial Affairs* Margaret C Conrads PhD
Open Mon 11 AM - 6 PM, Wed - Fri 11 AM - 9 PM, Sat - Sun 10 AM - 6 PM, cl Tues, Thanksgiving & Christmas
Collections: paintings; sculpture; works on paper; books; outdoor sculpture

CLARKSVILLE

M **UNIVERSITY OF THE OZARKS,** Stephens Gallery, 415 N College Ave, Walton Fine Arts Bldg Clarksville, AR 72830-2880. Tel 501-979-1000, 979-1349 (Gallery); Fax 501-979-1349; *Gallery Dir* Blaine Caldwell
Open Mon - Fri 10 AM - 3 PM & by special arrangement; No admis fee; Estab 1986
Collections: Gould Ivory Collection, Pfeffer Moser Glass Collection
Exhibitions: Monthly exhibitions
Activities: Educ dept; lect open to public; concerts; gallery talks; tours

L **Robson Library**, 415 N College Ave, Clarksville, AR 72830. Tel 479-979-1382; Fax 479-979-1355; Web: robson.ozarks.edu; *Library Dir* Stuart Stelzer
Open Mon-Thurs 8AM-12AM, Fri 8AM-4:30PM, Sat 1-5PM, Sun 3PM-12AM; Estab 1891
Library Holdings: Book Volumes 6,100, DVDs 70, Fiche, Periodical Subscriptions 10, Video Tapes 100

EL DORADO

A **SOUTH ARKANSAS ARTS CENTER,** 110 E Fifth St, El Dorado, AR 71730. Tel 870-862-5474; Fax 870-862-4921; Email info@saac-arts.org; Web: www.saac-arts.org; *Pres* George Maguire; *Exec Dir* Beth James; *VPres* Robert Allen
Open Mon - Fri 9 AM - 5 PM, Sat 10AM-3PM; No admis fee; Estab 1965 for the promotion, enrichment & improvement of the visual & performing arts by means of exhibits, lectures & instruction & through scholarships to be offered whenever possible; Gallery maintained. New 2,000 sq ft gallery; Mem: 450; dues individual $25, seniors minimum $15; board of dir meeting second Tues every month
Income: Financed by mem, city & state appropriation
Collections: Japanese block prints (including Hokusai, Utamarro, Hiroshige), regional watercolorists, Indian Jewelry (Hopi, Zuni, Navaho)
Exhibitions: Various art shows in this & surrounding states; gallery shows, ten guest artists annually. One show monthly, featuring regional or national artists
Publications: Newsletter, quarterly
Activities: Classes for adults & children; theater & dance workshops; guitar lessons; visual arts classes; lect open to public; gallery talks; competitions; scholarships offered

EUREKA SPRINGS

M **EUREKA FINE ART GALLERY,** 2 Pine St, Eureka Springs, AR 72632-3105. Tel 479-363-6000; Email eurekafineartgallery@gmail.com; Web: www.eurekafineartgallery.com; *Co-owner* Barbara Robinson; *Co-owner* Drew Gentle; *Co-owner* Charles Pierce; *Co-owner* Ernie Kilman; *Co-owner* Denise Ryan; *Co-owner* Larry Mansker; *Co-owner* John Willer; *Co-owner* John Rankine
Open daily 10 AM - 5 PM
Special Subjects: Photography, Sculpture
Collections: paintings; photographs; sculptures
Exhibitions: Temporary exhibits

FAIRFIELD BAY

NORTH CENTRAL ARKANSAS ART GALLERY, 110 Lost Creek Pkwy, Fairfield Bay, AR 72088. Tel 501-884-6100; Email chardon@artelco.com; Web: www.ncafae.org/galleries.html; *Art Coordr* Charlotte Rierson
Open Mon & Thurs - Fri 9 AM - 4 PM; No admis fee; Estab to provide the community with a space to view, purchase & display art
Special Subjects: Painting-American
Collections: works by local & national artists including paintings in oil, watercolor, acrylic & mixed media
Exhibitions: Temporary exhibits

FAYETTEVILLE

M **UNIVERSITY OF ARKANSAS,** Fine Arts Center Gallery, 116 Fine Arts Center, University of Arkansas Dept of Art Fayetteville, AR 72701. Tel 479-575-5202; Fax 479-575-2062; Email stk004@uark.edu; Web: art.uark.edu/fineartsgallery; *Gallery Dir* Sam King
Open Aug - May Mon - Fri 9 AM - 5:30 PM; subject to change, call for details; No admis fee; Estab 1950 as a teaching and community art gallery in fields of painting, drawing, sculpture and architecture; One gallery with moveable display panels covers 80 x 40 ft, gallery is part of center for art, music & theatre; Average Annual Attendance: 7,500
Income: Financed by state appropriation
Collections: Permanent collection of paintings, photographs, prints and sculpture, Seven original Alexander Calder mobiles
Exhibitions: 10-12 exhibitions per year, featuring a variety of media MFA thesis exhibs; faculty artists exhib on rotating basis; vis artists prog
Activities: Classes for adults; lects open to pub, 6-8 vis lectrs per year; concerts; gallery talks; competitions with awards; traveling exhibs 2-3 per yr

L **Fine Arts Library**, 365 N Mcllroy Ave, FNAR-104 Fayetteville, AR 72701-4002. Tel 479-575-4708; Email falib@uark.edu; Web: libinfo.uark.edu/fal/default.asp; *Librn* Phillip J Jones
Open Mon - Thurs 8 AM - 11 PM, Fri 8 AM - 6 PM, Sat 1 PM - 6 PM, Sun 2 PM - 11 PM; Estab 1951 to support the curriculum in art & architecture; Circ 5,000
Library Holdings: Book Volumes 33,000, CD-ROMs 60, DVDs 20, Exhibition Catalogs, Periodical Subscriptions 100
Special Subjects: Architecture, Art Education, Art History, Landscape Architecture, Interior Design

FORT SMITH

M **FORT SMITH REGIONAL ART MUSEUM,** 1601 Rogers Ave, Fort Smith, AR 72901. Tel 479-784-2787; Fax 479-784-9071; Email info@fsram.org; Web: www.fsram.org; *Gallery Mgr* Casey Seamans; *Educ Dir* Daleana Vaughan; *Marketing Asst* Melissa Carry; *Educ Asst* Natasha Luong
Open Tues - Sat 10 AM - 6 PM, Sun 1 PM - 5 PM, cl New Year's Day; Independence Day, Thanksgiving & day after; Christmas Eve & Day; No admis fee; Originated in 1948 as Ark. Assoc of University Women. Museum founded in Jan 2013; Rotating traveling exhibs, original exhibs, invitationals, permanent coll exhibits; Average Annual Attendance: 14,000; Mem: 400; dues $35-$5,000
Income: financed by grants, membership, contributions & museum store sales
Library Holdings: Auction Catalogs, Book Volumes, Original Art Works
Special Subjects: Drawings, Painting-American, Photography, Porcelain, Prints, Sculpture, Watercolors, Landscapes, Textiles
Collections: American painting, graphics & drawings, works of sculpture & photography, Boehm porcelain (largest collection in Ark), local & regional art
Exhibitions: Two-three exhib per month; competitions; traveling exhibits
Publications: Museum newsletter
Activities: Classes for adults, children & summer art camp; lects open to the pub; tours; competitions with awards; AIA Gulf States Region Merit Award & Historic Preservation of Arkansas Excellence in Preservation Award; scholarships offered; Outreach programs for at risk youth; sales shop sells original art, reproductions, prints, original jewelry, pottery; original art

HOT SPRINGS

M **THE FINE ARTS CENTER OF HOT SPRINGS,** 626 Central Ave Hot Springs, AR 71901; PO Box 6263, Hot Springs, AR 71902-6263. Tel 501-624-0489; Fax 501-624-0489; Email info@hsfac.org; Web: www.hsfac.org; *Exec Dir* Donna Dunnahoe; *Gallery Dir* Kaye Coombe
Open Tues & Sat 10 AM - 5 PM; No admis fee; Estab 1947 as a multi-disciplinary Arts Center, for education, creative activities & encouragement of community participation; Exhib Center, gallery, gift shop; Average Annual Attendance: 12,000; Mem: 250 mems; $35 annual mem fee, $100 artist mem fee
Income: Financed by individual & corporate mem, grants from the Arkansas Arts Council & National Endowment for the Arts
Collections: Photos - Hot Springs Bath Houses, Marilyn Monroe collection, Permanent collection of fine art
Exhibitions: regional, state & local artist exhibition
Publications: Class schedule brochures; monthly exhibit announcements; newsletters, 4 times per year; Short List collection of short stories; A Gathering of Artists II, Artists collective
Activities: Classes for adults & children in art; lects open to pub; 10 vis lectrs per yr; concerts; gallery talks; tours; sponsored competitions: Diamond, Photo & Regional; children's art schols offered; mus shop sells original art, pottery & woodcarvings, glass, jewelry, prints

L **NATIONAL PARK COMMUNITY COLLEGE LIBRARY,** 101 College Dr, Hot Springs, AR 71913-9173. Tel 501-760-4222; Fax 501-760-4106; Email sseaman@npcc.edu; *Dir* Sara Seaman
Open Mon - Thurs 7 AM - 9 PM, Fri 7 AM - 4:30 PM, Sat 9AM-1PM; Estab 1970
Income: Financed by state appropriation
Purchases: $50,000
Library Holdings: Book Volumes 750, Periodical Subscriptions 200, Video Tapes 150
Collections: Art history, pottery
Exhibitions: Rotating exhibitions

JONESBORO

M **ARKANSAS STATE UNIVERSITY-ART DEPARTMENT, JONESBORO,** Fine Arts Center Gallery, Caraway Rd, Jonesboro, AR; PO Box 1920, State University, AR 72467-1920. Tel 870-972-3050; Fax 870-972-3932; Email csteele@astate.edu; *Chair Art Dept* Curtis Steele; *Dir* Steven Mayes
Open weekdays Mon-Fri 10 AM - 5PM; No admis fee; Estab 1967 for educ objectives; recognition of contemporary artists & encouragement to students; Located in the Fine Arts Center, the well-lighted gallery measures 40 x 45 ft plus corridor display areas; Average Annual Attendance: 10,500
Income: $3956 (financed by state appropriation)
Collections: Contemporary paintings, contemporary sculpture, historical & contemporary prints, photographs
Publications: Exhibition catalogs
Activities: Lects open to public, 4-6 vis lectrs per yr; gallery talks; competitions; originate traveling exhibs

L **Library**, 108 Cooley Dr, Jonesboro, AR; PO Box 2040, State University, AR 72467-2040. Tel 870-972-3077; Fax 870-972-5706; *Dean* Dr Mary Moore; *Users Svcs Mgr* Anthony Phillips; *Reference Librn* Jeff Bailey
Library Holdings: Book Volumes 10,000, Cassettes, Fiche, Filmstrips, Kodachrome Transparencies, Motion Pictures, Periodical Subscriptions 79, Reels, Slides
Collections: Microfilm collection for 19th century photography

LITTLE ROCK

M **ARKANSAS ARTS CENTER,** 501 E 9th St, Little Rock, AR 72202; PO Box 2137, Little Rock, AR 72203-2137. Tel 501-372-4000; Fax 501-375-8053; Email info@www.arkansasartscenter.org; Web: www.arkansasartscenter.org; *Exec Dir* Todd A Herman, PhD; *Chief Cur* Brian Lang; *Cur Drawings* Ann Prentice Wagner,

PhD; *Registrar* Katie Hall; *CFO* Laine Harber; *Dir Develop* Kelly Fleming; *Dir Educ* Rana Edgar
Open Tues-Sat 10AM-5PM, Sun 11AM-5PM; No admis fee to galleries & Terry House Community Gallery, admis charged for theatre activities; Estab 1960 to further the develop, the understanding & the appreciation of the visual & performing arts; Circ Non-circulating, research only; Eight galleries; Average Annual Attendance: 640,000; Mem: 3,500; dues from benefactor $20,000 to basic $55; annual meeting in Aug
Income: Financed by endowment, mem, city & state appropriation & earned income & private corporate, state, local & federal grants
Library Holdings: Auction Catalogs, Audio Tapes, Book Volumes, CD-ROMs, Cards, Cassettes, Clipping Files, Compact Disks, DVDs, Exhibition Catalogs, Original Documents, Pamphlets, Periodical Subscriptions
Special Subjects: Ceramics, Crafts, Decorative Arts, Drawings, Glass, Jewelry, Metalwork, Painting-American, Painting-European, Prints, Renaissance Art, Watercolors, Woodcarvings, Sculpture
Collections: Drawings from the Renaissance to present, with major coll of American & European drawings since 1900, 19th & 20th century paintings & prints, 20th century sculpture & photographs, Oriental & American decorative arts, contemporary crafts & toys designed by artists
Publications: Members Bulletin, quarterly; annual membership catalog; annual report; catalogue selections from the permanent collection; exhibit catalogues & brochures
Activities: Classes for adults & children; dramatic progs; children's theatre; docent training; lects open to pub, 6-10 vis lectrs per yr; gallery talks; tours; competitions with awards; exten dept serving the state of Arkansas; artmobile; individual paintings & original objects of art lent to schools, civic groups & churches; lending collection contains motion pictures, original prints, paintings, 4300 phonorecords & 16,000 slides; book traveling exhibs; originates traveling exhibs; mus shop sells books, original art, reproductions, jewelry, crafts, cards & calendars

L **Elizabeth Prewitt Taylor Memorial Library**, 501 E 9th St, Little Rock, AR 72202; PO Box 2137, Little Rock, AR 72203-2137. Tel 501-396-0341; Fax 501-375-8053; Email library@arkansasartscenter.org; Web: www.arkansasartscenter.org; *Exec Dir* Todd Herman, PhD; *Chief Cur* Brian Lang; *Cur Drawings* Ann Wagner
Open Tues - Sat 10 AM - 5 PM, Sun 11 AM - 5 PM; No admis fee; photocopying charges apply; Estab 1963 to provide resources in the arts for students, educators & interested pub; For reference only
Library Holdings: Auction Catalogs, Book Volumes 5,500, Clipping Files, DVDs, Exhibition Catalogs, Motion Pictures, Pamphlets, Periodical Subscriptions 20, Photographs, Records, Video Tapes
Special Subjects: Afro-American Art, American Indian Art, American Western Art, Art History, Asian Art, Carpets & Rugs, Ceramics, Crafts, Decorative Arts, Drawings, Eskimo Art, Folk Art, Glass, Historical Material, History of Art & Archaeology, Latin American Art, Painting-American, Photography, Printmaking, Prints, Sculpture, Textiles, Watercolors
Publications: Delta Works
Activities: Classes for adults & children; dramatic progs; docent training; Junior Art Academy; tours; extension prog, state servs; artmobile; museum shop sells original art, apparel

M **HISTORIC ARKANSAS MUSEUM,** 200 E Third St, Little Rock, AR 72201. Tel 501-324-9351; Fax 501-324-9345; Email info@historicarkansas.org; Web: www.historicarkansas.org; *Cur Research* Swannee Bennett; *Dir Educ* Starr Mitchell; *Dir* William B Worthen Jr; *Dir Community Engagement* Ellen Korenblat; *Chmn* James M "Butch" Warren; *Pres* Wally Nixon; *Historic Site Specialist* David Etchieson; *Conservator* Andrew Zawacki; *Registrar* Lark Buckingham; *Fiscal Mgr* Rebecca Hochradel; *Coordr* Tricia Spione; *Security Supv* Mike Croy; *Mus Shop Mgr* Paige James
Open daily 9 AM - 5 PM, Sun 1 - 5 PM, cl New Year's, Easter, Thanksgiving, Christmas Eve & Christmas Day; Admis to mus houses adults $2.50, seniors (65+) $1.50, children $1, Museum Center & galleries free; Restoration completed 1941; Historic Arkansas Museum includes pre- Civil War homes, education space & galleries to interpret early Arkansas history; Average Annual Attendance: 50,000; Mem: Individual $35, family $50, supporting $100, sustaining $250, founder $500, cornerstone $1,000 & up; museum shop sells books, original art, reproductions, prints & handmade crafts
Income: Financed by state & private funding
Special Subjects: American Indian Art, Archaeology, Architecture, Carpets & Rugs, Ceramics, Costumes, Crafts, Decorative Arts, Drawings, Embroidery, Etchings & Engravings, Ethnology, Folk Art, Furniture, Glass, Historical Material, Laces, Manuscripts, Maps, Metalwork, Painting-American, Period Rooms, Porcelain, Portraits
Collections: Arkansas made guns & furniture, Audubon prints, furnishing of the period, prints & maps from the 19th century, silver coll, watercolors
Publications: Arkansas Made: The Decorative Mechanical & Fine Arts Produced in Arkansas 1819-1870, Vol I & Vol II; Exhibit catalogues; brochure; Newsletter, Collections: A Garden Heritage
Activities: Classes for children; Log House activities include educational prog for students & adults in candle dipping, cooking & needlework; reception ctr has exhibs & art gallery; individual paintings & original objects of art lent to other mus & cultural institutions; originate traveling exhibs to area mus & schools; mus store sells Arkansas made art & crafts

L **Library**, 200 E Third St, Little Rock, AR 72201. Tel 501-324-9351; Fax 501-324-9345; Email info@historicarkansas.org; Web: www.historicarkansas.org; *Dir* W B Worthen Jr; *Cur* Swannee Bennett; *Educ Dir* Starr Mitchell; *Develop Dir* Louise Terzia; *Communs Dir* Ellen Korenblat
Open Mon - Sat 9 AM - 5 PM, Sun 1 - 5 PM; Admis to galleries free, small charge for tours; Estab 1941 to preserve & promote Arkansas history; Arkansas Artist Gallery contains contemporary Arkansas artists with new display monthly, Knife Gallery contains Bowie Knife & history, 4 other galleries are dedicated to Arkansas made objects & history; Average Annual Attendance: 50,000; Mem: 400
Income: Financed by the state & private funds
Purchases: Arkansas made items for museum coll
Library Holdings: Audio Tapes, Book Volumes 1,000, Cassettes, Clipping Files, Framed Reproductions, Manuscripts, Original Art Works, Pamphlets, Periodical Subscriptions 8, Photographs, Prints, Reels, Reproductions, Slides
Collections: Arkansas-made decorative, mechanical & fine art
Exhibitions: Contemporary art; historical exhibits
Publications: Arkansas Made: The Decorative, Mechanical and Fine Art Produced in Arkansas 1819-1870 vol I & II
Activities: Classes for adults & children; dramatic progs; docent training; lects open to pub, 3 vis lectrs per yr; tours; exhibs openings; special events; individual paintings & original objects of art lent to other mus; mus shop sells books, original art, reproductions, prints

M **QUAPAW QUARTER ASSOCIATION, INC,** Villa Marre, Curran Hall, 615 E Capitol Ave Little Rock, AR 72202-2421; PO Box 165023, Little Rock, AR 72216-5023. Tel 501-371-0075; Fax 501-374-8142; Email qqa@quapaw.com; Web: www.quapaw.com; *Exec Dir* Rhea Roberts; *Operations Asst* Michelle Bilello
Open Mon - Fri 9 AM - 1 PM, Sun 1 - 5 PM, & by appointment; Admis adults $3, sr citizens & students $2; Estab 1966; The Villa Marre is a historic house mus which, by virtue of its extraordinary collection of late 19th century decorative arts, is a center for the study of Victorian styles; Average Annual Attendance: 5,000; Mem: 350; dues $25 & up; annual meeting in Nov
Income: $95,000 (financed by mem, corporate support, grants & fundraising events)
Special Subjects: Decorative Arts, Furniture, Textiles
Collections: Artwork by Benjamin Brantley, curios appropriate to an 1881 Second Empire Victorian home, late 19th & early 20th century furniture, textiles, 19 century maps, custom floorcloth
Publications: Quapaw Quarter Chronicle, bimonthly
Activities: Classes for adults & children; docent training; lects open to pub; 8-12 vis lectrs; tours; book traveling exhibs; originate traveling exhibs; sales shop sells books; magazines; prints & other items

L **Preservation Resource Center/ Historic Cannon Hall**, 615 E Capitol Ave, Little Rock, AR 72202; PO Box 165023, Little Rock, AR 72216. Tel 501-371-0075; Fax 501-374-8142; Web: www.quapaw.com; *Exec Dir* Roger D Williams; *Operations Asst* Michelle Bilello; *Exec Dir* Rhea Roberts
Open Mon - Sat 9 AM - 5 PM, Sun 1 - 5 PM; No admis fee, donations; Estab 1976 for the assembly of materials relevant to historic buildings & neighborhoods in the greater Little Rock area
Income: Financed by private donations
Library Holdings: Book Volumes 250, Clipping Files, Kodachrome Transparencies, Lantern Slides, Manuscripts, Maps, Pamphlets, Periodical Subscriptions 12, Photographs
Special Subjects: Maps, Manuscripts, Architecture, Photography
Collections: Architectural drawings
Activities: Lects open to pub; 4-10 vis lectrs per yr; tours; sales shop sells books, prints

SOCIETY FOR COMMERCIAL ARCHEOLOGY, PO Box 2500, Little Rock, AR 72203-2500. Tel 608-264-6560; Fax 608-264-7615; Email office@sca-roadside.org; Web: www.sca-roadside.org; *Pres* Nancy Sturm; *VPres* Michael Hirsch
Estab 1976 to promote pub awareness, exchange information & encourage selective conservation of the commercial landscape; Mem: 800; dues institutional $40, individual $25; annual meetings
Income: Financed by mem & dues
Publications: Journal, two times a year; newsletter, quarterly

M **UNIVERSITY OF ARKANSAS AT LITTLE ROCK,** Art Galleries, Dept of Art, 2801 S University Little Rock, AR 72204-1000. Tel 501-569-8977; Fax 501-569-8775; Email becushman@uair.edu; *Cur Asst* Nathan Larson; *Gallery Dir* Brad Cushman
Open Mon - Fri 9 AM - 5 PM, Sat 1-10PM, Sun 2 - 5 PM; No admis fee; Estab 1976 as an acad resource for the university; Three gallery spaces in Fine Art Building on university campus. 2,500 sq ft, 650 sq ft, 900 sq ft, respectively. Maintains reference library; Average Annual Attendance: 2,000
Income: Financed by university
Special Subjects: Etchings & Engravings, Painting-American, Photography, Prints, Sculpture, Woodcuts
Collections: Graphic Arts, prints, Photography, Works on Paper, drawings
Activities: Lects open to pub, 6-8 vis lectrs per yr; competitions; book traveling exhibs 3-5 per yr

L **UNIVERSITY OF ARKANSAS AT LITTLE ROCK,** Art Library and Galleries, 2801 S University, Fine Arts Bldg, Rm 202 Little Rock, AR 72204-1000. Tel 501-569-8976; Fax 501-683-7022; Email lmgrace@ualr.edu; Web: http://ualr.edu/art; *Chmn* Tom Clifton; *Visual Resources Cur* Laura Grace; *Gallery Cur* Brad Cushman; *Asst Gallery Cur* Nathan Larson
Open Mon - Fri 9 AM - 5 PM, Sat 10AM-1PM, Sun 1 - 4 PM; No admis fee; Estab 1978 for educational purposes; Gallery I, 2,500 sq ft, is a two story space; Gallery II, 500 sq ft, is glassed on two sides; Gallery III is a hallway for student works
Income: Financed by state funds & private donations
Library Holdings: Book Volumes 940, Clipping Files, Exhibition Catalogs, Periodical Subscriptions 15, Video Tapes 445
Collections: Photographs & other works on paper
Activities: Lects open to pub, 3 vis lectrs per yr; gallery talks; student competitions with awards; scholarships offered; originate traveling exhibs

MAGNOLIA

M **SOUTHERN ARKANSAS UNIVERSITY,** Art Dept Gallery & Magale Art Gallery, 100 E University, SAU Box 1309 Magnolia, AR 71753-2181. Tel 870-235-4000; Email rsstout@saumag.edu; Web: www.saumag.edu/art; *Chmn Art Dept* Scotland Stout; *Prof* Steven Ochs; *Pres* Steven G Gamble
Open Mon - Thurs 8 AM - 10 PM, Fri 8 AM - 5 PM, Sat 10 AM - 4 PM, Sun 2 - 10:30 PM (McGale Gallery), Mon, Wed & Fri 8 AM - 5 PM (Brinson Gallery); No admis fee; Estab 1970; Magale Library Art Gallery, foyer type with 120 running ft exhibition space, floor to ceiling fabric covered; Average Annual Attendance: 2,000; Scholarships
Income: Financed partially by state funds

Special Subjects: Prints
Collections: American printmakers
Exhibitions: Various professional exhibits
Activities: Classes for adults & children; lect open to public; gallery talks; tours; scholarships & fels offered; individual paintings & original objects of art lent to schools, nonprofit organizations

MONTICELLO

M **DREW COUNTY HISTORICAL SOCIETY,** Museum, 404 S Main, Monticello, AR 71655. Tel 870-367-7446, 367-5746; *Dir* Thomas Gray; *Pres* Jack Bennett; *Treas* Kittie S Hoofman; *VPres* Rhonda Bryant
Open Fri & Sat 2PM - 5PM; No admis fee; Estab 1971; Average Annual Attendance: 3,000; Mem: dues benefactor $1,000, patron $500, corporate $200, friends of mus $100, individual with journal $25, individual $15; 160 members
Income: Financed by endowment, mem, city & county appropriation, fundraisers
Special Subjects: American Indian Art, American Western Art, Antiquities-Assyrian, Antiquities-Persian, Archaeology, Architecture, Bookplates & Bindings, Bronzes, Carpets & Rugs, Ceramics, Coins & Medals, Costumes, Crafts, Decorative Arts, Dolls, Drawings, Embroidery, Etchings & Engravings, Flasks & Bottles, Folk Art, Furniture, Glass, Graphics, Historical Material, Ivory, Jade, Jewelry, Juvenile Art, Laces, Landscapes, Leather, Manuscripts, Maps, Metalwork, Military Art, Miniatures, Painting-American, Painting-Dutch, Painting-Italian, Period Rooms, Pewter, Photography, Porcelain, Portraits, Posters, Pottery, Pre-Columbian Art, Primitive art, Stained Glass, Tapestries, Textiles, Watercolors, Woodcarvings, Woodcuts
Collections: Antique toys & dolls, Civil War artifacts, Indian artifacts, Handwork & clothing from early 1800s, Woodworking tools, Farm implements, log cabins, china
Exhibitions: Antique Quilts, Trunks, Paintings by Local Artists; Leather Parlor Furniture from late 1800s
Publications: Drew County Historical Journal, annually
Activities: 4 vis lectrs per yr; tours; mus shop sells books & magazines

MORRILTON

M **RIALTO COMMUNITY ARTS CENTER,** The Gallery, 213 E Broadway, Morrilton, AR 72110-3403; PO Box 176, Morrilton, AR 72110. Tel 501-477-9955; Email rialtomorrilton@gmail.com; Web: rialtomorrilton.com; *Gallery Dir* George Hoelzeman
Mon - Thurs 5 PM - 8 PM; Estab 1911 to deliver community arts programming
Special Subjects: Painting-American, Photography
Collections: Work by local artists
Exhibitions: Temporary exhibits
Activities: Art programming; events; dance & theatre performances

MOUNTAIN VIEW

L **OZARK FOLK CENTER, ARKANSAS STATE PARK,** Ozark Cultural Resource Center, 1032 Park Ave, Mountain View, AR 72560-6008. Tel 870-269-3851; Fax 870-269-2909; Web: www.ozarkfolkcenter.com; *Archival Asst* Tricia Hearn
Call for hours; No admis fee; The Park was estab in 1973 to demonstrate various aspects of traditional culture of the Ozark Mountain region, the Resource Center was estab in 1975 to preserve the artifacts aspects & documentary history of the Ozark Region culture, crafts & music; The Resource Center is maintained for pub reference only; Average Annual Attendance: 200
Income: $70,000 (financed by state appropriation & auxiliary comt)
Library Holdings: Audio Tapes, Book Volumes 10,000, CD-ROMs, Cassettes, Clipping Files, Compact Disks, DVDs, Exhibition Catalogs, Filmstrips, Kodachrome Transparencies, Manuscripts, Maps, Memorabilia, Motion Pictures, Original Art Works, Pamphlets, Periodical Subscriptions 50, Photographs, Prints, Records, Reels, Slides, Video Tapes
Special Subjects: Architecture, Art Education, Art History, Constructions, Costume Design & Constr, Crafts, Decorative Arts, Drawings, Embroidery, Folk Art, Furniture, Glass, Graphic Arts, Handicrafts, Historical Material, Laces, Landscape Architecture, Landscapes, Manuscripts, Photography, Portraits, Textiles, Video, Woodcarvings
Collections: Traditional Ozark crafts, music folios & sheet music, 30 yrs of Live Folk Center performances, Stan French recorded music collection, The William K McNeil Collection
Activities: Lect open to public; concerts; tours; awards; workshops; sales shop sells books, magazines, slides

PINE BLUFF

A **ARTS & SCIENCE CENTER FOR SOUTHEAST ARKANSAS,** 701 Main, Pine Bluff, AR 71601. Tel 870-536-3375; Fax 870-536-3380; Email lshoults@asc701.org; Web: www.asc701.org; *Exec Dir* Dr Lenore Shoults; *Cur* Courtney Taylor
Open Tues - Fri 10 AM - 5 PM, Sat 1 PM - 4 PM; No admis fee; Opened in 1968 in Civic Center Complex; mission is to provide for the practice, teaching, performance, enjoyment, & understanding of the Arts & Sciences, opened new facility 1994; 22,000 sq ft facility containing four galleries & a 232 seat theatre, instructional studio; Average Annual Attendance: 33,000; Mem: 783; dues family $50
Income: $490,000 by state, municipal & membership dues
Library Holdings: Book Volumes, CD-ROMs, Cassettes, Clipping Files, Exhibition Catalogs, Original Art Works, Photographs, Sculpture, Video Tapes
Special Subjects: Afro-American Art, Bronzes, Collages, Drawings, Etchings & Engravings, Painting-American, Photography, Prints, Sculpture, Watercolors, Landscapes
Collections: Photographs by: Matt Bradley, J C Coovert of the Southern Cotton Culture, early 1900s, John M Howard Memorial Collection of Works by African American Artists, art deco/nouveau bronze sculptures, small works on paper (Arkansas artists), works on paper by local, national & international artists, Southern Mississippi Delta Art, Elsie Mistie Sterling Collection of Botanical Paintings, Howard S Stern Collection
Exhibitions: Art Gallery Exhibitions; Biennial Regional Competition; science exhibitions; annual cultural project
Activities: Classes for adults & children; dramatic progs; docent training; lects open to pub, 3-5 vis lectrs per yr; concerts; gallery talks; tours; sponsoring of competition; schols; exten prog for 10 counties of Southeast Arkansas; book traveling exhibs, 1-2 per yr

M **PINE BLUFF/JEFFERSON COUNTY HISTORICAL MUSEUM,** 201 E 4th Ave, Pine Bluff, AR 71601-4401. Tel 501-541-5402; Fax 501-541-5405; Email jcmuseum@ipa.net; Web: pbjcmuseum.com; *Dir* Sue Trulock; *Cur* Lola Gordon; *Registrar* Rebecca Phillips
Open Mon - Fri 9 AM - 5 PM, Sat 10 AM - 2 PM; No admis fee; Estab 1980 to collect, preserve & interpret artifacts showing the history of Jefferson County; Restored Union train station; Average Annual Attendance: 20,000; Mem: 300; Dues $10 - $1,000 ann.
Income: $27,000 (financed by county Quortum Ct appropriation)
Special Subjects: Historical Material, American Indian Art, Costumes, Dolls, Flasks & Bottles, Miniatures
Collections: Clothing dating from 1870, personal artifacts, photographs, tools & equipment, Quapau Indian artifacts, Antique Dolls - Local Black History
Exhibitions: Bottle Collection; Made in Pine Bluff AR; exhibit of dolls; Quapaw Indian Artifacts; Settlers Exhibit; Civil War Exhibit; World War I; World War II; Local Black History exhibit; Boeu & Currow - Antique Bottles
Publications: The Museum Record, quarterly newsletter
Activities: Lect open to public, 50 vis lectrs per year; gallery talks; docent led tours anytime

SILOAM SPRINGS

M **SAGER CREEK ARTS CENTER,** 301 E Twin Springs, PO Box 1127 Siloam Springs, AR 72761. Tel 479-524-4000; Email scac@cox-internet.com; *Exec Dir* Mary Ellen Mathers
Center offers affordable, quality entertainment and cultural events

SPRINGDALE

M **ARTS CENTER OF THE OZARKS,** 214 S Main, Springdale, AR 72765-7204. Tel 501-751-5441; Fax 501-927-0308; Email acozarks@swbell.net; Web: www.artscenteroftheozarks.org; *Dir Visual Arts* Lindsay Moover; *Dir Theatre* Harry Blundell; *Dir* Kathi Blundell
Open Mon - Fri 9 AM - 5 PM, Sat 9AM-3PM; No admis fee; Estab 1968, merged with the Springdale Arts Center to become Arts Center of the Ozarks in 1973 to preserve the traditional handcrafts, to promote all qualified contemporary arts & crafts, to help find markets for artists & craftsmen; Local & regional artists; Mem: 900; dues $20 & up
Income: Financed by mem & state appropriations
Exhibitions: Exhibitions change monthly
Publications: Arts Center Events, monthly; newsletter, bimonthly
Activities: Adult & children's workshops; instruction in the arts, music, dance & drama run concurrently with other activities; eight theater productions per year; concerts, arts & crafts

M **CITY OF SPRINGDALE,** Shiloh Museum of Ozark History, 118 W Johnson Ave, Springdale, AR 72764-4313. Tel 479-750-8165; Fax 479-756-7732; Email shiloh@springdalear.gov; Web: www.shilohmuseum.org; *Dir* Allyn Lord; *Outreach Coordr* Susan Young; *Exhib Designer* Curtis Morris; *Coll Mgr* Carolyn Reno; *Librn* Marie Demeroukas; *Secy* Kathy Plume; *Educ Colls Asst* Aaron Loehudorf; *Photographer* Kris Johnson; *Maintenance* Marty Powers; *Educ Mgr* Judy Costello; *Educ Asst* Carly Squyres
Open Mon - Sat 10 AM - 5 PM; No admis fee; Estab 1968 to exhibit history & culture of Ozarks Arkansas; Displays in main exhibit hall & six historic outbuildings; Average Annual Attendance: 51,618; Mem: 650; dues begin at $10
Income: $642,400 (financed by endowment, mem, city appropriation, private & pub grants)
Library Holdings: Book Volumes, Clipping Files, Manuscripts, Maps, Periodical Subscriptions, Photographs, Prints
Special Subjects: American Indian Art, Ceramics, Crafts, Drawings, Embroidery, Flasks & Bottles, Folk Art, Furniture, Glass, Gold, Historical Material, Leather, Manuscripts, Maps, Painting-American, Period Rooms, Photography, Pottery, Primitive art, Textiles, Woodcarvings
Collections: Folk Arts, Ozarks Photographers, Charles Summey Oils, Essie Ward Primitive Paintings
Exhibitions: Essie Ward; Charles Summey; Peggy McCormack
Publications: Newsletter, quarterly
Activities: Progs & workshops for adults & children; lects open to pub, 10 vis lectrs per yr; lending coll contains 500 items; retail store sells books, magazines & original art

STUTTGART

A **GRAND PRAIRIE ARTS COUNCIL, INC,** Arts Center of the Grand Prairie, 108 W 12th St, Stuttgart, AR 72160-5210; PO Box 65, Stuttgart, AR 72160-0065. Tel 870-673-1781; Email Artsool@centurytel.net; *Pres* Marianne Maynard; *Ex Dir* Charles "Chuck" Law
Open Mon - Fri 10 AM - 12:30 PM & 1:30 - 4:30 PM, cl Sat & Sun; No admis fee; Estab 1956 & incorporated 1964 to encourage cultural develop in the Grand Prairie area, to sponsor the Grand Prairie Festival of Arts held annually in Sept at Stuttgart.

Estab as an arts center for jr & sr citizens; Average Annual Attendance: 2,500; Mem: 250; dues $25 & up; monthly meetings
Income: Financed by mem, donations & grants
Collections: Permanent collection started by donations
Exhibitions: Monthly exhibitions of Arkansas artists
Publications: Festival invitations; newsletter, monthly; programs
Activities: Classes for adults & children; dramatic progs; lects open to pub, 4-6 vis lectrs per yr; gallery talks; competitions with awards; monthly gourmet coffee house featuring various types of music & comedy; originate traveling exhibs

VAN BUREN

M **CENTER FOR ART & EDUCATION,** 104 N 13th St, Van Buren, AR 72956-4512. Tel 479-474-7767; Email info@art-ed.org; Web: www.art-ed.org; *Exec Dir* Jane Owen
Open Tues - Fri 10 AM - 4 PM; Admis free; Estab 1976; Two galleries, main gallery & studio gallery; Average Annual Attendance: 10,000; Mem: Dues $50 individual, $100 family
Library Holdings: Book Volumes
Special Subjects: Glass, Landscapes, Metalwork, Miniatures, Painting-American, Religious Art
Activities: Classes for adults & children; lects open to pub; 2 vis lectrs per yr; gallery talks; tours; competitions; schols; mus shop sells books, magazines, original art, reproductions & prints

CALIFORNIA

ALISO VIEJO

M **SOKA UNIVERSITY,** Founders Hall Art Gallery, 1 University Dr, Aliso Viejo, CA 92656. Tel 949-480-4081; Fax 949-480-4260; Email info@soka.edu; Web: www.soka.edu
Open Mon - Fri 9 AM - 5 PM; No admis fee; Estab May 2001; 8,000 sq ft; 2 floors
Collections: Works by national & international artists; paintings; photographs; sculpture
Activities: Lects open to pub; 2 vis lectrs per yr; tours

APTOS

A **SAVING & PRESERVING ARTS & CULTURAL ENVIRONMENTS,** 9053 Soquel Dr Ste 205, Aptos, CA 95003-4034. Tel 323-463-1629; Email info@spacearchives.org; *Dir* Jo Farb Hernandez
Open by appointment only; Estab 1978 for documentation & preservation of folk art environments; Mem: Dues $15-$250
Income: Financed by membership, state, grants
Collections: Archival material about America's contemporary folk art environments
Exhibitions: Several exhibitions per year
Publications: Occasional newsletter
Activities: Lect open to public, 6 vis lectrs per year; gallery talks; tours; lending collection contains 20,000 photographs; originates traveling exhibs; sales shop sells books, magazines, prints

L **Spaces Library & Archive,** 9053 Soquel Dr Ste 205, Aptos, CA 95003-4034. Tel 831-662-2907; Email info@spacesarchives.org; Web: www.spacesarchives.org; *Dir* Jo Farb Hernandez; *Archivist* Stacy Mualler
Open by appointment only; Estab 1978 to provide reference for scholars, artists, preservations concerned with art environments; For lending & reference
Income: Financed by government & pvt grants, volunteers, usage fees, curatorial fees
Library Holdings: Audio Tapes, Book Volumes 1500, CD-ROMs, Cassettes, Clipping Files, Compact Disks, DVDs, Exhibition Catalogs, Kodachrome Transparencies, Manuscripts, Maps, Memorabilia, Original Art Works, Original Documents, Other Holdings, Pamphlets, Periodical Subscriptions, Photographs, Prints, Records, Reels, Sculpture, Slides, Video Tapes
Special Subjects: Architecture, Art History, Collages, Constructions, Decorative Arts, Film, Folk Art, Historical Material, Intermedia, Landscape Architecture, Mexican Art, Mosaics, Photography, Posters, Sculpture, Video
Collections: Watts Tower Collection - photographs, documentation, archive, letters, clippings, history, Seymour Rosen Photographs, Robert Foster Photographs
Exhibitions: Divine Disorder: Art Environments in California; Singular Spaces: Spanish Art Environment, Ronald Gasowski Photographs, Jo Farb Hernandez Photographs & Documentation of Spanish Art Environments
Activities: Lects; originate traveling exhibs to nonprofit galleries & museums; mus shop sells books, magazines & prints

BAKERSFIELD

M **BAKERSFIELD ART FOUNDATION,** Bakersfield Museum of Art, 1930 R St, Bakersfield, CA 93301-4815. Tel 661-323-7219; Fax 661-323-7266; Web: www.csub.edu/bma; *Exec Dir/CEO* Bernard J Herman; *Asst Dir* David Gordon; *Cur* Emily Falke
Open Tues - Fri 10 AM - 4 PM, Sat - Sun Noon - 4 PM, cl Mon; Admis adults $5, seniors $4, students & children under 12 $2, children 6 & under free; Estab to provide the facilities & services of an accredited art museum which will nurture & develop the visual arts in Kern County; Mus is a one story building encompassing 5 galleries adjacent to Central Park; Average Annual Attendance: 20,000; Mem: 900; dues $20-60
Income: Financed by corporate, state & local public, & private nonprofit sources
Special Subjects: Painting-American
Collections: California art & artists
Activities: Educ prog; classes for adults & children; docent training; lects open to pub; gallery talks; tours; juried competitions with prizes; schols; book traveling exhibs; originate traveling exhibs; mus shop sells books, magazines, original art, gifts, crafts & art-related items

M **BUENA VISTA MUSEUM OF NATURAL HISTORY,** 2018 Chester Ave, Bakersfield, CA 93301-4420. Tel 661-324-6350; Fax 661-324-7522; Email bvmnh@sharktoothhill.com; Web: www.sharktoothhill.com; *Contact* Bob Smith
Open Thurs - Sat 10 AM - 5 PM, also by appt; Admis adults $3, children, seniors & students with ID $2; group rates available; mus promotes scientific & educ aspects of earth history with emphasis on paleontology & anthropology in Kern County; Mem: memberships available
Special Subjects: Historical Material, Anthropology
Collections: The Bob & Mary Ernst Collection
Exhibitions: Sharktooth Hill, Kern County, CA; San Joaquin Valley Through Time; McKittrick Tar Seeps; Mount St Helens: 20 Years Later; San Andreas Fault; Yosemite Valley
Publications: Sharkbites, newsletter
Activities: Geology field trips; workshops; events; mus related items for sale

M **CALIFORNIA STATE UNIVERSITY, BAKERSFIELD,** Todd Madigan Gallery, 9001 Stockdale Hwy, 15FA Bakersfield, CA 93311-1099. Tel 661-654-2238; Fax 661-654-2539; Web: www.csub.edu/art/gallery; *Dir* Joey Kotting
Open acad yr Tues - Thurs 1 PM - 6 PM, Sat 1 PM - 5 PM, cl univ breaks & holidays
Collections: paintings; sculpture; photographs

M **KERN COUNTY MUSEUM,** 3801 Chester Ave, Bakersfield, CA 93301-1345. Tel 661-852-5000; Fax 661-322-6415; Web: kcmuseum.org; *Asst Dir* Jeff Nickell; *Dir* Carola Rupert Enriquez; *Cur* Lori Wear
Open Mon - Sat 10AM-5PM; Admis adults $8, sr citizens $7, children 3-12 $6, under 3 free; Estab 1945 to collect & interpret local history & culture, mainly through a 14 acre outdoor mus. Also has Lori Brock Children's Discovery Center; One main building, 1929 Chamber of Commerce Building, houses changing exhibitions on assorted topics; modern track lighting, temporary walls; Average Annual Attendance: 103,000; Mem: 650; dues family $60
Income: $1.7 million (financed by county appropriation, earned income & non-profit foundation)
Purchases: Archival, occasionally decorative arts
Library Holdings: Manuscripts, Maps, Memorabilia, Motion Pictures, Original Documents, Other Holdings, Pamphlets, Periodical Subscriptions, Photographs, Prints, Records, Video Tapes
Special Subjects: Archaeology, Architecture, Costumes, Decorative Arts, Ethnology, Historical Material, Laces, Maps, Period Rooms, Photography
Collections: 60-structure outdoor museum covering 14 acres, Photographic Image Collection, Material Culture, Paleontology, Natural History
Publications: Brochure on the Museum; The Forgotten Photographs of Carleton E Watkins
Activities: Classes for adults & children; docent training; lects open to pub; concerts; tours; Candlelight Christmas & Heritage celebrations; competitions with awards; book traveling exhibitions 2 per year; gift shop sells books, reproductions, slides, prints & handicrafts; junior mus located at Children's Discovery Center

L **Library,** 3801 Chester Ave, Bakersfield, CA 93301-1345. Tel 661-852-5000; Fax 661-322-6415; Email kcmuseum@kern.org; Web: www.kcmuseum.org; *Cur* Jeff Nickell; *Dir* Carola Rupert Enriquez; *Educ Prog* Jackie Brouillette; *VChmn* Bob Shore; *Mus Shop Mgr* Erica Hinojos
Open Mon - Fri 8 AM - 5 PM by appointment only; Estab 1950 to support the work of the mus; Open for reference only by appointment
Library Holdings: Book Volumes 2,200, Clipping Files, Filmstrips, Manuscripts, Memorabilia, Pamphlets, Photographs, Video Tapes
Special Subjects: Costume Design & Constr, Ethnology, Furniture, Historical Material, Crafts, Decorative Arts, History of Art & Archaeology, Maps, Period Rooms, Restoration & Conservation, Textiles
Collections: More than 200,000 photos relating to Kern County
Publications: Courier, quarterly newsletter
Activities: Classes for adults & children; docent training; lect open to public; concerts; tours; gallery talks; gift shop sells books, reproductions; Lori Brock Children's Discovery Ctr

BERKELEY

A **BERKELEY ART CENTER,** 1275 Walnut St, Berkeley, CA 94709-1406. Tel 510-644-6893; Fax 510-540-0343; Email info@berkeleyartcenter.org; Web: www.berkeleyartcenter.org; *CEO & Dir* Jill Berk Jiminez; *Pres (V)* Susan Klee; *Program Coordr* Jeanne Rehrig
Open Wed - Sun Noon - 5 PM, cl Mon - Tues, holidays & during installations; No admis fee; Estab 1967 as a community art center; Average Annual Attendance: 12,400; Mem: 400; dues $30 - $2500; annual meeting Jan 1
Income: Financed by city appropriation and other grants
Collections: prints
Exhibitions: Rotating loan exhibitions & shows by Northern Calif artists; Annual Exhibitions: Members Exhibition, Youth Arts Festival & The National Juried Exhibition
Activities: Lects open to public, 8 vis lectrs per yr; concerts; gallery talks; competition with prizes; original objects of art lent to nonprofit & educational institutions; originate traveling exhibs; mus shop sells books, magazines, original art & prints

A **BERKELEY CIVIC ARTS PROGRAM,** 2118 Milvia St, Ste 200, Berkeley, CA 94704. Tel 510-705-8183; Fax 510-883-6554; Email mamfor@ci.berkeley.ca.us; Web: www.ci.berkeley.ca.us; Others TDD 510-644-6915; *Civic Arts Coordr* Mary Ann Merker
Estab 1980. Provides grants to art organizations, cultural service contracts, community outreach, bus & technical assistance to artists & organizations, information referrals to the arts community; conducts on-going efforts to promote

the importance of the arts & actively participates in regional & national local art agency develop
Income: $264,500
Exhibitions: Exhibits 14 different showings annually by artists & art organizations in the Addison Street storefront windows
Publications: Arts Education Resource Directory; arts events list; quarterly newsletter

L **BERKELEY PUBLIC LIBRARY,** Art & Music Department, 2090 Kittredge St, Art & Music Dept Berkeley, CA 94704-1427; 2031 Bancroft Way, Berkeley, CA 94704. Tel 510-981-6241; Web: www.berkeleypubliclibrary.org; *Librn* Emily Foster; *Librn* Wendy Hyman; *Librn* Deborah Carton
Open Mon noon - 8 PM, Tues 10 AM 8 PM, Wed - Sat 10 AM - 6 PM, Sun 1 - 5 PM; No admis fee
Library Holdings: Book Volumes 30,000, Clipping Files, Compact Disks 20,000, Periodical Subscriptions 85, Records 6,000, Slides 22,000
Exhibitions: Exhibitions by local artists & arts organizations. Annual quilt show. Annual Staff art show
Activities: Classes for adults, dramatic programs; Lectures open to the public; concerts

A **KALA INSTITUTE,** Kala Art Institute, 2990 San Pueblo Ave, Berkeley, CA 94702; 1060 Heinz Ave, Berkeley, CA 94710-2719. Tel 510-549-2977; Fax 510-540-6914; Email kala@kala.org; Web: www.kala.org; *Artistic Dir* Yuzo Nakano; *Exec Dir* Archana Horsting; *Gallery Cur & Communs Dir* Mayumi Hamanaka; *Dir Develop* Ellen Lake; *Bus Mgr* Wendy Neu; *Art Sales Mgr* Andrea Voinot; *Youth Art Progs Mgr* Jamila Dunn; *Prog Mgr Artists Residencies* Carrie Hott; *Digital Media & Facilities Mgr* Jon Zax; *Print Studio Mgr* Paper Buck; *Custom Printing Mgr* Unai San Martin
Open Tues - Fri noon - 5 PM, Sat noon - 4:30 PM; No admis fee; Estab 1974 to provide equipment, space, exhibition opportunities to artists; Maintains Ray Abel Memorial Library of Fine Arts Books; Average Annual Attendance: 5,000; Mem: 900; mem open to artists with proficiency in printmaking; mem prog (Friends of Kala) 90 mems
Income: $1,175,000 (financed by mem, city & state appropriation, art sales, classes & private foundations)
Collections: Kala Institute Archive, Works on Paper
Exhibitions: On going: Works on Paper
Activities: Classes for adults & children; lects open to pub; 10 vis lectrs per yr; gallery talks; tours; 8 fels given per yr; scholarships & fels offered; book traveling exhibs; originate traveling exhibs 1 per yr; sales shop sells books, prints & original art

M **UNIVERSITY OF CALIFORNIA, BERKELEY,** Berkeley Art Museum & Pacific Film Archive, 2155 Center St, Berkeley, CA 94704; 2120 Oxford St, Berkeley, CA 94720-2250. Tel 510-642-0808; Fax 510-642-4889; Email bampfa@berkeley.edu; Web: bampfa.org; *Dir & Chief Cur* Lawrence Rinder; *Dir Educ & Academic Relations* Sherry Goodman; *Dir Registration* Lisa Calden; *Film Coll Mgr* Mona Nagai; *Cur Film* Kathy Geritz; *Sr Film Cur* Susan Oxtoby
Open Wed - Fri 11 AM - 7 PM, Sat & Sun 11 AM - 9 PM, cl Mon & Tues; Admis $13, Non-UC Berkeley students, disable, & seniors (65+) $11; Estab 1963, new mus building opened in 2016; Mus designed by Diller Scofidio & Renfro features galleries, two film theaters (233 seats). & four study centers; Average Annual Attendance: Gallery 100,000, Pacific Film Archive 100,000; Mem: 2800; dues vary
Income: $6,300,000 (financed by university sources, federal & foundation grants, earned income & private donations)
Library Holdings: Audio Tapes, Book Volumes, CD-ROMs, Cards, Cassettes, Clipping Files, DVDs, Exhibition Catalogs, Filmstrips, Manuscripts, Memorabilia, Motion Pictures, Original Art Works, Original Documents, Other Holdings, Pamphlets, Photographs, Prints, Records, Reels, Sculpture, Slides, Video Tapes
Special Subjects: African Art, Afro-American Art, Architecture, Asian Art, Drawings, Folk Art, Latin American Art, Painting-American, Painting-British, Painting-European, Photography, Posters, Prints, Sculpture
Collections: Gift of 45 Hans Hoffman paintings housed in the Hans Hoffman Gallery, pre-20th century paintings & sculpture, Chinese & Japanese paintings, 20th century European & American paintings & sculpture, over 7000 films & video tapes, 16th-20th century works on paper, conceptual art study center, American Art; Conceptual Art; Contemporary Art
Publications: The Calendar, bi-monthly; catalogs; handbills; exhibition brochures; Matrix artists sheets
Activities: Educ dept; classes for adults & children; docent training; lects open to pub & mems only, 15 vis lectrs per yr; concerts; gallery talks; tours; on-site performances; film programs for classes & research screening; film study center & library; 3 book traveling exhibs per yr; originate traveling exhibs to other art museums; mus shop sells books, prints, craft art, souvenirs; rental facilities available, cafe

M **Phoebe Apperson Hearst Museum of Anthropology**, 103 Kroeber Hall No 3712, Berkeley, CA 94720-3712. Tel 510-642-3681, 642-3682; Fax 510-642-6271; Email pahma-admin@berkeley.edu; Web: hearstmuseum.berkeley.edu; *Dir* Benjamin W Porter, PhD
Open Wed - Sat 10 AM - 4:30 PM, Sun Noon - 4 PM, cl univ holidays; Admis adults $4, seniors $2, children $2, no admis fee Thurs; Cal ID holder: free; Estab 1901 as a research mus for the training & educating of undergraduate & graduate students, a resource for scholarly research & to collect, preserve, educate & conduct research; Average Annual Attendance: 20,000
Income: Financed principally by state appropriations, private donations, and revenue
Special Subjects: Afro-American Art, Afro-American Art, American Indian Art, American Western Art, Anthropology, Antiquities-Assyrian, Antiquities-Egyptian, Antiquities-Etruscan, Antiquities-Greek, Antiquities-Roman, Archaeology, Asian Art, Flasks & Bottles, Ceramics, Coins & Medals, Crafts, Decorative Arts, Eskimo Art, Ethnology, Folk Art, Furniture, Glass, Gold, Islamic Art, Jade, Latin American Art, Maps, Mexican Art, Photography, Porcelain, Portraits, Pottery, Pre-Columbian Art, Primitive art, Reproductions, Sculpture, Southwestern Art, Textiles, Woodcarvings
Collections: Over four million objects of anthropological interest, both archaeological & ethnological. Ethnological colls from Africa, Oceania, North America (California, Plains, Arctic & Sub-Arctic), Archaeological Colls from Egypt, Peru, California, Africa & Oceania
Publications: Classics in California Anthropology; Museum News, annual
Activities: Family days; classes for children; Docent training;; lects open to pub, 10 vis lectrs per yr; gallery talks; tours

L **Pacific Film Archive**, 2625 Durant Ave, Berkeley, CA 94720-2251. Tel 510-642-1412, 642-1437; Fax 510-642-4889; *Library Head* Nancy Goldman; *Film Coll Mgr* Mona Nagai; *Assoc Film Cur* Kathy Geritz; *Cur Film* Edith Kramer
Open Mon - Fri 1 - 5 PM; nightly film screenings 6 - 11 PM; Estab 1971, the Archive is a cinematheque showing a constantly changing repertory of films; a research screening facility; a media information service & an archive for the storage & preservation of films
Income: Financed by earned box office income, grants, students fees & benefits
Library Holdings: Book Volumes 5,500, Clipping Files 60,000, Motion Pictures 6,000, Other Holdings Posters 7,000; Stills 25,000, Periodical Subscriptions 75, Photographs
Special Subjects: Film
Collections: Japanese film coll, Soviet Silents, experimental & animated films
Publications: Bi-monthly calendar
Activities: Nightly film exhibition; special daytime screening of films; lect, 50-57 vis filmmakers per yr

L **Architecture Visual Resources Library**, 494 Wurster Hall, Berkeley, CA 94720-1800; 232 Wurster Hall (MC 1800), Berkeley, CA 94720-1800. Tel 510-642-3439; Fax 510-642-8655; Email maryly@berkeley.edu; Web: www.mip.berkeley.edu/spiro (image database), www.arch.ced.berkeley.edu/resources/avre, www.lib.berkeley.edu/arch; *Library Asst* Tracy Farbstein; *Photographer* Steven Brooks; *Librn* Maryly Snow
Open Mon - Fri 9AM-5PM, after completion of new user orientation; Admis for outside borrowers $150 per semester; Estab 1905 for instructional support for the Department of Architecture. Library permits circulation on a 24 hour basis for educational presentations. No duplication of slides permitted; Circ 46,000; Average Annual Attendance: 300
Income: Financed by state & donor funds
Library Holdings: Kodachrome Transparencies, Lantern Slides, Other Holdings, Photographs, Slides
Special Subjects: Architecture, Landscape Architecture
Collections: Denise Scott Brown & William C Wheaton Collections: City Planning, Herwin Schaefer Collection: visual design, architecture & topography instructional circulating coll, Harold Stump world architecture slide coll, Ray Lifchez slide collection, Joseph Esherick travel slides collection

L **Environmental Design Library**, 210 Wurster Hall, Berkeley, CA 94720-6000. Tel 510-642-4818; Fax 510-642-8266; Email envi@library.berkeley.edu; Web: www.lib.berkeley.edu/ENVI; *Head* Elizabeth Byrne; *Planning & Instruction Librn* David Eifler
Open Aug- May Mon - Thurs 9 AM - 9 PM, Fri 9 AM - 5 PM, Sat 1 - 5 PM, Sun 1 - 5 PM; Estab 1903; Circ 91,000; 3 exhibs per year
Income: Pub/state
Library Holdings: Book Volumes 210,000, CD-ROMs, Fiche, Periodical Subscriptions 700, Reels, Video Tapes
Special Subjects: Architecture, Landscape Architecture
Collections: Beatrix Jones Farrand Collection, Architecture, city & regional planning, landscape architecture
Exhibitions: Three times per year
Publications: On website

M **UNIVERSITY OF CALIFORNIA, BERKELEY,** The Magnes Collection of Jewish Art & Life, The Magnes, 2121 Allston Way Berkeley, CA 94720-6000. Tel 510-643-2526; Email magnes@berkeley.edu; Web: www.magnes.berkeley.edu; *Dir* George Breslauer; *Cur* Francesco Spagnolo; *Registrar, Exhib Coordr & Rights Mgr* Julie Franklin; *Asst Cur* Zoe Lewin; *Asst Cur* Shir Kochavi; *Prog & Events Coordr* Lisa Davis; *Asst Registrar* Rebecca Hisiger; *Preparator* Ernest Jolly
Call for hours; No admis fee; Estab 1962 to preserve, collect & exhibit Jewish artifacts & art from around the world; the Judah L Magnes mus also contained the Blumenthal Rare Books & Manuscripts Library & the Western Jewish History Center Archives on the Jewish community in the Western United States since 1849. Collection transferred to UC Berkeley's Bancroft Library in 2010, to open to the pub in fall 2011 upon completion of new facility
Library Holdings: Auction Catalogs, Audio Tapes, Book Volumes, Clipping Files, Exhibition Catalogs, Manuscripts, Motion Pictures, Periodical Subscriptions, Photographs, Records, Video Tapes
Special Subjects: Calligraphy, Carpets & Rugs, Ceramics, Coins & Medals, Collages, Costumes, Crafts, Decorative Arts, Drawings, Embroidery, Etchings & Engravings, Folk Art, Furniture, Gold, Graphics, Historical Material, Judaica, Laces, Manuscripts, Metalwork, Painting-American, American Western Art, Art History, Religious Art, Painting-German, Painting-Israeli, Painting-Polish, Painting-Russian, Photography, Posters, Prints, Sculpture, Textiles, Watercolors
Collections: Hanukkah lamps, Synagogue art & objects, spice boxes, graphics, manuscripts, prints, rare books, textiles, genre paintings, art & ceremonial objects from Sephardic & Indian Jewish communities, Jewish Ceremonial Art

L **The Magnes Collection of Jewish Art and Life**, The Bancroft Library, University of California Berkeley, CA 94720-6000. Tel 510-642-2526; Email magnes@library.berkeley.edu; Web: www.magnes.org; *Cur* Francesco Spagnolo; *Head Admin Serv* Erik Nelson
Estab 1966 as a center for the study & preservation of Judaica; Circ Non-circ
Library Holdings: Book Volumes 12,000, Clipping Files, Exhibition Catalogs, Filmstrips, Manuscripts, Memorabilia, Motion Pictures, Other Holdings Original documents, Pamphlets, Periodical Subscriptions 15, Reproductions, Slides
Special Subjects: Art History, Bookplates & Bindings, Calligraphy, Cartoons, Illustration, Judaica, Manuscripts, Maps
Collections: Community colls from Cochin, Czechoslovakia, Egypt, India & Morocco, Holocaust Material (Institute for Righteous Acts), Karaite Community (Egypt), Passover Haggadahs (Zismer), 16th to 19th century rare printed editions, books & manuscripts, Ukrainian programs (Belkin documents)
Exhibitions: Jewish Illustrated Books

BEVERLY HILLS

M **ACADEMY OF MOTION PICTURE ARTS & SCIENCES,** The Academy Gallery, 8949 Wilshire Blvd, Beverly Hills, CA 90211-1972. Tel 310-247-3000; Fax 310-247-3610; Email gallery@oscars.org; Web: www.oscars.org; *Gallery Mgr* Julie Gumpert; *Gallery Dir* Ellen Harrington; *Gallery Staff* Claire Lockhart; *Chief Preparator* Alex Yust
Open Tues - Fri 10 AM - 5 PM, Sat & Sun Noon - 6 PM; No admis fee; Estab 1970; Rotating exhibitions on motion picture history & contemporary filmmaking; Average Annual Attendance: 40,000
Library Holdings: Audio Tapes, Book Volumes, Clipping Files, Exhibition Catalogs, Kodachrome Transparencies, Lantern Slides, Manuscripts, Motion Pictures, Original Art Works, Photographs, Reproductions
Collections: Gallery borrows regularly from the Academy library's colls of archival posters, photos, & documents
Exhibitions: Rotating exhibits
Publications: Exhibition catalogs
Activities: Seminars on producing & screen writing; lects open to pub; 6 vis lectrs per year; gallery talks; tours; Academy Awards; Nicholl Fel in screenwriting offered; approx 2 book traveling exhibs per yr; originates traveling exhibs that circulate to accredited museum facilities

L **BEVERLY HILLS PUBLIC LIBRARY,** Fine Arts Library, 444 N Rexford, Beverly Hills, CA 90210. Tel 310-288-2237; Fax 310-247-0536; Email mstark@beverlyhills.org; Web: www.bhpl.org; *Fine Arts Librn* Mary Stark
Open Mon - Wed 10 AM - 8 PM, Thurs - Sat 10 AM - 6 PM, Sun Noon - 5 PM; No admis fee; Estab 1973 to make art materials available to the general public; The library concentrates on 19th & 20th century American & West European art, & Southern CA art
Income: Financed by city appropriation and Friends of Library
Library Holdings: Auction Catalogs, Book Volumes 22,822, Compact Disks 11,528, DVDs 4,143, Exhibition Catalogs, Fiche, Original Art Works, Original Documents, Periodical Subscriptions 200
Special Subjects: Advertising Design, Afro-American Art, American Western Art, Antiquities-Byzantine, Antiquities-Egyptian, Antiquities-Greek, Antiquities-Oriental, Antiquities-Persian, Antiquities-Roman, Architecture, Art History, Asian Art, Bronzes, Calligraphy, Cartoons, Ceramics, Coins & Medals, Commercial Art, Crafts, Decorative Arts, Drafting, Drawings, Etchings & Engravings, Fashion Arts, Film, Furniture, Glass, Graphic Arts, Graphic Design, Handicrafts, History of Art & Archaeology, Illustration, Interior Design, Islamic Art, Jewelry, Landscape Architecture, Oriental Art, Painting-American, Painting-British, Painting-Dutch, Painting-European, Prints, Painting-French, Painting-German, Painting-Italian, Painting-Japanese, Painting-Russian, Painting-Spanish, Period Rooms, Photography, Portraits, Posters, Pottery, Printmaking, Sculpture, Silver, Southwestern Art, Woodcuts, Religious Art, Tapestries, Textiles, Theatre Arts, Watercolors
Collections: Artists Books
Exhibitions: Various exhib
Activities: Classes for adults, literary; 10 vis lectrs per yr; judged one of the top twelve libraries in the state by Library Journal in 2009

C **PLAYBOY ENTERPRISES, INC,** 9346 Civic Center Dr, Beverly Hills, CA 90210-3604. Tel 312-751-8000; Fax 312-751-2818; *Cur & Bus Develop Dir* Aaron Baker
Open to pub by appointment only in groups; Estab 1953 to gather & maintain works commissioned for reproduction by Playboy Magazine
Library Holdings: Auction Catalogs, Book Volumes, Exhibition Catalogs, Kodachrome Transparencies, Manuscripts, Memorabilia, Original Art Works, Original Documents, Photographs, Sculpture, Slides, Video Tapes
Collections: Selected works from 4000 illustrations & fine art pieces, works include paintings & sculpture representing 20th Century artists such as Robert Ginzel, Roger Hane, Larry Rivers, James Rosenquist, Seymour Rosofsky, Roy Schnackenberg, George Segal, Andy Warhol, Robert Weaver, Tom Wesselman, Karl Wirsum, Roger Brown, Ed Paschke, Don Lewis & others
Exhibitions: Playboy Redux; The Great Indoors; Mr Playboy's Wild Ride
Publications: Catalogs pertaining to Beyond Illustration - The Art of Playboy; The Art of Playboy - from the First 25 Years
Activities: Lects; tours; annual illustration awards; individual paintings & original objects of art lent to museums & schools; originate traveling exhibs to galleries, universities, museums & cultural centers

L **Library,** 9346 Civic Center Dr, Ste 200 Beverly Hills, CA 90210-3604. Tel 312-751-8000, Ext 2420; Fax 312-751-2818; *Librn* Mark Durand
Library Holdings: Book Volumes 10,000, Clipping Files, Exhibition Catalogs, Original Art Works, Periodical Subscriptions 75, Photographs

BONITA

M **BONITA HISTORICAL SOCIETY,** Bonita Museum and Cultural Center, 4355 Bonita Rd Bonita, CA 91902-1351. Tel 619-267-5141; Fax 619-267-2143; Email bonitamuseum@sbcglobal.net; Web: bonitahistoricalsociety.org; *Exec Dir* Julie Gay; *Treas* Barb Scott
Open Wed - Sat 10 AM - 4 PM; No admis fee; 2 large galleries for local history & rotating art History anthropology; Average Annual Attendance: 10,000; Mem: 300; $30 individual; gen meeting in Nov
Library Holdings: Book Volumes
Special Subjects: American Western Art, Anthropology, Archaeology, Carpets & Rugs, Ceramics, Costumes, Decorative Arts, Dolls, Embroidery, Ethnology, Folk Art, Furniture, Glass, Jewelry, Latin American Art, Maps, Painting-American, Period Rooms, Photography, Porcelain, Portraits, Posters, Pottery, Primitive art, Sculpture, Southwestern Art, Textiles, Watercolors, Woodcarvings
Collections: Local history objects, photos, Audi Lawson Collection, Ellen Magi Collection, personal family items from 1920-2000, prehistoric archaeological objects
Activities: Classes for adults & children; docent training; lects open to pub; gallery talks; tours; sponsoring of competitions; mus shop sells books, original art, reproductions, prints

BREA

M **CITY OF BREA,** Art Gallery, One Civic Center Circle, Brea, CA 92821. Tel 714-990-7730; Fax 714-990-7736; Email breagallery@cityofbrea.net; Web: www.breagallery.com; *Educ Dir* Tina Hasenberg; *Coordr* Claudia Sandoval
Open Wed - Sun noon - 5 PM; cl Mon, Tues, holidays; Admis adults $2, children 12 & under free; Estab 1980; 6300 sq ft exhib space; Average Annual Attendance: 7,000
Income: nonprofit
Special Subjects: Ceramics, Drawings, Glass, Graphics, Jewelry, Landscapes, Military Art, Painting-American, Photography, Portraits, Posters, Pottery, Prints, Sculpture, Textiles, Watercolors
Exhibitions: Made in California (annual juried show); National Watercolor Society Juried Exhib
Activities: Classes for adults & children; docent training; lect open to public; tours; gallery talks; workshops; made in California Art Awards $500, $350, $200, $100; mus shop sells original art, prints & jewelry

BURBANK

L **WARNER BROS STUDIO RESEARCH LIBRARY,** 4000 Warner Blvd, Bldg 169 Burbank, CA 91522. Tel 818-954-6000; Fax 818-567-4366; *Library Admin* Phill Williams; *Research Librn* Barbara Poland
Open Mon - Fri 9 AM - 5 PM; Estab 1928 for picture & story research
Income: Financed by endowment
Library Holdings: Book Volumes 35,000, Clipping Files, Pamphlets, Periodical Subscriptions 85, Photographs
Special Subjects: Costume Design & Constr, Fashion Arts, Film, Interior Design
Collections: Art & Architecture History, Costumes, Interior Design, Military & Police, Travel & Description

CAMARILLO

M **STUDIO CHANNEL ISLANDS ART CENTER,** 2222 Ventura Blvd, Camarillo, CA 93010. Tel 805-383-1368; Email sciartcenter@verizon.net; Web: www.studiochannelislands.org; *Exec Dir* Karin Geiger
Open Tues 11AM-3PM, Wed-Fri 11AM-5PM, Sat 10AM-3PM
Collections: works by regional, nat & international artists
Activities: Classes for adults & children; docent training; lects open to the pub; gallery talks; tours; fels; awards, Studio Channel Islands Art Center Award for Excellence in Art Studies; mus shop sells original art

CARMEL

M **CARMEL MISSION & GIFT SHOP,** 3080 Rio Rd, Carmel, CA 93923-9144. Tel 831-624-1271; Fax 831-624-0658; Web: www.carmelmission.org; *Shop Mgr* Kristine Silveria; *Cur* Richard J Menn
Open Mon - Sat 9:30 AM - 4:30 PM, Sun 10:30 AM - 4:30 PM, cl Thanksgiving & Christmas; No admis fee; donations accepted; Estab 1770
Collections: California's first library, founded by Fray Junipero Serra, 1770, library of California's first college, founded by William Hartnell, 1834, Munras Memorial Collection of objects, papers, furnishings of early California, large coll of ecclesiastical art of Spanish colonial period, large coll of ecclesiastical silver & gold church vessels, 1670-1820, paintings, sculpture, art objects of California Mission period
Activities: Sales shop sells religious articles, souvenir books & postcards

CARMICHAEL

PASTEL SOCIETY OF THE WEST COAST
For further information, see National and Regional Organizations

CARSON

M **UNIVERSITY ART GALLERY AT CALIFORNIA STATE UNIVERSITY, DOMINGUEZ HILLS,** 1000 E Victoria St, Carson, CA 90747-0001. Tel 310-243-3334; Email kzimmerer@csudh.edu; Web: www.cah.csudh.edu/dnp/art_gallery/index.asp; *Gallery Dir* Kathy Zimmerer; *Instructional Support Technician* Gregory Mocilnikar
Open Mon - Thurs 10:00 AM - 4 PM; No admis fee; Estab 1973 to exhibit faculty, student, contemporary & historical California art & multi-cultural exhibits; 2,000 sq ft gallery, 18' high ceilings; Average Annual Attendance: 10,000
Income: Financed by yearly grants from CSUDH Student Assoc; support from Friends of the Gallery, City of Carson; external grants
Library Holdings: Audio Tapes, Exhibition Catalogs, Original Documents, Slides
Special Subjects: Art History
Exhibitions: A Tradition of Pride: African American Quilters of Los Angeles; 21 Artists Create Books, African Identities in Textiles & Art; Portraits of the Human Experience; Local Not Local: Arabic & Iranian Typography Made in California; Urban Transformations: The Contemporary Landscape; Peeling Back; Altered Objects; Heated Exchange: Contemporary Encaustic
Publications: Exhibition catalogue published one time per yr; yearly newsletter
Activities: Classes for children; lects open to pub, 5 vis lectrs per yr; gallery talks; demonstrations; gallery tours; schols; book traveling exhibs 1 every other yr; originates traveling exhibs (Painted Light) to Irvine Mus, Autry National Center

CHERRY VALLEY

M **RIVERSIDE COUNTY MUSEUM,** Edward-Dean Museum & Gardens, 9401 Oak Glen Rd, Cherry Valley, CA 92223-3739. Tel 951-845-2626; Fax 951-845-2628;

Email edm-events@rivcoeda.org; Web: www.edward-deanmuseum.org; *Mus Mgr* Stacey Chester
Open Thurs - Sat 10 AM - 5 PM; Admis adults $5, seniors & students $2, children under 12 free; Built in 1957 & given to the county of Riverside in 1964; The South Wing of the gallery displays antiques & decorative arts as permanent collections; the North Wing has changing exhibits including contemporary artists; Average Annual Attendance: 20,000; Mem: 250; monthly meetings
Income: Financed by county funding
Library Holdings: Memorabilia, Original Documents, Sculpture
Special Subjects: Decorative Arts, Oriental Art, Watercolors
Collections: 17th & 18th Century European & Oriental decorative arts, David Roberts Collection
Publications: Museum catalog
Activities: Classes for children; docent training; lects open to pub; tours; outdoor art shows; cultural festivals; concerts; gallery talks; original objects of art lent to local universities & colleges; mus shop sells books, magazines, original art, reproductions & prints

L **Library**, 9401 Oak Glen Rd, Cherry Valley, CA 92223-3799. Tel 909-845-2626; Fax 909-845-2628; *Librn* Margaret Mueller
Open by appointment for reference only
Library Holdings: Book Volumes 2,300, Cards, Manuscripts, Original Art Works, Periodical Subscriptions 6, Prints
Special Subjects: Art History, Asian Art, Ceramics, Costume Design & Constr, Decorative Arts, Furniture, Glass, History of Art & Archaeology, Jade, Painting-British, Painting-European, Porcelain, Watercolors

CHICO

M **1078 GALLERY,** 820 Broadway St, Chico, CA 95928. Tel 530-343-1973; Email info@1078gallery.org; Web: www.1078gallery.org; *Chair* Amanda Riner
Pop-up shows are available until a permanent gallery space is found; Estab 1981 as a nonprofit artist run arts organization showing contemporary art exhibitions & installations by artists of cultural & geographic diversity; Mem: dues $25-$200
Income: Financed by members, donors & programming

M **CALIFORNIA STATE UNIVERSITY, CHICO,** University Art Gallery, Art Dept, Chico, CA 95929-0820. Tel 530-898-5864; Email jtannen@csuchico.edu; *Chmn* Jason Tannen
Open Mon - Fri 10 AM - 4 PM, Sun Noon - 4 PM; No admis fee; Estab to afford broad cultural influences to the massive North California region
Income: Financed by state appropriations & private funds
Collections: University Art Coll includes Masters of Graduate Artwork, Study coll of fine art print
Exhibitions: Varies every 4 months: local artist
Activities: Lects open to public, 6-12 vis lectrs per yr; competitions with awards; individual & original objects of art lent to offices on campus

L **Meriam Library**, First & Hazel, Chico, CA 95929-0295. Tel 530-898-5862; Fax 530-898-4443; Web: www.csuchico.edu/library; *Dir* Carolyn Dusenbury
Open Mon-Thurs 7:30AM-11:45PM, Fri 7:30AM-4:45PM, Sat noon-4:45PM, Sun noon-11:45PM
Library Holdings: Audio Tapes, Book Volumes 900, Cards, Cassettes, Fiche, Filmstrips, Micro Print, Motion Pictures, Original Art Works, Periodical Subscriptions 72, Photographs, Prints, Reels, Reproductions, Sculpture, Video Tapes

M **Associated Students, 3rd Floor Art Gallery**, Bell Memorial Union, 3rd Fl, 2nd & Chestnuts Sts Chico, CA 95929; PO Box 7570, Chico, CA 95927-7570. Tel 530-898-3380; Email mhoag@csuchico.edu; Web: as.csuchico.edu; *Exec Dir* David Buckley; *Prog Coordr* Marilyn Hoag
Open Mon - Thurs 7 AM - 10 PM, Fri 7 AM - 7 PM, Sat 9 AM - 7 PM, Sun noon - 10 PM; No admis fee; Estab 1945; 100 linear ft of enclosed area & two gallery halls; Average Annual Attendance: 1,000
Income: Financed by associated students & university
Exhibitions: Student work year round

M **Janet Turner Print Museum, CSU, Chicago**, 400 W 1st St, Meriam Library, CSU Chico Chico, CA 95929-0820. Tel 530-898-4476; Fax 530-898-5581; Email csullivan@.csuchico.edu; Web: www.theturner.org; *Cur, Head of Colls* Catherine Sullivan; *Coll Mgr* Adria Crossen Davis; *Resource Mgr* Reed Applegate; *Prof Emeritus Art History Research* Dr Yoshio Kusaba; *Curatorial Asst* Trinity Connelly; *Curatorial Asst* Willow Starkey; *Prof Emeritus Art History Research* James McManus
Open Mon - Sat 11 AM - 4 PM during academic yr; No admis fee; Estab 1981; Located in Meriam Library; displays 6 thematic exhibs per acad yr from the Print Museum's Collection of over 3,000 original prints. Display 6 exhibs in Ayres Hall; Average Annual Attendance: 4,000; Mem: 40; dues $2-$100
Income: $33,000 (financed by endowment, mem & state appropriation)
Purchases: Contemporary prints, mixed media, historic prints
Library Holdings: Auction Catalogs, Book Volumes, Clipping Files, DVDs, Exhibition Catalogs, Memorabilia, Original Art Works, Periodical Subscriptions, Photographs, Reproductions, Slides, Video Tapes
Special Subjects: Afro-American Art, American Indian Art, American Western Art, Asian Art, Eskimo Art, Etchings & Engravings, Graphics, Hispanic Art, Latin American Art, Medieval Art, Mexican Art, Oriental Art, Prints
Collections: General coll of prints historical to contemporary, international in scope, includes all techniques, printmaking making, library, books
Publications: Exhib catalogs
Activities: Educ dept classes for children; docent exhib tours; lect to CSU Chico classes; lects open to pub; 3 vis lectrs per yr; competitions with prizes; 4 purchase awards for Nat'l Print Compt Exhib; gallery talks; tours; scholarships offered; original objects of art lent in traveling exhibs; lending collection contains 2000 original prints; originate traveling exhibs to other CSU system colleges; sales shop sells cards, catalogs & cards

CHULA VISTA

M **SOUTHWESTERN COLLEGE,** Art Gallery, 900 Otay Lakes Rd, Chula Vista, CA 91910-7297. Tel 935-421-6700; Fax 935-421-6372; Email pturley@swc.cc.ca.us; Web: www.swccd.edu; *Gallery Dir* G Pasha Turley
Open Mon - Tues & Fri 10 AM - 2 PM, Wed - Thurs 6 - 9 PM; No admis fee; Estab 1961 to show contemporary artists' work who are of merit to the community & the school, & as an educational service; Gallery is approx 3,000 sq ft; Average Annual Attendance: 10,000
Income: Financed by city and state appropriations
Collections: Permanent collection of mostly contemporary work
Exhibitions: (1999) Gang of Five, recent works; Painting (David Beck Brown) Allied Craftsman; De La Torre Brothers, The Printers Craft Photos, Linda McCartney, Ceicel Beattes
Activities: Classes for adults; lects open to pub, 3-5 vis lectrs per year; gallery talks; competitions, State Art Festival; individual paintings & original objects of art lent; lending collection contains color reproductions, photographs & original art works; junior mus

CITY OF INDUSTRY

M **WORKMAN & TEMPLE FAMILY HOMESTEAD MUSEUM,** 15415 E Don Julian Rd, City of Industry, CA 91745-1029. Tel 626-968-8492; Fax 626-968-2048; Email info@homesteadmuseum.org; Web: www.homesteadmuseum.org; *Dir* Karen Graham Wade; *Asst Dir* Paul Spitzzeri; *Pub Prog Mgr* Alexandra Rasic; *Asst Pub Prog Mgr* Lillian Choy; *Facilities Coordr* Robert Barron; *Vol Coordr* Steve Dugan; *Colls Coordr* Michelle Muro; *Progs Coordr* Gennie Slobe
Open Wed-Sun 1-4 PM; group tours of 10+ by appointment; No admis fee; Estab 1981 to collect & interpret Southern California history from 1830 to 1930; Contemporary exhibition gallery; mid-19th century Workman Family House; late 19th century water tower; 1922-27 Spanish Colonial Revival Temple Family Residence; Average Annual Attendance: 18,000
Income: $800,000 (financed by city appropriation)
Special Subjects: Architecture, Decorative Arts, Furniture, Historical Material, Metalwork, Stained Glass
Collections: California ceramic tile, La Casa Nueva stained glass, Southern California architecture
Exhibitions: La Casa Nueva: A 1920s Spanish-Style Mansion
Activities: Classes for adults docent training; lects open to pub; 3 vis lectrs per yr; concerts; tours; mus shop sells books & reproductions

L **Research Library**, 15415 E Don Julian Rd, City of Industry, CA 91745-1029. Tel 626-968-8492; Fax 626-968-2048; Email info@homesteadmuseum.org; Web: www.homesteadmuseum.org; *Coll Mgr & Library Head* Paul Spitzzeri
Open by appt only; Estab 1981; Circ 2000; For reference only
Income: $60,000 (financed by city appropriation)
Library Holdings: Book Volumes, CD-ROMs, Clipping Files, Compact Disks, DVDs, Maps, Pamphlets, Periodical Subscriptions 20, Photographs 500, Prints, Reproductions, Slides 2,500, Video Tapes
Special Subjects: Architecture, Crafts, Decorative Arts, Historical Material, Interior Design, Restoration & Conservation, Stained Glass

CLAREMONT

M **THE POMONA COLLEGE MUSEUM OF ART,** 333 N College Way, Claremont, CA 91711-4429. Tel 909-621-8283; Fax 909-621-8989; Email kathleen.howe@pomona.edu; Web: www.pomona-edu/museum; *Cur* Rebecca McGrew; *Assoc Dir & Registrar* Steve Comba; *Admin Asst* Barbara Coldiron; *Dir* Kathleen Howe; *Mus Coordr* Justine Bae; *Cur Acad Progs* Terri Geis
Open acad yr Tues - Fri noon - 5 PM, Sat - Sun noon - 5 PM, cl Mon; No admis fee; Estab 1958 to present balanced exhibs useful not only to students of art history & studio arts, but also to the general pub; Average Annual Attendance: 20,000
Income: Financed by Pomona College, support group & endowment grants
Special Subjects: African Art, American Indian Art, Asian Art, Decorative Arts, Drawings, Etchings & Engravings, Graphics, Painting-American, Painting-Italian, Photography, Prints, Renaissance Art, Sculpture, Watercolors, Woodcuts, Oriental Art
Collections: Samuel H Kress Collection of Renaissance paintings, Old Master & contemporary graphics
Exhibitions: Exhibs include: historical, contemporary, faculty, student shows and project series
Publications: Art Publications List, annual
Activities: Lects open to public, 2-3 vis lectrs per yr; gallery talks; tours; individual paintings & original objects of art lent to qualified museums & galleries; originates traveling exhibs to other museums

M **SCRIPPS COLLEGE,** Ruth Chandler Williamson Gallery, 1030 Columbia Ave, Claremont, CA 91711-3948. Tel 909-607-3397; Fax 909-607-4691; Email kdelman@scrippscol.edu; Web: www.scrippscollege.edu/williamson-gallery; *Dir* Mary Davis McNaughton; *Coll Mgr, Registrar* Kirk Delman; *Admin Asst* Jennifer Anderson; *Digital Specialist* Colleen Salomon
Open Wed - Sun 1 -5 PM, cl nat & col holidays; No admis fee; Estab 1993 to present balanced exhibitions useful not only to students of art history & studio arts, but also the general public; Average Annual Attendance: 5,000; Mem: 10,000
Income: Financed by Scripps College, support group & endowment grants
Special Subjects: African Art, Afro-American Art, Antiquities-Egyptian, Antiquities-Greek, Antiquities-Roman, Archaeology, Asian Art, Bronzes, Calligraphy, Ceramics, Costumes, Dioramas, Drawings, Enamels, Glass, Graphics, Landscapes, Marine Painting, Mexican Art, Oriental Art, Painting-American, Painting-French, Painting-Japanese, Photography, Pre-Columbian Art, Primitive art, Prints, Prints, Sculpture, Tapestries, Textiles, Tapestries, Watercolors, Woodcuts
Collections: Dr & Mrs William E Ballard Collection of Japanese Prints, Mrs James Johnson Collection of Contemporary American, British, Korean, Mexican & Japanese Ceramics, Dorothy Adler Routh Collection of Cloisonne, Wagner Collection of African Sculpture, General Edward Young Collection of American Paintings, Fred & Estelle Marer Contemporary Ceramics Collection

Exhibitions: Rotating exhibitions
Publications: Art Publications List
Activities: Lects open to pub, 2-3 vis lectrs per yr; gallery talks; films; tours; intermuseum loans; book traveling exhibs biennially; originate traveling exhibs

M **SCRIPPS COLLEGE,** Clark Humanities Museum, 1030 Columbia Ave, Claremont, CA 91711-3948. Tel 909-607-3606; Fax 909-607-7143; *Admin Asst* Nancy Burson; *Dir* Eric Haskell
Open Mon - Fri 9 AM - Noon & 1 - 5 PM, cl holidays & summer; No admis fee; Estab 1970 to present multi-disciplinary exhibits in conjunction with Scripps College's humanities curriculum & to maintain a study collection; Mus has large room with storage & study area; reception desk
Income: Pvt income
Special Subjects: Afro-American Art, Oriental Art, Sculpture, Textiles
Collections: Nagel Collection of Chinese, Tibetan Sculpture & Textiles, Wagner Collection of African Sculpture
Exhibitions: Four to seven exhibits
Activities: Lect open to public; gallery talks

CONCORD

A **CALIFORNIA WATERCOLOR ASSOCIATION,** Gallery Concord, 1765 Galindo, Concord, CA 94518; PO Box 4631, Walnut Creek, CA 94596-0631. Tel 925-691-6140; Email info@californiawatercolor.org; Web: www.californiawatercolor.org; *Pres* Bruce Stangeland; *VPres* Eileen Libby; *Dir Budget* Marilyn Miller; *Dir Communs* Samantha McNally; *Dir Workshops* Wendy Oliver; *Dir of Outreach* Nan Lovington; *Dir Mem* Sue Johnston; *Dir Programs* Pamela Miller; *Dir Workshops* Susan Lenoir; *Dir California Shows* Lynda Moore
Open Thurs - Sun 11 AM - 4 PM; No admis fee; Estab 1968; Maintains art gallery at Gallery Concord in Concord; Average Annual Attendance: 2,700; Mem: 800; dues $45; monthly meetings every third Wed
Income: Financed by mem dues
Library Holdings: DVDs, Exhibition Catalogs, Framed Reproductions, Original Art Works, Slides, Video Tapes
Exhibitions: Annual National Watercolor Exhibition plus 6-7 mem exhibits per yr
Publications: Annual catalog; monthly newsletter
Activities: Classes for adults & children; docent training; Workshops; 6-7 watercolor workshops per yr; Plein Air Paint Outs; lects open to pub, 10 vis lectrs per yr; vis lectrs 4 workshops per yr; gallery talks; tours; competitions & cash awards; mem shows & nat exhib juried with awards; scholarships offered; lending collection contains DVDs & 1500 slides; originate traveling exhibs; gallery shop sells original art, reproductions, prints, greeting cards

CORTE MADERA

A **MARIN COUNTY WATERCOLOR SOCIETY,** 138 Willow Ave, Corte Madera, CA 94925-1433. Tel 415-924-8191; Email marinwatercolors@gmail.com; Web: www.marincountywatercolorsociety.com; *Bulletin Ed* Jacqueline Hensel; *Show Dir* Pat Lawrence; *Membership* Tania Walters
Estab 1970 to provide a way for members to share painting experiences in outdoor landscape, urban landscape, seascape; Mem: 180; open to painters, ranging from beginner to professional, interest in watercolor, in Marin County & San Francisco Bay area; dues $20
Exhibitions: Marin County Watercolor Society; exhibit throughout the area in various locals
Publications: Monthly bulletin
Activities: Ruth Alexander Stewart Award (each exhibit); lects open to pub; 2 vis lectrs peryr

CUPERTINO

M **DE ANZA COLLEGE,** Euphrat Museum of Art, 21250 Stevens Creek Blvd, Cupertino, CA 95014-5797. Tel 408-864-8836; Web: www.deanza.edu; *Dir Arts & Schools Prog* Diana Argabrite; *Dir* Jan Rindfleisch
Open Tues & Thurs 11 AM - 4 PM, Wed 7 - 9 PM; No admis fee; Estab 1971; 1700 sq ft contemporary gallery located on De Anza College Campus; Average Annual Attendance: 10,000
Income: $175,000 (financed by mem, grants, endowment, college)
Publications: Art Collectors in & Around Silicon Valley; Art of the Refugee Experience; Art, Religion & Spirituality; Content Contemporary Issues; The Power of Cloth (Political Quilts 1845-1986); Staying Visible: The Importance of Archives
Activities: Classes for children; docent progs; lects open to pub; competition with awards; sales shop sells books

CYPRESS

M **CYPRESS COLLEGE,** Fine Arts Gallery, 9200 Valley View St, Cypress, CA 90630-5897. Tel 714-826-2220; Fax 714-527-8238; *Secy* Maureen King; *Dir* Betty Disney
Open Mon & Thurs 10 AM - 2 PM, Tues & Wed 6 - 8 PM, cl Fri, except by appointment; No admis fee; Estab 1969 to bring visually enriching experiences to the school & community; Average Annual Attendance: 5,000
Income: Financed by school budget, donations & sales
Collections: Donor gifts, purchase awards, student works
Publications: Exhibition catalogs
Activities: Lects open to public, 2 vis lectrs per year; competitions; scholarships

DAVIS

M **PENCE GALLERY,** 212 D St, Davis, CA 95616-4513. Tel 530-758-3370; Fax 530-758-4670; Email penceassistant@sbcglobal.net; Web: www.pencegallery.org; *Board Pres* Bill Roe; *Asst Dir* Eileen Hendren; *Dir & Cur* Natalie Nelson; *Gallery Asst* Tim Barrera; *Designer* Sohyung Choi
Open Tues-Sun 11:30AM-5PM, 2nd Fri 6PM-9PM; No admis fee; Estab 1975 to foster & stimulate awareness of the arts & cultural heritage of California through changing exhibitions of art & objects of artistic, aesthetic & historical significance; State of the art museum with 3 galleries & conference rooms available for rent and functions; Average Annual Attendance: 17,000; Mem: Dues: gallery circle $2500, cur circle $1000, benefactor $500, patron $250, sponsor $100, family $75, individual $45
Income: $270,000 (financed by fund raisings)
Library Holdings: Auction Catalogs, Book Volumes, Exhibition Catalogs
Exhibitions: Twelve rotating exhibitions per yr, exploring contemporary California art
Publications: Pence Events, quarterly newsletter
Activities: Classes for adults & children; docent training; lects open to pub; 2 visiting lectrs per year; concerts; gallery talks; tours; Community Art awards; scholarships offered; sales shop sells books, original art & prints

DESERT HOT SPRINGS

M **PUEBLO MUSEUM,** (Cabot's Old Indian Pueblo Museum), 67616 E Desert View Ave, Desert Hot Springs, CA 92240-4114; PO Box 104, Desert Hot Springs, CA 92240-0104. Tel 760-329-7610; Fax 760-329-2738; Email cabotsmuseum@roadrunner.com; Web: www.cabotsmuseum.org; *Board Pres* Mike Chedester; *Board VPres* John Mahoney; *Board CFO* Paul Hietter; *Board Secy* Linda Stevens; *Dir* Ginger Ridgway; *Registrar* Peggy Pourtemour
Open Tues - Sat Oct - May 9 AM - 4 PM, June - Sep 9 AM - 1 PM; Admis adults $11, sr citizens & under 12 $9; Estab 1939 as museum & home; 1100 sq ft art gallery representing contemporary artists through a variety of media. Artifacts of past cultures & Americana along with Native American work; Average Annual Attendance: 10,000; Mem: 2500; dues Household $50, Individual $35
Income: Financed by donations, grants
Purchases: Cahuilla baskets, Navajo blankets & rugs acquired
Library Holdings: Book Volumes, Cassettes, Clipping Files, Kodachrome Transparencies, Memorabilia, Original Art Works, Original Documents, Pamphlets, Photographs, Prints, Records, Reproductions, Sculpture
Special Subjects: American Western Art, American Indian Art, Architecture, Costumes, Drawings, Eskimo Art, Etchings & Engravings, Furniture, Historical Material, Painting-American, Period Rooms, Photography, Portraits, Pottery, Primitive art, Sculpture, Southwestern Art, Textiles, Woodcarvings
Exhibitions: Select weekend exhibits of Art Fairs with Blacksmith Exhib, artists working on their crafts; Indian Monument carved by Peter Toth (1978); Hopi-Style Pueblo Home & Museum of Cabot Yerxa
Activities: Classes for adults & children; docent training; lects open to pub; concerts; gallery talks; tours; mus shop sells books, magazines, original art, reproductions, prints, ceramics, jewelry

EL CAJON

M **GROSSMONT COMMUNITY COLLEGE,** Hyde Art Gallery, 8800 Grossmont College Dr, Bldg 25 El Cajon, CA 92020-1798. Tel 619-644-7299; Fax 619-644-7922; Email alex.decosta@gcccd.edu; Web: hydeartgallery.com; *Dept Chair* Dr Marion De Koning; *Gallery Dir* Alex DeCosta; *Visual Arts & Humanities Dead* Susan Schwarz
Open Mon & Thurs 10 AM - 6 PM & by appointment, cl Fri - Sun & legal holidays; No admis fee; Estab 1970 as a co-curricular institution which cooperates with & supports the Art Department of Grossmont College & which provides a major cultural resource for the general pub in the eastern part of the greater San Diego area; Two galleries, one 30 x 40 ft; one 30 x 20 ft; Average Annual Attendance: 20,000
Income: Financed through College
Special Subjects: Photography, Pottery, Prints
Collections: Prints, photographs, clay objects, large Tom Holland painting, Marje Hyde, Steve Gibson, Pablo Picasso, Ansel Adams, Andy Warhol
Publications: Exhibition catalogs; posters
Activities: Lects open to public, 6 vis lectrs per yr; concerts; student awards from ann art council auction; original objects of art lent to institutions; lending collection photographs; originate traveling exhibs

ESCONDIDO

M **CALIFORNIA CENTER FOR THE ARTS,** Escondido Museum, 340 N Escondido Blvd, Escondido, CA 92025-2600. Tel 760-839-4120 (museum), 839-4138 (office); Fax 760-743-6472 (office); Email oluther@ci.escondido.ca.us; Web: www.artcenter.org; *Mus Dir* Olivia Luther; *Registrar* Mary Johnson; *Cur Asst* Tara Smith
Open Tues - Sat 10 AM - 4 PM, Sun 1 PM - 5 PM, cl Mon & major holidays; Admis adults $5, seniors & active military $4, youth 12 - 18 & students $3, children under 12 & mem free; free admis first Wed of every month during an exhibition; Estab 1994; committed to presenting contemporary art; Average Annual Attendance: 8,500; Mem: Dues $50-$10,000
Income: Financed by grants, funds & mem
Library Holdings: Book Volumes, Exhibition Catalogs, Periodical Subscriptions, Video Tapes
Special Subjects: Landscapes, Painting-American, Sculpture
Collections: Collection of decorative arts, Paintings, photography & sculpture from 1900 to present
Exhibitions: Exhibits draw on a distinct theme or idea in contemporary art
Publications: Exhibition specific catalogues
Activities: Classes for children & adults; docent training; lects open to pub; concerts; gallery talks; tours; individual paintings & original objects of art lent; book traveling exhibs; mus shop sells books, original art, reproductions, prints, ceramics, glass, decorative items & jewelry

EUREKA

A **HUMBOLDT ARTS COUNCIL,** Morris Graves Museum of Art, 636 F St, Eureka, CA 95501-1012. Tel 707-442-0278; Fax 707-442-2040; Web: www.humboldtarts.org; *Exec Dir & Cur* Jemima Harr
Open Wed - Sun Noon - 5 PM; No admis fee; Estab 1966 to encourage, promote & correlate all forms of activity in the visual & performing arts & to make such activity a vital influence in the life of the community; Gallery has 7 spaces rotating 41 exhib; Average Annual Attendance: 26,000; Mem: 700; dues $30; annual meeting in Apr
Income: $10,000 (financed by mem)
Collections: Art Bank, other purchase & donated works of art, photograph coll, Premier Coll of North Coast Art (traveling display), traveling import museum exhibits, Morris Graves Collection
Exhibitions: Annual Youth Art Exhibit
Activities: Classes for children & adults, music & dance performances, docent training; concerts; competitions, lects for mems, gallery talks, tours; scholarships offered; individual paintings & original objects of art lent; originate traveling exhibs; museum shop sells books, magazines, original art, reproductions, prints

FREMONT

M **CITY OF FREMONT,** Olive Hyde Art Gallery, 123 Washington Blvd, Fremont, CA 94539-5209; PO Box 5006, Fremont, CA 94537-5006. Tel 510-791-4357, 791-4324 (Dir); Fax 510-494-4753; Email gkim@fremont.gov; Web: www.fremont.gov; *Gallery Cur & Recreation Supvr* Gloria Kim
Open Thurs - Sun 12 - 5 PM; No admis fee; Estab 1964 for community exposure to artistic awareness; Historical former home of Miss Olive Hyde, a well-known San Franciscan art patron. This is the only fine arts gallery open to the public between Hayward & San Jose, located across from the Historical Mission San Jose in Fremont. Exhibits are displayed in 1000 sq ft of space; Average Annual Attendance: 10,000
Income: $20,000 (financed by city appropriation)
Special Subjects: Cartoons, Ceramics, Collages, Crafts, Decorative Arts, Dolls, Drawings, Drawings, Embroidery, Enamels, Etchings & Engravings, Furniture, Glass, Graphics, Jewelry, Landscapes, Mexican Art, Miniatures, Painting-American, Painting-American, Photography, Prints, Sculpture, Textiles, Watercolors, Photography, Porcelain, Portraits, Pottery, Sculpture
Exhibitions: 7 exhibits per year in fine arts, crafts, photography, textiles, sculpture; local, regional, national & international artists; Special traveling exhibits every few years
Publications: Full color exhibit postcards
Activities: Classes for adults & children; docent progs; gallery talks; tours; lects open to both the pub & mems only, 10 vis lectrs per yr; competitions with cash prizes & awards; tours; schols offered; book traveling exhibs 1 per yr; originate traveling exhibs

FRESNO

M **FRESNO ARTS CENTER & MUSEUM,** 2233 N First St, Fresno, CA 93703. Tel 559-441-4220; Fax 559-441-4227; Email fam@qnis.net; Web: www.fresnoartmuseum.org; *Exec Dir* Michael Mazur; *Cur* Jacqueline Pilar
Open Tues - Sun 11AM-5PM, Thurs 11AM-8PM; Admis adults $4, students & seniors $2, children 16 & under, school tours & mus mem free, Sat free to pub; Estab 1949 as a visual arts gallery to provide Fresno & its environs with a community oriented visual arts center; The Center exhibits works of internationally known artists & arranges shows of local artists. Three galleries plus entry for exhibits; Average Annual Attendance: 98,000; Mem: 2500; dues $25; annual meeting in May
Income: Financed by mem & fundraising efforts
Special Subjects: Mexican Art, Oriental Art
Collections: Works of prominent California artists, contemporary American artists, Mexican folk art, Mexican graphic arts, permanent coll, National & International artists, extensive Pre-Columbian folk art
Exhibitions: Rotating exhibits every 3 months
Activities: Classes for adults & children; docent training; lects open to pub, 12 vis lectrs per yr; gallery talks; concerts; tours; competitions; scholarships offered; individual paintings & objects of art lent to city & county offices & other institutions; lending collection contains framed reproductions, original art works, original prints & slides; book traveling exhibs; originates traveling exhibs; mus shop sells books, magazines, original art, reproductions, prints, cards & local crafts

M **FRESNO METROPOLITAN MUSEUM,** 205 E River Park Cir, Ste 410, Fresno, CA 93720-1572. Tel 559-441-1444; Fax 559-441-8607; Email marketing@fresnomet.org; Web: www.fresnomet.org; *Exec Dir* Dana Thorpe; *Dir Mktg & Mem* Candice Pendergrass
Open Tues - Sun 11 AM - 5 PM; Admis adults $8, seniors & students $5, children 3-12 $3, members & children under 3 free; Estab 1984 to increase the availability of fine & educational arts to the Fresno area; Mus is housed in a refurbished 1922 newspaper plant, two stories, with other floors marked for develop; equipped with elevators & facilities for the handicapped; Average Annual Attendance: 100,000; Mem: 5000; dues $30-$1000
Income: $1,300,000 (financed by mem, donations, service fees & grants)
Collections: Frank & Mary Alice Diener Collection of ancient snuff bottles, Oscar & Maria Salzer Collection of still life & trompe l'oeil paintings, Oscar & Maria Salzer collection of 16th & 17th century Dutch & Flemish paintings, Charles Small Puzzle Collection
Publications: MetReport, monthly
Activities: Children's classes & summer day camps; dramatic progs; docent training; lects open to pub; tours; individual paintings & original objects of art lent; book traveling exhibs; originate traveling exhibs; mus shop sells books & prints

M **GALLERY 25,** Art Gallery, 2223 S Van Ness Ave, Fresno, CA 93721-3430. Tel 559-264-4092; Web: www.gallery25.org; *Dir* Michael McKee
Open 1st Thurs each month 5 PM - 8 PM Fri - Sun noon - 4 PM; No admis fee; Estab 1974; cooperative art gallery; Contemporary art of central California; Average Annual Attendance: 5,000; Mem: 25; dues $720 ann; qualifications, highest quality contemporary art
Income: Self financed by mem dues & sales
Collections: works by contemporary artists
Exhibitions: Rotating monthly exhibs
Activities: Gallery talks; sales shop sells books, magazines, original art, prints & jewelry

FULLERTON

M **CALIFORNIA STATE UNIVERSITY, FULLERTON,** Visual Arts Galleries, 800 N State College Blvd, Fullerton, CA 92634-3559; PO Box 6850, Visual Arts Dept Fullerton, CA 92834-6850. Tel 657-278-3471 (Dept); 278-7750 (Gallery); Fax 657-278-2390; Email mmcgee@fullerton.edu; Web: www.fullerton.edu/arts/; *Cur* Mike McGee
Open Mon - Fri 8 AM - 5 PM, cl Sat & Sun; No admis fee; Estab 1963 to bring to the campus carefully developed art exhibits that instruct, inspire & challenge the student to the visual arts; to present to the student body, faculty & community exhibits of historical & aesthetic significance; to act as an educational tool, creating interaction between various departmental disciplines & promoting pub relations between campus & community; Visual Arts Galleries comprised of the Begovich Gallery, East Gallery, West Gallery & Exit Gallery; 4-5 exhibits each year stemming from the Museum Studies & Exhibition Design Program. Undergraduate & graduate students have the opportunity to focus within a professionally oriented program directed toward the mus profession. Activity incorporates classes, art gallery & local mus. The Department of Art & the Art Gallery are the holders of the permanent collection; Average Annual Attendance: 15,000-20,000
Income: Financed by state appropriation, grants & donations
Collections: Contemporary Lithographs (Gemini), works by artists in the New York Collection for Stockholm executed by Styria Studio, lithographs by Lita Albuquerque, Coy Howard, Ed Rusha & Alexis Smith, Pre-Columbian artifacts, environmental & site-specific sculpture by Lloyd Hamrol, Ray Hein, Bernard Rosenthal, Michael Todd, Jay Willis, Smithsonian Collection of American Art, Jene Isaacson Collection
Publications: Exhibition catalogs
Activities: Lects open to public, 8-10 vis lectrs per yr; workshops; production of slide/sound interpretation programs in conjunction with specific exhibitions; gallery talks; tours; scholarships offered; exten dept 4-6 major exhibs per yr; originate traveling exhibs

M **FULLERTON COLLEGE ART GALLERY,** 321 E Chapman Ave, Bldg 1000 Fullerton, CA 92832-2011. Tel 714-922-7131; Fax 714-992-7320; Email bsolomon@fullcoll.edu; Web: art.fullcoll.edu; *Gallery Dir & Art Instr* Beth Solomon Marino
Open Mon - Thurs 10 AM - 2 PM, selected evenings 5 PM - 7 PM; No admis fee; Estab 1913 (Fullerton Col); 1750 sq ft with movable walls (7 rotating exhibs per yr); Average Annual Attendance: 3,500
Collections: paintings, photographs, sculpture, prints
Publications: Visions Catalogue of Collection
Activities: Classes for adults; lects open to pub; 3 vis lectrs per yr; gallery talks; tours; schols; lending of original objects of art to CSU, Fullerton & Orange Coast Community Col; sales shop sells original art, prints

A **MUCKENTHALER CULTURAL CENTER,** 1201 W Malvern, Fullerton, CA 92633. Tel 714-738-6595; Fax 714-738-6366; Email info@themuck.org; Web: www.muckenthaler.org; *Center Adminr* Zoot Velasco; *Exhib & Educ Adminr* Matt Leslie
Open Wed - Fri 10 AM - 4 PM, Sat - Sun Noon - 4 PM, By appt Tues; Admis free; Estab 1966 for the promotion & develop of a public cultural center for the preservation, display & edification in the arts; Gallery is a National Historic Building, contains 2500 sq ft & is on 8 1/2 acres of land; outdoor theatre facilities; Average Annual Attendance: 65,000; Mem: 600; dues $10 & up; annual meeting in Apr
Income: $230,000 (financed by endowment, mem & city appropriation)
Publications: Exhibition catalogs
Activities: Classes for adults & children; dramatic progs; docent training; lects open to pub; 12 vis lectrs per yr; concerts; gallery talks; tours; book traveling exhibs; mus shop sells original art, reproductions, prints & gifts

GILROY

M **GAVILAN COMMUNITY COLLEGE,** Art Gallery, 5055 Santa Teresa Blvd, Gilroy, CA 95020-9599. Tel 408-846-4946; Fax 408-846-4927, 846-4801; Web: www.Gavilan.cc.ca.us; *Gallery Adv & Humanities Div Dir* Kent Child; *Prof Art & New Technology* Jane Edberg
Open Mon - Fri 8 AM - 5 PM; No admis fee; Estab 1967 to serve as a focal point in art exhibs for community col district & as a teaching resource for the art dept; Gallery is in large lobby of college library with 25 ft ceiling, redwood paneled walls & carpeted floor
Income: Financed through college
Collections: Over 25 paintings purchased as award purchase prizes in college art competitions
Exhibitions: Monthly exhibits of student & local artists; Ann Gavilan Student Show, HS Student Exhib
Activities: Lending collection contains books, cassettes, color reproductions, film strips, Kodachromes, paintings, sculpture

GLEN ELLEN

M **JACK LONDON STATE HISTORIC PARK,** House of Happy Walls, 2400 London Ranch Rd, Glen Ellen, CA 95442-9749. Tel 707-938-5216; Fax

707-938-4827; *Supv Ranger* Greg Hayes; *Ranger* Cheryl Lawton; *Ranger* Angie Nowicki
Open daily 10 AM - 5 PM, summers 10 AM - 7 PM, cl New Year's Day, Thanksgiving, Christmas; Admis $10-$20 per bus, $3 per car, seniors $2; Estab 1959 for the interpretation of the life of Jack London; the fieldstone home was constructed in 1919 by London's widow; The collection is housed on two floors in the House of Happy Walls, and is operated by Calif Dept of Parks & Recreation; Average Annual Attendance: 100,000
Income: Financed by state appropriation
Collections: Artifacts from South Sea Islands, original illustrations, Portrait of activity during Jack London's residence
Activities: Tours; sales shop sells some of London's books

GLENDALE

M **FOREST LAWN MUSEUM,** 1712 S Glendale Ave, Glendale, CA 91205. Tel 800-204-3131; Fax 323-551-5329; Email museum@forestlawn.com; Web: www.forestlawn.com; *Mus Opers Supv* Elizabeth Bloess; *Exhib Designer* Joan Adan
Open Tues - Sun 10 AM - 5 PM; No admis fee; Estab 1951 as a community mus offering educ & culture through assn with the architecture and the art of world masters; Two galleries of permanent collection, museum store & rotating exhibit gallery; Average Annual Attendance: 50,000
Special Subjects: American Western Art, Antiquities-Greek, Antiquities-Roman, Architecture, Bronzes, Ceramics, Coins & Medals, Decorative Arts, Drawings, Enamels, Furniture, Glass, Gold, Islamic Art, Ivory, Jade, Jewelry, Landscapes, Latin American Art, Manuscripts, Medieval Art, Mosaics, Painting-Polish, Photography, Religious Art, Renaissance Art, Reproductions, Sculpture, Silver, Stained Glass
Collections: American Western Bronzes, Ancient Biblical and Historical Coins, Crucifixion by Jan Styka (195 x 45 ft painting), Resurrection (Robert Clark), painting, reproductions of Michelangelo's greatest sculptures, stained glass window of the Last Supper by Leonardo da Vinci, originals and reproductions of famous sculptures, paintings, and documents
Exhibitions: Four changing exhibits every year, see website
Activities: Community events; History Comes Alive Program; originate traveling exhibs; mus shop sells books, original art reproductions, prints, objects that reflect the collection

M **GLENDALE PUBLIC LIBRARY,** (Brand Library & Art Galleries) Brand Library & Art Center, 1601 W Mountain St, Glendale, CA 91201-1200. Tel 818-548-2051; Fax 818-548-5079; Email info@brandlibrary.org; Web: www.brandlibrary.org; *Sr Library Supvr* Cathy Billings; *Librn* Blair Whittington; *Librn* Caley Cannon
Open Mon - Thurs 10 AM - 8 PM; Fri - Sun 10 AM - 5 PM; No admis fee; Estab 1956 to exhibit Southern California artists as part of an art & music library; Circ 170,000; Large gallery, foyer gallery, glass & concrete sculpture ct; Average Annual Attendance: 100,000; Mem: 375; dues $15 - $500
Income: Financed by city & state appropriations
Library Holdings: Auction Catalogs, Book Volumes 106,000, Compact Disks, DVDs, Exhibition Catalogs, Periodical Subscriptions, Records 6,000, Video Tapes
Special Subjects: Woodcuts, Furniture, Watercolors, Textiles, Tapestries, Stained Glass, Southwestern Art, Silver, Sculpture, Religious Art, Prints, Primitive art, Pre-Columbian Art, Pottery, Advertising Design, Aesthetics, Afro-American Art, American Indian Art, American Western Art, Anthropology, Architecture, Art History, Asian Art, Bronzes, Calligraphy, Carpets & Rugs, Cartoons, Ceramics, Collages, Commercial Art, Conceptual Art, Costume Design & Constr, Crafts, Decorative Arts, Display, Drawings, Embroidery, Enamels, Eskimo Art, Etchings & Engravings, Fashion Arts, Folk Art, Glass, Posters, Graphic Arts, Graphic Design, Handicrafts, History of Art & Archaeology, Illustration, Industrial Design, Interior Design, Islamic Art, Ivory, Jade, Jewelry, Landscape Architecture, Landscapes, Latin American Art, Leather, Lettering, Manuscripts, Maps, Marine Painting, Metalwork, Mexican Art, Miniatures, Mixed Media, Mosaics, Oriental Art, Photography, Porcelain, Portraits
Collections: Indexes & other guides to art & music literature, books, catalogue raisonne, scores, CDs & DVDs
Exhibitions: 4-6 exhibits per year
Activities: Los Angeles Opera Talks; lects open to pub; 4 - 6 vis lectrs; concerts; gallery talks; tours; competitions, children's art & music programs; book group; dance series

M **MUSEUM OF NEON ART,** 216 S Brand Blvd, Glendale, CA 91204; PO Box 631, Glendale, CA 91209-0631. Tel 818-696-2149; Email info@neonmona.org; Web: www.neonmona.org; *Exec Dir* Kim Koga
Open Thurs - Sat noon - 7 PM, Sun Noon - 5 PM, cl New Year's Day, Thanksgiving Day, Christmas Day; Admis adults $10, seniors $8, students $5, children 12 & under free; Estab 1981 to exhibit, document & preserve works of neon, electric & kinetic art; Consists of large main gallery for group or theme exhibitions & a small gallery for solo shows; Average Annual Attendance: 15,000; Mem: 300; dues $35 & up; annual meetings in Dec
Income: Financed by mem, donations, admis fees, gifts & grants
Collections: Antique electrical signs, contemporary neon art
Exhibitions: Ladies of the Night; Victoria Rivers: Neon/Fabric Construction; Electro-Kinetic Box Art.
Publications: Transformer, quarterly
Activities: Classes for adults; lects open to pub; concerts; gallery talks; tours; book traveling exhibs; originates traveling exhibs; mus shop sells books, magazines, original art, reproductions, prints, slides, electronic jewelry & posters

HALF MOON BAY

M **COASTAL ARTS LEAGUE MUSEUM,** 300 Main St, Half Moon Bay, CA 94038. Tel 650-726-6335; Web: www.coastalartsleague.com
Open Thurs - Mon 11 AM - 5 PM; No admis fee
Special Subjects: Ceramics, Painting-American, Photography, Pottery, Restorations, Sculpture, Watercolors
Collections: Paintings; photographs; sculpture; ceramics
Exhibitions: International photography juried show; juried & invitational exhibs -high school yearly show
Activities: Mus related items for sale

HAYWARD

M **CALIFORNIA STATE UNIVERSITY, EAST BAY,** University Art Gallery, 1233 Art & Education Bldg, CSUEB Hayward, CA 94542. Tel 510-885-3299; Fax 510-885-2281; Web: www.csueastbay.edu/artgallery; *Dir* Philip Hofstetter
Open Mon - Thurs 12:30 PM - 3:30 PM; No admis fee; Estab 1970 to provide a changing exhibition program for the university & general public; Gallery contains 2,200 sq ft; Average Annual Attendance: 11,000
Publications: Usually one catalog a yr; flyers for each show

M **C E Smith Museum of Anthropology,** 4047 Meiklejohn Hall, California State University East Bay Hayward, CA 94542; Anthropology Dept M13097, CSU East Bay Hayward, CA 94542. Tel 510-885-3104; Fax 510-885-3353; Email george.miller@csueastbay.edu; Web: class.csueastbay.edu/anthropologymuseum; *Dir* George Miller PhD; *Assoc Dir* Marjorie Rhodes-Ousley
Open Mar - June Mon - Fri 10 AM - 4 PM; No admis fee; Estab 1974 as a teaching museum; Three connected galleries; one main entrance from center room; alarm system; smoke detectors; Average Annual Attendance: 2,500; Mem: 200
Income: $22,000 (financed by state appropriation)
Special Subjects: African Art, Anthropology, Archaeology, Ethnology, Pre-Columbian Art, Southwestern Art, Textiles
Collections: Krone Collection: Philippine artifacts, Lee Collection: Hopi Kachinas, baskets, Navajo Mat
Publications: Seasons of the Kochina, ed L J Bean; The Ohlone Past & Present, ed L J Bean
Activities: Educ prog; classes for adults; college classes; tours; Lect open to pub, 4 vis lectrs per yr; tours

M **HAYWARD AREA FORUM FOR THE ARTS,** Sun Gallery, 1015 E St, Hayward, CA 94541-5210. Tel 510-581-4050; Fax 510-581-3384; Email sungallery@comcast.net; Web: www.sungallery.org; *Admin Asst* Christine Bender; *Exec Dir* Dorsi Diaz
Open Thurs - Sun 11 AM - 5 PM, cl major holidays; No admis fee; Estab 1975; Exhibition gallery, gallery shop & teaching studio; Average Annual Attendance: 5,000; Mem: dues sustaining $65, family $50, single $35, senior citizen $25
Income: Financed by city, corporate & foundation grants, county & mem funds
Library Holdings: Audio Tapes, Book Volumes, CD-ROMs, Cards, Cassettes, Clipping Files, Kodachrome Transparencies, Original Art Works, Prints, Sculpture, Slides, Video Tapes
Collections: Contemporary art by Northern California artists
Exhibitions: San Francisco Alumni Association exhibition (photography); recent works in Monotype; contemporary Mexican painters (from Santiago Garza collection); Jack & Marilyn da Silva (metalware); art programs for the physically limited; Roger Hankins (painting, assemblage); Dicksen Schneider; Southern Alameda County Art Educators; Corita Kent; Artistas del Grupo Hermes (paintings, drawings); Recent Work in Metal; Artists With Creative Growth; The Picture: As Object, As Image (painting, assemblage, photography); Shrine & Koan (painting, sculpture); Corita & Southern Alameda County Art Educators (multi-media); HAFA members exhibition (multi-media); Art in the News (photojournalists, editorial cartoonists); Forms In Space (2-D, 3-D); Felted Fibers; The Hottest Show in Town: Exhibit featuring art by firefighters; A Cut Above: Art created by cutting; An Annual Children's Book Illustrator Exhibit; The Wild, Wild West
Activities: Classes for adults & children; docent training; summer art camp; lects open to pub, 6-8 vis lectrs per yr; gallery talks; tours; sponsoring competitions; awards, 2015 Environmental Award from City of Hayward; scholarships offered; individual paintings & original objects of art lent to city offices; mus shop sells original art, prints, magazines, reproductions, books & crafts

HUNTINGTON BEACH

M **HUNTINGTON BEACH ART CENTER,** 538 Main St, Huntington Beach, CA 92648-5134. Tel 714-374-1650; Fax 714-374-5304; Email deangel@surfeity-hb.org ; *Dir* Kate Hoffman; *Dir Programming* Darlene DeAngelo
Open Wed-Sat noon-6PM; No admis fee; Estab 1995 to provide community art center; Three large galleries, store gallery, studio & one educational gallery; Average Annual Attendance: 3,000; Mem: 300
Activities: Classes for adults & children; performance art venue; lect open to public; Sun jazz concerts; sales shop sells books & magazines

INDIO

M **COACHELLA VALLEY HISTORY MUSEUM,** 82-616 Miles Ave, Indio, CA 92201. Tel 760-342-6651; Fax 760-863-5232; Email erin@cvhm.org; Web: coachellavalleymuseum.org; *Pres* William H Claire; *Archivist/Cur* Erica M Ward; *Office Admin* Janice Woodside
Open Oct - May Thurs - Sat 10 AM - 4 PM, Sun 1 - 4 PM, cl holidays; Admis adults $10, senior citizens & students $8, children 6-12 $5, children under 5 & members free; Estab Oct 1984; Average Annual Attendance: 4,200; Mem: 380
Income: Financed by mems, donations & bequeathments
Library Holdings: Book Volumes, Original Documents, Photographs
Collections: works by local artists
Exhibitions: Monthly local art show, reception first Sun ea month
Publications: quarterly newsletter, Scratches in the Sand; annual magazine, The Periscope; pictorial history book
Activities: Summer art classes for adults & children 8-12; docent prog; lects open to pub; vis lectrs 3 per yr; guided tours; school tours; mus shop sells books, original art, toys, DVDs

IRVINE

M **CITY OF IRVINE,** Irvine Fine Arts Center, 14321 Yale Ave, Irvine, CA 92604-1901. Tel 949-724-6880; Fax 949-552-2137; Web: www.irvinefinearts.org; *Dir* Wendy Shields; *Youth Prog Coordr* Andrea Becerra; *Adult Prog Coordr* Katy Metz
Open Mon - Thurs 10 AM - 9 PM, Fri 10 AM - 5 PM, Sat 9AM-5PM; No admis fee; Estab 1980 to promote awareness of the value & function of the arts in the community; Gallery contains 5000 sq ft; Average Annual Attendance: 65,000; Mem: 250; dues $25 - $100
Income: $800,000 (financed by city appropriation, grants & donations)
Exhibitions: Solo & group themed exhibitions of local, national & international contemporary artists
Publications: Inside Irvine, quarterly
Activities: Classes for adults & children; docent progs; open studios; 2 arts festivals per year; lects open to pub, competitions, scholarships; sales shop sells original art

M **IRVINE MUSEUM,** 18881 Von Karman Ave Ste 100, Irvine, CA 92612-1559. Tel 949-476-0294; Fax 949-476-2437; Web: www.irvinemuseum.org; *Exec Dir* Jean Stern; *Cur Educ* Dora James; *Bookstore Mgr* Don Bridges; *Visitor Svcs* Leslee Fitzgibbons
Open Tues - Sat 11 AM - 5 PM; No admis fee; Estab 1992 to promote the California Impressionist Period; Average Annual Attendance: 19,000
Special Subjects: Painting-American
Collections: Paintings of the California Impressionist Period, 1890-1930, California Impressionist paintings
Exhibitions: Exhibits change every 4 months; traveling exhibs
Publications: Exhibit catalogs
Activities: Classes for children; docent progs; mus shop sells books

M **UNIVERSITY OF CALIFORNIA, IRVINE,** Beall Center for Art + Technology, and University Art Gallery, 712 Arts Plaza, Univ of Calif Irvine Irvine, CA 92697-2775. Tel 949-824-6206; Fax 949-824-2450; Email syoungha@uci.edu; Web: www.beallcenter.uci.edu; *Dir* Joseph S Lewis III; *Asst Dir* David Familian; *Prog Dir* Samantha Younghans-Haug
Open Oct - June, Tue & Wed Noon - 5 PM, Thurs - Sat Noon - 8 PM; No admis fee; Estab 2000; focus on experimental media arts & contemporary art; 2 galleries totaling 5,000 sq ft; Average Annual Attendance: 5,000
Income: Financed by state appropriations & by pvt and corporate donors
Publications: Exhibition catalogs; mailers
Activities: Educ prog; family art days; robotics summer camps for children; lects open to pub; 2 vis lectrs per yr; performances; gallery talks; tours; field trips

KENTFIELD

M **COLLEGE OF MARIN,** Art Gallery, 835 College Ave, Kentfield, CA 94904-2551. Tel 415-485-9494; Web: www.marin.edu; *Dir* Julie Gustafson
Open Mon - Fri 9 AM - 5 PM, also during all performances for drama, music & concert; No admis fee; Estab 1970 for the purpose of educ in the col district & community; Gallery is housed in the entrance to Fine Arts Complex, measures 3600 sq ft of unlimited hanging space; has portable hanging units & locked cases; Average Annual Attendance: 100-450 daily
Income: Financed by state appropriation & community taxes
Collections: Art student work, miscellaneous coll
Exhibitions: Faculty & Art Student; Fine Arts & Decorative Arts
Publications: Catalogs, 1-2 per year
Activities: Gallery Design-Management course; gallery talks; tours

LA JOLLA

M **JOSEPH BELLOWS GALLERY,** 7661 Girard Ave, La Jolla, CA 92037. Tel 858-456-5620; Fax 858-456-5621; Email info@josephbellows.com; Web: www.josephbellows.com; *Dir* Joseph Bellows; *Dir* Mike Mulno; *Special Projects* Carol Lee Brosseau; *Remote Preparator* Shigeto Miyata; *Account* Tracey Davis
Open Tues - Sat 10 AM - 5 PM; Estab 1998
Special Subjects: Photography
Collections: historic & contemporary work with an emphasis on American work; photography
Exhibitions: Temporary exhibits

L **LIBRARY ASSOCIATION OF LA JOLLA,** Athenaeum Music & Arts Library, 1008 Wall St, La Jolla, CA 92037-4418. Tel 858-454-5872; Fax 858-454-5835; Email athdir@pacbell.net; Web: www.ljathenaeum.org; *Exec Dir* Erika Torri; *Prog Dir* Judith Oishei; *Asst to Dir* Maura Walters; *Librn* Kathi Bower-Peterson; *Pub Rels* Stephanie Shepherd; *School Dir* Cornelia Feye; *Jazz Coordr* Daniel Atkinson
Open Tues, Thurs, Fri & Sat 10 AM - 5:30 PM, Wed 10 AM - 8:30PM; No admis fee; Estab 1899 to provide the La Jolla & San Diego communities with library resources in music & arts & an on going schedule of cultural programs, classes, concerts & exhibitions; Circ 30,000; changing exhibitions every six weeks; Average Annual Attendance: 130,000; Mem: 2300; dues $40-$15,000; annual meeting third Tues in July
Income: $1,700,000 (financed by mem dues, endowment, fund raisers, gifts, admis & tuitions)
Purchases: of books $50,000
Library Holdings: Audio Tapes 4,000, Book Volumes 18,000, CD-ROMs 200, Cassettes 4000, Clipping Files 2500, Compact Disks 12,000, DVDs 1,000, Exhibition Catalogs, Other Holdings Sheet Music, Artists' Books 1500, Pamphlets, Periodical Subscriptions 85, Photographs, Records 8000, Video Tapes 3000
Special Subjects: Advertising Design, Aesthetics, Afro-American Art, Architecture, Art History, Asian Art, Bookplates & Bindings, Bronzes, Photography
Collections: Collection of artists books, works by regional, nat & international artists; paintings; sculpture; drawings; photographs
Exhibitions: Changing exhibitions every six weeks; Permanent Art Coll Works by artists who have exhibited at the Athenaeum
Publications: Bimonthly newsletter, qtr school brochure, occasional exhib catalogues, catalogs on artists' book artists: Ed Ruscha, Ida Applebroog, Allen Ruppersberg, John Baldessari, Bruce Newman
Activities: Classes for adults & children; lect open to public, 15 vis lectrs per year; concerts; library tours; panel discussions; vis artists workshops; outreach programs for children; qtr book sales; competitions with prizes; 1st, 2nd, 3rd awards for juried shows; original artists books lent to qualified mus & institutions; sales shop sells books, cards, craft items

M **MUSEUM OF CONTEMPORARY ART SAN DIEGO LA JOLLA,** 700 Prospect St, La Jolla, CA 92037-4291. Tel 858-454-3541; Fax 858-454-6985; Email info@mcasd.org; Web: www.mcasd.org; *Pres Bd Trustees* Matthew Strauss; *David C Copley Dir* Dr Hugh Davies, PhD; *Deputy Dir & CFO* Charles Castle; *Advancement Dir* Edie Nehls; *Chief Cur* Kathryn Kanjo
Open at LaJolla & Downtown locations: Thurs - Tues 11 AM - 5 PM, 3rd Thurs 11 AM - 7 PM, cl Wed; Gen admis $10, seniors & students 26 & over w/ ID $5, military families & ages 25 and under w/ ID free; Estab 1941 to collect, preserve, & present post-1950 art; Maintains two locations, a 500 seat auditorium, 16,000 sq ft total exhibition space
Income: $5,400,000 financed by endowment, mem, city, & state appropriation, grants from the National Endowment for the Arts, Institute of Mus Services & private foundations
Library Holdings: Audio Tapes, Clipping Files, Exhibition Catalogs, Pamphlets, Periodical Subscriptions, Slides
Publications: VIEW; quarterly newsletter; exhibition catalogues; gallery guides
Activities: Classes for adults and children, docent training; Lects open to pub, gallery talks, tours, and internships offered; books traveling exhibs 1 per year; originates traveling exhibs 2 per year; mus shop sells books

A **QUINT PROJECTS,** 7547 Girard Ave, La Jolla, CA 92037; 5171 Santa Fe St, Stes H, B & A San Diego, CA 92117. Tel 858-454-3409; Fax 858-454-3421; Email info@quintgallery.com; Web: quintgallery.com; *Owner* Mark Quint; *Dir* Sarah Trujillo-Porter; *Project Mgr* Shawn Bigbee; *Mktg* Nina Howard
Open Thurs 10 AM - 6 PM, Fri - Sat 10 AM - 4 PM; other times by appt; No admis fee; Estab 1981; 3000 sq ft interior exhib space; Average Annual Attendance: 1000
Library Holdings: Cards, Compact Disks, DVDs, Framed Reproductions, Kodachrome Transparencies, Original Art Works, Original Documents, Pamphlets, Photographs, Prints, Sculpture, Slides, Video Tapes
Special Subjects: Prints, Posters, Sculpture
Collections: Contemporary art, Estate of Manny Farber, Minimal Abstract, Light & Space Art, Installations, Site-Specific Art
Publications: Kelsey Brookes: Psychodelic Space; Robert Irwin: Projects & Exhibitions; Ryan McGinnes: Women: New (Re)Presentations
Activities: Lects open to pub; 5 vis lectrs per yr; concerts; gallery talks; tours; Mus shop sells books; original art; prints

M **THUMBPRINT GALLERY,** 920 Kline St, Ste 104 La Jolla, CA 92037. Tel 858-354-6294; Email info@thumbprintgallerysd.com; Web: www.thumbprintgallerysd.com; *Co-Owner* Paul Ecdao; *Co-Owner* Johnny Tran
Open Fri Noon - 6 PM, Sat - Sun Noon - 4 PM; Estab 2009; curates monthly & pop-up exhibs with a focus on contemporary pop-culture & urban art; engages a community that appreciates and supports local, national, and international artists
Collections: Contemporary art
Exhibitions: Monthly exhibits; pop-up exhibits

M **UNIVERSITY OF CALIFORNIA, SAN DIEGO,** Stuart Collection, 9500 Gilman Dr, La Jolla, CA 92093-0010. Tel 858-534-2117; Fax 858-534-9713; Email mbeebe@ucsd.edu; Web: www.stuartcollection.ucsd.edu; *Project Dir* Mathieu Gregoire; *Dir* Mary Livingstone Beebe; *Prog Asst* Jane Zwerneman
Open 24 hours, 7 days a week; No admis fee; Estab 1981 to commission outdoor sculptures for UCSD campus; Maintains small library; Average Annual Attendance: 38,000 per day; Mem: Friends of the Stuart Collection $2,000 per yr
Income: Staff raises all funds; salaries paid by UCSD
Purchases: 18 commissioned sculptures
Special Subjects: Architecture, Drawings, Sculpture
Collections: Outdoor sculptures, 18 works
Publications: Landmarks: Sculpture commissions for the Stuart Collection at the University of California, San Diego, pub 2001
Activities: Lects for mems only; 1-2 vis lectrs per yr; tours by appointment; support groups; Americans for the Arts Public Art Network Award-2011; San Diego Architectural Foundation Grand Orchid-2013

M **UNIVERSITY OF CALIFORNIA-SAN DIEGO,** University Art Gallery, 9500 Gilman Dr, Mail Code 0327 La Jolla, CA 92093-0327. Tel 858-534-0419; Fax 858-822-3548; Email uag@ucsd.edu; Web: www.universityartgallery.ucsd.edu; *Asst Dir* Merete Kjaer
Open Tues - Fri 11 AM - 5 PM; No admis fee; Estab 1967; Size 2800 sq ft; Average Annual Attendance: 15,000
Income: Financed by state appropriations, member contributions & student registration fees
Exhibitions: 5 exhib per yr incl MFA plus on campus & off site projects
Activities: Classes for children & docent training; lects open to public, 3-4 vis lectrs per yr; gallery talks; tours; fels; originate traveling exhibs

LAGUNA BEACH

M **LAGUNA ART MUSEUM,** 307 Cliff Dr, Laguna Beach, CA 92651-1696. Tel 949-494-8971; Fax 949-494-1530; Web: www.lagunaartmuseum.org; *Bus Mgr* Peter Salomon; *Cur Historical Art* Janet Blake; *Registrar* Dawn Minegar; *Exec Dir* Malcolm Warner; *Deputy Dir* Genny Boccardo-Dubay; *Cur Educ* Marinta Skupin; *Dir Special Events* Sarah Strozza; *Director of Design and Installation* Tim Schwab; *Head Security* Joel Woodard; *Asst Cur of Educ* Irin Mahoparn; *Membership & Devel Officer* Kate Ambrose; *Admin Coordr* Kristin Anthony; *Director of Communication* Cody Lee; *Grants Officer* Kristin Kelly; *Visitor Services Manager* Lailani Yamanishi

Open Mon - Tue, Fri - Sun 11 AM - 5 PM, Thurs 11 AM - 9 PM; cl Wed & major holidays; Admis adults $7, seniors & students $5, children under 12 free; Estab 1918; the museum of California art.; Two large galleries, six small galleries, mus store & offices; Average Annual Attendance: 50,000; Mem: 1800; dues $60 - $10,000; annual meeting in Sept
Income: Financed by endowment & mem
Library Holdings: Auction Catalogs, Book Volumes, Exhibition Catalogs, Pamphlets, Periodical Subscriptions, Photographs
Special Subjects: American Western Art, Ceramics, Drawings, Landscapes, Painting-American, Photography, Portraits, Sculpture
Collections: American Art with focus on contemporary & early 20th century California painting, California Art
Exhibitions: Rotating exhibits
Activities: Classes for adults & children; docent training; lects open to public, 12 vis lectrs per yr; concerts; gallery talks; tours; Wendt Award; book traveling exhibs; originate traveling exhibs; sales shop sells books, original art, prints; reproductions

L **LAGUNA COLLEGE OF ART & DESIGN,** Dennis & Leslie Power Library, 2222 Laguna Canyon Rd, Laguna Beach, CA 92651-1136. Tel 949-376-6000x225; Fax 949-376-6009; Email libcheckout@lcad.edu; Web: www.lcad.edu; *Head Librn* Jennifer Martinez Wormser; *Library Services Specialist* Christa Jech
Open Mon - Thurs 9 AM - 8 PM, Fri 9 AM - 5 PM; No admis fee; Estab 1961; Circ 6,600; For lending only to students & faculty; Average Annual Attendance: 40,000
Income: Financed through Institute
Purchases: $20,000
Library Holdings: Auction Catalogs, Audio Tapes, Book Volumes 20,643, CD-ROMs, Clipping Files, DVDs 2,065, Exhibition Catalogs 400, Manuscripts, Original Art Works, Periodical Subscriptions 82, Photographs, Slides 23,787, Video Tapes 172
Special Subjects: Advertising Design, American Western Art, Art Education, Art History, Cartoons, Ceramics, Commercial Art, Drawings, Etchings & Engravings, Fashion Arts, Film, Graphic Arts, Graphic Design, History of Art & Archaeology, Illustration, Mixed Media, Painting-American, Photography, Portraits, Printmaking, Video, Aesthetics, Afro-American Art, Asian Art, Bookplates & Bindings, Bronzes, Conceptual Art, Costume Design & Constr, Decorative Arts, Industrial Design, Jewelry, Islamic Art, Landscapes, Latin American Art, Lettering, Mexican Art, Oriental Art, Posters, Pre-Columbian Art, Primitive art, Religious Art, Sculpture, Southwestern Art, Stage Design, Woodcuts
Publications: Catalog, annual; newsletters, semi-annual

LONG BEACH

A **ARTS COUNCIL FOR LONG BEACH,** (Public Corporation for the Arts), 350 Elm Ave, Long Beach, CA 90802-2415. Tel 562-570-1930; Fax 562-432-5175; Email info@artspca.org; Web: www.artspca.org; *Exec Dir* Joan Van Hooten
Open Mon - Thurs 9 AM - 5 PM, cl Fri, Sat & Sun; No admis fee; Estab 1977, nonprofit, official arts adv council for city of Long Beach
Income: $750,000 (financed by endowment, mem, city appropriation, private corporations & foundations)
Publications: Quarterly events calendar
Activities: Enrichment & alternative arts progs; technical assistance; individual & community art grants, Smithsonian Week

M **BARBARA & RAY ALPERT JEWISH COMMUNITY CENTER,** Pauline & Zena Gatov Gallery, 3801 E Willow St, Long Beach, CA 90815-1791. Tel 562-426-7601; Fax 562-424-3915; Email elunt@alpertjcc.org; Web: www.alpertjcc.org; *Pres* Steve Gordon; *Exec Dir* Jeff Antonoff; *Gallery Dir* Eve Lunt; *Prog Dir* Susan Paletz
Open Mon - Sun 10 AM - 6 PM; No admis fee; Estab 1960 to provide a showcase for Jewish artists, Judaica & a forum for socially conscious art from the greater Long Beach community; The gallery is located in the main promenade of the building; panels & shelves are for exhibit displays; Average Annual Attendance: 5,000; Mem: Varied
Income: Financed by mem & gallery sales
Special Subjects: Judaica
Collections: Max Gatov Yad Coll, Milton Hebald Terracotta Figure of Mendelson
Exhibitions: Annual Youth Art Show; Biannual Art for Social Justice Exhibit; monthly exhibits throughout the year; paintings, photography, portraits, sculpture, biannual col art exhibit
Publications: Community Chronicle, monthly
Activities: Classes for adults & children; dramatic progs; lects open to pub; concerts; gallery talks; tours; competitions with awards; Judaic library; full serv fitness ctr

A **CALIFORNIA STATE UNIVERSITY,** Long Beach Foundation, 6300 State University Dr Ste 332, Long Beach, CA 90815. Tel 562-985-5537; Fax 562-985-7951; Email mstephens@csulb.edu; Web: www.foundation.csulb.edu; *CEO* Mary Stephens; *COO* Brian Nowlin; *CFO* Alan Ray; *Dir Grants & Contracts* Denise Bell
Open Mon - Fri 8 AM - 5 PM; Estab 1955 existing solely to advance the mission of the University. Serves to complement & strengthen the University's teaching, research, scholarly, creative & pub service goals
Activities: Lect open to pub, 8 vis lectrs per yr; grants offered

M **CALIFORNIA STATE UNIVERSITY, LONG BEACH,** University Art Museum, 1250 Bellflower Blvd, Long Beach, CA 90840-0004. Tel 562-985-5761; Fax 562-985-7602; Email uam@csulb.edu; Web: www.csulb.edu/uam; *Reg & Cur Permanent Coll* Angela Barker; *Asst Cur* Elizabeth Hanson; *Assoc Dir* Ilee Kaplan; *Interim Dir* Brian Trimble; *Educ Asst* Christina Alegria; *Pub Relations Dir* Sarah G Vinci
Open Tues-Sun noon-5PM, Thurs noon-8PM, cl Mon & university holidays; Admis general pub $4, children under 12 free, UAM mems, CSULB students, faculty & staff free; Estab 1949 to be an acad & community visual arts resource; Contemporary art; Average Annual Attendance: 50,000; Mem: 300
Income: Financed by university appropriation & private funding
Purchases: Site specific sculpture, works of art on paper
Special Subjects: Drawings, Photography, Prints, Sculpture
Collections: 1965 Sculpture Symposium
Exhibitions: Jim Dine Figure Drawings: 1975-1979; Kathe Kollwitz at the Zeitlin Bookshop 1937: CSULB 1979; Roy Lichtenstein: Ceramic Sculpture; Nathan Oliveira Print Retrospective; Lucas Samaras: Photo Transformations; George Segal: Pastels 1957 - 1965; Frederick Sommer at Seventy-five; The Photograph as Artifice; Renate Ponsold-Robert Motherwell: Apropos Robinson Jeffers; Francesco Clemente Recent Works; Paul Wonner: Recent Works; Jacques Hurtubise: Oeuvres Recentes-Recent Works; Bryan Hunt: A Decade of Drawings; Anders Zorn Rediscovered; Robert Longo: Sequences-Men in the Cities; A Collective Vision: Clarence White & His Students; Hirosada: Osaka Printmaker; Eric Fischl; Scenes Before the Eye; Lorna Simpson; Imagenes Liricas: New Spanish Visions; James Rosenquist: Time Dust, The Complete Graphics 1962 - 1992; The Great American Pop Art Store: Multiples of the Sixties
Publications: Exhibition catalogs & brochures, 3-4 per year
Activities: Classes for adults & children; docent training; lects open to pub, 3-5 vis lectrs per yr; concerts; gallery talks; tours; book traveling exhibs 1-2 per yr; originate traveling exhibs to qualified mus; mus shop sells books, magazines, original art reproductions, jewelry & objects

L **University Library**, 1250 Bellflower Blvd, Long Beach, CA 90840-1901. Web: www.csulb.edu/library; *Dean Lib & Acad Tech* Roman V Kochan; *Arts Libr* Leslie Anderson
Open Mon-Thurs 7:45AM-11PM, Fri 7:45AM-5PM, Sat 10AM-5PM, Sun 12:30PM-11PM; Estab 1949 for delivery of information & related services to the campus & surrounding communities; Circ 340,248; For lending & reference
Income: Financed by state appropriation
Purchases: $17,722
Library Holdings: Book Volumes 1,022,263, Cards, Cassettes, Exhibition Catalogs, Fiche, Filmstrips, Motion Pictures, Other Holdings Art vols 37,000, Pamphlets, Periodical Subscriptions 116, Prints, Records, Reels, Reproductions, Slides, Video Tapes
Special Subjects: Art Education, Art History, Asian Art, Photography, Prints, Video
Collections: Modern Photography Collection (Edward Weston, Ansel Adams): original photographic prints, Kathe Kollwitz Collection: original prints

L **CITY OF LONG BEACH,** Long Beach Public Library, 101 Pacific Ave, Long Beach, CA 90822. Tel 562-570-7500; Fax 562-570-7408; Email lbpl_comments@lbpl.org; Web: www.lbpl.org; *Dir Libr Servs* Glenda Williams
Open Tues 12 - 8 PM, Wed 12 - 6 PM, Thurs 12 - 7 PM, Fri & Sat 10 AM - 5 PM; Estab 1897
Income: Financed by municipality
Library Holdings: Audio Tapes 20,000 (Books), Book Volumes, CD-ROMs, Clipping Files, Compact Disks, DVDs, Pamphlets, Periodical Subscriptions, Records, Video Tapes
Special Subjects: Asian Art, Display, Historical Material
Collections: Lorraine & Earl Burns Miller Special Collections Room housing fine arts books with an emphasis on Asian Art, the Bertrand Smith Sr coll & Marilyn Horne Archives
Exhibitions: (ongoing exhibs)

M **LONG BEACH MUSEUM OF ART FOUNDATION,** Long Beach Museum of Art, 2300 E Ocean Blvd, Long Beach, CA 90803-2442. Tel 562-439-2119; Fax 562-439-3587; Email ronn@lbma.com; Web: www.lbma.org; *Exec Dir* Ron Nelson; *Dir Educ & Visitor Svcs* Lisa Marsh; *Exhibs Preparator* Seija Rohkea
Open Thurs 11 AM - 8 PM, Fri - Sun 11 AM - 5 PM, cl New Year's, July 4, Thanksgiving & Christmas; Admis adults $7, seniors & students with ID $6, mems & children under 12 free, & free on Fri; Opened in 1951 as a Municipal Art Center under the city library department; in 1957 the Long Beach City Council changed the center to the Long Beach Museum of Art; managed by Foundation since 1985; Eight galleries & a screening room with changing exhibitions & selections from Permanent Collection; Average Annual Attendance: 100,000; Mem: 850; dues circle $1000 - $5000, educ benefactor $500, patron $150, family $75, individual $50, student, senior or educator $40
Income: Financed by annual contribution from the City of Long Beach, through grants from private foundations & through individual & corporate contributions
Special Subjects: Asian Art, Ceramics, Crafts, Decorative Arts, Drawings, Enamels, Etchings & Engravings, Graphics, Landscapes, Latin American Art, Painting-American, Painting-American, Photography, Porcelain, Prints, Prints, Sculpture, Sculpture, Silver, Textiles, Watercolors
Collections: Permanent Coll: 3,000+ paintings, sculpture, prints, drawings, works on paper, crafts, photography & decorative art objects, with 300 years of ceramics, early 20th century European art, California Modernism & contemporary art of California with emphasis on West Coast & California modern & contemporary art, sculpture garden, Milton Wichner Collection: incl Kandinsky, Jawlensky, Feininger, Moholy-Nagy, LBMA Video Archive at the Getty Research Institute
Exhibitions: 5 rotating exhibitions per yr
Publications: Announcements; exhibit catalogs; quarterly bulletin; Masterworks: Defining a New Narrative
Activities: Classes & workshops for adults, families & children; docent training; volunteer & membership progs; screening & lect series open to pub; concerts; gallery talks; tours; book traveling exhibs; loans to mus; mus shop sells books, jewelry, cards & other items

L **Long Beach Museum of Art**, 2300 E Ocean Blvd, Long Beach, CA 90803. Tel 562-439-2119; Fax 562-439-3587; Email haln@lbma.com; Web: www.lbma.org; *Dir* Harold Nelson
Open 11 AM - 5 PM Tues - Sun; Admis $5; Estab 1950 to enrich lives and promote understanding by bringing people together to celebrate the arts; Open for staff reference with restricted lending of books, publications & slides; Average Annual Attendance: 65,000; Mem: 200; dues $40
Library Holdings: Book Volumes 3200, Clipping Files, Exhibition Catalogs, Periodical Subscriptions 8, Video Tapes
Special Subjects: Art History, Drawings, Painting-American, Ceramics, Decorative Arts
Exhibitions: Annual Children's Cultural Festival, fall each yr
Publications: Quarterly newsletter

Activities: Classes for adults & children; docent training; artmaking workshops; lects open to pub; 1-3 vis lectrs per yr; concerts; gallery talks; tours; artmobile to other mus; 1-4 book traveling exhibs per yr; originate traveling exhibs to US & foreign mus; mus shop sells books, original art, reproductions, prints

M **MUSEUM OF LATIN AMERICAN ART,** 628 Alamitos Ave, Long Beach, CA 90802-1513. Tel 562-437-1689; Fax 562-216-4190; Email frontdesk@molaa.org; Web: www.molaa.org; *Cur* Edward Hayes Jr; *Development* Gina Adams; *Registrar* Susan Bolanos; *Director PR/Media* Susan Golden
Open Tues - Thurs, Sat & Sun 11 AM - 5 PM, Fri 11 AM - 9 PM; Admis $10, students & seniors $7, children under 12 free; Estab 1996 to research, collect & exhibit contemporary Latin American art; Maintains reference library; Average Annual Attendance: 60,000; Mem: 2200; dues $60 individual, $80 family
Income: Financed by endowment, mem & grants
Library Holdings: Auction Catalogs, Audio Tapes, Clipping Files, Exhibition Catalogs, Kodachrome Transparencies, Pamphlets, Periodical Subscriptions, Slides, Video Tapes
Special Subjects: Latin American Art, Mexican Art, Sculpture, Bronzes, Ceramics, Collages, Drawings, Etchings & Engravings, Glass, Graphics, Hispanic Art, Portraits, Prints, Watercolors, Woodcarvings, Woodcuts, Landscapes, Photography
Collections: Robert Gumbiner Foundation Collection, contemporary Latin American art-paintings & sculpture produced since 1945, Molka's Collection
Publications: History of Contemporary Latin American Art
Activities: Classes for adults & children; docent training; lects open to pub; concerts; family day of events, including lect, workshops, music, film; exhibs 6 per yr; originates traveling exhibs to museums in the USA; sales shop sells books, original art, prints, lithographs, contemporary fine art, folk art & jewelry

M **PACIFIC ISLAND ETHNIC ART MUSEUM,** 695 Alamitos Ave Long Beach, CA 90802-1514. Tel 562-216-4170; Fax 562-435-3052; Email info@pieam.org; Web: www.pieam.org; *Founder* Robert Gumbiner
Open Wed - Sun 11 AM - 5 PM, cl Mon - Tues, New Year's Day, Independence Day, Thanksgiving & Christmas; Admis general $5, seniors 62+ & students with ID $3, mem & children under 12 free; Estab 2010 to integrate Pacific Island cultures, focusing on Micronesia, into a living arts coll; Mem: dues $15-$1,000
Special Subjects: Textiles, Jewelry
Collections: 1,000 works of cultural art & artifacts including carving traditions, fiber, textile arts, body ornamentation & performing arts
Exhibitions: Rotating exhibits
Activities: Educ progs; tours

LOS ALTOS

M **GALLERY 9,** 143 Main St, Los Altos, CA 94022-2912. Tel 415-941-7969; Web: www.gallery9losaltos.com; *Treas* Charles W Halleck; *Exhibits Chmn* Carol Hake; *Staff* Jean Pell Morton; *Publicity* Louise Freund
Open Tues - Sat 11:30 AM - 5:30 PM; No admis fee; Estab 1970 to exhibit local fine art; Average Annual Attendance: 1,200; Mem: 30; dues $520; meetings first Mon each month
Exhibitions: Exhibit changes each month. Member artists featured once every two years
Activities: Sales shop sells original art

LOS ANGELES

M **AUTRY NATIONAL CENTER,** Museum of the American West, Griffith Park, 4700 Western Heritage Way, Los Angeles, CA 90027-1462. Tel 323-667-2000; Fax 323-660-5721; Email vservices@theautry.org; Web: theautry.org; *Pres & CEO* W. Richard West Jr.
Open Tues - Fri 10 AM - 4 PM, Sat - Sun 10 AM - 5 PM, cl Mon; Summer Hrs: Jul - Aug Thurs & 1st Thurs in Sep mus & store 10 AM - 8 PM, cl Mon; cl Jul 4, Labor Day, Thanksgiving, Christmas Day; Admis adults $14, seniors & students w/ID $10, children 3-12 $6, mems & children under 3 free, active military, vets, peace officers & park rangers free, 2nd Tues of month free; discounts available; Estab 1988, merged 2003 with Southwest Museum of the American Indian & Women of the West Museum to form Autry National Ctr; Maintains Autry Library
Special Subjects: American Indian Art, American Western Art
Collections: Women of the West
Activities: Classes for children & adults; family activities; docent training; lects open to pub & for mems only; tours; theater performances; concerts; festivals; book signings & discussions; mus shop

L **Braun Research Library**, 234 Museum Dr, Los Angeles, CA 90065-5000. Tel 323-221-2164; Fax 323-224-8223; Email rroom@theautry.org; Web: theautry.org/research/braun-research-library; *Head Librn & Archivist* Anna Liza Pasas
Open by appointment; Estab 1907; For reference only; Average Annual Attendance: 175,000; Mem: Dues individual $55, dual $65, family $75, family plus grandparents $125, Turquoise $175
Library Holdings: Auction Catalogs, Audio Tapes, Book Volumes 50,000, CD-ROMs, Cards, Cassettes, Clipping Files, Compact Disks, Exhibition Catalogs, Fiche, Filmstrips, Framed Reproductions, Kodachrome Transparencies, Lantern Slides, Manuscripts, Maps, Memorabilia, Motion Pictures, Original Art Works, Original Documents, Pamphlets, Periodical Subscriptions 300, Photographs, Prints, Records, Reels, Reproductions, Slides, Video Tapes
Special Subjects: American Indian Art, American Western Art, Anthropology, Archaeology, Architecture, Bookplates & Bindings, Eskimo Art, Ethnology, Historical Material, Latin American Art, Manuscripts, Maps, Mexican Art, Photography, Pre-Columbian Art, Religious Art, Watercolors
Collections: George Wharton James's Collection, Joseph Amasa Munk Papers, Charles F Lummis Manuscript Collection, Frederick Webb Hodge Papers, Gene Autry Papers, Meihle Sepulveda Family Papers
Activities: Lects open to pub; 4 vis lectrs per yr; tours; mus shop

M **Southwest Museum of the American Indian, Mt. Washington Campus**, 234 Museum Dr, Los Angeles, CA 90065-5000. Tel 323-221-2164; Fax 323-224-8223; Web: www.theautry.org; *Ahmanson Cur of Native American History & Culture* Kim Walters; *Asst Cur* Paige Bardolph
Open Sat 10 AM - 4 PM; Estab 1907, opened 1914; Museum & Braun Research Library; Mem: Individual $55, dual $75, family $125, family plus $175, turquoise $250, copper (shell) 500, silver $1,250, gold $2,500
Special Subjects: Afro-American Art, Anthropology, Archaeology, Eskimo Art, Ethnology, Folk Art, Hispanic Art, History of Art & Archaeology, Latin American Art, Manuscripts, Maps, Military Art, Mixed Media, Painting-American, Photography, Pottery, Pre-Columbian Art, Scrimshaw, Southwestern Art
Collections: Native American, Spanish Colonial

L **Autry Library**, Griffith Park, Los Angeles, CA 90027; 4700 Western Heritage Way, Los Angeles, CA 90027-1462. Tel 323-667-2000x349; Email rroom@theautry.org; Web: theautry.org
Open Mon - Fri 9 AM - 5 PM by appt only, cl holidays; Opened 1995
Library Holdings: Audio Tapes, Book Volumes, Other Holdings
Special Subjects: American Western Art, Historical Material
Collections: Fred Rosenstock Coll of Western Americana: 21,000+ works on paper incl books, manuscripts, diaries, visual material, Dime Novel Coll: dating from 1880's - 1960's, Saddle & Western Wear Trade Catalogs Coll: dating from 1880's - 1960's, Gene Autry Archive: coll documenting the career & business interests of the Western star, media phenomenon, & Mus founder, Western TV Script & Photographic Stills Coll: 1,200+ scripts with annotations by producers, editors, cinematographers & actors, & Stills documenting Western TV series from 1949 - 1990's, Dude Ranch Brochures: dating from 1920's - 1960's, Collections Online digital database

M **THE BROAD,** 221 S Grand Ave, Los Angeles, CA 90012. Tel 213-232-6200; Email info@thebroad.org; Web: www.thebroad.org; *Dir & Chief Cur* Joanne Heyler; *Dir Mus Opers* Jeannine Guido
Open Tues & Wed 11 AM - 5 PM, Thurs & Fri 11 AM - 8 PM, Sat 10 AM - 8 PM, Sun 10 AM - 6 PM, cl Mon, Thanksgiving Day & Christmas Day; No admis fee; 120,000 sq ft contemporary art museum located in downtown Los Angeles
Collections: 2,000 piece Broad Collection of postwar & contemporary art

M **CALIFORNIA AFRICAN-AMERICAN MUSEUM,** 600 State Dr, Exposition Park Los Angeles, CA 90037-1267. Tel 213-744-7432; Fax 213-744-2050; Web: www.caamuseum.org; *Exec Dir* George O. Davis; *Deputy Dir & Chief Cur* Naima J. Keith; *Cur History* Tiffini Bowers; *Cur Visual Arts & Prog Mgr* Mar Hollingsworth; *Cur Visual Arts & Prog Mgr.* Vida L. Brown; *Cur Educ* Sonia Brown; *Registrar Colls* Susan Guadamuz; *Exhib Supv* Edward Garcia; *Fiscal Officer* Roberta Saligumba
Open Tues - Sat 10 AM - 5 PM, Sun 11 AM - 5 PM, cl Mon, New Year's Day, Thanksgiving, Christmas Day; No admis fee; parking fees apply; Estab 1977, opened 1981 to examine, collect, preserve & display art, history & culture of Blacks in The Americas with concentration on Blacks in California; renovated 2001 - 2003; 44,000 sq ft facility incl 3 full size exhib galleries, a theater gallery, a 14,000 sq ft Sculpture Court, exhib design & storage areas, research library, conference center/ special events rm & admin offices; Mem: Dues student $25, individual $40, family $75, friend $100, patron $250, supporting $500, benefactor $1000
Library Holdings: Book Volumes, CD-ROMs, Cassettes, Clipping Files, Compact Disks, DVDs, Exhibition Catalogs
Special Subjects: African Art, Afro-American Art
Collections: Academic & Naturalistic Landscape of the 19th c, Modern & Contemporary Art, Contemporary Art from the African Diaspora, Traditional African Art, History Collection
Exhibitions: African American Journey West: Permanent Collection
Publications: Calendar of Events, every 2 months; exhibition catalogs
Activities: Classes for children; weekends at the museum; docent training; lect open to pub; gallery talks; films; symposia

L **Research Library**, 600 State Dr, Los Angeles, CA 90037-1267. Tel 213-744-7432; Fax 213-744-2050; Email dmciver@caamuseum.org; Web: www.caamuseum.org; *Librn* Denise L McIver; *Exec Dir* George O Davis
Open during mus hrs & by appt; No admis fee; donations accepted for photocopying; For reference & research only
Library Holdings: Auction Catalogs, Audio Tapes, Book Volumes 4,000, CD-ROMs, Cassettes, DVDs, Exhibition Catalogs, Micro Print, Periodical Subscriptions 100, Records, Video Tapes
Special Subjects: Afro-American Art, Architecture, Art History, Decorative Arts, Drawings, Ethnology, Folk Art, Furniture, Painting-American, Sculpture, Historical Material, Islamic Art
Collections: Literature & Popular Writings by authors incl: Zora Neale Hurston, Maya Angelou, Langston Hughes, Text book of the Madame CJ Walker School of Beauty Culture, 1855 Ed of My Bondage & My Freedom by Frederick Douglas, Multi-vol Encyclopedia of African-American Culture & History, Access to 3 major daily newspapers, Older issues of selected African-American newspapers incl Chicago Defender & Pittsburgh Courier, Museum in Black Collection, Bernard C Parks, Sr Collection, Mary Jane Hewitt Collection
Publications: Museum Notes, quarterly
Activities: Docent training; lects open to pub; gallery talks; tours

M **CALIFORNIA SCIENCE CENTER,** 700 Exposition Park Dr, Los Angeles, CA 90037-1210. Tel 323-724-3623; Fax 213-744-2034; Email 4info@cscmail.org; Web: www.casciencectr.org; *Cur World Ecology* Chuck Kopczak; *Deputy Dir Educ* Ron Rohovit; *Technology Cur* David Bibas; *Deputy Dir Exhib* Diane Perlov; *Sr VPres Develop & Mktg* William Harris; *Aerospace Cur* Kenneth E Phillips; *CFO* Cynthia Pygin; *Deputy Dir Opers* Tony Budrovich; *VPres Retail Opers* Kent Jones; *Deputy Dir Admin* Cheryl Tateishi
Open daily 10 AM - 5 PM, cl New Year's Day, Thanksgiving, Christmas Day; No admis fees to permanent galleries; A dynamic destination where families, school groups, adults & children can explore the wonders of science though interactive exhibits, live demonstrations & innovative programs; Three permanent exhibit galleries - Creative World (showcases the wonders & consequences of human innovation); World of Life (probes the commonalities of the living world); Air & Space (features hands-on exhibits coupled with real air & space craft). Also, a Special Exhibits Gallery hosts 3-4 exhibits a yr; Average Annual Attendance: 1,800,000; Mem: 6,850, $65-$550 per yr
Income: Financed by state appropriation and California Science Center Foundation

Exhibitions: Various exhib
Publications: Notices of temporary exhibits, maps, pamphlets
Activities: Formal science-art educ progs for school groups & public, teacher training; lects open to pub, 3 vis lectrs per yr, competitions; scholarships offered; originates traveling exhibs; mus shop sells books, science toys & videos

M **CALIFORNIA STATE UNIVERSITY, LOS ANGELES,** Fine Arts Gallery, 5151 State University Dr, Los Angeles, CA 90032-4226. Tel 323-343-4023; Fax 323-343-4045; *Dir* Dr. Mika Cho
Open Mon - Thurs Noon - 5 PM; No admis fee; Estab 1954 as a forum for advanced works of art & their makers, so that educ through exposure to works of art can take place; Gallery has 3500 sq ft, clean white walls, 11 ft high ceilings with an entry & catalog desk; Average Annual Attendance: 30,000
Income: Financed by endowment & state appropriation
Exhibitions: Various exhib
Publications: Exhibition catalogs, three per year
Activities: Educ dept; lect open to public, 10-20 vis lectrs per year; gallery talks; exten dept

M **Luckman Gallery**, 5151 State University Dr, Los Angeles, CA 90032-8116. Tel 323-343-6604; Fax 323-346-6423; Email info@luckmanarts.org; Web: www.luckmanarts.org; *Exec Dir* Wendy Baker
Open Mon-Thurs & Sat 12PM-5PM
Collections: works by contemporary artists from around the world

M **CITY OF LOS ANGELES,** Cultural Affairs Dept, 201 N Figueroa St, Ste 1400 Los Angeles, CA 90012-2637. Tel 213-202-5500; Fax 213-202-5517; Web: www.culturela.org; *Gen Mgr* Danielle Brazell; *Asst Gen Mgr* Daniel Tarica; *Dir Mktg & Devel* Will Caperton y Montoya; *Pub Art Dir* Felicia Filer; *Grants Administration Div Dir* Joe Smoke
Activities: Classes for adults & children; grants prog; folk arts prog

M **CRAFT AND FOLK ART MUSEUM (CAFAM),** 5814 Wilshire Blvd, Los Angeles, CA 90036-4501. Tel 323-937-4230; Fax 323-937-5576; Email info@cafam.org; Web: www.cafam.org; *Exec Dir* Suzanne Isken; *Cur Exhib* Holly Jerger; *Cur Public Engagement* Andres Payan; *Mgr Exhibitions & Communications* Sasha Ali; *Mgr Devel* Sonia Mak-Shahbazi
Open Tues - Wed & Fri 11 AM - 5 PM; Thurs 11 AM - 7 PM; Sat - Sun Noon - 6 PM; Admis adults $7, seniors & students $5, children under 10 free; Founded in 1973 by the late Edith Wyle; champions cultural understanding by encouraging curiosity about our diverse world. Nonprofit org; Mus exhibs contemporary craft, international folk art and art highlighting diverse cultures and pub progs for all visitors; Mem: Donor $2500; Dir Circle $1000; Patron $500; Contributor $250; Assoc & Believer $100; Family $60; Individual $45; Senior/Student $35
Special Subjects: African Art, Afro-American Art, American Indian Art, Anthropology, Art Education, Asian Art, Carpets & Rugs, Ceramics, Coins & Medals, Collages, Costumes, Crafts, Decorative Arts, Dioramas, Drawings, Embroidery, Etchings & Engravings, Ethnology, Folk Art, Furniture, Glass, Graphics, Hispanic Art, Islamic Art, Jewelry, Judaica, Latin American Art, Leather, Manuscripts, Metalwork, Mexican Art, Mosaics, Oriental Art, Porcelain, Posters, Pottery, Primitive art, Prints, Sculpture, Silver, Southwestern Art, Tapestries, Textiles, Woodcarvings, Woodcuts
Activities: School tours; internships; family art workshops; theatrical performances; craft workshops, progs & special events, classes for adults & children; lects open to pub; concerts, gallery talks & tours; books, original art, crafts, clothing, housewares & mus related items for sale

M **CULTURAL AFFAIRS DEPARTMENT,** Los Angeles Municipal Art Gallery, 4800 Hollywood Blvd, Los Angeles, CA 90027-5302. Tel 323-644-6269; Fax 323-644-6271; Email lamag@lacity.org; Web: www.culturala.org/lamag/home.html; *Dir* Isabelle Lutterodt; *Cur* Steven Wong; *Mus Educator* Marta Feinstein
Open Thurs - Sun Noon - 5 PM; No admis fee; Estab 1952 to promote, interpret & present the art of emerging, mid career & established artists of Southern CA; 10,000 sq ft exhib space; Average Annual Attendance: 15000
Income: City of Los Angeles
Library Holdings: Exhibition Catalogs, Kodachrome Transparencies, Pamphlets, Slides, Video Tapes
Publications: Annual COLA Fel Catalog
Activities: Gallery talks; COLA Award, Lorser Fietelson & Helon Lundebero Feitelson Fel; currently engaged in outreach through exhibs & events at other sites

A **CULTURAL AFFAIRS DEPARTMENT CITY OF LOS ANGELES,** Barnsdall Art Center & Junior Arts Center, 4800 Hollywood Blvd, Los Angeles, CA 90027. Tel 213-485-4474; Email info@barnsdall.org; Web: www.barnsdall.org; *Dir* Isti Haroh Glasgow; *Teacher Outreach Coordr* Laura Stickney; *Coordr Handicapped Svcs* Dr Mary J Martz; *Sunday Coordr* Nicolette Kominos; *International Child Art Coordr* Patty Sue Jones
Open Tues - Sun 10 AM - 5 PM; No admis fee; Estab 1967 to stimulate & assist in the develop of art skills & creativity; The gallery offers exhibitions of interest to children & young people & those who work with the young; Average Annual Attendance: 80,000; Mem: 400; dues vary ; annual meeting June 1
Income: Financed by city appropriation & Friends of the Junior Arts Center
Collections: Two-dimensional works on paper, 8mm film by former students
Exhibitions: 12 exhibitions a year
Publications: Schedules of art classes, quarterly; exhibition notices
Activities: Art classes for young people in painting, dramatic progs drawing, etching, general printmaking, photography, filmmaking, photo silkscreen, ceramics, film animation; workshops for teachers; lectrs, 2-4 vis lectrs per yr; films; musical instrument making, design, video festivals for students & the general pub; gallery talks; tours; schols offered

L **Library**, 4814 Hollywood Blvd, Los Angeles, CA 90027. Tel 323-644-6275; 644-6295; Fax 323-644-6277; Email jacbac@schglobal.net; Web: www.juniorartscenter.org, www.barnsdallartcenter.org; *Dir BAC Educ* Livija Lapaite; *Office Mgr* Nancy Jung
Open Mon - Sat 10 AM - 5 PM; No admis fee; Estab as reference library; Circ Non-circulating; Open to public
Library Holdings: Book Volumes 700, Slides 15,000
Special Subjects: Art Education, Art History, Crafts
Activities: Classes for adults & children

A **EL PUEBLO DE LOS ANGELES HISTORICAL MONUMENT,** 125 Paseo de la Plaza, Ste 400 Los Angeles, CA 90012-2959. Tel 213-485-8437; Fax 213-485-0428; Email elpueblovc@lacity.org; Web: elpueblo.lacity.org; *Gen Mgr* Christopher Espinosa; *Asst Gen Mgr* Lisa Sarno
Open daily 9 AM - 4 PM; No admis fee; Estab 1781 as a living memorial to the history & traditions of Los Angeles life, preserving for the public forever the architecture & characteristics of the history & the diverse peoples associated with the City's founding & evolution; Collection of five museums ea telling & interpreting the story of Los Angeles through time; Average Annual Attendance: 500,000
Special Subjects: Asian Art, Ceramics, Crafts, Folk Art, Hispanic Art, Historical Material, Latin American Art, Leather, Maps, Mexican Art, Oriental Art, Period Rooms, Photography
Collections: El Pueblo Movement Collection, El Pueblo Photo Archive
Activities: Docent training; dramatic progs; lects open to pub; five vis lectrs per yr; gallery talks; tours; concerts; mus shop sells books

A **FELLOWS OF CONTEMPORARY ART,** 970 N Broadway Ste 208, Los Angeles, CA 90012. Tel 213-808-1008; Fax 213-808-1018; Email foca@focala.org; Web: www.focala.org; *Exec Dir* Tom McKenzie; *Chair* Donna Gottlieb
Open Mon. - Fri 10-5; Estab 1975 to support contemporary California art by initiating & sponsoring exhibitions & videos at selected institutions; Mem: 150; nomination process for membership
Income: Financed by mem dues
Exhibitions: At least one major exhibition per year
Publications: Exhib catalogs
Activities: One day educ progs; guest speakers; domestic & international tours

A **FREDERICK R WEISMAN ART FOUNDATION,** 275 N Carolwood Dr, Los Angeles, CA 90077-3535. Tel 310-277-5321; Fax 310-277-5075; Email tours@weismanfoundation.org; Web: www.weismanfoundation.org; *Dir* Billie Milam Weisman; *Registrar* Mary Ellen Powell
Open Mon - Fri 10:30 AM - 2 PM by appointment only; No admis fee; Estab 1982 as a nonprofit foundation focusing on exhibition & tours; Circ Catalogue Available; House setting; 2 floors, 1 gallery; Average Annual Attendance: 10,000
Income: Financed by endowment
Library Holdings: Auction Catalogs, Exhibition Catalogs, Kodachrome Transparencies, Original Art Works, Original Documents, Periodical Subscriptions, Photographs, Sculpture, Slides
Special Subjects: Architecture, Painting-American, Painting-European, Painting-Japanese, Sculpture, Ceramics, Etchings & Engravings, Painting-Dutch, Painting-German, Painting-Russian, Photography, Prints
Collections: Contemporary Art: Installation Work, Mixed Media, Painting, Sculpture, Works on Paper
Exhibitions: Frederick R. Weisman permanent collection
Publications: Workshop publication, semi-annual
Activities: Docent training; art purchase; tours; lend original art objects to Major US & European Museums; traveling shows available on request; organize traveling exhibs by request; mus shop sells books

A **GALLERY 825/LOS ANGELES ART ASSOCIATION,** Gallery 825, 825 N LaCienega Blvd, Los Angeles, CA 90069-4707. Tel 310-652-8272; Fax 310-652-9251; Email gallery825@laaa.org; Web: www.laaa.org; *Exec Dir* Peter Mays
Open Tues - Sat 10 AM - 5 PM; No admis fee; Estab 1925; Gallery 825/LAAA is a 501(c)(3) nonprofit arts organization supporting southern California artists with an emphasis on emerging talent; Average Annual Attendance: 5,000; Mem: 230; dues $150; annual meeting in Apr; must reside in southern California to exhibit
Exhibitions: Graphics, Painting & Sculpture by Southern California Artists, monthly
Publications: Announcements of exhibitions & lectures, monthly; newsletter, quarterly
Activities: Classes for adults; lects open to pub; gallery talks

L **THE GETTY CENTER,** Trust Museum, 1200 Getty Center Dr, Los Angeles, CA 90049-1657. Tel 310-440-7300; Fax 310-440-7751; Email gettymuseum@getty.edu; Web: www.getty.edu; Telex 82-0268; *Dir.* Timothy Potts
Open Mon - Fri 10 AM - 5:30 PM, Sat 10 AM - 9 PM; No admis fee, parking reservations required, call 310-440-7300; Estab 1983 for the purpose of advancing research in art history & related disciplines; The mus building is a re-creation of an ancient Roman villa & consists of 47 galleries; Average Annual Attendance: 400,000
Income: Financed by Foundation
Library Holdings: Book Volumes 800,000, Exhibition Catalogs, Fiche, Pamphlets, Periodical Subscriptions 1500, Reels
Collections: Art historical archives, photo archives
Publications: Calendar, monthly; Museum Journal, annually
Activities: Docent training; slide show for children; classroom materials; research scholar prog by invitation only, 20 vis scholars per yr; original objects of art lent to other mus for special exhibs; mus shop sells books, reproductions, slides & mus publs

M **The J Paul Getty Museum**, 1200 Getty Center Dr, Suite 1000 Los Angeles, CA 90049-1687. Tel 310-440-7300; Fax 310-440-7751; Email visitorservices@getty.edu; Web: www.getty.edu; *Dir* Timothy Potts; *Assoc Dir Colls* Richard Rand; *Head Admin* Robin Weissberger; *Asst Dir Pub Affairs* John Giurini; *Assoc Dir Exhibs* Carolyn Marsden-Smith; *Asst Dir Educ, Pub Progs & Interpretive Media* Lisa Clements
Open Tues - Fri & Sun 10 AM - 5:30 PM, Sat 10 AM - 9 PM, cl Mon, New Year's Day, July 4th, Thanksgiving, Christmas Day; No admis fee; parking $15 per car, $10 after 3 PM, no parking reservations required, call 310-440-7300; Estab 1974; international cultural & philanthropic organization serving both general audiences & specialized professionals. Seeks to further knowledge of visual arts & nurture critical seeing by collecting, preserving, exhibiting & interpreting works of art; The museum is designed around an open central courtyard surrounded by 5 2-story pavilions; Average Annual Attendance: 1,600,000

Income: Financed by J Paul Getty Trust
Library Holdings: Auction Catalogs, Book Volumes 500,000, Exhibition Catalogs, Fiche, Original Art Works, Pamphlets, Periodical Subscriptions 1500, Photographs, Reels, Slides
Collections: Greek & Roman antiquities, French decorative arts, Western European paintings, drawings, sculpture, illuminated manuscripts, decorative arts, 19th & 20th century photographs, European & American
Publications: Calendar, quarterly; Museum Journal, annually; Trust Report, annual
Activities: Classes for adults & children; docent/volunteer training; school progs; professional develop prog; community collaboration workshops; dramatic progs; lects open to pub; seminars; concerts; gallery talks; performances; architecture & garden tours; orientation film; storytelling; artist demonstrations; gallery games; schols & fels offered; mus shop sells books, reproductions, prints, slides, postcards, gift cards, calendars, mugs, clothing, educational toys, stationery

M **The J Paul Getty Museum - Getty Villa**, Malibu, CA; 1200 Getty Center Dr Ste 1000, Los Angeles, CA 90049-1687. Tel 310-440-7300; Email visitorservices@getty.edu; Web: www.getty.edu; *Dir* Dr Timothy Potts
Open Thurs - Mon 10 AM - 5 PM, cl Tues & select Wed; No admis fee, advance timed ticket required per adult, gen admis ticket allows 1 adult & 3 children ages 15 & under in 1 car; parking $15 per car or motorcycle, free after 5 PM; Estab 2006 as second location for J Paul Getty Mus; museum & cultural center dedicated to study the arts & cultures of ancient Greece, Rome & Etruria; Opened following completion of renovation project; Average Annual Attendance: 1,600,000
Income: Financed by J Paul Getty Trust
Collections: Houses 44,000 works of art from J Paul Getty Museum's coll on Greek, Roman & Etruscan antiquities, over 1,200 items on view

C **GOLDEN STATE MUTUAL LIFE INSURANCE COMPANY,** Afro-American Art Collection, 1999 W Adams Blvd, Los Angeles, CA 90018-3595; PO Box 26894, San Francisco, CA 94126-6894. Tel 323-731-1131 exten 237; Fax 323-733-0320; Email info@gsmlife.com; Web: www.gsmlife.com; *Mktg & Pub Rels Mgr* Becky Ganther
Open to pub by appointment through pub relations staff asst; Estab 1965 to provide a show place for Afro-American Art; to assist in the develop of ethnic pride among the youth of our community; Collection displayed throughout building; Average Annual Attendance: 400
Income: Financed by the Company
Collections: Drawings, lithographs, paintings and sculpture
Publications: Afro-American Art Collection Brochure; Historical Murals Brochure
Activities: Tours by appointment

M **HEBREW UNION COLLEGE,** Skirball Cultural Center, 2701 N Sepulveda Blvd, Los Angeles, CA 90049-6833. Tel 310-440-4500; Fax 310-440-4728; Email info@skirball.org; Web: www.skirball.org; *Sr Cur* Erin Clancey; *Dir Music & Educ* Sheri Bernstein; *Prog Dir* Andrew Horwitz; *Learning for Life* Adele Lander Burke; *Chief of Staff* Kathryn Girard
Open Tues-Fri noon-5PM, Sat-Sun 10AM-5PM; Admis general $12, students & seniors $9, children 2-12 $7, children 2 & under free; Estab 1972 to interpret American Jewish experience & nurture American Jewish identity & encourage cultural pluralism; 4000 years of Jewish historical experience and American democratic values; Average Annual Attendance: 250,000; Mem: 6500; dues $65-$1500
Income: Financed by mem admis, private & pub grants, programs & fees
Library Holdings: Book Volumes
Special Subjects: Archaeology, Architecture, Coins & Medals, Collages, Costumes, Crafts, Decorative Arts, Dolls, Drawings, Embroidery, Etchings & Engravings, Ethnology, Folk Art, Furniture, Glass, Graphics, Historical Material, Jewelry, Judaica, Juvenile Art, Laces, Landscapes, Manuscripts, Medieval Art, Metalwork, Oriental Art, Prints, Sculpture
Collections: American Jewish Ethnographic Collection: 5000+ items, 2000 archaeological objects from the Near East, primarily Israeli, Biblical Archaeology, 6000 ceremonial objects, primarily Western European, but some exotic Oriental & Indian pieces as well, Chinese Torah & India Torah cases, Judaica collection, 4000 prints & drawings from Western Europe, spanning 4-5 centuries
Exhibitions: Vision & Values; Jewish Life from Antiquity to America; Changing exhibitions: Noah's Ark Galleries
Publications: Exhibition brochures & catalogs
Activities: Classes for adults & children; dramatic progs; docent training; film series; lects open to pub, 5 vis lectrs per yr; concerts; gallery talks; tours; book traveling exhibs 5-8 per yr; originate traveling exhibs; mus shop sells books, original art, reproductions, prints, jewelry & children's items

M **INSTITUTE OF CONTEMPORARY ART, LOS ANGELES,** (Santa Monica Museum of Art), 1717 E 7th St, Los Angeles, CA 90021. Tel 310-284-8100; Email info@theicala.org; Web: www.theicala.org; *Exec Dir* Elsa Longhauser; *Dir Educ* Asuka Hisa
Wed - Fri 11 - 7, Sat - Sun 11 - 6, cl Mon, Tues & holidays; No admis fee; Admis by suggested donation, general $5, artists, students & seniors $3; Estab 1984, programming began 1988; Organizes exhibs of contemporary art in all mediums and across disciplines; Average Annual Attendance: 35,000; Mem: starts at $55 per yr
Special Subjects: African Art, Afro-American Art, Architecture, Asian Art, Ceramics, Drawings, Painting-American, Painting-Australian, Painting-Canadian, Painting-Dutch, Painting-Flemish, Painting-French, Painting-German, Painting-Israeli, Painting-Italian, Painting-Japanese, Painting-New Zealand, Painting-Polish, Painting-Russian, Painting-Scandinavian, Painting-Spanish, Photography, Portraits, Pottery, Prints, Sculpture, Watercolors
Activities: Educ prog; classes for adults & children; outreach progs; workshops; lects open to pub; gallery talks; tours; concerts; mus shop sells books, reproductions, prints, and various merchandise

M **JAPANESE AMERICAN CULTURAL & COMMUNITY CENTER,** George J Doizaki Gallery, 244 S San Pedro St, Ste 505, Los Angeles, CA 90012-3895. Tel 213-628-2725; Fax 213-617-8576; Email info@jaccc.org; Web: www.jaccc.org; *Dir.* Michelle Moreno
Open Tues - Fri 10 AM - 5 PM, Sat - Sun 10 AM - 4 PM; Admis $3; Estab 1980; 6,000 sq ft; Average Annual Attendance: 30,000; Mem: 1500; dues $35 and up
Income: Financed through mem, grants & donations
Exhibitions: Exhibitions rotate every six weeks

M **JAPANESE AMERICAN NATIONAL MUSEUM,** 100 N Central Ave, Los Angeles, CA 90012. Tel 213-625-0414; Fax 213-625-1770; Email hnrc@janm.org; Web: www.janm.org; *VPres External* Carol Komatsuka; *Dir Develop* Cheryl Ikemiya; *VPres* Nahan Gluck; *Dir Retail & Visitors* Maria Kwong; *Treas* Thomas Decker; *VChmn* George Takei; *Dir Support Svcs* Clement Hanami; *Dir National Program* Cayleen Nakamura; *Mgr Human Resources* Myrna Mariona
Open Tues, Wed & Fri - Sun 11 AM - 5 PM, Thurs Noon - 8 PM, cl Mon, Jul 4, Thanksgiving, Christmas & New Year's Days; Office open Tues - Fri 9 AM - 5 PM; Admis adults $12, seniors, students w/ID & youth (6-17) $6, mems and children 5 & under free, every Thurs 5 - 8 PM & every 3rd Thurs of month free; group discounts available; Estab 1992 to share the Japanese American experience; Contains several galleries in new pavilion & 2 spaces in historic building; Average Annual Attendance: 160,000; Mem: dues $15 - $100
Collections: Collection of art work made in America's concentration camps during WWII by Japanese Americans, Henry Sugimoto
Publications: Japanese American National Museum Magazine
Activities: Classes for adults & children; dramatic progs; docent training; performances; lects open to pub; concerts; gallery talks; tours; individual paintings & original objects of art lent to other mus; book traveling exhibs 1-5 per yr; originate traveling exhibs to Smithsonian Museum, Bishop Museum, Ellis Island Museum; mus shop sells books, magazines, reproductions, clothing, videos & prints

M **KOHN GALLERY,** 1227 N Highland Ave, Los Angeles, CA 90038. Tel 323-461-3311; Email info@kohngallery.com; Web: www.kohngallery.com; *Dir & Ptnr* Samantha Glaser-Weiss
Open Tues - Fri 10 AM - 6 PM, Sat 11 AM - 6 PM; Estab 1985
Collections: works by artists from California, New York & Europe; paintings; sculpture

M **LA COUNTY MUSEUM OF ART,** 5814 Wilshire Blvd, Los Angeles, CA 90036-4501. Tel 323-857-6010; *Librn* Joan Beneditti; *Dir* Joan Bruin
Open Mon., Tues & Thurs 11 AM - 5 PM, Fri 11 AM - 8 PM, Sat - Sun 10 AM - 7 PM, cl Wed, Thanksgiving, Christmas Day; Admis adults $15, students & seniors $10, children 17 & under and members free; Estab 1973 as The Egg & The Eye Gallery
Special Subjects: Asian Art, Costumes, Crafts, Dolls, Embroidery, Ethnology, Folk Art, Furniture, Glass, Hispanic Art, Latin American Art, Mexican Art, Pottery, Southwestern Art, Textiles
Collections: Contemporary American Crafts, Contemporary Design, International Folk Art including Japanese, East Indian & Mexican works, masks of the worlds, Industrial Design, International Folk Art
Exhibitions: Annual International Festival of Masks; Intimate Appeal: The Figurative Art of Beatrice Wood; Ed Rossbach: 40 Years of Exploration & Innovation in Fiber Art
Publications: Quarterly calendar
Activities: Classes for adults & children; docent training; lects open to pub, 5 vis lectrs per yr; gallery talks; tours; community outreach programs; book traveling exhibs 1-2 per yr; originate traveling exhibs; mus shop sells books, magazines, original art, reproductions, prints, jewelry, folk art, ceramics, glass

L **Edith R Wyle Research Library of The Craft & Folk Art Museum**, 5905 Wilshire Blvd, Los Angeles, CA 90036-4597. Tel 323-857-6118; Fax 323-857-6216; Email benedetti@lacma.org; Web: www.lacma.org; *Librn* Joan M Benedetti
Open by appointment only; Estab 1975 to support & supplement the documentation & information activities of the Craft & Folk Art Museum in regard to contemporary crafts, international folk art, design. Visual material collected equally with print; For reference only
Income: Financed by the museum
Library Holdings: Book Volumes 5000, Clipping Files, Exhibition Catalogs, Kodachrome Transparencies, Memorabilia, Other Holdings Posters, Pamphlets, Periodical Subscriptions 18, Photographs, Slides
Special Subjects: Aesthetics, Ceramics, Costume Design & Constr, Decorative Arts, Ethnology, Folk Art, Glass, Historical Material, Industrial Design, Metalwork, Mixed Media
Collections: Artists' files - self taught and contemporary crafts artists, 12 V F Drawers of Ephemera

M **LACE (LOS ANGELES CONTEMPORARY EXHIBITIONS),** 6522 Hollywood Blvd, Los Angeles, CA 90028-6210. Tel 323-957-1777; Fax 323-957-9025; Email info@welcometolace.org; Web: www.welcometolace.org; *Exec Dir* Sarah Russin; *Asst Dir* Fiona Ball; *Operations Manager* Andrew Friere; *Cur* Daniela Lieja Quintanar
Open (gallery) Wed - Sun noon - 6 PM; (office) Mon - Fri 10:30 AM - 6:30 PM; No admis fee; Estab 1978, interdisciplinary contemporary visual arts ctr; Circ 50,000; 3,500 sq ft; Average Annual Attendance: 30,000; Mem: 500; dues $50+
Income: Financed by private & public contributions; earned income initiatives
Library Holdings: Auction Catalogs 28, Audio Tapes 100, Book Volumes 100, CD-ROMs 50, Cards 300, Clipping Files, DVDs 100, Exhibition Catalogs 200, Framed Reproductions 2, Original Art Works 30, Original Documents 100, Pamphlets 100, Photographs 40, Prints 25, Sculpture 20, Slides, Video Tapes
Special Subjects: Architecture, Art Education, Art History, Calligraphy, Conceptual Art, Drawings, Historical Material, Illustration, Mixed Media
Collections: Contemporary Art
Publications: Exhibit catalogs
Activities: Classes for adults & children; dramatic progs; docent training; panel discussions; film screenings; performances; lects open to public & for mem only; 40 vis lectrs per year; concerts; gallery talks; tours; educational programs; workshops for various target audiences; originates traveling exhibs; mus shop sells books, magazines, original art, prints & limited edition artworks

M **LOS ANGELES COUNTY MUSEUM OF ART,** 5905 Wilshire Blvd, Los Angeles, CA 90036-4598. Tel 323-857-6000; Fax 323-857-6214; Email publicinfo@lacma.org; Web: www.lacma.org; *CEO & Wallis Annenberg Dir* Michael Govan; *Co-Chair* Elaine P Wynn; *Co-Chair* Tony P Ressler; *VP Educ &*

Pub Progs Jane Burrell; *VP & Gen Counsel* Fred Goldstein; *VP Devel* Sr VPres Educ & Public Progs Morello; *CFO* Ann Rowland; *Sr Deputy Dir Art Admin & Colls* Nancy Thomas
Open Mon - Tues & Thurs 11 AM - 5 PM, Fri 11 AM - 8 PM, Sat - Sun 10 AM - 7 PM, cl Wed, Thanksgiving & Christmas; People residing outside L.A. County Admis adults $25, seniors (65+) & students with ID $21 mus members, children 17 & under free; People residing in L.A. County Admis adults $20, seniors (65+) & students with ID $16 mus members, children 17 & under free, After 3pm Mon-Fri free; Estab 1910 as Division of History, Science & Art; estab separately in 1961, for the purpose of acquiring, researching, publishing, exhibiting & providing for the educational use of works of art from all parts of the world in all media, dating from prehistoric times to the present; Maintains reference library; Average Annual Attendance: 825,000; Mem: 80,000; dues $60 & up
Income: $30,000,000 (financed by endowment, mem & county appropriation)
Special Subjects: Asian Art, Costumes, Decorative Arts, Drawings, Islamic Art, Painting-American, Painting-European, Prints, Religious Art, Sculpture, Textiles
Collections: American art, ancient & Islamic art, contemporary art, decorative arts, European painting & sculpture, Far Eastern art, Indian & South Asian art, textiles & costumes, modern art, prints & drawings, photography
Publications: Members Calendar, monthly; exhib catalogs, 6-8 yearly; exhib educ brochures, 6 yearly; permanent collection catalogs, 3 yearly
Activities: Classes for adults & children; dramatic progs; docent training; lects open to pub, 50 vis lectrs per yr; concerts; gallery talks; tours; films; individual paintings & original objects of art lent to other AAM-accredited mus for special exhibs; lending collection contains original art work, original prints, paintings & 130,000 slides; originate traveling exhibs; mus shop sells books, magazines, reproductions, prints, gifts, posters, postcards, calendars & jewelry

L **Allan C Balch Art Research Library**, 5905 Wilshire Blvd, Los Angeles, CA 90036-4504. Tel 323-857-6118; Fax 323-857-4790; Email library@lacma.org; Web: www.lacma.org; *Head Librn* Alexis Curry; *Sr Librn* Pauline Wolstencroft; *Serials & Electronic Resources Librn* Douglas Cordell
Open by appointment; No admis fee; Estab 1965 to support research needs of mus staff & outside scholars, pub by appointment; Circ Non-circulating; For reference only
Income: Financed through the museum
Library Holdings: Auction Catalogs, Audio Tapes, Book Volumes 250,000, CD-ROMs, Cassettes, Clipping Files, Exhibition Catalogs, Fiche, Manuscripts, Other Holdings Artists' Files; Auction catalogs 35,000, Pamphlets, Periodical Subscriptions 450, Slides, Video Tapes
Special Subjects: Afro-American Art, Antiquities-Assyrian, Archaeology, Architecture, Art History, Asian Art, Bronzes, Ceramics, Coins & Medals, Conceptual Art, Crafts, Decorative Arts, Drawings, Enamels, Etchings & Engravings, Fashion Arts, Furniture, Glass, Gold, Graphic Arts, Handicrafts, History of Art & Archaeology, Interior Design, Islamic Art, Latin American Art, Mexican Art, Mosaics, Painting-American, Painting-Dutch, Painting-European, Painting-Flemish, Painting-German, Painting-Italian, Painting-Spanish, Photography, Pottery, Pre-Columbian Art, Primitive art, Prints, Religious Art, Restoration & Conservation, Sculpture, Silver, Textiles, Woodcuts

L **Robert Gore Rifkind Center for German Expressionist Studies**, 5905 Wilshire Blvd, Los Angeles, CA 90036-4504. Tel 323-857-6165; Fax 323-857-4752; Email rifkind@lacma.org; Web: www.lacma.org; *Cur* Timothy Benson; *Asst Registrar* Christine Vigiletti; *Librn* Julia Kim
Open by appointment; Circ Non-circulating; Reference library
Library Holdings: Book Volumes 6000, Exhibition Catalogs, Original Art Works, Prints
Special Subjects: Art History, Decorative Arts, Drawings, Etchings & Engravings, Graphic Arts, Painting-German, Photography, Portraits, Posters, Printmaking, Prints, Sculpture, Watercolors, Woodcuts
Collections: German expressionist prints, drawings, books & periodicals
Publications: Publications relating to German Expressionist studies
Activities: Schols offered; individual graphics & illustrated books; periodicals lent to qualified institutions; book traveling exhibs

L **LOS ANGELES PUBLIC LIBRARY,** Art, Music, Recreation & Rare Books, 630 W Fifth St, Los Angeles, CA 90071-2002. Tel 213-228-7235; Fax 213-228-7239; Email art@lapl.org; Web: www.lapl.org; *Sr Librn* Mary McCoy; *Dept Mgr* Ani Boyadjian
Open Mon-Thurs 10 AM - 8 PM, Fri & Sat 10 AM - 5:30 PM, Sun 1PM - 5 PM; No admis fee; Estab 1872
Income: Financed by municipality
Library Holdings: Book Volumes 200,000, Clipping Files, DVDs, Exhibition Catalogs, Original Art Works, Other Holdings Prints including original etchings, woodcuts, lithographs & drawings, Periodical Subscriptions 800, Photographs, Prints, Video Tapes
Special Subjects: Aesthetics, Afro-American Art, American Indian Art, American Western Art, Antiquities-Assyrian, Architecture, Art History, Asian Art, Bronzes, Calligraphy, Carpets & Rugs, Cartoons, Ceramics, Coins & Medals, Collages, Commercial Art, Conceptual Art, Constructions, Costume Design & Constr, Crafts, Decorative Arts, Dioramas, Dolls, Drafting, Drawings, Embroidery, Enamels, Eskimo Art, Etchings & Engravings, Ethnology, Fashion Arts, Flasks & Bottles, Folk Art, Furniture, Glass, Gold, Goldsmithing, Graphic Arts, Graphic Design, Handicrafts, Historical Material, History of Art & Archaeology, Industrial Design, Interior Design, Intermedia, Islamic Art, Ivory, Jade, Jewelry, Judaica, Laces, Landscape Architecture, Landscapes, Leather, Lettering, Manuscripts, Maps, Marine Painting, Metalwork, Mexican Art, Miniatures, Mixed Media, Mosaics, Oriental Art, Painting-American, Painting-Australian, Painting-British, Painting-Canadian, Painting-Dutch, Painting-European, Painting-Flemish, Painting-French, Painting-German, Painting-Israeli, Painting-Italian, Painting-Japanese, Painting-New Zealand, Painting-Polish, Painting-Russian, Painting-Scandinavian, Painting-Spanish, Period Rooms, Pewter, Photography, Porcelain, Portraits, Posters, Pottery, Pre-Columbian Art, Primitive art, Printmaking, Prints, Religious Art, Reproductions, Restoration & Conservation, Scrimshaw, Sculpture, Silver, Southwestern Art, Stage Design, Stained Glass, Tapestries, Textiles, Video, Watercolors, Woodcarvings, Woodcuts, Advertising Design
Collections: scores, orchestral scores, & many special colls, Japanese & California Prints, Bullfighting, Culinary History
Exhibitions: Museum's Artists Scrapbooks, NY Public Artist's File

M **LOYOLA MARYMOUNT UNIVERSITY,** Laband Art Gallery, One LMU Dr MS8346, Los Angeles, CA 90045. Tel 310-338-2880; Fax 310-338-6024; Email cpeter@lmu.edu; Web: www.cfa.lmu.edu/laband
Open Wed - Sun Noon - 4 PM; No admis fee; Estab 1971 to hold exhibitions; The new gallery which opened in 1984, is 40 ft by 50 ft with 20 ft ceilings, track lighting & closeable skylights; Average Annual Attendance: 10,000
Special Subjects: Ceramics, Ethnology, Folk Art, Hispanic Art, Latin American Art, Photography, Religious Art
Exhibitions: Biennial national exhibitions of the Los Angeles Printmaking Society; Annual exhibitions vary
Publications: Catalogs, 2-3 per year
Activities: Lects open to public, 4-5 vis lectrs per yr; concerts; gallery talks; films; competitions with awards; originate traveling exhibs

M **MOUNT SAINT MARY'S COLLEGE,** Jose-Drudis-Biada Art Gallery, 12001 Chalon Rd, Art Dept Los Angeles, CA 90049-1526. Tel 310-476-2237, 954-4360 (Gallery); Fax 310-476-9296; Email JBaral@msmc.la.edu; Web: msmu.edu/resources-culture/art-gallery; *Gallery Dir* Jody Baral
Open Wed - Sat Noon - 5 PM; No admis fee; Estab to present works of art of various disciplines for the enrichment of students & community; Primarily Los Angeles and Southern California artists
Income: Financed by College
Collections: Collection of works by Jose Drudis-Blada
Exhibitions: Gene Mako Collection; Sedivy & Zokosky: Recent Paintings; Works on Paper; Drucker: Constructions; Geer Installation; Primarily Los Angeles and Southern California Artists
Publications: Exhibitions catalogs, 1 per year
Activities: Lect open to public, 2-3 vis lectrs per year; scholarships

M **MUSEUM OF AFRICAN AMERICAN ART,** 4005 S Crenshaw Blvd, 3rd Fl Macys Los Angeles, CA 90008-2534. Tel 323-294-7071; Fax 323-294-7084; Email info@maaala.org; Web: www.maaala.org; *Founder* Samella Lewis, PhD; *Pres* Berlinda Fontenot-Jamerson; *VPres* Alfonzo Dave Jr
Open Thurs - Sun noon - 5PM; No admis fee donations welcome; Estab 1975 as a national resource dedicated to the presentation of the rich cultural heritage of people of African descent; educates the broadest possible audience; serves as a vehicle through which it promotes & fosters scholarship in art history with a particular interest in the contemporary & historical contributions of African American artists; Mem: Dues $40
Special Subjects: African Art, Afro-American Art
Collections: Arts of the African & African-descendant people, Soapstone Sculpture of Shona, People of Southeast Africa, Makonde Sculpture of East Africa, Traditional Sculpture of West Africa, Sculpture, Paintings, Ceramics of the Caribbean & the South American Peoples, Contemporary North American Artists, Palmer Hayden Coll
Activities: Dramatic progs; poetry readings; lects for mem only; gallery talks; mus shop sells books, original art, reproductions & prints

M **THE MUSEUM OF CONTEMPORARY ART (MOCA),** MOCA Grand Avenue, 250 S Grand Ave, Los Angeles, CA 90012-3007. Tel 213-626-6222 (General); 621-1741 (Vis Svcs); Fax 213-620-8674; Web: www.moca.org; *Dir* Philippe Vergne; *Dir Visitor Engagement* Catherine Arias; *Sr Cur* Bennett Simpson; *Chief Communs Officer* Sarah L Stifler
Open Mon, Wed & Fri 11AM-6PM, Thurs 11AM-8PM, Sat & Sun 11AM-5PM; Admis general $15, seniors $10, students with ID $8, children under 12, members, jurors with ID & Thurs 5 - 8 PM free; Estab 1979, emphasizing the arts since mid century, encompassing traditional & non-traditional media; MOCA Grand designed by Arata Isozaki opened in 1986, Geffen Contemporary at MOCA designed by Frank Gehry, 1983 (one of three locations where MOCA collections are displayed); digital gallery; Average Annual Attendance: 300,000; Mem: dues $70-$750
Income: $16,500,000 (financed by donations, admis fees, grants (private, corporate, NEA), mem & sales)
Library Holdings: Book Volumes 30000, Exhibition Catalogs, Periodical Subscriptions 60
Special Subjects: Architecture, Drawings, Graphics, Hispanic Art, Latin American Art, Mexican Art, Painting-American, Photography, Prints, Sculpture, Watercolors
Collections: El Paso Collection, Barry Lowen Collection, Panza Collection, Ralph M Parsons Foundation Photography Collection, Rita & Taft Schreiber Collection, Scott D F Spiegel Collection, Marcia Simon Weisman Collection, Lannan Foundation Collection, Sam Francis Collection, Joseph & Robert Cornell Memorial Foundation Collection
Exhibitions: Various exhib; 15th Jan, 2017) Doug Aitken: Electric Earth; 6th Feb, 2017) Michalene Thomas: Do I Look Like a Lady?
Publications: The Contemporary, quarterly
Activities: Classes for adults & children; docent training; dramatic progs; family workshops; engagement party; lects open to public; lects mems only; gallery talks; tours; competitions with awards; individual paintings lent to other institutions; originate traveling exhibs; mus shop sells books, magazines, original art, reproductions, posters & gifts, clothing, street banners, phone accessories, jewelry

M **The Geffin Contemporary at Moca**, 152 N Central Ave, Los Angeles, CA 90012-3911. Tel 213-626-6222 (General); 621-1741 (Vis Svcs); Fax 213-620-8674; Web: www.moca.org
Open Mon, Wed & Fri 11 AM - 5 PM, Thurs 11 AM - 8 PM, Sat & Sun 11 AM - 5 PM, cl Tues, Wed, New Year's Day, July 4, Thanksgiving & Christmas Day; Admis general $15, seniors $10, students with ID $8, children under 12 & jurors with ID free; Estab 1979, opened 1983; A former police car warehouse in Little Tokyo renovated by noted California architect Frank O Gehry, this location offers 40,000 sq ft of exhibition space (one of three locations where MOCA collections are displayed)
Activities: Tours; mus store

M **Moca Pacific Design Center**, 8687 Melrose Ave, Red Bldg Ste 1600 West Hollywood, CA 90069. Tel 310-289-5223; Email info@moca.org
Open Tues - Fri 11 AM - 5 PM, Sat & Sun 11 AM - 6 PM, cl Mon, New Year's Day, July 4, Thanksgiving, Christmas Day; No admis fee; One of three locations where MOCA collections are displayed

Exhibitions: Rotating exhibs
Activities: Mus store

M **NATURAL HISTORY MUSEUM OF LOS ANGELES COUNTY,** 900 Exposition Blvd, Los Angeles, CA 90007-4057. Tel 213-763-3466, 763-3434; Fax 213-763-2999; Email glorez@nhm.org; Web: www.nhm.org; *Pres & Dir* Dr Lori Bettison-Varga; *Chief Deputy Dir* Dawn McDivitt; *CFO* Gretchen Humbert; *Sr VPres Advancement* Tom Jacobson; *Sr. VPres Research* Dr Luis M. Chiappe; *VPres Exhibitions* Gretchen Baker; *VPres Educ & Prog* Su Oh
Open daily 9:30 AM - 5 PM, cl New Year's Day, July 4, Thanksgiving Day, Christmas Day; Admis adults $12, seniors, college students & youth 13 - 17 yrs $9, children 3 - 12 $5, members & children under 2 free; Estab 1913 to collect, exhibit & research collection in history, art & science; now focuses on American history, science & earth science; Average Annual Attendance: 1,500,000; Mem: 11,000; dues $40-$100; annual meeting in Sept
Income: Financed by county appropriation & private donations
Special Subjects: American Western Art, Anthropology, Archaeology, Bookplates & Bindings
Collections: American historical works & decorative arts, California & western paintings & prints, pre-Columbian artifacts
Exhibitions: Permanent exhibits: American History Halls; Chaparral: A Story of Life from Fire; Dinosaur Fossils; Egyptian Mummy; Gem & Mineral Hall; Habitat Halls; Lando Hall of California & Southwest History; Marine Biology Hall; Megamouth; Pre-Columbian Hall; Ralph M Parsons Children's Discovery Center; Ralph M Parsons Insect Zoo; The Ralph W Schreiber Hall of Birds
Publications: Science Bulletin; Contributions in Science; Terra, bimonthly magazine
Activities: Classes for adults & children; docent training; lects open to pub; gallery talks; tours; artmobile; individual & original objects of art lent to recognized museums, educational galleries & similar institutions; lending collection contains 30,000 color reproductions, 8653 native artifacts, 35,670 slides, 5500 small mammals, historical & scientific models; originate traveling exhibs; mus & sales shops sell books, magazines, original art, reproductions, prints, slides & ethnic art objects

L **Research Library**, 900 Exposition Blvd, Los Angeles, CA 90007. Tel 213-744-3388; Email librarian@nhm.org; Web: www.nhm.org; *Chief Librn* Richard P Hulser
Open Mon - Fri 10 AM - 4 PM by appointment; No admis fee; Open to staff & pub by appointment for reference only
Library Holdings: Book Volumes 102,000, Clipping Files, Exhibition Catalogs, Memorabilia, Pamphlets, Periodical Subscriptions 350, Photographs, Prints, Reels 472, Slides
Special Subjects: Anthropology, Archaeology, Bookplates & Bindings, Coins & Medals, Decorative Arts, Dioramas, Dolls, Ethnology, Film, Folk Art, Maps, Pre-Columbian Art, Southwestern Art, Textiles

M **OCCIDENTAL COLLEGE,** Weingart Galleries, 1600 Campus Rd, Los Angeles, CA 90041-3314. Tel 323-259-2749 (art dept), 259-2714 (galleries); Email minta@edu; Web: www.oxy.edu; *Dir* Deena Selenow
Open Mon 1 PM - 6 PM, Tues - Wed & Fri 4 PM - 7 PM, Thurs noon - 4:30 PM, Sat - Sun noon - 5 PM; No admis fee; Estab 1938 to acquaint students & visitors with contemporary concerns in the visual arts; Average Annual Attendance: 80,000
Activities: Lect open to public; gallery talks

M **OTIS COLLEGE OF ART & DESIGN,** Ben Maltz Gallery, 9045 Lincoln Blvd, Los Angeles, CA 90045-3505. Tel 310-665-6905; Fax 310-665-6908; Email galleryinfo@otis.edu; Web: www.otis.edu/benmaltzgallery; *Dir Galleries & Exhibitions* Kate McNamara; *Gallery Mgr & Outreach Coordr* Kathy MacPherson; *Exhib Coordr & Gallery Registrar* Jinger Heffner; *Curatorial Programming Coord* Paulina Samborska
Open Tues - Fri 10 AM - 5 PM, Sat - Sun noon - 4 PM, cl Mon & major holidays, cl Jul 2 - 6 for Independence Day, Thanksgiving Day; No admis fee; Estab 1954 as a forum for contemporary art; Gallery is white drywall; 2700 sq ft; Average Annual Attendance: 20,000
Income: Financed by endowment
Special Subjects: Drawings, Photography, Sculpture
Collections: Contemporary art, Conceptual Art, Contemporary Painting
Publications: Catalogues for Tom Knechtel, Shahzia Sikander, Joan Tanner
Activities: Lects open to pub, 2-3 vis lectrs per yr; gallery talks; book traveling exhibs; originate traveling exhibs to other university museums & galleries

L **Millard Sheets Library**, 9045 Lincoln Blvd, Los Angeles, CA 90045-3505. Tel 310-665-6930; Email otislib@otisart.edu; *Dir* Sue Maberry
Open Mon - Fri 9 AM - 9 PM (during school session), Sat 9 AM - 5 PM; open to pub by appointment only; cl Sun; Estab 1918 as a visual arts library
Library Holdings: Audio Tapes, Book Volumes 30,000, Cassettes, Clipping Files, Exhibition Catalogs, Original Art Works, Pamphlets, Periodical Subscriptions 150, Records 150, Slides 100,000, Video Tapes 1000
Special Subjects: Costume Design & Constr, Decorative Arts, Graphic Arts, Mixed Media, Photography

A **PLAZA DE LA RAZA CULTURAL CENTER,** 3540 N Mission Rd, Los Angeles, CA 90031-3195. Tel 323-223-2475; Fax 323-223-1804; Email info@plazadelaraza.org; Web: www.plazadelaraza.org; *Exec Dir* Maria Jimenez-Torres; *Admin Office Asst* Gabriel Jiminez; *Groundskeeper* Arturo Moran; *Vol Coordr* Kay Rosser
Open Mon - Fri 9 AM - 8 PM, Sat 10 AM - 2 PM, cl Sun; No admis fee; Estab 1969 to preserve, promote & present Chicano/Mexican/Latino art & culture & promote new works; Boathouse Gallery houses Plaza's permanent collection of Latino art & also hosts temporary exhibits of the work of Chicano artists; Average Annual Attendance: 10,000; Mem: 100; dues $35 - $500
Income: $500,000 (financed by endowment, mem, city & state appropriation, grants from pvt & pub foundations)
Collections: Permanent collection of works by nationally known Latino visual artists
Exhibitions: Rotating exhibitions
Activities: Adult classes in folk arts, dance & music; children classes in music, dance, visual arts, theatre & folk arts; dramatic progs; competitions; retail store sells prints, original art, reproductions & crafts

A **SELF HELP GRAPHICS,** 1300 E 1st St, Los Angeles, CA 90033-3218. Tel 323-881- 6444; Fax 323-881-6447; Email info@selfhelpgraphics.com; Web: www.selfhelpgraphics.com; *Co Dir Prog & Operations* Joel Garcia; *Co Dir Advancement & Admin* Betty Avila; *Prog Coord* Alexa Kim
Open Wed -Fri 10 AM - 5 PM, Mon - Tues by appointment; No admis fee; Estab 1972 to provide art opportunities for Chicano & all artists; One gallery on first floor, 1,700 sq ft; Average Annual Attendance: 15,000
Income: Financed through donations & grants
Exhibitions: Rotating exhibitions, 10 -12 per yr

M **UNIVERSITY OF CALIFORNIA, LOS ANGELES,** Fowler Museum at UCLA, PO Box 951549, Los Angeles, CA 90095-1549. Tel 310-825-4361; Fax 310-206-7007; Email fowlerws@arts.ucla.edu; Web: www.fowler.ucla.edu; *Dir* Marla C Berns; *Registrar* Jeanette Saunders; *Head Conservator* Christian deBrer; *Dir Photog* Don Cole; *Dir Educa & Interpretation* Terri Geis; *Dir Exhibs* Sebastian Clough; *Dir Publications* Daniel R Brauer; *Cur African Arts* Erica Jones; *Asst Dir Develop* Michelle Klein; *HR Coordr* Roberto Salazar; *Dir Registration & Collections Mgr* Rachel Raynor; *Managing Ed* Deirdre O'Dwyer; *Mem Coordr* Lori LaVelle; *Deputy Dir* David Blair; *Mus Store Mgr* Kathy DiGenova
Open Wed noon - 8 PM, Thurs - Sun noon - 5 PM, cl Mon & Tues, New Year's Eve & Day, Thanksgiving, Christmas Eve & Day; No admis fee; Estab in 1963 to collect, preserve & make available for research & exhibition objects & artifacts from cultures considered to be outside the Western tradition; Circ Non-circulating; Changing exhibitions on view Wed - Sun Noon - 5 PM; Average Annual Attendance: 60,000; Mem: 607; dues individual $75, family $100, contributing $200, supporting $300, patron $500
Income: Financed by endowment, state appropriation & private donations
Special Subjects: African Art, American Indian Art, Anthropology, Archaeology, Asian Art, Eskimo Art, Ethnology, Folk Art, Hispanic Art, Islamic Art, Metalwork, Mexican Art, Photography, Pre-Columbian Art, Primitive art, Religious Art
Collections: Archaeological & ethnographic colls, 600,000 objects primarily from non-Western cultures - Africa, Asia, the Americas, Oceania, The Near East & parts of Europe
Publications: Exhibition catalogues; filmstrips; monographs; pamphlets; papers; posters; slide sets
Activities: Classes for adults & children; publications prog; lects open to pub, 1-3 vis lectrs per yr; concerts; gallery talks; tours; art workshops; symposiums; awards; book traveling exhibs; originate traveling exhibs; mus shop sells books, jewelry, magazines, textiles

M **Grunwald Center for the Graphic Arts at Hammer Museum**, 10899 Wilshire Blvd, Los Angeles, CA 90024-4343. Tel 310-443-7076; Fax 310-443-7099; Email info@hammer.ucla.edu; Web: www.hammer.ucla.edu; *Dir* Cynthia Burlingham; *Cur Assoc* Leslie Cozzi; *Assoc Registrar* Susan Chin
Open by appointment only; No admis fee; Estab 1956; Gallery serves the university & pub, program is integrated with the University curricula
Special Subjects: Graphics
Collections: Grunwald Center for the Graphic Arts: 45,000 prints, drawings, photographs & illustrated books from the 13th through 20th Centuries, including old master prints & drawings, Frank Lloyd Wright Collection of Japanese Prints, Tamarind Lithography Archive, The Rudolf L Baumfeld Collection of Landscape Drawings & Prints, Hammer Honore's Daumier Collection
Exhibitions: Three exhibitions annually
Publications: Exhibition catalogues; French Caricature; French Renaissance in Prints from the Bibliotheque nationale de France; The Rudolf L Baumfeld Collection of Landscape Drawings & Prints; Visionary States: Surrealist Prints from the Gilbert Kaplan Collection; The World From Here: Treasures of the Great Libraries of Los Angeles
Activities: Lects open to pub; gallery talks; tours daily; book traveling exhibs; originate traveling exhibs; mus shop sells books, magazines, original art, reproductions & various gift items

M **Hammer Museum**, 10899 Wilshire Blvd, Los Angeles, CA 90024. Tel 310-443-7000; Fax 310-443-7099; Email info@hammer.ucla.edu; Web: www.hammer.ucla.edu; *Dir* Ann Philbin
Open Tues - Fri 11 AM - 8 PM, Sat - Sun 11 AM - 5 PM, cl Mon, July 4, Thanksgiving, Christmas & New Year's Day; No admis fee; Estab 1990; Gallery serves the university & pub; program is integrated with the University curricula; Average Annual Attendance: 180,000; Mem: 3000; dues fellow $1000, patron $500, sustaining $250, participating $100, active $45, UCLA faculty, staff & senior citizens $25, students $20
Special Subjects: Painting-American, Painting-British, Painting-European, Painting-French, Sculpture
Collections: 300 paintings, including the Willitts J Hole Collection of the Italian, Spanish, Dutch, Flemish & English schools from the 15th-19th century, Franklin D Murphy Sculpture Garden: 70 sculptures from the 19th-20th centuries, including Arp, Calder, Lachaise, Lipchitz, Moore, Noguchi, Rodin & Smith, The Armand Hammer Collection includes approx 100 paintings, primarily 19th-century French artists, the Armand Hammer Daumier & Contemporaries Collection includes over 7000 works by 19th-century French artist Honore Daumier & his contemporaries
Exhibitions: 12 exhibs annually; operates in close conjunction with the UCLA Grunwald Center for the Graphic Arts
Publications: Exhibition catalogues; The Macchiaioli, California Assemblage; Silk Route & the Diamond Path; Chicano Art
Activities: Gallery talks; tours daily; book traveling exhibs; originate traveling exhibs; mus shop sells books & prints

L **Visual Resource Collection**, Department of Art History, 200 Dodd Hall Los Angeles, CA 90095-1417. Tel 310-825-3725; Fax 310-206-1903; Email ziegler@humnet.ucla.edu; *Dir* David Ziegler; *Asst Cur* Susan Rosenfeld
Library Holdings: Filmstrips, Lantern Slides 30,000, Slides 300,000
Special Subjects: Afro-American Art, American Indian Art, American Western Art, Antiquities-Assyrian, Archaeology, Architecture, Asian Art, Costume Design & Constr, Decorative Arts, Etchings & Engravings, Ethnology, Film, Folk Art, Furniture, Graphic Arts

L **Arts Library**, 1400 Public Affairs Bldg, Box 951392 Los Angeles, CA 90095-1392. Tel 310-206-5425; Fax 310-825-1303; Web: www.library.ucla.edu/libraries/arts; *Interim Head* Judy Consales; *Librn for Art* Robert Gore; *Librn for Film, TV & Theater* Diana King; *Architecture/Design Librn* Janine Henri; *Access Svcs Supvr* Alex Solodkaya; *Access Servs Asst* Cuauhtemoc Moncada; *Regional Manager* Robert Freel
Open Mon - Thurs 8 AM - 9 PM, Fri 8 AM - 5 PM, Sat 1 PM - 5 PM, Sun 1 - 5 PM, hours vary during intersession, summer & holidays; No admis fee; Founded 1952; Circ 26,836; Average Annual Attendance: 58,318
Library Holdings: Book Volumes 318,218, CD-ROMs 337, Cassettes 288, Compact Disks 40, DVDs 102, Exhibition Catalogs, Fiche 71,933, Other Holdings Ephemera files, Pamphlets 0, Periodical Subscriptions 1,987, Photographs, Reels 2,670, Video Tapes 24
Special Subjects: American Indian Art, American Western Art, Antiquities-Assyrian, Antiquities-Byzantine, Antiquities-Egyptian, Antiquities-Etruscan, Antiquities-Greek, Antiquities-Oriental, Antiquities-Persian, Antiquities-Roman, Architecture, Art History, Asian Art, Bronzes, Carpets & Rugs, Cartoons, Ceramics, Collages, Commercial Art, Costume Design & Constr, Crafts, Display, Drafting, Drawings, Eskimo Art, Etchings & Engravings, Fashion Arts, Film, Folk Art, Furniture, Glass, Gold, Goldsmithing, Graphic Arts, Graphic Design, History of Art & Archaeology, Illustration, Interior Design, Intermedia, Islamic Art, Ivory, Jade, Jewelry, Landscape Architecture, Landscapes, Latin American Art, Lettering, Manuscripts, Marine Painting, Metalwork, Mexican Art, Miniatures, Mixed Media, Oriental Art, Painting-American, Painting-Australian, Painting-British, Painting-Canadian, Painting-Dutch, Painting-European, Painting-Flemish, Painting-French, Painting-German, Painting-Israeli, Painting-Italian, Painting-Japanese, Painting-New Zealand, Painting-Polish, Painting-Russian, Painting-Scandinavian, Painting-Spanish, Photography, Porcelain, Portraits, Posters, Pottery, Pre-Columbian Art, Primitive art, Printmaking, Prints, Religious Art, Reproductions, Restoration & Conservation, Sculpture, Silver, Silversmithing, Stained Glass, Tapestries, Textiles, Theatre Arts, Video, Watercolors, Woodcarvings, Woodcuts

M **UNIVERSITY OF SOUTHERN CALIFORNIA,** USC Fisher Museum of Art, 823 Exposition Blvd, Los Angeles, CA 90089-0292. Tel 213-740-4561; Fax 213-740-7676; Email fmoa@usc.edu; Web: fisher.usc.edu; *Dir & Cur* Dr Selma Holo; *Assoc Dir* Kay Allen; *Coll Mgr & Registrar* Stephanie Kowalick; *Chief Preparator* Juan Rojas; *Admin Coord & Business Specialist* Raphael Gatchalian
Open Tues - Fri 12 - 4 PM, Sat noon - 5 PM, cl summer & university holidays; No admis fee; Estab 1939 as the art mus of the university; Fisher Gallery consists of five rooms, for changing exhibitions & 1 room for permanent collection exhibition; Average Annual Attendance: 12,000
Income: Financed by endowment & university subsidy
Special Subjects: American Western Art, Latin American Art, Mexican Art, Painting-American, Painting-British, Painting-Dutch, Painting-European, Painting-Flemish, Painting-French, Painting-Italian, Portraits, Portraits
Collections: Elizabeth Holmes Fisher Collection, Armand Hammer Collection, galleries house the permanent collections of paintings of 17th-century Dutch, Flemish & Italian, 18th-century British, 19th-century French & American landscape & portraiture schools, contemporary works by artists from Calif - emphasis on international art especially Mexico & Spain
Publications: Exhibition catalogs, three annually
Activities: Classes for adults & children; dramatic progs; docent training; lects open to pub; concerts; gallery talks; tours; individual paintings & original objects of art lent; lending collection contains original prints, paintings, sculpture; 1-2 book traveling exhibs per yr; originate traveling exhibs

L **Helen Topping Architecture & Fine Arts Library**, Watt Hall, 850 Bloom Walk, B-4, University Park Campus Los Angeles, CA 90089-0294. Tel 213-740-1956; Fax 213-749-1221, 740-8884; Email afa@usc.edu; Web: www.lib.usc.edu/info/afa; *Reference Center* Ruth Wallach
Open Mon - Thurs 9 AM - 10 PM, Fri 9 AM - 5 PM, Sun noon - 6 PM, summer hours Mon - Fri 9 AM - 5 PM, cl Sat; Estab 1925 to provide undergraduate & graduate level students & the teaching & research faculty materials in the areas of architecture & fine arts needed to achieve their objectives; Circ 65,000; Branch library in the central library system is supported by the university, lending library
Income: Financed by university funds
Purchases: $95,000
Library Holdings: Book Volumes 85,000, Clipping Files, Compact Disks, Exhibition Catalogs, Other Holdings Architectural drawings 1000; Artist's books 400, Pamphlets, Periodical Subscriptions 285, Reels, Slides 260,000, Video Tapes 150
Special Subjects: Antiquities-Roman, Architecture, Art History, Decorative Arts, Landscape Architecture, Latin American Art, Photography
Publications: Exhibit catalogs

L **Cinema-Television Library & Archives of Performing Arts**, University Library, Los Angeles, CA 90089-0182. Tel 213-740-8906; Fax 213-749-1221; Web: www.usc.edu\cinemaarts; *Dir* Robert Rosen
Open acad semester 8:30 AM - 10 PM; No admis fee; Estab 1960
Library Holdings: Audio Tapes, Book Volumes 18,000, Cards, Cassettes, Clipping Files, Manuscripts, Memorabilia, Pamphlets, Periodical Subscriptions 225, Records, Reels, Video Tapes
Special Subjects: Film, Video
Collections: Film & television: scripts, stills, posters, production records, correspondence

C **WELLS FARGO & CO,** History Museum, 333 S Grand Ave, Los Angeles, CA 90071-1504. Tel 213-253-7166; Fax 213-680-2269; Email wfmuseum.la@wellsfargo.com; *Mgr* Ileana Bonilla
Open Mon - Fri 9 AM - 5 PM, cl bank holidays; No admis fee; Museum estab to demonstrate impact of Wells Fargo on California & American West; 6500 sq ft; approx 1000 objects on display; Average Annual Attendance: 40,000
Income: Financed by private funds
Collections: Authentic 19th-century Concord Stagecoach, display of firearms, Dorsey Gold Collection of gold quartz ore, $50 gold piece, original Spanish language documents giving Los Angeles its city status in 1835, Perils of Road, Pony Express exhibit, two-pound gold nugget, Wells Fargo office
Exhibitions: Staging; mining; express; banking; South California
Publications: Various publications concerning Wells Fargo in US history
Activities: Dramatic progs; tours & off-site presentations; lects open to pub; mus shop sells books, reproductions of memorabilia & prints

MENDOCINO

A **MENDOCINO ART CENTER,** Gallery & School, 45200 Little Lake St, Mendocino, CA 95460; PO Box 765, Mendocino, CA 95460-0765. Tel 707-937-5818; Fax 707-937-1764; Email mendoart@mcn.org; Web: www.mendocinoartcenter.org; *Exec Dir* Peggy Templer
Open Wed-Sun 10AM-5PM; No admis fee; Estab 1959 as a rental-sales gallery for exhibition & sales of member work; also to provide workshops on all media; Three major gallery rooms, one gallery room available for rental of one-man shows; Average Annual Attendance: 25,000; Mem: 1000; dues $50
Income: Membership, donations, tui
Library Holdings: Book Volumes
Collections: Graphics, paintings & sculpture, Dorr Bothwell
Exhibitions: Rotate 6-8 per yr
Publications: Arts & Entertainment, monthly
Activities: Classes for adults & children; docent training; lect open to public, 4-10 vis lectrs per year; concerts; competitions; scholarships offered; individual paintings & original objects of art lent to bus & public places; sales shop sells books, original art, reproductions, prints & crafts

L **Library**, 45200 Little Lake St, Mendocino, CA 95460; PO Box 765, Mendocino, CA 95460-0765. Tel 707-937-5818; Fax 707-937-1764; Web: www.mendocinoartcenter.org; *Exec Dir* Peggy Templer
Open Tues - Sat 11 AM - 2 PM; No admis fee; Estab 1975 to provide members with access to art books & magazines; Circ 1350 books & 18 magazines; Lending library for members of Art Center only
Income: Financed by donations & mem
Library Holdings: Book Volumes 2500, Other Holdings Picture File, Periodical Subscriptions 4, Prints, Reproductions

MISSION HILLS

A **SAN FERNANDO VALLEY HISTORICAL SOCIETY,** 10940 Sepulveda Blvd, Mission Hills, CA 91346; PO Box 7039, Mission Hills, CA 91345-7039. Tel 818-365-7810; Web: www.sfvhs.com; *VPres & Cur* Dr Richard Doyle; *Pres* Carol Phelps
Open by appointment Mon 10 AM - 3 PM for tours; No admis fee; Estab 1943; The Soc manages the Andres Pico Adobe (1834) for the Los Angeles City Department of Recreation & Parks, where they house their collection; Average Annual Attendance: 500; Mem: dues life $100, active, sustaining & organization $15
Income: Financed by mem & donations
Collections: Historical material, Indian artifacts, paintings, costumes, decorative arts, manuscripts
Exhibitions: Permanent & temporary exhibitions
Publications: monthly newsletter, The Valley; guide
Activities: Lect; films; guided tours

L **Mark Harrington Library**, 10940 Sepulveda Blvd, Mission Hills, CA 91346; PO Box 7039, Mission Hills, CA 92346-7039. Tel 818-365-7810; *Pres & Cur* Dr Richard Doyle; *VPres* Jim Guleranson
Open by appointment; Estab 1970
Income: Financed by mem & gifts
Library Holdings: Book Volumes 1000, Cassettes, Clipping Files, Manuscripts, Memorabilia, Original Art Works, Pamphlets, Photographs, Prints
Collections: Citrus, Communities, Historical landmarks, Olive, Pioneers, San Fernando Mission, San Fernando Valley
Exhibitions: Regular exhibitions of valley history
Publications: The Valley, monthly newsletter

MONTEREY

M **CASA AMESTI,** 516 Polk St, Monterey, CA 93940-2810. Tel 831-372-8173, 372-2808; *Pres* Pam McCollough
Open Sat & Sun 2 - 4 PM, cl 2 wks July; Admis $3, children & members free; Bequeathed to the National Trust in 1953 by Mrs Frances Adler Elkins; It is an 1833 adobe structure reflecting phases of the history & culture of the part of California owned by Mexico, after the period of Spanish missions & before develop of American influences from the Eastern seaboard. It is a prototype of what is now known as Monterey style architecture. The Italian-style gardens within the high adobe walls were designed by Mrs. Elkins, an interior designer, & her bro, Chicago architect David Adler. The furnishings, largely European, collected by Mrs. Elkins are displayed in a typical 1930s interior. The property is a National Trust historic house. The Old Capital Club, a private organization, leases, occupies & maintains the property for social & educational purposes
Special Subjects: Historical Material
Collections: Elkins Collection of largely European furnishings
Activities: Monterey History & Art Assn volunteers provide interpretive services for visitors on weekends

A **MONTEREY HISTORY & ART ASSOCIATION,** 5 Custom House Plaza, Monterey, CA 93940. Tel 831-372-2608; Fax 831-655-3054; Web: www.montereyhistory.org; *Pres* Kathi Wojtkowski
No admis fee; Estab 1931; The Assoc owns the 1845 Casa Serrano Adobe, the 1865 Doud House, the 1845 Fremont Adobe, the Mayo Hayes O'Donnell Library & the newly constructed Stanton Center - Monterey's Maritime Mus & History Center. The Assoc celebrates the birthday of Monterey (June 3, 1770) with the Merienda each year on the Sat nearest that date. The Assoc commemorates the landing at Monterey by Commodore John Drake Sloat in 1846; Mem: 1800; dues individual life mem $500, sustaining couple $75, sustaining single $50, couple $25, single $15, junior $1
Income: Financed by mem, donations & fundraising activities

Collections: Costumes, manuscripts & paintings, sculpture, antique furniture, books, photographs
Exhibitions: Permanent & temporary exhibitions; Fourth Grade History & Art Contest
Publications: Noticias Del Puerto De Monterey, quarterly bulletin
Activities: Guided tours; competitions

M **Maritime Museum of Monterey**, 5 Custom House Plaza, Monterey, CA 93942. Tel 831-372-2608; Email accounting @montereyhistory.org; Web: www.mntmh.org; *Exec Dir* Mark Baer
Open Tues - Sun 10 - 5 PM; Admis adults $8, seniors, military $5, children under 12 free; Estab 1971, moved 1992 into new facility along waterfront; Maritime related artifacts & artwork; features operating light from Point Sur Lighthouse; Average Annual Attendance: 12,000; Mem: 1800; dues $20 - $100; annual meeting in Sept
Special Subjects: Marine Painting
Collections: Marine Artifacts, ship models, paintings, photographs, Fresnel First Order Lens from Point Sur, California (on loan from US Coast Guard)
Exhibitions: Permanent & temporary exhibitions
Activities: Classes for children; Lects open to pub, 12 vis lectrs per yr; concerts; gallery talks; tours; competitions with awards; mus shop sells books, prints, original art, reproductions, souvenirs, toys & gift items

L **Library**, 5 Custom House Plaza, Monterey, CA 93940-2430. Tel 831-372-2608; Fax 831-655-3054; *Librn* Faye Messinger
Open Wed, Fri, Sat & Sun 1:30 - 3:30 PM; No admis fee; Estab 1971; Open for research on the premises
Library Holdings: Book Volumes 2500, Manuscripts, Memorabilia, Original Art Works, Other Holdings Local History archive, Periodical Subscriptions 2, Photographs, Prints
Publications: Brochure of Museum with map

A **MONTEREY MUSEUM OF ART,** Monterey Museum of Art -Pacific Street, Monterey Museum of Art - La Mirada, 720 Via Mirada, Monterey, CA 93940; 559 Pacific St, Monterey, CA 93940-2805. Tel 831-372-5477; Fax 831-372-5680; Email info@montereyart.org; Web: www.montereyart.org; *Exec Dir* E Michael Whittington; *Dir Mktg Communs* Mary DeGroat; *Dir Educ* Terry Laurents; *Cur* Karen Crews Hendon
Open Wed - Sat 11 AM - 5 PM, Sun 1 - 4 PM, cl Mon, Tues, New Year's, Christmas & Thanksgiving; Admis non-member $10, full-time student with ID $5; Estab 1959, the mission of the Monterey Mus of Art is to educate and enrich the diverse Calif community. Inspiring awareness and thought through the arts, the Mus serves as a forum and catalyst for the discussion and debate of ideas. The Mus creates progs that engage visitors and uplift the human spirit; The museum's permanent collection includes Calif art, photography, Asian art & features significant bodies of work by Armin Hansen, William Ritschel, Ansel Adams & Edward Weston; Average Annual Attendance: 40,000; Mem: 2,000; dues $40-$1000 & above
Income: Financed by endowment, mem & fundraising functions
Library Holdings: Auction Catalogs, Book Volumes, Exhibition Catalogs, Original Documents, Periodical Subscriptions
Special Subjects: American Western Art, Antiquities-Oriental, Architecture, Asian Art, Bronzes, Ceramics, Decorative Arts, Drawings, Etchings & Engravings, Folk Art, Graphics, Landscapes, Miniatures, Painting-American, Pewter, Photography, Prints, Sculpture, Textiles, Watercolors, Woodcuts, Portraits
Collections: Armin Hansen Collection, William Ritschel Collection, Ansel Adams
Exhibitions: Theme shows
Publications: Weekly news - e-blast
Activities: Classes for adults & children; docent training; lects open to pub; vis lectrs; concerts; gallery talks; tours; in service training for teachers; outreach program; 3-4 traveling exhibs per year; originate traveling exhibs; mus shops sell books, reproductions, prints, jewelry, notecards, DVDs

L **MONTEREY PUBLIC LIBRARY,** Art & Architecture Dept, 625 Pacific St, Monterey, CA 93940-2866. Tel 831-646-3932; Fax 831-646-5618; Web: www.monterey.org/library; *Dir* Kim Bul-Burton
Open Mon 1-9PM, Tues-Wed 10AM-9PM, Thurs-Fri 10AM-6PM, Sat-Sun 1-5PM; Estab 1849
Income: Financed by mem & city appropriation
Purchases: $750,000
Library Holdings: Book Volumes 100,000, Cassettes 3000, Clipping Files, Manuscripts, Original Art Works, Periodical Subscriptions 379, Photographs, Reels 4000, Reproductions

M **SAN CARLOS CATHEDRAL,** 500 Church St, Monterey, CA 93940-3209. Tel 831-373-2628; Fax 831-373-0518; Web: www.sancarloscathedral.net; *Rector & Pastor* Rev. Emil Robu
Open daily 7:30 AM - 5 PM; No admis fee; Built in 1770, now a branch of the Monterey Diocese; The art museum is housed in the 1794 Royal Presidio Chapel
Special Subjects: Religious Art, Sculpture
Collections: Spanish religious paintings and sculpture of the 18th and 19th century
Activities: Classes for adults & children; lects open to pub, 1 vis lectr per yr; self-guided tours

MONTEREY PARK

M **EAST LOS ANGELES COLLEGE,** Vincent Price Art Museum, 1301 Avenida Cesar Chevez Ave, Monterey Park, CA 91754. Tel 323-265-8841; Fax 323-260-8173; Email vincentpriceartmuseum@elac.edu; Web: vincentpriceartmuseum.org; *Dir* Pilar Tompkins Rivas; *Musuem Preparator & Dir Asst* Victor Parra
Open Tues - Wed & Fri - Sat noon - 4 PM, Thurs noon - 7 PM, cl Sun & Mon; No admis fee; Estab 1958 as an institutional art gallery serving the East Los Angeles area
Income: Financed by the college, grants & donations
Special Subjects: African Art, American Indian Art, Renaissance Art
Collections: Includes art from Africa, Peruvian & Mexican artifacts dating from 300 B C, North American Indian Art, important works from the Renaissance to the present day, Leonard Baskin, Daumier, Delacroix, Durer, Garvarni, Hiroshige I, Rico Lebrun, Maillol, Picasso, Piranesi, Redon, Utrillo, Howard Warshaw, Anuskiewicz, Bufano, Rouault, Tamayo
Exhibitions: Annual Student Art Show; Selections from the private collection of the Vincent Price Art Collection

MORAGA

M **SAINT MARY'S COLLEGE OF CALIFORNIA,** Museum of Art, 1928 Saint Mary's Rd, Moraga, CA 94575; PMB 5110, Moraga, CA 94575-5110. Tel 925-631-4379; Email jrs6@stmarys-ca.edu; Web: www.stmarys-ca.edu/saint-marys-college-museum-of-art; *Registrar* Robin Bernhard; *Community Relations* Kyla Tynes
Open Wed - Sun 11 AM - 4:30 PM, cl Mon & Tues & between exhibitions; admis donation $5; Estab 1977 to exhibit a variety of the visual arts for the benefit of col community & gen pub audience; Maintains four galleries/rooms for temporary exhibitions, William Keith Room for permanent collection of 19th-century landscape painting; Average Annual Attendance: 14,000; Mem: 230; dues supporting $100 & up, family $75, individual $40; accredited by Am Assn Mus
Income: $275,000 (financed by college, donations, grants & earned income)
Purchases: 19th- & 20th-century California art
Special Subjects: African Art, Coins & Medals, Drawings, Etchings & Engravings, Ethnology, Graphics, Hispanic Art, Historical Material, Landscapes, Latin American Art, Medieval Art, Mexican Art, Painting-American, Photography, Pre-Columbian Art, Prints, Religious Art, Sculpture, Renaissance Art
Collections: 150 paintings by William Keith (1838-1911) & other 19th, 20th & 21st Century California art, African Oceanic & Latin American ethnographic objects, thematic print coll, Ethnographic Objects, Renaissance Sculpture-German Gothic Wood, Religious art, wine related art, ancient ceramics and coins
Publications: Exhibition catalogues, 1 - 2 per yr
Activities: Educ dept; class tours; lects open to pub, 4 vis lectrs per yr; gallery talks; tours; schols; individual paintings & original objects of art lent to mus; book traveling exhibs 2 per yr; originate traveling exhibs of William Keith Collection to mus; mus shop sells books, magazines, original art, reproductions, prints & jewelry

NEWHALL

M **LOS ANGELES COUNTY MUSEUM OF NATURAL HISTORY,** William S Hart Museum, 24151 San Fernando Rd, William S Hart Park Newhall, CA 91321-2908. Tel 661-254-4584; Fax 661-254-6499; Web: www.hartmuseum.org; *Adminr* Janis Ashley; *Coordr Educ* Kyle Harris
Open winter Wed - Fri 10 AM - 1 PM, Sat - Sun 11 AM - 4 PM; summer mid-June to mid-Sept Wed - Sun 11 AM - 4 PM; No admis fee; Estab through the bequest of William S Hart (1946) & opened 1958 for use as a public park & museum; The retirement home of William S Hart is maintained as it was during his lifetime, his extensive collection of Western art is on display throughout the house; Average Annual Attendance: 250,000; Mem: 250; dues $35; meetings second Wed of every month
Income: Financed by county appropriation & private donations
Special Subjects: Bronzes, Carpets & Rugs, Decorative Arts, Furniture, Glass, Historical Material, Painting-American, Period Rooms, Silver, Textiles, Watercolors, Woodcarvings
Collections: Frederic Remington Collection of Watercolor & Oil paintings, Charles M Russell Collection of Oil & Watercolor Paintings, Gouache, Pen & Ink, decorative arts, Navajo rugs, Charles Cristadoro Sculptures, Joe DeYong Paintings, Clarence Ellsworth Paintings, James M Flagg Paintings, Gene Hoback woodcarvings, Robert L Lambdin Paintings, Charles Schreyvogel Paintings
Activities: Classes for adults; docent training; school outreach prog; mus shop sells books, videotapes, souvenirs

NEWPORT BEACH

M **ORANGE COUNTY MUSEUM OF ART,** 850 San Clemente Dr, Newport Beach, CA 92660-6399. Tel 949-759-1122; Fax 949-759-5623; Email info@ocma.net; Web: www.ocma.net; *Cur* Sarah Bancroft; *Dir Develop* Patricia Falzon; *Opers Dir* Albert Lopez, Jr; *Dir* Dennis Szakacs
Open Wed-Sun 11AM-5PM, Thurs until 8PM, cl Mon, Tues, July 4, Thanksgiving, Christmas & New Year's Days; Admis adults $12, students w/ID & seniors $10, mems & children under 12 free, 2nd Sun of month free; Incorporated 1918 as Laguna Beach Art Assn, estab 1962 as a mus of the Art of our Time serving Orange County & Southern California, name changed in 1996; Building completed in 1977 contains four galleries of various sizes; 5000; 1600; 1200; 500 sq ft plus lobby & sculpture garden area; Average Annual Attendance: 100,000; Mem: 5500; dues supporting member $500, donor $100, general mem $45, student $25
Income: $2,500,000 (financed by special events, mem, government grants, private sector, sales from restaurant & bookstore)
Purchases: $100,000 year for works of art
Special Subjects: Ceramics, Drawings, Glass, Painting-American, Photography
Collections: Collections of Historical & contemporary American art, California artists from 1850 to present, 2,500 objects in coll, concentrating on California art from the early 20th c to present
Publications: Bimonthly calendar; exhibition catalogs; posters
Activities: Docent training; in-service training sessions for teachers, docent tours for school & adult groups; lects series, special guest lectrs & meet-the-artist programs; gallery talks; creative art workshops; concerts & performances; film & video programs; individual paintings & original objects of art lent to qualified art mus; lending collection contains original prints; paintings & sculptures; originates traveling exhibs; mus shop sells books, magazines, original art

NORTHRIDGE

M **CALIFORNIA STATE UNIVERSITY, NORTHRIDGE,** Art Galleries, 18111 Nordhoff St, Northridge, CA 91330-8299. Tel 818-677-2156; Fax 818-677-5910;

Web: www.csun.edu/artgalleries; *Dir* Jim Sweeters; *Exhib Coordr* Michelle Giacopuzzi; *Art Coll Registrar* Lucy Hernandez
Open Mon-Sat Noon - 4 PM, Thurs Noon-8 PM; No admis fee, donations accepted; Estab 1971 to provide a source of international & contemporary art for the university & the community at large; Exhibitions in Main Gallery have average duration of five weeks. West Gallery for weekly MA candidate solo exhibitions; Average Annual Attendance: 35,000; Mem: 300; Arts Council for CSUN; dues $35 annually, meet weekly
Income: $40,000 (financed by city & state appropriation, community support organizations)
Special Subjects: African Art, Afro-American Art, American Indian Art, American Western Art, Asian Art, Cartoons, Ceramics, Collages, Drawings, Etchings & Engravings, Folk Art, Graphics, Hispanic Art, Latin American Art, Maps, Mexican Art, Oriental Art, Painting-American, Painting-Australian, Painting-Japanese, Painting-Scandinavian, Painting-Spanish, Photography, Pre-Columbian Art, Prints, Sculpture, Southwestern Art, Textiles, Woodcuts, Illustration
Collections: University Foundation Art Collection
Publications: Exhibition catalogs, 1 per yr
Activities: Docent training; 2-3 art performances per year; workshops for adults; lects open to pub, 10-20 vis lectrs per yr; concerts; gallery talks; tours; competitions; student exhib cash awards $2,000 total; mus shop sells books, magazines, original art, prints, reproductions, slides, folk art objects, gifts, ceramics & jewelry

OAKLAND

L **CALIFORNIA COLLEGE OF THE ARTS,** Libraries, 5212 Broadway, Oakland, CA 94618-1426. Tel 510-594-3658; Email refdesk@cca.edu; Web: library.cca.edu, www.libraries.cca.edu; www.cca.edu; *Dir Libraries* Annemarie Haar; *Assoc Dir Libraries* Teri Dowling
Estab 1907; educates students to shape culture through the practice and critical study of the arts
Library Holdings: Book Volumes 57,000, DVDs 2,100, Original Art Works 650, Original Documents, Periodical Subscriptions 250, Photographs, Video Tapes 1,500
Special Subjects: Aesthetics, Architecture, Art History, Ceramics, Drawings, Film, Furniture, Glass, Graphic Design, Illustration, Industrial Design, Interior Design, Jewelry, Metalwork, Photography
Collections: Joseph Sinel Collection of pioneering work in industrial design, Capp Street Project Archives, Hamaguchi Study Print Collection, Emeryville Mudflat Ave documentation
Activities: Library Research Award; Student Book Art Award

M **CREATIVE GROWTH ART CENTER,** 355 24th St, Oakland, CA 94612-3126. Tel 510-836-2340; Fax 510-836-0769; Email info@creativegrowth.org; Web: www.creativegrowth.org; *Dir* Tom di Maria; *Studio Mgr* Matt Dostal; *Gallery Mgr* Sarah Galender Meyer; *Accnt* Haideh Vincent
Open Mon - Fri 10 AM - 4:30 PM, Sat 10 AM - 3 PM, other times by appointment; No admis fee; Estab 1974 to professionally exhibit the art of Creative Growth & art work by outsider & well-known artists; Average Annual Attendance: 5,000; Mem: $25 for 1 yr
Income: $900,000
Collections: Permanent collection includes art works in all media on traditional & contemporary subjects
Exhibitions: Individual & group shows; 9 exhibitions held per year in house gallery; 10 exhibitions in variety of locations
Publications: Creative Growth Art Center newsletter, 3-4 issues per year
Activities: Docent progs; lects open to pub, 6-8 vis lectrs per yr; competitions with awards; schols & fels offered; retail store sells prints, original art, reproductions

M **EAST BAY ASIAN LOCAL DEVELOPMENT CORP (EBALDC),** Asian Resource Gallery, 1825 San Pablo Ave, Ste 201 Oakland, CA 94612-1517. Tel 510-287-5353; Fax 510-763-4143; Email communications@ebaldc.org; Web: www.ebaldc.org; *Exec Dir* Joshua Simon
Open Mon - Fri 9 AM - 5 PM; No admis fee; Estab 1983 to promote Asian art & Asian artists; One gallery
Income: $3000 (financed by donations)
Special Subjects: Historical Material, Photography
Collections: Collection of photographs, paintings, mixed media, history exhibits on Asian groups from China, Japan & Korea
Exhibitions: Every month rotating exhibits include different artists in the Bay Area

L **LANEY COLLEGE LIBRARY,** Art Section, 900 Fallon St, Oakland, CA 94607-4893. Tel 510-464-3500; Fax 510-464-3264; Web: www.laney-peralta.cc.ca.us; *Head Librn* Evelyn Lord; *Ref* Phillippa Caldeira; *Acquisition & Technical Svcs* Autumn Sullivan
Open Mon - Thurs 8 AM - 9 PM, Fri 8 AM - 2 PM, Sat 8:30 AM - 1:30 PM, cl Sun; No admis fee; Estab 1954; Circ 78,000; Average Annual Attendance: 350,000
Library Holdings: Audio Tapes, Book Volumes 81,000, CD-ROMs, Cassettes, DVDs, Filmstrips, Kodachrome Transparencies, Lantern Slides, Motion Pictures, Other Holdings Compact discs; Laser discs, Periodical Subscriptions 300, Prints, Records, Reproductions, Slides, Video Tapes
Exhibitions: Exhibitions vary; call for details
Publications: Monthly newsletter

M **MILLS COLLEGE ART MUSEUM,** 5000 MacArthur Blvd, Aron Art Center Oakland, CA 94613-1301. Tel 510-430-2164 & 3250; Fax 510-430-3168; Email museum@mills.edu; Web: mcam.mills.edu; *Dir* Stephanie Hanor; *Mgr Exhibs & Colls* Luke Turner; *Prog Dir* Jayna Swartzman-Brosky
Open Tues & Thurs - Sun 11 AM - 4 PM, Wed 11 AM - 7:30 PM, cl Mon; No admis fee; Estab 1925 to show contemporary & traditional painting, sculpture & ceramics, exhibitions from permanent & loan collections; Gallery is Spanish colonial architecture & has 5500 sq ft main exhibition space, with skylight full length of gallery; Average Annual Attendance: 10,000
Income: Financed by college funds; grants & gifts
Purchases: Nagle, DeFeo, Bellows, Kales
Special Subjects: Drawings, Painting-American, Photography, Pottery, Prints, Southwestern Art, Textiles, Woodcarvings, Woodcuts
Collections: Asian & Guatemalan Collection (textiles), European & American Collection (prints, drawings & ceramics), Regional California Collection (paintings, drawings & prints), photographs, European & American Collection, Regional California Collection
Exhibitions: Five Internat. women artists
Publications: Annual bulletin; exhibition catalogs
Activities: Lects open to public, 8-10 vis lectrs per yr; gallery talks; tours; individual paintings & original objects of art lent; book traveling exhibs; originate traveling exhibs

M **OAKLAND MUSEUM OF CALIFORNIA,** Art Dept, 1000 Oak St at 10th St, Oakland, CA 94607-4892. Tel 510-238-2200, 238-3005; Fax 510-238-2258; Email dmpower@museumca.org; Web: http://museumca.org; *Exec Dir* Lori Fogarty
Open Wed - Thurs 11 AM - 5 PM, Fri 11 AM - 9 PM, Sat - Sun 10 AM - 6 PM, cl Mon & Tues, New Year's Day, Jul 4, Thanksgiving & Christmas; Admis general $15.95, seniors & students w/ID $10.95, youth 9-17 $6.95, mems, children 8 & under free; The Oakland Mus of California comprises three departments: Natural Sciences (formerly the Snow Mus of Natural History, founded 1922); History (formerly the Oakland Pub Mus, founded 1910); & the Art Department (formerly the Oakland Art Mus, founded 1916); The Oakland Mus occupies a 4 sq block, three-storied site on the south shore of Lake Merritt. Designed by Kevin Roche, John Dinkeloo & Assoc, the mus is a three-tiered complex of exhibition galleries, with surrounding gardens, pools, courts & lawns, constructed so that the roof of each level becomes a garden & a terrace for the one above. The Art Department has a large hall with 20 small exhibition bays for the permanent collection & 3 galleries for one-person or group shows as well as the Oakes Gallery; Average Annual Attendance: 500,000
Income: Financed by city funds, pvt donations & Oakland Mus of California Foundation
Special Subjects: Crafts, Drawings, Painting-American, Photography, Prints, Sculpture
Collections: Paintings, sculpture, prints, illustrations, photographs, by California artists & artists dealing with California subjects, in a range that includes sketches & paintings by early artist-explorers, gold Rush genre pictures, massive Victorian landscapes, examples of the California Decorative Style, Impressionist, Post-Impressionist, Abstract Expressionist, & other contemporary works
Publications: The Museum of California, quarterly; Oakland Museum of California, bimonthly calendar of exhibs & events
Activities: Classes for adults & children; family progs; docent training; teacher resources; lects open to pub; gallery talks; tours; individual paintings & original objects of art lent to other mus & galleries for specific exhibs; originate traveling exhibs; mus shop sells books, magazines, reproductions, prints, slides & jewelry

L **Library & Archives,** 1000 Oak St, Oakland, CA 94607-4892. Tel 510-318-8400; Fax 510-318-8416; Web: www.museumca.org; *Dir OMCA Lab* Barbara Henry
Open Wed- Sun 11 AM - 5 PM; Admis fee adults $12, seniors & students w/ID $9, youth 9-18 $6, children 8 & under & mems free; Estab 1969; Library maintains extensive files on California art & artists. For in-house use only, cl to the pub at this time
Income: Financed by city & state appropriation
Library Holdings: Auction Catalogs, Audio Tapes, Book Volumes, Cassettes, Clipping Files, Exhibition Catalogs, Lantern Slides, Memorabilia, Periodical Subscriptions 23, Photographs
Special Subjects: American Western Art, Ceramics, Crafts, Decorative Arts, Drawings, Folk Art, Glass, Graphic Arts, Jewelry, Landscapes, Painting-American, Photography, Portraits, Posters, Printmaking, Prints, Sculpture
Activities: Lects open to pub; gallery talks; tours; mus shop sells books

L **OAKLAND PUBLIC LIBRARY,** Art, Music, History & Literature Section, 125 14th St, Main Library Oakland, CA 94612-4397. Tel 510-238-3136; 238-3178; Email tdowns@oaklandlibrary.org; Web: www.oaklandlibrary.org; *Dir Library Svcs* Gerry Garzon; *Assoc Dir* Jamie Turbak; *Supvr Librn, Branches* Jenera Burton
Open Sun 1 PM - 5PM, Mon & Tues 10AM - 5:30PM, Wed & Thurs noon - 8PM, Fri noon - 5:30 PM, Sat 10AM - 5:30PM; Library cooperates with the Oakland Mus & local groups
Purchases: $30,000
Library Holdings: Audio Tapes, Book Volumes 1,010,000, Cassettes, Compact Disks, DVDs, Framed Reproductions, Other Holdings Posters, Periodical Subscriptions 2745, Records, Reproductions, Video Tapes
Special Subjects: Architecture, Ceramics, Decorative Arts, Graphic Arts, Historical Material, Maps, Metalwork, Photography
Collections: Picture Collections, Black History Collection, Family History & Genealogy Collection, Map Collection, Music Scores & Sheet Music Collections, Oakland History Room
Publications: Museum catalogs

M **PRO ARTS,** 150 Frank H. Ogawa Plaza, Oakland, CA 94612. Tel 510-763-4361; Fax 510-763-9470; Email info@proartsgallery.org; Web: www.proartsgallery.org; *Exec Dir* Natalia Mount; *Assoc Dir* Sarah Lockhart; *Gallery Mgr* Michelle Kim
Open Tues - Fri noon - 6 PM, special event weekends; No admis fee; Estab 1974 as a contemporary art exhibition space for static & non-static works, nonprofit; Gallery located in Frank Ogawa Plaza, downtown Oakland; Average Annual Attendance: 65,000; Mem: 1,000; dues $45 & up, monthly meetings
Income: Mem & grants
Exhibitions: Rotating exhibits every 2 months; on-site & off-site installations
Activities: Classes for children; gallery talks; community partnerships; youth arts initiative events; mus shop sells original art, reproductions & prints

OCEANSIDE

M **MISSION SAN LUIS REY DE FRANCIA,** Mission San Luis Rey Museum, 4050 Mission Ave, Oceanside, CA 92057-6402. Tel 760-757-3651; Fax 760-757-4613; Email museumcurator@sanluisrey.org; Web: www.sanluisrey.org; *Exec Dir* Fr David Gaa OFM; *Admin* Ed Gabarra; *Mus Cur* Bradford Claybourn

Open daily 10 AM - 4:00 PM; Admis family $25, adults $6, senior 65 and over & active military $5, youth $4, children 5 & younger free; Estab 1798 to protect, conserve & display artifacts which reflect the history of the mission; art & history; Average Annual Attendance: 60,000; Mem: Individual $60
Income: Financed by Franciscan Friars of Santa Barbara Province
Library Holdings: Memorabilia, Original Art Works, Original Documents, Photographs, Prints, Records, Sculpture
Special Subjects: American Indian Art, Archaeology, Architecture, Art History, Furniture, Historical Material, History of Art & Archaeology, Latin American Art, Mexican Art, Painting-American, Painting-European, Painting-Spanish, Religious Art, Restorations, Textiles
Collections: Artifacts from 18th century - present, furniture, paintings, statuary, 18th & 19th century religious vestments & vessels & other historical objects from early mission days in California, Spanish colonial and Rancho periods, Luseno Indian Baskets
Activities: Educ dept; docent training; 3 lects open to public; concerts; gallery talks; tours; individual paintings & original objects of art lent to qualified museums; sales of books, original art, prints, jewelry & artisan crafts

OJAI

M **BEATRICE WOOD CENTER FOR THE ARTS,** 8560 Ojai-Santa Paula Rd, Ojai, CA 93023-9351. Tel 805-646-3381; Fax 805-646-0560; Web: www.beatricewood.com; *Dir* Kevin Wallace
Open Fri-Sun 11AM-5PM
Collections: works by Beatrice Wood; sculpture; paintings

A **OJAI ART CENTER,** 113 S Montgomery, Ojai, CA 93023; PO Box 331, Ojai, CA 93024-0331. Tel 805-646-0117; Fax 805-646-0252; Email ojaiartcenter@aol.com; *Pres* Len Klaff; *Dir* Teri Mettala
Open Tues - Sun Noon - 4 PM; No admis fee; Estab 1936 to foster all art disciplines in community; Gallery is 40 x 50 ft, high ceilings, with a large hanging area; Average Annual Attendance: 60,000; Mem: 400; dues family $40, adult $30; annual meeting 1st Mon of Feb
Income: Financed by mem, class & special event fees
Exhibitions: Twelve monthly exhibitions; Annual Watercolor Competition
Publications: Newsletter, monthly; Rivertalk, ann poetry anthology
Activities: Classes for adults & children; dramatic progs; lects open to pub; concerts; gallery talks; competitions with awards; schols offered

ORANGE

M **CHAPMAN UNIVERSITY GUGGENHEIM GALLERY,** Moulton Center, One University Dr Orange, CA 92866-1005. Tel 714-997-6815
Open to public every day from 10 AM - 9:50 PM; Admis adults 30 RMB, students, senior citizens, military & handicapped 15 RMB, children under 1.3m in height & members no charge; admis after 6 PM adults 20 RMB, students 15 RMB; Establ Sept 2005
Collections: Paintings; sculpture; photographs
Activities: Special events & receptions

OROVILLE

M **BUTTE COLLEGE,** Art Gallery, 3536 Butte Campus Dr, Oroville, CA 95965-8399. Tel 530-895-2877; 895-2404; Fax 530-895-2414; Email oneilal@butte.edu; donnellyda@butte.edu; Web: www.butte.edu; *Co-Chair ADAD Dept* Alexandra O'Neil; *Co-Chair ADAD Dept* Daniel Donnelly
Open Mon - Thurs 10 AM - 4 PM, Wed until 7:30 PM; No admis fee, donations accepted; Estab 1981, a contemporary col art gallery; An educationally oriented exhib space with rotating shows featuring the work of student & local artists as well as nationally & internationally known artists; Average Annual Attendance: 5,000
Income: Financed by fundraising, art sales, district funding
Purchases: Graham Nash prints; Janet Turner prints; Robert Burride originals
Exhibitions: Annual Juried Student Art Exhibit; contemporary art of a local, regional & national orientation
Activities: Classes for adults; lect open to public, 5 vis lectrs per yr; gallery talks; sponsoring of competitions; schols available; sales shop sells original art, prints, artist cards & memorabilia, gallery souvenirs

OXNARD

M **CARNEGIE ART MUSEUM,** 424 S C St, Oxnard, CA 93030-5944. Tel 805-385-8157; Fax 805-483-3654; Web: www.carnegieam.org; *Cultural Arts Supv* Suzzane Bellah
Open Thurs - Sat 10 AM - 5 PM, Sun 1 - 5 PM; Admis $3 donation suggested; Estab 1980 as art museum & to house & manage City art coll; 5000 sq ft of gallery space; Average Annual Attendance: 20,000; Mem: 500, dues $25 & up
Income: financed by endowment, city appropriation, city & nonprofit support
Collections: California Art: 1920 to present
Exhibitions: Changing major exhibits quarterly
Publications: Master of the Miniature: The Art of Robert Olszewski; Municipal Art Collection Catalogue; Quechuan Rug Catalogue; Theodore Lukits Catalogue
Activities: Art classes, CAM Book Club; lects; poetry series; special events

M **CHANNEL ISLANDS MARITIME MUSEUM,** 3900 Bluefin Cr, Oxnard, CA 93035. Tel 805-984-6260; Fax 805-984-5970; Email office@cimmvc.org; Web: www.vcmm.org; *Exec Dir* Julia Chambers; *Cur Arts* Kate Crouse
Open daily 10 AM - 4 PM; Admis adults $7, seniors/students/military $5, children 6-17 $3, free admis 3rd Thurs of month; Estab 1991; Collection of maritime paintings (17th century - 20th century) and historic ship models; Average Annual Attendance: 25,000; Mem: 1000; dues variable
Income: $320,000 (financed by mem, contributions & grants)
Library Holdings: Book Volumes 3000
Special Subjects: Graphics, Historical Material, Manuscripts, Maps, Marine Painting, Painting-American, Painting-British, Painting-Dutch, Painting-European, Painting-Flemish, Photography, Prints, Scrimshaw, Watercolors, Etchings & Engravings
Collections: Nelson Maritime Arts Foundation Collection of Maritime Paintings, Prints & Ship Models (Dutch 17th century - Modern 20th century), Antique POW Bone models, Ship Models of the Age of Sail, Edward Marple Model Collection, McNish Scrimshaw, Nelson Library, William Fairburn Archives, LaJenelle, Whales
Exhibitions: Nautica: Annual Juried Maritime Show; international & local artists exhibit 4 times per year; Biennial Exhibit of the American Society of Marine Artists; Plein Air Festival Exhibit
Publications: Marple Exhibit Catalogue
Activities: Classes for adults & children; dramatic progs; docent training; lects open to pub, 12 - 18 vis lectrs per yr; gallery talks; tours; sponsoring of competitions; ship model guild meets monthly 3rd Tues; original objects of art lent to mus; originates traveling exhibs; mus shop sells books, original art, reproductions & prints

PACIFIC GROVE

A **PACIFIC GROVE ART CENTER,** 568 Lighthouse Ave, Pacific Grove, CA 93950-2624. Tel 831-375-2208; Email generalinfopgac@gmail.com; Web: www.pgartcenter.org; *Preparator* Mark Davy; *Pres Bd* Arthur Rogers; *VPres* Amanda Menefee; *Dir* Teresa Brown; *Gallery Asst* Jeanne Hamilton
Open Wed - Sat Noon - 5 PM, Sun 1 - 4 PM; No admis fee; Estab 1969 to promote the arts & encourage the artists of the Monterey Peninsula & California; Four galleries consist of 6000 sq ft of exhibition space, showing traditional & contemporary fine art & photography; galleries are available for classes & lects; Average Annual Attendance: 25,000; Mem: 550; dues bus & club $100, family $30, single $25; annual meeting in Nov
Income: Financed by grants, donations, mem. Dues & income from lease of studio space
Collections: Photography, painting
Exhibitions: Multiple exhibits every 7 weeks throughout the year
Publications: Newsletter every 7 weeks
Activities: Educ dept; classes for adults & children; dramatic progs; concerts; lects open to pub & for mems only; 3-4 vis lectrs per yr; concerts; gallery talks; competitions; tours; schols

PALM DESERT

M **IMAGO GALLERIES,** 45-450 Hwy 74, Palm Desert, CA 92260. Tel 760-776-9890; Fax 760-776-9891; Email info@imagogalleries.com; Web: www.imagogalleries.com; *Co-owner* Leisa Austin; *Co-owner* David Austin
Open Tues - Sat 10 AM - 5 PM & by appointment; Estab 1991; 18,000 sq ft gallery & 6,000 sq ft exterior sculpture garden
Special Subjects: Sculpture
Collections: works by contemporary artists; paintings; sculpture
Exhibitions: Temporary exhibits
Activities: Lects; fashion shows; performance arts; concerts

PALM SPRINGS

M **PALM SPRINGS ART MUSEUM,** 101 Museum Dr, Palm Springs, CA 92262-5659; PO Box 2310, Palm Springs, CA 92263-2310. Tel 760-322-4800; Fax 760-327-5069; Email info@psmuseum.org; Web: www.psmuseum.org; *Exec Dir* Steven A Nash, PhD; *Chief Cur* Katherine Hough; *Deputy Dir Art, Sr Cur* Daniell Cornell, PhD; *Deputy Dir Educ & Pub Progs* Robert Brasier; *Librn* Frank Lopez
Open Tues, Wed, Fri, Sat, Sun 10 AM - 5 PM, Thurs Noon - 8 PM, cl Mon; Admis adults $12.50, seniors $10.50, others $5; Estab 1938; Average Annual Attendance: 130,000; Mem: Dues individual $50, family/dual $85
Income: Financed by pvt funds
Library Holdings: Auction Catalogs, Audio Tapes, Book Volumes 12,000, CD-ROMs, Cassettes, Clipping Files, DVDs, Exhibition Catalogs, Manuscripts, Memorabilia, Original Documents, Pamphlets, Periodical Subscriptions 28, Photographs, Slides, Video Tapes
Special Subjects: American Indian Art, American Western Art, Art Education, Bronzes, Mexican Art, Mixed Media, Photography, Pre-Columbian Art, Sculpture
Exhibitions: Contemporary Glass, ongoing; A dialogue between Ancient and Modern: Selections from the Permanent Collection, ongoing
Publications: InSight, mem mag, quarterly; Spec exhibit catalogs ann
Activities: Classes for adults & children; docent training; dramatic progs; student visits to mus; out-reach art classes; on-site child/adult classes; lects open to pub & mem only; concerts; gallery talks; tours; competitions with awards; schols; exten dept serves pub schools; book traveling exhibs 4 per yr; originate traveling exhibs; mus shop sells books, reproductions, jewelry, educational children's toys, cards & artist-designed items

PALO ALTO

A **PALO ALTO ART CENTER,** 1313 Newell Rd, Palo Alto, CA 94303. Tel 650-329-2366; Fax 650-326-6165; Email artcenter@cityofpaloalto.org; Web: www.cityofpaloalto.org/artcenter; *Vol Coordr* Grace Abusharkh; *Studio Supv* Fanny Retsek; *Operations Mgr* Rebecca Barbee; *Dir Edu* Lucy Larson; *Dir* Karen Kienzle; *VChmn* Marsha Pugsley; *Mus Shop Mgr* Elizabeth Evans; *Coordr Child Art* Rebecca Passarello; *Coordr Family Progs & Outreach* Lauren Baines; *Mktg Coordr* Ken Heiman; *Coordr Exhib* Selene Foster; *Preparator* Keith Southern
Open Tues - Sat 10 AM - 5 PM, Thurs 10 AM - 9 PM, Sun 1 PM - 5 PM, cl Mon; No admis fee; Estab 1971 - your place to discover art, see, make & be inspired because everyone is an artist; Average Annual Attendance: 90,000; Mem: 700; dues $1000, $500, $250, $100, $80, $50
Income: $1,000,000 (financed by municipal funds, private donations & earned income)

Exhibitions: Exhibits rotate every 3 months
Activities: Classes for adults & children; docent training; lects open to pub, 6-8 vis lectrs per yr; gallery talks; tours; festivals; after hours events; rentals; birthday parties; vol opportunities; mus shop sells books, original art, ceramics, glass, jewelry, gifts, reproductions, prints & objects for sale related to exhibitions

M **PALO ALTO JUNIOR MUSEUM & ZOO,** 1451 Middlefield Rd, Palo Alto, CA 94301-3351. Tel 650-329-2111; Fax 650-473-1965; *Dir* Rachel Meyer
Open Tues - Sat 10 AM - 5 PM, Sun 1 - 4 PM, cl Mon, cl New Years, Easter, July 4, Thanksgiving & Christmas; No admis fee; Estab 1932, completely renovated in 1969; Average Annual Attendance: 150,000
Income: Financed by city appropriation
Collections: Interactive children's exhibits
Publications: Notes, monthly
Activities: Classes; self-guided tours; exten dept

PASADENA

A **ARMORY CENTER FOR THE ARTS,** 145 N Raymond Ave, Pasadena, CA 91103-3921. Tel 626-792-5101; Fax 626-449-0139; Email information@armoryarts.org; Web: www.armoryarts.org; *Exec Dir* Scott Ward; *Dir Gallery Progs* Irene Tsatos; *Gallery Progs Mgr* Sinead Finnerty-Pyne; *Dir Communs* Jon Lapointe; *Dir Devel* Elisa Laris; *Dir Fin & Opers* Slade Bellum
Open Gallery: Tues - Sun Noon - 5 PM; Office: Mon - Fri 9 AM - 5 PM; Admis $5 suggested donation, seniors, students & mems free; Estab 1974 for contemporary visual arts, exhibitions, performances & education; Average Annual Attendance: 35,000; Mem: 300; dues $35; annual meeting in Sept
Income: $1.3 million (financed by endowment, mem, city & state appropriation, foundations & corporations)
Special Subjects: Architecture, Bookplates & Bindings, Ceramics, Collages, Graphics, Juvenile Art, Painting-American, Photography, Portraits, Pottery, Prints, Sculpture, Watercolors, Woodcuts
Collections: Installation, Performance Art, Urban Design
Activities: Classes for adults & children; musical performances; lects open to pub; concerts; gallery talks; tours; fels; book traveling exhibs 1 per yr; originate traveling exhibs 1 per yr; mus shop sells books

L **ART CENTER COLLEGE OF DESIGN,** James Lemont Fogg Memorial Library, 1700 Lida St, Pasadena, CA 91103-1999. Tel 626-396-2233; Fax 626-568-0428; Email library@artcenter.edu; Web: hera.artcenter.edu; *VPres & Dir* Elizabeth Galloway; *Catalog Librn* Alison Holt; *Acquisitions Librn* George Porcari; *Circ Supv* Mark Von Schlegell; *Circ Supv* Nolina Burge; *Reference & Pub Servs Librn* Claudia Michelle Betty; *Photo Research Cur* Jennifer Faist
Open Mon - Thurs 8 AM - 10 PM, Fri 8 AM - 7PM; Estab to provide reference & visual resources for the designers who study & teach at Art Center College of Design; Circ 90,000
Income: Financed by institution & private grants
Purchases: $85,000 (books); $45,000 (periodicals); $30,000 (videos & slides)
Library Holdings: Book Volumes 65,000, Cassettes, Clipping Files 28,000, Exhibition Catalogs 1850, Motion Pictures 100, Periodical Subscriptions 450, Reproductions, Slides 90,000, Video Tapes 2200
Special Subjects: Advertising Design, Commercial Art, Graphic Design, Illustration, Industrial Design, Photography

M **Alyce de Roulet Williamson Gallery**, 1700 Lida St, Pasadena, CA 91103. Tel 623-396-2446, 623-396-2397; Fax 626-405-9104; Email stephen.nowlin@artcenter.edu; Web: www.williamsongallery.net; *Dir* Stephen Nowlin
Open Tues - Thurs & Sat 12 PM - 5 PM, Fri 12 PM - 9 PM, cl holidays
Collections: works of contemporary fine art & design

M **NORTON SIMON MUSEUM,** 411 W Colorado Blvd, Pasadena, CA 91105-1825. Tel 626-449-6840; Fax 626-796-4978; Email info@nortonsimon.org; Web: www.nortonsimon.org; *Pres* Walter W Timoshuk; *Chief Cur* Carol Togneri; *Dir External Affairs* Leslie C Denk; *Dir Opers* John Sudolcan
Open Mon & Wed - Thurs noon - 5 PM, Fri - Sat 11 AM - 8 PM, Sun 11 AM - 5 PM; Admis adults $15, seniors $12; members, children 18 & under & active military & students with ID free; Estab 1974; this museum brings collections of European paintings, prints & sculptures. Asian sculpture spanning 2000 yrs; Average Annual Attendance: 170,000; Mem: Dues $75-$1000
Income: Financed by endowment, mem, city appropriation, tours, admis, contributions, bookshop & grounds maintenance
Special Subjects: Asian Art, Bronzes, Graphics, Landscapes, Painting-American, Painting-European, Painting-Flemish, Painting-French, Photography, Portraits, Prints, Religious Art, Renaissance Art, Sculpture, Sculpture, Tapestries, Tapestries, Woodcuts
Collections: Art spanning 20 centuries: including paintings, sculptures & graphics from the early Renaissance through the 20th century, Indian & Southeast Asian sculpture
Publications: Masterpieces from the Norton Simon Museum; Handbook of the Norton Simon Museum & Coll Cats
Activities: Classes for adults; tours for children; private guided tours; lectrs open to pub; 10 vis lectrs; concerts; gallery talks; internships; mus shop sells books, reproductions, prints

M **PASADENA CITY COLLEGE,** Art Galleries, 1570 E Colorado Blvd, Center for the Arts (CA103) Visual, Performing & Media Arts Division Pasadena, CA 91106-2003. Tel 626-585-7238; Fax 626-585-7914; Email artgalleriespec@gmail.com; Web: www.pasadena.edu/campus-life/the-arts/the-galleries/index.php; *Gallery Dir* Mahara T Sinclaire
Open Mon & Tues 11AM - 5PM, Wed 11AM 7PM, Fri noon-3PM; No admis fee; Estab to show work that relates to class given at Pasadena City College; Gallery is housed in separate building; 1000 sq ft; Average Annual Attendance: 20,000; Mem: 2800
Income: Financed by the college
Collections: Small permanent collection of contemporary art, Contemporary Art
Exhibitions: Rotating exhibits & juried student show
Publications: Mailers for each show
Activities: Educ dept; lect open to public, 4 vis lectrs per year; gallery talks; competitions; scholarships; book traveling exhibitions occasionally

M **PASADENA MUSEUM OF CALIFORNIA ART,** 490 E Union St, Pasadena, CA 91101; 495 E Colorado Blvd, Pasadena, CA 91101-2024. Tel 626-568-3665; Fax 626-568-3674; Email info@pmcaonline.org; Web: www.pmcaonline.org; *Exec Dir* Jenkins Shannon; *Chmn* David Partridge; *Pub Rels* Emma Jacobson-Sive; *Treas* Ted McCarthy; *Gallery Mgr* Emmett Clements; *Exhib Mgr* Erin Aitali; *Exhib Designer* Sergio Gomez; *Mktg & Outreach Coordr* Alexis Kaneshiro; *Mem & Bookstore Assoc* Susan Wang
Open Wed - Sun 12 - 5 PM; cl New Years, Fourth of July, Thanksgiving & Christmas; Admis adults $7, seniors & students $5, children under 12 & mems no admis fee; Estab 2002 with the mission to educate & enrich the pub through the study & presentation of works of Calif art, design & architecture from 1850 - present; 11,000 sq ft exhib space; pvt nonprofit org; Average Annual Attendance: 35,000; Mem: dues Dir $500, Guild Level $200, Studio Level $50, Student & Senior $25
Special Subjects: American Western Art, Drawings, Furniture, Graphics, Landscapes, Painting-American, Photography, Portraits
Collections: Mus houses no perm coll; exhibs focus on Calif art, design & architecture from 1850 - present, paintings; prints; drawings; graphic arts; photographs
Activities: Guided tours; research in contemporary & historic Calif art; panel discussions; lects open to the public; 10 vis lectrs per yr; gallery talks; tours; exhibs: loan exhibs; traveling exhibs; Calif Design Biennial, Calif Air Club Gold Medal Exhib; mus shop sells books, prints, clothing, jewelry, design objects & other mus related items for sale

M **PASADENA MUSEUM OF HISTORY,** 470 W Walnut St, Pasadena, CA 91103-3562. Tel 626-577-1660; Fax 626-577-1662; Email info@pasadenahistory.org; Web: www.pasadenahistory.org; *Dir Exhib* Ardis Willwerth; *Exec Dir* Jeannette O'Malley; *Colls Mgr* Laura Verlaque
Open Wed - Sun Noon - 5 PM; Suggested donation adults $5, students & seniors $4, children under 12 free; Estab 1924 for the preservation & collection of historical data relating to Pasadena; Historical house with American Impressionist Art; 2 exhibit galleries, Finnish Farm House; Average Annual Attendance: 13,000; Mem: 1400; dues $50 - $1000
Income: $159,000 (financed through mem, endowment & contributions)
Library Holdings: Book Volumes 1500, Clipping Files, Manuscripts, Memorabilia, Original Art Works, Photographs 750,000
Special Subjects: Carpets & Rugs, Ceramics, Costumes, Crafts, Decorative Arts, Dolls, Embroidery, Folk Art, Furniture, Glass, Architecture, Decorative Arts, Historical Material, Landscapes, Painting-American, Period Rooms, Portraits, Silver, Textiles, Watercolors
Collections: Collection of documents & artifacts relating to Pasadena, Collection of paintings by California artists, European & American furniture (antiques & reproductions), over one million, rare books & manuscripts, Turn of the Century Life Style on Millionaire's Row, Costumes
Exhibitions: Calif Art Club Juries Exhib; 3-4 changing exhibits annually
Publications: Quarterly newsletter
Activities: Classes for adults; docent & junior docent training; lect open to public, 4-8 vis lectrs per year; gallery talks; tours; sales shop sells books, magazines, prints & gift items

L **PASADENA PUBLIC LIBRARY,** Fine Arts Dept, 285 E Walnut St, Pasadena, CA 91101-1598. Tel 626-744-4066; Web: www.pasadenapubliclibrary.net; *Dir* Jan Sanders; *Prin Librn & Information Access Servs* Beth Walker
Open Mon - Thurs 9 AM - 9 PM, Fri & Sat 9 AM - 6 PM, Sun 1 - 5 PM; No admis fee; Art dept estab 1927
Income: Financed by endowments & gifts, for materials only
Library Holdings: Audio Tapes 3,950, Book Volumes 15,636, Compact Disks 9,600, DVDs 2,377, Fiche, Other Holdings Audiobooks on CD 2,240, Periodical Subscriptions 60, Photographs, Video Tapes 3,500

M **SIDE STREET PROJECTS,** 730 N Fair Oaks Ave, Pasadena, CA 91109; PO Box 90432, Pasadena, CA 91109. Tel 626-798-7774; Fax 626-798-7747; Email info@sidestreet.org; Web: www.sidestreet.org; *Dir* Emily Hopkins; *Prog Dir* Michelle Glass; *Pres Bd Dir* Jon Lapointe
No admis fee; Estab 1992, became completely a mobile org in 2008
Exhibitions: Installations & projects by contemporary artists, local & international
Activities: Classes for adults & children; artmobile; lect open to public

M **UNIVERSITY OF SOUTHERN CALIFORNIA,** USC Pacific Asia Museum, 46 N Los Robles Ave, Pasadena, CA 91101-2009. Tel 626-449-2742; Fax 626-449-2754; Web: www.pacificasiamuseum.usc.edu; *Dir* Christina Yu Yu, PhD; *Educ Cur* Amelia Chapman; *Chief Develop Officer* Sandra Chen Lou; *Deputy Dir* Susana Smith-Bavtista, PhD; *Mktg & Pub Rels* Carol A Chaplin; *Asst Cur* Yeonsoo Chee; *Bus Mgr* Anthony Lee; *Sr Develop Assoc* Nadiya Conner; *Registrar* Annie Lee
Open Wed - Sun 10 AM - 6 PM, cl holidays; Admis adults & non-members $10, seniors & students $7, under 12, USC faculty, staff, students & alumni free; Estab 1971 to promote understanding of the cultures of the Pacific & Far East through exhibitions, lectures, dance, music & concerts. Through these activities, the mus helps to increase mutual respect & appreciation of both the diversities & similarities of Asian/Pacific & Western cultures; The building was designed by Marston, Van Pelt & Mayberry, architects for Grace Nicholson. The building is listed in the national register of historic places as the Grace Nicholson Building. There is 11,000 sq ft of exhibition space; Average Annual Attendance: 50,000; Mem: 900; dues associates $1,500-$10,000; plum blossom $500; chrysanthemum $250; lotus $100; bamboo $55; student $30
Library Holdings: Auction Catalogs, Book Volumes, Exhibition Catalogs, Memorabilia, Photographs
Special Subjects: Asian Art, Bronzes, Calligraphy, Ceramics, Coins & Medals, Decorative Arts, Folk Art, Furniture, Ivory, Jade, Miniatures, Painting-Japanese, Porcelain, Pottery, Prints, Sculpture, Tapestries, Textiles, Woodcarvings

Collections: Bronzes, Buddhist sculptures, Chinese & Japanese paintings & ceramics, Chinese textiles, Southeast Asian ceramics, Chinese, Japanese Prints, Asian Art, Himalayan Art
Publications: Exhibit catalogs
Activities: Classes for adults & children; docent training; lects open to pub; 22 vis lectrs per yr; gallery talks; tours; concerts; schols; original objects of art lent to other mus, East-West Bank & limited number of libraries; originate traveling exhibs to schools, libraries & other mus; mus shop sells books, original art, reproductions, prints, clothing jewelry & collectibles

POMONA

M **AMERICAN MUSEUM OF CERAMIC ART,** 399 N Garey Ave, Pomona, CA 91767-5431. Tel 909-865-3146; Fax 909-629-1067; Email frontdesk@ceramicmuseum.org; Web: www.ceramicmuseum.org; *Exec Dir* Beth Ann Gerstein; *Admin & Mem Mgr* Tiffany Zhu; *Asst Cur* Gino Ruzi; *Coll & Admin Clerk* Josh McCance; *Pres & Founder* David Armstrong; *Dir Advancement* Carolyn Wagner; *Mktg Mgr* Whitney Hanlon
Open Wed - Sun Noon - 5 PM, second Sat of each month Noon - 9 PM, cl New Year's Day, Thanksgiving, Christmas Eve & Day, July 4th; Admis adults $7, seniors & students $5, children & members free; Estab 2004; Average Annual Attendance: 15,000; Mem: 710
Income: 950,000; donations, grants, mem dues, gift store sales
Library Holdings: DVDs
Special Subjects: Ceramics, Decorative Arts, Folk Art
Publications: quarterly newsletter; exhib catalogues
Activities: Classes for adults & children; docent training; lects open to pub, lects for mems only, vis lectrs 12 per yr; gallery talks; tours; arts festivals; concerts; films; guided tours; competitions; hobby workshops; lectrs; loan exhib; theater; semi-annual event: Pottery Market; summer & winter member only events; temporary & traveling exhibs; mus shop sells books, magazines, original art, dvds & other items

M **LATINO ART MUSEUM,** 281 S Thomas St, Ste 105 Pomona, CA 91766-1740. Tel 909-484-2618, 909-620-6009; Email latinoartmuseum@msn.com; Web: www.lamoa.net; *Pres & Founder* Graciela H Nardi; *Treas* Mario Gee Lopez; *Secy* David Pion-Berlin
Call for hours; No admis fee; Estab 2001; Contemporary art; Average Annual Attendance: 1,200; Mem: 500
Income: Financed by mem, donations, grants
Library Holdings: Auction Catalogs, Book Volumes, CD-ROMs, Cards, Photographs, Prints, Reproductions, Sculpture
Special Subjects: Art Education, Ceramics, Collages, Conceptual Art, Drawings, Etchings & Engravings, Glass, Graphics, Hispanic Art, Jewelry, Landscapes, Latin American Art, Mexican Art, Miniatures, Mixed Media, Mosaics, Painting-European, Painting-Italian, Painting-Spanish, Pewter, Photography, Porcelain, Portraits, Posters, Pottery, Pre-Columbian Art, Prints, Sculpture, Silver, Stained Glass, Textiles, Watercolors, Woodcarvings, Woodcuts, Painting-European, Painting-French, Bronzes
Collections: Paintings; photographs; sculptures; books
Publications: Yearbooks, 2008, 2009, 2010, 2012, 2013 - 2015
Activities: Classes for adults & children; special events; rental facilities; docent training; art classes; lects open to pub; concerts; gallery talks; tours; organize traveling exhibs; mus shop sells books, magazines, original art, reproductions, prints & mus related items

QUINCY

M **PLUMAS COUNTY MUSEUM,** 500 Jackson St, Quincy, CA 95971-9412. Tel 530-283-6320; Fax 530-283-6081; Email pcmuseum@digitalpath.net; Web: www.countyofplumas.com/museum; *Asst Dir* Paul Russell; *Dir* Scott Lawson
Open winter Tues - Sat 10 AM - 4 PM; Admis fee adults $2, students $1; Estab 1964 to preserve the past for the enjoyment & edification of the present & future generations; 1878 historical home next door has been restored & opened to the pub with period rooms; Average Annual Attendance: 18,000; Mem: 700; general per yr $25; $35; $50; $1,000
Income: Financed by members & county budget
Purchases: $300
Library Holdings: Memorabilia, Photographs, Slides
Special Subjects: American Indian Art, Anthropology, Anthropology, Architecture, Asian Art, Bronzes, Carpets & Rugs, Ceramics, Ceramics, Coins & Medals, Costumes, Crafts, Decorative Arts, Dioramas, Dolls, Embroidery, Furniture, Furniture, Glass, Gold, Graphics, Historical Material, Historical Material, Jade, Metalwork, Painting-American, Painting-American, Photography, Porcelain, Silver, Stained Glass, Prints
Collections: Antique period furnishings, Indian (Maidu) artifacts, dolls, clothing, mining & logging artifacts, domestic, jewelry, guns, period furniture, Historic Home Museum adjacent, railroad coll, memorabilia, Variel Home, dolls, sculptures, antiques
Exhibitions: Various Local Artists
Publications: Plumas County Museum Newsletter, two times a year
Activities: Classes for children; docent training; lects open to public; 3 lectrs per yr; gallery talks; tours; sponsoring of competitions; museum shop sells books; original art & prints, reproductions & prints

L **Museum Archives,** 500 Jackson St, Quincy, CA 95971. Tel 530-283-6320; Fax 530-283-6081; Email pcmuseum@psln.com; Web: www.plumasmuseum.org; *CEO* Scott Lawson; *Bd Dir, Chmn* Don Clark
Open Tues - Sat 10 AM - 4 PM; Admis adults $2, 17 & under $1, children & members free; Estab 1964 to preserve Plumas County's rich heritage & history; Library for reference use only; Average Annual Attendance: 10,000; Mem: 550; dues $25 & up
Income: $80,000 (financed by memorial donations, mem, book store sales & personal donations)
Library Holdings: Auction Catalogs, Audio Tapes, Book Volumes 2000, CD-ROMs, Cassettes, Clipping Files, Compact Disks, DVDs, Exhibition Catalogs, Kodachrome Transparencies, Manuscripts, Maps, Memorabilia, Micro Print, Motion Pictures, Original Art Works, Original Documents, Other Holdings Negatives, Pamphlets, Periodical Subscriptions 1000, Photographs, Prints, Reels, Reproductions, Slides, Video Tapes
Special Subjects: Flasks & Bottles, Historical Material, Manuscripts
Collections: Indian jewelry, Maidu Indian Basket Collection, agriculture, bottles, china, crystal, dolls, furniture, logging, mining, musical instruments, railroad items, toys, Coburn Variel home
Activities: Classes for children; docent training; demonstrations; lect open to public; 5 vis lectrs per yr; gallery talks; tours; museum shop sells books, magazines, original art, reproductions, photographs

RANCHO PALOS VERDES

A **PALOS VERDES ART CENTER/BEVERLY G. ALPAY CENTER FOR ARTS EDUCATION,** 5504 W Crestridge Rd, Rancho Palos Verdes, CA 90275. Tel 310-541-2479; Fax 310-541-9520; Email info@pvartcenter.org; Web: www.pvartcenter.org; *Dir Educ Progs* Gail Phinney; *Exec Dir* Joe Baker; *Admin Dir* Bobbie Nowling; *Dir School of Art* Angela Hoffman; *Communs Dir* Scott Andrews
Open Mon - Fri 9 AM - 5 PM, Sat 10 AM - 4 PM, Sun 1 - 4 PM, cl major holidays; No admis fee; Estab 1931 to provide cultural enrichment through art educ, exhibitions & outreach; Changing exhibits in 4 galleries; Average Annual Attendance: 25,000; Mem: 1600; dues $25-$5000; annual meeting in June
Income: Financed by mem & pvt donations
Special Subjects: Calligraphy, Ceramics, Drawings, Jewelry, Photography, Prints, Sculpture
Exhibitions: Annual Juried All-media Show (June-Aug.); Annual Holiday Art Exhib, plus seven other exhibs
Publications: Exhibit catalogs; ARTifacts
Activities: Classes for children & adults; docent training; lect open to public; gallery talks; tours; competitions with awards; juried all-media; scholarships offered; sales shop sells original art

RANCHO SANTA FE

M **RANCHO SANTA FE ART GUILD,** PO Box 773, Rancho Santa Fe, CA 92067-0773. Web: www.ranchosantafeartguild.org; *Pres* Sandi Edwards; *VPres* Margot Wallace; *Secy* Carole Dowling
Mem: 50; mem qualifications, active artist; dues $50;
Income: Financed by dues & donations
Collections: Paintings; photographs; sculpture
Activities: Artist demonstrations; workshops; lects for mems only; 3 vis lectrs per yr

RED BLUFF

M **KELLY-GRIGGS HOUSE MUSEUM,** 311 Washington St, Red Bluff, CA; PO Box 9082, Red Bluff, CA 96080-6068. Tel 530-527-1129; *Pres* Linda Elsner; *Treas* Erick Frey; *Cur* Vivian Ogden
Open Thurs - Sun 1 - 4 PM, cl holidays, for groups any time by reservation; Admis donations accepted; Estab 1965, a Victorian history museum in a home built in 1880s; To preserve the past for present and future generations; Average Annual Attendance: 3,000; Mem: dues assoc $10, sustaining $50, supporting $100 annually, memoriam $100, life $200, patron $500, benefactor $1000
Income: mems, donations, fundraising events
Library Holdings: Book Volumes, DVDs, Memorabilia, Original Art Works, Original Documents, Pamphlets, Photographs
Special Subjects: American Indian Art, Antiquities-Oriental, Archaeology, Cartoons, Ceramics, Costumes, Dolls, Embroidery, Furniture, Glass, Hispanic Art, Jewelry, Laces, Leather, Painting-American, Period Rooms, Porcelain, Textiles, Historical Material
Collections: Collection of paintings spanning a century of art, Indian artifacts, antique furniture, Victorian costumes, Pendleton Collection
Exhibitions: Permanent and temporary exhibitions
Publications: Brochure; Kellygram (guides' newsletter and schedule)
Activities: Docent training; guided tours, lects 4-6 per yr

REDDING

M **TURTLE BAY EXPLORATION PARK,** 844 Sundial Bridge Dr, Redding, CA 96001; 1335 Arboretum Dr Ste A, Redding, CA 96003-3628. Tel 530-243-8850; Fax 530-243-8898; Email info@turtlebay.org; Web: www.turtlebay.org; *CEO* Michael Warren; *Cur* Julia Pennington; *CFO* Vickie Marler; *Develop Officer* Bev Stupek
Open Sun - Sat 9 AM - 5 PM (see website for seasonal hrs); Admis adults $16, seniors & children $12; Estab 1990 to interpret the complex relationships between people and their environments; Two temporary exhibition galleries, totaling 7,000 sq ft present changing contemporary art, history & natural science exhibits; outdoor art; Average Annual Attendance: 150,000; Mem: 6,000+; dues Family $80
Income: Financed by admis, mem, fundraising activities
Special Subjects: American Indian Art, American Western Art, Archaeology, Costumes, Historical Material, Manuscripts, Maps, Photography, Sculpture, Etchings & Engravings, Ethnology, Landscapes, Painting-American, Prints, Reproductions, Textiles, Watercolors
Collections: Native American baskets, Shasta County historical artifacts & documents, Contemporary Regional art, photography, Forest History
Exhibitions: Annual Art Competition; Bug-Eyed: Art, Culture, Insects; Realism Today: Audubon's Animals
Publications: Temporary exhib catalogs
Activities: Classes for adults & children; docent training; lects open to pub, vis lectrs; gallery talks; tours; Art Fair; lending collection; book traveling exhibs 3-5 per yr; originate traveling exhibs to other mus; mus shop sells books & original art, consignment from local craftspeople & artists, reproductions, gifts

L **Shasta Historical Society Research Library**, 1335 Arboretum Dr, Ste A, Redding, CA 96003. Tel 530-243-3720; *Librn* Linda Sharpe
Open Mon - Fri 10 AM - 4 PM; Open for reference only by appointment
Library Holdings: Periodical Subscriptions 64

REDLANDS

L **LINCOLN MEMORIAL SHRINE,** 125 W Vine St, Redlands, CA 92373-4761. Tel 909-798-7636, 798-7632; Fax 909-798-6566; Email heritage@akspl.org; Web: www.lincolnshrine.org; *Cur* Nathan Gonzales; *Assoc Archivist* Maria Carrillo; *VPres* Jack D Tompkins; *Dir* Don McCue
Open Tues - Sun 1 - 5 PM, other hours by appointment; cl Mon & holidays, except Lincoln's birthday; No admis fee; Estab 1932, operated as a section of A K Smiley Public Library; Reference use only; Average Annual Attendance: 17,500; Mem: 325; dues $25-$100
Library Holdings: Book Volumes 4500, Clipping Files, Filmstrips, Manuscripts, Maps, Memorabilia, Original Art Works, Original Documents, Pamphlets, Periodical Subscriptions, Photographs, Prints, Sculpture
Special Subjects: American Indian Art, Manuscripts, Maps, Historical Material
Collections: Sculptures, paintings, murals
Publications: Lincoln Memorial Assn Newsletter, quarterly
Activities: Docent training; lects open to public, 1 vis lectr per year; guided tours by appointment; Barondess Award, 1987; concerts; schols; mus shop sells pamphlets & postcards; books, reproductions & prints

A **REDLANDS ART ASSOCIATION,** Redlands Art Association Gallery & Art Center, 215 E State St, Redlands, CA 92373-5232. Tel 909-792-8435; Email gallery@redlandsartassociation.org; Web: www.redlands-art.org; *Pres* Gail Brownfield; *Gallery Mgr* Francis Wiley; *Publicity* Sandy Davies; *VPres* Tony Radcliffe; *Pres* Liz Coviello; *VPres* Maggie Macro
Open Mon - Sat 11 AM - 4:30 PM; No admis fee; Estab 1964 to promote interest in the visual arts & to provide a gallery for artists; Circ 200; 2 room bus site on main shopping st; Average Annual Attendance: 3,000; Mem: 250; dues $50; annual meeting in May; Artist, Art Appreciator
Income: Financed by dues, gifts, grants
Library Holdings: Book Volumes 400
Exhibitions: Multimedia mini juried show; Recycling Show; Plein Air Show; Photography Show; Featured Artist
Publications: Email newsletter
Activities: Classes for children & adults; lect open to public, 8 vis lectrs per year; tours; competitions with prizes; gallery talks; workshops; MCAEEF - educational awards to local educ establishments; scholarships offered; gallery shop sells original art, reproductions, glass, ceramics, jewelry & cards

M **SAN BERNARDINO COUNTY MUSEUM,** 2024 Orange Tree Lane, Redlands, CA 92374. Tel 909-798-8608; Fax 909-307-0539; Email museum@sbcounty.org; Web: www.sbcounty.org/museum; *Dir* Melissa Russo; *Curator History* Jennifer Dickerson; *Curator Anthropology* Tamara Serrao-Leiua
Open Tues - Sun 9 AM - 5 PM, cl New Year's Day, Thanksgiving, Christmas; Admis adults $10, seniors & active duty military $8, students with ID $7, children 5-12 $5, children under 5 & mus mem free; Estab 1952 for education; Maintains upper & lower dome galleries & foyer; Average Annual Attendance: 55,000; Mem: dues $25 - $150
Income: $280,000 (financed by mem)
Special Subjects: American Indian Art, American Western Art, Archaeology, Collages, Historical Material, Painting-American
Collections: Collection consists primarily of art from the S. California region; History; Art; Natural History; science.
Activities: Classes for adults & children; docent training; lects open to pub, 5-6 vis lectrs per yr; gallery talks; tours; art competitions with cash & purchase awards totaling $45,000 annually; book traveling exhibs; originate traveling exhibs; mus shop sells books, magazines, original art reproductions, prints & slides, jewelry, items pertaining to natural history

M **UNIVERSITY OF REDLANDS,** Peppers Art Gallery, 1200 E Colton Ave, Redlands, CA 92374-3755; PO Box 3080, Redlands, CA 92373-0999. Tel 909-793-2121; Fax 909-748-6293; *Chair Art Dept* Penny McElroy; *Admin Asst* Terri Hodgson
Open Tues - Fri 1 - 5 PM, Sat & Sun 2 - 5 PM, cl summer; No admis fee; Estab 1963 to widen students interest in art; Gallery is one large room with celestial windows & movable panels for display; Average Annual Attendance: 1,500
Income: Financed by endowment
Collections: Ethnic Art, graphics, a few famous artists works
Exhibitions: Exhibitions during fall, winter, spring
Publications: Exhibition catalogs & posters
Activities: Lect open to public, 4-5 vis lectrs per yr; gallery talks; tours; talent awards

RICHMOND

A **NATIONAL INSTITUTE OF ART & DISABILITIES (NIAD),** Florence Ludins-Katz Gallery, 551 23rd St, Richmond, CA 94804-1626. Tel 510-620-0290; Fax 510-620-0326; Email admin@niadart.org; Web: www.niadart.org; *Exec Dir* Deb Dyer; *Gallery Dir* Brian Stechschulte
Open Mon - Fri 9 AM - 4 PM or by appt; No admis fee; Estab 1984 to provide an art environment for people with developmental disabilities which promotes creative expression, independence, dignity and community integration; Maintains professional exhibition galleries which display the work of NIAD artists, often alongside the work of established artists from outside the NIAD setting in order to bring the art of NIAD artists to the attention of the general public; Average Annual Attendance: 1,000; Mem: 250; dues $15-$100
Collections: Gallery, books, pamphlets, posters, videotapes, CD-ROM
Exhibitions: NIAD artist work; 4 exhibs per yr; numerous exhibs nationally & internationally
Publications: Art & Disabilities, Freedom to Create, the Creative Spirit; Freedom to Create (videotape series)
Activities: Classes for adults with developmental disabilities; interdisciplinary visual art studio prog; professional training in art & disabilities field; research, training & technical assistance; gallery talks; tours; originate traveling exhibs of NIAD artist work to regional galleries, mus, colleges, community centers & bus; sales shop sells books, original art & prints

A **THE RICHMOND ART CENTER,** 2540 Barrett Ave, Civic Center Plaza Richmond, CA 94804-1600. Tel 510-620-6772; Fax 510-620-6771; Email admin@therac.org; Web: www.therichmondartcenter.org; *Exec Dir* Ric Ambrose
Open Tues - Sun 12 noon - 5 PM, cl Mon & holidays; No admis fee; Estab preliminary steps 1936-44; formed in 1944 to establish artists studios & community center for arts; to offer to the community an opportunity to experience & to improve knowledge & skill in the arts & crafts at the most comprehensive & highest level possible; A large gallery, small gallery & entrance gallery total 5000 sq ft & a rental gallery covers 1628 sq ft; an outdoor sculpture ct totals 8840 sq ft; Average Annual Attendance: 12,000; Mem: 1,000; dues $45 & up
Income: financed by indiv, businesses, foundations & city
Collections: Primarily contemporary art & crafts of Bay area
Exhibitions: Rotating: group theme, solo, invitational & juried annuals
Publications: Catalog for annual shows; newsletter, quarterly; show announcements for exhibitions
Activities: Classes for adults & children; lect open to public, 12 vis lectrs per year; gallery talks; tours; schols offered; outreach program for grades K-12 serving community; rental gallery, paintings & original objects of art lent to offices, bus & homes, members of Art Center

RIVERSIDE

M **RIVERSIDE ART MUSEUM,** 3425 Mission Inn Ave, Riverside, CA 92501-3368. Tel 951-684-7111; Fax 951-684-7332; Email ram@riversideartmuseum.org; Web: www.riversideartmuseum.org; *Exec Dir* Daniel Foster; *Assoc Dir* Andi Campognone; *Sr Cur* Peter Frank; *Educ Cur* Steve Thomas; *Sr Preparator* Christaan Von Martin
Open Mon - Sat 10 AM - 4 PM; Admis adults $5, mems free; Estab 1935 to display art, collect & preserve art created in the West; Three spaces - Main Gallery 72 ft x 35 ft; Upstairs Gallery 18 ft x 30 ft; Art Alliance Gallery 72 ft x 35 ft; Average Annual Attendance: 70,000; Mem: 1,200; dues life mem $10,000 & up, patron $2500, supporting $300, family $50, individual $35, senior citizens $10
Income: Financed by mem, grants & donations
Library Holdings: Book Volumes, Exhibition Catalogs
Collections: Mixture of media dating from the late 1800s to the present, 300 pieces, art by Southern California artists (past & present) living in the west (Andrew Molles Collection), Works on paper, Andrew Molles Collection
Exhibitions: Rotating exhibits
Publications: Artifacts, monthly
Activities: Classes for adults & children; docent training; internships; lects open to pub, 6 vis lectrs per yr; gallery talks; demonstrations; special events; sponsoring of competitions with prizes; tours; concerts; scholarships & fels offered; individual paintings & original objects of art lent; mus shop sells original art & books

L **Library**, 3425 Mission Inn Ave, Riverside, CA 92501-3368. Tel 909-684-7111; Fax 909-684-7332; Web: www.riversideartmuseum.org; *Dir* MJ Abraham; *Admin Dir* Kathy Smith; *Finance Mgr* Nichole Pingree; *Adult Educ Cur* Lee Tusman
Open Mon - Fri 10 AM - 4 PM; Admis $5 for non-mems, students $2; Open for reference upon request; Average Annual Attendance: 50,000; Mem: 1,200
Income: Financed by grants & donations
Library Holdings: Book Volumes 600, Exhibition Catalogs, Framed Reproductions, Pamphlets, Periodical Subscriptions 15, Photographs, Reproductions
Activities: Classes for adults & children, docent training; lects open to public; 2-4 vis lectrs per yr; concerts; gallery talks; tours; schol; lending of original objects of art to local business partnerships; mus sales shop sells books, original art, reproductions, & prints

M **RIVERSIDE METROPOLITAN MUSEUM,** 3580 Mission Inn Ave, Riverside, CA 92501. Tel 951-826-5273; Fax 951-369-4970; Email dbrennan@riversideca.gov; Web: www.riversideca.gov/museum; *Dir Mus* Ennette Morton; *Educ Cur* Teresa Woodard; *Cur Coll & Exhib* Brenda Focht
Open Tues-Wed & Fri 9 AM -5 PM, Thurs 9 AM- 9PM, Sat 10 AM - 5 PM, Sun 11 AM - 5 PM, cl Mon & major holidays; No admis fee, suggested donation $5; Estab 1924 to collect, preserve & display local & California prehistory, natural history & local history; Permanent galleries on local geology, paleontology, Indians, history & animals; Mem: 750; dues individual $20, family $30
Special Subjects: American Indian Art, Anthropology, Archaeology, Architecture, Carpets & Rugs, Dolls, Eskimo Art, Ethnology, Folk Art, Furniture, Photography, Pre-Columbian Art, Primitive art, Southwestern Art, Textiles
Collections: History photo archive, Indian art, Native American Basketry, historic house, 1891 Heritage House, photo & document archives, Citrus Label Art, Citrus Paraphernalia
Activities: Classes for children; docent training; lects open to members only, 6-10 vis lectrs per yr; tours; original objects of art lent to other pub mus & art galleries; nature lab; multicultural festival; mus shop sells books, original art, reproductions & prints

M **UCR ARTSBLOCK,** Sweeney Art Gallery, Watkins House, Riverside, CA 92521-0001. Tel 951-827-3755; Email karen.rapp@ucr.edu; Web: sweeney.ucr.edu; *Gallery Mgr* Jennifer Frias
Open Tues - Sat 11 AM - 4 PM; No admis fee; Estab 1963, gallery presents major temporary exhibitions; Gallery contains 2,000 sq ft; Average Annual Attendance: 5,000; Mem: dues patron $1,000 & up, supporting $500, contributor $100, family $45, individual $30, student $15
Income: $100,000 (financed by mem & state appropriation)
Purchases: $30,000 (print collection)
Collections: Works on paper-portfolios of prints, sculpture
Exhibitions: Main Gallery: Bas Jan Ader Retrospective

Publications: Exhibition catalogs
Activities: Lects open to pub, 2-3 vis lectrs per yr; book traveling exhibs 1-2 per yr; sales shop sells catalogs & posters

M **California Museum of Photography**, 3824 Main St, Riverside, CA 92501-3624. Tel 951-827-4787; Fax 951-827-4797; Web: www.artsblock.ucr.edu; *Exec Dir* Jonathan Green; *Assoc Dir* Emily Papavero; *CMP Cur Exhibs* Joanna Szupinska-Myers; *Dir Sweeney Art Gallery & Artistic Dir Culver Ctr* Tyler Stallings; *Cur Colls* Leigh Gleason
Open Tues - Sat 12 - 5 PM, first Sun of month, Oct - May 1 - 5 PM, first Thurs of month 6 - 9 PM; Admis $3, students & seniors free; Estab 2010 to provide a cultural presence, educ resource, community ctr & intellectual meeting ground for the univ & community; 8 galleries & large Atrium space; Average Annual Attendance: 40,000; Mem: 1,200; dues $35
Income: $800,000 (financed by university funds, grants, private donations & mem)
Library Holdings: Auction Catalogs, Audio Tapes, Book Volumes, CD-ROMs, Exhibition Catalogs, Lantern Slides, Manuscripts, Memorabilia, Original Art Works, Periodical Subscriptions, Photographs, Prints, Slides
Special Subjects: Art History, Painting-American, Photography, Prints, Sculpture, Posters
Collections: Coll of cameras photographic artifacts, Keystone-Mast Coll stereo negatives & prints, photographic prints by 20th century photographers, Ansel Adams/Fiat Lux Coll, Sweeney Coll of 1,500 works on paper & paintings
Publications: American Photography by Jonathan Green; Che Guevarra: Revolution & Icon by Trisha Ziff
Activities: Classes for adults & children; lects open to pub, 2 vis lectrs per yr; gallery talks; tours; competitions with awards; film series; symposia; original objects of art lent to other art institutions; lending collection contains 400,000 photographs; book traveling exhibs 3 per yr; originate traveling exhibs; mus shop sells books, prints & misc items

L **Tomas Rivera Library**, PO Box 5900, Riverside, CA 92517-5900. Tel 951-827-3220; Fax 951-827-2255; Email rivcirc@ucr.edu; Web: library.ucr.edu; *Art Selector* Krista Ivy; *Univ Librn* Steven Mandeville-Gamble
Open Mon - Thurs 7:30 AM - 12 AM, Fri 7:30 AM - 6 PM, Sat 9 AM - 5 PM; Open to faculty, students & staff
Library Holdings: Book Volumes 38,000, Cards, DVDs, Exhibition Catalogs, Fiche, Manuscripts, Motion Pictures, Original Art Works, Original Documents, Other Holdings, Periodical Subscriptions 172, Photographs, Slides, Video Tapes
Special Subjects: Architecture, Art History, Asian Art, Conceptual Art, Decorative Arts, Film, History of Art & Archaeology, Mixed Media, Painting-American, Painting-British, Painting-European, Painting-French, Painting-German, Painting-Italian, Painting-Scandinavian, Photography, Pre-Columbian Art, Sculpture, Video
Activities: Book Traveling Exhibs: 2 per yr

ROHNERT PARK

M **SONOMA STATE UNIVERSITY,** University Art Gallery, 1801 E Cotati Ave, Rohnert Park, CA 94928-3609. Tel 707-664-2295; Fax 707-664-2054; Email art.gallery@sonoma.edu; Web: www.sonoma.edu/artgallery/; *Dir* Michael Schwager; *Exhib Coordr* Carla Stone
Open Tues - Fri 11 AM - 4 PM, Sat & Sun Noon - 4 PM, cl summer; No admis fee; Estab 1978 to provide exhibitions of contemporary art to the university & Northern California community; 2500 sq ft of exhibition space designed to house monumental sculpture & painting; Average Annual Attendance: 5,000
Income: financed through University & private funds
Special Subjects: American Western Art, Cartoons, Ceramics, Collages, Drawings, Etchings & Engravings, Oriental Art, Painting-American, Photography, Portraits, Prints, Sculpture
Collections: Asian Collection of Prints, Garfield Collection of Oriental Art, Asnis Collection, Imagery Collection
Publications: Bulletins and announcements of exhibitions; exhibition catalog
Activities: Docent training; educ-outreach prog; lects open to the public; 5 vis lectrs per yr; gallery talks; tours; annual benefit auction; book traveling exhibs 1-2 per yr; originate traveling exhibs to national art mus; sales shop sells books, T-shirts & posters

SACRAMENTO

M **CALIFORNIA STATE PARKS,** State Indian Museum, 2618 K St, Sacramento, CA 95816-5104. Tel 916-324-0971; Email cmcgough@parks.ca.gov; Web: www.parks.ca.gov/indianmuseum; *Dir California State Parks* Lisa Mangat
Open daily 10 AM - 5 PM, cl New Years, Thanksgiving & Christmas; Admis adults $5, children 6-17 $3, children 5 & under free; Estab 1940; State historic park
Special Subjects: American Indian Art, Anthropology
Collections: Artifacts Collection from California Native Americans (basketry, hunting & fishing implements, regalia, musical instruments & photographs), Contemporary Native American Art
Exhibitions: Indian Arts & Crafts Holiday Fair; Native American Day; Honored Elders Day; every Sat in Nov
Publications: Native American Month
Activities: Classes for adults; docent training; lects open to public; 4-6 vis lectrs per yr; tours; competitions with awards; mus shop sells books, nature made jewelry, original art, reproductions, arts & crafts

M **CALIFORNIA STATE UNIVERSITY, SACRAMENTO,** Library - Central Reference Dept, Sacramento, CA. Tel 916-278-6218; Fax 916-278-7089; Web: www.lib.csus.edu; *Slide Librn, Arts Librn* Alicia Snee
Open Mon - Thurs 7:15 AM - 11 PM, Fri 7:15 AM - 7 PM, Sat 9 AM - 5 PM, Sun 11 AM - 10 PM (during school year), summer sessions vary during week; Estab 1947
Income: Financed through the University
Library Holdings: Audio Tapes, Cards, Cassettes, Clipping Files, Exhibition Catalogs, Fiche, Filmstrips, Pamphlets, Periodical Subscriptions 250, Reels, Reproductions, Slides
Publications: Women Artists: A Selected Bibliography; bibliographic handouts

M **The University Union Gallery**, University Union at Sac State, 6000 J St Sacramento, CA 95817-6017. Tel 916-278-6997; Fax 916-278-1750; Email uniongallery@csus.edu; Web: www.union.csus.edu; *Design, Identity & Studio Mgr* Rebecca Voorhees
Open Mon - Thurs 6:30 AM - 11 PM, Fri 6:30 AM - 9 PM, Sat 8 AM - 8 PM, Sun 10 AM - 11 PMhool year, summer hours vary; No admis fee; Estab 1975 to expose students to a variety of visual arts & techniques; The University Union Gallery is located on the second floor of the University Union. It has 85 running ft of display space. Gallery run by students; Average Annual Attendance: 8,250
Income: Student fees & commissions
Purchases: Works purchased for permanent collection annually from artists with a relationship, past or present, with the University
Collections: Various prints, photographs, paintings by students, sculpture by Yoshio Taylor: Tsuki; painting by Jack Ogden: American Grove; Bronze original by John Battenberg J G Sheds His Wolf's Clothing
Exhibitions: Annual student competition, other various exhibits encompassing a variety of media & subjects
Activities: Lect open to public, 1-2 vis lectrs per year; gallery talks; competitions

M **CROCKER ART MUSEUM,** 216 O St, Sacramento, CA 95814-5324. Tel 916-808-7000; Fax 916-808-7372; Email main@crockerart.org; Web: www.crockerartmuseum.org; *Chief Cur & Assoc Dir* Scott Shields; *Mus Store Mgr* Pam Pesetti; *Educ Dir* Stacy Shelnut-Hendrick; *Dir Advancement* Kerry Wood; *Dir Mktg* Christine Calvin
Open Tues - Sun 10 AM - 5 PM, Thurs 10 AM - 9 PM; cl Mon New Year's Day, Thanksgiving Day & Christmas Day; Admis adults $12, seniors, college students & military $8, youth (6-17) $6, children 5 & under free; Estab 1873; municipal art mus since 1885; original gallery building designed by Seth Babson completed in 1873; Crocker Mansion Wing opened in 1989; Teel Family Pavilion opened in 2010; Average Annual Attendance: 277,178; Mem: 12,800; dues $50 & up; annual meeting in June
Income: $8,506,066 (financed by Crocker Art Mus Assoc & city appropriation)
Library Holdings: Auction Catalogs, Book Volumes, CD-ROMs, Cassettes, Clipping Files, DVDs, Exhibition Catalogs, Manuscripts, Maps, Original Documents, Other Holdings Painting: India, Mogul, Iranian, Chinese, Pamphlets, Periodical Subscriptions, Photographs, Records, Slides, Video Tapes
Special Subjects: African Art, Afro-American Art, American Indian Art, American Western Art, Anthropology, Antiquities-Assyrian, Antiquities-Egyptian, Antiquities-Etruscan, Antiquities-Greek, Antiquities-Roman, Architecture, Art History, Asian Art, Baroque Art, Bookplates & Bindings, Bronzes, Calligraphy, Carpets & Rugs, Cartoons, Ceramics, Coins & Medals, Conceptual Art, Costumes, Crafts, Decorative Arts, Decorative Arts, Drawings, Embroidery, Etchings & Engravings, Etchings & Engravings, Folk Art, Folk Art, Furniture, Glass, Gold, Graphics, Illustration, Interior Design, Islamic Art, Jewelry, Landscape Architecture, Landscapes, Manuscripts, Maps, Marine Painting, Metalwork, Mexican Art, Miniatures, Mixed Media, Oriental Art, Painting-American, Painting-American, Painting-British, Painting-Dutch, Painting-European, Painting-European, Painting-Flemish, Painting-French, Painting-French, Painting-German, Painting-Italian, Painting-Japanese, Painting-Russian, Painting-Scandinavian, Painting-Spanish, Photography, Porcelain, Portraits, Posters, Pottery, Primitive art, Prints, Religious Art, Reproductions, Restorations, Sculpture, Silver, Southwestern Art, Textiles, Watercolors, Woodcuts, Photography
Collections: 19th century California painting, American decorative arts, contemporary California painting, sculpture & crafts, prints & photographs, European decorative arts, European painting 1500 - 1900, Old Master drawings, Oriental art, African Art Oceanic Art, International Ceramics
Publications: Art Letter, 4 times per year
Activities: Classes for adults & children; seminars for adults; children's progs; docent training, dramatic progs; lects for mems only; 12 vis lectrs per yr; concerts; tours; annual juried competitions; gallery talks; awards: Real Estate Project of the Year (2011) Sacramento Business Journal, Visionary Icon in Building Excellence (2011) Sacramento Downtown Partnership; Arts & Business Council of Sacramento - Arts & Business Partnership Award, 2014; individual paintings & original objects of art lent to other mus; Art travels to K-8 schools in seven surrounding counties; art ark; book traveling exhibs; originate traveling exhibs; mus shop sells books, mags, original art, cards, reproductions, prints & miscellaneous gifts

L **Research Library**, 216 O St, Sacramento, CA 95814-5324. Tel 916-808-8856; Fax 916-808-7372; Email library@crockerart.org; Web: www.crockerartmuseum.org; *Dir Educ* Stacey Shelnut-Hendrick
Open Tues - Wed 10 AM - 3 PM & by appt; Supports educ & research needs of mus staff & pub; Circ Non circ; Open for reference only to public, staff, docent, interns and others upon application
Library Holdings: Book Volumes 2000, Exhibition Catalogs, Fiche, Other Holdings Dissertations, Periodical Subscriptions 30
Special Subjects: Aesthetics, Afro-American Art, American Indian Art, American Western Art, Archaeology, Architecture, Art Education, Art History, Asian Art, Carpets & Rugs, Cartoons, Ceramics, Conceptual Art, Costume Design & Constr, Crafts, Decorative Arts, Drawings, Eskimo Art, Etchings & Engravings, Folk Art, Furniture, Glass, Graphic Arts, Graphic Design, Handicrafts, Historical Material, History of Art & Archaeology, Islamic Art, Landscape Architecture, Latin American Art, Manuscripts, Marine Painting, Mexican Art, Miniatures, Mixed Media, Oriental Art, Photography, Porcelain, Portraits, Pottery, Pre-Columbian Art, Primitive art, Printmaking, Prints, Religious Art, Restoration & Conservation, Scrimshaw, Sculpture, Stained Glass, Southwestern Art, Tapestries, Textiles, Watercolors, Woodcarvings, Woodcuts
Activities: Classes for adults & children; dramatic progs; docent training; lects open to pub, some open to members only, vis lectrs; concerts; tours; gallery talks; schols offered; artmobile; individual paintings lent; originates traveling exhibs to other mus; mus shop sells mus related items

M **LATINO CENTER OF ART AND CULTURE,** 2700 Front St, Sacramento, CA 95818. Tel 916-446-5133; Fax 916-446-1324; Email larazagaleria@gmail.com; Web: www.lrgp.org; *Exec Dir* Marie Acosta
Open Tues - Sat 12:30 PM - 6 PM, cl Sun & Mon; Estab 1972 as a Chicano art & culture center; 2,000 sq ft gallery; Average Annual Attendance: 30,000; Mem: 1,000; dues $15-$150
Special Subjects: Hispanic Art, Jewelry, Mexican Art

Collections: Permanent Coll
Activities: Classes for adults & children; lect open to public; gallery talks; tours

SAINT HELENA

M **NAPOLEONIC SOCIETY OF AMERICA,** Museum & Library, 3360 Saint Helena Hwy N, Saint Helena, CA 94574-9660. Tel 727-586-1779; Fax 727-581-2578; Email marengo@aol.com; Web: www.napoleonsociety.org; *Treas* Barbara Chambers; *Pres* Robert Snibbe
Open 9 AM - 5 PM; No admis fee; Estab 1983; Circ 1,500 worldwide; Mem: 1000; dues $48; annual meeting in Sept
Income: $309,199 (financed by mem)
Library Holdings: Book Volumes
Special Subjects: Historical Material, Miniatures, Painting-French, Porcelain, Bronzes, Prints
Publications: Member's Bulletin, quarterly
Activities: Lect open to public; gallery talks; fellowships; sales shop sells magazines, original art, reproductions, prints

M **ROBERT LOUIS STEVENSON MUSEUM,** 1490 Library Lane, Saint Helena, CA 94574-0409. Tel 707-963-3757; Fax 707-963-0917; Email rlsnhs@calicom.net; Web: www.silveradomuseum.org; *Dir* Edmond Reynolds; *Assoc Dir* Ann Kindred; *Cur* Dorothy Mackay-Collins
Open Wed-Sun noon-4PM; No admis fee; Estab 1968; the mus is devoted to the life & works of Robert Louis Stevenson, who spent a brief but important time in the area; the object is to acquaint people with his life & works & familiarize them with his stay; The mus has five wall cases & three large standing cases, as well as numerous bookcases; Average Annual Attendance: 5,500
Income: Financed by the Vailima Foundation, set up by Mr & Mrs Norman H Strouse
Special Subjects: Drawings, Etchings & Engravings, Furniture, Historical Material, Manuscripts, Photography, Portraits, Watercolors
Collections: Robert Louis Stevenson Collection: material relating to Stevenson & his immediate circle
Exhibitions: A different exhibition devoted to some phase of Stevenson's work is mounted every three months
Activities: Dramatic progs; docent training; lects open to pub 4 per yr; tours; sales desk sells books

L **Museum,** 1490 Library Lane Saint Helena, CA 94574; PO Box 23 Saint Helena, CA 94574-0023. Tel 707-963-3757; Fax 707-963-0917; Email office@stevensonmuseum.org; Web: stevensonmuseum.org; *Director* Barrett Dahl; *Admin Assistant* Presley Hubschmitt
Open Tues - Sat Noon - 4 PM; No admis fee; donations accepted; Estab 1970; Average Annual Attendance: 1,000
Income: Financed by Vailima Foundation
Purchases: Archival materials; acquisitions relating to Robert Louis Stevenson; artwork
Library Holdings: Audio Tapes, Book Volumes 3000, CD-ROMs, Cassettes, Compact Disks, DVDs, Kodachrome Transparencies 300, Manuscripts, Memorabilia, Motion Pictures, Original Art Works, Original Documents, Photographs, Prints, Sculpture, Video Tapes
Special Subjects: American Western Art, Drawings, Furniture, Sculpture, Manuscripts, Painting-American, Painting-British, Photography, Prints, Silver, Watercolors
Collections: First editions, variant editions, fine press editions of Robert Louis Stevenson, letters, manuscripts, photographs, sculptures, paintings and memorabilia
Exhibitions: Exhibits of 4 months duration 3 times a year
Publications: The Silverado Squatters; Prayers Written at Vailima; all books by Robert Louis Stevenson; biographies on RLS
Activities: Educ prog; Docent training; lectures open to pub; 3 vis lectrs per yr; tours; mus shop sells books

SALINAS

M **HARTNELL COLLEGE GALLERY,** 156 Homestead Ave, Salinas, CA 93901. Tel 831-755-6700, 755-6791; Fax 831-759-6052; Email gsmith@hartnell.cc.ca.us; *Dir* Gary T Smith
Open Mon 10 AM - 1 PM & 7 - 9 PM, Tues - Thurs 10 AM - 1 PM, cl Fri - Sun; No admis fee; Estab 1959 to bring to students & the community contemporary & historical works of all media; Main gallery is 40 x 60 ft, south gallery is 15 x 30 ft, brick flooring; Average Annual Attendance: 7,500
Collections: Approx 45 works on paper from the San Francisco Bay Area WPA, FSA photographs, Mrs Virginia Bacher Haichol Artifact Collection, Mrs Leslie Fenton Netsuke Collection
Exhibitions: Edward Weston; Claes Oldenburg; Edward Curtis; Oriental Porcelain from the Albert & Pat Scheopf Collection; Charles Russell & Frederick Remington; Russian Lacquer Boxes; Selections from the Hartnell Farm Security Admin Photography Collection; Christo: Wrapped Coast
Activities: Classes for adults; gallery management training; individual paintings & original objects of art lent to qualified institutions, professional galleries or museums; lending collection contains original art works; book traveling exhibs; originates traveling exhibs

SAN BERNARDINO

M **CALIFORNIA STATE UNIVERSITY, SAN BERNARDINO,** 5500 University Pkwy, San Bernardino, CA 92407-2397. Tel 909-880-5823, 880-7373 (Fullerton Mus); Fax 909-880-7068; Email artmuseum@csub.edu; Web: www.museum.csusb.edu; *Dir Gallery* Eva Kirsch; *Chmn Art Dept* Joe Moran
Open Tues -Wed & Fri-Sat 10AM-5PM, Thurs 10AM-7PM; No admis fee; Estab 1990s for the purpose of providing high quality exhibitions on varied subjects suitable for both campus & community; Gallery expanded into museum; Average Annual Attendance: 13,000
Income: Financed by mem, city & state appropriations
Collections: Egyptian Antiquities, African Collection, Asian Ceramics
Publications: Catalogs; pamphlets
Activities: Classes for adults; summer workshop for children; lects open to pub, 1-3 vis lectrs per yr; gallery talks; tours; competitions

A **SAN BERNARDINO ART ASSOCIATION,** National Orange Show Art Gallery, 689 South E St, San Bernardino, CA 92408. Tel 908-862-3668; Email erdogarz@roadrunner.com; Web: www.nosevents/com/about/art-gallery; *Contact* Ernie Garcia
Estab 2012 to periodically exhibit the National Orange Show Art Collection; Open to the public; maintains gallery of paintings & ceramics by local artists; Mem: 75; dues $20; meetings on first of each month
Exhibitions: Bimonthly exhibits
Publications: Newsletter
Activities: Classes for adults; artist presentations; lect open to public, 8 vis lectrs per year; gallery talks; competitions with awards; scholarships; individual paintings & original objects of art lent; sales shop sells original art, ceramics & photographs

SAN DIEGO

A **BALBOA ART CONSERVATION CENTER,** 1649 El Prado, San Diego, CA 92101-1662; PO Box 3755, San Diego, CA 92163-1755. Tel 619-236-9702; Fax 619-236-0141; Email info@bacc.org; Web: www.bacc.org; *Chief Exec & Chief Paper Conservator* Janet Ruggles; *Chief Paintings Conservator* Alexis Miller; *Registrar & Admin Asst* Emma Poggioli
Open Mon - Fri 9 AM - 5 PM, cl Sat - Sun; No admis fee; Estab 1975 for research & educ in art conservation; services in exams, treatment & consultation in art conservation; Mem: 18; nonprofit institutions are members, their members may contract for services; annual meeting in May
Income: $300,000 (financed by services performed)
Collections: Illustrative photographs, memorabilia, tools, equipment of profession, paintings for experimental & didactic purposes
Activities: Educ prog; regional workshop series on care of collections; lect open to public & some for members only; gallery talks; tours

M **CENTRO CULTURAL DE LA RAZA,** 2125 Park Blvd, San Diego, CA 92101-4753. Tel 619-235-6135; Fax 619-595-0034; Email thecentro@att.net; Web: centroculturaldelaraza.com; *Bd Pres* Tommy Ramirez; *Bd VPres* Sasha Cordova; *Secy* Aida Soria; *Treas* Monica Bernal
Open Tues - Sun noon - 4 PM; No admis fee, suggested donation $5; Estab 1970 to create, promote & preserve Mexican, Indian & Chicano art & culture; 2500 sq ft of gallery space with five sections & 8 X 15 ft walls; Average Annual Attendance: 65,000; Mem: 500; dues $10-$1000
Income: $150,000 (financed by mem, city & state appropriation, sales & services, private grants, National Endowment for the Arts)
Purchases: $1500
Collections: Historical artifacts of Mexican & Indian culture, contemporary artwork by Chicano artists
Exhibitions: Native American Contemporary Photography; solo exhibitions of local & regional artists; group shows; invitational group exhibitions
Publications: Exhibit catalogues, 3 per year; literary publications, 2 per year
Activities: Classes for adults & children; lects open to pub, 5-7 vis lectrs per yr; exten dept; lending collection includes 15 pieces of original art & prints; book traveling exhibs 1-2 per yr; originate traveling exhibs that circulate to other galleries & cultural centers; sales shop sells books, magazines, original art, reproductions, prints

M **MARITIME MUSEUM OF SAN DIEGO,** 1492 N Harbor Dr, San Diego, CA 92101-3309. Tel 619-234-9153; Fax 619-234-8345; Email info@sdmaritime.org; Web: www.sdmaritime.com; *Develop Dir* Kelli Lewis; *Pres & CEO* Raymond Ashley; *Colls Mgr* Kevin Schechan
Open daily 9 AM - 9 PM; Admis adults $18, active military & seniors $13, children 3 - 12 $8, children 2 & under free, discount to adult groups; Estab 1948 for preservation & educ of San Diego related maritime history; Maritime Mus in a fleet of 7 ships: Star of India (1863 bark), Berkeley (1898 ferryboat), Medea (1904 steam Yacht), HMS Surprise, American Submarine, Soviet Submarine; Californian; Average Annual Attendance: 180,000; Mem: 2400; dues Captain $5000, Captain's Table $1000 - $4000, 1st Mate $500 - $900, Boatswain $150 - $499, Crew $65, Mariner/ Individual $40, Apprentice/ Student & Navigator/ Senior $35
Library Holdings: Audio Tapes, Book Volumes, Cassettes, Clipping Files, Kodachrome Transparencies, Original Art Works, Original Documents, Other Holdings, Periodical Subscriptions, Photographs, Prints, Records
Special Subjects: Marine Painting
Collections: Antiques, maritime art, maritime artifacts, clothing, navigation instruments, antique ships
Exhibitions: Festival of Sail, annual Labor Day Weekend exhib; Tall Ships
Publications: Mains'l Haul, quarterly historical journal; Books: Euterpe, MEDEA The Classic Stream Yacht, Star of India, They Came by Sea, Transpac 1900-1979
Activities: Educ dept; classes for adults & children; docent training; lects for members & guests, 3 vis lectrs per yr; tours; special progs; competitions for children with awards; book traveling exhibs, 2 per yr; mus store sells books, magazines, original art, reproductions, prints, slides & related maritime items, including video tapes

M **MINGEI INTERNATIONAL, INC,** Mingei International Museum - Balboa Park & Mingei International Museum - Escondido, 1439 El Prado, San Diego, CA 92101-1617. Tel 619-239-0003; Fax 619-239-0605; Email website@mingei.org; Web: www.mingei.org; *Exec Dir & CEO* Rob Sidner; *Sr Mgr Colls & Registration* Barbara Hanson Forsyth; *Sr Develop Mgr* Caroline Nordquist; *Events Coordr* Martha Ehringer; *Chair* Courtney McGowen; *Treas* Howard Weiner; *Mgr Educ* Shannon Foley; *Mem & Mktg Mgr* Claire McKee; *Financial Mgr* Margaret Mays
Open Tues - Sun 10 AM - 5 PM; Admis adults $10, seniors, students with ID and children 6-17 $7, discounts to groups; Estab 1978 to further the understanding of arts of the people from all parts of the world; 41,000 sq ft mus, architecturally designed space, white interior, hardwood floors, track lighting. Maintains reference

library; Average Annual Attendance: 110,000; Mem: 2300; dues $35-$5000; annual meeting in May
Income: Financed by mem, endowment, city appropriation, grants & contributions
Library Holdings: Auction Catalogs, Audio Tapes, Book Volumes, Clipping Files, Exhibition Catalogs, Original Art Works, Pamphlets, Periodical Subscriptions, Sculpture, Slides, Video Tapes
Special Subjects: African Art, Afro-American Art, American Indian Art, Asian Art, Bronzes, Calligraphy, Carpets & Rugs, Ceramics, Costumes, Crafts, Decorative Arts, Dolls, Drawings, Embroidery, Enamels, Eskimo Art, Folk Art, Furniture, Glass, Hispanic Art, Islamic Art, Ivory, Jade, Jewelry
Collections: Traditional & Contemporary Folk Art, Craft & Design (in all media including textiles, ceramics, metals, woods, stone, paper, bamboo & straw), African, American, Ethiopian, East Indian, Indonesian, Japanese, Pakistani, Himalayan & Mexican Folk Art
Publications: Exhibition related publications
Activities: Docent training; lects open to pub, 10 vis lectrs per yr; films; gallery talks; tours; concerts; book traveling exhibs 1 per yr; originate traveling exhibs 1 per yr; mus shop sells books, magazines, original art

L **Reference Library,** 1439 El Prado, San Diego, CA 92101-1617. Tel 619-239-0003; Fax 619-239-0605; Email website@mingei.org
Open by appointment Tues - Fri 10 AM - Noon & 1 PM - 5 PM, cl Mon & major holidays
Income: Financed by endowments, city appropriation, contributions, grants
Library Holdings: Audio Tapes, Cassettes, Clipping Files, Exhibition Catalogs, Filmstrips, Framed Reproductions, Kodachrome Transparencies, Lantern Slides, Manuscripts, Memorabilia, Motion Pictures, Photographs, Slides, Video Tapes

M **MUSEUM OF CONTEMPORARY ART SAN DIEGO DOWNTOWN,** 1100 Kettner Blvd, San Diego, CA 92101; 700 Prospect St, La Jolla, CA 92037. Tel 858-454-3541; Email info@mcasd.org; Web: www.mcasd.org; *Communs & Mktg Mgr* Leah Straub; *Dir Expansion & Capital Campaign* Hugh M Davies PhD; *Deputy Dir & CFO* Charles Castle; *Dir & CEO* Kathryn Kanjo; *Advancement Dir* Elizabeth Yang-Hellewell
Open at LaJolla & Downtown locations: Mon - Tues 11 AM - 5 PM, Thurs - Sun 11 - 5 PM, cl Wed; Admis $10 general, seniors & students over 25 $5, ages 25 & under & military free; admis good 7 days at all MCASD locations; Estab 1941 to collect, preserve, & present post-1950 art; Maintains two locations, a 500 seat auditorium, 16,000 sq ft total exhibition space
Special Subjects: Drawings, Painting-American, Photography, Prints, Sculpture
Collections: More than 4,500 works created after 1950 representing all media & genres
Exhibitions: See web site
Publications: Catalogues & gallery guides for exhibitions; Quarterly newsletter
Activities: Classes for adults & children; gallery guide training; lects open to pub; artist talks; film series; TNT (Thurs Night Thing); tours; mus shop sells books

M **MUSEUM OF PHOTOGRAPHIC ARTS,** Edmund L. and Nancy K Dubois Library, 1649 El Prado, San Diego, CA 92101-1662. Tel 619-238-7559; Fax 619-238-8777; Email info@mopa.org; Web: www.mopa.org; *Exec Dir* Deborah Klochko; *Opers Mgr* John Hogan; *Exhibs Coordr* Karen Noble
Open Tues - Sun 10 AM - 5 PM, cl Mon, New Year's Day, Martin Luther King Day, Thanksgiving Day, Christmas Day; Admis pay what you wish; Estab 1983 to collect & exhibit photographic works of art; 3,500 sq ft; Average Annual Attendance: 75,000; Mem: 1500; dues $50 - $5,000
Income: $850,000 (financed by city, state, & federal appropriation, endowments, mem, grants & corporations)
Purchases: $20,000
Library Holdings: Book Volumes photography related, Exhibition Catalogs, Periodical Subscriptions
Special Subjects: Photography
Collections: Photographic collection includes examples from earliest to most recent photographs
Publications: Points of Entry
Activities: Classes for adults & children; docent training; educator workshop; summer workshops with guest artists; lects open to pub, 10-12 vis lectrs per yr; gallery talks; tours, concerts; Lou Stouman prize for photography; Century Award for Lifetime Achievement; book traveling exhibs 2 per yr; originate traveling exhibs; mus shop sells books, magazines, prints & photography related gifts

M **SAN DIEGO MUSEUM OF ART,** 1450 El Prado, Balboa Park San Diego, CA 92101-1618; PO Box 122107, San Diego, CA 92112-2107. Tel 619-232-7931; Fax 619-232-9367; Email information@sdmart.org; Web: www.sdmart.org; *Executive Director* Roxana Velasquez; *COO* Dieter Fenkart-Froeschl; *Deputy Dir, Curatorial Affairs & Education* Anita Feldman; *Assoc Cur European Art* Michael Brown; *Assoc Cur East Asian Art* Diana Y Chou
Open Mon - Tues & Thurs - Sat 10 AM - 5 PM, Sun Noon - 5 PM, cl Wed, New Years Day, Thanksgiving, Christmas & special hours select days, call for more info; Admis adults $15, military & seniors 65+ $10, students w/ID $8, youth 7-17 free, mems & children 6 & under free; family & group rates available; Estab 1925. Gallery built in 1926 by a generous patron in a Spanish Plateresque design; the West wing was added in 1966 & the East wing in 1974; Maintains multiple galleries, studio, classroom, offices, John M & Sally B Thornton Rotunda, May S Marcy Sculpture Garden & James S Copely Auditorium; Average Annual Attendance: 400,000; Mem: 33,200; dues benefactor's circle $10,000; dir's circle $5,000; curator's circle $3,000; patron's circle $1,500; sponsor $500; artfully social $300; friend of museum $200; household $100; dual $85; Individual $50
Income: Financed by investment income, contributions, admis, city & county appropriations & sales
Library Holdings: Auction Catalogs, Audio Tapes, Book Volumes, Clipping Files, Exhibition Catalogs, Manuscripts, Maps, Memorabilia, Original Art Works, Original Documents, Other Holdings, Pamphlets, Periodical Subscriptions, Photographs, Prints, Sculpture, Slides, Video Tapes
Special Subjects: Baroque Art, Decorative Arts, Furniture, Oriental Art, Painting-American, Painting-British, Painting-Dutch, Painting-European, Painting-Flemish, Painting-Italian, Painting-Spanish, Prints, Renaissance Art, Sculpture, Silver
Collections: Renaissance & Baroque paintings, with strong holdings in Spanish, 19th & 20th century American & European sculpture & paintings, Asian arts - sculpture, paintings, ceramics, decorative arts, American furniture & glass, English silver, Spanish Baroque, Flemish, Dutch & English schools, African, Oceanic & Native American Artworks Coll, Southern Asian & Persian Art Galleries
Exhibitions: Exhibits of pieces from the permanent collections rotating during the yr
Publications: Biennial Reports port; catalogs of collections; exhibition catalogs; membership calendar, monthly; gallery guide
Activities: Classes for adults & children; family activities; teacher resources; docent training; lects open to public; concerts; gallery talks; audio tours; subject tours; ASL tours; performances; films; competitions; originate traveling exhibs; sales shops sell books, reproductions, prints, cards, jewelry & ceramics

L **Art Library & Archives,** 1450 El Prado, Balboa Park San Diego, CA 92101-1618; PO Box 122107, San Diego, CA 92112-2107. Tel 619-696-1959; Email library@sdmart.org; Web: www.sdmart.org; *Library Servs Coordr* Loretta Deaver
Open to mems, qualified scholars & grad students by appt; Estab 1926 for curatorial research; Circ Non-circulating; Partnered with the San Diego Public Library. (for reference only)
Library Holdings: Auction Catalogs 18,000, Audio Tapes, Book Volumes 30,000, Cassettes, Clipping Files, Exhibition Catalogs, Manuscripts, Memorabilia, Original Art Works, Original Documents, Other Holdings Bound Periodicals: 15,000 vols, 540 titles, Pamphlets, Periodical Subscriptions 45, Photographs, Slides 15,000, Video Tapes
Special Subjects: Art History, Asian Art, Islamic Art, Latin American Art, Oriental Art, Painting-American, Painting-European, Painting-Italian, Painting-Japanese, Painting-Spanish, Prints, Religious Art, Sculpture, Watercolors, Photography
Collections: Bibliography of artists in exhibition catalogues, 30,000+ Artist Files, Online Databases, Papers from Bridges & Putnam families, Earle Grant, Pliny Munger, Dr Clarence & Mrs Ellis Spreckels Moore, Mr & Mrs Irving Snyder, & 1st mus dir Reginald Poland, Artist papers, letters & photographs incl: Robert Henri, Donal Hord, William Templeton Johnson, Alice Klauber, Alfred Mitchell, Walter Pach, Arthur Putnam, Roland Schneider, Florence Kemmler Schneider & Fritz Werner, Schneider-Kemmler Coll incl: 990 slide glass photographs & 300 autochromes c 1910's - 1930's, Scrapbook containing 200 images of China circa 1920 & 2 dozen rare panoramic photographs, 100 glass negatives of Arthur Putnam's bronze sculptures

L **SAN DIEGO PUBLIC LIBRARY,** Art, Music & Recreation, 820 E St, San Diego, CA 92101-6478. Tel 619-236-5810, press 1; 236-5800 (Reference); Fax 619-236-5811; Email artmusic@sandiego.gov; Web: www.sandiego.gov/public-library; *Music Librn* Victor Cardell; *Fine Art* Stephen Wheeler; *Supv Librn* Jacqueline Adams
Open Mon & Wed Noon - 8 PM, Tues, Thurs & Fri 9:30 AM - 5:30 PM, Sun 1 - 5 PM, cl Sat; No admis fee; Estab 1977 to exhib mus quality art in libraries of San Diego; Two gallery spaces: smaller gallery for student & classroom work; larger gallery is for invited guests; Average Annual Attendance: 8,000
Income: Financed by city and state appropriation
Purchases: $32,000
Library Holdings: Auction Catalogs, Audio Tapes, Book Volumes 100,000, CD-ROMs, Clipping Files, Compact Disks, DVDs, Exhibition Catalogs, Original Art Works, Other Holdings Postcards 10,000, Periodical Subscriptions 200, Records 11,000, Video Tapes
Collections: Former libraries of William Templeton Johnson, architect & Donal Hord, sculptor, emphasis is on Spanish, Mediterranean, Italian & French Renaissance architecture & Oriental art, sculpture & ceramics, books on the theatre including biographies of famous actors and actresses as well as histories of the American, London and European stages, gift of Elwyn B Gould, local theatre devotee, William Goe: chess collection

M **SAN DIEGO STATE UNIVERSITY,** University Art Gallery, 5500 Campanile Dr, San Diego, CA 92182-0001. Tel 619-594-1217; Fax 619-594-1217; Email artgallery@sdsu.edu; Web: www.artgallery.sdsu.edu; *Gallery Dir* Tina Yapelli; *Dir* Kotaro Nakamura
Open Mon - Thurs & Sat Noon - 4 PM, cl Fri & Sun; No admis fee; Estab 1977 to provide exhibitions of importance for the students, faculty & pub of the San Diego environment; for study & appreciation of art & enrichment of the University; 1 large gallery; Average Annual Attendance: 35,000; Mem: 270; dues $35
Income: Supported by student fees, SDSU Art Council & grants
Special Subjects: Crafts, Painting-American, Sculpture
Exhibitions: Contemporary national & international artists; 4 rotating exhibitions per year
Publications: Exhibit catalogs
Activities: Lects open to public, 4 vis lectrs per yr; gallery talks; book traveling exhibs 1 per yr; originate traveling exhibs; sales shop sells books & exhib catalogs

M **TIMKEN MUSEUM OF ART,** 1500 El Prado, San Diego, CA 92101-1620; 2550 5th Ave Ste 500, San Diego, CA 92103-6624. Tel 619-239-5548; Fax 619-531-9640; Email info@timkenmuseum.org; Web: www.timkenmuseum.org; *Dir Educ* Kristina Rosenberg; *Deputy Dir Develop & Endowments* Laurie Hawkins
Open Tues - Sat 10 AM - 4:30 PM, Sun 12 PM - 4:30 PM, cl Mon; No admis fee; Estab to display & preserve European Old Masters, 18th & 19th centuries American paintings & Russian icons; Six galleries; Average Annual Attendance: 200,000; Mem: 205 mem, dues vary
Income: financed by endowment & fund raising
Special Subjects: Baroque Art, Bronzes, Decorative Arts, Landscapes, Marine Painting, Painting-American, Painting-Dutch, Painting-European, Painting-Flemish, Painting-French, Painting-Italian, Painting-Russian, Painting-Spanish, Portraits, Religious Art, Sculpture, Tapestries
Collections: Dutch & Flemish, French, Spanish & American Italian paintings, Russian icons, all paintings owned by Putnam Collection are on permanent display
Publications: Gallery Guides; Exhibition Catalogues
Activities: Classes for adults & children; teacher workshops; art classes in schools; day trips; docent training; storytelling; lect; vis lectrs; gallery talks; tours available by request; lend original objects to other museums; two exhibs per yr; mus shop sells reproductions, postcards & catalogues

M **UNIVERSITY OF SAN DIEGO,** Founders' Gallery, 5998 Alcala Park, San Diego, CA 92110-2492. Tel 619-260-7516; Fax 619-260-6875; Email kpowers@sandiego.edu; Web: www.acusd.edu; *Gallery Dir* Derrick Cartwright PhD; *Exec Asst* Katherine Noland
Open (Hoehn) Mon - Fri noon - 5 PM, Sat noon - 4 PM; (KIPJ) Mon - Fri noon - 5 PM; (David W May) Tues - Thurs 1 PM - 4 PM; (Humanities Center) Mon - Fri noon - 5 PM; No admis fee; Estab 1971 to enrich the goals of the Fine Arts department & university by providing in-house exhibitions of all eras, forms & media & to share them with the community; Gallery has foyer, display area and patio, parking in central campus; Average Annual Attendance: 1,500
Income: Financed by Fine Arts department & private endowment
Special Subjects: Asian Art, Furniture, Sculpture, Tapestries, Textiles
Collections: 17th, 18th & 19th century French tapestries & furniture, South Asian textiles & costumes of 19th & 20th centuries, Tibetan & Indian looms, Gandhi spinning wheels, 19th-century French bronze sculpture, 20th-century paintings
Exhibitions: Seven shows each year
Publications: The Impressionist as Printmaker; Child Hassam 1859-1935; Arbol de la Vida, The Ceramic Art of Metepec
Activities: Educ dept; seminars in art history; lects open to public, 4 vis lectrs per yr; concerts; gallery talks; tours; awards; originate traveling exhibs

SAN FRANCISCO

L **ACADEMY OF ART,** University Library, 180 New Montgomery St, Fl 6 San Francisco, CA 94105; 79 New Montgomery St, San Francisco, CA 94105. Tel 415-618-3842; Fax 415-618-3981; Email library@academyart.edu; Web: library.academyart.edu; *Dir* Debra Sampson; *Asst Dir* Olga Nova; *Visual Resources Coordr* Miranda Lindelow; *Systems & Online Resources Librn* Brian Schumacher
Open Mon - Thurs 8 AM - 10 PM, Fri 8 AM - 7 PM, Sat - Sun 10 AM - 6 PM; No admis fee; Estab 1929
Library Holdings: Book Volumes 40,000, CD-ROMs, Clipping Files, DVDs, Exhibition Catalogs, Motion Pictures, Other Holdings Indexed image files, Periodical Subscriptions 300, Slides 100,000, Video Tapes
Special Subjects: Advertising Design, Fashion Arts, Graphic Design, Illustration, Industrial Design, Interior Design, Photography, Sculpture

M **ASIAN ART MUSEUM OF SAN FRANCISCO,** Chong-Moon Lee Ctr for Asian Art and Culture, 200 Larkin St, San Francisco, CA 94102-4734. Tel 415-581-3500; Fax 415-581-4700; Email pr@asianart.org; Web: www.asianart.org; *Dir Educ* Deb Clearwaters; *Cur Exhibs* Fan Zhang; *Conservator* Kathy Gillis; *Cur Korean Art* Hyonjeong Kim Han; *Librn* John Stucky; *Dir* Jay Xu; *Chief Cur* Forrest McGill; *Dir Communs & Bus Develop* Tim Hallman; *Cur Japanese Art* Laura Allen
Open Tues - Sun 10 AM - 5 PM, cl Mon, Thanksgiving Day, Dec 25 & Jan 1; Admis adults 18-64 $25, seniors (65+) $20, youth 13-17 & college students (with ID) $20, children under 12, mus mems, & active members of U.S. Armed Forces (+ 5 family members) free; Founded in 1966 by the City & County of San Francisco to collect, care for, exhibit & interpret the fine arts of Asia; 40,000 sq ft of exhibition space; Average Annual Attendance: 300,000; Mem: 20,000; dues $89 & up
Income: Financed by city & county appropriation & the Asian Art Mus Foundation
Library Holdings: Auction Catalogs, Audio Tapes, Book Volumes, CD-ROMs, Cassettes, Clipping Files, Compact Disks, Exhibition Catalogs, Fiche, Filmstrips, Manuscripts, Maps, Original Documents, Other Holdings, Pamphlets, Periodical Subscriptions, Photographs, Video Tapes
Special Subjects: Antiquities-Oriental, Antiquities-Persian, Asian Art, Bronzes, Calligraphy, Carpets & Rugs, Ceramics, Decorative Arts, Embroidery, Islamic Art, Ivory, Jade, Jewelry, Metalwork, Oriental Art, Painting-Japanese, Porcelain, Portraits, Pottery, Religious Art, Sculpture, Textiles, Woodcarvings, Architecture
Collections: Nearly 12,000 objects from China, Japan, Korea, India, Southeast Asia, The Himalayas & Middle East, Roy C Leventritt Collection
Publications: Exhibition catalogs; handbooks & catalogs on museum collections
Activities: Classes for adults & children; docent training; storytelling; school tours, dramatic programs; lects open to pub, 6 vis lectrs per yr; concerts; gallery talks; tours; original objects of art lent to other mus for exhibs; book traveling exhibs, 1 time per yr; originate traveling exhibs to other mus 1x a year; mus shop sells books, magazines, original art, reproductions & slides

L **C Laan Chun Library**, 200 Larkin St, San Francisco, CA 94102. Tel 415-581-3692; Fax 415-581-4703; Email jstucky@asianart.org; Web: www.asianart.org/collections/library; *Librn* John Carl Stucky
Open Mon - Fri 9 AM - 4 PM by appointment only; No fee for library patrons; Estab 1967; Circ Non-circulating; For reference only; Average Annual Attendance: 250-300
Income: Financed by city appropriation & private gifts
Library Holdings: Auction Catalogs, Audio Tapes, Book Volumes 40,000, CD-ROMs, Clipping Files, Compact Disks, DVDs, Exhibition Catalogs, Fiche, Manuscripts, Memorabilia, Other Holdings Subject Index, Pamphlets, Periodical Subscriptions 230, Photographs, Prints, Reproductions
Special Subjects: Antiquities-Oriental, Antiquities-Persian, Archaeology, Architecture, Art History, Asian Art, Bronzes, Calligraphy, Carpets & Rugs, Ceramics, Decorative Arts, Dolls, Drawings, Embroidery, Enamels, Folk Art, Furniture, Glass, Gold, Goldsmithing, Handicrafts, Historical Material, History of Art & Archaeology, Islamic Art, Ivory, Jade, Jewelry, Landscape Architecture, Leather, Metalwork, Miniatures, Oriental Art, Painting-Japanese, Porcelain, Pottery, Printmaking, Prints, Religious Art, Restoration & Conservation, Sculpture, Silver, Silversmithing, Tapestries, Textiles, Watercolors, Woodcarvings, Woodcuts
Collections: Documentary photograph colls of Chinese paintings & Khmer archaeological sites, exhibition catalogs; extensive subject index, Special colls of antique and rare books; a comprehensive research collection on Asian culture & cultural history
Activities: Classes for adults & children; dramatic programs; docent training; lects open to pub, lects for mems only; concerts; gallery talks; tours; mus sales shop sells books, magazines, original art, & reproductions

A **BAY AREA VIDEO COALITION, INC,** 2727 Mariposa St, Fl 2 San Francisco, CA 94110-1472. Tel 415-861-3282; Fax 415-861-4316; Email info@bavc.org; Web: www.bavc.org; *Interim Exec Dir* Jeremy O'Neal; *Progs Specialist* Lyndsey Florez; *Media Engagement Specialist* Jackelyn Perez; *Tech Mgr* Joel Tatum; *Sr Dir Engagement* Mindy Aronoff
Open Tues - Fri 10 AM - 6 PM, Sat - Sun 10 AM - 6 PM; Estab 1976; Gallery features video & new media technology, education & exhibitions
Publications: Mediamaker Handbook, annually
Activities: Classes for adults; cert progs; youth progs; lect open to public, 450 vis lectrs per yr; competitions with awards

C **BOSTON PROPERTIES LLC,** (Embarcadero Center Ltd), 4 Embarcadero Ctr, Lobby Level, San Francisco, CA 94111. Tel 415-772-0700; Fax 415-772-0554; *CEO* Owen D Thomas
Open to public at all hours; Estab 1971; Collection displayed throughout the Center complex; Center supports San Francisco DeYoung Museum, Fine Arts Museum Downtown Center, American Conservatory Theatre, San Francisco Symphony, San Francisco Center for the Performing Arts, and others
Collections: Willi Gutmann, Two Columns with Wedge, Nicholas Schoffer, Chronos XIV, Olga de Amaral, Columbia, Anne Van Kleeck, Blocks, Stacks, Louise Nevelson, Sky Tree, Jean Dubuffet, La Chiffonniere, John Portman Jr, The Tulip, Elbert Weinberg, Mistral, Charles O Perry, Eclipse, Armand Vaillancourt, 101 precast aggregate concrete boxes that allow visitors to walk over, under & through its waterfalls, Arnaldo Pomodoro, Colonna, Fritz Koenig, Untitled Bronze, Dimitri Hadzi, Creazione, Jules Guerin, Traders of the Adriatic, Arman, Hermes and Dyonisis, Arman, The University of Wisdom, Stephen DeStaebler, Torso with Arm Raised I, Bill Barrett, Baile Merengue, Zhengfu Lu, Rhythm of the Metropolis

M **CALIFORNIA COLLEGE OF THE ARTS,** CCAC Wattis Institute for Contemporary Arts, 360 Kansas St, San Francisco, CA 94103; 1111 8th St, San Francisco, CA 94107. Tel 415-355-9670; Fax 415-355-9676; Email wattis@cca.edu; Web: www.wattis.org; *Dir & Chief Cur* Anthony Huberman; *Graphic Designer* David Giordano; *CCA Communs Assoc* Laura Braun; *Cur & Head Progs* Kim Nguyen
Open Tues - Sat noon - 6 PM, cl Sun & Mon; No admis fee; Estab 1998; serves as a forum for the presentation & discussion of international contemporary art & curatorial practice; Newly renovated building contains galleries & event space; Average Annual Attendance: 20,000; Mem: 2500
Income: Financed by grants & tuition
Exhibitions: Rotating exhibits every 6-8 weeks
Publications: catalogs & limited editions
Activities: lects open to public, 20 vis lectrs per year; gallery talks; tours; screenings; organize traveling exhibs; mus shop sells books, prints

M **THE CALIFORNIA HISTORICAL SOCIETY,** 678 Mission St, San Francisco, CA 94105-4014. Tel 415-357-1848; Fax 415-357-1850; Email info@calhist.org; Web: www.californiahistoricalsociety.org; *Exec Dir & CEO* Anthea M Hartig; *Progs & Visitor Experience Mgr* Patty Pforte; *Dir Fin* Pam Garcia; *Develop & Admin Assoc* Myrna Alcaide
Open Tues - Fri 11 AM - 5 PM, cl Mon; Admis gen $5, mem & children free; Founded 1871, permanently estab 1922 to inspire & empower Californians to make the past a meaningful part of their lives; Mem: 4,500; dues $15-$250
Income: Financed by mem dues & contributions
Special Subjects: Drawings, Furniture, Watercolors, Graphics
Collections: Fine arts include California lithography & other graphics, furniture & artifacts to 1915, research materials both original & published on California & Western artists
Publications: California History, quarterly magazine
Activities: Classes for adults; docent training; progs; tours & films throughout the state; lects open to pub; concerts; gallery talks; tours; awards given for participation in the field of California history; exten prog serves Autry Museum, Los Angeles & Old Mill Gallery, San Marino; originates traveling exhibs

L **North Baker Research Library**, 678 Mission St, San Francisco, CA 94105-4014. Tel 415-357-1848; Fax 415-357-1850; Email info@calhist.org; Web: www.californiahistoricalsociety.org; *Archivist & Digital Archivist* Jamie Henderson; *Reference Librn* Frances Kaplan
Open Wed - Fri 1 PM - 5 PM; Estab 1871 to collect books, manuscripts, photographs, ephemera, maps and posters pertaining to California and Western history; Mem: 5,000 mem; dues starting at $60
Income: Private, non-profit
Library Holdings: Audio Tapes, Book Volumes 60,000, Cassettes, Clipping Files, Exhibition Catalogs, Fiche, Framed Reproductions, Kodachrome Transparencies, Lantern Slides, Manuscripts, Maps, Memorabilia, Original Art Works, Original Documents, Other Holdings 3-D artifacts, Pamphlets, Periodical Subscriptions 100, Photographs 500,000, Prints, Reels, Reproductions, Slides
Special Subjects: Advertising Design, American Western Art, Architecture, Bookplates & Bindings, Calligraphy, Cartoons, Drawings, Etchings & Engravings, Graphic Arts, Graphic Design, Historical Material, Illustration, Landscapes, Lettering, Manuscripts, Photography, Portraits, Posters, Printmaking, Prints, Watercolors, Woodcuts
Collections: Crocker Collections, Florence Keen Collection of Western Literature, Kemble Collection of Western Printing & Publishing
Publications: California History, quarterly; CHS Press Titles
Activities: Symposiums, website; lects open to pub, 12-15 lectrs per yr; tours; lending of original objects of art

M **CAPP STREET PROJECT,** Wattis Institute, 1111 Eighth St, San Francisco, CA 94107-2247. Tel 415-551-9210; Fax 415-551-9209; Email wattis@cca.edu; Web: www.wattis.org/capp; *Dir & Chief Cur* Anthony Huberman; *Cur & Head Progs* Kim Nguyen
Open Tues - Sat noon - 6 PM, cl Sun & Mon; Estab 1983 as a nonprofit arts organization providing three month residencies in San Francisco for installation art; Average Annual Attendance: 20,000
Collections: Installation Art, Public Art
Publications: Capp Street Project Catalog, biennially
Activities: Lects open to pub, 8-10 vis lectrs per yr; tours; originate traveling exhibs; mus store sells limited editions, merchandise

M **CARTOON ART MUSEUM,** 781 Beach Street, San Francisco, CA 94109-1254; P.O. Box 566, San Francisco, CA 94104-0566. Tel 415-227-8666; Fax

415-243-8666; Email office@cartoonart.org; Web: www.cartoonart.org; *Exec Dir* Summerlea Kashar; *Chmn* Ron Evans; *Cur* Andrew Farago; *Program Coordinator* Nina L. Taylor Kester
reopening spring 2017. See cartoonart.org for details; see cartoonart.org; Estab 1984 to preserve exhibit & study original cartoon art; 3000 sq ft exhibition space; Average Annual Attendance: 30,000; Mem: 500; dues individual $45
Library Holdings: Audio Tapes, Book Volumes, Clipping Files, Exhibition Catalogs, Video Tapes
Special Subjects: Afro-American Art, American Western Art, Cartoons, Drawings, Etchings & Engravings, Folk Art, Hispanic Art, Historical Material, Juvenile Art, Latin American Art, Manuscripts, Painting-American, Painting-Canadian, Painting-European, Painting-French, Photography, Portraits, Posters, Prints, Reproductions, Watercolors
Collections: 11,000 pieces of original cartoon art
Exhibitions: Rotating exhibits
Publications: Exhibition catalogs available at cartoonart.org/shop
Activities: Classes for adults, children & teens; lects open to pub, 4 vis lectrs per yr; gallery talks; tours; cartoon contests for children kindergarten through 12th grade with gift cert; individual paintings & original objects of art lent to other mus, galleries & corporations; lending collection contains color reproductions, original art works, original prints & paintings; retail store sells books, prints, magazines, gift items

M **CHILDREN'S CREATIVITY MUSEUM,** 221 Fourth St, San Francisco, CA 94103. Tel 415-820-3320; Fax 415-820-3330; Email info@creativity.org; Web: www.creativity.org; *Exec Dir* Carol Tang; *Assoc Dir Mktg* Pat Schultz Kilduff; *Dir Finance & Operations* Christine Fitzsimmons
Open Summer Tues - Sun 10 AM - 4 PM, Sept - June Wed - Sun 10 AM - 4 PM, other times by appointment; Admis adults $12, youth (3 - 18) $12, under 2 free; Estab 1998; urban renewal proj in the South of Market area by the SF Redevelopment Agency; Multimedia Arts & Tech; Average Annual Attendance: 100,000; Mem: 1,750
Collections: community & youth artwork, 1906 Charles Looff carousel
Activities: Art workshops; preschool workshops; youth docent internships; professional develop progs; live performances; mus shop

M **CHINESE CULTURE FOUNDATION,** Center Gallery, 750 Kearny St, 3rd Flr, San Francisco, CA 94108. Tel 415-986-1822; Fax 415-986-2825; Email info@cccsf.us; Web: www.cccsf.us; *Exec Dir* Mabel Teng; *Cur & Artistic Dir* Abby Chen; *Dir Educ & Engagement* Darin Ow-Wing
Open Tues - Sat 10 AM - 4 PM, cl Sun - Mon & holidays; No admis fee; Estab 1965 to promote the understanding & appreciation of Chinese & Chinese-American culture in the United States; Traditional & contemporary paintings, sculpture by Chinese & Chinese American artists, photographs & artifacts illustrating Chinese-American history & major international & cultural exchanges from China, Taiwan & Southeast Asia make the center a local & national focus of Chinese artistic activities; Average Annual Attendance: 60,000; Mem: 1,000; dues family $50, regular $35
Income: Financed by mem, city appropriation, grants & rental fees from auditorium
Special Subjects: Asian Art, Calligraphy, Decorative Arts, Folk Art, Jewelry, Oriental Art, Photography, Prints, Sculpture, Textiles, Watercolors, Woodcarvings
Collections: Painting: Chinese Genealogy
Exhibitions: In Search of Roots; Through Dust & Ruins: Photography by Tsung Woo Han; Urban Yearnings: Portraits of Contemporary China by Liu Qinghe, Su Xinping & Zhang Yajie
Publications: Chinese Culture Center Newsletter, quarterly; Exhibition catalogs
Activities: Classes for adults & children; dramatic progs; docent training; daily walking tour of Chinatown for school children & tourists; lects open to pub, 10 vis lectrs per yr; concerts; tours; film progs; mus shop sells books, original art, reproductions, prints, jewelry, pottery, jade, material & papercuts

A **EXPLORATORIUM,** Pier 15, San Francisco, CA 94111. Tel 415-528-4444; Email visit@exploratorium.edu; Web: www.exploratorium.edu; *Exec Dir* Chris Flink; *Dir Mktg, Communs, Frontline & Mem* Julie Nunn
Open Tues - Sun 10 AM - 5 PM, cl Mon except for MLK Day, Presidents Day, Memorial Day & Labor Day; Admis adults $29.95, seniors, people with disabilities, teachers, students & youth 13-17 $24.95, youth 4-12 $19.95, children under 4 & mem free; Estab 1969 to provide exhibits & art works centering around the theme of perception, which are designed to be manipulated & appreciated at a variety of levels by both children & adults; Average Annual Attendance: 1,100,000; Mem: 25,000; dues $45 & up
Income: Financed by national, city & state grants, private foundations, corporation contributions & earned income
Library Holdings: Motion Pictures
Collections: Over 650 exhibits incl Life Sciences, Bay Observation, Time & Motion, Seeing & Listening, Electricity & Magnetism, Creative Experimentation, Human Phenomena
Publications: The Exploratorium, bimonthly calendar; books, quarterly
Activities: Classes for adults & children; artists in residence prog, performing artists in residence prog & teachers training using artists & scientists in collaboration; docent training; lects open to pub; concerts; gallery talks; tours; fels; Webley Award for www.exploratorium.edu; originate traveling exhibs; mus shop sells books, magazines, reproductions, prints, slides & science related material

M **FINE ARTS MUSEUMS OF SAN FRANCISCO,** M H de Young Museum, 50 Hagiwara Tea Garden Dr, Golden Gate Park San Francisco, CA 94118-4502. Tel 415-750-3600; Email contact@famsf.org; Web: deyoung.famsf.org; *Dir* Max Hollein
Open Tues - Sun 9:30 AM - 5:15 PM, cl Mon, Thanksgiving, Christmas & New Years Days; Admis adults $15, seniors $12, students with valid ID $6, mems, children 17 & under free; admis to de Young Mus incl same-day admis to Legion of Honor; Estab 1971 as a mem organization for Fine Arts Museum of San Francisco & the Asian Art Mus of San Francisco & the Asian Art Mus of San Francisco; Mem: 110,000 households; dues $119 & up
Income: $2,770,000 (financed by mem & bookshop revenues)
Collections: American Paintings, American Decorative Art, African Art, Art of the Americas, Oceanic Art, Textile Arts
Publications: Triptych, bimonthly magazine
Activities: Educ prog Cultural Encounters on Fri nights; artist installations & demos; audio & docent-led tours; mus shop sells books, reproductions, prints & slides

M **Legion of Honor**, 100 34th Ave, Lincoln Park San Francisco, CA 94121-1677. Tel 415-750-3600, 863-3330 (public information); Email contact@famsf.org; Web: http://legionofhonor.famsf.org/; *Dir* Max Hollein; *Dir Mktg, Commun & Visitor Experience* Linda Butler
Open Tues - Sun 9:30 AM - 5:15 PM, cl Mon, Thanksgiving, Christmas & New Years Days; Admis adults $15, seniors $12, students with ID $6, mems, children 17 & under free; admis to Legion of Honor incl same-day admis to de Young Mus; Estab 1895 to provide museums of historic art from ancient Egypt to the 20th century; Two separate buildings are maintained one in the Golden Gate Part (de Young Mus) with 35 galleries & the other in Lincoln Park (California Palace of the Legion of Honor) with 22 galleries; Average Annual Attendance: 800,000; Mem: 50,000; dues patron $1000 sponsor $500, donor $250, contributing $125, family $70, participating $60
Income: Financed by pub-private partnership, city owned buildings
Special Subjects: African Art, Afro-American Art, American Indian Art, Antiquities-Assyrian, Antiquities-Byzantine, Antiquities-Egyptian, Antiquities-Etruscan, Antiquities-Greek, Antiquities-Roman, Bronzes, Carpets & Rugs, Ceramics, Costumes, Crafts, Decorative Arts, Drawings, Embroidery, Enamels, Eskimo Art, Etchings & Engravings, Furniture, Glass, Graphics, Ivory, Laces, Textiles
Collections: Rodin sculpture collection, Art from Central & South America & Mesoamerica, primitive arts of Africa, Oceania & the Americas
Activities: Classes for adults & children; docent training; lect open to public; concerts; gallery talks; tours; mus shop sells books, magazines, reproductions, prints & jewelry

L **Library**, 50 Hagiwara Tea Garden Dr, Golden Gate Park San Francisco, CA 94118-4502. Tel 415-750-7603
Open Mon - Fri by appt; Estab 1955 to serve mus staff in research on collections, conservation, acquisition, interpretations; Circ Non-circulating; Holdings on antiquities, European art & graphic arts housed at Legion of Honor; holdings on American art, African art, art of Oceana & Americas, textiles, periodicals, microform colls & exhib archival records housed at de Young Museum
Income: Financed by mem, city appropriation, donations
Library Holdings: Auction Catalogs, Book Volumes 50,000, Clipping Files, Exhibition Catalogs, Fiche, Periodical Subscriptions 125, Reels 8,000
Special Subjects: Decorative Arts, Graphic Arts, Painting-American, Painting-European, Photography, Pre-Columbian Art, Sculpture, Textiles
Collections: Microform: Smithsonian Institution's Archives of American Art, 19th c. periodicals, 18th - 20th c. auction catalogs, Original records: Exhib History Archive of the Fine Arts Mus of San Francisco

M **GALERIA DE LA RAZA,** Studio 24, 2857 24th St, San Francisco, CA 94110-4234. Tel 415-826-8009; Email info@galeriadelaraza.org; Web: www.galeriadelaraza.org; *Exec Dir* Ani Rivera; *Public Progs & Special Events Coordr* Reyes Segura; *Volunteer & Intern Coordr* Elizabeth Blancas
Open Wed - Sat Noon - 5 PM; No admis fee, donations accepted; Estab 1969 as a community gallery & mus to exhibit works by Chicano-Latino artists, contemporary as well as cultural folk art; Galeria Studio 24's mission is to foster public awareness and appreciation of Chicano/Latino art and serve as a laboratory where artists can explore contemporary issues in art, culture and civic society, while advancing intercultural dialogue. Galeria's artistic programs include visual arts exhibitions, the Digital Mural Program, the ReGeneration Project and our monthly Lunada series. Galeria also sponsors the Youth Media Project (YMP) an experiential youth arts education and mentorship program; Average Annual Attendance: 42,000; Mem: 300; dues $40
Income: Financed by California Arts Council, NEA, San Francisco Arts Commission, Grants for Arts, Miranda Lux Foundation, San Francisco Foundation, Walter & Elise Haas Foundation, van Loben Sels/RembeRock Foundation, Zellerbach Family Fund, Adobe/Silicon Valley Community Foundation, Anonymous Donor & Galeria Mems
Library Holdings: Cards, Exhibition Catalogs, Framed Reproductions, Memorabilia, Original Art Works, Original Documents, Photographs, Prints, Slides
Special Subjects: Folk Art
Collections: Chicano & Latino murals, Mexican & Latin American Folk art & contemporary art
Exhibitions: Changing monthly
Publications: Weekly email newsletters
Activities: Educ prog; classes for adults & children; lects open to pub, gallery talks; tours; Youth Media Lab-new media workshops & after school prog; musical events; LUNADAS: open mic & literary lounges; community events; mus shop sells books, original art, prints, cards, calendars & candles

A **INTERSECTION FOR THE ARTS,** 901 Mission St, Ste 301 San Francisco, CA 94103-3071. Tel 415-626-2787; Fax 415-626-1636; Web: www.theintersection.org; *Dir* Randy Rollison; *Dir Finance & Organization Develop* Yesenia Sanchez; *Dir Public Progs & Professional Develop* Marline Zaibak
Open Mon - Thurs 10 AM - 5 PM, Fri 10 AM - 1 PM; No admis fee; Estab 1965 to represent visual & performing arts; One gallery; Average Annual Attendance: 10,000
Income: Financed through foundation
Exhibitions: Rotating exhibitions, six per yr
Activities: Classes for adults & children; concerts; gallery talks; tours

A **JAPANTOWN ART & MEDIA WORKSHOP,** 1840 Sutter St, Ste 102, San Francisco, CA 94115. Tel 415-922-8700; Fax 415-922-8700
Open daily 10 AM - 5 PM; No admis fee; Estab 1977 as an Asian-American art center; Mem: 120; dues $20
Income: $100,000 (financed by endowment, mem, foundations, city & state appropriations)
Special Subjects: Asian Art, Graphics, Painting-Japanese, Posters
Collections: Silkscreen posters & other art works
Exhibitions: Layer Exhibition; Asia-American Film & Video Exhibit
Publications: Enemy Alien; Yoisho

Activities: Classes for adults & children; graphic design intern progs; concerts; competitions with awards; lending collection contains posters

M **THE LAB,** 2948 16th St, San Francisco, CA 94103-3613. Tel 415-864-8855; Fax 415-864-8855; Email thelabs@thelab.org; Web: www.thelab.org; *Dir* Dena Beard
Open Wed - Sat 1 PM - 6 PM; No admis fee; Estab 1983 to support the develop & presentation of experimental & interdisciplinary art of emerging or mid-career artists
Income: $130,000 (financed by mem, city & state appropriations, federal funding & private foundations)
Exhibitions: Installations; Interdisciplinary & Experimental Art
Activities: Lect open to public; concerts; dance; performance art events; visual art exhibitions

L **MECHANICS' INSTITUTE,** 57 Post St, San Francisco, CA 94104-5003. Tel 415-393-0113; Email dhunt@milibrary.org; Web: www.milibrary.org; *Library Director* Deborah Hunt; *Archivist* Diane Lai; *Exec Dir* Ralph Lewin; *Colls Mgr* Craig Jackson; *Head Tech Servs* Joel Webb; *Partnerships Librn* Taryn Edwards
Open Mon - Thurs 9 AM - 9 PM, Fri 9 AM - 6 PM, Sat 10 AM - 5 PM, Sun 1 - 5 PM; Estab 1854 to serve the needs of 5000 members with a general interest collection; Circ 59,047; Average Annual Attendance: 56,748; Mem: 5000; dues $120
Income: Financed by building rents, endowment, & membership fees
Library Holdings: Audio Tapes, Book Volumes 200,000, CD-ROMs, Cassettes 1200, Clipping Files, Compact Disks, DVDs, Fiche 35, Maps, Other Holdings Newspapers 60, Periodical Subscriptions 475, Photographs, Video Tapes 1300
Special Subjects: American Western Art, Architecture, Art History, Crafts, Decorative Arts, Embroidery, Etchings & Engravings, Fashion Arts, Furniture, Handicrafts, Painting-American, Painting-Australian, Painting-British, Painting-French, Painting-German
Activities: classes for adults; lects open to pub; 30 vis lectrs per year

M **THE MEXICAN MUSEUM,** Fort Mason Center, 2 Marina Blvd Bldg D San Francisco, CA 94123. Tel 415-202-9700; Email info@mexicanmuseum.org; Web: www.mexicanmuseum.org; *CEO* Dr Edgar De Sola; *Mus Opers Mgr* Vanessa Moreno; *Dir Educ* Diane Levy; *Visitor Servs* Horacio Zambrano
Open Thurs - Sun Noon - 4 PM; No admis fee; Estab 1975 to foster the exhibition, conservation & dissemination of Mexican & Mexican-American & Chicano culture for all people; Average Annual Attendance: 6,000
Income: Financed by state grants, corporate & individual support, earned income through gift shop, mem, educational tours & work shops
Library Holdings: Book Volumes, Exhibition Catalogs, Manuscripts, Maps, Original Art Works, Original Documents, Photographs, Prints
Special Subjects: American Western Art, Ceramics, Crafts, Dolls, Drawings, Embroidery, Etchings & Engravings, Folk Art, Hispanic Art, Jewelry, Latin American Art, Leather, Manuscripts, Mexican Art, Pewter, Photography, Portraits, Pottery, Pre-Columbian Art, Prints, Religious Art, Reproductions, Sculpture, Southwestern Art
Collections: Chicano, Colonial, Folk, Mexican, Mexican-American & Pre-Hispanic Fine Arts, Rare Books
Exhibitions: Highlights from the Permanent Coll
Publications: Exhibit catalogs
Activities: Classes for adults & children; docent training; dramatic progs; demonstrations & lectures; lects open to pub; gallery talks; tours; Website award by Web Marketing Assn 2002; mus shop sells books & original art

M **MISSION CULTURAL CENTER FOR LATINO ARTS,** 2868 Mission St, San Francisco, CA 94110-3908. Tel 415-821-1155; Fax 415-648-0933; Email info@missionculturalcenter.org; Web: www.missionculturalcenter.org; *Exec Dir* Jennie Emire Rodriguez; *Gallery Coord* Angelica A Rodriguez
Open Tues - Sat 10 AM - 5 PM; Admis fees for events & exhibs apply & vary; Estab 1977 to promote, preserve & develop the Latino cultural arts that reflect the living tradition & experiences of Chicano, Central & South American & Caribbean people; Houses a 142-seat theater; 2650 sq ft gallery exhibition space; spacious performing & visual art studios; state of the arts screen print facility; Average Annual Attendance: 5,000
Income: Financed by pub & pvt foundations, contributions & foundations
Collections: Latin America
Exhibitions: Rotating every month
Activities: Classes for adults & children in art, dance, music & self defense; workshops; internship progs; performances; festivals; films

M **MODERNISM,** 724 Ellis St, San Francisco, CA 94105. Tel 415-541-0461; Fax 415-541-0425; Email info@modernisminc.com; Web: www.modernisminc.com; *Pres* Martin Muller; *Dir* Danielle Beaulieu; *Registrar* David Peniston; *Gallery Asst* Lexi Paulson; *Gallery Asst* Allyson Beaulieu
Open Tues - Sat 10 AM - 5:30 PM; Estab 1979
Special Subjects: Painting-American, Photography, Sculpture
Collections: historical & contemporary paintings; photographs; sculpture
Exhibitions: Rotating exhibits; temporary exhibits
Activities: Art programming; Mus publications store offers books, catalogs & posters online

M **MUSEO ITALO AMERICANO,** Fort Mason Center, Bldg C San Francisco, CA 94123-1324; Fort Mason Center, 2 Marina B lvd, Bldg C San Francisco, CA 94123. Tel 415-673-2200; Fax 415-673-2292; Email info@sbcglobal.net; Web: www.museoitaloamericano.org; *Mng Dir* Paola Bagnatori; *Asst Mng Dir* Susan Filippo; *Cur* Mary Serventi Steiner
Open Tues - Sun noon - 4PM, Mon by appt; Admis free; Estab 1978 to research, preserve & display works of Italian & Italian-American artists & to foster educational programs for the appreciation of Italian & Italian-American art, history & culture; 3700 sq ft of exhibit space; The Fontana Gallery & The Lanzone Gallery; Average Annual Attendance: 25,000; Mem: 1034; dues $35-$1000
Income: Financed by mem, city appropriation, foundations & corporate contributions
Special Subjects: Historical Material, Landscapes, Painting-Italian, Photography, Sculpture, Watercolors
Collections: 20th Century paintings, sculptures, prints & photographs
Exhibitions: Rotating exhibits
Publications: Calendar of Events, monthly
Activities: Classes for adults & children; school outreach art prog; lects open to pub, concerts; awards; individual paintings & original objects of art lent to mus; mus shop sells books, magazines, original art, Italian pottery, blown glass & gift items

L **Library,** Fort Mason Center, Bldg C San Francisco, CA 94123-1324. Tel 415-673-2200; Fax 415-673-2292; Email museo@firstworld.net; Web: www.museoitaloamericano.com; *Cur* Valentina Fogher
Open Wed - Sun Noon - 5 PM; Estab 1978 to serve as a resource center of Italian & Italian-American culture & art
Library Holdings: Book Volumes 300

A **MUSEUM OF CONCEPTUAL ART,** Society of Independent Artists (SIA), 657 Howard St, San Francisco, CA 94105-3915. Tel 415-495-3193; Email tmarioni@earthlink.net; Web: tommarioni.com; *Dir* Tom Marioni; *Mgr Soc Independent Artists* Edward Stanton; *Curator* John Held Jr
Open by appointment; No admis fee; Estab 1970 for research, study & organization of exhibitions & events; Event Space; Average Annual Attendance: 5,000
Income: Financed by endowment
Library Holdings: Audio Tapes, Cassettes, DVDs, Exhibition Catalogs, Kodachrome Transparencies, Manuscripts, Original Art Works, Original Documents, Photographs, Prints, Sculpture, Slides, Video Tapes
Collections: Glass bottles, Conceptual Art
Exhibitions: Vito Acconci; Robert Barry; Bar Room Video; Chris Burden; Lowell Darling; Howard Fried; Paul Kos; Masashi Matsumoto; Restoration of Back Wall; Miniatures from San Francisco & Kyoto; Social Art, Cafe Society; Graduate Bartenders 2000-; Sound Effects
Publications: Vision, 1975-1982
Activities: Docent training; lects for mems only, 12 vis lectrs per yr; concerts; awards - NEA grants; NEA 1970's;; original traveling exhibs

L **Library,** 657 Howard St, San Francisco, CA 94105-3915. Tel 415-495-3193; Fax 415-495-3193; *Dir* Tom Marioni
For reference only
Library Holdings: Audio Tapes, Book Volumes 1200, Cassettes, Exhibition Catalogs, Filmstrips, Kodachrome Transparencies, Motion Pictures, Original Art Works, Other Holdings Original documents, Pamphlets, Photographs, Prints, Records, Reels, Sculpture, Slides, Video Tapes
Special Subjects: Calligraphy, Drawings, Etchings & Engravings, Period Rooms, Religious Art, Sculpture, Woodcuts
Exhibitions: Inspired by Leonardo

NATIONAL ALLIANCE FOR MEDIA ARTS & CULTURE
For further information, see National and Regional Organizations

M **PIER 24 PHOTOGRAPHY,** The Embarcadero, San Francisco, CA 94105. Tel 415-512-7424; Email info@pier24.org; Web: pier24.org; *Dir* Christopher McCall; *Assoc Dir* Allie Haeusslein; *Head Opers* Ry Allred; *Guest Servs Mgr* Mari Iki
Open Mon - Fri 9 AM - 5:15 PM by appointment; No admis fee; Estab to provide space for photographic works and engage the community; Historic site that yields few restrictions; design bridges storage & exhibition space
Special Subjects: Photography
Exhibitions: Temporary exhibits
Activities: Artist workshops; lects open to pub; art programming; competitions with awards; residencies

M **RANDALL JUNIOR MUSEUM,** 199 Museum Way, San Francisco, CA 94114-1499. Tel 415-554-9600; Fax 415-554-9609; Email info@randallmuseum.org; Web: www.randallmuseum.org; *Exec Dir* Chris Boettcher
Open Tues - Sat 10 AM - 5 PM, cl holidays; No admis fee; Estab 1937 as part of the San Francisco Recreation & Park Dept; Gallery is located in 16-acre park overlooking city; Average Annual Attendance: 80,000; Mem: 300; dues $30-$500; annual meeting in June
Special Subjects: Ceramics, Crafts, Drawings, Jewelry, Photography
Collections: Animals, Children's Art, Indian Artifacts, Insects, Minerals, Fossils, Live animal exhibit
Exhibitions: Festival on the Hill; Bug Day; Water Day; crafts fair
Publications: Class flyer 5 times per year; Hands-On newsletter, quarterly
Activities: Classes for adults & children; dramatic progs; docent training; lects open to pub; concerts; tours; competitions with awards; scholarships offered

A **SAN FRANCISCO AFRICAN-AMERICAN HISTORICAL & CULTURAL SOCIETY,** 762 Fulton St, Fl 2, San Francisco, CA 94102-4119. Tel 415-292-6172; Fax 415-440-4231; Email info@sfaahcs.org; Web: www.sfaahcs.org; *Exec Dir* W E Hoskins; *Pres* Al Williams; *Treasurer* Ellis Joseph
Open Tues - Sat 1 PM - 5 PM; No admis fee
Special Subjects: Ethnology

L **Library,** 762 Fulton St, San Francisco, CA 94123. Tel 415-292-6172; Fax 415-441-2847; Email aahs@sfpl.lib.ca.us; Web: www.sfblackhistory.org; *Pres* Alfred Williams; *Treas* Ellis Joseph; *Sec* Glenn Nance
Open Wed-Sat Noon-5 PM; No admis fee; 1955; For reference only & public library
Library Holdings: Audio Tapes, Book Volumes 5000, CD-ROMs, Framed Reproductions, Other Holdings Oral history, Photographs, Prints, Slides, Video Tapes
Collections: African-American newspapers, 1000 periodicals
Activities: Lects open to pub

M **SAN FRANCISCO ART INSTITUTE,** Walter and McBean Galleries, 800 Chestnut St, San Francisco, CA 94133-2299. Tel 415-749-4563; Fax 415-351-3516; Email exhibitions@artists.sfai.edu; Web: www.sfai.edu; *Cur Exhibs & Public Progs* Katie Hood Morgan
Open Tues 11 AM - 7 PM, Wed - Sat 11 AM - 6 PM; No admis fee; Estab 1969, to present exhibitions at the forefront of contemporary art practice; Walter McBean Galleries; two-levels, used for exhibitions of contemporary artists of international repute; Average Annual Attendance: 15,000

Income: Donations, tuition, grants
Exhibitions: Walter McBean (six exhibitions per year)
Publications: Exhibition catalogs
Activities: Classes for adults & children; lect open to public, 20 vis lectrs per year; gallery talks; tours; fels; scholarships & fels offered; exten dept; sales shop sells art supplies

L **Anne Bremer Memorial Library**, 800 Chestnut St, San Francisco, CA 94133. Tel 415-749-4562; Email library@sfai.edu; Web: www.stai.edu; *Catalog Asst* Claudia Marlowe; *Media Asst* Rebecca Alexander; *Librn* Jeff Gunderson
Open to researchers & pub by appt only; Open to students, alumni & faculty Mon - Thurs 8:30 AM - 7:30 PM, Fri 8:30 AM - 6 PM, Sat Noon - 5:30 PM; Estab 1871 to develop a collection & services which will anticipate, reflect & support the objectives & direction of an art education; Circ 9,750
Income: Tuition, donations
Library Holdings: Audio Tapes, Book Volumes 31,000, Cassettes 800, Compact Disks, DVDs, Exhibition Catalogs, Filmstrips, Kodachrome Transparencies, Manuscripts, Memorabilia, Motion Pictures, Original Documents, Pamphlets, Periodical Subscriptions 220, Photographs, Slides 125,000, Video Tapes 4,100
Special Subjects: Afro-American Art, Art History, Cartoons, Ceramics, Collages, Conceptual Art, Drawings, Etchings & Engravings, Film, Landscapes, Painting-American, Painting-Australian, Painting-British, Painting-Canadian, Painting-Dutch, Painting-European, Painting-Flemish, Painting-French, Painting-German, Painting-Israeli, Painting-Italian, Painting-Japanese, Painting-Polish, Painting-Russian, Painting-Scandinavian, Painting-Spanish, Photography, Posters, Printmaking, Prints, Sculpture, Video, Watercolors, Woodcuts
Collections: Archives documenting the history of the Art Institute 1871 - present, artists' books
Exhibitions: Artists' Book Contest; 60 years of photography at SFAI; 1960's Rock Posters; Larry Sultan & Mike Mandel; Western Roundtable on Modern Art; music & San Francisco Art; John Collier, Jr, photographer; Gems from David & Peggy Ross collection; Peter Selz - Diego Rivera
Activities: Poetry-Book Readings; current events roundtable

M **SAN FRANCISCO ARTS COMMISSION,** Gallery, 401 Van Ness Ave, Ste 126 San Francisco, CA 94102-4527. Tel 415-252-2244; Email art-info@sfgov.org; Web: www.sfartscommission.org/gallery; *Gallery Dir* Meg Shiffler; *Gallery Mgr* Cece Carpio
Open Tues - Sat 11 AM - 6 PM; No admis fee; Estab 1970; Exhib the work of bay area emerging artist; Average Annual Attendance: 20,000
Income: Financed by city appropriations & pvt donations
Exhibitions: Construct: Annual Installation Award Exhib
Activities: Educ prog; lect open to public; gallery talks; lending collection contains slides

A **SAN FRANCISCO ARTS EDUCATION PROJECT,** C/O Norse Auditorium, 135 Van Ness Ave San Francisco, CA 94102. Tel 415-551-7990; Fax 415-551-7994; Email info@sfartsed.org; Web: www.sfartsed.org; *Exec Dir* Chad S Jones; *Artistic Dir* Emily Keeler; *Prog Dir* Camille Olivier-Salmon; *Admin Coord* Kathleen Moore; *Accounting Mgr* Laura Bloch
Estab to provide participatory experience in the arts to children of San Francisco so they are better equipped to make use of their creative abilities in all aspects of their lives

A **SAN FRANCISCO CAMERAWORK,** 1011 Market St, 2nd Fl San Francisco, CA 94103. Tel 415-487-1011, (gallery) 415-425-8556; Email info@sfcamerawork.org; Web: www.sfcamerawork.org; *Exec Dir* Heather Snider; *Gallery Mgr* Kristina Graber
Open Tues - Thurs & Sat Noon - 6 PM, Fri Noon - 7 & by appt; Admis $5 adults, seniors & students $2, mems no admis fee; Estab 1973 to encourage & display contemporary photography & related visual arts through exhibitions, lectures, publications & commun services; Three galleries; Average Annual Attendance: 35,000; Mem: 1400; dues $50 & up
Income: Financed by government agencies & private contributions, mem
Library Holdings: Book Volumes, Cards, Exhibition Catalogs
Special Subjects: Photography
Publications: San Francisco Camerawork Quarterly
Activities: Lects open to pub, 6 per yr; workshops; gallery talks; Phelan Award; mentoring program; book traveling exhibs; mus shop sells books & magazines, postcards, original art, prints

A **SAN FRANCISCO CITY & COUNTY ARTS COMMISSION,** 401 Van Ness Ave, Ste 325, San Francisco, CA 94102; 401 Van Ness Ave, Ste 325 San Francisco, CA 94102. Tel 415-252-2255; Fax 415-252-2595; Web: sfartscommission.org; *Dir Cultural Affairs* Tom DeCaigny; *Deputy Dir* Rebekah Krell; *Dir Street Artist Prog* Howard Lazar; *Dir Pub Art Prog* Susan Pontious; *Mgr Civic Art Coll* Allison Cummings; *Dir Community Investments* Judy Nemzoff; *Pres* Kate Patterson
Call for hours; No admis fee; Estab 1932; Average Annual Attendance: 100,000; Mem: Consists of nine professional & three lay-members appointed by the Mayor with advice of art societies & five ex-officio members; monthly meetings
Collections: San Francisco Civic Art Coll
Activities: Pub Art Prog; gallery exhibs, pub meetings; sales shop sells original art, reproductions & prints

M **SAN FRANCISCO MARITIME NATIONAL HISTORICAL PARK,** Maritime Museum, 900 Beach St, San Francisco, CA 94109-1002. Tel 415-561-7000; Fax 415-556-1624; Email lynn_cullivan@nps.gov; Web: www.nps.gov/safr; *Prin Librn* David Hull; *Mgmt Asst* Lynn Cullivan; *Supt* William G Thomas; *Cur Maritime History* Steve Canright; *Chief Interpretation* Marc Hayman; *Supervisory Archivist* Lisbit Bailey
Open winter daily 10 AM - 4 PM, summer daily 10 AM - 6 PM; No admis fee for museum; Hyde St. Pier adults $5, children 16 & under no charge; Estab 1951; mus built in 1939; a Terrazzo & stainless steel structure with a nautical theme; Maintains reference library; Average Annual Attendance: 500,000
Income: Financed by federal funding, private support from National Maritime Mus Assoc
Purchases: A S Palmer Film Collection; Barbara Johnson Whaling Collection, books
Library Holdings: Audio Tapes, Book Volumes, Clipping Files, Fiche, Filmstrips, Manuscripts, Maps, Motion Pictures, Original Documents, Pamphlets, Periodical Subscriptions, Photographs, Prints, Reels, Video Tapes
Special Subjects: Costumes, Crafts, Drawings, Eskimo Art, Etchings & Engravings, Folk Art, Graphics, Historical Material, Ivory, Manuscripts, Maps, Marine Painting, Metalwork, Painting-American, Photography, Scrimshaw
Collections: Barbara Johnson Whaling Collection: books, A S Palmer Film Collection, paddlewheel ferry, paddlewheel tug, scow schooner, small craft, ship models, square-rigged sailing ship, steam schooner, steam tug, 3-mast schooner
Exhibitions: Tugboats; San Francisco Bay Ferryboats; Sparks, Waves and Wizards: Communications at Sea
Publications: Sealetter; booklets, irregular
Activities: Classes for adults & children; dramatic progs; docent training; lects open to pub, 4 vis lectrs per yr; concerts; tours; competitions; originate traveling exhibs to maritime museums; mus shop sells books, magazines, models & children's educational materials

L **Maritime Library**, Bldg E, Fort Mason Center, San Francisco, CA 94123-1314. Tel 415-561-7030; Email safr_maritime_library@nps.gov; Web: www.nps.gov/safr/historyculture/library-collections.htm; *Reference* Gina Bardi; *Technical Svcs* Heather Hernandez; *Library Technician* Mark Goldstein; *Chief of Cultural Resources* Robbyn Jackson; *Supt* Kevin Hendricks; *Colls Mgr* Keri Koehler
Open Mon -Fri 1 PM - 4 PM, by appointment only; No admis fee; historic ships $5, children 16 & under no charge; Estab 1951; streamlined modern structure with nautical theme; Open to the public for research on premises; Average Annual Attendance: 4,000,000
Library Holdings: Audio Tapes, Book Volumes 35,000, CD-ROMs, Cards, Cassettes, Clipping Files, Compact Disks, DVDs, Exhibition Catalogs, Fiche, Manuscripts, Maps, Memorabilia, Micro Print, Motion Pictures, Original Documents, Other Holdings Archives; Oral History; Vessel Plans, Pamphlets, Periodical Subscriptions 100, Photographs 250,000, Records, Reels, Video Tapes
Special Subjects: Historical Material, Marine Painting
Exhibitions: Cargo is King - permanent; A Walk Along the Waterfront (permanent)
Publications: Booklets, irregular, Maritime News
Activities: Docent training, interpretive sails on the bay; shanty sings; docent training; lects open to pub; concerts; tours

M **SAN FRANCISCO MUSEUM OF CRAFT AND DESIGN,** 2569 Third St, San Francisco, CA 94107. Tel 415-773-0303; Fax 415-773-0306; Email info@sfmcd.org; Web: www.sfmcd.com; *Exec Dir* JoAnn Edwards
Open Tues - Sat 11 AM - 6 PM, Sun noon - 5 PM, cl Mon; Suggested admis adults $8, seniors and students $6, children under 12 & first Tues of every month free
Collections: works of contemporary crafts & design

M **SAN FRANCISCO MUSEUM OF MODERN ART,** 151 3rd St, San Francisco, CA 94103-3159. Tel 415-357-4000; Fax 415-357-4037; Email visit@sfmoma.org; Web: www.sfmoma.org; *Dir ISS* Neal Benezra; *Deputy Dir Curatorial Affairs* Ruth Berson; *Cur Painting & Sculpture* Gary Garrels; *Dir Opers, Facilities & Security* Noah Bartlett; *Chief Content Officer* Chad Coerver; *Cur Photog* Corey Keller; *Chief HR Officer* Ed Lamberger; *Cur Media Arts* Rudolf Frieling; *Sr Cur Painting & Sculpture* Gary Garrels; *Dir Mus Store* Jana Machin; *Dir Mktg & Communs* Jennifer Northrop; *Deputy Dir Admin & Finance* Janet Alberti; *Dir Conservation & Colls* Jill Sterrett; *Interim Dir Develop* Samantha Leo; *Helen and Charles Schwab Dir* Neal Benezra
Open Mon - Tues & Fri - Sun 11 AM - 5:45 PM, Thurs 10 AM - 9 PM, cl Wed; Admis adults $25, seniors $22, ages 19 - 24 with ID $19, members, children 18 & under free; Estab 1935 to collect & exhibit art of the 20th century; Mus occupies its own 225,000 sq ft building; Average Annual Attendance: 750,000; Mem: 42,000; dues $65-$1000
Income: Financed by endowment, mem, city hotel tax, earnings & grants
Library Holdings: Auction Catalogs, Audio Tapes, Book Volumes, CD-ROMs, Cards, Cassettes, Clipping Files, Compact Disks, DVDs, Exhibition Catalogs, Fiche, Maps, Memorabilia, Motion Pictures, Original Art Works, Original Documents, Pamphlets, Periodical Subscriptions, Photographs, Prints, Records, Reels, Slides, Video Tapes
Special Subjects: Architecture, Painting-American, Photography, Sculpture
Collections: Clyfford Still Collection, painting, photography, sculpture architecture & design, media & video works
Exhibitions: Exhibits rotate
Publications: Monthly Calendar
Activities: Classes for adults & children; docent training; lects open to pub; lectrs mems only; 40 vis lectrs per yr; gallery talks; tours; competitions; originates traveling exhibs; Mus shop sells books, magazines, reproductions & prints

L **Library**, 151 Third St, San Francisco, CA 94103-3159. Tel 415-357-4120; Fax 415-357-4038; Email library@sfmoma.org; Web: www.sfmoma.org
Open to the pub Tues & Thurs 10 AM - 4 PM, by appointment only; Estab 1935
Income: Endowment, mem, earnings, grants
Library Holdings: Book Volumes 50,000, Exhibition Catalogs, Other Holdings Artists files; Exhibition archives, Periodical Subscriptions 400
Collections: Margery Mann Collection of books in the history of photography

M **Artist Gallery**, Fort Mason Ctr, 2 Marina Blvd, Bldg A San Francisco, CA 94123. Tel 415-441-4777; Fax 415-441-0614; Email artistsgallery@sfmoma.org; Web: www.sfmoma.org; *Corporate Art Coordr* Maria Medua; *Dir* Marian Parmenter; *Exhib Supv* Steve Pon; *Gallery Coordr* Michelle Nye; *Technical/Art Specialist* Renee de-Cossio; *Admin Asst* Julio Badel; *Art Installer/Driver* Ben Johnston
Open Mon - Fri 9 AM - 5 PM; No admis fee; Estab 1978 for the support & exposure of Northern California artists. Over 1200 artists represented; Rentals & sales
Income: Grants, contributions, endowment
Special Subjects: Collages, Drawings, Etchings & Engravings, Photography, Prints, Sculpture, Watercolors
Exhibitions: Eight exhibitions per year, all media; one person & group exhibitions
Activities: Artists gallery sells & rents original art

L **SAN FRANCISCO PUBLIC LIBRARY,** Art, Music & Recreation Center, 100 Larkin St, San Francisco, CA 94102-4705. Tel 415-557-4525; Fax 415-557-4524; Email artmusicrec@sfpl.org; Web: www.sfpl.org; *City Librn* Luis Herrera; *Mgr Art, Music, Bus & Technical Science* Mark Hall; *Librn II, Prog Mgr* Quindi Berger; *Librn II, Prog Mgr* Jason Gibbs
Open Mon & Sat 10 AM - 6 PM, Tues - Thurs 9 AM - 8 PM, Fri noon - 6 PM, Sun Noon - 5 PM; No admis fee; Estab 1878; Jewett Gallery (lower level), Skylight Gallery (6th flr)
Income: Financed by city & state appropriations
Library Holdings: Book Volumes 45,000, Cards, Clipping Files, DVDs, Exhibition Catalogs, Motion Pictures, Pamphlets, Periodical Subscriptions 250, Records, Reels
Activities: Classes for adults; lects open to pub; concerts; Sales shop sells books

L **SAN FRANCISCO STATE UNIVERSITY,** J Paul Leonard Library, 1630 Holloway, San Francisco, CA 94132. Tel 415-338-2188; Fax 415-338-6199; Email libweb@sfsu.edu; Web: www.library.sfsu.edu; *Art Librn* Darlene Tong
Open Mon - Thurs 8 AM - 10 PM, Fri 8 AM - 5 PM, Sat 10 AM - 6 PM, Sun noon - 9 PM; Estab 1899; Not available during bldg construction project
Library Holdings: Book Volumes 1,000,000, Compact Disks, DVDs, Exhibition Catalogs, Fiche, Framed Reproductions, Manuscripts, Memorabilia, Original Art Works, Other Holdings Bound per vol 132,000; Film & video 14,500; Graphic materials 98,000; Sound rec 57,000, Periodical Subscriptions, Photographs, Video Tapes
Special Subjects: Antiquities-Etruscan, Antiquities-Roman, Architecture, Art History, Graphic Design, Industrial Design, Intermedia
Collections: H Wilder Bentley Brush Painting Collection, Frank deBellis Collection on Italian Culture, John Magnani Collection of Arts & Crafts, Simeon Pelenc Collection of Paintings & Drawings, San Francisco Bay area television archives, visual materials from labor archives
Activities: Book traveling exhibs; originate traveling exhibs; sales shop sells books & reproductions

M **SOUTHERN EXPOSURE,** 3030 20th St, San Francisco, CA 94110-2780. Tel 415-863-2141; Fax 415-738-8018; Email director@soex.org; Web: www.soex.org; *Dir* Patricia Maloney; *Assoc Dir* Nick Wylie; *Projects & Exhibs Prog Dir* Valerie Lmus; *Artists in Educ Prog Dir* Maya Gomez; *Communs & Outreach Dir* Lisa Martin
Open Tues - Sat 12 PM - 6 PM; A non-profit organization committed to supporting visual artists since 1974; 28 ft ceilings; 2500 sq ft in three galleries; Average Annual Attendance: 25,000; Mem: 1800; dues $30-$2000 & up
Income: Financed by endowment, mem, contributions, grants
Collections: Juried Exhib (nationally recognized cur) Nov, Dec, Postcard Show
Activities: Artists in education prog (ages 12-21), performances, symposiums, internship prog; lects; Graue Award; Alternative Exposure Grants

M **TATTOO ART MUSEUM,** 841 Columbus Ave, San Francisco, CA 94133; 210 Clara Ave, Ukiah, CA 95482-4004. Tel 415-775-4991; Email lyletutt@pacific.net; Web: www.lyletuttle.com; *Consultant* Judith Tuttle; *Dir* Lyle Tuttle; *Mgr* Tanja Nixx
Open daily Noon - 9 PM; Estab 1974; Average Annual Attendance: 5,000
Special Subjects: Primitive art
Collections: Lyle Tuttle Collection, tattoo art, Memorabilia & Equipment, especially tattoo machines & primitive tools, George Burchett Collection
Publications: Magazine of the Tattoo Art Museum; Tattoo Historian, biannual
Activities: Lect open to public, 12 vis lectrs per year; awards; Tattoo Hall of Fame; individual paintings & objects of art lent

M **U GALLERY,** 3367 20th St, San Francisco, CA 94110. Tel 888-402-1722; Email sales@ugallery.com; Web: www.ugallery.com; *Co-Founder* Alex Farkas; *Co-Founder* Stephen Tanenbaum
Open Mon - Fri 9 AM - 5 PM; Estab 1991 to support culture in America; Curated online gallery; Average Annual Attendance: 600; Mem: 205
Income: privately financed
Special Subjects: Painting-American, Restorations, Painting-Polish, Furniture
Collections: Cyber Culture, Local Community, Psychotic
Exhibitions: Florescent Light; Saccadis Art; East Village Artist NYC
Activities: Lectrs for members only, 8 vis lectr per yr; concerts; mus shop sells original art & art objects

M **THE UNIVERSITY OF SAN FRANCISCO THACHER GALLERY,** Gleeson Library, 2130 Fulton St San Francisco, CA 94117-1080. Tel 415-422-5178; Email thachergallery@usfca.edu; Web: www.usfca.edu/thacher-gallery; *Dir* Glori Simmons; *Gallery Mgr* Nell Herbert
Open daily noon - 6 PM; No admis fee; Estab 1997 to encourage the coincidence of creativity, scholarship & community
Collections: Work by visiting artists, students & faculty; university art & rare book colls
Exhibitions: Temporary exhibits
Activities: Educ progs; student training; Artist talks; craft demonstrations; tours

C **WELLS FARGO BANK,** Wells Fargo History Museum, 420 Montgomery St, MAC A0101-106 San Francisco, CA 94163. Tel 415-396-2619; Fax 415-975-7430; Email wfmuseum.sf@wellsfargo.com; Web: www.wellsfargohistory.com; *Cur* Glen Myers
Open Mon - Fri 9 AM - 5 PM, cl Bank holidays; No admis fee; Estab 1960 to provide historical information on Wells Fargo, California & San Francisco; Permanent & special exhibitions open to the public; Average Annual Attendance: 50,000
Special Subjects: American Western Art, Gold, Historical Material, Jewelry, Maps, Painting-American, Photography, Prints, Reproductions, Sculpture
Collections: Wiltsee Collection of Postal Franks, California History, 19th & 20th Century Banking, San Francisco History
Exhibitions: Permanent: art & artifacts from gold rush, stagecoach travel, western art, banking history
Activities: Concerts; school tours featuring gold rush Calif era; mus shop sells books, stagecoach & gold rush souvenirs

M **YERBA BUENA CENTER FOR THE ARTS,** 701 Mission St, San Francisco, CA 94103-3138. Tel 415-978-2700; Fax 415-978-9635; Email hello@ybca.org; Web: www.ybca.org; *CEO* Deborah Cullinan; *COO* Scott Rowitz
Open Tues - Wed & Fri - Sun 11 AM - 6 PM, Thurs 11 AM - 8 PM, cl Mon; Admis $10; Estab 1993; contemporary art; Average Annual Attendance: 50,000; Mem: 2500
Special Subjects: Afro-American Art, Drawings, Hispanic Art, Juvenile Art, Latin American Art, Oriental Art, Painting-American, Sculpture
Exhibitions: Beautiful Losers; Cosmic Wonder; Erwin Wurm; Nick Cave; Yoshua Okon; Techno Craft; Audience as Subject, Song Doug
Activities: Docent training; workshops for children; teen employment & art training; lects open to pub; concerts; tours; gallery talks; originates traveling exhibs circulating to any art museum

SAN JACINTO

M **MT SAN JACINTO COLLEGE,** Fine Art Gallery, 1499 N State St, San Jacinto, CA 92583. Tel 951-487-3585; Email jknuth@msjc.edu; Web: www.msjc.edu/artgallery; *Gallery Cur* John Knuth
Open Mon - Thurs 10 AM - 4 PM; Estab to serve as an educational & cultural center that advocates creativity and diversity; Average Annual Attendance: 2,000
Special Subjects: Painting-American, Sculpture, Photography
Collections: paintings; sculpture; photographs
Exhibitions: Temporary exhibits
Activities: Artist talks

SAN JOSE

M **ROSICRUCIAN EGYPTIAN MUSEUM & PLANETARIUM,** Rosicrucian Order, AMORC, 1342 Naglee Ave, San Jose, CA 95126. Tel 408-947-3600; Fax 408-947-3638; Email info@egyptianmuseum.org; Web: www.egyptianmuseum.org; *Dir* Julie Scott; *Mgr, Supervisor* Lorraine Katich
Open Wed - Fri 9 AM - 5 PM, Sat & Sun 10 AM - 6 PM; Admis adults $9, seniors & students with ID $7, children 5-10 $5, under 5 free; Estab 1929, in present location 1966, to publicly show a collection of the works of ancient Egyptians, reflecting their lives & culture; Collections include Bronzes of Egyptian Gods & Goddesses; Funerary Models; full size walk-in tomb replica; human & animal mummies; Tel-El-Armana room with amulets, cosmetics & writing implements; jewelry, pottery & King Zoser's tomb complex; Mesopotamian collection - cuneiform tablets & seals from Babylon, Sumer & Assyria; Average Annual Attendance: 100,000
Income: Financed by Rosicrucian Order, AMORC
Purchases: Regular acquisitions of Egyptian antiquities
Special Subjects: Antiquities-Assyrian, Antiquities-Egyptian, Antiquities-Oriental, Jewelry
Collections: Collections include Bronzes of Egyptian Gods & Goddesses, Funerary Models, full size walk-in tomb replica, human & animal mummies, Tel-El-Armana room, amulets, cosmetics, writing implements, jewelry, pottery, scale model of King Zoser's tomb complex, Mesopotamian collection - cuneiform tablets & seals from Babylon
Exhibitions: Quarterly exhibitions in the Rotating Exhibits gallery featuring both Ancient and Modern Art
Publications: Treasures of the Rosicrucian Egyptian Museum, catalog; Rosecroixjournal.org

M **SAN JOSE INSTITUTE OF CONTEMPORARY ART,** 560 S First St, San Jose, CA 95113. Tel 408-283-8155; Fax 408-283-8157; Email info@sjica.org; Web: www.sjica.org; *Dir* Cathy Kimball
Open Tues - Fri 10 AM - 5 PM, Sat & Sun noon - 5 PM; No admis fee; Estab 1980, SJICA is a non-profit visual arts organization highlighting emerging & estab artists from the Greater Bay Area & beyond; 7500 sq ft facility includes gallery & on-site print center & admin offices; Average Annual Attendance: 25,000; Mem: 600; dues $35 & up
Income: Financed by mem & cultural grants
Library Holdings: Exhibition Catalogs, Pamphlets, Periodical Subscriptions
Collections: works by contemporary artists
Exhibitions: Monthly exhibition; Annual fall auction
Activities: Classes for adults; on-site print ctr offers workshops, open access prog, private individual & group workshops; Lect open to public; gallery talks; tours by appointment; print ctr artist-in residence print editions available for purchase

M **SAN JOSE MUSEUM OF ART,** 110 S Market St, San Jose, CA 95113-2383. Tel 408-271-2840; Fax 408-294-2977; Email info@sjmusart.org; Web: www.sanjosemuseumofart.org; *Deputy Dir* Deborah Norberg; *Dir Communs* Sherrill Ingalls; *Museum Store Mgr* Pat Downward; *Exec Dir* Susan Krane; *Dir Educ* Lucy Larson
Open Tues -Sun 11AM-5PM, cl Mon; Admis adults $8, seniors & students $5, SJMA mems & children 6 & under free; Estab 1969 to foster awareness, appreciation & understanding of 20th century art; An 1892 Richardson - Romanesque building with a striking contemporary new wing, totaling more than 18,000 sq ft of exhibition space; Average Annual Attendance: 100,000; Mem: 3,500; dues $50-$3,500
Income: Financed by City of San Jose, private sector contributions, state & federal government
Special Subjects: Photography, Prints, Sculpture, Drawings
Collections: Permanent Collection features work by nationally recognized artists, artists of the California region, American prints & sculptures, twentieth-century art
Publications: Tri-Annual Newsletter
Activities: Classes for adults & children; docent training; family progs; school outreach; lects open to pub, 13 vis lectrs per yr; concerts; gallery talks; tours; summer art studios; in-school art lessons; book traveling exhibs; originate traveling exhibs to other mus in the US; mus store sells books, magazines, reproductions, prints, jewelry, gifts, toys & cards

L **Library,** 110 S Market St, San Jose, CA 95113-2383. Tel 408-271-6840; Fax 408-294-2977; Email info@sjmusart.org; *Librn* Gloria Turk; *Chief Cur* Susan

Landauer; *Dir Visitor Experience & Interpreter* Margaret Maynard; *Sr Cur* JoAnne Northrup; *Deputy Dir* Deborah Norbert; *Dir Educ* Val DeLang; *Financial Officer* Lynn Schuyler-King; *Chief Design & Installations* Richard Karson; *Assoc Mktg & Commun* Stephanie Vidergar; *Asst Cur* Ann Wolfe; *Deputy Dir of Extended Affairs* Gary Gallagher Landis; *Pres* Deborah Rappaport; *Dir* Cindy Sylvester; *Cur Asst* Lyndsey Wylie
Open Tues - Sun 11 AM - 5 PM; no admis fee; Estab 1969; Open to the mus staff & volunteers for reference only; Average Annual Attendance: 200,000; Mem: 2600
Income: Financed by donations
Library Holdings: Book Volumes 3400, Clipping Files, Exhibition Catalogs 5950, Pamphlets, Periodical Subscriptions, Photographs, Video Tapes
Special Subjects: Art History, Painting-American
Collections: California and West Coast contemporary art
Publications: SJMA Frameworks, 6 times a year
Activities: Classes for adults; docent training; lects open to pub; lects for mem only; gallery talks, tours; mus shop sells books, reproductions, prints

M **SAN JOSE STATE UNIVERSITY,** Natalie & James Thompson Art Gallery, Dept of Art & Art History, San Jose State University San Jose, CA 95192-0089. Tel 408-924-4328; Fax 408-924-4326; Email jo.hernandez@sjsu.edu; Web: www.sjsu.edu; *Dir* Jo Farb Hernandez
Open Mon - 10 AM - 4PM, Tues 10 AM - 4 PM & 6-7:30 PM, Wed - Fri 10 AM - 4 PM; No admis fee; Estab 1960 as part of the university department; Gallery is 34 x 28 ft with 12 ft ceiling; Average Annual Attendance: 15,000
Income: Financed by state appropriations & private endowment
Collections: Coll of works by faculty, alumni & regional artists maintained by univ
Exhibitions: Contemporary Issues, Art & Art History
Publications: Exhibition catalogs; brochures; monthly announcement
Activities: Lects open to pub; over 30 per yr vis lectrs weekly during fall & spring semesters; concerts; gallery talks; tours; competition; scholarships offered; books traveling exhibs 0-1 per yr; originates traveling exhibs to other non-profit galleries & mus; sales shop sells books

L **Dr. Martin Luther King Jr. Library**, 150 E San Fernando St, San Jose, CA 95112-3580; 1 Washington Sq, San Jose, CA 95112-3613. Tel 408-808-2037; Fax 408-808-2009; Email edith.crowe@sjsu.edu; Web: sjlibrary.org; vrc-collections.sjsu.edu/vr_library/; *Visual Resources Cur* Stacy Barclay; *Art Reference Librn* Edith Crowe
Open Mon - Thurs 9 AM - midnight, Sun 7 PM - midnight
Income: Financed by state funds, student library fees & private donations
Purchases: $52,800
Library Holdings: Audio Tapes, Book Volumes 53,500, CD-ROMs, Cards, Cassettes, Compact Disks, Exhibition Catalogs, Fiche, Filmstrips, Framed Reproductions, Lantern Slides, Micro Print, Motion Pictures, Original Art Works, Periodical Subscriptions 87, Photographs, Prints, Records, Reels, Reproductions, Slides, Video Tapes

SAN LUIS OBISPO

L **CALIFORNIA POLYTECHNIC STATE UNIVERSITY,** College of Architecture & Environmental Design-Architecture Collection, 959 Higuera St, San Luis Obispo, CA 93401-3601. Tel 805-756-2165; Fax 805-756-5986; *Asst Dir* Vickie Aubourg
Open Mon - Fri 8:30AM-noon & 1PM-4:30PM; No admis fee; Estab 1969; 190,000 slides for reference; Circ 20,000 (slides)
Income: Financed by state appropriation
Library Holdings: Book Volumes 1000, Periodical Subscriptions 30
Special Subjects: Architecture, Constructions, Landscapes
Collections: Architecture & Landscape Architecture slide coll

L **CUESTA COLLEGE,** Harold J Miossi Art Gallery, Hwy 1, Room 7170 San Luis Obispo, CA 93405; PO Box 8106, San Luis Obispo, CA 93403. Tel 805-546-3202; Fax 805-546-3939; Email Bea_anderson@cuesta.edu; Web: www.my.cuesta.edu/artgallery; *Chair Fine Arts* Margaret Korisheli; *Fine & Performing Arts Support Coordr* Bea Anderson; *Outreach Develop Coordr* Emily Jagger; *Gallery Asst* Sabrina Jenkins
Open Mon - Fri noon - 4 PM; No admis fee; Estab 1966 to support the educational prog of the col; Contemporary fine art gallery featuring rotating exhibitions of national, regional & local artists; Average Annual Attendance: 10,000
Library Holdings: Audio Tapes, Book Volumes 3130, Cassettes, Fiche, Filmstrips, Motion Pictures, Pamphlets, Periodical Subscriptions 18, Records, Reels, Slides, Video Tapes
Special Subjects: Ceramics, Collages, Drawings, Painting-American, Prints, Sculpture, Watercolors, Woodcuts
Collections: 20 works of art primarily of California artists, 2 Japanese artists, works by contemporary artists
Activities: Educ dept, class for adults; lects open to pub, 3 vis lectrs per yr; concerts; gallery talks; tours; originate traveling exhibs

A **SAN LUIS OBISPO MUSEUM OF ART,** 1010 Broad St, San Luis Obispo, CA; PO Box 813, San Luis Obispo, CA 93406-0813. Tel 805-543-8562; Fax 805-543-4518; Email kkile@sloma.org; Web: www.sloma.org; *Exec Dir* Karen M Kile; *Exhib & Develop Dir* Ruta Saliklis; *Gallery Dir & Registrar* Wendy R Walter; *Community Engagement* Erica Ellis; *Youth Educ* Beth Mott; *Press Relations* Rebecca Leduc
Open every day July 4th-Labor Day 11AM-5PM, otherwise Wed - Mon 11AM-5PM; Admis free; Estab 1952 to promote the visual arts through educ, expression & interaction; Three galleries; Average Annual Attendance: 40,000; Mem: 830; dues $20 - $225
Income: $550,000+ (financed by mem, sales & donations)
Special Subjects: Ceramics, Crafts, Drawings, Glass, Jewelry, Landscapes, Painting-American, Photography
Collections: Permanent collection of regional artists
Publications: Newsletter, website
Activities: Classes for adults & children; lects & film nights; concerts; gallery talks; tours; sponsored competitions; exhibs in 3 galleries; scholarships; mus shop sells books, original art, reproductions, cards & jewelry

SAN MARCOS

M **PALOMAR COMMUNITY COLLEGE,** Boehm Gallery, 1140 W Mission Rd, San Marcos, CA 92069-1487. Tel 760-744-1150, Ext 2304; Fax 760-744-8723; Email jbigfeather@palomar.edu; Web: www.palomar.edu/art/boehmgallery.html; *Gallery Dir* Ingram Ober
Open Tues 10AM-4PM, Wed-Thurs 10AM-7PM, Fri-Sat 10AM-2PM; No admis fee; Estab 1964 to provide the community with fine art regardless of style, period or approach; The gallery is 35 x 35 ft, no windows, 18 in brick exterior, acoustic ceiling & asphalt tile floor; Average Annual Attendance: 50,000
Income: $8000 (exhibition budget). Financed by city & state appropriations
Collections: Contemporary art by nationally acclaimed artists, 16th - 20th century art, California artists
Activities: Lect open to public, 12 vis lectrs per year; competitions; individual paintings & original objects of art lent to reputable museums & galleries; lending collection contains original paintings, prints & sculpture

SAN MARINO

M **THE HUNTINGTON LIBRARY, ART COLLECTIONS & BOTANICAL GARDENS,** 1151 Oxford Rd, San Marino, CA 91108-1299. Tel 626-405-2100; Fax 626-405-0225; Email publicinformation@huntington.org; Web: www.huntington.org; *VPres Advancement* Randy Shulman; *CFO* Coreen A Rodgers; *Acting Dir Art Coll* Catherine Hess; *Dir Library* Sandra L. Brooke; *Dir Botanical Gardens* James Folsom; *VPres Communs* Susan Turner-Lowe; *Asst VPres Advancement* Randy Shulman
Open Mon, Wed - Sun 10 AM - 5 PM, cl Tues, New Year's Day, Independence Day, Thanksgiving, Christmas Eve & Christmas Day; Admis adults $25, seniors 65 & older & students 12-18 $21, youth 4-11 $13, groups of 15 or more $19, children under 4 free; Estab 1919 by the late Henry E Huntington as a free research library, art gallery, mus & botanical garden; exhibitions open to the pub in 1928 for educational & cultural purposes. Virginia Steele Scott Gallery for American art opened in 1984; Average Annual Attendance: 500,000; Mem: 15,000; supporters of the institution who give $60-$1000 annually are known as the Friends of the Huntington Library, Fellows give $2000 or more per year
Income: Financed by endowment & gifts
Special Subjects: Architecture, Baroque Art, Bronzes, Carpets & Rugs, Ceramics, Decorative Arts, Drawings, Etchings & Engravings, Furniture, Manuscripts
Collections: Ellesmere manuscript of Chaucer's Canterbury Tales, Gutenberg Bible on vellum, Birds of America by Audubon, Rich Collection: Rare Books & Manuscripts
Exhibitions: Rotating exhibits
Publications: The Calendar, bimonthly; Huntington Library Quarterly; various monographs & exhibition catalogs; Frontiers, semi-annually
Activities: Classes for children; docent training; lects open to pub, 25 vis lectrs per yr; concerts, gallery talks; tours; scholarships & fels offered; individual paintings lent; mus shop sells books, calendars, gift items, note cards, postcards, prints, puzzles, reproductions, slides

L **Library**, 1151 Oxford Rd, San Marino, CA 91108. Tel 626-405-2100; Fax 626-405-0398; Email publicinformation@huntington.org; Web: www.huntington.org; *Pres* Steven Kobik; *Exec Asst to Pres* Kathy Hacker; *VPres Advancement* George Abdo; *Dir Botanical Gardens* James Folsom; *Dir Educ* Susan Lafferty; *Assoc VPres Advancement* Suzy Moser; *Dir Colls* John Murdoch; *Dir Research & Educ* Robert C Ritchie; *Assoc VPres Operations* Laurie Sowd; *VPres Communs* Susan Turner-Lowe; *Dir Library* David Zeidberg
Open Mon, Wed, Thurs, & Fri Noon-4:30PM; Cl Tues and major holidays-New Year's Day, Independence Day, Thanksgiving, Christmas Eve, Christmas Day; Summer hours 10:30AM-4:30PM, cl Tues; Admis adults, $20, seniors, $15, students 12-18 $12, youth 5-11 $8, group rate $11 per person for groups of 15 or more, children under 5, & members free; Estab 1919, research & educational institution; 18th century British & French art & early 18th to early 20th century American art; Average Annual Attendance: 521,000; Mem: 25,000; dues Benefactor $1,250, Patron $600, Supporting $300, Sponsoring $200, Sustaining $100, Senior $80
Income: Financed by contributions, admis, endowment & earned income
Library Holdings: Book Volumes 682,094, Cards, Exhibition Catalogs, Fiche, Manuscripts, Memorabilia, Micro Print, Other Holdings Photographic archive 100,000, Pamphlets, Periodical Subscriptions 1200, Photographs, Prints, Reels
Special Subjects: American Western Art, Art History, Bronzes, Carpets & Rugs, Ceramics, Decorative Arts, Drawings, Etchings & Engravings, Furniture, History of Art & Archaeology, Illustration, Interior Design, Landscape Architecture, Landscapes, Manuscripts
Publications: Calendar; Frontiers Magazine; Annual Report; In Fact
Activities: Classes for adults & children; docent training; lects open to pub; 10-20 vis lectrs per yr; concerts; gallery talks; tours; scholarships; fel; lending of original objects of art to various orgs; originates traveling exhibs to various orgs; mus shop sells books, magazines, reproductions, prints, slides & gifts

L **UNIVERSITY OF SOUTHERN CALIFORNIA/THE GAMBLE HOUSE,** Greene & Greene Archives, Huntington Library 1151 Oxford Rd, San Marino, CA 91108. Tel 626-405-2232; Fax 626-796-6498; Email scheid@usc.edu; Web: www.usc.edu/dept/architecture/greeneandgreene; *Archivist* Ann Scheid
Open by appt; No admis fee; Estab 1968 as a concentrated collection of archival material on the work of architects Charles & Henry Greene; For research only; Average Annual Attendance: 100
Library Holdings: Auction Catalogs, Audio Tapes 5, Book Volumes 800, CD-ROMs 60, Clipping Files, Compact Disks 100, Exhibition Catalogs, Lantern Slides 50, Manuscripts 5,000, Memorabilia, Motion Pictures 5, Original Art Works 50, Original Documents 500, Other Holdings Drawings; Client files; Blueprints, Pamphlets, Photographs 3500, Records, Slides 800, Video Tapes 10
Special Subjects: Architecture, Decorative Arts, Landscape Architecture, Photography, Stained Glass
Collections: Art, architecture, and decorative arts of architects Charles Sumner Greene and Henry Mather Greene, Alfred Heineman Collection (architectural drawings, photographs, scrapbooks)

Publications: A New & Native Beauty: The Art & Craft of Greene & Greene; Seeing Greene & Greene: Architecture in Photographs
Activities: Docent training, vis col classes

SAN MIGUEL

M **MISSION SAN MIGUEL MUSEUM,** 755 Mission St, San Miguel, CA 93451; PO Box 69, San Miguel, CA 93451-0069. Tel 805-467-3256; Fax 805-467-2448; Email giftshop@missionsanmiquel.org; Web: www.missionsanmiquel.org; *Guardian* Max Hottle OFM; *Pastor* Pedro Umana OFM
Open daily 10 AM - 4:30 PM, cl New Year's, Easter, Thanksgiving & Christmas; Admis by donation; Estab 1797; The Mission fresco secco decorations date back to 1821; Average Annual Attendance: 25,000
Income: Financed by Franciscan Friars & donations
Special Subjects: Archaeology, Architecture, Dioramas, Historical Material, Manuscripts, Mexican Art, Painting-Spanish, Period Rooms, Religious Art, Reproductions, Restorations, American Indian Art
Collections: Spanish era art & artifacts
Activities: 4th grade tours; Tours; gift shop sells books, reproductions, prints, gifts & religious articles

SAN PEDRO

M **ANGELS GATE CULTURAL CENTER,** Gallery A & Gallery G, 3601 S Gaffey St, San Pedro, CA 90731-6969. Tel 310-519-0936; Fax 310-519-8698; Email artatgate@aol.com; Web: www.angelsgateart.org; *Exec Dir* Nathan Birnbaum; *Educ Dir* Jessica Maeson Yang
Open Tues - Sun 10 AM - 5 PM; No admis fee; Estab 1981 dedicated to innovation & cultural diversity; 3000 sq ft in Gallery A, 600 sq ft in Gallery G; Mem: 400; dues $25-1,000; annual meeting in Sept
Income: $250,000 (financed by mem, studio rentals, workshop tuition, donations & grants)
Activities: Classes for adults & children; internships; outreach workshops; docent training; artists in classrooms in local schools; lect open to public; dir tours; dialogue with artists; concerts; dance recitals; theatre productions; sales shop sells books, magazines, original art, prints, jewelry, handbags, cards & calendars

SAN RAFAEL

M **CITY OF SAN RAFAEL,** Falkirk Cultural Center, 1408 Mission Ave, San Rafael, CA 94901. Tel 415-485-3328, 485-3326; Fax 415-485-3404; Email jane.lange@ci.san-rafael.ca.us; Web: www.falkirkculturalcenter.org; *Cur* Beth Goldberg; *Dir* Jane Lange; *Pub Rels* Corey Bytof
Open Mon - Fri 1 PM - 5 PM, Sat 10 AM - 1 PM; No admis fee; Estab 1974 to provide classes, lectures, concerts for the city of San Rafael & surrounding region; Contemporary art gallery; Average Annual Attendance: 20,000; Mem: 50; dues bus/corporate $1000, fellow $500, advocate $250, steward $100, family $50, friend $30, sr citizen, student & artist $20
Income: Financed by City of San Rafael appropriation, rentals, classes & grants
Special Subjects: Restorations
Exhibitions: Annual juried exhibition, Dia de Los Muertos exhibition
Publications: Exhibition catalogues
Activities: Classes for adults & children; docent training; lect open to public, 6 vis lectrs per year; concerts; tours; juried annual competitions; bookstore sells books, prints, & poetry readings

A **MARIN SOCIETY OF ARTISTS INC,** 1515 3rd St, San Rafael, CA 94901-2710. Tel 415-454-9561; Email emailus@marinsocietyofartists.com; Web: www.marinsocietyofartists.org; *Resource Manager* Annalisa Price; *Pres* Debra Self; *VPres* Sue Lyttle; *Treasurer* Ronile Valenza; *Recording Secretary* Meg REilly
Wed-Sun Noon to 4PM; closed Mon & Tue; No admis fee; Estab 1927 to foster cooperation among artists & to continually develop pub interest in art; Circ Small library for mem only; Gallery is located in the town arts district. It is approx 3500 sq ft of well lighted exhibit space, plus 17 Artist studios.; Average Annual Attendance: 75,000; Mem: 300; dues tiered from $110 to $220; Two general member meetings annually
Income: Financed by mem, sale of art, & annual fundraiser, facilities rental
Exhibitions: One show per month; annual fundraiser
Publications: Weekly Member Newsletter; Monthly Patron Newsletter
Activities: Classes open to all, children & the blind; docent training; lect open to public, 2-3 vis lectrs per year; competitions with cash awards; sales shop sells original art, original prints, handcrafted jewelry ceramics & fiberworks

SANTA ANA

M **BOWERS MUSEUM,** 2002 N Main St, Santa Ana, CA 92706-2776. Tel 714-567-3600; Fax 714-567-3603; Email info@bowers.org; Web: www.bowers.org; *VPres Exhibit Design, Fabrication & Installation* Paul Johnson; *Pres* Dr Peter Keller; *CFO* Thuy Nguyen; *VPres Information Technology* Paul Dowdle
Open Tues - Sun 10 AM - 4 PM, cl Mon & holidays; Admis adults $13, students & seniors $10, under 12 years-old free; Estab 1936 to provide an active cultural arts museum for the community; Originally housed in an authentic California mission-style structure surrounding a courtyard fountain, devoted to the display of antique furniture, Indian relics & historical items of early California families, The museum has grown to encompass 90,000 sq ft. The new additions include major galleries, new collection storage rooms, admin offices, library & restaurant exhibiting the cultural arts of the world; Average Annual Attendance: 133,000; Mem: 7,000
Income: Financed by city appropriation, earned revenue & contributions
Special Subjects: African Art, American Indian Art, Asian Art, Pre-Columbian Art, Hispanic Art
Collections: Pre-Columbian Mesoamerica, Native N & S American art & artifacts, African & Oceanic art, California plein air paintings
Publications: Brochures; Quarterly Calendar; exhibition catalogs
Activities: Classes for adults & children; docent training; lects open to pub; films; gallery talks; tours; study clubs; paintings & original art objects lent to other mus; originates traveling exhibs; mus shop sells books, magazines, reproductions, slides, prints, jewelry, imported clothing, gift items; Kidseum 1801 N Main St Santa Ana, CA 92706

M **SANTA ANA COLLEGE,** Art Gallery, 1530 W 17th St, Santa Ana, CA 92706-3398. Tel 714-564-5615; Fax 714-564-5629; Email mccabe_caroline@sac.edu; Web: www.sac.edu/art; *Interim Gallery Dir* Phillip Marquez; *Gallery Coordr* Caroline McCabe; *Preparator* Wesley Schaffner
Open Mon - Thurs 10 AM - 2 PM, Wed 6:30 - 8:30 PM; No admis fee; Estab 1972 to educate students, staff, faculty & the community; Average Annual Attendance: 12,000
Income: Financed by Rancho Santiago Community College District budget
Exhibitions: Annual Juried Student Art Show; High School Art Show; Group exhibs, solo artists (professional)
Publications: Art Forum Newsletter, 6 per year
Activities: Classes for adults; dramatic progs; lects open to pub, 36-40 vis lectrs per yr; competitions with awards; concerts; gallery talks; tours; cash prizes for students during ann art show; schols offered

SANTA BARBARA

A **SANTA BARBARA CONTEMPORARY ARTS FORUM,** 653 Paseo Nuevo, Santa Barbara, CA 93101-3392. Tel 805-966-5373; Fax 805-962-1421; Web: www.sbcaf.org; Others TDD 805-965-9727; *Asst Dir* Rita Ferri; *VPres* Jeffrey Wyatt; *VPres* Keith Puccinelli; *Pres Bd Dir* Ian Smith; *Exec Dir* Miki Garcia; *Office Mgr* Yvonne Heine
Open Tues - Sat 11 AM - 5 PM, Sun Noon - 5 PM; Estab 1976; committed to the presentation of contemporary art; Klausner Gallery 2345 sq ft & Norton Gallery 378 sq ft; Mem: 921; dues start at $25
Income: $265,000 (financed by federal, state, county & city grants, corporate & private contributions, fund raising events)
Collections: Contemporary Art
Publications: Addictions; Carl Cheng: exhibit catalogues; Carroll Dunham: paintings; Focus/Santa Barbara; Jene Highstein: Gallery/Landscape; Teraoka Erotica
Activities: Classes for adults & children; docent training; lect open to public, 15 vis lectrs per year; gallery talks; tours; book traveling exhibs; originate traveling exhibs to other nonprofit galleries

M **SANTA BARBARA MUSEUM OF ART,** 1130 State St, Santa Barbara, CA 93101-2746. Tel 805-963-4364; Fax 805-966-6840; Email info@sbma.net; Web: www.sbma.net; *Dir* Larry J Feinberg; *Dir Devel* Coina Benesh; *Cur Educ* Patsy Hicks; *Registrar* Colonia Martinez; *Cur Asian Art* Susan Tai; *Chief Cur* Eik Kahng; *Cur Contemporary Art* Julie Joyce; *Curator of Photography & New Media* Charles Wylie
Open Tues, Wed, Fri, Sat & Sun 11 AM - 5 PM, Thurs 11 AM - 8 PM, cl Mon; Admis adults $10, seniors, students w/ID & children 6-17 $6, children under 6 no charge; Estab 1941 as an art mus with exhibitions & educ programs; 14 galleries totaling 16,500 sq ft of exhibition space. Maintains reference library; Average Annual Attendance: 167,000; Mem: 4000; dues benefactors' $3,000, dir $1500, cur $750, collectors' $500, gallery $250, assoc $125, general $60
Income: $2,600,000 (financed by earnings, including endowment, mem, grants, government & foundations & contributions)
Special Subjects: African Art, Antiquities-Greek, Antiquities-Roman, Asian Art, Drawings, Etchings & Engravings, Jade, Latin American Art, Oriental Art, Painting-American, Painting-European, Painting-French, Painting-Japanese, Painting-Spanish, Photography, Prints, Sculpture, Tapestries, Watercolors, Woodcuts
Collections: Preston Morton Collection of American Art, Henry Eichheim Collection, Alice F Schott Doll Collection
Publications: Bulletin, quarterly newsletter; exhibit & collection catalogs; Update, semi-annual periodical
Activities: Classes for adults & children; docent training; outreach classes & progs; lects open to pub, 4-6 vis lectrs per yr; concerts; gallery talks; tours; schols offered to children's art classes only; artmobile; individual paintings original objects of art lent to other mus only for exhibs; book traveling exhibs 3-5 per yr; originate traveling exhibs; mus shop sells books, original art, reproductions

L **Library,** 1130 State St, Santa Barbara, CA 93101-2746. Tel 805-963-4364; Fax 805-966-6840; Web: www.sbma.net; *Dir* Larry J Feinberg; *Dir Develop* Barbara Ben-Horin; *Chair Bd Trustees* John C Bishop; *Dir Educ* Patsy Hicks; *Spec Progs Coordr* Lisa Hill; *Mus Store Mgr* John Reilly; *Cur Contemporary Art* Julie Joyce; *Registrar* Sandy Davis; *CFO* James Hutchinson; *Cur Asian Art* Susan Shin-tsu Tai; *Librn* Heather Brodhead; *Chief Cur* Eik Kahng
Open to pub on an appointment basis; Admis adults $10, seniors (65+), students (with ID) & children 6-17 $6, under 6 free; 1941; For reference only
Income: Endowment, mem, grants, gov & foundation contributions
Library Holdings: Auction Catalogs, Audio Tapes, Book Volumes 25,000, Clipping Files, DVDs, Exhibition Catalogs, Manuscripts, Memorabilia, Other Holdings Oral History Recordings; Archives, Pamphlets, Periodical Subscriptions 20
Special Subjects: Antiquities-Assyrian, Art Education, Art History, Asian Art, Bronzes, Collages, Conceptual Art, Drawings, Etchings & Engravings, Glass, Handicrafts, Historical Material, History of Art & Archaeology, Prints, Landscapes, Latin American Art, Mexican Art, Mixed Media, Oriental Art, Painting-American, Painting-British, Painting-European, Painting-French, Painting-German, Painting-Italian, Photography, Portraits, Printmaking, Sculpture, Textiles, Watercolors, Woodcuts
Activities: Classes for adults & children; docent training; applied art classes for children & adults; lects open to pub; concerts; gallery talks; tours; schols; mus shop sells books, prints, jewelry, accessories, ceramics & art glass

L **SANTA BARBARA PUBLIC CENTRAL LIBRARY,** Faulkner Memorial Art Wing, 40 E Anapamu St, Santa Barbara, CA 93101-2722; PO Box 1019, Santa

Barbara, CA 93102-1019. Tel 805-962-7653, 564-5608 (library admin); Fax 805-962-6304; Web: www.santa-barbara.ca.us; *Lib Dir* Irene Macias
Open Mon - Thurs 10 AM - 9 PM, Fri & Sat 10 AM - 5:30 PM, Sun 1 - 5 PM; No admis fee; Estab 1930 & administered by the library trustees
Income: City funded
Library Holdings: Book Volumes 200,000, Cassettes 7800, Clipping Files, Fiche, Framed Reproductions, Micro Print, Pamphlets, Periodical Subscriptions 500, Records, Reels, Reproductions
Exhibitions: Local contemporary paintings & sculpture; Rotating exhibits
Activities: Lect, programs & meetings

M **UNIVERSITY OF CALIFORNIA, SANTA BARBARA,** Art, Design & Architecture Museum, Santa Barbara, CA 93106-9010; UC Santa Barbara, Santa Barbara, CA 93106-0001. Tel 805-893-2951; Fax 805-893-3013; Email museum@museum.ucsb.edu; Web: www.museum.ucsb.edu; *Designer* Mehmet Dogu; *Registrar* Susan Lucke; *Cur Architectural Drawings* Jocelyn Gibbs; *Asst to Dir & Outrreach Coordr* Lety Garcia; *Dir* Bruce Robertson; *Cur Exhibs & Asst Dir* Elyse A Gonzales; *Asst Designer* Todd Anderson; *Curatorial Asst* Rebecca Harlow
Open Wed - Sun Noon - 5 PM, Thurs until 8 PM; cl Mon, Tues & maj holidays; No admis fee; Estab 1959 & direct at both the needs of the university & the community; with a wide range of contemporary & historical exhibitions; Located on the UCSB campus, Arts Building complex; four galleries for changing exhibits; two which exhibit part of the permanent collection; Average Annual Attendance: 30,000; Mem: 100; dues vary; meeting dates vary
Income: Financed by university funds, grants, private donations
Library Holdings: Clipping Files, DVDs, Exhibition Catalogs, Filmstrips, Framed Reproductions, Memorabilia, Original Art Works, Other Holdings, Photographs, Prints, Sculpture, Slides, Video Tapes
Special Subjects: Architecture, Coins & Medals, Drawings, Etchings & Engravings, Ethnology, Graphics, Painting-American, Painting-Dutch, Painting-European, Photography, Posters, Religious Art, Renaissance Art, Sculpture, Watercolors
Collections: Collection of Architectural Drawings by Southern California Architects, including Irving Gill, R M Schindler, George Washington Smith & Kem Weber, Morgenroth Collection of Renaissance Medals & Plaquettes, Sedgwick Collection of 16th-18th Century Italian, Flemish & Dutch Artists, Ala Story Print Collection, Grace H Dreyfus Collection of Ancient Peruvian & Middle Eastern Art, Fernand Lungren Bequest
Publications: Exhibition catalogs, 1-2 per year
Activities: Classes for adults & children; docent training; lects for mems only; regular schedule of docent tours; gallery talks; 2-3 vis lectrs per yr; gallery talks; sponsoring of competitions; 1 - 2 per year; originate traveling exhibs to art museums; sales shop sells exhib catalogs, books, prints, slides, reproductions, t-shirts, gifts

L **Arts Library**, Santa Barbara, CA 93106-9010. Tel 805-893-2850; Fax 805-893-5879; Web: www.library.ucsb.edu; *Head Arts Library* Susan Moon; *Art Librn* Chizu Morihara; *Music Librn* Eunice Schroeder
Open Mon - Wed 9 AM - 10 PM, Thurs - Fri 9 AM - 5 PM, Sun 2 - 10 PM; cl Sat; Estab 1966 to support acad progs; Circ 28,700; Average Annual Attendance: 69,500
Income: Financed by state appropriation
Library Holdings: Auction Catalogs, Book Volumes 300,000, Compact Disks, DVDs, Exhibition Catalogs 100,000, Fiche 75,000, Other Holdings Auction Catalogs 50,000, Periodical Subscriptions 400, Photographs 5000, Reels 1400 (Microfilm), Video Tapes 225
Special Subjects: Afro-American Art, American Indian Art, American Western Art, Antiquities-Byzantine, Antiquities-Greek, Antiquities-Roman, Architecture, Art History, Asian Art, Decorative Arts, Drawings, Etchings & Engravings, Furniture, Graphic Arts, History of Art & Archaeology, Islamic Art, Latin American Art, Mexican Art, Oriental Art, Painting-American, Painting-Dutch, Photography, Portraits, Pottery, Pre-Columbian Art, Printmaking, Prints, Sculpture, Textiles, Video, Watercolors, Woodcuts
Publications: Catalogs of the Art Exhibition, Catalogs of the Arts Library, University of California, Santa Barbara; Cambridge, England, Chadwyck-Healey, 1978
Activities: Educ prog, docent training; teaching assistants; students; Tours

SANTA CLARA

M **SANTA CLARA UNIVERSITY,** de Saisset Museum, 500 El Camino Real, Santa Clara, CA 95053-0550. Tel 408-554-4528; Fax 408-554-7840; Email desaissetmuseum@scu.edu; Web: www.scu.edu/deSaisset/; *Acad Pres* Rev Michael Engh SJ; *Sr Vice Provost for Acad Affairs* Diane Jonte-Pace; *Dir* Rebecca M Schapp; *Sr Admin Asst* Kheuavanh Bouasavanh; *Coll Mgr* Stephanie Battle; *Asst Dir, Exhibs & Progs* Vacant; *Exhib Project Coordr* Chris Sicat
Open during exhibs Tues - Sun 11 AM - 4 PM, cl Mon; No admis fee; Estab 1955 as a major cultural resource in Northern California; 19,210 sq ft facility founded adjacent to Mission Santa Clara de Asis on Santa Clara Univ campus. Accredited by Amer Assoc of Mus & operated by the Univ; Average Annual Attendance: 25,000; Mem: dues presidential fellow $5,000, Locatelli fellow $2,500, de Saisset fellow $1,000, benefactor $500, patron $250, sponsor $100, friend $45
Income: Financed by endowment, mem, University operating budget, pvt funding & grants
Purchases: All media
Special Subjects: Painting-American, Sculpture, Graphics, Ceramics, Ivory, Silver, Tapestries, Furniture, Photography, African Art
Collections: 10,000+ objects: California history, Mission-era liturgical vestments, decorative arts, works on paper, painting & sculpture, new media, prints from Renaissance, Baroque, Rococo, 19th c & Modernist periods, contemporary works on paper, with emphasis on San Francisco Bay Area artists, California History Coll, Smith Anderson Editions archive, Andy Warhol Photographic Legacy Program
Exhibitions: 6 - 12 temp exhibs annually; Santa Clara Univ California History Coll, permanent exhib
Publications: Exhib announcements, quarterly; exhibition catalogs
Activities: Educ prog; docent training; workshops; family days; symposia; lects open to public; 8-12 vis lectrs per yr; gallery talks; tours; paintings lent to campus offices

M **TRITON MUSEUM OF ART,** 1505 Warburton Ave, Santa Clara, CA 95050-3791. Tel 408-247-3754; Fax 408-247-3796; Email staff@tritonmuseum.org; Web: www.tritonmuseum.org; *Exec Dir* Jill Meyers; *Chief Cur* Preston Metcalf; *Registrar* Stephanie Learmonth; *Dir Finance* Donna Tobkin; *Preparator* Bryan Callanta; *Cur Educ* Maria Ester Fernandez; *Develop Assoc* Johanna Kahn; *Facility Rental Mgr* Carmen Pascual; *Mktg/Design Assoc* Jennifer Dao
Open Tues - Sun 11 AM - 5 PM; No admis fee; Estab 1965 to offer a rich & varied cultural experience to members of the community through the display of 20th & 21st century American art, particularly artists of California & through related special events & programs; The mus consists of a state of the art facility designed by San Francisco architect Barcelon Jang. The building opened in Oct, 1987 & sits on a 7-acre park site with four Oriental/Spanish style pavilions & sculpture garden; Average Annual Attendance: 174,700; Mem: 1100; dues $20-$1000
Income: $700,000 (financed by endowment, mem, fundraisers, corporate sponsorships & city appropriation)
Library Holdings: Book Volumes, Exhibition Catalogs
Special Subjects: Ceramics, Glass, Painting-American, Prints, Sculpture, Photography, Portraits
Collections: Paintings by Frank Duveneck, Austen D Warburton Native American Art & Artifacts Collection, Theodore Wores Collection: oil paintings, Contemporary Work by California artists
Publications: Exhibition catalogs; newsletter, bimonthly
Activities: Educ progs for adults & children; art tours; lects open to pub; concerts; gallery talks; awards: Statewide; lectures for members only; Sponsoring of competitions; Photography winner, Statewide Painting winner; schols offered; lends original objects of art lent to local companies; mus shop sells original art, books, reproductions & prints; original art; jewelry; art supplies; ceramics

SANTA CLARITA

L **CALIFORNIA INSTITUTE OF THE ARTS LIBRARY,** 24700 McBean Pky, Santa Clarita, CA 91355. Tel 661-253-7885; Fax 661-254-4561; Email jgatten@calarts.edu; Web: www.calarts.edu; *Dean* Jeff Gatten; *Performing Arts Librn* Kathy Carbone; *Info Resources Librn* Susan Lowenberg; *Reference & Instruction Librn* Brena Smith; *Visual Arts Librn* Karen Baxter
Open Mon - Thurs 9 AM - midnight, Fri 9 AM - 9 PM, Sat 1 PM - 5 PM, Sun 1 PM - midnight; Estab 1965, first classes 1970, designed to be a community of practicing artists working in schools of art, design film, music, theater & dance
Income: Financed by endowment
Library Holdings: Book Volumes 98,375, CD-ROMs 122, Cassettes 2595, Compact Disks 7614, DVDs 4028, Exhibition Catalogs 14,887, Motion Pictures 1243, Pamphlets 2282, Periodical Subscriptions 344, Records 9193, Reels 5700, Slides 130,747, Video Tapes 4090
Special Subjects: Film, Theatre Arts, Video
Exhibitions: Student work, approx 20 per yr
Publications: California Institute of the Art Library Handbook
Activities: Schols & fels offered

SANTA CRUZ

M **MUSEUM OF ART & HISTORY, SANTA CRUZ,** 705 Front St, McPherson Center Santa Cruz, CA 95060-4508. Tel 831-429-1964; Fax 831-429-1954; Email admin@santacuzmah.org; Web: www.santacruzmah.org; *Interim Exec Dir* Paula Kenyon; *Cur Exhib* Susan Hillhouse; *Cur Educ* Ashley Adams
Open Tues - Sun 11 AM- 5 PM, 1st Fri of month 11 AM - 9 PM, cl Mon; Admis adults $5, students & seniors $3, children 12-17 $2, children under 12 & mus mems free, no admis fee first Fri of each month; Estab 1996 to promote understanding of contemporary art history & of Santa Cruz County; 2200 sq ft, 4 galleries, one permanent, 3 changing exhibition galleries; Average Annual Attendance: 21,000; Mem: 1400; dues benefactor circle $10,000, patron circle $5,000, pres circle $2,500, trustee circle $1,000, collector circle $500, art & history circle $250, dual/family $60, dual/family & seniors $50, individual $40, seniors $30, student/educator $20
Income: $100,000 (financed by endowment, mem, contributions, store income & county income)
Library Holdings: Book Volumes, Clipping Files, Exhibition Catalogs, Manuscripts, Maps, Memorabilia, Original Documents, Photographs, Prints, Slides, Video Tapes
Special Subjects: Architecture, Ceramics, Costumes, Decorative Arts, Dolls, Drawings, Embroidery, Etchings & Engravings, Folk Art, Furniture, Gold, Historical Material, Landscapes, Manuscripts, Maps, Painting-American, Photography, Pottery, Prints, Sculpture, Textiles, Watercolors
Collections: Contemporary art coll on paper, archival material, decorative costumes, textiles & 3-D objects, fine art of Santa Cruz County history, Contemporary Art, Santa Cruz County Photographs
Exhibitions: Where the Redwoods Meet the Sea: A History of Santa Cruz County & its people; Time & Place: 50 Years of Santa Cruz Studio Ceramics Art
Publications: Santa Cruz County History Journal, annually, catalogues; quarterly newsletter
Activities: Docent training, sch art & history progs; lects open to pub, 12 vis lectrs per yr; gallery talks; tours; originate traveling exhibs; mus shop sells books, original art, gifts & film series

A **SANTA CRUZ ART LEAGUE,** Center for the Arts, 526 Broadway, Santa Cruz, CA 95060-4622. Tel 831-426-5787; Fax 831-426-5789; Email info@scal.org; Web: www.scal.org; *Admin Dir* Doreen Davis; *Brd Pres* T. Mike Walker; *Graphics* Audrey Takeshita; *Exhibs* Keelin Sakel; *Staff Mem* Bella Frye; *Exec Dir* Valeria Miranda; *Admin Asst* Bob Bishop
Open Wed - Sat noon - 5 PM, Sun Noon - 4 PM, First Fri noon - 9 PM, cl Mon & Tues; No admis fee; Estab 1919, Incorporated 1949, to further interest in visual & arts performing in community; 2000 sq ft of gallery space, off-site exhibits, 65-seat performance hall; Average Annual Attendance: 10,000; Mem: 750; dues seniors & students $60, individual $85, family $135, bus partners $250-500
Income: Financed by donations, dues & grants
Collections: Local historical & contemporary works

Exhibitions: Annual Statewide Juried Show; Open Studios Preview; Annual High School Show; Luck-of-the-Draw Auction-Fundraiser; 14 exhibs per yr
Publications: Quarterly newsletter, exhibit catalogs
Activities: Classes for adults & children; classes in painting, drawing & sculpture; dramatic progs; docent training; concerts; lects open to pub; demonstration by professional artist; 12 vis lectrs per yr; concerts; gallery talks; competitions with awards; scholarships offered to senior high schools in Santa Cruz County; gift shop sells books, original art, ceramics, jewelry, reproductions & prints

M **UNIVERSITY OF CALIFORNIA AT SANTA CRUZ,** Eloise Pickard Smith Gallery, 1156 High St, Santa Cruz, CA 95064-1077. Tel 831-459-3606; *Dir* Linda Pope; *Gallery Mgr* Leslie Fellows
Open Tues - Sun 11 AM - 5 PM; No admis fee; Estab 1967; Art of the Monterey Bay Region; Average Annual Attendance: 4,000
Income: University Gallery
Activities: Docent training; gallery talks

M **Mary Porter Sesnon Art Gallery,** 1156 High St, Santa Cruz, CA 95064-1077. Tel 831-459-2314; Fax 831-459-3535; Email sesnon@ucsc.edu; Web: arts.ucsc.edu/sesnon; *Dir* Shelby Graham; *Asst Cur* Mark Shunney
Open Tues - Sat Noon - 5 PM; No admis fee; Estab 1971 for curricular support through exhibitions & programs; Contemporary art; Average Annual Attendance: 6,000
Income: $51,000 (financed by endowment, state appropriation, donor support & catalog sales)
Collections: Charles Griffin Farr
Publications: Exhibition catalogs, periodically
Activities: Lects open to pub, 3 vis lectrs per yr; gallery talks; originate traveling exhibs to other Univ Calif campuses

SANTA MONICA

A **18TH STREET ARTS COMPLEX,** 1639 18th St, Santa Monica, CA 90404-3807. Tel 310-453-3711; Fax 310-453-4347; Email office@18thstreet.org; Web: www.18thstreet.org; *Exec Dir* Jan Williamson; *Director of Development* Joy Kliewer; *Artistic Director* Anuradha Vikram; *Dir Communs & Outreach* Sue Bell Yank; *Asst. Operations Manager* Haroon Dasti
Open Mon - Fri 11 AM - 5:30 PM; No admis fee; Provides art services to the pub & services to artists & art organizations engaged with contemporary issues of community & diversity; Provocative contemporary art; Average Annual Attendance: 8,000
Income: Financed by grants, fundraisers, donations
Collections: High Performance Magazine Archives
Activities: Educ prog; lects open to pub; 4-8 vis lectrs per yr; gallery talks; tours; Fels

M **SANTA MONICA COLLEGE PERFORMING ARTS CENTER,** Pete & Susan Barrett Art Gallery, 1310 11th St, Santa Monica, CA 90401; 1900 Pico St, Santa Monica, CA 90405. Tel 310-434-3434; Fax 310-434-3646; Email mdartx@aol.com; Web: www.smc.edu/barrett; *Prof & Gallery Dir* Marian Winsryg
Open Tues - Fri noon - 5 PM, Sat 11 AM - 4 PM; No admis fee; Estab 1973 to provide a study gallery for direct contact with contemporary & historic works of art; Average Annual Attendance: 25,000
Income: Financed by mem, city & state appropriations
Collections: Southern California prints & drawings
Exhibitions: Rotating exhibitions every 3-4 weeks
Activities: Lect open to public; gallery talks; tours; original art objects lent

SANTA PAULA

M **SANTA PAULA ART MUSEUM,** 117 N 10th St Santa Paula, CA 93060-2877. Tel 805-525-5554; Fax 805-525-5540; Email info@santapaulaartmuseum.org; Web: www.santapaulaartmuseum.org; *Exec Dir* Jennifer Heighton; *Asst Dir* Julie Cluster; *Mus Educ* Meg Phelps
Open Wed - Sat 10 AM - 4 PM, Sun 12 PM - 4 PM; Admis adults $5, seniors $3, students free; Estab 2004; Featuring local art exhibs & the Santa Paula coll; Average Annual Attendance: 8000; Mem: 400 mems
Library Holdings: Memorabilia, Original Art Works, Photographs, Sculpture
Special Subjects: American Western Art, Decorative Arts, Hispanic Art, Historical Material, Landscapes, Mexican Art, Painting-American
Activities: Classes for children; docent training; 12 vis lectrs per yr; concerts; gallery talks; mus shop sells books, original art, reproductions & gifts

SANTA ROSA

M **MUSEUMS SONOMA COUNTY,** Art Museum of Sonoma County & History Museum of Sonoma County, 425 Seventh St, Santa Rosa, CA 95401-5202. Tel 707-579-1500; Fax 707-579-4849; Email info@museumsc.org; Web: museumsc.org; *Exec Dir* Jeff Nathanson; *History Cur* Eric Stanley; *Dir Pub Progs & Tours* Cynthia Leung; *Opers Mgr* Katie Azanza; *Develop & Mem* Alison Upham
Open Tues - Sun 11 AM - 5 PM, cl New Year's Day, Martin Luther King Jr Day, President's Day, Easter, Memorial Day, Independence Day, Labor Day, Thanksgiving & day after, Christmas Eve & Day; Admis adults $10, seniors & students $7, children under 12 & members free; Estab 1985 as mus of art & history; Circ 10 members (EBSCO); Rotating art & history exhibits; Average Annual Attendance: 13,184; Mem: 650; dues $50 & up
Income: Donation & mem based
Collections: Sonoma County & northern California history & culture, Tom Golden's Christo Collection, Carol Barnes Collection, fine art by artists working in Northern CA from 19th century to present, coll of work by Christo & Jeanne Claude, historic objects documenting the history of Sonoma County
Publications: newsletter, The Muse
Activities: Educ prog; classes for adults & children; docent training prog; lects; 25 vis lectrs per yr; guided tours; gallery talks; tours; films; arts festivals; family days; concerts; originate traveling exhibitions to other mus; mus shop sells books, original art, prints reproductions, toys, jewelry, notecards & AA supplies

M **SANTA ROSA JUNIOR COLLEGE,** Art Gallery, 1501 Mendocino Ave, Santa Rosa, CA 95401-4395. Tel 707-527-4298, 527-4011, Ext 4575; Fax 707-527-4532; Web: www.santarosa.edu; *Dir* Renata Breth
Open Tues - Fri & Sun Noon - 4 PM; No admis fee; Estab 1973; 1700 sq ft exhibit space with movable walls; Average Annual Attendance: 10,000
Exhibitions: Four exhibits during the school year generally of contemporary artists of national & local prominence & of emerging new artists
Activities: 1-2 vis lectrs per year; gallery talks

SARATOGA

A **MONTALVO CENTER FOR THE ARTS,** 15400 Montalvo Rd, Saratoga, CA 95070-6327; PO Box 158, Saratoga, CA 95071-0158. Tel 408-961-5800; Email info@montalvoarts.org; Web: www.montalvoarts.org; *Exec Dir* Angela McConnell; *Deputy Dir* Kelly Hudson
Open daily 8 AM - 5 PM; No admis fee; Estab 1930; administered by Montalvo Assn, Montalvo Arts Center is a nonprofit, mem supported org dedicated to fostering community engagement through multidisciplinary art; There are facilities for 10 artists-in-residence. The home of the late US Senator & Mayor of San Francisco, James Duval Phelan, was bequeathed as a cultural center & is conducted as a nonprofit enterprise by the Board of Trustees of the Montalvo Assn. Project Space Gallery & 2.5 mi of hiking trails & beautiful grounds available for event rentals; Average Annual Attendance: 200,000; Mem: 800; dues $60 & up
Income: $4,000,000 (financed by donation, grants & investments)
Exhibitions: 20 solo exhibitions per year of emerging artists in all media; occasional special or group exhibitions
Publications: Calendar, monthly
Activities: Educ & visual arts programs; classes for adults & children; Sally & Don Lucas Artists Residency Program; docent training; lects open to pub, 8 vis lectrs per yr; concerts; gallery talks; tours; competitions with awards; plays; winter workshops; Best Wedding Venue - Metro; fels & schols offered; mus shop sells books, original art, reproductions, prints & gift items

SAUSALITO

A **HEADLANDS CENTER FOR THE ARTS,** 944 Fort Barry, Sausalito, CA 94965. Tel 415-331-2787; Fax 415-331-3857; Email info@headlands.org; Web: www.headlands.org; *Residency Mgr* Holly Blake; *Exec Dir* Sharon Maidenberg; *Communs & Mktg Mgr* Amanda Davidson; *Facilities Mgr* Christopher Doyle
Open Mon - Fri 10 AM - 5 PM, Sun Noon - 5 PM, cl Sat; No admis fee; Estab 1982 to provide studio & living space for artists in the Marin Headlands, a National Park; 1,800 square ft Project Space - rotates monthly, March - Nov; Average Annual Attendance: 10,000; Mem: 500; dues $35 & up
Income: $900,000 (financed by endowment, city appropriation, donations from foundations & corporations)
Exhibitions: Front & Center annual exhib - Jan - Feb
Publications: Newsletter, three times a year
Activities: Lect open to pub; lect for members only; artist talks, lect & performances; 8 vis lectrs per year; concerts; gallery talks; artist residencies; film screenings; Tournesol Award (studio & grant awarded to a recent MFA painter); store sells notecard sets, limited edition prints, t-shirts & hoodies

SOLVANG

M **ELVERHOJ MUSEUM OF HISTORY AND ART,** 1624 Elverhoy Way, Solvang, CA 93464; PO Box 769, Solvang, CA 93464-0769. Tel 805-686-1211; Fax 805-686-1822; Email info@elverhoj.org; Web: www.elverhoj.org; *CEO* Esther Jacobsen Bates
Open Wed & Thurs 1 - 4 PM, Fri - Sun Noon - 4 PM & by appt, cl New Year's Day, Easter, Thanksgiving, Christmas Eve & Day; Suggested donation $3 per person; Former residence of one of Solvang's most artistic families, mus is devoted to local history & the Danish-American pioneer spirit of the town's founder. Nonprofit org; Average Annual Attendance: 11,200; Mem: Dues Patron $500; Benefactor $250; Bus $100; Couple or Family $50; Indiv $35
Special Subjects: Architecture, Decorative Arts, Painting-European, Porcelain, Silver, Art Education, Art History
Collections: Exhibs featuring local history & Danish culture, art gallery with changing exhibs, porcelain, silver
Publications: newsletter
Activities: Garden; ann events; Living History Days, juried shows; Danish language classes; children's workshops

M **WILDLING ART MUSEUM,** 1511 Mission Dr #8, Solvang, CA 93463-2607. Tel 805-688-1082; Fax 805-686-8339; Email info@wildlingmuseum.org; Web: www.wildlingmuseum.org; *Exec Dir* Elizabeth Knowles; *Pres* Patti Jacquemain; *Dir Develop* Kate Bennett; *Asst to Dir* Holly Cline; *Opers Mgr* Amy Mutza
Open Wed - Sun 11 AM - 5 PM, cl New Year's Day, Easter, Independence Day, Thanksgiving, Christmas; Admis by requested donation: adults $2, mems free, discounts to AAM mems; Estab 1997 to present art of America's wilderness; Average Annual Attendance: 4,300; Mem: 600
Income: Financed by pvt donations & admis
Library Holdings: Book Volumes, DVDs, Periodical Subscriptions
Special Subjects: American Indian Art, American Western Art, Bronzes, Drawings, Etchings & Engravings, Landscapes, Painting-American, Prints, Sculpture, Watercolors, Woodcuts
Collections: paintings, prints, drawings, photographs, sculpture
Publications: quarterly newsletter, The Fox Tale; brochures; exhib catalogs
Activities: Educ progs; artists workshops; art classes for children; lects open to pub; 5 vis lectrs per yr; gallery talks; tours; sponsoring of competitions; scholarships offered; mus shop sells books, magazines, reproductions, notecards, jewelry, toys, stuff animals

SONOMA

M **SONOMA VALLEY HISTORICAL SOCIETY,** Depot Park Museum, 270 First St W, Depot Park Sonoma, CA; PO Box 861, Sonoma, CA 95476-0861. Tel 707-938-1762; Email info@depotparkmuseum.com; Web: www.depotparkmuseum.org; *Dir* Sandi Hansen; *Treas* Jo Miller; *Secy* Jean Miller; *IT Tech/Mem Secy* Don Stevens; *Pres* Carol Page; *VPres* Newton Dal Poggetto; *IT Website* Dick Foster
Open Fri - Sun 1 - 4 PM; No admis fee, donations welcome; Estab 1979 (Depot Park Mus), 1937 (Sonoma Valley Historical Society); Old rail depot with three railroad cars, local history rooms, gift shop & book store, Indian Artifacts, Victorian exhibits, many Sonoma Valley artifacts, a pair of now-extinct CA Grizzly bear feet; Average Annual Attendance: 5,000-7,000; Mem: 280; dues $30 & up; ann & monthly meetings
Income: Financed by mem, donations small grants, gift shop
Library Holdings: Audio Tapes, Book Volumes, Cassettes, Clipping Files, DVDs, Framed Reproductions, Lantern Slides, Manuscripts, Maps, Memorabilia, Original Art Works, Original Documents, Other Holdings, Pamphlets, Periodical Subscriptions, Photographs, Prints, Records, Reels, Reproductions, Sculpture, Slides, Video Tapes
Collections: Raising of the Bear Flag, Victorian-era bedroom, dining room, kitchen; one room school house
Exhibitions: Rotating exhibitions: Famous Women of Sonoma Valley, Early baseball, trains, telegraph & Morse code, valley agriculture, Indian artifacts
Publications: newsletter, bimonthly; Sonoma Mission, Robert Smiley; Pioneer Sonoma, Robert Parmelee; Schools & Scows of Early Sonoma, Roger & George Emanuels; Saga of Sonoma; The Men of the Bear Flag Revolt & their Heritage, Barbara Warner; Images of America, Sonoma Valley, by Valerie Sherer Mathes, Diane Moll Smith, SVHS (Historical Society); A Short History of Sonoma by Lynn Downey
Activities: Classes for children; summer camps; docent training; school tours; caboose car tours; lects open to pub; 8 vis lectrs per yr; tours; schols; lending of original objects of art to Novato CA Historical Guild's Hamilton Mus; sales shop; books; reproductions; photos & antiques, gifts & children's items, local historical postcards, toys & jewelry

M **SONOMA VALLEY MUSEUM OF ART,** 551 Broadway, Sonoma, CA 95476-0322; PO Box 322, Sonoma, CA 95476. Tel 707-939-7862; Fax 707-939-1080; Email admin@svma.org; Web: www.svma.org; *Exec Dir* Kate Eilertsen; *Educ & Pub Progs Dir* Margie Maynard; *Exhibs & Mem Mgr* Flynn O'Brien; *Admin Mgr* Ron Richards; *Vis & Vol Coordr* Samantha Hull
Open Wed - Sun 11 AM - 5 PM during exhib times; Admis adults $5, children & members free; Estab 1998; Average Annual Attendance: 15,000
Library Holdings: Book Volumes
Special Subjects: Architecture
Activities: Classes for adults & children; lects open to the pub; 8-10 vis lectrs per yr; gallery talks; tours; mus shop sells books

STANFORD

M **STANFORD UNIVERSITY,** Cantor Arts Center at Stanford University, 328 Lomita Dr, Stanford, CA 94305-5006. Tel 650-498-1480; Fax 650-725-0464; Web: museum.stanford.edu; *Dir* Susan Dackerman; *Gift & Develop* Sheena Borja; *Special Events* Lorran Bronnar
Open Wed - Mon 11 AM - 5 PM, Thurs 11 AM - 8 PM, cl Tues, Thanksgiving & Christmas; No admis fee, donations accepted; Estab 1894 as a teaching mus & laboratory for University's Department of Art; 24 galleries plus sculpture gardens, courtyard, terraces with outdoor sculpture; Average Annual Attendance: 269,427; Mem: 3500; dues Friend $75, Family/Dual $100, Sponsor $200 Patron $300, Benefactor $600, Artists Circle $1,000, Connoisseurs Circle $2,500, New Founders Circle $5,000
Income: Financed by endowment, mem & university funds
Special Subjects: African Art, Afro-American Art, American Indian Art, Anthropology, Antiquities-Assyrian, Antiquities-Byzantine, Antiquities-Egyptian, Antiquities-Etruscan, Antiquities-Greek, Antiquities-Oriental, Antiquities-Persian, Antiquities-Roman, Asian Art, Baroque Art, Bookplates & Bindings, Calligraphy, Ceramics, Coins & Medals, Collages, Decorative Arts, Drawings, Etchings & Engravings, Furniture, Glass, Gold, Graphics, Hispanic Art, Historical Material, Islamic Art, Jewelry, Judaica, Landscapes, Latin American Art, Manuscripts, Maps, Marine Painting, Medieval Art, Metalwork, Mexican Art, Mosaics, Oriental Art, Painting-American, Painting-Australian, Painting-British, Painting-Canadian, Painting-Dutch, Painting-European, Painting-Flemish, Painting-French, Painting-German, Painting-Israeli, Painting-Italian, Painting-Spanish, Photography, Portraits, Pottery, Pre-Columbian Art, Primitive art, Prints, Religious Art, Renaissance Art, Sculpture, Watercolors, Woodcuts, Painting-Japanese, Painting-New Zealand, Painting-Polish, Painting-Russian, Painting-Scandinavian
Collections: Rodin Sculpture, Cypriote antiquities, prints & drawings since the Renaissance, Stanford Family Collection, American art of 19th & 20th centuries, European art 16th-20th century, photography including major holdings by Robert Frank & Eadweard Muybridge, Cesnola Collection, Robert Frank Photography Collection, Eadweard Muybridge Photography Collection, See website: museum. stanford.edu/collections.htm/
Exhibitions: Object Lessons: Art & Its Histories; New to the Cantor: Spencer Finch; (12th Oct, 2016-13th Mar, 2017) Highlights from the Marmor Collection; (12th Oct, 2016-24th Apr, 2017) New to the Cantor: Dasheill Manley; (16th Nov, 2016-20th Mar, 2017) The Wonder of Everyday Life: Dutch Golden Age Prints; (21st Dec, 2016-3rd Apr, 2017) The Conjured Life: The Legacy of Surrealism; (18th Jan, 2017-1st May, 2017) Muybridge/Paglen; (26th Apr, 2017-21st Aug, 2017) Creativity on the Line: Design and the Corporate World, 1950-1975
Publications: Exhib catalogues; Cantor Arts Center Journal
Activities: Docent training; family activities incl tours, art-making & sketching in the galleries; lects open to pub, 15 vis lectrs per yr; concerts; gallery talks; tours; 1-2 book traveling exhibs per yr; originate traveling exhibs to international mus

L **Art & Architecture Library,** 435 Lasuen Mall, #102 Stanford, CA 94305-2001. Tel 650-723-3408; Fax 650-725-0140; Email artlibrary@stanford.edu; Web: www.sul.stamford.edu/depts/art/about/index.html; *Head Librn* Alex Ross; *Deputy Librn* Peter Blank; *Ref Librn* Katie Keller; *Acting Head, VRC* Amber Ruiz
Open Mon - Thurs 9 AM - 10 PM, Fri & Sat 9 AM - 5 PM, Sun 1 - 10 PM; Circ 40,000; Library limited service to non-Stanford patrons
Library Holdings: Book Volumes 160,000, CD-ROMs, Exhibition Catalogs, Fiche, Periodical Subscriptions 560

STOCKTON

M **THE SAN JOAQUIN PIONEER & HISTORICAL SOCIETY,** The Haggin Museum, 1201 N Pershing Ave, Stockton, CA 95203-1604. Tel 209-940-6311; Fax 209-462-1404; Email info@hagginmuseum.org; Web: www.hagginmuseum.org; *Dir & Cur of History* Tod Ruhstaller; *Cur Educ* Lisa Cooperman; *Cur Coll* Kylee Denning; *Librn & Archivist* Kimberly Bray; *Develop Officer* Susan Obert; *Accnt* Karen Richards; *Mus Store Mgr* Patty Huntley; *Webmaster, Publicity* Eddie Hargreaves; *VPres* Bob Fay; *Facilities Supt* Ray Shermantine
Open Wed - Sun 1:30 PM - 5 PM, 1st & 3rd Thurs 1:30 PM - 9 PM; Admis adults $5, youth 10 - 17, seniors, students with ID $250, children under 10 with an adult and members free; Estab 1928 to protect, preserve & interpret historical & fine arts collections that pertain to the museum's disciplines; The mus covers 34,000 sq ft of exhibit space housing art & history collections; Average Annual Attendance: 45,000; Mem: 1600; dues $25 & up; annual meeting third Tues in Jan
Income: $1.2 million (financed by endowment, mem & foundation grant)
Library Holdings: Book Volumes, Cassettes, Clipping Files, Exhibition Catalogs, Kodachrome Transparencies, Lantern Slides, Manuscripts, Memorabilia, Motion Pictures, Other Holdings, Pamphlets, Photographs, Prints, Slides
Special Subjects: American Indian Art, American Western Art, Anthropology, Antiquities-Egyptian, Antiquities-Greek, Antiquities-Roman, Archaeology, Asian Art, Cartoons, Ceramics, Costumes, Decorative Arts, Dolls, Drawings, Eskimo Art, Etchings & Engravings, Furniture, Glass, Graphics, Historical Material, Jade, Landscapes, Latin American Art, Painting-American, Painting-Dutch, Painting-European, Painting-French, Painting-German, Painting-Spanish, Period Rooms, Photography, Pottery, Pre-Columbian Art, Watercolors, Oriental Art
Collections: Oriental & European decorative arts, Japanese woodblock prints, American Illustrators, Stockton/San Joaquin County History Collections
Exhibitions: 6 - 8 temporary exhibits per year; Stockton Art League Juried Exhibition; Robert T McKee Student Art Exhibition; Art and history related exhibitions
Publications: Museum Calendar, quarterly
Activities: Summer art classes for children; docent training; lects open to pub; 6-10 vis lectrs per yr; concerts; gallery talks; tours; competitions with awards; individual paintings & original objects of art lent; book traveling exhibs 2-3 per yr; mus shop sells books, reproductions, prints, postcards, posters, notecards, gift items

L **Petzinger Memorial Library & Earl Rowland Art Library,** 1201 N Pershing Ave, Victory Park Stockton, CA 95203-1604. Tel 209-940-6300; Fax 209-462-1404; Email info@hagginmuseum.org; Web: www.hagginmuseum.org; *Dir* Tod Ruhstaller; *Librn, Archivist* Kimberly D Bray
Open by appointment only; Appt fee $15; Estab 1941 to supply material to those interested in the research of California & San Joaquin County history as well as the history of Stockton; art reference library; For reference only
Income: $15,000 (financed by endowment for Historical Libraries)
Purchases: $400
Library Holdings: Book Volumes 7500, Cassettes, Clipping Files, Exhibition Catalogs, Kodachrome Transparencies, Lantern Slides, Manuscripts, Memorabilia, Motion Pictures, Other Holdings Original documents, Pamphlets, Photographs, Prints, Slides
Special Subjects: American Western Art, Historical Material, Painting-American, Painting-French
Collections: Earl Rowland Art Reference Library

M **UNIVERSITY OF THE PACIFIC,** Jeannette Powell Art Center, 3601 Pacific Ave, Stockton, CA 95211-0197. Tel 209-946-2011; Fax 209-946-2652; Web: www.uop.edu; *Pres* Donald DeRosa; *Chair* Barbara Flaherty
Open Mon - Fri 8:30 AM - 4:30 PM, Sat & Sun 1 - 6PM; No admis fee; Estab 1975 to expose the University community to various art forms; Gallery is 1200 sq ft with 80 ft wall space, well equipped ceiling spots and flat panels; Average Annual Attendance: 10,000
Income: Financed by student fees & sales
Exhibitions: Rotating schedule of contemporary California artists
Activities: Lect open to public, 3-4 vis lectrs per year; gallery talks; juried contests; awards; tours

SUNLAND

M **AMERICAN MUSEUM OF CARTOON ART, INC,** 8550 Day St, Sunland, CA 91040-1812. Tel 310-828-2919; Fax 310-453-3003; Email jeremykay@msn.com; Web: cartoonmuseum.com; *Dir & Cur* Jeremy Kay; *Assoc Dir* Jaeson Kay; *Treas* Liz Kay
Estab 1976 to preserve & display historic cartoon art; Circ 200 +; Maintains reference library; Average Annual Attendance: 150; Mem: 1,500; dues $50
Income: Financed by endowment, mem, city & state appropriation
Special Subjects: Cartoons
Collections: Animation Cartoons Art Comic Books Cartoon Art Historic Cartoons Art Newspaper Cartoon Art Original Cartoon Art
Publications: Annual Report
Activities: Classes for adults & children; docent training; community cartoon classes; lects open to pub, 150 vis lectrs per yr; originate traveling exhibs; sales shop sells books, magazines, original art, reproductions, prints & slides

SYLMAR

M **COUNTY OF LOS ANGELES,** Century Gallery, 13000 Sayre St, Sylmar, CA 91342-1913. Tel 818-362-3220; Fax 818-364-7755; *Dir* John Cantley

Open Mon - Fri 9 AM - 5 PM, Sat Noon - 4 PM; No admis fee; Estab 1977 for contemporary art exhibits & to bring educational value to the community; Average Annual Attendance: 7,500
Income: Financed by city, county & state appropriation
Exhibitions: Seven curated theme exhibits of contemporary art
Activities: Gallery talks; competitions

THOUSAND OAKS

M **CONEJO VALLEY ART MUSEUM,** PO Box 1616, Thousand Oaks, CA 91358-0616. Tel 805-373-0054, 373-0049; Fax 805-492-7677; Web: www.cvam.us; *CEO & VPres* Maria Dessornes
Open Wed & Fri - Sun Noon - 5 PM; No admis fee, donation suggested; Estab 1975 to exhibit works of nationally & internationally known artists; Average Annual Attendance: 10,000; Mem: 350; dues family $35, single $25
Income: Financed by mem, donations & grants
Collections: Large Serigraph by Ron Davis
Exhibitions: Artwalk; Juried Fine Art & Designer Crafts Outdoor Exhibition
Activities: Lects open to pub, 6 vis lectrs per yr; concerts; gallery talks; competitions with awards; scholarships offered; mus shop sells books, magazines, prints, jewelry & folk art

TORRANCE

M **EL CAMINO COLLEGE ART GALLERY,** 16007 Crenshaw Blvd, Torrance, CA 90506-0003. Tel 310-660-3010, 3011; Fax 310-660-3792; Email eccart-gallery@elcamino.edu; Web: www.elcamino.edu/commadv/artgallery/index.html; *Dir* Susanna Meiers
Open Mon & Tues 10 AM - 3 PM, Wed & Thurs 10 AM - 8 PM, Fri 10 AM - 2 PM; No admis fee; Estab 1970 to exhibit professional, historical & student art; Gallery has 2,300 sq ft of exhibit space located on the ground floor of the Art Building on campus; Average Annual Attendance: 5,000
Special Subjects: Prints, Sculpture
Collections: Small print coll, small sculpture coll
Exhibitions: Juried student exhibit; organizational & guild competitions; Shadow Pieces; Student Show; Taleteller
Publications: Exhibit catalogs
Activities: Classes for adults; docent training; lect open to public, 25 vis lectrs per year; concerts; gallery talks; tours; competitions with awards; scholarships offered through the Library; exten dept serves the South Bay Community; collections or parts of collections are exchanged; lending collection contains books & sculpture; sales shop sells original art & posters

M **TORRANCE ART MUSEUM,** 3320 Civic Center Dr, Torrance, CA 90503-5016. Tel 310-618-2376; Fax 310-618-2399; Web: www.torranceartmuseum.com; *Dir & Cur* Max Presneill; *Mgr Cultural Servs* Eve Rappoport
Open Tues - Sun 11 AM - 5PM; No admis fee; Estab 1978 to fill the need for arts in the community; Two galleries & a video darkroom; Average Annual Attendance: 5,980; Mem: dues $50-$5,000
Collections: Modern & contemporary artwork
Exhibitions: Temporary exhibits
Activities: Educ progs; classes for adults & children; interactive progs; Lects open to pub; artist talks; symposiums; concerts; tours; art programming; workshops; film screenings; events; Mus store sells books online

TURLOCK

M **CALIFORNIA STATE UNIVERSITY STANISLAUS,** University Art Gallery, 801 W Monte Vista Ave, Turlock, CA 95382. Tel 209-667-3186; Fax 209-667-3871; Email art_gallery@csustan.edu; Web: www.csustan.edu/art/gallery; *Dept Chair* Gordon Senior; *Gallery Dir* Dean De Cocker
Open Mon - Thurs Noon - 4 PM or by appointment; No admis fee; Estab 1967, for the purpose of community & cultural instruction; display, educate & foster contemporary art; Gallery is small, covering 200 running ft; Average Annual Attendance: 2,500
Income: Financed by state appropriation
Special Subjects: African Art, Asian Art, Drawings, Historical Material, Latin American Art, Painting-American, Photography, Pre-Columbian Art, Sculpture, Oriental Art
Collections: Permanent collection of graphics & small contemporary works, Ancient Egyptian & Greek artifacts, California Paintings 19th & 20th Century, contemporary paintings, Italian Renaissance Jewelry, Japanese artifacts, Pre-Conquest artifacts, Tamarind prints, William Wendt paintings (California landscapes)
Exhibitions: Exhibs annually including sr art show
Activities: Classes for adults; lects open to pub, 6 vis lectrs per yr; concerts; gallery talks; tours; lent to qualified museums & galleries & campus community; lending collection contains film strips, 35mm lantern slides, motion pictures, original art works, original prints; book traveling exhibs 1-2 per yr; originate traveling exhibitions to University Art Galleries

L **Vasche Library,** 1 University Cr, Vasche Library - Rm 185 Turlock, CA 95382-0299. Tel 209-667-3232; Fax 209-667-3164; Web: www.library.csustan.edu; *Dean Library Serv* Carl Bengston; *Library Admin Support Coordr* Loretta Blakeley
Open Mon - Thurs 7:30 AM - 11 PM, Fri 7:30 AM - 5 PM, Sat 9 AM - 5 PM, Sun 1 - 9 PM; Estab 1960, a regional state university
Purchases: $8,800
Library Holdings: Audio Tapes, Book Volumes 11,000, Cassettes, Fiche, Micro Print, Periodical Subscriptions 37, Reels, Video Tapes

UKIAH

A **ARTS COUNCIL OF MENDOCINO COUNTY,** 309 E Perkins St, Ukiah, CA 95482-4504. Tel 707-463-2727; Email director@artsmendocino.org; Web: www.artsmendocino.org; *Exec Dir* Alyssum Wier; *Pres* Hal Wagenet
Open by appointment; No admis fee; Estab 2000 to promote, introduce & benefit the arts in Mendocino County; Mem: 400; dues $25 regular mem; $25 artist mem
Income: $45,000 annual budget
Library Holdings: Book Volumes, Exhibition Catalogs
Special Subjects: Folk Art
Activities: Classes for adults & children; Artists-in-the-schools grant prog; Mendocino Cty Art Champion annual awards; mus shop sells original art

M **CITY OF UKIAH,** Grace Hudson Museum & The Sun House, 431 S Main St, Ukiah, CA 95482-4923. Tel 707-467-2836; Fax 707-467-2835; Email info@gracehudsonmuseum.org; Web: www.gracehudsonmuseum.org; *Dir* Sherrie Smith-Ferri; *Cur* Karen Holmes; *Preparator* Jen Lyon
Open Wed - Sat 10 AM - 4:30 PM, Sun Noon - 4:30 PM; Admis seniors/students $3, general $4, familie4s $10, first Friday of month free; Estab 1975; 3 permanent collection galleries, 1 changing exhibit gallery; Average Annual Attendance: 11,500
Income: $300,000 (financed by endowment, mem, city appropriation & grants)
Special Subjects: American Indian Art, American Western Art, Anthropology, Ethnology, Manuscripts, Painting-American
Collections: Hudson & Carpenter Family Collection, Grace Hudson Art Collection, Collection of Pomo Indian arts & material cult, Photographic & manuscript archives
Exhibitions: Grace Hudson (art); History & Anthropology of Native Americans; regional artists
Publications: exhibit catalogs
Activities: Classes for adults & children in docent progs; lects open to pub, 2-3 vis lectrs per yr; concerts; gallery talks; book traveling exhibs 1 per yr; originates traveling exhibs 1 per yr; mus shop sells books, magazines, original art, reproductions & jewelry

VALLEY GLEN

M **LOS ANGELES VALLEY COLLEGE,** Art Gallery, 5800 Fulton Ave, Valley Glen, CA 91401-4062. Tel 818-781-1200; Web: www.lavc.edu/arts/gallery.html; *Dean* Dennis Reed; *Gallery Mgr* Phung Huynh
Open Mon-Thurs 11AM - 2PM & 6-9 PM; No admis fee, donation requested; Estab 1960 to show changing exhibitions of ethnic, historical, & contemporary art; Single gallery
Income: $25,000 (financed by state appropriation & fundraising)
Exhibitions: Various exhib
Activities: Lects open to public, 2 vis lectrs per year; gallery talks; tours

VENICE

A **BEYOND BAROQUE FOUNDATION,** Beyond Baroque Literary Arts Center, 681 Venice Blvd, Venice, CA 90291-4805. Tel 310-822-3006; Fax 310-827-7432; Email bbproposals@gmail.com; Web: www.beyondbaroque.org; *Exec Dir* Richard Modiano; *Develop Dir/Mem* Lisa Lane; *Bookstore/Archive Mgr* Lenka Minkowski
Open Fri 11 AM - 6 PM & during events; Admis non-members $7, students $5, members free; Estab 1968 to promote & support literary arts projects, writers & artists in Southern Calif & nationally; Bookstore, theatre & gallery; Average Annual Attendance: 6,000; Mem: 1,000; dues $35 annually
Income: $150,000 (financed by grants from National Endowment for the Arts, California Art Council, City of Los Angeles, other government & private grants as well as donations from the public)
Collections: Literature, Poetry, Text Art
Activities: Classes for adults & children; all types of writing workshops; art lects open to public; weekly reading & performance series; art gallery; film program; music program; concerts

A **SOCIAL & PUBLIC ART RESOURCE CENTER,** (SPARC), 685 Venice Blvd, Venice, CA 90291-4805. Tel 310-822-9560; Fax 310-827-8717; Email info@sparcmurals.org; Web: www.sparcmurals.org; *Artistic Dir* Judith F Baca; *Exec Dir* Joel Arquillos; *Dir Educ* Julius Diaz; *Develop Dir* Lee Schube
Open Mon - Fri 10 AM - 4 PM, Sat - Sun 1 - 4 PM during some exhibitions only; Admis donations requested; Estab 1976 as a nonprofit multicultural art center that produces, exhibits, distributes & preserves public artworks; 1st fl in the Old Venice Police Sta; Average Annual Attendance: 10,000; Mem: 200; dues $25 & up; mem open to public
Income: Financed by government funding, mem & donations
Collections: Archive coll of over 60,000 mural images
Exhibitions: 4-6 exhibits per yr
Publications: California Chicano Muralists; Signs from the Heart
Activities: Classes for adults & children; lects open to pub, 6-10 vis lectrs per yr; gallery talks; mural tours; competitions; schols & fels offered; individual paintings & original objects of art lent to mus; lending coll contains books, framed reproductions, original art works, original paintings, paintings, photographs & slides; originate traveling exhibs; sales shop sells books, original art, reproductions, prints, slides, cards & postcards

VENTURA

M **MUSEUM OF VENTURA COUNTY,** 89 S California St, Ventura, CA 93001; 100 E Main St, Ventura, CA 93001-2698. Tel 805-653-0323; Fax 805-653-5267; Email marketing@venturamuseum.org; Web: www.venturamuseum.org; *Res Librn* Charles Johnson; *Exec Dir* Tim Schiffer; *Dir Mktg* Susan Gerrard; *Dir Develop* Robin Woodworth; *Cur Colls* Anna Rios-Bermudez; *Opers Mgr* Jeanne Scott; *Dir Educ* Wendy VanHorn; *Mgr Mus Store* Linden Royce; *Mem Asst* Danielle Martell;

Assoc Librn & Archivist Jennifer Maxon; *Asst Cur* Ariane Karakalos; *Bookkeeper* Izumi Kiesel; *Develop Asst* Suzy Dyer
Open Tues - Sun 11 AM - 6 PM, cl Mon; No general admis fee (some events require admis); Estab 1913 to collect, study, & interpret the history & art of Ventura County; Changing exhibits; Average Annual Attendance: 65,000; Mem: 2300; dues $45 - $500; annual meeting in Oct
Income: $100,000 (financed by endowment, mem, county appropriation)
Special Subjects: Historical Material, Painting-American
Collections: Farm implements & machines, fine arts, historical artifacts, historical figures, prehistoric artifacts, research library coll of 150,000 historic documents & rare glass plate images
Publications: Monthly newsletter; Journal of Ventura County History
Activities: Docent training & networking; school outreach; classes for adults & children; free family time activities third Sunday of month; lects open to pub; gallery talks; special events with each exhibit; mus shop sells books, original art, jewelry, and clothing

M **VENTURA COLLEGE,** Art Galleries, 4667 Telegraph Rd, Ventura, CA 93003-3899. Tel 805-648-8974; Fax 805-654-6466; *Dir Gallery* Kate Martin
Call ahead for hours; No admis fee; Estab 1970s to showcase faculty & student artworks, as well as prestigious artists from throughout the country; Gallery 2 & New Media Gallery
Activities: Originate traveling exhibs

WALNUT CREEK

M **DEAN LESHER REGIONAL CENTER FOR THE ARTS,** Bedford Gallery, 1601 Civic Dr, Walnut Creek, CA 94596-4299. Tel 925-295-1417; Fax 925-295-1486; Email galleryinfo@bedfordgallery.org; Web: www.bedfordgallery.org; *Cur* Carrie Lederer
Open Tues - Sun Noon - 5 PM, Thurs - Sat 6 - 8 PM (when there are performances in the LCA), cl Mon & national holidays; Admis adult $5, youth 13-17 $3, children 12 & under free; Estab 1963 to offer varied & educ changing exhibs to the community & surrounding area; Gallery contains 396 running ft, 3500 sq ft; Average Annual Attendance: 30,000; Mem: 1200; dues Diablo Regional Arts Assoc mem $35
Income: Funded by city, pub & pvt grants
Exhibitions: 5-6 exhibits on view at the gallery each year
Publications: The Diablo Arts Magazine, quarterly
Activities: Classes for adults & children; dramatic progs; docent training; lects open to pub, 4-5 vis lectrs per yr; concerts; gallery talks; tours; competitions; book traveling exhibs; organize traveling exhibs; sales shop sells original art, reproductions, prints, jewelry & other items

WEST HOLLYWOOD

M **NEW IMAGE ART,** 7920 Santa Monica Blvd, West Hollywood, CA 90046-5108. Tel 323-654-2192; Fax 323-654-2192; Email newimgart@aol.com; Web: www.newimagartgallery.com; *Dir* Marsea Goldberg; *Dir* Chris Johansen; *Dir* Joe Jackson; *Dir* Clayton Brothers; *Dir* Rich Jacobs; *Dir* Ed Templeton; *Dir* Scooter Rudolf; *Intern* Iya Muto
Open Wed-Sat 1-6PM; No admis fee; Estab 1995 to define the concept of New Image within the present avant-garde; Small alternative space in West Hollywood that shows a full season of primarily cutting edge American artists & street artists; Average Annual Attendance: 5,000
Income: pvt
Exhibitions: Cheryl Dunn, Barry McGee, Ed Templeton, Chris Johanson

WHITTIER

M **RIO HONDO COLLEGE ART GALLERY,** 3600 Workman Mill Rd, Whittier, CA 90601-1699. Tel 562-463-6652; Fax 562-908-3446; Email robert.miller@riohondo.edu; Web: www.riohondo.edu/arts; *Div Dean* Chris Guptill; *Gallery Dir* Robert A Miller
Open Mon - Fri 11 AM - 4 PM; No admis fee; Estab 1967 to bring to the col students a wide variety of art experiences that will enhance & develop their sensitivity & appreciation of art; Small gallery about 1,000 sq ft located within the art facility; Average Annual Attendance: 8,000
Income: Financed through college
Collections: Contemporary paintings and graphics by Southern California artists
Exhibitions: Landscapes by Paul Donaldson, Carl Aldana, James Urstrom; Sculptures by Joyce Kohl; Self Portraits by Selected California Artists; student shows and area high school honor show
Activities: Classes for adults; lect open to public; 2-4 vis lectr per yr; gallery talks

YOSEMITE NATIONAL PARK

M **YOSEMITE MUSEUM,** PO Box 577, National Park Service Yosemite National Park, CA 95389-0577. Tel 209-372-0281, 372-0297; Email yose_museum@nps.gov; Web: www.nps.gov/yose; *Chief Cur* Barbara L. Beroza; *Archivist* Paul Rogers; *Cur Collections* Greg Cox; *Research Libr* Virginia Sanchez; *Reg* Sara Hay
Open daily 9 AM - 5 PM; No admis fee; Estab 1926 to interpret the natural sciences & human history of the Yosemite area; Mem: 1700; dues $10 & up
Income: Financed by federal appropriation
Special Subjects: Photography, American Indian Art
Collections: Indian cultural artifacts, original paintings & photos of Yosemite, photographs (special coll on early Yosemite), pioneer artifacts, Yosemite related ephemera
Exhibitions: Rotating exhibits
Activities: Classes for adults & children; lects open to pub; paintings & original art objects lent on special exhibits only; lending collection contains prints, photographs; sales shop sells books, magazines, reproductions, prints, slides; junior mus

L **Research Library**, PO Box 577, Yosemite National Park, CA 95389-0577. Tel 209-372-0280; *Coll Cur* Barbara Beroza; *Registrar* Miriam Luchans; *Archivist* Brenna Lissoway
Open Mon - Sun 9 AM - 4 PM; No admis fee; 1890; national park; For reference only; Average Annual Attendance: 3,000,000
Income: Federal appropriation
Library Holdings: Book Volumes 10,000, Clipping Files, Exhibition Catalogs, Fiche, Lantern Slides, Manuscripts, Memorabilia, Pamphlets, Periodical Subscriptions 100, Photographs, Reels, Reproductions, Slides
Collections: Extensive art of Yosemite 1855-2007, Photographs, native basketry
Activities: Mus shop sells books, magazines, original art, & native crafts

YOUNTVILLE

M **NAPA VALLEY MUSEUM,** PO Box 3567, 55 Presidents Circle Yountville, CA 94599-3567. Tel 707-944-0500; Fax 707-945-0500; Web: www.napavalley.museum.org; *Exec Dir* Rick Deragon; *Office Mgr* Maureen Sweeney; *Mus Educ* Pat Alexander
Open Wed - Mon 10 AM - 5 PM, cl Tues; Admis adult $4.50, seniors & students $3.50, children $2.50; Estab 1971 for regional history, art & natural history; Average Annual Attendance: 12,000; Mem: 900; dues $35-$1000 & up; annual meeting 2nd Tues in June
Income: $750,000 (financed by endowment, mem, museum store, admis & grants)
Special Subjects: Painting-American, Photography, Watercolors
Collections: Henry Evans - linocut prints, Andrew Grayson Jackson - lithos, Sophie Alstrom Mitchell - watercolors, Charles O'Rear - photography, Agricultural Artifacts, American Indian Artifacts, Henry Evans Linocuts, Minerals & Fossil
Publications: Quarterly newsletter
Activities: Progs & classes for adults & children; dramatic progs; docent training; lects open to pub; exten dept serves local schools; book traveling exhibs 6 per yr; retail shop sells books, prints, magazines & gifts

COLORADO

ASPEN

M **ASPEN ART MUSEUM,** 637 E. Hyman Ave, Aspen, CO 81611-1922. Tel 970-925-8050; Fax 970-925-8054; Email info@aspenartmuseum.org; Web: www.aspenartmuseum.org; *Dir & Chief Cur* Heidi Zuckerman Jacobson; *Cur* Courtney Finn
Open Tues - Sun 10 AM - 8 PM, Thurs 5 - 7 PM, cl Mon; No admis fee; Estab 1979 to provide the community with a variety of cultural & educational experiences through exhibits, lectures & classes; 33,000 sq ft gallery; Average Annual Attendance: 15,000; Mem: 800; dues $50-$500; annual meeting in Aug
Income: $2,000,000 (financed by benefits, memberships, donations, grants)
Library Holdings: Audio Tapes, Book Volumes, Exhibition Catalogs, Periodical Subscriptions, Photographs, Slides, Video Tapes
Special Subjects: Sculpture, Manuscripts
Activities: Classes for adults & children; family workshops; docent training; lects, 8 vis lectrs per yr; gallery talks; tours; Aspen Award for Art; museum sleepovers; scholarships offered; mus shop sells books, cards, toys, hats, catalogs, t-shirts

M **BALDWIN GALLERY,** 209 S Galena St, Aspen, CO 81611. Tel 970-920-9797; Fax 970-920-1821; Email baldwingallery@baldwingallery.com; Web: www.baldwingallery.com; *Dir* Richard Edwards
Open Mon - Sat 10 AM - 6 PM Sun Noon - 5 PM; Estab 1994 to promote & display new work by renowned artists
Special Subjects: Painting-American, Drawings, Photography, Sculpture
Collections: works by estab & emerging artists; focus on contemporary American art
Exhibitions: Temporary exhibits

M **RED BRICK CENTER FOR THE ARTS,** 110 E Hallam St, Aspen, CO 81611-1458. Tel 970-429-2777; Email info@aspenart.org; Web: www.theredbrick.org; *Exec Dir* Debra Muzikar
Open Mon - Fri 10 AM - 6 PM, Sat 10 AM - 4 PM, cl Sun; Estab to provide space for art, workshops & activities
Collections: Work by local artists exclusively
Exhibitions: Temporary exhibits
Activities: Educ progs; classes for adults & children artist residencies; workshops; community events

BOULDER

A **BOULDER HISTORY MUSEUM,** Museum of History, 1206 Euclid Ave, Boulder, CO 80302-7224. Tel 303-449-3464; Fax 303-938-8322; Email ngeyer@boulderhistory.org; Web: www.boulderhistorymuseum.org; *Cur Costumes* Terri Schindel; *Assoc Dir* Wendy Gordon; *Exec Dir* Nancy Geyer; *Prog Mgr* Julie Schumaker; *Cur Coll* Pete Lundskow; *Dir Develop* Alan Browning
Open Tues - Fri 10 AM - 4 PM, Sat & Sun noon - 4 PM, cl Mon; Admis $5 adults, $3 seniors, $2 children; Estab 1944 to promote history of Boulder Valley; history of the Boulder area 1840s to present; Average Annual Attendance: 5,000; Mem: 400; dues $20 - $100; annual meeting in Spring
Income: $450,000 (financed by endowment & mem)
Purchases: Quilts, photographs, costumes, agricultural tools, glass, historical artifacts
Special Subjects: Historical Material
Collections: Costumes, Local Historical Material, Manuscripts & Photographs

Exhibitions: Period Kitchen & Sitting Room; 19th Century Businesses; Bicycles; Agriculture; Mining; Education
Publications: Biannual newsletter
Activities: Classes for adults & children, docent training; lects open to pub, 400 vis lectrs per yr; lending coll contains 5000 paintings; book traveling exhibs 2 per yr; retail store sells books & local history artifacts

A **BOULDER MUSEUM OF CONTEMPORARY ART,** 1750 13th St, Boulder, CO 80302-6226. Tel 303-443-2122; Fax 303-447-1633; Email info@bmoca.org; Web: www.bmoca.org; *Pres Bd Dir* Andrew McArthur; *Develop Co-Exec Dir* Penny Barnow; *Sr Cur* Joan Markowitz; *Assoc Cur* Kirsten Gerdes
Open Tues - Fri 11 AM - 5 PM, Sat 9 AM - 4 PM, Sun noon - 3 PM, Wed until 8PM, cl Mon & holidays; Admis exhibs $5, students & seniors $4, mem & children under 12 free, Saturdays, free.; Estab 1972 to explore the forefront of contemporary art & ideas, bringing together innovative exhibits, performances & educ to inspire & challenge; Three galleries totaling 5000 sq ft; lecture space; black box theater; exhibitions focus on contemporary, regional, national & international art; Average Annual Attendance: 20,000; Mem: 500; dues from $12-$1000; annual meeting in Oct
Income: Financed by contributions, mem, city support & grants
Publications: Weather Report; Art & climate change
Activities: Classes for adults & children; dramatic progs; docent training; poetry & performance art; pub theatre; lects open to pub, 3-5 vis lectrs per yr, also lects for members; concerts; gallery talks; tours; competitions with awards; mus shop sells books, magazines & mus materials

L **BOULDER PUBLIC LIBRARY & GALLERY,** Arts Gallery, 1000 Canyon Blvd, Boulder, CO 80302; PO Drawer H, Boulder, CO 80306. Tel 303-441-3100; Fax 303-442-1808, 441-4119; Web: www.boulder.lib.co.us; *Exhib Coordr* Gregory Ravenwood; *City of Boulder Arts Commission & Dir Cultural Programs* Donna Gartenmann; *Dir Library* Tony Tallent
Open Mon - Thurs 10 AM - 9 PM, Fri & Sat 10 AM - 6 PM, Sun Noon - 6 PM; Estab to enhance the personal develop of Boulder citizens by meeting their informational needs; Bridge Gallery, three shows change monthly; Average Annual Attendance: 300,000
Income: Financed by city appropriations, grants & gifts
Library Holdings: Audio Tapes, Cards, Cassettes, Clipping Files, Compact Disks, DVDs, Exhibition Catalogs, Fiche, Framed Reproductions, Manuscripts, Micro Print, Original Art Works, Pamphlets, Photographs, Prints, Reproductions, Sculpture, Slides, Video Tapes
Activities: Classes for adults & children; lect open to public; 7,500 lectrs per yr; concerts; gallery talks; tours; competitions; awards; sales shop sells books & magazines

M **DAIRY ARTS CENTER,** 2590 Walnut St, Boulder, CO 80302-5700. Tel 303-440-7826; Fax 303-440-7104; Email kharwood@thedairy.org; Web: thedairy.org; *Exec Dir* Melissa Fathman; *Visual Art Cur* Rebecca Cuscadew; *Cur Visual Arts* Rebecca Cuscaden
Open McMahon Gallery: Mon - Tues 9 AM - 6 PM, Wed - Fri 9 AM - 8 PM, Sat - Sun Noon - 6 PM; Polly Addison Gallery, Hand-Rudy Gallery & MacMillan Family Lobby: daily 9 AM - 8 PM; Suggested donation $5; Estab 1992 to supply local artists with work spaces & performers with venues; 42,000 sq ft; four galleries; Mem: dues individual $120, dual $180
Special Subjects: Film
Collections: Performing, cinematic & visual arts
Exhibitions: Temporary exhibits
Activities: Educ progs; classes for adults & children; lects open to pub

M **LEANIN' TREE MUSEUM & SCULPTURE GARDEN OF WESTERN ART,** 6055 Longbow Dr Boulder, CO 80301; PO Box 9500, Boulder, CO 80301-9500. Tel 303-530-1442 ext 4101; Fax 303-581-2152; Email info@leanintree.com; Web: www.leanintreemuseum.com; WATS 800-777-8716; *Founder* Edward P Trumble; *Pres* Tom Trumble
Open Mon - Fri 8 AM - 6 PM, Sat 9 AM - 5 PM, Sun 10 AM - 5 PM; No admis fee; Estab 1974; Two floors of paintings & bronzes with outdoor sculpture garden; Average Annual Attendance: 40,000
Purchases: Hollywood Indian #5, 1970 by Fritz Scholder (1937-2005); Board of Dir 2002 by James E Reynolds (1926-2010); Stealth Hunter by Robert Kuhn (1920-2007); On the Beach by Burt Proctor (1901-1980); Respect, bronze 1985 by Allan Houser (1914-1994); Apache Cradle Board, bronze 1994 by Allan Houser (1914-1994); Kachina Dream State, (acrylic 2003 by Dan Namingha (1950-); Seal Hunter, acrylic 2002 by Bob Kuhn (1920-2007)
Library Holdings: Book Volumes 1, Cards 2500, Framed Reproductions, Prints, Sculpture
Special Subjects: American Western Art, Bronzes, Painting-American, Sculpture, Southwestern Art, Watercolors
Collections: Contemporary Western cowboy & Indian art, Western bronze sculptures, paintings by major contemporary Western artists, 1950 to present day, outdoor sculpture garden
Activities: Self guided tours; guided tours of greeting card factory; mus shop sells books, reproductions, prints, mus related items, greeting cards, holiday cards, original art, posters, & gifts

M **UNIVERSITY OF COLORADO,** CU Art Museum, 1085 18th St, Boulder, CO 80309; 318 UCB, Boulder, CO 80309-0318. Tel 303-492-8300; Fax 303-735-4197; Email lisa.becker@colorado.edu; Web: cuartmuseum.colorado.edu; *Dir* Lisa Tamiris Becker; *Colls Mgr & Registrar* Kimberly Dorazewski-Smouse; *Assoc Colls Mgr & Registrar* Caitlin Rumery; *Exhibs, Facilities & Securities Mgr* Stephen Martonis; *Preparator* Pedro Caceres; *Mus Coordr* Jennifer Conrad
Open Mon - Fri 10 AM - 5 PM, Tues until 7 PM, Sat Noon - 4 PM, cl Sun; No admis fee, suggested donation $5; Estab 1939 to maintain & exhibit art collections & to show temporary exhibits; Visual Arts Complex maintains 5 galleries incl 2 Changing Exhib Galleries, 2 Permanent Exhib Galleries & a Video Gallery, as well as a study center, education/ workshop room & collection storage; Mem: Dues $45 - $10,000
Income: Financed through University, gifts & grants
Special Subjects: African Art, Antiquities-Greek, Antiquities-Roman, Asian Art, Ceramics, Coins & Medals, Drawings, Etchings & Engravings, Glass, Manuscripts, Painting-American, Photography, Pottery, Prints, Sculpture, Watercolors, Woodcarvings, Baroque Art, Renaissance Art
Collections: 19th & 20th century paintings & prints, The Colorado Collection, Ancient Greek Pottery Collection, Roman Glass Collection, Wilton Jaffee Roman Coin Collection, Collection of African Sculpture, Southeast Asian Pottery Collection, Medieval Manuscript Collection, Renaissance & Baroque Print & Drawing Collection, Ancient Iranian Pottery Collection, Japanese Ukiyo-e Collection, Southwest American & South American Santos & Bultos Collections
Publications: Exhib catalogs; brochures
Activities: Lects open to public; gallery talks; symposia; tours

L **Art & Architecture Library**, 1720 Pleasant St, Norlin Library, 184 UCB Boulder, CO 80309. Tel 303-492-7521; Fax 303-492-0935; Email reflib@colorado.edu; Web: ucblibraries.colorado.edu/art/index.htm; *Art & Architecture Librn* Yem Fong
Open by appointment. Please call first; Estab 1966 to support the university curriculum in the areas of fine arts, art history, environmental design, architecture, planning, landscape & interior design; For lending only
Income: Financed by state appropriation
Library Holdings: Auction Catalogs, Book Volumes 120,000, Compact Disks, DVDs, Exhibition Catalogs, Fiche 5950, Other Holdings MFA thesis statements; Museum & gallery publications, Periodical Subscriptions 500, Reels
Special Subjects: Afro-American Art, American Indian Art, American Western Art, Eskimo Art, Folk Art, History of Art & Archaeology, Latin American Art, Mexican Art, Oriental Art, Painting-American, Religious Art, Southwestern Art, Architecture, Dioramas

BRIGHTON

M **ADAMS COUNTY HISTORICAL SOCIETY,** Adams County Museum, 9601 Henderson Rd, Brighton, CO 80601-8127. Tel 303-659-7103; Fax 303-659-7988; Email adamscountymuseum@gmail.com; Web: adamscountymuseum.com
Open Tues - Sat 10 AM - 4 PM; Guided tours $3; For reference. Different artists & groups exhibited throughout the yr
Income: $50,000 (financed by mem, dues, craft shows, gifts & grants)
Library Holdings: Book Volumes, Clipping Files, Lantern Slides, Pamphlets, Records
Collections: American Antiques
Activities: Tours

CANON CITY

A **FREMONT CENTER FOR THE ARTS,** 505 Macon Ave, Canon City, CO 81212-3309; PO Box 1006, Canon City, CO 81215-1006. Tel 719-275-2790; Fax 719-275-4244; Email fca@fremontarts.org; Web: www.fremontarts.org; *Admin* Katrina Mann; *Treas* Jon Stone; *VPres* Dick Ploeger
Open Tues - Sat 10 AM - 4 PM; Admis $3; Estab 1947; Housed in historic U.S. Post Office bldg; Average Annual Attendance: 10,000; Mem: $350; dues $30, ann meeting in Feb
Income: Financed by mem, individual donations, local small bus, grants, fundraising
Library Holdings: Book Volumes, Clipping Files, Original Art Works, Photographs, Prints
Collections: permanent colls
Exhibitions: Exhibs change every month
Publications: Artifacts quarterly newsletter
Activities: Classes for adults & children; dramatic progs; docent training; lects open to public; concerts; gallery talks; competitions; monetary ribbons awards; sales shop sells books, reproductions, prints, CDs, original art & prints

CENTRAL CITY

A **GILPIN COUNTY ARTS ASSOCIATION,** 119 Eureka St, Central City, CO 80427-5952; PO Box 98, Central City, CO 80427-0098. Tel 303-642-0991; Email info@gilpinarts.org; Web: www.gilpinarts.org; *Pres* Susan Snodgrass; *Gallery Mgr* Diane Sill
Open June 1-Aug 15 Tues-Sun noon-6PM, open until 8PM on opera nights, Aug 23-Oct 4 Fri-Sun 10AM-6PM; No admis fee; Estab 1947 to offer a juried exhibition of Colorado artists & to support the local school arts program; Six wings on two floors; outdoor sculpture garden; memorial fountain in Newbury Wing sculpted by Angelo di Benedetto; gallery is open June - Sept 15; oldest juried art exhibition in Colorado; nonprofit organization; Average Annual Attendance: 25,000; Mem: 200; dues $1000; annual meeting, third Sun in Aug
Income: Financed by mem, sales & entry fee
Purchases: Over $60,000 annually
Publications: Annual exhibit catalog
Activities: Juried competitions with awards; sponsor elementary & secondary school art program

COLORADO SPRINGS

AMERICAN NUMISMATIC ASSOCIATION
For further information, see National and Regional Organizations

L **ARJUNA LIBRARY,** Digital Visual Dream Laboratory & Acoustic Studio, 1404 E Bijou, Colorado Springs, CO 80909-5520. Tel 719-473-0360; Email pfuphoff@earthlink.net; Web: home.earthlink.net/~pfuphoff/; *Exec Dir (Arjuna Lib) & Ed in Chief, Journal of Regional Criticism* Ct. Pf. Joseph A Uphoff Jr
Estab 1983; For reference only
Library Holdings: Book Volumes 2100, CD-ROMs 250, Compact Disks 450, DVDs 700, Manuscripts, Original Art Works, Other Holdings Flash Drives, Terrabyte Portable Hand Drives, Periodical Subscriptions, Photographs, Records 150, Sculpture, Slides 1400, Video Tapes 100 clips (computer hard drive)

Special Subjects: Aesthetics, Archaeology, Calligraphy, Ceramics, Coins & Medals, Conceptual Art, Decorative Arts, Drawings, Historical Material, Illustration, Manuscripts, Oriental Art, Painting-American, Painting-British, Painting-European, Painting-French, Painting-German, Portraits, Sculpture, Stage Design
Collections: Eshkol-Wachman Movement Notation Studies, Manuscripts & Proceedings, Differential Logic, Mathematical Surrealistic Theory, Mathematical Proceedings in Criticism for Drama. Poetics, Dance, Martial Arts & Yoga, Metamathematics, Calculus, Logical Integration Abstract Algebra, Poetry Reading, Videos & Portraits, JPG Digital Photos, Regional Poetry History
Exhibitions: Type Programming Mail Art Exhib; Internet Group Shows, Internet JPG Exhibs; Media & Mail Art Blogs; You Tube, Digital Video Clips; DVD Movies
Publications: Journal of Regional Criticism, irregular
Activities: Trending Poems; Hello Poetry (Hello Poetry Computer); Poetry West Essays, Colorado Springs Fresh Ink (The Gazette); awards: Ryosuke Cohen, Brain Cell Life Form, Featured File, International Union of Mail Artists; The Uphoff Residence designated a Wildlife Habitat; monthly poetry & open microphone readings; Hear Here (719 on Facebook)

M **COLORADO SPRINGS FINE ARTS CENTER,** Taylor Museum, 30 W Dale St, Colorado Springs, CO 80903-3210. Tel 719-634-5583; Fax 719-634-0570; Email info@csfineartscenter.org; Web: www.csfineartscenter.org; *Mus Dir* Rebecca Tucker Ph.D.; *Dir Educ* Kris Stanec; *Cur Modern & Contemporary Art* Joy Armstrong; *Dir Communs & Mktg* Dori Mitchell; *Collections Mgr & Registrar* Michael Howell
Open Tues - Sun 10 AM - 5 PM, cl Mon; Admis adults $10, seniors, military w/ID, students w/ID & youth ages 5-17 $8.50, mems & children 4 & under free; Estab 1936 as a forum, advocate & programmer of visual & performing arts activities & art school for the community; 132,286 sq ft of gallery space, original bldg designed by John Gaw Meem in 1936, recent addition designed by David Owen Tryba; comprised of Blessing Gallery, Duff Gallery, Manley Gallery, Loo Gallery, East Events Gallery, Dickinson Gallery, Lane Gallery & Courtyard Corridor; Average Annual Attendance: 75,000; Mem: 8,000; dues $30-$750; annual meeting in Dec
Income: $2,174,000 (financed by endowment, mem, bus & industry contributions, revenue producing enterprises, city, state & federal appropriations)
Library Holdings: Auction Catalogs, Audio Tapes, Book Volumes 27,000, Clipping Files, Exhibition Catalogs, Memorabilia, Pamphlets, Periodical Subscriptions 50, Video Tapes
Special Subjects: American Indian Art, American Western Art, Anthropology, Bronzes, Ceramics, Drawings, Folk Art, Glass, Graphics, Hispanic Art, Landscapes, Latin American Art, Mexican Art, Painting-American, Sculpture, Southwestern Art, Photography, Portraits, Pottery, Pre-Columbian Art, Prints, Religious Art, Silver, Textiles, Watercolors, Woodcarvings
Collections: American paintings, sculptures, graphics & drawings with emphasis on art west of the Mississippi, ethnographic collections, fine arts collections, 19th - 21st c American Art, Taylor Collection of Southwestern Art: incl anthropology, Spanish Colonial Art & Native American Art
Publications: Artsfocus, bimonthly calendar; educational programs and tours; exhibition catalogs; gallery sheets; scholarly publications; catalogue of the collections
Activities: Docent training & presentations; internships; lects open to pub & mems only; gallery talks; tours; concerts; films; competitions; Governors Award for Excellence in the Arts; art lent to AAM accredited mus; mus shop sells books, original art, reproductions & prints

M **Bemis School of Art,** 818 Pelham Pl, Colorado Springs, CO 80903; 30 W Dale St, Colorado Springs, CO 80903-3210. Tel 719-475-2444; Fax 719-634-0570; Email bemis@csfineartscenter.org; Web: www.csfineartscenter.org; *Dir* Tara Sevanne Thomas, MA; *Asst Dir* Jeremiah Houck
Open Mon-Thurs 9AM-5PM, Fri 9AM-3PM; Estab 1919 as Broadmoor Art Academy, incorporated 1936 into John Gaw Meem's Fine Arts Ctr, later housed in own facility; 7 art studios
Special Subjects: Art History, Ceramics, Drawings, Jewelry, Mosaics, Photography, Sculpture, Watercolors
Activities: Classes for adults & children; art classes for pre-school arts prog; gifted & talented classes (gr 3-6) in visual arts & drama; creative dramatics

M **UNITED STATES FIGURE SKATING ASSOCIATION,** World Figure Skating Museum & Hall of Fame, 20 First St, Colorado Springs, CO 80906. Tel 719-635-5200 Ext 450; Fax 719-635-9548; Email information@worldskatingmuseum.org; Web: www.worldskatingmuseum.org; *Sr Dir, External Relations* Barbara Reichert; *Archivist* Karen Cover
Open Tues - Fri 10 AM - 4 PM, cl New Year's Day, Independence Day, Veterans Day, Thanksgiving & day after, Christmas Eve & Day; Admis adults $5, sr citizens & children 6-12 $3, children under 6 free; Estab 1965 as the international repository for the sport of figure skating; Maintains 10,000 sq ft exhibition area. Managed by OS Figure Skating; Average Annual Attendance: 7,000
Library Holdings: Audio Tapes, CD-ROMs, Cassettes, Clipping Files, DVDs, Exhibition Catalogs, Filmstrips, Framed Reproductions, Memorabilia, Motion Pictures, Original Art Works, Original Documents, Pamphlets, Photographs, Prints, Records, Reels, Video Tapes
Special Subjects: Art History, Bronzes, Ceramics, Costumes, Decorative Arts, Drawings, Etchings & Engravings, Gold, Historical Material, Manuscripts, Painting-Dutch, Painting-European, Painting-German, Pewter, Photography, Porcelain, Portraits, Posters, Prints, Restorations, Sculpture
Collections: Skating in Art, the Gillis Grafstrom Collection, costumes of the champions, Pierre Brunet Collection, National, World & Olympic protocols, Gladys McFerron Collection, Dorothy Stevens Collection, 2010 US Champions, World Synchronized Skating, Kloss Photo Collection
Exhibitions: Sonja Henie Remembered; 1961 World Figure Skating Team Memorial
Publications: Skating Magazine; Figure Skating: A History by James R Hines
Activities: Docent training; 2-3 special events per yr; gallery talks; tours for adults & children; competitions with awards; local summer reading sponsor with prizes; video tape showings; US & World Hall of Fame induction & reception; selected donations to local skating organizations, clubs & members; exten prog serves local library & airport with satellite exhibs; originates traveling exhibs, 3-4 per yr, to local library & airport; gift shop sells reproductions, books, magazines, branded skating items; branded items

M **UNIVERSITY OF COLORADO AT COLORADO SPRINGS,** Gallery of Contemporary Art, 1420 Austin Bluffs Pkwy, Colorado Springs, CO 80918-3733. Tel 719-262-3567; Fax 719-262-3183; Email clynn@uccs.edu; Web: www.galleryuccs.org
Open Thurs - Sun 1 PM - 6 PM, other times by appointment; No admis fee; Estab 1981 to organize & host group exhibitions primarily of contemporary art by artists of international, national & regional significance; 2,800 sq ft of exhibition space; adjoining classroom, auditorium & workshop/storage room; Average Annual Attendance: 7,000; Mem: Renewals: Jul 1 yearly
Income: $150,000 (financed by state appropriation, private donations & grants)
Special Subjects: Afro-American Art, American Indian Art, American Western Art, Asian Art, Crafts, Drawings, Etchings & Engravings, Folk Art, Glass, Landscapes, Latin American Art, Mexican Art, Photography, Prints, Sculpture, Southwestern Art, Textiles, Watercolors, Woodcuts
Exhibitions: 6 to 7 group exhibitions annually based on themes or surveys of particular mediums
Activities: Classes for adults & children; docent training; mus training prog; lects open to pub, lects open to members only; 10 vis lectrs per yr; concerts; gallery talks; tours; book traveling exhibs

CRESTED BUTTE

M **CENTER FOR THE ARTS PIPER GALLERY,** 606 6th St, Crested Butte, CO 81224-1819; PO Box 1819, Crested Butte, CO 81224-1819. Tel 970-349-7487; Fax 970-349-5626; Email info@crestedbuttearts.org; Web: www.crestedbuttearts.org/Piper-Gallery; *Exec Dir* Jenny Birnie; *Visual Arts Prog Dir* Melissa Mason
Call for hours; Estab 1986; 6,000 sq ft center
Special Subjects: Photography, Pottery, Painting-American
Collections: Local & regional artwork including photography, pottery & oil pastels
Exhibitions: Temporary exhibits

CRIPPLE CREEK

M **CRIPPLE CREEK DISTRICT MUSEUM,** 500 E Bennett Ave, Cripple Creek, CO 80813-1210; PO Box 1210, Cripple Creek, CO 80813-1210. Tel 719-689-9540; Email director@cripplecreekmuseum.com; Web: www.cripple-creek.org; *Dir* Richard Tremayne
Open Fall & Summer daily 10 AM - 5 PM, Spring & Winter weekends only; Admis adults $7, children 7 - 12 & military $5, children under 7 free; Estab 1953 as a showplace for local artists; One room, 50 ft x 20 ft, second room 25 ft x 25 ft; Average Annual Attendance: 35,000; Mem: 80 mem; dues $50-500
Income: Financed by donations
Library Holdings: Audio Tapes, Book Volumes, CD-ROMs, Cassettes, Clipping Files, Compact Disks, DVDs, Framed Reproductions, Manuscripts, Maps, Memorabilia, Original Art Works, Original Documents, Pamphlets, Periodical Subscriptions, Photographs, Prints, Records, Reproductions, Sculpture, Slides, Video Tapes
Special Subjects: American Indian Art, American Western Art, Bookplates & Bindings, Cartoons, Ceramics, Coins & Medals, Costumes, Crafts, Decorative Arts, Dioramas, Dolls, Drawings, Embroidery, Etchings & Engravings, Flasks & Bottles, Folk Art, Furniture, Glass, Gold, Historical Material, Jewelry, Laces, Leather, Manuscripts, Manuscripts, Maps, Miniatures, Painting-American, Period Rooms, Photography, Porcelain, Portraits, Posters, Pottery, Primitive art, Prints, Religious Art, Reproductions, Restorations, Sculpture, Southwestern Art, Stained Glass, Tapestries, Watercolors, Woodcarvings, Woodcuts
Collections: Archival Coll, small coll of locally produced paintings
Exhibitions: Permanent Gold Ore exhibit; Permanent art, jewelry, & sculptures
Activities: Classes for children; docent training; lects open to pub; lects mems only; 2 vis lectrs per yr; tours; first place Gold Rush Days Parade 2011; first place in floats, Donkey Derby Days Parade 2011; True West Magazine Top Ten Western Museum list 2010 & 2011; sales shop sells books, magazines, original art, reproductions, prints & slides

DENVER

M **BLACK AMERICAN WEST MUSEUM & HERITAGE CENTER,** 3091 California St, Denver, CO 80205-3044. Tel 720-242-7428; Web: bawmhc.org; *Chmn* Daphne Rice-Allen; *Gen Asst* Denise Leadon
Open Fri & Sat 10 AM - 2 PM; Admis adults $10, seniors $9, students $8, children $7; Estab 1971; Blacks in the Western United States; Average Annual Attendance: 10,000; Mem: 300; dues vary; annual meeting in Feb
Income: $200,000 (financed by mem, donations, gift shop sales, rentals & grants)
Activities: Docent training; classes for adults & children; lects open to pub; tours; originates traveling exhibs; mus shop sells prints & reproductions

M **COLORADO PHOTOGRAPHIC ARTS CENTER,** 3636 Chestnut Pl, Denver, CO 80216-3630. Tel 303-837-1341; Email info@cpacphoto.org; Web: www.cpacphoto.org; *Exec Dir* Samantha Johnston; *Bd Chair* Keith Brenner
Tues-Friday 11 AM -5 PM , Sat Noon - 4 PM; No admis fee; Estab 1963 to foster the art of photography; Average Annual Attendance: 4,000; Mem: Senior/Student $35, Individual $45
Income: $150,000 (financed by grants, mem dues, donations, classes & workshops)
Library Holdings: Book Volumes, Cards, Exhibition Catalogs, Memorabilia, Original Art Works, Periodical Subscriptions
Special Subjects: Photography
Collections: Permanent collection, 500-600 photographs
Exhibitions: Local & regional exhibits; occasional national & international exhibits
Activities: Classes for adults; student gallery talks; lect open to pub & members, 4-5 vis lectrs per year; gallery talks; competitions with awards, Hal Gould Vision in

Photography Award; exhibits; workshops & tours; awards for juried members show; sales shop sells books, prints & original art

A **COLORADO WATERCOLOR SOCIETY,** PO Box 100003, Denver, CO 80250-0003. Tel 303-972-4001; Email president@coloradowatercolorsociety.org; Web: www.coloradowatercolorsociety.org; *Pres* Sydney Eitel
Estab 1954
Exhibitions: Colorado State Watermedia Exhibit; New Trends Show; Members Show
Publications: Monthly newsletter
Activities: Various workshops; lects open to pub; 10 vis lectrs per yr

M **CORE,** New Art Space, 900 Santa Fe Dr, Denver, CO 80204. Tel 303-297-8428; Web: www.coreartspace.com
Open Wed & Sat Noon - 6 PM, Fri Noon - 9 PM, Sun 1 PM - 4 PM; No admis fee; Estab 1982 to provide showing opportunities to members & non members; a nonprofit co-op gallery; Average Annual Attendance: 15,000; Mem: 24 mems
Library Holdings: Kodachrome Transparencies, Memorabilia, Original Art Works, Photographs, Prints, Sculpture, Slides
Activities: gallery talks; rental space available for three-week runs; 3 week 2 person mem shows

M **DENVER ART MUSEUM,** 100 W 14th Ave Pkwy, Denver, CO 80204-2713. Tel 720-865-5000; Fax 720-913-0001; Email info@denverartmuseum.org; Web: www.denverartmuseum.org; *Chmn* J Landis Martin; *Frederick & Jan Mayer Dir* Christoph Heinrich; *Deputy Dir & Chief Mktg Offier* Andrea Kalivas Fulton
Open Mon - Sun 10 AM - 5 PM, Fri 10 AM - 8 PM; Admis adults $13, sr citizens & students $10, children 18 and under & members free; Estab 1893, original bldg opened 1971, to provide a number of permanent & rotating art collections for pub viewing, as well as a variety of art educ programs & services; Hamilton Bldg added 2006; The seven story North Building contains 210,000 sq ft of space, 117,000 of which is exhibit space; the Hamilton Bldg contains 146,000 sq ft, inc 53,000 sq ft of exhib galleries; Average Annual Attendance: 600,000; Mem: 35,500; dues family $50, individual $35; annual meeting in Apr
Income: Financed by mem, city & state appropriations & private funding
Special Subjects: African Art, American Indian Art, American Western Art, Antiquities-Oriental, Architecture, Asian Art, Baroque Art, Bronzes, Ceramics, Decorative Arts, Drawings, Eskimo Art, Folk Art, Furniture, Glass, Gold, Islamic Art, Jade, Jewelry, Judaica, Landscapes, Landscapes, Latin American Art, Medieval Art, Metalwork, Mexican Art, Oriental Art, Painting-American, Painting-British, Painting-European, Painting-French, Painting-Italian, Painting-Japanese, Photography, Portraits, Pottery, Pre-Columbian Art, Religious Art, Renaissance Art, Restorations, Scrimshaw, Sculpture, Silver, Textiles, Tapestries, Southwestern Art
Collections: American art, contemporary art, design & architecture, European art, Native American art, Native arts, New World art, Oriental art, Western art
Publications: Calendar, monthly; catalogues for exhibitions
Activities: Classes for adults & children; dramatic progs; docent training; lects open to pub, 10 vis lectrs per yr; concerts; gallery talks; tours; book traveling exhibs 2-3 per yr; originate traveling exhibs to national & international museums & galleries; mus shop sells books, magazines, original art, reproductions, prints, jewelry, rugs & children's art projects

L **Library,** 100 W 14th Ave Pkwy, Denver, CO 80204-2713. Tel 720-913-0100; Fax 720-913-0001; Web: www.denverartmuseum.org
Open by appointment; Reference only
Library Holdings: Auction Catalogs, Book Volumes 25,000, Clipping Files, Exhibition Catalogs, Manuscripts, Memorabilia, Pamphlets, Periodical Subscriptions 50, Photographs
Special Subjects: Afro-American Art, American Indian Art, American Western Art, Anthropology, Archaeology, Asian Art, Folk Art, History of Art & Archaeology, Islamic Art, Latin American Art, Pre-Columbian Art, Southwestern Art
Collections: Native American

L **DENVER PUBLIC LIBRARY,** Reference, 10 W 14th Ave Pkwy, Denver, CO 80203. Tel 720-865-1111; Fax 720-865-1481; Web: www.denverlibrary.org; *Mgr Reference* Karen Kelley; *Mgr Western History & Genealogy* Jim Kroll
Open Mon - Tues 10 AM - 8 PM, Wed - Fri 10 AM - 6 PM, Sat 9 AM - 5 PM, Sun 1 - 5 PM; No admis fee; Estab 1889
Income: Financed by city & county taxes
Library Holdings: Audio Tapes, Book Volumes 80,000, Cassettes, Clipping Files, Compact Disks, DVDs, Exhibition Catalogs, Fiche, Manuscripts, Maps, Memorabilia, Original Art Works, Other Holdings Original documents, Periodical Subscriptions 100, Photographs 14,752, Prints 1384, Reels, Reproductions, Sculpture, Video Tapes
Special Subjects: American Western Art, Painting-American, Photography
Collections: Western art
Exhibitions: Frequent exhibitions from the book & picture collections
Activities: Lects open to pub; tours

M **EMMANUEL GALLERY,** 10th & Lawrence Mall, Auraria Campus Denver, CO 80010; PO Box 173364, Auraria Campus Box 177 Denver, CO 80217-3364. Tel 303-315-7431; Email emmanuelgallery@ucdenver.edu; Web: www.emmanuelgallery.org; *Dir & Cur* Jeff Lambson
Open Mon - Wed & Fri 10 AM - 5 PM, Thurs 10 AM - 7 PM, Sat noon - 4 PM; No admis fee; Estab 1976; Gallery is in the oldest standing church structure in Denver which has been renovated for exhibit space. This historic gallery supports the Community College of Denver, Metropolitan State College of Denver, the University of Colorado Denver as well as local, national & international artists; Average Annual Attendance: 10,000
Income: Financed by above colleges & Auraria Higher Education Center
Library Holdings: Sculpture
Collections: works by regional, nat & international artists
Exhibitions: Various exhib by students, faculty & artists
Activities: Lects open to pub; 2 vis lectrs per yr, gallery talks, tours, outreach progs

M **HISTORY COLORADO CENTER MUSEUM,** 1200 Broadway, Denver, CO 80203. Tel 303-447-8679; Fax 303-866-2711; Email information@chs.state.co.us; Web: www.coloradohistory.org; *Executive Director* Steve Turner; *Publications Ed* Steve Grinstead; *Dir Mktg &Communs* Kelly Williams
Open daily 10 AM - 5 PM, cl New Year's Day, Thanksgiving & Christmas; Admis adult $12, seniors (65 & older) & students (12-22 with ID) $10, children (6-12) $8, children (5 & under) & mems free; Estab 1879 to collect, preserve & interpret the history of Colorado; Average Annual Attendance: 203,640; Mem: 8000
Special Subjects: American Indian Art, American Western Art, Anthropology, Archaeology, Carpets & Rugs, Ceramics, Coins & Medals, Costumes, Decorative Arts, Dioramas, Dolls, Ethnology, Furniture, Hispanic Art, Historical Material, Manuscripts, Maps, Painting-American, Prints, Sculpture, Silver, Southwestern Art, Textiles
Collections: William H Jackson Photo Collection
Exhibitions: Destination Colorado; Colorado Stories, Denver A-Z; Living West; We Heart RMNP; El Movimiento: The Chicano Movement in Colorado
Publications: Colorado History, quarterly; Colorado History Now, monthly
Activities: Classes for children; docent training; lects open to pub; lectrs; gallery talks; tours; individual paintings & original objects of art lent to qualified museums; lending collection contains film strips & motion pictures; mus shop sells books, magazines, original art, reproductions, prints & souvenirs

L **Stephen H Hart Library,** 1200 Broadway, Ste 400, Denver, CO 80203. Tel 303-866-2305; Fax 303-866-4204; Email cosearch@state.co.us; Web: www.historycolorado.org; *Ref Librn* Barbara Dey; *Photo Librn* Sarah Everhart; *Cataloger* Pat Fraker
Open Wed - Sat 10 AM - 2 PM; Estab 1879 to preserve the history of Colorado; Open to public for reference; Average Annual Attendance: 5,000 visit reading rm; Mem: 7000; dues $30; annual meeting in Dec
Income: Financed by state agency, endowments & mus admis
Library Holdings: Audio Tapes 600, Book Volumes 45,000, Clipping Files 250, Lantern Slides, Manuscripts 9,000,000, Maps 5,000, Memorabilia, Motion Pictures, Original Art Works, Original Documents, Other Holdings Colorado Newspapers on Microfilm 2500; Maps 5000, Pamphlets, Periodical Subscriptions 600, Photographs 600,000, Prints, Reels, Video Tapes
Special Subjects: American Indian Art, American Western Art, Anthropology, Archaeology, Architecture, Art History, Carpets & Rugs, Ceramics, Coins & Medals, Costume Design & Constr, Crafts, Decorative Arts, Dioramas, Dolls, Drawings, Etchings & Engravings, Ethnology, Fashion Arts, Furniture, Handicrafts, Historical Material, Landscapes, Manuscripts, Maps, Mexican Art, Painting-American, Photography, Portraits, Posters, Pottery, Silver, Southwestern Art, Textiles, Watercolors
Collections: 600,000 photographs Colorado Western History, Aultman Photo Studio, Denver Rio Grande Photo & Manuscripts, William Henry Jackson Glass Plate Negatives of Views West of the Mississippi
Publications: Colorado Heritage, Colorado History, History Now newsletter
Activities: Classes for children; docent training; speakers bureau; historical treks; workshops; lects open to pub, 12 vis lectrs per yr; tours; Bancroft award; individual paintings & original objects of art lent to other mus; mus shop sells books, magazines, reproductions, prints, cards & gifts

M **KIRKLAND MUSEUM OF FINE & DECORATIVE ART,** 1311 Pearl St, Denver, CO 80203-2518. Tel 303-832-8576; Fax 303-832-8404; Email info@kirklandmuseum.org; Web: www.kirklandmuseum.org; *Dir* Hugh Grant; *Deputy Cur* Christopher Herron; *Deputy Dir* Gerald Horner; *Educ Mgr & Historian* Maya Wright; *Registrar* Becca Goodrum; *Visitor Servs Mgr* Charlotte Otto; *Vol Prog Mgr* Megan Sullivan; *Colls Mgr* Rebecca Gates; *Mktg & Outreach Mgr* Renee Albiston; *Librn* Lily Baird
Temporarily closed to visitor until early 2018, when we will reopen in a new bldg at 12th & Brannock in Denver. Vance Kirkland Studio Bldg will be relocated to the new site.; Estab 1996 to promote the life & works of Vance Kirkland (1904-1981); Retrospective & individual works 19th & 20th Century, decorative arts, Colorado art; Average Annual Attendance: 14,000; Mem: 500; student, senior, teacher $30, individual $35, dual $45, individual & guest $50, arts & crafts $100, art nouveau $250, bauhaus $500, art deco $1,000, modern $2,500
Income: Privately funded
Library Holdings: Auction Catalogs, Book Volumes
Special Subjects: American Western Art, Architecture, Bronzes, Carpets & Rugs, Ceramics, Decorative Arts, Drawings, Enamels, Etchings & Engravings, Furniture, Glass, Landscapes, Metalwork, Portraits, Posters, Pottery, Prints, Sculpture, Silver, Watercolors, Woodcarvings, Prints
Collections: Decorative Art from 1875-1990, Colorado Art from 1875-1990, Vance Kirkland 1904-1981 painting retrospective
Publications: Exhibition catalogs
Activities: Docent training; lects for mem only; gallery talks; tours; mus shop sells books, magazines & original art

A **LA NAPOULE ART FOUNDATION,** Chateau de la Napoule, 1673 Hudson St, Denver, CO 80220. Tel 603-436-3040; Fax 603-430-0025; Email LNAF@clews.org; Web: www.LNAF.org; *Pres* Christopher S Clews; *Exec Dir* Noele M Clews; *Chair Residency Comt* Natasha Gallaway; *Chair Pub Rels Comt* Christina Clews
Open Feb 7 - Nov 7 daily 10 AM - 6 PM, Nov 8 - Feb 10 Mon - Fri 2 PM - 5 PM, Sat & Sun 10 AM - 5 PM; Admis $5; Estab 1950 as an American organization to build Franco-American relations through a wide range of educational & artistic programs; Foundation's programs & artists' residencies take place year-round at the architecturally significant Chateau de la Napoule, located West of Cannes on the shores of the Mediterranean. The Chateau houses the permanent collection of 20th century sculptor, Henry Clews & changing contemporary exhibitions fill the Strawbridge Gallery; Average Annual Attendance: 40,000
Income: Financed by private & pub funds, governmental agencies, private foundations & individuals
Library Holdings: Book Volumes, Clipping Files, Exhibition Catalogs, Framed Reproductions, Lantern Slides, Manuscripts, Maps, Memorabilia, Original Art Works, Original Documents, Other Holdings, Photographs, Prints, Reproductions, Sculpture, Slides
Special Subjects: Antiquities-Oriental, Architecture, Bronzes, Ceramics, Decorative Arts, Drawings, Etchings & Engravings, Furniture, Historical Material, Landscapes, Manuscripts, Maps, Painting-American, Painting-European,

Painting-Italian, Period Rooms, Porcelain, Portraits, Posters, Pottery, Sculpture, Stained Glass, Watercolors, Woodcarvings
Collections: Henry Clews Collection: paintings and sculpture of the 20th-century artist, Staffordshire Pottery of James & Ralph Clews
Exhibitions: on-going exhibitions: architecture of the chateau, extensive gardens; 3 exhibits per year of contemporary art & sculpture; exhibits of resident artists; garden sculpture
Activities: Classes for children & adults in USA & France; artist residencies in France, summer cultural events including concerts & opera; awards, residencies for artists, biennial Prix de La Napoule for sculpture tours & 3 vis lectrs per year; books, reproductions, prints & Chateau-related items

M **METROPOLITAN STATE UNIVERSITY OF DENVER,** Center for Visual Art, 965 Santa Fe Dr, Denver, CO 80204-3936. Tel 303-294-5207; Fax 303-294-5210; Email cva@msudenver.edu; Web: msudenver.edu/cva; *Mng Dir & Cur* Cecily Cullen; *Exec Dir* Deanne Pytlinski; *Gallery Mgr* Jenna Miles; *Educ Dir* Talya Dornbush
Open to public Tues - Fri 11 AM - 6 PM, Sat 12 - 5 PM, cl all major holidays; No admis fee, donations accepted; Estab 1990 for temporary exhibitions of contemporary art; 5000 sq ft; Average Annual Attendance: 32,000; Mem: 300; annual meeting in July; D & E; Scholarships
Income: $350,000 (financed by mem, state appropriation, grants & revenues)
Special Subjects: Afro-American Art, American Indian Art, Hispanic Art, Southwestern Art
Publications: Quarterly newsletter
Activities: Classes for adults, teens & children; lects open to pub, 8 vis lectrs per yr; gallery talks; tours; book traveling exhibs 1-2 per yr; originate traveling exhibs 5 per yr
Ent Req: GED

M **MIZEL MUSEUM,** 400 S Kearney St, Denver, CO 80224-1238. Tel 303-394-9993; Fax 303-394-1119; Email details@mizelmuseum.org; Web: www.mizelmuseum.org; *Chmn Bd* Larry Mizel; *Mng Dir* Georgina Kolber; *Dir Educ* Penny Nisson
Open by appt only; No admis fee; 1982 to tell the continuum of the Jewish people within a multicultural content through the arts; Average Annual Attendance: 40,000
Library Holdings: Book Volumes 400
Collections: ritual & religious synagogue artifacts, contemporary Judaica, multicultural educational exhibits
Exhibitions: Bridges of Understanding; Immigrant Adventure; Mystical Masks of Many Cultures; Tikkun Olam
Publications: newsletter; educ brochure; email blasts
Activities: Workshops; art classes for adults & children; organized educ prog; docent prog; guided tours; lect; films; Community Cultural Enrichment Award; progs in the schools; schools

M **MUSEO DE LAS AMERICAS,** 861 Santa Fe Dr, Denver, CO 80204-4344. Tel 303-571-4401; Fax 303-607-9761; Email gloria@museo.org; Web: www.museo.org; *Exec Dir* Maruca Sulazar; *Dir Devel* Christy Costello; *Opers Mgr* Claudia Moran
Open Tue - Fri 10 AM - 5 PM, Sat - Sun noon - 5 PM; Admis adults $5, students & seniors $3, members & children under 13 free; Estab 1991 to collect, preserve & interpret Latin American art, history & culture; Circ 25,000; Contemporary, Pre-Columbian & Folk Art Galleries; Average Annual Attendance: 20,000; Mem: 800; dues $15 - $1,000
Income: $550,000 (financed by mem, foundation, corporation, pub funding & store revenue)
Library Holdings: Auction Catalogs, Audio Tapes, Book Volumes, CD-ROMs, Cassettes, Compact Disks, DVDs, Exhibition Catalogs, Framed Reproductions, Original Art Works, Original Documents, Other Holdings, Photographs, Prints, Records, Reproductions, Sculpture, Slides, Video Tapes
Special Subjects: American Western Art, Anthropology, Archaeology, Architecture, Baroque Art, Bronzes, Ceramics, Coins & Medals, Crafts, Drawings, Embroidery, Etchings & Engravings, Ethnology, Folk Art, Furniture, Glass, Gold, Graphics, Hispanic Art, Historical Material, Jade, Jewelry, Latin American Art, Leather, Maps, Metalwork, Mexican Art, Painting-American, Painting-Spanish, Photography, Porcelain, Portraits, Posters, Pottery, Prints, Religious Art, Reproductions, Sculpture, Silver, Southwestern Art, Tapestries, Textiles, Watercolors, Woodcarvings, Woodcuts
Collections: Tragew, Hamilton, Bloodworth, Pelliser & Bass Coors
Exhibitions: Eppie Archuleta: Master Weaver of the San Luis Valley; Cuba Siempre Vive; Alberto Gironela: Madonna Series; Luis Jimenez: Man On Fire
Publications: Notitas Newsletter, quarterly
Activities: Classes for adults & children; docent training; lects open to pub, 6 vis lectrs per yr; concerts; gallery talks; tours; 2009 Mayor's Award for Excellence in the Arts; book traveling exhibs 5 per yr; mus shop sells books, magazines, reproductions, prints, original art, textiles, curios, historical objects & clothing

M **MUSEUM OF CONTEMPORARY ART DENVER,** 1485 Delgany St, Denver, CO 80202-1100. Tel 303-298-7554; Fax 303-298-7553; Email info@mcadenver.org; Web: mcadenver.org/about; *Dir & Chief Animator* Adam Lerner; *Dir Programming & Chief of Fictions* Sarah Kate Baie; *Deputy Dir* Laura Huff; *Assoc Dir Devel & Chief Matchmaker* Michael McNeill
Open Tues - Thurs Noon - 7 PM, Fri Noon - 9 PM, Sat 10 AM - 5 PM, Sun 10 AM - 5 PM; Admis adults $8, students & seniors $5, members & children under 18 free; Estab 1997 to educate & inspire artists, students & the general public about important new developments in visual arts - regional, national or international; Mem: Dues $45+
Activities: Workshops; lects open to pub; tours, symposiums; mus shop sells books, magazines, & prints

M **PIRATE-CONTEMPORARY ART,** 3655 Navajo, Denver, CO 80211; 1370 Verbena, Denver, CO 80220. Tel 303-458-6058; Email info@pirateartonline.org; Web: www.pirateartonline.org; *Dir* Phil Bender
Open by appt Fri 5 PM - 10 PM, Sat & Sun Noon - 5 PM; No admis fee; Estab 1980; gallery displays contemporary art; Average Annual Attendance: 2,000; Mem: 30
Income: Financed by mem, grants & donations
Exhibitions: Member Artists Exhibit Yearly; Member solo exhibs & Day of the Dead show in Nov
Activities: Community outreach prog; sales shop sells original art, hats, t-shirts, buttons & bumper stickers

M **ROBISCHON GALLERY,** 1740 Wazee Street, Denver, CO 80202. Tel 303-298-7788; Fax 303-298-7799; Email mail@robischongallery.com; Web: www.robischongallery.com; *Owner & Dir* Jim Robischon; *Owner & Dir* Jennifer Doran; *Registrar & Gallery Mgr* Debra Malik Demosthenes; *Preparator* Lee Puckett; *Social Media & Pub Rels* Laura Leffler
Open Tues - Fri 11 AM -6 PM, Sat Noon - 5 PM; Estab 1976 to produce exhibs of regional, national, and international artists; addresses ongoing artistic global dialogue surrounding Middle Eastern & Chinese contemporary art; Formal & separate exhib spaces
Special Subjects: Photography, Sculpture
Collections: Paintings, video, installation
Exhibitions: Temporary exhibits

M **SPARK GALLERY,** 900 Santa Fe Dr, Ste 1 Denver, CO 80204-3937. Tel 720-889-2200; Email info@sparkgallery.com; Web: www.sparkgallery.com; *Co-Dir* Kate McGuinness; *Sec* Elaine Ricklin; *Treas* Annalee Schorr; *Mem Coordr* Barbara Carpenter
Open Thurs & Sat Noon - 5 PM, Friday Noon - 9 PM, Sun 1 PM - 4 PM; Estab 1979; Mem: dues $60
Special Subjects: Photography, Sculpture
Collections: Works by regional, nat & international artists; paintings; sculpture; drawings; photographs
Exhibitions: Temporary exhibits

A **THINK 360 ART COMPLETE EDUCATION,** (Young Audiences Inc) Colo Chapter, 135 Park Ave W, Denver, CO 80205-3209. Tel 720-904-8890; Fax 720-904-8894; Email info@think360arts.org; Web: www.think360arts.org; *Interim Executive Director* Mike Johnson; *Educ Dir* Jason Diminich; *Program Director* Lares Feliciano; *Develop & Mktg Coordr* Juliana Fajardo
Open Mon - Fri 8 AM - 4 PM; Admis fee varies per event, see program catalog; Estab to strive to make the arts an essential part of the educ of every Colorado child enabling students & their teachers to experience the arts, to learn from professional artists & to understand the role of the arts in the creative process & in educational excellence; Average Annual Attendance: 7,000
Income: Grant funded
Activities: Classes for adults and children; family progs

M **WALKER FINE ART,** 300 W 11th Ave #A, Denver, CO 80204. Tel 303-355-8955; Fax 303-623-0553; Email info@walkerfineart.com; Web: www.walkerfineart.com; *Owner* Bobbi Walker; *Gallery Mgr* Libby Garon; *Administrative Manager* Abbey Arit; *Event Coordr* Eliza Ross
Open Tues - Fri 11 AM - 5 PM, other times by appointment; free; 2002; Contemporary art, abstraction & realism through mixed media, experimental photog, sculpture installation
Special Subjects: Ceramics, Drawings, Jade, Landscapes, Metalwork, Painting-American, Photography, Porcelain, Portraits, Pottery, Prints, Reproductions, Sculpture, Watercolors, Woodcarvings, Woodcuts
Exhibitions: rotating group exhibits every 8 weeks
Activities: lectures opent to the public

DURANGO

M **DURANGO ARTS CENTER,** (Barbara Conrad Art Gallery) Barbara Conrad Art Gallery, 802 E 2nd St, Durango Arts Center Durango, CO 81301-5426. Tel 970-259-2606; Fax 970-259-6571; Email peter@durangoarts.org; Web: www.durangoarts.org; *Exec Dir* Cristie M Scott; *Exhibits Dir* Peter Hay
Open Tues - Sat 10 AM - 5 PM; No admis fee; Average Annual Attendance: 100,000; Mem: 1,200
Library Holdings: Book Volumes, DVDs, Exhibition Catalogs, Memorabilia, Original Art Works, Other Holdings, Pamphlets, Periodical Subscriptions, Prints
Special Subjects: Aesthetics, American Indian Art, American Western Art, Art Education, Art History, Ceramics, Conceptual Art, Crafts, Decorative Arts, Drawings, Embroidery, Folk Art, Glass, Graphic Arts, Landscapes, Latin American Art, Mixed Media, Mosaics, Painting-American, Photography, Prints, Southwestern Art, Tapestries, Textiles, Watercolors, Woodcuts
Exhibitions: Ten exhibs annually (juried shows & curated exhibs)
Activities: Classes for adults & children; dramatic progs; docent training; ten plus visiting lectrs per year; gallery talks; sponsoring of competitions (juried shows), Concerts, Tours; mus shop sells books, original art, folk art, fine craft, jewelry, textiles, prints

ERIE

NATIONAL COUNCIL ON EDUCATION FOR THE CERAMIC ARTS (NCECA)
For further information, see National and Regional Organizations

EVERGREEN

M **JEFFERSON COUNTY OPEN SPACE,** Hiwan Homestead Museum, 4208 S. Timbervale Dr Evergreen, CO 80439; 700 Jefferson County Pkwy, Ste 100 Evergreen, CO 80401. Tel 303-271-5925; Fax 303-670-7746; Email trock@jeffco.us; Web: www.jeffco.us/open-space; *Adminr* John Steinle
Open office Mon-Fri 7:30AM-5:30PM, mus Sept-May noon-5PM, June-Aug 11AM-5PM; No admis fee; Estab 1975 to collect, preserve & exhibit Jefferson County history; History House furnished to 1900; 25 rm log mansion with original furnishings & displays on local history; maintains reference library; Average Annual Attendance: 18,000

Income: Financed by county taxes
Special Subjects: American Indian Art, American Western Art, Architecture, Costumes, Decorative Arts, Dolls, Folk Art, Furniture, Historical Material, Mexican Art, Painting-American, Religious Art, Southwestern Art, Textiles
Collections: Decorative & fine arts, manuscripts, Native American Arts & Crafts, Photographs, Textiles
Exhibitions: Seasonally rotating exhibitions
Publications: The Record, quarterly
Activities: Classes for children; docent training; historic lect series open to pub, 4 vis lectrs per yr

FORT COLLINS

M **CENTER FOR FINE ART PHOTOGRAPHY,** 400 N College Ave, Fort Collins, CO 80524-2409. Tel 970-224-1010; Email coordinator@c4fap.org; Web: www.c4fap.org; *Exec Dir* Hamidah Glasgow; *Progs Mgr* Sunshine Divis; *Progs Asst* Ren Burke
Open Tues - Fri 10 AM - 6 PM, Sat 11 AM - 5 PM, cl Sun - Mon; No admis fee; Estab 2004 to advocate for a greater comprehension of photography's visual, emotional & social impacts; 3,400 sq ft; three galleries; Mem: dues $57-$1,000
Special Subjects: Photography
Collections: Photography
Exhibitions: 10 international group exhibs per year
Activities: Educ progs; artist talks; workshops; Mus shop sells prints, exhib catalogs & posters

M **COLORADO STATE UNIVERSITY,** Curfman Gallery, 8033 Campus Delivery, Lory Student Ctr Fort Collins, CO 80523-8033. Tel 970-491-2810; Fax 970-491-3746; Email curfman@lamar.colostate.edu; Web: www.curfman.colostate.edu; *Dir* Matthew S Helmer; *Dir* Stanley Scott
Open Mon - Thurs 9 AM - 9 PM, Fri 9 AM - 9:30 PM, Sat 12 - 4 PM; No admis fee; Estab 1969 to exhibit multi-cultural works from all over the world plus student works; Average Annual Attendance: 50,000
Collections: African Collection
Exhibitions: Rotating Exhibits
Activities: Lects open to public; vis lectrs per year varies; gallery talks; awards Best of CSU & Best of Fort Collins

M **FORT COLLINS MUSEUM OF ART, INC,** 201 S College Ave, Ste 101, Fort Collins, CO 80524-3182. Tel 970-482-2787; Fax 970-482-0804; Email info@ftcma.org; Web: www.ftcma.org; *Gen Mgr* Gloria Boresen; *Vol & Event Coordr* Kali Dhayatker; *Exec Dir* Lisa Hatchadoorian; *Mktg & Design Coordr* Alicia Atchison; *Educ Coordr* Beth Gherardi; *Resource Devel Dir* De Dahlgren; *Registrar & Preparator* Cheryl Rogers
Open Wed - Fri 10 AM -5 PM, Sat & Sun 12 PM - 5 PM; Admis adults $5, students with ID & seniors $4, youth 7 - 18 $1, mem & children 6 & under free; Estab 1983 a non-profit art mus dedicated to educ & exhibition of visual art; one gallery, 3000 sq ft housed in former 1911 post office on historic register; Average Annual Attendance: 19,000; Mem: 500, various levels
Income: $325,000 (financed by mem, fundraisers, grants & sponsorships)
Exhibitions: Rocky Mountain Biennial Competition; Rotating exhibitions
Publications: Catalogs
Activities: Classes for adults, teens & children; docent training; lects open to pub, 2 vis lectrs per yr; gallery talks; tours; competitions; book traveling exhibs 1 per yr; originates traveling exhibs; mus shop sells books, original art, prints

FORT MORGAN

M **FORT MORGAN HERITAGE FOUNDATION,** 414 Main St, Fort Morgan, CO 80701-2143; PO Box 184, Fort Morgan, CO 80701-0184. Tel 970-542-4010; Fax 970-542-4012; Email fortmorganmuseum@ftmorganmus.org; Web: www.ftmorganmus.org; *Pres Heritage Foundation* Don Ostwald; *VPres* Gerald Danford; *Publ Cur* Nickki Cooper; *Educ* Andrew Dumohoo; *Dir* Marne Jurgemeyer; *Mus Tech* Joyce Martinez
Open Mon - Fri 10 AM - 5 PM, Tues-Thurs 10AM-8PM, Fri 10AM-5PM, Sat 11AM-5PM; No admis fee; Estab 1975 to interpret the history & culture of the area; Mus exhibits on a temporary basis fine art exhibits, both local artists & traveling exhibits; Average Annual Attendance: 10,000; Mem: 275; dues $10-$500; annual meeting fourth Thurs in Jan
Income: $110,000 (financed by endowment, mem, city appropriation & local, state & federal grants)
Library Holdings: Clipping Files, Filmstrips, Kodachrome Transparencies, Lantern Slides, Maps, Memorabilia, Original Documents, Photographs, Records, Video Tapes
Special Subjects: Historical Material, Anthropology, Archaeology, Costumes, Manuscripts, Painting-American
Collections: Hogsett Collection, primarily cultural & historical material, Native Arts, Howard Rollin Bird Paintings
Activities: Classes for adults & children; dramatic progs; docent progs; 14 lectrs for mems only; AAM accredited awards; books, prints & original art

GEORGETOWN

M **COLORADO MOUNTAIN ART GALLERY,** 406 6th St, Georgetown, CO 80444; c/o CAE, PO Box 2737 Evergreen, CO 80437. Tel 303-569-2787; Email info@coloradomountainartgallery.com; Web: www.coloradomountainartgallery.com; *Gallery Dir* Jennifer Benedict-Johnson; *Exec Dir* Stephen Summer
Open Jan - April: Mon - Fri 11 AM - 4 PM, Sat & Sun 10 AM - 5 PM; May - Dec: daily 10 AM - 5 PM; No admis fee; Estab 2010; Co-op space housing the work of more than 60 Colorado-based fine & craft artists
Collections: Oil, acrylic, pastel, water color & mixed media art, photography, crafts & jewelry
Exhibitions: monthly changing local artist
Activities: Sales shop sells prints, cards & reproductions

GLENWOOD SPRINGS

M **GLENWOOD CENTER FOR THE ARTS,** 601 E 6th St, Glenwood Springs, CO 81601. Tel 970-945-2414; Email info@glenwoodarts.org; Web: glenwoodarts.org; *Exec Dir* Brie Carmer
Open Mon - Fri 9 AM - 5 PM, Sat - Sun Noon - 4 PM; Estab to create opportunities for creative & enjoying art; Mem: dues $25-$100
Special Subjects: Pottery, Painting-American, Mixed Media
Collections: Local artists & work including fine art, visual art, mixed media, collage, pottery & performing arts
Exhibitions: Temporary exhibits
Activities: Educ progs; classes for adults & children; workshops

GOLDEN

M **CLEAR CREEK HISTORY PARK,** 923 10th St, Golden, CO 80401-1025. Tel 303-278-3557; Fax 303-278-8916; Email info@clearcreekhistorypark.org; Web: www.clearcreekhistorypark.org
Open May & Sept: Sat 10 AM - 4:30 PM, June, July & Aug: Tues - Sat 10 AM - 4:30 PM; Founded 1999; History mus & living history park; vol hrs 3250; Average Annual Attendance: 9610
Special Subjects: Furniture
Collections: Six relocated homestead structures including 2 cabins, barn, chicken coop, and a one-room schoolhouse, historic & reproduction items with emphasis on furnishings, personal artifacts, recreational artifacts, tools & equip for materials
Publications: Dear Friends, quarterly newsletter; The Friendly Reminder, monthly newsletter
Activities: Organized educ progs for adults & children; docent prog; training prog; guided tours; concerts

A **FOOTHILLS ART CENTER, INC,** 809 15th St, Golden, CO 80401-1813. Tel 303-279-3922; Fax 303-279-9470; Email epapenfus@foothillsartcenter.org; Web: www.foothillsartcenter.org; *Exec Dir* Reilly Sanborn; *Cur* Michael Chavez; *Opers Mgr* Esther Papenfus
Open Mon - Sat 10- AM - 5 PM, Sun 1 - 4 PM, cl holidays; Admis adults $3, seniors $2, mem & students free; Estab 1968 to provide a cultural center which embraces all the arts, to educate & stimulate the community in the appreciation & understanding of the arts, to provide equal opportunities for all people to participate in the further study & enjoyment of the arts & to provide artists & artisans with the opportunity to present their work; Housed in the former First Presbyterian Church of Golden, the original structure was built in 1872, the manse (a part of the whole layout) was built in 1892; there are five galleries, an outdoor sculpture garden and classrooms; Average Annual Attendance: 40,000; Mem: 1,200; dues $35; annual meeting in Dec
Income: $670,000 (financed by donated & earned income)
Special Subjects: American Indian Art, American Western Art, Architecture, Bronzes, Ceramics, Collages, Crafts, Decorative Arts, Drawings, Etchings & Engravings, Folk Art, Hispanic Art, Historical Material, Juvenile Art, Landscapes, Latin American Art, Miniatures, Painting-American, Photography, Portraits, Posters, Pottery, Pre-Columbian Art
Exhibitions: North American Sculpture Exhibitions; Rocky Mountain National Watermedia Exhibition; numerous open juried competitions
Publications: Bimonthly newsletter; catalogs of major national shows
Activities: Classes for adults & children; lects open to pub, 8 vis lectrs per yr; concerts; gallery talks; tours, competitions with awards; individual paintings & original objects of art lent to bus; mus shop sells original art

GRAND JUNCTION

M **MUSEUM OF WESTERN COLORADO,** Museum of the West, 462 Ute Ave, Grand Junction, CO 81501; PO Box 20000, Grand Junction, CO 81502-5020. Tel 970-242-0971; Fax 970-242-3960; Email info@wcmuseum.org; Web: www.wcmuseum.org; www.colosys.net/uranium; *Cur Archives & Librn* Michael J Menard; *Dir* Peter Booth; *Bus Mgr* Carla Hatch; *Cur Paleontology* Julia McHugh; *Maintenance* Fred Espinosa; *Facilities Mgr* Don Kerven; *Maintenance* Dan Rosenbaum; *Cur History* David Bailey; *Asst Dir Opers & Pub Rels, Cur Cross Orchard, Gift Shop Mgr* Kay Fiegel
Open Mon - Fri 10 AM - 4 PM, cl Sun, Christmas wk & major holidays; Admis adults $5.50, seniors $4.50, children $3.50, free for group mem; Estab 1965 to collect preserve, interpret social & natural history of Western Colorado; Mem: dues benefactor $1000, patron $500, sponsor $150, contributor & bus $50, family $25, retired adult $15
Income: Financed by Mesa County, admis, gift shop revenues, grants, mem, donations, programs & special events
Library Holdings: Audio Tapes, Book Volumes 3500, Cassettes 2500, Compact Disks, DVDs, Lantern Slides 15, Manuscripts 300, Memorabilia, Micro Print, Motion Pictures, Original Art Works, Pamphlets 200, Periodical Subscriptions 15, Photographs 18,000, Reels 47, Slides 14,000
Special Subjects: American Indian Art, American Western Art, Anthropology, Archaeology, Crafts, Decorative Arts, Ethnology, Furniture, Historical Material, Landscapes, Manuscripts, Manuscripts, Maps, Painting-American, Restorations, Sculpture, Southwestern Art, Military Art
Collections: Frank Dean Collection, Al Look Collection, Warren Kiefer Railroad Collection, Wilson Rockwell Collection, artwork, books, manuscripts & photographs on the history & natural history of Western Colorado, Mesa County Oral History Collection
Exhibitions: Rotating exhibits & pieces from permanent collection
Publications: A Bibliography of the Dinosauria; Cross Orchards Coloring Book; Dinosaur Valley Coloring Book; Familiar Insects of Mesa County, Colorado; Footprints in the Trail; Mesa County, Colorado: A 100 Year History; Mesa County Cooking with History; More Footprints in the Trail; Museum Times, monthly newsletter; Paleontology & Geology of the Dinosaur Triangle

Activities: Classes for adults & children; dramatic programs; docent training; lects open to pub, 20+ vis lectrs per yr; concerts; gallery talks; tours; Cross Ranch Apple Jubilee; Cross Ranch Artisan's Festival; slides/tape & video tape presentations; sales shop sells books, magazines, original art, reproductions

A **WESTERN COLORADO CENTER FOR THE ARTS,** The Art Center, 1803 N Seventh, Grand Junction, CO 81501. Tel 970-243-7337; Fax 970-243-2482; Email info@gjartcenter.org; Web: www.gjartcenter.org; *Events & Commun* Lee Borden; *Artist in Res* Terry Shepherd; *Gift Shop & Mem Mgr* Laurie Lester; *Children's Progs Mgr* Rachel Egelston; *Exec Dir* Camille Silverman; *Cur & Adult Educ* Avery Glassman
Open Tues - Sat 9 AM - 4 PM; Admis $3 for non-members; Art Center - Mus incorporated in 1952 to provide an appropriate setting for appreciation of & active participation in the arts; Three changing exhibition galleries of 2000 sq ft each; permanent collection gallery; six studio classrooms; auditorium; Average Annual Attendance: 30,000; Mem: 1200; dues family $50, individual $35; annual meeting in Nov
Income: Financed by endowment, mem, tuition, gifts & grants
Collections: Ceramics, needlework, paintings, Navajo weavings & pottery
Exhibitions: Changing exhibits only in gallery; exhibits change monthly
Publications: Newsletter for members, monthly; catalog of permanent collections
Activities: Classes for adults & children; docent training; lect open to public; 12 vis lectrs per year; concerts; gallery talks; tours; competitions; schols; sales shop sells books, magazines, original art, reproductions, Southwest Indian & contemporary fine art & craft items & notecards

L **Library,** 1803 N Seventh, Grand Junction, CO 81501. Tel 970-243-7337; Fax 970-243-2482; Web: www.gjartcenter.org; *Chief Exec Officer* Mikkel Kelly; *Pres* Robbie Breaux
Open Tues - Sat 9 AM - 4 PM; Admis $3, free on Tues; Estab 1953; Open to members & pub for reference; Average Annual Attendance: 28,000; Mem: 1,150
Library Holdings: Book Volumes 1000, Exhibition Catalogs
Special Subjects: Anthropology, Ethnology, Decorative Arts, Painting-American, Photography, Prints, Sculpture
Collections: works by Western artists; Navajo blankets & rugs; Anasazi pottery; contemporary Colorado paintings & ceramics
Publications: bimonthly newsletter
Activities: Educ progs for adults & children; Lectures open to the public; gallery talks; tours; yes; Books; original art; prints

GREELEY

M **MADISON & MAIN GALLERY,** 927 16th St, Greeley, CO 80631-5511. Tel 970-351-6201; Email madisonmaingallery@gmail.com; Web: www.madisonandmaingallery.com; *Treas* Susan B Anderson
Open Mon - Sat 10 AM - 4 PM; No admis fee; Estab 1987 as an artists' cooperative; Mem: dues $100 & up
Income: $30,000 (financed by art sales)
Special Subjects: Ceramics, Jewelry, Textiles, Watercolors, Stained Glass, Photography
Collections: Clay, jewelry, textiles, watercolors, pastels, stained glass, marble, photography & paper
Exhibitions: Six shows per year plus work of members & consignees
Activities: Artist demonstrations

M **UNIVERSITY OF NORTHERN COLORADO,** Mariani Gallery, 8th Ave & 18th St, Greeley, CO 80639; University of Northern Colorado Galleries, Campus Box 30, Guggenheim Hall Greeley, CO 80639. Tel 970-351-2184, 2143; Fax 970-351-2299; Email joan.shannonmiller@unco.edu; Web: www.arts.unco.edu/visarts/visarts_galleries.html; *Gallery Dir* Joan Shannon-Miller
Open Mon - Fri noon - 5 PM, Sat 10 AM - 2 PM; No admis fee; Estab 1973, to provide art exhibitions for the benefit of the University & the surrounding community; Remodeled space 2001; Average Annual Attendance: 20,000
Income: Financed by endowment & city & state appropriations
Exhibitions: UNC Faculty Exhibition; UNC Student Exhibition
Publications: Schedule of Exhibitions, quarterly
Activities: Gallery talks; competitions with awards

GUNNISON

M **GUNNISON ARTS CENTER,** 102 S Main St, Gunnison, CO 81230. Tel 970-641-4029; Web: www.gunnisonartscenter.org; *Dir Opers* Carlie Kenton; *Educ Dir* Alysa Vandenheuver; *Events Dir* Sarah Rozell; *Visual Arts Dir* Kerry Curtis
Open Tues - Fri Noon - 6 PM, Sat 10 AM - 2 PM, cl Sun - Mon; No admis fee
Activities: Classes for adults & children; dramatic progs; concerts; gallery talks; sales shops sells original art, handmade items & prints

M **WESTERN STATE COLLEGE OF COLORADO,** Quigley Hall Art Gallery, 101 Quigley Hall, Gunnison, CO 81231-0001. Tel 970-943-3093, 943-0120 (main); Fax 970-943-2329; Email acaniff@western.edu; Web: www.western.edu; *Art Area Coordr* Lee Johnson; *Dir Gallery* Harry Heil; *Chmn* Al Caniff
Open Mon - Fri 1 - 5 PM; No admis fee; Estab 1967 for the purpose of exhibiting student, staff & traveling art; Nearly 300 running ft composition walls, security lock-up iron grill gate is contained in the gallery; Average Annual Attendance: 7,500
Income: Financed by state appropriation
Special Subjects: Prints, Painting-American
Collections: Original paintings and prints
Exhibitions: Rotating exhibits
Activities: Competitions; originates traveling exhibs

HOLYOKE

M **PHILLIPS COUNTY MUSEUM,** 109 S Campbell Ave, Holyoke, CO 80734-1501. Tel 970-854-2129; Fax 970-854-3811; Email pcmuseum@pctelcom.coop; Web: www.rootswebancestry.com/~copchs/index.htm; *Pres* Carol Haynes; *Treas* Hilda Hassler; *Secy* Leona Oltjenbruns; *VPres* Diane Rahe
Open Tues - Sat 10 AM - 4 PM; No admis fee; Estab 1929 as an educational & cultural museum to impart an appreciation of local history & to display objects of art from all over the world; Average Annual Attendance: 5,000; Mem: 250; dues $3-$5; annual meeting first Fri in May
Income: Financed by endowment, mem & city appropriation
Special Subjects: Ceramics, Glass, Painting-American
Collections: China, glassware, paintings, Indian artifacts, Civil War memorabilia, Thomas Alva Edison Historical Display, Civil War Collection

LA JUNTA

M **KOSHARE INDIAN MUSEUM, INC,** 115 W 18th St, La Junta, CO 81050-3302; PO Box 580, La Junta, CO 81050-0580. Tel 719-384-4411; Fax 719-384-8836; Email koshare@ria.net; Web: kosharehistory.org; *Office Mgr* Linda Root; *Gift Shop Mgr* Jo Ann Jones; *Develop Dir* Linda Powers; *Coll Mgr* Jo Anne Kent
Open noon-5PM, call for appointment on Mon & Thurs; Admis adults $5, students 7-17 $3, seniors $3, children 6 and under free; Estab 1949 for the exhib of Indian artifacts & paintings; 15,000 sq ft display space. For reference to members only or by special arrangement; Average Annual Attendance: 100,000; Mem: 250; annual meeting second Tues in Dec; dues start at $25 & up
Income: Financed by donations & shows
Special Subjects: American Indian Art, American Western Art, Archaeology, Bronzes, Carpets & Rugs, Crafts, Decorative Arts, Eskimo Art, Folk Art, Hispanic Art, Ivory, Jewelry, Leather, Mexican Art, Painting-American, Portraits, Pottery, Prints, Scrimshaw, Textiles, Watercolors, Woodcarvings
Collections: Indian arts & crafts, of & by Indians, Taos Ten, prominent southwestern artists
Exhibitions: Exhibits change monthly
Activities: Classes for children; tours; paintings & original art works lent to qualified mus; book traveling exhibs; mus shop sells books, original art, reproductions, souvenirs, Indian jewelry & pottery

L **Library,** 115 W 18th, La Junta, CO 81050. Tel 719-384-4411; Fax 719-384-8836; Email koshare@ria.net; Web: www.ruralnet.net/-koshare, www.koshare.org; *Dir Progs* Joe Clay
Open by appt only; No admis fee; Estab 1949 for educ through art & youth prog; Open for reference only; Average Annual Attendance: 18,000
Income: Donations, grants
Library Holdings: Book Volumes 1700, Clipping Files
Special Subjects: American Indian Art, American Western Art, Anthropology, Archaeology, Eskimo Art, History of Art & Archaeology, Pottery, Primitive art, Southwestern Art
Collections: Baskets, Clothing, Kachinas, Paintings, Pots, Textiles
Activities: Classes for children; dramatic progs; Boy Scouts of America-Koshare Indian Dancers; concerts; gallery talks; tours; individual paintings & original objects of art lent to other mus; book traveling exhibs; mus shop sells books, original art, reproductions, prints, slides, jewelry, kachinas, pots & videos

LEADVILLE

A **LAKE COUNTY CIVIC CENTER ASSOCIATION, INC,** Heritage Museum & Gallery, 102 E 9th St, Leadville, CO 80461-3302; PO Box 962, Leadville, CO 80461-0962. Tel 719-486-1878, 486-1421; *Pres Board Dirs* Ray Stamps; *VPres* Ted Mullings
Open Memorial Day-Labor Day 10 AM-6 PM. Also open May, Sept & Oct on limited hours daily; Admis adults $4, sr citizens $3.50, children 6 - 16 $3, under 6 free, members free; Estab 1971 to promote the preservation, restoration & study of the rich history of the Lake County area & to provide display area for local & non-local art work & also to provide an educational assistance both to public schools & interested individuals; The Museum & Gallery own no art work, but display a variety of art on a changing basis; Average Annual Attendance: 9,000; Mem: 160; dues $20-$250; annual meeting Feb
Collections: Diorama of Leadville history, mining & Victorian era artifacts, Victorian furniture
Exhibitions: Changing displays of paintings, photography and craft work
Publications: The Tallyboard, newsletter, quarterly
Activities: Lect open to pub; competitions; sales shop sells books, slides, papers, postcards, rock samples

M **TABOR OPERA HOUSE MUSEUM,** 308 Harrison Ave, Leadville, CO; 30709 Stampede Run, Buena Vista, CO 81211-8149. Tel 719-486-8409; Email info@taboroperahouse.net; Web: taboroperahouse.net; *Owner* Sharon Bland
Open June - Oct Mon - Sat 10 AM - 5:00 PM, Nov - May by appointment only; Admis adults $5, children 6-11 $2.50, under 6 free; Tours adults $8, combined tour adults $5; Estab 1955 as a historic theatre museum
Collections: Costumes, paintings
Exhibitions: Original scenery live shows
Activities: Lect; living history tours for students; films; concerts; arts festivals; sales shop sells books, cards, pictures, prints & souvenirs

LITTLETON

M **ARAPAHOE COMMUNITY COLLEGE,** Colorado Gallery of the Arts, 2500 W College Dr, Littleton, CO 80160-1956; PO Box 9002, Littleton, CO 80160-9002. Tel 303-797-5649; Fax 303-797-5935; Web: www.arapahoe.com; *Chmn* Scott Engel; *Gallery Coordr* Trish Sangelo
Open Mon - Fri Noon - 5 PM, Tues 5 - 7 PM; No admis fee; Gallery contributes significantly to the cultural growth of the Denver-metro area
Income: funded by school appropriations
Special Subjects: Costumes

LOVELAND

M **LOVELAND MUSEUM/GALLERY,** 503 N Lincoln, Loveland, CO 80537. Tel 970-962-2410, 2770; Fax 970-962-2910; Email akelek@ci.loveland.co.us; Web: www.cityofloveland.org/museum; *Mktg Coordr* Kim Akeley-Charron; *Dir Cultural Svcs* Susan Ison; *Bus Svcs* Suzanne Janssen; *Coordr Educ* Jenni Dobson; *Cur History* Jennifer Cousino; *Cur Art* Maureen Corey; *Graphic Design* Michelle Standiford; *Exhibs Preparator* Quinn Johnson; *Registrar* Robert Hoot; *Office Support Specialist* Mary Shada
Open Tues, Wed & Fri 10 AM - 5 PM, Thurs 10 AM - 7 PM, Sat 10 AM - 4 PM, Sun Noon - 4 PM; No admis fee; Estab 1946 to preserve & interpret history of Loveland area; 4000 sq ft; features local, state, national & international art exhibitions; Average Annual Attendance: 50,000; Mem: 120; dues individual $30
Income: Financed by city appropriation
Library Holdings: Book Volumes, CD-ROMs, Exhibition Catalogs, Memorabilia, Original Documents, Pamphlets, Sculpture, Slides
Special Subjects: American Indian Art, American Western Art, Anthropology, Archaeology, Architecture, Bronzes, Costumes, Decorative Arts, Dioramas, Dolls, Drawings, Embroidery, Folk Art, Furniture, Glass, Historical Material, Jewelry, Laces, Manuscripts, Painting-American, Period Rooms, Photography, Sculpture, Textiles
Collections: Archaeology, art, dioramas, historical material, period rooms, sugar beet industry, textiles, tools, valentines, western, photography
Exhibitions: Bureau of Reclamation Relief Map of Big Thompson Project; Great Western Sugar Company Exhibit; pioneer cabin; Fireside History Gallery
Publications: Exhibition catalogues; history books; newsletter
Activities: Classes for adults & children; dramatic progs; art workshops; poetry readings; lects open to pub, 20 vis lectrs per yr; concerts; gallery talks; tours & sponsoring of competitions; schols; inter-mus loan progs containing cassettes, filmstrips, motion pictures, nature artifacts, original works of art & slides; book traveling exhibs 2-3 per yr; originate traveling exhibs; mus shop sells books, magazines, original art, reproductions & prints

MESA VERDE NATIONAL PARK

L **MESA VERDE NATIONAL PARK,** Research Library, PO Box 8, Mesa Verde National Park, CO 81330-0008. Tel 970-529-5014; Fax 970-529-5013; Web: www.nps.gov/meve; *Supv Ranger* Rosemarie Salazar
Call for appointment; Admis $10; Estab 1906; Average Annual Attendance: 250
Income: $35,800 (financed by endowment)
Library Holdings: Audio Tapes, Book Volumes 10,000, Manuscripts, Maps, Original Documents, Video Tapes
Special Subjects: Anthropology, Archaeology, Ethnology, Historical Material, Manuscripts, Pottery, Restoration & Conservation
Collections: American Indians, Anthropology, Archaeology, Ethnology, Forest Fires, Mary Colter Collection

PUEBLO

M **ROSEMOUNT MUSEUM, INC,** 419 W 14th St, Pueblo, CO 81003-2707. Tel 719-545-5290; Fax 719-545-5291; Email cwainright@rosemount.org; Web: www.rosemount.org; *Exec Dir* Deb Darrow; *Colls Mgr* Susan Kittinger; *Maintenance* Roger Cain; *Office Mgr* Carolyn Wainright
Open Tues - Sat 10 AM - 3:30 PM (last tour), cl Sun, Mon and Jan; Admis adults $6, sr citizens $5, children 6-16 $4, under 6 free; Estab 1968 as a historic house museum to narrate late Victorian life in the west; 37-room Victorian mansion contains 80 percent of original furnishings including many decorative objects & art from late 19th century; Average Annual Attendance: 10,000; Mem: 500; dues $15-$500; annual meeting in Apr
Income: $270,000 (financed by endowment, mem, rental, gift shop, auxiliary organization, fundraisers, admis, donations & grants)
Library Holdings: Auction Catalogs, Book Volumes, Cards, Clipping Files, Kodachrome Transparencies, Lantern Slides, Manuscripts, Memorabilia, Original Art Works, Prints, Reproductions, Sculpture, Video Tapes
Special Subjects: Antiquities-Egyptian, Furniture, Stained Glass
Collections: Permanent collections are displayed in a 37-room Victorian mansion; intact collections of the American Aesthetic Movement, Collections include furnishings, decorative objects, paintings, sculpture, drawings, photographs, all pertaining to the life of the Thatcher Family, Andrew McClelland Collection of World Curiosities, Thatcher Family Collection
Publications: Rosemount News, quarterly
Activities: Classes for adults & children; dramatic progs; docent training; lects open to pub, vis lectrs varies per yr; special theme & holiday events; tours; Best Museum in Pueblo-2000; El Pomar Award of Excellence; mus shop sells books, prints, & decorative art objects

A **SANGRE DE CRISTO ARTS & CONFERENCE CENTER,** 210 N Santa Fe, Pueblo, CO 81003. Tel 719-295-7200; Fax 719-295-7230; Email mail@sdc-arts.org; Web: www.sdc-arts.org; *Exec Dir* Dan Lere; *Cur Visual Arts* Christel Dussart; *Facilities & Beverage Mgr* Lorrie Marquez; *Mktg Specialist* Nicki Hart; *Cur Educ* Jackie Henderson; *Admin Asst* Kathy Berg; *Cur Children's Mus* Donna Stinchcomb; *Asst Cur Children's Mus* Joleen Ryan; *Controller* Rochelle Spoone; *Mem & Box Office Mgr* Cheryl Califano; *Asst Mem & Box Office Mgr* Dan Masterson; *Asst Cur Visual Arts & Colls Mgr* Gabe Wolff; *Asst Educ Cur* Diane Pirraglia; *Artistic Dir for School of Dance* Stephen Wynne; *Mktg Asst* Jenny Kemp; *Accounting Asst* Julie Gallery
Open (box office) Mon - Fri 9 AM - 5 PM; (galleries) Tues - Sat 11 AM - 4 PM; Admis $4; Estab 1972 to promote the educational & cultural activities related to the fine arts in Southern Colorado including four gallery spaces & a hands on children's museum, a conference area with over 7000 sq ft of rentable space for conventions, receptions, meetings, including a 500 seat theater; The Helen T White Gallery provides four gallery spaces with changing exhibitions by local, regional & international artists, including the Francis King Collection of Western Art, Buell Children's Mus displays over 2 dozen hands-on exhibits; Average Annual Attendance: 220,000; Mem: 3800; dues $15-$1500
Income: $993,000 (financed by mem, city & County appropriation, grants, grants, private underwriting, donations & in-kind services)
Library Holdings: Book Volumes, Exhibition Catalogs, Framed Reproductions, Original Art Works, Periodical Subscriptions, Sculpture
Special Subjects: American Western Art, Bronzes, Ceramics, Collages, Drawings, Folk Art, Hispanic Art, Landscapes, Mexican Art, Photography, Pottery, Sculpture, Southwestern Art, Watercolors, Woodcuts
Collections: Francis King Collection of Western Art, Contemporary, Gene Kloss Collection, Santo Collection, Molas
Exhibitions: Converted art inspired by car culture; Own Your Own (Nov - Jan)
Publications: Town & Center Mosaic, four times a yr; Catalogue of Francis King Collection; West By Southwest book, collections of the Francis King Collection of Western Art, Collection of Intaglio Prints by Gene Kloss, Ruth Gast Collection of Santos; annual report exhibition catalogues; brochures for workshop & dance classes, quarterly; performance arts series, children's series, children's museum; Catalogue Under Western Skies (30 yrs of collecting selections from the colls of the Sangre de Cristo Arts & Conference Center)
Activities: Year-round workshop prog, wide selection of disciplines for children & adults; docent training; dramatic programs; special facilities for ceramics, painting & photography; school of dance; artists-in-residence; lect & seminars coinciding with exhibs; Visiting lect 3 per yr; gallery talks; tours; Theatre Arts - Town & Gown Performing Arts Series; Children's Playhouse Series; outdoor summer concerts, Repertory Theatre Company presenting 2 performances a year, resident modern dance company; concerts; sponsoring of competitions; cash awards to representing the West artists; scholarships offered; individual paintings & objects of art lent to museums, galleries & art centers; lending of original objects of art to community businesses & municipal offices, collection contains 575 original art works, 130 original prints, 445 paintings, photographs, nature artifacts & sculptures; book traveling exhibs 4 per yr; originates traveling exhibs to other institutions; sales shop sells hand-crafted & imported gifts & southwestern artifacts, posters, books, jewelry, magazines, original art, reproductions, prints, slides; Buell Children's Museum

M **UNIVERSITY OF SOUTHERN COLORADO,** College of Liberal & Fine Arts, 2200 Bonforte Blvd, Pueblo, CO 81001-4990. Tel 719-549-2100; Fax 719-549-2120; Web: www.colostate-pueblo.edu; *Art Dept Chmn* Roy Sonnema; *Dir Gallery* Dennis Dolton
Open daily 10 AM - 4 PM; No admis fee; Estab 1972 to provide educational exhibitions for students attending the University; Gallery has a 40 x 50 ft area with 16 ft ceiling; vinyl covered wooden walls; carpeted & adjustable track lighting; Average Annual Attendance: 6,000
Income: Financed through University & student government
Special Subjects: American Indian Art, Drawings, Prints
Collections: Basketry of the Plains Indian, clothing of the Plains Indian, Orman Collection of Indian Art of the Southwest including Indian blankets of the Rio Grande & Navajo people, pottery of the Pueblo Indians (both recent & ancient)
Exhibitions: Art Director's Club of Denver Exhibition; Art Resources of South Colorado; Colorado Invites
Publications: Catalogs
Activities: Lects open to pub; individual paintings & original objects of art lent; book traveling exhibs 2-6 per yr; originates traveling exhibs

SNOWMASS VILLAGE

A **ANDERSON RANCH ARTS CENTER,** 5263 Owl Creek Rd, Snowmass Village, CO 81615; PO Box 5598, Snowmass Village, CO 81615-5598. Tel 970-923-3181; Fax 970-923-3871; Email info@andersonranch.org; Web: www.andersonranch.org; *Exec Dir* Nancy Wilhelms; *Assoc Dir & Artistic Dir Ceramics* Doug Casebeer; *Artistic Dir, Painting, Drawing & Printmaking* Elizabeth Ferrill; *Artistic Dir, Photog, New Media, Chair of Workshop & Artists-in-Residence Progs* Andrea Wallace; *Artistic Dir, Sculpture* Jose Ferreira
Open Mon - Fri 9 AM - 5 PM; No admis fee; Estab 1966 to feature Ranch artists; Gallery features rotating exhibs of 2-D & 3-D works by Ranch artists; Average Annual Attendance: 5,000
Income: $2,000,000 (financed by private donations, grants & tuition)
Special Subjects: Ceramics, Drawings, Etchings & Engravings, Photography, Pottery, Prints, Sculpture
Collections: Print collection of contemporary pieces by acclaimed artists
Publications: Workshops catalog, annual
Activities: Classes for adults & children; lects open to pub; schols offered; sales shop sells books, original art, refreshments, clothing & art supplies

TRINIDAD

M **ARTHUR ROY MITCHELL MEMORIAL INC,** A.R. Mitchell Museum, 150 E Main St, Trinidad, CO 81082; PO Box 95, Trinidad, CO 81082-0095. Tel 719-846-4224; Fax 719-846-2004; Email mitchellmuseum@qwestoffice.net; Web: armitchell.org; *Co-Dir* Paula Little; *Co-Dir* Joanie Hessling
Open yearly Mon - Sat 10 AM - 4 PM, & May - Sept also open Sun Noon - 4 PM; Admis adults $3; children under 12 & mem no admis fee; Estab 1981 to preserve & display art of the American West; 15,000 sq ft gallery space; Average Annual Attendance: 3000; Mem: 950; dues $30 - $1000
Income: $50,000 (financed by endowment, mem, donations, gifts, grants & gift shop)
Special Subjects: American Indian Art, American Western Art, Carpets & Rugs, Ceramics, Decorative Arts, Folk Art, Hispanic Art, Historical Material, Jewelry, Landscapes, Painting-American, Photography, Portraits, Pottery, Religious Art, Sculpture, Southwestern Art, Watercolors
Collections: Harvey Dunn Collection, A R Mitchell Collection, Almeron Newman Collection of photography, The Aultman Collection of photography, Benjamin Wittick Collection of Photography, Hispanic Religious art (Santos); saddles; guns
Exhibitions: 3 special exhibs per yr
Activities: Educ prog; classes for adults & children; lects open to pub, concerts; gallery talks; tours; competitions with prizes; individual paintings & original

objects of art lent to & other mus; book traveling exhibs; originate traveling exhibs; mus shop sells books, original art, reproductions & Indian jewelry

CONNECTICUT

AVON

A **FARMINGTON VALLEY ARTS CENTER,** 25 Arts Center Lane Avon, CT 06001. Tel 860-678-1867; Email info@artsfvac.org; Web: www.artsfvac.org; *Dir Educ* Carol Kaplan; *Exec Dir* Roy David; *Gallery Mgr & Admin Dir* Sandy Buerker; *Sr Admin* Lisa Pichnarcik
Open Mon 10 AM - 2 PM; Tues - Fri 10 AM - 4 PM, Sat noon - 4 PM; No admis fee; Estab 1974 to provide a facility with appropriate environment & programs that serves as a focal point for public awareness of & participation in the visual arts through quality arts education, exposure to dedicated artists & exposure to high quality crafts; The Fisher Gallery (1300 sq ft) displays and sells fine craft and art and offers educational programming. Esther B Drezner Visitors' Gallery showcases artists' work in a variety of medium. Exhibs of local & regional artists represented; Average Annual Attendance: 2,000; Mem: 1,000; dues family $60, individual $35, teens & srs $25
Income: $500,000 (financed by class tuition, gallery, mem, grants, tuitions, donations from corporations & individuals special event earning)
Library Holdings: Original Art Works, Pamphlets, Photographs, Prints, Sculpture
Special Subjects: Ceramics, Decorative Arts, Drawings, Jewelry, Photography, Sculpture, Painting-American, Etchings & Engravings, Glass, Portraits, Pottery, Silver
Collections: Handicrafts, Mixed Media, Painting, Silversmithing, Textile Design, Weaving, Wood, Metal & Glass Work, Ceramics, Jewelry, Wearable art
Exhibitions: American craftspeople featured in Fisher Gallery; on-site studio artists featured in Visitor's Gallery
Activities: Classes for adults & children, educational outreach progs; 20 studios for rent; career advancement prog for artists; summer arts camp; lects open to pub; 4 vis lectrs per yr; gallery talks; tours; visits to artists' studios; annual holiday exhib of fine crafts; sales shop sells original art

BLOOMFIELD

C **CIGNA CORPORATION,** CIGNA Art Collection, 900 Cottage Grove Rd L9, Bloomfield, CT 06002-2920. Tel 860-226-3844; *Mgr* Sarah A Polirer
Open by appointment; No admis fee; Estab 1925
Income: Financed by company
Special Subjects: Afro-American Art, Architecture, Ceramics, Collages, Crafts, Decorative Arts, Dioramas, Drawings, Etchings & Engravings
Collections: Over 4,000 American fine and decorative art pieces; fire fighting and marine related objects; manuscripts

BRIDGEPORT

M **THE BARNUM MUSEUM,** 820 Main St, Bridgeport, CT 06604-4912. Tel 203-331-1104; Fax 203-331-0079; Email dsaviello@basnum.museum.org; Web: www.barnum-museum.org; *Cur* Kathleen Maher; *Exec Dir* Lawrence A Fisher; *Dir Develop* Susan J Agamy; *Educ Dir* J Knoedler; *Pub Rels Dir* KP Greaser; *Chmn (V)* Craig Frew; *Educ Progs* Ken Blinn; *Mus Shop Mgr* Debbie Saviello
Open Tues - Sat 10 AM - 4:30 PM, Sun Noon - 4:30 PM; Admis adults $7, college students & sr citizens $4 & children $4; Estab 1893 to exhibit the life & times of P T Barnum; Average Annual Attendance: 20,000; Mem: 400; dues family $45, individual $25
Income: Financed by City of Bridgeport, corporate individual, mem & endowments
Collections: Tom Thumb Collection, Jenny Lind Collection of Photos
Publications: The Barnum Herald newsletter, twice per year
Activities: Tours; films; school & pub progs; workshops; lects open to pub; book traveling exhibs 1 per yr; originate traveling exhibs; sales shop sells books, souvenirs

M **CITY LIGHTS GALLERY,** 265 Golden Hill St, Bridgeport, CT 06604-4915. Tel 203-334-7748; Email citygallerybpt@gmail.com; Web: www.citylightsgallery.org; *Exec Dir* Suzanne Kachmar; *Gallery Mgr* Steve Gerber
Open Wed - Fri 11:30 AM - 5 PM, Sat Noon - 4 PM or by appt; No admis fee; Estab 2004 to provide exposure to local artists & advocate the positive effects art can have on community
Collections: Paintings, photographs & sculpture
Exhibitions: 10 exhibits annually
Activities: Workshops; outreach progs

M **DISCOVERY MUSEUM,** 4450 Park Ave, Bridgeport, CT 06604-1098. Tel 203-372-3521; Fax 203-374-1929; Email hawkins@discoverymuseum.org; Web: www.discoverymuseum.org; *Pres* Paul Audley; *Dir Admin* Lynn Hamilton; *Develop* Cynthia Manning; *Acting Cur* Wendy Kelly; *Sr VPres* Linda Markin
Open Tues - Sat 10 AM - 5 PM, Sun Noon - 5 PM, cl major holidays; Admis adults $7, children, sr citizens & col students $5.50, children under 3 & members free; Estab 1958 to provide exhibitions & educational programs in the arts & sciences for a regional audience; Average Annual Attendance: 100,000; Mem: 1500; dues $20-$1000; annual meeting in June
Income: Financed by mem dues
Special Subjects: Painting-American, Furniture
Collections: Paintings, prints & works on paper, Historic house
Exhibitions: Temporary & permanent exhibitions; hands-on physical science exhibits; Hands-on Art Gallery; Challenger Space Station; Fine Art Gallery; Planetarium
Activities: Classes for children; docent training; lects open to pub, 4 vis lectrs per yr; concerts; tours; competitions with awards; scholarships; planetarium shows; individual paintings & original objects of art lent to other local and regional mus; book traveling exhibs 1 per yr; mus shop sells books, reproductions, cards, calendars, gifts, jewelry, dishware & toys for children & adults

M **HOUSATONIC COMMUNITY COLLEGE,** Housatonic Museum of Art, 900 Lafayette Blvd, Bridgeport, CT 06604-4704. Tel 203-332-5203; 332-5052; Fax 203-332-5123; Email rzella@hcc.commnet.edu; Web: www.housatonicmuseum.org; *Dir* Robbin Zella
Open Sep - May Mon - Fri 8:30 AM - 5:30 PM, Thurs until 7 PM, Sat 9 AM - 3 Pm, Sun Noon - 4 PM, subject to chg during holidays; Jun - Aug Mon - Fri 8:30 AM - 5:30 PM, Thurs until 7 PM, Sat 9 AM - 3 PM, Sun noon - 4 PM, gallery cl during col holidays; No admis fee; Mus estab 1967; Burt Chernow Galleries host a range of contemporary & historic shows; Average Annual Attendance: 12,000
Income: Financed by state & local funding, public & private foundation grants & donations
Library Holdings: Audio Tapes, Book Volumes, CD-ROMs, Clipping Files, Exhibition Catalogs, Original Art Works, Periodical Subscriptions, Photographs, Prints, Sculpture
Special Subjects: Drawings, Painting-American, Sculpture
Collections: Extensive 19th & 20th Century drawings, paintings & sculpture: Avery, Baskin, Calder, Cassat, Chagall, Daumier, DeChirico, Derain, Dubuffet, Gottlieb, Lichtenstein, Lindner, Marisol, Matisse, Miro-Moore, Pavia,, Picasso, Rauchenberg, Rivers, Shahn, Vasarely, Warhol, Wesselmann & others, extensive ethnographic collections, including Africa, South Seas & others, smaller holdings from various historical periods
Exhibitions: Several exhibitions per year
Publications: Exhibition catalogs
Activities: Classes for adults; college art courses; lects open to pub, 4-6 vis lectrs per yr; concerts; gallery talks; tours; sponsors competitions; scholarships offered; individual paintings & original objects of art lent to accredited mus; limited lending collection contains 2000 paintings, 25,000 slides, sculpture, original art works, original prints; book traveling exhibs; originate traveling exhibs to other universities; exhibs include Beyond Recognition, Ecce Homo, Monuments & Memory; mus shop sells books, t-shirts, posters

L **Library,** 900 Lafayette Blvd, Bridgeport, CT 06604-4704. Tel 203-332-5070; Fax 203-332-5132; *Dir* Bruce Harvey
Open Mon - Wed & Fri 8:30 AM - 5:30 PM, Thur 8:30 AM - 7 PM; No admis fee; Libr Estab 1967; Extensive art section open to students & community; Average Annual Attendance: 5,000
Income: state, fed & pvt
Library Holdings: Book Volumes 30,000, Fiche

M **UNIVERSITY OF BRIDGEPORT GALLERY,** 380 University Ave, Bridgeport, CT 06604-5692. Tel 203-576-4239; Fax 203-576-4512; Web: www.bridgeport.edu/art; *Art Dept Chmn* Thomas Juliusburger; *Assoc VPres of Univ Rels* James Garland
No admis fee; Estab 1972
Collections: Contemporary art, prints
Activities: Lects open to pub; gallery talks; concerts; individual paintings & original objects of art lent; originates traveling exhibs

BROOKFIELD

M **BROOKFIELD CRAFT CENTER, INC,** Gallery, 286 Whisconier Rd, Brookfield, CT 06804-0122; PO Box 122, Brookfield, CT 06804-0122. Tel 203-775-4526; Fax 203-740-7815; Email info@brookfieldcraft.org; Web: www.brookfieldcraft.org; *Exec Dir* Howard Lasser
Open Tues - Fri 1 - 5 PM, Sat 11 AM - 5 PM, Sun noon - 4 PM, cl Mon; No admis fee; Estab 1954 to provide a wide spectrum of craft educ & exhib to the local & national audiences; Contemporary American craft for exhib & sale; Average Annual Attendance: 15,000; Mem: 500; dues-$50
Exhibitions: Contemporary craft exhibitions changing every 8 weeks
Publications: Catalogs
Activities: Classes for adults & children; lects open to pub; schols offered; book traveling exhibs to other craft organizations; sales shop sells books, original art & handmade craft items

BROOKLYN

M **NEW ENGLAND CENTER FOR CONTEMPORARY ART,** 7 Putnam Pl, Brooklyn, CT 06234; PO Box 302 7, Brooklyn, CT 06234-0302. Tel 860-774-881302; Fax 860-774-4840; Web: www.museum-necca.org; *Dir* Henry Riseman; *Assoc Dir* Paul Sorel; *Cur Chinese Art* Xue JianXin
Open Wed - Fri 10 AM - 4 PM, Sat & Sun 1 PM - 5 PM, cl Christmas; No admis fee; Estab 1975; Mem: dues corporate $100, supporting $50, family $15, individual $10, senior citizen $6
Income: Financed by state appropriations, mem, contributions & gifts
Collections: Contemporary paintings & sculpture, print coll by Russian artists, woodblock print coll from the People's Republic of China
Exhibitions: Rotating and traveling exhibits
Activities: Classes for adults & children; lect; tours; films; gallery talks; originate traveling exhibs; sales shop sells paintings, prints & books

CHESHIRE

M **BARKER CHARACTER, COMIC AND CARTOON MUSEUM,** 1188 Highland Ave, Rte 10, Cheshire, CT 06410. Tel 203-699-3822; Fax 203-250-6770; Email fun@barkeranimation.com; Web: www.barkermuseum.com; *Co-Founder* Herbert Barker, DHL; *Co-Founder* Gloria Barker; *Cur* Judy Fuerst
Open Wed - Sat noon - 4 PM, cl holidays; tours available by appt for those 8 years of age & up; Admis adults $5, children 17 & under $3, children 3 & under free; Estab 1998; Comic strip & cartoon memories from childhood are captured here; advertising memorabilia amassed by Herb & Gloria Barker. Though none of the

museum's coll is for sale, exhibs contain the current market value; Average Annual Attendance: 50,000
Special Subjects: Cartoons, Miniatures, Costumes, Dolls, Glass, Jewelry
Collections: Official California Raisins Museum, Official Celebriducks Museum, featuring extensive coll of rubber ducks, Disney, Hanna-Barbera, Warner Bros, Charles Fazzino & many other colls of memorabilia, Roy Rogers lunch box, Ronald McDonald phone, Charlie McCarthy puppet, Flintstones Band Toy, Lone Ranger Gun, Mickey & Minnie hand car, advertising memorabilia, rare recent acquisitions
Activities: Field trips by advance reservation

COS COB

M **BUSH-HOLLEY HISTORIC SITE & STOREHOUSE GALLERY,** Greenwich Historical Society, 39 Strickland Rd, Cos Cob, CT 06807-2727. Tel 203-869-6899; Fax 203-861-9720; Email bbishop@greenwichhistory.org; Web: www.greenwichhistory.org; *Chmn* Davidde Strackbein; *Exec Dir* Debra L Mecky, PhD; *Mktg & Communs Dir* Barbara Bishop; *Archivist* Christopher Shields; *Educ Cur* Anna Greco; *Cur & Exhib Coordr* Karen Frederick
Open Storehouse Gallery & Historic Site: Wed - Sun noon - 4 PM; Docent-led tours 1, 2 & 3 PM; special tours available by appt; Admis adults $10, sr citizens & students $8, mems & children 6 and under free; free first Wed ea month; Estab 1931 to collect & preserve the history of Greenwich, CT; National historic landmark; home of the first art colony in CT; gallery, lib, & archives at CosCob Art Colony; rotating art & history exhib; Average Annual Attendance: 16,000; Mem: Leadership circle $2500, benefactor $1000, patron $500, donor $250, sponsor $100, family/dual $65, individual & senior $40
Income: Financed by contributions, mem, special events, fees
Library Holdings: Auction Catalogs, Audio Tapes, Book Volumes, CD-ROMs, Cards, Cassettes, Clipping Files, Compact Disks, DVDs, Exhibition Catalogs, Fiche, Filmstrips, Framed Reproductions, Kodachrome Transparencies, Lantern Slides, Manuscripts, Maps, Memorabilia, Micro Print, Motion Pictures, Original Art Works, Original Documents, Other Holdings, Pamphlets, Periodical Subscriptions, Photographs, Prints, Records, Reels, Reproductions, Slides, Video Tapes
Special Subjects: Architecture, Art Education, Art History, Crafts, Decorative Arts, Decorative Arts, Etchings & Engravings, Etchings & Engravings, Folk Art, Furniture, Historical Material, Painting-American, Painting-American, Period Rooms, Photography, Porcelain, Pottery, Textiles, Drawings, Maps, Prints
Collections: American Impressionist art coll, Greenwich history
Publications: e-mail newsletter monthly; annual report; pamphlets
Activities: Classes for adults & children; docent training; dramatic programs; field trips; lects open to pub; vis lectrs 5-6 per yr; gallery talks; tours; guided tours of Bush-Holley house; Preservation Awards; concerts; mus shop sells books, magazines, prints, gift & stationery

COVENTRY

M **NATHAN HALE HOMESTEAD MUSEUM,** 2299 South St, Coventry, CT 06238-0760; Connecticut Landmarks, 59 S Prospect St Hartford, CT 06106. Tel 860-742-6917; Email hale@ctlandmarks.org; Web: www.ctlandmarks.org; *Site Admin* Bev York
Open mid-May to mid-Oct Wed - Sun noon - 4 PM; Admis Family $15, adults $7, senior $6, children $4, children under 6 no admis fee; Mus is on the grounds in which Revolutionary War hero Nathan Hale uttered his final words "I only regret that I have but one life to lose for my country." Georgian-style house was built by the Hale family in 1776, situated on over 500 acres of forest land; Average Annual Attendance: 3,500 ann
Library Holdings: Book Volumes, Records
Special Subjects: Historical Material, Painting-American, Period Rooms, Portraits, Reproductions, Textiles
Collections: Georgian house built in 1776 on site, portraits of Hale
Activities: Educ progs; classes for children; birthday parties; summer camp; trails; horseback riding; 18th century demonstration garden; hands-on activities; dramatic progs; docent training; gallery talks; tours; sales shop sells books, prints & mus related items

DANBURY

M **DANBURY SCOTT-FANTON MUSEUM & HISTORICAL SOCIETY, INC,** 43 Main St, Danbury, CT 06810-8011. Tel 203-743-5200; Fax 203-743-1131; Email dmhs@danburyhistorical.org; Web: www.danburyhistorical.org; *Dir* Levi Newsome; *Cur Specialist* Brigid Durkin; *Research Specialist* Kathleen Zuris
Call for information; No admis fee; donations welcome; Estab June 24, 1941 as historic house. Merged with Mus & Arts Center by Legislative Act 1947; Operates the 1785 John & Mary Rider House as a mus of early Americana & the 1790 Dodd Hat Shop with exhibits relating to hatting. Huntington Hall houses frequently changing exhibits. Ives Homestead, located at Rogers Park in Danbury is to be restored & opened to the pub as a memorial to American composer Charles Edward Ives. Marian Anderson Studio - a memorial to famous Afro-American singer; Average Annual Attendance: 5,000; Mem: 500; dues student $2 up to life $1000; annual meeting in May
Income: Financed by endowment & mem
Special Subjects: Textiles
Collections: Quilt Collection, Batting Collection, Early 1800s men's & women's clothing, Early American Furniture
Publications: Newsletter, quarterly; reprints
Activities: Classes for adults & children; dramatic progs; lects open to pub; concerts; open house; special exhibits; gallery talks; tours; slide shows

L **Library,** 43 Main St, Danbury, CT 06810. Tel 203-743-5200; Web: www.danburyhistorical.org; *Dir* Levi Newsome; *Cur Specialist* Brigid Durkin; *Research Specialist* Kathleen Zuris
Call for information; Historic information & photographs for reference only
Library Holdings: Clipping Files, Manuscripts, Memorabilia, Other Holdings City Directories, Photographs
Collections: Charles Ives Photograph Collection

A **WOOSTER COMMUNITY ART CENTER,** 91 Miry Brook Rd, Danbury, CT 06810-7417. Tel 203-744-4825; *Asst Dir* Judy Kagan; *Exec Dir* Nancy M Rogers
Open Mon - Fri 9:30 AM - 6 PM, cl Sat & Sun; Estab 1965 as a Community Art Center; Reception center gallery 500 sq ft; Average Annual Attendance: 1,500; Mem: 100; dues family $50, individual $35
Exhibitions: Faculty Exhibits; Art exhibits change monthly in Lobby Gallery, Area artists exhibit artwork in varied media, indoor & outdoor photography, painting & sculpture
Publications: Arts News (newsletter), 3 times per yr
Activities: Classes for adults & children; lects open to public, 5 vis lectrs per yr; scholarships & fels offered; originate traveling exhibs; sales shop sells art supplies

L **Library,** 91 Miry Brook Rd, Danbury, CT 06810-7417. Tel 203-744-4825; *Exec Dir* Nancy M Rogers
For reference only
Library Holdings: Book Volumes 2000, Periodical Subscriptions 3, Slides 2200

DERBY

M **OSBORNE HOMESTEAD MUSEUM,** 500 Hawthorne Ave, Derby, CT 06418; PO Box 435, Derby, CT 06418-0435. Tel 203-734-2513; Fax 203-922-7833; Email susan.d.robinson@ct.gov; Web: www.ct.gov/deep/kellogg; *Dir* Diane Chisnall Joy; *Environmental Educ* Susan Quincy; *Office Mgr* Donna Kingston; *Maintainer* Marguerite Heneghan; *Mus Educ* Susan Robinson
Open Museum: May - Oct Thurs & Fri 10 AM - 3 PM, Sat 10 AM - 4 PM, Sun 12 PM - 4 PM; Kellogg Estate Gardens: Spring - Autumn Mon - Sat 9 AM - 4:30 PM; Holiday Tours: Thurs - Sun 10 AM - 4 PM first Fri after Thanksgiving Day - Sat before Christmas; Mus celebrates life & times of Frances Osborne Kellogg, noted industrialist, agriculturalist & conservationist who was dedicated to preserving land for future generations
Special Subjects: Furniture, Historical Material
Collections: period furniture, fine art, history of the Osborne family
Activities: School, teacher & scout progs; hands-on activities; bird walks; adjacent state park; formal gardens; holiday tours

ESSEX

A **ESSEX ART ASSOCIATION, INC,** 10 N Main St, Essex, CT 06426-1030; PO Box 193, Essex, CT 06426-0193. Tel 860-767-8996; Web: www.essexartassociation.com; *Treas* Robert Gantner; *Pres* Rob DeBartolo; *Admin Dir* Lesley Braren
Open daily 1 - 5 PM May - Oct, cl Tues; No admis fee; Estab 1946 as a nonprofit organization for the encouragement of the arts & to provide & maintain suitable headquarters for the showing of art; Maintains a small, well-equipped one-floor gallery; Average Annual Attendance: 2,500; Mem: 360; elected artists $45; assoc artists $35; supporting members $30
Income: Financed by mem & donations
Exhibitions: 6 annual exhibits per yr; 5 exhibits for EAA; 1 exhib for Valley Regional High School Scholarship Award Show
Activities: $10,200 misc awards per yr

FAIRFIELD

A **FAIRFIELD HISTORICAL SOCIETY,** Fairfield Museum & History Center, 370 Beach Rd, Fairfield, CT 06824-6639. Tel 203-259-1598; Fax 203-255-2716; Email info@fairfieldhs.org; Web: www.fairfieldhistory.org; *CEO* Michael Jehle; *Dir Educ* Christine Jewell; *Prog & Vol Coordr* Walter Matis; *Libr Dir* Elizabeth Rose
Open Mon - Fri 10 AM - 4 PM, Sat - Sun 12 PM - 4 PM; Admis fee adults $5, children & seniors $3; Estab 1902 to collect, preserve & interpret artifacts & information relating to the history of Fairfield & the surrounding region; Changing exhibitions and permanent collections display; Average Annual Attendance: 25,000; Mem: 3000; dues $30-$1,000; annual meeting in Oct
Income: $850,000
Library Holdings: Audio Tapes, Book Volumes, Clipping Files, Lantern Slides, Manuscripts, Maps, Memorabilia, Original Art Works, Original Documents, Pamphlets, Periodical Subscriptions, Photographs, Prints, Records
Special Subjects: Archaeology, Architecture, Ceramics, Costumes, Crafts, Decorative Arts, Dolls, Drawings, Embroidery, Etchings & Engravings, Folk Art, Furniture, Glass, Historical Material, Laces, Landscapes, Marine Painting, Painting-American, Photography, Portraits, Posters, Prints, Silver, Textiles, Manuscripts, Maps, Restorations
Collections: Ceramics, furniture, jewelry, paintings, photographs, prints, silver, local history, textiles & costumes, Local History, Archaeology, Kansas postcard series
Publications: Newsletter
Activities: Classes for adults & children; docent training; dramatic progs; lects open to pub; 10-15 vis lectrs per yr; gallery talks; tours; volunteer training; individual paintings & original objects of art lent to other Fairfield County mus; mus shop sells books, prints, reproductions, original art

L **Library,** 370 Beach Rd, Fairfield, CT 06824-6639. Tel 203-259-1598; *Librn* Dennis Barrow
Open Tues - Sat 10 AM - 4:30 PM, Sun 1 - 4:30 PM; Open to the pub for reference only; Mem: User fee $3
Library Holdings: Audio Tapes, Book Volumes 10,000, Cassettes, Clipping Files, Fiche, Lantern Slides, Manuscripts, Memorabilia, Motion Pictures, Other Holdings Diaries; Documents; Maps, Pamphlets, Periodical Subscriptions 12, Photographs, Records, Reels, Slides, Video Tapes
Special Subjects: Architecture, Historical Material, Landscape Architecture, Manuscripts, Maps, Photography, Video
Activities: Classes for adults

M **FAIRFIELD UNIVERSITY,** Art Museum, 1073 N Benson Rd, Fairfield, CT 06824-5171. Tel 203-254-4046; Fax 203-254-5529; Email museum@fairfield.edu; Web: www.fairfield.edu/museum; *Dir* Dr. Linda Wolk-Simonlwolk-simon@fairfield.edu; *Asst Dir* Carey Mack

Webercweber@fairfield.edu; *Cur of Education & Academic Engagment* Dr. Michelle DiMarzomdimarzo@fairfield.edu; *Kress Interpretive Fellow* Dr. Sarah Cantor; *Cur of the Plaster Cast Collection* Dr. Katherine Schwab
Open Bellamine Hall Galleries: Tues - Sat 11 AM - 4 PM ; Walsh Gallery: Wed - Sat 12 PM - 4 PM; No admis fee; Estab 1990; Multi-purpose space with state of the art security & environmental controls requirement; 2200 sq ft; Average Annual Attendance: 7,000; Mem: free membership program
Income: Financed by endowment & university funds
Special Subjects: Afro-American Art, Archaeology, Baroque Art, Painting-American, Posters, Prints, Renaissance Art
Collections: permanent collection - ancient to contemporary
Exhibitions: Thematic & social context art exhibitions; modern & contemporary art
Publications: Educational materials; exhibition catalogues
Activities: Adult classes; docent training; lects open to pub; gallery talks; tours

M **SACRED HEART UNIVERSITY,** Gallery of Contemporary Art, 5151 Park Ave, Fairfield, CT 06825-1000. Tel 203-365-7650; Fax 203-396-8361; Email gevass@sacredheart.edu; Web: artgallery.sacredheart.edu; *Dir* Sophia Gevas
Open Mon - Thurs noon - 5:00 PM, Sun Noon - 4 PM; No admis fee; Estab 1989 for the purpose of exhibiting contemporary artists in a wide range of media; Average Annual Attendance: 3,000
Income: university support & annual fundraisers
Purchases: Occasional purchasing of works & commissions of large scale site specific works for new buildings
Collections: Contemporary works, all media, Art Walk, sculpture on loan & commissioned permanent works
Publications: 2 brochure catalogues per yr
Activities: Art talks for high school students & community groups; middle school student workshops; lects open to pub, 2-3 vis lectrs per yr; gallery talks; book traveling exhibs 1 per 3-5 yrs; originates traveling exhibs to other university galleries

FARMINGTON

M **FARMINGTON VILLAGE GREEN & LIBRARY ASSOCIATION,** Stanley-Whitman House, 37 High St Farmington, CT 06032. Tel 860-677-9222; Web: www.stanleywhitman.org; *Dir* Lisa Johnson; *Educ Coordr* Debbie Andrews; *Tour Interpreter* Peter Devlin; *Admin Asst* Jo-Ann B Silverio
Open May - Oct Wed - Sun Noon - 4 PM; Nov - Apr, Sat & Sun Noon - 4 PM & by appointment; Admis adults $5, sr citizens $4, children $2, mems free; Estab 1935 to collect, preserve, educate about 18th century Farmington; A separate building, has space for art exhibits. Maintains reference library; Average Annual Attendance: 5,000; Mem: 200; dues $18-$500
Income: Financed by endowment interest, special events, mem & admis
Purchases: $186,000
Library Holdings: Original Documents, Photographs
Special Subjects: Archaeology, Architecture, Bookplates & Bindings, Ceramics, Coins & Medals, Costumes, Crafts, Decorative Arts, Dolls, Drawings, Embroidery, Etchings & Engravings, Folk Art, Furniture, Glass
Collections: American decorative arts, ceramics, costumes & textiles, 18th century decorative arts, dooryard & herb garden, furniture, glass, household utensils, photographs, weaving equipment
Exhibitions: Permanent & changing exhibitions
Publications: A Guide to Historic Farmington, Connecticut; A Short History of Farmington, Connecticut
Activities: Classes for adults & children; dramatic progs; docent training; family & school progs; children's hands-on tour; lects open to pub, 3 vis lectrs per yr; gallery talks; tours; lending collection contains cassettes, over 1000 photographs & 300 slides; mus shop sells books, toys, games & cards

M **HILL-STEAD MUSEUM,** 35 Mountain Rd, Farmington, CT 06032-2304. Tel 860-677-4787; Fax 860-677-0174; Email cagenelloc@hillstead.org; Web: www.hillstead.org; *Dir & CEO* Sue Sturtevant, Ed.D; *Mus Shop Mgr* Priscilla Ramage; *Dir Educ & Curatorial Svcs* Marcie Jackson; *Dir Communs* Cynthia Cagenello; *Vol Pres* M Timothy Corbett; *Dir Opers* David Perbeck; *Finance Dir* Becky Hendricks; *Dir Develop* Dougla Pyrke; *Cur* Melanie Bourbeau; *Dir Poetry Festival* Mimi Madden
Open: call for hours; Admis adults $12, discounts for AAA & AAM members, members no charge; Estab 1947 to house French & American impressionist painting, plus Japanese woodblock prints; Colonial Revival style house designed by Theodate Pope in collaboration with McKim, Mead & White & built in 1901 for industrialist Alfred Atmore Pope. Set on 150 acres including a sunken garden designed by Beatrix Farrand, the house contains Mr. Pope's early collection of French Impressionist paintings & decorative arts; Average Annual Attendance: 46,000; Mem: 1300; dues family $75, individual $50; annual meeting in June
Income: Financed by endowment, mem, contributions, individual, corporate & foundations, admis & sales
Library Holdings: Exhibition Catalogs, Memorabilia, Original Documents, Photographs
Special Subjects: Antiquities-Greek, Architecture, Asian Art, Bronzes, Carpets & Rugs, Ceramics, Decorative Arts, Drawings, Etchings & Engravings, Furniture, Glass, Historical Material, Landscapes, Painting-American, Painting-French, Period Rooms, Photography, Porcelain, Portraits, Pottery, Pre-Columbian Art, Prints, Sculpture, Silver, Textiles, Watercolors, Woodcuts
Collections: Paintings by Cassatt, Degas, Manet, Monet & Whistler, prints by Durer, Piranesi, Whistler & other 19th century artists, American, English & other European furniture, Oriental & European porcelain, Japanese prints
Exhibitions: Rotating exhibits
Publications: Catalog of Hill-Stead Paintings; Theodate Pope Riddle, Her Life & Work; Hill-Stead Museum House Guide; Hill-Stead: The Country Place of Theodate Pope Riddle; Wonders Revealed: Rarely seen original prints from Hill-Stead's collection
Activities: Classes for adults & children; docent training; dramatic progs; poetry seminars; nature walks; farmers market; lects open to pub, 5-10 vis lectrs per yr; concerts; gallery talks; tours; competition with awards; mus shop sells books, magazines, reproductions, slides, CDs, poetry, tapes & videos; holiday boutique

GOSHEN

M **GOSHEN HISTORICAL SOCIETY,** 21 Old Middle St, Goshen, CT 06756; PO Box 457, Goshen, CT 06756-0457. Tel 860-491-9610, 491-3129; Email (cur) jvnkuq@juno.com; Web: www.goshenhistoricalct.org; *Pres & Cur* Henrietta C Horvay; *VPres* Marcia Barker
Open Apr - Oct Tues 10 AM - Noon, by appointment; No admis fee; Estab 1955 to interpret the past & present of our area; Average Annual Attendance: 400; Mem: 150; meetings in May & Oct
Income: Financed by mem & donations
Special Subjects: American Indian Art, Historical Material, Photography
Collections: Collection of Indian art, farm tools, household items used through town's history & photographs, quilts
Exhibitions: Exhibits focused on 275 years of town's history; Goshen in Civil War; Lucas Ledgers
Activities: Classes for children & visits mus; gallery talks; tours; lects open to pub, 2 vis lectrs per mon June - Aug; lending of objects of art to other historical societies & libraries; mus shop sells books & other mus related items

GREENWICH

M **THE BRANT FOUNDATION ART STUDY CENTER,** 941 North St, Greenwich, CT 06831. Tel 203-869-0611; Email info@brantfoundation.org; Web: brantfoundation.org; *Dir* Allison Brant; *Assoc Dir* Zoe Larson
Open Mon - Fri 10 AM - 4 PM by appointment; No admis fee; Estab 2009 to promote education and appreciation of contemporary art & design by making works available to institutions & individuals for study & examination
Income: Financed by endowment
Collections: Works by emerging & estab contemporary artists
Activities: Classes for adults & children; numerous events & workshops; lects open to pub; gallery talks; tours; individual works of art lent

M **BRUCE MUSEUM, INC,** One Museum Dr, Greenwich, CT 06830-7100. Tel 203-869-0376; Fax 203-869-0963; Email info@brucemuseum.org; Web: brucemuseum.org; *Exec Dir* Peter C Sutton; *Deputy Dir* Susan Ball; *Cur Sci* Daniel Ksepka; *Dir Finance* Bill Ference; *Dir Exhibitions* Anne von Stuelpnagel; *Dir Institutional Advancement* Whitney Lucas Rosenberg
Open Tues - Sun 10 AM - 5 PM, cl Mon & major holidays; Admis adults $7, sr citizen & student $6, Tues free, mem & children under 5 free; Estab 1908 by Robert M Bruce. Expanded & completely renovated in 1992. Museum features changing exhibits in fine & decorative arts & natural sciences; Interdisciplinary shows in four galleries; small reference library for staff use only; Average Annual Attendance: 70,000; Mem: 2900; dues individual $60, student $35, senior $40, sr couple $60, family & dual $65, young friend $150, patron $250, benefactor $750, Robert Bruce Circle $2,000; annual meeting in June
Special Subjects: American Indian Art, Archaeology, Baroque Art, Carpets & Rugs, Cartoons, Ceramics, Costumes, Decorative Arts, Dioramas, Drawings, Etchings & Engravings, Ethnology, Landscapes, Maps, Marine Painting, Miniatures, Oriental Art, Painting-American, Painting-British, Painting-European, Painting-Flemish, Photography, Portraits, Pre-Columbian Art, Prints, Prints, Sculpture, Sculpture, Textiles
Collections: 19th & 20th century American paintings; costumes, North American Indian ethnology, Orientalia, American natural history, Major mineral collection, Photography; Works on paper; Decorative arts; Sculpture
Exhibitions: Changes in Our Land (ongoing)
Publications: Exhibition Catalogs, 3 per yr; calendar of events, newsletter, 4 per yr; e-newsletter, 50 per yr
Activities: Classes for adults & children; docent training; public progs; family days, films, performance art, mus outreach & afterschool progs; lects open to pub, 30-40 vis lectrs per yr; concerts; gallery talks; tours; festival awards; individual paintings & original objects of art lent to other mus; 30 mile radius - Brucemobile; originate 1-3 book traveling exhibs per yr; originate traveling exhibs; mus shop sells books, stationery & gifts; Seaside Center located at Greenwich Point Park (seasonal)

M **DAHESH MUSEUM OF ART,** 96 Lewis St, Greenwich, CT 06830-6631. Tel 212-759-0606; Fax 203-861-9634; Email info@daheshmuseum.org; Email museumshop@daheshmuseum.org; Web: www.daheshmuseum.org; *Dir* Flora Kaplan; *Pres* Mervat Zahid; *CFO* William Ignatowich; *VPres* Steven Simkin; *VPres, Sec & Treas* Amira Zahid
Estab 1987; Maintains reference library; Average Annual Attendance: 20,000
Special Subjects: Bronzes, Drawings, Etchings & Engravings, Graphics, Landscapes, Painting-British, Painting-European, Painting-French, Sculpture, Watercolors
Collections: European 19th & 20th Century Acad Art (paintings, sculpture & works on paper)
Publications: Dahesh Muse, newsletter 3 per year
Activities: Lects open to pub, 20 vis lectrs per yr; mus shop sells books, prints, reproductions, jewelry, figurines, stationery, educational toys & gifts

A **GREENWICH ART SOCIETY INC,** 299 Greenwich Ave, Greenwich, CT 06830-2501. Tel 203-629-1533; Fax 203-629-3414; Email admin@greenwichartsociety.org; Web: www.greenwichartsociety.org; *Co-VP Dir of Classes & Office Mgr* Mary Newcomb; *Pres & Co-VP Dir of Classes* Anna Patalano; *Co-Treas* Arnold Braff; *Admin Staff* Jill Foster
Open Office: 9:30 - 12:30 PM weekdays; Greenwich Art Society Gallery: weekdays 10 AM - 5 PM, Sat 12 - 4 PM, Sun 1 - 4 PM, except July & Aug; no admis fee; Estab 1912 as a nonprofit organization to further art educ & to awaken & stimulate broader interest in the visual arts in the town of Greenwich; Art Center studio is used for classes & Greenwich Art Society Gallery meetings & exhibitions; Mem: 350; dues regular $50, student 21 & under $25
Income: Financed by mem fees & contributions, classes tuitions
Library Holdings: Book Volumes

Exhibitions: Winter Exhibition: Bendheim Gallery, 299 Greenwich Ave, Greenwich, CT; Summer Exhibition: Flinn Gallery, Greenwich Library, 101 W Putnam Ave
Publications: The History of the Greenwich Art Society, booklet; bulletin of program for the year & class schedule
Activities: Day & evening classes for adults, special classes for children; critiques & demonstrations; lect open to public; art outreach progs to underserved students

M **Bendheim Gallery**, 299 Greenwich Ave, Greenwich, CT 06830-6504. Tel 203-862-6750; Fax 203-862-6753; Email info@greenwicharts.org; Web: www.greenwicharts.org/index.asp

L **GREENWICH LIBRARY,** 101 W Putnam Ave, Greenwich, CT 06830-5387. Tel 203-622-7900; Fax 203-622-7939; Web: www.greenwichlibrary.org; *Acting Dir* Barbara Ormerod-Glynn
Open Mon - Fri 9 AM - 9 PM, Sat 9 AM - 5 PM, Sun 1 - 5 PM Oct - May; Estab 1878 to provide free & convenient access to the broadest possible range of information & ideas; Circ 1,063,950; Hurlbutt Gallery features exhibits of paintings, prints, sculpture, photos, antiques & objects d'art, sponsored by Friends of the Greenwich Library
Income: $3,378,992 (financed by city appropriation)
Purchases: Art & Music $19,925, video $39,913, records & audio cassettes $46,285
Library Holdings: Book Volumes 313,824, Cassettes 6550, Framed Reproductions 326, Other Holdings Art related books 16,990; Compact discs 10,000, Periodical Subscriptions 600, Video Tapes 10,000
Collections: Book arts coll (fine press books)
Exhibitions: Six different exhibits per year
Publications: Monthly book lists
Activities: Lects open to pub, 3-5 vis lectrs per yr; individual paintings lent to Greenwich residents; lending collection contains approx 438 items

GROTON

M **ALEXEY VON SCHLIPPE GALLERY OF ART,** 1084 Shennecossett Rd, Groton, CT 06340-6097. *Dir & Cur* Julia Pavone

HAMDEN

L **PAIER COLLEGE OF ART, INC,** Library, 20 Gorham Ave, Hamden, CT 06514-3902. Tel 203-287-3031; Fax 203-287-3021; Email paier.admin@snet.net; Web: www.paiercollegeofart.edu; *Pres* Jonathan E Paier; *VPres* Daniel Paier; *Dir Library* Beth R Harris
Open Mon & Tues 11 AM-7 PM, Wed & Thurs 9 AM-5 PM, Fri 9 AM-Noon; No admis fee; Estab 1946, library estab 1978
Library Holdings: Book Volumes 11,600, Clipping Files, Exhibition Catalogs, Pamphlets, Periodical Subscriptions 68, Prints, Reproductions, Slides 16,000, Video Tapes 120
Special Subjects: Advertising Design, Architecture, Art History, Calligraphy, Commercial Art, Conceptual Art, Decorative Arts, Drawings, Folk Art, Graphic Arts, Graphic Design, History of Art & Archaeology, Illustration, Interior Design, Lettering
Collections: Children's books (400), Reference pictures (30,000)

HARTFORD

A **ARTISTS COLLECTIVE INC,** 1200 Albany Ave, Hartford, CT 06112-2104. Tel 860-527-3205; Fax 860-527-2979; Email info@artistscollective.org; Web: artistscollective.org; *Founding Exec Dir* Dollie McLean; *Founder* Jackie McLean
Admis fees for special performances vary, see website; Estab 1970
Income: $690,000
Activities: Classes for children; dramatic progs; workshops; concerts

M **CHARTER OAK CULTURAL CENTER,** 21 Charter Oak Ave, Hartford, CT 06106-1801. Tel 860-310-2588; Fax 860-524-8014; Email yashiras@charteroakcenter.org; Web: www.charteroakcenter.org; *Exec Dir* Rabbi Donna Berman; *CFO & Mng Dir* Rebecca Scorso; *Admin Coordr* Yashira Santiago
Open Tues - Fri 10 AM - 5 PM; No admis fee; Estab in the late 1970s to foster multicultural arts; Mem: dues $150-$1,000
Collections: Multicultural art
Exhibitions: Temporary exhibits
Activities: Arts programming; performance art

A **CONNECTICUT HISTORICAL SOCIETY,** 1 Elizabeth St, Hartford, CT 06105-2213. Tel 860-236-5621; Fax 860-236-2664; Email ask-us@chs.org; Web: www.chs.org; *CEO & Exec Dir* Jody Blankenship; *Chief Admin Officer* Kevin Hughes; *Chief Cur* Ilene Frank
Open Tues - Thurs noon - 5 PM; Fri - Sat 9 AM - 5 PM; Admis adults $8, seniors & students $6, children 5 & under $4, mems free, group discounts available; Estab 1825 to collect & preserve materials of Connecticut interest & to encourage interest in Connecticut history; Exhibition space totals 6500 sq ft, half of which is devoted to permanent exhibitions, the other half to changing exhibits; Average Annual Attendance: 43,000; Mem: 1200; dues $40 individual, $50 family; annual meeting in May
Income: Financed by endowment & mem
Library Holdings: Auction Catalogs, Audio Tapes, Book Volumes, CD-ROMs, Cards, Cassettes, Clipping Files, Compact Disks, DVDs, Exhibition Catalogs, Fiche, Filmstrips, Framed Reproductions, Kodachrome Transparencies, Lantern Slides, Manuscripts, Maps, Memorabilia, Micro Print, Motion Pictures, Original Art Works, Original Documents, Other Holdings, Pamphlets, Periodical Subscriptions, Photographs, Prints, Records, Reels, Reproductions, Sculpture, Slides, Video Tapes
Special Subjects: Decorative Arts, Furniture
Collections: Historical Collections, Frederick K & Margaret R Barbour Furniture Collection, George Dudley Seymour Collection of Furniture, Morgan P. Brainard Tavern Signs, costumes, textiles & housewares
Exhibitions: Making Connecticut; See website for changing exhibs
Publications: Newsletter: CHS Magazine, 3 times per year
Activities: Classes for adults & children, dramatic progs, docent training; lects open to pub, 12 vis lectrs per yr; gallery talks; tours; fels offered; lending collection contains books, original objects of art lent to qualified institutions; originate traveling exhibs; mus shop sells books, mags, reproductions, prints, various items made in CT

L **Library**, 1 Elizabeth St, Hartford, CT 06105-2213. Tel 860-236-5621; Fax 860-236-2664; Email education_assistant@chs.org; Web: www.chs.org; *Dir Exhibs & Colls* Andrea V Papacz; *Research & Colls Assoc* Tasha Caswell; *Research & Colls Assoc* Sierra Dixon; *Research & Colls Assoc* Molly Woods
Open Tues - Thurs noon - 5 PM; Sat 9 AM - 5 PM; Admis adults $33 (3 visits), seniors $27 (3 visits), students $27 (5 visits); 1825; 2 permanent galleries, 1 temporary gallery & library; Mem: 1200
Library Holdings: Book Volumes Monographs & Serials: 100,000, Manuscripts 3,000,000, Other Holdings Objects: 38,000; Graphics 240,000
Collections: Genealogical Research Collection
Activities: Docent training; lects open to pub, 10 vis lectrs per yr; gallery talks; tours

L **CONNECTICUT STATE LIBRARY,** Museum of Connecticut History, 231 Capitol Ave, Hartford, CT 06106-1548. Tel 860-757-6535; Fax 860-757-6521; Email dnelson@cslib.org; Web: www.cslib.org; *Cur* David J Corrigan; *Cur* Patrick Smith; *Mus Adminr* Dean Nelson
Open Mon - Fri 9 AM - 4 PM, Sat 9 AM - 2 PM, cl holidays; No admis fee; Estab 1910 to collect, preserve & display artifacts & memorabilia reflecting the history & heritage of Connecticut; For reference only; Average Annual Attendance: 21,000
Income: State funding
Library Holdings: Book Volumes 500,000, Cassettes, Clipping Files, Fiche 50,000, Manuscripts, Memorabilia, Motion Pictures, Original Art Works, Other Holdings Original documents 100,000,000, Pamphlets, Photographs, Prints, Reels, Video Tapes
Special Subjects: Coins & Medals
Collections: Collection of Firearms, Portraits of Connecticut's Governors, Connecticut Collection - Industrial & Military History
Exhibitions: Changing exhibits
Activities: Classes for children

L **HARRIET BEECHER STOWE CENTER,** 77 Forest St, Hartford, CT 06105-3296. Tel 860-522-9258; Fax 860-522-9259; Email info@stowecenter.org; Web: www.harrietbeecherstowecenter.org; *Exec Dir* Katherine Kane; *Project Cur* Cynthia Cormier; *Bus Mgr* Maria Agramonte-Gomez; *Colls Mgr* Elizabeth Burgess; *Dir Mktg* Vivian Nabeta; *Dir Educ & Visitor Servs* Shannon Burke; *Enterprise & Sales Mgr* Aqua Drakes
Open Mon - Sat 9:30 AM - 5 PM, Sun Noon - 5 PM, cl Columbus Day - Memorial Day; Admis adults $14, sr citizen $12, children $8, children under 5 free; Estab 1941 to maintain & open to the pub the restored Harriet Beecher Stowe House; The Foundation operates the Stowe Library, oversees a publishing program of reprints of H B Stowe's works & new books & provides workshops & lect; Average Annual Attendance: 22,000; Mem: 150; dues sustaining $150, supporting $50, family $30, individual $20; fall & spring meetings
Library Holdings: Book Volumes, Clipping Files, Exhibition Catalogs, Framed Reproductions, Lantern Slides, Manuscripts, Original Art Works, Pamphlets, Periodical Subscriptions, Photographs
Special Subjects: Architecture, Graphic Arts, Historical Material, Manuscripts, Painting-American, Period Rooms, Watercolors
Collections: 19th Century Decorative Arts, Domestic Furnishing, Fine Arts, Wallpaper & Floor Treatment Sample Collections
Exhibitions: A Moral Battle Cry for Freedom: Uncle Tom's Cabin (ongoing); Reforming the Season: Christmas & 19th Century Reformer (annually-Dec)
Publications: The Journal newsletter, quarterly
Activities: Workshops for adults & teachers; educ prog; docent training; Teachers Institute; lects open to pub; concerts; 1-2 vis lectrs per yr; gallery talks; tours; Stowe Prize & Stowe Student Prize; paintings & original decorative, domestic or fine art objects lent to institutions; mus shop sells books, reproductions, prints, slides, fabrics, Victorian gift items & garden materials

L **Library**, 77 Forest St, Hartford, CT 06105. Tel 860-522-9258; Fax 860-522-9259; Email info@stowecenter.org; Web: www.harrietbeecherstowecenter.org; *Exec Dir* Katherine Kane; *Educ & Visitor Svcs* Shannon Burke
Open Sun noon - 5 PM, Mon - Sat 9:30 AM - 5 PM; Admis adults $14, seniors & students $12, children (5-16) $8; library free by appointment; Estab 1941 to concentrate on the architecture, decorative arts, history & literature of the United States in the 19th century emphasizing a Hartford neighborhood known as Nook Farm, and the Beecher/Stowe families; Circ Non-circulating; Reference only for gen pub, students, staff & academia; Average Annual Attendance: 24,000
Library Holdings: Book Volumes 15,000, Clipping Files, Exhibition Catalogs, Fiche, Lantern Slides 60, Manuscripts, Maps, Memorabilia, Original Art Works, Original Documents, Other Holdings Original documents 160,000, Pamphlets 5000, Periodical Subscriptions, Photographs 5000, Prints, Reels 100, Sculpture, Slides 3500
Special Subjects: Architecture, Decorative Arts, Furniture, Historical Material, Landscape Architecture, Photography, Restoration & Conservation, Textiles
Collections: Architecture & Decorative Arts of 19th Century: books, plans, drawings, trade catalogs, Hartford 19th Century Literary Community, Nook Farm & Residents, Mark Twain, Harriet Beecher Stowe, Chas Dudley Warner, William Gillette, letters & documents of the Stowe family, Stowe family artifacts, 19th-Century artwork, Uncle Tom's Cabin memorabilia
Activities: Programs for adults & children; lects open to pub & for members only; concerts; book club; gallery talks; tours; sponsoring of competitions; Stowe Prize for books; mus shop sells books, magazines, reproductions & prints

M **MARK TWAIN HOUSE MEMORIAL,** 351 Farmington Ave, Hartford, CT 06105-4401. Tel 860-247-0998 (admin office), 247-0998 ext 26 (visitor center); Fax 860-278-8148; Email info@marktwainhouse.org; Web: www.marktwainhouse.org; *Exec Dir* Pieter Roos; *Chief Cur* Tracy Brindle
Open Mon - Sun 9:30 AM - 5:30 PM, first Thurs of the month 9:30 AM - 8 PM, cl Tues Jan - Apr; Admis adults $20, seniors $18, children 6-16 $12, children under 6

free; Estab 1929 to foster an appreciation of the legacy of Mark Twain as one of our nation's culturally defining figures; to demonstrate the continuing relevance of his work, life & times; Maintains Historic House Mus with period interiors, mus room of memorabilia. National Historic Landmark status, US Dept of Interior; Average Annual Attendance: 65,000; Mem: 900; dues $35-$5000; annual meeting in Nov
Income: financed by members, donations, admis fees
Special Subjects: Ceramics, Decorative Arts, Furniture, Glass, Painting-American, Period Rooms, Photography, Sculpture, Silver, Stained Glass, Textiles, Woodcarvings
Collections: Mark Twain memorabilia (photographs, manuscripts), period & original furnishings, Tiffany Glass Collection, Lockwood deForest Collection, Candace Wheeler Collection
Exhibitions: National Symposia; Rotating exhibits; Orientation exhibitions
Publications: Exhibition catalogues
Activities: Classes for adults & children; symposia; internship progs; docent training; lects open to pub, 6 vis lectrs per yr; concerts; gallery talks; tours; college internships offered; individual paintings & original objects of art lent to approved mus & organizations; lending collection contains books, color reproductions, prints, paintings, photographs, sculpture & slides; mus shop sells books, reproductions, prints, slides, gifts & Mark Twain memorabilia

L **Research Library**, 351 Farmington Ave, Hartford, CT 06105. Tel 860-247-0998 (admin office); Fax 860-278-8148; Web: www.marktwainhouse.org; *Chief Cur* Tracy Brindle; *Asst Cur* Mallory Howard
Open Mon - Fri 9:30 AM - 4 PM; For reference only
Library Holdings: Auction Catalogs, Audio Tapes, Book Volumes 6000, CD-ROMs, Cassettes, Clipping Files, Exhibition Catalogs, Fiche, Filmstrips, Framed Reproductions, Lantern Slides, Manuscripts, Memorabilia, Motion Pictures, Original Art Works, Original Documents, Other Holdings, Pamphlets, Periodical Subscriptions 22, Photographs, Records, Reels, Reproductions, Sculpture, Slides, Video Tapes

M **OLD STATE HOUSE,** 800 Main St, Hartford, CT 06103-2301. Tel 860-522-6766; Fax 860-522-2812; Email info@shareCT.org; Web: www.cga.ct.gov; *Exec Dir* Sally Whipple; *Head Educ* Brian Cofrancesco; *Coord Visitor Servs* Renee Goldstein; *Mktg Mgr* Chris Zaccaro
Open Mon - Fri 10 AM - 5 PM; Admis general $6, students $3, seniors & Children $3, children under 6, active military & veterans free; Estab 1975 to preserve oldest state house in the nation & present variety of exhibitions on historic & contemporary subjects; Former exec wing is used for exhibitions of contemporary artists & craftsmen, paintings, decorative arts on a rotating basis; Average Annual Attendance: 200,000; Mem: 1500; dues life $1000, family $15, individual $10; annual meeting in the fall
Income: Financed by endowment, mem & appeals
Collections: Connecticut portraits, documents, Restored Senate Chamber
Activities: Educ dept; classes for adults & children; dramatic progs; lects open to pub, 25 vis lectrs per yr; concerts; gallery talks; tours; individual paintings & original objects of art lent to mus for special exhibs; mus shop sells books, magazines, original art, reproductions, prints, slides, Connecticut arts & crafts

M **REAL ART WAYS (RAW),** 56 Arbor St, Hartford, CT 06106-1222. Tel 860-232-1006; Fax 860-233-6691; Email info@realartways.org; Web: www.realartways.org; *Exec Dir* Will K Wilkins; *Visual Arts Coordr* Neil Daigle-Orians; *Mem Coordr* Paige Usher-Rankin
Open daily 2 PM - 9 PM; Admis suggested donation; Estab 1975 to present artists of many disciplines working at the forefront of creative activity in their respective fields; 1 fl; Mem: Annual dues vary
Income: Financed by mem and donations
Special Subjects: Photography, Prints, Sculpture
Collections: Contemporary Art
Exhibitions: Rotating exhibitions
Activities: Classes for children, summer art workshop; lects open to pub, 5 vis lectrs per yr; concerts; gallery talks; tours; book traveling exhibs 2 per yr; originate traveling exhibs to qualified institutions

M **TRINITY COLLEGE,** Austin Arts Center, Widener Gallery, 300 Summit St, Hartford, CT 06106-3186. Tel 860-297-2199; Fax 860-297-5380; Email austinartsinfo@trincoll.edu; Web: www.trincoll.edu/depts/aac/; *Cur* Felice Caivano
Open daily 1 PM - 6 PM, cl Sun; No admis fee; Estab 1965; A building housing the teaching & performing aspects of music, theater dance & studio arts at a liberal arts college. Widener Gallery provides exhibition space mainly for student & faculty works, plus outside exhibitions; Average Annual Attendance: 12,000
Income: Financed by college appropriation
Collections: Edwin M Blake Memorial & Archive, College Collection, Samuel H Kress Study Collection, George Chaplin Collection, George F McMurray Collection
Exhibitions: Rotating exhibitions
Activities: Classes for adults; dramatic progs; lects open to pub, 6-8 vis lectrs per yr; concerts; lending collection contains 500 original art works & 100,000 slides

M **WADSWORTH ATHENEUM MUSEUM OF ART,** 600 Main St, Hartford, CT 06103-2990. Tel 860-278-2670; Fax 860-527-0803; Email info@wadsworthatheneum.org; Web: www.thewadsworth.org; *Dir & CEO* Thomas J Laughman; *Cur Contemporary Art* Patricia Hickson; *Cur European Decorate Arts* Linda Roth; *Assoc Cur American Paintings & Sculpture* Erin Monroe; *Cur Film & Theater* Deborah Gaudet; *Chief Conservator* Ulrich Birkmaier; *CFO* Cindy Martinez; *Head Mus Design* Cecil Adams; *Dir Mktg* Kim Hugo; *Interim Dir Develop* Nancy S Harvin; *Dir Educ* Anne Rice
Open Wed - Fri 11 AM - 5 PM, Sat - Sun 10 AM - 5 PM, cl Mon & Tues; Admis $15 adults, $12 seniors 62 & up, $5 students (18+ w/ID) $5; free children 17 & under; free for Hartford Residents; Estab 1842 by Daniel Wadsworth; Collections comprise more than 50,000 works of European and American fine and decorative arts. Highlights include Hudson River School landscapes, 17th century American furniture, European baroque paintings, French & German porcelain, French & American impressionists, modern & contemporary masters & African American art & history; Average Annual Attendance: 140,000; Mem: 6,000; dues $45 & up; annual meeting in Nov
Income: Financed by private funds
Library Holdings: Auction Catalogs, Audio Tapes, Book Volumes, CD-ROMs, Cassettes, Clipping Files, Compact Disks, DVDs, Exhibition Catalogs, Manuscripts, Other Holdings, Pamphlets, Periodical Subscriptions, Slides, Video Tapes
Special Subjects: African Art, Afro-American Art, American Indian Art, Archaeology, Architecture, Baroque Art, Ceramics, Costumes, Crafts, Decorative Arts, Drawings, Embroidery, Furniture, Jewelry, Laces, Latin American Art, Maps, Mosaics, Painting-American, Painting-Australian, Painting-British, Painting-Canadian, Painting-Dutch, Painting-European, Painting-Flemish, Painting-French, Painting-German, Painting-Israeli, Painting-Italian, Porcelain, Prints, Sculpture, Silver, Stained Glass, Textiles, Woodcarvings, Woodcuts
Publications: Newsletter, quarterly to members; collections and exhibitions catalogs
Activities: Docent training; workshops for families & adults; free community events; lects & gallery talks; lects open to pub; concerts; gallery tours; outside lect; members' exhibition previews & various special events; seminars; schols & fels; lending original objects of art to other mus; mus shop sells books, reproductions, prints, photographs, cards, toys, accessories & gifts; cafe

L **Auerbach Art Library**, 600 Main St, Hartford, CT 06103-2990. Tel 860-838-4115; Fax 203-527-0803; Email amy.kilkenny@wadsworthatheneum.org; *Head Library & Archives* Amy Kilkenny
Open Wed & Thurs 11 AM - 5 PM, cl Tues & Fri; Estab 1934 as a reference service to the mus staff, members & pub; to provide materials supporting work with mus collection; For reference only
Library Holdings: Auction Catalogs, Book Volumes 49,000, Clipping Files, Exhibition Catalogs, Fiche, Lantern Slides, Pamphlets, Periodical Subscriptions 150, Records, Reels
Special Subjects: Afro-American Art, American Indian Art, Archaeology, Architecture, Art Education, Art History, Asian Art, Ceramics, Conceptual Art, Costume Design & Constr, Crafts, Decorative Arts, Embroidery, Enamels, Etchings & Engravings, Fashion Arts, Film, Furniture, Graphic Arts, Handicrafts, Historical Material, History of Art & Archaeology, Illustration, Industrial Design, Jewelry, Painting-American, Painting-Australian, Painting-British, Painting-Canadian, Painting-Dutch, Painting-European, Painting-Flemish, Painting-French, Painting-German, Painting-Italian, Painting-Russian, Painting-Spanish, Silver
Collections: Sol Lewitt (contemporary art), Elizabeth Miles (English silver), Watkinson Collection (pre-1917 art reference)

KENT

M **DEPARTMENT OF ECONOMIC & COMMUNITY DEVELOPMENT,** State of Connecticut DECD Eric Sloane Museum, Route 7, 31 Kent-Cornwall Rd. Kent, CT 06757; PO Box 917, Kent, CT 06757-0917. Tel 860-927-3849; Fax 860-927-2152; Email ericsloane.museum@ct.gov; Web: www.cultureandtourism.org; *Dir Mus* Karin Peterson; *Mus Asst* Barbara Russ; *Deputy Commissioner* Christopher (Kip) Bergstrom
Check website for hrs; Admis adults $8, sr citizens $6, children $5; Estab 1969 to collect, preserve, exhibit historic American tools, implements & artwork of Eric Sloane (1905-1985); Artists re-created studio & display gallery; Average Annual Attendance: 5,000
Income: Financed by state appropriation
Special Subjects: Archaeology, Dioramas, Historical Material, Landscapes, Painting-American, Portraits, Posters, Painting-American
Collections: Eric Sloane Collection (artwork), American tools & implements, Sloane's Studio
Activities: Lects open to pub; 1-2 vis lectrs per yr; gallery talks; sales shop sells books, prints & gifts

A **KENT ART ASSOCIATION,** Gallery, 21 S Main St, Kent, CT 06757; PO Box 202, Kent, CT 06757-0202. Tel 860-927-3989; Fax 860-927-4218; Email info@kentart.org; Web: www.kentart.org; *VPres* Will Kefauver; *Second VPres* Ruth Newquist; *Treas* Beth Dooley; *Pres* Carolyn Fisher
Open during exhibitions Thurs - Sun; No admis fee; Estab 1923, incorporated 1935; Maintains gallery for changing exhibitions; Average Annual Attendance: 2,000; Mem: 400; dues life $200, patron $40, sustaining $25, assoc $15; annual meeting in Oct; qualifications for mem open
Income: Financed by mem, donations
Exhibitions: Spring Show; Member's Show; President's Show; Elected Artist Show
Publications: Exhibition catalogues, 4 per year
Activities: Lect; demonstrations

LITCHFIELD

A **LITCHFIELD HISTORY MUSEUM,** 7 South St, Litchfield, CT 06759-4005; PO Box 385, Litchfield, CT 06759-0385. Tel 860-567-4501; Fax 860-567-3565; Email cfields@litchfieldhistoricalsociety.org; Web: www.litchfieldhistoricalsociety.org/museum.html; *Cur* Judith Loto; *Educ Coordr* Rebecca Martin; *Dir* Catherine Keene Fields
Open mid Apr - Nov Tues - Sat 11 AM - 5 PM, Sun 1 - 5 PM; Admis $5, children under 14 free; seniors & children 6 & over $3; Estab 1896, incorporated 1897 for the preservation & interpretation of local historical collections; A gallery of portraits by Ralph Earl is maintained; Average Annual Attendance: 12,000; Mem: 450; dues benefactor $500, donor $250, contributing $100, family $40, individual $25; annual meeting second Fri in Sept
Income: $220,000 (financed by endowment, mem & fundraising)
Special Subjects: Costumes, Decorative Arts, Embroidery, Folk Art, Furniture
Collections: American & Connecticut fine & decorative arts, pewter, costumes, textiles, paintings, silver, pottery & graphics, furniture, textiles, household goods
Exhibitions: Changing exhibitions on area art & history
Activities: Classes for adults & children; docent training; curriculum units; workshops; lects open to pub, 4 vis lectrs per yr; gallery talks; tours; individual & original objects of art lent to accredited mus with board approval; sales shop sells books, reproductions & prints

L **Ingraham Memorial Research Library**, 7 South St, Litchfield, CT 06759-4005; PO Box 385, Litchfield, CT 06759-0385. Tel 860-567-4501; Fax 860-567-3565; Web: w.litchfieldhistory.org; *Dir* Catherine Keene Fields

Open Tues - Fri 10 AM - Noon & 1 - 4 PM, 1 Sat a month; No admis fee; Estab 1896 as a center of local history & genealogy study; Reference only; Mem: Same as society
Income: $10,000 (financed by endowment & mem)
Library Holdings: Book Volumes 10,000, Clipping Files, Exhibition Catalogs, Manuscripts, Memorabilia, Other Holdings Original documents 50,000, Pamphlets, Periodical Subscriptions 10, Photographs, Prints, Reels
Collections: 40,000 manuscripts in local history
Exhibitions: Several rotating exhibitions per year

MERIDEN

A **ARTS & CRAFTS ASSOCIATION OF MERIDEN INC,** Gallery 53, 53 Colony St, Meriden, CT 06451-3210. Tel 203-235-5347; Email info@gallery53.org; Web: www.gallery53.org
Open Tues - Fri Noon - 4 PM, Sat 10 AM - 2 PM; No admis fee; Estab 1907 to encourage appreciation of the arts in the community; One floor gallery to hold exhibits & art work studios above with meeting room; Average Annual Attendance: 1,800; Mem: 300; dues $35 & up; annual meeting in June
Income: Financed by mem & fund raising, class fees
Collections: Permanent collection of paintings & sculptures includes works by Eric Sloan, Emile Gruppe, Stow Wengenroth as well as works by Meriden artists
Exhibitions: Annual Members Show; Photography Show; Student Show; One man & group shows; theme shows & alternating exhibits of works from permanent collection
Activities: Classes for adults & children; dramatic progs; lects open to pub, 8 vis lectrs per yr; workshops; gallery talks; tours; competitions with awards; schols offered; individual paintings & original objects of art lent to banks & public buildings; originate traveling exhibs; sales shop sells original art & crafts

L **Gallery 53**, 53 Colony St, Meriden, CT 06451-0348. Tel 203-235-5347; Fax 203-866-0015; Email gallary53ct@gmail.com; Web: www.gallery53.org; *Pres* Laura LeClair; *VPres* Christine Webster; *Gallery Dir* Rita Sarris
Open Tues - Fri Noon - 4 PM, Sat 10 AM - 2 PM; No admis fee; Estab 1907 to promote the arts; Gallery changes exhibits every 4 wks approx; shows work of art groups, individual painters, photographers, school students; permanent collection of paintings
Income: Non-profit
Library Holdings: Book Volumes 650
Collections: Indiana Thomas Book Collection
Activities: Educ prog; classes for adults & children; gallery talks; schols offered; sales shop sells original art, prints, pottery, jewelry, accessories

MIDDLETOWN

M **WESLEYAN UNIVERSITY,** Davison Art Center, 301 High St, Middletown, CT 06459-3232. Tel 860-685-2500; Fax 860-685-2501; Web: www.wesleyan.edu/dac; *Cur* Clare Rogan
Open Tues - Sun 12 - 4 PM; No admis fee; Part of the collection was presented to Wesleyan University by George W & Harriet B Davison. Since 1952 the collection with its reference library has been housed in an addition to the historic Alsop House; collection of works on paper; rotating exhibitions
Special Subjects: Drawings, Etchings & Engravings, Photography, Prints, Woodcuts
Collections: The print collection, extending from the 15th century to present day, includes Master E S, Nielli, Mantegna, Pollaiuolo, Durer, Cranach, Rembrandt, Canaletto, Piranesi, Goya, Millet, Meryon, Jim Dine, & others, Japanese & contemporary American prints, 1840s to present, photographs
Exhibitions: Regularly changing exhibitions of prints, drawings, photographs & other works on paper
Publications: Exhibition catalogues
Activities: Lects open to public, gallery talks; tours; collection contains 25,000 original prints, drawings & photographs; originates traveling exhibs

L **OLIN Memorial Library**, 252 Church St, Middletown, CT 06459. Tel 860-685-3326; *Art Librn* Susanne Javorski
Open Mon - Thurs 8:30 AM - 2 PM, Fri 8:30 AM - 11 PM, Sat 10 AM - 10 PM, Sun 10 AM - 2 AM; Estab 1950 as research/reference coll primarily supporting university courses in art history & studio arts
Library Holdings: Book Volumes 50,000, Periodical Subscriptions 125
Collections: Print Reference Collection (books pertaining to the history of the graphic arts)

A **Friends of the Davison Art Center**, 301 High St, Middletown, CT 06459-0487. Tel 860-685-2500; Fax 203-685-2501; *Pres* Mariah Klaneski Reisner
Estab 1961 for the support & augmentation of the activities & acquisition fund of the Davison Art Center by its members
Income: Financed by mem dues & contributions
Purchases: Photographs, Prints
Activities: Gallery talks

M **Ezra & Cecile Zilkha Gallery**, Ctr for the Arts, Middletown, CT 06459-0001. Tel 860-685-2695; Fax 860-685-2061; Web: www.wesleyan.edu/cfalzilkha/home.html; *Cur Exhib* Nina Felshin
Open Tues - Sun Noon - 4 PM, cl Mon & acad vacations; No admis fee; Estab 1973 to exhibit contemporary art; Exhibitions of contemporary art; Average Annual Attendance: 15,000
Income: Financed by contributions
Exhibitions: Changing exhibitions of contemporary art
Publications: Exhibition catalogs & brochures
Activities: Educ Dept; lects open to public, 6 vis lectrs per yr; gallery talks; tours; sales shop sells catalogs

MYSTIC

A **MYSTIC ART ASSOCIATION, INC,** Mystic Museum of Art, 9 Water St, Mystic, CT 06355-2592. Tel 860-536-7601; Fax 860-536-0610; Web: www.mysticmuseumofart.org; *Pres* Alex Bancroft; *Treas* Michele Kirk; *Exec Dir* George G King; *Secy* David Madacs; *Corp Rels & Events Mgr* Andrea Frickman; *Deputy Dir Pub Engagement & Opers* Dawn Salerno; *Dir Finance* Judith Flora; *Asst to the Dir & Exhibs Coordr* Erika Neenan; *Graphic Designer* James Kaczman; *Facilities Mgr* Tony Saccone
Open Jan - April Tues - Sun 11 AM - 5 PM; May - Dec daily 11 AM - 5 PM; No admis fee; $3 suggested donation, children & members free; Estab 1913 to maintain an art mus to promote cultural educ, local philanthropic & charitable interests; The assoc owns a historic building on the bank of Mystic River with spacious grounds; five galleries, handicap access, air conditioned, new educational wing opened Spring of 1999; Average Annual Attendance: 20,000; Mem: 1000, artist mem must have high standards of proficiency & be juried in four shows; dues active $40; meeting held in Apr
Income: Financed by mem, grants & leases
Collections: Mystic Art Colony Paintings, including artwork by Charles Harold Davis, Henry Ward Ranger & Robert Brackman, Mystic Art Colony Collection
Exhibitions: Juried Members' Show (all media); Annual Regional (all media)
Publications: News Views, monthly
Activities: Classes for adults & children; international workshop; photography lab; lects open to pub, 2 vis lectrs per yr; concerts; gallery talks; tours; competitions with awards; juried shows; curated exhibs; scholarships offered; exten dept serves New London County; individual paintings & original objects of art lent to historical societies & museums; New London County; sales shop sells original art & prints

NEW BRITAIN

M **CENTRAL CONNECTICUT STATE UNIVERSITY,** Art Dept Museum, 1615 Stanley St, New Britain, CT 06050-2439. Tel 860-832-2633; Fax 860-832-2634; Email ro-mimi.gallery@hotmail.com; Web: www.art.ccsu.edu
Open Mon-Wed 1-4PM, Thus 1-7PM; No admis fee; Estab to collect, display & interpret works of art & ethnic materials relating to the art educ program; Center will be constructed within two years & collection will be on display in center, whole collection will not be on permanent display
Income: Financed by the univ
Exhibitions: Changing exhibitions every month
Activities: Lect open to public; gallery talks

M **NEW BRITAIN MUSEUM OF AMERICAN ART,** 56 Lexington St, New Britain, CT 06052-1412. Tel 860-229-0257; Fax 860-229-3445; Email nbmaa@nbmaa.org; Web: www.nbmaa.org; *Dir & CEO* Min Jung Kim; *Assoc Dir Develop* Amanda Shuman; *Dir Finance & HR* Tom Bell; *Collections Mgr* Keith Gervase; *Mgr Facility & Security* Paul Grzyb; *Mgr Visitor & Volunteer Experience* Kaitlyn M. Way
Open Sun - Wed & Fri 11 AM - 5 PM, Thurs 11 AM - 8 PM, Sat 10 AM - 5 PM; Admis adults $15, sr citizens $12, students $10, children under 12 & Sat 10 AM - noon no charge; Estab 1903 to exhibit, collect & preserve American art; 43,000 sq ft Chase Family Bldg, plus 17,346 sq ft addition: 22 galleries, 3 art studios, auditorium/multi purpose space; state-of-the-art collections storage, HVAC & security systems; cafe & terrace, mus shop & 105 off-st parking spaces. 10,000 sq ft Landers House: hands-on space called ArtLab for Pre-K through grade 5, library & admin offices; Average Annual Attendance: 90,000; Mem: 5,221; dues Chairman's Circle $10,000, Director's Circle $5,000, Leadership Circle $2,500, American Art Circle $1,000, Collector's Circle $500, Artist's Circle $250, Friends Circle $100, Household $80, Household Senior $75, Individual $50, Individual Senior $45, student/educator $40; ann mtg in mid-Oct
Income: Financed by contributions, grants, sponsorships, earned income (admis prog fees, shop revenue, facility rental, exhib loan fees) & endowment
Purchases: Purchases art objects for the collection
Library Holdings: Exhibition Catalogs, Original Art Works, Photographs, Prints, Sculpture
Special Subjects: Afro-American Art, American Indian Art, American Western Art, Bronzes, Cartoons, Ceramics, Collages, Drawings, Etchings & Engravings, Jewelry, Landscapes, Marine Painting, Painting-American, Photography, Porcelain, Portraits, Posters, Prints, Sculpture, Watercolors, Woodcuts
Collections: American Art, Colonial & Federal Portraits, 19th Century Still-Life, American Impressionists, 20th Century Art, The Eight, Social Realists & Early Moderns, Stieglitz Group, Precisionists, Geometric Abstraction, Surrealism, Abstract Expressionism, Pop Art, Photo-Realism, Super Realism & Op Art, Thomas Hart Benton's The Arts of Life in America, Illustration & New Media, Shaker Art
Exhibitions: 15-20 changing exhibs per yr, in addition to the display of the permanent collection
Publications: Newsletter, quarterly; calendar, quarterly; annual report; New Britain Museum of American Art: Highlights of the Collection: Volume I; New Britain Museum of American Art: Highlights of the Collection: Volume II; New Britain Museum of American Art: Highlights of the Collection: Volume III; The Sanford B. D. Law Memorial Illustration Collection; Exhibs catalogues & brochures
Activities: Educ dept; docent training; classes for adults & children; lects open to pub, concerts; gallery talks; tours; teacher workshops; sponsor competitions; original objects of art lent to other mus; originates traveling exhibs; mus shop selling books, original art, reproductions, prints, slides & postcards & gifts

NEW CANAAN

M **NEW CANAAN HISTORICAL SOCIETY,** 13 Oenoke Ridge, New Canaan, CT 06840. Tel 203-966-1776; Fax 203-972-5917; Email newcanaan.historica@gmail.com; Web: www.nchistory.org; *Exec Dir* Janet Lindstrom; *Assistant* Michael Murphy; *Assistant* Donna Dearth
Open Town House & Library: Tues - Fri 9:30 AM - 4:30 PM, Sat 9:30 AM - 12:30 PM; Restored Museums: by appointment; Admis by suggested donation, $5; Estab 1889 to bring together & arrange historical events & genealogies, collect relics, form a museum & library; Society consists of seven museums & library. Rogers' studio contains sculpture groups by John Rogers. Exhibit room houses changing displays of costumes, photos & paintings; Average Annual Attendance: 5,000; Mem: 800; dues family $50, individual $40; meetings second Mon in Mar, June, Sept, Dec
Income: Financed by mem & contributions

Library Holdings: Audio Tapes, Book Volumes, Clipping Files, Fiche, Manuscripts, Maps, Original Art Works, Original Documents, Photographs, Slides, Video Tapes
Special Subjects: Costumes, Decorative Arts, Dolls, Flasks & Bottles, Historical Material, Landscape Architecture, Manuscripts, Maps, Painting-American, Period Rooms, Pewter, Portraits, Scrimshaw, Sculpture, Textiles, Architecture
Collections: Costume coll, including fans, purses & shoes, document colls, pewter, period furniture, photo coll, Rogers' sculpture groups, quilts, paintings, house files
Exhibitions: Costume & History; permanent exhibition of Rogers' sculptures; changing exhibits of art by Silvermine artists; Costume exhibits (changing)
Publications: New Canaan Historical Society Annual; Philip Johnson in New Canaan; John Rogers (1829-1904) & the Rogers Groups by John Rogers (1945-present); Portrait of New Cannan; New Cannan: Texture of a Community; other titles upon request
Activities: Seminars; children's classes; docent training; summer camp; lects open to pub, 4-6 vis lectrs per yr; concerts, tours; Bayles Award (summer interim) Award to New Canaan High School Junior for outstanding achievement in history; mus sells New Canaan Historical Society Annual, Christmas ornaments, maps, postcards & stationery

L **NEW CANAAN LIBRARY,** H. Pelham Curtis Gallery, 151 Main St, New Canaan, CT 06840-5514. Tel 203-594-5000; Fax 203-594-5026; Email reference@newcanaanlibrary.org; Web: www.newcanaanlibrary.org; *Dir* David Bryant; *Chair Art Comt* Suzanne Salomon
Open Mon - Thurs 9 AM - 8 PM, Fri & Sat 9 AM - 5 PM, Sun Noon - 5 PM except summer; Estab 1877; H. Pelham Curtis Gallery organizes 8 shows per year; Average Annual Attendance: 2,000; Mem: Art Comt - 20 members, no dues, 1st Thursday each month
Income: $1,293,000 (financed by mem, city & state appropriation)
Library Holdings: Audio Tapes, Book Volumes 146,000, CD-ROMs, DVDs, Other Holdings Audio & Video tapes 7338, Periodical Subscriptions 407
Special Subjects: Crafts, Landscape Architecture, Oriental Art, Painting-American, Painting-European, Painting-Japanese, Photography, Sculpture, Video
Collections: Alfandari Collection-European from fall of Rome to Impressionism, Chinese-Japanese art, general collection of art books & videos
Activities: Lectrs open to the public, 2 visiting lectrs per year, concerts, exhibit-related classes for children

M **PHILIP JOHNSON GLASS HOUSE, NATIONAL TRUST FOR HISTORIC PRESERVATION,** 199 Elm St, Visitor Center New Canaan, CT 06840. Tel 203-594-9884; Fax 203-594-9885; Web: www.philipjohnsonglasshouse.org; *Cur & Colls Mgr* Irene Shum Allen
Open for Tours May-Nov, Wed-Mon; Admis rates for tours vary, see website; Estab 2007. Not recommended for children under 10
Library Holdings: Auction Catalogs, Audio Tapes, Book Volumes, Compact Disks, DVDs, Maps, Memorabilia, Other Holdings, Photographs, Records, Slides, Video Tapes
Special Subjects: Architecture, Landscapes
Collections: Architecture (modern), Fine Art (Modern & Contemporary), Furniture & Design (Modern & Contemporary), Library & Archives
Publications: Pairings (2007); Glan House (Anonline 2008); Modern Views (Anonline 2010)
Activities: Educ prog; outgoing loan prog; publication prog; mus shop sells books, prints, & other items

M **SILVERMINE ARTS CENTER,** Silvermine Galleries, 1037 Silvermine Rd, New Canaan, CT 06840-4398. Tel 203-966-5617, ext 20; Fax 203-972-7236; Email sacgallery@silvermineart.org; Web: www.silvermineart.org; *Dir of Operations* Barbara Lianarducci; *Dir School* Anne Connell; *Gallery Dir* Jeffrey Mueller; *Gallery Manager* Jennifer Burbank
Open Tues - Sat 11 AM - 5 PM, Sun 1 - 5 PM, Mon by appointment; No admis fee, suggested donation $2; Estab 1922, incorporated 1924 as an independent art center to foster, promote & encourage activities in the arts & art educ; to provide a place for member artists & invited artists to show & sell their work; to offer the community a wide variety of artistic, cultural & educational activities; Five exhibition galleries featuring one-person shows, regional & national juried artists; Average Annual Attendance: 20,000; Mem: 300; mems juried in by a panel of guild artists; dues $150 & up
Income: Financed by mem, sale of art, contributions & tuitions
Collections: Permanent print collection containing purchase prizes from International Print Exhibition
Exhibitions: Rotating exhibits every 5-6 weeks
Publications: Exhibition catalogs; member newsletter, quarterly
Activities: Classes for adults & children; workshops; outreach education;; lects open to pub, 10 vis lectrs per yr; concerts; gallery talks; tours; competitions with awards; scholarships offered; individual paintings & original objects of art lent to corporations & banks; lending collection contains books & original prints; originate traveling exhibs; mus shop sells books, ceramics, jewelry; prints

NEW HAVEN

M **KNIGHTS OF COLUMBUS SUPREME COUNCIL,** Knights of Columbus Museum, 1 State St, New Haven, CT 06511-6702. Tel 203-865-0400; Fax 203-865-0351; Web: www.kofcmuseum.org; *Dir* Kathryn Cogan; *Cur & Registrar* Bethany Sheffer; *Archivist* Vivian Lea Solek; *Gift Shop Mgr* Olga Lapaeva
Open daily 10 AM - 5 PM; cl Good Friday, Holy Saturday, Easter, Thanksgiving, Christmas Eve & Day; No admis fee; Estab 1982 as a corporate history museum revealing the history & activities of the Knights of Columbus; 77,000 sq ft bldg; 170 ft wall of history; Average Annual Attendance: 50,000
Special Subjects: Baroque Art, Bronzes, Ceramics, Coins & Medals, Costumes, Decorative Arts, Dioramas, Embroidery, Folk Art, Furniture, Glass, Graphics, Ivory, Latin American Art, Manuscripts, Maps, Mexican Art, Mosaics, Painting-American, Painting-Canadian, Painting-Dutch, Painting-European, Painting-Italian, Painting-Polish, Painting-Russian, Porcelain, Posters, Prints, Religious Art, Renaissance Art, Reproductions, Sculpture, Silver, Stained Glass, Textiles, Woodcarvings, Watercolors
Collections: Fine & decorative arts, Fine Arts, Colonial Mexican Art
Exhibitions: Christopher Columbus; Founder Father Michael J McGivney; gifts & items from Knights of Columbus state & local councils; Knights of Columbus War Activities; Tributes (interactions with the Catholic Church & the Vatican); rotating loan exhibits; Three loan exhibits per yr
Publications: Postcards; museum tour brochures; posters; exhib catalog
Activities: Lect open to the public; Christmas tree festival for children; 1 - 2 vis lectrs per yr; gallery talks; tours; Christmas tree festival prizes; corporate archives research history of Knights of Columbus; individual paintings & original objects of art lent under special arrangements & careful consideration; mus shop sells books, original art, reproductions, prints, religious items, medals, tapes, videos & jewelry

M **NEW HAVEN MUSEUM,** Whitney Library, 114 Whitney Ave, New Haven, CT 06510-1238. Tel 203-562-4183; Fax 203-562-2002; Email Info@newhavenmuseum.org; Web: www.newhavenmuseum.org; *Exec Dir* Margaret Anne Tockarshewsky
Open Tues - Fri 10 AM - 5 PM, Sat noon - 5 PM, cl Mon & major holidays; Admis adults $4, sr citizens $3, students $2, children 12 & under & members free; Estab 1862 for the preservation, exhibition & research of local history; 8 galleries; Average Annual Attendance: 10,000; Mem: 500; annual meeting in Nov
Income: (financed by private contributions)
Library Holdings: Book Volumes, Clipping Files, Exhibition Catalogs, Kodachrome Transparencies, Manuscripts, Maps, Memorabilia, Micro Print, Original Documents, Other Holdings, Pamphlets, Periodical Subscriptions, Photographs, Slides
Special Subjects: Afro-American Art, Architecture, Bookplates & Bindings, Ceramics, Coins & Medals, Costumes, Decorative Arts, Drawings, Embroidery, Etchings & Engravings, Flasks & Bottles, Folk Art, Furniture, Glass, Hispanic Art, Historical Material, Landscapes, Manuscripts, Maps, Marine Painting, Painting-American, Period Rooms, Pewter, Photography, Portraits, Prints, Reproductions, Silver, Textiles, Woodcarvings, Woodcuts, Watercolors
Collections: 18th & 19th Century Coll of portraits of the New Haven area personages, maritime coll of shops paintings, paintings by local artists Durrie, Jocelyn, Moulthrop
Exhibitions: Permanent exhibition includes paintings by local artists such as Jocelyn, Moulthrop & George H Durrie; landscape portraits; maritime historical paintings; New Haven Illustrated: From Colony, Town to City; Maritime New Haven; Ingersoll Collection of Furniture & Decorative Arts; Two changing exhibitions per year minimum
Publications: Newsletter
Activities: Classes for adults & children; hands-on progs; docent training; lects open to pub, 4 vis lectrs per yr; slideshows; concerts; gallery talks & tours; individual paintings & objects of art lent to other approved mus; mus shop sells books, reproductions, prints, antiques, collectibles & journals, children's toys, posters, postcards, videos, CDs

M **SOUTHERN CONNECTICUT STATE UNIVERSITY,** Art Dept, 501 Crescent St, New Haven, CT 06515-1330. Tel 203-392-6652, Ext 5974; Fax 203-392-6658; Web: www.southernct.edu; *Dir* Cort Sierpinski
Open Mon - Fri 8 AM - 10 PM; Estab 1976 to build a collection of works of art for educational purposes, gallery developing now; Mem: 750
Income: $10,000 (financed by mem, state appropriation & fundraising)
Special Subjects: African Art, Pre-Columbian Art
Collections: African & Pre-Columbian art
Activities: Travelogues; lects open to pub, 6 vis lectrs per yr; gallery talks; national & international tours; original objects of art lent to admin offices

M **YALE UNIVERSITY,** Yale University Art Gallery, 1111 Chapel St, New Haven, CT 06520-8271. Tel 203-432-0600; Fax 203-432-9523; Email artgalleryinfo@yale.edu; Web: artgallery.yale.edu; *Dir* Stephanie Wiles; *Cur Ancient Art* Susan Matheson; *Cur American Painting & Sculpture* Mark Mitchell; *Cur American Decorative Arts* Patricia Kane; *Registrar* Lynne Addison; *Mem* Linda Jerolmon; *Cur Educ* Ryan Hill; *Cur Modern & Contemporary Art* Pamela Franks; *Cur Asian Art* Denise Patry Leidy; *Dir Communs* Joellen Adae; *Cur European Art* Laurence Kanter; *Cur African Art* Barbara Plankensteiner; *Dir Publs* Tiffany Sprague; *Cur Indo-Pacific Art* Ruth Barnes; *Cur Photography* Judy Ditner; *Cur Numismatics* Benjamin Hellings
Open July - Aug Tues - Fri 10 AM - 5 PM, Sat - Sun 11 AM -5 PM, Sept - June Tues - Wed & Fri 10 AM - 5 PM, Thurs 10 AM - 8 PM, Sat - Sun 11 AM - 5 PM, cl Mon, New Year's Day, Independence Day, Thanksgiving, Christmas Eve & Day; No admis fee; Estab 1832 to exhibit works of art from ancient times to present; Three buildings designed by Louis Kahn (1953), Egerton Swartwout (1926), Peter Bonnet Wight (1866); Average Annual Attendance: 220,000; Mem: 10,000; free
Income: Financed by endowment, mem & annual fundraising
Special Subjects: Antiquities-Greek, Antiquities-Roman, Oriental Art, Painting-American, Painting-European, Sculpture, Silver, African Art, Afro-American Art, American Western Art, Asian Art, Ceramics, Coins & Medals, Decorative Arts, Etchings & Engravings, Furniture, Glass, Gold, Islamic Art, Ivory, Jade, Jewelry, Landscapes, Medieval Art, Metalwork, Miniatures, Mosaics, Painting-British, Painting-Dutch, Painting-Flemish, Painting-French, Painting-German, Painting-Italian, Painting-Japanese, Period Rooms, Pewter, Photography, Porcelain, Portraits, Pottery, Pre-Columbian Art, Prints, Religious Art, Renaissance Art, Watercolors, Woodcarvings, Woodcuts
Collections: American & European painting & sculpture, Chinese painting & ceramics, Dura-Europos Archaeological Collection, Garvan Collection of American Decorative Arts, History paintings & miniatures by John Trumbull, Japanese painting & ceramics, Jarves Collection of Italian Renaissance Painting, Societe Anonyme Collection of Twentieth century art, Stoddard Collection of Greek Vases, 20th Century Art, 25,000 prints, drawings & photographs, Charles B Benenson Collection of African Art, Indo-Pacific Art, Coins and Medals
Publications: Exhibition catalogues; Collection catalogues; Yale University Art Gallery Bulletin, catalogue raisonnes; artist's books
Activities: Classes for adults & children; family progs; evening lects; gallery tours three times per wk; gallery talks; concerts; tours; fels; originate traveling exhibs; books; postcards; t-shirts

M **Yale Center for British Art,** 1080 Chapel St, New Haven, CT 06510-2302; PO Box 208280, New Haven, CT 06520-8280. Tel 203-432-2800; Fax 203-432-9628;

Email ycba.info@yale.edu; Web: www.yale.edu/ycba; *Dir* Amy Meyers; *Deputy Dir* Constance Clement; *Chief Librn* Kraig Binkowski; *Chief Cur Rare Books & Manuscripts* Elisabeth Fairman; *Deputy Dir Research & Educ and Cur Sculpture* Martina Droth; *Deputy Dir Collections* Scott Wilcox; *Chief Cur Art Collections* Matthew Hargraves
Open Tues - Sat 10 AM - 5 PM, Sun Noon - 5 PM, cl Mon, New Year's Day, Independence Day, Thanksgiving, Christmas Eve & Day; No admis fee; Estab 1977 to foster appreciation & knowledge of British art; to encourage interdisciplinary use of the collections; Circ Non-circulating library; 3 floors of gallery space exhibiting permanent colls & special exhibs; Average Annual Attendance: 100,000; Mem: 850; dues individual $50
Income: Financed by endowment, annual gifts, mem & mus shop
Library Holdings: Auction Catalogs, Audio Tapes, Book Volumes, CD-ROMs, Cards, Cassettes, Clipping Files, Compact Disks, DVDs, Exhibition Catalogs, Fiche, Filmstrips, Framed Reproductions, Kodachrome Transparencies, Lantern Slides, Manuscripts, Maps, Memorabilia, Micro Print, Motion Pictures, Original Art Works, Original Documents, Other Holdings, Pamphlets, Periodical Subscriptions, Photographs, Prints, Records, Reproductions, Sculpture, Slides, Video Tapes
Special Subjects: Architecture, Bookplates & Bindings, Drawings, Etchings & Engravings, Landscapes, Manuscripts, Maps, Marine Painting, Miniatures, Painting-British, Portraits, Prints, Sculpture, Watercolors
Collections: Paintings & sculpture, drawings, prints, rare books
Publications: exhibition catalogues
Activities: Classes for adults & children; dramatic progs; docent training; student guides; lects & symposia, 10 vis lectrs per yr; concerts, gallery talks; tours; films; fels; individual paintings & objects of art lent to other mus; lending collection contains rare books, original art works, original prints & paintings; book traveling exhibs; originate traveling exhibs; mus shop sells books, reproductions, slides, postcards, exhibs catalogs, glass, ceramics, jewelry & other items

L **Yale Center for British Art Reference Library**, 1080 Chapel St, New Haven, CT 06520-2302; PO Box 208280, New Haven, CT 06520-8280. Tel 203-432-2818; Fax 203-432-9613; Email bacref@pantheon.yale.edu; Web: www.yale.edu/ycba
Open Tues - Fri 10 AM - 4:30 PM, Sat 1 - 4:30 PM when Yale is in session; No admis fee; Estab 1977 to support collection of British Art and related fields of architecture, history, literature and the performing arts; Reference library & photo archive
Library Holdings: Auction Catalogs, Book Volumes 20,000, CD-ROMs, Cards, Exhibition Catalogs, Fiche 75,000, Pamphlets, Periodical Subscriptions 70, Photographs 200,000, Reels 860, Video Tapes
Collections: British Art from age of Holbein to present
Activities: Classes for adults & children; docent training

L **The Robert B. Haas Family Arts Library**, 180 York St, New Haven, CT 06511-8924; PO Box 208318, New Haven, CT 06520-8318. Tel 203-432-2645; Fax 203-432-0549; Email art.library@yale.edu; Web: www.library.yale.edu/arts; *Dir* Heather Gendron
Open acad yr Mon - Thurs 8:30 AM - 11 PM, Fri 8:30 AM - 5 PM, Sat 10 AM - 6 PM, Sun 2 PM - 11 PM; Summer Mon & Wed - Fri 8:30 AM - 5 PM, Tues 8:30 AM - 7 PM; Estab 1868. Serves Schools of Art, Drama & Architecture, History of Art Department & the Yale University Art Gallery; William H Wright special collections exhib area
Library Holdings: Book Volumes 115,000, Exhibition Catalogs, Other Holdings Digital Images, Photographs & Color Prints 183,000, Slides 825,000
Collections: Faber Birren Collection of Books on Color, Arts of the Book Collection, Yale Bookplate Collection
Publications: Faber Birren Collection of Books on Color: A Bibliography

L 121 Wall St, New Haven, CT 06511; P.O. Box 280240, New Haven, CT 06520-8240. Tel 203-432-2977; Fax 203-432-4047; Email beinecke.library@yale.edu; Web: www.library.yale.edu/beinecke
Open Mon 10 AM - 7 PM, Tues - Thurs 9 AM - 7 PM, Fri 9 AM - 5 PM, Sat noon - 5 PM, Sun noon - 4 PM; No admis fee; Estab 1963; Non-circulating
Library Holdings: Book Volumes 600,000, Clipping Files, Manuscripts, Maps, Memorabilia, Original Art Works, Original Documents, Pamphlets, Photographs, Prints, Sculpture
Special Subjects: Afro-American Art, American Indian Art, American Western Art, Art History, Bookplates & Bindings, Calligraphy, Drawings, Etchings & Engravings, Graphic Arts, Graphic Design, Historical Material, History of Art & Archaeology, Illustration, Islamic Art, Judaica
Collections: Osborn Collection of English literary & historical manuscripts from the Anglo-Saxon period to 20th century, Coll of America Literature of 19th & early 20th century writings, German Literature Coll of rare books & first editions of 17th-20th century, Western Americana Coll of books, manuscripts, maps, art, prints & photographs of Trans-Mississippi West through world War I, General coll of Early Books & Manuscripts includes Greek & Roman papyri, medieval & Renaissance manuscripts, modern books & manuscripts in English literature & history from 17th-20th century
Publications: Exhibition catalogs
Activities: Lects open to pub, 10-15 vis lectrs per yr; concerts; schols & fels offered; sales shop sells books

NEW LONDON

M **LYMAN ALLYN ART MUSEUM,** 625 Williams St, New London, CT 06320-4199. Tel 860-443-2545; Fax 860-442-1280; Email info@lymanallyn.org; Web: www.lymanallyn.org; *Dir* Samuel Quigley; *Dir Educ* Caitlin Healy; *Dir External Affairs* Vera Harsh; *Registrar & Dir Exhibs* Jane LeGrow
Open Tues - Sat 10 AM - 5 PM, Sun 1 - 5 PM; cl Mon & major holidays; Admis adults $10, seniors & students (over 18) $7, Students (under 18) $5, children under 12 & New London residents free; Estab 1926 for the educ & enrichment of the community & others; The museum is housed in a handsome Neo-Classical building designed by Charles A Platt; Average Annual Attendance: 20,000; Mem: 300; dues range from individual $50 - benefactor $1,000
Library Holdings: Auction Catalogs, Book Volumes, Exhibition Catalogs, Periodical Subscriptions
Special Subjects: Decorative Arts, Dolls, Furniture, Landscapes, Oriental Art, Painting-American, Painting-European, Painting-French, Painting-Italian, Prints, Silver
Collections: American Impressionist Paintings, Connecticut Decorative Arts, Contemporary, Modern & Early American Fine Arts, collection of 30,000 works, European Paintings & Works on Paper, Over 15,000 objects from ancient times to the present; artworks from Africa, Asia, the Americas, & Europe
Exhibitions: Temporary exhibitions of American Art from public & private collections; The Devotion Family of 18th Century Connecticut; Connecticut Women Artists; Impressionist Paintings from the Lyman Allyn Collection; At Home & Abroad: The Transcendental Landscapes of Christopher Pearce Cranch; Walter Wick: Games & Toys in the Attic; Portions of Museum's permanent coll on view in the American Stories exhib galleries featuring many of the museum's most prized examples of American art
Publications: New London County Furniture from 1640-1840; New London Silver; Selection of Lyman Allyn publications, book
Activities: Educ prog; classes for adults & children; docent training; school tours & progs; bus trips; homeschool progs; lects open to pub; lects for mems only; concerts; gallery talks; tours; scholarships; individual paintings & original objects of art lent; mus shop sells books, reproductions, cards & gifts

L **Hendel Library**, 625 Williams St, New London, CT 06320. Tel 860-443-2545; Fax 860-442-1280; Web: www.lymanallyn.conncoll.edu; *Librn* Lissa Van Dyke
Open Tues - Sat 10 AM - 5 PM, Sun 1 - 5 PM; Admis for mems & by appointment only; Estab 1932 to provide an art reference library as an adjunct to the material in the Lyman Allyn Art Museum; Reference only; Average Annual Attendance: 1,500
Income: financed by Harriet Allen trust
Library Holdings: Book Volumes 4500, Clipping Files, Exhibition Catalogs, Fiche, Pamphlets, Periodical Subscriptions 32, Photographs, Reproductions, Slides
Special Subjects: Decorative Arts
Collections: Decorative arts, furniture, drawings
Activities: Docent training; lects open to pub, 2 vis lectrs per yr; gallery talks; tours

A **NEW LONDON COUNTY HISTORICAL SOCIETY,** Shaw Mansion, 11 Blinman St, New London, CT 06320-5677. Tel 860-443-1209; Fax 860-443-1209; Email info@nlchs.org; Web: www.nlhistory.org; *Pres* Nancy Steenburg; *Exec Dir* Steve Manuel; *Assoc Dir* Kayla Carrell
Open Wed - Fri 1 - 4 PM, Sat by appointment only; Admis $5 for tours; Estab 1870 for preservation of New London County history; Maintains reference library; paintings throughout historic house; Average Annual Attendance: 3,000; Mem: 350; dues family $40, individual $30, sr citizen & student $20; progs 2nd Sun of most months
Income: $100,000 (financed by endowment, mem, admis & research fees)
Purchases: Manuscripts; artifacts
Library Holdings: DVDs, Original Documents, Photographs, Slides, Video Tapes
Special Subjects: Ceramics, Coins & Medals, Costumes, Decorative Arts, Dolls, Drawings, Embroidery, Eskimo Art, Folk Art, Furniture, Historical Material, Manuscripts, Maps, Marine Painting, Miniatures, Painting-American, Period Rooms, Pewter, Photography, Scrimshaw, Textiles, Porcelain
Collections: Six Portraits by Ralph Earle, furniture & decorative arts owned by Shaw & Perkins families, furniture made in New London County, miscellaneous portraits, miniatures, photographs, rare maps, Textile Collection, Goddard Furniture-Newport; newspapers
Exhibitions: Ongoing; New London in the Revolution; Remember Me-Civil War Photographs
Publications: NLCHS Newsletter, quarterly
Activities: Lect open to public, 10 vis lectrs per year; dramatic programs; docent training; tours; community events; Connecticut Humanities Council; mus shop sells books & gifts

M **UNITED STATES COAST GUARD MUSEUM,** 15 Mohegan Ave, US Coast Guard Academy New London, CT 06320-8100. Tel 860-444-8511; Fax 860-701-6700; Web: www.uscg.mil/hq/cg092/museum
Open Mon - Fri 9 AM - 4:30 PM, Sat 10 AM - 5 PM, Sun Noon - 5 PM; No Admis fee; Estab 1967 to preserve historical heritage of the US Coast Guard, US Life Saving Service, US Lighthouse Service & Revenue Cutter Service; Average Annual Attendance: 20,000
Income: Financed by federal appropriations and private donations
Special Subjects: American Indian Art, Ceramics, Coins & Medals, Costumes, Decorative Arts, Drawings, Eskimo Art, Etchings & Engravings
Collections: Ship & aircraft models, paintings, photographs & manuscripts representing the Coast Guard, military artifacts from WWI, WWII & Vietnam
Activities: Paintings & original objects of art lent to federal museums & qualified organizations for educational purposes only

NORFOLK

M **NORFOLK HISTORICAL SOCIETY INC,** Museum, 13 Village Green Norfolk, CT 06058; PO Box 288, Norfolk, CT 06058-0288. Tel 860-542-5761; Email norfolkhistorical@sbcglobal.net; Web: www.norfolkhistoricalsociety.org; *Pres* Barry C Webber; *Cur* Ann Havemeyer
Open June-Oct Sat-Sun 1PM-4PM, Nov-May 1st Thurs of month 1PM-5PM, also open by appt anytime; No admis fee; Estab 1960
Special Subjects: Architecture, Costumes, Furniture, Historical Material, Maps, Photography, Portraits
Collections: Marie Kendall Photography Collection (1884 - 1935), era during which she worked in Norfolk, Collection of works by Alfredo S G Taylor, noted architect - his blueprints, drawings, photographs plus documents for 40 of his buildings in Norfolk listed as a Thematic Group in the National Register of Historic Places, Small collection of Connecticut clocks, Fine 1879 dollhouse with elegant original furnishings, photographs & memorabilia of the Norfolk Downs, one of the very first New England golf courses (1897)
Exhibitions: Norfolk General Stores, Post Offices & Early Norfolk Merchants
Publications: Exhibition catalogs; books, pamphlets & maps, publishes at irregularly intervals
Activities: Historic Howe tours; walking tours; gallery talks; slide shows; Connecticut League of History Org Award of Merit (AASLH)

NORWALK

M **LOCKWOOD-MATHEWS MANSION MUSEUM,** 295 West Ave, Norwalk, CT 06850-4002. Tel 203-838-9799; Fax 203-838-1434; Email info@lockwoodmathewsmansion.com; Web: www.lockwoodmathewsmansion.com; *Exec Dir* Susan Gilgore, PhD; *Cur* Kathleen Motes Bennewitz; *Facility Coordr* Stephen Kostes; *Social Media & Mktg Asst* Elizabeth Gorenbergh; *Manager, Museum Services* Melissa Feliciano
Open Wed - Sun Noon - 4 PM; gift shop open Wed - Sun noon - 4PM; Admis adults $10, seniors $8, students $5, children under 8 free; Built between 1864 - 1868 to completely restore this 19th century 66 room Victorian mansion as a historic house mus. Now a registered National Historic Landmark. Can be rented for private parties & corporate events; National Historic Landmark; Average Annual Attendance: 20,000; Mem: 300; annual meeting in June
Income: State and federal budgets, private funds
Library Holdings: Audio Tapes, Cards, Cassettes, DVDs, Framed Reproductions, Maps, Memorabilia, Original Art Works, Pamphlets, Photographs, Prints, Reproductions
Special Subjects: Architecture, Costumes, Decorative Arts, Etchings & Engravings, Furniture, Glass, Historical Material, Painting-American, Painting-French, Period Rooms, Restorations, Sculpture
Collections: Furniture original to the mansion, 19th century decorative arts, painting & textiles
Exhibitions: The Stairs Below The Mansion's Dome
Publications: Newsletter, bi-mothly
Activities: Classes for adults & children; docent training; lects open to pub; 7 visiting lects per year; exhibit gallery talks; tours; performing arts; story & play reading; Young Writers Competition Award; the Lockwood-Matthews Mansion Museum/Ernest Hemingway/Young Writers' Competition; mus shop sells books, magazines, reproductions, prints & decorative accessories

M **NORWALK COMMUNITY COLLEGE,** Art Galleries & Collection, 188 Richards Ave, Norwalk, CT 06854. Tel 203-857-7000; Email shardesty@ncc.commnet.edu; Web: www.ncc.commnet.edu/aad/facilities; *Dir* Susan Hardesty
Open Mon - Thurs 7 AM - 10 PM, Fri & Sat 8 AM - 5 PM; No admis fee; Two galleries and an art collection for the college community
Special Subjects: Painting-American, Prints, Photography, Sculpture, Mixed Media
Collections: Contemporary art by more than 600 nationally & internationally known artists
Exhibitions: Rotating exhibits
Activities: Educ progs; Lects open to pub; gallery talks; art invitationals

C **XEROX CORPORATION,** Art Collection, 45 Glover Ave # 1, Norwalk, CT 06850-1203. Tel 203-968-3000; Fax 203-968-3330; *VPres Xerox Foundation* Joseph M Cahalan; *Prog Mgr* Evelyn Shockley
Open by appointment, Mon - Fri 9 AM - 5 PM; No admis fee; Collection on display at Xerox Headquarters
Collections: The art collection represents a broad spectrum of American fine art as well as art forms from other countries. The works range from abstraction to realism & consist of sculpture by David Lee Brown located in the lobby, fiberwork by Gerhardt Knodel located in the dining facility, collages, etchings, lithographs, graphics, mezzotints, mono-prints, montages, pastels, photography, pochoir, silkscreens, watercolors & xerography

NORWICH

M **NORWICH FREE ACADEMY,** Slater Memorial Museum, 108 Crescent St, Norwich, CT 06360-3500. Tel 860-887-2506; Fax 860-885-0379; Email info@slatermuseum.org; Web: www.slatermuseum.org; *Dir* Vivian Zoe; *Asst Dir* Leigh Thomas; *Vis Ctr Mgr* Sheena Emma
See website; Admis adults $3, senior citizens $2, students w/ID 12-18 children under 12 free; Estab 1888; The Slater collection is housed in a 1886 Neo-Romanesque building on the campus of the Norwich Free Academy. The adjacent Converse Gallery was built in 1906; Average Annual Attendance: 10,000; Mem: patron $100, contributing $50, family $35, individual $25, senior citizen $15
Income: Financed by endowment, Friends of Slater Museum & admissions
Purchases: John Denison Crocker's Shepherdess O/C; Frank Gardner Hale brooch silver/stones
Library Holdings: Book Volumes, Clipping Files, Exhibition Catalogs, Manuscripts, Memorabilia, Original Documents, Pamphlets, Photographs, Prints, Slides
Special Subjects: African Art, Afro-American Art, American Indian Art, Anthropology, Antiquities-Assyrian, Antiquities-Byzantine, Antiquities-Egyptian, Antiquities-Etruscan, Antiquities-Greek, Antiquities-Oriental, Antiquities-Persian, Antiquities-Roman, Architecture, Asian Art, Bronzes, Carpets & Rugs, Cartoons, Ceramics, Coins & Medals, Collages, Costumes, Crafts, Decorative Arts, Dolls, Drawings, Embroidery, Enamels, Eskimo Art, Etchings & Engravings, Ethnology, Flasks & Bottles, Folk Art, Furniture, Glass, Gold, Graphics, Hispanic Art, Historical Material, Islamic Art, Ivory, Jade, Jewelry, Judaica, Juvenile Art, Laces, Landscapes, Leather, Manuscripts, Maps, Marine Painting, Metalwork, Miniatures, Mosaics, Oriental Art, Painting-American, Painting-European, Painting-Flemish, Painting-French, Painting-German, Painting-Italian, Painting-Japanese, Painting-Spanish, Period Rooms, Pewter, Photography, Porcelain, Portraits, Pottery, Prints, Religious Art, Renaissance Art, Reproductions, Restorations, Scrimshaw, Sculpture, Silver, Silversmithing, Stained Glass, Tapestries, Textiles, Watercolors, Woodcarvings, Woodcuts
Collections: Vanderpoel Collection of Asian Art, American Art & Furniture from the 17th - 20th Centuries, Greek, Roman & Renaissance Plaster Cast Collection, Original 1888 collection of Plaster Casts of Archaic, Egyptian, Greek, Roman & Renaissance marbles & bronzes, Norwich-related fine & decorative art & industrial (maritime, armaments) artifacts, European, African & 20th C American art
Exhibitions: Special exhibitions on view in Converse Gallery - six per year; Annual Connecticut artists juried exhibition; In New Contiguous Atrium - Changing Exhibs; John Meyer of Norwich; Around the World on the Yacht Eleanor
Publications: Catalogue of the Plaster Cast Collection; Charlotte Fuller Eastman, Artist & Teacher; Greek Myths for Young People; Gualtieri, a Retrospect; NORWICH, a Photographic Essay; Renaissance Art for Young People; John Meyer of Norwich: An African Original, Crockers Norwich
Activities: Classes for children; docent training; orientation video; lects open to pub; gallery talks; guided & walking tours; school group & adult group tours; 6 vis lectrs per yr; films; competitions with awards; CT League of History Organizations Award of Merit; CT Artists' Juried show; exhib cash awards; Katherine Forest Crafts Foundation Award for Excellence in Fine Craft; extension prog to Connecticut area schools; lending original objects of art to area businesses & other mus; 1-2 book traveling exhibs; Joan Meyer of Norwich: An American Original; mus shop sells books, magazines, original art by local artists, reproductions, prints, crafts, CT made items, jewelry, cosmetics, souvenirs

OLD LYME

L **LYME ACADEMY COLLEGE OF FINE ARTS,** Krieble Library, 84 Lyme St, Old Lyme, CT 06371-2333. Tel 860-434-5232; Fax 860-434-8725; Web: www.lymeacademy.edu
Lending to students & faculty only
Library Holdings: Book Volumes 6000, Exhibition Catalogs, Pamphlets, Periodical Subscriptions 40, Slides 10,000, Video Tapes 60
Publications: Brochure; catalog
M **Chauncy Stillman Gallery**
Open Mon - Sat 10 AM - 4 PM; No admis fee; Internal & external exhibs, student & faculty

A **LYME ART ASSOCIATION, INC,** 90 Lyme St, Old Lyme, CT 06371-2367. Tel 860-434-7802; Email info@lymeartassociation.org; Web: www.lymeartassociation.org; *Pres* Katherine Simmons; *Exec Dir* Joseph Newman; *Bus Mgr* Laurie Pavlos; *Gallery Mgr* Jocelyn Zallinger; *Dir Develop* Gary Parrington
Open Mon - Sat 10 AM - 5 PM, Sun 1 - 5 PM; No admis fee, donations accepted; Estab 1914 to promote art & advance representational art educ; Four large sky-lighted galleries are maintained. Building designed by Charles Platt & built in 1920 by early Lyme Impressionist artists; Average Annual Attendance: 12,000; Mem: 800; elected artist members $75, assoc artist members & friends $45
Income: Financed by mem & assoc members dues, donations & sales commissions
Library Holdings: Book Volumes, Cards, Exhibition Catalogs, Memorabilia, Original Art Works, Original Documents, Sculpture, Video Tapes
Special Subjects: Architecture, Painting-American, Drawings, Etchings & Engravings, Landscapes, Marine Painting, Portraits, Sculpture
Exhibitions: Eight annual exhibs featuring representational fine art by mem & invited artists
Publications: Weekly e-newsletter; The Early Years: 1902-1930 of LAA, catalog; Elected Artists of the Lyme Art Association
Activities: Classes for adults & children; art workshops; lects open to pub, 5 - 6 vis lectrs per yr; concerts; gallery talks; competitions with awards; schols offered; originates bus trips; sales shop sells original art

M **LYME HISTORICAL SOCIETY,** Florence Griswold Museum, 96 Lyme St, Old Lyme, CT 06371-1426. Tel 860-434-5542; Fax 860-434-9778; Web: www.florencegriswoldmuseum.org; *Dir* Rebekah Beaulieu; *Cur* Amy Kurtz Lansing
Open Tues - Sat 10 AM - 5 PM, Sun 1 - 5 PM; Admis adults $10, seniors $9, students $8, children 12 & under free; Estab 1953 as a research facility for mus programs & for the pub; Changing exhibitions throughout the year
Library Holdings: Book Volumes, Cassettes, Clipping Files, Exhibition Catalogs, Kodachrome Transparencies, Manuscripts, Memorabilia, Motion Pictures, Pamphlets, Periodical Subscriptions 25, Photographs, Prints, Reproductions, Slides
Special Subjects: Etchings & Engravings, Historical Material, Landscapes, Painting-American, Period Rooms, Photography, Sculpture
Collections: Old Lyme Art Colony Paintings, Hartford Steam Boiler Collection of American art, Clara Champlain Griswold Toy Collection, Evelyn McCurdy Salisbury Ceramic Collection
Exhibitions: The Art Colony at Old Lyme; Walker Evans Photographs; Clark Voorhees 1971 - 1933; Old Lyme: The American Barbizon; Dressed for Any Occasion: Patterns of Fashion in the 19th Century; Thomas W Nason, 1889 - 1971, The Notable Women of Lyme; The Whites of Waterford: An American Landscape Tradition; Childe Hassam in Connecticut; En Plein Air: The Art Colonies of East Hampton & Old Lyme; The Harmony of Nature; Frank Vincent DuMond; Wilson Irvine & The Poetry of Light; The American Artist in Connecticut; May Night: Willard Metcalf at Old Lyme; The Finishing Touch
Publications: The Connecticut Impressionists at Old Lyme; The Lieutenant River; The Lymes Heritage Cookbook; Hamburg Cove: Past & Present; The Lyme Ledger, quarterly; Report of the Lyme Historical Society, annually; Miss Florence & The Artists of Old Lyme; A New Look at History
Activities: Classes for adults & children; docent training; lects open to pub; concerts; gallery talks; tours; mus shop sells books, magazines, original art, reproductions & prints
L **Library,** 96 Lyme St, Old Lyme, CT 06371. Tel 860-434-5542; Fax 860-434-9778; Web: www.flogris.org; *Registrar* Laurie Bradt; *Dir* Jeffrey Andersen
Open Mon - Sat 10 AM - 5 PM, Sun 1 - 5 PM; No admis fee; Estab 1953 as a research facility for mus programs & for the pub; Open to the public for reference by appointment
Purchases: $1500
Library Holdings: Book Volumes 1600, Cassettes, Clipping Files, Exhibition Catalogs, Kodachrome Transparencies, Manuscripts, Memorabilia, Motion Pictures, Pamphlets, Periodical Subscriptions 25, Photographs, Prints, Reproductions, Slides
Special Subjects: Historical Material, Landscapes, Painting-American
Collections: Connecticut Impressionism, Lyme Art Colony, Hartford Steam Boiler Fire Art Collections
Activities: Classes for adults and children; docent training; lects open to pub; gallery talks; tours; mus shop sells books, reproductions, prints

RIDGEFIELD

M **ALDRICH MUSEUM OF CONTEMPORARY ART,** 258 Main St, Ridgefield, CT 06877-4933. Tel 203-438-4519; Fax 203-438-0198; Email general@aldrichart.org; Web: www.aldrichart.org; *Dir* Alyson Baker; *Exhib Dir* Richard Klein; *Dir Communs* Pamela Ruggio; *Progs Dir* Tracey Moore
Open Tues - Sun Noon - 5 PM, cl Mon, New Year's Day, Easter, Independence Day, Thanksgiving & Christmas Day, open Martin Luther King Jr Day, President's Day, Memorial Day & Labor Day & Columbus Day, group visits by appointment; Admis adults $10, college students & seniors $5, mems, K-12 teachers & children under 18 free, active duty military & family with ID free through Blue Star Prog, Tues free all day; Estab 1964 for the presentation of contemporary art; to stimulate public awareness of contemporary art through exhibitions & educ programs; to advance creative thinking by connecting today's artists with individuals & communities in unexpected ways; Renovated colonial building with modern addition: 26,000 sq ft exhib space comprise 15 galleries incl screening room, sound gallery, 22 ft high proj space, 100-seat performance area, Educ Ctr & sculpture garden; Average Annual Attendance: 18,000; Mem: 1100; dues $100 & up
Income: Financed by mem, federal & state grants, corporate & private foundations
Special Subjects: Prints
Exhibitions: Rotating exhibits 4-6 per yr
Publications: Exhibition brochures; quarterly calendars; monthly, e-newsletters
Activities: Classes for adults & children; docent training; pub progs for schools, teachers, children, families, teens & adults; events; performances; workshops & more; lects open to pub; lects for mems only; concerts; gallery talks; tours; schols; book traveling exhibs; organize traveling exhibs; mus shop sells books, magazines; prints & designs

STAMFORD

L **FERGUSON LIBRARY,** 1 Public Library Plaza, Stamford, CT 06904. Tel 203-964-1000; Fax 203-357-9098; Email admin@ferg.lib.ct.us; Web: www.fergusonlibrary.org; *Pres* Ernest A DiMattia Jr; *Dir Admin Servs* Nicholas Bochicchio Jr; *Dir Human Resources & General Counsel* George Nichols Esq; *Bus Office Supv* Marie Giuliano; *Dir Computer Svcs* Gary Giannelli; *Dir Develop & Communs* Linda Auellar; *Dir User Servs* Alice Knapp
Open Mon - Thurs 11 AM - 8 PM, Fri 11 AM - 6 PM, Sat 10 AM - 5 PM, mid Sept - mid May Sun 1 - 5 PM; Estab 1880 as a public library dedicated to serving the information needs of the community
Income: Financed by city appropriation
Purchases: $8000 (art & music books), $50,000 (video cassettes), $22,000 (tapes & compact discs)
Library Holdings: Book Volumes 366,200, Cassettes, Compact Disks, DVDs, Framed Reproductions, Motion Pictures, Other Holdings Audio-Visual Materials 34,537, Records, Slides, Video Tapes
Collections: Photography of Old Stamford
Exhibitions: Painting, sculpture, photography & posters under sponsorship of Friends of Ferguson Library
Publications: Focus on Ferguson quarterly newsletter, Art Currents for the Whitney Museum, Musical Notes for the Stamford Symphony and the Connecticut Grand Opera
Activities: Classes for adults & children; lects open to pub; concerts

M **STAMFORD MUSEUM & NATURE CENTER,** 39 Scofieldtown Rd, Stamford, CT 06903-4096. Tel 203-322-1646; Fax 203-322-0408; Email info@stamfordmuseum.org; Web: www.stamfordmuseum.org; *Dir* Melissa Mulrooney
Open Mon - Sat 9 AM - 5 PM, Sun & holidays 1 - 5 PM, cl Thanksgiving, Christmas & New Year's Day; Admis adults $8, Stamford residents $3, Children accompanied by adult $4, mem free; Estab 1936, Art Department 1955; Museum has an art wing for changing exhibitions of 19th & 20th century art; Average Annual Attendance: 250,000; Mem: 3000; dues $35 & up; annual meeting in June
Income: Financed by mem, private & corporate donations & city appropriation
Special Subjects: American Indian Art, Crafts, Drawings, Painting-American, Photography, Prints, Sculpture
Collections: American crafts, American Indian drawings, photography, prints, 19th & 20th century painting, sculpture
Exhibitions: Annual Connecticut Artists; Four Winners Exhibition; Ellen Lanyon: Strange Games; Private Expressions: Personal Experiences; Color: Pure & Simple; American Art at the Turn of the Century; American Printmaking; The Natural Image; New American Paperworks; Connecticut Craftsmen; Bernstein; Button; Johnson; Margolies; Krushenick; Fiberforms; Contemporary Iroquois Art
Publications: American Art: American Women; Animals; brochures; exhibit catalogs; Folk Art: Then & Now; monthly newsletter
Activities: Educ dept, classes for adults & children in art, dance, nature & science; docent training; lects open to pub, 12 vis lectrs per yr; concerts; gallery talks; tours; competitions with awards; individual paintings & original objects of art lent to other mus; originate traveling exhibs; mus shop sells books, magazines, slides, & 19th century collectibles & gifts

STORRS

M **UNIVERSITY OF CONNECTICUT,** William Benton Museum of Art, 245 Glenbrook Rd, Unit 3140 Storrs, CT 06269-2140. Tel 860-486-4520; Fax 860-486-0234; Email nancy.stula@uconn.edu; Web: benton.uconn.edu; *Exec Dir* Nancy Stula; *Opers & Progs* Karen Sommer; *Educ* Alison Golomb; *Registrar & Asst Cur* Rachel Zilinski; *Prep* Kerry Smith; *Visitor Servs & Museum Store* Samantha Smith
Open during exhibitions Tues - Fri 10 AM - 4:30 PM, Sat & Sun 1 - 4:30 PM, cl Mon; No admis fee; Estab 1966, a mus of art, operating as an autonomous department within the University, serving the students, faculty & general pub; contributing to the field at large through research, exhibitions & publications & by maintaining a permanent collection of over 3500 objects; The main gallery measures 36 x 116 ft, galley II 33 x 36 ft; Average Annual Attendance: 36,000; Mem: 600; dues $25 & up
Income: $700,000 (financed by mem, state appropriation, grants & gifts & donations)
Special Subjects: Graphics, Painting-American, Painting-European, Sculpture
Collections: American painting & graphics 19-20th Century, German & French graphics late 19th & 20th Century, selected 17th & 18th Century European paintings, sculptures & graphics, Western European & American c 1600 to present, paintings, graphics, contemporary photography
Publications: Exhibition catalogs, annually
Activities: Lects open to pub, 5-8 vis lectrs per yr; gallery talks; tours; individual paintings & original objects of art lent to accredited institutions for exhib purposes; lending collection contains original prints, paintings & sculpture; book traveling exhibs; originate traveling exhibs; sales shop sells books, original art, prints, reproductions & mus related art objects & jewelry

M **Jorgensen Auditorium**, 2132 Hillside Rd, Storrs, CT 06269-3104; Unit 3104, Storrs, CT 06269-3104. Tel 860-486-4228; Fax 860-486-6781; Email rock@jorg.anj.uconn.edu; Web: www.jorgensen.ct-arts.com; *Dir* Rodney Rock; *Operations Dir* Gary Yakstis
Open Mon - Fri 8 AM - 5 PM, cl Sat & Sun; No admis fee; Estab 1967 to present work by leading contemporary North American artists. Serves the pub as well as the university community; The gallery is 2872 square ft; Average Annual Attendance: 25,000; Mem: 500 Friends of Jorgensen
Exhibitions: Various exhibitions, call for details
Activities: Gallery talks

L **Art & Design Library**, Box U-5AD, Storrs, CT 06269-1005; 369 Fairfield Rd - Unit 1005, Univ of Connecticut Libraries Storrs, CT 06269-9001. Tel 860-486-2787; Fax 860-486-3593; Email tom.jacoby@uconn.edu; *Art & Design Librn* Thomas J Jacoby
Open Mon - Thurs 10 AM - 10 PM, Fri 10 AM - 5 PM, Sat Noon - 5 PM, Sun 2 - 10 PM; No admis fee; Estab 1979 to support the Department of Art, Art History, Landscape Architecture & William Benton Mus of Art; Circ 16,000
Income: Financed by state appropriation & private funds
Library Holdings: Auction Catalogs, Book Volumes 70,000, Exhibition Catalogs, Fiche, Periodical Subscriptions 180
Special Subjects: Afro-American Art, American Indian Art, Anthropology, Antiquities-Byzantine, Antiquities-Etruscan, Antiquities-Greek, Antiquities-Roman, Asian Art, Etchings & Engravings, Folk Art, Latin American Art, Painting-American, Painting-European, Restoration & Conservation, Theatre Arts

STRATFORD

M **STRATFORD HISTORICAL SOCIETY,** Catharine B Mitchell Museum, 967 Academy Hill, Stratford, CT 06615-6328; Box 382, Stratford, CT 06615. Tel 203-378-0630; Fax 203-378-2562; Email judsonhousestfd@aol.com; *Cur* Carol Lovell
Open Wed, Sat & Sun 11 AM - 4 PM, June - Oct; Admis adults $3, seniors & children $1; Estab 1925 to preserve Stratford's past; Mus contains local history; Judson House, 1750 house with period furnishings; Average Annual Attendance: 1,500; Mem: 400; dues $12; meetings in Sept, Nov, Jan, Mar & May, last Fri of month
Income: Financed by endowment, fundraising & mem
Library Holdings: Book Volumes 4,000, Cards, Clipping Files, Kodachrome Transparencies, Manuscripts, Maps, Memorabilia, Original Art Works, Original Documents, Pamphlets, Photographs, Slides
Special Subjects: American Indian Art, Architecture, Ceramics, Dolls, Drawings, Embroidery, Folk Art, Furniture, Glass, Manuscripts, Maps, Marine Painting, Oriental Art, Painting-American, Period Rooms, Pewter, Photography, Porcelain, Portraits, Posters, Primitive art, Prints, Silver, Textiles, Watercolors
Collections: Local Indians, 18th century house with period furnishings, collection of baskets, ceramics, cooking items, paintings, quilts, military items & weapons, clothing, textiles & furniture
Exhibitions: Permanent and changing exhibitions
Publications: Newsletter
Activities: Classes for children; dramatic progs; docent training; lects open to pub, 5 vis lectrs per yr; tours; individual paintings & original objects of art lent to accredited mus & galleries; lending collection contains books, original art, paintings, photographs & slides; mus shop sells books, reproductions, cards, prints & souvenirs

L **Genealogical Library**, 967 Academy Hill, Stratford, CT 06615; Box 382, Stratford, CT 06615. Tel 203-378-0630; Fax 203-378-2562; Email judsonhousetfd@aol.com; *Cur* Carol W Lovell
Open Tues & Thurs 11 AM - 4 PM; No admis fee; Estab 1925 for preservation and dissemination of items of history of Stratford, Conn; For reference & genealogical research
Income: Financed by mem & city appropriation
Library Holdings: Audio Tapes, Book Volumes 1000, Cassettes, Clipping Files, Exhibition Catalogs, Filmstrips, Kodachrome Transparencies, Manuscripts, Memorabilia, Original Art Works, Pamphlets, Photographs, Prints, Reproductions, Slides, Video Tapes
Special Subjects: American Indian Art, Art History, Ceramics, Drawings, Flasks & Bottles, Folk Art, Furniture, Glass, Manuscripts, Marine Painting, Miniatures, Oriental Art, Painting-American, Period Rooms, Pewter
Collections: Ceramics, Clothing, Textiles, Furniture

WASHINGTON DEPOT

A **WASHINGTON ART ASSOCIATION,** 4 Bryan Plaza, Washington Depot, CT 06794; PO Box 173, Washington Depot, CT 06794-0173. Tel 860-868-2878; Fax 860-868-3447; Email washington.art.assoc@snet.net; Web: www.washingtonart.org; *Admin* Ginger Nelsen; *Asst Admin* Patricia Andersen
Open Tues - Sat 10 AM - 5 PM, Sun noon - 5 PM, cl Mon; No admis fee; Estab 1952 to promote an understanding and appreciation of art & to encourage & facilitate the study and practice of the arts; Three connected galleries for individual & group shows; Average Annual Attendance: 12,000; Mem: 850; dues $35 & up; annual meeting Aug

Income: $32,000 (financed by membership, contributions, commissions, endowment & fund raising events)
Library Holdings: Book Volumes 800, Clipping Files, Exhibition Catalogs, Periodical Subscriptions 2
Exhibitions: Monthly juried exhibitions by regional & nationally known artists
Publications: Events Bulletin, quarterly
Activities: Classes & workshops for adults & children; lect open to pub, 3-4 vis lectr; members show Apr ea yr

WATERBURY

M **MATTATUCK HISTORICAL SOCIETY,** Mattatuck Museum, 144 W Main St, Waterbury, CT 06702-1298. Tel 203-753-0381; Fax 203-756-6283; Email info@mattatuckmuseum.org; Web: www.mattatuckmuseum.org; *Cur* Cynthia Roznoy, PhD
Open Tues - Sat 10 AM - 5 PM, Sun Noon - 5 PM, cl Mon; Admis $7, seniors & students $6, under 16 free; Estab 1877 to collect & preserve the arts, history of America with an emphasis on Connecticut; American art with a focus on Connecticut from Colonial Period to present day; Average Annual Attendance: 45,000; Mem: 550; dues $40-$5000; annual meeting in June
Income: Financed by endowment, mem & grants
Library Holdings: Book Volumes, Exhibition Catalogs, Maps, Photographs
Special Subjects: Ceramics, Decorative Arts, Glass, Historical Material, Landscapes, Painting-American, Photography, Portraits, Sculpture, American Western Art, Drawings, Etchings & Engravings, Textiles
Collections: American art, regional history
Publications: Annual Report
Activities: Classes for adults & children; dramatic progs; docent training; lects open to the public; 8 vis lectrs per year; gallery talks; group tours by appointment; competitions; art and historical objects lent to other mus; Originates traveling exhibs to small and midsize museums throughout the New England corridor; mus shop sells books, original art, reproductions, prints, decorative arts

L **SILAS BRONSON LIBRARY,** 267 Grand St, Waterbury, CT 06702-1981. Tel 203-574-8225; Fax 203-574-8055; Web: www.bronsonlibrary.org; *Dir* Emmett McSweeney
Open Mon - Thurs 9 AM - 8 PM, Fri 9 AM - 5:30 PM, Sat 10 AM - 2 PM; Estab 1869 to provide a free public library for the community; A spotlighted gallery wall & locked glass exhibition case used for art exhibits; Average Annual Attendance: 300,000
Income: Financed by endowment & city appropriation
Library Holdings: Audio Tapes 1964, Book Volumes 207,463, Cassettes 5028, Periodical Subscriptions 2464, Video Tapes 4996
Exhibitions: Local artists in various media; High school art students
Publications: Books & Happenings, monthly newsletter
Activities: Lect open to the public; concerts; individual framed art prints lent

WEST HARTFORD

M **NOAH WEBSTER HOUSE, INC,** Noah Webster House & West Hartford Historical Society, 227 S Main St, West Hartford, CT 06107-3453. Tel 860-521-5362; Fax 860-521-4036; Email comments@noahwebsterhouse.org; Web: www.noahwebsterhouse.org; *Dir Educ* Jennifer DiCola Matos; *Office Mgr* Abigail Perkins; *Dir* Christopher Dobbs; *Coordr Pub Programs* Sarah Mocko; *Mus Shop Mgr* Pattie Whittel; *Asst Cur/Archivist* Sheila Daley
Open Thurs - Mon 1 PM - 4 PM; Admis adult $7, sr citizens & AAA members $5, children 6-college $4, children 5 & under no charge; Estab 1965 to preserve & promote 18th-century daily life, Noah Webster & West Hartford history; Average Annual Attendance: 15,000; Mem: 325; dues $25 & up, annual meeting in May
Exhibitions: Permanent Noah Webster exhibit & temporary exhibits on West Hartford history
Publications: The Spectator, quarterly member newsletter
Activities: Classes for adults & children; docent training; family progs; school & scout progs; lects open to pub; tours; competitions with prizes; lending collection; sales shop sells books, reproductions, prints & educational items

M **SAINT JOSEPH COLLEGE,** Art Gallery, University of Saint Joseph, 1678 Asylum Ave, West Hartford, CT 06117-2791. Tel 860-231-5399; Fax 860-231-5754; Email artgallery@usj.edu; Web: www.usj.edu/artgallery; *Dir, Cur* Ann H Sievers; *Coll Mgr, Registrar* Rochelle L R Oakley
Open Tues, Wed, Fri & Sat 11 AM - 4 PM, Thurs 11 AM - 7 PM, Sun 1PM-4PM, cl Mon; No admis fee; Estab 1937, the gallery opened 2001 in The Carol Autorino Ctr for the Arts & Humanities. It's a resource for the acad community & gen pub through its acad prog, permanent coll & loan exhibs; Average Annual Attendance: 5,000
Special Subjects: Drawings, Etchings & Engravings, Landscapes, Latin American Art, Marine Painting, Mexican Art, Painting-American, Photography, Prints, Watercolors, Woodcuts, Portraits
Collections: Paintings ea 20th Century American Artists, Original Prints from artists dating from the 15th-century to the present, Japanese woodblock prints, Thomas Nast wood engravings
Publications: Exhibition brochures
Activities: Docent training; lects open to public; 1 vis lectrs per year; gallery talks, opening receptions

L **UNIVERSITY OF HARTFORD,** Mortensen Library, 200 Bloomfield Ave, West Hartford, CT 06117-1599. Tel 860-768-4364; Fax 860-768-5165; Email bigazzi@hartford.edu; *Art Reference Librn* Anna Bigazzi
Open Mon - Thurs 8 AM - 12 AM, Fri 8 AM - 6 PM, Sat 10 AM - 6 PM, Sun Noon - 12 AM; Estab 1964
Purchases: $5000
Library Holdings: Exhibition Catalogs, Pamphlets, Periodical Subscriptions 80, Reproductions, Video Tapes
Special Subjects: Afro-American Art, American Indian Art, Art History, Conceptual Art, Decorative Arts, Drawings, Graphic Arts, History of Art & Archaeology, Mexican Art, Oriental Art, Portraits, Pre-Columbian Art, Primitive art, Sculpture, Watercolors

M **UNIVERSITY OF HARTFORD,** Joseloff Gallery, 200 Bloomfield Ave, Harry Jack Gray Ctr West Hartford, CT 06117-1545. Tel 860-768-4090; Fax 860-768-5159; Email gaumond@hartford.edu; Web: www.joseloffgallery.org; *Dir* Zina Davis; *Gallery Mgr* Lisa Gaumond
Open Tues - Fri 11 AM - 4 PM, Sat & Sun Noon - 4 PM; No admis fee; Comprehensive exhibition program focusing on established & emerging artists
Income: financed by the college
Collections: 20th-century & contemporary art in all media, Rotating exhibitions
Activities: Classes for adults

L **Anne Bunce Cheney Art Collection**, 200 Bloomfield Ave, Mortensen Library West Hartford, CT 06117-1545. Tel 860-768-4397; Fax 860-768-4274; Email bigazzi@hartford.edu; Web: www.library.hartford.edu; *Art Reference Librn* Anna Bigazzi
Open Mon - Thurs 8 AM - 1:30 AM, Fri 8 - 6 PM, Sat 10 AM - 6 PM, Sun Noon -1:30 AM; Estab 1964
Income: Financed through university library
Library Holdings: Book Volumes 20,500, Exhibition Catalogs, Pamphlets, Periodical Subscriptions 80, Reproductions 17,600
Special Subjects: Advertising Design, Aesthetics, American Indian Art, Archaeology, Art History, Ceramics, Drawings, Etchings & Engravings, Furniture, Graphic Arts, History of Art & Archaeology, Judaica, Oriental Art, Photography, Sculpture

WESTPORT

A **NEW YORK SOCIETY OF WOMEN ARTISTS, INC,** 19A Darbrook Rd, Westport, CT 06880-3611. Tel 203-329-9179; Email sraushenbusch@earlthlink.net; Web: www.anny.org, www.nyswa.com; *Pres* Stephanie Rauschenbusch; *VPres* Elisa Pritzker; *Exec VPres* Benice Catchi; *Treas* Joyce Pommer; *Recording Sec* Marlene Wiedenbaum; *Recording Sec* Olga Poloukhine
Admis $45; Estab 1920 for the advancement of women's art; Affiliated with Pleiades Gallery in Chelsea, NY; Mem: 60; mem open to superior artists; dues $100; meetings in Nov & May
Income: Financed by jury selection
Special Subjects: Drawings, Prints, Sculpture
Collections: Art Education, Art History, Conceptual Art, Mixed Media, Printmaking

M **WESTPORT ARTS CENTER,** 51 Riverside Ave, Westport, CT 06880. Tel 203-222-7070; Email info@westportartscenter.org; Web: www.westportartscenter.org; *Exec Dir* Peter Van Heerden; *Dir Visual Arts* Helen Klisser During; *Visual Arts Coordr* Jill Sarver
Open Mon-Fri 10AM-4PM, Sat-Sun noon-4PM; No admis fee
Collections: contemporary art; paintings; sculpture

L **WESTPORT PUBLIC LIBRARY,** 20 Jesup Rd, Westport, CT 06880-4329. Tel 203-291-4840; Fax 203-227-3829; Email ref@westportlibrary.org; Web: www.westportlibrary.org; *Dir* Maxine Bleiweis; *Asst Dir & COO* Paul R Mazzaccaro
Open Mon - Thurs 9 AM - 9 PM, Fri 9 AM - 6 PM, Sat 9 AM - 5 PM, Sun 1 - 5 PM; No admis fee; Estab 1907; Circ 839,613; Art display kiosks in library with exhibits; Average Annual Attendance: 591,516
Income: $5,649,157, 82% town appropriation, 18% contributions, endowments and other
Purchases: $521,178
Library Holdings: Book Volumes, Compact Disks, DVDs, Original Art Works, Periodical Subscriptions, Video Tapes
Collections: Picture collection (for pictorial research by artists, illustrators, & designers), Famous Artists School Publications
Publications: 5 per year newsletter
Activities: Lect open to public

WETHERSFIELD

M **WETHERSFIELD HISTORICAL SOCIETY INC,** Museum, 150 Main St, Wethersfield, CT 06109-3126. Tel 860-529-7656; Fax 860-563-2609; *Dir* Brenda Milkofsky
Open Tues - Sat 10 AM - 4 PM, Sun 1 - 4 PM; Estab 1932 to preserve local history; Two changing exhibit rooms; Average Annual Attendance: 18,000; Mem: 800; dues family $35, individual $23; annual meeting in mid-May
Income: $190,000 (financed by endowment, mem, programs & fundraising)
Special Subjects: Archaeology, Costumes, Folk Art, Furniture, Historical Material, Maps, Painting-American, Period Rooms, Photography, Textiles
Collections: Local history/culture
Exhibitions: Changing monthly exhibits
Publications: Newsletter, quarterly
Activities: Children's progs; docent progs; lects open to pub, 4 vis lectrs per yr; book traveling exhibs 8 per yr; retail store sells books & prints

L **Old Academy Library**, 150 Main St, Wethersfield, CT 06109. Tel 860-529-7656; Fax 860-563-2609; Email society@wethhist.org; Web: www.wethhist.org; *Interim Dir* Jose Fiak
Open Tues - Fri 9 AM - 4 PM & by appointment; Estab 1932; Mem: 1000; dues vary
Income: $250,000 (financed by endowment, mem, programs, donations & rentals)
Library Holdings: Book Volumes 2000, Original Documents, Photographs
Special Subjects: Historical Material
Collections: Wethersfield history & genealogy
Exhibitions: Wethersfield History; Legendary People, Ordinary Lives (permanent)
Publications: Newsletter, quarterly
Activities: Classes for adults & children; docent progs; lects open to pub, 3 - 4 vis lectrs per yr; concerts; gallery talks; tours; book traveling exhibs 4 per yr; retail store sells books, prints & more

WHITNEYVILLE

A **NEW HAVEN PAINT & CLAY CLUB, INC,** PO Box 6314, Whitneyville, CT 06517-6314. Tel 203-624-8055; Email jciravolo97@gmail.com; Web: www.elyhouse.org; *Pres* Jeanne Ciravolo; *VPres* Sheila Kaczmarek; *VPres* Bill Meddick
Estab 1900 to provide opportunities for artists in New England to exhibit their work, inc in 1928; Mem: 270; open to artists working in any media whose work has been accepted two times in the Annual Juried Show; dues life $100, active $20, assoc $10; annual meeting in May
Purchases: $3000
Collections: 280 2-D pictures & 14 sculptures
Exhibitions: Annual Mar-Apr Exhibition (New England & New York artists); Annual Fall Exhibition (active members only); Permanent Collection
Publications: Exhibition catalogs; newsletter
Activities: Lects open to pub, 1 vis lectr per yr; lects at annual meeting; awards $500 members show, $4500 juried exhibition; scholarships; individual paintings & original objects of art lent to local organizations

WILTON

M **NATIONAL PARK SERVICE,** Weir Farm National Historic Site, 735 Nod Hill Rd, Wilton, CT 06897-1309. Tel 203-834-1896; Fax 203-834-2421; Email wefa_interpretation@nps.gov; Web: www.nps.gov/wefa; *Supt* Linda Cook
Open 9:00 AM - 5 PM Wed-Sun May -Oct; 10AM - 4PM Thurs-Sun, Nov -Apr; Grounds open every day from dawn to dusk; No admis fee; Estab 1990; Visitor center has changing exhibits in two small rooms; Average Annual Attendance: 10,000
Special Subjects: Architecture, Decorative Arts, Etchings & Engravings, Furniture, Historical Material, Landscapes, Painting-American, Watercolors
Collections: American Impressionist paintings, Decorative Arts Collection, Finding Aid for the Dorothy Weir Young Research Papers (1813-1947), Finding Aid for the Weir Family Papers (1746-1962), Finding Aid for the Burlingham/Weir Archive of the Metropolitan Museum of Art, American Impressionist Paintings, J Alden Weir Archive & Manuscripts Collection
Activities: Classes for children; visiting & resident artist prog for professional artists; lects open to pub, 5 vis lectrs per yr; tours; mus shop sells books & prints

WINDSOR

M **THE LOOMIS CHAFFEE SCHOOL,** Mercy Gallery, 4 Batchelder Rd, Windsor, CT 06095-3028. Tel 860-687-6030; 687-6104

DELAWARE

DOVER

M **BIGGS MUSEUM OF AMERICAN ART,** 406 Federal St, Dover, DE 19901; PO Box 711, Dover, DE 19903-0711. Tel 302-674-2111; Fax 302-674-5133; Email admin@biggsmuseum.org; Web: www.biggsmuseum.org; *Cur* Ryan Grover; *Dir* Charles A Guerin; *Chm (V)* Marcia Dewitt; *Mus Mgr* Ellen Arthur; *Mktg Mgr* Stephanie Adams
Open Tues - Sat 9 AM - 4:30 PM, Sun 1 PM - 4:30 PM, cl New Year' Day, Easter, Thanksgiving, Christmas; Visit website for admis fees; Estab 1989; Includes 25 galleries; Average Annual Attendance: 20,000; Mem: Dues: Individual $40, Artist $60, Family $75, Reciprocal $125, Curator's Circle $250, Director's Circle $500, Sewell's Circle $1,000.
Income: financed by endowment, mem, state appropriation, foundations & contributions
Purchases: $50,000
Library Holdings: Auction Catalogs, Book Volumes, Clipping Files, Exhibition Catalogs, Kodachrome Transparencies, Memorabilia, Periodical Subscriptions, Photographs, Slides
Special Subjects: Ceramics, Furniture, Painting-American, Portraits, Sculpture, Silver, Textiles, Watercolors, Decorative Arts, Prints, Drawings, Graphics
Collections: Biggs Collection of American Representational Paintings & Decorative Arts from the Delaware Valley, Delaware Silver Study Ctr
Publications: Quarterly newsletter; bi-monthly calendar; 2-vol catalogue The Sewell
Activities: Adult & children's activities; docent training; school tours; lects open to pub, 10 vis lectrs per yr; gallery talks; classes for children; art workshops; competitions; mus shop sells book & postcards

M **DELAWARE DIVISION OF HISTORICAL & CULTURAL AFFAIRS,** 102 S State St, Dover, DE 19901; 21 The Green, Dover, DE 19901. Tel 302-739-5316; Fax 302-739-6712; Web: www.destatemuseum.org; *Cur Coll* Ann Baker Horsey; *Cur Educ* Madeline Dunn; *Coll Mgr* Claudia Leister; *Cur Archaeology* Charles Fithian; *Mgr* Lynn Riley; *Site Adminstr* Beverly Laing
Open John Dickinson Plantation: Tues - Sat 10 AM - 3:30 PM, Apr - Dec 1:30 - 4:30 PM; Johnson Victrola Museum, Meeting House Galleries I & II: Tues - Sat 10 AM - 3:30 PM; Old State House, Zwaanendael, New Castle Courthouse: Tues - Sat 8:30 AM - 4:30 PM, Sun 1:30 - 4:30 PM; State Visitor Ctr (Dover): Mon - Sat 8:30 AM - 4:30 PM, Sun 1:30 - 4:30 PM; No admis fee; Historic house museums were opened in the 1950s, Zwaanendael Museum 1931, to reflect the pre-historic & historic develop of Delaware by exhibiting artifacts & interpreting the same through various facilities-those of early times; Average Annual Attendance: 100,000
Income: $2,400,000 (state appropriations)
Library Holdings: Book Volumes, Cassettes, Compact Disks, Exhibition Catalogs, Manuscripts, Maps, Memorabilia, Original Art Works, Original Documents, Periodical Subscriptions, Photographs, Records
Special Subjects: Archaeology, Architecture, Glass, Historical Material, Painting-American, Period Rooms, Portraits, Posters, Silver, Ceramics, Textiles
Collections: Meeting House Galleries I & II: Prehistoric & Historic Archaeology, Museum of Small Town Life: Main Street Delaware, John Dickinson Plantation: Decorative arts, furniture & Dickinson family objects, New Castle Court House: Portraits of famous Delawareans, archaeological artifacts, furniture & maps, Old State House: legislative judicial & governmental furniture & decorative arts, Zwaanendael Museum: HMB Debraak Artifacts, Commemorative gifts to the State of Delaware from Holland, china, glass, & silver, Johnson Victrola Museum: Talking machines, Victrolas, early recordings & Johnson memorabilia associated with the Victor Talking Machine Company (RCA), Victor Talking Machine Company Phonographs & Records, HMS DeBraak, 18th century British Warship, Maritime Archaeology
Publications: Delaware State Museum Bulletins; Delaware History Notebook; miscellaneous booklets & brochures
Activities: Classes for adults & children; docent training; special educational progs for school groups & adults which reflect the architecture, government, educ & aspects of social history relevant to Delaware; lects open to pub; gallery talks; tours; Nat Tourism award; individual paintings are lent to governmental facilities; in-service progs relating to Delaware history are offered to Delaware teachers; internship; lending of original objects of art to other mus; originate traveling trunk prog circulated to elementary schools; mus shop sells books, magazines, prints, original art & Delaware souvenirs

MILLSBORO

M **NANTICOKE INDIAN MUSEUM,** Rte 24, Millsboro, DE 19966; 27073 John J Williams Hwy, Millsboro, DE 19966-4642. Tel 302-945-7022 (Museum), 302-945-3400 (Tribal Office); Fax 302-947-9411; Email info@nanticokeindians.org; Web: www.thelongneckpage.com/nia
Open Summer: Tues - Sat 10 AM - 4 PM; Jan - April: Thurs - Sat 10 AM - 4 PM, Sun noon - 5 PM; Admis adults $2, children $1; 1984; Mus mission is to tell the story of the Nanticoke Native Americans, people who have faced many obstacles throughout history
Special Subjects: Historical Material, Pottery, Costumes, Woodcarvings, Photography
Collections: Stone artifacts, carvings, pottery, traditional clothing, mus library houses large coll of Native American books, photos & video presentations
Activities: Ann Nanticoke Indian Powwow celebration

NEWARK

M **UNIVERSITY OF DELAWARE,** University Museums, 30 N College Ave, 208 Mechanical Hall Newark, DE 19716. Tel 302-831-8037; Fax 302-831-8057; Email museums@udel.edu; Web: library.udel.edu/special; *Dir* Janis A Tomlinson, PhD; *Cur Mineralogical Mus* Sharon Fitzgerald PhD; *Colls Mgr* Janet G Broske; *Preparator & Facilities Coordr* Brian Kamen
Open Thurs - Sun noon - 5 PM, Wed noon - 8 PM, cl Mon, Tues, late July & Aug & during Univ vacations; No admis fee; Estab 1978 to enhance the educational & scholarly mission of the Univ of Delaware; enriches cultural life beyond the campus through presentation of the work of recognized artists & through outreach programs; 3 art galleries in Old College & Mechanical Hall, Mineralogical Museums; Average Annual Attendance: 6,000
Special Subjects: African Art, Antiquities-Byzantine, Antiquities-Egyptian, Antiquities-Greek, Antiquities-Roman, Drawings, Eskimo Art, Etchings & Engravings, Graphics, Landscapes, Painting-American, Pottery, Prints, Sculpture, Textiles
Collections: 19th & 20th century American works on paper, Pre-Columbian textiles & ceramics, African Artifacts, early 20th century photographs, Contemporary Canadian Prints and Inuit Drawings, African-American Art, Paul R Jones Collection of African American 20th Century Art, Mineralogical collection
Publications: Exhibit catalog; brochures
Activities: Lects open to pub, 4 vis lectrs per yr; gallery talks; tours; individual & original objects of art lent to other mus & universities; mus shop sells books

L **Morris Library**, 181 S College Ave, Newark, DE 19717-5267. Tel 302-831-2965, 831-2231; Fax 302-831-1046; Web: www.udel.edu/library; *Vice Provost & May Morris Dir Libraries* Susan Brynteson; *Subject Librn (Art & Art History)* Susan A Davi; *Head Reference Dept* Shirley Branden; *Asst Dir Library Collections* Craig Wilson; *Asst Dir Library Pub Serv* Sandra Millard; *Asst Dir Library Technical Servs* M Dina Giambi; *Asst Dir Library Computing Systems* Gregg Silvis; *Asst Dir Library Admin Servs* Paul Anderson
Open Fall and Spring Mon - Thur 8 AM - 12 AM, Fri 8 AM - 8 PM, Sat 9 AM - 8 PM, Sun 11 AM - 12 AM
Income: Financed through the University
Purchases: $113,150
Library Holdings: Audio Tapes, Book Volumes 2,704,986, Cards, Cassettes 7735, Compact Disks, DVDs 2,199, Exhibition Catalogs, Fiche, Filmstrips 1646, Manuscripts 2952, Micro Print, Motion Pictures, Pamphlets, Periodical Subscriptions 12,532, Photographs, Prints, Records, Reels, Slides, Video Tapes 14,204
Collections: American art & architecture, early 20th century European art, material on ornamental horticulture, ARTstor

ODESSA

L **CORBIT-CALLOWAY MEMORIAL LIBRARY,** 115 High St, PO Box 128 Odessa, DE 19730-0128. Tel 302-378-8838; Fax 302-378-7803; Email corbit@infinet.com; Web: www.corbitlibrary.org; *Dir* Steven J Welch
Open Mon & Sat 1 - 9 PM, Wed & Fri 10 AM - 5 PM, Wed until 9 PM, Sat 9 AM - 1 PM; No admis fee; Estab 1847
Library Holdings: Audio Tapes, Book Volumes 21,000, Periodical Subscriptions 58, Slides, Video Tapes
Collections: Delawareana

REHOBOTH BEACH

A **REHOBOTH ART LEAGUE, INC,** 12 Dodds Lane, Henlopen Acres Rehoboth Beach, DE 19971-1668. Tel 302-227-8408; Fax 302-227-4121; Web: www.rehobothartleague.org; *Pres Board* Marcia DeWitt; *Dir* Lawrence Sweigert; *Gallery Mgr* Nick Serratare
Open Mon - Sat 9AM-4PM, Sun noon-4PM; No admis fee; Estab 1938 to provide art educ & creative arts in Rehoboth Beach community & Sussex County, Delaware; Two galleries, the Corkran & the Tubbs built for exhibitions; plus Homestead, c 1743, gallery & studio; Average Annual Attendance: 10,000; Mem: 1200; dues $50 & up
Income: Financed by mem, donations, fund raising & sales of paintings
Special Subjects: Etchings & Engravings, Historical Material, Marine Painting, Painting-American
Collections: Small permanent collection from gifts (1,000+), includes many Ethel P B Leach, Orville Peats & Howard Pyle
Exhibitions: Annual Members Fine Arts Crafts Exhibition; Annual Members Fine Arts Exhibition; Outdoor Fine Art; Individual and visiting artist exhibits throughout the year
Publications: Brochure of yearly events; calendar of classes
Activities: Classes for adults & children; docent training; lect open to public, 3 vis lectrs per year; concerts; gallery talks; competitions with awards; Regional Juried Show, Member Fine Art, Young at Art; serves disadvantaged communities via Sussex County, DE; lending coll extended to Biggs Mus, Dover DE; sales shop sells books, original art & prints

WILMINGTON

A **CHRISTINA CULTURAL ARTS CENTER, INC,** 705 N Market St, Wilmington, DE 19801-3008. Tel 302-652-0101; Fax 302-652-7480; Email info@ccacde.org; Web: www.ccacde.org; *Exec Dir* H Raye Jones-Avery; *Educ Dir* Kim Graham; *Dir Fin* Jo Anne Jackson; *Visual Arts* Milton Downing
Open Mon - Fri 9 AM - 9 PM, Sat 9 AM - 5 PM; No admis fee; Estab to bring professional arts training & educ to a broad spectrum of the community with an emphasis on serving low income families

M **DELAWARE ART MUSEUM,** 2301 Kentmere Pkwy, Wilmington, DE 19806-2096. Tel 302-571-9590, 866-232-3714; Fax 302-571-0220; Email info@delart.org; Web: www.delart.org; *Exec Dir & CEO* Samuel Sweet; *Cur Illustrations & Outlook Exhibs* Mary F Holahan; *Cur Bancroft Coll* Margaretta S Frederick; *Chief Cur & Cur American Art* Heather Campbell Coyle; *Cur Contemporary Art* Margaret Winslow; *Dir Devel & External Affairs* Molly Giordano; *Dir Educ* Saralyn Rosenfield; *Opers Mgr* AJ Schwander
Open Wed - Sun 10 AM - 4 PM, Thurs 10 - 8 PM, cl Mon, Tues, New Year's Day, July 4, Thanksgiving & Christmas Day; Admis family of 2 adults & 4 youth $25, adults $12, seniors $10, college students with ID & youth ages 7-18 $6, mems & children 6 & under free, Sun free to all; Blue Star admis for military & families; other discounts available; Incorporated 1912 as the Wilmington Soc of Fine Arts; present building expanded 1987; a privately funded, non-profit cultural & educational institution dedicated to the increase of knowledge & pleasure through the display & interpretation of works of art & through classes designed to encourage an understanding of & a participation in the fine arts; Nine galleries are used for exhibitions; 8 usually hold permanent or semi-permanent exhibitions which change at six week intervals; maintains Copeland Sculpture Garden; Average Annual Attendance: 20,000; Mem: 3200; dues Dir Cir $1500-$10000, benefactor $500, sponsor $250, family $70-$125, individual $50; annual meeting in Mar
Income: Financed by endowment, mem & grants
Purchases: $20,000
Library Holdings: Auction Catalogs, Book Volumes, Clipping Files, DVDs, Exhibition Catalogs, Fiche, Filmstrips, Manuscripts, Original Documents, Periodical Subscriptions, Photographs, Prints, Reels, Slides
Special Subjects: Decorative Arts, Etchings & Engravings, Graphics, Landscapes, Painting-American, Painting-British, Photography, Portraits, Posters, Prints, Sculpture
Collections: Copeland Collection of Work by Local Artists, American paintings & sculpture, including many Howard Pyle works & complete etchings & lithographs of John Sloan, Bancroft Collection, Phelps Collection, Works by Edward Hopper, George Segal & Robert Motherwell
Exhibitions: 6 or more every yr
Publications: DAM Magazine, quarterly
Activities: Classes for adults & children; docent training; workshops; studio art progs; outreach; art camp; mem events; lects open to pub; concerts; gallery talks; tours; fellowships; fellowship available; exten dept serving schools & community groups offering two-week programs in visual educ; originate traveling exhibs; mus shop sells books, original art, reproductions

L **Helen Farr Sloan Library**, 2301 Kentmere Pky, Wilmington, DE 19806. Tel 302-571-9590 (Mus); 351-8540 (Librn); Fax 302-571-0220; Email rdieleuterio@delart.org; Web: www.delart.org; *Head Librn* Rachael DiEleuterio
Open Wed - Fri 10 AM - 4 PM by appt only; Estab 1923; Open to public for reference only
Library Holdings: Auction Catalogs, Book Volumes 40,000, Clipping Files, DVDs, Exhibition Catalogs, Lantern Slides, Manuscripts, Maps, Memorabilia, Original Art Works, Original Documents, Pamphlets, Periodical Subscriptions, Photographs, Prints, Reproductions, Slides, Video Tapes
Special Subjects: Art History, Illustration, Painting-American, Crafts, Decorative Arts, Manuscripts, Painting-British, Photography, Posters, Prints
Collections: John Sloan Archives and Library, Howard Pyle Archives and Library, Samuel Bancroft Pre-Raphaelite Library, Everett Shinn Archives, Frank Schoonover Archives
Activities: Adopt-A-Book sponsor prog

M **DELAWARE CENTER FOR THE CONTEMPORARY ARTS,** 200 S Madison St, Wilmington, DE 19801-5100. Tel 302-656-6466; Fax 302-656-6944; Email info@thedcca.org; Web: www.thedcca.org; *Exec Dir* Joseph J Gonzelez; *Interim Cur Contemporary Art* Katherine Page; *Cur Coordr* J Gordon; *Dir Educ* Jennifer Polillo; *Develop Mgr* Jillian E Decker; *Dir Special Events* Megan Mika; *Mktg* Tatiana Michels; *Dir Security & Opers* Antonio Calzada-Charma; *Assoc Dir Admin* Helen Page
Open Tues & Sun Noon - 5 PM, Wed Noon - 7 PM, Thurs - Sat 10 AM - 5 PM; Admis suggested adults $10, children under 18 $5; Estab 1979 to promote growth & develop of contemporary arts in Delaware; 35,000 sq ft comprising 7 galleries, 26 artists studios, an auditorium, classroom & gift shop; Average Annual Attendance: 18,000; Mem: Dues $40 general & up
Exhibitions: Art Auction; Rotating exhibitions every 6-8 weeks
Publications: Exhibition catalogs & brochures
Activities: Classes for adults & children; outreach progs; docent training; lects open to pub; symposia; concerts; mus shop sells books, magazines & original art

M **DELAWARE HISTORICAL SOCIETY,** Delaware History Museum and Center for African American Heritage, 504 N Market St, Wilmington, DE 19801; 505 N Market St, Wilmington, DE 19801. Tel 302-655-0637; Fax 302-655-7844; Email deinfo@dehistory.org; Web: dehistory.org; *Chief Cur* Leigh Rifenburg; *Cur Objects* Jennifer Potts; *CEO* Scott W Loehr; *Head Mus Progs* Rebecca Fay
Open Wed - Sat 11 AM - 4 PM; Admis fee adults $6, seniors, military & students $5, children $4; Estab 1864 to preserve, collect & display material related to Delaware History; Delaware History Mus & Old Town Hall Mus are the main mus galleries for the Delaware Historical Society; Mem: 1400; dues $45; annual meeting in Oct
Collections: Regional decorative arts, children's toys, costumes, distinctively Delaware, photos, art objects; textiles, Delaware African American
Exhibitions: Core Exhibits: One State, Many Stories & The Center for African American Heritage
Publications: Delaware History, twice a year
Activities: Classes for adults & children; lects open to pub, 3-7 vis lectrs per yr; concerts; gallery talks; tours; originate traveling exhibs in conjunction with other history mus; mus shop sells books, reproductions, prints

M **Read House and Gardens**, 42 The Strand, New Castle, DE 19720. Tel 302-322-8411; Web: www.hsd.org; *Dir Library Progs* Brenton Grom
Open Wed - Fri 11 AM - 4 PM, Sat 10 Am - 4 PM, Sun 11 AM - 4 PM, by appointment only Jan - March, cl major holidays.; Admis adults $7, students & seniors 65 & over $6, children under 10 free; Estab 1976; period rooms in the Georgian-Federal mansion with garden installed in 1847; Average Annual Attendance: 20,000; Mem: 1200; dues $10 & up
Special Subjects: Architecture, Decorative Arts, Furniture, Landscapes, Portraits
Collections: Federal Period decorative arts & architecture
Activities: Classes for children; family-oriented programming; lects open to pub, walking tours; sales shop sells books & crafts

L **Library**, 505 N Market St, Wilmington, DE 19801. Tel 302-655-7161; Fax 302-655-7844; Email deinfo@dehistory.org; Web: dehistory.org; *CEO* Scott W Loehr; *Chief Cur* Leigh Rifenburg; *Asst CEO* Michele Anstine
Open Mon 11 AM - 7 PM, Tues & Thurs 9 AM - 1 PM, Fri 9 AM - 5 PM, cl Wed; estab 1864; Circ non-circulation; reference only; Average Annual Attendance: 1,200; Mem: 1400; $45 per yr; Annual meeting in Oct
Income: $1,500,000 (financed by endowment, annual support & grants)
Purchases: $15,000
Library Holdings: Audio Tapes, Book Volumes 75,000, Cassettes, Clipping Files, Exhibition Catalogs, Fiche, Filmstrips, Kodachrome Transparencies, Lantern Slides, Manuscripts, Maps, Memorabilia, Motion Pictures, Original Art Works, Original Documents, Pamphlets, Periodical Subscriptions 73, Photographs, Prints, Records, Reels, Reproductions, Slides, Video Tapes
Collections: Manuscript; photography; maps; books
Publications: Delaware History; twice a yr
Activities: Classes for adults; gallery talks; tours; lects open to pub; History Makers award; mus shop

M **THE NEMOURS FOUNDATION,** Nemours Mansion & Gardens, 1600 Rockland Rd, Wilmington, DE 19803-3607. Tel 302-651-6912; Fax 302-651-6370; Email tours@nemours.org; Web: www.nemoursmansion.org
Open Tues - Sat 10 AM - 5 PM, Sun Noon - 5 PM, cl Mon; Admis $17, senior, active military & student with ID $15, children (5-16) $7, children under 5 free; Estab 1977; 300 acre estate of Alfred I du Pont; 72 room modified Louis XVI chateau built 1909 - 10; formal French-style gardens and natural woods; Average Annual Attendance: 20,000
Income: Financed by pvt funding
Special Subjects: Furniture, Tapestries, Bronzes, American Western Art, Carpets & Rugs, Ceramics, Decorative Arts, Drawings, Enamels, Glass, Landscapes, Marine Painting, Painting-American, Painting-British, Painting-Dutch, Painting-European, Painting-Flemish, Painting-French, Painting-German, Painting-Italian, Painting-Spanish, Porcelain, Portraits, Pottery, Prints, Religious Art, Renaissance Art, Sculpture, Silver, Tapestries, Watercolors
Collections: Collection of European furniture, tapestries, & paintings dating back to the 15th century, Oriental rugs, objects d'art, Household goods

WINTERTHUR

M **WINTERTHUR MUSEUM,** Winterthur Museum, Garden & Library, 5105 Kennett Pike, Winterthur, DE 19735-0002. Tel 302-888-4600; 800-448-3883; Fax 302-888-4820; Email pressroom@winterthur.org; Web: www.winterthur.org; *Dir* Dr David P Roselle; *Dir Museum Affairs* J Thomas Savage; *Estate Historian & Cur Garden Objects* Jeff Groff; *Dir Colls* Linda Eaton; *Dir Develop* Robert Davis; *Dir Library, Colls Management & Acad Progs* Greg Landrey; *Dir Garden & Estate* Chris Strand; *Dir & CFO* Robert Necarsulmer
Open Tues - Sun 10 AM - 5 PM, cl Mondays, Thanksgiving, Christmas; Admis $20, sr, student & group discounts, guided tours of mus additional fee; Opened 1951, a nonprofit, educ corporation; Collection of 90,000 objects made used in America between 1640-1860 including furniture, textiles, paintings, prints, ceramics, brass, pewter, needlework & much more; Average Annual Attendance: 150,000; Mem: 13,000 individuals & families, dues vary
Income: nonprofit corporation
Library Holdings: Auction Catalogs, Audio Tapes, Book Volumes, Cards, Exhibition Catalogs, Fiche, Manuscripts, Maps, Original Documents, Other Holdings, Pamphlets, Periodical Subscriptions, Photographs, Prints

Special Subjects: Bookplates & Bindings, Carpets & Rugs, Ceramics, Decorative Arts, Drawings, Embroidery, Etchings & Engravings, Folk Art, Glass, Historical Material, Jewelry, Landscapes, Maps, Painting-American, Porcelain, Prints, Sculpture, Textiles, Watercolors, Manuscripts
Collections: Antique furniture, silver, needlework, textiles, painting, prints, ceramics and glass, interior architecture
Publications: Winterthur portfolio
Activities: Classes for adults & children; 2 grad prog; lects; concerts; gallery talks; tours; seminars; film; competitions with awards; fels; exten prog for regional area, original art lent to other mus & institutions; book traveling exhibs 1-2 per year; originate traveling exhibs to select mus Winter and Fall Institutes; mus shop sells books, reproductions, plants

DISTRICT OF COLUMBIA

WASHINGTON

M **ADDISON/RIPLEY FINE ART,** 1670 Wisconsin Ave NW, Washington, DC 20007. Tel 202-338-5180; Fax 202-338-2341; Email info@addisonripleyfineart.com; Web: www.addisonripleyfineart.com; *Owner* Christopher Addison; *Dir* Romy Silverstein
Open Tues - Sat 11 AM - 5:30 PM, other times by appointment
Collections: works by contemporary artists; paintings; sculptures; photographs; fine art prints

AMERICAN ALLIANCE OF MUSEUMS
For further information, see National and Regional Organizations

M **AMERICAN ARCHITECTURAL FOUNDATION,** The Octagon Museum, 740 15th St, #225, Washington, DC 20005-1019. Tel 202-638-3105 (information), 638-3221 (museum); Fax 202-879-7764; Web: www.archfoundation.org; *Dir* Eryl J Wentworth; *Cur Exhibits* Linnea Hamer; *Cur Coll* Sherry Birk
Open Tues - Sun 10 AM - 4 PM, cl Mon; Admis adults $5, seniors & students $3; groups over 10 charges $3 per person except student & seniors groups $1 per person; Opened as house mus in 1970; formerly a federal townhouse designed by the first architect of the United States Capitol, Dr William Thornton for Col John Taylor III to serve as a winter home; used by President & Mrs Madison as temporary White House during war of 1812; Furnished with late 18th & early 19th centuries decorative arts; changing exhibition program in second floor galleries; Average Annual Attendance: 35,000
Collections: Permanent collection of furniture, paintings, ceramics, kitchen utensils
Publications: Competition 1792-Designing a Nation's Capitol, 1976 book; exhibition catalogs; Octagon being an Account of a Famous Residence: Its Great Years, Decline & Restoration, 1976 book; William Thornton: A Renaissance Man in the Federal City, book; The Architect & the British Country House, book; Architectural Records Management, 1985 booklet; the Architecture of Richard Morris Hunt, 1986 book; Building the Octagon, 1989 book; Ambitious Appetites: Dining, Behavior & Patterns of Consumption in Federal Washington, 1990 book; In the Most Fashionable Style: Making a Home in the Federal City, 1991 book; Creating the Federal City, 1774-1800: Potomac Fever, 1988 book; The Frame in American, 1700-1900: A survey of Fabrication, Techniques & Styles, 1983 catalog; Robert Mills, Architect, 1989 book; Sir Christopher Wren: The Design of St Paul's Cathedral, 1987 book; & exhibit catalogs
Activities: Educ dept; docent training; lects open to pub, 6 vis lectrs per yr; tours; mus shop sells books & gift items

M **Museum,** 1735 New York Ave, NW, Washington, DC 20006-5292. Tel 202-626-7500; Fax 202-879-7764; Web: www.aaspages.org; *VPres* Melissa Houghton
Open to the pub for reference but primarily used by staff; Mem: 350; dues $30-$50
Income: mem & contributions
Special Subjects: Archaeology, Decorative Arts

M **AMERICAN ART MUSEUM,** Smithsonian Institution, 8th & F Sts NW, Washington, DC 20004; MRC 970 Box 37012, Washington, DC 20013-7012. Tel 202-633-7970; Email AmericanArtInfo@si.edu; Web: americanart.si.edu; *Dir* Stephanie Stebich; *Chief Cur* Virginia M Mecklenburg; *Deputy Chief Cur* E. Carmen Ramos
Open 11:30 AM - 7 PM daily, cl Dec 25; No admis fee; Estab 1829 & later absorbed by the Smithsonian Institution, it was designated the National Gallery of Art in 1906. The museum's name was changed to the National Collection of Fine Art in 1937 & in 1980, to the National Museum of American Art. With the largest collection of American art in the world, it is the leading center for study of the nation's heritage. On Oct 27, 2000 its name was officially changed to the Smithsonian American Art Museum; Circ 100,000; Bureau of the Smithsonian Institution; Average Annual Attendance: 1,625,000
Library Holdings: Book Volumes, CD-ROMs, Exhibition Catalogs, Pamphlets, Periodical Subscriptions
Special Subjects: Afro-American Art, American Indian Art, American Western Art, Decorative Arts, Drawings, Etchings & Engravings, Folk Art, Furniture, Glass, Gold, Graphics, Hispanic Art, Jewelry, Landscapes, Marine Painting, Painting-American, Photography, Portraits, Primitive art, Stained Glass, Textiles, Watercolors, Woodcarvings, Woodcuts
Collections: All regions, cultures & traditions in the United States are represented in the museum's holdings, research resources, exhibitions & public programs. Colonial portraiture, 19th century landscapes, American impressionism, 20th century realism & abstraction, New Deal projects, sculpture, photography, graphic arts, works by African Americans, contemporary art & the creativity of self-taught artists are featured in the galleries, Major collections include those of Harriet Lane Johnston (1906), William T Evans (1907), John Gellatly (1929), the SC Johnson & Son Collection (1967), Container Corporation of America Collection (1984), Sara Roby Foundation Collection (1984), Herbert Waide Hemphill Jr Collection (1986) & the Patricia & Phillip Frost Collection, Research resources include 300,000 listings on the Inventory of American Painting & Sculpture, Container Corporation of America Collection, William T Evans Collection, Patricia & Phillip Frost Collection, John Gellatly Collection, Herbert Waide Hemphill Jr Collection, SC Johnson & Son Collection, Harriet Lane Johnston Collection, Sara Roby Foundation Collection, Levin Collection
Exhibitions: A representative selection of works from the collection are on permanent display in the galleries, providing a comprehensive view of the varied aspects of American art. Many temporary exhibitions, approx 12 per year, are originated by the staff. They include both studies of individual artists & thematic studies; Luce Foundation Ctr & Conservation Ctr visible storage holds over 3,300 works on view
Publications: American Art, journal; calendar of events; quarterly member newsletter; major exhibitions are accompanied by authoritative publications; smaller exhibitions are accompanied by checklists & often brochures
Activities: The museum carries on an active prog with schools & the general pub, offering imaginative participatory tours for children, as well as lect & symposia for adults. A research prog in American art is maintained for vis scholars & training is carried on through internships in general mus practice & conservation; docent training; concerts; gallery talks; tours; sponsoring of competitions; Charles C Eldridge Prize for distinguished schol in American art; Lucelia Artist Award; Patricia & Phillip Frost Essay award; fels offered; circulates exhibs throughout the United States on a regular basis; mus shop sells books, magazines, original art, reproductions & prints; Renwick Gallery branch mus

L **Library,** Victor Bldg, Ste 2100, 750 9th St NW Washington, DC 20560-4505; PO Box 37012, MRC 975 Washington, DC 20013-7012. Tel 202-633-8230; Fax 202-633-8232; Email AAPGLibrary@si.edu; Web: library.si.edu; *Head Librn* Anne Evenhaugen; *Reference Librn* Alexandra Reigle
Open Mon - Fri 10 AM - 5 PM, cl Federal holidays; No admis fee; Estab 1964 to serve the reference & research needs of the staff & affiliated researchers of the National Museum of American Art, The National Portrait Gallery, the Archives of American Art & other Smithsonian bureaus; Research facility open to Smithsonian staff & fellows, researchers, & students. Branch of the Smithsonian Institution Libraries; shared with National Portrait Gallery
Income: Financed by federal appropriation
Library Holdings: Auction Catalogs, Book Volumes, CD-ROMs, Clipping Files, DVDs, Exhibition Catalogs, Fiche, Manuscripts, Other Holdings Catalogues Raisonne; Dissertations; Scrapbooks, Pamphlets, Periodical Subscriptions, Reels, Video Tapes
Special Subjects: Painting-American
Collections: Ferdinand Perret Art Reference Library: coll of scrapbooks of clippings & pamphlets, special section on California art & artists consisting ring binders on art & artists of Southern California, vertical file drawers of material on art & artists, with increasing emphasis on American art & artists, Online Digital Coll, Living Portrait Artists' File

M **Renwick Gallery,** Pennsylvania Ave NW at 17th St, Washington, DC 20006; MRC 510 Box 37012, Washington, DC 20013-7012. Tel 202-633-7970; Email AmericanArtInfo@si.edu; Web: americanart.si.edu/renwick; *Cur-in-Charge* Abraham Thomas; *Cur of Craft* Nora Atkinson; *Chief Admin* Robyn Kennedy
Open daily 10 AM - 5:30 PM, cl Dec 25; No admis fee; Designed in 1859 by architect James Renwick, Jr as the original Corcoran Gallery of Art, the building was renamed for the architect in 1965 when it was transferred by the Federal government to the Smithsonian Institution for restoration; Restored to its French Second Empire elegance after 67 years as the United States Ct of Claims, the building has two public rooms with period furnishings, the Grand Salon & the Octagon Room, as well as eight areas for its permanent collection & temporary exhibitions of American crafts, design & decorative arts; Average Annual Attendance: 575,000
Special Subjects: Crafts, Period Rooms, Decorative Arts
Publications: Major exhibitions are accompanied by publications, smaller exhibitions by checklists & brochures
Activities: Docent training; film progs; lects & workshops emphasizing the creative work of American craft artists; tours; concerts

AMERICAN ASSOCIATION OF UNIVERSITY WOMEN
For further information, see National and Regional Organizations

AMERICAN INSTITUTE OF ARCHITECTS
For further information, see National and Regional Organizations

M **AMERICAN UNIVERSITY,** Museum at the Katzen, Katzen Arts Center, 4400 Massachusetts Ave NW Washington, DC 20016-8031. Tel 202-885-1300; Fax 202-885-1140; Email museum@american.edu; Web: www.american.edu/cas/museum; *Dir & Cur* Jack Rasmussen, PhD; *Chief Preparator* Bruce Wick
Open Tues - Sun 11 AM - 4 PM; No admis fee; Programming will focus on Contemporary Art; 3-floor, 30,000 sq/ft gallery space; Mem: dues $50 - $2,5000
Special Subjects: Drawings, Etchings & Engravings, Painting-American, Painting-European, Posters, Prints, Sculpture, Watercolors, Woodcuts
Collections: Katzen Collection of 19th & 20th century American & European paintings
Activities: Lects open to pub; individual paintings & original objects of art lent to museums & university galleries; originates traveling exhibs

M **ANACOSTIA COMMUNITY MUSEUM,** Smithsonian Institution, 1901 Fort Pl SE, Washington, DC 20020-3298. Tel 202-633-4820; Email acminfo@si.edu; Web: anacostia.si.edu; *Interim Dir* Lisa Sasaki; *Deputy Dir* Sharon Reinckens; *Registrar* Grant Czubinski; *Chief Cur* Samir Meghelli; *Coll Mgr* Miriam Doutriaux
Open daily 10 AM - 5 PM, cl Dec 25; No admis fee; Estab 1967, as a nonprofit federally chartered corporation to record & research African, Black American & Anacostia history & urban problems; the first federally funded, community-based museum; Bureau of the Smithsonian Institution; Average Annual Attendance: 24,000
Income: Financed by federally funded bureau of Smithsonian Institute
Special Subjects: Afro-American Art, African Art
Collections: Afro-American history, exhibits & artifacts of the Black Diaspora in the Western Hemisphere, Black Diaspora Exhibits & Artifacts, Griffith Family Collection, Lillian Evans-Tibbs Collection, Lorenzo Dow Turner Collection, fine art holdings incl the work of James Wells, James Porter, John Robinson, Sam

Gilliam, Nelson Stevens, Benny Andrews & folk artists Leslie Payne & Charles Smith, artifacts, photographs, archival documents, media, & art objects
Exhibitions: (Indefinite) Separate & Unequaled: Black Baseball in the District of Columbia
Publications: Educational booklets; exhibit programs; museum brochures accompany each major exhibit
Activities: Programs for children & adults; Museum Academy Prog offers after-school & summer opportunities; lects; tours; gallery talks; art festivals; performances; demonstrations; competitions; exten dept serves groups unable to visit the museum; originates traveling exhibs

L **Library,** 1901 Fort Pl SE, Rm 215 Washington, DC 20020. Tel 202-633-4862; Fax 202-287-3183; Email wilderb@si.edu; Web: library.si.edu; *Librn* Baasil Wilder; *Circulation & Interlibrary Loan Tech* Carol Heard
Open by appointment Mon - Fri 10 AM - 3:30 PM; Open to public for research on the premises; call for appointment
Library Holdings: Book Volumes 5,000, Periodical Subscriptions 100

M **ARCHIVES OF AMERICAN ART,** Smithsonian Institution, 750 9th St NW, Victor Bldg Ste 2200 Washington, DC 20001-4524; PO Box 37012 MRC 937, Washington, DC 20013-7012. Tel 202-633-7940 (General); 633-7950 (Ref); Fax 202-633-7994 (Ref); Email edwardsth@si.edu; Web: www.aaa.si.edu; *Dir* Kate Haw; *Deputy Dir* Liza Kirwin; *Assoc Dir, Advancement* Melissa Rollenhagen Cristal; *Registrar* Susan Cary; *Head, Colls Processing* Erin Kinhart; *Head, Digital Opers* Karen Weiss
Open Mon - Fri 9 AM - 5 PM; No admis fee; Since 1954, the Archives of American Art has provided researchers worldwide with access to the largest collection of primary source materials documenting the history of the visual arts in America from the Colonial period to the present. Among the collection's 14.6 million items are letters and diaries of artists and collectors; manuscripts of critics and scholars; records of museums, galleries and schools; photographs of art world figures and events; works of art on paper, and oral and video history interviews. A research institute of the Smithsonian since 1970, the Archives fulfills its ongoing mission to collect, preserve and make accessible for study the documentation of this country's rich artistic legacy. As a result, the Archives had played a pivotal role in expanding scholarship and illuminating the history of art in American for the benefit of future generations; Bureau of the Smithsonian Institution; Mem: 2,000; dues benefactor $2,500, fellow $1000, patron $500, sponsor $250, assoc $125, sustaining $65
Income: Financed by a combination of federal appropriation, private contributions & foundation grants
Special Subjects: Manuscripts
Collections: More than 14.6 million documents, diaries, letters, manuscripts, records of museums, galleries, & schools, works of art on paper; and oral & video history interviews, Copies of the Archives microfilm can be viewed at alternate institutions: Boston Public Library, Boston, MA; Amon Carter Museum Library, Fort Worth, TX; De Young Museum, San Francisco, CA; Huntingdon Library, San Marino, CA
Publications: Finding aids & guides, video: From Reliable Sources - The Archives of American Art
Activities: Various members' events, including trips, tours, gallery talks and special fundraising events; lects open to pub; lending of original material to mus and other arts organizations; mus shop by mail sells books & journals
—**New York Research Center,** 300 Park Ave S, Ste 300 New York, NY 10010. Tel 212-399-5015; Fax 212-307-4501; Web: www.aaa.si.edu
Open Mon - Fri 9 AM - 5 PM; No admis fee; Estab 1956 to collect papers of artists, critics, dealers & collectors; 3,000 sq ft
Collections: Letters, diaries, artwork, writings, photographs & oral histories of the American art world
Activities: Lects open to members only, 1,500 vis lectrs per year; gallery talks

M **ART MUSEUM OF THE AMERICAS,** 201 18th St, NW, Washington, DC 20006; 1889 F St, NW, Washington, DC 20006. Tel 202-370-0147; Email artmus@oas.org; Web: www.museum.oas.org; *Cur Permanent Coll & Educ* Adriana Ospina; *Dir* Pabol Zuniga
Open Tues - Sun 10 AM - 5 PM, cl holidays; No admis fee; Estab 1976 by organization of American States to bring about an awareness & appreciation of contemporary Latin American art; The mus maintains an art gallery with the focus on contemporary Latin American art; Average Annual Attendance: 100,000
Special Subjects: Drawings, Prints, Sculpture
Collections: Contemporary Latin American & Caribbean art including paintings, prints, drawings & sculpture
Activities: Lects open to public, 10 vis lectrs per yr; gallery talks; tours; paintings & original art objects lent to museums & educational institutions; originate traveling exhibs; sales shop sells films on Latin American art & artists

L **Archive of Contemporary Latin American Art,** 201 18th St NW, Washington, DC 20006; 1889 F St NW, Washington, DC 20006. Tel 202-458-6016; Fax 202-458-6021; Web: museum.oas.org; *Cur* Adriana Ospina
Open by appt only; No admis fee; Maintain archives of Latin Am artists and gen pub; Open to scholars for research only
Library Holdings: Audio Tapes, Book Volumes 200, Clipping Files, Exhibition Catalogs, Fiche, Memorabilia, Pamphlets, Photographs, Reels, Reproductions, Slides, Video Tapes
Special Subjects: Aesthetics, Art History, Film, Latin American Art, Mexican Art, Painting-Spanish

A **ART PAC,** 408 Third St SE, Washington, DC 20003. Tel 202-546-1804; Fax 202-543-2405; *Treas* Robert J Bedard
Estab 1981 to lobby for art's legislation & assist federal candidates supporting the arts; Mem: dues $40
Income: Financed by mem
Publications: Newsletter/ART PAC News, quarterly
Activities: Legislator of the Year Award

A **ART RESOURCES INTERNATIONAL,** 5813 Nevada Ave NW, Washington, DC 20015-2547. Tel 202-363-6806; Fax 202-244-6844; Email helen@artresources.org; *Exec Dir* Donald H Russell; *Dir Spec Projects* Helen M Brunner
Estab 1987 to provide consulting to foundations and organizations in strategic planning and institutional change; management of exhib, public prog, publ & coll
Special Subjects: Painting-American, Photography, Prints, Sculpture
Collections: Book Arts, Media Arts, Public Sculpture

M **ARTS CLUB OF WASHINGTON,** James Monroe House, 2017 I St NW, Monroe & MacFeely Galleries Washington, DC 20006-1804. Tel 202-331-7282; Fax 202-857-3678; Email membership@artsclubofwashington.org; Web: www.artsclubofwashington.org; *Pres* Judith Viggers Nordin; *Gen Mgr* Yann Henrotte
Open Tues - Fri 10 AM -5 PM; No admis fee; Founded 1916. The James Monroe House (1803-1805) was built by Timothy Caldwell of Philadelphia. It is registered with the National Register of Historic Places, the Historical Survey 1937 & 1968 & the National Trust for Historic Preservation; James Monroe, fifth President of the United States, resided in the house while he was Secretary of War & State. During the first six months of his Presidency (1817-1825) the house served as the Exec Mansion, since the White House had been burned in the War of 1812 & had not yet been restored. Garden, banquet rooms & formal galleries, parlors, stair halls serve as galleries; Average Annual Attendance: 10,000; Mem: 350; annual meeting in Apr
Income: Financed by mem, catering functions, fundraising, gallery sales, pub programs
Purchases: Obtained through gifts & bequests
Library Holdings: Original Art Works, Original Documents, Pamphlets, Sculpture
Collections: Washington, DC art
Exhibitions: Solo shows in two galleries, Oct - July, third gallery coming soon
Publications: Monthly news bulletin to members, promotional material, brochures
Activities: Classes for adults; pub progs vary; literary; musical & dramatic; lect open to public & for members, 12-24 vis lectrs per year; concerts; gallery talks; book awards; scholarships offered

ASSOCIATION OF COLLEGIATE SCHOOLS OF ARCHITECTURE
For further information, see National and Regional Organizations

A **THE ASSOCIATION OF INTERNATIONAL PHOTOGRAPHY ART DEALERS,** 2025 M St NW, Ste 800 Washington, DC 20036. Tel 202-367-1158; Fax 202-367-2158; Email info@aipad.org; Web: www.aipad.org; *Exec Dir* Meredith Robertson; *Sr Opers Coordr* Sarah Langan; *Show Mgr* Kelly Sapp; *Artistic Dir* Beatrice Andrieux
Estab 1979 to encourage public support of fine art photography by acting as a collective voice for the dealers of fine art photography and through communication & education that enhances the confidence of the public, museums, institutions & others responsible for fine art photography dealers; Mem: Membership: 24 galleries
Publications: On Collecting Photography
Activities: Photography workshops; gallery talks; annual show in April

M **B'NAI B'RITH INTERNATIONAL,** B'nai B'rith Klutznick National Jewish Museum, 2020 K St NW, Fl 7 Washington, DC 20006-1806. Tel 202-857-6647; Fax 202-857-6601; Email museum@bnaibrith.org; Web: www.bnaibrith.org; *Curatorial Consultant* Cheryl Kempler
Open by appt through email request; Suggested donation adults $5, children under 12 free; Estab 1957 to exhibit & preserve Jewish art & culture; Permanent collection gallery including life & holiday cycles; Average Annual Attendance: 40,000; Mem: 1000; dues $45-$5000
Income: General operations financed by parent organization; private & corporate donations; programs & exhibitions financed by mus members
Special Subjects: Judaica
Collections: Permanent collection of Jewish ceremonial & folk art, archives of B'nai B'rith, contemporary paintings, lithographs, photographs, sculptures
Exhibitions: Jews in Sports
Publications: Exhibitions brochures & catalogues; members newsletter, semi-annual; permanent collection catalogue
Activities: Classes for adults & children; docent training; lects open to pub; 1 vis lectrs per yr; concerts; gallery talks; tours; individual paintings lent to museums; originate traveling exhibs

L **CATHOLIC UNIVERSITY OF AMERICA,** Humanities Library, Mullen Library, 620 Michigan Ave, NE, Washington, DC 20064-0001. Tel 202-319-5070; Email lib-circulation@cua.edu; Web: libraries.cua.edu; *Librn* Stephen Connaghan
Open Mon - Thurs 8 AM - 11:30 PM, Fri 8 AM - 10 PM, Sat 9 AM - 10 PM, Sun 11 AM - 11:30 PM; No admis fee; Estab 1958 to offer acad resources & services that are integral to the work of the institution
Library Holdings: Book Volumes 14,000
Collections: Various collections

M **CORCORAN GALLERY OF ART,** 500 17th St NW, Washington, DC 20006-4899. Tel 202-639-1700; Web: www.corcoran.org; *Pres & Dir* David C Levy; *Deputy Dir & Chief Cur* Jack Cowart; *Cur Contemporary Art* Terrie Sultan; *Registrar* Nancy Swallow; *Cur Photo & Media Arts* Philip Brookman; *Bechhoefer Cur American Art* Sarah Cash; *Cur Educ* Susan Badder
Open Wed - Sun 10 AM - 5 Pm, Thurs until 9 PM, cl Mon, Thanksgiving, Christmas & New Year's Days; Admis adults $10, seniors & students $8, mems, children under 12 active military free, Free Summer Saturdays; Founded 1869 primarily for the encouragement of American art; The nucleus of the collection of American Paintings was formed by its founder, William Wilson Corcoran, early in the second half of the 19th century. In 1925 a large wing designed by Charles A Platt was added to house the European collection bequeathed by Senator William Andrews Clark of Montana. The Walker Collection, formed by Edward C and Mary Walker, added important French Impressionists to the collection upon its donation in 1937; Average Annual Attendance: 400,000; Mem: 4500; dues fellow $1000, contributing $500, sponsor $295, supporting $160, family $100, dual $90, sr dual $80, individual $60, sr individual $50, national $45, student $30
Special Subjects: Antiquities-Greek, Bronzes, Decorative Arts, Drawings, Furniture, Painting-American, Painting-British, Painting-Dutch, Painting-European, Painting-Flemish, Painting-French, Photography, Stained Glass, Tapestries, Watercolors

Collections: The American coll of paintings, watercolors, drawings, sculpture & photography from the 18th through 20th centuries, European coll includes paintings & drawings by Dutch, Flemish, English & French artists, 18th century French salon, furniture, laces, rugs, majolica, Gothic & Beauvais tapestries, Greek antiquities, 13th century stained glass window & bronzes by Antoine Louise Barye, triptych by Andrea Vanni, Walker Collection of French Impressionists, Clark European Collection
Publications: Calendar of Events (for members); Corcoran Shop Catalogue
Activities: Classes for adults, youth & children; summer camps; family progs; educator workshops & resources; pre-college classes; docent training; internships; lects open to public; concerts; gallery talks; tours; performances; films; mems only events; originates traveling exhibs; mus shop sells books, magazines, reproductions, prints & slides

L **Corcoran Library**, 500 17th St NW, Washington, DC 20006-4804. Tel 202-478-1544; Fax 202-628-1544; Email library@corcoran.org; Web: www.corcoran.edu/library; *Libr Dir* Mario Ascenio; *Circ Mgr* Shawana Snell; *Digital Assets & Media Librn* Jacqueline Protka; *Tech Svcs Assoc* Patricia L Reid
Open during school yr Mon - Thurs 8:30 AM - 8 PM, Fri 8:30 AM - 5 PM, Sat 10 AM - 4 PM, cl Sun & Thanksgiving; Research & lending resource for mus & school, staff, faculty & student. Provides interlibrary loan to other institutions & open for pub use by appointment only. Located on 2nd fl in hemicycle
Library Holdings: Book Volumes 35,000, DVDs, Exhibition Catalogs, Other Holdings Online Database Subscriptions: 14, Periodical Subscriptions 190, Slides 32,000, Video Tapes
Special Subjects: Advertising Design, Afro-American Art, Art History, Commercial Art, Drawings, Etchings & Engravings, Furniture, Graphic Design, Lettering, Painting-American, Photography, Pottery, Printmaking, Prints, Religious Art, Graphic Arts
Collections: Artists books

A **CULTURE CAPITAL,** (Cultural Alliance of Greater Washington), 923 F St NW, Ste 303 Washington, DC 20004-1479; 975 F St NW, Washington, DC 20004-1479. Tel 202-393-2161; Fax 202-393-2595; Email jpayne@culturecapital.org; Web: www.cultural-alliance.org; *Pres* Jennifer Cover Payne; *VPres* Eileen Rappoport; *Treas* Steven Cupo; *Website Admin* Laura Bloomquist
Open Mon-Fri 9 AM - 5 PM; Estab 1978 to increase appreciation & support for the arts in Washington DC region; Mem: 647; mem open to artists, arts adminr or patron; dues individual $60, organization-scaled to annual income; annual meeting in the fall
Income: $82,663 (financed by mem & donations $563,849)
Activities: Classes for adults; lects open to public for fee, free to members

M **DAR MUSEUM,** National Society Daughters of the American Revolution, 1776 D St NW, Washington, DC 20006-5303. Tel 202-628-1776; Fax 202-628-0820; Email museum@dar.org; Web: www.dar.org/museum; *Dir & Chief Cur* Heidi Campbell-Shoaf
Open Mon - Fri 8:30 AM - 4 PM, Sat 9 AM - 5 PM, cl Sun; No admis fee; Estab 1890 for collection & exhibition of decorative arts used in America from 1700-1840; for the study of objects & the preservation of Revolutionary artifacts & documentation of American life; There are 33 period rooms which reflect the decorative arts of particular states, also a mus which houses large collections grouped by ceramics, textiles, silver, glass, furniture & paintings; Average Annual Attendance: 12,000; Mem: 215,000; dues $15 - $17; annual meeting in Apr
Income: $200,000 (financed by mem)
Special Subjects: Carpets & Rugs, Ceramics, Coins & Medals, Costumes, Decorative Arts, Dolls, Embroidery, Furniture, Glass, Jewelry, Miniatures, Painting-American, Period Rooms, Pewter, Porcelain, Portraits, Pottery, Silver, Textiles
Collections: Ceramics, furniture, glass, paintings, prints, silver, textiles
Exhibitions: Special exhibitions arranged & changed periodically, usually every 6 months
Activities: Classes for adults & children; docent training; lects open to pub; tours; paintings & original art works lent to mus & cultural institutions for special exhibs; mus shop sells books, stationery, dolls & handcrafted gift items

L **Library**, 1776 D St NW, Washington, DC 20006-5303. Tel 202-879-3241; Fax 202-628-0820; Email museum@dar.org; Web: www.dar.org/museum, dar.org/library; *Dir & Chief Cur* Heidi Campbell-Shoaf; *Colls Mgr* Anne Ruta; *Cur Historic Furnishings* Patrick Sheary; *Cur Costumes & Textiles* Alden O'Brien; *Cur Educ* Marilyn Sklar
Open Mon - Fri 8:30 AM - 4:00 PM, Sat 9:00 AM - 5:00 PM, cl Sun; No admis fee; Estab 1890; collects objects made or used in America prior to 1840; Open to pub; rotating exhibs in main gallery; permanent colls in Yochim Gallery; museum library open to pub; Average Annual Attendance: 23,000
Income: Pvt donations
Library Holdings: Book Volumes 3000, Periodical Subscriptions 10
Collections: American Decorative Arts and Fine Arts
Activities: Classes for adults & children; school progs; Christmas open house; docent training; vol; Girl Scout progs; school progs; lects open to pub; 4 vis lectrs per yr; gallery talks; tours of 32 period rooms; exten prog serves mus nationwide; mus shop sells books, reproductions, prints & slides

M **DISTRICT OF COLUMBIA ARTS CENTER (DCAC),** 2438 18th St NW, Washington, DC 20009-2004. Tel 202-462-7833; Fax 419-821-9622; Email info@dcartscenter.org; Web: www.dcartscenter.org; *Dir* B Stanley; *Gallery Mgr* Michael Mattason; *Office Mgr* Becky Lallande
Open Wed - Sat 2 - 7 PM; No admis fee; Estab 1989 to support new & emerging artists; 800 sq ft; Average Annual Attendance: 5,000; Mem: 500; dues $30
Income: $250,000 (financed by mem, city appropriation & foundations)
Activities: Classes for adults; dramatic progs; lects open to pub, 5 vis lectrs per yr; gallery talks

M **DUMBARTON OAKS,** Dumbarton Oaks Museum, 1703 32nd St NW, Washington, DC 20007-2934. Tel 202-339-6960; Fax 202-625-0283; Email museum@doaks.org; Web: www.doaks.org; *Dir* Jan M Ziolkowski; *Cur & Mus Dir* Gudrun Buhl; *Dir Gardens & Grounds* Jonathan Kavalier
Open Tues - Sun 11:30 AM - 5:30 PM, cl Mon & federal holidays; Gardens open Mar 15 - Oct 31; Admis to mus free; garden admis Mar 15 - Oct 31 general $8, Nov 1 - Mar 14 free; Conveyed in 1940 to Harvard University by Mr & Mrs Robert Woods Bliss as a research center in the Byzantine & Medieval humanities & subsequently enlarged to include Pre-Columbian studies & studies in landscape architecture; Average Annual Attendance: 15,000
Special Subjects: Antiquities-Byzantine, Decorative Arts, Furniture, Mosaics, Painting-American, Painting-European, Pre-Columbian Art, Religious Art, Sculpture, Textiles, Antiquities-Roman, Antiquities-Greek
Collections: Byzantine Dept: devoted to early Christian & Byzantine mosaics, textiles, bronzes, sculpture, ivories, metalwork, jewelry, glyptics & other decorative arts of the period, Pre-Columbian Dept: devoted to sculpture, textiles, pottery, gold ornaments & other objects from Mexico, Central & South America, dating from 800 BC to early 16th century, House Collection: European & American paintings, sculpture & decorative arts; historic interiors, Asian, European & American artworks, & interior furnishings
Publications: Handbooks & catalogs of the Byzantine & pre-Columbian collection; scholarly publications in Byzantine, pre-Columbian & landscape architecture studies
Activities: Lect; conferences; garden tours; mus tours; concerts by subscription; fellowships; mus shop sells books & reproductions

L **Dumbarton Oaks Research Library**, 1703 32nd St NW, Washington, DC 20007. Tel 202-339-6968; Fax 202-625-0279; Web: www.doaks.org/library-archives; *Dir Libr* Daniel Boomhower; *Head Cataloger* Sandra Parker Provenzano; *Pre-Columbian Studies Librn* Bridget Gazzo; *Interlibrary Loan Librn* Ingrid Gibson; *Rare Book Librn* Linda Lott; *Byzantine Studies Librn* Deborah Stewart
Open (application for access is required) to scholars with weekday reader status: Mon - Fri 9 AM - 5 PM; Open to scholars with reader status: Mon - Fri 8 AM - 10 PM, Sat - Sun 9 AM - 10 PM; Rare Book Coll open by appt only Mon - Fri 9:30 AM - 12:30 PM & 1:30 PM - 4:30 PM
Library Holdings: Book Volumes 215,000, CD-ROMs, Exhibition Catalogs, Fiche, Manuscripts, Maps, Memorabilia, Micro Print, Motion Pictures, Original Art Works, Original Documents, Other Holdings Mus Catalogs, Pamphlets, Periodical Subscriptions 550, Photographs, Prints, Reels, Reproductions, Slides, Video Tapes
Special Subjects: Anthropology, Archaeology, Art History, Decorative Arts, Mosaics, Pre-Columbian Art, Sculpture, Manuscripts
Collections: Dumbarton Oaks Census of Early Christian and Byzantine Objects in American Collection, Photographs Collection, Rare Book Collection, Pre-Columbian Library Collection: 2,000+ vols

L **Image Collections and Fieldwork Archives**, 1703 32nd St NW, Washington, DC 20007. Tel 202-339-6972; Email icfa@doaks.org; Web: www.doaks.org/library-archives/icfa; *Mgr Image Coll & Fieldwork Archives* Bettina Smith; *Cataloger* Kimball Clark
Open Mon - Fri 9 AM - Noon & 1-5 PM to approved scholars by written request, see website; Estab to support scholarship in Byzantine, Garden & Landscape, & Pre-Columbian studies by acquiring, preserving, cataloging & providing access to images in a variety of media & documentation of archaeological surveys & excavations both textual & visual
Library Holdings: Kodachrome Transparencies, Lantern Slides, Manuscripts, Motion Pictures, Original Documents, Photographs, Records, Slides
Special Subjects: Antiquities-Byzantine, Archaeology, Architecture, Art History, History of Art & Archaeology, Landscape Architecture, Manuscripts, Photography, Pre-Columbian Art, Textiles
Collections: See online inventory
Exhibitions: See website

M **FEDERAL RESERVE BOARD,** Art Gallery, 20th & C Sts NW, Washington, DC 20551-0001. Email firearts@frb.gov; Web: www.federalreserve.gov/finearts; *Dir* Stephen Bennett Phillips; *Fine Arts Prog Asst* Rhonda Gray-Young; *Fine Arts Prog Asst* Nikki Pisha
Open Mon - Fri 10 AM - 3:30 PM advance reservation required, cl Federal holidays; No admis fee; Estab 1975 to promote art in the work place; Two story atrium space with travertine marble walls.
Income: Operating expenses by the Federal Reserve Board
Purchases: By donation
Special Subjects: Architecture, Collages, Drawings, Etchings & Engravings, Hispanic Art, Landscapes, Latin American Art, Marine Painting, Painting-American, Painting-Australian, Photography, Prints, Sculpture
Collections: American & European paintings, works on paper & photographs
Publications: Exhibition catalogs

L **FOLGER SHAKESPEARE LIBRARY,** 201 E Capitol St SE, Washington, DC 20003-1094. Tel 202-544-4600; Fax 202-544-4623; Email info@folger.edu; Web: www.folger.edu; *Dir* Dr Michael Witmore; *Head Coll Info Servs* Dr Erin Blake; *Project Coord* Rachel B Dankert
Open Mon - Sat 10 AM - 5 PM, Sun noon - 5 PM; No admis fee to exhibs; Estab 1932 as a private, independent research library & international center for the study of all aspects of the European Renaissance & civilization in the 16th & 17th centuries; Maintains an exhibition gallery & a permanent display of Shakespearean items, with changing topical exhibits of books, manuscripts, paintings & porcelain
Income: Financed by endowment, grants, gifts & earned income
Library Holdings: Audio Tapes, Book Volumes 160,000, Exhibition Catalogs, Filmstrips, Manuscripts 60,000, Memorabilia, Motion Pictures, Original Art Works 3800, Other Holdings Rare books 135,000, Pamphlets, Periodical Subscriptions 180, Photographs 3000, Prints 20,000, Records, Reels 10,000, Reproductions, Sculpture, Slides
Collections: Shakespeare, playbills & promptbooks, Continental & English Renaissance, 1450-1700, manuscripts; paintings; works of art on paper; prints & engravings
Exhibitions: See website for current exhibs
Publications: The Folger Edition of the Complete Plays of William Shakespeare; Shakespeare Quarterly; Folger Magazine 3 times per year
Activities: Educ prog; classes for children; dramatic progs; docent training; seminars for advanced graduate students; lects open to public; lects open to mems; 20 vis lectrs per year; concerts; gallery talks; tours; fels offered; sales shop sells books, reproductions, music

M **FREER GALLERY OF ART & ARTHUR M SACKLER GALLERY,** Freer Gallery of Art, Jefferson Dr at 12th St, Washington, DC 20560; 1050 Independence

Ave SW, PO Box 37012 MRC 707 Washington, DC 20013-7012. Tel 202-633-1000 (General); Fax 202-357-4911; Email publicaffairsAsia@si.edu; Web: www.freersackler.si.edu; *Acting Dir* Richard Kurin; *Chief Cur* Massumeh Farhad
Open daily 10 AM - 5:30 PM, cl Dec 25; No admis fee; Estab 1923 to exhibit 19th-century & early 20th-century American art; Italian-Renaissance-Style gallery constructed of granite & marble; A permanent installation in the gallery is the Peacock Room, a dining room once part of a London townhouse & lavishly decorated with a blue & gold peacock design by James McNeill Whistler in 1876; Eugene & Agnes E Meyer Auditorium provides a venue for free public programs, including concerts of Asian music & dance, films, lectures, chamber music & dramatic presentations. Bureau of the Smithsonian Institution; Connected by an underground exhib space to the neighboring Arthur M Sackler Gallery; Average Annual Attendance: 200,000
Income: Financed by endowment, federal appropriation, gifts & purchases
Special Subjects: American Western Art, Ceramics, Manuscripts
Collections: James McNeill Whistler Collection, art from China, Japan, Korea, South & Southeast Asia & the Near East, Buddhist sculpture, Chinese paintings, Indian & Persian manuscripts, Japanese folding screens, Korean ceramics
Activities: Classes for adults & children; dramatic progs; docent training; teacher workshops; lects open to pub, 5-6 vis lectrs per yr; concerts; gallery talks; tours; films; schols offered; originate traveling exhibs; mus shop sells books, magazines, original art, reproductions, prints, slides, textiles, music, ceramics & jewelry

M **Arthur M Sackler Gallery**, 1050 Independence Ave SW, Washington, DC 20560; PO Box 37012 MRC 707, Washington, DC 20013-7012. Tel 202-633-1000 (General); Fax 202-357-4911; Email publicaffairsAsia@si.edu; Web: www.freersackler.si.edu; *Acting Dir* Richard Kurin; *Chief Cur* Massumeh Farhad
Open daily 10 AM - 5:30 PM, cl Dec 25; No admis fee; Estab 1987 for exhibition, research & educ on the arts of Asia; Bureau of the Smithsonian Institution; Connected by an underground exhib space to the neighboring Freer Gallery of Art; Average Annual Attendance: 92,000
Income: Financed by endowment & federal appropriation
Special Subjects: Anthropology, Antiquities-Assyrian, Antiquities-Byzantine, Antiquities-Egyptian, Antiquities-Oriental, Antiquities-Persian, Antiquities-Roman, Archaeology, Architecture, Asian Art, Bookplates & Bindings, Bronzes, Calligraphy, Ceramics, Coins & Medals, Collages, Costumes, Crafts, Decorative Arts, Drawings, Embroidery, Enamels, Etchings & Engravings, Furniture, Glass
Collections: Arthur M Sackler Collection (ancient Near Eastern ceramics & metalware, Chinese bronzes & jades, Chinese paintings & lacquerware, sculpture from South & Southeast Asia), Vever Collection (Islamic arts of the book, 11th-19th century), arts of village India, contemporary Chinese ceramics, Indian, Chinese, Japanese & Korean paintings, 19th & 20th century Japanese prints & contemporary porcelain, photography
Publications: Asian Art & Culture, annual; Arthur M Sackler Gallery Calendar, bi-monthly
Activities: Classes for adults & children; dramatic progs; docent training; teacher workshops; lects open to pub, 5-6 vis lectrs per yr; concerts; gallery talks; tours; films; schols offered; originate traveling exhibs; mus shop sells books, magazines, original art, reproductions, prints, slides, jewelry, cards, gifts, ceramics, music & textiles

L **Library**, Arthur M Sackler Gallery, Rm 2058 Washington, DC 20560-0112. Tel 202-633-0477; Fax 202-786-2936; Email YOSHIRE@si.edu; Web: library.si.edu; *Head Librn* Reiko Yoshimura; *Librn* Kathryn D Phillips; *Librn* Yue Shu; *Librn* Mike Smith
Open Mon - Fri 10 AM - 5 PM, cl Federal holidays; Branch of Smithsonian Institution Libraries
Library Holdings: Audio Tapes, Book Volumes 65,000, Cassettes, Clipping Files, Exhibition Catalogs, Fiche, Filmstrips, Kodachrome Transparencies, Lantern Slides, Manuscripts, Memorabilia, Motion Pictures, Other Holdings Sales catalogs, Pamphlets, Periodical Subscriptions 500, Photographs, Prints, Reels, Reproductions, Slides, Video Tapes
Special Subjects: Archaeology, Architecture, Art Education, Art History, Asian Art, Bookplates & Bindings, Bronzes, Calligraphy, Carpets & Rugs, Ceramics, Decorative Arts, Embroidery, Enamels, Etchings & Engravings, Flasks & Bottles, Jade, Metalwork, Painting-Japanese, Sculpture, Glass
Collections: Contains approx 80,000 monograph vols & 1,400 serials titles, with almost half its printed resources in Chinese, Japanese, or Korean, Japan Art Catalog Project Collection, Rare Book Collection, Paul Marks Collection on James McNeill Whistler, Conservation Library in Freer Gallery, containing research materials on conservation & restoration of Asian art

M **GEORGE WASHINGTON UNIVERSITY,** (Textile Museum) The George Washington Museum and The Textile Museum, 701 21st St NW, Washington, DC 20052. Tel 202-994-5200; Email museuminfo@gwu.edu; Web: www.textilemuseum.org; *Co-Chair* Dr Bruce P Baganz; *Co-Chair* Douglas E Evelyn; *Dir* Dr John Wetenhall; *Sr Cur* Sumru Belger Krody
Open Mon & Fri 11 AM - 5 PM, Wed - Thurs 11 AM - 7 PM, Sat 10 AM - 5 PM, Sun 1 PM - 5 PM, cl Tues & university holidays; No admis fee, suggested donation $8; Estab 1925 to further the understanding of mankind's creative achievements in textile arts; Mus is devoted to international handmade textile arts, Washington area maps & documents & university collections; Average Annual Attendance: 30,000; Mem: 3000; dues Individual $60
Income: Financed by endowment, mem & grants
Library Holdings: Auction Catalogs, Book Volumes, Cassettes, Exhibition Catalogs, Kodachrome Transparencies, Lantern Slides, Pamphlets, Periodical Subscriptions, Slides, Video Tapes
Special Subjects: Carpets & Rugs, Historical Material, Textiles, Decorative Arts, Embroidery
Collections: Collection of oriental carpets including, Caucasian, Chinese, Egyptian (Mamluk), Persian, Spanish & Turkish, Collections of African, Chinese, Coptic, India, Indonesian, Islamic, pre-Columbian Peruvian & textiles of traditional cultures of Americas, Arthur D Jenkins Library of textile arts, maps, documents & manuscripts on the development of Washington, DC
Publications: The Textile Museum Members Magazine, quarterly membership newsletter
Activities: Workshops for adults & children; seminars & demonstrations; docent training; family programming; fall symposium; evening events; lects open to pub, 10 vis lectrs per yr; gallery talks; tours; Georg Hewitt Myers Award given ann; individual textiles & original objects of art lent; originate traveling exhibs to Seattle Art Museum; mus shop sells books, magazines, original art, ethnographic textiles, jewelry & one of a kind items

L **Arthur D Jenkins Library**, 701 21st St NW, Washington, DC 20052. Tel 202-994-5200; Email museumlibrary@gwu.edu; Web: museum.gwu.edu/library; *Librn* Lynora Williams
Open Wed & Thurs 1 PM - 4 PM and by appointment; No admis fee; Estab 1925 as a reference library dealing with ancient & ethnographic textiles & rugs of the world; Average Annual Attendance: 1,000
Income: Financed by endowment, mem & gifts
Library Holdings: Auction Catalogs, Book Volumes 20,000, CD-ROMs, Cassettes, Clipping Files, DVDs, Exhibition Catalogs, Manuscripts, Other Holdings Monographs; Serials, Pamphlets, Periodical Subscriptions 164, Photographs, Slides, Video Tapes
Special Subjects: American Indian Art, Anthropology, Antiquities-Assyrian, Antiquities-Byzantine, Antiquities-Oriental, Antiquities-Persian, Archaeology, Architecture, Art Education, Art History, Asian Art, Carpets & Rugs, Costume Design & Constr, Crafts, Decorative Arts, Embroidery, Eskimo Art, Ethnology, Fashion Arts, Handicrafts, History of Art & Archaeology, Islamic Art, Jewelry, Laces, Latin American Art, Leather, Metalwork, Mexican Art, Oriental Art, Pre-Columbian Art, Primitive art, Tapestries, Textiles
Collections: Art, Costume, Cultural History, Rugs, Costumes & Textiles of the traditional Cultures of the Americas, Asia, Africa, the Middle East & the Pacific Rim; Textile processes; fashion
Publications: Annual Bibliography of Textile Literature (co-published by the Textile Mus & Textile Soc of Am) compiled & edited by Mary E Mallia, librn; online library catalog, TextileMuse

M **THE GEORGE WASHINGTON UNIVERSITY,** Luther W Brady Art Gallery, 805 21st St NW, Washington, DC 20052. Tel 202-994-1525; Fax 202-994-1632; Email lutherbradyart@gmail.com; Web: www2.gwu.edu/~bradyart; *Dir & Chief Cur* Lenore D Miller; *Asst Dir* Olivia Kohler
Open Tues - Fri 10 AM - 5 PM; No admis fee; Estab 2001 to enhance graduate & undergraduate programs in fine art & research in art history; documentation of permanent collections; feature historical & contemporary exhibitions related to university art dept programs; Average Annual Attendance: 10,000
Special Subjects: Graphics, Painting-American, Photography, Prints, Sculpture, Historical Material
Collections: Joseph Pennell Collection of Prints, W Lloyd Wright Collection of Washingtoniana, graphic arts from the 18th, 19th & 20th centuries, with special emphasis on American art, works pertaining to George Washington, U S Grant Collection
Publications: Exhibition catalogs
Activities: Lect open to public; gallery talks; tours; individual paintings & original objects of art lent

M **GEORGETOWN UNIVERSITY,** Art Collection, 3700 O St NW, Washington, DC 20057-1104. Tel 202-687-1469; Fax 202-687-7501; Email llw@georgetown.edu; Web: www.library.georgetown.edu/dept/speccoll/guac; *Asst Cur* Christen Runge; *Cur* Lulen Walker
Call for hours; No admis fee; University estab 1789; The collection is on the Georgetown University campus in Healy Hall (1879)
Income: Financed by University budget
Special Subjects: Graphics, Historical Material, Mosaics, Painting-American, Religious Art, Sculpture, Silver, Portraits
Collections: Works by Van Dyck, Giordano & Gilbert Stuart
Exhibitions: 4 exhibitions per yr of graphic art held in Lauinger Library
Activities: Educ progs for undergraduate students; gallery talks, guided tours; art festivals, temporary exhibs

L **Lauinger Library - Special Collections Division**, 3700 O St NW, Washington, DC 20057-1174. Tel 202-687-1469; Fax 202-687-7501; Email artcollection@georgetown.edu; Web: www.library.georgetown.edu/special-collections/art/carroll-parlor; *Spec Coll Librn* John Buchtel; *Art Coll Cur* Lulen Walker; *Asst Cur* Christen Runge
Open weekdays; check hours on website or call; Estab 1975 to support Georgetown's acad progs; 3 exhibitions per yr of fine prints in Library; permanent collection of paintings, sculpture & dec arts in Carroll Parlor of Healy Bldg
Library Holdings: Original Art Works, Photographs, Prints, Sculpture
Special Subjects: Bookplates & Bindings, Cartoons, Decorative Arts, Drawings, Etchings & Engravings, Illustration, Landscapes, Latin American Art, Mosaics, Painting-American, Painting-British, Painting-Flemish, Painting-French, Painting-German, Painting-Italian, Painting-Spanish, Period Rooms, Prints, Religious Art, Sculpture, Woodcuts, Watercolors
Collections: Editorial Cartoon Collection - American Originals, c 1910 to Present, Elder Collection - Artist Self-Portraits, Prints, Drawings, Watercolors, Paintings, c 1925-1975, Jesuit Collection - American Fine Prints, c 1900-1950, Eric F Menke Collection - Prints, Drawings, Watercolors, Paintings, Murphy Collection - American fine prints, c 1900-1950, Eric Smith Collection - Original Editorial Cartoon, Lynd Ward Collection - Prints, Drawings, Watercolors, Paintings, c 1925-1980, Printmakers' Collections: John DePol, Werner Drewes, Isac Friedlander, Norman Kent, Clare Leighton, William E C Morgan, Barry Moser, Philip Riesman, Prentiss Taylor, Ralph Fabri Collection, Old Masters Paintings, 19th Century American Paintings & Sculpture
Publications: Issued with many spec exhibs

HERITAGE PRESERVATION
For further information, see National and Regional Organizations

M **HILLWOOD MUSEUM & GARDENS FOUNDATION,** (Marjorie Merriweather Post) Hillwood Estate Museum & Gardens, 4155 Linnean Ave NW, Washington, DC 20008-3806. Tel 202-686-5807; Fax 202-966-7846; Email info@hillwoodmuseum.org; Web: www.hillwoodmuseum.org; *Pres* Marci DeWitt; *Exec Dir & CEO* Kate Markert; *Dir Collections & Co-Chair Exhibs* Estella Chung; *Chief Cur & Co-Chair Exhibs* Wilfried Zeisler; *Exec Admin* Jan Jensen; *Dir Opers & HR* Michael Dudich; *Dir Develop* Judith Paska; *Head Interpretation* Audra Kelly; *Dir Horticulture* Brian Barr; *Head Security* Victor Braschnewitz; *Asst Cur*

Costumes & Textiles Howard Kurtz; *Head Merchandising* Lauren Salazar; *Dir Facilities Mgmt* Donald Rogers
Open Tues - Sat 10 AM - 5 PM, cl Jan & nat holidays; Admis adults $18, seniors $15, students $10, children (6-18) $5. children under 6 & mem free; Estab 1977 to enlighten & engage visitors; Georgian-style mansion, home of the late Marjorie Merriweather Post, situated on 25 acres, 13 of which are formal gardens; auxiliary bldg Dacha currently housing temp exhibs; Average Annual Attendance: 44,162; Mem: 1,650; dues $60-$500, circles $1000-$2500
Income: Financed by endowment, operating income & grants
Purchases: Active acquisitions program in Russian & Western European decorative arts
Library Holdings: Auction Catalogs, Book Volumes, Clipping Files, Exhibition Catalogs, Fiche, Kodachrome Transparencies, Manuscripts, Maps, Memorabilia, Motion Pictures, Original Documents, Pamphlets, Periodical Subscriptions, Photographs, Prints, Records, Reels, Slides, Video Tapes
Special Subjects: Asian Art, Bookplates & Bindings, Bronzes, Carpets & Rugs, Ceramics, Coins & Medals, Costumes, Crafts, Decorative Arts, Drawings, Embroidery, Enamels, Etchings & Engravings, Flasks & Bottles, Folk Art, Furniture, Glass, Gold, Graphics, Historical Material, Ivory, Jade, Jewelry, Judaica, Laces, Landscapes, Leather, Manuscripts, Maps, Marine Painting, Metalwork, Military Art, Miniatures, Oriental Art, Painting-American, Painting-British, Painting-Dutch, Painting-European, Painting-French, Painting-Italian, Painting-Russian, Pewter, Photography, Porcelain, Portraits, Posters, Pottery, Prints, Religious Art, Renaissance Art, Sculpture, Silver, Tapestries, Textiles, Watercolors, Woodcarvings, Woodcuts
Collections: Western European & French fine & decorative arts, furnishings & American memorabilia, Russian fine & decorative arts, Asian decorative arts, Art Research Library, Archives & Visual Resources relating to coll & Marjorie Merriweather Post, mus found
Publications: The Hillwood Post newsletter, triennial, 1998 catalogue A Taste for Splendor: Russian Imperial and European Treasures from the Hillwood Mus; Hillwood Collection Series of 5 books: Faberge at Hillwood, Russian Icons at Hillwood, Sevres Porcelain at Hillwood, Russian Imperial Porcelain at Hillwood & Russian Glass at Hillwood; Art of the Russian North; French Furniture in the Collection of Hillwood Museum & Gardens; What Became of Peter's Dream? Court Culture in the Reign of Nicholass II co-published with Middlebury College Museum of Art in Middlebury, VT; Tradition in Transition: Russian Icons in the Age of the Romanovs; Hillwood: Thirty Years of Collecting 1977-2007
Activities: Classes for adults & children; docent training; lects open to pub; 10 vis lectrs per yr; concerts; gallery talks; tours; originates traveling exhibs for art mus; mus shop sells books, gifts, reproductions, prints & jewelry

M **HIRSHHORN MUSEUM & SCULPTURE GARDEN,** Smithsonian Institution, Independence Ave at 7th St SW, Washington, DC 20560; PO Box 37012 MRC Code 350, Washington, DC 20013-7012. Tel 202-633-4674; Fax 202-633-8835; Email hmsginquiries@si.edu; Web: hirshhorn.si.edu; *Dir* Melissa Chiu; *Deputy Dir* Jaya Kaveeshwar; *Chief Cur* Stephane Aquin
Open daily 10 AM - 5:30 PM, The Plaza 7:30 AM - 5:30 PM, Sculpture Garden 7:30 AM- dusk; cl Dec 25; No admis fee; Estab 1966 under the aegis of the Smithsonian Institution; building designed by Gordon Bunshaft of the architectural firm of Skidmore, Owings & Merrill. Opened in 1974; Bureau of the Smithsonian Institution; Average Annual Attendance: 559,000; Mem: Dues $100 - $25,000
Income: Financed by federal funds
Library Holdings: Auction Catalogs, Audio Tapes, Book Volumes, Cassettes, Clipping Files, Exhibition Catalogs, Pamphlets, Periodical Subscriptions, Video Tapes
Special Subjects: Afro-American Art, Collages, Drawings, Latin American Art, Painting-American, Painting-European, Sculpture
Collections: American art beginning with a strong group of Thomas Eakins & going on to De Kooning, Gorky, Hartley, Hopper, Johns, Elizabeth Murray, Rothko, Frank Stella, Warhol, European paintings & mixed media work of the last 5 decades represented by Bacon, Balthus, Kiefer & Korenellis, Leger, Miro, Polke & Richter, extensive sculpture collection includes works by Bourgeois, Brancusi, Calder, Cragg, Giacometti, Hessi, Merz, Moore, Oldenburg & Shea, David Smith, 12,000 paintings, sculptures, mixed media works, drawings & prints, the nucleus donated to the nation by Joseph H Hi emphasizing contemporary art & the develop of modern art from the latter half of the 19th century to present, Contemporary Art
Publications: Exhibit catalogs; Family Guide; collection catalogs; seasonal events calendar, three times per yr
Activities: Classes for children; workshops for adults; docent training; workshops for teachers; outreach; free summer concerts; lects open to pub, 4 vis lectrs per yr; gallery talks; tours; individual paintings & original objects of art lent to accredited mus that meet security & conservation standards, loans, subject to approval by cur; lending contains original art works, original prints & sculpture; book traveling exhibs 1-2 per yr; originate traveling exhibs 1-2 per yr; mus shop sells books, reproductions, slides, jewelry by artists, CD's & sculptural toys

L **Library,** Hirshhorn Museum, 4th Fl, 700 Independence Ave SW Washington, DC 20560-0001; PO Box 37012, MRC 361 Washington, DC 20013-7012. Tel 202-633-2776; Email HMSGLibrary@si.edu; Web: library.si.edu; *Librn* Jacqueline Protka
Open Mon - Fri 10 AM - 5 PM; No admis fee; Estab 1974; Circ 9,500 (est); Branch of Smithsonian Institution Libraries (for reference only by appointment)
Income: Financed through the Smithsonian Institution
Library Holdings: Audio Tapes, Book Volumes 62,000, Clipping Files, DVDs, Exhibition Catalogs, Memorabilia, Other Holdings Auction Catalogs, Periodical Subscriptions 35, Photographs
Special Subjects: Afro-American Art, Art History, Collages, Conceptual Art, Drawings, Etchings & Engravings, Film, Latin American Art, Mixed Media, Painting-American, Painting-European, Photography, Printmaking, Prints, Sculpture, Video, Woodcuts
Activities: Museum shop

M **HISTORICAL SOCIETY OF WASHINGTON DC,** The City Museum of Washington DC, 801 K St NW, Mount Vernon Sq Washington, DC 20001-3746. Tel 202-249-3955; Fax 202-417-3823; Email info@historydc.org; Email library@historydc.org; Web: www.dchistory.org; *Dir Library & Colls* Anne McDonough
Open exhibs Tues - Sun 10 AM - 5 PM; Admis free; Estab 1894 to preserve & interpret local history of Washington, DC; Permanent and changing exhibitions on the history of Washington DC. Maintains reference library; Average Annual Attendance: 350,000; Mem: 1,800; dues $50 - $5000
Income: $2.5 million (financed by endowment, mem, grants & earned income)
Library Holdings: Audio Tapes, Book Volumes, Clipping Files, Fiche, Lantern Slides, Manuscripts, Maps, Memorabilia, Original Art Works, Original Documents, Pamphlets, Photographs, Prints, Sculpture
Special Subjects: Architecture, Decorative Arts, Historical Material
Collections: Photographs, Prints, Paintings, Maps, Decorative Arts, Ephemera, Archives
Exhibitions: Washington Perspectives; Digging History and Washington Stories; City of Sports; Taking a Closer Look; Chinatown; Mount Vernon Square
Publications: Washington History, semi-annual magazine
Activities: Classes for adults & children; dramatic progs; docent training; lects open to pub, 12 vis lectrs per yr; tours; sponsoring competitions; awards; originate traveling exhibs to local organizations, libraries & schools; mus shop sells books, reproductions, prints, crafts & souvenirs

L **Library,** 801 K St NW, Washington, DC 20001. Tel 202-383-1850, 383-1800; Fax 202-383-1872; Email info@historydc.org; Web: www.historydc.org; *Dir Library & Colls* Anne McDonough
Open Mon - Thurs 10 AM - 4 PM by prior appointment; No admis fee; Estab 1894 for collection of materials related to Washington, DC history; For reference only; Average Annual Attendance: 1500; Mem: 1,800; dues $50 - $5000; annual meeting
Income: $700,000 financed by grants, membership & earned income
Library Holdings: Book Volumes 14,000, Cards, Clipping Files, Exhibition Catalogs, Fiche, Lantern Slides, Manuscripts, Memorabilia, Original Art Works, Original Documents, Pamphlets, Photographs, Prints, Reels, Slides
Special Subjects: Archaeology, Architecture, Art History, Decorative Arts, Drawings, Etchings & Engravings, Historical Material, History of Art & Archaeology, Landscape Architecture, Manuscripts, Painting-American, Photography, Portraits, Prints
Collections: Photographs, Prints, Paintings, Maps, Decorative Arts, Archives, Books, Ephemera
Exhibitions: Window to Washington (permanent exhib)
Publications: Washington History, semi-annual magazine
Activities: Workshops; teacher training; lects open to pub; 2-4 vis lectrs per yr; gallery talks; tours; schols; mus shop sells books, magazines, original art, reproductions & prints

M **HOWARD UNIVERSITY,** Gallery of Art, 2455 6th St NW, College of Fine Arts Washington, DC 20059-0001. Tel 202-806-7040; Fax 202-806-6503; Web: www.galleryofart.howard.edu; *Asst Dir* Scott Bakersbaker@howard.edu; *Registrar* Eileen Johnstonejohnston@howard.edu; *Assoc Dir* Dr. Gwendolyn H Everettgeverett@howard.edu
Open Mon-Fri 9:30 AM - 5 PM, Sun 1 PM - 4 PM; No admis fee; Estab 1928 to stimulate the study & appreciation of the fine arts in the University & community; Three air-conditioned art galleries are in Childers Hall, James V Herring Heritage Gallery, James A Porter Gallery & the Student Gallery along with Gumbel Print Room, Lois Jones Gallery; Average Annual Attendance: 26,000
Income: School funding
Special Subjects: Renaissance Art, Painting-Italian, African Art, Prints, Watercolors, Sculpture, Graphics, Afro-American Art
Collections: University collection of painting, sculpture & graphic arts by Afro-Americans, Agnes Delano Collection of Contemporary American Watercolors & Prints, Irving R Gumbel Collection of prints, Kress Study Collection of Renaissance paintings & sculpture, Alain Locke Collection of African art, Era Katz Collection of Theatrical Marquis 1970's-1980's
Exhibitions: Changing tri-monthly exhibits; acad exhibits; ann student show
Publications: Catalogue of the African & Afro-American collections; exhibition catalogues; informational brochures; Native American Arts (serial)
Activities: Bimonthly gallery lect & community programs

L **Architecture & Planning Library,** 2366 Sixth St NW, Washington, DC 20059. Tel 202-806-7773; Web: www.howarduniversity.edu; *Cur* Sarah Humber
Open Mon - Fri 8:30 AM - 5 PM; No admis fee; Estab for students & staff covering aspects of architecture & Afro American design
Library Holdings: Book Volumes 27,000, CD-ROMs, Filmstrips, Lantern Slides, Other Holdings Documents 600, Periodical Subscriptions 400, Photographs, Reels 1,300, Slides 29,000
Collections: Dominick Collection of pre-1900 books & periodicals on architecture, K Keith Collection of books & photographs on indigenous African architecture

A **THE JOHN F KENNEDY CENTER FOR THE PERFORMING ARTS,** 2700 F St NW, Washington, DC 20566; PO Box 101510, Arlington, VA 22210-4510. Tel 202-416-8000; 467-4600; Fax 202-416-8421; Web: www.kennedy-center.org; *Chmn* David M Rubenstein; *Pres* Deborah F Rutter
Open Mon - Sat 10 AM - 9 PM, Sun noon - 9 PM (box office); No admis fee for building, ticket prices vary; The Center opened in Sept 1971. Facilities include the 2200-seat Opera House, 2750-seat Concert Hall, 1130-seat Eisenhower Theater, 500-seat Terrace Theater, 200-seat family theater & 350-seat Theater Lab. Estab in 1958 by Act of Congress as the National Cultural Center. The Center is the sole official memorial in Washington to President Kennedy. Although the Center does not have an official collection, gifts in the form of art objects from foreign countries are on display throughout; Bureau of the Smithsonian Institution; Administered by a separate Bd of Trustees; Average Annual Attendance: 2,000,000 ticketed, 2,500,000-3,000,000 visitors; Mem: Friends of the Kennedy Center 40,000; dues from $60 & up
Publications: Kennedy Center News, bimonthly
Activities: Classes for adults & children; dramatic progs; performing arts series for young audiences; lects open to pub, 50 vis lectrs per yr; concerts; tours

M **THE KREEGER MUSEUM,** 2401 Foxhall Road NW, Washington, DC 20007. Tel 202-337-3050; Fax 202-337-3051; Email visitorservices@kreegermuseum.org; Web: www.kreegermuseum.org; *Dir* Helen Chason; *Opers Mgr* Ivan Delgado; *Head Educ* David Hawkins; *Head Pub Rels & Mem* Sarah Hines; *Head Coll Mgmnt, Visitor Svcs & Pvt Events* Joanna Baker

Open Tues - Sat 10 AM - 4 PM, cl Sun & Mon; Suggested donation adults $10, students, seniors & military $8; Estab 1994; Designed by Philip Johnson, it showcases the Kreeger's permanent collection of 19th & 20th century paintings & sculpture; Average Annual Attendance: 15,000
Income: Financed by David Lloyd Kreeger Foundation
Library Holdings: Auction Catalogs, Book Volumes, Exhibition Catalogs
Special Subjects: African Art, Architecture, Drawings, Landscapes, Painting-American, Painting-French, Painting-German, Painting-Spanish, Sculpture
Activities: Classes for adults & children; docent training; lect open to public; concerts; gallery talks; tours

L **LIBRARY OF CONGRESS,** Prints & Photographs Division, 101 Independence Ave SE, Madison Bldg, LM 337 Washington, DC 20540-4730. Tel 202-707-6394; Fax 202-707-6647; Web: www.loc.gov/rr/print; *Librn of Congress* Carla Hayden; *Dir Colls & Svcs and Chief of Prints & Photographs* Helena Zinkham; *Head Reference Section* Barbara Natanson
Open Mon - Fri 8:30 AM - 5 PM; No admis fee; Estab 1897; Circ 96,000; For reference only; Average Annual Attendance: 1,900,000
Income: Financed by congressional appropriation, gifts & endowments
Purchases: Fine prints, photographs, posters, architectural drawings, historical prints & drawings, cartoons
Library Holdings: Auction Catalogs, Audio Tapes, Book Volumes, CD-ROMs, Cards, Cassettes, Clipping Files, Compact Disks, DVDs, Exhibition Catalogs, Fiche, Filmstrips, Framed Reproductions, Kodachrome Transparencies, Lantern Slides, Manuscripts, Maps 4,562,267, Memorabilia, Micro Print, Motion Pictures, Original Art Works, Original Documents, Other Holdings Architectural items 2,000,000; Fine prints; Master photographs; Photographic images 10,500,000; Popular & applied graphic art item 20,000; Posters 100,000, Pamphlets, Periodical Subscriptions, Photographs, Prints, Records, Reels, Reproductions, Sculpture, Slides, Video Tapes
Collections: Archive of Hispanic Culture, Japanese Prints, Pennell Collection of Whistleriana, Civil War drawings, prints, photographs & negatives, early American lithographs, pictorial archives of early American architecture, Historic American Buildings Survey, Historic American Engineering Record, Cabinet of American Illustration, original fine prints of all schools & periods, Yanker Collection of Propaganda posters, originally designed posters for all periods, dating 1840s - present, Seagram County Court House Collection: Swann Collection of Caricature & Cartoon, American Political Cartoons, Collection of photographs & photographic negatives incl: the Brady-Handy Collection, Farm Security Administration Collection, Alexander Graham Bell Collection, Arnold Genthe, J C H Grabill, F B Johnston, Tony Frissell, Detroit Photographic Co, W H Jackson Collection, George Grantham Bain Collection, H E French Washington Photographs, Matson Near Eastern Collection, NY Work-Telegram & Sun, US News & World Report, Presidential, geographical, biographical & master photograph groupings, captured German photographs of the WW II period & panorama photographs & the Look magazine archive, early 20th Century architecture photograph coll Gottscho-Schleisner
Exhibitions: Permanent collection
Publications: New Field of Vision; Norton/Library of Congress Visual Sourcebooks; A Century of Photographs, 1846-1946; American Prints in the Library of Congress; American Revolution in Drawings & Prints; Eyes of the Nation: A Visual History of the United States; Graphic Sampler; Historic America: Buildings, Structures & Sites; Historic American Buildings Survey; Middle East in Pictures, Prints & Photographs: An Illustrated Guide; Viewpoints; Spec Collections in the Library of Congress; Fine Prints in the Library of Congress: The Poster Collection in the Library of Congress; Popular & Applied Graphic Art in the Library of Congress
Activities: Docent training; lects open to pub; concerts; gallery talks; tours; orientations; fels offered; sales shops sell books, magazines, reproductions

MARJORIE MERRIWEATHER POST FOUNDATION OF DC
For further information, see Hillwood Museum & Gardens Foundation

M **MAURINE LITTLETON GALLERY,** 1667 Wisconsin Ave NW, Washington, DC 20007. Tel 202-333-9307; Fax 202-342-2004; Email info@littletongallery.com; Web: www.littletongallery.com; *Dir* Harvey K Littleton
Open by appointment only
Collections: works by contemporary glass artists; sculpture; ceramics

M **MERIDIAN INTERNATIONAL CENTER,** Cafritz Galleries, 1624 Crescent Pl NW, Washington, DC 20009-4004. Tel 202-667-6800; Fax 202-667-1465; Email info@meridian.org; Web: www.meridian.org; *Chmn* Carlos M Gutierrez; *Pres & CEO* Stuart W Holliday
Open Wed - Sun 2 - 5 PM; No admis fee; Estab 1960 to promote international understanding through exchange of people, ideas & the arts; 3000 sq ft, 5 rooms in renovated historic mansion; Average Annual Attendance: 50,000; Mem: donations
Income: Financed by endowment, contributions, arts: private support, grants & corporate support
Publications: Exhibit catalogues; Meridian newsletter, 3 per year
Activities: Docent training; lects open to pub, 2-3 vis lectrs per yr, concerts, tours; originates traveling exhibs

M **NATIONAL ACADEMY OF SCIENCES,** Arts in the Academy, 2101 Constitution Ave, NW, Washington, DC 20418-0007; 500 5th St NW, Rm NAS 271 Washington, DC 20001-2736. Tel 202-334-2415; Fax 202-334-1690; Email cpnas@nas.edu; Web: www.cpnas.org; *Dir* JD Talasek; *Sr Prog Assoc* Alana Quinn
Open Mon - Fri 9 AM - 5 PM, cl weekends & holidays; No admis fee; Exhib of Science Related Art; Two small galleries within operating office building; Average Annual Attendance: 5,000
Income: Organizational endowment
Activities: Lect open to public; concerts

M **NATIONAL AIR AND SPACE MUSEUM,** Smithsonian Institution, Independence Ave at 6th St SW, Washington, DC 20560-0310; PO Box 37012, Office of Public Affairs MRC 321 Washington, DC 20013-7012. Tel 202-633-2214; Fax 202-633-8174; Email NASMVisitorServices@si.edu; Web: airandspace.si.edu; *John & Adrienne Mars Dir* Gen. Ellen R Stofan; *Deputy Dir* Christopher Browne; *Dir Advancement* Laura Gleason; *Assoc Dir* Meg Caulk; *Assoc Dir* Rick Flansburg; *Chief Cur* Peter L Jakab; *Assoc Dir* Michelle Lamberton
Open daily 10 AM - 5:30 PM, cl Dec 25; No admis fee; Estab 1946 to memorialize the national develop of aviation & space flight; One gallery comprised of 5,000 sq ft devoted to the theme, Flight & the Arts. Bureau of the Smithsonian Institution; Average Annual Attendance: 4,700,000; Mem: Dues $35 - $10,000
Income: Financed through the Smithsonian Institute
Special Subjects: Drawings, Painting-American, Prints, Sculpture
Collections: Paintings, prints & drawings include: Alexander Calder, Lamar Dodd, Richard Estes, Audrey Flack, Francisco Goya, Lowell Nesbitt, Robert Rauschenberg, James Wyeth, major sculptures by Richard Lippold, Alejandro Otero, Charles Perry, Stuart M Speiser Collection of Photo Realist Art
Exhibitions: Exhibitions change annually
Publications: Various publications relating to aviation & space science
Activities: Educ dept; handicapped services; regional resource prog; lects open to pub, 15-20 vis lectrs per yr; concerts; gallery talks; tours; schols offered; individual paintings & original objects of art lent to nonprofit educational institutions; book traveling exhibs; originate traveling exhibs; mus shop sells books, magazines, reproductions, prints, slides, posters, stamp covers, kites, models & jewelry

L **Regional Planetary Image Facility,** Rm 3773 MRC 315, PO Box 37012 Washington, DC 20013-7012. Tel 202-633-2480; Fax 202-786-2566; Web: airandspace.si.edu/research/resources/rpif/; *Dir* Dr Tom Watters; *Data Mgr* Rose Aiello; *Data Asst* Jennifer O'Brien
Open Mon - Fri 10 AM - 4 PM to researchers by appt only; No admis fee; Estab to act as a reference library providing planetary science researchers with access to the extensive collection of image data obtained from planetary missions; At Center for Earth & Planetary Studies within Smithsonian National Air & Space Mus
Library Holdings: CD-ROMs, Original Documents, Photographs

NATIONAL ARCHITECTURAL ACCREDITING BOARD, INC
For further information, see National and Regional Organizations

NATIONAL ASSEMBLY OF STATE ARTS AGENCIES
For further information, see National and Regional Organizations

NATIONAL ENDOWMENT FOR THE ARTS
For further information, see National and Regional Organizations

M **NATIONAL GALLERY OF ART,** Constitution Ave at 4th St NW, Washington, DC 20565; 2000B S Club Dr, Landover, MD 20785-3228. Tel 202-737-4215; Email d-lenoir@nga.gov; Web: www.nga.gov; Others 202-842-6176 (TDD); *Dir* Earl A Powell III; *Deputy Dir* Franklin Kelly; *Dean, Center for Advanced Study in Visual Arts* Elizabeth Cropper; *Chief Librn* Neal Turtell; *Spec Events Officer* Carol Kelley; *Cur Northern Baroque Painting* Arthur Wheelock; *Cur Renaissance Painting* David Brown; *Cur Sculpture & Decorative Arts* C.D. Dickerson; *Educ Div Head* Lynn Russell; *Chief Design & Installation* Mark Leithauser; *Chief Photographic Svcs* Sarah Greenough; *Chief Horticulture* Cynthia Kaufmann; *Chief Conservation* Mervin Richard; *Deputy Chief and Senior Archivist* Michele Willens; *Secy & Gen Counsel* Nancy Breuer; *Treas* William McClure; *Registrar* Michelle Fondas; *Music Dept Specialist* Danielle Hahn; *Chief Develop & Corporate Rels Officer* Christine Meyers; *Chmn Board Trustees* Sharon Rockefeller; *Chief of Communicaitons* Anabeth Guthrie
Open Mon - Sat 10 AM - 5 PM; Sun 11 AM - 6 PM; cl Christmas & New Years Day; No admis fee; Estab 1937 for the people of the U.S. by a joint resolution of Congress accepting the gift of financier, pub servant and art collector Andrew W Mellon; Affiliate of the Smithsonian Institution; Governed by a separate Board of Trustees composed of 5 Trustees & the Secretary of State, Secretary of the Treasury, US Chief Justice & the Secretary of the Smithsonian Institution; Average Annual Attendance: 4,100,000
Income: Financed by private endowment & federal appropriation
Library Holdings: Auction Catalogs, Clipping Files, Exhibition Catalogs, Fiche, Filmstrips, Lantern Slides, Manuscripts, Original Documents, Periodical Subscriptions, Photographs, Prints, Records, Reels, Sculpture
Collections: More than 130,000 paintings, drawings, prints, photographs, sculpture, decorative arts & furniture traces the development of Western art from the Middle Ages to the present
Exhibitions: Temporary exhibitions from collections both in the United States & abroad
Publications: exhibition catalogs; annual report; Bulletin; the conservation division's biennial journal, Facture; CASVA's annual report, Center; symposia series, Studies in the History of Art; seminar paper series; seasonal highlights brochure; e-newsletters
Activities: Classes for adults & children; family program; weekend classic cinema, documentary, avant garde & area premiers program; docent led tours; gallery talks by museum educators & specialists for adults; lects open to the pub; Sunday lects by distinguished quest speakers & members of the staff are given throughout the year; A W Mellon Lect in the Fine Arts; concerts programs; special tours are arranged for groups; films on art are presented on a varying schedule; DVDs on gallery exhibs & collections; exten dept provides art loans to museums around the world; mus shop sells books, reproductions, stationary; jewelry; home decor; CDs & DVDs, stationary, kids

L **Library,** Constitution Ave at 4th St NW, Washington, DC 20565; 2000B S Club Dr, Landover, MD 20785-3228. Tel 202-842-6511; Email library@nga.gov; Web: www.nga.gov/resources/dldesc.shtm; *Exec Librn* Neal Turtell; *Head Reader Svcs* Lamia Doumato; *Reference Librn* John Hagood; *Admin Librn* Roger Lawson; *Chief, Library Image Coll* Gregory P J Most
Open Mon Noon - 4:30 PM, Tues - Fri 10 AM - 4:30 PM, cl Federal holidays; Estab 1941 to support the national curatorial, educational & research activities & serve as a research center for graduate & undergraduate students, vis scholars & researchers in the visual arts. Supports the research programs of the Center for Advanced Study in the Visual Arts; For reference only
Income: Financed by federal appropriations & trust funds
Library Holdings: Auction Catalogs, Book Volumes 425,000, Clipping Files, Exhibition Catalogs, Fiche, Manuscripts, Micro Print, Other Holdings Vertical Files 125,000, Pamphlets, Periodical Subscriptions 990, Photographs, Reels, Slides
Collections: Art exhibition, art auction & private art coll catalogs, artist monographs, Leonardo da Vinci, catalogues raisonne, Over 300,000 books,

periodicals, & documents on the history, theory, & criticism of art and architecture, with emphasis on Western art from the Middle Ages to the present (particularly Italian, Dutch, Flemish, German, French, Spanish, & British schools) & American art from the colonial era to the present
Publications: NGA Library Guide, 2012
Activities: Library tours on request

L **Department of Image Collections**, Constitution Ave at 4th St NW, Washington, DC 20565; 2000B S Club Dr, Landover, MD 20785. Tel 202-842-6026; Fax 202-789-3068; Email image-collections@nga.gov; Web: www.library.nga.gov/imagecollections/; *Dep Chief & Architecture Specialist* Andrea Gibbs; *Italian Specialist* Melissa Beck Lemke; *Modern Specialist* Meg Melvin; *Circ Asst* Carrie Scharf; *American Specialist* Andrew L Thomas; *French Specialist* Nicholas A Martin; *Spanish Specialist* Thomas A O'Callaghan Jr; *Chief* Gregory P J Most; *Conserv* Sarah Wagner; *Spec Projects Specialist* Lisa M Coldiron; *Northern & Central Europe Specialist* Molli E Kuenstner
Open Mon Noon - 4:30 PM, Tues - Fri 10 AM - 4:30 PM, cl federal holidays; Slide Library (estab 1941) & Photographic Archives (estab 1943) merged in 2004 to Dept of Image Collections; Circ 30,000; The Department of Image Collections is a study and research collection of images documenting European and American art and architecture
Library Holdings: Book Volumes, CD-ROMs 200, Fiche 7,500,000, Lantern Slides, Other Holdings, Photographs 7,700,000, Prints 2,000, Slides 150,000
Special Subjects: Architecture, Art History, Bronzes, Ceramics, Decorative Arts, Drawings, Furniture, Manuscripts, Oriental Art, Painting-American, Painting-British, Painting-Dutch, Painting-European, Painting-Flemish, Painting-French, Painting-German, Painting-Italian, Painting-Russian, Portraits, Pre-Columbian Art, Prints, Religious Art, Sculpture, Silver, Watercolors
Publications: Manual for Classifying and Cataloging Images; Guide to the National Gallery of Art Photo Archives

L **Index of American Design**, Constitution Ave at 6th St NW, Washington, DC 20565. Tel 202-842-6605; Fax 202-842-6859; Email c-ritchie@nga.gov; Web: www.nga.gov/collection/gallery/iad.htm; *Asst Cur* Ruth Fein; *Asst Cur* Carlotta Owens
Open daily 10 AM - Noon & 2 - 4 PM; No admis fee; Acquired by National Gallery in 1943 to serve as a visual archive of American decorative arts, late 17th through 19th centuries; Visual archive produced between 1935 &1942; Study room with National Gallery print galleries available for exhibitions; offices; storeroom
Library Holdings: Fiche, Original Art Works Watercolors 18,000, Photographs
Special Subjects: Architecture, Ceramics, Costume Design & Constr, Decorative Arts, Folk Art, Furniture, Glass, Jewelry, Religious Art, Silver, Textiles, Woodcarvings, Watercolors
Collections: 18,000 watercolor renderings of American decorative arts objects from the colonial period through the 19th c
Activities: Online slide tours; original objects of art lent to institutions complying with National Gallery lending rules; lending collection contains 11 slide programs available through National Gallery dept of exten programs

NATIONAL LEAGUE OF AMERICAN PEN WOMEN
For further information, see National and Regional Organizations

M **NATIONAL MUSEUM OF AFRICAN AMERICAN HISTORY AND CULTURE,** Smithsonian Institution, 1400 Constitution Ave NW, Washington, DC 20560. Tel 844-750-3012; Email nmaahcinfo@si.org; Web: nmaahc.si.edu; *Founding Dir* Lonnie G Bunch III; *Deputy Dir* Kinshasha Holman Conwill; *Assoc Dir Curatorial Affairs* Dr Rex Ellis
Open daily 10 AM - 5:30 PM, cl Christmas Day; No admis fee; Estab 2003 to document African American life, art, history & culture; Average Annual Attendance: 1,400,000; Mem: Dues $25 - $5,000
Collections: Coll includes 36,000 artifacts, American South, American West, Civil Rights, Clothing & Dress, Communities, Education, Family, Literature, Military, Music, Politics, Religious Groups, Segregation, Slavery

M **NATIONAL MUSEUM OF AFRICAN ART,** Smithsonian Institution, 950 Independence Ave SW, Washington, DC 20560-0708; PO Box 37012 MRC 708, Washington, DC 20013-7012. Tel 202-633-4600; Fax 202-357-4879; Email nmafaweb@si.edu; Web: africa.si.edu; *Dir* Gus Casely-Hayford; *Deputy Dir & Chief Cur* Christine Mullen Kreamer; *Head Registar* Clarissa Fostel; *Cur Educ* Deborah Stokes
Open daily 10 AM - 5:30 PM, cl Dec 25; No admis fee; Estab 1964 to foster public understanding & appreciation of the diverse cultures & artistic achievements in Africa; museum joined the Smithsonian Institution in 1979. Moved in 1987 to the Smithsonian's new museum complex, the Quadrangle on the National Mall; Bureau of the Smithsonian Institution; Average Annual Attendance: 98,000; Mem: Dues $100 - $10,000
Library Holdings: Video Tapes
Special Subjects: African Art
Collections: More than 11,860 traditional & contemporary objects from throughout the African continent, The Walt Disney-Tishman African Art Coll
Exhibitions: Permanent Exhibitions: Images of Power & Identity; The Art of the Personal Object; The Ancient West African City of Benin, AD 1300-1897; The Ancient Nubien City of Kerma, 2500-1500 BC; Ceramic Art at the National Museum of African Art
Publications: Booklets; exhibition catalogs; multimedia slide kit; pamphlets; videotapes
Activities: Classes for adults & children; docent training; lects open to pub; concerts; gallery talks; films; tours; residency fellowship program; book several traveling exhibs per yr; originates traveling exhibs; mus sales shop sells books, magazines, reproductions, prints, slides, quality crafts, original art, cassettes & CD's, jewelry & other imports from Africa

L **Warren M Robbins Library**, 950 Independence Ave SW, Rm 2138 Washington, DC 20560; PO Box 37012 MRC 708, Washington, DC 20013-7012. Tel 202-633-4680; Fax 202-357-4879; Email AskaLibrarian@si.edu; Web: library.si.edu; *Librn* Janet L Stanley; *Libr Technician* Karen F Brown
Open Mon - Fri 9 AM - 5:15 PM; Estab 1971 to provide major resource center for African art & culture; Library is part of the Smithsonian Institution Libraries system; Branch of Smithsonian Institution Libraries (for reference only)
Income: Financed through Smithsonian budget
Library Holdings: Auction Catalogs, Audio Tapes, Book Volumes 32,000, Clipping Files, DVDs, Exhibition Catalogs, Maps, Pamphlets, Periodical Subscriptions, Video Tapes
Special Subjects: Archaeology, Crafts, Pottery, Printmaking, Sculpture, Textiles, Architecture, Photography

L **Eliot Elisofon Photographic Archives**, 950 Independence Ave SW, Washington, DC 20560; PO Box 37012 MRC 708, Washington, DC 20013-7012. Tel 202-633-4690; Fax 202-357-4879; Email elisofonarchives@si.edu; Web: africa.si.edu
Open Tues - Thurs 10 AM - 4 PM by appt; No admis fee; fees for use of archive images; Estab 1973; devoted to the collection, preservation & dissemination of visual materials that encourage & support the study of the arts, cultures & history of Africa
Library Holdings: Lantern Slides, Maps, Motion Pictures 120,000 ft of film, Other Holdings, Photographs 80,000, Slides 180,000
Collections: Eliot Elisofon Coll: over 50,000 black-and-white negatives & photographs, 30,000 color slides, & 120,000 feet of motion picture film and sound materials, Constance Stuart Larrabee Coll: over 5,000 black-and-white photographs taken in South Africa between 1936 & 1983, Henry Drewal & Margaret Thompson Drewal Coll: over 10,000 slides depicting Yoruba art & culture, Historical coll of over 13,000 postcards, Special colls include late 19th- & early 20th-century photographic albums, Total archives coll contains approximately 300,000 items, incl rare collections of glass plate negatives, lantern slides, stereographs, postcards, maps & engravings

M **NATIONAL MUSEUM OF AMERICAN HISTORY,** Smithsonian Institution, Constitution Ave NW, Btwn 12th & 14th Washington, DC 20560; PO Box 37012, MRC 010 Washington, DC 20013-7012. Tel 202-633-1000; Email info@si.edu; Web: americanhistory.si.edu; *Interim Dir* Susan Fruchter; *Deputy Dir External Affairs* Kari Fantasia; *Deputy Dir Experience Design* Andrea E Lowther; *Head, Colls Mgmnt & Registrar* Joshua M Gorman
Open daily 10 AM - 5:30 PM, cl Dec 25; No admis fee; Estab 1964 as Mus of History & Tech, name changed 1980, reopened 2008 following renovation; The Mus is devoted to the collection, care, study & exhibition of objects that reflect the experience of the American people, as well as sharing & honoring the cultural achievements of Native Americans from North, Central & South America. West Wing renovations 2012-2015. Bureau of the Smithsonian Institution; Average Annual Attendance: 3,200,000; Mem: Dues $50 - $5,000 & up
Special Subjects: American Indian Art, Etchings & Engravings, Sculpture
Collections: Agriculture, armed forces, automobiles, ceramics, locomotives, musical instruments, numismatics, political history, textiles, popular culture, domestic life, technology information, electricity, science, medicine
Exhibitions: Several rotating exhibitions per year; The American Presidency; A Glorious Burden; Within These Walls...; America on the Move; Star-Spangled Banner-The Flag that inspired the National Anthem; Price of Freedom: Americans at War; Julia Child's Kitchen; The First Ladies; Gunboat Philadelphia; American Stories
Publications: Exhibition brochures & catalogs; related research publications
Activities: Activities for adults & children; docent training; internship & fellowship progs; lects open to pub; concerts; gallery talks; tours; lending original objects to Smithsonian affiliated mus; originate traveling exhibs to affiliated mus; mus shop sells books, magazines, reproductions, prints, souvenirs, jewelry, clothing

L **Library**, National Museum of American History, Rm 5016 Washington, DC 20560-0001. Tel 202-633-3865; Fax 202-633-3427; Email AskaLibrarian@si.edu; Web: library.si.edu; *Head, History & Culture Dept* William E Baxter; *Head Librn* Trina Brown
Open Mon - Thurs 9 AM - 5 PM, Fri noon - 5 PM by appt, cl federal holidays; Library is part of the Smithsonian Institution Libraries system; Open to staff & vis scholars
Income: Financed through SIL budgets
Library Holdings: Book Volumes 120,000, Fiche 20,000, Reels 8,000
Special Subjects: Carpets & Rugs, Decorative Arts, Furniture, Graphic Design, Historical Material, Metalwork, Photography, Pottery, Silver, Textiles

M **NATIONAL MUSEUM OF NATURAL HISTORY,** Smithsonian Institution, 10th St & Constitution Ave NW, Washington, DC 20560; PO Box 37012, Smithsonian Institution Washington, DC 20013-7012. Tel 202-633-1000; Email naturalexperience@si.edu; Web: naturalhistory.si.edu; *Sant Dir* Dr Kirk Johnson; *Assoc Dir Devel* Dr Sandra Lovinguth; *Asst Dir Colls* Carol Butler; *Asst. Dir Communs* Jim Wood; *Asst Dir Science Prog Admin* Dr Wendy Wiswall; *Asst Dir Exhibs* Mike Lawrence; *Asst Dir Facilities Opers* Chun-Hsi Wong
Open daily 10 AM - 5:30 PM, cl Christmas Day; No admis fee; Estab 1910 to inspire curiosity, discovery & learning about the natural world through unparalleled research, collections, exhibitions and education outreach programs; Comprised of 1.5 million total sq ft with 325,000 sq ft devoted to exhib & pub space. Bureau of the Smithsonian Institution; Average Annual Attendance: 3,700,000
Income: Financed through the Smithsonian Institute
Collections: 126 million piece coll including 30 million insects, 4.5 million plants, 7 million fish, 2 million cultural artifacts, including 400,000 photographs, Botany, Entomology, Invertebrate & Vertebrate Zoology, Analytical Biology, Mineral Sciences, Paleobiology, Anthropology
Exhibitions: Exhibitions change annually
Publications: Various publications relating to natural history
Activities: Educ dept; handicapped services; regional resource prog; Lects open to pub; schols offered; book traveling exhibs; originate traveling exhibs; mus shop sells books, magazines, reproductions, prints, posters, models & jewelry

M **NATIONAL MUSEUM OF THE AMERICAN INDIAN,** Smithsonian Institution, 4th St & Independence Ave SW, Washington, DC 20560; PO Box 23473, Washington, DC 20026-3473. Tel 202-633-1000; 800-242-NMAI (6624); Fax 202-633-6920; Email nmai-info@si.edu; Web: americanindian.edu; *Dir* Kevin Gover Jr
Open Daily 10 AM - 5:30 PM; cl Dec 25; No admis fee; Estab 1989; opened Sept 21, 2004; Average Annual Attendance: 781,000; Mem: Dues $25 - $5,000 & up
Library Holdings: Auction Catalogs, Audio Tapes, Book Volumes, CD-ROMs, Cards, Cassettes, Clipping Files, Compact Disks, DVDs, Exhibition Catalogs, Fiche, Filmstrips, Framed Reproductions, Kodachrome Transparencies,

Manuscripts, Maps, Memorabilia, Micro Print, Motion Pictures, Original Art Works, Original Documents, Other Holdings, Pamphlets, Periodical Subscriptions, Photographs, Prints, Records, Reels, Reproductions, Sculpture, Slides, Video Tapes
Special Subjects: American Indian Art, American Western Art, Anthropology, Archaeology, Cartoons, Ceramics, Coins & Medals, Collages, Crafts, Decorative Arts, Dolls, Drawings, Embroidery, Eskimo Art, Etchings & Engravings, Ethnology, Folk Art, Glass, Gold, Graphics, Hispanic Art, Historical Material, Landscapes, Latin American Art, Leather, Manuscripts, Maps, Military Art, Miniatures, Mosaics, Painting-American, Painting-Canadian, Painting-European, Painting-French, Painting-German, Painting-Spanish, Photography, Porcelain, Portraits, Posters, Pottery, Pre-Columbian Art, Primitive art, Prints, Religious Art, Reproductions, Sculpture, Silver, Southwestern Art, Textiles, Tapestries, Watercolors, Woodcarvings
Collections: Approx 266,000 catalog records (825,000 items representing over 12,000 yrs of history & more than 1,200 indigenous cultures throughout the western hemisphere, Mus holdings include photographic archive (approx 324,000 images from the 1860s to present, Media archive (approx 12,000 items) including film & audiovisual colls, Paper archives (approx 1,500 linear feet) comprised of records dating from the 1860s to present
Publications: American Indian Magazine - qtr
Activities: Educ progs; docent training; outreach progs; internships; lects open to pub; concerts; gallery talks; tours; sponsored competitions; seminars; symposia; schols; fels; mus shop sells books, magazines, original art, reproductions, prints, CDs, DVDs, cards, specialty items & souvenirs

L **Archive Center**, 4220 Silver Hill Rd, Cultural Resources Center Suitland, MD 20746-2863. Tel 301-238-1400; Fax 301-238-3038; Email nmaiarchives@si.edu; Web: americanindian.si.edu/explore/collections/archive/; *Head Archivist* Michael Pahn; *Asst Head Archivist* Emily Moazami; *Reference Archivist* Nathan Sowry
Open Mon - Fri 9:30AM - 4:30 PM to researchers by appt only; No admis fee; Archives housed in the NMAI Cultural Resources Center
Library Holdings: Audio Tapes, Book Volumes, Compact Disks, Lantern Slides, Manuscripts, Maps, Memorabilia, Motion Pictures, Original Documents, Photographs, Slides, Video Tapes
Special Subjects: Photography
Collections: Paper Archives: contains approx 1500 ft of records & special colls from 1830s on, documenting the history of NMAI & MAI; official records incl correspondence, memoranda, photographs, & audio material pertaining to MAI founder & staff; other records include unpublished manuscripts, field notebooks with original drawings, site diagrams, maps, scrapbooks, photographs, object coll listings, exhibit planning materials, & correspondence pertaining to research expeditions, collecting projects, & collectors; Maintains Board of Trustees records, annual reports, & copies of NMAI publications; Special colls incl National Congress of the American Indian (NCAI) Archives, Leuman Maurice Waugh Papers, Reuben Snake Papers, & ARROW, Inc. records, Photo Archives: approx 324,000 images, negatives, vintage prints, transparencies, lantern slides, glass-plate negatives, color slides & digital photos documenting Native American culture & history from the mid-19th c to present; incl historic scenes, portraits, field photographs of mus ethnographic & archaeological expeditions in Mexico & North, South & Central America, & recordings of contemporary Native American artists, Media Archives: 12,000+ video tapes, motion picture films, & audio recordings, from 1902 to the present representing communities from N & S America in interviews, performances, cinematic films, & documentary recordings; contemporary Native American cinema; variety of formats incl motion picture film, analog & digital video tape recordings, & audio recordings on wax cylinders, phonograph discs, audio tape, & CDs falling into 3 categories - archival recordings, mus progs documentation, & Native Cinema study collection

M **NATIONAL MUSEUM OF WOMEN IN THE ARTS,** 1250 New York Ave NW, Washington, DC 20005-3970. Tel 202-783-5000; Fax 202-393-3235; Email media@nmwa.org; Web: www.nmwa.org; *Dir* Susan Fisher Sterling; *Dir of Library & Research Center* Lynora Williams; *Dir Communs & Mktg* Amy Mannarino
Open Mon - Sat 10 AM - 5 PM, Sun 12 PM - 5 PM, cl Thanksgiving, Christmas & New Year's Days, group tours by appointment; Admis adults $10, seniors (65+) & students $8, youth 18 & under and NMWA members free, 1st Sun of month free; Estab 1981 to promote knowledge & appreciation of women artists through exhibits, publications, educ programs & library services; Maintains library; Average Annual Attendance: 100,000; Mem: 16,000
Income: Private non-profit
Library Holdings: Audio Tapes, Clipping Files, Exhibition Catalogs, Slides, Video Tapes
Special Subjects: Afro-American Art, American Indian Art, American Western Art, Asian Art, Calligraphy, Ceramics, Costumes, Crafts, Decorative Arts, Etchings & Engravings, Jewelry, Landscapes, Latin American Art, Painting-American, Photography
Collections: Over 4,500 works by women artists from 16th c. to present. Incl paintings, sculpture & pottery, 600 unique & limited edition artists' books, Women silversmiths, Botanical prints
Exhibitions: Selections from the permanent collection (indefinitely)
Publications: Exhibit catalogs, women artists (Oct 2000); Women in the Arts, quarterly magazine
Activities: Classes for adults & children; dramatic progs; docent training; films; teacher progs; lects open to pub; lects for mems only; concerts; gallery talks; tours; library fellows award; individual paintings & original objects of art lent; book exhibs 1 per yr; originate traveling exhibs; mus shop sells books, prints & reproductions, jewelry, crafts

L **Library & Research Center**, 1250 New York Ave NW, Washington, DC 20005. Tel 202-783-7365; Fax 202-393-3234; Web: www.nmwa.org; *Dir of Libr & Res Ctr* Heather Slania
Open Mon - Fri 10 AM - 5 PM, by appointment to researchers only; No admis fee
Library Holdings: Audio Tapes, Book Volumes 16,000, Cassettes, DVDs, Exhibition Catalogs, Manuscripts, Memorabilia, Original Art Works, Original Documents, Other Holdings Artists files, Pamphlets, Periodical Subscriptions, Photographs, Prints, Reproductions, Slides, Video Tapes
Special Subjects: Asian Art, Bookplates & Bindings, Bronzes, Calligraphy, Ceramics, Crafts, Decorative Arts, Drawings, Embroidery, Etchings & Engravings, Jewelry, Laces
Collections: Irene Rice Pereira Library, Collection of Artists' Books, Collection of Bookplates, Archives of the International Festival of Women Artists in Copenhagen, Denmark, 1980, Frida Kahlo letters
Activities: Classes for adults & children; docent training; Lects open to pub; concerts; gallery talks; tours; competitions; Mellor Prize; original objects of art & individual paintings lent to mus; book traveling exhibs 2-3 per yr; originate traveling exhibs to mus; mus shop sells books, magazines, original art; reproductions, prints, slides, artisan crafts

M **THE NATIONAL PARK SERVICE, UNITED STATES DEPARTMENT OF THE INTERIOR,** Statue of Liberty National Monument & The Ellis Island Immigration Museum, 1849 C St NW, Dept of Interior Washington, DC 20240-0001. Tel 212-363-3200; Fax 212-363-6302; Email stli_social_media@nps.gov; Web: www.nps.gov/stli; *Cur Coll* Geraldine Santoro; *Supervisory Archivist* George Tselos; *Chief Cur* Diana Pardue; *Library Technician* Barry Moreno; *Library Technician* Jeff Dosik; *Cur Exhibs & Media* Judy Giuriceo
Open daily 9 AM - 5 PM; No admis fee, donations accepted; Estab 1972; Exhibit areas in base of Statue of Liberty & in Ellis Island Immigration Museum; Average Annual Attendance: 4,000,000
Library Holdings: Audio Tapes, Book Volumes, CD-ROMs, Clipping Files, DVDs, Filmstrips, Kodachrome Transparencies, Manuscripts, Maps, Motion Pictures, Periodical Subscriptions, Photographs, Prints, Records, Slides, Video Tapes
Special Subjects: Archaeology, Architecture, Cartoons, Ceramics, Coins & Medals, Costumes, Decorative Arts, Embroidery, Etchings & Engravings, Folk Art, Furniture, Graphics, Historical Material, Judaica, Manuscripts, Painting-American, Photography, Posters, Prints, Religious Art, Restorations, Sculpture, Textiles
Collections: Ellis Island Collection, Statue of Liberty Collection, Furniture Art Work, oral histories, prints, manuscripts, films & videos, books, periodicals, historic structures
Exhibitions: Ellis Island Exhibits; Statue of Liberty exhibit
Activities: Classes for children; dramatic progs; docent training; lects open to pub; gallery talks; tours; individual paintings & original objects of art lent to other mus; book traveling exhibs; sales shop sells books, magazines, reproductions, original art, prints & slides

M **NATIONAL PORTRAIT GALLERY,** Smithsonian Institution, 8th & F Sts, NW, Washington, DC 20001; PO Box 37012, Victor Bldg, Ste 410, MRC 973 Washington, DC 20013-7012. Tel 202-633-8300; Fax 202-633-8243; Email npgnews@si.edu; Web: npg.si.edu; *Dir* Kim Sajet; *Head Communs* Concetta Duncan
Open daily 11:30 AM - 7:00 PM; cl Dec 25; No admis fee; Estab by Act of Congress in 1962 as a mus of the Smithsonian Institution for the exhibition & study of portraiture depicting men & women who have made significant contributions to the history, develop & culture of the people of the United States; History of America through the individuals who have shaped its culture. Gallery portrays poets & presidents, visionaries & villains, actors & activists whose lives tell the American story. Bureau of the Smithsonian Institution; Average Annual Attendance: 1,600,000
Income: Financed by federal appropriation & private contributions
Special Subjects: Bronzes, Cartoons, Drawings, Historical Material, Miniatures, Painting-American, Photography, Portraits, Posters, Prints, Sculpture, Watercolors, Woodcarvings, Woodcuts, Etchings & Engravings
Collections: Portraits of significant Americans, preferably executed from life, in all media: oils, watercolors, charcoal, pen & ink, daguerreotypes, photographs; video, portraits of American Presidents, 1800 original works of art from the Time Magazine Cover coll, more than 5000 glass plate negatives by Mathew Brady & studio in the Meserve Coll
Publications: Large-scale, richly illustrated publications accompany major shows & provide comprehensive analysis of exhibition themes; documentary, audio & visual materials designed to be used as teaching guides; American portraiture
Activities: Classes for adults & children; dramatic progs; Outreach progs for elementary & secondary schools, senior citizens groups, docent training; lects open to the pub; scheduled walk-in tours for special groups, adults, families & schools; films; Cultures In Motion, (special musical & dramatic events); gallery talks; organize traveling exhibs; mus shop sells books, magazines, reproductions, recordings, jewelry, gifts, clothing & housewares

L **Library**, 750 9th St NW, Victor Bldg, Ste 2100 Washington, DC 20560; PO Box 37012, MRC 975 Washington, DC 20013-7012. Tel 202-633-8230; Fax 202-633-8232; Email AAPGLibrary@si.edu; Web: library.si.edu; *Head Librn* Anne Evenhaugen; *Reference Librn* Alexandra Reigle
Open Mon - Fri 10 AM - 5 PM, cl Federal holidays; Branch of Smithsonian Institution Libraries; shared with American Art Mus
Library Holdings: Book Volumes 100,000, Clipping Files, Exhibition Catalogs, Fiche, Manuscripts, Periodical Subscriptions 800, Reels, Reproductions

M **NATIONAL POSTAL MUSEUM,** Smithsonian Institution, 2 Massachusetts Ave NE, Washington, DC 20002; PO Box 37012 MRC 570, Washington, DC 20013-7012. Tel 202-633-5555; Web: postalmuseum.si.edu; *Dir* Elliot Gruber; *Dir Advancement* Michelle Buhr; *Colls Mgr* Beth Heydt; *Mgr Pub Rels & Internet Affairs* Marty Emery; *Dir Education* Matthew White; *Registrar* Ted Wilson; *Winton M Blount Research Chair* Susan Smith; *Head Cur, History Dept* Nancy Pope
Open daily 10 AM - 5:30 PM, cl Dec 25; No admis fee; Coll estab 1886, housed in Arts & Industries Bldg from 1908 - 1963, housed in National Mus of American History from 1964 - 1992, until creation of Natl Postal Mus in 1990 & mus opening in 1993; Located on the lower level of the historic City Post Office Building, which was constructed in 1914 and served as the Washington, DC, post office from 1914 through 1986. Museum occupies 75,000 sq ft of the bldg with 23,000 sq ft of exhib space; Average Annual Attendance: 371,000
Income: Financed by US Postal Svc, annual federal appropriation via the Smithsonian Institution, & gifts from pvt individuals, foundations, & corporations
Library Holdings: Exhibition Catalogs, Memorabilia, Original Documents, Other Holdings, Pamphlets, Periodical Subscriptions, Photographs, Prints, Reproductions, Sculpture
Exhibitions: Permanent exhibs incl: Binding the Nation; Customers & Communities; Moving the Mail; Philatelic Gallery; Multiple online exhibs; Postal

Inspectors: The Silence Service; Collecting History; Systems at Work; Mail Call; Networking a Nation: Star Route Service
Activities: Classes for adults & children; docent training; lects open to pub; gallery talks; tours; symposia; Smithsonian Philatelic Achievement Awards; stamp shop; mus store sells books

L **Library**, 2 Massachusetts Ave NE, MRC 570, Rm 106 Washington, DC 20560-0570. Tel 202-633-5543; Fax 202-633-8876; Email wilderb@si.edu; Web: library.si.edu; *Librn* Baasil Wilder
Open Mon - Fri 10 AM - 3:30 PM & 3rd Sat of month 10 AM - 4 PM; cl Federal holidays; No admis fee; 6,000 sq ft
Library Holdings: Book Volumes 40,000, Other Holdings Journals; Catalogs; Archival Documents
Collections: Postal & Philatelic Files Online, Butler & Carpenter Correspondence, Railway Mail Service, Aerial Mail Service, Highway Post Office, Panama Canal Zone Post Office, Frederick J Melville working papers, Thaddeus P Hyatt working papers

M **NATIONAL TRUST FOR HISTORIC PRESERVATION,** 2600 Virginia Ave NW, Ste 1000 Washington, DC 20037-1922. Tel 202-588-6000; Fax 202-588-6038; Email info@nthp.org; Web: www.preservationnation.org; *Pres* Stephanie Meeks; *Dir Interpretation* Max Van Balgooy; *Architect* Barbara Campagna; *Dir Mus Coll* Terri Anderson; *VPres* James Vaughan; *Admin Dir* Lyn Moriarity
Open to the pub, hours & fees vary with the property, cl Christmas, New Year's, call for information; Founded 1949, the National Trust for Historic Preservation is the only national, nonprofit, private organization chartered by Congress to encourage pub participation in the preservation of sites, buildings & objects significant in American history & culture; Its services, counsel & educ on preservation & historic property interpretation & admin, are carried out at national & regional headquarters in consultation with adv in each state & U S Territory; Mem: 265,000; dues sustaining $100, active $20, student $15
Income: Financed by mem dues, contributions & matching grants from the US Department of the Interior, National Park Service, under provision of the National Historic Preservation Act of 1966
Special Subjects: Decorative Arts, Furniture
Collections: Fine & decorative arts furnishing nine historic house museums: Chesterwood, Stockbridge, MA, Cliveden, Philadelphia, PA, Decatur House & Woodrow Wilson House, Washington, DC, Drayton Hall, Charleston, SC, Lyndhurst, Tarrytown, NY, Oatlands, Leesburg, VA, The Shadows-on-the-Teche, New Iberia, LA, Woodlawn/Pope-Leighey Plantation House, Mt Vernon, VA. (For additional information, see separate listings)
Publications: Preservation Magazine, bi-monthly

M **Decatur House**, 748 Jackson Pl NW, Washington, DC 20006-4912. Tel 202-842-0920; Fax 202-842-0030; *Exec Dir* Paul Reber
Open Tues - Fri 10 AM - 3 PM, Sat & Sun Noon - 4 PM, cl Mon; No admis fee; Estab 1958, bequeathed to National Trust for Historic Preservation by Mrs Truxton Beale to foster appreciation & interest in the history & culture of the city of Washington, DC; The House is a Federal period townhouse designed by Benjamin Henry Latrobe & completed in 1819; Average Annual Attendance: 19,000; Mem: National Trust members
Income: Financed by endowment & mem
Special Subjects: Period Rooms, Furniture
Collections: Furniture & memorabilia of the Federal period, Victorian house furnishings
Exhibitions: Special exhibits
Activities: Lect open to public, 2-3 vis lectrs per year; concerts; individual paintings & original objects of art lent; sales shop sells books, magazines, reproductions, prints & Christmas decorations

M **NAVAL HISTORICAL CENTER,** National Museum of the US Navy, Washington Navy Yard, 901 M St SE Washington, DC 20374-5060; 805 Kidder Breese SE, Washington Navy Yard Washington, DC 20374-5060. Tel 202-433-4882; Fax 202-433-8200; Web: www.history.navy.mil; *Cur* Dr Edward Furgol; *Art Coll Cur* Gale Munro; *Pub Affairs Officer* Shejal Pulivarti; *Dir* Jim Bruns; *Educ & Pub Progs* Laura Hockensmith
Open Mon - Fri 9 AM - 5 PM, Sat - Sun 1 - 5PM; No admis fee & parking; Estab 1961 to present history & preserve heritage of US Navy; 48,000 sq ft exhibit area; Average Annual Attendance: 150,000
Income: Financed by federal appropriations
Special Subjects: Archaeology, Architecture, Asian Art, Bronzes, Calligraphy, Cartoons, Ceramics, Coins & Medals, Costumes, Decorative Arts, Dioramas, Drawings, Embroidery, Etchings & Engravings, Folk Art, Furniture, Glass, Graphics, Ivory, Leather, Manuscripts, Maps, Marine Painting, Metalwork, Military Art, Miniatures, Painting-American, Photography, Porcelain, Portraits, Posters, Prints, Scrimshaw, Sculpture, Silver, Watercolors, Woodcuts
Collections: History of US Navy from 1775 to Space Age, Naval Art, Paintings, Prints, Watercolors, Naval Artifacts, Fighting Top of Constitution, WW II Corsair (744 plane)
Exhibitions: Changing art exhibitions; Polar Exploration; Perry & Japan
Activities: Docent training; tours; concerts; internships; 10 vis lectrs per yr; individual paintings & original objects of art lent to pub institutions; mus shop sells books, reproductions, prints, postcards, jewelry, t-shirts, models & nautical accessories

M **THE PHILLIPS COLLECTION,** 1600 21st St NW, Washington, DC 20009-1090. Tel 202-387-2151; Fax 202-319-0070; Email communications@phillipscollection.org; Web: www.phillipscollection.org; *Dir & CEO* Dorothy M Kosinski; *Deputy Dir Curatorial & Academic Affairs* Klaus Ottmann; *Dir Budgeting & Reporting* Cherie Nichols; *Deputy Dir Develop & Opers* Kara Mullins; *Dir Educ* Suzanne Wright; *Chief Information Officer* Darci Vanderhoff
Open Tues - Sat 10 AM - 5 PM, Sun noon - 6:30 PM, Thurs unil 8:30 PM, cl Mon & holidays; Admis price varies with each exhib and includes admis to the permanent coll; discounts to seniors & students; Open to the pub 1921 to show & interpret the best of contemporary painting in the context of outstanding works of the past; to underscore this intent through the presentation of concerts & lectures; The original building, a Georgian Revival residence designed in 1897 by Hornblower & Marshall, was added to in 1907 & renovated in 1983-84. A modern annex connected by a double bridge to the old gallery was opened to the public in 1960 & renovated in 1987-89. In Apr 2006 the Phillips celebrated the opening of its new Sant Bldg which adds 30,000 sf of expanded gallery spaces, a 180 seat auditorium, new educational spaces & more; Average Annual Attendance: 150,000; Mem: 9,000; dues corporate mem $10,000; individual $60-$50,000 & up
Income: $12,000,000 (financed by endowment, mem, contributions, grants, sales, rental fees & exhibition fees)
Library Holdings: Auction Catalogs, Book Volumes, Clipping Files, Exhibition Catalogs, Periodical Subscriptions, Photographs
Special Subjects: Etchings & Engravings, Folk Art, Graphics, Painting-American, Painting-European, Painting-French, Painting-Italian, Painting-Russian, Painting-Scandinavian, Painting-Spanish, Photography, Portraits, Prints, Watercolors, Woodcuts
Collections: 19th & 20th century American & European painting with special emphasis on units of particular artists such as Bonnard, Braque, Cezanne, Daumier, de Stael, Dufy, Rouault & Americans such as Avery, Dove, Gatch, Knaths, Marin, O'Keeffe, Prendergast, Rothko & Tack. The best known painting is Renoir's Luncheon of the Boating Party
Publications: magazine, three times annually & books
Activities: Classes for adults & children; docent training; lects open to pub, 35 vis lectrs per yr; weekly concerts Oct-May; gallery talks; tours; Duncan Phillips award; individual paintings & original objects of art lent to select national & international mus; book traveling exhibs 3-5 per yr; originate traveling exhibs to national & international mus; mus sales shop sells books, magazines, reproductions, prints, slides, jewelry & original crafts

L **Library**, 1600 21st St NW, Washington, DC 20009. Tel 202-387-2151, Ext 212; Fax 202-387-2436; Email kschneider@phillipscollection.org; Web: www.phillipscollection.org; *Head Librn* Karen Schneider; *Archives Asst* Colleen Henessey
Open to the pub: Tues & Thurs 2 PM - 5 PM; open for research Mon - Fri 10 AM - 4:30 PM; Estab 1978; Available to serious students, researchers & mus professionals, by appointment. Reference only; Average Annual Attendance: 60; Fellowships
Library Holdings: Book Volumes 10,000, Clipping Files, Exhibition Catalogs, Filmstrips, Lantern Slides, Manuscripts, Other Holdings Vertical files, Pamphlets, Periodical Subscriptions 6, Reels 60
Special Subjects: Aesthetics, Afro-American Art, Art Education, Art History, Asian Art, Collages, Decorative Arts, Drawings, Eskimo Art, Etchings & Engravings, Folk Art, Furniture, Graphic Arts, History of Art & Archaeology, Latin American Art, Leather, Lettering, Manuscripts, Mexican Art, Painting-American, Painting-British, Painting-Canadian, Painting-European, Painting-French, Painting-German, Painting-Italian, Painting-Japanese, Photography, Portraits, Primitive art, Printmaking, Prints, Restoration & Conservation, Sculpture, Watercolors, Woodcuts
Activities: Classes for adults & children; lects open to pub; 10 lectrs per yr; concerts; gallery talks; tours; awards, Duncan Phillips book award; sales shop sells books, original art, reproductions & prints, decorative art and jewlery

L **PUBLIC LIBRARY OF THE DISTRICT OF COLUMBIA,** Art Division, 901 G St NW, Martin Luther King Memorial Library Washington, DC 20001-4531. Tel 202-727-1291; Fax 202-727-1129; Email george-mckinley.martin@dc.gov; Web: www.dclibrary.org; *Chief Art Div* George-McKinley Martin; *Librn* Patricia Wood; *Librn* S Michele Casto
Open winter & summer Mon - Thurs 9:30 AM - 9 PM, Fri 9:30 AM - 5:30 PM, Sat 9:30 AM - 5:30 PM, Sun 1 - 5 PM; No admis fee
Income: Financed by city government appropriation
Library Holdings: Auction Catalogs, Book Volumes 48,961, Clipping Files, Exhibition Catalogs, Original Art Works, Original Documents, Pamphlets, Periodical Subscriptions 95, Reels
Special Subjects: Aesthetics, Afro-American Art, American Indian Art, American Western Art, Antiquities-Assyrian, Antiquities-Byzantine, Antiquities-Egyptian, Antiquities-Etruscan, Antiquities-Greek, Antiquities-Oriental, Architecture, Art History, Asian Art, Bronzes, Calligraphy
Collections: Reference & circulating books & periodicals on architecture, painting, sculpture, photography, graphic & applied arts, extensive pamphlet file including all art subjects, with special emphasis on individual American artists & on more than 1400 artists active in the area, circulating picture collection numbering over 81,519 mounted reproductions
Exhibitions: Special exhibitions held occasionally

L **Audiovisual Division**, 901 G St NW, Rm 226, Martin Luther King Memorial Library Washington, DC 20001-4531. Tel 202-727-1265; Fax 202-727-1129; Email www.avdcpl@yahoo.com; *Chief* Eric White; *Film & Video Librn* Turner Freeman
Open Mon - Thurs 10 AM - 9 PM, Fri 10 AM - 5:30 PM, Sun 10 AM - 5:30 PM
Purchases: 16 mm, VHS
Library Holdings: Cassettes, Motion Pictures, Other Holdings Books-on-tape, Periodical Subscriptions 15, Records, Video Tapes

M **SAINT JOHN PAUL II NATIONAL SHRINE,** 3900 Harewood Rd NE, Washington, DC 20017-1505. Tel 202-635-5400; Fax 202-635-5411; Email info@jp2cc.org; Web: www.jp2cc.org; *Exec Dir* Patrick E Kelly
Open Mon - Sat 10 AM - 5 PM, Sun 12 - 5 PM; Admis suggested donations families $15, seniors & students $4, discounts to member
Collections: paintings, statues, Catholic Church history, Papal & Polish heritage, photographs
Activities: Lect; children's activities

M **SMITHSONIAN INSTITUTION,** Smithsonian Institution Building (The Castle), 1000 Jefferson Dr, SW, Washington, DC 20560-0008; PO Box 37012, SI Building, Room 153, MRC 010 Washington, DC 20013-7012. Tel 202-633-1000; Email info@si.edu; Web: www.si.edu; *Secy* Dr David J Skorton; *COO & Under Secy Finance & Admin* Albert Horvath; *Provost & Under Secy for Museums Educ & Research* John Davis
Open daily 10 AM - 5:30 PM, cl Dec 25; No admis fee; Estab 1846, when James Smithson bequeathed his fortune to the United States, under the name of the Smithsonian Institution, an establishment in Washington for the increase & diffusion of knowledge. To carry out the terms of Smithson's will, the Institution performs fundamental research; preserves for study & reference approx 140 million

items of scientific, cultural & historical interest; maintains exhibits representative of the arts, American history, aeronautics & space exploration; technology; natural history & engages in progs of educ & national & international cooperative research & training; The Smithsonian Institution is the world's largest museum complex composed of 14 museums & the National Zoo in Washington, DC & the Cooper-Hewitt, National Design Museum & the National Museum of the American Indian in New York City; see separate listings for complete information on the bureaus listed below; Average Annual Attendance: 815,000 (The Castle); 20,900,000 (all Smithsonian museums); Mem: Several programs, call for info
Income: Financed by federal appropriations & private monies
Special Subjects: African Art, American Indian Art, Asian Art, Ceramics, Crafts, Decorative Arts, Portraits
Publications: Smithsonian magazine
Activities: Classes for adults & children; dramatic progs; docent training; lects open to pub; concerts; gallery talks; tours; awards; schols & fels; for information call Smithsonian Institution Traveling Exhibs at 202-357-3168; mus stores sell books, magazines, original art, reproductions, prints, slides & gifts

—Anacostia Community Museum
See separate listing in Washington, DC

—National Portrait Gallery
See separate listing in Washington, DC

—Arthur M Sackler Gallery
See separate listing in Washington, DC

—Freer Gallery of Art
See separate listing in Washington, DC

—National Museum of African Art
See separate listing in Washington, DC

—National Museum of the American Indian
See separate listing in Washington, DC

—National Postal Museum
See separate listing in Washington, DC

—Archives of American Art
See separate listing in Washington, DC

—Cooper-Hewitt National Design Museum
See separate listing in New York, NY

—Hirshhorn Museum & Sculpture Garden
See separate listing in Washington, DC

—John F Kennedy Center for the Performing Arts
See separate listing in Washington, DC; Administered under a separate Board of Trustees

—National Air & Space Museum
See separate listing in Washington, DC

—American Art Museum
Includes the Renwick Gallery. See separate listing in Washington, DC

—National Gallery of Art
See separate listing in Washington, DC

—National Museum of American History
See separate listing in Washington, DC

M **THE SOCIETY OF THE CINCINNATI AT ANDERSON HOUSE,** 2118 Massachusetts Ave NW, Washington, DC 20008-3640. Tel 202-785-2040; Fax 202-785-0729; Email admin@societyofthecincinnati.org; Web: www.societyofthecincinnati.org; *Dir Library* Ellen McCallister Clark; *Deputy Dir & Cur* Emily L Schulz; *Exec Dir* Jack D Warren Jr; *Mus Vis Svcs Coordr* Caren Pauley
Open Museum: Tues - Sat 1 - 4 PM; Library: Mon - Fri 10 AM - 4 PM by appointment; No admis fee; Museum estab 1938. Serves as the National Headquarters Museum & Library of the Society of the Cincinnati. Collects, preserves & interprets the history of American Revolution, the Society of Cincinnati & Anderson House & its occupants; Historic house museum of Anderson House, a 1905 beaux-arts mansion & the Winter residence of Larz Anderson III & his wife Isabel Weld Perkins from 1905-1937. One temp exhib gallery displays two changing exhib each yr; Average Annual Attendance: 10,000
Library Holdings: Auction Catalogs, Book Volumes, CD-ROMs, Clipping Files, Compact Disks, DVDs, Exhibition Catalogs, Fiche, Framed Reproductions, Manuscripts, Maps, Memorabilia, Motion Pictures, Original Art Works, Original Documents, Pamphlets, Periodical Subscriptions, Photographs, Prints, Video Tapes
Special Subjects: Antiquities-Roman, Asian Art, Baroque Art, Bronzes, Carpets & Rugs, Ceramics, Coins & Medals, Costumes, Decorative Arts, Dioramas, Etchings & Engravings, Furniture, Glass, Historical Material, Ivory, Jade, Jewelry, Manuscripts, Maps, Military Art, Miniatures, Oriental Art, Painting-American, Painting-British, Painting-European, Painting-French, Painting-Japanese, Period Rooms, Porcelain, Portraits, Prints, Renaissance Art, Sculpture, Silver, Tapestries, Textiles, Watercolors, Bookplates & Bindings, Graphics, Posters, Drawings, Metalwork, Religious Art
Collections: Original furnishings & collections of Larz & Isabel Anderson & objects related to the history of the Society of the Cincinnati & the American Revolution, the history of the art of war in the 18th century
Publications: Why America Is Free: The Insignia of the Society of the Cincinnati by Minor Myers, Jr (1998); Exhibition catalogs & brochures; Liberty without Anarchy: A History of the Society of the Cincinnati (2004)
Activities: Docent training; lects open to pub, 4-8 vis lectrs per yr; concerts; tours; Clement Ellis Conger Internship; Mass Society of the Cincinnati Internship; Cox Book Prize given every 3 yrs to author of distinguished work of American history in era of American Revolution; Tyree-Lamb Library Fel award annually; lends original object of art to qualified mus & other institutions; public concert series; other public progs; mus shop sells books, note cards & Anderson House ornament, DVDs, post cards

M **STUDIO GALLERY,** 2108 R St NW, Washington, DC 20008-1900. Tel 202-232-8734; Email director@studiogallerydc.com; Web: www.studiogallerydc.com; *Director* Stacey Blomstrom; *Co-Director* Camila Rondon; *Treas* Steven Marks
Open Wed - Fri 1 - 6 PM, Sat 11 AM - 6 PM; No admis fee; Estab 1964 as a showcase for local artists; Fine contemporary art; Average Annual Attendance: 20,000; Mem: 30; monthly meetings
Income: Nonprofit
Collections: Many private coll in the DC Metropolitan area
Exhibitions: Rotating monthly exhibitions
Activities: Outreach progs; yoga nights; music & dance performances, author talks, artist talks; community service to underserved youth; lects open to pub; 8 vis lectrs per yr; gallery talks; concerts; tours; individual paintings & original works of art lent

M **SUPREME COURT OF THE UNITED STATES,** Office of the Curator, 1 1st St NE, US Supreme Court Bldg Washington, DC 20543-0001. Tel 202-479-3298; Fax 202-479-2926; Email curator@supremecourt.gov; Web: www.supremecourt.gov; *Cur* Catherine E Fitts; *Assoc Cur* Matthew Hofstedt; *Visitor Prog Mgr* Nikki Peronace
Open Mon - Fri 9 AM - 4:30 PM, cl federal holidays; No admis fee; Cur Office estab 1973; Exhibit space on ground floor; portrait collection displayed on ground floor & in restricted areas of the bldg; Average Annual Attendance: 300,000
Library Holdings: Audio Tapes, Clipping Files, Exhibition Catalogs, Manuscripts, Memorabilia, Original Art Works, Original Documents, Photographs, Prints, Records, Sculpture, Slides, Video Tapes
Special Subjects: Historical Material, Miniatures, Photography, Portraits, Prints, Sculpture
Collections: Portraits of former Justices, marble busts of the Chief Justices and certain Assoc Justices, historic images such as photos, etchings & drawings of the Justices & the architecture of the building, memorabilia, archival & manuscript materials on the Supreme Ct history, 18th & 19th centuries American & English furniture & decorative arts
Exhibitions: Permanent & temporary exhibits
Publications: Exhibit brochures
Activities: Docent training; courtroom lect every hour on the half hour open to pub; continuously running film describing the functions of the Supreme Court; individual paintings & original objects of art lent to mus & historical organizations; mus shop operated by Supreme Ct Historical Society sells gift items, books, reproductions, prints & other items

L **TRINITY COLLEGE LIBRARY,** 125 Michigan Ave NE, Washington, DC 20017-1090. Tel 202-884-9350; Fax 202-884-9241; Email libraryreference@trinitydc.edu; Web: www.trinitydc.edu/library; *Librn* Trisha Smith; *Public Servs Librn* Bridgette Comanda; *Access Servs Librn* Alexander Salopek
Open during school semesters Mon - Fri 8:30 AM - 10 PM, Sat 8:30 AM - 5 PM, Sun 1 PM - 9 PM; Estab 1897 as an undergraduate col library, serving the college community
Income: $253,548 (financed by college budget)
Library Holdings: Book Volumes 200,000, Cassettes, Periodical Subscriptions 600, Reels, Slides

M **UNITED STATES CAPITOL,** Architect of the Capitol, Washington, DC 20515. Tel 202-225-6827; Fax 202-228-4602; Web: www.aoc.gov; *Architect of the Capitol* Alan M Hantman; *Cur* Dr Michele Cohen; *Photo Branch* Michael Dunn
Open Mon - Sat 9 AM - 4:30 PM; No admis fee; Cornerstone layed 1793. Capitol is working building with mus value; Restored historic chambers; paintings & sculptures scattered through rooms & halls of Congress; reference library; Average Annual Attendance: 1,500,000
Income: Financed by United States Congressional appropriation & appropriate donations
Library Holdings: Book Volumes
Special Subjects: Architecture, Bronzes, Decorative Arts, Etchings & Engravings, Landscapes, Manuscripts, Painting-American, Period Rooms, Portraits, Prints, Restorations, Sculpture, Stained Glass, Watercolors
Collections: Works by Andrei, Brumidi, Crawford, Cox, Franzoni, French, Greenough, Leutze, Peale, Powers, Rogers, Trumbull, Vanderlyn, Weir, 800 paintings & sculptures, manuscripts, 70,000 photographs & 120,000 architectural drawings, The Nat Statuary Hall Collection
Exhibitions: Capital Visitor Center, changes periodically; Congressional Student Annual Exhibition
Publications: Constantino Brumidi, History of the United States Capitol
Activities: US Capitol Guide Service tours; fellowships

A **UNITED STATES COMMISSION OF FINE ARTS,** 401 F St NW, National Building Museum Ste 312 Washington, DC 20001-2637. Tel 202-504-2200; Fax 202-504-2195; Email cfastaff@cfa.gov; Web: www.cfa.gov; *Secy* Thomas Leubke
Open Mon - Fri 9 AM - 5 PM; Estab by Act of Congress in 1910 to advise the President, members of congress & various governmental agencies on matters pertaining to the appearance of Washington, DC. The Commission of Fine Arts is composed of seven members who are appointed by the President for four-year terms. Report issued periodically, principally concerned with architectural review; Plans for all new projects in DC under the direction of the Federal & District of Columbia Governments which affect the appearance of the city & all questions involving matters of design with which the Federal Government may be concerned must be submitted to the Commission for comment & advice before contracts are made. Also gives advice on suitability of designs of private buildings in certain parts of the city adjacent to the various departments & agencies of the District & Federal Governments, the Mall, Rock Creek Park & Georgetown
Income: Financed by annual appropriations enacted by Congress
Publications: 15 publications on area architecture, 1964-1978; Commission of Fine Arts, 1910-1985

M **UNITED STATES DEPARTMENT OF STATE,** Diplomatic Reception Rooms, M/FA - Rm 8213, 2201 C St NW Washington, DC 20520-0099. Tel 202-647-1990; Email touroffice@state.gov; Web: diplomaticrooms.state.gov; *Dir* Marcee F Craighill
Open for three public tours by reservations only Mon - Fri 9:30 AM, 10:30 AM & 2:45 PM; No admis fee; Estab 1961 to entertain foreign dignitaries; These rooms allow foreign & American visitors to view furniture & art of the American & Federal periods. Furnished in 18th & early 19th Century American furniture, silver, Chinese export porcelain, antique Oriental rugs, American portraits & paintings, Tour Mon - Fri; Average Annual Attendance: 100,000

Income: Financed by private donations, foundation & corporate grants & loans of furnishings & paintings
Special Subjects: Carpets & Rugs, Furniture, Painting-American, Porcelain, Silver
Collections: American furniture 1740-1825, American portraits & paintings, American silver, Chinese export porcelain
Exhibitions: Rotating exhibits
Publications: Treasures of the US Dept of State; PBS documentary film: America's Heritage; Becoming a Nation

M **UNITED STATES DEPARTMENT OF THE INTERIOR,** Interior Museum, 1849 C St NW, MS-2266, Dept of the Interior Washington, DC 20240-0001. Tel 202-208-4743; Fax 202-208-1535; Email museum_services@nbc.gov; Web: www.doi.gov/interiormuseum
Open Mon - Fri 8:30 AM - 4:30 PM, cl federal holidays; some areas require reservations to view artwork; No admis fee; Estab 1938 to explain through works of art & other media the history, aims & activities of the Department; Museum occupies one wing on the first floor of the Interior Department Building; Average Annual Attendance: 26,000
Income: Federally funded
Special Subjects: Eskimo Art, Painting-American, Sculpture, Watercolors, American Indian Art, Archaeology, Dioramas, Ethnology, Maps
Collections: Colburn Collection of Indian basketry, collection of Indian, Eskimo, South Sea Islands & Virgin Islands arts & crafts, documents, maps, charts, etc, Gibson Collection of Indian materials, Indian arts & crafts, murals, dioramas of Interior history scenes, oil paintings of early American survey teams by William Henry Jackson, watercolor & black & white illustrations, wildlife paintings by Walter Weber
Exhibitions: Changing exhibits gallery at museum entrance has new exhibits every three months; Permanent exhibits include: Overview of Interior history & activities; architectural history of the headquarters building; interpretation of a turn of the century totem pole
Activities: Educ dept; lect open to public, 10-12 vis lectrs per year; gallery talks; tours

M **UNITED STATES NAVY,** Art Gallery, 822 Sicard St SE, Washington Navy Yard Washington, DC 20374-5060; 805 Kidder Breese St SE, Washington Navy Yard Washington, DC 20374-5060. Tel 202-433-3815; Web: www.history.navy.mil; *Cur* Samuel Cox
By appointment; No admis fee; Estab 1800 to document history of US Navy & Naval personnel; Exhibs merged into the Navy museum, research facilities available
Income: Financed by Naval History & Heritage Command
Special Subjects: Cartoons, Etchings & Engravings, Marine Painting, Military Art, Painting-American, Posters, Prints, Watercolors, Woodcuts
Collections: Graphic arts, paintings, sketches, Sculptures
Exhibitions: US Naval History; Traveling Exhibits
Publications: United States Navy Combat Art
Activities: Internships; individual paintings & original objects of art lent to AAM accredited museums & US military museums officially recognized by their service; originate traveling exhibs; sales shop sells reproductions, prints, slides & brochures

A **UNITED STATES SENATE COMMISSION ON ART,** United States Capitol Bldg, Rm S-411, Washington, DC 20510-7102. Tel 202-224-2955; Fax 202-224-8799; Email curator@sec.senate.gov; Web: www.senate.gov; *VChmn* Thomas A Daschle; *Cur* Melinda K Smith; *Museum Specialist* Richard L Doerner; *Admin* Scott M Strong; *Staff Asst* Clare Colgrove; *Historic Preservation Off* Kelly Steele; *Assoc Registrar* Jamie Arbolino; *Colls Mgr* Deborah Wood
Open daily 9 AM - 4:30 PM; No admis fee; Commission estab 1968 to acquire, supervise, hold, place & protect all works of art, historical objects & exhibits within the Senate wing of the United States Capitol & Senate Office Buildings; Average Annual Attendance: 3,000,000
Income: Financed by United States Senate appropriation
Collections: Paintings, sculpture, historic furnishings & memorabilia located within the Senate wing of the Capitol & Senate Office Buildings, Preservation Projects: Old Senate & Old Supreme Court Chamber restored to their appearances 1850
Exhibitions: Senate Art & Stamps; The Supreme Court of the United States, the Capitol Years 1801-1935; Isaac Bassett, The Venerable Doorkeeper, 1831-1895; The Political Cartoons from Puck
Publications: The Senate Chamber 1810-1859; The Supreme Court Chamber 1810-1860; A Necessary Fence: The Senate's First Century; An Assembly of Chosen Men: Popular Views of the Senate's Chambers 1847-1886; U S Senate graphic Arts Collection: An Illustrated Checklist; Brumidi Corridor; Vice Presidential Bust Collection
L **Reference Library,** United States Capitol Bldg, Rm S-411, Washington, DC 20510-7102. Tel 202-224-2976; Email curator@sec.senate.gov; Web: senate.gov/curator/index.html
Open daily 9 AM - 4:30 PM; A reference collection on fine & decorative arts; supplemented by the United States Senate Library
Income: $1000 (financed by United States Senate appropriation to the Commission)
Library Holdings: Book Volumes 250,000, Cards, Clipping Files, Exhibition Catalogs, Manuscripts, Memorabilia, Pamphlets, Periodical Subscriptions 30, Photographs, Slides
Special Subjects: Architecture, Decorative Arts

WASHINGTON SCULPTORS GROUP
For further information, see National and Regional Organizations

M **WESLEY THEOLOGICAL SEMINARY, HENRY LUCE III CENTER FOR THE ARTS & RELIGION,** Dadian Gallery, 4500 Massachusetts Ave, NW, Washington, DC 20016. Tel 202-885-8608; Fax 202-885-8550; Email artsandreligion@wesleyseminary.edu; Web: www.wesleyseminary.edu/lcar; *Cur* Kiki McGrath; *Dir* Deborah Sokolove; *Program Admin* Amy Gray
Open Mon - Fri 10 AM - 4:30 PM; No admis fee; Estab 1989 to provide visual demonstration of intrinsic relationship between art & religion; Average Annual Attendance: 5,000
Income: $50,000 (financed by gifts & grants, subsidized partly by parent institution)
Collections: Gifts from Artists, WTS Collection, Contemporary Art
Exhibitions: 5 - 7 Exhibs per yr ranging from group to solo shows
Activities: Classes for adults; dramatic progs; poetry readings; dance & music concerts; lects open to pub, 5 vis lectrs per yr; gallery talks; lending collection contains paintings & art objects; book traveling exhibs; originate traveling exhibs

M **WHITE HOUSE,** 1600 Pennsylvania Ave NW, Washington, DC 20502-0001. Tel 202-456-7041; Fax 202-456-6820; Web: www.whitehouse.gov; *Asst Cur* Lydia Tederick; *Coll Mgr* Donna Hayashi-Smith; *Asst Cur* Melissa Naulin; *Asst Cur* Monica McKiernan
Open Tues - Thurs 7:30 AM - 1 PM & Fri - Sat 7:30 AM - 1:30 PM for tours, Visitor Ctr open 7:30 AM - 4 PM. Passes must be requested from your Congress Person along with security information. Date of Birth and SS# must be submitted; No admis fee
Income: Financed by federal government appropriation
Special Subjects: Architecture, Decorative Arts, Furniture, Glass, Historical Material, Manuscripts, Metalwork, Painting-American, Period Rooms, Porcelain, Portraits, Prints, Sculpture
Collections: 18th & 19th century period furniture, 18th, 19th & 20th century paintings & prints, glassware, manuscripts, porcelain, sculpture
Publications: Art in the White House: A Nation's Pride; The First Ladies; The Living White House; The President's House: A History; The Presidents of the United States; White House Glassware: Two Centuries of Presidential Entertaining; The White House: An Historic Guide; White House History, magazine; The White House: Historic Furnishings & First Families

M **WOODROW WILSON HOUSE,** 2340 S St, NW, Washington, DC 20008. Tel 202-387-4062; Fax 202-483-1466; Email faucella@woodrowwilsonhouse.org; Web: www.woodrowwilsonhouse.org; *Interim Exec Dir* Carrie Willar; *Mgr Bus & Opers* John Pucher
Open (March - Dec) Wed - Sun 10 AM - 4 PM, cl Mon - Tues & major holidays, (Jan - Feb) Fri - Sun 10 AM - 4 PM, cl Mon - Thurs & major holidays; Admis adults $10, $8 seniors, $5 students, National Trust members & under 12 free; Estab 1963, owned by the National Trust for Historic Preservation, it works to foster interest & appreciation of the 28th President, Woodrow Wilson; Wilson House is a 1915 Georgian-Revival townhouse designed by Waddy B Wood, with formal garden. From 1921 it served as the home of President & Mrs Wilson; Average Annual Attendance: 16,000; Mem: 350; dues $50 & up
Income: Financed by endowment, mem, admis, sales & fundraising
Special Subjects: Architecture, Decorative Arts, Furniture, Historical Material, Painting-American, Period Rooms
Collections: Early 20th century art, furnishings, clothing, presidential memorabilia, decorative arts
Publications: Woodrow Wilson News, quarterly
Activities: Lects open to pub; 5-6 vis lectrs per yr; concerts; tours; individual paintings & objects of art lent to qualified mus; mus shop sells books, reproductions, prints & slides

ZENITH GALLERY, 1429 Iris St NW, Washington, DC 20012-1409. Tel 202-783-2963; *Dir* Margery Goldberg
Open Mon - Fri 10 AM - 6 PM, Sat 11 AM - 6 PM, Sun Noon - 5 PM

FLORIDA

BOCA RATON

A **BOCA RATON MUSEUM OF ART,** 501 Plaza Real, Boca Raton, FL 33432-3982. Tel 561-392-2500; Fax 561-391-6410; Email info@bocamuseum.org; Web: www.bocamuseum.org; *Pres* Dalia Stiller; *Exec Dir* Steven Maklansky; *Dir Educ* Claire Clum; *Dir Art School* Rebecca Sanders; *Dir Finance* Linda Ursillo; *Asst Exec Dir* Valerie Johnson; *Dir Admin* Roberta Stewart; *Registrar* Martin Hanahan; *Spec Events & Vols* Belle Forino; *Communs Coordr* Inga Ford; *Cur* Marisa J Pascucci; *Cur* Kathleen Goncharov; *Asst Cur* Kelli Bodle; *Mktg & Pub Rels Assoc* Austin Modine
Open Tues, Wed, Thurs & Fri 10 AM - 6 PM, Sat & Sun Noon - 6 PM, cl Mon & holidays; Admis adults $8, seniors $6, students with ID $4, discounts to groups, members & children under 12 Wed 5 PM - 9 PM no charge, admis may change for special exhibits; Estab 1951 to foster & develop the cultural arts; Large Main Gallery, mus shop contained in one building. Second building houses art school & storage. 4500 sq ft expansion houses a permanent collection; Average Annual Attendance: 200,000; Mem: 4300; dues individual $80, family & dual $100; contributing $150, supporting $300, sustaining $600, dir's circle $2,500, trustee's circle $5,000, pres's circle $10,000, benefactor's circle $25,000; annual meeting in Apr
Income: Financed by mem, fundraising, art school & grants
Library Holdings: Auction Catalogs, Book Volumes, Clipping Files, Exhibition Catalogs, Pamphlets, Slides
Special Subjects: African Art, Archaeology, Asian Art, Ceramics, Decorative Arts, Drawings, Etchings & Engravings, Folk Art, Graphics, Hispanic Art, Islamic Art, Landscapes, Latin American Art, Mexican Art, Painting-American, Painting-European, Photography, Portraits, Posters, Pre-Columbian Art, Primitive art, Prints, Sculpture, Watercolors
Collections: Photography from 19th century to present, John J Mayers Collection, works by Braque, Demuth, Glackens, Matisse & Picasso
Exhibitions: Changes every 6-8 weeks; state-wide competition & show; annual outdoor art festival
Publications: Exhibition catalogues; quarterly member magazine
Activities: Classes for adults & children; docent training; children's gallery educ progs, art trips; lects open to pub; 5 vis lectrs per yr; concerts; gallery talks; tours; juried exhibs; national outdoor art festival with awards given for Best in Show & Merit; individual paintings & original objects of art lent; 6-10 book traveling

exhibs; originate various traveling exhibs; mus shop sells books, original art, reproductions, prints, gift items

L **Library**, 501 Plaza Real, Mizner Park Boca Raton, FL 33432. Tel 561-392-2500; Fax 561-391-6410; Email info@bocamuseum.org; Web: www.bocamuseum.org; *Exec Dir* Irvin Lippman; *Dir Develop* Roberta Kjelgaard; *Dir Finance* Linda Ursillo; *Dir The Art School* Walter O'Neill; *Dir Innovations, Mktg & Communications* Inga Ford; *Cur Exhibs & Audience Engagement* Kathy Goncharov; *Cur Educ* Claire Clum; *Cur 20th Century & Contemporary Art* Marisa Pascucci; *Chief Registrar* Martin Hanahan
Open Tues, Wed & Fri 10 AM - 5 PM, Thu 10 AM - 8 PM, Sat & Sun noon - 5 PM, cl Mon; Admis adults $12, seniors $10, students no admis fee; Estab 1940; Circ 10,000; 5,500+ works in permanent collection; Average Annual Attendance: 200,000; Mem: 2,300
Library Holdings: Book Volumes 10,000, Exhibition Catalogs
Special Subjects: Afro-American Art, American Western Art, Asian Art, Ceramics, Collages, Decorative Arts, Drawings, Etchings & Engravings, Folk Art, Glass, Graphic Arts, Landscapes, Latin American Art, Painting-American, Painting-European, Painting-French, Painting-German, Painting-Israeli, Painting-Italian, Painting-Russian, Painting-Spanish, Photography, Portraits, Posters, Pre-Columbian Art, Primitive art, Prints, Sculpture, Woodcuts
Collections: Contemporary Art, Pre-Columbian, Photography, Modern Masters, African, Sculpture
Publications: catalogs; monthly newsletter
Activities: Classes for adults & children; docent training; art school; lects open to pub, 12 vis lectrs per yr; concerts; gallery talks; tours; ann Art Fest

M **FLORIDA ATLANTIC UNIVERSITY,** University Galleries/Ritter Art Gallery/ Schmidt Center Gallery, 777 Glades Rd, Boca Raton, FL 33431-6496. Tel 561-297-2660; 297-2966; Fax 561-297-2166; Email wfaulds@fau.edu; Web: www.fau.edu/galleries; *Dir University Galleries* W Rod Faulds
Open Tues - Fri 1 PM - 4 PM, Sat 1 - 5 PM; No admis fee; Estab 1983 to present a wide range of innovative contemporary art exhibitions and related pub prog & to provide exhibit space for faculty & students; Two 2,500 sq ft spaces & public spaces for projects/installations; Average Annual Attendance: 15,000; Mem: 200
Income: Financed by Univ (state) appropriations, student activities fees & pvt/pub grants
Collections: AE Beanie Backus paintings
Exhibitions: Annual Juried Student Show; traveling exhibitions
Publications: Exhibit catalogues
Activities: Artist in residence progs with university dept of art; docent training for university art students; lects open to pub; concerts; gallery talks; readings; tours; competitions with awards; book 1 - 3 traveling exhibs per yr; originates traveling exhibs to other university galleries

BRADENTON

A **ART CENTER MANATEE,** 209 Ninth St W, Bradenton, FL 34205. Tel 941-746-2862; Fax 941-746-2319; Email acm@artcentermanatee.org; Web: www.artcentermanatee.org; *Assoc Dir* Mary Roff; *Pres* Andi Franco; *Mktg* Peggy Haynes
Open year round Mon, Fri & Sat 9 AM - 5 PM, Tues, Wed & Thurs 9 AM - 6 PM; cl holidays & 2 wks in Aug; No admis fee; Estab 1937 to offer opportunities in further educ in the visual arts by providing space for exhibitions, classes, demonstrations, critiques & the exchange of ideas & information by vis artists; Circ 3,000; Searle Gallery: 2,000 sq ft; Kellogg Gallery: 2,500 sq ft; Reid-Hodges Gallery: 2,024 sq ft; Average Annual Attendance: 40,000; Mem: 1,000+; dues $20 & up; annual meeting in Nov
Library Holdings: Book Volumes, Cassettes, Clipping Files, Exhibition Catalogs, Original Art Works, Pamphlets, Photographs, Records, Slides, Video Tapes
Exhibitions: Work by members & local artists one person shows & circulating exhibitions changing at three week intervals from Oct to May
Activities: Art school instruction in painting, drawing, clay techniques & variety of handcrafts; creative develop for children; special art progs; classes for adults & children; lects open to pub, 5 vis lectrs per yr; gallery talks; tours; sponsoring of competitions; schols available; sales shop sells original arts & prints

CORAL GABLES

M **UNIVERSITY OF MIAMI,** Lowe Art Museum, 1301 Stanford Dr, Coral Gables, FL 33146-2009. Tel 305-284-3535; Fax 305-284-2024; Email eli2@miami.edu; Web: www.lowemuseum.org; *Dir* Jill Deupi; *Asst Dir Collections & Exhibitions* Eugenia Incer; *Cur* Jodi Sypher
Open Tues - Sat 10 AM - 4 PM, Sun Noon - 4 PM, cl Mon & univ holidays; Admis general $12.50, seniors & students $8, members, University of Miami students & children under 12 free, group rates available; Estab 1952 to bring outstanding exhibitions & collections to the community & to the University; gallery maintained; Maintains reference library; wheelchair accessible; Average Annual Attendance: 95,000; Mem: Mem dues: Academic $40, Cintas Individual $60, Kress Family $120, Sustaining $225, Contributor $500
Special Subjects: African Art, Afro-American Art, American Indian Art, American Western Art, Anthropology, Antiquities-Egyptian, Antiquities-Greek, Antiquities-Roman, Asian Art, Baroque Art, Ceramics, Drawings, Eskimo Art, Etchings & Engravings, Glass, Hispanic Art, Jade, Landscapes, Latin American Art, Medieval Art, Mexican Art, Oriental Art, Painting-American, Painting-British, Painting-Dutch, Painting-European, Painting-Flemish, Painting-French, Painting-German, Painting-Italian, Painting-Spanish, Period Rooms, Photography, Porcelain, Portraits, Pottery, Primitive art, Prints, Religious Art, Renaissance Art, Scrimshaw, Sculpture, Silver, Southwestern Art, Textiles, Woodcarvings
Collections: Washington Allston Trust Collection, Virgil Barker Collection of 19th & 20th Century American Art, Alfred I Barton Collection of Southwestern American Indian Art, Esso Collection of Latin American Art, Samuel H Kress Collection of Renaissance & Baroque Art, Samuel K Lothrop Collection of Guatemalan Textiles, Cintas Foundation Collection of Spanish Old Master Paintings
Exhibitions: Varied, changing exhibitions throughout the year; student exhibs; sculpture; Cuban American art
Publications: Exhibition catalogs; newsletter, bimonthly
Activities: Classes for children; docent training; lects open to pub, 7-8 vis lectrs per yr; concerts; gallery talks; tours; individual paintings & original objects of art lent to other mus; book 3-5 traveling exhibs per yr; originate traveling exhibs; mus shop sells books, magazines, gift items

CORAL SPRINGS

M **CORAL SPRINGS MUSEUM OF ART,** 2855 Coral Springs Dr, Coral Springs, FL 33065-3825. Tel 954-340-5000; Fax 954-346-4424; Email bknicely@coralsprings.org; Web: www.coralspringsmuseum.org; *Exec Dir* Bryan W Knicely
Open Mon - Wed, Fri - Sat 10 AM - 5 PM, cl major holidays; Admis adults $6, seniors & tours $5, students $3, children 5 & under & members free, discounts to AAM members; Estab 1997; 8,000 sq ft exhibition galleries; Average Annual Attendance: 31,000
Collections: contemporary art
Activities: Classes for adults & children; artist in res prog; docent training; lects open to pub; 7-10 vis lectrs per yr; guided tours; gallery talks; sponsoring of competitions; mus shop sells books, original art, prints, & mus related items

DADE CITY

L **PIONEER FLORIDA MUSEUM ASSOCIATION, INC,** Pioneer Florida Museum & Village, PO Box 335, Dade City, FL 33526-0335. Tel 352-567-0262; Fax 352-567-1262; Email curator@pioneerfloridamuseum.org; Web: www.pioneerfloridamuseum.org
Open Tues - Sat 10 AM - 5 PM, cl Sun & Mon; Admis adults $5, seniors $4, students 6-18 $2; Estab 1961 to preserve & promote Pioneer life; Average Annual Attendance: 12,000; Mem: 400; dues life family $250, life individual $150, family $35, individual $25; annual meeting last Sun in Oct
Income: $80,000 (financed by endowment, mem, state appropriation, special events, donations, memories & grants)
Activities: Tours; annual special events festivals; mus shop sell books & prints

DAVIE

M **BROWARD COMMUNITY COLLEGE - A. HUGH ADAMS CAMPUS,** Fine Arts Gallery, 3501 SW Davie Rd, Bldg 3 Davie, FL 33314. Tel 954-201-6984; *Contact Person* Barbara Ryan
Open Mon - Fri 9 AM - 2 PM Sat 11 AM - 2 PM; No admis fee
Collections: Paintings; sculpture; photographs

DAYTONA BEACH

M **DAYTONA STATE COLLEGE,** Southeast Museum of Photography, 1200 W International Speedway Blvd, Daytona Beach, FL 32114-2817; PO Box 2811, Daytona Beach, FL 32120-2811. Tel 386-506-4475; Fax 386-506-4487; Email museum1@daytonastate.edu; Web: www.smponline.org; *Dir* Kevin R Miller; *Mktg & Communs* Cassie Brown; *Educ Dept* Christina Katsolis; *Colls Mgr* Melissa Reamer; *Lead Mus Technician* Alexis Rogers; *Exhib Coordr* Juliana Romnes
Open Tues, Thurs, Fri 11 AM - 5 PM, Wed 11 AM - 7 PM, Sat & Sun 1 - 5 PM, PM, June, July & Dec Tues - Sun noon - 4 PM, cl Mon, summer recess (July 31 - Aug 17), winter recess (Dec 17 - Jan 11), Easter Sun, Independence Day, Thanksgiving weekend (Thurs - Sun); No admis fee; Estab 1992; Specialist photography museum; contemporary, historical, new media; Average Annual Attendance: 22,999; Mem: 3,000
Income: Financed by college sponsored annual budget $500,000
Special Subjects: Photography
Collections: Photographic Collection of Karsch, Chartier-Bresson, Friedlander, Perlmutter
Activities: Classes for adults & children; summer photo camps for kids; lects open to pub; 10 vis lectrs per yr; tours; scholarships; organize traveling exhibs: Lee Dunkel, Bastienne Schmidt; mus shop sells books, photo postcards, catalogs & cameras

M **HALIFAX HISTORICAL SOCIETY, INC,** Halifax Historical Museum, 252 S Beach St, Daytona Beach, FL 32114-4407. Tel 386-255-6976; Fax 386-255-7605; Email mail@halifaxhistorical.org; Web: www.halifaxhistorical.org; *Pres* Ruth Trager; *VPres* Walter Snell; *VPres* Michael Link, Ph.D; *VPres* Warren Trager; *Recording Secy* Beth Mindlin; *Treas* E Holmes Davis; *Exec Advisor* Virginia Buckner; *Mus Dir* Fayn (no e) LeVeille; *Admin Asst* Leigh Finner
Open Tues - Fri 10:30 AM - 4:30 PM, Sat 10 AM - 4 PM; Admis adults $5, children 12 & under $1, Thurs by donation, Sat children 12 & under free; Estab 1949 to preserve & share local history of the Halifax Country area, east Volusia County; (101 years old) 1910 Merchants Bank Building in historic downtown Daytona Beach, FL; Average Annual Attendance: 3,000; Mem: 365 (approx); dues $35 individual, $45 family, and up; annual meeting 2nd Sat in Jan
Income: Financed by dues, donations, grants, gift shop, fund raising
Library Holdings: Audio Tapes, Book Volumes, Cards, Cassettes, Clipping Files, Compact Disks, Original Documents, Pamphlets, Photographs, Records, Reels, Reproductions, Slides, Video Tapes
Special Subjects: American Indian Art, Ceramics, Coins & Medals, Costumes, Dioramas, Dolls, Drawings, Embroidery, Flasks & Bottles, Folk Art, Furniture, Glass, Historical Material, Laces, Maps
Collections: The Models of Lawson Diggett, artifacts of World War II, 18th century Spanish & English artifacts, Indian projectiles, canoe, pottery, racing memorabilia, Victorian clothing & furniture, Charles Grove Burgoyne Collection, Bill McCoy Collection, Local artifacts dating back to 2500-5000 BC
Exhibitions: Grandma's Attic; Permanent & rotating exhibitions; Three new exhibits a yr of various subjects in the exhibit changing area

Publications: Biannual Halifax Herald; quarterly newsletters
Activities: Educ dept; dramatic prog; lects for mems only, 30-40 vis lectrs per yr; recognition plaques; tours; book traveling exhibs 4 per yr; mus shop sells books, reproductions, prints & other various items

M **THE MUSEUM OF ARTS & SCIENCES INC,** 352 S Nova Rd Daytona Beach, FL 32114. Tel 386-255-0285; Fax 386-255-5040; Web: www.moas.org; *Cur History & Science* James Zacharias; *Dir* Andrew Sandall; *Director of Operations* Sara Tucker Craig; *Chief Cur* Ruth Grim; *Mktg Dir* Jenelle Cooianne; *Director of Development* Stephanie Mason-Teague; *Director of Sales & Special Events* Alexandra Middleton; *Director of Astronomy* Seth Mayo
Open Mon-Sat 10AM-5PM, Sun 11AM-5PM; Admis $12.95, students & seniors $10.95, children 6-17 $6.95, members and children under 5 free; Estab 1971; 90,000 sq ft of exhibition galleries, hall gallery & lobby gallery are maintained: Mus includes Planetarium, A Frischer Sculpture Garden, Gallery of American Art, Root Hall & Gallery, Gallery of African Art, Gallery of Florida History & Prehistory of Florida Gallery. Maintains reference library, Gallery of Cuban art, Gallery of Chinese Art, Galleries of Decorative Arts; childrens museum added in 2008; Average Annual Attendance: 240,000; Mem: 5,000; annual meeting in Dec
Income: $2,500,000 (financed by endowment, mem, city & county appropriations, donations, earned income)
Purchases: American Art 1720-2004. American Decorative Arts, Chinese Art, Cuban Art, European Art, African Art
Library Holdings: Auction Catalogs, Book Volumes, Exhibition Catalogs, Manuscripts, Maps, Photographs, Sculpture
Special Subjects: African Art, Afro-American Art, American Indian Art, American Western Art, Anthropology, Antiquities-Greek, Antiquities-Oriental, Antiquities-Persian, Archaeology, Architecture, Baroque Art, Bronzes, Calligraphy, Carpets & Rugs, Ceramics, Coins & Medals, Decorative Arts, Drawings, Enamels, Etchings & Engravings, Ethnology, Folk Art, Furniture, Glass, Gold, Graphics, Hispanic Art, Ivory, Jade, Jewelry, Landscapes, Latin American Art, Manuscripts, Maps, Marine Painting, Medieval Art, Oriental Art, Painting-American, Painting-Australian, Painting-British, Painting-Dutch, Painting-European, Painting-French, Painting-German, Painting-Italian, Painting-Russian, Painting-Spanish, Pewter, Photography, Porcelain, Portraits, Posters, Pottery, Pre-Columbian Art, Primitive art, Prints, Religious Art, Renaissance Art, Sculpture, Sculpture, Silver, Stained Glass, Textiles, Watercolors, Woodcuts, Asian Art
Collections: Aboriginal Art including Florida Indian, American Art 1620-1900, American Fine Art, American Illustration: Norman Rockwell, Cuban Collection, Florida Contemporary Collection
Exhibitions: Center for Florida History; The Levine Collection of Gems and Jewelry; Colonial Cuba: The Lithographs of Eduardo LaPlante; Treasures from the age of Napoleon; American Paintings 1800-1900
Publications: Arts & Sciences Magazine, 4 times per year; catalogs, monthly; A Treasury of American Art; Cuba: A History in Art; Coast to Coast: Contemporary Landscape in Florida; Reflections: Paintings of Florida from 1865 - 1965 From the Collection of Cici & Hyatt Brown; Great Masters of Cuban Art: Ramos Collection
Activities: Classes for adults and children; docent training; social events; lects open to pub, 15 vis lectrs per yr; gallery talks; concerts; tours; competitions with awards; schols offered; exten dept serves Volusia County; artmobile individual paintings & original objects of art lent to other mus, municipalities & public spaces; lending collection contains 2000 nature artifacts, 1000 original art works, 1000 original prints, 250 paintings, 100 photographs & sculptures; book traveling exhibs 4 per yr; originate traveling exhibs to Fla & national AAM accredited mus; mus shop sells books, magazines, original art, reproductions, prints

L **Library**, 352 S Nova Rd, Daytona Beach, FL 32114-4512. Tel 386-255-0285; Web: www.moas.org; *Librn* Marge Sigerson
Open Tues - Fri 9 AM - 4 PM; Open to mems & school children; reference library
Income: Financed by Mus
Purchases: Periodicals & reference materials
Library Holdings: Book Volumes 10,000, Clipping Files, Exhibition Catalogs, Manuscripts, Original Art Works, Periodical Subscriptions 2000, Photographs, Prints, Slides, Video Tapes
Special Subjects: Aesthetics, Afro-American Art, American Indian Art, American Western Art, Anthropology, Archaeology, Architecture, Art Education, Art History, Asian Art, Bronzes, Calligraphy, Ceramics, Decorative Arts, Drawings
Collections: General Fulgencio Batista Cuban Collection, Antique Coin Books

DELAND

M **MUSEUM OF ART - DELAND FL, INC,** 600 N Woodland Blvd, Deland, FL 32720-3447. Tel 386-734-4371; Fax 386-734-7697; Email tanner@mdartdeland.org; Web: www.mdartdeland.org; *CEO* George Bolge; *Exhibitions* David Fithian; *Dir Develop* Pattie Pardee; *Educ Cur* Pam Coffman; *Dir Finance & Opers* Dorothy Dansberger; *Dir Mktg* Lisa Habermehl; *Mgr Special Events, Guest Servs & Mem* Suzi Tanner
Open Tues - Sat 10 AM - 4 PM, Sun 1 - 4 PM, cl Mon; Admis adults $5, children under 12 free; Estab 1951 to provide art educ & exhibits; Lower gallery: 12 ft carpeted walls, 3100 sq ft; upper gallery: 12 ft carpeted walls, 2100 sq ft, classrooms, interdisciplinary space; Average Annual Attendance: 90,000; Mem: 800; dues family $60, individual $35
Income: $600,000 (financed by mem, state appropriation & Volusia County & earned income & donations)
Purchases: $10,000 - $20,000
Library Holdings: Book Volumes, Cards, Clipping Files, Compact Disks, DVDs, Exhibition Catalogs, Maps, Memorabilia, Original Art Works, Pamphlets, Periodical Subscriptions, Photographs, Prints, Records, Sculpture, Slides, Video Tapes
Special Subjects: Ceramics, Drawings, Etchings & Engravings, Folk Art, Glass, Graphics, Hispanic Art, Jewelry, Juvenile Art, Landscapes, Latin American Art, Metalwork, Painting-American, Photography, Porcelain, Portraits, Posters, Prints, Sculpture, Textiles, Watercolors, Woodcuts
Collections: Contemporary Florida Artists 1900 - Present
Exhibitions: Rotating exhibs; Legendary Florida-Ongoing Exhib; Touring Exhibs
Activities: Classes for adults & children; docent progs; spring & summer art camp for children & teens; outreach; K-12 art integration; Artist workshops in various media; family fun Saturdays (free event for families featuring hands-on art activities); AMP (art, media & performance) series; lects open to pub; lectrs for members only; 10-20 vis lectrs per yr; concerts; gallery talks; tours; competitions with awards; scholarships; Dorothy Johnson Award given annually to & in honor of local arts supporter in Volusia Cty, FL; sponsor art festival; lending of original objects of art to Arts in Public Places & outdoor sculpture program; touring exhibs; book traveling exhibs 1 per yr; originate traveling exhibs 5 per yr; Florida artists; sales shop sells books, original art, reproductions, prints, slides, crafts & gift items; Evans C & Betty Drees Johnson Children's Art Ctr

DELRAY BEACH

M **CORNELL MUSEUM OF ART AND AMERICAN CULTURE,** 51 N Swinton Ave, Delray Beach, FL 33444-2631. Tel 561-243-7922; Fax 561-243-7022; Email gadams@delraycenterforthearts.org; Web: www.oldschool.org; *Dir* Gloria Rejune Adams; *Mus Asst* Melanie Johanson
Open Tues - Sat 10 AM - 4:30 PM, Sun 1 - 4:30 PM; cl Mon yr round & major holidays; Admis adults $8, seniors (over 65) & students with ID $6, children under ten free; Estab 1990; Large spacious rooms, wooden floors; Average Annual Attendance: 30,000; Mem: Dues $30 regular, family & friends $75; annual meeting in Jan
Income: Grants from State of Florida; private donors; memberships, TDC, city of Delray Beach, CRA
Library Holdings: Auction Catalogs, Book Volumes, Clipping Files, Exhibition Catalogs, Memorabilia, Original Art Works, Original Documents, Pamphlets, Periodical Subscriptions, Photographs, Prints, Sculpture, Slides
Special Subjects: African Art, American Indian Art, Antiquities-Etruscan, Bronzes, Drawings, Etchings & Engravings, Folk Art, Furniture, Painting-American, Painting-British, Painting-European, Painting-Spanish, Photography, Pre-Columbian Art, Sculpture
Collections: Teaching collection
Exhibitions: Rotating exhibs every 4 or 5 months; Crest Galleries
Activities: Classes for adults & children; docent training; Kickin Arts; photography school; lects open to pub; 6 vis lectrs per yr; concerts; gallery talks; tours; Florida cultural institutions prog award; sponsoring of competitions; schols offered; lending collection available; book traveling exhibs 1-2 per yr; originate traveling exhibs; mus shop sells books, magazines, original art, reproductions, prints, slides, jewelry, pottery

M **PALM BEACH COUNTY PARKS & RECREATION DEPARTMENT,** Morikami Museum & Japanese Gardens, 4000 Morikami Park Rd, Delray Beach, FL 33446-2305. Tel 561-495-0233; Fax 561-499-2557; Email morikami@pbcgov.org; Web: www.morikami.org; *Cultural Dir* Thomas Gregersen; *Dir Educ* Reiko Nishioka; *Museum Store Mgr* Sallie Chisolm; *Admin Assoc* Debbie Towers; *Horticulture Supv* Heather Grzybek; *Coll Cur* Veljko Dujin; *Adminr* Bonnie White Lemay; *Dir Advancement* Amy Hever; *Cur Japanese Art* Susanna Brooks Lavallee
Call for hours & admis prices; Estab 1977 to preserve & interpret Japanese culture & Japanese-American culture; Five small galleries in Japanese style bldg & two larger galleries in main museum bldg; Average Annual Attendance: 150,000; Mem: 2700; annual meeting Apr
Income: $3,500,000 (financed by mem & county appropriation)
Purchases: $9000
Library Holdings: Auction Catalogs, Book Volumes, Clipping Files, Exhibition Catalogs, Periodical Subscriptions
Special Subjects: Anthropology, Asian Art, Costumes, Crafts, Decorative Arts, Dolls, Ethnology, Folk Art, Graphics, Historical Material, Painting-Japanese, Photography, Pottery, Woodcuts, Porcelain
Collections: Archived colls pertaining to the Yamato Colony, Japanese Fine Arts (hanging scrolls, folding screens, paintings, textiles, prints, ceramics), Japanese Folk Arts (dolls, tools, home furnishings, folk figures, miniature buildings, toys)
Publications: Newsletter, quarterly; Calendar bi-monthly; Exhibition catalogs 1-2 per yr
Activities: Classes for adults & children; docent training; lects for mem only; 4-6 vis lectrs per yr; concerts; tours; book traveling exhibs, 2-3 per yr; originate traveling exhibs; mus shop sells books, magazines, reproductions, prints & slides

L **Donald B Gordon Memorial Library**, 4000 Morikami Park Rd, Morikami Museum Delray Beach, FL 33446-2305. Tel 561-495-0233; Fax 561-499-2557; Email morikami@co.palm-beach.fl.us; Web: www.morikami.org; *Coll Cur* Noelle Shuey Altamirano
Open by appointment Tues - Sun 10 AM - 5 PM, cl Mon & holidays; Admis adults $9, seniors $8, children 6-18 & college students $6, mems & children under 6 free; Estab 1977 to provide printed & recorded materials on Japan; For reference only; Average Annual Attendance: 250,000; Mem: 2300. Dues based on tiered levels
Income: Financed by donations
Purchases: $1000
Library Holdings: Auction Catalogs, Book Volumes 4500, Clipping Files, Exhibition Catalogs, Periodical Subscriptions 25
Special Subjects: Anthropology, Antiquities-Oriental, Architecture, Art History, Asian Art, Calligraphy, Ceramics, Commercial Art, Costume Design & Constr, Crafts, Decorative Arts, Dolls, Drawings, Enamels, Etchings & Engravings, Ethnology, Film, Folk Art, Furniture, Graphic Arts, Historical Material, Ivory, Miniatures, Oriental Art, Painting-Japanese, Photography, Porcelain, Pottery, Prints, Textiles, Religious Art, Sculpture
Collections: Memorabilia of George S Morikami
Exhibitions: Permanent exhib on Yamato colony and authentic tea house
Publications: My Morikami, published 3 times per year
Activities: Classes for adults & children; docent training; guided tours; outreach progs; lects open to pub; 2 vis lectrs per yr; gallery talks; tours; mus shop sells books, magazines, reproductions, jewelry, textiles, children's items, decorative items

FORT LAUDERDALE

L **ART INSTITUTE OF FORT LAUDERDALE,** Technical Library, 1799 SE 17th St, Fort Lauderdale, FL 33316-3000. Tel 954-463-3000, Ext 541; 800-275-7603; Fax 954-463-1339; Email webadmin@ail.edu; Web: www.artinstitute.edu; *Library-LRC Dir* Diane Rider; *Librn* Rick Fought; *Assoc Dir* Art McKinney
Open Mon - Thurs 8 AM - 8 PM, Fri 8 AM - 5 PM; Estab 1973 as a technical library for the applied & fine arts
Purchases: $8000
Library Holdings: Audio Tapes, Book Volumes 1200, Cassettes 50, Clipping Files 2000, Filmstrips, Kodachrome Transparencies, Motion Pictures, Periodical Subscriptions 157, Video Tapes 600
Activities: Educ dept; lect open to public; competitions; scholarships & fels offered; sales shop sells books, prints & supplies

A **BROWARD COUNTY BOARD OF COMMISSIONERS,** Broward Cultural Div, 100 S Andrews Ave, FL 6 Fort Lauderdale, FL 33301-1830. Tel 954-357-7457; Fax 954-357-5769; Email culturaldiv@broward.org; Web: www.broward.org/arts; *Dir* Earl F Bosworth; *Admin Asst* Rowena Nocom; *Grants Admin* James Shermer; *Grants Financial Analyst* Susan Schultz; *Community Develop Dir* Jody Horne-Leshinsky; *Community Develop Arts Educ* Grace Kewl-Durfey; *Pub Art Admin* Leslie Fordham
Estab 1976 to enhance the cultural environment of Broward County through develop of the arts; develops & distributes gov & pvt resources for the visual arts, performing arts, literary arts, museums & festivals; acts as the liaison between cultural organizations, all levels of gov & the pvt sector in encouraging & promoting cultural develop
Publications: Annual Calendar; Arts Education Directory; Cultural Directory; Cultural Quarterly; Cultural Treasures of Broward County Brochure; Voices & Venues Newsletter, bi-monthly
Activities: Schols & grants offered

M **MUSEUM OF ART, FORT LAUDERDALE,** One E Las Olas Blvd, Fort Lauderdale, FL 33301-1807. Tel 954-525-5500; Fax 954-524-6011; Email receptionist@moafl.org; Web: www.moafl.org; *Dir of Retail* Douglas Ratcliff; *Exec Dir & Pres* Irvin Lippman; *Chief Cur* Annegreth Hill
Open Tues - Wed 11 AM - 6 PM, Thurs11 AM - 8 PM, Sun noon - 5 PM, cl Mon; Admis adults $10, seniors, children 6-17, and military $7, members, children 5 and under, and college students with ID free; Estab 1958 to bring art to the community & provide cultural facilities & programs; Library, exhib space & auditorium are maintained; Average Annual Attendance: 100,000; Mem: 3500; dues corporate $5000, $2500 & $1000, benefactor $1000, patron $500, contributing $250, sustaining $125, family-dual $65, individual $50
Income: Financed by public grants, private philanthropy
Library Holdings: Book Volumes, Exhibition Catalogs, Pamphlets, Periodical Subscriptions, Prints, Slides
Special Subjects: Ceramics, Graphics, Painting-American, Sculpture, Latin American Art, Painting-American, Painting-Dutch, Period Rooms, Pre-Columbian Art, Primitive art, Sculpture
Collections: Golda & Meyer B Marks Cobra Art Collection, William Glackens Collection, American & European paintings, sculpture & graphics from late 19th century-present, Pre-Columbian & historic American Indian ceramics, basketry & stone artifacts, Modern Cuban Collection, West African tribal sculpture, Warhol, Picasso, Dali
Publications: quarterly newsletter, season calendar
Activities: Educ prog; classes for children; docent training; slide lect prog in schools by request; lects open to pub, 3 vis lectrs per yr; gallery talks; tours; films; competitions; individual paintings & original objects of art lent to other mus; mus shop sells books, original art, reproductions, prints

L **Library**, One E Las Olas Blvd, Fort Lauderdale, FL 33301-1807. Tel 954-525-5500; Fax 954-524-6011; Email museumofart@hotmail.com; Web: www.museumofart.org; *Cur Educ* Fran Mulcahy; *Dir of Develop* Lynn Mandeville; *Dir Finance* Robert Granson
Open Tues - Sat 10 AM - 5 PM, Sun Noon - 5 PM; Founded 1958; 35,000 sq ft gallery space
Library Holdings: Book Volumes 7500, Periodical Subscriptions 15, Slides
Collections: William Glackens; Cobra; Contemporary Cuban Collections
Activities: Classes for adults & children; docent training; lects open to pub; originates traveling exhibs; mus shop sells books & novelty items

M **MUSEUM OF DISCOVERY & SCIENCE,** 401 SW Second St, Fort Lauderdale, FL 33312-1707. Tel 954-467-6637; Fax 954-467-0046; Email information@mods.net; Web: www.mods.org; *Pres* Kim L Cavendish
Open Mon-Sat 10AM-5PM, Sun noon-6PM, Imax times and prices differ; Admis adults $10, seniors $9, children 2-12 $8, special group rates available, members free; Estab 1977 to increase science literacy; Average Annual Attendance: 534,000; Mem: 5500; dues $75; annual meeting in Sept
Income: $5,500,000
Special Subjects: Graphics, Prints
Exhibitions: Choose Health; Florida EcoScapes; Gizmo City; Great Gravity Clock; KidScience, No Place Like Home; Science Fair; Sound; Space Base; Runways to Rockets; Living in the Everglades
Publications: Explorations, quarterly
Activities: Classes for adults & children; camps; sleepovers; outreach progs; films daily; docent training; lects open to pub, some to mems only, 8-10 vis lectrs per yr; gallery talks; tours; book traveling exhibs 5 per yr; originate traveling exhibs to other mus; mus shop sells books, original art, reproductions, prints & science related activities

FORT MYERS

M **EDISON STATE COLLEGE,** Bob Rauschenberg Gallery at Edison State College, 8099 College Pkwy, Fort Myers, FL 33919. Tel 239-489-9313; Fax 239-489-9482; Email RBishop@Edison.edu; Web: bobrauschenberggallery.com; *Cur & Dir* Ron Bishop; *Asst* Lindsay Wollard
Open Mon - Fri 10 AM - 4 PM, Sat 11 AM - 3 PM, cl Sun & holidays; No admis fee; Estab 1979 to provide exhibitions of national & regional importance & related educational programs; Main gallery 2000 sq ft, high security; adjunct performing arts hall gallery; Average Annual Attendance: 10,000
Income: Financed by endowment & state appropriation
Exhibitions: Rotating exhibits
Activities: Tours for adults & children; docent training; lect open to public, 4 vis lectrs per year; concerts; gallery talks; tours; annual art show awards; scholarships & fels offered; book traveling exhibs 2 - 4 per year; originate traveling exhibs to other museums in Florida; sales shop sells reproductions, prints, posters & catalogs

FORT PIERCE

M **A.E. BACKUS MUSEUM & GALLERY,** 500 N Indian River Dr, Fort Pierce, FL 34950-3080. Tel 772-465-0630; Fax 772-468-6204; Email info@backusmuseum.com; Web: www.backusmuseum.com; *Dir* Kathleen P Fredrick; *Mktg Dir* Robin Dannahower; *Exhib Coordr* Georgina Love; *Social Media & Comms* Corinne Fredrick
Open Oct-June Wed-Sat 10AM - 4 PM, Sun noon-4PM; July-Sept by appointment; Admis $5, discounts to AAA & AARP mems; Estab 1960; visual arts facility; Permanent coll of A.E. Backus, changing exhibs; Average Annual Attendance: 30,000; Mem: 1,110
Income: (financed by mem, admis, fundraising & mus shop)
Special Subjects: Ceramics, Drawings, Glass, Jewelry, Landscapes, Painting-American, Photography, Prints, Reproductions, Watercolors, Woodcarvings, Woodcuts
Collections: Works by A.E. Backus, Painting by the Florida Highwaymen, Indian River School
Activities: docent training; lects open to the pub; 4-6 vis lectrs per yr; gallery talks; tours; sponsoring competitions; lending of original works of art; sales shop sells books, original art, reproductions

GAINESVILLE

M **CITY OF GAINESVILLE,** Thomas Center Galleries - Cultural Affairs, 302 NE Sixth Ave, Bldg A, Gainesville, FL 32061-5476; PO Box 490, Sta 30, Gainesville, FL 32627-0490. Tel 352-393-8532; Fax 352-334-3299; Email etlingrh@cityofgainesville.org; Web: www.gvlcultralaffairs.org; *Cultural Affairs Progs Coordr* Russell Etling
Open Mon - Fri 9 AM - 5 PM, Sat & Sun 1 - 4 PM; No admis fee; Estab 1979 to increase local arts awareness; Two small galleries in a historic building; Average Annual Attendance: 9,000
Income: $8,000 (financed by city appropriation, grants & donations)
Special Subjects: Folk Art, Furniture, Glass, Graphics, Historical Material, Landscapes, Latin American Art, Oriental Art, Painting-American, Period Rooms, Photography, Portraits, Pottery, Textiles, Watercolors, Woodcarvings, Woodcuts
Exhibitions: Contemporary American Artists, predominantly Floridian; 6 shows per year in main gallery; 8 shows per year in mezzanine gallery; regional history; photography; antiquities; cultural memorabilia
Publications: Exhibition brochures
Activities: Lect open to public, 4 vis lectrs per year; gallery talks; tours; competitions with prizes; workshops & receptions for artists

M **UNIVERSITY OF FLORIDA,** University Gallery, 400 SW 13th St, Gainesville, FL 32601; PO Box 115803, Gainesville, FL 32611-5803. Tel 352-273-3000; Fax 352-846-0266; Email galleries@arts.ufl.edu; Web: www.arts.ufl.edu/galleries; *Dir* Amy Vigilante; *Coordr* Yue Zhang
Open Tues 10 AM - 8 PM, Wed - Fri 10 AM - 5 PM, Sun 1 - 5 PM, cl Mon, Sat & holidays; No admis fee; Estab 1965 as an arts exhibition gallery, open 11 months of the year, showing monthly exhibitions with contemporary & historical content; Gallery located in independent building with small lecture hall, limited access & completely secure with temperature & humidity control, adjustable track lighting; display area is in excess of 3000 sq ft; Average Annual Attendance: 8,000; Mem: 50; dues professional $100 & up, family $50, individual $25
Income: $97,000 (financed by state appropriation & community mem)
Purchases: $2,000
Special Subjects: Folk Art, Latin American Art, Oriental Art, Painting-American, Painting-British, Pre-Columbian Art, Prints
Collections: Contemporary Art
Exhibitions: Changing monthly exhibitions; Annual University of Florida Art Faculty (January); Annual student juried exhibition; MFA thesis exhibitions
Publications: Exhibition catalogs; periodic bulletins
Activities: Lects open to pub; gallery talks; Henri Theil Memorial Purchase Award; exten dept serves area schools; lending collection contains cassettes, original art works, photographs & slides; originate traveling exhibs

L **Architecture & Fine Arts Library**, 201 Fine Arts Bldg A, Gainesville, FL 32611; PO Box 117017, Gainesville, FL 32611-7017. Tel 352-273-2805; Fax 352-846-2747; Web: www.uflib.ufl.edu/afa; *Architecture Fine Arts Bibliographer & Head Librn* Ann Lindell
Open Mon - Thurs 8 AM - 10 PM, Fri 8 AM - 5 PM, Sat 1 - 5 PM, Sun 2 - 10 PM; Estab 1853 as a state art & architecture information center
Library Holdings: Auction Catalogs, Book Volumes 104,000, CD-ROMs, Exhibition Catalogs, Fiche, Manuscripts, Pamphlets, Periodical Subscriptions 600, Photographs, Reels, Reproductions, Video Tapes
Special Subjects: Advertising Design, Afro-American Art, American Indian Art, American Western Art, Architecture, Asian Art, Decorative Arts, Folk Art, Gold, Graphic Arts, History of Art & Archaeology, Intermedia, Interior Design, Landscape Architecture, Latin American Art
Collections: Rare book collection

M **Samuel P Harn Museum of Art**, 3259 Hull Road, Gainesville, FL 32611-2700; PO Box 112700, Gainesville, FL 32611-0001. Tel 352-392-9826; Fax 352-392-3892; Email twroath@harn.ufl.edu; Web: www.harn.ufl.edu; *Dir* Lee Anne Chesterfield, PhD; *Cur Contemporary Art* Kerry Oliver-Smith; *Chief Cur & Cur Modern Art* Dulce Roman; *Dir Educ & Cur Academic Progs* Eric Segal; *Dir Mktg*

& Public Relations Tami Wroath; *Dir Develop* Kelly C Harvey; *Cur Photography* Carol McCusker; *Cur African Art* Susan Cooksey
Open Tues - Fri 11 AM - 5 PM, Sat 10 AM - 5 PM, Sun 1 PM - 5 PM; No admis fee; Estab 1990 to collect, preserve, display & interpret art; One of the Southeast's largest university art museums with almost 90,000 square feet. Also a museum store off the Galleria (entrance). Maintains a reference library available to visitors & staff; Average Annual Attendance: 90,000
Special Subjects: Pottery, Asian Art, Bronzes, Ceramics, Collages, Drawings, Hispanic Art, Landscapes, Latin American Art, Painting-American, Photography, Pre-Columbian Art, Prints, Sculpture, Watercolors, Painting-European, Primitive art, Textiles, Woodcarvings
Collections: African Art, Contemporary Art, Modern Art, Photography
Publications: Inform, bi-monthly newsletter
Activities: Classes for adults & children; docent training; lects open to pub; concerts; gallery talks; tours; individual paintings & objects of art lent; senior outreach prog; book traveling exhibs; originate traveling exhibs; mus shop sells books, magazines, original art, reproductions & prints

HOLLYWOOD

M **ART & CULTURE CENTER OF HOLLYWOOD,** Art Gallery/Multidisciplinary Cultural Center, 1650 Harrison St, Hollywood, FL 33020-6806. Tel 954-921-3274; Fax 954-921-3273; Email info@artandculturecenter.org; Web: www.artandculturecenter.org; *Exec Dir* Joy Satterlee; *Asst Dir* Susan Rakes; *Mktg Dir* Alesh Houdek; *Dir Develop* Jeff Rusnak; *Publ Relations & Community Partnership Mgr* Leo Sarmiento; *Theater Mgr* Chad Harris
Open Tues - Fri 10 AM - 5 PM, Sat & Sun noon - 4 PM; Admis nonmembers $7, seniors, students & children 4-13 $4, center mems & children age 3 & younger with an adult free; Estab 1975 as a private non-profit corporation for the study, educ & enjoyment of visual & performing arts; Great Gallery, major exhibit space, is 6300 sq ft with 400 running ft; group tours are also held there. Two Hall galleries. Maintains reference library. Gallery hosts at least a dozen thought-provoking, stimulating contemporary art exhibs each yr; Average Annual Attendance: 60,000; Mem: 617; dues $30-$1,000; no annual meeting
Income: $1.3 million (financed by pub funding, foundations, pvt contributions, contracts & mem)
Library Holdings: Book Volumes, Exhibition Catalogs
Special Subjects: Antiquities-Byzantine, Antiquities-Egyptian, Antiquities-Etruscan, Antiquities-Greek, Antiquities-Oriental, Antiquities-Persian, Antiquities-Roman, Architecture, Art Education, Art History, Asian Art, Bronzes, Calligraphy, Cartoons, Ceramics, Coins & Medals, Collages, Conceptual Art, Crafts, Decorative Arts, Drawings, Enamels, Etchings & Engravings, Flasks & Bottles, Folk Art, Furniture, Glass, Gold, Graphics, History of Art & Archaeology, Illustration, Interior Design, Islamic Art, Ivory, Jade, Jewelry, Judaica, Landscapes, Latin American Art, Maps, Metalwork, Mexican Art, Miniatures, Mixed Media, Mosaics, Oriental Art, Painting-American, Painting-Australian, Painting-British, Painting-Dutch, Painting-European, Painting-Flemish, Painting-French, Painting-German, Painting-Italian, Painting-Japanese, Painting-Polish, Painting-Russian, Painting-Scandinavian, Painting-Spanish, Photography, Porcelain, Portraits, Posters, Pottery, Pre-Columbian Art, Primitive art, Religious Art, Reproductions, Restorations, Sculpture, Silver, Tapestries, Textiles, Watercolors, Woodcarvings, Woodcuts, African Art
Collections: 19th & 20th century American & contemporary Florida artists, Contemporary paintings & sculpture, Ethnographic arts
Publications: Exhibition brochures/catalogs
Activities: Classes for adults & children; volunteer training; summer camp for ages 4-18; free admis days; distance learning offered to schools; dramatic progs; children & youth arts progs; lects open to pub; 4 vis lectrs per yr; gallery talks; concerts; group tours; competitions with awards; Exceptional Service & Outstanding Contributions to Art Education

HOLMES BEACH

M **ISLAND GALLERY WEST,** 5368 Gulf Dr, Holmes Beach, FL 34217-1775. Tel 941-778-6648; Web: www.amisland.com/gallery
Open Mon - Sat 10 AM - 5 PM; No admis fee; Estab 1991 to exhibit & sell local artists' work; Art work by local & regional artists working in a wide variety of media; Mem: 30; juried in by current artist members
Activities: Artist demonstrations Sat 10AM-Noon; mus shop sells original art

INDIAN ROCKS BEACH

M **GULF BEACH ART CENTER,** 1515 Bay Palm Blvd, Indian Rocks Beach, FL 33785-2827. Tel 727-596-4331; Fax 727-596-4331; Email arts1515@gmail.com; Web: www.beachartcenter.org; *Exec Dir* Anna Kuhlman
Open Mon - Fri 9 AM - 4 PM, cl major Holidays; No admis fee, donations accepted; Estab 1978 - Mission is to offer creative education experiences in the visual arts that stimulate awareness & appreciation of the arts.
Income: Not-for profit: donations, fund raisers & mem & class fees
Library Holdings: Book Volumes 300
Collections: paintings
Publications: newsletter
Activities: Classes for adults & children; educ prog; workshops; art festivals

JACKSONVILLE

M **CUMMER MUSEUM OF ART & GARDENS,** Museum & Library, 829 Riverside Ave, Jacksonville, FL 32204-3336. Tel 904-356-6857; Fax 904-353-4101; Web: cummermuseum.org; *Acting Dir* Holly Keris
Open Tues 10 AM - 9 PM, Wed - Sat 10 AM - 4 PM, Sun noon - 4 PM; Admis adults $10, seniors, military & students $6, members & children 5 & under free; Estab 1961 to engage & inspire through the arts, gardens & educ; 14 galleries of paintings & decorative arts sited on 2-1/2 acres of formal gardens; Average Annual Attendance: 164,000; Mem: 3,200; dues $50-$750
Income: Financed by donations, city funds, endowments, membership & grants
Library Holdings: Book Volumes 6,000, Exhibition Catalogs, Periodical Subscriptions, Slides
Special Subjects: Asian Art, Baroque Art, Ceramics, Decorative Arts, Etchings & Engravings, Graphics, Landscapes, Medieval Art, Oriental Art, Painting-American, Painting-British, Painting-Dutch, Painting-European, Painting-Flemish, Painting-French, Painting-Israeli, Painting-Japanese, Porcelain, Portraits, Pre-Columbian Art, Prints, Renaissance Art, Sculpture, Tapestries, Watercolors, Woodcuts, Ivory, Jade
Collections: Netsuke, Inro & porcelains, Early Meissen porcelain, European & American painting, sculpture, graphic arts & decorative arts
Exhibitions: (14th Jun, 2016-12th Feb, 2017) Lift: Contemporary Expressions of the African American Experience; (4th Mar, 2017-20th Jul, 2017) An American in Venice: James McNeill Whistler and His Legacy; (27th Jan, 2017-23rd Apr, 2017) Masterworks of Academic Art from the Dahesh Museum Collection; (19th May, 2017-3rd Sep, 2017) Ink, Silk, and Gold: Islamic Treasures from the Museum of Fine Arts, Boston; (17th Dec, 2016-25th Jun, 2017) The World War I Etchings of James McBey; (11th Jul, 2017-4th Feb, 2018) A Collector's Eye: Celebrating Joseph Jeffers Dodge; (5th Nov, 2016-4th Oct, 2017) Chasing Shadows: David Ponsler; (13th Oct, 2016-7th Jan, 2018) Bijoux Parisiens: French Jewelry from the Petit Palais, Paris
Publications: A Legacy in Bloom: Celebrating a Century of Gardens at The Cummer; Eugene Savage: The Seminole Paintings; Early Meissen Porcelain: The Work Collection at the Cummer; The Art of Empathy: The Mother of Sorrows in Northern Renaissance Art & Devotion
Activities: Educ prog; classes for adults & children; dramatic programs; docent training;; lects open to pub; concerts; gallery talks; tours; book traveling exhibs; originate traveling exhibs; mus shop sells books & original art

M **FLORIDA STATE COLLEGE AT JACKSONVILLE,** South Gallery, Wilson Center for the Arts, 11901 Beach Blvd Jacksonville, FL 32246-6624. Tel 904-646-2023; Fax 904-646-2336; Email ellewis@fccj.edu; Web: www.facebrook.com/southgalery; *Gallery Coordr* Lynn Lewis
Open Mon - Thurs 10 AM - 4 PM, Fri 10 AM - 2 PM; No admis fee; Estab 1985
Collections: FCCJ Permanent Collection
Exhibitions: George Merritt Milton; Student Annual Juried School; Toshiko Takaezu; Joyce Tennyson; Hiram Williams; Arnold Newman; Brooks Jensen
Activities: Classes for adults & children; lects open to public; 3 vis lectrs per yr; gallery talks

L **JACKSONVILLE PUBLIC LIBRARY,** Fine Arts & Recreation Dept, 303 N Laura St Jacksonville, FL 32202. Tel 904-630-2665; Fax 904-630-2431; Web: www.jpl.coj.net; *Interim Dir* Jennifer Giltrop
Open Mon & Thurs - Sat 10 AM - 6 PM, Tues - Wed 11 AM - 7 PM, Sun 1 PM - 5 PM; No admis fee; Estab 1905 to serve the pub by giving them free access to books, films, recordings, pamphlets, periodicals, maps, plus informational services & free programming
Income: Financed by city appropriation
Library Holdings: Book Volumes 48,000, Motion Pictures 2000, Other Holdings Compact discs 6000, Periodical Subscriptions 200, Records 10,000, Slides 3500, Video Tapes 6000
Publications: Annual Report

M **JACKSONVILLE UNIVERSITY,** Alexander Brest Museum & Gallery, 2800 University Blvd, Jacksonville, FL 32211. Tel 904-256-7374; Fax 904-256-7375; Email jbenedi@ju.edu; *Dir* Jim Benedict
Open Mon - Fri 9 AM - 4:30 PM; No admis fee; Estab 1972 to exhibit decorative arts collection; Two galleries exhibiting decorative arts & Pre-Columbian art & artifacts. Three galleries contain contemporary art on rotating schedule; Average Annual Attendance: 12,000
Income: Financed by endowment & private funds
Special Subjects: African Art, Antiquities-Persian, Asian Art, Bronzes, Carpets & Rugs, Ceramics, Coins & Medals, Decorative Arts, Drawings, Furniture, Glass, Gold, Ivory, Jade, Oriental Art, Painting-American, Porcelain, Pre-Columbian Art, Sculpture, Watercolors, Woodcarvings, Enamels, Etchings & Engravings, Painting-Dutch, Painting-Flemish, Religious Art, Woodcuts, Textiles
Collections: Porcelain, Ivory, Pre-Columbian, Steuben, Tiffany
Publications: Museum catalog
Activities: Classes for adults; docent training; lects open to public, 4-6 vis lectrs per yr; gallery talks; competitions

M **MUSEUM OF CONTEMPORARY ART JACKSONVILLE,** 333 N Laura St, Jacksonville, FL 32202-3505. Tel 904-366-6911; Fax 904-366-6901; Email hellomoca@unf.edu; Web: mocajacksonville.unf.edu; *Dir* Caitlin Doherty; *Cur* Jaime Desimone; *Registrar* Alyssa Hockenberry
Open Tues - Sat 11 AM - 5 PM, Thurs 5 PM - 9 PM, Sun Noon - 5 PM; Admis adults $8, seniors, military & students with ID $5, UNF students, children under 2 & mems free, Artwalk free & Sun free for families; Estab 1948 as an art center for the greater Jacksonville area; Average Annual Attendance: 100,000; Mem: 3200; dues luminary $500, family $100, dual $75, individual $50; annual meeting spring
Income: Financed by mem
Special Subjects: Painting-American, Pre-Columbian Art, Prints, Sculpture, Photography
Collections: Pre-Columbian art, Permanent Coll: 800+ works of art incl painting, printmaking, sculpture & photography from 20th c, primarily 1960 - present
Publications: Calendar, monthly; exhibition catalogues
Activities: Classes for adults & children; docent training; art enrichment prog; dramatic progs; lects open to pub, 10 vis lectrs per yr; concerts; gallery talks; tours; competitions; scholarships offered; book traveling exhibs; originate traveling exhibs; mus shop sells books, magazines, original art, reproductions, prints, jewelry & children's toys

M **MUSEUM OF SCIENCE & HISTORY,** 1025 Museum Circle, Jacksonville, FL 32207. Tel 904-396-6674; Fax 904-396-5799; Email cslingluff@themosh.org; Web:

www.themosh.org; *Pres* Maria Hane; *Sr VPres* Mike Hornsby; *Dir Planetarium & School Progs* Eddie Whisler
Open Mon - Thurs 10 AM - 5 PM, Fri 10 AM - 8 PM, Sat 10 AM - 6 PM, Sun Noon - 5 PM; Admis $12.50 , seniors, military & youth $10, children under 3 free; Estab 1941; Lobby & three floors contain exhibit areas, classrooms & studios; Average Annual Attendance: 225,000; Mem: 2000; member families dues vary
Income: Financed by admission, earned revenue & pvt support grant
Special Subjects: Historical Material
Collections: Historical, Live Animal Collection, Physical Science Demonstrations
Exhibitions: Alexander Brest Planetarium (16th largest in US); health; science; wildlife
Publications: Teacher's Guide, annually; brochures, online newsletters; annual report
Activities: Classes for children; dramatic progs; docent training; lects open to pub; tours; mus shop and sales shop selling books, prints, museum-oriented items and toys for children

JUPITER

M **EDNA HIBEL ART FOUNDATION,** Hibel Museum of Art, 5353 Parkside Dr, John D. MacArthur Campus Jupiter, FL 33458-2906. Tel 561-622-5560; Fax 561-622-4881; Email hibelgalleryjupiter@gmail.com; Web: www.hibelartmuseum.org; *Dir* Nancy Walls; *Exec Trustee* Edna Hibel Plotkin; *Dir Educ* Carol Davis; *Prog Coordr* Susan Babila; *Dir Sales* Helene Plotkin
Open Tues - Fri 11 AM - 4 PM, in season concerts & teas one time/mo Sun & Mon; No admis fee; Estab 1977 to extend the appreciation of the art of Edna Hibel, specifically, & visual art in general; 10 galleries & spaces devoted to paintings, lithographs, sculpture & porcelain art by artist Edna Hibel, features antique furniture, snuff bottles, paper weights & art book collections. Maintains reference library; Average Annual Attendance: 2,000; Mem: Meeting Jan
Income: $40,000 (financed by donations, mem, mus gift shop sales, art camp & private donations)
Purchases: $30,000
Library Holdings: Book Volumes, DVDs, Memorabilia, Original Documents, Photographs, Sculpture
Special Subjects: Archaeology, Dioramas, Dolls, Drawings, Etchings & Engravings, Furniture, Glass, Graphics, Historical Material, Jade, Jewelry, Landscapes, Painting-American, Porcelain, Portraits, Primitive art, Prints, Renaissance Art, Sculpture, Watercolors, Reproductions
Collections: English & Italian 18th Century furniture, 18th & 19th Century paperweights, 19th & 20th Century library art books, Paintings, Porcelain Art, Lithographs, Serigraphs, Sculpture by Edna Hibel, Porcelain Dolls, Archaeological antiquities & prehistoric minerals, fossils & geodes, Craig Collection of Edna Hibel's Work, 18th & 19th Century fans
Publications: Exhibition catalogs; exhibition posters
Activities: Classes for children; docent training; summer art camp (7 wks June-July); lects open to pub; concerts; gallery talks; tours; sponsoring of competitions; scholarships; mus shop sells books, reproductions, original art, prints, trivits, soaps, plates & porcelain

L **Hibel Museum Gallery**, 5353 Parkside Dr, Jupiter, FL 33458-2906. Tel 561-622-1380; Fax 561-622-3475; Email info@hibelmuseum.org; Email nancy@hibelmuseum.org; Web: www.hibelmuseum.org; *Dir Educ* Carol Davis; *Dir* Nancy Walls; *Prog Coordr* Adra Farriss
Open Tues - Fri 11:30 AM - 3:30 PM Nov - Apr; Tues - Fri 12 PM - 3 PM Apr - Oct; Sat by appointment; No admis fee; Estab 2003, displaying & selling the art of Edna Hibel to support the Hibel Museum of Art; For reference only; Average Annual Attendance: 1,000
Income: Financed through sales & Edna Hibel Art Foundation
Library Holdings: Audio Tapes, Book Volumes 500, Cassettes, Clipping Files, DVDs, Exhibition Catalogs, Framed Reproductions, Memorabilia, Original Art Works, Pamphlets, Photographs, Prints, Reproductions, Sculpture, Slides, Video Tapes
Activities: Classes for adults & children; docent training; lects open to pub, 2 vis lectrs per yr; lect to school classes & cultural activities for elementary school children; concerts; gallery talks; tours; book traveling exhibs 4-5 per yr; sales shop sells books, reproductions & original art, prints, collectable art plates, gift boxes, jewelry, posters, stone lithographs & serigraphs

KEY WEST

M **KEY WEST ART & HISTORICAL SOCIETY,** East Martello Museum & Gallery, 3501 S Roosevelt Blvd, Key West, FL 33040-5209. Tel 305-296-3913; Fax 305-296-6206; Email cpennington@kwahs.org; Web: www.kwahs.org; *Pres* Bob Feldman; *Exec Dir* Claudia Pennington; *Dir Opers* Diane Rippe; *Museum Store Mgr* Linda Hardy
Open daily 9:30AM-4:30PM; Admis $6 adults, children 7-15 $3, active military free, seniors and local residents $5, children under 6 free; Estab 1962 to preserve history of the Florida Keys; 2300 square feet Civil War fort, last standing Martello fort in country; Average Annual Attendance: 25,000; Mem: 2000; dues $40, family $100, student $40; annual meeting in Apr
Income: Financed by mem, donations, admis & gift shop sales
Special Subjects: Folk Art
Collections: Carvings & paintings of Mario Sanchez, junkyard art of Stanley Papio
Exhibitions: History of Key West
Publications: Martello; two newsletters
Activities: Art & music series for adults & children; lects open to pub, 6 vis lectrs per yr; children's competitions with prizes; individual paintings & original objects of art lent to qualifying mus; book traveling exhibs; mus shop sells books, reproductions, prints, postcards, children's educ material

M **OLD ISLAND RESTORATION FOUNDATION INC,** Oldest House in Key West, 322 Duval St, Key West, FL; PO Box 689, Key West, FL 33041-0689. Tel 305-294-9501; Fax 305-294-4509; Email oirf@oirf.org; Web: www.oirf.org; *Adin* Teri Beard
Open Mon, Tues, Thurs - Sat 10 AM - 4PM; No admis fee; Estab 1976 to present the history of Key West's oldest house; Furnished period house with paintings throughout; Average Annual Attendance: 14,000; Mem: 200; dues $95-$500; annual meeting in Apr
Income: $36,000 (financed through donations & fundraising)
Purchases: $2,000 (19th century dining table)
Special Subjects: Ceramics, Costumes, Dioramas, Dolls, Folk Art, Furniture, Marine Painting, Painting-American, Period Rooms, Textiles, Woodcarvings, Historical Material, Period Rooms
Collections: Oil on canvas by Edward Moran, All Sailing Ships & Scenes, Watercolors by Marshall Joyce, Watercolors by unknown artists, Orlon canvas by W W Cowell, Polychrome on wood, Mario Sanchez
Exhibitions: Rotating exhibitions
Activities: Classes for children; docent training; sponsoring of competitions; restoration grants; schols; tours;

LAKE WORTH

A **CULTURAL COUNCIL OF PALM BEACH COUNTY,** 601 Lake Ave, Lake Worth, FL 33460-3810. Tel 561-471-2901; Fax 561-687-9484; Email rblades@palmbeachculture.com; Web: www.palmbeachculture.com; *Pres & CEO* Rena Blades; *Dir Fin* Kathleen Alex; *Dir Grants* Jan Radusky; *Mgr Arts & Cultural Educ* Shawn Berry; *Mem & Special Events Mgr* Debbie Calabria; *Grants Coordr* Margaret Granda; *Dir Develop* Mary Lewis; *Admin Asst* Autumn Oliveras; *Web & eMktg Mgr* Daniel Boudet; *Bookkeeper* Jean Brasch; *Develop Assoc* Kristen Smiley; *Mktg Coordr* Theresa Louckes; *Mgr Artist Servs* Nichole Hickey; *Vis Servs Coordr* Marlon Foster
Open Tues - Sat 10 AM - 5 PM; No admis fee; Estab 1978 by Alex W Dreyfoos Jr as the Palm Beach County Council of the Arts to develop, coordinate, & promote the arts & cultural activities throughout Palm Beach County; recognized by the Board of County Commissioners as the county's adv agency for cultural develop & administers a portion of local tourist develop funds under contract with county government; Average Annual Attendance: 6,886; Mem: 545; dues $50-1,000
Income: Financed by donations
Publications: Art and Culture Magazine; Arts and Culture Map; Calendar of Events; Cultural Caravan; Treasures Brochure; Teachers Guide to Cultural Organizations in Palm Beach County
Activities: Teachers workshops; teachers guide to organizations; artist in residency program; Ubertalli Award (for visual artists); Fyfe Award (for performing artists)

LAKELAND

M **ARTS ON THE PARK,** Lakeland Center for Creative Arts, 845 Mississippi Ave, Lakeland, FL 33801-5520. Tel 863-680-2787; Email info@artsontheparklakeland.org; Web: artsontheparklakeland.org; *Exec Dir* Christine Boring; *Pres* Karen Seggerman; *VPres* Tim Gallagher
Open Tues-Sat noon-4PM, open late Fri nights, cl holidays; No admis fee; Estab 1979 to encourage Florida artists through shows & competitions; 1600 sq ft ground floor, plus second floor galleries in Lakeland's Munn Park Historic District; Average Annual Attendance: 30,000; Mem: 1200; dues sponsor $100-$999, individual $40, senior citizens $30
Income: $80,000 (financed by mem dues, sponsorships, grants, city, bus & industry)
Exhibitions: Monthly shows; Upstairs gallery is monthly rental
Publications: Constant contact email
Activities: Classes for adults & children; Docent training; lects open to pub, concerts; competitions with awards; juried shows; scholarships; exten dept serves county; originate traveling exhibs; sales shop sells original art, jewelry

M **FLORIDA SOUTHERN COLLEGE,** Melvin Art Gallery, 111 Lake Hollingsworth Dr, Lakeland, FL 33801-5698. Tel 863-680-4743, 680-4111; Fax 863-680-4147; Email apaxson@flsouthern.edu; Web: www.flsouthern.edu; *Prof Art History & Chmn Div Fine & Performing Arts* James Rogers, PhD; *Assoc Prof Art, Chmn Dept Art & Art History, Dir Studio Prog* William Otremsky, MFA; *Asst Prof Art & Dir Foundation Prog* Kelly Sturhahn, MFA; *Asst Prof Art & Dir Graphic Design Prog* Samuel Romero, MFA; *Adjunct Asst Prof Art History* Nadine Pantano, PhD; *Adjunct Prof Art* Joseph Mitchell, MFA; *Adjunct Instr Art* Eric Blackmore, BFA; *Adjunct Asst Prof Art Educ* Jacquelyn Hanson, MFA; *Prof Emerita* Beth Ford, MA; *Gallery Coordr* Jenna Rice, BFA; *Adjunct Prof Art* Patricia Lamb, MFA
Open Mon - Fri 9 AM - 4 PM when col is in session; No admis fee; Estab 1971 as a teaching gallery; Large 3,000 sq ft main gallery; small one room adjacent gallery; Average Annual Attendance: 3,000-5,000
Library Holdings: Slides
Special Subjects: Drawings, Etchings & Engravings, Folk Art, Glass, Landscapes, Painting-American, Photography, Portraits, Prints
Collections: Brass Rubbings Coll in Roux Library, Laymon Glass Collection in Annie Pfeiffer Chapel, permanent coll in various offices & buildings, Drawing & Painting Coll by Tibor Pataky
Publications: The Art of Downing Barnitz by James G Rogers Jr, William Meek, Alexander Bruce
Activities: Lects open to public, 3 vis lectrs per yr; gallery talks; concerts; sponsoring of competitions; John R Reuter Award, Florida Art Award

M **POLK MUSEUM OF ART,** 800 E Palmetto St, Lakeland, FL 33801-5529. Tel 863-688-7743; Fax 863-688-2611; Email VisitorServices@PolkMuseumofArt.org; Web: www.polkmuseumofart.org; *Exec Dir & Chief Cur* Claire Orologas; *Admin Mgr* Marilyn Wilson; *Educ Mgr* Ellen Chastain; *Deputy Dir* Palemeschia "Pal" Rivers Powell; *Visitor Servs & Retail Mgr* Terry Aulisio
Open Tues - Sat 10 AM - 5 PM, Sun 1 - 5 PM, cl Mon & major holidays; No admis fee; Estab 1966 series of galleries for temporary and permanent exhibitions; 8 galleries with rotating exhibs; permanent Pre-Columbian gallery; Average Annual Attendance: 140,000; Mem: 1,500; dues platinum patron $5,000, gold patron $2,500, patron $1,000, advocate $250, sponsor $100, family $60, individual $40; annual meeting in June

Income: Financed by mem, cities of Lakeland, Bartow, Auburndale & Winter Haven, Polk County School Board, grants, endowment & special projects
Library Holdings: Auction Catalogs, Book Volumes, Exhibition Catalogs, Periodical Subscriptions 28, Photographs, Prints, Slides
Special Subjects: African Art, Afro-American Art, Antiquities-Assyrian, Asian Art, Carpets & Rugs, Ceramics, Collages, Decorative Arts, Drawings, Folk Art, Glass, Gold, Juvenile Art, Latin American Art, Oriental Art, Painting-American, Photography, Pre-Columbian Art, Prints, Sculpture, Silver, Textiles
Collections: 15th-19th Century European Collection of ceramics, Pre-Columbian Collection, assorted decorative arts, Asian arts, contemporary paintings, photographs, prints & sculpture featuring American artists, South African textiles & fibers, Ellis Verink Collection
Exhibitions: Changing exhibitions; 9 student gallery exhibitions including 12th Congressional District Competition; Permanent display of Pre-Columbian art; temporary displays of student, contemporary and historic art
Publications: Exhib catalogues and gallery guides, quarterly newsletter, ann report
Activities: classes for adults & children; dramatic programs; docent training; workshops; lects open to pub; gallery talks; tours; competitions with awards; lifetime art achievement award; outreach programs; annual outdoor art festival; Family Day; sculpture competition; schols & fels offered; exten prog serves children of Polk City, Florida; book traveling exhibs 2 per yr; originate traveling exhibs to other mus in Florida; mus shop sells books, original art, reproductions, prints, jewelry, home decorative objects

LEESBURG

M **LEESBURG CENTER FOR THE ARTS,** 429 W Magnolia St, Leesburg, FL 34749; PO Box 492857, Leesburg, FL 34749-2857. Tel 352-365-0232; Fax 352-315-1152; Email director@leesburgcenterforthearts.com; Web: www.leesburgcenterforthearts.com; *Exec Dir* Amy Padgett Griffin
Open 10 AM - 5 PM; Estab to provide community with art education & cultural events; Mem: dues $30
Collections: Local artists
Activities: Educ progs; art programming; artists demonstrations; cultural events

MAITLAND

M **ART AND HISTORY MUSEUMS - MAITLAND,** 231 W Packwood Ave, Maitland, FL 32751-5553. Tel 407-539-2181; Fax 407-539-1198; Email RCmailMAC@aol.com; Web: www.maitlandartcenter.org; *Educ Coordr* Ann E Spalding; *Prog Coordr* Dawn Feavyour; *Cur Coll* Richard D Colvin; *CEO & Exec Dir* James G Shepp; *Staff Coordr* Carol B Shurtleff; *2nd VChmn* Priscilla Cockerell; *Treas* Renae Vaughn; *VChmn* Stockton Reeves; *Secy* Belinda Townsend; *Community Relations* Pamela Wells; *1st VChmn* Wallace G Harper; *Mus Store Mgr* Diedre Peeler
Open Mon - Fri 9 AM - 4:30 PM, Sat & Sun Noon - 4:30 PM, cl major holidays; Admis adults $3, students 12-22 & Maitland residents $2; Estab 1938 to promote exploration & educ in the visual arts & contemporary crafts; listed in National Register of Historic Places; Four galleries totaling 202 running ft; Average Annual Attendance: 60,000; Mem: 625; dues $20-$1000; annual meeting in Sept
Income: Financed by mem, city & state appropriations, donations, special events, endowment
Special Subjects: Collages, Crafts, Drawings, Eskimo Art, Etchings & Engravings, Glass, Graphics, Landscapes, Painting-American, Photography, Porcelain, Posters, Pottery, Prints, Sculpture, Watercolors, Woodcarvings, Woodcuts
Collections: Architectural work including 6-acre compound & memorial chapel designed by Smith, graphics, paintings & sculptures of Andre Smith, etchings & drawings
Publications: Exhibit catalogs; quarterly class schedules; quarterly newsletter
Activities: Classes for adults & children; docent training; lects open to pub, 2 vis lectrs per yr; concerts; gallery talks; tours; individual paintings & original objects of art lent to museums & art centers; book traveling exhibs 1 per yr; originate traveling exhibs to mus, art centers, libraries & universities; mus shop sells original art, reproductions, cards, jewelry & children's items

L **Maitland Art Center**, 231 W Packwood Ave, Maitland, FL 32751-5553. Tel 407-539-2181; Fax 888-316-5729; Email info@artandhistory.org; Web: artandhistory.org; *CEO* Andrea Bailey Cox; *Chief Curator* Rebecca Sexton Larson; *Marketing Director* Rae Ward; *Operations Director* Danielle Thomas; *Development Director* Jennifer Grozio
Open Tues - Sun 11 AM - 4 PM; History Museum Thurs- Sun 12-4PM; cl major holidays; Admis non members $3, 65 & older $2, students $1, members no fee; Estab 1970 to promote knowledge & educ in American Art; Open for reference; Average Annual Attendance: 60,000; Mem: 926
Income: Financed by City of Maitland, mem, tuition, special events, grants, contributions, gallery donations
Library Holdings: Book Volumes 4500, Exhibition Catalogs, Periodical Subscriptions 10, Slides, Video Tapes
Special Subjects: Painting-American, Photography, Porcelain, Portraits, Posters, Pottery, Printmaking, Prints, Sculpture, Watercolors, Woodcarvings, Woodcuts
Collections: Works by Andre Smith (1880 - 1959), exhibiting artists
Exhibitions: 31st Dec, 2016) John Petrey & Derek Gores: Marking 40 Years of the Rotary Arts Festival; (13th Jan, 2017-19th Feb, 2017) Meditations, Mapping and Memories; (3rd Mar, 2017-16th Apr, 2017) Art31: Borrowed Light; (28th Apr, 2017-2nd Jul, 2017) Architects as Artists
Activities: Educ prog; classes for adults & children;; lects open to pub, 3 vis lectrs per yr; concerts; gallery talks; tours; originate traveling exhibs

MELBOURNE

M **FOOSANER ART MUSEUM,** (Brevard Art Museum), 1463 Highland Ave, Melbourne, FL 32935-6562. Tel 321-674-8916; Fax 321-674-8910; Email info@brevardartmuseum.org; Web: www.foosanerartmuseum.org; *Dir Univ Mus* Carla Funk; *Admin Asst to Dir Univ Mus* Tama Johnson; *Mgr Vis Servs* Tina Murray; *Dir Colls* Sarah Smith; *Coll Mgr* Jose Marquez; *Cur Educ* Sara Petrosky
Open Wed - Sat 10 AM - 4 PM; No admis fee; Estab 1978 to exhibit art for the educ, information, & enjoyment of the pub; Exhibition facility with approx 6000 sq ft of exhibition space; Average Annual Attendance: 25,000; Mem: dues patron $150 & up, general $55, senior $25
Income: $400,000 (financed by mem, city & county appropriation, corporate gifts & grants)
Library Holdings: Auction Catalogs, Audio Tapes, Book Volumes, CD-ROMs
Collections: Contemporary regional & national artists, drawings, paintings, prints of Ernst Oppler, Chase Collection, Clyde Butcher Photographs, Shared Vision Collection
Exhibitions: Rotating exhibs of international, national & regional artists
Publications: Quarterly newsletter; calendar for members; handouts & catalogues for changing exhibitions
Activities: Classes for adults & children; docent training; lects open to pub, 10 vis lectrs per yr; concerts; gallery talks; tours; schols offered; book traveling exhibs 3-4 per yr; originate traveling exhibs to qualifying institutions; mus shop sells books, original art, jewelry

MIAMI

M **AVANT GALLERY,** 270 Biscayne Blvd Way, Ste 102 Miami, FL 33131. Tel 786-220-8600; Email info@avantgallery.com; Web: avantgallery.com; *Founder & Dir* Dmitry Prut
Open Mon - Wed 11 AM - 8 PM, Thurs - Sat 11 AM - 12 AM, Sun 11 AM - 6 PM; Estab 2007 to act as a positive presence for contemporary fine arts
Special Subjects: Photography, Sculpture, Interior Design

M **BAKEHOUSE ART COMPLEX, INC,** 561 NW 32nd St, Miami, FL 33127-3749. Tel 305-576-2828; Fax 305-576-0316; Email info@bacfl.org; Web: bacfl.org; *Exec Dir* Bibi Baloyra; *Opers Mgr* Beatriz Calderon
Open daily Noon - 5 PM; No admis fee; Estab 1986; 2600 sq ft gallery; Average Annual Attendance: 6,500
Special Subjects: Painting-Australian, Painting-Spanish, Portraits, Restorations
Exhibitions: 20 exhibs per yr, contact for more information
Activities: Classes for adults, children & advanced artists; lect open to public; 4-6 vis lectrs per year; panel discussions; concerts; tours; competitions with awards; scholarships & fels; individual painting & original object of art lent to city facilities & developers; retail store sells original art

M **FLORIDA INTERNATIONAL UNIVERSITY,** The Patricia & Phillip Frost Art Museum, Modesto Maidique Campus, 10975 SW 17th St Miami, FL 33199. Tel 305-348-2890; Fax 305-348-2762; Email artinfo@fiu.edu; Web: frost.fiu.edu; *Dir* Jordana Pomeroy; *Educ Cur* Miriam Machado; *Chief Registrar* Debbye Kirschtel-Taylor; *Mgr Strategic Initiatives* Maryanna Ramirez; *Finance & HR Mgr* Marina Garcia, MPA; *Bldg Opers Mgr* Julio Alvarez; *Curatorial Asst* Ashlye Valines; *Sr Vis Svcs Mgr* Jacquelyne Velken
Open Tues - Sat 10 AM - 5 PM, Sun noon - 5 PM, cl Mon; No admis fee; Estab 1977; 46,000 sq ft bldg, 9 galleries; Average Annual Attendance: 50,000; Mem: dues $20-$1,000
Income: Financed by state appropriation & supported by Friends of the Art Mus, private foundations & municipal councils
Library Holdings: DVDs, Exhibition Catalogs
Special Subjects: Sculpture, Architecture, Latin American Art
Collections: Cintas Foundation Collection, The Metropolitan Museum & Art Center Collection, Betty Laird Perry Emerging Artist Collection & Sculpture Park
Publications: Exhibition catalogues
Activities: Dade County Public Schools Museum Educ Program; classes for children; docent training; summer camp; teacher workshops; lect open to public, lects for mems only, 4-5 visiting lectrs per year; gallery talks; tours of Sculpture Park; mus sales shop sells books, catalogs, exhibit/program merchandise

M **MIAMI-DADE COLLEGE,** Kendal Campus, Art Gallery, 11011 SW 104th St M-123, Miami, FL 33176-3393. Tel 305-237-7700; Fax 305-237-2901; Email museum@mdc.edu; Web: www.mdcmoad.org; *Exec Dir & Chief Cur* Rina Carvajal
Closed through spring 2018; No admis fee; Estab 1970 as a teaching laboratory & pub service; Average Annual Attendance: 15,000
Income: Financed by state appropriation
Special Subjects: African Art, Afro-American Art, Drawings, Etchings & Engravings, Folk Art, Historical Material, Latin American Art, Painting-American, Painting-Spanish, Photography, Photography, Prints, Sculpture, Woodcuts
Collections: Contemporary American paintings, photographs, prints, sculpture includes: Beal, Boice, Bolotowsky, Christo, Ferrer, Fine, Gibson, Henry, Hepworth, Hockney, Judd, Komar, Lichtenstein, Marisol, Melamid, Michals, Motherwell, Nesbitt, Oldenburg, Parker & Pearlstein, Bedia, Schnabel
Exhibitions: Fritz Bultman; Connie Fox; Philip Gieger; John Hull; William King; Melissa Weinman; Richard Williams; Magdalena Abakanowicz; Diane Lechleitner; Kay Walking Stick
Publications: 6 catalogs per year
Activities: Lects open to pub, 4-6 vis lectrs per yr; concerts; gallery talks; individual paintings & original objects of art lent; lending collection contains original art works, original prints, paintings, photographs, sculpture; originates traveling exhibs

M **MIAMI-DADE COLLEGE,** MDC Museum of Art & Design, 600 Biscayne Blvd, Freedom Tower, 2nd fl Miami, FL 33132. Tel 303-237-7700; Email Museum@mdc.edu; Web: mdcmoad.org; *Executive Director and Chief Curator* Rina Carvajal; *Director of Campus Galleries* Wanda Texon; *Director of Campus Galleries* Jessica Broadsky; *Executive Administrative Assistant* Carolina Salazar; *Membership + Events Coordinator* Elizabeth Buege; *Registrar* Vickie Pierre; *Collection Specialist* Patricia Duany; *Museum Exhibition Coordinator* William Iverson; *Lead Preparator* Robert Perez; *Museum Front Desk Associate + Volunteer Coordinator* Sierra Manno; *Front Desk Associate + Tour Coordinator* Cristie Alfonso; *Museum Studies Program Coordinator* Melissa Diaz; *CINTAS Coordinator* Laurie Escobar
Open Wed-Sun noon-5 PM; No admis fee; Established August 2012; With more than 17,000 square feet of exhibition space, the Museum is known for it's

presentation of exhibits by emerging artists, as well as major figures in modern, post-modern, and contemporary art.; Average Annual Attendance: 45,000+; Mem: Individual $45, Benefactor $250, MOA+D Creative Society $500, Museum Circle $1,000
Income: $299,000, as part of Wolfson Campus Galleries (financed by annual grants & state appropriation)
Special Subjects: Etchings & Engravings, Hispanic Art, Landscapes, Latin American Art, Painting-American, Photography, Posters, Pottery, Pre-Columbian Art, Reproductions
Collections: Centre Gallery - Youth Matters, Endurance: The Information (The History of the Body in performance Arts, Inter-American Gallery - Linda Matalon: Gathering & protecting, Carol Sun
Publications: Exhibition catalogs
Activities: Educ packets; workshops; symposia; classes for adults & children; docent training;; lects open to pub, 12 vis lectrs per yr; concerts; gallery talks; tours; book traveling exhibs 3 per yr; originate traveling exhibs 1 per yr; Exhibition catalogues

L **MIAMI-DADE PUBLIC LIBRARY,** 101 W Flagler St, Miami, FL 33130-1504. Tel 305-375-2665; Web: mdpls.org; *Dir* Ray Baker
Open Mon - Sat 10 AM - 6 PM; No admis fee; Estab 1947 to provide the informational, educational and recreational needs of the community; Gallery maintained, Artmobile maintained
Income: Financed by special millage
Library Holdings: Cassettes 2000, Clipping Files, Exhibition Catalogs, Fiche, Framed Reproductions 800, Motion Pictures 5500, Original Art Works 1200, Pamphlets, Periodical Subscriptions 100, Photographs, Prints, Records 4000, Reels, Reproductions, Video Tapes 6000
Special Subjects: Afro-American Art, Latin American Art
Collections: African American original graphics, Latin American original graphics, Oriental collection of original graphics, Creole Collection
Publications: Exhibition catalogs
Activities: Lects open to public; concerts; gallery talks; tours; exten dept; artmobile; reproductions lent; book traveling exhibs, 1-2 per yr; originate traveling exhibitions, permanent collection of works on paper

NATIONAL YOUNGARTS FOUNDATION(National Foundation for Advancement in the Arts)
For further information, see National and Regional Organizations

M **NEW WORLD SCHOOL OF THE ARTS,** Gallery, 25 NE Second St, Miami, FL; 300 NE Second Ave, Miami, FL 33132-2297. Tel 305-237-3620; Email mcuesta@mdcc.edu; *Dean Visual Arts* Maggy Cuesta
Open 9 AM - 5 PM; No admis fee; Estab 1990 to exhibit contemporary art & design; Major gallery in downtown Miami showing contemporary art & design from USA & abroad & faculty & student art work
Income: Financed by county & state appropriation
Publications: Exhibition catalogs
Activities: High School & BFA progs; lects open to pub, 25 vis lectrs per yr; concerts; gallery talks; tours; juried student exhibitions; schols offered; book traveling exhibs 2 per yr; originate traveling exhibs 1 per yr

M **PEREZ ART MUSEUM MIAMI,** 1103 Biscayne Blvd, Miami, FL 33132. Tel 305-375-3000; Fax 305-375-1725; Email info@pamm.org; Web: www.pamm.org; *Dir* Franklin Sirmans
Open Tues - Wed & Fri - Sun 10 AM - 6 PM, Thurs 10 AM - 9 PM; cl Mon, Thanksgiving & Christmas; Admis adults $16, youth, seniors with ID & students with ID $12; members, children under 6, active military with ID, 1st Thurs & 2nd Sat of month no admis fee; Estab 2013; 200,000 sq ft of programmable space
Collections: Paintings, sculpture
Activities: Tours

M **RUBELL FAMILY COLLECTION AND CONTEMPORARY ARTS FOUNDATION,** 95 NW 29th St, Miami, FL 33127. Tel 305-573-6090; Email info@rfc.museum; Web: rfc.museum; *Dir* Juan Roselione-Valadez; *Colls Mgr* William Vargas; *Archivist & Assoc Registrar* Laura Randall
See website for hours; Adults $10, students & seniors $5, US military & under 18 free
Collections: works by contemporary artists; paintings; sculpture

A **SOUTH FLORIDA CULTURAL CONSORTIUM,** Miami Dade County Dept of Cultural Affairs, 111 NW First St Ste 625, Miami, FL 33128-1964. Tel 305-375-4634; Fax 305-375-3068; Email culture@miamidade.gov; Web: www.miamidadearts.org; *Exec Dir* Michael Spring; *Deputy Dir* Deborah J Margol; *Chief Arts Educ* Francine M Anderson; *Cur & Artist Mgr* Amanda Sanfilippo
Open Mon - Fri 9 AM - 5 PM; Estab 1976 to provide planning, coordination, promotion & advocacy, as well as funding support & technical assistance to & marketing for Dade County's & South Florida's cultural organizations & activities; create a nurturing environment for the develop of cultural excellence & diversity; address the needs of cultural community that includes the visual & performing arts, history, historic preservation & folklife, the sciences, festivals & special events, & the literary & media arts

M **VIZCAYA MUSEUM & GARDENS,** 3251 S Miami Ave, Miami, FL 33129-2897. Tel 305-250-9133; Fax 305-285-2004; Email vizcayainformation@vizcaya.org; Web: www.vizcaya.org; *Exec Dir* Joel M Hoffman
Open Sun- Mon 9:30 AM - 4:30 PM, cl Thanksgiving & Christmas Day; Admis $18, seniors 62 & over $12, students with ID & visitors using wheelchairs $10, children 6-12 $6, US veterans & military with ID, children 5 & under free; Estab 1952 to preserve & interpret art & design in historical contexts; Vizcaya is a house mus with a major collection of European decorative arts & elaborate formal gardens. The Hour, formerly the home of James Deering, was completed in 1916 & contains approx 70 rooms; The Vizcaya Village, in the process of renovation, includes eleven national historic landmark bldgs; Average Annual Attendance: 185,000; Mem: 1500; dues $35 & up; annual meeting third Wed in Apr
Special Subjects: Antiquities-Oriental, Antiquities-Roman, Bronzes, Carpets & Rugs, Ceramics, Decorative Arts, Furniture, Period Rooms, Renaissance Art, Sculpture, Tapestries, Textiles
Collections: Italian & French Furniture of the 16th-18th & early 19th centuries, Notable Specialized Collections of Carpets. Tapestries, Furniture, Roman Antiques & Bronze Mortars, 16th-19th Centuries Decorative Arts, Archives
Publications: Vizcayan Newsletter, quarterly
Activities: Tours for children; docent training; lects open to pub; concerts; tours; individual paintings & original objects of art lent to accredited mus; mus shop sells books, magazines, original art, reproductions, prints & slides

L **Vizcaya Volunteer Guides Library,** 3251 S Miami Ave, Miami, FL 33129. Tel 305-250-9133, Ext 2242
Open to mus volunteers & students of the decorative arts for reference only
Income: Financed by donations
Library Holdings: Book Volumes 4000, Cassettes, Exhibition Catalogs, Kodachrome Transparencies, Memorabilia, Other Holdings Archival material, Periodical Subscriptions 18, Photographs, Slides
Special Subjects: Decorative Arts, Furniture, Interior Design
Collections: Slide collection for reference & teaching

MIAMI BEACH

M **BASS MUSEUM OF ART,** 2100 Collins Ave, Miami Beach, FL 33139-1919. Tel 305-673-7530; Fax 305-673-7062; Email scubina@bassmuseum.org; Web: www.bassmuseum.org; *Exec Dir & Chief Cur* Silvia Karmen Cubina; *Asst Dir* Jean Ortega; *Chief Preparator/Exhib Technician* Jan Galliardt; *Registrar & Exhib Mgr* Chelsea Guerdat; *Dir Individual Giving & Special Events* Denise Wolpert; *Dir External Affairs* Megan Riley; *Dir Educ* Adrienne von Lates; *Admin Asst to Exec Dir* Elisa Alonso
Open Wed - Sun Noon - 5 PM, cl Mon & Tues; Admis adults $8, students & seniors $6; Estab 1963 for the collection & exhibition of works of art. Collection features European art, architectural drawings & contemporary art; The museum is a two-story 1930 art deco structure with a new wing designed by Arata Isozaki; Average Annual Attendance: 40,000; Mem: 1,000; dues student $25, $50 ind, $75 family, sustaining $125, contributing $250, donor $500, silver dir cir $1000, gold dir cir $2500, platinum dir cir $5000
Income: $1,900,000 (financed by city, mem & grants from state, county & federal government)
Library Holdings: Book Volumes, Cassettes, Exhibition Catalogs
Special Subjects: Antiquities-Oriental, Baroque Art, Ceramics, Decorative Arts, Furniture, Painting-American, Painting-British, Painting-Dutch, Painting-European, Painting-Flemish
Collections: Permanent collection of European textiles, Old Master paintings, Baroque sculpture, Asian art, ecclesiastical artifacts, 19th & 20th century graphics, paintings & architectural drawings & arts, Photography
Exhibitions: (Ongoing) Selections from the Collection
Publications: Quarterly magazine; exhibition catalogues; permanent collection catalogue
Activities: Docent Training; family days; lects open to pub; 10 vis lectrs per year; concerts; films; gallery talks; tours; individual & original objects of art lent to other museums; originate traveling exhibs; sales shop selling books, original art, reproductions, prints

A **THE WOLFSONIAN-FLORIDA INTERNATIONAL UNIVERSITY,** 1001 Washington Ave, Miami Beach, FL 33139-5099. Tel 305-531-1001; Fax 305-531-2133; Email info@thewolf.fiu.edu; Web: www.wolfsonian.org; *Dir* Tim Rodgers
Open Mon - Tues, Thurs & Sat 10 AM - 6 PM, Fri 10 AM - 9 PM, Sun noon - 6 PM, cl Wed; Admis adults $12, seniors, students and children 6-18 $8, Wolfsonian members, children under 6, State Univ System of Florida students, faculty & staff free; Estab 1986; Average Annual Attendance: 30,000; Mem: dues $50 & up
Library Holdings: Book Volumes, Manuscripts, Memorabilia, Other Holdings, Pamphlets, Prints
Special Subjects: Architecture, Bookplates & Bindings, Coins & Medals, Decorative Arts, Dioramas, Drawings, Furniture, Glass, Graphics, Historical Material, Manuscripts, Maps, Photography, Porcelain, Portraits, Posters, Prints, Sculpture, Silver, Stained Glass, Textiles, Watercolors
Collections: Architecture & Design Arts, Decorative & Propaganda Arts (pertaining to period 1885-1945), Fine Arts, Rare & Reference Library
Exhibitions: Art and Design in the Modern Age; Agitated Images: John Heartfield & German Photomontage 1920-1938; Fashioning the Modern French Interior: Pochoir Portfolios in the 1920s; A Bittersweet Decade: The New Deal in America, 1935; Thoughts on Democracy: American Streamlined Design: The World of Tomorrow
Publications: The Journal of Decorative and Propaganda Arts
Activities: Classes for adults & children; lects for mem only, concerts, gallery talks, tours, schols, fellowships; 1 - 2 book traveling exhibs per yr; mus shop sells books, prints, reproductions, prints, design objects, housewares, movies

M **WORLD EROTIC ART MUSEUM,** 1205 Washington Ave, Miami Beach, FL 33139. Tel 305-532-9336; Fax 305-695-1209; Email missnaomi@weam.com; Web: www.weam.com; *Owner, Cur* Naomi Wilzig; *Gen Mgr* Geovanni Gonzalez; *Art Dir* Helmut Schuster; *Mktg* Robert Harbour
Open daily Mon - Thurs 11 AM - 10 PM, Fri - Sun 11 AM - midnight; Admis adults $15, seniors $14, students $13.50; Estab 2005. Children not allowed admission; Historical exhibition of erotic art through the ages; Average Annual Attendance: 35,000; Mem: $100 annual-new campaign
Income: Privately financed
Library Holdings: Book Volumes 250, Kodachrome Transparencies
Special Subjects: Afro-American Art, American Indian Art, Antiquities-Assyrian, Antiquities-Byzantine, Antiquities-Egyptian, Antiquities-Etruscan, Antiquities-Greek, Antiquities-Oriental, Antiquities-Persian, Antiquities-Roman, Asian Art, Bronzes, Cartoons, Ceramics, Coins & Medals, Decorative Arts, Dolls, Eskimo Art, Etchings & Engravings, Ethnology, Flasks & Bottles, Folk Art, Furniture, Glass, Gold, Hispanic Art, Ivory, Jade, Jewelry, Judaica, Leather, Metalwork, Mexican Art, Miniatures, Oriental Art, Painting-American,

Painting-European, Painting-French, Painting-German, Painting-Israeli, Painting-Italian, Painting-Russian, Period Rooms, Pewter, Photography, Porcelain, Posters, Pre-Columbian Art, Religious Art, Reproductions, Scrimshaw, Sculpture, Silver, Stained Glass, Watercolors, Tapestries, Woodcuts
Collections: Personal collection of Naomi Wilzig, Josephine Baker - Black History Month - Feb 2011
Activities: Lects open to pub; award - Key to the City -enhancing cultural atmosphere; tours; mus shop sells books, prints & giftware

MIAMI LAKES

M **JAY I KISLAK FOUNDATION,** 7900 Miami Lakes Dr W, Miami Lakes, FL 33016. Tel 305-364-4208; Fax 305-821-1267; Email foundation@kislak.com; Web: www.KislakFoundation.org; *Dir* Arthur Dunkelman
Open Mon-Fri by appointment; No admis fee; One large gallery
Collections: Pre-Columbian art & artifacts; rare books & manuscripts, Polar
Publications: Columbus to Catherwood (book)
Activities: Classes for children; open to Miami-Dade County pub schools

NAPLES

M **DEBRUYNE FINE ART,** (Naples Art Gallery), 275 Broad Ave S, Naples, FL 34102-7028. Tel 941-262-4551; Fax 239-262-4051; Email info@debrynefineart.com; Web: www.debruynefineart.com; *Co-Pres* Suzanne DeBruyne; *Co-Pres* Paul DeBruyne
Open Mon - Thurs 10 AM - 5 PM, Fri & Sat 10 AM - 8 PM, Sun Noon - 5 PM; No admis fee; Estab 1965 to present works of prominent American artists for display in home or office; Contains foyer with fountain & four additional gallery rooms & sculpture garden; 4600 sq ft of gallery space; Average Annual Attendance: 15,000
Income: $1,000,000 (financed by sales)
Exhibitions: Jenness Cortez, Marilyn Simandle, EJ Paprocki, Edouard Cortes (1882-1969)
Publications: Exhibit brochures

NORTH MIAMI

M **MUSEUM OF CONTEMPORARY ART,** 770 NE 125th St, North Miami, FL 33161-5654. Tel 305-893-6211; Fax 305-891-1472; Email info@mocanomi.org; Web: www.mocanomi.org; *Registrar* Kim Stillwell; *Dir* Bonnie Clearwater; *Prog Mgr* Jeremy T Chestler
Open Tues - Sat 11 AM - 5 PM, Sun Noon - 5 PM; Admis adults $5, students & seniors $3, under 12, members, and residents free; Estab 1981 to feature national, international & Florida artists; 1 main gallery; Average Annual Attendance: 30,000; Mem: 2000; dues $25-$1,000
Income: Financed by mem, city appropriation, private donations, corporations foundations
Special Subjects: African Art, Afro-American Art, Architecture, Ceramics, Collages, Drawings, Etchings & Engravings, Furniture, Glass, Graphics, Hispanic Art, Jewelry, Landscapes, Latin American Art, Painting-American
Collections: Contemporary Art
Exhibitions: 8-10 rotating exhibits
Publications: Catalogs; newsletter, quarterly
Activities: Classes for adults & children; docent training; lects open to pub; concerts; gallery talks; tours; schols offered; originate traveling exhibs & performances; mus shop sells books, magazines, original art

NORTH MIAMI BEACH

M **ANCIENT SPANISH MONASTERY,** (Saint Bernard Foundation & Monastery), 16711 W Dixie Hwy, North Miami Beach, FL 33160-3714. Tel 305-945-1461; Fax 305-945-4052; Email info@spanishmonastery.com; Web: www.spanishmonastery.com; *Cur* Dr Gregory Mansfield; *Gift Shop Mgr* Carolina Del Vecchio; *Dir Concerts* Herman Whitfield III
Open Mon-Sat 10 AM - 4:30 PM, Sun 11 AM - 4:30 PM; Admis adults $10, seniors $5, student with ID $5, under 5 free; Estab 1133 AD; A reconstruction of a monastery built in Segovia, Spain, in 1133, with original stones brought to the United States by William Randolph Hearst; Average Annual Attendance: 50,000
Income: Financed by members & donations of visitors
Library Holdings: Original Art Works, Original Documents, Photographs, Sculpture
Special Subjects: Historical Material, Religious Art, Medieval Art, Sculpture, Stained Glass
Collections: Historic and Religious Material, paintings, sculpture
Activities: Classes for adults & children; docent training; lects open to the pub; 6-8 vis lectrs per yr; concerts; gallery talks; tours; arts festivals; mus shop sells books, magazines, original art, reproductions, prints, slides, jewelry & religious objects

OCALA

M **COLLEGE OF CENTRAL FLORIDA,** Appleton Museum of Art, 4333 E Silver Springs Blvd, Ocala, FL 34470-5001. Tel 352-291-4455; Fax 352-291-4460; Email ormej@cf.edu; Web: www.appletonmuseum.org; *Dir* Cindi Morrison, Ph.D; *Graphic Design, Web & PR Coordinator* Hjunjee Kramer; *Staff Asst III* Joyce Orme; *Mgr Mem, Events & Fundraisers* Colleen Harper; *Registrar* David Reutter; *Coordr Facilities* Russell Days; *Coordr Finance Servs* Kathleen Balboni; *Asst Dir* Victoria Billig
Open Tues - Sat 10 AM - 5 PM, Sun 12 - 5 PM, cl New Year's Day, Thanksgiving, Christmas; Admis call for fees; Estab 1987; Average Annual Attendance: 50,000
Library Holdings: Book Volumes, Video Tapes
Special Subjects: African Art, Antiquities-Egyptian, Antiquities-Etruscan, Antiquities-Greek, Antiquities-Persian, Antiquities-Roman, Asian Art, Coins & Medals, Drawings, Etchings & Engravings, Flasks & Bottles, Furniture, Glass, Jewelry, Landscapes, Manuscripts, Marine Painting, Painting-American, Painting-European, Painting-French, Photography, Pre-Columbian Art, Prints, Sculpture, Textiles
Collections: Permanent colls of European, American & Contemporary Art, African, Asian & Pre-Columbian artifacts
Exhibitions: Temp exhibs throughout yr
Publications: Artifacts newsletter, 3 times per yr
Activities: Educ progs; classes for adults & children; docent training; lects open to pub; 5-7 visiting lectures per year; guided tours; films; concerts; gallery talks;; Scholarships; Up to 4 traveling exhibitions per year; originates traveling exhibs to other AAM accredited institutions; mus shop sells books, magazines, original art, reproductions, prints

M **FLORIDA STATE UNIVERSITY AND CENTRAL FLORIDA COMMUNITY COLLEGE,** The Appleton Museum of Art, 4333 NE Silver Springs Blvd, Ocala, FL 34470-5000. Tel 352-236-7100; Fax 352-236-7137; Email ormej@of.edu; Web: www.appletonmuseum.org; *Deputy Dir Finance/Admin* Jim Rosengren; *Facilities Dir* Russell Days; *Dir Curatorial Affairs* Dr Leslie Hammond; *Assoc Educ/Vol Coordr* Margie Shambaugh; *Assoc Dir* Sandra Talarico; *Coordr* Colleen Harper
Open Tues - Sat 10 AM - 5 PM, Sun Noon - 5PM; Admis adults $6, seniors & students with ID $4, children under 10 free; Estab 1987 to provide cultural & educational programs; Average Annual Attendance: 50,000; Mem: 3500; dues $15-2500
Income: $1,000,000 (financed by endowment, mem & state appropriation)
Special Subjects: African Art, Antiquities-Egyptian, Antiquities-Etruscan, Antiquities-Greek, Antiquities-Persian, Antiquities-Roman, Asian Art, Bronzes, Carpets & Rugs, Decorative Arts, Furniture, Glass, Islamic Art, Ivory, Jade, Landscapes, Maps, Marine Painting, Medieval Art, Metalwork, Oriental Art, Painting-American, Painting-European, Painting-French, Painting-German, Porcelain, Portraits, Pre-Columbian Art, Religious Art, Sculpture, Textiles, Watercolors
Collections: Appleton Museum of Art Collection, Antiquities, Asian, Pre-Columbian & African, Decorative Arts, European Painting & Sculpture
Publications: Gallery guides; museum catalog; quarterly newsletter
Activities: Educ dept; classes for adults & children; docent training; lects open to pub, 10 vis lectrs per yr; concerts; gallery talks; tours; individual paintings & original objects of art lent to other institutions; lending collection contains books, photographs & slides; book traveling exhibs 8-10 per yr; originate traveling exhibs to state institutions; mus shop sells books, original art, reproductions, posters & jewelry

ORLANDO

M **MENNELLO MUSEUM OF AMERICAN ART,** 900 E Princeton St, Orlando, FL 32803-1437. Tel 407-246-4278; Fax 407-246-4329; Email mennello.museum@cityoforlando.net; Web: www.mennellomuseum.com; *Exec Dir* Shannon Fitzgeraldshannon.fitzgerlad@cityoforlando.net; *Office Mgr* Kim Robinson; *Cur Educ* Geneive Bernard; *Media Coordr* Lindy Sheperd
Open Tues - Sat 10:30 AM - 4:30 PM, Sun Noon - 4:30 PM, cl Mon; Admis adults $5, seniors (55+) & students $4, children under 12 & active military free; Estab 1998; American art; Average Annual Attendance: 27,000; Mem: 300, dues $25 and up
Income: $535,000 (financed by city appropriation) & friends board
Purchases: $50,000
Library Holdings: Auction Catalogs 150, Audio Tapes 1,000, Book Volumes 400, CD-ROMs, Cassettes, Clipping Files, Compact Disks, DVDs, Exhibition Catalogs, Kodachrome Transparencies 400, Manuscripts, Memorabilia, Original Art Works, Original Documents, Pamphlets, Periodical Subscriptions 10, Photographs, Records, Reproductions, Sculpture, Slides, Video Tapes
Special Subjects: Afro-American Art, American Indian Art, American Western Art, Bronzes, Ceramics, Collages, Decorative Arts, Drawings, Etchings & Engravings, Folk Art, Glass, Graphics, Hispanic Art, Landscapes, Painting-American, Photography, Scrimshaw, Sculpture, Silver, Southwestern Art, Textiles, Watercolors, Woodcarvings, Woodcuts, Pottery, Prints
Collections: American Art
Publications: Exhibit catalogs; Members magazine
Activities: Classes for adults & children; dramatic programs; docent training; lects open to pub, 3 vis lectrs per yr; concerts; gallery talks; tours; sponsoring of competitions; book traveling exhibs 3 per yr; originate traveling exhibs to other museums, SAAM, Fenimore; mus shop sells books, magazines, original art work, reproductions, prints & other items

M **ORLANDO MUSEUM OF ART,** 2416 N Mills Ave, Orlando, FL 32803-1483. Tel 407-896-4231; Fax 407-896-9920; Email info@omart.org; Web: www.omart.org; *Cur* Hansen Mulford; *Cur of Educ* Jane Ferry; *Registrar* Andrea Long; *Mktg Dir* Randy Ross; *Grants Mgr* Dan Calleja; *Finance Dir* Dana Dougherty; *Dir* Glen Gentele; *Opers Dir* Alex Garcia; *Opers Mgr* German Silva; *Assoc Cur Educ* Casey Goldman; *Facility Rental Mgr* Casey Hall; *Exec Asst* Morgan Crew; *Mem Mgr* Irene Cardozo; *Develop Dir* Jake White; *Assoc Cur* Azela Santana
Open Tues - Fri 10 AM - 4 PM, Sat & Sun Noon - 4 PM, cl Mon; Admis adults $8, seniors & college students $7, students 6-18 $5; ages 5 & younger and OMA members no charge; Estab 1924 to encourage the awareness of & participation in the visual arts. Accredited by the American Assoc of Museums; 81,884 sq ft mus; seven galleries including exhibitions of 19th & 20th Century American Art, Pre-Columbian & African Art; Average Annual Attendance: 341,066; Mem: 2900; dues $40 & up; annual meeting in Sept
Income: Financed by mem, United Arts of Central Florida, Inc & State of Florida
Library Holdings: Auction Catalogs, Book Volumes, Clipping Files, Exhibition Catalogs, Pamphlets, Periodical Subscriptions
Collections: 19th & 20th Century American painting, sculpture, prints & photography, Pre-Columbian from Central & South America, African Art, Contemporary Art
Publications: Members Magazine, 4 times per year; mem newsletter, 12 times per year; exhibition catalogues

Activities: Educ prog; classes for adults & children; docent training; concerts, gallery talks, tours; schols offered; originate traveling exhibs; mus shop sells books, reproductions, art exhibit & art related merchandise; original art; prints

L **Orlando Sentinel Library**, 2416 N Mills Ave, Orlando, FL 32803-1483. Tel 407-896-4231; Fax 407-896-9920; Email info@omart.org; Web: www.omart.org; *Cur* Hansen Mulford; *Cur of Educ* Jane Ferry; *Registrar* Andrea Long; *Mktg Dir* Randy Ross; *Grants Mgr* Dan Calleja; *Finance Dir* Dan Dougherty; *Dir* Glen Gentele; *Opers Dir* Alex Garcia; *Opers Mgr* German Silva; *Assoc Cur Educ* Casey Goldman; *Facility Rental Mgr* Casey Hall; *Exec Asst* Morgan Crew; *Mem Mgr* Irene Cardozo; *Develop Dir* Jake White; *Assoc Cur* Azela Santana
Open Tues - Fri 10 AM - 4 PM, Sat & Sun Noon - 4 PM, cl Mon & Holidays; Admis adults $8, seniors & students $7, children between 6 & 18 $5; Estab 1924; Average Annual Attendance: 100,000
Library Holdings: Auction Catalogs, Book Volumes 3600, Clipping Files, Exhibition Catalogs, Pamphlets, Periodical Subscriptions 10
Special Subjects: Aesthetics, American Western Art, Art Education, Art History, Ceramics, Decorative Arts, Furniture, Glass, History of Art & Archaeology, Landscape Architecture, Mexican Art, Painting-American, Pre-Columbian Art, Prints, Calligraphy
Collections: Contemporary Art, 19th & 20th Century American painting, sculpture, prints & photography, Pre-Columbian Art from Central & South America, African Art
Activities: Educ prog; classes for adults and children; docent training; lects open to pub; concerts; gallery talks; tours; schols; originate traveling exhibs; mus shop sells books, reproductions, art exhibit & art related merchandise, original art & prints

L **UNIVERSITY OF CENTRAL FLORIDA LIBRARIES,** PO Box 162666, Orlando, FL 32816-2666. Tel 407-823-2564; Fax 407-823-2529; Web: www.library.ucf.edu; *Dir* Barry B Baker; *Assoc Dir Admin* Frank R Allen; *Head of Acquisitions* Mary Page; *Head Spec Coll* Laila Miletic-Vejzovic
Open in spring Mon - Thurs, 7:45 AM - 1 AM, Fri 7:45 AM - 7 PM, Sat 9 AM - 7 PM, Sun Noon - 1 AM; summer Mon - Thurs & Sun, 7:45 AM - 11 PM; Estab 1968
Collections: Bryant West Indies Collection, artifacts, original paintings, rare books, Caribbean Art, Leonardo Nierman Collection

M **VALENCIA COMMUNITY COLLEGE,** Art Gallery-East Campus, 701 N Econlockhachee Trail, Orlando, FL 32825-6404; PO Box 3028, Orlando, FL 32802-3028. Tel 407-299-5000, Ext 2298; Fax 407-249-3943; Web: www.valencia.cc.fl.us; *Pres* Sanford Shugart; *Gallery Cur* David Walsh
Open Mon - Fri 8:30 AM - 4:30 PM; No admis fee; Estab 1982
Income: Financed by state appropriation, grants & private donations
Purchases: $1500
Collections: Permanent collection: Mixed Media, Small Works: Mixed Media
Activities: Individual paintings & original objects of art lent; lending collection contains 250 items; originate traveling exhibs 2 per yr

ORMOND BEACH

M **ORMOND MEMORIAL ART MUSEUM AND GARDENS,** 78 E Granada Blvd, Ormond Beach, FL 32176-6534. Tel 904-676-3347; Fax 904-676-3344; Email omam78e@aol.com; Web: www.ormandartmuseum.org; *Dir* Ann Burt; *Educ Specialist* Jeanne Malloy; *Admin Asst* Vanessa Elliott; *Dir* Susan Tucker
Open Mon - Fri 10AM-4PM; Admis general $2; Estab 1946 to house the symbolic oil paintings of Malcolm Fraser; Four connecting rooms opens to two galleries; Average Annual Attendance: 15,000; Mem: 1000; dues $20-$1,000; monthly meetings & annual meeting in Sept
Income: $238,000 (financed by endowment, mem & city appropriation)
Collections: Malcolm Fraser Symbolic Paintings - permanent collection, Catherine Combs lusterware, Florida landscapes
Exhibitions: Paintings, photography, crafts, sculpture & multi-media exhibits
Publications: Halifax Magazine
Activities: Classes for adults & children; lects open to pub; workshops & children's events; private tours available; gallery tours

PALM BEACH

M **HENRY MORRISON FLAGLER MUSEUM,** 52 Cocoanut Row, Palm Beach, FL 33480-4037; P0 Box 969, Palm Beach, FL 33480-0969. Tel 561-655-2833; Fax 561-655-2826; Email mail@flaglermuseum.us; Web: www.flaglermuseum.us; *Dir* John Blades; *Chief Cur* Tracy Kamerer; *Educ Dir* Allison Goff; *Dir Mem Svcs* Sarah Brutschy; *Facilities Mgr* Bill Fallacaro; *Bus Mgr* Susan Present; *Pub Affairs Dir* David Carson; *Mus Store & Cafe Mgr* Kristen Cahill
Open Tues - Sat 10 AM - 5 PM, Sun Noon - 5 PM, cl Mon; Admis adults $18, youth 13-17 $10, children 6-12 $3, under 6 free, reserved groups 20+ $14; Estab 1959 for preservation & interpretation of the Whitehall mansion, the 1902 residence built for Standard Oil partner & pioneer developer of Florida's east coast, Henry Morrison Flagler; Fifty-five room historic house with restored rooms & special collections, special events & exhibitions. Accredited by the American Assoc of Museums; Average Annual Attendance: 80,000; Mem: 1500; dues $75-$10,000
Income: Financed by endowment, mem & admis
Special Subjects: Architecture, Carpets & Rugs, Decorative Arts, Furniture, Glass, Historical Material, Laces, Painting-American, Painting-European, Period Rooms, Sculpture, Silver, Textiles
Collections: Original family furnishings, china, costumes, furniture, glassware, paintings, silver, sculptures, extensive lace collection, private railcar
Exhibitions: Various temporary exhibits
Publications: Flagler Museum, An Illustrated Guide; Inside Whitehall Magazine, quarterly; exhibit catalogs
Activities: Classes for children; docent training; mentor program; summer camps; lects open to pub; 8 vis lectrs per yr; gallery talks; concerts; tours; books 1-2 traveling exhibs per yr; mus shop sells books, reproductions & prints, gifts

A **THE SOCIETY OF THE FOUR ARTS,** 2 Four Arts Plaza, Palm Beach, FL 33480. Tel 561-655-7227; Fax 561-655-7233; Web: www.fourarts.org; *Pres* Dr David W Breneman; *Exec VPres* Nancy Mato
Open Dec - mid - Apr Mon - Sat 10 AM - 5 PM, Sun 1 - 5 PM; Admis adults $5, children 14 and under free; Estab 1936 to encourage an appreciation of the arts by presentation of exhibitions, lectures, concerts, films & programs for young people & the maintenance of a fine library & gardens; Five galleries for exhibitions, separate general library, gardens & auditorium; Average Annual Attendance: 100,000 (galleries & library); Mem: Dues $1,300 per yr
Income: Financed by endowment, mem, city appropriation toward maintenance of library & contributions
Library Holdings: Auction Catalogs, Audio Tapes, Book Volumes, CD-ROMs, Compact Disks, DVDs, Exhibition Catalogs, Periodical Subscriptions
Publications: Calendar; schedule of events, annual, quarterly newsletter
Activities: Classes for adults & children; programs for young people; dramatic programs; lects open to pub; vis lectrs min 50 per yr; concerts; gallery talks; films; tours

L **Gioconda & Joseph King Library**, 3 Four Arts Plaza, Palm Beach, FL 33480. Tel 561-655-2766; Fax 561-659-8510; Email kinglibrary@fourarts.org; Web: www.fourarts.org; *Art Reference Librn* Nila Bent; *Librn* Joanne Rendon
Open Mon - Fri 10 AM - 5 PM, cl Sat May - Nov; No admis fee; Estab 1936; Circ Non-circulating collection; Mem: Dues $25 family, $12 mems
Income: Financed by endowment, mem & city appropriation
Library Holdings: Auction Catalogs 1,000, Book Volumes 10,000, Exhibition Catalogs 5,000, Periodical Subscriptions 70, Video Tapes 50
Special Subjects: Aesthetics, Afro-American Art, American Indian Art, American Western Art, Antiquities-Assyrian, Antiquities-Byzantine, Antiquities-Egyptian, Antiquities-Etruscan, Antiquities-Greek, Antiquities-Oriental, Antiquities-Persian, Antiquities-Roman, Architecture, Art Education, Art History, Asian Art, Bronzes, Carpets & Rugs, Cartoons, Ceramics, Conceptual Art, Costume Design & Constr, Crafts, Decorative Arts, Dolls, Drawings, Embroidery, Eskimo Art, Etchings & Engravings, Fashion Arts, Folk Art, Furniture, Glass, Graphic Design, Handicrafts, History of Art & Archaeology, Interior Design, Islamic Art, Ivory, Jade, Jewelry, Laces, Landscape Architecture, Landscapes, Latin American Art, Marine Painting, Metalwork, Miniatures, Mixed Media, Mosaics, Oriental Art, Painting-American, Painting-British, Painting-Dutch, Painting-European, Painting-Flemish, Painting-French, Painting-German, Painting-Israeli, Painting-Italian, Painting-Japanese, Painting-Russian, Painting-Scandinavian, Painting-Spanish, Photography, Porcelain, Portraits, Pottery, Primitive art, Printmaking, Prints, Religious Art, Restoration & Conservation, Sculpture, Silver, Silversmithing, Stained Glass, Tapestries, Textiles, Video, Watercolors, Woodcuts
Collections: John C Jessup Collection, Henry P McIntosh Collection, James I Merrill Collection, Addison Mizner Collection: 300+ reference books & scrapbooks
Publications: Booklist, semi annual
Activities: Library tours; 4 vis lectrs per yr; book talks with authors

PANAMA CITY

M **VISUAL ARTS CENTER OF NORTHWEST FLORIDA,** 103 W 5th St, Panama City, FL 32401-2603. Tel 850-769-4451; Fax 850-785-9248; Email vacexhibitions@knology.net; Web: www.vac.org.ch; *Exec Dir* Vicki Middlemas
Open Tues-Sat 10AM-6PM, Sun noon-6PM; Admis adults $3.50, seniors & military $2.50, student $1.50, children under 6, mem & every Tues free; The Center occupies the old city hall, jail & fire station on the corner of Fourth St & Harrison Ave in downtown Panama City. Main gallery hosts contemporary artists, juried competitions & mus coordinated collections. The lower galleries feature emerging artists & community sponsored competitions & collections; Impressions Gallery for children; Average Annual Attendance: 20,000; Mem: 540; family $60, individual $35, student $15
Income: Financed by mem, grants & corporate sponsors
Collections: Permanent collection contains works of artists from Northwest Florida
Exhibitions: Rotating exhibits of all types of art
Publications: Images, newsletter, every 3 months
Activities: Classes for adults & children; docent progs; gallery talks; tours; competitions with prizes; individual paintings & original objects of art lent to bus; book traveling exhibs 2 per yr; junior mus

PEMBROKE PINES

M **BROWARD COMMUNITY COLLEGE - SOUTH CAMPUS,** Art Gallery, 7200 Hollywood Blvd, Bldg 69 Pembroke Pines, FL 33024-7225. Tel 954-201-8895; Fax 954-963-8934; Email directorskbelan@broward.edu; *Gallery Dir* Dr Kyra Belan
Open Mon - Fri 10 AM - 2 PM; No admis fee; Estab 1991 to offer contemporary art exhibs & cultural enrichment activities to col students & to the surrounding community; Gallery is 31 ft x 31 ft with a glass wall & high ceilings
Income: Financed by grants
Exhibitions: Studio Art Club Annual Juried Exhibition
Activities: Lect open to public, 6 vis lectrs per year; competitions

PENSACOLA

A **HISTORIC PENSACOLA PRESERVATION BOARD,** T.T. Wentworth Jr. Florida State Museum, Historic Pensacola Village, 120 Church St Pensacola, FL 32501; PO Box 12866, Pensacola, FL 32576-2866. Tel 850-595-5985; Fax 850-595-5989; Email lrobertson@historicpensacola.org; Web: www.historicpensacola.org; *Interim Exec Dir* Malinda Horton; *Chief Cur* Wanda Edwards; *Bus Mgr* Marsha Clark
Open Tues - Sat 10 AM - 4 PM; Admis adults $6, seniors $5, children 4-16 $2.50; Estab 1967 to preserve, maintain & operate for the educ & enjoyment of the pub certain bldgs & objects of historical interest in Pensacola & the surrounding areas (northwest Florida); Multi-building complex includes two museums & three historic houses; main gallery includes history of develop of West Florida as well as area for temporary exhibits; Average Annual Attendance: 50,000; Mem: 350; dues $35 per year basic family membership
Income: $650,000 from state, supplemented with funding from city & county governments & earned income from rentals, store sales, admissions & memberships

Collections: Archives, costumes, decorative arts, Early 19th & 20th century local artists, Marine lumbering & farming tools & equipment, T.T. Wentworth Jr collection of historical artifacts & documents, Manual G Runyan Art Collection
Activities: Docent training; classes for adults & children; sales shop sells books, reproductions & local crafts; historical toys & souvenirs; Discovery Gallery, 120 Church St Pensacola, FL 32501

M **PENSACOLA MUSEUM OF ART,** 407 S Jefferson St, Pensacola, FL 32502-5901. Tel 850-432-6247; Fax 850-469-1532; Email info@pensacolamuseumofart.org; Web: www.pensacolamuseumofart.org; *Exec Asst* Kate Moloney; *Exec Dir* Melissa Morgan; *Assoc Cur* Leah Griffin; *Educ Coordr* Patrick Jennings; *Registrar & Preparator* Nicholas J Christopher; *Develop Coordr* Kate Sutley; *Exec Dir* Sonya Davis; *Asst to Dir* Hillary Hughes; *Dir Finance* Jessica Hyche; *Interim Educ Coordr* Betsy Walker; *Graphic Design & Mktg Coordr* Amber Johnson; *Patrons' Serv & Vol Coordr* Amy Schnupp
Open Tues - Fri 10 AM - 5 PM, Sat & Sun 12 - 5 PM, cl Mon & national holidays; Admis adults $5, students & military $2, members free; Estab 1954 to further & disseminate art history & some studio instruction with regard to the general pub & to increase knowledge & appreciation thereof; Mus is a historical building, old city jail built in 1908 & has 13,000 sq ft of exhibition area; Average Annual Attendance: 85,000; Mem: 850; dues $20-$500; annual meeting in Oct
Income: Financed by mem
Special Subjects: African Art, Decorative Arts, Etchings & Engravings, Folk Art, Glass, Painting-American, Photography, Portraits, Prints, Watercolors, Woodcuts
Collections: Art, African pieces, contemporary art, glass, 20th & 21st century works, all media
Exhibitions: Changing loan exhibitions
Publications: Quarterly newsletter
Activities: Educ prog; classes for adults & children; docent training; lects open to pub, lectrs varies; gallery talks; tours; individual paintings & original objects of art lent to other mus or galleries; extension prog serves Escambia & Santa Rosa County Schools, Univ of West Florida; book traveling exhibs 9 per yr; originate traveling exhibs to regional mus; mus shop sells books, magazines, original art, reproductions, prints, jewelry, cards, stationery, children's items & puzzles

L **Harry Thornton Library**, 407 S Jefferson St, Pensacola, FL 32501-5901. Tel 850-432-6247; Fax 850-469-1532; Email info@pensacolamuseumofart.org; Web: www.pensacolamuseumofart.org; *VPres* Margaret N Lorren; *Exec Asst* Sandra J Gentry; *Cur Educ* Vivian L Spencer; *Asst Cur & Registrar* Heather Roddenberry; *Exec Dir* Maria Butler
Open Tues - Fri 10 AM - 5 PM, Sat 10 AM - 4 PM, cl Sun & Mon & national holidays; Estab 1968 to provide reference material for public & members; Reference library
Income: Financed by mem, city appropriation & grants by state & federal government
Purchases: $250
Library Holdings: Audio Tapes, Book Volumes 1500, Exhibition Catalogs, Periodical Subscriptions 10, Slides
Special Subjects: Afro-American Art, Glass, Painting-American, Photography, Sculpture
Collections: Complete set of E Benezit's Dictionnaire des Peintres, Sculpteurs, Dessinateurs et Graveurs, Encyclopedia of World Art and other art references books
Publications: Exhibitions catalogs; newsletter, 10 per year
Activities: Classes for adults & children; docent training; lects open to pub, lectrs varies; concerts; gallery talks; purchase & category awards

M **PENSACOLA STATE COLLEGE,** Visual Arts Gallery, Anna Lamar Switzer Center for Visual Arts, 1000 College Blvd, Bldg 15 Pensacola, FL 32504-8998. Tel 850-484-1000, 850-484-2550; Fax 850-484-2564; Email vspencer@pensacolastate.edu; Web: www.pensacolastate.edu/visarts; *Dir* Vivian Spencer
Open Mon - Thurs 8 AM - 9 PM, Fri 8 AM - 3:30 PM, cl weekends; No admis fee; Estab 1970 for educ & curation; Average Annual Attendance: 60,000; Mem: Anna Society $250, $500, $1,000, $50, $24
Income: Financed by state appropriation
Library Holdings: CD-ROMs, Clipping Files, Compact Disks, DVDs, Exhibition Catalogs, Framed Reproductions, Kodachrome Transparencies, Manuscripts, Original Art Works, Original Documents, Other Holdings, Pamphlets, Periodical Subscriptions, Photographs, Prints, Reproductions, Sculpture, Slides, Video Tapes
Collections: Contemporary ceramics, glass, drawings, paintings, prints, photographs, sculpture, student work
Publications: Catalog, brochure or poster for each exhibition
Activities: Educ prog; classes for adults; lects open to pub, lects for mems only; 5 vis lectrs per yr; workshops; gallery talks; tours; competitions with awards given; schols offered; individual paintings & original objects of art lent to other mus & lending collection contains original art works; originates traveling exhibs

M **UNIVERSITY OF WEST FLORIDA,** Art Gallery, 11000 University Pkwy, Bldg 82 Pensacola, FL 32514-5732. Tel 850-474-2696; Email artgallery@uwf.edu; Web: www.uwf.edu/art/art_gallery.cfm; *Dir* Amy Bowman
Open Mon - Tues, Thurs - Fri 10 AM - 5 PM; No admis fee; Estab 1970 to hold exhibitions of contemporary artwork that enhances the educational mission of the university; Galleries include a foyer gallery 10 x 40 ft & a main gallery of 1500 sq ft. It is fully air-conditioned walls are dry wall with full facilities for construction & display; Average Annual Attendance: 14,000
Income: Financed by state appropriation
Special Subjects: Photography, Prints
Collections: Photographs & prints by a number of traditional & contemporary artists
Activities: Lect open to public, 6 vis lectrs per year; gallery talks; tours; films; competitions with awards; films; scholarships offered; individual paintings & original objects of art lent to university offices; book traveling exhibitions

L **Library**, 11000 University Pkwy, Bldg 32 Pensacola, FL 32514-5750. Tel 850-474-2213; Fax 850-474-3338; Email ddebolt@uwf.edu; Web: www.library.uwf.edu/speccoll; *Dir Spec Coll* Dean DeBolt
Open Mon - Fri 8 AM - 4:30 PM; Estab 1967
Income: Financed by state appropriations & Friends of the Library
Library Holdings: Book Volumes 8200, Filmstrips, Memorabilia, Periodical Subscriptions 150
Collections: Includes colls of papers about Gulf Coast artists & art organizations

SAFETY HARBOR

M **SAFETY HARBOR MUSEUM AND CULTURAL ARTS CENTER,** (Safety Harbor Museum of Regional History), 329 Bayshore Blvd S, Safety Harbor, FL 34695. Tel 727-724-1572; Email sschafer@cityof safetyharbor.com; rsandersonsutlen7@tampabay.rr.com; Web: www.safetyharbormuseum.org; *Cur* Robert S Anderson; *Dir* Shannon Schaffer
Open Tues-Wed 10AM-4PM, Thurs 1PM-7:30PM, Fri 10AM-4PM; Admis adults $4, children $2 (12 to 18), seniors & child 7-18 $3; Estab 1977 to promote, encourage, maintain & operate a mus for the preservation of knowledge & appreciation of Florida's history; to display & interpret historical materials & allied fields; Indian art in the form of murals, pottery & artifacts; Average Annual Attendance: 6,500
Income: $2,000 (financed by mem, grants & donations)
Special Subjects: American Indian Art, Archaeology, Dioramas, Historical Material, Maps
Collections: Florida archaeological artifacts & historical memorabilia
Exhibitions: 2-4 Temporary exhibits; rotating art exhibits
Activities: Classes for adults & children; Docent training; lects open to pub, 6-8 vis lectrs per yr; gallery talks; tours; originate traveling exhibs; sales shop sells books & Native American reproductions

SAINT AUGUSTINE

A **CITY OF SAINT AUGUSTINE,** PO Box 210, Saint Augustine, FL 32085-0210. Tel 904-825-5033; Fax 904-825-5096; Email hpht@aug.com; Web: www.historicstaugustine.com; *Cur* John Powell; *Chmn* William R Adams
Open daily 9 AM - 5:15 PM, cl Christmas; Admis to six buildings adults $6.50, students $2.50, children under 6 free; Estab 1959 to depict daily life in the 1740s (Spanish) through its living history mus; Average Annual Attendance: 94,000
Collections: Spanish artifacts, fine & decorative arts, restored & reconstructed colonial buildings from the 18th & 19th centuries
Exhibitions: Permanent & temporary exhibitions
Publications: Brochures & booklets

M **LIGHTNER MUSEUM,** 75 King St, Museum-City Hall Complex, PO Box 334 Saint Augustine, FL 32085. Tel 904-824-2874; Fax 904-824-2712; Email lightner@aug.com; Web: www.lightnermuseum.org; *Cur* Barry W Myers; *Registrar* Irene L Lawrie; *Visitors Svcs* Helen Ballard; *Exec Dir* Robert W Harper III; *VChmn* Edward G Mussallem; *Mus Shop Mgr* Janice Phelan; *Asst to Dir* Helen C Amato; *Bus Mgr* Angela Blankenship
Open 9 AM - 5 PM, cl Christmas; Admis adults $10, students $2, children under 12 free when accompanied by adult; Estab 1948; Average Annual Attendance: 100,000
Income: Financed by admis
Library Holdings: Auction Catalogs, Book Volumes, Clipping Files, Exhibition Catalogs, Memorabilia, Original Art Works, Pamphlets, Periodical Subscriptions 10, Photographs, Prints, Reproductions, Sculpture
Special Subjects: African Art, American Indian Art, Anthropology, Antiquities-Egyptian, Antiquities-Greek, Antiquities-Oriental, Antiquities-Roman, Asian Art, Bronzes, Carpets & Rugs, Ceramics, Coins & Medals, Costumes, Decorative Arts, Dolls, Drawings, Embroidery, Enamels, Etchings & Engravings, Folk Art, Furniture, Glass, Graphics, Hispanic Art, Ivory, Jade, Judaica, Laces, Landscapes, Metalwork, Military Art, Oriental Art, Painting-American, Painting-French, Painting-German, Painting-Italian, Painting-Japanese, Porcelain, Pottery, Sculpture, Silver, Stained Glass, Textiles, Watercolors, Woodcarvings
Collections: 19th century material culture, decorative arts, & fine arts
Publications: Lost Colony: The Artists of St Augustine
Activities: Classes for adults & children; dramatic progs; docent training; concerts; gallery talks; sales shop sells books, magazines & reproductions

A **SAINT AUGUSTINE ART ASSOCIATION AND ART GALLERY,** 22 Marine St, Saint Augustine, FL 32084-4438. Tel 904-824-2310; Fax 904-824-0716; Email info@staaa.org; Web: www.staaa.org; *Pres* Diane Bradley; *Treas* Audra Lester; *Exec Dir* Elyse Brady; *Vpres* Vincent Celestino
Open Tues - Sat Noon - 4 PM, Sun 2 - 5 PM, cl Mon & holidays; No admis fee; Estab 1924, incorporated 1934 as a non-profit organization to further art appreciation in the community by exhibits & educ, also to provide a gallery where artists may show their work & pub & tourists may see them free; 3600 sq ft of exhibition space with carpeted walls & track lighting; Average Annual Attendance: 10,000; Mem: 600; dues $50 & up; annual meeting in Mar
Income: Financed by mem dues, donations, arts & crafts festivals
Library Holdings: Book Volumes, DVDs, Lantern Slides, Original Art Works, Original Documents, Other Holdings Artifacts, Photographs, Sculpture, Video Tapes
Special Subjects: Painting-American
Collections: Donations of art works by St Augustine artists or members representing St Augustine, Permanent Collection of St Augustine-Lost Colony
Exhibitions: Rotating monthly shows on different themes; National juried "Nature & Wildlife" show $5,000 prize money, $2,500 1st place
Activities: Classes for adults & children; docent training; workshops; Mon night sketch group; lect open to public; concerts; gallery talks; tours; competitions with prizes; $300 Best of Show for 9 exhibs; $500 Best of Show for Honors Show; additional cash prizes; concerts, weddings & meetings on a rental basis; original art sales

M **SAINT AUGUSTINE HISTORICAL SOCIETY,** Oldest House Museum Complex, 14 Saint Francis St, Saint Augustine, FL 32084; 271 Charlotte St, Saint Augustine, FL 32084-5033. Tel 904-824-2872; Fax 904-824-2569; Email sahsdirector@bellsouth.net; Web: www.oldesthouse.org; *Dir* Dannie Helm; *Mus Store Mgr* Jean Scerbo; *Library Mgr* Charles Tingley

Open daily 9 AM - 5 PM; cl Christmas Day, Thanksgiving Day, Easter; Admis adults $8, seniors $7, students $4; Estab 1883 to preserve the Spanish heritage of the United States through exhibits in historic mus with collection of furnishings appropriate to the periods in Saint Augustine history (1565 to date); Maintains a research library, rotating exhibits gallery; Average Annual Attendance: 58,000; Mem: 600; dues $35; annual meeting in 3rd Tues in Jan
Income: Financed by admis, grants, endowment, mus store, donations
Library Holdings: Audio Tapes, Book Volumes, Clipping Files, Exhibition Catalogs, Fiche, Manuscripts, Maps, Memorabilia, Motion Pictures, Original Art Works, Original Documents, Pamphlets, Periodical Subscriptions, Photographs, Prints, Slides
Special Subjects: American Indian Art, Anthropology, Archaeology, Architecture, Art Education, Art History, Ceramics, Coins & Medals, Costumes, Decorative Arts, Dolls, Folk Art, Furniture, Glass, Hispanic Art, Historical Material, History of Art & Archaeology, Interior Design, Landscapes, Manuscripts, Maps, Painting-American, Painting-Spanish, Period Rooms, Photography, Porcelain, Portraits, Pottery, Pre-Columbian Art, Reproductions, Sculpture, Silver, Watercolors
Collections: Archaeological material recovered from this area, both aboriginal & colonial, period furnishings: Spanish America (1565-1763 & 1783-1821), British (1763-1783), American (1821-present), materials relating to Florida history
Publications: El Escribano, annual; East Florida Gazette, bi-ann; St Augustine News, bimonthly
Activities: Classes for adults; elder hostels; continuing education for architects & interior designers; summer camp; lects open to pub; gallery talks; tours; 5 vis lectrs per yr; individual paintings lent to mus & galleries; mus shop sells books, reproductions, original art, prints & gift items relating to St Augustine history

L **Library**, 6 Artillery Ln, Saint Augustine, FL 32084; 271 Charlotte St, Saint Augustine, FL 32084. Tel 904-825-2333; Fax 904-824-2569; Email sahslibrary @bellsouth.net; Web: www.oldesthouse.org; *Exec Dir* Susan R Parker, PhD; *Library Dir* Charles Tingley; *Assoc Librn* Judith Foxworth; *Asst Librn* Judy Drapeau
Open Tues - Fri 9 AM - 4:30 PM, 3rd Sat of each month 9 AM - 12:30 PM, cl holidays; No admis fee; 1883; Circ Non-circulating; Research library
Income: Financed by endowment & admis from Oldest House
Library Holdings: Audio Tapes, Book Volumes 10,000, CD-ROMs, Cassettes, Clipping Files, Compact Disks, DVDs, Fiche, Kodachrome Transparencies, Manuscripts, Maps, Memorabilia, Micro Print, Motion Pictures, Original Art Works, Original Documents, Other Holdings Original documents, Pamphlets, Periodical Subscriptions 40, Photographs, Prints, Records, Reels, Reproductions, Sculpture, Slides, Video Tapes
Special Subjects: American Indian Art, Anthropology, Archaeology, Architecture, Art History, Ceramics, Coins & Medals, Costume Design & Constr, Decorative Arts, Etchings & Engravings, Film, Furniture, Glass, Historical Material, History of Art & Archaeology, Manuscripts, Maps, Painting-American, Painting-Spanish, Period Rooms, Photography, Portraits, Posters, Pottery, Prints, Religious Art, Restoration & Conservation, Video, Watercolors, Woodcuts
Collections: Paintings of early artists & of early Saint Augustine, 200 linear feet of maps, photographs, documents & photostats of Spanish archival materials touching directly on Saint Augustine's history during the early Spanish, British & American periods (1565 to present), M J Heade Flower Studies, portraits by Sawer, PA
Publications: East Florida Gazette, semiannually; El Escribano, annually
Activities: Dramatic progs; docent training; Lects open to public, 8 vis lectrs per yr; tours; Historic Community Volunteer Service Award; lend original objects of art to Lightner Museum & Norton Museum of Art; originates traveling exhib to libraries, community ctrs & schools; museum shop sells books, reproductions, prints, slides, jewelry & games

SAINT PETERSBURG

M **FLORIDA CRAFTART,** 501 Central Ave, Saint Petersburg, FL 33701-3703. Tel 727-821-7391; Email info@floridacraftart.org; Web: www.floridacraftart.org; *Exec Dir* Katie Deits; *Bus Mgr* Janie Lorenz; *Develop* Rhonda Sanborn; *Gallery Mgr* Liz Rogers
Open Mon - Sat 10 AM - 5:30 PM, Sun Noon - 5 PM; Estab 1951 to establish fine craft as a serious art form; 2,500 sq ft retail gallery; Mem: dues $30-$5,000
Special Subjects: Ceramics, Woodcarvings, Metalwork, Glass, Jewelry, Mixed Media
Collections: Crafts including clay, fiber, wood, metal, glass, jewelry & mixed media.
Exhibitions: Temporary exhibits
Activities: Workshops; tours

M **MUSEUM OF FINE ARTS, SAINT PETERSBURG, FLORIDA, INC,** 255 Beach Dr NE, Saint Petersburg, FL 33701-3498. Tel 727-896-2667; Fax 727-894-4638; Email webmonkey@fine-arts.org; Web: www.fine-arts.org; *Interim Mus Dir* Roger Zeh; *Chief Cur* Dr Jennifer Hardin; *Interim Cur Educ* John E Schloder; *Dir Devel* Judy Whitney; *Dir Pub Rels* David Connelly
Open Mon - Sat 10 AM - 5 PM; Sun noon - 5 PM; Admis adults $17, seniors $15, youth & college students with ID & youth 7 - 18 $10, mems & children ages 6 & under free; Estab 1962, opened 1965 to increase & diffuse knowledge & appreciation of art; to collect & preserve objects of artistic interest; to provide facilities for research & to offer popular instruction & opportunities for aesthetic enjoyment of art; 25 galleries of works from the collection incl period rooms; Average Annual Attendance: 100,000; Mem: 4000; dues fine arts sustainer $1000, pelican dual $350, pelican single $250, patron $200, family $125, general dual $100, individual $60, educator $45, student $35; annual meeting in May
Income: $1,200,000 (financed by endowment, mem, fundraising, city & state grants) & admis
Purchases: 2.8 million
Library Holdings: Auction Catalogs, Book Volumes, Exhibition Catalogs, Periodical Subscriptions
Special Subjects: African Art, American Indian Art, American Western Art, Antiquities-Assyrian, Antiquities-Byzantine, Antiquities-Egyptian, Antiquities-Etruscan, Antiquities-Greek, Antiquities-Oriental, Antiquities-Persian, Antiquities-Roman, Art History, Asian Art, Bronzes, Ceramics, Decorative Arts, Drawings, Etchings & Engravings, Folk Art, Furniture, Glass, Gold, Hispanic Art, Latin American Art, Painting-American, Painting-British, Painting-Canadian, Painting-Dutch, Painting-European, Painting-Flemish, Painting-French, Painting-German, Painting-Italian, Painting-Japanese, Painting-Spanish, Period Rooms, Pewter, Photography, Portraits, Pre-Columbian Art, Prints, Religious Art, Sculpture, Silver, Watercolors, Woodcuts
Collections: Art: African, Ancient, Asian, Native American & Pre-Columbian, decorative arts, 19th & 20th Century photographs, paintings, Steuben glass, prints, sculpture, 17th, 18th, 19th, & 20th c European Art, 18th, 19th & 20th c American Art
Publications: Mosaic, quarterly newspaper; brochures & exhibition catalogs; catalog of the collection
Activities: Classes for adults & children; docent training; dramatic programs; free admis days; lects open to pub; 4-5 visiting lectrs per yr; films; tours; performing arts; dance; concerts; gallery talks; theatre; storytellers; individual paintings & original objects of art lent to other accredited mus in Greater Tampa Bay Region; artmobile; lending collection contains color reproductions, films on art; originate traveling exhibs to accredited museums and university galleries; mus shop sells books, museum reproductions, prints, mus replicas, jewelry, pottery & crafts by local & national artisans, stationery, cards, children's art educational games & puzzles, t-shirts with museum logo

L **Art Reference Library**, 255 Beach Dr NE, Saint Petersburg, FL 33701. Tel 727-896-2667; Fax 727-894-4638; Web: www.fine-arts.org
Open Tues - Thurs 10 AM - Noon, 1 - 4:45 PM; Estab 1962 as reference library
Income: Financed by grants & contributions
Library Holdings: Book Volumes 25,000, Exhibition Catalogs 3,000, Periodical Subscriptions 25
Special Subjects: Decorative Arts, Painting-American, Painting-British, Painting-Dutch, Painting-European, Painting-Flemish, Painting-French, Painting-Italian, Painting-Spanish, Photography, Sculpture, Gold

M **SALVADOR DALI MUSEUM,** 1 Dali Blvd, Saint Petersburg, FL 33701-3920. Tel 727-823-3767; Fax 727-894-6068; Email info@thedali.org; Web: www.thedali.org; *Exec Dir* Charles (Hank) Hine
Open Mon - Sat 10AM - 5:30PM, Thurs until 8PM, Sun Noon - 5:30PM, cl Thanksgiving & Dec 25, extended hrs between Christmas & New Years; Admis adults $24, seniors, teachers with ID, police, military & firemen $22, students 18 & up with ID & children ages 13-17 $17, children 6-12 $10, children five & under free; Estab 1971 to share the private Dali Collection of Mr & Mrs A Reynolds Morse with the pub; formerly in Cleveland, Ohio, the museum re-opened Mar 7, 1982 in Saint Petersburg, Fla; Average Annual Attendance: 215,000; Mem: 1,500; dues individual $40
Income: Financed by private collector, State University Systems & donations
Collections: 96 oils and 5 large masterworks by Dali make up a retrospective of his work from 1914 to the present, over 100 watercolors & drawings, 1,300 graphics, photographs, sculptures & objects d'art
Publications: Dali Draftsmanship; Guide to Works by Dali in Public Museums; Introduction to Dali; Dali-Picasso; Poetic Homage to Gala-Dali; Dali Primer; Dali's World of Symbols: Workbook for Children; Dali Newsletter; exhibition catalogues
Activities: Adult classes; docent training; lects open to pub, 2 vis lectrs per yr; film series; gallery talks; tours; mus shop sells books, reproductions, prints, slides, postcards

L **Library**, 1 Dali Blvd, Saint Petersburg, FL 33701-3920. Tel 727-823-3767; Fax 727-894-6068; Email info@the dali.org; Web: www.thedali.org; *Deputy Dir & Cur* Joan R Kropf; *Dir* Dr Charles Hine; *Cur Exhibs* Dr William Jeffett; *Deputy Dir* Kathy White; *Mktg* Kathy Grief; *Cur Educ* Peter Tush
Open Mon - Fri 10AM - 5:30 PM, Thurs until 8PM, Sun Noon - 5:30 PM; Admis Adults $21, seniors & military $19, children 13-18 $15, Children 6-12 $7, children 5 & under free, Thurs after 5 pm $5; Estab 1982 for research purposes; Permanent collection & temporary exhibitions; contains 5000 references to Dali in books, periodicals & newspapers; Average Annual Attendance: 300,000; Mem: 1000; dues individual $60; family $100
Income: Financed privately by Salvador Dali Foundation; public/grants
Library Holdings: Auction Catalogs, Audio Tapes, Book Volumes 32, Cassettes, Clipping Files, Compact Disks, DVDs, Exhibition Catalogs, Framed Reproductions 1028, Kodachrome Transparencies 3000, Manuscripts, Memorabilia, Motion Pictures 10, Original Art Works 165, Original Documents, Other Holdings Illustrated editions, Pamphlets, Periodical Subscriptions 20, Photographs, Prints 750, Reproductions, Sculpture, Slides, Video Tapes 50
Collections: Films & Tapes on or by Dali
Publications: Pollock to Pop: America's Brush with Dalí; Jordi Colomer: Arabian Stars
Activities: Classes for adults & children; docent training; jr & teen docent training; lects for members only; 10 vis lectrs per yr; gallery talks; tours; concerts; lending original objects of art to national gallery of Victoria, Melbourne, Australia; artmobile; Urban Recreation Center summer program; mus shop sells books; reproductions; prints & varied items of clothing, mugs, jewelry, etc

SARASOTA

A **ART CENTER SARASOTA,** 707 N Tamiami Trail, Sarasota, FL 34236. Tel 941-365-2032; Fax 941-366-0585; Email lisa@artsarasota.org; Web: www.artsarasota.org; *COO* Sarah Ford; *Develop & Commun* Lisa Berger; *Exec Coordr* Emma Thurgood; *Educ Coordr* Elizabeth Hillmann
Open Tues - Sat 10 AM - 4 PM, cl Sun & Mon; Admis donation $3; Estab 1926, incorporated 1940, to promote the educational & cultural advantages of Sarasota in the field of contemporary art; Four galleries: front galleries for curated shows; 2 galleries curated shows, 1 gallery student shows, 1 gallery juried exhib; Average Annual Attendance: 26,000; Mem: 800; dues $75 & up; annual meeting each Oct
Income: Financed by mem, donations & educ prog
Library Holdings: Book Volumes
Exhibitions: 20 exhibitions annually including curated & member exhibitions - every 6 wks in 4 galleries
Publications: Bulletin, monthly; yearbook
Activities: Classes for adults & children; workshops; lects open to pub; 10 vis lectrs per yr; concerts; gallery talks; tours; demonstrations; sponsoring of competitions;

cash awards for juried shows; scholarships offered; originate traveling exhibs; mus shop sells books, original art, reproductions & prints; members gallery & holiday art bazaar

M **FLORIDA STATE UNIVERSITY,** John & Mable Ringling Museum of Art, 5401 Bay Shore Rd, Sarasota, FL 34243-2161. Tel 941-359-5700; Fax 941-359-5745; Email info@ringling.org; Web: www.ringling.org; *Exec Dir* Steven High; *Chief Registrar* Mari Carpenter
Open daily 10 AM - 5 PM, Thurs until 8 PM, cl Thanksgiving, Christmas & New Year's Day; Admis adults $25, seniors $23, students & children 6-17 $5, active US military $15, FL teachers w ID $10, children under 5 & members free; Estab 1928; Bequeathed to the State of Florida by John Ringling & operated by the state; built in Italian villa style around sculpture garden on 60 plus landscaped acres; original 19th century theater from Asolo, near Venice, in adjacent building; Ringling Residence & Circus Galleries on grounds; Average Annual Attendance: 400,000 paid; Mem: 8,600; dues friend $75, associate $100, contributor $175, sponsor $500, colleague $1,000, curators circle $2,500, directors circle $5,000, chairmen's circle $10,000
Library Holdings: Auction Catalogs, Book Volumes, Exhibition Catalogs, Periodical Subscriptions
Special Subjects: Coins & Medals, Decorative Arts, Drawings, Glass, Painting-American, Painting-British, Painting-Dutch, Painting-European, Painting-Flemish, Painting-French, Painting-German, Painting-Italian, Period Rooms, Photography, Prints, Sculpture, Renaissance Art
Collections: Archaeology of Cyprus, Baroque pictures, especially those of Peter Paul Rubens, developing collection of 19th & 20th century painting, sculpture, drawings & prints, Bickel, Palmer, studio glass, Asian art
Exhibitions: Veronese, Luke DuBois: Now
Publications: Calendar, bi-monthly; Collection Catalogues; Exhibition Catalogues; Newsletter, quarterly
Activities: Educ dept; classes for adults & children; docent training; state services; lects open to public & some for members only; 8 vis lectrs per yr; concerts; gallery talks; tours; fels; exten dept serves the state; individual paintings & original objects of art lent to affiliates & other qualified museums nationally & internationally on board approval; lending collection contains 1000 individual paintings, 1000 objects of art; originate traveling exhibs to affiliates; museum shop sells books, reproductions, prints & slides

L **The John and Mable Ringling Museum of Art Library**, 5401 Bay Shore Rd, Sarasota, FL 34243. Tel 941-359-5700, Ext 2700; Fax 941-360-7370; Email library@ringling.org; Web: www.ringling.org; *Head Librn* Linda R McKee; *Assoc Librn* Artis Wick; *Asst Librn* Megan Oliver; *Cataloguer* Arwen Spinosa
Open Mon - Fri - 5 PM; Estab 1946; Reference only; Mem: Friends of Ringling Mus Library, $100 annual dues
Library Holdings: Auction Catalogs 15,000, Book Volumes 85,000, Clipping Files 5,000, DVDs 300, Exhibition Catalogs, Other Holdings Art auction catalogues; Rare books, Periodical Subscriptions 135, Video Tapes 200
Special Subjects: Art Education, Art History, Asian Art, Ceramics, Drawings, Painting-Dutch, Painting-Flemish, Painting-Italian, History of Art & Archaeology
Collections: John Ringling Library of rare books, circus books, Willy Pogany, Fan Books, James Turrell books; Chick Austin Library, Bickel, Palmer
Activities: Classes for adults & children; book club; lects open to pub; lects for Friends mems; 4 vis lectrs per yr; mus shop sells books & reproductions

M **JMW TURNER MUSEUM,** 930 N Tamiami Trail, Ste 807 Sarasota, FL 34236-4070. Tel 941-343-8320; Email info@jmwturnermuseum.org; Web: jmwturnermuseum.org; *Dir, Stockholm, Sweden* Isis Marina Graham; *Treas, Sarasota, FL* Douglass Montrose-Graem; *Trustee, London* Dr Selby Whittingham; *Trustee, Canada* Bridget Robinson; *Trustee, Sarasota, FL* Senator Bob Johnson; *Trustee* Michael R Pender Jr, CPA; *Webmaster* Ben Gallaher
Open by appointment only; Admis $25; Estab 1973 to promote JMW Turner & Thomas Moran; 501(c)3; Maintains reference library; currently in the process of re-estab a permanent home in Sarasota FL; Mem: over 1000; dues $100, students $5; annual meeting in Dec
Library Holdings: Auction Catalogs, Book Volumes, Cards, Exhibition Catalogs, Original Art Works, Original Documents, Photographs, Prints, Slides, Video Tapes
Special Subjects: American Western Art, American Western Art, Art Education, Art History, Bookplates & Bindings, Carpets & Rugs, Drawings, Etchings & Engravings, Furniture, Graphics, History of Art & Archaeology, Illustration, Landscape Architecture, Landscapes, Manuscripts, Maps, Marine Painting, Marine Painting, Mixed Media, Oriental Art, Painting-American, Painting-American, Painting-British, Painting-European, Photography, Portraits, Posters, Prints, Religious Art, Reproductions, Restorations, Sculpture, Watercolors
Collections: JMW Turner - Works on Paper, Thomas Moran - Works on Paper, Please refer to website for additional colls
Exhibitions: Please see website for mus & galleries
Publications: Turner's Cosmic Optimism; Triple Turner Treat (ebook); Please see website for additional publs
Activities: Classes for adults & children; lects open to pub; concerts; top 99 art mus in America (Atlantic Monthly); organize traveling exhibs to other mus; mus shop sells books & original art; reproductions; prints, A Strong & Mighty Wind by Douglas Graem

L **RINGLING COLLEGE OF ART & DESIGN,** Verman Kimbrough Memorial Library, 2700 N Tamiami Trail, Sarasota, FL 34234. Tel 941-359-7587; Fax 941-359-7632; Email library@ringling.edu; Web: www.lib.ringling.edu; *Visual Resources Librn* Allen Novak; *Technical Servs Librn* Janet Thomas
Open Mon - Thurs 8 AM - 11 PM, Fri 8 AM - 6 PM, Sat Noon - 6 PM, Sun 10 AM - 11 PM; Estab 1931 to serve the curriculum needs of an undergraduate, visual arts col; Circ 38,000; Average Annual Attendance: 78,593
Income: $246,441 (financed by library assoc, parent institution & capital expense)
Purchases: $231,551
Library Holdings: Book Volumes 52,696, CD-ROMs 280, Compact Disks 899, DVDs 8,678, Exhibition Catalogs 345, Other Holdings 129,338 Digital Images, Periodical Subscriptions 295, Video Tapes 394
Special Subjects: Advertising Design, Aesthetics, Afro-American Art, American Indian Art, American Western Art, Anthropology, Archaeology, Architecture, Art History, Asian Art, Bookplates & Bindings, Calligraphy, Cartoons, Commercial Art, Conceptual Art, Decorative Arts, Drawings, Etchings & Engravings, Film, Furniture, Graphic Arts, Graphic Design, History of Art & Archaeology, Illustration, Interior Design, Islamic Art, Landscape Architecture, Landscapes, Latin American Art, Lettering, Mixed Media, Painting-American, Painting-Australian, Painting-British, Painting-Canadian, Painting-Dutch, Painting-European, Painting-Flemish, Painting-French, Painting-German, Painting-Israeli, Painting-Italian, Painting-Japanese, Painting-New Zealand, Painting-Polish, Painting-Russian, Painting-Scandinavian, Painting-Spanish, Photography, Porcelain, Portraits, Posters, Pottery, Pre-Columbian Art, Printmaking, Prints, Sculpture, Southwestern Art, Textiles, Theatre Arts, Video, Watercolors, Woodcuts

STUART

M **HISTORICAL SOCIETY OF MARTIN COUNTY,** Elliott Museum, 825 NE Ocean Blvd, Stuart, FL 34996-1626. Tel 772-225-1961; Fax 772-225-2333; Email info@elliottmuseumfl.org; Web: www.elliottmuseumfl.org; *Pres & CEO* Jennifer Esler; *Cur* Janel Hendrix; *Dir Fin* Amy Martin; *Coll Coordr* LaVaine Wrigley; *Fin Asst / DBA* Kelly Mangan; *Dir Develop* Diane Kimes; *Rental Coordr* Ericah Brinson; *Mem Coordr* Martha Parker
Open daily 10 AM - 5 PM; cl Easter, Thanksgiving & Christmas Day; Admis adult $12, senior, group & military $10, children (2-12 yrs) $6, children under 2 free
Library Holdings: Auction Catalogs, Audio Tapes, Book Volumes, Cards, Clipping Files, DVDs, Exhibition Catalogs, Kodachrome Transparencies, Manuscripts, Maps, Memorabilia, Original Art Works, Original Documents, Pamphlets, Periodical Subscriptions, Photographs, Prints, Records, Sculpture, Slides, Video Tapes
Special Subjects: Painting-American, Archaeology, Decorative Arts, Dolls, Furniture, Glass, Period Rooms
Collections: Contemporary American artists (realistic), Walter Brightwell, Nina D Buxton, Cecilia Cardman, E I Couse, James Ernst, Jo Gabeler, Diana Kan, Hui Chi Mau, Rose W Traines, antiques, Automobiles & historic fashions
Activities: Art classes for adults & children, docent training, annual classic car show; lects open to pub; concerts; yearly lect series; local school tours; art studio & summer art camps; mus shop sells books, reproductions, original art, jewelry, educational toys

TALLAHASSEE

A **FLORIDA DEPARTMENT OF STATE, DIVISION OF CULTURAL AFFAIRS,** Florida Council on Arts & Culture, 500 S Bronough St, RA Gray Bldg Tallahassee, FL 32399-0250. Tel 850-245-6470; Fax 850-245-6497; Web: www.florida-arts.org; Telex 488-5779; *Arts Adminr* Morgan Lewis; *Dir* Sandy Shaughnessy; *Arts Admin* Timothy Storhoff
Open 8 AM - 5 PM; No admis fee; Estab 1969 to advise the Secretary of State in fostering the arts in Florida; Gallery for innovation and the arts
Collections: Florida Department of State Art Collection
Exhibitions: Capitol Complex Exhibition
Activities: Fels offered to individual artists

A **FLORIDA FOLKLIFE PROGRAMS,** 500 S Bronough St, Bureau Historic Preservation Tallahassee, FL 32399-2147. Tel 850-245-6333; Fax 850-922-0496; Email tbucuvalas@dos.state.fl.us; WATS 800-847-7278; *Bureau Chief* Fred Gaske; *Folk Arts Coordr* Dr Tina Bucuvalas; *Folklife Adminr* Gregory Hansen
Open Mon - Fri 9AM-4:30PM, Sat 10AM-4:30PM, Sun noon-4:30PM; No admis fee; Estab 1979 to encourage local folk artisans to appreciate this important art form; The Bureau is under Secretary of Jim Smith & carries on a year-round calendar of folk activities in an effort to encourage statewide pub interests & participation in the folk arts & folklore
Activities: Classes for adults & children; lects open to public; concerts; Florida Folk Heritage Award; apprenticeships offered; originate traveling exhibs

L **Library**, 500 S Bronough St, Grey Bldg, Rm 402 Tallahassee, FL 32399-1800. Tel 850-245-6333; Email blaine.waide@dos.myflorida.com; Web: www.flheritage.com/preservation/folklife; WATS 800-847-7278; *Folk Arts Coordr* Blaine Waide
Open to pub for reference Mon - Fri 8 AM - 5 PM
Library Holdings: Audio Tapes, Book Volumes 500, Cards, Cassettes, Clipping Files, Exhibition Catalogs, Filmstrips, Kodachrome Transparencies, Manuscripts, Original Art Works, Pamphlets, Periodical Subscriptions 10, Photographs, Records, Slides, Video Tapes
Special Subjects: Ethnology, Folk Art
Collections: Folklife
Activities: Folklife apprenticeship prog; Fla Folk Heritage awards; Folklife Days; Music in the Sunshine State radio series

M **FLORIDA STATE UNIVERSITY,** Museum of Fine Arts, 530 W Call St, 250 Fine Arts Building Tallahassee, FL 32306-1140. Tel 850-644-6836; Fax 850-644-7229; Email apalladinocraig@fsu.edu; Web: www.mofa.fsu.edu; *Sr Preparator* Wayne Vonada; *Cur Educ* Viki D Thompson Wylder; *Registrar & Book Designer* Jean Young; *Dir & Ed-in-Chief* Allys Palladino-Craig; *Communs Coordr* Liz McLendon; *Fiscal Officer* Ellen Agrella
Open Mon - Fri 9 AM - 4 PM, Sat & Sun 1 - 4 PM (Fall & Spring semesters); cl school holidays; No admis fee; Estab 1950; Three upper galleries; two lower galleries, one for permanent collection; sculpture courtyard; Average Annual Attendance: 58,000; Mem: 325, friends of the Gallery & Artists' League
Income: Financed by state appropriations, grants & private sector
Library Holdings: Book Volumes 300, Exhibition Catalogs 600, Original Art Works 4000, Prints, Sculpture
Special Subjects: Painting-American, Sculpture
Collections: Asian prints, Carter Collection of Pre-Columbian Art, Walmsley Collection of Historic Prints and contemporary American graphics, photography & paintings, European & American painting, Mooney Collection of West African Art
Publications: Exhibition catalogues; Athanor, art history journal
Activities: Educ dept; docent training; K-12, Senior and adult and special needs audiences; lects open to public, 15 vis lectrs per yr; gallery talks; tours; AAM

accredited; exten dept; individual paintings & original objects of art lent by appropriate request; originate traveling exhibs to museums in Florida and nationally

M **LEMOYNE ART FOUNDATION,** Center for the Visual Arts, 125 N Gadsden St, Tallahassee, FL 32301-1507. Tel 850-222-8800; Fax 850-224-2714; Email curator@lemoyne.org; Web: www.lemoyne.org; *Pres* Kelly Dozier; *Exec Dir* Hillary Brett; *Cur* Lesley Marchessault; *Events, Gift Shop* Sheri Sanderson; *Educ Dir* Amanda Wilke; *Educ Dir* Jennifer Infinger
Open Tues - Sat 10 AM - 5 PM; Sun 1 - 5 PM; cl Mon; Admis adults $1, members & children under 12 free, Sun free; Estab 1964 as a non-profit organization to serve as gallery for contemporary, quality art of Florida artists; sponsor the visual arts in Tallahassee; an educational institution in the broadest sense; Built c. 1840, the Meginniss-Munroe House is home to LeMoyne's five galleries and gallery shop; Average Annual Attendance: 103,881; Mem: 900; dues $30-$5000
Income: Financed by mem, sales, grants & fund raisers
Special Subjects: Afro-American Art, Ceramics, Collages, Crafts, Decorative Arts, Drawings, Painting-American, Portraits, Posters, Pottery, Prints, Sculpture, Stained Glass, Textiles, Watercolors
Collections: Contemporary Artists, Karl Zerbe Serigraphs, Nancy Reid Grunn Encaustics, George Milton
Exhibitions: LeMoyne Holiday Show; Chain of Park's Festival
Publications: Newsletter, bi-monthly; exhibit catalogs
Activities: Classes for adults & children, summer art camp & workshops; lects open to public, 4 vis lectrs per year; gallery talks; tours; competitions; individual paintings and original objects of art lent to bus and members; lending collection contains original art works, original prints; paintings and sculpture; Artisans Gallery sells original fine art, craft items & prints, books

M **TALLAHASSEE MUSEUM OF HISTORY & NATURAL SCIENCE,** 3945 Museum Dr, Tallahassee, FL 32310-6325. Tel 850-575-8684; Fax 850-574-8243; Email rdaws@tallahasseemuseum.org; Web: www.tallahasseemuseum.org; *Dir Educ* Jennifer Golden; *Cur Coll & Exhib* Linda Deaton; *Animal Cur* Michael Jones; *Dir* Russell S Daws
Open Mon - Sat 9 AM - 5 PM; Sun 12:30 - 5 PM; Admis adults $9, seniors & students with ID $8.50,children 4-15 $6, members free; Estab 1957 to educate children & adults about natural history, native wildlife, North Florida history, art & culture; Facilities include 1880's farm, historic buildings, exhibit & class buildings, 40 acres of nature trails & animal habitats; Average Annual Attendance: 120,000; Mem: 5000; dues $60; annual meeting third Thurs in Oct
Income: $1,900,000 (financed by mem, fundraisers, admis & government appropriation)
Special Subjects: Archaeology, Architecture, Ceramics, Costumes, Crafts, Folk Art, Historical Material, Period Rooms, Pottery, Reproductions, Decorative Arts, Dolls, Embroidery
Collections: Pre-Columbia Florida Indian Pottery, historic buildings, furnishings, natural history & science
Exhibitions: Changing exhibit on art, clothing, crafts, history & science; permanent or semi-permanent (3 years) exhibits on local history & natural history
Publications: Newsletter, monthly
Activities: Classes for adults & children; docent training; lects open to pub, 8-12 vis lectrs per yr; concerts; gallery talks; tours; scholarships offered; extension prog serves North Florida, South Georgia & Southeastern Alabama; mus shop sells books & original art

L **Museum**, 3945 Museum Dr, Tallahassee, FL 32310. Tel 850-575-8684; Fax 850-574-8243; Email rdaws@tallahasseemuseum.org; Web: www.tallahasseemuseum.org; *CEO & Exec Dir* Russell S Daws; *Chief Cur* Linda Deaton
Open Mon - Sat 9 AM - 5 PM, Sun 11 AM - 5 PM; Admis adults $9, children $6; Estab 1957; Open to members; historical bldgs; Average Annual Attendance: 130,000; Mem: 4,000 mems; dues range from $25 - $1,000
Income: $2,560,158 (financed by earned income, donations, grants & special events)
Purchases: $2,523,633
Library Holdings: Book Volumes 500, Periodical Subscriptions 12
Special Subjects: Afro-American Art, Anthropology, Architecture, Ceramics, Costume Design & Constr, Decorative Arts, Dolls, Folk Art, Historical Material, Period Rooms, Photography, Pottery, Prints, Textiles
Collections: Ivan Gundrum Pre-Columbian Florida Indian Artifacts (reproductions) representing the Weeden Island culture 500 - 1500 AD, 14 historic structures of regional significance, 8,500 historical artifacts & natural history specimens, Natural Science Colls, Living Colls
Publications: Monthly Tallahassee Museum Newsletter
Activities: Classes for adults & children; concerts; 2-5 book traveling exhibs; 2-6 book traveling exhibs per yr; mus shop sells books

TAMPA

C **CASPERS, INC,** Art Collection, 4908 W Nassau St, Tampa, FL 33607-3827. Tel 813-287-2231; Fax 813-289-7850; *Pres* Chuck Peterson; *Mktg Mgr* Steve Scott; *CEO* Joseph Casper
Open Mon - Fri 8 AM - 5 PM; Estab 1981 to enhance the employees' environment
Collections: Collection features works by artists with some relationship to Florida

A **CITY OF TAMPA,** Public Art Program, 306 E. Jackson St, Tampa, FL 33602-5208. Tel 813-274-8531; Fax 813-274-8732; Email robin.nigh@tampagov.net; *Admin* Robin Nigh
Estab 1985 to visually enhance & enrich the public environment for both residents & visitors of Tampa; Mem: Public Art Comt meets monthly
Collections: wide variety of public art
Publications: Public Art Brochure; Save Outdoor Sculpture

M **TAMPA MUSEUM OF ART,** 120 W Gasparilla Plz, Tampa, FL 33602-1500. Tel 813-274-8130; Fax 813-274-8732; Web: www.tampamuseum.com; *Chief Cur* Elaine Gustafson; *Preparator* Bob Hellier; *Registrar* Devon Larsen; *Dir* Ken Rollins; *Cur Educ* Dawn Johnson; *Dev* Steve Klihdt; *Mktg* Meredith Elarfi
Open Tues, Wed, Thurs, Fri & Sat 10 AM - 5 PM, Sun 11 AM - 5 PM; Admis adults $8, seniors $7, students & children 6-18 $3, under 6 free; Estab 1970 to educate the pub through the display of art; 7 galleries with antiquities, sculpture, photography & paintings; Average Annual Attendance: 82,500; Mem: 1950; dues $35
Income: $2,400,000 (financed by local government, grants, mem & contributions)
Library Holdings: Auction Catalogs, Exhibition Catalogs, Periodical Subscriptions
Special Subjects: Antiquities-Etruscan, Antiquities-Greek, Antiquities-Roman, Bronzes, Ceramics, Coins & Medals, Crafts, Drawings, Etchings & Engravings, Folk Art, Glass, Latin American Art, Painting-American, Photography, Prints, Sculpture, Textiles, Watercolors, Woodcuts
Collections: Greek & Roman antiquities, 20th - 21st century painting, sculpture & photography, 19th century photography & sculpture, C Paul Jennewein Collection, Otto Neumann Collection
Exhibitions: Rotating exhibits every 8-10 weeks
Publications: Catalogs; Newsletter, bi-monthly; school calendar
Activities: Classes for adults & children; docent training; films; workshops; lects open to pub; concerts; gallery talks; tours; individual paintings & original objects of art lent to fellow mus; book traveling exhibs 10 per yr; originate traveling exhibs to other mus; mus shop sells books, original art, reproductions, prints, jewelry, toys, t-shirts, cards & stationary

L **Judith Rozier Blanchard Library**, 120 W Gasparilla Plz, Tampa, FL 33602-1500. Web: www.tampamuseum.org; *Cur Educ* Dawn Johnson
Open by appt. Contact the curatorial staff of the museum; No admis fee; For reference only
Library Holdings: Book Volumes 7801, Exhibition Catalogs 700, Other Holdings CD ROM programs, Pamphlets, Periodical Subscriptions 32, Slides
Publications: Art Muse Quarterly Newsletter
Activities: training

M **UNIVERSITY OF SOUTH FLORIDA,** Contemporary Art Museum, 4202 E Fowler Ave, CAM 101 Tampa, FL 33620-0007. Tel 813-974-4133; Fax 813-974-5130; Email caminfo@arts.usf.edu; Web: www.arts.usf.edu/museum; *Dir* Margaret A Miller; *Deputy Dir* Alexa A Favata
Open Mon - Fri 10 AM - 5 PM, Sat 1 - 4 PM; No admis fee; Estab 1961 to provide exhibitions of contemporary art; Mus located on W Holly Dr on Tampa Campus; Average Annual Attendance: 55,000; Mem: dues corporate $1000-$100,000, private $5-$1000
Income: Financed by state appropriation, grants, mem fees & corporate art program
Special Subjects: African Art, Drawings, Painting-American, Photography, Posters, Pre-Columbian Art, Prints, Sculpture
Collections: African art, Pre-Columbian artifacts, art bank collection of loan traveling exhibitions (approx 60 small package exhibitions), contemporary photography, contemporary works on paper, painting, sculpture
Publications: Exhibition catalogs
Activities: Docent training; lects open to pub, 4 vis lectrs per yr; gallery talks; tours; through Art Bank program original prints are lent to institutions, universities & arts organizations; book traveling exhibs 2 per yr; originate traveling exhibs to universities, galleries & colleges; mus shop sells books, magazines, artists' created jewelry, architecture related products

L **Library**, 4202 E Fowler Ave LIB 122, Tampa Campus Tampa, FL 33620-5400. Tel 813-974-2729; Fax 813-974-9875; Web: www.lib.usf.edu; *Adminr* Jim Gray; *Art Reference Librn* Ilene Frank
Open Mon - Thurs 7:30 AM - 1 AM, Fri 7:30 AM - 9 PM, Sat 10 AM - 8 PM, Sun Noon - 1 AM; Open to students & pub
Income: Financed by state appropriations & grants
Library Holdings: Audio Tapes, Book Volumes 930,000, Cards, Cassettes, Clipping Files, Fiche, Filmstrips, Framed Reproductions, Manuscripts, Motion Pictures, Pamphlets, Periodical Subscriptions 5450, Photographs, Prints, Reels, Reproductions, Video Tapes
Special Subjects: Historical Material
Collections: Rare art books

M **UNIVERSITY OF TAMPA,** Henry B Plant Museum, 401 W Kennedy Blvd, Tampa, FL 33606-1450. Tel 813-254-1891, Ext 22; Web: www.plantmuseum.com; *Cur & Registrar* Susan Carter; *Museum Relations* Jeannette Twachtmann; *Cur Educ* Amy Franklin-David; *Museum Store Mgr* Sue Gauthier; *Dir* Cynthia Gandee; *Mgr Operations & Mem* Heather Brabham; *Cur Asst* Alexandra Fernandez
Open Tues - Sat 10 AM - 4 PM, Sun Noon - 4 PM, cl holidays; Admis suggested donation $5 & $2 for children under 12; Estab 1933 in the former Tampa Bay Hotel built in 1891, to explain the importance of the Tampa Bay Hotel & Henry Plant to the area; This building which contains Victorian furnishings & artifacts, original to the Tampa Bay Hotel, is now on the register as a National Historical Landmark built by the railroad industrialist H B Plant; Average Annual Attendance: 25,000; Mem: 500
Income: Financed by city appropriation, University of Tampa, mem & donations
Special Subjects: Furniture, Porcelain
Collections: Late Victorian furniture & objects d'art of same period, Venetian mirrors, Wedgwood, Oriental porcelains
Exhibitions: Exhibits relating to 19th century life; Plant system railroads & steamships, Annual Christmas Stroll
Publications: Henry B Plant Museum, Today & Moments In Time, a pictorial history of the Tampa Bay Hotel; Tampa Bay Hotel: Florida's First Magic Kingdom (video); member newsletter, quarterly; series of Jean Stallings; educational series about Henry Plant & Victorian period
Activities: Docent training; lects open to pub & lects for members only; mus store sells books, original art reproductions, Victorian style gifts, antique estate jewelry, estate silver, linens

M **Scarfone/Hartley Gallery**, 401 W Kennedy Blvd, Tampa, FL 33606-1450. Tel 813-253-6217; Fax 813-258-7497; Email dcowden@ut.edu; Web: www.utarts.com; *Dir of Galleries* Dorothy Cowden; *Pres of the Univ* Ron Vaughn
Open Tues - Fri 10 AM - 4 PM, Sat 1 - 4 PM, cl June - July; No admis fee; Estab 1977 to exhibit works of art as an extension of the classroom & to utilize the space for pub functions which would benefit from the artistic environment created by showing current trends of all art forms of artistic merit; 4,000 sq ft of exhib space; Average Annual Attendance: 12,000; Mem: 75; donation dues $25-$1000
Income: Financed by donations & fundraisers

Collections: Contemporary artists
Exhibitions: Studio F; Electronics Alive - Biennial digital invitational
Publications: Exhibition brochures, 10 times a yr
Activities: Classes for adults; lects open to pub; 10 vis lectrs per yr; gallery talks; student annual juried awards; scholarships offered; lend artwork to other art or educational institutions; lending collection contains 100 pieces of original art; originate traveling exhibs to mus & galleries

TEQUESTA

M **LIGHTHOUSE ARTCENTER MUSEUM & SCHOOL OF ART,** 373 Tequesta Dr, Gallery Sq N Tequesta, FL 33469-3027. Tel 561-746-3101; Email info@lighthousearts.org; Web: www.lighthousearts.org; *Exec Dir & School of Art Interim Dir* Katie Deits; *Dir Finance* Julie Alexander; *Dir Events* Sheila McDonald-Bell; *Cur & Asst to Dir* Barbara Broidy; *Educ Coordr* Robyn D Eckersley; *School of Art Admin Asst* Penny Robb; *Instruction & Youth Progs* Cara McKinley; *Visitor Relations* Sheri Gancz; *Visitor & Vol Relations* Evelyne Bates; *Mem Data Mgt* Sarah Nastri
Open Mus Mon-Fri 10 AM - 4 PM, Sat 10 AM - 2 PM; School of Arts Mon - Sat 9 AM - 5 PM; Admis mus: $5 for non-mems, free for mems,; Estab 1964 to create pub interest in all forms of the fine arts; Average Annual Attendance: 90,000; Mem: 1,000; dues $75; annual meeting in Oct
Income: financed by membership, donations, grants
Library Holdings: Book Volumes
Special Subjects: Calligraphy, Ceramics, Collages, Drawings, Landscapes, Painting-American, Photography, Pottery, Sculpture, Watercolors, Art History, Painting-American, African Art
Collections: Museum Coll of paintings & sculpture
Exhibitions: Temporary & traveling exhibitions; Celebration of the Arts juried exhibit
Publications: Calendar of Events, monthly; Newsletter, quarterly
Activities: Classes for adults & children; docent training; workshops; Formal Beaux Art Ball; lects open to pub, 6 vis lectrs per year; concerts; gallery talks; tours; competitions with awards; scholarships offered; organize traveling exhibs to art centers & mus; mus shop sells books, original art, greeting cards & ceramics

L **Not Profit Art Center,** 373 Tequesta Dr, Gallery Sq N Tequesta, FL 33469-3027. Tel 561-746-3101; Fax 561-746-3241; Email info@lighthousearts.org; Web: www.lighthousearts.org; *Exec Dir* Katie Deits
Open Mon - Sat 10 AM - 4:30 PM; Library estab 1964; Exhibitions, cultural events, museum store; Average Annual Attendance: 50,000; Mem: $75 & up annually
Income: financed by membership, donations, sponsorships & grants
Library Holdings: Book Volumes 600, Clipping Files, Exhibition Catalogs, Original Art Works, Pamphlets, Periodical Subscriptions 10, Prints
Special Subjects: Ceramics, Landscapes, Painting-American, Watercolors
Collections: Permanent collection of American artists
Activities: Educ prog; classes for adults & children; docent training; artbridge outreach; lects open to pub; 1,500 vis lectrs per year; concerts; gallery talks; tours; sponsoring of competitions; schols offered; mus shop sells original art

VALPARAISO

M **HERITAGE MUSEUM ASSOCIATION, INC,** The Heritage Museum of Northwest Florida, 115 Westview Ave, Valparaiso, FL 32580-1387. Tel 850-678-2615; Fax 850-678-4547; Email heritagemuseum@co.okaloosa.fl.us; Web: www.heritage-museum.org; *Exec Dir* Michelle A Severino; *Adminr Mgr* Gina Marini; *Curatorial Asst* Michael Weech
Open Tues - Sat 10AM-4PM; Admis adults $2; HMNF members & children under 4 free; Estab 1971 to collect, preserve, & display items related to the history & develop of the area; Average Annual Attendance: 19,000; Mem: 240; dues senior & student $15; individual $35; family $50
Income: $50,000 (financed by mem, city & county appropriation, fundraising & donations)
Library Holdings: Audio Tapes, Cassettes, Compact Disks, DVDs, Manuscripts, Maps, Memorabilia, Original Art Works, Original Documents, Other Holdings, Photographs, Prints, Records, Reproductions, Video Tapes
Special Subjects: American Indian Art, Anthropology, Archaeology, Crafts, Dolls, Embroidery, Folk Art, Glass, Historical Material, Laces, Maps, Pottery, Silver, Textiles
Collections: Paleo & archaic stone artifacts, pioneer household utensils, agricultural implements, artisans' tools, tools used in the turpentine & lumber industries, photos & files of research materials, Art History, Flasks & Bottles, Handicrafts, Paleo & Archaic Stone Artifacts
Publications: Heritage Press electronic newsletter; Teacher's Resource & Field Trip Guide
Activities: Adult & children's classes; docent progs; lects open to pub & for mems, 6 vis lectrs per yr; original objects of art lent to mus & for special school & college exhibits; book traveling exhibs, 4 per yr; originate traveling exhib; mus shop sells books, magazines, original art, prints & original handcrafts

VENICE

M **VENICE ART CENTER,** 390 Nokomis Ave S, Venice, FL 34285-2416. Tel 941-485-7136; Fax 941-484-4361; Email info@veniceartcenter.com; Web: www.veniceartcenter.com; *Exec Dir* Mary Moscatelli; *Prog Coordr* Carol Sikora
Open Mon - Sat 9 AM - 5 PM; Estab 1956 to foster an appreciation for visual arts in the community & provide educational resources; 5,000 sq ft; Mem: dues student $20, individual $65, couple $75, family $100
Library Holdings: 1,000 art & fine craft books
Special Subjects: Jewelry, Ceramics, Drawings, Photography, Watercolors, Sculpture, Pottery
Collections: Visual arts by local artists
Exhibitions: Temporary exhibits
Activities: Educ progs; classes for adults & children; teacher training, outreach & resources; lects open to pub; art programming; workshops; integrated art events; events

VERO BEACH

M **VERO BEACH MUSEUM OF ART,** 3001 Riverside Park Dr, Vero Beach, FL 32963-1874. Tel 772-231-0707; Fax 772-231-0938; Email info@verobeachmuseum.org; Web: www.verobeachmuseum.org; *Exec Dir* Lucinda H Gedeon PhD; *Dir Educ* J Marshall Adams; *Dir Develop* Robyn P Orzel; *Cur Coll & Exhibs* Jay Williams; *Registrar* Dana Twersky; *Mus Store Mgr* Jo Anne Miller; *Dir Mktg & Communs* Sophie Bentham Wood
Open Memorial Day to Labor Day Tues - Sat 10 AM - 4:30 PM, Sun 1 - 4:30 PM, Sept - May Mon - Sat 10 - 4:30 PM, Sun 1 - 4:30 PM, cl New Year's Day, Memorial Day, Independence Day, Labor Day, Thanksgiving, Christmas Day; Admis call for fees; Estab 1986; Average Annual Attendance: 82,000; Mem: 5390; annual meeting in Apr
Library Holdings: Auction Catalogs, Audio Tapes, Book Volumes 5,000, DVDs, Exhibition Catalogs, Periodical Subscriptions
Special Subjects: Bronzes, Collages, Drawings, Etchings & Engravings, Glass, Painting-American, Photography, Portraits, Prints, Sculpture, Watercolors, Woodcuts
Collections: 20th-century American art & European art, 21st-century American & International art
Publications: exhibition catalogues; quarterly magazine; annual report; public programs brochures; class schedule; e-newsletter
Activities: Classes for adults & children; docent training; Art instructional studios; museum school; lects open to pub; lects for mems only; arts festivals; guided tours; concerts; gallery talks; sponsor competitions; schol; awards, accredited by Amer Assoc of Mus; lends original objects of art to other museums; originates traveling exhibs to various members of AAM & AAMD; mus shop sells books, art related items, children's toys & gifts

WEST PALM BEACH

M **HISTORICAL SOCIETY OF PALM BEACH COUNTY,** The Richard and Pat Johnson Palm Beach County History Museum, 300 N Dixie Hwy, Suite 471 West Palm Beach, FL 33401; PO Box 4364, West Palm Beach, FL 33402-4364. Tel 561-832-4164; Fax 561-832-7965; Email info@historicalsocietypbc.org; Web: www.hspbc.org; *Dir Research & Archives* Debi Murray; *Office Mgr* Sharon Poss; *Pres & CEO* Jeremy W Johnson CAE; *Cur Colls* Benjamen Salata; *Cur Educ* Rose Gualtieri; *Dir Mktg & Special Events* Jillian Markwith; *Dir Research* Nicholas Golubov; *Mem Assoc* Lise Steinhauer
Open Tues - Sat 10 AM - 5 PM; No admis fee; Estab 1937 to preserve & disseminate history of Palm Beach County; Average Annual Attendance: 12,000; Mem: 1000; dues $50-$2,500; annual meeting in Apr
Income: $900,000 (financed by mem, donations & grants)
Library Holdings: Audio Tapes, Book Volumes, CD-ROMs, Clipping Files, Framed Reproductions, Manuscripts, Maps, Memorabilia, Original Art Works, Original Documents, Pamphlets, Photographs, Prints, Records
Special Subjects: Archaeology, Architecture, Historical Material, Manuscripts
Collections: Addison Mizner architectural drawings, History of Palm Beach County, other local architect drawings
Publications: Tustenegee
Activities: Docent training; lects open to public, 5 vis lectrs per year; tours; Judge James R Knott Award for excellence in historical research-public history; Fannie James Award; original objects of art lent to qualified non-profit organizations; lending collection contains film strips, framed reproductions, original art works, original prints, photographs, slides & artifacts from permanent collection; traveling trunks; civic tabs; mus shop sells books, reproductions, original art, prints & gift items

M **NORTHWOOD UNIVERSITY,** Jeannette Hare Art Gallery, 2600 N Military Trail, Turner Education Bldg West Palm Beach, FL 33409-2999. Tel 561-478-5538; Fax 561-640-3328; *Arts Coordr* Samara Strauss; *Mus Shop Mgr* Katherine Kress
Open Mon-Fri 9AM-6PM, Sat & Sun noon-6PM; No admis fee; Estab 1959 to provide aesthetic, creative & spiritual elements as part of a bus education; Average Annual Attendance: 10,000
Collections: Art About the Automobile, International Costume Collection, Tamassy Collection of Old Masterworks on Paper, Wally Findlay Collection
Publications: Arts Report, annual; exhibition catalogues
Activities: Lects open to pub, 4 vis lectrs per year; book traveling exhibitions 3-4 per year

M **NORTON MUSEUM OF ART,** 1451 S Olive Ave, West Palm Beach, FL 33401-7162. Tel 561-832-5196; Email info@norton.org; Web: www.norton.org; *Exec Dir & CEO* Hope Alswang; *Cur Chinese Art* Laurie Barnes; *Dir Curatorial Affairs, Cur Contemporary Art* Cheryl Brutvan; *Cur Photography* Tim Wride; *Cur Educ* Glenn Tomlinson; *Assoc Cur Educ* Erica Ando; *Asst Curatorial* Rachel Gustafson; *Dir Communs* Scott Benarde; *Cur American Art* Ellen Roberts
Open Tues - Wed & Fri - Sun noon - 5 PM, Thurs noon - 9 PM, cl Mon & major holidays; No admis fee; Estab 1941 by Ralph and Elizabeth Norton to present exhibition related lectures, concerts, and programs for children & adults; Over 30 galleries displaying the permanent collection & special exhibs; Average Annual Attendance: 100,000; Mem: 11,000
Income: Financed by endowment, mem, city appropriation, Palm Beach County Tourist Develop Council, donations & fundraising events
Library Holdings: Book Volumes 3,800, Exhibition Catalogs, Kodachrome Transparencies, Memorabilia, Pamphlets, Periodical Subscriptions 30, Photographs
Collections: Norton Museum of Art mems magazine
Publications: Exhibition catalogs; Visions magazine, 3 times per yr; Images magazine, 6 times per yr
Activities: Educ dept; classes for adults & children; family & youth progs; dramatic progs; docent training; internships; teacher resources; lects open to pub, lects for

mems only, 8 vis lectrs per yr; films; concerts; gallery talks; general tours; adult tours; competitions with awards; IMLS Medal of Honor; individual paintings & original objects of art lent to mus around the world; PACE progressive after school community arts education; books traveling exhibs 3-5 per yr; originate traveling exhibs; mus shop sells books, magazines, reproductions, prints & slides

M **ROBERT & MARY MONTGOMERY ARMORY ART CENTER,** Armory Art Center, 1700 Parker Ave, West Palm Beach, FL 33401. Tel 561-832-1776; Fax 561-832-0191; Email workshops@armoryart.org; Web: www.armoryart.org; *Acting Exec Dir* Nancy Albano Lambrecht; *Dir Mktg* Jeanne Martin; *Dir Exhibs* Hans Evers
Open Mon-Fri 10AM-4PM, Sat 10AM-2PM, cl Sun; Admis $5 suggested donation; Estab 1986; 3 galleries showing local, national & international artists; Average Annual Attendance: 5,000; Mem: dues student $25, individual $50
Exhibitions: (see website)
Activities: Educ prog; classes for adult & children; lects open to pub; 20-30 vis lectrs per yr; gallery talks; tours; museum shop sells original art

M **SOUTH FLORIDA FAIR,** Yesteryear Village, 9067 Southern Blvd, South Florida Fair West Palm Beach, FL 33421; PO Box 210367, West Palm Beach, FL 33421-0367. Tel 561-790-5232; Fax 561-753-2124; Web: www.southfloridafair.com/yesteryearvillage.html; *CEO & Dir* Rick Vymlatil; *VPres & COO* Vicki Chouris; *VPres & COO* Matt Wallsmith; *VPres & CFO* Carol Hammond
Open Tues - Sun 10 AM - 5 PM; Office Hours: Mon - Fri 9 AM - 5 PM; Nov 2015 - March 2016 call for hours; Admis adults $10, seniors $7, children $5, under age 5 free; Estab 1990; mus contains 30 restored bldgs, schoolhouse, church, blacksmith, gen store & more

WHITE SPRINGS

M **FLORIDA DEPARTMENT OF ENVIRONMENTAL PROTECTION,** Stephen Foster Folk Culture Center State Park, 11016 Lillian Saunders Dr, Hwy 41, White Springs, FL 32096; PO Drawer G, White Springs, FL 32096. Tel 386-397-2733; Fax 386-397-4262; Web: www.floridastateparks.org/stephenfoster; *Park Mgr* Manny Perez; *Event Coordr* Elaine McGrath; *Park Svc Specialist* Andrea Thomas; *Asst Park Mgr* Stephanie McClain
Open 8 AM - Sunset daily; Admis per vehicle $5 up to 8 people, children under 6 free, each additional passenger $2; Estab 1950 as a memorial to Stephen Collins Foster; operated by the State of Florida Dept of Environmental Protection, Division of Recreation & Parks; Mus contains eight dioramas of Foster's best known songs. The North wing holds a collection of 19th century furniture & musical instruments; the 200 foot tall Foster Tower, world's largest tubular bell system and a collection of pianos; Average Annual Attendance: 100,000
Special Subjects: Dioramas, Folk Art, Furniture, Jewelry, Period Rooms, Historical Material
Collections: Dioramas, furniture, minstrel materials, musical instruments, pianos
Activities: Classes for adults & children; numerous events & workshops; lects open to pub; concerts; tours; awards; sales shop sells books, original art, prints, crafts, handmade items, music, jellies, jams & honey

WINTER PARK

M **ALBIN POLASEK MUSEUM & SCULPTURE GARDENS,** 633 Osceola Ave, Winter Park, FL 32789-4429. Tel 407-647-6294; Fax 407-647-0410; Email info@polasek.org; Web: www.polasek.org; *Exec Dir* Debbie Komanski; *Operations Coordinator* Marnie Vanture; *Cur* Rachel Frisby; *Development Coordinator* Lane Epps; *Events Coordinator* Kim Ruffler
Open year-round, Tues - Sat 10 AM - 4 PM, Sun 1 PM - 4 PM;; Admis adults $5, seniors $4, student $3, mem & under 12 free; Estab 1961 to promote legacy of internationally known sculptor Albin Polasek; Retirement home, galleries and pvt chapel in a 3 acre sculpture garden; Average Annual Attendance: 21,000; Mem: dues student/teacher& senior $35, individual $45, family $100; dual $65
Income: $200,000 (financed by endowment, mem & gifts)
Purchases: $3000
Library Holdings: Book Volumes, Periodical Subscriptions
Special Subjects: Painting-American, Painting-European, Sculpture, Bronzes, Drawings, Furniture, Historical Material, Portraits, Religious Art, Reproductions, Stained Glass, Woodcarvings
Collections: Sculpture of Albin Polasek, Works of Augustus St Gaudens, Charles Grafly, Alphonse Mucha & Charles Hawthorne, Sculpture by Ruth Sherwood
Publications: On View Newsletter
Activities: Classes for adults & children; docent training; lects open to pub; gallery talks; tours; concerts; mus shop sells books, original art, reproductions, prints, note cards, magnets & Moravian items

A **ARCHITECTS DESIGN GROUP INC,** 333 N Knowles Ave, Winter Park, FL 32789; PO Box 1210, Winter Park, FL 32790-1210. Tel 407-647-1706; Fax 407-645-5525; Email adg@adgusa.org; Web: www.adgusa.org; *Pres* I S K Reeves V FAIA; *Mktg Dir* Tonya Cranin
Open by appointment 9 AM - 3 PM; Estab 1971 to exhibit Native American antique art; Corporate headquarters for architecture firm
Collections: Antique American Indian Art, Florida Contemporary Art, Native American Art
Activities: Originate traveling exhibs to museums & cultural institutions in the Southeast

M **CHARLES MORSE MUSEUM OF AMERICAN ART,** Charles Hosmer Morse Museum of American Art, 445 North Park Ave, Winter Park, FL 32789. Tel 407-645-5311; Fax 407-647-1284; Email information@morsemuseum.org; Web: www.morsemuseum.org; *Dir* Laurence Ruggiero
Open Tues - Thurs, Fri 9:30 AM - 8 PM Sat 9:30 AM - 4 PM Nov - Apr, 9:30 AM - 4 PM May - Oct, Sun 1 - 4 PM, cl Mon & major holidays except Easter & July 4; Admis adults $3, students $1, children under 12 free; all visitors free Fri 4 - 8 PM Nov - Apr; Estab by Jeannette Genius McKean & developed by her & her husband Hugh F. McKean, committed to the cultural enrichment of their community; The mus consists of 19 galleries, includes a major collection of American art pottery & representative collections of late 19th & early 20th century American painting, graphics & decorative art; Average Annual Attendance: 60,000; Mem: 1,169; dues student or teacher $5, individual $15, family $25, contributing $50, benefactor $100, sustaining $1000
Income: private endowment
Collections: World's most comprehensive collection of works by Louis Comfort Tiffany, including Tiffany jewelry, pottery, paintings, art glass, stained-glass windows & lamps, & the chapel interior designed for the 1893 Worlds' Columbian Exposition in Chicago
Publications: INSIDER, monthly newsletter to members
Activities: Docent training; lects open to pub; 4-5 vis lectrs per yr; concerts; gallery talks; tours; exten prog to Central Florida; artmobile to area schools

NATIONAL CARTOONISTS SOCIETY
For further information, see National and Regional Organizations

M **ROLLINS COLLEGE,** George D & Harriet W Cornell Fine Arts Museum, 1000 Holt Ave, Winter Park, FL 32789-4409. Tel 407-646-2526; Fax 407-646-2524; Web: cfam.rollins.edu; *Registrar & Collections Mgr* Leslie Cone; *Exec Asst* Sandy Todd; *Dir* Dr Ena Heller; *Cur* Dr Jonathan F Walz; *Donor & Guest Relations Liaison & Educ Cur* Dana Thomas
Open Tues - Fri 10 AM - 4 PM, Sat & Sun 12 PM - 5 PM, cl Mon; Admis adults $5, free to mem & students; AAM accredited museum located on Rollins College Campus in Winter Park; The mus houses the college's permanent collection of more than 5000 works & provides a focus for the arts in Central Florida. Mus consists of the McKean, the Yust, Myers, Clive, & Zollo galleries; Average Annual Attendance: 43,000; Mem: Dues Benefactor $1,000+, Salon $500-999, Patron $200-$499, Contributing $100-199, Basic $60-99, Individual Student, Educator or Young Professional $30-$59
Income: $520,000 (funded by endowment & grants)
Purchases: Over 500 contemporary American & European artworks
Special Subjects: Afro-American Art, American Indian Art, Anthropology, Antiquities-Egyptian, Antiquities-Etruscan, Antiquities-Roman, Archaeology, Asian Art, Baroque Art, Bronzes, Cartoons, Ceramics, Coins & Medals, Collages, Costumes, Crafts, Decorative Arts, Folk Art, Painting-American, Painting-Russian, Pewter, Photography, Portraits, Primitive art, Prints, Sculpture, Textiles, Painting-European
Collections: Smith Watch Key Collection: 1200 keys, Bloomsbury Collection of Kenneth Curry
Exhibitions: Rembrandt van Rijn, Sordid and Sacred: The Beggars in Rembrandt's Etchings, Selections from the John Villarino Collection; L C Armstrong: The Paradise Triptychs; Jack R Smith: Portraits of American Poets
Publications: Exhibit catalogs, 3 per year; newsletter, 5 per year
Activities: Classes for adults & children, docent training; lects open to pub, 10-15 vis lectrs per yr; gallery talks; tours; originate traveling exhibs

GEORGIA

ALBANY

M **ALBANY MUSEUM OF ART,** 311 Meadowlark Dr, Albany, GA 31707-5704. Tel 229-439-8400; Fax 229-439-1332; Email info@albanymuseum.com; Web: www.albanymuseum.com; *Exec Dir* Paula Williams; *Mem & Fin Mgr* Veronica Parrish; *Special Events Mgr* Savannah Hughes; *Interim Exhibs Mgr* Michael Mallard; *Dir Educ & Prog Plng* Chloe Hinton
Open Tues - Thurs 10 AM - 5 PM; no admis fee; Estab 1964; new museum facility opened 1983; Average Annual Attendance: 20,000; Mem: 3,000; dues Student no charge; Family/Individual/Military $75; Supporting Member $100; Patron Couple $250; Benefactor $500; Collectors Circle $1,000
Income: $625,000 (financed by state, federal & foundation grants, mem & special events)
Library Holdings: Auction Catalogs, Book Volumes, Exhibition Catalogs, Pamphlets, Periodical Subscriptions, Video Tapes
Special Subjects: African Art, Afro-American Art, Antiquities-Egyptian, Antiquities-Greek, Antiquities-Roman, Painting-American, American Indian Art, Decorative Arts, Drawings, Folk Art, Furniture, Historical Material, Jewelry, Photography, Portraits, Portraits
Collections: African Collection, Art of the Southern Region, 20th Century American Art, African Collection, Ancient Art, Twentieth Century American Art
Publications: Quarterly Magazine; exhibition catalogs
Activities: Classes for adults & children; workshops; docent training; lects open to pub, 6 vis lectrs per yr; concerts; gallery; films; talks; tours; sponsoring of competitions; Children's Art Fair; individual paintings & original objects of art lent to other museums; originate traveling exhibs to other museums; mus shop sells books, magazines, reproductions

AMERICUS

M **GEORGIA SOUTHWESTERN STATE UNIVERSITY,** JEC Gallery & FAB Gallery, 800 Georgia Southwestern State University Dr, Americus, GA 31709-4376. Tel 912-931-2204; Fax 912-931-2927; Email tonia.hughes@gsw.edu; *Sr Lectr* Tonia Hughes
Open Mon - Fri 8 AM - 5 PM; No admis fee; Estab 1971; Fine arts
Activities: Educ prog; lects open to pub; gallery talks; tours; schols offered; junior mus, Fine Arts Building Gallery
Tuition: Res $1,200 per sem: non-res $2,700 per sem

ATHENS

M **LYNDON HOUSE ART,** 293 Hoyt St, Athens, GA 30601; PO Box 1868, Athens, GA 30603-1868. Tel 706-613-3623; Fax 706-613-3627; *Dir* Claire Benson; *Cur* Nancy Lukasiewicz; *Lyndon House Art Foundation* Dan Hope
Open Tues 11 AM - 8 PM, Wed - Fri 11 AM - 5 PM, cl legal holidays; No admis fee; Average Annual Attendance: 12,000
Collections: decorative arts, period furnishings
Publications: periodic catalogs
Activities: Educ progs; workshops; art courses; internships; lects; gallery talks; arts festivals

M **UNIVERSITY OF GEORGIA,** Georgia Museum of Art, 90 Carlton St, Athens, GA 30602-1502. Tel 706-542-4662; Fax 706-542-1051; Email mlachow@uga.edu; Web: www.georgiamuseum.org; *Museum Dir* William Eiland; *Deputy Dir* Annelies Mondi; *Dir Communs* Hillary Brown; *Chief Preparator* Todd Rivers; *Dir Devel* Heather Malcolm; *Cur Decorative Art* Dale Couch; *Bus Mgr* Lisa Conley; *Cur Pierre Daura* Lynn Boland; *Head Registrar* Tricia Miller; *Pub Rels Coordr* Michael Lachowski; *Cur American Art* Sarah Kate Gillespie; *Larry D & Brenda A Thompson Cur of African American & African Diasporic Art* Dr Shawnya Harris; *Assoc Cur Educ* Callan Steinmann; *Assoc Cur Educ* Sage Kincaid; *Art Handler* Larry Forte; *Museum Shop Mgr* Amy Miller
Open Tues, Wed, Fri & Sat 10 AM - 5 PM, Thurs 10 AM - 9 PM, Sun 1 PM - 5 PM; No admis fee; Estab 1945; open to the pub 1948 as a fine arts mus; 22 exhib galleries. Maintains reference library & study centers in the humanities (4 archives); Average Annual Attendance: 80,000; Mem: 700; dues $35 - $10,000; ann meeting May
Income: Financed through univ, mem & grants
Purchases: American & European prints & paintings
Library Holdings: Auction Catalogs, Book Volumes, CD-ROMs, Pamphlets, Periodical Subscriptions
Special Subjects: African Art, Afro-American Art, American Western Art, Asian Art, Baroque Art, Bookplates & Bindings, Bronzes, Carpets & Rugs, Ceramics, Coins & Medals, Collages, Costumes, Crafts, Decorative Arts, Drawings, Embroidery, Etchings & Engravings, Folk Art, Furniture, Glass, Gold, Graphics, Hispanic Art, Historical Material, Jewelry, Laces, Landscapes, Latin American Art, Manuscripts, Marine Painting, Metalwork, Mexican Art, Miniatures, Painting-American, Painting-British, Painting-European, Painting-French, Painting-Italian, Painting-Polish, Painting-Spanish, Photography, Porcelain, Portraits, Posters, Pottery, Prints, Religious Art, Renaissance Art, Sculpture, Silver, Southwestern Art, Stained Glass, Tapestries, Textiles, Watercolors, Woodcarvings, Woodcuts
Collections: American & European Paintings (19th & 20th century), European & American Graphics, Japanese Graphics, 15th century to the present, Alfred H & Eva Underhill Holbrook Collection of American Art, Samuel H Kress Study Collection, The Paulson Collection of Ancient Near Eastern Coins, Larry D & Brenda A Thompson coll of African American art
Exhibitions: Check website
Publications: Georgia Museum of Art Bulletin; quarterly newsletter; exhibition catalogs & brochures; gallery notes; calendar
Activities: Classes for adults & children; docent training; senior citizen progs; volunteer docents prog; lects open to pub, 10-12 vis lectrs per yr; concerts; tours; gallery talks; competitions with awards; M Smith Griffith Volunteer of the Yr award; individual paintings & original objects of art lent to other museums & galleries; Senior Outreach Program; State of 6A; original traveling exhibs; mus shop sells books & original art

L **University of Georgia Libraries**, 320 S Jackson St, Athens, GA 30602-5002. Tel 706-542-7463; Web: www.libs.uga.edu; *Art Librn* Marilyn Healey
Open by appointment; Reference library only
Income: Financed by state appropriation
Library Holdings: Audio Tapes, Book Volumes 58,500, Cards, Cassettes, Clipping Files, Exhibition Catalogs, Fiche, Manuscripts, Micro Print, Motion Pictures, Pamphlets, Periodical Subscriptions 265, Photographs, Records, Reels, Slides, Video Tapes
Collections: Rare books & manuscripts collection, illustration archives on microfiche, stereographs from William C Darrah Collection, private press coll, handmade paper colls

L **Dept of Art Lamar Dodd School of Art**, 270 River Rd Athens, GA 30602. Tel 706-542-1618, 542-1600 (art dept); Fax 706-542-0226; Web: art.uga.edu/index; *Slide Librn* Janet Williamson; *Dir* Carmon Colangelo
Open 8 AM - 5 PM and by special arrangement; Estab 1955 to house slides & AV equipment for use by faculty & students for classroom lecturing; Reference & instructional library
Library Holdings: Cassettes, Slides 165,000, Video Tapes
Special Subjects: American Western Art, Antiquities-Assyrian, Archaeology, Asian Art, Ceramics, Coins & Medals, Decorative Arts, Etchings & Engravings, Furniture, Islamic Art, Latin American Art, Mexican Art, Oriental Art, Painting-American, Photography

ATLANTA

M **ALTERNATE ROOTS, INC,** 115 Martin Luther King Jr Dr SW, Atlanta, GA 30303-3030. Tel 404-577-1079; Fax 404-577-7991; Email info@alternateroots.org; Web: www.alternateroots.org; *Exec Dir* Carlton Turner; *Mng Dir* Ashley Walden Davis; *Opers Mgr* Paige Heurtin; *Opers Assoc* Kerry Lee; *Communs Mgr* Nicole Gurgel-Seefeldt; *Progs Mgr* Wendy Shenefelt; *Communs Develop* Joseph Thomas
Open Mon - Fri 10 AM - 6 PM; Estab 1976 to support the creation & presentation of original performing art that is rooted in a particular community or place, tradition or spirit; Mem: 250; dues introductory $20, satellite $50, voting $65; annual meeting
Income: Financed by grants, mem, private contributions
Activities: Classes for adults

M **THE APEX MUSEUM,** 135 Auburn Ave NE, Atlanta, GA 30303-2567. Tel 404-523-2739; Fax 404-523-3248 (call first); Email info@apexmuseum.org; Web: www.apexmuseum.org; *Pres, Dir & Founder* Dan Moore Sr; *Chmn Emeritus* Mr Billye Aaron; *Gallery Coordr* Michelle Mitchell
Open Tues - Sat 10 AM - 5 PM, Sun - Mon & major holidays; Admis adults $7, seniors & students $5; Estab 1978 to preserve & present black history; Average Annual Attendance: 75,000
Collections: African American art, Sankoya wood & brass artifacts
Publications: The APEX Times; Black Codes in Georgia
Activities: Guided tours; lects; awarded best non-profit in 2008; mus-related items for sale

M **ATLANTA CONTEMPORARY ART CENTER,** 535 Means St NW, Atlanta, GA 30318. Tel 404-688-1970; Fax 404-577-5856; Email info@thecontemporary.org; Web: atlantacontemporary.org; *Exec Dir* Veronica Kessenich; *Board Chair* Randy Gue; *Cur* Daniel Fuller
Open Tues - Wed 11 AM - 5 PM; Thurs 11 AM - 8 PM; Fri - Sat 11 AM - 5 PM, Sun 12 PM - 4 PM, cl Mon; No admis fee; Estab 1973 as a non-collecting institution dedicated to the creation, presentation & advancement of contemporary art by emerging & established artists; Average Annual Attendance: 8,000; Mem: 800; dues $25 - $5,000
Income: $560,000
Library Holdings: Auction Catalogs, Clipping Files, DVDs, Exhibition Catalogs, Memorabilia, Periodical Subscriptions
Exhibitions: Exhibs quarterly
Publications: Artist books; exhib catalogs; e-news, weekly
Activities: Classes for adults & children; art trips; lects open to pub, gallery talks; concerts; tours; media programs; internship programs; Nexus Award; originate traveling exhibs; sales shop sells Nexus artist books, magazines, prints, contemporary catalogs

M **ATLANTA HISTORICAL SOCIETY INC,** Atlanta History Center, 130 W Paces Ferry Rd, Atlanta, GA 30305. Tel 404-814-4000; Fax 404-814-4186; Web: www.atlantahistorycenter.com; *Colls Mgr* Erica Hague; *Dir Develop Events* Katherine Hoogerwerf; *COO* Paul Carriere; *Pres & CEO* Sheffield Hale
Open Mon - Sat 10 AM - 5:30 PM, Sun Noon - 5:30 PM, Library/Archives open Tues - Sat 10 AM - 5 PM; Admis adult $21.50, seniors & students $18, youth 4-12 $9, children 3 & under free; Estab 1926, dedicated to presenting the stories of Atlanta's past, present & future through exhibits, programs, collections & research; Atlanta History Museum with exhibits, shop, cafe, classrooms, 100 seat theater; two National Historic Register houses: Swan House, a 1928 classically styled mansion with original furnishings & the 1840's Tullie Smith Farm with outbuildings & livestock; 1890s Victorian playhouse; 33 acres of gardens & woodland trails labeled for self-guided tours; McElreath Hall, housing an extensive library/archives; member's room & a 400 seat auditorium; Average Annual Attendance: 175,000; Mem: 6000; dues $30-$1000; annual meeting
Income: $6,000,000 (financed through endowment, county appropriation, donations, admis & shop sales, cafe sales & facility rental)
Purchases: $22,500
Special Subjects: Architecture, Costumes, Decorative Arts, Dioramas, Dolls, Historical Material, Manuscripts, Maps, Period Rooms, Photography, Textiles
Collections: costumes & textiles, general Atlanta history, Burrison Folklife Collection, Thomas S Dickey Civil War Ordnance Collection, DuBose Civil War Collection, Philip Trammell Shutze Collection of Decorative Arts
Exhibitions: Metropolitan Frontiers: Atlanta, 1835-2000; Shaping Traditions: Folk Arts in a Changing South; Turning Point: The American Civil War;
Publications: Atlanta History: A Journal of Georgia & the South, quarterly; Atlanta History Center News, quarterly; Atlanta History Programs Calendar, quarterly
Activities: Classes for adults & children; family progs; docent progs; lects open to pub, 15 vis lectrs per yr; symposia; workshops; special events; guided tours; originate traveling exhibs; retail store sells books, prints, magazines, slides, original art, reproductions, folk crafts, educational toys & Atlanta history memorabilia

M **ATLANTA INTERNATIONAL MUSEUM OF ART & DESIGN,** Museum of Design Atlanta, 1315 Peachtree St NE, Atlanta, GA 30309-7515. Tel 404-979-6455; Fax 404-856-5960; Email info@museumofdesign.org; Web: www.museumofdesign.org; *Exec Dir* Laura Flusche; *Educ Coordr* Blair Banks
Open Tues - Wed, Fri & Sun noon - 6 PM, Thurs noon - 8 PM, Sat 10 AM - 6 PM, cl Mon; Admis adults $10, seniors & military $8, children 6-17 & college students $5, children under 5 free; Estab 1989 to promote the study & impact of design on everyday life; Includes 3 galleries; Average Annual Attendance: 15,000; Mem: 700; dues $50 & up
Income: $1,000,000 (financed by endowment, mem, city & state appropriation & corporate sponsorship)
Special Subjects: Architecture, Jewelry, Graphics, Metalwork, Posters
Exhibitions: The Furniture of Eero Saarinen: Designs for Everyday Living; Marcel Breuer: Design & Architecture; ATLANTA: Beyond Bricks & Sticks; LoveNests: Photographs & Objects
Publications: Exhibit catalogue
Activities: Classes for adults & children; docent training; family workshops; 1st Thursdays Downtown Atlanta Arts Walk; lects open to pub, 3 vis lectrs per yr; originate traveling exhibs 1 per yr to Metro-Atlanta community; sales shop sells books & original art

L **ATLANTA-FULTON PUBLIC LIBRARY,** Central Library Art Gallery, One Margaret Mitchell Sq NW, Atlanta, GA 30303. Tel 404-730-1700; Fax 404-730-1757; Email librarycomments@fultoncountyga.gov; Web: www.afpls.org; *Dir* Dr Gabriel Morley; *Gallery Coordr* Chera Baugh
Open Mon - Thurs 10 AM - 8 PM, Fri & Sat 9 AM - 6 PM, Sun 2 - 6 PM; Estab 1950 to provide materials in the fine arts; Some exhibit space maintained; Average Annual Attendance: 2500
Income: Financed by county & state appropriation
Library Holdings: Book Volumes 9,000, Compact Disks 7500, DVDs 100, Video Tapes 200
Exhibitions: exhibitions change monthly
Activities: Lects open to pub; concerts; gallery talks; book traveling exhibs 1-2 per yr

M **CENTER FOR PUPPETRY ARTS,** 1404 Spring St NW at 18th, Atlanta, GA 30309-2820. Tel 404-873-3089; Fax 404-873-9907; Email info@puppet.org; Web: www.puppet.org; *Exec Dir* Barbara Wylly; *Exec Dir* Bill Wylly; *Cur Exhibs* Kelsey Fritz; *Educ Progs* Aretta Baumgartner; *Dir Devel* Heather Karellas
Open Tues - Fri 9 AM - 5 PM, Sat 10 AM - 5 PM, Sun Noon - 5 PM; Admis general $12.50, mems free; Estab 1978 to educate pub of the art of puppetry; Puppetry - National & International Exhibits displayed in 9 rooms with hands-on displays includes 1 special exhibit which changes every 6 months; Mem: dues $25 - $1,000 & up
Income: $1,300,000 (financed by endowment, mem, city & state appropriations)
Special Subjects: African Art, Afro-American Art, Asian Art, Costumes, Folk Art, Historical Material, Latin American Art, Photography, Posters, Pre-Columbian Art, Religious Art, Restorations, Woodcarvings
Collections: Collection of puppets from around the globe, Puppetry
Exhibitions: Permanent Collection: Puppet Power Wonders (800 puppets)
Publications: Articles, brochures, catalogs & reports
Activities: Classes for adults & children; docent training; lects open to pub, 2-3 vis lectrs per yr; gallery talks; tours; schols offered; lending collection contains original objects of art & photographs; book traveling exhibs 3 per yr; originate traveling exhibs 2 per yr; mus shop sells books & puppets

L **Museum & Library,** 1404 Spring St NW, Atlanta, GA 30309-2820. Tel 404-881-5130; Fax 404-873-9907; Web: www.puppet.org; *Exec Dir* Barbara Wylly; *Exec Dir* Bill Wylly; *Exhibs Dir* Kelsey Fritz
Open mus Tues - Fri 9 AM - 5 PM, Sat 10 AM - 5 PM, Sun noon - 5 PM, cl Mon; library open by appointment; Admis museum $12.50; Estab 1978
Library Holdings: Audio Tapes, Book Volumes 1,500, Cassettes, Clipping Files, Exhibition Catalogs, Framed Reproductions, Memorabilia, Original Art Works, Pamphlets, Photographs, Prints, Records, Reproductions, Slides, Video Tapes
Collections: Coll of over 3,000 puppets from around the world, including over 400 objects from the Jim Henson Coll
Activities: Classes for adults & children; docent training; tours; mus shop

A **CITY OF ATLANTA,** Office of Cultural Affairs, 233 Peachtree St, NE, Harris Tower Atlanta, GA 30303-1504. Tel 404-546-6815; Fax 404-546-9473; Email mdprothro@atlantaga.gov; Web: www.ocaatlanta.com; *Art Prog Mgr* Monica D Prothro
Estab 1974 to improve the social fabric & quality of life for Atlanta's citizens & visitors by supporting the arts & cultural activities & by nurturing the arts community
Activities: Contracts for art services; music progs; pub art progs; special projects

M **Gallery 72,** 72 Marietta St, Atlanta, GA 30303. Tel 404-546-3220; Email gallery72@atlantaga.gov; Web: www.ocaatlanta.com; *Dir* Camille Russell Love; *Pub Art Mgr* Dorian McDuffie; *Gallery 72 Project Coordr* Kevin Sipp
Open Mon - Fri 10 AM - 5 PM; No admis fee; Estab to present contemporary fine art produced by regional, national & international professional artists; focused primarily on Atlanta-based artists; goal: display work that is stimulating & innovative & that presents a new perspective or cross-collaboration with other art disciplines; 3,000 sq ft space divided into north & south galleries; Average Annual Attendance: 30,000
Income: Financed by prog of the Mayor's Office of Cultural Affairs
Exhibitions: 5-6 exhibs per yr
Publications: Catalogs: Larry Walker: Four Decades (2001) & Beverly Buchanan: Habitats & Shotgun Shacks (2000)
Activities: Workshops for adults & childrens; dramatic progs; lects open to pub; forums, demonstrations & performances in collaboration with service agencies; concerts; gallery talks; tours; awards: Best New Gallery in Atlanta 2014, Best Recycled Space 2014, AIA Georgia 2014 Citation Design Award

M **Atlanta Cyclorama & Civil War Museum,** Atlanta History Center, 130 W Paces Ferry Rd, NW Atlanta, GA 30305. Tel 404-658-7625; Fax 404-658-7045; Email info@atlanticyclorama.org; Web: www.atlantahistorycenter.com; *Pres & CEO* Sheffield Hale; *VPres Mktg & Communs* Hillary Hardwick
Open Mon - Sat 10 AM - 5:30 PM, Sun noon - 5:30 PM; Admis adults $21.50, seniors & students $18, youth 4-12 $9, children under 4 free; Estab 1886; Located in Grant Park & listed in the National Historic Register; 184-seat revolving platform; Average Annual Attendance: 100,000
Income: The self-sustaining Cyclorama functions as an enterprise
Special Subjects: Costumes, Historical Material, Painting-American
Collections: Civil War artifacts, lifelike figures in Civil War costume & period props, panoramic painting depicting the Battle of Atlanta, The Locomotive Texas
Activities: Scavenger hunts; Sales shop sells books, videos & Civil War era souvenirs

M **Chastain Arts Center & Gallery,** 135 W Wieuca Rd NW, Atlanta, GA 30342-3221. Tel 404-252-2927; Fax 404-851-1270; Email chastainarts@atlantaga.gov; Web: www.ocaatlanta.com/chastain; *Facility Mgr* Karen Lowe; *Project Coordr* Rachel Ballard
Open summer Mon & Fri 9:30 AM - 5 PM, Tues -Thurs 9:30 AM - 9 PM, Fri - Sat 9:30 AM - 5 PM, cl Sun; Estab 1968 to advance city art educational progs and to display art by local, regional & national artists & designers and arts organizations; Located in Chastain Park; oldest City-operated arts facility in Atlanta; Average Annual Attendance: 2,000
Special Subjects: Drawings, Jewelry, Pottery, Prints
Activities: Educ prog; classes for adults & children; workshops; gallery talks; sales shop sells original art

M **Gilbert House,** 2238 Perkerson Rd SW, Atlanta, GA 30315-6216. Tel 404-817-6815; Fax 404-853-7643
Open by appointment; Tues - Fri 10 AM - 5 PM; Estab 1984; Built in 1865 by Jeremiah Gilbert immediately after the Civil War; registered historic landmark located on 12 acres
Activities: Art classes for adults & children; exhibs of art work

L **Public Art Program,** 233 Peachtree St NE, Ste 1700 Atlanta, GA 30303-1563. Tel 404-546-6815; *Exec Dir* Camille Love
Estab 1977 to administer the development & management of public art projects for the Atlanta City government; sole caretaker of Public Art Collection for the City of Atlanta; Offers open files on all Hotline presenters: listings of available studio space in Atlanta, health insurance policies for self-employed artists, sets of grant guidelines from National Endowment for the Arts & local arts funding agencies, as well as information on pub art commissions nationwide
Collections: 127 public art works
Activities: Art in educ prog; professional develop workshops; arts hotline; materials for the arts prog

A **DECORATIVE ARTS COLLECTION MUSEUM,** 1406 Woodmont Ln, Atlanta, GA 30318; PO Box 18028, Atlanta, GA 30316. Tel 404-351-1151; Email info@dpmuseum.org; Web: www.decorativeartscollection.org
Open by appointment only; Estab 1982 to preserve & collect items of decorative painting & educate the public about the art form; Average Annual Attendance: 500; Mem: 1,000
Income: Financed by mem & gifts
Library Holdings: Book Volumes, Original Documents, Photographs, Slides
Special Subjects: Decorative Arts, Painting-American, Painting-Canadian, Painting-Dutch, Painting-Japanese, Painting-Russian, Painting-Scandinavian, Porcelain, Watercolors
Collections: Decorative Arts Collection - antique & contemporary decorative art, various media
Publications: Friends, newsletter, twice a year
Activities: Classes for adults and children; industry contribution recognition awards; DAC juried art awards; lending collection; originate traveling exhibs; sales shop sells books, magazines, jewelry & original art

M **EMORY UNIVERSITY,** Michael C Carlos Museum, 571 S Kilgo Circle, Atlanta, GA 30322-1120. Tel 404-727-4282; Fax 404-727-4292; Email jadanie@emory.edu; Web: www.carlos.emory.edu; *Assoc Dir* Catherine Howett Smith; *Dir Exhib & Collections* Joseph Gargasz; *Dir Educ* Elizabeth S Hornor; *Dir* Bonnie Speed
Open Tues - Fri 10 AM - 4 PM, Sat 10 AM - 5 PM, Sun Noon - 5 PM; Admis adults $8, students, seniors & children 6-17 $6, children under 6 & mem free; Estab 1919; Mus redesigned in 1985 by Michael Graves, Post-Modernist architect; 15,400 sq ft; permanent exhibition galleries & special exhibition galleries; Average Annual Attendance: 120,000; Mem: 1,400; dues individual $50, Dual $75, Family $100, Doric $150, Ionic $300, Corinthian $600
Income: $2,500,000
Special Subjects: African Art, Antiquities-Egyptian, Antiquities-Etruscan, Antiquities-Greek, Antiquities-Roman, Archaeology, Asian Art, Ceramics, Etchings & Engravings, Glass, Jade, Jewelry, Latin American Art, Manuscripts, Mexican Art, Oriental Art, Photography, Pottery, Pre-Columbian Art, Sculpture, Watercolors, Woodcarvings
Collections: Art collection from Renaissance to present, African, classical Greek & Egyptian, Old World art & archaeology, including works from Egypt, Mesopotamia, ancient Palestine, Pre-Columbian, American Indian & Far Eastern holdings, Works on Paper, Asian, African
Publications: Exhibition catalogues
Activities: Classes for adults & children; classes for teachers; docent training; lects open to pub; 10 vis lectrs per yr; concerts; gallery talks; tours; schols & fels offered; exten dept; original objects of art lent to other institutions; book traveling exhibs 2-4 per yr; originate traveling exhibs; mus shop sells books, magazines, original art, reproductions, prints, gifts, jewelry, CD ROMs, videos & catalogues

A **GEORGIA COUNCIL FOR THE ARTS,** Georgia's State Art Collection, 260 14th St NW, Ste 401, Atlanta, GA 30318-5360. Tel 404-685-2787; Fax 404-685-2788; Web: www.gaarts.org; *Exec Dir* Karen L Paty
Open (office) Mon - Fri 8 AM - 5 PM; gallery by appointment only; No admis fee; Estab 1968 as a state agency providing funding to non-profit, tax-exempt organizations for arts programming & support; Art work of Georgians; Mem: 24 members appointed by governor; meetings four times per yr
Income: $3,900,000 (financed by state appropriation plus federal funding)
Publications: Guide to Programs, annual (one for organizations & one for artists)

L **GEORGIA INSTITUTE OF TECHNOLOGY,** College of Architecture Library, Georgia Institute of Technology, Atlanta, GA 30332-0155. Tel 404-894-4877; Email archhelp@library.gatech.edu; Web: www.library.gatech.edu/architect/; *Head Librn* Cathy Carpenter; *Info Assoc* Corinne Kennedy
Open Mon - Thurs 8 AM - 10 PM, Fri 8 AM - 6 PM, Sat 10 AM - 6 PM, Sun Noon - 10 PM
Income: Financed by state appropriation
Library Holdings: Book Volumes 33,800, Periodical Subscriptions 160, Reels

A **GEORGIA LAWYERS FOR THE ARTS,** 887 W Marietta St, NW, Ste J-101 Atlanta, GA 30318-5266. Tel 404-873-3911; Fax 404-873-3911; Email gla@glarts.org; Web: www.glarts.org; *Exec Dir* Meredith Ragains; *Dir of Vol Services* Katherine B B Russell Esq
Open Mon - Fri 9 AM - 5 PM by appointment only; No admis fee; Estab 1975 to provide legal services & educational programming to artists and arts organizations in Georgia; Mem: Dues individual artists $40, nonprofit arts organizations $75
Collections: Copyrights, fundraising, art law related to literature
Publications: An Artists Handbook on Copyright; Handbook on the Georgia Print Law; Art Law in Georgia: A Guide for Artists and Art Organizations
Activities: Educ prog; classes for adults; network of volunteer attorneys who provide free legal services to low income artists; lects open to pub; 50-60 vis lectrs per yr; workshops and seminars on legal issues

L **GEORGIA STATE UNIVERSITY,** School of Art & Design, Visual Resource Center, 520 Art & Humanities Bldg, Atlanta, GA 30302-3965. Tel 404-651-5233; Fax 404-651-1779; Email aengland@gsu.edu; Web: www.gsu.edu; *Cur* Ann England
Open Mon - Fri 8:30 AM - 5 PM; No admis fee; Estab 1970 to make visual & literary resource materials available for study, teaching & research; Average Annual Attendance: 20,000
Library Holdings: Book Volumes 300, Exhibition Catalogs, Original Art Works, Pamphlets, Periodical Subscriptions 18, Reproductions, Slides 255,000, Video Tapes 45
Special Subjects: Aesthetics, Afro-American Art
Collections: Rare book collection, original prints emphasis impressionism, 19th - early 20th century artists, extensive Pre-Columbian slide collection, History of textile, Metalsmithing & jewelry making, History of photography

Activities: Lects open to public, 5-10 vis lectrs per year; films; artist's slide presentations; discussions

M **Ernest G Welch Gallery**, 10 Peachtree Center Ave Rm 117, University Plaza Atlanta, GA 30303-3003; PO Box 4107, School of Art & Design Atlanta, GA 30302-4107. Tel 404-413-5230; Fax 404-413-5261; Email cfarnell@gsu.edu; Web: artdesign.gsu.edu/artgallery; *Gallery Dir* Cynthia Farnell
Open Mon - Fri 10 AM - 6 PM; No admis fee; Two galleries for student and facility exhibits, national and international traveling shows.
Publications: Catalogues
Activities: Lects open to public; gallery talks; tours

M **HAMMONDS HOUSE MUSEUM,** 503 Peeples St, SW, Atlanta, GA 30310. Tel 404-612-0481; Fax 404-752-8733; Email business@hammondshouse.org; Web: www.hammondshouse.org; *Interim Exec Dir* Leatrice Ellzy-Wright; *Facilities Mgr & Security* Wendell Hurst; *Mem & Vol Coordr* Donna Watts-Nunn; *Exec Asst* Audrey M Johnson
Open Wed - Fri 10 AM - 6 PM, Sat - Sun 1 PM - 5 PM; cl Mon & nat holidays; Admis $5, senior citizens, students & children $3, free for mem; guided tours $6 per person; Estab 1988; Original artwork displayed throughout early 19th c. Eastlake Victorian venue; Average Annual Attendance: 10,000; Mem: 400; dues $15 & up
Income: Financed by grants, donations, mem, earned income
Library Holdings: Audio Tapes, CD-ROMs, Cassettes, DVDs, Exhibition Catalogs, Filmstrips, Original Art Works, Original Documents, Photographs, Prints, Sculpture, Slides, Video Tapes
Special Subjects: African Art, Afro-American Art, Collages, Decorative Arts, Folk Art, Furniture, Historical Material, Photography, Posters, Prints, Woodcuts
Collections: More than 350 art works from mid-19th century artists, Haitian paintings, African sculptures & masks, Recordings of artist talks
Exhibitions: 4 - 6 major changing exhibs in main gallery space w/ additional exhibs in AARL satellite space
Activities: Educ prog; classes & workshops for adults & children; Kids Eye View Programs; teacher workshops; Wine & Words book series; docent training; lects; multiple vis lects; film screenings, workshops, booksignings; garden concerts; gallery talks; tours; awards & grants; partner programming with Auburn Avenue Research Library; mus shop sells books, magazines, original art, prints,

M **HIGH MUSEUM OF ART,** 1280 Peachtree St NE, Atlanta, GA 30309-3502. Tel 404-733-4400; 733-4444; Web: www.high.org; *Dir* Randall Suffolk; *Asst Cur Photography* Gregory Harris; *Cur Modern & Contemporary* Michael Rooks; *Cur African Art* Carol Thompson; *Cur American Art* Stephanie Heydt; *Cur Folk & Self-Taught Art* Katherine Jentleson; *Cur Decorative Arts & Design* Sarah Schleuning
Open Tues - Thurs 10 AM - 5 PM, Fri 10 AM - 9 PM, Sun noon - 5 PM, cl Mon & major holidays; Gen admis $7.25 children under 6 & mems free; Estab 1926 to make the best in the visual arts available to the Atlanta public in exhibitions & supporting programs; Four floors (46,000 sq ft) exhibition space; top floor for traveling exhibitions; semi-flexible space (moveable walls); ramp & elevator for accessibility; Average Annual Attendance: 500,000; Mem: 39,000; dues $45 & up
Income: $7,500,000 (financed by endowment, mem, Members Guild of the High Museum of Art, city & state appropriations, museum shop sales, grants & foundations, ticket sales & operating income)
Library Holdings: Auction Catalogs, Book Volumes 14,000, Clipping Files, Exhibition Catalogs, Periodical Subscriptions 50, Slides
Special Subjects: Afro-American Art, American Western Art, Architecture, Art Education, Art History, Ceramics, Conceptual Art, Crafts, Decorative Arts, Drawings, Etchings & Engravings, Folk Art, Photography
Collections: American painting & sculpture, European painting & sculpture, 20th Century painting, photography & sculpture, African & Sub-Saharan Art, Works on Paper, 18th & 19th Century decorative art featuring Herter Brothers, William Whitehead & John Henry Belter, contemporary crafts, 20th Century furniture, regional historical decorative arts & English ceramics, 19th Century American landscape paintings, contemporary art since 1970, Western art early Renaissance - present, decorative arts, graphics, sculpture, 19th - 20th century photography, Modern & Contemporary Art
Publications: HighLife, bi-monthly mem magazine; exhibition catalogues
Activities: Workshops for adults, children & families; docent training; teacher resources; lects open to pub; family days; tours; concerts; book signings; performing arts programs; senior citizen programs; gallery talks; speakers bureau; originates traveling exhibs; two mus shops sell books, reproductions, slides, prints, stationery, children's books & toys, crafts, jewelry & gift items

L **SAVANNAH COLLEGE OF ART & DESIGN - ATLANTA,** ACA Library of Atlanta, 1600 Peachtree St NW, Atlanta, GA 30309-2403; PO Box 77300, Atlanta, GA 30357-1300. Tel 404-253-3196; Email ref_atl@scad.edu; Web: www.scad.edu/life/libraries/; *Head Librn* Teresa Burk; *Vis Resources Librn* Mary Murphy; *Ref Librn* Caley Cannon; *Cataloging Librn* Jenny Wang
Open Mon - Thurs 8 AM - 5 PM, Fri noon - 5 PM, Sat & Sun noon - 8 PM; No admis fee; Estab 1950 to provide art information & research facility to the Atlanta College of Art community & the southeast art community; Circ 12,000
Library Holdings: Book Volumes 32,000, Clipping Files, DVDs 10, Exhibition Catalogs, Other Holdings Artists' books 1,500, Periodical Subscriptions 185, Slides 98,000, Video Tapes 400
Special Subjects: Graphic Design, Interior Design, Art History, Drawings, Painting-American, Photography
Collections: Artists' Books, rare books, circulating art books
Activities: Classes for adults & children; films; vis artists program; JoAnne Paschall award for student artists' book competition

M **SYMMES SYSTEMS,** Photographic Investments Gallery, 3977 Briarcliff Rd NE, Atlanta, GA 30345-2647. Tel 404-320-1012; *Pres* Edwin C Symmes Jr
Open by appointment; No admis fee; Estab 1979 to display & produce traveling exhibits of classical photography
Collections: 19th century photographic images in all media, 20th century black & white & color photos by masters
Exhibitions: 19th Century Albumen Prints of Westminster Cathedral; Netsuke: An Insight into Japan; Color Photography by E C Symmes; 19th & 20th Century Images of China.
Activities: Lects open to pub; original objects of art lent; lending collection contains 1500 19th century Albumen prints; originate traveling exhibs; mus shop sells original art

AUGUSTA

M **GERTRUDE HERBERT INSTITUTE OF ART,** 506 Telfair St, Augusta, GA 30901-2310. Tel 706-722-5495; Fax 706-722-3670; Email ghia@ghia.org; Web: www.ghia.org; *Dir* Heather Williams; *Admin Mgr* Mollie Story; *Educ Dir* Dorothy Eckmann; *Preparator* John Eckert
Open Mon - Fri 10 AM - 5 PM, Sat by appointment, groups by special appointment, cl Sun & all major holidays; No admis fee; donations accepted; Estab 1937 for the advancement & encouragement of art & educ in art; Main gallery located on second fl of historic home; Average Annual Attendance: 5,000; Mem: 400
Library Holdings: Book Volumes 400
Special Subjects: Graphics, Painting-American, Sculpture, Drawings, Photography, Prints
Exhibitions: Circulating exhibitions; monthly exhibitions; one-person and group exhibitions; The National Annual Juried Exhibition
Activities: Classes for adults & children; docent training; outreach to area schools; lect open to public, 4 vis lectrs per year; gallery talks; tours; competitions with awards, Agnes Markwalter Youth Award, Sense of Place; scholarships offered; book traveling exhibitions

C **MORRIS COMMUNICATIONS CO. LLC,** Corporate Collection, 725 Broad St, Augusta, GA 30901-1336; PO Box 936, Augusta, GA 30903-0936. Tel 706-724-0851; Fax 706-722-7125; *Chmn & CEO* W S Morris III; *Fine Art Mgr* Louise Keith Claussen
Collections: Alaskan Art, American Paintings, Western Bronzes, Wildlife (birds), European Paintings

M **MORRIS MUSEUM OF ART,** One Tenth St, Augusta, GA 30901-1134. Tel 706-724-7501; Fax 706-724-7612; Web: www.themorris.org; www.southernsoulandsong.org; *Exec Dir & Chief Cur* Kevin Grogan; *Cur Educ* Matt Porter; *Registrar* Stacey Thompson; *Store Mgr & Buyer* Christy Dove; *Dir Mktg & Pub Rels* Nicole McLeod; *Librn & Archivist* Cary Wilkins; *Exhibition Designer & Preparator* Dwayne Clark; *Dir External Affairs* Phyllis Giddens; *Creative Dir* Todd Beasley; *Security Officer* Bill Lay; *Vis Svcs & Educ Programs Coord* Brooke Shivers; *Mem Svcs Coord* Jenna Blitch
Open Tues - Sat 10 AM - 5 PM, Sun Noon - 5 PM; Admis adults $5, seniors 65+, military, students, & children 13-17 $3, children 12 & under & mem free; Estab 1992; 40,000 sq ft facility on 3 floors; 18,000 sq ft of gallery space; 16 galleries; Average Annual Attendance: 40,000; Mem: dues $15-$5000
Income: Financed by endowment, mem, grants, gifts & fundraising activities
Purchases: Southern Art permanent collection
Library Holdings: Auction Catalogs, Audio Tapes, Book Volumes 9,000, CD-ROMs, Cassettes, Clipping Files, Compact Disks, DVDs, Exhibition Catalogs, Filmstrips, Kodachrome Transparencies, Manuscripts, Maps, Memorabilia, Motion Pictures, Original Art Works, Original Documents, Pamphlets, Periodical Subscriptions, Photographs, Records, Reproductions, Slides, Video Tapes
Special Subjects: Afro-American Art, Archaeology, Architecture, Art Education, Art History, Collages, Conceptual Art, Crafts, Decorative Arts, Drawings, Drawings, Etchings & Engravings, Folk Art, Furniture, Glass, Graphics, Historical Material, Illustration, Landscape Architecture, Landscapes, Landscapes, Marine Painting, Painting-American, Painting-American, Photography, Porcelain, Portraits, Portraits, Pottery, Primitive art, Prints, Textiles, Watercolors, Woodcarvings, Woodcuts, Sculpture
Collections: The first museum in the country dedicated to celebrating and exploring the art and artists of the American South. The museum has a permanent collection of some 5,000 works of art. It is a broad-based survey collection, encompassing a history of painting in the South, ranging from the late Colonial Era to the present., library & archives: 18,000 vols, 20,000 vertical files; 500 films; video; slides; artist papers
Exhibitions: A Southern Collection: Masterworks from a Permanent Collection of Painting in the South
Publications: Exhibition catalogs, books
Activities: Educ dept; classes for adults & children; dramatic progs; Southern circuit tour of independent filmmakers; docent training; film programs; readings; classic film prog; lects open to pub, 12-18 vis lectrs per yr; 18 concerts; gallery talks; tours; competitions with awards; "Combining Voices" Youth Literary competition; Porter Fleming Literary Competition Awards; Smithsonian Affiliations Internship; exten prog serves central Savannah River area; individual paintings lent to mus; book traveling exhibs, 2-3 per yr; originate traveling exhibs circulate principally to Southeastern mus; mus shop sells books, magazines, original art, reproductions, prints, slides, gift items, crafts, food items

BAINBRIDGE

M **FIREHOUSE CENTER FOR THE ARTS,** Institution for Savings Art Gallery, 119 Water St, Bainbridge, GA 39817-3620; c/o Phyllis Lucas, Pres, 293 Rivervale Dr Bainbridge, GA 39817-7437. Tel 229-243-1010; Email bainbridgefirehouse@gmail.com; Web: bainbridgeart.com; *Artistic Dir* Ali White; *Admin Dir* Gerard Kwilecki
Open Mon - Fri 12 PM - 4 PM, Sat - Sun 1 PM - 5 PM; groups by appointment; Estab to enhance community life through the arts; Mem: dues $35-$250
Special Subjects: Sculpture, Photography
Collections: Paintings; sculpture; photographs
Exhibitions: Temporary exhibits
Activities: Educ progs; classes for adults & children; art programming; workshops; events

BRUNSWICK

A **GOLDEN ISLES ARTS & HUMANITIES ASSOCIATION,** 1530 Newcastle St, Brunswick, GA 31520-6805. Tel 912-262-6934; Fax 912-262-1029; Email info@goldenislearts.org; Web: www.goldenislesarts.org; *Exec Dir* Heather Heath; *Educ Dir* Jacob Demlow
Open Wed - Fri 9 AM - 5 PM, Sat 10 AM - 2 PM; Estab 1989 as a county coordinating arts council & presenter; The Ritz Theatre Lobby; Average Annual Attendance: 10,000; Mem: 700; dues family $50, single $35; annual meeting in Oct
Income: $285,000 (financed by mem, programs, services & grants)
Activities: Children's classes; dramatic progs; lects open to pub, 4-5 vis lectrs per yr; photographic & visual arts competitions; ribbons & cash awards; concerts; schols offered; book traveling exhibs 1 per yr

CARTERSVILLE

M **BOOTH WESTERN ART MUSEUM,** 501 Museum Dr, Cartersville, GA 30120; PO Box 3070, Cartersville, GA 30120-1702. Tel 770-387-1300; Fax 770-387-1319; Web: www.boothmuseum.org; *Exec Dir* Seth Hopkins; *Devel* Tom Roberson; *Educ* Lisa Wheeler; *Pub Rels* Tara Currier; *Treas* Cathy Lee Eckert; *Registrar* Nikki Morris; *Cur* Jeff Donaldson; *Libm & Archivist* Liz Gentry; *Mus Shop Mgr* Macra Adair; *Security* Ken Wade
Open Tues - Wed & Fri - Sat 10 AM - 5 PM, Thurs 10 AM - 8 PM, Sun 1 - 5 PM; Admis adults $10, seniors 65 & over & military $8, students $7, discounts to groups of 15 or more, children 12 & under & members no charge; Estab 2000; Western art, Civil War art, presidential photographs; Average Annual Attendance: 48,000; Mem: Dues individual $50, family $95, friend $150, museum package $200, contributor $250, patron $500, curator $1,000, collector's circle $2,500, dir circle $5,000 & up
Library Holdings: Auction Catalogs 200, Book Volumes 12,200, CD-ROMs 300, DVDs 200, Exhibition Catalogs 300, Motion Pictures 200, Periodical Subscriptions 50, Video Tapes 200
Special Subjects: Afro-American Art, American Western Art, Bronzes, Drawings, Graphics, Historical Material, Landscapes, Military Art, Painting-American, Photography, Portraits, Posters, Pottery, Prints, Sculpture, Southwestern Art, Watercolors
Collections: Western American art & culture, Presidential letters & portraits, Western movie posters, contemporary Civil War art
Publications: quarterly newsletter, The Booth Bulletin
Activities: Demonstrations; discussions; docent prog; lects; 25 vis lectrs per yr; concerts; galley talks; guided tours; sponsoring competitions; Lifetime Achievement award; exten prog NW Georgia; book traveling exhibitions 8 per yr; mus shop sells books, magazines, original art, reproductions & prints

M **TELLUS NORTHWEST GEORGIA SCIENCE MUSEUM,** 100 Tellus Museum Dr Cartersville, GA 30120; PO Box 3663, Cartersville, GA 30120-1712. Tel 770-386-0576; Fax 770-386-0600; Email info@tellusmuseum.org; Web: www.tellusmuseum.org; *Dir & Cur* Jose Santamaria; *Educ* Terry Everett; *Asst Dir* Mary Vinson; *Registrar & Archivist* Cherry Johnson; *Guest Svcs* Conilia Dover
Open Tues - Sat 10 AM - 5 PM, Sun 1 - 5 PM; cl Mon & maj holidays; Admis adults $4, seniors $3.50, children $3; Estab 1982; Average Annual Attendance: 21,685; Mem: dues Corporate $250 - $1000, Sponsor $250, Friend $100, Family $50, Indiv $25, Student $20
Library Holdings: Book Volumes 1500, Periodical Subscriptions 3000
Collections: Exhibits related to geological objects: minerals, fossils, rocks, gems & mining artifacts. Emphasis on minerals & fossils from the state of Georgia & its mining heritage.
Exhibitions: Rockfest: Outdoor gem & mineral show with free admis to mus; Holiday Open House: free activities, refreshments & admis
Publications: Weinman Mineral Museum News, Quarterly
Activities: Educ progs for adults & children

COLUMBUS

M **THE COLUMBUS MUSEUM,** 1251 Wynnton Rd, Columbus, GA 31906-2899. Tel 706-748-2562; Fax 706-748-2570; Email information@columbusmuseum.com; Web: www.columbusmuseum.com; *Director of Curatorial Affairs & Curator of American Art* Jonathan Frederick Walz; *Curator of History/Exhibition Coordinator* Rebecca Bush; *Assistant Collections Manager* Lauren Fleming; *Asst to Dir* Patricia Butts; *Director of Education* Abbie Edens; *Community Programs Coordinator* Christy Barlow; *Collections Manager* Aimee Brooks; *Community Outreach and Volunteer Coordinator* Kirsten Dunn; *Director* Marianne Richter; *Youth and Family Programs Coordinator* Jessamy South; *Director of Development* Carmen Overton; *Marketing and Media Manager* Mercedes Parham; *Membership Manager* Autumn Amos; *Event Sales Manager* Kelly Cargill; *Graphic Designer* Marcolm Tatum; *Social Media and Online Coordinator* Kiara McClellan; *Development Assistant* Laura Narr; *Deputy Director for Operations* Kimberly Beck; *Accounting Specialist II* Paula Evans; *Information Assistant* Mary Goff; *Museum Shop Associate* Cole Trahan; *Visitor Services Representative* Nick Decker; *Visitor Services Representative* Liliana Harrell; *Security Chief* Rick McGowan; *Security Deputy* Larry Hunter; *Security Deputy* Al Johnson
Open Tues - Sat 10 AM - 5 PM, Sun 1 - 5 PM, Thurs 10 AM - 8 PM, cl Mon & legal holidays; No admis fee; Estab 1953 to build a permanent collection; encourage work by Georgia & Southern artists; establish loan shows & traveling exhibitions in all fields of American art & history; 11,000 sq ft history gallery, 2,000 sq ft interactive gallery, 25,000 sq ft art gallery. Maintains reference library; Average Annual Attendance: 48,000; Mem: 2900; dues $45 - $5,000; annual meeting in May
Library Holdings: Auction Catalogs, Book Volumes, DVDs, Memorabilia, Periodical Subscriptions
Special Subjects: African Art, Afro-American Art, American Indian Art, Archaeology, Architecture, Asian Art, Ceramics, Collages, Costumes, Crafts, Decorative Arts, Dolls, Drawings, Eskimo Art, Etchings & Engravings, Ethnology, Folk Art, Furniture, Glass, Graphics, Historical Material, Historical Material, Ivory, Jade, Jewelry, Landscapes, Maps, Marine Painting, Metalwork, Oriental Art, Painting-American, Painting-British, Period Rooms, Photography, Porcelain, Portraits, Posters, Pottery, Pre-Columbian Art, Primitive art, Prints, Sculpture, Silver, Tapestries, Textiles, Watercolors, Woodcarvings, Woodcuts
Collections: American art from all periods & all media, Artifacts relating to the culture of the Chattahoochee Valley & Southeastern United States, permanent coll includes Landscapes, Paintings & Portraits by Early & Contemporary American Painters, with strong Coll of American drawings & primitive arts, American firearms, quilts & textiles, Southern folk art
Publications: Annual report; gallery guides; newsletter, quarterly; web news
Activities: Classes for adults & children; docent training; workshops; lects open to pub, 5-7 vis lectrs per yr; concerts; gallery talks; tours; TripAdvisor Award of Excellence;; scholarships offered; individual paintings & original objects of art lent to qualified institutions which are recognized & meet facilities accreditation standards; book traveling exhibs 6-10 per yr; originate traveling exhibs to other mus; mus shop sells books, original art, reproductions, jewelry & children's toys & gift items; junior mus

M **COLUMBUS STATE UNIVERSITY,** Norman Shannon and Emmy Lou P Illges Gallery, 4225 University Ave, Dept of Art Columbus, GA 31907-5679. Tel 706-507-8312; Fax 706-571-4353; Email israel_hannah@columbusstate.edu; Web: art.columbusstate.edu; *Gallery Dir* Hannah Israel
Open Mon - Fri 9 AM - 5 PM; No admis fee; Average Annual Attendance: 6,000
Income: $11,000 (financed by student activities)
Purchases: Permanent collection
Library Holdings: Auction Catalogs, Audio Tapes, Book Volumes, CD-ROMs, Video Tapes
Exhibitions: Annual art students show; faculty show; regional guest artist & nationally prominent artists
Publications: newsletters
Activities: Classes for adults & col students; workshops for adults & children 12-14; lects open to pub, lects for mems, 1-5 vis lectrs per yr; tours; gallery talks; competitions with awards; fels offered; Artbeat; sculpture walk; mus shop sells slides

DALTON

A **CREATIVE ARTS GUILD,** 520 W Waugh St, Dalton, GA 30722-3474. Tel 706-278-0168; Fax 706-278-6996; Email cagarts@creativeartsguild.org; Web: www.creativeartsguild.org; *Exec Dir* Terry Tomasello; *Visual Arts & Gallery Dir* Bradley Wilson; *Arts in Educ Dir* Renee Rector; *Bookkeeper* Carol Cofield; *Admin Asst & Rental Coordr* Crystal Coker
Open Mon - Thurs 9 AM - 7 PM, Fri 9 AM - 4:30 PM, others by appt; No admis fee; Estab 1963 to build & maintain an environment supportive of the arts in NW Georgia; Average Annual Attendance: 130,000; Mem: 1,000; dues family $35, annual meeting in June
Income: $500,000 (financed by mem, commissions, grants, tuitions & fund raising events)
Library Holdings: Book Volumes
Collections: Permanent collection of regional art
Exhibitions: Changing monthly shows of crafts; graphics; photography; original art; sculpture; fiber
Publications: Bulletins to members, monthly
Activities: Classes for adults & children; dramatic progs; visual & performing arts programs for schools; concerts; gallery talks; competitions with awards; arts & crafts festivals; individual paintings & original objects of art lent to area schools & organizations

DECATUR

M **AGNES SCOTT COLLEGE,** Dalton Art Gallery, 141 E College Ave, Dana Fine Arts Bldg Decatur, GA 30030-3770. Tel 404-471-5361; Email daltongallery@agnesscott.edu; Web: daltongallery.agnesscott.edu; *Chmn Art Dept* Donna Sadler; *Printmaker* Anne Beidler; *Art Historian* Roger Rothman
Open Mon - Fri 10 AM - 9 PM, Sat 9 AM - 5 PM, Sun 2 - 5 PM; No admis fee; Estab 1965 to enhance art program; Gallery consists of four rooms, 300 running ft of wall space, light beige walls & rug; Dana Fine Arts Bldg designed by John Portman
Income: Financed by endowment
Collections: Clifford M Clarke Collection, Harry L Dalton Collection, Steffen Thomas Collection, Ferdinand Warren Collection
Exhibitions: 4 exhibitions per yr
Activities: Lect open to public

DUBLIN

M **LAURENS COUNTY HISTORICAL SOCIETY,** Dublin-Laurens Museum, 311 Academy Ave, PO Box 1461 Dublin, GA 31040-5219. Tel 478-272-9242; Email history@nlamerica.com; *Dir* Scott B Thompson Sr
Open Tues - Fri 1 - 4:30 PM; No admis fee; Estab 1967; Average Annual Attendance: 5,000; Mem: 500; dues $15-$200 graduating
Income: $25,000 (financed by mem, city & county appropriation, contributions)
Collections: Indian Artifacts; Art Originals-Lila Moore Keen
Exhibitions: Historical Photographs
Publications: Laurens County Historical Society Newsletter, quarterly

FORT BENNING

M **NATIONAL INFANTRY MUSEUM & SOLDIER CENTER,** Patriot Park, Fort Benning, GA 31905; 1775 Legacy Way, Columbus, GA 31903-3600. Tel 706-685-5800; 653-9234; Web: www.nationalinfantrymuseum.com
Open Mon - Sat 9 AM - 5 PM, Sun 11 AM - 5 PM, cl Christmas Day & New Year's Day; No admis fee, donations accepted; 190,000 sq ft facility with galleries & Soldier Center with IMAX, restaurant & mus store; Mem: Dues 1775 society

$1000, patron $300, individual/family $50, ret military/ educator $35, active military/ student $25
Collections: Over 30,000 artifacts tracing Infantry history, Era Galleries trace Infantry history from the Revolutionary War to present day
Exhibitions: The Last 100 Yards; The Fort Benning Gallery; The Family Support Gallery; Entering the International Stage; A World Power; The Cold War; The Sole Superpower; Hall of Valor; Officers Candidate School of Honor; Ranger Hall of Honor
Activities: Lects; tours; seminars

FORT VALLEY

L **FORT VALLEY STATE COLLEGE,** H A Hunt Memorial Library, 1005 State College Dr, Fort Valley, GA 31030-3298. Tel 478-825-6342; Fax 912-825-6916; Email fvsclib@uscn.cc.uga.edu; Web: www.fvsu.edu/academics/library; *Dept Head* Frank Mahitas
Open Mon-Thurs 8AM-midnight, Fri 8AM-5PM, Sat 1PM-5PM, and Sun 3PM-10PM; No admis fee; Estab 1939
Income: Financed by state assistance
Special Subjects: Afro-American Art, Art Education, Art History, Historical Material
Collections: Afro - American Art, Graphic Arts
Exhibitions: History of College
Activities: Classes for adults; lending collection contains books

HAWKINSVILLE

M **HAWKINSVILLE/PULASKI COUNTY ARTS COUNCIL,** Hawkinsville Old Opera House, 42 Lumpkin St, Hawkinsville, GA 31036; PO Box 266, Hawkinsville, GA 31036-0266. Tel 912-783-1884; Fax 912-783-2333; Email info@hawkinsvilleoperahouse.com; Web: hawkinsvilleoperahouse.com
Open Mon - Fri 10 AM - 4 PM; Varies per show
Collections: Paintings, photographs & sculpture by Georgia artists
Activities: Concerts; tours

JEKYLL ISLAND

M **JEKYLL ISLAND MUSEUM,** Stable Rd, Jekyll Island, GA 31520; 381 Riverview Dr, Jekyll Island, GA 31527-0874. Tel 912-635-2119; 635-2122; Fax 912-635-4420; Email jekyllisland@compuserve.com; Web: www.jekyllisland.com; *Exec Dir Jekyll Island* Bill Donohue; *Dir Mus & Historic Preservation* F Warren Murphey; *Cur Educ* Gretchen Greminger; *Chief Cur* John Hunter
Open Memorial Day - Labor Day Mon - Sun 9:30 AM - 5 PM, Labor Day - Memorial Day Mon - Sun 9:30 AM - 4 PM; Admis adults $10, students 6-18 years $6; Estab 1954; Average Annual Attendance: 51,000
Income: Financed by fees & admis
Special Subjects: Furniture, Portraits, Stained Glass
Collections: 1890 Furniture, Tiffany Stained Glass Windows, portraits
Activities: Programs for adults & children; lects open to pub; tours; mus shop sells books, reproductions, slides & turn-of-the century related items

LAGRANGE

M **LAGRANGE ART MUSEUM,** (Chattahoochee Valley Art Museum), 112 Lafayette Pkwy, LaGrange, GA 30240. Tel 706-882-3267; Fax 706-882-2878; Email info@lagrangeartmuseum.org; Web: www.lagrangeartmuseum.org; *Exec Dir* Karen Briggs; *Bus Mgr* Debbie Howard; *Mem Coordr* Lauren Oliver; *Educ Coordr* Sallie Keith
Open Tues - Fri 9 AM - 5 PM, Sat 11 AM - 5 PM, cl Sun & Mon; Admis free to Troup county residents; Estab 1963 to provide visual art experience & educ to people of West Georgia; 100 year old former Troup County Jail refurbished for use as galleries having about 350 running ft of wall space & 7000 sq ft of floor space on two floors; Average Annual Attendance: 8,200; Mem: 300; dues $25 - $5,000; annual meeting in Jan
Income: $350,000 (financed by mem, foundation grant, civic organizations & fundraisers)
Purchases: $10,000, Purchase Awards, LaGrange National Competition, Southeast Regional/Folk Art
Special Subjects: Afro-American Art, American Indian Art, Carpets & Rugs, Ceramics, Drawings, Etchings & Engravings, Folk Art, Graphics, Juvenile Art, Marine Painting, Painting-American, Photography, Pottery, Prints, Stained Glass, Textiles, Watercolors, Woodcarvings, Woodcuts
Collections: Contemporary American art of all types & media
Exhibitions: Rotating exhibitions, four per yr
Activities: Classes for adults & children; lects open to pub; 1-2 visiting lectures per year; gallery talks; tours; competitions with awards, Purchase Awards - La Grange Southeast Regional Competition; Creative Youth Art League Competition;; individual paintings & original objects of art lent to bus patrons in a 5 county area; originate traveling exhibs to museums across US; mus shop sells prints, original art & reproductions

M **LAGRANGE COLLEGE,** Lamar Dodd Art Center Museum, 601 Broad St, LaGrange, GA 30240-2955. Tel 706-882-2911; Fax 706-884-6567; *Dir* John D Lawrence
Open Mon-Fri 8:30AM-4:30PM during school; Estab 1988
Collections: 20th Century Photography, American Indian Collection, Retrospective Collection
Exhibitions: Two shows every six weeks

MACON

M **MUSEUM OF ARTS & SCIENCES, INC,** 4182 Forsyth Rd, Macon, GA 31210-4869. Tel 478-477-3232; Fax 478-477-3251; Email lfisher@masmacon.com; Web: www.masmacon.org; *Dir* Susan Welsh; *Opers Dir* Lisa Gant Fisher; *Cur Educ* Susan Mays; *Cur Science* Paul Fisher; *Museum Shop Mgr* Beth Fisher
Open Tues - Sat 10 AM - 5 PM, Sun 1 - 5 PM; Admis adults $10, seniors $8, students $7, children $5, members free; Estab 1956 as a general art & science museum with a planetarium; South Gallery 50 ft x 60 ft; North Gallery 25 ft x 35 ft; Hall Gallery 8 ft x 32 ft; Newberry Hall 1759 sq ft; Average Annual Attendance: 64,261; Mem: 2200; dues $20-$1000
Special Subjects: Archaeology, Drawings, Painting-American, Painting-European, Prints, Sculpture, Ceramics
Collections: American art with emphasis on the Southeast drawings, paintings, prints & sculpture, gems & minerals, doll coll, quilt coll, ethnographic
Publications: Museum Muse, quarterly newsletter; catalogues
Activities: Classes for adults & children; docent training; lects open to pub, 2-6 vis lectrs per yr; concerts; gallery talks; guided tours; movies; special events; summer children's camps; individual paintings & original objects of art lent to other mus; book traveling exhibs, 5 - 10 per yr; originate traveling exhibs to schools or appropriate institutions in Georgia & Southeast; mus shop sells books, magazines, original art, reproductions, prints, small educational toys, t-shirts, gem & minerals, gift items, rocks, shells, science kits

M **TUBMAN AFRICAN AMERICAN MUSEUM,** 310 Cherry St, Macon, GA 31201; PO Box 6671, Macon, GA 31208-6671. Tel 478-743-8544; Fax 478-743-9063; Email guestservices@tubmanmuseum.com; Web: www.tubmanmuseum.com; *Exec Dir* Dr Andy Ambrose; *Dir Educ* Trenda Byrd; *Dir Exhib* Jeff Bruce
Open Tues - Sat 9 AM - 5 PM; Admis $10 adults, $8 sr citizens, students & military, $6 children; Estab 1981, to educate people about African American art, history & culture, while promoting racial harmony; Nine galleries, one mural entitled from Africa to America; Average Annual Attendance: 65,000; Mem: 500; dues $20 - $2,500; annual meeting in Dec
Income: Financed by endowment, mem, city & state appropriation, store
Special Subjects: African Art, Afro-American Art, Ceramics, Coins & Medals, Collages, Costumes, Crafts, Drawings, Etchings & Engravings, Flasks & Bottles, Folk Art, Furniture, Historical Material, Jewelry, Metalwork, Painting-American, Photography, Porcelain, Portraits, Pottery, Prints, Sculpture, Textiles, Woodcarvings, Woodcuts, Primitive art
Collections: African & African-American art & artifacts, 70 foot long mural is signature possession, Medal of Honor, Sgt Rodney Davis, From Africa to America
Exhibitions: Rotating exhibits every 2 1/2 months; Harriet Tubman exhib; African American Inventors exhib
Activities: Classes for adults & children; dramatic progs; docent training; festival last Sun in Apr; black-tie fundraiser All That Jazz in Nov; lects open to pub, 1-7 vis lectrs per yr; gallery talks; tours; Act of Courage Awards (annual), Shelia award (biannual); schols & fels offered; lending of original objects of art; originate traveling exhibs via outreach program sending teachers & exhibs to schools, after-school progs & community ctrs; mus shop sells books, magazines, original art, prints, reproductions, apparel, jewelry & African crafts

L **Keil Resource Center,** PO Box 6671, Macon, GA 31208-6671. Tel 912-743-8544; Fax 912-743-9063; Web: www.tubmanmuseum.org
Open Mon - Fri 9 AM - 5 PM; Estab 1987; For reference only
Income: Financed by endowment, mem, city & state appropriations, store
Library Holdings: Book Volumes 2500, Video Tapes
Special Subjects: Afro-American Art, Art Education, Art History, Film, Folk Art, Mixed Media, Painting-American, Photography, Pottery, Printmaking, Prints, Sculpture, Textiles, Theatre Arts

MADISON

M **MADISON MUSEUM OF FINE ART,** 290 Hancock St, Madison, GA 30650; PO Box 814, Madison, GA 30650-0814. Tel 706-485-4530; Email mbechtell@prodigy.net; Web: madisonmuseum.org; *CEO, Pres & Dir* Michele Bechtell; *Chmn* MC Bechtell; *Secy* Sean Gallagher
Open Mon - Sat 1 - 5 PM; Admis by donation; Fine art history museum; Average Annual Attendance: 6,000
Special Subjects: African Art, Antiquities-Oriental, Ceramics, Drawings, Etchings & Engravings, Folk Art, Landscapes, Painting-American, Painting-European, Painting-Flemish, Painting-French, Painting-Italian, Porcelain, Pottery, Prints, Religious Art, Sculpture, Stained Glass
Collections: paintings, sculpture garden
Publications: quarterly newsletter
Activities: Classes for adults & children; docent prog; lects open to the pub; concerts; films; art festivals; gallery talks; tours; lending of original objects of art; mus shop

M **MORGAN COUNTY FOUNDATION, INC,** Madison-Morgan Cultural Center, 434 S Main St, Madison, GA 30650-1640. Tel 706-342-4743; Fax 706-342-1154; Email cultural@mail.morgan.public.lib.ga.us; Web: www.madisonmorgancultural.org; *Chmn Bd* Sarah Burbach; *Admin Dir* Rhonda Smith; *Dir Visual Arts* Angela Nichols; *Interim Dir* Tina Lilly; *Dir* Kimberly Brown; *Dir Mktg* Theresa Dickinson; *Dir Prog* Rebecca Bonas; *Dir Visual Arts* Deanna Lamar
Open Tues - Sat 10 AM - 5 PM, Sun 2 - 5 PM; Admis fee adults $3, seniors $2.50, students $2, members free; Estab 1976 to enhance the educational & cultural life of Georgia & the Southeast; Four galleries for changing exhibits, housed in former classrooms (approx 25 ft x 35 ft) of historic 1895 school facility; heart pine floors, no daylight, tungsten track lighting only, with heat, air conditioning & electronic security; Average Annual Attendance: 30,000; Mem: 1500; dues $15-$1,000; annual meeting second Mon in July
Income: $460,000 (financed by endowment, mem, state grants, admis fees for services & sponsorship contributions)

Exhibitions: Usually two simultaneous exhibits, each 8-12 wks, of work by regional artists &/or collections of museums & private collections from the region or across the nation; Annual Juried Regional Art Exhibit
Publications: Exhibit brochures & catalogs, 4-5 per yr; Madison Georgia - An Architectural Guide
Activities: Performing arts progs; docent training; gallery tours; demonstrations; lects open to pub, 5-10 vis lectrs per yr; concerts; gallery talks; competitions with awards; book traveling exhibs 5-10 per yr; originate traveling exhibs; mus shop sells books, original art & reproductions

MARIETTA

M **MARIETTA-COBB MUSEUM OF ART,** 30 Atlanta St NE, Marietta, GA 30060-1975. Tel 770-528-1444; Fax 770-528-1440; Email info@mariettacobbartmuseum.org; Web: www.mariettacobbartmuseum.org; *Exec Dir* Sally Macaulay; *Dir Fin & Opers* Jennifer Fox
Open Tues - Fri 11 AM - 5 PM, Sat 11 AM - 4 PM, Sun 1 - 4 PM; Admis adults $8, seniors & students (6-18 with ID) $5, mems & children (under 6) no charge; Estab 1990 to provide the communities of Cobb County, the city of Marietta & visitors to the area exposure to the visual arts through a diversity of visual art experiences, educational services & outreach activities based upon visiting exhibitions & the acquisition, conservation & exhibition of a permanent collection focused on American Art; Galleries 1-3 on main floor, gallery 4-5 on second level; Average Annual Attendance: 15,000; Mem: 600; dues individual $35 & up
Income: Financed by mem & donations, grants, foundations grants, county grants, city grants
Special Subjects: Painting-American, Prints, Sculpture
Collections: Collection of 400 works of art focusing on 19th & 20 century American Art
Activities: Classes for adults & children; docent training; art camp; lects open to pub; concerts; competitions; individual paintings & original objects of art lent to other mus; mus shop sells original art; junior mus

MOULTRIE

M **COLQUITT COUNTY ARTS CENTER,** 401 7th Ave SW, Moultrie, GA 31768-4633. Tel 229-985-1922; Fax 229-890-6746; Web: www.colquittcountyarts.com; *Visual Arts Dir* Jane Simpson; *Dir* Jeff Ophime; *Asst Dir* Lin Sheffield; *Cur* Candace Underwood
Open Mon - Fri 10 AM - 5:30 PM Sat 10 AM - 2 PM; No admis fee
Collections: Paintings, photographs & sculpture by national & international artists
Activities: Educ programs; special events; annual events; theater productions

MOUNT BERRY

M **BERRY COLLEGE,** Moon Gallery, PO Box 580, Mount Berry, GA 30149-2289. Tel 706-238-2219; Fax 706-236-7835; Web: http://www.berry.edu/academics/humanities/finearts/page.aspx?id=2823; *Pres* Stephen R Briggs; *Dept Chair* Dr. Stan Pethel; *Dir* Jere Lykins
Open Mon - Sat 10 AM - 5 PM, Sun 1 - 5 PM; Admis adults $5, children 6-12 $3; Estab 1972; Medium size gallery, carpeted floors & walls, tracking spots; Average Annual Attendance: 3,500
Exhibitions: Guest lecturer & juror for student Honors show
Activities: Classes for adults & children; lects open to pub, 6-8 vis lectrs per yr; gallery talks; competitions with awards; scholarships offered; individual paintings & original objects of art lent; lending collection contains books, cassettes, color reproductions, 20 original prints, paintings, records, photographs & 5000 slides; book traveling exhibs; originate traveling exhibs

L **Memorial Library**, 2277 Martha Berry Hwy NW, Mount Berry, GA 30149. Tel 706-236-2221; Fax 706-236-9596; Email lfoldes@berry.edu; Web: berry.edu; *Prof Art* Dr T J Mew III; *Dir* Lance Foldes
Open Mon - Thurs 8 AM - 12 AM, Fri 8 AM - 8 PM, Sat 1 - 6 PM, Sun 1 PM - 12 AM during acad yr, Mon - Thurs 8 AM - 10 PM, Fri 8 AM - 5 PM during summer; Estab 1926 for educational purposes
Library Holdings: Audio Tapes, Book Volumes 350, Cassettes, Clipping Files, Exhibition Catalogs, Filmstrips, Manuscripts, Memorabilia, Motion Pictures, Original Art Works, Pamphlets, Periodical Subscriptions 25, Photographs, Prints, Records, Slides, Video Tapes
Special Subjects: Ceramics

PEACHTREE CITY

M **AMERICAN PRINT ALLIANCE,** 302 Larkspur Turn, Peachtree City, GA 30269-2210. Tel 770-486-6680; Email director@printalliance.org; Web: www.printalliance.org; *Dir* Carol Pulin PhD; *Community Coordr* Valerie Dibble
Estab 1992 to provide educ & resource information for the promotion of the print arts; Internet gallery for prints, paperwork, & artists' books; Average Annual Attendance: 18,000 plus 120,000 internet vis per yr; Mem: 15 councils; mem open to non-profit printmakers' councils: dues $100, individual $32-$38, student $19
Income: Financed by mem & journal subscriptions
Exhibitions: Memorial Portfolio: September 11th; Soap Box Prints: For the Environment; Soap Box Prints 2: Prints, Politics & Democracy; On-going traveling exhibs
Publications: Contemporary Impressions, semi-annual; Guide to Print Workshops in Canada & The United States
Activities: Conferences; lect open to pub; originate traveling exhibs 1 per yr to museums, colleges, universities, community & arts centers & other public bldgs; online mus shop sells original prints

POOLER

AMERICAN SOCIETY FOR AESTHETICS
For further information, see National and Regional Organizations

RABUN GAP

M **HAMBIDGE CENTER FOR CREATIVE ARTS & SCIENCES,** 105 Hambidge Ct, Rabun Gap, GA 30568-1525; PO Box 339, Rabun Gap, GA 30568-0339. Tel 706-746-5718; Fax 706-746-9933; Email center@hambidge.org; Web: www.hambidge.org; *Exec Dir* Jamie Badoud; *Operations Manager* Christine Jason
Open Feb - Dec; No admis fee; Estab 1934, residency prog since 1988; Listed on the National Register of Historic Places, 600 acres; Average Annual Attendance: 120; Mem: 775, variable dues
Income: Nonprofit organization
Special Subjects: Folk Art, Crafts
Exhibitions: Fine Craft Exhibs, Annual Georgia Pottery Show
Activities: 2-8 week residencies for professional artists/authors; ceramic workshops; speakers' forums open to public; guided nature walks; historic mill; anagama pottery firings; lects open to pub; 4 vis lectrs per yr; Sales shop sells books, original art, prints

SAINT SIMONS ISLAND

A **GLYNN VISUAL ARTS, INC GLYNN VISUAL ARTS,** (Glynn Art Association), 106 Island Dr, Saint Simons Island, GA 31522-3780. Tel 912-638-8770; Fax 912-634-2787; Email info@glynnvisualarts.org; Web: wwwglynnvisualarts.org; *Pres* Sue Cansler; *Dir* Susan Ryles; *VPres* Deborah Wright; *Treas* Marie Dodd; *Secy* Will Gallagher; *Office Mgr* Laura Dunn; *Pottery Dir* Debbie Craig
Open Mon -Sat 9 AM - 5 PM; No admis fee; Estab 1953; 1,100 sq ft, largest portion devoted to local art, smaller portion for one man exhibits, traveling shows & competitions; Average Annual Attendance: 8,000; Mem: 600; dues $50-$1,000; annual meeting in Apr
Income: $300,000 (financed by mems & commission on sales of art)
Library Holdings: Book Volumes
Special Subjects: Crafts, Drawings, Glass, Porcelain, Pottery, Prints, Silver, Woodcarvings
Exhibitions: Miniature competition from all over & more than 100 local artists; Exhibs rotate six week intervals (two galleries)
Publications: The Canvas, monthly newsletter
Activities: Classes for adults & children; docent training; lect open to public, 3-4 vis lectrs per year; gallery talks; competitions with prizes; awards, Coastal Nat, Fall Festival; scholarships & fels offered; sales shop sells books, prints & original art

SAVANNAH

M **SHIPS OF THE SEA MARITIME MUSEUM,** 41 Martin Luther King, Jr Blvd Savannah, GA 31401. Tel 912-232-1511; Fax 912-234-7363; Email contact@shipsofthesea.org; Web: www.telfair.org; *Exec Dir* Tony Pizzo; *Asst Dir* Karl DeVries; *Gift Shop Mgr* Eileen Lewis
Open Tues - Sun 10 AM - 5 PM; Admis adults $7, seniors & students $5; Estab 1966 to promote Savannah's maritime history & preserve William Scarbrough house; Average Annual Attendance: 50,000
Income: Financed privately
Special Subjects: Historical Material, Marine Painting, Painting-American, Scrimshaw
Collections: Figureheads, maritime antiques, paintings, porcelains, scrimshaw, ship models, Maritime antiques; ship models
Exhibitions: Savannah & Civil War at Sea; Steamship Company (Savannah Line)
Publications: Exhibit catalogues, Flotsam & Jetsam; William Scarbrough's House
Activities: Educ Prog; classes for children; lects open to pub; concerts; tours; mus shop sells books & magazines, gift shop

M **TELFAIR MUSEUMS,** 121 Barnard St, Savannah, GA 31401-3612; PO Box 10081, Savannah, GA 31412-0281. Tel 912-790-8800; Fax 912-232-6954; Email info@telfair.org; Web: www.telfair.org; *Dir & CEO* Lisa Grove; *Exec Asst* Margo Jackson; *Cur Fine Arts & Exhibit* Courtney McNeil; *Cur Decorative Arts & Historic Sites* Shannon Brawning-Mullis; *Senior Cur Educ* Harry DeLorme; *Asst Cur* Beth Moore; *Registrar* Jessica M Estes; *Financial Officer* Joey Rudder; *Dir Develop* Molly Taylor
Open Sun & Mon noon - 5 PM; Tues - Sat 10 AM - 5 PM; 3 site pass $20, seniors & military $18, students $5, children under 12 free; Estab 1875 to collect & to preserve, exhibit & interpret; Circ Non-lending 5,000 publications, 18 periodicals; Telfair Academy: 4 galleries 2400 sq ft, Rotunda gallery 3400 sq ft, Sculpture gallery 2700 sq ft, Jepson Center 64,000 sq ft of display & interactive galleries; Average Annual Attendance: 188,000; Mem: 4500; dues $45-$10,000; annual meeting in Apr
Income: Financed by endowment, mem, city & state appropriation, banks & corporate foundations & federal government
Library Holdings: Auction Catalogs, Book Volumes, Exhibition Catalogs
Special Subjects: Decorative Arts, Painting-French, Painting-German, Period Rooms, Portraits
Collections: American decorative arts, American & European artists, Late 18th century to present, 19th & 20th century American & European paintings, works on paper
Exhibitions: Special & traveling exhibitions
Publications: The Octagon Room; We Ain't What We Used to Be; Christopher P H Murphy (1869-1939): A Retrospective; Nostrums for Fashionable Entertainments: Dining in Georgia 1800-1850; Classical Savannah: Fine and Decorative Arts 1800-1840; Looking Back: Art in Savannah 1900-1960; Ladies, Landscapes and Loyal Retainers: Japanese Art from a Private Collection; Frederick Carl Frieseke: The Evolution of an American Impressionist; Southern Melodies: A Larry

Connatser Retrospective; GA Triennial; Freedom's March; Palliser; Dutch Utopia: American Artists in Holland 1880-1914
Activities: Classes for adults; classes for children; docent training; progs & classes for children; lects open to pub, 6 vis lectrs per year; concerts; gallery talks; tours; Effingham County; Chatham County; parks & playgrounds; individual paintings & original objects of art lent to other mus internationally; lending collection contains over 4000 original art works, over 100 sculptures, 2,186 fine arts and 1,968 decorative; book traveling exhibs 6-10 per yr; originate traveling exhibs to other art mus throughout US; mus shop sells books, reproductions, prints, posters, postcards; original art

—**Telfair Academy of Arts & Sciences Library**, 121 Barnard St, Savannah, GA 31401-3612; PO Box 10081, Savannah, GA 31412-0281. Tel 912-790-8800; Fax 912-232-6954; Email hadaways@telfair.org; Web: www.telfair.org; *CFO* Shelly Cannady; *Dir Mktg & Pub Rels* Kristen Boylston; *Cur Educ* Harry DeLorme; *Cur Fine Arts & Exhibits* Hollis Koons McCullough; *Registrar* Jessica Mumford; *Mus Shop Mgr* Lisa Ocampo; *Admin* Sandra S Hadaway; *Designer & Preparator* Milutin Pavlovic; *VPres & Bd of Trustees* John Kennedy III; *Asst Cur* Elizabeth Moore; *Dir Develop* Barbara Evans; *Asst Cur* Courtney McGowan
Open Jepson Ctr & Telfair Acad: Sun noon-5PM, Mon 10AM-5PM, cl Tues, Wed-Sat 10AM-5PM; Owens Thomas House: Sun 1PM-5PM, Mon noon- 5PM, Tues-Sat 10AM-5PM; Admis adults $10, seniors $8, students $5, children 5-12 $4, children under 5 free, members free, group rates; adult tours $7, college group $6, K-12 student groups $4, family with two adults and two kids $25; Estab 1875 to collect, preserve, exhibit, & interpret the objects in its collection of fine & decorative arts & its National Historic Landmark buildings; Circ 4,000; For reference only, for scholars & the public; Average Annual Attendance: 144,500; Mem: 1420; dues grand benefactor $10,000; benefactor $5,000; sponsor $2,500; grand patron $1,500; patron $1,250; sustainer $1,000; friend $600; supporting $300; donor $100; family $60; individual $35; special $25
Income: 2,000,000 (financed by membership, grants, fundraising events & endowments)
Purchases: 40,000
Library Holdings: Book Volumes 3,500, Exhibition Catalogs, Periodical Subscriptions 130
Exhibitions: 4-6 traveling exhibitions per year
Publications: Quarterly newsletter; exhibition brochures & catalogs
Activities: Originate traveling exhibs to local institutions, also to NY & willing to lend nationwide

SUWANEE

A **HANDWEAVERS GUILD OF AMERICA,** 1255 Buford Highway, Ste 211, Suwanee, GA 30024. Tel 678-730-0100; Fax 678-730-0836; Email hga@weavespindye.org; Web: www.weavespindye.org; *Exec Dir* Elizabeth Williamson; *Ed* Sally Orgren
Open Mon - Thurs 10 AM - 5 PM; No admis fee; Estab 1969 to promote fiber arts; Mem: 4,000; dues $40; annual meeting in summer; interest in fiber arts req
Income: Financed by mem dues, contributions, advertising & conferences
Library Holdings: Book Volumes, Exhibition Catalogs, Original Documents
Special Subjects: Carpets & Rugs, Crafts, Decorative Arts, Embroidery, Laces, Leather, Tapestries, Textiles
Exhibitions: Small Expressions (annual) spring/summer exhibit
Publications: Shuttle, Spindle & Dyepot, quarterly publication for members
Activities: Fiber progs for adults; lects open to mems & pub for fee, 1 vis lectr per yr; gallery talks; tours; Exhib Awards & HGA Award, awards to selected fiber art shows; schols & fels offered; originate traveling exhibs to fiber guilds; e-shop on website sells books

VALDOSTA

M **VALDOSTA STATE UNIVERSITY,** Art Gallery, 1500 N Patterson St, Valdosta, GA 31698-0001. Tel 229-333-5835; Fax 229-259-5121; Email kgmurray@valdosta.edu; Web: www.valdosta.edu/art; *Dir Gallery* Karin Murray; *Acting Head Art Dept* A Blake Pearce; *Cur* Dick Bjornseth
Open Mon - Thurs 10 AM - 4 PM, Fri 10 AM - 3 PM; No admis fee; Estab 1970 for educational purposes serving students, faculty, community & region; Gallery is an open rectangular room with approx 122 running ft of exhibition space; Average Annual Attendance: 20,000
Income: Financed by state appropriations
Special Subjects: African Art
Collections: African art, Lamar Dodd
Exhibitions: 8-9 exhibitions per year; national juried Valdosta works on paper exhibition; faculty show
Activities: Classes for adults; dramatic progs; docent training; lects open to pub, 3-5 vis lectrs per yr; Valdosta State Orchestra; concerts; gallery talks; tours; competitions; vis artists; demonstrations; scholarships offered; originate traveling exhibs

WAYCROSS

M **OKEFENOKEE HERITAGE CENTER, INC,** 1460 N Augusta Ave, Waycross, GA 31501-4954. Tel 912-285-4260; Fax 912-283-2858; Email okeheritage@gmail.com; Web: www.okefenokeeheritagecenter.org; *Executive Director* Elizabeth Welch; *Vis Coordr* Betty Callahan
Open Tues - Sat 9 AM - 2 PM; Admis $7, children 6-18 $5, children under 5 no charge; Estab 1975 to house displays on arts & history; Four gallery areas; Average Annual Attendance: 10,000; Mem: 350; dues bus $10,000, guardian $5,000, corporate patron $3,000, sponsor & corporate sponsor $1,000, donor & bus donor $500, friend & bus friend $300, heritage club $100, family $60, individual $36
Income: $85,000 (financed by endowment, mem, grants, contributions, admis, special activities, gift shop)
Special Subjects: African Art, Afro-American Art, American Indian Art, Crafts, Painting-American, Prints, Historical Material, Period Rooms, Dioramas, Dolls, Furniture, Pottery
Collections: 1912 Baldwin Steam Locomotive train & caboose, 1830's Homestead, 1870's house exhibit, 1890's print shop, prints, crafts, paintings, photographs; Native American History; Gram Parson's exhibit
Exhibitions: Annual art show (Sept); Sacred Harp (Permanent); Individual Artists Children Art Show
Publications: Quarterly exhibit catalogues; newsletter
Activities: Classes for adults & children; demonstrations; workshops; lects open to pub; concerts; gallery talks; tours; competitions; purchase awards; book traveling exhibs; mus shop sells books, original art, reproductions, prints, gifts, souvenirs & train memorabilia

HAWAII

HAWAII VOLCANOES NATIONAL PARK

M **VOLCANO ART CENTER GALLERY,** Crater Rim Drive, Next to Kilauea Visitor Center Hawaii Volcanoes National Park, HI; P.O. Box 129, Volcano, HI 96785-0129. Tel 866-967-7565 (Gallery), 808-967-7565 (Gallery); 967-8222 (Admin Dept); Fax 808-967-7511 (Gallery); 967-8512 (Admin Dept); Email gallery@volcanoartcenter.org; Web: www.volcanoartcenter.org; *Exec Dir* Michael A Nelson; *Gallery Mgr* Emily C Weiss; *Brd Chmn* Hugh Jenkins
Open Gallery: daily 9 AM - 5 PM; Admin: Mon - Fri 8:30 AM - 5 PM; No admis fee; park entrance fees apply; Estab 1974 as a non-profit organization; Mem: 1800, dues range from $42, ann meeting every Oct
Income: Gallery sales, grants, memberships & donations
Special Subjects: Art Education, Ceramics, Crafts, Decorative Arts, Drawings, Etchings & Engravings, Furniture, Glass, Graphics, Jewelry, Photography, Posters, Pottery, Primitive art, Prints, Scrimshaw, Sculpture, Silver, Stained Glass, Tapestries, Textiles, Watercolors, Woodcarvings, Woodcuts
Publications: E-newsletter/website
Activities: Environmental forest stewardships; lects open to pub; 1-4 vis lectrs per yr; performances; concerts; gallery talks; tours; sponsoring competitions; mus shop sells books, magazines, original art, reproductions, prints

HILO

M **EAST HAWAII CULTURAL CENTER,** Hawaii Museum of Contemporary Art, 141 Kalakaua St, Hilo, HI 96720. Tel 908-961-5711; Email admin@ehcc.org; Web: www.ehcc.org; *Exec Dir* Mike Marshall
Open Tues - Sat 10 AM - 4 PM, Tues - Fri 10 AM - 4 PM; No admis fee; suggested donation $5; Estab to provide the community with an outlet for creative & cultural expression; Mem: dues $25-$75
Special Subjects: Pottery
Collections: Contemporary art
Exhibitions: Temporary exhibits
Activities: Concerts; gallery talks; tours; art programming; workshops; dance & theatre performances; cultural events; Mus shop sells prints; gifts; contemporary crafts; furniture

M **WAILOA ARTS & CULTURAL CENTER,** 200 Piopio St, Wailoa River State Recreation Area Hilo, HI 96720-4274; Division of State Parks, 75 Aupuni St Rm 204 Hilo, HI 96720-4245. Tel 808-933-0416; Fax 808-933-0417; Email wailoaartculturalcenter@gmail.com; *CEO & Dir* Codie King
Open Mon - Tues & Thurs - Fri 8:30 AM - 4:30 PM, Wed Noon - 4:30 PM, cl holidays; No admis fee; Estab 1967; located in Wailoa River State Recreation Area; Average Annual Attendance: 30,000
Library Holdings: Book Volumes
Collections: works by local artists, Big Island history & culture
Activities: Demonstrations; seminars; workshops; classes; outreach progs; school tours; concerts; live performances

HONOLULU

A **ASSOCIATION OF HAWAII ARTISTS,** PO Box 10202, Honolulu, HI 96816-0202. Tel 808-239-6066; Fax 808-923-1062; Email ahahawaii@gmail.com; Web: associationhawaiiartists.com; *Pres* Jenee Wonderlich; *VPres* Priscilla Hall; *Corresp Secy* Linda Umstead; *Recording Secy* Sylvia Lewis
Estab 1926 to promote congeniality & stimulate growth by presenting programs; to contribute to the cultural life of the State of Hawaii; Average Annual Attendance: 1,000; Mem: 250; dues $17-$35; monthly meeting every second Tues
Income: Financed by mem
Publications: Paint Rag, monthly
Activities: Lect open to public, 2-3 vis lectrs per year; demonstrations; competitions with cash awards, plaques & rosettes

M **BERNICE PAUAHI BISHOP MUSEUM,** 1525 Bernice St, Honolulu, HI 96817-2704. Tel 808-847-3511; Fax 808-848-4147; Email ask@bishopmuseum.org; Web: www.bishopmuseum.org; *Interim Pres & CEO* Linda Lee Kuuleilani Farm
Open daily 9 AM - 5 PM, cl Thanksgiving & Christmas Day; Admis adult $22.95, seniors 65 & over $19.95,children 4-17 $14.95, children 3 & under no charge; Estab 1889 to preserve & study the culture & natural history of Hawaii; Mem: Dues $35 - $1,000
Exhibitions: Awesome Treasures of Hawaii & the Pacific: A Hands-On Adventure; Treasures; Ocean Planet

L **Library & Archives**, 1525 Bernice St, Honolulu, HI 96817-0916. Tel 808-848-4148; Fax 808-847-8241; Email library@bishopmuseum.org; Web: www.bishopmuseum.org; *Head Librn* Duane Wenzel; *Archivist* DeSoto Brown; *Reference Librn* Patty Belcher; *Librn* Janet Short; *Archivist* Ron Schaeffer; *Reference Archivist* Judy Kearney

Open Tues & Thurs 1 PM - 4 PM, Sat 9 AM - Noon; Admis adults $17.95, youth & seniors (65 & over) $14.95, children (3 & under) no charge; Estab 1889 to stimulate awareness & appreciation of the natural & cultural world of Hawaii & the Pacific; Average Annual Attendance: 200,000; Mem: 10,000; dues $35- $65
Library Holdings: Book Volumes 40,000, Manuscripts 3,500, Photographs 1,000,000
Special Subjects: Anthropology, Archaeology, Ethnology, Folk Art, Historical Material, History of Art & Archaeology
Collections: Books, Insect Specimens, Journals, Manuscripts, Pacific & Hawaiian Cultural Objects, Photographs, Plant Specimens, Zoological Specimens, Maps, Fine Art, Moving Images
Activities: Classes for adults & children; docent training; lects open to pub; concerts; gallery talks; tours; competitions with awards; originate traveling exhibs; mus shop sells books; original art & reproductions

M **HONOLULU MUSEUM OF ART,** 900 S Beretania St, Honolulu, HI 96814-1495. Tel 808-532-8700; Fax 808-532-8787; Email info@honolulumuseum.org; Web: www.honolulumuseum.org; Cable HONART; *Dir* Sean O'Harrow; *Chmn* Violet S W Loo; *Deputy Dir Admin & Opers* Allison Wong; *Dir Fin* Tania Ginoza; *Dir Develop* Cara Mazzei; *Dir Security* Mike Chock; *Dir Human Resources* Sharon Stillman
Open Tues - Sun 10 AM - 4:30 PM, cl Mon & major holidays; Admis adults $20, Hawaii res $10, children 18 & under & mems free; Estab 1927 as the only art museum of a broad general nature in the Pacific; to provide Hawaii's people of many races with works of art representing their composite cultural heritage from both East and West; Circ 45,000; Main building is a Registered National Historic Place; Average Annual Attendance: 255,000; Mem: 7,000; dues $55 & up
Income: $8,261,641
Library Holdings: Auction Catalogs 12,000, Book Volumes 45,000, Clipping Files 56, Exhibition Catalogs 2,000, Periodical Subscriptions 40
Special Subjects: African Art, American Indian Art, American Western Art, Asian Art, Bronzes, Ceramics, Costumes, Decorative Arts, Etchings & Engravings, Folk Art, Furniture, Islamic Art, Jade, Landscapes, Medieval Art, Oriental Art, Painting-American, Painting-European, Painting-Flemish, Painting-French, Painting-Italian, Painting-Japanese, Photography, Porcelain, Pre-Columbian Art, Prints, Prints, Religious Art, Renaissance Art, Textiles
Collections: Kress Collection of Italian Renaissance Painting
Exhibitions: Approx 50 temporary exhibitions annually
Publications: Art Books and Pamphlets; Catalog of the Collection; Catalogs of Spec Exhibs
Activities: Classes for adults & children; docent training; lectr; concerts; sponsoring of competitions; films & videos illustrating contemporary & historic range of the medium; guided tours; gallery talks; arts festivals; workshops; music programs; research in Asian & Western Art; lending collection contains paintings, prints, textiles, reproductions, photographs, slides and ethnographic objects (about 21,000); sales shop sells books, original art, reproductions, prints, jewelry, stationary/note cards & gifts

L **Robert Allerton Art Library,** 900 S Beretania St, Honolulu, HI 96814-1495. Tel 808-532-8754; Fax 808-681-7331; Email library@honolulumuseum.org; Web: www.honolulumuseum.org; *Librn* Sachiyo Kawaiaea
Open Wed 10 AM - 4 PM & by appointment; No admis fee; Estab 1927; Circ Non-circulating research library; Reference library for staff & members
Library Holdings: Auction Catalogs, Book Volumes 50,000, Clipping Files, Exhibition Catalogs, Pamphlets, Periodical Subscriptions 42
Special Subjects: Art History, Oriental Art

M **KING KAMEHAMEHA V JUDICIARY HISTORY CENTER,** 417 S King St, Honolulu, HI 96813-2943. Tel 808-539-4999; Fax 808-539-4996; Email info@jhchawaii.net; Web: www.jhchawaii.net; *Exec Dir* Matt Mattice; *Educ Specialist* Keahe Davis; *Program Specialist* Teri Skillman; *Asst Educ Specialist* David Cypriano
Open Mon - Fri 8 AM - 4 PM; No admis fee; Estab to interpret the history of Hawaii's courts & legal system; Average Annual Attendance: 57,110; Mem: 320; dues $25 - $3,000
Income: Financed by appropriation
Library Holdings: DVDs, Memorabilia, Original Documents, Other Holdings
Special Subjects: Architecture, Furniture, Manuscripts, Maps
Collections: Art (paintings, prints), Artifacts, Documents (judicial & legal), furniture
Exhibitions: The Monarchy Courts; Martial Law in Hawaii 1941 - 1944; Restored Court Room 1913; Who's Who in the Courtroom
Activities: Educ prog; classes for children; dramatic prog; lects open to pub; tours; mus shop sells books, postcards & DVDs

M **UNIVERSITY OF HAWAII AT MANOA,** The Art Gallery & The John Young Museum of Art, 2535 McCarthy Mall, Honolulu, HI 96822-2233. Tel 808-956-6888; Fax 808-956-9659; Email gallery@hawaii.edu; Web: www.hawaii.edu/artgallery; *Assoc Dir* Sharon Tasaka; *Design Asst* Wayne Kawamoto; *Dir* Rod Bengston
Open Mon - Fri 10 AM - 4PM; Sun Noon - 4PM; cl Sat & holidays; No admis fee; Estab 1976 to present a program of regional, national & international exhibitions; Gallery is a teaching tool for all areas of specialization. It is located in the center of the art building & is designed as a versatile space with a flexible installation system that allows all types of art to be displayed; Average Annual Attendance: 50,000
Income: Financed by state govt, grants, pvt contributions
Collections: Japanese, European, American & Polish posters, Asia Pacific Collection
Publications: Exhibition catalogs
Activities: Classes for adults; lects open to public; 4-6 vis lectrs per yr; gallery talks; tours; competitions; scholarships & fels offered; book traveling exhibs; 1 biennially; originate traveling exhibs to public and university museums; sales shop sells exhibit catalogs

KANEOHE

M **HAWAII PACIFIC UNIVERSITY,** Art Gallery, 45-045 Kamehameha Hwy, Kaneohe, HI; 1164 Bishop St, Honolulu, HI 96813. Tel 808-544-0228; Fax 808-544-1424; Email jishaque@hpu.edu; Web: www.hpu.edu; *Admin* Joan Ishaque; *Cur* Sanit Khewhok
Open Mon - Sat 8 AM - 5 PM; No admis fee; Estab 1983 as a cultural & acad resource for students & community; 12,000 sq ft; Average Annual Attendance: 8,500
Income: Financed by college funds & private donations
Exhibitions: 6 exhibitions per year featuring contemporary artists working in Hawaii
Activities: Lect open to public; gallery talks; competitions

LAHAINA

A **LAHAINA ARTS SOCIETY,** Art Organization, 648 Wharf St Ste 103, Lahaina, HI 96761-1272. Tel 808-661-0111, 661-3228; Fax 808-661-9149; Email info@lahaina-arts.com; Web: www.lahaina-arts.com; *Pres* Don McCann; *Exec Dir* Amy Fry; *Exec Dir Lahaina Arts Assoc* Priscilla Gonsalves
Open daily 9 AM - 5 PM; No admis fee; Estab 1967 as a nonprofit organization interested in perpetuating culture, art & beauty by providing stimulating art instruction, lectures & art exhibits, exhibiting exclusively local Maui artists; Gallery located in old Lahaina Courthouse; Main Gallery is on ground floor; Old Jail Gallery is in the basement; Average Annual Attendance: 50,000; Mem: 80; dues $100; annual meeting June
Income: financed by mem
Exhibitions: Exhibits once a month
Publications: Newsletter, monthly; exhibition catalogs
Activities: Classes for children; lect for members only; gallery talks; competitions with scholarships; workshops; scholarships offered; gallery sells local original art, prints, cards, ceramics, handcrafted jewelry & sculptures

M **WHALERS VILLAGE MUSEUM,** 2435 Ka'anapali Pkwy, Lahaina, HI 96761. Tel 808-661-4567, 808-661-5992 (Info); Web: www.whalersvillage.com
Open daily 9:00AM - 10 PM; History-oriented mus brings to life Lahaina's whaling era (1825 - 1860) as told through the eyes of an ordinary sailor & whaleman and illustrates the challenges of daily life on the sea. Nonprofit org
Special Subjects: Sculpture, Anthropology, Archaeology, Decorative Arts, Folk Art, Historical Material, Photography, Scrimshaw
Collections: 19th-century scrimshaw, pictures carved on whale teeth & bone, antique ornaments & utensils made from whale ivory & bone, one of the world's largest scale models of a whaling ship on display, photo murals & interpretive graphics
Activities: Self-guided tours; informational videos shown throughout the day; scrimshaw, jewelry, books & mus related items for sale

LAIE

A **POLYNESIAN CULTURAL CENTER,** 55-370 Kamehameha Hwy, Laie, HI 96762-1113. Tel 808-293-3005; Fax 808-293-3022; Email culturalexpert@polynesia .com; Web: www.polynesia.com; *Pres & CEO* Alfred Grace
Open Mon - Sat 12 noon - 9 PM, cl Sun, Thanksgiving, New Year's & Christmas; Admis adults $49.95, children (5-11) $39.95; Estab 1963 by the Church of Jesus Christ of Latter Day Saints as an authentic Polynesian village; Center is a 42 acre living museum with two amphitheaters, it represents villages of Hawaii, Samoa, Tonga, Fiji, Tahiti, New Zealand & the Marquesas; Average Annual Attendance: 700,000
Income: Financed by admis
Collections: Decorative arts, ethnic material, graphics, paintings & sculpture
Publications: Brochures
Activities: Classes for adults & children; workshop training in Polynesian arts & crafts; 2 hr Polynesian Show of Cultures nightly; lect open to public; scholarships offered

LIHUE

M **KAUAI MUSEUM ASSOCIATION, LTD,** 4428 Rice St, Lihue, HI 96766-1338. Tel 808-245-6931; Fax 808-245-6864; Email museum@kausimuseum.org; Web: www.kauaimuseum.org; *Exec Dir* Jane Gray; *Mem Mgr/Admin* Lyah Kama-Drake; *Cur* Chris Faye
Open Mon - Sat 10 AM - 5 PM, cl Sun; Admis adults $10, seniors $8, students $6, children 12 - 6 $2, children 6 & under free; Estab 1960 to provide the history through the permanent exhibit, the Story of Kauai & through art exhibits; ethnic cultural exhibits in the Wilcox Building to give the community an opportunity to learn more of ethnic backgrounds; Average Annual Attendance: 30,000; Mem: 1,700; dues $25-$1,000; annual meeting in Feb
Income: Financed by mem dues, government grants
Library Holdings: DVDs, Filmstrips, Framed Reproductions, Manuscripts, Maps, Original Art Works, Original Documents, Photographs, Prints, Records, Reproductions, Sculpture, Video Tapes
Collections: Hawaiian coll with emphasis on items dealing with the island of Kauai, school art exhibits, ethnic & heritage displays, 50 year old quilts, Niihau shells, Leis, Necklaces, bracelets, earrings
Exhibitions: Downstairs: Hawaiian History; Quilts; Upstairs
Publications: Hawaiian Quilting on Kauai; Early Kauai Hospitality; Amelia; Moki Goes Fishing; Kauai: The Separate Kingdom; Kauai Museum Quilt Collection
Activities: Classes for adults & children; dramatic progs; docent training; lects open to pub, lects open to mems; 100 vis lectrs per yr; concerts; tours; gallery talks; sponsor competitions; awards: living treasures, children's art contest & May Day contest; educ outreach to schools; lending of original objects of art by request; book traveling exhibs 3 per yr; originates traveling exhibs 5 yrs in advance; mus shop

sells books, magazines, original art, reproductions, prints, quilts, novelties, Niihau shells, Kauai made products

MAKAWAO MAUI

M **HUI NO'EAU VISUAL ARTS CENTER,** Gallery and Gift Shop, 2841 Baldwin Ave, Makawao Maui, HI 96768-9642. Tel 808-572-6560; Fax 808-572-2750; Email info@huinoeau.com; Web: www.huinoeau.com; *Exec Dir* Caroline Killhour
Open Mon - Sat 10 AM - 4 PM; No admis fee; Estab 1934 to encourage & promote the develop of artistic expression & creativity in the individual & to stimulate a broader appreciation & understanding of the visual arts as a vital language in our culture; 1,000 sq ft exhibit space in historic living & dining areas; Average Annual Attendance: 30,000; Mem: 1,050; dues $40
Income: Financed by endowment, mem, state appropriation & earned income
Special Subjects: Ceramics, Drawings, Etchings & Engravings, Historical Material, Jewelry, Landscapes, Marine Painting, Metalwork, Painting-American, Photography, Porcelain, Pottery, Prints, Textiles, Watercolors
Collections: Fiber Art, Woodworking
Publications: Hui News, bi-monthly; Hui brochure
Activities: Classes for adults & children; visitor prog; Hawaiian culture & art; lects open to pub, 12 vis lectrs per yr; competitions with awards; gallery talks; tours; schols offered; book traveling exhibs 1-2 per yr; originate traveling exhibs 1-2 per yr; retail store sells books, original art, reproductions & prints

PAIA

M **MAUI CRAFTS GUILD,** 120 Hana Hwy, Paia, HI 96779; PO Box 790609, Paia, HI 96779-0609. Tel 808-579-9697; Fax 808-579-8694; Email info@mauicraftsguild.com; Web: www.mauicraftsguild.com
Open daily 10 AM - 6 PM; Estab 1983 to provide a quality gallery outlet for crafts; Cooperative & share running gallery
Collections: Works by local artists including ceramics, sculpture, prints, textiles, photographs & baskets

WAILUKU

M **MAUI HISTORICAL SOCIETY,** Hale Hoike ike at the Bailey House, 2375A Main St, Wailuku, HI 96793-1661. Tel 808-244-3326; Email info@mauimuseum.org; Web: www.mauimuseum.org; *Exec Dir* Naomi Lake-Farm; *Archives* Marianne Klaus
Open Mon - Sat 10 AM - 4 PM, cl Sun; Admis Donation requested adults $7, seniors $5, children (7-12) $2, 6 & under free; Estab 1957 to preserve the history of Hawaii, particularly Maui County; housed in former residence of Edward Bailey (1814-1903); Average Annual Attendance: 21,000; Mem: 300; dues $40-$200; annual meeting in Aug
Income: $200,000 (financed by mem, gift shop purchases & admis fees)
Library Holdings: Auction Catalogs, Book Volumes, Cassettes, Compact Disks, Exhibition Catalogs, Framed Reproductions, Manuscripts, Maps, Memorabilia, Micro Print, Original Documents, Photographs, Records
Special Subjects: Archaeology, Furniture, Landscapes
Collections: Landscape Paintings (1860-1900), Paintings of Hawaiian Scenes by Edward Bailey, Prehistoric Hawaiian Artifacts
Exhibitions: Exhibits depicting missionary life, throughout the year
Publications: Hale Ho'ike'ike Journal
Activities: Classes for adults & children; docent training; Tai Chi; lects open to pub, 4-6 vis lectrs per yr; monthly Hawaiian music concerts; tours; sponsoring competitions, Ann Art Contest; extension prog serves educ loan prog; lending original objects of art to pub & private schools; originate traveling exhibs to schools & other mus; mus shop sells books, original art, reproductions, prints, CD's, slides & arts & crafts

WAIPAHU

M **HAWAII OKINAWA CENTER,** 94-587 Ukee St, Waipahu, HI 96797-4214. Tel 808-676-5400; Fax 808-676-7811
Open Mon - Fri 8:30 AM - 5 PM, Sat 9 AM - 3 PM; cl during major holidays
Collections: Local history & culture; Okinawa crafts including pottery, doll making, & fabrics; early plantation & immigration

IDAHO

BOISE

M **BOISE ART MUSEUM,** 670 Julia Davis Dr, Boise, ID 83702. Tel 208-345-8330; Fax 208-345-2247; Email info@boiseartmuseum.org; Web: www.boiseartmuseum.org; *Cur Educ* Terra Feast; *Cur Art* Nicole Herden; *Exec Dir* Melanie Fales; *Pres Bd Trustees* Cheryl Thompson; *Registrar* Eileen Wiedenheft; *Mus Store Mgr* Nora Sweeney; *Facilities Mgr & Preparator* Corey Clyne; *Fin Mgr* Caren Massari; *Coordr Mem* Rebecca Mulberry; *Curatorial & Facilities Asst* Josephine Backus; *Develop Mgr* Britney Whiting-Looze; *Event Coordr* Heather Lie; *Mus Resources Coordr* Hana Van Huffel
Open Tues - Sat 10 AM - 5 PM, (1st Thurs 10 AM - 8 PM), Sun Noon - 5 PM, cl Mon & holidays; Admis general $6, seniors $4, grades K - 12 $3, children under 6 free, discounts to mus professionals, first Thurs of month admis by donation; Estab 1931, inc 1961, mus opened 1937; Art Mus offers exhibs, educational progs & community events; Average Annual Attendance: 55,500; Mem: 2,000; dues seniors $35, individual $45, family $60, family plus $90, advocate $125, contributing $250, sustaining $500, patron $1,000, benefactor $2500, grand benefactor $5,000; annual meetings in May
Income: Financed by mem, grants, private & corporate donations, fund raisers
Special Subjects: Asian Art, Bronzes, Painting-American, Photography, Porcelain, Portraits, Prints, Sculpture, Watercolors, Woodcuts
Collections: African Sculpture (masks), American Ceramics, American, European & Asian Collections of Painting, Sculpture, American Realism, Photography, collection of works by Northwest Artists, Contemporary Prints
Publications: Annual report; quarterly bulletin; occasional catalogs & posters of exhibitions
Activities: Classes in art for adults & children; docent training; docent tours; performances; outdoor arts festival; lects for mems only; 5 vis lectrs per yr; gallery talks; tours; originate traveling exhibs statewide & Northwest region 6 per yr; mus shop sells books, original art, reproductions, cards & jewelry

A **IDAHO COMMISSION ON THE ARTS,** 2410 Old Penitentiary Rd, PO Box 83720 Boise, ID 83720-0008. Tel 208-334-2119; Fax 208-334-2488; Email info@arts.idaho.gov; Web: www.arts.idaho.gov; *Exec Dir* Michael Faison; *Dir Community Develop* Michelle Coleman; *Dir Artist Svcs* John McMahon; *Dir Communs* Jocelyn Robertson; *Dir Arts Educ* Ruth Piispanen; *Dir Folk & Traditional Arts* Steven Hatcher; *Deputy Dir* Stuart Weiser; *Grants Specialist* Jade Carson
Open 8 AM - 5 PM; No admis fee; Estab 1966 to promote artistic develop within the state & to make cultural resources available to all Idahoans
Library Holdings: DVDs, Pamphlets, Video Tapes
Activities: Governors arts awards

M **IDAHO HISTORICAL MUSEUM,** 2205 Old Penitentiary Rd, Idaho State Historical Society Boise, ID 83712-8250. Tel 208-334-2682; Fax 208-334-2774; Email jody.ochoa@ishs.idaho.gov; Web: www.state.id.us/ishs; *Registrar* Jody Ochoa; *Cur* Joe Toluse; *Museum Adminr* Kenneth J Swanson
Open Mon - Sat 9 AM - 5 PM, Sun & holidays 1 - 5 PM; Admis adults $4, seniors $2, children under 6 $1; Estab 1881; Average Annual Attendance: 100,000; Mem: Dues $500 life mem, $100 bus, $25 patron, $15 couple, $10 individual
Income: Financed by donations and mem
Special Subjects: Archaeology, Costumes, Decorative Arts, Furniture, Period Rooms, Textiles
Collections: History artifacts
Exhibitions: Story of Idaho
Activities: Classes for children; dramatic progs; docent training; lects open to pub; tours; competitions; individual paintings & original objects of art lent to agencies & institutions; lending collection contains 7 slide progs; book traveling exhibs; originate traveling exhibs to state schools & libraries; mus shop sells books & gifts

CALDWELL

M **THE COLLEGE OF IDAHO,** Rosenthal Art Gallery, 2112 Cleveland Blvd, Caldwell, ID 83605-4432; PO Box 60, Caldwell, ID 83606. Tel 208-459-5321; Fax 208-459-5175; Email gclaassen@collegeofidaho.edu; *Prof Art* Steven M Fisher; *Assoc Prof Art* Lynn Webster; *Dir* Dr Garth Claassen
Open Tues - Thurs 1 PM - 4 PM or by appointment; No admis fee; Estab 1980
Income: Financed by college funds
Special Subjects: Painting-American, Prints
Collections: Luther Douglas, Sand Paintings, Paintings, Prints Collection
Exhibitions: Temporary & traveling exhibitions on an inter-museum loan basis
Publications: Exhibit Brochures
Activities: Lect; gallery talks; guided tours; films

COEUR D ALENE

M **THE ART SPIRIT GALLERY,** 415 Sherman, Coeur D Alene, ID 83814. Tel 208-765-6006; Email contactus@theartspiritgallery.com; Web: www.theartspiritgallery.com; *Owner* Steve Gibbs; *Gallery Asst* Blair Williams; *Gallery Asst* Kasey Davis; *Gallery Asst* Teresa Runge
Open June - Sept: daily 11 AM - 6 PM; Oct - May: Tues - Sat 11 AM - 6 PM; No admis fee; Estab 1997; Original fine art by regional artists
Collections: Paintings; drawings; sculpture; pottery
Exhibitions: New exhib opens 2nd Friday of every month

EMMETT

M **GEM COUNTY HISTORICAL SOCIETY AND MUSEUM,** Gem County Historical Village Museum, 501 E 1st St, Emmett, ID 83617-3005. Tel 208-365-9530, 4340; Email mdavis@gemcountymuseum.org; Web: www.gemcountymuseum.org; *Dir & Cur* Meg Davis
Open Wed 1-5PM, Thurs & Fri 10:30 AM - 5PM, Sat 1PM - 5 PM; No admis fee, donations accepted; Opened in 1973 with the focus being the interpretation of life in early Gem County beginning with the Native Americans who first inhabited the land to the contributions of the trappers, miners, and settlers. Nonprofit org; Average Annual Attendance: 1,500-2,000; Mem: Dues Gold $1,000; Silver $500; Copper $250; Garnet $100; Opal $50; Benefactor $25; Family $15; Individual $10
Income: Financed by mem, grants, endowments
Library Holdings: Audio Tapes, Book Volumes, Manuscripts, Maps, Memorabilia, Original Documents, Pamphlets, Periodical Subscriptions, Photographs, Prints, Video Tapes
Special Subjects: Archaeology, Costumes, Dolls, Embroidery, Ethnology, Flasks & Bottles, Folk Art, Furniture, Furniture, Glass, Gold, Historical Material, Laces, Manuscripts, Painting-American, Period Rooms, Period Rooms, Photography, Photography, Portraits, Primitive art, Prints
Collections: Large coll of photographs, full-sized period displays of a general store, a turn-of-the-century parlor, a laundry room, and a combined doctor's and dentist's office, special tribute to the men and women who have served in the armed forces, several pianos, office machines, and other local items, Hunt Memorial House, a turn-of-the-century cottage holding the belongings of former Governor and Mrs Frank W Hunt, Little Red Schoolhouse, Bunkhouse which houses tribute to birds

indigenous to the county as well as a tribute to the cattle & sheep industry, blacksmith's shop with variety of tools, reading & research library
Activities: Special events; ladies social, Feb; River Through Time-hands on History, 1st weekend in Oct; cemetery tour to be announced; lects open to the pub; tours; mus shop sells books, reproductions, prints

FORT HALL

M **SHOSHONE BANNOCK TRIBES,** Shoshone Bannock Tribal Museum, I-15, Exit 80, Fort Hall, ID 83203; PO Box 306, Fort Hall, ID 83203-0306. Tel 208-237-9791; Fax 208-237-4318; Email rdevinney@shoshonebannocktribes.com; Web: www.sho-ban.com; *Mgr & Coordr* Rosemary A Devinney
Open June - Aug daily 10 AM - 5 PM; Sept - May Mon - Fri 10 AM - 5 PM; cl on all Tribal Holidays; Admis adults $3.50, children $1, no admis fee for Native Americans with Tribal ID; group rates (5 minimum); Mus was built in 1985 and was cl for several years. It re-opened in 1993 by volunteers with the help of community mems who donated & loaned many photos and precious heirlooms to the mus; Learn all about the Shoshone-Bannock people who live on the Fort Hall Indian Reservation in Southeastern Idaho
Income: By the Shoshone-Bannock tribal government
Special Subjects: American Indian Art, Bronzes, Crafts, Dioramas, Historical Material, Jewelry, Photography, Prints
Collections: photographs, displays & exhibs dating back to 1895, authentic arts & crafts made by tribal mems, reference books on the Shoshone-Bannock people as well as other North American tribes, artifacts from archeological excavations
Exhibitions: Tribal History; Photographs; Beadwork; Paintings; Family History
Activities: Mus shop sells books, prints, music, beadwork & crafts

IDAHO FALLS

M **THE ART MUSEUM OF EASTERN IDAHO,** 300 S Capital Ave, Idaho Falls, ID 83402-3952. Tel 208-524-7777; Fax 208-529-6666; Email admin@theartmuseum.org; Web: www.theartmuseum.org; *Pres* Lexie French; *VPres* Lisa Schultz; *Dir* Miyai Abe Griggs; *Secy* Kim Southwick; *Treas* Eric Liester; *Educ Dir* Alexa Stanger; *Bus Mgr* Jessica Livesay; *Edu Asst* Liz Johnson; *Museum Coordinator* Jesse Martin
Open Tues - Sat 11 AM - 5 PM, Thurs 11AM - 8 PM; Admis family $10, adult $4, Youth $2, 5 & under free; Estab 2002; Mus serves southeastern ID through the coll, preservation & exhibition of works of art by ID artists; Average Annual Attendance: 24,000; Mem: Dues Benefactor $2,500; Dir Club $1,000; Patron $500; Sustaining $250; Supporting $100; Family $50; Contributing $35
Library Holdings: Book Volumes
Special Subjects: African Art, American Western Art, Drawings, Etchings & Engravings, Hispanic Art, Mexican Art, Painting-American, Portraits, Primitive art, Watercolors, Woodcuts
Collections: Original paintings, etchings & lithographs from internationally known and local artists
Activities: Classes for adults & children; children's events; ann events; elementary school art exhib; lects open to public; 10 vis lectrs per yr; concerts; tours; gallery talks; sponsoring of competitions; originates traveling exhibs to Idaho galleries; mus shop sells books, original art & prints

M **WILLARD ARTS CENTER,** Carr Gallery, Colonial Theater, 450 A St Idaho Falls, ID 83402-3617; 498 A St Idaho Falls, ID 83402-3617. Tel 208-522-0471; Fax 208-522-0413; Email bnewton@idahofallsarts.org; Web: www.idahofallsarts.org; *Exec Dir* Brandi Newton; *Technical Dir* Brad Higbee; *Develop Dir* Brandie Leonard; *Office Mgr* Amber Carmichael; *Accnt* Courtney Archibald; *Mktg Dir* Andrea Todd
Open Carr Gallery Mon-Fri 11AM-5PM, Sat 10AM-4PM; No admis fee; Estab to promote visual & performing arts in eastern Idaho; Average Annual Attendance: 10,000; Mem: Dues $50
Collections: Artwork by local, national & international artists, Blake G. Hall Community Gallery
Exhibitions: Rotating exhibs quarterly; 3 day free art festival for families, annually
Publications: Arts Alive! regional art calendar, pub 3 times per yr
Activities: Educ prog; classes for adults & children; workshops; docent training; concerts; gallery talks; tours; support of arts/ achievement in arts awards

KETCHUM

M **GAIL SEVERN GALLERY,** 400 1st Ave N, Ketchum, ID 83340. Tel 208-726-5079; Fax 208-726-5092; Email info@gailseverngallery.com; Web: www.gailseverngallery.com; *Owner & Dir* Gail Severn
Open Mon - Sat 9 AM - 5 PM, Sun Noon - 5 PM; Estab to facilitate museum exhibitions, participate in international art fairs & publish artist books & catalogs; 8,000 sq ft houses four distinct exhib spaces; outdoor sculpture court & garden
Collections: Works by young, mid career & established artists
Exhibitions: Temporary exhibits

MOSCOW

M **APPALOOSA MUSEUM AND HERITAGE CENTER,** 2720 W Pullman Rd, Moscow, ID 83843-4024. Tel 208-882-5578; Fax 208-882-8150; Email museum@appaloosa.com; Web: www.appaloosamuseum.org; *Pres* King Rockhill; *Dir* Jennifer Hamilton
Open Mon - Fri 10 AM - 5 PM, Sat 10 AM - 4 PM; No admis fee donations appreciated; Estab 1974 to collect, preserve, study & exhibit those objects that illustrate the story of the Appaloosa Horse; Average Annual Attendance: 5,000; Mem: 33,000; annual meeting in May
Income: $38,000 (financed by grants from Appaloosa Horse Club, shop sales & fundraising)
Purchases: $1,600
Library Holdings: Audio Tapes 30, Book Volumes 500, Framed Reproductions 10, Maps 10, Original Art Works 40, Original Documents 100, Photographs 15,000, Prints 200, Reproductions, Sculpture 20, Video Tapes 30
Special Subjects: American Indian Art, American Western Art, Bronzes, Costumes, Crafts, Drawings, Landscapes, Leather, Manuscripts, Maps, Painting-American, Photography, Prints, Reproductions
Collections: Bronzes by Shirley Botoham, Less Williver, Don Christian & William Menshew, reproductions of Chinese, European & Persian Art relating to Appaloosas, reproductions of Charles Russell art, original Western by George Phippen, Reynolds, Native American Items, saddle & other tack art work, Trace History of Appaloosa Horses from prehistoric times to present, Early Indian Art
Exhibitions: live horse exhibit
Publications: quarterly newsletter
Activities: Educ programs; programs for children; lects open to pub, 1-2 vis lectrs per yr; gallery talks; tours; trail ride; auction; mus shops sells books, jewelry, cards & games, toys, clothing & Appaloosa Horse reproductions, original art & prints

POCATELLO

M **IDAHO STATE UNIVERSITY,** John B Davis Gallery of Fine Art, 921 8th Ave, Pocatello, ID 83209-8004. Tel 208-236-2361; Fax 208-282-4791; Email adamjef2@isu.edu; Web: www.isu.edu/departments.art; *Chair* Jeffrey Adams; *Dir Gallery* Ryan Babcock
Open Mon - Fri 11 AM - 6 PM; No admis fee; Estab 1956 to exhibit art; Gallery contains 130 running ft of space with 8 ft ceilings; Average Annual Attendance: 2,600
Income: $2600 (financed by city appropriation)
Purchases: $350
Collections: Permanent collection
Exhibitions: Big Sky Biennial Exhibit; Regional Group Graduate Exhibit; exhibitions & national exhibitions; MFA Thesis Exhibits, bi-weekly one-man shows; student exhibits
Activities: Lects talks; tours; competitions with awards; scholarships offered; exten dept serves surrounding communities; individual paintings lent to school offices & community; originate traveling exhibs

M **The Transition Gallery**, 921 S 8th Ave, Earl R Pond Student Union Pocatello, ID 83209. Tel 208-282-3451

M **Mind's Eye Gallery**, 921 S 8th Ave, Rendezvous Complex Pocatello, ID 83209. Tel 208-282-3451

M **POCATELLO ART CENTER,** 444 N Main St, Pocatello, ID 83204-5070. Tel 208-232-0970; Email pocartctr@da.net; Web: pocatelloartctr.org
Estab to serve as a community center for the visual arts; Mem: dues $15-$100
Special Subjects: Photography, Jewelry, Porcelain
Collections: Paintings, photographs, jewelry & porcelain art
Exhibitions: Rotating exhibits; temporary exhibits
Activities: Classes for adults & children; workshops

TWIN FALLS

M **HERRETT CENTER FOR ARTS & SCIENCES,** (College of Southern Idaho) Jean B King Art Gallery, 315 Falls Ave, Twin Falls, ID 83301; PO Box 1238, Twin Falls, ID 83303-1238. Tel 208-732-6655; Fax 208-736-4712; Email herrett@csi.edu; Web: www.csi.edu; *Dir* James Woods; *Colls Mgr* Phyllis Oppenheim; *Art Gallery Mgr* Milica Popovic; *Exhibits Mgr* Joey Heck; *Display Technician* Nick Peterson; *Office Mgr* Wilma Titmus
Open Labor Day - Memorial Day; Tues & Fri 9:30 AM - 9 PM, Sat 1 - 9 PM; No admis fee; Estab 1965; Art Gallery, Natural History Gallery, four anthropology galleries (700-2400 sq ft); Average Annual Attendance: 37,000
Special Subjects: American Indian Art, Anthropology, Archaeology, Decorative Arts, Eskimo Art, Pre-Columbian Art
Collections: Pre-Columbian, Prehistoric & Ethnographic Indian Artifacts
Exhibitions: Exhibits change every 5-6 weeks
Activities: Classes for adults & children; lects open to pub, vis lectrs; gallery talks; tours; original objects of art lent to other pub institutions; originate traveling exhibs to schools, libraries & mus; mus shop sells books, original art, prints, mus replicas & novelties

WEISER

M **SNAKE RIVER HERITAGE CENTER,** 2295 Paddock Ave, Weiser, ID 83672-1195; PO Box 307, Weiser, ID 83672-0307. Tel 208-549-0205; Email info@weisermuseum.com; Web: www.weisermuseum.com; *Pres* Lynn Isaacson; *VPres* Wesley Higgins; *Treas* Dick Bergquist; *Secy* Jeri Kleppin
Open summer (last weekend in June thru last weekend in Aug): Fri - Sat 10 AM - 1 PM & by appointment, (under construction); Admis by donation; Estab 1962 to preserve the history of Washington County, Idaho; Housed in a 1920 five story, solid concrete building of the Intermountain Institute, founded in 1899; Average Annual Attendance: 750; Mem: 100+; dues $25.00, lifetime $300
Income: $30,000 (financed by mem, county appropriation, gifts & fundraising)
Library Holdings: Audio Tapes, Book Volumes, Cards, Cassettes, DVDs, Framed Reproductions, Manuscripts, Maps, Memorabilia, Original Art Works, Original Documents, Other Holdings, Periodical Subscriptions, Photographs, Prints, Records, Reproductions, Sculpture, Slides
Collections: Washington County memorabilia & artifacts of Snake River Country, Baseball Hall of Famer Walter Johnson's Collection, Arrow Heads, Telephone Pioneers Communication Room, Display of 1925 Seth Thomas Clock weighing 1200 lbs, Historical automobile garages room
Exhibitions: Shoshone Indian Display; Vintage Fashion Collection
Publications: Museum newsletter; annual report
Activities: Classes for adults & children; dramatic progs; historical tours; concerts; gallery talks; tours; mus sales shop sells books, original art, reproductions, prints, reproductions of early pioneer textiles, VCR tapes, DVDs, & clothing reproductions

ILLINOIS

ALTON

M **ALTON MUSEUM OF HISTORY & ART, INC,** Loomis Hall, 2809 College Ave Alton, IL 62002-4743. Tel 618-462-2763; Email altonmuseum@gmail.com; Web: www.altonmuseum.com; Facebook; *Pres Emeritus* Dr. Norman Showers; *Secy* John Langley; *Gift Shop Chmn* Lois Lobbig; *Pres* Brian Combs; *VPres & Hostess* Patti Culp; *Treas* Lois Mitchell; *Researcher* Charlene Johnson; *Researcher/Editor* Brad Combs
Open Wed - Sat 10 AM - 4 PM, Sun 1 - 4 PM; Admis adult $5, children 12 and under $1 - group, senior + veterans discounts; Estab 1971 to collect, preserve & exhibit local history; Second location: The Koenig House, 829 E Fourth St, Alton, IL 62002 (by appointment); Average Annual Attendance: 14,000; Mem: 250; dues $15-$100; annual meeting 2nd Wed in Apr
Income: $30,000-40,000 (financed by mem, endowment & tours; admis; grants)
Library Holdings: Audio Tapes, Book Volumes, CD-ROMs, Cards, Cassettes, Clipping Files, Compact Disks, DVDs, Framed Reproductions, Lantern Slides, Manuscripts, Maps, Original Art Works, Original Documents, Pamphlets, Periodical Subscriptions, Photographs, Records, Reels, Sculpture, Video Tapes
Special Subjects: Bronzes, Drafting, Afro-American Art, Architecture, Coins & Medals, Dioramas, Dolls, Drawings, Folk Art, Furniture, Glass, Graphics, Historical Material, Laces, Landscapes, Manuscripts, Maps, Painting-American, Primitive art, Prints, Restorations, Sculpture, Watercolors, Woodcarvings
Collections: Architecture of Lost Alton, 19th Century Textiles/clothing, Lovejoy, early industry, early glass blowing, Robert Wadlow's life & memorabilia, Shurtleff College, Western Military Academy; Monticello Col
Exhibitions: changing art exhibits throughout the year
Publications: Newsletter
Activities: Classes for adults & children; docent training; lects open to pub, 12 vis lectrs 2nd Fri of every month; gallery talks; tours;; mus shop sells books, reproductions, prints, post cards, t-shirts

AURORA

M **AURORA REGIONAL FIRE MUSEUM,** 53 N. Broadway, Aurora, IL 60505; PO Box 1782, Aurora, IL 60507-1782. Tel 630-256-4140; Email ed@auroraregionalfiremuseum.org; Web: www.auroraregionalfiremuseum.org; *Executive Director* Brian Failing
Open Thurs - Fri 12-4 PM; Sat 10-4 PM; $3 Children; $5 adults; Estab 1990; housed in Central Fire Station built in 1894; preserves & presents the history of firefighting in Aurora & surrounding communities; Average Annual Attendance: 3000 by estimate
Library Holdings: Original Documents, Photographs
Special Subjects: Historical Material
Collections: 300 various firefighting periodicals; 100 fire service books; 50 local firefighting-related scrapbooks
Publications: Fire Museum News, quarterly newsletter
Activities: Formal educ for adults & children; films; lects; ann event: Fire Engine Muster; mus related items for sale

M **AURORA UNIVERSITY,** Schingoethe Center for Native American Cultures & The Schingoethe Art Gallery, 347 S Gladstone Ave, Dunham Hall, 1400 Marseillaise Aurora, IL 60506-4877. Tel 630-844-5402; Fax 630-844-6529; Web: www.aurora.edu/museum; *Cur Coll* Elizabeth Easto; *Dir* Meg Bero
Open Wed- Fri 10 AM - 4 PM, Sun 1- 4 PM, cl Sat; No admis fee; Estab 1990 to advance cultural literacy about Native peoples; Two permanent exhibit galleries with rotating displays from the mus collection; total of 3,500 sq ft; Average Annual Attendance: 10,000; Mem: 50; dues donor $50 - $500, individual $20
Income: $150,000 (financed by mem & endowment)
Special Subjects: American Indian Art, Archaeology, Eskimo Art, Ethnology, Folk Art, Latin American Art, Mexican Art, Pre-Columbian Art, Southwestern Art, Textiles
Collections: Ethnographic material from North, Central & South America, Native American Fine Art, Prehistoric & Pre-Columbian material, Inuit Art
Publications: Spreading Wings; quarterly newsletter to membership
Activities: Summer workshops for adults & children; outreach materials for educators; docent progs; lects open to pub; mus shop sells books, original art & reproductions

BISHOP HILL

M **ILLINOIS HISTORIC PRESERVATION AGENCY,** Bishop Hill State Historic Site, PO Box 104, Bishop Hill, IL 61419-0104. Tel 309-927-3345; Fax 309-927-3343; Email bishophill@mymctc.net; Web: www.bishophill.com; *Asst Site Mgr* Ed Safiran; *Site Mgr* Martha J Downey
Open Wed - Sun Mar - Oct 9 AM - 5 PM, Nov - Feb 9 AM - 4 PM; Admis suggested donation adults $4, ages 17 & younger $2, family $10; Estab 1946 to preserve & interpret the history of Bishop Hill Colony 1846-1861; Restored Colony Church, 1848 & restored Colony Hotel, 1860, Bishop Hill Mus 1988, Folk paintings of Olof Krans; Average Annual Attendance: 51,000
Income: Financed by state appropriation
Special Subjects: Archaeology, Architecture, Carpets & Rugs, Crafts, Decorative Arts, Folk Art, Furniture, Painting-American, Portraits, Primitive art, Restorations, Textiles, Historical Material
Collections: Bishop Hill Colony artifacts-agricultural items, furniture, household items, textiles & tools, Olof Krans Collection of Folk Art Paintings

BLOOMINGTON

M **ILLINOIS WESLEYAN UNIVERSITY,** Merwin & Wakeley Galleries, PO Box 2900, Bloomington, IL 61702-2900. Tel 309-556-3822; Fax 309-556-3976; Email clozar@iwu.edu; Web: www2.iwu.edu/art/galleries; *Dir* Carmen Lozar
Open Mon - Fri Noon - 4 PM, Tues 7 - 9 PM, Sat & Sun 1 - 4 PM; Estab 1945
Income: Financed by endowment & mem
Special Subjects: Drawings, Painting-American, Prints
Collections: 250 drawings, paintings & prints including works by Baskin, Max Beckmann, Helen Frankenthaler, Philip Guston, John Ihle, Oliviera, Larry Rivers & Whistler
Exhibitions: Rotating exhibits
Publications: Exhibition Posters; Gallery Schedule, monthly;
Activities: Dramatic progs; lects open to pub, 5 vis lectrs per yr; concerts; tours; competitions with awards; original objects of art lent, on campus only; book traveling exhibs; originates traveling exhibs

L **Sheean Library,** 1312 Park St, Bloomington, IL 61701-1773. Tel 309-556-3003; Fax 309-556-3706; Email bdelvin@titan.iwu.edu; Web: www.iwu.edu/library; *Fine Arts Librn* Robert C Delvin
Open Mon - Thurs 7:45 AM - 1:30 AM; Fri 7:45 AM - 10 PM; Sat 10 AM - 10 PM; Sun 11 AM - 1:30 AM
Income: Financed by endowment
Library Holdings: Slides 35,000

A **MCLEAN COUNTY ART ASSOCIATION,** McLean County Arts Center, 601 N East St, Bloomington, IL 61701-3094. Tel 309-829-0011; Fax 309-829-4928; Email info@mcac.org; Web: www.mcac.org; *Exec Dir* Douglas C Johnson; *Cur* Claire Hedden; *Educ Coordr* Joseph Hooten; *Project Coordr* Ian Carey
Open Tues 10 AM - 7 PM, Wed - Fri 10 AM - 5 PM, Sat Noon - 4 PM, Dec only Sun Noon - 4 PM; No admis fee; Estab 1922 to enhance the arts in McLean County. Provides display galleries, sales & rental gallery featuring local professional artists; Brandt Gallery is 2500 sq ft hosting local shows & traveling exhibits; Average Annual Attendance: 10,000; Mem: 600; annual meeting first Fri in May
Income: Financed by mem, art & book sales
Collections: Small permanent collection with concentration on Midwestern artists
Exhibitions: Annual Amateur Competition & Exhibition; Annual Holiday Show & Sale; 10-2 other exhibits, local & traveling
Publications: Quarterly newsletter
Activities: Classes for adults & children; lect open to public; 8 vis lectrs per yr; gallery talks; tours; competitions with awards; schols; artmobile to rural youth; gift shop sells fine crafts & original art, conservation framing shop

M **MCLEAN COUNTY HISTORICAL SOCIETY,** McLean County Museum of History, 200 N Main, Bloomington, IL 61701. Tel 309-827-0428; Fax 309-827-0100; Email marketing@mchistory.org; Web: www.mchistory.org; *Librn* William Kemp; *Cur* Susan Hartzold; *Exec Dir* Greg Koos; *Dir Educ* Candace Summers; *Dir Mktg* Jeff Woodard; *Educ Prog Coordr* Hannah Johnson; *Registrar* Tod Eagleton; *Dir Develop* Beth Whisman; *Develop Asst* Amelia Hill; *Dir Vols* Deb VanAntwerp; *Asst Vol Coordr* Betty Turchirollo; *Develop Asst* Laura Lacy; *Archivist* George Perkins; *Mgr, Bloomington - Normal Vis Center* Barb Adkins; *Educ Outreach Coordr* Anthony Bowman; *Cur Digital Humanities* Torii More
Open Mon - Sat 10 AM - 5 PM, Tues 10 AM - 9 PM; Admis adults $5, seniors $4, students & mems free, Tues free; Estab 1892 to promote history of McLean County; Maintain long term exhibits, changing exhibits and traveling exhibits; Average Annual Attendance: 34,000; Mem: 1300
Income: $750,000; Financed by mem, endowment, earned income & government
Purchases: $2,000
Library Holdings: Book Volumes 10,000, CD-ROMs, Clipping Files, Fiche, Kodachrome Transparencies, Lantern Slides, Manuscripts, Maps, Memorabilia, Motion Pictures, Original Art Works, Original Documents, Other Holdings, Pamphlets, Periodical Subscriptions, Photographs, Prints, Records, Reels, Sculpture, Slides, Video Tapes
Special Subjects: Anthropology, Archaeology, Architecture, Carpets & Rugs, Ceramics, Coins & Medals, Costumes, Crafts, Decorative Arts, Dolls, Drawings, Embroidery, Ethnology, Flasks & Bottles, Folk Art, Furniture, Glass, Historical Material, Jewelry, Laces, Manuscripts, Maps, Painting-American, Photography, Porcelain, Portraits, Posters, Pottery, Prints, Sculpture, Textiles, Antiquities-Assyrian
Collections: Civil War, Illinois History, local history, Material Culture, Folk Art, Portraits, Photography, Textiles; personal items; household
Exhibitions: Encounter on the Prairie
Activities: Classes for adults & children; senior citizen progs; dramatic progs; lects open to pub; 12 vis lectrs per yr; galley talks; tours; concerts; exten prog with Central Illinois Elementary Schools & retirement communities; originates traveling exhibs to mus in Midwest; mus shop sells books, reproductions & prints

CARBONDALE

M **SOUTHERN ILLINOIS UNIVERSITY CARBONDALE,** University Museum, 1000 Faner Dr, MC 4508 SIUC Carbondale, IL 62901-4328. Tel 618-453-5388; Fax 618-453-7409; Email museum@siu.edu; Web: www.museum.siu.edu; *Dir* Dona Bachman; *Cur Anthro* Susannah Munson; *Cur Exhibs* Alison Erazmus
Open Tues - Fri 10 - 4 PM, Sat 1 PM - 4 PM; No admis fee; Estab 1874 to reflect the history & cultures of Southern Illinois & promote the understanding of the area; to provide area schools & the University with support through educational outreach programs; to promote the fine arts, humanities & sciences; 10,000 sq ft in 9 gallery spaces, 3 devoted to permanent collections; Average Annual Attendance: 10,000; Mem: Dues $10 - $1,000
Income: Financed by state appropriated budget, federal, state & private grants, donations & University Mus patrons
Special Subjects: African Art, Afro-American Art, Anthropology, Bronzes, Ceramics, Costumes, Decorative Arts, Dioramas, Etchings & Engravings, Ethnology, Folk Art, Furniture, Glass, Historical Material, Landscapes, Photography, Pre-Columbian Art, Primitive art, Prints, Sculpture, Watercolors, Woodcarvings

Collections: Decorative Arts, European & American paintings, drawing & prints from 13th-21st century with emphasis on 19th & 20th century, photography, sculpture, blacksmithing & art & crafts, Oceanic Collection, Southern Illinois history, 20th century sculpture, metals, ceramics, Asiatic holdings, archaeology, costumes, textiles, geology
Exhibitions: A variety of changing exhibitions in all media; ethnographic arts; fine & decorative arts; history & the sciences
Publications: Annual report; seasonal museum newsletter; exhibition catalogs
Activities: Classes for children; gallery talks; lects open to pub

L **Morris Library**, 605 Agriculture Dr, Mailcode 6632 Carbondale, IL 62901-4310. Tel 618-453-2818; Fax 618-453-8109; Email lkoch@lib.siu.edu; Web: www.lib.siu.edu
Primarily lending
Income: Financed by college funds, gifts, pub & private grants
Library Holdings: Book Volumes 35,000, Cards, Cassettes 475, Exhibition Catalogs, Fiche, Periodical Subscriptions 180, Records, Reels

CHAMPAIGN

M **PARKLAND COLLEGE,** Parkland Art Gallery, 2400 W Bradley Ave, Champaign, IL 61821-1899. Tel 217-351-2485; Fax 217-373-3899; Web: www.parkland.edu/gallery; *Gallery Dir* Lisa Costello
Open Mon - Thurs 10 AM - 7 PM, Fri 10 AM - 3 PM, Sat noon - 2 PM; No admis fee; Estab 1981 to exhibit contemporary fine art; Average Annual Attendance: 10,000
Income: Nonprofit, supported by Parkland College & in part by Illinois Arts Council, a state agency
Collections: Student, Foundation
Exhibitions: State of the Art - Biennial National Watercolor Invitational; Midwest Ceramics Invitational - Biennial, 2-person shows; solo exhibits
Publications: Bi-annual exhibition catalogs & brochures
Activities: Local high school art student seminar; art expedition day trips to Chicago, Indianapolis & St Louis; lects open to public; 18 vis lectrs per year; gallery talks; tours; awards given to works of excellence in student exhibits; originate traveling exhibitions

M **UNIVERSITY OF ILLINOIS AT URBANA-CHAMPAIGN,** Krannert Art Museum and Kinkead Pavilion, 500 E Peabody Dr, Champaign, IL 61820-6913. Tel 217-333-1861; Fax 217-333-0883; Email kam@illinois.edu; Web: www.kam.illinois.edu; *Assoc Dir* Claudia Corlett-Stahl; *Registrar & Exhib Dir* Christine Saniat; *Coordr Communs & Mktg* Julia Nucci Kelly; *Dir Educ* Anne Sautman; *Sr Cur & Cur Global African Art* Allyson Purpura; *Sr Dir Advancement* Brenda Nardi; *Cur European & American Art* Maureen Warren; *Cur Modern & Contemp Art* Amy Powell; *Collections Mgr* Kimberly Sissons; *Design & Instillation Specailist* Walter Wilson
Open academic year: Mon - Sat 9 AM - 5 PM, Thurs until 9 PM, cl Sun; No admis fee; Estab 1961 to house & administer the art collections of University of Illinois, to support teaching & research programs & to serve as an area art mus; Gallery is 48,000 sq ft, with 30,000 devoted to exhibition space; Average Annual Attendance: 138,000; Mem: 500; dues $15 & up
Income: Financed by mem, state appropriation & grants
Library Holdings: Auction Catalogs, Book Volumes, DVDs, Exhibition Catalogs, Maps, Original Art Works, Pamphlets, Periodical Subscriptions, Photographs, Prints, Reels, Sculpture, Slides, Video Tapes
Special Subjects: African Art, Afro-American Art, American Indian Art, American Western Art, Antiquities-Assyrian, Antiquities-Byzantine, Antiquities-Egyptian, Antiquities-Greek, Antiquities-Oriental, Antiquities-Roman, Asian Art, Baroque Art, Bronzes, Calligraphy, Ceramics, Collages, Decorative Arts, Drawings, Embroidery, Enamels, Etchings & Engravings, Folk Art, Furniture, Glass, Gold, Graphics, Hispanic Art, Islamic Art, Ivory, Jade, Jewelry, Landscapes, Manuscripts, Marine Painting, Medieval Art, Metalwork, Mexican Art, Miniatures, Oriental Art, Painting-American, Painting-British, Painting-Dutch, Painting-European, Painting-Flemish, Painting-French, Painting-German, Painting-Italian, Painting-Japanese, Painting-New Zealand, Painting-Spanish, Pewter, Photography, Porcelain, Portraits, Posters, Pottery, Pre-Columbian Art, Primitive art, Prints, Religious Art, Renaissance Art, Sculpture, Silver, Southwestern Art, Stained Glass, Tapestries, Textiles, Watercolors, Woodcarvings, Woodcuts
Collections: American paintings, sculpture, prints & drawings, Ancient Near Eastern Classical & Medieval Art, European & American Decorative Arts, Trees Collection of European & American Painting, Moore Collection of European & American Decorative Arts, Olsen Collection of Pre-Columbian Art, African Art (Encounters: The Arts of Africa)
Publications: Catalogs, 1 or 2 annually
Activities: Classes for children; docent training; Art-to-Go Outreach; lects open to pub; free concerts; gallery talks; tours; 15-20 vis lectrs per yr; AAMC Award for excellence (Encounters: The Arts of Africa); individual paintings & original objects of art lent to mus & university galleries; educ lending library; book traveling exhibs; originate traveling exhibs; mus cafe

M **Spurlock Museum**, 600 S Gregory, Urbana, IL 61801. Tel 217-333-2360; Fax 217-244-9419; Email kflesher@illinois.edu; Web: www.spurlock.illinois.edu; *Dir* Prof Susan Frankenberg; *Dir Educ* Elisabeth Stone; *Collections Mgr* Christa Deacy-Quinn; *Registrar* Jennifer White; *Information Technology* Jack Thomas; *Educ Coordr* Beth Watkins; *Asst Educator* Kim Sheahan; *Asst Coll Mgr* John Holton; *Head of Security* Harold Bush; *Asst Registrar* Amy Heggemeyer; *Prog Coordr* Karen Flesher; *Spec Events Coordr & Vol Coordr* Brian Cudianat; *Educ Prog Coordr* Brook Taylor; *Coll Coordr* Melissa Sotelo
Open Tues noon - 5 PM, Wed - Fri 9 AM - 5 PM, Sat 10 AM - 4 PM, Sun noon - 4 PM; No admis fee; Estab 1911; Five permanent galleries covering Africa, ancient Egypt, Mesopotamia, the Americas, the ancient Mediterranean, East & Southeast Asia, Oceania & Europe; Average Annual Attendance: 19,000; Mem: 300
Income: $860,000 (university)
Special Subjects: African Art, Anthropology, Antiquities-Egyptian, Antiquities-Greek, Antiquities-Roman, Asian Art, Ceramics, Coins & Medals, Glass, Historical Material, Judaica, Archaeology, Ethnology
Collections: Original & reproduction artifacts of Greek, Roman, Egyptian, Mesopotamian, African, Asian & European cultures, including sculpture, pottery, glass, implements, coins, seals, clay tablets, inscriptions, manuscripts & items of everyday life
Exhibitions: 30th Apr, 2017) Medieval Irish Masterpieces in Modern Reproductions
Activities: Classes for adults & children; docent training; lects open to pub; concerts; workshops; gallery talks; tours; accredited with The American Assoc of Mus; original objects of art lent for special shows in established mus; outreach programs within 100 miles of mus; book 1 traveling exhibs per yr

L **Ricker Library of Architecture & Art**, 608 E Lorado Taft Dr, 208 Architecture Bldg Champaign, IL 61820-6922. Tel 217-333-2290; Fax 217-244-5169; Web: www.library.uiuc.edu/arx; *Librn* Dr Jane Block; *Asst Librn* Jing Liao
Open Mon - Thurs 8:30 AM - 8 PM, Fri 8:30 AM - 5 PM, Sat 1 AM - 5 PM, Sun 1 - 10 PM; Estab 1878 to serve the study & research needs of the students & faculty of the university & the community; Circ 50,000; Ricker Library lends material through UIUC Interlibrary Loan
Income: (financed by state appropriation, blanket order, gifts & UIUC Library Friends)
Library Holdings: Book Volumes 45,000, CD-ROMs, Clipping Files, Exhibition Catalogs, Fiche, Pamphlets, Periodical Subscriptions 350, Photographs, Reels, Reproductions, Sculpture, Video Tapes
Special Subjects: Architecture, Art Education, Art History, Asian Art, Ceramics, Collages, Conceptual Art, Crafts, Decorative Arts, Drawings, Graphic Design, Handicrafts, History of Art & Archaeology, Illustration, Interior Design
Collections: Architectural Folio, Prairie School Architects, Ricker Papers, Frank Lloyd Wright
Publications: Acquisitions list, 4 per year; annual periodicals list

CHARLESTON

M **EASTERN ILLINOIS UNIVERSITY,** Tarble Arts Center, 2010 9th St, Charleston, IL 61920-3099; 600 Lincoln Ave, Charleston, IL 61920-3099. Tel 217-581-2787; Fax 217-581-7138; Email tarble@eiu.edu; Web: www.eiu.edu/tarble; *Dir & Chief Cur* Rehema C Barber; *Asst Dir* Michael Schuetz; *Dean* Anita Shelton
Open Tues - Fri 10 AM - 5 PM, Sat - Sun 1 - 4 PM, cl Mon, during installations periods & major holidays; No admis fee; Estab 1982 to encourage the understanding of & participation in the arts; Main Gallery consists of fifteen 20 ft x 20 ft modular units with natural & incandescent lighting; Brainard Gallery, 20 ft x 50 ft; Gallery 40 ft x 20 ft; eGallery 20 ft x 40 ft; Average Annual Attendance: 16,000; Mem: 200; dues $50 - $1,000
Income: Financed by state appropriation, mem contributions, sales & rental commissions, grant & foundation funds
Library Holdings: Audio Tapes, Kodachrome Transparencies, Original Documents, Other Holdings, Photographs, Reels, Slides, Video Tapes
Special Subjects: Drawings, Etchings & Engravings, Folk Art, Landscapes, Watercolors, Woodcuts, Painting-American, Prints, Sculpture
Collections: Contemporary works on paper by Midwest artists, American Scene Works on Paper, Paul Turner Sargent paintings, Contemporary American Art, Indigenous Contemporary Illinois Folk Arts
Exhibitions: Solo exhibitions & group shows.; Annual Exhibitions: Art Faculty Exhibition, All-Student Show (juried, undergraduate), Graduate Art Exhibition (group thesis), Drawing/Watercolor: Illinois (biennial juried competition), Children's Art Exhibition; Folk Arts from the Collection; 9/16-5/18Heather Hart; 2/17-9/18Diana Al-Hadid
Publications: Exhibition catalogs
Activities: Classes & workshops for children & adults; dramatic progs; docent training; lects open to pub, 4-6 vis lectrs per yr; concerts; gallery talks; tours; drawing/watercolor: Illinois biennial purchase & merit awards; individual paintings & original objects of art lent to qualified professional galleries, arts centers & mus; book traveling exhibs 2-4 per yr; originate traveling exhibs; sales shop sells books, original art & craft pieces; Sales/Rental Gallery rents & sells original works

CHICAGO

M **ARC GALLERY AND EDUCATIONAL FOUNDATION,** 2156 Damen Ave Ste 1, Chicago, IL 60647-6483. Tel 773-252-2232; Email info@arcgallery.org; Web: www.arcgallery.org; *Pres* Carolyne King; *VPres* Cheri Reif Naselli; *Treas* Nancy Fritz; *Secy* Ruti Modlin; *VPres* Ann O'Brien; *Assoc Dir Devel* Monica J Brown
Open Wed - Sat noon - 6 PM, Sun noon - 4 PM; No admis fee; Estab 1973 for the exhib of alternative artworks & educ to the pub about contemporary art; Women run gallery and educational foundation; Mem: 20; mem open to female professional artists; juried entry; dues $60 per month
Income: Grants, contributions & mem support
Special Subjects: Painting-American, Sculpture
Collections: Installation-Site Specific
Exhibitions: ARC National Show & Solo Shows, 77 exhibitions annually, seven per month in seven separate galleries, group shows, member shows
Activities: Educ dept; community outreach progs; workshops & discussions for adults; lects open to pub; gallery talks; tours; juried exhibs & awards; scholarships; originate traveling exhibs

A **THE ART INSTITUTE OF CHICAGO,** 111 S Michigan Ave, Chicago, IL 60603-6492. Tel 312-443-3600; Fax 312-443-0849; Web: www.artic.edu; *Chmn Bd Trustees* Robert Levy; *Pres & Eloise W Martin Dir* James Rondeau; *Pres, School of the Art Inst* Elissa Tenny; *Exec VPres, Gen Coun, Secy* Julia E Getzels; *Exec VPres, Finance* Alexandra Holt
Open Mon - Wed & Fri - Sun 10:30 AM - 5 PM, Thurs 10:30 AM - 8 PM, cl Thanksgiving, Christmas & New Year's Day; Admis adults $25, seniors, students & children $19, mems & children 13 & under no charge; Estab & incorporated 1879 to found, build, maintain & operate museums of fine arts, schools & libraries of art, to form, preserve & exhibit collections of objects of art of all kinds & to carry on appropriate activities conducive to the artistic develop of the community. Maintains reference library; Average Annual Attendance: 1,790,000; Mem: 145,000; dues life $2,500, family $75, individual $60, national assoc $50 & students $40
Income: $125,000,000 (financed by endowments, gifts, grants, auxiliary activities & others)

Library Holdings: Auction Catalogs, Book Volumes 425,000, CD-ROMs, Clipping Files, Compact Disks, Exhibition Catalogs, Fiche, Original Documents, Pamphlets, Periodical Subscriptions 1500, Slides 450,000
Special Subjects: African Art, Afro-American Art, American Indian Art, Antiquities-Egyptian, Architecture, Asian Art, Baroque Art, Bronzes, Ceramics, Collages, Decorative Arts, Enamels, Etchings & Engravings, Folk Art, Glass, Gold, Hispanic Art, Islamic Art, Laces, Latin American Art, Medieval Art, Oriental Art, Pewter, Prints, Sculpture
Collections: Paintings, sculpture, Asian art, prints & drawings, photographs, decorative arts, architectural fragments, tribal arts & textiles, The painting coll reviews Western art, with a sequence of French Impressionists & Post Impressionists, the print coll illustrates the history of printmaking from the 15th-20th centuries with important examples of all periods. It is particularly rich in French works of the 19th century including Meryon, Redon, Millet, Gauguin & Toulouse-Lautrec, textiles are displayed in the Agnes Allerton Textile Galleries which includes a study room & new conservation facilities, colls also include African, Oceanic & ancient American objects, The Architecture Coll includes 19th & 20th century drawings & architectural fragments in the Institute's permanent coll including the more than 40,000 architectural drawings from the Burnham Library of Architecture, The Columbus Drive Facilities include the reconstructed Trading Room from the Chicago Stock Exchange, Arthur Rubloff Paperweight coll is on view, the America Windows, monumental stained glass windows designed by Marc Chagall are on view in the gallery overlooking McKinlock Ct, decorative arts & sculpture range from medieval to the twentieth century, the Asian coll contains a coll of Ukiyo-e prints
Publications: News & Events every two months; catalogs; Ann Report
Activities: Classes & workshops for adults & children; teacher training; docent training; performances; lects open to pub; concerts; gallery walks & talks; guided lect tours; individual paintings & original objects of art lent to mus around the world; originate traveling exhibs to selected mus; mus shop sells books, reproductions, prints, slides, decorative accessories, crafts, jewelry, greeting cards & postcards; jr mus at Kraft Educ Center

L **Ryerson & Burnham Libraries**, 111 S Michigan Ave, Chicago, IL 60603-6492. Tel 312-443-3666; Fax 312-443-0849; Email ryerson@artic.edu; Web: www.artic.edu; *Head Technical Svcs* Anne Champagne; *Exec Dir* Douglas Litts; *Head Reader Servs* Autumn Mather; *Institutional Archivist* Bart Ryckbosch
Open Mon - Wed & Fri 1 - 5 PM, Thurs 10:30 AM - 8 PM; Mus admis req if non-mem; Estab 1879; Circ 60,000; Open to all mus visitors, staff of mus, students & faculty of the School of Art Institute & vis scholars & cur, for reference only; Average Annual Attendance: 10,000
Income: $1,860,000
Purchases: $600,000
Library Holdings: Auction Catalogs, Audio Tapes, Book Volumes 500,000, CD-ROMs, Cassettes, Clipping Files, Compact Disks, Exhibition Catalogs, Fiche, Kodachrome Transparencies, Lantern Slides, Manuscripts, Maps, Memorabilia, Original Art Works, Original Documents, Pamphlets, Periodical Subscriptions 1,100, Photographs, Prints, Reels, Reproductions, Slides, Video Tapes
Special Subjects: Architecture, Art History, Asian Art, Bronzes, Carpets & Rugs, Ceramics, Conceptual Art, Crafts, Decorative Arts, Drawings, Embroidery, Enamels, Folk Art, Furniture, Glass, Gold, Goldsmithing, Graphic Arts, Ivory, Jade, Jewelry, Laces, Latin American Art, Marine Painting, Metalwork, Mexican Art, Painting-American
Collections: Burnham Archive, Louis Sullivan, Frank Lloyd Wright & D H Burnham Collections, Percier & Fontaine Collection, Chicago Art & Artists Scrapbook, Mary Louise Reynolds Collection, Bruce Goff Archive, Collins Archive of Catalan Art & Architecture, Bertrand Goldberg Archive, Irving Penn Archive
Publications: Architectural Records In Chicago, research guide; Burnham Index to Architectural Literature (1990); Art Through the Pages (2008)
Activities: Classes for adults; docent training; lects for mems only; mus shop sells books, magazines, reproductions & prints

M **Kraft Education Center/Museum Education**, 111 S Michigan Ave, Chicago, IL 60603. Tel 312-443-3680; Fax 312-443-0084; Web: www.artic.edu; *Dir Museum Educ* Robert Eskridge
Open Mon - Wed & Fri 10:30 AM - 4:30 PM, Thur 10:30 AM - 8 PM; Admis adults $12, children, students & sr $7; Estab 1964; The new center includes a main exhibition gallery, family room, classrooms, a Teacher Resource Center, a seminar room, an auditorium, conference room & staff offices
Income: Financed by grants, gifts & endowment; renovation financed by Kraft General Foods & the Woman's Board; exhibitions supported by grants from John D & Catherine T MacArthur Foundation & NEA
Exhibitions: Faces, Places, and Inner Spaces: Interactive Exhibit
Publications: Family Self Guides & teacher packets to permanent collections & spec exhibs; gallery games; yearly publs; Volunteer Directory; Information for Students & Teachers; quarterly brochures on family programs, teachers' services, school & general programs
Activities: Docent training; teacher & family workshops; lects open to the pub; gallery walks & games; tours; performances; artist demonstrations

L **Crown Family Educator Resource Center**, 111 S Michigan Ave, Chicago, IL 60603. Tel 312-443-3719; Email erc@artic.edu; Web: www.artic.edu/resource-center; *Dir Teacher Progs* Sarah Alvarez; *School Progs Asst* Tyler Blackwell
Open Tues & Wed 1 - 5 PM, Thurs 1 - 7 PM, Sat 10:30 AM - 4:30 PM; Open for reference; Average Annual Attendance: 4,000
Library Holdings: Book Volumes 1500, CD-ROMs, Cassettes, Compact Disks, Exhibition Catalogs, Pamphlets, Periodical Subscriptions, Reproductions, Slides, Video Tapes
Special Subjects: Art Education, Art History
Activities: Classes for adults; progs/professional develop for educ; gallery games; architectural walks; student self-guides; exten program in Chicagoland, 100 mile radius of mus; mus shop sells books, magazines, reproductions, prints & slides

A **The Woman's Board of the Art Institute of Chicago**, 111 S Michigan Ave, Chicago, IL 60603-6110. Tel 312-443-3629; Fax 312-443-1041; Web: www.artic.edu; *Pres* Francie Corner
Open Mon - Fri 9 AM - 5 PM; Mus admis fee req for access; Estab 1952 to supplement the Board of Trustees in advancing the growth of the Institute & extending its activities & usefulness as a cultural & educational institution; Used by mem only; Mem: 82; annual meeting May
Income: Financed by contributions

A **Auxiliary Board of the Art Institute of Chicago**, 111 S Michigan Ave, Chicago, IL 60603. Tel 312-443-3674; Fax 312-443-1041; *Pres* Paulita Pike
Open Mon - Fri 9 AM - 5 PM; Estab 1973 to promote interest in programs & activities of the Art Institute among younger men & women; Mem: 60; dues $500; annual meeting in June

A **Antiquarian Society of the Art Institute of Chicago**, 111 S Michigan Ave, Chicago, IL 60603. Tel 312-443-3641; Fax 312-443-1041; Email theantiquariansociety@artic.edu; *Admin* Dawn Yingst
Open daily 9 AM - 5 PM; Estab 1877; Support American Arts & European Decorative Arts; Mem: 600; by invitation; annual meeting in Nov
Income: Financed by donations, benefits, annual dues
Exhibitions: Preview of Charles Rennie Mackintosh
Publications: Antiquarian Society Catalogue, every 10 years
Activities: Lects & seminars for members; tours; trips

A **Dept of Prints & Drawings**, 111 S Michigan Ave, Chicago, IL 60603-6110. Tel 312-443-3660; Fax 312-443-0085; Email pdstudy@artic.edu; Web: www.artic.edu; *Prince Trust Interim Chair & Cur Prints & Drawings* Victoria Sancho Lobis; *Cur* Mark Pascale; *Coll Mgr* Emily Vokt Ziemba; *Dept Coord* Judith Broggi; *Paper Conservator* Harriet Stratis; *Conservation Tech* Christine Conniff-O'Shea; *Conservation Tech* Mardy Sears; *Assoc Paper Conservator* Kristi Dahm
Open by appointment; Estab & incorporated 1922 to study prints & drawings & their purchase for the institute; Mem: 260; dues $100 - $1,000
Income: Financed by mem contributions
Special Subjects: Cartoons, Collages, Drawings, Etchings & Engravings, Graphics, Manuscripts, Posters, Prints, Watercolors, Woodcuts
Activities: Lects; gallery talks

A **Society for Contemporary Art**, 111 S Michigan Ave, Chicago, IL 60603. Tel 312-443-3630; Fax 312-443-1041; Email info@scaaic.org; Web: www.scaaic.org; *Pres* Nancy A Lauter
Estab & incorporated 1940 to assist the Institute in acquisition of contemporary works; Mem: 160; dues $150 - $1,000; annual meeting in May
Income: Financed by mem contributions
Activities: Lects; seminars & biennial exhibs at the Institute; 8 vis lectrs per yr

A **Department of Asian Art**, 111 S Michigan Ave, Chicago, IL 60603. Tel 312-443-3834; Fax 312-443-9281; Email asianart@artic.edu; Web: www.artic.edu; *Pritzker Chmn Asian Art & Cur Chinese Art* Tao Wang; *Assoc Cur Chinese Art* Elinor Pearlstein; *Assoc Cur Japanese Art* Janice Katz; *Assoc Cur Indian, SE Asian, Himalayan & Islamic Art* Madhuvanti Ghose; *Cur Islamic Art* Daniel Walker; *Asst Cur Chinese Art* Lu Zhang
Estab 1922 as Dept Oriental Art; affiliate group, Asian Art Council, estab in 1925 to promote interest in the Institute's collection of Asian art; Mem: 50; dues $50
Collections: Chinese paintings, furniture, bronze, jade, ceramics, Japanese paintings, ceramics, Clarence Buckingham Collection of Japanese Woodblock Prints, Buddhist art, Indian and southeast Asian paintings and sculpture, Korean ceramics, Islamic arts
Activities: Lects open to pub; symposia on exhibs; lects mems only

A **Department of Textiles, Textile Society**, 111 S Michigan Ave, Chicago, IL 60603. Tel 312-443-3696; Fax 312-214-4304; Web: www.artic.edu; *Cur Emerita* Christa Thurman; *Cur & Chair* Christopher Monkhouse; *Conservator* Lauren Chang; *Dept Specialist* Isaac Facio; *Asst Cur* Odile Joassin
Open daily 10:30 AM - 4 PM by appointment only; Admis $18 for mus; Estab 1968 to promote appreciation of textiles through lectures, raising of funds, special publications & exhibitions for the Department of Textiles; Changing gallery for permanent coll; Mem: 130, Textile Society; dues $50
Income: Membership fees, funds raised by the soc for periodic purchases
Purchases: Ongoing acquisitions through purchase & gift
Special Subjects: Architecture, Asian Art, Baroque Art, Bronzes, Carpets & Rugs, Ceramics, Coins & Medals, Decorative Arts, Drawings, Embroidery, Enamels, Etchings & Engravings, Folk Art, Furniture, Glass, Gold, Graphics, Hispanic Art, Jewelry, Laces, Landscapes, Latin American Art, Manuscripts, Medieval Art, Metalwork, Mexican Art, Miniatures, Oriental Art, Painting-American, Painting-British, Painting-Dutch, Painting-European, Painting-German, Painting-Italian, Period Rooms, Pewter, Photography, Porcelain, Portraits, Posters, Pottery, Pre-Columbian Art, Prints, Sculpture, Silver, Southwestern Art, Stained Glass, Tapestries, Textiles, Watercolors, Woodcarvings, Woodcuts

A **THE ARTS CLUB OF CHICAGO,** 201 E Ontario St, Chicago, IL 60611-3204. Tel 312-787-3997; Fax 312-787-8664; Email information@artsclubchicago.org; Web: www.artsclubinchicago.org; *Facilities & Gallery Mgr* Adam Mikos; *Pres* Helyn Goldenberg; *Exec Dir* Janine Mileaf
Open Tues - Fri 11 AM - 6 PM, Sat 10 AM - 3 PM; No admis fee; Estab 1916 to maintain club rooms for members & provide public galleries for changing exhibitions; Gallery has 230 running ft of wall space; Average Annual Attendance: 15,000; Mem: 1,200; annual meeting in Nov
Income: Financed by mem dues
Purchases: Occasional purchases gifts & bequests
Library Holdings: Audio Tapes, Book Volumes, Exhibition Catalogs
Collections: Modern Collection incl Braque, Calder, Noguchi, Picabia, Picasso, Contemporary Coll incl Polke, Katz, Doig
Exhibitions: 3 exhibs per yr
Publications: Exhibition Catalogs
Activities: Lects open to members only; concerts; vis lectrs 100 per yr; gallery talks

L **Reference Library**, 201 E Ontario St, Chicago, IL 60611. Tel 312-787-3997; Fax 312-787-8664; *Dir* Kathy Cottong
Open Mon - Fri 11 AM - 6 PM; No admis fee; Estab 1916; Contemporary art; Average Annual Attendance: 20,000; Mem: 1,200
Library Holdings: Book Volumes 3750, Exhibition Catalogs, Periodical Subscriptions 8
Activities: Lects for members only

M **BALZEKAS MUSEUM OF LITHUANIAN CULTURE,** 6500 S Pulaski Rd, Chicago, IL 60629-5136. Tel 773-582-6500; Fax 773-582-5133; Email info@balzekasmuseum.org; Web: www.balzekasmuseum.org; *Exec Dir & Pres* Stanley Balzekas Jr; *Dir Educ & Edit* Karile Vaitkute; *Office Mgr* Rita Striegel; *Cur Folk Art* Frank Zapolis; *Art Dir* Rita Janz; *Dir Genealogy Dept* Robert Balzekas; *Chmn Numismatic* Frank Passic; *Cur Cartography* Edward Pocius; *Dir Periodicals*

Coll Irene Norbut; *Librn* Irena Pumputiene; *Chmn Mem, Com Rels & Mus Shop Mgr* Regina Vasiliauskiene; *Dir Intl Prog* Rasa Rudzykte
Open daily 10 AM - 4 PM; Admis adults $5, seniors & students $4, children 12 & under $2, discounts AAM & ICOM mems; mems no charge; Estab 1966 as a repository for collecting and preserving Lithuanian cultural treasures; Main Gallery 40 x 100; two other galleries 20 x20 & 10 x 15; Average Annual Attendance: 44,000; Mem: 2700; dues individual $30, family $40, supporting $50, genealogy $75, patron $100, organizations $250, sponsor $1,000, life $5,000
Income: $10,000 (financed by mem & donations)
Library Holdings: Book Volumes, CD-ROMs, Cards, Cassettes, Clipping Files, Compact Disks, DVDs, Exhibition Catalogs, Filmstrips, Framed Reproductions, Manuscripts, Maps, Motion Pictures, Original Art Works, Original Documents, Pamphlets, Periodical Subscriptions, Photographs, Prints, Records, Reproductions, Sculpture, Slides, Video Tapes
Special Subjects: Archaeology, Ceramics, Coins & Medals, Costumes, Crafts, Decorative Arts, Drawings, Embroidery, Folk Art, Graphics, Jewelry, Maps, Photography, Prints, Religious Art, Stained Glass, Tapestries, Textiles, Textiles, Watercolors, Woodcarvings, Woodcuts
Collections: Amber, archeology, archives, coins, fine art, folk art, graphics, maps, numismatics, paintings, philately, photography, rare books, rare maps, textiles, wooden folk art, Textiles, Wooden folk art, Maps, Paintings, Graphics
Exhibitions: Various exhibits of paintings, graphics & sculpture
Publications: Lithuanian Museum Review, quarterly
Activities: Classes for adults & children; docent progs; demonstrations; folk art workshops; lects open to mem, 20 vis lectrs per yr; gallery talks; tours; man or woman of the year award; original objects of art lent to other museums & galleries; lending collection contains books, nature artifacts, original art works, paintings, photographs & slides; book 5 traveling exhibs per yr; originate traveling exhibs to mem; mus shop sells books, magazines, original art, reproductions, prints, folk art, amber jewelry, souvenirs & t-shirts

L **Research Library,** 6500 S Pulaski Rd, Chicago, IL 60629. Tel 773-582-6500; Fax 773-582-5133; Email info@balzckasmuseum.org; Web: www.balzckasmuseum.org; *Pres* Stanley Balzekas; *Librn* Robert A Balzekas
Open daily 10 AM - 4 PM; Estab 1966 to preserve Lithuanian-American culture & history; Circ Non-circulating; Open to pub for reference only; Average Annual Attendance: 40,000
Income: Grants
Library Holdings: Audio Tapes, Book Volumes 40,000, Cards, Cassettes, Clipping Files, Exhibition Catalogs, Framed Reproductions, Manuscripts, Maps, Memorabilia, Micro Print, Original Art Works, Original Documents, Pamphlets, Photographs, Prints, Records, Reels, Reproductions, Sculpture, Slides, Video Tapes
Special Subjects: Anthropology, Archaeology, Architecture, Art History, Decorative Arts, Ethnology, Folk Art, Furniture, Graphic Arts, Historical Material, History of Art & Archaeology, Maps, Photography, Prints, Manuscripts, Sculpture, Textiles, Watercolors, Woodcarvings, Woodcuts
Collections: Reproductions of Lithuanian artists, Information on Lithuanian artists & their works, original art work: painting, sculpture & rare maps, folk art, archeological, audiovisual and film, photographs
Exhibitions: Exhibs vary; No Home to Go To: The Story of Baltic Displaced Persons 1944-1952
Publications: Lithuanian Museum Review
Activities: Classes for adults & children in a variety of Lithuanian crafts; lects for mems only; vis lectrs 5 per yr; gallery talks; tours; concerts; originates traveling exhibs 20 per yr; mus sales shop sells books, magazines, original art, reproductions, prints, slides

M **CHICAGO ARCHITECTURE FOUNDATION,** 224 S Michigan Ave, Chicago, IL 60604-2505. Tel 312-922-3432; Fax 312-922-0481; Email info@architecture.org; Web: www.architecture.org; *Pres & CEO* Lynn J Osmond; *CFO* Matthew Biecker; *VPres Educ & Experiences* Gabrielle Lyon; *VPres Opers & Bus Strategy* Michael Malak; *VPres Devel* Lynne Considine Nieman; *Dir Interpretation & Research* Jen Masengarb
Open Mon - Sat 9 AM - 7 PM; 65 free walking tours; paid tours $20 - $49; Estab in 1966; comprehensive program of tours, lectures, exhibitions & special events to enhance pub awareness & appreciation of Chicago architecture; Average Annual Attendance: 200,000; Mem: 7000; dues $55 - $1,500
Income: Financed by mem, shop & tour center, foundation, government & private grants
Special Subjects: Architecture
Exhibitions: City Space
Publications: In Sites Newsletter, quarterly
Activities: Classes for adults; docent training; lect open to public, vis lectrs; citywide tours; competitions; sales shop sells books, magazines, architecturally inspired gift items, stationery & posters

M **CHICAGO ARTISTS COALITION,** 217 N Carpenter, Chicago, IL 60607-1712. Tel 312-491-8888; Email cac@chicagoartistscoalition.org; Web: www.chicagoartistscoalition.org; *Exec Dir* Caroline Older; *Dir Exhibs & Residencies* Teresa Silva; *Dir Devel* Stephanie Lentz; *Dir Educ* Penny Duff; *Dir Strategic Partnerships & Spec Projects* Mary DeYoe
Open Mon - Fri 9 AM - 5 PM, Sat 12 PM - 6 PM; Estab 1974 to provide a sustainable marketplace for entrepreneurial artists & creatives & to empower & connect the artistic community through professional develop trainings, exhib & residency initiatives & advocacy; 2,500 sq ft gallery space with natural light & soaring ceilings; Average Annual Attendance: 5,000 (est); Mem: 300; dues $45 - $250; no qualifications for mem
Income: $600,000 (operating budget) financed by contributed funding by foundations, corporate sponsors, government sources, individual & other contributed revenue including earned income through prog fees & other initiatives
Exhibitions: The Annual
Activities: Classes for adults; Lect open to public, 8 -10 vis lectrs per year; gallery talks; tours; Special Achievement Award for Service to the Visual Arts in Chicago, Maker Grant

M **CHICAGO CHILDREN'S MUSEUM,** 700 E Grand Ave, Ste 127 Chicago, IL 60611-3577. Tel 312-527-1000; Fax 312-527-9082; Web: www.chicagochildrensmuseum.org; *Pres & CEO* Jennifer Farrington; *VPres Educ Prog & Experience Devel* Natalie Bortoli; *VPres Mktg* Twania Brewster; *VPres Institutional Giving* Stacia Whitmore; *VPres Devel* Stephanie Lieber; *VPres HR* Catherine Patyk; *VPres Exhibits & Bldg Opers* Peter Williams
Open daily 10 AM - 5 PM, Thurs 10 AM - 8 PM; Admis adults & children $14. seniors $13, mems & children under 1 no charge; Estab 1982 to inspire discovery & self-expression in children through interactive exhibits & programs; Average Annual Attendance: 500,000; Mem: dues $145 - $500
Income: $6,500,000 (financed by mem, foundation, corporate, government, individual support, earned income)
Exhibitions: Safe 'N' Sound; Under Construction; Water Ways; Inventing Lab; Infotech Arcade; Treehouse Trails; Play Maze
Activities: Classes for adults & children; docent progs; retail store sells books, prints, educational toys & games, music, videotapes, sweatshirts, t-shirts

A **CHICAGO HISTORY MUSEUM,** 1601 N Clark St, Chicago, IL 60614-6038. Tel 312-642-4600; Fax 312-266-2077; Email info@chicagohistory.org; Web: www.chicagohistory.org; *Pres* Gary Johnson; *Exec VP & Chief Historian* Russell Lewis; *VPres External Rels* David Deyhie; *VPres Finance* Cheryl Obermeyer; *VPres Interpretation & Educ* John Russick
Open Mon, Wed - Sat 9:30 AM - 4:30 PM, Tues 9:30 AM - 7:30 PM, Sun Noon - 5 PM; Admis adults $16, seniors & students 13-22 w/ID $14, mems & children under 13 free, Mon free; Estab 1856 to collect, interpret & present the rich, multi-cultural history of Chicago & Ill as well as selected areas of Am history to the public; Maintains galleries & Research Ctr; Average Annual Attendance: 175,000; Mem: 8500; dues Core $70 & $90, Premium $100, & $120
Income: $7,200,000 (financed by endowment, mem, city & state appropriations & public donations)
Library Holdings: Audio Tapes, Book Volumes, Manuscripts, Original Documents, Photographs, Prints, Video Tapes
Special Subjects: Architecture, Costumes, Decorative Arts, Historical Material, Manuscripts, Painting-American, Photography, Prints, Sculpture
Collections: Over 23 million objects, images, & documents, 2 million photographic items, Chicago History, Early American History, Chicago Daily News Photo Collection, Oral History, Film & Video Coll, 100,000 Books & Published Materials
Exhibitions: Chicago: Crossroads of America, Facing Freedom, Secret Lives of Objects
Publications: Books, Calendar of Events & newsletter, quarterly; catalogs; Chicago History, quarterly
Activities: Classes for adults; lect open to public, 15-20 vis lectrs per year; gallery talks; tours; sales shop selling books, magazines, prints, reproductions, gifts, apparel, food

L **Research Center,** 1601 N Clark St, Chicago, IL 60614-6038. Tel 312-642-4600; Fax 312-266-2077; Email research@chicagohistory.org; Web: www.chicagohistory.org
Call for hours; No admis fee to Research Center; children under 6 not admitted; photocopying fees apply
Collections: ARCHIE online catalog, Electronic Encyclopedia of Chicago, Chicago Daily News Database, Online resources for research topics: History Fair, architecture & building history, family history, Online exhibs incl Lincoln at 200: Lincoln & the West: 1809-1860 & The Fiery Trial: Abraham Lincoln & The Civil War, Louis Sullivan at 150, The Great Chicago Fire & The Web of Memory, The Dramas of Haymarket, Wet With Blood, Studs Terkel, History Files website

L **CHICAGO PUBLIC LIBRARY,** Harold Washington Library Center, 400 S State St, Chicago, IL 60605-1203. Tel 312-747-4300; Email art@chipublib.org; Web: www.chipublib.org; *Commissioner* Brian Bannon; *Librn & Head Art Dept* Robert Sloane; *Art Reference Librn* Carol LeBras; *Art Librn* Leslie Petterson
Open Mon - Thurs 9 AM - 9 PM, Fri & Sat 9 AM - 5 PM, Sun 1 - 5 PM; No admis fee; Estab 1872 as a free public library & reading room; The original building was built in 1897. New location of central library. The Harold Washington Library Center was opened to the public in 1991
Income: Financed by city & state appropriation
Library Holdings: Book Volumes 175,000, CD-ROMs, Clipping Files, Compact Disks, DVDs 250, Exhibition Catalogs, Fiche 6192, Memorabilia, Motion Pictures, Original Art Works, Original Documents, Other Holdings Videodiscs, Pamphlets, Periodical Subscriptions 515, Photographs, Records, Reels, Reproductions, Sculpture, Slides, Video Tapes 1500
Special Subjects: Architecture, Decorative Arts, Bookplates & Bindings
Collections: Dance collection: folk dance index, Chicago dance collection, Ann Barzel dance film archive, Fine Arts collection: Chicago Artists' Archive, Picture Collection, Van Damm Collection of New York theater photographs 1919-1961, Chicago Stagebills, Chicago Reader motion picture stills
Exhibitions: Rotating exhibs by Chicago artists
Activities: Dance & art progs; lect open to pub; concerts; gallery talks; documentary film series; tours; sponsored competitions

M **CHICAGO STATE UNIVERSITY,** President's Gallery, 9501 S King Dr, Cook Admin Bldg, 3rd Fl Chicago, IL 60628. Tel 773-995-3984; Web: www.csu.edu; *Co-Cur* Juarez Hawkins; *Co-Cur* Thomas Lucas
Open Mon - Fri 8 AM - 6 PM; No admis fee
Collections: Paintings & photographs
Exhibitions: Exhibs four to five times per yr
Activities: Lectures; demonstrations; workshops; special events

M **CITY OF CHICAGO DEPT. OF CULTURAL AFFAIRS & SPECIAL EVENTS,** Clarke House Museum, 1827 S Indiana Ave, Chicago, IL 60616-1308. Tel 312-744-3316; Email clarkehousemuseum@cityofchicago.org; Web: www.clarkehousemuseum.org; *Cur* Becky LaBarre
Open Wed, Fri & Sat 1 PM & 2:30 PM; No admis fee; Estab 1982; Chicago's oldest building & only Greek Revival structure. House was built in 1836 & includes period rooms; Average Annual Attendance: 4,500
Library Holdings: Auction Catalogs 600, Book Volumes
Special Subjects: Architecture, Ceramics, Decorative Arts, Flasks & Bottles, Furniture, Glass, Historical Material, Maps, Period Rooms, Portraits, Pottery, Prints, Restorations, Silver
Collections: Early 19th century period furniture & decorative objects, Clarke, Chrimes & Ford Family Archives

Publications: Clarke House: Chicago's Oldest Building (2011)
Activities: Classes for adults & children; docent training; classes for children; lects open to public, 4 vis lectrs per year; concerts; tours; sales shop sells books & magazines

M **DUSABLE MUSEUM OF AFRICAN AMERICAN HISTORY,** 740 E 56th Pl, Chicago, IL 60637-1495. Tel 773-947-0600; Fax 773-947-0677; Web: www.dusablemuseum.org; *Pres & CEO* Perri Irmer; *COO* Troy Ratliff; *VPres Planning, Educ & Mus Experience* Lee Bay; *Dir Pub Prog & Educ* Clinee Hedspeth; *Archivist & Spec Cols Librn* Skyla Hearn, MLIS; *Registrar* Kate Swisher; *Visitor Svcs Mgr* Whitney Hamilton; *Assoc Dir Membership & Vol Servs* Erica Griffin
Open Tues - Sat 10 AM - 5 PM, Sun Noon - 5 PM; Admis adults $10, students w/ID & seniors w/ID $7, children 6-11 $3, children under 5 free; Estab 1961 as history & art museum on African American history; Mem: Dues student & senior citizen $25, individual $40, family $60
Special Subjects: Afro-American Art, Photography, Prints, Sculpture
Collections: Historical archives, paintings, photographs, prints, sculpture
Publications: Books of poems, children's stories, African & African-American history; Heritage Calendar, annual
Activities: Lect; guided tours; book traveling exhibitions; sales shop sells curios, sculpture, prints, books & artifacts

M **FIELD MUSEUM,** 1400 S Lake Shore Dr, Chicago, IL 60605-2496. Tel 312-922-9410; Fax 312-922-0741; Web: www.fieldmuseum.org; *Pres & CEO* Richard Lariviere; *Gen Counsel* Lori Breslauer; *VPres Institutional Advancement* Charles Katzenmeyer
Open daily 9 AM - 5 PM, cl Christmas; Admis adults $24, sr citizens & students $21, children 3-11 $17; Estab 1893 to preserve & disseminate knowledge of natural history; 22 anthropological exhibition halls, including a Hall of Primitive Art are maintained; Average Annual Attendance: 1,400,000; Mem: 25,000; dues $60 & $125
Income: Financed by endowment, mem, city & state appropriations & federal & earned funds
Special Subjects: Primitive art
Collections: Anthropological, botanical, geological & zoological colls totaling over 30,000,000 artifacts & specimens, including 100,000 art objects from North & South America, Oceania, Africa, Asia & prehistoric Europe
Exhibitions: Permanent exhibitions: Ancient Egypt Exhibition; Prehistoric Peoples Exhibition; Dinosaur Hall; The American Indian; Pacific Exhibition
Publications: In the Field, monthly; Fieldiana (serial)
Activities: Classes for adults & children; lects open to pub, 25 vis lectrs per yr; concerts; gallery talks; tours; exten dept serving Chicago area; original objects of art lent to qualified museum or other scholarly institutions; originates traveling exhibs; mus shop selling books, magazines, prints, slides

L **Library,** 1200 S Lake Shore Dr, Chicago, IL 60605-2402. Tel 312-665-7887; Fax 312-427-7269; Email harlow@fieldmuseum.org; *Librn & Spec Coll Librn* Benjamin Williams
Open Mon - Fri 8:30 AM - 4:30 PM
Library Holdings: Book Volumes 250,000, Periodical Subscriptions 4000
Special Subjects: American Indian Art, Anthropology, Antiquities-Egyptian, Archaeology, Asian Art
Collections: Rare Book Room housing 6500 vols

M **GLESSNER HOUSE MUSEUM,** 1800 S Prairie Ave, Chicago, IL 60616-1320. Tel 312-326-1480; Email info@glessnerhouse.org; Web: www.glessnerhouse.org; *Exec Dir & Cur* William Tyre; *Tour Coord* Gwendolyn Carrion; *Admin* Michele Rudnick
Open Wed - Sun 11 AM - 4 PM; Admis adults $15, students & seniors (60 & up) $12, children (5-12) $8; Estab. 1966 house saved from demolition; to engage diverse audiences in exploring urban life & design through preservation & interpretation of the historic home of John & Frances Glessner. Glessner House Museum works to increase public awareness, understanding, and appreciation for the history, culture and architecture of Chicago as represented in the lives & home of the of the Glessner household and the surrounding Prairie Ave Historic District; Late 19th c. Arts & Crafts Home designed by H. H. Richardson; Average Annual Attendance: 8,000; Mem: 200; dues $25 & up
Income: Non-profit; financed by mem, tours, programs, grants & rentals
Special Subjects: Architecture, Bookplates & Bindings, Bronzes, Calligraphy, Carpets & Rugs, Ceramics, Costumes, Decorative Arts, Embroidery, Etchings & Engravings, Furniture, Glass, Historical Material, Manuscripts, Metalwork, Period Rooms, Photography, Porcelain, Prints, Reproductions, Restorations, Silver, Textiles, Woodcarvings, Ceramics
Collections: William DeMorgan Ceramics, Emile Galle Glass, Morris & Co Textiles, English arts & crafts, Isaac Scott Collection
Exhibitions: Richardson & His Works (permanent); Simmering Gallery of Prairie Avenue History (permanent)
Publications: The Glessner Journal, quarterly
Activities: Classes for adults & children; docent training; dramatic progs; lects open to pub, 4-8 vis lectrs per yr; gallery talks; forum discussions; symposia; tours; original objects of art lent to galleries which are mounting exhibs on architecture & decorative arts exhibs; lending collection contains architectural ornaments; mus shop sells books, magazines, prints, stationery & small gift items

M **HYDE PARK ART CENTER,** 5020 S Cornell Ave, Chicago, IL 60615. Tel 773-324-5520; Fax 773-324-6641; Email generalinfo@hydeparkart.org; Web: www.hydeparkart.org; *Exec Dir* Kate Lorenz; *Deputy Dir* Hilesh Patel; *Dir Exhibs & Residency* Allison Peters Quinn; *Dir Educ* Mike Nourse; *Mktg & Communs Coordr* Tracy Montes; *Finance & Opers Mgr* Eileen Truong; *Dir Devel* Aaron Rodgers; *Preparator* Andi Crist
Open Mon - Thurs 9 AM - 8 PM, Fri - Sat 9 AM - 5 PM, Sun noon - 5 PM; No admis fee; Estab 1939 to stimulate an interest in art; Average Annual Attendance: 45,000; Mem: 500; dues family $55, individual $45, artist, senior & student $30
Income: $600,000 (financed by endowment, mem, city & state appropriation, foundations, corporations & private contributions)
Special Subjects: Ceramics, Crafts, Drawings, Etchings & Engravings, Folk Art, Painting-American, Photography, Sculpture, Watercolors, Textiles
Exhibitions: (see website for details)
Publications: Quarterly newsletter, exhibition catalogues
Activities: Classes for adults & children; lect open to public; gallery talks; scholarships offered; exten prog serves South & West sides of Chicago; sales shop sells original art

M **INTUIT: THE CENTER FOR INTUITIVE & OUTSIDER ART,** 756 N Milwaukee Ave, Chicago, IL 60642-5939. Tel 312-243-9088; Fax 312-243-9089; Email intuit@art.org; Web: www.art.org; *Exec Dir* Debra Kerr; *Sr Mgr Exhibs & Devel & Chief Cur* Alison Amick; *Sr Mgr Learning & Engagement* Melissa Smith; *Educ Mgr* Joel Javier; *Devel Coordr* Claire Fassnacht; *Mktg Coordr* Annaleigh Wetzel
Open Tues - Wed, Fri - Sat - 11 AM - 6 PM, Thurs 11 AM - 7:30 PM, Sun noon - 5 PM; cl Mon; Voluntary admis $5; Estab 1991 to educate the public on outsider art; Maintains reference library & 2 display galleries; Average Annual Attendance: 10,000; Mem: 650; dues $25 - $2,500
Income: $400,000 (financed by mem & grants)
Library Holdings: Auction Catalogs, Audio Tapes, Book Volumes, Cards, Cassettes, Clipping Files, Compact Disks, DVDs, Exhibition Catalogs, Fiche, Kodachrome Transparencies, Lantern Slides, Manuscripts, Memorabilia, Micro Print, Original Documents, Other Holdings, Pamphlets, Periodical Subscriptions, Photographs, Records, Slides, Video Tapes
Special Subjects: Afro-American Art, Primitive art, Cartoons, Drawings, Folk Art
Collections: Outsider Art, Henry Darger Room Collection, studio evocation/ reproduction
Publications: The Outsider, ann
Activities: Classes for adults & children; docent training; dramatic progs; lects open to pub; 12 vis lectrs per yr; concerts, gallery talks, tours; films; teacher fellowship prog; lending of original objects of art to Chicago Public Schools; approx once per yr; mus shop sells books, magazines, clothes, CDs, DVDs, jewelry

M **LOYOLA UNIVERSITY CHICAGO,** Loyola University Museum of Art, 820 N Michigan Ave, Chicago, IL 60611. Tel 312-915-7600; Fax 312-915-6388; Email luma@luc.edu; Web: www.luc.edu/luma; *Registrar* Mary Albert; *Cur* Natasha Ritsma; *Head Preparator* Tim Duncan; *Mem & Visitor Servs Mgr.* Theolyn Patterson
Open Tues 11 AM - 8 PM, Wed - Sat 11 AM - 6 PM; Admis general $9, seniors (65 & up) $6, students (w/ID) $3; Estab 1969 to display the permanent university collection of Medieval, Renaissance & Baroque decorative arts & paintings & rotating exhibs; Circ 4,000 titles; Average Annual Attendance: 30,000; Mem: 350; dues $50 - $1,000
Income: Financed by donations, endowment, mem & university support & earned income
Library Holdings: Auction Catalogs, Book Volumes 4,000, CD-ROMs, Cards, DVDs, Exhibition Catalogs
Special Subjects: Anthropology, Bronzes, Conceptual Art, Crafts, Decorative Arts, Enamels, Etchings & Engravings, Gold, Islamic Art, Ivory, Latin American Art, Painting-European, Painting-Flemish, Painting-French, Painting-German, Painting-Italian, Painting-Russian, Pewter, Pottery, Prints, Religious Art, Sculpture, Sculpture, Silver, Stained Glass, Tapestries, Textiles, Textiles, Woodcuts, Antiquities-Assyrian, Architecture, Baroque Art, Ceramics
Collections: Decorative arts, furniture, liturgical objects, paintings, sculptures & textiles
Publications: Exhibition catalogs
Activities: Educ dept, classes for adults & children; docent training; lect open to public, 20 vis lectrs per yr; concerts; gallery talks; tours on request; paintings & original objects of art lent to qualified museums; lending collection contains original art works, paintings & sculpture; organize traveling exhibs to univ mus; mus shop sells books, reproductions & jewelry

M **MUSEUM OF CONTEMPORARY ART CHICAGO,** 220 E Chicago Ave, Chicago, IL 60611-2644. Tel 312-280-2660; Fax 312-397-4095; Email info@mcachicago.org; Web: www.mcachicago.org; *Pritzker Dir* Madeleine Grynsztejn; *James W Alsdorf Chief Cur* Michael Darling; *Deputy Dir* Janet Alberti; *Dir Cols & Exhibs* Anne Breckenridge Barrett; *Chief Registrar* Meridith Gray; *Dir Devel* Lisa Key; *Manilow Sr Cur & Dir Global Initiatives* Omar Kholeif; *Chief Content Officer* Susan Chun; *Polk Bros Assoc Dir Educ* Marissa Reyes; *Design Dir* Dylan Fraccareta; *Dir Visitor Experience* Patricia Fraser; *Spec & Rental Events Coordr* Kristi Widgery
Open Tues & Fri 10 AM - 9 PM, Wed, Thurs, Sat & Sun 10 AM - 5 PM, cl Mon, Thanksgiving, Christmas & New Year's Day; Suggested admis adults $15, students & seniors $8; Estab 1967 as a forum for contemporary arts in Chicago; Average Annual Attendance: 280,000; Mem: 8500, dues circle $1,500+, advocate $1000+, assoc $500+, contributor $250+, friend $150+, household $85, individual $70,
Income: $14,000,000 (financed by endowment, mem, pub & private sources)
Special Subjects: Afro-American Art, Asian Art, Collages, Drawings, Oriental Art, Painting-American, Painting-German, Painting-Italian, Photography, Prints, Sculpture
Collections: Permanent coll: 2,500+ objects of 20th century & contemporary art, constantly growing through gifts & purchases, Examples of visual art from 1945 - present, focusing on surrealism, minimalism, conceptual photography & work by Chicago-based artists
Publications: Bimonthly calendar, exhibition catalogs, membership magazine
Activities: Classes for adults & children; family progs; docent training; teacher workshops; community outreach; lects; gallery talks; tours; performance; films; book traveling exhibs; originate traveling exhibs; mus shop sells books, designer jewelry & other gifts, magazines, original art & reproductions

L **Library,** 220 E Chicago Ave, Chicago, IL 60611. Tel 312-397-3894; Fax 312-397-4099; Email library@mcachicago.org; Web: www.mcachicago.org/Learn/Library; *Library Dir* Mary Richardson
Open by appointment Mon - Fri 9:30 AM - 4 PM; Estab 1967; Library collection, non-circulating; for reference
Income: Financed by endowment, mem, pub & pvt sources
Library Holdings: Book Volumes 19,000, Cassettes, Other Holdings exhibition records, ephemera, Periodical Subscriptions, Photographs, Video Tapes
Special Subjects: Art History, Conceptual Art

M **MUSEUM OF CONTEMPORARY PHOTOGRAPHY,** Columbia College Chicago, 600 S Michigan Ave, Chicago, IL 60605. Tel 312-663-5554; Fax 312-369-8067; Email mocp@colum.edu; Web: www.mocp.org; *Exec Dir* Natasha Egan; *Deputy Dir & Chief Cur* Karen Irvine; *Head Opers* Stephanie Conaway; *Mgr Mktg & Community Engagement* Marisa Fox; *Cur Academic Progs & Cols* Kristin Taylor; *Video Prog Coordr* Kate Bowen; *Audience Devel Coordr* George Chen
Open Mon - Fri 10 AM -5 PM, Thurs until 8 PM, Sun Noon - 5 PM; Admis suggested donation $5; Estab 1976 to exhibit, collect & promote contemporary photog; 4000 sq ft on two levels; newly designed 1500 sq ft main exhibition gallery permits a spacious installation of 200 photographs; upper level gallery can accommodate an additional 200-300 prints; Average Annual Attendance: 50,000; Mem: 450; dues $20-2500
Special Subjects: Photography
Collections: Contemporary American photography, including in-depth holdings of works by Harold Allen, Harry Callahan, Barbara Crane, Louise Dahl-Wolfe, Dorothea Lange, Danny Lyon, Barbara Morgan, David Plowden, Anne Naggle & Joel Peter-Witkin
Exhibitions: Rotate exhibitions five times per yr
Publications: Exhibit catalogs
Activities: Educ dept: classes at Chicago Public Schools; teen after school prog; lects open to pub, 10 vis lectrs per yr; gallery talks; tours; lending collection contains photographs; book traveling exhibs 2 per yr; originate traveling exhibs; mus shop sells books, prints

L **Library,** 624 S Michigan Ave, Chicago, IL 60605. Tel 312-369-7900; Fax 312-369-8062; Email askalibrarian@colum.edu; Web: library.colum.edu; *Dean of Lib* Jan Chindlund; *Head Technical Serv & Coll Mgr* Dennis McGuire; *Head Access Serv & Assessment* Jennifer Sauzer; *Head Ref & Instruction* Arlie Sims; *Head Archives & Colls* Heidi Marshall
Open Mon - Thurs 7:30 AM - 10 PM, Fri 7:30 AM - 8 PM, Sat 9 AM - 5 PM, Sun 10 AM - 5 PM; Estab 1893 to provide library & media services & materials in support of the curriculum & to serve the col community as a whole; Circ 101,902; For lending & reference
Library Holdings: Book Volumes 295,000, Other Holdings Serials 550, Audio 23,800, Film/Video 22,000, E-Books 61,290, Full-text Journals 63,990, Audio 23,800, Film/Video 22,000, Research Databases 180, Digital Images 351,600
Special Subjects: Commercial Art, Film, Graphic Arts, Graphic Design, Interior Design, Photography, Theatre Arts, Video, Painting-American
Exhibitions: Art in the Library Exhibit ongoing quarterly exhibits; Alumni on Five Biannual Exhibs
Activities: Lectures open to pub; 2 visiting lectrs per year

M **MUSEUM OF SCIENCE & INDUSTRY,** 57000 Lake Shore Dr, Chicago, IL 60637-2093. Tel 773-684-1414; Fax 773-684-7141; Email contact@msichicago.org; Web: www.msichicago.org; *Pres & CEO* David Mosena; *VPres Mktg & Communs* Matthew Simpson; *VPres Educ & Guest Servs* Mary Krinock
Open Mon - Sun 9:30 AM - 4 PM, cl Dec 25; see website for extended hours; Admis adults $18, children 3-11 $11, mem free, certain days free see website for details; parking fees; Estab 1926 to further pub understanding of science, technology, industry, medicine & related fields; Visitor-participation exhibits depicting scientific principles, technological applications & social implications in fields of art science; Omnimax Theater; Average Annual Attendance: 2,000,000; Mem: 59,470; dues premier $180, family $115, individual $80, senior & student $55
Income: $16,200,000 (financed by endowment, mem, city & state appropriation, contributions & grants from companies, foundations & individuals)
Publications: AHA quarterly
Activities: Classes for adults & children; dramatic progs; field trips; summer camps; teacher workshops; Snoozeum; lects open to pub; tours; competitions; outreach activities; lending collection contains communications, transportation & textile equipment; book traveling exhibs; originate traveling exhibs; mus shop sells books, magazines, prints, slides, postcards & souvenirs

M **NATIONAL MUSEUM OF MEXICAN ART,** 1852 W 19th St, Chicago, IL 60608-2706. Tel 312-738-1503; Fax 312-738-9740; Email info@nationalmuseumofmexicanart.org; Web: nationalmuseumofmexicanart.org; *Pres* Carlos Tortolero; *Assoc Dir, Registrar* Raquel Aguinaga-Martinez; *Dir Visual Arts & Chief Cur* Ceareo Moreno; *Dir Opers* Alex Alvarado; *Chief Devel Officer* Barbara Engelskirchen; *Bus Dir* Eimy Rosales; *Permanent Coll Cur* Rebecca Meyers
Open Tues - Sun 10 AM - 5 PM; No admis fee; Estab 1982; Average Annual Attendance: 110,000; Mem: 1,500; dues educators $30, individuals $40, sr couple 450. household $60
Income: $4,000,000 (financed by mem, city, state & federal appropriation, corporations & foundations)
Special Subjects: Folk Art, Latin American Art, Mexican Art, Photography, Prints
Collections: Mexican prints, photography & folk art collection, Latino art collection
Exhibitions: Jose Guadalupe Posada; rotating 4 per year
Activities: Classes for children in docent progs; lects open to pub, 4 vis lectrs per yr; mus shop sells books, original art, folk art & prints

M **THE NATIONAL MUSEUM OF PUERTO RICAN ARTS & CULTURE,** 3015 W Division St, Chicago, IL 60622. Tel 773-486-8345; Fax 773-486-8806; Email info@nmprac.org; Web: www.nmprac.org; *CEO & Pres* Billy Ocasio; *Dir Exhibs & Educ Prog* Bianca Ortiz Declet
Open Tues - Fri 10 AM - 5 PM, Sat 10 AM - 2 PM; No admis fee
Library Holdings: Book Volumes, Pamphlets, Photographs, Sculpture, Video Tapes
Special Subjects: Folk Art, Graphics, Sculpture, Architecture
Activities: Three vis lectrs per yr; concerts; mus shop sells books, magazines, original art & reproductions

M **NATIONAL VETERANS ART MUSEUM,** 4041 N Milwaukee Ave, 2nd Fl Chicago, IL 60641. Tel 312-326-0270; Email info@nvam.org; Web: www.nvam.org; *Exec Dir* Brendan Foster; *Gallery Coordr* Destinee Oitzinger; *Asst Educ Coordr* Monica Tantoco; *Programming Asst* Monserrat Wisdom
Open Tues - Sat 10 AM - 5 PM; No admis fee; Estab 1981; Average Annual Attendance: 7,500; Mem: 200; dues $100 - $5,000+
Income: grants, donations, membership, some sponsorship
Special Subjects: Ceramics, Collages, Drawings, Military Art, Painting-American, Photography, Sculpture, Watercolors
Collections: paintings, photographs, sculpture, drawings, mixed media
Publications: newsletter, Transmissions
Activities: Classes for adults & children; docent training; lects open to the pub; lects for members only; 2 - 5 vis lects per yr; gallery talks; tours; Mus shop sells books; reproductions; prints; apparel; gift items

L **THE NEWBERRY,** 60 W Walton St, Chicago, IL 60610-3380. Tel 312-943-9090; Fax 312-255-3513; Web: www.newberry.org; *Pres & Librn* David Spadafora; *Roger & Julie Baskes VPres Cols & Library Svcs* Alice Schreyer; *VPres Finance & Admin* James Burke; *VPres Research & Acad Progs* D Bradford Hunt; *VPres Develop* Katy Hall; *Dir Communs & Mktg* Alex Teller; *Dir Dept Exhibs & Maj Projects* Diane Dillon; *Dir Col Servs* Alan Leopold; *Dir Conservation Servs Dept* Lesa Dowds; *Dir Reader Servs Dept* Will Hansen; *Dir Dept Digital Initiatives & Servs* Jennifer Thorn Dalzin; *Dir Dept Pub Engagement* Karen Christianson; *Dir IT* Drin Gyuk; *Dir HR* Judy Rayborn; *Dir Office Events & Vol* Chayla Bevers Ellison
Open Tues - Thurs 10 AM - 6 PM, Fri & Sat 9 AM - 5 PM; Tours Thurs 3 PM, Sat 10:30 AM; No admis fee; Estab 1887 for research in the history & humanities of Western Civilization; Circ Non-circulating; For reference only. Maintains two small galleries for exhibitions; Mem: 1950; dues $35; annual meeting in Oct
Income: $4,500,000 (financed by endowment, mem, gifts, federal, corporate & foundation funds)
Purchases: $400,000
Library Holdings: Audio Tapes, Book Volumes, Cards, Clipping Files, Exhibition Catalogs, Fiche, Manuscripts, Memorabilia, Motion Pictures, Original Art Works, Pamphlets, Periodical Subscriptions, Photographs, Records, Reels, Video Tapes
Special Subjects: American Indian Art, American Western Art, Art History, Ethnology, Graphic Arts, History of Art & Archaeology, Manuscripts, Maps, Southwestern Art, Religious Art
Collections: American History & Culture, American Indian & Indigenous Studies, Chicago and the Midwest, Genealogy & Local History, History of the Book, Manuscripts & Archives, Maps, Travel & Exploration, Medieval Renaissance & Early Modern Studies, usic, Postcards, Religion
Publications: A Newberry Newsletter, quarterly; Center for Renaissance Studies Newsletter, 3 times per yr; Mapline, quarterly newsletter; Meeting Ground, bi-annual newsletter; Origins, quarterly newsletter
Activities: Classes for adults; dramatic progs; docent training; lects open to pub, some open to members only, 35 vis lectrs per yr; concerts; gallery talks; tours; schols & fels offered; individual paintings & original objects of art lent to mus & libraries on restricted basis; book traveling exhibs 1-2 per yr; sales shop sells books, reproductions, slides

M **NORTH PARK UNIVERSITY,** Carlson Tower Art Gallery, 2543 W Cullom Ave, Chicago, IL 60618-1501. Tel 773-244-5611; Email tlowly@northpark.edu; Web: www.northpark.edu; *Dir Gallery* Tim Lowly
Open Mon - Fri 9 AM - 9 PM, occasional weekend evenings; No admis fee; Educational develop of aesthetic appreciation
Special Subjects: Religious Art
Collections: Original contemporary Christian, Illinois & Scandinavian art
Activities: Classes for adults; lect open to public, 1-2 vis lectrs per year; concerts; exten dept serves Chicago; book traveling exhibs, 1-2 per year

M **NORTHEASTERN ILLINOIS UNIVERSITY,** Fine Arts Center Gallery, 5500 N Saint Louis Ave, Art Dept Chicago, IL 60625-4625. Tel 773-442-4944; Fax 773-442-4920; Email h-weber@neiu.edu; Web: www.neiu.edu; *Dir* Heather Weber
Open by appointment Mon - Thurs 10 AM - 4 PM, Fri 10 AM - Noon; No admis fee; Estab Feb 1973 for the purpose of providing a link between the University & the local community on a cultural & aesthetic level, to bring the best local & midwest artists to this community; Gallery is located in the Fine Arts Center on the University campus; Average Annual Attendance: 8,000
Income: Financed by Department of Art funds and personnel
Exhibitions: Various exhib
Publications: Postcard announcements; brochures; catalogs
Activities: Lects open to pub; 4-6 vis lectrs per yr; gallery talks; tours

M **PALETTE & CHISEL ACADEMY OF FINE ARTS,** 1012 N Dearborn St, Chicago, IL 60610-2804. Tel 312-642-4400; Fax 312-642-4317; Email fineart1012@sbcglobal.net; Web: www.paletteandchisel.org; *Pres* Val Yachik; *Exec Dir* William Ewers
Open Mon - Fri 10:30 AM - 6:30 PM, workshops are open to the pub on a regular basis; No admis fee; Estab & incorporated 1895 to provide a meeting/work place for the visual arts; Building contains galleries, classrooms, studios & library; Mem: 430; dues $360; patron & nonresident mem available
Collections: Permanent Collection: works by James Montgomery Flagg, J Jeffery Grant Permanent Collection, Alphonse Mucha, Richard Schmid Permanent Collection, James Montgomery Flagg Permanent Collection
Exhibitions: Five Members Award Shows; guest artists & organizations frequently exhibited
Publications: The Quick Sketch, monthly
Activities: Educ events; classes for artists; lect open to public; tours; competitions with awards; scholarships offered

M **POLISH MUSEUM OF AMERICA (PMA),** 984 N Milwaukee Ave, Chicago, IL 60642-4101. Tel 773-384-3352; Email pma@polishmuseumofamerica.org; Web: www.polishmuseumofamerica.org; *Pres* Richard Owsiany; *Mng Dir* Malgorzata Kot; *Head Archivist* Halina Misterka; *Head Librn* Iwona Bozek; *Mem Coordr & Graphic Designer* Lisa Terlecki; *Historian* Jan M Lorys; *Photo Coll Cur* Julita Siegel; *Archivist & Librn* Teresa Sromek
Open Wed 11 AM - 7 PM, Fri - Tues 11 AM - 4 PM, cl Thurs; Admis adults $10, seniors & students $8.50, mems $6; Estab 1935 & opened 1937, to preserve the artistic, cultural, historic & literary heritage of Polish Americans and Poles throughout the world; A specialized mus & gallery containing works of Polish

artists & Polish-American culture artists is maintained; Average Annual Attendance: 10,000; Mem: 1,500; dues $25
Income: Financed by donations, memberships & grants
Special Subjects: Coins & Medals, Costumes, Decorative Arts, Etchings & Engravings, Folk Art, Historical Material, Maps, Military Art, Miniatures, Painting-Polish, Prints, Religious Art, Reproductions, Sculpture, Silver, Tapestries, Watercolors
Collections: Originals dating to beginning of 20th century, a few older pieces, Pulaski at Savannah (Batowski), works of Polish artists, Polish-American artists & works on Polish subject, Nikifor, Jan Styka, Wojciech Kossak, paintings from the coll of the Polish Pavilion from 1939 World's Fair in NY, large coll of Paderewski memorabilia, including the last piano he played on, prints & posters coll
Exhibitions: Modern Polish Art; folk art; militaria
Publications: Exhibit Catalogs; Art Collection Catalog
Activities: Classes for adults & children; docent training; workshops; lects open to pub, 5 vis lectrs per yr; tours; concerts; gallery talks; sponsoring of competitions; mus shop sells books, original art, reproductions, prints, Polish Folk items, amber, crystal, merchandise & Polish gifts: ornaments, jewelry, t-shirts

L **The Polish Museum of America Library (PMAL),** 984 N Milwaukee Ave, Chicago, IL 60642-4101. Tel 773-384-3352; Email pma@polishmuseumofamerica.org; Web: www.polishmuseumofamerica.org/library; *Head Librn Spec Cols* Iwona Bozek; *Librarian* Krystyna Grell; *Archivist & Librn* Teresa Sromek
Open Mon, Tues & Fri 10 AM - 4 PM, Wed 1 - 7 PM, Sat 11 AM - 4 PM; No admis fee; Estab 1935, for reference only; interlibrary circulation; Exhibit space: Stephen & Elizabeth Ann Kusmierczak Art Gallery; Maritime Room, Paderewski Room, Art Deco Corridor; Average Annual Attendance: 3,000
Income: Donations & mem
Library Holdings: Audio Tapes, Book Volumes 100,000, Cassettes, Clipping Files, DVDs, Exhibition Catalogs, Fiche, Filmstrips, Framed Reproductions, Manuscripts, Maps, Memorabilia, Motion Pictures, Original Art Works, Other Holdings Newspapers, Pamphlets, Periodical Subscriptions 125, Photographs 20,000, Prints, Records, Reels, Reproductions 1000, Sculpture, Slides 2000, Video Tapes
Special Subjects: Architecture, Coins & Medals, Costume Design & Constr, Crafts, Decorative Arts, Dolls, Embroidery, Ethnology, Fashion Arts, Film, Folk Art, Graphic Arts, Historical Material, Judaica, Manuscripts, Maps, Painting-American, Painting-Polish, Photography, Portraits, Posters, Stained Glass, Textiles, Theatre Arts, Woodcarvings, Woodcuts
Collections: Haiman, Paderewski, Polish Art, Graphical Art, Posters, paintings, sculpture, 1939 New York World's Fair - Polish Pavilion, Music coll: song sheets, records, piano rolls, manuscripts, Genealogy materials, Immigration Coll, Polonia Coll
Publications: Art Collection catalog
Activities: Docent training; workshops; lects open to pub; concerts; tours; sponsoring of competitions; schols; book traveling exhibs to institutions in the US & Poland; organize traveling exhibs; mus shop sells books, reproductions

PRINT COUNCIL OF AMERICA
For further information, see National and Regional Organizations

A **THE RENAISSANCE SOCIETY,** University of Chicago, 5811 S Ellis Ave, Cobb Hall, 4th Fl Chicago, IL 60637. Tel 773-702-8670; Fax 773-702-9669; Email info@renaissancesociety.org; Web: renaissancesociety.org; *Exec Dir & Chief Cur* Solveig Ovstebo; *Dir Finance & Opers* Jessica Cochran; *Dir Devel* Colleen Kelly; *Dir Publs & Registrar* Karen Reimer; *Dir Communs* Anne Searle Jones; *Chief Preparator* Pierre Sondeijker; *Asst Cur* Karsten Lund; *Devel Assoc* Julia DeRose
Open Tues - Fri 10 AM - 5 PM, Sat & Sun Noon - 5 PM, cl summer; No admis fee; Founded 1915 to advance the understanding & appreciation of the arts in all forms; Non-collecting mus of contemporary art; Average Annual Attendance: 32,000; Mem: 500; dues $50; annual meeting in June
Exhibitions: Four changing exhibitions per yr
Publications: Exhibit catalogs
Activities: Educ dept; lect open to public; concerts; gallery talks; tours; film programs; performances; mus shop sells editions, books

L **SAINT XAVIER UNIVERSITY,** Robert and Mary Rita Murphy Stump Library, 3700 W 103rd St, L-228, Ward Academic Center Chicago, IL 60655-3105. Tel 773-298-3352; Fax 773-779-5231; Email ask@sxu.libanswers.com; Web: www.sxu.edu; *Dir* David Stern; *Assoc Librn* James Kusik
Open Mon - Thurs 7:30 AM - Midnight, Fri 7:30 AM - 7 PM, Sat Noon - 7 PM, Sun Noon - Midnight; Estab 1847
Income: Financed by college funds & contributions
Library Holdings: Book Volumes 160,600, Cards, Kodachrome Transparencies, Motion Pictures, Original Art Works, Periodical Subscriptions 890, Records, Slides 10,000, Video Tapes
Collections: Permanent art collection

L **SCHOOL OF THE ART INSTITUTE OF CHICAGO,** Video Data Bank, 112 S Michigan Ave, Chicago, IL 60603-6105. Tel 312-345-3550; Fax 312-541-8073; Email info@vdb.org; Web: www.vdb.org; *Dir* Albina Manning
Open Mon - Fri 9 AM - 5 PM; No admis fee; Estab 1976 to distribute, preserve & promote videos by & about contemporary artists; Average Annual Attendance: 500,000
Income: Financed by grants & earned income
Library Holdings: Video Tapes 6000
Special Subjects: Art History, Film, Mixed Media, Painting-American, Painting-British, Painting-German, Photography, Sculpture, Video
Collections: Video Tapes: Early Video History, Independent Video/Alternative Media, Latin/South America, Media Literacy, On Art & Artists
Publications: Annual catalog of holdings

L **SCHOOL OF THE ART INSTITUTE OF CHICAGO,** John M Flaxman Library, 37 S Wabash Ave, 6th Fl Chicago, IL 60603. Tel 312-899-5097; Fax 312-899-1851; Email flaxman@artic.edu; *Exec Dir* Claire Eike; *Col Management Librn* Sylvia Choi; *Spec Coll Mgr* Kayla Anderson; *Spec Col Librn* Anne-Dorothee Boehme; *Research & Access Servs Librn* Holly Stec Dankert; *Digital Servs Librn* Christopher Day; *Media Preservation & Digitization Librn* Carolyn Faber; *Reference & Instruction Librn* Nick Ferreira; *Reference & Instruction Librn* Mackenzie Salisbury
Open Mon - Thurs 9 AM - 7:30 PM, Fri 9 AM - 4 PM, Sat & Sun Noon - 6 PM; Estab 1967 to provide a strong working collection for School's programs in the visual & related arts; Circ 54,002; Average Annual Attendance: 80,000
Income: 701,445 (financed by the operational budgets of the school of Art Institute of Chicago)
Purchases: $189,870
Library Holdings: Audio Tapes 1,000, Book Volumes 65,000, CD-ROMs 75, Cassettes 700, Clipping Files, Compact Disks 1,000, DVDs 100, Exhibition Catalogs, Fiche, Filmstrips 750, Motion Pictures 663, Other Holdings 4,000, Periodical Subscriptions 350, Records 100, Video Tapes 1,000
Collections: Joan Flasch Artists Book Collection, 16mm Film Study Collection, Tony Zwicker Archives, Warren Menaker Thought Books series, Randolph Street Gallery Archives, Correspondence Art digital library

SOCIETY OF ARCHITECTURAL HISTORIANS
For further information, see National and Regional Organizations

M **SPERTUS INSTITUTE OF JEWISH STUDIES,** 610 S Michigan Ave, Chicago, IL 60605-1901. Tel 312-322-1700; Fax 312-922-3934; Email info@spertus.edu; Web: www.spertus.edu; *Pres & CEO* Hal M Lewis, PhD; *Cur Colls & Exhibs* Ionit Behar; *Colls Mgr* Kathy Bloch; *Colls Asst* Tom Gengler
Open Sun 10 AM - 5 PM, Mon - Wed 9 AM - 5 PM, Thurs 9 AM - 6 PM, cl Fri 9 AM - 3 PM; No admis fee; Estab 1967 for interpreting & preserving the 3,500-year-old heritage embodied in Jewish history; Circ 1,000; Changing exhibs of art & artifacts from the Jewish experience; Average Annual Attendance: 35,000; Mem: dues SpertusNet & senior $50, individual $60, household $75, assoc $100
Income: Financed by contributions & subsidy from Spertus Institute
Library Holdings: Auction Catalogs, Audio Tapes, Book Volumes, CD-ROMs, Cassettes, Clipping Files, Compact Disks, DVDs, Exhibition Catalogs, Fiche, Framed Reproductions, Manuscripts, Maps, Motion Pictures, Original Documents, Other Holdings, Pamphlets, Periodical Subscriptions, Photographs, Records, Reels, Slides, Video Tapes
Special Subjects: Antiquities-Greek, Antiquities-Oriental, Antiquities-Roman, Archaeology, Architecture, Bookplates & Bindings, Carpets & Rugs, Cartoons, Ceramics, Coins & Medals, Crafts, Decorative Arts, Decorative Arts, Drawings, Enamels, Etchings & Engravings, Folk Art, Glass, Graphics, Historical Material, Jewelry, Judaica, Manuscripts, Maps, Metalwork, Mixed Media, Oriental Art, Painting-American, Painting-British, Painting-Canadian, Painting-European, Painting-German, Painting-Israeli, Painting-Polish, Painting-Russian, Pewter, Photography, Porcelain, Portraits, Posters, Prints, Religious Art, Sculpture, Silver, Stained Glass, Tapestries, Textiles, Watercolors, Woodcarvings, Woodcuts, Painting-American
Collections: Permanent collection of sculpture, paintings & graphic art, ethnographic materials spanning centuries of Jewish experience, a permanent Holocaust memorial, Judaica, paintings, ceremonial silver, textiles, archaeology
Publications: Spec publs with exhibits; Calendar of Events
Activities: Classes for adults; dramatic progs; lects open to pub, 20 vis lectrs per yr; concerts; gallery talks; tours; individual paintings & original objects of art lent to other mus & institutions; originate traveling exhibs to other mus; mus shop sells books, original art, reproductions, prints, objects for Jewish home, children's toys & clothing

L **Asher Library**, 610 S Michigan Ave, Chicago, IL 60605-1906. Tel 312-322-1712; Fax 312-922-0455; Email resources@spertus.edu; Web: www.spertus.edu; *Librn* Gail Goldberg
Open Sun noon - 4 PM, Mon 10 AM - 6 PM, Wed 10 AM - 4 PM; Library of Jewish studies; Reference library open to public. Includes Badona Spertus Art Library
Library Holdings: Auction Catalogs, Audio Tapes, Book Volumes 100,000, Cassettes, DVDs, Exhibition Catalogs, Fiche, Manuscripts, Pamphlets, Periodical Subscriptions 556, Photographs, Records, Reels, Slides, Video Tapes
Special Subjects: Archaeology, Architecture, Calligraphy, Cartoons, Ceramics, Coins & Medals, Folk Art, Glass, Historical Material, Judaica, Manuscripts, Maps, Painting-Israeli, Photography, Porcelain, Portraits, Posters, Printmaking, Religious Art, Sculpture, Silver, Stained Glass

M **SWEDISH AMERICAN MUSEUM,** 5211 N Clark St, Chicago, IL 60640-2101. Tel 773-728-8111; Fax 773-728-8870; Email museum@samac.org; Web: swedishamericanmuseum.org; *Exec Dir* Karin Moen Abercrombie; *Cur* Keith Ulrich; *Educ Mgr* Stacey Nyman; *Mem & Community Engagement Mgr* Caroline Gerbaulet-Vanasse; *Commun Mgr* Angelica Farzaneh-Far
Open Mon - Fri 10 AM - 4 PM, Sat & Sun 11 AM - 4 PM; Admis families $10, adults $4, students children & seniors $3, mems free; Estab 1976 to display Swedish arts, crafts, artists, scientists, and artifacts connected with United States, especially Chicago; Material displayed in the four story museum in Andersonville, once a predominantly Swedish area in Chicago; Average Annual Attendance: 40,000; Mem: 1800; dues $15-$500
Income: $700,000 (financed by mem & donations)
Special Subjects: Carpets & Rugs, Ceramics, Coins & Medals, Costumes, Crafts, Decorative Arts, Embroidery, Etchings & Engravings, Folk Art, Furniture, Glass, Historical Material, Jewelry, Manuscripts, Painting-Scandinavian, Photography, Porcelain, Portraits, Pottery, Religious Art, Prints, Stained Glass, Textiles, Watercolors, Woodcarvings
Collections: Artifacts used or made by Swedes, photographs, oils of or by Swedes in United States
Exhibitions: Dream of America, permanent exhib; Brunk Children's Museum of Immigration, 3rd fl; special art exhibits in the 1st fl gallery - 4/yr
Publications: FLAGGAN quarterly
Activities: Classes for adults & children; docent training; lects open to pub, 3-4 vis lectrs per yr; concerts; gallery talks; tours; awards; individual paintings lent; book traveling exhibs 2-3 per yr; mus shop sells books, magazines, reproductions, prints, gifts, Swedish linen & items; junior mus named Children's Museum of Immigration

M **TRUMAN COLLEGE ART GALLERY,** 300 E Normal St, Chicago, IL 60621. Tel 312-989-6059; Email hcook@truman.edu; Web: ww.truman.edu; *Gallery Dir* Heidi Cook

Open Mon - Thurs 8:30 AM - 7 PM, Fri 8:30 - 5 PM, Sat Noon - 4:30 PM; No admis fee; Estab a space to host exhibs of faculty & student art, art historical exhibs and exhibs of regional contemporary art.
Collections: Paintings; photographs

M **UKRAINIAN INSTITUTE OF MODERN ART,** 2320 W Chicago Ave, Chicago, IL 60622-4722. Tel 773-227-5522; Email info@uima-chicago.org; Web: uima-chicago.org; *Cur* Adrienne Kochman; *Asst Cur* Olivia Rozdolsky; *Develop & Opers Mgr* Victoria Cooper
Open Wed - Sun Noon - 4 PM; No admis fee; donations accepted; Estab 1971 to introduce the public to nationally & internationally recognized artists engaged with contemporary art; Two galleries, rotating & permanent exhibs; Average Annual Attendance: 8,000; Mem: 160; dues $30 & up
Library Holdings: CD-ROMs, Exhibition Catalogs, Original Art Works, Original Documents, Other Holdings, Periodical Subscriptions, Photographs, Prints, Reels, Sculpture
Special Subjects: Bronzes, Ceramics, Drawings, Embroidery, Etchings & Engravings, Painting-American, Painting-Canadian, Painting-French, Painting-Japanese, Photography, Sculpture, Tapestries, Textiles, Watercolors, Woodcarvings, Woodcuts
Collections: Kowalsky Coll, over 500 artworks, Permanent Colls (1,000 Artworks)
Exhibitions: 5-6 exhibs per year; Temporary & permanent exhibits
Publications: 5-6 yearly catalogs for temporary exhibits; permanent coll catalog
Activities: 4-6 classical music & jazz performances; 4 literary events; poetry & fiction readings; collaborative events; concerts; tours; lects open to pub; lects for mems only; 4-5 vis lectrs per yr; concerts; mus shop sells books, original art, prints, exhibition catalogs

L **UKRAINIAN NATIONAL MUSEUM & LIBRARY,** 2249 W Superior St, Chicago, IL 60612-1327. Tel 312-421-8020; Fax 773-772-2883; Email info@ukrainiannationalmuseum.org; Web: ukrainiannationalmuseum.org; *Pres* Lydia Tkaczuk; *Admin* Orysia Kourbatov; *Cur* Maria Klimchak; *Tour Guide* Halyna Parasiuk
Open Thurs - Sun 11 AM - 4 PM; Suggested donation $5; Estab 1954, to collect & preserve Ukrainian cultural heritage; Average Annual Attendance: 6,000; Mem: 200; dues $40; annual meeting in Jan-Feb; sales shop sells forms of folk art
Income: Financed through mem & donations
Library Holdings: Book Volumes 20,000, Cards, Clipping Files, Framed Reproductions, Kodachrome Transparencies, Manuscripts, Memorabilia, Original Art Works, Pamphlets, Periodical Subscriptions, Photographs, Sculpture, Slides
Special Subjects: Embroidery, Folk Art, Portraits, Pottery, Tapestries, Textiles, Woodcarvings
Collections: Ukrainian Folk Art
Exhibitions: Ukrainian Holodomor - Genocide
Activities: Classes for adults; tours; lending collection contains 18,000 books; originates traveling exhibs; mus shop sells books, magazines, original art

M **UNIVERSITY OF CHICAGO,** Reva and David Logan Center for the Arts, 915 E 60th St, Chicago, IL 60637. Tel 773-702-2787; Email arts@uchicago.edu; Web: arts.uchicago.edu; *Dir* Bill Michel
Exhibitions: Graduate MFA & Undergraduate Exhibitions
Activities: Special performances; schols offered

M **Smart Museum of Art**, 5550 S Greenwood Ave, Chicago, IL 60637-1506. Tel 773-702-0200; Fax 773-702-3121; Email smart-museum@uchicago.edu; Web: www.smartmuseum.uchicago.edu; *Chief Preparator* Rudy Bernal; *Sr Cur* Richard A Born; *Asst Guest Servs & Opers Mgr* Paul Bryan; *Dir Educ & Interpretation* Michael Christiano; *Exec Asst Leadership Support* Cindy Hansen; *Head Registrar* Sara Hindmarch; *Dana Feitler Dir* Anthony G Hirschel; *Study Rm Supvr & Campus Art Coordr* Alice Kain; *Guest Servs & Opers Mgr* Kate Kelly; *Consulting Cur* Wu Hung; *Cur & Assoc Dir Academic Initiatives* Anne Leonard; *Assoc Cur Contemp Art* Jessica Moss
Open Tues - Sun 10 AM - 5 PM, Thurs until 8 PM; No admis fee; Estab 1974 to assist the teaching & research programs of the University of Chicago by maintaining a permanent collection & presenting exhibitions & symposia of scholarly & general interest; Gallery designed by E L Barnes; exhibit space covers 9500 sq ft & also contains print & drawing study room, Elden Sculpture Garden; Average Annual Attendance: 60,000; Mem: 650; dues individual $40
Income: Financed by mem, university, special funds, corporations, foundations & government grants
Special Subjects: Antiquities-Greek, Antiquities-Roman, Asian Art, Baroque Art, Collages, Decorative Arts, Drawings, Etchings & Engravings, Furniture, Glass, Graphics, Oriental Art, Painting-American, Painting-British, Painting-Dutch, Painting-European, Painting-Flemish, Painting-French, Painting-German, Painting-Italian, Painting-Japanese, Pewter, Photography, Portraits, Prints, Religious Art, Renaissance Art, Sculpture, Silver, Watercolors, Woodcuts
Collections: American, Ancient, Baroque, decorative arts, drawings, Medieval, Modern European, Oriental & Renaissance paintings, photographs, prints, sculpture, Asian, contemporary
Publications: Looking and Listening in Nineteenth-Century France; Displacement: Three Gorges Dam and Contemporary Chinese Art; Echoes of the Past: The Buddhist Cave Temples of Xiangtangshan; Heartland
Activities: Classes for adults & children; docent training; lects open to pub, 5-6 vis lectrs per yr; concerts; gallery talks; tours; individual paintings & original objects of art lent to professional art mus; book traveling exhibs 1-3 per yr; originate traveling exhibs to professional art mus; sales shop sells books, post cards, posters, jewelry & photographs

M **Oriental Institute**, 1155 E 58th St, Chicago, IL 60637-1540. Tel 773-702-9514; Fax 773-702-9853; Email oi-museum@uchicago.edu; Web: www.oi.uchicago.edu; *Registrar* Helen McDonald; *Head Archivist* Anne Flannery; *Research Assoc* Jack Green; *Head of Conservation* Laura D'Alessandro; *Dir* Christopher Woods
Open Tues & Thurs - Sun 10 AM - 5 PM, Wed 10 AM - 8 PM, Cl Mon; No admis fee (suggested donation adults $10, children under 12 $5); Estab 1919 as a research institute & mus of antiquities excavated from Egypt, Mesopotamia, Assyria, Syria, Palestine, Persia, Anatolia & Nubia, dating from 7000 years ago until the 18th Century AD; 8 permanent galleries & 1 special exhibits gallery; Average Annual Attendance: 62,000; Mem: 2650; dues $50 & up
Income: Financed by parent institution, admis donations, federal, state grants & proceeds from sales
Special Subjects: Antiquities-Assyrian, Antiquities-Egyptian, Archaeology, Architecture, Bronzes, Ceramics, Costumes, Dioramas, Dolls, Furniture, Glass, Gold, Historical Material, Islamic Art, Ivory, Jewelry, Leather, Manuscripts, Medieval Art, Photography, Pottery, Religious Art, Sculpture, Textiles, Watercolors, Antiquities-Persian
Collections: Ancient Near Eastern antiquities from pre-historic times to the beginning of the present era plus some Islamic artifacts, Egypt: colossal statue of King Tut, mummies, Iraq, Assyrian winged human-headed bull (40 tons), Mesopotamia temple & house interior, reconstructions, sculpture, jewelry, Iran: Persepolis bull, column & capital, Palestine: Megiddo ivories & horned alter
Publications: Annual report; News & Notes, monthly; museum guidebook; brochures
Activities: Classes for adults & children; dramatic progs; docent training; family progs; lects open to pub; 10 vis lectrs per yr; gallery talks; tours; competitions with awards; original objects of art lent to mus & institutions; lending collection contains Kodachromes, original art works & mini mus boxes; book traveling exhibs; sales shop sells books, magazines, original art, reproductions, prints, slides, items of jewelry, clothing, household furnishings from the Near East
—**Oriental Institute Research Archives**, 1155 E 58th St, Chicago, IL 60637-1540. Tel 773-702-9537; Fax 773-702-9853; Email oi-library@uchicago.edu; Web: www.oi.uchicago.edu; *Librn* Charles E Jones
Open daily 10 AM-4 PM by appointment; Circ Non-circulating; Open to staff, students & members for reference
Library Holdings: Audio Tapes, Book Volumes 38,000, Cards, Cassettes, Clipping Files, Exhibition Catalogs, Fiche, Kodachrome Transparencies, Lantern Slides, Manuscripts, Memorabilia, Motion Pictures, Pamphlets, Periodical Subscriptions 500, Photographs, Reels, Slides
Special Subjects: Anthropology, Antiquities-Assyrian, Antiquities-Byzantine, Antiquities-Egyptian, Antiquities-Greek, Antiquities-Persian, Archaeology, Asian Art, Historical Material, History of Art & Archaeology, Islamic Art, Textiles

L **Visual Resources Collection**, 5540 S Greenwood, Chicago, IL 60637-1506. Tel 773-702-0261; Fax 773-702-5901; Web: www.humanities.uchicago.eduhumanitiesartslide.htmlartfulprojectslide; *Cur* John L Butler-Ludwig
Open Mon - Fri 9 AM - 5 PM, cl Sat & Sun; Estab 1938; Circ Restricted circulation-faculty & students; For reference only
Library Holdings: Lantern Slides 88,000, Other Holdings 500,000, Photographs 740,000, Slides 386,000

L **Max Epstein Archive**, 1100 E 57th St, Chicago, IL 60637-1502. Tel 773-702-7080; Fax 773-702-5901; *Cur* Meg Klinkow
Open Mon - Fri 9 AM - 5 PM, cl Sat & Sun; Estab 1938; Circ Non-circulating; For reference only
Income: Financed by gifts & donations
Library Holdings: Book Volumes 55,500, Other Holdings Mounted photographs of art; catalogued & mounted photographs added annually 8000; auction sales catalogs, Union Catalog of Art Books in Chicago
Collections: Photographs of architecture, sculpture, painting, drawing & decorative arts illustrating Far Eastern, South Asian & Western art history, illustrated Bartsch Catalogue, DIAL Index, Marburger Index, Papal Medals Collection, Courtauld Institute Illustrated Archive, Courtauld Photo Survey, Armenia Architecture, Dunlap Society Architecture, Willoughby Collection

M **UNIVERSITY OF ILLINOIS AT CHICAGO,** Gallery 400, 400 S Peoria St, Art & Exhibition Hall (MC034) Chicago, IL 60607-7032. Tel 312-996-6114; Fax 312-355-3444; Email gallery400@uic.edu; Web: gallery400.uic.edu; *Dir* Lorelei Stewart; *Asst Dir* Erin Nixon
Open Tues - Fri 10 AM - 6 PM, Sat Noon - 6 PM, other times by appointment; No admis fee; Estab 1983; 2,900 sq ft loft exhibition space & additional 1300 square ft hall for lectures, films & video screenings; Average Annual Attendance: 10,000
Income: $250,000 (financed by state & federal grants, college of A&A, private donations & foundations)
Library Holdings: DVDs, Exhibition Catalogs, Periodical Subscriptions, Video Tapes
Special Subjects: Photography, Posters, Prints, Sculpture
Collections: works by local & nat artists
Publications: The Alchemy of Comedy...Stupid by Edgar Arceneaux
Activities: Lects open to pub, 18 vis lectrs per yr; gallery talks; tours; book traveling exhibs average 1 every 2 yr; originates traveling exhibs 1 per yr, Univ galleries, artist organizations

M **WOMAN MADE GALLERY,** 2150 S Canalport #4A-3, Chicago, IL 60608. Tel 312-738-0400; Fax 312-738-0404; Email general@womanmade.org; Web: womanmade.org; *Exec Dir* Deb Flagel
Open Thurs & Fri Noon - 6 PM, Sat & Sun Noon - 4 PM; No admis fee; Estab 1992 to provide exhib opportunities for women artists; Mem: dues $25 - $100
Collections: Works by women artists
Activities: Rental facilities; special events; museum-related items for sale

DANVILLE

M **VERMILION COUNTY MUSEUM SOCIETY,** 116 N Gilbert St, Danville, IL 61832-8506. Tel 217-442-2922; Fax 217-442-2001; Email vermilioncounty@att.net; Web: www.vermilioncountymuseum.org; *Dir* Susan Richter; *Bookkeeper* Wendy Wilder; *Pres* Donald Richter
Open Tues - Sat 10 AM - 5 PM, cl Sun, Mon & major holidays; Admis 18 yrs & older $5, children 13-17 $1, under 13 yrs, school & scout groups free; Estab 1964 in 1855 doctor's residence & courthouse replica bldg; Average Annual Attendance: 5,500; Mem: 1,001; dues life $450, patron $75, bus $100, family $30, organization & individual $25, seniors $20, students & schools $15
Income: Financed by endowment fund, mem.
Library Holdings: Book Volumes, Clipping Files, Manuscripts, Maps, Original Documents, Pamphlets, Periodical Subscriptions, Photographs, Prints, Records, Slides, Video Tapes

Special Subjects: American Indian Art, Decorative Arts, Furniture, Historical Material, Manuscripts, Maps, Period Rooms, Restorations
Collections: Costumes, decorative arts, graphics, historical material, paintings, sculpture, furniture, local historical artifacts, Lincoln artifacts, medical equipment
Publications: Heritage, quarterly magazine; newsletter, bimonthly
Activities: Classes for children; dramatic progs; historical school prog; lects open to pub, 2 vis lectrs per yr; tours; children competitions; mus shop sells books, magazines, original art, prints, reproductions & handmade items

L **Library,** 116 N Gilbert St, Danville, IL 61832. Tel 217-442-2922; Fax 217-442-2001; Email susricht@aol.com; Web: www.vermilioncountymuseum.org; *Dir* Susan E Richter; *Pres* Donald Richter; *Bookkeeper* Wendy Wilder
Open Tues - Sat 10 AM - 5 PM, cl Sun, Mon & major holidays; Admis 18 yrs & older $5, children 13-17 $1, under 13 yrs, school & scout groups free; Estab 1964 in 1855 doctor's residence & courthouse replica bldg; Circ 1,001; Open to the public for reference; Average Annual Attendance: 5,500; Mem: dues life $450, bus $100, patron $75, family $30, organization & individual $25, seniors $20, students & schools $15
Income: Financed by endowment fund
Library Holdings: Book Volumes 400, Clipping Files, Manuscripts, Maps, Original Documents, Pamphlets, Periodical Subscriptions, Photographs, Prints, Records, Slides, Video Tapes
Collections: Medical equipment, furniture, photographs, arrowheads, historical materials, paintings, sculpture, local historical artifacts, Lincoln artifacts
Publications: The Heritage of Vermilion County, quarterly; bimonthly newsletter
Activities: Historical school prog

DEKALB

A **ILLINOIS ALLIANCE FOR ARTS EDUCATION (IAAE),** 315 Dresser Rd, DeKalb, IL 60115. Tel 312-750-0589; Fax 312-750-9113; Email barbarah@tbc.net; Web: www.illinoisalliance4artsed.org; *Exec Dir* Barbara Heimerdinger; *Pres* Becky Blaine
Open daily 9 AM - 5 PM; Estab 1972 to safeguard and expand arts educ for all Illinois students; Mem: 150, dues $45 for individuals, $100 for institutions
Income: $200,000 (financed by nat, state and local govt, also pvt foundations, corporate gifts & the Kennedy Center Alliance for Arts Educ Network)
Publications: Finding Dollar$, a Statewide Guide for Artists & Schools to Locate Funds for Arts Educ Progs; Integrated Curriculum Arts Project, lesson plan book
Activities: Arts integration workshops for pub school teachers; conferences & professional develop workshops for teachers & adminrs; ArtSmart prog to raise pub awareness of importance of arts educ; annual service recognition awards

M **NORTHERN ILLINOIS UNIVERSITY,** NIU Art Museum, Altgeld Hall, 1st Fl, West End, 1425 W Lincoln Hwy DeKalb, IL 60115-2828. Tel 815-753-1936; Fax 815-753-7897; Web: www.niu.edu/artmuseum; *Dir* Jo Burke; *Assistant Director* Peter Olson; *Coordinator, Marketing + Education* Stuart Henn
Open Tues - Fri 10 AM - 5 PM, Sat Noon - 4 PM; No admis fee; Estab 1970; Multiple rooms, totalling 3,500 square feet; Average Annual Attendance: 10,000; Mem: 100; $10, 15, 25, 45, 100, 250, 500
Income: Financed by state appropriation & grants from public agencies & private foundations
Special Subjects: Asian Art, Etchings & Engravings, Painting-American, Watercolors, Woodcuts
Collections: Contemporary & Modern paintings, prints, sculptures, & photographs, Burmese Art, Native American Art
Exhibitions: temporary exhibits, Sept - May
Activities: Lect open to public; gallery talks; tours; original objects of art lent to accredited museums; book traveling exhibitions

L **The University Libraries,** University Libraries, 1425 W Lincoln Hwy DeKalb, IL 60115-2828. Tel 815-753-0616; *Arts Librn* Charles Larry
Open Mon - Thurs 7:30 AM - 10 PM, Sat 9 AM - 10 PM, Sun 1 PM - 2 AM; Estab 1977 to provide reference service & develop the collection
Library Holdings: Book Volumes 47,000, Cards, Exhibition Catalogs, Fiche, Motion Pictures, Other Holdings Art book titles 975; Rare bks 250, Periodical Subscriptions 164, Reels, Slides, Video Tapes

DECATUR

M **MILLIKIN UNIVERSITY,** Perkinson Gallery, 1184 W Main St, Decatur, IL 62522-2084. Tel 217-424-6227; Fax 217-424-3993; Email jschietinger@millikin.edu; Web: www.millikin.edu; *Gallery Dir* Jim Schietinger; *Art Dept Chair* Lyle J Salmi
Open Mon - Fri Noon - 5 PM; No admis fee; Estab 1970; Gallery has 3200 sq ft & 224 running ft of wall space
Income: Financed by university appropriation
Special Subjects: Drawings, Painting-American, Prints, Sculpture, Watercolors
Collections: Drawings, painting, prints, sculpture, watercolors
Exhibitions: Annual Senior Group Exhibition; Millikin National Works on Paper.
Publications: Monthly show announcements
Activities: Lect; guided tours; gallery talks

EDWARDSVILLE

L **SOUTHERN ILLINOIS UNIVERSITY,** Lovejoy Library, 30 Hairpin Dr, Edwardsville, IL 62026-1063. Tel 618-650-2000; Fax 618-650-2381; Web: www.siue.edu; *Friends of Lovejoy Librn* Kyle Moore
Open Mon - Thurs 8 AM - 11:30 PM, Fri 8 AM - 9 PM, Sat 9 AM - 5 PM, Sun 1 - 9 PM; Estab 1957, as a source for general University undergraduate & graduate instruction, & faculty research
Library Holdings: Book Volumes 500,000, Fiche, Motion Pictures, Other Holdings Illustrated sheet music covers, Periodical Subscriptions 6000, Records, Reels, Slides, Video Tapes
Special Subjects: Advertising Design, Aesthetics, Afro-American Art, American Indian Art, American Western Art, Anthropology, Archaeology, Architecture, Art Education, Art History, Asian Art, Bookplates & Bindings, Bronzes, Calligraphy, Carpets & Rugs
Exhibitions: Louis Sullivan Collection of Terra Cotta
Activities: Photography contest; tours; scholarships

ELMHURST

M **ELMHURST ART MUSEUM,** 150 Cottage Hill Ave, Elmhurst, IL 60126-3329. Tel 630-834-0202; Fax 630-834-0234; Email info@elmhurstartmuseum.org; Web: www.elmhurstartmuseum.org; *Asst Cur* Emily Barney; *Controller* Heather Pastore; *Asst Exec Dir* Stephanie Grow; *Visitor Svcs Coordr* Jeff Francik; *Educ Coordr* Amy Janken; *Develop Mktg Coordr* Stuart W Henn
Open Tues, Thurs & Sat 10 AM - 4 PM, Wed 1 - 8 PM, Fri & Sun 1 - 4 PM; Admis adult $7, seniors & students $5, children under 12 free, members & Tues free; Opened 1997 to exhibit contemporary art, Chicago vicinity to national; Three exhibition galleries, 1 artists' guild gallery & entrance gallery; Average Annual Attendance: 35,000; Mem: 1200; dues individual $40 for 1 yr
Income: Financed by endowment, mem, corporate sponsorships, city & state appropriation
Special Subjects: Afro-American Art, American Western Art, Architecture, Asian Art, Ceramics, Drawings, Etchings & Engravings, Folk Art, Historical Material, Ivory, Juvenile Art, Painting-American, Painting-Dutch, Painting-French, Portraits, Prints, Sculpture, Watercolors, Woodcarvings, Woodcuts
Collections: Contemporary Art-American & Chicago vicinity
Exhibitions: Annual competitions; children's exhibits; one person & group shows; permanent collections; traveling exhibits
Activities: Classes for adults & children; docent training; lects open to pub, 10-12 vis lectrs per yr; concerts; gallery talks; tours; competitions with awards; individual paintings & objects of art lent to other mus & the Federal Reserve; book traveling exhibs 2-3 per yr; mus shop sells books, magazines, original art, reproductions, prints & gift items

M **LIZZADRO MUSEUM OF LAPIDARY ART,** 220 Cottage Hill Ave, Elmhurst, IL 60126-3351. Tel 630-833-1616; Email info@lizzadromuseum.org; Web: www.lizzadromuseum.org; *Exec Dir* John S Lizzadro; *Dir* Dorothy Asher
Open Tues - Sat 10 AM - 5 PM, Sun 1 - 5 PM, cl Mon; Admis adults $5, sr citizens $4, students $3, ages 7-12 yrs $2, under 7, active military, mems & Fri no charge; Estab 1962 to promote interest in the lapidary arts & the study & collecting of minerals & fossils; Main exhibit area contains hardstone carvings, gemstone materials, minerals; lower level contains earth science exhibits, gift shop; Average Annual Attendance: 30,000; Mem: 350; dues $30 per yr
Income: Financed by endowment
Special Subjects: Asian Art, Dioramas, Ivory, Jade, Mosaics, Oriental Art
Collections: Hardstone Carving Collection
Exhibitions: Educational exhibits, push button exhibits, rotating special exhibits
Publications: Newsletter & calendar of events 4 times per yr
Activities: Classes for adults & children; lects open to pub, 12 vis lectrs per year; educational films; tours; demonstrations; gallery talks; book 3-4 traveling exhibs per yr; originate traveling exhibs to libraries & universities; sales shop sells books, magazines, hardstone & gemstone souvenirs

ELSAH

M **PRINCIPIA COLLEGE,** School of Nations Museum, 1 Maybeck Pl, Elsah, IL 62028. Tel 618-374-2131, Exten 5236; Fax 618-374-5122; Web: www.prin.edu/upper/museum; *Cur* Nancy Boyer-Reehlin
Open Tues & Fri by appointment only
Special Subjects: American Indian Art, Asian Art, Ceramics, Crafts, Decorative Arts, Dolls, Glass, Metalwork, Textiles
Collections: American Indian coll including baskets, bead work, blankets, leather, pottery, quill work and silver, Asian art coll includes arts and crafts, ceramics, textiles from China, Japan and Southeast Asia, European colls include glass, metals, snuff boxes, textiles and wood, costumes and dolls from around the world
Exhibitions: Changing exhibits on campus locations; permanent exhibits in School of Nations lower floor
Activities: Special programs offered throughout the year; objects available for individual study

EVANSTON

L **C G JUNG CENTER,** 817 Dempster St, Evanston, IL 60201-4303. Tel 847-475-4848; Fax 847-475-4970; Web: www.cgjungcenter.org; *Asst Dir & Ed* Mary Nolan; *Exhibit Coordr* Barbara Zaretsky; *Librn & AV Production Mgr* Mark Swanson; *Exec Dir* Peter Mudd
Open Mon - Thurs 10 AM - 4 PM; No admis fee; Estab 1965; For reference only
Library Holdings: Audio Tapes, Book Volumes 4000, Clipping Files, Exhibition Catalogs, Manuscripts, Motion Pictures, Pamphlets, Reproductions, Slides, Video Tapes
Special Subjects: American Indian Art, Anthropology, Archaeology, Asian Art, Ethnology, Film, Folk Art, History of Art & Archaeology, Islamic Art, Judaica, Oriental Art, Pre-Columbian Art, Religious Art
Collections: Archive for Research in Archetypal Symbolism (ARAS), photographs & slides
Publications: Transformation, quarterly

A **EVANSTON ART CENTER,** 1717 Central St, Evanston, IL 60201-1507. Tel 847-475-5300; Fax 847-475-5330; Web: www.evanstonartcenter.org; *Exec Dir* Norah Diedrich; *Pres* Linda Kaufman
Open Mon-Sat 10 AM-4 PM, & 7-10 PM, Sun 1-4 PM; No admis fee; Estab 1929 as a community visual arts center with exhibits, instructions & programs; Focuses primarily on changing contemporary arts exhibitions with emphasis on emerging & under-recognized Midwest artists; Average Annual Attendance: 35,000; Mem: 1800; dues $30, annual meeting in Aug
Income: Financed by state & city arts councils & mem

Exhibitions: Primarily artists of the Midwest, all media
Publications: Concentrics, quarterly; exhibition catalogs
Activities: Classes for adults & children, outreach progs, teaching cert renewal; lects

M **EVANSTON HISTORICAL SOCIETY,** Charles Gates Dawes House, 225 Greenwood St, Evanston, IL 60201-4713. Tel 847-475-3410; Fax 847-475-3599; Email evanstonhs@northwestern.edu; Email evanstonhs@nwu.edu; Web: www.evanstonhistorycenter.org; *Cur* Eden Juron Pearlman; *Develop Officer* Kim Olson-Clark; *Educ Officer* Leslie Goddard
Open Thurs - Sun 1 - 5 PM; Admis $5, seniors & children $3; Estab 1898 to collect, preserve, exhibit & interpret Evanston's history; Average Annual Attendance: 4,000; Mem: 1,050; dues $25-$500; annual meeting in June
Income: Financed by mem & private donations
Special Subjects: American Indian Art, Architecture, Carpets & Rugs, Ceramics, Costumes, Crafts, Decorative Arts, Dioramas, Dolls, Furniture, Glass, Historical Material, Jewelry, Laces, Landscapes, Manuscripts, Maps, Metalwork, Military Art, Painting-American, Period Rooms, Photography, Porcelain, Portraits, Posters, Sculpture, Silver, Stained Glass, Textiles
Collections: Collections reflecting the history of Evanston & its people, especially since the mid 1800s, including costumes & archival material
Exhibitions: Charles Gates Dawes House permanent exhibit; other rotating exhibits year round; Evanston Tackles the Woman Question, the Story of Evanston women who influenced the National Women's Movement; The Sick Can't Wait, the story of Evanston Community Hospital; Your Presence Is Requested, the Story of African-American Social Organization
Publications: TimeLines, mem newsletter, quarterly; annual report
Activities: Docent training; school outreach & in-house educational progs; lects open to pub; gallery talks; tours; individual paintings & original objects of art lent to other cultural institutions; lending collection contains 60 paintings & 30 sculptures; originate traveling exhibs; mus shop sells books & mus & Victorian related gifts

M **NORTHWESTERN UNIVERSITY,** Mary & Leigh Block Museum of Art, 40 Arts Cir Dr, Evanston, IL 60208-2410. Tel 847-491-4000; Fax 847-491-2261; Email block-museum@northwestern.edu; Web: www.blockmuseum.northwestern.edu; *Dir* Lisa Graziose Corrin; *Assoc Dir Cur Affairs* Kathleen Bickford Berzock; *Dir of Engagment/ Cur Public Practice* Susy Bielak; *Snr Mgmt Mktg & Comm* Lindsay Bosch; *Snr Registrar* Kristina Bottomley; *Asst Mgr of Visitor Svcs* Aaron Chatman; *Comm Coord* Caroline Claflin
Open Tues & Sat - Sun 10 AM - 5 PM, Wed - Fri 10 AM - 8 PM; No admis fee; Estab 1980 as visual arts venue for univ & surrounding communities; 4 galleries for rotating & permanent displays; Average Annual Attendance: 40,000; Mem: Block Builders $100-$999; Block Leadership Circle $1,000
Income: Financed by mem, college, grants
Special Subjects: Prints, Photography
Collections: 5,000 works of art from medieval to contemporary, focusing on prints & photographs
Activities: Classes for adults & children; lects open to pub & mems only, 10-15 vis lectrs per yr; gallery talks; tours; fels offered; book traveling exhibs, 3-4 per yr; originate traveling exhibs circulated through other museums & galleries; mus shop sells books, exhib & coll related gifts

L **Art Collection, University Library**, 1970 Campus Dr, Evanston, IL 60208-2300. Tel 847-491-7484, 491-6471; Fax 847-467-7899; Email r-clement@northestern.edu; Web: www.library.northwestern.edu/art; *Head Art Coll* Russell T Clement; *Pub Svcs Librn* Lindsay King
Open Mon - Thurs 8:30 AM - 10 PM, Fri & Sat 8:30 AM - 5 PM, Sun 1 - 10 PM; No admis fee; Estab 1970 as a separate library collection. Serves curriculum & research needs of the Art History and Art Theory & Practice departments
Income: Financed through the university & endowment funds
Library Holdings: Book Volumes 125,000, Exhibition Catalogs
Special Subjects: Architecture, Art History, Etchings & Engravings, Graphic Arts, History of Art & Archaeology, Painting-American, Painting-Dutch, Painting-European, Painting-Flemish, Painting-French, Painting-German, Painting-Italian, Photography, Prints, Sculpture, Illustration

GALENA

M **CHICAGO ATHENAEUM,** Museum of Architecture & Design, 601 S Prospect St, Galena, IL 61036-2519. Tel 847-777-4444; Fax 815-777-2471; Email info@chicagoathenaeum.org; Web: www.chi-athenaeum.org; *Dir & Pres* Christian K Narkiewicz-Laine; *Dir of Design* Timothy A Patula; *Dir Exhib Installation & Architect* Alexander Kozionnyi; *Chmn* Neil Kozokoff; *VPres* Ioannis Karalias; *Secy* Belinda Shastal
Open call for new hrs; Admis non mems $3, seniors & students $2, mems are free; Estab 1988; dedicated to all areas in the art of design - architecture, industrial & product design, graphics & urban planning; One floor of temporary exhibits; Average Annual Attendance: 500,000; Mem: 2500; dues $50-$250
Income: Financed by mem, grants & pvt & pub funding
Special Subjects: Architecture, Decorative Arts, Furniture, Glass, Graphics, Photography, Posters, Textiles
Collections: Architectural Drawings & Models, International Collection, Design-Chicago (1910-1960) Collection, Design-International Product & Graphic Collection, Japanese Graphic Design Collection, Industrial Design, Japanese Graphic Design, Contemporary Art Collection, Contemporary Fabric & Textile
Exhibitions: Large Scale Pub Sculpture; Landmark Chicago; American Architectural awards, Good Design
Activities: Seminars; lects open to pub, 15 vis lectrs per yr; competitions; book traveling exhibs 8 per yr; originate traveling exhibs 6 per yr; mus shop sells glass, toys, jewelry, fashion, book & international high design

GALESBURG

A **GALESBURG CIVIC ART CENTER,** 114 E Main St, Galesburg, IL 61401-4601. Tel 309-342-7415; Email info@galesburgarts.org; Web: www.galesburgarts.org; *Office Mgr* Lynn Miller; *CEO & Archivist* Heather L Norman; *Pres* Jim Straub
Open Tues - Fri 10:30 AM - 4:30 PM, Sat 10:30 AM - 3 PM, cl all holidays; No admis fee, donations accepted; Estab 1923 as a non-profit organization for the furtherance of art; The main gallery has about 129 feet of wall space for the hanging of exhibits. The sales-rental gallery runs on a commission basis & is open to professional artists as a place to sell their work under a consignment agreement; Average Annual Attendance: 6,000; Mem: 450; dues begin at $20; annual meeting second Wed in June
Income: Financed by members, grants & fundraisers
Collections: Permanent coll of approx 400 pieces
Exhibitions: GALEX - national juried competition all media; Regional/national artists in a variety of media (change monthly); Art-in-the-Park annual fair
Publications: The Artifacts newsletter
Activities: Classes for adults & children; Art Fair; Film Festival; gallery talks; tours; competitions with awards; lending collection contains original art works, paintings, photographs & sculpture; sales shop sells original art, prints, etc

GREENVILLE

M **GREENVILLE COLLEGE,** Richard W Bock Sculpture Collection, Almira College House, 315 E College Ave, Greenville, IL 62246-0159. Tel 618-664-1840, ext 6724; Email sharon.grimes@greenville.edu; Web: www.greenville.edu; *Dir & Cur* Sharon Grimes
Open Wed 1-4PM, Fri 1-5PM, Sat 10AM-2PM & by appointment, cl summer & holidays; No admis fee, donations accepted; Estab 1975 to display an extensive collection of the life work of the American sculptor in a restored home of the mid-19th century period; Five large rooms and two floors have approx 1800 sq ft of exhib space; Average Annual Attendance: 2,500
Income: Financed by endowment, college appropriation, gifts and donations
Special Subjects: Drawings, Furniture, Oriental Art, Painting-American, Posters, Sculpture
Collections: Furniture and furnishings of the 1850-1875 era, late 19th and early 20th century drawing, painting and sculpture, Frank Lloyd Wright artifacts, designs and drawings
Publications: Exhibit catalog; general museum brochures
Activities: Lects open to pub, 1-2 vis lectrs per yr; gallery talks; individual paintings and original objects of art lent to mus only; lending collection contains original art works, paintings, photographs, sculpture and drawings; originates traveling exhibs; mus shop sells books, magazines

L **The Richard W Bock Sculpture Collection & Art Library**, 315 E College Ave, Greenville, IL 62246-0159. Tel 618-664-1840, ext 6724; Web: www.greenville.edu; *Librn* Sharon Davis
Open by appt only; For reference only, students & academia only
Library Holdings: Book Volumes 1000, Exhibition Catalogs, Memorabilia, Records

HIGHLAND PARK

M **THE ART CENTER OF HIGHLAND PARK - TAC,** 1957 Sheridan Rd, Highland Park, IL 60035. Tel 847-432-1888; Fax 847-432-9106; Email info@theartcenterhp.org; Web: www.theartcenterhp.org; *Exec Dir* Michele Cohen
Open Mon - Thurs 9 AM - 5 PM, Fri 9 AM - 4:30 PM, Sat 9 AM - 3:30 PM, Sun by appointment; Estab 1960 to provide the community with education in visual arts; Modern & contemporary work by emerging & established regional artists; Mem: 500
Collections: Contemporary art
Exhibitions: Temporary exhibits
Activities: Educ progs; classes for adults & children; scholarships; Gallery talks; tours; art programming; workshops; integrated art events; facilitation of public art projects; arts festivals

JACKSONVILLE

M **THE ART ASSOCIATION OF JACKSONVILLE,** The David Strawn Art Gallery, 331 W College, Jacksonville, IL 62650-2474; PO Box 1213, Jacksonville, IL 62651-1213. Tel 217-243-9390; Web: www.strawnartgallery.org; *Dir* Kelly M Gross; *Pres* Linda Standley
Open Sept - May, Tues - Sat 4 - 6 PM, Sun 1 - 3 PM; No admis fee; Estab 1873, endowed 1915, to serve the community by offering monthly shows of visual arts and weekly classes in a variety of media. The two main rooms house the monthly exhibitions and a third large room houses a collection of Pre-Columbian pottery; The Gallery is in a large building, previously a private home; Average Annual Attendance: 1,800; Mem: 470; dues $15 & up; annual meeting July
Income: Financed by endowment & mem
Special Subjects: Pottery, Pre-Columbian Art
Collections: Pre-Columbian Pottery, pottery discovered in the Mississippi Valley, Miriam Cowger Allen Doll Collection
Exhibitions: Strawn family antique - permanent exhib; year-round permanent exhib
Activities: Classes for adults & children, art educ; lects workshops open to pub, 9 vis lectrs per yr, 9 gallery talks per season, tours on demand, educ schols; educ schols

JOLIET

M **JOLIET JUNIOR COLLEGE,** Laura A Sprague Art Gallery, 1215 Houbolt Rd, J Bldg Joliet, IL 60431-8938. Tel 815-280-2423 (Gallery Dir); 280-2223 (Fine Arts Office); Fax 815-280-6739; Web: www.jjc.edujjc.edu/info/fine-arts-events; *Prof of Art Gallery Dir* Joe B Milosevich; *Assoc Prof Art* Eric Gorder; *Prof Art* Meaghan Callan; *Prof Art* Giselle Atterberry
Open summer semesters: Mon - Thurs 8 AM 0 8 PM; fall & spring semesters: Mon - Fri 8 AM - 8 PM; No admis fee; Estab 1978, to present exhibs related to acad progs, the col & the community; Gallery, approx 30 x 60 ft; located on first floor of

Spicer-Brown Hall/J-bldg; solo & group exhibs of regional & nat artists working in all media
Income: Financed by college appropriations
Purchases: Permanent coll JJC student art (ann purchases)
Collections: Permanent collection of student work, annual
Exhibitions: 5-6 exhibs ann (see website
Publications: Exhibs post card announcements printed for all shows
Activities: Lect open to public, 2-3 vis lectrs per year; gallery talks; tours; sponsor student competitions with awards

LAKE FOREST

L **LAKE FOREST LIBRARY,** Fine Arts Dept, 360 E Deerpath, Lake Forest, IL 60045-2200. Tel 847-234-0636; Fax 847-234-1453; Email fsong@lakeforestlibrary.org; Web: lakeforestlibrary.org; *Adult Svcs Coordr* Felicia Song; *Graphic Artist* Kathe Stoepel; *Admin Librn* Kaye Grabbe
Open Mon - Thurs 9 AM - 9 PM, Fri - Sat 9 AM - 5 PM, Sun 1 - 5 PM (Sept - May); No admis fee; Estab 1898 to make accessible to the residents of the city, books & other resources & services for educ, information & recreation; Circ 500,000; Gallery exhibits small local shows
Income: $3,954,995 (financed by city 96% & state 1% appropriations & local library generated income 3%)
Special Subjects: Architecture, Landscape Architecture
Collections: Folk art, painting, landscape architecture
Exhibitions: local artist & student shows - spring
Publications: Lake Forest Library Newsletter, four times per year
Activities: Annual 10-12 $5,000 student art awards

LE ROY

L **J T & E J CRUMBAUGH MEMORIAL PUBLIC LIBRARY,** 405 E Center, PO Box 129 Le Roy, IL 61752-0129. Tel 309-962-3911; Email crumbaughlibrary@yahoo.com; *Librn* Lois Evans; *Circ* Fae Morris
Open Mon - Sat 10 AM - 5 PM; No admis fee; Estab 1927
Library Holdings: Book Volumes 14,000, Other Holdings Genealogy Files 655; Local History Scrapbooks 72, Periodical Subscriptions 50, Reels 59
Special Subjects: Historical Material
Collections: Books, genealogy, local history
Publications: JT&EJ Crumbaugh Spiritualist Church & Memorial Library - 1998 (updated every 10 years); Tracing Your Roots (updated every 2 years)
Activities: Classes for children; summer reading prog; holiday story times & progs

LOMBARD

L **HELEN M PLUM MEMORIAL LIBRARY,** 110 W Maple St, Lombard, IL 60148-2514. Tel 630-627-0316; Fax 630-627-0336; Web: www.plum.lib.il.us; *Adult Servs* Donna Slyfield; *Dir* Robert A Harris
Open Mon - Fri 9 AM - 9 PM, Sat 9 AM - 5 PM, Sun 1 -5 PM; No admis fee; Estab as a pub library
Income: $2,243,693 (financed by local government)
Purchases: $434,451
Library Holdings: Audio Tapes, Book Volumes 210,815, CD-ROMs, Cassettes, Compact Disks, DVDs, Fiche, Filmstrips, Micro Print, Pamphlets, Periodical Subscriptions 358, Prints, Records, Sculpture, Slides, Video Tapes
Special Subjects: Art History, Crafts, Decorative Arts, Folk Art, Handicrafts, Painting-American
Publications: Brochure, annual
Activities: Lect open to public; original objects of art lent to public

MACOMB

M **WESTERN ILLINOIS UNIVERSITY,** Western Illinois University Art Gallery, 1 University Circle Macomb, IL 61455. Tel 309-298-1587; Fax 309-298-2400; Email JR-Graham@wiu.edu; Web: www.wiu.edu/artgallery; *Pres* Alvin Goldfarb; *Cur Exhib* John R Graham
Open Mon - Fri 9 AM - 4 PM & Tues 6 - 8 PM; No admis fee; Estab 1945 to present art as an aesthetic and teaching aid; Building has three galleries with 500 running ft; Average Annual Attendance: 9,000
Income: Financed through state appropriation
Special Subjects: Ceramics, Drawings, Graphics, Painting-American, Prints, Sculpture, Watercolors, Woodcuts
Collections: WPA & 20th Century: Prints, Drawing, Paintings & Ceramics, Old Masters Prints
Activities: Classes for adults; lects open to pub, 8 vis lectrs per yr; gallery talks; tours; competitions with awards; individual paintings lent; lending collection contains 100 paintings; originates traveling exhibs

MOLINE

C **DEERE & COMPANY,** One John Deere Pl, Moline, IL 61265. Tel 309-765-8000; Fax 309-765-4735; *Colls Mgr* Nathan Augustine
Estab 1964 to complement the offices designed by Eero Saarinen & Kevin Roche; to provide opportunities for employees & visitors to view & enjoy a wide variety of art pieces from many parts of the world; Collection displayed at Deere & Company Headquarters
Collections: Artifacts, paintings, prints, sculpture & tapestries from over 25 countries
Activities: Concerts; tours

MOUNT VERNON

M **CEDARHURST CENTER FOR THE ARTS,** Mitchell Museum, 2600 Richview Rd, Mount Vernon, IL 62864; PO Box 923, Mount Vernon, IL 62864. Tel 618-242-1236; Fax 618-242-9530; Email mitchellmuseum@cedarhurst.org; Web: www.cedarhurst.org; *Dir Visual Arts* Rusty Freeman; *Exec Dir* Sharon Bradham; *Dir Operations* Greg Hilliard; *Mus Gift Shop Mgr & Historian* Sarah Lou Bicknell; *CFO* Heather Owens; *Staff Coordr* Linda Wheeler; *Dir Commun* Sarah Sledge; *Dir Educ* Jennifer Sarver; *Dir Shrode Art Center* Carrie Gibbs; *Dir Develop* Hillary Esser
Open Tues - Sat 10 AM - 5 PM, Sun 1 - 5 PM, cl Mon & national holidays; Admis fee for non-mems for special events & exhibs, free admis each Thurs; Estab 1973 to present exhibitions of paintings, sculpture, graphic arts, architecture & design representing contemporary art trends; to provide continued learning & expanded educ; Marble faced structure houses three galleries for exhibition, 3000 sq ft & 1300 sq ft; flexible designs; Shrode Art Center Gallery; Average Annual Attendance: 50,000; Mem: 800; dues individual $35, family $60, patron $125, sponsor $250, benefactor $500, guarantor $1,000; annual meeting in Nov
Income: Financed by endowment, mems & contributions
Special Subjects: Glass, Ivory, Jade, Painting-American, Silver, Woodcarvings, Graphics, Sculpture
Collections: Paintings by late 19th & early 20th century American artists, some drawings & small sculptures, silver, small stone, wood & ivory carvings, jade, small bronzes, 85 acre Cedarhurst Sculpture Park
Publications: Form Beyond Function: Recent Sculpture by North American Metalsmiths; quarterly newsletter; Recent Graphics from American Print Shops; Sculpture at Cedarhurst, catalogue; Kathleen Holmes: Bedtime Stories; Harold Gregor's Illinois
Activities: Classes for adults & children; dramatic progs; docent training; workshops; demonstrations; field trips; lects open to pub, 8-10 vis lectrs per yr; concerts; gallery talks; tours; competitions with awards; scholarships offered; book traveling exhibs 1 per yr; originate traveling exhibs to qualified mus & college galleries with adequate staff & facilities; mus shop sells books, original art, regional glass & ceramics & jewelry

L **Cedar Hurst Library**, Richview Rd, Mount Vernon, IL 62864; PO Box 923, Mount Vernon, IL 62864-0019. Tel 618-242-1236; Fax 618-242-9530; Email mitchell@midwest.net; Web: www.cedarhurst.org; *Librn* Rhonda Sparks
Open Tues - Sat 10 AM - 5 PM; Open to public for reference only
Library Holdings: Audio Tapes, Book Volumes 1250, Exhibition Catalogs, Kodachrome Transparencies, Pamphlets, Periodical Subscriptions 20, Records, Slides, Video Tapes
Special Subjects: Painting-American

NAPERVILLE

L **NORTH CENTRAL COLLEGE,** Oesterle Library, 320 E School Ave, Naperville, IL 60540. Tel 630-637-5700; Fax 630-637-5716; Web: www.noctrl.edu; *Technician* Belinda Cheek; *Pub Servs Librn* Ted Schwitzner; *Reference Librn* Carol Murdoch; *Dir* Carolyn A Sheehy
Open Mon - Thurs 8 AM - midnight, Fri 8 AM - 8 PM, Sat 9 AM - 5:30 PM, Sun Noon - 11 PM; Estab 1861 to provide acad support; For lending & reference. Art Gallery houses 4-5 exhibitions per yr
Library Holdings: Audio Tapes, Book Volumes 120,000, Cassettes, Clipping Files, Compact Disks, Fiche, Filmstrips, Manuscripts, Memorabilia, Motion Pictures, Original Art Works, Pamphlets, Periodical Subscriptions 751, Photographs, Records, Reels, Video Tapes
Collections: Sang Collection of Fine Bindings

NILES

M **THE BRADFORD GROUP,** 9333 Milwaukee Ave, Niles, IL 60714. Tel 847-966-2770; Fax 847-581-8639
Open Mon - Fri 8:30 AM - 4:30 PM; No admis fee; Estab 1978 to house and display limited-edition collector's plates for purposes of study, educ and enjoyment
Income: Financed by The Bradford Exchange
Special Subjects: Porcelain
Collections: 800 Limited-Edition Collector's Plates

NORMAL

M **ILLINOIS STATE UNIVERSITY,** University Galleries, 110 Ctr For Visual Arts, Beaufort St Campus Box 5600 Normal, IL 61790-5600. Tel 309-438-5487; Fax 309-438-5161; Email Gallery@ilstu.edu; Web: www.cfa.ilstu.edu/galleries; *Dir* Barry Blinderman; *Cur* Bill Conger; *Reg* Tracy Berner; *Cur* Kendra Paitz
Open Tues 9:30 AM - 9 PM, Wed - Fri 9:30 AM - 4:30 PM, Sat - Mon Noon - 4 PM; No admis fee; Estab 1973 to provide changing exhibits of contemporary art for the students & community at large; The main gallery I contains rotating exhibitions; galleries II & III display student & faculty work, graduate exhibitions, studio area shows & works from the permanent collection; Average Annual Attendance: 10,000
Income: Financed by university & Illinois Arts Council
Library Holdings: Exhibition Catalogs, Original Art Works, Prints, Sculpture
Special Subjects: Ceramics, Collages, Drawings, Painting-American, Photography, Prints, Sculpture
Collections: Contemporary art emphasis, prints & drawings
Exhibitions: Oliver Herring, Student Annual, Julia Fish
Publications: Exhibition catalogs
Activities: Lects open to pub, 3 - 4 vis lectrs per yr; gallery talks; tours; individual paintings & original objects of art lent for other exhibs; lending collection contains original art works, original prints, paintings, photographs & sculpture; originate traveling exhibs; mus shop sells books

L **Museum Library**, 201 N School St, Campus Box 8900 Normal, IL 61790-8900. Tel 309-438-3451; *Cur* Debra Risberg
Museum library open to scholars, students & staff

Library Holdings: Book Volumes 150, Periodical Subscriptions 8
Special Subjects: Decorative Arts, American Indian Art, Pre-Columbian Art

M **Normal Editions Workshop**, 5620 School of Art, Normal, IL 61790-5620. Tel 309-438-7530; Fax 309-438-2215; Email normaleditionsworkshop@ilstu.edu; Web: www.normaleditions.illinoisstate.edu/; *Interim Dir* Veda Rives
Open Mon-Thurs 9AM-5PM, other times by appointment; No fee; Estab 1976
Library Holdings: Original Art Works, Prints
Collections: Works by emerging & estab artists
Activities: Lects open to pub; 2 vis lectrs per yr; Best Graduate & Undergraduate Printmaking awards at the student annual exhib; schols; organize traveling exhibs for galleries, mus & schools; sales shop sells books, original art & prints

OAK BROOK

C **MCDONALD'S CORPORATION,** Art Collection, 2915 Jorie Blvd, Oak Brook, IL 60523-2126. Tel 630-623-3585; Fax 630-623-6428; Email cheryl.ogilvie@us.mcd.com; Web: www.mcdonalds.com; *Cur* Susan Pertl; *Cur* Cheryl Ogilvie
Open to group tours by appointment; No admis fee; Estab 1971; Walking tour through corporate campus
Income: Financed through McDonald's Corporation
Special Subjects: Glass, Landscapes, Painting-American, Sculpture
Collections: Collection of contemporary paintings & sculpture by established & emerging artists, glass sculptures
Activities: Lect; The Spirit of McDonald's Competition; individual paintings & original objects of art lent; lending collection consists of more than 1000 pieces

PALATINE

AMERICAN SOCIETY OF ARTISTS, INC
For further information, see National and Regional Organizations

PARIS

M **BICENTENNIAL ART CENTER & MUSEUM,** 132 S Central Ave, Paris, IL 61944-1729. Tel 217-466-8130; Fax 217-466-8130; Email parisartcenter@frontier.com; Web: www.parisartcenter.com; *Exec Dir* Susan Stafford; *Treas* Ann Staats; *Chmn & Pres (V)* Tom Hebermehl
Open Tues - Fri 10 AM - 4 PM; No admis fee; Estab 1975 to encourage & bring art to area; Five galleries, 234 running ft; Average Annual Attendance: 4,179; Mem: 325; annual meeting in Oct
Income: $30,000 (financed by mem, contributions & fundraising)
Collections: Paintings & sculptures primarily 20th century period, including extensive collection of Alice Baber works
Exhibitions: Annual Fall Art Show; Annual Paint Illinois; changing exhibits each month
Publications: Monthly newsletter
Activities: Classes for adults & children; docent training; gallery talks; tours; judged competitions; scholarships offered; lending library

PARK RIDGE

M **BRICKTON ART CENTER,** 306 Busse Hwy, Park Ridge, IL 60068. Tel 847-823-6611; Fax 847-823-6622; Email bricktondirector@gmail.com; Web: www.bricktonartcenter.org; *Exec Dir* Theresa Blackborn; *Outreach Dir* Alyssa Kulak-Harris; *Brd Pres* Anna Mana Hallagan; *Gallery Dir* Kristin Haas
Open Mon-Thurs 10AM - 5PM, Fri 10AM - 4PM, Sat 10AM - 2PM, cl Sun; Mem: 200
Income: Membership, donations & classes
Special Subjects: Art Education, Art History, Conceptual Art, Drawings, Landscapes, Mixed Media, Photography, Watercolors
Activities: Classes for adults & children; dramatic progs; lects open to pub; gallery talks; schs

PEORIA

M **BRADLEY UNIVERSITY,** Heuser Art Center, 1501 W Bradley Ave, Peoria, IL 61625-0003. Tel 309-677-2967; Fax 309-677-3642; Email gwill@bradley.edu; Web: www.art.bradley.edu; *Gallery Dir* Erin Buczynski; *Chmn Art Dept* Gary Will
Open Mon-Tues 9 AM - 7 PM, Fri 9 AM - 4 PM; No admis fee; Exhibition space 639 sq ft; Average Annual Attendance: 2,000
Income: Financed by University, Illinois Arts Council
Library Holdings: Audio Tapes 100, Book Volumes 10,000, Exhibition Catalogs 300, Photographs, Prints, Sculpture, Slides, Video Tapes 100
Collections: 1500 contemporary print & drawings
Exhibitions: Rotating exhibits; Purchase prizes Bradley Nat Print & Drawing Exhib; Central Time Ceramics - Biennial Exhib
Activities: Classes for adults; docent training; lects open to pub; gallery talks; tours; competitions with awards; master print program; individual paintings lent on campus

M **CONTEMPORARY ART CENTER,** 305 SW Water St, Peoria, IL 61602. Tel 309-674-6822; Email artcentr@mtco.com; Web: www.peoriacac.org; *Pres* Joe Borsberry; *VPres* Linda Miller; *Secy* Karen Zichterman; *Exec Dir* William Butler
Open Tues - Sat 11 AM - 5 PM; Estab 1994 to create a space where artists could create and foster discussion of contemporary art; 3,000 sq ft; Mem: dues $25-$10,000
Special Subjects: Sculpture, Mixed Media, Photography, Prints, Drawings
Collections: Contemporary art including sculpture, painting, print & drawing, mixed media & photography
Exhibitions: Temporary exhibits
Activities: Classes for adults; events

A **PEORIA ART GUILD,** 203 Harrison Peoria, IL 61602. Tel 309-637-2787; Fax 309-637-7334; Email info@peoriaartguild.org; Web: www.peoriaartguild.org; *Dir* Joshua Cox
Open Mon - Thurs 10 AM - 3 PM; No admis fee, donations appreciated; Estab 1878 to encourage develop & appreciation of the visual arts; 3000 sq ft floor space; Average Annual Attendance: 40,000; Mem: 400; dues $50
Income: Financed by mem, sales, private donations, five art fairs
Collections: Framed & unframed 2-D design, ceramics, sculpture, jewelry, weaving & wood designs, winning works from the Bradley National Print & Drawing Exhibition, 150 featured artists from the US and international
Exhibitions: One-person shows; group theme shows, shows annually; Marsha S. Glaten; Anthony Swan, photojournalism
Activities: Classes for adults & children; workshops; lect open to public, 5-6 vis lectrs per year; gallery talks; tours; awards; individual paintings rented to bus & members of the community; lending collection contains original art work, prints, paintings, photographs & sculptures; sales shop sells original art & prints

M **PEORIA HISTORICAL SOCIETY,** 611 SW Washington St, Peoria, IL 61602-5104. Tel 309-674-1921; Fax 309-674-1882; Web: peoriahistoricalsociety.org; *Exec Dir* Walter C Ruppman; *Board Pres* Mark Johnson; *Coll Mgr* Robert Killion
Open Judge John C Flanagan House: Mar - Dec Wed - Sun 1 - 4 PM & by appt; Pettengill-Morron House: by appt only; Admis adults $7, children 15 & under $3; Estab 1934 to acquire, preserve & display artifacts & records relating to the history of Peoria & the Central Illinois Valley; to encourage & support historical research & investigation & to promote & sustain pub interest in history of Peoria & the Central Illinois Valley; Two historic house museums: Flanagan House is post-colonial, Pettengill-Morron house is Victorian; Library housed in Special Collections Ctr of Bradley Univ; Average Annual Attendance: 10,000; Mem: 700; dues $25 & up; annual meeting in May
Income: Financed by mem, endowments; private gifts & grants
Library Holdings: Audio Tapes, Book Volumes, CD-ROMs, Cards, Cassettes, Clipping Files, Framed Reproductions, Kodachrome Transparencies, Manuscripts, Maps, Memorabilia, Original Art Works, Original Documents, Other Holdings, Pamphlets, Periodical Subscriptions, Photographs, Prints, Records, Reproductions, Sculpture, Slides, Video Tapes
Special Subjects: Period Rooms, Pottery
Collections: Household items & artifacts from 1840, Peoria Pottery, Lincoln artifacts, Civil War, WW I & II, Peoria bus, French exploration; fur trade
Exhibitions: Rennick Award (art works relating to historic sites), History Fair; Victorian Mourning Rituals; Peoria's Past Rediscovered; English exploration
Publications: Bi-monthly Newsletter to members
Activities: Educ prog; docent training; internship progs; lects open to pub, 7 vis lectrs per yr; competitions with prizes; tours; Historic Preservation award; Regional History Fair winner, Centenarians & Volunteer of Yr awards; exten prog serves mus, cultural & educational institutions; originates traveling exhibs to regional bus & educational institutions; boutique at Pettengill-Morron House (The Butler's Pantry); sells books & gifts

M **PEORIA RIVERFRONT MUSEUM,** (Lakeview Museum of Arts & Sciences), 222 SW Washington St, Peoria, IL 61602-2500. Tel 309-686-7000; Fax 309-863-3054; Email info@peoriariverfrontmuseum.org; Web: www.peoriariverfrontmuseum.org; *Cur* Kristan McKinsey; *VPres Educ* Ann Schmitt; *Pres & CEO* Sam Gappmayer
Open Tues - Sat 10 AM - 5 PM, Sun noon - 5 PM, cl Mon; Admis adults $11, seniors $10, students $9, children 3 & under free; Estab 1965, new building opened 1965, to provide enjoyment & educ by reflecting the historical, cultural & industrial life of the Central Illinois area; Average Annual Attendance: 250,000; Mem: 3,000; qualification for mem: Smithsonian Affiliate
Income: $2,500,000
Library Holdings: Book Volumes, DVDs, Exhibition Catalogs
Special Subjects: Archaeology, African Art, Folk Art, Posters, Primitive art, Southwestern Art, Tapestries, Textiles, Woodcarvings
Collections: Archaeological, decorative arts, Regional American Fine & Folk Art, paintings & graphics, fine arts, anthropology, natural sciences
Exhibitions: Changing exhibitions dealing with the arts, sciences & history
Publications: Mems bulletin; Explore More, exhibition catalogues
Activities: Classes for adults & children; docent training; lects open to pub; concerts; gallery talks; tours; competitions with awards; individual & original objects of art lent to sister institutions; 2-3 per yr book traveling exhibs; organize traveling exhibs to mus; mus store sells books, magazines, original art, reproductions, prints & craft items

QUINCY

A **QUINCY ART CENTER,** 1515 Jersey St, Quincy, IL 62301-4250. Tel 217-223-5900; Fax 217-223-6950; Email lrabe@quincyartcenter.org; Web: www.quincyartcenter.org; *Exec Dir* Julie D Nelson; *Dir Educ* Jennifer Teter; *Asst Direct Publ Coordr* Lana Rabe; *Exhibs Prep* Libby Tournear; *Graphic Designer* Shannon Larson
Open Mon - Fri 9 AM - 4 PM, Sat & Sun 1 - 4 PM; cl holidays; Admis adults $3, seniors & students $1,mems free, Thurs free; Estab 1923, incorporated 1951 to foster pub awareness & understanding of the visual arts; Mid sized Sinnock 1945 Gallery - Art Modern Style renovated historic carriage house; large contemporary gallery in 1989-1990 wing; Average Annual Attendance: 18,000; Mem: 500; dues $25 & up
Income: Financed by grants, donations, mem fees & Beaux Art Ball, foundations, special events, individual donations
Purchases: Four new pottery wheels for studio
Library Holdings: Book Volumes
Special Subjects: Crafts, Drawings, Etchings & Engravings, Landscapes, Marine Painting, Mexican Art, Painting-American, Painting-European, Period Rooms, Portraits, Posters, Prints, Sculpture, Watercolors, Woodcuts, Photography
Collections: Donenberg Collection, Early 20th century midwestern art, Small coll 20th century African American Art
Publications: Calendar, brochures &/or catalogs for temporary exhibitions

Activities: Classes & workshops for adults & children; art mentor training; art mentor programs; lects open to pub; gallery talks; tours; competitions with awards; artists presented in solo & two-person exhibits; scholarships offered; inter-museum loan

A **QUINCY SOCIETY OF FINE ARTS,** 300 Civic Ctr Plaza, Ste 244, Quincy, IL 62301-4162. Tel 217-222-3432; Email art@artsqcy.org; Web: www.artsqcy.org; *Exec Dir* Lenny Bart
Open Mon - Fri 10 AM - 3 PM; Estab 1947 as a community arts council to coordinate & stimulate the visual, performing & Arts in educ in Quincy & Adams County; Mem: 48 art organizations; non-profit, arts & humanities
Income: Financed by endowment, mem & contribution, Illinois Arts Council, National Endowment for the Arts
Library Holdings: Book Volumes, Maps, Photographs
Publications: Cultural Calendars, monthly; pamphlets & catalogs; Arts Quincy, monthly
Activities: Workshops for adults & students in visual & performing arts; George Irwin Arts Awards & Arts/Quincy Student Art Awards

M **QUINCY UNIVERSITY,** The Gray Gallery, 1800 College Ave, Quincy, IL 62301-2699. Tel 217-228-5371; Web: www.quincy.edu; *Dir Gallery* Robert Lee Mejer
Open Mon - Thur 8 AM - 10 PM, Fri 8 AM - 6 PM, Sat 1 - 5 PM, Sun 1 - 10 PM; No admis fee; Estab 1968 for cultural enrichment & exposure to contemporary art forms in the community; Exhibitions are held in the Brenner library foyer & The Gray Gallery; Average Annual Attendance: 6,000
Income: Financed through the coll & student activities assoc
Special Subjects: Drawings, Prints
Collections: 19th century Oriental & European prints, permanent coll of student & faculty works, 20th century American prints & drawings
Exhibitions: Watercolors by Bruce Bobick; Waterbase Monotypes Dennis Olsen
Publications: Brochures, 1-2 times annually; gallery calendars, annually
Activities: Lects open to public, 1 vis lectr per year; gallery talks; tours; student show with awards; individual paintings & original objects of art lent; slide reviews of potential artists/shows; book traveling exhibs 1-2 per year

L **Brenner Library,** 1800 College Ave, Quincy, IL 62301-2699. Tel 217-222-8020; Fax 217-228-5354; Email qulib@darkstar.rsa.lib.il.ms; Web: www.quincy.edu; *Dean of Library* Pat Tomczak
Open by appointment only; Reference only for pub; lending for faculty & students
Income: $1,600 (financed by college revenues)
Purchases: $1,600 annually for books
Library Holdings: Book Volumes 7890, Cassettes, Exhibition Catalogs, Filmstrips, Lantern Slides, Motion Pictures, Periodical Subscriptions 20, Prints, Records, Slides, Video Tapes

ROCK ISLAND

M **AUGUSTANA COLLEGE,** Augustana College Art Museum, NW Corner Seventh Ave & 38th St, Rock Island, IL 61201; 639 38th St, Rock Island, IL 61201-2296. Tel 309-794-7469; Fax 309-794-7678; Email dr.prestonthayer@augustana.edu; Web: www.augustana.edu; *Dir Gallery* Preston Thayer
Open Tues - Sat Noon - 4 PM; No admis fee; Estab 1973 for the display of visual arts exhibits commensurate with a liberal arts col curriculum; Main gallery serves as an entrance to large auditorium; lower gallery is smaller than main gallery; two galleries total 217 ft wall space; Art Collection Gallery, opened in 1999 is located off lower gallery; Average Annual Attendance: 50,000
Income: $53,785
Purchases: $3000
Special Subjects: African Art, American Indian Art, Ceramics, Decorative Arts, Etchings & Engravings, Painting-American, Portraits, Pottery, Sculpture, Textiles, Watercolors, Woodcuts, Prints, Tapestries, Woodcarvings
Collections: Contemporary, Eastern & Western prints, Swedish American Art, Modern Oriental, Native American
Publications: Exhibit catalogs
Activities: Classes for children; lect open to public; 3-4 vis lectrs per year; concerts; gallery talks; tours; competitions with prizes; individual paintings & original objects of art lent upon requests considered on individual basis; book traveling exhibitions, 2-3 per year

A **QUAD CITY ARTS INC,** 1715 2nd Ave, Rock Island, IL 61201. Tel 309-793-1213; Fax 309-793-1265; Email info@quadcityarts.com; Web: www.quadcityarts.com; *Exec Dir* Carmen Darland; *Visual Arts Dir* Dawn Wohlford-Metallo; *Performing Arts & Arts in Educ Dir* Susan Wahlmann; *Community Arts Dir* Jessi Black; *Communs Mgr* Rebecca Green
Open Tues - Fri 10 AM - 5 PM, Sat 11 AM - 5 PM, Mon by appt only, cl Sun & major holidays; No admis fee; Estab 1970 in IL & chartered in 1974 in IA to bring visual arts to the people; Maintains Quad City Arts Gallery & Quad City International Airport Gallery; Average Annual Attendance: 12,800; Mem: Dues seniors, students & educators $25, individual $35, household $50, orchestra $100 - $249, cast $250 - $499, choreographer $500 - $999, playwright $1000+
Activities: Classes for youth; public sculpture prog; literary progs; Vanguard events; vis artist series; lect open to public; concerts; gallery talks; tours; sales shop sells original art & prints

ROCKFORD

A **ROCKFORD ART MUSEUM,** 711 N Main St, Rockford, IL 61103-7204. Tel 815-968-2787; Fax 815-316-2179; Email staff@rockfordmuseum.org; Web: www.rockfordartmuseum.org; *Financial Officer* Dave Schroepfer; *Educ Coordr & Mus Asst* Stacy Sauer; *Exec Dir* Linda Dennis; *Cur* Patty Rhea; *Communs Coordr* David Dixon; *Pub Rels & Spec Events* Sarah McNamara; *Registrar* Jeremiah Blankenbaker
Open Mon-Sat 10 AM - 5 PM, Sun Noon-5 PM; Admis adults $5, seniors $3, students & children free; Estab 1913 to enrich the quality of life by communicating the pleasure, appreciation & meaning of the visual arts through a prog of exhib, interpretation, educ & coll; 17,000 sq ft exhibition space; Average Annual Attendance: 40,000; Mem: 1000
Income: Financed by mem, grants, state appropriation & private donations
Collections: Permanent collection 19th & 20th century American oil paintings, graphics, sculpture, photography, ceramics, glassware, textiles, watercolors & mixed media
Exhibitions: Annual Greenwich Village Art Fair; Annual Young Artist's Exhibition; numerous one-person and group shows; Rockford-Midwestern Show (biennial)
Publications: Exhibition brochures & catalogs; magazine, quarterly
Activities: Classes for adults & children; docent training; artist-in-residence; mus school prog; lects open to pub, 5 vis lectrs per yr; gallery talks; tours; competitions with cash awards; book traveling exhibs; mus shop sells books, original art, reproductions, prints, jewelry, ceramics & crafts

M **ROCKFORD UNIVERSITY,** Art Gallery, 5050 E State St, Clark Arts Center Rockford, IL 61108-2311. Tel 815-226-4105; Fax 815-394-5167; Email cwarzecha@rockford.edu; Web: www.rockford.edu/artslectures/artgallery; *Dir* Christina Warzecha
Open Mon, Wed & Fri 3 PM - 6 PM or by appointment; No admis fee; Estab 1970
Collections: Paintings, sculpture, digital & mixed media
Exhibitions: Temporary exhibits
Activities: Gallery & group tours; lects open to pub, 6 vis lectrs per yr; art programming; originate traveling exhibs 1 per yr

SKOKIE

L **SKOKIE PUBLIC LIBRARY,** 5215 Oakton, Skokie, IL 60077. Tel 847-673-7774; Fax 847-673-7797; Email tellus@skokielibrary.info; Web: www.skokielibrary.info; *Dir* Carolyn Anthony; *Mktg & Progs* Christie Robinson
Open Mon - Fri 9 AM - 9 PM, Sat 9 AM - 6 PM, Sun noon - 6 PM; No admis fee; Estab 1941 as a general pub library serving the residents of Skokie; reciprocal borrowing privileges offered to members of pub libraries in reading across Illinois Library System; Art gallery is maintained; Average Annual Attendance: 800,000
Income: $11,664,243 (financed by independent tax levy)
Purchases: $1,136,669
Library Holdings: Book Volumes 342,452, Clipping Files, Compact Disks 43,897, Framed Reproductions, Original Art Works 20, Other Holdings 95,279 w/DVDs incl, Pamphlets, Periodical Subscriptions 1807, Reproductions, Sculpture 12
Special Subjects: Architecture, Art History, Crafts, Dolls, Embroidery, Handicrafts, Painting-American, Painting-European, Sculpture, Watercolors
Exhibitions: Sendak & Co children's book art; Resistance & Remembrance: The Story of the White Rose; Following the Tracks: Photographs of Railroad Tramps by Dale Wickum
Activities: Classes for adults & children, dramatic progs; lect open to public; 15 vis lectrs per yr; concerts; gallery talks; tours

SPRINGFIELD

M **ILLINOIS STATE MUSEUM,** ISM Lockport Gallery, Chicago Gallery & Southern Illinois Art Gallery, Spring & Edwards St, Springfield, IL 62706; 502 S Spring St, Springfield, IL 62706-5000. Tel 217-782-7386; Email robert.sill@illinois.gov; Web: www.museum.state.il.us; *Interim Dir* Michael Wiant PhD; *Interim Dir Art & History* Robert Sill; *Preparator* Philip Kennedy; *Assoc Cur ISM Chicago Gallery* Douglas Stapleton; *Gallery Mgr Lockport* John Lustig
Open Mon - Sat 9 AM - 4:30 PM, Sun Noon - 5 PM; No admis fee; Estab 1877 as mus of natural history, art added in 1928. Collection, exhibition & publication of art produced by or of interest to Illinois & its citizens. Three major changing exhibitions annually; Circ Research lib; Changing exhibition space: Springfield Art Gallery 3000 sq ft; Arts of Science Gallery (six changing exhibitions), 1364 sq ft; permanent collection galleries present fine, decorative & ethnographic arts, 6400 sq ft, permanent exhibit of Illinois Decorative Arts, At Home in The Heartland 3000 sq ft; Average Annual Attendance: 250,000; Mem: 650; dues $35-$1000
Income: $966,000. Art Section & four gallery sites financed by state appropriations & private gifts
Purchases: $5000
Library Holdings: Auction Catalogs, Audio Tapes, Book Volumes 36,000, CD-ROMs, Exhibition Catalogs, Manuscripts, Maps, Original Art Works, Original Documents, Periodical Subscriptions 900 (historical holdings only), Sculpture
Special Subjects: African Art, Afro-American Art, American Indian Art, American Western Art, Anthropology, Archaeology, Art History, Ceramics, Collages, Crafts, Decorative Arts, Dioramas, Dolls, Drawings, Embroidery, Enamels, Eskimo Art, Etchings & Engravings, Ethnology, Flasks & Bottles, Folk Art, Furniture, Glass, Gold, Graphics, Hispanic Art, History of Art & Archaeology, Ivory, Laces, Landscapes, Leather, Maps, Miniatures, Mosaics, Oriental Art, Painting-American, Period Rooms, Pewter, Photography, Porcelain, Portraits, Posters, Pottery, Pre-Columbian Art, Primitive art, Prints, Scrimshaw, Sculpture, Silver, Southwestern Art, Stained Glass, Tapestries, Watercolors, Woodcuts, Religious Art, Woodcarvings
Collections: Fine art including ceramics, metal work, textiles, glass, furniture, quilts, dolls, Decorative art including paintings, sculpture, prints, drawings, photography, contemporary crafts, folk art; quilts; dolls
Exhibitions: Exhibitions featuring contemporary & historical paintings, sculpture, photography, graphics, decorative arts & history, with emphasis on Illinois material
Publications: Living Museum (also in Braille), quarterly; exhibit & collection catalogs; Biennial report; Impressions, bimonthly members publication
Activities: Educ prog; classes for adults & children; dramatic progs; docent training; lects & symposia open to pub; 45+ vis lectrs per yr; concerts; gallery talks; tours; competitions with awards; film series; internships; individual paintings lent to other mus, historical sites & galleries; book traveling exhibs; sales shop sells books, original art & work of IL artisans

L **Library,** 502 S Spring, Springfield, IL 62706-5000. Tel 217-782-6623; Fax 217-524-0496; Web: www.museum.state.il.us

Open by appointment only Mon - Fri 9 AM - 4 PM; Estab to provide informational materials & services to meet the requirements of the mus staff in fields pertinent to the purpose & work of the mus
Income: Financed by state appropriation
Purchases: varies
Library Holdings: Book Volumes 30,000, Clipping Files, Manuscripts, Pamphlets, Periodical Subscriptions 900 (historical holdings), Video Tapes
Special Subjects: Anthropology, Archaeology, Art Education, Art History, Decorative Arts, Dolls, Ethnology, History of Art & Archaeology, Manuscripts
Collections: Anthropology and Ornithology, Decorative Arts, Fine Art-Illinois, Natural History

A **SPRINGFIELD ART ASSOCIATION OF EDWARDS PLACE,** 700 N Fourth St, Springfield, IL 62702. Tel 217-523-2631, 523-3507; Fax 217-523-3866; Email office@springfieldart.org; Web: www.springfieldart.org; *Exec Dir* Betsy Dollar; *Coll Cur* Erika Holst; *Educ Coordr* Erin Svendson; *Library Dir* Jan Arnold; *Office Mgr* Charlotte Kane; *Develop Coordr* Mary Beth Burke
Open Daily 9 AM - 5 PM, Sat 10 AM - 3 PM; No admis fee to gallery, library, studios; Edwards Place $5; Estab 1913 to foster appreciation of art, to instruct people in art & to expose people to quality art; Circ 400; 9-12 curated exhibits each yr featuring local, regional & nationally juried work in all media; Average Annual Attendance: 4,200; Mem: 800; dues $55-$1000; monthly meeting
Income: $200,000 (financed by mem & grants, interest, tuition & benefits)
Library Holdings: Book Volumes, CD-ROMs, DVDs, Periodical Subscriptions, Video Tapes
Collections: American decorative arts, American paintings, antique toys, prints, sculpture
Exhibitions: 3 to 4 exhibitions are scheduled annually with one juried exhibition; work is borrowed from museum & artist nationwide
Publications: Membership brochures, quarterly; newsletters
Activities: Classes for adults & children; dramatic progs; docent training; art outreach prog in school in community; monthly lects; musical prog; lects open to pub, 6 vis lectrs per yr; concerts; gallery talks; tours; schols offered; lends original objects upon request to other mus & institutes exhibs; book traveling exhibs

L **Michael Victor II Art Library**, 700 N Fourth, Springfield, IL 62702. Tel 217-523-2631; Fax 217-523-3866; Email mvlibrary@springfieldart.org; Web: springfieldart.org; *Library Dir* Jan Arnold
Open weekdays 9 AM - 5 PM, Sat 10 AM - 3 PM, cl Sun; Estab 1965 to provide total community with access to art & art related books
Library Holdings: Book Volumes 7000, CD-ROMs, DVDs, Exhibition Catalogs, Pamphlets, Periodical Subscriptions 20, Reproductions, Video Tapes
Special Subjects: Aesthetics, Afro-American Art, American Indian Art, American Western Art, Architecture, Art Education, Art History, Asian Art, Calligraphy, Carpets & Rugs, Cartoons, Ceramics, Collages, Commercial Art, Conceptual Art
Activities: Classes for children; lect series, 8 vis lectrs per yr; film prog

VERNON HILLS

M **CUNEO MANSION & GARDENS,** 1350 N Milwaukee, Vernon Hills, IL 60061. Tel 847-362-3042; Fax 847-362-4130; Email cuneomansion@luc.edu; Web: luc.edu/cuneo/about; *Dir* Lisa Cushing-Davis
Open Tues - Sun 10 AM - 5 PM; Estab 1991; 100-acre estate
Income: $300,000 (financed by endowment, mem & admis)
Special Subjects: Decorative Arts, Painting-Italian, Period Rooms, Tapestries
Collections: Architecture, decorative arts, furniture, paintings, fine art
Activities: Acad progs; lects open to pub; tours

WATSEKA

M **IROQUOIS COUNTY HISTORICAL SOCIETY MUSEUM,** Old Courthouse Museum, 103 W Cherry, Watseka, IL 60970. Tel 815-432-2215; Fax 815-432-2215; Email ichs2215@mchsi.com; Web: www.iroquoiscountyhistoricalsociety.com; *Pres & Chmn Mgmt Comt* Rolland Light; *VPres* Jean Hiles; *Treas* Bob Ficke; *Art Gallery Chmn & Secy* Marilyn Wilken; *Office Mgr* Judy Ficke
Open Mon - Fri 10 AM - 4 PM, Sat by appointment only - call ahead or 1st Sat of Mon 10 AM - 2 PM; Donation adults $2, children $.50; Estab 1967 to further the interest in history, art & genealogy; One room for county artists; Average Annual Attendance: 10,000; Mem: 800; dues annual $15 - $150 life
Income: Financed by donations by visitors, artists, memberships & art comt sells crafts
Library Holdings: Book Volumes, Fiche, Maps, Memorabilia
Special Subjects: Archaeology, Coins & Medals, Costumes, Crafts, Decorative Arts, Dioramas, Dolls, Flasks & Bottles, Furniture, Glass, Manuscripts, Maps, Historical Material, Period Rooms
Collections: Paintings, prints, posters & pictures, Iroquois Co memorabilia & artifacts
Exhibitions: Art work by local artists - display changes every 2 months
Publications: Genealogical Stalker, quarterly; Iroquois County Historical Society newsletter, quarterly; historic reprints
Activities: Lects open to pub; concerts; gallery talks; tours; competitions with awards; mus shop sells books, T-shirts & misc postcards

WHEATON

A **DUPAGE ART LEAGUE SCHOOL & GALLERY,** 218 W Front St, Wheaton, IL 60187-5111. Tel 630-653-7090; Fax 630-681-0975; Email tanyaberley@yahoo.com; Web: www.dupageartleague.org; *VPres Educ & Pres Emeritus* Tanya Berley; *VPres Exhibits* Kay Wahlgren; *VPres Mem* Tammy Proctor; *VPres Buildings & Grounds* Jim Karszewski; *VPres Activities* Stephanie Dalton; *Pres* Diana Mitchell; *VPres Finance* Bob Wahlgren; *Secy* Marguerite Paris; *VPres Office Mgmt* Yvonne Thompson; *VPres Publicity & Promotion* Sally Hines
Open Mon - Fri 9 AM - 5 PM, Sat 9 AM - 2 PM; No admis fee; Estab 1957 primarily as an educational organization founded to encourage artists & promote high artistic standards through instruction, informative programs & exhibits; Two galleries are maintained where members exhibit & sell their work; Mem: 450; dues $40; annual meeting in May
Income: Financed through mem, gifts & donations
Library Holdings: Book Volumes
Exhibitions: Monthly exhibits; nine juried shows per yr; holiday gift gallery; Fine Art Gallery with monthly exhibits of local artists (Gallery I), one-man or one-woman shows (Gallery II), Fine Crafts (Gallery III)
Publications: Monthly newsletter
Activities: Classes for adults & children; progs; demonstrations; lects open to pub, 8 vis lectrs per yr; gallery talks; competitions; awards; schols offered; individual paintings & original objects of art lent to local libraries & bus; sales shop sells original art & fine crafts (jewelry, ceramics, woodworks fiber & glass)

WINNETKA

A **NORTH SHORE ART LEAGUE,** 620 Lincoln Ave, Winnetka, IL 60093-2308. Tel 847-446-2870; Fax 847-446-4306; Email info@northshoreartleague.org; Web: www.northshoreartleague.org; *Exec Dir* Linda Nelson
Open Mon - Fri 9 AM - 5 PM; No admis fee; Estab 1924, inc 1954, to promote interest in creative art through education, exhibition opportunities, scholarship & art programs; Year-round gallery exhibs; Mem: 500; dues $45; annual meeting in June
Income: Financed by mem dues, shows & tuition from classes, contributions
Exhibitions: Printworks (March); Watercolor Show (May); Art in the Village (June); Members show (Sept); Inchworks (Nov); 10 one man shows throughout the year
Publications: Art League News, quarterly
Activities: Classes for adults & children; lect for mems only & lects open to pub; tours; sponsor juried competitions with awards; scholarships offered for children

INDIANA

ANDERSON

A **ANDERSON FINE ARTS CENTER,** The Anderson Center for the Arts, 32 W 10th, Anderson, IN 46016-1409; PO Box 1218, Anderson, IN 46015-1218. Tel 765-649-1248; Fax 765-649-0199; Email dstapleton.taca@sbcglobal.net; Web: www.andersonart.org; *Exec Dir* Deborah McBratney-Stapleton; *Educ Coordr* Holly Renneker; *Exhib Cur* Tim Swain; *Admin Asst* Cheryl Mitchell
Open Tues - Fri Noon - 5 PM, Sat 10 AM - 5 PM, Sun 2 - 5 PM, cl Mon & national holidays; Admis adults $2, sr citizens $1.50, students $1, family rate $5, Tues & 1st Sun of month free; Estab 1967 to serve the community by promoting & encouraging interest in the fine arts through exhibs, progs & educ activities & the develop of a permanent coll; Three galleries contain 1705 sq ft; also a small sales & rental gallery & a studio/theatre; Average Annual Attendance: 30,000; Mem: 700; dues master $1000 or more, benefactor $500-$999, sustaining $250-$499, patron $125-$249, family $60-$124, individual $40-$59; annual meeting in May
Income: Financed by mem, endowments, grants, individual & corporate contributions
Collections: Midwestern & 20th century American prints, paintings & drawings, Contemporary American Art
Exhibitions: Annual Indiana Artists - Local Exhibit; annual photo exhibits; one-man shows - Local Artist, National Artist, International Artists
Publications: Calendar of Events, quarterly; catalogue of the permanent collection; exhibition catalogs
Activities: Classes for adults & children; dramatic progs; docent training; educational outreach; lects open to pub, 4-6 vis lectrs per yr; concerts; gallery talks; tours; competitions with awards; individual paintings & original objects of art lent to bus, educational facilities & other mus; lending collection contains 300 original art works, 150 original prints, 300 paintings, 10 sculpture & 1000 slides, extension progs serving senior explorations - nursing homes in Madison County; book traveling exhibs; mus shop sells books, original art, reproductions, prints, slides, pottery, handcrafted items, glass, fine cards & note papers, frame shop

BLOOMINGTON

L **INDIANA UNIVERSITY,** Fine Arts Library, 1133 E 7th St, Museum 251 Bloomington, IN 47408-7509. Tel 812-855-3314; Fax 812-855-3443; Email antmwhite@indiana.edu; Web: www.indiana.edu/~libfinea; *Head Librn* Tony White; *Reference Technical Assoc* Mary Buechley; *Technical Svcs Asst* Edwin Cheek; *Branch Coordr* Nicole Beatty
Estab c1940; Circ 50,000; For lending
Income: Financed by state & student fees
Library Holdings: Auction Catalogs, Book Volumes 150,000, CD-ROMs, Cassettes, Clipping Files 50,000, Compact Disks, Exhibition Catalogs, Fiche 24,000, Periodical Subscriptions 390, Slides 25,000, Video Tapes 200
Special Subjects: Advertising Design, Aesthetics, Afro-American Art, American Indian Art, American Western Art, Anthropology, Antiquities-Byzantine, Antiquities-Etruscan, Antiquities-Greek, Antiquities-Oriental, Antiquities-Roman, Archaeology, Architecture, Art History, Asian Art, Bronzes, Calligraphy, Carpets & Rugs, Cartoons, Ceramics, Collages, Commercial Art, Conceptual Art, Crafts, Decorative Arts, Drawings, Enamels, Eskimo Art, Etchings & Engravings, Fashion Arts, Folk Art, Furniture, Gold, Goldsmithing, Graphic Arts, Graphic Design, Handicrafts, Historical Material, History of Art & Archaeology, Illustration, Interior Design, Islamic Art, Jade, Jewelry, Landscape Architecture, Latin American Art, Lettering, Manuscripts, Marine Painting, Metalwork, Mexican Art, Mixed Media, Oriental Art, Painting-American, Painting-Australian, Painting-British, Painting-Canadian, Painting-Dutch, Painting-European, Painting-Flemish, Painting-French, Painting-German, Painting-Israeli, Painting-Japanese, Painting-New Zealand, Painting-Russian, Painting-Scandinavian, Painting-Spanish, Photography, Portraits, Posters, Pottery, Pre-Columbian Art, Primitive art,

Printmaking, Prints, Religious Art, Restoration & Conservation, Sculpture, Silversmithing, Southwestern Art, Stained Glass, Tapestries, Textiles, Video, Watercolors, Woodcarvings, Woodcuts

M **INDIANA UNIVERSITY,** Eskenazi Museum of Art, 1133 E Seventh St, Bloomington, IN 47405-7509. Tel 812-855-5445; Fax 812-855-1023; Email iuam@indiana.edu; Web: www.artmuseum.iu.edu; *Dir* David Brenneman; *Assoc Dir Develop* Patricia Winterton; *Editorial* Mariah Keller; *Assoc Dir Curatorial Services & Cur African & Oceanic Pre-Columbian Art* Diane Pelrine; *Cur Ancient Art* Juliet Istrabadi; *Cur 19th & 20th Century Art* Jenny McComas; *Asst Dir* Steve Cook; *Cur Works on Paper* Nan Brewer; *Cur Asian Art* Judy Stubbs
Open Tues - Sat 10 AM - 5 PM, Sun Noon - 5 PM, cl Mon; No admis fee; Estab 1941 to serve as a teaching & cultural resource for the University community & the public at large; Gallery has 3 permanent exhibitions: Western Art, Medieval - present; Africa, Asian, Oceania & Americas; special exhibits (temporary & travelling); Average Annual Attendance: 40,000
Income: Financed by col & grants
Special Subjects: African Art, American Western Art, Antiquities-Assyrian, Antiquities-Byzantine, Antiquities-Egyptian, Antiquities-Etruscan, Antiquities-Greek, Antiquities-Oriental, Antiquities-Persian, Antiquities-Roman, Asian Art, Baroque Art, Bronzes, Calligraphy, Carpets & Rugs, Ceramics, Coins & Medals, Drawings, Etchings & Engravings, Ethnology, Primitive art, Prints
Collections: African, ancient to modern, Far Eastern, Oceanic, the Americas, prints, drawings, photographs & sculpture
Exhibitions: 5 rotating exhibs per yr
Publications: Guide to the collection, exhibition catalogs, occasional papers, newsletter
Activities: Classes for adults & children; docent training; lects open to pub; gallery talks; tours; concerts series; competition with awards; book traveling exhibs, 1-2 per yr; originates traveling exhibs, mainly other universities & art mus; mus shop sells books, magazines, reproductions, prints, slides

M **The Mathers Museum of World Cultures,** 416 North Indiana Ave, Bloomington, IN 47405; 601 E Eighth St, Bloomington, IN 47408. Tel 812-855-6873; Fax 812-855-0205; Email mathers@indiana.edu; Web: www.indiana.edu/~mathers/home; *Conservator* Judith Sylvester; *Asst Dir* Judith Kirk; *Cur Coll* Deeksha Nagar; *Bus Mgr* Sandra Warren; *Dir* Geoffrey W Conrad; *Cur Educ* Ellen Sieber; *Co-Cur Exhibs* Elaine Gaul; *Co-cur of Exhibits* Matthew Sieber; *Registrar* Theresa Harley-Wilson
Open Tues - Fri 9 AM - 4:30 PM, Sat & Sun 1 - 4:30 PM; No admis fee; Estab 1964 as Indiana University Mus, institute renamed in 1983. Mus of World Cultures housing over 30,000 artifacts; Mem: Dues $25-$45
Income: Financed by mem & col
Special Subjects: Anthropology, Historical Material, Folk Art
Collections: Anthropology, folklore & history with colls of American primitives, Latin American primitives & folk art
Exhibitions: Museum features changing exhibitions
Publications: Papers & monograph series
Activities: Docent prog; mus training classes; lects; tours; film series; school loan collection

CARMEL

M **EVAN LURIE FINE ART GALLERY,** 30 W Main St, Carmel, IN 46032. Tel 317-844-8400; Fax 317-844-8460; Email info@evanluriegallery.com; Web: www.evanluriegallery.com; *Dir* Evan Lurie
Open Tues - Sun 11 AM - 7 PM; 5,200 sq ft
Special Subjects: Sculpture, Photography
Collections: Contemporary abstract & neo-realism paintings, sculpture & photography
Exhibitions: Rotating exhibits
Activities: Lects open to pub; gallery walks; community & private events; public art collaborations

CHESTERTON

M **CHESTERTON ART CENTER,** 115 S 4th St, Chesterton, IN 46304-2344. Tel 219-926-4711; Email gallery@chestertonart.com; Web: www.chestertonart.com; *Exec Dir* Wendy Marciniak
Open Mon - Fri 11 AM - 4 PM, Sat 10 AM - 2 PM, cl Sun; Estab as a nonprofit association for art appreciation & educ; Mem: 500; dues $25
Collections: Regional artwork
Exhibitions: Temporary exhibits
Activities: Educ progs; classes for adults & children

ELKHART

M **MIDWEST MUSEUM OF AMERICAN ART,** 429 Main St, Elkhart, IN 46516-3210. Tel 574-293-6660; Fax 574-293-6660; Email mdwstmsmam@aol.com; Web: www.midwestmuseum.us; *Cur Exhib & Educ* Brian D Byrn; *Admin Gallery Coordr* Randall Roberts
Open Tues - Fri 10 AM - 4 PM, Sat - Sun 1 - 4 PM; Admis adults $5, students $4, family (3 or more) $10; Estab 1978 to provide high quality exhibitions, educational programs & permanent collection of 19th & 20th century American art for the public; Nine galleries on two floors (approx 9500 sq ft of exhibit space); Average Annual Attendance: 25,000; Mem: 710; dues $10-$250
Income: $100,000 (financed through mem, grants, foundations, contributions)
Library Holdings: Auction Catalogs, Audio Tapes, Book Volumes, CD-ROMs, Cards, Cassettes, Clipping Files, DVDs, Exhibition Catalogs, Original Art Works, Photographs, Prints, Sculpture, Slides, Video Tapes
Special Subjects: Bronzes, Ceramics, Collages, Decorative Arts, Drawings, Etchings & Engravings, Folk Art, Glass, Graphics, Landscapes, Latin American Art, Painting-American, Photography, Portraits, Pottery, Primitive art, Prints, Sculpture, Southwestern Art, Watercolors, Woodcuts
Collections: Paintings: Arthur Bowen Davies, Joan Mitchell, Robert Natkin, Grant Wood, Red Grooms, Carl Olaf Seltzer, Norman Rockwell, LeRoy Neiman, Roger Brown, Art Green, George Luks, Glen Cooper Henshaw, Pennerton West, Robert Reid, Sculpture: Felix Eboigbe, Frederick MacMonnies, Fritz Scholder, Overbeck Art Pottery Collection, Jaune Quick-To-See, Norman Rockwell lithograph
Exhibitions: 6 temporary or changing exhibs annually
Publications: Midwest Museum Bulletin, quarterly
Activities: Classes for adults and children; docent training; lects open to pub, 52 vis lectrs per yr; concerts; gallery talks; tours; competitions with awards; regional juried competition & national youth art awards; scholarships; individual paintings & original objects of art lent to other mus only; originate traveling exhibs to other mus & university galleries; mus shop sells books, magazines, original art, reproductions, prints & original crafts

L **RUTHMERE MUSEUM,** Robert B. Beardsley Arts Reference Library, 302 E Beardsley Ave, Elkhart, IN 46514-2719. Tel 574-264-0330; Fax 574-266-0474; Email jjohns@ruthmere.org; Web: www.ruthmere.org/library.asp; *Cur* Jennifer Johns
Open Library open by appointment only; Museum open Tues - Sat 10 AM - 4 PM, Sun 1 PM - 4 PM; Admis adults $10, students $4; Campus Pass: adult $13; Estab 1973 as a reference library/historic house mus; Circ Non-circulating/lending; Average Annual Attendance: 12,000; Mem: 260; dues Patron & Higher levels $100; Family $75; Individual 50
Income: Financed by mems
Library Holdings: Auction Catalogs, Book Volumes 1800, Periodical Subscriptions 15, Slides
Special Subjects: Architecture, Art History, Decorative Arts, Landscape Architecture, Landscapes, Painting-American, Porcelain, Pottery, Restoration & Conservation, Sculpture, Stained Glass, Bronzes
Collections: Fine Art Coll within the house (Samuel Rodins, F B Morse, William Morris Hunt, William Ordway Partridge, Camille Claudel
Activities: Educ classes; docent training; lects open to pub; concerts; gallery talks; tours

EVANSVILLE

A **ARTS COUNCIL OF SOUTHWESTERN INDIANA,** The Bower-Suhrheinrich Foundation Gallery, 318 Main St Ste 101, Evansville, IN 47708-1451. Tel 812-422-2111; Fax 812-492-4312; Email mjschenk@artswin.evansville.net; Web: www.artswin.evansville.net; *Exec Dir* Mary Jane Schenk; *Activities & Communs Dir* Shannon L Hurt; *Pres Bd Dir* Dirck Stahl
Open Mon-Fri 9AM-5PM; No admis fee; Estab 1970 to increase the awareness & accessibility of the arts in Southwestern Indiana through community programs, arts in educ & festivals; serves as an umbrella organization for over 50 cultural organizations, providing technical assistance, marketing & linkage with local, state & national arts organizations; Average Annual Attendance: 5,000; Mem: 550; $20 & up
Income: Financed by endowment, mem, city appropriation & state appropriation, sales
Exhibitions: Business/Arts Month; titles vary: new exhibs every six weeks
Publications: Artist directory; artist registry; Arts Talk Newsletter, quarterly; cultural calendar; cultural directory; media directory
Activities: Classes for general community; arts-in-education prog; artist residencies in elementary schools; art workshops; lects open to pub; concerts; festivals; outreach program provided to six rural counties; Awards include Mayor's Arts award, Young Artist of the Year, Artist of the Year, Arts in Education, Arts Advocate of the Year, Corporate Arts Award, Regional Arts Awards; mus shop sells books, original art, reproductions, prints, ceramics, pottery, jewelry, cards

M **EVANSVILLE MUSEUM OF ARTS, HISTORY & SCIENCE,** 411 SE Riverside Dr, Evansville, IN 47713-1098; PO Box 3435, Evansville, IN 47733-3435. Tel 812-425-2406, 421-7506 (TTY); Fax 812-421-7509; Email info@emuseum.org; Web: evansvillemuseum.org; *Pres Bd Dir* Bill Bartelt; *Dir Emeritus* John W Streetman III; *Cur Educ* Karen Malone; *Cur Coll* Mary Bower; *Registrar* Elizabeth Fuhrman Bragg; *Dir Science Experiences* Mitch Luman; *Dir* Bryan W Knicely; *Cur History* Tom Lonnberg
Open Tues - Wed & Fri - Sat 11 AM - 5 PM, Thurs 11 AM - 8 PM, Sun Noon - 5 PM, cl Mon; Admis adult $10, youth $8; Estab 1926 to maintain & perpetuate a living mus to influence & inspire the taste & cultural growth of the community, to provide facilities for the collection, preservation & exhibition of objects, data & programs related to the arts, history, science & technology; First Level: Koch Immersive Theater; 19th century village of homes, shops, offices & town hall, America at War Gallery, two science & technology galleries, classrooms; Second Level: furnished Gothic Room with linefold paneling; Sculpture Gallery: galleries for Dutch & Flemish art, 18th century English art, 19th & 20th century American & European art, Anthropology Gallery; three galleries for temporary exhibits; Average Annual Attendance: 100,000; Mem: 1,730; Dues Contributor $60-$99; Patron $100-$249; Donor $250-$499; Director's Assoc $500-$999; President's Circle $1,000-2,499; Founder's Society $2,500-$4,999; Benefactor $5,000 & above
Income: $1,295,000 (financed by mem, city & state appropriations)
Special Subjects: African Art, Anthropology, Antiquities-Egyptian, Decorative Arts, Dolls, Etchings & Engravings, Ethnology, Folk Art, Furniture, Glass, Manuscripts, Maps, Oriental Art, Painting-American, Painting-British, Painting-Dutch, Painting-European, Painting-Flemish, Period Rooms, Sculpture, Tapestries, Textiles, Watercolors, Woodcuts
Collections: 19th & 20th Century Indiana Art, 20th Century American Still Life, World War II artifacts
Publications: Catalogs of exhibitions; Members Magazine, biannual
Activities: Classes for adults & children; docent training; family activities (super Sat); lects open to pub; 10 visiting lectures per year; gallery talks; tours; sponsoring of competitions; MidStates Arts Competition; Organizes Traveling Exhibitons; Books; original art

M **UNIVERSITY OF EVANSVILLE,** Krannert Gallery & Peterson Gallery, 1800 Lincoln Ave, Evansville, IN 47722-0001. Tel 812-488-2043; Fax 812-488-2101;

Email bb32@evansville.edu; *Chmn Art Dept* Stephanie Frusier; *Dean Arts & Sciences* Jean Beckman; *Gallery Dir* William Brown
Open Mon - Sat 10 AM - 4 PM; No admis fee; Krannert Gallery was estab 1969-70 to bring to the University & pub communities exhibitions which reflect the contemporary arts, ranging from crafts through painting & sculpture; Peterson Gallery has larger open space & higher ceilings; Pub access exhibition space 80 x 40 & located in Fine Arts Building; Melvin Peterson Gallery located in Studio Bldg; Average Annual Attendance: 100 per month
Income: Financed by Department of Art funds
Purchases: private collections
Collections: Dicke Collection, Permanent Collections
Exhibitions: Drawing Exhibition; Indiana Ceramics; New Acquisitions; Student Scholarship Exhibition; Undergraduate BFA Exhibition; Faculty Exhibition; Painting Invitational; Sculpture Invitational; Evansville Artists Guild Show; Photography Exhibition; Various invitationals to other univ; Quilting Exhibit
Activities: Lect open to public, 4 vis lectrs per year; gallery talks; tours; competitions with awards; individual paintings & original objects of art lent to university community

L **University Library,** 1800 Lincoln Ave, Evansville, IN 47722. Tel 812-488-2486; Fax 812-488-6987; Email kb4@evansville.edu; Web: www.libraries.evansville.edu; *Librn* William F Louden; *Head Reference Librn* Randy Abbott
Open Mon - Thurs 7:45 AM - midnight, Fri 7:45 AM - 6 PM, Sat 10 AM - 6 PM, Sun noon-midnight
Special Subjects: Cartoons
Collections: Knecht Cartoon Collection

L **WILLARD LIBRARY,** Dept of Fine Arts, 21 First Ave, Evansville, IN 47710. Tel 812-425-4309; Fax 812-421-9742, 425-4303; Email willard@willard.lib.in.us; Web: www.willard.lib.in.us; *Dir* Greg Hager; *Spec Coll* Lyn Martin; *Children's Librn* Rhonda Mort; *Adult Librn* Eva Sanford
Open Mon - Tues 9 AM - 8 PM, Wed - Fri 9 AM - 5:30 PM, Sat 9 AM - 5 PM, Sun 1 - 5 PM; Estab 1885
Income: $5000 (financed by endowment & city appropriation)
Library Holdings: Book Volumes 7500, Original Art Works, Periodical Subscriptions 16, Photographs, Records

FORT WAYNE

L **ALLEN COUNTY PUBLIC LIBRARY,** Art, Music & Audiovisual Services, 900 Webster St, Fort Wayne, IN 46802-3602. Tel 219-421-1200 Ext 1210; Fax 219-422-9688; Email ask@acpl.info; Web: www.acpl.lib.in.us; *Assoc Dir* Steven Fortriede; *Art, Music & Av Mgr* Stacey Huxhold; *Dir* Jeffrey R Krull
Open Mon - Thurs 9 AM - 9 PM, Fri & Sat 9 AM - 6 PM, Sun noon - 5 PM; Estab 1968 to provide a reference coll of the highest quality & completeness for the community & its colleges, a place where local artists & musicians could exhibit their works & perform to provide a circulating collection of slides & musical scores sufficient to meet the demand; The gallery is reserved for painting, sculpture, graphics, photography, ceramics & other art crafts
Income: $253,699 (financed by local property taxes)
Library Holdings: Audio Tapes, Book Volumes 85,000, Cassettes 9000, Compact Disks 17,000, DVDs 2000, Exhibition Catalogs, Memorabilia, Motion Pictures, Periodical Subscriptions 52, Records, Slides 25,000, Video Tapes 11,000
Special Subjects: Art History, Ceramics, Crafts, Decorative Arts, Drawings, Graphic Arts, Graphic Design, Landscape Architecture, Painting-American, Photography, Portraits, Prints, Sculpture, Video, Watercolors
Exhibitions: Exhibits monthly
Activities: Lect open to public, vis lectr; concerts; lending collection contains books, slides, videos, CDs, cassettes & books-on-tape; sales shop sells books, posters, videos, CDs & cassettes

M **ARTLINK, INC,** Auer Center for Arts & Culture, 300 E Main St, Fort Wayne, IN 46802-1919. Tel 260-424-7195; Fax 260-424-8453; Email info@artlinkfw.com; Web: www.artlinkfw.com; *Exec Dir* Deb Washler; *Gallery & Educ Coordr* Rebecca Stockert; *Gallery Receptionist* Diane Groenert; *Gallery Asst* Suzanne Galazka
Open Tues - Fri 10 AM - 5 PM, Sat noon - 6 PM, Sun noon - 5 PM; Admis non-mem $2, mem free; Estab 1979 to promote the work of emerging & mid-career artists as well as educational opportunities for the community; 3,000 sq ft main gallery in renovated Auer Center for Arts & Culture, home of four not-for-profit arts organizations.; Average Annual Attendance: 14,000; Mem: 730; dues $10-$200, individual $30; individual artist $25
Income: Financed by mem, Arts United, Indiana Arts Commission, foundations & donations
Publications: Genre newsletter, quarterly; annual print show catalogue
Activities: Educ prog; classes for adults, summer classes for children; docent training; workshops 2-3 per yr; lects open to pub, 2-3 vis lectrs per yr; competitions with awards; sponsoring of competitions; mus shop sells original art, reproductions & prints

A **ARTS UNITED OF GREATER FORT WAYNE,** 300 E Main St, Fort Wayne, IN 46802-1920. Tel 260-424-0646; Fax 260-424-2783; Web: www.artsunited.org; *Exec Dir* James Sparrow; *Dir Community Develop* Dan Ross; *Dir Resource Develop* Susan Mendenhall
Open Mon - Fri 8 AM - 5 PM; No admis fee; Estab 1955 to raise funds for cultural organizations in Fort Wayne & to foster a positive atmosphere for arts growth
Income: Financed by pub allocations & private donations
Collections: Bicentennial Collection
Publications: Discovery, quarterly newspaper; fine arts calendar
Activities: Own & manage the Performing Arts Center, umbrella organization for 57 arts organizations

M **FORT WAYNE MUSEUM OF ART, INC,** 311 E Main St, Fort Wayne, IN 46802-1997. Tel 260-422-6467; Fax 260-422-1374; Email mail@fwmoa.org; Web: www.fwmoa.org; *Dir* Charles A Shepard III; *Dir Bus & Fin* Lon R Braun; *Deputy Dir Admin & Communs* Amanda Martin; *Registrar* Leah Reeder; *Dir Security & IT* Scott Tarr; *Assoc Cur Exhibs* Joslyn Elliott
Open Tues - Wed & Fri - Sat 10 AM - 6 PM, Thurs 10 AM - 8 PM, Sun Noon - 5 PM; Admis fee adults $7, students (K-college) $5, family $20; Estab 1922 to heighten visual perception of American fine arts & perception of other disciplines; 8 galleries incl sculpture court & hands-on children's gallery; Average Annual Attendance: 100,000; Mem: 900; dues $40 for an individual & up; annual meeting in June
Income: Financed by endowment, mem, Arts United & grants
Library Holdings: Book Volumes, Periodical Subscriptions
Special Subjects: Painting-American, Prints, Sculpture
Collections: Hamilton Collection (paintings & sculpture), Thieme Collection (paintings), Weatherhead Collection (contemporary paintings & prints), contemporary pieces by living America artists, paintings, sculptures & works on paper from 1850 to present by artists from the US & Europe, works by significant regional artists, Steven Sorman archives, Natl repository for Coll of the American Cut Glass Assn's brilliant cut glass
Publications: exhib catalogs; ann report
Activities: Docent training; 5 vis lectrs; lects open to pub; gallery talks; tours; scholastic art & writing awarded - NEIN, NW OH region; artmobile for area schools; book traveling exhibs 2 per yr; originate traveling exhibs to natl art centers & museums; mus shop sells books, reproductions, prints, fine crafts & original art

M **UNIVERSITY OF SAINT FRANCIS, SCHOOL OF CREATIVE ARTS,** John P Weatherhead Gallery & Lupke Gallery, 2701 Spring St, Fort Wayne, IN 46808-3994. Tel 260-399-7700, ext 8001; Fax 260-399-8171; Email rcartwright@sf.edu; Web: www.sf.edu/art; *Dean* Rick Cartwright; *Gallery Dir* Justin Johnson; *Coordr* Molly McGowen
Open Mon - Fri 9 AM - 5 PM, Sat 10 AM - 5 PM, Sun 1 - 5 PM; No admis fee; Estab 1965 to provide art programs to students & community; Weatherhead Gallery, approx 1,000 sq ft, is located in the Rolland Art Center; Lupke Gallery, approx 700 sq ft, is located in the North Campus facilities; Average Annual Attendance: 20,000
Activities: Classes for adults & children, dramatic progs; lects open to pub, 4 vis lectrs per yr, tours, competitions with awards, gallery talks, concerts, schols; originates traveling exhibs

FRANKFORT

M **FRANKFORT COMMUNITY PUBLIC LIBRARY,** Anna & Harlan Hubbard Gallery, 208 W Clinton St, Frankfort, IN 46041-1899. Tel 765-654-8746; Fax 765-654-8747; Email fcpl@accs.net; Web: www.fcpl.accs.net; *Arts Dir* Flo Caddell
Open Mon - Thurs, 9 AM - 8 PM, Fri & Sat 9 AM - 5 PM; open Sun, Sept - May, 1 - 5 PM
Library Holdings: Audio Tapes, Book Volumes, CD-ROMs, Clipping Files, DVDs, Fiche, Filmstrips, Original Art Works, Periodical Subscriptions, Photographs, Prints, Records, Sculpture, Video Tapes
Special Subjects: Bronzes, Folk Art, Painting-American, Prints
Collections: Bronzes, folk art, Indiana art, paintings, prints, Works by Harlan Hubbard, Konrad Juestel & Victor Colby
Exhibitions: Friends Ann Christmas Art Exhib & Sale (2nd weekend in Nov)
Activities: Classes for adults & children; exhibits; concerts; gallery talks; tours

HAMMOND

M **PURDUE UNIVERSITY CALUMET,** Library Gallery, 2200 169th St, Hammond, IN 46323-2094. Tel 219-989-2400; Fax 219-989-2070; Email univrel@calumet.purdue.edu; Web: www.calumet.purdue.edu/library/current.html; *Interim Libr Dir* Karen M Corey
Open Mon - Thurs 8 AM - 9:30 PM, Fri 8 AM - 5 PM, Sat 10 AM - 4 PM, Sun 1 - 5 PM; No admis fee; Estab 1976 to present varied art media to the university community & general public; Average Annual Attendance: 25,000
Income: $3000
Collections: 19th century Chinese Scroll coll, 1930 art deco bronze sculptured doors from City Hall
Exhibitions: Area Professional Artists & Students Shows; group shows; traveling shows (Smithsonian Institution, French Cultural Services, Austrian Institute)
Activities: Book traveling exhibs

HUNTINGTON

M **HUNTINGTON UNIVERSITY,** Robert E Wilson Art Gallery, 2303 College Ave, Merillat Center for the Arts Huntington, IN 46750-1237. Tel 260-359-4272; Fax 260-359-4249; Email bmichel@huntington.edu; Web: www.huntington.edu/mca/gallery/default.htm; *Gallery Dir* Ms Barbara Michel
Open Mon - Fri 9 AM - 5 PM; No admis fee; Estab 1990 to provide community with art exhibits & support col art prog; Gallery is 25 x 44 ft; Average Annual Attendance: 3,000
Income: $5,000 (financed by college & gifts)
Collections: Robert E Wilson Collection of Paintings & Sculpture, Huntington University - Permanent Student Art Collection
Activities: Art in the schools; gallery talks; vis lectrs 300 per yr; student exhib awards; book traveling exhibs three per yr

INDIANAPOLIS

M **THE CHILDREN'S MUSEUM OF INDIANAPOLIS,** 3000 N Meridian St, Indianapolis, IN 46208-4716; PO Box 3000, Indianapolis, IN 46206-3000. Tel 317-334-4000; Fax 317-921-4019; Email customerservice@childrensmuseum.org; Web: www.childrensmuseum.org; *Pres & CEO* Dr Jeffrey Patchen; *Chief Devel Officer* Amy Kwas; *CFO* Andy Bawel; *VP Human Resources & Organizational Devel* Katy Allen; *VP Mktg & External Rels* Lisa Townsend; *VP Opers & Gen Counsel* Brian Statz; *VP Experience Development & Family Learning* Jennifer Pace-Robinson; *Pub Rels Coordr* Kim Harms; *Chief Tech Officer* David Donaldson

Open 10 AM - 5 PM; Admis fee adults $22.50, senior 60 & over $21.50, children 2-17 $18.50, under 2 free; Estab 1925 to create learning experiences across science, art, humanities that have the power to transform lives of children & families; Family learning in sciences, arts & humanities; Average Annual Attendance: 1,300,000; Mem: 34,000 households; dues family $164
Income: $30,000,000 (funded by endowment, mem, fundraising, admissions)
Library Holdings: Auction Catalogs, Audio Tapes, Cassettes, Compact Disks, DVDs, Fiche, Filmstrips, Lantern Slides, Memorabilia, Motion Pictures, Original Art Works, Original Documents, Photographs, Prints, Records, Sculpture, Slides, Video Tapes
Special Subjects: African Art, Anthropology, Antiquities-Byzantine, Antiquities-Egyptian, Antiquities-Greek, Antiquities-Roman, Archaeology, Asian Art, Cartoons, Maps, Ceramics, Coins & Medals, Costumes, Decorative Arts, Dioramas, Dolls, Drawings, Embroidery, Enamels, Eskimo Art, Etchings & Engravings, Ethnology, Flasks & Bottles, Folk Art, Furniture, Glass, Hispanic Art, Historical Material, Islamic Art, Ivory, Jade, Jewelry, Judaica, Juvenile Art, Leather, Manuscripts, Maps, Medieval Art, Metalwork, Mexican Art, Miniatures, Painting-American, Painting-Australian, Pewter, Photography, Porcelain, Posters, Pottery, Pre-Columbian Art, Religious Art, Scrimshaw, Sculpture, Silver, Stained Glass, Tapestries, Textiles, Woodcarvings, Woodcuts
Collections: Toys and artifacts from around the world, Caplan Collection, Max Simon Comic Book Collection
Exhibitions: Permanent Exhibs: Dinosphere: Now You're in Their World; All Aboard!; Chihuly Fireworks of Class; National Geographic Treasures of the Earth; Take Me There: China; Power of Children; Playscape; Carousel Wishes & Dreams; ScienceWorks; Beyond Spaceship Earth
Publications: Mem newsletter: Extra!
Activities: Children's classes; dramatic progs; vol intern training; lects open to pub; The Power of Children Awards; exten prog serves state of Indiana; book traveling exhibs, 1 per yr; originates traveling exhibs to other mus & science centers; retail store sells books, original art, reproductions, prints, & educational toys

M **EITELJORG MUSEUM OF AMERICAN INDIANS & WESTERN ART,** 500 W Washington, Indianapolis, IN 46204. Tel 317-636-9378; Fax 317-275-1400; Web: www.eiteljorg.org; *Registrar* Christa Barleben; *Pres & CEO* John Vanausdall; *VPres & Chief Curatorial Officer* James H Nottage; *VPres Pub Progs & Vis Experience* Martha L Hill PhD; *Develop Mgr* Sally Dickson; *Dir Mktg & Communs* Bert Beiswanger
Open Mon - Sat 10 AM - 5 PM, Sun Noon - 5 PM; cl New Year's Day, Thanksgiving & Christmas Day; Admis adults $13, seniors (65 & over) $11, children (5-17) $7, children under 5, mems, & IUPUI free; Estab 1989; the mus is dedicated to inspiring an appreciation & understanding of the art, history & cultures of the American West & the indigenous peoples of North America. The Eiteljorg Mus collects & preserves Western art & Native American art & cultural objects of the highest quality & serves the pub through exhibs, educational progs, cultural exchanges & entertaining special events; Average Annual Attendance: 101,000; non-circulating; Mem: 3000; dues $50 individual, $60 family
Income: Financed through mem, grants & donations
Library Holdings: Audio Tapes, Book Volumes, DVDs, Exhibition Catalogs, Fiche, Manuscripts, Maps, Other Holdings, Pamphlets, Periodical Subscriptions, Video Tapes
Special Subjects: American Indian Art, American Western Art, Bronzes, Decorative Arts, Drawings, Eskimo Art, Etchings & Engravings, Jewelry, Landscapes, Painting-American, Photography, Portraits, Pottery, Prints, Scrimshaw, Sculpture, Southwestern Art, Textiles, Watercolors
Collections: American art of the West, 19th century to the present, strongest in Taos Society artists & early modernists in the West, Native American cultural arts of North America, from pre-contact to the present, Contemporary Native American fine art coll of particular importance
Exhibitions: Exhibitions rotate four times per yr
Publications: Out of the West: The Gund Collection of Western Art; Art Quantum: The Eiteljorg Fellowship for Native American Fine Art; Diversity & Dialogue: The Eiteljorg Fellowship for Native American Fine Art; Generations: The Helen Cox Kersting Collection of Southwestern Cultural Arts
Activities: Classes for adults & children; dramatic progs; docent training; educ coll; gallery interpreting; lects open to pub; gallery talks; tours; concerts; mus shop sells books, magazines, original art, prints, jewelry; reproductions

A **HOOSIER SALON PATRONS ASSOCIATION, INC,** Art Gallery & Membership Organization, 711 E 65th St, #202, Indianapolis, IN 46220-1609. Tel 317-253-5340; Fax 317-253-5468; Email hoosiersalon@iquest.net; Web: hoosiersalon.org; *Exec Dir* Jim May; *Pres* Marilyn Shank; *Carmel Gallery Mgr* Michael Sinon; *New Harmony Gallery Mgr* Linda Volz
Open (Carmel Gallery) Wed - Thurs Noon - 6 PM, Fri - Sat Noon - 9 PM; (New Harmony Gallery) Tues - Sun 1 - 4 PM; No admis fee; Estab 1925 to promote work of Indiana artists; 1,800 sq ft featuring artwork by Indiana artists; Average Annual Attendance: 60,000; Mem: 600 (artists), 450 (patrons); dues patrons $75 & up, artists $40 artists eligible after 1 yr residence in Indiana
Income: Financed by mem, art sales, grants, gifts & patrons
Collections: Paintings, prints, sculpture
Exhibitions: 6-7 special exhib per yr at galleries in Indianapolis & New Harmony, IN
Publications: Annual Salon Exhibition Catalog; History of the Hoosier Salon; Hoosier Salon Newsletter, four times a year
Activities: Educ dept includes CD Rom "Landscape Painting in Indiana; A Modern Art"; gallery talks & tours at annual exhibit; juried competition with awards 40 awards in 2004 total value $28,050; original prints & paintings lent to qualified organizations; originate traveling exhibs circulating to 30 sites around the state of IN, usually 20 works in 6 groups; sales shop sells books, prints, original art & sculpture

M **INDIANA LANDMARKS,** Morris-Butler House, 1204 N Park Ave, Indianapolis, IN 46202. Tel 317-639-4534; Fax 317-639-6734; Email specialevents@indianalandmarks.org; Web: www.indianalandmarks.org; *Dir Volunteers & Heritage Experiences* Gwendolen Nystrom; *Pres* Marsh Davis; *Dir Heritage Educ & Info* Suzanne Rollins Stanis
Open for events & rentals (no tours); Available for events & rentals (no tours); Home built 1865 & restored by Indiana Landmarks. Estab in 1969 to document age of picturesque eclecticism in architecture & interior decoration. Interpretation, exhibition & preservation of Victorian Indianapolis architecture, culture, history & society (1865-1901); Facilities for receptions & meetings. All paintings by Indiana artists and/or previously owned by Mid-Victorian homeowners (1865-1901); Average Annual Attendance: 4,000; Mem: Annual dues $35 - $100
Income: Financed by private funds & rental & event fees
Special Subjects: Architecture, Carpets & Rugs, Ceramics, Decorative Arts, Furniture, Glass, Laces, Landscapes, Painting-American, Painting-Italian, Period Rooms, Porcelain, Portraits, Primitive art, Prints, Restorations, Sculpture, Silver, Textiles, Watercolors
Collections: Rococo, Renaissance & Gothic Revival furniture, paintings by early Indiana artists, Victorian ceramics, silver & glass, Victorian textiles
Activities: Available for events & rentals (no tours)

L **Information Center Library,** 1201 Central Ave, Indianapolis, IN 46202. Tel 317-639-4534; Fax 317-639-6734; Email sstanis@indianalandmarks.org; Web: www.indianalandmarks.org; *Pres* Marsh Davis; *Educ & Information Dir* Suzanne Stanis
Open by appointment Mon - Fri 8:30 AM - 4 PM; For reference only
Income: Financed by pvt funds & admis fees
Library Holdings: Audio Tapes, Book Volumes 3000, Clipping Files, DVDs, Kodachrome Transparencies, Periodical Subscriptions 100, Slides
Special Subjects: Architecture, Historical Material, Interior Design, Landscape Architecture, Restoration & Conservation, Decorative Arts, Landscapes
Activities: Classes for adults & children; docent training; lects open to pub; tours; sponsoring of competitions

M **INDIANA STATE MUSEUM,** 650 W Washington St, Indianapolis, IN 46204-2185. Tel 317-232-1637; Fax 317-232-7090; Email museumcommunication@indianamuseum.org; Web: www.indianamuseum.org; *CEO & Pres* Cathy Ferree; *Chmn Bd Trustees* William A Browne Jr; *Chief Mktg Officer* Amy Ahlersmeyer; *Chief Develop Officer* Kate Harvey; *VPres Mktg & Commun* Julie A Shaefer; *Exhib Develop* Cathy Donnelly; *Chief Cur Cultural History* Dale Ogden; *Chief Cur Nat History* Ron Richards
Open Mon - Fri 10 AM - 5 PM, Sat 10 AM - 5 PM, Sun 11 AM - 5 PM; Admis adults $14.95, seniors $13.95, students $12.95, children (3-17) $9.95, children under 3 free; members free; Estab 1869 for collections; current mus building opened 1967 to collect, preserve & interpret the natural & cultural history of the state; Numerous galleries; Average Annual Attendance: 35,721; Mem: 1200; dues individual premier $65; family & grandparent $80; patron $115
Income: Financed by state appropriation
Special Subjects: Anthropology, Archaeology, Architecture, Ceramics, Costumes, Decorative Arts, Dolls, Furniture, Historical Material, Manuscripts, Painting-American, Photography, Sculpture, Silver, Textiles
Publications: Brochures for individual historic sites
Activities: Educ prog; classes for children; docent training; in-school progs; lects open to pub, 4 vis lectrs per yr; concerts; gallery talks; tours; exten prog statewide; I-Reach lends to various organizations; 1-2 book traveling exhibs; mus shop selling books, reproductions & prints

M **INDIANA UNIVERSITY - PURDUE UNIVERSITY AT INDIANAPOLIS,** Herron Galleries, 735 W New York St, Indianapolis, IN 46202-5222. Tel 317-278-9419; Fax 317-278-9471; Email herron4u@iupui.edu; Web: www.herron.iupui.edu/galleries; *Gallery Dir & Cur* Max Weintraub
Open Year-round Mon - Fri 10 AM - 5 PM, Wed 10 AM - 8 PM, Sat 10 AM - 5 PM, cl Sun, summer: MON - Fri 10 AM - 5 PM, Sat 1 PM - 5 PM; No admis fee; School & gallery estab 1902 to educate about the visual arts, provide exhibition opportunities to students & faculty, and to present exhibs by regional, national, and international contemporary artists; Eleanor Prest Reese and Robert B. Berkshire Dorit & Gerald Paul Galleries: 3,000 sq ft, 22 ft ceiling, bamboo floors; Marsh Gallery: 1,100 sq ft, 16 ft ceiling, finished concrete floor; Basile Gallery 500 sq ft, 15 ft ceiling, finished concrete floor; Average Annual Attendance: 30,000
Income: Financed by state appropriation, grants & private support
Activities: lects open to pub; 15-20 vis lectrs/films per yr; gallery talks; tours; competitions; awards; exten dept serving Indianapolis & surrounding communities; facilitators of civic art projects; book traveling exhibs 1 per yr; originate traveling exhibs to other univ galleries mall/mid-size mus
—**Herron School of Art Library,** 735 W New York St, Indianapolis, IN 46202-5222. Tel 317-278-9484; Fax 317-278-9497; Email herron@iupui.com; Web: www.ulib.iupui.edu/herron; *Dir* Sonja Staum; *Circ Mgr* Praseth Kong; *Visual Resource Specialist* Danita Davis
Open (during acad yr) Mon - Thurs 8 AM - 6PM, Fri 8 AM - 5 PM; Estab 1970 as a visual resource center for the support of the curriculum of the Herron School of Art
Income: Financed by state appropriation
Library Holdings: Audio Tapes 615, Book Volumes 27,500, Clipping Files, DVDs, Exhibition Catalogs, Lantern Slides, Other Holdings Laser disc, Pamphlets, Periodical Subscriptions 100, Photographs, Prints, Reproductions, Slides 160,000, Video Tapes 1,500
Special Subjects: Advertising Design, Afro-American Art, American Indian Art, American Western Art, Antiquities-Greek, Architecture, Art Education, Art History, Ceramics, Collages, Commercial Art, Conceptual Art, Crafts, Display, Drawings

A **INDIANAPOLIS ART CENTER,** Marilyn K. Glick School of Art, 820 E 67th St, Indianapolis, IN 46220-1139. Tel 317-255-2464; Fax 317-254-0486; Email info@indplsartcenter.org; Web: www.indplsartcenter.org; *Pres & Exec Dir* Patrick Flaherty; *Dir Mktg & Communs* Shannon Bennett; *Office Mgr* Elise Howell; *Dir Develop* Emily Hunter; *Dir Educ & Outreach* Michelle Winkelman; *Dir Finance* Susan Meyer
Open Mon - Fri 9 AM - 10 PM, Sat 9 AM - 6 PM, Sun Noon - 6 PM; No admis fee; Estab 1934 to engage, enlighten & enhance community through art educ, participation & observation; Art Center houses 5 galleries: Churchman-Fehsenfeld Gallery, Allen W Clowes Gallery & Sarah M Hurt Gallery; Frank M Basile Exhibition Hall; Ruth Lilly Library; also has a 9.5 acre sculpture garden called Arts Park; Average Annual Attendance: 325,000; Mem: 2200; dues family $125, individual $85, senior $80, student $55

Income: Financed by endowment, mem, city & state appropriation
Exhibitions: 35-45 exhibs per yr - visit www.indplsartcenter.org or pflaherty@indplsartcenter.org for list
Publications: Paper Canvas, quarterly; quarterly program & class schedule; periodic exhibition catalogues
Activities: Over 90 art classes offered for all ages & skill levels in all medias; summer fine arts camps; workshops; gallery talks; tours; competitions with awards; scholarships offered; sales shop sells books, original art & prints

L **INDIANAPOLIS MARION COUNTY PUBLIC LIBRARY,** Central Library, One Library Sq, 40 E Saint Clair St Indianapolis, IN 46204; PO Box 211, Indianapolis, IN 46206-0211. Tel 317-275-4100; Fax 317-269-5229; Web: www.imcpl.org; *CEO* Jackie Nytes
Open Mon - Wed 10 AM - 8 PM, Thurs 10 AM - 6 PM, Fri 10 AM - 5 PM, Sat 10 AM - 5 PM, Sun Noon - 5 PM; No admis fee; Estab 1873
Income: Financed by state appropriation and county property tax
Library Holdings: Book Volumes 25,000, Cassettes, Clipping Files, DVDs, Exhibition Catalogs, Periodical Subscriptions 200, Video Tapes
Collections: Julia Connor Thompson Collection on Finer Arts in Homemaking
Activities: Lect open to public; concerts; tours

M **INDIANAPOLIS MUSEUM OF CONTEMPORARY ART,** 216 E South St, Indianapolis, IN 46204. Tel 317-790-5757; Fax 317-634-1977; Email info@indymoca.org; Web: www.indymoca.org
Open daily 9 AM - 7 PM; No admis fee; Estab 2001; Average Annual Attendance: 25,000; Mem: Individual $50; Family $75; Ally $125.
Activities: Formal educ programs; concerts; films; lects

M **MARIAN UNIVERSITY,** Allison Mansion, 3200 Cold Spring Rd, Indianapolis, IN 46222-1997. Tel 317-955-6120; Fax 317-955-6407; Web: www.marian.edu; *Dir Special Events* Katie Smith; *Special Events Coordr* Kortni Wright
Open by appointment; Estab 1970; house in the National Register of Historical Places since 1936; The interior of the mansion is oak, walnut & marble. The grand stairway in the main hall leads to the balcony overlooking the hall, all hand-carved walnut. A private collection of 17th century paintings
Income: Financed by donations
Collections: 17th century paintings
Activities: Concerts; tours; corporate meeting site; rent to pub

M **NEWFIELDS,** (Indianapolis Museum of Art), 4000 Michigan Rd, Indianapolis, IN 46208-4196. Tel 317-923-1331; Fax 317-931-1978; Email info@discovernewfields.org; Web: www.discovernewfields.org; *Melvin and Bren Simon Dir & CEO* Charles L Venable; *Deputy Dir Public Progs & Audience Engagement* Preston Bautista; *Deputy Dir Institutional Advancement* Kim Gattle; *COO* Katie Haigh; *Deputy Dir Mktg & External Affairs* Gary Stoppelman; *CFO* Jerry Wise; *Deputy Dir Horticulture & Natural Resources* Jonathan Wright
Open Sun, Tues - Wed 11AM - 5 PM, Thurs - Sat 11 AM - 8 PM cl Mon, Thanksgiving, Christmas, and New Years Day; Admis free; Estab 1883; IMA serves the creative interests of its communities by fostering exploration of art, design, & the natural environment. The IMA promotes these interests through the coll, presentation, interpretation & conservation of its artistic, historic & environmental assets; Museum's 152 acre campus includes an encyclopedia art museum, the historic Lilly House, and a 26 acre Oldfields Estate; also includes 100 Acres: The Virginia B Fairbanks Art & Nature Park; IMA owns the Miller House & Garden in Columbus, IN; Average Annual Attendance: 380,000; Mem: 10,000
Income: Financed by corporations, foundations, private individuals & endowment
Special Subjects: Bronzes, Ceramics, Decorative Arts, Drawings, Furniture, Jade, Oriental Art, Painting-American, Painting-European, Period Rooms, Porcelain, Portraits, Prints, Textiles, Watercolors
Collections: J M W Turner Collection of prints, watercolors & drawings, W J Holliday Collection of neo-impressionist art & paintings, Clowes Fund Collection of Old Master paintings, Eli Lilly Collection of Chinese art, European & American painting & sculpture, contemporary art, textiles & costumes, decorative arts, Eteljorg Collection of African Art
Publications: Brochures; handbook of permanent collections; quarterly magazine; catalogues for IMA-organized exhibs; Every Way Possible: 125 Years of the Indianapolis Museum of Art; Oldfields
Activities: Classes for adults & children; docent training; lects open to pub, 15-30 vis lectrs per yr; musical performance; gallery talks; tours; films; 2009 National Medal for Mus & Libr Svcs; book traveling exhibs 12-20 per yr; originate traveling exhibs; mus shop sells books, reproductions, prints, jewelry, & gifts

L **Stout Reference Library,** 4000 Michigan Rd, Indianapolis, IN 46208. Tel 317-920-2647; Fax 317-926-8931; Email library@imamuseum.org; Web: imamuseum.org; *Head of Lib & Archives* Alba Fernandez-Keys; *Catalog/Reference Librn* Deborah Evans-Cantrell; *Archivist* Jennifer Whitlock
Open Library: Tues, Wed, Fri 2 - 5 PM, Thurs 2 - 8 PM; No admis fee; Estab 1908 to serve needs of Mus staff & public; For reference only
Income: Financed by endowment, mem, city appropriation & federal grants
Library Holdings: Auction Catalogs, Book Volumes 60,000, Clipping Files, DVDs, Exhibition Catalogs, Original Documents, Other Holdings Artists Files 30,000, Pamphlets, Periodical Subscriptions 490, Reels, Video Tapes
Special Subjects: Asian Art, Carpets & Rugs, Textiles
Collections: Indiana Artists
Publications: Exhibition catalogs as needed; Indianapolis Museum of Art Bulletin, irregularly; newsletter, bimonthly; 100 Masterpieces
Activities: Classes for adults

M **UNIVERSITY OF INDIANAPOLIS,** Christel DeHaan Fine Arts Gallery, 1400 E Hanna Ave, Indianapolis, IN 46227-3697. Tel 317-788-3253; Fax 317-788-6105; Email jviewegh@uindy.edu; Web: www.uindy.edu; *Gallery Coordr* Mark Ruschman; *Asst Gallery Coordr* Hazel Augustin
Open Mon - Fri 9 AM - 9 PM; No admis fee; Estab 1964 to serve the campus & community; Average Annual Attendance: 6,000
Income: Financed by institution support
Purchases: $15,000
Special Subjects: Calligraphy, Ceramics, Coins & Medals, Drawings, Etchings & Engravings, Folk Art, Graphics, Historical Material, Landscapes, Metalwork, Painting-American, Photography, Portraits, Prints, Sculpture, Watercolors, Woodcarvings
Collections: Art Department Collection, Krannert Memorial Collection
Exhibitions: Student, faculty & local artists exhibits
Publications: Announcements; annual catalog & bulletin
Activities: Classes for adults; lect open to public; concerts; gallery talks; competitions with prizes; scholarships offered

LAFAYETTE

M **ART MUSEUM OF GREATER LAFAYETTE,** 102 S Tenth St, Lafayette, IN 47905. Tel 765-742-1128; Fax 765-742-1120; Email info@artlafayette.org; Web: www.artlafayette.org; *Dir* Kendall Smith; *Cur* Michael Atwell; *Brd Pres* Jeff Love
Open Tues - Sun 11 AM - 4 PM, cl Mon & major holidays; No admis fee; Estab 1909 to encourage & stimulate art & to present exhibitions of works of local, regional & national artists & groups as well as representative works of American & foreign artists; 3 galleries with changing exhibs; 1 permanent coll gallery; Average Annual Attendance: 25,000; Mem: 900; dues $35 & up; annual meeting in Oct
Income: Financed by art assoc foundation, endowment, mem, school of art & special events
Special Subjects: Afro-American Art, American Indian Art, Ceramics, Crafts, Decorative Arts, Drawings, Etchings & Engravings, Folk Art, Graphics, Hispanic Art, Painting-American, Photography, Porcelain, Portraits, Pottery, Prints, Religious Art, Sculpture, Southwestern Art, Textiles, Watercolors, Woodcarvings, Woodcuts
Collections: Permanent collection of over 900 works of art obtained through purchase or donation since 1909, American art coll specializing in Hoosier artist's work, Laura Anne Fry American Art Pottery & Art Glass, Akeley Collection of Mexican Modernists
Exhibitions: See website for current exhibitions
Publications: Annual report; bi-monthly calendar; exhibition catalog; quarterly newsletter
Activities: Classes for adults & children; docent training; lects open to pub; tours; competitions with awards; scholarships & fels offered; mus shop sells work of local artists

MADISON

M **JEFFERSON COUNTY HISTORICAL SOCIETY MUSEUM,** 615 W First St, Madison, IN 47250. Tel 812-265-2335; Email info@jchshc.org; Web: www.jchshc.org; *Pres* Nick Schultz; *Dir* John Nyberg; *Mus Educator* Joanne Spiller; *Office Mgr* Diana Hand
Open Mon - Sat 10 AM - 4:30 PM, cl Jan & Feb; Admis $6; Estab 1900 to preserve & display art & artifacts worthy of note & pertinent to local area history & culture; Museum has a permanent gallery of Civil War & steamboating, other gallery has rotating exhibits; Average Annual Attendance: 2,000; Mem: 400; family $35, single $25
Collections: William McKendree Snyder Collection, paintings, portraits, Jefferson County artifacts-textiles, primitives, 1895 Madison Railroad Station
Publications: Beloved Madison
Activities: Classes for children; mus shop sells books

MUNCIE

M **BALL STATE UNIVERSITY,** David Owsley Museum of Art, 2021 W Riverside Ave, Muncie, IN 47306. Tel 765-285-5242; Fax 765-285-4003; Email artmuseum@bsu.edu; Web: www.bsu.edu/artmuseum; *Dir* Robert LaFrance; *Dir Educ* Tania Said; *Exhibs Designer Preparator* Randy Salway
Open Mon - Fri 9 AM - 4:30 PM, Sat & Sun 1:30 PM - 4:30 PM, cl legal holidays; No admis fee; Estab 1936 as a university & community art museum; 12 galleries, sculpture court & mezzanine; Average Annual Attendance: 29,000
Income: Financed by university, community & federal government
Special Subjects: African Art, American Indian Art, American Western Art, Antiquities-Egyptian, Antiquities-Etruscan, Antiquities-Greek, Antiquities-Oriental, Antiquities-Roman, Architecture, Asian Art, Baroque Art, Ceramics, Coins & Medals, Decorative Arts, Drawings, Etchings & Engravings, Ethnology, Furniture, Glass, Renaissance Art, Painting-American, Painting-European, Prints
Collections: 18th, 19th & 20th c European & American Art, David T Owsley Collection of Ethnographic Art
Publications: Exhibition catalogs
Activities: Art for lunch talks; children's activity sheets; docent training; educ prog; lects open to pub, 10 vis lectrs per yr; gallery talks; tours; sponsoring of competitions; individual paintings & original objects of art lent to qualified mus; book traveling exhibs 2 per yr; mus shop sells posters, postcards & catalogues

L **Architecture Library,** McKinley at Neely, College of Architecture & Planning Muncie, IN 47306-0160. Tel 765-285-5857, 285-5858; Fax 765-285-3726; Email aetrendler@bsu.edu; Web: www.bsu.edu/library/collections/archlibrary; *Librn* Amy Trendler; *Asst Librn* Helen Ulrich; *Visual Resources Cur* Cindy Turner
Open Mon - Thurs 7:30 AM - 10 PM, Fri 7:30 AM - 6 PM, Sat 9 AM - 5 PM, Sun 1 - 10 PM; hours vary during acad vacations, interims & summer sessions; Estab 1965 to provide materials necessary to support the acad progs of the College of Architecture & Planning; Average Annual Attendance: 45,000
Income: Financed through University
Library Holdings: Book Volumes 24,000, CD-ROMs 100, DVDs 250, Other Holdings Student theses & 70,000 digital images, Periodical Subscriptions 100, Slides 110,000, Video Tapes 34
Special Subjects: Architecture, Decorative Arts, Drafting, Drawings, Furniture, Graphic Design, Industrial Design, Interior Design, Landscape Architecture, Restoration & Conservation

MUNSTER

M **SOUTH SHORE ARTS,** 1040 Ridge Rd, Munster, IN 46321-1876. Tel 219-836-1839; Fax 219-836-1863; Web: southshoreartsonline.org; *Exec Dir* John

Cain; *Pres* Liz Valavanis; *Dir Finance & Admin* Susan Anderson; *Gallery Mgr* Mary McClelland; *Dir Mktg & Develop* Tricia Hernandez; *Dir Educ* Linda Eyermann; *Educ Coordr* Kimberly McKinley; *Spec Projects Mgr* Jennifer Vinovich; *Mus Shop Mgr* Jackie Wicklund; *Asst Mus Shop Mgr* Andrea Miller
Open Mon - Fri 10 AM - 5 PM, Sat 10 AM - 4 PM, Sun noon - 4 PM; Admis adults $3, students $2, members no charge; Estab 1969; 5,000 sq ft exhib space
Library Holdings: Book Volumes
Special Subjects: Photography, Prints, Sculpture
Collections: regional art
Publications: quarterly newsletter
Activities: Educ progs; docent prog; lects; guided tours; concerts; arts festivals; theater; mus shop

NASHVILLE

A **BROWN COUNTY ART GALLERY FOUNDATION,** One Artist Dr, Nashville, IN 47448-8010; PO Box 443, Nashville, IN 47448-0443. Tel 812-988-4609; Email brncagal@aol.com; Web: www.browncountyartgallery.org; *Pres* Dr Emanuel Klein; *VPres* Sara Hess; *Secy* Richard Hess; *Treas* Kim Cornelius; *Museum Coordr* Richard Halvorson; *Gallery Mgr* Juanita Moberly; *Gallery Mgr* Pam Crawford; *Grants & Fund-raising Adv to Bd* Susanne Gaudin; *Legal Affairs Adv to Bd* Sharon A Wildey
Open Fri, Sat & Sun 10 AM -5 PM; Sun 2 - 5 PM Jan & Feb only; cl Thanksgiving, Christmas & New Years; No admis fee; Estab 1926 to unite artists and laymen in fellowship; to create a greater incentive for develop of art and its presentation to the public; to estab an art gallery for exhibition of work of members of the Assn; 6 gallery rooms; Average Annual Attendance: 35,000; Mem: 30 artists; 200 supporting members; for foundation mem art patron, for assn mem professional artist; dues life $1,000, individual $20; annual meeting in May
Income: Financed by mem & foundation
Library Holdings: Auction Catalogs, Book Volumes, Memorabilia, Original Documents, Photographs, Sculpture, Video Tapes
Special Subjects: Painting-American, Prints, Watercolors
Collections: 81 paintings & pastels by the late Glen Cooper Henshaw, over 200 paintings by early Brown County Artists
Exhibitions: Three exhibits each year by the artist members & paintings from permanent collection
Publications: Annual catalog
Activities: Classes for adults & children; docent training; lect open to public, various vis lectrs per year; gallery talks; tours; sales shop sells books, original art, reproductions, prints & videos

M **T C STEELE STATE HISTORIC SITE,** 4220 TC Steele Rd, Nashville, IN 47448. Tel 812-988-2785; Fax 812-988-8457; Email tcsteeleshs@indianamuseum.org; Web: www.tcsteele.org; *Historic Site Mgr* Andrea Smith de Tarnowsky; *Prog Develop* Cate Whetzel
Open Tues - Sat 9 AM - 5 PM, Sun 1 - 5 PM, cl Mon & most holidays; Admis adults $7, sr citizens $6, children & teens $4, group tour rate $1 discount; Estab 1945 to protect, collect & interpret the art & lives of T C & Selma Steele; 2,400 sq ft incl historic home setting, with 80 T C Steele paintings on display at any one time; Average Annual Attendance: 17,000; Mem: Support organization, The Friends of TC Steele
Income: Financed by state appropriation & admissions
Special Subjects: Ceramics, Decorative Arts, Furniture, Historical Material, Landscapes, Painting-American, Textiles, Period Rooms, Portraits
Collections: 347 paintings, historic furnishing, decorative arts, photos, books, restored historic gardens. No purchases, all part of donated estate
Activities: Classes for adults & children; docent training; Artists in Residence prog; lects open to pub; concerts; gallery talks; tours; annual special events; sponsoring of competitions; individual paintings & original objects of art lent to other mus & universities; lending collection contains original art works & paintings; framed reproductions; mus shop sells books, reproductions, prints & gift items relations to site/collections

NEW ALBANY

M **CARNEGIE CENTER FOR ART & HISTORY,** 201 E Spring St, New Albany, IN 47150-3422. Tel 812-944-7336; Fax 812-981-3544; Email info@carnegiecenter.org; Web: www.carnegiecenter.org; *Pres* Terry Ginkins; *Coordr Pub Progs & Engagement* Albartus Gorman; *Cur* Daniel Pfalzgraf; *Pub Rels* Delesha Thomas
Open Tues - Sat 10 AM -5:30 PM; No admis fee; Estab 1971, to exhibit regional professional artists' work on a monthly basis & to promote the arts & history of our community; Two galleries are maintained, approx dimensions: 21 x 30 ft & 21 x 30 ft; Average Annual Attendance: 24,000; Mem: 400; dues $30 - $1,000; annual meeting in Jan
Income: Financed through NAFC Public Library
Library Holdings: Memorabilia, Original Art Works
Special Subjects: Dioramas, Folk Art, Painting-American, Portraits, Sculpture, Textiles
Collections: Permanent collection of historical items
Exhibitions: Ordinary People Extraordinary Courage: The Men and Women of the Underground Railroad; Remembered: The Life of Lucy Higgs Nichols (permanent); Rotating contemporary exhibs; New Albany Public Art Project
Publications: Bulletins; Exhibit catalog
Activities: Classes for adults & children; lect open to public; 12 vis lectrs per yr; concerts; gallery talks; tours; competitions with awards, AAM Bronze Muse Award 2007, AASLH Leadership in History 2007; extension prog includes outreach presentations of underground railroad film off-site

NEW HARMONY

M **UNIVERSITY OF SOUTHERN INDIANA,** New Harmony Gallery of Contemporary Art, 506 Main St, New Harmony, IN 47631; PO Box 627, New Harmony, IN 47631-0627. Tel 812-682-3156; Email skrhoades@usi.edu; Web: www.nhgallery.com; *Asst Dir* Sara Rhoades
Open Tues - Sat 10 AM - 5 PM, Sun Noon - 4 PM (Apr-Dec), cl Mon; No admis fee; Estab 1975 for exhibition of contemporary midwest art & artists; Midwestern contemporary art; consignment gallery; Average Annual Attendance: 25,000
Income: Financed by contributions & grants
Collections: Univ Southern Ind Collection
Exhibitions: 8 exhibitions per year
Activities: Classes for adults; lects open to pub, gallery talks; workshops; sales shop sells original art & prints

NOTRE DAME

M **SAINT MARY'S COLLEGE,** Moreau Galleries, Moreau Center for the Arts, Notre Dame, IN 46556. Tel 574-284-4655; Fax 574-284-4715; Email khoefle@saintmarys.edu; Web: www.moreauartgalleries.com; *Gallery Dir* Krista Hoefle
Open Mon - Fri 10 AM - 4 PM, cl weekends; No admis fee; Estab 1956 for educ, community-related exhibits & contemporary art; Gallery presently occupies three spaces; all exhibits rotate; Average Annual Attendance: 6,000
Income: Financed through college
Special Subjects: Prints
Collections: Cotter Collection, Dunbarton Collection of prints, Norman LaLiberte Collection, various media
Exhibitions: Rotating exhibitions
Publications: Catalogs, occasionally
Activities: Lects open to pub; tours; concerts; gallery talks; competitions with awards; individual paintings & original objects of art lent; originate traveling exhibs

M **UNIVERSITY OF NOTRE DAME,** Snite Museum of Art, 100 Moose Krause Circle, Notre Dame, IN 46556-0368; PO Box 368, Notre Dame, IN 46556-0368. Tel 574-631-5466; Fax 574-631-8501; Web: sniteartmuseum.nd.edu; *Interim Dir* Ann M Knoll; *Cur European Art* Cheryl K Snay, PhD; *Cur Educ & Pub Progs* Sarah Martin; *Exhib Coordr* Ramiro Rodriguez
Open Tues - Fri 10 AM - 5 PM, Thurs 10 AM - 7:30 PM, Sat noon - 5 PM, cl Sun, Mon and major holidays; No admis fee; Estab 1842; Wightman Memorial Art Gallery estab 1917; O'Shaughnessy Art Gallery estab 1952; Snite Museum estab 1980 to educate through the visual arts; Galleries consist of 35,000 sq ft; Average Annual Attendance: 43,557; Mem: 354; dues from $25 - $1,000; annual meeting in May
Income: Supported by university budget and endowment funds
Special Subjects: African Art, American Indian Art, Baroque Art, Drawings, Oriental Art, Painting-American, Painting-British, Painting-European, Painting-French, Painting-Italian, Photography, Porcelain, Pre-Columbian Art, Prints, Sculpture, Afro-American Art, American Western Art, Antiquities-Egyptian, Antiquities-Greek, Antiquities-Persian, Antiquities-Roman, Decorative Arts, Etchings & Engravings, Furniture, Glass, Gold, Hispanic Art, Landscapes, Latin American Art, Manuscripts, Medieval Art, Pottery, Pre-Columbian Art, Stained Glass, Religious Art, Silver, Watercolors, Woodcuts
Collections: 18th & 19th century American, English, 17th, 18th & 19th Century French paintings & Master drawings, Kress Study Collection, 19th century French oils, Reilly Collection of Old Master Drawings through 19th century, Feddersen Collection of Rembrandt Collections, James Scholz Collection of 19th century European Photographs
Exhibitions: 6-8 special exhibits per academic year
Publications: Exhibition catalogs, 3-5 times per yr; Calendar of Events, semi-annually
Activities: Tours for adults & children, docent training; lects open to pub, 1-3 vis artists per yr; gallery talks; tours; bus trips to other museums; summer music series; original objects of art lent to qualified institutions

L **Architecture Library**, 117 Bond Hall, Notre Dame, IN 46556-5652. Tel 574-631-6654; Fax 574-631-9662; Email library.archlib.1@nd.edu; Web: www.architecture.library.nd.edu; *Library Supv* Deborah Webb; *Architecture Librn* Jennifer Parker
Open Mon - Thurs 8 AM - 10 PM, Fri 8 AM - 6 PM, Sat 10 AM - 5 PM, Sun 1 - 10 PM, intersessions Mon - Fri 8 AM - 5 PM; Estab 1930 as a branch of the university library
Income: Funding by University
Library Holdings: Book Volumes 28,000, CD-ROMs 6, Fiche, Lantern Slides 4,500, Periodical Subscriptions 119, Reels, Video Tapes 100
Special Subjects: Antiquities-Greek, Antiquities-Roman, Architecture, Furniture, Historical Material, Interior Design, Landscape Architecture, Restoration & Conservation
Collections: Furniture book coll, Rare books on architecture

PORTLAND

M **ARTS PLACE, INC,** (Jay County Arts Council) Hugh N Ronald Memorial Gallery, 131 E Walnut St, Portland, IN 47371-2108; PO Box 804, Portland, IN 47371-0804. Tel 219-726-4809; Fax 219-726-2081; Email artsland@jayco.net; Web: www.artsland.org; *Exec Dir* Eric Rogers; *Dir Admin* Julie Swoveland; *Dir Develop* Lisa Vogler; *Dir Visual Arts* Kimberly Anderson; *Sales & Mktg* Sophia Benedict
Open Mon - Fri 10 AM - 9 PM; No admis fee; Estab 1967; Local, regional, national & international contemporary art in a wide range of media; Average Annual Attendance: 15,000; Mem: 800
Exhibitions: Contemporary regional art
Activities: Classes for adults & children; dramatic progs; awards during juried exhibs; schols offered; originate traveling exhibs 4-8 per yr

RICHMOND

M **EARLHAM COLLEGE,** Leeds Gallery, 801 National Rd W, Richmond, IN 47374-4095. Tel 765-983-1400; Fax 765-983-1304; Web: www.earlham.edu; *Dir of Events Coordr* Lynn Knight
Open Mon-Fri 9AM-6PM, Sat-Sun 1PM-8PM; No admis fee; Estab 1847 as a liberal arts col; Leeds Gallery estab 1970
Collections: Regional artist: George Baker, Bundy (John Ellwood), Marcus Mote, prints by internationally known artists of 19th & 20th centuries, regional artists, rotating colls from all areas
Activities: Dramatic progs; lects open to pub, 5-6 vis lectrs per yr; concerts; individual paintings & original objects of art lent; originates traveling exhibs; sales shop sells books

M **Ronald Gallery**, 801 National Rd W, Richmond, IN 47374-4095. Tel 765-983-1410; *Cur* Julia May
Open Mon-Thurs 8AM-midnight, Fri 8AM-10PM, Sat 10AM-10PM, Sun noon-midnight
Collections: over 3,000 paintings, prints & sculptures

A **RICHMOND ART MUSEUM,** 350 Hub Etchison Pkwy, Richmond, IN 47375; PO Box 816, Richmond, IN 47375. Tel 765-966-0256; Fax 765-973-3738; Email shaun@richmondartmuseum.org; Email lance@richmondartmuseum.org; Web: www.richmondartmuseum.org; *Exec Dir* Shaun T Dingwerth; *Educ Dir* Lance Crow
Open Tues - Fri 11 AM - 5:30 PM, Sat 10 AM - 4 PM, cl Sun & Mon; No admis fee; Estab 1898 to promote creative ability, art appreciation & art in pub schools; Circ non-circulating; Maintains an art gallery with four exhibit rooms: two rooms for permanent collection & two rooms for current exhibits; Average Annual Attendance: 22,000; Mem: 600; dues students $10 - $1,000; annual meeting in Nov
Income: Financed by mem, grants, donations
Special Subjects: Ceramics, Painting-American, Photography, Prints, Pottery, Sculpture, Southwestern Art, Tapestries, Textiles, Watercolors, Woodcuts
Collections: Regional & state art, American, European, Oriental art, Overbeck Pottery
Exhibitions: Annual Area Artists Exhibition; Hands-On Exhibition for grade school children; High School Art Exhibition
Publications: Art in Richmond - 1898-1978; quarterly newsletter; Richmond Group Artists, by Shaun Dingwerth
Activities: Classes for adults & children; docent training; lects open to pub, 4 vis lectrs per yr; gallery talks; tours; competitions with merit & purchase awards; scholarships offered; individual paintings & original objects of art lent to corporations that annually support the museum or to other galleries for exhib; lending collection contains books, original art works, original prints & photographs; originate traveling exhibs; mus shop sells books, original art & prints

L **Israel D. Edelman Library**, 350 Hub Etchison Pkwy, Richmond, IN 47374; PO Box 816, Richmond, IN 47375. Tel 765-966-0256; Fax 765-973-3738; Email shaund@rcs.k12.in.us; Web: www.richmondartmuseum.org; *Exec Dir* Shaun T Dingwerth; *Educ Dir* Lance Crow
Open Tues - Sat 10 AM - 5 PM; No admis fee; est 1898; Circ Non-circ; Open to pub; library primarily for reference & art research; Average Annual Attendance: 22,000; Mem: 500
Library Holdings: Audio Tapes, Book Volumes 800, Exhibition Catalogs
Special Subjects: Art History, Ceramics, Decorative Arts, Graphic Arts, Landscapes, Painting-American, Painting-British, Painting-Dutch, Painting-European, Painting-Flemish, Photography, Pottery, Printmaking, Reproductions, Sculpture
Collections: Richmond Group artists, American Impressionists, Overbeck Pottery
Publications: The Richmond Group Artists
Activities: Classes for adults & children; lects open to pub; gallery talks

ROCHESTER

M **FULTON COUNTY HISTORICAL SOCIETY INC,** Fulton County Museum (Tetzlaff Reference Room), 37 E 375 N, Rochester, IN 46975-9718. Tel 574-223-4436; Fax 574-224-4436; Email fchs@rtcol.com; Web: www.fultoncountyhistory.org; *Dir Museum* Melinda Clinger; *Pres* Fred Oden Jr; *Treas* Lola Riddle; *Cataloger* Peggy Van Meter; *Cataloger* Annette Wise; *Pres Emerita* Shirley Willard
Open Mon - Sat 9 AM - 5 PM, cl holidays; No admis fee; Estab 1963 to preserve Fulton County & Northern Indiana history; 64 X 184 ft; new exhibit quarterly, 40 ft addition in 2001; 100 ft meeting rm added in 2008; Average Annual Attendance: 45,000; Mem: 400; dues $20; annual meeting third Mon in Nov
Income: $106,000 (financed by mem, sales & festivals, grants & donations)
Library Holdings: Audio Tapes, Book Volumes, CD-ROMs, Cards, Cassettes, Clipping Files, Compact Disks, DVDs, Exhibition Catalogs, Filmstrips, Framed Reproductions, Kodachrome Transparencies, Lantern Slides, Manuscripts, Maps, Memorabilia, Motion Pictures, Original Art Works, Original Documents, Other Holdings, Pamphlets, Periodical Subscriptions, Photographs, Prints, Records, Reels, Reproductions, Sculpture, Slides, Video Tapes
Special Subjects: American Indian Art, Coins & Medals, Costumes, Dioramas, Dolls, Folk Art, Furniture, Historical Material, Jewelry, Manuscripts, Maps, Painting-American, Period Rooms, Photography, Porcelain, Portraits, Posters, Pottery, Prints, Textiles, Woodcarvings
Collections: Antiques, Elmo Lincoln, first Tarzan, old farm equipment, old household furniture, Woodland Indians, Genealogy, Ogle Library, DAR, Chief White Eagle Library, Manitou Chapter DAR, John Tombaugh World War II Collection, Jack Overmyer Civil War Collection, Fulton County, IN authors
Exhibitions: Traditional & Indian Crafts; Round Barn Festival; Trail of Courage; Redbud Trail; Living History Village of 14 Bldgs (Loyal Indiana) portrays 1900-1925
Publications: Fulton County Images, newsletter; Fulton County Folk Finder, newsletter; Potawatomi Trail of Death Assn, newsletter; Fulton County Historical Power Assn, newsletter; Rochester - a pictorial history; Fulton Country Folks vol 1 + 2
Activities: Classes for adults & children; dramatic progs; docent progs; Indian dances; living history festivals; classes for children in summer; lects open to pub, 3 vis lectrs per yr; gallery talks; tours; competitions with prizes; Vol of Yr; Benefactor of Yr; retail store sells books, prints, magazines, original art & reproductions, Indian crafts, traditional crafts

SOUTH BEND

A **SOUTH BEND REGIONAL MUSEUM OF ART,** 120 S Saint Joseph St, South Bend, IN 46601-1902. Tel 574-235-9102; Fax 574-235-5782; Email info@southbendart.org; Web: www.sbrma.org; *Chief Cur* Bill Tourtillotte; *Exec Dir* Susan R Visser
Open Tues - Fri 11 AM - 5 PM, Sat & Sun noon - 5 PM; Admis non-mems $35 mems free; Estab in 1947 for museum exhibitions, lectures, film series, workshops, and studio classes; The Art Center is located in a three-story building designed by Philip Johnson. There are four galleries: the Warner Gallery features traveling shows or larger exhibits organized by the Art Center & the Art League Gallery features one or two-person shows by local or regional artists; also a community & permanent gallery; Average Annual Attendance: 50,000; Mem: 1,000; dues sustaining $100, family $60, active $40, student & senior citizens $30
Income: Financed by mem, corporate support, city & state appropriations
Special Subjects: Afro-American Art, Ceramics, Collages, Crafts, Drawings, Folk Art, Photography, Pottery, Prints, Sculpture, Textiles, Woodcarvings, Woodcuts, Painting-American
Collections: European and American paintings, drawings, prints and objects, 20th century American art with emphasis on regional and local works
Exhibitions: 4 rotating exhibits
Publications: Checklists; exhibition catalogues; quarterly newsletter
Activities: Studio classes for adults & children; docent training & tours; outreach educational prog conducted by Art League; workshops; lects open to pub, 3 vis lectrs per yr; gallery talks; artist studio tours; competitions with prizes; film series; paintings and original works of art lent to accredited mus; lending collection contains prints, paintings, records and sculptures; mus shop sells gift items and original works of art

L **Library**, 120 S Saint Joseph St, South Bend, IN 46601. Tel 574-235-9102; Fax 574-235-5782; Email sbrma@sbt.infi.net; *Exec Dir* Susan R Visser
No admis fee for members; non-members $3; Estab 1947 to provide art resource material to members of the Art Center
Library Holdings: Book Volumes 1100, Exhibition Catalogs, Motion Pictures, Periodical Subscriptions 63, Records
Special Subjects: Afro-American Art, Ceramics, Collages, Crafts, Drawings, Folk Art, Painting-American, Photography, Pottery, Prints, Sculpture, Textiles, Woodcarvings, Woodcuts
Activities: Educ prog; classes for adults & children; docent training; lects open to pub, 4 vis lectrs per yr; concerts; gallery talks; tours; sponsoring of competitions; scholarships; mus shop sells books, original art

TERRE HAUTE

M **INDIANA STATE UNIVERSITY,** University Art Gallery, Ctr Performing & Fine Arts, Terre Haute, IN 47809; 200 N 7th St, Terre Haute, IN 47809-1902. Tel 812-237-3720; Fax 812-237-4369; Email mvandenberg@isugw.indstate.edu; Web: www.indstate.edu/artgallery
Open Mon - Wed & Fri, 11 AM - 4 PM, Thurs 11AM- 8 PM, Sat noon-4PM; No admis fee; Contemporary gallery
Collections: Paintings & sculpture
Exhibitions: Changing exhibitions of national & regional contemporary art during school terms; periodic student & faculty exhibitions
Activities: Lect

M **SWOPE ART MUSEUM,** 25 S Seventh St, Terre Haute, IN 47807-3692. Tel 812-238-1676; Fax 812-238-1677; Email info@swope.org; Web: www.swope.org; *Exec Dir & Cur Exhibs* Susan Baley; *Develop Asst* Michelle Adler; *Dir Community Engagement* Hilda Andres; *Facilities Mgr* Jim Dawnson; *Office & Publ Mgr* Kristi Finley; *Registrar & Preparator* Edward Trover
Open Tues - Sun 10 AM - 5 PM, Fri until 8 PM; No admis fee; Estab 1942 to present free of charge American art of the 19th & 20th centuries; Average Annual Attendance: 12,000; Mem: 500; dues individual $40; annual meeting third Wed in Sept
Income: $300,000 (financed by mem & trust fund, annual donations & grants)
Purchases: Caprice 4 by Robert Motherwell; Girl With Cat by William Zorzach; Young Man Playing Double Flute by Ben Shahn; Still Life with Fruit by Barton S. Hays
Library Holdings: Book Volumes, Clipping Files
Special Subjects: American Western Art, Painting-American, Prints, Sculpture
Collections: American art of 19th & 20th centuries, James Farrington Cooking Art, Gilbert Wilson Art
Exhibitions: Listed on mus website
Publications: Membership newsletter; catalogs to spec exhibs
Activities: Classes for children; docent training; lects open to pub, 10 vis lectrs per yr; concerts; gallery talks; tours; competitions with awards; individual paintings & original objects of art lent to other museums; originate traveling exhibs; mus shop sells books, original art, reproductions, note cards, gift items & prints

L **Research Library**, 25 S Seventh St, Terre Haute, IN 47807-3692. Tel 812-238-1676; Fax 812-238-1677; Email info@swope.org; Web: www.swope.org; *Cur Colls & Exhibs* Elizabeth (Lisa) Petrulis; *Commun Mgr* Kristi Finley; *Exec Dir* Marianne Richter; *Coll Mgr* Jennifer Lanman; *Develop Asst* Michelle Adler
Open Tues - Fri 10 AM - 5 PM; No admis fee; Estab 1942; Circ 1,200; Open to pub; Average Annual Attendance: 12,000; Mem: 500; dues $40; ann meeting 4th Mon in Sept
Income: $337,072 (financed by endowments, sales, individuals, corporations, sponsorships, foundations, federal & state support, fund raising, donations, memorial contributions)
Purchases: John Rogers Cox, White Cloud; Mary Fairchild MacMonnies, Garden in Giverny; Frederick Puckstuhl, Evening; William Edouard Scott, Etaples; Carl Woolsey, Rod to the Village; Abraham Walkowitz, Abstraction; Isadore Duncan, Untitled; Ben Shahn, Young Man Playing Double Flute; Barton S. Hayes, Still Life with Fruit

Library Holdings: Book Volumes 1182, Clipping Files, Periodical Subscriptions 3, Video Tapes 9
Special Subjects: Aesthetics, Afro-American Art, American Indian Art, Architecture, Art Education, Art History, Ceramics, Drawings, Etchings & Engravings, Furniture, Glass, Graphic Arts, Graphic Design, Historical Material, History of Art & Archaeology, Industrial Design, Landscape Architecture, Landscapes, Painting-American, Photography, Printmaking, Prints, Sculpture, Watercolors, Woodcuts
Collections: American 19th & 20th century art works, Gilbert Wilson art, James Farrington Cooking Art
Publications: Newsletter 2 times per yr; Laurette E McCarthy - Swope Art Museum: Selected Works from the Collection
Activities: Classes for adults & children; docent training; lects open to pub, 8-16 vis lectrs per yr; gallery talks; tours; merit & purchase awards for Ann Wabash Valley Juried Exhib; exten prog to Vigo County School District; lending of original objects of art to mus; sales gallery shop sells reproductions, T-shirts, sweatshirts, postcards, caps, bags & button

UPLAND

M **TAYLOR UNIVERSITY,** Metcalf Art Gallery, 236 W Reade Ave, Art Dept Upland, IN 46989-1001. Tel 765-998-2751, Ext 5322; Fax 765-998-4680; Email visualarts@tayloru.edu; Web: www.taylor.edu/academics/acaddepts/art; *Chmn* Jonathan Bouw
Open Mon - Fri 8 AM - 5 PM, cl Sun; No admis fee; Estab 2003 as an educational gallery
Income: Financed by educational funding
Exhibitions: Visiting Artists Exhibits
Activities: Gallery talks; schols offered

VALPARAISO

M **VALPARAISO UNIVERSITY,** Brauer Museum of Art, 1709 Chapel Dr, Valparaiso, IN 46383-4520. Tel 219-464-5365; Fax 219-464-5244; Web: www.valpo.edu/brauer-museum-of-art; *Assoc Cur & Registrar* Gloria Ruff; *Dir & Cur* Gregg Hertzlieb
Open Tues, Thurs & Fri 10 AM - 5 PM, Wed 10AM - 8:30 PM, Sat & Sun Noon - 5 PM, cl Mon; No admis fee; Estab 1953 to present significant art to the University community & people of Northwest Indiana; Average Annual Attendance: 10,000
Income: $18,000 (financed by membership)
Purchases: $45,000
Special Subjects: Drawings, Painting-American, Prints, Religious Art
Collections: 19th, 20th & 21st Century American Paintings, Prints & Drawings
Exhibitions: Rotating Exhibits
Activities: Docent training; lects open to pub; gallery talks; tours; individual paintings and original objects of art lent to museums and art centers

VEVAY

M **SWITZERLAND COUNTY HISTORICAL SOCIETY INC,** Life on the Ohio: River History Museum, 208 E Market St, Vevay, IN 47043-1233. Tel 812-427-3560; Email swcomuseums@embarqmail.com; Web: www.switzcomuseums.org; *Exec Dir* Martha Bladen; *Pres* Sundra Whitham; *Treas* Anita Danner; *Secy* Joyce Benbow
Open daily noon - 4PM; No admis fee; Estab 2004 to exhibit & educate the history of Switzerland County as it relates to the historic Ohio River through the steamboat era; River history mus; Average Annual Attendance: 3,000; Mem: 400; dues vary; quarterly meetings
Income: Financed through memberships, donations, grants & volunteer hours
Library Holdings: Book Volumes, Clipping Files, Original Documents, Other Holdings Genealogy Reference Materials, Photographs
Special Subjects: Landscapes, Manuscripts, Maps, Marine Painting, Painting-American, Watercolors, Woodcuts
Collections: Steamboat models, Pilot Wheel, Extensive coll of photos & documents, Historical colls, Distribution & transportation artifacts, Tools & equip for materials, Original paintings & prints with river themes
Exhibitions: Delta Queen, steamboat memorabilia, ongoing
Activities: Tours; mus shop sells books, reproductions, prints

M **Switzerland County Historical Museum,** 210 E Market St, Vevay, IN 47043-1233; 208 E Market St, Vevay, IN 47043-1233. Tel 812-427-3560; Email swcomuseums@embarqmail.com; Web: switzcomuseums.org; *Exec Dir* Martha Bladen; *Pres* Sundra Whitham; *Treas* Anita Danner; *Secy* Joyce Benbow
Open noon - 4 PM; No admis fee; Estab 1925 to unite those people interested in the history of Switzerland County, IN & surrounding region for its protection, preservation & promotion; Average Annual Attendance: 3,000; Mem: 400; dues vary by category; quarterly meetings
Income: Financed by memberships, donations, grants, volunteer hours
Library Holdings: Clipping Files, Manuscripts, Maps, Memorabilia, Original Documents, Other Holdings Genealogy & Family History Files, Periodical Subscriptions, Photographs
Special Subjects: American Indian Art, Archaeology, Architecture, Ceramics, Decorative Arts, Flasks & Bottles, Folk Art, Furniture, Glass, Historical Material, Manuscripts, Maps, Painting-American, Porcelain, Portraits, Pottery, Religious Art, Restorations, Stained Glass, Woodcuts
Collections: Early Swiss settlement, Indian artifacts, Tools & primitive farm equipment, Dolls, military, domestic arts
Activities: Classes for children; quilting prog & exhibits; 3 vis lectrs per yr; concerts; tours; lending of original objects of art to pub library & visitor's ctr; originate traveling exhibs, ann trunk show of IN history to public schools; mus shop sells books, reproductions, prints

WEST LAFAYETTE

M **PURDUE UNIVERSITY GALLERIES,** 1396 Physics Bldg, West Lafayette, IN 47907-2036; 525 Northwestern Ave, Physics Bldg Room 205 Lafayette, IN 47907-2036. Tel 765-494-3061; Fax 765-496-2817; Email gallery@purdue.edu; Web: www.purdue.edu/galleries; *Asst Dir* Michael Atwell; *Dir Gallery* Craig Martin; *Admin Asst* Mary Ann Anderson
Open Mon - Sat 10 AM - 5 PM, Thurs 10 AM - 8 PM, Sun 1 - 5 PM; No admis fee; Estab 1978 to provide aesthetic & educational programs for art students, the university & greater Lafayette community; Galleries are located in three different bldgs to provide approx 5000 sq ft of space for temporary exhibitions; Average Annual Attendance: 15,200
Income: Financed through the university & private & corporate contributions
Special Subjects: American Indian Art, Ceramics, Drawings, Etchings & Engravings, Mexican Art, Oriental Art, Photography, Pre-Columbian Art, Prints, Woodcuts
Collections: American Indian baskets, photographs, Contemporary paintings, prints, sculpture, ceramics, Pre-Columbian textiles, Art of the Americas
Exhibitions: By faculty, students, regionally & nationally prominent artists
Publications: Exhibit catalogs
Activities: Classes for adults & children; lects open to public; 3-34 vis lectrs per yr; gallery talks; competitions with awards, tours; exten program serving professional mus and galleries; book traveling exhibs, 1-2 per yr; originates traveling exhibs

IOWA

AMES

M **IOWA STATE UNIVERSITY,** Brunnier Art Museum, 290 Scheman Bldg, University Museums, Iowa State University Ames, IA 50011. Tel 515-294-3342; Fax 515-294-7070; Email museums@muse.adp.iastate.edu; *Dir* Lynette Pohlman; *Educ Coordr* Matthew DeLay; *Admin Spec* Janet McMathon; *Assoc Cur* Dana Michels; *Develop Secy* Susan Olson; *Cur Historic House* Eleanor Ostendorf; *Educ Asst* Jackie Wilson
Open Tues, Wed & Fri 11 AM - 4 PM, Thurs 11 AM - 4 PM & 5 - 9 PM, Sat & Sun 1 - 4 PM, cl Mon; No admis fee; Estab 1975, to provide a high level of quality, varied & comprehensive exhibits of national & international scope & to develop & expand a permanent decorative arts collection of the western world; Gallery is maintained & comprised of 10,000 sq ft of exhibit space, with flexible space arrangement; Average Annual Attendance: 50,000; Mem: 400 mems; $40 ann dues
Income: $400,000 (financed through state appropriations & grants)
Special Subjects: American Indian Art, Ceramics, Decorative Arts, Dolls, Enamels, Furniture, Glass, Jade, Oriental Art, Porcelain, Posters, Pottery, Prints
Collections: Permanent collection of ceramics, dolls, furniture, glass, ivory, wood, sculpture, fine arts
Publications: Christian Petersen, Sculptor
Activities: Classes for children; docent training; lects open to pub, 10 - 15 vis lectrs per yr; book traveling exhibs, 3-4 per yr; originates traveling exhibs; mus shop sells books, magazines, catalogs, jewelry, dolls, glass & original works

A **OCTAGON CENTER FOR THE ARTS,** 427 Douglas Ave, Ames, IA 50010-6281. Tel 515-232-5331; Fax 515-232-5088; Email rpayne@octagonarts.org; Web: www.octagonarts.org; *Pres* Susan Christensen; *VPres* Mark Peterson; *Treas* Nancy Marion; *Educ Dir* Beth Weninger; *Shop Mgr* Ruth Wiedemeyer; *Exec Dir* Kathy Stevens; *Mktg Dir* Amy Streich; *Cur* Heather Straszheim
Open Tues - Sat 10 AM - 5 PM, Sun 2 - 5 PM; Admis suggested donation or contribution, family (up to five people) $3, individual $2; Estab 1966 to provide year-round classes for all ages; exhibitions of the work of outstanding artists local, regional & worldwide & also special programs in the visual & performing arts; Average Annual Attendance: 33,000; Mem: 365, open to anyone interested in supporting or participating in the arts; dues $15-$500 & up; annual meeting in May; individual $35, household $50, supporter $100, founders $300 & up
Income: $375,000 (financed by mem, city and state appropriations, class fees and fund raising)
Collections: Feinberg Collection of Masks from Around the World
Exhibitions: Octagon Arts Festival-art festival of over 125 Midwest artists; clay, fiber, glass, wood exhibition
Publications: Exhibition catalogs; newsletter, quarterly
Activities: Classes in the arts for adults & children; special classes for senior citizens & physically & emotionally challenged; outreach progs; lects open to pub, 5-8 vis lectrs per yr; gallery talks; tours; competitions with awards; scholarships offered; book traveling exhibs; mus shop sells books, original art, prints & original fine crafts

ANAMOSA

A **PAINT 'N PALETTE CLUB,** Grant Wood Memorial Park & Gallery, 17314 Hwy 64, Anamosa, IA 52205; 673 Bolton Manor Rd, Springville, IA 52336-9733. Tel 319-462-2680; Email lshaffer@netins.net; *Cur* Wilbur Evarts
Open June 1 - Oct 15; Sun 1 - 4 PM; other times for groups & organizations; No admis fee (donations accepted); Estab 1955 to maintain Antioch School, the school attended by a famous Iowa artist from 1897-1901 Grant Wood; school restored to 1900 vintage; to provide a studio & gallery for local artists & for pub enjoyment. A log cabin art gallery on the grounds of the Grant Wood Memorial Park contains the work of some local & vis artists; Showcases works by local outsider artists. Most subject matter is rural, & this regionalist theme is echoed through natural surroundings; Average Annual Attendance: 3,000; Mem: 32, members must have art experience; dues $15
Income: Financed by dues and donations
Library Holdings: Audio Tapes, Maps, Memorabilia, Original Art Works, Pamphlets, Prints
Special Subjects: Folk Art, Landscapes, Painting-American, Posters

Collections: Prints of Grant Wood, Iowa's most famous artist, original amateur art, arts and crafts, postcards, memorabilia
Exhibitions: Special exhibits throughout the season; Annual Art Show; additional exhib 2nd Sun in Jun, annually; Annual Grant Wood Art Festival 2nd Sun June
Publications: Bulletin, monthly
Activities: Occasional classes for adults; summer instruction by professional painter; lects open to public, 1-2 vis lectrs per year; tours; competitions; films; lending of original objects of art; sales shop sells prints, original art, prints, reproductions, postcards & commemorative coins

ARNOLDS PARK

M **IOWA GREAT LAKES MARITIME MUSEUM,** 243 W Broadway, Arnolds Park, IA 51360; PO Box 609, Arnolds Park, IA 51331-0609. Tel 712-332-5264; Fax 712-332-2186; Email mary@arnoldspark.com; Web: www.okobojimuseum.org; *CEO & Dir* Steven R Anderson; *Chmn* Rick Johnson; *Cur* Mary Kennedy
Open daily 9 AM - 9 PM; cl Easter, Thanksgiving & Christmas; No admis fee, donations accepted; Estab 1987; Pvt nonprofit org; 6000 sq ft exhib space; theater capacity 150; wheelchair available; FT paid 2, FT volunteers 1, PT vols 12. Maritime & antique mus that provides a look at the history of the Iowa Great Lakes region; Average Annual Attendance: 75,000; Mem: dues Lifetime $1000, Benefactor $100, Captain $50, Gen $25
Library Holdings: Book Volumes (150) local history, Periodical Subscriptions (1500) wooden boat magazines
Collections: Artifacts; recreational artifacts; tools & equip for materials; furnishings; personal artifacts; photographs, Wooden boats from the Iowa Great Lakes area, steamships, sand pales, fishing lures & paddlefish
Publications: Biannual newsletter: The Steam Whistle
Activities: Formal educ for adults; lects; guided tours

BELMOND

M **JENISON-MEACHAM MEMORIAL ART CENTER & MUSEUM,** 1179 Taylor Ave, Belmond, IA 50421-7568. Tel 641-444-3557; 444-4635

BURLINGTON

A **ART GUILD OF BURLINGTON,** Art Center of Burlington, 301 Jefferson St, Burlington, IA 52601-5333. Tel 319-754-8069; Fax 319-754-4731; Email tammy@artcenterofburlington.com; Web: www.artcenterofburlington.com; *Pres Bd Dirs* Rachel Lindeen; *Exec Dir* Tammy McCoy; *Communs Dir* Hillaurie Fritz-Bonar; *Program Coordinator* Nicole Kamrath
Open Mon - Wed 10 AM - 5 PM, Thurs& Fri 10 AM - 8 PM, Sat 10 AM - 4 PM; No admis fee; Estab 1966 with the mission enhance the arts through educ exhibs & performance progs in the Burlington area; Historic Downtown bldg; Average Annual Attendance: 8,000; Mem: 450; dues benefactor $1,000, down to student $15
Income: Financed by mem & donations
Library Holdings: Book Volumes, Video Tapes
Exhibitions: Exhibitions of regional professional artists
Publications: Monthly newsletter
Activities: Classes for adults, teens & children; docent training; special workshops; lects open to public; gallery talks; tours; Juried Art Show; gallery exhibits; sales shop sells original art, prints

CEDAR FALLS

M **CITY OF CEDAR FALLS, IOWA,** James & Meryl Hearst Center for the Arts & Sculpture Garden, 304 W Seerley Blvd, Cedar Falls, IA 50613-4050. Tel 319-273-8641; Fax 319-273-8659; Email Martin.Arthur@cedarfalls.com; Web: www.thehearst.org; *Supervisor* Martin Arthur; *Educ Coordr* Olivia Randolph; *Cur, Registrar* Emily Drennan; *Sr Svcs Coordr* Gail LeFlore
Open Tues - Fri 9 AM - 5 PM, Tues & Thurs evenings 5 - 9 PM, Sat & Sun 1 - 4 PM; No admis fee; Estab 1989; Municipal arts center serving the Cedar Valley in Iowa; Average Annual Attendance: 45,000; Mem: 275; dues $35 - $1,000, Friends of the Hearst req; annual meeting in June
Income: $500,000 (financed by city appropriation, individual contributions, program fees & grants)
Library Holdings: Clipping Files, Exhibition Catalogs, Manuscripts, Memorabilia, Original Art Works, Original Documents, Other Holdings, Sculpture
Special Subjects: Ceramics, Drawings, Etchings & Engravings, Graphics, Landscapes, Manuscripts, Painting-American, Photography, Portraits, Posters, Pottery, Prints, Reproductions, Sculpture, Woodcuts
Collections: Book by Creative Education, complete set of illustrations for Legend of Sleepy Hollow, Gary Kelley Illustrations, children's book illustration, A number of Animals illustrations by Chris Wormell, cover of The Nutcracker by the artist Roberto Innocenti, public art in community, Hearst Sculpture Garden, permanent coll, Mid-western artists coll
Exhibitions: Developing Expressions; First 50; 14 Exhibits per year
Publications: Quarterly class brochure; This Month at the Hearst; spec collection & membership brochures, annual
Activities: Classes for adults & children;; lects open to pub, 4 vis lectrs per yr; concert; gallery talks;r poetry readings; contemporary music series; chamber music series; sponsoring of competitions; schols & fellowships offered; exten dept serves 30 mile radius; individual paintings & original objects of art lent to art organizations & mus; book traveling exhibs every 1.5 yrs; originate traveling exhibs to regional art mus; mus shop sells books, original art, reproductions, prints & gen merchandise related to coll

M **UNIVERSITY OF NORTHERN IOWA,** UNI Gallery of Art, 1601 W 27th St, Cedar Falls, IA 50614-0362. Tel 319-273-2077; Fax 319-273-7333; Email GalleryOfArt@uni.edu; Web: www.uni.edu/art/gallery.html; *Dir* Darrell Taylor
Open Mon - Thurs 10 AM - 7 PM, Fri - Sat noon - 5 PM; also by appointment; No admis fee; Estab 1978 to bring to the University & the community at large the finest quality of art from all over the world; The 5,000 sq ft gallery is divided into five separate exhibition rooms; high security mus space with climate control & a highly flexible light system; the Gallery adjoins a pub reception space & a 144 seat auditorium; the facility also has a newly renovated coll storage facility, a work shop, a general storage room & a fully accessible loading dock; Average Annual Attendance: 12,000
Income: Financed by state appropriation
Purchases: 20th century art work
Library Holdings: DVDs, Exhibition Catalogs, Original Art Works, Photographs, Prints, Sculpture
Special Subjects: Painting-American, Painting-European
Collections: 20th century American & European Art
Exhibitions: 8 rotating & 8 mini-exhibs per yr
Publications: Exhibition catalogs
Activities: Volunteer training; lects open to public, 5 vis lectrs per year; performances; gallery talks; tours; competitions; ann juried student art exhib Merit & Purchase Awards; competition with awards; individual paintings & original objects of art lent to comparable orgs & institutions; traveling exhibs

L **Fine & Performing Arts Collection Rod Library,** 1227 W 27th St, Cedar Falls, IA 50613-3675. Tel 319-273-6252; Fax 319-273-2913; Web: www.library.uni.edu/collections/fine-performing-arts; *Head Colls & Mus* Kate Martin; *Fine & performing Arts* Angela Pratesi; *Fine & Performing Arts* Julie Ann Beddow; *Dean of Library Svcs* Christopher Cox
Open Mon - Thurs 7:30 AM - 10:50 PM, Fri 7:30 AM - 5 PM, Sat noon - 5PM, Sun noon-10:50 PM; No admis fee; Main Library estab 1964, additions 1975 & 1995; to serve art & music patrons; Circ 3,200; For lending & reference; Average Annual Attendance: 9,300; Mem: 12,000 students
Income: Financed by state
Purchases: $18,000
Library Holdings: Audio Tapes, Book Volumes, Cassettes, Clipping Files, Compact Disks, DVDs, Exhibition Catalogs, Framed Reproductions, Original Art Works, Other Holdings, Pamphlets, Periodical Subscriptions, Photographs, Prints, Records, Reproductions, Sculpture, Video Tapes
Special Subjects: Art History, Textiles
Exhibitions: Continual Exhibs
Activities: Educ prog; acad; lects open to pub; number of vis lectrs per yr vary; tours; sponsoring of competitions

CEDAR RAPIDS

M **AFRICAN AMERICAN MUSEUM OF IOWA,** 55 12th Ave SE, Cedar Rapids, IA 52401. Tel 319-862-2101; Fax 319-862-2105; Email information@blackiowa.org; Web: www.blackiowa.org; *Dir* Michael Kates; *Cur* Brianna Wright; *Develop Dir* Grant Stevens; *Educ Dir* Michelle Poe; *Facilities Coordr* Katherine Smith
Open Mon - Sat 10 AM - 4 PM; Admis adults $4, children, youth & students $3; Estab 1994; Mus with permanent & changing exhibits about Iowa's rich African American heritage.; Average Annual Attendance: 54,000; Mem: Platinum $400+, Golden $200-$399, Century $100-$199, Family $50-$99, Indiv $35-$49, Student & Seniors $25-$34
Income: Grants, donations, mems, endowment & rentals
Library Holdings: Book Volumes 1,500, Clipping Files, Compact Disks, DVDs, Manuscripts, Original Documents, Periodical Subscriptions 200, Photographs, Prints
Special Subjects: African Art, Afro-American Art, Dioramas, Historical Material, Manuscripts, Maps
Collections: African-Americans in Iowa; also includes an archive
Publications: Griot, quarterly newsletter; annual report
Activities: Formal educ progs for adults & children; docent prog; guided tours; lects; loan exhibs; participatory, temp & traveling exhibs; Ann Events: Juneteenth, Banquet, Kwanzaa Journey to Freedom; History Makers Gala; exten prog for all of Iowa; mus shop sells books, prints & objects

M **CEDAR RAPIDS MUSEUM OF ART,** 410 Third Ave SE, Cedar Rapids, IA 52401. Tel 319-366-7503; Fax 319-366-4111; Email info@crma.org; Web: www.crma.org; *Exec Dir* Sean Ulmer; *Develop* Joanne Wzontek; *Dir Opers* Deanna Clemens Pedersen; *Assoc Cur* Kate Kunau; *Preparator* Judy Frauenholtz; *Educ Dir* Erin Thomas; *Registrar* Jaci Falco; *Communs Coordr* Lori Tofanelli; *Bldg Suprv* Carlis Faurot; *Retail & Vis Svcs Mgr* Lou Wendel
Open Tues, Wed, Fri, Sun noon - 4 PM, Thurs noon - 8 PM, Sat 10 AM - 4 PM; Admis adults $7, sr citizens $6, children 6-18 $3, AAM, CRMA, NARM indiv mems & children under 5 free; Estab 1895; First & second floors maintain changing exhibits & the Permanent Collection; Average Annual Attendance: 38,000; Mem: 1000; dues Turner soc $1000, Cone Wood soc $500, benefactor $250, patron $125, family $60, individual $40, students & senior citizens $30, educator $30
Income: Financed by endowment, mem & revenues
Library Holdings: Book Volumes, Exhibition Catalogs
Special Subjects: American Western Art, Antiquities-Roman, Ceramics, Coins & Medals, Decorative Arts, Drawings, Eskimo Art, Landscapes, Painting-American, Photography, Portraits, Pottery, Prints, Sculpture, Watercolors, Afro-American Art, American Indian Art
Collections: Coll of artworks by Grant Wood, Marvin Cone & Mauricio Lasansky, print coll, Roman antiquities, Midwestern art
Exhibitions: Midwestern Visions: Grant Wood, Marvin Cone and Beyond (permanent exhib); Art in Roman Life (permanent exhib); Mauricio Lasansky: Master Printmaker (permanent exhib)
Activities: Classes for adults & children; docent training; lects open to pub; gallery talks; tours; individual paintings & original objects of art lent to other mus; originate traveling exhibs; mus shop sells books, original art, reproductions, prints; Grant Wood Studio & Visitor Ctr

L **Herbert S Stamats Library**, 410 Third Ave SE, Cedar Rapids, IA 52401. Tel 319-366-7503; Fax 319-366-4111; Email info@crma.org; Web: www.crma.org
Open Tues, Wed, Fri & Sun noon - 4 PM, Thurs noon - 8 PM, Sat 10 AM - 4 PM; Admis adults $5, seniors & college students $4, children 18 & under & mems free; Estab Art Assn 1905; first and second floors of mus maintain permanent &

changing exhib; Average Annual Attendance: 30,000; Mem: 700; dues - family $60, individual $40, senior/student $30, NARM mems free
Income: endowment, grants & memberships
Library Holdings: Book Volumes 3000, Cassettes, Filmstrips
Special Subjects: Art Education, Art History, Antiquities-Roman, Ceramics, Painting-American, Prints
Collections: Grant Wood, Marvin Cone
Publications: Clary Illian: A Potter's Potter
Activities: Classes for adults & children; docent training; lects open to pub; 18-22 vis lectrs per yr; concerts; gallery talks; tours; mus shop sells books, original art, reproductions, prints

M **COE COLLEGE,** Eaton-Buchan Gallery & Marvin Cone Gallery, 1220 First Ave NE, Cedar Rapids, IA 52402. Tel 319-399-8217; Fax 319-399-8557; Email dchance@coe.edu; Web: www.coe.edu; *Chmn Art Dept* John Beckelman; *Gallery Dir* Delores Chance
Open daily 3 - 5 PM; No admis fee; Estab 1942 to exhibit traveling exhibitions & local exhibits; Two galleries, both 60 x 18 ft with 125 running ft of exhibit space & 430 works on permanent exhibition; Average Annual Attendance: 5,000
Income: $7,090 (financed through college)
Collections: Coe Collection of art works, Marvin Cone Collection, Hinkhouse Collection of contemporary art, Grant Wood Collection, Works of nearly 300 artists spanning several centuries & 5 continents, Conger Metcalf Collection of Paintings
Exhibitions: Circulating exhibits; one-person & group shows of regional nature
Publications: Exhibition brochures, 8-10 per year
Activities: Lects open to public, 5-6 vis lectrs per yr; gallery talks; tours; competitions; individual paintings & original objects of art lent to colleges & local galleries; lending collection contains original art work, original prints, paintings, sculpture & slides; originates traveling exhibs

M **Stewart Memorial Library & Gallery**, 1220 First Ave NE, Cedar Rapids, IA 52402-5092. Tel 319-399-8023; 8585; Fax 319-399-8019; Email jjack@coe.edu; Web: www.coe.edu; *Dir Library Svcs* Jill Jack
Open Mon - Thurs 8 AM - midnight, Fri 8 AM - 6 PM, Sat 9 AM - 6 PM, Sun 1 PM - 12 AM; June - Aug Mon - Fri 8 AM - 4 PM; Grant Wood, Marvin Cone, Conger Metcalf galleries; various artists
Collections: 200 permanent coll works

M **MOUNT MERCY UNIVERSITY,** White Gallery, 1330 Elmhurst Dr NE, Cedar Rapids, IA 52402-4797. Tel 319-363-8213; Fax 319-363-5270; Email vanallen.david@mcleodusa.net; *Dir* Andrew Castro
Open Mon - Thurs 7 AM - 9 PM; No admis fee; Estab 1970 to show work by a variety of fine artists. The shows are used by the art department as teaching aids. They provide cultural exposure to the entire community; One room 22 x 30 ft; two walls are glass overlooking a small courtyard; Average Annual Attendance: 1,000
Income: Financed through the college
Purchases: $300
Collections: Small collection of prints & paintings
Exhibitions: Annual High School Art Exhibit; Senior Thesis Exhibit
Publications: Reviews in Fiber Arts; American Craft & Ceramics Monthly
Activities: Classes for adults; dramatic progs; lects open to pub; gallery talks; competitions with awards; 3 vis lectrs per yr; scholarships; lending original objects of art: campus locations; sales shop: original art, prints, Mexican folk art

L **Library**, 1330 Elmhurst Dr NE, Art Dept Cedar Rapids, IA 52402-4797. Tel 319-363-8213, Ext 244; Fax 319-363-9060; Email library@mtmercy.edu; Web: www.mtmercy.edu; *Dir Lib Srvs* Marilyn Murphy
Open Mon-Thurs 8 AM - midnight, Fri 8 AM - 6 PM, Sat 9 AM - 5 PM, Sun 1 PM - midnight; No admis fee; Estab 1928; Circ 35,000; Ref library & circ
Income: By the college
Library Holdings: Audio Tapes, Book Volumes 2000, Cards, Cassettes, Exhibition Catalogs, Fiche, Filmstrips, Framed Reproductions, Kodachrome Transparencies, Lantern Slides, Micro Print, Motion Pictures, Original Art Works, Pamphlets, Periodical Subscriptions 38, Photographs, Prints, Records, Reels, Reproductions, Sculpture, Slides, Video Tapes

CHARLES CITY

M **CHARLES CITY ARTS CENTER,** 301 N Jackson St, Charles City, IA 50616-2006. Tel 641-228-6284; Email charlescityarts@gmail.com; Web: www.charlescityarts.org; *Dir* Jacqueline Davidson
Open Wed - Fri 1 PM - 6 PM, Sat 10 AM - 2 PM; No admis fee; Mem: Mem $25-$1,000 & up
Income: Financed by mem, grants, private donations & endowment fund
Collections: Regional artwork
Exhibitions: Monthly exhibits
Activities: Educ progs; classes for adults & children; art programming; workshops; performance art; cultural events

M **CHARLES CITY LIBRARY,** Mooney Art Collection, 106 Milwaukee Mall, Charles City, IA 50616. Tel 641-257-6319; Fax 641-257-6325; Email director@charles-city.lib.ia.us; Web: www.charles-city.lib.ia.us/artgal; *Library Dir* Kim Jones
Open Mon - Thurs 10 AM - 8 PM, Fri 10 AM - 5 PM, Sat 1 PM - 5 PM; No admis fee; Estab 1994 to bring collection to the public
Special Subjects: Prints
Collections: 77 classic art prints
Exhibitions: Permanent exhibit

CLEAR LAKE

M **CLEAR LAKE ARTS CENTER,** 17 S 4th St, Clear Lake, IA 50428. Tel 641-357-1998; Fax 641-357-0547; Email clac@cltel.net; Web: www.clartscenter.com; *Exec Dir* Paual Chenchar Hanus, MFA; *Gift Shop Mgr* Renae Quandt; *Office Mgr* Shane Treslan; *Educ Coordr* Linda Dlouhy
Open Tues - Sat 10 AM - 5 PM; No admis fee; Estab 1977 to promote interest in visual, literary & performing arts; Mem: dues $25-$1,000
Special Subjects: Photography, Drawings, Mixed Media, Ceramics
Collections: Photography, drawings, paintings, mixed media & ceramics
Exhibitions: Temporary exhibits
Activities: Classes for adults & children; mus shop sells books, original art

CLINTON

M **CLINTON ART ASSOCIATION,** River Arts Center, 229 Fifth Ave S, Clinton, IA 52733-0132. Tel 563-243-3300, 242-8055; Email mthayes9@msn.com; Web: www.clintonarts.com; *Pres* Ronald Blatchley; *VPres & Publicity* Martha Hayes; *Treas* Nancy Bergess
Open Wed - Sun 1 - 4 PM, cl Christmas & New Year; No admis fee; Estab 1968 to bring visual art to the community; Art gallery, classrooms, pottery studio, permanent coll, community theater in downtown location; Average Annual Attendance: 16,000; Mem: 420; dues single membership $30; annual meeting
Income: Financed by mem & through grants from the Iowa Arts Council
Special Subjects: Painting-American, Photography, Etchings & Engravings, Sculpture, Prints, Pottery, Woodcarvings, Woodcuts, Glass
Collections: Painting (watercolor, oil, acrylic, pastel), beaded loin cloth, photographs, lithograph, engraving, sculptures, etching, prints, pottery, fabric, pencil, wood, slate, Ektaflex Color Printmaking System, glass, ink, lucite, rugs, woodcarving
Exhibitions: Rotating exhibits
Publications: Newsletter, quarterly
Activities: Classes for adults & children in watercolor, oil, drawing, photography & pottery making; docent training; dramatic progs & other; lect open to public; 2-3 vis lectrs per yr; gallery talks; tours; schols; lending collection contains books; sales shop sells original art, prints & stationery, reproductions

CORNING

M **CORNING CENTER FOR THE FINE ARTS,** 706 Davis Ave, Corning, IA 50841-1451. Tel 641-322-4549; Web: www.corningfinearts.com
Open Wed - Fri 10 AM - 5 PM, Sat 10 AM - 4 PM; No admis fee; Estab to provide community & tourists with an artistic cultural experience; 1,500 sq ft
Collections: Fine art & artisan crafted items
Exhibitions: Temporary exhibits
Activities: Educ progs; classes for adults & children; artist residencies

DAVENPORT

M **FIGGE ART MUSEUM,** 225 W 2nd St, Davenport, IA 52801-1804. Tel 563-326-7804; Fax 563-326-7876; Email vbenson@figgeartmuseum.org; Web: www.figgeartmuseum.org; *Exec Dir* Tim Schiffer; *Dir Educ* Melissa Mohr; *Dir Develop* Raelene Pullen; *Annual Giving Coord* Tessa Pozzi; *Outreach Coordr* Laura Wriedt
Open Tues - Sat 10 AM - 5 PM, Thurs 10 AM - 9 PM, Sun noon - 5 PM, cl Mon & holidays; Admis adults $7, seniors & students with ID $6, children ages 4-12 $4, mems free; Estab 1925 as a mus of art & custodian pub collection & an educ center for the visual arts, renamed in 1963, relocated 2003, reopened 2005; Consists of three levels including a spacious main gallery, exhibition area & two additional floors with galleries; six multipurpose art studios & ceramic gallery, studio workshop & an outdoor studio-plaza on the lower level; 114,000 sq ft facility designed by David Chipperfield; Average Annual Attendance: 100,000; Mem: 600; dues household $40 & up
Income: $900,000 (financed by private & city appropriation)
Special Subjects: Painting-American, Painting-British, Painting-European, Painting-French, Painting-German, Oriental Art, Mexican Art
Collections: American Coll: 19th & 20th c works, Midwest Regionalist Coll incl Grant Wood, Thomas Hart Benton, John Steuart Curry, European Coll, Mexican Colonial Coll, Haitian Coll
Exhibitions: Beverly Pepper: The Moline Makers; Byron Burford; Mississippi Corridor; Grandma Moses; Selections: The Union League of Chicago Collection; Thomas Eakins (photographs); Joseph Sheppard; Mauricio Lasansky; Sol LeWitt; Stephen Antonakos - Neons; Frederic Carder: Portrait of a Glassmaker; Paul Brach Retrospective; David Hockney (photographs); Rudie (holograms); McMichael Canadian Collection; Kassebaum Medieval & Renaissance Ceramics; Collected Masterworks: The International Collections of the Davenport Museum of Art; Mexico Nueve; A Different War: Vietnam In Art; Judaica: Paintings by Nathan Hilu & Ceramics by Robert Lipnick; Faith Ringgold: 25 Year Survey
Publications: Quarterly newsletter; biennial report; Focus 1: Michael Boyd - Paintings from the 1980s; Focus 2: Photo Image League - Individual Vision/ Collective Support; Focus 3: A Sense of Wonder - The Art of Haiti; Focus 4: Artists Who Teach: Building our Future; Haitian Art: The Legend & Legacy of the Naive Tradition; Three Decades of Midwestern Photography, 1960 - 1990
Activities: Classes for adults, teens, children & families; docent training; lects open to pub; concerts; gallery talks; tours; competitions with prizes; scholarships & fels offered; book traveling exhibs organized & circulated; originate traveling exhibs; mus shop sells books, posters, notecards, t-shirts, jewelry, scarves, original art, gifts & other items; Arterarium environmental installation

L **Art Reference Library**, 225 W 2nd St, Davenport, IA 52801-1804. Tel 563-326-7804; Fax 563-326-7876; Web: www.figgeartmuseum.org; *Cur* Michelle Robinson; *Dir Educ* Ann Marie Hayes
Open Tues - Sat 10 AM - 5 PM, Sun 1 - 5 PM, cl Mon; Admis adults $7, seniors & students $6, children under 12 $4; mus mem free; Estab 1925 as first municipal art mus in Iowa; Circ non-circulating library; Open for reference; Average Annual Attendance: 50,000; Mem: $65 household; $35 individuals; $25 teachers
Library Holdings: Auction Catalogs, Book Volumes 6000, Kodachrome Transparencies, Periodical Subscriptions 20, Video Tapes
Special Subjects: American Western Art, Decorative Arts, Drawings, Etchings & Engravings, Landscapes, Mexican Art, Mixed Media, Painting-American, Painting-Dutch, Painting-European, Painting-Flemish, Painting-French, Painting-German, Painting-Italian, Photography, Portraits, Religious Art, Sculpture, Stained Glass, Silver, Woodcuts

Collections: 3,500 works of art (American, European, Haitian & Mexican-Colonial)
Exhibitions: Treasures of Mexican Colonial Painting, Marcus Burlee; Tracing the Spirit: Ethnographic Essays on Haitian Art, Karen McCarthy Brown; Grant Wood: An American Master Revealed
Activities: Classes for adults & children; docent training; continuing education classes for teachers; lects open to pub; 12 vis lectrs per yr; gallery talks; tours; sponsored competitions with awards; schol offered; originates traveling exhibs to art mus; mus shop sells books, decorative art, furniture, reproductions & gift items related to collections & traveling exhibs

M **PUTNAM MUSEUM OF HISTORY AND NATURAL SCIENCE,** 1717 W 12th St, Davenport, IA 52804-3597. Tel 563-324-1933; Fax 563-324-6638; Email museum@putnam.org; Web: www.putnam.org; *Pres & CEO* Kimberly Findlay; *Chief Cur* Eunice Schlichting; *IMAX Theater Mgr* Dean K Fich; *Dir Visitor Svcs* Beth Knaack; *Exhibits Mgr* Michael Murphy; *Dir Mktg* Lori Arquello; *Dir Finance* Kim Nickels; *Cur Natural Science* Christine Chandler; *Dir Educ* Donna Murray; *Mus Shop Mgr* Sue Folwell; *Cur Hist & Anthropology* Christina Kastell
Open Mon - Sat 10AM-5PM, Sun noon-5PM; coll by appt; Admis adults $6, sr citizens $5, ages 3-12 $4, members & children 2 & under free; Estab 1867 as Davenport Academy of Natural Sciences; To provide educational & enriching experiences through interpretive exhibits & mus programming; Average Annual Attendance: 170,000
Income: $3,000,000 (financed by contributions, grants, endowments, mem & earned income)
Library Holdings: Book Volumes 25,000, Lantern Slides, Motion Pictures, Original Art Works, Photographs, Prints, Records
Special Subjects: Antiquities-Egyptian, Antiquities-Etruscan, Antiquities-Greek, Antiquities-Oriental, Antiquities-Persian, Antiquities-Roman, Archaeology, Asian Art, Carpets & Rugs, Ceramics, Coins & Medals, Costumes, Decorative Arts, Dolls, Drawings, Embroidery, Furniture, Glass, Historical Material, Manuscripts, Maps, Prints, Silver, Textiles, Watercolors
Collections: Natural history, American Indian, pre-Columbian, anthropology, arts of Asia, Near & Middle East, Africa, Oceanic, botany, ethnology, paleontology, decorative arts, local history
Exhibitions: Permanent & changing exhibition programs
Activities: Formally organized educ progs for children & adults; films; lects; gallery talks; guided tours; IMAX Theatre presentations; individual paintings & original objects of art lent to mus & educational organizations for special exhibs only; book traveling exhibs 6 per yr; originate traveling exhibs; mus store sells books, original art, prints, miscellaneous collections-related merchandise for children & adults

DECORAH

M **LUTHER COLLEGE,** Fine Arts Collection, 700 College Dr, Decorah, IA 52101-1041. Tel 563-387-1300; Fax 563-387-1132; Email ellika03@luther.edu; *Gallery Coordr* David Kamm; *Cur* Kate Elliott
Open Sept - June 8 AM - 5 PM; No admis fee; Estab 1900; Five galleries on campus; Average Annual Attendance: 10,000
Income: $4000
Special Subjects: American Western Art, Antiquities-Greek, Antiquities-Roman, Bronzes, Carpets & Rugs, Ceramics, Drawings, Enamels, Eskimo Art, Etchings & Engravings, Painting-American, Painting-Scandinavian, Portraits, Posters, Pottery, Pre-Columbian Art, Primitive art, Religious Art, Sculpture, Southwestern Art, Watercolors, Woodcarvings, Woodcuts, Landscapes, Photography, Prints
Collections: Gerhard Marcks Collection (drawings, prints & sculpture), Marguerite Wildenhain Collection (drawings & pottery), Inuit sculpture, pre-Columbian pottery, Scandinavian immigrant painting, contemporary & historical Prints
Publications: Occasional catalogs & brochures
Activities: Lect open to public; gallery talks; lending collection contains individual paintings & original objects of art; book traveling exhibitions 12 per year

M **VESTERHEIM NORWEGIAN-AMERICAN MUSEUM,** 523 W Water St, Decorah, IA 52101; PO Box 379, Decorah, IA 52101-0379. Tel 563-382-9681; Fax 563-382-8828; Email info@vesterheim.org; Web: vesterheim.org; *Chief Cur* Lauran Gilbertson; *Exec Dir* Chris Johnson; *Dir Retail Svcs* Ken Koop; *Ed* Charlie Langton; *Registrar & Librn* Jennifer Kovarik; *Dir Admin* Marcia McKelvey; *Develop Dir* Shawna Wagner; *Educ Specialist-Folk Art* Darlene Fossum Martin; *Chair* Lorie Reins Schweer; *Bookkeeper* Kathy Wilbur; *Mem Mgr* Peggy Sersland; *Vol Coordr* Martha Griesheimer
Open May-Oct daily 9 AM- 5 PM, Nov-Apr daily 10 AM to 4 PM; Admis adults $10, seniors $8, youth $5, members free; Estab 1877, Vesterheim embodies the living heritage of Norwegian immigrants to America. Sharing this cultural legacy can inspire people of all backgrounds to celebrate tradition; Main Building with four floors of exhib, plus numerous historic buildings including two from Norway; Average Annual Attendance: 13,000; Mem: 5600; dues basic mem $35
Income: $1,800,000 (financed by endowment, mem, donations, admis, sales)
Library Holdings: Auction Catalogs 10, Audio Tapes 10, Book Volumes, CD-ROMs 5, Cassettes 25, Clipping Files, DVDs 10, Exhibition Catalogs, Filmstrips, Lantern Slides, Manuscripts, Maps, Memorabilia, Original Art Works 2,200, Original Documents, Pamphlets, Periodical Subscriptions 70, Photographs, Prints, Records, Reels, Reproductions, Sculpture, Video Tapes 100
Special Subjects: Architecture, Carpets & Rugs, Ceramics, Coins & Medals, Costumes, Crafts, Decorative Arts, Dolls, Drawings, Embroidery, Etchings & Engravings, Flasks & Bottles, Folk Art, Furniture, Glass, Historical Material, Jewelry, Laces, Landscapes, Leather, Manuscripts, Maps, Marine Painting, Metalwork, Miniatures, Painting-American, Painting-Scandinavian, Period Rooms, Period Rooms, Pewter, Photography, Photography, Porcelain, Porcelain, Portraits, Portraits, Pottery, Prints, Religious Art, Reproductions, Sculpture, Silver, Tapestries, Textiles, Watercolors, Woodcarvings, Woodcuts
Collections: folk art; furnishings; textiles; machinery; tools; historic buildings; reference & special collections libraries; archives
Exhibitions: exhibitions rotate, please check exhibition schedule on museum's website
Publications: Vesterheim Magazine, semi annual; Time Honored Norwegian Recipes; Rosemaling Letter, 3 times per yr; Vesterheim: Samplings from the Collection; Rosemaler's Recipes Cookbook; Ole Goes to War: Men from Norway Who Fought in America's Civil War; Marking Time: The Primstav Murals of Sigmund Aarseth
Activities: Educ prog; classes for adults; children's educ prog; docent training; lects open to pub; gallery talks; tours; sponsoring of competitions; Vesterheim gold medal award; Silos & Smokestacks-People's Choice for "Site of the Year" National Heritage Area (SSNHA); periodic book traveling exhibs; originate traveling exhibs for cultural institutions; mus shop sells art & craft supplies, books, original art, prints, related gift items, woodenware, artist supplies for rosemaling & woodworking

DES MOINES

M **EDMUNDSON ART FOUNDATION, INC,** Des Moines Art Center, 4700 Grand Ave, Des Moines, IA 50312-2002. Tel 515-277-4405; Web: www.desmoinesartcenter.org; *Pres Board Trustees* James Wallace; *Dir* Jeff Fleming; *Sr Cur* Alison Ferris; *Cur* Laura Burkhalter; *Dir Develop* Tiffany Nagel Spinner; *Dir Mem Experiences* Debra Kurtz; *Dir Educ* Jull Featherstone; *Retail Opers Dir* Sarah Jane Shimasaki
Open Tues - Wed & Fri 11 AM - 4 PM, Thurs 11 AM - 9 PM, Sat 10 AM - 4 PM, Sun Noon - 4 PM, cl Independence Day, Thanksgiving, Christmas, New Year's Eve & Day; No admis fee; Estab 1948 for the purpose of displaying, conserving & interpreting art; Large sculpture galleries in I M Pei-designed addition; the main gallery covers 36 x 117 ft area. New Meier wing, opened 1985, increased space for exhibitions 50 percent
Income: $4,000,000 (financed by endowment, mem, gifts, grants, shop sales, tuition & state appropriation)
Library Holdings: Auction Catalogs, Book Volumes, CD-ROMs, Clipping Files, Exhibition Catalogs, Original Documents, Periodical Subscriptions, Slides
Special Subjects: African Art, Graphics, Painting-American, Sculpture
Collections: African art, graphics, American & European sculpture & painting of the past 200 years
Publications: Bulletin, bimonthly; catalogs of exhibitions
Activities: Classes for adults & children; docent training; lects open to pub, 6 vis lectrs per yr; concerts; gallery talks; tours; competitions; traveling exhibs organized & circulated; mus shop sells books, original art, prints & postcards

L **Des Moines Art Center Library,** 4700 Grand Ave, Des Moines, IA 50312-2099. Tel 515-277-4405; Web: www.desmoinesartcenter.org
Open by appointment only; Estab 1948 for research of permanent collection, acquisitions, exhibition preparation, class preparation & lectures; Open to the public for reference by appointment
Library Holdings: Auction Catalogs, Book Volumes 14,700, CD-ROMs, Clipping Files, Exhibition Catalogs, Original Documents, Periodical Subscriptions 70, Slides

M **POLK COUNTY HERITAGE GALLERY,** Heritage Art Gallery, Polk County Office Bldg, 111 Court Ave Des Moines, IA 50309-2218. Tel 515-286-2242; Email pcheritagegallery@gmail.com; Web: polkcountyheritagegallery.org
Open Mon - Fri 11 AM - 4:30 PM; No admis fee; Estab 1980; exhib space for visual art in the Polk County office building built in 1908 & on the register of historic places; Average Annual Attendance: 4,000
Exhibitions: Greater Des Moines Exhibited (annually, winter); Iowa Exhibited (annually, spring)
Activities: Cash awards for two annual competitions

L **PUBLIC LIBRARY OF DES MOINES,** Central Library Information Services, 1000 Grand Ave, Des Moines, IA 50309-2380. Tel 515-283-4152, Ext 3; Email reference@dmpl.org; Web: www.desmoineslibrary.com; *Dir* Greg Head; *Deputy Dir* Linda Roe; *Mgr* Sarah Scholten
Open Sept - May Mon-Wed 9 AM - 8 PM, Thurs - Fri 9 AM - 6 PM, Sun 1 PM - 5 PM; June - Aug Mon-Wed 9 AM - 8 PM, Thurs - Fri 9 AM - 6 PM; No admis fee; Estab 1866, dept estab 1970 to serve art & music patrons
Income: Financed by city appropriation
Library Holdings: Book Volumes 4500, Periodical Subscriptions 12, Video Tapes

M **SALISBURY HOUSE FOUNDATION,** Salisbury House and Garden, 4025 Tonawanda Dr, Des Moines, IA 50312-2909. Tel 515-274-1777; Web: www.salisburyhouse.org; *Executive Director* Kit Curran
Open Tues - Sat 10 AM - 5 PM; Sun noon - 4 PM; Guided: adults $12, seniors $11, veterans & active military $4, youth $2; Self-Guided: adults $8, seniors 65 & over $7, youth $2, children 5 & under, veterans & active military free; Estab 1954 as a historic house museum; Historic Mansion is modeled after the King's House in Salisbury, England & contains Tudor era furniture, classic paintings & sculpture from East & West, tapestries, Oriental rugs; Average Annual Attendance: 30,000; Mem: dues $35 - $100
Income: Financed through admis, mem, contributions, cultural programs, private & corporate function facility fees, endowment & grants
Library Holdings: Book Volumes, Cards, Clipping Files, Kodachrome Transparencies, Manuscripts, Memorabilia, Original Art Works, Original Documents, Prints
Special Subjects: American Indian Art, Asian Art, Bronzes, Carpets & Rugs, Ceramics, Costumes, Decorative Arts, Furniture, Historical Material, Manuscripts, Metalwork, Oriental Art, Painting-American, Painting-British, Period Rooms, Porcelain, Portraits, Sculpture, Southwestern Art, Tapestries, Textiles
Collections: Collection of paintings by Genth, Lillian, Joseph Stella, Sir Thomas Lawrence, Van Dyck, Brussels Brabant tapestries, sculpture by Archipenko, Bourdelle, Chinese, Indian & Oriental (Persian) rugs
Exhibitions: Permanent collection
Activities: Docent training, workshops, dramatic progs; lects open to pub, 4 vis lectrs per yr; concerts; tours; individual paintings & original objects of art lent; lending collection contains motion pictures, original art works, paintings; mus shop sells reproductions, brochures, postcards, stationery, books, prints & videos

DUBUQUE

M **DUBUQUE MUSEUM OF ART,** 701 Locust St, Dubuque, IA 52001-6817. Tel 563-557-1851; Fax 563-557-7826; Email info@dbqart.com; Web: www.dbqart.com; *Exec Dir* David Schmitz; *Pres* Russell Knight; *Dir Educ* Margaret Buhr; *Assoc Cur & Registrar* Stacy Peterson
Open Tues - Fri 10 AM - 5 PM, Sat & Sun 1 - 4 PM, cl Mon; Admis gen $6, seniors 65 & up $5, students $3, mem & children under 19 free; Estab 1874, to preserve, collect, exhibit, interpret & teach the fine arts to those in the Dubuque area & surrounding communities; Average Annual Attendance: 9,450; Mem: 400; dues $15-$4000; annual meeting in May
Income: Financed by dues & donations
Collections: Permanent collection consists of regional & historic art, drawings, paintings, prints, sculptures & watercolor, Grant Wood, Edward S Curtis, Arthur Geisert
Exhibitions: Ceramics, drawing, paintings, sculptures
Publications: Art News, quarterly
Activities: Classes for adults & children; lects open to pub, 12-14 vis lectrs per yr; concerts; gallery talks; tours; competitions with awards; mus shop sells books, misc. children's gift items & jewelry

EPWORTH

M **DIVINE WORD COLLEGE,** Father Weyland SVD Gallery, 102 Jacoby Dr SW, Epworth, IA 52045-7716. Tel 319-876-3353; Fax 319-876-3353; Email jrudd@dwci.edu; Web: www.dwci.edu; *Asst Prof Art* Jeremy Rudd
Open Mon - Sun 9 AM - 5 PM; No admis fee; Estab 1985; Carpeted walls, track lighting
Exhibitions: Art of Africa & Papua New Guinea; 5 exhibits each year

FAIRFIELD

L **FAIRFIELD ART ASSOCIATION,** 200 N Main, Fairfield, IA 52556; PO Box 904, Fairfield, IA 52556-0016. Tel 641-472-5374; Email suzan1252@aol.com; *Dir* Suzan Kessel; *Pres* Terry M Klein; *VPres* Cindy Travers
Open Mon - Sat 9 AM - 5 PM; No admis fee; Estab 1966; Large gallery in new Arts & Convention Center; Average Annual Attendance: 20,000
Income: Financed by endowment & mem
Library Holdings: Cards, Original Art Works, Periodical Subscriptions 180
Collections: Graphics, paintings
Exhibitions: New exhibits monthly
Activities: Classes for adults & children; dramatic progs; lects open to pub; competitions; gallery talks; tours; schols offered; sales shop sells original art & prints

A **MAHARISHI UNIVERSITY OF MANAGEMENT,** Department of Art, 1000 N 4th St, c/o MUM Dept of Art Fairfield, IA 52557-0001. Tel 641-472-7000 Ext 5035; Email art@mum.edu; Web: www.mum.edu; *Dir* Ceyrona Kay; *Office Mgr* Betsy Henry
Open Mon - Sat 10 AM - 4 PM; No admis fee; Estab 1965 as teaching galley & to foster develop of the arts in the region; One gallery 20 ft X 44 ft for exhibition of contemporary & modern art; 20 artist studios; theater for lectures & performances; classrooms for teaching visual arts courses; Average Annual Attendance: 1,000
Income: Financed by Maharishi University of Management
Collections: Contemporary art in all media
Exhibitions: Regional & in-state artists; student shows
Publications: Exhibit catalogues
Activities: University classes; lects open to public, 6 vis lectrs per year; gallery talks

FORT DODGE

M **BLANDEN MEMORIAL ART MUSEUM,** 920 Third Ave S, Fort Dodge, IA 50501. Tel 515-573-2316; Fax 515-573-2317; Web: www.blanden.org; *Educ & Asst Dir* Eric Anderson; *Bus Office* Pamela Kay; *Security & Maintenance* Paul Goodman
Open Tues - Sat 11 AM - 5 PM; cl Sun, Mon & holidays; No admis fee-donations accepted; Estab 1930 as a permanent municipal, non-profit institution, educational & aesthetic in purpose; the mus interprets, exhibits & cares for a permanent collection & traveling exhibitions; Houses works of art in permanent collection; Average Annual Attendance: 17,000; Mem: 600; dues $25-$1,000
Income: $500,000 (financed by city & state appropriation, mem, Blanden Charitable Foundation & private support)
Library Holdings: Book Volumes, Clipping Files, Exhibition Catalogs, Memorabilia, Original Documents, Other Holdings, Pamphlets, Periodical Subscriptions, Photographs, Prints
Special Subjects: Antiquities-Egyptian, Antiquities-Greek, Antiquities-Roman, Architecture, Baroque Art, Bronzes, Bronzes, Calligraphy, Ceramics, Etchings & Engravings, Historical Material, Medieval Art, Oriental Art, Painting-American, Painting-European, Painting-German, Painting-Spanish, Period Rooms, Photography, Porcelain, Portraits, Posters, Pre-Columbian Art, Prints, Renaissance Art, Sculpture, Sculpture, Textiles, Woodcarvings, Woodcuts, African Art
Collections: Arts of China & Japan, 15th - 20th Century Works on Paper, Pre-Columbian & African Art, Regional Art, Twentieth century American & European masters, paintings & sculpture, Beckman, Chagall, Miro/City of Fort Dodge History
Publications: Annual report; exhibition catalogues; handbook of the permanent collection; membership information; quarterly bulletin
Activities: Educ prog; classes for adults & children; docent training; dramatic progs; volunteer training (front desk); lects open to pub, 4-6 vis lectrs per yr; concerts; gallery talks; tours; competitions with awards; scholarships offered; exten outreach art appreciation prog; loans to art mus meeting necessary professional requirements including climate conditions, security & other physical needs specifications of the art collection; lending of original objects of art to State College/Spain; book traveling exhibs; originate traveling exhibs; mus shop sells books; magazines; artist work

GRINNELL

M **GRINNELL COLLEGE,** Faulconer Gallery, 1108 Park St, Grinnell, IA 50112-1643. Tel 641-269-4660; Fax 641-269-4626; Email wright1@grinnell.edu; Web: www.grinnell.edu/faulconergallery; *Dir* Lesley Wright; *Assoc Dir* Dan Strong; *Cur Acad & Community Outreach* Tilly Woodward; *Exhib Designer* Milton Severe; *Cur Coll* Kay Wilson; *Admin Asst* Conni Gause
Open daily 11 AM - 5 PM; No admis fee, donations accepted; Estab 1999 as a college gallery of distinction. Faulconer Gallery promotes learning through artistic excellence & creative collaboration; 7,400 sq ft gallery designed by Cesar Pelli; print & drawing study room
Income: $75,000 (financed by endowment)
Purchases: $140,000 (from endowed funds)
Special Subjects: African Art, Drawings, Etchings & Engravings, Graphics, Photography, Prints, Watercolors, Woodcuts
Collections: Works of Art on Paper
Exhibitions: Sandy Skoglund: Raining Popcorn; Layers of Brazilian Art; John Wilson: A Retrospective; William Kentridge Prints; Scandinavian Photography 1: Sweden; Scandinavian Photography 2: Denmark; Hin: The Quiet Beauty of Japanese Bamboo Art; Where Are You From: Contemporary Portuguese Art; Of Fables & Folly: Diane Victor, Recent Work; Sandow Birk's American Quran; Civil War Era Drawings from the Becker Collection; Robert Polidori: Selected Works 1985-2009; From Wunderkammer to the Modern Museum; Complex Conversations: Willie Cole Sculptures & Wall Works; Edward Burtynsky: Water; Dark Commander: The Art of John Scott
Publications: Exhibition catalogs
Activities: Classes for children; lects open to pub; concerts; gallery talks; tours; book traveling exhibs 2-4 per yr; organize traveling exhibs occasionally to other col mus

INDIANOLA

M **SIMPSON COLLEGE,** Farnham Gallery, 701 N "C" St, Indianola, IA 50125. Tel 515-961-1486; Fax 515-961-1498; Email richmond@simpson.edu; Web: www.simpson.edu; *Head Art Dept* David Richmond; *Asst Prof* Justin Nostrala
Open Mon - Fri 8 AM - 4:30 PM; No admis fee; Estab 1982 to educate & inform the public; Two small gallery rooms each 14 ft, 4 in x 29 ft; Average Annual Attendance: 1,200
Income: college fees
Collections: Small permanent collection being started
Activities: Classes for adults; lects open to pub, 4 vis lectrs per yr; gallery talks; scholarships offered; individual paintings lent; originate traveling exhibs

IOWA CITY

M **UNIVERSITY OF IOWA,** University of Iowa Museum of Art, 150 N Riverside Dr, 100 OMA Iowa City, IA 52242. Tel 319-335-1727; Fax 319-335-3677; Email uima@uiowa.edu; Web: uima.uiowa.edu; *Interim Dir* Jim Leach; *Sr Cur* Kathleen Edwards; *Cur Educ* Dale William Fisher; *Mgr Exhibs & Collections* Katherine Wilson; *Cur Arts of African, Oceania & Americas* Cory Gundlach
Open Tues, Wed & Fri 10 AM - 5 PM, Thurs 10 AM - 9 PM, Sat - Sun noon - 5 PM; cl Mon & univ holidays; No admis fee; Estab 1969 to collect, exhibit & preserve for the future, works of art from different cultures; to make these objects as accessible as possible to people of all ages in the state of Iowa; to assist the pub, through educational programs & publications, in interpreting these works of art & expanding their appreciation of art in general; Temporary UIMA@IMU visual classroom opened after 2008 flood; Average Annual Attendance: 50,000; Mem: Friend less than $100; Contributor $100-$249; Curator's Circle $250-$499; Sponsor $500-$999; Director's Circle $1,000-$2,499; Advocate $2,500-$4,999; Patron $5,000-$9,999; Wilke Society $10,000 & up
Income: Financed by state appropriation & private donations
Special Subjects: African Art, American Indian Art, Antiquities-Etruscan, Asian Art, Ceramics, Decorative Arts, Drawings, Etchings & Engravings, Graphics, Islamic Art, Jade, Oriental Art, Painting-American, Painting-French, Painting-German, Photography, Pottery, Pre-Columbian Art, Prints, Sculpture, Silver, Textiles, Watercolors, Woodcarvings, Woodcuts, Metalwork, Religious Art
Collections: African & Pre-Columbian art, Chinese & Tibetan bronzes, Oriental jade, 19th & 20th century European & American paintings & sculpture, prints, drawings, photography, silver, Elliott Collection of 20th Century European Art, Mauricio Lasansky Print Collection
Exhibitions: The Elliott Collection of 20th Century European paintings, silver & prints; a major collection of African sculpture; many changing exhibs each yr, both permanent collection, original & traveling exhibitions
Publications: Magazine 2 times per yr; exhibition catalogs
Activities: Classes for adults; docent training; K-12 & senior living community art outreach/educ progs; lects open to pub; lects for mems only; 10-20 vis lectrs per yr; concerts; gallery talks; tours; works of art lent to other museums; traveling exhibs; originate traveling exhibs; sales shop sells posters, postcards, catalogs, mugs, tote bags, t-shirts, anniversary book, notecards, magnets

L **Art Library**, W 145 Art Bldg, Iowa City, IA 52242; 1375 Highway 1 W, W 145 Art Bldg Iowa City, IA 52246-4233. Tel 319-335-3089; Email art-lib@uiowa.edu; Web: www.lib.uiowa.edu/art/index; *Head Librn* Rijn Templeton
Open Mon - Thurs 8:30 AM - 8:30 PM, Fri 8:30 AM - 5 PM, Sat 1 - 5 PM, SUN 1 - 7 PM; call for seasonal hours; Estab 1937 to support the University programs, community & state needs; Circ 40,000
Income: Financed by state appropriation
Library Holdings: Book Volumes 100,000, CD-ROMs, Clipping Files, Exhibition Catalogs, Fiche, Memorabilia, Pamphlets, Periodical Subscriptions 230, Reels

KEOKUK

A **KEOKUK ART CENTER,** 210 N 5th St, Keokuk, IA 52632-5614. Tel 319-524-8354; Email tseabold@keokukartcenter.org; Web: www.keokukartcenter.org; *Dir* Thomas Seabold
Open Tues - Sat 9 AM - 4PM & by appointment; No admis fee; Estab 1954 to promote art in tri-state area; Gallery maintained in Keokuk Public Library, 210 N Fifth St; Average Annual Attendance: 2,000; Mem: dues sustaining $50, patron $25, family $12, individual $6, student $2; annual meeting first Mon in May
Collections: Paintings, sculpture
Exhibitions: Changing exhibits
Publications: Newsletter, quarterly
Activities: Classes for adults & children; docent training; lects open to public; gallery talks; tours; competitions with cash awards; scholarships; book traveling exhibs; originate traveling exhibs

MARSHALLTOWN

A **CENTRAL IOWA ART ASSOCIATION, INC,** 709 S Center St Ste 1, Marshalltown, IA 50158. Tel 641-753-9013; Email ciaa@iowatelecom.net; Web: www.uiowa.edu/uima
Open Mon - Thurs 11 AM - 5 PM; Estab 1942, incorporated 1959; The large auditorium has changing monthly exhibitions of varied art; glass cases in corridor & studio display contemporary ceramics of high quality; Average Annual Attendance: 3,000; Mem: 330; dues $15; annual meeting Dec/Jan
Income: Financed by mem, contributions & United Way
Special Subjects: American Indian Art, Bronzes, Ceramics, Etchings & Engravings, Porcelain, Pottery, Primitive art, Sculpture, Watercolors, Woodcarvings
Collections: Fisher Collection-Utrillo, Cassatt, Sisley, Vuillard, Monet, Degas, Signac, Le Gourge, Vlaminck and Monticelli, sculpture-Christian Petersen, Rominelli, Bourdelle, ceramic study collection-Gilhooly, Arneson, Nagle, Kottler, Babu, Geraedts, Boxem, Leach, Voulkos, traditional Japanese wares
Exhibitions: Monthly art & crafts in Fisher Community Center Auditorium
Publications: Newsletter, monthly; brochures
Activities: Classes for adults & children in ceramics, sculpture, jewelry, painting; lects open to public, 3 vis lectrs per yr; gallery talks; tours; awards; individual paintings & original objects of art lent; book traveling exhibs; originate traveling exhibs; sales shop sells original art, reproductions, prints, pottery, wood, fiber & metal

L **Art Reference Library**, 709 S Center St Ste 1, Marshalltown, IA 50158-2876. Tel 641-753-9013; Fax 641-753-9013; Email ciaa@iowatelecom.net; Web: www.cenraliowaartassociation.org; *Bd Pres* Renaie Hutzel
Open mid Apr - mid Oct 11 Am - 5 PM daily, mid Oct - mid Apr Mon - Fri 11 AM - 5 PM; No admis fee; Estab 1958 for fine art collecting classes; For reference only; Average Annual Attendance: 5,000; Mem: 400
Income: Grants, memberships & donations
Library Holdings: Book Volumes 700, Cassettes, Original Art Works, Photographs, Sculpture, Slides
Special Subjects: Ceramics, Painting-French
Collections: 18 Impressionist & Post-Impressionist works, including Degas, Matisse, Casatt & Pisarro, 119 ceramics pieces, including Levine, Arruson, Voulkos, W M Daley
Exhibitions: Exhibitions change monthly
Activities: Classes for adults & children; docent training; 25 vis lectrs per yr; concerts; tours; gallery talks; schol; sales shop sells original art

M **FISHER ART GALLERY,** 709 S Center St, Marshalltown, IA 50158-2876. Tel 515-753-9013; Email ciaa@iowatelecom.net; Web: www.centraliowaartassociation.org
Open 11 AM - 5 PM weekdays, Sat & Sun 1-5 PM or by appointment; cl holidays; 19 French Impressionist & Post Impressionist works; Average Annual Attendance: 500
Special Subjects: Art Education, Art History, Ceramics, Landscapes, Painting-American, Painting-French
Collections: 114 piece ceramic study collection
Activities: Classes for adults & children; docent training; sales shop sells art supplies

MASON CITY

M **CITY OF MASON CITY,** Charles H MacNider Art Museum, 303 Second St SE, Mason City, IA 50401-3988. Tel 641-421-3666; Fax 641-422-9612; Email mlinskeydeegan@masoncity.net; Web: www.macniderart.org; *Dir* Edith M Blanchard; *Assoc Cur & Registrar* Mara Linskey-Deegan
Open Tues, Wed, Fri, Sat 9 AM - 5 PM; Tues & Thurs extended evening hrs until 9 PM; cl Sun & Mon; No admis fee; Estab 1964, opened 1966 to provide experience in the arts through develop of a permanent collection, through scheduling of temporary exhibitions, through the offering of classes & art instruction, through special programs in film, music & other areas of the performing arts. The mus was estab in an English-Tudor style of brick & tile, enhanced by modern, design coordinated additions; It is located in a scenic setting, two & a half blocks from the main thoroughfare of Mason City. Gallery lighting & neutral backgrounds provide a good environment for exhibitions; Average Annual Attendance: 19,480; Mem: 435; dues from contributions $25-$1000 or more
Income: $492,550 (financed by mem, city appropriation & grants)
Library Holdings: Book Volumes 1500, Clipping Files, Exhibition Catalogs, Motion Pictures, Periodical Subscriptions 30, Slides, Video Tapes
Special Subjects: Afro-American Art, American Indian Art, American Western Art, Cartoons, Ceramics, Collages, Drawings, Etchings & Engravings, Glass, Landscapes, Marine Painting, Metalwork, Painting-American, Painting-American, Period Rooms, Photography, Photography, Portraits, Pottery, Pottery, Prints, Prints, Sculpture, Sculpture, Southwestern Art, Stained Glass, Textiles, Watercolors, Woodcuts
Collections: Permanent collection with an emphasis on American art, with some representation of Iowa art, contains paintings, prints, sculpture, pottery, artists represented include Baziotes, Birch, Benton, Burchfield, Bricher, Calder, Cropsey, De Staebler, Dove, Flannagan, Francis, Gottlieb, Graves, Guston, Healy, Hurd, Lasansky, Levine, Marin, Maurer, Metcalf, Sloan & Oliveira, Bil Baird: World of Puppets
Publications: Annual report; newsletter, quarterly; occasional exhibit fliers or catalog
Activities: Classes for adults & children; docent training; lects open to pub; 5 vis lectrs per yr; concerts; gallery talks; tours; competitions; individual paintings & original objects of art lent to other mus & art centers; mus shop sells original art, jewelry & cards

L **MASON CITY PUBLIC LIBRARY,** 225 Second St SE, Mason City, IA 50401. Tel 641-421-3668; Fax 641-423-2615; Email librarian@mcpl.org; Web: www.mcpl.org; *Dir* Mary Markwalter; *Reference* Barbara Madson; *Art Librn* Kenneth Enabnit; *Reference* Katrina Bowen
Open Mon - Wed 8:30 AM-8:30 PM, Thurs-Sat 9:30 AM-5:30 PM, cl Sun; No admis fee; Estab 1869 to service pub in providing reading material & information; Circ 197,635; Monthly exhibits of local & regional artists located in main lobby of library
Income: Financed by city, county appropriation & Federal Revenue Sharing
Library Holdings: Book Volumes 110,000, Cassettes, Clipping Files, Fiche, Filmstrips 350, Framed Reproductions, Memorabilia, Motion Pictures, Original Art Works, Other Holdings Original documents, Pamphlets, Periodical Subscriptions 325, Prints, Records, Reels
Collections: Permanent collection of regional artists, signed letters of authors
Exhibitions: Rotating exhibitions; Monthly exhibitions
Activities: Exten dept serves general public; gallery holdings consist of art works & reproductions paintings which are lent to public

MOUNT VERNON

M **CORNELL COLLEGE,** Peter Paul Luce Gallery, McWethy Hall, 600 First St SW Mount Vernon, IA 52314-1098. Tel 319-895-4491; Fax 319-895-4519; Email scoleman@cornell.college.edu; Web: www.cornell-iowa.edu; *Pres* Jonathan Brand; *Dept Chair* Susannah Biondo-Gemmell; *Dean* Joseph Dieker; *Bus Officer* Anissa Wolfe; *Coord Exhibs* Susan Coleman; *Dir Pub Info* DeeAnn Rexroat
Open academic year: Mon - Fri 9 AM - 4 PM, Sun 2 - 4 PM; Summer by appt; No admis fee; Estab in 2002 with a gift from the Henry Luce Foundation Inc to display student works as well as professional artists; Average Annual Attendance: 5,000
Income: Financed by Cornell College with endowment from Henry Luce Foundation Inc
Special Subjects: American Indian Art, Baroque Art, Carpets & Rugs, Painting-American, Drawings, Prints
Collections: Sonnenschein Collection of European Drawings of the 15th - 17th Century, Thomas Nast Collection, Whiting Collection of Early Phoenician Glass 4th to 5th Century, Bertha Jacques Print Collection, Powers Ceramics Collection
Exhibitions: 4 exhibits per year plus 10-20 student thesis shows
Publications: Hugh Lifton, The Cornell Years (2001); Cultural Expressions in Clay, The Work of Doug Hanson (2012)
Activities: Lects open to pub, 3 vis lectrs per yr; gallery talks; tours

MUSCATINE

M **MUSCATINE ART CENTER,** 1314 Mulberry Ave, Muscatine, IA 52761-3429. Tel 563-263-8282; Fax 563-263-4702; Email art@muscatineiowa.gov; Web: www.muscatineartcenter.org; *Dir* Melanie Alexander; *Registrar* Virginia Cooper; *Office Coordr* Lynn Bartenhagen
Open Tues - Fri 10 AM - 5 PM, Thurs until 7 PM, Sat & Sun 1 - 5 PM, cl Mon & legal holidays; No admis fee; Estab 1965 to collect, preserve & interpret work of art & objects of historical & aesthetic importance; Average Annual Attendance: 30,000; Mem: 500; Friends of Muscatine Art Center, ann mtg July; dues individual $30, family $50, contributing $100, patron $250, sustaining $500, benefactor $1,000
Income: Financed by city appropriation & Muscatine Art Center Support Foundation
Special Subjects: Carpets & Rugs, Costumes, Decorative Arts, Drawings, Glass, Graphics, Historical Material, Landscapes, Maps, Oriental Art, Painting-American, Painting-French, Period Rooms, Portraits, Pottery, Prints, Sculpture, Textiles, Watercolors
Collections: Muscatine History, Button Collection, Paperweight Collection, American painting prints, especially Mississippi River views, Gilmore Collection of French Impressionists
Publications: Newsletter, quarterly
Activities: Classes for children; docent training; lects open to public, 12 vis lectrs per yr; concerts; gallery talks; tours; schols; individual paintings & original objects of art lent to qualified museums for exhib purposes; book traveling exhibs 2 per yr; originate traveling exhibs 1-2 per yr

OKOBOJI

M **PEARSON LAKES ART CENTER,** 2201 Hwy 71, Okoboji, IA 51355; PO Box 255, Okoboji, IA 51355-0255. Tel 712-332-7013; Fax 712-332-7014; Email info@lakesart.org; Web: www.lakesart.org; *Dir Visual Arts* Morgan Aalgaand; *Dir Educ* Holly Zinn; *Dir Performing Arts* Rachelle Fratzke
Open June - Aug Mon - Sat 10 AM - 4 PM, Sept - May Tues - Sat 10 AM - 4 PM; No admis fee; Average Annual Attendance: 20,000
Special Subjects: Painting-American, Painting-Russian, Portraits, Sculpture
Collections: works by international & national artists
Activities: Educ progs for adults & children, dramatic progs, docent training; lects open to public, 3 vis lectrs per yr; musical & theater events; festivals; film series; readings, concerts; gallery talks; tours; sponsoring of exhib; schols avail; mus shop sells books, original art & prints

ORANGE CITY

M **NORTHWESTERN COLLEGE,** Te Paske Gallery, 101 7th St SW, Dept of Art Orange City, IA 51041-1923. Tel 712-737-7000, 707-7004; Fax 712-737-3777; Email rein@nwciowa.edu; Web: www.nwciowa.edu; *Rotation Exhib Coordr* Rein Vanderhill; *Prof Sculpture* Arnold Carlson; *Prof Graphic Design* Phil Scorza
Open Mon - Sat 8 AM - 12 PM; No admis fee; Estab 1968 to promote the visual arts in northwest Iowa and to function as a learning resource for the col and community; 78 linear feet wall, 10' wall height; Average Annual Attendance: 2,000
Income: Financed by school budget
Special Subjects: Etchings & Engravings
Collections: Approx 75 original works of art, etchings, woodcuts, serigraphs, lithographs, mezzotints, paintings, sculpture & ceramics by modern & old masters of Western World & Japan, Fine Art Permanent Collection of Northwestern College (Iowa), Stegeman Collection of Japanese Woodcut Prints (19th & 20th c)
Exhibitions: Contemporary American Artists Series; student shows
Activities: Lects open to public, 2-3 vis lectrs per year; gallery talks; competitions

M **Denler Art Gallery**, 3003 Snelling Ave N, Totino Fine Arts Center, 2nd Fl Saint Paul, MN 55113-1501. Tel 651-631-5110 (main); Web: art.nwc.edu/denler; *Dir* Luke Aleckson
Call for hours
Special Subjects: Painting-American, Photography, Sculpture

OTTUMWA

L **AIRPOWER MUSEUM LIBRARY,** 22001 Bluegrass Rd, Ottumwa, IA 52501-8569. Tel 641-938-2773; Fax 641-938-2093; Email antiqueairfield@sirisonline.com; Web: www.antiqueairfield.com
Estab 1971
Library Holdings: Filmstrips, Photographs, Video Tapes
Special Subjects: Drawings, Film, Maps, Photography, Video
Collections: Aviation Collection, blueprints, books, brochures, clothing, drawings, films, lithographs, maps, models, paintings, periodicals, photographs, videos
Publications: Airpower Museum bulletin, annual

SIOUX CITY

M **LOREN D. CALLENDAR GALLERY,** 607 4th St, Sioux City, IA 51101-1634. Tel 712-279-6174; Fax 712-252-5615; Email scpm@sioux-city.org
Open Tues - Sat 10 AM - 5 PM, Sun 1 PM - 5 PM; cl holidays; No admis fee, donations welcomed
Collections: Photographs; Sioux City history

A **SIOUX CITY ART CENTER,** 225 Nebraska St, Sioux City, IA 51101-1712. Tel 712-279-6272; Fax 712-255-2921; Email aharris@sioux-city.org; Web: www.siouxcityartcenter.org; *Bd Trustees* Gregory Jones; *Board Dirs Pres* Stacie Anderson; *Dir* Al Harris-Fernandez, MFA; *Admin Asst & Contact* Kjersten Welch; *Cur* Todd Behrens; *Educ Specialist* Debra Marqusec
Open Tues, Wed, Fri & Sat 10 AM - 4 PM, Thurs 10 AM - 9 PM, Sun 1 - 4 PM, cl Mon & holidays; No admis fee; Estab 1938 to provide art experiences to the general pub; Four exhibition galleries consisting of nationally known artists from the midwest regional area; includes a permanent collection gallery & changing exhibitions; Average Annual Attendance: 30,000; Mem: 725; dues $15-$5000; monthly meetings
Income: Financed by mem, city & state appropriation
Special Subjects: Drawings, Etchings & Engravings, Landscapes, Painting-American, Photography, Prints, Sculpture, Watercolors, Ceramics, Portraits
Collections: Permanent collection of over 700 works, consists of paintings & prints of nationally known regional artists, contemporary photography & sculpture & crafts, Art from the upper Midwest
Publications: Annual Report; quarterly newsletter; class brochures, quarterly; exhibition catalogs; exhibition announcements
Activities: Classes for adults & children; docent training; workshops; outreach progs to schools; ArtSplash Festival of the Arts; Sculpt Siouxland; lects open to pub; gallery talks; tours; concerts; competitions; awards given in conjunction with juried exhibs & YAM; scholarships offered; original objects of art & individual paintings lent to qualified institutions with approved facilities & security; one book traveling exhib per yr; originates traveling exhibs; mus shop sells books, magazines, original art, prints, jewelry & property items

STORM LAKE

M **WITTER GALLERY,** 609 Cayuga St, Storm Lake, IA 50588-2239. Tel 712-732-3400; Email wittergallery@yahoo.com; Web: www.thewittergallery.org; *Pres* Judy Ferguson; *VPres* Bruce Ellingson; *Dir* Ron Stevenson
Open Tues - Fri 1- 5 PM, Thurs 1 - 6 PM, Sat 10AM - 2 PM; No admis fee; Estab 1972 to encourage the appreciation of fine arts & to support fine arts educ, exhibits, lectures & workshops; Gallery occupies a wing of the Storm Lake Pub Library building. It has about 1800 sq ft of floor space & 120 linear ft of hanging wall space; Average Annual Attendance: 10,000; Mem: 300; dues sponsor $250, supporting $100, sustaining $50, active $25
Income: $20,000 (financed by endowment, mem, city appropriation, fundraising projects)
Library Holdings: Exhibition Catalogs, Memorabilia, Original Art Works, Original Documents, Photographs, Slides
Special Subjects: Prints
Collections: Paintings & collected artifacts of Miss Ella Witter, prints by Dorothy D Skewis
Exhibitions: Iowa Women in Art: Pioneers of the Past- touring exhibition of work by Ella Witter and Dorothy Skewis
Publications: Witter Gallery News & Events, The Palette Monthly
Activities: Classes for adults & children; art appreciation progs in area schools; lects open to pub, 10 vis lectrs per yr; gallery talks; concerts; tours; biennial juried competition with cash awards; originate traveling exhibs; gift gallery sells notecards & original art - pottery, jewelry, prints, silk scarves

WATERLOO

M **WATERLOO CENTER OF THE ARTS,** 225 Commercial St, Waterloo, IA 50701-1313. Tel 319-291-4490; Fax 319-291-4270; Email museum@waterloo-ia.org; Web: www.waterloocenterforthearts.org; *Dir* Cammie V Scully; *Educ Dir* Bonnie Winninger; *Dir Mktg* Shannon Farlow; *Cur* Kent Shankle
Open Tues-Sat 10AM-5PM, Sun 1PM-5PM; No admis fee; Estab 1947 to initiate further awareness, appreciation, & support of the arts by a diverse audience; Maintains reference library; Average Annual Attendance: 110,000, plus junior art gallery attendance of 16,000; Mem: 500; dues individual $40 & up
Income: Financed by city funds, mem, grants & donations
Special Subjects: Afro-American Art, Ceramics, Decorative Arts, Painting-American, Prints, Sculpture, Woodcarvings
Collections: American decorative Arts, Contemporary American art, Haitian/ Caribbean paintings & sculpture
Exhibitions: Rotating exhibits & an interactive children's museum
Activities: classes for adults & children, docent training, birthday parties; lects open to pub; concerts; gallery talks; tours; schols; serves area with 45 miles of waterloo; lends original objects of art to other museums; mus shop sells prints, books, magazines, original art, children's merchandise, & jewelry; junior museum

WEST BRANCH

L **NATIONAL ARCHIVES & RECORDS ADMINISTRATION,** Herbert Hoover Presidential Library - Museum, 210 Parkside Dr, West Branch, IA 52358-9685; PO Box 488, West Branch, IA 52358-0488. Tel 319-643-5301; Fax 319-643-6045; Email hoover.library@nara.gov; Web: www.hoover.archives.gov; *Library Dir* Tom Schwartz; *Reference Archivist* Matt Schaefer; *Cur Mus* Marcus Eckhardt; *Educ Specialist* Elizabeth Dinschel; *Admin Officer* Kathy Grace; *A/V Archivist* Lynn Smith; *Archivist* Craig Wright; *Registrar* Karen Maxville
Open daily 9 AM - 5 PM, cl Thanksgiving, Christmas, New Year's Day; Admis adults $10, over age 62 $5, children 6-15 $3, ages 5 and under free; Estab 1962 as a research center to service the papers of Herbert Hoover & other related manuscript collections; a museum to exhibit the life & times of Herbert Hoover from his 90 years of public service & accomplishments; Average Annual Attendance: 50,000
Income: Financed by federal appropriation
Library Holdings: Audio Tapes, Book Volumes 23,041, Clipping Files, Manuscripts, Memorabilia, Motion Pictures, Original Art Works, Original Documents, Other Holdings Original documents; Still photographs, Pamphlets, Periodical Subscriptions 30, Photographs, Records, Reels, Slides
Special Subjects: Historical Material, Manuscripts
Collections: 64 Chinese porcelains, oil paintings, 190 Original Editorial Cartoons, 340 posters, 26 World War I Food Administration, 464 World War I Painted and Embroidered Flour Sacks
Exhibitions: Permanent exhibits on Herbert & Lou Henry Hoover; subjects related to Hoover & the times; temporary exhibits cover subjects related to the memorabilia collection, the decades & activities of Hoover's life & state & national interest
Activities: Classes for children; docent training; lects open to pub, 2-3 vis lectrs per yr; concerts; tours; schols; sales shop sells books, prints, reproductions; slides & medals

WINTERSET

M **WINTERSET ART CENTER,** 216 S John Wayne Dr, Winterset, IA 50273; PO Box 325, Winterset, IA 50273-0325. Tel 515-462-4600; Web: wintersetartcenter.org; *Chmn* Margaret Ripperger; *Pub Rels* Barbara Cook
Open Mon - 9 AM - 2 PM, other times by appointment, cl Christmas & New Year; No admis fee; Average Annual Attendance: 3,000
Collections: works by local & regional artists
Activities: Educ progs; classes for adults & children; hobby workshops; arts festivals; tours; lending of original objects of art; book traveling exhibs; organize traveling exhibs to local venues; Mus shop sells original art

KANSAS

ABILENE

L **NATIONAL ARCHIVES AND RECORDS ADMINISTRATION,** Eisenhower Presidential Library, 200 SE Fourth St, Abilene, KS 67410; PO Box 339 Abilene, KS 67410-0339. Tel 785-263-6700; Fax 785-263-6715; Email eisenhower.library@nara.gov; Web: www.eisenhower.archives.gov; *Dir* Karl Weissenbach; *Cur* William Snyder; *Registrar* Matthew Thompson; *Communs Dir* Samantha Kenner
Open daily 9 AM - 4:45 PM, cl Thanksgiving, Christmas & New Year's; Admis $12, sr citizens $9, under 16 free; Estab 1945; Average Annual Attendance: 190,000
Income: Financed by Federal Government appropriation & private 501c3 foundation
Library Holdings: Audio Tapes, Book Volumes 22,850, Cassettes, Clipping Files, Filmstrips, Manuscripts, Maps, Memorabilia, Micro Print, Motion Pictures, Original Art Works, Original Documents, Photographs, Prints, Records, Reels, Sculpture, Slides, Video Tapes
Special Subjects: American Western Art, Asian Art, Calligraphy, Carpets & Rugs, Cartoons, Ceramics, Coins & Medals, Decorative Arts, Drawings, Historical Material, Ivory, Manuscripts, Maps, Painting-American, Portraits, Prints, Reproductions, Sculpture, Textiles, Watercolors

Collections: Research Library and Museum contains papers of Dwight D Eisenhower and his assoc, together with items of historical interest connected with the Eisenhower Family. Mementos and gifts of General Dwight D Eisenhower both before, during, and after his term as President of the United States
Activities: Educ dept; docent training; lects open to pub, 5 vis lectrs per yr; concerts; libr tours; film series open to pub first three wks of Mar every yr; individual paintings & original objects of art lent; lending collection contains original art work & prints, paintings & sculpture; originate traveling exhibs; mus shop sells books, magazines, prints, reproductions, slides & other items

ALMA

M **WABAUNSEE COUNTY HISTORICAL MUSEUM,** 227 Missouri Ave, Alma, KS 66401; PO Box 387, Alma, KS 66401-0387. Tel 785-765-2200; Email wabcomuseum@emarqmail.com; Web: www.wabaunsee.org; *Cur* Alan Winkler
Open Tues - Sat 10 AM - 4 PM; No admis fee; suggested donation; Estab 1968 for the purpose of preserving art & artifacts in Wabaunsee County; Paintings are hung throughout the museum in available space. Maintains reference library; Average Annual Attendance: 1,800; Mem: 340; yr $25; annual meeting first Sat in June
Income: $25,000 (financed by mem, donations & endowment)
Library Holdings: Audio Tapes, Compact Disks, DVDs, Maps, Memorabilia, Original Art Works, Photographs
Collections: General Louis Walt display, blacksmith shop, clothing, farm tools & equipment, Native American artifacts, Mainstreet USA-historical town, 1923 Reo fire truck, postal display, organization display case, 1918-1965, leather-making display, early day doctor's office, 1880 school room, Paintings by local artist August Ohst (1851-1939), genealogy records, photo panels, local artist Maude Mitchell, 1875-1957, Civil War Display (Wm Meyers Diary, Colt 45 pistol, GAR badges)
Publications: Stories of the Past, Historical Society newsletter, quarterly
Activities: Classes for children; hist tours fall; mus quilters on Tues & Wed; sales shop sells books, postcards

ASHLAND

M **CLARK COUNTY HISTORICAL SOCIETY,** Pioneer - Krier Museum, 430 W 4th St, Ashland, KS 67831; PO Box 862, Ashland, KS 67831-0862. Tel 620-635-2227; Fax 620-635-2227; Email pioneer@ucom.net; Web: www.pioneer-krier.com; *Dir* Tony Maphet
Open Tues-Fri 10AM-noon, 1PM-4PM; Admis donations requested; Estab 1948 to collect & preserve Southwest Kansas history; Maintains reference library; Average Annual Attendance: 2,000; Mem: Dues: lifetime $25; annual meeting in Feb
Income: $42,000 financed by mem, county taxes & donations)
Special Subjects: American Indian Art, Archaeology, Carpets & Rugs, Coins & Medals, Dioramas, Dolls, Etchings & Engravings, Furniture, Glass, Historical Material, Laces, Manuscripts, Maps, Metalwork, Painting-American, Period Rooms, Photography, Porcelain, Portraits, Reproductions, Southwestern Art, Tapestries, Textiles, Woodcarvings
Collections: Archeological coll, Barbed Wire Coll, Early Settlers Coll, Elephant Coll, Gun Coll, Implement Seat coll - Memorabilia of five famous people from Clark County, Kansas, Track Stars, Jerome C Berryma 1921-1925, Wes Santee 1950's, Aerobatic Champion Harold Krier, Notre Dame Coach Jesse Harper, World Renowned Counter-Tenor Rodney Hardesty, Implement Seat Coll
Publications: Notes on Early Clark County, Kansas, book; Kings & Queens of the Range, book; Cattle Ranching South of Dodge City - The Early Years (1870 - 1920), book
Activities: Demonstrations & group tours; historical tours; book traveling exhibs, 1 - 2 per yr; mus shop sells books, original art, reproductions

ATCHISON

M **MUCHNIC FOUNDATION & ATCHISON ART ASSOCIATION,** Muchnic Gallery, 704 N 4th St, Atchison, KS 66002-1924. Tel 913-367-4278; Fax 913-367-2939; Email atchisonart@gmail.com; Web: www.atchisonart.org; *Cur* Deborah Geiger
Open Mar - Dec Wed & Sat - Sun 1PM - 5PM; Admis $2; Estab 1970 to bring fine arts to the people of Atchison; 19th century mansion with art gallery inside; Average Annual Attendance: 3,000; Mem: 210; board meeting third Mon of month
Income: Financed by Muchnic Foundation, Atchison Art Asn art shows
Purchases: $7,000
Special Subjects: Painting-American, Period Rooms
Collections: Paintings by regional artists: Don Andorfer, Thomas Hart Benton, John Stuart Curry, Raymond Eastwood, John Falter, Jim Hamil, Wilbur Niewald, Jack O'Hara, Roger Shimomura, Robert Sudlow, Grant Wood, Jamie Wyeth, Walter Yost
Activities: Classes for adults & children; docent training; lects open to pub; tours; scholarships & fels offered; individual paintings lent to local museums; book traveling exhibs 3 per yr; originate traveling exhibs; sales shop sells books, original art & prints

BALDWIN CITY

M **BAKER UNIVERSITY,** Old Castle Museum, 515 5th St, Baldwin City, KS 66006; PO Box 65, Baldwin City, KS 66006-0065. Tel 785-594-8380; Fax 785-594-2522; Email brenda.day@bakeru.edu; *Dir* Brenda Day
Open Mon-Fri 8AM-noon; Admis by donation; Estab 1953 to display items related to life in early Kansas; Average Annual Attendance: 1,500
Income: Financed by endowment, University & donations
Special Subjects: Historical Material, Pewter, Pottery
Collections: Country store, Indian artifacts & pottery, 19th century print shop, quilts, silver & pewter dishes & table service, tools, old quilts, old cameras, Santa Fe Trail Artifacts
Exhibitions: John Brown material; Indian Pottery; Indian artifacts; old guns
Activities: Lect open to public

CHANUTE

M **MARTIN AND OSA JOHNSON SAFARI MUSEUM, INC,** 111 N Lincoln Ave, Chanute, KS 66720-1819. Tel 620-431-2730; Fax 620-431-2730; Email osajohns@safarimuseum.com; Web: www.safarimuseum.com; *Dir* Conrad G Froehlich; *Cur* Jacquelyn L Borgeson Zimmer; *Store & Office Mgr* Shirley Rogers-Naff
Open Tues - Sat 10 AM - 5 PM, Sun 1 - 5 PM; Admis adults $6, students & seniors $4, children 6-12 $3, children under 6 free; Estab 1961 to be the repository of the Johnson Archives; Average Annual Attendance: 5,000; Mem: 165; dues $10-$500
Income: $180,000 (financed by mem, city appropriation, donations & gift shop)
Special Subjects: African Art
Collections: Fine art-natural history subjects, Martin & Osa Johnson-films, photos, manuscripts, Ethnographic-African, Borneo, South Pacific
Exhibitions: Johnson Exhibition, Imperato African Gallery, Selsor Art Gallery (special exhibit space); Traveling exhibits including Married to Adventure
Publications: Wait-A-Bit News, quarterly newsletter
Activities: Educ dept; classes for adults & children; docent training; lect open to public, vis lectrs; tours; sponsoring of competitions; Barbara Enlow Henshall award for vol serv; mus boxes for school use; individual paintings & original objects of art lent to qualified institutions; mus shop sells books, prints, original art, imported carvings, brass, fabric & ethnic toys

M **Imperato Collection of West African Artifacts**, 111 N Lincoln Ave, Chanute, KS 66720. Tel 620-431-2730; Fax 620-431-2730; Email osajohns@safarimuseum.com; Web: www.safarimuseum.com; *Dir* Conrad G Froehlich; *Cur* Jacquelyn Borgeson
Open Tues - Sat 10 AM - 5 PM, Sun 1 - 5 PM; Admis adults $6, seniors & students $4, children 6-12 $3, children under 6 free; Estab 1974; Average Annual Attendance: 5,000; Mem: 165; $35 dues
Income: $180,000 (financed by members, city, donations, gift shop)
Collections: West African sculpture including masks, ancestor figures & ritual objects, household items, musical instruments
Exhibitions: African culture exhibit of East & West African items; ceremonial masks
Publications: Collection catalogs
Activities: Classes for adults & children; docent training; Tours; pub lects & gallery talks; ann mus volunteer award; exhibit & progs at Walt Disney World & other sites; traveling exhibs to mus, zoos, galleries; mus shop sells books, original art, reproductions, prints

M **Johnson Collection of Photographs, Movies & Memorabilia**, 111 N Lincoln Ave, Chanute, KS 66720. Tel 620-431-2730; Fax 620-431-2730; Email osajohns@safari.museum.com; Web: www.safarimuseum.com; *Dir* Conrad G Froehlich; *Cur* Jacquelyn Borgeson
Open Tues - Sat 10 AM - 5 PM, Sun 1 - 5 PM; Admis adults $6, seniors & students $4, children 6-12 $3, children under 6 free; Estab 1961; Average Annual Attendance: 5,000; Mem: 165; $35 dues
Income: $180,000 (financed by members, city, donations, gift shop)
Collections: Photographs & movie footage of the South Seas, Borneo & East Africa between 1917-1936, Manuscript material, archival collection, & artifacts collected by the Johnsons, Photos & films licensed for commercial & non-profit uses
Activities: Classes of adults & children; docent training; pub lects, tours & gallery talks; ann mus volunteer award; exhibit & progs at Walt Disney World & other sites; traveling exhibs to mus, zoos, galleries; mus shop sells books, original art, reproductions & prints

M **Selsor Art Gallery**, 111 N Lincoln Ave, Chanute, KS 66720. Tel 620-431-2730; Fax 620-431-2730; Email osajohns@safarimuseum.com; Web: www.safarimuseum.com; *Dir* Conrad G Froehlich; *Cur* Jacquelyn Borgeson
Open Tues - Sat 10 AM - 5 PM, Sun 1 - 5 PM; Admis adults $6, seniors & students $4, children 6-12 $3, children under 6 free; Estab 1981; Average Annual Attendance: 5,000; Mem: 165; $35 dues
Income: $180,000 (financed by members, city, donations, gift shop)
Collections: Original paintings, scratch boards & sketches, bronze, ivory & amber sculpture, lithographs
Exhibitions: Rotating exhibits
Activities: Classes for adults & children; docent training; Tours; objects of art lent to qualified institutions; pub lects; ann mus volunteer award; exhibit & progs at Walt Disney World & other sites; traveling exhibs to mus, zoos & galleries; mus shop sells books, reproductions, prints

L **Scott Explorers Library**, 111 N Lincoln Ave, Chanute, KS 66720. Tel 620-431-2730; Fax 620-431-2730; Email osajohns@safarimuseum.com; Web: www.safarimuseum.com; *Dir* Conrad G Froehlich; *Cur* Jacquelyn Borgeson; *Librn* Jane Martin; *Librn* Carla White
Open Tues - Sat 10 AM - 5 PM, Sun 1 - 5 PM; Estab 1980 for research and reference
Library Holdings: Book Volumes 10,000

COTTONWOOD FALLS

M **FLINT HILLS GALLERY,** 321 Broadway St, Cottonwood Falls, KS 66845-2884. Tel 620-273-8235; Fax 620-273-8235; Email judithamackey@gmail.com; Web: www.flinthillsgallery.com; *Artist* Judith Mackey
Open Mon - Sat 10 AM - 4 PM; Estab 1987; Studio of Judith Mackey, artist of the Flint Hills Tallgrass Prairie

EL DORADO

M **BUTLER COMMUNITY COLLEGE,** Erman B. White Gallery, 901 S Haverhill Rd, El Dorado, KS 67042-3225. Email vharing@butlercc.edu; Email tcoates1@butlercc.edu; *Co-Dir* Valerie Haring; *Co-Dir* Trisha Coates
Estab 1927 to make a scope of art mediums available for experience
Special Subjects: Prints, Painting-American, Prints, Drawings, Sculpture, Ceramics, Architecture, Jewelry, Photography

Collections: Paintings, prints, drawings, sculptures, ceramics, architecture, hand crafted jewelry & photography by regional & national artists.
Exhibitions: Temporary exhibits

M **COUTTS MUSEUM OF ART, INC,** 110 N Main St, El Dorado, KS 67042-2016. Tel 316-321-1212; Fax 316-321-1215; Email rseel@couttsmuseum.org; Web: couttsmuseum.org; *Exec Dir* Rod Seel; *Admin Asst* Tennielle Montgomery
Open Tues - Fri 9 AM - 5 PM, Sat Noon - 4 PM; No admis fee; Estab 1970 as a Fine Arts museum; Fine art & antiques; Average Annual Attendance: 6,000; Mem: 300, $55 per couple, quarterly 3rd Thurs
Income: Financed by endowment & gifts
Special Subjects: American Indian Art, American Western Art, Asian Art, Carpets & Rugs, Cartoons, Ceramics, Collages, Decorative Arts, Drawings, Etchings & Engravings, Folk Art, Furniture, Glass, Landscapes, Latin American Art, Mexican Art, Miniatures, Oriental Art, Painting-American, Painting-British, Painting-European, Painting-French, Painting-Russian, Painting-Spanish, Photography, Portraits, Prints, Reproductions, Sculpture, Southwestern Art, Watercolors
Collections: Frederic Remington sculpture coll completed in 1992 (recasts), Western & Contemporary Western, Two & Three-Dimensional Designs, William Dickerson, Prairie Printmakers
Exhibitions: Annual All County Student Art Show; rotating 4-6 wks; 10-11 exhibits a year, changing every 4 weeks; Paint the Parks Annual Exhibit (Nat Parks)
Publications: Quarterly newsletter
Activities: Classes for children; dramatic pros; docent training; lects open to pub, 4-6 vis lectrs per yr; concerts; gallery talks; tours; competitions with awards; schols offered; individual paintings & original objects of art lent; book traveling exhibs 1-2 per yr; organize traveling exhibs; other exhib venues; museum shop sells books, original art, reproductions, prints

EMPORIA

M **EMPORIA STATE UNIVERSITY,** Norman R Eppink Art Gallery, 1 Kellogg Circle, Emporia, KS 66801. Tel 620-341-5246 or 341-5689; Fax 620-341-6246; Email reichenb@emporia.edu; Web: www.emporia.edu/art/; *Assoc Prof of Art & Galleries Dir* Roberta Eichenberg
Open Mon - Fri 9 AM - 4 PM, cl university holidays; No admis fee; Estab 1939 to bring a variety of exhibitions to the campus; Main Gallery is 25 x 50 ft & has a 50 ft wall for hanging items; adjacent gallery is 16 x 50 ft; display gallery contains eighteen 40 inch x 28 inch panels; Average Annual Attendance: 10,000
Income: Financed by state, grant & endowment funds
Purchases: Annual purchase of contemporary drawings from the Annual National Invitational Drawing Exhibition & varied works from invited exhibiting artists
Library Holdings: Slides
Collections: Artifacts, contemporary drawings and paintings, sculpture
Publications: Exhibition catalogs
Activities: Univ classes; lects open to pub, 8 vis lectrs per yr; concerts; gallery talks; tours; scholarships offered; individual paintings & original objects of art lent to university offices; book traveling exhibs 4-6 per yr; originate traveling exhibs to schools

HAYS

M **FORT HAYS STATE UNIVERSITY,** Moss-Thorns Gallery of Arts, 600 Park St, Hays, KS 67601-4099. Tel 785-628-4247; Fax 785-628-4087; Email ctaylor@fhsu.edu; Web: www.fhsu.edu; *Chmn* Leland Powers; *Secy* Colleen Taylor
Open Mon - Fri 8:30 AM - 4 PM, weekends on special occasions; summer hours: Mon - Thurs 8 AM - 4:30 PM; No admis fee; Estab 1953 to provide constant changing exhibitions for the benefit of students, faculty & other interested people in an educ situation; Rarick Hall has 2200 sq ft with moveable panels that can be used to divide the gallery into four smaller galleries; Average Annual Attendance: 5,000; Mem: 88
Income: Financed by state appropriation
Purchases: $2000
Special Subjects: Drawings, Painting-American, Prints
Collections: Regionalist Collection (1930s), Oriental Scroll Collection, Vyvyan Blackford Collection
Publications: Exhibitions brochures; Art Calendar, annually
Activities: Lects open to public, 4 vis lectrs per yr; gallery talks; tours; competitions with prizes; concerts; exten dept servs western Kansas

L **Forsyth Library**, 600 Park St, Hays, KS 67601. Tel 785-628-4431; Fax 785-628-4096; Email dmludwig@fhsu.edu; Web: www.fhsu.edu/library; *Office Asst* Janet Basgall; *Coordr Research & Teaching* Masyn Phoenix; *Dean* Deborah Ludwig; *Coordr Coll Analysis & Develop* Heath Bogart
Open Mon - Thurs 7:30AM - Midnight, Fri 7:30 AM - 7 PM, Sat 10 AM - 5 PM, Sun 1 PM-Midnight; Academic Library
Library Holdings: Book Volumes 6000, Exhibition Catalogs, Filmstrips, Periodical Subscriptions 1100
Collections: Ethnic Studies Collection, Western Collection

M **HAYS ARTS CENTER,** 112 E 11th St, Hays, KS 67601-3604. Tel 785-625-7522; Email bmeder1038@aol.com; Web: www.haysartcouncil.org; *Exec Dir* Brenda K. Meder
Call for hours; Estab as a nonprofit community arts agency serving Hays, KS and the surrounding area
Special Subjects: Photography, Painting-American, Sculpture
Collections: Contemporary art
Exhibitions: Rotating exhibits
Activities: Educ progs; classes for adults & children;; Lects open to pub; lects for mems only; concerts; gallery talks; tours; art programming; workshops; competitions with awards; public art projects; arts festivals; performance art; cultural events; art invitationals; film screenings

HUTCHINSON

A **HUTCHINSON ART ASSOCIATION,** Hutchinson Art Center, 405 N Washington, Hutchinson, KS 67501. Tel 620-663-1081; Fax 620-663-6367; Email hutchart2@hac.kscoxmail.com; Web: www.hutchartcenter.net; *Pres* Susan Isaac; *Dir* Mark L Rassetti
Open Tues - Fri 9 AM - 5 PM, Sat & Sun 1 - 5 PM; No admis fee; Estab 1949 to bring exhibitions to the city of Hutchinson & maintain a permanent collection; Three galleries & educational area; Average Annual Attendance: 10,000; Mem: 500; dues $20-$5,000; monthly meetings
Income: Financed by mem & endowment
Special Subjects: Ceramics, Glass, Metalwork, Prints, Watercolors
Collections: Permanent collection of watercolors, prints, ceramics, glass, wood, oils & metals
Exhibitions: Two all-member shows per yr; one traveling show per month
Activities: Classes for adults & children; docent training; tours; schols offered; book traveling exhibitions; sales shop sells original art & books

INDEPENDENCE

M **INDEPENDENCE HISTORICAL MUSEUM & ART CENTER,** 123 N 8th & Myrtle, Independence, KS 67301-3501; PO Box 294, Independence, KS 67301-0294. Tel 620-331-3515; Email museum123@cableone.net; Web: www.independencehistoricalmuseum.org; *Mus Coordr* Sylvia Augustine; *Pres* Joy Barta; *1st VPres* Kym Kays; *2nd VPres* Mike Flood; *Secy* Donna Dittmer; *Treas* Randy Hoffman
Open Tues - Sat 10 AM - 4 PM; Admis adults $5, students (6-18) $3, children 5 & under free; Estab 1882 to secure an art collection for the community; The mus has a large gallery which contains original paintings; Indian art & artifacts; military room, Western room; country store, period bedroom, early 1900 kitchen, children's room, historical oil room, & blacksmith shop; Average Annual Attendance: 6,000; Mem: 275; dues $30 - $5,000; monthly meeting Sept - May
Income: Financed by mem, bequests, gifts, art exhibits, various projects & donations
Library Holdings: Cards, Clipping Files, Compact Disks, Maps, Memorabilia, Original Documents, Photographs, Prints, Sculpture
Special Subjects: American Indian Art, American Western Art, Anthropology, Archaeology, Coins & Medals, Dolls, Drawings, Furniture, Furniture, Glass, Glass, Historical Material, Historical Material, Landscapes, Landscapes, Leather, Manuscripts, Maps, Maps, Metalwork, Mexican Art, Miniatures, Period Rooms, Period Rooms, Photography, Porcelain, Portraits, Posters, Pottery, Primitive art, Prints, Reproductions, Sculpture, Southwestern Art, Tapestries, Textiles, Watercolors, Woodcarvings
Collections: American Indian Collection, William Inge Memorabilia Collection, Bill Kurtis, Alf Landon
Exhibitions: Annual Art Exhibit: Quilt Affair; various artists & craftsmen exhibits; Photography Show; Baseball exhibit
Publications: Museum Messenger, monthly members newsletter
Activities: Classes for adults & children; docent training; lectrs open to pub, 2 vis lectrs per yr; gallery talks; tours; competitions with awards; mus shop sells books, reproductions, original art, prints, calendars, KS items, T-shirts & caps

JUNCTION CITY

M **JUNCTION CITY ARTS COUNCIL GALLERY,** 107 W 7th St, Junction City, KS 66441-2942; PO Box 403 Junction City, KS 66441-0403. Tel 785-762-2581; Email jcartscouncil1@gmail.com; Web: www.junctioncityac.org; *Pres* Sally Jardine; *VPres* Emily Vierya; *Secy* Sherry Frewerd; *Treas* Stan Gauntt
Estab 1974 to unite individuals & organizations with an interest in promoting & developing art & culture; Mem: dues $25-$2,500
Activities: Classes for adults & children

LAWRENCE

M **UNIVERSITY OF KANSAS,** Spencer Museum of Art, 1301 Mississippi St, Univ of Kansas Lawrence, KS 66045-7500. Tel 785-864-4710; Fax 785-864-3112; Email spencerart@ku.edu; Web: www.spencerart.ku.edu; *Assoc Dir* Stephen Goddard; *Communs Mgr* Elizabeth Kanost; *Dir Educ* Kristina Walker; *Cur European & American Art* Susan Earle; *Graphic Designer* Jeffrey Mckee; *Dir* Saralyn Reece Hardy; *Exhib Designer* Richard Klocke; *Assoc Dir Schools & Educ Engagement* Amanda Martin Hamon; *Dir Advancement & Planning* Alexis Fekete-Shukla; *Head Coll Mgmt* Sofia Galarza Liu; *Coll Mgr* Angela Watts; *Dir Internal Opers* Jennifer Talbott; *Database Mgr & Archivist* Robert Hickerson; *Cur, Works on Paper* Kate Meyer; *Cur Global Cont & Asian Art* Kris Ercums; *Assoc Dir Public Engagement* Amy Duke; *IT Support Technician* Jared Johanning; *Exhib Technician* Dan Coester; *Exhib Technician* Doug Bergstrom; *Outreach Coord* Celka Straughn; *Creative Svcs Mgr* Ryan Waggoner; *Asst to the Dir* Brittany Nanney
Open Tues, Fri & Sat 10 AM - 4 PM, Wed & Thurs 10 AM - 8 PM, Sun Noon - 4 PM, cl Mon; No admis fee; donations accepted; Dedicated in Spooner Hall 1928, Spencer dedicated 1978. The Museum has traditionally served as a laboratory for the visual arts, supporting curricular study in the arts & art history. Primary emphasis is placed on acquisitions & publications, with a regular schedule of changing exhibitions; Museum has a two level Central Ct, seven galleries devoted to the permanent collections & five galleries for temporary exhibitions; altogether affording 29,000 sq ft; Average Annual Attendance: 117,690; Mem: 400; Dues $50
Income: Financed by mem, state appropriation & state & federal grants, contributions & foundations
Library Holdings: Auction Catalogs, Book Volumes
Special Subjects: African Art, Asian Art, Baroque Art, Bronzes, Calligraphy, Carpets & Rugs, Drawings, Embroidery, Etchings & Engravings, Glass, Graphics, Medieval Art, Painting-American, Painting-British, Painting-Dutch, Painting-European, Painting-Italian, Painting-Japanese, Photography, Prints, Renaissance Art, Sculpture, Silver, Textiles, Watercolors, Woodcuts

Collections: American paintings, ancient art, Asian art, graphics, Medieval art, 17th & 18th century art, especially German, 19th century European & American art, 20th century European & American art, Ethnographic coll: African, North American, Japanese Painting & Prints, Chinese Paintings & Sculpture
Publications: Calendar, monthly; Murphy Lectures, annually; The Register of the Spencer Museum of Art, annually; exhibition catalogs, 1-2 per year
Activities: Classes for children; docent training; international artist in residency prog; lects open to pub, 12 & more vis lectrs per yr; concerts; gallery talks; tours; internships offered; book traveling exhibs; originates traveling exhibs; mus shop sells books, reproductions, prints, slides, posters, postcards, jewelry & gifts

L **Murphy Library of Art & Architecture**, 1425 Jayhawk Blvd, University of Kansas Lawrence, KS 66045-7594. Tel 785-864-3020; Fax 785-864-4608; Email scraig@ukans.edu; Web: www.2ku.eduårtlib; *Librn* Susan V Craig
Open during school yr, Mon - Thurs 8 AM - 10 PM, Fri 8 AM - 6 PM, Sat Noon - 5 PM, Sun 1 - 10 PM; Estab 1970 to support acad progs & for research; Circ Open to faculty, students & pub; some restrictions on circulating items
Library Holdings: Book Volumes 110,000, CD-ROMs, Exhibition Catalogs, Fiche, Other Holdings Auction catalogs, Pamphlets, Periodical Subscriptions 700, Reels
Special Subjects: Architecture, Art Education, Art History, Asian Art, Decorative Arts, Graphic Design, Painting-American, Painting-Dutch, Painting-Flemish, Painting-Japanese, Photography, Prints, Textiles

L **Architectural Resource Center**, 1465 Jayhawk Blvd, School of Architecture & Urban Design Lawrence, KS 66045-7594. Tel 785-864-3244; Fax 785-864-5393; Email u-stammler@ku.edu; *Dir* Ursula Stammler
Open Mon - Fri 10 AM - 5 PM, Sun - Thurs 7:30 PM - 9:30 PM; Slide Library, estab 1968, is primarily a teaching tool for faculty, but also accessible to students; Donald E & Mary Bole Hatch Architectural Reading Room, estab 1981, is adjacent to studios in School of Architecture & supports the immediate reference needs of students; For reference only
Income: Financed by endowment & state appropriation
Library Holdings: Book Volumes 3000, Periodical Subscriptions 30, Slides 82,000
Special Subjects: Architecture

LEAVENWORTH

M **CARNEGIE ARTS CENTER,** 121 Cherokee St, Leavenworth, KS 66048-2816. Tel 785-890-6442; Email gldarts@st-tel.net; Web: goodlandarts.org; *Dir* Carolyn Singleton
Open Tues - Thurs Noon - 4 PM, Sat 10 AM - 4 PM, cl Fri & Sun; Estab 1978 to create opportunities for the community to experience a variety of art forms in an accessible & affordable way; dues $20-$500
Exhibitions: Monthly exhibits
Activities: Classes for adults & children; workshops; recitals; art demonstrations; lects; concerts

LIBERAL

M **BAKER ARTS CENTER,** 624 N Pershing Ave, Liberal, KS 67901-3115. Tel 620-624-2810; Fax 620-624-7726; Email tonismith@bakerartscenter.org; Web: www.bakerartscenter.org; *Dir* Toni Smith; *Arts Admin Asst* Kim Bryant; *Office Mgr* Emily Castaneda
Open Tues - Fri 9 AM - noon & 1 PM - 5 PM, Sun 1 PM - 3 PM; No admis fee; Estab 1984 to support the arts; Mem: dues $35-$1,000
Library Holdings: Book Volumes 2,000, 1,000 reference portfolios
Special Subjects: Watercolors, Sculpture, Photography
Collections: Oil, acrylic & watercolor painting, sculpture & photography
Exhibitions: Temporary exhibits
Activities: Classes & workshops

LINDSBORG

M **BETHANY COLLEGE,** Mingenback Art Center, 335 E Swensson, Lindsborg, KS 67456. Tel 785-227-3380, Ext 8145; Email kahlerc@bethanylb.edu; Web: www.bethanylb.edu; *Assoc Prof* Mary Kay; *Prof* Dr Bruce Kahler; *Asst Prof* Frank Shaw; *Prof* Ed Pogue; *Prof* Caroline Kahler; *Instr* Jim Turner
Open daily 8 AM - 5 PM, cl summer & holidays; No admis fee; Estab 1970 as an educational gallery for student & professional exhibitions; Materials are not for pub display, for educational reference only; Average Annual Attendance: 1,500
Income: Financed by collections
Special Subjects: Ceramics, Sculpture, Watercolors
Collections: Oil paintings, watercolors, prints, etchings, lithographs, wood engravings, ceramics & sculpture
Exhibitions: Autumn Exhibition; Messiah Exhibition; Rotating exhibs; Graduating Sr Exhibits
Activities: Classes for adults; lect open to public, 2 vis lectrs per year; Kaymeyer Visiting Artist Lecture Series; gallery talks; competitions with prizes; portfolio-based performance awards; scholarships offered

L **Wallerstedt Library**, 235 E Swensson, Lindsborg, KS 67456. Tel 785-227-3380, Ext 8165; Fax 785-227-2860; Email carsond@bethanylb.edu; Web: www.bethanylb.edu/home; *Dir* Denise Carson; *Inter-Library Loan Librn* Brittney Read; *Librn* Lucy Walline
Open Mon - Thurs 7:30 AM - 10:30 PM, Fri 7:30 AM - 5 PM, Sat 1PM-5PM, Sun 3PM-10:30PM; Estab 1881; For reference only
Library Holdings: Book Volumes 121,000, Exhibition Catalogs

M **BIRGER SANDZEN MEMORIAL GALLERY,** 401 N 1st St, Lindsborg, KS 67456-1813; PO Box 348, Lindsborg, KS 67456-0348. Tel 785-227-2220; Fax 785-227-4170; Email fineart@sandzen.org; Web: www.sandzen.org; *Dir* Ronald Michael; *Cur* Cori North; *Sandzen Foundation Pres & CEO* Dr Bryce Loder; *VPres* Kenneth Warren; *Secy* Judy Langley; *Treas* John Levin
Open Tues - Sat - 10 AM - 5 PM, Sun 1 - 5 PM; No admis fee; Estab 1957 to permanently exhibit the paintings & prints by the late Birger Sandzen, teacher at Bethany College for 52 years along with art exhibitions and special exhibitions by regional and nationally recognized artists; Nine exhibition areas; Average Annual Attendance: 17,200; Mem: 350; dues $30-$5,000; annual meeting May for Board of Dir
Income: Financed by admis fees, sales & mem, invested endowment
Library Holdings: Book Volumes, Cards, Clipping Files, Exhibition Catalogs, Memorabilia, Original Documents, Pamphlets, Periodical Subscriptions, Photographs, Slides, Video Tapes
Special Subjects: Art History, Asian Art, Oriental Art, Photography, Painting-American, Ceramics, Jade, Prints, Sculpture, Watercolors, Woodcuts
Collections: H V Poor, Lester Raymer, Birger Sandzen, John Bashor, Elmer Tomasch, Doel Reed & Carl Milles, Prairie Print Maker Society prints
Publications: Birger Sandzen: An Illustrated Biography; The Graphic Work of Birger Sandzen; Sandzen & the New Land, catalogue; color reproductions & posters of Sandzen oils
Activities: Classes for children; docent training; lects open to pub, 3 - 7 vis lectrs per yr; concerts; gallery talks open to pub; chamber music concerts; tours; lending of original objects of art to art museums; 1-2 book traveling exhibs per yr; originates traveling exhibs to art museums & cultural organizations; sales shop sells books, reproductions, prints & cards; consignment art sales

LOGAN

M **DANE G HANSEN MEMORIAL MUSEUM,** PO Box 187, Logan, KS 67646-0187. Tel 785-689-4846; Fax 785-689-4892; Email hansenmuseum@ruraltel.net; Web: www.hansenmuseum.org; *Dir* Shirley A Henrickson
Open Mon - Fri 9 AM - Noon & 1 - 4 PM, Sat 9 AM - Noon & 1 - 5 PM, Sun & holidays 1 - 5 PM, cl Thanksgiving, Christmas & New Year's; No admis fee; Estab 1973; Traveling exhibitions; Average Annual Attendance: 9,000; Mem: 300; dues sustaining $50, patron $25, benefactor $10
Collections: Coins, guns, paintings, sculptures
Activities: Classes for adults & children; lect open to public; concerts; gallery talks; tours; 6 traveling book exhibitions per year

LUCAS

M **GRASSROOTS ART CENTER,** 213 S Main St, Lucas, KS 67648; PO Box 304, Lucas, KS 67648-0304. Tel 785-525-6118; Email grassroots@wtciweb.com; Web: www.grassrootsart.net; *Exec Dir* Rosslyn Schultz; *Staff Asst* Peg Gilbert; *Staff Asst* Alice Sutton
Open May - Sept Mon - Sat 10 AM - 5 PM, Sun 1 PM - 5 PM; Oct & Apr Thurs - Mon 1 PM - 4 PM, Nov - Mar Thurs - Sat 1 PM - 4 PM, cl holidays (winter months); Admis adults $7, children 6-12 $3, discounts to groups of 10+; Estab 1991 to preserve, document, educate, exhibit self taught, outsider, recycled art & folk art of the region; Outsider art; Average Annual Attendance: 7,000; Mem: 321; mtgs 2nd Mon; various levels
Income: Admission, mem, donations, gift area sales & grants
Library Holdings: Audio Tapes, Book Volumes, CD-ROMs, DVDs, Original Art Works, Photographs, Slides, Video Tapes
Special Subjects: Folk Art, Metalwork, Miniatures, Mosaics, Textiles, Woodcarvings
Collections: Self taught artists
Exhibitions: Dennis Clark: Imaginative Cities
Publications: Newsletter May & Oct
Activities: Art classes for adults & children; docent training; lects open to pub; vis lectrs 2 per yr; gallery talks; tours; 8 Wonders of Kansas Art & KS Governor's Tourism awards; lending original art to galleries by request; mus shop sells books & original & recycled art

MANHATTAN

L **KANSAS STATE UNIVERSITY,** Paul Weigel Library of Architecture Planning & Design, 323 Seaton Hall, College of Architecture Planning & Design Manhattan, KS 66506-2900. Tel 785-532-5968; Web: www.lib.k-state.edu/branches/arch; *Library Asst* Judy Wyatt; *Ref Librn* Ann Scott; *Librn* Jeff Alger
Open Mon - Thurs 8 AM - 10 PM, Fri 8 AM - 5 PM, Sat 1- 5 PM, Sun 2 - 10 PM; No admis fee; Estab 1917; Circ 29,861
Income: $40,000 (financed by state appropriations & gifts)
Library Holdings: Book Volumes 38,806, Clipping Files, Fiche, Periodical Subscriptions 225, Reels
Special Subjects: Architecture, Drafting, Graphic Design, Historical Material, Landscape Architecture, Restoration & Conservation
Publications: Subject catalog

M **RILEY COUNTY HISTORICAL SOCIETY & MUSEUM,** Riley County Historical Museum, 2309 Claflin Rd, Manhattan, KS 66502-3421. Tel 785-565-6490; Fax 785-565-6491; Email ccollins@rileycountyks.gov; Web: www.rileycountyks.gov/index.asp; *Cur Archives & Libr* Linda Glasgow; *Dir & Cur* D Cheryl Collins; *Cur Exhibits* Allana Saenger; *Cur Coll & Registrar* Corina Hugo
Open Tues - Fri 8:30 AM - 5 PM; Sat & Sun 2 - 5 PM; No admis fee, donations accepted; Estab 1916 to exhibit history & current & historical arts & crafts; Maintains reference library & exhibit galleries; Average Annual Attendance: 25,000; Mem: 1000; dues life $300, patron $100+, sustainer $75 - $99, sponsor $ 50 - $74, friend $10 - $49; dinner meetings in Jan, Apr, July & Oct
Income: Mus financed by Riley County budget; Society a pvt dues org
Special Subjects: Architecture, Carpets & Rugs, Coins & Medals, Costumes, Decorative Arts, Dolls, Flasks & Bottles, Folk Art, Furniture, Glass, Historical Material, Laces, Manuscripts, Maps, Period Rooms, Porcelain, Portraits, Posters, Pottery, Prints, Textiles, Decorative Arts
Collections: Photo Collections, Riley County History Artifacts
Exhibitions: Household Work Week; The Land & the People - standing exhib
Publications: RCHS Newsletter, 10 times per year; Tracing Traditions, a coloring book for children; The Architects & Buildings of Manhattan, Kansas by Dr Patricia

J O'Brien; This Land is Our Land by Donald Parrish; Rural Schools of Riley Co, Kansas by Bogart, Brannon, Setterquist, Setterquist & Tippin
Activities: Classes for children: hands on tours using educational coll; Docent progs & training; lects open to pub; tours; originate traveling exhibs to schools & club meetings; mus shop sells books, Kansas crafts, wood cuts & KS themed items

L **Seaton Library**, 2309 Claflin Rd, Manhattan, KS 66502. Tel 785-565-6490; Fax 785-565-6491; Email ccollins@rileycountyks.gov; *Library Archivist* Linda Glasgow; *Dir* D Cheryl Collins; *Exhibits* Allana Saenger; *Registrar* Corina Hugo
By appointment only; No admis fee; Estab 1976; research library; Reference, non-circulating collection
Income: Financed by Riley County
Library Holdings: Audio Tapes, Book Volumes 4000, Clipping Files, Lantern Slides, Manuscripts, Maps, Memorabilia, Motion Pictures, Original Documents, Pamphlets, Periodical Subscriptions, Photographs, Slides, Video Tapes
Special Subjects: Architecture, Historical Material, Manuscripts, Maps
Collections: Photo Collection, Family files, maps, club records, school records, bus records, county government & city records
Activities: Mus shop sells books

MCPHERSON

M **MCPHERSON COLLEGE GALLERY,** 1600 E Euclid, Friendship Hall McPherson, KS 67460-3847. Tel 316-241-0731; Fax 316-241-8443; Web: www.mcpherson.edu; *Dir* Wayne Conyers
Open Mon - Fri 8 AM - 10 PM; No admis fee; Estab 1960 to present works of art to the col students & to the community; A long gallery which is the entrance to an auditorium, has four showcases & 11 panels 4 x 16 ft; Average Annual Attendance: 2,500
Income: Financed through college
Special Subjects: Painting-American, Prints, Watercolors
Collections: Oils, original prints, watercolors
Exhibitions: change monthly
Activities: Classes for adults; scholarships offered; book traveling exhibitions

M **MCPHERSON MUSEUM AND ARTS FOUNDATION,** 1111 E Kansas Ave McPherson, KS 67460. Tel 620-241-8464; Fax 620-241-2676; Email director@mcphersonmuseum.com; Web: www.mcphersonmuseum.com; *Dir* Anna Ruxlow
Open May - Sept Mon - Fri 8 AM - 5 PM, Sat -Sun 1 PM - 5 PM; Sept - May Mon - Fri 8 Am - 5 PM, Sat 1 PM - 5 PM; Admis adults $5, seniors & students $3, children under 4 & mems no charge; Estab 1984; Birger Sandzen prints on display year round; one annual feature art exhibit; Average Annual Attendance: 4,500; Mem: 200, dues $25 - $50
Income: Financed by city appropriation & pvt donations
Special Subjects: African Art, American Indian Art, Anthropology, Antiquities-Oriental, Archaeology, Asian Art, Costumes, Decorative Arts, Dolls, Folk Art, Furniture, Glass, Historical Material, Landscapes, Painting-American, Textiles, Woodcarvings, Pottery, Prints
Collections: Fossils of mammoths, mastodons, saber tooth tigers & many other fossils, oriental & African coll, Pioneer artifacts & Native American Pottery, Sandzen Prints, folk art collection, Folk art carvings of artist Anna Larkin
Exhibitions: 4 feature exhibits per year, including 1 art exhibit
Publications: McPherson Museum & Art Foundation newsletter, The Diamond
Activities: Sponsor Wordfest, an annual writer's conference; sponsor writers' group; summer music series (6 concerts); educ prog; classes for adults & children; winter lect series (7 lects); lects open to pub, 7 vis lectrs per year; concerts; tours; sponsoring of competitions; mus shop sells books, original art & reproductions

MONTEZUMA

M **STAUTH FOUNDATION & MUSEUM,** Stauth Memorial Museum, 111 N Azetec St, Montezuma, KS 67867-0396; PO Box 396, Montezuma, KS 67867. Tel 620-846-2527; Fax 620-846-2810; Email stauthm@ucom.net; Web: www.stauthmemorialmuseum.org; *Dir & Financial Dir* Kim Legleiter
Open Tues - Sat 9 AM - Noon & 1 - 4:30 PM, Sun 1:30 - 4:30 PM; No admis fee; Estab 1996; Four galleries; Average Annual Attendance: 4,000
Income: $95,000 (financed by endowment & donations)
Library Holdings: Maps National Geo 1945-present, Slides
Special Subjects: African Art, Asian Art, Bronzes, Ceramics, Coins & Medals, Costumes, Decorative Arts, Dolls, Embroidery, Enamels, Eskimo Art, Etchings & Engravings, Flasks & Bottles, Folk Art, Furniture, Glass, Ivory, Jewelry, Latin American Art, Maps, Metalwork, Oriental Art, Photography, Posters, Scrimshaw, Sculpture, Woodcarvings, Textiles
Collections: Coins-foreign, decorative arts, jewelry-foreign, natural history coll, slides-over 10,000, musical instruments, Remington bronze miniatures & other western bronze miniatures, North American Big Game Specimen
Exhibitions: Around The World with Claude & Donald Stauth; The Ralph Fry Wildlife Collection; Wall Western Collection; Special exhibitions gallery
Activities: Classes for children; lects open to pub; 2-3 vis lectrs per yr; tours; book traveling exhibs 7 - 8 per yr

NORTH NEWTON

L **BETHEL COLLEGE,** Mennonite Library & Archives, 300 E 27th St, North Newton, KS 67117-1716. Tel 316-284-5304; Fax 316-284-5843; Email mla@bethelks.edu; Web: www.bethslks.edu/mla/index.php; *Archivist* John D Thiesen; *Librn* Barbara A Thiesen; *Asst Archivist* James Lynch
Open Mon - Thurs 10 AM - 5 PM; No admis fee; Estab 1936 to preserve resources related to Mennonite history for the use of researchers
Income: $70,000 (financed by college & church conference support)
Library Holdings: Audio Tapes, Cassettes, Clipping Files, Exhibition Catalogs, Fiche, Filmstrips, Framed Reproductions, Kodachrome Transparencies, Lantern Slides, Manuscripts, Memorabilia, Motion Pictures, Original Art Works, Pamphlets, Photographs, Prints, Records, Reels, Reproductions, Slides, Video Tapes
Special Subjects: Ethnology, Historical Material, Manuscripts, Painting-American, Painting-Dutch, Painting-German, Photography, Religious Art
Collections: 500 paintings and etchings by Mennonite artists, Photographs of Hopi and Cheyenne Indians
Publications: Mennonite Life, on-line only
Activities: Lects

NORTON

C **FIRST STATE BANK,** They Also Ran Gallery, 105 W Main St, Norton, KS 67654-1947; PO Box 560, Norton, KS 67654-0560. Tel 785-877-3341; Fax 785-877-5808; Email firstate@ruraltel.net; Email theyalsoran@firstatebank.com; Web: www.firstatebank.com, www.theyalsoran.com; *Chmn* Norman L Nelson; *Pres* John P Engelbert; *Contact* Lee Ann Shearer
Open Mon - Fri 9 AM - 3 PM, Sat 8:30 AM - 11:30 AM; No admis fee; Estab 1965 as a gallery of those who ran for President of the United States & lost; 60 portraits & biographies; Average Annual Attendance: varies
Income: through the bank
Special Subjects: Historical Material
Collections: Also Ran Gallery, Take Off Elephants
Exhibitions: Permanent
Publications: Take off brochure available
Activities: Tours

OVERLAND PARK

M **KANSAS CITY JEWISH MUSEUM OF CONTEMPORARY ART - EPSTEN GALLERY,** 5500 W 123rd St, Overland Park, KS 66209. Tel 913-266-8414; *Prog & Develop Asst* Abby Rufkahr; *Exec Dir* Eileen Garry; *Cur* Marcus Cain
Open Tues-Fri 11AM-4PM, Sat-Sun 1PM-4PM; No admis fee, donations accepted
Collections: works by contemporary artists

RUSSELL

M **DEINES CULTURAL CENTER,** 820 N Main St, Russell, KS 67665-1932. Tel 785-483-3742; Fax 785-483-4397; Email info@deinesculturalcenter.org; Web: www.deinesculturalcenter.org; *Dir* Shannon Trevethan; *Cur* Mathew Miller
Open Tues - Fri 12--5PM, Sat-Sun 1PM-5PM; No admis fee; Estab 1990 to promote the arts & humanities; Average Annual Attendance: 2,500; Mem: 175; dues $25
Income: $30,000 (financed by mem & city appropriation)
Special Subjects: Ceramics, Collages, Dolls, Etchings & Engravings, Folk Art, Historical Material, Jewelry, Juvenile Art, Painting-American, Photography, Pottery, Prints, Sculpture, Watercolors, Woodcuts, Landscapes
Collections: E Hubert Deines Wood Engravings, Various regional artists
Exhibitions: Monthly exhibits
Activities: Classes for adults & children; recitals; lects open to pub; book traveling exhibitions 1 per year; mus shop sells original art

SALINA

M **SALINA ART CENTER,** 242 S Santa Fe, Salina, KS 67401-3932; PO Box 743, Salina, KS 67402-0743. Tel 785-827-1431; Fax 785-827-0686; Email info@salingartcenter.org; Web: www.salinaartcenter.org; *Dir Community Develop* Wendy Moshier; *Communs Coordr* Pamela Harris; *Comm Coordr* Libby Shoup; *Gallery Mgr* Joshua Smith
Open Tues, Wed, Fri & Sat noon - 5 PM, Thurs noon - 7 PM, Sun 1- 5 PM, cl Mon; No admis fee; Estab 1979 as an international & national private non-profit, non-collecting contemporary art & educ center; One floor, 50 ft x 150 sq. ft.; Average Annual Attendance: 50,000; Mem: 500; dues $40 basic
Income: $350,000 (financed by mem & private donations)
Exhibitions: Contemporary Art; changing exhibitions; Annual Juried Show
Publications: Brochures; newsletters
Activities: Classes for adults & children; docent progs; lects open to pub, 6-8 vis lectrs per yr; competitions; traveling exten dept serves rural Kansas; book traveling exhibs 4 per yr; originate traveling exhibs 5 per yr

SCOTT CITY

M **KEYSTONE GALLERY,** 401 US 83, Scott City, KS 67871-8013. Tel 620-872-2762; Web: www.keystonegallery.com; *Artist* Charles Bonner; *Photographer* Barbara Shelton; *Web Designer* Logan Bonner
Call for hours; Admis fee $5; Estab 1991 as an art gallery & fossil mus; displays of fossils & Western Kansas paintings; Average Annual Attendance: 5,000
Special Subjects: American Western Art, Graphics, Historical Material, Jewelry, Photography, Sculpture
Collections: Local history & culture; paintings; fossils; period artifacts; photographs
Activities: Gallery talks; tours; mus shop sells books; original art; prints, minerals & fossils

TOPEKA

M **KANSAS STATE HISTORICAL SOCIETY,** Kansas Museum of History, 6425 SW Sixth Ave, Topeka, KS 66615-1099. Tel 785-272-8681; Fax 785-272-8682; Email KansasMuseum@kshs.org; Web: www.kshs.org; *Exec Dir* Jennie Chinn; *Cur of Decorative Art* Blair Tarr; *Dir Mus* Mary W Madden
Open Tue - Sat 9 AM - 5 PM, Sun 1 - 5 PM, cl Mon, state holidays, New Year's & Christmas; Admis adults $8, students $6, mems & children 5 & under free; Estab 1875 to collect, preserve & interpret the historical documents & objects of Kansas

history; Average Annual Attendance: 40,000; Mem: 3400; dues life $1000, special $50 - $1000, family $35, individual $25, student $15; meetings in spring & fall
Income: financed by endowment & state
Special Subjects: Cartoons, Historical Material
Collections: Regional collection for period from middle 19th century to present, especially portraiture, native art, political cartoons & folk art
Exhibitions: Rotating Exhibits
Publications: Kansas History: Journal of the Central Plains, quarterly; exhibit catalogs
Activities: Classes for adults & children; dramatic progs; docent training; history lab; online resources include collection's virtual database, Kansas Memory; lects open to pub, tours; limited schols available for student groups; exten dept serves entire state of Kansas; traveling trunks on Kansas topics; sales shop sells books, prints, cards, slides, postcards, folk art, crafts, souvenirs and jewelry

M **TOPEKA & SHAWNEE COUNTY PUBLIC LIBRARY,** Alice C Sabatini Gallery, 1515 SW Tenth St, Topeka, KS 66604-1374. Tel 785-580-4515; Fax 785-580-4496; Email gallery@tscpl.org; Web: www.tscpl.org; *Art Coll Cur* Sherry L Best; *Exec Dir* Gina Millsap; *Art Exhibit Cur* Zan Popp; *Gallery Assoc* Betsy Knab Roe; *Special Colls/Art Librn* Brea Black; *Pub Servs Mgr* Stephanie L Hall
Open Mon - Fri 9 AM - 9 PM, Sat 9 AM - 6 PM, Sun 12 - 9 PM; No admis fee; Estab 1870 to serve the city & the Northeast Kansas Library System residents with public information, both educational & recreational; to be one of the areas cultural centers through services from the Gallery within the library; Circ Public library circulation, over 2 million items; Gallery reopened in 2001 with a 1864 sq ft plus space, professional lighting, security system; gallery furniture; Average Annual Attendance: 20,000+; Mem: 90; dues $30 per yr
Income: Financed by city, county & property taxes
Purchases: Contemporary arts
Library Holdings: Audio Tapes, Book Volumes, CD-ROMs, Cassettes, Clipping Files, Compact Disks, DVDs, Exhibition Catalogs, Fiche, Lantern Slides, Maps, Memorabilia, Micro Print, Original Art Works, Original Documents, Pamphlets, Periodical Subscriptions, Photographs, Prints, Sculpture, Slides, Video Tapes
Special Subjects: African Art, American Indian Art, American Western Art, Architecture, Asian Art, Bronzes, Carpets & Rugs, Ceramics, Drawings, Enamels, Etchings & Engravings, Glass, Jewelry, Landscapes, Latin American Art, Metalwork, Mexican Art, Oriental Art, Painting-American, Pottery, Primitive art, Prints, Religious Art, Watercolors, Woodcarvings
Collections: 19th Century Chinese Decorative Arts, Hirschberg Collection of West African Arts, Johnson Collection of Art, Contemporary American Ceramics, Glass paperweight coll, New Mexican Woodcarving, Rare Book Room, Regional painting, drawing & prints, Wilder Collection of Art Nouveau Glass & Ceramics, Books as art
Exhibitions: Juried national Topeka Competition of 3D contemporary works; Juried National Printmaking competition; Permanent collections, children's & group exhibits
Publications: Creative Expression in Rural West Africa; Rookwood Pottery: One Hundred Year Anniversary
Activities: Docent training; lects open to pub, concerts; gallery; talks; tours by request; special programs for exhibits; competitions with awards; cash & purchase awards for Competitions; Institute for Museum and Library Svcs: Mus assessment program grant; individual paintings & original objects of art lent to other qualified mus; mus shop sells used books

M **WASHBURN UNIVERSITY,** Mulvane Art Museum, 17th & Jewell Sts, Topeka, KS 66621-0001; 1700 SW College Ave, Topeka, KS 66621-0001. Tel 785-670-1124; Fax 785-670-1329; Email mulvane.info@washburn.edu; Web: www.washburn.edu/mulvane; *Dir* Connie Gibbons; *Cur* Julia Myers; *Admin Asst* Delene Van Sickle; *Cur Educ* Kandis Barker; *Preparator* Michael Allen; *Asst Cur Educ* Jane Hanni; *Mus Receptionist* Jan Bychinski
Open Tues 10 AM - 7 PM, Wed, Thurs & Fri 10 AM - 5 PM, Sat 1 - 4 PM, cl holidays; No admis fee; Estab 1922; Building gift of Joab Mulvane: provides six galleries with 600 running ft of hanging space with temperature & humidity controlled; Average Annual Attendance: 120,000; Mem: 400; dues individual $50, family/director's circle $125
Income: $450,000 (Financed by Washburn Univ endowed funds & Friends of The Mulvane Art Mus, Inc)
Purchases: $10,000
Special Subjects: Asian Art, Ceramics, Etchings & Engravings, Glass, Graphics, Painting-American, Prints, Sculpture, Southwestern Art, Watercolors, Woodcuts
Collections: 18th-19th Century Japanese Fine & Decorative Art, 19th & 20th Century American Art, 16th-20th Century European Prints
Exhibitions: Contemporary Mountain-Plains regional painting, prints, sculpture, ceramics; changing exhibitions include a Kansas Artist Exhibit & Annual Mountain-Plains Art Fair
Publications: Exhibition brochures
Activities: Classes for adults & children; outreach progs: Art Beginning in Childhood; Art in School, Art After School; docent training; lects open to pub, 4-6 vis lectrs per yr; gallery talks; tours; scholarships; individuals painting & original objects of art lent to accredited art mus; book traveling exhibs; mus shop sells books, original art, reproductions, jewelry, note cards, toys, unusual gifts for all ages

WAMEGO

M **THE COLUMBIAN THEATRE FOUNDATION, INC,** Columbian Theatre Museum & Art Center, 521 Lincoln Ave, Wamego, KS 66547. Tel 785-456-2029; Fax 785-456-9498; Email boxoffice@columbiantheatre.com; Web: www.columbiantheatre.com; *Exec Dir* Clint Stueve; *Mktg Asst* Alyssa Smith; *Box Office Coordr* Rhonda Jacques; *Production Manager* Libby Stratton; *Event Coordr* Tara Jackson
Open Tues-Fri 10 AM - 5 PM, Sat 10AM-3PM, cl Mon; No admis fee, suggested donation $5; Estab 1994; Curated by the Columbian artist group; offers variety of area artist's work; Average Annual Attendance: 24,000; Mem: 200; dues $50-$1500
Income: $300,000 (financed by mem, grants, gifts, earned income (ticket sales) & underwriters)
Special Subjects: Architecture, Decorative Arts, Historical Material, Painting-American
Collections: A 20-painting coll from the Columbian Exposition, the 1893 Chicago World's Fair, representing 60 percent of the decorative art from the Government Building. Includes 6 large oil on canvas paintings (restored & on display) by Ernest Theodore Behr
Exhibitions: Swogger gallery houses an average of 6-8 rotating exhibits per year featuring artists & collections from or pertaining to the region &/or the mission of the Columbian
Activities: Dramatic progs; dinners; children's Summer Theatre Academy; gallery/ building tours; gift shop sells local items

WICHITA

M **FRIENDS UNIVERSITY,** Riney Fine Arts Center Gallery, Riney Fine Arts Bldg, 2100 University Ave Wichita, KS 67213-3379. Tel 316-295-5537; Email artgallery@friends.edu; *Fine Arts Events Coordr* Megan Berry
Open Mon - Fri 8 AM - 6 PM; No admis fee; Estab 1963 to bring art-craft exhibits to campus as an educational learning experience & to supply the local community with first class exhibits; 1224 sq ft of exhibit space; Average Annual Attendance: 20,000
Activities: 4 vis lectrs per yr; gallery talks; tours; monthly art exhibs & receptions; exten dept

L **Edmund Stanley Library,** 2100 University Ave, Wichita, KS 67213. Tel 316-295-5880; Fax 316-295-5080; Email askalibrarian@friends.edu; Web: www.friends.edu/academics/library; *Library Dir* Max M Burson; *Reference Librn* Kathy Delker
Open semester Mon - Thurs 7:45 - 10 PM, Fri 7:45 - 4 PM, Sat 9 AM - 5 PM, Sun 3 PM - 10 PM; summer Mon - Thurs 7:45 AM - 7 PM, Fri 7:45 - Noon, cl Sat - Sun; Admis free for community card to check out books; Estab 1979; 500 sq ft of exhibition space, ideal for crafts & locked cases
Library Holdings: Audio Tapes, Book Volumes, Cassettes, Compact Disks, DVDs, Fiche, Filmstrips, Maps, Memorabilia, Original Art Works, Original Documents, Pamphlets, Periodical Subscriptions 90, Photographs, Sculpture 10, Slides, Video Tapes

M **GALLERY XII,** 412 E Douglas Ave, Ste A, Wichita, KS 67202. Tel 316-267-5915; Email wichitagallery12@yahoo.com; Web: www.wichitagalleryXII.com; *Pres* Tom Montgomery; *VPres* Jan Butler; *Secy* Martha Wherry; *Member* Susan Fellows; *Member* Judy Dove
Open Mon - Sat 10 AM - 4 PM, final Fri of month 5:30 PM - 10 PM; No admis fee; Estab 1977 as art cooperative; Gallery specializes in original art by Kansas artists; Average Annual Attendance: 10,000; Mem: dues $400; 22 mem; local artists juried by current mems
Income: financed by mem
Library Holdings: Original Art Works, Photographs, Prints, Sculpture, Slides
Publications: Edition of 20 hand-pulled black & white lithographs
Activities: Gallery talks; sponsoring of competitions; crazy 8 invitational; scholastic art awards;; exten program serves local nonprofit organizations; local source for pub & pvt schools - field trips, tours & lab; originates traveling exhibs to nonprofits in Kansas; gallery sells original art by Kansas artists, photographs

A **KANSAS WATERCOLOR SOCIETY,** Mark Arts, 9112 E Central, Wichita, KS 67206. Tel 316-634-2787; Fax 316-634-0593; Email katy@narkartsks.com; Web: www.markartsks.com; *Exec Dir* Katy Dorrah
Open Tues -Sun 1 PM - 5 PM; No admis fee; Estab 1970 to promote watercolor in Kansas; Mem: 185; dues $20
Income: Financed by mem, entry fees, patrons & Kansas Arts Commission
Exhibitions: Rotating exhibits
Publications: Newsletter, quarterly
Activities: Demonstrations & workshops; lects open to public; gallery talks; tours; competitions with awards; originates traveling exhibs

A **MARY R KOCH ARTS CENTER,** Mark Arts, 9112 E Central, Wichita, KS 67206. Tel 316-634-2787; Fax 316-634-0593; Web: www.markartsks.com; *Bd Pres* Karla Fazio; *Treas* William Tinker Jr; *Exec Dir* Katy Dorrah; *Dir Exhibs* Dimitris Skliris; *Dir Educ* Lauren Baldwin
Open Tues - Sun 1 - 5 PM, cl national holidays; No admis fee; Estab 1920, incorporated 1932, as an educational & cultural institution; Gallery contains 1000 running ft of exhibit space; up to five exhibits each six-week period; Average Annual Attendance: 55,000; Mem: 1250; dues $35 & up
Income: Financed by private contributions
Collections: Prints and drawings, paintings, sculpture, American decorative arts & contemporary crafts
Exhibitions: Exhibitions change each six weeks; one man shows; special programs; Biennial National Craft Exhibit
Publications: 6 newsletters per year
Activities: Visual & performing arts classes for adults & children; theatre productions; docent training; lects open to public, up to 6 vis lectrs per yr; gallery talks; classic film series; competitions with awards; scholarships; individual paintings & original objects of art lent to other art museums; book traveling exhibs; originate traveling exhibs; sales shop sells books & original art

M **MID-AMERICA ALL-INDIAN CENTER,** Indian Center Museum, 650 N Seneca, Wichita, KS 67203. Tel 316-350-3340; Email ascott@wichita.gov; Web: www.theindiancenter.org; *Exec Dir* April Scott
Open Tues - Sat 10 AM - 4 PM; Admis adults $7, seniors $5, children 6-12 $3, under 6 free; Estab 1976 to preserve the Indian heritage, culture & traditions; Average Annual Attendance: 70,000; Mem: 400; dues benefactor $500 & up, patron $250 - $499, friend $100 - $249, contributor $50 - $99, family $35 - $49, individual $25 - $34
Income: Financed by admis, donations, mem & gift shop sales
Library Holdings: Book Volumes
Special Subjects: American Indian Art
Collections: Native American arts & artifacts, Plains beadwork, Northwest Coast & Eskimo crafts, Southwest pottery, paintings, sculpture, carvings & basketry,

Mildred Manty Memorial Collection, Ray Meadows Collection, Lincoln Ellsworth Collection
Exhibitions: Four changing exhibits per yr, prehistory or specialty exhibits; three dimensional traditional art; two & three dimensional contemporary art
Activities: Classes for adults & children; docent training; lects open to pub; gallery talks; tours; mus shop sells books, magazines, original art, reproductions & prints

L **Black Bear Bosin Resource Center**, 650 N Seneca, Wichita, KS 67203. Tel 316-262-5221
Open Tues - Sat 10 AM - 5 PM by appointment only; Reference only
Income: financed by donations, gifts
Library Holdings: Book Volumes 400, Filmstrips, Motion Pictures, Pamphlets, Slides
Collections: Indian art & history

M **WICHITA ART MUSEUM,** 1400 W Museum Blvd, Wichita, KS 67203-3296. Tel 316-268-4921; Fax 316-268-4980; Email info@wichitaartmuseum.org; Web: www.wichitaartmuseum.org; *Dir* Patricia McDonnell; *Registrar* Leslie Servantez; *Educ Cur* Courtney Spousta
Open Tues - Sat 10 AM - 5 PM, Sun Noon - 5 PM, cl Mon & holidays; Admis adults $7, seniors & adult students $5 youth 5-17 $3, under 5 free & free Sat; Founded 1935; brings people, ideas & American art together to enrich lives & build community; Facility designed by Clarence S Stein, 1935 with addition in Oct 1977 designed by Edward Larrabee Barnes; expanded & renovated, opened 2003. Maintains reference library; Average Annual Attendance: 62,028; Mem: dues $30 up
Library Holdings: Auction Catalogs, Book Volumes 10,000, Clipping Files, Exhibition Catalogs, Manuscripts, Original Documents, Pamphlets, Periodical Subscriptions
Special Subjects: Drawings, Mexican Art, Painting-American, Porcelain, Pre-Columbian Art, Sculpture, Southwestern Art, Textiles, Watercolors, Woodcarvings
Collections: Roland P Murdock, American Art, M C Naftzger Collection of Charles M Russell (paintings, drawings & sculpture), Kurdian Collection of Pre-Columbian Mexican Art, Virginia & George Ablah Collection of British Watercolors, L S & Ida L Naftzger Collection of Prints & Drawings, Gwen Houston Naftzger Collection of Boehm & Doughty Porcelain Birds, Florence Naftzger Evans Collection of Porcelain & Faience, F. Price Cossman Collection of Steuben Glass, Elizabeth S Navas Papers, Howard E Wooden Papers
Exhibitions: (20th May, 2017-10th Sep, 2017) Glass Exhibition; (19th Nov, 2016-30th Jul, 2017) Printmaking is...
Publications: Catalog of Roland P Murdock Collection; bimonthly newsletter; exhibition brochures & catalogues; Toward an American Identity: Selections from the Wichita Art Mus; Wichita Art Museum: 75 Years of American Art
Activities: Classes for children; docent training; tours of collection; lects open to pub; concerts; gallery talks; tours; exten prog to teachers & parents; lending of items from Art Resource Center (books & visual materials)

L **Emprise Bank Research Library**, 1400 W Museum Blvd, Wichita, KS 67203. Tel 316-268-4918; Fax 316-268-4980; Email library@wichitaartmuseum.org; Web: www.wichitaartmuseum.org; *Librn* Joyce Norris; *Dir* Patricia McDonnell; *Registrar* Leslie Servantez; *Cur Educ* Courtney Spousta
Open by appointment Tues & Thurs 10 AM - 2:30 PM; Estab 1963 as research library for mus staff; Reference only
Library Holdings: Auction Catalogs, Book Volumes 10,000, Clipping Files, Exhibition Catalogs, Manuscripts, Other Holdings Auction catalogs; Museum handbooks, Pamphlets, Periodical Subscriptions 15, Video Tapes
Special Subjects: American Indian Art, American Western Art, Art History, Decorative Arts, Drawings, Etchings & Engravings, Folk Art, Landscapes, Painting-American, Pre-Columbian Art, Prints, Sculpture, Watercolors
Collections: Elizabeth S Navas Papers, Howard E Wooden Papers, Chris Paulsen Polk Papers
Exhibitions: Storytelling: Highlights & Insights from the Wichita Art Museum; (19th Nov, 2016-30th Jul, 2017) Printmaking is...
Activities: Classes for children; docent training; lects open to pub; gallery talks; tours; mus shop sells books, original art, reproductions & gifts

L **WICHITA PUBLIC LIBRARY,** 223 S Main St, Wichita, KS 67202-3795. Tel 316-261-8500; Email admin@wichita.lib.ks.us; Web: www.wichitalibrary.org; *Dir* Cynthia Berner
Open Mon - Thurs 10 AM - 8 PM, Fri & Sat 10 AM - 6 PM, Sun 1 - 5 PM; No admis fee; research charges apply; Estab 1876 & grown to be informational center & large free public library to improve the community with educational, cultural & recreational benefits through books, recordings, films, art works & other materials; Circ 1,100,000
Income: Financed by local taxes
Library Holdings: Framed Reproductions, Motion Pictures, Records, Reels
Special Subjects: Advertising Design, Afro-American Art, American Indian Art, American Western Art, Architecture, Coins & Medals, Crafts, Decorative Arts, Film, Folk Art, Furniture, Glass, Graphic Arts
Collections: Kansas Book Collection, John F Kennedy Collection, Harry Mueller Philately Book Collection
Exhibitions: Preview of Academy Award Short Subjects; Rotating exhibits
Activities: Progs for adults, teens, children & families; tech training classes; reference & research svcs; lect; tours; book discussions; films; talks; concerts; crafts

M **WICHITA STATE UNIVERSITY,** Ulrich Museum of Art, 1845 Fairmount, Wichita, KS 67260-0046. Tel 316-978-3664; Fax 316-978-3898; Email ulrich@wichita.edu; Web: www.ulrich.wichita.edu; *Dir* Bob Workman; *Pub Rels & Mktg Mgr* Jennifer Lane; *Mem & Special Events Mgr* Carolyn Copple; *Designer & Preparator* James Porter; *Cur Modern & Contemporary Art* Sally Frater
Open Tues - Fri 11 AM - 5 PM, Sat & Sun 1 - 5 PM, cl Mon & national/univ holidays; No admis fee; Estab 1974. Collecting, preserving, exhibiting & interpreting modern & contemporary art; 5 galleries on 2 floors, 18 ft ceiling, 10,000 sq ft exhibition space; Average Annual Attendance: 18,000; Mem: 400
Special Subjects: Afro-American Art, American Indian Art, Bronzes, Drawings, Etchings & Engravings, Furniture, Hispanic Art, Landscapes, Marine Painting, Painting-American, Photography, Prints, Sculpture, Portraits, Watercolors, Woodcuts
Collections: Over 7,000 works of contemporary & modern works of art, Martin H Bush Outdoor Sculpture Coll
Activities: Classes for adults and children; docent training; lects open to pub; 12 vis lecrts per yr; gallery talks; concerts; tours; scholarships; 1-2 book traveling exhibs per yr

WINFIELD

L **SOUTHWESTERN COLLEGE,** Deets Library - Art Dept, 100 College St, Winfield, KS 67156-2499. Tel 620-229-6225, 866-734-1275; Fax 620-229-6382; Email gzuck1@swcart.edu; Web: www.sckans.edu/library; *Lib Dir* Veronica McAsey
Open school year Mon - Thurs 7:45 AM-12AM, Fri 7:45AM-5PM, Sat noon-4PM, Sun 3PM-12AM; Estab 1885 as a four-year liberal arts col; Circ 77,000
Income: Financed by college budget
Library Holdings: Book Volumes 77,000, Exhibition Catalogs, Fiche, Periodical Subscriptions 120, Reels
Collections: Arthur Covey Collection of paintings, mural sketches, etchings, lithographs, drawings and watercolors, Cunningham Asian Arts Collection of books, catalogues & exhibition catalogs
Publications: databases
Activities: Tours

KENTUCKY

ASHLAND

C **ASHLAND INC,** PO Box 391, Ashland, KY 41114-0001. Tel 606-329-3333; Fax 606-329-3559; *Corporate Art Admin* Tim Heaberlin
Open by appt only; Estab 1972, primary function is decorative art, but also to establish a creative atmosphere; to enhance community cultural life; Collection displayed in public areas of corporate office buildings
Collections: Mainly contemporary printmaking, emphasis on Americans, paintings, sculpture, wall hangings
Activities: Tours; competitions, sponsorship consists of purchase awards for local art group & museum competitions; provides purchase & merit awards for certain museum & university competitions; individual objects of art lent; originate traveling exhibs to museums, colleges, universities & art centers in general marketing areas

BEREA

M **BEREA COLLEGE,** Doris Ulmann Galleries, CPO 2162, Berea, KY 40404. Tel 859-985-3083; Fax 859-985-3541; Email meghan_doherty@berea.edu; Web: www.dulmanngalleries.berea.edu; *Dir & Cur* Dr Meghan C Doherty
Open Mon - Thurs 8 AM - 6 PM, Fri 8 AM - 5 PM, Sun 1 - 5 PM, cl col holidays; No admis fee; Estab 1936 for educational purposes; Gallery with rotating & permanent colls.; Average Annual Attendance: 1,500; Mem: None; open free to pub & researchers
Income: Financed by college budget
Library Holdings: CD-ROMs, Periodical Subscriptions 25, Prints
Special Subjects: African Art, Archaeology, Art History, Asian Art, Ceramics, Prints, Textiles, Textiles, Photography
Collections: General
Activities: student learning; Lect open to public, 4 vis lectrs per year; gallery talks; tours; competitive exhibs; lending of original objects of art

A **KENTUCKY GUILD OF ARTISTS & CRAFTSMEN INC,** 210 N Broadway, Ste 3 Berea, KY 40403-1505; PO Box 291, Berea, KY 40403. Tel 859-986-3192; Fax 859-986-0334; Email info@kyguild.org; Web: www.kyguild.org; *Dir* Jeannette Rowlett; *Prog Admin Mgr* Glenna Combs; *Prog Asst* Susan England
Open Mon - Fri 9 AM - 5 PM; Admis adults $5, children 12 and under free; Estab 1961 for the pursuit of excellence in the arts & crafts & to encourage the pub appreciation thereof; Average Annual Attendance: 8,000; Mem: 350; must be a Kentucky resident & be juried for exhibiting status; dues exhib mem $50
Income: $80,000 (financed by grants, contributions, corporate donations, admis & mem fees)
Publications: The Guild Record, 4 times per yr; Online Update - electronic newsletter; Art & Craft Insight Network = Art & Craft Learning Opportunities
Activities: Classes for adults & children; docent training; workshops; lect open to public; demonstrations; competitions with awards; 2 ann retail fairs; originates traveling exhibs to KY & surrounding states

BOWLING GREEN

M **CAPITOL ARTS ALLIANCE,** Houchens Gallery, 416 E Main St, Bowling Green, KY 42101; PO Box 748, Bowling Green, KY 42102-0748. Tel 270-782-2787; Fax 270-782-2804; Email gallery@capitolarts.com; Web: www.capitolarts.com; *Gallery Dir* Lynn Robertson; *Exec Dir* Karen Hume
Open Mon - Fri 9 AM - 4 PM; No admis fee; Estab 1981 as a community arts center; Main floor Ervin G Houchens & upper level Mezzanine Gallery
Exhibitions: Rotating exhibitions selected annually by a review panel including an All State Juried Exhibition; Youth Art (K-6th grade); Women In the Arts; Scholastic (9th-12th grade); Annual Jack E. Lunt Memorial Exhib
Activities: Classes for children; dramatic progs; summer arts camp, school day performances; concerts, tours; competitions with awards, All KY Juried Exhibition-12 awards, Best of Show $500, Honor $250, merit $100; scholarships given

M **WESTERN KENTUCKY UNIVERSITY,** Kentucky Library & Museum, 1 Big Red Way, Bowling Green, KY 42101-5730. Tel 270-745-5083; Fax 270-745-6264; Web: www.wku.edu/library/dlsc/; *Dept Head* Timothy Mullin; *Libr Coordr* Connie Mills; *Librn* Jonathan Jeffery; *Manuscript Librn* Pat Hodges; *Univ Archivist* Sue Lynn McDaniel; *KY Spec* Nancy Baird; *Exhib Cur* Donna Parker; *Coll Cur* Sandy Staebell
Open Mon-Fri 8:30AM-4:30PM, Sat 9:30AM-4PM; Admis fee $2; Estab 1939 to preserve KY's cultural heritage; Open to the public; Average Annual Attendance: 18,000; Mem: 400, $50
Library Holdings: Audio Tapes, Book Volumes 70,000, Cassettes, Clipping Files, Framed Reproductions, Kodachrome Transparencies, Lantern Slides, Manuscripts, Maps, Memorabilia, Original Art Works, Other Holdings Broadsides; Maps; Postcards, Pamphlets, Periodical Subscriptions 1800, Photographs, Records, Reels, Slides
Special Subjects: Costumes, Decorative Arts, Folk Art
Collections: Ellis Collection of steamboat pictures, Gerard Collection of Bowling Green Photographs, McGregor Collection of rare books, Neal Collection of Utopian materials, Kentucky Genealogy Collection, Collections of and about Shakers and other religious den, Collections about state and national politics and politicians, literary figures, wars, bus, every day life and univ archives, Felts Log House
Activities: Classes for adults & children, dramatic progs; lects open to pub, gallery talks, sponsoring of competitions; sells books, prints, gifts

M **University Gallery**, 1906 College Heights Blvd, Ivan Wilson Center for Fine Arts Rm 441 Bowling Green, KY 42101-1000. Tel 270-745-3944, 2592; Fax 270-745-5932; Email art@wku.edu; Web: www.wku.edu/art/, www.wku.edu/dept/academic/ahss/art.html; *Dept Head* Kim Chalmers; *Gallery Dir* Kristina Arnold
Open Mon - Fri 8:30 AM - 4:30 PM; No admis fee; Estab 1973 for art exhibitions relating to university instruction & regional cultural needs; Average Annual Attendance: 12,000
Income: Financed by state appropriation
Exhibitions: Annual student & faculty shows

CRESTVIEW

M **THOMAS MORE COLLEGE,** Eva G Farris Art Gallery, 333 Thomas More Pkwy, Crestview, KY 41017-3495. Tel 859-344-3420, 344-3419; Fax 859-344-3345; *Dir* Barb Rauf
Open Mon - Thurs 9AM-9PM, Fri 9AM-4:30PM, Sat 10AM-4:30PM, Sun noon-5PM; No admis fee; Estab for cultural & educational enrichment for the institution & area; Average Annual Attendance: 2,000
Special Subjects: Ceramics, Drawings, Graphics, Photography, Sculpture
Exhibitions: Full acad season of exhibitions
Activities: Lects open to public, 4 vis lectrs per year; gallery talks; schols & fels offered; book traveling exhibs

DANVILLE

M **MCDOWELL HOUSE & APOTHECARY SHOP,** (Ephraim McDowell-Cambus-Kenneth Foundation), 125 S Second St, Danville, KY 40422. Tel 859-236-2804; Email mcdowellhouse1@att.net; Web: www.mcdowellhouse.com; *Dir* Carol Senn; *Asst Dir & Educ Dir* Lauren Clontz; *Admin Asst* Linda Thygesen; *Gift Shop Mgr* Barbara McCumber
Open Mon - Sat 10 AM - Noon & 1 - 4 PM, Sun 2 - 4 PM, cl Mon Nov 1 - Mar 1; Admis adults $7, sr citizens $5, students $1.50, children under 12 $1, group rates by phone; Estab 1935 to preserve the home of the Father of Abdominal Surgery in Danville, 1795 - 1830; Average Annual Attendance: 5,000; Mem: 600; dues $25-$1,000 & up
Income: $60,000 (financed by endowment, mem, private contribution from groups & individuals)
Special Subjects: Architecture, Carpets & Rugs, Coins & Medals, Decorative Arts, Dolls, Drawings, Embroidery, Furniture, Glass, Historical Material, Jewelry, Maps, Miniatures, Painting-American, Period Rooms, Pewter, Portraits, Pottery, Silver, Porcelain, Flasks & Bottles, Folk Art, Restorations
Collections: All furnishings pre-1830, apothecary collection: late 18th & early 19th Century, 320 pieces, portraits & folk art, 1795-1830, Shelby Family: 2 fancy chairs, baby high chair; McDowell Family: English silver
Publications: Annual newsletter
Activities: Docent training; summer children's prog; lects open to pub, 5 vis lectrs per yr; tours; sales shop sells books, prints, slides, pewter mugs, DVDs, videos of tours

DAWSON SPRINGS

M **DAWSON SPRINGS MUSEUM AND ART CENTER,** 127 S Main St, Dawson Springs, KY 42408; PO Box 107, Dawson Springs, KY 42408-0107. Tel 270-797-3503; *Exec Dir* Sylvia Lynn Thomas; *Chmn* Shirley Menser
Open Feb - Dec Tues - Sat 1 - 4 PM, cl major holidays; No admis fee; 535 sq ft exhibit space; Average Annual Attendance: 2,200
Library Holdings: Book Volumes 70
Collections: Dawson Springs history, Japanese art
Publications: Brochure, The Dawson Springs Museum & Art Center
Activities: Book traveling exhibs

FORT KNOX

M **PATTON MUSEUM FOUNDATION,** General George Patton Museum and Center of Leadership, PO Box 25, Fort Knox, KY 40121-0025; 4554 Fayette Ave, Fort Knox, KY 40121-0208. Tel 502-624-3812; Fax 502-624-2364; Email knox.museum@conus.army.mil; Web: www.generalpatton.org; *CEO* Robert Keats
Open Tues - Fri 10 AM - 4:30 PM, Sat 10 AM - 5:30 PM, cl Sun & Mon; No admis fee; Estab 1975 to preserve historical materials relating to Cavalry & Armor & to make these properties available for public exhibit & research. The Museum is administered by the US Army Armor Center, Fort Knox & is one of the largest in the US Army Museum System; Galleries feature a variety of armored equipment & vehicles, weapons, art & other memorabilia which chronologically present the develop of the Armor branch from the beginning of mechanization to the present
Income: Financed through state
Collections: Military Equipment Relating to Mech Cavalry & Armor
Exhibitions: Permanent & rotating exhibitions
Activities: Retail store sells books & prints

FRANKFORT

M **KENTUCKY HISTORICAL SOCIETY,** Old State Capitol & Annex, 100 W Broadway, Frankfort, KY 40601-1931. Tel 502-564-1792; Fax 502-564-4701; Web: www.history.ky.gov; *Exec Dir* Kent Whitworth; *Pub Rels & Mktg* Laura Coleman
Open Tues-Sat 10AM-6PM; Admis adults $4, youth 6-18 $2, children 5 and under free; Estab 1836 as a general history & art mus emphasizing the history, culture & decorative arts of the Commonwealth of Kentucky & its people; The Old Capitol Galleries located in the Old State House consist of two rooms totaling 2740 sq ft which are used by the Mus to display its fine arts exhibitions, painting, silver, furniture & sculpture, one temporary exhibits gallery in Old Capitol Annex; Average Annual Attendance: 250,000; Mem: 5000; dues for life $300 individual $35
Income: $7 million (financed by state appropriation)
Special Subjects: Historical Material, Period Rooms
Collections: Kentucky & American furniture coverlets, furniture, paintings, quilts, silver, textiles
Exhibitions: 3 - 4 exhibitions per year
Publications: The Register, The Bulletin, quarterly
Activities: Lects open to pub, 4 vis lectrs per yr; tours; individual paintings & original objects of art lent to qualified mus; lending collection consists of original art works, original prints; paintings; sculpture & historical artifacts; book traveling exhibs; originates traveling exhibs; mus shop sells books & reproductions

L **Library**, 100 W Broadway, Frankfort, KY 40601-1931. Tel 502-564-1792 ext 4460; Fax 502-696-3846; Email Refdesk@ky.gov; Web: http://history.ky.gov
No admis fee; Reference library
Library Holdings: Book Volumes 90,000, Other Holdings Microfilm: 16,000

M **KENTUCKY NEW STATE CAPITOL,** Division of Historic Properties, 700 Louisville Rd, Frankfort, KY 40601-3304. Tel 502-564-3000, Ext 222; Tour Desk: 502-564-3449; Fax 502-564-6505; *Cur* Lou Karibo
Open Mon - Fri 8:30AM-3:30PM, Sat 10AM-2PM, Sun 1-4PM; No admis fee
Income: Funded by state appropriation
Collections: First Lady, Miniature Dolls, Oil Paintings of Chief Justices, Statues of Famous Kentuckians including Abraham Lincoln & Jefferson Davis
Publications: Brochures; exhibition catalogs
Activities: Tours; sales shop sells books, reproductions & prints

M **KENTUCKY STATE UNIVERSITY,** Jackson Hall Gallery, 400 E Main St, Art Dept Frankfort, KY 40601-2334. Tel 502-597-5995, 597-5994; Email JAlexandra@qwmail.kysu.edu; Web: www.kysu.edu; *Area Head* John Bater
Open Mon - Fri 8 AM - 4:30 PM; No admis fee; Estab 1886 to present exhibition of African art; Gallery; Average Annual Attendance: 1,000
Income: Financed through small grants & university appropriations
Library Holdings: Book Volumes 500
Collections: A small coll of student & faculty work, African Art
Exhibitions: Rotating exhibits
Activities: Lects open to pub, 2 vis lectrs per yr; competitions; schols offered; book traveling exhibs 2-3 per yr

M **LIBERTY HALL HISTORIC SITE,** Liberty Hall Museum, 202 Wilkinson St, Frankfort, KY 40601-1826. Tel 502-227-2560; Fax 502-227-3348; Email director@libertyhall.org; Web: www.libertyhall.org; *Cur* Kate Hesseldenz; *Exec Dir* Julienne Foster Jones; *Educ* Vicky Middleswarth; *Tour Admin* Rebecca Shipp; *Office Mgr & Bookkeeper* Judy Isaacs; *Mktg & Spec Events Coordr* Chris Harp
Open March - Dec Mon - Sat 1:30 PM tour; Admis adults $6, students/children 5-18 $3, children 4 & under free; Estab 1937 as an historic museum; A Georgian house built in 1796, named Historic Landmark in 1972; Average Annual Attendance: 5,000; Mem: 250; $50 ann dues
Income: Privately funded non-profit institution
Library Holdings: Book Volumes 4000, Lantern Slides, Manuscripts, Maps, Original Art Works, Original Documents, Pamphlets, Photographs 900
Special Subjects: Architecture, Costumes, Decorative Arts, Furniture, Period Rooms, Painting-American, Photography, Portraits, Silver, Textiles, Watercolors
Collections: 18th century furniture, china, silver, portraits, original Kentucky 19th century art work, 19th century clothing & textiles; archives
Publications: Palladium newsletter
Activities: Classes for adults & children; dramatic progs; docent training; 6 vis lectrs per yr; concerts; guided tours; ann seminars; gallery talks; fels offered; mus shop sells books & prints

L **Library**, 202 Wilkinson St, Frankfort, KY 40601-1826. Tel 502-227-2560; Fax 502-227-3348; Email libhall@dcr.net; Web: www.libertyhall.org; *Exec Dir* Sara Farley Harger; *Treas* Helen Chenery; *Educ Coordr* Megan Canfield; *VPres* Katherine M Davis
Open by appointment only; No admis fee; Estab 1965; Non-circulating library; Average Annual Attendance: 100
Income: Privately funded nonprofit institution
Library Holdings: Book Volumes 2000
Collections: Books belonging to John Brown, Kentucky's first US senator & builder of Liberty Hall

M **Orlando Brown House**, 202 Wilkinson St, Frankfort, KY 40601-1826. Tel 502-227-2560; Fax 502-227-3348; Web: www.libertyhall.org; *Dir* Julienne Foster Jones; *Cur* Kate Hesseldenz
Open for tours Mon -Sat 1:30; Admis adults $6, youth 5-18 $3, children 4 & under free; Estab 1956; Built in 1835 by architect Gilbert Shryock; Average Annual Attendance: 2,500
Income: Privately funded non-profit institution

Collections: Paul Sawyier paintings, original furnishings
Activities: Classes for adults & children; dramatic progs; lects; guided tours; mus shop sells books, prints, jewelry

GEORGETOWN

M **GEORGETOWN COLLEGE,** Georgetown College Fine Art Galleries, 400 E College St, Georgetown, KY 40324. Tel 502-863-8106, 863-8399; Email galleries@georgetowncollege.edu; Web: www.georgetowncollege.edu/galleries; *Gallery Director, Curator of Collections* Samantha Simpson; *Art Dept Chair* Daniel Graham
Open Mon - Fri Noon - 4:30 PM or by appointment; No admis fee; Estab 1959 as educational gallery with various mediums & styles; Gallery consists of 3 temporary spaces; Average Annual Attendance: 1,200
Income: Financed by college & grants
Special Subjects: African Art, Anthropology, Antiquities-Egyptian, Antiquities-Greek, Antiquities-Oriental, Asian Art, Ceramics, Drawings, Folk Art, Graphics, Glass, Historical Material, Painting-American, Painting-European, Painting-French, Painting-German, Painting-Italian, Painting-Japanese, Sculpture, Photography, Portraits, Pre-Columbian Art, Renaissance Art, Restorations, Sculpture, Crafts
Collections: Contemporary graphics, contemporary painting & sculpture, crafts, artifacts
Exhibitions: Rotating exhibits; student shows; Jacobs Gallery (permanent)
Activities: Classes for children; lects open to public; 6 vis lectrs per year; gallery talks; tours; schols & fels offered; exten dept; individual paintings & original objects of art lent to museums

HARRODSBURG

M **OLD FORT HARROD STATE PARK MANSION MUSEUM,** S College St, Harrodsburg, KY 40330; PO Box 156, Harrodsburg, KY 40330-0156. Tel 859-734-3314; Fax 859-734-0794; Email joan.huffman@ky.gov; Web: www.parks.kg.gov/findparsk/recparks/fh; *Park Supt* Joan Huffman
Open daily 9 AM - 5:00 PM; Admis $4.50 adults; $2.50 children; winter rates $2 adults, $1 children; seniors $4; Estab 1925; History museum, Union, Confederate & Lincoln memorabilia; music & gun collection; Average Annual Attendance: 30,000
Income: State agency
Special Subjects: Period Rooms
Collections: Antique China, Confederate Room, Daniel Boone & George Rogers Clark Room, furniture, gun collection, Indian artifacts, Lincoln Room, musical instruments, silver
Exhibitions: Permanent collection
Activities: Dramatic progs; concerts; tours; awards for top 10 events; one Smithsonian exhibit; sells books, original art, reproductions & prints

M **SHAKER VILLAGE OF PLEASANT HILL,** 3501 Lexington Rd, Harrodsburg, KY 40330-8846. Tel 859-734-5411, 800-734-5611; Fax 859-734-7278; Email lcurry@shakervillageky.org; Web: www.shakervillageky.org; *Pres & CEO* Madge B Adams; *VChmn Bd* G Watts Humphrey
Open Apr-Oct 10AM-5PM, Nov-Mar 10AM-4:30PM; Admis April-Oct adults $14, youth $12-17 $7, child 6-11 $5, Nov-Mar adult $7, youth 12-17 $3.50, child 6-11 $2.50; Estab 1961 to restore, preserve & interpret the architecture, artifacts & culture of Shakers; 2800 acres, 34 historic buildings (1805-1855); Primary exhibition building: 40 room Centre family dwelling (1824-1834); stone, three story dwelling full of artifacts & furniture of Shakers; Shaker Life Exhib with permanent & changing exhib gallery; Average Annual Attendance: 80,000; Mem: 1200; dues family $50, annual meeting in Feb
Income: Financed by mem, endowment, inn & lodging, sales, village-generated income
Special Subjects: Archaeology, Architecture, Costumes, Crafts, Decorative Arts, Folk Art, Furniture, Historical Material, Manuscripts, Religious Art, Textiles
Collections: Shaker culture including furniture, textiles, manuscripts, cultural artifacts, architecture, period rooms & shops
Publications: Pleasant Hill & Its Shakers; The Gift of Pleasant Hill; Keepsake Art Calendar; Two Cookbooks
Activities: Classes for adults & children; dramatic progs; docent training; self-guided village tours; guided tours; lects open to pub, 15-25 vis lectrs per yr; concerts; tours; lending collection contains videos; mus shop sells reproductions, prints & slides

HIGHLAND HEIGHTS

M **NORTHERN KENTUCKY UNIVERSITY,** Galleries, Art Galleries, Northern KY Univ Highland Heights, KY; 100 Nunn Dr, Art Galleries Newport, KY 41099. Tel 859-572-5148; Fax 859-572-6501; Email knight@nku.edu; Web: artscience.nku.edu/departments/art/galleries.html; *Dir Exhib & Colls* David Knight
Open Mon - Fri 9 AM - 9 PM or by appt, cl Sat, Sun & major holidays; No admis fee; Estab 1968, new location 1990, to provide an arts center for the University & community area; Main Gallery & 3rd Floor Gallery maintained, the smaller is 15 X 30; Average Annual Attendance: 20,000
Income: Financed by university & state funds
Special Subjects: Folk Art, Photography, Prints, Sculpture
Collections: Permanent collection of Red Grooms Monumental Sculpture in Metal, Donald Judd Monumental Sculpture, earth works, other outdoor sculpture, prints, painting, photographs, folk art
Exhibitions: Annual Juried Student Exhibition; state, regional & natl visiting artists
Publications: Bulletins, 4-5 per year
Activities: Lects open to pub, 3-5 vis lectrs per yr; gallery talks; tours; individual paintings & original objects of art lent to univ mems to be used in their offices only; lending coll contains 379 prints, paintings, photographs & ceramics; traveling exhibs to Univ & Col

LEXINGTON

ASSOCIATION OF MEDICAL ILLUSTRATORS
For further information, see National and Regional Organizations

M **BODLEY-BULLOCK HOUSE MUSEUM,** 200 Market St, Lexington, KY 40507-1030. Tel 859-259-1266; Email nr_travel@nps.gov; Web: www.cr.nps.gov/nr/travel/lexington/bod.htm
Open by appt year-round; cl holidays; Mus housed in historic mansion built in 1814 for Lexington Mayor Thomas Pindell. House was later sold to General Thomas Bodley, a veteran of the War of 1812. House served as headquarters for both Union & Confederate forces during Civil War. House was purchased in 1912 by Dr Waller Bullock, an accomplished sculptor
Special Subjects: Furniture, Historical Material
Activities: Tours by appt

M **HEADLEY-WHITNEY MUSEUM,** 4435 Old Frankfort Pike, Lexington, KY 40510-9657. Tel 859-255-6653; Fax 859-255-8375; Email hwmuseum@headley-whitney.org; Web: www.headley-whitney.org; WATS 800-310-5085; *Dir & Cur* Amy Gundrum Greene; *Dir Educ* Jacqueline Beck
Open Wed - Fri 10 AM - 5 PM, Sat & Sun Noon - 5 PM, cl Dec - March; Admis adults $10, senior & students $8, children 5 & under free; Estab 1968 in central Kentucky for the care collection, preservation & interpretation of the decorative & fine arts; Five principal galleries are maintained which include the work of the founder, jewelry designer, George W Headley III & temporary exhibits on the decorative & fine arts; Average Annual Attendance: 17,950; Mem: 600; dues individual $55, family $85, benefactor $400, patron $150, dir circle $2,500
Income: Financed by admis, mem, benefits, grants, contributions, trust, affiliated with Smithsonian
Library Holdings: Auction Catalogs, Original Art Works, Original Documents, Periodical Subscriptions
Special Subjects: Asian Art, Bronzes, Ceramics, Decorative Arts, Glass, Gold, Ivory, Jade, Jewelry, Miniatures, Oriental Art, Porcelain, Textiles, Portraits, Sculpture, Silver
Collections: Bibelots, jewelry, gemstones, Kentucky Silver
Exhibitions: Quarterly exhibitions
Publications: The Jewel newsletters quarterly, for mem
Activities: Classes for adults & children; outreach progs; lects open to pub, concerts; gallery talks; tours; international bibelot contest; book traveling exhibs; mus shop sells books, prints, jewelry, rocks gems, loose jewels

A **LEXINGTON ART LEAGUE, INC,** 209 Castlewood Dr, Loudoun House Lexington, KY 40505-3629. Tel 859-254-7024, 800-914-7990; Fax 859-254-7214; Email info@lexingtonartleague.org; Web: www.lexingtonartleague.org; *Exec Dir* Stephanie Harris; *Events & Mem Dir* Mark Mozingo; *Develop Dir* Lee Erik Eachus; *Education & Community Engagement Dir* Logan Dennison
Open (tours) Mon - Fri 9 AM - 5 PM; No admis fee; Estab 1957, to encourage an active interest in the visual arts among its members & community as a whole; Three visual art galleries; Project Space has installation & work in new media; Average Annual Attendance: 200,000; Mem: 700; open to all interested in visual arts; dues $45; annual meeting in May
Income: Financed by mem, art fairs, donations, grants
Library Holdings: Book Volumes, Periodical Subscriptions
Exhibitions: Changing monthly exhibitions; member, group, one person exhibitions
Publications: Annual Membership Book; email newsletter
Activities: Classes for adults; lects open to pub, 4 vis lectrs per yr; gallery talks; competitions; juried awards for most exhibits; scholarships offered; originate traveling exhibs

M **LIVING ARTS & SCIENCE CENTER, INC,** 362 N Martin Luther King Blvd, Lexington, KY 40508-1889. Tel 859-252-5222; Fax 859-255-7448; Email info@lasclex.org; Web: www.lasclex.org; *Exec Dir* Heather Lyons; *Discovery Educ Dir* Katherine Bullock; *Art Educ Coordr* Mollie Rabiner; *Art Gallery Dir* Jeffrey Nichols
Open Mon - Fri 8:30 AM - 5 PM, cl holidays; No admis fee; Estab 1968 to provide enrichment opportunities in the arts & sciences; Gallery features 6-8 exhibits per yr of regional art; Average Annual Attendance: 25,000; Mem: 400; dues $35-1000; annual meetings
Income: Financed by grants, fundraising events, memberships, tuition & sponsorships
Exhibitions: Rotating exhibitions; Two science exhib per year
Publications: Exhibition catalogs
Activities: Classes for adults & children; field trips for over 7500 school children; after school art classes at elementary schools; festivals; lect open to public; tours; children's art, artist-in-residence; sponsoring of competitions; class scholarships offered; programs for at-risk & underserved; state of Kentucky, Wow: Wonders on Wheels Mobile Art Programs; book traveling exhibitions once per year; sales shop sells original art, reproductions, prints & notecards

M **TRANSYLVANIA UNIVERSITY,** Morlan Gallery, 300 N Broadway, Mitchell Fine Arts Ctr Lexington, KY 40508-1797. Tel 859-233-8142; Fax 859-233-8797; Email afisher@mail.transy.edu; Web: transy.edu/morlan; *Dir* Andrea Fischer
Open Mon - Fri Noon - 5 PM; No admis fee; Estab 1978 to exhibit contemporary art; Gallery is housed in Mitchell Fine Arts Building on Transylvania University's campus located in Lexington, KY; Average Annual Attendance: 3,000
Income: Financed by endowment
Special Subjects: Historical Material, Portraits
Collections: 19th century natural history works, 19th century portraits, decorative arts
Exhibitions: Temporary exhibitions, primarily contemporary works, various media
Activities: Lects open to pub, 2-4 vis lectrs per yr; concerts; gallery talks; tours; competitions; originate traveling exhibs

L **UNIVERSITY OF KENTUCKY,** Hunter M Adams Architecture Library, 200 Pence Hall, Lexington, KY 40506-0001. Tel 859-257-1533; Fax 859-257-4305;

Email fharders@pop.uky.edu; Web: libraries.uky.edu/design; *Library Technician* Lalana Powell; *Librn* Faith Harders
Open Mon - Thurs 8 AM - 7 PM, Fri 8 AM - 6 PM, cl Sat - Sun, summer Mon - Fri 8 AM - 4:30 PM; Estab 1963
Library Holdings: Audio Tapes, Book Volumes 34,000, Cassettes, Fiche 1903, Other Holdings Architectural drawing, Periodical Subscriptions 91, Reels 606, Sculpture
Special Subjects: Architecture, Furniture, Interior Design

M **THE UNIVERSITY OF KENTUCKY ART MUSEUM,** 405 Rose St & Euclid Ave, Singletary Center for the Arts Lexington, KY 40506-0241. Tel 859-257-5716; Fax 859-323-1994; Email artmuseum@uky.edu; Web: finearts.uky.edu/art-museum; *Registrar* Barbara Lovejoy; *Preparator* Alan Rideout; *Dir* Stuart Horodner; *Publ & Pub Rels* Dorothy Freeman; *Cur Coll & Exhibs* Janie Welker; *Vis Servs Mgr* Michaela Miles; *Mem Coordr* Lyndi Van Deursen
Open Tues - Thurs 10 AM - 5 PM, Fri 10 AM - 8 PM, Sat - Sun noon - 5 PM, cl Mon & university holidays; No admis fee; Estab 1976 to collect, preserve, exhibit & interpret world art for the benefit of the university community & the region; New building completed & opened Nov 1979; 20,000 sq ft of galleries & work space; Average Annual Attendance: 24,000; Mem: 450; dues $45 - $1,000
Income: $325,000 (financed by state appropriation & gifts)
Special Subjects: African Art, Afro-American Art, American Indian Art, Antiquities-Oriental, Antiquities-Persian, Antiquities-Roman, Asian Art, Baroque Art, Bronzes, Carpets & Rugs, Cartoons, Ceramics, Coins & Medals, Collages, Costumes, Crafts, Decorative Arts, Drawings, Embroidery, Enamels, Etchings & Engravings, Ethnology, Flasks & Bottles, Folk Art, Furniture, Glass, Graphics, Islamic Art, Ivory, Jade, Jewelry, Landscapes, Latin American Art, Marine Painting, Medieval Art, Metalwork, Mexican Art, Miniatures, Oriental Art, Painting-American, Painting-British, Painting-Dutch, Painting-European, Painting-Flemish, Painting-German, Painting-Italian, Painting-Japanese, Painting-Spanish, Photography, Porcelain, Portraits, Posters, Pottery, Pre-Columbian Art, Primitive art, Prints, Religious Art, Renaissance Art, Sculpture, Silver, Tapestries, Textiles, Watercolors, Woodcarvings, Woodcuts
Collections: European & American paintings, sculpture & graphics, 15th-21st Century, photographs, Pre-Columbian, African & Asian artifacts, decorative arts
Publications: Museum Newsletter; exhibitions catalogs; posters, family guide
Activities: Classes for adults & children; docent training; lects open to pub, 8 vis lectrs per yr; gallery talks; tours; book traveling exhibs 8 per yr; mus shop sells original art, reproductions, jewelry & exhibit-related merchandise

L **Lucille Little Fine Arts Library**, 160 Patterson Dr, Lexington, KY 40506-0224. Tel 859-257-2800; Fax 859-257-4662; Email falib@email.ukg.edu; Web: www.libraries.uky.edu/falib; *Librn* Meg Shaw; *Dir* Gail Kennedy
Open Mon-Thur 7:30 AM-11 PM, Fri 7:30 AM-6 PM, Sat 10 AM-6 PM, Sun 10 AM-11 PM; Open to students, faculty & general public
Library Holdings: Auction Catalogs, Book Volumes 53,000, Clipping Files, DVDs, Fiche 812, Original Art Works, Pamphlets, Periodical Subscriptions 202, Reels 223, Video Tapes 24
Special Subjects: Art Education, Art History, Photography, Theatre Arts

L **Photographic Archives**, Margaret King Library Annex, King Bldg 0039 Lexington, KY 40506-0039. Tel 859-257-8611, 257-9611; Fax 859-257-1563; Email sclibraryrefdesk@lsv.uky.edu; Web: www.uky.edu/libraries/scdp; *Dir Spec Coll & Archives* William J Marshall; *Photographic Archivist* Lisa R Carter
Open Mon-Fri 8AM-5PM; Estab for reference & loan purposes for general pub, staff & students; Circ Non-circulating
Library Holdings: Audio Tapes, Book Volumes 100,000, Exhibition Catalogs, Motion Pictures, Other Holdings Manuscript materials, Periodical Subscriptions 60
Collections: Over 350,000 photographs documenting the history of photography as well as Kentucky, Appalachia & surrounding areas

LOUISVILLE

M **21C MUSEUM,** 700 W Main St, Louisville, KY 40202-2634. Tel 502-217-6300; Fax 502-217-6347; Web: www.21cmuseumhotels.com; *Museum Mgr* Karen Gillenwater
Call for hours; No admis fee; Five 19th-century warehouses; 9,000 sq ft
Collections: works by regional, national & international artists
Exhibitions: Rotating exhibits

M **CONRAD-CALDWELL HOUSE MUSEUM,** 1402 St James Ct, Louisville, KY 40208. Tel 502-636-5023; Fax 502-636-1264; Email conradcaldwellhouse@gmail.com; Web: www.conradcaldwell.org; *Exec Dir* Kate Meador
Open Tours Sun & Wed - Fri 1 PM & 3 PM, Sat 11 AM, 1 PM & 3 PM; also by appt; Admis adults $10, seniors $8, students $6, children under 8 free; Estab as mus in 1987; purchased & operated by St James Ct Historic Foundation; With its woodwork, stained glass, gargoyles & arches, mansion defines Richardsonian-Romanesque architecture. Mansion was built for Theophilus Conrad, who made his fortune in the tanning bus. House was purchased by the Caldwell family in 1905 and it later served as the Rose Anna Hughes Presbyterian Retirement Home; Mem: dues individual $50; Family $100; Supporter $250; Patron $500; Corporate $2,500
Special Subjects: Furniture, Historical Material, Period Rooms
Activities: Tours; facilities can be rented for special events

A **EMBROIDERERS GUILD OF AMERICA,** Margaret Parshall Gallery, 1355 Bardstown Rd, #157 Louisville, KY 40204-1355. Tel 502-589-6956; Fax 502-584-7900; Email egahq@egausa.org; Web: www.egausa.org; *Exec Dir* Anita Streeter; *Mem Coordr* Tonya Parks; *Accnt* Paula Kirk
Open Mon - Fri 9 AM - 4:30 PM; No admis fee; Estab 1958; Permanent & special exhibs of a wide range of embroidery; Mem: 16,000; dues $40; annual meeting in fall; interest in embroidery & needle arts
Income: Financed by endowment & mem
Library Holdings: Auction Catalogs, Book Volumes, Kodachrome Transparencies, Manuscripts, Memorabilia, Original Art Works, Original Documents, Slides, Video Tapes
Special Subjects: Embroidery, Textiles, American Indian Art, American Western Art, Costumes, Crafts, Decorative Arts, Dolls
Collections: 900 Embroidery Pieces
Exhibitions: Through the Needle's Eye; varied throughout the yr
Publications: Needle Arts Magazine
Activities: Classes for adults & children; lects for mems only; originates traveling exhibs to mus & galleries; mus shop

L **Dorothy Babcock Memorial Library**, 1355 Bardstown Rd, Ste 157 Louisville, KY 40204-1353. Tel 502-589-6956; Fax 502-584-7900; *Office Mgr* Bonnie Key
Lending & reference library for members only
Library Holdings: Slides, Video Tapes
Special Subjects: Embroidery, Tapestries, Textiles

A **THE FILSON HISTORICAL SOCIETY,** 1310 S Third St, Louisville, KY 40208. Tel 502-635-5083; Fax 502-635-5086; Email research@filsonhistorical.org; Web: www.filsonhistorical.org; *Pres & CEO* Craig Buthod; *Mgr Collections Access* Jennie Cole; *Cur Coll* Jim Holmberg
Open Mon - Fri 9 AM - 5 PM, first Sat of month 9AM-4PM, cl national holidays; Research fee for non-mem $10; Estab 1884 to collect, preserve & publish historical material, especially pertaining to Kentucky, the upper South & the OH Valley; Changing exhibits; Average Annual Attendance: 20,000; Mem: 4,500; dues $50 & up
Income: Financed by mem dues & private funds
Purchases: All historical materials, including appropriate paintings
Library Holdings: Book Volumes, Clipping Files, DVDs, Fiche, Manuscripts, Maps, Motion Pictures, Original Art Works, Original Documents, Pamphlets, Periodical Subscriptions, Photographs, Prints, Sculpture, Video Tapes
Collections: Books & manuscripts, collection of portraits of Kentuckians, artifacts, textiles, silver, photographs, maps, prints, artist research colls
Publications: Ohio Valley History; The Filson History Quarterly 75 vol, The Filson News Mag
Activities: Classes for adults & children; dramatic progs; family history; reading & discussion groups; dramatic progs for children; tours of historic sites; lects; public & acad conferences; lects open to pub, 45-50 vis lectrs per yr; gallery talks; concerts; tours; Filson Historical Society High School Essay Contest; schols & fellowships offered; fellowships & internships on a competitive basis; individual paintings & original objects of art lent to accredited mus & historical societies in KY & OH Valley region; mus shop sells books, magazines, reproductions, prints

L **Reference & Research Library**, 1310 S Third St, Louisville, KY 40208. Tel 502-635-5083; Fax 502-635-5086; Email filson@filsonclub.org; Web: www.filsonclub.org; *Librn* Judith Partington
Open Mon - Fri 9 AM - 5 PM, 1st Sat of every month 9AM-4PM; Estab 1884 to collect, preserve & publish Kentucky historical material & assoc material
Income: Financed by endowments, mem & gifts
Library Holdings: Book Volumes 55,000, Clipping Files, Manuscripts, Memorabilia, Original Art Works, Pamphlets, Photographs, Prints, Reels, Sculpture
Collections: Civil War Collection
Exhibitions: Portraits of Kentuckians
Publications: Filson Club History Quarterly; Series & Series 2 publication (40 vols)
Activities: Lects open to pub 6-10 per yr; tours; individual paintings & original objects of art lent to other organizations for special exhibits; mus shop sells books, reproductions & prints

M **KENTUCKY DERBY MUSEUM,** 704 Central Ave Gate 1, Louisville, KY 40201-1212. Tel 502-637-1111; Fax 502-636-5855; Email info@derbymuseum.org; Web: www.derbymuseum.org
Open Summer Mon - Sat 8 AM - 5 PM, Sun 11 AM - 5 PM, Winter Mon - Sat 9 AM - 5 PM, Sun. 11 AM - 5 PM, cl Kentucky Oaks & Kentucky Derby Day, Thanksgiving, Christmas Eve & Day; Admis adults $15, sr citizen $14, children 5-14 $8, children under 5 free; Estab 1985 to expand appreciation for Kentucky Derby & Thoroughbred racing; 2 floors of interactive exhibs designed to share the fun of the Kentucky Derby experience; Average Annual Attendance: 200,000; Mem: 1100; dues $25-$2000
Income: $3,500,000 (financed by Earned revenues)
Special Subjects: Bronzes, Costumes, Flasks & Bottles, Glass, Manuscripts, Painting-American, Photography, Sculpture
Collections: Archives from industry, Kentucky Derby memorabilia, 19th & 20th century Equine Art, Thoroughbred Racing Industry Collection (artifacts)
Exhibitions: Permanent exhibits about Derby & Thoroughbred Racing Industry; Barbaro: Heart of a Winner
Publications: Inside Track newsletter, quarterly
Activities: Classes for children; lects for mem only, 4 vis lectrs per yr; gallery talks; competitions with prizes; individual paintings lent to qualified mus; originate traveling exhibs; originate traveling exhibs statewide; mus shop sells books, original art, prints

M **KENTUCKY MUSEUM OF ART AND CRAFT,** (Kentucky Art & Craft Gallery), 715 W Main St, Louisville, KY 40202-2633. Tel 502-589-0102; Fax 502-589-0154; Email admin@kentuckyarts.org; Web: www.kmacmuseum.org; *Exec Dir* Aldy Milliken; *Cur* Joey Yates; *Communs Mgr* Emily Miles; *Educ* Joanna Miller; *Shop Sales Mgr* Julia Comer; *Develop Dir* Michelle Staggs
Open Tues - Sat 10 AM - 6 PM, Sun 10 AM - 5 PM; Admis adults $8, seniors & military $5, children (0-5) free, (6-12) $2, students $4; Estab 1981 to advance & perpetuate Kentucky's art & craft heritage; Works by over 400 Kentucky makers & artisans displayed & sold in restored 19th century building; Average Annual Attendance: 65,000; Mem: 427; dues $500, $200, $75 & $40
Income: Financed by mem dues, state appropriation, corporations, foundations & fund-raising events
Library Holdings: Book Volumes, CD-ROMs, Exhibition Catalogs, Original Art Works, Periodical Subscriptions, Photographs, Slides
Special Subjects: Afro-American Art, Ceramics, Collages, Costumes, Crafts, Decorative Arts, Drawings, Folk Art, Furniture, Glass, Graphics, Jewelry, Juvenile Art, Mosaics, Oriental Art, Painting-American, Photography, Portraits, Pottery, Prints, Sculpture, Silver, Southwestern Art, Tapestries, Textiles, Watercolors, Woodcarvings, Primitive art
Collections: Small collection of contemporary American folk art

Exhibitions: Rotating exhibits
Publications: Matthew Ronay The Third Attention, forward by Aldy Milliken & Ying Kit Chan & John Begley; Essays by Matthew Drutt & John R Hale
Activities: Docent training; annual: 8-10 exhibs; avg 100 field trips; 3-4 vis lectrs per yr; 37 maker workshops; 1 winter, 1 spring & 9 summer camps; 12 musical performances; 3 special event fundraisers; 13 traveling mobile museum suitcases; 2 artist in residence; community events; group tours; Alma Lesch Award; extension prog to surrounding area public schools; 2 book traveling exhibs per yr; kmac shop sells original art & functional objects

A **LOUISVILLE VISUAL ART,** 1538 Lytle St, Louisville, KY 40203. Tel 502-584-8166; Fax 502-584-7976; Email info@louisvillevisualart.org; Web: www.louisvillevisualart.org; *Executive Director* Lindy Casebier; *Education Coordinator* Annette Cable; *Dir Creative Design* Amy Chase; *Dir Educ & Outreach* Jackie Pallesen; *Outreach Prog Mgr* Ehren Reed; *Facility & Gallery Mgr* Keith Waits
Open Mon - Thurs 9 AM - 4 PM; No admis fee; Established 1909 to provide programs for local and regional artists and children. As a creative hub now established in the Portland Neighborhood, they are dedicated to engaging and encouraging artists through programming such as Artebella Daily, Open Studio Weekend, and weekly calls forartists. LVA is shaping and inspiring the next generation of creative leaders by providing quality instruction to over 5,500 students annually through Children's Fine Art Classes and outreach programs in schools and community centers.; Currently no regular gallery schedule. In 2015 LVA purchased a 32,000 sq ft building. In 2017 it will launch a capital campaign to renovate this facility to accommodate all aspects of programming including exhibits.; Average Annual Attendance: 200,000; Mem: 5000; dues $25 and up; monthly meeting of Board of Dir
Income: $750,000 (financed by endowment, mem, state appropriation, Louisville Fund for the Arts, grants, rental of space & annual fundraising events)
Exhibitions: Curating exhibits in remote locations such as Louisville's Metro Hall and private businesses; Artist's Studio Tour weekend event each fall; Limited Pending renovation but emphasis on LVA programming, local and regional art
Publications: Exhibit catalogs
Activities: Classes & workshops for adults & children; docent training, Children's fine art classes for elementary middle and high school students since 1925; lects open to pub, 50 vis lectrs per yr; concerts; gallery talks; tours; competitions with awards; scholarships offered; exten dept serves Jefferson, Bullitt, Oldham & Shelby Counties in Kentucky & Clark, Floyd & Harrison Counties in Indiana; individual paintings & original objects of art lent to prospective buyers; open doors, mural art program, Studio 2000, Future is now mentorship program, internships for college credit available; book traveling exhibs 1-2 per yr; originate traveling exhibs; sales shop sells magazines, original art, prints, jewelry, pottery, glass & hand crafted items

M **RIVERSIDE, THE FARNSLEY-MOREMEN LANDING,** 7410 Moorman Rd, Louisville, KY 40272-4572. Tel 502-935-6809; Fax 502-935-6821; Web: www.riverside-landing.org; *CEO & Dir* Patti Linn; *Vol Chmn* Reba Doutrick; *Mus Shop Mgr* Heather French
Open March - Nov Tues - Sat 10 AM - 4:30 PM, Sun 1 - 4:30 PM; Dec - Feb Tues - Sat 10 AM - 4:30 PM, cl New Year's Day, Thanksgiving Day & the day after & Christmas Day; Admis family $15, adults $6, seniors $5, students & children 6-12 $3, mems no admis fee; Estab 1993; 300-acre historic farm site with focus on the restored 1837 Farnsley-Moremen House. The museum's mission is to promote, preserve, restore & interpret historic farm life on the Ohio River. 200-capacity auditorium; 3000 sq ft exhib space; 3rd congressional dist; FT Paid 4, PT Paid 3, PT vols 60+; Average Annual Attendance: 25,341; Mem: dues Family $35, Indiv $20
Collections: coll of printed materials on local history, reproduction toys & games, and other site-specific publs, structures; furnishings; archaeological specimens; decorative arts; tools & equipment for materials
Publications: Riverside Review, quarterly newsletter
Activities: Formal educ progs for adults & children; docent prog; concerts; lects; guided tours; Ice Cream Social; Riverside Heritage Festival; Plant & Herb Sale; A Riverside Christmas; research in historic interiors & decorative arts for the 1840s - 1880s in Louisville, KY; mus related items for sale

M **SOUTHERN BAPTIST THEOLOGICAL SEMINARY,** Joseph A Callaway Archaeological Museum, 2825 Lexington Rd, Louisville, KY 40280-0001. Tel 502-897-4011, 4132; Fax 502-897-4880; Email jdrinkard@sbts.edu; Web: www.sbts.edu; *Librn* Bruce Keisling
Open Mon - Fri 8 AM - 4:30 PM; No admis fee; Estab 1961
Income: Financed by the seminary & donations
Special Subjects: Antiquities-Assyrian, Antiquities-Byzantine, Antiquities-Egyptian, Archaeology, Pottery, Religious Art, Sculpture, Textiles
Collections: Biblical archeology, coptic religious materials, glass, materials excavated from Jericho, AI & Jerusalem, mummy, numismatics, ostraca, pottery, sculpture, textiles, copy of the Rosetta Stone
Exhibitions: Rotating exhibits
Activities: Guided tours; films

M **THE SPEED ART MUSEUM,** 2035 S Third St, Louisville, KY 40208-1812. Tel 502-634-2700; Fax 502-636-2899; Email info@speedmuseum.org; Web: www.speedmuseum.org; *Dir* Stephen Reily; *COO* Paul Esselman; *Cur Decorative Arts & Design* Scott Erbes
Open Wed - Sat 10 AM - 5 PM, Sun 12 PM - 5 PM, cl Mon & Tues; Adults $18, children 4-17, $12, seniors, military & students with valid ID $12; children 3 & under free; Estab 1925, opened 1927 for the collection & exhibition of works of art of all periods & cultures, supported by a full special exhibition program & educational activities; Galleries are arranged to present painting, sculpture & decorative arts of all periods & cultures; special facilities for prints & drawings; Average Annual Attendance: 180,000; Mem: 4,000; dues individual $70; Family $100; Reciprocal $140; Supporter $250
Income: Financed by endowments, donations, grants, ticket sales & memberships
Special Subjects: African Art, Afro-American Art, American Indian Art, American Western Art, Antiquities-Egyptian, Antiquities-Etruscan, Antiquities-Greek, Antiquities-Persian, Antiquities-Roman, Architecture, Asian Art, Baroque Art, Bronzes, Carpets & Rugs, Cartoons, Ceramics, Coins & Medals, Collages, Costumes, Crafts, Decorative Arts, Dolls, Drawings, Embroidery, Enamels, Etchings & Engravings, Flasks & Bottles, Folk Art, Furniture, Glass, Gold, Ivory, Jade, Jewelry, Laces, Landscapes, Leather, Manuscripts, Maps, Marine Painting, Medieval Art, Metalwork, Mexican Art, Miniatures, Mosaics, Painting-American, Painting-Australian, Painting-British, Painting-Canadian, Painting-Dutch, Painting-European, Painting-Flemish, Painting-French, Painting-German, Painting-Israeli, Painting-Italian, Painting-Japanese, Painting-Polish, Painting-Russian, Painting-Scandinavian, Painting-Spanish, Period Rooms, Pewter, Photography, Porcelain, Portraits, Posters, Pottery, Prints, Religious Art, Renaissance Art, Sculpture, Silver, Stained Glass, Tapestries, Textiles, Watercolors, Woodcarvings, Woodcuts
Collections: Comprehensive permanent coll, Coll spans 6,000 yrs of human creativity
Publications: The Speed Art Museum: Highlights from the Collection; newsletter, bi-annually; Bulletin, occasional
Activities: Classes for children, ArtSparks; docent training; summer camps; teacher progs; lects open to pub, 4 vis lectrs per yr; concerts; gallery talks; tours; mus shop sells books & museum-related items

L **Art Reference Library**, 2035 S Third St, Louisville, KY 40208. Tel 502-634-2710; Fax 502-636-2899; Email library@speedmuseum.org; Web: www.speedmuseum.org; *Librn* Allison Gillette
Open Wed, Thurs, Sat 10 AM - 5 PM, Fri 10 AM - 9 PM, Sun noon - 5 PM; Library (by appointment only), cl Mon & Tues; Admis fee adults $10, seniors (65+) $8, children 3-17 $5, children under 3 free; 1927; Circ Non-circulating library; Collection is extensive, spanning 6000 yrs
Income: Financed by general budget
Library Holdings: Auction Catalogs, Book Volumes 2500, Clipping Files, Exhibition Catalogs, Manuscripts, Other Holdings Vertical files 23, Pamphlets, Periodical Subscriptions 13
Special Subjects: Aesthetics, Afro-American Art, American Indian Art, Antiquities-Egyptian, Antiquities-Greek, Antiquities-Oriental, Antiquities-Roman, Architecture, Art History, Asian Art, Bronzes, Ceramics, Conceptual Art, Constructions, Costume Design & Constr, Crafts, Decorative Arts, Drawings, Etchings & Engravings, Folk Art, Furniture, Glass, Historical Material, History of Art & Archaeology, Landscapes, Oriental Art, Painting-American, Painting-British, Painting-Canadian, Painting-Dutch, Painting-European, Painting-Flemish, Painting-French, Painting-German, Painting-Italian, Photography, Porcelain, Pottery, Prints, Sculpture, Silver, Silversmithing, Tapestries, Textiles, Watercolors, Woodcuts, Latin American Art
Collections: Frederick Weygold's Indian Collection, African Art, Ancient Art, Native American Art, American Art, European Art, Contemporary Art
Publications: Index to J B Speed Art Museum bulletins, index to dealers catalogs; J B Speed Handbook
Activities: Classes for adults & children; docent training; Lects open to pub; lects for members only; concerts; gallery talks; tours; mus shop sells books, prints

M **UNIVERSITY OF LOUISVILLE,** Hite Art Institute, 104 Schneider Hall, Belknap Campus Louisville, KY 40292-0001. Tel 502-852-6794; Fax 502-852-6791; Web: www.art.louisville.edu; *Chmn* James Grubola; *Gallery Dir* John Begley; *Art History Prog Head* Linda Gigante
Open Mon - Fri 8:30 AM - 4:30 PM, cl Sat 10 AM - 2 PM, Sun 1 - 6 PM; No admis fee; Estab 1935 for educ & enrichment; There are three galleries: Morris Belknap Gallery, Dario Covi Gallery, Gallery X; Average Annual Attendance: 35,000
Income: Financed by endowment & state appropriation
Special Subjects: Drawings, Prints
Collections: Teaching collection
Publications: Exhibition catalogs
Activities: Lects open to public, 9-12 vis lectrs per yr; gallery talks; tours; Winthrop Allen Memorial Prize for creative art; scholarships offered; original objects of art lent to other departments on campus & to other exhibitions; lending collection includes Kentucky regional art, prints & drawings, alumni; book traveling exhibs

L **Margaret M Bridwell Art Library**, Schneider Hall, Louisville, KY 40292-0001. Tel 502-852-6741; Email gail.gilbert@louisville.edu; Web: louisville.edu/library/art; *Dir Art Library* Gail R Gilbert
Open Mon - Thurs 8 AM - 9 PM, Fri 8 AM - 5 PM, Sat 10 AM - 3 PM, Sun 1 - 8 PM, summer Mon-Fri 8AM-5PM, Sat 10AM-1PM; Estab 1956 to support the programs of the art department; For reference only
Income: Financed by endowment & state appropriation
Purchases: $125,000
Library Holdings: Book Volumes 93,000, CD-ROMs 323, Clipping Files, DVDs 606, Exhibition Catalogs, Fiche 2,500, Manuscripts, Memorabilia, Pamphlets, Periodical Subscriptions 310, Video Tapes 506
Special Subjects: Afro-American Art, Antiquities-Byzantine, Antiquities-Etruscan, Antiquities-Greek, Antiquities-Roman, Archaeology, Architecture, Art Education, Art History, Decorative Arts, Drawings, Etchings & Engravings, Glass, Graphic Design, History of Art & Archaeology, Interior Design, Painting-American, Painting-British, Painting-European, Painting-Flemish, Painting-French, Painting-German, Painting-Italian, Painting-Spanish, Photography, Pottery, Printmaking, Prints, Sculpture, Textiles, Watercolors, Woodcuts, Posters
Collections: Original Christmas cards, Ainslie Hewett bookplate coll, artist's books, Morton Woodblock collection; Brecher Tobacco & chewing gum card collection

L **Ekstrom Library Photographic Archives**, 2301 S 3rd St, Ekstrom Library Louisville, KY 40292-0001. Tel 502-852-6752; Fax 502-852-8734; Email special.collections@louisville.edu
Open Mon - Fri 9 AM - 5 PM; No admis fee; Estab 1967 to collect, preserve, organize photographs & related materials; primary emphasis on documentary photography; Circ Restricted circ; Four exhibits per year
Income: Financed through the University & revenue
Library Holdings: Book Volumes 1000, Clipping Files, Exhibition Catalogs, Photographs 1,200,000, Reels 200
Collections: Antique Media & Equipment, Lou Block Collection, Will Bowers Collection, Bradley Studio - Georgetown, Theodore M Brown - Robert J Doherty Collection, Caldwell Tank Co Collection, Caulfield & Shook, Inc, Lin Caulfield Collection, Cooper Collection, Flexner Slide Collection, Erotic Photography, Fine Print Collection, Arthur Y Ford Albums, Forensic Photographic Collection, Vida Hunt Francis Collection, K & IT Railroad Collections, Mary D Hill Collections,

Griswold Collections, Joseph Krementz Collection, Kentucky Mountain Schools Collection, The Macauley Theater Collection, Manvell Collection of Film Stills, Boyd Martin Collection, Kate Matthews Collection, J C Rieger Collections, Roy Emerson Stryker Collections, A W Terhune Collection, Joseph & Joseph Collection, Andre Jeneut Collection
Publications: Exhibition catalogues; collections brochures; guide to spec collections
Activities: Lects open to public, vis lectrs per yr varies; gallery talks; educational groups; individual prints lent to museums & galleries; book traveling exhibs; originates traveling exhibs; sales shop sells reproductions, prints, slides & postcards, reference and research services

L **Visual Resources Center**, Lutz Hall, Rm 104, Louisville, KY 40292-0001. Tel 502-852-5917; Email amy.fordham@louisville.edu; Web: louisville.edu; *Cur Visual Resources* Amy Fordham
Open Mon - Fri 8:30 AM - 4:30 PM; Estab 1930s to provide comprehensive collection of slides for use in the university instructional program; 300,000 catalogued slides primarily illustrating history of western art for faculty & students of fine arts; Circ restricted
Library Holdings: Clipping Files, Kodachrome Transparencies, Other Holdings Computer Digital Image Bank, Slides 350,000
Special Subjects: Architecture, Painting-American, Photography, Pottery
Collections: American Studies, Calligraphy, Manuscript of Medieval Life

MAYSVILLE

M **MAYSVILLE,** (Mason County Museum) Kentucky Gateway Museum Center, 215 Sutton St, Maysville, KY 41056-1109. Tel 606-564-5865; Fax 606-564-4372; Email communications@kygmc.org; Web: www.kygmc.org; *Pres* Dee Werline; *Dir* Dawn C Browning; *Librn* Myra Hardy; *Bus Mgr* Gayle H McKay; *Dir Pub Rels* Lynn David; *Educ Coordr* Dr James Shires; *Cur Books & Art* Sue Ellen Grannis; *VPres* Kent Kalb; *Accounting* Joyce Weigott; *Libr Asst* Cay Chamness; *Receptionist* Marion Browning; *Reference Tech* Paula Ruble; *Cur Miniatures* Kaye Browning
Open Tues - Fri 10 AM - 5 PM, Sat 10 AM - 4 PM, Sun 1-4PM; Admis adults $10, children $2; Estab 1878 to maintain historical records & artifacts for area; Average Annual Attendance: 3,000; Mem: 450; dues $25-$50
Income: $150,000 (financed by endowment and members)
Special Subjects: Anthropology, Archaeology, Architecture, Ceramics, Coins & Medals, Costumes, Decorative Arts, Dioramas, Dolls, Drawings, Embroidery, Etchings & Engravings, Flasks & Bottles, Folk Art, Furniture, Glass, Historical Material, Jewelry, Laces, Landscapes, Manuscripts, Maps, Marine Painting, Miniatures, Painting-American, Photography, Portraits, Posters, Pottery, Sculpture, Silver, Textiles, Watercolors, Woodcarvings, Prints, Reproductions
Collections: Paintings & maps related to area, genealogical library, KSB Miniatures Collection
Publications: Quarterly Newsletter
Activities: Classes for children; lects open to pub, 5 vis lectrs per yr; gallery talks; tours; individual paintings & original objects of art lent to different museums; book traveling exhibs, 2-4 per yr; mus shop sells books, reproductions, prints, postcards, souvenirs, miniatures, toys, jewelry

MOREHEAD

M **MOREHEAD STATE UNIVERSITY,** Kentucky Folk Art Center, 102 W First St, Morehead, KY 40351. Tel 606-783-2204; Fax 606-783-5034; Email m.collinswor@morehead-st.edu; Web: www.kyfolkart.org; *Cur* Adrian Swain; *Dir* Matt Collinsworth
Open Mon - Sat 9 AM - 5 PM, Sun 1 - 5 PM; Admis adults $3, seniors $2; Estab 1985 to promote contemporary folk art; Includes two galleries: Lovena & William Richardson Gallery which houses Collection & the Garland & Minnie Adkins Gallery housing rotating exhibits; Average Annual Attendance: 10,000; Mem: 400; dues $15-$5000; annual meeting in Sept
Income: $335,000 (financed by mem, state appropriations, grants & earnings
Purchases: $5000 (African-American, Kentucky)
Special Subjects: Afro-American Art, Folk Art, Painting-American, Pottery, Primitive art, Sculpture, Textiles, Watercolors, Woodcarvings
Collections: Kentucky Folk Art, Kentucky Self-Taught Art
Exhibitions: Kentucky Folk Art from permanent collection; Kentucky Quilts: Roots & Wings
Publications: KFAC Newsletter, quarterly
Activities: Classes for adults & children; dramatic progs; docent training; lects open to pub; 10 vis lectrs per yr; individual paintings & original objects of art lent; lending collection contains 800 items; book traveling exhibs 2 per yr; originate traveling exhibs; sales shop sells books, magazines, original art, prints

M **MOREHEAD STATE UNIVERSITY,** Claypool-Young Art Gallery, Claypool Young Bldg, 150 University Blvd Morehead, KY 40351-1684. Tel 606-783-5446; Fax 606-783-5048; Email j.reis@moreheadstate.edu; Web: www.moreheadstate.edu; *Chmn* Jean Petsch; *Dir* Jennifer Reis
Open Mon - Fri 8 AM - 4 PM, by appointment; No admis fee; Estab 1969 as univ art gallery; An exhibition gallery is maintained for traveling exhibitions, faculty & student work. The Claypool-Young Art Gallery is tri-level with 2344 sq ft of exhibition space; Average Annual Attendance: 8,000
Income: Financed by appropriation
Special Subjects: Prints
Collections: Permanent coll: prints by major contemporary figures, several works added each year through purchase or bequest. Additions to lending coll include: The Maria Rilke Suite of lithographs by Ben Shahn consisting of 23 pieces, the Laus Pictorum Suite by Leonard Baskin, consisting of 14 pieces, & three lithographs by Thomas Hart Benton: Jesse James, Frankie & Johnny, & Huck Finn
Exhibitions: A large number of group & thematic exhibits; 8 exhibits per yr, student shows & regional shows
Activities: Educ dept; classes for adults & children; lects open to public; 6-10 vis lectrs per yr; concert; gallery talks; tours; competitions; Bluegrass Biennial: Kentucky Exhib awards

MORGANFIELD

M **JAMES D VEATCH CAMP BRECKINRIDGE MUSEUM & ARTS CENTER,** 1116 N Village Rd, Morganfield, KY 42437; PO Box 60, Morganfield, KY 43437-0060. Tel 270-389-4420; *Dir* Vicki Ricketts
Open Tues - Fri 10 AM - 3 PM, Sat 10 AM - 4 PM, Sun 1 PM - 4 PM
Special Subjects: Painting-American, Photography
Collections: Military history; local history; murals
Exhibitions: Permanent & temporary exhibits
Activities: Educ progs; classes for adults & children; lects open to pub; concerts; gallery talks; integrated art events; facilitation of public art projects; cultural events

MURRAY

M **MURRAY STATE UNIVERSITY,** Art Galleries, 604 Fine Arts Bldg, Corner of 15th & Olive Sts Murray, KY 42071-3342. Tel 270-762-3052; Fax 270-762-3920; Email becky.atkinson@murraystate.edu
Open Mon - Fri 8 AM - 5 PM, Sat & Sun 1 - 4 PM, cl University holidays; No admis fee; Estab 1971; Gallery houses the permanent art collection of the University; the Main Gallery is located on the sixth floor & its dimensions are 100 x 40 ft; the Upper Level is divided into three small galleries that may be used as one or three; the Curris Center Art Gallery is also part of the offerings; Average Annual Attendance: 12,000
Income: Financed by state appropriation and grants
Special Subjects: Drawings, Etchings & Engravings, Furniture, Juvenile Art, Painting-American, Photography, Portraits, Prints, Sculpture, Textiles
Collections: Asian Collection (given by Asian Cultural Exchange Foundation), Collection of Clara M Eagle Gallery, WPA prints, drawings, Magic Silver Photography Collection, Harry L Jackson Print Collection
Exhibitions: Biennial Magic Silver Show (even years); Annual Student Exhibition; Biennial Faculty Exhibitions (odd years); Contemporary Regional Arts
Publications: Brochures and posters for individual shows
Activities: Vis artists; workshops; demonstrations; lects open to public, 8 vis lectrs per yr; gallery talks; tours; competitions with merit & purchase awards; exten dept serving Jackson Purchase Area of Kentucky; individual paintings & original objects of art lent; lending collection consists of original prints, paintings, photographs & sculpture; books traveling exhibs; originates traveling exhibs

OWENSBORO

M **BRESCIA UNIVERSITY,** Anna Eaton Stout Memorial Art Gallery, 717 Frederica St, Owensboro, KY 42301-3019. Tel 270-685-3131; Email maryt@brescia.edu; *Chair, Div Fine Art* Sr Mary Diane Taylor; *Prof of Art & Gallery Dir* David Stratton; *Asst Prof of Art* Frank Krevens
Open Mon - Fri 8 AM - 4:30 PM, Sat 8 AM - Noon; No admis fee; Estab 1950; Gallery space is 20 x 30 ft, walls are covered with neutral carpeting; Average Annual Attendance: 4,000
Activities: Lects open to public, 2-3 vis lectrs per year; competitions with awards; schols offered; book traveling exhibs; originate traveling exhibs

M **OWENSBORO MUSEUM OF FINE ART,** 901 Frederica St, Owensboro, KY 42301. Tel 270-685-3181; Fax 270-685-3181; Email info@omfa.us; Web: www.omfa.us; *Dir* Mary Bryan Hood; *Director of Development & Marketing* Jason Hayden; *Bus Mgr* Horace Hardison; *Registrar* John Dunham; *Admin Asst* Sharon Hagerman; *Edu Coordr* Rocky Cecil
Open Tues - Thurs 10 AM - 4 PM, Fri 10 AM - 7 PM, Sat & Sun 1 PM - 4 PM, cl Mon & national holidays; No admis fee, donations suggested: Adult $2, Children under 13 $1; Estab 1977 to showcase regional, national & international art & to promote the cultural history of Kentucky through acquisition & exhib of artists with connections to the state through birth, educ & residency; Three Wings: Decorative Arts in restored pre-Civil War mansion; temporary & permanent collection exhibition galleries; stained glass gallery; atrium sculpture ct & two outdoor sculpture parks; Average Annual Attendance: 70,000; Mem: 800; dues $25-$10,000
Income: Financed by pvt & pub sectors supplemented by foundation grants & major fundraising events
Library Holdings: Auction Catalogs, Audio Tapes, Book Volumes, Cassettes, Clipping Files, DVDs, Exhibition Catalogs, Kodachrome Transparencies, Slides, Video Tapes
Special Subjects: African Art, Afro-American Art, American Indian Art, American Western Art, Architecture, Asian Art, Bronzes, Carpets & Rugs, Ceramics, Collages, Crafts, Decorative Arts, Drawings, Etchings & Engravings, Folk Art, Furniture, Glass, Graphics, Hispanic Art, Juvenile Art, Landscapes, Oriental Art, Painting-American, Painting-Australian, Painting-British, Painting-French, Period Rooms, Photography, Porcelain, Portraits, Pottery, Prints, Religious Art, Sculpture, Stained Glass, Textiles, Watercolors, Woodcarvings, Woodcuts, Silver, Southwestern Art
Collections: 14th-18th century European drawings, graphics, decorative arts, 19th-20th century American, French & English paintings, sculpture & stained glass, 20th century studio glass, American folk Art, monumental outdoor sculpture
Publications: Exhibition catalogues; newsletters
Activities: Classes for adults & children; docent training; seminars & critiques led by major American artists; performing arts events; children's art gallery & interactive art studio; lects open to pub, 6 vis lectrs per yr; concerts; gallery talks; tours; competitions with awards; pre-tour visits to the classroom; film series; book traveling exhibs 3-5 per yr; sales shop sells books, original art & decorative arts objects; Young ar Art Gallery - children's art

PADUCAH

M **THE NATIONAL QUILT MUSEUM,** (The National Quilt Museum: Museum of the American Quilter's Society), 215 Jefferson St, PO Box 1540 Paducah, KY 42002-1540. Tel 270-442-8856; Fax 270-442-5448; Email info@quiltmuseum.org; Web: www.quiltmuseum.org; *Exec Dir* Frank Bennett; *Cur & Registrar* Judy

Schwender; *Dir Pub Rels* Amanda Ball; *Cur Educ* Becky Glasby; *Bus Mgr* Stacy Canter
Open Mon - Sat 10 AM - 5 PM yr round, Apr 1 - Oct 31 also open Sun 1 PM - 5 PM; Admis adult $11, seniors 60 & over $9, student 13-college $5, group rates available, children 12 & under & school groups free; Estab 1991; Three climate controlled galleries - Gallery A (7000 sq ft) displays selection from Mus Collection. Gallery B (2900 sq ft) and Gallery C (3500 sq ft) display temporary exhibits of contemporary & antique quilts; Average Annual Attendance: 45,000; Mem: 2,000 Friends of the Museum; donations of $40 and above
Income: $882,702; financed by private & corporate donations & grants including Kentucky Arts Council grant
Library Holdings: Book Volumes, Compact Disks, DVDs, Exhibition Catalogs
Special Subjects: Crafts, Decorative Arts, Embroidery, Folk Art, Textiles
Collections: Quilts made in 1980 to present, Education Coll & Paul D Pilgrim Coll, Miniature Quilt Coll
Exhibitions: 10 - 12 exhibs each yr incl antique, contemporary & special topics & curated exhibs
Publications: NQM Friends, quarterly newsletter; New Quilts from an Old Favorite, annual; Coll of Quilts from the National Quilt Museum
Activities: Classes for adults & children; docent training; lects open to pub & some for mem only; occasional vis lectrs; gallery talks; tours; sponsoring of competitions; schols offered; exten prog serves the school &community groups in the region, off-site, lending slide show, & trunk with art samples to quilt guilds & schools; college credit offered for adult quilt class; book traveling exhibitions 6-8 times per yr; originate traveling exhibs circulate to quilt & art mus; mus shop sells books, magazines, original art, reproductions, prints & fine crafts in all media

M **RIVER HERITAGE MUSEUM,** 117 S Water St, Paducah, KY 42001-0787. Tel 270-575-9958; Fax 270-444-9944; Web: www.riverheritagemuseum.org; *Exec Dir & Mus Shop Mgr* Julie Harris; *Develop Mem & Pub Rels* Nate Heider; *Vol Chmn* Ken Wheeler; *Educ* E J Abell
Open Apr - Nov Mon - Sat 9:30 AM - 5 PM, Sun 1 PM - 5 PM; cl at noon on Christmas Day; cl Easter, Thanksgiving Day & Christmas Day; Admis adults $5, seniors $4.50, tours & groups $4, children $3, mems no admis fee; Estab 1990; mus explores the history & significance of the river & the impact it has on people's lives through its use of state-of-the-art interactive exhibs, music stations, films, colls & aquariums; Average Annual Attendance: 10,600; Mem: dues Captain $1000, Pilot $500, Engineer $250, Crew $100, First Mate $50, Deckhand $25
Collections: Riverboat; steamboat; towboat; paddlewheel models; river memorabilia; nautical memorabilia; Civil War artifacts
Publications: The Anchor, quarterly newsletter
Activities: Events: Marine Industry Day; Sand In the City; River Trek; films; guided tours; participatory exhibs; rental gallery; school loan svc; mus shop sells books, clothing, jewelry, educ toys & related items

A **YEISER ART CENTER INC,** 200 Broadway, Paducah, KY 42001. Tel 270-442-2453; Fax 270-442-0828; Email info@theyeiser.org; Web: www.theyeiser.org; *Exec Dir* Teri Moore
Open Tues - Sat 10 AM - 4 PM, cl Sun, Mon & major holidays; Admis by donation; Estab 1957 as a nonprofit cultural and educational institution to provide the community and the membership with visual art exhibitions, classes and related activities of the highest quality; Average Annual Attendance: 16,000; Mem: 600; monthly programs & mem meetings
Income: $150,000 (financed by mem fees, donations, commissions & grants)
Purchases: $100,000
Collections: Primarily regional/contemporary with some 19th century works on paper & Japanese prints, teaching coll, Collection includes R Haley Lever, Matisse, Goya, Emil Carlsen, Philip Moulthrop, Ron Isaacs
Exhibitions: Fantastic Fibers, Annual national Fibers Exhibit; National State Annual Competition; changing exhibitions of historical & contemporary art of regional, national & international nature
Publications: Fantastic Fibers, annual catalog; exhibit catalog; monthly newsletter
Activities: Classes for adults & children; dramatic progs; docent training; lects open to pub, 12 vis lectrs per yr; gallery talks; tours; competitions with awards; sponsoring of competitions; scholarships offered; individual and original objects of art lent to qualified institutions; lending collection contains original art works, prints and paintings; originate traveling exhibs; mus shop sells books, original art, prints, gifts & unique items

PARIS

M **HISTORIC PARIS - BOURBON COUNTY, INC,** Hopewell Museum, 800 Pleasant St, Paris, KY 40361-1734. Tel 859-987-7274; Fax 859-987-8107; Email hopewellmuseum@yahoo.com; Web: www.hopewellmuseum.org; *Exec Dir* Leah W Craig
Open Wed-Sat Noon-5 PM, Sun 2 PM-4 PM; Admis $3, free to mems & students; Estab 1994 to display Kentucky fine art & Bourbon County history; Six gallery rooms & a hall; building originally constructed in Beaux Arts Style as a post office; Average Annual Attendance: 2,500; Mem: 200; dues $45
Income: $95,000; (financed by mem, donations & pledges)
Special Subjects: Costumes, Crafts, Decorative Arts, Furniture, Glass
Collections: Bourbon County History (books, clothing, furniture, photography, others), Kentucky Fine Art (paintings), Bourbon County History, Kentucky Fine Art
Exhibitions: Victorian Children's Room; Civil War; Main Street Views-photography of Doris Ullman; Agricultural Heritage Exhibit
Activities: Classes for children; dramatic progs; docent training; lects open to pub, 3-5 vis lectrs per yr; mus shop sells books & prints

WHITESBURG

C **APPALSHOP INC,** Appalshop, 91 Madison St, Whitesburg, KY 41858. Tel 606-633-0108; Orders: 800-545-7467; Fax 606-633-1009; Email info@appalshop.org; Web: www.appalshop.org; *Mng Dir & Gallery Dir* Beth Bingman; *Theater Dir* Dudley Cocke; *Communs Dir* Mark Kidd; *Mktg & Sales* Derek Mullins
Open Mon - Fri 9 AM - 5 PM; Admis fee for special events; Estab 1969 as the Community Film Workshop of Appalachia, part of a national program to train poor & minority young people in the skills of film & television production, now an incorporated nonprofit media arts center; In 1982 a renovated 13,000 sq ft warehouse, became the Appalshop Center with offices, video & radio editing suites, a 150 seat theater, an art gallery & educational facilities. A community radio station was added in 1987
Income: financed by grants & contributions
Publications: Newsletter, annual
Activities: Films, plays, music & educational progs to schools, college, mus, libraries, churches, festivals, conferences & community in the region, throughout the US & in Europe, Asia & Africa; classes for children; lect open to pub; concerts; originate traveling exhibs circulating to colleges in eastern Kentucky; sales shop sells music & films

WILMORE

M **ASBURY COLLEGE,** Student Center Gallery, One Macklem Dr, Wilmore, KY 40390-1198. Tel 859-858-3511; Fax 859-858-3921; Email kbarker@asbury.edu; Web: www.asbury.edu/art; *Prof Art History* Dr Linda Stratford; *Photography & Graphic Arts, Dept Chair* Prof Keith Barker; *Painting & Drawing* Prof Chris Sigre-Lewis; *Prof Ceramics Sculpture* Margaret Parks Smith
Open 8 AM - 11 PM Mon - Sat; No admis fee; Estab 1976 for the purpose of exhibiting the works of national, local, and student artists; Track lighting in a 20 x 20 ft space; Average Annual Attendance: 2,000; Mem: Christians in the Visual Arts (CIVA)
Income: Financed by college funds
Special Subjects: Ceramics, Drawings, Etchings & Engravings, Glass, Landscapes, Painting-American, Photography, Portraits, Pottery, Prints, Religious Art, Sculpture, Stained Glass, Watercolors, Woodcuts
Collections: Ongoing permanent collection of varied media
Exhibitions: 8-10 per year
Activities: Classes for adults; lects open to public, 4 vis lectrs per year; gallery talks; tours; schols offered

LOUISIANA

ABBEVILLE

M **ALLIANCE CENTER MUSEUM AND ART GALLERY,** 200 N Magdalen Sq, Abbeville, LA 70510-4645. Tel 337-898-4114
Open Tues & Sat 10AM-3PM, Wed-Fri 10AM-5PM
Collections: local history & culture; genealogy; photographs; documents; period artifacts; paintings

ALEXANDRIA

M **LOUISIANA STATE UNIVERSITY AT ALEXANDRIA,** University Gallery, 8100 Hwy 71 S, Alexandria, LA 71302-9119. Tel 318-473-6449; Email rdeville@lsua.edu; Web: www.lsua.edu; *Dir University Gallery* Roy V de Ville
Open Mon - Fri 10 AM - 3 PM; No admis fee; Estab 1960 as university art department gallery; Gallery located in student union for both students & public. Meets all state & university guidelines for climate control; Average Annual Attendance: 800
Income: Financed by university
Exhibitions: Local & student art shows
Publications: University Gallery Catalogue, quarterly
Activities: Docent training; lects open to pub, 3-4 vis lectrs per yr; concerts; galley talks; competitions; schols; individual paintings & original objects of art lent

BAKER

M **HERITAGE MUSEUM & CULTURAL CENTER,** 1606 Main St, Baker, LA 70704-0707; PO Box 707, Baker, LA 70704-0707. Tel 225-774-1776; Fax 225-775-5635; Email bakermuseum@bellsouth.net; Web: www.bakerheritagemuseum.org
Open Mon - Sat 10 AM - 4 PM; No admis fee, donations accepted; Estab 1974 in a restored c.1906 local residence; mus collects, preserves, documents & exhibits items relating to local history. Nonprofit org
Special Subjects: Historical Material, Restorations, Coins & Medals, Crafts, Costumes
Exhibitions: Mus has traveling box exhibits including: The Ballot Box, The Money Box, The Sewing Box, The Music Box, The Letter Box, The Hat Box, The Memory Box & The Way We See It
Publications: Musings, community newsletter
Activities: Guided tours; Educ progs; Christmas displays; speakers; originates traveling exhibs

BATON ROUGE

M **BATON ROUGE GALLERY,** (East Baton Rouge Parks & Recreation Commission) Center For Contemporary Art, 1515 Dalrymple Dr, Baton Rouge, LA 70808-1037. Tel 225-383-1470; Email info@batonrougegallery.org; Web: www.batonrougegallery.org; *Exec Dir* Jason Andreasen; *Special Facility Mgr* Jennifer Poulter; *Develop Dir* Jennifer Dewey
Open Tues - Sun Noon - 6 PM, cl Mon; No admis fee; Estab 1966 to educate & promote contemporary art; Nonprofit, cooperative, contemporary gallery made up of general members from community & artist members; Average Annual Attendance: 15,000; Mem: 56 artist mems meet semi-annually

Special Subjects: Afro-American Art, Ceramics, Etchings & Engravings, Hispanic Art, Landscapes, Painting-American, Photography, Sculpture, Watercolors
Collections: Southern regional artists based around Baton Rouge & throughout Louisiana
Exhibitions: Rotating mothly exhibitions; Surreal Salon (ann juried exhib in January)
Publications: The Art & Artists of Baton Rouge Gallery (2012)
Activities: Classes for adults & children;; lects open to pub; concerts; gallery talks; tours; competitions with awards; individual paintings & original objects of art lent to State of Louisiana; mus shop sells books & original art

M **LOUISIANA ARTS & SCIENCE MUSEUM,** PO Box 3373, Baton Rouge, LA 70821-3373; 100 River Rd S, Baton Rouge, LA 70802-5730. Tel 225-344-5272; Fax 225-344-9477; Email lasm@lasm.org; Web: www.lasm.org; *Asst Dir* Sam Losavio; *Dir Interpretation & Museum Cur* Elizabeth Weinstein; *Audience Engagement & PR Mgr* Hayley Westphal; *Events Coordr* Leslie Charleville; *Pres & Exec Dir* Carol S Gikas; *Planetarium Mgr* Sheree Westerhaus; *Planetarium Producer* Jay Lamm; *Dir Develop & Communs* Keith Dixon
Open Tues - Fri 10 AM - 3 PM, Sat 10 AM -5 PM, Sun 1 PM - 5 PM; Admis adults $9, children (3-12) & seniors (65+) $6, free for members; Estab 1960. General mus - art & science; Housed on the banks of the Mississippi River, the Louisiana Art & Science Mus (LASM) offers educational entertainment for visitors of all ages, including exhibs of internationally renowned artists, innovative programming in the state-of-the-art Pennington Planetarium, interactive art & science galleries for children & an Ancient Egypt Gallery; Average Annual Attendance: 80,000; Mem: 1200; Dues $20-$1000
Income: Financed by mem, city appropriation & donations
Special Subjects: African Art, Antiquities-Egyptian, Antiquities-Greek, Antiquities-Roman, Bronzes, Ceramics, Costumes, Dolls, Drawings, Eskimo Art, Folk Art, Graphics, Landscapes, Painting-American, Painting-European, Pottery, Prints, Sculpture, Textiles
Collections: 18th & 20th century European & American paintings, contemporary photographs, Clementine Hunter paintings, Ivan Mestrovic, sculpture, Egyptian artifacts, Eskimo graphics & soapstone carvings, North American Indian crafts, Tibetan religious art
Exhibitions: Discovery Depot, a participatory gallery that introduces children to art; Irene W Pennington Planetarium; Ancient Egyptian Gallery
Publications: LASM Calendar, quarterly
Activities: Classes for children; workshops, YouthALIVE; lects open to pub, 7 vis lectrs per yr; gallery talks; tours; individual paintings & original objects of art lent to other mus & galleries; book traveling exhibs 8-10 per yr; originate traveling exhibs; mus shop sells books, magazines, original art, reproductions, slides, educational toys & t-shirts

L **Library**, 100 S River Rd, Baton Rouge, LA 70802; PO Box 3373, Baton Rouge, LA 70821-3373. Tel 225-344-5272; Fax 225-344-9477; Web: www.lasm.org; *Exec Dir* Carol S Gikas; *Asst Dir* Sam Losavio
Open Tues - Fri 10 AM - 3 PM, Sat 10 - 4 PM, Sun 1 PM - 4 PM, cl Mon; Estab 1971; Small reference library open to staff only. Two floor gallery for changing exhibitions; Average Annual Attendance: 69,000; Mem: 2000
Library Holdings: Book Volumes 1000, Exhibition Catalogs, Pamphlets, Periodical Subscriptions 32, Slides, Video Tapes
Special Subjects: Painting-European, Painting-American, Photography, Sculpture
Collections: 18th-20th American & European art, 2d largest coll of Ivan Mestrovic in U.S.
Publications: LASM Quarterly membership newsletter; exhibition catalogues
Activities: Classes for adults & children; docent training; lects open to pub, 6 vis lectrs per yr; gallery talks; workshops; school group programs; exten art programs in local schools; 8-10 traveling exhibs

M **LOUISIANA STATE UNIVERSITY,** Museum of Art, 100 Lafayette, Baton Rouge, LA 70801. Tel 225-389-7200; Fax 225-389-7219; Email artmuseum@lsu.edu; Web: www.lsumoa.org; *Exec Dir* Daniel Stentson; *Asst Dir Coll* Fran Huber
Open Tues - Sat 10 AM - 5 PM, Thurs 10 AM - 8 PM, Sun 1 PM - 5 PM; Admis adults (13 & older) $5, children (under 13) & mem free; Estab 1959 to collect, conserve, exhibit & protect the works of art entrusted to its care; 19,500 sq ft; Average Annual Attendance: 55,000; Mem: 1200; dues $25 - $1,000
Income: Financed by LSU, state, fundraising & earned
Purchases: 20th century - 21st century American art
Library Holdings: Auction Catalogs 150, Book Volumes 2,100, Exhibition Catalogs 250, Original Art Works 4,250, Photographs, Prints, Sculpture
Special Subjects: Ceramics, Decorative Arts, Drawings, Furniture, Glass, Graphics, Jade, Painting-American, Painting-British, Photography, Sculpture, Silver, Watercolors
Collections: Hogarth & Caroline Durieux Graphics Collection, Newcomb Crafts: 19th century lighting devices, New Orleans Silver, early Baton Rouge Subjects
Publications: Catalogues; newsletter
Activities: Classes for adults & children; docent training; lects open to pub; gallery talks; tours; originate traveling exhibs; mus shop sells books, magazines, original art, reproductions, prints, slides, jewelry, cards, games

L **Library**, 114 Memorial Tower, Baton Rouge, LA 70803-0001. Tel 225-388-5652; Email libcirc@lsu.edu; Web: www.lib.lsu.edu; *Dean LSU Libraries* Stanley Wilder
Open Mon - Thurs 24 hrs, Fri midnight - 8 PM, Sat 10 AM - 5 PM, Sun 11 AM - midnight, cl university holidays; No admis fee; Reference library; Average Annual Attendance: 7,500
Library Holdings: Book Volumes 700, Clipping Files, Exhibition Catalogs, Original Art Works, Photographs, Prints, Sculpture
Special Subjects: Drawings, Painting-American, Painting-British, Decorative Arts
Exhibitions: English period rooms 17th & 19th century; American period rooms 18th & 19th centuries; Collection of Newcomb Crafts; New Orleans made Silver; Hogarth Prints; Works by Caroline Durieux; 18th century lighting devices
Publications: Exhibit catalogs
Activities: Lects for members only, 1-2 per yr; tours; individual paintings & objects of art lent to other museums

M **Student Union Art Gallery**, LSU Box 25123, 210 LSU Student Union Baton Rouge, LA 70803. Tel 225-578-5162; Fax 225-578-4329; Email unionartgallery@lsu.edu; Web: www.lsu.edu; *Gallery Dir* Judith R Stahl
Open Mon - Fri 9 AM - 4:30 PM, Sat during home football games Noon - 4 PM; No admis fee; Estab 1964, designed for exhibitions for university & community interests; Gallery is centrally located on the main floor of the LSU Student Union with 3000 sq ft; Average Annual Attendance: 55,000
Income: Financed by fundraising, grants & university support
Purchases: To be determined by Accession Comt
Special Subjects: Graphics, Painting-American, Photography, Prints, Stained Glass, Woodcuts
Collections: Contemporary American Art, European Viennese Realism
Exhibitions: Annual National Art Competition; 8 annual rotating exhibits; state & student competition; curated exhibits & travelling art shows
Publications: Brochures and postcards for exhibits, exhibit catalogs, semester calendars & e-newsletters
Activities: Educ prog; docent training; lects open to public, 4 vis lectrs per yr; concerts; gallery demonstrations; competitions with awards, national $5,000, state $3,000, student $1,800; interactive activities

M **School of Art - Glassell Gallery**, Shaw Center for the Arts, 100 Lafayette St Baton Rouge, LA 70801-1201. Tel 225-389-7180; Fax 225-389-7185; Email artgallery@lsu.edu; Web: www.glassellgallery.org; *Dir Galleries* Kristin Malia Krolak
Open Tues - Fri 10 AM - 5 PM, Sat & Sun noon - 5 PM; No admis fee; Mem: Dues patron $1000, benefactor $500, contributor $250, supporter $100, artist $50, student $20
Special Subjects: Drawings, Graphics, Prints
Collections: Department coll
Activities: Lects open to public, 2 vis lectrs per yr; gallery talks; tours; sponsoring of competitions; scholarships & fels offered; lending of original art to local bus; book traveling exhibs, 2 per yr; originate traveling exhibs

L **Middleton Library**, 141 Middleton Library, Baton Rouge, LA 70803. Tel 225-578-6897; Email cargill@lsu.edu; Web: www.lib.lsu.edu; *Dean Libraries* Stanley Wilder; *Colls & Materials Selector Librn* Tom Diamond; *Head Resource Description & Metadata Servs* Linda Smith Griffin; *Asst Cur Manuscripts* Melissa Smith; *Exhibs Coordr* Leah Wood Jewett
No admis fee; Estab 1958
Library Holdings: Auction Catalogs, Book Volumes 15,000, CD-ROMs, DVDs, Exhibition Catalogs, Maps, Other Holdings Vertical files 8 drawers, blueprints, Periodical Subscriptions 100, Video Tapes
Special Subjects: Architecture, Art History, Decorative Arts, Graphic Design, Interior Design, Landscape Architecture, Asian Art, Printmaking, Sculpture
Activities: Educ prog; library instruction; virtual tour

M **LOUISIANA STATE UNIVERSITY SCHOOL OF ART,** (Alfred C Glassell Jr Exhibition Gallery) Alfred C Glassell Jr Exhibition Gallery, LSU School of Art, Shaw Center for the Arts, 100 Lafayette St Baton Rouge, LA 70801. Tel 225-389-7180; Email artgallery@lsu.edu; *Dir* K Malia Krolak; *Asst Dir* Renee Smith
Open Tues - Fri 10 AM - 5 PM, Sat - Sun noon - 5 PM; No admis fee
Collections: works by local, national & international contemporary artists

COLUMBIA

M **THE SCHEPIS, LOUISIANA ARTISTS MUSEUM,** 106 Main St, Columbia, LA 71418; PO Box 743 Columbia, LA 71418-0743. Tel 318-649-9931; Email schepismuseum@bellsouth.net; *Asst Mgr* Robin Kolb
Open 10 AM - 4:30 PM, cl Sat & Sun; Estab to provide community with art education
Exhibitions: Rotating exhibits
Activities: Drama, writing & painting workshops

COVINGTON

A **ST TAMMANY ART ASSOCIATION,** 320 N Columbia, Covington, LA 70433-2918. Tel 985-892-8650; Fax 985-898-0976; Email info@sttammanyartassociation.org; Web: www.sttammanyartassociation.org; *Exec Dir* Kim Bergeron; *Art House Coordr* Peggy DesJardins
Open Tues - Fri 10 AM - 4 PM, Sat 11 AM - 4 PM, cl Sun & Mon; Estab 1958 to provide arts education & exhibs to the community; Mem: 800; dues $30-$1,200
Collections: Work by regional and national artists
Exhibitions: Temporary exhibits
Activities: Educ progs; classes for adults & children

CROWLEY

A **CROWLEY ART ASSOCIATION,** The Gallery, 220 N Parkerson Ave, Crowley, LA 70526-5003; PO Box 2003, Crowley, LA 70527-2003. Tel 337-783-3747; Fax 337-783-3747; Email gallerythe@bellsouth.net; Web: crowleyartgallery.com; *Pres* Isabella dela Houssaye; *VPres* Virginia Duson; *Treas* Shirley Griffin; *Secy* Hurley Gautreaux
Open daily 10 AM - 4 PM; No admis fee; Estab 1980 to promote art in all forms; 1,100 sq ft; Average Annual Attendance: 3,000; Mem: 250; dues $25; monthly meetings; mem qualifications: interest in & production of art
Income: Financed by mem, fundraisers & grants
Exhibitions: Juried Art Show; International Rice Festival Arts & Crafts Show
Publications: Monthly newsletter
Activities: Classes for adults & children; lects open to pub, 3 vis lectrs per yr; competitions; sales shop sells original art, prints & Cajun crafts

FRANKLIN

M **ST MARY CHAPTER LOUISIANA LANDMARKS SOCIETY,** Grevemberg House Museum, 407 Sterling Rd (Hwy 322), Franklin, LA 70538; PO Box 400, Franklin, LA 70538-0400. Tel 337-828-2092; Fax 337-828-2028; Email info@grevemberghouse.com; Web: www.grevemberghouse.com; *Vol Pres* Katie

Seim; *Pub Rels & Treas* Margaret Todd; *Archivist* Margie L Luke; *Lead Interpreter* Craig Landry; *VPres* Victoria Simoneaux; *Secy* Betty Veeder
Open daily 10 AM - 4 PM; cl New Year's Day, Good Friday, Easter Sunday, Thanksgiving Day, Christmas Eve & Day; Admis adults $10 seniors, students & group rates $8, children $5, mems no admis fee; Estab 1972; 1851 Greek-revival townhouse that showcases 19th c life in south Louisiana; listed on National Register of Historic Places; managed by St Mary Landmark's 17-mem vol Bd of Trustees; Average Annual Attendance: 500; Mem: dues Corinthian $1000, Queen Anne $500, Victorian $250; Gothic $100; Conservator $75; Pillar $60; Foundation $35
Income: corporate and personal dues; public and private grants; fundraisers
Special Subjects: Decorative Arts, Dolls, Furniture, Historical Material, Painting-American, Period Rooms, Portraits
Collections: Antique furnishings from the period of 1820 - 1870 based on items listed in the estates of Gabriel and Frances Wikoff Grevemberg, with exceptions allowed for items of local historic significance from other periods
Publications: Landmark Lagniappe, semiannual newsletter
Activities: Research in the translation of Grevemberg family papers from French to English; mid-19th c south Louisiana graveyards; lects open to pub; 1-2 vis lectrs per yr; Victorian Christmas Celebration; guided tours; St Mary Landmarks Historic Preservation Award; mus shop sells books, prints, notecards, tote bags, sugarcane, jewelry

JENNINGS

M **ZIGLER ART MUSEUM,** 154 N Main St, Jennings, LA 70546-5846. Tel 337-824-0114; Fax 337-824-0120; Email zigler-museum@charter.net; Web: www.ziglerartmuseum.org; *Cur* Dolores Spears; *Pres Bd Trustees* Gregory Marcantel; *VPres* Wendell Miller; *Treas* Burt Tietje
Open Tues - Sat 10 AM - 4 PM, Sun 1 - 4 PM; Admis fee adults $5, children & students $2; Estab 1963 to place the art of western civilization & the area in a historical context; West Wing has permanent collection of American & European paintings & sculptures. East Wing contains a gallery of wildlife art. Central galleries are reserved for a new art exhibit each month; Average Annual Attendance: 20,000
Income: Income from private foundation
Purchases: 29 paintings by William Tolliver; One painting by Vlaminck; One painting by Whitney Hubbard; One painting by van Dyck; One painting by Herring
Special Subjects: Afro-American Art, American Indian Art, Asian Art, Bronzes, Ceramics, Dioramas, Drawings, Etchings & Engravings, Glass, Landscapes, Marine Painting, Miniatures, Painting-American, Painting-British, Painting-Dutch, Painting-European, Painting-Flemish, Woodcarvings, Painting-German, Painting-Italian, Painting-Japanese, Painting-Polish, Photography, Porcelain, Portraits, Pottery, Prints, Religious Art, Sculpture, Woodcuts, Woodcuts
Collections: Bierstadt, Chierici, Constable, Crane, Gay, Heldner, George Inness Jr, Pearce, Pissarro, Frank Smith, Vergne, Whistler, Gustave Wolff, Robert Wood, J Chester Armstrong Sculpture Collection, Tolliver Collection: 29 pieces
Exhibitions: Rotating exhibits
Publications: Brochure
Activities: Classes for adults & children; docent training; lects open to pub; gallery talks; tours; individual paintings & original objects of art lent; originates traveling exhibs that travel to other museums; mus shop sells books, magazines, original art, reproductions, prints, Indian baskets & hand-painted porcelain

LAFAYETTE

M **LAFAYETTE MUSEUM ASSOCIATION,** Lafayette Museum-Alexandre Mouton House, 1122 Lafayette St, Lafayette, LA 70501-6838. Tel 337-234-2208; Fax 337-234-2208; *Pres LMA* Gail Dehart; *VPres* Mimi Francez
Open Tues - Sat 10 AM - 4 PM, cl Sun & Mon; Admis free suggested donation $5 general, seniors $3, students $2; Estab 1954 as a historical house; Historic home restored & authentically furnished with period antiques, original artwork & historic documents; Average Annual Attendance: 3,000
Income: $40,000 (financed by donations from friends of the mus, grants)
Library Holdings: Book Volumes, DVDs, Framed Reproductions, Memorabilia, Original Art Works, Original Documents, Photographs, Records
Special Subjects: Historical Material
Collections: Historical Costumes & Dress, Documents, Furnishings, Objects
Exhibitions: Mardi Gras costumes during season; Quilts Exhibits, Historical Exhibits (dates & subjects vary)
Activities: School tours; French tours; lects open to pub; 4 vis lectrs per yr; cookbooks & postcards for sale

M **LAFAYETTE SCIENCE MUSEUM & PLANETARIUM,** 433 Jefferson St, Lafayette, LA 70501-7013. Tel 337-291-5544; Fax 337-291-5464; Email kkrantz@lafayettela.gov; Web: www.lafayettesciencemuseum.org; *Cur Planetarium* David Hostetter; *Admin Asst* Karen Miller; *Museum & Planetarium Tech* Paul McCasland; *Dir* Kevin Krantz; *Cur Exhibs* Blake Lagneaux; *Colls Cur* Deborah Clifton; *Asst Cur* Charlotte Guillot; *Receptionist* Likassina Brown; *Tour Scheduling* Edi Gilbert
Open Mus Tues-Fri 9AM-5PM, Sat 10AM-6PM, Sun 1-6PM, call for planetarium show times; Admis adults $5, seniors 65 & over $3, children 4 - 17 yrs $2, children 3 & under free; Estab 1969 to provide a focus on the physical world in order to benefit the citizens of the community; 5,800 sq ft of exhibition space, interior walls constructed as needed; Average Annual Attendance: 65,000; Mem: 300; annual meeting in Oct
Income: $650,000 (financed by mem & city & parish appropriation)
Purchases: $4000
Library Holdings: Audio Tapes, Book Volumes, CD-ROMs, Cassettes, Clipping Files, Compact Disks, DVDs, Exhibition Catalogs, Kodachrome Transparencies, Manuscripts, Maps, Memorabilia, Original Art Works, Original Documents, Pamphlets, Periodical Subscriptions, Photographs, Prints, Records, Reels, Reproductions, Video Tapes
Special Subjects: Afro-American Art, Anthropology, Archaeology, Bookplates & Bindings, Costumes, Crafts, Dioramas, Drawings, Embroidery, Etchings & Engravings, Ethnology, Folk Art, Furniture, Graphics, Historical Material, Landscapes, Manuscripts, Maps, Painting-American, Photography, Posters, Primitive art, Prints, Restorations, Sculpture, Tapestries, Textiles, Woodcarvings
Collections: Acadian artifacts, Audubon prints, Historical Louisiana maps, Louisiana Indian artifacts, Louisiana moths & butterflies, Louisiana shells, Louisiana Landscape Art, Louisiana Related Harper's Weekly Prints, Meteorites, Rocks, Minerals, Fossils
Exhibitions: Titanic; Star Wars; Dinosaurs; Giant Worlds; Mars Quest; Lafayette; Water World; Leaving Earth: Story of Space Travel; Geology; Insects
Activities: Classes for adults & children; self-guided tours; concerts; lending collection contains 20 nature artifacts, original art works, 400 photos, 1000 slides, 200 Louisiana Indian & Acadian artifacts to home schools, scouts; book traveling exhibs

M **UNIVERSITY OF LOUISIANA AT LAFAYETTE,** Paul and Lulu Hilliard University Art Museum, 710 E Saint Mary Blvd, Lafayette, LA 70503; PO Box 42571, Lafayette, LA 70504-2571. Tel 337-482-2278; Fax 337-262-1268; Email artmuseum@louisiana.edu; Web: hillardmuseum.org; *Dir* Lou Anne Greenwald; *Asst Dir* Cami Joseph; *Registrar* Misty Taylor; *Mgr Mktg & Mem* Jolie Johnson; *Cur* Laura Blereau; *Educator* Olivia Morgan; *Security* Jacob Spaetgens
Open Tues, Thurs & Fri 9 AM - 5 PM, Wed 9 AM - 8 PM, Sat 10 AM - 5 PM; Admis adults $5, seniors $4, youth $3; Estab 1968 as an art mus, for educ of the population of the region; Three galleries totaling 11,000 sq ft built in 2003; Average Annual Attendance: 25,000; Mem: 350; dues $25 - $1,000
Income: $600,000 (financed by mem & state appropriation)
Purchases: Lowe Collection of Outsider Art
Special Subjects: Afro-American Art, Antiquities-Egyptian, Architecture, Ceramics, Coins & Medals, Collages, Decorative Arts, Drawings, Etchings & Engravings, Folk Art, Furniture, Glass, Graphics, Landscapes, Miniatures, Oriental Art, Painting-American, Photography, Portraits, Pottery, Primitive art, Prints, Sculpture, Silver, Watercolors, Woodcuts
Collections: Henry Botkin Collection, Cohn Collection-19th & 20th Century Japanese Prints, Louisiana Collection-19th & 20th Century Art, all media, Lowe Collection-Outsider Art, 19th & 21st Century Art, Contemporary Russian Art
Publications: Books; exhibition catalogues
Activities: Educ programs; docent training; lects open to pub; 15 vis lectrs per yr; concerts; gallery talks; tours; book traveling exhibs, 4 per yr; originate traveling exhibs one per yr circulating to art mus, univ mus, & others; mus shop sells books, magazines original art, prints, posters, jewelry, post cards

LAKE CHARLES

M **IMPERIAL CALCASIEU MUSEUM,** 204 W Sallier St, Lake Charles, LA 70601-5844. Tel 337-439-3797; Fax 337-439-6040; Email impmuseum@bellsouth.net; Web: www.imperialcalcasieumuseum.org; *Dir* Susan H Reed
Open Tues-Sat 10AM-5PM; Admis adults $2, students $1; Estab Mar 1963 by the Junior League of Lake Charles & housed in City Hall; After several moves in location, the mus is now housed in a building of Louisiana Colonial architecture which incorporates in its structure old bricks, beams, balustrades & columns taken from demolished old homes. In Dec 1966 admin was assumed by the Fine Arts Center & Mus of Old Imperial Calcasieu Mus, Inc, with a name change in 1971. Site of the building was chosen for its historic value, having been owned by the Charles Sallier family, the first white settler on the lake & the town named for him. The mus depicts the early history of the area; Average Annual Attendance: 12,500; Mem: 350; dues $50-$1500
Income: Financed by mem
Special Subjects: Period Rooms
Collections: Artifacts of the Victorian Period, especially Late Victorian, John James Audubon
Exhibitions: American Indian Artifacts in Calcasieu Collections; Antique Quilts & Coverlets; Calcasieu People & Places in 19th Century Photographs; Christmas Around The World; special exhibitions every six weeks, with smaller exhibits by other organizations at times
Activities: Docent training, Classes for adults & children; lects open to general public, 2-3 vis lectrs per yr; gallery talks; tours; book traveling exhibs 1 per yr; originate traveling exhibs; sales shop sells books, original art & Prints

M **Gibson-Barham Gallery**, 204 W Sallier St, Lake Charles, LA 70601. Tel 337-439-3797; Fax 337-439-6040; *Coordr* Mary June Malus
Open Tues - Sat 10 AM - 5 PM, Sun 1 - 5 PM, cl Mon; Admis adults $2, students $1; Estab 1963 to collect & display history & artifacts at five parishes in the original Imperial Land Grant; 1000 running ft; Average Annual Attendance: 10,000; Mem: 300; dues $50
Income: financed by membership, donations
Special Subjects: American Indian Art, Carpets & Rugs, Ceramics, Coins & Medals, Costumes, Crafts, Decorative Arts, Dolls, Drawings, Embroidery, Etchings & Engravings, Folk Art, Furniture, Graphics, Historical Material, Jewelry, Laces, Manuscripts, Maps, Painting-American, Period Rooms, Pewter, Photography, Pottery, Prints
Exhibitions: 6-10 rotating exhibitions per year
Activities: Lects open to public, 2 vis lectrs per yr; gallery talks; tours; individual paintings & original objects of art lent to established museums or collectors; book traveling exhibs 3-4 per yr; originate traveling exhibs; sales shop sells books & original art

L **Gibson Library**, 204 W Sallier St, Lake Charles, LA 70601. Tel 337-439-3797; Fax 337-439-6040; *Coordr* Mary June Malus
Open Mon - Fri 10 AM - 5 PM, Sat & Sun 1 - 5 PM; No admis fee; Estab 1971, to display early school books & bibles; Circ non-circulating; Reference Library; Mem: Part of museum
Income: Financed by mem, memorials & gifts
Library Holdings: Audio Tapes, Book Volumes 100, Cassettes, Memorabilia, Original Art Works, Pamphlets, Periodical Subscriptions 100, Photographs, Sculpture, Slides, Video Tapes
Special Subjects: Crafts, Decorative Arts, Drafting, Folk Art, Furniture, Historical Material, Manuscripts, Maps, Painting-American, Period Rooms, Pewter, Photography, Porcelain, Pottery, Prints

Collections: Audubon animal paintings, Audubon bird paintings, Calcasieu photographs, Boyd Cruise
Exhibitions: History of Imperial Calcasieu Parish, with settings & objects

M **MCNEESE STATE UNIVERSITY, DEPT OF VISUAL ARTS,** (Abercrombie Gallery) Abercrombie Gallery and Grand Gallery, McNeese State University, Ryan & Sale Sts Lake Charles, LA 70609. Tel 337-475-5060; Fax 337-475-5927; Web: mcneeseartonline.org; *Dir* Lynn Reynolds; *Coordr* Heather Ryan Kelley
Mon - Fri 9 AM - 4:30 PM; No admis fee
Purchases: Awards from Annual Works on Paper Exhibition
Collections: works by local, regional, & national contemporary artists
Exhibitions: (1st Apr, 2016-31st May, 2016) 30th Annual McNeese Natl Works on Paper; Annual Faculty Exhibition; Senior Thesis Show
Publications: catalog, Works on Paper
Activities: 4 vis lects per year; gallery talks; Works on Paper Award

LEESVILLE

M **MUSEUM OF WEST LOUISIANA,** 803 S Third St, Leesville, LA 71446. Tel 337-239-0927; Web: www.museumofwestla.org
Open Tues - Sun 1 - 5 PM; other times by appt; No admis fee, donations accepted; Opened in 1987 for the purpose of preserving & displaying artifacts illustrative of the history, culture, folk art & resources of Vernon Parish and the West Central area of the Louisiana Territory. Nonprofit org; Mem: different levels of annual mem dues
Special Subjects: Archaeology, Decorative Arts, Dolls, Furniture, Military Art, Folk Art
Collections: Archaeological artifacts, logging implements, railroad memorabilia, quilts, clothing, cooking & household items, furniture & special displays, POW paintings & WWII memorabilia, children's toys & dolls
Activities: Pioneer Park is available for special events; mus related items for sale

MADISONVILLE

LAKE PONTCHARTRAIN BASIN MARITIME MUSEUM, 133 Mabel Dr, Madisonville, LA 70447-9301. Tel 985-845-9200; Fax 985-845-9201; Email info@lpbmaritimemuseum.org; Web: www.lpmaritimemuseum.org; *CEO & Dir* Nixon Adams
Open Tues - Sat 10 AM - 4 PM, Sun 12 PM - 4 PM, cl Thanksgiving, Christmas Eve & Day; Admis adults & seniors $2, mems & age 12 & under no admis fee; Unique nautical & cultural heritage of Lake Pontchartrain, research in archeological survey of shipwrecks in the Lake Pontchartrain (pvt nonprofit mus; maintains library; vols available for inter-library loan); Average Annual Attendance: 1000 - 9999; Mem: dues Supporting $500, Friend $100, Family $25
Exhibitions: Madisonville Wooden Boat Festival, ann festival held the third weekend in Oct, 10 AM - 6 PM

MINDEN

L **WEBSTER PARISH LIBRARY,** 521 East & West Sts, Minden, LA 71055. Tel 318-371-3080; Fax 318-371-3081; *Dir* Beverly Hammett; *Librn* Eddie Hammontree
Open Ferguson Stewart Building Mon-Fri 8AM-5PM, Main Mon, Wed, Thurs 8:15AM-8PM, Tues, Fri, Sat 8:15AM-5PM; Estab 1929 to serve as headquarters & main branch for county; Circ 145,508
Income: $221,353 (financed by parish tax)
Library Holdings: Book Volumes 60,000, Cassettes, Clipping Files, Filmstrips, Framed Reproductions, Original Art Works, Pamphlets, Periodical Subscriptions 800, Photographs, Records, Reels, Slides, Video Tapes
Activities: Exten dept serves the elderly; individual paintings lent to registered borrowers, lending collection contains 54 art prints & 50 b & w photographs depicting parish history

MONROE

M **NORTHEAST LOUISIANA CHILDREN'S MUSEUM,** 323 Walnut St, Monroe, LA 71201-6711. Tel 318-361-9611; Fax 318-361-9613; Email nelcm@nelcm.org; Web: www.nelcm.org
Open Tues - Fri 9 AM - 2 PM, Sat 10 AM - 5 PM; Admis $5 per person; Group Rate: $3 per person for groups of 15 or more
Exhibitions: The Kids' Cafe: sponsored by the Louisiana Restaurant Assoc, exhib recreates a true-to-life restaurant environment where each child can explore the different types of jobs found in a restaurant; Health Hall: children may drive an ambulance to the ER, listen to a patient's heart & check out his x-ray, as well as learn about how the body works; The Think Tank: visitor is challenged to use problem-solving skills to figure out puzzles, utilize creativity in putting on a puppet show, as well as explore The Gravity Wall; Stuffee: 9-ft soft sculptured doll sponsored by the Ouachita Medical Alliance Society, whose internal organs are removable & teach us how our body works; Toddler Town: a picket fence-surrounded area designated for toddlers, features soft blocks & educational toys
Activities: Monthly events; Birthday Parties & events; Summer Drop-Off Days for children ages 4 - 8; traveling & permanent exhibs; educational-related items for sale

M **OUACHITA RIVER ART GALLERY,** 204 Williamsburg Dr, Monroe, LA 71203. Email b-jmcdaniel@comcast.net; Web: www.ouachitariverartgallery.com; @ouchita.artgallery
Physical gallery is closed; artwork available for purchase on Facebook
Special Subjects: Painting-American, Woodcarvings, Pottery, Jewelry, Glass, Photography
Collections: Features art by regional artists including paintings, woodturning, pottery, jewelry, glass & photography

M **TWIN CITY ART FOUNDATION,** Masur Museum of Art, 1400 S Grand St, Monroe, LA 71202-2012. Tel 318-329-2237; Fax 318-329-2847; Email info@masurmuseum.org; Web: www.masurmuseum.org; *Dir* Evelyn Stewart; *Cur Colls & Exhibs* Benjamin Hickey; *Cur Educ* Jenny Burnham
Open Tues - Fri 9 AM - 5 PM, Sat noon - 5 PM; No admis fee; Estab 1963 to encourage art in all media & to enrich the cultural climate of this area; Gallery has 485 running ft hanging space; Average Annual Attendance: 20,000; Mem: 380; dues $20 - $1,000
Income: $225,000 (financed by mem & appropriations)
Special Subjects: Painting-American, Photography, Prints, Sculpture, Watercolors, Woodcuts
Collections: Contemporary art all media, approx 500 works
Publications: Brochures of shows, monthly
Activities: Classes for adults & children; lects open to pub, 4 vis lectrs per yr; tours; competitions; book traveling exhibs

M **UNIVERSITY OF LOUISIANA AT MONROE,** Bry Gallery, 700 University Ave, Bry Hall Monroe, LA 71203-3708. Tel 318-342-1375; Fax 318-342-1369; Email tresner@ulm.edu; Web: www.ulm.edu/art/gallery/welcome.html; *Head* Gary Ratcliff, MFA; *Gallery Dir* Cliff Tresner; *Asst Gallery Dir* Dara Engler
Open Mon-Thurs 8 AM - 4:30 PM, Fri 8AM-noon; No admis fee; Estab 1931; Gallery is 45 x 26 sq ft with 14 ft ceilings; Average Annual Attendance: 8,000
Collections: Kit Gilbert, Pave Brou of New Orleans
Activities: Classes for adults & children; docent training; 6 vis lectrs per yr; gallery talks

NEW IBERIA

M **NATIONAL TRUST FOR HISTORIC PRESERVATION,** Shadows-on-the-Teche, 317 E Main St, New Iberia, LA 70560-3728. Tel 337-369-6446; Fax 337-365-5213; Email shadows@shadowsontheteche.org; Web: www.shadowsontheteche.org; *Dir* Patricia Kahle; *Cur Educ* Catherine Schramm
Open Mon - Sat 9 AM - 5 PM, cl major holidays; Admis adults (18-64) $10, seniors (65 & over) $8, students (6-17) $6.50; The Shadows is a property of the National Trust for Historic Preservation. Preserved as a historic house mus: operated as a community preservation center, it is a National Historic Landmark. On the Bayou Teche, it faces the main street of modern New Iberia, but is surrounded by 2 1/2 acres of landscaped gardens shaded by live oaks. Built in 1834, the Shadows represents a Louisiana adaptation of classical revival architecture. The life & culture of a 19th century southern Louisiana sugar plantation are reflected in the possessions of four generations of the Weeks family on display in the house, which was restored during the 1920s by Weeks Hall, great-grandson of the builder; Average Annual Attendance: 16,000; Mem: 250
Income: Financed by mem in Friends of the Shadows, admis fees & special events
Special Subjects: Architecture, Decorative Arts, Furniture, Landscapes, Period Rooms, Photography, Portraits, Restorations, Textiles
Collections: Paintings by Louisiana's itinerant artist Adrien Persac & period room settings (1830s-60s), paintings by Weeks Hall, furnishings typical of those owned by a planter's family between 1830 and 1865
Activities: Classes for children; docent training; lects open to pub; 1-2 vis lectrs per yr; interpretive programs which are related to the Shadows historic preservation program; tours; awards, Plein Air Competition; mus shop sells books, original art and prints

NEW ORLEANS

A **ARTS COUNCIL OF NEW ORLEANS,** 935 Gravier St Ste 850, New Orleans, LA 70112. Tel 504-523-1465; Fax 504-529-2430; Email dee@artscouncilofneworleans.org; Web: www.artsneworleans.org; *Pres & CEO* Kim Cook; *Deputy Dir* Nick Stillman; *Artist Servs Dir* Gene Meneray; *Artist Servs Mgr* Joycelyn Reynolds; *Mktg & Communs Dir* Lindsey Glatz; *Mem Mgr* Dolita Brown; *Major Gifts & Foundation Officer* Mary Len Costa; *Spec Projects & Pub Art Dir* Morgana King; *Spec Projects Mgr* Nori Clemens; *Research Fellow* Heidi Schmalbach; *People & Community Practice Mgr* Morgan Sasser
Open 9 AM - 5 PM; Estab 1975 to support & expand the opportunities for diverse artistic expression & to bring the community together in celebration of rich multicultural heritage; provides a variety of Cultural Planning, Advocacy, Public Art, Economic Develop, Arts Education, Grants & Service Initiatives focused on its vision of New Orleans as a flourishing cultural center; Ground floor gallery; Average Annual Attendance: 1,000; Mem: Memberships offered at $75, $250 & $500 levels
Activities: Lect open to public & members; workshops

M **CALLAN CONTEMPORARY,** 518 Julia St, New Orleans, LA 70130. Tel 504-525-0518; Fax 504-525-0516; Email borislava@callancontemporary.com; Email stevencallan@callancontemporary.com; *Dir* Borislava Callan; *Owner* Steven Callan
Open Tues-Sat 10AM-5PM, other times by appointment; Contemporary abstract & figurative paintings, sculptures & installations by emerging & internationally recognized artists
Collections: works by contemporary artists; paintings; sculpture

M **COLLINS C. DIBOLL ART GALLERY,** 4th Fl Monroe Library, 6363 St Charles Ave New Orleans, LA 70118-6143; 6363 St Charles Ave, Campus PO Box 906 New Orleans, 70118. Tel 504-864-7248; Email gallery@loyno.edu; Web: www.loyno.edu/dibollgallery; *Gallery Dir* Karoline Schleh
Open Mon - Sat 10 AM - 4 PM; No admis fee
Collections: Paintings

A **CONFEDERATE MEMORIAL HALL,** Confederate Museum, 929 Camp St, New Orleans, LA 70130-3907. Tel 504-523-4522; Fax 504-523-8595; Email Memhall@aol.com; Web: www.confederatemuseum.com; *Chmn Memorial Hall Comt* Dr Keith Cangelosi; *Cur* Pat Ricci
Open Mon - Sat 10 AM - 4 PM; Admis adults $5, students & sr citizens $4, children $2; Estab 1891 to collect & display articles, memorabilia & records surrounding the

Civil War; Gallery is maintained in a one story brick building; one main hall paneled in cypress, one side hall containing paintings of Civil War figures & display cases containing artifacts; Average Annual Attendance: 15,000; Mem: 2000; dues benefactor $500, patron $250, assoc $100, support $50, gen $25, student $10; annual meeting Mar
Income: Financed by mem & admis
Publications: Louisiana Historical Assn Newsletter; Louisiana History, quarterly
Activities: Lect open to public; competitions; sales shop sells books, reproductions & novelties

A **CONTEMPORARY ARTS CENTER,** 900 Camp St, New Orleans, LA 70130-3908. Tel 504-528-3805 (Admin), 3800 (Tickets & Info); Fax 504-528-3828; Email info@cacno.org; Web: www.cacno.org; *Dir & CEI* Neil A Barclay
Open Thurs - Sun 11 AM - 5 PM, hours vary for special events, cl holidays; Admis $8, seniors & students $6, members free; Estab 1976 to support experimentation & innovative products of work in visual arts & performing arts. Interdisciplinary arts center; Average Annual Attendance: 100,000; Mem: 3000; dues $25 & up; annual meeting in June
Special Subjects: Glass
Exhibitions: Prospect 3; EN Mas: Carnival & Performance Art
Publications: Radcliffe Bailey Recent Works Catalog
Activities: Classes for children; docent training; lect open to public; 10 vis lectrs per yr; concerts; gallery talks; tours; awards, Sweetarts Awards; organize traveling exhibs to Independent Curators International; museum shop sells books, magazines, original art & prints

M **THE HISTORIC NEW ORLEANS COLLECTION,** Williams Research Center, 410 Chartres St, New Orleans, LA 70130-2102. Tel 504-598-7171; Fax 504-598-7168; Email wrc@hnoc.org; Web: www.hnoc.org; *Chmn* Mary Louise Christovich; *Dir The Historic New Orleans Collection* Priscilla Lawrence; *Dir Mus Prog* John Lawrence; *Dir Williams Research Ctr* Dr Alfred Lemmon; *Pub Rel Dir* Teresa Devlin; *Dir Publications* Jessica Dormon; *Senior Librn* Pamela D Arceneaux; *Historian & Cur* John Magill; *Manuscripts* Mark Cave
Open Tues - Sat 9:30AM - 4:30PM, Sun 10:30 AM - 4:30PM; No admis fee to Gallery, admis to Williams Residence & Louisiana History Galleries, tour by guide $5; Main bldg constructed in 1792 by Jean Francois Merieult; renovated by Koch & Wilson to accommodate the Louisiana History galleries which house a collection of paintings, prints, documents, books & artifacts relating to the history of Louisiana from the time of its settlement, gathered over a number of years by the late L Kemper Williams & his wife. The foundation was estab in 1966 with private funds to keep original collection intact & to allow for expansion; Research Center for State & Local History/Mus; Average Annual Attendance: 45,000
Library Holdings: Book Volumes 18,000, CD-ROMs, Clipping Files, Compact Disks, Exhibition Catalogs, Fiche, Manuscripts, Maps, Memorabilia, Motion Pictures, Original Art Works, Original Documents, Other Holdings Broadside 200, Pamphlets 10,000, Periodical Subscriptions 30, Photographs, Prints, Records, Slides, Video Tapes
Special Subjects: Historical Material, Manuscripts, Photography
Collections: Charles L Franck, photographs (1900-1955); Dan Leyrer, photographs (1930-1970); Clarence Laughlin, photographs (1935-1965); James Gallier Jr & Sr, architectural drawings (1830-1870); Morries Henry Hobbs, prints (1940); B Lafon, drawings of fortifications (1841); B Simon lithographs of 19th-century bus, Alfred R & William Waud, drawings of Civil War & post-war; maps, paintings, photographs, prints, three-dimensional objects; Civil War Collection
Exhibitions: Various exhibs
Publications: Guide to Research at the Historic New Orleans Collection; exhibition brochures & catalogs; historic publications, monograph series; quarterly newsletter; Guide to The Vieux Carre Survey, a guide to a collection of material on New Orleans
Activities: Docent training; lects open to pub; tours; competitions with awards; gallery talks; concerts; awards Kemper and Leila Williams Prize in Louisiana History; fels; individual paintings & original objects of art lent to mus, institutions, foundations, libraries & research centers; mus shop sells books, original art, magazines, reproductions, prints, slides & ephemera; research collections

M **Royal Street Galleries**, 533 Royal St, New Orleans, LA 70130-2113. Tel 504-523-4662; Fax 504-598-7108; Email wrc@hnoc.org; Web: www.hnoc.org; *Exec Dir* Priscilla Lawrence; *CFO* Michael Cohn; *Coll Mgr* Warren J Woods; *Dir Develop & External Affairs* Jack Pruitt Jr; *Dir Mus Progs* John H Lawrence; *Cur Educ* Sue Laudeman; *Sr Cur* Judith H Bonner; *Head Photographer* Keely Merritt; *Head Preparator* Scott Ratterree; *Head Docent* Bunny Hinckley
Open Tues - Sat 9:30 AM - 4:30 PM, Sun 10:30 AM - 4:30 PM, cl holidays; No admis fee to gallery, admis to Williams Residence & Louisiana History Galleries, tour by guide $3; Main bldg constructed in 1792 by Jean Francoise Merieult; renovated by Koch & Wilson to accommodate the Louisiana History Galleries which house a coll of paintings, prints, documents, books & artifacts relating to the history of Louisiana from the time of its settlement, gathered over a number of years by the late L Kemper Williams & his wife; Foundation estab 1966 with pvt funds to keep original coll intact & allow for expansion; Complex comprised of museum & historic French Quarter bldgs: Williams Gallery, Louisiana History Gallery, Williams Residence, Merieult House, Counting House, Maisonette, Townhouse, Louis Adam House & Creole Cottage; Average Annual Attendance: 45,000
Income: Financed by endowment
Special Subjects: American Western Art, Architecture, Bookplates & Bindings, Decorative Arts, Drawings, Embroidery, Etchings & Engravings, Folk Art, Furniture, Glass, Manuscripts, Painting-American, Photography, Portraits, Prints, Silver, Watercolors, Maps
Collections: Charles L Franck, photographs (1900-1955), Dan Leyrer, photographs (1930-1970), Clarence Laughlin, photographs (1935-1965), James Gallier Jr & Sr, architectural drawings (1830-1870), Morries Henry Hobbs, prints (1940), B Lafon, drawings of fortifications (1841), B Simon, lithographs of 19th-c bus, Alfred R & William Waud, drawings of Civil War & post-War, maps, paintings, photographs, prints, 3-D objects, Civil War Collection
Publications: Guide to Research at the Historic New Orleans Collection; exhib brochures & catalogs; historic publications; monograph series; newsletter, quarterly; Guide to The Vieux Carre Survey, a guide to the collection of material on New Orleans
Activities: Docent training; lects open to pub; tours; competitions with awards; gallery talks; concerts; film screenings; awards Kemper & Leila Williams Prize in Louisiana History; fels; individual paintings & original objects of art lent to mus, institutions, foundations, libraries & research ctrs; mus shop sells books, original art, magazines, reproductions, prints, slides & ephemera; research collections

M **LONGUE VUE HOUSE & GARDENS,** 7 Bamboo Rd, New Orleans, LA 70124-1007. Tel 504-488-5488; Fax 504-486-7015; Email info@longuevue.com; Web: www.longuevue.com; *Dir* Tony Chauveaux; *Asst Dir* Mary E D'Aquin Fergusson; *Cur* Lenora Costa; *Dir Programs* Edna Lanieri; *Operations & Sales* Daniel Kane; *Operations & Sales* Anna Bell Jones; *Head Gardener* Amy Graham; *Dir Finance* Patrick Nedd; *Mktg & Commun* Summer Duperon; *Dir Develop* Jen Glick
Open Mon - Sat 10 AM - 5 PM, Sun 1 - 5 PM, last house tour 4 PM; Admis adults $12, seniors $10, students & children $8, under 3 free; Estab 1968 to preserve & interpret Longue Vue House & Gardens; Period 1930-40 house & gardens; Average Annual Attendance: 51,000; Mem: 1700; dues family $75, individual $35, biannual meetings in spring & fall
Income: $1,240,000 (financed by endowment, fundraising & admis)
Library Holdings: Audio Tapes, Book Volumes, Cassettes, Clipping Files, Exhibition Catalogs, Filmstrips, Kodachrome Transparencies, Manuscripts, Memorabilia, Motion Pictures, Original Art Works, Original Documents, Pamphlets, Periodical Subscriptions, Photographs, Sculpture, Slides
Special Subjects: Architecture, Carpets & Rugs, Cartoons, Ceramics, Costumes, Decorative Arts, Dolls, Drawings, Embroidery, Furniture, Glass, Historical Material, Judaica, Landscapes, Painting-American, Painting-German, Painting-Israeli, Painting-Russian, Period Rooms, Pewter, Pottery, Prints, Sculpture, Silver, Textiles, Porcelain
Collections: 18th - 19th century English & American furniture, textile coll of 18th - 20th century English, French, & American fabrics, needlework, Karabagh & Aubusson rugs, 19th - 20th century French wallpapers, 18th - 20th century British ceramics, Chinese exports, contemporary & modern art, including Vasarely, Gabo, Picasso, Michel, Agam, Hepworth, & Laurens
Exhibitions: Rotating exhibits
Publications: The Art of the Craftsmen: Ruppert Kohlmaier; The Decorative Arts at Longue Vue; The Queen's Table
Activities: Classes for adults & children; docent training; lects open to pub, 25 vis lectrs per yr; gallery talks; tours; original objects of art lent to other like institutions contingent on facilities; mus shop sells books, original art, reproductions, prints, slides, decorative arts

M **LOUISIANA DEPARTMENT OF CULTURE, RECREATION & TOURISM,** Louisiana State Museum, 751 Chartres St, New Orleans, LA 70116-3205; PO Box 2448, New Orleans, LA 70176-2448. Tel 504-568-6968; Fax 504-568-4995; Web: www.lsm.crt.state.la.us; *Chmn* Rosemary Ewing; *Dir Cur Serv* Jeff Rubin; *Registrar* Jennae Biddiscombe; *Mus Dir* Sam Rykels; *Dir Coll* Greg Lambousey
Open Tues - Sun 10 AM - 4:30PM; Admis adults $6, seniors & students $5, children 12 & under free, educational groups free by appointment; Estab 1906, to collect, preserve & present original materials illustrating Louisiana's heritage; Gallery is maintained & has eight historic buildings in New Orleans with facilities in Patterson, Natchitoches, Thibodaux & Baton Rouge containing paintings, prints, maps, photographs, decorative arts, furniture, costumes & jazz; Average Annual Attendance: 320,000; Mem: 3000; dues $20-$35; annual meeting in May
Income: $9,000,000 (financed by state appropriation)
Special Subjects: Afro-American Art, Architecture, Bronzes, Ceramics, Costumes, Decorative Arts, Decorative Arts, Dolls, Drawings, Etchings & Engravings, Ethnology, Folk Art, Furniture, Glass, Graphics, Historical Material, Jewelry, Manuscripts, Maps, Marine Painting, Military Art, Miniatures, Painting-American, Period Rooms, Photography, Portraits, Posters, Pottery, Primitive art, Prints, Sculpture, Silver, Textiles, Watercolors, Woodcarvings
Collections: Carnival costumes (2000 items), Colonial documents (500,000 folios), decorative art (8000 items), flat textiles (1000 items), historic costumes (6000 items), jazz & Louisiana music (40,000 objects), Louisiana silver (300), maps & cartography (3000), Newcomb pottery & allied arts (750), paintings (1500 canvases), photography (70,000 images), post Colonial manuscripts (500,000), prints (3000 works), rare Louisiana books (40,000), Sculpture (125 works)
Exhibitions: 8 -12 rotating exhibitions per year
Publications: Louisiana's Black Heritage; Louisiana Portrait Gallery. Vol I; A Social History of the American Alligator; A Medley of Cultures: Louisiana History at the Cabildo; exhibit catalogs
Activities: Classes for adults & children; docent training; dramatic progs; lects open to pub, 6-10 vis lectrs per yr; tours; concerts; gallery talks; individual paintings & original objects of art lent to mus; book traveling exhibs 2-3 per yr; originate traveling exhibs to Louisiana museums, libraries, & community centers; mus shop sells books, original art, reproductions, prints, maps & crafts

L **Louisiana State Museum**, 751 Chartres Ave, ; PO Box 2448, New Orleans, LA 70116-2448. Tel 504-568-6968; Fax 504-568-6969; Email ism@crt.state.la.us; Web: louisianastatemuseum.org; *Dir* Mark A Tullos Jr; *Dir Curatorial Svcs* Dawn Hammatt; *Dir Mktg & Pub Rels* Marvin McGraw; *Deputy Dir* Robert Wheat
Open 10 AM - 4 PM Tue - Sun; Admis adults $6, students, seniors, active military $4; Estab 1906, to collect materials related to Louisiana history & culture; Nine mus located in New Orleans, Baton Rouge & North Louisiana; Average Annual Attendance: 500,000
Library Holdings: Book Volumes 40,000, Clipping Files, Manuscripts, Maps, Original Art Works, Original Documents, Other Holdings Non-circulating Louisiana historical material, Pamphlets, Periodical Subscriptions 5, Records, Reels, Sculpture, Slides
Collections: Coll of over 500,000 objects in costumes, textiles, science & technology, maps & manuscripts, material culture, visual arts, jazz, aviation, sports
Activities: Classes for adults & children; docent training; lects open to pub; 100 vis lectrs pr yr; concerts; gallery talks; tours; sponsoring of competitions; lending of original objects of art to mus regionally & nationally; three book traveling exhibs per yr; originate traveling exhibs to mus; mus shop sells books, reproductions, prints

M **NEW ORLEANS ACADEMY OF FINE ARTS,** Academy Gallery, 5256 Magazine St, New Orleans, LA 70115-1852. Tel 504-899-8111; Fax 504-897-6811;

Email patsya@noafa.com; Web: noafa.com; *Pres* Dorothy J Coleman; *Dir Academy* Auseklis Ozolis; *Gallery Dir & Adminr* Patsy Baker Adams
Open Mon - Fri 9 AM - 4 PM, Sat 10 AM - 4 PM; No admis fee; Estab 1978 to provide instruction in the classical approaches to art teaching adjunct to school; Average Annual Attendance: 300
Income: Financed by the academy & endowments
Exhibitions: Rotating exhibits
Activities: Classes for adults; lects open to mems only, 3 vis lectrs per yr; acad awards in painting, drawing, sculpture

M **NEW ORLEANS ARTWORKS AT NEW ORLEANS GLASSWORKS & PRINTMAKING STUDIO,** 727 Magazine St, New Orleans, LA 70130-3629. Tel 504-529-7279; Fax 504-539-5417 (call before faxing); Email neworleansglassworks@gmail.com; Web: www.neworleansartworks.com; *Pres* Geriod Baronne
Open Mon - Sat 10AM - 5 PM; No admis fee; Estab 1990 to educate visitors about glassworking, printmaking & book binding; 25,000 sq ft front room collectors' gallery with daily demonstrations in the glass, print & book arts studio; Average Annual Attendance: 20,000; Mem: approx 3,500; dues $40, monthly meetings
Income: Financed by mem, sale of art works, national & international corporate funding, tax deductible donations & grants
Library Holdings: Auction Catalogs, Cards, Exhibition Catalogs, Memorabilia, Original Art Works, Other Holdings, Prints, Sculpture
Special Subjects: Decorative Arts, Enamels, Etchings & Engravings, Furniture, Metalwork, Prints, Sculpture
Exhibitions: Gilles Chambrier; Curtiss Brock; Josh Cohen; Fabienne Picaud; Richard Royal; Pino Signoretto; Paul Stankard; Frank Van Denham; Udo Zembok; Dan Schreiber; Terri Walker; Stephen Williams; Jim Mongrain; Jason Christian; Kyle Herr
Activities: Classes for adults & children; classes in torchworking, copper enameling; two-hour short courses; design & wine glasses; hands-on daily glass & print demonstrations in working artist studio; lects open to pub; 4 vis international master artists per year; 6 vis lectrs per yr first Sat of each month; tours; extension prog first Sat of month; dinner receptions while master glassblowers and artists create pieces, tours & demonstrations in their studios; book traveling exhibs at leading museums & universities; sales shop sells original art, books, glasswork & prints made in the glass sculpture & printmaking studio, bookbinding, bronze pours, papermaking, repair of broken glass, commissions available

M **NEW ORLEANS MUSEUM OF ART,** 1 Collins Diboll Cir, City Park New Orleans, LA 70124-4603; PO Box 19123, New Orleans, LA 70179-0123. Tel 504-658-4100; Fax 504-658-4199; Email palexander@noma.org; Web: www.noma.org; *Dir* Susan M Taylor; *Cur Decorative Arts & Design* Mel Buchanan; *Deputy Dir Curatorial Affairs & Cur Asian Art* Lisa Rotondo-McCord; *Head Registrar* Jennifer Ickes; *Librn* Sheila Cork; *Sculpture Garden Mgr* Pamela Buckman; *Deputy Dir Admin & Fin* Gail Asprodites; *Mus Shop Mgr* Christina Lossi; *Ed Mus Publications* David Johnson; *Cur Photog, Prints & Drawings* Russell Lord; *Cur Contemporary & Modern Art* Katie Pfohl; *Cur Educ* Tracy E Kennan; *IT Mgr* Karl Oelkers; *Dir Develop* Jenni Daniel
Open Tues - Thurs 10 AM - 6 PM, Fri 10 AM - 9 PM, Sat 10 AM - 5 PM, Sun 11 AM - 5 PM, cl Mon; Admis adults $12, seniors & active military $10, students $8, children 7-12 $6, children 6 & under free; Estab 1910; building given to city by Isaac Delgado, maintained by municipal funds & private donations to provide a stimulus to a broader cultural life for the entire community. Stern Auditorium, Ella West Freeman wing for changing exhibitions; Wisner Educ wing for learning experiences; Delgado Building for permanent display shop; 135,000 sq ft space, three fl; Average Annual Attendance: 220,000; Mem: 7,000; dues $65-$20,000; annual meeting in Nov
Income: Financed by mem, city appropriation, federal, state & foundation grant, corporate contributions & individual donations
Special Subjects: African Art, Afro-American Art, American Indian Art, Asian Art, Bronzes, Decorative Arts, Folk Art, Furniture, Glass, Graphics, Oriental Art, Painting-American, Painting-Dutch, Painting-European, Painting-Flemish, Painting-French, Painting-Japanese, Period Rooms, Photography, Porcelain, Portraits, Pre-Columbian Art, Sculpture, Silver, Latin American Art
Collections: Kress Collection of Italian Renaissance & Baroque Painting, Chapman H Hyams Collection of Barbizon & Salon Paintings, Edgar Degas works, 20th century English & Continental art, including Surrealism & School of Paris, Melvin P Billups Glass Collection, 19th & 20th century United States & Louisiana painting & sculpture, Latter- Schlesinger Collection of English & Continental Portrait Miniatures, Victor Kiam Collection of African, Oceanic American Indian, & 20th century European & American Painting & Sculpture, The Matilda Geddings Gray Foundation Collection of Works by Peter Carl Faberge, Rosemonde E & Emile Kuntz Federal & Louisiana Period Rooms, 16th - 20th century French art, Bert Piso Collection of 17th century Dutch painting, Imperial Treasures by Peter Carl Faberge from the Matilda Geddings Gray Foundation Collection, Morgan-Whitney Collection of Chinese Jades, Rosemonde E & Emile Kuntz Rooms of Late 18th - Early 19th Century American Furniture, Stern-Davis Collection of Peruvian Painting, Sydney & Walda Besthoff Sculpture Garden
Publications: Arts Quarterly; catalogs of New Orleans Museum of Art organized exhibitions; History of New Orleans Museum of Art
Activities: Classes for adults & children; docent training; teacher workshops; art therapy prog; internships; Taylor Scholars Prog; lects open to pub, 10 vis lectrs per yr; concerts; gallery talks; tours including multi-language; competitions incl Cox Art Contest; Isaac Delgado Memorial Award ann to outstanding art patron; individual paintings & original objects of art lent in metropolitan New Orleans; book traveling exhibs 5 per yr to schools and libraries; originate traveling exhibs to other art mus in USA and Europe; mus shop sells books, original art, reproductions, prints, cards, slides, toys & jewelry

L **Felix J Dreyfous Library,** 1 Collins Diboll Cir, New Orleans, LA 70124-4603; PO Box 19123, New Orleans, LA 70179-0123. Tel 504-658-4100; Fax 504-658-4199; Web: www.noma.org; *Librn* Sheila Cork
Admis non-LA residents $8, adults $7, seniors 65 & over $4, children 3 & under free; Estab 1971 to provide information for reference to the cur, mus members & art researchers; Open Wed-Sun 10 AM - 4:30 PM; Average Annual Attendance: 100,000
Income: Financed by mem, donations & gifts
Library Holdings: Audio Tapes, Book Volumes 20,500, Cassettes, Clipping Files, Exhibition Catalogs, Fiche, Memorabilia, Pamphlets, Periodical Subscriptions 50, Reels, Slides, Video Tapes
Special Subjects: Photography
Collections: WPA Project - New Orleans Artists
Activities: Mus shop sells collectibles; books; jewelry & art related items

M **OGDEN MUSEUM OF SOUTHERN ART, UNIVERSITY OF NEW ORLEANS,** 925 Camp St, New Orleans, LA 70130-3907. Tel 504-539-9650; Fax 504-539-9602; Email info@ogdenmuseum.org; Web: www.ogdenmuseum.org; *Dir* William Andrews; *Deputy Dir/Music Cur* Libra LaGrone; *Educ* Ellen Balkin; *Cur* Bradley Sumrall; *Pub Relations* Sarah Story; *Security* Monica Barre; *Chair* Allison Kendrick; *Cur Center for So Craft & Design* William Pritchard; *Mem Coordr* Amelia Whittington
Open Wed - Mon 10 AM - 5PM & Thurs 6PM - 8PM after hrs; cl New Year's Day, Mardi Gras Day, Memorial Day, July 4th, Labor Day, Thanksgiving & Christmas; Admis adults $10, seniors $8, students $5, discount to groups, free admis for Louisiana residents on Thurs 10 AM - 5PM; Founded 1994, Grand Opening 2003; Mus showcases the visual art & culture of the American south. Pub nonprofit org; FT paid 16, PT paid 6, interns 6, docents & vols approx 50; Average Annual Attendance: 50,000 - 99,999; Mem: 1,800; dues vary
Special Subjects: Afro-American Art, Architecture, Ceramics, Costumes, Crafts, Decorative Arts, Drawings, Embroidery, Etchings & Engravings, Folk Art, Furniture, Glass, Graphics, Landscapes, Painting-American, Photography, Portraits, Posters, Pottery, Primitive art, Prints, Religious Art, Sculpture, Textiles, Watercolors, Woodcarvings, Woodcuts
Collections: Coll showcases the visual art of the southern states & WA DC from 1733 - present, Center for Southern Craft and Design
Activities: Educ prog; docent training; classes for adults & children; dramatic progs; docent training; live music by Southern musicians every Thurs night: Ogden After Hours; summer camps for children; lects open to pub; lects for mems only; 4 vis lectrs per yr; guided tours; concerts; gallery talks; sponsoring of competitions; hobby workshops; Sunday afternoon programming: Sundays At the O; schols; fels; organize traveling exhibs to mus; Mus shop sells books, magazines, original art, reproductions, prints, crafts & many other items

M **TULANE UNIVERSITY,** University Art Collection, 7001 Freret St, Tulane University Library New Orleans, LA 70118-5549. Tel 504-865-5685; Fax 504-865-5761; Web: tulane.edu; *Cur* Joan G Caldwell
Open Mon - Fri 9 AM - 4:45 PM, cl school holidays & Mardi Gras; No admis fee; Estab 1980
Special Subjects: Decorative Arts, Drawings, Graphics, Historical Material, Manuscripts, Maps, Photography, Pottery, Prints, Religious Art, Sculpture, Watercolors
Collections: Linton-Surget Collection, La Artists, Modern British Prints, 19th & 20th Century paintings, photograph coll
Activities: Gallery talks; tours; original objects of art lent to other institutions; book traveling exhibs; originate traveling exhibs

L **Architecture Library,** 7001 Freret St, Howard-Tilton Memorial Library New Orleans, LA 70118-5549. Tel 504-865-5391; Fax 504-862-8966; Email arch@tulane.edu; Web: www.architecture.tulane.edu/facilities/the-architecture-library; *Unit Supervisor* Alan Velasquez; *Library Technician* Joshua Windham
Open vary according to acad calendar; Estab 1971; For reference only; Average Annual Attendance: 8415
Income: Donations
Purchases: Architecture trade catalogs
Library Holdings: Book Volumes 26,000, Periodical Subscriptions 249
Special Subjects: Architecture

L **Southeastern Architectural Archive,** 6801 Freret St, New Orleans, LA 70118-5549. Tel 504-865-5699; Email seaa@tulane.edu; Web: seaa.tulane.edu; *Archivist* Kevin Williams
Open Mon - Fri 9 AM - noon, 1 - 5 PM; cl Tulane Univ Holidays; Estab 1979; preservation & conservation of architectural records associated with New Orleans & Louisiana; Average Annual Attendance: 765
Income: Donations
Library Holdings: Book Volumes, Lantern Slides, Maps, Original Art Works, Original Documents, Other Holdings, Photographs, Prints, Sculpture, Slides, Video Tapes Drafting/Architectural Office Tools & Supplies
Special Subjects: Architecture, Drawings, Landscape Architecture, Maps
Collections: (more than 135 colls)
Exhibitions: See Website for online exhibits
Activities: Classes for adults

M **TULANE UNIVERSITY,** Newcomb Art Museum, 6823 St Charles Ave, Woldenberg Art Center #81 New Orleans, LA 70118-5665. Tel 504-865-5328; Fax 504-865-5329; Email museum@tulane.edu; Web: www.newcombartmuseum.tulane.edu; *Dir* Monica Ramirez-Montagut PhD; *External Affairs* Miriam Taylor; *Coord Interpretation & Pub Engagement* Tom Friel; *Colls Mgr & Exhibs Registrar* Sierra Polisar
Open Tues - Fri 10 AM - 5 PM, Sat 11 AM - 4 PM; cl New Year's Eve & Day, Mardi Gras, Thanksgiving; Christmas Eve & Day; No admis fee; Gallery estab 1996 to present inspiring exhibs & progs that engage communities both on & off campus; Average Annual Attendance: 10,000; Mem: Please refer to website for info
Income: Financed by endowment, membership & university support
Purchases: Newcomb pottery
Special Subjects: Decorative Arts, Photography, Pottery, Sculpture
Collections: Newcomb pottery: Louisiana arts & crafts
Publications: Exhibition catalogs
Activities: Lects open to pub, 2-4 vis lectrs per yr; gallery talks; tours; film series

M **UNIVERSITY OF NEW ORLEANS,** Fine Arts Gallery, 2000 Lakeshore Dr, New Orleans, LA 70122-3520. Tel 504-280-6493; Fax 504-280-7346; Email finearts@uno.ed; Web: www.uno.edu; *Gallery Dir* Doyle Gertjejansen
Open Mon - Fri 8:30 AM - 4:30 PM; No admis fee; Estab 1974 to expose the students & community to historic & contemporary visual arts; Gallery consists of

1800 sq ft, 165 lineal ft of wall space, 20 ft ceilings, natural & artificial lighting; Average Annual Attendance: 15,000
Income: Financed by state appropriation
Exhibitions: Rotating exhibits
Activities: Cr & non-cr classes for adults in conjunction with Univ of New Orleans; lects open to public, 20 vis lectrs per year

L **Earl K Long Library**, 2000 Lakeshore Dr, New Orleans, LA 70122-3520. Tel 504-280-6549; Fax 504-280-7277; Web: www.library.uno.edu; *Chmn Reference Svcs* Robert T Heriard
Open Mon-Thurs 8AM-11AM; Fri 8AM-8PM, Sat 9AM-6PM, Sun Noon-8PM; Estab 1958 for scholarly & professional research; Circ 110,140; For lending & reference
Income: $2,401,104 (financed by state appropriation)
Purchases: $797,407
Library Holdings: Book Volumes 394,729, Cards, Fiche, Other Holdings Art per subs 250; Art vols 12,974, Periodical Subscriptions 4500, Reels

OPELOUSAS

M **OPELOUSAS MUSEUM OF ART, INC (OMA),** 106 N Union St, Opelousas, LA 70570-6267. Tel 337-942-4991; Fax 337-942-4930; Email omamuseum@aol.com; Web: http://auction.lpb.org/oma.htm; *Cur* Keith J Guidry
Open Tues - Fril - 5 PM, Sat 9 AM - 5 PM, cl Sun & Mon; Admis adults $3, accompanying children & mems free; Estab 1997 to display traveling art exhibitions; Shows exhibitions from major museums, private collections & community & local exhibitions; Average Annual Attendance: 3,500; Mem: 500+
Special Subjects: Afro-American Art, American Indian Art, American Western Art, Architecture, Collages, Decorative Arts, Drawings, Etchings & Engravings, Folk Art, Hispanic Art, Juvenile Art, Landscapes, Latin American Art, Maps, Marine Painting, Medieval Art, Mexican Art, Military Art, Painting-American, Painting-Canadian, Painting-French, Painting-German, Painting-Israeli, Painting-Italian, Painting-Spanish, Photography, Historical Material
Activities: Lects open to pub; lect for members only; 6 vis lectrs per yr; tours; book traveling exhibs 4 per yr; originate traveling exhibs 2 per yr

PATTERSON

M **WEDELL-WILLIAMS MEMORIAL AVIATION MUSEUM,** LA 90 in Kemper Williams Park, 118 Cotton Rd Patterson, LA 70392; P.O. Box 2448, New Orleans, LA 70176. Tel 985-399-1268; Web: www.lsm.crt.state.la.us/wedellex.htm
Open Tues - Sat 9 AM - 5 PM; Admis adults $3, students $2, seniors, military, & children 12 and under free; Estab by the Legislature as the state's official aviation mus, mus is named after Jimmie Wedell & Harry Williams, two Louisiana aviators who formed an air service in 1928; Mus is committed to preserving & presenting artifacts & documents reflecting aviation history in Louisiana
Special Subjects: Historical Material
Collections: Airworthy replica of Wedell's "44" racer, 1939 D175 Beechcraft, Presidential Aero-Commander 680 that was used during the Eisenhower administration, race trophies from the 1930s, the state's largest coll of model airplanes, vintage hot air balloon basket
Activities: Model airplane-building classes; astronomy workshop for children

PORT ALLEN

M **WEST BATON ROUGE PARISH,** West Baton Rouge Museum, 845 N Jefferson Ave, Port Allen, LA 70767-2417. Tel 225-336-2422; Fax 225-336-2448; Email contact_us@wbrmuseum.org; Web: www.westbatonrougemuseum.com; *Dir* Julia Rose; *Educ Cur* Jeannie Giroir Luckett; *Admin Asst* Alice LeBlanc; *Cur* Lauren Davis
Open Tues - Sat 10 AM - 4:30 PM, Sun 2 - 5 PM; Admis adults $4 seniors & students $2, West Baton Rouge Parish residents free; Estab 1968 to foster interest in history, particularly that of West Baton Rouge Parish; to encourage research, collection & preservation of material illustrating past & present activities of the parish; to operate one or more museums; to receive gifts & donations; to accept exhibits & historical materials on loan; A large room housing a scale model of a sugar mill (one inch to one ft, dated 1904) & parish memorabilia; restored French Creole cottage (c 1830); a room 31 X 40 ft for art exhibits; restored plantation quarters cabin (1850); Average Annual Attendance: 18,000; Mem: 300; dues $10; annual meeting in Jan
Income: $250,000 (financed by mem, gifts & millage levied on parish)
Library Holdings: Original Documents, Pamphlets, Photographs, Prints
Special Subjects: Architecture, Costumes, Crafts, Furniture, Furniture, Manuscripts, Maps, Period Rooms, Photography, Pottery, Restorations, Drawings, Painting-American, Prints, Sculpture
Collections: Art coll of parish artifacts, c1830 French Creole Cottage, contemporary Louisiana (drawings, paintings, prints & sculpture), early 19th century furnishings, historic photographs & family papers, Newcomb Pottery Coll, duck decoys, c1880s Share Cropper Cabins (2), early 20th century shot gun dwelling
Exhibitions: Gallery with six shows yearly
Publications: Ecoutez, 4 times a yr
Activities: Classes for children; docent training; lects open to pub, 1 vis lectr per yr; tours; book traveling exhibs semi-annually; mus shop sells books, magazines, original art, reproductions & prints

SAINT MARTINVILLE

M **LONGFELLOW-EVANGELINE STATE COMMEMORATIVE AREA,** 1200 N Main St, Hwy 31 Saint Martinville, LA 70582-3516. Tel 337-394-4284, 394-3754, 888-677-2900; Fax 337-394-3553; Email longfellow@crt.state.la.us; Web: www.crt.state.la.us; *Site & Cur Mus* Suzanna Laviolette; *Mgr* Reinaldo Barnes
Open daily 9 AM - 5 PM, cl Thanksgiving, Christmas & New Year; Admis adults $2, adults over 61 free, children under 13 free, all school groups free; Estab 1934 to display & describe 19th century French lifeways & folk items; Artworks are displayed in a 19th century plantation home, in the interpretive center of the site & in the 18th century cabin; Average Annual Attendance: 26,000
Income: Financed by state appropriations
Special Subjects: Architecture, Ceramics, Coins & Medals, Crafts, Decorative Arts, Dolls, Embroidery, Folk Art, Furniture, Glass, Historical Material, Laces, Landscapes, Painting-American, Painting-French, Period Rooms, Pewter, Photography, Porcelain, Portraits, Pottery, Prints, Religious Art, Reproductions, Textiles
Collections: Early 19th century portraits, 18th, 19th & 20th centuries textile arts, local craft & folk art, Louisiana cypress furniture, 19th century antiques, religious art of the 19th century, wood carvings, Plantation House, Acadian Art
Exhibitions: Attakapas Trade Days (Fall); Creole Holidays (Dec); Plantation Days (Spring)
Activities: Dramatic progs; docent training; lects open to pub, 4 vis lectrs per yr; tours; workshops

SHREVEPORT

M **CENTENARY COLLEGE OF LOUISIANA,** Meadows Museum of Art, 2911 Centenary Blvd, Shreveport, LA 71104-3335; PO Box 41188, Shreveport, LA 71134-1188. Tel 318-869-5040; Fax 318-869-5730; Email meadows@centenary.edu; Web: www.centenary.edu/meadows; *Dir* Sean FitzGibbons
Open Sept - April Mon - Fri 10 AM - 5 PM; cl New Year's Day, Easter. Memorial Day, Labor Day, Thanksgiving, Christmas; No admis fee; Estab 1976 to house the Indo-China Collection of Drawings & Paintings by Jean Despujols; main gallery on first floor 25 x 80 ft; other galleries 25 x 30 ft; track lights and no windows; Average Annual Attendance: 2,500
Income: Financed by endowment
Special Subjects: Ethnology, Painting-French, Costumes, Drawings, Eskimo Art, Etchings & Engravings, Landscapes, Mexican Art, Photography, Prints, Sculpture, Textiles, Watercolors, Woodcuts
Collections: 360 works in Indo-China Collection, dealing with Angkor Region, The Cordillera, Gulf of Siam, Laos, The Nam-Te, The Thai, Upper Tonkin, Vietnam
Exhibitions: Rotating exhibits
Publications: Partial Catalog of Permanent Collection with 21 color plates
Activities: Intern training; lects open to pub; gallery talks; tours; individual paintings & original objects of art lent to qualified mus; mus shop sells books & reproductions

M **THE MULTICULTURAL CENTER OF THE SOUTH,** 520 Spring St Shreveport, LA 71101-3257; PO Box 305 Shreveport, LA 71101-0305. Tel 318-424-1380; Fax 318-424-1384; Email jgatlin-mccs@comcast.net; Web: www.mccsouth.org; *Dir Progs* Janice Gatlin; *Curriculum Specialist* Priscilla Metoyer
Open to pub Tues - Fri 10 AM - 4 PM; Sat by appointment for large groups; Admis adults $3, students & seniors $2; Estab 1999; 16 cultural exhibs; Average Annual Attendance: 1500

M **R W NORTON ART FOUNDATION,** R W Norton Art Gallery, 4747 Creswell Ave, Shreveport, LA 71106-1899. Tel 318-865-4201; Fax 318-869-0435; Email gallery@rwnaf.org; Web: www.rwnaf.org; *Pres Bd* M Lewis Norton; *Secy-Treas & Dir Pub Rels* Ruth Norton; *Bldg & Grounds Supt* Gerry Ward; *Dir Research & Rare Coll* Everl Adair; *Educ Dir* Emily Boykin; *Tour Coordr* Ashleigh Newberry-Mills; *Events Designer* Emily Feazel
Open Tues - Fri 10 AM - 5 PM, Sat & Sun 1 - 5 PM, cl Mon & holidays; No admis fee; Estab 1946, opened 1966. Founded to present aspects of the develop of American & European art & culture through exhibition & interpretation of fine works of art & literature, both from the Gallery's own collections & from those of other institutions & individuals; American & European art spanning over four centuries spotlighting art of the American West by Frederic Remington and Charles Russell; Average Annual Attendance: 17,000
Income: Financed by endowment
Library Holdings: Auction Catalogs, Audio Tapes 12,000, Book Volumes, Exhibition Catalogs, Original Documents, Pamphlets, Periodical Subscriptions
Special Subjects: American Western Art, Miniatures, Painting-American, Painting-European, Portraits, Pottery, Sculpture, Silver, Tapestries
Collections: American miniatures & colonial silver, contemporary American & European painting & sculpture, painting & sculpture relating to Early American history, Paintings by 19th century American artists of the Hudson River School, Portraits of famous confederate leaders, 16th Century Flemish tapestries, Wedgwood collection, paintings & sculpture by western American artists Frederic Remington & Charles M Russell, Frederic Remington Collection, Charles M Russell Collection
Publications: Announcements of spec exhibs; catalogs (60 through 2007); catalogs of the Charles M Russell Collection & of the Wedgwood Collection; electronic newsletter
Activities: Educ dept; docent training; classes for children; lects open to pub; vis lectrs 3 per yr; gallery talks; tours; serves elderly in nursing homes; book traveling exhibs 2 per yr; mus shop sells exhibition catalogs, catalogs of permanent collection

L **Library**, 4747 Creswell Ave, Shreveport, LA 71106-1899. Tel 318-865-4201; Fax 318-869-0435; Email jb@rwnaf.org; Web: www.rwnaf.org; *Secy-Treas* Jerry Bloomer
Open by appointment only; No admis fee; Estab 1946 to acquire and make available for public use on the premises, important books, exhibition catalogs, etc relating to the visual arts, literature, American history and genealogy, as well as other standard reference and bibliographic works for reference only; Circ Non-circulating; A mus of Am & European art spanning over 4 centuries; Average Annual Attendance: 20,000 - 30,000
Income: Financed by endowment
Library Holdings: Auction Catalogs, Book Volumes 12,000, Clipping Files, Exhibition Catalogs, Manuscripts, Memorabilia, Other Holdings Original documents; Auction catalogs, Pamphlets, Periodical Subscriptions 100, Photographs, Reels, Slides

Special Subjects: American Western Art, Architecture, Art History, Bronzes, Ceramics, Coins & Medals, Decorative Arts, Dolls, Drawings, Etchings & Engravings, Glass, Goldsmithing, Graphic Arts, History of Art & Archaeology, Illustration, Landscapes, Manuscripts, Marine Painting, Metalwork, Miniatures, Painting-American, Painting-British, Painting-European, Painting-Flemish, Painting-French, Painting-German, Pewter, Photography, Porcelain, Portraits, Pottery, Printmaking, Prints, Sculpture, Silver, Silversmithing, Southwestern Art, Stained Glass, Watercolors
Collections: James M Owens Memorial Collection of Early Americana (725 volumes on Colonial history, particularly on Virginia), large coll of books on Frederic Remington & Charles M Russell
Activities: Conduct tours & slide progs; sales of collection & special exhib catalogs

M **SECRETARY OF STATE MUSEUM DIVISION,** Louisiana State Exhibit Museum, 3015 Greenwood Rd, Shreveport, LA 71109; PO Box 38356, Shreveport, LA 71133-8356. Tel 318-632-2020; Fax 318-632-2056; Email lsem@sos.louisiana.gov; Web: www.laexhibitmuseum.org; *Dir* Wayne Waddell; *Cur* Nita Cole; *Asst Dir* Rodney Clements; *Pub Info Officer* Cynthia Grogan
Open Mon - Fri 9 AM - 4 PM; No admis fee; Estab 1939 to display permanent & temporary exhibitions demonstrating the state's history, resources & natural beauty; Art Gallery is maintained; Average Annual Attendance: 200,000
Income: Financed by state appropriation
Special Subjects: American Indian Art, Anthropology, Archaeology, Dioramas, Historical Material, Pottery, Architecture, Painting-American
Collections: Archaeology, dioramas, historical artifacts, Indian artifacts, murals, natural history
Publications: brochures
Activities: Classes for children; docent training; pub Archaeology prog; lects open to pub, 4-6 vis lectrs per yr; gallery talks; films; concerts; tours; competitions sponsored; book traveling exhibs, 3 per yr

L **SOUTHERN UNIVERSITY LIBRARY,** 3050 Martin Luther King Jr Dr, Attn Library Shreveport, LA 71107. Tel 318-674-3400; Fax 318-670-6403; Web: www.susla.edu; *Dir* Orella R Brazile
Open Mon-Thurs 8AM-9PM, Fri 8AM-5PM, Sat 9AM-1PM Summer Mon-Fri 8AM-5PM; Estab 1967 to supplement the curriculum & provide bibliographic as well as reference service to both the acad community & the pub
Library Holdings: Book Volumes 48,789, Cassettes 1121, Clipping Files, Fiche 24,308, Filmstrips 414, Framed Reproductions, Motion Pictures 59, Original Art Works, Pamphlets 750, Periodical Subscriptions 379, Prints, Records 293, Reels, Reproductions 12, Sculpture, Slides 22,874, Video Tapes 240
Collections: Black Collection, pictures, clippings & books, Louisiana Collection, Black Ethnic Archives (local people)
Exhibitions: Show Local Artists Exhibitions

M **SOUTHERN UNIVERSITY MUSEUM OF ART IN SHREVEPORT,** 3050 Martin Luther King Jr Dr, Shreveport, LA 71107.

SORRENTO

M **LOUISIANA POTTERY,** 6470 Hwy 22, Cajun Village Sorrento, LA 70778. Tel 225-675-5572; Email lapottery@cox.net; Web: www.louisianapottery.com; *Owner* Judy L Starrett
Open Tues-Sun 10AM-5PM; No admis fee; Apr, 1999; Fine hand-crafted wares made by Louisiana artisans; Mem: 135+ artists represented
Collections: pottery; etchings; hand-blown glass; pine needle baskets; hand-carved wooden ducks & boats; books; original art
Exhibitions: Permanent coll - exhib on site Pat Wagner, creating beauty for the World
Activities: Classes for adults & children; 2 vis lectrs per yr; organize traveling exhibs open; sales shop sells books, magazines, original art, pottery & clay sculpture

MAINE

ALNA

M **WISCASSET, WATERVILLE & FARMINGTON RAILWAY MUSEUM (WW&F),** 97 Cross Rd, Alna, ME 04535; PO Box 242, Alna, ME 04535-0242. Tel 207-882-4193; Email info@wwfry.org; Web: www.wwfry.org; *Pres* Stephen Suppa; *Finance Dir* James Patten; *Publicity* Gordon Davis; *Archivist* Bruce Wilson; *Mem Chmn* Frances Hernandez; *Mus Gift Shop Mgr* Linda Zeller
Open Memorial Day - Columbus Day: Sat & Sun 9 AM - 5 PM; after Columbus Day - before Memorial Day: Sat 9 AM - 5 PM; Admis adults $7, children $4; Estab 1989; Operating restored two-ft gauge railroad with mus & shops (pvt nonprofit org; vol hrs 25,000; 1st Maine Congressional Dist); Average Annual Attendance: 1000 - 9999; Mem: Dues Indiv Life $300, Indiv Annual $30
Income: $200,000 - Financed by donations, gift shop sales, tickets
Library Holdings: Book Volumes, Clipping Files, DVDs, Framed Reproductions, Manuscripts, Maps, Memorabilia, Original Documents, Photographs
Collections: Numerous books, photos, documents, artifacts, and original railroad equip from 2-ft gauge railroad
Publications: WW&F Newsletter, six times per yr; WW&F Musings, 128-pg book
Activities: Docent prog; guided tours; training progs for professionals; films; ann picnic; Christmas trains

AUGUSTA

M **UNIVERSITY OF MAINE AT AUGUSTA,** The Danforth Gallery, 46 University Dr Augusta, ME 04330. Tel 207-621-3243; Fax 207-621-3293; Email peter.precourt@maine.edu; *Dir* Karen Adrienne
Open Mon - Thurs 9 AM - 5 PM, Fri 9 AM - 4 PM; No admis fee; Estab 1970 to provide changing exhibitions of the visual arts for the university students and faculty and for the larger Augusta-Kennebec Valley community; the principal exhibition area is a two level gallery; Average Annual Attendance: 3,000
Income: Financed by university budget
Library Holdings: Book Volumes, CD-ROMs, DVDs, Exhibition Catalogs, Original Art Works, Periodical Subscriptions, Sculpture
Collections: Drawings, paintings, outdoor sculpture
Exhibitions: Five major art exhibits
Activities: Lects open to pub; 2-3 vis lectrs per year; gallery talks; tours; annual awards to art & architecture students in annual exhib

BANGOR

M **UNIVERSITY OF MAINE,** Museum of Art, 40 Harlow St, Bangor, ME 04401-5102. Tel 207-561-3350; Fax 207-561-3351; Web: www.umma.umaine.edu; *Asst Mus Coordr & Mem Mgr* Kathryn Jovanelli; *Dir* George Kinghorn; *Educ Coordr* Kat Johnson; *Registrar/Preparator* Shawn Lefevre; *Mus Tech* Aaron Pyle
Open Tues - Sat 10 AM - 5 PM; No admis fee; Estab 1946 to add to the cultural life of the university student; to be a service to Maine artists; to promote good & important art, both historic & modern; The mus is located in downtown Bangor's Historic Norumbega Hall; Average Annual Attendance: 14,000
Income: Financed by state appropriation to university, donations & grants
Special Subjects: Drawings, Etchings & Engravings, Painting-American, Photography, Portraits, Posters, Prints, Watercolors, Woodcuts
Collections: The Mus of Art's permanent coll has grown to a stature which makes it a nucleus in the state for historic & contemporary art. It includes more than 6000 original works of art & is particularly strong in American mid-20th century works
Publications: Biennial catalogs & exhibition notes, newsletter
Activities: Classes for adults and children; lects open to pub & mems only, 1-2 vis lectrs per yr; gallery talks, tours; Vincent Hart gen "Access to the Arts + Museum on the Road" programs; young curators program; scholarships & fels offered

BATH

M **MAINE MARITIME MUSEUM,** 243 Washington St, Bath, ME 04530-1638. Tel 207-443-1316; Fax 207-443-1665; Web: www.bathmaine.com; *Exec Dir* Amy Lent Jr; *Dir Library* Nathan Lipfert; *Cur* Christopher Hall
Open daily 9:30 AM - 5 PM, cl New Year's Day, Thanksgiving, Christmas; Admis adults $9.50, children under 17 $6.50, under 6 free, seniors $8.50, group rates available; Estab 1964 for the preservation of Maine's maritime heritage; Several galleries; Average Annual Attendance: 65,000; Mem: 1800; dues $25 & up; annual meeting in Sept.
Income: Financed by mem, gifts, grants & admis
Special Subjects: Marine Painting
Collections: Marine art, navigational instruments, ship models, shipbuilding tools, shipping papers, traditional watercraft
Exhibitions: Historical Percy & Small Shipyard; Lobstering & the Maine Coast; Maritime History of Maine; small watercraft; other rotating exhibits
Publications: Rhumb Line, quarterly
Activities: Classes for adults & children; docent training; lects open to pub, 20 vis lectrs per yr; group tours; concerts; gallery talks; individual paintings & original objects of art lent to non-profit institutions with proper security & climate control; Mus shop sells books, reproductions, prints & related novelties

L **Archives Library,** 243 Washington St, Bath, ME 04530. Tel 207-443-1316; Fax 207-443-1665; Email lipfert@maritime.org; Web: www.mainemaritimemuseum.org; *Senior Cur* Nathan Lipfert; *Registrar* Kelly Page
Open Tues & Thurs 9:30AM-3PM; Admis $12; Estab 1964; Circ Non-circ; Small reference library; Average Annual Attendance: 1,800
Income: Financed by mem, admis, gifts & grants
Library Holdings: Auction Catalogs, Audio Tapes 220, Book Volumes 14,000, Cassettes, Clipping Files, Kodachrome Transparencies, Lantern Slides, Manuscripts 2,000 lin ft, Maps 1,000, Memorabilia, Motion Pictures, Original Art Works, Other Holdings vessel plans-42,000 sheets, Pamphlets, Periodical Subscriptions 50, Photographs 130,000, Reels 620, Slides, Video Tapes 482
Special Subjects: Historical Material, Manuscripts, Maps, Marine Painting, Painting-American, Painting-Australian, Scrimshaw, Painting-European
Collections: Sewall Ship Papers, shipbuilding firms bus papers, vessel plans, nautical charts
Exhibitions: Maritime History of Maine, Lobstering & the Maine Coast
Activities: Classes for adults; docent training; boat building shop; lects open to public; lects for members only; concerts; tours; Mariner's Award; White House "Preserve America Stewards" award (2010); mus shop sells books, magazines, original art, reproductions & prints

BIDDEFORD

M **HEARTWOOD COLLEGE OF ART,** Main Gallery, 2 Main St, Bldg 18, Ste 230, North Dam Mill Biddeford, ME 04005. Tel 207-307-2171; Email hca@heartwoodcollege.org; Web: www.heartwoodcollegeofart.org; *Pres* Berri Kramer; *Dean* Susan Wilder
Call for hours; Showcases works by MFA candidates and local artists
Activities: Educ progs; classes for adults; ; artist residencies; co-op prog; artist workshops; lects open to pub; gallery talks; art programming; workshops; competitions with awards; integrated art events; facilitation of public art projects; cultural events; art invitationals

BLUE HILL

M **PARSON FISHER HOUSE,** Jonathan Fisher Memorial, Inc, 44 Mines Rd, Rte 15, Blue Hill, ME 04614; PO Box 537, Blue Hill, ME 04614-0537. Tel 207-374-2459; Fax 207-374-5082; Email info@jonathanfisherhouse.org; Web: www.jonathanfisherhouse.org; *Pres* Eric Linnell; *Adminr* Sandra Linnell

Open Thurs, Fri, & Sat 1-4PM; Admis $2; Estab 1965 to preserve the home & memorabilia of Jonathan Fisher. The house was designed & built by him in 1814; Average Annual Attendance: 300; Mem: 260; dues endowment $1000, contributing $100, sustaining $25, annual $10; annual meeting in Aug
Income: Financed by admis fees, dues, gifts & endowment funds
Purchases: Original Fisher paintings or books
Collections: Furniture, Manuscripts, Paintings & Articles made by Fisher
Exhibitions: Annual Arts & Crafts Fair
Activities: Lects open to public, 1-2 vis lectrs per year; individual paintings & original objects of art lent to state museum or comparable organizations for exhibit; sales shop sells reproductions

BOOTHBAY HARBOR

A **BOOTHBAY REGION ART FOUNDATION INC,** One Townsend Ave, Boothbay Harbor, ME; PO Box 124, Boothbay Harbor, ME 04538-0124. Tel 207-633-2703; Email braf@boothbayartists.org; Web: www.boothbayartists.org; *Pres* Sarah G Smith; *VPres* Jennifer Litchfield; *Gallery Mgr* June Rose
Open Apr 15 - Oct 12 Mon - Sat 11 AM - 5 PM, Sun Noon - 5 PM; No admis fee; Estab 1967, originated to help develop an art curriculum in the local schools, presently functions to bring art of the region's artists to enrich the culture of the community; Store front gallery providing exhibit space in heart of Boothbay Harbor; includes prints, drawings, pastels, oils & watercolors; Average Annual Attendance: 6,000; Mem: 250; dues $25 & up; annual meeting third Tues in Oct
Income: Financed by mem, contributions & commissions
Exhibitions: Seven juried & invitational shows of graphics, paintings & sculpture by artists of the Boothbay Region
Activities: Adult & children workshop, Jan, Feb & Mar (fee); two schols offered ea yr to post graduates attending college for visual art studies

BRUNSWICK

M **BOWDOIN COLLEGE,** Peary-MacMillan Arctic Museum, 9500 College Station, Brunswick, ME 04011-9112. Tel 207-725-3416; Fax 207-725-3499; Email jtanzer@bowdoin.edu; Web: www.bowdoin.edu/arctic-museum; *Dir* Susan A Kaplan; *Asst Dir* Julie J Santorella; *Cur & Registrar* Genevieve LeMoine; *Exhib Technician* Steven T Bunn; *Museum Outreach Coord* James Tanzer
Open Tues - Sat 10 AM - 5 PM, Sun 2 - 5 PM, cl Mon & national holidays; No admis fee; Estab 1967; Museum consists of 3 galleries containing ivory, fur & soapstone Inuit artifacts, Arctic exploration equipment, natural history specimens, prints & paintings; Average Annual Attendance: 14,709
Special Subjects: American Indian Art, Anthropology, Eskimo Art, Ethnology, Historical Material, Ivory, Leather, Maps, Painting-American, Painting-Canadian, Photography, Primitive art, Sculpture
Collections: Drawing & exploration films
Activities: Educ progs; docent training; lects open to pub, 3-7 vis lectrs per yr; tours; individual paintings & original objects of art or ethnographic objects lent to other museums; mus shop sells books, cards & original native art, reproductions, prints, stationary, jewelry, t-shirts

M **Museum of Art,** 9400 College Station, Brunswick, ME 04011-8494. Tel 207-725-3275; Fax 207-725-3762; Email artmuseum@bowdoin.edu; Web: www.bowdoin.edu/art-museum; *Asst Dir* Caroline Baljon; *Cur* Joachim Homann; *Registrar & Colls Mgr* Laura Latman; *Preparator* Jose Ribas; *Assoc Dir Mus & Fin Ops* Leslie Bird; *Co-Dir* Anne Collins Goodyear; *Co-Dir* Frank H Goodyear
Open Tues - Sat 10 AM - 5 PM, Thurs 10 AM - 8:30 PM, Sun noon - 5 PM, cl Mon & holidays; No admis fee; Estab 1891-1894; 14 galleries containing paintings, medals, sculpture, decorative arts, works on paper & antiquities; Average Annual Attendance: 35,000; Mem: dues $50 & up
Special Subjects: Antiquities-Assyrian, Antiquities-Etruscan, Antiquities-Greek, Antiquities-Roman, Asian Art, Ceramics, Coins & Medals, Collages, Decorative Arts, Drawings, Painting-American, Painting-Dutch, Painting-European, Painting-Flemish, Painting-French, Painting-German, Pewter, Photography, Portraits, Pre-Columbian Art, Prints, Silver, Textiles, Watercolors, Woodcarvings, Woodcuts, Sculpture
Collections: Kress Study Collection, Molinari Collection of Medals & Plaquettes
Exhibitions: 14 - 20 temporary exhibitions per year; three major exhibitions per year
Activities: Docent training; lects open to pub, 3 vis lectrs per yr; gallery talks; tours; individual paintings & original objects of art lent to accredited mus; book traveling exhibs 3 per yr; originate traveling exhibs to other accredited mus; mus shop sells books, reproductions, slides, jewelry

DAMARISCOTTA

M **RIVER ARTS,** (Round Top Center for the Arts Inc) Arts Gallery, 170 Main St, Damariscotta, ME 04543; PO Box 1316, Damariscotta, ME 04543-1316. Tel 207-563-1507; Email info@riverartsme.org; Web: www.riverartsme.org
Open Mon - Sat 10 AM - 4PM, Sun Noon - 4PM; No admis fee; Mem: dues steward $1,000; patron $500; contributor $125; household $75; individual $60; student & senior $25
Special Subjects: Painting-American
Collections: All facets & eras of visual arts history, classical music coll, theatre script coll
Publications: Catalogues, gallery booklets & newsletters
Activities: Classes for adults & children; dramatic progs; lects open to pub, 5-10 vis lectrs per yr; mus shop sells prints, crafts & paintings

DEER ISLE

M **HAYSTACK MOUNTAIN SCHOOL OF CRAFTS,** 89 Haystack School Dr, Deer Isle, ME 04627-0518; PO Box 518, Deer Isle, ME 04627-0518. Tel 207-348-2306; Fax 207-348-2307; Email haystack@haystack-mtn.org; Web: www.haystack-mtn.org; *Chmn Bd* Kristin Mitsu Shiba; *Dir* Paul Sacaridiz; *Pres* Matt Hutton; *Treas* Miguel Gomez-Ibanez; *Develop* Ginger Aldrich
Open tours Wed 1PM, June-August; Admis adults $5; Estab 1950 to provide craft educ workshops & residency; Average Annual Attendance: 500
Income: pvt funding
Library Holdings: Book Volumes, Exhibition Catalogs, Kodachrome Transparencies, Maps, Memorabilia, Slides, Video Tapes
Special Subjects: Ceramics, Jewelry, Crafts, Decorative Arts, Embroidery, Porcelain, Furniture, Glass, Gold, Graphics, Metalwork, Mixed Media, Silver, Southwestern Art, Textiles, Woodcarvings, Woodcuts, Printmaking
Exhibitions: Seasonal - Spring Summer
Publications: Annual brochure
Activities: One & two week summer sessions in ceramics, graphics, glass, jewelry, weaving, blacksmithing, papermaking, furniture, sculpture & fabrics; lects open to pub, 40 vis lectrs per yr; scholarships & fellowships offered

L **Center for Community Programs Gallery,** PO Box 518, Deer Isle, ME 04627-0518. Tel 207-348-2306; Fax 207-348-2307; Email haystack@haystack-mtn.org; Web: www.haystack-mtn.org; *Dir* Paul Sacaridiz; *Asst Dir* Ellen Wieske; *Develop Dir* Ginger Aldrich
Open June-Aug; Wed, Fri-Sun 1-5pm; Estab 2007 for community programs & exhibs; Contemporary craft; Average Annual Attendance: 1,000
Income: Privately financed
Library Holdings: Book Volumes 1000, Exhibition Catalogs, Kodachrome Transparencies, Maps, Memorabilia, Periodical Subscriptions 10, Slides, Video Tapes
Special Subjects: Ceramics, Crafts, Decorative Arts, Embroidery, Enamels, Furniture, Glass, Gold, Goldsmithing, Graphic Arts, Graphic Design, Handicrafts, Jewelry, Metalwork, Mixed Media, Porcelain, Pottery, Printmaking, Silver, Silversmithing, Textiles, Woodcarvings, Woodcuts
Exhibitions: fall, spring, & summer exhibs
Publications: Monograph series
Activities: Classes for adults & children, community programs; lects open to pub; 40 vis lectrs per yr; AIA 25 year award, ACC Gold Medal award; National Historic Register; schols and fels offered; mus shop sells books

EASTPORT

M **TIDES INSTITUTE & MUSEUM OF ART,** 43 Water St Eastport, ME 04631-1532; PO Box 161 Eastport, ME 04631-0161. *Dir* Hugh French

ELLSWORTH

M **HANCOCK COUNTY TRUSTEES OF PUBLIC RESERVATIONS,** Woodlawn: Museum, Gardens & Park, 19 Black House Dr, Ellsworth, ME 04605; PO Box 1478, Ellsworth, ME 04605-1478. Tel 207-667-8671; Fax 207-667-7950; Email director@woodlawnmuseum.org; Web: www.woodlawnmuseum.org; *Pres* Terry Carlisle; *Exec Dir* Joshua C Torrance
Open May & Oct Tues - Sun 1 - 4 PM, June - Sept Tues - Sat 10 AM - 5 PM, Sun 1 - 4 PM; Admis adults $10, children & students $3; Estab 1929; Historical estate operated by the Hancock County Trustees of Pub Reservations; Average Annual Attendance: 10,000; Mem: 450
Income: Financed by private trust fund, donations admis, & special events
Library Holdings: Maps, Original Documents, Pamphlets, Photographs, Prints, Slides
Special Subjects: Carpets & Rugs, Ceramics, Decorative Arts, Embroidery, Etchings & Engravings, Folk Art, Furniture, Glass, Jewelry, Landscape Architecture, Landscapes, Manuscripts, Maps, Miniatures, Painting-American, Painting-American, Painting-British, Painting-European, Period Rooms, Photography, Portraits, Prints, Silver, Textiles, Watercolors, Woodcarvings, Tapestries
Collections: fine examples of American & European fine & decorative arts in original setting, carriages & sleighs
Publications: Colonel John Black of Ellsworth (1781 - 1856); David Cobb an American Patriot; Legacy of the Penobscot Million; Quarterly newsletter; Woodlawn: A Look Within
Activities: Classes for adults & children; docent training; dramatic prog; craft workshops; Ellsworth Antiques Show at Woodlawn; lects open to pub; 6 vis lectrs per yr; concerts; gallery talks; tours; fellowships; mus shop sells books, prints & reproductions

M **THE NEW ENGLAND MUSEUM OF TELEPHONY, INC,** The Telephone Museum, 166 Winkumpaugh Rd, Ellsworth, ME 04605; PO Box 1377, Ellsworth, ME 04605-1377. Tel 207-667-9491; Email switchboard@downeast.net; Web: ellsworthme.org/ringring; *Pres & Dir* Martin Harriss; *Finance Dir* Bryan T McLellan; *VPres & Dir* Doug Kirkpatrick; *Secy & Dir* Stan St Onge
Open Jul - Sept Sat - Sun 1 PM - 4 PM, open by appt June & Oct, cl Nov - June; Admis adults $10, children $5; Estab 1983; Mus traces the history of telecommunications through hands-on working exhibs of telephone switching systems. By illustrating the technical, social & corporate evolution of the telephone network the mus provides a basis for understanding modern communication systems; Average Annual Attendance: approx 350; Mem: dues The LongLines Club (life members) $1,000, Sustaining $250, Participating $100, Org $75, Family $50, Indiv $30
Special Subjects: Historical Material
Collections: Technical documents; personal & corporate papers; manuals & reference materials, Large-scale electro-mechanical telephone switching systems; switchboards; telephone sets; central office equip; outside plant equip
Publications: The Pole Line, biannual newsletter; Subscriber Directory, annual; The Telephone: A Love/Hate Relationship, Aug 2004; Military Communications, Aug 2004; Telstar and Andover, Maine, Aug 2004
Activities: Lects; guided tours; ann Telephone Fair (Open House); spec exhibs; project days: allows mus mems to work on equip restoration projs; research in early telephone lines in Hancock Co, Maine; children's workshops; mus shop sells books, telephone wire baskets, t-shirts, toys, puzzles, DVDs, projects

FRYEBURG

M **FRYEBURG ACADEMY,** The Palmina F & Stephen S Pace Galleries of Art, 745 Main St, Leura Hill Eastman Performing Arts Ctr Fryeburg, ME 04037. Tel 207-831-0959; Email jday@fryeburgacademy.com; Web: www.fryeburgacademy.com; *Dir* John Day
Open Tues & Thurs 10 AM - 1 PM
Special Subjects: Painting-American, Sculpture, Drawings, Ceramics, Photography
Activities: Educ progs; artist workshops; gallery talks; tours; art programming; workshops; live performances

HALLOWELL

A **KENNEBEC VALLEY ART ASSOCIATION,** Harlow Gallery, 160 Water St, Hallowell, ME 04347-1315. Tel 207-622-3813; Email kvaa@harlowgallery.org; Web: www.harlowgallery.org; *Exec Dir* Deborah Fahy; *Board Member* Lisa Rigoulot; *Treasurer* Diana Scully; *Bd President* Susan MacPherson; *Gallery Manager* Cassie Bouton; *PR & Documentation Specialist* Allison McKeen; *Bd Secy* Anne Young; *Admin Asst* Nancy Bixler; *VPres* Helene Farrar; *Bd Mem* Sally Wagley
Open Wed - Sat noon - 6 PM; No admis fee; Estab 1959; supports artistic development of member artists, providing workshops, lectrs, demonstrations; space available to artists' groups for mtgs & events; Single gallery on ground level having central entrance & two old storefront windows which provide window display space; Average Annual Attendance: 7,000; Mem: 350; dues $40-$80; meetings see website
Income: Financed by mem, dues, donations, art sales & rent
Exhibitions: Monthly exhibitions include individual, member shows & juried shows
Publications: Newsletter, bimonthly
Activities: Classes for adults & children, poetry readings; weekly figure drawing sessions & other artists groups; docent training; lects open to pub, 10 vis lectrs per year; gallery talks; concerts; sponsoring of competitions; scholarships offered

HOULTON

M **AROOSTOOK COUNTY HISTORICAL & ART MUSEUM,** 109 Main St, Houlton, ME 04730-2123. Tel 207-532-6687; Email houltonmuseum@yahoo.com; Web: houltonmuseum.wixsite.com/acham
Open Tues - Fri 1 PM - 4 PM or by appointment; Estab 1938 to preserve Aroostook County's history & artistic tradition
Special Subjects: Photography, Military Art
Collections: Artifacts, photographs & documents from the Ricker Classical Institute & Ricker College, items from from the Aroostook War, the Civil War, Spanish American War, World Wars I & II & the Korean War, including an antique gun collection, flags, uniforms & artifacts, Sarah Houlton Kitchen display, E. B. White Collection; photographs, Houlton Prisoner-of-War Camp
Exhibitions: Permanent exhibits; temporary exhibits

KENNEBUNK

M **BRICK STORE MUSEUM,** 117 Main St, Kennebunk, ME 04043-7088. Tel 207-985-4802; Email info@brickstoremuseum.org; Web: www.brickstoremusuem.org; *Registrar* Kathryn Hussey; *Exec Dir* Cynthia Walker; *Colls Mgr* Leanne Hayden; *Develop Coordr* Deborah Williams
Open Tues - Fri 10 AM - 4:30 PM, Sat 10 AM - 1 PM; Admis families $20, adult $7.50, senior $6, children $3; Estab 1936 to preserve & present history & art of southern Maine; Non-circulating reference library only; Average Annual Attendance: 5,500; Mem: 450; dues vary
Library Holdings: Audio Tapes, Book Volumes 4000, Cards, Clipping Files, Compact Disks, Exhibition Catalogs, Fiche, Filmstrips, Framed Reproductions, Manuscripts, Maps, Memorabilia, Original Art Works, Original Documents, Other Holdings Architectural drawings & plans, Pamphlets, Periodical Subscriptions, Photographs, Prints, Reels, Reproductions, Sculpture, Video Tapes
Special Subjects: Architecture, Bookplates & Bindings, Carpets & Rugs, Coins & Medals, Costumes, Decorative Arts, Dioramas, Dolls, Flasks & Bottles, Furniture, Glass, Historical Material, Laces, Landscapes, Maps, Marine Painting, Painting-American, Painting-Dutch, Porcelain, Portraits, Textiles, Sculpture
Collections: Art Library of Edith Cleaves Barry, Maritime - Kenneth Roberts, Booth Tarkington & Maine authors in general, Papers of Architect William E Barry, 40,000 items: photographs, documents, fine art & decorative arts, Abbott Graves paintings, John Brewster Jr paintings, William Badger paintings
Exhibitions: Permanent exhibs of furniture decorative arts; Collectors (2016); Medical History (2016)
Publications: Architectural Walking Tour Book
Activities: Docent training; classes for adults & children; history camp, architectural walking tours, field trips; lects open to pub, 10 vis lectrs per yr; concerts; tours; gallery talks; Edith Barry book award for excellence in art; Joyce Butler Book award for excellence in hist; individual paintings & original objects to other nonprofit mus; originate traveling exhibs to schools & senior citizen groups; mus shop sells books, reproductions

KINGFIELD

M **STANLEY MUSEUM, INC,** 40 School St, Kingfield, ME 04947; PO Box 77, Kingfield, ME 04947-0077. Tel 207-265-2729; Fax 207-265-4700; Email maine@stanleymuseum.org; Web: www.stanleymuseum.org; *Dir* Debbie Smith; *Archivist* Jim Merrick
Open Tues - Sun 1 - 4 PM May 1 - Oct 31, Tues - Fri 1 - 4 PM Nov 1 - Apr 30; Admis adults $4, children $2, seniors $3; Estab 1981; Average Annual Attendance: 3,000; Mem: 500; dues $45-$1,000; annual meeting in July
Income: $100,000 (financed by endowment, mem, donations & grants)
Library Holdings: Auction Catalogs, Clipping Files, Compact Disks, DVDs, Framed Reproductions, Lantern Slides, Memorabilia, Original Art Works, Original Documents, Photographs, Prints, Reproductions
Special Subjects: Photography, Drawings, Furniture, Painting-American
Collections: Chansonetta Stanley Emmons (photography, glass plate negatives), Raymond W Stanley Archives, Collection of Steam cars, photography & violins
Activities: Classes for adults & children in dramatic & docent progs; lects open to pub, 10 vis lectrs per yr; tours; awards, Stanley Mus Schol; original objects of art lent to other mus & galleries; mus shop sells books, magazines, reproductions, prints & gift items

LEWISTON

M **BATES COLLEGE,** Museum of Art, 75 Russell St, Olin Arts Ctr Lewiston, ME 04240-6044. Tel 207-786-6158; Fax 207-786-8335; Email museum@bates.edu; Web: www.bates.edu/museum; *Cur Coll* Bill Low; *Educ Cur* Anthony Shostak; *Dir* Dan Mills; *Educ Fellow* Catherine Jones; *Coll Manager* Curie Audette
Open Mon - Sat 10 AM - 5 PM, Mon & Wed until 7:30 PM during acad yr; cl major holidays; No admis fee; Estab in the Olin Arts Center, Oct 1986 to serve Bates College & the regional community; Average Annual Attendance: 25,000; Mem: Please see website
Special Subjects: Afro-American Art, Ceramics, Drawings, Etchings & Engravings, Oriental Art, Painting-American, Painting-British, Painting-French, Painting-Italian, Photography, Posters, Pre-Columbian Art, Prints, Sculpture
Collections: Marsden Hartley Memorial Collection, 19th & 20th Century American & European Collection, Modern & contemporary works on paper; photography; contemporary Chinese art, art about Maine by artists of nat & international significance
Exhibitions: Wenda Gu; Cryptozoology; Green Horizons
Publications: Documenting China: Contemporary Photography and Social Change; Cryptozoology; Robert Indiana; Charlie Hewitt; Starstruck: The Fine Art of Astrophotography; Xiaoze Xie: Amplified Moments; Tale Spinning
Activities: School progs; life drawing classes weekly; lects open to pub, 4-6 vis lectrs per yr; gallery talks; tours; loan to mus; organize traveling exhibs to college mus & acad galleries; mus shop sells books, film series

LIBERTY

M **DAVISTOWN MUSEUM,** Liberty Location, 58 Main St # 4, Liberty, ME 04949; PO Box 346, Liberty, ME 04949-0346. Tel 207-589-4900; Fax 207-589-4900; Email curator@davistownmuseum.org; Web: www.davistownmuseum.org; *Cur* HG Skip Brack; *Dir Educ* Judith Brown; *Technical Dir* Sett Balise; *Web & Office Mgr* Beth Sundberg
Open Mar - Dec 11 AM - 5 PM; always by appt; No admis fee, donations accepted; Regional tool, history & art mus located in Liberty Village, Maine; features colonial & 18th - 19th century hand tools; mus is forum for the work of local & regional artists
Library Holdings: Auction Catalogs, Book Volumes, Exhibition Catalogs, Original Art Works, Original Documents, Photographs, Prints, Sculpture
Special Subjects: Crafts, Furniture, Historical Material, Metalwork, Painting-American, Photography, Pottery, Sculpture
Collections: Extensive coll of 18th & 19th century tools, outdoor flower garden, contemporary Maine sculpture, sculpture garden exhibiting the work of over a dozen Maine artists on 2 1/2 acres of field, located at the Hulls Cove site
Publications: Hand Tools in History Series
Activities: Ann art exhib featuring local artists; mus shop sells books, original art, prints

MILLINOCKET

M **NORTH LIGHT GALLERY,** 256 Penobscot St, Millinocket, ME 04462-1510. Tel 207-723-4414; Email artnorthlight@gmail.com; Web: www.artnorthlight.com; *Founder* Marsha Donahue
Open Mon - Tues 9 AM - 5 PM, cl Wed through mid month & Sun; Estab 2004
Special Subjects: Prints, Crafts
Collections: Originals, prints & high-end crafts
Exhibitions: Rotating exhibits

MONHEGAN

M **MONHEGAN MUSEUM,** Monhegan Museum of Art & History, 1 Lighthouse Hill, Monhegan, ME 04852. Tel 207-596-7003; Email museum@monheganmuseum.org; Web: www.monheganmuseum.org; *Pres* Edward L Deci; *Cur Annual Exhibs* Emily Grey; *Chief Cur* Jennifer Pye
Open daily 11:30 AM - 3:30 PM (July-Aug), June 24 - 30 & Sept 1 - 30, 1:30 PM - 3:30 PM daily; Suggested donation $4; Estab 1968 to preserve the history of Monhegan Island; Housed in the historic Monhegan Island Light Station; Average Annual Attendance: 6,000; Mem: 300; dues $25-$1,000
Income: $170,000 (financed by endowment, mem, donations, rental, interest & fundraisers)
Special Subjects: Historical Material, Landscapes, Marine Painting, Painting-American, Period Rooms, Photography, Prints
Collections: Art, natural history, social history & fishing industry exhibits all related to Monhegan Island, Natural History, Social History
Activities: Mus shop sells books, reproductions & prints

NEW GLOUCESTER

M **UNITED SOCIETY OF SHAKERS,** Shaker Museum, 707 Shaker Rd, New Gloucester, ME 04260-2652. Tel 207-926-4597; Email usshakers@aol.com; Web: www.shaker.lib.me.us; *Dir & Cur* Michael S Graham; *Librn/Archivist* Charles Rand

Open Mon - Sat 10 AM - 4:30 PM Memorial Day - Columbus Day; Admis for tours; adults $10, children 6-12 yrs $2, under 6 free with adult; Estab 1931, incorporated 1971, to preserve for educational & cultural purposes Shaker artifacts, publications, manuscripts & works of art; to provide facilities for educational & cultural activities in connection with the preservation of the Shaker tradition; to provide a place of study & research for students of history & religion; 4 historic bldgs
Library Holdings: Auction Catalogs, Audio Tapes, Book Volumes, Cassettes, Clipping Files, DVDs, Exhibition Catalogs, Kodachrome Transparencies, Lantern Slides, Manuscripts, Maps, Memorabilia, Motion Pictures, Original Art Works, Original Documents, Pamphlets, Photographs, Prints, Records, Slides, Video Tapes
Special Subjects: Architecture, Ceramics, Coins & Medals, Costumes, Crafts, Decorative Arts, Dolls, Drawings, Embroidery, Folk Art, Glass, Historical Material, Historical Material, Landscapes, Leather, Manuscripts, Maps, Miniatures, Period Rooms, Pewter, Photography, Porcelain, Portraits, Posters, Pottery, Prints, Religious Art, Textiles, Watercolors, Flasks & Bottles
Collections: Drawings & paintings by Shaker artists, Shaker textiles, community industries, furniture, manuscripts, metal & wooden ware, Radical Christian; herbal collection
Exhibitions: Creating Chosen Land (architectural history)
Publications: The Shaker Quarterly, annual
Activities: Classes for adults; workshops in summer for herb dyeing, oval box making, cultivating, weaving, spinning, photography, baskets; lects open to pub; concerts; tours; individual paintings & original objects of art lent to institutions mounting exhibs; originate traveling exhibs; mus shop sells books, magazines, prints, slides, herbs produced in the community, yarn from flock, woven items

L **The Shaker Library**, 707 Shaker Rd, New Gloucester, ME 04260-2652. Tel 207-926-4597; Email brooksl@shaker.lib.me.us; Web: www.shaker.lib.me.us; *Dir & Cur* Michael Graham; *Archivist & Librn* Charles E Rand
Open Mon - Thurs 8:30AM-4:30PM, appointments required; Estab 1882; For reference only
Library Holdings: Audio Tapes, Book Volumes 12,000, Cassettes, Clipping Files, Exhibition Catalogs, Filmstrips, Kodachrome Transparencies, Manuscripts, Maps, Micro Print 317, Motion Pictures, Original Art Works, Original Documents, Other Holdings Ephemera, Periodical Subscriptions 57, Photographs, Prints, Records, Reels 353, Slides, Video Tapes
Special Subjects: Architecture, Crafts, Folk Art, Furniture, Historical Material, History of Art & Archaeology, Manuscripts, Maps, Mixed Media, Photography, Posters, Textiles, Video, Woodcuts, Archaeology, Period Rooms
Collections: Shaker, Radical Christian
Publications: The Shaker Quarterly
Activities: Classes for adults & children; lects open to public; concerts

OAKLAND

M **MACARTNEY HOUSE MUSEUM,** 25 Main St, Oakland, ME 04963; Oakland Area Historical Society, PO Box 59 Oakland, ME 04963-0059. Tel 207-465-7549; Email meporters@myfairpoint.net; Web: www.rootsweb.ancestry.com; *Pres* Alberta Porter; *Vol Treas* Richard Lord; *Cur* Ruth W Wood
Open Jun - Aug Wed 1:30 - 4:30 PM; No admis fee, donations accepted; Estab 1979; Historical period home specializing in Oakland area history. Pvt nonprofit org; Mem: dues Life $50, Family $7.50, Indiv $5
Activities: Classes for children; tours

OGUNQUIT

M **BARN GALLERY,** Shore Rd & Bourne Ln, Ogunquit, ME 03907; PO Box 794, Ogunquit, ME 03907-0529. Tel 207-646-8400; Email oacbarngallery@gmail.com; Web: www.barngallery.org; *Pres* Deirdre O'Flaherty; *Treas* Nancy R Davison; *Gallery Mgr* Hana Harding
Open Mon - Sat 11 AM - 5 PM, Sun late May - Columbus Day 1 - 5 PM; No admis fee except for auction, workshops & concerts; Estab 1959 to exhibit the finest local art; Not for profit artist run educ & sales gallery; Average Annual Attendance: 6,500; Mem: Juried artist & patron mem (see website)
Income: Financed by donations, grants & management fees
Exhibitions: Four sets of exhibs by mems of Ogunquit art assoc per season
Publications: Printed catalogs; checklists
Activities: Classes for adults; lects open to pub; gallery talks

M **OGUNQUIT MUSEUM OF AMERICAN ART,** 543 Shore Rd, Ogunquit, ME 03907-0815; PO Box 815, Ogunquit, ME 03907-0815. Tel 207-646-4909; Fax 207-646-6903; Email ogunquitmuseum@aol.com; Web: www.ogunquitmuseum.org; *Dir & Cur* Michael Culver
Open May-Oct 31, Daily 10am-5pm; Admis adults $10, sr citizens $9, students $9, children under 12 free; Estab 1953 to exhibit, collect & preserve American art; Museum consists of five interior galleries with 6000 sq ft; central gallery provides an expansive view of the Atlantic Ocean & the rockbound coast; outdoor sculpture garden; Average Annual Attendance: 16,000; Mem: 600; dues Directors Circle from $10,000, benefactor $5000, Stakeholder $2500, partner's circle $1000, sustainer $500, supporter $250, assoc $150, household $75, individual $50
Income: Financed by endowment, mem, donations
Purchases: works by Will Barnet, Gertrude Fiske, Robert Henri, Winslow Homer, Edward Hopper, Jack Levine, Fairfield Porter
Library Holdings: Exhibition Catalogs, Original Documents, Photographs, Slides, Video Tapes
Special Subjects: Drawings, Painting-American, Sculpture
Collections: Paintings, drawings & sculpture by 20th Century contemporary Americans, including Marsh, Burchfield, Hartley, Lachaise, Tobey, Kuhn, Strater, Graves, Levine & Marin
Publications: Exhibition catalog, annually; Museum Bulletin
Activities: Educ dept; docent training; lects open to pub, 8 vis lectrs per yr; gallery talks; tours; concerts; individual paintings & original objects of art lent to other mus; lending collection contains 2,000+ original art works; originate traveling exhibs; mus shop sells books, magazines, original art, reproduction prints, posters, postcards, museum catalogs & art books

L **Reference Library**, 543 Shore Rd, Ogunquit, ME 03907; PO Box 815, Ogunquit, ME 03907-0815. Tel 207-646-4909; Fax 207-646-6903; Email ogunquitmuseum@aol.com; Web: ogunquitmuseum.org; *Dir & Cur* Michael Culver; *Bd Pres* Timothy Ellis
Open July - Oct 31, Mon - Sat 10:30 AM - 5 PM, Sun 2 - 5 PM; Admis adults $5, seniors $4, students $3; Estab 1953; For reference only; Average Annual Attendance: 13,000; Mem: 780, dues $30 - $5,000
Income: financed by endowments, memberships, donations
Library Holdings: Book Volumes 400, Clipping Files, Exhibition Catalogs, Manuscripts, Memorabilia, Pamphlets, Photographs, Reproductions
Activities: Docent training; lects open to pub, 6 vis lectrs per yr; concerts; gallery talks; tours; mus shop sells books, reproductions & prints

PEMAQUID POINT

A **PEMAQUID GROUP OF ARTISTS,** Pemaquid Art Gallery, Lighthouse Park, Pemaquid Point, ME; 1311 Bristol Rd, c/o Barbara Applegate Bristol, ME 04539. Tel 207-677-2752; Email pjsfarrell@gmail.com; Web: www.pemaquidartgallery.com; *Pres* Sally Loughridge; *Vice Pres* Jan Kilburn; *Secy* Peggy Farrell; *Treas* Barbara Applegate
Open daily 10 AM - 5 PM; No admis fee; $2 to enter Pemaquid Lighthouse Park; Estab 1929 to exhibit & sell paintings, sculpture, carvings by members & to give scholarships & passes to Portland Museum of Art, Maine; Maintains an art gallery, open Jun - Oct; Average Annual Attendance: 10,000; Mem: 26; must be residents of the Bristol Peninsula, Damariscotta or Newcastle & pass jury; dues $80; annual meeting in Oct
Income: Financed by dues, patrons, commissions on paintings & sculpture
Purchases: Office equipment
Exhibitions: Summer members exhibition
Activities: Schols offered; gallery sells original art

PORTLAND

L **MAINE COLLEGE OF ART,** Joanne Waxman Library, 522 Congress St, Portland, ME 04101-3378. Tel 207-775-5153; Fax 207-772-5069; Email library@meca.edu; Web: http://meca.edu/library; *Library Dir* Shiva Darbandi; *Library Assit* Amy Shinn; *Library Asst* Linda Smallwood
Open by appointment; Estab 1973, to support the curriculum & serve the needs of students & faculty; Circ 340; circulation 12,000; Lending library; Mem: Membership fee for non-MECA $50 per yr; patrons over 65 $25 per yr
Library Holdings: Book Volumes 42,000, CD-ROMs, Compact Disks, DVDs 480, Exhibition Catalogs, Original Art Works 25, Other Holdings Ephemera Files, Pamphlets, Periodical Subscriptions 103
Special Subjects: Advertising Design, Aesthetics, Afro-American Art, American Indian Art, American Western Art, Anthropology, Archaeology, Architecture, Art Education, Art History, Asian Art, Bookplates & Bindings, Bronzes, Calligraphy, Cartoons, Ceramics, Collages, Commercial Art, Conceptual Art, Constructions, Costume Design & Constr, Crafts, Decorative Arts, Display, Drafting, Drawings, Embroidery, Enamels, Eskimo Art, Etchings & Engravings, Ethnology, Fashion Arts, Film, Folk Art, Furniture, Glass, Gold, Goldsmithing, Graphic Arts, Graphic Design, Handicrafts, History of Art & Archaeology, Illustration, Intermedia, Islamic Art, Ivory, Jade, Jewelry, Landscape Architecture, Landscapes, Latin American Art, Lettering, Manuscripts, Maps, Marine Painting, Metalwork, Mexican Art, Mixed Media, Mosaics, Oriental Art, Painting-American, Painting-Australian, Painting-British, Painting-Canadian, Painting-Dutch, Painting-European, Painting-Flemish, Painting-French, Painting-German, Painting-Italian, Painting-Japanese, Painting-Polish, Painting-Russian, Painting-Scandinavian, Painting-Spanish, Pewter, Photography, Porcelain, Portraits, Posters, Pottery, Pre-Columbian Art, Primitive art, Printmaking, Prints, Religious Art, Sculpture, Silversmithing, Southwestern Art, Stained Glass, Tapestries, Textiles, Watercolors, Woodcarvings, Woodcuts
Collections: 42,000 titles, special coll of rare books & artist books

M **The Institute of Contemporary Art**, 522 Congress St, Portland, ME 04101. Tel 207-699-5029; Email ica@meca.edu; Web: www.meca.edu/ica; *Dir* Erin Hutton; *Exhibs Coord* Nikki Rayburn
Open Wed & Sun 11 AM - 5 PM, Thurs 11 AM - 7 PM, Fri 11 AM - 5 PM; No admis fee; Gallery estab 1983 to present temporary exhibs of contemporary art & design; Newly renovated 3300 sq ft gallery located on first floor of Beaux Arts building; Average Annual Attendance: 20,000
Income: $38,700
Special Subjects: African Art, Conceptual Art, Sculpture, Painting-American, Photography, Prints
Collections: Contemporary Art-National & International, Video
Publications: Exhibition catalogues, 2 yearly
Activities: Tours of exhibitions; classes for children; docent training; lects open to pub; 6 vis lectrs per yr; gallery talks; tours; Originates traveling exhibs

A **MAINE HISTORICAL SOCIETY,** 489 Congress St, Portland, ME 04101-3414. Tel 207-774-1822; Fax 207-775-4301; Email info@mainehistory.org; Web: www.mainehistory.org, www.mainememory.net; *Exec Dir* Stephen Bromage; *Chief Cur* Kate McBrien; *Cur Library Colls* Nicholas Noyes; *Dir Digital Engagement* Kathy Amoroso
Admis charged; Estab 1822 to collect, preserve & teach the history of Maine; the Soc owns & operates a historical research library & the Wadsworth - Longfellow House of 1785; Average Annual Attendance: 15,000; Mem: 2,700; dues $15 & up; annual meeting in May or June
Income: Donations, admis, dues
Library Holdings: Manuscripts, Maps, Original Documents, Other Holdings, Pamphlets, Periodical Subscriptions, Photographs, Prints
Special Subjects: Historical Material
Collections: Architecture, books archival, material culture, photographs, special coll-prints
Exhibitions: Changing exhibs on Maine history
Publications: Maine Historical Society, quarterly; tri-annual monograph

Activities: Classes for adults; docent training; lects open to pub, 4 vis lectrs per yr; gallery talks; tours; individual paintings & original objects of art lent; mus shop sells books, reproductions & prints

M **Wadsworth-Longfellow House**, 489 Congress St, Portland, ME 04101. Tel 207-774-1822; Fax 207-775-4301; Email info@mainehistory.org; Web: www.mainehistory.org; *Exec Dir* Steve Bromage
Open May - Oct Mon - Sat 10:30 AM - 4 PM, Sun noon - 4 PM; Admis adults $15, seniors and students $6, children (6-17) $3, children under 5 & mem free; Average Annual Attendance: 19,000; Mem: Part of the society
Income: Financed by donations, admis, dues & endowment income
Library Holdings: Manuscripts, Maps, Original Documents, Periodical Subscriptions, Photographs
Special Subjects: Architecture, Ceramics, Costumes, Decorative Arts, Embroidery, Furniture, Landscapes, Manuscripts, Miniatures, Period Rooms
Collections: Maine furniture, glass, historic artifacts, paintings, photographs, pottery, prints, textiles, Maine artists, Maine portraits, seascapes
Publications: Quarterly, spec publs
Activities: Classes for adults; docent training; lects open to pub; individual paintings & original objects of art lent to mus; mus shop sells books, reproductions, prints

L **Library and Museum**, 489 Congress St, Portland, ME 04101. Tel 207-774-1822; Fax 207-775-4301; Email info@mainehistory.org; Web: www.mainehistory.org; *Reference Historian* William D Barry; *Archivist & Cataloger* Nancy Noble; *Cur Library Colls* Nicholas Noyes; *Dir Library Servs* Jamie K Rice; *Mus Cur* Kate McBrien
Open Tues - Sat 10 AM - 4 PM; Admis $10; Estab 1822; Circ Non-circ; For reference only; Average Annual Attendance: 5,500; Mem: 2,500
Income: Part of society
Library Holdings: Auction Catalogs, Audio Tapes, Book Volumes 100,000, CD-ROMs, Cards, Cassettes, Clipping Files, Compact Disks, Exhibition Catalogs, Fiche, Lantern Slides, Manuscripts 2,000,000, Maps 5,000, Memorabilia, Motion Pictures, Original Art Works, Original Documents, Other Holdings, Pamphlets, Periodical Subscriptions, Photographs, Prints, Reels, Sculpture, Slides
Special Subjects: American Indian Art, Architecture, Cartoons, Costume Design & Constr, Decorative Arts, Folk Art, Goldsmithing, Graphic Arts, Historical Material, Interior Design, Marine Painting, Miniatures, Painting-American, Photography, Printmaking
Publications: Maine History Society Newsletter
Activities: Classes for adults & children; docent training; lects open to pub; 3-5 vis lectrs per yr; gallery talks; tours; fellowships; Baxter Award; Ring Award; NW Allen Award; Maine statewide; mus shop sells books, reproductions & prints

M **MHS Museum**, 489 Congress St, Portland, ME 04101. Tel 207-774-1822; Fax 207-775-4301; Email info@mainehistory.org; Web: www.mainehistory.org; *Exec Dir* Steve Bromage
Open May - Oct, daily 10 AM - 5 PM; winter hours Mon-Sat 10 AM - 5 PM, Sun noon - 5 PM; Admis adults $8; students & seniors $7; children 6-17 & under $2,; Estab 1822 to preserve & promote the understanding of Maine history; Changing exhibitions; one or two exhibitions at a time; Average Annual Attendance: 17,000; Mem: 2,500; dues $40; annual meeting in the Spring
Income: Mem, donations, grants, admissions
Library Holdings: Book Volumes, Fiche, Manuscripts, Maps, Memorabilia, Original Art Works, Original Documents, Pamphlets, Periodical Subscriptions, Photographs
Special Subjects: Archaeology, Costumes, Decorative Arts, Folk Art, Historical Material, Painting-American, Glass
Collections: Archaeological artifacts, costumes, decorative arts, folk art, history artifacts, paintings, books, manuscripts, maps, photos
Exhibitions: Rotating 1-2 times per yr
Publications: Maine History, qtr
Activities: Classes for adults & children; docent training; lects open to pub, 5 vis lectrs per yr, gallery talks; tours; individual paintings & original objects of art lent to other mus & historical societies; lending collection contains original art works, books, photographs, slides, paintings & sculptures; book traveling exhibs; originate traveling exhibs; mus shop sells books, reproductions & prints

M **PORTLAND MUSEUM OF ART,** 7 Congress Sq, Portland, ME 04101-1119. Tel 207-775-6148; Fax 207-773-7324; Email info@portlandmuseum.org; Web: www.portlandmuseum.org; *Chief Cur* Jessica May; *Registrar* Erin Damon; *Deputy Dir & CFO* Elena Henry; *Dir* Mark Bessire
Open Mon - Wed 10 AM - 6 PM, Thurs - Fri 10 AM - 8 PM, Sat-Sun 10 AM - 6 PM; Admis adults $15, sr citizens $13, students $10, youth 14 & under free; Estab 1882 as a non-profit educational institution based on the visual arts & critical excellence; The Museum includes the McLellan-Sweat House, built in 1800, a Registered National Historic Landmark; the LDM Sweat Memorial Galleries, built in 1911; & the Charles Shipman Payson Building, built in 1983, designed by Henry N Cobb. This building is named for Mr Charles Shipman Payson, whose gift of 17 Winslow Homer paintings spurred expansion; Average Annual Attendance: 150,000; Mem: 9,000; dues $50+
Income: $6,000,000 (financed by endowment, mem, private & corporate donations, grants from national, state & municipal organizations)
Special Subjects: Decorative Arts, Glass, Painting-American, Painting-European, Prints, Sculpture
Collections: 19th & 20th century American & European paintings, neo-classic American sculpture, contemporary prints, State of Maine Collection of artists assoc with Maine including Winslow Homer, Andrew Wyeth & Marsden Hartley, American decorative arts of the Federal period, American glass
Exhibitions: Visit website
Publications: Mem mag, monthly; exhibition catalogs; general information brochure
Activities: Classes for adults & children; docent training; lects open to pub; lects for mems only; tours; gallery talks; concerts; films; competitions; members' openings of exhibs; mus shop sells books, reproductions, prints, posters, cards, jewelry, gifts & items by Maine artists & artisans

L **PORTLAND PUBLIC LIBRARY,** Art - Audiovisual Dept, 5 Monument Sq, Portland, ME 04101-4072. Tel 207-871-1700; Fax 207-871-1703; Email reference@portlandpubliclibrary.org; Web: www.portlandlibrary.com; *Dir* Sarah Campbell; *Art & AV Librn* Tom Wilsbach; *AV Mgr* Patti Delois
Open Mon - Thurs 10 AM - 7 PM, Fri 10 AM - 6 PM, Sat 10 AM - 5 PM; Estab 1867 as the public library for city of Portland; Circ 51,700
Income: Financed by endowment, city & state appropriation
Purchases: $32,000
Library Holdings: Book Volumes 18,000, Compact Disks, DVDs, Exhibition Catalogs, Fiche, Motion Pictures, Original Art Works, Pamphlets, Periodical Subscriptions 35, Records, Sculpture, Video Tapes
Collections: Costume Book Collection, Maine Sheet Music, Press Books - Anthoensen Press, Mosher Press, The Drummond Collection of Opera
Exhibitions: Monthly exhibits concentrating on Portland & Maine artists
Activities: Lects open to pub

M **UNIVERSITY OF NEW ENGLAND,** Art Gallery, 716 Stevens Ave, Portland, ME 04103-2693. Tel 207-221-4499; Fax 207-523-1901; Email azill@une.edu; Web: www.une.edu/artgallery; *Dir* Anne B Zill
Open Wed & Fri - Sun Noon - 5 PM, Thurs Noon - 7 PM; Estab 1976; Mem: Dues $15 - $1,000
Special Subjects: Painting-American, Photography, Drawings
Collections: 19th century oils & primitives, contemporary art, bronze plaques, fine photography
Exhibitions: Permanent & temporary exhibits
Activities: Educ progs; artist workshops; lects open to pub; gallery talks; tours; art programming; conferences; workshops

M **VICTORIA MANSION - MORSE LIBBY HOUSE,** 109 Danforth St, Portland, ME 04101-4504. Tel 207-772-4841; Fax 207-772-6290; Email information@victoriamansion.org; Web: www.victoriamansion.org; *Dir* Thomas B Johnson; *Cur* Arlene Palmer Schwind
Open Nov 24 - Jan 7 daily 11 AM - 4:30 PM, Mon until 6:30; May 1 - Oct 31 Sat 10 AM - 3:45 PM, Sun 1 - 4 PM; Admis adults $16, seniors $14, students, $7, children 6-17 $5, under 6 free; Estab 1941 Italian Villa, Victorian Period architecture built by Henry Austin of New Haven, Connecticut in 1858-1860; interiors by Gustav Herter; Average Annual Attendance: 20,000; Mem: 360; dues $35; annual meeting in Apr
Income: $480,000 (financed by endowment, mem, grants & contributions
Library Holdings: Manuscripts, Memorabilia, Original Documents, Photographs, Slides
Special Subjects: Architecture, Carpets & Rugs, Ceramics, Decorative Arts, Furniture, Glass, Historical Material, Manuscripts, Painting-American, Period Rooms, Photography, Porcelain, Portraits, Restorations, Sculpture, Stained Glass, Textiles, Silver
Collections: Mid 19th Century Decorative Arts (luxury) & Architecture, Original Interior-Exterior & Original Furnishings, Gifts of the Victorian Period, Porcelain tableware
Exhibitions: Christmas Opening Exhibition
Activities: Docent training; lects open to pub, 2-4 vis lectrs per yr; tours; mus shop sells books, original art, reproductions, jewelry, textiles, stationary, &Victorian style gifts

PRESQUE ISLE

M **NORTHERN MAINE MUSEUM OF SCIENCE,** 181 Main St, University of Maine at Presque Isle Presque Isle, ME 04769. Tel 207-768-9482; Web: www.umpi.maine.edu/info/nmms/museum.htm; *Dir* Kevin McCartney, PhD; *Cur Chemistry* Michael Knopp, PhD; *Cur Herbarium* Robert J Pinette, PhD; *Cur Colls* Jeanie McGowan; *Cur Outdoor Areas* Chad Loder; *Cur Mathematics* Richard Rand, PhD; *Cur Mathematics* Richard Kimball; *Asst Cur Mathematics* Frank Kitteredge; *Asst Cur Physics* Alan Dearborn; *Asst Cur Entomology* Beth Taylor; *Cur Colls (Emeritus)* Earl Oman; *Asst Cur Agriculture (Emeritus)* Alvin Reeves, PhD
Mus mission is to support science educ in northern Maine by means of exhibs & progs for educators & students
Special Subjects: Anthropology, Archaeology
Collections: The Maine Solar System Model built by the People of Aroostook County, Maine, whale vertebrae & jawbone, dinosaur & miscellaneous animal & insect models, meteorology station, Coral Reef exhib & mural, mineral & rock exhibs
Activities: Tours; Library of Traveling Trunks; Campus Nature Trail

RANGELEY

M **RANGELEY LAKES REGION LOGGING MUSEUM,** PO Box 154, Rangeley, ME 04970-0154; 221 Stratton Rd, Rangeley, ME 04970. Tel 207-864-5595; Email myocom@gmu.edu; Web: http://mason.gmu.edu/~myocom; *Vol Mus Folklorist, Cur & Archivist* Dr Margaret Yocom; *Vol Pres & Dir* Rodney C Richard Sr; *Festival Coordr* Stephen A Richard; *Vol Treas* Laura Haley; *Vol Secy* Lucille Richard
Open Jul - Labor Day Sat & Sun 11 AM - 2 PM; No admis fee, donations accepted; Estab 1979; mus preserves & celebrates the heritage of logging in the western mountains of Maine; collects & displays artifacts that speak of the history & folklife of logging; Average Annual Attendance: under 500 by estimate; Mem: dues Indiv $5
Special Subjects: Folk Art, Historical Material
Collections: Tools & equipment for logging; folk culture; paintings; photographs; letters; journals; botanicals (nonliving); quilts; knitting; woodcarvings
Publications: Logging in the Maine Woods: The Paintings of Alden Grant, book by Yocom; Working the Woods, book by Yocom & Mundell
Activities: 2-day logging festival; Craft Show & Sale; Auction; lects; group visits; mus related items for sale

ROCKLAND

M **WILLIAM A FARNSWORTH LIBRARY & ART MUSEUM,** Museum, 16 Museum St, Rockland, ME 04841-2867. Tel 207-596-6457; Fax 207-596-0509;

Email writeus@farnsworthmuseum.org; Web: www.farnsworthmuseum.org; *Dir* Christopher B Crosman; *Assoc Dir* Victoria Woodhull; *Coll Cur* Helen Ashton Fisher
Open Summer: daily, 10AM - 5PM, Wed until 8 PM; Winter: Wed -Sun 10AM - 5PM, cl Mon & Tues; Admis Rockland Campus: $12, seniors & students 17 & older $10, Rockland Campus & Olson House: $17, seniors & students 17 & older $15, Olson House only $10, seniors & students 17 & older $8; Estab 1948 to house, preserve & exhibit American art; Twelve galleries house permanent & changing exhibitions; Average Annual Attendance: 79,000; Mem: 2500; dues $50 individual, $75 dual
Income: Financed by pvt donations, grants, dues
Special Subjects: Decorative Arts, Painting-American, Painting-European
Collections: American Art, two historic houses; emphasis on Maine art; works on paper; prints; sculpture; photography; decorative artifacts; manuscripts
Publications: Exhibition catalogs & brochures 6-8 per year; quarterly newsletter for members
Activities: Classes for adults & children; docent training; interactive computer progs; lects open to pub, 6-10 vis lectrs per yr; concerts; gallery talks; tours; films; outreach progs; scholarships; individual paintings & original objects of art lent to other mus & galleries; originate traveling exhibs; mus shop sell books, reproductions, notecards, educational toys & contemporary design objects; Julia's Gallery for Young Artists

L **Library**, 16 Museum St Rockland, ME 04841-2867. Tel 207-596-6457; Fax 207-596-0509; Email farnsworth@midcoast.com; Web: www.farnesworthmuseumart.org; *Dir* Christopher B Crosman; *Assoc Dir* Victoria Woodhull; *Cur 19th & 20th Century* Pamela Belanger; *Coll Cur* Helen Ashton Fisher
Open Summer: daily, 10-5; Winter: Tues-Sun 10-5; please call for shoulder season hours; Admis $9 gen, Rockland res, mems, 17 & younger free; Estab 1948; Circ non-circulating; Art reference only. Archives on American artists, including papers of Louise Nevelson, Andrew Wyeth, N C Wyeth, George Bellows, Robert Indiana & Waldo Peirce; Average Annual Attendance: 75,000; Mem: 2,500 - Dues $50 individual, $75 dual
Income: Income from pvt donations, grants, dues
Library Holdings: Auction Catalogs, Audio Tapes, Book Volumes 4000, Clipping Files, Exhibition Catalogs, Kodachrome Transparencies, Manuscripts, Maps, Memorabilia, Motion Pictures, Original Art Works, Other Holdings American artists' file, Pamphlets, Periodical Subscriptions 13, Photographs, Prints, Sculpture, Slides, Video Tapes
Special Subjects: Art History, Etchings & Engravings, Folk Art, Marine Painting, Painting-American, Printmaking, Prints, Watercolors
Collections: American art with an emphasis on Maine Art, paintings, works on paper, prints, sculpture, photography, decorative arts, artifacts & manuscripts, N.C., Andrew, James Wyeth
Publications: Maine in America: American Art at the Farnsworth Museum
Activities: Classes for adults & children; docent training; interactive computer progs; lects open to pub; 6-10 vis lectrs per yr; concerts; gallery talks; tours; scholarships offered; exten progs to Maine schools statewide; originate traveling exhibs; mus shop sells books, reproductions; Julia's Gallery for Young Artists

ROCKPORT

A **CMCA-CENTER FOR MAINE CONTEMPORARY ART,** Art Gallery, 162 Russell Ave, Rockport, ME 04856; PO Box 1767, Rockland, ME 04841-1767. Tel 207-236-2875; Fax 207-236-2490; Email info@cmcnow.org; Web: www.cmcanow.org; *Dir* Suzette McAvoy; *Operations & Communs Mgr* Paula Blanchard; *Admin Asst* Jean Thompson
Open Tues - Sat 10 AM - 5 PM, Sun 1 PM - 5 PM May to Dec; Admis free to mems, suggested donation $5; 1952; to advance contemporary art in Maine through exhibitions & educational programs; Gallery building was an old livery stable & fire station overlooking Rockport Harbor; Average Annual Attendance: 15,000; Mem: 500; dues $30-$50; annual meeting in April
Income: Financed by mem, contributions, grants, an art auction, craft sale & gallery shop
Exhibitions: Seasonal: varied exhibitions of contemporary Maine art; Annual Juried Craft Fair; Biennial Juried Exhibition
Publications: Email newsletter; exhibition catalogues; brochures
Activities: Art lab classes for adults & children; professional develop for artists; lects open to pub; 3-6 lects per yr; films; concerts; gallery talks; tours; mus shop sells books, original art, prints, gift merchandise

A **ROCKPORT COLLEGE,** Maine Photographic Workshops, PO Box 200, Rockport, ME 04856-0200. Tel 207-236-8519; Fax 207-236-2558; Email info@theworkshops.com; *Founder & Dir* David H Lyman
Open Mon - Sun 9 AM - 5 PM & 7 - 9 PM June - Aug; Admis lectures $3; Estab 1973 as photographic center; Contains four separate spaces for the display of vintage & contemporary photographers; Average Annual Attendance: 10,000; Mem: 1,400; dues $20; annual meetings Nov
Income: $2,000,000 (financed by mem, tuitions, sales & accommodations)
Special Subjects: Prints
Collections: Eastern Illustrating Archive containing 100,000 vintage glass plates, The Kosti Ruohomaa Collection, prints of Life photographers, Master Work Collection, Paul Caponigro Archive
Exhibitions: Forty photographic exhibitions
Publications: The Work Print, bi-monthly newsletter; Catalogues - Programs, semi-annual
Activities: Classes for adults & children; dramatic progs; lects open to pub, 50 vis lectrs per yr; competitions with awards; schols offered; lending collection contains photographs; book traveling exhibs; originate traveling exhibs; sales shop sells books, magazines, original art, reproductions, prints, photographic equipment & supplies

L **Carter-Haas Library**, PO Box 200, Union Hall Rockport, ME 04856-0200. Tel 207-236-8314; Fax 207-236-2558; Email library@theworkshops.com; *Library Mgr* Rachel Jones
Open Mon - Wed 1 - 10 PM, Thurs 10 AM - 3 PM; Estab 1975 to support student studies
Purchases: $5,000
Library Holdings: Audio Tapes, Book Volumes 6,500, Cards, Cassettes, Clipping Files, Exhibition Catalogs, Filmstrips, Framed Reproductions, Kodachrome Transparencies, Lantern Slides, Memorabilia, Micro Print, Motion Pictures, Original Art Works, Pamphlets, Periodical Subscriptions 45, Photographs, Records, Reproductions, Slides, Video Tapes
Special Subjects: Film, Photography
Activities: Schols offered

SACO

M **SACO MUSEUM,** (York Institute Museum), 371 Main St, Saco, ME 04072-1520. Tel 207-283-3861; Fax 207-283-0754; Email traiselis@sacomuseum.org; Web: www.sacomuseum.org; *Coll Mgr* Carolyn Parsons Roy; *Educ & Pro Mgr* Zoe B Thomas; *Mus Dir* Tara Raiselis
Open Tues, Wed, Thurs noon-4PM, Fri noon-8PM, Sat 10AM-4PM, Sun June-Dec only noon-4PM; Admis adults $5, seniors $3, students & groups $2; Estab 1866 as a museum of regional history & culture; Permanent collections feature Maine furniture, decorative arts & paintings. Special exhibitions on regional art, social history & student art; Average Annual Attendance: 10,000
Income: Financed by endowment, private & corporate contributions, federal, state & municipal support
Special Subjects: Archaeology, Architecture, Ceramics, Coins & Medals, Costumes, Decorative Arts, Dolls, Folk Art, Furniture, Glass, Landscapes, Manuscripts, Maps, Metalwork, Miniatures, Painting-American, Period Rooms, Pewter, Photography, Porcelain, Portraits, Sculpture, Silver, Textiles, Watercolors
Collections: Federal period Maine books, ceramics, decorative arts, glass, manuscripts, maps, natural history paintings, pewter, sculpture, silver
Publications: Saco Revisited, Arcadia Publishing, 2010; I My Needle Ply with Skill: Main schoolgirl needlework of the Federal Era, 2013; From the Elegant to the Everyday: 200 yrs of fashion in northern New England 2014
Activities: Classes for adults & children; art workshops; dramatic progs; docent training; lects open to pub, 1-2 vis lectrs per month; concerts; gallery talks; historic walking tours; house tour; individual paintings & original objects of art lent to other mus; mus shop sells books

SEARSPORT

M **PENOBSCOT MARINE MUSEUM,** 40 E Main St, Searsport, ME 04974-3351; PO Box 498, Searsport, ME 04974-0498. Tel 207-548-2529, store 548-0334; Fax 207-548-2520; Email museumoffices@pmm-maine.org; Web: www.penobscotmarinemuseum.org; *Exec Dir* Liz Lodge
Open Memorial Day weekend - mid Oct, Mon - Sat 10 AM - 5 PM, Sun Noon - 5 PM; Admis adults $12, seniors (65+) $10, youth 7-15 $8, 6 & under free; Estab 1936 as a memorial to the maritime record of present & former residents of the State of Maine in shipbuilding, shipping & all maritime affairs; The Museum consists of eight historic buildings, including the Old Town Hall (1845), Nickels-Colcord Duncan House (1880); Fowler True Ross House (1825); Cap Merithew House; Dutch House; two new buildings: Stephen Phillips' Memorial Library (1983) & Douglas & Margaret Carver Memorial Art Gallery (1986) & Educ Center; Average Annual Attendance: 15,000; Mem: 800; dues $45 & up
Income: Financed by endowment, mem, grant, gifts & admis
Special Subjects: Historical Material, Period Rooms, Photography, Porcelain, Scrimshaw, Marine Painting
Collections: Marine Artifacts, China Trade Exports, paintings & prints, Ship Models, small water craft, decorative arts, ceramics, glass, textiles & extensive archives, photography archives
Exhibitions: Permanent exhibit: Marine Painting of Thomas & James Buttersworth; Working the Bay; Gone Fishing: Maine's Sea Fisheries
Publications: Searsport Sea Captains, 1989; Lace & Leaves: The Art of Dolly Smith, 1994 (exhibit catalogue); annual report; newsletter, 3 times per year
Activities: Classes for adults & children; docent training; maritime-based literacy curriculum; lects open to pub; awards: accredited; AAM; scholarships offered; individual paintings & original objects of art lent to other institutions in accordance with museum policies; originate traveling exhibs; sales shop sells Marine books, magazines, original art & reproductions & prints

L **Stephen Phillips Memorial Library**, 11 Church St, PO Box 498 Searsport, ME 04974-0498. Tel 207-548-2529; Fax 207-548-2520; Email cgood@pmm-maine.org; Web: www.penobscotmarinemuseum.org; *Colls Mgr* Cipperly Good
Open by appointment; No admis fee; Estab 1936 to support research at Penobscot Marine Museum and to serve the public; Open for reference to researchers; Average Annual Attendance: 1,050; Mem: 1,000; dues $20 and up
Library Holdings: Audio Tapes, Book Volumes 12,000, Cassettes, Clipping Files, Compact Disks, DVDs, Exhibition Catalogs, Fiche, Filmstrips, Manuscripts, Maps 3,000, Memorabilia, Motion Pictures, Original Art Works, Original Documents, Other Holdings Nautical charts, Pamphlets, Periodical Subscriptions 40, Photographs 60,000, Prints, Records, Reels, Slides, Video Tapes
Special Subjects: Maps, Marine Painting, Photography, Scrimshaw, Painting-American, Painting-European
Publications: The Bay Chronicle newsletter
Activities: Classes for adults & children; lects open to pub; 12 vis lectrs per yr; mus shop sells books & prints

SOUTHPORT

M **HENDRICKS HILL MUSEUM,** 417 Hendricks Hill Rd, Rte 27, Southport, ME 04576; PO Box 3, Southport, ME 04576-0003. Tel 207-633-1102; *Pres* Richard Snyder; *Treas* Joyce Duncan
Open July 1 - Labor Day Tues, Thurs & Sat 11 AM - 3 PM; also open by appt in Sept; No admis fee, donations accepted; Mus is housed on farmhouse built in 1810; 11 rooms of household furnishings, archival material & fishing equipment dating from 1850 - 1960; separate boatshop houses boats, tools & ice harvesting equipment
Special Subjects: Furniture, Historical Material

Collections: Genealogical material, photographs & postcards depicting Southport Island life
Activities: Reference room with Southport Town Reports

SOUTHWEST HARBOR

M **WENDELL GILLEY MUSEUM,** 4 Herrick Rd, Southwest Harbor, ME 04679-4431; PO Box 254, Southwest Harbor, ME 04679-0254. Tel 207-244-7555; Email info@wendellgilleymuseum.org; Web: www.wendellgilleymuseum.org; *Pres* Eleanor T M Hoagland; *Exec VPres* Robert L Hinckley; *Exec Dir* Nina Z Gormley; *VPres* Carol L Weg; *Carver-in-Residence* Steven Valleau; *Educator* Jennifer Linforth
Open June, Sept & Oct Tues - Sun 10 AM - 4 PM, July - Aug Tues - Sun 10 AM - 5 PM, May, Nov & Dec Fri - Sun 10 AM - 4 PM; Admis adults $5.00; Estab 1981 to house collection of bird carvings & other wildlife related art; Gallery occupies 3000 sq ft on one floor of a solar heated building; handicapped access; Average Annual Attendance: 21,000; Mem: 2000; dues $35-$1000; annual meeting in Jan
Income: $219,000 (financed by mem, admis, sales & fundraising events)
Special Subjects: Folk Art, Prints, Woodcarvings
Collections: Decorative wood carvings of birds & working decoys by Wendell Gilley, Birds of America, 1972 ed J J Audubon, Birds of Mt Desert Island by Carroll S Tyson (prints), Photos by Eliot Porter
Exhibitions: Bird Carvings by Wendell Gilley (rotating); Audubon prints (rotating); Ann temporary contemporary & historical art exhibits
Publications: The Eider, bi-annual newsletter
Activities: Classes for adults & children; films; lects open to pub, gallery talks; tours; schols offered; original objects of art lent to qualified institutions; book traveling exhibs 1 per yr; mus shop sells books, original art, carving tools, gift items, jewelry, posters & toys

WATERVILLE

M **COLBY COLLEGE,** Museum of Art, 5600 Mayflower Hill, Waterville, ME 04901-4799. Tel 207-859-5600; Fax 207-859-5606; Email museum@colby.edu; Web: www.colby.edu/museum; *Asst Dir* Greg Williams; *Dir* Daniel Rosenfeld; *Cur* Sharon Corwin
Open Tues - Sat 10 AM - 4:30 PM, Sun 12 - 4:30 PM, cl major holidays; No admis fee; Estab 1959 to serve as an adjunct to the Colby College Art Program & to be a mus center for Central Maine; Average Annual Attendance: 20,000; Mem: Friends of Art at Colby, 700; dues $25 & up
Income: Financed by college funds, mem & donations
Collections: Bernat Oriental ceramics & bronzes, American Heritage coll, The Helen Warren & Willard Howe Cummings Collection of American Art, American Art of the 18th, 19th & 20th centuries, Jette Collection of American painting in the Impressionist Period, John Marin Collection of 25 works by Marin, Adelaide Pearson Collection, Pre-Columbian Mexico, Etruscan art, Paul J Schupf Wing For the Works of Alex Katz, William J Pollock Collection of American Indian Art
Publications: Exhibition catalogs; periodic newsletter
Activities: Docent training; lects open to pub; gallery talks; tours; individual paintings lent to other museums; originate traveling exhibs; mus shop sells books, note cards, postcards & posters

L **Bixler Art & Music Library**, 5660 Mayflower Hill, Waterville, ME 04901. Tel 207-859-5660; Fax 207-859-5105; Email mericson@colby.edu; Web: colby.edu/bixler; *Librn* Margaret Ericson; *Library Coordr* Robin Duperry
Open acad yr Mon - Thurs 8 AM - 12 AM, Fri 8 AM - 6 PM, Sat 10 AM - 6PM, Sun 10 AM - 12 AM; No admis fee; Estab 1959 as a study space and arts collections, computer lab facilities and seminar rooms; Circ 14,000 vols/yr; For reference & acad lending to college community & Maine residents; Average Annual Attendance: 85,000
Library Holdings: Book Volumes 45,000, CD-ROMs, Compact Disks 10,000, DVDs 1,500, Other Holdings Music, Periodical Subscriptions 90, Records 1,800
Special Subjects: Afro-American Art, Architecture, Art History, Asian Art, Painting-American, Religious Art, Photography, American Western Art, Antiquities-Greek, Folk Art, Landscapes
Activities: docent training, library instruction for art curriculum

M **THOMAS COLLEGE,** Art Gallery, 180 W River Rd, Waterville, ME 04901-5097. Tel 207-859-1362; Fax 207-877-0114; *Pub Rels Dir* Mark Tardif; *Admin Asst* Nancy Charette
Open Mon - Fri 8 AM - 4 PM; No admis fee; Estab 1968 for presentation of instructional shows for student & community audiences; Displays various works by local artists; Average Annual Attendance: 1,500
Income: Financed through college funds
Exhibitions: Monthly & bimonthly exhibitions by local artists

L **Mariner Library**, 180 W River Rd, Waterville, ME 04901. Tel 207-859-1319; Fax 207-877-1114; Email charetten@thomas.edu; Web: www.thomas.edu/library; *Librn* Steven Larochelle; *Asst Librn* Cynthia Mitchell
Open Mon - Thurs 8 AM - 10 PM, Fri 8 AM - 4:30 PM, Sun 2 - 9 PM, cl Sat; For reference only
Income: state appropriation; funded by college
Library Holdings: Book Volumes 21,500, Periodical Subscriptions 400, Slides

M **WATERVILLE HISTORICAL SOCIETY,** Redington Museum, 62 Silver St, Unit B, Waterville, ME 04901. Tel 207-872-9439; Web: www.rediingtonmuseum.org; *Resident Custodian* Bryan Finnemore; *Resident Custodian* Bonny Finnemore; *Librn* Tina Serdjenian; *Pres Historical Society* Frederic P Johnson; *VPres* Stephen R McGraw; *Secy* Kate O'Halloran; *Treas* James Violette Jr; *Cur* Sarah Sugden
Open Memorial Day - Labor Day Tues - Sat 10 AM - 3 PM; tours 10 & 11 AM, 1 & 2 PM; Admis adults $5, children 18 & under free; Estab 1903; 1814 federal style bldg on nat register of historic places; Average Annual Attendance: 500; Mem: 250; dues friend $100, family $40, single $20; annual meeting second Thurs in June
Income: Financed by mem & limited endowment
Special Subjects: Costumes, Decorative Arts, Dolls, Flasks & Bottles, Furniture, Glass, Historical Material, Manuscripts, Maps
Collections: Early Silver & China, 18th & 19th century furniture, 19th century apothecary, portraits of early local residents, Victorian clothing, Indian artifacts, Early photos, tools & toys
Activities: Lect open to public, tours

WISCASSET

A **LINCOLN COUNTY HISTORICAL ASSOCIATION, INC,** Pownalborough Courthouse, 133 Federal St, Wiscasset, ME 04578. Tel 207-882-6817; Email lcha@wiscasset.net; Web: www.lincolncountyhistory.org; *Exec Dir* Jay Robbins
Open July & Aug Tues - Sat 10 AM - 4 PM, Sun Noon - 4 PM, June & Sept Sat 10 AM - 4 PM, Sun Noon - 4 PM; Admis adults $4, children 18 & under free; Incorporated 1954, to preserve buildings of historic interest; Average Annual Attendance: 700; Mem: 350; dues $25 & up; ann meeting in July
Income: Financed by dues, fundraisers, admis, bequests & donations
Special Subjects: American Indian Art, American Western Art, Archaeology, Architecture, Crafts, Decorative Arts, Embroidery, Flasks & Bottles, Folk Art, Furniture, Glass, Historical Material, Manuscripts, Maps, Painting-American, Period Rooms, Porcelain, Pottery, Reproductions, Restorations, Scrimshaw, Textiles, Woodcarvings
Collections: Furniture, hand tools, household articles, textiles
Publications: Newsletter; occasional monographs
Activities: School progs & docent training; lects open to pub approx 250 per yr; tours; gallery talks; slide shows; mus shop sells books, original art, reproductions

L **Library**, 133 Federal St, Wiscasset, ME 04578. Tel 207-882-6817; *Dir* Anne R Dolan
Open by appointment for reference & research
Library Holdings: Book Volumes 200

M **1811 Old Lincoln County Jail & Lincoln County Museum**, 133 Federal St, Wiscasset, ME 04578. Tel 207-882-6817; Email lcha@wiscasset.net; Web: www.lincolncountyhistory.org; *Exec Dir* Jay Robbins
Open July & Aug Tues - Sat 10 AM - 4 PM, Sun Noon - 4 PM, June & Sept Sat 10 AM - 4 PM, Sun Noon - 4 PM, Oct-May by appointment; Admis adults $4, children 18 & under free; Estab 1954 for historical preservation; Average Annual Attendance: 1,500; Mem: 350; dues $20 & up, annual meeting in Oct
Income: Financed by mem, donations, restricted funds & bequests
Special Subjects: American Indian Art, American Western Art, Archaeology, Architecture, Ceramics, Costumes, Crafts, Decorative Arts, Embroidery, Folk Art, Furniture, Glass, Historical Material, Maps, Painting-American, Period Rooms, Pewter, Photography, Porcelain, Portraits, Prints, Reproductions, Restorations, Scrimshaw, Silver, Textiles, Watercolors, Woodcarvings
Collections: Early American tools, jail artifacts, quilts, prison equipment, samplers, textiles, Scrimshaw, Ephemera, Photographs, Baskets, Fans
Exhibitions: shows once a year
Publications: Lincoln County Chronicle - Newsletter
Activities: Docent training; lects open to pub, over 2 vis lectrs per yr; tours; gallery talks; mus shop sells books; original art; reproductions; cards; postcards

M **Maine Art Gallery**, 15 Warren St, Wiscasset, ME 04578. Tel 207-882-7511; Email meartgallery@gwi.net; Web: www.maineartgallery.org; *Bd Pres* Sally Loughridge Bush; *Gallery Mgr* Kay Liss; *Treas* Marcia Mansfield; *Asst Mgr* Michele Roberge
Open early May thru late Nov daily 10 AM - 4 PM, Sun 11 AM - 4 PM, cl Winter; No admis fee, donations appreciated; Estab 1958 as a cooperative, non-profit gallery created by the Artist Members of Lincoln County Cultural & Historical Assoc to exhibit the work of artists living or working in Maine; Gallery occupies a red brick federal two-story building built in 1807 as a free Academy. The building is now on National Historical Register; Average Annual Attendance: 6,000; Mem: 200; dues $35; bd meets 4 times per year
Income: Financed by patrons, art sales & fundraising
Exhibitions: Summer Exhibition: A juried show in parts of 4 weeks featuring approx 100 painters & sculptors living or working in Maine; 6 exhibitions per year, 1 juried show, 1 members show, 4 invitational or from show proposals
Activities: Classes for adults; lects open to pub; gallery talks; school art classes; visits

MARYLAND

ANNAPOLIS

M **HAMMOND-HARWOOD HOUSE ASSOCIATION, INC,** Hammond-Harwood House, 19 Maryland Ave, Annapolis, MD 21401-1626. Tel 410-263-4683; Fax 410-267-6891; Email hhhcurator@gmail.com; Web: www.hammondharwoodhouse.org; *Exec Dir* Shawn M Herne; *Asst Dir* Rachel Lovett; *Museum Shop Mgr* Nancy Farmer
Open April - Dec Tues - Sat noon - 5 PM, Sun Noon - 4 PM; Jan - March by appt; cl New Year's Day, Thanksgiving, Christmas; Admis adults $10, students & seniors $8, children $5, mems & children under 6 no charge; Estab 1938 to preserve the Hammond-Harwood House (1774), a National Historic Landmark; to educate the pub in the arts & architecture of Maryland in the 18th century; Average Annual Attendance: 13,004; Mem: 350; dues varied; meeting May & Nov
Income: Financed by endowment, mem, attendance & sales
Library Holdings: Audio Tapes, Clipping Files, Manuscripts, Original Art Works, Original Documents, Photographs, Prints, Slides
Special Subjects: Architecture, Baroque Art, Ceramics, Decorative Arts, Dolls, Drawings, Embroidery, Furniture, Glass, Historical Material, Landscapes, Manuscripts, Maps, Marine Painting, Metalwork, Miniatures, Oriental Art, Painting-American, Painting-British, Period Rooms, Pewter, Porcelain, Prints, Silver, Portraits
Collections: Paintings by C W Peale, Chinese export porcelain, English & American furnishings, especially from Maryland, prints, English & American silver, colonial architectural interiors designed by William Buckland
Publications: Maryland's Way (Hammond-Harwood House cookbook); Hammond-Harwood House Guidebook

Activities: Interpretive progs; docent training; classes for adults; classes for children; docent training; lects open to pub; lectrs for mems only; concerts; gallery talks; tours; special architecture tours; individual paintings & original objects of art lent to bona fide mus within reasonable transporting distance; mus shop sells books, magazines, reproductions & prints

M **MARYLAND HALL FOR THE CREATIVE ARTS,** Chaney Gallery, 801 Chase St, Annapolis, MD 21401-3530. Tel 410-263-5544; Fax 410-263-5114; Email cmanucy@mdhallarts.org; Web: www.marylandhall.org; *Exec Dir* Linnell R Bowen; *Dir Exhibs* Sigrid Trumpy
Open Mon - Sat 9 AM - 5 PM; No admis fee; Estab 1979 to exhibit work of contemporary regional artists; Two room post modern space with 100 ft of wall space & 1100 sq ft of floor area. Contemporary grid-track lighting. Second gallery 450 sq ft, track lighting, also outdoor sculpture; Average Annual Attendance: 7,000; Mem: 2,000; dues $25 & up
Income: Financed by local, state & special grant funds
Special Subjects: Afro-American Art, Drawings, Photography, Sculpture, Watercolors, Woodcarvings, Woodcuts
Exhibitions: Rotating exhibitions, 12-15 per yr
Publications: Postcards
Activities: Classes for adults & children; dramatic progs; concerts; gallery talks; competitions

M **ST JOHN'S COLLEGE,** Elizabeth Myers Mitchell Art Gallery, 60 College Ave, Annapolis, MD 21401. Tel 410-626-2556; Fax 410-263-4828; Email hydee.schaller@sjc.edu; Web: www.sjc.edu/mitchellgallery; *Exhibit Preparator* Neal Falanga; *Outreach Coordr* Lucinda Edinberg; *Dir* Hydee Schaller
Open Sept - May Tues - Sun Noon - 5 PM, Fri 6:45 - 7:45 PM; No admis fee; Estab 1989 to present museum quality exhibits & educational progs for the greater Annapolis area; Two adjoining galleries; one gallery of 1300 sq ft, rectangle with corner windows and one gallery of 525 sq ft, rectangular, no windows; Average Annual Attendance: 10,000; Mem: 800 members; 427 memberships; dues $50-$1000
Exhibitions: Please refer to our website: www.stjohnscollege.edu/events/Mitchell Gallery
Publications: Catalogs; exhibition programs; gallery guides
Activities: Educ dept offers studio courses in painting, life drawing; workshops for children; sculpture for adults & children; docent training; lectrs open to pub, 6 vis lectrs per yr; gallery talks; tours; concerts; sponsoring of competitions; American Alliance of Museums accreditation (2015); book traveling exhibs 2-4 per yr; originate traveling exhibs

M **UNITED STATES NAVAL ACADEMY,** USNA Museum, 118 Maryland Ave, Annapolis, MD 21402-1321. Tel 410-293-2108; Fax 410-293-5220; Web: www.usna.edu/museum; *Sr Cur* James W Cheevers; *Cur Ship Models* Robert F Sumrall; *Cur Robinson Coll* Sigrid Trumpy; *Exhibit Specialist* Robert Chapel; *Dir* Dr J Scott Harmon; *Registrar* Donald Leonard; *Research Assoc* Grant Walker
Open Mon - Sat 9 AM - 5 PM, Sun 11 AM - 5 PM; No admis fee; Estab 1845 as Naval School Lyceum for the purpose of collecting, preserving & exhibiting objects related to American naval history; Mus contains two large galleries totaling 9000 sq ft, with other exhibits in other areas of the campus; Average Annual Attendance: Approx 250,000
Income: Financed by federal government appropriations & private donations
Purchases: $36,170
Special Subjects: Ceramics, Coins & Medals, Drawings, Manuscripts, Metalwork, Painting-American, Prints, Sculpture, Silver
Publications: Collection catalogs & spec exhib brochures, periodically
Activities: Lects; tours upon request; individual paintings & original objects of art lent to other museums & related institutions for special, temporary exhibs; originate traveling exhibs

BALTIMORE

M **ALBIN O KUHN LIBRARY & GALLERY,** Univ Maryland Baltimore County Campus, 1000 Hilltop Circle Baltimore, MD 21250-0001. Tel 410-455-2232; Email aok@umbc.edu; Web: www.umbc.edu/aok/main/index.html; *Spec Coll Librn* Susan Graham; *Cur Exhibs* Emily Hauver
Open (gallery) Mon - Fri 10 AM - 4:30 PM, Thurs until 8 PM, Sat - Sun Noon - 5 PM; (library) Aug - Dec, Mon - Thurs 8 AM - 12 AM, Fri 8 AM - 6 PM, Sat 10 AM - 6 PM, Sun 12 PM - 12 AM; Estab 1973 to promote scholarly exhibitions of original works of art & historic materials for UMBC & the greater Baltimore & Maryland region; 300 running ft to 4,500 sq ft; Average Annual Attendance: 5,000
Library Holdings: Auction Catalogs, Exhibition Catalogs, Manuscripts, Original Art Works, Original Documents, Photographs
Special Subjects: Manuscripts, Photography
Collections: 2,000,000 photographs
Exhibitions: Three to four exhibitions annually of photographs, rare books, manuscripts & historic artifacts
Publications: Music of the Mind: Jaromir Stephan Photographs & Digital Images
Activities: Classes for adults & children; lects open to public, 1 vis lectrs per yr; gallery talks; tours; symposia

M **BALTIMORE CITY COMMUNITY COLLEGE,** Art Gallery, 2901 Liberty Heights Ave, Fine & Applied Arts Dept Baltimore, MD 21215-7807. Tel 410-462-8000; Fax 410-462-7614; Web: www.bccc.edu; *Coordr Arts* Carlton Leverette
Open Mon - Fri 10 AM - 4 PM; No admis fee; Estab 1965 to bring to the Baltimore & col communities exhibs of note by regional artists & to serve as a showplace for the artistic productions of the col art students & faculty; Consists of one large gallery area, approx 120 running ft, well-lighted through the use of both natural light (sky domes) & cove lighting which provides an even wash to the walls
Income: Financed through the college
Special Subjects: Graphics, Painting-American
Collections: Graphics from the 16th century to the present, paintings by notable American artists & regional ones
Exhibitions: Groups shows & three-man shows representing a broad cross section of work by regional artists; art faculty show; three-man show featuring graphic designs & paintings; exhibition of portraits by 15 artists; annual student show
Publications: Gallery announcements
Activities: Lect open to public; gallery talks

M **THE BALTIMORE MUSEUM OF ART,** 10 Art Museum Dr, Baltimore, MD 21218-3827. Tel 443-573-1700; Fax 443-573-1582; Email abrown@artbma.org; Web: www.artbma.org; *Dir* Christopher Bedford; *COO* Christine Dietze; *Dep Dir Develop* Judith Gibbs; *Chief Cur* Asma Naeem; *Sr Cur Prints, Drawings and Photographs* Andaleeb Badiee Banta; *Cur American Art* Virginia Anderson; *Sr Cur Contemp Art* Kristen Hileman; *Sr Cur European Painting & Sculpture* Katherine Rothkopf; *Cur Textiles* Anita Jones; *Dir Retail Operations* Greg Ferrara; *Sr Dir Communications & Mktg* Anne Brown; *Librn* Emily Rafferty
Open Wed - Sun 10 AM - 5 PM, cl Mon, Tues & major holidays; No admis fee; some exhibitions may be ticketed; Estab 1914 to house & preserve art works, to present art exhibitions, art-related activities & offer educational programs & events; The original building was designed by John Russell Pope in 1929; addition in 1982 with cafe, auditorium & traveling exhibition galleries; sculpture gardens opened in 1980 & 1988; wing for Contemporary Art opened in 1994, maintains reference library; Average Annual Attendance: 208,976; Mem: 9,859; dues $55 & up
Income: $14,435,660 (financed by city, state, county & Federal appropriation; corporate, individual & foundation gifts; mem, earned revenue & endowment income)
Library Holdings: Auction Catalogs, Book Volumes, CD-ROMs, Cassettes, Clipping Files, Exhibition Catalogs, Fiche, Lantern Slides, Manuscripts, Memorabilia, Micro Print, Motion Pictures, Original Art Works, Original Documents, Other Holdings, Pamphlets, Periodical Subscriptions, Photographs, Prints, Reels, Reproductions
Special Subjects: African Art, Afro-American Art, American Indian Art, American Western Art, Antiquities-Egyptian, Architecture, Asian Art, Ceramics, Decorative Arts, Drawings, Furniture, Gold, Jewelry, Latin American Art, Mexican Art, Mosaics, Painting-American, Painting-European, Painting-Israeli, Painting-Spanish, Photography, Portraits, Pre-Columbian Art, Prints, Renaissance Art, Sculpture, Silver, Textiles
Collections: Cone Collection: featuring works of Matisse & Picasso & other 20th century American & European artists, George A Lucas Collection: drawings, esp19th c French
Exhibitions: Imagining Home; 29th Jan, 2017) Matisse/Diebenkorn; 18th Jun, 2017) Shifting Views: People & Politics in Contemporary African Art
Publications: Exhibition catalogs; members newsletter; posters & postcards; gallery guides; family guides
Activities: Classes for adults & children; docent training; lects open to pub; concerts; films; gallery talks; tours; individual paintings & original objects of art lent to other art mus regionally to internationally; lending collection contains original art works, original prints, paintings, photographs & sculpture; book traveling exhibs; 1 per yr; originate traveling exhibs; mus shop sells books, reproductions, slides, jewelry & children's gifts

L **E Kirkbride Miller Art Library,** 10 Art Museum Dr, Baltimore, MD 21218-3827. Tel 443-573-1778; Fax 443-573-1781; Email bmalibrary@artbma.org; Web: www.artbma.org; *Head Librn & Archivist* Emily Rafferty
Open by appointment
Library Holdings: Book Volumes 60,000, Clipping Files, Exhibition Catalogs, Lantern Slides, Manuscripts, Other Holdings 15,000, Pamphlets, Periodical Subscriptions 302, Video Tapes
Special Subjects: Afro-American Art, American Indian Art, Carpets & Rugs, Ceramics, Decorative Arts, Drawings, Embroidery, Eskimo Art, Etchings & Engravings, Furniture, Glass, Laces, Painting-American, Painting-Australian, Painting-European, Photography, Porcelain, Pottery, Primitive art, Printmaking, Prints, Sculpture, Tapestries, Textiles, Woodcuts

L **ENOCH PRATT FREE LIBRARY OF BALTIMORE CITY,** 400 Cathedral St, Fine Arts Dept Baltimore, MD 21201-4401. Tel 410-396-5430 (General); 396-5490 (Fine Arts & Music Dept); Fax 410-396-1409 (Fine Arts & Music Dept); Email far@prattlibrary.org; Web: www.prattlibrary.org; *Dir* Carla Hayden; *Chief State Library Resource Center* Wesley Wilson
Open Oct - May, Mon - Wed 10 AM - 7 PM, Thurs - Sat 10 AM - 5 PM, Sun 1 - 5 PM; No admis fee; Estab 1882 to provide materials, primarily circulating on the visual arts and music; Exhibition space in display windows, interior display cases, corridors and special departments
Income: Financed by city and state appropriation
Library Holdings: Book Volumes 97,000, Filmstrips, Framed Reproductions, Other Holdings Framed prints; Unframed pictures, Records, Reproductions, Slides
Publications: Book lists, periodically
Activities: Lect & film showings

M **EUBIE BLAKE NATIONAL JAZZ INSTITUTE AND CULTURAL CENTER,** 847 N Howard St, Ste 323 Baltimore, MD 21201. Tel 410-225-3130; Fax 410-225-3139; Email info@eubieblake.org; Web: www.eubieblake.org; *Artistic Dir* Troy Burton; *Admin Asst* Kennedy McDaniel
Open Wed - Fri 1 PM - 6 PM, Sat 11 AM - 3PM, cl Sun - Tues; Admis varies, call for more info; Estab 1983; Two galleries feature works by local and regional artists; Average Annual Attendance: 10,000; Mem: 100; dues $20; annual meeting in Feb
Income: $2,300,000 (financed by mem, city & state appropriation)
Special Subjects: Afro-American Art
Collections: Paintings, photography, illustration & mixed media
Exhibitions: Monthly exhibits
Publications: Ragtime, quarterly newsletter
Activities: Classes for children; dramatic progs; lects open to pub; 4 vis lectrs per yr; competitions; concerts; tours; mus shop sells books, original art & prints

M **GOUCHER COLLEGE,** Rosenberg & Silber Art Gallery, 1021 Dulaney Valley Rd, Baltimore, MD 21204. Tel 410-337-6477; 337-6367 (Art Coll); Fax 410-337-6405; Email laura.amussen@goucher.edu; Email sonja.sugerman@goucher.edu; Web: www.goucher.edu/learn/undergraduate-programs/studio-art/art-galleries; *Exec Dir & Cur* Laura Amussen; *Visual Resources & Art Coll Cur* Sonja Sugerman

Open (Rosenberg Gallery) Mon - Fri 9 AM - 5 PM during the acad calendar & on evenings & weekends of pub events; Silber Gallery: Tues - Sun 11 AM - 4 PM during the acad calendar; Art Coll: by appointment only; No admis fee; Estab 1964 to display temporary & continuously changing exhibitions of contemporary & historically important visual arts; Gallery spaced located in the lobby of the Kraushaar Auditorium; 144 running ft of wall space; Average Annual Attendance: 125,000
Income: Financed privately
Collections: Ceramics, coins, drawings, paintings, prints, sculpture, photography, Art coll consisting of permanent teaching coll comprised of fine & decorative art & artifacts displayed around the campus & Pres's house
Publications: Exhibit brochures, 9 per year
Activities: Lects open to public; opening receptions; gallery talks & artists talks; original objects of art lent to qualified museums & educational institutions; book traveling exhibitions 1 per year

M **GOYA CONTEMPORARY,** 3000 Chestnut Ave, Mill Ctr, #214 Baltimore, MD 21211. Tel 410-366-2001; Fax 410-235-8730; Email gallery@goyacontemporary.com; Web: goyacontemporary.com; *Founder* Martha Macks-Kahn; *Exec Dir & Cur* Amy Eva Raehse; *Registrar* Emily Vollherbst; *Gallery Asst* Sara Havekotte
Open Tues & Fri 10 AM - 6 PM, Sat Noon - 5 PM, cl holidays; Estab to promote contemporary & art culture through curatorial practice, catalogs, print publishing, and encouraging artistic coll
Collections: Contemporary art
Exhibitions: Temporary exhibits

M **JOHNS HOPKINS UNIVERSITY,** Archaeological Museum, 3400 N Charles St, 150 Gilman Hall Baltimore, MD 21218-2608. Tel 410-516-0383; Fax 410-516-5218; Email archmuseum@jhu.edu; Web: archaeologicalmuseum.jhu.edu; *Dir Near Eastern & Egyptian Art* Dr Betsy Bryan; *Colls Tech* Jennifer Torres; *Registrar & Colls Mgr* Kate Gallagher; *Cur & Conservator* Sanchita Balachandran
Mon - Fri 10:30 AM - 1:30 PM
Special Subjects: Antiquities-Egyptian, Antiquities-Roman
Collections: Egyptian through Roman material 3500 BC to 500 AD

M **Evergreen Museum & Library**, 4545 N Charles St, Baltimore, MD 21210. Tel 410-516-0341; Fax 410-516-0864; Email evergreenmuseum@jhu.edu; Web: museums.jhu.edu/evergreen.php; *Dir & Cur* Julia Rose; *Assoc Dir Commun & Mktg* Heather Stalfort; *Visitor Servs Coordr* Nancy Powers
Open Tues - Fri 11 AM - 4 PM, Sat & Sun Noon - 4 PM, Last tour daily at 3 PM; Admis fee adults $8, seniors $7, students $5, free mem & children under 6; Estab 1952 for promotion of cultural & educational functions & research; Formerly the residence of Ambassador John W Garrett which he bequeathed to the University; Average Annual Attendance: 10,000; Mem: 200; dues $25 - $250
Income: Evergreen House Found; John Hopkins Univ
Library Holdings: Book Volumes, Other Holdings
Special Subjects: American Western Art, Antiquities-Egyptian, Antiquities-Greek, Antiquities-Persian, Antiquities-Roman, Architecture, Art History, Asian Art, Bookplates & Bindings, Bronzes, Carpets & Rugs, Ceramics, Ceramics, Coins & Medals, Decorative Arts, Decorative Arts, Drawings, Drawings, Enamels, Etchings & Engravings, Etchings & Engravings, Ethnology, Furniture, Furniture, Glass, Hispanic Art, Historical Material, History of Art & Archaeology, Interior Design, Islamic Art, Jade, Landscape Architecture, Landscapes, Landscapes, Manuscripts, Maps, Metalwork, Mexican Art, Miniatures, Mosaics, Oriental Art, Painting-American, Painting-American, Painting-French, Painting-French, Painting-German, Painting-Russian, Painting-Spanish, Porcelain, Portraits, Pottery, Silver, Stained Glass
Collections: Leon Baskt-designed private theatre, American and European Ceramics, American art glass, 19th and 20th century European paintings, American, European, and Middle Eastern Decorative and Applied Arts, Japanese Inro Nesuke and lacquerwares, Chinese porcelains, 30,000 Vol John Work Garret Libr, Laurence Hall Fowler architectural drawing collection
Exhibitions: Changing exhibitions
Publications: Raoul Dufy at Evergreen and the Evolution of Alice Warder Garret as a Patron of Contemp Art, 2007; Leon Basket at the Evergreen House: A Collection Built Around a Friendship, 2004
Activities: Classes for adults; classes for children; docent training; dramatic programs; lects open to pub; 4 vis lectrs per year; concerts; gallery talks; tours; individual paintings & original objects of art lent to other mus, national & international; mus shop sells books, reproductions & prints; original art

L **George Peabody Library**, 17 E Mount Vernon Pl, Baltimore, MD 21202-2308. Tel 410-659-8179; Fax 410-659-8137; *Librn* Carolyn Smith
Open Tues - Thurs 10 AM - 5 PM, Fri 10 AM - 3 PM, Sat 10 AM - 1 PM
Library Holdings: Book Volumes 250,000
Special Subjects: Architecture, Decorative Arts
Collections: British History, art and architecture, decorative arts, religion, travel, geography, maps

M **Homewood Museum**, 3400 N Charles St, Baltimore, MD 21218-2680. Tel 410-516-5589; Fax 410-516-7859; Email homewoodmuseum@jhu.edu; Web: www.museums.jhu.edu; *Dir* Winston Tab; *Programs Coordr* Judith Proffitt; *Assoc Dir Communs & Mktg* Heather Egan Stalfort; *Assoc Dir Develop* Elizabeth Courtmanche
Open Tues -Fri 11 AM - 4 PM, Sat - Sun Noon - 4 PM; Admis fee $8, seniors $7, students $5, free mem & children under 6; Estab 1987; a historic house mus; Restored Federal Period country seat of Charles Carroll, Jr, with period furnishings; Average Annual Attendance: 10,000; Mem: 350; annual dues $50
Special Subjects: Archaeology, Architecture, Ceramics, Decorative Arts, Period Rooms, Pewter, Porcelain, Restorations, Silver, Textiles, Furniture, Glass, African Art
Collections: English & American decorative arts of the late 18th & early 19th Century
Activities: Docent Training; Lectures open the public; concerts; internships offered; mus shop sells books, original art, object reproductions, prints, slides, exclusive Homewood items & jewelry

M **MARYLAND ART PLACE,** 218 W Saratoga St, Fl 2 Baltimore, MD 21201-3532. Tel 410-962-8565; Fax 410-244-8017; Email map@mdartplace.org; Web: www.mdartplace.org; *Exec Dir* Amy Cavanaugh Royce; *Pres* Christopher Janian; *Prog Mgr & Registry Coordr* Naomi Davidoff
Open Tues - Sat Noon - 5 PM; No admis fee; Estab 1981, to provide opportunities for artists to exhibit work, nurture & promote new ideas & forms; Three galleries within one floor; Average Annual Attendance: 30,000; Mem: 4000; dues $30 & up
Income: $450,000 (financed by mem, federal, state & corporate appropriation)
Special Subjects: Ceramics, Collages, Drawings, Folk Art, Graphics, Hispanic Art, Landscapes, Painting-American
Exhibitions: Varies
Publications: Annual catalogs; exhibition brochures, 4-6 per year; quarterly newsletter
Activities: Annual public forum; professional develop; lects open to pub, 4 vis lectrs per yr; gallery talks; tours; competitions; originate traveling exhibs 1-2 per yr

M **MARYLAND HISTORICAL SOCIETY,** Museum of Maryland History, 201 W Monument St, Baltimore, MD 21201-4601. Tel 410-685-3750; Fax 410-385-2105; Web: www.mdhs.org; *Chief Cur* Alexandra Deutsch; *Dir* Patricia Anderson
Open Thurs - Sat 10 AM - 5 PM; Admis adults $9, seniors $7, students & children (3-18) $6; children under 3 & mem free; Estab 1844 to collect, display & interpret the history of the State of Maryland; Average Annual Attendance: 70,000; Mem: dues family $60, individual $50; annual meeting in June
Income: Financed by endowment, mem, city & state appropriations
Library Holdings: Audio Tapes, Book Volumes, Clipping Files, Compact Disks, DVDs, Exhibition Catalogs, Filmstrips, Framed Reproductions, Kodachrome Transparencies, Lantern Slides, Manuscripts, Maps, Memorabilia, Motion Pictures, Original Documents, Other Holdings, Pamphlets, Periodical Subscriptions, Photographs, Records, Reproductions, Slides
Special Subjects: Architecture, Glass, Metalwork, Painting-American, Porcelain, Pottery, Silver, Textiles
Collections: Architectural drawings, crystal & glassware, ethnic artifacts, all of Maryland origin or provenance, metalwork, paintings, both portrait & landscape, porcelain & pottery, silver, textiles & costumes, furniture
Exhibitions: Continually changing exhibitions reflecting the history & culture of the state
Publications: Maryland Historical Society Magazine, quarterly; MDHS/news 3 times per yr
Activities: Classes for adults & children; docent training; lects open to pub; 12 vis lectrs per yr; concerts; gallery talks; tours; competitions with awards; exten dept; individual paintings & original objects of art lent to other organizations in State of Maryland; originate traveling exhibs; mus shop sells books, original art, prints

L **Library**, 201 W Monument St, Baltimore, MD 21201-4601. Tel 410-685-3750 ext 359; Fax 410-385-2105; Email reference@mdhs.org; Web: www.mdhs.org/library; *Special Colls Archivist* Damon Talbot; *Pres & CEO* Mark Letzer; *Chief Registrar & Assoc Cur Fashion Archives* Allison Tolman; *CFO* Dennis Elder; *Sr Reference Librn* Francis O'Neill; *Mus Shop Mgr* Leila Warshaw
Open Wed - Sat 10 AM - 5 PM; Estab 1844; Library for reference only; Average Annual Attendance: 70,000; Mem: 6,500
Library Holdings: Audio Tapes, Book Volumes 70,000, Cassettes, Clipping Files, Exhibition Catalogs, Fiche, Filmstrips, Kodachrome Transparencies, Lantern Slides, Manuscripts, Memorabilia, Motion Pictures, Pamphlets, Periodical Subscriptions 125, Photographs, Prints, Records, Reels, Reproductions, Slides, Video Tapes

M **MORGAN STATE UNIVERSITY,** James E Lewis Museum of Art, 1700 E Cold Spring Lane, Baltimore, MD 21251. Tel 443-885-3030; Fax 410-319-4024; Email jelmamuseum@morgan.edu; Email laura.brown@morgan.edu; Web: www.jelmamuseum.org; *Dir & Cur* Gabriel S Tenabe; *Assoc Dir* Robin Howard; *Asst Admin* Laura Brown
Open Tues - Fri 10 AM - 4 PM, Sat - Sun Noon - 4 PM, cl Mon, Easter, Thanksgiving, Christmas; No admis fee; Estab 1950; Average Annual Attendance: 5,000
Income: $5,500
Collections: 19th & 20th centuries American & European sculpture, graphics, paintings, decorative arts, archaeology, African & New Guinea Sculptures
Publications: Monthly catalogs
Activities: Lects open to pub, vis lectrs; lending collection contains Kodachromes; originate traveling exhibs

L **Library**, 1700 E Cold Spring Lane, Baltimore, MD 21251. Tel 443-885-3477; Fax 443-885-8246; Email library.reference@morgan.edu; Web: www.morgan.edu/library; *Dir* Richard Bradberry PhD
Open Mon - Thurs 8 AM - 12 AM, Fri 8 AM - 9 PM, Sat 9 AM - 6 PM, Sun 1 - 12 AM
Library Holdings: Book Volumes 8800, DVDs, Photographs

M **NATIONAL MUSEUM OF CERAMIC ART,** 2406 Shelleydale Dr, Baltimore, MD 21209-3242. Tel 410-764-1042; *Adminr* Shirley B Brown; *Pres* Richard Taylor; *VPres* Bruce T Taylor, MD; *Secy & Treas* Robert B Brown
Estab 1994 to exhibit ceramic art & glass & develop educational progs; Average Annual Attendance: 9,000; Mem: 478; dues $25-$150; meetings in Oct & Apr
Income: Financed by mem, city & state appropriation & grants
Special Subjects: Art Education, Ceramics, Crafts, Decorative Arts, Glass, Illustration, Pottery
Exhibitions: Annual April/May Exhib
Activities: Classes for adults & children; ceramic art after school programs in middle schools across the Baltimore Metropolitan area; original objects of art lent

M **NATIONAL SOCIETY OF COLONIAL DAMES OF AMERICA IN THE STATE OF MARYLAND,** Mount Clare Museum House, 1500 Washington Blvd, Carroll Park Baltimore, MD 21230-1727. Tel 410-837-3262; Fax 410-837-0251; Email director@mountclare.org; Web: www.mountclare.org; *Dir* Rose Gallenberger
Open Thurs - Sun 11 AM - 4 PM; Admis adults $8, seniors $7, children (2-12) $6; Estab 1917 to preserve the home of Charles Carroll, Barrister & teach about the colonial period of Maryland history. Maintained by the National Soc of Colonial Dames of America; Rooms of the house are furnished with 18th & early 19th century decorative arts, much of which belonged to the Carroll family who built the house in 1760 & has been designated a National Historic Landmark; Average Annual Attendance: 5,000; Mem: 14,000; dues vary

Income: Financed by admis, gift shop sales & contributions from pub & private sectors
Library Holdings: Book Volumes
Special Subjects: Architecture, Ceramics, Costumes, Decorative Arts, Dolls, Embroidery, Etchings & Engravings, Flasks & Bottles, Folk Art, Furniture, Glass, Gold, Graphics, Historical Material, Ivory, Jewelry, Laces, Landscapes, Manuscripts, Metalwork, Military Art, Miniatures, Painting-American, Period Rooms, Pewter, Portraits, Pottery, Primitive art, Prints, Silver, Tapestries, Textiles, Watercolors, Reproductions, Restorations
Collections: American paintings, 18th & early 19th century English & American furniture, English silver, Irish crystal, Oriental export porcelain, other English & American decorative arts, rare books
Exhibitions: Special exhibs periodically, see website
Publications: Brochure on Mount Clare; Mount Clare: Being an Account of the Seat Built by Charles Carroll, Barrister Upon His Lands at Patapsco; booklet on the house; others pertaining to collection & Maryland
Activities: Classes for adults & children; docent training; school tours; traveling trunk shows; colonial camp; lects open to pub, 4 vis lectrs per yr; gallery talks; tours; original objects of art lent to historical societies by request; mus shop sells books, magazines, original art, reproductions, gift items, souvenirs & historical replicas

L **Library**, 1500 Washington Blvd, Carroll Park Baltimore, MD 21230-1727. Tel 410-837-3262; Fax 410-837-0251; Email director@mountclare.org; Web: www.mountclare.org; WATS www.users.errolls/mountclaremuseumhouse.org
Open by appointment only; Admis free; Estab 1917; Circ 1,500; Open to members & the pub for reference only; Average Annual Attendance: 5,000; Mem: 14,000; application dues vary
Income: Private finance
Library Holdings: Book Volumes 1000, Clipping Files, Exhibition Catalogs, Framed Reproductions, Kodachrome Transparencies, Lantern Slides, Manuscripts, Maps, Memorabilia, Original Art Works, Original Documents, Other Holdings, Pamphlets, Periodical Subscriptions, Photographs, Prints, Slides
Special Subjects: American Western Art, Anthropology, Archaeology, Architecture, Art Education, Art History, Asian Art, Carpets & Rugs, Ceramics, Costume Design & Constr, Decorative Arts, Dolls, Drawings, Embroidery, Etchings & Engravings, Flasks & Bottles, Folk Art, Furniture, Glass, Gold, Goldsmithing, Handicrafts, Historical Material, History of Art & Archaeology, Ivory, Jewelry, Landscape Architecture, Metalwork, Miniatures, Painting-American, Period Rooms, Pewter, Porcelain, Portraits, Pottery, Primitive art, Prints, Restoration & Conservation, Silver, Silversmithing, Textiles
Collections: 18th century furniture, decorative arts, part of the library of Charles Carroll, Barrister-at-law, builder of the house, 1756, art; photos
Publications: Library of rare book; out of print; MD history; MD genealogy
Activities: Classes for adults & children; docent training; social & material culture progs; lects open to pub; 4 vis lectrs per yr; tours; Congressional schols; history essay award; extension prog to Maryland & mid-Atlantic; traveling trunk to schools; mus shop sells book, magazines

M **NORMAN AND SARAH BROWN ART GALLERY,** Jewish Community Center, 5700 Park Heights Ave Baltimore, MD 21215. Tel 410-542-4900 ext 239; Web: www.jcc.org; *Dir Baltimore Jewish Film Festival* Claudine Davison
Open Mon - Tues 11 AM - 5 PM, Wed - Thurs 3 PM - 5 PM, Fri noon - 2:30, Sun noon - 5 PM
Collections: Paintings; prints; sculpture; photographs; documents; drawings; books
Activities: Community center; classrooms; garden; museum-related items for sale

A **SCHOOL 33 ART CENTER,** 1427 Light St, Baltimore, MD 21230-4528. Tel 443-263-4350; Fax 410-837-6947; Email school33@promotionandarts.com; Web: www.school33.org; *Dir Cultural Affairs* Randi Vega; *Asst Dir Cultural Affairs* Krista Green; *Exhibs Mgr* Melissa Webb; *Cultural Affairs Assoc* Flannery Winchester
Open Wed - Sat 11 AM - 4 PM; No admis fee; Estab 1979
Activities: Classes for adults & children

A **STAR-SPANGLED BANNER FLAG HOUSE ASSOCIATION,** Flag House & 1812 Museum, 844 E Pratt St, Baltimore, MD 21202-4495. Tel 410-837-1793; Fax 410-837-1812; Email info@flaghouse.org; Web: www.flaghouse.org; *Exec Dir* Amanda Davis
Open Tues - Sat 10 AM - 4 PM; Admis adults $9, seniors & military $8, students K-12 $6, children under 6 & mems no charge; Estab 1927 for the care & maintenance of 1793 home of Mary Pickersgill, maker of 15 stars, 15 stripes flag used at Fort McHenry during Battle of Baltimore, war of 1812, which inspired Francis Scott Key to pen his famous poem, now our national anthem; also to conduct an educational program for pub & private schools; Mus houses artifacts, portraits & library. 1793 house furnished & decorated in Federal period to look as it did when Mary Pickersgill was in residence; Average Annual Attendance: 13,127; Mem: 500; dues ind $30, family $50; annual meeting in Apr
Income: Financed by mem, admis, special events fund-raisers & sales from mus shop
Collections: Original antiques of Federal period
Publications: The Star (newsletter), quarterly
Activities: Classes for children; dramatic progs; docent training; lects open to pub, 10 vis lectrs per yr; tours; competition with cash awards; original objects of art lent to Pickersgill Retirement Home; mus sales shop sells books, reproductions, prints, slides, Baltimore souvenirs, flags from all nations, maps, country crafts & small antiques

M **Museum**, 844 E Pratt St, Baltimore, MD 21202-4495. Tel 410-837-1793; Fax 410-837-1812; Email info@flaghouse.org; Web: www.flaghouse.org
Open Tues - Sat 10 AM - 4 PM; Admis $3-$5; Estab 1927; Mem: 500; dues $30; annual meeting in Apr
Income: mem, admis, special events fundraisers, sales from museum shop
Special Subjects: Porcelain
Collections: House furnished in authentic federal period furniture & artifacts, books, photographs & documents
Publications: The Star, quarterly
Activities: Lects open to pub, 5 vis lectrs per yr; mus shop sells books & flags of all descriptions

M **UNITED METHODIST HISTORICAL SOCIETY,** Lovely Lane Museum, 2200 Saint Paul St, Baltimore, MD 21218-5805. Tel 410-889-4458; Email archives-history@bwcumc.org; Web: www.lovelylanemuseum.com; *Dir of Librn* James Reaves; *Asst Librn* Wanda Hall; *Exec Secy* Edwin Schell
Estab 1855; a religious collection specializing in Methodism; The main mus room contains permanent exhibits; three other galleries are devoted largely to rotating exhibits; Average Annual Attendance: 4,000; Mem: 417; dues $25-$300; annual meeting in May
Income: $58,000 (financed by mem & religious den)
Purchases: $868
Library Holdings: Clipping Files, Manuscripts, Maps, Memorabilia, Original Documents, Pamphlets, Periodical Subscriptions, Photographs, Prints, Slides
Special Subjects: Archaeology, Bookplates & Bindings, Calligraphy, Decorative Arts, Historical Material, Manuscripts, Maps, Photography, Portraits, Religious Art
Collections: Archaeological items from Evans House, Artifacts with Methodist significance, medallions, Methodist Library & Archives, oil portraits & engraving of United Methodist leader, quilts, Papers of Leading Methodists
Publications: Third Century Methodism, quarterly; annual report
Activities: Docent training; lects open to pub, 1-2 vis lectrs per yr; tours; competitions with awards; individual paintings & original objects of art lent to institutions able to provide proper security upon application & approval by Board of Dir; originate traveling exhibs to United Methodist Churches & Conferences; mus shop sells books, prints, reproductions

L **Library**, 2200 Saint Paul St, Lovely Lane Museum Baltimore, MD 21218-5805. Tel 410-889-4458; Email archives-history@bwcumc.org; *Asst Librn* Betty Ammons; *Librn* Suni Johnson
No admis fee; Estab 1855 specializing in United Methodist history & heritage; Open to general pub for reference; Average Annual Attendance: 4,000; Mem: 600
Income: $43,000
Purchases: $700
Library Holdings: Audio Tapes, Book Volumes 4000, Cassettes, Clipping Files, Filmstrips, Kodachrome Transparencies, Lantern Slides, Manuscripts, Memorabilia, Micro Print, Motion Pictures, Original Art Works, Other Holdings Archives, Pamphlets, Periodical Subscriptions 17, Photographs, Prints, Records, Reels, Reproductions, Sculpture, Slides, Video Tapes
Special Subjects: Archaeology, Architecture, Bookplates & Bindings, Etchings & Engravings, Film, Prints, Religious Art, Historical Material, Manuscripts, Maps, Painting-American, Portraits, Posters, Textiles
Publications: Third Century Methodism, 3 per year
Activities: Tours

M **UNIVERSITY OF MARYLAND, BALTIMORE COUNTY,** Center for Art Design and Visual Culture, 1000 Hilltop Circle, Baltimore, MD 21250-0002. Tel 410-455-3188; Email sgardner@umbc.edu; Web: cadvc.umbc.edu; *Exec Dir* Symmes Gardner; *Research Prof & Chief Cur* Maurice Berger; *Cur Colls & Outreach* Sandra Abbott; *Bus Mgr* Janet Magruder
Open Tues - Sat 10 AM - 5 PM, cl New Year's Eve & Day; Christmas Eve, Day & week; Estab 2003 to present exhibs & pub programs
Collections: paintings; sculpture; drawings; printmaking; graphic design; digital art; video; film; architecture; art history
Exhibitions: Rotating exhibits
Publications: Books; catalogs
Activities: Educ progs; artist workshops; lects open to pub; gallery talks; tours; art programming; workshops; integrated art events

M **WALTERS ART MUSEUM,** 600 N Charles St, Baltimore, MD 21201-5185. Tel 410-547-9000; Fax 410-783-7969; Email info@thewalters.org; Web: www.thewalters.org; *Chair Bd Trustees* Ellen N. Bernard, PhD; *Exec Dir* Dr Julia Marciari-Alexander, PhD; *Cur Renaissance & Baroque Art* Joaneath Spicer; *Deputy Dir Mus Advancement* Joy Heyman; *COO* Kathleen Basham; *Communs Mgr* Gabriella Souza; *Asst Cur 18th-19thc Art* Jo Briggs
Open Wed - Sun 10 AM - 5 PM, Thurs 10 - 9 PM, cl Mon, Tues & federal holidays except New Year's Day, MLK Jr Day & Easter Sunday; No admis fee for permanent coll; special coll fees apply, discounted rates for adult & college groups of 10+; Estab 1931 by the will of Henry Walters & opened in 1934 as an art mus. Hackerman House Mus of Asian Art opened in 1990; A Renaissance revival mus of 1905 with a contemporary wing of five floors opened in 1974, covering 126,000 sq ft of exhibition space with auditorium, library & conservation laboratory; Average Annual Attendance: 190,000; Mem: 4600; dues $55 & up
Income: $15 (financed by endowment, mem, city & state appropriation, grants & admis
Library Holdings: Auction Catalogs, Book Volumes, CD-ROMs, Compact Disks, Exhibition Catalogs, Kodachrome Transparencies, Maps, Photographs, Prints, Slides
Special Subjects: Antiquities-Assyrian, Antiquities-Byzantine, Antiquities-Egyptian, Antiquities-Etruscan, Antiquities-Greek, Antiquities-Oriental, Antiquities-Persian, Antiquities-Roman, Asian Art, Baroque Art, Decorative Arts, Islamic Art, Ivory, Jewelry, Medieval Art, Oriental Art, Painting-American, Painting-British, Painting-European, Painting-French, Religious Art, Renaissance Art, Sculpture, Porcelain
Collections: The Collection covers the entire history of art from Egyptian times to the beginning of the 20th century. It includes important groups of Roman sculpture, Etruscan, Byzantine & medieval art
Publications: Bulletin, bi-monthly; journal, annually; exhibition catalogues
Activities: Classes for adults & children; dramatic progs; docent training; seminars; lects open to pub; concerts; gallery talks; tours; films; fellowships offered; exten dept serves Baltimore City & nearby counties; book traveling exhibs 3-4 per yr; originate traveling exhibs to mus throughout the world; mus shop sells books, reproductions, slides, Christmas cards, notepaper, gifts

L **Library**, 600 N Charles St, Baltimore, MD 21201-5185. Tel 410-547-9000; Fax 410-783-7969; Email lherbert@thewalters.org; Web: www.thewalters.org/research/library.asp; *Head of Library* Chris Henry
Open Mon - Fri 9:30 AM - 4:30 PM (by appointment); No admis fee - only special exhibs; Estab 1934 serves staff of the mus & open to the pub by appointment; Non-circulating
Income: $154,000
Purchases: $73,000

Library Holdings: Auction Catalogs, Book Volumes 104,000, DVDs, Maps, Photographs, Reproductions
Special Subjects: American Western Art, Antiquities-Assyrian, Archaeology, Architecture, Ceramics, Decorative Arts, Drawings, History of Art & Archaeology, Painting-American, Religious Art, Restoration & Conservation, Sculpture, Silver, Silversmithing, Stained Glass
Activities: Classes for adults & children; docent training; Lects open to pub; 6 vis lectrs per yr; concerts; gallery talks; tours; mus shop sells books, reproductions, prints, cards & jewelry

CHESTERTOWN

A **HISTORICAL SOCIETY OF KENT COUNTY,** 101 Church Alley, Chestertown, MD 21620; PO Box 665, Chestertown, MD 21620-0665. Tel 410-778-3499; Email director@kentcountyhistory.org; Web: www.kentcountyhistory.com; *Exec Dir* Diane Daniels
Open Tues-Fri 10AM-4PM, Sat May-Oct 1 - 4PM; Admis adults $3 children & students free; Estab 1936; dedicated to the collection & presentation of county history; Headquarters are in the early 18th century Geddes-Piper House (c 1784), beautifully restored and furnished; Average Annual Attendance: 2,000; Mem: 700; dues family $50, single $30; annual meeting in Apr
Income: Financed by mem & donations
Special Subjects: Embroidery, Furniture, Manuscripts, Maps, Painting-American, Period Rooms
Collections: Furniture, pictures, Indian artifacts, fans, Chinese porcelain teapots, Maps, Portraits, Archival library (genealogy)
Exhibitions: Permanent house museum
Activities: Lect for members & community; vis lectrs 5 per yr; tours; open house with traditional costuming; sales shop sells books & maps

M **WASHINGTON COLLEGE,** Kohl Gallery, 300 Washington Ave, Gibson Ctr for the Arts Chestertown, MD 21620. Tel 410-778-6499; Email kohl_gallery@washcoll.edu; Web: www.washcoll.edu/about/campus/kohl-gallery/; *Contact* Donald McColl
Open Wed - Fri 1 PM - 6 PM, Sat - Sun 11 AM - 4 PM, cl Mon & Tues; No admis fee; 1,200 sq ft gallery equipped with environmental controls
Income: Financed by Washington College parents Benjamin and Judy Kohl
Collections: Fine art
Exhibitions: Visiting exhibits, including student & faculty shows

CHEVY CHASE

C **RITZ-CARLTON HOTEL COMPANY,** Art Collection, 4445 Willard Ave, Ste 800 Chevy Chase, MD 20815. Tel 301-547-4700; Fax 801-468-4069; Web: www.ritzcarlton.com; *Design Coordr* Marilyn Bowling; *Pres & CEO* Simon Cooper
Activities: Lect open to public on request; sales shop sells books & reproductions

COLLEGE PARK

M **UNIVERSITY OF MARYLAND, COLLEGE PARK,** The Art Gallery, 1202 Art-Sociology Bldg, College Park, MD 20742. Tel 301-405-2763; Fax 301-314-7774; Email ag210@umail.umd.edu; Web: www.artgallery.umd.edu; *Dir* John Shipman; *Arts Admin Mgr* Jewell Watson
Open during exhibs Mon - Sat 11 AM - 4 PM, cl summer & between exhibs; No admis fee, donations accepted; Estab 1966 to present historic & contemporary exhibitions; Gallery has 4000 sq ft of space, normally divided into one large & one smaller gallery; Average Annual Attendance: 8,000
Income: Financed by university & department funds, grants, catalog sales, traveling exhibitions
Special Subjects: African Art, Painting-American, Prints, Sculpture, Drawings
Collections: 20th century paintings, prints & drawings, including WPA mural studies, paintings by Warhol, Prendergast & Gottlieb, prints by Hundertwasser, Appel, Kitaj, Rivers & Chryssa, 20th century Japanese prints by Hiratsuka, Kosaka, Matsubara, Iwami, Ay-O & others, West African sculpture, Andy Warhol Collection
Exhibitions: Masters of Fine Arts Thesis Exhibitions; Regional Artists & National Artists
Publications: Exhibition catalogs, 1 - 2 per year
Activities: Lects; symposiums & films open to public; 2-3 vis lectrs per yr; gallery talks; tours; individual paintings & original objects of art lent; lending collection contains original art work & print, paintings, photographs & sculpture; one book traveling exhib every other yr; originate traveling exhibs; exhib catalogs sold in gallery

L **Art Library**, Art-Sociology Bldg, College Park, MD 20742. Tel 301-405-9061; Fax 301-314-9725; Web: www.lib.umd.edu/umcp/art/art.html; *Reference Librn* Louise Green; *Library Asst* Amrita Kaur; *Library Technical Asst* Warren Stephenson; *Head Art Library* Lynne Woodruff; *Library Technical Asst* Bonnie Cawthorne
Open Mon - Thurs 8:30 AM - 10 PM, Fri 8:30 AM - 5 PM, Sat 1 AM - 5 PM, Sun 1 - 10 PM; Estab 1979 in new building to serve the needs of the art & art history departments & campus in various art subjects
Income: Financed by university library system
Library Holdings: Book Volumes 95,000, CD-ROMs 30, Exhibition Catalogs, Fiche, Periodical Subscriptions 234, Reels, Reproductions 33,000
Special Subjects: Advertising Design, Afro-American Art, American Indian Art, Graphic Arts, Photography
Collections: Art & Architecture in France, Index photographic de l'art de France, Index Iconologicus, Decimal Index to art of Low Countries, Marburg index, Index of American Design, Deloynes Collections, Southeast Asia Collection
Publications: Bibliography; Checklist of Useful Tools for the Study of Art; Western Art; Asian Art
Activities: Tours

L **Architecture Library**, College Park, MD 20742-7011. Tel 301-405-6317 (architecture), 405-6320 (Libr Colls); Web: www.lib.umb.edu/arch/architecture.html; *Head* Anita Carrico
Open Mon - Thurs 8:30 AM - 10 PM, Fri 8:30 AM - 5 PM, Sat 1 - 5 PM, Sun 1 - 10 PM; Estab 1967 for lending & reference; Circ 25,000
Library Holdings: Book Volumes 37,000, Clipping Files, Fiche 200, Filmstrips, Other Holdings Bd per 6200, Periodical Subscriptions 180, Reels 600
Special Subjects: Architecture, Interior Design, Landscape Architecture
Collections: World Expositions: books & pamphlets on buildings, art work & machinery
Publications: Architecture Library (brochure), annual; Access to Architectural Literature: Periodical Indexes, annual

L **National Trust for Historic Preservation Library Collection**, Hornbake Library, College Park, MD 20742-0001. Tel 301-405-6320, 405-3300; Fax 301-314-2709; Email nt_library@umail.umd.edu; Web: www.lib.umd.edu/ntl; *Librn* Sally Sims Stokes; *Prog Management Specialist* Kevin Hammett
Open Mon - Fri 10 AM - 5 PM; Circ For reference only; Accessible via Maryland Room in Hornbake Library
Income: Financed by the University of Maryland
Library Holdings: Audio Tapes, Book Volumes 11,000, Cassettes, Clipping Files, Fiche, Manuscripts, Motion Pictures, Pamphlets, Periodical Subscriptions 300, Photographs, Video Tapes
Special Subjects: Architecture, Historical Material, Period Rooms, Restoration & Conservation

M **Stamp Gallery**, 1220 Stamp Student Union, Adele Stamp Memorial Union College Park, MD 20742. Tel 301-314-8493; Email stampgallery@umd.edu; Web: www.thestamp.umd.edu/gallery; *Cur & Coordr* Jackie Milad
Open Fall & Spring: Mon - Thurs 10 AM - 8 PM, Fri 10 AM - 6 PM, Sat 11 AM - 4 PM; Summer: Mon - Thurs 10 AM - 6 PM, Fri -Sat 11 AM - 4 PM
Special Subjects: Photography
Collections: Contemporary Art

COLUMBIA

M **AFRICAN ART MUSEUM OF MARYLAND,** 5430 Vantage Point Rd Ste B, Columbia, MD 21044-2642. Tel 410-730-7106; Fax 410-730-7105; Email africanartmuseum@aol.com; Web: www.africanartmuseum.org; *Dir* Doris Hillian Ligon; *Events Coordr* Carole L Oduyoye; *VChmn Bd Trustees* Jean W Toomer
Open Tues - Fri 10 AM - 4 PM, Sun 1 - 4 PM & by appointment; Admis adults $3, seniors 55+ $2, AAA guests $1.50, children 12 & under $1, AAAMM mems free; Estab 1980; better understanding of African art & culture; Exhibits African Art: traditional and contemporary; Average Annual Attendance: 40,000; Mem: 300; dues family $50, individual $25, students & senior citizens $20; dues annually; interest in African Art & Culture req
Income: Financed by memberships, grants, corporate support, endowment
Library Holdings: Auction Catalogs, Book Volumes, DVDs, Motion Pictures, Original Documents, Photographs, Sculpture, Slides, Video Tapes
Special Subjects: African Art, Antiquities-Egyptian, Archaeology, Architecture, Art Education, Bronzes, Ceramics, Costumes, Crafts, Decorative Arts, Ethnology, Historical Material, Islamic Art, Ivory, Jewelry, Maps, Photography, Textiles, Furniture
Collections: African art consisting of household items, jewelry, masks, musical instruments, sculpture & textiles, 202 Gold Weights Harold Courlander Coll
Exhibitions: 2-3 exhibits per yr
Publications: Museum Memos, quarterly; The Quartet jazz quarterly
Activities: Workshops & classes for adults, children & families; docent training; lects open to pub, 5 or more vis lectrs per yr; concerts; gallery talks; ann tours to Africa; Akua'ba & Dir's awards given; Legacy in the Arts-Howie Award; original objects of art lent to other mus, institutions & trustees; originates traveling exhibs; mus shop sells books, magazines, original art, reproductions, prints, jewelry, clothing, textiles & crafts

M **HOWARD COMMUNITY COLLEGE,** The Rouse Company Foundation Gallery, 10901 Little Patuxent Pkwy, Columbia, MD 21044. Tel 443-518-1200; *Asst to Dir* Chaya Shapiro; *Art Dir* Rebecca Bafford
Open Mon - Fri 10 AM - 8 PM, Sat - Sun 12 PM - 5 PM, cl univ holidays
Collections: paintings; sculpture; photographs

CUMBERLAND

M **ALLEGANY ARTS COUNCIL THE SAVILLE GALLERY,** (The Saville Gallery), 9 N Centre St, Cumberland, MD 21502. Tel 301-777-2787; Fax 301-777-7719; Email arts@allconet.org; Web: www.alleganyartscouncil.org
Open Mon-Fri 9AM-5PM, Sat 11AM-4PM; May-Nov only Sun 11 AM-4PM; No admis fee
Collections: works by local, regional, & national artists

M **ALLEGANY COUNTY HISTORICAL SOCIETY,** Gordon-Roberts House, 218 Washington St, Cumberland, MD 21502-2827. Tel 301-777-8678; Fax 301-777-8678; Email info@gordon-robertshouse.com; Web: www.gordon-robertshouse.com; *Pres* Sue Morgan; *Pres. Emeritus* Nancy Cotton; *Treas* Karen Sword; *Exec Dir* Evan Slonaker; *Secy* Virginia Schry; *Assistant Director* Lindsay M. Lindsay
Open Wed - Sat 10 AM - 5 PM; Admis $7, seniors $6, children under 12 $5, Veterans - free; Estab 1937, preserve and promote local history; 1867 Victorian house, each room furnished with furniture, antiques, pictures, paintings, changing exhibits; Average Annual Attendance: 3,000; Mem: 500; dues individual $20, couple $30; meetings in March, Sept & Nov
Library Holdings: Book Volumes, Maps, Original Documents, Photographs, Prints, Slides
Special Subjects: Architecture, Carpets & Rugs, Ceramics, Costumes, Decorative Arts, Dolls, Furniture, Glass, Historical Material, Laces, Landscapes, Manuscripts, Maps, Painting-American, Period Rooms, Pewter, Photography, Porcelain, Portraits, Prints, Restorations, Tapestries, Textiles, Watercolors, Drawings, Etchings & Engravings, Pottery, Silver

Collections: period clothing & furnishings, Paintings, Books, Textiles, Weaponry
Exhibitions: (1st Feb, 2017-28th Feb, 2017) Smithsonian Traveling Exhibit: The Way We Worked
Publications: Quarterly newsletter
Activities: Classes for adults & children; docent training; dramatic progs; lects for mem only; lects open to the public; tours; competitions; concerts; 2 vis lectrs per yr; educational trunk show for elementary schools; lending of art objects to other museums, including the Allegany Museum, and Allegany Arts Council; originate traveling exhibs to area schools; mus shop sells books, prints, teapots & tea accessories, toys

M **CUMBERLAND THEATRE,** Lobby for the Arts Gallery, corner of Johnson & Fayette Sts, Cumberland, MD 21502; 101 N Johnson St, Cumberland, MD 21502-2918. Tel 301-759-4990; Fax 301-777-7092; Email boxoffice@cumberlandtheatre.com; Web: www.cumberlandtheatre.com; *Asst Dir* Greg Malloy
Open daily Noon - 8 PM; No admis fee; Estab 1987 to showcase artists & educate audiences; 24 x 30 ft, well-lighted & equipped for work of all sizes; Average Annual Attendance: 24,000; Mem: 29; ann meeting in Nov; meeting monthly
Income: $260,000 (financed by mem, city & state appropriation)
Exhibitions: Juried exhibits accompany the theatrical season
Activities: Dramatic progs; book traveling exhibs 2 per yr; originate traveling exhibs 22 per yr; mus shop sells original art

EASTON

M **ACADEMY ART MUSEUM,** 106 South St, Easton, MD 21601-2949. Tel 410-822-2787; Fax 410-822-5997; Email academy@academyartmuseum.org; Web: www.academyartmuseum.org; *Director* Dennis McFadden; *Chair* Carolyn Williams; *Curator* Anke Van Wagenberg; *Director of Finance* Mabel Williams; *Director of Advancement* Damika Baker; *Director of Programs & Design* Janet Hendricks; *Director of ArtReach & Community Programs* Constance Del Nero; *Supervisor of Buildings & Grounds* Edward Robinson; *Visitor Services Manager* Tracey Mullery
Open daily Mon-Thurs 10 AM - 8 PM, Fri-Sun 10AM - 4PM, cl Thanksgiving, Christmas and New Year's Day; Admis fee $3; free to members; Estab 1958 to promote the knowledge, appreciation & practice of all the arts; a private nonprofit art museum; The museum campus includes three 19th-century historical structures connected during two expansion programs. The 35,000 sq. ft. facility includes six galleries, five educational classrooms, performance hall and a 3,000 volume resource library.; Average Annual Attendance: 55,000; Mem: 1,500; dues Lifetime $7,500, Advocate $500, Sustainer $250, Friend $125, Family $80, Individual $500
Income: Financed by mem, contributions, government, corporate & foundation grants, admis, tuitions, endowment & investments
Library Holdings: Book Volumes, Exhibition Catalogs
Special Subjects: Drawings, Etchings & Engravings, Landscapes, Painting-American, Prints, Sculpture, Watercolors, Woodcuts
Collections: Coll focus includes 19th and 20th century works on paper, painting and sculpture. Sampling of artists represented in the coll include Pierre Bonnard, James McNeill, Whistler, Robert Rauschenberg, Jim Dine, James Rosenquist, Robert Motherwell, Richard Diebenkorn, Gene Davis, Anne Truitt, The Ashcan School, Marc Chagall, Pablo Picasso, Joan Miro, Reign van Rembrandt & more.
Exhibitions: The Academy mounts a number of exhibitions per year featuring local, regional & nationally known artists
Publications: Academy. Printed quarterly; Exhibition catalogues
Activities: Classes in drawing, painting, sculpture, fine crafts plus weekend workshops & open studio sessions; dance & music classes for all ages; children's summer arts prog in all disciplined & arts media; lects open to pub, 8 vis lectrs per yr; gallery talks; concerts; tours; dramatic progs; annual members shows with prizes awarded; sponsored competitions; exten dept serving regional schools & Eastern Shore of Maryland; book traveling exhibs 1-2 per yr

ELLICOTT CITY

A **HOWARD COUNTY ARTS COUNCIL,** 8510 High Ridge Rd, Ellicott City, MD 21043-7502. Tel 410-313-2787; Fax 410-313-2790; Email info@hocorts.org; Web: www.hocoarts.org; *Exec Dir* Coleen West
Open office: Mon - Fri 9 AM - 5 PM; gallery: Mon - Fri 10 AM -8 PM, Sat 10 AM - 4 PM, Sun noon - 4 PM; No admis fee; Estab 1981 to serve pub fostering arts, artists & art organizations; Two exhibition galleries, 2000 sq ft; 10-12 exhibitions annually, studios, classrooms, black box theater, meeting rm; Average Annual Attendance: 50,000; Mem: Dues $25-$500; annual meeting in Sept
Income: $1,200,000 (financed by pub & pvt funds, spec events & earned income
Exhibitions: Changing exhibs every 6 weeks
Activities: Classes for adults & children; dramatic progs, theatrical productions & dance studio; summer camp; lects open to pub; 3-4 lectrs per yr; concerts; gallery talks; tours; sponsoring of competitions; juror's awards; schols offered; sales shop sells original art

FORT MEADE

M **FORT GEORGE G MEADE MUSEUM,** 4674 Griffin Ave, Fort Meade, MD 20755-7047. Tel 301-677-6966; Fax 301-677-2953; Email robert.johnson31@conus.army.mil; Web: www.ftmeade.army.mil/museum.index.htm; *Exhibits Specialist* Barbara Taylor; *Museum History Specialist* David Manning; *Cur* Robert S Johnson
Open Wed - Sat 11 AM - 4 PM, Sun 1 - 4 PM, cl Mon, Tues & holidays; No admis fee; Estab 1963 to collect, preserve, study & display military artifacts relating to the United States Army, Fort Meade & the surrounding region; Average Annual Attendance: 40,000
Income: Financed by federal funds
Special Subjects: Cartoons, Costumes, Graphics, Historical Material, Manuscripts, Maps, Military Art, Photography, Posters, Textiles
Collections: World War I, World War II & Civil War Periods, Military Art Collection
Exhibitions: Development of Armor, 1920-1940; History of Fort George G Meade
Activities: Lects open to pub, 4 vis lectrs per year; gallery talks; tours; living history programs

FREDERICK

M **DELAPLAINE VISUAL ARTS EDUCATION CENTER,** 40 S Carroll St, Frederick, MD 21701. Tel 301-698-0656; Fax 301-663-1080; Email info@delaplaine.org; Web: www.delaplaine.org; *Exec Dir & CEO* Catherine Moreland; *Dir Develop & Communs* Duane Doxzen; *Dir Opers* Marilyn Orsinger; *Gift Gallery Mgr* Jean Frank; *Staff Asst* Padraig Higgins; *Dir Educ* Virginia Rose Kane; *Vol Coordr* Margie Mott; *Special Projects Mgr* Tim Ryan; *Exhibits Mgr* Diane Sibbison; *Instruction Mgr* Janet Ibrahim
Open Mon - Sat 9 AM - 5 PM, Sun 11 AM - 5 PM, cl New Year's Day, Easter, Memorial Day, Independence Day, Labor Day, Thanksgiving, Christmas; No admis fee; Estab 1986 to provide the Frederick region with educational opportunities & experiences in the visual arts through classes, exhibits & progs; Kline Gallery/F&M Gallery: main floor 1,500 sq ft combine, drywall & brick with hanging system; Side Gallery: main floor 240 sq ft; Gardiner Gallery: main Floor, 1,800 sq ft, wall space only; Hall Gallery 2nd floor, 150 sq ft wall space only; New Gallery 2nd floor, 240 sq ft; Average Annual Attendance: 85,000 visitors; Mem: 1,400 mems; dues family $50; individual $30
Library Holdings: Book Volumes 4,000
Collections: photographs; paintings; sculpture
Exhibitions: 50 exhibs ann including: The National Juried Quilt Exhibit; The National Juried Photography Exhibit; The Annual Juried Exhibit; The Frederick County Art Assoc Members' Exhibit; The Frederick All-County Student Art Exhibit & numerous other exhibs
Publications: Spring, Summer, Fall & Winter catalogs
Activities: Classes for adults & children; variety of art enrichment progs for the community including: Creative Outlet, Art Night, The Community Supported Art Project, Easels in Frederick, Focus at the Delaplaine, Local Color, Art Carnival & Frederick Festival of Arts; Community Outreach Progs; lects open to pub; 5 vis lectrs per yr; schols, M&T Senior Schol in Arts; awards; mus shop sells original art, reproductions, prints

FROSTBURG

M **FROSTBURG STATE UNIVERSITY,** The Stephanie Ann Roper Gallery, 101 Braddock Rd, Fine Arts Bldg Frostburg, MD 21532-2303. Tel 301-687-4797; Fax 301-687-3099; Email ddavis@frostburg.edu; *Chair* Dustin P Davis; *Admin Asst* Sharon Gray
Open Sun - Wed 1 - 4 PM; No admis fee; Estab 1972 for educational purposes; Average Annual Attendance: 1,000
Income: Financed by state appropriation
Special Subjects: Folk Art, Prints
Collections: Folk art, prints
Activities: Educ dept; lect open to public, 5 vis lectrs per year; gallery talks; competitions with awards; book traveling exhibitions 4 per year

L **Lewis J Ort Library,** 1 Susan Eisel Dr, Frostburg, MD 21532-2342. Tel 301-687-4395; Fax 301-687-7069; Email lmessman@frostburg.edu; *Dir* Dr Lea Messman-Mandicott; *Exhib Librn* Mary Jo Price
Open Mon - Fri 8 AM - 12 AM, Sat 11 AM - 6 PM & Sun 1 PM - 12 AM
Library Holdings: Audio Tapes, Book Volumes 500,000, Cassettes, DVDs, Exhibition Catalogs, Fiche, Filmstrips, Kodachrome Transparencies, Maps, Motion Pictures, Periodical Subscriptions 1300, Photographs, Prints, Reproductions, Slides, Video Tapes
Collections: poster coll Communist USA 1920's to present

GERMANTOWN

M **BLACKROCK CENTER FOR THE ARTS,** 12901 Town Commons Dr, Germantown, MD 20874. Tel 301-528-2260; Fax 301-528-2266; Email info@blackrockcenter.org; Web: www.blackrockcenter.org; *Gallery Dir* Anne Burton
Open Mon - Sat 10 AM - 5 PM, cl Sun; Estab early 1990s to promote community arts; 30,878 sq ft; Mem: dues $65-$10,000
Exhibitions: Temporary exhibits
Activities: Educ progs; classes for adults & children; tours; artists talks; performance art; workshops

GRANTSVILLE

M **SPRUCE FOREST ARTISAN VILLAGE,** 177 Casselman Rd, Grantsville, MD 21536. Tel 301-895-3332; Email info@spruceforest.org; Web: spruceforest.org; *Contact* April Hershberger
Open May - Oct Mon - Sat 10 AM - 5 PM; No admis fee; Average Annual Attendance: 60,000
Special Subjects: Painting-American, Sculpture, Pottery
Collections: Paintings, pottery, sculpture
Activities: Educ progs; classes for adults; artist residencies; artist workshops; lects open to pub; gallery talks; tours; workshops; public art projects; arts festivals; cultural events

HAGERSTOWN

M **VALLEY ART ASSOCIATION,** Mansion House Art Center, 501 Highland Way, Hagerstown, MD 21740. Tel 301-797-2867; Web: valleyartassoc.com; *Pres* Hal Mason; *Gallery Dir* Susan McNally
Open Fri - Sat 11 AM - 4 PM, Sun 1 PM - 5 PM; Estab 1938; Circa 1849 mansion
Special Subjects: Painting-American, Sculpture

Collections: Oil, watercolor, pastel, acrylic, tempera & encaustic paintings, etchings, silk screens, lithographs, wood block prints, collages & carvings
Exhibitions: Permanent, rotating & temporary exhibits
Activities: Educ progs; classes for adults; artist workshops; lects open to pub; tours; gallery talks; public art projects; cultural events

M **WASHINGTON COUNTY ARTS COUNCIL,** Gallery, 34 S Potomac St, Hagerstown, MD 21740-5513. Tel 301-791-3132; Email info@washingtoncountyarts.com; Web: www.washingtoncountyarts.com; *Exec Dir* Mary Anne Burke; *Gallery Mgr* Chris Brewer
Open Tues-Fri 11 AM - 5 PM, Sat 10 AM - 4 PM; Admis free; Estab 1968; Exhib gallery & the gallery shop representing local artists
Income: financed by mem, donations, grants, fundraisers, sponsorships
Collections: works by regional artists
Exhibitions: Exhibs change monthly

M **WASHINGTON COUNTY MUSEUM OF FINE ARTS,** 401 Museum Dr, City Park Hagerstown, MD 21740-6271; PO Box 423 Hagerstown, MD 21741-0423. Tel 301-739-5727; Fax 301-745-3741; Email info@wcmfa.org; Web: www.wcmfa.org; *Pres* Bradley Pingrey; *Assoc Cur* Jennifer Smith; *Registrar* Linda Dodson; *Educator* Amy Hunt; *Dir* Rebecca Massie Lane
Open Tues - Fri 9 AM - 5 PM, Sat 9 AM - 4 PM, Sun 1 - 5 PM, cl Mon; No admis fee; Estab 1930 to exhibit, interpret & conserve art; The mus consists of eleven galleries; Average Annual Attendance: 70,000; Mem: 980; dues $30 & up
Income: Financed by local government, mem & donations
Special Subjects: Drawings, Glass, Jade, Laces, Oriental Art, Painting-American, Prints, Sculpture
Collections: American pressed glass, sculpture, 19th & early 20th century American art
Exhibitions: Exhibits drawn from the Permanent Collection - 19th & 20th Century American Art
Publications: American Pressed Glass; Old Master drawings; bi-monthly bulletin; catalogs of major exhibitions; catalog of the permanent collection
Activities: Classes for adults & children; dramatic progs; docent training; lects open to pub, 10 vis lectrs per yr; concerts; gallery talks; tours; competitions with awards; original objects of art lent to accredited mus; originate traveling exhibs; sales shop sells books & original art

HYATTSVILLE

A **PYRAMID ATLANTIC,** 4318 Gallatin St, Hyattsville, MD 20781. Tel 301-608-9101; Fax 301-608-9102; Email hello@pyramid-atlantic.org; Web: www.pyramidatlanticartcenter.org; *Dir* Jose Dominguez; *Artistic Dir* Gretchen Schermerhorn; *Gallery Dir* Kristina King
Open Tues - Sat 10 AM - 6 PM, Sun noon - 5 PM, cl Mon; No admis fees; Estab 1981; Mem: Dues $40 - $500
Collections: works by nat & international artists

LAUREL

M **MARYLAND-NATIONAL CAPITAL PARK & PLANNING COMMISSION,** Montpelier Arts Center, 9652 Muirkirk Rd, Laurel, MD 20708-2605. Tel 301-377-7800, 410-792-0664; Fax 301-377-7801; Email montpelier.arts@pgparks.com; Web: www.pgparks.com; *Dir* Sonya Kitchens; *Asst Dir* Susanne Fields-Kuehl; *Technical Dir* Beth Crisman
Open daily 10 AM - 5 PM; No admis fee; Estab 1979 to serve artists regionally & to offer high quality fine arts experiences to pub; Main Gallery houses major invitational exhibitions by artists of regional & national reputation; Library Gallery houses local artists' exhibitions; Resident Artists' Gallery provided to artists who rent studio space; Small library of donated volumes; Average Annual Attendance: 56,000; Mem: 83; 50 individuals; 30 families
Income: $300,000 (financed by county appropriation, grants, classes & studio rentals)
Library Holdings: Book Volumes, Periodical Subscriptions
Publications: Exhibit catalogs; promotional invitations; jazz concerts
Activities: Educ prog; classes for adults & children; workshops in specialized areas; lects open to pub, 3-4 vis lectrs per yr; gallery talks; concerts (14 jazz, 7 blues & folk, 4 classical recitals); tours; competitions with exhibs awards/honorariums; book traveling exhibs, annually; originate traveling exhibs; Jazzmont label produces and sells jazz CD's

LEONARDTOWN

M **NORTH END GALLERY,** 41652 Fenwick St, Leonardtown, MD 20650. Tel 301-475-3130; Web: www.northendgallery.com
Open Tues - Sat 11 AM - 5 PM, Sun 12 PM - 4 PM; Estab 1986 to promote traditional & contemporary arts
Special Subjects: Watercolors, Sculpture, Pottery, Jewelry, Decorative Arts, Stained Glass, Photography
Collections: Oils, acrylics, watercolors, hand-pulled serigraphs, sculpture, pottery, jewelry, decorative art, stained glass, painted silk & photography
Exhibitions: Monthly exhibits
Activities: Annual Event: Community Show in summer

MARBURY

M **MATTAWOMAN CREEK ART CENTER,** Smallwood State Park, Marbury, MD 20658; PO Box 258, Marbury, MD 20658-0258. Tel 301-743-5159; Email mattawomanart@aol.com; Web: www.mattawomanart.org; *Pres* Edwin Thiedeman; *Coordr* Mary DeMarco-Logue
Open Gallery: Fri - Sun 11 AM - 4 PM; Office: Tues & Thurs 11 AM - 3 PM; cl Thanksgiving; Christmas; No admis fee, donations appreciated; Non-profit art gallery; a variety of art classes yearly; Mem: Any adult interested in the visual arts
Collections: works by regional artists; paintings; sculpture
Exhibitions: 9-10 Exhibs per yr
Activities: Classes for adults; docent training; lects open to pub; gallery talks; sales shop sells books, original art, prints, jewelry & sculpture

MOUNT AIRY

M **SWETCHARNIK ART STUDIO,** 7044 Woodville Rd, Mount Airy, MD 21771-7934. Tel 301-829-0137; Email sara@swetcharnik.com; Web: www.swetcharnik.com; *Dir & Artist* William Swetcharnik; *Project Coordr & Artist* Sara Morris Swetcharnik
Open by appointment; No admis fee; donations accepted; Estab1980; Artwork by Sara Morris Swetcharnik & William Swetcharnik; Average Annual Attendance: 5,000
Library Holdings: Book Volumes, Exhibition Catalogs, Reproductions, Sculpture
Special Subjects: Decorative Arts, Drawings, Photography, Sculpture
Collections: Works by Sara & William Swetcharnik
Activities: Formal educ progs; guided tours; lects open to pub; Fulbright grants; alumni award; loan, temporary & traveling exhibs; mus shop sells books, original art & reproductions

ROCKVILLE

M **JEWISH COMMUNITY CENTER OF GREATER WASHINGTON,** Jane L & Robert H Weiner Judaic Museum, 6125 Montrose Rd, Rockville, MD 20852-4857. Tel 301-881-0100; Fax 301-881-5512; Web: www.jccgw.org; *Pres* Steven Lustig; *Exec Dir* Michael Witkes; *Gallery Dir* Karen Falk; *Art Gallery Mgr* Phyllis Altman; *CEO* Toni Goodman; *Chief Operating Officer* Michael Feinstein; *Prog Dir* Tracey Dorfmann
Open Mon - Thurs Noon - 4 PM & 7:30 - 9:30 PM, Sun 2 - 5 PM; No admis fee; Estab 1925 to preserve, exhibit & promulgate Jewish culture; Center houses mus & Goldman Fine Arts Gallery; Average Annual Attendance: 25,000
Income: Financed by endowment, corporate, private & pub gifts, grants & sales
Exhibitions: Monthly exhibits, Sept-June; Fine art, fine craft, documentary photography; seven to eight temporary exhibitions yearly including Israeli Artists & American & emerging artist
Publications: Exhibition catalogues; brochures
Activities: Classes for adults & children; docent training; lects open to pub; concerts; gallery talks; tours; book traveling exhibs; originate traveling exhibs; mus shop sells books, original art, reproductions & prints

SAINT MICHAELS

M **CHESAPEAKE BAY MARITIME MUSEUM,** 213 N Talbot St, Saint Michaels, MD 21663; PO Box 636, Navy Point Saint Michaels, MD 21663-0636. Tel 410-745-2916; Fax 410-745-6088; Email comments@cbmm.org; Web: www.cbmm.org; *Pres* Langley Shook; *Cur* Pete Lesher
Open daily 10 AM - 6 PM (Summer), 10 AM - 5 PM (Fall), 10 AM - 4 PM (Winter); cl New Year's Day, Thanksgiving, Christmas; Admis adults $13, seniors $9, children $5; Estab 1965 as a waterside mus dedicated to preserving the maritime history of the Chesapeake Bay; Consists of twenty buildings on approx 18 acres of waterfront property including Hooper's Strait Lighthouse, 1879; Average Annual Attendance: 63,000; Mem: 7000; dues $55 - $125
Income: Financed by mem, admis & endowment
Library Holdings: Audio Tapes 300, Book Volumes 9800, Clipping Files, Manuscripts, Maps, Original Art Works, Original Documents, Pamphlets, Periodical Subscriptions 17, Photographs 55,000, Prints, Slides, Video Tapes
Special Subjects: Folk Art, Historical Material, Marine Painting, Photography, Woodcarvings, Manuscripts, Prints, Watercolors
Collections: Paintings, ship models, vessels including skipjack, bugeye, log canoes, & many small crafts, waterfowling exhibits, working boat shop
Publications: Beacons of Hooper Strait (2000)
Activities: Classes for adults & children; docent training; lects open to pub, 4 vis lectrs per yr; concerts; tours; individual paintings & original objects of art lent to other mus; 1-2 book traveling exhibs per yr; mus shop sells books, magazines, reproductions, prints

L **Howard I Chapelle Memorial Library**, PO Box 636, Navy Point Saint Michaels, MD 21663-0636. Tel 410-745-2916; Fax 410-745-6088; Web: www.cbmm.org; *Cur* Pete Lesher; *Coll Mgr* Lynne Phillips
Open by appointment; Estab 1965 for preservation of Chesapeake Bay maritime history & culture; Non-circulating research facility; Average Annual Attendance: 100
Income: Financed by endowment
Library Holdings: Auction Catalogs, Audio Tapes 300, Book Volumes 9800, Cards, Clipping Files, Manuscripts, Pamphlets, Periodical Subscriptions 17, Photographs 55,000
Special Subjects: Folk Art, Marine Painting, Woodcarvings, Maps
Collections: Ships plans, registers, manuscripts; oral histories
Activities: Classes for adults & children; docent training; lects open to pub; 4 vis lectrs per yr; 1-2 book traveling exhibs per yr; mus shop sells books, magazines & prints

SALISBURY

M **SALISBURY UNIVERSITY,** (Ward Foundation) Ward Museum of Wildfowl Art, 909 S Schumaker Dr, Salisbury, MD 21804. Tel 410-742-4988; Fax 410-742-3107; Email ward@wardmuseum.org; Web: www.wardmuseum.org; *Exec Dir* Lora Bottinelli; *Educ Dir* Mark Bushman; *Dir Outreach* Rose Taylor; *Gift & Mem Coordr* Sarah Maciarello; *Registrar* Barbara Gehrm; *Cur & Folklorist* Dr Kristin Sullivan; *Controller* Kevin Evans; *Facilities Dir* Adam Schultz; *Event Dir* Shaina Adkins; *Vol Coordr* Mary Kline
Open Mon - Sat 10 AM - 5 PM, Sun Noon - 5 PM; Admis adults $7, seniors $5, students $3, family $17, mem & SU faculty, staff & students free; Estab 1968 as a

non-profit organization dedicated to preservation & conservation of wildfowl carving; Over 30,000 sq ft with 10 galleries includes interactive theatre, walking audio tour, mus store, observation deck & more; Average Annual Attendance: 30,000; Mem: 2000; dues family $60, individual $35
Income: $1,000,000 (financed by mem, city & state appropriations, grants, donations, gift shop sales)
Library Holdings: Auction Catalogs 200, Audio Tapes 200, Book Volumes 300, Cassettes 200, Clipping Files, DVDs, Exhibition Catalogs 50, Memorabilia, Original Art Works, Pamphlets, Periodical Subscriptions, Photographs, Prints, Records, Reproductions, Slides, Video Tapes
Special Subjects: Anthropology, Crafts, Decorative Arts, Folk Art, Painting-American, Photography, Prints, Sculpture, Watercolors, Woodcarvings, Art History
Collections: Decoys & decorative bird carvings, fowling skiffs & firearms
Exhibitions: Ward World Championship Wildfowl Carving Competition & Art Festival (last weekend of April ann); Chesapeake Wildfowl Expo (2nd wk of October ann); Art in Nature Photo Festival (Aug annual)
Publications: Ward Museum Journal, bi-annual
Activities: Classes for adults & children, docent training; teacher training; lects open to pub; 3 vis lectrs per yr; tours; competition with awards; carving workshops held in Apr, June & Feb; mus shop sells books, magazines, original art, reproductions, prints, decoys & birding items; hand crafted jewelry

M **SALISBURY UNIVERSITY,** Salisbury University Art Galleries, 1101 Camden Ave, Salisbury, MD 21801-6860. Tel 410-548-2547; Fax 410-548-3002; Email eckauffman@salisbury.edu; Web: www.salisbury.edu/universitygalleries; *Dir of Galleries* Elizabeth Kauffman
See website for hours; No admis fee; Estab 1967 to provide a wide range of art exhibitions to the University & community, with emphasis on educational value of exhibitions; Average Annual Attendance: 8,000
Income: Financed mainly by Salisbury State University with additional support from the Maryland State Arts Council, The Salisbury/Wicomico Arts Council & other agencies
Special Subjects: Prints
Exhibitions: Annual faculty & student shows; wide range of traveling exhibitions from various national & regional arts organizations & galleries; variety of regional & local exhibitions; speakers & special events; sculpture gardens
Publications: Announcements
Activities: Workshops for children, students & gen pub; film series; lects open to pub, 1-2 vis lectrs per yr

L **SU Libraries Guerreri Academic Commons**, 1101 Camden Ave, Salisbury, MD 21801. Tel 410-543-6130; Fax 410-543-6203; Web: www.salisbury.edu/library; *Dean of Libraries & Instructional Resources* Dr Beatriz Hardy
Open Mon - Thurs 8 AM - 2 AM, Fri 8 AM - 10 PM, Sat 10 AM - 8 PM, Sun 11 AM - 2 AM; Estab 1925, to support the curriculum of Salisbury University; Circ 2,500; Library has total space of 221,000 sq ft; Average Annual Attendance: 371,966
Library Holdings: Audio Tapes 340, Book Volumes 205,155, Cassettes 495, Clipping Files, Compact Disks 148, DVDs 1,002, Fiche 636,809, Original Art Works 14, Periodical Subscriptions 697, Reels 9,227, Video Tapes 113

SOLOMONS

M **CALVERT MARINE MUSEUM,** PO Box 97, Solomons, MD 20688-0097. Tel 410-326-2042; Fax 410-326-6691; Email mccormmj@co.cal.md.us; Web: www.calvertmarinemuseum.com; *Registrar* Robert J Hurry; *Exhib Designer* Carey Crane; *Master Woodcarver* Skip Edwards; *Cur Maritime History* Richard J Dodds; *Cur Estuarine Biology* David Moyer; *Cur Paleontology* Stephen Godfrey; *Dir* C Douglass Alves Jr; *Deputy Dir* Sherrod A Sturrock; *Bus Mgr* Roxie Welch; *Develop Dir* Vanessa Gill
Open Mon - Sun 10 AM - 5 PM; Admis $9, seniors 55 & over, active military & AAA mems $7, children 5-12 $4; 5,500 sq ft gallery is maintained on maritime history of the region; three permanent exhibits covering marine fossils of the Miocene Epoch, the Maritime history of southern MD; three to four shows per yr; 14 tank aquariums exploring the ecology of the Chesapeake Bay; Average Annual Attendance: 78,000; Mem: 2,500; dues family $60, individual $40
Purchases: $1000
Special Subjects: Archaeology, Historical Material, Manuscripts, Maps, Marine Painting, Watercolors, Woodcarvings
Collections: Joseph S. Bohannon Folk Art Steamboat Painting Colls, E.C. Tufnell Ship Portrait Painting Coll, Louis J. Feuchter Waterscape Painting Coll, C. Leslie Oursler Painting & Drawing Coll, August H. O. Rolle Waterfront Painting Coll, Leonard Vosburgh Painting Coll, A.B. Chesley Boat Drawing Coll, Otto Muhlenfeld Steamboat Painting Coll
Publications: Bugeye Times, quarterly newsletter; Thrills & Spills: The Golden Era of Powerboat Racing in southern Md; Boats for Work, Boats for Pleasure: The Last Era of Wood Boatbuilding in southern MD; Islands in a River: Solomons & Broomes Island, MD; Miocene Shark Teeth from Around the Chesapeake Bay; Working the Water: The Commercial Fisheries of Maryland's Patuxent River; Fossils of Calvert Cliffs; I Remember - Recollections of Pepper Langley: Growing up in Solomons; Cradle of Invasion: A History of the U.S. Naval Amphibious Training Base, Solomons, MD 1942-1945; Tankers in the Patuxent: The Esso Fleet Lay-Up Site in the 1930s; Early Chesapeake Single-Log Canoes: A Brief History & Introduction to Building Techniques; It Ain't Like It Was Then: The Seafood Packing Industry of southern MD; The Patuxent Ghost Fleet 1927-1941; Solomons Mines: A History of the U.S. Naval Mine Warfare Test Station Solomons, MD, 1942-1947; The Othello Affair: The Pursuit of French Pirates on Patuxent River, MD; Calvert Marine Museum, Solomons, MD; Solomons Island & Vicinity: An Illustrated History & Walking Tour; Sirenians & Sirens: Sea Cows & Mermaids
Activities: 898.Classes for adults and children; docent training; lects open to pub, concerts; tours; mus store sells books, magazines, original art, prints, reproductions, hand crafts

L **Library**, 14150 Solomons Island Rd, Solomons, MD 20688; PO Box 97, Solomons, MD 20688-0097. Tel 410-326-2042 exten 14; Fax 410-326-6691; Email information@calvertmarinemuseum.com; Web: www.calvertmarinemuseum.com/library; *Librn* Paul Berry; *Registrar* Robert J Hurry
Open Mon - Fri 9 AM - 4:30 PM, cl weekends; Estab 1970; Library open for research and reference, local maritime history, paleontology; Average Annual Attendance: 100
Income: $2500 (finance by Calvert County government, mem, gift shop, donations & grants)
Purchases: $1000
Library Holdings: Audio Tapes 10, Book Volumes 7,500, CD-ROMs 15, Cassettes 15, Clipping Files, DVDs 12, Exhibition Catalogs, Fiche 10, Manuscripts, Maps, Memorabilia, Micro Print, Original Art Works, Pamphlets, Periodical Subscriptions 40, Photographs 12,500, Prints, Records, Reproductions, Slides 10,000, Video Tapes 175
Special Subjects: Archaeology, Historical Material, Manuscripts, Maps, Marine Painting, Woodcarvings, Prints
Collections: marine/maritime paintings, ship models
Activities: Classes for children; lects open to pub, 3-4 vis lectrs per yr; concerts; mus shop sells books, prints, ship models & jewelry

ST MARY'S CITY

M **ST MARY'S COLLEGE OF MARYLAND,** The Dwight Frederick Boyden Gallery, SMC, St Mary's City, MD 20686; 18952 E Fisher Rd, Saint Mary's College St Mary's City, MD 20686-3002. Tel 240-895-4246; Fax 240-895-4958; Email mebraun@smcm.edu; Web: www.smcm.edu/boydengallery; *Dir* Mary E Braun; *Gallery Asst* Daniel Holden
Open Mon - Fri 11AM-5PM; No admis fee; 1600 sq ft exhibition space for temporary exhibits of art; five bldgs with art hung in public areas; Average Annual Attendance: 2,500
Income: Financed by St Mary's College
Purchases: Collection is from donation
Special Subjects: African Art, Afro-American Art, Antiquities-Greek, Antiquities-Roman, Asian Art, Ceramics, Costumes, Crafts, Decorative Arts, Drawings, Etchings & Engravings, Landscape Architecture, Marine Painting, Painting-American, Painting-Dutch, Painting-Flemish, Painting-French, Painting-Japanese, Photography, Portraits, Posters, Prints, Sculpture, Textiles, Watercolors, Woodcarvings, Woodcuts
Collections: Study, developmental, Long Term Loan, SMC, Permanent
Activities: Lects open to pub; gallery talks; tours; competitions sponsored; individual paintings & original objects of art lent to local, nonprofit organizations; lending collection contains original art works & prints, paintings & sculptures; originates traveling exhibs

TAKOMA PARK

L **MONTGOMERY COLLEGE OF ART & DESIGN LIBRARY,** 7600 Takoma Ave CF 120, Takoma Park, MD 20912. Tel 301-649-4454; Fax 301-649-2940; Email mcadlibrary@aol.com; Web: www.mcadmd.org; *Head Librn* Kate Cooper
Open Mon - Fri 9 AM - 5 PM; Estab 1977 to facilitate & encourage learning by the students & to provide aid for the faculty; Circ 8000; College maintains Gudelsky Gallery
Purchases: $7000
Library Holdings: Auction Catalogs, Book Volumes 12,000, Cassettes 50, Clipping Files, Motion Pictures, Periodical Subscriptions 35, Slides 30,000, Video Tapes
Special Subjects: Afro-American Art, Antiquities-Assyrian, Antiquities-Byzantine, Antiquities-Egyptian, Antiquities-Etruscan, Antiquities-Greek, Antiquities-Roman, Architecture, Art History, Calligraphy, Decorative Arts, Drawings, Graphic Arts, Graphic Design, History of Art & Archaeology
Activities: Classes for adults & children

TOWSON

M **TOWSON UNIVERSITY,** Center for the Arts Gallery, 1 Fine Arts Dr., Towson, MD 21204; 8000 York Rd, Towson, MD 21252-0002. Tel 410-704-2333; Fax 410-704-2810; Email elehman@towson.edu; Web: www.towson.edu/main/artsculture/artexhibitions/galleries.asp; *Dir* Dr Erin Lehman; *Cur* Dr J Susan Isaacs
Open Tues - Sat 11 AM - 8 PM; No admis fee; Estab 1973 to provide a wide variety of art exhibitions, primarily contemporary work, with national importance; The main gallery is situated in the fine arts building directly off the foyer. It is 30 x 60 ft with 15 ft ceiling & 15 x 30 ft storage area; Average Annual Attendance: 10,000
Income: $31,000 (financed by state appropriation, cultural services fees & private gifts, University + grants)
Special Subjects: Historical Material, Maps, Marine Painting, Prints, Sculpture, Ceramics, Collages, Costumes, Drawings, Etchings & Engravings, Photography, Textiles
Exhibitions: Cross Pollinated: Hybrid Art Abuzz; Reference Material - Fall 2016
Publications: Calendar, each semester; exhibition posters & catalogs
Activities: Classes for adults & children; community & museum educ; docent training; lect open to public, 8 vis lectrs per year; concerts; gallery talks; book traveling exhibitions 1 per year

M **Asian Arts & Culture Center**, 8000 York Rd, Center for the Arts-Towson University Towson, MD 21252-0001. Tel 410-704-2807; Fax 410-704-4032; Web: www.towson.edu/asianarts; *Dir* Joanna Pecore
Open during acad yr Mon - Sat 11 AM - 4 PM; No admis fee; Estab 1972 to provide an area to display the Asian art collections of the University & present art & culture programs on Asia through-out school year; The gallery is located on the second floor of the Fine Arts Building; Average Annual Attendance: 10,000; Mem: Dues Dragon Circle $1,000 & up, Phoenix Circle $500-$999, Tiger Soc $250-$499, Crane Club $100-$249, general mem $30-$99
Income: Financed by membership, grants & corporate sponsorship
Special Subjects: Antiquities-Oriental, Asian Art, Bronzes, Ceramics, Costumes, Decorative Arts, Folk Art, Furniture, Ivory, Metalwork, Oriental Art, Painting-Japanese, Porcelain, Pottery, Sculpture, Textiles, Prints
Collections: Approx 600 objects from Asia

Exhibitions: Permanent collection; special loan exhibs; exhibs on contemporary art of Asia; student produced exhibs
Publications: Asian Arts & Culture Center newsletter, biannual
Activities: Classes for adults & children; lect open to public; gallery talks; tours; workshops; concerts; performances; academic projects; 0-2 book traveling exhibs

WESTMINSTER

M **MCDANIEL COLLEGE,** (Western Maryland College) Esther Prangley Rice Gallery, 2 College Hill, Dept of Art & Art History, Peterson Hall Westminster, MD 21157-4303. Tel 410-857-2595; Fax 410-386-4657; Email igalliera@mcdaniel.edu; Web: www.mcdaniel.edu; *Dir* Steven Pearson; *Cur* Izabel Galliera
Open Mon - Wed & Fri 10 AM - 4 PM, Thurs 10 AM - 8 PM, Sat noon - 5 PM; call in advance; No admis fee; Estab to expose students to original works by professional artists; Top floor of Peterson Hall/Art Bldg
Income: Financed by college funds
Collections: Permanent collection of international artifacts, Egyptian, African, Native American, Asian, Prints (Picasso, Daumier, Mark Tobey)
Exhibitions: Rotating artist and one student show per yr
Activities: Lects open to pub; vis lectrs; gallery talks

MASSACHUSETTS

AMESBURY

M **THE BARTLETT MUSEUM,** 270 Main St, Amesbury, MA 01913; PO Box 692, Amesbury, MA 01913-0016. Tel 978-388-4528; Email museum@bartlettmuseum.org; Web: www.bartlettmuseum.org; *Cur* Hazele Kray; *Pres* John McCone; *Treas (V)* Wayne Gove; *Mus Shop Mgr* Gina Moscardini
Open Memorial Day - Labor Day Fri & Sun 1 - 4 PM, Sat 10 AM - 4 PM; Estab 1968; Two-room Victorian-style Ferry School built in 1870. Name later changed to The Bartlett School in honor of Josiah Bartlett, signer of America's Declaration of Independence, near whose home the school was sited; Mem: dues patron $100 & up, contributing $25, family $15, individual $5, student $1
Special Subjects: Architecture, Costumes, Dioramas, Furniture, Historical Material, Manuscripts, Maps, Painting-American, Period Rooms, Portraits, Sculpture, Silver
Collections: Natural science artifacts, Genealogy
Activities: Workshops

AMHERST

M **AMHERST COLLEGE,** Mead Art Museum, 41 Quadrangle Dr, Amherst, MA 01002; PO Box 5000, Amherst, MA 01002-5000. Tel 413-542-2335; Fax 413-542-2117; Email mead@amherst.edu; Web: www.amherst.edu/mead; *Dir & Chief Cur* David E Little, PhD; *Cur Russian & European Art* Galina Mardilovich; *Security Officer* Jerry Devine; *Preparator* Timothy Gilfillan; *Colls Mgr* Stephen S Fisher; *Study Room Supv & European Print Specialist* Miloslava Hruba; *Cur American Art* Vanja V Malloy, PhD
Open acad season Tues - Thurs & Sun 9 AM - midnight, Fri - 9 AM - 8 PM, Sat 9 AM - 5 PM, academic recess Tues - Sun 9 AM - 5 PM, first Thurs of month open till 8 PM; No admis fee; Estab 1949; The Mead Art Museum houses the art coll of Amherst college spanning 5,000 yrs & encompassing the achievements of many world cultures; Average Annual Attendance: 21,000; Mem: 500; annual meetings in the spring
Special Subjects: African Art, Afro-American Art, Antiquities-Assyrian, Antiquities-Byzantine, Antiquities-Egyptian, Antiquities-Etruscan, Antiquities-Greek, Antiquities-Oriental, Antiquities-Persian, Antiquities-Roman, Archaeology, Asian Art, Baroque Art, Bronzes, Ceramics, Collages, Decorative Arts, Drawings, Etchings & Engravings, Flasks & Bottles, Furniture, Glass, Hispanic Art, Historical Material, Ivory, Jade, Jewelry, Landscapes, Latin American Art, Maps, Medieval Art, Metalwork, Mexican Art, Miniatures, Mosaics, Oriental Art, Period Rooms, Pewter, Photography, Porcelain, Portraits, Posters, Pottery, Pre-Columbian Art, Prints, Religious Art, Renaissance Art, Reproductions, Sculpture, Silver, Stained Glass, Textiles, Watercolors, Woodcarvings, Woodcuts
Collections: Western European & Oriental Collections, African Art; Oriental Art; American Art; Ancient Art; English; Russian Art
Publications: American Art at Amherst: A Summary Catalogue of the Collection at the Mead Art Gallery; American Watercolors & Drawings from Amherst College; Mead Museum Monographs; catalogues for major exhibitions; Mead Art Museum at Amherst College Collection Guide; Picturing Enlightenment: Tangka in the Mead Art Museum; Reinventing Tokyo
Activities: Classes for adults & children; educ dept; docent training; Mellon faculty seminars; lect open to public, 5-10 vis lectrs per year; gallery talks; tours; concerts; Wise prize for fine art; individual paintings & original objects of art lent for exhibition only to other museums; mus shop sells books, magazines, reproductions, prints, postcards, vintage colls

L **Robert Frost Library**, PO Box 5000, Amherst, MA 01002-5000. Tel 413-542-2677; Fax 413-542-2662; *Reference & Fine Arts Librn* Michael Kasper
Open Mon - Thurs 8 AM - 1 AM, Fri 8 AM - midnight, Sat 9:30 AM - 11 PM, Sun 10 AM - 1 AM; Circulating to Amherst College students & five college faculty
Library Holdings: Book Volumes 40,000, Exhibition Catalogs, Fiche, Periodical Subscriptions 82, Slides

ARTS EXTENSION SERVICE
For further information, see National and Regional Organizations

L **JONES LIBRARY, INC,** 43 Amity St, Amherst, MA 01002-2285. Tel 413-259-3090; Fax 413-256-4096; Email info@joneslibrary.org; Web: www.joneslibrary.org; *Dir* Sharon Sharry; *Reference* Matt Berube; *Head Borrower Servs* Linda Wentworth
Open Mon 1 - 5:30 PM, Wed 9 AM 5:30 PM, Tues & Thurs 9 AM - 9:30 PM, Fri & Sat 9 AM - 5:30 PM, Sun 1 - 5 PM; call for appointment for special colls; No admis fee; Estab 1919 as a public library; Circ 520,000; Burnett Gallery - exhibs by local artists; permanent art coll of oil paintings & sculpture; special coll of prints & photographs; Average Annual Attendance: 400,000; Mem: Open to public, no fee
Income: Financed by endowment & town appropriation & state aid
Library Holdings: Audio Tapes, Book Volumes 185.000 (all subjects), Cassettes, Clipping Files, Compact Disks, DVDs, Framed Reproductions, Manuscripts, Memorabilia, Original Art Works, Pamphlets, Periodical Subscriptions 150, Photographs, Records, Reels, Sculpture, Slides
Collections: Ray Stannard Baker, Emily Dickinson, Robert Frost, Julius Lester, Harlan Fiske Stone, Sidney Waugh Writings, local history & genealogy, Burnett Family, Clifton Johnson
Exhibitions: Permanent collection & rotating exhibits on local history
Activities: Classes for children; lects open to public; concerts; tours; sales shop sells tote bags, t-shirts, magazines

M **UNIVERSITY OF MASSACHUSETTS, AMHERST,** University Gallery, 151 Presidents Dr (Ofc 2), Fine Arts Ctr, University of Massachusetts Amherst, MA 01003-9311. Tel 413-545-3670; Fax 413-545-2018; Email ugallery@acad.umass.edu; Web: www.umass.edu/fac/universitygallery; *Gallery Mgr* Craig Allaben; *Coll Registrar* Justin Griswold; *Dir* Loretta Yarlow; *Educ Cur* Eva Fierst
Open Tues - Fri 11 AM - 4:30 PM, Sat & Sun 2 - 5 PM during school yr; No admis fee; Estab 1975; Main Gallery 57-1/2 x 47 ft, East Gallery 67-1/2 x 20-1/2 ft, West Gallery 56-1/2 x 23-1/2 ft, North Gallery 46-1/2 x 17-1/2 ft; Average Annual Attendance: 15,000; Mem: 150; dues $25 & up
Income: University
Special Subjects: Drawings, Etchings & Engravings, Painting-American, Photography, Pottery, Prints, Sculpture, Southwestern Art
Collections: 20th century American works on paper including drawings, prints & photographs
Publications: Exhibition catalogs
Activities: Lects open to public, 2-3 vis lectrs per yr; gallery talks; tours; individual art works from the permanent collection loaned to other institutions; originate traveling exhibs; peer institutions/museums

M **Herter Art Gallery**, 125A Herter Hall, Amherst, MA 01003. Tel 413-545-0976; *Contact* Trevor Richardson

L **Dorothy W Perkins Slide Library**, 130 Hicks Way, 221 Barlett Hall Amherst, MA 01003-9269. Tel 413-545-3314; Fax 413-545-3880, 3135; Web: www.umass.edu; *Cur Visual Coll* Nathalie Bridegam
Open Mon - Fri noon - 4 PM; Graduate student reference slide library; Circ 60,000 (slides); campus only
Library Holdings: Other Holdings Interactive video disks; Magnetic disks 50; Study Plates 7000, Slides 270,000

ANDOVER

A **ANDOVER HISTORICAL SOCIETY,** 97 Main St, Andover, MA 01810-3803. Tel 978-475-2236; Fax 978-470-2741; Email andover@historical.org; Web: www.andoverhistorical.org; *Exec Dir* Elaine Clements; *Mus Educ* Sarah Syct
Open Jan 1 - July 31, Tues - Sat 10 AM - 4 PM, cl Mon & Aug; Admis adults $4, student & seniors $2; 1911; 1819 period rm, museum & barn as well as research lib & archives; Average Annual Attendance: 8,335
Library Holdings: Auction Catalogs, Book Volumes, Clipping Files, Manuscripts, Original Art Works, Pamphlets, Photographs, Prints, Sculpture
Special Subjects: Costumes, Furniture, Historical Material, Jewelry, Manuscripts, Maps, Painting-American, Period Rooms, Photography, Portraits
Exhibitions: Amos Blanchard Home, Contemporary Andover Artist Series, quarterly changing exhibits
Activities: Adult, 3rd grade school children & family day progs; lects; walking tours; house & garden tours; originate traveling exhibs; mus shop sells books, original art & prints

A **NORTHEAST DOCUMENT CONSERVATION CENTER, INC,** 100 Brickstone Sq, Andover, MA 01810-1494. Tel 978-470-1010; Fax 978-475-6021; Email nedcc@nedcc.org; Web: www.nedcc.org; *Registrar* Jonathan Goodrich; *Develop & Pub Rels Coordr* Julie Martin; *Mgr Financial Servs* Joanne Masse; *Admin Asst* Juanita Singh
Open Mon - Fri 8:30 AM - 4:30 PM; Estab 1973 to improve preservation programs of libraries, archives, mus & other historical & cultural organizations; to provide services to institutions that cannot afford in-house conservation facilities or that require specialized expertise; & to provide leadership to the preservation field; Headquarters located in a fire-proof 1920's mill building with masonry construction, including concrete floors 8" thick; 20,000 sq ft; state-of-the-art security systems & environmental controls

M **PHILLIPS ACADEMY,** Addison Gallery of American Art, Chapel Ave, Andover, MA 01810; 180 Main St, Andover, MA 01810-4161. Tel 978-749-4015; Fax 978-749-4025; Email addison@andover.edu; Web: www.addisongallery.org; *Dir* Judith F Dolkart; *Dir Devel* David A Freilach; *Registrar* James M Sousa; *Assoc Dir & Cur* Susan Faxon
Open Tues - Sat 10 AM - 5 PM, Sun 1 - 5 PM, cl Mon, Aug & holidays; No admis fee; Estab 1931 in memory of Mrs Keturah Addison Cobb, to enrich permanently the lives of the students by helping to cultivate & foster in them a love for the beautiful. The gift also includes a number of important paintings, prints & sculpture as a nucleus for the beginning of a permanent collection of American art; Maintains small reference library for on site use only; Average Annual Attendance: 35,000; non-circulating libraries; Mem: 500, dues $50-10,000
Income: Financed by endowment & gifts
Purchases: American art
Library Holdings: Book Volumes, Exhibition Catalogs, Other Holdings, Photographs, Reproductions, Slides
Special Subjects: Drawings, Painting-American, Photography, Prints, Sculpture, Silver, Watercolors, Woodcuts, American Western Art, Decorative Arts, Furniture, Glass, Graphics

Collections: 18th, 19th & 20th centuries drawings, paintings, prints, sculpture, photographs, film, videotapes
Publications: Sheila Hicks! 50 Years; William Wegman; American Vanguards; Alfred Maurer
Activities: Educ Program, classes for children; lects open to public; lects for mems only; 8-10 vis lectrs per year; gallery talks; fellowships; book traveling exhib: 2-3; originates traveling exhibs for nat and internat mus; mus shop sells books, original art, reproductions & other gift items

ARLINGTON

M **ARLINGTON CENTER FOR THE ARTS,** 41 Foster St, Gibbs Ctr Arlington, MA 02474-6813. Tel 781-648-6220; Email info@acarts.org; Web: www.acarts.org; *Exec Dir* Linda Shoemaker; *Dir Educ & Prog* Sarah Buyer; *Operations Mgr* Pam Shanley; *Prog & Mktg Coordr* Michael Mahin; *Office Admin* Lorraine Kilby
Open Mon - Fri 9 AM - 5 PM; Estab 1988 as a space for artist collaboration & art educ; Mem: dues $25-$50
Collections: Work by local artists
Exhibitions: Temporary exhibits
Activities: Educ progs; classes for adults & children; workshops; performances; special events

ATTLEBORO

M **ATTLEBORO ARTS MUSEUM,** 86 Park St, Attleboro, MA 02703-2335. Tel 508-222-2644; Fax 508-226-4401; Email office@attleboroartsmuseum.org; Web: www.attleboroartsmuseum.org; *Pres Bd Trustees* Nancy Aleo; *Exec Dir* Mim Brooks Fawcett
Open Tues - Sat 10 AM - 4 PM, cl Sun & Mon; No admis fee, donations accepted; Estab 1927 to exhibit the works of contemporary New England artists, as well as the art works of the museum's own collection. These are pub openings plus several competitive exhibits with awards & an outdoor art festival; Three galleries with changing monthly exhibits of paintings, drawings, sculpture, ceramics, jewelry, glass, metals & prints; Average Annual Attendance: 7,800; Mem: 230; dues life mem & corporate $1000, patron $500, benefactor $250, sponsor & supporting $125, assoc $40, family $ 50, artist mem $35 student & senior citizen $25
Income: Financed by mem, gifts, local & state grants
Library Holdings: Auction Catalogs, Audio Tapes, Cards, Clipping Files, Original Art Works, Original Documents, Pamphlets, Periodical Subscriptions, Photographs, Prints, Records, Sculpture, Slides
Special Subjects: Painting-American, Prints
Collections: Paintings & prints
Exhibitions: Holiday Show; Annual Area Artist Exhibit; Individual & Group Exhibits of Various Media & Subject; Competitive Painting Show; Fall Members Show; Competitive Photography Show; Selections from the Permanent Collection; Hi-art
Publications: Newsletter, every 2 months
Activities: Classes for adults & children; workshops; lects open to pub; vis lectrs; 2 concerts per yr; gallery talks; tours; competitions, schols offered; painting & photography; 1st, 2nd, 3rd place awards & Honorable Mention; original objects of art lent; mus shop sells photograph albums, ceramics & jewelry

BEVERLY

M **BEVERLY HISTORICAL SOCIETY,** Cabot, Hale & Balch House Museums, 117 Cabot St, Beverly, MA 01915-5196. Tel 978-922-1186; Email info@beverlyhistory.org; Web: www.beverlyhistory.org; *Dir & Cur* Susan J Goganian; *Pres* Dan Lohnes
Open Cabot Museum: yearly Tues & Thurs - Sat 10 AM - 4 PM, Wed 1 - 9 PM; Balch House: June - Oct; Hale House June - Oct; Admis adults $5, seniors & students $4, children under 16 free; 1891; The Balch House built in 1636 by John Balch contains period furniture. The Hale House was built in 1694 by the first minister, John Hale. Cabot House built in 1781-82 by prominent merchant & private owner, John Cabot; Average Annual Attendance: 2,000; Mem: 450; dues families $50, single $30; annual meeting in March
Special Subjects: Archaeology, Ceramics, Decorative Arts, Embroidery, Folk Art, Furniture, Glass, Historical Material, Maps, Marine Painting, Painting-American, Pewter, Photography, Porcelain, Portraits, Posters, Pottery, Prints, Textiles
Collections: 120 paintings containing portraits, folk & Revolutionary War scenes, 1000 pieces furniture, toys, doll houses, military & maritime items & pewter, books, manuscripts & photographs
Exhibitions: Beverly and the American Revolution
Publications: Quarterly newsletter
Activities: Docent training; lect open to pub & some for members only; gallery talks by arrangement; tours; individual paintings & original objects of art lent to other museums & libraries; sales shop sells books, reproductions & postcards

L **Library,** 117 Cabot St, Beverly, MA 01915. Tel 978-922-1186; Email info@beverlyhistory.org; Web: www.beverlyhistory.org; *Dir* Susan Goganian; *Cur* Darren Brown
Open Tues, Thurs-Sat 10 AM - 4 PM, Wed 1 PM - 9 PM; Admis adults $5, children under 16 free; Estab 1891; Mem: 500/50family
Library Holdings: Audio Tapes, Book Volumes 4100, Clipping Files, Manuscripts, Maps, Memorabilia, Motion Pictures, Original Art Works, Original Documents, Pamphlets, Periodical Subscriptions 8, Photographs, Prints, Sculpture, Slides, Video Tapes
Special Subjects: Archaeology, Architecture, Ceramics, Coins & Medals, Costume Design & Constr, Crafts, Decorative Arts, Drawings, Embroidery, Folk Art, Furniture, Glass, Historical Material, Lettering, Manuscripts, Maps, Marine Painting, Painting-American, Pewter, Photography, Sculpture, Pottery, Prints, Silver, Textiles, Watercolors, Landscapes
Collections: 800,000+ objects & documents connected to Beverly history
Activities: mus shop sells books, reproductions & prints

BOSTON

ARCHAEOLOGICAL INSTITUTE OF AMERICA
For further information, see National and Regional Organizations

A **ARTS & BUSINESS COUNCIL OF GREATER BOSTON, INC,** Volunteer Lawyers for the Arts of MA, 15 Channel Center St, Ste 103 Boston, MA 02210. Tel 617-350-7600; Fax 888-412-7610; Email mail@artsandbusinesscouncil.org; Web: www.artsandbusinesscouncil.org; *Exec Dir* James F Grace; *Assoc Dir* David Holland
Open Mon - Fri 9 AM - 5 PM; Estab 1989 to provide legal services, advice and educational programming to artists and cultural organizations in Massachusetts
Income: Financed in part by the Massachusetts Cultural Council, a state agency & by the Boston Bar Assoc; earned income; sponsorships; individual donations
Activities: Lect open to public; legal referral program

A **BOSTON ARCHITECTURAL COLLEGE,** McCormick Gallery, 320 Newbury St, Boston, MA 02115-2703. Tel 617-585-0100; Fax 617-585-0110; Email communication@the-bac.edu; Web: the-bac.edu; *Pres* Glen LeRoy; *Dir Admin Operations* Patti Vaughn
Open Mon - Fri 8 AM - 10:30 PM, Sat & Sun 8 AM - 8 PM; No admis fee; Estab 1889 for educ of architects & designers; Small exhibition space on first floor; Average Annual Attendance: 2,000; Mem: Annual meetings of institutes of higher education in September
Activities: Classes for adults; lects open to pub, 16 vis lectrs per yr; competitions; exten dept servs professional architects; originates traveling exhibs

L **Library,** 320 Newbury St, Boston, MA 02115. Tel 617-585-0155; Fax 617-285-0151; Email library@the-bac.edu; Web: the-bac.edu/library; *Library Dir* Susan Lewis; *Assoc Library Dir* Kristen Liberman
Open Mon - Thurs 10 AM - 10:30 PM, Fri & Sat 10 AM - 5 PM, Sun Noon - 7 PM; No admis fee; 1889 to create a place to learn & relax with those in architecture & related fields; Circ 13,500; Open to pub
Income: $168,000
Library Holdings: Book Volumes 2000, CD-ROMs 200, Manuscripts 15, Original Art Works 5, Periodical Subscriptions 125, Sculpture 12, Slides 25,000
Collections: 18th, 19th & early 20th centuries architectural books from the colls of practicing architects, 20th century architecture, interior design & landscape arch
Activities: Classes for adults; 3 vis lectrs per yr; multiple awards

L **BOSTON ATHENAEUM,** 10 1/2 Beacon St, Boston, MA 02108-3703. Tel 617-227-0270; Fax 617-227-5266; Email cure@bostonathenaeum.org; Web: www.bostonathenaeum.org; *Stanford Calderwood Dir* Dr Elizabeth Barker; *Susan Morse Hilles Sr Cur Paintings & Sculpture & Dir Exhibs* David Dearinger; *Cur Prints & Photos* Catharina Slautterback; *Chief Conservator* Dawn Walus; *Dir Opers* Robert West; *Dir Bus Opers & Augusta Thomas Dir Finance* Christopher Boudrot; *Ann C and David J Brober Curator of Rare Books, Manuscripts & Maps* Stanley Cushing
Open to pub Tues Noon - 8 PM, Wed - Sat 10 AM - 4 PM; mem hours Mon - Thurs 9 AM - 8 PM, Fri & Sat 9 AM - 5 PM; Admis general (13 & up) $10; 1807; Mem: dues $220 - $700
Library Holdings: Auction Catalogs, Book Volumes 550,000, CD-ROMs, Clipping Files, Exhibition Catalogs, Manuscripts, Maps, Memorabilia, Original Art Works, Original Documents, Pamphlets, Periodical Subscriptions 400+, Photographs, Prints, Reels, Reproductions, Sculpture
Collections: 19th century Boston prints & photographs, American & European painting & sculpture, World War I posters, George Washington's Library
Exhibitions: 3 art exhibitions per year, open to the public
Activities: Tours for pub & mem only; seminars

M **BOSTON CENTER FOR THE ARTS,** Mills Gallery, 551 Tremont St, Boston, MA 02116. Tel 617-426-5000; Email info@bcaonline.org; Web: www.bcaonline.org; *Pres & CEO* Gregory Ruffer; *Dir Visual Arts* Randi Hopkins
Open Wed & Sun noon - 5 PM, Thurs - Sat noon - 9 PM; Estab to present contemporary works by emerging & established artists & curators
Special Subjects: Photography, Mixed Media, Drawings
Collections: Contemporary art
Exhibitions: Temporary exhibits
Activities: Educ progs; artist workshops; gallery talks; tours; competitions with awards; six exhibs per yr; dance & theater performances

A **THE BOSTON PRINTMAKERS,** at Lesley University, College of Art & Design, 29 Everett St Boston, MA 02138. Tel 617-735-9898; Email info@bostonprintmakers.org; Web: www.bostonprintmakers.org; *Pres* Renee Covalucci; *VPres* Sharon Hayes; *Treas* Susan Denniston; *Secy* Bob Tomolillo
Estab 1947 to aid printmakers in exhibiting their work; to bring quality work to the public; Average Annual Attendance: 15,000; Mem: 250; dues $40; mem by jury selection; annual meeting April; North American Printmaker
Income: Financed by mem, entry fees, and commission on sales
Exhibitions: Prints, artist books, etchings, lithograph, mixed media, monotypes, serigraph & woodcut; biennial open, juried North American print biennial and Arches biennial student exhibition, contemporary Cuban printmakers
Publications: Exhibition catalogs; 60 Years of North American Prints 1947-2007 by David Acton
Activities: Lects open to pub; gallery talks; competitions with awards and prizes; purchase & materials awards at biennial; individual paintings and original objects of art lent to local museums, galleries, libraries and schools including Duxbury Art Complex Museum, Boston Public Library, DeCordova Museum; book 5 traveling exhibs per yr; originates traveling exhibs to galleries at libraries, universities and schools

L **BOSTON PUBLIC LIBRARY,** Central Library, 700 Boylston St, Copley Sq Boston, MA 02116-2813. Tel 617-536-5400; Email ask@bpl.org; Web: www.bpl.org; *Pres* David Leonard; *Director of Library Svcs.* Michael Colford; *Chief of Collections* Laura Irmscher; *Chief Financial Officer* Ellen Donaghey; *Central Library Mgr.* Anna Fahey-Flynn; *Dir. of Neighborhood Svcs.* Priscilla Foley; *Dir. of Strategic Partnerships* Ben Hires; *Chief of Communications* Lisa Pollack; *Dir. of Opers.* Eamon Shelton

Open Mon - Thurs 9 AM - 9 PM, Fri & Sat 9 AM - 5 PM, Sun (Oct - May) 1 - 5 PM; No admis fee; Estab library 1848; Circ Reference only; Building contains mural decorations by Edwin A Abbey, John Elliott, Pierre Puvis de Chavannes, & John Singer Sargent; bronze doors by Daniel Chester French; sculptures by Frederick MacMonnies, Bela Pratt, Louis Saint Gaudens; paintings by Copley & Duplessis; & bust of John Deferrari by Joseph A Coletti; Average Annual Attendance: 2,500,000
Income: Financed by city & state appropriation
Library Holdings: Book Volumes 6,000,000 (entire library), Clipping Files, Exhibition Catalogs, Fiche, Lantern Slides, Manuscripts, Memorabilia, Original Art Works, Original Documents, Other Holdings Architectural Drawings, 700,000, Pamphlets, Periodical Subscriptions 16,704 (entire library), Photographs, Prints, Reels, Reproductions, Sculpture
Special Subjects: Aesthetics, Archaeology, Architecture, Art History, Bookplates & Bindings, Calligraphy, Cartoons, Costume Design & Constr, Crafts, Decorative Arts, Dioramas, Drawings, Etchings & Engravings, Fashion Arts, Graphic Arts, Handicrafts, Illustration, Interior Design, Landscape Architecture, Latin American Art, Manuscripts, Maps, Miniatures, Photography, Printmaking, Prints, Restoration & Conservation, Stained Glass, Watercolors, Woodcuts
Publications: Exhibition catalogues
Activities: Classes for adults & children; lect open to public; concerts; tours

L **Arts Reference Department**, 700 Boylston St, Boston, MA 02116-2813. Tel 617-536-5400; Email fineartsref@bpl.org; Web: www.bpl.org; *Cur Arts Dept* Kim Tenney; *Cur Fine Arts* Eve Griffin; *Sr Music Reference Librn* Charlotte Kolczynski; *Cur Music* Liz Berndt-Morris; *Sr Fine Arts Reference Librn* Sarah Hagan
Open Mon - Thurs 9 AM - 9 PM, Fri & Sat 9 AM - 5 PM, Sun 1 - 5 PM; Estab for visual, design, decorative arts & music reference collections and services; Circ Non-circ
Library Holdings: Book Volumes, Clipping Files, Exhibition Catalogs, Fiche, Lantern Slides, Manuscripts, Memorabilia, Original Art Works, Original Documents, Other Holdings Architectural drawings, Pamphlets, Periodical Subscriptions, Photographs, Reels
Special Subjects: Architecture, Art History, Ceramics, Decorative Arts, Etchings & Engravings, Painting-American, Porcelain, Pottery, Prints, Stained Glass
Collections: Connick Stained Glass Archives, Maginnis & Walsh architectural drawings, Peabody & Stearns Architectural Drawings, W G Preston Architectural Drawings, Archives of American Art (unrestricted) Microfilm, Society of Arts & Crafts, Boston, Archives, Vertical files on local artists, galleries, museums societies, Vertical & image files on Boston's built-environment, Clarence Blackall scrapbooks & sketchbooks, Allen A Brown Music Collection
Activities: Educ prog; Bibliographic instruction; student & public orientations

M **Albert H Wiggin Gallery & Print Department**, Copley Sq, Boston, MA 02117; 700 Boylston St, Boston, MA 02117-2813. Tel 617-536-5400; Email prints@bpl.org; Web: www.bpl.org; *Head Spec Colls* Beth Prindle
Open (by appointment) Mon - Thurs 9 AM - 9 PM, Fri & Sat 9 AM - 5 PM, Sun 1 - 5 PM; Admis free
Library Holdings: Book Volumes 3600, Clipping Files, Exhibition Catalogs, Lantern Slides 6,623, Memorabilia, Original Art Works 150,000, Photographs 1.2 mil, Prints
Special Subjects: Architecture, Photography, Prints, Drawings, Etchings & Engravings, Historical Material, Portraits, Posters, Prints, Watercolors, Woodcuts
Collections: Collection of 18th, 19th & 20th century French, English & American prints & drawings, including the Albert H Wiggin Collection, 20th century American prints by Boston artists, 19th century photographs of the American West & India & Middle East, Boston Pictorial Archive, paintings, postcards, Boston Herald Traveler Photo Morgue, ephemera, Chromolithographs of Louis Prang & Co, Historic American Collection
Exhibitions: Eight or nine per year drawn from the print department's permanent collections
Activities: Lect open to public, 1-2 vis lectrs per year; internships offered

L **Rare Book & Manuscripts Dept**, 700 Boylston St, McKim Bldg, 3rd Fl Boston, MA 02116-2813. Tel 617-859-2225; Email rare_books@bpl.org; Web: www.bpl.org/research/rb; *Head Spec Colls* Elizabeth Prindle; *Reference Librn* Sean Casey; *Chief Conservator* Christopher Letizia; *Cur Manuscripts* Kimberly Reynolds
Currently closed for inventory & capital improvements through 2019; Estab 1934; Average Annual Attendance: 1,400
Income: Financed by trust funds
Purchases: Books, manuscripts, maps, prints & photographs relevant to our current subject strengths
Library Holdings: Book Volumes 600,000, Lantern Slides, Manuscripts, Memorabilia, Micro Print, Periodical Subscriptions 4, Photographs, Reels
Special Subjects: Antiquities-Greek, Antiquities-Roman, Bookplates & Bindings, Calligraphy, Coins & Medals, Costume Design & Constr, Etchings & Engravings, Ethnology, Fashion Arts, Landscape Architecture, Historical Material, Manuscripts
Collections: FEER World's Fair Collection, Americana, book arts, Boston theater, history of printing, juvenilia, landscape & gardening, theater costume design, Boston history, Colonial & Revolutionary America, library of John Adams, antislavery, library of John Adams, Medieval Manuscripts, Barton Collection of Shakespeare
Exhibitions: Exhibits change every 3-4 months & feature books, manuscripts, maps & prints that make up department collections;
Activities: Seminars; lect open to public, 3 vis lectrs per year; concerts; tours; sales shop sells postcards & pamphlets

M **BOSTON UNIVERSITY ART GALLERIES,** The Faye G, Jo & James Stone Gallery, 855 Commonwealth Ave, Boston, MA 02215-1303. Tel 617-353-3329; Fax 617-353-4509; Email gallery@bu.edu; Web: www.bu.edu/art; *Mng Dir* Josh Buckno; *Artistic Dir* Lynne Cooney
Open Tues - Sun Noon - 5 PM, Thurs until 8 PM, cl Boston Univ holidays & intersessions; No admis fee; Estab 1960; One exhibition space, 250 running ft, 2500 sq ft
Collections: Contemporary & New England Art
Exhibitions: Rotating 8 week Exhib
Publications: Annual exhibition catalogs
Activities: Lects open to pub; 2-3 vis lectrs per yr; gallery talks; book traveling exhibs 1 per yr; originate traveling exhibs

M **Rubin-Frankel Gallery**, Florence & Chafetz Hillel House, 213 Bay State Rd, Fl 2 Boston, MA 02215-1499. Tel 617-353-7634; Fax 617-353-7660; Email sarahy@bu.edu; Web: www.bu.edu/hillel/about/gallery; *Educator* Sarah Young
Open Mon - Thurs & Sat 9 AM - 9 PM, Fri 9 AM - 11 PM
Special Subjects: Judaica, Painting-American, Painting-Israeli, Photography, Prints, Religious Art, Sculpture, Tapestries, Watercolors
Collections: paintings; drawings; sculpture; photographs

M **THE BOSTONIAN SOCIETY,** Old State House Museum, 206 Washington St, Boston, MA 02109-1773. Tel 617-720-1713; Fax 617-720-3289; Email oldstatehouse@bostonhistory.org; Web: www.bostonhistory.org; *Exec Dir* Nathaniel Sheidley; *Coll Mgr* Sira Dooley Fairchild; *Dir Educ & Exhibs* Kathy Mulvaney; *Dir Facilities & Historic Preservation* Matt Ottinger
Open daily 9 AM - 5 PM, Memorial Day to Labor Day 9 AM - 9 PM; Admis adults $10, seniors & students $8.50; Estab 1881 to collect & preserve the history of Boston; Average Annual Attendance: 100,000; Mem: 1250; dues supporter $150, family $80, individuals $50, seniors $40, student/teacher $25
Income: Financed by endowment, mem, admis, grants, state & federal appropriations
Library Holdings: Book Volumes, Lantern Slides, Manuscripts, Maps, Memorabilia, Original Documents, Other Holdings, Pamphlets, Periodical Subscriptions, Photographs, Prints, Reproductions, Slides
Special Subjects: Ceramics, Coins & Medals, Decorative Arts, Drawings, Folk Art, Manuscripts, Maps, Marine Painting, Painting-American, Portraits, Prints, Scrimshaw, Sculpture, Watercolors, Architecture, Costumes, Furniture, Historical Material, Military Art
Collections: Paintings & artifacts relating to Boston history, Maritime art, Revolutionary War artifacts, prints
Exhibitions: Ongoing exhibitions
Publications: Proceedings of The Bostonian Society; The Bostonian Society Newsletter
Activities: Classes for children; lects open to pub; concerts; gallery talks; walking tours; Boston History Award; individual paintings & original objects of art lent to other mus; mus shop sells books, decorative arts, reproductions, prints & toys

L **Library**, 15 State St, 3rd Fl Boston, MA 02109-3502; 206 Washington St, Old State House Boston, MA 02109-1702. Tel 617-720-1713; Fax 617-720-3289; Email library@bostonhistory.org; Web: www.bostonhistory.org; *Colls Mgr* Sira Dooley Fairchild
Open Tues - Thurs 10 AM - 3:30 PM; Admis nonmembers $10; college students $5; Estab 1881 to collect & preserve material related to the history of Boston; For reference only; Mem: dues benefactor $500, supporter $100, family & individual $50, sr 62 & over $40, student $25
Library Holdings: Book Volumes 7500, Clipping Files, Fiche, Lantern Slides, Manuscripts, Maps, Memorabilia, Original Art Works, Other Holdings Documents; Ephemera; Postcards; Scrapbooks, Pamphlets, Periodical Subscriptions 10, Photographs 30,000, Prints 2000, Reproductions, Slides 3000
Special Subjects: Historical Material, Manuscripts, Maps, Photography, Prints
Publications: Bostonian Society Newsletter, quarterly; monthly e-news
Activities: Educ prog; classes for adults & children; lects open to pub, over 6 vis lectrs per yr for members only; concerts; gallery talks; tours; Boston History Award; mus shop sells books, reproductions & prints

M **BROMFIELD ART GALLERY,** 450 Harrison Ave, Boston, MA 02118. Tel 617-451-3605; Email info@bromfieldgallery.com; Web: www.bromfieldgallery.com; *Gallery Dir* Gary Duehr
Open Wed - Sat Noon - 5 PM; No admis fee; Estab 1975 to exhibit contemporary art with an emphasis on New England artists; Two galleries, approx 500 sq ft; Average Annual Attendance: 3,000; Mem: 20; dues $750; monthly meetings
Income: Financed by mem and sales
Activities: Lect open to public, 5 vis lectrs per year; gallery talks; sponsoring of competitions

M **CHASE YOUNG GALLERY,** 450 Harrison Ave No 57, Boston, MA 02118. Tel 617-859-7222; Email kate@chaseyounggallery.com; Web: www.chaseyounggallery.com; *Dir* Kate Kostopoulos; *Dir* Jane Young
Open Tues - Sat 11:30 AM - 5 PM; Estab 1990 to exhibit a wide variety of contemporary artists with a specific focus on innovative painting mediums
Collections: contemporary paintings, sculpture, & photographs

A **CITY OF BOSTON ARTS & CULTURE,** City Hall Galleries, 1 City Hall Sq, Rm 802 Boston, MA 02201-2029. Tel 617-635-3914; Email arts@boston.gov; Web: www.boston.gov/arts; *Chief, Arts & Culture* Julie Burros; *Exhibs Dir & Cur* John Crowley
Open Mon - Fri 8:30 AM - 5:30 PM; No admis fee; Estab 1965 to showcase Boston art & its cultural heritage; gallery space throughout City Hall bldg, incl Mayor's Art Gallery, Scollay Square Gallery & Mayor's Neighborhood Gallery; Average Annual Attendance: 100,000; Mem: none
Purchases: Artwork available to public for purchase
Special Subjects: Afro-American Art, Archaeology, Ceramics, Crafts, Juvenile Art, Painting-American, Photography, Sculpture
Exhibitions: Jan-Feb Black History Month; March - Women's History; Apr-May Boston Public Schools Ann Art Show; June-Dec Juried Art Show
Publications: Catalog and guide to the art work owned by the City of Boston, in preparation; Passport to Public Art
Activities: Competitions, 12 lects, concerts, gallery talks & tours

EMBARCADERO CENTER LTD
For further information, see Boston Properties, LLC

M **GIBSON SOCIETY, INC,** Gibson House Museum, 137 Beacon St, Boston, MA 02116-1504. Tel 617-267-6338; Fax 617-267-5121; Email info@thegibsonhouse.org; Web: www.thegibsonhouse.org; *Museum Admin* Michelle Coughlin; *Cur* Wendy Swanton; *Cur* Meghan Gelardi Holmes; *Museum Asst* Barbara Callahan

Open year round by tour only Wed - Sun 1, 2 & 3 PM; Admis adults $9, seniors & students $6, children $3; Estab 1957 as a Victorian House museum; memorial to Gibson family & Boston's Back Bay; Victorian time capsule, early Back Bay Town House, eight rooms with Victorian & Edwardian era furnishings; Average Annual Attendance: 2,300
Income: Financed by trust fund & admis
Special Subjects: Period Rooms
Collections: Decorative arts, paintings, sculpture, Victorian period furniture, objects assoc with Gibson & related families
Activities: Lect open to public, 6-10 vis lectrs per year; holiday open house; galley talks; guided tours; summer lect series July & Aug, Thurs 5:30 PM; original objects of art lent to museums & galleries; sales shop sells books, prints & postcards

A **THE GUILD OF BOSTON ARTISTS,** 162 Newbury St, Boston, MA 02116-2889. Tel 617-536-7660; Email bostonguild@gmail.com; Web: guildofbostonartists.org; *Pres* Jean Lightman; *Gallery Dir* Alex Ciesielski; *Asst Dir* Daniel Lloyd-Miller
Open Tues - Sat 10:30 AM - 5:30 PM, other times by appt; No admis fee; Estab & incorporated 1914, nonprofit art assn; Exhibiting 53 of New England's finest contemporary realist painters; front gallery features continual show of general membership; President's gallery showcases solo or group themed shows; Mem: 53+ artist members - ann dues $775; $100 assoc mems & patron mems $100 ann; student mems $35 ann; artist mems meeting in Apr, must live in New England & work in form of traditional, representational painting or sculpture. No qualifications for assoc or patron mems. Student mems must show proof of full time study under professional artist
Income: Sales, donations, rental of studios
Exhibitions: Rotating exhibitions; Annual Regional Juried Exhibition (non-mem); Annual Members Juried Exhibition
Publications: American Art Review; Fine Art Connoisseur; Artscope Magazine
Activities: Artist demonstrations, painting workshops & classes for adults & children; lect open to public, receptions, gallery talks & tours; concerts; various awards at both juried exhibitions

A **HISTORIC NEW ENGLAND,** (Society for the Preservation of New England Antiquities), 141 Cambridge St, Harrison Gray Otis House Boston, MA 02114-2799. Tel 617-227-3956; Email info@historicnewengland.org; Web: www.historicnewengland.org; *Pres & CEO* Carl R Nold; *Exec VPres & COO* Diane Viera; *VPres Advancement* Jennifer Kent; *Dir Finance* Wendy Gus; *Team Leader, Preservation Svcs* Carissa Demore; *Team Leader, Visitor Experience* Peter Gittleman; *Team Leader, Property Care* Benjamin Haavik; *Team Leader, Coll Svcs* Julie Solz
Open Wed - Sun 11 AM - 4:30 PM; Admis $10, discounts to senior citizens, ICOM, AAA, AAM, WGBH members, members no charge; Estab & incorporated 1910, the Otis House serves as both headquarters & mus for Historic New England; owns over 36 historic houses throughout New England; Average Annual Attendance: 208,368; Mem: 7,870; dues national $35, individual $50, household $60
Income: financed by members, grants
Special Subjects: Architecture, Decorative Arts, Furniture, Landscapes, Period Rooms, Photography, Textiles
Collections: American & European decorative arts & antiques with New England history, photographs, houses
Publications: Historic New England Magazine (3xs)
Activities: Classes for adults & school children; lects open to pub, 5-10 vis lectrs per yr; tours; awards book prize, prize for collecting works on paper, Community Preservation Grants; originate traveling exhibs; mus shop sells books/merchandise

L **Library and Archives,** Harrison Gray Otis House, 141 Cambridge St Boston, MA 02114-2702. Tel 617-994-5909; Email archives@historicnewengland.org; Web: www.historicnewengland.org; *Cur Library & Archives* Lorna Condon; *IT Officer* David Dwiggins
Open Mon - Fri & the first Sat of April, May, June, Oct, Nov & Dec 9:30 AM - 4:30 PM; Admis nonmembers $5, mems free; Estab 1910 to document New England architecture and material culture from the 17th century to the present with emphasis on 19th & 20th centuries; For reference; Mem: 6500; dues individual $45, household $55
Library Holdings: Auction Catalogs, Audio Tapes, Book Volumes, Cards, Clipping Files, Exhibition Catalogs, Fiche, Filmstrips, Kodachrome Transparencies, Lantern Slides, Manuscripts, Maps, Memorabilia, Original Art Works, Original Documents, Pamphlets, Periodical Subscriptions, Photographs, Prints, Slides, Video Tapes
Special Subjects: Advertising Design, Architecture, Bookplates & Bindings, Decorative Arts, Drafting, Drawings, Etchings & Engravings, Graphic Design, Historical Material, Interior Design, Landscape Architecture, Manuscripts, Period Rooms, Photography
Collections: 123,00 object & 1,500,000 million archival materials, 35,000 architectural drawings, 10,000 books including rare, 10,000 newspaper clippings, 450,000 photographs & negatives, 2,500 prints, 800 maps & atlases, 700 drawings & watercolors, 1,000 linear ft manuscripts
Activities: Internships; lects open to pub; tours; Historic New England book prize & Collector's prize; mus shop sells books & reproductions

A **INQUILINOS BORICUAS EN ACCION (IBA),** Villa Victoria Center for the Arts, 405 Shawmut Ave, Boston, MA 02118-2029. Tel 617-927-1707; Fax 617-536-5816; Email info@ibaboston.org; Web: www.ibaboston.org; *CEO* Vanessa Calderon-Rosado; *COO* Mayra Negron-Rivera; *CFO* Karla Jaramillo; *Sr Prog Dir* Rafael Medina
Open Mon - Fri 9 AM - 5 PM; La Galeria open by appointment; Free and open to the pub; Estab 1968 to support the development & empowerment of the Villa Victoria community in Boston's south end; Maintains La Galeria at Villa Victoria Ctr for the Arts; Average Annual Attendance: 900
Activities: Classes for children; lects open to the pub; concerts; gallery talks; tours

M **INSTITUTE OF CONTEMPORARY ART/BOSTON,** 25 Harbor Shore Dr, Boston, MA 02210-2172. Tel 617-478-3100; Email info@icaboston.org; Web: www.icaboston.org; *Ellen Matilda Poss Dir* Jill Medvedow; *Dir Exhibs* Abby Newbold; *Barbara Lee Chief Cur* Eva Respini; *Chief Preparator* Tim Obetz; *Sr Registrar* Alison Hatcher; *Dir Educ* Monica Garza; *CFO & COO* Michael Taubenberger; *Bill T Jones Dir Performing & Media Arts* David Henry; *Dir Retail* Liz Adrian; *Dir Develop* Katie Mayshak; *IT Dir* Maurice Haddon
Open Tues - Wed & Sat - Sun 10 AM - 5 PM, Thurs - Fri 10 AM - 9 PM, cl Thanksgiving, Christmas & New Year's; Admis adults $15, seniors $13, students $10, mems & youth 17 & under free; New England's premier contemporary art museum, the ICA presents provocative exhibitions by national and international artists that explore the ideas, issues and images of our times. For over 65 years the ICA has been the first to show many of the most innovative and inspired artists from around the world; Mem: 1600; dues $65 & up; annual meeting in Sept
Income: Financed by mem, gifts & grants, earned income
Publications: Exhibition catalogs
Activities: Educ dept; classes for adults & children; docent training; lects open to pub, 20 vis lectrs per yr; film series; video; concerts; gallery talks; tours; performances; competitions; ICA Artist prize; book traveling exhibs annually; originate traveling exhibs, circulating to other national & international contemporary art mus; mus shop sells books, magazines, t-shirts, catalogs, cards, posters

M **ISABELLA STEWART GARDNER MUSEUM,** 25 Evans Way, Boston, MA 02115-5538. Tel 617-566-1401; Fax 617-566-7653; Email information@isgm.org; Web: www.gardnermuseum.org; *Norma Jean Calderwood Dir* Peggy Fogelman
Open Mon & Wed - Sun 11 AM - 5 PM, Thurs until 9 PM; cl Tues, Independence Day, Patriot's Day, Thanksgiving, Christmas & New Year's Day; Admis adults $15, seniors $12, college students with current ID $10, children under 18 free; Estab 1903, the mus houses Isabella Stewart Gardner's various collections; Mus building is styled after a 16th century Venetian villa; all galleries open onto a central, glass-roofed courtyard, filled with flowers that are changed with the seasons of the year; Average Annual Attendance: 225,000; Mem: 5,750; dues $35 & up
Income: Financed by endowment, fundraising, mem donations & door charge
Special Subjects: Antiquities-Greek, Antiquities-Roman, Oriental Art, Painting-American, Painting-Dutch, Painting-Flemish, Painting-French, Painting-Italian
Collections: Gothic & Italian Renaissance, Roman & classical sculpture, Dutch & Flemish 17th century, Japanese screens, Oriental & Islamic ceramics, glass, sculpture, 19th century American and French paintings, major paintings of John Singer Sargent & James McNeill Whistler
Publications: Guide to the Collection; Oriental & Islamic Art in the Isabella Stewart Gardner Museum; Drawings - Isabella Stewart Gardner Museum; Mrs Jack; Sculpture in the Isabella Stewart Gardner Museum; Textiles - Isabella Stewart Gardner Museum; children's books - Isabella Stewart Gardner Museum; Fenway Court; History & Companion Guide; Spec Exhibition Catalogs
Activities: Progs for children; lects open to pub; concerts; gallery talks; tours; sales shop selling books, reproductions, prints, slides, postcards & annual reports, jewelry, gifts

L **Isabella Stewart Garden Museum Library & Archives,** 25 Evans Way, Boston, MA 02115-5538. Tel 617-264-6003; Email archives@isgm.org; Web: www.gardnermuseum.org
Open by appointment Mon, Wed, Fri & Sat; Estab 1903; Open to scholars who need to work with mus archives; building designed in style of 15th century Venetian palace; Mem: 3000
Income: endowments & mem donations
Library Holdings: Auction Catalogs, Book Volumes 800, Clipping Files, Exhibition Catalogs, Manuscripts, Memorabilia, Periodical Subscriptions 19, Photographs
Special Subjects: Art History
Collections: Objects spanning 30 centuries, 1,000 rare books spanning 6 centuries including papers of museum founder, rich in Italian Renaissance painting
Exhibitions: Rotating exhibits
Activities: Educ prog; lects open to pub, 6-8 vis lectrs per yr; symposia; concerts; gallery talks; tours; sales shop sells books, gifts, reproductions, prints, slides & postcards

M **KAJI ASO STUDIO,** Gallery Nature & Temptation, 40 Saint Stephen St, Boston, MA 02115-4510. Tel 617-247-1719; Fax 617-247-7564; Email administrator@kajiasostudio.com; Web: www.kajiasostudio.com; *Exec Dir* Kate Finnegan
Tues 7 - 9 PM, Fri 1 -5 PM & by appointment; No admis fee; Estab 1973 to foster new/emerging artists representational to abstract-positive feeling; Two rooms on 1st floor 10' x 14' in historic brownstone; track lighting; Mem: 40; monthly dues $150
Exhibitions: Watercolor, Oil, Drawing, Ceramic, Japanese Calligraphy & Sumi Painting
Publications: Dasoku Journal of Arts, biannual
Activities: Classes for adults; lects open to pub; concerts; gallery talks; tours

L **MASSACHUSETTS COLLEGE OF ART AND DESIGN,** Library, 621 Huntington Ave, Boston, MA 02115-5801. Tel 617-879-7150; Fax 617-879-7110; Email library@massart.edu; Web: massart.edu/library; *Librn* Greg Wallace; *Visual Resources Dir* Caitlin Pereira
Open Mon - Thurs 8 AM - 9 PM, Fri 8 AM - 6 PM, Sat & Sun 11 AM - 5 PM
Library Holdings: Audio Tapes, Book Volumes 35,000, Cards, Cassettes, Compact Disks, DVDs, Exhibition Catalogs, Fiche 8,000, Filmstrips, Memorabilia, Motion Pictures, Original Art Works, Pamphlets, Periodical Subscriptions 491, Photographs, Prints, Records, Sculpture, Slides
Special Subjects: Art Education, Art History

M **Bakalar & Paine Galleries,** 621 Huntington Ave, South Hall Boston, MA 02115-5801. Tel 617-879-7337; Fax 617-879-7340; Email galleryinfo@massart.edu; Web: massart.edu/galleries; *Dir & Cur* Lisa Tung
Open Mon - Sat noon - 6 PM, Wed noon - 8 PM; No admis fee; Largest free contemporary art space in New England
Collections: works by contemporary artists

A **MASSACHUSETTS HISTORICAL SOCIETY,** 1154 Boylston St, Boston, MA 02215-3631. Tel 617-536-1608; Fax 617-859-0074; Email collections@masshist.org; Web: www.masshist.org; *Pres* Catherine Allgor; *VPres Colls* Brenda Lawson; *Dir Communs* Carol Knauff; *Dir Progs* Gavin Kleespies; *Asst Dir Develop* Audrey Wolfe; *Cur Art & Artifacts* Anne E Bentley; *Dir Research* Katheryn Viens

Open Mon - Sat 10 AM - 4 PM; No admis fee; Estab 1791 as the nation's first historical society; Art works by appt only; for library hours see www.masshist.org/events; Average Annual Attendance: 3,000
Income: Financed by endowment, grants, individual gifts
Special Subjects: Historical Material, Manuscripts
Collections: Archives, historical material, paintings, sculpture
Exhibitions: Temporary exhibitions
Publications: Journal
Activities: Educ prog; teacher progs; lects open to pub; special exhibits for members & their guests

L **Library**, 1154 Boylston St, Boston, MA 02215-3631. Tel 617-536-1608; Fax 617-859-0074; Email library@masshist.org; Web: www.masshist.org; *Stephen T Riley Librn* Peter Drummey; *Dir Library* Elaine Heavey; *Reproductions Coordr* Sabina Beauchard; *Sr Library Asst* Rakashi Chand
Open Mon - Fri 9 AM - 4:45 PM, Sat 9 AM - 4 PM; No admis fee; Estab 1791; Galleries, progs, research library; Average Annual Attendance: 8,000
Income: Endowment, grants & individual gifts
Library Holdings: Book Volumes 250,000, Fiche, Manuscripts 3500, Maps, Original Art Works, Original Documents, Photographs, Prints
Special Subjects: Coins & Medals, Manuscripts, Maps, Miniatures, Painting-American, Photography, Portraits, Prints, Historical Material
Publications: Portraits in the Massachusetts Historical Society, Boston 1988 (one edition)
Activities: Lects open to pub; lects for mems only; gallery talks; tours; exhibs; fels

M **MUSEUM OF AFRICAN AMERICAN HISTORY,** 46 Joy St, Boston, MA 02114-4005; 14 Beacon St, Ste 401 Boston, MA 02108-3742. Tel 617-725-0022; Fax 617-720-5225; Email history@maah.org; Web: maah.org; *Exec Dir* Marito Rivero; *Dir Educ* L'Merchie Frazier; *Dir Capital Improvements of Facility Opers* Dana Parcon; *Donor Rels Mgr* Nancy Cao
Open Mon - Sat 10 AM - 4 PM; Admis adults $10, student & seniors $8, children under 12 no charge; Estab in 1967 as a nonprofit educ institution founded to study the social history of New England's Afro American communities & to promote an awareness of that history by means of educational programs, publications, exhibits & special events. The African Meeting House, the Abiel Smith School, the African Meeting House on Nantucket, & the Black Heritage Trail are the chief artifacts of the mus of African American History; 2 galleries; Mem: 200; dues Legacy Society $1000, William Lloyd Garrison Leader $500, Frances E. W. Harper Partner, Josephine Ruffin Preservation $125, Hamilton Smith Family $75, Lewis Hayden Individual $35
Income: Financed by grants, mem & donations
Library Holdings: Auction Catalogs, Book Volumes, Exhibition Catalogs, Maps, Memorabilia, Original Art Works, Pamphlets, Photographs, Prints, Reproductions, Sculpture, Video Tapes
Collections: 18 & 19th Century African American History, Hamilton Sutton Smith Glass Plate Negatives
Exhibitions: Rotating exhibits
Activities: Educ progs; classes for adults & children; lects open to pub; lectrs for mems only; 4 vis lectrs per yr; concerts; gallery talks; tours; individual sculptures & original objects of art lent; book traveling exhibs; mus shop sells books, magazines, original art, reproductions, prints, slides & gifts

M **MUSEUM OF FINE ARTS,** 465 Huntington Ave, Boston, MA 02115-5523. Tel 617-267-9300; Fax 617-247-6880; Email tickets@mfa.org; Web: www.mfa.org; *Ann & Graham Gund Dir* Matthew Teitelbaum; *CBO & Deputy Dir* Katie Getchell; *Deputy Dir* Maria Muller; *CFO & Deputy Dir* Mark Kerwin; *Chief Director's Office* Kristin Ferguson; *Chief Exhibs Strategy* Edward Saywell
Open Mon - Tues & Sat - Sun 10 AM - 5 PM, Wed - Fri 10 AM - 10 PM, cl New Year's Day, Patriots Day, Independence Day, Thanksgiving Day, Christmas Day; Admis adults $25, seniors (65+) & students (18+) $23, youths 7-17 $10 free weekends, weekdays after 3 PM & Boston public school holidays, children 6 and under free; Estab & incorporated in 1870; present building opened 1909; Collection of nearly 500,000 works of art from Ancient Egyptian to contemporary; Average Annual Attendance: 1,200,000; Mem: 67,000; dues $75 - $3,000
Special Subjects: Antiquities-Egyptian, Antiquities-Greek, Antiquities-Roman, Decorative Arts, Oriental Art, Period Rooms, Porcelain, Prints, Sculpture, Silver
Collections: Ancient Nubian & Near Eastern art, Art of Africa, Oceania & Ancient Americas, Chinese, Japanese & Indian art, Egyptian, Greek & Roman art, European & American decorative & minor arts, including period rooms, porcelains, silver, Western & Asian tapestries, costumes & musical instruments, master paintings of Europe & America, print coll from 15th century to present, sculpture, Contemporary
Exhibitions: Specially organized exhibitions are continually on view (www.mfa.org/exhibitions)
Publications: (www.mfa.org/collections/publications)
Activities: Classes for adults & children; docent training; lects open to pub; lects for mems only; concerts; gallery talks; tours; films; book traveling exhibs; organize traveling exhibs; mus shop sells books, magazines, original art, reproductions, prints & slides

L **William Morris Hunt Memorial Library**, 300 Massachusetts Ave, Horticulture Hall, Fl 2 Boston, MA 02115; 465 Huntington Ave, Boston, MA 02115-5523. Tel 617-369-3378; Fax 617-369-4257; Email libstaff@mfa.org; Web: www.mfa.org/collections/libraries-and-archives; *Susan Morse Hilles Dir Library & Archives and Museum Historian* Maureen Melton; *Head Librn* Deborah Barlow Smedstad
Open Mon - Fri 1 - 5 PM; No admis fee; Estab 1870 to house, preserve, interpret & publish its collections; Circ Non-circulating; For reference only; Average Annual Attendance: 1,000,000; Mem: 59,000
Income: Institution
Library Holdings: Auction Catalogs 50,000, Book Volumes 320,000, CD-ROMs, Clipping Files, Exhibition Catalogs, Fiche, Pamphlets 117,000, Periodical Subscriptions 650, Reels
Special Subjects: Carpets & Rugs, Ceramics, Decorative Arts, Drawings, Etchings & Engravings, Furniture, Painting-American, Prints, Sculpture, Textiles, Mosaics, Painting-European, Restoration & Conservation
Activities: Classes for adults & children; docent training; dramatic progs; lects open to pub; concerts; gallery talks; tours; book traveling exhibs

M **MUSEUM OF THE NATIONAL CENTER OF AFRO-AMERICAN ARTISTS,** 300 Walnut Ave, Boston, MA 02119-1369. Tel 617-442-8614; Fax 617-445-5525; Email info@ncaaa.org; Web: ncaaa.org; *Dir & Cur* Edmund B Gaither; *Asst to the Dir* Carol Murray
Open Tues - Sun 1 - 5 PM; Admis adults $5, seniors & students $4; Estab 1969 to promote visual art heritage of Black people around the globe; Suite of three special exhibition galleries; suite of three African Art Galleries; suite of three permanent collection galleries; one local artist gallery; Average Annual Attendance: 10,000; Mem: 250; dues $20-$1,000
Income: $250,000 (financed by private gifts, contracts, etc)
Special Subjects: Afro-American Art
Collections: Early 19th & 20th Century Afro-American Prints & Drawings, visual fine arts of the black world, Caribbean Collection
Exhibitions: Aspelpa: A Nubian King's Burial Chamber
Publications: Newsletter, quarterly
Activities: Dramatic progs; lects open to pub, 6 vis lectrs per yr; concerts; gallery talks; tours; competitions with awards (Edward Mitchell Barrister Award); book traveling exhibs; originates traveling exhibs; sales shop sells books, magazines, prints and small sculpture

M **NATIONAL ARCHIVES & RECORDS ADMINISTRATION,** John F Kennedy Presidential Library & Museum, Columbia Point, 220 Morrissey Blvd Boston, MA 02125. Tel 617-514-1600; Fax 617-514-1652; Web: www.jfklibrary.org; *Dir* Warren Finch; *Deputy Dir* James Roth; *Dir Archives* Karen Adler Abramson; *Cur* Stacey Bredhoff; *Dir Educ & Pub Progs* Nancy McCoy
Open daily 9 AM - 5 PM, cl holidays; Admis adults $14, seniors & college students w/ID $12, youth 13-17 & military $10, mems and children 12 & under free; Estab 1964 to preserve collections of Kennedy papers & other material pertaining to his career; to educate public about J F Kennedy's career & political system; to make materials available to researchers; Library is a nine-story building overlooking Boston Harbor, has two theaters & an exhibition floor; Average Annual Attendance: 220,000
Income: Financed by federal government & national archives trust fund
Library Holdings: Audio Tapes, Book Volumes, Cards, Cassettes, Fiche, Filmstrips, Lantern Slides, Memorabilia, Micro Print, Motion Pictures, Original Art Works, Pamphlets, Photographs, Prints, Reproductions, Slides, Video Tapes
Special Subjects: Historical Material
Collections: 48,000,000 documents & personal papers of John F Kennedy, Robert Kennedy & many others assoc with life & career of John F Kennedy, 7,550,000 ft of film relating to political career, 200,000 photographs, 1300 oral histories, 22,000 paintings & museum objects (personal), manuscripts of Ernest Hemingway, 10,000 photographs of him with family & friends, 800 glass plates coll of Josiah Johnson Hawes
Activities: Classes for children; docent training; lects open to pub; 24 vis lectrs per yr; tours; Profiles in Courage awards; fels & research grants; mus shop sells books, reproductions, prints and slides

M **NICHOLS HOUSE MUSEUM, INC,** 55 Mount Vernon St, Boston, MA 02108-1330. Tel 617-227-6993; Fax 617-723-8026; Email info@nicholshousemuseum.org; Web: www.nicholshousemuseum.org; *Exec Dir* Linda Marshall; *Progs & Colls Coordr* Laura Cunningham; *Communs & Admin Assoc* Charlotte Wittmann; *Visitor Experience & Research Assoc* Victoria Johnson
Open Apr 1 - Oct 31 Tues - Sat 11 AM - 4 PM, Nov 1 - Mar 31 Thurs - Sat 11 AM - 4 PM, cl most major holidays; Admis $10, children 12 & under free; Estab 1961; Historic house museum offers a unique glimpse of late 19th, early 20th century life of Boston's Beacon Hill; original federal design attributed to architect Charles Bulfinch; Average Annual Attendance: 3,000; Mem: 280; dues individual $45, family $75, friend $125, sponsor $300; annual meeting in May
Income: $133,000 (financed by endowment, admis sales, donations, grants, mem)
Special Subjects: Decorative Arts, Period Rooms, Carpets & Rugs, Furniture, Prints, Tapestries, Textiles
Collections: Decorative Arts Collection, Portraits, Oriental Rugs, Sculptures by Augustus Saint-Gaudens
Activities: Docent training; lects open to pub; tours; INLS 2002 Conservation Project; NEH 2002 Conservation Project; mus shop sells books

M **ROBERT KLEIN GALLERY,** 38 Newbury St, 4th Fl Boston, MA 02116. Tel 617-267-7997; Fax 617-267-5567; Email inquiry@robertkleingallery.com; Web: www.robertkleingallery.com; *Owner* Robert Klein; *Dir* Hank Hauptmann
Open Tues - Fri 10 AM - 5:30 PM, Sat 11 AM - 5 PM, other times by appointment; No admis fee; Estab 1980; Fine art photography gallery specializing in 19th century, 20th century & contemporary artists
Collections: photographs, photography books

A **THE SOCIETY OF ARTS & CRAFTS,** 100 Pier 4 Blvd, Ste 200 Boston, MA 02110-1974. Tel 617-266-1810; Fax 617-266-5654; Email director@societyofcrafts.org; Web: www.societyofcrafts.org; *Exec Dir* Fabio J Fornandez; *Gallery Mgr* George Summers; *Develop Dir* Patricia Salic; *Assoc Cur* Luiza deCamargo
Open Mon by appointment, Tues - Sat 10 AM - 6 PM, Thurs 10 AM - 9 PM; No admis fee; Estab 1897 to promote high standards of excellence in crafts & to educate the pub in the appreciation of fine craftsmanship; Two galleries, second level exhibitions; Average Annual Attendance: 8,000; Mem: 700; dues family/dual $60, single $35
Income: financed by mem, gallery sales, grants
Exhibitions: Juried exhibitions presented year round
Publications: Mass Crafts, guide to crafts in central New England, annual
Activities: Lect open to public, vis lectr; gallery talks; awards; sales shop sells fine handmade crafts in ceramics, wood, glass, metal & fiber

M **SUFFOLK UNIVERSITY,** Gallery, Sawyer Bldg, 6th Fl, 8 Ashburton Pl Boston, MA 02108. Tel 617-573-8785; Email gallery@suffolk.edu; Web: www.suffolk.edu/nesad; *Dir & Cur* Deborah Davidson
Open Mon - Fri 11 AM - 4 PM & by appointment; No admis fee; Estab as main exhibition space for the New England School of Art & Design reflecting a wide range of art and design representing all fields of study offered by the school
Income: Financed by Suffolk Univ

Special Subjects: Advertising Design, Architecture, Commercial Art, Decorative Arts, Drafting, Drawings, Furniture, Graphic Design, Illustration, Interior Design, Landscape Architecture
Activities: Student, faculty & alumni and thesis exhibs throughout the yr

M **USS CONSTITUTION MUSEUM,** Charlestown Navy Yard, Bldg 22, Boston, MA 02129; PO Box 291812, Boston, MA 02129-0215. Tel 617-426-1812; Fax 617-242-0496; Email museumlearning@ussconstitutionmuseum.org; Web: ussconstitutionmuseum.org; *Pres* Anne Grimes Rand; *Dir Colls & Learning* Sarah Watkins; *Dir Exhibits* Robert Kiihne
Open April - Oct daily 9 AM - 6 PM; Nov - Mar daily 10 AM - 5 PM; Admis by suggested donation adults $5 - $10, children $3 - $5, family $20 - $25; Estab 1972 to collect, preserve & display items relating to the sailing frigate USS Constitution; Average Annual Attendance: 300,000; Mem: 800; dues $30 - $2,500; annual meeting in the fall
Income: $3,000,000 (financed by endowment, mem, admis, gift shop, federal, state & private grants)
Special Subjects: Ceramics, Coins & Medals, Costumes, Drawings, Etchings & Engravings, Flasks & Bottles, Furniture, Glass, Graphics, Historical Material, Jewelry, Manuscripts, Manuscripts, Maps, Marine Painting, Marine Painting, Military Art, Photography, Photography, Portraits, Posters, Prints, Reproductions, Silver, Textiles, Watercolors, Woodcarvings
Collections: Documents relating to the sailing frigate USS Constitution, Personal possessions of crew members, Shipbuilding & navigational tools, Souvenirs depicting Old Ironsides, USS Constitution images (paintings, prints & photos), Historic naval uniforms, Naval weapons, USS Constitution models
Exhibitions: Old Ironsides in War & Peace; Annual Juried Ship Model Show; All Hands on Deck; War of 1812 Discovery Center; Making "Old Ironsides" new; Forest to Frigate
Publications: Chronicle; Men of Iron; Old Ironsides Activity book
Activities: Family progs; educator workshops; interactive games & activities; lects open to public; concerts; gallery talks; tours; awards: Samuel Eliot Morison Award; Charles Francis Adams Award; Don Turner Award; Old Ironsides Exemplary Service Award; mus shop sells books, reproductions, prints, souvenirs, apparel gifts & ship models

L **WENTWORTH INSTITUTE OF TECHNOLOGY,** Douglas D Schumann Library & Learning Commons, 550 Huntington Ave, Boston, MA 02115-5998. Tel 617-989-4040; Fax 617-989-4091; Email circdesk@wit.edu; Web: www.library.wit.edu; *Dir* Kevin Kidd; *Head Reference & Instruction Librn* Marianne Thibodean; *Reference & Instruction Coordr* Dan Neal; *Head Librn Access & Organization* Priscilla Biondi; *Library Admin Servs Coordr* Malissa Redmond; *Cataloger* Kurt Oliver
Open Mon - Thurs 7 AM - Midnight, Fri 7 AM - 6 PM, Sat 10 AM - 6 PM, Sun 11 AM - Midnight; No admis fee; Estab as a dynamic, technology-driven space for students and faculty to collaborate & learn
Library Holdings: Audio Tapes, Book Volumes 75,000, Clipping Files, DVDs, Memorabilia, Micro Print, Periodical Subscriptions 600, Photographs, Video Tapes
Special Subjects: Architecture, Art History, Drafting, Historical Material, Industrial Design, Interior Design, Landscape Architecture

BROCKTON

L **BROCKTON PUBLIC LIBRARY,** Joseph A Driscoll Art Gallery, 304 Main St, Brockton, MA 02301-5300. Tel 508-580-7890; Fax 508-580-7898; Email emarcus@cobma.us; Web: www.brocktonpubliclibrary.org; *Dir* Elizabeth A. Marcus; *Head Adult Serv* Lucia M Shannon; *Asst Dir* Keith Choquette
Open Mon, Tues noon - 8 PM, Wed - Sat 9 AM - 5 PM; No admis fee; Estab 1913; Special room for monthly art exhibitions; Average Annual Attendance: 20,000
Library Holdings: Book Volumes 202,000
Collections: W C Bryant Collection of 19th & 20th century American paintings, chiefly by New England artists, gifts of 20th century paintings which includes four paintings by Hendricks Hallett & an oil painting by Mme Elisabeth Weber-Fulop, loan coll of 20th century painters from the Woman's Club of Brockton, mounted photographs of Renaissance art & watercolors by F Mortimer Lamb
Exhibitions: Monthly exhibitions by local & nationally known artists

M **FULLER CRAFT MUSEUM,** 455 Oak St, Brockton, MA 02301-1340. Tel 508-588-6000; Fax 508-587-6191; Email director@fullercraft.org; Web: www.fullercraft.org/; *Dir* Wyona Lynch-McWhite; *Dir Educ* Noelle Foye; *CFO* Martin Gredinger
Open Tues - Sun 10 AM - 5 PM, Wed 10 AM - 9 PM; Admis adults $8, seniors & students $5, mem & children 12 & under Free, Wed 5 - 9 PM Free; Estab 1969 to provide a variety of craft exhibitions & educ programs of regional & national interest; The center houses six galleries; Average Annual Attendance: 23,000; Mem: Mem: 2,000
Income: $784,000 (financed by endowment, mem, gifts & government grants)
Special Subjects: African Art, Bookplates & Bindings, Carpets & Rugs, Ceramics, Collages, Crafts, Decorative Arts, Drawings, Embroidery, Enamels, Etchings & Engravings, Furniture, Glass, Graphics, Jewelry, Laces, Leather, Metalwork, Miniatures, Mosaics, Painting-American, Photography, Portraits, Pottery, Pre-Columbian Art, Prints, Sculpture, Silver, Watercolors, Woodcuts, Stained Glass, Tapestries, Textiles, Woodcarvings
Collections: Contemporary American art, Early American & Sandwich glass, contemporary regional crafts, Sandwich Glass Collection
Exhibitions: Avg 12 exhibs organized per yr
Publications: Quarterly newsletter & calendar of events
Activities: Classes for adults & children; dramatic progs; docent training; special progs for children; lects, open to pub & mem only, 4 vis lectrs per yr; gallery talks; tours; concerts; individual paintings & original objects of art lent to accredited mus of the American Assn of Museums; lending collection contains paintings & art; book traveling exhibs 2 per yr; originate traveling exhibs 2 per yr; mus shop sells book, original art, reproductions, prints, contemporary crafts, t-shirts & mugs

L **Library,** 455 Oak St, Brockton, MA 02301-1340. Tel 508-588-6000; Fax 508-587-6191; Web: www.fullermuseum.org; *Exec Dir* Wyona Lynch-McWhite
Open to members, staff & students
Library Holdings: Book Volumes 500, Exhibition Catalogs, Pamphlets

BROOKLINE

M **GATEWAY ARTS,** Gateway Gallery, 62 Harvard St, Brookline, MA 02445. Tel 617-734-1577; Fax 617-734-3199; Email gatewayarts@vinfen.org; Web: www.gatewayarts.org; *Dir* Rae Edelson; *Artistic Dir* Stephen De Fronzo; *Prog Dir* Ted Lampe
Open Mon - Fri 9 AM - 4:30 PM, Sat Noon - 5 PM, cl Sun; Estab 1973 to provide day service to adults with disabilities
Special Subjects: Drawings, Graphic Design, Mixed Media, Ceramics, Jewelry
Collections: Fabric & decorative painting, drawing, graphic design, mixed media sculpture, ceramics, sewing, jewelry, performance arts
Exhibitions: Temporary exhibits
Activities: Educ progs; classes for adults; Mus shop sells gifts & card; jewelry; clothing

CAMBRIDGE

A **CAMBRIDGE ART ASSOCIATION,** 25 Lowell St, Cambridge, MA 02138-4725. Tel 617-876-0246; Fax 617-876-1880; Email info@cambridgeart.org; Web: www.cambridgeart.org; *Dir* Kathryn Schultz; *Dir Sales & Rental* Susan Vrotsus; *Asst to Dir* Jodi Hays Gresham
Open Mon - Fri 9 AM - 6 PM, Sun 9 - 1 PM, cl Aug; No admis fee; Estab 1944 to exhibit, rent & sell members' work & to encourage an interest in fine arts & crafts in the community; 2 gallery spaces located in & near Harvard Sq; Mem: 575; dues artist $75, friends $40, students $15; jury of artist mems meets 4 times per yr to review work, slides & resumes
Income: Financed by dues, sale of art, annual appeal & endowment
Exhibitions: Invited shows in Rental Gallery & Craft Gallery; foreign exhibition each year; members' juried exhibitions in Main Gallery every month; National Prize Show (June)
Publications: Newsletter, quarterly
Activities: Classes for members; lect & demonstrations; competitions with prizes

M **CAMBRIDGE ARTS COUNCIL,** CAC Gallery, 344 Broadway, 2nd fl, Cambridge, MA 02139. Tel 617-349-4380; Fax 617-349-4669; Email hsu@mlittman@cambridgema.gov; Web: www.cambridgeartscouncil.org; *Exec Dir* Jason Weeks; *Dir Pub Art* Lillian Hsu; *Dir Community Arts* Julie Madden; *Dir Mktg & Pub Rels* Mara Littman; *Pub Arts Admin* Jeremy Gaucher
Open Mon & Wed 8:30 AM - 8 PM, Tues & Thurs 8:30 AM - 5 PM, Fri 8:30 AM - Noon; No admis fee; Estab 1974 by city ordinance & inc 1976 as public nonprofit. As the official arts agency for the City of Cambridge, MA, it's mission is to ensure arts remain vital for people living, working & vis Cambridge.; Exhibs are designed to support and present the work of local, national and international artists and explore the relationship between visual art, pub art and civic dialogue; Average Annual Attendance: 2,500
Exhibitions: 6-8 exhibitions annually; Exhibition focus: contemporary public art & community engagement
Activities: Progs for Public Art Youth Council; Lect open to pub; gallery talks; tours; rotating collection to municipal bldgs & offices only

L **CAMBRIDGE HISTORICAL COMMISSION, CITY OF CAMBRIDGE,** Research Library on Architectural and Social History of Cambridge, Mass, 831 Massachusetts Ave, 2nd Floor, Cambridge, MA 02139. Tel 617-349-4683; Fax 617-349-3116; Email histcomm@cambridgema.gov; Web: www.cambridgema.gov/historic; *Exec Dir* Charles M Sullivan; *Preservation Planner* Sarah L Burks; *Dir Survey* Susan E Maycock; *Asst Dir* Kathleen L Rawlins; *Archivist* Emily Gonzalez; *Preservation Adminr* Samantha Paull
Open Mon 8:30 AM - 8 PM, Tues - Thurs 8:30 AM - 5 PM, Fri 8:30 Am - noon, research by appointment; No admis fee; Estab 1963; Circ Non-circulating
Income: $490,000 (financed by city appropriation)
Library Holdings: Book Volumes 1000, Clipping Files, Kodachrome Transparencies, Manuscripts, Maps, Memorabilia, Original Art Works, Original Documents, Pamphlets, Periodical Subscriptions, Photographs, Prints, Slides
Special Subjects: Architecture, Historical Material
Collections: Architectural & social history of Cambridge
Publications: Architectural History Series: Mid Cambridge (1967); Cambridgeport (1971); Old Cambridge (1973); Northwest Cambridge (1977); Photographic History of Cambridge (1984); East Cambridge (1988); Building Old Cambridge (2016); Oral Histories: Photographic History of Cambridge (1984); In Our Own Words: Stories of North Cambridge (1997); Crossroads: Stories of Central Square, Mass. (2001); All in the Same Boat: 20th Century Stories of East Cambridge (2005); Common Cause, Uncommon Courage: World War II and the Home Front in Cambridge (2009); We are the Port: Stories from Area 4 (2014)
Activities: Staff offers educational & informational talks & tours for children and adults including Cambridge Discovery Day; annual Cambridge Preservation Awards program; historic preservation grants to nonprofit institutions and institutions with historic properties; assists homeowners, architects, students and genealogists with research

M **HARVARD UNIVERSITY,** Harvard Art Museums, 32 Quincy St, Cambridge, MA 02138-3845. Tel 617-495-9400; Web: www.harvardartmuseums.org; *Dir* Martha Tedeschi; *Deputy Dir* Maureen Donovan; *Dir Center for the Technical Study of Modern Art* Narayan Khandekar; *Head Div Acad & Pub Progs* Jessica Levin Martinez; *Expedition Admin* Bahadir Yildirm; *Archivist* Megan Schwenke; *Dir Colls Management* Jennifer Allen; *Dir Communs* Daron Manoogian; *Dir Digital Infrastructure & Emerging Tech* Jeff Steward; *Dir Facilities Planning & Mgmt* Peter Atkinson; *Dir Institutional Advancement* Thomas Woodward; *Dir Security* Stephen St. Laurent; *Dir Vis Servs* Sanja Kugat
Open daily 10 AM - 5 PM; cl major holidays (see website for details); Admis adults $15, seniors (65+) $13, non-Harvard students (18+) $10, youth 18 & Cambridge residents free; Estab 1895; Renovated & expanded facility, uniting Fogg, Busch-Reisinger & Arthur M. Sackler Museums; 43,000 sq ft gallery space; 300

seat lecture hall; art study center; classrooms; pub educ room; shop & cafe; Average Annual Attendance: 170,000; Mem: 3,500+; dues $60 & up
Income: Financed by endowment, mem & federal grants
Collections: Combined colls of the Fogg, Busch-Reisinger & Arthur M. Sackler Museums range from ancient world to the present & from the Americas, Europe, North Africa, the Mediterranean & Asia
Publications: Digital magazine; gallery guides; catalogues & other books
Activities: Classes for adults & children; lects open to pub; gallery talks; tours; seminars; concerts; fels; lending of original objects of art to other exhibs & museums; organize traveling exhibs to other museums; mus shop sells books, magazines, reproductions, prints, stationary, jewelry, art supplies, textiles & more

—**Busch-Reisinger Museum**, 32 Quincy St, Cambridge, MA 02138-3836; 485 Broadway, Cambridge, MA 02138. Tel 617-495-9400; Fax 617-495-9936; Email am_webmaster@harvard.edu; Web: www.harvardartmuseums.org; *Acting Cur* Linda Muir; *Cur Asst* Joanna Wendel; *Cur Intern* Clelia Pozzi
Open Mon - Sat 10 AM - 5 PM, Sun 1 - 5 PM, cl national holidays; Admis adults $9, seniors $7, students $6, under 18 & Sat AM free; Estab 1901 & opened in 1920, it has one of most important & extensive collections of Central & European art outside of Europe, ranging from the Romanesque to the present day. This coll serves the teaching prog of the Dept of Fine Arts, outside scholars & the gen pub; Werner Otto Hall contains 7 galleries, 6 for German Art (1880-1980), 1 for rotating exhibits; Average Annual Attendance: 83,696; Mem: 2,700; dues individual $35
Special Subjects: Painting-European, Renaissance Art, Sculpture
Collections: 18th Century Painting Coll, Late Medieval, Renaissance & Baroque Sculpture Coll, 16th Century Porcelain Coll, 20th Century German Works Coll, largest coll of Bauhaus material outside Germany, drawings, paintings, prints, sculpture
Publications: Newsletter
Activities: Classes for children; lects open to pub; concerts; gallery talks; tours; symposia; individual paintings & original objects of art lent to other museums, considered on request; book traveling exhibs 1-2 per yr; originate traveling exhibs; Mus shop sells books, reproductions, prints & small gift items

—**William Hayes Fogg Art Museum**, 1805 Cambridge St., Cambridge, MA 02138. Tel 617-495-9400; Fax 617-495-9936; Email artmuseums@fas.harvard.edu; *Deputy Dir* Frances A Beane; *Cur Drawings* William W Robinson; *Cur Prints* Marjorie B Cohn; *Cur Painting* Ivan Gaskell
Open Mon - Sat 10 AM - 5 PM, Sun 1 - 5 PM, cl national holidays; Admis adults $5, seniors $4, students $3, Sat AM free; University estab 1891; mus estab 1927; serves both as a pub mus & as a laboratory for Harvard's Dept of Fine Arts, which trains art history mus professionals; The Straus Center for Conservation operates a training program for conservators & technical specialists; Average Annual Attendance: 83,696; Mem: 2,700; dues $35 & up
Income: Financed by endowment, mem & federal grants
Special Subjects: Antiquities-Egyptian, Antiquities-Greek, Antiquities-Oriental, Antiquities-Roman, Bronzes, Ceramics, Decorative Arts, Drawings, Jade, Painting-American, Painting-European, Photography, Prints, Sculpture, Silver
Collections: Maurice Wertheim Collection of Impressionist & Post-Impressionist Art, European & American paintings, sculpture, decorative arts, photographs, prints & drawings, English & American silver, Wedgwood
Exhibitions: (Permanent) Circa 1874: The Emergence of Impressionism; France & The Portrait, 1799-1870; Subliminations: Art & Sensuality in the Nineteenth Century.
Publications: Annual report; newsletter, 4 - 5 per year
Activities: Docent training; lects open to pub; concerts; gallery talks; tours; individual paintings & original objects of art lent to other museums, considered on individual basis; book traveling exhibs 1-2 per yr; originate traveling exhibs; Mus shop sells books, reproductions, prints & small gift items

—**Arthur M Sackler Museum**, 485 Broadway, Cambridge, MA 02138-3845. Tel 617-495-9400; Fax 617-495-9936; Email artmuseums@fas.harvard.edu; *Deputy Dir* Frances A Beane; *Cur Chinese Art* Robert Mowry; *Cur Ancient Art* David Gordon Mitten
Open Mon - Sat 10 AM - 5 PM, Sun 1 - 5 PM; Admis adults $9, seniors $7, Students $6; Estab 1985 to serve both as a pub mus & a laboratory for Harvard's Dept of Fine Arts, which trains art historians & mus professionals
Special Subjects: Antiquities-Egyptian, Asian Art, Bronzes, Ceramics, Islamic Art, Jade, Jewelry, Manuscripts, Metalwork, Prints, Sculpture, Textiles
Collections: Ancient coins, Asian bronzes, ceramics, jades, painting, prints & sculpture, Egyptian antiquities, Greek red & black figure vases, Greek & Roman bronze & marble sculpture, Greek, Roman & Near Eastern jewelry & metalwork, Islamic & Indian ceramics, illuminated manuscripts, metalwork, paintings & textiles
Exhibitions: (Permanent) Serveran Silver Coinage
Activities: Mus shop sells books, prints & reproductions

L **Fine Arts Library**, 1805 Cambridge St, Littauer Ctr Harvard University North Yard Cambridge, MA 02138-3001. Tel 617-495-3373; Fax 617-496-4889; Email altenhof@fas.harvard.edu; Web: http://hcl.harvard.edu/libraries/finearts/
Open to Harvard Community Mon - Thurs 9 AM - 10 PM, Fri 9 AM - 6 PM, Sat 10 AM - 5 PM, Sun 1-6 PM during school yr

L **Frances Loeb Library**, 48 Quincy St, Graduate School of Design - Gund Hall Cambridge, MA 02138-3000. Tel 617-495-9163; Fax 617-496-5929; Web: www.gsd.harvard.edu/loeb_library; *Librn* Hugh Wilburn
Open Mon - Thurs 8:30 AM - 10 PM, Fri 8:30 AM - 6 PM, Sat 10 AM - 6 PM, Sun noon - 8 PM; Estab 1900 to serve faculty & students of graduate school of design; Circ 55,000
Income: $1,100,000 (financed by endowment & tuition)
Purchases: $208,381
Library Holdings: Audio Tapes 350, Book Volumes 266,852, Cassettes 326, Clipping Files, Exhibition Catalogs, Fiche, Filmstrips 65, Kodachrome Transparencies, Lantern Slides, Manuscripts, Memorabilia, Motion Pictures, Original Art Works, Other Holdings Drawings, Pamphlets, Periodical Subscriptions 1100, Photographs, Records, Reels, Slides 169,515, Video Tapes
Special Subjects: Architecture
Collections: Cluny Collection, Curutchet Collection (Le Corbusier's built works), Edward Larrabee Barnes Collection, Charles Elliot Collection, Daniel Kiley Collection, John C Olmsted Collection, H H Richardson Collection, Charles Mulford Robinson Collection, Hugh Stubbins Collection, Joseph Luis Sert Collection, Jesse Tarbox Beals Photographic Collection, Richard Marsh Bennett Collection, John S Bolles Collection, Walter Frances Bogner Collection, Grady E Clay Collection, Arthur Coleman Comey Papers, George Roseborough Collins Collection in Linear City Planning, CIAM Collection, Arland Augustus Dirlam Architectural Drawings Collection, Robin Evans Collection, Jorge Ferrari Hardoy Collection
Activities: Tours

M **Semitic Museum**, 6 Divinity Ave, Cambridge, MA 02138-2020. Tel 617-495-4631; Fax 617-496-8904; Email semiticm@fas.harvard.edu; Web: www.fas.harvard.edu./~semitic; *Asst Dir* Joseph A Greene; *Asst Cur* Adam Aja; *Cur Cuneiform Coll* Piotr Steinkeller; *Dir* Lawrence Stager; *Dir Publ* Michael Coogan
Open Mon - Fri 10 AM - 4 PM, Sun 1 - 4 PM, cl Sat & holiday weekends; No admis fee, donations accepted; Estab 1889 to promote sound knowledge of Semitic languages & history; an archaeological research mus; Average Annual Attendance: 3,000-5,000; Mem: 250; dues $35 & up
Income: Financed by endowment, mem, private research grants, gifts
Special Subjects: Antiquities-Byzantine, Antiquities-Egyptian, Antiquities-Greek, Antiquities-Persian, Antiquities-Roman, Archaeology, Coins & Medals, Costumes, Islamic Art
Collections: Excavated archaeological & excavation archives materials from Egypt, Mesopotamia, Syria-Palestine, Cyprus, Arabia, North Africa, ethnographic coll (Ottoman period)
Exhibitions: Ancient Cyprus: The Cesnola Collection; Nuzi & The Hurrians: Fragments from a Forgotten Past; The Houses of Ancient Israel: Domestic, Royal, Divine; Ancient Egypt: Magic and the Afterlife
Publications: Harvard Semitic Series; exhibit catalogs; Harvard Semitic Monographs; Semitic Museum Newsletter; Studies in the Archaeology & History of the Levant
Activities: Classes for adults & children; docent training; teacher workshop; lect-film series; tours; lects open to pub, 4-6 vis lectrs per yr; gallery talks; tours; children's vacation prog; scholarships offered; exten dept serves Harvard University; original objects of art lent to universities & museums; Mus shop sells books, reproductions & magazines

M **LESLEY UNIVERSITY,** Roberts Gallery, 1801 Mass Ave, Cambridge, MA 02140; 29 Everett St, Cambridge, MA 02138-2702. Tel 617-585-6600; Email robinson@lesley.edu; Web: www.lesley.edu/exhibitions; *Dir Gallery & Exhib* Bonnell Robinson; *Assoc Dir* Andrew Mroczak
Mon - Fri 9 AM - 6 PM, Sat & Sun noon - 5 PM; No admis fee; Estab 1969 to present major contemporary & historical exhibitions of the work of established & emerging artists & to show work by students & faculty of the Institute; 3,000 sq ft of gallery space across three galleries: Roberts, Raises, Van Dernoot; Average Annual Attendance: 4,000
Exhibitions: Works from the Collaboration of Richard Benson & Callaway Editions; Luis Gonzalez Palma (Guatemalan photographer); Contemporary Book Design; Edward Sorel; Pedro Meyer; Edward Gorell; Chuck Close; Magnuw Photographers; Irving Penn: Beyond Beauty
Activities: Classes for adults & children; professional progs in fine & applied arts & photography; lects open to pub, 5 vis lectrs per yr; lect series coordinated with exhibitions; gallery talks; tours; competitions, local & regional; exten dept serves Greater Boston area; individual paintings & original objects of art lent to other galleries; curate & mount exhibitions for major public spaces

L **College of Art & Design Library**, 700 Beacon St, Boston, MA 02215; 29 Everett St, Cambridge, MA 02138. Tel 617-585-6670; Fax 617-585-6720; Email aib_circ@lesley.edu; Web: www.lesley.edu; *Head Librn* Carrie L McDade; *Library Asst* Raye Yankavskas
Open Mon - Thurs 8:30 AM - 9:30 PM, Fri 8:30 AM - 5:30 PM, Sat Noon - 6 PM, Sun 2 - 8 PM; Estab 1969 to support school curriculum
Library Holdings: Book Volumes 10,000, CD-ROMs 5, DVDs, Exhibition Catalogs, Other Holdings Vertical File, Periodical Subscriptions, Slides, Video Tapes
Special Subjects: Afro-American Art, American Indian Art, Antiquities-Egyptian, Pre-Columbian Art, Architecture, Art Education, Art History, Asian Art, Cartoons, Ceramics, Collages, Commercial Art, Constructions, Crafts, Drawings, Etchings & Engravings, Graphic Arts, Graphic Design, History of Art & Archaeology, Illustration, Intermedia, Latin American Art, Metalwork, Painting-American, Painting-British, Painting-Dutch, Painting-European, Painting-Flemish, Painting-French, Painting-German, Painting-Italian, Painting-Japanese, Painting-Russian, Painting-Scandinavian, Photography, Portraits, Posters, Pottery, Primitive art, Printmaking, Prints, Religious Art, Sculpture, Video, Watercolors, Woodcarvings
Activities: Classes for adults; lects open to pub; 6 vis lectrs per yr; gallery talks, sponsoring competitions, schols, fellowships

M **LONGFELLOW NATIONAL HISTORIC SITE,** Longfellow House - Washington's Headquarters, 105 Brattle St, Cambridge, MA 02138-3407. Tel 617-876-4491; Fax 617-497-8718; Email FRLA_longfellow@nps.gov; Web: www.nps.gov/long; *Coll Mgr* David Daly; *Supt* Myra Harrison; *Site Mgr* Beth Law; *Archives Specialist* Chris Wirth; *Park Ranger* Garrett Cloer
Open daily 10 AM - 4:30 PM (June-Oct); No admis fee; Estab 1972 to acquaint the pub with the life, work & time of the American poet Henry W Longfellow & as a memorial to George Washington; Average Annual Attendance: 40,000
Income: Financed by US Department of the Interior
Library Holdings: Book Volumes, Manuscripts, Memorabilia, Original Art Works, Original Documents, Pamphlets, Photographs, Prints, Sculpture
Special Subjects: Period Rooms
Collections: Paintings, sculpture, prints, letters, furniture & furnishings once belonging to Henry W Longfellow & his daughter Alice, 19th century photographic coll including views of China & Japan, American, European & Asian Colls
Activities: Classes for adults & children; lect open to public; 5 vis lectrs per yr; concerts; tours; gallery talks; fels; individual paintings & original objects of art lent to qualified institutions; mus shop sells books, reproduction & slides

M **MASSACHUSETTS INSTITUTE OF TECHNOLOGY,** List Visual Arts Center, 20 Ames St, Wiesner Bldg E 15 - 109 Cambridge, MA 02142-1308. Tel 617-253-4680; Fax 617-258-7265; Email mlinga@mit.edu; Web: www.listart.mit.edu; *Registrar* Alison Hatcher; *Admin Officer* David Freilach;

Gallery Mgr Tim Lloyd; *Dir* Paul C Ha; *Pub Art Cur* Alise Upitis; *Outreach Coordr* Courtney Klemens; *Cur* Henriette Huldisch; *Mktg* Mark Linga
Open Tues - Sun Noon - 6 PM, Thurs Noon - 8 PM; No admis fee; Estab 1963 to organize exhibitions of contemporary art in all media; Contemporary Art gallery; Average Annual Attendance: 15,000
Income: Financed by MIT, pub & private endowments, art councils, corporations & individuals
Special Subjects: Drawings, Painting-American, Photography, Prints, Sculpture
Collections: Major public sculpture, paintings, drawings, prints, photographs & site-specific commissions all publicly sited through the campus. All collections are being enlarged through donations & purchases
Exhibitions: 8-9 exhibitions per year of contemporary art in all mediums
Publications: Exhibition catalogs, artists' books
Activities: Educ Dept; tours; films; lects open to pub, 10 vis lectrs per yr; gallery talks; Vera List Prize for Writing on the Visual Arts; lending collection of original art to student, faculty & admin staff; Student Loan Print Collection of over 600 pieces; book traveling exhibs 2 per yr; mus shop sells exhibs catalogues

M **MIT Museum**, 265 Massachusetts Ave, Bldg N51 Cambridge, MA 02139. Tel 617-253-5927; Fax 617-253-8994; Email museum@mit.edu; Web: web.mit.edu/museum; *Dir* John Durant; *Assoc Dir* Mary Leen; *Cur Hart Nautical Coll* Kurt Hasselbalch; *Cur Science & Technology* Deborah Douglas; *Registrar* Joan Whitlow; *Cur Architecture & Design* Gary Van Zante; *Mgr Exhibs* Donald Stidsen; *Emerging Technologies Coordr* Seth Riskin; *Dir Cambridge Science Festival* PA J'Arbeloff; *Dir Pub Rels & Mktg* Josie Patterson; *Dir Programs* Brindha Muniappan; *Dir Exhibs* Alexander Goldowsky; *Dir Technology* Allan Doyle
Open daily 10 AM - 5 PM (except for major holidays); Admis for people outside MIT community adults $10, youth 5-17, students & seniors $5, free admis last Sun of each month; Estab 1971 as a mus facility to document, interpret & communicate the activities & achievements of MIT; Main exhibition facility & one campus galleries; Average Annual Attendance: 100,000; Mem: not applicable
Income: Financed by University, outside funding & earned income
Special Subjects: Architecture, Drawings, Historical Material, Maps, Marine Painting, Photography, Portraits, Watercolors, Prints
Collections: Architectural drawings, biographical information, holograms, maritime, objects d'art, paintings, photographs, portraits, scientific instruments & apparatus, Nautical Prints
Publications: Gallery exhibition notes; collection catalogs
Activities: Progs for adults, children & families, after school camps; lects open to pub, 1-2 vis lectrs per yr; gallery talks; tours; individual paintings & original works lent to other mus; originate traveling exhibs; mus shop sells books, prints, MIT - & exhibit-related items, toys, games & gift items
—**Hart Nautical Galleries & Collections**, 55 Massachusetts Ave, Cambridge, MA 02139; 265 Massachusetts Ave, Cambridge, MA 02139. Tel 617-253-5942; Fax 617-258-9107; Email kurt@mit.edu; Web: http://web.mit.edu/museum/; *Cur* Kurt Hasselbalch
Open daily 9 AM - 7 PM; reference open Mon - Fri 10 AM - 5 PM by appointment only; Estab 1922 to preserve history of naval architecture, shipbuilding & related nautical technology; Galleries include permanent exhibit of ship models & MIT Ocean Engineering exhibit; Average Annual Attendance: 16,000
Income: Financed by University & pvt gifts
Special Subjects: Maps, Marine Painting
Activities: Individual paintings & original objects of art lent to qualified mus; lending collection contains prints, slides & models; mus shop sells books

L **Rotch Library of Architecture & Planning**, 77 Massachusetts Ave, Rm 7-238, Cambridge, MA 02139-4307. Tel 617-258-5592, 258-5599; Fax 617-253-9331; Web: www.mit.edu; *Head of GIS* Lisa Sweeney; *Librn Urban Studies, Planning & Real Estate* Peter Cohn; *Librn Architecture & Visual Arts* Jolene De Verges; *Librn Architecture & Visual Arts* Jennifer Friedman; *Librn Urban Studies & Planning* Heather McCann; *Librn Aga Khan Prog* Omar Khalidi; *Aga Khan Cataloger* Yahya Melhem
Open Mon - Thurs 8:30 AM - 11 PM, Fri 8:30 AM - 7 PM, Sat 1 - 6 PM, Sun 2 - 10 PM; Mon - Fri 10 AM - 6 PM when school is not in session; Estab 1868 to serve the students & faculty of the School of Architecture & Planning & other members of the MIT community
Library Holdings: Audio Tapes, Book Volumes 236,873, CD-ROMs, Cassettes, Compact Disks, DVDs 619, Exhibition Catalogs, Fiche, Kodachrome Transparencies, Lantern Slides, Maps 3,000, Motion Pictures, Original Documents, Pamphlets 33,000, Periodical Subscriptions 1944, Photographs, Reels, Slides, Video Tapes
Special Subjects: Architecture, Art History, Conceptual Art, Drafting, Drawings, Film, Glass, Graphic Arts, Graphic Design, Historical Material, History of Art & Archaeology, Illustration, Industrial Design, Interior Design, Islamic Art, Landscape Architecture, Latin American Art, Maps, Painting-American, Painting-British, Painting-European, Painting-German, Photography, Sculpture, Printmaking, Stained Glass, Video

A **MOBIUS INC,** 55 Norfolk St, Cambridge, MA 02139-2614. Tel 617-945-9481; Email info@mobius.org; Web: www.mobius.org; *Dir* Daniel S DeLuca
Open check event schedule or email for appointment; Estab 1977; Artist group & centers for experimental art in all media
Activities: Concerts gallery talks; organize traveling exhibs to galleries & art spaces

M **PHOTOGRAPHIC RESOURCE CENTER, INC,** Lunder Arts Center, Lesley University, 1801 Massachusetts Ave, Office 312 Cambridge, MA 02140; 411A Highland Ave #317, Somerville, MA 02144. Tel 617-975-0600; Email info@prcboston.org; Web: www.prcboston.org; *Pres* John Bunzick; *Acting Exec Dir* Bruce Myren
(see website for hours); Admis: suggested donation $3, mems & students of mem schools no charge; Estab 1976; The PRC is a vital forum for the exploration, interpretation, celebration of new work, ideas & methods in photography; Average Annual Attendance: 2,500; Mem: 1,000; dues $50 - $250
Library Holdings: Auction Catalogs, Book Volumes 4000, Clipping Files, Exhibition Catalogs, Periodical Subscriptions
Special Subjects: Historical Material, Photography, Art History
Activities: Photography workshops with guest artists; classes for adults; lects open to pub, gallery talks; sponsoring of competitions; fels; mus shop sells books, original art & prints

CHATHAM

M **CHATHAM HISTORICAL SOCIETY,** The Atwood House Museum, 347 Stage Harbor Rd, Chatham, MA 02633; PO Box 709, Chatham, MA 02633-0709. Tel 508-945-2493; Email info@chathamhistorical.org; Web: www.chathamhistoricalsociety.org; *Chmn* Steve Burlingame; *Exec Dir* Danielle Jeanbz; *Admin* Margaret Martin; *Head Archivist* Mary Ann Gray
Open July - Sept Tues - Sat 10 AM - 4 PM; June and Oct varies; Admis $10, students 7 - 18 $5, members & children under 7 free; Estab 1923 to preserve local Chatham history; Eleven Galleries. Murals Barn houses Alice Stallknecht murals of Chatham people, Portrait Gallery houses Frederick Wight paintings of local sea captains; Fishing Gallery offers paintings by Harold Brett, Frederick Wight; Atwood House houses Giddings Ballou portraits; Average Annual Attendance: 3,700; Mem: 950; ann meeting in Aug
Income: Financed by mem dues, donations & grants
Purchases: Local historical artifacts & paintings
Library Holdings: Audio Tapes, Book Volumes, CD-ROMs, Compact Disks, DVDs, Manuscripts, Maps, Original Art Works, Pamphlets, Periodical Subscriptions, Photographs, Video Tapes
Special Subjects: Carpets & Rugs, Ceramics, Costumes, Decorative Arts, Dolls, Drawings, Embroidery, Folk Art, Furniture, Glass, Historical Material, Ivory, Landscapes, Manuscripts, Maps, Marine Painting, Painting-American, Period Rooms, Photography, Porcelain, Portraits, Pottery, Religious Art, Scrimshaw, Stained Glass, Textiles, Watercolors, Woodcarvings, Architecture
Collections: Giddings Ballou portraits, Harold Brett, paintings, Harold Dunbar, Wendell Rogers paintings, Frederick Wight, paintings, Sandwich Glass, 17th & 18th century furnishings, antique tools, china, items brought back by Chatham sea captains, maritime paintings, ship models, Crowell miniature decoys & sea shells from around the world, Parian Ware, Sandwich glass, Transfer ware, map & sea charts, Alice Stallknecht murals, fishing equipment, lantern room with Fresnel lens
Exhibitions: Exhibits change every year; Dressing Through Time; Chatham and the Military
Publications: The Atwood log, quarterly newsletter; Three Centuries in a Cape Cod Village
Activities: Classes for adults & children; Docent training; talks & slideshows; lects open to pub; 9 vis lectrs per yr; tours; gallery talks; Bringing History to Life Award; mus shop sells books, reproductions, prints & gifts; original art;

CHESTNUT HILL

M **BOSTON COLLEGE,** McMullen Museum of Art, 140 Commonwealth, Devlin Hall 108 Chestnut Hill, MA 02467-3800. Tel 617-552-8587; Fax 617-552-8577; Email artmuseum@bc.edu; Web: www.bc.edu/sites/artmuseum; *Dir* Nancy Netzer; *Multimedia & Design Serv* John McCoy; *Exhib Design, Coll Mgmt & Curatorial Affairs* Diana Larsen; *Mgr Publications & Exhibs* Kate Shugert
Open Mon - Wed & Fri 10 AM - 8 PM, Thurs 10 AM - 8 PM, Sat & Sun 12 PM - 5 PM; No admis fee; Estab 1986 to enhance the teaching mission of the University & extend it to a wider audience; Two floors; flexible galleries; Maintains lending & reference library; Average Annual Attendance: 50,000; Mem: 200; dues $50 & up
Income: Financed through University funds & donations
Collections: Old Master Paintings, Modern, Irish Paintings, American Art
Exhibitions: Rotating exhibitions
Publications: Catalogues
Activities: Classes for adults; docent training; lects open to pub, 10 vis lectrs per yr; concerts; gallery talks; tours; scholarships offered; individual paintings & original objects of art lent to other exhibs; book traveling exhibs 3 per yr; originates traveling exhibs to other museums

COHASSET

M **COHASSET HISTORICAL SOCIETY,** Pratt Building (Society Headquarters), 106 S Main St, Cohasset, MA 02025; PO Box 627, Cohasset, MA 02025-0627. Tel 781-383-1434; Fax 781-383-1190; Email cohassethistory@yahoo.com; Web: www.cohassethistoricalsociety.org; *Exec Dir* Lynne DeGiacomo; *Historian* Rebecca Bates-McArthur; *Pres* Kathleen L O'Malley
Open Mon - Fri 10 AM - 4 PM; Admis by donations; Estab 1928; Paintings & artifacts of local significance are displayed in various rooms; Cohasset Historical Society's library & archives, costumes, textile coll located here; Average Annual Attendance: 2,000; Mem: 400; dues sustaining $50, family $35, single $25; annual meetings in Oct & Apr
Library Holdings: Book Volumes 1000, DVDs 100, Lantern Slides 100, Manuscripts 50, Maps 100, Memorabilia 5000, Original Art Works 50, Original Documents 5000, Pamphlets 50, Periodical Subscriptions 5, Photographs 3500, Slides 1000, Video Tapes 25
Special Subjects: Ceramics, Costumes, Decorative Arts, Dolls, Furniture, Historical Material, Manuscripts, Maps, Painting-American, Textiles, Dioramas, Embroidery, Marine Painting
Collections: Works of art; historical artifacts & archives; costumes; textiles; theatre, Maritime Museum located at 4 Elm St, Cohasset, Historic House at 4 Elm St, Cohasset
Exhibitions: Dec Christmas Exhibit; Two additional exhibits per year
Publications: Historical Highlights, newsletter 4 times per yr; Images of America; Cohasset (2004)
Activities: Lect open to public Sept - Jun, 6 vis lectrs per yr; tours; mus shop sells books

M **Cohasset Maritime Museum**, 4 Elm St, Cohasset, MA 02025; 106 S Main St, Cohasset, MA 02025. Tel 781-383-1434; Fax 781-383-1190; Email cohassethistory@yahoo.com; Web: www.cohassethistoricalsociety.org; *Historian* Rebecca Bates-McArthur; *Exec Dir* Lynne DeGiacomo; *Pres* Kathleen L O'Malley

Open mid-June - end of Aug Wed - Fri 1 PM - 4 PM, Sat 10 AM - 2 PM; Admis by donation; Estab 1957 to display the seafaring history of Cohasset; Average Annual Attendance: 800; Mem: 370
Special Subjects: Historical Material, Marine Painting, Portraits
Collections: Local maritime history, fishing gear of 19th century, ship models, lifesaving, shipwreck memorabilia, pictures & charts

M **Captain John Wilson Historical House**, 4 Elm St, Cohasset, MA 02025. Tel 781-383-1434; Fax 781-383-1190; Email cohassethistory@yahoo.com; Web: cohassethistoricalsociety.org; *Pres* Kathleen L O'Malley; *Exec Admin* Lynne DeGiacomo
Open mid-June - Labor Day 1:30 - 4:30 PM, cl Sat, Sun, Mon; No admis fee - Donations welcome; Estab 1928; Historic house mus; Average Annual Attendance: 1,000; Mem: 400; Dues - sustaining $50, family $35, single $25
Income: Financed by dues, donations & grants, in-kind serv & goods
Library Holdings: Auction Catalogs, Book Volumes 200, Clipping Files, Lantern Slides, Manuscripts, Maps, Memorabilia, Original Art Works, Original Documents, Other Holdings, Pamphlets, Periodical Subscriptions, Photographs 2000, Prints, Reels 3, Reproductions, Slides 2000, Video Tapes 25
Special Subjects: Historical Material
Collections: Old household furnishings, toys, kitchenware & artwork from the old homes of Cohasset, Wilson family artifacts
Publications: Qu newsletter; Historical Highlights
Activities: Classes for adults & children; lects open to public; 8 lects per year; gallery talks, tours, schols; mus shop sells books

M **SOUTH SHORE ART CENTER,** 119 Ripley Rd, Cohasset, MA 02025-1744. Tel 781-383-2787; Fax 781-383-2964; Email info@ssac.org; Web: www.ssac.org; *Dir* Sarah Hannan
Open Mon-Sat 10AM-4PM, Sun 12PM-4PM
Collections: works by regional & nat contemporary artists; paintings; sculpture
Activities: Classes for adults & children; gallery tours

CONCORD

A **CONCORD ART ASSOCIATION,** 37 Lexington Rd, Concord, MA 01742-2570. Tel 978-369-2578; Fax 978-371-2496; Email gallery@concordart.org; Web: www.concordart.org; *Cur* Betsy Adams; *Pres* John S Tilney; *Dir* Lili Oh
Open Tues - Sat 10 AM - 4:30 PM, Sun Noon - 4 PM, cl Mon; No admis fee; Estab 1916 for the encouragement of art & artists; Housed in a 1740 house with four galleries, rent out to weddings & meetings; Average Annual Attendance: 10,000; Mem: 1000; dues life member $500, bus & patron $100, family $75, individual $50, artist $40, student $20, sr citizen $25, corporate $1000
Income: Financed by mem
Collections: Bronze sculptures, colonial glass
Exhibitions: Changing exhibition per year
Publications: Exhibition notices
Activities: Classes for adults and children; lect open to public, 4-6 vis lectrs per year; tours; competitions with prizes; original objects of art lent; room for mems use

M **CONCORD MUSEUM,** 200 Lexington Rd, Concord, MA 01742-3711; PO Box 146, Concord, MA 01742-0146. Tel 978-369-9763; Fax 978-369-9660; Email cm1@concordmuseum.org; Web: www.concordmuseum.org; *Cur* David Wood; *Exec Dir* Peggy Burke; *Dir Mktg & PR* Emer McCourt; *Coll Mgr* Adrienne Donohue; *Bus Mgr* Michelle Guerhin
Open Apr - May & Sept - Dec Mon - Sat 9 AM - 5 PM, Sun Noon - 5 PM, Jun - Aug 9 AM - 5 PM daily; Admis adults $10, seniors & students $8, children $5, members & children under 5 free; Estab 1886 to further public understanding & appreciation of Concord's history & its relationship to the cultural history of the nation by collecting, preserving & interpreting objects used or made in the Concord area. The museum serves as a center of learning and cultural enjoyment for the region & as a gateway to the town of Concord for visitors from around the world; Twenty galleries & period rooms including six Why Concord? history galleries; Average Annual Attendance: 45,000; Mem: 1200; dues $50 & up
Income: $1,300,000 (financed by mem, admis, grants, endowment & giving)
Special Subjects: Archaeology, Ceramics, Costumes, Decorative Arts, Furniture, Historical Material, Metalwork, Painting-American, Period Rooms, Pewter, Portraits, Silver, Textiles, Sculpture
Collections: Coll incl: the lantern that hung in the church steeple on the night of Paul Revere's ride, Thoreau's possessions, including the desk where he penned Walden and Civil Disobedience, and Emerson's Study. The museum's collections contain many 17th-19th-century furniture, clocks, silver, ceramics & needlework.
Publications: Newsletter, quarterly; Concord: Climate for Freedom by Ruth Wheeler; Forms to Sett On: A Social History of Concord Seating Furniture; Musketaquid to Concord: The Native & European Experience; Native American Source Book: A Teacher's Guide to New England Natives; The Concord Museum: Decorative Arts from a New England Collection; An Observant Eye: The Thoreau Collection at the Concord Museum
Activities: Classes for adults & children; docent training; lects open to pub; 8 vis lectrs per yr; concerts; gallery talks; tours; mus shop sells books, reproductions, prints, gift items & crafts which complement the mus collection

A **LOUISA MAY ALCOTT MEMORIAL ASSOCIATION,** Orchard House, 399 Lexington Rd, Concord, MA 01742-3712; PO Box 343, Concord, MA 01742-0343. Tel 508-369-4118; Fax 508-369-1367; Email info@louisamayalcott.org; *Dir Educ* Cara Shapiro; *Cur* Patty Bruttomesso; *Dir* Lisa A Simpson
Open Apr - Oct Mon - Sat 10 AM - 4:30 PM, Sun noon - 4:30 PM, Nov - Mar Mon - Fri 11 AM - 3 PM, Sat 10 AM - 4:30 PM, Sun 1 - 4:30 PM, cl Easter, Thanksgiving, Christmas & Jan 1 - 15; Admis adults $9, seniors & students $8, children $5, family rate $25; Estab 1911, preservation of house & family effects for educational purposes; Historic House Museum. Maintains reference library; Average Annual Attendance: 45,000; Mem: 500; dues family $40, individual $25
Income: Financed by mem, admis, gift shop sales, donations & grants
Special Subjects: Architecture, Costumes, Decorative Arts, Dioramas, Dolls, Drawings, Furniture, Glass, Manuscripts, Period Rooms, Photography, Porcelain, Portraits, Prints, Sculpture, Silver, Textiles, Watercolors
Collections: Books & photographs of Alcott's, Household furnishings, House where Little Women was written, Louisa May Alcott's paintings & sketches
Publications: Exhibit catalogs
Activities: Classes for adults & children; dramatic progs; living history performances; lects open to pub, 5 vis lectrs per yr; tours; original objects of art lent to other mus; lending collection contains books, original art works, original prints, paintings, photographs & sculpture; sales shop sells books, magazines, prints & exclusive reproductions

COTUIT

M **CAHOON MUSEUM OF AMERICAN ART,** 4676 Falmouth Rd, PO Box 1853 Cotuit, MA 02635-1853. Tel 508-428-7581; Fax 508-420-3709; Email rwaterhouse@cahoonmuseum.org; Web: www.cahoonmuseum.org; *Dir & Cur* Richard Waterhouse; *Mus Store Mgr* Susan Quinlan-Brown; *Bus Mgr* Agnes Maloney; *Mem Coordr* Christy Laidlaw
Open Tues - Sat 10 AM - 4 PM, Sun 1 PM - 4 PM, cl Jan & major holidays; No admis fee for members & children under 12; Estab 1984; A stately 1775 Georgian colonial farmhouse maintained with period furnishings stenciled floorboards, numerous fireplaces, a 200-year old beehive oven & wall stenciling; Average Annual Attendance: 10,000; Mem: 500; dues patron $1000, sponsor $500, assoc $250, contributor $100, family/dual $50, individual $30, adults $25, student $15
Income: $350,000 financed by fundraisers, memberships, admissions, annual appeal, mus shop
Special Subjects: Folk Art, Landscapes, Marine Painting, Portraits
Collections: Primitive paintings of Ralph and Martha Cahoon, 19th and early 20th Century American Art including works by James E. Buttersworth, William Matthew Prior, William Bradford & John J. Enneking
Exhibitions: Six - eight yearly exhibitions
Publications: Spyglass Newsletter, quarterly
Activities: Classes for adults; lect open to public; docent tours SmART! field trip program for elementary school classes; gallery talks; mus store sells books, prints, jewelry, gifts

M **COTUIT CENTER FOR THE ARTS,** 4404 Rte 28, Cotuit, MA 02635; PO Box 2042, Cotuit, MA 02635. Tel 508-428-0669; Email info@cotuitcenterforthearts.org; Web: www.artsonthecape.org; *Dir* David Kuehn
Open Summer: daily 10 AM - 4 PM; Winter: Mon - Sat 10 AM - 4 PM; cl Sun; Admis ticket prices vary; no charge for gallery; Estab 1995; 2 levels of space; Average Annual Attendance: 50,000; Mem: 1300; fees vary by level
Collections: works by contemporary artists
Exhibitions: Exhibs vary changing every 3-7 wks
Activities: Classes for adults & children; Dramatic progs; lects open to pub; 2 vis lectrs per yr; concerts; gallery talks; tours; sales shop sells original art

CUMMINGTON

M **TOWN OF CUMMINGTON HISTORICAL COMMISSION,** Kingman Tavern Historical Museum, 41 Main St, Cummington, MA 01026; PO Box 10, Cummington, MA 01026-0010. Tel 413-634-5527; *Chmn* Stephen Howes; *VChmn* Donald Pearce; *Secy* Stephanie Pasternak; *Archivist* Sondra Huntley
Open 2 - 5 PM, Jul & Aug; Admis donation suggested; Estab 1968 to have & display artifacts of Cummington & locality; 17 rm house with artifacts of Cummington & area including 17 miniature rms, two flr barn, tools, equipment, carriage shed, cider mill; Average Annual Attendance: 300; Mem: 7, appointed by selectmen
Income: $30,000 (financed by endowment & donations)
Library Holdings: Cards, Clipping Files, Memorabilia, Original Documents, Photographs
Collections: Art of WWII Refugees, paintings of local New England artists
Publications: Only One Cummington, history of Cummington; Vital Records, Town of Cummington 1762 - 1900
Activities: Demonstrators; lects open to pub; 2 vis lectrs per yr; mus shop; books

DEERFIELD

M **HISTORIC DEERFIELD, INC,** 80 Old Main St, Deerfield, MA 01342-0321; PO Box 321, Deerfield, MA 01342-0321. Tel 413-774-5581; Fax 413-775-7220; Email info@historic-deerfield.org; Web: www.historic-deerfield.org; *Chair* Anne K Groves; *Pres* Philip Zea; *VPres Mus Affairs* Anne Lanning; *Cur Chair* Amanda E Lange; *Cur Furniture* Joshua Lane
Open Daily 9:30 AM - 4:30 PM; Admis adults $12, children 6 - 17 $5, children 5 & under free; Estab 1952 to collect, study & interpret artifacts related to the history of Deerfield, the culture of the Connecticut Valley & the arts in early American life; Maintains 11 historic house museums, Flynt Center of Early New England life; Average Annual Attendance: 30,000; Mem: dues $40 and higher; annual meeting 2nd or 3rd Sun in Sep
Income: $1,923,527 (financed by endowment, mem, rental, royalty & museum store income)
Purchases: $163,694
Special Subjects: Ceramics, Costumes, Decorative Arts, Embroidery, Furniture, Furniture, Glass, Maps, Painting-American, Period Rooms, Pewter, Pottery, Silver, Textiles, Silver
Collections: American & English silver, American & European textiles & costume, American needlework, American pewter, Chinese export porcelain, early American household objects, early American paintings & prints, early New England furniture, English ceramics, American furniture, Powder horns, English creamware
Exhibitions: Into the Woods: Crafting Early American Furniture; Celebrating the Fiber Arts
Publications: Historical Deerfield Magazine; Annual Report
Activities: Classes for adults, children & families; docent training; lects open to pub, 17 vis lectrs per yr; gallery talks; tours; scholarships & fels; mus shop sells books, reproductions, slides & local crafts

L **Henry N Flynt Library**, 84B Old Main St, Deerfield, MA 01342; PO Box 321, Deerfield, MA 01342-0341. Tel 413-775-7125; Fax 413-775-7223; Email library@historic-deerfield.org; Web: www.historic-deerfield.org/library; *Librn* David C Bosse; *Asst Librn* Martha Noblick; *Asst Librn* Heather Harrington
Open Mon - Fri 9 AM - 5 PM; No admis fee; Estab 1970 to support research on local history & genealogy & the museum collections; also for staff training; For reference & research on early New England & Connecticut River Valley
Income: Grants & Historic Deerfield budget
Purchases: 500 vols per year
Library Holdings: Auction Catalogs, Audio Tapes, Book Volumes 23,000, Cards, Clipping Files, Compact Disks, DVDs, Exhibition Catalogs, Fiche, Filmstrips, Manuscripts, Maps, Original Documents, Pamphlets, Periodical Subscriptions 110, Reels 550, Video Tapes 25
Special Subjects: Architecture, Ceramics, Decorative Arts, Folk Art, Furniture, Glass, Historical Material, Landscape Architecture, Landscapes, Painting-American, Porcelain, Pottery, Silver, Silversmithing, Textiles, Manuscripts
Collections: Decorative Arts, Works dealing with the Connecticut River Valley
Publications: Research at Deerfield, An Introduction to the Memorial Libraries, irregular
Activities: Mus sales shop sells books, reproductions, prints & slides

A **POCUMTUCK VALLEY MEMORIAL ASSOCIATION,** Memorial Hall Museum, 8 Memorial St, Deerfield, MA 01342; PO Box 428, Deerfield, MA 01342-0428. Tel 413-774-7476; Fax 413-774-5400; Email tneumann@deerfield.history.museum; Web: www.deerfield-ma.org; *Pres* Carol Letson; *Dir & CEO* Timothy C Neumann; *Cur* Suzanne Flint; *Dir Youth Progs* Lynne Manring; *Libr* David Bosse; *Mus Shop Mgr* Tom Mershon
Open May Sat - Sun 10:30 AM - 4:30 PM, June - Oct Tues - Sun 11 AM - 4:30 PM; Admis adults $6, students 6-21 & children $3; Estab 1870 to collect the art & other cultural artifacts of Connecticut River Valley & western Massachusetts; Maintains 15 galleries; Average Annual Attendance: 52,292; Mem: dues annual $40, family $60; annual meeting last Tues in Feb
Income: $1,400,000 (financed by endowment, mem, sales & fundraising)
Special Subjects: American Indian Art, Architecture, Ceramics, Costumes, Crafts, Decorative Arts, Embroidery, Etchings & Engravings, Folk Art, Furniture, Glass, Historical Material, Landscapes, Manuscripts, Maps, Miniatures, Painting-American, Period Rooms, Pewter, Photography, Portraits, Pottery, Primitive art, Textiles
Collections: Folk art, furniture, Indian artifacts, paintings, pewter, textiles, tools, toys, dolls
Activities: Classes for children; dramatic progs; lects open to pub; concerts; tours; individual paintings & original objects of art lent to other mus; lending collection contains original art works, original prints, paintings & artifacts; mus shop sells books, original art, reproductions & slides; Old Deerfield Children's Museum, Main St, Deerfield, MA 01342

DENNIS

M **CAPE COD MUSEUM OF ART INC,** 60 Hope Lane Rt 6A Dennis Village, Dennis, MA 02638; PO Box 2034, Dennis, MA 02638-5034. Tel 508-385-4477; Fax 508-385-7533; Email info@ccmoa.org; Web: www.ccmoa.org; *Exec Dir* Edith A Tonelli, PhD; *Mgr Exhib* Michael Giaquinto; *Mem & Registrar* Angela Bilsky; *Bus Mgr* Lilian O'Brien
Open May - Oct Mon - Sat 10 AM - 5 PM, Sun noon - 5 PM; Oct -May Tues - Sat 10 AM - 5 PM, Thurs eves until 8 PM; Admis adults $9, mem & ages 18 & under free; Estab 1981 for art & artists associated with & influencing the cultural history of Cape Cod, the Islands & southeastern Massachusetts; Six permanent collection galleries, temporary exhibitions; maintains reference library; Average Annual Attendance: 35,000; Mem: 2,000; dues $50-$5000
Income: $1,000,000 (financed by endowment, mem, events to earned income)
Purchases: New England Torso, bronze by Gilbert Franklin
Library Holdings: Book Volumes, Clipping Files, Exhibition Catalogs, Memorabilia, Original Documents, Periodical Subscriptions, Slides
Special Subjects: Bronzes, Ceramics, Etchings & Engravings, Glass, Graphics, Painting-American, Prints, Sculpture, Watercolors, Woodcarvings, Woodcuts
Collections: Artists assoc with Cape Cod that influenced Cape Cod cultural history, Sculpture garden
Publications: Art Matters Quarterly; exhibit catalogues
Activities: Classes for adults & children; docent training; lects open to pub; 15 vis lectrs; concerts; gallery talks; tours; sponsoring of competitions; awards, Muse Award; individual paintings & original objects of art lent; 1-2 book traveling exhibs per yr; organize traveling exhibs to other mus; mus shop sells books, magazines & prints, original art, reproductions

DUXBURY

M **ART COMPLEX MUSEUM,** Carl A Weyerhaeuser Library, 189 Alden St, Duxbury, MA 02331; PO Box 2814, Duxbury, MA 02331-2814. Tel 781-934-6634 ext 16; Fax 781-934-5117; Email info@artcomplex.org; Web: www.artcomplex.org; *Communs Coordr* Laura Doherty; *Colls Mgr* Maureen Wengler; *Asst to Dir* Mary Curran; *Dir & CEO* Charles A Weyerhaeuser; *Librn* Cheryl O'Neill; *Contemporary Cur* Craig Bloodgood; *Consulting Cur* Alice R M Hyland; *Community Coordr* Doris Collins; *Grounds & Maint* William Thomas; *Coordr Educ* Sally Dean Mello; *Colls Asst* Kyle Turner; *Accnt* Mary Wallace; *Preparator* Sue Aygarn-Kowalski
Open Wed - Sun 1 - 4 PM; No admis fee, donations accepted; Estab 1971 as a center for the arts; Circ Non-circulating; Three galleries - Bengtz, Phoenix, Rotations; Average Annual Attendance: 10,000
Income: Financed by endowment
Library Holdings: Auction Catalogs, Book Volumes 7,000, Clipping Files, DVDs, Exhibition Catalogs, Manuscripts, Pamphlets, Periodical Subscriptions 15, Video Tapes
Special Subjects: Asian Art, Prints, Art History, Ceramics, Painting-American, Painting-European, Painting-Japanese, Etchings & Engravings, Printmaking
Collections: American paintings, prints & sculpture, European paintings & prints, Asian art, Shaker furniture & other objects
Publications: Complexities (newsletters); exhibit catalogues
Activities: Educ dept; classes for adults & children; workshops for children & adults; Japanese Tea Ceremony presentations; lects open to pub; concerts; gallery talks; tours of vis groups; Gold Star Award from MA Cultural Council; lending of original objects of art to museums & traveling exhibs

L **Library,** 189 Alden St, Duxbury, MA 02332-2801; PO Box 2814, Duxbury, MA 02331-2814. Tel 718-934-6634; *Dir* Charles Weyerhaeuser; *Librn* Cheryl O'Neill
Open Wed-Sun 1 PM-4 PM; Estab 1971; Circ Non-circulating; Open to the pub for reference; Average Annual Attendance: 12,000
Income: Financed by endowment
Library Holdings: Book Volumes 5000, Clipping Files, Exhibition Catalogs, Pamphlets, Periodical Subscriptions 20, Slides, Video Tapes
Special Subjects: Asian Art, Prints
Activities: Docent reading group

ESSEX

M **ESSEX HISTORICAL SOCIETY AND SHIPBUILDING MUSEUM,** 66 Main St, Essex, MA 01929; PO Box 277, Essex, MA 01929-0005. Tel 978-768-7541; Email info@essexshipbuildingmuseum.org; Web: www.essexshipbuildingmuseum.org; *Pres* Harold Burnhan; *Treas* Marcia Hubbard; *Vice Pres* David Brown; *Dir Educ* Nancy Dudley; *Secretary* Mary Katherine Taylor; *Director of Tours* Justin Demetri; *Facilities Manager* Jeff Lane; *Yard & Property Manager* Christopher Stepler
Open Nov - May, Weekends 10 AM - 5 PM; June - Oct, Wed - Sun 10 AM - 5 PM; Admis adults $7, seniors $6, children $5; Estab 1976 to preserve & interpret Essex history with special emphasis on its shipbuilding industry; Maintains reference library; Average Annual Attendance: 4,500; Mem: 600; dues $35, annual meeting in June
Special Subjects: Archaeology, Crafts, Decorative Arts, Drawings, Historical Material, Landscapes, Maps, Marine Painting, Photography, Prints, Woodcarvings
Collections: Collection of ship building tools, documents, paintings, plans & photographs, models-both scale & builders, fishing schooner hulls, shipyard site 300 years old, Shipbuilding
Exhibitions: Five rigged ship models & 15 builder's models on loan from the Smithsonian Institution's Watercraft Collection; Frame-Up (ongoing); Caulker's Art (ongoing).
Publications: A list of vessels, boats & other craft built in the town of Essex 1860-1980, a complete inventory of the Ancient Burying Ground of Essex 1680-1868; Essex Electrics, 1981; Dubbing, Hooping & Lofting, 1981
Activities: Classes for adults & children; lects open to pub, 8-10 vis lectrs per r; gallery talks; tours; mus shop sells books, prints, original art, reproductions, & audio-video cassettes, t-shirts, models, plans, magazines & notecards

FALL RIVER

M **FALL RIVER HISTORICAL SOCIETY,** 451 Rock St, Fall River, MA 02720-3398. Tel 508-679-1071; Fax 508-675-5754; Web: www.lizzieborden.org; *Pres* Elizabeth Denning; *VPres* Andrew Mann Lizak; *Cur* Michael Martins
Open Tues - Fri (Apr - Nov) Tours 10 & 11 AM, 1, 2 & 3 PM, (June - Sept) Tours 1, 2, 3 & 4 PM, open house day after Thanksgiving Day before New Year's Day; Admis adults $5, children 6-14 $3.00, children under 6 free; Estab 1921 to preserve the social & economic history of Fall River; Average Annual Attendance: 6,000; Mem: 659; dues $45 family, $25 individual
Income: Financed by endowment, mem
Special Subjects: Costumes, Decorative Arts, Painting-American
Collections: Fall River School Still Life Paintings & Portraits, Antonio Jacobsen marine paintings, Period costumes, furs, fans, Victorian furnishings & decorative arts, Victorian Decorative Stenciling: A Lost Art Revived
Exhibitions: Still Life painting by 19th Century Artists of the Fall River School
Activities: Small private tours for local schools; lect open to public, 4 vis lectrs per year; individual paintings lent; shop sells books, prints, postcards, paperweights

FITCHBURG

M **FITCHBURG ART MUSEUM,** 185 Elm St, Fitchburg, MA 01420-7503. Tel 978-345-4207; Fax 978-345-2319; Email info@fitchburgartmuseum.org; Web: www.fitchburgartmuseum.org; *Dir Devel* Rebecca Wright; *Dir* Nick Capasso; *Bus Mgr* Sheryl Demers; *Dir Educ* Laura Howick; *Dir Corporate Mem Svcs* Jane Keough; *Dir Docents* Ann Descoteaux; *Dir Mktg* Kledia Spiro; *Cur* Mary Tinti
Open Wed - Fri noon - 4 PM, Sat - Sun 11 AM - 5 PM; cl Mon & Tues; Admis fee $9, seniors & students $5; Estab 1925; Three building complex, twelve galleries & two entrance halls, offices & admin; Average Annual Attendance: 24,000; Mem: 1156; dues $25 - $1000+; annual meeting Dec
Income: Financed by endowment & mem
Special Subjects: African Art, Afro-American Art, Antiquities-Egyptian, Antiquities-Greek, Antiquities-Roman, Costumes, Decorative Arts, Drawings, Drawings, Furniture, Hispanic Art, Landscapes, Latin American Art, Painting-American, Prints, Painting-American, Photography, Pre-Columbian Art
Collections: American & European paintings, prints, drawings & decorative arts, African, Egyptian, Greek, Roman, Asian art & antiquities
Exhibitions: Rotating exhibits
Publications: Exhibitions catalogs; event notices
Activities: Classes for adults & children; docent training; lect open to public, 12 vis lectrs per year; gallery talks; tours; competitions with awards; scholarships; individual paintings & original objects of art lent to colleges & museums; mus shop sells books, reproductions & jewelry

FRAMINGHAM

M **DANFORTH MUSEUM OF ART,** Danforth Museum of Art, 123 Union Ave, Framingham, MA 01702-8291. Tel 508-620-0050; Fax 508-872-5542; Email

dmadev@conversent.net; Web: www.danforthnuseum.org; *Dir* Katherine French; *Dir Fin & Opers* Mary Kiely; *Dir Educ* Pat Walker; *Cur Asst* Kristina Wilson
Open Wed, Thurs & Sun Noon - 5 PM, Fri & Sat 10 AM - 5 PM. cl Mon & Tues; Admis adults $11, seniors $9, students $8, mems & children under 17 free; Estab 1975 to provide fine arts & art-related activities to people of all ages in the South Middlesex area; There are seven galleries, including a children's gallery with hands-on activities; Average Annual Attendance: 30,000; Mem: 1500; dues individual $45, family $60, friend $100, supporter $250, sponsor $500, patron $1000, seniors get $10 off any category, annual meeting in Oct
Income: Financed by mem, Framingham State College & Town of Framingham, federal & state grants; foundations & corporate support
Special Subjects: Drawings, Painting-American, Prints, Watercolors, Ceramics, Crafts, Glass, Painting-American, Photography, Pottery
Collections: Old master & contemporary prints, drawings & photography, 19th & 20th c American art by: Gilbert Stuart, James McNeill Whistler, Charles Sprague Pearce, Meta Vaux Warrick Fuller, Albert Bierstadt, Yves Tanguy, Karl Knaths, Thomas Hart Benton & Faith Ringgold, African & Oceanic art
Exhibitions: Varied program of changing exhibitions, traveling shows, selections from the permanent collection, in a variety of periods, styles & media
Publications: Newsletter; exhibition brochures & catalogues, museum school brochure
Activities: Classes for adults & children; docent training; progs for area schools; workshops; teacher development; family progs; lects open to pub; concerts; gallery talks; tours; trips; receptions; competitions; book traveling exhibs 2-3 per yr; originate traveling exhibs to other mus & galleries nationally; mus shop sells original art & reproductions; junior gallery

L **Library**, 123 Union Ave, Framingham, MA 01701-8291. Tel 508-620-0050; Fax 508-872-5542; Email kfrench@danforthmuseum.org; Web: www.danforthmuseum.org; *Dir* Katherine French; *Mus Educ* Pat Walker
Open Wed, Thurs, Sun 12 PM - 5 PM, Fri - Sat 10 AM - 5 PM; Admis adults $8, seniors & students $7; Estab 1975 as an educational resource of art books & catalogues; For reference only; research as requested; Average Annual Attendance: 40,000; Mem: 1,400; dues family $60, individual $45
Library Holdings: Auction Catalogs, Book Volumes 6500, Clipping Files, Exhibition Catalogs, Pamphlets, Video Tapes
Special Subjects: American Indian Art, Painting-American
Collections: Meta Warrick Fuller
Activities: Classes for adults & children; docent training; lects; 15 vis lectrs per yr; concerts; gallery talks; tours; competitions; juried exhib awards; purchase awards; schols & fels offered; mus shop sells books, magazines, original art, reproductions & prints

GARDNER

M **MOUNT WACHUSETT COMMUNITY COLLEGE,** East Wing Gallery, 444 Green St, Gardner, MA 01440-1378. Tel 978-632-6600, Ext 168; Web: www.mwcc.mass.edu; *Chmn Dept Art* Gene Cauthen; *Painting Prof* John Pacheco; *Ceramics Prof* Joyce Miller; *Adjunct Faculty* Joslin Stevens; *Adjunct Faculty* Susan Montgomery; *Adjunct Faculty* Keith Hollingwood
Open Mon - Thurs 8 AM - 9 PM, Fri 8 AM - 5 PM; No admis fee; Estab 1971 to supply resources for a two-year art curriculum; develop an art collection; Well-lighted gallery with skylights & track lighting, white paneled walls; two open, spacious levels with Welsh tile floors; Average Annual Attendance: 8,000-10,000
Income: Financed by city & state appropriations
Purchases: Pottery by Makato Yabe, print by Bob Roy, 17 student paintings, ten student prints, five student ceramic works, eight student sculpture, two bronze works
Collections: Approx 100 works, framed color art posters & reproductions, prints, ceramic pieces, student coll
Exhibitions: Annual student competition of painting, sculpture, drawing, ceramics, printmaking; local, national & international artists & former students' works
Publications: Annual brochure
Activities: Continuing educ classes for adults & children; lect open to public, 8-10 vis lectrs per year; gallery talks; tours; competitions with awards; exten dept serves Mount Wachussett

L **La Chance Library**, 444 Green St, Gardner, MA 01440. Tel 978-630-9125, 888-884-6922; Fax 978-630-9556; Web: www.mwcc.mass.edu; *Coordr, Library Svcs* Jess Mynes
Open Mon - Thurs 7:30 AM - 7:30 PM, Fri 7:30 AM - 4 PM, (when school is in session); Estab 1964; Circ 12,998; Lending library
Income: Financed by state appropriation
Library Holdings: Book Volumes 55,000, CD-ROMs, DVDs, Exhibition Catalogs, Memorabilia, Periodical Subscriptions 82
Exhibitions: Periodic exhibitions

GLOUCESTER

M **CAPE ANN MUSEUM,** 27 Pleasant St, Gloucester, MA 01930-5909. Tel 978-283-0455; Fax 978-283-4141; Email rondafaloon@capeannmuseum.org; Web: www.capeannmuseum.org; *Dir* Ronda Faloon; *Pres* John Cunningham; *Mus Shop Mgr* Cara White
Open Tues - Sat 10 AM - 5 PM, Sun 1 - 4 PM, cl major holidays; Admis adults $10, seniors, students & Cape Ann residents $8, mems & children under 18 free; Estab 1873 to foster appreciation of the quality & diversity of life on Cape Ann past & present; Fine arts, decorative arts & American furniture; Fisheries/maritime galleries; granite industry gallery; 1804 furnished house; maintains reference library; Average Annual Attendance: 25,000; Mem: dues $50-$5,000
Income: Financed by memberships, donations, admissions & endowment
Library Holdings: Auction Catalogs, Audio Tapes, Book Volumes, CD-ROMs, Clipping Files, Compact Disks, DVDs, Exhibition Catalogs, Manuscripts, Maps, Memorabilia, Original Documents, Pamphlets, Periodical Subscriptions, Photographs
Special Subjects: American Western Art, Art Education, Art History, Bronzes, Coins & Medals, Decorative Arts, Dioramas, Dolls, Drawings, Embroidery, Etchings & Engravings, Furniture, Historical Material, Jade, Landscapes, Manuscripts, Maps, Marine Painting, Painting-American, Painting-American, Period Rooms, Pewter, Photography, Porcelain, Portraits, Pottery, Prints, Sculpture, Silver, Textiles, Watercolors
Collections: Fitz Henry Lane Collection: paintings, 20th Century: Maurice Prendergast, John Sloan, Stuart Davis, Marsden Hartley, Milton Avery, Granite Industry of Cape Ann, Maritime & Fishing Industry, 20th Century Sculpture-Walker Hancock, Paul Manship, Folly Cove Designs-Textiles
Exhibitions: Charles Hopkinson
Activities: Classes for adults & children; outreach to area schools; on-site progs for students; docent training; lects open to pub; vis lectrs 4 per yr; concerts; gallery talks; tours; individual paintings & original objects of art lent to mus, galleries & local bus; mus shop sells books, magazines, reproductions, original art, prints, slides, jewelry, postcards, note paper & Cape Ann related items

L **Library**, 27 Pleasant St, Gloucester, MA 01930. Tel 978-283-0455; Fax 978-283-4141; Web: www.capeannmuseum.org; *Dir* Ronda Faloon
Open Tues - Sat 10 AM - 5 PM, Sun 1 - 4 PM; Admis adults $10, seniors & students $8, Cape Ann residents & students under 18 free; Estab 1876; Reference only; Average Annual Attendance: 20,000
Income: mem, donations, admissions, sales
Library Holdings: Auction Catalogs, Book Volumes 3000, Clipping Files, Exhibition Catalogs, Manuscripts, Memorabilia, Motion Pictures, Original Art Works, Original Documents, Pamphlets, Photographs, Prints, Records, Reproductions, Sculpture
Special Subjects: Art History, Decorative Arts, Historical Material, Manuscripts, Maps, Marine Painting, Painting-American, Period Rooms, Photography, Porcelain, Portraits, Sculpture, Silver, Watercolors
Collections: Fitz Henry Lane Collection, 20th century art, fisheries/maritime, granite quarrying
Activities: Classes for children; full schedule of progs; lects open to pub; concerts; gallery talks; tours; mus shop sells books, magazines, reproductions, prints

M **HAMMOND CASTLE MUSEUM,** 80 Hesperus Ave, Gloucester, MA 01930-5299. Tel 978-283-7673, 283-7620; Fax 978-283-1643; Web: www.hammondcastle.org; *Acting Dir & Cur* John W Pettibone; *VPres* Craig Lentz
Open daily June - Aug 10 AM - 6 PM, weekends Sept - May 10 AM - 3 PM; Admis adults $6.50, seniors & students $5.50, children between 4 & 12 $4.50; Estab 1931 by a famous inventor, John Hays Hammond Jr. Incorporated in 1938 for the pub exhib of authentic works of art, architecture and specimens of antiquarian value and to encourage and promote better educ in the fine arts, with particular reference to purity of design and style; Built in style of a medieval castle with Great Hall, courtyard and period rooms, Dr Hammond combined elements of Roman, Medieval and Renaissance periods in his attempt to recreate an atmosphere of European beauty; Average Annual Attendance: 60,000
Income: Financed by tours, concerts, special events & rentals
Collections: Rare collection of European artifacts, Roman, Medieval and Renaissance Periods
Publications: Exhibition catalogs; Hammond Biography
Activities: Classes for children; docent training; educational & teacher workshops; lect open to public; concerts; self-guided & group tours; exten dept servs neighboring schools; sales shop sells books, reproductions, crafts, jewelry, art cards & postcards

A **NORTH SHORE ARTS ASSOCIATION, INC,** 11 Pirate's Lane, Gloucester, MA 01930. Tel 978-283-1857; Email arts@nsarts.org; Web: www.nsarts.org; *Pres* George Martin; *VPres* Kathy Moore; *VPres* Dolores Erikson Reid; *Treas* Mary Kathryn Gray; *Gallery Dir* Suzanne Gilbert
Open daily 10 AM - 5 PM, Sun Noon - 5 PM, May 1 - Oct 31; No admis fee; Estab 1922 by the Cape Ann Artists to promote American art by exhibitions; Gallery owned by assn; maintains reference library; Average Annual Attendance: 8,000; Mem: 375; dues artist $75, patron $50, assoc $40; juried membership
Income: Financed by dues, contributions & rentals
Library Holdings: Cards, Exhibition Catalogs, Original Art Works, Original Documents, Pamphlets, Periodical Subscriptions, Prints, Reproductions, Sculpture
Special Subjects: Painting-American
Collections: Member paintings
Exhibitions: 4 summer exhibs in addition to solo exhibs; hosts national shows on even numbered yrs
Publications: Calendar of Events; exhibit catalogs; brochures
Activities: Classes for adults & children; dramatic progs; docent training; art auctions; children's festival; lects open to pub, 4 vis lectrs per yr; concerts; gallery talks; sponsored competitions; schols; lending of original objects of art to other mus; sales shop sells books, original art & members cards

GREAT BARRINGTON

M **BARD COLLEGE AT SIMON'S ROCK,** Hillman-Jackson Gallery, 84 Alford Rd, Great Barrington, MA 01230-2499. Tel 413-644-4400; Fax 413-528-7365; Email mcherin@simons-rock.edu; Web: www.simons-rock.edu; *Cur* Margaret Cherin
Open daily; No admis fee; Estab 1966 as a liberal arts col; 25 ft x 16 ft gallery
Income: Financed by the college
Exhibitions: A continuing exhibition program of professional faculty & student works in drawing, painting, photography, sculpture & ceramics;
Activities: Gallery talks; tours; Juror's prize for annual juried student show; faculty prize

L **Library**, 84 Alford Rd, Great Barrington, MA 01230. Tel 413-528-7274, 413-528-0771; Email goodkind@simons rock.edu; Web: www.simons-rock.edu; *Librn* Joan Goodkind
Open Mon - Tues 8:30 AM - 2 AM, Wed - Fri 8:30 AM - Midnight, Sat 11 AM - Midnight, Sun 11 AM - 2 AM; No admis fee; Estab 1964; 20 ft x 30 ft
Income: Financed by the college
Library Holdings: Book Volumes 60,500, Cassettes, Fiche, Periodical Subscriptions 350, Records, Reels
Exhibitions: In the Atrium Gallery, exhibits change monthly

HADLEY

M **PORTER-PHELPS-HUNTINGTON FOUNDATION, INC,** Historic House Museum, 130 River Dr, Hadley, MA 01035-9782. Tel 413-584-4699; Web: www.pphmuseum.org; *Pres* Thomas N Harris; *VPres* Dan Huntington Fenn; *Exec Dir* Susan J Lisk
Open May 15 - Oct 15 Sat - Wed 1 - 4:30 PM; Admis fee $5, children under 12 $1; Estab 1948; Historic house built in 1752; twelve rooms house the accumulated belongings of ten generations of one family; carriage house; corn barn; historic gardens; sunken garden; Average Annual Attendance: 5,500; Mem: 500; dues $25 - $1,000; ann meeting in Dec
Income: $65,000 (financed by endowment, grants, programs & mem)
Special Subjects: Decorative Arts, Architecture, Costumes, Drawings, Furniture, Glass, Historical Material, Jewelry, Manuscripts, Maps, Miniatures, Painting-American, Pewter, Photography, Porcelain, Portraits, Prints, Scrimshaw, Silver, Textiles, Watercolors
Collections: Porter-Phelps-Huntington family collection of 17th, 18th & 19th century furniture, paintings, papers, decorative arts, clothing collection, Porter-Phelps - Hunting Family Paper on deposit at Amherst College Special Collections & Archives
Exhibitions: Annual rotating exhibits by regional artists
Activities: Dramatic progs; history institute for teachers; lects open to pub, 1 vis lectr per yr; concerts; tours; individual paintings & objects of art lent to other mus; mus shop sells books, cards & pamphlets

HARVARD

M **FRUITLANDS MUSEUM, INC,** 102 Prospect Hill Rd, Harvard, MA 01451-1348. Tel 978-456-3924; Fax 978-456-8078; Email education@fruitlands.org; Web: www.fruitlands.org; *Cur* Michael Volmar, PhD; *Dir Educ* Maggie Green; *Dir Develop* Kerry Castorano; *Exec Dir* Wyona Lynch-McWhite
Open mid-April 1 thru - Oct Daily 10 AM - 4 PM, weekends & holidays 10 AM - 5 PM, cl Tuesdays; Admis adults $12, seniors & college students $10, ages 5 & under no charge; Estab 1914, incorporated 1930 by Clara Endicott Sears. Fruitlands was the scene of Bronson Alcott's Utopian experiment in community living; The Fruitlands Farmhouse contains furniture, household articles, pictures, handcrafts, books & valuable manuscript collection of Alcott, Lane & Transcendental group. The Shaker House, built in 1794 by the members of the former Harvard Shaker Village, was originally used as an office. Moved to its present location, it now forms the setting for the products of Shaker Handicrafts & Community Industries. Native American Mus contains ethnological exhibs. Art gallery contains portraits by itinerant artists of the first half of the 19th century & landscapes by Hudson River School & rotating exhibits; Average Annual Attendance: 11,000; Mem: 700; dues senior/students $30, individual $55, family $70, Patron $250, Fruitlands Benefactor $500; annual meeting in June
Income: Financed by earned income, Sears Trust, mem fees, gifts & grants
Purchases: Books, paintings & ethnographic materials
Library Holdings: Original Art Works, Original Documents, Photographs, Records, Sculpture
Special Subjects: American Indian Art, Dioramas, Dolls, Drawings, Embroidery, Eskimo Art, Etchings & Engravings, Folk Art, Furniture, Landscapes, Manuscripts, Maps, Painting-American, Period Rooms, Sculpture, Sculpture
Collections: Hudson River Landscapes, Philip Sears Sculpture Collection, Shaker Handcraft Furniture, household articles & pictures
Publications: The View Newsletter, 3 times/yr
Activities: Art classes for adults & children; lects open to pub, 2-4 vis lectrs per yr; concerts; gallery talks; competitions; individual & original objects of art lent to other mus in the area; lending collection includes original art works, prints, paintings; book traveling exhibs; mus shop sells books, reproductions, prints & handcrafted gifts

L **Library,** 102 Prospect Hill Rd, Harvard, MA 01451. Tel 978-456-3924; Fax 978-456-8078; Email mvolmar@fruitlands.org; Web: www.fruitlands.org; *Cur* Michael A Volmar PhD
Open yr round by appointment; Estab 1914 for staff resource & scholarly research
Library Holdings: Book Volumes 10,000, Filmstrips, Manuscripts, Memorabilia, Motion Pictures, Original Art Works, Periodical Subscriptions 10, Photographs, Records, Reels, Slides, Video Tapes
Special Subjects: Art History

HAVERHILL

L **HAVERHILL PUBLIC LIBRARY,** Special Collections, 99 Main St, Haverhill, MA 01830-5092. Tel 978-373-1586 ext 642; Fax 978-373-8466; Web: www.haverhillpl.org; *Cur Spec Coll* Greg Laing
Open Tues & Fri 10 AM - 1 PM, 2 - 5 PM; No admis fee; Estab 1873
Income: Financed by private endowment
Library Holdings: Audio Tapes, Book Volumes 8650, Cassettes, Clipping Files, Kodachrome Transparencies, Lantern Slides, Manuscripts, Motion Pictures, Original Art Works, Periodical Subscriptions 16, Photographs, Prints, Video Tapes
Special Subjects: Manuscripts, Photography, Prints
Collections: Illuminated manuscripts, mid-19th century photographs, work by Beato and Robertson, Bourne, Frith, Gardner, Naya, O'Sullivan, and others, small group of paintings including Joseph A Ames, Henry Bacon, Sidney M Chase, William S Haseltine, Thomas Hill, Harrison Plummer, Winfield Scott Thomas, Robert Wade
Exhibitions: Changing exhibits

HOLYOKE

M **HISTORIC HOLYOKE AT WISTARIAHURST & CITY OF HOLYOKE,** 238 Cabot St, Holyoke, MA 01040-3904. Tel 413-322-5660; Fax 413-534-2344; Email wistariahurst@gmail.com; Web: www.wistariahurst.org; *Dir* Kate Preissler; *Event Coordr* Sara English; *Cur & City Hist* Penni Martorell
Open year-round Sat, Sun & Mon noon - 4 PM; Admis adults $7, seniors $5, members & children under 12 free; Historic house museum estab to share history of Holyoke 1850-1930; Includes art gallery showcasing works by local artists; Average Annual Attendance: 1,400; Mem: 200; dues $30 indv, $50 family; annual meeting Oct
Income: Financed by city appropriation, donations & grants
Library Holdings: Book Volumes, Original Documents, Other Holdings, Pamphlets, Photographs, Records
Special Subjects: Architecture, Costumes, Decorative Arts, Embroidery, Ethnology, Furniture, Glass, Historical Material, Historical Material, Landscapes, Landscapes, Manuscripts, Maps, Miniatures, Oriental Art, Period Rooms, Portraits, Restorations, Textiles, Stained Glass
Collections: Late 19th & early 20th centuries furniture, paintings, prints, decorative arts & architectural details, period rooms, History of Holyoke 1850-1930, Native American ethnographic material, Historical Landscape Tour, Textile Collection, Holyoke Rotary papers, Vega Collection
Publications: Museum newsletter (Spring & Fall)
Activities: Progs for adults & children; school progs; dramatic progs; docent training; visual arts gallery; cultural performances; lects open to pub; 25 vis lectrs per yr; concerts; gallery taks; tours; mus shop sells books, original art; reproductions; prints & other items

IPSWICH

M **THE TRUSTEES OF RESERVATIONS,** The Mission House, 290 Argilla Rd, Castle Hill Ipswich, MA 01938-2647. Tel 978-921-1944; Fax 978-921-1948; Email history@ttor.org; Web: www.thetrustees.org; *Chmn (V)* Elliot M Surkin; *Dir Devel* Ann Powell; *Communs* Michael Triff; *Dir Historic Resources* Susan C S Edwards; *Dir Finance & Admin* John McCrane; *Dir Land Conservation* Wesley Ward; *Exec Dir* Andrew Kendall; *Bd Pres (V)* Janice Hunt
Open Memorial Day through Columbus Day Daily 10 AM - 5 PM; Admis adults $5, children 6-12 $2.50; Built 1739, the home of John Sergeant, first missionary to the Stockbridge Indians, it is now an Early American Mus containing an outstanding collection of Colonial furnishings. Mus opened in 1930; Average Annual Attendance: 3,000
Special Subjects: Period Rooms
Publications: Yearly brochure

LAWRENCE

M **ESSEX ART CENTER,** 56 Island St, Lawrence, MA 01840. Tel 978-685-2343; Fax 978-688-0276; Email info@essexartcenter.com; Web: essexartcenter.com; *Exec Dir* John Budzyna; *Sidell Gallery Dir & Registrar* Sara Hidalgo; *Educ Dir* Maria Sanchez Kouassi; *Beland Gallery Dir & Special Projects* Cathy McLaurin
Open Mon - Fri 10 AM - 6 PM; Estab to foster artistic potential in the surrounding community; Two professional galleries, a Communit Artist gallery, four spacious classrooms, a media lab & ceramics room; large open studio on ground level used for adult classes & events
Collections: Sidell Gallery shows local artist's work across a great variety of mediums, Beland Gallery displays work by emerging and mid-career artists; new media and multidisciplinary art forms
Exhibitions: 12 gallery exhibits annually
Activities: Educ progs; classes for adults & children; events; film screenings; art programming

LEXINGTON

M **NATIONAL HERITAGE MUSEUM,** 33 Marrett Rd, Lexington, MA 02421-5703. Tel 781-861-6559; Fax 781-861-9846; Email info@monh.org; Web: www.nationalheritagemuseum.org; Others TTY: 781-274-8539; *Dir Exhibits* Hilary Anderson; *Dir Admin & Finance* June Cobb; *Designer* Mike Rizzo; *Dir Coll* Aimee Newell; *Archivist* Catherine Swanson; *Mgr Lib* Jeffrey Croteau
Open Tues - Sat 10 AM - 4:30 PM, Sun Noon - 4:30PM, Library open Tues - Sat 10 AM - 4 PM, cl Sun; No admis fee; Estab 1972 as an American history museum, including art and decorative art; Four modern galleries for changing exhibs, flexible lighting & climate control. Two galleries of 3000 sq ft, two 1500 sq ft; Average Annual Attendance: 58,000; Mem: 225; dues benefactor $500, assoc mem $250, contributing $100, family $60, individual $40, senior and student $30
Income: $2,900,000 (financed by endowment & appeal to Masons)
Library Holdings: Auction Catalogs, Audio Tapes, Book Volumes, Cassettes, Compact Disks, DVDs, Exhibition Catalogs, Kodachrome Transparencies, Manuscripts, Maps, Original Documents, Other Holdings, Pamphlets, Periodical Subscriptions, Photographs, Records, Slides, Video Tapes
Special Subjects: Decorative Arts, Painting-American, Historical Material
Collections: General American & American Paintings, American decorative art, objects decorated with Masonic, patriotic & fraternal symbolism, Masonic Collection
Exhibitions: Images of Women in WWI posters opens; Pets in America opens; The Art of the Needle: Master. Quilts from the Shelburne Mus opens; Raymond Loewy: Designs for a consumer Culture opens; Telephones opens
Publications: Exhibition catalogs
Activities: Docent training; lects open to pub; 12 vis lectrs per yr; concerts; gallery talks; tours for school groups; paintings and art objects lent; originate traveling exhibs; mus shop sells books and a variety of gift items related to exhibit prog; mus courtyard cafe

LINCOLN

M **DECORDOVA SCULPTURE PARK & MUSEUM,** (DeCordova Museum & Sculpture Park), 51 Sandy Pond Rd, Lincoln, MA 01773-2699. Tel 781-259-8355; Fax 781-259-3650; Email info@decordova.org; Web: www.decordova.org; *Mus Dir* John Ravenal; *Deputy Dir External Affairs* Bruce Smith; *Sr Cur* Jennifer Gross; *Assoc Cur Contemporary Art* Sarah Montross; *Registrar* Lynn Hermann Traub; *Cur*

Educ Emily Silet; *Preparator* Anderson Heagy; *Head Visitor Svcs* Holly Berube; *Dep Dir Opers* David A Duddy; *Leadership Ann Giving Officer* Nocolas Kane; *Dir Corp Rel & Art Loan Prog* Sharon Glennon; *Dep Dir Learning & Engagement* Julie Bernson; *Mem Coordr* Amber Price; *Acctg Mgr* Nicole Solari
Open Mon - Sun 10 AM - 5 PM & on select holidays; Admis adults $14, children 6-12 free, students $10, seniors $12, mems, res, military & children 12 & under free; discounts available; Estab 1948, opened 1950 to exhibit, to interpret, collect & preserve modern & contemporary American art; Maintains multiple galleries with climate control, cafe, library & Sculpture Garden; Average Annual Attendance: 125,000; Mem: 3,500; dues Dir's Cir $2,500, Julian Club $1,000, patron $600, sponsor $300, school & friend $150, household $90, household teacher $80, individual $60
Income: Financed by endowment, individual/corporate mem, foundation & government grants
Library Holdings: Book Volumes 3,000, Exhibition Catalogs, Other Holdings Museum Catalogs, Periodical Subscriptions 10
Special Subjects: Etchings & Engravings, Glass, Graphics, Landscapes, Painting-American, Photography, Portraits, Prints, Sculpture, Woodcuts, Painting-American
Collections: 3,000+ artworks of various media, 20th century American painting, graphics, sculpture & photography, American Art, with emphasis on New England
Publications: Exhib catalogs; newsletter
Activities: Classes for adults & children; docent training; teacher training, outreach & resources; Sculpture on Site prog; Teen to Screen video prog; lects open to pub, 4 vis lectrs per yr; concerts; gallery talks; guided tours; arts festivals; outreach progs; exten prog serves Boston area; individual paintings & original objects of art lent to corporate program members & schools; book traveling exhibs 2-3 per yr; originate traveling exhibs; mus shop sells books, magazines, original art, art supplies, handcrafted gifts, jewelry, wearable art & contemporary crafts

M **Sculpture Park,** 51 Sandy Pond Rd, Lincoln, MA 01773-2699. Tel 781-259-3626; Fax 781-259-3650; Email info@decordova.org; Web: www.decordova.org; *Mus Dir* Dennis Kois; *Cur Dept Asst* Jenn Schmitt
Open daily dawn to dusk; Admis joint with mus admis; Estab 1985, name changed 1989; acts as outdoor sculpture exhibition space & recreation area for Lincoln & the surrounding Boston area metropolitan communities; 35 acres with approx 75 artworks at any given time; Average Annual Attendance: 125,000
Special Subjects: Sculpture
Collections: First Tier: outdoor sculpture from the DeCordova Permanent Collection, incl 20th c sculpture from artists such as George Rickey, Alexander Liberman & Nam June Paik, Second Tier: large-scale outdoor sculptures on loan, currently from artists Ursula von Rydingsvard, William Tucker, Mark diSuvero, Sol LeWitt, Chakaia Booker & Jim Dine, Third Tier: site-specific, temporary, long-term (1-5 yrs) outdoor sculpture & installations designed for specific sites in the park, incl works by Steven Siegel, Ronald Gonzalez, Carlos Dorrien & Rick Brown
Activities: Tours

LOWELL

M **AMERICAN TEXTILE HISTORY MUSEUM,** 491 Dutton St, Lowell, MA 01854-4289. Tel 978-441-0400; Fax 978-441-1412; Email maghiarian@athm.org; Web: www.athm.org; *Pres & CEO* Jonathan Stevens; *Dir Finance & Admin* Steven Jackson; *Dir Advancement* Todd Smith; *Cur* Karen Herbaugh; *Librn* Jane Ward; *Registrar* Stephanie Hebert; *Educ Coordr* Kathy Hirbour; *Exhib Consultant* Diane Fagan Affleck; *Consulting Libr* Clare Sheridan; *Vis Servs Rep* Denise Webb; *Coordr Mem & Develop* Michelle Aghiarian
Open Wed - Sun 10 AM - 4 PM; Admis adults ages 17+ $10, children ages 6-16 & seniors 62+ $8, mems & children under 6 free; Estab 1960 to preserve artifacts, documents & records of the American textile industry; Textile & social history exhib & special exhib gallery; Average Annual Attendance: 43,478; Mem: 1,082 4-5 events; Student/senior $40; Individual $50; Dual $65; Family $100; Contributing $150; Supporting $250
Income: Financed by endowment & annual fund
Library Holdings: Audio Tapes, Book Volumes, Exhibition Catalogs, Lantern Slides, Manuscripts, Motion Pictures, Original Art Works, Original Documents, Other Holdings Engineering & architectural plans, Pamphlets, Periodical Subscriptions, Photographs, Records, Slides, Video Tapes
Special Subjects: Historical Material, Manuscripts, Photography, Prints, Textiles, Costumes
Exhibitions: Textile Revolution: An Exploration through Space and Time
Publications: Exhib catalogs; Linen Making in America
Activities: Classes for adults & children; docent training; pub progs; vacation & summer workshops; lects open to pub; gallery talks; special exhibs; sales desk sells textiles, books, prints & postcards; fiber art

L **Osborne Library,** 491 Dutton St, Lowell, MA 01854. Tel 978-441-0400; Fax 978-441-1412; Email jward@athm.org; Web: www.athm.org; *Librn* Jane Ward
Open Mon - Fri 9 AM - 5 PM; Admis $10; Estab 1960; For reference only
Income: Financed by endowment
Library Holdings: Auction Catalogs, Audio Tapes, Book Volumes 30,000, CD-ROMs, Cassettes, DVDs, Exhibition Catalogs, Lantern Slides, Manuscripts, Maps, Memorabilia, Motion Pictures, Original Art Works, Original Documents, Other Holdings Ephemera; Trade literature, Pamphlets, Periodical Subscriptions 50, Photographs, Prints, Reels, Sculpture, Video Tapes
Special Subjects: Architecture, Carpets & Rugs, Decorative Arts, Fashion Arts, Industrial Design, Manuscripts, Painting-American, Photography, Prints, Textiles, Maps
Collections: Books; pamphlets; manuscripts; broadsides; serials; trade material; photographs; prints; advertising; ephemera; on-line catalog; insurance maps
Publications: Checklist of prints and manuscripts

M **THE BRUSH ART GALLERY & STUDIOS,** 256 Market St, Lowell, MA 01852-1877. Tel 978-459-7819; *Exec Dir* E Linda Poras
Open Tues - Fri 11 AM - 5 PM; Estab 1982; Nonprofit; in national historic park. Gallery with changing exhibitions plus 13 artist studios; Average Annual Attendance: 200,000; Mem: dues $25-$40
Income: Financed by mem, grants, fundraising & sales
Activities: Classes for adults & children; lect open to public; schols offered; sales shop sells original art

M **THE LOADING DOCK GALLERY,** 122 Western Ave Lowell, MA 01851-1433. Tel 978-596-1576; Email loadingdockgallery122@gmail.com; Web: www.theloadingdockgallery.com
Open Wed - Sat 12 PM - 5:30 PM, Sun Noon - 4 PM; Estab 2007 to facilitate opportunities for artists & audiences to; Mem: dues $90
Special Subjects: Jewelry, Pottery, Prints
Collections: Original fine art, handcrafted gift items, jewelry, greeting cards, handmade soap & lotions, pottery, prints & art-to-wear
Exhibitions: Rotating exhibits

A **LOWELL ART ASSOCIATION, INC,** Whistler House Museum of Art, 243 Worthen St, Lowell, MA 01852-1874. Tel 978-452-7641; Fax 978-454-2421; Email mlally@whistlerhouse.org; Web: www.whistlerhouse.org; *President/Executive Dir.* Sara M Bogosian; *Mgr Curatorial Services* Brooke Baerman
Open Wed - Sat 11 AM - 4 PM; Admis Adults $10, Seniors $7, Children under 12 free; Estab 1878 to preserve the birthplace of James McNeill Whistler; to promote the arts in all its phases & to maintain a center for the cultural benefit of all the citizens of the community; Contemporary gallery; Average Annual Attendance: 6,000; Mem: 500; dues family $60, adults $45, senior citizens $30, students $25, artist members $40
Income: Financed by endowment, mem, admis, grants & earned income
Library Holdings: Book Volumes, Cards, DVDs, Exhibition Catalogs, Maps, Memorabilia, Pamphlets, Photographs, Sculpture
Special Subjects: Painting-American, Portraits, Prints
Collections: Mid 19th through early 20th century American Art: Hibbard, Benson, Noyes, Spear, Paxton, Phelps, Whistler etchings & lithographs, Gorky, Sculptures, Antique Lace, Antique Furniture, Chinese Bone China
Exhibitions: Galleries of works from permanent collection & exhibits by contemporary artists; Quilt Exhibitions
Publications: Brochures; S P Howes: Portrait Painter, catalog; Christmas in Landmark Homes
Activities: Classes for adults & children; docent training; lects open to pub, 8 vis lectrs per yr; concerts; gallery talks; tours; progs of historical interest; scholarships; book traveling exhibs 1-2 per yr; originate traveling exhibs to small mus & schools; mus shop sells books, magazines, original art, reproductions, prints & postcards, Whistler Paraphenalia

LYNN

M **LYNN ARTS,** 25 Exchange St, Lynn, MA 01901-1423. Tel 781-598-5244; Fax 781-599-8926; *Contact* Susan Halter

MAGNOLIA

M **CRANE COLLECTION, GALLERY OF AMERICAN PAINTING AND SCULPTURE,** 2 Old Salem Path, Magnolia, MA 01930-5275. Tel 978-526-1698; Fax 781-235-4181; Email bonnie@cranecollection.com; Web: www.cranecollection.com; *Owner, Dir & Pres* Bonnie L Crane
Open by appointment; No admis fee; Estab 1983 to exhibit 19th & early 20th century American paintings; Art gallery with changing inventory, on Boston's North Shore; Average Annual Attendance: 7,500
Library Holdings: Auction Catalogs, Book Volumes, Exhibition Catalogs, Original Art Works, Sculpture
Special Subjects: Painting-American, Period Rooms
Collections: 19th century & early 20th century American paintings & sculptures, including Hudson River School, Boston School & regional artists, outstanding contemporary artists of region
Exhibitions: Boston School: Then & Now; Summer Scenes II; Bruce Crane; Tonalism; Inspiration of Cape Ann; City Scenes; Little Picture Show; American Barbizon; Interiors; Russian Light I, II & III
Publications: The Gentle Art of Still Life; Russian Light

MALDEN

L **MALDEN PUBLIC LIBRARY,** Art Dept & Gallery, 36 Salem St, Malden, MA 02148-5291. Tel 781-324-0218, 381-0238; Fax 781-324-4467; Email maldensup@sbln.lib.ma.us; Email mbln@lib.ma.us; Web: www.mbln.lib.ma.us/malden/index.htm; *Dir & Librn* Dina G Malgeri
Open Mon - Thurs 9 AM - 9 PM, Fri & Sat 9 AM - 6 PM, cl Sun; No admis fee; Estab 1879, incorporated 1885 as a public library and art gallery; Circ 239,493; Maintains three galleries, the main gallery being the Ryder Gallery, and the others known as the Upper & Lower Galleries
Income: $421,530 (financed by endowment, city and state appropriations)
Library Holdings: Exhibition Catalogs, Framed Reproductions, Manuscripts, Memorabilia, Original Art Works, Pamphlets, Photographs, Prints, Reproductions, Sculpture
Activities: Lect open to pub, 6-12 vis lectrs per yr; concerts; gallery talks; tours

MARBLEHEAD

A **MARBLEHEAD ARTS ASSOCIATION, INC,** 8 Hooper St, King Hooper Mansion Marblehead, MA 01945-3213. Tel 781-631-2608; Email info@marbleheadarts.org; Web: www.marbleheadarts.org; *Exec Dir* Kristina Fisher; *Asst Dir* Betsy Hundahl; *Pres* Melissa Fisher; *VPres* Michele Martin; *Secy* Kristen Ueukerman; *Treas* Sara Bolduc; *Pres* Claudia Kaufman
Tues-Fri & Sun Noon-5pm; Saturday 10am - 5pm; No admis fee; Estab 1922. Owns & occupies the historic King Hooper Mansion, located in historic Marblehead; Located in the historic King Hooper Mansion; contains six galleries of exhibits by association mems & guest artists that change every 6 weeks and educ programs. classes, and special events are offered throughout the year.; Average Annual

Attendance: 3000; Mem: 500 assoc, artist, & corporate mems; mem upon application (open); jury process for artist mem acceptance; dues assoc $50, family $100, senior over 65 $40, student to age 23 $25, Artist Mem $75, donor rem supporter $125, donor mem Patron $250, Donor Mem Benefactor $500
Income: Financed by mem & mansion rentals, gallery & shop sales, tuition fees & programs
Special Subjects: Etchings & Engravings, Prints
Collections: Works of: Sam Chamberlain, Claire Leighton, Lester Hornby, Sam Thal, Nason, Grace Albee & Phillip Kappel from the 1940s series: Friends of Contemporary Prints, Paintings by Mary Bradish Titcomb, Orlando Rouland, William Haseltine, Harry Powers, & Frank Flanagan
Exhibitions: Annual Town Show; Annual Member Show; Monthly Exhibits in six galleries of local and regional artists displaying over 1200 pieces of art annually
Publications: Newsletter, monthly, Annual Report (annually), Program Brochure (every 6 months)
Activities: Classes for adults & children; drama programs; workshops; demonstrations; lects open to pub, 3 vis lectrs per yr; fall lect series; musical performances; gallery talks; competitions with awards; annual fundraising events; schols offered; mus sales shop sells books, original art, reproductions, prints, fine crafts, glass, jewelry, greeting cards

M **MARBLEHEAD MUSEUM & HISTORICAL SOCIETY,** 170 Washington St, Marblehead, MA 01945-3340. Tel 781-631-1768; Fax 781-631-0917; Email info@marbleheadmuseum.org; Web: www.marbleheadmuseum.org; *Dir* Pam Peterson; *Cur* Karen MacInnis
Open June 1 - Oct 31 Tues - Sat 10 AM - 4 PM; Nov - May Tues - Fri 10 AM - 4 PM; Average Annual Attendance: 2,500; Mem: 700; dues based on sliding scale
Library Holdings: Audio Tapes, Book Volumes, Kodachrome Transparencies, Lantern Slides, Manuscripts, Maps, Memorabilia, Original Art Works, Original Documents, Other Holdings, Pamphlets, Photographs, Slides
Special Subjects: Architecture, Carpets & Rugs, Ceramics, Coins & Medals, Costumes, Decorative Arts, Dolls, Embroidery, Furniture, Historical Material, Marine Painting, Period Rooms, Portraits, Folk Art, Jewelry, Maps, Photography, Porcelain, Silver, Textiles, Watercolors
Collections: Folk Art Paintings
Exhibitions: 2 or 3 per yr-changing exhibs of a variety of Marblehead subjects & media
Activities: Educ prog; classes for adults & children; lect open to the pub; approx 4 vis lectrs per yr; walking tours

M **John Orne Johnson Frost Gallery**, 170 Washington St, Marblehead, MA 01945. Tel 781-631-1768; Fax 781-631-0917; Email info@marbleheadmuseum.org; Web: www.marbleheadmuseum.org/; *Dir* Pam Peterson; *Cur* Karen MacInnis
Open Tues - Sat 10 AM - 4 PM June - Oct; Open Tues - Fri 10 AM - 4 PM Nov - May; cls Christmas week; No admis fee; 1920s folk art paintings & models by J O J Frost depicting life in Marblehead & fishing at sea in the past; Average Annual Attendance: 2,700; Mem: 700; dues based on sliding scale
Income: Financed by endowment, mem, & admis
Collections: Ceramics, decorate arts, documents, dolls, folk art, furniture, glass, military items, nautical items, period rooms, portraits, ship paintings, textiles
Exhibitions: Permanent exhibit; Rotating exhibit
Publications: Semi-annual newsletter
Activities: Classes for children; docent training; workshops; lect open to public, 4 vis lectrs per year; gallery talks; tours; mus shop sells books, magazines, prints & postcards

M **Jeremiah Lee Mansion**, 161 Washington St, Marblehead, MA 01945; 170 Washington St, Marblehead, MA 01945. Tel 781-631-1768; Fax 781-631-0917; Email info@marbleheadmuseum.org; Web: www.marbleheadmuseum.org; *Dir* Pam Peterson; *Cur Colls* Emilia Emig; *Asst Dir* Cheri Grishin
Open June 1 - Oct 31 Tues - Sat 10 AM - 4 PM; Admis adults $10, mems & children under 12 free; Built 1768; mansion purchased 1909; Georgian-style three-story mansion made of woodcut blocks to simulate stone with elegant rococo interior carving & original hand-painted English wallpaper depicting Roman ruins; 18th-century-style-garden; top floor has been converted to a museum of Marblehead history; Average Annual Attendance: 2,500; Mem: 800; dues based on sliding scale
Income: Financed by endowment, mem & admis
Special Subjects: Architecture, Carpets & Rugs, Ceramics, Coins & Medals, Costumes, Decorative Arts, Dolls, Embroidery, Folk Art, Furniture, Historical Material, Jewelry, Maps, Marine Painting, Painting-American, Period Rooms, Porcelain, Portraits, Silver, Textiles, Watercolors
Collections: Ceramics, decorative arts, documents, dolls, folk art, furniture, glass, military items, nautical items, period rooms, portraits, ship paintings & textiles
Activities: Architecture classes for adults; classes for children; docent training; lect open to public, vis lectr; gallery talks; house or mansion tours; walking tours; sales shop sells books

L **Archives**, 170 Washington St, Marblehead, MA 01945. Tel 781-631-1768; *Cur* Karen MacInnis
Open Tues - Fri 10 AM - 4 PM; Admis non-members $5, members free; Estab 1898 to collect & maintain artifacts of Marblehead history; No galleries. Art & decorative art displayed in historic 1768 mansion; Average Annual Attendance: 4,000; Mem: 700; dues on a sliding scale
Income: Financed by mem fees & donations
Library Holdings: Auction Catalogs, Audio Tapes, Book Volumes, CD-ROMs, Cassettes, Clipping Files, Framed Reproductions, Kodachrome Transparencies, Lantern Slides, Manuscripts, Maps, Memorabilia, Motion Pictures, Original Art Works, Original Documents, Other Holdings, Pamphlets, Periodical Subscriptions, Photographs, Prints, Reproductions, Slides, Video Tapes
Special Subjects: Historical Material, Manuscripts
Collections: Archives
Publications: Members semiannual newsletter
Activities: Classes for adults & children; docent training; lect open to public, 3 vis lectrs per year; tours; sales shop sells books, original art, reproductions, prints & postcards

MARION

A **MARION ART CENTER,** Cecil Clark Davis Gallery, 80 Pleasant St, Marion, MA 02738; PO Box 602, Marion, MA 02738-0011. Tel 508-748-1266; Fax 508-748-2759; Email marionartcenter@verizon.net; Web: www.marionartcenter.org; *Pres* Patricia White; *Dir* Wendy Bidstrup; *VPres* Joy Horstmann; *Secy* Kate Marvel; *Treas* Eric Strand
Open Tues - Fri 1 - 5 PM, Sat 10 AM - 2 PM; No admis fee; Estab 1957 to provide theater, concerts & visual arts exhibitions for the community & to provide studio art, theater arts, music & dance classes for adults & children; Two galleries, 125 ft of wall space, 500 sq ft floor space; indirect lighting; entrance off Main St; Average Annual Attendance: 2,000; Mem: 650; dues angel $1,000, patron $500, donor $250, sponsor $100, family $50, basic $25; annual meeting in Jan
Income: Financed by mem dues, donations & profit from ticket & gallery sales
Collections: Cecil Clark Davis (1877-1955), portrait paintings
Exhibitions: Monthly one person & group shows; Arts in the Park - one day outdoor festival in July
Publications: Annual mem folder; monthly invitations to opening; quarterly newsletter
Activities: Classes for adults & children; dramatic progs, pvt lessons in piano & voice; lects open to pub; concerts; gallery talks; competitions; schols; sales shop sells fine crafts, small paintings, prints, cards, original art and reproductions

MEDFORD

M **TUFTS UNIVERSITY,** Tufts University Art Gallery, 40 Talbot Ave, Aidekman Arts Center Medford, MA 02155. Tel 617-627-3518; Fax 617-627-3121; Email art gallery@tufts.edu; Web: www.artgallery.tufts.edu; *Dir* Amy Ingrid Schlegel PhD; *Preparator & Registrar* Doug Bell; *Colls Registrar* Laura McCarty; *Publs Coordr* Jeanne Koles; *Colls Assoc Registrar* John Rossetti; *Educ Outreach Coordr* Dorothee Perin; *Exhib Coordr* Lissa Cramer
Open Tues - Wed & Fri - Sun 11 AM - 5 PM, Thurs 11 AM - 8 PM, cl holidays & Aug; No admis fee; suggested donation $3; Estab 1991; 7,000 sq ft of exhibit space over 4 galleries; Average Annual Attendance: 8,000; Mem: Contemporary Arts Circle Friends Group
Special Subjects: Antiquities-Egyptian, Antiquities-Greek, Antiquities-Roman, Painting-American, Photography, Prints
Collections: Primarily 19th & 20th centuries American paintings, prints & drawings, contemporary paintings, photographs & works on paper
Exhibitions: Approx ten shows annually, three of which are thesis exhibits of candidates for the MFA degree offered by Tufts in affiliation with the School of the Boston Museum of Fine Arts; New media wall, sculpture ct; Annual summer exhibition of local artists
Publications: Catalogues & brochures
Activities: Docent training; tours for adults; lects open to pub, 4 vis lectrs per yr; gallery talks; tours; intra-univ art loan prog; originate traveling exhibs

MILTON

M **CAPTAIN FORBES HOUSE MUSEUM,** 215 Adams St, Milton, MA 02186-4215. Tel 617-696-1815; Fax 617-696-1815; Email info@forbeshousemuseum.org; Web: forbeshousemuseum.org
Open Sun 1 - 4 PM; Admis $10, seniors & students $8, children under 5 free; Estab 1964 as a Historic House museum; for preservation, research, education: 19th century through Forbes family focus; Average Annual Attendance: 1,000; Mem: 400; dues life member $1,000, benefactor $500, sponsor $250, donor $100, friend $50, family $50, individual $30
Income: $250,000 (financed by endowment, mem & fundraising)
Library Holdings: Book Volumes 2500, Exhibition Catalogs, Manuscripts, Memorabilia, Micro Print, Original Art Works, Pamphlets, Periodical Subscriptions 6, Photographs, Prints
Special Subjects: Decorative Arts, Period Rooms, Porcelain
Collections: Abraham Lincoln Civil War Collections & Archives, Forbes Family Collection of China trade & American furnishings
Exhibitions: Annual Abraham Lincoln essay contest for grades K - 8th grade
Activities: Classes for adults & children; docent training; lects open to pub, 3 vis lectrs per yr; tours; competitions & awards; lending collection contains decorative arts, Lincoln memorabilia, original art works, original prints & sculpture; mus sells books & cards

NANTUCKET

A **ARTISTS ASSOCIATION OF NANTUCKET,** 19 Washington St & 1 Gardner Perry Ln, Nantucket, MA 02554; PO Box 1104, Nantucket, MA 02554-1104. Tel 508-228-0722; Fax 508-228-9700; Email aanoff@verizon.net (office); Email anngallery@verizon.net (gallery); Web: www.nantucketarts.org; *Pres (V)* Katie Frinkle Legge; *Gallery Dir* Robert Foster; *Admin* Meghan Valero; *Dir Arts Prog* Liz Hunt O'Brien
Open spring daily Noon - 5 PM, summer daily 10 AM - 6 PM; No admis fee; Estab 1945 to provide a place for Nantucket artists of all levels & styles to show their work & encourage new artists; Maintains one gallery: at 19 Washington St, 2 fls; Average Annual Attendance: 50,000 - 70,000; Mem: 600; dues patron $50 - $500, artist $100; annual meeting Aug
Income: $75,000 - $100,000 (financed by mem, fundraising & commissions, large patron gifts)
Library Holdings: Auction Catalogs, Book Volumes, Clipping Files, Exhibition Catalogs, Original Art Works, Periodical Subscriptions
Collections: 600 pieces, most by Nantucket artists, Wet Paint Auction
Exhibitions: Annual Craft Show; juried shows; changing one-person & group member shows during summer; occasional off-season shows
Publications: Monthly newsletter; annual brochure
Activities: Classes for adults & children; workshops; lect open to public, 5-6 vis lectrs per year; gallery talks, competitions with awards; scholarships; individual

paintings & original objects of art lent to local hospital & public offices; sales shop sells original art, prints & lithographs

M **EGAN MARITIME INSTITUTE,** Shipwreck & Lifesaving Museum, 158 Polpis Rd, Nantucket, MA 02554; PO Box 2923, Nantucket, MA 02584. Tel 508-228-2505; Fax 508-228-7069; Email egan@eganmaritime.org; Web: www.eganmaritime.org; *Exec Dir* Pauline Proch; *Asst Dir & Cur* Lisa Lazarus
Open Memorial Day - Columbus Day daily 10 - 5 PM; Admis adults $10, seniors & students $7, youth 6 - 17 $5, children under 6 free; Average Annual Attendance: 3,000
Income: Financed by the foundation
Special Subjects: Architecture, Decorative Arts, Etchings & Engravings, Historical Material, Landscapes, Manuscripts, Maps, Marine Painting, Painting-American, Painting-British, Photography, Portraits, Watercolors
Collections: 19th & 20th century marine paintings, ship models
Exhibitions: Nantucket Spirit; The Life and Art of Elizabeth R. Coffin
Publications: Millhill Press-book
Activities: Adult classes; lect open to public, 7-10 vis lectrs per year; lending collection contains paintings & objects of art; sales shop sells books & prints

M **NANTUCKET HISTORICAL ASSOCIATION,** Historic Nantucket, 15 Broad St, Nantucket, MA 02554-3502; PO Box 1016, Nantucket, MA 02554-1016. Tel 508-228-1894; Fax 508-228-5618; Email nhainfo@nha.org; Web: www.nha.org; *Exec Dir* Jean M Weber; *Cur Library & Archives* Georgen Gilliam; *CEO* Frank D Milligan; *Dir Develop* Jean Grimmer; *Museum Shop Mgr* Georgina Winton; *VPres* Arie Kopelman; *Chief Cur* Niles Parker
Open June - Oct 10 AM - 5 PM; Admis a visitor pass to all buildings, adults $10, children 5-14 $5, individual building admis $2-$5; Estab 1894 to preserve Nantucket & maintain history; Historic Nantucket is a collection of 10 historic buildings & 3 museums throughout the town, open to the pub & owned by the Nantucket Historical Assoc. Together they portray the way people lived & worked as Nantucket grew from a small farming community to the center of America's whaling industry; maintains reference library; Mem: 3000; dues $30-$1000; annual meeting in July
Income: Financed by endowment, contributions, events, mem & admis
Special Subjects: Painting-American
Collections: Portraits, Oil Paintings, Watercolors, Needlework Pictures, baskets, furniture, photographs, scrimshaw, textiles, whaling tools & all other manner of artifacts related to Nantucket & Maritime History, all objects exhibited in our historic houses & museums which cover the period 1686-1930
Publications: Art on Nantucket; Historic Nantucket, quarterly, magazine for members
Activities: Classes for children; docent training; lects open to pub, 24 vis lectrs per yr; concerts; gallery talks; tours; research fels offered; mus shop sells books, reproductions, prints, slides, period furniture, household items, silver, bone & ivory scrimshaw, candles & children's toys

NEW BEDFORD

M **NEW BEDFORD ART MUSEUM/ARTWORKS!,** 608 Pleasant St, New Bedford, MA 02740-6204. Tel 508-961-3072; Email info@newbedfordart.org; Web: newbedfordart.org; *Studio Educ & Outreach Dir* Deb Smook; *Educ Prog Asst* Alanna Boucher; *Develop Mgr* Meg Albert
Open Wed - Sun Noon - 5 PM, Thurs Noon - 9 PM; Admis adults $5, seniors & students $3, mem & children under 17 when accompanied by an adult free; Estab 2014; Mem: dues $35-$500
Collections: Has featured contemporary & historic artwork as well as local, national & international artists
Exhibitions: Temporary exhibits
Activities: Educ progs; classes for adults & children; outreach & resources; artist talks; performances; video & film screenings

L **NEW BEDFORD FREE PUBLIC LIBRARY,** Special Collections Dept: Art Collection, 613 Pleasant St, New Bedford, MA 02740-6203. Tel 508-979-1787; Fax 508-979-1614; Email jhodson@sailsinc.org; Web: www.ci.new-bedford.ma.us/nbfpl.htm; *Cur Art* Janice Hodson; *Head Spec Colls* Jodi Goodman
Open Mon - Thurs 9 AM - 9 PM, Fri & Sat 9 AM - 5 PM; Art Room open Tues - Wed 1 PM - 5 PM, Thurs 1 PM - 5 PM & 6 PM - 9 PM, Fri 9 Am - 5 PM, Sat 9 AM - Noon, 1 PM - 5 PM; cl Sun & holidays; No admis fee; Estab 1852; Circ non-circulating; 19th & 20th Century Am & European art; Average Annual Attendance: 4500
Income: Financed by endowment, city, & state appropriation
Library Holdings: Auction Catalogs, Book Volumes, CD-ROMs, Cassettes, DVDs, Exhibition Catalogs, Fiche, Filmstrips, Framed Reproductions, Kodachrome Transparencies, Lantern Slides, Manuscripts, Maps, Memorabilia, Motion Pictures, Original Art Works, Original Documents, Pamphlets, Periodical Subscriptions, Photographs, Prints, Records, Reels, Sculpture, Slides, Video Tapes
Special Subjects: American Western Art, Art History, Decorative Arts, Etchings & Engravings, Handicrafts, Historical Material, Landscapes, Maps, Marine Painting, Painting-American, Painting-Dutch, Painting-German, Photography, Portraits, Prints, Silver, Textiles, Watercolors, Woodcarvings, Woodcuts, Miniatures, Archaeology, Asian Art, Illustration, Posters
Collections: Paintings by Clifford Ashley, Albert Bierstadt, F D Millet, William Wall, Dodge MacKnight, William Bradford, R Swain Gifford, Ralph Fasenella, John James Audubon's Birds of America Folio, maritime art; landscapes; portraiture; auction catalogs; rare books; early study prints; Japanese Woodblock Prints, Hudson River School painters
Activities: Art progs for children & adults; lects open to pub; vis lectrs; gallery talks; tours; internships offered; objects of art lent to museums for special exhibits

M **OLD DARTMOUTH HISTORICAL SOCIETY,** New Bedford Whaling Museum, 18 Johnny Cake Hill, New Bedford, MA 02740. Tel 508-997-0046; Fax 508-997-0018; Web: www.whalingmuseum.org; *Chief Cur* Christina Connett; *Dir Colls* Jordan Berson
Open Jan - Mar Tues - Sat 9 AM - 4 PM, Sun 11 AM - 4 PM; select galleries open until 8 PM every 2nd Thurs of month; April - Dec daily 9 AM - 5 PM; select galleries open until 8 PM every 2nd Thurs of month; Admis adult $17, senior 65+ $15, students 19+ $10, child & youth $7, children 3 and under free; free on AHA! nights (see calendar for more details); Estab 1903 to collect, preserve & interpret objects including printed material, pictures & artifacts related to the history of the New Bedford area & American whaling; Average Annual Attendance: 100,000; Mem: 3,000; dues $50-$1,000; annual meeting in May
Income: $3,849,000 (financed by endowment, mem, private gifts, grants, special events & admis)
Special Subjects: Costumes, Crafts, Decorative Arts, Dolls, Drawings, Embroidery, Etchings & Engravings, Ethnology, Folk Art, Furniture, Glass, Historical Material, Ivory, Laces, Manuscripts, Maps, Marine Painting, Miniatures, Painting-American, Photography, Portraits, Prints, Restorations, Scrimshaw, Sculpture
Collections: Paintings, watercolors, drawings, prints, photographs, scrimshaw, furniture, glass marine memorial biographic recordings, whaling equipment, ship models, including 89 foot 1/2 scale model of whaler Lagoda
Exhibitions: 66 Ft Skeleton of Blue Whale; Two Brothers Gowlart; changing exhibits every 6 months; Energy & Enterprise: Industry and the City of New Bedford
Publications: Bulletin from Johnny Cake Hill, quarterly; exhibition catalogs; calendar, quarterly
Activities: Classes for adults & children; docent training; lects open to pub, 12 vis lectrs per yr; gallery talks; tours; individual paintings & original objects of art lent to other mus; lending collection contains microfilm, nature artifacts, original art works, original prints, paintings, photographs & sculptures; originates traveling exhibs; mus shop sells books, magazines, reproductions, prints, slides & gift items

L **Whaling Museum Library**, 18 Johnny Cake Hill, New Bedford, MA 02740. Tel 508-997-0046; Fax 508-997-0018; Web: www.whalingmuseum.org
Open by appointment only Mon - Fri 10 AM - Noon & 1 - 5 PM, first Sat of each month; For reference only
Income: Financed by private gifts & grants
Library Holdings: Book Volumes 15,000, Clipping Files, Exhibition Catalogs, Filmstrips, Manuscripts, Memorabilia, Pamphlets, Periodical Subscriptions 12, Reels

NEWBURYPORT

M **HISTORICAL SOCIETY OF OLD NEWBURY,** Cushing House Museum, 98 High St, Newburyport, MA 01950-3053. Tel 978-462-2681; Email info@newburyhistory.org; Web: www.newburyhistory.org; *Executive Director* Susan Edwards; *Assistant Director* Emily Shafer
Open Office: Tues - Fri yr round 10 AM - 4 PM, Tours: Wed - Fri 10 AM - 4 PM, Sat & Sun noon - 4 PM (June 1 - Oct 31; Admis adults $5, kids under 12 free; Estab 1877 to preserve heritage of Old Newbury, Newbury, Newburyport & West Newbury; Average Annual Attendance: 3,000; Mem: 600; dues patron $500, benefactor $250, sustaining $100, friend $75, family $50, individual $30
Income: $50,000 (financed by dues, tours, endowments, fund-raisers)
Library Holdings: Auction Catalogs, Book Volumes, Exhibition Catalogs, Manuscripts, Maps, Memorabilia, Original Art Works, Original Documents, Other Holdings, Pamphlets, Periodical Subscriptions, Photographs, Prints, Reproductions, Slides
Special Subjects: Architecture, Decorative Arts, Embroidery, Furniture, Historical Material, Manuscripts, Painting-American, Period Rooms, Textiles
Collections: China, dolls, furniture, glass, miniatures, needlework, paintings, sampler coll, silver, military & other historical material representative of over three centuries of Newbury's history
Publications: Old-Town & The Waterside, 200 years of Tradition & Change in Newbury, Newburyport & West Newbury - 1635-1835
Activities: Classes for adults; docent training; lects open to pub, 8 vis lectrs per yr; gallery talks; tours for children;; scholarships & fels offered; exten dept serves Merrimack Valley; individual paintings & original objects of art lent to nonprofit cultural institutions; mus shop sells books

M **NEWBURYPORT MARITIME SOCIETY, INC,** Custom House Maritime Museum, 25 Water St, Newburyport, MA 01950-2754. Tel 978-462-8681; Email info@thchmm.org; Web: www.thechmm.org; *Chmn* Thomas Gould; *Exec Dir* Michael Mroz; *Assoc Dir* Dee McManvs; *Cur* Kevin MacDonald
Open Jan - Apr: Sat 10 AM - 4 PM, Sun & holiday Mon noon - 4PM May - Dec: Tues - Sat 10 AM - 4 PM, Sun Noon - 4 PM, holiday Mon noon - 4 PM; Admis adults $7, seniors & students $5, military & children under 6 free; Estab 1975 to exhibit the maritime heritage of Newburyport & the Merrimack Valley; 7 galleries housed in an 1835 Custom House designed by Robert Mills. The structure is on the National Register of Historic Places; Average Annual Attendance: 17,000; Mem: 400; dues $40 & up; annual meeting in Apr
Income: Financed by mem, admis, fundraisers, gifts & grants
Library Holdings: Book Volumes, Manuscripts, Maps, Original Documents, Photographs, Prints
Special Subjects: Decorative Arts, Ethnology, Marine Painting, Historical Material, Manuscripts, Maps, Painting-American, Photography, Portraits
Collections: Coll of portraits, ship models & decorative art objects 1680-1820, original coll of ethnographic items owned by Newburyport Marine Society Members, half hull models of Merrimack River Valley Ships, portraits of sea captains, navigational instruments & models, core exhibits on populations, natural resources, urban seaport, coast guard
Exhibitions: See website for activities & events
Publications: Year round news & event emails
Activities: Classes for children; docent training; lects open to pub, lects for mems ony; 15 vis lectrs per yr; concerts; tours; mus shop sells books, original art & prints

NEWTON

M **HISTORIC NEWTON,** (Jackson Homestead), 527 Washington St, Newton, MA 02458-1433. Tel 617-796-1450; Fax 617-552-7228; Email cstone@newtonma.gov; Web: www.historicnewton.org; *Cur Manuscripts* Sara Goldberg; *Dir* Cindy Stone

Open Tues - Sat 11 AM - 5 PM, Sun Noon - 5 PM; Admis adult $5, children & seniors $3; Estab 1950 to encourage inquiry into Newton, MA within the broad context of American history; Permanent & temporary exhibitions highlight Newton's role as one of the country's earliest railroad suburbs & the Homestead as a station on the Underground Railroad; Average Annual Attendance: 7,500
Income: Mem, grants & contributions
Library Holdings: Audio Tapes, Book Volumes, Cards, Cassettes, Clipping Files, Exhibition Catalogs, Lantern Slides, Manuscripts, Maps, Memorabilia, Original Art Works, Original Documents, Photographs, Slides, Video Tapes
Special Subjects: Archaeology, Ceramics, Costumes, Dolls, Drawings, Embroidery, Furniture, Historical Material, Landscapes, Manuscripts, Maps, Painting-American, Pewter, Photography, Portraits, Silver, Textiles
Collections: Costumes, furniture, household & personal items, paintings, textiles, tools, toys, archives of papers, photographs & maps
Activities: Classes for adults & children; special progs & events; docent training; lects open to pub, 8 per yr; gallery talks; tours; awards, Historic Presentation; mus shop sells books, reproductions & prints

NEWTONVILLE

M **NEW ART CENTER IN NEWTON,** 61 Washington Park, Newtonville, MA 02460-1915. Tel 617-964-3424; Fax 617-630-0081; Email info@newartcenter.org; Web: newartcenter.org; *Exec Dir* Dan Elias; *Exhibs Coordr* Leah Hamilton French; *Registrar* Marte Humbert
Open Tues - Fri 1 PM - 6 PM or by appointment; Estab 1977 to provide art education through an inclusive approach; Mem: dues $500
Collections: Paintings, photography, sculpture
Exhibitions: Temporary exhibits
Activities: Educ progs; classes for adults & children; workshops

NORTH EASTON

L **AMES FREE-EASTON'S PUBLIC LIBRARY,** 53 Main St, North Easton, MA 02356-1452. Tel 508-238-2000; Fax 508-238-2980; Email info@amesfreelibrary.org; Web: www.amesfreelibrary.org; *Reference Librn & Adult Svcs* Steven Somerdin; *Children's Librn* Catherine Coyne; *Exec Dir* Annalee Bundy; *Asst Dir* Madeline Miele Holt; *Admin Asst* Michelle DuPrey; *Circ & Interlibrary Loan* Joan Roan; *Cataloger* Anne Marie Large; *Computer Instr* Whitney Anderson; *Serials Technician* Lorraine Robinacci; *Circ Asst* Amy Dean
Open Mon & Thurs 10 AM - 8 PM, Tues & Wed 1 - 8 PM, Fri - Sat 10 AM - 5 PM; No admis fee; Estab 1879; Circ 97,000
Income: $684,760 (financed by local endowment) & public funds
Purchases: $90,110
Library Holdings: Audio Tapes 187, Book Volumes 56,000, Cassettes, Clipping Files, Periodical Subscriptions 137, Video Tapes
Special Subjects: Architecture, Decorative Arts
Collections: Architecture (Richardsonian), Decorative Arts
Activities: Classes for adults & children; dramatic prog; story hours; storytellers; booktalks

NORTH GRAFTON

M **WILLARD HOUSE & CLOCK MUSEUM, INC,** 11 Willard St, North Grafton, MA 01536-2011. Tel 508-839-3500; Fax 508-839-3599; Email cynthia@willardhouse.org; Web: www.willardhouse.org; *VPres* Sumner Tilton; *Dir* Patrick Keenan; *Pres* Richard Currier; *Conservator* David Gow
Open Wed - Sat 10 AM - 4 PM, Sun 1 - 4 PM, cl Mon & holidays; Admis adults $7, seniors $6, children $3; Estab 1971 for educ in the fields of history, horology, decorative arts & antiques; Maintains nine rooms open in house mus; Average Annual Attendance: 1,500; Mem: 200; dues $25 individual, $40 family
Income: Financed by endowment, mem, admis, gifts & sales
Library Holdings: Auction Catalogs, Book Volumes, Memorabilia, Original Documents, Pamphlets, Periodical Subscriptions, Photographs, Prints, Slides
Special Subjects: Architecture, Calligraphy, Carpets & Rugs, Ceramics, Coins & Medals, Costumes, Decorative Arts, Dolls, Embroidery, Folk Art, Furniture, Glass, Gold, Historical Material, Jewelry, Painting-American, Period Rooms, Pewter, Portraits, Restorations, Silver, Textiles
Collections: Native American Artifacts Collection, Willard Clockmaking Family Collection, furnishings, memorabilia & portraits, 18th & 19th Century Early Country Antique Furniture Collection, 19th Century Embroidery Collection, 18th & 19th Century Firearms Collection, 19th Century Children's Toy Collection, 19th Century Costume Collection, 19th Century Oriental Rug Collection, Willard Clockmaking Collection
Exhibitions: Annual Clock Collectors Workshop; Annual Christmas Open House
Publications: Mem newsletter, biannual
Activities: Classes for adults & children; docent training; lects open to pub; 1 vis lectr per yr; tours; mus shop sells books, magazines, clocks, antiques, jewelry

NORTHAMPTON

L **FORBES LIBRARY,** 20 West St, Northampton, MA 01060-3798. Tel 413-587-1011, 587-1013; Fax 413-587-1015; Email art@forbeslibrary.org; Web: www.forbeslibrary.org; *Arts & Music Librn* Faith Kaufmann
Open Mon 1 - 9 PM, Tues 9 AM - 6 PM, Wed 9 AM - 9 PM, Thurs 1 - 5 PM, Fri - Sat 9 AM - 5 PM, cl Sun & holidays; Estab 1894 to serve the community as a general public library and a research facility; Circ 292,950; Houses Hosmer Gallery and Calvin Coolidge Presidential Library & Museum. Gallery and exhibit cases for regional artists, photographers and craftspeople
Library Holdings: Audio Tapes, Book Volumes 40,000, Cassettes 2000, Compact Disks 4000, DVDs 200, Exhibition Catalogs, Original Art Works, Original Documents, Periodical Subscriptions 52, Photographs, Prints, Reels, Video Tapes 2000
Special Subjects: Posters, Photography
Collections: Bien edition of Audubon Bird Prints, Library of Charles E Forbes, Walter E Corbin Collection of Photographic Prints & Slides, Connecticut Valley History, Genealogical Records, Official White House Portraits of President Calvin Coolidge & Grace Anna Coolidge, World War I & II Poster Collection, Local History Photograph Collection & Print Collection
Exhibitions: Monthly exhibits of works by regional artists, photographers and crafts people; Calvin Coolidge Presidential Library & Mus
Activities: Films; readings; lects open to public; Concerts; Gallery talks; exten dept serves elderly & house bound

M **HISTORIC NORTHAMPTON MUSEUM & EDUCATION CENTER,** 46 Bridge St, Northampton, MA 01060-2428. Tel 413-584-3669, 584-6011; Fax 413-584-7956; Email hstnhamp@jauanet.com; Web: www.historic-northampton.org; *Exec Dir* Kerry Buckley
Open Tues - Fri 10 AM - 4 PM, weekends Noon - 4 PM, cl Mon & holidays; Estab 1905 to collect, preserve & exhibit objects of human history in Northhampton & Connecticut Valley; The mus maintains three historic houses from about 1728, 1798 & 1813; a barn from about 1825 with newly added educ center; a non-circulating reference library; Average Annual Attendance: 9,500; Mem: 500; dues bus $100 - $500, individual $20 - $100; annual meeting in Nov
Income: $95,000 (financed by endowment, mem, gifts)
Special Subjects: Costumes, Decorative Arts, Furniture, Photography, Textiles
Collections: Collections focus on material culture of Northampton & the upper Connecticut River Valley, costumes, textiles, ca. 1900 Howes Brothers photographs, archaeological artifacts from on-site excavation, decorative arts, oil paintings of local personalities & scenes, Collection of costumes, textiles, furniture & decorative art
Publications: Newsletter, quarterly; booklets on local subjects; brochures & flyers
Activities: Classes for adults & children; docent progs; workshops; internships; lects open to pub; gallery talks; schols offered; mus shop sells books, merchandise related to mus's collections, reproductions of collection items, maps, period toys & games

M **NORTHAMPTON CENTER FOR THE ARTS,** 17 New South St, Northampton, MA 01060; PO Box 366, Northampton, MA 01061-0366. Tel 413-584-7327; Fax 413-582-9014; Email ncfa@nohoarts.org; Web: nohoarts.org; *Exec Dir* Penny Burke
Call for hours; Estab 1983 to promote arts in the community
Collections: Culturally diverse performance art including theater, music, art & dance
Activities: Educ progs; performance art

M **SMITH COLLEGE,** Museum of Art, 20 Elm St at Bedford Terrace, Northampton, MA 01063. Tel 413-585-2760; Fax 413-585-2782; Email artmuseum@ais.smith.edu; Web: www.smith.edu/artmuseum; Others TTY 413-585-2786; *Dir & Chief Cur* Jessica Nicoll; *Registrar & Coll Mgr* Deborah Diemente; *Cur Prints, Drawings & Photographs* Aprile Gallant; *Mem & Mktg Dir* Margi Caplan; *Communs Coord* Martha Ebner; *Mus Store Mgr* Justin Thomas; *Exhib Coordr* Kelly Holbert; *Dir Asst* Louise Krieger; *Preparator* Nikolas Asikis; *Assoc Educ* Taiga Ermansons; *Assoc Dir Acad Progs & Public Educ* Maggie Lind Newey; *Assoc Educator School & Family Progs* Gina Hall; *Mgr Security & Guest Servs* Ann Mayo; *Asst Mgr Security & Guest Servs* Rick Turschman
Open Tues - Wed & Fri - Sat 10 AM - 4 PM, Thurs 10 AM - 8 PM, Sun noon - 4 PM, 2nd Fri 10 AM - 8 PM, cl Mon & Holidays; Admis adults $5, seniors (65 & over) $4, college students, youth (18 & under) free; free second Friday of month 4 PM - 8 PM; Collection founded 1879; Hillyer Art Gallery built 1882; Smith College Museum of Art estab 1920; Tryon Art Gallery built 1926; present Smith College Museum of Art in Tryon Hall opened 1973; renovated and expanded 2003; Average Annual Attendance: 34,000; Mem: 1200; dues student $20, educator $35, individual $50, family/household $75, contributor $150, sustainer $500, patron $1,000
Special Subjects: Decorative Arts, Drawings, Painting-American, Painting-European, Photography, Prints
Collections: Examples from most periods and cultures with special emphasis on European and American paintings, sculpture, drawings, prints, photographs and decorative arts of the 17th-20th centuries
Exhibitions: Temporary exhibitions and installations 12-24 annually
Publications: Catalogues
Activities: Lect; gallery talks; guided tours; audio tours; concerts; individual works of art lent to other institutions; mus shop sells publications, post and note cards, posters, art-related merchandise

L **Hillyer Art Library**, Elm St at Bedford Terrace, Northampton, MA 01063. Tel 413-585-2940; Fax 413-585-6975; Email hillinfo@smith.edu; Web: www.smith.edu/libraries/libs/hillyer/; *Librn* Barbara Polowy; *Art Library Asst* Lisa DeCarolis
Open Mon - Thurs 9 AM - 11 PM, Fri 9 AM - 9 PM, Sat 10 AM - 9 PM, Sun Noon - Midnight; Estab 1918 to support courses offered by art department of Smith College; Circ 23,500; For reference use only
Income: Financed by endowment
Library Holdings: Auction Catalogs 10,000, Book Volumes 125,000, CD-ROMs 300, Exhibition Catalogs, Periodical Subscriptions 180
Special Subjects: Antiquities-Etruscan, Antiquities-Greek, Antiquities-Oriental, Antiquities-Roman, Architecture, Art History, Drawings, Etchings & Engravings, History of Art & Archaeology, Painting-American, Painting-British, Painting-European, Painting-Italian, Painting-Spanish, Sculpture

NORTON

M **WHEATON COLLEGE,** Beard and Weil Galleries, 26 E Main St, Norton, MA 02766-2311. Tel 508-286-3578; Fax 508-286-3565; Email amurray@wheatonma.edu; Web: www.wheatoncollege.edu/acad/art/gallery; *Dir* Ann H Murray; *Prog Coordr for the Arts* Betsy Cronin; *Asst Prof Mus Studies/Art History & Cur Permanent Coll* Leah Niederstadt
Open Mon - Sat 12:30 - 4:30 PM except during col vacations; No admis fee; Estab 1960, gallery program since 1930 to provide a wide range of contemporary one-person & group shows as well as exhibitions from the permanent collection of

paintings, graphics & objects; Gallery is of fireproof steel-frame, glass & brick construction; Average Annual Attendance: 5,000
Income: Financed by college budget & occasional grants
Purchases: Marble portrait bust of Roman boy; Etruscan antefix head; Head of Galienus, Roman c 260 AD; Cycladic Figurine, 2500-1100 BC Greek Black Figure Amphora, 6th c BC; DuBourg Book of Hours, 1475-1490
Library Holdings: Auction Catalogs, Book Volumes, Exhibition Catalogs, Original Documents
Special Subjects: African Art, American Indian Art, Antiquities-Byzantine, Antiquities-Etruscan, Antiquities-Greek, Antiquities-Roman, Asian Art, Baroque Art, Bronzes, Ceramics, Coins & Medals, Decorative Arts, Drawings, Embroidery, Etchings & Engravings, Flasks & Bottles, Glass, Graphics, Ivory, Laces, Landscapes, Manuscripts, Marine Painting, Mosaics, Painting-American, Painting-British, Painting-Dutch, Painting-French, Painting-German, Pre-Columbian Art, Prints, Sculpture, Stained Glass, Textiles, Watercolors, Woodcarvings, Woodcuts
Collections: 19th & 20th centuries prints, drawings, paintings & sculpture, Wedgewood, 18th & 19th centuries glass, ancient bronzes, sculptures & ceramics, Cass Wedgewood Collection
Exhibitions: Changing exhibitions
Publications: Exhibition catalogs; Prints of the 19th Century: A Selection from the Wheaton College Collection; The Art of Drawing; The Art of the Print & The Art of Painting and Sculpture: Selections from the Permanent Collection; The Realist Impulse: Paintings & Sculpture from the Wheaton Col Collection, c 1830-1940; Dorothea Rockburne: Astronomy Drawings
Activities: Lects open to pub, 5-8 vis lectrs per yr; concerts; gallery talks; tours; sponsoring of competitions; individual paintings & original objects of art lent to colleges, other museums & galleries; originate traveling exhibs

OAK BLUFFS

A **MARTHA'S VINEYARD CENTER FOR THE VISUAL ARTS,** PO Box 168, Oak Bluffs, MA 02557. Tel 508-736-9743; Web: artmv.org; *Pres* Chris Dreyer; *VPres* Holly Alaimo; *Secy, Treas* Renee Balter
Estab 1991; centered on grant giving to Vineyard-area artists
Income: Financed by mem, donations, grant from local cultural council
Exhibitions: July - Aug weekly shows of member art
Publications: Arts Directory, annually
Activities: Classes & workshops; scholarships offered; originate traveling exhibs

PAXTON

M **ANNA MARIA COLLEGE,** Saint Luke's Gallery, 50 Sunset Ln, Moll Art Ctr Paxton, MA 01612-1106. Tel 508-849-3318; Web: www.annamaria.edu/; *Chmn Art Dept* Alice Lambert
Open Mon - Fri 1 - 5 PM, Sat 2 - 4 PM, Sun 1 - 4 PM; No admis fee; Estab 1968 as an outlet for the art student and professional artist, and to raise the artistic awareness of the general community; Main Gallery is 35 x 15 ft with about 300 sq ft of wall space; Average Annual Attendance: 500
Income: Financed by the college
Special Subjects: Furniture, Painting-American, Sculpture
Collections: Small assortment of furniture, paintings, sculpture
Exhibitions: Annual senior art exhibit; local artists; faculty & students shows
Publications: Exhibit programs
Activities: Educ Dept; lect open to public; individual paintings & original objects of art lent to campus offices

PEMBROKE

NEW ENGLAND WATERCOLOR SOCIETY
For further information, see National and Regional Organizations

PITTSFIELD

L **BERKSHIRE ATHENAEUM,** Reference Dept, One Wendell Ave, Pittsfield, MA 01201. Tel 413-499-9480 ext 4; Fax 413-499-9489; Email pittsref@cwmars.org; Web: www.berkshire.net/PittsfieldLibrary; *Dir* Ron Latham; *Supv Reference* Madeline Kelly; *Music & Arts Specialist* Mary Ann Knight
Open Mon & Fri 9 AM - 5 PM, Tues - Thurs 9 AM - 9 PM, Sat 10 AM - 5 PM; reduced hours July & Aug; No admis fee; Estab 1872
Income: Financed by city & state appropriations
Library Holdings: Book Volumes, Cassettes 300, Compact Disks, Other Holdings Compact Discs 2,000, Periodical Subscriptions 15-20, Video Tapes
Collections: Mary Rice Morgan Ballet Collection: a reference room of programs, artifacts, prints, original art, rare & current books on dance & costume design
Activities: Lects open to pub, concerts

M **BERKSHIRE MUSEUM,** 39 South St, Pittsfield, MA 01201-6169. Tel 413-443-7171, ext 10; Fax 413-443-2135; Email pr@berkshiremuseum.org; Web: www.berkshiremuseum.org; *Exec Dir* Van Shields; *Dir Finance & Admin* Jon C Provost; *Dir Develop* Nina Garlington; *Dir Educ & Progs* Craig Langlois; *Bldg & Security Mgr* Brian Warner; *Mus Shop Mgr* Tracey Rock; *Dir Commun* Lesley Ann Beck
Open to pub Mon - Sat 10 AM - 5 PM, Sun Noon - 5 PM, cl New Year's Day, Memorial Day, Independence Day, Labor Day, Thanksgiving & Christmas; Admis Adults $10, children 3-18 $5, members & children under 2 free; Estab 1903 as a mus of art, natural science & history; Maintains reference library for staff & teachers; Average Annual Attendance: 82,000; Mem: 2000; dues single $45, dual $60, family $75, special members $100-$500, corporate members $200 & up, Crane Society $1,000 & up
Income: Financed by endowment, mem, fundraising & gifts
Special Subjects: American Indian Art, American Western Art, Anthropology, Antiquities-Egyptian, Antiquities-Etruscan, Antiquities-Greek, Ceramics, Coins & Medals, Costumes, Decorative Arts, Dioramas, Dolls, Drawings, Etchings & Engravings, Ethnology, Folk Art, Furniture, Glass, Jewelry, Landscapes, Painting-American, Painting-British, Painting-Dutch, Painting-Flemish, Painting-Italian
Collections: Paintings of the Hudson River School (Inness, Moran, Blakelock, Martin, Wyant, Moran, Church, Bierstadt & others), early American portraits, Egyptian, Babylonia & Near East arts, grave reliefs from Palmyra, Paul M Hahn Collection of 18th-Century English & American Silver, Old Masters (Pons, de Hooch, Van Dyck & others), contemporary painting & sculpture, three Norman Rockwell paintings
Publications: Schedule of events, quarterly; annual report
Activities: Classes for adults & children; lects open to pub, 20 vis lectrs per yr; concerts; gallery talks; tours; sponsoring of competitions; scholarships; individual paintings & original objects of art lent to corporate & individual members; originate traveling exhibs primarily to New England institutions; mus shop sells gifts, books, original art, reproductions, jewelry, toys & games

M **CITY OF PITTSFIELD OFFICE OF CULTURAL DEVELOPMENT,** Lichtenstein Center for the Arts, 28 Renne Ave, Pittsfield, MA 01201-4720. Tel 413-499-9348; Fax 413-442-6803; Email cultural@pittsfieldch.com; Web: www.discoverpittsfield.com; *Dir* Jennifer Glockner; *Admin Asst* Shiobbean Lemme
Open Wed - Sat 11 AM 4 PM; No admis fee; Estab 1976; Three story 100 yr old brownstone, municipal gallery; Average Annual Attendance: 56,000
Income: $100,000 (financed by endowment, mem, city, state & federal appropriations)
Special Subjects: Crafts, Drawings, Glass, Hispanic Art, Landscapes, Painting-American, Photography, Pottery, Prints, Sculpture, Tapestries, Textiles, Watercolors, Woodcuts
Exhibitions: Doe, Warner Freidman, Dave Novak, Jay Tobin, Daniel Balvez, John Dilg, Sally Fine, Linda Bernstein, David Merritt
Publications: The Berkshire Review
Activities: Classes for adults & children; dramatic progs; docent training; lects open to pub, 12 vis lectrs per yr; concerts; gallery talks; tours; competitions; schols & fels offered; artmobile; lending collection contains paintings, art objects; book traveling exhibs 12 per yr; originate traveling exhibs 12 per yr; mus shop sells books, prints, magazines, slides, original art, pub murals

M **HANCOCK SHAKER VILLAGE, INC,** 1843 W Housatonic St, Pittsfield, MA 01202; PO Box 927, Pittsfield, MA 01202-0927. Tel 413-443-0188; Fax 413-447-9357; Email info@hancockshakervillage.org; Web: www.hancockshakervillage.org; *CEO* Jennifer Trainer; *Cur Coll* Lesley Herzberg; *Dir Educ* Cindy Dickerson; *Shaker Mercantile Buyer* Nadia Dole
Open April-Nov; Admis adults $20, teens $8, mems & children under 12 no charge; Estab 1960 for the preservation & restoration of Hancock Shaker Village & the interpretation of Shaker art, architecture & culture. Period rooms throughout the village; Circ no circulation; Exhibition Gallery contains Shaker inspirational drawings & graphic materials; Average Annual Attendance: 60,000; Mem: dues vary, start at $60
Income: Financed by mem, donations
Special Subjects: Anthropology, Archaeology, Architecture, Crafts, Decorative Arts, Dolls, Drawings, Folk Art, Furniture, Furniture, Historical Material, Manuscripts, Maps, Period Rooms, Portraits, Posters, Prints, Textiles
Collections: Shaker architecture, furniture & industrial material, Shaker inspirational drawings, Buildings; furniture; farm & crafts artifacts; inspirational drawings; over 22,000 shaker objects, textiles
Exhibitions: Gather up the Fragments: The Andrews Shaker Collection
Publications: Newsletter, quarterly; specialized publications
Activities: Classes for adults & children; docent training; workshops; seminars; lects open to pub; vis lectrs 6 per yr; gallery talks; tours; sponsor competitions; schols & fels; individual paintings & original objects of art lent to qualified mus with proper security & environmental conditions; lent to New York State Museum for Quiet Revolutionaries exhibit thru 2016; originates traveling exhibs to Portland Mus Art, Stamford Mus & Nature Center, & more; mus shop sells books, magazines, reproductions, prints, oval boxes, wood items toys & food

PLYMOUTH

M **PILGRIM SOCIETY,** Pilgrim Hall Museum, 75 Court St, Plymouth, MA 02360-3823. Tel 508-746-1620; Fax 508-746-3396; Email donna.curtin@pilgrimhall.org; Web: www.pilgrimhallmuseum.org; *Pres* Suzanne Giovanetti; *Dir & Librn* Donna D Curtin; *Archivist* Rebecca Piccirillo; *Group Tour Coordinator* Karen Yourell; *Develop Dir* Robin Nutter; *Museum Shop Manager* Carol Reynolds
Open daily 9:30 AM - 4:30 PM, cl Jan & Christmas Day; Admis family $25, adults $8, seniors $7, AAA $6, children $5; Estab 1820 to depict the history of the Pilgrim Colonists in Plymouth Colony; Average Annual Attendance: 27,000; Mem: 600; dues $35; annual meetings in Dec
Income: Financed by endowment, mem & admis
Special Subjects: Ceramics, Decorative Arts, Embroidery, Furniture, Furniture, Glass, Manuscripts, Painting-American, Pewter, Portraits, Silver, Stained Glass
Collections: Arms & armor, decorative arts, furniture & paintings relating to the Plymouth Colony settlement (1620-1692) & the later history of Plymouth
Exhibitions: Permanent collections; exhibitions change year round
Activities: docent training; Lects open to pub, 6 vis lectrs per yr; tours; mus shop sells books, magazines, reproductions, prints, slides, ceramics, souvenir wares

L **Library,** 75 Court St, Plymouth, MA 02360. Tel 508-746-1620; Fax 508-746-3396; *Dir* Ann Berry; *Assoc Dir & Cur* Stephen O'Neill
Open by appointment only; No admis fee; Estab 1820 to collect material relative to the history of Plymouth; For reference only
Library Holdings: Audio Tapes, Book Volumes 10,000, Cassettes, Clipping Files, Exhibition Catalogs, Kodachrome Transparencies, Lantern Slides, Manuscripts, Memorabilia, Motion Pictures, Original Art Works, Pamphlets, Periodical Subscriptions 5, Photographs, Prints, Records, Reels, Reproductions, Sculpture, Slides
Special Subjects: Historical Material, Manuscripts

A **PLYMOUTH ANTIQUARIAN SOCIETY,** 126 Water St, Plymouth, MA 02361; PO Box 3773, Plymouth, MA 02361-3773. Tel 508-746-0012; Email pasm@verizon.net; Web: www.plymouthantiquariansociety.org; *Pres* Rose Stearns; *Exec Dir* Donna Curtin
Open June - Aug 2 - 6 PM, days vary, call for more information; Admis adults $6, children (5-14) $3; Estab 1919 to maintain & preserve the three museums: Harlow Old Fort House (1677), Spooner House (1747) & Antiquarian House (1809); Average Annual Attendance: 5,000; Mem: 550; dues Individual $25, family $40; annual meeting in Nov
Income: Financed by mem & donations
Special Subjects: Costumes, Decorative Arts, Embroidery, Furniture, Historical Material, Manuscripts, Painting-American, Period Rooms, Portraits, Textiles
Collections: American furniture & decorative arts, costumes & textiles, toys & dolls
Activities: Classes for adults & children; lect open to pub; concerts; tours; sales shop sells books, reproductions & antiques; open for special events, call for more information

PROVINCETOWN

A **FINE ARTS WORK CENTER,** Hudson D. Walker Gallery, 24 Pearl St, Provincetown, MA 02657-1500. Tel 508-487-9960; Fax 508-487-8873; Email general@fawc.org; Web: www.fawc.org; *Exec Dir* Michael Roberts; *Summer Prog Dir* Cyndi Wish; *Visual Coordr* James Stanley; *Writing Coordr* Matthew Null; *Admin Coordr* Naya Bricher
Open Mon - Fri 9 AM - 5 PM; No admis fee; Maintains Hudson D Walker Gallery
Activities: Summer workshop prog; summer classes for adults; senior writers progs; Returning Res Prog; fels offered

A **PROVINCETOWN ART ASSOCIATION & MUSEUM,** 460 Commercial St, Provincetown, MA 02657-2415. Tel 508-487-1750; Fax 508-487-4372; Email info@paam.org; Web: www.paam.org; *Exec Dir* Christine McCarthy; *Registrar* Peter Macara; *Archivist & Preparator* Jim Zimmerman; *Educ Coordr* Lynn Stanley; *Mem Coordr* Annie Longley; *Educ Asst* Grace Ryder-O'Malley
Open daily Mon - Thurs 11 AM - 8 PM, Fri 11 AM - 10 PM, Sat & Sun 11 AM - 5 PM; Admis adults $10, mems free; Estab in 1914 to promote & cultivate the practice & appreciation of all branches of the fine arts, to hold temporary exhibitions, forums & concerts for its members & the pub; Five galleries are maintained; Average Annual Attendance: 50,000; Mem: 2,000; mem open; dues $50 ann
Income: $1,100,000 (financed by mem, private contributions, state agencies, earned income & others)
Library Holdings: Auction Catalogs, Audio Tapes, Book Volumes, CD-ROMs, Compact Disks, DVDs, Exhibition Catalogs, Kodachrome Transparencies, Memorabilia, Original Art Works, Photographs, Prints, Reproductions, Slides, Video Tapes
Special Subjects: Collages, Etchings & Engravings, Graphics, Marine Painting, Painting-American, Photography, Prints, Sculpture, Watercolors, Woodcuts
Collections: Permanent collection consists of artists work who have lived or worked on the Lower Cape, Permanent collection mem, Blanche Lazzell: The Hofmann Drawings, Ross Moffelt, Nancy Webb; LaForge Bailey; William Freed; Lillian Orlowsky
Exhibitions: Edna Boies Hopkins; Hans Hofmann & his students; Ciro Cozzi; Paula Kotis photographs; Jack Tworkov; Will Barnett; Robert Motherwell; Paul Resika; Maurice Freeman
Publications: Exhibitions catalogues & newsletters
Activities: Classes for adults & children; docent training; lects open to pub, 8 vis lectrs per yr; concerts; gallery talks; tours; film series; competitions; schol; Leed Certification (Silver) US Green Buildings Commission award; AIA Award of Merit; BSA Design Award; Green Good Design Award, AIA Sustainable Design Award, Top Ten Art Green Projects Award; individual paintings & original objects of art lent to other mus; book traveling exhibs; originate traveling exhibs; mus shop sells books, magazines, original art, prints, reproductions

L **Library,** 460 Commercial St, Provincetown, MA 02657. Tel 508-487-1750; Fax 508-487-4352; Email Info@paam.org; Web: www.paam.org; *Exec Dir* Christine McCarthy
Open yr round, check for times; Admis non mem $10; Estab 1914; Average Annual Attendance: 52,000; Mem: 2000; dues individual $50
Library Holdings: Auction Catalogs, Book Volumes 500, Clipping Files, Compact Disks, Exhibition Catalogs, Memorabilia, Pamphlets, Photographs
Special Subjects: Drawings, Etchings & Engravings, Landscapes, Painting-American, Photography, Portraits, Sculpture, Prints, Watercolors, Woodcuts
Collections: Memorabilia of WHW Bicknell, Provincetown Artists, Outer Cape American Art from 1900 - Present, Edward Hopper Drawings
Activities: Classes for adults & children; lects open to pub, 8 vis lectrs per yr; concerts; gallery talks; tours; original art objects lent to mus; originate traveling exhibs to other mus; mus shop sells books, magazines, original art, reproductions, prints

M **THE SCHOOLHOUSE GALLERY,** 494 Commercial St, Provincetown, MA 02657-2414. Tel 508-487-4800; Email mike@galleryschoolhouse.com; Web: www.galleryschoolhouse.com; *Owner & Dir* Mike Carroll; *Design Consultant* Stephen Magliocco
Open Fri - Sat 11 AM - 5 PM, Sun 11 AM - 4 PM by appointment; Estab 1998 to facilitate artist collaboration
Special Subjects: Painting-American, Photography, Prints
Collections: Modern & contemporary painting, photography & printmaking
Exhibitions: Temporary exhibits
Activities: Educ progs; community progs

QUINCY

M **ADAMS NATIONAL HISTORIC PARK,** 135 Adams St, Quincy, MA 02169-1749. Tel 617-773-1177; Fax 617-471-7562; Email ADAM_Visitor_Center@nps.gov; Web: www.nps.gov/adam; *Supt* Marianne Peak; *Cur* Kelly Cobble
Open daily Apr 19 - Nov 10 9 AM - 5 PM; Admis adults $5, children under 16 admitted free if accompanied by an adult; Estab 1946; The site consists of three houses, part of which dates to 1731; a library containing approx 14,000 books, a carriage house, a woodshed & grounds which were once owned & enjoyed by four generations of the Adams family; Average Annual Attendance: 81,000
Income: Financed by Federal Government
Library Holdings: Clipping Files, Maps, Original Art Works, Original Documents, Pamphlets, Photographs, Slides
Special Subjects: Bookplates & Bindings, Ceramics, Decorative Arts, Furniture, Historical Material, Period Rooms, Portraits
Collections: Original furnishings belonging to the four generations of Adams who lived in the house between 1788 and 1937
Activities: Classes for children; dramatic progs; docent training; lect (4per yr); concerts; tours; sales shop sells books, reproductions & prints

ROCKPORT

A **ROCKPORT ART ASSOCIATION,** 12 Main St, Old Tavern Rockport, MA 01966-1513. Tel 978-546-6604; Fax 978-546-9767; Email rockportart@verizon.net; Web: www.rockportartassn.org; *Pres* David Curtis; *Exec Dir* Abby Battis
Open summer daily 10 AM - 5 PM, Sun Noon - 5 PM, winter daily 10 AM - 4 PM, Sat 10 AM - 5 PM, Sun Noon - 5 PM; No admis fee; Estab 1921 as a non-profit educational organization established for the advancement of art; Four galleries are maintained in the Old Tavern Building; two large summer galleries are adjacent to the main structure; Average Annual Attendance: 75,000; Mem: 1300; mem open to Cape Ann resident artists (minimum of one month), must pass mem jury; contributing mem open to public; photography mem subject of resident/jury restrictions
Income: Financed by endowment, mem, gifts, art programs & sales
Collections: Permanent collection of works by Cape Ann artists of the past, especially those by former members
Exhibitions: Special organized exhibitions are continually on view; fifty exhibitions scheduled per year
Publications: Quarry Cookbook; Rockport Artists Book 1990; Reprints (recent); Rockport Artists Book 1940; Rockport Sketch Book
Activities: Classes & workshops for adults & children; lects open to pub; painting lectr/demonstrations; Tavern Door shop sells books, cards & notes by artist members

A **SANDY BAY HISTORICAL SOCIETY & MUSEUMS,** Sewall Scripture House-Old Castle, 40 King St & Castle Lane, Rockport, MA 01966-1460; PO Box 63, Rockport, MA 01966-0063. Tel 978-546-9533; *Cur* Cynthia Peckham
Open mid-June to mid-Sept; Admis $3, mem free; Estab 1925 to preserve Rockport history; Sewall Scripture House built in 1832, Old Castle built c 1700; Average Annual Attendance: 300; Mem: 500; dues $10; annual meeting first Fri in Sep
Income: $15,000 (financed by endowment & mem)
Collections: Extensive Granite Tools & Quarry Materials, 55 local paintings in oil, prints, watercolor, old quilts, samplers, textiles, Genealogical reference libr
Exhibitions: A Town That Was; Some Rockporters Who Were (for the Sesqui-centennial of the town); Deceased Artists
Publications: Mem bulletins, 3-4 annually; brochures
Activities: Docent training, monthly progs; tours

SALEM

M **PEABODY ESSEX MUSEUM,** Corner Essex & New Liberty, Salem, MA 01970; 161 Essex St, East India Sq Salem, MA 01970-3783. Tel 978-745-9500; Fax 978-744-6776; Email information@pem.org; Web: pem.org; *Exec Dir* Dan L Monroe; *Deputy Dir* Lynda Roscoe Hartigan; *Chief Cur Affairs* Kathy Fredrickson; *Chief Coll Svcs & Library Dir* John D Childs; *CFO* Nathalie Apchin; *Chief Mktg Officer* Jay Finney
Open Tues - Sun 10 AM - 5 PM, 3rd Thurs every month 10 AM - 9 PM; cl Mon, Thanksgiving, Christmas, New Year's Day, open select Mon holidays; Admis adults $20, seniors $18, students $12, youth 16 & under & residents of Salem, Mass free; ticket fees for special exhibs; Estab 1799; The recently transformed Peabody Essex Museum presents art and culture from New England and around the world. In addition to its vast collections, the museum offers changing exhibitions and a hands-on education center. The museum campus features numerous parks, period gardens, and 24 historic properties, including Yin Yu Tang, the only example of Chinese vernacular architecture in the United States; Average Annual Attendance: 150,000; Mem: 4200; dues $30-$65; annual meeting in Nov
Income: $6,000,000 (financed by endowment, mem, gifts & admis)
Special Subjects: African Art, American Indian Art, Architecture, Asian Art, Ceramics, Decorative Arts, Furniture, Ivory, Marine Painting, Oriental Art, Painting-American, Photography, Porcelain, Scrimshaw, Sculpture, Textiles, Drawings
Collections: American Art & Architecture, African Art, Asian Export Art, Chinese Art, Indian Art, Japanese Art, Korean Art, Maritime Art & History, Native American Art, Oceanic Art, Photography, Over 1 million works of art, primarily from 16th c - present
Publications: Peabody Essex Museum Collections, quarterly; The American Neptune, quarterly; The Review of Archaeology, semiannually; Connections, member's magazine, quarterly; occasional books
Activities: Classes for adults & children; docent training; lects open to public; originates traveling exhibs: Candice Breitz's, The Woods; mus shop sells books, reproductions, prints, furniture, jewelry, ceramics

L **Phillips Library,** 132 Essex St, Salem, MA 01970-3701. Tel 978-745-9500; Fax 978-741-9012; Email pem@pem.org; Web: pem.org; *Dir Phillips Libr* Sidney Berber
Open Wed 10 AM - 5 PM, Thurs 1-5 PM; For reference only
Library Holdings: Book Volumes 400,000, Clipping Files, Exhibition Catalogs, Fiche, Kodachrome Transparencies, Lantern Slides, Manuscripts, Memorabilia,

Motion Pictures, Original Art Works, Pamphlets, Periodical Subscriptions 200, Slides
Special Subjects: American Indian Art, Anthropology, Archaeology, Architecture, Asian Art, Bookplates & Bindings, Ceramics, Crafts, Decorative Arts, Etchings & Engravings, Ethnology, Folk Art, Furniture, Glass, Ivory
Collections: The library supports the entire range of the collections of this international & multi-disciplinary museum of arts & cultures
Publications: Peabody Essex Museum Collections; Monographic Series, annual; The American Neptune, quarterly journal of maritime art & history

M **Andrew-Safford House**, 13 Washington Sq W, Salem, MA 01970; 161 Essex St, East India Salem, MA 01970. Tel 978-745-9500; Email pem@pem.org; Web: pem.org; *Cur* Dean Lahikainen
Open Mon - Sat 10 AM - 5 PM, Sun Noon - 5 PM, cl Mon, Nov - Mar; Admis adults $8.50, seniors & students $7.50, children 6-16 $5, children under 6 free; Built in 1818-1819 & purchased by the Institute in 1947 for the purpose of presenting a vivid image of early 19th century urban life; It is the residence of the Institute's director

M **Peirce-Nichols House**, 80 Federal St, Salem, MA 01970; 161 Essex St, East India Sq Salem, MA 01970-3726. Tel 978-745-9500; Email pem@pem.org; Web: pem.org
Open Mon - Sat 10 AM - 5 PM, Sun Noon - 5 PM, Nov - Mar cl Mon; Admis adults $8.50, seniors & students $7.50, children 6-16 $5, children under 6 free; Built in 1782 by Samuel McIntire; Maintains some original furnishings & a counting house

M **Cotting-Smith-Assembly House**, 138 Federal St, Salem, MA 01970; 161 Essex St, East India Square Salem, MA 01970-3726. Tel 978-744-2231; Fax 978-744-0036; Email pem@pem.org; Web: pem.org; *Exec Dir* Dan L Monroe
Open Mon - Sat 10 AM - 5 PM, Noon - 5 PM, Nov - Mar cl Mon; Admis adults $8.50, seniors & students $7.50, children 6-16 $5, children under 6 free; Built in 1782 as a hall for social assemblies; remodeled in 1796 by Samuel McIntire as a home residence; Not open to pub

SANDWICH

M **HERITAGE MUSEUMS & GARDENS,** 67 Grove St, Sandwich, MA 02563-2110. Tel 508-888-3300; Fax 508-888-9535; Email info@heritagemuseums.org; Web: www.heritagemuseumsandgardens.org; *Dir* Stewart Goodwin; *Deputy Dir Mus Prog & Svcs* Sunnee Spencer; *Deputy Dir Admin* Lucy Bukowski; *Asst Dir* Nancy Tyrer; *Cur Military History* James Cervantes; *Cur Botanical Science* Jeanie Gillis; *Dir Exhib & Coll* Jennifer Younginger; *Cur Antique Auto Mus* Robert Rogers; *Dir* Gene A Schott; *Dir Devel* Wendy Perry
Open Jan & Feb weekends, Mar, Apr, Nov & Dec Wed - Sun 10 AM - 4 PM, May - Oct Daily 10 AM - 6 PM; Admis adults $12, seniors $10, children $6; Estab 1969 as a mus of Americana. Heritage Museums & Gardens is a Massachusetts charitable corporation; Maintains three galleries which house collections; Average Annual Attendance: 100,000; Mem: $2000; dues $45-$1000
Income: Financed by endowment, mem & admis
Special Subjects: American Indian Art, Folk Art, Primitive art, Scrimshaw
Collections: American Indian artifacts, folk art, primitive paintings, Scrimshaw, Antique Automobiles, Folk Art, Fine Arts, Tools, Weapons, Military Miniatures, Native American Art
Exhibitions: Landscape Paintings; Antique & Classic Automobiles; Hand painted Military Miniatures & Antique Firearms; Restored 1912 Charles I D Looff Carousel; Currier & Ives prints.
Publications: Exhibit catalogues; quarterly newsletter
Activities: Classes for adults & children; dramatic progs; docent training; lects, 7-10 vis lectrs per yr; concerts; gallery talks; tours; exten dept serving Cape Cod area; individual paintings & original objects of art lent; lending coll includes, original prints, paintings & nature artifacts; 1-2 book traveling exhibs; mus shop sells books, magazines, original art, reproductions & prints

M **THE SANDWICH HISTORICAL SOCIETY, INC & SANDWICH GLASS MUSEUM,** Sandwich Glass Museum, 129 Main St, Sandwich, MA 02563; PO Box 103, Sandwich, MA 02563-0103. Tel 508-888-0251; Fax 508-888-4941; Email katie.campbell@sandwichglassmuseum.org; Web: www.sandwichglassmuseum.org; *Exec Dir* Katharine H Campbell; *Cur* Dorothy Hogan-Schofield; *Retail Mgr* Robert Lee Ward
Open Feb - Mar, Wed - Sun 9:30 AM - 4 PM, Apr - Dec daily 9:30 AM - 5 PM, cl New Year's Day, Easter, Thanksgiving, Christmas Eve & Day; Admis adults $9, children 6-14 $2, mems no charge; Estab 1907 to collect, preserve local history; 16 galleries of Sandwich glass; Average Annual Attendance: 70,000; Mem: 605; dues indiv $25, family $35, sustaining indiv $60, family sustaining $75. sponsor $125, patron $275 ; meeting dates: third Thurs in Feb, Apr, June, Aug & Oct
Income: $482,000 (financed by endowment, mem, admis & retails sales)
Library Holdings: Auction Catalogs, Book Volumes, Clipping Files, Exhibition Catalogs, Kodachrome Transparencies, Manuscripts, Maps, Photographs, Prints, Reproductions, Slides
Special Subjects: Ceramics, Decorative Arts, Dioramas, Embroidery, Flasks & Bottles, Furniture, Glass, Historical Material, Jewelry, Maps, Painting-American, Period Rooms, Reproductions, Portraits, Posters
Collections: Glass-Sandwich, American, European, Artifacts relating to the history of Sandwich
Exhibitions: Exhibitions vary; call for details
Publications: Acorn, bi-ann; The Cullet, bi-ann
Activities: Classes for adults & children; docent training; lects open to pub; 2 vis lectr per yr; gallery talks; walking tours of Sandwich; book traveling exhibs 1-2 per yr; mus shop sells books, original art, reproductions, contemporary glass art, jewelry, perfumes, paperweights, art glass & ornaments

SOUTH HADLEY

M **MOUNT HOLYOKE COLLEGE,** Art Museum, Lower Lake Rd, South Hadley, MA 01075-1499. Tel 413-538-2245; Fax 413-538-2144; Email artmuseum@mtholyoke.edu; Web: www.mtholyoke.edu/artmuseum; *Bus & Events Mgr* Debbie Davis; *Coll Mgr* Linda Delone Best; *Mus Technician* Jacqueline Finnegan; *Coordr Acad Affairs* Ellen Alvord; *Curatorial Asst* Hannah Blunt; *Digitization Specialist* Laura Shea; *Art Adv Bd Fellow* Taylor Anderson; *Asst Cur Educ* Kendra Weisbin; *Asst Cur Visual & Material Culture* Aaron Miller; *Florence Finch Abbott Dir* John Stomberg; *Senior Admin Asst* Maggie Finnegan
Open Tues - Fri 11 AM - 5 PM, Sat - Sun 1 - 5 PM, cl Mon & certain Col holidays, same schedule yr-round; No admis fee; Estab 1876, mus now occupies a building dedicated in 1970. In addition to its permanent collections, mus also organizes special exhibitions of international scope; Art mus with 8 galleries houses the permanent collection & special exhibitions; Average Annual Attendance: 15,000; Mem: Dues $10-$2500
Income: Financed by endowment, mem & college funds
Special Subjects: Antiquities-Egyptian, Antiquities-Greek, Antiquities-Roman, Asian Art, Drawings, Painting-American, Painting-European, Pre-Columbian Art, Prints, Sculpture, Medieval Art
Collections: Asian art, European & American paintings, sculpture, photographs, prints & drawings, Egyptian, Greek, Roman, Pre-Columbian, Ancient coins (mostly Greek & Roman)
Exhibitions: 2-4 rotating special exhibitions per yr
Publications: Newsletter, bi-annually; exhibition catalogues
Activities: Educ dept; lects open to pub, 5-6 vis lectrs per yr; concerts; gallery talks; tours; "Jane Hammond: Paper Work" catalog awarded prize for design; excellence by the Assn of American Univ Presses; fels; individual paintings lent to qualified mus; book traveling exhibs 1-2 per yr; originate traveling exhibs to qualified mus; mus shop sells books, magazines, reproductions, mugs, tote bags & posters

L **Art Library**, 50 College St, South Hadley, MA 01075-6404. Tel 413-538-2225; Fax 413-538-2370; Email sperry@mtholyoke.edu; Web: www.mtholyoke.edu; *Dir* Susan L Perry
Open to college community only
Library Holdings: Book Volumes 15,550, Periodical Subscriptions 64, Slides

SPRINGFIELD

A **SPRINGFIELD CITY LIBRARY,** 220 State St, Springfield, MA 01103-1772. Tel 413-263-6828; Fax 413-263-6825; Web: www.springfieldlibrary.org; *Dir* Emily Bader; *Asst Dir* Lee Fogerty; *Head Adult Information Svcs* John Clark
Open Mon & Wed 11 AM - 8 PM, Tues 9 AM - 6 PM, Fri & Sat 9 AM - 5 PM, Sun 12 PM - 5 PM; cl holidays; No admis fee; Estab 1857, Department opened 1905; Circ 611,893 (totals for system); In addition to the City Library system, the Springfield Library & Mus Assn owns & administers, as separate units, the George Walter Vincent Smith Mus, the Springfield Mus of Fine Arts, the Science Mus & the Connecticut Valley Historical Mus; Average Annual Attendance: 1,100,000; Mem: 3,400; $35 & up
Library Holdings: Audio Tapes 36,000, Book Volumes 700,000, Video Tapes 26,500
Exhibitions: Occasional exhibitions from the library's collections & of work by local artists

M **SPRINGFIELD COLLEGE,** William Blizard Gallery, Visual & Performing Arts Dept, 263 Alden St Springfield, MA 01109-3788. Tel 413-747-3000, 748-0204; Fax 413-748-3580; *Chmn* Ronald Maggio; *Dir Gallery* Holly Murray
Open Mon - Fri 9 AM - 4 PM, Fri 8 AM - 8 PM, Sat 9 AM - 8 PM, Sun Noon - 12 AM; Estab 1998 to bring a wide range of quality exhibits in all areas of the visual arts to the Springfield College campus & surrounding community
Income: Financed by William Simpson Fine Arts Comt
Library Holdings: Book Volumes, Cassettes, Filmstrips, Micro Print, Motion Pictures, Original Art Works, Periodical Subscriptions, Prints, Video Tapes
Exhibitions: Rotating exhibits monthly
Activities: Lect open to public; gallery talks

M **SPRINGFIELD MUSEUMS,** Michele & Donald D'Amour Museum of Fine Arts, 21 Edwards St, Springfield, MA 01103-1548. Tel 413-263-6800; Fax 413-263-6814; Email info@springfieldmuseums.org; Web: www.springfieldmuseums.org; *Pres* Holly Smith-Bove; *Dir* Heather Haskell; *VPres* Kathleen Simpson
Open Tues - Sat 10 AM - 5 PM, Sun 11 AM - 5 PM, cl Mon & major holidays; Admis adults $18, seniors & college students $12, children $9.50 (includes admis to four museums); Estab 1934 to collect, preserve & exhibit fine & decorative arts; Average Annual Attendance: 110,000; Mem: 3200; dues $45 & up; annual mtg in Sept
Income: Financed by mem, admis & prog fees; local, state, federal grants, pvt foundations & corporate sponsorships
Special Subjects: Graphics, Oriental Art, Painting-American, Painting-British, Painting-Dutch, Painting-European, Painting-French, Painting-Italian, Primitive art, Renaissance Art, Sculpture, Woodcuts, Prints
Collections: Japanese woodblock prints, Currier & Ives American Print Collection
Exhibitions: Special exhibitions, historic to contemporary are continually on view in addition to permanent collection; changing exhibitions
Publications: Handbook to the American & European Collection, Museum of Fine Arts, Springfield; exhibition catalogs; Selections from the American Collections; Legacy of Currier & Ives: Shaping the American Spirit catalog
Activities: Classes for adults & children; docent progs; outreach progs; lects open to pub; book traveling exhibs 6-8 per yr; mus shop sells books, gift items & scientific objects

M **Connecticut Valley Historical Society**Tel 413-263-6800; Fax 413-263-6898; Web: www.quadrangle.org; *Head Library & Archive Coll* Margaret Humbertson; *Pres & Exec Dir* Joseph Carvalho; *VPres Mktg & Develop* Susan Davison; *Vice Pres Finance* Richard Dunbar
Open Wed-Fri Noon - 4 PM, Sat & Sun 11 AM - 4 PM; Admis adults $7, seniors & college students $5, children $3, under 6 free. Includes admis to all four mus at Quadrangle; Estab 1927 to interpret history of Connecticut River Valley; Average Annual Attendance: 463,493; Mem: Mem: 3645; dues $35 & up; annual meeting in Sept
Special Subjects: Painting-American, Folk Art, Decorative Arts, Portraits, Furniture, Silver, Historical Material, Embroidery, Pewter

Collections: Decorative arts of Connecticut Valley, including furniture, paintings & prints, pewter, firearms, glass, silver, early games; Genealogy Library
Exhibitions: Many exhibits pertaining to history & decorative arts of Connecticut River Valley
Publications: Say Goodbye to the Valley
Activities: Classes for adults & children; lects open to pub; lects for mems only; gallery talks; tours; book traveling exhibs 1-2 per yr; mus shop sells books, note cards, genealogy shirts & tote bags

M **George Walker Vincent Smith Art Museum**, 21 Edwards St, Springfield, MA 01103-1548. Tel 413-263-6800; Fax 413-263-6884; Email info@springfieldmuseums.org; Web: www.springfieldmuseums.org; *Exec Dir & Pres* Joseph Carvalho; *Dir* David Stier; *CFO* Holly Smith-Bove; *Dir Museum Educ & Institutional Advancement* Kathleen Simpson
Open Tues - Sat 10 AM - 5 PM, Sun 11 AM - 5 PM; Admis adults $18, seniors & college students $12, child $9.50 (includes admis to four museums); Estab 1899 to collect, preserve & exhibit material related to art, history, & science colls; Average Annual Attendance: 221,000; Mem: 3200; dues $45 & up; annual meeting in Sept
Income: Financed by mem, admis & prog fees; local, state, federal grants, pvt foundations & corporate sponsorships
Special Subjects: African Art, American Indian Art
Collections: Aquarium, Dinosaur Hall, Exploration Center, habitat groupings of mounted animals, Planetarium, live animal eco-center
Activities: Classes for adults & children; docent progs; outreach progs; lects open to pub; book traveling exhibs 2-3 per yr; mus shop sells books & gift items & scientific objects

STOCKBRIDGE

M **NATIONAL TRUST FOR HISTORIC PRESERVATION,** Chesterwood, 4 Williamsville Rd, Stockbridge, MA 01262; PO Box 827, Stockbridge, MA 01262-0827. Tel 413-298-3579; Fax 413-298-1065; Email chesterwood@savingplaces.org; Web: chesterwood.org; *Exec Dir* Donna Hassler; *Office Mgr* Lisa I Reynolds
Open Memorial Day to Columbus Day 10 AM - 5 PM; Admis adults $18, seniors $17, grounds only $10, NTHP members, military & children 13-17 $9, Friends of Chesterwood & children under 13 free; Estab 1955 to preserve the country home & studio of Daniel Chester French; Chesterwood, a National Trust Historic Site, is the country home, studio & gardens of America's foremost public sculptor Daniel Chester French (1850-1931), sculptor of the Lincoln Memorial, Minute Man & leading figure of the American Renaissance. The 122 acre property includes: the sculptor's studio (1898) & residence (1900-1901), both designed by Henry Bacon, architect of the Lincoln Memorial; Barn Gallery, a c1825 barn adapted for use as an exhibition space & a museum gift shop; a 1909 garage adapted as an exhib space & country place garden with woodland walls laid out by French; Average Annual Attendance: 14,000; Mem: Dues & mem levels $50-$2,500
Special Subjects: Architecture, Bronzes, Decorative Arts, Furniture, Landscapes, Painting-American, Painting-European, Painting-Italian, Portraits, Sculpture, Textiles
Collections: American Renaissance, Daniel Chester French Collection: sculpture by or owned by the artist, memorabilia, plaster models, marble & bronze casts of French's work & paintings, Chesterwood Archives were re-located to the Chapin Library at Williams College, Williamstown, MA
Exhibitions: Daniel Chester French: Sculpting an American Vision
Activities: Dramatic programs; lects open to pub; 5-7 vis lects per yr; concerts; tours; traveling exhibs; mus shop sells books, reproductions, prints

M **NORMAN ROCKWELL MUSEUM,** 9 Glendale Rd, Rte 183, Stockbridge, MA 01262. Tel 413-298-4100; Fax 413-298-4142; Email inforequest@nrm.org; Web: www.nrm.org; *Chmn* Robert Horvath; *Pres* Alice Carter; *COO* Jill Gellert; *Chief Adv Officer* Michelle Clarkin; *Deputy Dir & Chief Cur* Stephanie Haboush Plunkett; *Deputy Dir Audience & Bus Devel* Margit Hotchkiss; *Dir HR* Holly Coleman; *Mgr Media Svcs* Jeremy Clowe; *Dir Digital Learning & Engagement* Rich Bradway; *Dir Colls & Registration* Martin Mahoney; *Dir of Visitor Experience* Laura Berliner; *Education & Outreach Manager* Patrick O'Donnell; *Merchandise Sales Mgr.* Michael Duffy; *Mgr Traveling Exhibs* Mary Melius; *Mgr Facilities* David Slick; *Registrar & Image Svcs* Thomas Mesquita; *Mgr IT* Frank Kennedy; *Cur Educ* Thomas Daly; *Mgr Visitor Svcs* Carolyn Grogan; *Educ & Outreach Mgr* Patrick O'Donnell; *Sls & Mktg Coord* Ellen Swan Mazzer
Open May - Oct daily 10 AM - 5 PM, Nov - Apr Mon - Fri 10 AM - 4 PM, Sat & Sun 10 AM - 5 PM, cl Thanksgiving, Christmas, New Year's Day; Admis adults $20, college students $10, mems & children 18 & under no charge; Estab 1967 to collect, manage, preserve, study, interpret & present to the public material pertaining to the life & career of Norman Rockwell while featuring the work of other illustrators; Consists of a main building (1993), situated on 36 acres in a country setting with galleries for permanent & changing exhibitions, classrooms, the Norman Rockwell Reference Center, meeting room & store. Norman Rockwell Studio is located on the museum site. Terrace Cafe open May-Oct; Average Annual Attendance: 125,000; Mem: 1,569, dues $50 & up; annual meeting in Sept
Income: Financed by admis, mem, donations, sales & grants
Library Holdings: Auction Catalogs, Audio Tapes, Book Volumes, CD-ROMs, Cards, Cassettes, Clipping Files, Compact Disks, DVDs, Exhibition Catalogs, Fiche, Filmstrips, Framed Reproductions, Kodachrome Transparencies, Lantern Slides, Manuscripts, Maps, Memorabilia, Micro Print, Motion Pictures, Original Art Works, Original Documents, Other Holdings, Pamphlets, Periodical Subscriptions, Photographs, Prints, Records, Reels, Reproductions, Sculpture, Slides, Video Tapes
Special Subjects: Drawings, Painting-American, Photography, Portraits
Collections: Largest permanent collection of original Rockwell art (more than 900 original paintings & drawings), artifacts & furnishings of Norman Rockwell's studio, archives including bus letters, memorabilia, negatives & photographs, Norman Rockwell Collection, American Illustration - William Steig, George Bridgman, Edmund Ward, Al Parker, JC Leyendecker, James Montgomery Flagg, Thomas Fogarty, Famous Artists School, Robert Cunningham
Exhibitions: Norman Rockwell Highlights from the Permanent Collection; (11th Nov, 2017-28th May, 2018) Never Abandon Imagination: The Fantasy Art of Toni Diterlizzi; (14th Feb, 2018-10th Jun, 2018) Gloria Stoll Karn: Pulp Romance; (9th Jun, 2018-28th Oct, 2018) Keepers of the Flame: Parrish, Wyeth, Rockwell and the Narrative Tradition
Publications: Norman Rockwell: A Definitive Catalogue; The Portfolio, quarterly newsletter; Programs & Events, quarterly calendar, Pictures for the American People, American Chronicles, Peter Rockwell: A Sculptors Retrospective; Baseball, Rodeos & Automobiles: The Art of Murray Tinkelman (2014); The Unknown Hopper: Edward Hopper as Illustrator (2014); Mort Kunstler: The Art of Adventure (2011); Masters of the Golden Age: Harvey Dunn & His Students; Jerry Pinkney: Imaginings An Interactive Guide (2015); Roz Chast: Cartoon Memoirs (2015)
Activities: Classes for adults & children; docent training; lects open to pub; gallery talks; tours; educator's seminars, art workshops for adults & children; school programs; family days; special performances & events; free admis days; schols, fels & internships offered; individual paintings & original objects of art lent to qualifying not for profit educational institutions; originate traveling exhibs; mus shop sells books, prints, reproductions & gift items

L **Library**, 9 Route 183, Stockbridge, MA 01262; PO Box 308, Stockbridge, MA 01262. Tel 413-298-4100; 931-2251; Fax 413-298-4145; Email inforequest@nrm.org; Web: www.nrm.org; *Archivist* Venus Van Ness
Open by appointment; Admis to libr incl in mus admis; 1993
Library Holdings: Auction Catalogs, Audio Tapes, Book Volumes 300, Cassettes, Clipping Files, DVDs, Exhibition Catalogs, Kodachrome Transparencies, Lantern Slides, Manuscripts, Memorabilia, Motion Pictures, Original Documents, Periodical Subscriptions 10, Photographs, Prints, Records, Reproductions, Slides, Video Tapes
Special Subjects: Advertising Design, Art History, Commercial Art, Graphic Arts, Illustration, Painting-American, Art Education
Collections: Norman Rockwell Archives, Al Parker Archives, Tom Lovell Archives, Illustration Ephemera
Activities: Educ prog; classes for adults & children; lects open to pub; gallery talks; schols offered; originates traveling exhibs; mus shop sells books, magazines, reproductions, & prints

SUDBURY

M **LONGFELLOW'S WAYSIDE INN MUSEUM,** 72 Wayside Inn Rd, Sudbury, MA 01776-3206. Tel 978-443-1716, 800-339-1776; Fax 978-443-8041; Email innkeeper@wayside.org; Web: www.wayside.org; *Chmn Trustees* Richard Davidson; *Innkeeper* Robert H Purrington
Open daily 9 AM - 8 PM cl Christmas Day & July 4th; No admis fee, donations accepted; Estab 1716 as one of the oldest operating Inns in America. The ancient hostelry continues to provide hospitality to wayfarers from all over the world; 18th century period rooms including Old Barroom, Longfellow Parlor, Longfellow Bed Chamber, Old Kitchen, Drivers and Drovers Chamber. Historic buildings on the estate include Redstone School of Mary's Little Lamb fame, grist mill, and Martha Mary Chapel; Average Annual Attendance: 170,000
Income: Nonprofit organization
Special Subjects: Decorative Arts, Furniture, Painting-American, Period Rooms, Prints
Collections: Early American furniture and decorative arts, Howe family memorabilia, paintings, photographs of the Inn, prints, historic papers
Exhibitions: Various exhibits
Activities: Classes for adults; colonial crafts demonstrations and workshops; lect open to public, 5 vis lectrs per year; tours; sales shop selling books, original art, reproductions & prints

TAUNTON

M **OLD COLONY HISTORICAL SOCIETY,** Museum, 66 Church Green, Taunton, MA 02780. Tel 508-822-1622; Fax 508-880-6317; Email info@oldcolonyhistorymuseum.org; Web: www.oldcolonyhistorymuseum.org; *Dir* Katherine M MacDonald; *Cur Colls* Bronson Michaud; *Community Prog Coord* Saria Sweeney; *Asst to Dir* Elizabeth Bernier
Open Tues - Sat 10 AM - 4 PM; Admis adults $4, seniors & children 12-18 $2, mems no charge; Estab 1853 to preserve & perpetuate the history of the Old Colony in Massachusetts; Four exhibition halls; Average Annual Attendance: 5,025; Mem: 700; dues $10-$250; annual meeting third Thurs in Apr
Income: $120,000 (financed by endowment, mem, service fees, grants)
Special Subjects: Furniture, Silver, Textiles
Collections: Fire fighting equipment, furniture, household utensils, Indian artifacts, military items, portraits, silver, stoves
Publications: Booklets; pamphlets
Activities: Classes for adults & children; docent training; workshops; lects open to pub, 8-10 vis lectrs per yr; fels offered; mus shop sells books & souvenirs

L **Library**, 66 Church Green, Taunton, MA 02780. Tel 508-822-1622; *Library Asst* Greta Smith; *Dir* Katheryn P Viens
Open Tues - Sat 10 AM - 4 PM; Admis genealogy $5, other research $2; Estab 1853; For reference only; research services available for a fee
Library Holdings: Audio Tapes, Exhibition Catalogs, Manuscripts, Memorabilia, Pamphlets, Periodical Subscriptions 10, Photographs, Prints, Reels, Slides
Special Subjects: Architecture, Art History, Ceramics, Coins & Medals, Decorative Arts, Dolls, Flasks & Bottles, Folk Art, Furniture, Glass, Manuscripts, Maps, Metalwork, Painting-American, Pewter

TYRINGHAM

M **SANTARELLA MUSEUM & GARDENS,** 75 Main Rd, Tyringham, MA 01264; PO Box 466, Tyringham, MA 01264-0466. Tel 413-243-3260; Fax 413-243-9178; *Dir* Hope C Talbert
Open 10 AM - 5 PM (May - Oct), cl Tues & Wed; Admis $4, children under 6 free; Estab 1996 to exhibit & sell paintings, prints & sculptures by recognized artists, including world masters; The building was designed as a sculpture studio by the late Sir Henry Kitson; Average Annual Attendance: 15,000
Income: Financed privately
Special Subjects: Architecture, Bronzes, Decorative Arts, Sculpture
Collections: Santarella Sculpture Gardens, Henry Hudson-Kitson Studios

Exhibitions: One-person shows by established artists; Outdoor sculpture exhibitions (various artists)
Activities: Lects open to pub; 2 vis lectrs per yr; gallery talks; tours; mus shop sells books, original art, reproductions & prints

WALTHAM

M **BRANDEIS UNIVERSITY,** Rose Art Museum, 415 South St Stop 069, Waltham, MA 02453-2728. Tel 781-736-3434; Fax 781-736-3439; Email roseartmuseum@brandeis.edu; Web: www.brandies.edu/rose; *Head Prep* Roy Dawes; *Dir & Chief Cur* Luis A Croquer
Open Wed - Sun 11 AM - 5 PM; No admis fee; Estab 1961 to exhibit and collect modern and contemporary art; Sept - June revolving displays of Brandeis Art; Average Annual Attendance: 10,000; Mem: 250; $50 & up
Purchases: William Kentridge; Barry McGee; Robin Rhode
Special Subjects: American Indian Art, Asian Art, Pre-Columbian Art, Prints
Collections: The permanent collections consist of African art, contemporary art (post World War II), modern art (1800 to World War II), including the Riverside Museum Collections & the Teresa Jackson Weill Collection, pre-modern art (before 1800), Mr & Mrs Edward Rose Collection of early ceramics, Helen S Slosberg Collection of Oceanic art, Teresa Jackson Weill Collection
Publications: Exhibition catalogs
Activities: Classes for children; docent training; lect open to public; gallery talks; concerts; tours; individual paintings & original objects of art lent to students & individuals within the university; lending collection contains original art works, original prints, paintings; book traveling exhibitions 1 per year

L **Leonard L Farber Library**, 415 South St, Norman & Rosita Creative Arts Ctr Waltham, MA 02453-2728; PO Box 9110, Waltham, MA 02254-9110. Tel 781-736-4681; Fax 781-736-4675; *Librn* Darwin Scott
Open Mon - Thurs 8:30 AM - Noon, Fri 8:30 AM-8 PM, Sat 11 AM -8 PM, Sun 11 AM-Midnight; Estab 1948 to provide materials & services for the teaching, research & pub interest in the arts of the Brandeis community; For lending & reference
Library Holdings: Book Volumes 40,000, Cards, Cassettes, Exhibition Catalogs, Fiche, Micro Print, Periodical Subscriptions 130, Photographs, Records, Reels
Special Subjects: Art History
Collections: collection of books on Daumier, Dr Bern Dibner Collection of Leonardo da Vinci - Books, Benjamin A & Julia M Trustman Collection of Honore Daumier Prints (4,000)
Exhibitions: Rotating exhibition of Daumier Prints

WELLESLEY

M **WELLESLEY COLLEGE,** Davis Museum & Cultural Center, 106 Central St, Wellesley, MA 02181-8203. Tel 781-283-2051; Fax 781-283-2064; Web: www.davismuseum.wellesly.edu; *Dir* David Mickenberg; *Dir Museum Develop & Mem* Nancy Gunn; *Assoc Dir* Dennis McFadden; *Registrar* Bo Mompho; *Cur* Elizabeth Wyckoff; *Cur* Dabney Hailey; *Cur* Elaine Mehalakes
Open Tues & Fri - Sat 11 AM - 5 PM, Wed 11 AM - 8 PM, Sun 1 - 5 PM; cl New Year's Day, Thanksgiving and Dec 24 - Jan 2; No admis fee; Estab 1889, dedicated to acquiring a collection of high quality art objects for the primary purpose of teaching art history from original works; Main gallery houses major exhibitions; Corridor Gallery, works on paper; Sculpture Ct, permanent installation, sculpture, reliefs, works on wood panel; Average Annual Attendance: 18,000; Mem: 650; dues donor $100, contributor $50, regular $25
Income: Financed by mem, through college & gifts
Special Subjects: African Art, Antiquities-Greek, Antiquities-Roman, Baroque Art, Drawings, Etchings & Engravings, Hispanic Art, Landscapes, Latin American Art, Medieval Art, Painting-American, Painting-British, Painting-European, Painting-Flemish, Painting-Italian, Painting-Spanish, Photography, Portraits, Pre-Columbian Art, Prints, Religious Art, Renaissance Art, Sculpture, Watercolors, Woodcuts
Collections: Paintings, sculpture, graphic & decorative arts, Asian, African, ancient, medieval, Renaissance, Baroque, 19th & 20th century European & American art, photography, prints, drawings
Publications: Exhibition catalogs; Wellesley College Friends of Art Newsletter, annually
Activities: Docent training; lects open to pub & members only; gallery talks; tours; VTS viewing sessions for students; lending collection contains original prints; book traveling exhibs; originate traveling exhibs; sales shop sells catalogs, postcards & notecards

L **Art Library**, 106 Central St, Wellesley, MA 02481-8203. Tel 781-283-3258; Fax 781-283-3647; Email artlib@wellesley.edu; Web: www.wellesley.edu; *Art Librn* Brooke Henderson
Circ 18,000
Income: Financed by College appropriation
Library Holdings: Book Volumes 67,000, CD-ROMs 61, Exhibition Catalogs, Fiche 1700, Pamphlets, Periodical Subscriptions 158
Special Subjects: Antiquities-Roman, Archaeology, Architecture, Art History, Asian Art, Decorative Arts, History of Art & Archaeology, Oriental Art, Painting-American, Painting-European, Painting-Italian, Photography

WELLFLEET

M **WELLFLEET HISTORICAL SOCIETY & MUSEUM, INC,** 266 Main St, Wellfleet, MA 02667; PO Box 58, Wellfleet, MA 02667-0058. Tel 508-349-2954; Email info@wellfleethistoricalsociety.org; Web: www.wellfleethistoricalsociety.org; *Pres* Brad Williams; *Cur* Joan Hopkins Coughlin; *Treas* Dawn Rockman; *VPres* Deidre Portnoy; *Secy* William Carlson
Open late June - early Oct, Wed, Thurs & Sat - 2 - 5 PM, Tues & Fri 10 AM - Noon; No admis fee; Estab 1951; Average Annual Attendance: 1,200; Mem: 350; dues $20; 12 general meetings per yr
Income: $25,000 (financed by mem); grants & awards
Purchases: $5,000
Special Subjects: Dolls
Collections: Books, china & glass, documents, Indian artifacts, paintings & photographs, personal memorabilia of Wellfleet, pewter, shellfish & finfish exhibit, shop models, shipwreck & marine items
Publications: Beacon, annual
Activities: Classes for children; lects open to public, 5 vis lectrs per year; walking tours during summer; mus shop sells books & prints

WENHAM

A **WENHAM MUSEUM,** 132 Main St, Wenham, MA 01984-1520. Tel 978-468-2377; Fax 978-468-1763; Web: www.wenhammuseum.org; *Pres* Elizabeth Stone; *Office Admin* Felicia Connolly; *Doll Cur* Diane Hamblin; *Cur* Bar Browdo; *Dir* Emily Stearns
Open Tues - Sun 10 AM - 4 PM, cl Mon & major holidays; Admis adults $5, seniors $4, children $2 & up $3, mem free; Estab 1921 as Historical Soc, incorporated 1953, to acquire, preserve, interpret & exhibit collections of literary & historical interest; to provide an educational & cultural service & facilities; Maintains three permanent galleries & one gallery for changing exhibits; Average Annual Attendance: 10,000; Mem: 650; dues family $55, individual $30; annual meeting Apr
Income: Financed by endowment, mem, earned income
Collections: Dolls, doll houses, figurines, costumes & accessories 1800-1960, embroideries, fans, needlework, quilts, toys
Exhibitions: Ice Cutting Tool Exhibit; 19th Century Shoe Shops; Still Lifes; Quilts Old & New; Samplers; Tin & Woodenware; Weavers; Wedding Dresses
Publications: Annual report; newsletter
Activities: Classes for children; lects open to pub; gallery talks; tours; mus shop sells books, miniatures, original needlework, dolls & small toys

L **Timothy Pickering Library**, 132 Main St, Wenham, MA 01984. Tel 978-468-2377; Fax 978-468-1763; Email info@wenhammuseum.org; Web: www.wenhammuseum.org; *Exec Dir* Lindsay Diehl; *Mus Shop Mgr* Diane McMahon
Open by appointment; Open to members & the pub for reference
Income: Endowments, earned income, mem
Library Holdings: Book Volumes 2200, Manuscripts, Memorabilia, Pamphlets, Photographs

WEST NEWTON

M **BOSTON SCULPTORS AT CHAPEL GALLERY,** The Second Church in Newton, 60 Highland St West Newton, MA 02465-2405. Tel 617-244-4039; Web: www.bostonsculptors.com; *Dir* Julie Scaramella
Open Wed - Sun 1 - 5:30 PM; No admis fee; Estab 1992 as an alternate venue for contemporary sculpture; Collaborative gallery operated by 20 sculptors; Mid-career sculptors by invitation; Average Annual Attendance: 5,000 - 7,000; Mem: 20
Income: Dues & sales
Exhibitions: Group & solo invitations - Sept - June
Activities: Lect open to public, gallery talks: Best of Boston Award; mus shop sells original art & postcards

WESTFIELD

M **WESTFIELD ATHENAEUM,** Jasper Rand Art Museum, 6 Elm St, Westfield, MA 01085-2997. Tel 413-568-7833; Fax 413-568-1558; Email pcramer@exit3.com; Web: www.ci.westfield.ma.us/athen.html; *Pres* James Rogers; *Treas* Mark Morin; *Dir* Patricia T Cramer; *Asst Dir* Donald G Buckley
Open Mon - Thurs 8:30 AM - 8 PM, Fri & Sat 8:30 AM - 5 PM, cl Sat in July & Aug; No admis fee; Estab 1927 to provide exhibitions of art works by area artists & other prominent artists; Gallery measures 25 x 30 x 17 feet, with a domed ceiling & free-standing glass cases & wall cases; Average Annual Attendance: 13,500; Mem: Annual meeting fourth Mon in Nov
Income: Financed by endowment
Exhibitions: Changing exhibits on a monthly basis

WESTON

M **REGIS COLLEGE FINE ARTS CENTER,** Carney Gallery, 235 Wellesley St, Weston, MA 02493-1545. Tel 781-768-7034 (Dir); Fax 781-768-7030; Email fac@regiscollege.edu; Web: www.regiscollege.edu; *Dir* Steven B Hall; *Assoc Dir* Nancy Rosata; *Technical Dir* Andre Schiff
Open Mon - Fri 10 AM - 4 PM; No admis fee; Estab 1993 and houses the music, art and theater depts as well as the Casey Theatre & Carney Gallery; Carney Gallery is one room, 26 x 40 ft; Average Annual Attendance: 1,500
Income: Financed by college
Exhibitions: Rotate every 6 wks, focus on works of contemporary women artists
Activities: Classes for adults; lects open to pub; 1-4 vis lectrs per year, gallery talks

WILLIAMSTOWN

M **CLARK ART INSTITUTE,** 225 South St, Williamstown, MA 01267-2878. Tel 413-458-2303; Email info@clarkart.edu; Web: www.clarkart.edu; *Director* Michael Conforti; *Sr Cur of Paintings & Sculpture* Richard Rand; *Dir Exhibs & Colls & Cur Decorative Arts* Kathleen Morris; *Cur Prints, Drawings & Photog* James A Ganz; *Cur American Art* Marc Simpson; *Asst Cur Paintings* Sarah Lees; *Dir Research & Academic Prog* Michael Ann Holly; *Assoc Dir Research & Academic Prog* Mark Ledbury; *Cur Educ* Michael Cassin; *Asst Cur Educ* Danielle Steinmann
Open daily July & Aug 10 AM - 5 PM; Tues - Sun rest of year 10 AM - 5 PM, cl Mon, Patriot's Day, Thanksgiving, Christmas & New Year's Day; Gen admis $20, children under 18 & students (w/ valid ID) free; Estab 1955 as a mus of fine arts with galleries, art research library & pub events in auditorium; Intimately scattered galleries in a rural setting; Average Annual Attendance: 200,000; Mem: 6,500; dues $60 & up

Library Holdings: Auction Catalogs, Book Volumes, CD-ROMs, Exhibition Catalogs, Periodical Subscriptions, Slides
Special Subjects: Ceramics, Decorative Arts, Drawings, Etchings & Engravings, Flasks & Bottles, Furniture, Glass, Landscapes, Painting-American, Painting-British, Painting-Dutch, Painting-European, Painting-Flemish, Painting-French, Painting-Italian, Photography, Porcelain, Portraits, Posters, Prints, Religious Art, Sculpture, Silver, Watercolors, Woodcuts
Collections: English and American silver, Dutch, Flemish, French, Italian Old Master paintings from the 14th-18th centuries, French 19th century paintings, especially the Impressionists, 19th century sculpture, Old Master prints & drawings, selected 19th century American artists (Homer & Sargent), Early photography, American furniture, British Art
Exhibitions: The Permanent Collection & Traveling Exhibitions
Publications: Calendar of Events, quarterly; Journal, annually; miscellaneous exhib catalogues; Research Academic Program Volumes
Activities: Classes for adults & children; docent training; dramatic programs; lects open to pub & mem only, 20+ vis lectrs per yr; concerts; gallery talks; tours for school children; Awards, Clark Prize for Excellence in Arts Writing; fels available; individual paintings & original objects of art lent to other mus whose facilities meet criteria, for exhibs of acad importance; book traveling exhibs 1-2 per yr; organize traveling exhibs circulating to global selected partners; mus shop sells books, original art, reproductions, prints, slides, jewelry, glass, games, puzzles, gifts

L **Library**, 225 South St, Williamstown, MA 01267-2878; PO Box 8, Williamstown, MA 01267-0008. Tel 413-458-2303 ext 350; Fax 413-458-9542; Email library@clarkart.edu; Web: www.clarkart.edu/library; *Librn* Susan Roeper
Open Mon - Fri 9 AM - 5 PM, cl holidays; Estab 1962; For reference only; Average Annual Attendance: 14,000
Purchases: $260,000
Library Holdings: Auction Catalogs, Book Volumes 270,000, Exhibition Catalogs, Fiche, Other Holdings Auction sale catalogues 40,000, Periodical Subscriptions 640, Photographs, Reels, Reproductions
Collections: Mary Ann Beinecke Decorative Art Collection, Duveen Library, Juynboll Collection

M **WILLIAMS COLLEGE,** Museum of Art, 15 Lawrence Hall Dr, Ste 2 Williamstown, MA 01267-2584. Tel 413-597-2429; Fax 413-597-5000; Email wcma@williams.edu; Web: wcma.williams.edu; *Dep Dur Curatorial Affairs* Lisa Dorin; *Asst to Dir* Amy Tatro; *Assoc Dir Academic & Public Engagement* Sonnet K Coggins; *Assoc Dir Mus Budget & Opers* Barbara Palmer; *Sr Mus Registrar Colls & Exhibs* Diane Hart; *Cur Acad Progs* Elizabeth Gallerani; *Chief Preparator* Nathan Ahern; *Assoc Registrar* Rachel Tassone; *Senior Curator of American Art* Kevin M Murphy; *Interim Mgr Student & Visitor Engagement* Hadley DesMeules; *Preparator* Richard H Miller; *Visitor Services Coordinator* Hadley DesMeules
Open Sept - May: every day 10 AM - 5 PM, cl Wed; June - Aug: every day 10 AM - 5 PM, Thurs 10 AM - 8 PM; No admis fee; Estab 1926 for the presentation of the permanent collection & temporary loan exhibitions for the benefit of the Williams College community & the general pub; Original 1846 Greek Revival building designed by Thomas Tefft; 1983 & 1986 additions & renovations designed by Charles Moore & Robert Harper of Centerbrook Architects & Planners. Building also houses Art Department of Williams College; Average Annual Attendance: 35,000
Special Subjects: African Art, Afro-American Art, Antiquities-Assyrian, Antiquities-Byzantine, Antiquities-Egyptian, Antiquities-Etruscan, Antiquities-Greek, Antiquities-Oriental, Antiquities-Persian, Antiquities-Roman, Asian Art, Baroque Art, Cartoons, Collages, Decorative Arts, Drawings, Etchings & Engravings, Folk Art, Furniture, Historical Material, Islamic Art, Landscapes, Latin American Art, Medieval Art, Oriental Art, Painting-American, Painting-British, Painting-European, Painting-Flemish, Painting-French, Painting-German, Painting-Italian, Painting-Japanese, Painting-Spanish, Photography, Portraits, Posters, Pre-Columbian Art, Prints, Religious Art, Renaissance Art, Sculpture, Watercolors, Woodcuts
Collections: Ancient & medieval art, Asian & African art, modern & contemporary art, 18th-20th century American art, 20th century American photography
Publications: Brochures; exhibition catalogs, 3-4 per year
Activities: Student Gallery Guides; lects open to pub, 10 vis lectrs per yr; gallery talks; tours; Fulkerson Leadership in the Arts award; individual paintings & original objects of art are lent to other mus; Walls Williams Art Loan for Living; Student Art loan program;; book traveling exhibs 1 per yr; originate traveling exhibs to mus; mus shop sells books, jewelry, magazines, posters & postcards

L **Sawyer Library**, 55 Sawyer Library Dr, Williamstown, MA 01267-2562. Tel 413-597-2501; Fax 413-597-4106; Email david.pilachowski@williams.edu; Web: www.williams.edu/library/sawyer; *Librn* David Pilachowski; *Asst Librn* Betty Milanesi
Open Mon - Thurs 8 AM - 10 PM, Sat 9 AM - 10 PM, Sun 9 AM - 2 AM; No admis fee
Income: Financed by endowments, gifts, Williams College
Library Holdings: Book Volumes 697,023, Periodical Subscriptions 3024, Slides 22,800

L **Chapin Library**, Sawyer Library, 26 Hopkins Hall Dr Williamstown, MA 01267. Tel 413-597-4200; Fax 413-597-2929; Email chapin.library@williams.edu; Web: chapin.williams.edu; *Librn* Wayne G Hammond
Open Mon - Fri 10 AM - 5 PM; No admis fee; Library estab 1923; For reference only; Average Annual Attendance: 5,000
Income: Financed by Williams College, endowments & gifts
Library Holdings: Auction Catalogs, Audio Tapes, Book Volumes 55,000, Cassettes, Clipping Files, Compact Disks, DVDs, Exhibition Catalogs, Kodachrome Transparencies, Manuscripts, Maps, Memorabilia, Motion Pictures, Original Art Works, Original Documents, Pamphlets, Periodical Subscriptions 10, Photographs, Prints, Records, Sculpture, Slides, Video Tapes
Special Subjects: Advertising Design, Architecture, Art History, Bookplates & Bindings, Calligraphy, Cartoons, Coins & Medals, Commercial Art, Costume Design & Constr, Decorative Arts, Drawings, Etchings & Engravings, Ethnology, Fashion Arts, Film, Furniture, Graphic Arts, Graphic Design, Historical Material, History of Art & Archaeology, Illustration, Industrial Design, Interior Design, Judaica, Landscape Architecture, Lettering, Manuscripts, Maps, Photography, Portraits, Posters, Printmaking, Prints, Restoration & Conservation, Sculpture, Stage Design, Theatre Arts, Woodcuts
Collections: Pauline Baynes; Samuel "Erewhon" Butler; John DePol; CB Falls; Julio Granda; Herman & Helena Rosse; Frank Lloyd Wright; Leo Wyatt; Chesterwood Archives (Daniel Chester French Etal); Artist's Books; Illustrated Books; Posters; Historic Prints, Photographs & medallions

A **WILLIAMSTOWN ART CONSERVATION CENTER,** 227 South St, Williamstown, MA 01267-2891. Tel 413-458-5741; Fax 413-458-2314; Email wacc@williamstownart.org; Web: www.williamstownart.org; *Dir* Thomas J Branchick; *Objects Conservator & Dept Head* Helene Gillette-Woodard; *Furniture Conservator & Dept Head* Hugh Glover; *Paper Conservator* Rebecca Johnston; *Paintings Conservator* Montserrat Le Mense; *Paintings Conservator* Sandra Webber; *Paper Conservator & Dept Head* Leslie Paisley; *Paintings Conservator & Internatl Projs Specialist* Cynthia Luk
Open Mon - Fri 9 AM - 5 PM; Estab 1977
Income: $1,000,000 (financed by state appropriation & earned income)
Activities: Progs for undergrad, grad & post grad; internships; fellowships; apprentice training; lect open to public, 2-4 vis lectrs per year; IIC Keck Award 1996

WINCHESTER

M **ARTHUR GRIFFIN CENTER FOR PHOTOGRAPHIC ART,** Griffin Museum of Photography, 67 Shore Rd, Winchester, MA 01890-2821. Tel 781-729-1158; Fax 781-721-2765; Email agcfpa@gis.net; Web: www.griffincenter.org; www.griffinmuseum.org; *Exec Dir* Paula Tognarelli; *Assoc Dir* Frances Jakubek; *Gallery Monitor* Martha Stone
Open Tues - Thurs 11 AM - 5 PM, Fri 11 AM - 4 PM, Sat & Sun noon - 4 PM; Admis $7, seniors $3; Estab 1992 to promote historic & contemporary photography through photographic exhibitions; 1,500 sq ft modern gallery for photography; 4 satellite galleries, 58 shows per year; Average Annual Attendance: 5,000; Mem: 4,000
Income: Mem, entrance fee & photo sales
Special Subjects: Photography
Collections: Photographic works of Arthur Griffin
Exhibitions: Annual Juried Photography Show; over 58 shows per year
Activities: Classes for adults & children; lects open to pub, 12-20 vis lectrs per yr; gallery talks; juried competitions; original objects of art lent; book traveling exhibs; originate traveling exhibs to mus & galleries; mus shop sells books, original art & prints, magazines

WORCESTER

AMERICAN ANTIQUARIAN SOCIETY
For further information, see National and Regional Organizations

L **BECKER COLLEGE,** William F Ruska Library, 61 Sever St, Worcester, MA 01615-2195. Tel 508-791-9241, Ext 211; Fax 508-849-5131; Email plummer@go.becker.edu; *Asst Dir* Sharon Krauss; *Catalog & Reference Librn* Alice Baron; *Dean Library* Bruce Plummer
Open Mon - Thur 8 AM - 9 PM, Fri 8 AM - 5 PM, Sat 11 AM - 3 PM, Sun 2 PM - 10 PM; Estab 1887
Library Holdings: Slides, Video Tapes
Special Subjects: Graphic Design, Interior Design
Collections: Graphic Design, Interior Design
Publications: Acquisition List; Faculty Handbook, annual

M **CLARK UNIVERSITY,** The Schiltkamp Gallery/Traina Center for the Arts, 950 Main St, Worcester, MA 01610-1477. Tel 508-793-7113; Fax 508-793-8844; Web: www.clarku.edu; *Dir* Sarah Buie
Open Mon - Fri 9 AM - 5 PM; Sat Noon - 5 PM; Sun Noon - 10 PM; No admis fee; Estab 1976 to provide the Clark community & greater Worcester community the opportunity to view quality exhibitions of art, primarily, but not exclusively, contemporary; First floor foyer of the Traina Center for the Arts; Average Annual Attendance: 2,000
Income: Financed through the University
Exhibitions: Six to eight exhibitions per year of, primarily emerging artists & well-known artists
Publications: Announcements of exhibitions
Activities: Exhibitions; art events; gallery talks; lects open to pub; 4-6 lectrs per year

L **COLLEGE OF THE HOLY CROSS,** Dinand Library, One College St, Worcester, MA 01610-2349. Tel 508-793-3372; Fax 508-793-2372; Email kreilly@holycross.edu; Web: www.holycross.edu, academics.holycross.edu/libraries; *Director* Karen Reilly; *Assoc Dir* Karen Reilly
Open Sun - Thurs 8:30 AM - 1 AM, Fri & Sat 8:30 AM - 11 PM; mid-May - Sept summer hours Mon - Fri 8:30 AM - 4:30 PM; Estab 1843 to support the acad study & research needs of a liberal visual arts department
Library Holdings: Book Volumes 637,000 for all campus, Compact Disks, DVDs, Exhibition Catalogs, Original Art Works, Periodical Subscriptions 900, Sculpture, Slides 94,000
Special Subjects: Antiquities-Byzantine, Antiquities-Greek, Architecture, Art Education, Art History, Commercial Art, Decorative Arts, Fashion Arts, Film, Graphic Arts, Industrial Design, Painting-American, Theatre Arts
Exhibitions: Various exhibitions
Publications: Art reference bibliographies, semi-annual

M **WORCESTER ART MUSEUM,** 55 Salisbury St, Worcester, MA 01609-3196. Tel 508-799-4406; Fax 508-798-5646; Email information@worcesterart.org; Web: worcesterart.org; *Pres* Lis Kirby Gibbs; *The C. Jean and Myles McDonough Dir* Matthias Waschek; *Dir Educ & Experience* Marnie Weir; *Dir Operations* Francis Pedone; *Dir Strategic Initiatives* Nora Maroulis; *Dir Curatorial Affairs & Cur European Art* Jon L. Seydl; *Chief Preparator & Exhib Designer* Patrick Brown; *Asst Chief Cur Prints, Drawings & Photography* Nancy Kathryn Burns; *Chief Registrar* Gareth Salway; *Cur Asian Art* Vivian Li; *Special Events Mgr* Janice

Potter; *Librn* Deborah Aframe; *Mus Shop Mgr* Susan Giordano; *Cafe Mgr* Laurie Krohn
Open Wed - Sun 10 AM - 4 PM, until 8 PM on 3rd Thurs of month, cl Mon, Tues & holidays; Admis adults $16, seniors & college students with ID $14, children 4-17 $6, mems, military & children under 18 free, 1st Sat of month 10 AM - noon free to all; Estab Museum 1896, School 1898. The Mus and School were founded for the promotion of art and art educ in Worcester; for the preservation and exhib of works and objects of art and for instruction in the industrial, liberal and fine arts. There are 42 galleries housed in a neoclassical bldg. The Higgins Educ Wing, built in 1970, houses studios and classrooms and contains exhib space for shows sponsored by the Educ Dept; Circ 53,000; Average Annual Attendance: 100,000; Mem: 4400, dues $65 - $105; ann meeting in Nov
Income: $8.4 million (financed by endowment, mem, private corporate contributions & government grants)
Library Holdings: Auction Catalogs, Book Volumes, Exhibition Catalogs, Pamphlets, Periodical Subscriptions, Slides
Special Subjects: Antiquities-Egyptian, Antiquities-Oriental, Antiquities-Roman, Asian Art, Baroque Art, Ceramics, Coins & Medals, Decorative Arts, Drawings, Etchings & Engravings, Jade, Landscapes, Medieval Art, Mosaics, Painting-American, Painting-British, Painting-Dutch, Painting-Flemish, Painting-French, Pre-Columbian Art, Prints, Religious Art, Renaissance Art, Sculpture, Silver, Watercolors, Woodcuts
Collections: John Chandler Bancroft Collection of Japanese Prints, American Paintings of 17th - 20th Centuries, British Paintings of 18th and 19th Centuries, Dutch 17th & 19th Century Paintings, Egyptian, Classical, Oriental & Medieval Sculpture, French Paintings of 16th - 19th Centuries, Flemish 16th - 17th Century Paintings, Italian Paintings of the 13th - 18th Centuries, Mosaics from Antioch, Pre-Columbian Collection, 12th Century French Chap House, Paul Revere Silver & Engravings
Publications: American Portrait Miniatures: The Worcester Art Museum Collection; In Battle's Light: Woodblock Prints of Japan's Early Modern Wars; Calendar of Events, quarterly; The Second Wave: American Abstractions of the 1930s & 1940s; A Spectrum of Innovation: American Color Prints, 1890 - 1960; Paths to Impressionism: French & American Landscape Paintings; Photography at the Worcester Art Museum: Keeping Shadows
Activities: Classes for adults & children; docent training; lects open to pub, 7-10 vis lectrs per yr; symposia; concerts; gallery talks; tours; scholarships offered; originates traveling exhibs; mus shop sells books, reproductions, jewelry & exhib related merchandise

L **Library**, 55 Salisbury St, Worcester, MA 01609-3196. Tel 508-799-4406, Ext 3070; Fax 508-798-5646; Email library@worcesterart.org; Web: www.worcesterart.org; *Librn* Debby Aframe; *Asst Librn* Christine Clayton
Open Wed - Fri 11 AM - 5 PM, Sat 10 AM - 5 PM Sept - May & by appointment during acad yr; Estab 1909 to provide resource material for the Mus Depts; Maintains non-circulating collection only
Library Holdings: Auction Catalogs, Book Volumes 50,000, Exhibition Catalogs, Other Holdings Auction & sale catalogues, Pamphlets, Periodical Subscriptions 100, Slides
Special Subjects: Advertising Design, Aesthetics, Afro-American Art, American Indian Art, American Western Art, Anthropology, Antiquities-Assyrian, Antiquities-Byzantine, Antiquities-Egyptian, Antiquities-Etruscan, Antiquities-Greek, Antiquities-Oriental, Antiquities-Persian, Antiquities-Roman, Archaeology, Art Education, Art History, Asian Art, Bookplates & Bindings, Bronzes, Calligraphy, Carpets & Rugs, Coins & Medals, Collages, Commercial Art, Conceptual Art, Constructions, Crafts, Decorative Arts, Dioramas, Display, Dolls, Drafting, Drawings, Embroidery, Enamels, Eskimo Art, Etchings & Engravings, Ethnology, Fashion Arts, Film, Flasks & Bottles, Folk Art, Furniture, Glass, Goldsmithing, Graphic Arts, Graphic Design, Handicrafts, Historical Material, History of Art & Archaeology, Illustration, Industrial Design, Interior Design, Intermedia, Islamic Art, Ivory, Jade, Jewelry, Judaica, Laces, Landscape Architecture, Landscapes, Latin American Art, Leather, Lettering, Manuscripts, Maps, Marine Painting, Metalwork, Mexican Art, Painting-American, Painting-European, Painting-Flemish, Miniatures, Mixed Media, Mosaics, Oriental Art
Exhibitions: Periodic book displays related to museum exhibitions and special library collections
Activities: Tours

M **WORCESTER CENTER FOR CRAFTS,** Krikorian Gallery, 25 Sagamore Rd, Worcester, MA 01605-3914. Tel 508-753-8183; Fax 508-797-5626; Email wcc@worcestercraftcenter.org; Web: www.worcestercraftcenter.org; *Exec Dir* Barbara Walzer; *Pub Rels & Mktg* Amy Black; *Develop* David Leach
Open Mon, Wed, Fri 10AM - 5:30 PM, Tues & Thurs 10AM-7:30PM, Sat 10 AM - 5 PM, cl Sun; No admis fee; Estab 1856 for educational exhibits of historic & contemporary crafts; Professionally lighted & installed 40 x 60 gallery with six major shows per yr in main gallery; Average Annual Attendance: 20,000; Mem: 1000; dues $40 & up
Income: Financed by mem, grants, contributions & endowment
Special Subjects: Crafts
Collections: Collection contains 200 books, 2000 Kodachromes, 300 photographs
Exhibitions: 10 exhibits per yr; major exhibit focus on 3-D art, reflects work from studio-visual art
Publications: On-Center, newsletter; school for professional crafts brochures; 3 course catalogs, yearly
Activities: Classes for adults & children; weekend professional workshops; 2 yr full-time progs in professional crafts; lects open to pub, 4 vis lectrs per yr; gallery talks; tours; schols & fels offered; City Outreach Prog brings crafts to pub schools; book traveling exhibs 2 per yr; originates traveling exhibs anywhere in Massachusetts; supply shop & gift shop sell books, original craft objects

MICHIGAN

ADRIAN

M **SIENA HEIGHTS COLLEGE,** Klemm Gallery, Studio Angelico, 1247 E Siena Heights Dr, Adrian, MI 49221-1755. Tel 517-264-7860; Fax 517-264-7739; Email creising@sienahts.edu; Web: www.sienaheights.edu/~art; *Dir* Dr Peter Barr
Open Tues- Fri 9 AM - 4 PM, Sun Noon - 4 PM, cl major holidays & summers; No admis fee; Estab 1970's to offer cultural programs to Lenawee County & others; Average Annual Attendance: 6,000
Income: Funded by college
Exhibitions: Invitational Artists Shows; major national culturally-based exhibitions; professional artists & student shows; fall semester 3 month-long solo or group exhibitions
Activities: Classes for adults; lects open to public, gallery talks; tours; performances; scholarships offered

L **Art Library**, 1247 E Siena Heights Dr, Adrian, MI 49221-1755. Tel 517-264-7152; Fax 517-264-7711; Email sbeck@sienahts.edu; Web: www.sienahts.edu/~libr/library.htm; *Pub Servs Librn* Melissa M Sissen; *Cataloging* Mark Dombrowski
Open Mon - Fri 8:30 AM - 11 PM, Sat Noon - 5 PM, Sun 1 - 11 PM
Income: Funded by college
Library Holdings: Audio Tapes, Book Volumes 10,000, Cards, Cassettes, Clipping Files, Fiche, Filmstrips, Pamphlets, Periodical Subscriptions 35, Photographs, Records, Reels, Slides, Video Tapes

ALBION

M **ALBION COLLEGE,** Bobbitt Visual Arts Center, 611 E Porter, Albion, MI 49224. Tel 517-629-0246; Fax 517-629-0752; Email art@albion.edu; Web: www.albion.edu; *Prof* Lynne Chytilo, MFA; *Prof Emer* Frank Machek, MFA; *Prof Emeritus* Douglas Goering, MFA; *Prof* Dr Bille Wickre, PhD; *Prof* Anne McCauley, MFA; *Assoc Prof & Dept Chair* Michael Dixon; *Asst Prof* Ashley Feagin
Open Mon - Thurs 9 AM - 9 PM, Fri 9 AM - 5 PM, Sat 10 AM - 2 PM; No admis fee; Estab 1835 to offer art educ at col level & gen art exhib prog for campus community & pub; Maintains one large gallery & one print gallery; Average Annual Attendance: 500
Income: Privately funded
Library Holdings: Lantern Slides, Manuscripts, Original Art Works, Prints, Sculpture
Special Subjects: African Art, Asian Art, Carpets & Rugs, Ceramics, Decorative Arts, Etchings & Engravings, Folk Art, Furniture, Glass, Prints, Southwestern Art, Painting-American, Textiles, Woodcuts
Collections: African Art, ceramics, glass, prints
Exhibitions: From the Print Collection; Pieces from the Permanent Collection; various one-person & group exhibitions, contemporary artists
Activities: Lects open to pub, 4-8 vis lectrs per yr; gallery talks; competitions with awards; scholarships offered; individual paintings & original objects of art lent to acad institutions, museums & galleries; lending collection contains 2350 original prints; originate traveling exhibs

ALPENA

M **BESSER MUSEUM FOR NORTHEAST MICHIGAN,** (Jesse Besser Museum), 491 Johnson St, Alpena, MI 49707-1496. Tel 989-356-2202; Fax 989-356-3133; Email sanderson@bessermuseum.org; Web: www.bessermuseum.org; *Dir* Janet Smoak, PhD
Open Mon - Sat 10 AM - 5 PM, Sun Noon - 4 PM; Admis adults $5, seniors, students & children $3; Estab assoc 1962, building open to pub 1966, an accredited mus of history, science & art serving northern Michigan; Mus has a research library, a planetarium, a Foucault Pendulum, Indian artifact collection, Ave of shops, lumbering exhibits & preserved furnished historical buildings on grounds. Also on grounds, sculptured fountain by artist Glen Michaels. Three galleries are utilized for shows, traveling exhibits, & changing exhibitions of the Museum's collection of modern art & art prints, decorative arts & furniture. There are 260 running ft of wall space on lower level, 1250 sq ft & 16 45 sq ft on upper level galleries; Average Annual Attendance: 25,000
Income: Financed by Besser Foundation, federal & state grants, private gifts & donations, Museums Founders Soc, Operation Support Grant from Michigan Council for the Arts, & other sources
Special Subjects: American Indian Art, Archaeology, Ceramics, Costumes, Crafts, Decorative Arts, Dioramas, Dolls, Drawings, Etchings & Engravings, Folk Art, Furniture, Glass, Graphics, Laces, Landscapes, Manuscripts, Maps, Marine Painting, Painting-American, Photography, Porcelain, Posters, Pottery, Prints, Anthropology, Textiles
Collections: Art prints, Clewell pottery, contemporary Native American art, maps of the Great Lakes, modern art, photography
Exhibitions: Changing exhibitions of all major collecting areas & touring exhibits; Northeast Michigan Juried Art
Activities: Classes for adults & children; art workshops; seminars; docent training; lects open to pub, 5 vis lectrs per yr; gallery talks; tours; competitions with awards; book traveling exhibs 8 per yr; originate traveling exhibs; mus shop sells books, magazines, original art, handicrafts

L **Philip M Park Library**, 491 Johnson St, Alpena, MI 49707-1496. Tel 517-356-2202; Fax 517-356-2202; Email cwitulski@bessermuseum.org; Web: www.bessermuseum.org; *Dir* Christine Witulski; *Exhibs Dir* Randy Shultz
Open Tues - Sat 10 AM - 5 PM; Admis adults $5, children 5 - 7 & seniors $3; Museum estab 1966; Art, history & science exhibits; Average Annual Attendance: 25,000
Library Holdings: Book Volumes 4200, Cassettes, Clipping Files, Exhibition Catalogs, Fiche, Manuscripts, Maps, Original Documents, Pamphlets, Periodical Subscriptions 46, Photographs, Prints, Reels, Slides, Video Tapes

Special Subjects: American Indian Art, Architecture, Art History, Ceramics, Decorative Arts, Dolls, Flasks & Bottles, Folk Art, Glass, Painting-American, Pottery, Printmaking, Prints, Restoration & Conservation
Collections: History, art, & science
Activities: Educ prog; classes for adults & children; docent training; gallery talks, tours, competitions

ANN ARBOR

A **ANN ARBOR ART CENTER,** Art Center, 117 W Liberty, Ann Arbor, MI 48104. Tel 734-994-8004, ext 110; Fax 734-994-3610; Email a2artcen@aol.com; Web: www.annarborartcenter.org; Telex
101; *CEO & Pres* Marsha Chamberlin; *Gallery Dir* Terry Browning; *Dir Operations* Eric Wolff
Open Mon - Fri 10 AM - 6 PM, Sat 10 AM - 6 PM, Sun Noon - 5:30 PM; Estab 1909 to provide for the well-being of the visual arts through programs that encourage participation in & support for the visual arts, as well as foster artistic development; Maintains 750 sq ft of exhibit gallery space with monthly shows; & 1300 sq ft sales - rental gallery next to exhibit areas; classes in studio art & art appreciation; special events; Average Annual Attendance: 52,000; Mem: 1300; dues vary; annual meeting in Feb
Income: Financed by mem, Michigan Council for the Arts grant, rental of studios & retail sales
Exhibitions: 8 juried & nonjuried shows throughout yr
Publications: Class catalog, quarterly; gallery announcements, monthly; lecture listings, quarterly; newsletter, quarterly
Activities: Classes for adults & children; artist workshops on professional development; lect open to public, 4-6 vis lectrs per year; gallery talks; tours; competitions with prizes; scholarships offered; exten dept lends individual paintings & original objects of art to organizations & community facilities; sales shop sells original art & fine contemporary crafts

A **ARTRAIN, INC,** 1100 N Main St Ste 106, Ann Arbor, MI 48104-1059. Tel 734-747-8300; Fax 734-747-8530; Email info@artrainusa.org; Web: www.artrainUSA.org; *Chmn* Burt Althaver; *Exec Dir* Debra Polich
No admis fee; Estab 1971 to tour major art exhibits throughout the nation & provide catalyst for community arts development; Traveling art museum in a train; consists of converted railroad cars with large walls & cases; Average Annual Attendance: 122,000
Income: Financed by endowment, state appropriation, individual foundation & corporation campaigns
Publications: Exhibition catalogs; newsletter
Activities: Classes for children; docent training; lects open to pub; competitions; book traveling exhibs; mus shop sells exhibs related items

A **MICHIGAN GUILD OF ARTISTS & ARTISANS,** Michigan Guild Gallery, 118 N Fourth Ave, Ann Arbor, MI 48104. Tel 734-662-3382; Fax 734-662-0339; Email info@theguild.org; Web: www.michiganguild.org; *Gallery Coordr* Esther Kirshenbaum; *Gallery Coordr* Pamela Stoddard; *Exec Dir* Debra Clayton; *Receptionist* Audrey Libke
Open Mon - Fri 9 AM - 5 PM; No admis fee; Estab with no percentage, small artist fee for artists who have never had an exhib locally & artists with new, unshown work; Small, street level; highly thought of locally; Average Annual Attendance: 2,000; Mem: 1100; dues $45-$75; annual meeting in July
Income: Financed by mem fees & art fair fees
Publications: Mem newsletter, bi-monthly
Activities: Educ dept provides workshops; lect open to public; concerts; member art shown in pub places

M **UNIVERSITY OF MICHIGAN,** Museum of Art, 525 S State St, Ann Arbor, MI 48109-1354. Tel 734-764-0395; Fax 734-764-3731; Email umma.info@umich.edu; Web: www.umma.umich.edu; *Dir* Christina Olsen; *Deputy Dir Educ* Ruth Slavin; *Deputy Dir Devel & External Relations* Carrie Throm
OpenTues - Sat 11 AM - 5 PM, Sun noon - 5 PM; No admis fee, $10 suggested donation; Estab 1946, as a university art mus & mus for the Ann Arbor community; Average Annual Attendance: 225,000; Mem: 1400; dues individual $50
Income: Financed by state appropriation other federal and state agencies, and private donations
Special Subjects: African Art, Afro-American Art, American Western Art, Asian Art, Baroque Art, Etchings & Engravings, Landscapes, Medieval Art, Painting-American, Painting-European, Painting-Flemish, Painting-Italian, Painting-Japanese, Photography, Porcelain, Portraits, Prints, Religious Art, Renaissance Art, Restorations, Sculpture, Stained Glass, Tapestries, Watercolors
Collections: Arts of the Western World from the Sixth Century AD to the Present, Asian, Near Eastern, African & Oceanic, including ceramics, contemporary art, decorative art, graphic arts, manuscripts, painting, sculpture, James McNeill Whistler Collection
Publications: Bulletin of the Museum of Art & Archaeology, irregular; bimonthly Insight, Catalogues & Gallery Brochures, irregular
Activities: Classes for adults & children, dramatic programs, visiting writers series, film series, Educ dept; docent training; community days; lects open to pub, vis lectrs; gallery talks; tours; concerts; individual paintings & original objects of art lent to other mus; originate traveling exhibs to national & international mus; mus shop sells publications, posters, postcards & gifts, original art, prints

M **Kelsey Museum of Archaeology**, 434 State St, Ann Arbor, MI 48109-1390. Tel 734-764-9304; Fax 734-763-8976; Web: www.lsa.umich.edu/kelsey; *Dir* Sharon C Herbert; *Cur* Elaine K Gazda; *Assoc Cur* Janet Richards; *Assoc Cur* Terry Wilfong; *Assoc Dir & Assoc Cur Educ* Lauren E Talalay; *Conservator* Suzanne Davis; *Exhibit Preparator* Scott Meier; *Coordr of Mus Visitor Programs* Todd Gerring; *Cur* Margaret Root; *Conservator* Claudia Chemello; *Communs Ed* Margaret Lourse; *Mus Coll Mgr* Michelle Fortenot; *Mus Coll Mgr* Sebastian Encina; *Adminr* Helen Baker; *Assoc Prof* Nicholas Terrenato; *Assoc Prof* Christopher Ratte
Open Tues - Fri 9 AM - 4 PM, Sat - Sun 1-4 PM, cl Mon & univ holidays; No admis fee; Estab 1928; Seven galleries are maintained; Average Annual Attendance: 37,000
Income: State, Grants, Tuition
Special Subjects: Antiquities-Egyptian, Antiquities-Greek, Antiquities-Roman, Bronzes, Ivory, Pottery, Sculpture, Textiles
Collections: Objects of the Graeco-Roman period from excavations conducted by the University of Michigan in Egypt & Iraq, Greece, Etruria, Rome & provinces: sculpture, inscriptions, pottery, bronzes, terracottas, Egyptian antiquities dynastic through Roman, Roman & Islamic glass, bone & ivory objects, textiles, coins, 19th century photographs
Publications: Biannual newsletter; Bulletin of the Museums of Art & Archaeology, irregular; Kelsey Museum Studies Series, irregular
Activities: Educ dept; classes for children; lects open to pub, 4 vis lectrs per yr; tours, gallery talks; original objects of art lent to other mus upon request; book traveling exhibs; originate traveling exhibs to mus with similar collections; Mus shop sells books, reproductions

M **Jean Paul Slusser Gallery**, 2000 Bonisteel Dr, School of Art & Design Ann Arbor, MI 48109-2069. Tel 734-936-2082; Fax 734-615-6761; Email slussergallery@umich.edu; Web: www.umich.edu/~webteam/SOAD/; *Dir* Mark Nielsen
Open Tues & Thurs Noon - 8 PM, Wed, Fri, Sat & Sun 11 AM - 4 PM; No admis fee; Estab 1974; Gallery is located on the main floor of the Art & Architecture Building. Comprised of 3600 sq ft of exhibition space; Average Annual Attendance: 11,000
Income: Financed by School of Art general fund
Collections: Artifacts of the School's history, works by faculty & alumni of the University of Michigan School of Art
Exhibitions: Emese Benczur; Olafur Eliasson; Annika Eriksson; Anna Gaskell; Liam Gillick; Carsten Holler; Pierre Huyghe; Koo Jeong-a; Aernout Mik; Manfred Pernice; Stephanie Rowden; Superflex; Apolonija Sustersic; Elin Wikstrom; Andrea Zittel
Publications: catalogues
Activities: Lects open to pub, 11 vis lectrs per yr; gallery talks; books 2 traveling exhibs per yr; sales shop sells books

L **Asian Art Archives**, 525 S State St, Ann Arbor, MI 48109-1354. Tel 734-764-5555; Fax 734-647-4121; Email wholden@umich.edu; *Sr Assoc Cur* Wendy Holden
Open Mon - Fri 9 AM - 5 PM; Estab 1962 for study & research. Contains 180,000 black & white photographs of Asian art objects or monuments. Library also houses the Asian Art Photographic Distribution, a nonprofit bus selling visual resource materials dealing with Chinese & Japanese art. Houses Southeast Asia Art Foundation Collection of 100,000 slides & photographs of Southeast Asian art; For research only
Income: $5000 (financed by endowment, federal funds)
Purchases: $4000 - $5000
Library Holdings: Book Volumes 50, Clipping Files, Exhibition Catalogs, Fiche 10,000, Other Holdings Black/white negatives 26,000, Photographs 80,000, Reels, Reproductions 3000, Slides
Special Subjects: Architecture, Art History, Asian Art, Bronzes, Calligraphy, Ceramics, Coins & Medals, Decorative Arts, Glass, Gold, Graphic Arts, Islamic Art, Ivory, Jade, Landscapes
Collections: National Palace Museum, Taiwan, photographic archive, Chinese art, painting, decorative arts, Southeast Asian Art Archive, sculpture, architecture, Islamic Art Archive, Asian Art Archive, Chinese & Japanese arts, painting
Publications: Newsletter, East Asian Art & Archaeology (three issues per year)

L **Fine Arts Library**, 855 S University Ave, 260 Tappan Hall Ann Arbor, MI 48109-1357. Tel 734-764-5405; Fax 734-764-5408; Email finearts@umich.edu; Web: www.lib.umich.edu/finearts; *Head Fine Arts Library, Head Librn* Deirdre Spencer; *Information Resources Specialist* Jessica DuVerneay; *Information Resources Asst* Myrtle Hudson; *Information Resources Supv* Nancy Damm
Open Mon - Thurs 8 AM - 10 PM, Fri 8 AM - 5 PM, Sat 1 PM - 6 PM, Sun 1 - 10 PM, summer hours Mon - Thurs 8 AM - 8 PM, Fri 8 AM - 5 PM, Sun 1 - 5 PM, cl Sat; Estab 1949, to support the acad programs of the History of the Art Department, including research of faculty & graduate students; Circ 17,200
Income: Financed by state appropriation
Library Holdings: Book Volumes 100,000, CD-ROMs, Compact Disks, Exhibition Catalogs, Fiche, Filmstrips, Other Holdings Marburger index of photographic documentation of art in Germany, Pamphlets, Periodical Subscriptions 232, Reels
Special Subjects: Afro-American Art, American Indian Art, American Western Art, Antiquities-Assyrian, Antiquities-Byzantine, Antiquities-Egyptian, Antiquities-Etruscan, Antiquities-Greek, Antiquities-Oriental, Antiquities-Persian, Antiquities-Roman, Art History, Asian Art, Bronzes, Calligraphy, Carpets & Rugs, Cartoons, Ceramics, Conceptual Art, Decorative Arts, Embroidery, Film, Folk Art, Furniture, History of Art & Archaeology, Islamic Art, Ivory, Jade, Jewelry, Judaica, Latin American Art, Mexican Art, Miniatures, Mixed Media, Mosaics, Oriental Art, Painting-American, Painting-British, Painting-Dutch, Painting-European, Painting-Flemish, Painting-French, Painting-German, Painting-Israeli, Painting-Italian, Painting-Japanese, Painting-Russian, Painting-Spanish, Photography, Porcelain, Portraits, Pottery, Primitive art, Prints, Religious Art, Sculpture, Silver, Stained Glass, Tapestries, Textiles, Watercolors
Activities: Educ prog; library instruction

L **Department of the History of Art, Visual Resources Collection**, 855 S University Ave, 110 Tappan Hall Ann Arbor, MI 48109-1357. Tel 734-764-5400; Fax 734-647-4121
Open by appt only for Asian Art archives; Estab 1911, as a library for teaching & research collection of slides & photos of art objects; limited commercial distribution; nonprofit slide distribution projects; (Asian Art Photographic Distribution; Univ of Mich Slide Distribution); For in-house research only
Income: Financed by state appropriation
Library Holdings: Lantern Slides, Photographs 200,000, Reproductions, Slides 290,000
Special Subjects: History of Art & Archaeology
Collections: Islamic Archives, Palace Museum Archive (Chinese painting), Romanesque Archive (sculpture & some architecture concentrating on Burgundy, Southwestern France, Spain & southern Italy), Southeast Asian & Indian Archives
Activities: Materials lent only to University of Michigan faculty & students; archive materials may not be circulated, restrictions apply

L **Media Union Library**, 2281 Bonisteel Blvd, Ann Arbor, MI 48109-2094. Tel 734-647-5735; Fax 734-764-4487; Email mu.ref@umich.edu; Web: www.lib.umich.edu…mmu\; *Visual Resources Librn & Selector Art & Design,*

Architecture & Urban Planning Librn Rebecca Price; *Head Librn & Dir Arts & Engineering Librs* Michael D Miller; *Art & Design Field Librn* Annette Haines
Open 24 hours daily for students, 8 AM - 10 PM for non-students; Estab to support the teaching & research activities of the School of Art & the College of Architecture & Urban Planning
Library Holdings: Audio Tapes, Book Volumes 75,000, CD-ROMs 120, Cards, Cassettes 100, Clipping Files, DVDs 10, Exhibition Catalogs, Fiche, Filmstrips, Kodachrome Transparencies, Lantern Slides 17,000, Manuscripts, Maps 100, Micro Print, Original Art Works, Other Holdings Digital Images 20,000, Pamphlets, Periodical Subscriptions 400, Photographs 30,000, Reels, Sculpture, Slides 105,000, Video Tapes 1350
Special Subjects: Tapestries
Activities: 1500 computer workstations with various software

BATTLE CREEK

M **ART CENTER OF BATTLE CREEK,** 265 E Emmett St, Battle Creek, MI 49017-4601. Tel 269-962-9511; Fax 269-969-3838; Email artcenterofbc@yahoo.com; Web: www.artcenterofbattlecreek.org; *Exec Dir* Linda Holderbaum; *Assistant to Executive Director* Michelle Dunkelberger
Open Tues- Fri 10 AM - 5 PM, Sat 11AM-3PM, cl Aug & legal holidays; Admis adults $3, seniors & students $2; Estab 1948 to offer classes for children & adults & to present monthly exhibitions of professional work; Two galleries of varying sizes with central vaulted ceiling gallery, track lighting & security; Average Annual Attendance: 30,000; Mem: 750; dues $15; annual meeting in Sept
Income: Financed by mem, endowment fund, grants, UAC, special projects, tuition, sales of artwork
Special Subjects: Costumes, Textiles, Decorative Arts, Photography, Prints, Drawings, Graphics, Sculpture, Calligraphy
Collections: Michigan Art Collection featuring 20th century Michigan artists
Exhibitions: Group & Solo Shows: Paintings; Photography; Prints; Sculpture; Crafts; American Art 40s & 50s; Artist's competitions
Publications: Newsletter, bi-monthly
Activities: Classes for adults & children; docent training; workshops & progs; lects open to pub, 5 vis lectrs per yr; gallery talks; tours; competitions with prizes; scholarships offered; individual paintings & original objects of art lent to qualified institutions; book traveling exhibs 1-2 per yr; originate traveling exhibs to mus & art centers; mus shop sells original art by Michigan artists; KidSpace hands-on gallery

L **Michigan Art & Artist Archives**, 265 E Emmett St, Battle Creek, MI 49017-4601. Tel 616-962-9511; Fax 616-969-3838; Email artcenterofbc@yahoo.com; Web: www.artcenterofbattlecreek.org; *Exec Dir* Linda Holderbaum; *Asst to Exec Dir* Michelle Dunkelberger
Open Tues - Fri - 10 AM - 5 PM, Sat 11 AM - 3 PM; Admis adults $3, seniors & students $2, free Thurs; Estab 1946; 2 exhib galleries; Average Annual Attendance: 10,000; Mem: 300
Library Holdings: Book Volumes 550, Clipping Files, Exhibition Catalogs, Original Art Works, Periodical Subscriptions 12, Photographs, Sculpture, Slides
Special Subjects: Afro-American Art, American Indian Art, Antiquities-Egyptian, Art History
Collections: MI-Art, Michigan Art Coll - 200 pieces of 2-D + 3-D work by Michigan Arts
Exhibitions: Exhibs change monthly
Activities: Classes for adults & children; docent training; lects open to pub; gallery talks; tours; sponsoring of competitions; sales shop; original art

BAY CITY

M **BAY COUNTY HISTORICAL SOCIETY,** Historical Museum of Bay County, 321 Washington Ave, Bay City, MI 48708-5837. Tel 989-893-5733; Fax 989-893-5741; Web: www.bchsmuseum.org; *Exec Dir* Gay McInerney
Open Mon - Fri 10 AM - 5 PM, Sat Noon - 4 PM; No admis fee; Estab 1919 to preserve, collect, & interpret the historical materials of Bay County; 2 new permanent galleries; 1 features 7 period rooms; the other interactive displays - Selling Mrs. Consumer & Bay City: Seaport to the World; Average Annual Attendance: 60,000; Mem: 500; dues corporate $500, patron $100, small bus $50, sustaining $25; annual meeting in Apr
Income: Financed by mem, gift shop, county funds
Special Subjects: American Indian Art, Anthropology, Archaeology, Crafts, Decorative Arts, Historical Material, Landscapes, Period Rooms, Photography, Textiles
Collections: Hand crafts, photographs, portraits, quilts, Patrol Craft Sailor Assn National Collections, mid-1800 - post WW II historical material, native American materials & paintings, sugar beet history (memorabilia & materials)
Publications: Anishinabe - People of Saginaw; Ghost Towns & Place Names; Historic Architecture of Bay City, Michigan; Vanished Industries; Women of Bay County
Activities: Classes for adults & children; home tours; historical encampment; living history progs; traveling displays & educational kits; lects open to pub, 2-3 vis lectrs per yr; gallery talks; tours; mus shop sells books, reproductions, hand crafts, historical gifts

BIRMINGHAM

A **BIRMINGHAM BLOOMFIELD ART CENTER,** Art Center, 1516 S Cranbrook Rd, Birmingham, MI 48009-1855. Tel 248-644-0866; Fax 248-644-7904; Web: www.bbartcenter.org; *Pres & CEO* Annie Van Gelderen; *VP Progs* Cynthia K Mills; *VP Finance* Gwenn Rosseau; *Educ* Debra Callahan; *Exhib* Amy Kantgias
Open Mon - Thurs 9 AM - 6 PM, Fri & Sat 9 AM - 5 PM; No admis fee; Estab 1957 to provide a community-wide, integrated studio-gallery art center; to enhance life within our region by promoting the appreciation and understanding of the arts; 4 gallery spaces; Average Annual Attendance: 30,000; Mem: 2000; dues $50 & up; annual meeting in May
Income: $1,500,000 (financed by mem, tuitions, special events funding & donations)
Collections: Sol LeWitt Wall Drawing
Exhibitions: Annual Michigan Fine Arts Competition; juried exhibits & competitions; local high school exhibit; local and regional artist groups; traveling exhibition
Publications: Class brochure; bi-annual newsletter
Activities: Classes for adults & children; competitions with prizes; holiday shop; children's art camps and interdisciplinary art camps; annual festival; scholarships offered; gallery shop sells original art

BLOOMFIELD HILLS

M **CRANBROOK ART MUSEUM,** 39221 Woodward Ave, Bloomfield Hills, MI 48303; Box 801, Bloomfield Hills, MI 48303-0801. Tel 248-645-3323; Fax 248-645-3324; Email artmuseum@cranbrook.edu; Web: www.cranbrook.edu; *Admin Mgr* Kim Larsen; *Preparator* Mark Baker; *Dir* Greg Wittkopp; *Registrar* Roberta Frey Gilboe; *Cur. Education* Kelly S. Lyons; *Cur. Art & Design* Laura Mott
See website for hours; Estab 1930; Modern and contemporary art, crafts, architectural and design museum; Average Annual Attendance: 37,000; Mem: 900; dues family $75, individual $50
Special Subjects: Architecture, Ceramics, Crafts, Decorative Arts, Drawings, Etchings & Engravings, Furniture, Graphics, Metalwork, Painting-American, Photography, Porcelain, Pottery, Prints, Sculpture, Silver, Tapestries, Textiles
Collections: Artists associated with Cranbrook Academy of Art: ceramics by Maija Grotell, architectural drawings & decorative arts by Eliel Saarinen, porcelains by Adelaide Robineau, sculpture by Carl Milles, contemporary paintings, 19th century prints, study coll of textiles, Shuey Collection: paintings and sculptures by Albers, Dubuffet, Judd, de Kooning, Lichtenstein, Martin, Motherwell, Rauschenberg, Riley, Stella, Warhol and more
Exhibitions: 13 exhibitions annually of contemporary art, architecture & design
Activities: Docent training; dramatic progs; lects open to pub, 18 vis lectrs per yr; gallery talks; tours; concerts; individual paintings & original objects of art lent to other institutions; book traveling exhibs 1-2 per yr; originate traveling exhibs & circulate to other mus national & international; mus shop sells books, magazines, original art, reproductions, gift items & cards

L **Library**, 39221 Woodward Ave, Bloomfield Hills, MI 48303-0801; PO Box 801, Bloomfield Hills, MI 48303-0801. Tel 248-645-3355; Fax 248-645-3464; Web: www.cranbrookart.edu/library; *Dir Library* Judy Dyki; *Librn* Mary Beth Kreiner; *Library Asst* Elizabeth Dizik
Open Mon & Thurs 9 AM - 8 PM, Fri 9 AM - 5 PM, Sat & Sun 1 PM - 5 PM; Estab 1928 to support research needs of Art Academy & Mus; Library is for Academy students, faculty & staff; open to pub for reference only
Income: Financed by academy
Library Holdings: Audio Tapes, Book Volumes 29,000, Cassettes 800, Clipping Files, DVDs 1,600, Exhibition Catalogs, Other Holdings Masters theses, Periodical Subscriptions 190, Video Tapes 1,400
Special Subjects: Architecture, Art History, Ceramics, Graphic Arts, Metalwork, Photography, Printmaking, Sculpture

BYRON CENTER

M **VAN SINGEL FINE ARTS CENTER,** Van Singel Art Gallery, 8500 Burlingame SW, Byron Center, MI 49315. Tel 616-678-6801; Fax 616-878-6820; Email cindiford11@gmail.com; Email kathyrichards@bcpslc12.net; Web: vsfac.com; *Cur, Contact* Cindi Ford; *House Mgr* Kathy Richards
Open Mon - Fri noon - 5 PM; Free; Estab 1998
Activities: dramatic programs; concerts

DAVISBURG

M **THE ART CAFE,** 7700 Dilley Rd, Davisburg, MI 48350-2639. Tel 248-210-0862; Email staff@artcafeonline.org; Web: www.artcafeonline.org; *Exec Dir* Cora Smilkovich; *Treas* Kurt C Kohl; *Secy* Andrew Sumner
Admis. donations accepted; Estab. 12/03 to provide a space for artists to create & exhibit art with an outreach component to promote emerging & established art & native art awareness; Exhibit space onsite & outreach exhibits
Activities: Classes for adults; concerts; gallery talks tours; sponsoring of competitions; awards

DEARBORN

M **ACCESS,** Arab American National Museum, 13624 Michigan Ave, Dearborn, MI 48126-3519. Tel 313-582-AANM; Fax 313-582-1086; Email aanm@accesscommunity.org; Web: www.arabamericanmuseum.org; *Dir* Devon Akmon
Open Wed - Sat 10 AM - 6 PM, Sun 12 - 5 PM, cl Mon & Tues, New Year's Day, Thanksgiving Day & Christmas Day; Admis adults $8, seniors 62 & up, students w/ ID & children 6 - 12 $4, children 5 & under no admis fee; 2005. Mus maintains library & resource center; Average Annual Attendance: 35,000; Mem: 3,000; $75 family, twice yr
Library Holdings: Audio Tapes, CD-ROMs, Compact Disks, DVDs, Manuscripts, Maps, Motion Pictures, Original Documents, Pamphlets, Periodical Subscriptions, Photographs
Special Subjects: Calligraphy, Ceramics, Costumes, Decorative Arts, Drawings, Ethnology, Furniture, Glass, Graphics, Historical Material, Islamic Art, Jewelry, Manuscripts, Maps, Metalwork, Mosaics, Oriental Art, Photography, Posters, Pottery, Religious Art, Reproductions, Sculpture, Textiles, Woodcarvings
Collections: Art, three-dimensional artifacts, documents, personal papers, photographs
Exhibitions: "Coming to America" is an exhibit that examines the history of Arab American immigration from 1500 to the present, with spec emphasis on waves of

immigration since the 1800s; "Living in America" focuses on the life of Arab Americans in the US at different time periods, and examines such topics as family life, religion, activism and political involvement, institution-building, work, and leisure.; Making an Impact highlights the contributions of individuals and community organizations; Rotating/temporary exhibits
Activities: Adult & children classes; docent training; lects open to pub; concerts; tours avail by appt; awards: Arab American National Museum Book Award; mus shop sells books, reproductions & prints

M **DEARBORN COMMUNITY ARTS COUNCIL,** Padzieski Art Gallery, 15801 Michigan Ave, Dearborn, MI 48126-2904. Tel 313-943-3095; Fax 313-943-2368; Email rvaldez@ci.dearborn.mi.us; Web: dcacarts.org; *Exec Dir* Ralph Valdez
Open Tues - Fri Noon - 6 PM; Estab 1989 as the city's first public art gallery; Mem: dues $20-$750
Collections: Features local & regional artists
Exhibitions: Rotating exhibits
Activities: Educ progs; classes for children; Community progs & events

C **FORD MOTOR COMPANY,** Henry Ford Museum & Greenfield Village, 20900 Oakwood Blvd, Dearborn, MI 48124-4088. Tel 313-982-6001; Web: www.hfmgv.org; *Dir Media & Film Relations* Wendy Metrou; *Mgr* Kate Storey; *Mgr* Carrie Nolan
Open daily 9:30 AM - 5 PM, cl Christmas & Thanksgiving; Admis adult $15, seniors (62+ & active military) $14, youth (5-12) $11, child 4 & under free; Estab 1929

DETROIT

M **CENTRAL UNITED METHODIST CHURCH,** Swords Into Plowshares Peace Center & Gallery, 33 E Adams St, Detroit, MI 48226. Tel 313-963-7575; Fax 313-963-2569; Email swordsintoplowshares313@gmail.com; Web: www.swordsintoplowsharesdetroit.org; *Dir* Clara Lawrence
Open Thurs - Sat 1 PM - 5 PM; No admis fee; Estab 1985 to use the arts for peace in the world; Main gallery 1,475 sq ft, height 13 ft 7 inches; multipurpose gallery 1,043 sq ft, height 7 ft 8 inches; second floor balcony gallery 357 sq ft, height 7 ft 3 inches. Maintains reference library; Average Annual Attendance: 7,000; Mem: 1800 supporters
Income: Financed by endowment, individuals, city & state appropriation, grants, sales, local churches
Library Holdings: Audio Tapes, Book Volumes, CD-ROMs, Cassettes, Clipping Files, Compact Disks, Exhibition Catalogs, Kodachrome Transparencies, Lantern Slides, Memorabilia, Original Art Works, Photographs, Reproductions, Sculpture, Slides, Video Tapes
Special Subjects: Afro-American Art, American Indian Art, Architecture, Calligraphy, Cartoons, Ceramics, Embroidery, Etchings & Engravings, Folk Art, Graphics, Landscapes, Maps, Painting-American, Painting-Australian, Painting-Canadian, Painting-French, Painting-German, Painting-Israeli, Painting-Japanese, Posters, Pottery, Prints, Religious Art, Reproductions, Woodcarvings
Collections: Peace Art Collection (permanent)
Publications: Harbinger Newsletter, 3-4 times per year; periodic exhibit catalogs
Activities: Classes for adults & children; docent training; 4 -6 concerts per yr; lects open to pub; concerts; gallery talks; tours; individual paintings & original objects of art lent to groups, events; book traveling exhibs, 4-5 exhibits per yr; traveling exhibs to churches, other galleries & events; mus shop sells books, original art, reproductions, prints, cards, t-shirts, posters & buttons

L **COLLEGE FOR CREATIVE STUDIES,** College of Art & Design Library, Manoogian Visual Resource Center, 301 Frederick Douglass Dr Detroit, MI 48202-4034. Tel 313-664-7642; Fax 313-664-7880; Email bwalker@collegeforcreativestudies.edu; Web: www.ccscad.edu; *Dir* Beth Walker
Open Mon - Thurs 8 AM - 10 AM, Fri 8 AM - 6 PM, Sat 10 AM - 5 PM, Sun 1 PM - 7 PM; Estab 1966 to serve students & faculty of an undergraduate art school. Primarily a how-to, illustrative collection
Income: Financed by private school
Library Holdings: Book Volumes 23,000, Exhibition Catalogs, Periodical Subscriptions 72, Slides 70,000
Special Subjects: Advertising Design, Crafts, Graphic Design, Industrial Design, Photography

M **DETROIT ARTISTS MARKET,** 4719 Woodward Ave, Detroit, MI 48201-1307. Tel 313-832-8540; Fax 313-832-8543; Email info@detroitartistsmarket.org; Web: www.detroitartistsmarket.org
Open Tues - Sat 11 AM - 6 PM; No admis fee, donations accepted; Estab 1932 to educate pub & promote, exhibit & sell artwork by local Michigan artists; Average Annual Attendance: 10,000; Mem: 500; dues $25 - $2500
Income: $340,000 (financed by endowment, mem, state appropriation, mini-grants, MCA, contributions, percent of art work sales)
Exhibitions: Small Group Exhibition; All Media Juried Exhibition; The Garden Sale.; Art For The Holidays; Scholarship Show
Publications: catalogs for targeted exhibs; artists' statements & show information for exhibs
Activities: Educ prog; lects open to pub; tours; gallery talks; competitions with awards; schols offered; exten prog lends original objects of art to movie productions & local businesses; sales shop sells magazines, original art, prints & unique gift items

M **DETROIT INSTITUTE OF ARTS,** 5200 Woodward Ave, Detroit, MI 48202-4094. Tel 313-833-7900; Fax 313-833-3756; Web: www.dia.org; *Cur & Department Head Contemporary Art* Laurie Ann Farrell; *Co-Chief Cur* Nii Quarcoopome; *Dir Educ* Jennifer Czajkowski; *Head Conservator* Ellen Hanspach-Bernal; *Sr Cur European Paintings, Sculpture & Decorative Arts* Alan Darr; *Dir* Salvador Salart-Pans; *Cur Film* Elliot Wilhelm; *Cur African American Art* Valerie Mercer; *Cur American Art* Kenneth Meyers; *CFO* Robert Bowen
Open Tues - Thurs 9 AM - 4 PM, Fri 9 AM - 10 PM, Sat - Sun 10 AM - 5 PM, cl Mon, Tues & holidays; Admis adults $14, seniors $9, college students (w/ school ID) $8, youth 6-17 $6, children 5 & under & mems free, Detroit residence free on Fri; Estab & incorporated 1885 as Detroit Mus of Art; chartered as municipal department 1919 & name changed; original organization continued as Founders Soc Detroit Institute of Arts; present building opened 1927; Ford Wing addition completed 1966; Cavanagh Wing addition opened 1971. In 1998 the Founders Soc signed a 20 yr operating agreement with City of Detroit to run the DIA as a 501(c)(3) org; Average Annual Attendance: 500,000; Mem: 32,000 households; dues Chair Assoc $10,000, Dirs Assoc $5,000, Sustaining Assoc $3,000, Assoc $2,000, Conservator $1,000, Contributor $600, Patron $300, Affiliate $180, Family Plus $110, Individual $65, Senior Citizen (age 62 & over) $60
Library Holdings: Auction Catalogs, Audio Tapes, Book Volumes, Cassettes, Clipping Files, Compact Disks, DVDs, Exhibition Catalogs, Manuscripts, Original Documents, Pamphlets, Periodical Subscriptions, Photographs, Reels, Slides, Video Tapes
Special Subjects: African Art, Afro-American Art, Antiquities-Assyrian, Antiquities-Byzantine, Antiquities-Egyptian, Antiquities-Etruscan, Antiquities-Greek, Antiquities-Oriental, Antiquities-Persian, Antiquities-Roman, Archaeology, Architecture, Asian Art, Baroque Art, Bronzes, Calligraphy, Carpets & Rugs, Ceramics, Coins & Medals, Collages, Costumes, Crafts, Decorative Arts, Drawings, Embroidery, Enamels, Eskimo Art, Etchings & Engravings, Flasks & Bottles, Furniture, Glass, Gold, Graphics, Hispanic Art, Islamic Art, Ivory, Jade, Jewelry, Judaica, Laces, Landscapes, Latin American Art, Leather, Manuscripts, Maps, Marine Painting, Medieval Art, Metalwork, Mexican Art, Military Art, Miniatures, Mosaics, Oriental Art, Painting-American, Painting-Australian, Painting-British, Painting-Dutch, Painting-European, Painting-Flemish, Painting-German, Painting-Israeli, Painting-Italian, Painting-Japanese, Painting-New Zealand, Painting-Polish, Painting-Russian, Painting-Scandinavian, Painting-Spanish, Period Rooms, Pewter, Photography, Porcelain, Portraits, Posters, Pottery, Pre-Columbian Art, Prints, Religious Art, Renaissance Art, Restorations, Scrimshaw, Sculpture, Silver, Stained Glass, Tapestries, Textiles, Watercolors, Woodcarvings, Woodcuts
Collections: Robert H Tannahill Collection of Impressionist & Post Impressionist paintings, German Expressionist Art, African, Oceanic & New World Cultures, Elizabeth Parke Firestone Collection of 18th Century Silver, William Randolph Hearst Collection of Arms & Armor & Flemish Tapestries, Grace Whitney-Hoff Collection of Fine Bindings, Paul McPharlin Collection of Theatre & Graphic Arts
Publications: Exhibition catalogues; bulletin; annual report; collection catalogues
Activities: Classes for adults & children; dramatic progs; docent training; lects open to pub; gallery talks; tours; concerts, Detroit film theatre; scholarships & fels offered; book traveling exhibs; originate traveling exhibs; mus shop sells books, calendars, games, jewelry, prints, slides & t-shirts

L **Research Library & Archives**, 5200 Woodward Ave, Detroit, MI 48202. Tel 313-833-3460; Fax 313-833-6405; Email mketcham@dia.org; Web: www.dia.org; *Dept Head* Maria Ketcham
Open by written request only; Estab 1905 to provide material for research, interpretation & documentation of mus collection; For reference only
Income: Financed by city & memberships
Library Holdings: Auction Catalogs, Book Volumes 185,000, Exhibition Catalogs, Other Holdings, Pamphlets, Periodical Subscriptions 150
Special Subjects: Afro-American Art, American Indian Art, Antiquities-Assyrian, Antiquities-Byzantine, Antiquities-Egyptian, Antiquities-Etruscan, Antiquities-Greek, Antiquities-Oriental, Antiquities-Persian, Antiquities-Roman, Archaeology, Architecture, Art History, Asian Art, Bookplates & Bindings, Bronzes, Carpets & Rugs, Ceramics, Coins & Medals, Conceptual Art, Decorative Arts, Drawings, Etchings & Engravings, Film, Folk Art, Furniture, Glass, Graphic Arts, History of Art & Archaeology, Islamic Art, Ivory, Latin American Art, Manuscripts, Marine Painting, Mexican Art, Painting-American, Painting-Australian, Painting-British, Painting-Canadian, Painting-Dutch, Painting-European, Painting-Flemish, Painting-French, Painting-German, Painting-Israeli, Painting-Italian, Painting-Japanese, Painting-New Zealand, Painting-Polish, Painting-Russian, Painting-Scandinavian, Painting-Spanish, Pewter, Photography, Porcelain, Portraits, Pottery, Pre-Columbian Art, Printmaking, Sculpture, Silver, Theatre Arts, Woodcuts
Collections: Albert Kahn Architecture Library, Paul McPharlin Collection of Puppetry, Grace Whitney-Hoff Collection of Fine Bindings

L **DETROIT PUBLIC LIBRARY,** Art & Literature Dept, 5201 Woodward Ave, Detroit, MI 48202-4093. Tel 313-833-1470; Fax 313-833-1474; Email dir@detroitpubliclibrary.org; Web: www.detroitpubliclibrary.org; *Exec Dir* Jo Anne Mondowney; *Interim Dir Public Servs* Margaret Gillis Bruni; *Asst Dir for Tech Servs* J Randolph Call; *Asst Dir Mktg* Atiim J Funchess
Open Tues & Wed Noon - 8 PM, Thurs - Sat 10 AM - 6 PM; Estab 1865. Serves residents of Michigan with circulating and reference materials; Ann fee for library card for non- Detroit res $100
Income: Financed by city and state appropriation
Library Holdings: Book Volumes 81,000, Clipping Files, Exhibition Catalogs, Pamphlets, Periodical Subscriptions 550, Photographs
Special Subjects: Afro-American Art, American Western Art, Architecture, Art History, Calligraphy, Ceramics, Decorative Arts, Etchings & Engravings, Furniture, Industrial Design, Landscape Architecture, Painting-American, Photography, Sculpture
Activities: Tours

M **DETROIT REPERTORY THEATRE GALLERY,** 13103 Woodrow Wilson, Detroit, MI 48238. Tel 313-868-1347; Fax 313-259-8242; Email detrepth@aol.com; Web: www.detroitreptheatre.com; *Dir* Bruce E Millan
Open (box office) Mon - Fri 10 AM - 5 PM, Sat 10 AM - 1 PM; Estab 1957 to show Detroit Art; 1 fl in lobby of theater; Average Annual Attendance: 30,000
Income: Financed by endowment & state appropriation
Special Subjects: Afro-American Art, Collages, Decorative Arts, Drawings, Etchings & Engravings, Folk Art, Photography, Portraits, Prints, Reproductions, Textiles, Watercolors, Woodcarvings, Woodcuts
Collections: works by Detroit-area artists; 2-D works
Exhibitions: One person shows for emerging Detroit Area Artists; Amy Kelly, Robert Hyde, Jay Jurma, Kris Essen, Kathy Arkley, Renee Dooley, Albert Nassar, Sabrina Nelson; New exhibit for every show
Publications: Exhibition catalogs

Activities: Adult classes; dramatic progs

M **NATIONAL CONFERENCE OF ARTISTS,** Michigan Chapter Gallery, 18100 Meyers Rd, NW Activities Center Detroit, MI 48235-1497. Tel 313-342-1786; Email info@ncamich.org; Web: www.ncamich.org; *Gallery Dir* Esther Vivian Brewer; *Proj Dir* Raymond Wells; *Museum Liaison* Shirley Woodson; *Emerging Arts Prog* Oni Akilah; *International Project* Jide Aje; *Mem Chair* Eileen Monteiro
Open Tues - Wed & Sat Noon - 5 PM & by appointment; No admis fee; Estab 1972 to promote cultural support for artists & community through visual arts; Art gallery exhibs emerging & contemporary master artists; Average Annual Attendance: 4,500; Mem: 300; dues $50; monthly meetings & forums every 1st Sat of the month
Income: $50,000 (financed by mem, city & state appropriation, corporate, National Endowment for the Arts & private donations)
Library Holdings: Auction Catalogs, Exhibition Catalogs
Special Subjects: African Art, Afro-American Art
Collections: Documentation of African American Artists: Books, Journals, Slides, Photographs, Periodicals, Audio Tapes, Video Tapes
Publications: NCA Newsletter, quarterly
Activities: Classes for adults & children; docent progs; lects open to pub, gallery talks, tours, 6 vis lectrs per yr; annual award: Excellence in the Visual Arts; schols; originate traveling exhibs 3 per yr to art centers, universities & mus; sales shop sells art videos, books, original art, art journals & prints

M **PEWABIC SOCIETY INC,** Pewabic, 10125 E Jefferson, Detroit, MI 48214. Tel 313-626-2000; Fax 313-626-2100; Email info@pewabic.org; Web: www.Pewabic.org; *Exec Dir* Steve McBride; *Bd Chair* Catherine Dobrowitsky; *VChair* Rick Portwood
Open Mon - Sat 10 AM - 6 PM, Sun Noon - 4 PM; No admis fee; Estab 1903 to continue its tradition of leadership in the areas of ceramic production & education; Average Annual Attendance: 40,000; Mem: 1200; dues $75 family, $50 individual
Income: Financed by mem, donations & grants
Special Subjects: Ceramics
Collections: The work of the founder (Mary Chase Stratton)
Exhibitions: 4 annually - vary each year
Activities: Classes for adults & children; residencies & internships; lects open to pub; tours; competitions; original objects of art lent; originate traveling exhibs to libraries & mus; sales shop sells original art

M **THE SCARAB CLUB,** Gallery, 217 Farnsworth St, Detroit, MI 48202. Tel 313-831-1250; Fax 313-831-6815; Email tericson@scarabclub.org; Web: scarabclub.org; *Gallery Dir* Treena Flannery Ericson
Open Wed - Sun Noon - 5 PM, cl Memorial Day, Independence Day, Labor Day, Thanksgiving & Christmas Eve through New Year's Day; Estab 1907 to nurture & celebrate visual, literary & performing arts; Mem: dues $50-$1,000
Special Subjects: Decorative Arts
Collections: Canvas, paper, murals
Exhibitions: Temporary exhibits; fashion show
Activities: Educ progs for adults & children; internships; sketch sessions; reading series; events

M **WAYNE STATE UNIVERSITY,** Community Arts Gallery, 150 Community Arts Bldg, Detroit, MI 48202. Tel 313-577-2980; Fax 313-577-3491; Email art@wayne.edu; Web: art.wayne.edu; *Dir Galleries & Special Prog* Thomas Pyrzewski
Open Tues - Thurs 10 AM - 6 PM, Fri 10 AM - 7 PM; Estab 1956
Collections: Features art by prominent Michigan artists
Exhibitions: Temporary exhibits

EAST LANSING

M **MICHIGAN STATE UNIVERSITY,** Eli & Edythe Broad Art Museum, 547 E Circle Dr, East Lansing, MI 48824; 556 E Circle Dr, Rm 344 East Lansing, MI 48824. Tel 517-884-4800; Email eebam@msu.edu; Web: broadmuseum.msu.edu; *Dir* Marc-Olivier Wahler; *Deputy Dir Admin* Bill Matt; *Assoc Cur* Carla Acevedo-Yates; *Assoc Cur* Steven Bridges; *Chief Preparator* Brian Kirschensteiner; *Creative Content Coordr* Madeline Rosemurgy; *Mgr Exhibs & Opers* Jayne Goeddeke; *Dir Educ* Michelle Word
Open Tues - Sun noon - 7 PM, cl Mon; No admis fee; Estab 1959; The former Kresge Art Museum.; Average Annual Attendance: 30,000; Mem: 500; dues $15 - $1000
Income: Financed by Michigan State University, endowment funds.
Purchases: Paolo di Giovanni Fei triptych, 1985; John Marin watercolor, 1986; Gaston Lachaise, 1987; Jasper Johns; Duane Hanson, 1998; Chuck Close prints, 1999; Sol Lewitt portfolio, 2008; Jan Van Goyen painting, 2009
Special Subjects: African Art, Afro-American Art, Antiquities-Assyrian, Antiquities-Byzantine, Antiquities-Egyptian, Antiquities-Etruscan, Antiquities-Greek, Antiquities-Oriental, Antiquities-Persian, Antiquities-Roman, Asian Art, Baroque Art, Bronzes, Calligraphy, Ceramics, Coins & Medals, Collages, Decorative Arts, Drawings, Enamels, Eskimo Art, Etchings & Engravings, Ethnology, Glass, Graphics
Collections: Work from neolithic period to present, European paintings & sculpture, American paintings & sculpture, prints from 1500 to present, Small Asian, African, pre-Columbian collections, photography; figurative Expressionist painting
Exhibitions: Shows making up a yearly calendar of about 10 exhibitions supplementing the permanent collection; special exhibits; faculty and student shows
Publications: Kresge Art Museum Bulletin; Exhibition calendar & publications
Activities: Docent training; workshops; lects open to public; 8 vis lectrs per yr; gallery talks; tours; cell phone tours; scholarships offered; individual paintings & original objects of art lent to qualified institutions, museums or galleries; book traveling exhibs 2-3 per yr; originate traveling exhibs to other art museums nationally; sales shop sells books, prints, cards & miscellaneous items

ESCANABA

M **WILLIAM BONIFAS FINE ARTS CENTER AND GALLERY,** 700 First Ave S, Escanaba, MI 49829. Tel 906-786-3833; Fax 906-786-3840; Web: www.bonifasarts.org; *Adminr* Susan Roll; *Gallery Dir* Pasgua Warstler
Open Tues - Fri 10 AM - 5:30 PM, Sat 10 AM - 3 PM; No admis fee; Estab 1974 to advance the arts in the area; 40 x 80, lower gallery inside Center; additional upper gallery; Mem: Dues patron $50 & up, family $50, individual $35
Collections: Local artists working shows & regional artwork
Exhibitions: Northern Exposure; Smithsonian Matthew Brady Photographs; Michigan Watercolor Society; Regional & Touring Exhibits; exhibits that reflect the culture and history of Michigan's Upper Peninsula
Publications: Arts News quarterly
Activities: Classes for adults & children; dramatic progs; docent training; lects open to pub, 2-3 vis lectrs per yr; tours; concerts; gallery talks; sponsor competitions; awards in connection with annual regional competition; scholarships offered; individual paintings & original objects of art lent to arts organizations & bus in return for promotional assistance; book traveling exhibs to 6-8 area schools per yr

FLINT

M **BUCKHAM FINE ARTS PROJECT,** Buckham Gallery, 134-1/2 W Second St, Flint, MI 48502. Tel 810-239-6233; Email manager@buckhamgallery.org; Web: www.buckhamgallery.org; *Pres* Ken Hakala; *Dir* Meghan Kelly
Open Thurs - Sat noon - 5:30 PM; No admis fee; Estab 1984 to present contemporary arts; 40 x 60 ft gallery with 14 ft arched ceiling, no permanent interior walls; Average Annual Attendance: 5,000; Mem: 52; dues $75 or $180; Meetings 4th Thurs of each month
Income: $90,000 (financed by mem, state appropriation, grants, gifts, commissions from sales)
Exhibitions: New exhibitions on rotating monthly basis, 12 each year
Activities: Exhibitions; performances; readings; lects open to pub; 2 vis lectrs per yr; competitions with prizes; gallery talks; extension prog, GVRC - youth detention; book traveling exhibs 1 per yr; sales shop sells books, original art, prints; reproductions; gallery merch;

M **FLINT INSTITUTE OF ARTS,** 1120 E Kearsley St, Flint, MI 48503-1915. Tel 810-234-1695; Fax 810-234-1692; Email info@flintarts.org; Web: www.flintarts.org; *Exec Dir* John B Henry III; *Develop Officer* Tracey Stewart; *Cur Educ* Monique Desormeau; *Dir Finance & Admin* Michael Melenbrink; *Art School Dir* Donovan Entrekin; *Cur Colls & Exhibs* Tracee Glab; *Dir Mem & Guest Relations* Sarah Mullane
Open Mon - Fri noon - 5 PM, Sat 10 AM - 5 PM, Sun 1 - 5 PM; Admis adults $10, students & seniors $8, discounts to AAM & ICOM members, children under 12 & members no charge; Estab 1928 with a mission to advance the understanding & appreciation of art for all through colls, exhibs & educ progs; 1 large temporary & 9 rotating permanent collection; Average Annual Attendance: 146,725; Mem: 4,745
Income: 4.4 million; financed by endowments, grants, contributions & earned income, including memberships
Library Holdings: Book Volumes 8,750
Special Subjects: African Art, American Indian Art, Asian Art, Baroque Art, Bronzes, Ceramics, Collages, Decorative Arts, Drawings, Embroidery, Eskimo Art, Etchings & Engravings, Flasks & Bottles, Folk Art, Furniture, Glass, Graphics, Ivory, Jade, Laces, Landscapes, Leather, Metalwork, Mexican Art, Mosaics, Oriental Art, Painting-American, Painting-British, Painting-Dutch, Painting-European, Painting-Flemish, Painting-French, Painting-German, Painting-Italian, Painting-Spanish, Photography, Porcelain, Portraits, Pottery, Pre-Columbian Art, Prints, Religious Art, Renaissance Art, Sculpture, Silver, Tapestries, Textiles, Watercolors, Woodcarvings, Woodcuts
Collections: American & European Fine Arts, Native American, African, Chinese, Japanese, & Pre-Columbian Art
Exhibitions: (6th May, 2017-30th Jul, 2017) Auguste Rodin the Human Experience; (22nd Jan, 2017-15th Apr, 2017) Women of a New Tribe
Publications: Exhibition catalogs; bimonthly magazine for members & public
Activities: Classes for adults & children; docent training; lects open to the public; lects for mems only; gallery talks; tours; schols awarded; exten program serves ArtReach, Art on the Go (senior centers & nursing homes); books traveling exhibs 3-4 per yr; originates traveling exhibs to mus & galleries; mus shop sells books, original art, reproductions, prints, gift items

L **Library,** 1120 E Kearsley St, Flint, MI 48503-1915. Tel 810-234-1695; Fax 810-234-1692; Web: www.flintarts.org; *Exhib Coordr* Kristie Everett Zamora; *Dir* John B Henry III; *Develop Dir* Deborah Gossel; *Cur Educ* Monique Desormeau; *Bus Mgr* Michael Melenbrink
Open Tues - Sat 10 AM - 5 PM, Sun 1 - 5 PM; No admis fee, donations accepted; Estab 1928; Average Annual Attendance: 85,000
Library Holdings: Book Volumes 4500, Exhibition Catalogs, Periodical Subscriptions 19
Special Subjects: American Indian Art, Architecture, Asian Art, Ceramics, Crafts, Decorative Arts, Drawings, Etchings & Engravings, Folk Art, Furniture, Oriental Art, Painting-American, Painting-European, Photography, Pottery
Collections: American & European Fine Arts, Native American, African, Chinese & Japanese
Publications: Bimonthly magazine; exhibit catalogs
Activities: Classes for adults & children; docent training; film series; museum art school; annual art fair; lects open to pub, 8 vis lectrs per yr; concerts; gallery talks; tours; exten program lends original objects of art to other mus; 1 book traveling exhib per yr; mus shop sells books

GRAND RAPIDS

M **CALVIN COLLEGE,** Center Art Gallery, 3201 Burton St SE, Grand Rapids, MI 49546-4388; Covenant Fine Arts Center, 1795 Knollcrest Cir SE Grand Rapids, MI 49546-4388. Tel 616-526-6271; Fax 616-526-8551; Web: www.calvin.edu/centerartgallery; *Dir Exhibs* Joel Zwart

Open Sept - May Mon - Tues 9 AM - 5 PM, Wed - Fri 9 AM - 9 PM, Sat 10 AM - 4 PM; summer by appointment; No admis fee; Estab 1974 & relocated 2010, to provide the art students, & the col community & the pub at large with challenging visual monthly exhibs; Gallery is spread over 3 exhib spaces totaling 3,800 sq ft, with HVAC control & proper lighting.; Average Annual Attendance: 10,000
Income: Financed through private budget
Special Subjects: Ceramics, Drawings, Prints, Sculpture, Textiles, Asian Art, Etchings & Engravings, Graphics, Hispanic Art, Historical Material, Islamic Art, Landscapes, Painting-American, Painting-Dutch, Photography, Porcelain, Portraits, Posters, Pottery, Prints, Religious Art, Sculpture, Watercolors, Woodcuts
Collections: Dutch 17th & 19th centuries paintings & prints, Japanese prints, contemporary American paintings, prints, drawings, sculpture, weaving & ceramics
Exhibitions: Invitational exhibits by various artists, exhibits of public & private collections & faculty & student exhibits
Publications: Various exhibition brochures & catalogs
Activities: Classes for adults; lect open to public; concerts; gallery talks; competitions; scholarships offered; book traveling exhibitions, 1-2 per year

M **GRAND RAPIDS ART MUSEUM,** 101 Monroe Center St NW, Grand Rapids, MI 49503-2801. Tel 616-831-1000; Fax 616-831-1001; Email info@artmuseumgr.org; Web: www.artmuseumgr.org; *Dir & CEO* Dana Friis-Hansen; *CFO & COO* Robert L Branch; *Chief Cur* Ron Platt; *Registrar* Julie Burgess
Open Mon - Sat noon - 8 PM, Sun noon - 6 PM; Admis adults $5, students (w/ID) & seniors, youth 6-17, children under 6 & GRAM members free; Museum allocated a 1910 Beaux Arts former post office & courthouse, renovated & opened in Sept 1981; Average Annual Attendance: 94,500; Mem: 2500; dues corporate benefactor $2500, corporate patron $1000, corporate donor $600, corporate $300, benefactor $2500, grand patron $500-$1000, Masters $1000, Beaux Arts $500, collections patron $300, sponsor $350, donor $150, Arts Alive/Friends of Art $100, patron $74, family $50, individual $35, full-time student $15; annual meeting in Sept
Income: $919,000 (financed by endowment, mem, state appropriation & federal grants)
Purchases: $30,000
Special Subjects: African Art, Afro-American Art, American Indian Art, American Western Art, Antiquities-Egyptian, Ceramics, Coins & Medals, Collages, Costumes, Crafts, Etchings & Engravings, Folk Art, Furniture, Glass, Graphics, Metalwork, Miniatures, Oriental Art, Painting-American, Painting-Dutch, Painting-Japanese, Painting-Polish, Painting-Russian, Painting-Scandinavian, Painting-Spanish
Collections: American & European 19th & 20th Centuries paintings, prints & photographs, Renaissance to Contemporary drawings, 20th Century design & decorative arts, German expressionist paintings, master prints of all eras, Renaissance paintings, sculpture
Publications: Catalogs of major exhibitions; quarterly newsletter
Activities: Classes for adults & children; dramatic progs; docent training; lects open to pub, 7-10 vis lectrs per yr; concerts; gallery talks; tours; competitions with awards; exten dept serves elementary schools; individual paintings & original objects of art lent to mus; lending collection contains books, original art works, original prints, paintings, photographs, sculpture & slides; book traveling exhibs; originate traveling exhibs; mus & sales shops sells books, magazines, original art, reproductions, gift items & prints; Gram for Kids

L **Reference Library,** 101 Monroe Center St NW, Grand Rapids, MI 49503. Tel 616-242-5030; Fax 616-831-1001; Email cbuckner@artmuseumgr.org; Web: www.artmuseumgr.org; *Assoc Cur* Cindy Buckner; *Cur Asst* Julie Conklin
Open Tues - Sat 1 PM - 4 PM; Estab 1969; Reference only lib
Income: Financed by mem, gifts, museum general budget allowance
Purchases: $2000
Library Holdings: Auction Catalogs, Book Volumes 8,000, Clipping Files, DVDs, Exhibition Catalogs 10,000, Pamphlets, Periodical Subscriptions 5, Video Tapes
Special Subjects: Aesthetics, Afro-American Art, American Western Art, Art Education, Art History, Bronzes, Ceramics, Drawings, Etchings & Engravings, Photography, Prints, Woodcuts, Architecture, Furniture, Painting-American, Painting-European, Watercolors
Activities: Docent Training; three times a year; museum shop sells books

L **GRAND RAPIDS PUBLIC LIBRARY,** 111 Library St NE, Grand Rapids, MI 49503-3268. Tel 616-988-5400; Fax 616-988-5419; Email kcorrado@grpl.org; Web: www.grpl.org; *Library Dir* Marcia Warner; *Asst Library Dir* Marla Ehlers; *Mktg & Communs Mgr* Kristen Krueger-Corrado; *Reference & Adult Svcs Coordr* Asante Cain; *Tech Svcs & Circ Coordr* Rebecca Near; *Info Sys Mgr* William Ott
Open Mon - Thurs 9 AM - 9 PM, Fri & Sat 9 AM - 6 PM & Sun (Labor Day - Memorial Day) 1 - 5 PM; No admis fee; Estab 1871 to provide information & library materials for people in Grand Rapids, expansion in 1967, renovation 1997-2003; Circ 1,523,566; Average Annual Attendance: 950,000
Income: Financed by city & state appropriations
Library Holdings: Book Volumes, CD-ROMs, Cassettes, Clipping Files, Compact Disks, DVDs, Fiche, Filmstrips, Lantern Slides, Manuscripts, Maps, Memorabilia, Micro Print, Original Art Works, Original Documents, Pamphlets, Periodical Subscriptions, Photographs, Prints, Records, Reels, Reproductions, Video Tapes
Special Subjects: Furniture
Collections: The Furniture Design Collection
Activities: Classes for adults & children; lects open to pub; 20 vis lectrs per yr; tours; sales shop sells books & magazines

M **GRAND RAPIDS PUBLIC MUSEUM,** 272 Pearl NW, Grand Rapids, MI 49504-5371. Tel 616-929-1700; Fax 616-929-1780; Email info@grpm.org; Web: www.grpm.org; *Pres & CEO* Dale Robertson; *Exec Asst* Leslie Milstead; *CFO & VPres Admin* Karen Wilburn; *VPres Mktg & Pub Rels* Kate Moore; *VPres Educ* Mike Posthumus; *VPres Devel* Gina Schulz
Open Mon, Wed - Sat 9 AM - 5 PM, Tues 9 AM - 8 PM, Sun Noon - 5 PM, cl New Year's Day, Easter, Memorial Day, Labor Day, Thanksgiving, Christmas; Admis adults $8, seniors $7, Kent Co adults $5, Kent Co seniors, college students with ID & children 7-17 $3, Kent Co children no charge; Estab 1854 for the interpretation of environment, history & culture of West Michigan & Grand Rapids; Maintains non-circulating reference library; 150,000 sq ft museum (Van Andel Museum Center) with 9600 sq ft temporary gallery; 140,000 sq ft research center, historic house museum; Average Annual Attendance: 247,371; Mem: 6,000; dues $35-$65; annual meeting in May
Income: $6,500,000 (financed by endowment, mem, city & state appropriations, grants, contributions & foundations)
Library Holdings: Audio Tapes, Book Volumes, Clipping Files, Exhibition Catalogs, Filmstrips, Lantern Slides, Manuscripts, Maps, Memorabilia, Motion Pictures, Original Art Works, Original Documents, Other Holdings, Pamphlets, Photographs, Prints, Records, Slides
Special Subjects: American Indian Art, Anthropology, Antiquities-Egyptian, Archaeology, Asian Art, Carpets & Rugs, Ceramics, Coins & Medals, Costumes, Decorative Arts, Dioramas, Dolls, Drawings, Etchings & Engravings, Ethnology, Flasks & Bottles, Furniture, Glass, Graphics, Historical Material, Ivory, Laces, Manuscripts, Maps, Oriental Art, Painting-American, Period Rooms, Pewter, Photography, Porcelain, Portraits, Pottery, Pre-Columbian Art, Prints, Textiles
Collections: Costumes & household textiles, Decorative arts, Ethnology, Furniture of the 19th & 20th centuries, Industrial & agricultural artifacts, Anthropology; Paleontology
Exhibitions: Permanent exhibitions: West Michigan Habitats; Newcomers: People of this Place; Streets of Old Grand Rapids; Anishinabek: People of this Place
Publications: Museum, quarterly; Discoveries, monthly; exhibition catalogs
Activities: Classes for adults & children; dramatic progs; docent training; classes in film, music & dance; summer camps; lects open to pub; 20 vis lectrs per yr; concerts; gallery talks; tours; individual paintings, objects of art & historical & anthropological artifacts lent to nonprofit educational institutions; book traveling exhibs 2 per yr; originate traveling exhibs; mus shop sells books, magazines, original art, reproductions, prints, publications & catalogs; gifts

L **KENDALL COLLEGE OF ART & DESIGN,** Kendall Gallery, 17 Fountain St NW, Grand Rapids, MI 49503-3194. Tel 616-451-2787; Fax 616-451-9867; Email kcadgallery@ferris.edu; Web: www.kcad.edu; *Dir Exhibitions* Sarah Joseph
Open Mon - Sat 10 AM - 5 PM; No admis fee; Estab to serve Kendall students & faculty, as well as surrounding community; Focus on contemporary art by nat and international artists; Average Annual Attendance: 8,506
Income: Financed by tuition
Special Subjects: Art History, Asian Art, Ceramics, Commercial Art, Drafting, Folk Art, Graphic Arts, History of Art & Archaeology, Interior Design, Landscapes, Painting-American, Photography, Pre-Columbian Art, Prints, Sculpture
Activities: Lects open to public; 7-12 vis lectrs per year; gallery talks; sponsoring competitions

M **KENDALL COLLEGE OF ART & DESIGN,** Urban Institute for Contemporary Arts, 2 W Fulton, Grand Rapids, MI 49503. Tel 616-454-7000; Fax 616-454-9395; Email info@uica.org; Web: www.uica.org; *Exec Dir* Miranda Krajniak; *Assoc Dir* Megan Bylsma; *Film Coordr* Nick Hartman; *Develop Officer* Kristen Taylor; *Exhibs Cur* Heather Duffy; *Community Prog Coordr* Katherine Williams
Open Tues - Sat noon - 9 PM, Sun noon - 6 PM, cl Mon; Admis $6, mems free; Estab 1976, dedicated to the development of a vital cultural community; Visual arts gallery-multi disciplinary arts center, movie theatre; Average Annual Attendance: 15,000; Mem: 650; dues families $75, individuals $40, students $25
Income: Financed by grants, donations, mem, ticket sales, studio rental & fundraising events
Publications: Quarterly newsletter
Activities: Classes for children; docent training; lects open to pub; gallery talks; tours; mus shop sells books, original art, prints, local handmade gifts

GROSSE POINTE SHORES

M **EDSEL & ELEANOR FORD HOUSE,** 1100 Lake Shore Rd, Grosse Pointe Shores, MI 48236-4106. Tel 313-884-4222; Fax 313-884-5977; Email info@fordhouse.org; Web: www.fordhouse.org; *Pres* Kathleen Stiso Mullins; *VPres Communs* Ann Fitzpatrick; *VPres Finance & Admin* Robert Seestadt; *Dir Interpretation & Progs* Christopher Shires; *Group Tour Sales Dir* Donna Buchanan; *Dir Develop* Bernadette Banko; *Cur* Josephine Shea; *Colls Mgr* Megan Callewaert
Open Tues - Sat 10 AM - 4 PM Sun noon - 4 PM (Apr - Dec); Jan - Mar: please call for tour schedule; Admis adults $12, seniors $11, children $8; Estab 1978 to help educate public on local history, fine & decorative arts; The Edsel & Eleanor Ford House experience is an authentic witness to the past that inspires, educates & engages visitors through exploration of its unique connections to art, design, history & environment while celebrating family traditions & community relationships; Average Annual Attendance: 50,000
Income: Financed by endowment, admissions, sponsors & grants
Special Subjects: Antiquities-Persian, Architecture, Asian Art, Carpets & Rugs, Costumes, Decorative Arts, Drawings, Furniture, Glass, Metalwork, Mexican Art, Painting-American, Painting-French, Period Rooms, Porcelain, Sculpture, Ceramics, Painting-Italian
Collections: Fine art, decorative arts including French & English antique furniture, ceramics, textiles; interior modern rooms by Walter Dorwin Teague; Jens Jensen landscape
Exhibitions: Rotating exhibits
Publications: Edsel & Eleanor Ford House Book
Activities: Classes for adults & children; seasonal children's programs; docent training; lects open to pub, house & grounds tours; concerts; books traveling exhibs occasionally; mus shop sells books, gifts; Cotswold Cafe

HOLLAND

M **HOPE COLLEGE,** DePree Art Center & Gallery, 160 E 12th St, Holland, MI 49422-3609. Tel 616-395-7500; Fax 616-395-7499; Email art@hope.edu; Web: www.hope.edu/academic/art; *Dir* Dr Heidi Kraus; *Mgr* Steve Nelson; *Admin* Kristin Underhill
Open Mon - Sat 10 AM - 5 PM, Sun 1 - 5 PM; No admis fee; Estab as a place for the col & community to enjoy art; Acad gallery featuring historical and contemporary exhibs; Average Annual Attendance: 5,000
Collections: 625 items of Western & Non-Western art

Publications: Exhibition catalogs, e.g. Going Dutch: Contemporary Artists and the Dutch Tradition
Activities: Lect open to public; gallery talks

INTERLOCHEN

L **INTERLOCHEN CENTER FOR THE ARTS,** PO Box 199, Interlochen, MI 49643-0199. Tel 231-276-7420; *Head Librn* Sandra Besselsen
Open daily 8 AM - 5 PM & 6:30 - 9:30 PM; Estab 1963; Circ 9000; Special music library with over 50,000 titles
Library Holdings: Book Volumes 23,000, Periodical Subscriptions 140
Publications: Interlochen Review, annual
Activities: Dramatic progs; lects open to pub; concerts; tours; competitions; awards; schols & fels offered; originate traveling exhibs

JACKSON

M **ELLA SHARP MUSEUM,** 3225 Fourth St, Jackson, MI 49203. Tel 517-787-2320; Fax 517-787-2933; Email info@ellasharp.org; Web: www.ellasharp.org; *Exec Dir* Amy Reimann
Open Tues - Wed & Fri - Sat 10 AM - 5 PM, Thurs 10 AM - 7 PM, cl Sun, Mon & holidays; Admis adults $5, children 5-12 $3, children under 5 free; Estab 1965 to promote the understanding & appreciation of art & history through exceptional exhibs, interpretation of historical bldgs & engaging educ progs.; 3 permanent galleries: Jackson History Gallery, Andrews Gallery of Wildlife Art, Never Enough Time Clock Gallery; 3 rotating exhibs; Average Annual Attendance: 18,000; Mem: 1,165; dues $40, $50, $60, $125; annual meeting in June
Income: Financed by endowment & mem along with grants & sponsorships
Special Subjects: Ceramics, Costumes, Decorative Arts, Maps, Photography, Sculpture, Woodcarvings
Collections: China, coverlets & quilts, furniture from Victorian period, items related to Jackson history, wildlife art, (contact mus for further information)
Exhibitions: Rotating exhibits; outdoor sculptures
Publications: Online & print newsletter
Activities: Classes for adults & children; docent training; four seasonal festivals; lects open to pub, 10+ vis lectrs per yr; gallery talks; tours; competitions; awards; schols offered; art objects lent to schools; lending collection contains photographs; gift shop, Granary Restaurant; original art, reproductions, gifts, archives

KALAMAZOO

M **KALAMAZOO INSTITUTE OF ARTS,** 314 S Park St, Kalamazoo, MI 49007-5102. Tel 269-349-7775, ext 3001; Fax 269-349-9313; Email museum@kiarts.org; Web: www.kiarts.org; *Exec Dir* Belinda A Tate; *Dir Finance & Personnel* George Baltmanis; *Registrar* Corey Gross; *Dir Mus Educ* Susan Eckhardt; *Dir Develop* Cindy Kole; *School Dir* Denise Lisiecki; *Dir Facilities* Ron Boothby; *Coordr Mktg* Katie Houston; *Mem Coordr* Cindy Trout; *Librn* Malcolm McBryde; *Gallery Shop Mgr* Karyn Juergens; *Vol Coordr* Sandy Linabury; *Exec Asst* Laura Wilson; *Asst Cur Youth & Family Progs* Candie Waterloo
Open Tues, Wed & Sat 11 - 5, Thurs & Fri 11 - 8, Sun 12 - 5, cl Mon & major holidays; non-mems $5, students $2, free to mems; Incorporated 1924 to further interest in the arts, especially in the visual arts; new building opened in 1998; Four permanent collection galleries & four temporary exhibition galleries devoted to pieces from the permanent collection; Average Annual Attendance: 55,000; Mem: 2500; dues student $35; individual $55; family $85; sustaining $125; donor $175; patron $250; benefactor $500; dir circle: founder $1,000-$2,499; leader $2,500-$4,999; visionary $5,000 & up
Income: $800,000 (financed by endowment, private donations, corporate & foundation grants, state & federal grants & mem)
Library Holdings: Auction Catalogs, Book Volumes, CD-ROMs, Cards, Clipping Files, Compact Disks, DVDs, Motion Pictures, Original Documents, Periodical Subscriptions, Prints, Records, Reproductions, Slides, Video Tapes
Special Subjects: African Art, Bronzes, Ceramics, Drawings, Etchings & Engravings, Hispanic Art, Landscapes, Latin American Art, Painting-American, Photography, Portraits, Pre-Columbian Art, Prints, Watercolors, Woodcarvings, Woodcuts
Collections: 19th & 20th-century American art; 20th-century European art; 15th to 20th-century graphics; ceramics; small sculpture; photography; works on paper
Exhibitions: Various rotating exhib call for information
Publications: Exhibition catalogs, issued irregularly; e-newsletters, weekly; magazines, quarterly
Activities: Classes for adults & children; docent training; mus educ dept; lects open to pub; tours; 12 vis lectrs per yr; gallery talks; competitions with awards;; scholarships; exten dept serves Southwest Michigan; individual paintings lent for selected mus exhibs; Lending collection contains photographs, paintings, prints & ceramics; originate traveling exhibs; gallery shop sells books, magazines, original art, reproductions, prints, slides, craft items, jewelry & cards

L **The Mary & Edwin Meader Fine Arts Library**, 314 S Park St, Kalamazoo, MI 49007-5102. Tel 269-349-7775; Fax 269-349-9313; Email museum@kiarts.org; Web: www.kiarts.org; *Head Librn* Malcolm McBryde; *Dir of School* Denise Lisiecki; *Dir Museum Educ* Susan Eckhardt; *Dir Develop* Joe Bower; *Dir Colls & Exhibs* Vicki Wright; *Dir Finance & Personnel* George Baltmanis; *Exec Dir* Belinda Tate
Open Thur & Fri 11 AM - 8 PM, Tues, Wed & Sat - 11 AM - 5 PM, Sun 12 PM - 5 PM; Admis adults $5, students $2, 12 & younger, active military & KIA mems free; Estab 1924 to stimulate the creation & appreciation of visual arts; Library estab 1961 as a reference for staff, school faculty & mems; Circ 1,100; 10 galleries for temporary exhibitions & permanent collection; library for public reference only, open to members for circulation (1,100 items annually); Average Annual Attendance: 65,000; Mem: 2700; dues $25 & up; annual meeting in Sept
Income: Privately financed through donation & membership sales
Library Holdings: Auction Catalogs, Book Volumes 10,500, Clipping Files 1000, Compact Disks, DVDs, Exhibition Catalogs, Pamphlets, Periodical Subscriptions 52, Slides 10,000, Video Tapes 200
Special Subjects: Art History, Ceramics, Etchings & Engravings, Folk Art, Jewelry, Lettering, Painting-American, Painting-British, Painting-European, Photography, Pottery, Printmaking, Watercolors, Woodcuts
Collections: Art on paper, ceramics, watercolors, sculpture, 20th century American art, German Expressionist prints, Photographs
Publications: Exhibit catalogues; biennial reports
Activities: Classes for adults & children; docent training; pub progs; lects; tours; gallery talks; sponsors competitions; scholarships; sales shop sells books, original art, stationery, children's items & jewelry

M **WESTERN MICHIGAN UNIVERSITY GWEN FROSTIC SCHOOL OF ART,** Richmond Center for Visual Arts, 1903 W. Michigan Ave, Department of Art Kalamazoo, MI 49008-5200. Tel 269-387-2455; Fax 269-387-2477; Email indra.lacis@wmich.edu; Web: www.wmich.edu/art/exhibitions/exhibitions/index.html; *Exhib Dir* Indra Lacis; *Registrar* Mindi Bagnall
Open Mon - Thurs 10AM-6PM, Fri 10AM-9PM, Sat Noon -6PM; No admis fee; Estab 1965 to provide visual enrichment to the university & Kalamazoo community. The School of Art Galleries are located in the Richmond Center for Visual Arts; Sculpture Tour is a rotating outdoor exhibit of traveling sculpture for which a catalog is available. 10,000 sq ft of exhib space with special features for lightening, data, and projection capabilities; Average Annual Attendance: 12,000; Mem: 350; annual member fees
Income: Financed by state appropriation, 1 program support 1, corporate foundations
Special Subjects: Prints
Collections: Contemporary print coll, 19th & 20th century American & European Art
Exhibitions: Rotating exhibition on contemporary arts
Publications: Sculpture Tour 92-93, 93-94, 94-95, 96-97, 98-99, 00-01, 01-06, 08-09; Sculptural Concepts Exhib Catalog 2008; Charismatii Abstraction 2008; Heroes Like Us 2010
Activities: Classes for adults; lect open to public, 12 vis lectrs per year; gallery talks; tours; awards; scholarships offered; collection contains 2000 original art works, 750 original prints; exhibitions 7 per yr; Univ galleries & museums

LAKESIDE

M **LAKESIDE STUDIO,** 15486 Red Arrow Hwy, Lakeside, MI 49116; PO Box 3, Three Oaks, MI 49128-0003. Tel 269-469-3022; Fax 269-469-1011; Email lakesidegal@triton.net; Web: www.lakesidegalleries.com; *Exec Dir* John Wilson
Open daily 10 AM - 5 PM; No admis fee; Estab 1968, international; Represents international artists, American, Soviet, Chinese, Dutch work done by Artists-in-Residence
Income: Financed by pvt ownership
Exhibitions: Rotating exhibits
Activities: Award placement in Artist-in-Residence Prog through selection process; mus shop sells original art

LANSING

M **LANSING ART GALLERY,** 119 N Washington Sq, Lansing, MI 48933. Tel 517-374-6400; Fax 517-374-6385; Email lansingartgallery@gmail.com; Web: www.lansingartgallery.org; *Pres* Mary Cusack; *Exec Dir* Barb Whitney; *Prog Mgr* Jane Kramer; *Gallery Coordr* Sara Pulver
Open Tues - Fri 10 AM - 4 PM, Sat & 1st Sun of the month 1 - 4 PM; No admis fee; Estab 1965 as a nonprofit gallery to promote the visual arts in their many forms to citizens of the greater Lansing area; Maintains large exhibit area, gallery shop & rental gallery; Average Annual Attendance: 25,000; Mem: 500; dues $25-$2500; annual meeting in June
Income: $250,000 (financed by mem, sales, grants, contributions & fees)
Publications: Image, quarterly
Activities: Classes for adults; classes for children; docent training; lect open to public, 5 vis lectrs per year; gallery talks; tours; competitions with awards; scholarships; individual paintings & original objects of art available for lease or purchase, including original art works, original prints, paintings, photographs & sculpture; book traveling exhibitions, 1-2 per year; mus shop sells books, original art, sculpture

LELAND

M **LEELANAU HISTORICAL MUSEUM,** 203 E Cedar St, Leland, MI 49654-5015; PO Box 246, Leland, MI 49654-0246. Tel 231-256-7475; Fax 231-256-7650; Email info@leelanauhistory.org; Email leemuse@traverse.com; Web: www.leelanauhistory.org; *Cur* Laura Quackenbush
Call for hours; Admis adults $2, student $1; Estab 1959 for the preservation & exhibition of local history; One gallery for temporary exhibits of traditional & folk arts, 40 ft x 20 ft; Average Annual Attendance: 5,000; Mem: 550; dues $25; annual meeting in Aug
Income: $160,000 (financed by endowment, mem, fundraising & activities & grants)
Special Subjects: American Indian Art, Crafts, Folk Art, Historical Material, Laces, Manuscripts, Ethnology
Collections: Collections of local paintings, both folk & fine art, Leelanau County Native American baskets, birch bark crafts
Publications: Lee Muse newsletter, quarterly
Activities: Educ dept; sales shop sells books, reproductions, local crafts & original needlework kits

MARQUETTE

M **NORTHERN MICHIGAN UNIVERSITY,** De Vos Art Museum, 1401 Preque Isle Ave, Marquette, MI 49855. Tel 906-227-1481, 227-2194; Fax 906-227-2276;

Email mmatusca@nmu.edu; Web: www.art.nmu.edu/devosartmuseum; *Mus Dir & Cur* Melissa Matuscak
Open Mon - Fri 10 AM - 5 PM, Sun 1 - 4 PM; No admis fee; Estab 1975 to bring exhibits of the visual arts to the University, community & the upper peninsula of Michigan; Museum covers approx 5000 sq ft of space, built in 2005 by HGA Architects; Average Annual Attendance: 10,000; Mem: 130; dues & mtgs vary
Income: $6500 (financed by University funds)
Collections: Contemporary printing & sculpture, student coll, Japanese & American illustration, Japanese prints & artifacts, permanent coll
Exhibitions: Average of 4-5 major exhibits each yr of regional, nat & internat contemporary art in all media.
Publications: Exhibit Announcement, monthly
Activities: Educ dept; lects open to pub, 5 vis lectrs per yr; gallery talks; tours; competitions; individual paintings & original objects of art lent; originates traveling exhibs

MIDLAND

A **ARTS MIDLAND GALLERIES & SCHOOL,** 1801 W St Andrews, Midland, MI 48640. Tel 989-631-5930; Fax 989-631-7890; Email info@mcfsta.org; Web: www.mcfta.org; *Dir* B B Winslow; *Prog Coordr* Cheryl Gordon; *Admin Asst* Emmy Mills; *Studio School Coordr & Registrar* Armin Mersmann
Open Mon - Sun 10 AM - 6 PM; No admis fee; Estab 1956 to generate interest in & foster understanding & enjoyment of the visual arts; Exhibition space consists of three galleries, one 40 x 80 ft & two smaller 20 x 40 ft space; spot tracking lighting; Average Annual Attendance: 20,000; Mem: 550; dues family $45, senior citizen $30; annual meeting in fall; monthly board meetings
Income: $200,000 (financed by endowment, mem, grants, fees for services, fundraising events)
Exhibitions: Great Lakes Regional Art Exhibition; Annual All Media Juried Competition & Exhibition (open to all Michigan artists age 18 & over); Annual Juried Summer Art Fair; Juried Holiday Art Fair
Publications: Calendar of events; quarterly newsletter for members; yearly report
Activities: Classes for adults & children; docent training; workshops; Picture Parent; lects open to public, 4 vis lectrs per yr; gallery talks; self-guiding tours; tours; juried art fairs; competitions with awards; scholarships offered; book traveling exhibs 5-10 per yr; originate traveling exhibs

L **GRACE A DOW MEMORIAL LIBRARY,** Fine Arts Dept, 1710 W Saint Andrews, Midland, MI 48640. Tel 989-837-3430; Fax 989-837-3468; Web: www.gracedowlibrary.org/; *Dir* Melissa Barnard; *Chair* Cherie Hutter
Open Mon - Fri 9 AM - 9 PM, Sat 10 AM - 5 PM; during school year, Sun 1 - 5 PM; No admis fee; Estab 1955 as a pub library; Maintains art gallery
Income: Financed by city appropriation & gifts
Library Holdings: Audio Tapes, Book Volumes 12,000, Cassettes, Clipping Files, Framed Reproductions, Motion Pictures, Original Art Works, Other Holdings Compact Discs, Pamphlets, Periodical Subscriptions 80, Prints, Records, Reproductions, Video Tapes
Collections: Alden P Dow Fine Arts Collection
Exhibitions: Exhibits from local artists, art groups & schools
Activities: Films

M **MIDLAND CENTER FOR THE ARTS,** Alden B Dow Museum of Science & Art, 1801 W Saint Andrews Rd, Midland, MI 48640-2656. Tel 989-631-5930; Fax 989-631-7890; Web: www.mcfta.org; *Dir* Bruce Winslow; *Pres* Mike Hayes; *Bus & Opers Mgr* Emmy Mills; *Museum School Mgr* Armin Mersmann
Open seasonally; Admis adults $9, children $6; Estab 1971; Average Annual Attendance: 179,000; Mem: 1,800; dues family $75
Income: varies according to exhibs(financed by endowment & mem)
Special Subjects: Art Education
Collections: Contemporary visual art
Activities: Educ outreach prog to schools in the area; classes for adults & children; docent progs; lects open to pub, 3 vis lectrs per yr; gallery talks; tours; sponsor competitions, schols; mus shop sells books, magazines, original art & prints

MONROE

A **MONROE COUNTY COMMUNITY COLLEGE,** Fine Arts Council, 1555 S Raisinville Rd, Monroe, MI 48161-9746. Tel 734-384-4153; Fax 734-457-6023; Email vmaltese@monroeccc.edu; Web: www.monroeccc.edu; *Dean* Vinnie Maltese; *Assoc Prof Art* Gary Wilson; *Asst Prof Art* Theodore Vassar; *Adjunct Instr Art* Daniel Stuart
Open Mon & Tues 8:30 AM - 7 PM, Wed - Fri 8:30 AM - 4:30 PM; No admis fee; Estab 1967 to promote the arts; Average Annual Attendance: 120
Income: $3000 (financed by endowment, mem & county appropriation)
Activities: Classes for children; gallery talks; competitions with awards; schols

MOUNT CLEMENS

A **ANTON ART CENTER,** 125 Macomb Pl, Mount Clemens, MI 48043-5650. Tel 586-469-8666; Fax 586-469-4529; Web: www.theartcenter.org; *Exec Dir* Jennifer Callans
Open Tues - Sat 10 AM - 5 PM, Sun noon-4PM; No admis fee; Estab 1969 to foster art appreciation and participation for people of Macomb County; The only public facility of its kind in the northeast Detroit metro area; The Center has two rooms, 17 x 27 ft, connected by lobby area in the former Carnegie Library Bldg, a Historical State Registered building; Average Annual Attendance: 10,000; Mem: 500; dues individual $25; annual meeting in June
Income: Financed by mem, city & state appropriation, commissions from sales, class fees & special fundraising events
Exhibitions: Annual season of exhibitions both regional & statewide by established & emerging Michigan artists
Publications: Newsletter, quarterly
Activities: Classes for adults and children; docent training; tours; competitions; gallery & gift shops sell original art

MOUNT PLEASANT

M **CENTRAL MICHIGAN UNIVERSITY,** University Art Gallery, 132 Wightman Hall, CMU Mount Pleasant, MI 48859. Tel 989-774-3800, 774-7457; Fax 989-774-2278; Email goche1as@cmich.edu; Web: www.uag.cmich.edu; *Gallery Dir* Anne Gochenour
Open Tues - Fri 11 AM - 6 PM, Sat 11 AM - 3 PM, cl school holidays; No admis fee; Estab 1970 to serve Mount Pleasant & university community; offer nat and international artists exhibs of contemporary art; Corner of Franklin & Preston Streets. 290 linear ft of wall space & 2100 sq ft of unobstructed floor space; Average Annual Attendance: 10,000
Income: Financed by Dept of Art & Design, CMU
Library Holdings: Book Volumes, CD-ROMs, Cards, Clipping Files, DVDs, Exhibition Catalogs, Kodachrome Transparencies, Manuscripts, Maps, Original Art Works, Prints
Collections: Twentieth Century Anishinabe Art - The Olga Denison Collection, modern & contemporary prints
Publications: Subverting the Market: Artwork on the Web Exhib Catalogue; Twentieth Century Anishinabe Art
Activities: Educ prog; docent training; mus studies prog instruction; collaborate with pub schools; part of art dept curriculum; lects open to pub, 2-4 vis lectrs per yr; gallery talks; tours; competitions; annual award for juried student exhib; originates traveling exhibs to colleges & universities

MUSKEGON

M **MUSKEGON MUSEUM OF ART FOUNDATION,** (Muskegon Museum of Art) Muskegon Museum of Art, 296 W Webster Ave, Muskegon, MI 49440-1282. Tel 231-720-2571; Fax 231-720-2585; Email mgawron@mpsk12.net; Web: www.muskegonartmuseum.org; *Exec Dir* Judith Hayner; *Sr Cur & Dir Colls & Exhib* Art Martin; *Cur Educ* Cathy Mott; *Communs, Pub Rels & Vol Coordr* Marguerite Curran-Gawron; *Assoc Cur & Mgr Coll* Pending; *Develop Officer* Kirk Hallman
Open Tues - Wed & Fri - Sat 11 AM - 5 PM, Thurs 11 AM - 8 PM, Sun noon - 5 PM; Admis adults 18 & over $8, students 17 & over (w/ID) $5, children 17 & under & mems free; check website for special admis fees; Estab 1912; Permanent coll & changing exhib galleries; Average Annual Attendance: 29,000; Mem: 995; Chmn's Society $10,000, Coll's Cir $5,000, Hackley Guild $2,500, Ambassador $1,000, Benefactor $500, Patron $300, Friend $150, Mem + Guest & Household $70, Artist or Educ $50, Student $30
Income: Privately funded
Special Subjects: Asian Art, Bronzes, Cartoons, Ceramics, Collages, Crafts, Decorative Arts, Drawings, Etchings & Engravings, Glass, Graphics, Landscapes, Marine Painting, Marine Painting, Miniatures, Painting-American, Painting-British, Painting-Dutch, Painting-European, Painting-European, Painting-Flemish, Painting-French, Painting-German, Painting-Italian, Photography, Photography, Portraits, Prints, Sculpture, Watercolors, Woodcuts, Posters, Textiles, Woodcarvings, Woodcuts
Collections: Significant holdings of American and European Art
Publications: Pictures of the Best Kind: The First Century of the Muskegon Museum of Art; exhib catalogues
Activities: Classes for adults & children; docent training; lects open to pub, 15-30 vis lectrs per yr; concerts; gallery talks; tours; sponsoring of competitions; individual & original objects of art lent to qualified museums; 1-5 book traveling exhibs; originate traveling exhibs to US art mus 1-2 per yr; mus shop sells books, original art, jewelry, gifts, handcrafts & reproductions

OLIVET

M **OLIVET COLLEGE,** Armstrong Collection, 320 S Main St, Olivet, MI 49076-9406. Tel 269-749-7000 Ext 7661; Fax 269-749-7178; Web: www.olivetcollege.edu; *Dir* Donald Rowe; *Chmn Arts & Comm Depts* Gary Wortheimer
Call for hours; Estab 1960 to collect artifacts & display for educational purposes; Average Annual Attendance: 1,200
Special Subjects: Primitive art, Prints, Sculpture
Collections: American Indian, Mesopotamian, Philippine & Thai Artifacts, Modern American Prints, Primitive Art, Sculpture
Exhibitions: Invitational shows; one-man shows; student shows; traveling shows

L **Library,** Corner of Main & College Sts, Olivet, MI 49076; 320 S Main St, Olivet, MI 49076-9406. Tel 616-749-7608; Fax 616-749-7178; Web: www.olivet.edu; *Library Dir* Mary Jo Blackport
Open during school yr Mon - Thurs 8 AM - Noon, Fri 8 AM - 5 PM, Sat 11 AM - 5 PM, Sun 2 - 11 PM
Library Holdings: Book Volumes 78,000, Micro Print

ORCHARD LAKE

M **ST MARY'S GALERIA,** 3535 Indian Trail, Orchard Lake, MI 48324. Tel 248-683-0345; *Dir* Marian Owczarski
Open Mon - Fri upon request, first Sun of the month Noon - 5 PM & anytime upon request; No admis fee; Estab to house major Polish & Polish-American art; Average Annual Attendance: 6,700
Special Subjects: Painting-Polish
Collections: Contemporary Polish Painting, Sculpture by Marian Owczarski, History of Polish Printing: Rare Books & Documents, Polish Folk Art, Polish Tapestry, Paintings of A Wierusz Kowalski, Watercolors by J Falat, Watercolors by Wojciech Gierson, Louvre by Night, a sketch by Aleksander Gierymski, oil paintings by Jacek Malczewski, lithographs by Irene Snarski & Barbara Rosiak
Exhibitions: Various exhib

Activities: Lect open to public; concerts; gallery talks; tours; competitions for youngsters & artists

OWOSSO

M **SHIAWASSEE ARTS CENTER,** 206 Curwood Castle Dr, Owosso, MI 48867-2723. Tel 989-723-8354; Fax 989-729-9134; Email sac@shiawasseearts.org; Web: www.shiawasseearts.org; *Exec Dir* Piper Brewer; *Exhibs Dir* Karen Marumoto; *Arts Educ Dir* Linda Ruehle; *Mktg Specialist* Emma Tomkins; *Gallery Asst* Delaney Asbridge
Open Mon - Fri Noon - 5 PM, Sat - Sun Noon - 4 PM; No admis fee; Estab to encourage participation in and appreciation of the arts among the community; Mem: dues $15-$500
Collections: Features local, statewide & national artists
Exhibitions: Temporary exhibits
Activities: Educ progs; classes for adults & children; workshops; art programming; Mus shop sells jewelry, paintings, prints, pottery metal work, hand-blown glass, scarves & note cards

PETOSKEY

M **CROOKED TREE ARTS COUNCIL,** Virginia M McCune Community Arts Center, 461 E Mitchell St, Petoskey, MI 49770-2623. Tel 231-347-4337; Fax 231-347-5414; Web: www.crookedtree.org; *Dir* Liz Ahrens
Open Mon - Sat 10 AM - 5 PM; No admis fee; Estab 1981 as a non-profit arts council & arts center; 40 ft x 25 ft exhibition gallery featuring monthly shows, modern lighting & security systems; 85 x 45 ft gallery featuring work of Michigan artists on consignment; Average Annual Attendance: 50,000; Mem: 1600; dues family $50, individual $30; annual meeting in Sept
Income: $300,000 (financed by endowment, city & state appropriation, ticket sales, tuition income, fundraisers)
Exhibitions: Monthly exhibits
Publications: Art news, bimonthly
Activities: Classes for adults & children; dramatic progs; docent progs; music & dance classes; 3 competitions per yr (crafts, fine arts, photography); cash prizes; book traveling exhibs 7 per yr; sales shop sells original art, reproductions, prints, art postcards

PONTIAC

A **CREATIVE ARTS CENTER,** 47 Williams St, Pontiac, MI 48341-1759. Tel 248-333-7849; Fax 248-333-7841; Email cpaster@aol.com; Web: www.pontiac.mi.us/cac; *Exec Dir* Carol Paster; *Chmn (V)* John Manfredi
Open Wed - Sat 10 AM - 5 PM, cl holidays; No admis fee; Estab 1965 to present the best in exhibitions, educational activities, & community art outreach; Main gallery is a two story central space with carpeted walls; Clerestory Gallery is the second floor balcony overlooking the main gallery; Average Annual Attendance: 3,000; Mem: 160; dues organizational $50, general $35, artists & citizens $20, annual meeting in Mar
Income: Financed by endowment, mem, city & state appropriation, trust funds, United Way, Michigan Council for the Arts
Exhibitions: Temporary exhibits of historic, contemporary & culturally diverse works
Publications: Biannual newsletter, Creative Arts Center
Activities: Classes for adults & children; dramatic progs, music, dance, visual arts progs; lects open to pub, 30 vis lectrs per yr; gallery talks; concerts; tours; competitions with awards; schols offered; book traveling exhibs semi-annually; originate traveling exhibs; sales shop sells books & original art work

PORT HURON

M **PORT HURON MUSEUM,** 1115 Sixth St, Port Huron, MI 48060. Tel 810-982-0891; Fax 810-982-0053; Email info@phmuseum.org; Web: www.phmuseum.org; *Exec Dir* Susan Bennett; *Dir Bus Opers* Anita Varty; *Dir Educ, Coll & Exhibs* Katherine Bancroft; *Vol Srvcs Coordr* Stacie Fraley
Open daily 11AM - 4PM, cl Mon & Tues; Admis adults $7, seniors & students $5, 4 & under free; Estab 1968 to preserve area historical & marine artifacts; exhibit living regional artists; exhibit significant shows of national & international interest. Maintains reference library; Two galleries are maintained for loaned exhibitions & the permanent collection; also a decorative arts gallery & a sales gallery; Average Annual Attendance: 40,000; Mem: 900; dues family $45, individual $35, seniors $25, students $15
Income: $200,000 (financed by endowment, mem, city appropriation, state & federal grants & earned income through program fees)
Special Subjects: American Indian Art, Anthropology, Archaeology, Carpets & Rugs, Cartoons, Costumes, Decorative Arts, Dolls, Embroidery, Folk Art, Furniture, Glass, Jewelry, Landscapes, Maps, Marine Painting, Painting-American, Painting-Canadian, Painting-European, Photography, Portraits, Prints, Silver, Textiles, Watercolors
Collections: Civil War Collection, Thomas Edison Collection
Exhibitions: Blue Water Art
Publications: Quarterly newsletter
Activities: Classes for adults & children; dramatic progs; docent training; lects open to pub; tours; festivals; book traveling exhibs, 2 per yr; mus shop sells books, magazines, original art; prints

M **SAINT CLAIR COUNTY COMMUNITY COLLEGE,** Jack R Hennesey Art Galleries, 323 Erie St, Port Huron, MI 48060; PO Box 5015, Port Huron, MI 48061-5015. Tel 810-989-5709; Fax 810-984-2852; Email dkorff@stclair.cc.mi.us; Web: www.sc4.edu; *Coordr Galleries & Exhibits* David Korff
Open Mon - Fri 8 AM - 4:30 PM; No admis fee; Estab 1975 to serve the community as an exhib site & to serve the faculty & students of the col as a teaching tool; Maintains three galleries connected by common hall with approx 2,000 sq ft; Average Annual Attendance: 3,000
Special Subjects: Metalwork, Painting-American, Prints, Sculpture, Woodcarvings
Collections: Paintings, print, and sculpture (wood and metal)
Activities: Educ dept; lect open to public; concerts; competitions with awards; scholarships offered; book traveling exhibitions, one per year or as funds permit

ROCHESTER

M **OAKLAND UNIVERSITY,** Oakland University Art Gallery, 371 Wilson Blvd, 208 Wilson Hall Rochester, MI 48309-4486. Tel 248-370-3005; Fax 248-370-4368; Email goody@oakland.edu; Web: www.oakland.edu, www.ouartgallery.org; www.oakland.edu/ouag; *Dir* Dick Goody
Open Tues - Sun Noon - 5 PM, evenings in conjunction with Meadow Brook Theater Performances through the intermission; No admis fee; Estab to provide exhib schedule that emphasizes excellence in fine arts, provide exhib opportunities for emerging & mid career Mich artists & raise awareness & enthusiasm about contemporary art in South Eastern Mich; 2400 sq ft space across hallway from theatre; Average Annual Attendance: 16,000; Mem: Various levels; $15-1,000; AAM required
Income: Financed by university budget, mem, contributions & outside grant funding
Special Subjects: African Art, Asian Art, Collages, Photography
Collections: Art of Africa, Oceania and Pre-Columbian America, contemporary art and Sculpture Park, Oriental art, numerous fine prints
Exhibitions: Minimum of 6 exhibs annually
Publications: Exhibition catalogs
Activities: Lect open to public; 6-10 visiting lectures per year; symposiums; gallery talks; slide presentations in conjunction with exhibitions; paintings & original art objects lent within university; on loan exhibs

M **PAINT CREEK CENTER FOR THE ARTS,** 407 Pine St, Rochester, MI 48307-1933. Tel 248-651-4110; Fax 248-651-4757; Email general@pccart.org; Web: www.pccart.org; *Exec Dir* Tami Salisbury; *Mgr Art Educ* Alex Wilson; *Mgr Galleries & Digital Media* Jenny Creech; *Officer Mgr & Program Coordr* Jessica Ann Bauer; *Accountant* Sue Wood; *Social Media & Mem Coordr* Kelly Bradsher
Open Mon - Thurs 9 AM - 7 PM, Fri 9 AM - 5 PM, Sat 9 AM - 4 PM; Estab 1983 to foster arts and artistic excellence & create opportunities for artists
Collections: Features contemporary art by artists in the Michigan area
Exhibitions: 6 - 8 exhibits per year
Activities: Educ progs; classes for adults & children; gallery talks

ROYAL OAK

M **DETROIT FOCUS,** PO Box 843, Royal Oak, MI 48068-0843. Tel 248-541-2210; Email director@detroitfocus.org; Web: http://www.detroitfocus.org/; *Dir* Michael Sarnacki; *Co-Dir* Gene Baskin
Open by appointment; No admis fee; Estab 1978 as an exhibition space for Michigan visual artists; Foundation
Income: $21,000 (financed by mem, city & state appropriation, fundraising)
Exhibitions: Juried exhibitions, visual & performance art
Publications: Detroit Focus Quarterly; exhibition catalogues
Activities: Lects open to pub, 5 vis lectrs per yr; competitions with awards; originate traveling exhibs

M **DETROIT ZOOLOGICAL INSTITUTE,** Wildlife Interpretive Gallery, 8450 W 10 Mile, PO Box 39 Royal Oak, MI 48068-0039. Tel 248-398-0903; Fax 248-398-0504; *Cur Educ* Gerry Craig
Open daily 10 AM - 5 PM (Summer), 10 AM - 4 PM (Winter); No admis fee with zoo admis; Estab 1995 to celebrate & interpret humans' relationship with animals; The permanent art collection of the Wildlife Interpretive Gallery is displayed on the mezzanine level of the main rotunda, under the glass dome. Commissioned works are on display throughout the building. A temporary art gallery has 4 shows annually focusing on fine arts or educ exhibits; Average Annual Attendance: 1,200,000; Mem: 55,000; dues $50-$500
Special Subjects: African Art, Antiquities-Egyptian, Antiquities-Persian, Asian Art, Ceramics, Embroidery, Eskimo Art, Metalwork, Painting-American, Photography, Pre-Columbian Art, Prints, Sculpture, Tapestries, Textiles
Activities: Classes for adults & children; dramatic progs; lects open to pub, 4-6 vis lectrs per yr; exten services to schools with performing arts prog; book traveling exhibs 4 per yr; originate traveling exhibs 1-2 per yr

SAGINAW

M **SAGINAW ART MUSEUM,** 1126 N Michigan Ave, Saginaw, MI 48602-4795. Tel 989-754-2491; Fax 989-754-9387; Email staff@saginawartmuseum.org; Web: www.saginawartmuseum.org; *Exec Dir* Stacey Gannon; *Assoc Cur* Eric Birkle; *Event Coordr* Emily Korn
Open Tues - Sat noon - 5 PM; Admis $5, seniors 65 & students with ID $3, children under 16 free; Estab 1947; Circ 1100 non-lending; 4,000 sq ft gallery with 550 running feet; 9 additional small galleries; Average Annual Attendance: 15,000; Mem: 700; dues $25-$1,000
Income: Grants, local business
Library Holdings: Auction Catalogs, Book Volumes, Exhibition Catalogs, Memorabilia, Original Documents, Other Holdings Archives of Michigan artists, Pamphlets, Periodical Subscriptions, Video Tapes
Special Subjects: American Indian Art, American Western Art, Antiquities-Etruscan, Antiquities-Oriental, Architecture, Asian Art, Bronzes, Carpets & Rugs, Ceramics, Collages, Costumes, Crafts, Decorative Arts, Drawings, Embroidery, Etchings & Engravings, Folk Art, Glass, Graphics, Hispanic Art, Historical Material, Laces, Landscapes, Marine Painting, Medieval Art, Military Art, Oriental Art, Painting-American, Painting-British, Painting-Dutch, Painting-European, Painting-French, Painting-German, Painting-Japanese, Painting-Polish, Painting-Russian, Photography, Porcelain, Portraits, Posters,

Pottery, Prints, Religious Art, Sculpture, Southwestern Art, Tapestries, Textiles, Watercolors, Woodcarvings, Woodcuts
Collections: African, Asian & Ancient Near East, painting & sculpture; 18th - 21st century American, European, Asian painting, sculpture & decorative art; late 19th to early 20th century photography, Eanger Irving Couse, Corot, Inness, Cropsey, Minor, Arneson, Held, Blakelock
Publications: Annual report; Quarterly newsletter
Activities: Classes for adults & children; docent training; progs: Art Goes to School, Art Across the Curriculum; lects open to pub; 6-12 vis lectrs per yr; concerts; gallery talks; tours, awards: 2004 American Architecture Award from Chicago Athenaeum, 2005 NY AIA Merit Award, 2005 Michigan AIA Honor Award; exten dept serves mid-Michigan region; lending of original objects of art to AAM accredited institutions; 1-2 book traveling exhibitions per year; originates traveling exhibs; books; original art; jewelry; apparel; novelties

SAINT JOSEPH

M **KRASL ART CENTER,** 707 Lake Blvd, Saint Joseph, MI 49085-1398. Tel 269-983-0271; Fax 269-983-0275; Email info@krasl.org; Web: www.krasl.org; *Exec Dir* Julia Gourley; *Dir Exhibs & Colls* Tami Miller; *Dir Community Rels* Joshua Nowicki; *Dir Admin & Gift Shop Mgr* Patrice Rose; *Dir Krasl Art Fair on the Bluff & Special Events* Sara Shambarger; *Educ Progs Coordr* Rebecca Hunt
Open Mon - Wed & Fri - Sat 10 AM - 4 PM, Thurs 10 AM - 9 PM, Sun 1 - 4 PM; No admis fee; Estab 1980 with the mission to bring people & art together; 3 galleries; 200 running ft; Average Annual Attendance: 29,000; Mem: 1015; dues $25 & up; annual meeting 1st wk in Nov
Income: $1,000,000 (financed by earned income, endowment, membership, state appropriations & foundations)
Library Holdings: Book Volumes, DVDs, Exhibition Catalogs, Periodical Subscriptions, Slides, Video Tapes
Special Subjects: Sculpture
Collections: Krasl Art Center Sculpture Collection
Publications: Krasl Newsletter, bimonthly; exhibit catalogs; collection catalogs
Activities: Classes for adults & children; docent training; lect open to pub; 10-12 vis lectrs per yr; concerts; gallery talks; tours; scholarships offered; 1-3 book traveling exhibs; mus shop sells books, original art & prints

TRAVERSE CITY

M **CROOKED TREE ARTS CENTER - TRAVERSE CITY,** Gallery, 322 Sixth St, Traverse City, MI 49684-2414. Tel 231-941-9488; Fax 231-941-0886; Email tc@crookedtree.org; Web: www.crookedtree.org; *Pres* Liz Ahrens; *Assoc Dir* Megan Kelto; *Educ & Outreach Coord* Kristi Wodek
Open Mon, Tues, Thurs & Fri 9 AM - 5 PM, Wed, Sat & Sun 10 AM - 5 PM; No admis fee; Estab 1971 to sponsor and encourage activities in the arts for the residents of Charlevoix & Emmet counties; Average Annual Attendance: 50,000; Mem: 2,000; dues $20 - $2,500
Special Subjects: Painting-American, Photography, Sculpture, Ceramics, Textiles
Collections: Contemporary art
Exhibitions: Rotating exhibits
Activities: Educ progs; classes for adults & children; docent training; artist workshops; lects open to pub; concerts; gallery talks; tours; workshops; competitions with awards; public art projects; performance art; outreach progs; film screenings; dance & theater performances; cultural events; art festivals; mus shop sells original art

M **NORTHWESTERN MICHIGAN COLLEGE,** Dennos Museum Center, 1701 E Front St, Traverse City, MI 49686. Tel 231-995-1055; Fax 231-995-1597; Email dmc@nmc.edu; Web: www.dennosmuseum.org; *Dir Mus* Eugene A Jenneman; *Registrar* Kim Hanninen; *Museum Shop Mgr* Terry Tarnow; *Opers Mgr* Megan Heator; *Educ Cur* Jason Dake
Open Mon - Sat 10 AM - 5 PM, Sun 1 - 5 PM, Thurs until 8PM; Admis adults $6, children $4, family $20 (subject to change with exhib); Estab 1991; 40,000 sq ft complex features three changing exhibit galleries & a sculpture ct; a hands on Discovery Gallery; & a Gallery of Inuit Art, the museum's major permanent collection. The 367 seat Milliken Auditorium offers theater & musical performances throughout the year; Average Annual Attendance: 60,000; Mem: 1200; dues $40 individual, $60 family, and up; Scholarships
Income: $900,000 (financed by earned income/endowment)
Collections: Canadian Inuit sculpture & prints
Activities: Classes for adults & children, docent training; lect open to public, 12-15 vis lectrs per year; concerts; Governor's Award for Arts & Culture; gallery talks; tours; individual paintings & original objects of art lent to mus; lending coll contains original art works & original prints; originate traveling exhibs to mus; mus shop sells books, magazines, original art, reproductions & prints

TROY

M **MUSEUM OF NEW ART,** 2461 Rochester Ct, Troy, MI 48083. Tel 248-210-7560; Email detroitmona@gmail.com; Web: detroitmona.wixsite.com/mona; *Creative Dir* Jef Bourgeau; *Project Dir* Paul Smith; *Cur* Jessica Hopkins
Estab 1996 to examine the potential for exhibition-making to be an independent, alternative exercise in art
Collections: Contemporary art
Exhibitions: Temporary exhibits

WHITEHALL

M **ARTS COUNCIL OF WHITE LAKE,** Gallery, Nuveen Center, 106 E Colby St Whitehall, MI 49461-1009. Tel 231-894-2525; Email director@artswhitelake.org; Web: artswhitelake.org; *Exec Dir* Jennifer Diamond
Open Tues - Fri 10 AM - 5 PM, Sat 11 AM - 3 PM; Estab 1985 to foster and facilitate an artistic, cultural environment
Collections: Features work by local & regional artists
Exhibitions: Temporary exhibits
Activities: Educ progs; classes for adults & children; art walk; workshops

YPSILANTI

M **EASTERN MICHIGAN UNIVERSITY,** Ford Gallery, 114 Ford Hall, Bldg 114 Ypsilanti, MI 48197-2251. Tel 734-487-0465, 1077; Fax 734-487-2324; Email gtom@emich.edu; Web: art.emich.edu; *Dept Head* Colin Blackely; *Dir Gallery* Gregory Tom
Open Mon & Thurs 10 AM - 5 PM, Tues & Wed 10 AM - 7 PM, Fri & Sat 10 AM - 2 PM; No admis fee; Estab 1925, in present building since 1982, for educational purposes; Art Dept gallery is maintained displaying staff & student exhibitions from a wide variety of sources; also on large, well-lighted gallery with lobby & a satellite student-operated gallery are maintained
Income: Financed by state appropriation
Purchases: $500
Exhibitions: Seven changing exhibitions annually; Annual Faculty Exhibition; Annual Juried Student Exhibition; Biannual Michigan Drawing Exhibition
Publications: Exhibition catalogs
Activities: Classes for adults; lects open to pub; gallery talks; competitions

L **Art Dept Slide Collection**, 214 Ford Hall, Ypsilanti, MI 48197-2251. Tel 734-487-1268; Fax 734-487-2324; Email cpawloski@emich.edu; Web: webstage.emich.edu/art; *Visual Resource Librn* Carole Pawloski
Open 8 AM - 5 PM; Estab 1978 to foster slide circulation for art faculty
Library Holdings: Lantern Slides, Slides 100,000, Video Tapes
Special Subjects: Afro-American Art, American Indian Art, American Western Art, Furniture, History of Art & Archaeology, Mexican Art, Oriental Art, Painting-American, Pre-Columbian Art, Restoration & Conservation
Collections: 100,000 art slides, 4,000 digital images
Activities: Classes for adults; lectrs open to pub & lectrs for mems only; gallery talks; exten prog serves entire univ

MINNESOTA

AITKIN

M **THE JAQUES ART CENTER,** 121 Second St NW, Aitkin, MN 56431. Tel 218-927-2363; Fax 218-927-4729; Email info@jaquesart.com; Web: jaquesart.com
Open Tues-Sat 11AM-4PM; No admis fee; Estab 1995; art of Francis Lee Jacques & contemporary artists; Carnegie Bldg - nat historic place/exhib galleries; Average Annual Attendance: 4,000; Mem: 350; open to all
Income: Donations, grants, fundraisers
Library Holdings: Original Art Works
Collections: paintings, sculptures, photographs
Activities: Classes for adults & children; sponsoring competitions, Plein Air Painting Comp; Honorable Peoples Choice; 1 book traveling exhib; mus shop sells books, magazines, reproductions, prints & creative arts by regional artisans

BLOOMINGTON

M **ARTISTRY,** (Bloomington Art Center) Inez Greenberg Gallery, 1800 W Old Shakopee Rd, Bloomington, MN 55431-3071. Tel 952-563-8575; Fax 952-563-8576; Email info@artistrymn.org; Web: www.artistrymn.org; *Exec Dir* Andrea Specht; *Visual Arts Dir* Rachel Daly; *Dir Publicity* Nancy Lamberger
Open Mon - Fri 8 AM - 10 PM, Sat 9 AM - 5 PM, Sun 1 - 10 PM, cl holidays; No admis fee; Estab 1976 to serve emerging & established local artists; Circ 13,000; Inez Greenberg Gallery, 1800 sq ft; Atrium Gallery, single artist shows; Average Annual Attendance: 69,000; Mem: 500; dues individual $40, household $55
Income: (financed by mem, programming, city appropriation); 1.5 million
Exhibitions: Ongoing
Activities: Classes for adults & children in visual, literary & dramatic progs; lects open to pub, 1-2 vis lectrs per yr; gallery talks; tours; competitions with prizes; annual members' juried exhib; annual mems juried awards; sales shop sells books, original art, reproductions & prints

M **MHIRIPIRI GALLERY,** 9001 Penn Ave S, Bloomington, MN 55431-2225. Tel 952-285-9684; Fax 952-848-0306; Email rexandjulie@shonasculpturemhiripir.com; Web: www.shonasculpturemhiripir.com; *Co-Owner* Julie Mhiripiri; *Co-Owner* Rex Mhiripiri
Open 10 AM - 6 PM & by appt; Estab 1986; commercial art gallery 5,200 sq ft
Special Subjects: Sculpture
Collections: Stone sculpture
Exhibitions: Permanent exhibits; temporary exhibits

BRAINERD

M **CROW WING COUNTY HISTORICAL SOCIETY,** PO Box 722, Brainerd, MN 56401-0722. Tel 218-829-3268; Fax 218-828-4434; Email history@co.crow-wing.mn.us; Web: www.crowwinghistory.org; *Exec Dir* Mary Lou Moudry
Open Tues-Sat 10AM-3PM, cl holidays; Admis adults $3; Estab 1927 to preserve & interpret county history; Average Annual Attendance: 6,000; Mem: 350; dues $15-$250; annual meeting in Apr
Income: $60,000 (financed by mem, county, state grants, private donations)
Special Subjects: Archaeology, Architecture, Carpets & Rugs, Costumes, Dolls, Drawings, Embroidery, Etchings & Engravings, Furniture, Glass, Jewelry, Manuscripts, Maps, Painting-American, Photography, Portraits

Exhibitions: N.P. Railroad; Sarah Thorp Heald & Freeman Thorp Paintings: Home & Community: Rotating Artifacts Reflecting Country Life; American Indian Tools & Beadwork; When Lumber Was King; Mining; 19th & Early 20th Century Furnishings
Publications: The Crow Wing County Historian, quarterly newsletter
Activities: Docent training; lects open to pub; tours; competitions with awards; mus shop sells books, Victorian items, American Indian items, notecards & stationery, archival supplies

BROOKLYN PARK

M **NORTH HENNEPIN COMMUNITY COLLEGE,** Joseph Gazzuolo Fine Arts Gallery, 7411 85th Ave N, Brooklyn Park, MN 55445-2231. Tel 763-424-0779, 424-0775; Fax 763-424-0929; Email will.agar@nhcc.mnscu.edu; Web: www.nhcc.edu; *Dir* Will Agar
Open Mon, Thurs & Fri 8 AM - 4:30 PM, Tues & Wed 8 AM - 7 PM; No admis fee; Estab 1966 to make art available to students & community; Rectangular 30x15 feet white walled, stone floor, panelled wooden ceiling with track lighting; Average Annual Attendance: 8,000
Income: Financed by state appropriation & foundation grants
Purchases: Yearly student & local artist purchases
Collections: Student works & local artists in Minnesota
Exhibitions: Mid-West Artist on regular basis
Activities: Lects open to pub; concerts; gallery talks; tours; student show with prizes; individual paintings & original objects of art lent to faculty members on campus; book traveling exhibs 1-2 per year; sales shop sells books

COLLEGEVILLE

M **ST JOHNS UNIVERSITY,** Alice R Rogers/Target Galleries, SJU Art Center, Collegeville, MN 56321; BAC, 37 S College Ave, Saint Joseph, MN 56374-2001. Tel 320-363-2701, 320-363-5792 (office); Fax 320-363-6097; Email tdietzel@csbsju.edu; Web: www.csbsju.edu/fine-arts; *Dir Exhibs* Tracy Doreen Dietzel, MFA
Open Thurs noon - 9 PM, Fri - Wed noon - 6 PM; No admis fee; Univ estab 1857, gallery estab 1991; 2 secured fully equipped galleries
Income: Financed by college
Exhibitions: contemporary artworks from established & emerging regional, national & international artists. Solo & group shows change every 6-8 weeks
Activities: Lects open to pub; 10-16 vis lectrs per yr

COMFREY

M **JEFFERS PETROGLYPHS HISTORIC SITE,** 27160 County Rd 2, Comfrey, MN 56019. Tel 507-628-5591; Fax 507-628-5593; Email jefferspetroglyphs@mnhs.org; Web: www.mnhs.org/places/sites/jp; *Site Mgr* Tom Sanders; *Site Supervisor* Pam Jensen
Open Memorial weekend to Labor Day Mon & Thurs - Sat 10 AM - 5 PM, Sun noon - 5 PM; Admis adults $7, seniors $6, children 6 - 17 $5, group of 10 or more with advanced reservation $4, children under 6 & MHS members free; Estab 1966; Historical site; sacred site to the American Indians; mus concentrates on American Indian history & spirituality which dates back to the plain's Archaic Period (7000 BC - 600 AD); mus situated on over 160 acres of prairie. 1300 sq ft exhib space; theater capacity 50; nonprofit, governed by state; Average Annual Attendance: 7,000; Mem: Dues North Star Circle $1000, Sustaining $500, Contributing $250, Assoc $145, Household plus $95, Household $75, Sr Household of two adults 65 & over plus Indiv $65, Indiv $50, Sr Indiv $45
Collections: Over 2000 carvings on quartzite rock ranging from 5000 - 10,000 yrs old that are symbols of thunderbirds, bison, turtles, lightning strikes, humans & other figures, book vols on Native American history & culture, book vols on prairie flowers & grasses
Publications: The Jeffers Petroglyphs, book
Activities: Research in archaeology, geology, petroglyphs, and prairie grasses & flowers; training progs for professional mus workers; educ progs for children, college students & adults; guided tours; Native American books, jewelry, soap, dreamcatchers & other mus related items for sale

DULUTH

M **SAINT LOUIS COUNTY HISTORICAL SOCIETY,** St. Louis County Historical Society, 506 W Michigan St, Duluth, MN 55802-1517. Tel 218-733-7580; Fax 218-733-7585; Email history@thehistorypeople.org; Web: www.thehistorypeople.org; *Exec Dir* JoAnne Coombe
Open Winter, Mon - Sat 10 AM - 5 PM, Sun 1 PM - 5 PM; Summer 9:30AM-6PM Daily; Admis adults 13 yrs & older $12, children 3-13 $6, 2 and under free; Estab in 1922. Housed in the Saint Louis County Heritage & Arts Center along with Minnesota Ballet, Duluth Playhouse, Duluth Art Institute, & Lake Superior Railroad Mus; Soc exhibit areas consist of three galleries interspersed in viewing areas & Veterans Memorial Hall Mus; Average Annual Attendance: 120,000; Mem: 400; dues $30 & up
Income: $634,238 (financed by pub support, dues, earned profit, & volunteer service)
Purchases: $707,734
Library Holdings: Audio Tapes, Book Volumes, Cards, Cassettes, Clipping Files, Filmstrips, Manuscripts, Maps, Memorabilia, Original Art Works (in artifact coll), Original Documents, Other Holdings Military, Pamphlets, Periodical Subscriptions, Photographs, Records, Reels, Reproductions, Slides, Video Tapes
Special Subjects: American Indian Art, Ceramics, Coins & Medals, Costumes, Dolls, Embroidery, Flasks & Bottles, Folk Art, Furniture, Glass, Historical Material, Laces, Miniatures, Painting-American, Pottery, Reproductions, Stained Glass, Textiles, Watercolors, Woodcarvings
Collections: E Johnson Collection, drawings, paintings, Ojibwe & Sioux beadwork, quill work, basketry, Logging Exhibit, Herman Melheim hand-carved furniture, Priley Collection (carved figures)
Exhibitions: Changing exhibits on topics related to the history of northeastern Minnesota & Lake Superior region
Publications: Books & pamphlets on topics related to the history of northeastern Minn; semi-annual newsletter
Activities: Workshops; lect; 12-15 vis lectrs per yr; annual dinners; veterans' march; antique appraisals; various fundraising events; exhib openings/receptions; schols; sales shop sells books, prints & gift items

M **UNIVERSITY OF MINNESOTA DULUTH,** Tweed Museum of Art, 1201 Ordean Ct, Duluth, MN 55812-2496. Tel 218-726-7823; Fax 218-726-8503; Email tma@d.umn.edu; Web: www.d.umn.edu/tma/; *Dir* Ken Bloom; *Registrar* Camille Doran; *Preparator* Anneliese Verhoeven; *Head of Security* Scott Stevens; *Communs Mgr* Christine Strom; *Store Mgr & Exec Sec.* Kathy Sandstedt; *Sir Graphic Designer* Mike Cousino
Open Tues 9 AM - 8 PM, Wed - Fri 9 AM - 4:30 PM, Sat & Sun 1 - 5 PM, cl Mon & univ holidays; No admis fee; donations family $5, individual $2, seniors & students free; Estab 1950 to serve both the univ & community as a center for exhib of works of art & related activities; Nine galleries within the mus; Average Annual Attendance: 35,000; Mem: 500; dues $10-$1000
Income: Financed by mem, state appropriation & foundation
Purchases: 50% (state; 20% income & endowments) 15% private foundations; 15% members
Library Holdings: Auction Catalogs 300, Audio Tapes 50, Book Volumes 2,000, CD-ROMs 50, Clipping Files 500, Exhibition Catalogs, Periodical Subscriptions 5, Slides 1000, Video Tapes 300
Special Subjects: American Indian Art, Drawings, Etchings & Engravings, Painting-American, Painting-Canadian, Painting-European, Painting-French, Photography, Pottery, Prints, Renaissance Art, Textiles, Watercolors, Woodcuts, Sculpture
Collections: Jonathan Sax Collections of 20th Century American Prints, George P Tweed Memorial Art Collections: 5,000 paintings with emphasis on Barbizon School & 19th Century American, Glenn C Nelson international ceramics, George Morrison Collection, Potlatch Collection of Royal Canadian Mounted Police Illustrations, Richard E & Dorothy Rawlings Nelson Collection of American Indian Art, Wiiken Contemporary Glass Collection
Exhibitions: 8-10 major exhibits annually; 31st May, 2017) Whose Song Shall I Sing?; (1st Jan, 2017-31st Mar, 2017) Sinew; (1st Apr, 2017-30th Apr, 2017) Annual Student Exhibition; (1st Jun, 2016)Graphic Ceramics; through Spring 2017From the Beginning: Selections from the Original Alice Tweed Tuohy & George Tweed Collection; through summer 2017Reframing Ophelia; Selections of Native Art from the Tweed Museum Collection; Midwestern Moderns; 31st Jan, 2017) Un-Typing Casta
Publications: European Paintings in the Tweed Museum of Art by David Stark; American Painting in the Tweed Museum of Art by J Gray Sweeney; Luis Gonzalez Palma; Frank Big Bear; From Dreams May We Learn: Paintings & Drawings by Rabbett Before Horses (2007); Perspectives and Parallels: Expanding Interpretive Foundations with American Indian Curators and Writers (2014); The Way of Cheng-Khee Chee: Paintings 1974-2014 (2015); Robert Minichiello: Spontaneous Acts (2015); Jeffrey T. Larson: Domestic Space (2016)
Activities: Classes for adults & children; docent training; lects open to pub, 10 vis lectrs per yr; gallery talks; tours; individual paintings & original objects of art lent to qualifying mus & institutions; originates traveling exhibs to national & international mus & galleries; mus shop sells books, magazines, original art, reproductions, prints, gift items

EDINA

M **EDINA ART CENTER,** Margaret Foss Gallery, 4701 W 64th St, Edina, MN 55435-1501. Tel 952-903-5780; Fax 952-903-5781; Email artcenter@edinamn.gov; Web: www.edinaartcenter.com; *Gen Mgr* Michael Frey
Open Mon - Thurs 9 AM - 8 PM, Fri 9 AM - 5 PM, Sat 9 AM - 1 PM, cl Sun; Estab to promote the arts and art appreciation in the community; Mem: dues $35-$500
Special Subjects: Ceramics, Jewelry, Photography
Collections: Ceramics, jewelry, paintings & photography
Exhibitions: Temporary exhibits
Activities: Educ progs; classes for adults & children; art programming; workshops; cultural events

FARIBAULT

M **PARADISE CENTER FOR THE ARTS,** 321 Central Ave, Faribault, MN 55021. Tel 507-332-7372; Web: www.paradisecenterforthearts.org; *Exec Dir* Ryan Heinritz
Open Tues - Sat noon - 5 PM, Thurs until 8 PM; Admis free except for ticketed events; Estab 2007; multidisciplinary center for the arts, theatre, music, gallery, education; 3 galleries; Carlander Family Gallery, Lois Varnesh Boardroom Gallery & Cory Lynn Creger Memorial Gallery; Mem: 500; dues: family $60, individual $45
Income: Financed by donations, mem, ticketed events, fundraisers & grants
Exhibitions: View all exhibs at www.paradisecenterforthearts.org
Activities: Classes for adults & children; dramatic progs; concerts; gallery talks; tours; sales shop sells original art

FOUNTAIN

A **FILLMORE COUNTY HISTORICAL SOCIETY,** Fillmore County History Center, 202 County Rd, Fountain, MN 55935. Tel 507-268-4449; Email fchc@frontier.com; Web: fillmorecountyhistory.wordpress.com; *Exec Dir* Debra Richardson
Open Tues - Sat 9 AM - 4 PM; No admis fee, donations accepted, library fees; Estab 1934 to preserve & illustrate the written & photographic history; Average

Annual Attendance: 8,000; Mem: 350; dues $5-$150; annual meeting second Sat in Oct
Income: $50,000 (financed by mem, county appropriations, donations)
Purchases: An Original Bernard Pietenpol Airplane
Library Holdings: Memorabilia, Original Documents, Photographs, Records
Collections: Bue Photography, Antique Agricultural Equipment, Hand Made Wooden Tools, Vintage Clothing & Tractors
Exhibitions: Rotation exhibitions
Publications: Rural Roots, quarterly
Activities: Lects open to pub; 4 vis lectrs per yr; gift shop sells books

FRANCONIA

M **FRANCONIA SCULPTURE PARK,** 29836 St Croix Trail, Franconia, MN 55074. Tel 651-257-6668; Email info@franconia.org; Web: www.franconia.org; *Artistic Dir & CEO* John Hock; *Office Mgr* Joy Fusco; *Develop & Communs Mgr* Tessa Enroth; *Educ & Prog Coordr* Kendra Douglas
Open dawn - dusk; No admis fee; Estab 1996 to serve as ab artist residency program & open-air sculpture space; 43-acre outdoor sculpture park
Special Subjects: Sculpture
Collections: Sculptures
Exhibitions: Permanent exhibit
Activities: Educ progs; classes for children; artist residencies; interactive progs; tours; art programming; workshops

FRIDLEY

M **BANFILL-LOCKE CENTER FOR THE ARTS,** 6666 E River Rd, Fridley, MN 55432-4229. Tel 763-574-1850; Fax 763-502-6946; Email info@banfill-locke.org; Web: banfill-locke.org; *Exec Dir* Jeffrey Ebeling
Open Tues - Sat 10 AM - 4 PM; No admis fee; Estab 1979 to inspire & enrich its community through the arts
Collections: Features work by local & regional artists
Exhibitions: Temporary exhibits
Activities: Educ progs; classes for adults & children; artist residencies; Mus shop sells cards, jewelry, gifts & pottery

GLENWOOD

M **POPE COUNTY HISTORICAL SOCIETY,** Pope County Museum, S Hwy 104, Glenwood, MN 56334; 809 S Lakeshore Dr, Glenwood, MN 56334. Tel 320-634-3293; Email popecountymuseum@gmail.com; Web: www.popecountymuseum.com; *Cur* Merlin Peterson; *Archivist* Brent Gulsvig; *Collections Mgr* Ann Grady
Open Tues - Sat 10 AM - 5 PM; Admis adults $3, students $1.50, children $.50; Estab 1932 to display & preserve artifacts & genealogy files; 8,000 sq ft & seven historic buildings; Average Annual Attendance: 4,500; Mem: 400; dues $10; annual meeting
Income: $100,000 (financed by county appropriation, admis & gifts)
Library Holdings: Audio Tapes, Book Volumes, Clipping Files, Maps, Memorabilia, Original Art Works, Original Documents, Other Holdings, Photographs, Slides
Special Subjects: American Indian Art, Architecture, Costumes, Crafts, Decorative Arts, Dolls, Drawings, Embroidery, Eskimo Art, Furniture, Glass, Historical Material, Landscapes, Manuscripts, Metalwork, Painting-American, Painting-Scandinavian, Period Rooms, Photography, Portraits, Religious Art, Woodcarvings, Southwestern Art, Textiles
Collections: Native American Arts & Crafts; Pioneer History; Local History
Publications: Semi-annual newsletter
Activities: Educ dept; classes for children; guided tours for students; lects open to pub; 2 lects per yr; gallery talks; sales shop sell books & prints

INTERNATIONAL FALLS

M **KOOCHICHING MUSEUMS,** 214 Sixth Ave, International Falls, MN 56649. Tel 218-283-4316; Fax 218-283-8243; *Exec Dir* Edgar Oerichbauer
Open Mon - Fri 9 AM - 5 PM; Admis adults $2, students $1; Estab 1958 to collect, preserve & exhibit the material & social cultures of Koochiching County, North Central Minnesota & the southern border portions of southern Ontario; 2 mus; The Koochiching Historical Society & The Bronco Mus; Mem: 500; dues $15-$1000
Income: Financed by county, mem, admis funds & grants
Special Subjects: Coins & Medals, Crafts, Dolls, Embroidery, Furniture, Glass, Jewelry, Laces, Landscapes, Manuscripts, Maps, Painting-American, Period Rooms, Photography, Porcelain, Portraits, Pottery, Textiles
Collections: 100 paintings relating to the history of the region, including many by local artists & six of which were commissioned for the museum, various small collectors, football memorabilia
Exhibitions: Permanent coll
Publications: Koochiching Chronicle, quarterly
Activities: Classes for adults & children; dramatic progs; lects open to pub; tours; originate traveling exhibs; sales shop sells books, Indian craft items, post cards, unique gifts

LANESBORO

M **LANESBORO ARTS CENTER,** 103 Parkway Ave N, Lanesboro, MN 55949-0152; PO Box 152, Lanesboro, MN 55949-0152. Tel 507-467-2446; Email info@lanesboroarts.org; Web: lanesboroarts.org; *Exec Dir* John Davis; *Gallery Dir* Robbie Brokken; *Prog Dir* Adam Wiltgen; *Advancement Dir* Kara Maloney
Open (Jan - April) Tues - Sat 10 AM - 5 PM (May) Tues - Sat 10 AM - 5 PM, Sun 11 AM - 4 PM, (Memorial Day - October 31) Mon - Thurs 10 AM - 5 PM, Fri - Sat 10 AM - 7 PM, Sun 11 AM - 4 PM (Nov - Dec) Tues - Sat 10 AM - 5 PM, Sun 11 AM - 3 PM; Estab 1980 as an arts council; Mem: dues $35-$1,000
Collections: Work by regional & emerging artists
Exhibitions: Temporary exhibits
Activities: Educ progs; classes for adults & children

LE SUEUR

M **LESUEUR MUSEUM,** 709 N 2nd St, Le Sueur, MN 56058; c/o LCHS, PO Box 123 Le Center, MN 56057-0123. Tel 507-267-4091; Email info@lesueurcountyhistory.org; Web: www.lesueurcountyhistory.org; *Coord* Kathy Burns
Open year round by appt; No admis fee, donations accepted
Special Subjects: Historical Material
Exhibitions: Green Giant & Canning; Agriculture; Genealogy; Veterinary Medicine; War in the Valley

LITTLE FALLS

M **CHARLES A LINDBERGH HISTORIC SITE,** 1620 Lindbergh Dr S, Little Falls, MN 56345; 345 W Kellog Blvd, Minnesota Historic Society Saint Paul, MN 55102-1906. Tel 320-616-5421; Fax 320-616-5423; Email lindbergh@mnhs.org; Web: www.mnhs.org; *Historic Site Mgr* Charles D Pautler
Open Memorial Day - Labor Day: Thurs - Sat 10 AM - 5 PM, Sun 12 - 5 PM; cl Mon -Wed except holidays; open by appt year-round; Admis adults $7, seniors $6, students $5, children $4; spec rates for grps; mems no admis fee; Estab 1969; Childhood home of Charles A Lindbergh where he lived from 1902-1920; also contains visitor ctr which has state-of-the-art exhibs on Lindbergh's life & that of his wife, Anne Morrow Lindbergh; visitors can take guided tour of the 1906 home, tour three levels of mus exhibs & galleries in the visitor ctr & see films containing footage from Lindbergh's life. 2500 sq ft exhib space; 50-capacity theater with large screen; one classroom; nonprofit org governed both privately and by state govt; Average Annual Attendance: 14,000
Collections: 200 books vols on politics 1870 - 1920, 100 book vols of children's books, 50 vols on secondary reference resources, over 100 folders & research on Lindbergh & aviation
Exhibitions: Comprehensive exhibs on Lindbergh & his family, as well as the WPA
Activities: Lects; research in Lindbergh's aviation 1924 - 1927, Lindbergh's involvement in the anti-war effort 1939 - 1940; gen aviation history 1903 - 1940; Lindbergh's Pacific War experience 1944; guided tours; films; hobby workshops; participatory & traveling exhibs; spec events: Children's Day, Family Fun Day, Air Show, Film Festival; Lindbergh & aviator books, souvenirs, children's items & other mus related items for sale

MANKATO

M **MANKATO AREA ARTS COUNCIL,** Carnegie Art Center, 120 S Broad St, Mankato, MN 56001-3611. Tel 507-625-2730; Email artctr@hickorytech.net; Web: www.thecarnegiemonkato.com; *Gallery Coordr* Hope Cook; *Gift Shop Coordr* Janet Husar
Open Thurs 1 - 7 PM, Fri 1 - 4 PM, Sat 11 AM - 5 PM; No admis fee; Estab 1980 to provide exhibition space for regional artists; Three galleries (Rotunda Gallery, Cook Gallery & Fireplace Gallery) housed in historic Carnegie Library; library of author Maud Hart Lovelace; Average Annual Attendance: 5,000; Mem: 200; dues $25 individual & up; annual meeting in Nov
Exhibitions: Monthly regional shows by visual artists
Activities: Gallery exhibs; tours of Art Center & historic Carnegie Library on request; studio rental; studio art classes for adults; annual CAC juried exhib; gift shop sells handmade work by local & regional artists

M **MINNESOTA STATE UNIVERSITY, MANKATO,** 228 Wiecking Ctr, Mankato, MN 56001-6062. Tel 507-389-6412; Email harlan.bloomer@mnsu.edu; Web: www.mnsu.edu; *Dir* Harlan Bloomer
Open Mon - Fri 9AM-4PM; No admis fee; Estab 1979 to provide cultural enrichment in the visual arts to the campus & community through a prog of exhibs from local, regional & national sources & student exhibs; Gallery has 150 running ft of carpeted display area, track lighting & climate controlled
Income: Financed by univ
Special Subjects: Bookplates & Bindings, Crafts, Drawings, Painting-American, Prints
Collections: American bookplates, contemporary prints, drawings, paintings, photographs, sculpture & crafts, student works in all media

MAPLEWOOD

C **3M,** Art Collection, 2501 Hudson Rd, 3M Center Maplewood, MN 55144-1000. Tel 651-733-1110; Fax 651-737-4555; *Cur, Art Coll* Charles Thames
Estab 1902, dept estab 1974; Concourse Gallery provides changing exhibitions drawn from the collection
Collections: Collection of paintings, drawings, sculpture, watercolors, original prints, photographs & textiles
Publications: Exhibition brochures
Activities: Tours by appointment only & must be scheduled two weeks in advance; individual paintings & original objects of art lent to scholarly exhibitions

MINNEAPOLIS

AMERICAN CRAFT COUNCIL
For further information, see National and Regional Organizations

M **AMERICAN SWEDISH INSTITUTE,** 2600 Park Ave, Minneapolis, MN 55407-1090. Tel 612-871-4907; Fax 612-871-8682; Email info@asimn.org; Web: www.asimn.org; *Pres & CEO* Bruce Karstadt; *Cur Exhibs & Colls* Curt Pederson; *Visitor Servs & Volunteer Coordr* Robert Nicholl
Open Tues & Thurs - Sat 10 AM - 5 PM, Wed 10 AM - 8 PM, Sun noon - 5 PM, cl Mon & national holidays; Admis adults $10, seniors $7, students & children 6-18 $5, mem & children under 6 free; Estab & incorporated 1929 to preserve, collect, procure & exhibit objects related to Swedish-Americans in the Midwest from 1845; Building donated by Swan J Turnblad & contains, in a home setting, a coll of Swedish artifacts, plus many items of gen cultural interest pertaining to Scandinavia. The Grand Hall is paneled in African mahogany. Throughout the mansion there are eleven porcelain tile fireplaces; Average Annual Attendance: 50,000; Mem: 5000; dues, life $3000, patron $150, sustaining $100, family (husband, wife & all children under age 18, living at home) $50, regular (single) $35, non-resident single, or husband & wife outside of fifty mile radius of Twin Cities $35, students attending school, below the age of 18 $20, other mem levels available
Library Holdings: Book Volumes, Clipping Files, Fiche, Lantern Slides, Manuscripts, Maps, Memorabilia, Motion Pictures, Original Documents, Other Holdings, Photographs, Video Tapes
Special Subjects: Architecture, Ceramics, Crafts, Folk Art, Glass, Painting-Scandinavian, Porcelain, Sculpture, Tapestries, Woodcarvings, Period Rooms, Textiles
Collections: Paintings, sculpture, tapestries, ceramics, china, glass, pioneer items & textiles, immigration related objects
Publications: ASI Posten (newsletter), bimonthly
Activities: Classes for adults & children; dramatic progs; docent training; lect open to public; concerts; gallery talks; tours; scholarships offered; individual paintings lent to other museums; book traveling exhibs 1-2 per year; bookstore sells books, magazines, original art, reproductions & prints

A **ARTS MIDWEST,** 2908 Hennepin Ave Ste 200, Minneapolis, MN 55408-1954. Tel 612-341-0755; Fax 612-341-0902; Email yumiko.inomata@artsmidwest.org; Web: www.artsmidwest.org; Others TDD 612-341-0901; *Exec Mgr* Emily Anderson; *Develop Mgr* Emma Bohmann; *Sr Prog Dir* Angela Urbanz; *VPres Strategy & Prog* Adam Perry; *Prog Dir* Sharon Rodning Bash
Estab 1985, provides funding programs, conferences & publications to individuals & organizations in Illinois, Indiana, Iowa, Michigan, Minnesota, North Dakota, Ohio, South Dakota & Wisconsin. Works in collaboration with corporations, foundations, state government arts agencies, the National Endowment for the Arts & art enthusiasts to connect the arts to audiences, enabling individuals & families to share in & enjoy the arts & cultures of the region & the world
Publications: Inform, bimonthly newsletter; Insights on Jazz, booklets; Midwest Jazz, quarterly newsmagazine
Activities: Conferences

C **FEDERAL RESERVE BANK OF MINNEAPOLIS,** 90 Hennepin Ave, Minneapolis, MN 55401-2171. Tel 612-204-6065; Fax 612-204-6070; Email keithjablonski@mpls.frb.org; *Cur* Keith Jablonski
Open by appointment with Cur; Estab 1973 to enhance the working environment of bank; to support the creative efforts of ninth district artists; Collection displayed throughout the bank in offices, lounges, public areas and work areas
Collections: Regional collection consists of works by artists living & working in the Ninth Federal Reserve District

M **HIGHPOINT CENTER FOR PRINTMAKING,** 912 W Lake St, Minneapolis, MN 55408. Tel 612-871-1326; Email info@highpointprintmaking.org; Web: www.highpointprintmaking.org; *Exec Dir* Carla McGrath; *Artistic Dir* Cole Rogers

M **INTERACT CENTER FOR THE VISUAL & PERFORMING ARTS,** Interact Gallery, 1860 Minnehaha Ave W, Minneapolis, MN 55104. Tel 651-209-3575; Fax 651-209-3579; Email info@interactcenter.com; Web: www.interactcenter.com; *Artistic/Exec Dir* Jeanne Calvit; *Dir Opers* Glenis Zempel
Estab 1996; Space hosts professional public exhibitions and special exhibition events

M **INTERMEDIA ARTS,** 2822 Lyndale Ave S, Minneapolis, MN 55408-2108. Tel 612-871-4444; Email info@intermediaarts.org; Web: www.intermediaarts.org; *Exec Dir* Eyenga Bokamba; *Dir Youth Develop* Michael Hay; *Dir Creative Leadership Opers & Policy* Tisidra Jones; *Develop & Communs Mgr* Jessie Roelofs
Open Tues - Fri Noon - 6 PM; Suggested donation $3-$10; Estab 1973; 2,000 sq ft space used for installations, screenings & performances; Average Annual Attendance: 5,000
Income: Financed by donations, grants & earned income
Library Holdings: Book Volumes, Cassettes, DVDs, Other Holdings Caroline Holbrook Poetry Library, Video Tapes
Special Subjects: African Art, Afro-American Art, American Indian Art, American Western Art, Architecture, Cartoons, Ceramics, Collages, Decorative Arts, Drawings, Embroidery, Etchings & Engravings, Folk Art, Graphics, Hispanic Art, Islamic Art, Landscapes, Latin American Art, Metalwork, Mexican Art, Mosaics
Exhibitions: Exhibition supporting New Works in Media & interdisciplinary Arts; Exhibs change regularly in partnership with local artists & arts groups
Activities: Professional develop for artists; classes for adults & teens; grants progs; lects open to pub; approx 300 vis lectrs per yr; gallery talks; tours; fels; concerts; community-based progs to build understanding among people through art

M **JUXTAPOSITION ARTS,** 2007 Emerson Ave N, Minneapolis, MN 55411-2507. Tel 612-588-1148; Email info@juxtaposition.org; Web: juxtapositionarts.org; *CEO* DeAnna Cummings; *Chief Cultural Producter* Roger Cummings
Estab 1995 to engage youth artists and support their creative careers
Exhibitions: Temporary exhibits
Activities: Educ progs; classes for adults & children; artist residencies; tours; community events

A **MIDWEST ART CONSERVATION CENTER,** 2400 3rd Ave S, Minneapolis, MN 55404. Tel 612-870-3120; Fax 612-870-3118; Email macc@preserveart.org; Web: www.preserveart.org; *Sr Paper Conservator* Elizabeth Buschor; *Dir Preservation Svcs* Elisa Redman; *Objects Conservator* Nicole Grabow; *Sr Paintings Conservator* Kristy Jeffcoat; *Contract Textile Conservator* Beth McLaughlin; *Exec Dir* Colin D Turner; *Chief Conservator & Sr Objects Conservator* Megan Emery; *Paper Conservator* Liz Sorkin; *Sr Paintings Conservator* Kristy Jeffecoat; *Office Mgr* Jenny Wollner
Open Mon - Fri 8:30 AM - 5 PM; Estab 1977 for art conservation & education; Non-profit org; Mem: 170; dues $50-600; annual meeting in the Fall
Income: $1,000,000 (financed by mem, earned income & grants)

L **MINNEAPOLIS COLLEGE OF ART & DESIGN,** Library, 2501 Stevens Ave S, Minneapolis, MN 55404. Tel 612-874-3791; Fax 612-874-3704; Email library@mcad.edu; Web: intranet.mcad.edu/library; *Technical Svcs Librn* Kay Kroeff-Streng; *Visual Resources Librn* Allan Kohl; *Dir* Amy Naughton Becker
Open Mon - Thurs 8:30 AM - 10 PM, Fri 8:30 AM - 5 PM, Sat Noon - 5 PM, Sun Noon - 10 PM; No admis fee (students only); Estab to provide library & materials in support of the curriculum of the College; includes a library & slide library; Circ 21,000, circulation limited to students, staff, alumni & faculty; Average Annual Attendance: 90,000
Income: Financed by student tuition, grants & gifts
Library Holdings: Book Volumes 55,000, CD-ROMs, Clipping Files, Compact Disks, DVDs, Exhibition Catalogs, Pamphlets, Periodical Subscriptions 175, Records, Slides 145,000, Video Tapes
Special Subjects: Art History, Film, Graphic Design, Illustration, Photography

M **MINNEAPOLIS INSTITUTE OF ART,** 2400 Third Ave S, Minneapolis, MN 55404. Tel 888-642-2787; Fax 612-870-3004; Web: www.artsmia.org; *Chief Advancement Officer* Julianne Amendola; *Dir Learning Innovation* Karleen Gardner; *Chief Digital Officer* Douglas Hegley; *Deputy Dir & COO* Patricia J Grazzini; *Dir & Pres* Kaywin Feldman; *Deputy Dir & Chief Cur* Matthew Welch; *Chief of Staff* Michele Nichols; *Chief Engagement Officer* Kristin Prestegaard
Open Tues - Wed & Sat 10 AM - 5 PM, Thurs & Fri 10 AM - 9 PM, Sun 11 AM- 5 PM, cl Mon, Thanksgiving, Christmas Eve, Christmas Day & July 4; No admis free (special exhibs may require tickets); Estab 1883 to foster the knowledge, understanding & practice of the arts; The first gallery was opened in 1889 & the original bldg was constructed in 1911-15. The south wing was added in 1926 & the entire structure features the classical elements of the day. The mus was expanded to twice the original size in 1972-74 & has incorporated modern themes designed by Kenzo, Tange & URTEC of Tokyo; Average Annual Attendance: 789,961; Mem: 21,000; Basic membership ($0-$149); Investors ($150-$499), Partners ($500-$2,499), Patrons ($2,500-$9,999)
Income: Financed by endowment, mem, county & state appropriations & admis
Special Subjects: Painting-European, Painting-American, Sculpture, Decorative Arts, Period Rooms, Photography, Drawings, Prints, African Art, American Indian Art, Oriental Art, Antiquities-Greek, Antiquities-Roman, Pre-Columbian Art
Collections: Over 89,000 works of art representing more than 20,000 years of world history, European masterworks by Rembrandt, Poussin, van Gogh; modern & contemporary paintings & sculpture by Picasso, Matisse, Mondrian, Stella & Close, Decorative arts, Modernist design, photographs, prints, drawings, Asian, African & Native American art, Chinese and Japanese coll
Exhibitions: Rotating exhibitions
Publications: Annual Report
Activities: Classes for adults & children; docent training; workshops; lects open to pub, 15 vis lectrs per yr; concerts; gallery talks; tours; paintings & original art objects lent to other professional arts organizations; originate traveling exhibs; mus shop sells books, magazines, original art, reproductions, prints, slides & jewelry

L **Art Research & Reference Library**, 2400 Third Ave S, Minneapolis, MN 55404. Tel 612-870-3117; Fax 612-870-3004; Web: www.artsmia.org; *Head Librn* Janice Lea Lurie; *Asst Librn* Jessica McIntyre
Open Tues - Fri 11:30 AM - 4:30 PM, hours vary around holidays; Estab 1915 to provide a reference collection based around the museum's collection of works of art; Has exhibitions of books & prints. For reference only
Library Holdings: Auction Catalogs, Book Volumes 50,000, Exhibition Catalogs, Pamphlets, Periodical Subscriptions 125
Collections: Leslie Collection: History of Books & Printing, Minnich Collection: Botanical, Floral & Fashion Books, institutional archives
Publications: Imperial Silks by Robert Jacobsen; Chaining the Sun: Portraits by Jeremiah Gurney, by Christian Peterson; Classical Chinese Furniture in the Minneapolis Institute of Arts by Robert Jacobsen; Progressive Design in the Midwest by Jennifer Komar Olivarez

A **Friends of the Institute**, 2400 Third Ave S, Minneapolis, MN 55404. Tel 612-870-3045; Fax 612-870-3004; Web: www.artsmia.org; *Pres* Suzanne Payne
Open Mon - Fri 8:30 AM - 4:30 PM; Estab 1922 to broaden the influence of the Institute in the community & to provide volunteer support within the mus; Mem: 1900; annual meeting in May
Activities: Coordinates docent prog, mus shop, sales & rental gallery, speaker's bureau, information desk, special lect, exhibs & fundraising projects

M **MUSEUM OF RUSSIAN ART,** 5500 Stevens Ave S, Minneapolis, MN 55419. Tel 612-821-9045; Email info@tmora.org; Web: tmora.org; *Dir* Vladimir von Tsurikov; *Cur* Maria Zavialova
Open Mon - Fri 10 AM - 5 PM, Sat 10 AM - 4 PM. Sun 1 PM - 5 PM; Admis adults $10, seniors 65+ $8, children 14+ & students $5, children under 13 & mem free; Average Annual Attendance: 40,000
Library Holdings: Book Volumes 500
Collections: Russian art
Publications: semiannual newsletter
Activities: Seminars; children's educational events; lects; rental facilities; mus shop

M **SOAP FACTORY,** 514 Second St SE, Minneapolis, MN 55414-2105. Tel 612-623-9176; Email info@soapfactory.org; Web: www.soapfactory.org; *Exec Dir* Bill Mague; *Gallery Dir* Kate Arford; *Mktg & Outreach Coord* Joni Van Bockel
Currently under rennovation; No admis fee; Estab 1989 to provide budding artists with a supportive exhibition space; Mem: Historic 130-year-old, 48,000 sq ft wood & brick warehouse
Special Subjects: Sculpture, Video
Collections: Visual arts including sculpture, installation, new media, video & performance art

Exhibitions: Temporary exhibits
Activities: Artist residencies

M **SOO VISUAL ARTS CENTER,** 2909 Bryant Ave S, Minneapolis, MN 55408-4966. Tel 612-871-2263; Email info@soovac.org; Web: www.soovac.org; *Exec Dir* Carolyn Payne; *Assoc Dir* Alison Hiltner; *Gallery Asst* Britt Omann
Open Wed 11 AM - 5 PM, Thurs - Fri 11 AM - 7 PM, Sat & Sun 11 AM - 4 PM; Estab 2001 to enforce the view that art is critical to a community's health & success; Mem: dues $50-$500 & up
Exhibitions: Temporary exhibits

M **THRIVENT FINANCIAL FOR LUTHERANS,** Gallery of Religious Art, 625 Fourth Ave S, Minneapolis, MN 55415. Tel 612-844-6433; Fax 612-844-8458; Email artcollection@thrivent.com; Web: www.thrivent.com/offers/art.html; *Cur* Joanna Reiling Lindell
Open Mon - Fri 9:30 AM - 4 PM; No Admis fee; Estab 1982 as a cultural & educational gallery; Art is exhibited in a modest sized gallery & in the corporate library
Income: Financed by mem, gifts, donations
Collections: Bing & Grondahl Plate Collection, Martin Luther Commemorative Medals 16th-20th centuries, collection restricted to religious prints & drawings (15th-20th centuries)
Exhibitions: 8-10 Exhibitions per year
Activities: Originate traveling exhibs

M **TRAFFIC ZONE CENTER FOR VISUAL ART,** 250 3rd Ave North, Suite 500 Minneapolis, MN 55401. Tel 612-419-0107; Email trafficzoneart@gmail.com; Web: trafficzoneart.com; *Asset Mgr* Jean Kramer-Johnson
Open Mon - Sat 9 AM - 5 PM; Estab 1992; Housed in a restored six-story warehouse
Special Subjects: Painting-American, Photography, Prints, Sculpture, Ceramics
Collections: Paintings, photography, prints, sculptures, ceramics
Exhibitions: Quarterly exhibits
Activities: Classes for adults & children; presentations; workshops

M **UNIVERSITY OF MINNESOTA,** Katherine E Nash Gallery, 405 21st Ave S Minneapolis, MN 55455. Tel 612-624-7530; Fax 612-625-7881; Email artdept@umn.edu; Web: nash.umn.edu; *Dir* Nick Shank
Open Tues - Sat 11 AM - 7 PM, cl Sun, Mon, national holidays, winter & spring breaks; No admis fee; Provides educational exhibition space; Student exhibits
Special Subjects: Ceramics, Metalwork, Painting-American, Photography, Prints, Sculpture
Exhibitions: Rotating exhibitions every 3-4 weeks
Activities: Lect open to public, 5-8 vis lectrs per year; gallery talks; purchase awards; McKnight Fel

M **UNIVERSITY OF MINNESOTA,** Frederick R Weisman Art Museum, 333 E River Rd, Minneapolis, MN 55455. Tel 612-625-9494; Fax 612-625-9630; Email waminfo@unm.edu; Web: www.weisman.umn.edu; *Dir & Chief Cur* Lyndel King; *Registrar* Annette Van Aken; *Cur* Diane Mullin; *Bldg & Tech Opers Asst* Shane Davis; *Accounts Supvr* Carol Stafford; *Develop Dir* Patti Phillips
Open Tues, Thurs & Fri 10 AM - 5 PM, Wed 10 AM - 8 PM, Sat & Sun 11 AM - 5 PM, cl Mon; No admis fee; Estab 1934; the progs of the Weisman Art Museum are geared to meet broad objectives of an all-Univ mus, as well as the specific teaching & research needs of various University of Minnesota depts; Average Annual Attendance: 130,000; Mem: 1,200
Income: Financed by state appropriation, grants & gifts
Special Subjects: Drawings, Painting-American, Prints, Sculpture
Collections: Paintings, drawings & prints by American artists working in the first half of the 20th century, & contains notable works by Avery, Biederman, Dove, Feininger, Hartley, MacDonald-Wright, Marin, Maurer, Nordfeldt & O'Keeffe, print coll includes works by artists of all schools & periods, Ceramic colls include ancient American Indian Pottery, ancient Chinese & Korean objects, ancient Greek vases, German, French & English 18th & 19th century porcelain, international 20th century ceramics
Exhibitions: The Weisman Art Museum stresses a program of major loan exhibitions, held concurrently with smaller exhibitions organized for specific teaching purposes or from the permanent collection
Activities: Docent training; concerts; tours; lending prog to Univ, staff & students of Minnesota faculty of framed two-dimensional material; mus shop sells books, magazines, reproductions, cards

M **The Studio/Larson Gallery**, 2017 Buford Ave, St Paul Student Center Saint Paul, MN 55108-6180. Tel 612-625-0214, 624-3742; Fax 612-624-9124; Email larsonart@umn.edu; Web: www.sua.umn.edu/arts/events; *Prog Dir* Tricia Schweitzer; *Visual Arts Comt Chair* Jackie Beutell; *Visual Arts Comt Chair* Ruby Brayman; *Visual Arts Comt Chair* Alex Wendt; *Visual Arts Comt Chair* Miluzka McCarthy
Open Mon - Wed 10 AM - 5 PM, Thurs noon - 8 PM, Fri 10 AM -7 PM; No admis fee; Estab 1976 to make art accessible to univ community & gen pub; Average Annual Attendance: 30,000
Income: Financed by student fees
Exhibitions: 7-10 Exhibitions, annually
Activities: Educ dept; lects; gallery talks

L **Arts & Architecture Collections**, 309 19th Ave S, Minneapolis, MN 55455-0438. Tel 612-624-1638, 624-0303; Email ultan004@umn.edu; Web: lib.umn.edu; *Arts, Architecture & Landscape Architecture Librn* Deborah K Ultan
Open Mon - Fri 7 AM - 9 PM, Sat 9 AM - 5 PM, Sun Noon - 9 PM; Estab 1950 to serve undergraduate & graduate teaching programs in Art History, Fine Arts, Architecture, Landscape Architecture & Humanities to PhD level & in Studio Art to MA level; to provide art related books to other departments & to the entire acad community
Library Holdings: Book Volumes 150,000, Cassettes 52, Exhibition Catalogs 5000, Fiche 7000, Pamphlets, Periodical Subscriptions 339
Special Subjects: Architecture, Art History, Intermedia, Landscape Architecture, Mixed Media, Theatre Arts
Exhibitions: Annual book exhibs of rare art materials & special collections
Activities: Lects; tours

L **Architecture & Landscape Library**, 89 Church St SE, East Bank Minneapolis, MN 55455-0148. Tel 612-624-3321; Fax 612-625-5597; Email arlalib@umn.edu; Web: arch.lib.umn.edu; *Library Head* Deborah Ultan
Open Mon - Fri 9 AM - 9 PM, Sat & Sun 1 - 6 PM; Circ 20,641; Used as a reference lending library
Income: Financed by University
Library Holdings: Book Volumes 38,000, Periodical Subscriptions 165, Reels 244, Video Tapes
Special Subjects: Architecture, Interior Design, Landscape Architecture

L **Children's Literature Research Collections**, 222 21st Ave S, 113 Andersen Library Minneapolis, MN 05545-4403. Tel 612-624-4576; Fax 612-625-5525; Email asc-clrc@umn.edu; Web: www.lib.umn.edu/clrc; *Cur* Lisa Von Drasek
Open Mon - Fri 8:30 AM - 4:30 PM; refer to website for extended hrs; No admis fee; Estab 1949 to collect children's books, manuscripts & illustrations for use by researchers & for exhibits; For reference & research only
Income: Financed by endowment, University of Minnesota libraries
Library Holdings: Audio Tapes, Book Volumes 140,000, Cassettes, Clipping Files, Exhibition Catalogs, Fiche, Filmstrips, Manuscripts, Original Art Works, Original Documents, Other Holdings Toys, Pamphlets, Periodical Subscriptions 37, Photographs, Records, Slides, Video Tapes
Special Subjects: Drawings, Illustration, Lettering, Manuscripts, Painting-American, Photography, Posters, Watercolors
Collections: Figurine Coll
Publications: Kerlan Newsletter, 4 times per yr
Activities: Classes for adults; lects open to pub, 2 vis lectrs per yr; competitions with awards; fels; annual Kerlan Award; schols offered; individual paintings lent to art galleries; traveling exhibits; lending coll contains books, original art work, manuscript material; book traveling exhibs 6 per yr; originate traveling exhibs in Sweden, Spain & US; sales shop sells notecards, posters, books, keepsakes & catalogs, publs

M **The Bell Museum of Natural History**, 10 Church St SE, Minneapolis, MN 55455-0145. Tel 612-624-7389; Email andria@umn.edu; Web: www.bellmuseum.umn.edu
Estab 1872 to explore the diversity of life in the natural world; Dioramas, Discovery Room, temporary exhibits gallery; Average Annual Attendance: 60,000; Mem: 600; dues $20-$35
Special Subjects: Dioramas, Drawings, Etchings & Engravings, Painting-American, Prints, Watercolors
Collections: Owen T Gromme Collection, Francis Lee Jaques Collection, three separate Audubon colls, works by other artist-naturalists, natural history art (wildlife)
Exhibitions: Exotic Aquatics; Francis Lee Jaques-Images of the North Country; The Peregrine Falcon-Return of an Endangered; The Photography of Jim Brandenburg; 18 touring exhibits
Publications: Imprint & Calendar, quarterly
Activities: Classes for adults & children; docent training; lects open to public, 2 vis lectrs per year; gallery talks; tours; competitions; lends to other non-profit art museums; lending coll contains original art works, original prints, paintings & sculpture; originate traveling exhibs to libraries, art mus, nature centers, environmental learning centers & schools

M **WALKER ART CENTER,** 1750 Hennepin Ave, Minneapolis, MN 55403. Tel 612-375-7600; Fax 612-375-7618; Email info@walkerart.org; Web: www.walkerart.org; *Pres* Monica Nassif
Open Galleries & Box Office: Tues, Wed & Sun 11 AM - 5 PM, Thurs until 9 PM, Fri & Sat 11 AM - 6 PM, cl Mon & major holidays; Sculpture Garden: daily 6 AM - Midnight; Admis adults $15, seniors (62+) $13, students $10, active military $7.50, mems & children 18 & under free, admis to Sculpture Garden free; Estab 1879 by T B Walker, reorganized 1939 as Walker Art Center, Inc; building erected 1927; new museum building opened 1971; expanded in 2005; The Center consists of nine galleries, three sculpture terraces, the Center Bookshop 11 acre Sculpture Garden, Conservatory & the Gallery 8 Restaurant; Average Annual Attendance: 906,605; Mem: 8000; dues household $45, individual & special $25; annual meeting in Sept
Income: Financed by corporate & individual contributions, endowment, mem, state & federal appropriation, grants, book shop, museum admis & prog ticket sales
Special Subjects: Drawings, Painting-American, Photography, Prints, Sculpture
Collections: Joseph Beuys Collection, Jasper Johns Collection, Sigmar Polke Collection, Complete Archive of Tyler Graphics: Contemporary Print Collection, Edmond R Ruben Film Study Collection, Visual Arts Study Coll, Minneapolis Sculpture Garden
Exhibitions: Selections from Permanent Collection
Publications: Brochures; calendar of events; exhibition catalogs
Activities: Classes for adults & children; docent training; internships; lects open to pub, 25 vis lectrs per yr; concerts; gallery talks; school & adults tours; films; individual paintings & original objects of art lent to mus; book traveling exhibs; originates traveling exhibs; mus shop selling books, magazines, posters, jewelry & gift items

L **Library and Archives**, 1750 Hennepin Ave, Minneapolis, MN 55403-1169. Tel 612-375-7680; Fax 612-375-8502; Email library.archives@walkerart.org; Web: www.walkerart.org; *Librn* Margit Wilson; *Archivist* Jill Vuchetich; *Visual Resources Librn* Barbara Economon
Open by appointment to outside researchers; Circ Non-circulating; Average Annual Attendance: 700 outside researchers
Library Holdings: Audio Tapes 2000, Book Volumes 35,000, Cassettes, Clipping Files, Compact Disks, Exhibition Catalogs, Lantern Slides, Motion Pictures, Original Documents, Other Holdings Artists' Books 1500, Periodical Subscriptions 110, Photographs, Slides, Video Tapes
Special Subjects: Art History, Decorative Arts, Drawings, Film, Graphic Arts, Graphic Design, Industrial Design, Intermedia, Painting-American, Painting-Australian, Painting-British, Painting-Dutch, Painting-European, Painting-Flemish, Painting-French, Painting-German, Painting-Israeli, Painting-Japanese, Painting-New Zealand, Painting-Polish, Painting-Russian, Painting-Scandinavian, Photography, Prints, Sculpture, Painting-Spanish
Collections: Catalogs dating back to 1940, Rosemary Furtak Artist Book Collection

MOORHEAD

M **HISTORICAL AND CULTURAL SOCIETY OF CLAY COUNTY,** (Heritage Hjemkomst Interpretive Center) Hjemkomst Center, 202 First Ave N, Moorhead, MN 56560; PO Box 157, Moorhead, MN 56561-0157. Tel 218-299-5511; Fax 218-299-5510; Web: www.hjemkomst-center.com; *Exec Dir* Maureen Kelly Jonason; *Dir Visitor Svcs* Markus Kraeger; *Events Coordr* Tim Jorgenson; *Commun Coordr* Michelle Kittleson; *Cur* Lisa Vedaa; *Archivist* Mark Peihl
Open Mon - Sat 9 AM - 5 PM, A Tues 9 AM - 8 PM, Sun Noon - 5 PM; Admis adults $7, sr citizens $6, youths 5-17 $5; Estab 1986 to interpret River Valley heritage & Clay county history through interdisciplinary exhibits & programs; 7000 sq ft exhibition area for traveling exhibits; Average Annual Attendance: 40,000; Mem: Dues $30; annual meeting in May
Income: $410,000 (financed by mem & attendance & Clay County appropriations)
Special Subjects: Anthropology, Folk Art
Collections: Clay County Artifacts and Archives, Tom Arp Collection
Exhibitions: Focus on humanities, but are supplemented by art and/or science exhibits
Publications: Hourglass quarterly
Activities: Docent progs; lects open to pub, concerts, gallery talks, tours; Clay County library exhibits; book traveling exhibs 3 per yr; sales shop sells books, prints, Scandinavian items, reproductions, original art

NORTHFIELD

M **CARLETON COLLEGE,** Art Gallery, One N College St, Northfield, MN 55057. Tel 507-222-4469, 4342; Fax 507-646-7042; Email lbradley@carleton.edu; Web: apps.carleton.edu/campus/gallery/info; *Dir & Cur* Laurel Bradley PhD; *Registrar* James F Smith
Open during exhibs Mon-Wed noon-6PM, Thurs & Fri noon-10PM, Sat & Sun noon-4PM; No admis fee; Estab 1971 for art exhibitions & programs emphasizing quality & interdisciplinary ideas; One gallery 30 x 40 ft, secure; Average Annual Attendance: 5,000
Income: $100,000 (financed by parent organization)
Special Subjects: Antiquities-Greek, Antiquities-Roman, Asian Art, Painting-American, Photography, Prints, Woodcuts
Collections: American Paintings, Asian Objects, Photographs (1945-Present), Prints European & American (19th-20th century)
Activities: Lects open to pub, 10 vis lectrs per yr; book traveling exhibs 1-2 per yr; originates traveling exhibs

A **NORTHFIELD ARTS GUILD,** 304 Division St, Northfield, MN 55057. Tel 507-645-8877; Fax 507-645-6201; Email nfldarts@rconnect.com; Web: www.northfieldartsguild.org; *Visual Arts Specialist* Toni Bennett Easterson; *Theater Specialist* Ann Etter; *Literary Arts Specialist* Paula Granquist; *Pres & Dance Specialist* Mary Hahn; *Music Specialist* David Wolff
Open Office Mon-Fri 10AM-1PM & 2PM-5PM, Gallery & Gift Shop Mon-Sat 10AM-5PM, Thurs until 8PM; Estab 1958 as a non-profit organization which offers classes & programming in visual arts, theater, music, dance & literary art; Mem: 570 households
Publications: NAG Notes, quarterly
Activities: Classes for adults & children; dramatic progs; dance school; lects open to pub; concerts; gallery talks; schols offered; mus shop sells books, original art

M **SAINT OLAF COLLEGE,** Flaten Art Museum, 1520 St Olaf Ave, Dittmann Center Northfield, MN 55057-1574. Tel 507-786-3556; Fax 507-786-3776; Email beckerj@stolaf.edu; Web: www.stolaf.edu/collections/flaten/; *Dir* Jane Becker Nelson; *Registrar* Mona Weselmann
Open Mon, Tues, Wed & Fri 10 AM - 5 PM, Thurs 10 AM - 8 PM, Sat & Sun 2 - 5 PM; cl during col breaks; No Admis fee; Estab 1976; 2500 flexible sq ft, shows regional, national, international work, no unsolicited shows; Average Annual Attendance: 10,000
Library Holdings: Exhibition Catalogs, Original Art Works, Photographs, Prints, Sculpture
Special Subjects: African Art, Asian Art, Bronzes, Carpets & Rugs, Ceramics, Drawings, Etchings & Engravings, Landscapes, Miniatures, Oriental Art, Painting-American, Painting-British, Painting-European, Painting-Italian, Painting-Japanese, Painting-Russian, Painting-Scandinavian, Painting-Spanish, Photography, Portraits, Pottery, Pre-Columbian Art, Prints, Religious Art, Sculpture, Tapestries, Textiles, Watercolors, Woodcuts
Collections: Chris Janer prints & paintings, Nygaard sculpture, Contemporary and traditional paintings, sculpture, prints, work by Norwegian artists, Japanese Prints, Southwestern Native American Pottery, Richard N. Tetlie European & American paintings, drawings, prints, sculpture & photography, Andy Warhol Polaroids & b/w photographs
Publications: Exhibit announcements every 5-6 weeks; Occasional catalogs
Activities: Supports acad progs & classes; lects open to pub, 4-6 vis lectrs per yr; concerts; gallery talks; tours; lend original objects of art to nearby educational institutions; book traveling exhibs 1 per yr; organize traveling exhibs to Macalester College (MN)

OWATONNA

A **OWATONNA ARTS CENTER,** 435 Garden View Lane, Owatonna, MN 55060; PO Box 134, Owatonna, MN 55060-0134. Tel 507-451-0533; Fax 507-446-0198; Email info@oacarts.org; Web: oacarts.org; *Dir & Cur* Silvan A Durben; *Pres* Ray Lacina; *VPres* Doug Parr; *Develop & Bus Dir* Megan Proft; *Educ Coordr* Christina Spencer
Open Tues - Sun 1 - 5 PM; No admis fee except for specials; Estab 1974 to preserve local professional artists' work & promote the arts in the community; The West Gallery (32 x 26 x 12 ft) & the North Gallery (29 x 20 x 12 ft) provide an interesting walk through space & a versatile space in which to display two & three dimensional work; the two galleries can be combined by use of moveable panels & the Sculpture Garden which was completed in 1979 of multi-level construction; Average Annual Attendance: 17,000; Mem: 400; dues basic $50 & up, sustaining $200 & up
Income: $102,000 (financed by mem & fund raising activities plus sustaining fund from industries & bus)
Collections: Marianne Young World Costume Collection of garments & jewelry from 27 countries, painting, prints, sculpture by local professional artists, 2 Bronzes by John Rood, Paul Grandland, steel sculpture by Hammel, print coll of Adolph Den
Exhibitions: Annual Christmas Theme Display; Annual Outdoor Arts Festival; Annual Steele County Show; Festival of the Arts - July
Publications: Newsletter to members & other arts organizations
Activities: Classes for adults & children; 2 vis lectrs per year; festivals; concerts; gallery talks; tours; schols offered; original objects of art & Costume Collection lent to other arts organizations

L **Library**, 435 Dunnell Dr, Owatonna, MN 55060; PO Box 134, Owatonna, MN 55060-0134. Tel 507-451-0533; Fax 612-224-8854; *Dir* Silvan Berben; *Admin Asst* Julie Enzenaurer
Open Tues - Sat 1 PM - 5 PM by appointment; Open to members only; for reference
Library Holdings: Book Volumes 255

PARK RAPIDS

M **NEMETH ART CENTER,** 301 Court Ave, Park Rapids, MN 56470-1421. Tel 218-616-2064; Web: www.nemethartcenter.org; *Director* Michael Dagen; *Chair of the Board* LouAnn Muhm
Call for hours; No admis fee; Estab 1977 to provide a cultural and educational center to house a permanent study collection of old school European paintings & to house traveling exhibitions for the benefit of persons of all ages through contact & work with art in its many forms; Maintains Great Gallery, Members Gallery, four Revolving Galleries & studio; Average Annual Attendance: 2,000; Mem: 120; dues family $50, individual $25
Income: $25,000 (financed by mem, individual & corporate grants & gifts)
Special Subjects: African Art, Painting-European, Period Rooms
Collections: 160 Nigerian arts, crafts & artifacts, 40 Old School European paintings, 18 Contemporary Prints, 10 Contemporary paintings & artwork, 19 Drawings of Native American Children
Exhibitions: Annual Juried High School Fine Arts Exhibition
Activities: Classes for adults & children; docent training; lects open to pub, 2-3 lectrs per yr; concerts; gallery talks; tours; competitions; book traveling exhibs 5-6 per yr; originate traveling exhibs; mus shop selling original art, books, reproductions, prints and other memorabilia

ROCHESTER

A **ROCHESTER ART CENTER,** 40 Civic Center Dr SE, Rochester, MN 55904-3773. Tel 507-282-8629; Fax 507-282-7737; Email info@rochesterartcenter.org; Web: www.rochesterartcenter.org; *Exec Dir* Shannon Fitzgerald; *Facility Dir/Exhib Preparator* Phillip Ahnen; *Pub Programs Dir* Naura Anderson; *Chief Cur* Kris Douglas; *Event Mgr* Emily Tweten; *Develop Dir* Sandy Thompson; *Educ Coordr* Jason Pearson; *Admin Opers Dir* Joan Lovelace
Open Wed - Sat 10 AM - 5 PM, Thurs 10 AM - 9 PM, Sun Noon - 5 PM, cl Mon & Tues; Admis adults $5, seniors $3, students, children, res of Olmstead Co, mems & families in military free; Estab 1946, today the Rochester Art Center presents significant contemporary art exhibs; community-oriented pub progs; arts educ progs for pre-K, K-12, col & univ, & Life-Long Learning; & is a premier gathering place for community events; Maintains 4 galleries: Judy & Burton Onofrio Main Gallery, 3rd Floor Emerging Artists Gallery, Accent Gallery & ArtSpeak; Average Annual Attendance: 20,000; Mem: 750; dues $30 - $2,500
Income: city & state appropriations, fund raising & class tuition, private donations, corporate & foundation grants
Exhibitions: Varied exhibits in Contemporary Fine Arts & Crafts
Publications: Quarterly newsletter
Activities: Classes for adults & children; docent training; lects open to public; concerts, gallery talks; tours; scholarships; originate traveling exhibs; sales shop sell books, jewelry & gift items

SAINT CLOUD

M **SAINT CLOUD STATE UNIVERSITY,** Atwood Memorial Center Gallery, 720 4th Ave S, 118 Atwood Memorial Center Saint Cloud, MN 56301-4498. Tel 320-308-2205; Fax 320-308-1669; Email upbvisualarts@stcloudstate.edu; Web: www.stcloudstate.edu/atwood; *Arts Advisor & Asst Dir* Janice Courtney; *Prog Dir* Jessica Ostman
Open Mon - Fri 8 AM - 7 PM, Sat & Sun 9 AM - 5 PM; No admis fee; Estab 1967 as a university student union facility; Gallery curated by the UPB Visual Arts Committee, designed for maximum exposure of art by local, regional, national & international artists
Income: Financed by student enrollment fee assessment
Collections: Collections of artists work from Minnesota & some national
Exhibitions: Monthly exhibits in various media
Activities: Artists' residencies, lect & workshops that coincide with exhibs; gallery talks

M **Kiehle Gallery**, 720 4th Ave S, 102 Kiehle Visual Arts Center Saint Cloud, MN 56301-4442. Tel 320-308-4283; Fax 320-308-2232; Email art@stcloudstate.edu; Web: www.stcloudstate.edu/art; *Gallery Dir* Bill Gorcica
Open Mon - Fri 8 AM - 4 PM; No admis fee; Estab 1974 to expose col community to ideas & attitudes in the field of visual arts; The gallery has 1600 sq ft of enclosed multi use gallery floor space & 2500 sq ft outside sculpture ct; Average Annual Attendance: 15,000
Income: Financed by student fund appropriation
Activities: Lects open to public, 5 vis lectrs per yr; gallery talks; competitions; individual paintings & original objects of art lent to other departments on campus; lending collection contains original prints, paintings, photographs & sculpture; originates traveling exhibs

A **VISUAL ARTS MINNESOTA,** 913 W St Germain Saint Cloud, MN 56301; PO Box 972, Saint Cloud, MN 56302-0972. Tel 320-257-3108; Fax 320-257-3111; Email vam@visualartsminnesota.org; Web: www.visualartsminnesota.org; *Exec Dir* Kerry K Osberg
Estab 1973 to serve as an advocate & a resource for visual artists, art groups, educators & the community; Mem: 100; dues $20-$250
Income: Grants, pvt support (nonprofit)
Collections: Works donated by artists or friends/family of artists popular at various times in the community, collection can be loaned for a small fee
Exhibitions: Essential Art Show with awards; High School Art Competition; Children's Art Exhibit, Art ala Carte with awards
Publications: Ann newsletter
Activities: Artists critiques; scholarships offered; individual painting & original objects of art lent for public display; lending collection contains original artwork, original prints, sculptures & slides; sales shop sells books & original art

SAINT JOSEPH

M **COLLEGE OF SAINT BENEDICT,** Gorecki Gallery & Gallery Lounge, 37 S College Ave, Benedict Arts Center Saint Joseph, MN 56374-2001. Tel 320-363-5792; Fax 320-363-6097; Email jdubbeldeekuhn@csbsju.edu; Web: www.csbsju.edu/finearts
Open Mon - Sat 10 AM -9PM; Sun noon-9PM; No admis fee; Estab 1963; contemporary artworks from established & emerging regional, national, & international artists; Average Annual Attendance: 15,000
Income: Financed by college
Special Subjects: Ceramics, Drawings, Mixed Media, Photography, Prints, Sculpture
Collections: Contemporary coll of crafts, drawings, paintings, prints and sculpture, East Asian Coll of ceramics, crafts, drawings, fibers and prints, Miscellaneous African, New Guinea, Indian and European
Exhibitions: Ongoing exhibitions every 6-8 weeks; contemporary artworks in all media, bookarts
Activities: Lects open to pub, gallery talks; tours; concerts; competitions with awards; individual paintings & original objects of art lent to dept faculty & staff members of the college

SAINT PAUL

M **ARCHIVES OF THE ARCHDIOCESE OF ST PAUL & MINNEAPOLIS,** 226 Summit Ave, Saint Paul, MN 55102-2121. Tel 651-291-4485; Fax 651-290-1629; Email archives@archspm.org; *Archivist* Steven T Granger
Estab 1987 to collect & preserve materials of archival value relating to the Catholic Church of the Archdiocese of Saint Paul & Minneapolis
Income: Financed by Diocesan funds
Special Subjects: Religious Art
Collections: Artifacts, documents, letters, painting, papers & photographs
Activities: Lects, 2 vis lectrs per yr

M **FILMNORTH,** 550 Van Dalia St, Saint Paul, MN 55114-1943. Tel 651-644-1912; Fax 651-644-5708; Web: myfilmnorth.org; *Exec Dir* Andrew Peterson; *Deputy Dir & Educ Dir* Reilly Tillman; *Dir Technical & Facilities Opers* Max Becker
Open Mon - Fri 10:30 AM - 5:30 PM; Estab to give artists agency & support career success; Mem: dues $55-$200
Special Subjects: Film
Collections: Film & media
Exhibitions: Temporary exhibits
Activities: Educ progs; classes for adults & children; outreach & resources; art programming; conferences; film screenings

M **HAMLINE UNIVERSITY STUDIO ARTS & ART HISTORY DEPTS,** Gallery, 1536 Hewitt Ave, Drew Fine Arts Center Saint Paul, MN 55104-1205. Tel 651-523-2396; Fax 651-523-3066; Email jschlink01@hamline.edu; Web: www.hamline.edu/cla/acad/depts_programs/art_art_history/index.html; *Dir Exhibs* John-Mark T Schlink; *Registrar* Kimberly Arleth; *Student Asst* Loren Hextall
Open Mon - Fri 10 AM - 4 PM, cl holidays; Display of original modern works from BC to 21st century; extensive color slide library of paintings, architecture, sculpture, minor arts & graphics, prints, ceramics
Publications: Icons of Perfection: Figurative Sculpture from Africa

M **MACALESTER COLLEGE,** Macalester College Art Gallery, 1600 Grand Ave, Saint Paul, MN 55105-1899. Tel 651-696-6416; Fax 651-696-6266; Email gallery@macalester.edu; Web: www.macalester.edu; *Gallery Dir & Cur* Jehra Patrick
Open Mon - Fri 10 AM - 4 PM, Thurs until 8 PM, Sat & Sun Noon-4 PM, cl June 5 - Sept 15, national holidays & school vacations; No admis fee; Estab 1964 as a col facility to bring contemporary art exhibs to the students, faculty & community; Average Annual Attendance: 18,000
Special Subjects: African Art, Asian Art, Ceramics, Painting-American, Painting-European, Painting-German, Photography, Porcelain, Pottery, Prints, Sculpture, Tapestries, Textiles
Collections: African Art, Asian & British Ceramics, Oriental Art, contemporary & historical prints, paintings, sculpture & crafts
Exhibitions: Temporary, traveling & student exhibitions with special emphasis on international & multi-cultural
Activities: Lects open to pub; concerts; gallery talks; tours; competitions with awards; individual paintings & original objects of art lent; lending collections contains original prints, paintings & sculpture; book traveling exhibs; originates traveling exhibs; sales shop sells art books & supplies

L **DeWitt Wallace Library,** 1600 Grand Ave, Saint Paul, MN 55105. Tel 651-696-6345; Web: www.macalester.edu; *Dir Library* Teresa Fishel
Open Sep-May daily 8AM-Noon; No admis fee; Estab 1964; Circ 66,531
Library Holdings: Book Volumes 273,668, Cards, Cassettes, Fiche, Framed Reproductions, Pamphlets, Periodical Subscriptions 1311, Reels
Special Subjects: Art History
Activities: Individual paintings & original objects of art lent to faculty & staff of the college

M **MINNESOTA HISTORICAL SOCIETY,** Minnesota State Capitol Historic Site, 75 Rev Dr Martin Luther King Jr Blvd, Saint Paul, MN 55155-1605. Tel 651-296-2881; Fax 651-297-1502; Web: www.mnhs.org/statecapitol; *Historic Site Mgr* Brian Pease; *Prog Mgr* Linda Cameron; *Tour Registrar* Candice Christensen; *Site Supv* Jaymie Korman
Open Mon - Fri 9 AM - 5 PM with the last tour at 3 PM; Sat 10 AM - 3 PM with the last tour at 2 PM; Sun 1 - 4 PM, last tour at 3 PM; cl all holidays except President's Day; No admis fee to mus; Special Event fees: adults $8, seniors $7, children 6 - 12 $5, educ grps $2 - $5, mems $2 discount; Estab 1969; Minn State Capitol bldg designed by renowned 19th-century architect Cass Gilbert; 377,000 sq ft exhib space. Nonprofit org; Average Annual Attendance: 205,508; Mem: North Star Circle $1000, Sustaining $500, Contributing $250, Assoc $125, Household $65, Sr Household & Indiv $55, Sr Indiv $45
Special Subjects: Architecture, Decorative Arts, Furniture, Military Art, Painting-American, Portraits, Restorations, Sculpture
Collections: Over 800 pieces of orig 1905 furniture, works of art throughout the capitol that includes 33 canvas murals, 16 paintings, 15 plaques, 30 statues/busts, 37 governor's portraits and 21 historic battle flags, over 200 vols on historical info on the state capitol
Publications: Minnesota History, quarterly magazine
Activities: Year-round progs on four themes of the capitol: Art, Architecture, Minn History & State Govt; formal educ for adults, students & children; guided tours; temporary exhibs; books, postcards, small gifts & other mus related items for sale; cafe on-site (legislative session only)

M **MINNESOTA MUSEUM OF AMERICAN ART,** The Pioneer Endicott, 141 E 4th St, Suite 101 Saint Paul, MN 55101. Tel 651-797-2571; Fax 651-797-4748; Email info@mmaa.org; Web: www.mmaa.org; *Exec Dir* Kristin Makholm; *Administrative Assoc* Anna Lavanger
Open Thus 11 AM - 6 PM, Fri 11 AM - 6 PM, Sat & Sun 10 AM - 4 PM; No admis fee; Estab 1927 as the Saint Paul Gallery & School of Art; Average Annual Attendance: 50,000; Mem: 800; dues household $60, individual $40
Income: $350,000 (financed by endowment, individual contributions, mem, foundation & government grants)
Library Holdings: Audio Tapes, Book Volumes, CD-ROMs, Cassettes, Clipping Files, Compact Disks, Exhibition Catalogs, Pamphlets, Periodical Subscriptions, Slides
Special Subjects: Bronzes, Ceramics, Collages, Crafts, Drawings, Etchings & Engravings, Glass, Painting-American, Photography, Portraits, Posters, Pottery, Prints, Sculpture, Watercolors
Collections: American Art, contemporary art of the Upper Midwest, Paul Manship, Late 19th & 20th Century Art, Native American, George Morrison
Publications: Annual report
Activities: docent training;; lects open to public; gallery talks; tours; City Pages: Best Museum; originated traveling exhibs to midsized art museums

L **SAINT PAUL PUBLIC LIBRARY,** Central Adult Public Services, 90 W Fourth St, Saint Paul, MN 55102. Tel 651-266-7000; Email central.library@ci.stpaul.mn.us; Web: www.stpaul.lib.mn.us; *Library Dir* Jane Eastwood; *Communs & Digital Servs Dir* Phoebe Larson
Open Mon Noon - 8 PM, Tues - Fri 9 AM - 5:30, Sat 11 AM - 5 PM, Sun 1 - 5 PM; Estab 1882; Circ 92,642
Income: Financed by city appropriation
Purchases: $42,700
Library Holdings: Book Volumes 16,000, Clipping Files, Exhibition Catalogs, Other Holdings Compact discs 4000, Periodical Subscriptions 95, Video Tapes 4500
Collections: Field coll of popular sheet music

M **SAINT PAUL'S WESTERN SCULPTURE PARK,** Western Sculpture Park, 381 Wabasha St N Saint Paul, MN 55102; c/o Public Art Saint Paul, 351 Kellogg Blvd E Saint Paul, MN 55101. Tel 651-290-0921; Fax 651-292-0345; Email pasp@publicartstpaul.org; Web: publicartstpaul.org; *Exec Dir* Colleen Sheehy; *Contact* Kathy Graves
Open daily from dawn to dusk; No admis fee
Collections: contemporary sculpture
Activities: Classes for children

M **UNIVERSITY OF MINNESOTA,** Paul Whitney Larson Gallery, 364 McNeal Hall, 1985 Buford Ave Saint Paul, MN 55108. Tel 612-624-7434; Fax 612-624-8749; Email gmd@umn.edu; Web: goldstein.design.umn.edu; *Dir* Lin Nelson-Mayson
Open Mon - Fri 9 AM - 6 PM, Sat & Sun 1 PM - 5 PM; No admis fee; Estab 1979 to bring art of great variety into the daily lives of students & university community; Intimate gallery featuring traditional & contemporary visual arts
Income: Financed by student fees
Publications: Annual report & activity summary
Activities: Mus shop sells jewelry

M **Goldstein Museum of Design,** 241 McNeal Hall, 1985 Buford Ave Saint Paul, MN 55108-6134; 364 McNeal Hall, Saint Paul, MN 55108. Tel 612-624-7434; Fax 612-625-5762; Email gmd@umn.edu; Web: www.goldstein.design.umn.edu; *Dir* Lin Nelson-Mayson; *Asst Cur* Jean McElvain; *Registrar* Eunice Haugen; *Admin Asst* Barbara Lutz
Open Tues - Fri 10 AM - 5 PM, Thurs 10 AM - 5 PM, Sat & Sun 1:30 - 4:30 PM; No admis fee; donations welcome; Estab 1976, collects, exhibits & researches design; Average Annual Attendance: 14,000; Mem: 315; mem $20 & up
Income: Financed by private gifts, mem & grants
Library Holdings: Book Volumes, Clipping Files, Exhibition Catalogs, Periodical Subscriptions
Special Subjects: Architecture, Carpets & Rugs, Ceramics, Costumes, Crafts, Decorative Arts, Embroidery, Folk Art, Furniture, Glass, Graphics, Interior Design, Laces, Leather, Metalwork, Pewter, Porcelain, Pottery, Silver, Tapestries, Textiles, Textiles

Collections: Historic apparel & accessories, 20th century designer apparel & accessories, historic & contemporary decorative arts, furniture, textiles, graphic commun
Publications: Exhibition catalogs
Activities: Educ dept classes for adults; lects open to pub, 3-5 vis lectrs per yr; gallery talks; tours; College of Design Senior award; collection objects lent to other institutions; book traveling exhibs to general mus, 1 per yr; originate traveling exhibs to academic museums & galleries; mus shop sells books & notecards

A **WOMEN'S ART REGISTRY OF MINNESOTA GALLERY,** 550 Rice St, Saint Paul, MN 55103-2116. Tel 651-292-1188; Email board@thewarm.org; Web: www.thewarm.org; *Board Pres* Tara Tieso
Estab 1975; Office only; Mem: 170; dues $60; women artists
Income: Financed by mem, grants for projects & operating expenses
Collections: Members work on display in one area
Exhibitions: Local & national exhibitions; Annual Juried Members Exhibit
Publications: e-warm-ups, biweekly online publication
Activities: Educ dept; Fresh Art; Mentor Prog; lects open to pub; 1 vis lectrs per yr; gallery talks; competitions with awards; juror awards for juried mem exhibs; individual paintings lent & original objects of art lent to non-profit groups for fee

SPRING GROVE

M **BLUFF COUNTRY ARTISTS GALLERY,** 111 W Main St, Spring Grove, MN 55974. Tel 507-498-2787; Email bcagallery@springgrove.coop; Web: bluffcountryartistsgallery.org; *Bd Pres* Mary Zaffke; *Secy* Joanne Griffin; *Treas* Linda Nerstad Kemp
Open Wed - Fri Noon - 5 PM, Sat 10 AM - 4 PM, cl Sun - Tues; Estab to provide artist with a platform for selling their work and make it available to consumers; Mem: dues $10-$250
Collections: Features work by regional artists
Exhibitions: Temporary exhibits
Activities: Educ prog

WAYZATA

M **MINNETONKA CENTER FOR THE ARTS,** 2240 N Shore Dr, Wayzata, MN 55391-9347. Tel 952-473-7361 x 160; Fax 952-473-7363; Email information@minnetonkaarts.org; Web: www.minnetonkaarts.org; *Exec Dir* Roxanne Heaton; *Exhibs Dir & Retail Mgr* Robert Bowman; *Communs Dir* Gregory Collins; *Registrar* Anicka Schanilec
Open Mon, Wed & Fri - Sat 9 Am - 4 PM, Tues & Thurs 9 AM - 9:30 PM, cl Sun; Estab to make art accessible to all community members, especially through visual arts educ & outreach; Mem: dues $60-$1,000
Collections: Work by established & emerging artists
Exhibitions: Temporary exhibits
Activities: Educ prog; classes for children & adults; outreach

WHITE BEAR LAKE

M **WHITE BEAR CENTER FOR THE ARTS,** Gallery, 1280 N Birch Lake Blvd, White Bear Lake, MN 55110. Tel 651-407-0597; Fax 651-429-1569; Email wbca@whitebeararts.org; Web: whitebeararts.org; *Exec Dir* Suzi Hudson; *Prog Dir* Danielle Cezanne; *Events & Mem Coordr* Lori Swanson; *Develop Coordr* Andy Vollbrecht
Open Mon - Fri 9 AM - 4 PM, Tues & Thurs 6:30 PM - 8:30 PM, Sat 10 AM - 3 PM; Estab to facilitate diverse arts experiences; Mem: dues $40-$60
Collections: Features work by local artists
Exhibitions: Rotating exhibits
Activities: Educ progs; classes for adults & children; workshops

WINONA

L **WILLET HAUSER ARCHITECTURAL GLASS INC,** 1685 Wilkie Dr, Winona, MN 55987. Tel 800-533-3960; Fax 877-495-9486; Email info@willethauser.com; Web: www.willethauser.com; *Owner* John Phillips Jr
Open by appointment; No admis fee; Estab 1898 as the largest stained glass studio in the United States; For reference only
Special Subjects: Antiquities-Assyrian, Antiquities-Byzantine, Antiquities-Egyptian, Antiquities-Etruscan, Antiquities-Greek, Antiquities-Oriental, Antiquities-Persian, Antiquities-Roman, Architecture, Art History, Calligraphy, Costume Design & Constr, History of Art & Archaeology, Illustration, Stained Glass, Mosaics, Photography, Printmaking, Restoration & Conservation
Collections: Lumiere Watercolor Collection
Publications: Black & White Photos of works in progress, Design & slides of installations
Activities: Lect open to pub; gallery talks; tours; internships offered; individual paintings & original objects of art lent; lending coll contains photographs, Kodachromes & motion pictures; originates traveling exhibs

WORTHINGTON

A **NOBLES COUNTY ART CENTER,** 407 12th St, Worthington, MN 56187; PO Box 343, Worthington, MN 56187-0343. Tel 507-372-8245; Email noblearts@knology.net; *Co-Dir* Martin Bunge; *Co-Dir* Jean Bunge; *Pres* Tricia Mikle
Open Mon - Fri 2 - 4:30 PM, cl Sat, Sun & holidays; No admis fee; Estab 1960 to nourish the arts & to bring arts & cultures of other communities & nations, civilizations to Nobles County & the surrounding area so residents become more universal in their thinking; Circ 300; Located on the ground floor; handicapped accessible; Average Annual Attendance: 3,000; Mem: 100; dues $10-$500; annual meeting in Jan
Income: Financed by mem dues, donations, memorial gifts, county appropriation bequest & grants
Collections: International art
Exhibitions: Two juried fine art shows per year; annual student exhibition; the work of area artists; new exhibit every month
Publications: Gallery, monthly newsletter; monthly press releases
Activities: Classes for adults & children; lects open to public; concerts; gallery talks; tours; competitions with awards; originate traveling exhibs

MISSISSIPPI

BAY SAINT LOUIS

M **ALICE MOSELEY FOLK ART AND ANTIQUE MUSEUM,** 1928 Depot Way, Bay Saint Louis, MS 39520-3217. Tel 228-467-9223; Email alicemoseley@gmail.com; Web: www.alicemoseley.com; *Cur* W L Tim Moseley
Open Mon - Sat 10 AM - 4 PM, cl Sun & major holidays; No admis fee; Estab to increase public awareness of Alice Moseley's art & life; promote tourism & the arts
Special Subjects: Glass, Painting-American
Collections: 50 paintings by Alice Moseley, folk art, vintage bottles, Majolica vases, depression glass, antique objects
Activities: Tours

BELZONI

M **CATFISH CAPITAL VISITORS CENTER AND MUSEUM,** 111 Magnolia St, Belzoni, MS 39038; PO Box 385, Belzoni, MS 39038-0385. Tel 800-408-4838; 662-247-4838; Fax 662-247-4805; Email catfish@belzonicable.com; Web: www.belzonims.com; *Exec Dir* Steve Anderson
Open Mon - Fri 9 AM - 5 PM; No admis fee
Collections: local history & culture; photographs; paintings; personal artifacts; sculpture

M **THE ETHEL WRIGHT MOHAMED STITCHERY MUSEUM,** 307 Central St, Belzoni, MS 39038-3603; PO Box 254, Belzoni, MS 39038-0254. Tel 662-247-3633; Fax 662-247-1433; Email hwilson493@aol.com; Web: www.mamasdreamworld.com; *Cur* Carol Mohamed Ivy; *Asst Cur* Amy Harris Hawkins; *Asst Cur & Webmaster* Hazel Mohamed Wilson
Open by appt only; Admis adults $2, children & bus driver no admis fee; Mus is former home of Ethel Wright Mohamed, award-winning artist who lived from 1906-1992 and was also known as "Mississippi's Grandma Moses of Stitchery"; mus contains stitchery created by the artist that centered on her family & life
Special Subjects: Decorative Arts, Tapestries, Folk Art
Collections: Coll of stitchery & sketches
Publications: My Life in Pictures, by Ethel Wright Mohamed
Activities: Guided tours; mus shop sells reproductions, prints & cards

CLARKSDALE

M **DELTA BLUES MUSEUM,** (Carnegie Public Library), 1 Blues Alley, Clarksdale, MS 38614-4336; PO Box 459, Clarksdale, MS 38614-0459. Tel 662-627-6820; Fax 662-627-7263; Email info@deltabluesmuseum.org; Web: www.deltabluesmuseum.org; *Group Tour Mgr* Maie Smith; *Gift Shop Mgr* Richard Crisman; *Dir* Shelley Ritter
Open Nov-Feb Mon-Sat 10AM-5PM, Mar-Oct Mon-Sat 9AM-5PM; Admis $10 adults; $8 student and seniors; group rates available; Estab 1979 to preserve & promote understanding of MS Delta blues music & heritage; 9000 sq ft of exhibits; Average Annual Attendance: 25,000
Income: $383,000 (financed by gift shop, federal & state grants, mem & corporate donors)
Library Holdings: Audio Tapes, Book Volumes, CD-ROMs, Cassettes, Compact Disks, DVDs, Framed Reproductions, Memorabilia, Original Art Works, Pamphlets, Photographs, Prints, Records, Sculpture
Special Subjects: Afro-American Art, Architecture, Costumes, Crafts, Folk Art, Maps, Painting-American, Photography, Portraits, Posters, Pottery, Primitive art, Sculpture
Collections: Books & tapes, Interpretative exhibits, memorabilia, photography & art (sculpture, paintings), recordings, stage & music, videos
Exhibitions: All Shook Up; Bancas to Blues: West African Stringed Instrument traditions & the origin of pre-civil War American Music; MS Roots of American Music; Vintage American Guitar Collection; Blues Booze & BBQ; Give My Poor Heart Ease; Paramount Portraits Vol 1& 2
Publications: Delta Blues Museum Brochure
Activities: Monthly Blues performances; classes for adults; classes for children; music lessons; Traveling Trunk; lects open to pub, 10 vis lectrs per yr; lending of original objects of art to schools- traveling trunk; books traveling exhibs 1-2 per yr; mus shop sells books, magazines, original art, reproductions, prints, T-shirts

CLEVELAND

M **DELTA STATE UNIVERSITY,** Fielding L Wright Art Center, 1003 W Sunflower Rd, Cleveland, MS 38733-0001. Tel 662-846-4729; Fax 662-846-4726; Web: www.deltastate.edu; *Exhib Chmn* Patricia Brown; *Chmn Dept* Ronald G Koehler
Open Mon - Thurs 8 AM - 8:30 PM, Fri 8 AM - 4 PM, cl weekends & school holidays; No admis fee; Estab 1968 as an educational gallery for the benefit of the students, but serves the entire area for changing art shows; it is the only facility of this nature in the Mississippi Delta Region; Three gallery areas; Average Annual Attendance: 3,600
Income: Financed by state appropriation

Collections: Delta State University permanent coll, Photography Study Coll, Ruth Atkinson Holmes Collection, Marie Hull Collection, Smith-Patterson Memorial Collection, Whittington Memorial Collection, Joe & Lucy Howorth Collection, John Miller Photography Collection, James Townes Medal Collection
Publications: Announcements of exhibitions, monthly during fall, winter & spring; exhibit catalogs
Activities: Lects open to public, 10 vis lectrs per yr; gallery talks; tours; competitions; exten dept serving the Mississippi Delta Region; individual paintings & original objects of art lent to offices of campus; lending collection contains color reproductions, film strips, motion pictures, original art works, 30,000 slides; originates traveling exhibs

L **Roberts LaForge Library**, Le Flore Cir, Cleveland, MS 38733-0001. Tel 662-846-4440; Fax 662-846-4443; Email refdesk@deltastate.edu; Web: www.library.deltastate.edu; *Dir Library Svcs* Terry S Latour; *Asst Dir* Jeff H Slagell
Open Mon-Thurs 7:30 AM-10 PM, Fri 7:30 AM-4 PM, Sat 10 AM-5 PM, Sun 2 PM-10 PM; No admis fee; Estab as gen acad library covering all topics for students & staff; Mabelle Smith and William Mountjoy Garrad Collection of Art
Income: col funding
Library Holdings: Audio Tapes, Book Volumes 7500, CD-ROMs, Cards, Cassettes, Clipping Files, Compact Disks, DVDs, Exhibition Catalogs, Fiche, Filmstrips, Framed Reproductions, Kodachrome Transparencies, Micro Print, Original Art Works, Periodical Subscriptions 31, Photographs, Prints, Records, Reels, Sculpture, Slides 381, Video Tapes 78
Special Subjects: Art Education, Art History, Drawings, Etchings & Engravings, Film, Graphic Design, Historical Material, History of Art & Archaeology, Illustration, Interior Design, Painting-European, Photography, Portraits, Pottery, Printmaking
Collections: Sculptures & paintings for variety of Mississippi Delta artists

KAPPA PI INTERNATIONAL HONORARY ART FRATERNITY
For further information, see National and Regional Organizations

COLUMBUS

M **COLUMBUS HISTORIC FOUNDATION,** (Columbus & Lowndes County Historical Society) Blewett-Harrison-Lee Museum, 316 7th St, Columbus, MS 39710-1300. Tel 662-329-3533, 800-327-2686; Fax 662-329-1027; Web: www.historic-columbus.org; *Cur* Carolyn Neault; *CAS Gen* Steph D Lee
Open Fri 10 AM - 4 PM or by appointment; Admis $5, students free; Estab 1960 for a memorabilia 1832-1907 pertaining to Lowndes County preserved & exhibited; Average Annual Attendance: 2,000; Mem: 210; dues $5; annual meeting third Thurs in Sept
Income: $600 (financed by mem, bequests, donations, memorials, sale of souvenirs)
Special Subjects: Historical Material
Collections: 100 years of artifacts, books, china, crystal, clothes, flags, furniture, jewelry, pictures, portraits, swords, wedding gowns
Activities: Docent training; tours for school children; awards; mus shop sells books & souvenirs

M **MISSISSIPPI UNIVERSITY FOR WOMEN,** Fine Arts Gallery, 1100 College St, MuW-70, Columbus, MS 39701-5800. Tel 662-329-7341, 662-241-6976; Fax 662-241-7815; Email aswills@muw.edu; *Recorder* Shawn Dickey; *Cur* Alex Stelioeswills
Open Mon - Fri 2 AM - Noon, 1 -4PM every day the univ is open; No admis fee; Estab 1948, new bldg 1960, renovated 1998; 3 galleries with 350 running ft wall space, the main gallery with 173 ft wall space covered with fabric; Average Annual Attendance: 1,200
Income: Financed by state appropriation & private funds
Special Subjects: Drawings, Painting-American, Prints
Collections: American Art, paintings, sculpture, photographs, drawings, ceramics, prints, Permanent collection of Mississippi artists
Exhibitions: Frequent special and circulating exhibitions; Selections from permanent collection, periodically
Activities: Visiting artists prog; workshops; lects open to pub, 4 vis lectrs per yr; gallery talks; tours; scholarships; individual paintings & original objects of art lent to offices & pub student areas on the campus; lending collection contains 400 original prints, 300 paintings, 100 records; book traveling exhibs; originate traveling exhibs

GREENWOOD

M **COTTONLANDIA MUSEUM,** 1608 Hwy 82 W, Greenwood, MS 38930-2725. Tel 662-453-0925; Fax 662-455-7556; Email cottonlandia@bellsouth.net; Web: www.cottonlandia.org/museum.asp; *Exec Dir* Robin Seage Person; *Mus Shop Mgr* Lyllian Tubbs; *Pres* Tommy Ellett; *Pres (V)* Jean Codney; *Interim Dir* Dave Freeman; *Educ & Art Coordr* Jennifer Whites
Open Mon - Fri 9 AM - 5 PM, Sat - Sun 2 - 5 PM; Admis adults $5, seniors 65 & over $3.50, students $3, children 3-18 $2; Estab 1969 as a mus for tourism & learning facility for schools; Two well lighted rooms plus available space in mus for temporary & competition, permanent hangings in some corridors; Average Annual Attendance: 7,500; Mem: 270; dues vary; annual meeting early Nov
Income: Financed by mem, county appropriation, donation & admis
Library Holdings: Book Volumes, Clipping Files, Original Documents, Periodical Subscriptions, Photographs
Collections: Permanent collection of works of past Cottonlandia Collection, competition winners, other accessions by Mississippi Artists
Exhibitions: Temporary exhibs change every two months
Activities: Classes for adults; lects open to pub; gallery talks; tours; competitions with awards; individual paintings lent; lending collection contains nature artifacts; mus shop sells books, original art, reproductions, prints & natural stone jewelry

HATTIESBURG

L **UNIVERSITY OF SOUTHERN MISSISSIPPI,** McCain Library & Archives, 118 College Dr #5148, Hattiesburg, MS 39406-0002. Tel 601-266-4345; Web: www.lib.usm.edu/mccain.html; *Dir* Kay L Wall, MLS; *Cur* Ellen Ruffin; *Archivist* Diane Ross; *Librn* Peggy Price
Open Mon - Fri 8 AM - 5 PM; No admis fee; University estab 1912, library estab 1976; For reference only
Collections: Cleanth Brooks Collection, de Grummond Children's Literature Research Collection (historical children's literature & illustrations), Earnest A Walen Collection, Genealogy Collection
Publications: Juvenile Miscellany, 2 times per year

M **UNIVERSITY OF SOUTHERN MISSISSIPPI,** Museum of Art, Dept of Art & Design, 118 College Dr, #5033 Hattiesburg, MS 39406-0001. Tel 601-266-5200; Email artmuseum@usm.edu; Web: www.usm.edu/visualarts/museum.php; *Dir* Dr. Jan Siesling; *Asst Dir* Mark Rigsby
Open Jan - May & Sept - Dec: Tues - Fri 10 AM - 5 PM, Sat 10 AM - 4 PM; June - Aug: Tues - Fri noon - 5 PM; No admis fee
Collections: Regional, international, historical & contemporary artwork

JACKSON

M **MISSISSIPPI MUSEUM OF ART,** 380 S Lamar St, Jackson, MS 39201-4007. Tel 601-960-1515; Fax 601-960-1505; Web: www.msmuseumart.org; *Dir* Betsy Bradley; *Interim Chief Cur* Jochen Wierich
Open Tues - Sat 10 AM - 5 PM, Sun noon - 5 PM, cl Mon; hours subject to change during major exhibs; No admis fee, may vary by exhib; Chartered in 1911; Estab 1978; Average Annual Attendance: 40,000; Mem: 1400; dues Chairman's Rembrandt $5,000, Director's Rembrandt $2500, Rembrandt Soc $1200, Young Rembrandt $600, curator $500, partner $250, supporting $100, family/dual $60, senior family or dual $50, individual $45, senior $35
Income: $2.7M (financed by endowment, mem, contributions, pub sector grants & appropriations, earned income)
Purchases: Birney Imes III (45 color photographs), Arthur B Davies, Georgia O'Keeffe, Hale Woodruff, John Sloan
Library Holdings: Book Volumes, Clipping Files, Exhibition Catalogs, Memorabilia, Pamphlets, Periodical Subscriptions
Special Subjects: Asian Art, Drawings, Etchings & Engravings, Folk Art, Glass, Painting-American, Painting-European, Painting-Italian, Photography, Pre-Columbian Art, Primitive art, Prints, Sculpture, Textiles, Watercolors, Woodcuts
Collections: American art by artists incl: Albert Bierstadt, Arthur B Davies, Robert Henri, George Inness, Georgia O'Keeffe, Reginald Marsh, Thomas Sully & James McNeill Whistler, Mississippi Coll incl works by 19th c painter G Ruder Donoho, photographer & writer Eudora Welty, & outsider artists Theora Hamblett, Elizabeth Wright Mohammed & Sultan Rogers in addition to contemporary & historical works by Mississippi artists & quilt coll, 19th c British paintings by Thomas Lawrence & Thomas Sully, European Coll incl impressions by Picasso, Joan Miro, Marc Chagall & Rembrandt
Publications: Bi-annual newsletter; selected exhibition catalogs; Four Dog Blues Band, a children's book; The Mississippi Story
Activities: Classes for adults & children; docent training; weekend activities for children; community progs; lects open to pub, some for members only, 3 vis lectrs per yr, 10 vis artists per yr; tours; competitions; music series; concerts; receptions; Scholastic Art Awards; scholarships offered; individual paintings & original objects of art lent to qualifying mus & other institutions & educational/cultural centers; lending collection contains 3500 original art works, 700 original prints, 300 paintings, 150 photographs & 50 sculptures; book traveling exhibs; originate traveling exhibs to other mus, art, educational & cultural institutions, Mississippi, Affiliate Network; mus shop sells books, magazines, reproductions, prints, posters, slides, paper goods, designer items, Mississippi crafts, jewelry, pottery

L **Howorth Library**, 201 E Pascagoula St, Jackson, MS 39201. Tel 601-960-1515; Fax 601-960-1505; Email mmart@netdoor.com; Web: www.msmuseumart.org; *Asst Cur Educ* Lianne Takemori; *VChmn* Chuck Dunn; *Auxiliary VPres* Margo Heath; *Dir Finance* Sheryl Trim; *Registrar* Tobin Fortenberry; *Dir* Betsy Bradley; *Office Mgr* Sonya Croins; *Chief Preparator* LC Tucker; *Dir Develop* Shari Veazey; *Asst to Dir* Nina Moss; *Visitor Info Center* Annette French; *Asst Preparator* Melvin Johnson; *Deputy Dir Prog* Rene Paul Barilleaux; *Mus Shop Mgr* Erdell Hart
Open Mon - Fri 10 AM - 5 PM by appointment; For reference only, open to the general pub
Income: Museum funded
Library Holdings: Book Volumes 10,000, Clipping Files, Exhibition Catalogs, Pamphlets, Periodical Subscriptions 12, Slides, Video Tapes
Collections: Walter Anderson Collection on Slides, Marie Hull Collection of Art Reference Books, Metropolitan Miniature Album, E Benezit Vol 1 - 14, 1999
Activities: Classes for children; docent training; lects open to pub; concerts; gallery talks; tours; sponsoring of competitions; 5 vis lectrs per yr

LAUREL

M **LAUREN ROGERS MUSEUM OF ART,** 565 N 5th Ave, Laurel, MS 39440; PO Box 1108, Laurel, MS 39441-1108. Tel 601-649-6374; Fax 601-649-6379; Email info@lrma.org; Web: www.lrma.org; *Registrar* Tommie Rodgers; *Mktg Dir* Holly Green; *Dir* George Bassi; *Bus Mgr* Jo-Lyn Helton; *Develop Dir* Allyn Boone; *Cur* Jill Chancey; *Cur Educ* Mandy Buchanan; *Outreach Educ Coordr* Angie King; *Visitor Svcs Coordr* Lizabeth Brumley
Open Tues - Sat 10 AM -4:45 PM, Sun 1 - 4 PM, cl Mon; No admis fee; Estab 1923 as a reference & research library & mus of art for pub use & employment; Six smaller galleries open off large American Gallery; these include European Gallery, Catherine Marshall Gardiner Basket collection, Gibbons Silver Gallery plus 2 temporary exhibit galleries; Average Annual Attendance: 20,000; Mem: Dues $15-$2500
Income: Financed by endowment (Eastman Memorial Foundation), mem, donations, fundraising, events government appropriations, grants

Library Holdings: Auction Catalogs, Book Volumes, Cards, DVDs, Exhibition Catalogs, Original Documents, Periodical Subscriptions, Video Tapes
Special Subjects: Bookplates & Bindings, Painting-American, Painting-European, Period Rooms, Prints, Silver
Collections: European Artists of the 19th century, 18th-century English Georgian Silver, 19th- & 20th-century American Paintings, Native American, Native American Baskets
Exhibitions: Annual schedule of exhibitions by regional & nationally recognized artists; collections exhibits
Publications: Gibbons Silver Catalog; Jean Leon Gerome Ferris, 1863-1930: American Painter Historian; Handbook of The Collections; Mississippi Portraiture; By Native Hands: Woven Treasures from the Lauren Rogers Mus Art; The Floating World: Ukiyo-e Prints from the Wallace B Rogers Collection
Activities: Workshop for adults & children; musical concerts; docent training; lects open to pub; concerts; gallery talks; tours; individual art objects lent to AAM accredited mus or galleries; mus shop sells books, prints, Choctaw baskets, silver, jewelry, toys, Mississippi arts & crafts & t-shirts

L **Library**, PO Box 1108, Laurel, MS 39441-1108. Tel 601-649-6374; Fax 601-649-6379; Email lrmalibrary@c-gate.net; Web: www.lrma.org; *Head Librn* Donnelle Conklin
Open Tues - Sat 10 AM - 4:45 PM, Sun 1 - 4 PM, cl Mon; Estab 1923; Circ Non-circ; For reference only; Mem: Membership: part of museum
Income: Financed by endowment (Eastman Memorial Foundation), mem, donations
Library Holdings: Auction Catalogs, Book Volumes 11,000, Cassettes, Clipping Files, Exhibition Catalogs, Manuscripts, Memorabilia, Pamphlets, Periodical Subscriptions 60, Photographs, Reproductions, Slides 500, Video Tapes
Special Subjects: Painting-American, Painting-European, Prints, Silver
Collections: Museum archives
Publications: by Native Hands: Woven treasures from the Lauren Rogers Mus of Art

MERIDIAN

M **MERIDIAN MUSEUM OF ART,** Seventh St at Twenty-Fifth Ave, PO Box 5773 Meridian, MS 39301; PO Box 5773, Meridian, MS 39302-5773. Tel 601-693-1501; Email meridianmuseum@bellsouth.net; Web: meridianmuseum.org; *Dir* Kate Cherry; *Educ Dir* Marsha Iverson
Open Wed - Sat 11 AM - 5 PM, cl Sun, Mon & Tues; No admis fee; Estab 1970 to provide exhibition space for local, state & nationally known artists. Mus has four galleries; Housed in a national landmark building, the mus offers over twenty exhibitions annually in four galleries; Average Annual Attendance: 10,500; Mem: 500; dues $60-$10,000; annual mem meeting mid-Jan
Income: Financed by mem & appropriation
Library Holdings: Original Art Works, Sculpture
Special Subjects: Decorative Arts, Drawings, Landscapes, Painting-American, Photography, Portraits, Pottery, Prints, Sculpture, Watercolors
Collections: 20th century Southern fine arts & photography, 18th century European portraits, contemporary & traditional crafts & decorative arts
Exhibitions: Annual Bi-State; People's Choice Art Competition; Mem Invitational Exhibits
Activities: Classes for adults & children; youth art classes held each summer & after school; symposia lects open to pub; gallery talks; tours; competitions with awards; original objects of art lent to mus, traveling shows & offices in the city; book traveling exhibs 2 per yr; originate traveling exhibs for circulation to mus & galleries; muse & crafts

OCEAN SPRINGS

M **WALTER ANDERSON MUSEUM OF ART,** 510 Washington Ave, Ocean Springs, MS 39564-4632. Tel 228-872-3164; Fax 228-875-4494; Email wama@walterandersonmuseum.org; Web: www.walterandersonmuseum.org; *Exec Dir* Rosemary Roosa; *Dir Colls & Exhibs* Mattie Codling; *Opers Mgr* Julie Franc; *Finance Mgr* Donna Cobb; *Gift Shop Mgr* Josie Gardner; *Educ Dir* Heather Rumfelt; *Weekend Mgr* Genie Martz; *Dir Develop* Cory Christy
Open Mon - Sat 9:30 AM - 4:30 PM, Sun 12:30 PM - 4:30 PM; Admis $10 adults, $8 seniors, $8 students, $5 children (4 & under free); Estab 1991 to exhibit the works of Walter Anderson & other artists; The museum includes a main galleria & 4 galleries; Average Annual Attendance: 15,000; Mem: 800; dues $20-$1,000
Income: Financed by mem, attendance, grants, fundraisers, shop proceeds & donations
Library Holdings: Audio Tapes, Book Volumes, Clipping Files, DVDs, Exhibition Catalogs, Motion Pictures, Original Documents, Pamphlets, Periodical Subscriptions, Photographs, Prints, Video Tapes
Special Subjects: Art Education, Art History, Drawings, Painting-American, Photography, Pottery, Reproductions, Watercolors, Woodcarvings, Sculpture, Woodcuts, Furniture, Ceramics
Collections: Work of Walter Inglis Anderson, ceramics, textiles, wood carving, works of art on paper, linoleum blocks & prints, Peter & Mac Anderson (brothers of Walter) Collection, furniture, oil paintings, education collection; adjunct collection
Publications: Motif, quarterly newsletter
Activities: Classes for adults & children; docent training; lects open to mems & to pub, 5-15 vis lectrs per yr; concerts; gallery talks; tours; schols; Governor's Award for Excellence in Art; awards, Certificate of Excellence, Jackson City Chamber; 3 state educational outreach progs; lending of original art to Beau Rivage Casino Resort; 3 book traveling exhibs per yr; organize traveling exhibs for mus & other cultural institutions; mus shop sells books, prints, reproductions, games & educational materials

OXFORD

M **UNIVERSITY OF MISSISSIPPI,** University Museum & Historic Houses, University Ave & Fifth St, Oxford, MS 38655; PO Box 1848, University, MS 38677-1848. Tel 662-915-7073; Fax 662-915-7035; Email museums@olemiss.edu; Web: www.olemiss.edu; *Dir* Robert Saarniorsaarnio@olemiss.edu; *Rowan Oak Cur* William Griffithwgriffit@olemiss.edu; *Educ Cur* Emily Dean McCauleyesdean@olemiss.edu; *Coll Mgr* Melanie Antonellimjmunns@olemiss.edu; *Mem, Events & Communs Coordr* Kate Wallaceksw@olemiss.edu; *Assoc Dlr of Devel* Angela Barlow Brownambarlow@olemiss.edu; *Fin & Admin Mgr* Michelle Perrymgperry@olemiss.edu; *Security* Mike Hashgmhash@olemiss.edu
Open Tues - Sat 10 AM - 6 PM, cl Sun, Mon & univ holidays; No admis fee for permanent exhibs; special exhibs require admis fee; Estab 1977 to collect, conserve & exhibit objects related to history of the University of Mississippi & to the cultural & scientific heritage of the people of the state & region; Main gallery contains 3000 sq ft with 12 ft ceilings for permanent collections & 800 sq ft with 18 ft ceilings for temporary exhibits; each of the four galleries of the Mary Buie Mus contains 400 sq ft for permanent collection; Lawrence & Fortune Galleries; Walton Young Historic House; Average Annual Attendance: 14,000; Mem: 150
Income: $190,000 (financed by state appropriation)
Special Subjects: African Art, Afro-American Art, Anthropology, Antiquities-Greek, Antiquities-Roman, Asian Art, Decorative Arts, Dolls, Drawings, Etchings & Engravings, Folk Art, Furniture, Glass, Historical Material, Jewelry, Painting-American, Photography, Porcelain, Portraits, Prints, Sculpture, Silver, Textiles, Watercolors, Woodcarvings
Collections: Theora Hamblett Collection (paintings, glass, drawings), Fulton-Meyer Collection of African Art, Millington-Barnard Collection of 19th Century Scientific Instruments, David Robinson Collection of Greek & Roman antiquities
Publications: Department essays; exhibit catalogs
Activities: Classes for adults & children; children's hands-on gallery; lects open to pub, 15 vis lectrs per yr; gallery talks; tours; school outreach program; mus shop sells books, magazines, original art, reproductions, prints, souvenirs related to collections

M **University Gallery**, 85 Cross St, 116 Meek Hall University, MS 38677; PO Box 1848, University, MS 38677-1848. Tel 662-915-7193; Fax 662-915-5013; Email art@olemiss.edu; Web: www.olemiss.edu/; *Chair & Prof* Dr Nancy L Wicker
Open daily 8:30 AM - 4:30 PM; No admis fee; Estab 1954 as a teaching gallery; Average Annual Attendance: 1,000
Income: Financed by state appropriation & tuition
Collections: Faculty & student work, some work purchased from traveling exhibitions
Exhibitions: Faculty, students, alumni & visiting artists
Activities: Lects open to pub, 6-8 vis lectrs per yr; gallery talks; individual paintings & original objects of art lent to departments within the University; lending collection contains original art works, original prints, paintings & sculpture

M **UNIVERSITY OF MISSISSIPPI,** Rowan Oak, Home of William Faulkner, 916 Old Taylor Ave, Oxford, MS 38655; PO Box 1848, Univ of Miss University, MS 38677-1848. Tel 662-234-3284; Fax 662-915-7035; Email wgriffit@olemiss.edu; Web: www.olemiss.edu; *Cur* William Griffith
Open Aug 2 - May 31 Tues - Sat 10 AM - 4 PM, Sun 1 - 4 PM; Jun 1 - Aug 1, open Mon - Sat 10 AM - 6 PM, Sun 1 - 6 PM; cl New Year's Day, Jul 4, Thanksgiving, Christmas Eve & Day; Admis adults, seniors & students $5, free to children & college & univ students; Estab 1977; Rowan Oak was home of William Faulkner from 1930 - 1962; house & grounds have been recently restored & are a National Historic Landmark as well as Literary Landmark owned & maintained by the Univ of MS. Nonprofit org; Average Annual Attendance: 23,000 by accurate count
Collections: Furnishings, personal artifacts

RAYMOND

M **HINDS COMMUNITY COLLEGE DISTRICT,** Marie Hull Gallery, 501 E Main St, PO Box 1100 Raymond, MS 39154-1100. Tel 601-857-3275; Web: www.hindscc.edu, www.hindscc.edu/locations-facilities/marie-hull-art-gallery/; *Dept Chair and Gallery Director* Sarah Teasley
Open Sept - May Mon - Thurs 8 AM - 3 PM, Fri 8 AM - Noon, cl school holidays; No admis fee; Estab 1971 as a community service & cultural agent for the visual arts; Main gallery measures 60 x 60 ft; an adjacent gallery 8 x 45 ft; reception area 15 x 25 ft; Average Annual Attendance: 2,500
Income: $2,900 (financed by Art Department budget)
Collections: Permanent collection of state artist, with 400 pieces in prints, sculptures & paintings
Exhibitions: Sponsors 6 exhibits during college session
Activities: Lects open to public, 3 vis lectrs per yr; gallery talks; tours; sponsor competitions; schols & fels offered

RIDGELAND

M **CRAFTSMEN'S GUILD OF MISSISSIPPI, INC,** Mississippi Craft Center, 950 Rice Rd, Ridgeland, MS 39157-3040. Tel 601-856-7546; Fax 601-856-7531; Email info@mscrafts.org; Web: www.craftsmensguildofms.org; *Opers Mgr* Sheri Cox; *Exec Dir* Nancy Perkins; *Gallery Mgr* Sheri Cox; *CFO* Tomeka Hall-Cheathan; *Educ Coordr* Drew Brunson
Open Mon - Sat 9 AM - 5 PM, Sun 12 PM - 5 PM; No admis fee; Estab 1973 to provide access to & educ in fine crafts to the pub & to provide a marketing venue for juried mem artists; A 20,000 square foot contemporary bldg just off the Natchez Trace Pkwy Nat Park; Average Annual Attendance: 100,000; Mem: 375; mem by Standards Comt evaluation; dues $100 - $125; annual meeting in Dec
Income: Financed by sales & grants
Library Holdings: Original Art Works, Periodical Subscriptions, Photographs, Sculpture
Special Subjects: Afro-American Art, American Indian Art, Bronzes, Carpets & Rugs, Ceramics, Collages, Costumes, Crafts, Dolls, Embroidery, Enamels, Etchings & Engravings, Folk Art, Furniture, Glass, Gold, Ivory, Jade, Jewelry, Laces, Leather, Miniatures, Mosaics, Pewter, Porcelain, Pottery, Scrimshaw, Sculpture, Stained Glass, Textiles, Woodcarvings, Prints
Collections: Choctaw Indian crafts created by members, crafts created by members, Choctaw Indian Crafts, Traditional craft permanent collection; contemporary permanent collection

Exhibitions: Monthly exhibits in George Berry Gallery
Activities: Classes for adults & children; craft demonstration, lect & festivals; docent training; lects open to pub, 3 vis lectrs per yr; gallery talks; Gov's Leadership in Arts Award 2006; MS Travel Attraction of the Year by MS Tourism Assn 2010 & 2011; Best Place to Buy Unique Gifts by Best of Jackson 2010 & 2014; artmobile; original objects of art lent by negotiation in response to requests; lending collection contains original art works, photographs & slides; originate traveling exhibs; sales shop sells books, magazines, prints & original art, primarily original craft objects (Native American to contemporary)

STONEVILLE

A **MISSISSIPPI ART COLONY,** PO Box 387, Stoneville, MS 38756-0387. Tel 888-452-5332; Web: www.msartcolony.com; *Dir* Mrs Jamie Tate; *Pres* Bryon Myrick; *VPres* Keith Alford; *Treas* Evelyn Breland; *Secy* Patty Pilic
Estab 1948 to hold workshops at least twice yearly, for painting & drawing instruction and occasionally other areas; to organize juried show, with prizes awarded, that travels state of Mississippi between workshops; Average Annual Attendance: 50; Mem: $200; annual dues $20
Income: Financed by mem
Exhibitions: Two travel exhibitions each year; Painting workshops
Publications: Bulletin, newsletter
Activities: Annual fall workshop last week in Sept, $300; competitions judged; awards; scholarships; traveling exhibs in Mississippi museums

TOUGALOO

M **TOUGALOO COLLEGE,** Tougaloo Art Collection, 500 W County Line Rd, Tougaloo, MS 39174-9799. Tel 601-977-7743; Email jgilbert@tougaloo.edu; Web: tougaloocollege.edu; *Pres* Beverly Wade Hogan; *VPres Acad Affairs* Dr Bettye Parker Smith; *Dir, Cur* Johnnie Mae Maberry; *Chair* Prof Jesse Primer
Open by appointment; No admis fee; Estab 1963 to service the community & the metropolitan Jackson area; Bennie G Thompson Bldg; Average Annual Attendance: 2,500
Income: Financed by endowment & department budget
Collections: Afro-American, African, International Print Collection with emphasis on European art, New York School (abstract, expressionism, minimal art, surrealism), African Oceania Genevieve McMillan Collection
Exhibitions: African Collection; Afro-American Collection; Faculty & Student Show; Local artists; Art Colony Exhibit, Visiting Artists Special Exhibits
Publications: Mississippi Museum of Art, African Tribal Art; Calder-Hayter-Miro; G M Designs of the 1960s; Hans Hofmann, Light Prints; brochure; catalog; newspaper of spec events
Activities: Classes for adults; dramatic progs; docent training; lects open to pub, 3 vis lectrs per yr; concerts; gallery talks; tours by appointment; schols offered; exten dept; individual paintings & original objects of art lent to libraries, universities & mus; lending collection contains 8000 lantern slides, 700 original art works, 350 original prints, 140 paintings, 150 sculpture, industrial designs & typography; book traveling exhibs; originate traveling exhibs; mus shop sells original art

L **Coleman Library,** 500 W Count Line Rd, Tougaloo, MS 39174-9700. Tel 601-977-7706; Fax 601-977-7714; Web: www.tougaloo.edu/library/index.htm; *Dir Library Svcs* Charlene Cole
Open Mon - Fri 8 AM - 4PM, Sat noon - 4 PM, Sun 5 -11 PM; No admis fee; Estab 1963; Open to students & faculty
Income: Financed by rental fees
Library Holdings: Audio Tapes, Book Volumes 135,000, Cards, Cassettes, Clipping Files, Exhibition Catalogs, Fiche, Filmstrips, Framed Reproductions, Kodachrome Transparencies, Manuscripts, Memorabilia, Motion Pictures, Original Art Works, Pamphlets, Periodical Subscriptions 432, Photographs, Prints, Records, Reels, Reproductions, Sculpture, Slides
Special Subjects: Advertising Design, Aesthetics, Afro-American Art, American Indian Art, American Western Art, Anthropology, Antiquities-Egyptian, Antiquities-Greek, Antiquities-Oriental, Antiquities-Persian, Antiquities-Roman, Archaeology, Folk Art, Glass, Graphic Arts
Collections: Tracy Sugerman (wash drawings, civil rights studies 1964), African masks & sculpture
Exhibitions: Four major exhibits per year
Publications: Tougaloo College Art Collections
Activities: Lects open to pub, 2 vis lectrs per yr; symposium; gallery talks; tours

TUPELO

C **BANCORP SOUTH,** (Bank of Mississippi) Art Collection, 1 Mississippi Plaza, Tupelo, MS 38802-4926; PO Box 789, Tupelo, MS 38802-0789. Tel 662-680-2000; *Pres* Aubrey B Patterson Jr; *Chief Financial Officer* Nash Allen
Estab to encourage local artists & provide cultural enrichment for customers & friends; Works displayed throughout building
Purchases: $500
Collections: Oils, prints, watercolors

M **GUMTREE MUSEUM OF ART,** 211 W Main St, Tupelo, MS 38804; PO Box 786, Tupelo, MS 38802-0786. Tel 662-844-2787; Fax 662-844-9751; Email tina@gumtreemuseum.com; Web: www.gumtreemuseum.com; *Exec Dir & Pub Rels* Tina Lutz; *Chmn* Nancy Difee; *Asst* George Maynard
Open Tues - Fri 10 AM - 4 PM, Sat 10 AM - 2 PM, cl New Year's Day, Independence Day, Thanksgiving, Christmas; No admis fee, donations accepted; Average Annual Attendance: 13,200
Collections: paintings, drawings
Activities: Educ prog; study clubs; lect; guided tours

L **LEE COUNTY LIBRARY,** 219 N Madison, Tupelo, MS 38804. Tel 662-841-9029; Fax 662-840-7615; Email lils@li.lib.ms.us; Web: www.li.lib.ms.us; *Technical Servs Librn* Barbara Anglin; *Dir* Jan Willis; *Reference Librn* Brian Hargett; *Bookmobile Librn* Ann Grimes
Open Mon - Thurs 9:30 AM - 8:30 PM, Fri & Sat 9 AM - 5 PM, cl Sun; Estab 1941 to provide books & other sources of information to serve the intellectual, recreational & cultural needs of its users; Maintains art gallery; The Mezzanine Gallery & Helen Foster Auditorium are used as exhibit space for works by University Art students, local professional artists & traveling exhibitions
Income: Financed by city, state & county appropriations
Library Holdings: Book Volumes 200,000, Cassettes, Fiche, Framed Reproductions, Photographs, Prints, Records, Sculpture, Video Tapes
Collections: The Tupelo Gum Tree Festival purchase prizes, these include paintings and pottery
Activities: Children's summer reading series: Children's series Thurs at 10am; Helen Foster lect series every Apr with renowned authors

MISSOURI

ARROW ROCK

M **ARROW ROCK STATE HISTORIC SITE,** 4th and Van Bruen St, Arrow Rock, MO 65320; PO Box 1, Arrow Rock, MO 65320-0001. Tel 660-837-3330; Fax 660-837-3300; Email dspasso@4mail.dns.state.mo.ks; Web: www.mostateparks.com/arrowrock; *Adminr* Mike Dickey
Open daily 7 AM-10 PM, Dec-Feb: Fri-Sun from 10 AM - 4 PM, Visitor Ctr open 10 AM - 4 PM.; No admis fee; Estab 1923 to preserve, exhibit & interpret the cultural resources of Missouri, especially those assoc with George Caleb Bingham & his era in central Missouri; The 1837 home of G C Bingham serves as a mus house & the 1834 Tavern; Average Annual Attendance: 80,000
Income: Financed by state appropriation
Collections: Bingham Collection, Central Missouri Collection (textiles, furnishing & glass of the 19th century)
Exhibitions: Annual Art Fair; Annual Summer Workshop Exhibit; Annual Craft Festival
Publications: Friends of Arrow Rock Letter, quarterly
Activities: Classes for children; tours

BOLIVAR

M **THE ELLA CAROTHERS DUNNEGAN GALLERY OF ART,** 511 N Pike, Bolivar, MO 65613; PO Box 468, Bolivar, MO 65613. Tel 417-326-3438; Email dunnegan@windstream.net; Web: www.dunnegangallery.com; *Dir* Jo Roberts
Open Mon, Wed & Fri 1 - 4 PM; special hours for special shows; No admis fee; Fine arts mus
Collections: Paintings, sculpture
Activities: Book 2 traveling exhibs per yr

CAPE GIRARDEAU

L **SOUTHEAST MISSOURI STATE UNIVERSITY,** Kent Library, 1 University Plz, MS 4600 Cape Girardeau, MO 63701-4710. Tel 573-651-2235; Fax 573-651-2666; Email scron@semoum.semo.edu; Web: www.library.semo.edu; *Lib Dir* Ed Buis
Open Mon - Thurs 7:30AM-11:30PM, Fri 7:30AM-6PM, Sat 11AM-5PM; No admis fee; Exhibition areas on second & third levels; Atrium Gallery on fourth level. The Jake K Wells Mural, 800 sq ft covers the west wall of the library foyer, depicting the nature & the development of the southeast region of the state
Income: Financed by the univ & grants
Library Holdings: Book Volumes 400,000
Collections: Charles Harrison Collection (rare books including some of the finest examples of the book arts), books & manuscripts from the 13th to the 20th centuries
Exhibitions: Exhibits by local artists
Activities: Tours

CLAYTON

A **ST LOUIS ARTISTS' GUILD & GALLERIES,** 12 N Jackson Ave, Clayton, MO 63105. Tel 314-727-6266; Fax 314-727-9190; Email guild-info@stlouisartistsguild.org; Web: www.stlouisartistsguild.org; *Exec Dir* Kathryn Nahorski; *Exhibs & Educ* Carrie Keasler; *Exhibs & Educ Asst* Amy Firestone Rosen
Open Tues - Fri 10 AM - 6 PM, Sat 10 AM - 4 PM, cl Sun, Mon & holidays; No admis fee; Estab 1886 for the purpose of promoting excellence in the arts; Maintains reference library; Average Annual Attendance: 30,000; Mem: 900+, dues $55
Income: Financed by mem
Special Subjects: Afro-American Art, Bronzes, Cartoons, Ceramics, Crafts, Drawings, Furniture, Glass, Painting-American, Photography, Portraits, Pottery, Prints, Sculpture, Silver, Watercolors, Woodcarvings, Woodcuts
Exhibitions: 15-20 exhibits per yr
Publications: Quarterly newsletter
Activities: Classes for adults & children; lects open to pub, 5 vis lectrs per yr; gallery talks; tours; competitions with awards; workshops; sales shop sells original art

CLINTON

M **HENRY COUNTY MUSEUM & CULTURAL ARTS CENTER,** 203 W Franklin St, Clinton, MO 64735-2008. Tel 660-885-8414; Email hcmus1@centurylink.net; Web: www.henrycountymuseum.org; *Dir* Brenda Dehn; *Asst Dir* Betty Maxwell

Open Mon - Sat, 10 AM - 4 PM; Admis adults $5, students under 12 free; Estab 1976; Turn of the 20th-century museum; museum complex includes: 1856 Dog Trot Log Cabin, 1852 2-story brick home, 1886 Anheuser-Bush Bldg, 1880's One Room School; Average Annual Attendance: 4,500; Mem: 600; dues $15 individual, $25 family; semi-annual meetings
Income: Financed by members
Library Holdings: Clipping Files, Maps, Memorabilia, Original Art Works, Original Documents, Photographs, Records, Slides
Special Subjects: American Indian Art, Antiquities-Greek, Antiquities-Oriental, Antiquities-Persian, Archaeology, Architecture, Asian Art, Bronzes, Carpets & Rugs, Costumes, Decorative Arts, Dolls, Drawings, Embroidery, Eskimo Art, Ethnology, Furniture, Glass, Historical Material, Jewelry, Leather, Maps, Metalwork, Military Art, Miniatures, Mosaics, Oriental Art, Painting-American, Painting-French, Painting-Japanese, Period Rooms, Pewter, Photography, Porcelain, Portraits, Posters, Pottery, Pre-Columbian Art, Prints, Religious Art, Sculpture, Stained Glass, Textiles, Watercolors, Woodcarvings, Woodcuts
Collections: Paintings of Mr & Mrs Louis Freund, Ike Parker Collection: Callie Hart, over 250 pieces of Thomas Clark sculptures
Exhibitions: Louis Freund WPA Work at all Times; Thomas F. Clark at all times
Activities: Classes for adults & children; docent training; 3 vis lectrs per yr; tours; sponsoring of competitions; Heritage Award; schols available; book traveling exhibs, 1-2007, Between Fences, from MO Humanities; mus shop sells books, magazines, original art, reproductions & prints

COLUMBIA

A **STATE HISTORICAL SOCIETY OF MISSOURI,** 1020 Lowry, Columbia, MO 65201-7298. Tel 573-882-7083; Fax 573-884-4950; Email shsofmo@umsystem.edu; Web: shs.umsystem.edu; *Exec Dir* Dr Gary R Kremer; *Vol Pres* Stephen N Limbaugh Jr; *Art Cur* Dr Joan Stack; *Mus Preparator Chief* Greig Thompson
Open Tues-Fri 8 AM - 4:45 PM, Sat 8 AM - 3:30 PM; No admis fee; Estab 1898 to collect, preserve, make accessible & publish materials pertaining to the history of Missouri & the Middle West; Circ Non-circulating; Major art gallery 54 ft x 36 ft; corridor galleries; Average Annual Attendance: 5,233; Mem: 4,864; dues $30 individual, $50 household; annual meeting in fall
Income: Financed by state appropriation, membership dues & private giving
Library Holdings: Book Volumes, Clipping Files, Lantern Slides, Manuscripts, Maps, Original Art Works, Original Documents, Pamphlets, Periodical Subscriptions, Photographs, Prints, Records, Reels, Slides, Video Tapes
Special Subjects: Cartoons, Drawings, Historical Material, Manuscripts, Painting-American, Photography, Portraits, Prints, Watercolors, Maps
Collections: Works by Thomas Hart Benton, George C Bingham, Karl Bodmer, Fred Geary, Carl Gentry, William Knox, Roscoe Misselhorn, Frank B Nuderscher, Charles Schwartz, Fred Shane, Frederick Sylvester, contemporary artists coll containing work of over fifty outstanding Missouri related artists, original cartoon coll of works by Tom Engelhardt, Daniel Fitzpatrick, Don Hesse, Bill Mauldin, S J Ray and others
Publications: Missouri Historical Review, quarterly; R Douglas Hurt & Mary K Dains, eds; Thomas Hart Benton: Artist, Writer & Intellectual (1989); Lynn Wolf Gentzler, ed, "But I Forget That I am a Painter and not a Politician": The Letters of George Caleb Bingham (2011)
Activities: Lects open to public; tours; 8-10 vis lectrs per yr; gallery talks; individual paintings lent, loans based on submitted requests; sales shop sells books & prints

L **Gallery and Library,** 1020 Lowry St, Columbia, MO 65201-7207. Tel 573-882-7083; Fax 573-884-4950; Email shsofmo@umsystem.edu; Web: www.shs.umsystem.edu; *Exec Dir* Dr Gary R Kremer; *VPres* Dick Franklin; *Art Cur* Dr Joan Stock
Open Library: Mon, Wed - Fri 8 AM - 4:30 PM, Tues 8 AM - 9 PM, Sat 9 AM - 4:30 PM; Gallery: Mon, Wed - Sat 9 AM - 4 PM, Tues 5 PM - 8 PM; No admis fee, donations accepted; Estab 1898; Open to public; Mem: 5,167; $20 individual, $30 family
Income: Financed by state appropriation
Library Holdings: Audio Tapes, Book Volumes 460,000, Cassettes, Clipping Files, Exhibition Catalogs, Fiche, Kodachrome Transparencies, Manuscripts, Maps 4,405, Original Art Works, Original Documents, Pamphlets, Periodical Subscriptions 984, Photographs, Prints, Records, Reels, Slides, Video Tapes
Special Subjects: Historical Material, Manuscripts, Maps, Photography
Collections: George Caleb Bingham Collection, Thomas Hart Benton Collection, Karl Bodmer: 90 colored engravings, Bay Collection of Middle Western America
Activities: Lects open to public; gallery talks; tours; sales shop sells books, prints, notecards & t-shirts

M **STEPHENS COLLEGE,** Lewis James & Nellie Stratton Davis Art Gallery, 1200 Broadway, Columbia, MO 65215-0001. Tel 573-876-7627; Fax 573-876-7248; Email irene@stephens.edu; *Dir* Robert Friedman; *Cur* Irene Alexander
Open Mon - Fri 10 AM - 4 PM, cl school holidays & summer; No admis fee; Estab 1964 to provide exhibs of art for the gen interest of the local community & for the educ of the student body in gen; Average Annual Attendance: 500
Income: $2000 (financed by endowment)
Special Subjects: Graphics, Painting-American, Primitive art, Sculpture
Collections: Modern graphics, modern paintings, primitive sculpture
Exhibitions: Elizabeth Layton's Drawing on Life; Ron Meyers: Ceramics; Margaret Peterson Paintings; Burger Sandzen exhibit
Activities: Lects open to public, 6 vis lectrs per year; gallery talks; exhibs; competitions with awards

M **UNIVERSITY OF MISSOURI,** Museum of Art & Archaeology, 1 Pickard Hall, Columbia, MO 65211-1420. Tel 573-882-3591; Fax 573-884-4039; Email museumuser@missouri.edu; Web: maa.missouri.edu; *Cur European & American Art* Mary Pixley; *Cur Ancient Art* J Benton Kidd; *Registrar* Jeffrey Wilcox; *Cur Educ* Cathy Callaway; *Preparator* Barb Smith; *Fiscal Officer & Admin Assoc* Carol Geisler; *Dir* Alex Barker; *Asst Dir* Bruce Cox; *Academic Coordr* Arthur Mehrhoff; *Graphic Designer* Kristie Lee
Open Tues - Fri 9 AM - 4PM, Sat & Sun Noon - 4 PM, Thurs open til 8 PM, cl Mon & holidays; No admis fee; Estab 1957 to exhibit a study collection for students in Art History & Archaeology; a comprehensive collection for the enjoyment of the general area of Missouri; Housed in renovated 1890's building. Ten galleries for permanent collection & special exhibitions; Average Annual Attendance: 35,000; Mem: 600
Income: $1,088,667 (financed by mem, grants & state appropriation)
Special Subjects: African Art, Afro-American Art, Antiquities-Assyrian, Antiquities-Byzantine, Antiquities-Egyptian, Antiquities-Etruscan, Antiquities-Greek, Antiquities-Oriental, Antiquities-Persian, Antiquities-Roman, Archaeology, Asian Art, Baroque Art, Bronzes, Ceramics, Ceramics, Collages, Drawings, Enamels, Etchings & Engravings, Folk Art, Glass, Gold, Islamic Art, Ivory, Jade, Jewelry, Landscapes, Landscapes, Manuscripts, Medieval Art, Mosaics, Oriental Art, Painting-American, Painting-British, Painting-Dutch, Painting-European, Painting-Flemish, Painting-French, Painting-Japanese, Photography, Portraits, Pottery, Pre-Columbian Art, Primitive art, Prints, Religious Art, Sculpture, Textiles, Watercolors, Woodcuts
Collections: Ancient Art-Egypt, Western Asia, Greek & Roman, European & American painting & sculpture, Early Christian-Byzantine & Coptic, Modern paintings & sculpture, Prints & drawings, African, Pre-Columbian, Oriental-Chinese & Japanese, South Asian-Indian, Thai, Tibetan, Nepalese
Exhibitions: Weinberg Gallery of Ancient Art, ongoing; European and American Gallery of Art, ongoing; Barton Gallery of Modern and Contemporary Art, ongoing; Collecting for a New Century: Recent Acquisitions, Black Women in Art and the Stories They Tell, Ran In-Ting's Watercolors: East and West Mix in Images of Rural Taiwan, A Midwestern View: The artists of the Ste. Genevieve Art Colony, Love, Life, Death and Mourning: Remembrance in Portraits by George Caleb Bingham, The Mediterranean Melting Pot: Commerce and Cultural Exchange in Antiquity, The Sacred Feminine: Prehistory to Postmodernity, Narratives of Process and Time in the Prints of Jorg Schmeisser
Publications: Muse, annually; exhibition catalogues; Museum Magazine, 2 per yr; calendars, 12 per yr; Glen Lukens: Innovations in Clay, Testament of Time; Antiquities from the Holy Land; Golden Treasures by Akelo: The Voyage of a Contemporary Italian Goldsmith in the Classical World
Activities: Classes for adults & children; docent training; workshops on conservation; lects open to pub, 5-10 vis lectrs per yr; tours; gallery talks, concerts; original objects of art lent to institutions; book traveling exhibs 2-3 per yr; originate traveling exhibs; mus shop sells books, prints, reproductions, slides, gifts & jewelry

L **Art, Archaeology & Music Collection,** MU Libraries, University of Missouri, Room 104, Ellis Library Columbia, MO 65201; 1020 Lowry St Stop 1, Ellis Library Columbia, MO 65201-5149. Tel 573-882-4581; Fax 573-882-8044; *Librn* Michael Muchow; *Music* Anne Barker; *Reference Desk Coordr* Cynthia Cotner
Open Mon-Thurs 8AM-11PM, Fri 8AM-6PM, Sat 9 AM-6PM, Sun Noon-11PM; Estab 1841 to house material for the faculty & students of the University
Income: Financed by state appropriation
Library Holdings: Book Volumes 81,000, CD-ROMs, Exhibition Catalogs, Fiche, Periodical Subscriptions 300, Records, Reels, Video Tapes

FAYETTE

M **CENTRAL METHODIST UNIVERSITY,** Ashby-Hodge Gallery of American Art, 411 Central Methodist Sq, Fayette, MO 65248-1104. Tel 660-248-6324 or 6304; Fax 660-248-2622; Email jegeist@centralmethodist.edu; Web: www.centralmethodist.edu; *Cur* Denise Gebhardt; *Registrar* Dr Joe Geist
Open Tues - Thurs & Sun 1:30-4:30 PM, other times by appointment; No admis fee; Estab 1993; focus on American art; Average Annual Attendance: 5,000; Mem: 800
Purchases: Lithographs: Coney Island-Paul Cadnus; Color Prints: River at Asot Neg-Maxfield Parrish; Wooden Sculpture: Scene From Pittsburgh-Joseph Falsetti; Barrel & Sack Corn - Alfred Montgomery; Still Life with Strawberries - August Laux; in 2012: etching by Stephen Maxwell Pamuk, etching by Joseph Meers, lithograph by Donald Roberts & Morea Soyer, The Hunt by Leroy Neiman
Special Subjects: Painting-American, Photography, Sculpture, Watercolors
Collections: Ashby Collection of American Art, Dr Robert Bussabarger, Brother Mel Meyer, SM, Edna Schenk
Exhibitions: Salvador Dali
Activities: Docent training; 2 vis lectrs per yr; tours

FENTON

L **MARITZ, INC,** Library, 1400 S Highway Dr, Fenton, MO 63099-0001. Tel 636-827-1501; Fax 636-827-3006; *Mgr* Jan Meier
Estab 1968; Circ 12,000; For reference & lending
Library Holdings: Book Volumes 7500, Periodical Subscriptions 250
Special Subjects: Graphic Arts, Illustration

FULTON

M **NATIONAL CHURCHILL MUSEUM,** 501 Westminster Ave, Fulton, MO 65251-1299. Tel 573-592-5369; Fax 573-592-5222; Web: www.nationalchurchillmuseum.org; *Asst Dir* Kit Freudenberg; *Educ Cur* Amanda Plybon; *Archivist/Cur* Amy Cantone; *Vis Servs & Mus Store Mgr* Becky McCue; *Mktg Specialist* Collin Shaw
Open daily 10AM-4:30PM, cl Thanksgiving, Christmas & New Year's; Admis adults $7.50, seniors $6.50, college students $5.50, youth 12-18 $5.50, children 6-11 $4.50, children 5 & under free; Estab 1969 to commemorate life & legacy of Winston Churchill including 1946 vis to Westminster College to deliver the Iron Curtain speech; Permanent exhib redesigned 2006 with hands-on displays & videos re: Churchill's life & world history. Special exhibs gallery changes quarterly. 17th century Christopher Wren church donated & restored on site in 1960's; Average Annual Attendance: 22,000; Mem: 900
Income: Financed by endowment, mem, admis, friends fundraising, gift shop sales
Special Subjects: Historical Material, Maps
Collections: Churchill & family memorabilia, including documents, manuscripts & photographs, Churchill oil paintings, rare maps

Exhibitions: Churchill paintings; Iron Curtain speech memorabilia
Publications: The Churchillian qtrly magazine; The Dispatch Box e-newsletter
Activities: Churchill classes for WC students; docent training; lects open to pub; concerts; tours; 2009 designated by US Congress as America's National Churchill Museum; schols & fels offered; individual paintings & original objects of art lent to other mus & libraries; book traveling exhibs 2-4 per yr; originate traveling exhibs; mus shop sells books, original art, reproductions, prints, slides, Churchill busts & memorabilia, English china, posters, collectible English toy soldiers

M **WILLIAM WOODS UNIVERSITY,** Cox Gallery, 1 University Ave, Fulton, MO 65251-2388. Tel 573-592-4245/4244; Fax 573-592-1623; Email nicole.petrescu@williamwoods.edu; Web: www.williamwoods.edu; *Gallery coordr* Nicole Petrescu; *Div Chair* Dr Caroline Boyer Ferhat
Open Mon - Fri 9 AM - 6 PM while in session, cl Univ Holidays; No admis fee; Estab 1967 to be used as a teaching aid for the Kemper Art Center; Maintains 3200 sq ft sky-lighted gallery with a mezzanine
Income: Financed by endowment
Activities: Classes for children; lects open to pub, 2 vis lectrs per yr; tours; gallery talks; schols

INDEPENDENCE

M **CHURCH OF JESUS CHRIST OF LATTER-DAY SAINTS,** Independence Visitors' Center, 937 W Walnut, Independence, MO 64050. Tel 816-836-3466; Fax 816-252-6256; Email vcindependence@ldschurch.org; Web: www.lds.org; *Dir* Barrie G McKay
Open daily 9 AM - 9 PM; No admis fee; Estab 1971 as a Visitors' Center of Church of Jesus Christ of Latter Day Saints beliefs & history in Missouri, Ohio & Illinois; Average Annual Attendance: 50,000
Income: Financed by The Church of Jesus Christ of Latter Day Saints
Special Subjects: Religious Art, Portraits, Woodcuts
Collections: Large 15 ft marble Christus statue, painting, computer reproductions, Short movies about Church history & life experiences of Jesus Christ
Exhibitions: Paintings; movies; audio-visual shows; historical maps exhibits; special flag display; log cabin 1800s (original)
Publications: Brochures
Activities: Lect open to public; free guided tours

L **NATIONAL ARCHIVES & RECORDS ADMINISTRATION,** Harry S Truman Museum and Library, 500 West Hwy 24, Independence, MO 64050-1798. Tel 816-833-1400; Fax 816-833-4368; Email truman.library@mara.gov; Web: www.trumanlibrary.org; *Acting Dir* Michael Devine; *Mus Cur* Clay Bauske
Open Mon - Sat 9 AM - 5 PM, Thurs 9 AM - 9 PM, Sun Noon - 5 PM; Admis adults $8, seniors $7, children 6-15 $3, under 6 free; Estab 1957 to preserve & make available for study & exhibition the papers, objects & other materials relating to President Harry S Truman & to the history of the Truman admin; Gravesite of President & Mrs Truman in the courtyard. Admin by the National Archives & Records Administration of the Federal Government; Average Annual Attendance: 150,000
Income: Financed by federal appropriation, federal trust fund & private donations
Library Holdings: Audio Tapes, Book Volumes 40,000, Clipping Files, Framed Reproductions, Manuscripts, Memorabilia, Motion Pictures, Original Art Works, Other Holdings Documents, Pamphlets, Periodical Subscriptions 23, Photographs, Prints, Records, Reels, Sculpture, Slides
Collections: Papers of Harry S Truman, his assoc, and of officials in the Truman administration, Portraits of President Truman, paintings, prints, sculptures & artifacts presented to President Truman during the Presidential & Post-Presidential periods, original political cartoons, mural by Thomas Hart Benton
Exhibitions: Permanent & temporary exhibits relating to the life & times of Harry S Truman; the history of the Truman administration; the history & nature of office of the Presidency
Publications: Historical materials in the Truman Library
Activities: Educ dept; lect; conferences & commemorative events; tours to tour groups; film series; research grants; sales shop sells books, reproductions, slides & postcards

M **WORNALL MAJORS HOUSE MUSEUMS,** The 1859 Jail, Marshal's Home & Museum, 114 S Main St, Ste 103, Independence, MO 64050-3703; PO Box 4241, Independence, MO 64051-4241. Tel 816-252-1892; Fax 816-461-1897; Web: www.jchs.org; *Exec Dir* Steve Noll
Open Mon - Sat 10 AM - 5 PM, Sun 1 - 4 PM, Mar, Nov & Dec Mon 10 AM - 4 PM, cl Jan & Feb; Admis adults $4.00, sr citizens $3.50, children 6-16 $1, under 5 free, group rates available; Estab 1958 for interpretation of Jackson County history; 1859 Federal town house of county marshal, attached limestone jail which served as federal headquarters during the Civil War. Restored historical interior c 1860s. Restored cell of Frank James c 1882; Average Annual Attendance: 12,000; Mem: 1,000; dues $20-$1,000
Income: Financed by mem, tours, fundraising events
Special Subjects: Historical Material, Period Rooms
Collections: Jackson County history, 1800-present, home furnishings of mid-19th century in restored areas
Exhibitions: Permanent exhibits on Jackson County history; changing exhibits
Publications: Jackson County Historical Society Journal, bi-annual
Activities: Classes for children; docent training; lects open to pub; tours; mus shop sells books

L **Research Library & Archives**, 6115 Wornall Ave, Kansas City, MO 64113; 112 W Lexington Ave Ste 103, Independence, MO 64050-2843. Tel 816-444-1858; Web: www.wornallmajors.org; *Exec Dir* Kerrie Nichols
Open Tues - Fri 10 AM - 4 PM, Sat 10 AM - 1 PM; No admis fee; Estab 1966; Gallery collects, preserves, & makes available for research exhibition & education materials that relate to Jackson County history; Mem: $20-1,000
Income: Financed by mem, fees, donations, sales
Library Holdings: Audio Tapes, Book Volumes 2000, Clipping Files, Filmstrips, Kodachrome Transparencies, Lantern Slides, Motion Pictures, Periodical Subscriptions 15, Photographs, Reels, Slides, Video Tapes
Collections: Photograph collection for reference, extensive manuscript collection

M **John Wornall House Museum**, 6115 Wornall Rd, Kansas City, MO 64113. Tel 816-444-1858; Fax 816-361-8165; Email director@wornallmajors.org; Web: www.wornallmajors.org; *Dir* Kerrie Nichols
Open Wed - Sat 10 AM - 4 PM, Sun 1 - 4 PM; Admis adults $8, sr citizens & students $6, children 5-12 $5, children 4 & under free, group rates available; Estab 1972 restored to interpret the daily lives of prosperous frontier farm families between 1830-1875 in early Kansas City; House was used as field hospital by both armies during the Civil War. Built in 1858; opened to pub in 1972; Average Annual Attendance: 7,000; Mem: 200: dues $25-500
Income: Financed by mem, tours & fund raisings
Special Subjects: Decorative Arts, Furniture, Architecture, Maps
Collections: Home furnishings of prosperous farm families, Civil War Period Collection
Exhibitions: Special exhibitions on subjects dealing with interpretation of home & Civil War period
Activities: Classes for adults & children; docent training; tours; lects open to pub; 2-3 vis lectrs per yr; mus shop sells books, holiday & gift items

JEFFERSON CITY

M **MISSOURI DEPARTMENT OF NATURAL RESOURCES,** Missouri State Museum, Jefferson Landing SHS, Jefferson City, MO 65101; PO Box 176, Division of State Parks Jefferson City, MO 65102-0176. Tel 573-751-2854; Fax 573-526-2927; Web: www.mostateparks.com; *Mus Dir* Kurt Senn; *Asst Dir* Linda Endersby; *Interpretive Progs & Tours* Chris Sterman; *Cur Exhibs* Julie Kemper; *Cur Collections* Kate Keil
Open daily 8 AM - 5 PM, cl New Years, Easter, Thanksgiving, Christmas; No admis fee; Estab 1920; History art & natural history of Missouri; Average Annual Attendance: 250,000
Income: Financed by state sales tax, affiliated with Missouri Department of Natural Resources
Special Subjects: Anthropology, Costumes, Historical Material, Painting-American
Collections: Art murals by T H Benton, Berninghaus, Frank Brangwyn, N C Wyeth, historical material and natural specimens representing Missouri's natural and cultural resources, Indian artifacts, History hall
Exhibitions: Permanent & temporary exhibits
Publications: Pamphlets
Activities: Guided tours of Capitol; audio-visual presentations; gallery tours; state parks & historic sites; books

M **Elizabeth Rozier Gallery**, 101 Jefferson St, Union Hotel Jefferson City, MO 65101-3054; PO Box 176, Division of State Parks Jefferson City, MO 65102-0176. Tel 573-751-2854; Fax 573-526-2927; *Dir* Kurt Senn; *Asst Dir* Linda Endersby; *Cur* Julie Kemper
Open 10 AM - 4 PM, Tues - Sat; No admis fee; Estab 1981 to provide art, crafts & history educational exhibits; Located in mid-nineteenth century building with a large & small gallery; Average Annual Attendance: 6,000
Income: Financed by state sales tax affiliated with Missouri Dept of Natural Resources
Special Subjects: Historical Material
Exhibitions: New exhibit every month
Activities: Lects open to pub; 2 vis lectrs per yr; gallery talks; tours

JOPLIN

A **GEORGE A SPIVA CENTER FOR THE ARTS,** 222 W Third St, Joplin, MO 64801. Tel 417-623-0183; Fax 417-623-3805; Email spiva@spivaarts.org; Web: www.spivaarts.org; *Bd Pres* Brandon Davis; *2nd Bd VPres* Chad Greer; *Exhibs Coordr* Shaun Conroy; *Bookkeeper* Rhea Cooper; *Asst Dir* Kerstin Landwer
Open Tues - Sat 10 AM - 5 PM, Sun 1 - 5 PM, cl Mon & national holidays; No admis fee - donations are appreciated; Estab 1948, incorporated 1959, as a non-profit, to provide cultural, educational & artistic exhibits & progs to increase public's appreciation of art; 3 galleries for Nat/International & local artist exhibits; Average Annual Attendance: 15,000; Mem: 600; dues $20-$1000; annual meeting in Nov
Library Holdings: Book Volumes, Clipping Files, Exhibition Catalogs, Periodical Subscriptions
Collections: Permanent collection
Exhibitions: PhotoSpiva; Annual Membership Show
Publications: Calendar; newsletter
Activities: Classes for adults & children; vol training; dramatic progs; lects open to public, 3 vis lectrs per year; tours; concerts; gallery talks; competitions with awards; mus shop sells books, original art, gifts

L **WINFRED L & ELIZABETH C POST FOUNDATION FOUNDATION,** Post Art Library, 300 S Main St, Joplin, MO 64801-2384. Tel 417-782-7678; Email jhsullivan@postartlibrary.org; Web: www.postartlibrary.org; *Dir* Jill Sullivan
Open Mon, Tues, Thurs + Fri 10-6; Wed + Sat 10-4, cl Sun & holidays; No admis fee; Estab 1981 to provide information on the fine & decorative arts to members of the community; historic preservation of local history; Circ circulating; Located in a wing of the Joplin Public Library. Includes art gallery + library resources.; Average Annual Attendance: 6,500
Income: Financed by private endowment
Library Holdings: Book Volumes 3500, Clipping Files, Exhibition Catalogs, Original Art Works, Pamphlets, Periodical Subscriptions 25, Photographs, Reproductions, Sculpture
Special Subjects: Sculpture, Architecture, Art History, Decorative Arts, Furniture, Historical Material, Photography
Collections: 16th-17th Century Antiques & Artworks, Joplin, Missouri historic architecture coll, fine arts books colls
Exhibitions: Monthly exhibits of works by area artists
Publications: From Lincoln Logs to Lego Blocks: How Joplin Was Built by Leslie Simpson; Now and Then and Again: Joplin Historic Architecture by Leslie Simpson; Joplin: Post Card History by Leslie Simpson
Activities: Educ dept; film & slide progs; lects open to pub; concerts; tours; lects to civic groups offsite; mus shop sells books, notecards

KANSAS CITY

M **AVILA UNIVERSITY,** Thornhill Art Gallery, 11901 Wornall Rd, Dallavis Ctr Kansas City, MO 64145-1007. Tel 816-501-3762; Fax 816-501-2459; Email thornhillgallery@avila.edu; Web: www.avila.edu; *Gallery Dir* Marci Aylward; *Office Mgr* Janine Urness
Open Mon - Thurs 9 AM - 3 PM & by appointment; No admis fee; Estab 1978; Gallery space 60 x 35 ft is maintained with carpeted floor and walls and track lighting; Average Annual Attendance: 2,000
Income: Financed through school budget
Collections: Avila University Art Collection
Exhibitions: Japanese Woodblock Prints, Faculty Biennial
Activities: Lect open to public; gallery talks; sponsoring of competitions; originate traveling exhibits with the Mid-America Arts Alliance

M **BELGER ARTS CENTER,** 2100 Walnut St, Kansas City, MO 64108. Tel 816-474-3250; Fax 816-221-1621; Email mdickens@belgerartscenter.org; Web: www.belgerartscenter.org; *Exec Dir* Evelyn Craft Berger
Open Wed - Fri 10 AM-4 PM, Sat noon to 4 PM, other times by appointment; Estab 2000; The center hosts contemporary art exhibs featuring the work of notables from the Belger Collection. The annual exhib schedule also includes rotating & solo group exhibs of national & international contemporary artists; Average Annual Attendance: 7,000
Special Subjects: Ceramics, Decorative Arts, Etchings & Engravings, Landscapes, Painting-American, Prints, Sculpture
Collections: works by contemporary artists
Activities: Groups of 10 to 30 may schedule free docent-led tours & hands-on activities; gallery talks; tours

C **COMMERCE BANCSHARES, INC,** Fine Art Collection, Commerce Bank, 922 Walnut St, Art Dept KC Art Kansas City, MO 64106-1871. Tel 816-760-7885; Fax 816-234-2356; Email robin.trafton@commercebank.com; *CEO & Pres* David W Kemper; *Cur* Robin Trafton
Open Mon - Sat 8 AM - 5 PM; No admis fee; Estab 1964; 125 ft barrel vaulted gallery with 13 ft ceiling to exhibit mus quality paintings
Collections: American Art
Activities: Individual paintings lent on restricted basis

C **HALLMARK CARDS, INC,** Hallmark Art Collection, 2501 McGee, Kansas City, MO 64141. Tel 816-545-6993; Email info@hallmarkartcollection.com; Web: www.hallmarkartcollection.com; *Cur* Joe Houston
Visitors Center: call for hours; Estab 1949; Corporate art collection
Special Subjects: Drawings, Photography, Prints, Ceramics
Collections: Hallmark Art Collection, illustration art
Publications: Exhibition catalogs
Activities: Lects; individual objects of art lent to reputable institutions for temporary exhibs; originate traveling exhibs

L **Creative Library**, 2501 McGee, No 146, Kemo, MO 64108. Tel 816-274-5525; Fax 816-274-7245
Open to Hallmark personnel only; Estab to provide pictorial research
Income: Financed by corp funds
Library Holdings: Book Volumes 22,000, Periodical Subscriptions 150
Special Subjects: Illustration
Collections: Old & rare collection

M **KANSAS CITY ARTISTS COALITION,** 201 Wyandotte, Kansas City, MO 64105. Tel 816-421-5222; Fax 816-459-0806; Email information@kansascityartistscoalition.org; Web: www.kansascityartistscoalition.org; *Exec Dir* Janet F Simpson; *Asst Dir* Marissa Starke
Open Wed - Sat 11 AM - 5 PM; No admis fee; Estab 1975 to promote contemporary art & artists from Kansas City & the Midwest; nonprofit organization; Average Annual Attendance: 19,000; Mem: 800; dues $45
Collections: Contemporary Art
Exhibitions: Exhibs of high-quality, innovative work by emerging & mid-career artists; exhib series features a diverse combination of local, regional & national artists
Publications: Forum, online
Activities: Res prog; exhibs & lects open to pub; gallery talks; competitions with awards; workshops; schols & grants available; Money for Artists Promotion (MAP) Grant; Lighton International Artists Exchange Prog (LIAEP)

A **KANSAS CITY MUNICIPAL ART COMMISSION,** 414 E 12th St, City Hall, 17th Fl Kansas City, MO 64106-2702. Tel 816-513-3422; Fax 816-513-2523; Email elizabeth.bowman@kcmo.org; Web: www.kcmo.gov/art; *Public Art Administrator* Liz Bowman
Estab 1926. Administers the One-Percent-for-Art Program in Kansas City, setting aside one percent of all construction costs for new building & renovation projects for artwork
Exhibitions: Shown at various pub locations, such as libraries, col campuses & museums on a rotating basis
Activities: Originate traveling exhibs

L **KANSAS CITY PUBLIC LIBRARY,** 14 W 10th St, Kansas City, MO 64105-1702. Tel 816-701-3400; Fax 816-701-3401; Web: www.kclibrary.org; *Exec Dir* R Crosby Kemper III; *Dir Central Libr* Lillie Brack
Open Mon - Wed 9 AM - 9 PM, Thurs 9 AM - 6 PM, Fri 9 AM - 5 PM, Sat 10 AM - 5 PM, Sun 1 - 5 PM; No admis fee

M **LEEDY-VOULKOS ART CENTER,** 2012 Baltimore Ave, Kansas City, MO 64108-1914. Tel 816-474-1919; Fax 816-221-8474; Web: www.leed-voulkos.com; *Exec Dir* James Leedy; *Managing Dir* Holly Swangstu
Open Wed - Sat 11 AM - 5 PM or by appointment; Estab 1985 to showcase contemporary arts & crafts; 10,000 sq ft of exhib space; Average Annual Attendance: 50,000
Exhibitions: Showcase contemporary art in all media-changing exhibits every six weeks
Activities: Classes for adults & children; 4 vis lectrs per yr; gallery talks; mus shop sells books & original art

M **LIBERTY MEMORIAL MUSEUM & ARCHIVES,** The National Museum of World War I, 2 Memorial Dr., Kansas City, MO 64108-4616. Tel 816-888-8100; Email info@nwwone.org; Web: www.libertymemorialmuseum.org; *Archivist* Jonathan Casey; *Cur* Doran L Cart
Open Winter Tues - Sun 10 AM - 5 PM, Summer Sun - Fri 10 AM - 5 PM, Sat. 9 AM - 5 PM; Admis prices vary per exhibit; Estab 1919 to exhibit World War I memorabilia; Two rectangular spaces 45 x 90 ft; permanent & temporary exhibits; expanded mus space of 32,000 sq ft; Average Annual Attendance: 62,000; Mem: 1000+; ann meeting Nov
Income: Financed by city appropriation & pvt donations
Purchases: 1917 Harley Davidson Army Motorcycle
Library Holdings: Kodachrome Transparencies, Lantern Slides, Manuscripts, Maps, Memorabilia, Motion Pictures, Original Art Works, Original Documents, Other Holdings, Periodical Subscriptions, Photographs, Prints, Records, Reels, Sculpture, Slides, Video Tapes
Special Subjects: Coins & Medals, Costumes, Drawings, Etchings & Engravings, Historical Material, Manuscripts, Maps, Military Art, Painting-American, Painting-French, Painting-German, Photography, Posters, Prints
Collections: WWI: books, documents, militaria, original sketches & paintings, photos, posters, sheet music, Soldiers' Art & Crafts, Sheet Music Covers, World War I Covers
Exhibitions: Trench Warfare; Aviation; Artillery; Medical Care; Uniforms; Women at War
Publications: Quarterly newsletter
Activities: Children's progs; lect open to pub; 2-4 vis lectrs per yr; mus shop sells books, reproductions, postcards & posters

MID AMERICA ARTS ALLIANCE & EXHIBITS USA
For further information, see National and Regional Organizations

M **THE NELSON-ATKINS MUSEUM OF ART,** 4525 Oak St, Kansas City, MO 64111-1873. Tel 816-751-1278; Email ask@nelson-atkins.org; Web: www.nelson-atkins.org; *Dir & CEO* Julian Zugazagoitia; *COO* Karen Christiansen; *Chair Board of Trustees* Shirley Helzberg; *Dir Cur Affairs* Catherine Futter
Open Wed & Sat - Sun 10 AM - 5 PM, Thurs & Fri 10 AM - 9 PM, cl Mon - Tues, New Year's Day, July 4, Thanksgiving, Christmas Eve & Day; Adults $18, seniors $15, students $10, children 12 & under free; Estab 1933 as a gen mus serving the greater Kansas City region; Circ 135,000; Encyclopedic mus with art from ancient to contemporary & modern; maintains reference library; Average Annual Attendance: 400,000; Mem: 11,000; dues $50 - $10,000
Income: Financed by endowment, mem & contributions
Library Holdings: Auction Catalogs, Book Volumes, Other Holdings, Periodical Subscriptions
Special Subjects: African Art, Afro-American Art, American Indian Art, American Western Art, Antiquities-Assyrian, Antiquities-Egyptian, Antiquities-Greek, Antiquities-Roman, Asian Art, Baroque Art, Calligraphy, Carpets & Rugs, Ceramics, Costumes, Decorative Arts, Drawings, Etchings & Engravings, Glass, Hispanic Art, Ivory, Jewelry, Landscapes, Medieval Art, Period Rooms, Photography, Pottery, Prints, Restorations, Sculpture, Woodcuts, Bronzes, Furniture, Painting-American
Collections: Burnap Collection: English pottery, Oriental ceramics, paintings, sculpture, bronze, Egyptian tomb sculpture, American painting, period rooms & furniture, Hallmark Photographic Collection, Donald J Hall Sculpture Park, African, American Indian & Asian Art
Publications: Explore art calendar, 6 times per yr; Member magazine, 2 times per yr
Activities: Classes for adults & children; dramatic progs; docent training; lects open to pub, 50 vis lectr per yr; gallery talks; tours; concerts; individual paintings and original objects of art lent to qualified organizations & exhibs; organize various traveling exhibs; mus shop sells books, magazines, original art, reproductions & slides

L **Spencer Art Reference Library**, 4525 Oak St, Kansas City, MO 64111-1873. Tel 816-751-1216; Fax 816-751-0498; Web: www.nelson-atkins.org; *Head Lib Svcs* Marilyn Carbonell; *Sr Librn & Pub Svcs* Dr. Amelia Nelson; *Archives Asst* Tara Laver
Open Tues by appointment, Wed 10 AM - 5 PM, Thurs - Fri 10 AM - 6 PM, Sat - Sun 1 - 4 PM; No admis fee; For reference only; library instruction for college & univ classes in art & art hist; topical book displays and readings
Library Holdings: Auction Catalogs 42,254, Audio Tapes, Book Volumes 127,277, Cassettes, Clipping Files 8,379, DVDs 286, Exhibition Catalogs, Fiche, Manuscripts, Original Documents, Other Holdings Archives: 96 coll; Per titles 1,200; 48,198 vols, Pamphlets, Periodical Subscriptions 650, Photographs, Slides 119,738, Video Tapes
Special Subjects: American Indian Art, American Western Art, Antiquities-Egyptian, Antiquities-Etruscan, Antiquities-Greek, Antiquities-Oriental, Antiquities-Roman, Archaeology, Art Education, Art History, Asian Art, Ceramics, Decorative Arts, Etchings & Engravings, Furniture, Historical Material, History of Art & Archaeology, Illustration, Jade, Landscape Architecture, Metalwork, Mixed Media, Oriental Art, Painting-American, Painting-British, Painting-Dutch, Painting-European, Painting-Flemish, Painting-French, Painting-German, Painting-Italian, Painting-Japanese, Pewter, Photography, Porcelain, Portraits, Posters, Pottery, Primitive art, Printmaking, Prints, Religious Art, Restoration & Conservation, Sculpture, Silver, Southwestern Art, Video, Woodcuts
Collections: Chinese Art; Auction Catalogs

M **Creative Arts Center**, 4525 Oak St, Kansas City, MO 64111-1873. Tel 816-751-1236; Fax 816-561-7154; Web: www.nelson-atkins.org; *CEO & Cur* Julian Zugazagoitia
Open Wed 10 AM - 4 PM, Thurs & Fri 10 AM - 9 PM, Sat 10 AM - 5 PM, Sun noon - 5 PM; cl Mon & Tues, New Year's Day, Independence Day, Thanksgiving, Christmas Eve & Day; No admis fee
Activities: Art classes for children ages 3-18 & adults; workshops for schools; family workshops & events; tours

C **UMB FINANCIAL CORPORATION,** PO Box 419226, Kansas City, MO 64141-6226. Tel 816-860-7000; Fax 816-860-7610; Email carol.sturn@umb.com; Web: www.umb.com; *Chmn* Mariner Kemper
Estab 1947 to display classic & contemporary art for viewing by patrons & employees; Collection is displayed in lobbies & customer access areas in various UMB Banks in Oklahoma, Colorado, Kansas, Missouri & Illinois
Collections: Americana Collection, including American portraits (George Caleb Bingham, Benjamin Blythe, Gilbert Stuart, Charles Wilson Peale), regional coll (William Commerford, Peter Hurd, J H Sharp, Gordon Snidow), modern art (Fran Bull, Olive Rush, Wayne Thiebaud, Ellsworth Kelly)
Activities: Objects of art lent to galleries for spec exhibits

M **UNIVERSITY OF MISSOURI-KANSAS CITY,** Gallery of Art, 5100 Rockhill Rd, 205C Fine Arts Bldg Kansas City, MO 64110-2446. Tel 816-235-1501; Fax 816-235-5507; Email art@umkc.edu; Web: cas.umkc.edu/art/gallery.cfm; *Dir* Craig Subler
Open Mon, Wed, Fri, & Sat 11AM-4PM; No admis fee; Estab 1977 to bring a broad range of art to both students and the community; 1,725 sq ft; Average Annual Attendance: 5,000; Mem: 100; dues $50
Income: Financed by endowment, city & state appropriation, contribution
Publications: Exhib catalogues
Activities: Adult classes; lect open to pub; book traveling exhibs; originate traveling exhibs that circulate to museums & galleries in US & abroad

MARYVILLE

M **NORTHWEST MISSOURI STATE UNIVERSITY,** DeLuce Art Gallery, 800 University Dr, Dept of Fine & Performing Arts Maryville, MO 64468-6015. Tel 660-562-1326; Fax 660-562-1346; Email gwillms@mail.nwmissouri.edu; Web: wwwnwmissouri.edu/dept/art/index.htm; *Chmn Dept Fine & Performing Arts* Dr Joe Kreizinger; *Olive DeLuce Art Gallery Coll Cur* Philip Laber; *Olive DeLuce Art Gallery Coordr* Glenn Williams
Open Mon 6 - 9 PM, Tues - Sat 1 - 5 PM, Sun 1:30 - 5 PM; No admis fee; Estab 1965 to provide exhibitions of contemporary works in all media as part of the learning experiences in the visual arts; Gallery is maintained with 150 running ft exhib space with high security, humidity-controlled air conditioning & flexible lighting; Average Annual Attendance: 6,000
Income: Financed by state appropriation & external grants
Collections: Percival DeLuce Memorial Collection consisting of American paintings, drawings, prints and decorative arts, some European furniture and prints
Exhibitions: Rotating exhibits
Activities: Classes for adults; lects open to pub, 6 vis lectrs per yr; gallery talks; tours; schols offered; individual & original objects of art lent within the institution; lending coll contains original art works, original prints, paintings & drawings; book traveling exhibs 3 per yr

MEXICO

M **AUDRAIN COUNTY HISTORICAL SOCIETY,** Graceland Museum & American Saddlehorse Museum & Fire Brick Industry Museum, 501 S Muldrow Ave, Mexico, MO 65265-2082. Tel 573-581-3910; Email lpratt@audrain.org; Web: www.audrain.org; *Exec Dir* Kathryn Adams; *Exec Dir* Lori Pratt; *Asst Dir* Janice Robison; *Bd Pres* Tony Robertson
Open Tues - Sat 10 AM - 4 PM, Sun 1-4 PM, cl Mon, Jan & holidays; Admis $5, children 12 & under $3; Estab 1959; Average Annual Attendance: 2,500; Mem: 600; dues $15 & up
Income: $25,000 (financed by endowment & mem)
Library Holdings: Book Volumes, Cards, Clipping Files, Framed Reproductions, Maps, Memorabilia, Original Documents, Photographs, Prints, Records
Special Subjects: Ceramics, Decorative Arts, Etchings & Engravings, Furniture, Glass, Historical Material, Historical Material, Maps, Painting-American, Prints, Period Rooms
Collections: Currier & Ives, Photographs, Lusterware, Dolls, Tom Bass Artifacts, Historical Items, period furniture, artwork, saddles, Tom Bass horse memorabilia, fire brick items from industry leaders, bells, clothing, 3 faced glass trophies, ribbons
Activities: Mus shop sells books & original art

L **MEXICO-AUDRAIN COUNTY LIBRARY,** 305 W Jackson, Mexico, MO 65265. Tel 573-581-4939; Fax 573-581-7510; Email mexicoaudrain@netscape.net; Web: mexico-audrain.lib.mno.us/mexico-audrain; *Children's Librn* Aletha Taylor; *Acquisitions Librn* Ruth Taylor; *Dir* Ray Hall; *Head Librn* Christal Brunner
Open winter hours, Mon - Thurs 9 AM -8PM, Fri 9 AM - 5:30 PM, Sat 9AM-1PM; summer hours Mon, Tues, Thurs, & Fri 9AM-5:30PM, Wed 9AM-8PM, Sat 9AM-1PM; No admis fee; Estab 1912 to provide library services to the residents of Audrain County, Missouri; Exhibit room with different exhibits each month; children's dept has a continuously changing exhibit
Income: Financed by donations
Library Holdings: Book Volumes 112,529, Filmstrips, Kodachrome Transparencies, Motion Pictures, Other Holdings Art print reproductions; Newspapers, Periodical Subscriptions 127, Records
Collections: Audrain County history, paintings by Audrain County artists
Exhibitions: Local Federated Women's Club sponsored a different exhibit each month during the fall, winter & spring, these included local artists, both adult & young people, & recognized artists of the area; The Missouri Council of the Arts also provide traveling exhibits that we display
Activities: Classes for children; story hour (one hour, four days a wk); individual paintings & original objects of art lent

OSAGE BEACH

NATIONAL OIL & ACRYLIC PAINTERS SOCIETY
For further information, see National and Regional Organizations

RAYTOWN

THE STAINED GLASS ASSOCIATION OF AMERICA
For further information, see National and Regional Organizations

SAINT CHARLES

M **FOUNDRY ART CENTRE,** 520 N Main Center, Saint Charles, MO 63301-2181. Tel 636-255-0270; Fax 636-925-0345; Web: www.foundryartcentre.org; *Exec Dir & Exhibs Mgr* Melissa Whitwam, MFA; *Gallery Asst* Bruce Alves, MFA; *Events Mgr* Melanie Sanders; *Educ Mgr* Evan Wagman; *Media Coordr* Logan Rohlf; *Facility Mgr* David Helling
Open Tues - Thurs 10 AM - 8 PM, Fri - Sat 10 AM - 5 PM, Sun Noon - 4 PM, cl Mon; No admis fee; Estab 2004 to connect people with the arts; 5,200 square feet of exhibition space to host international exhibitions; Average Annual Attendance: 74,000; Mem: dues $30-$500
Exhibitions: New exhibitions showcased every 6 weeks
Activities: Classes for adults & children; lects open to the public; concerts; gallery talks; tours; scholarships; Mus shop sells original art; prints

M **LINDENWOOD UNIVERSITY,** Harry D Hendren Gallery, 209 Southkings Hwy, School of Fine and Performing Arts Saint Charles, MO 63301-1693. Tel 636-949-4862; Fax 636-949-4610; Email etillinger@lindenwood.edu; Web: www.lindenwood.edu; *Chmn* Dr Elaine Tillinger; *Dean Fine Arts & Performing Arts* Dean Marsha H Parker
Open Mon - Fri 9 AM - 5 PM, Sat & Sun 1 - 4 PM; No admis fee; Estab 1969 as a col exhib gallery; Gallery is approx 3,600 sq ft with skylight & one wall of side light; 2 additional galleries; Lindenwood Univ Cultural Ctr off campus; Studio East on campus; Average Annual Attendance: 4,000
Income: Financed by endowment
Special Subjects: Prints
Collections: Contemporary American & European prints in various media including Works by Paul Jenkins, William Hayter, Will Barnet, Mauricio Lazansky, Werner Drewes, William Sett
Exhibitions: Rotating Exhibits
Activities: Lects open to pub, 5-6 vis lectrs per yr; gallery talks; tours; original objects of art lent; lending coll contains photographs; originates traveling exhibs through the Missouri State Council on the Arts; artist workshops at Daniel Boone Village (owned by Univ)

SAINT JOSEPH

M **THE ALBRECHT-KEMPER MUSEUM OF ART,** 2818 Frederick Ave, Saint Joseph, MO 64506-2903. Tel 816-233-7003; Fax 816-233-3413; Email frontdesk@albrecht-kemper.org; Web: www.albrecht-kemper.org; *Exec Dir* Brett Knappe PhD; *Registrar & Exhibs Mgr* Megan Benitz; *Mktg & Communs Mgr* Christy George; *Dir Special Events* Laura Lawson; *Guest Servs* Bee Burgiss-Hill
Open Tues - Fri 10 AM - 4 PM, Sat & Sun 1 - 4 PM, cl Mon & major holidays; Admis adults $5, seniors 65 & over $2, students $1, mem & children 6 & under free, group rates available; Estab 1913 to increase pub knowledge & appreciation of the arts; Repository of 18th, 19th, 20th Century American art, serving as a cultural arts center for Northwest Missouri; Average Annual Attendance: 17,000; Mem: 550; dues $35 & up, students $15; ann meeting in Apr
Income: Financed by mem & fundraising events
Special Subjects: American Indian Art, American Western Art, Drawings, Etchings & Engravings, Landscapes, Marine Painting, Painting-American, Prints, Watercolors, Woodcuts
Collections: Collections of American Art consisting of paintings by George Bellows, Thomas Hart Benton, Albert Bierstadt, Alfred Bricher, William Merritt Chase, Francis Edmonds, George Hall, Robert Henri, Edward Hopper, George Inness, Eastman Johnson, Fitz Hugh Lane, Ernest Lawson, William Paxton, Rembrandt Peale, John Sloan, Gilbert Stuart, Andrew Wyeth, drawings by Leonard Baskin, Isabel Bishop, Paul Cadmus, Kenneth Callahan, William Gropper, Gabor Peterdi, Robert Vickrey & John Wilde, prints by John Taylor Arms, George Catlin, Thomas Nason, sculpture by Deborah Butterfield, L E Gus Shafer & Ernest Trova
Publications: Annual report including catalog of year's acquisitions, exhibition catalogs & brochures; Art Matters Quarterly
Activities: Classes for adults & children; docent training; lect open to pub; performances & progs in fine arts theater; concerts; gallery talks, tours, competitions; individual paintings & original objects of art lent to other museums; originate traveling exhibs to other museums; mus shop sells books, magazines & misc items

L **Bradley Art Library**, 2818 Frederick Ave, Saint Joseph, MO 64506. Tel 816-233-7003; Fax 816-233-3413; Web: www.albrecht-kemper.org; *Dir* Terry Oldham
Open museum hrs; Non-circulating art reference library open to the pub
Library Holdings: Book Volumes 2,500, Periodical Subscriptions

A **ALLIED ARTS COUNCIL OF ST JOSEPH,** 118 S Eighth St, Saint Joseph, MO 64501. Tel 816-233-0231; Fax 816-233-6704; Email artstaff@stjoearts.org; Web: www.stjoearts.org; *Exec Dir* Teresa Fankhauser; *Opers Mgr* Cathy Ketter; *Prog Coordr* Tammy Santos
Open Mon - Fri 8 AM - 5 PM; No admis fee; Estab 1963 to bring the Arts & people together; Remote at Heartland Hospital; Mem: 1800
Income: Financed by state appropriation
Activities: Classes for children; Biennial Artist awards

M **MISSOURI WESTERN STATE UNIVERSITY,** Gallery 206 Foyer Gallery, 4525 Downs Dr, Thompson E Potter FA Bldg Saint Joseph, MO 64507-2246. Tel 816-271-4282; Fax 816-271-4181; Email gallery@missouriwestern.edu; Web: www.missouriwestern.edu/art/art-gallery; *Gallery Director* Rebecca Foley; *Chmn Dept Art* Peter Hriso
Open Mon - Fri 8:30 AM - 4:30 PM; No admis fee; Estab 1971 to bring an awareness of contemporary directions in art to students & to the community; Foyer

gallery is in front of building, next to theater; 120 ft long, 30 ft wide, with 25 ft high ceiling; rug paneling on walls;; Average Annual Attendance: 10,000
Income: Financed by state appropriation
Exhibitions: Invitational or juried art exhibs; student and faculty exhibs
Activities: Classes for adults; lects open to pub, 4 vis lectrs per yr; gallery talks; tours

M **SAINT JOSEPH MUSEUM, INC.,** 3406 Frederick Ave, Saint Joseph, MO 64508-2913; PO Box 8096, Saint Joseph, MO 64508-8096. Tel 816-232-8471; Fax 816-232-8482; Email sjm@stjosephmuseum.org; Web: www.stjosephmuseum.org; *Dir* Sara Wilson; *Cur* Sarah Elder; *Mktg* Kathy Reno; *Security* Robert Culbertson; *Cur* Cole Klawuhn; *Bookkeeper* Anita Sontheimer; *Gift Shop* Joy Sanders; *Coll Mgr* Trevor Tutt
Open Mon - Sat 9 AM - 5 PM, Sun 1 - 5 PM; Library open by appointment only; Admis adults $6, seniors $5, students $4; Estab 1927 to increase & diffuse knowledge & appreciation of history, art & the sciences & to aid the educational work that is being done by the schools of Saint Joseph & other educ organizations; Two locations: 3406 Frederick Ave and 11th & Charles, St. Joseph, MO; Average Annual Attendance: 25,000; Mem: 200
Income: Contracted as the Municipal Museum of St Joseph
Special Subjects: Afro-American Art, American Indian Art, American Western Art, Anthropology, Archaeology, Architecture, Ceramics, Dolls, Ethnology, Painting-American, Period Rooms, Photography, Southwestern Art, Stained Glass
Collections: More than 200,000 objects
Exhibitions: Glore Psychiatric Museum; Civil War Medicine; Native American Galleries; Doll Exhibit; Black Archives; Historic Architecture; Missouri River
Publications: The Happenings (newsletter), bimonthly
Activities: Classes for children; docent training; craft prog; field trips; Super Science Saturday; lect open to pub; gallery talks; tours; 10 vis lectrs per yr; Black Archives Hall of Fame; lending of original objects of art to other institutions; 2 book traveling exhibs per yr; mus shop sells books & magazines

SAINT LOUIS

M **AMERICAN KENNEL CLUB,** Museum of the Dog, 1721 S Mason Rd, Saint Louis, MO 63131-1518. Tel 314-821-3647; Fax 314-821-7381; Email info@museumofhedog.com; Web: www.museumofthedog.org; *Cur & Mgr* Barbara Jedda McNab
Open Tues - Sat 10 AM - 4PM, Sun 1 - 5PM, cl Mon & holidays; Admis adults $6, seniors $4, children 5-14 $1; Estab 1984; Average Annual Attendance: 12,000; Mem: 650; dues $25 & up; ann meeting in Oct
Purchases: Kathy Jacobson - Dog Walking in Central Park
Special Subjects: Cartoons, Ceramics, Drawings, Etchings & Engravings, Folk Art, Historical Material, Painting-American, Painting-British, Painting-European, Period Rooms, Porcelain, Portraits, Posters, Pottery, Reproductions, Primitive art, Prints, Sculpture, Silver, Watercolors, Woodcarvings, Woodcuts
Collections: Fine Art: art, artifacts & literature dedicated to the dog
Exhibitions: Artists' Registry Exhibition
Publications: SIRIUS, quarterly newsletter
Activities: Classes for adults; docent progs; lect open to pub; book traveling exhibs 2 per yr; mus shop sells books & prints

L **Reference Library**, 1721 S Mason Rd, Saint Louis, MO 63131-1518. Tel 314-821-3647; Fax 314-821-7381; Email dogarts@aol.com; Web: www.akc.org
Open Tues - Sat 10 AM - 4 PM, Sun 1 - 5 PM; Admis adults $3, sr citizens $1.50, children $1; Estab 1982; For reference only; Average Annual Attendance: 10,000; Mem: 800; dues from patron $1,000 to individual $35
Income: $400,000 (financed by endowment, mem & gift shop sales)
Library Holdings: Book Volumes 2000, Cassettes, Exhibition Catalogs, Framed Reproductions, Memorabilia, Motion Pictures, Original Art Works, Periodical Subscriptions 10, Photographs, Prints, Sculpture, Slides, Video Tapes
Collections: Fine Arts Collection; paintings, drawings & sculptures; decorative arts
Publications: Newsletter, SIRIUS (3 times per yr)
Activities: Fun Day activities for children; Guest Dog of the Week events; gallery talks; tours; sales shop sells books, magazines, jewelry, wearables & luggage

M **ART SAINT LOUIS,** 1223 Pine St, Saint Louis, MO 63103-2527. Tel 314-241-4810; Fax 314-241-6933; Email info@artstlouis.org; Web: www.artstlouis.org; *Assoc Dir* Robin Hirsch
Open Mon & Sat 10AM-4PM, Tues-Fri 10AM-5PM. Cl holidays; No charge
Collections: paintings; sculpture

A **ARTS & EDUCATION COUNCIL OF GREATER SAINT LOUIS,** 3547 Olive St, Saint Louis, MO 63103. Tel 314-289-4000; Email info@keeparthappening.org; Web: keeparthappening.org; *Pres & CEO* Cynthia Prost; *VPres Opers* Susan Rowe Jennings; *VPres Devel* Kate Francis
Estab 1963 to coordinate, promote & assist in the development of cultural & educ activities in the Greater St. Louis area; to offer planning, coordinating, promotional & fundraising service to eligible organizations & groups, thereby creating a valuable community-wide assoc; Mem: 150
Income: Financed by funds from pvt sector
Exhibitions: Saint Louis Arts Awards
Publications: Ann report; calendar of cultural events, quarterly; quarterly newsletter

M **ATRIUM GALLERY,** 4814 Washington Blvd, Ste 110 Saint Louis, MO 63108-1833. Tel 314-367-1076; Fax 314-367-7676; Email atrium@earthlink.net; Web: www.atriumgallery.net; *Dir* Carolyn Miles
Open Thurs - Sat 10 AM - 5 PM, Tues & Wed by appointment; No admis fee; Estab 1986; Commercial gallery featuring contemporary artists who are active regionally & nationally featuring one-person shows
Income: Financed by donations
Activities: Buffet luncheon/lects art series; 8 vis lectrs per yr; salon progs featuring talks by exhibiting artists, 6 progs per yr

M **CENTER OF CREATIVE ARTS (COCA),** Millstone Gallery, 524 Trinity Ave, Saint Louis, MO 63130. Tel 314-725-6555; Fax 314-725-6222; Email info@cocastl.org; Web: www.cocastl.org; *Exec Dir* Kelly Pollock
Open Mon - Fri 9 AM - 9 PM, Sat 9 AM - 6 PM, Sun 11 AM - 6 PM; Estab 1986 to serve as a visual & performing arts center for the community
Exhibitions: Temporary exhibits
Activities: Classes for adults & children; performance art; dance & theatre performances

M **CHATILLON-DEMENIL HOUSE FOUNDATION,** Chatillon-DeMenil Mansion, 3352 DeMenil Pl, Saint Louis, MO 63118. Tel 314-771-5828; Fax 314-771-3475; Email info@demenil.org; Web: www.demenil.org; *Dir* Andrew M Cooperman; *Facilities Mgr* Kevin O'Neill; *Sales & Events Mgr* Curtis Galloway
Open Wed - Fri 11 AM - 2 PM, Sat 11 AM - 3 PM; Admis adults $8, children (under12) $5; Estab 1965 to educate & inform the community on 19th century life & culture; Average Annual Attendance: 8,000; Mem: 500; dues $15 - $1,000; ann meeting in Dec
Income: Financed by mem, grants & donations; tour fees; site rentals; gift shop
Special Subjects: Coins & Medals, Architecture, Decorative Arts, Furniture, Historical Material, Painting-American, Period Rooms, Porcelain, Portraits, Silver, Glass, American Western Art, Photography, Textiles
Collections: Decorative art from c1770 through 19th century, period rooms with furnishings, paintings, 1904 St. Louis World's Fair
Exhibitions: Historic Photos-French & Indian Families in American West; Victorian Mourning Event; Victorian Home Crafts
Publications: Newsletter, quarterly
Activities: Educ progs; docent training; lects open to pub; tours; retail store sells books, reproductions, eclectic merchandise; prints; CDs

M **CONCORDIA HISTORICAL INSTITUTE,** 804 Seminary Pl, Saint Louis, MO 63105-3014. Tel 314-505-7900; Fax 314-505-7901; Email chi@lutheranhistory.org; Web: www.concordiahistoricalinstitute.org; *Archivist* Rev Todd Zittlow; *Museum Cur* Rebecca Wells; *Exec Dir* Dr Daniel Harmelink
Open Mon - Fri 8:30 PM - 4 PM, cl international holidays; Admis suggested donation $6; Estab 1847, to collect & preserve resources on the history of Lutheranism in America. Affiliated with The Lutheran Church, Missouri Synod; Average Annual Attendance: 3,000; Mem: 700; dues Individual & Organizational $50; Director's Circle $1,000
Special Subjects: African Art, Asian Art, Coins & Medals, Costumes, Crafts, Etchings & Engravings, Furniture, Hispanic Art, Manuscripts, Painting-American
Collections: Church archives & vast historical materials, crafts, handcrafts, Reformation & Lutheran coins & medals, Works by Lutheran artists & paintings & artifacts for Lutheran worship, Native artwork from Foreign Mission Fields, especially China, India, Africa & Papua New Guinea
Exhibitions: Temporary exhibitions
Publications: Concordia Historical Institute Quarterly; Historical Footnotes; various e-newsletters
Activities: Lect open to pub; competitions with awards; Distinguished Service Award & awards of commendation for exemplary works in North American Lutheran history; sales shop sells books, slides & craft items; Concordia Historical Institute Mus on Lutheran History, 1333 S Kirkwood Rd, St Louis, Mo 63122, 8:15 AM - 3:30 PM

A **CONTEMPORARY ART MUSEUM ST LOUIS,** 3750 Washington Blvd, Saint Louis, MO 63108-3612. Tel 314-535-4660; Fax 314-535-1226; Email info@camstl.org; Web: www.camstl.org; *Exec Dir* Lisa Melandri; *Chief Cur* Wassan Al-Khudhairi; *Registrar* Jessi Cerutti
Open Wed - Sun 10 AM - 5 PM, Thur & Fri until 8 PM, cl Mon - Tues; No admis fee; Estab 1980 to promote & advocate contemporary arts; Multi-disciplinary visual arts center, maintains cafe; Average Annual Attendance: 35,000; Mem: 600; dues $55 & up
Publications: Exhibit catalogs; newsletter, quarterly; ann magazine
Activities: Educ outreach; workshops; Artreach; family, teen & student progs; lects open to public, 12 - 15 vis lectrs per year; concerts; gallery talks; tours; Great Rivers Biennial award; book traveling exhibs to mus & not for profits w/ contemporary art progs; mus shop sells books, magazines, prints & branded items

M **CRAFT ALLIANCE CENTER OF ART & DESIGN,** (Craft Alliance), 6640 Delmar Blvd, Saint Louis, MO 63130-4503. Tel 314-725-1177; Fax 314-725-2068; Email gallery@craftalliance.org; Web: www.craftalliance.org; *Educ Dir* Luanne Rimel; *Interim Exec Dir* Jim Weidman; *Dir Exhibs* Stefanie Kirkland; *Dir Develop & Communs* Jackie Chambers
Open Tues - Thurs 10 AM - 5 PM, Fri & Sat 10 AM - 6 PM, Sun 11 AM - 5 PM; No admis fee; Estab 1964 for exhib & sales of craft objects; 1500 sq ft; Average Annual Attendance: 60,000; Mem: 750; $50 minimum dues per yr; Scholarships
Income: Financed by mem, Missouri Arts Council, St Louis Arts & Educ Council, Regional Arts Commission
Exhibitions: Monthly exhibits by nat & international artists
Publications: Mem newsletter; Winter-Spring, Summer & Fall catalogs
Activities: Classes for adults & children; vis artists prog; outreach; lects open to pub; gallery talks; tours; sales shop sells original art

M **The Kranzberg Arts Center**, 501 N Grand, Saint Louis, MO 63103. Tel 314-753-3539; Web: kranzbergartscenter.org; *Exec Dir* Chris Hansen; *Dir Gallery* Diana Hansen
Open Wed - Thurs 11 AM - 6 PM, Fri 11 AM - 9 PM, Sat 10 AM - 5 PM, Sun noon - 5 PM
Activities: Classes for adults & children; lects open to pub; gallery talks; tours; schols

M **LAUMEIER SCULPTURE PARK,** 12580 Rott Rd, Saint Louis, MO 63127-1212. Tel 314-615-5278; Fax 314-615-5288; Email info@laumeier.org; Web: www.laumeier.org; *Chmn Bd Trustees* Ramsey Maune; *Cur Educ* Karen Mullen; *Special Events Mgr* Scott Layne; *Chief Preparator* Marty Linson; *Admin & Volunteer Coordr* Julia Norton; *Interim Dir* Stephanie Riven; *Cur Exhib* Dana Turkovic; *Mktg/Commun Mgr* Lauren Kistner
Open Park: daily 8 AM - 30 mins past sunset; Museum: open daily 10 AM - 4 PM, cl Christmas day & Art Fair weekend; No admis fee except special events; Estab

1976 to exhibit contemporary sculpture by internationally acclaimed artists; Circ non-circulating research lib & archives; 5 indoor galleries feature changing exhib 2 per yr; Average Annual Attendance: 350,000; Mem: 1,000; dues Visionary $5000 & up, Laumeier Society $2,500 & up, Collector's Circle $1,000 - $2,499, Dir Circle $500, Sculptor's Forum $250, Casting Circle $125, Family $65, Friends $45, ArtLink $20
Income: Financed by mem, corporate gifts & grants
Library Holdings: Audio Tapes, Book Volumes, Clipping Files, Compact Disks, DVDs, Exhibition Catalogs, Original Documents, Periodical Subscriptions, Video Tapes
Special Subjects: Art History, Landscape Architecture, Restorations, Sculpture
Collections: Contemporary Art, monumental & site specific sculpture & related works, representative examples of Vito Acconci, Mark di Suvero, Jackie Ferrara, Charles Ginnever, Michael Heizer, Alexander Liberman, Beverly Pepper & Ursula Von Rydingsvard, Ernest Trova sculptures, Tony Tasset; Joseph Havel; Mary Miss
Publications: Objectivity, quarterly newsletter
Activities: Classes for adults & children; docent training; lects open to pub; concerts; guided tours; lects; temp indoor & outdoor art exhib; perm installations; art fair; special events; mus shop sells books, original art, jewelry, toys, souvenirs

M **MARYVILLE UNIVERSITY SAINT LOUIS,** Morton J May Foundation Gallery, 650 Maryville University Dr, Saint Louis, MO 63141-7299. Tel 314-529-9381; Fax 314-529-9940; Email artgallery@maryville.edu; Web: www.maryville.edu, www.facebook.com/muartgallery; *Gallery Dir* John Baltrushunas
Open during Univ Library hrs (check website for times or call 314-529-9595); No admis fee; Estab to show work of regional, national artists & designers; Average Annual Attendance: 3,000
Income: $4,500 (university)
Library Holdings: Book Volumes, Exhibition Catalogs, Kodachrome Transparencies, Periodical Subscriptions, Records, Slides, Video Tapes
Special Subjects: Painting-American
Activities: Curating experience for advanced students; lects open to pub, 3-4 vis lectrs per yr; gallery talks; sponsoring of competitions; individual paintings & original objects of art lent to organizations, art guilds & schools

M **MISSOURI HISTORICAL SOCIETY,** Missouri History Museum, Lindel & De Baliviere in Forest Park, 5700 Lindell Blvd Saint Louis, MO 63112-0040. Tel 314-746-4599; Fax 314-454-3162; Email info@mohistory.org; Web: mohistory.org; *Pres* Frances Levine; *Mng Dir Admin & Opers* Karen M Goering; *Mng Dir Develop* Yvette LeGear Hartsfield; *CFO* Benjamin Washington; *Mng Dir Mus Svcs* Katherine Van Allen
Open daily 10 AM - 5 PM, Tues until 8 PM; No admis fee; fees apply to special exhibs; Estab 1866 to col & preserve objects & information relating to the history of St Louis, Missouri & the Louisiana Purchase Territory; Circ 6000; dues from $45 & up; Average Annual Attendance: 200,000; Mem: 5500; dues from $55; ann meeting Sept; Scholarships; Fellowships
Income: Financed by pvt endowment, mem, special events, city & county taxes
Special Subjects: Historical Material
Collections: 19th & 20th century art of St Louis and the American West, paintings, photographs, prints
Exhibitions: Lindbergh Memorabilia; St Louis Memory & History: 1904 Worlds Fair; 5 rotating exhibs per yr
Publications: MHS magazine, bimonthly, mems only pub; Voices, online; Gateway, ann journal
Activities: Classes for adults & children; dramatic progs; docent training; outreach prog festivals; lects open to pub; concerts; gallery talks; tours; individual paintings & original objects of art lent to qualified mus & galleries that meet AAM standards; book traveling exhibs; originate traveling exhibs; Sales shop sells books, prints, slides, souvenirs, china

M **PHILIP SLEIN GALLERY,** 4735 McPherson Ave, Saint Louis, MO 63108-1918. Tel 314-361-2617; Email director@philipsleingallery.com; Web: www.philipsleingallery.com; *Co-Owner* Philip Slein; *Co-Owner* Tom Bussmann
Open Tues - Sat 10 AM - 5 PM, other times by appointment
Collections: works by regional & nat artists; painting; drawings; printmaking; photographs; sculpture

M **SAINT LOUIS ART MUSEUM,** 1 Fine Arts Dr, Forest Park Saint Louis, MO 63110-1331. Tel 314-721-0072; Fax 314-721-6172; Email members@slam.org; Web: www.slam.org; *Dir* Brent Benjamin; *Asst Dir* Jeanette T Fausz
Open Tues - Sun 10 AM - 5 PM, Fri until 9 PM, cl Mon, Thanksgiving & Christmas Day; No admis fee except for featured exhibitions; admis fee for featured exhibs free on Fridays; Estab 1879, originally called St Louis School & Mus of Fine Arts, an independent entity within Washington Univ; Mus contains over 30,000 works of art. Collections include works from virtually every culture & time period; Average Annual Attendance: 450,000; Mem: 15,000; dues $65 - $25,000
Income: Property tax provides 60% of operating income & balance from grants & pvt donations
Library Holdings: Auction Catalogs, Audio Tapes, Book Volumes 109,000, CD-ROMs, Cassettes, Clipping Files, Compact Disks, DVDs, Exhibition Catalogs, Fiche, Lantern Slides, Memorabilia, Original Documents, Pamphlets, Periodical Subscriptions 220, Slides 75,000, Video Tapes 300
Collections: African, American, Ancient & Islamic, Asian, Contemporary, Decorative Arts & Design, European Art to 1800, Modern, Oceanic, Pre-Columbian & American Indian, Prints, Drawings & Photographs, ancient Chinese bronzes, 20th century German painting, Henri Matisse's Bathers with a Turtle, George Caleb Bingham's Election Series, Hans Holbein the Younger's Mary, Lady Guilford, Vincent van Gogh's Stairway at Auvers, Bartolomeo Manfredi's Appollo and Marsyas
Publications: Biennial report, quarterly magazine and program guide, exhibition catalogs
Activities: Classes for adults & children; docent training; lects open to pub, 30 vis lectrs per yr; lects for members only; concerts; gallery talks; tours; competitions with prizes; exten dept serves state of Missouri; individual paintings & original objects of art lent to other museums; book traveling exhibs; originates traveling exhibs; mus shop sells books, magazines, prints & reproductions

L **Richardson Memorial Library,** 1 Fine Arts Dr, Forest Park Saint Louis, MO 63110-1331. Tel 314-655-5252; Fax 314-721-4911; Email library@slam.org; Web: www.slam.org; *Head Librn* Marianne L Cavanaugh; *Archivist* Norma Sindelar; *Pub Serv Librn* Clare Vasquez; *Technical Servs Librn* Christopher Handy
Open Tues - Fri 10 AM - 5 PM; No admis fee; Estab 1915 to provide reference & bibliographical service to the mus staff & the adult pub; to bibliographically support the colls owned by the mus; For research only; Average Annual Attendance: Non-circulating
Income: Financed by endowment & city appropriation
Library Holdings: Auction Catalogs, Book Volumes 109,000, CD-ROMs, Clipping Files, DVDs, Exhibition Catalogs, Fiche, Manuscripts, Original Documents, Pamphlets, Periodical Subscriptions 167, Photographs, Reels
Special Subjects: Afro-American Art, American Indian Art, Antiquities-Greek, Antiquities-Oriental, Antiquities-Roman, Art History, Asian Art, Carpets & Rugs, Decorative Arts, Etchings & Engravings, Ethnology, Furniture, Glass, Painting-American, Photography
Collections: Museum Archives, includes records of Louisiana Purchase Expo (1904) & papers of Morton D May

L **SAINT LOUIS PUBLIC LIBRARY,** 1301 Olive St, Saint Louis, MO 63103. Tel 314-241-2288; Email webref@slpl.org; Web: www.slpl.org; *Mgr Fine Arts Dept* Mary Enns Frechette
Open Mon - Thurs 10 AM - 9 PM, Fri & Sat 10 AM - 6 PM, Sun 1 - 5 PM (1st fl only); Estab Art Dept in 1912
Library Holdings: Book Volumes 115,000, Clipping Files 500, Exhibition Catalogs, Original Art Works 4, Pamphlets, Periodical Subscriptions 45
Special Subjects: Afro-American Art, Architecture, Art History, Decorative Arts, Graphic Arts, Illustration, Interior Design, Photography, Crafts
Collections: Steedman Architectural Library
Activities: Occasional exhibits of materials from the Steedman Architectural Library

M **SHELDON ART GALLERIES,** 3648 Washington Blvd, Saint Louis, MO 63108-3610. Tel 314-533-9900; Fax 314-533-2958; *Dir* Olivia Lahs-Gonzales; *Gallery Coordinator and Education Manager* Rebecca Gunter; *Gallery Visitor Servs* Paula Lincoln
Open Tues 12 PM - 8 PM, Wed - Fri 12 PM - 5 PM, Sat 10 AM - 2 PM, cl New Year's Eve & Day, Independence Day, Thanksgiving Day, Christmas Eve & Day; Free; 1998; Average Annual Attendance: 70,000+
Special Subjects: Painting-American, Photography, Sculpture, Architecture, Printmaking, African Art, Afro-American Art, American Indian Art, American Western Art, Asian Art, Costumes, Decorative Arts, Ethnology, Folk Art, Hispanic Art, Islamic Art, Juvenile Art, Latin American Art, Painting-German, Painting-Israeli, Painting-Italian, Painting-Japanese, Painting-Spanish, Pre-Columbian Art
Collections: Hartenberger World Music Collection (World Musical Instruments)
Publications: Printmaking in St. Louis Now, 2016; The City at 250: A Celebration of St. Louis in Photographs, 2014; Imagining the Founding of St. Louis, 2014; The Sheldon: 100 Moments-A Celebration of the 100th Anniversary, 2012; Our Vision: Young Photographers Capture Sheldon Moments, 2012; Ralston Crawford and Jazz, 2011; Larry Fink: Attraction and Desire 50 Years in Photography, 2011; Nothin' But the Blues: Art and Writing by Area Students, 2010; Herb Snitzer: Photographs from the Last Years of Metronome, 2008; Josephine Baker: Image and Icon, 2006; City of Gabriels: The History of Jazz in St. Louis, 1895-1973, 2006; Leon Hicks: Iconic Caper/Dancing, 2007
Activities: Workshops for children; teacher & professional development workshops; Concerts; Gallery Talks; Tours; Organizes traveling exhibits to art museums; Museum Shop sells Books, jewelry, clothing

M **TROVA FOUNDATION,** Philip Samuels Fine Art, 1011 E Park Industrial, Saint Louis, MO 63130. Tel 314-727-2444; Fax 314-727-6084; Email rgiancola@universalsewing.com; *Dir* Clifford Samuels; *Pres* Philip Samuels
Open Mon - Fri by appointment only; Estab 1988; Contemporary painting, collage, drawing & sculpture

M **UNIVERSITY OF MISSOURI, SAINT LOUIS,** Gallery 210, 1 University Blvd, 44 Arnold Grobman Dr Saint Louis, MO 63121-4400. Tel 314-516-5976; Fax 314-516-5816; Email suhret@umsl.edu; Web: gallery210.umsl.edu; *Dir* Terry Suhre
Open Tues - Sat 11 AM - 5 PM; Estab 1972 to exhibit contemporary art of national importance & to provide visual enrichment to campus & community; Average Annual Attendance: 5,000
Income: Financed by state appropriation & grants
Publications: Exhibition catalogs: Color Photography; Light Abstractions
Activities: Educ dept on art history; lect open to pub; originate traveling exhibs

M **WASHINGTON UNIVERSITY,** Mildred Lane Kemper Art Museum, 1 Brookings Dr, Campus Box 1214 Saint Louis, MO 63130-4862. Tel 314-935-4523; Fax 314-935-7282; Email kemperartmuseum@wustl.edu; Web: www.kemperartmuseum.wustl.edu; *Dir & Chief Cur* Sabine Eckmann; *Assoc Cur* Meredith Malone; *Exhibs Preparator* Ron Weaver; *Dir Develop* Michael Adrio; *Assistant Director for Collections & Exhibitions* Mark Ryan; *Assoc Registrar Colls* Kim Broker; *Asst Registrar* Kristin Good; *Head of Publications* Jane Neidhardt; *Mgr Mktg, Communs & Visitor Servs* Ida McCall; *Admin Coordr* Melissa Meinzer; *Head of Educ & Community Engagement* Allison Taylor; *Univ Acad Prog Coordr* Rochelle Caruthers; *Cur Pub Art* Leslie Markle; *Assoc Cur* Allison Unruh
Open daily 11 AM - 5 PM, cl Tues & university holidays.; No admis fee; Estab 1881, present building opened 1960, for the students of Washington University & the community at large to share resources, enrich environment, preserve exhibits, acquire & research art; A modern building containing two fls of gallery space for exhibit of the permanent coll & special exhibs. Also houses a library of art, archaeology, architecture & design; Average Annual Attendance: 40,215
Income: Financed by univ & pvt support
Special Subjects: American Indian Art, Antiquities-Egyptian, Antiquities-Greek, Asian Art, Baroque Art, Ceramics, Coins & Medals, Drawings, Etchings & Engravings, Landscapes, Painting-American, Painting-British, Painting-Dutch, Painting-European, Painting-French, Painting-German, Painting-Italian, Painting-Japanese, Painting-Spanish, Photography, Portraits, Posters, Prints,

Religious Art, Renaissance Art, Sculpture, Woodcarvings, Woodcuts, American Western Art
Collections: Emphasis on modern artists, including Miro, Ernst, Picasso, Leger, Beckman, many Old Masters, 19th & 20th, 21st century European & American paintings, sculpture, drawings & prints
Publications: Exhibition catalogs
Activities: Educ prog; docent training; lects open to pub, 15-20 vis lectrs per yr by artists, art historians & architects; symposia; music concerts; gallery talks; tours; films; individual paintings & original objects of art lent to other museums; originate traveling exhibs to other museums; primarily American & European venues (i.e. McNay Museum/San Antonio, TX & Opelvillen, Russelsheim, Germany; sales shop sells books, exhib catalogs, postcards, gifts

L **Kenneth & Nancy Kranzberg Art & Architecture Library**, One Brookings Dr, Campus Box 1061 Saint Louis, MO 63130. Tel 314-935-5268; Fax 314-935-4362; Email artarch@wumail.wustl.edu; Web: library.wustl.edu/units/artarch/; *Art & Architecture Librn* Rina Vecchiola; *Subject Librn for Art & Architecture* Jennifer Atkins; *Library Assoc* Sarah Weeks; *Library Assoc* James Gardner
Open Mon - Thurs 8:30 AM - 9 PM, Fri 8:30 AM - 5 PM, Sat Noon - 5 PM, Sun 1 PM - 9 PM, cl nights & weekends during vacations & intercessions; Supports the acad progs of the School of Art, the School of Architecture & the Department of Art History & Archaeology
Income: Financed through the university
Library Holdings: Book Volumes 101,000, DVDs 50, Exhibition Catalogs, Periodical Subscriptions 310, Reproductions, Video Tapes 550

SAINTE GENEVIEVE

M **STE GENEVIEVE MUSEUM,** 3rd & Merchant, Sainte Genevieve, MO 63670; PO Box 88, Sainte Genevieve, MO 63670. Tel 573-883-9622; Email ffrsg@att.net; Email info@historicstegen.org; Web: stegenevievemuseum.wordpress.com; historicstegen.org; *Pres* Mickey Koetting
Open Mon - Sat 10 AM - 4 PM, Sun noon - 4 PM, Nov - Mar noon - 4 PM; Admis adults $2, students (hs & below) $.50; Estab 1935; Average Annual Attendance: 8,000; Mem: Dues bus $50, family $25, individual $10
Income: Financed by mem, admis, sales
Special Subjects: American Indian Art, Archaeology, Coins & Medals, Dolls, Embroidery, Historical Material, Jewelry, Laces, Maps
Collections: Indian artifacts; salt spring kettles, hair jewelry, guns, quilts, cookware
Activities: Mus shop sells books

SEDALIA

M **DAUM MUSEUM OF CONTEMPORARY ART,** 3201 W 16th St, State Fair Community College Sedalia, MO 65301-2188. Tel 660-530-5888; Fax 660-530-5890; Email info@daummuseum.org; Web: www.daummuseum.org; *Dir* Thomas Piche Jr; *Pres* Dr Joanna Anderson; *Mus Coordr* Marcia Teter; *Cur Educ* Victoria Weaver; *Registrar* Matthew Clause
Open Tues - Fri 11 AM - 5 PM, Sat - Sun 1 - 5 PM; No admis fee; Average Annual Attendance: 26,000
Special Subjects: Ceramics, Collages, Drawings, Etchings & Engravings, Landscapes, Painting-American, Photography, Porcelain, Prints, Sculpture, Textiles, Watercolors, Woodcuts
Collections: Contemporary art spanning the last 60 yrs
Activities: Docent training; art & lect series; lects open to pub; 3 vis lectrs per yr; gallery talks; tours

SPRINGFIELD

A **SOUTHWEST MISSOURI MUSEUM ASSOCIATES INC,** Springfield Art Museum, 1111 E Brookside Dr, Springfield, MO 65807-1829. Tel 417-837-5700; Fax 417-837-5704; Email artmuseum@springfieldmo.gov; printsusa@ci.springfield.mo.us; Web: www.ci.springfield.mo.us/egov/art/index.html; *Dir* Jerry Berger
Open Tues, Wed, Fri, Sat 9 AM - 5 PM, Thurs 9 AM - 8 PM, Sun 1PM-5PM, cl Mon; Admis donation; Estab 1928 to inform & interest citizens in appreciation of art & to maintain an art mus as an essential pub institution; Mem: 1300; dues sustaining life $1000, life $500, supporting $50, family $40, at large $30, art group: resident $20, exten groups $10
Income: $14,000 (financed by mem)
Publications: Bimonthly newsletter, in cooperation with the Museum
Activities: Gift shop sells books, original art, prints, reproductions, stationery & gift items; maintain a sales gallery

M **SPRINGFIELD ART MUSEUM,** 1111 E Brookside Dr, Springfield, MO 65807-1899. Tel 417-837-5700; Fax 417-837-5704; Email artmuseum@springfieldmo.gov; Web: www.springfieldmo.gov/art/index.html; *Cur Coll* Chalen Phillips; *Dir* Jerry A Berger; *Mus Educ* Dan Carver; *Librn* Susan Potter; *Exec Secy* Tyra Knox; *Cur Exhibs* Sarah Buhr
Open Tues - Sat 9 AM - 5 PM, Thurs until 8 PM, Sun 1 - 5 PM, cl Mon & city & national holidays; No admis fee, donations accepted; Estab 1928 to encourage appreciation & foster educ of the visual arts; Mus has four temporary exhib galleries for traveling & spec exhibs totaling approx 7500 sq ft; wing opened in 1994 with 13,400 sq ft including four galleries for the permanent coll; 400-seat auditorium & sales gallery; new wing w/ 10,000 sq ft including 4 new galleries and new lib opened in 2008; Average Annual Attendance: 50,000; Mem: 1,300; dues $15-$1000; ann meeting second Wed in May
Income: $1,000,000 (financed by mem, city & state appropriations)
Purchases: $70,000
Library Holdings: Auction Catalogs, Book Volumes, Exhibition Catalogs, Periodical Subscriptions, Video Tapes
Special Subjects: Asian Art, Ceramics, Collages, Decorative Arts, Drawings, Etchings & Engravings, Folk Art, Furniture, Glass, Landscapes, Painting-American, Painting-Dutch, Painting-Spanish, Photography, Portraits, Pottery, Prints, Sculpture, Silversmithing, Southwestern Art, Watercolors, Woodcarvings, Woodcuts, Afro-American Art, American Indian Art, American Western Art, Art History, Bronzes, Mixed Media, Painting-British, Painting-Japanese
Collections: American & European decorative arts, American drawing & photography, American painting & sculpture of all periods, American prints of all periods with emphasis on the 20th Century, European prints, drawings & paintings from the 17th-20th Centuries
Activities: Classes for adults & children; lects open to pub; concerts; gallery talks; tours; competitions with awards; originate traveling exhibs; mus shop sells books, original art, reproductions, pottery, jewelry, cards, stationery & t-shirts

L **Library**, 1111 E Brookside Dr, Springfield, MO 65807-1899. Tel 417-837-5700; Fax 417-837-5704; Web: www.springfieldmo.gov/art/; *Librn* Susan Potter
Open Tues - Sat 9 AM - Noon & 1 - 5 PM; No admis fee; Estab 1928 to assist those persons interested in securing information regarding art & artists, craftsmen from ancient times to the present; Circ 971; Lending & reference library; Average Annual Attendance: 2,060
Income: Financed by city
Purchases: $6,000 (library acquisitions), $60,000 (artwork acquisitions)
Library Holdings: Auction Catalogs, Audio Tapes, Book Volumes 5615, Cassettes, Clipping Files, Exhibition Catalogs, Filmstrips, Manuscripts, Other Holdings Art access kits; Exhibition cards; slide kits, Pamphlets, Periodical Subscriptions 53, Slides, Video Tapes
Special Subjects: Afro-American Art, American Indian Art, American Western Art, Archaeology, Architecture, Art Education, Art History, Bronzes, Ceramics, Decorative Arts, Folk Art, Watercolors
Collections: American & European paintings, prints & sculpture-primarily 19th & 20th century
Exhibitions: Prints USA - a biennial print juried exhib
Publications: Exhib catalogs; bimonthly newsletter; watercolor USA Catalog, annually
Activities: Classes for adults & children; docent training; lects open to pub, 2 vis lectrs per yr; gallery talks; tours; competitions with prizes; lending coll contains 6000 books, 446 slide sets; sales of books, original art

WARRENSBURG

M **UNIVERSITY OF CENTRAL MISSOURI,** Gallery of Art & Design, 217 Clark St, Art Center Rm 215B Warrensburg, MO 64093. Tel 660-543-4498; Fax 660-543-8786; Email gallery@ucmo.edu; Web: www.ucmo.edu/gallery; *Gallery Dir* Christian H Cutler
Open Mon - Fri 8 AM - 5 PM, Thurs 8 AM - 8 PM, Sat noon - 4 PM; No admis fee; Estab 1984 for the purpose of educ through exhib; Small outer gallery & large main gallery located in the University Art Center; Average Annual Attendance: 8,000
Income: Financed by state appropriation & univ funding
Collections: University permanent coll
Activities: Classes for adults; Lects open to public; 2-3 vis lectrs per yr; concerts; gallery talks; tours; competitions with awards; Book 1-2 traveling exhibs per yr

WEBSTER GROVES

M **WEBSTER UNIVERSITY,** Cecille R Hunt Gallery, 8342 Big Bend Blvd, Webster Groves, MO 63119. Tel 314-968-7171; Email langtk@websteruniv.edu; Web: www.webster.edu/depts/finearts/art/; *Dept Chair* Tom Lang
Open Mon - Fri 10 AM - 4 PM, Sat 10 AM - 2 PM, cl Christmas; No admis fee; Estab 1950; Average Annual Attendance: 4,000
Income: Financed by col funds, donations & contributions
Exhibitions: Exhibs of local, national & international artists in all media; rotating exhibits
Publications: Monthly news releases; exhibition catalogs; books
Activities: Lects open to pub, 6 vis lectrs per yr; competitions with awards; Hunt Awards for student shows; individual paintings & original objects of art lent

L **Emerson Library**, 101 Edgar Rd, St Louis, MO 63119; 470 E Lockwood Ave, Saint Louis, MO 63119. Tel 800-985-4279; Fax 314-968-7113; Email emilyscharf99@webster.edu; Web: www.library.webster.edu; *Instruction & Liaison ServLibrn* Emily Scharf
Open Mon - Sun 8 AM - Midnight; For reference & lending
Income: Financed by col funds
Library Holdings: Book Volumes 300,000, Cassettes, DVDs, Exhibition Catalogs, Motion Pictures, Periodical Subscriptions 1235, Photographs, Prints, Records, Slides, Video Tapes

WEST PLAINS

M **HARLIN MUSEUM,** 505 Worcester Ave, West Plains, MO 65775-2709; PO Box 444, West Plains, MO 65775-0444. Tel 417-256-7801; Email staff@harlinmuseum.com; Web: harlinmuseum.com
Collections: Lennis L Broadfoot
Publications: Pioneers of the Ozarks, book on Broadfoot art & personal papers, auth Lennis L Broadfoot

WESTON

M **NATIONAL SILK ART MUSEUM,** 423 Main St, Weston, MO 64098. Tel 816-536-5955; Email info@nationalsilkart museum.com; Web: www.nationalsilkartmuseum.com; *Cur* John Pottie; *Cur* Venessa Pottie
Call for hours; No admis fee; 2003; Circ 7,800; Art Gallery; Average Annual Attendance: 4,500; Mem: 57; $30
Income: Memberships; donations
Library Holdings: Auction Catalogs, Book Volumes, Clipping Files, Framed Reproductions, Memorabilia, Original Art Works, Original Documents, Other Holdings, Photographs, Prints, Reproductions
Special Subjects: Decorative Arts, Embroidery, Historical Material, Portraits, Religious Art, Tapestries, Art Education, Art History, History of Art & Archaeology, Oriental Art, Restoration & Conservation, Textiles

Collections: more than 600 French, English & German silk tapestries by artists from the 19th & 20th centuries
Activities: Gallery talks; tours; lects open to pub; books; original art; reproductions; prints

MONTANA

ANACONDA

A **COPPER VILLAGE MUSEUM & ARTS CENTER,** 401 E Commercial, Anaconda, MT 59711. Tel 406-563-2422; Fax 406-563-2422; Email copper_village@hotmail.com; Web: coppervillageartcenter.com; *Dir* Mary Lynn McKenna; *Grant Writer* Susan Lanes; *Pres* Mike Hale
Open Tues - Fri 10 AM - 4 PM, open Sat by appointment; No admis fee; Estab 1971 as Community Arts Center, gallery & regional historical mus; Features local artists & traveling shows; Average Annual Attendance: 15,000; Mem: 150; dues $10 - $100
Income: Financed by endowment, mem, fundraising events & individual donations
Library Holdings: Auction Catalogs, Exhibition Catalogs, Memorabilia, Original Art Works, Original Documents
Collections: Permanent coll holds paintings & prints
Exhibitions: Monthly exhibits of local, national & international art work
Publications: Quarterly newsletters, brochures
Activities: Classes for adults & children; dramatic progs; docent training; lects open to pub, 4 vis lectrs per yr; concerts; gallery talks; tours; awards; schols; book traveling exhibs 1 per yr; originate traveling exhibs which circulate to Montana Galleries; mus shop sells book & prints

L **Library**, 401 E Commercial, Anaconda, MT 59711. Tel 406-563-2422; *Dir* Carol Jette
Open Tues - Sat 10 AM - 4 PM, cl Mon & holidays; Library open to the pub for reference
Library Holdings: Book Volumes 45, Clipping Files, Memorabilia, Motion Pictures, Pamphlets, Periodical Subscriptions 11, Reproductions, Sculpture, Slides
Publications: Newsletters, quarterly; brochures
Activities: Book traveling exhibs

BILLINGS

M **MONTANA STATE UNIVERSITY AT BILLINGS,** Northcutt Steele Gallery, 1500 University Dr, Billings, MT 59101-0245. Tel 406-657-2903; Fax 406-657-2187; Email leanne.gilbertson@msu-billings.edu; Web: www.msubillings.edu/gallery; *Gallery Dir* Leanne Gilbertson
Open Mon - Fri 8 AM - 4:00 PM & by appt; No admis fee; Located on the 1st fl of the library bldg
Income: Financed by univ
Collections: MSU-Billings permanent collection, Opal Leonard Coll of Chinese & Japanese Art, Helen & Paul Covert Collection
Exhibitions: Ann faculty & student exhib; visiting artists; Independent Student Exhibition with awards
Activities: Vis artist prog; lects open to pub; 4 vis lectrs per yr; awards for ann juried student exhib

A **YELLOWSTONE ART MUSEUM,** 401 N 27th St, Billings, MT 59101-1290. Tel 406-256-6804; Fax 406-256-6817; Email artinfo@artmuseum.org; Web: www.artmuseum.org; *Exec Dir* Robyn G Peterson; *Educ Dir* Mary Serbe; *Senior Cur* Bob Durden; *Fin & Admin Dir* John Greenberger; *Registrar* Kelly Price; *Asst Cur* Amanda Daniel; *Develop Dir* Ryan Cremer
Open Tues - Wed & Sat 10 AM - 5 PM, Thurs & Fri 10 AM - 8 PM, Sun 11 AM - 4 PM, cl Mon; Admis adults $6, seniors, students & children $4, mems free; Estab 1964 to offer a broad prog of art exhibs, both historical & contemporary, of the highest quality, to provide related educ progs; two large galleries & five smaller ones in a large brick structure, plus pub accessible storage vault; Average Annual Attendance: 40,000; Mem: 1,000; dues $40 & up; ann meeting in July
Income: $1,700,000 (financed by mem, contributions, county appropriations, grants, mus shop & fundraising events)
Purchases: Current work by regional artists
Library Holdings: Auction Catalogs, Book Volumes, CD-ROMs, Cards, Cassettes, Exhibition Catalogs, Memorabilia, Original Art Works, Original Documents, Periodical Subscriptions, Photographs, Prints, Sculpture, Slides
Special Subjects: American Indian Art, American Western Art, Archaeology, Bronzes, Ceramics, Collages, Drawings, Furniture, Glass, Graphics, Historical Material, Landscapes, Manuscripts, Metalwork, Painting-American, Painting-European, Photography, Portraits, Sculpture, Watercolors, Prints
Collections: Poindexter Collection of Abstract Expressionism, Contemporary Regional Artists, Will James, Montana Modernism, Dorothy & Herbert Vogel Collection
Exhibitions: 10 - 12 changing exhibitions per yr
Publications: Newsletter; exhib catalogues, 4-6 per yr
Activities: Classes for adults & children; docent training; lects open to pub, 6-8 vis lectrs per yr; concerts; gallery talks; tours; sponsoring of competitions; awards, President's Awards for Service to the Arts; individual paintings & original art objects lent to museums & art centers; Art Suitcase prog goes out to all 4th & 5th grade students including rural areas; President's award for service to the arts; lending of original objects of art to qualified mus; 1-3 book traveling exhibs; originate traveling exhibs circulate to other qualified museums; 1-6 book traveling exhibs per yr; sales shop sells books, magazines, original art, reproductions, prints, handmade jewelry, textiles, clothing, home furnishings, gifts & consignment art gallery; junior mus on site, Young Artists' Gallery

M **YELLOWSTONE COUNTY MUSEUM,** (Peter Yegen Jr Yellowstone County Museum), 1950 Terminal Cir, Billings, MT 59105-1988. Tel 406-256-6811; Fax 406-254-6031; Email ycm@tctwest.net; Web: www.ycmhistory.org; *Dir* Benjamin Nordlund; *Cur* Kathryn Barton
Open Tue - Sat 10:30 AM - 5:30 PM; No admis fee; Estab 1953; 5,000 sq ft, 2 fls, 25,000 artifacts; Average Annual Attendance: 15,000; Mem: Dues: corporate $250, founder $100, family $50, individual $35, senior/student $20
Income: $32,000 (financed by county, mem, memorials, donations & grants)
Special Subjects: Textiles, Decorative Arts, Pottery, Portraits, Painting-American, Furniture, Folk Art, Flasks & Bottles, Drawings, Dioramas, American Indian Art, American Western Art, Anthropology, Archaeology, Ceramics, Coins & Medals, Photography
Collections: Dinosaur bones, Montana Pioneers, Native American, Northern Pacific Steam Switch Engine, Yellowstone Valley, Photographs, Ranching Artifacts, Roundup Wagon, Sheep Wagon
Exhibitions: Indian artifacts; Western memorabilia; firearms, Clark/Corps of Discovery Canoe Camp, Ghost Dance
Publications: Cabin Chat, quarterly newsletter
Activities: tours, 2 vis lects per yr; mus shop sells books, reproductions, prints, jewelry, toys, souvenirs

BOZEMAN

M **MONTANA STATE UNIVERSITY,** Museum of the Rockies, 600 W Kagy Blvd, Bozeman, MT 59717-2730. Tel 406-994-2251; Fax 406-994-2682; Email museum@montana.edu; Web: www.museumoftherockies.org; *Exec Dir* Sheldon McKamey; *Cur History* Michael Fox; *Security Chief* Ronda Harrison; *Dir Philantrhopy* Kathryn Hohmann; *Cur Art & Photog* Steve Jackson; *Cur Paleontology* John Scannella; *Exhibs & Paleo Dir* Patrick Leiggi; *Dir Finance* Kristi Mills; *Mktg Dir* Alicia Thompson; *Interim Store Mgr & Buyer* John Olsen
Open Memorial Day - Labor Day daily 8 AM - 6 PM, Sept - May daily 9 AM - 5 PM, cl New Year's Day, Thanksgiving, Christmas; Adults $14.50, seniors 65 & over $13.50, MSU students with valid ID $10, youth 5-17 $9.50, children 4 & under no charge; Estab in 1958 to interpret the physical & cultural heritages of the Northern Rockies region; Average Annual Attendance: 179,000; Mem: 4200; dues $25-$1,000
Income: Financed by MSU, fundraising, grants & revenue
Special Subjects: American Indian Art, American Western Art, Anthropology, Archaeology, Bronzes, Carpets & Rugs, Cartoons, Ceramics, Collages, Decorative Arts, Dolls, Drawings, Embroidery, Etchings & Engravings, Ethnology, Folk Art, Furniture
Collections: Art Works by R E DeCamp, Edgar Paxton, C M Russell, O C Seltzer, William Standing, geology, paleontology, astronomy, archaeological artifacts, history & western art, regional native Americans
Exhibitions: Rotation Gallery features changing exhibs
Publications: Quarterly newsletter; papers
Activities: Classes for adults & children; docent training; progs in science, history & art; lect open to pub, 20 vis lectrs per yr; planetarium shows; field trips; field schools; gallery talks; tours; traveling portable planetarium, book traveling exhibs; originate traveling exhibs; mus shop sells books, magazines, original art, reproductions, prints, slides, crafts, toys, hats, t-shirts, stationery

M **Helen E Copeland Gallery**, 213 Haynes Hall, Bozeman, MT 59717. Tel 406-994-4501; Fax 406-994-3680; Email ella.watson@montana.edu; Web: www.hecgallery.com; *Gallery Dir* Ella Watson; *Dir School of Art* Vaughan Judge
Open Mon - Fri 9 AM - 5 PM when school is in session; No admis fee; Estab 1974 to present exhibitions of national interest & educate students; Gallery space adjacent to offices & studio classrooms on 2nd fl; archives; Average Annual Attendance: 5,000
Income: Financed by univ appropriation
Special Subjects: American Indian Art, American Western Art, Anthropology, Ceramics, Costumes, Crafts, Decorative Arts, Dolls, Drawings, Etchings & Engravings, Folk Art, Historical Material, Jewelry, Landscapes, Mexican Art, Oriental Art, Painting-American, Porcelain, Posters, Pre-Columbian Art, Prints, Sculpture, Southwestern Art, Tapestries, Textiles, Watercolors
Collections: Japanese Patterns, Native American Ceramics, WPA Prints, Contemporary prints, small paintings, ceramic artifacts, early-mid 20th century textiles
Exhibitions: 7-8 exhibs ann including graduate & undergraduate exhibs; BFA Thesis, MFA Thesis, Geometric Alajamaia, Douglas Russell, Right to Decide
Activities: internships on gallery-archive management; Lect open to pub, 8-12 vis lectrs per yr; gallery talks; competitions; individual paintings lent to univ offices; book traveling exhibs; originate traveling exhibs to Montana Galleries, forums; Waller-Voblonsky Gallery @ Melvin Graduate Studios 2998 West Lincoln St, Bozeman, MT 59718

L **Creative Arts Library**, 207 Cheever Hall, Creative Arts Complex Bozeman, MT 59717; PO Box 173320, Bozeman, MT 59717-3320. Tel 406-994-4091; Fax 406-994-2851; Email jjthull@montana.edu; Web: www.lib.montana.edu/collections/cal.php; *Ref Librn* Jim Thull
Open Mon - Thurs 8 AM - 10 PM, Fri 8 AM - 5 PM, Sat 10AM-5PM, Sun 10AM-10PM; Estab 1974 to support the Schools of Architecture & Art
Income: Financed by state appropriation
Library Holdings: Book Volumes 30,000, Other Holdings Matted reproductions, Periodical Subscriptions 150

BROWNING

M **MUSEUM OF THE PLAINS INDIAN & CRAFTS CENTER,** Junction of 2 & 89 W, Browning, MT 59417; PO Box 410, Browning, MT 59417-0410. Tel 406-338-2230; Fax 406-338-7404; Email mpi@3rivers.com; Web: www.iacb.doi.gov; *Cur* David Dragonfly
Open June - Sept, daily 9 AM - 5 PM, Oct - May Mon - Fri 10 AM - 4:30 PM, cl New Year's Day, Thanksgiving Day and Christmas; Admis Jun - Sept adults $4, groups of 10 or more $3 per person, children (6-12) $1; Estab 1941 to promote the development of contemporary Native American arts & crafts, administered and operated by the Indian Arts and Crafts Board, US Dept of the Interior; New exhib every 4 months; Average Annual Attendance: 80,000; Mem: Friends of the Museum $25 fee
Income: Financed by federal appropriation

Special Subjects: American Indian Art, American Indian Art, Bronzes, Ceramics, Crafts, Dioramas, Dolls, Drawings, Eskimo Art, Photography, Prints, Sculpture, Sculpture, Stained Glass, Textiles, Woodcarvings, Woodcuts, Etchings & Engravings
Collections: Contemporary Native American arts & crafts, historic works by Plains Indian craftsmen & artists
Exhibitions: Historic arts created by the tribal peoples of the Northern Plains; Traditional costumes of Northern Plains men, women & children; Art forms related to the social & ceremonial aspects of the regional tribal cultures; One-Person exhibs of Native American artists & craftsmen; Architectural decorations, including carved wood panels by sculptor John Clarke & a series of murals by Victor Pepion
Publications: Continuing series of brochures for one-person shows, exhib catalogues
Activities: Gallery talks; tours; demonstrations of Native American arts & crafts; originates traveling exhibs; Pikuni gift shop sells books, original art, prints

BUTTE

M **BUTTE SILVER BOW ARTS FOUNDATION,** 128 W Granite, Butte, MT 59701. Tel 406-723-1150; Email gretchen@bsbarts.org; Web: www.bsbarts.org; *Exec Dir* Gretchen Miller
Open Mon - Fri 8 AM - 4 PM, Sat 10:30 AM - 3:30 PM, cl Sun; Estab 1977 to promote the arts, culture & heritage of Butte; Foundation housed in a local coffee house and offers art exhibits, literary & poetry readings and acoustic music; Mem: 350; dues Bus: benefactor $1000, patron $750, sustaining $500, contributing $100, active $10; Individual: benefactor $1000, patron $500, sustaining $100, contributing $50, family $25, active $10; ann meeting Jan
Collections: Contemporary regional art, Elizabeth Lochrie Coll of Native American Portraits
Exhibitions: Exhibs change every 3 months
Publications: Newsletter
Activities: Classes for adults & children, dramatic progs; lect open to pub, 10 vis lectrs per yr; gallery talks; tours; book traveling exhibs 4 per yr; art supply store sells original art, reproductions, prints & recitals

CHESTER

M **LIBERTY VILLAGE ARTS CENTER & GALLERY,** 410 Main St, Chester, MT 59522; PO Box 269, Chester, MT 59522-0269. Tel 406-759-5652; Fax 406-759-5652; Email lvac@mtintouch.net; Web: www.libertyvillagearts.org; *Treas* Laurie S Lyders; *Dir* Patricia Aaberg
Open Tues & Fri 11 AM - 2 PM, Wed & Thurs 12:30 PM - 4:30 PM; other times by request; cl New Years, Easter, Thanksgiving & Christmas; No admis fee; Estab 1976 to provide community with traveling exhibs & educ center; Renovated Catholic Church c 1910; Average Annual Attendance: 1,500-2,000; Mem: 70; dues patron $100 & up, Friend of the Arts $50-$99, family $25, individual $20; ann meeting in Oct
Collections: Works by local artists, paintings & quilts
Exhibitions: Traveling exhibs
Activities: Classes for adults & children; workshops; film series; lect open to pub, 3 vis lectrs per year; gallery talks; competitions with awards; book traveling exhibs; originate traveling exhibs; mus shop sells books, original art & prints

COLSTRIP

M **SCHOOLHOUSE HISTORY & ART CENTER,** 400 Woodrose St, Colstrip, MT 59323; PO Box 430, Colstrip, MT 59323-0430. Tel 406-748-4822; Email shac@bhwi.net; Web: www.schoolhouseartcenter.com; *Exec Dir* Lu Shomale
Open Memorial Day to Labor Day Tues - Sat 11 AM - 5 PM, Fall & Spring Mon - Fri 11 AM - 5 PM; No admis fee
Collections: photographs, period artifacts
Activities: Educ progs; art classes; children's activities; mus shop

DILLON

M **THE UNIVERSITY OF MONTANA - WESTERN,** Art Gallery Museum, 710 S Atlantic, Dillon, MT 59725-3958. Tel 406-683-7232; WATS 800-WMC-MONT; *Dir* Randy Horst
Open Tues - Fri Noon - 4:30 PM; No admis fee; Estab 1970 to display art works of various kinds, used as an educ facility; Located in the south end of Old Main Hall houses the Seidensticker Wildlife Coll of taxidermy; Average Annual Attendance: 7,000
Income: Financed through col funds
Collections: Seidensticker Wildlife Trophy Collection
Activities: Educ dept

L **Lucy Carson Memorial Library**, 710 S Atlantic St, Dillon, MT 59725-3511. Tel 406-683-7541; Fax 406-683-7493; Email m.shultz@wmc.edu; Web: www.wmc.edu/academics/library; *Library Dir* Mike Shultz
Open Mon - Thurs 7:30 AM - 11 PM, Fri 7:30 AM - 5 PM, Sat 11 AM - 5 PM, Sun 3 - 10PM; Library open to the pub
Income: Financed by coll & state
Library Holdings: Book Volumes 4500, Cassettes, Compact Disks, DVDs, Fiche, Filmstrips, Framed Reproductions, Lantern Slides, Maps, Memorabilia, Micro Print, Motion Pictures, Original Art Works, Original Documents, Periodical Subscriptions 12, Photographs, Prints, Reels, Reproductions, Sculpture, Slides, Video Tapes 140
Collections: Emerick Arts Collection

DRUMMOND

M **OHRMANN MUSEUM AND GALLERY,** 6155 Hwy 1, Ohrmann Designs Drummond, MT 59832. Tel 406-288-3319; Email ohrmann@blackfoot.net; Web: www.ohrmannmuseum.com; *Artist & Owner* Bill Ohrmann
Open daily 10 AM - 5 PM; Located 2 1/2 miles S of Drummond on Hwy 1, mus houses the paintings, woodcarvings, bronzes & steel sculptures of Bill Ohrmann; Average Annual Attendance: 2,000
Special Subjects: Painting-American, Bronzes, Woodcarvings
Activities: Artist's works available for sale

EAST GLACIER PARK

M **THE JOHN L. CLARKE WESTERN ART GALLERY & MEMORIAL MUSEUM,** 900 Montana Hwy 49, East Glacier Park, MT 59434; PO Box 141, East Glacier Park, MT 59434-0141. Tel 406-226-9238; Web: www.eastglacierpark.info; *Owner & Mgr* Dana Turvey
Open May - Sept: Mon - Sat 10 AM - 7 PM, Sun 10 AM - 5 PM; No admis fee; Estab 1977
Income: Probate
Special Subjects: American Indian Art, American Western Art, Bronzes, Painting-American, Photography, Prints, Sculpture, Watercolors, Woodcarvings, Woodcuts
Collections: Wood carvings & paintings by John L. Clarke, 28 Montana Artists represented, Contemporary Artists related to Glacier National Park

GLENDIVE

M **FRONTIER GATEWAY MUSEUM,** I-94, Exit 215 (201 State St), Glendive, MT 59330; PO Box 1181, Glendive, MT 59330-1181. Tel 406-377-8168; Email frontiermuseum@ymail.com; Web: www.frontiergatewaymuseum.org; *Cur* Fayette Miller; *Treas* Patty Atwell; *1st VPres* Audre Avilla; *2nd VPres* Rosanne Bos; *Pres* Mark Geiger; *Asst Cur* Trena Kuehn
Open Memorial Day - Labor Day Mon - Sat 9 AM - noon & 1 - 5 PM, Sun & holidays 1 - 5 PM; cl mid-Sept to mid-May; No admis fee, donations accepted; Founded 1963; Gen historical mus of Glendive & Dawson Counties in MT; 10,080 sq ft exhib space situated in 7 bldgs on one acre; Average Annual Attendance: 1785; Mem: dues Life $75, ann $10
Income: $10,000 (financed by memberships, memorials, county allotted)
Library Holdings: Book Volumes 650, Clipping Files 33 drawers, Maps 263, Photographs 7 file drawers
Special Subjects: Historical Material, Period Rooms, Photography
Collections: Prehistoric to contemporary coll consists of fossils, mammoth, mastodon, buffalo, Indians, cattlemen, homesteads, small towns, fashions, personal artifacts; tools & equipment for materials; paleontological items; structures; folk culture; technology; furnishings, HO train collection
Publications: Report to the Membership, ann newsletter
Activities: Open house; tours; demonstrations; lects; hobby workshops; mus related souvenirs for sale & books

GREAT FALLS

M **C M RUSSELL MUSEUM,** 400 13th St N, Great Falls, MT 59401-1498. Tel 406-727-8787; Fax 406-727-2402; Email info@cmrussell.org; Web: www.cmrussell.org; *Exec Dir* Thomas Figarelle; *Dir Art & Philanthropy* Duane Braaten
Open Summer: Tues - Sun 10 AM - 5 PM; Winter: Wed - Sun 10 AM - 5 PM; Admis adults $9, students $4, seniors $7, children under 5 free; Estab 1953 to preserve art of Charles M Russell, western painter; Mus includes Russell's home & original studio; has seven galleries of Western art & photographs & Indian artifacts. Maintains reference library; Average Annual Attendance: 50,000; Mem: 1,750; dues $30 - $500 & up
Income: Financed by operating budget
Library Holdings: Auction Catalogs, Clipping Files, Memorabilia, Micro Print, Original Documents, Other Holdings, Pamphlets, Periodical Subscriptions, Photographs, Records
Special Subjects: American Indian Art, American Western Art, Anthropology, Archaeology, Bronzes, Cartoons, Decorative Arts, Drawings, Etchings & Engravings, Ethnology, Folk Art, Historical Material, Latin American Art, Manuscripts, Mexican Art, Painting-American, Period Rooms, Photography, Portraits, Pottery, Pre-Columbian Art, Prints, Reproductions, Sculpture, Southwestern Art
Collections: Works by Charles M Russell & other Western works including Seltzer, Couse, Wieghorst, Sharp, Heikka, Reiss, Farny, Historical & contemporary, Contemporary & western art, Native American art
Exhibitions: Traveling exhibs of western art; permanent exhibs; The Bison: American Icon, Heart of Plains Indian Culture
Publications: Quarterly magazine; monthly e-newsletter
Activities: Classes for adults & children; docent training; lects for mems only & lects open to pub; 0-6 vis lectrs per yr; gallery talks; tours; individual paintings & original objects of art lent to qualified museums; book traveling exhibs 1 per yr; mus store sells books, magazines, reproductions, prints, jewelry, pottery

L **Frederic G Renner Memorial Library**, 400 13th St N, Great Falls, MT 59401. Tel 406-727-8787; Fax 406-727-2402; Email smcgowan@cmrussell.org; Web: www.cmrussell.org/library; *Registrar* Sheryl Foxman; *Cur* Emily Wilson Burt; *Educ & Progs Mgr* Eileen Laskowski; *Librn* Kathyrn Kramer
Open by appointment only; Admis Adults $9, seniors $7, children & students $4, under 5 free; Library estab 1965 to provide research material on Western art & artists, primarily C M Russell & The History of Montana & The West; Museum estab 1953 to showcase CM Russell's work; Circ 3,700; For reference only; Average Annual Attendance: 56,000; Mem: 2,000, $35 - $2,500
Income: (financed by pvt contributions)
Library Holdings: Auction Catalogs, Audio Tapes, Book Volumes 3,500, CD-ROMs, Clipping Files, DVDs, Exhibition Catalogs, Kodachrome Transparencies, Manuscripts, Memorabilia, Micro Print, Motion Pictures, Original Documents, Pamphlets, Periodical Subscriptions 4, Photographs, Prints, Reproductions, Slides, Video Tapes
Special Subjects: American Indian Art, American Western Art, Art History, Bronzes, Carpets & Rugs, Ceramics, Etchings & Engravings, Ethnology, Historical

Material, Landscapes, Painting-American, Photography, Prints, Sculpture, Southwestern Art, Watercolors, Woodcarvings
Collections: Yost Archival Collection, Flood Archival Collection, Taliaferro Reference Notes, Joseph Henry Sharp Collection of Indian Photographs, Fred Renner Collection
Publications: Russell's West Quarterly, quarterly; Studio Talk, monthly
Activities: Classes for adults & children; dramatic prog; docent training; Native American classes; summer day camps; lects open to pub & members; 6 vis lectrs per year; concerts; gallery talks; tours; fel; sponsoring of competitions; Trigg award; mus shop sells books, magazines, original art, reproductions, prints, slides, clothing, souvenirs & children's items; Discovery Gallery: Hands-on Experience for Children & Families

M **CASCADE COUNTY HISTORICAL SOCIETY,** The History Museum, 422 2nd St S, Great Falls, MT 59405-1816. Tel 406-452-3462; Fax 406-461-3805; Email info@thehistorymuseum.org; Web: www.thehistorymuseum.org; *Exec Dir* Jim Meinert; *Colls Admin* Ashleigh McCann
Open Tues- Fri 10 AM - 5 PM; No admis fee; Estab 1976 to preserve & interpret the history of the Central Montana area & the diverse area heritage; The historical mus is housed in the Internal Harvester building built in 1929. We have the regional archival research center for North Central Montana and a large collection that supports regional history exhibits; Average Annual Attendance: 82,000; Mem: Dues benefactor $500; patron $250; sponsor $125; sustainer $75; historian $35. Bd dirs meeting held monthly on 4th Thurs
Income: $200,000 (financed by mem dues, donations, memorials, & grants)
Purchases: 1925 Chickering 9 foot piano for historical events
Library Holdings: Auction Catalogs, Audio Tapes, Book Volumes, Cards, Cassettes, Clipping Files, Exhibition Catalogs, Framed Reproductions, Kodachrome Transparencies, Lantern Slides, Manuscripts, Maps, Memorabilia, Motion Pictures, Original Art Works, Original Documents, Pamphlets, Periodical Subscriptions, Photographs, Prints, Records, Reproductions, Sculpture, Slides, Video Tapes
Collections: Art, documents, manuscripts, photographs, objects reflecting the history of the local area, clothing, furniture & memorabilia from Great Falls & Cascade County
Exhibitions: Exhibits from the permanent colls, changed quarterly; Celebrate Central Montana; Handcrafted: An Expression of American Tradition
Activities: Classes for adults & children; docent training; lect open to public, 10-15 vis lectrs per yr; gallery talks; tours; sponsoring of competitions; Community Heritage Preservation Award; individual paintings & original objects of art lent to other museums in central Montana; lending of original objects of art to fellow museums; book traveling exhibs 1 per yr; originate traveling exhibs to schools & smaller area town bus in Montana; mus shop sells books, magazines, original arts, reproductions

M **PARIS GIBSON SQUARE,** Museum of Art, 1400 First Ave N, Great Falls, MT 59401. Tel 406-727-8255; Fax 406-727-8256; Email info@the-square.org; Web: www.the-square.org; *Exec Dir* Tracy Houck; *Cur Art* Kristi Scott; *Dir Educ* Sarah Justice
Open Mon - Fri 10 AM - 5 PM, Tues evening 5 PM - 9 PM, Sat Noon - 5 PM, cl Sun; No admis fee; Estab 1976 to exhibit contemporary art; Maintains 7 galleries of assorted sizes and dimensions; Average Annual Attendance: 25,000; Mem: 550-650; mem open to pub; dues $35 & up; ann meetings in June
Income: $670,000 (financed by mem, grants, contributions & county mill)
Special Subjects: American Indian Art, Ceramics, Collages, Decorative Arts, Drawings, Etchings & Engravings, Folk Art, Painting-American, Photography, Portraits, Pottery, Primitive art, Prints, Sculpture, Watercolors, Woodcarvings, Woodcuts, Porcelain
Collections: Contemporary regional & national artists, Montana folk-art sculptures (polychromed wood), Lee Steen
Exhibitions: Various exhibs
Publications: Artist postcards, catalogs; quarterly newsletter
Activities: Classes for adults, children & disabled; docent training; Native American Contemporary Art Suitcase Museum; lect open to pub, 6-12 vis lectrs per yr; gallery talks; tours; schols & fels offered; individual paintings & original objects of art lent to other museums; lending coll contains original art works, original prints, paintings & photographs; book traveling exhibs 1-2 per yr; originate traveling exhibs to regional art institutions

HAMILTON

M **RAVALLI COUNTY MUSEUM,** 205 Bedford St, Old Court House Hamilton, MT 59840-2853. Tel 406-363-3338; Email rcmuseum@qwestoffice.net; Web: www.ravallimuseum.org; *Dir* Tamar Stanley; *Hist* Bill Whitfield; *Cur* Tara Gallagher; *Graphic Design & Mktg* Sarah Monson; *Exhibits* Noellynn Pepos; *Acctg* Paula Frickey
Open Tues - Fri 10 AM - 4 PM, Sat 9 AM - 1 PM, cl Sun & Mon; Admis adults $3, family $6, seniors & students $1; Estab 1979 to preserve the history of the Bitterroot Valley; Museum contains Flathead Indian exhibit, Discovery room encompasses Native Am lifestyles in the Bitterroot Valley, Lewis & Clark travelling through the Bitterroot, The Salish Indians; pioneer rooms, rotating exhibits in old ct room; extensive archives; natural history exhibit; children's exhibit; Average Annual Attendance: 24,000; Mem: 425; dues business $100 & up, family $50, individual $40; meetings third Mon each month
Income: heritage events & donations
Purchases: $5000
Library Holdings: Audio Tapes, Book Volumes, CD-ROMs, Cards, Cassettes, Clipping Files, Compact Disks, DVDs, Exhibition Catalogs, Fiche, Filmstrips, Framed Reproductions, Kodachrome Transparencies, Manuscripts, Maps, Memorabilia, Micro Print, Original Art Works, Original Documents, Other Holdings, Pamphlets, Periodical Subscriptions, Photographs, Prints, Records, Reels, Reproductions, Slides, Video Tapes
Collections: Home furnishings reflecting early life of the Bitterroot Valley, Native American, Railroad, Bertie Lord Collection, Ernst Peterson Collection, ranching & agricultural items, military
Exhibitions: Special Exhibits of historical Interest; Special Local Collection Exhibit; Veterans Exhibit; Lewis & Clark Exhibit
Publications: Bitter Root Trails One, Two, Three, Bitter Root Historical Society; McIntosh Apple Cookbook; Historic Survey of Hamilton Buildings 1890-1940; The Yellow Pine; Newsletter; The Bitterrooter, George Hayes, Rocky Mountain Spotted Fever in Western Montana; Anatomy of a Pestilence-Dr Robert Philip; Bitter Root Trails IV
Activities: Educ dept; classes for adults & children; art classes; docent training; cultural progs; free family activities; concerts; tours; gallery talks; competitions with awards; local institutions, libraries & banks; mus shop sells books, original art, reproductions, prints, porcelain, jewelry & gifts featuring Lewis & Clark; children's exhibit

HARDIN

M **BIG HORN COUNTY HISTORICAL MUSEUM,** 1163 3rd St E, Hardin, MT 59034. Tel 406-665-1671; Fax 406-665-3068; Email info@bighorncountymuseum.org; Web: bighorncountymuseum.org; *Dir* Diana Scheidt; *Pres* Beth Mehling; *Treas* Merna Kincaid; *Mus Shop Mgr & Mus Asst* Joan Miller; *Asst Dir* Bonnie Stark
Open Memorial Day to Labor Day: daily 8 AM - 6 PM, Sept - May Mon - Fri 9 AM - 5 PM; historic bldgs cl Oct - Apr; mus cl New Year's Day, Thanksgiving Day, Christmas Day; Adult $6, seniors (60 & over) $5, student $3; bus tours $100, children (6 & under), school groups, & mems no admis fee; donations accepted; Estab 1979; mus is located on 35-acre former vegetable farm that was donated to Big Horn County in 1979 & features orig farmhouse & barn; authentic historic structures have been restored & placed on site; Average Annual Attendance: 10,000 - 25,000 by estimate; Mem: dues Lifetime $500, Bus $50, Family $25, Indiv $15
Special Subjects: Historical Material
Collections: Includes items of historical significance related to the development of Big Horn County, MT from 1900 to modern times with emphasis on the cultures of people who have settled in the area, including The Crow Indians, Northern Cheyenne Indians, Japanese, German, Russian, Korean & Norwegian cultures, historic structures; horse-drawn equipment; restored tractor; farm equipment; furnishings; photographs & personal artifacts, hundreds of book vols on the Plains Indians, hundreds of local publs, Kenneth F Roahen - Photographs - Will James Studio
Publications: On the Bighorn, quarterly newsletter
Activities: Tractor Show; Auction; Hands on For Students; classes for children; guided tours; mus shop sells books, reproductions, prints & gifts

HELENA

M **HOLTER MUSEUM OF ART,** 12 E Lawrence St, Helena, MT 59601-4019. Tel 406-422-6400; Fax 406-442-2404; Email holter@holtermuseum.org; Web: www.holtermuseum.org; *Cur Educ* Sondra Hines; *Exec Dir* Karen Bohlinger; *Cur Art* Yvonne Seng
Open Tues - Sat 10 AM - 5:30 PM, Sun noon - 4 PM; Admis by donation; Estab 1987 to educate & enhance the quality of life of constituents; Average Annual Attendance: 32,000; Mem: 1,000; dues individual $50, guardian $50-$1,000; ann meeting in fall
Income: $700,000 (financed by endowment, mem & state appropriation)
Library Holdings: Audio Tapes, Book Volumes, Exhibition Catalogs, Pamphlets, Photographs, Slides, Video Tapes
Special Subjects: American Indian Art, Ceramics, Folk Art, Glass, Jewelry, Landscapes, Metalwork, Painting-American, Photography, Porcelain, Pottery, Sculpture, Textiles, Watercolors, Woodcarvings
Collections: Contemporary Northwest Regional Art in all mediums
Exhibitions: ANA
Publications: Monthly newsletter
Activities: Classes for adults & children; docent training; lect open to pub, 8 vis lectrs per yr; gallery talks; tours; youth electrum $750 awards; national Juried exhib; schols offered; book traveling exhibs 4 per yr; originate traveling exhibs 2 per yr; mus shop sells books, original art, prints, ceramics, jewelry, mixed media arts

A **MONTANA HISTORICAL SOCIETY,** 225 N Roberts, Helena, MT 59601-4514; PO Box 201201, Helena, MT 59620-1201. Tel 406-444-2694; Fax 406-444-2696; Email jbottomly@mt.gov; Web: www.montanahistoricalsociety.org; *Dir* Bruce Whittenberg; *Sr Cur* Jennifer Bottonly-O'looney; *Archivist* Jodie Foley; *Mus Shop Mgr* Rod Coslit; *Cur Colls* Amanda Trunn; *Preservation Officer* Mark Baumler; *Publ Mgr* Molly Holz; *Pub Rels* Tom Cook; *Educ* Deb Mitchell; *Cur History* Maggie Ordon; *Research Center Dir* Molly Kruckenberg; *Devel Officer* Susan Near; *Central Servs Adminr* Denise King
Open Mon - Fri 8 AM - 5 PM, Sat 9 AM - 5 PM, cl Sun & holidays; Admis general $5; Estab 1865 to collect, preserve & present articles relevant to history & heritage of Montana & the Northwest; Mackay Gallery of C M Russell Art; temporary exhibits gallery; Montana Homeland; Average Annual Attendance: 93,000; Mem: 4000; dues $60
Income: $545,000 (financed by State of Montana General Fund, pvt gifts & grants, federal grants, earned revenue)
Library Holdings: Auction Catalogs, Clipping Files, Exhibition Catalogs, Manuscripts, Maps, Memorabilia, Original Documents, Photographs
Special Subjects: American Indian Art, American Western Art, Archaeology, Architecture, Bronzes, Costumes, Decorative Arts, Ethnology, Furniture, Historical Material, Leather, Painting-American, Photography, Portraits, Posters, Sculpture, Textiles, Watercolors
Collections: Haynes Collection of Art, Photographs & Artifacts, Mackay Collection of C M Russell Art, Poindexter Collection of Abstract Art, Montana artists, late 19th & 20th century Western art, Bob Scriver - the artist's coll
Exhibitions: Montana Homeland; changing temporary exhibits
Publications: Montana, Magazine of Western History, quarterly; Montana Post (newsletter), quarterly
Activities: Educ progs for adults & children; docent training; lect open to pub, 30 vis lectrs per yr; gallery talks, tours; individual paintings & original objects of art lent to museums, galleries, historical societies; lending coll includes 300 color transparencies, 200 original art works, 500,000 photographs, 40 sculptures, 1000

slides; originates traveling exhibs; sales shop selling books, magazines, prints, reproductions, slides

L **Library**, 225 N Roberts, Helena, MT 59620; PO Box 201201, Helena, MT 59620-1201. Tel 406-444-1799; Fax 406-444-2696; Email gashmore@state.mt.us; Web: www.montanahistoricalsociety.org; *Head Librn & Archivist* Charlene Porsild; *Photograph Cur* Delores Morrow; *Cur Coll* Kirby Lambert
Open Mon - Fri 8 AM - 5 PM by appointment; For reference and research only
Income: Financed by State of Montana
Library Holdings: Book Volumes 4000, Clipping Files, Exhibition Catalogs, Manuscripts, Pamphlets, Periodical Subscriptions 100, Photographs
Special Subjects: American Indian Art, American Western Art, Anthropology, Archaeology, Ethnology, Historical Material, Manuscripts, Painting-American, Photography
Collections: Late 19th & 20th century art
Publications: Montana: The Magazine of Western History, quarterly

KALISPELL

A **HOCKADAY MUSEUM OF ART,** 302 2d Ave E, Kalispell, MT 59901-4942. Tel 406-755-5268; Fax 406-755-2023; Email information@hockadaymuseum.org; Web: www.hockadaymuseum.org; *Exec Dir* Tracy Johnson; *Dir Educ* Kathy Martin; *Mgr of Museum Operations* Sharon Staso; *Commun & Mktg Dir* Brian Eklund; *Advising Cur* Mark Norley; *Coll Admin* James Udick
Open Tues - Sat 10 AM - 5 PM; Admis adults $5, seniors $4, students $2, mems & children K-12 free; Estab 1968 to enrich the cultural life of the community and region and preserve the artistic legacy of Montana and Glacier National Park; Mus is housed in the former Carnegie Library in downtown Kalispell; has six spacious exhib galleries & a gift gallery; classroom; Average Annual Attendance: 20,000; Mem: 750; dues $35 & up; annual meeting in March
Income: Financed by mem, contributions, grants, exhib sponsors, corporate donations & city funds
Special Subjects: American Indian Art, American Western Art, Bronzes, Ceramics, Drawings, Etchings & Engravings, Glass, Islamic Art, Landscapes, Painting-American, Photography, Posters, Pottery
Collections: Focus on the art and culture of Montana and the artists of Glacier National Park
Exhibitions: (Permanent) Crown of the Continent
Publications: Exhib catalogs; Quarterly "Art Matters"; annual reports
Activities: Classes for adults & children; docent training; lect open to pub, 3 per yr; gallery talks; tours; sponsoring of competitions; schols offered; ext prog serving Flathead, Lake, Lincoln & Glacier Counties; originate traveling exhibs to Museum and Art Gallery Directors Assn of Montana (MAGDA); mus shop sells books, original art, reproductions, prints

LEWISTOWN

A **LEWISTOWN ART CENTER,** 323 W Main St, Lewistown, MT 59457; PO Box 1018, Lewistown, MT 59457-1018. Tel 406-535-8278; Fax 406-535-6024; Email lewistownartcenter@gmail.com; Web: www.lewistownartcenter.org; *Exec Dir* Linda Tullis; *Educ Dir* Leah Granzke; *Gift Shop Coordr* Suzanne Carter
Open Tues - Fri 11:30 AM - 5:30 PM, Sat 10 AM -4 PM; No admis fee; Estab 1971 for advancement & educ in the arts. The gallery exhibs change monthly showing a variety of local, state artwork; A sales gallery features Montana artists & local artists; Average Annual Attendance: 5,000; Mem: 350; dues $25 & up; ann meeting in Aug
Income: $100,000 (financed entirely by mem, donations, sponsorships by local bus, art grants, sales from gift shop, auction & market room)
Special Subjects: Painting-American, Photography, Porcelain, Posters, Pottery, Prints, Reproductions, Sculpture, Silver, Stained Glass, Textiles, Watercolors
Collections: Collection of art work from artists from Central Montana, bronze & all other mediums
Exhibitions: In-state shows; 12 gallery shows per yr; ongoing exhibition by various artists at Central Montana Medical Center
Publications: Newsletter, quarterly
Activities: Arts classes & workshops for adults & children; lects open to pub, concerts, 1-2 vis lectrs per yr; gallery talks; schols; competitions with awards; art educ offered; sales shop sells books, magazines, original art, reproductions, prints, sculpture, pottery, wall hangings, jewelry, fiber arts, Montana made consignment

LIVINGSTON

M **LIVINGSTON CENTER FOR ART & CULTURE,** 119 S Main St, Livingston, MT 59047-2668. Tel 406-222-5222; Email admin@livingstoncenter.org; Web: livingstoncenter.org; *Exec Dir* Kathy Bekedam
Open Tues - Sat Noon - 4 PM; Estab to engage community in the arts; Mem: dues $25-$2,501 & up
Exhibitions: Temporary exhibits
Activities: Classes for adults & children; scholarships

MILES CITY

A **WATERWORKS ART MUSEUM,** 85 Waterplant Rd, Miles City, MT 59301-4032; PO Box 1284, Miles City, MT 59301-1284. Tel 406-234-0635; Fax 406-234-0637; Email ccartc@midrivers.com; Web: www.wtrworks.org; *Exec Dir* Dixie Rieger; *Educ Dir* Mark Sanders; *Admin Asst* De Nice Curry
Open Tues - Sun 1 - 5 PM, cl holidays; Summer hours 9 AM - 5 PM; No admis fee; Estab 1977 to provide an arts prog of exhibits and educ activities to residents of Southeastern Montana; Maintains The WaterWorks Gallery, located in the former holding tanks of the old Miles City Treatment Plant; Average Annual Attendance: 20,000; Mem: dues benefactor $500, patron $300, sponsor $150, sustaining $100, bus $100, contributing $75, family $50, individual $30, student $15, sr citizens $25
Income: Financed by mem, fundraising events & grants
Library Holdings: Original Art Works, Photographs, Prints
Special Subjects: Painting-American, Photography, Pottery, Prints, Sculpture, Southwestern Art, Stained Glass, Watercolors, Woodcarvings, Woodcuts, Historical Material
Collections: Vintage photographic coll, includes ES Curtis, LA Huffman, E Cameron, Historical & Contemporary Montana Artists
Exhibitions: Changing exhibs every 4-8 wks
Publications: Biannual exhibit catalogs; quarterly newsletter
Activities: Classes for adults, children & disabled srs; lect open to pub, 10 vis lectrs per yr; gallery talks (speakers bureau); artmobile, serving art classes through artist-in-schools & communities program; 100 mile radius (30,000 sq miles) in 11 counties of SE Montana; traveling exhibs; mus store sells books & original art; Pottery

MISSOULA

M **HISTORICAL MUSEUM AT FORT MISSOULA,** 3400 Captain Rawn Way, Missoula, MT 59804. Tel 406-728-3476; Fax 406-543-6277; Email ftmslamuseum@montana.com; Web: www.fortmissoulamuseum.org; *Dir Educ* Kristjana Eyjolfsson; *Exec Dir* Matt Lautzenheiser; *Develop Dir* Jessie Colt Rogers; *Mus Aide* Sharon Garner; *Asst Dir* Carolyn Thompson; *Cur Colls* Nicole Webb
Open Memorial Day to Labor Day Mon - Sat 10 AM - 5 PM, Sun Noon - 5 PM, Labor Day to Memorial Day Tues - Sun Noon - 5 pm; Admis adults $4, seniors $3, students $2, children under 6 free; Estab July 4, 1976 to collect and exhibit artifacts related to the history of western Montana; Changing gallery, 900 sq ft used for temporary exhibits; Meeting room gallery, 200 sq ft; Permanent gallery, 1200 sq ft; Average Annual Attendance: 45,000; Mem: 300; dues $30 & up; quarterly meetings; Scholarships; Fellowships
Income: $450,000 (financed by mem, county appropriation & fundraising events)
Special Subjects: American Western Art, Archaeology, Architecture
Collections: Forest industry artifacts from Western Montana, Fort Missoula & the military presence in Western Montana, Missoula history
Exhibitions: The Road to Today: 250 Years of Missoula County History, changing exhibs, building exhib
Publications: The Military History of Fort Missoula; Missoula: The Way It Was; Purple & Gold: Missoula County High School, 1905-1965
Activities: Classes for adults & children; docent training; Forestry Day; 4th of July Celebration; lect open to pub; 3-5 vis lectrs per yr; gallery talks; tours; Dale & Coby Johnson Volunteer Award; fels offered; book traveling exhibs; originates traveling exhibs to mus & art galleries; mus shop sells books, magazines, original art & post cards

M **MISSOULA ART MUSEUM,** 335 N Pattee, Missoula, MT 59802. Tel 406-728-0447; Email museum@missoulaartmuseum.org; Web: www.missoulaartmuseum.org; *Exec Dir* Laura Millin; *Director of Development* Cassie Strauss; *Assoc Cur* John Calsbeek; *Dir Finance & Admin* Tracy Cosgrove; *Vis Servs & Retail* Cassidy Tucker; *Registrar* Jennifer Reifsneider; *Sr Cur* Brandon Reintjes; *Mktg & Communs* Bethany O'Connell; *Educ Cur* Renee Taaffe
Open Tues - Sat 10 AM - 5 PM; No admis fee; Estab 1975 to collect, preserve & exhibit international art; to educate through exhibits, art school, special progs & forums; Housed in renovated Carnegie Library (1903) featuring soft-panel covered walls; moveable track lighting; approx 3500 sq ft of exhibit space on two floors; fire and security alarm systems; meeting rooms; Average Annual Attendance: 25,000; Mem: 1,200
Income: $500,000 (financed by mem, grants, fundraising events & ann permissive mill levy by Missoula County)
Purchases: Contemporary Art of Western United States
Library Holdings: Auction Catalogs, Audio Tapes, Book Volumes, CD-ROMs, Cards, Cassettes, Clipping Files, DVDs, Exhibition Catalogs, Sculpture
Special Subjects: African Art, Afro-American Art, American Indian Art, American Western Art, Architecture, Bronzes, Calligraphy, Ceramics, Collages, Crafts, Decorative Arts, Embroidery, Eskimo Art, Etchings & Engravings, Ethnology, Jewelry, Landscapes, Metalwork, Painting-American, Photography, Porcelain, Portraits, Primitive art, Prints, Sculpture, Woodcarvings, Woodcuts
Collections: Contemporary Art of Western United States with an emphasis on Montana, Contemporary Art of Western Montana
Exhibitions: Paintings, Prose, Poems & Prints: Missouri River Interpretations; 23rd Annual Art Auction Exhib; Jacob Lawrence: Thirty Years of Prints (1963-1993); Beth Lo: Sabbatical Exhib.; Narrative Painting; Talking Quilts: Possibilities in Response; Jim Todd: Portraits of Printmakers; David Regan: WESTAF Fellowship Winner; Art Museum of Missoula Permanent Coll; Lucy Capehart: Interiors; Devin Leonardi: In Memorium; Willem Volkersz: Paper Trail
Publications: Exhibit catalogs; membership newsletter; mailers & posters advertising shows
Activities: Classes for adults & children; dramatic progs; docent training; lect open to pub & for mems only, concerts; gallery talks; tours; MAM award; artmobile; lending of original objects of art; book traveling exhibs; originate traveling exhibs to museums in region; mus shop sells books

M **ROCKY MOUNTAIN MUSEUM OF MILITARY HISTORY,** Fort Missoula, Bldg T-310, Missoula, MT 59807; PO Box 7263, Missoula, MT 59807-7263. Tel 406-549-5346; Email info@fortmissoula.org; Web: www.fortmissoula.org; *Pres* Gary R Lancaster; *Exec Dir* Tate Jones; *VPres* Hayes Otoupalik; *VPres* Stan Cohen
Open June 1 - Labor Day: daily noon - 5 PM; day after Labor Day - end of May Sun noon - 5 PM; Admis no charge, donations accepted; Mus bldgs constructed in 1936 by the US Fourth Infantry Regiment & the Civilian Conservation Corps. Pvt nonprofit org; Mus promotes the commemoration & study of the US armed svcs, from the Frontier Period to the War on Terrorism; strives to impart a greater understanding of the roles played by America's service men & women through this period of dramatic social change; Mem: dues $25
Collections: Wide coll of documents & artifacts, ranging from Civil War artillery to Vietnam-era anti-tank missiles, home of Montana Civilian Conservation Corps aka "The Tree Army"

M **UNIVERSITY OF MONTANA,** Gallery of Visual Arts, Social Sciences Bldg, 1st Fl, University of Montana Missoula, MT 59812; 32 Campus Dr, School of Art

Missoula, MT 59812-0003. Tel 406-243-2813; Fax 406-243-4968; Email gallery.visarts@umontana.edu; Web: http://www.umt.edu/art/galleries
Open Mon - Thurs 11 AM - 4 PM; No admis fee; Estab 1981 to present faculty, student & outside exhibs of contemporary emphasis for community interest; Gallery has 220 linear ft, 2,200 sq ft; adjustable lighting; Average Annual Attendance: 15,000
Exhibitions: Various rotating exhibits call for details
Activities: Internships for gallery management; lects open to pub, 4-8 vis lectrs per yr; gallery talks; tours; competitions; campus art awards

M **Montana Museum of Art & Culture**, Main Hall, Room 006, University of Montana Missoula, MT 59812. Tel 406-243-2019; Fax 406-243-2797; Email museum@umontana.edu; Web: www.umt.edu/montanamuseum; *Dir* Barbara Koostra; *Registrar* Jeremy Canwell; *Program & Publ Coordr* Jessica Vizzutti
Open Wed, Thurs & Sat noon - 3 PM, Fri noon - 6 PM; June - Aug: cl Sun - Tues; Sep - May: Tues, Wed, Sat noon - 3 PM, Thurs, Fri noon - 6 PM, cl Sun, Mon; Admis general $5; Mus acquires & preserves art that expresses the spirit of the American West & its relationship to the broader world. As a univ & state mus, MMAC presents exhibs & educational programs that explore local, regional & global themes; The coll of the Montana mus of Art & Culture has been in existence since 1894. Currently with more than 10,000 works in its permanent coll, MMAC is home to one of the oldest & most prominent colls in the Rocky Mountain northwest; Average Annual Attendance: 50,000-60,000
Income: State, grants
Library Holdings: Auction Catalogs, Book Volumes, Kodachrome Transparencies, Pamphlets, Slides, Video Tapes
Special Subjects: Ceramics, Furniture, Painting-American
Collections: The Rudy Autio Contemporary Ceramic Collection, The Fra Dana Collection of American Impressionists, Pop Art & Contemporary Prints, Contemporary Native American Art, Bill & Polly Nordeen Collection of Western Art, New Deal Prints, Stella Duncan Collection of European Paintings, Cappadocia Collection of Southeast Asian Textiles, Henry Meloy Collection, Edgar S Paxton Collection, University of Montana Public Art Works
Publications: Contemporary Native American Art: Reflections after Lewis & Clark; The Original Man: The Life & Work of Montana Architect A J Gibson
Activities: Classes for adults & children; docent training; internships for coll & gallery management; lect open to pub; gallery talks; tours; Campus Art Award; original objects of art lent to Montana Art Gallery Dir Assn mems & to Wildling Art Mus, Los Olivos, CA; loans of historical objects to Montana museums; lending coll contains original prints, paintings & photographs; book traveling exhibs 1-3 per yr; originate traveling exhibs to Oregon Historical Society, National Cowboy and Western Heritage Mus, CM Russell Mus, Booth Mus of Western Art, Yellowstone Art Mus, Plains Art Mus, Three Affiliated Tribes Mus, Washington State Capitol Mus; mus shop sells books, reproductions & prints

PRYOR

M **CHIEF PLENTY COUPS MUSEUM STATE PARK,** PO Box 100, Pryor, MT 59066-0100. Tel 406-252-1289; Fax 406-252-6668; Email plentycoups@plentycoups.org; Web: www.plentycoups.org; *Dir* Rich Furber
Open May 1 - Sept 30 daily 10 AM - 5 PM; Admis $1 per person (park entrance fee includes mus); Estab 1972; Average Annual Attendance: 10,000
Income: Financed by state appropriation; affiliated with Montana Fish, Wildlife & Parks
Special Subjects: American Indian Art, Ethnology, Historical Material
Collections: Ethnographic materials of the Crow Indians, paintings, drawings, prehistoric artifacts
Exhibitions: Crow clothing and adornment; Pro Life Ways
Publications: Newsletter, annually
Activities: Fishing day for children; lect open to pub; 8 vis lectrs per yr; tours; sales shop sells books, magazines, original art, reproductions, prints, stationery notes, Crow crafts & beadwork

SIDNEY

M **MONDAK HERITAGE CENTER,** History Library, 120 Third Ave SE, Sidney, MT 59270. Tel 406-433-3500; Fax 406-433-3503; Email mdhc@richland.org; Web: www.mondakheritagecenter.org; *Exec Dir* Benjamin L Clark; *Admin Asst* Leann Pelvit
Open year round Tues-Fr 10AM-4PM, Sat 1-4PM, cl Jan; No admis fee; Estab 1972 to preserve history of area & further interest in fine arts; For reference only; Average Annual Attendance: 7,000; Mem: Annual meeting Sep
Income: Financed by county appropriations, mem dues, grants & donations
Library Holdings: Audio Tapes, Book Volumes 2,000, Cassettes, Clipping Files, Fiche, Lantern Slides, Manuscripts, Maps, Memorabilia, Original Documents, Pamphlets, Periodical Subscriptions, Photographs, Records, Video Tapes
Special Subjects: American Western Art, Dolls, Historical Material, Painting-American, Period Rooms, Woodcuts
Publications: MonDak Historical & Arts Society Newsletter, quarterly
Activities: Classes for adults & children; lects open to pub & mem only, 10 vis lectrs per yr; concerts; gallery talks; tours; competitions; schols; book traveling exhibs, 8 per yr

M **Museum**, 120 3rd Ave SE, Sidney, MT 59270-4324. Tel 406-433-3500; Fax 406-433-3503; Email mdhc@richland.org; Web: www.themondak.org; *Exec Dir* Kim Simmonds; *Educ Coordr* Jessica Newman
Open Tues - Fri 10 AM - 4 PM, Sat 1 - 4 PM; No admis fee; Estab 1967 as mus, for cultural events & shows; Average Annual Attendance: 10,000; Mem: Annual meeting Sep
Income: Financed by County Mill levy, memberships, & donations
Library Holdings: Audio Tapes, Book Volumes 1500, Cards, Clipping Files, Exhibition Catalogs, Fiche, Manuscripts, Maps, Memorabilia, Original Art Works, Original Documents, Other Holdings, Pamphlets, Periodical Subscriptions, Photographs, Reels
Special Subjects: American Western Art, Archaeology, Dolls, Furniture, Historical Material
Collections: Local history & art
Exhibitions: Regularly changing exhibs
Publications: newsletter, quarterly
Activities: Classes for adults & children; docent training; traveling trunks for children; lects open to pub & mem only; concerts; gallery talks; tours; competitions; schools; book travelling exhibs, 6-8 per yr; mus shop sells books, original art, prints, regional arts, crafts & local art & crafts

THREE FORKS

M **THREE FORKS AREA HISTORICAL SOCIETY,** Headwaters Heritage Museum, 202 S Main, Three Forks, MT 59752; PO Box 116, Three Forks, MT 59752-0116. Tel 406-285-4778; Email museumthreeforks@aol.com; Web: www.tfhistory.org; *Vol Dir, Cur & Mus Shop Mgr* Robin Cadby-Sorensen; *Vol Pres* Pat O'Brien Townsend; *Vol Treas* Patrick Finnegan; *Vol Secy* Richard Townsend; *Mem Chairperson* Joan Burwell
Open Jun 1 - Sept 30 Mon-Sat 9 AM - 5 PM, Sun11AM-3PM; other times by appt; No admis fee, donations accepted; Estab 1979 (Historical Society); Mus: 1982; Mus was constructed in 1910 and originally housed one of the first banks in Three Forks and contains thousands of artifacts & memorabilia depicting the local history of the Headwaters of the Missouri area; upstairs rooms depict a turn-of-the-century kitchen, schoolroom, blacksmith shop, railroad room, beauty shop & more. pvt nonprofit org; Average Annual Attendance: 2,500; Mem: dues Gen Mem $25, Gallatin Patron $125, Madison Patron $250, Jefferson Patron $500, Missouri Patron $1,000, Headwaters Patron $5,000
Special Subjects: Bronzes, Dolls, Flasks & Bottles, Furniture, Historical Material, Period Rooms, Photography, Portraits
Collections: Colls are from the local families of the Missouri Headwaters area, largest brown trout caught in Montana, fur trapp, anvil, barbed wire coll, misc artifacts from 1900s - 1950s, fossils; rocks; arrowheads; maps; agricultural tools; photographs; costumes; furnishings; papers & more, railroad press & hat shop
Publications: Headwaters History, 1983; Selected Papers of the 2010 Fur Trade Symposium at the Three Forks
Activities: Lects; guided tours; loan exhibs; traveling exhibs; docent prog; Ann Events: Journey of Discovery; Christmas Stroll; children's tours; mus shop sells books, postcards, souvenirs, prints & mus related items for sale

VICTOR

M **VICTOR HERITAGE MUSEUM,** Blake & Main St, Victor, MT 59875; PO Box 610, Victor, MT 59875-0610. Tel 406-642-3997; *Pres* Mark K Hafer
Open Memorial Day - End of Aug: Tues - Sat 1 - 4 PM, cl holidays; No admis fee, donations accepted; Estab 1989 on land that was donated by Alvin & Ruth Cote; mus focuses on history of the town of Victor from the early 1900s, including mining, railroad & Native American history. Pvt nonprofit org; Average Annual Attendance: 500 by estimate; Mem: dues Family $10
Collections: Permanent displays of items & artifacts that relate to Victor's history that are supplemented by thematic displays that change each yr, structures; personal artifacts; folk culture; distribution & transportation artifacts; tools & equip for commun; tools & equip for materials
Activities: Research on the Victor area & its residents prior to the 1930s; Ann event: Chocolate-Tasting Party, a fundraiser taking place on the first Mon in Dec

WHITEFISH

M **STUMPTOWN ART STUDIO,** Whitefish Gallery, 145 Central Ave, Whitefish, MT 59937. Tel 406-862-5929; Fax 406-862-5029; Email info@stumptownartstudio.org; Web: www.whitefishgallerynights.org
Open Mon - Sat 10 AM - 6 PM, Sun Noon - 5 PM; Estab 1995; Mem: dues $35-$5,000
Collections: painting; sculpture; photographs
Exhibitions: Temporary exhibits
Activities: Classes for adults & children; artist residencies; docent program; art programming; community projects

NEBRASKA

ALLIANCE

M **CARNEGIE ARTS CENTER,** 204 W 4th St, Alliance, NE 69301-3332. Tel 308-762-4571; Fax 308-762-4571; Email art@carnegieartscenter.com; Web: www.carnegieartscenter.com; *Gallery Dir* Rose Pancost; *Administrative Assistant* Kyren Conley; *Office Asst* Ray Schleyer; *Sales Manager of Sales Gallery* Jelinda Nye
Open Tues - Sat 10 AM - 4 PM, Sun 1 PM - 4 PM; Free; Estab 1993; Fine arts: exhibits, workshops & special events; Average Annual Attendance: 2,500-2,800
Collections: Paintings; various art exhibits
Activities: Classes for adults & children; Concerts; Tours; Scholarships; TripAdvisors Top rated art center; Sales shop; original art

ASHLAND

M **GENE RONCKA WILLOW POINT GALLERY/MUSEUM,** 1431 Silver St Ashland, NE 68003-1845. Tel 402-944-3613; Fax 402-944-3613; Email gr35419@windstream.net; Web: www.generoncka.com; *Artist* Gene Roncka; *Gallery Dir* Mary Roncka; *Sales Assoc* Marge Anderson; *Sales Assoc* Melissa Poulter; *Sales* Frank Demeter
Open Mon - Sat 10 AM - 5:30 PM, Sun 1 PM - 4 PM; No admis fee; Estab1994 - art sales; Gene Roncka art sales, framing, big game collection; Average Annual Attendance: 8,000

Activities: Tours; mus shop sells original art, reproductions & prints

AURORA

M **PLAINSMAN MUSEUM,** 210 16th St, Aurora, NE 68818-3009. Tel 402-694-6531; Email plainsman@hamilton.net; Web: www.plainsmanmuseum.org; *Exec Dir* Tina Larson; *Bldg Supvr* Norm Schachenmeyer; *Communs* Dawn Marie Moe
Open Tues - Sat 9 AM - 4 PM, cl New Year's Day, Easter, Thanksgiving, Christmas; Admis adults $7, seniors $5, youth 5-16 $3, children under 5 no charge; Estab 1935 to tell the story of Hamilton County, Nebraska, focusing on the time from 1860 -1950; Free-standing panels in area of Historical Mus (5 large folding panels). Maintains reference library; Average Annual Attendance: 4,000; Mem: 350; dues indiv $20, family $30, Century Club $100, lifetime $1,000; ann meeting Dirs meet 3rd Thurs of every month
Income: $100,000 (financed by mem, county allowance & individual donations)
Library Holdings: Book Volumes, Clipping Files, Lantern Slides, Manuscripts, Maps, Original Documents, Periodical Subscriptions, Photographs, Prints
Special Subjects: Coins & Medals, Dolls, Embroidery, Folk Art, Furniture, Glass, Historical Material, Jewelry, Laces, Leather, Maps, Mosaics, Painting-American, Period Rooms, Photography, Portraits, Textiles, Woodcarvings
Collections: One large pen & ink mural (20 ft x 8 ft) by Larry Guyton, 13 Wesley Huenefeld murals, Sidney E King Collection of murals, two large murals by Ernest Ochsner, Six Pioneer Scene Mosaic floor murals, Ted Bergren woodcarvings, Early Terrance Duren drawings
Publications: Events Past & Upcoming, Plainsman newsletter, 4 times yearly
Activities: Lect open to pub; concerts; gallery talks; tours; mus shop sells books, original art

CAMBRIDGE

M **CAMBRIDGE MUSEUM,** 612 Penn St Cambridge, NE 69022; Box 129, Cambridge, NE 69022. Tel 308-697-4385; Email bettyboop1-39@hotmail.com; *Cur* Betty Kruger; *Pres* Marilyn Kester; *Sec* Mae Groshong; *Board Mem* Arla Mae Pearson; *Board Mem* Loyd Thompson; *Board Mem* Roy Patterson; *Board Mem* Wanda Warwick
Open Apr - Sep Tues - Sun 1 - 5 PM, Oct - Mar Sat - Sun 1 PM - 5 PM; No admis fee, donations accepted; Estab 1938 to give local people & tourists a place to learn about history; Average Annual Attendance: 1,074; Mem: 6
Income: Financed by donations
Purchases: $75 (Norris House painting)
Special Subjects: American Indian Art, American Western Art, Archaeology, Coins & Medals, Costumes, Furniture, Maps, Period Rooms, Pottery, Dolls, Embroidery, Historical Material, Landscapes, Painting-American
Collections: Painting by Musi Muse, Paintings by Leonna Cowels & Gale Kasson, Clare Heumphreus Bettridge, Gary Hobbs, Henriette Johnson, Dorothy Lendall, Donna Flammang, Tea pot coll (159); bell coll (98); glass dog coll (130), Old license Plates (2 leather license Plates), American Indian arrow points & artifacts
Exhibitions: Rotating exhibits
Activities: Classes for children; scavenger hunts; twice a year entertainment by Nebraska Humanities; local people displaying large collection of Indian relics; lect open to pub - 1 per yr; schols ($500); originate traveling exhibs 1 per yr

CHADRON

M **CHADRON STATE COLLEGE,** Memorial Hall Main Gallery & Memorial Hall Gallery 239, 1000 Main St, Chadron, NE 69337-2690. Tel 308-432-6380; Fax 308-432-7784; Email sjohns@csc.edu; Web: www.csc.edu; *Coordr Conf* Shellie Johns; *Chair Performing & Visual Arts* Richard Bird
Open Mon - Fri 8 AM - 4 PM; No admis fee; Estab 1967 to offer opportunities for national recognized artists, students, faculty & local artists to present their works; to bring in shows to upgrade the cultural opportunities of students & the general pub; Main gallery has space for traveling & larger shows; Gallery 239 suffices for small shows; Average Annual Attendance: 5,000
Income: Financed by college budget, fine art student fee & state appropriation
Library Holdings: Book Volumes, CD-ROMs, Compact Disks, DVDs, Manuscripts, Maps, Memorabilia, Motion Pictures, Original Art Works, Pamphlets, Photographs, Prints, Records, Sculpture, Slides, Video Tapes
Collections: Chadron Foundation Art Collection
Activities: Docent training; lects open to pub, 3 vis lectrs per yr; gallery talks; tours; concerts; individual objects of art lent to campus bldgs; 4 book traveling exhibs per yr; circulate to regn bus & libraries; mus shop sells books, original art & prints

CHAPPELL

L **CHAPPELL MEMORIAL LIBRARY AND ART GALLERY,** 289 Babcock Ave, Chappell, NE 69124-0248; PO Box 248, Chappell, NE 69124-0248. Tel 308-874-2626; *Head Librn* Dixie Riley; *Asst Librn* Doris McFee
Open Tues - Thurs 1 - 5 PM, Tues & Thurs evening 7 - 9 PM, Sat 2 - 5 PM; No admis fee; Estab 1935 by gift of Mrs Charles H Chappell
Income: Financed by city of Chappell
Library Holdings: Book Volumes 10,398, Periodical Subscriptions 31
Collections: Aaron Pyle Collection, permanent personal coll of art works from many countries, a gift from Mrs Charles H Chappell
Exhibitions: Rotating Exhibits
Activities: Gallery talks; library tours

DAVID CITY

M **BONE CREEK MUSEUM OF AGRARIAN ART,** 575 "E" St, David City, NE 68632. Tel 402-367-4488; Email artinfo@bonecreek.org; Web: www.bonecreek.org; *Cur* Amanda Mobley Guenther; *Colls Mgr & Office Mgr* Gabrielle Comte
Open Wed, Fri & Sat 10 AM - 4 PM, Thurs 10 AM - 8 PM, Sun 1 PM - 4 PM; cl major holidays; No admis fee; Estab 2007; Nat center for preserving, viewing, learning about exceptional Agrarian art
Income: pvt & limited pub
Library Holdings: Exhibition Catalogs, Framed Reproductions, Manuscripts, Memorabilia, Original Art Works, Original Documents, Other Holdings, Photographs, Prints, Records, Sculpture
Special Subjects: American Indian Art, American Western Art, Ceramics, Drawings, Etchings & Engravings, Folk Art, Graphics, Landscapes, Latin American Art, Manuscripts, Military Art, Painting-American, Photography, Posters, Pottery, Primitive art, Prints, Sculpture, Woodcuts, Southwestern Art, Watercolors
Collections: Agrarian art; Dale Nichols, Thomas Hart Benton, Robert Bateman, Birger Sandzen, Robert Gwathmey, Thomas Mangelsen, Luigi Lucioni, John Steuart Curry, Mark L Moseman
Publications: Dale Nichols: Transcending Regionalism, exhib catalog; Robert Lougheed: Beyond Cowboys, Fields of the Heart, exhib catalog; Jen Terry: Upstate New York Farmstead, exhib catalog
Activities: Educ prog, classes, tours & field trips for adults & children; lects open to pub, 4-5 vis lectrs per yr; gallery talks; tours; Nebraskaland Foundation's Rising Star Award; sales shop sells books & prints

FREMONT

M **GALLERY 92 WEST / FREMONT AREA ART ASSOCIATION,** 92 W 6th St, Fremont, NE 68025-4956. Tel 402-721-7779; Email gallery92west@92west.org; Web: www.92west.org; *Exec Dir* Barbara Gehringer
Open Tues - Sun 1 - 4 PM, cl Mon; No admis fee; Estab 1960 to promote the appreciation & development of visual art
Exhibitions: Temporary exhibits
Activities: Classes for adults & children; workshops

GERING

M **OREGON TRAIL MUSEUM ASSOCIATION,** Scotts Bluff National Monument, Hwy 92 W, Gering, NE 69341; PO Box 27, Gering, NE 69341-0027. Tel 308-436-4340, 9700; Fax 308-436-7611; Web: www.NPS.gov/scbl; *Admin Mgr* John Kussack; *Bus Mgr* Jolene Kaufman; *Historian* Dean Knudsen; *Supt* Valerie J Naylor
Open June - Sept 8 AM - 8 PM, Oct - May 8 AM - 5 PM, cl Christmas & New Year's Day; Admis $5 per vehicle; Estab 1919 to preserve & display Oregon Trail landmark, artifacts, art & natural resources; 3 exhibit rooms; Average Annual Attendance: 120,000; Mem: 75; dues $10, renewal $5
Income: Financed by sales of Oregon Trail Museum Assn
Collections: Watercolors, drawings, & photographs by William H Jackson, surface finds from the Oregon Trail vicinity, paleontological specimens from within Monument boundaries
Exhibitions: 6 exhibits depicting geological, prehistoric, archaeological, ethnological history of the area; 15 exhibits depicting history of western migration from 1840-1870s; photos, drawings & paintings by W H Jackson; 2 dioramas depicting interaction between white men & buffalo
Publications: The Overland Migration; brochures & handbooks
Activities: Slide presentation of history of Oregon Trail & Scotts Bluff; Living History presentation of life on the trail; lect open to pub; mus shop sells books, prints, slides, postcards

HASTINGS

M **HASTINGS MUSEUM OF NATURAL & CULTURAL HISTORY,** (Hastings Museum), 1330 N Burlington Ave, Hastings, NE 68901; PO Box 1286, Hastings, NE 68902-1286. Tel 402-461-4629; Fax 402-461-2379; Email hastingsmuseum@alltel.net; Web: www.hastingsmuseum.org; *Educ* Russanne Erickson; *Cur & Coll* Teresa Kreutzer-Hodson; *Vol Coordr* Kaitlyn Karr
Mon - Sat 9 AM - 7 PM; Sun 1 PM - 6 PM; Admis adults $7, seniors (60+) $6, children (3-12) $5, tots free, large format films additional; Estab 1927 for a program of service & exhibits to augment & stimulate the total educative prog of schools & the gen pub; Animal displays in natural habitat settings; IMAX Theater open daily; Average Annual Attendance: 65000; Mem: 5100; premier $175, $325, $600, family $55, individual $45
Income: Financed by city appropriation & pvt donations
Special Subjects: Coins & Medals, Dioramas, Furniture, Glass, American Indian Art, American Western Art, Decorative Arts, Dioramas, Historical Material
Collections: Discover the Dream: Kool-Aid, Gun Collection, Animal Mounts, Cars, Native American & Pioneer
Exhibitions: Nature Nook, open yr round; World's Largest Display of Whooping Cranes
Publications: Museum Up Close, semi-ann
Activities: Classes for adults & children; lects open to pub, vis lectrs varies per yr; exten prog serving pre-k; traveling exhibs one per Summer; mus shop sells books & selected gift items; Reproductions

HOLDREGE

M **PHELPS COUNTY HISTORICAL SOCIETY,** Nebraska Prairie Museum, N Hwy 183, Holdrege, NE 68949-0164; PO Box 164, Holdrege, NE 68949-0164. Tel 308-995-5015; Fax 308-995-2241; Email prairie995@gmail.com; Web: www.nebraskaprairie.org; *Pres* Dr Bob Butz; *VPres* Eileen Schrock; *Treas & Exec Dir* Dan Christensen; *Secy* Warner Carlson; *Genealogy Librn* Sandra Slater

Open Mon - Sat 9 AM - 5 PM, Sun 1 - 5 PM, cl Jan 1, July 4, Thanksgiving, Easter, Christmas Eve & Christmas; Admis (suggested) adults $5, children $2; Estab 1966 for preservation of County history & artifacts; Thomas F. Naegele Gallery, over 60 works depicting live in German POW camps in the US; Average Annual Attendance: 9,500; Mem: 450; dues life $1,000, family ann $30, ann $20; ann meeting in May
Income: Financed by mem, county mill levy, state contributions & estate gifts
Library Holdings: Book Volumes, Clipping Files, Fiche, Maps, Original Documents, Other Holdings genealogy information, Photographs, Records
Special Subjects: Anthropology, Architecture, Bronzes, Carpets & Rugs, Ceramics, Coins & Medals, Costumes, Crafts, Dolls, Embroidery, Historical Material, Period Rooms, Pottery, Sculpture, Woodcarvings
Collections: Agriculture equipment, china, furniture, historical items, photos, POW, military, Native American
Publications: Centennial History of Holdrege, 1883; History of Phelps County, 1873-1980; Holdrege Centennial Coloring Book; Prisoners On The Plains; Stereoscope, quarterly
Activities: Classes for children; docent training; pow film; lect open to pub, 4 vis lectrs per yr; tours; book traveling exhibs; mus shop sells books, magazines, labels, souvenir plates, original art & reproductions

L **Donald O. Lindgren Library**, 2701 Burlington, Holdrege, NE 68949-0164; PO Box 164, Holdrege, NE 68949-0164. Tel 308-995-5015; Fax 308-995-2241; Web: www.nebraskaprairie.org; *Genealogy Librn* Sandra Slater; *Office Mgr* Cheryl Mill; *Pres* Dr Robert Butz; *Exec Dir* Dan R Van Dyke
Open May - Oct Mon - Fri, 9 AM - 5 PM; Nov - Apr Mon - Fri, 9 AM - 4 PM, Sat - Sun 1 PM - 5 PM; Admis donations only; Estab 1966 for historic preservation & educ; Average Annual Attendance: 10,000; Mem: 400; dues $30; ann meeting in May
Income: $100,000 (financed by taxes, investment earnings & contributions
Library Holdings: Audio Tapes, Book Volumes 1000, Cassettes, Clipping Files, Fiche, Kodachrome Transparencies, Lantern Slides, Manuscripts, Motion Pictures, Original Documents, Pamphlets, Periodical Subscriptions, Photographs, Prints, Video Tapes
Special Subjects: Coins & Medals, Crafts, Dioramas, Dolls, Embroidery, Historical Material, Period Rooms, Porcelain, Posters, Pottery
Collections: The Thomas F. Naegele Gallery contains 60 paintings depicting life in the POW camps at Atlanta & Indianola, Nebraska
Publications: The Stereoscope, quarterly
Activities: Classes for adults & children; docent training; lect open to public, 4 vis lectrs per year; tours; ext prog to schools; sales shop sells books, magazines, original art, reproductions, prints, toys, jewelry & ceramics

LEXINGTON

M **DAWSON COUNTY HISTORICAL SOCIETY,** Museum, PO Box 369, Lexington, NE 68850-0369. Tel 308-324-5340; Fax 308-324-5340; Email dcmuseum@atcjet.net; Web: www.dchsmuseum.com/index.html; *Pres* Gail Hall; *Treas* Jan Wightman; *Sec* Barb Knapple; *Dir* Barbara Vondras; *Staff Asst* Carol Nelson
Open Mon - Sat 9 AM - 5 PM, Sun by appt only; No admis fee; Estab 1958 to preserve Dawson County's heritage; Art gallery features exhibits by local artists; exhibits change monthly; Average Annual Attendance: 6,000; Mem: 450; dues life $150, family $20, individual $12.50
Income: Financed by endowment, mem, grants, county appropriation
Special Subjects: Furniture, Textiles
Collections: Agricultural Equipment, Furniture, Glassware, Household Implements, Quilts, Tools, Agricultural Equipment, Glassware
Exhibitions: 1919 McCave Aeroplane; Restored Country Schoolhouse; Restored Train Engine & Depot; Log Cabin Gallery Show monthly exhibit
Publications: Dawson County Banner newsletter, quarterly
Activities: Docent progs; lect open to pub, 3 vis lectrs per yr; book traveling exhibs 2 per yr; retail store sells books, original art

LINCOLN

A **LINCOLN ARTS COUNCIL,** 1701 S 17th St, Ste 1A Lincoln, NE 68502-2641. Tel 402-434-2787; Fax 402-434-2788; Email info@artscene.org; Web: www.artscene.org; *Pres* Christine Wilcox; *Office & Prog Mgr* Lori McAlister; *Exec Dir* Deborah Weber
Open Mon-Fri 9:30 AM - 4:30 PM; Estab 1966 to promote & encourage arts in Lincoln & serves as central information & advocacy source for the arts in the capital city; Mem: 60 arts
Income: Financed by pvt contributions, grants, city of Lincoln contract & Nebraska Arts Council
Publications: Artscene arts calendar, bimonthly; pub art guide, gallery guide

M **NEBRASKA STATE CAPITOL,** 1445 K St, Lincoln, NE 68509-4924; PO Box 94696, Lincoln, NE 68509-4696. Tel 402-471-0448; Fax 402-471-6952; Email hello@capitol.org; Web: www.capitol.org; *Capitol Adminr* Robert C Ripley; *Preservation Architect* Thomas L Kaspar; *Tourism Supvr* Roxanne E Smith; *Archivist* Karen Wagner
Open Mon - Fri 8 AM - 5 PM, Sat & holidays 10 AM - 5 PM, Sun 1 - 5 PM, cl Thanksgiving, Christmas & New Year's Day; Stone carvings of BAS reliefs; mosaic tile vaulting & fl panels; painted & mosaic murals; vernacular architectural ornamentation; Average Annual Attendance: 100,000
Income: Financed by state appropriation & pvt donations
Purchases: Eight murals commissioned to complete Capitol Thematic Prog
Special Subjects: Architecture, Decorative Arts, Furniture, Historical Material, Leather, Painting-American, Posters, Restorations, Sculpture, Tapestries, Woodcarvings
Collections: Lee Lawrie, building sculptor, Hildreth Meiere, mosaicist, muralists - Augustus V Tack, Kenneth Evett, James Penny, Elizabeth Dolan, Jean Reynal, Reinhold Marxhausen, F John Miller, Charles Clement, Stephen C Roberts
Publications: A Harmony of the Arts - The Nebraska State Capitol
Activities: Univ of Nebraska lect & service organization lect; guided tours; sales shop sells books, reproductions, prints, original art & Nebraska related items

M **NEBRASKA WESLEYAN UNIVERSITY,** Elder Gallery, 5000 Saint Paul Ave, Department of Art Lincoln, NE 68504-2760. Tel 402-466-2371, 465-2230; Fax 402-465-2179; Web: www.nebrwesleyan.edu; *Dir* Dr Donald Paoletta; *Gallery Preparator* Regina O'Reere
Open Tues - Fri 10 AM - 4 PM, Sat & Sun 1 - 4 PM; No admis fee; Estab 1966 as a cultural addition to col & community; Average Annual Attendance: 10,000
Special Subjects: Painting-American, Prints, Sculpture
Collections: Campus coll, permanent coll of prints, paintings & sculpture
Exhibitions: Annual Fred Wells National Juried Exhib; Nebraska Art Educators; faculty show; students shows; other changing monthly shows
Activities: Classes for adults

M **NOYES ART GALLERY,** 119 S Ninth St, Lincoln, NE 68508. Tel 402-475-1061; Email allgood52@gmail.com; Web: www.noyesartgallery.com; *Dir* Julia Noyes; *Asst* Tom Marshall; *Cur* Janna Harsch; *IT* Lisa Gustafson; *Designer* Karen Bowling; *Designer* Drew Curtright; *Mgr* Kye Halsted; *Studio Mgr* Kevin Baker; *FOCUS Chair* Gayle Kuhlman
Open Mon - Sat 10 AM - 5 PM, Nov - Dec 24 Mon - Sun 10 AM -5 PM, first Fri 10 AM - 9 PM; No admis fee; Estab 1993 as a commercial, cooperative profit organization to exhibit, promote & sell works by 80 regional artists; Located in a 100 yr old building near downtown Lincoln; main fl includes over 1200 sq ft exhibit area, office, storage & kitchen; second floor contains rented artist studios & classrooms; Mem: Guest artists & co-op artists apply
Income: 20,000; Financed by mem, commissions on sales
Library Holdings: Book Volumes, Cards, Photographs, Prints, Reproductions, Sculpture
Special Subjects: Asian Art, Baroque Art, Bronzes, Cartoons, Ceramics, Collages, Crafts, Decorative Arts, Drawings, Enamels, Folk Art, Furniture, Glass, Graphics, Landscapes, Metalwork, Miniatures, Mosaics, Painting-American, Painting-Japanese, Painting-Russian, Photography, Portraits, Pottery, Religious Art, Sculpture, Silver, Stained Glass, Textiles, Watercolors, Woodcarvings
Exhibitions: Monthly exhibits of gallery & visiting artists' work; Special monthly & private openings
Publications: Exhibit announcements, monthly
Activities: Classes for adults & children; docent training; music & poetry readings; lect open to pub; 4 competitions with awards; gallery talks; tours; concerts; 4 book traveling exhibs per yr; originates traveling exhibs to statewide libraries, churches & museums; mus shop sells original art

M **UNIVERSITY OF NEBRASKA, LINCOLN,** Sheldon Memorial Art Gallery & Sculpture Garden, PO Box 880300, Lincoln, NE 68588-0300. Tel 402-472-2461; Fax 402-472-4258; Web: www.sheldonartgallery.org; *Dir & Chief Cur* Wally Mason; *Assoc Registar* Genevieve Ellerbee; *Registar* Stacey Walsh; *Develop Dir* Laura Reznicek; *Visitor Servs Mgr* Janelle Stevenson
Open Mon - Wed & Sat 10 AM - 5 PM, Thurs - Fri 10 AM - 7 PM, Sun noon - 5 PM; No admis fee; Estab 1888 to exhibit the permanent colls owned by the Univ & to present temporary exhibs on an ann basis. These activities are accompanied by appropriate interpretive progs; The Sheldon Gallery, a gift of Mary Frances & Bromley Sheldon, was opened in 1963 & is the work of Philip Johnson. Facilities in addition to 15,000 sq ft of exhib galleries, include an auditorium, a print study, mems room a 25-acre outdoor sculpture garden; Average Annual Attendance: 125,000; Mem: dues $50 & up
Income: Financed by endowment, state appropriation & Nebraska Art Assoc
Purchases: $200,000
Special Subjects: Bronzes, Ceramics, Decorative Arts, Drawings, Folk Art, Graphics, Painting-American, Photography, Portraits, Prints, Sculpture, Watercolors
Collections: Frank M Hall Collection of contemporary paintings, sculpture, prints, drawings, photographs & ceramics, Nebraska Art Assn Collection of American paintings & drawings, University Collections, Permanent collection includes more than 12,000 objects in various media
Publications: Exhib catalogs & brochures; sculpture coll catalogue
Activities: Educ dept; docent training; lect open to pub, 3-5 vis lectrs per yr; tours; exten dept serves State of Nebraska; individual paintings & original objects of art lent to campus offices & other institutions in US & abroad; originate traveling exhibs; gift shop sells reproductions of works of original art within the permanent coll, prints, jewelry, ceramics & unique gifts

L **Architecture Library**, PO Box 880300, Lincoln, NE 68588-0300. Tel 402-472-1208; Fax 402-472-0665; Email archmail@unl.edu; Web: libraries.unl.edu/architecture-library; *Prof & Digital Arts Coordr* Kay Logan-Peters
Open Mon - Thurs 8 AM - 9 PM, Fri 8 AM - 5 PM, Sat 1 PM - 5 PM, Sun 1 PM - 9 PM; slides open Mon-Fri 8 AM - 5 PM; Estab to provide acad support for students & faculty in architectural concentration; Circ 21,000
Purchases: $25,000
Library Holdings: Audio Tapes, Book Volumes 65,000, Cassettes, Clipping Files, Exhibition Catalogs, Fiche, Filmstrips, Periodical Subscriptions 203, Photographs, Records, Reels, Slides 100,000, Video Tapes
Special Subjects: Architecture
Collections: American Architectural Books (microfilm), Architecture: Urban Documents (microfiche), Fowler Collection of Early Architectural Books (microfilm), National Register of Historic Places (microfiche), Historic American Building Survey Measure & Drawings, Slide coll

M **Eisentrager Howard Gallery**, Stadium Dr and T St (1st fl), Richards Hall 120 Lincoln, NE 68588-0114. Tel 402-472-5522; Email eisentragerhowardgallery@unl.edu; Web: arts.unl.edu/art/eisentrager-howard-gallery; *Dept Dir* Robert Ladislas Derr
Open Mon - Thurs 12:30 PM - 4:30 PM; call to confirm hours; No admis fee; Estab 1985 to exhibit contemporary art by national artists; student & faculty exhibs; 2,300 sq ft with 238 running ft of exhib space in two spacious rooms; track lights; Average Annual Attendance: 8,000
Collections: Coll of UNL Student Work from BFA & MFA degree prog
Exhibitions: Undergrad, grad & faculty exhibs
Publications: Exhib catalogs

M **UNIVERSITY OF NEBRASKA-LINCOLN,** Great Plains Art Museum, Hewit Place, 1155 Q St Lincoln, NE 68588-0250; PO Box 880250, Lincoln, NE 68588-0250. Tel 402-472-6220; Fax 402-472-0463; Email cgps@unl.edu; Web: www.unl.edu/plains/great-plains-art-museum; *Cur* Melynda Seaton; *Cur Asst* Naomi Szpot
Open Tues - Sat 10 AM - 5 PM; No admis fee; Estab 1980 to promote educ & gen awareness of Western art with an emphasis on Great Plains; Circ non-circulating, on-site research only; Three galleries rotating 8-12 exhibits per year & maintaining a research space and lib of Western Americana with approx 7,000 vols; Average Annual Attendance: 10,000; Mem: 150; dues $25 - $1000
Income: Financed by endowment, mem & state appropriation
Library Holdings: Book Volumes, Exhibition Catalogs, Manuscripts, Original Documents
Special Subjects: American Indian Art, American Western Art, Bronzes, Drawings, Landscapes, Painting-American, Photography, Portraits, Posters, Prints, Sculpture, Watercolors, Woodcuts
Collections: Broder Collection of 20th century American Indian paintings, Christlieb Collection of bronze sculpture, paintings & works on paper including drawings, prints & photographs depicting western subjects, Dwight and John Kirch Collection, Charles W Guildman Collection
Publications: Exhib catalogs & brochures
Activities: Lect open to pub, 6 vis lectrs per yr; tours; gallery talks; individual paintings & original objects of art lent; lending coll contains 1600 items; lends original objects of art to mus of schools with common region of interest; traveling exhibs to schools throughout Nebr; sales shop sells books, original art & reproductions

MCCOOK

M **HIGH PLAINS MUSEUM,** 423 Norris Ave, McCook, NE 69001-2003. Tel 308-345-3661; *Chmn Bd* Russell Dowling
Open Tues - Sat 1 - 5 PM, Sun 2 PM - 4 PM, cl Mon & holidays; No admis fee, donations accepted; Estab 1963 to preserve the items pertaining to local history & to interpret them for the pub; Mus is located in new building. New additions include complete pioneer kitchen; railroad section (inside & out); complete Old Time Pharmacy; 1942 Airbase; George W Norris Room; Governors From Nebraska; Average Annual Attendance: 5,000; Mem: 210; mem qualification is art display by local art club; dues $5 - $200; ann meeting in Apr
Income: Financed by mem & donations
Library Holdings: Memorabilia, Original Art Works, Pamphlets, Photographs, Records 33 1/2 phonograph records, Sculpture, Video Tapes
Collections: Paintings made on the barracks walls of prisoner of war camp near McCook, paintings donated by local artists, model railroad, displays pertaining to life of Southwest Nebraska
Exhibitions: Art Exhibit
Publications: Flyer, 3-page pamphlet describing hours & show displays
Activities: Lect open to pub, 8 vis lectrs per yr; competitions; lending coll contains books, framed reproductions & motion pictures; mus shop sells books, postcards, rings for children, petrified wood, arrowheads, medallions

MINDEN

M **HAROLD WARP PIONEER VILLAGE FOUNDATION,** 138 E Hwy 6, Minden, NE 68959-2500. Tel 308-832-1181; Fax 308-832-1181; Email manager@pioneervillage.com; Web: www.pioneervillage.org; *Pres* Harold Warp; *Gen Mgr* Marshall Nelson
Open Winter daily 9AM-4:30PM, Summer daily 8AM-6PM; Admis adults $14, children $7, children under 6 no charge; Estab 1953 to preserve man's progress from 1830 to present day; Foundation includes a 90-unit motel, 350-seat restaurant & 135-site campground; Elm Creek Fort; The People's Store; Bloomington Land Office; fire house; Lowell Depot; country school; sod house; China house; church; merry-go-round; horse barn; homes & shops building; antique farm machinery building; antique tractor & 350 autos & trucks; livery stable; agricultural building, blacksmith shop; Pony Express barn; Pony Express station; home appliance building; hobby house; John Roger statuary; William Jackson paintings; Albert Tilburne paintings; Average Annual Attendance: 40,000
Special Subjects: Historical Material
Collections: Airplanes, automobiles, bath tubs, bicycles, boats, clocks, fire wagons, guns, harvesters, horse drawn rigs, kitchens, lighting, locomotives, musical instruments, numismatics, paintings, plows, rare china, sculpture, street cars, telephones, threshers, toys, tractors, trucks
Publications: 500 Fascinating Facts; History of Man's Progress (1830-present); Pioneer Cookbook; Sister Clara's Letters (Over Our Hill-Past Our Place)
Activities: Classes for adults; elder hostel; docent training; children's progs, Holiday & Pioneer life in the Midwest; lect for mems only; tours; mus shop sells books, reproductions, prints & slides

NEBRASKA CITY

M **KIMMEL-HARDING-NELSON CENTER FOR THE ARTS,** 801 Third Corso, Nebraska City, NE 68410-2819. Tel 402-874-9600; Email info@khncenterforthearts.org; Web: www.khncenterforthearts.org; *Dir* Holly McAdams Olson; *Asst Dir* Shelli Rasmussen
Open Mon - Fri 10 AM - 5 PM; Estab 2001
Collections: Works by previous visual artist residents including 300 works of art, literature & music, Books, manuscripts, musical recordings
Exhibitions: Temporary exhibits
Activities: Artist residencies; open studios

M **NEBRASKA GAME AND PARKS COMMISSION,** Arbor Lodge State Historical Park & Morton Mansion, 2600 Arbor Ave, Nebraska City, NE 68410-1072; PO Box 15, Nebraska City, NE 68410-0015. Tel 402-873-7222; Fax 402-874-9885; Email ngpc.arbor.lodge @nebraska.gov; Web: outdoornebraska.org; *Asst Supt* Mark Kemper; *Supt* Randall Fox
Open mid Apr - End of Oct Mon - Sun 11AM - 5 PM; Admis adults $5, children 3-12 $2, children 2 & under free; Estab 1923; Art coll of mems of the J S Morton family & outdoor scenes spread through a 52-room mansion; Average Annual Attendance: 90,000
Income: Financed by state appropriation
Special Subjects: Afro-American Art, American Western Art, Architecture, Bronzes, Carpets & Rugs, Costumes, Dolls, Furniture, Furniture, Historical Material, Historical Material, Jewelry, Landscapes, Leather, Painting-American, Period Rooms, Photography, Portraits, Sculpture, Stained Glass, Woodcarvings
Activities: Lect open to pub; tours; awards; Arbor Day Tree plantings on last weekend in Apr; Apple Jack Fine Art show & sale 3rd Sat & Sun in Sept; living history demonstrations 4th & 5th Sun in Sept, 1st & 2nd Sun in Oct; mus shop sells books, magazines, prints, Arbor Day tree pins, postcards, nature crds, DVD's & t-shirts

NORFOLK

M **NORFOLK ARTS CENTER,** 305 N 5th St Norfolk, NE 68701-4092. Tel 402-371-7199; Fax 402-371-1971; Email info@norfolkartscenter.org; Web: www.norfolkartscenter.org; *Exec Dir* Kara Weander-Gaster
Open Tues - Fri 10 AM - 6 PM, Sat 10 AM - 4 PM; No admis fee; Estab 1978
Exhibitions: Midwest Regional Artist exhibs
Activities: Classes for adults & children; dramatic progs; teacher resources; concerts; gallery talks; tours; competitions; sales shop sells original art, jewelry, crafts

OMAHA

M **ARTISTS' COOPERATIVE GALLERY,** 405 S 11th St, Omaha, NE 68102-2805. Tel 402-342-9617; Email artistscoopgallery@gmail.com; Web: artistscoopomaha.com
Open Sun & Tues - Thurs noon - 6 PM, Fri - Sat 11 AM - 10 PM; No admis fee; Estab 1975 to be gathering place for those interested in visual art; to display quality local, contemporary art; to offer progs, panels & discussions on related issues to the pub; Gallery contains 4000 sq ft consisting of large open area with 1 small, self-contained gallery; Average Annual Attendance: 30,000; Mem: 35; dues $450 yearly; monthly meetings, work at gallery
Income: $30,000
Special Subjects: Painting-American
Exhibitions: Each month a different show features 2 - 4 mems of the gallery with a major show. Dec features an all-mem show; exchange exhibits & special exhibits are featured by arrangement
Activities: Metro area senior high art exhibits; lect open to pub, 2 vis lectrs per yr; concerts; gallery talks; tours; originate traveling exhibs to other cooperative galleries

M **BEMIS CENTER FOR CONTEMPORARY ARTS,** 724 S 12th St, Omaha, NE 68102-3202. Tel 402-341-7130; Fax 402-341-9791; Email info@bemiscenter.org; Web: www.bemiscenter.org; *Devel Dir* Ellie Novak; *Residency Prog Mgr* Holly Kranker
Open Wed - Sat 11 AM - 5 PM; No admis fee; Estab 1981; Maintains reference library, 3 galleries & 13 live/work studios; Average Annual Attendance: 20,000
Library Holdings: Auction Catalogs, Book Volumes, DVDs, Exhibition Catalogs, Periodical Subscriptions, Video Tapes
Special Subjects: Ceramics, Decorative Arts, Sculpture, Photography
Collections: Aesthetics, Art History, Film, Bemis Collection
Publications: Monthly e-news
Activities: Lect open to pub, 25-30 vis lectrs per yr; concerts; gallery talks; tours; awards; educ progs; schols offered; individual paintings & original objects of art lent to museums & galleries

M **CREIGHTON UNIVERSITY,** Lied Art Gallery, 2500 California Plaza, Omaha, NE 68178-0303. Tel 402-280-2261; Fax 402-280-2320; Email liedartgallery@creighton.edu; Web: www.creighton.edu/liedgallery; *Gallery Dir* Jess Benjamin
Open Mon - Fri 11 AM - 1 PM & 5 PM - 6 PM, Sat - Sun 1 PM - 4 PM; No admis fee; Mus estab 1973; Gallery handles 5-8 exhibitions per acad yr; space provided for student thesis exhibits; 149 running ft; Average Annual Attendance: 2,000
Income: $8,000 (financed by school's gen funding)
Special Subjects: Ceramics, Drawings, Graphics, Painting-American, Photography, Pottery, Sculpture, Prints
Collections: Ceramics, drawings, graphics, paintings, photography, pottery & sculpture, printmaking
Exhibitions: Senior Thesis Exhibits; Creighton University Faculty Exhibit
Activities: Lect open to pub, 1-5 vis lectrs per yr; gallery talks; book traveling exhibs

M **EL MUSEO LATINO,** 4701 S 25th St, Omaha, NE 68107-2728. Tel 402-731-1137; Fax 402-733-7012; Email info@elmuseolatino.org; Web: elmuseolatino.org
Open Mon, Wed & Fri 10 AM - 5 PM, Tues & Thurs 1 - 5 PM, Sat 10 AM - 2 PM, cl New Year's Eve & Day, Independence Day, Thanksgiving, Christmas; Admis adults $5, college students $4, senior citizens & students K-12 $3.50, children under 5 & members free; Estab May 5, 1993; Average Annual Attendance: 50,000
Library Holdings: Book Volumes 500
Collections: Latin American art & history
Activities: Workshops for adults & children; docent prog; bilingual prog; lect; concerts; guided tours; gallery talks; museum shop

M **HOT SHOPS ART CENTER,** 1301 Nichols St, Omaha, NE 68102-4212. Tel 402-342-6452; Email manager@hotshopsartcenter.com; Web: www.hotshopsartcenter.com; *Bldg Mgr* Tim Barry
Open Mon - Fri 9 AM - 6 PM, Sat - Sun 11 AM - 5 PM; Estab 1999 to provide artists with a studio & space to collaborate

Special Subjects: Ceramics, Stained Glass, Jewelry, Sculpture, Metalwork, Photography, Mixed Media
Collections: Painting, ceramics, stained glass, jewelry, sculpture, metal casting, photography & mixed media
Exhibitions: Temporary exhibits
Activities: Classes for adults & children

M **JOSLYN ART MUSEUM,** 2200 Dodge St, Omaha, NE 68102-1292. Tel 402-342-3300; Fax 402-342-2376; Web: www.joslyn.org; *Exec Dir & CEO* Jack F Becker; *Chief Cur* Toby Jurovics
Open Tues - Wed & Fri - Sun 10 AM - 4 PM, Thurs 10 AM - 8 PM, cl Mon and major holidays; Admis gen admis free, additional charge for some special exhibs; Estab in 1931; Nebraska's largest general art mus. Emphasis on 19th-C European & American art; Average Annual Attendance: 180,000; Mem: 2,700+ mem households
Special Subjects: African Art, American Indian Art, American Western Art, Antiquities-Egyptian, Antiquities-Greek, Antiquities-Oriental, Antiquities-Roman, Architecture, Asian Art, Bronzes, Coins & Medals, Decorative Arts, Drawings, Etchings & Engravings, Furniture, Glass, Graphics, Historical Material, Ivory, Jade, Landscapes, Medieval Art, Painting-American, Painting-British, Painting-Dutch, Painting-European, Painting-Flemish, Painting-French, Painting-Italian, Painting-Russian, Painting-Spanish, Photography, Portraits, Pottery, Prints, Renaissance Art, Sculpture, Watercolors, Woodcuts, Textiles
Collections: 11,000+ works comprising ancient through modern art with emphasis on 18th & 19th c American & European art, incl Greek pottery, Renaissance & Baroque masterworks by Rembrandt, Titian, El Greco, Veronese, Jacob Van Ruisdael & Claude Lorrain, portraits by James Peale, Mary Cassatt & Thomas Eakins, genre paintings by Severin Roesen, Eastman Johnson & William M Harnett, 20th c paintings by Grant Wood, Thomas Hart Benton, George Ault, Jackson Pollock, Kenneth Noland & Helen Frankenthaler, contemporary works by Robert Irwin, Donald Judd, George Segal & Martin Puryear, American West holdings by Alfred Jacob Miller & 400 watercolors & drawings by Swiss artist Karl Bodmer, paintings of Plains chiefs by Charles Bird King & Henry Inman
Publications: Members calendar, quarterly; exhib catalogs; art books
Activities: Classes for adults & children; docent training; special events; reading & art progs; lects open to pub; lects for mems only; 15-20 vis lectrs per yr; concerts; gallery talks; tours; awards fully-accredited by American Assoc of Mus; teacher resource prog serves State of Nebraska & Southwest Iowa; remote classroom to serve worldwide; lend original objects of art to other major mus; 8-10 book travel exhibs per yr; travel exhibs to mus worldwide; mus shop sells books, original art, reproductions & prints

M **OMAHA CHILDREN'S MUSEUM,** 500 S 20th St, Omaha, NE 68102-2505. Tel 402-342-6164; Fax 402-342-6165; Email info@ocm.org; Web: www.ocm.org; *Exec Dir* Lindy Hoyer; *Chief Mus Officer* Jeff Barnhart
Open Tues - Sat 10 AM - 4 PM, Sat 9 AM - 5 PM, Sun 11 AM - 5 PM, cl Mon; Admis adults & children $12, seniors $11, mem & children under 2 free; Purpose, to engage the imagination & create excitement about learning; Average Annual Attendance: 253,000; Mem: 2500 families; dues $45
Income: Financed by mem, admis, grants, donations from individuals, foundations & corporations
Exhibitions: Hands-on exhibits which promote learning in the arts, science & humanities; traveling exhibits; workshops by local professional educators & artists
Publications: Bimonthly calendar; mus newsletter, quarterly
Activities: Classes for children; summer camp; exten dept serves local metro area; book traveling exhibs 2-3 per yr; mus shop sells books, educational games & toys

M **UNIVERSITY OF NEBRASKA AT OMAHA,** UNO Art Gallery, 6001 Dodge St, Dept Art & Art History, WFA Rm 129 Omaha, NE 68182-0012. Tel 402-554-2796; Fax 402-554-3436; Email unoartgallery@unomaha.edu; Web: www.artgallery.unomaha.edu; *Coordr* Denise Brady
Open Mon - Thurs 10 AM - 3 PM by appointment (call ahead); No admis fee; Estab 1967 to heighten cultural & aesthetic awareness in the metropolitan & midlands area; 2 galleries - 1500 sq ft & 675 sq ft hexagon; Average Annual Attendance: 5000
Income: Financed by state appropriation
Special Subjects: Prints
Collections: University Visiting Printmaker's Coll
Exhibitions: Six exhibs during academic yr, including student, faculty & regional/national contemporary artists; see website
Activities: Lect open to pub, 4 vis lectrs per yr; gallery talks; tours; competitions; schols

SCOTTSBLUFF

M **WEST NEBRASKA ART CENTER,** Gallery, 106 E 18th St, Scottsbluff, NE 69361-2423. Tel 308-632-2226; Email donna@thewnac.com; Web: www.thewnac.com; *Contact* Donna Thompson
Open Tues - Sat 9 AM - 5 PM, Sat - Sun 1 PM - 5 PM, cl Mon; Estab 1967 to promote community & diversity in the arts; Mem: dues $25-$5,000
Collections: Features visual art by local, national & international artists
Exhibitions: Monthly exhibits
Activities: Educ progs

SEWARD

M **CONCORDIA UNIVERSITY,** Marxhausen Art Gallery, 800 N Columbia Ave, Seward, NE 68434-1500. Tel 402-643-3651, Ext 7435; Web: www.cune.edu/finearts/art; *Dir* James Bockelman
Open Mon - Fri 11 AM - 4 PM, Sat & Sun 1 PM - 4 PM; No admis fee; Estab 1959 to provide the col & community with a wide variety of original art; both monthly exhibs & permanent coll serve primarily an educational need; spacious gallery has additional showcases
Income: Financed by col funds
Special Subjects: Ceramics, Prints
Collections: Ceramics, Contemporary Original Prints
Exhibitions: One & two artists exhibs; shows drawn from Permanent Coll & Annual Student Exhibs; The Art of Cartoons; Animal Show; The Computer & its Influence on Art & Design; Part II; Rotating exhibits
Activities: Gallery talks; original objects of art lent; lending coll of framed reproductions, original prints & paintings; book traveling exhibs, 6 per yr

WAYNE

M **WAYNE STATE COLLEGE,** Nordstrand Visual Arts Gallery, Peterson Fine Arts Bldg, Room 203, Anderson Dr, Wayne State Campus Wayne, NE 68787; 1111 Main St, Art Dept Wayne, NE 68787-1172. Tel 402-375-7000; Fax 402-375-7204; *Chmn Art* Prof Pearl Hansen; *Prof* Marlene Mueller; *Prof* Wayne Anderson
Open Mon - Fri 8AM-4PM; No admis fee; Estab Jan 1977 to provide art students with a space to display work; to enhance student's educ by viewing incoming regional professional work; to enrich cultural atmosphere of col & community; Small gallery, carpeted floors & walls, ceiling spotlights on tracts; Average Annual Attendance: 800
Income: Financed by city & state appropriation, as well as Wayne State Foundation
Library Holdings: Audio Tapes, Book Volumes, Slides
Special Subjects: Prints
Collections: Wayne State Foundation Print Collection
Activities: Lects open to pub, 1-2 vis lectrs per yr; competitions; tours

NEVADA

ELKO

M **NORTHEASTERN NEVADA MUSEUM,** 1515 Idaho St, Elko, NV 89801-4021. Tel 775-738-3418; Fax 775-778-9318; Email info@museumelko.org; Web: www.museumelko.org; *Dir* Claudia Wines; *Archivist* Toni Mendive; *Registrar* Katie Taylor; *Exhibs Coordr* Tracy Beatty
Open Tues-Sat 9AM-5PM, Sun 1 - 5PM; Admis adults $5, seniors 65 and over $3, students $3, children 3-12 $1, children under 3 free; Estab 1968; gen mus concentrating on Northeastern Nevada; also area cultural center; Gallery is 4000 sq ft, 12 exhibits per yr local, state, regional & national artists; Average Annual Attendance: 20,000; Mem: 1300; dues $25 - $1000; ann meeting date varies
Income: Financed by grants, contributions, dues, sales shop & memorials
Special Subjects: American Western Art, Historical Material, Painting-American, Photography, Watercolors
Collections: History, Pre-History, Natural History, Art, Wildlife Exhibit
Exhibitions: Will James art & books (permanent); Ansel Adams photos (permanent); Edward Borein Western Art (permanent), Edward Western photos (permanent)
Publications: Historical, quarterly; Northeastern Nevada Historical Society Quarterly
Activities: Classes for adults & children; lect open to pub; concerts; gallery talks; tours; coll of 5,000 photographs; 1,700 books; mus shop sales books, magazines, reproductions, prints & local craft items

ELY

M **NEVADA NORTHERN RAILWAY MUSEUM,** 1100 Ave A, Ely, NV 89301; PO Box 150040, Easy Ely, NV 89315-0040. Tel 775-289-2085, 866-407-8326; Email info@nnry.com; Web: www.nevadanorthernrailway.net; *CEO & Exec Dir* Mark S Bassett; *Mus Shop Mgr* Heather Barber; *Cur* Joan Bassett
Open daily June - Aug 8 AM - 6:30 PM, Sept - May 8 AM - 5 PM, cl Tues; cl Thanksgiving, Christmas Eve & Day, New Year's Eve & Day; Admis adults $6, children 4-12 $3; Estab 1985; site of the orig railroad serving the mining district; consists of a rail yard with 48 structures, 3 steam locomotives, 13 diesel locomotives & many other rail cars; Average Annual Attendance: 10,000 - 49,999 by estimate; Mem: 2,300; dues Leader $10,000, Benefactor $5,000, Supporter $2,500, Friend $1,000, Sustaining $250, Centennial $100, Family $50, Active $30
Special Subjects: Historical Material, Period Rooms, Restorations
Collections: Railroad equipment; buildings & artifacts related to NV Northern Railroad; mining rail equipment from the White Pine County mines
Publications: Ghost Tracks, quarterly newsletter
Activities: Railroad Camp; Memorial Day Members weekend; Polar Express; docent prog; formal educ for adults; guided tours; temp exhibs; mus related items for sale

LAS VEGAS

M **BELLAGIO RESORT & CASINO,** Bellagio Gallery of Fine Art, 3600 Las Vegas Blvd S, Las Vegas, NV 89109-4339. Tel 702-693-7871, 888-488-7111; Email fineartgallery@bellagioresort.com; Web: www.bellagio.com/bgfa
Open daily 10 AM - 8 PM; Admis adults $18, NV residents, seniors 65 & over, students, teachers & military $16; children 12 & under free; estab 1998; temporary exhib space
Special Subjects: Photography, Sculpture
Activities: Intern prog; school group tours; school & lib outreach; book traveling exhibs, 2 per yr; mus shop sells books, exhib merchandise (postcards, magnets etc)

M **LAS VEGAS NATURAL HISTORY MUSEUM,** 900 Las Vegas Blvd N, Las Vegas, NV 89101. Tel 702-384-3466; Fax 702-384-5343; Email dino@lvnhm.org; Web: www.lvnhm.org; *Exec Dir* Marilyn Gillepsie
Open daily 9 AM - 4 PM; Admis adults $12, seniors, military & students $10, children $6, children under 2 & mems free; Estab 1989; Gallery has a classroom & a children's hands-on room
Special Subjects: African Art

Collections: Art (prints), fossils, live animals, mounted animals, teaching coll, Murals of Wildlife & Habitats, Wildlife Art
Publications: Newsletter, quarterly
Activities: Classes for adults & children; docent training; lect open to pub; book traveling exhibs annually; sales shop sells books & educ toys

L **LAS VEGAS-CLARK COUNTY LIBRARY DISTRICT,** 1401 E Flamingo Rd, Las Vegas, NV 89119-5256. Tel 702-734-7323; Web: www.lvccld.org; *Exec Dir* Ronald R Heezen; *Branch Mgr* Marie Nicholl-Lynam
Open Mon - Thurs 10 AM - 8 PM, Fri-Sun 10 AM - 6 PM; No admis fee; Estab 1965 to provide information in all its varieties of form to people of all ages; nine branch libraries, including three art galleries; Circ 1,770,951; Galleries provide regularly rotating art exhibs of regional & national repute as well as ten solo shows per yr, & a regional mixed media competition every spring
Library Holdings: Audio Tapes, Cassettes, Clipping Files, Fiche, Filmstrips, Framed Reproductions, Motion Pictures, Original Art Works, Pamphlets, Periodical Subscriptions 586, Photographs, Prints, Records, Reels, Reproductions, Sculpture
Collections: Model ship collection, Nevada materials
Exhibitions: Art-a-Fair; Nevada Watercolor Society; All Aboard: Railroads, Memorabilia; Neon: Smithsonian Exhibition; Expressions in Fiber; Graham & Breedlove; Sand & Water; Dottie Burton; Woodworks: Christian Brisepierre & Jack Daseler; KNPR Craftworks; It's a Small, Small World: Dollhouses, Kimberly House
Publications: Exhib brochures, monthly; library prog, bimonthly
Activities: Lect open to pub; concerts; tours; competitions with awards; exten dept & regional servs dept serving the area; individual paintings & original objects of art lent; book traveling exhibs; originate traveling exhibs; used book store sells books, magazines, original art & handcrafts

M **Flamingo Gallery**, 833 Las Vegas Blvd N, Las Vegas, NV 89101. Tel 702-507-3500; Web: www.lvccld.org; *Acting Branch Mgr* Sam Kushner
Open Mon - Thurs 10 AM - 8 PM, Fri - Sun 10 AM - 6 PM; No admis fee; Estab 1970; Gallery is located in Clark County Library, main gallery has 80 running ft of exhibit space, upstairs gallery is used for photographic displays
Income: Financed by tax support, federal & state grants
Exhibitions: Art-A-Fair (judged and juried); Spirit Impressions; The Potter & the Weaver; Nevada Watercolor Society Annual exhibit
Publications: Bimonthly library calendar of events
Activities: Classes for adults & children; dramatic progs; string quartet; feature films; lect open to pub, 10 vis lectrs per yr; concerts; Art-A-Fair competition; monetary awards

M **UNIVERSITY OF NEVADA, LAS VEGAS,** Donna Beam Fine Art Gallery, 4505 S Maryland Pky, Las Vegas, NV 89154-5002. Tel 702-895-3893; Email donnabeamfineartgallery@unlv.edu; Web: donnabeamgallery.unlv.edu; *Dir* Jerry Schefcik
Open Mon - Fri 9 AM - 5 PM, Sat 10 AM - 2 PM, cl Sun & holidays; No admis fee; Estab 1962 to exhibit contemporary art; Gallery measures 1400 sq ft, 175 linear ft with track lighting; Average Annual Attendance: 10,000
Income: Financed by mem & appropriation
Special Subjects: Painting-American, Photography, Prints
Collections: General coll of about 300 objects of all media. Works are from the United States & the 2nd half of the 20th century, Dorothy & Herbert Vogel Collection: Fifty Works for Fifty States, Nevada
Activities: Classes for adults & children; docent training; lect open to pub, 3 vis lectrs per yr; gallery talks; juried competitions with cash awards; individual painting & original objects of art lent; lending coll includes 150 original art works; book traveling exhibs 1 per yr; originate traveling exhibs to other universities & galleries

M **THE WALKER AFRICAN AMERICAN MUSEUM & RESEARCH CENTER,** 705 W Van Buren Ave, Las Vegas, NV 89106. Tel 702-752-6043 (call for appt), 702-752-6043 (call for appt); Email walkeraamuseum1@yahoo.com; *Founder & Cur* Gwendolyn Walker
Open by appointment; Estab 1993; Mus is designed to promote & preserve the history of people of African descent (locally, nat & internat) with a concentration on the history of Black & African Americans in Nevada; Mem: Dues Supporting $100; Mem $25
Income: Financed by mem dues & donations
Library Holdings: Book Volumes 600, Cassettes, Clipping Files, Framed Reproductions, Memorabilia, Original Art Works, Original Documents, Other Holdings, Pamphlets, Photographs, Prints, Records, Reproductions, Video Tapes
Special Subjects: African Art, Afro-American Art, Ceramics, Coins & Medals, Collages, Costumes, Crafts, Decorative Arts, Dioramas, Dolls, Drawings, Folk Art, Graphics, Historical Material, Ivory, Jewelry, Juvenile Art, Manuscripts, Maps, Miniatures, Photography, Photography, Porcelain, Portraits, Posters, Pottery, Pre-Columbian Art, Prints, Reproductions, Collages
Collections: Books, documents, artifacts, news articles, photographs, dolls, stamps & ann publs of local & state history, Interchangeable, Moulin Rouge, Dr M L King, Pres Barack Obama, local political
Publications: Black Pioneers of Nevada, ann booklet; From the Kitchen to the Boardroom: Nevada's Black Women, book; Courage, Strength & Faith: Nevada's Black Men, booklet publishes every other yr; cookbook
Activities: Classes for adults & children; African-American Cultural Arts Festival; films; research in early bus owned by African-Americans in NV; lects open to public; tours; gallery talks; sponsoring of competitions; mus shop sells books, magazines, reproductions, prints, stamps, Kwanzaa supplies, dolls, figurines & related items

MESQUITE

M **MESQUITE FINE ARTS CENTER & GALLERY,** 15 W Mesquite Blvd, Mesquite, NV 89027-4754. Tel 702-346-1338; Fax 702-346-1339; Email warts@gmail.com; Web: www.mesquitefineartscenter.com; *Pres* Katherine Cole; *VPres* Kathleen Birkholz
Open Mon - Sat 10 AM - 4 PM, cl holidays; 0; Estab 2003; Fine art by local artists; Mem: 200; dues $35 yr; 3rd Mon of every month
Income: Dues, sale commission, donation, grants, city of Mesquite NV art council
Purchases: Gallery operation & improvement for bldg & landscaping
Exhibitions: Lucky 13, Nov - Dec
Publications: Mem application brochure
Activities: Educ progs; classes for adults & children; brown bag lects (1st Tues each month); monthly art reception; docent training; ann student art exhib; lects open to pub; gallery talks; schols; awards, Outside Venue-display art at local bus; mus shop sells books, original art, reproductions

NORTH LAS VEGAS

M **LEFT OF CENTER ART GALLERY & STUDIO,** 2207 W Gowan, North Las Vegas, NV 89032-7961. Tel 702-647-7378; Fax 702-647-7340; *Dir* Vicki Richardson
Call for hours
Collections: works by national and local artists

RENO

M **NEVADA MUSEUM OF ART,** 160 W Liberty St, Reno, NV 89501-1916. Tel 775-329-3333; Fax 775-329-1541; Email art@nevadaart.org; Web: www.nevadaart.org; *Exec Dir & CEO* David B Walker; *Dir Communs* Amanda Horn; *Sr Cur & Deputy Dir* Ann M Wolfe; *Dir Educ* Marisa Cooper; *Dir Center for Art & Environ* William L Fox; *Deputy Dir & COO* Amy Oppio; *Mng Dir Mus Advancement* Casey Burchby; *Dir Special Projects* Heidi Loeb
Open Wed & Fir - Sun 10 AM - 6 PM, Thurs 10 AM - 8 PM; Admis adults $10, students & seniors $8, children 6 - 12 $1, Washoe & Douglas Co high school students with valid ID, children under 5 & mems free; Estab 1931 to collect, conserve & exhibit 19th & 20th century American art with an emphasis on artwork which articulates our interaction with the land & environment. The colls are divided into 5 focus areas including The Altered Landscape Coll; The facility is a 60,000 sq ft state of the art building built in 2003 which holds 12 exhibs simultaneously; Mem: dues $35 - $10,000; Scholarships
Income: Financed by endowment, mem, federal & pvt foundation grants, individual grants & earned income
Library Holdings: Auction Catalogs, Audio Tapes, Book Volumes, CD-ROMs, Cards, Cassettes, Compact Disks, DVDs, Exhibition Catalogs, Maps, Memorabilia, Original Art Works, Pamphlets, Periodical Subscriptions, Photographs, Prints, Sculpture, Video Tapes
Special Subjects: American Indian Art, American Western Art, Bronzes, Ceramics, Drawings, Etchings & Engravings, Glass, Landscapes, Leather, Manuscripts, Marine Painting, Painting-American, Painting-European, Photography, Portraits, Prints, Sculpture, Textiles, Watercolors, Woodcarvings, Woodcuts, Architecture, Art History, Art Education, Decorative Arts, Landscape Architecture
Collections: E L Wiegand Art Collection (emphasis on the American work ethic), Altered Landscape Collection (photography), Contemporary Collection, Historical Collection, Sierra Nevada Great Basin Collection, CA&E Archive Collection, Robert S & Dorothy J Keyser Art of the Greater West
Exhibitions: Rotating exhibs every 3 months
Publications: Annual Report; brochures; calendar; event calendar; newsletter, bimonthly; postcards for events; Art of Tahoe
Activities: Educ programs; classes for adults & children; hands-on exhibs; docent training; lects open to pub; 3-5 vis lectrs per yr; gallery talks; tours; concerts; competitions; awards, Silver Telly, Trip Advisor, Best of Northern Nevada; schols offered; outreach services to schools, sr citizens & other community groups in Greater Reno-Carson-Tahoe area; exchange prog with other mus; 1-2 book traveling exibs; originate traveling exhibs to Oakland Mus of California; mus shop sells books, original art, prints, stationery, jewelry & other items

L **CA & E Research Library**, 160 W Liberty St, Reno, NV 89501-1916. Tel 775-329-3333; Fax 775-329-1541; Email art@nevadaart.org; Web: www.nevadaart.org; *Exec Dir & CEO* David B Walker
Open Wed - Sun 11 AM - 2 PM; Admis adults $10, $8 students & seniors, $1 children 6-12, children five and under free; New 55,000 sq ft facility designed by Will Bruder opened in 2003
Library Holdings: Book Volumes 1400, Clipping Files, Exhibition Catalogs, Manuscripts, Memorabilia, Pamphlets, Periodical Subscriptions 6, Photographs, Reproductions
Special Subjects: Advertising Design, Aesthetics, Afro-American Art, American Indian Art, American Western Art, Anthropology, Antiquities-Byzantine, Antiquities-Egyptian, Antiquities-Etruscan, Antiquities-Greek, Antiquities-Oriental, Antiquities-Roman, Archaeology, Architecture, Art Education
Collections: Focus on art and environment, Altered landscape photography, Sierra Nevada/Great Basin, Contemporary, Historical
Activities: Classes for adults & children; docent training; mus school on site; lects open to pub; concerts; gallery talks, tours; mus shop

A **SIERRA ARTS FOUNDATION,** Sierra Arts Gallery, 17 S Virginia St, Reno, NV 89501. Tel 775-329-2787; Email tracey@sierraarts.org; Web: www.sierraarts.org; *Exec Dir* Tracey Oliver; *Prog Mgr* Tia Flores; *Galleries Cur Assoc* Eric Brooks; *Pub Rels & Mktg Assoc* Alexa Solis
Open Mon - Fri 10 AM - 5 PM, Fri - Sat by appt; No admis fee; Estab 1971 as a nonprofit, pvt community arts agency, advocates for & supports the arts; Contemporary works by emerging artists; Mem: dues $35 - $5,000; Fellowships
Income: Financed by endowment, corporate & individual mem, grants & fundraising activities
Exhibitions: 6-wk exhibs of contemporary artworks throughout the yr
Publications: Art Resource Guide; Artist Registry, current list of culture organizations, facilities list & media list; Encore, monthly community arts magazine; Master Calendar; Services Booklet
Activities: Classes for children in elementary school; classes for at-risk youths in local detention facility shelter for runaway kids & alternative high school; dramatic prog; lects open to pub; concerts; gallery talks; tours; sponsoring of competitions; grants offered; fels & schols available; exten dept; Endowment Income Grants Program for local individual artists; sales shop sells original art on consignment

M **STREMMEL GALLERY,** 1400 S Virginia St, Reno, NV 89502-2806. Tel 775-786-0558; Email info@stremmelgallery.com; Web: stremmelgallery.com; *Exec Dir* Peter Stremmel; *Gallery Dir* Turkey Stremmel
Open Mon - Fri 9 AM - 5 PM, Sat 10 AM - 3 PM; cl holidays
Collections: works by contemporary artists

M **UNIVERSITY OF NEVADA, RENO,** Sheppard Contemporary & University Galleries, Church Fine Arts Complex, 1664 N Virginia St Reno, NV 89557. Tel 775-784-6682; Fax 775-784-6655; Email bakerprindle@unr.edu; Web: www.unr.edu/art; *Dir, Univ Galleries* Paul Baker Prindle
Open Tues & Wed noon - 4 PM, Thurs - Fri noon - 8 PM, Sat 10 AM - 8 PM; No admis fee; Estab 1960; Sheppard Contemporary has 1800 sq ft finished exhib space & additional galleries including student exhib spaces; Scholarships
Special Subjects: Asian Art, Baroque Art, Ceramics, Costumes, Drawings, Etchings & Engravings, Folk Art, Furniture, Glass, Illustration, Landscapes, Latin American Art, Painting-American, Photography, Portraits, Pottery, Prints, Sculpture, Southwestern Art, Textiles, Watercolors, Woodcarvings, Woodcuts
Collections: Local & regional Nevada artists, works on paper from16th century, Valentine's Day Benefit
Exhibitions: Annual Student Exhibition
Publications: Exhibit catalogs
Activities: Lect open to pub, 6-10 vis lectrs per yr; gallery talks; tours; competitions with awards; poetry readings; curators conversations; studio arts; Sheppard Contemporary on the road studio visits across Nevada

SEARCHLIGHT

M **SEARCHLIGHT HISTORIC MUSEUM & MINING PARK,** 300 Michael Wendell Way, Searchlight, NV 89046; PO Box 36, Searchlight Museum Guild Searchlight, NV 89046-0036. Tel 702-297-1642; Web: searchlighthistoricmuseum.org; *Founder* Jane Bunker Overy; *Pres* Jan Roy; *VPres* Deanna Miller; *Secy* Pat Hattersley; *Treas* Val Roxberg
Open Mon - Fri 9 AM - 5 PM, Sat 9 AM - 1 PM, cl Sun & Holidays; available upon notice for pvt tour groups; No admis charge, donations accepted; Estab 1989; Through the use of photos & exhibs, the Searchlight Historic Mus tells the story of early mining days of Searchlight & it's former residents. Names include Clara Bow, Rex Bell, Edith Head, Louis Meyer, John MacReady, Lt William Nellis & U S Senator Harry Reid; Average Annual Attendance: 1000 - 9999; Mem: Dues Lifetime Assessor $5000 & up; Lifetime Recorder $1000 - $4999; Sponsorship $500; Grubstaker $100; Miner $75; Surveyor $50; Prospector $25; Promoter $15; Founder $5
Collections: Gold Mining memorabilia, historic photos & maps, early mining town piano, Clara Bow's clothing trunk & several of her hats as well as some of Rex Bell's clothing, both available on a rotating basis

NEW HAMPSHIRE

CENTER SANDWICH

M **SANDWICH HISTORICAL SOCIETY,** 4 Maple St, Center Sandwich, NH 03227; PO Box 244, Center Sandwich, NH 03227-0244. Tel 603-284-6269; Email sandwhichhistory@gmail.com; Web: sandwichhistorical.org; *Pres* Geoff Burrows; *Mus Shop Mgr* Jennifer Wright; *Admin Asst* Jenny Vierus
Open late June - late Sept Wed - Sat 10 AM - 4 PM, otherwise by appointment only; Admis donations accepted; Estab 1917; Four bldgs, including period house & school house, transportation mus & mus of home occup & trade equipment; Average Annual Attendance: 1,500; Mem: 350
Income: Mems, donations & grants
Library Holdings: Audio Tapes, Book Volumes, CD-ROMs, Cassettes, Fiche, Filmstrips, Manuscripts, Maps, Memorabilia, Original Documents, Other Holdings Sandwich NH History & Family Genealogics, Pamphlets, Periodical Subscriptions, Photographs, Prints, Slides, Video Tapes
Collections: Paintings by Albert Gallatin Hoit (oil & water), Paintings by E Wood Perry (oil), Furniture, Horse-drawn vehicles, Yearly seasonal featured exhibits, Textiles
Exhibitions: (1st Jul, 2017-30th Sep, 2017) Sandwich Center + Lower Corner 100th Anniversary of the Sandwich Historical Society
Publications: Annual Excursion Bulletin; newsletter, 3 per yr
Activities: Excursions, tours; school outreach; jr historian progs; lects open to pub; 1-3 vis lectrs per yr; gallery talks; mus shop sells books, magazines, reproductions, prints, maps & postcards

CONCORD

M **KIMBALL JENKINS ESTATE,** 266 N Main St, Concord, NH 03301-5053. Tel 603-225-3932; Email arts@kimballjenkins.com; Web: www.kimballjenkins.com; *Exec Dir* Rob Fried; *Dir Outreach & Develop* Althea Barton; *Mng Dir* Ryan Linehan; *Business Mgr* Rachel Young; *Events Coordr* Dawn Beauchesne; *Facilities Mgr* Ko Dustin; *Studio Mgr* Matthew Montague
Open Mon - Thurs 10 AM - 4 PM, other times by appointment; Estab to serve as a space for learning and participating in the visual arts; Mem: dues $35-$1,000
Collections: paintings; sculpture; photographs
Exhibitions: Temporary exhibits
Activities: Educ progs; classes for adults & children; interactive progs; Lects open to pub; tours; art programming; workshops; cultural events

M **LEAGUE OF NEW HAMPSHIRE CRAFTSMEN,** Grodin Permanent Collection Museum, 49 S Main St (Suite 100), Concord, NH 03301-5080. Tel 603-224-3375; Fax 603-225-8452; Email nhleague@nhcrafts.org; Web: www.nhcrafts.org; *Dir* Susie Lowe-Stockwell; *Finance Dir* Prudence Gagne; *Opers Mgr* Terri Wiltse
Open Mon - Fri 8:30 AM - 4:30 PM, Sat 10 AM - 4 PM during exhibs; Admis free; Estab 1932 to encourage the economic development & educ of the crafts; gallery displaying exhibits of mems' works; Over 1500 volumes on a variety of fine craft technique & history; Average Annual Attendance: 5,000; Mem: 800 juried mems; must be res of New Hampshire or within 10 miles of Ntl border& make work by hand; Scholarships
Income: Financed by grants, memberships, fundraising
Special Subjects: Bronzes, Calligraphy, Carpets & Rugs, Ceramics, Collages, Crafts, Decorative Arts, Dolls, Embroidery, Enamels, Etchings & Engravings, Folk Art, Furniture, Glass, Gold, Historical Material, Jewelry, Leather, Metalwork, Miniatures, Mosaics
Collections: Permanent coll museum over 300 lots fine craft 1930-present
Exhibitions: Annual Craftsmen's Fair; Living with Crafts; Annual Juried Exhibit
Publications: Newsletter, quarterly
Activities: Classes for adults; exhibs; competitions with awards; lending collection of books; traveling exhibs & various exhibs throughout the yr

L **Kira Fournier Resource Library Center**, 49 S Main St (Suite 100), Concord, NH 03301. Tel 603-224-3375; Fax 603-225-8452; Web: www.nhcrafts.org; *Dir* Susie Lowe-Stockwell
Open to members
Income: Financed by league operating funds
Library Holdings: Book Volumes 1100, Cassettes, Periodical Subscriptions 30
Special Subjects: Art Education, Art History, Bronzes, Calligraphy, Carpets & Rugs, Ceramics, Crafts, Dolls, Embroidery, Enamels, Folk Art, Furniture, Glass, Goldsmithing, Handicrafts, Jewelry, Leather, Metalwork, Mixed Media, Mosaics

A **NEW HAMPSHIRE HISTORICAL SOCIETY,** New Hampshire Historical Society Museum, 30 Park St, Concord, NH 03301-4956. Tel 603-228-6688; Fax 603-224-0463; Email jdesmarais@nhhistory.org; Web: www.nhhistory.org; *Dir Educ & Pub Progs* Elizabeth Dubrulle; *Dir Coll & Exhibs* Wesley Balla; *Colls Mgr* Douglas Copeley
Open Tues - Sat 9:30 AM - 5 PM, Sun Noon - 5 PM; July 1-Oct 15 & Dec also open Mon 9:30 AM - 5:30 PM; Admis adults $7, children under 18, full-time students, active military & their families no charge; Estab 1823 to collect, preserve & make available books, manuscripts & artifacts pertaining to the history of New Hampshire; gallery maintained; Exhib gallery maintained; Average Annual Attendance: 23,189; Mem: 4,000; dues $75-$1,500; ann meeting first Sat in May
Purchases: $20,000
Library Holdings: Auction Catalogs, Book Volumes, Clipping Files, Exhibition Catalogs, Manuscripts, Maps, Memorabilia, Original Art Works, Prints
Special Subjects: Ceramics, Furniture, Photography, Silver, Textiles, Painting-American
Collections: Artifacts made or used in New Hampshire including colls of glass, furniture, metals, paintings, silver & textiles, fine and decorative arts, historical memorabilia
Exhibitions: New Hampshire Through Many Eyes (ongoing exhib)
Publications: Historical New Hampshire, biannual; exhib catalogs; quarterly newsletter
Activities: Classes for adults & children; docent training; lects open to pub; 8 vis lectrs per yr; over 50 pub progs per yr; progs & tours for children; gallery talks; bus tours; 1 book traveling exhib; originates traveling exhibs to mus & libraries, local historical societies; exhibs include: Before Their Times: Child Labor Through the Lens of Lewis Hine & Soldiers, Sailors, Slaves & Ships: The Civil War Photographs of H P Moore; mus shop sells books, magazines, reproductions, prints, gifts & crafts, The White Mountains of New Hampshire

L **New Hampshire Historical Society Library**, 30 Park St, Concord, NH 03301-6384. Tel 603-228-6688; Fax 603-224-0463; Email wballa@nhhistory.org; Web: www.nhhistory.org; *Pres* William H Dunlap; *Library Dir* Sarah Gauigan; *Dir Colls & Exhibs* Wesley Balla; *Reference Librn/Archivist* Malia Ebel
Open Tues - Fri 9:30 AM - 5 PM; Admis non-members, $7 per day; Estab 1823; Discovering New Hampshire & White Mountain Painting Gallery; Average Annual Attendance: 20,000; Mem: 4,500; dues $50, $75
Library Holdings: Auction Catalogs, Audio Tapes, Book Volumes 50,000, Cassettes, Exhibition Catalogs, Manuscripts, Maps, Memorabilia, Motion Pictures, Original Documents, Other Holdings Newspapers, Pamphlets, Periodical Subscriptions 100, Photographs, Records, Reels, Slides, Video Tapes
Special Subjects: Art History, Crafts, Decorative Arts, Historical Material, Landscapes, Manuscripts, Maps, Painting-American, Portraits, Posters, Pottery, Metalwork, Prints, Painting-American
Collections: History & genealogy of New Hampshire & New England, American art, New Hampshire & New England art & decorative arts, Historical New Hampshire, scholarly journal, biannual
Exhibitions: Discovering New Hampshire; White Mountain Painting Gallery
Activities: Classes for adults & children; docent training; lects open to pub; 4 vis lectrs per yr; concerts; tours; book traveling exhibs; originates traveling exhibs; shop sells books, New Hampshire products, gift items

M **SAINT PAUL'S SCHOOL,** Art Center in Hargate, 325 Pleasant St, Concord, NH 03301-2591. Tel 603-229-4643; Fax 603-229-5696; Email ccallahan@sps.edu; Web: www.sps.edu; *Gallery Asst* Mary Gaudette; *Dir Art Center* Colin J Callahan
Open Tues - Sat 9 AM - 4 PM, during school yr; No admis fee; Estab 1967 to house the Art Dept of St Paul's School, to provide a cultural center for the school community as well as central New Hampshire; Secure gallery, 50 X 40 ft; Average Annual Attendance: 5,000
Income: Financed by endowment
Collections: Collection represents varied periods & nationalities, chiefly gifts to the school, drawings, graphics, painting & sculpture
Activities: Lect & classes for students & school community only; gallery receptions & lects open to pub; tours; original objects of art lent to qualifying institutions

L **Ohrstrom Library**, 325 Pleasant St, Concord, NH 03301-2591. Tel 603-229-4862; Fax 603-229-4888; Email brettew@sps.edu; Web: www.sps.edu/library; *Librn* Robert H Rettew
Open Mon - Fri 7:30 AM - 10 PM, Sat 8 AM - 10 PM, Sun 10 AM - 10 PM; Estab 1967 for art reference only; Circ 600
Income: $1000 (financed by endowment)
Purchases: Approx $1000

Library Holdings: Book Volumes 50,000, Exhibition Catalogs, Periodical Subscriptions 150, Reproductions, Slides

CORNISH

M **SAINT-GAUDENS NATIONAL HISTORIC SITE,** 139 Saint-Gauden Rd, Cornish, NH 03745-4232. Tel 603-675-2175; Fax 603-675-2701; Email saga@valley.net; Web: www.sgnhs.org; *Supt & Cur* John H Dryfhout; *Cur* Henry Duffy; *Chief Ranger* Gregory Schwarz
Open May 22- Oct 31 daily 9 AM - 4:30 PM; Admis ages 17+ $6; Estab 1926, transferred to Federal Government (National Park Service) in 1965 to commemorate the home, studios & works of Augustus Saint-Gaudens (1848-1907), one of America's foremost sculptors. The site has historically (1907) furnished rooms, studios & gardens displaying approx half of the work of Augustus Saint-Gaudens; Average Annual Attendance: 40,000; Mem: Friends of Saint-Gaudens Memorial
Income: Financed by federal appropriation (National Park Service)
Purchases: Works by Augustus Saint Gaudens; original furnishings of the Cornish Property
Library Holdings: Auction Catalogs, Book Volumes, CD-ROMs, Cassettes, Clipping Files
Special Subjects: Furniture, Period Rooms, Sculpture
Collections: Historic furnishings & sculpture, plaster, bronze & marble works by Augustus Saint-Gaudens
Publications: Catalogs & books, exhib checklists, postcards, pamphlets, handbooks
Activities: Gallery talks; tours; original objects of art lent to museums; book traveling exhibs; originate traveling exhibs; mus shop sells books & slides

L **Library,** 139 Saint-Gaudens Rd, Cornish, NH 03745-4232. Tel 603-675-2175; Fax 603-675-2701; Web: www.nps.gov/saga; *Supt* Rick Kendall; *Supv Interpretation* Gregory C Schwarz; *Cur & Div Chief* Henry J Duffy; *Mus Technician* Elizabeth Rodriguez
Open by appointment only; Museum open Memorial Day weekend - Oct 31 9:30 AM - 4:30 PM; Admis ages 16+ $7; Estab 1964, National Park; Circ Non-circulating; Sculpture by Augustus Saint-Gaudens; work of Cornish Colony artists; Average Annual Attendance: 40,000
Income: Financed by federal appropriations
Library Holdings: Audio Tapes, Book Volumes 1400, Clipping Files, Exhibition Catalogs, Manuscripts, Memorabilia, Original Art Works, Pamphlets, Photographs, Sculpture, Slides, Video Tapes
Special Subjects: Architecture, Art Education, Art History, Asian Art, Bronzes, Carpets & Rugs, Cartoons, Ceramics, Coins & Medals, Costume Design & Constr, Decorative Arts, Drawings, Furniture, Glass, History of Art & Archaeology, Jewelry, Landscape Architecture, Landscapes, Manuscripts, Maps, Painting-French, Period Rooms, Portraits, Prints, Religious Art, Sculpture, Tapestries, Textiles, Watercolors
Collections: Sculpture of Cornish Colony, Textiles; decorative arts; furnishings relating to Augustus Saint-Gaudens, Prints of Stephen Parrish paintings
Activities: Classes for adults & children; classes in sculpture; lects open to pub; concerts; gallery talks; tours; lend original objects of art to other mus; mus shop sells books, prints & other items

DURHAM

M **UNIVERSITY OF NEW HAMPSHIRE,** Museum of Art, 30 Academic Way, Paul Creative Arts Ctr Durham, NH 03824-2617. Tel 603-862-3712, 3713 (outreach); Fax 603-862-2191; Email museum.of.art@unh.edu; Web: www.unh.edu/moa; *Dir* Kristina Durocher; *Educ & Communs Mgr* Sara Zela; *Admin Asst* Cynthia Farrell; *Exhibs & Colls Mgr* Laura Calhoun
Open Mon - Wed 10 AM - 4 PM, Thurs 10 AM - 8 PM, Sat & Sun 1 - 5 PM, Sept-May only; No admis fee; Estab 1960 renovated 1973, teaching coll for univ faculty & students outreach & pub service functions for the non-univ community; Circ 40,000 students per yr; Upper mezzanine & lower level galleries with a total of 3800 ft of exhib space; 900 ft storage room to house permanent coll & temporary loans; additional storage & office space; Average Annual Attendance: 7,000; Mem: 191
Income: $220,000 (financed by state, mem, sales, interest & private support)
Library Holdings: Original Art Works 1,882
Special Subjects: Drawings, Etchings & Engravings, Landscapes, Painting-American, Photography, Prints
Collections: 19th century American landscapes, 19th century Japanese prints & 20th century works on paper
Exhibitions: Temporary exhibs; The Museum of Art features exhibs ranging from historical to contemporary from Sept through May each yr
Publications: Exhib catalogs
Activities: Educ prog for area schools; workshops; docent training; children's art camp; lect open to pub; 15 vis lectrs per yr; concerts; gallery talks; tours; fellowships; lending of original objects of art to other museums; book traveling exhibs 1-3 per yr; originate traveling exhibs; mus shop sells books, posters, notecards & postcards

L **Dept of the Arts Slide Library,** 30 Academic Way, Paul Creative Arts Ctr Durham, NH 03824-2617. Tel 603-862-1366; Fax 603-862-2191; Web: www.unh.edu; *Slide Librn* Barbara Steinberg
Open daily 8 AM - 4:30 PM; Estab as a teaching coll for the univ; Slides do not circulate off-campus
Library Holdings: Slides 132,000

EXETER

M **PHILLIPS EXETER ACADEMY, FREDERICK R. MAYER ART CENTER,** Lamont Gallery, 11 Tan Lane, Exeter, NH 03833; 20 Main St, Exeter, NH 03833-2460. Tel 603-777-3461; Fax 603-777-4371; Email gallery@exeter.edu; Web: www.exeter.edu/arts/9140.aspx; *Prin* Thomas E Hassan; *Interim Dir* Sara B Zela
Open Mon 1 - 5 PM, Tues - Sat 9 AM - 5 PM; No admis fee; Estab 1953 to provide an Art Center & studios for art instruction dedicated to the memory of Thomas William Lamont II, lost in action in 1945. The Lamont gallery forms an exhib & teaching space which through exhibs & progs seek to create an appreciation to the visual arts & to integrate the arts into the curriculum of Phillips Exeter Academy.; Four bays with moveable walls to alter number & size of bays, sky lit with sol-r-veil screen; Average Annual Attendance: 3500
Exhibitions: Exhibits change every 4-6 weeks
Activities: Classes for Academy students; dramatic progs; lects open to pub, 5 vis lectrs per yr; gallery talks; one book traveling exhibs per yr

HANOVER

M **DARTMOUTH COLLEGE,** Hood Museum of Art, 6 E Wheelock St, Hanover, NH 03755-4008. Tel 603-646-2808, 2900; Fax 603-646-1400; Email hood.museum@dartmouth.edu; Web: www.hoodmuseum.dartmouth.edu; *Senior Cur Colls & Acad Programming* Katherine Hart; *Deputy Dir* Juliette Bianco; *Security & Bldg Mgr* Gary Alafat; *Cur Educ* Lesley Wellman; *Cur American Art* Barbara J MacAdam; *Registrar* Kathleen O'Malley; *Assoc Registrar* Cynthia Gilliland; *Lead Preparator* John Reynolds; *Bus Mgr* Nancy A McLain; *Gift Shop Mgr* Mary Ellen Rigby; *Bus Asst* Stephanie Foornier; *Exec Asst* Tracy Hoanes; *Data Mgr* Deborah Haynes; *Coordr Pub Rels* Alison Sharp; *Head Publishing & Communs* Nils Nadeau; *Exhibitions Designer* Patrick Dunfey; *School & Family Programs Coordr* Neely McNulty; *Preparator* Matthew Zayatz; *Asst Cur Educ* Rebecca Karp; *Tour Coordr* Kate George; *Coordr Acad Prog* Amelia Kohl; *Prog & Exec Coordr* Sharon Reed; *Develop Mem Coordr* Julie Ann Otrs; *Dir* Michael Taylor
Open Tues - Sat 10 AM - 5 PM, Wed 10 AM - 9 PM, Sun Noon - 5 PM, cl Mon; No admis fee; Estab 1772 to serve the Dartmouth community & Upper Valley region; New building, designed by Charles Moore & Chad Floyd of Centerbrook, completed in 1985, houses ten galleries; Average Annual Attendance: 40,000; Mem: 2,015; dues $100 - $5,000; ann meeting in July
Income: Financed through Dartmouth College, endowment income, contributions & grants
Special Subjects: African Art, Afro-American Art, American Indian Art, American Western Art, Anthropology, Antiquities-Assyrian, Antiquities-Egyptian, Antiquities-Etruscan, Antiquities-Greek, Asian Art, Baroque Art, Bronzes, Ceramics, Coins & Medals, Costumes, Decorative Arts, Drawings, Eskimo Art, Etchings & Engravings, Furniture, Glass, Landscapes, Latin American Art, Mexican Art, Mosaics, Painting-American, Painting-Australian, Painting-British, Painting-Dutch, Painting-European, Painting-Flemish, Painting-French, Painting-Italian, Pewter, Photography, Portraits, Posters, Pre-Columbian Art, Prints, Religious Art, Renaissance Art, Sculpture, Silver, Tapestries, Watercolors, Woodcuts
Collections: 65,000 fine art objects, Native American, African, Asian & Pre-Columbian art, Oceanic Collection
Exhibitions: Approx fifteen temporary exhibs per yr on a wide range of subjects. Exhibs include those organized by the mus, traveling exhibs & exhibs drawn from permanent colls
Publications: Hood Quarterly; exhib catalogues; ann gen brochure; gallery brochures; ann report; school programs brochure; teacher manuals; family guide brochures, A Space for Dialogue
Activities: Classes for adults & children; family days; docent training; dramatic progs; teacher training; teacher workshops; Dartmouth student workshops & panels; classes for Dartmouth students & for medical students; lects open to pub, 24 vis lectrs per yr (mix of vis & faculty); symposia; films; concerts; gallery talks; tours; awards: Volunteer of the Yr (Natl arts/humanities month), Friendship Fund Award (teacher who demonstrated exemplary use of visual arts in curriculum); schols; fels; individual paintings & original objects of art lent to other museums & campus depts; book traveling exhibs 1-2 per yr; originate traveling exhibs for mus in US & Internationally; mus shop sells books, cards, posters, original art, reproductions & jewelry

L **Sherman Art Library,** Hinman Box 6025, Carpenter Hall Hanover, NH 03755-4008. Tel 603-646-2305; Fax 603-646-1218; Email sherman.library.reference@dartmouth.edu; Web: www.dartmouth.edu/~library/sherman; *Librn* Barbara E Reed
Open Mon - Thurs 8 AM - midnight, Fri 8 AM - 6 PM, Sat 9 AM - 6 PM, Sun 1 PM - midnight, during school terms (reduced hours in summer & during intersessions); Estab 1928
Library Holdings: Book Volumes 110,000, CD-ROMs, Exhibition Catalogs, Fiche 100,000, Other Holdings Videodiscs, Pamphlets, Periodical Subscriptions 530, Reels 111
Special Subjects: Architecture, Photography

M **Hopkins Center for the Arts,** 2 E Wheelock St, Hanover, NH 03755. Tel 603-646-2422

HOOKSETT

M **SOUTHERN NEW HAMPSHIRE UNIVERSITY,** McIninch Art Gallery, 2500 N River Rd, Robert Frost Hall Hooksett, NH 03106. Tel 603-629-4622; Email m.gallery@snhu.edu; Web: www.snhu.edu; *Gallery Dir* Debbie Disston
Open Mon - Sat 10 AM - 3 PM, Thurs 5 PM - 8 PM. cl Sun; No admis fee
Exhibitions: Temporary exhibits

HOPKINTON

M **NEW HAMPSHIRE ANTIQUARIAN SOCIETY,** Hopkinton Historical Society, 300 Main St, Long Memorial Bldg Hopkinton, NH 03229-2627. Tel 603-746-3825; Email nhas@tds.net; Web: www.hopkintonhistory.org; *Exec Dir* Heather Mitchell
Open Thurs & Fri 9AM - 4PM, Sat 9AM-1PM; No admis fee; Estab 1859 to preserve local & state historical genealogical records & colls & to provide the community with cultural & historical progs of local significance; Gallery houses artifacts pertaining to local history; maintains a reference library; Average Annual Attendance: 2,000; Mem: 425; dues $25 - $500; ann meeting in Jan

Library Holdings: Audio Tapes, CD-ROMs, Cassettes, Clipping Files, Compact Disks, Lantern Slides, Manuscripts, Maps, Memorabilia, Original Art Works, Original Documents, Other Holdings, Pamphlets, Photographs, Prints, Records
Special Subjects: Archaeology, Architecture, Ceramics, Coins & Medals, Costumes, Crafts, Decorative Arts, Dolls, Drawings, Embroidery, Etchings & Engravings, Folk Art, Furniture, Glass, Historical Material, Landscapes, Manuscripts, Maps, Military Art, Painting-American, Photography, Portraits, Posters, Restorations, Pottery, Silver, Textiles, Watercolors
Collections: Early American furniture, clothing, china, portraits, local historical material
Exhibitions: Annual history exhibit; annual art show featuring works of regional artists; rotate 2 per yr
Activities: Educ prog; classes for adults & children; pub progs; lect open to pub, 6 vis lectrs per yr; concerts; gallery talks; tours; competitions; individual paintings & original objects of art lent; mus shop sells books, artisan wares, gifts, cards, magnets & T-shirts

KEENE

M **HISTORICAL SOCIETY OF CHESHIRE COUNTY,** 246 Main St, Keene, NH 03431-4143; PO Box 803, Keene, NH 03431-0803. Tel 603-352-1895; Fax 603-352-9226; Email hscc@hsccnh.org; Web: www.hsccnh.org; *Exec Dir* Alan Rumrill, MLS; *Educ Dir* Jennifer Carroll; *Admin Asst* Katharine Schillemat; *Develop Coordr* Andrea Cheeney; *Develop Dir* Richard Swanson
Open Tues, Thurs - Fri 9 AM - 4 PM, Wed 9 AM - 9 PM, Sat 9 AM - Noon (1st & 3rd Sat only); No admis fee; Estab 1927 to collect, preserve & share history of southwest New Hampshire; Average Annual Attendance: 12,000; Mem: 900; dues $25- $200; ann meeting fourth Mon in Apr
Income: $295,000 (dues, donations, grants, fees for programs)
Purchases: $1,000
Library Holdings: Audio Tapes, Book Volumes, CD-ROMs, Cassettes, Compact Disks, DVDs, Manuscripts, Maps, Memorabilia, Original Documents, Pamphlets, Periodical Subscriptions, Photographs, Prints, Reproductions, Slides, Video Tapes
Special Subjects: Archaeology, Architecture, Ceramics, Coins & Medals, Flasks & Bottles, Furniture, Glass, Historical Material, Landscapes, Manuscripts, Maps, Painting-American, Period Rooms, Pewter, Photography, Portraits, Pottery, Sculpture, Silver, Textiles, Watercolors, Art History
Collections: Archival colls, books, furniture, glass, maps, photos, pottery, silver, toys, paintings
Publications: Newsletter, 5 times a yr.
Activities: Classes for adults & children; docent training; lects open to pub, 6 vis lectrs per yr; concerts; gallery talks; tours; book traveling exhibs 1-2 per yr; mus shop sells books, reproductions, original art, colonial toys; DVDs & local artisans crafts

M **KEENE STATE COLLEGE,** Thorne-Sagendorph Art Gallery, Wyman Way, Keene, NH 03435-3501; 229 Main St, Keene, NH 03435. Tel 603-358-2720; Fax 603-358-2238; Email thorne@keene.edu; Web: www.keene.edu/tsag; *Dir* Brian Wallace; *Admin Asst* Colleen Johnson
Open Sept - May Sun - Wed Noon - 5 PM, Thurs & Fri noon - 7 PM, Sat Noon - 8 PM, June - July Wed, Thurs, Sat, Sun Noon - 5 PM, Fri 3 PM - 8 PM; No admis fee; Estab 1965 to provide a year-round calendar of continuing exhibs; to sponsor related progs of artistic & educ interest & to maintain small permanent coll displayed on campus; Two adjacent galleries occupy space in new facility opened in 1993 on campus; Average Annual Attendance: 9,000
Income: Financed by endowment, state appropriation & college budget
Special Subjects: Painting-American, Prints, African Art
Collections: Paintings & Prints of Historical Interest included: Pierre Alechinsky, Milton Avery, Chuck Close, Robert Mapplethorpe, Paul Pollero, Gregorio Prestopino, George Rickey, Sidney Twardowicz, Artists of National Prominence including Jules Olitski, Paintings by Dublin Art Colony Artists, Dublin Art Colony
Publications: Small catalogs or brochures to accompany exhibits
Activities: Classes for children; docent training; lects open to pub, 1-2 vis lectrs per yr; gallery talks; competitions & awards; originates book traveling exhibs; originates traveling exhibs regionally

MANCHESTER

M **THE CURRIER MUSEUM OF ART,** 150 Ash St, Manchester, NH 03104-4380. Tel 603-669-6144; Fax 603-669-7194; Email visitor@currier.org; Web: www.currier.org; *Dir & CEO* Alan Chong; *Graphic Design & Social Media Specialist* Vanessa De Zorzi; *Librn & Archivist* Meghan Petersen; *Dir Colls & Exhibs* Andrew Spahr; *Asst Cur* Samantha Cataldo; *Dir Finance* Sherry McNeil; *Registrar* Karen Papineau; *Guest Experience & Retail Mgr* Heidi Norton; *Chief Preparator & Exhib Design* Jeff Allen; *Cur* Dr K Sundstrom; *Dir Art Educ* Bruce McColl
Open Sun - Mon & Wed - Fri 11 AM - 5 PM, 1st Thurs of each month until 9 PM, Sat 10 AM - 5 PM, cl Tues; Admis adults $15, seniors $13, students $10, youth (13-17), mem & children under 13 free; Estab & incorporated 1915 by will of Mrs Hannah M & Governor Moody Currier, which included endowment, building opened in 1929; Circ Non-circulating; Building contains nine galleries, library & auditorium, two pavilions. Currier Art Center offers after-school & Sat classes for adults & children; Average Annual Attendance: 60,000; Mem: 3800; dues $50 & up
Income: Financed by endowment
Library Holdings: Auction Catalogs, Book Volumes 15,000, CD-ROMs, Clipping Files, Exhibition Catalogs, Lantern Slides, Manuscripts, Pamphlets, Periodical Subscriptions, Photographs, Records, Slides, Video Tapes
Special Subjects: African Art, American Indian Art, American Western Art, Architecture, Asian Art, Baroque Art, Bookplates & Bindings, Ceramics, Drawings, Embroidery, Enamels, Etchings & Engravings, Folk Art, Glass, Historical Material, Landscapes, Manuscripts, Medieval Art, Oriental Art, Painting-American, Painting-British, Painting-Dutch, Painting-Flemish, Painting-French, Painting-German, Painting-Italian, Painting-Russian, Painting-Spanish, Pewter, Photography, Porcelain, Portraits, Prints, Renaissance Art, Silver, Tapestries, Textiles, Watercolors, Woodcarvings, Sculpture
Collections: American Furniture, glass & textiles 18th - 20th century, American Paintings & Sculpture 18th century to present, European Paintings, prints & sculpture, 13th - 20th century, European Masters 13th - 20th century, Fine American Decorative Art 17th - 19th century including furniture, glass textiles & silver, Frank Lloyd Wright designed residence, Zimmerman House, opened seasonally for tours
Publications: Bulletin, semiannually; calendar, quarterly; exhib catalogs, occasionally; Ann Report
Activities: Classes for adults & children; docent training; lect open to pub, 10 vis lectrs per yr; concerts; gallery talks; tours; school progs & outreach presentations for 4th & 5th graders; individual paintings & original objects of art lent to art institutions worldwide; lending coll contains original art works, original prints, paintings, photographs & sculpture; book traveling exhibs 2 per yr; originate traveling exhibs to art museums; mus shop sells books, jewelry, prints & reproductions

L **Library,** 201 Myrtle Way, Manchester, NH 03104. Tel 603-669-6144 x 127; Web: www.currier.org; *Librn* Michele Turner
Open Wed - Fri 1 - 4:30 PM
Library Holdings: Auction Catalogs, Book Volumes 15,000, Clipping Files, Exhibition Catalogs, Periodical Subscriptions 26
Special Subjects: Architecture, Decorative Arts, Folk Art, Photography
Collections: Frank Lloyd Wright, general photography coll

M **FRANCO-AMERICAN CENTRE,** 100 St Anselm Dr, Manchester, NH 03102-1308. Tel 603-641-7114; Fax 603-669-0644; Email info@facnh.com; Web: www.facnh.com
Open by appointment only; Estab 1990 to promote French history, culture & education; Mem: dues $10-$100
Collections: French heritage & culture; paintings; photographs; personal artifacts; period furnishings; sculpture
Exhibitions: Temporary exhibits
Activities: Classes for adults & children

L **MANCHESTER CITY LIBRARY,** 405 Pine St, Manchester, NH 03104-6199. Tel 603-624-6550, ext 334; Fax 603-624-6559; Web: www.manchester.lib.nh.us; *Lib Dir* Denise Van Zanten; *Branch Mgr* Sarah Basbas; *Head of Info Svcs* Lichen Rancourt; *Deputy Dir* Dee Santoso
Open Mon, Tues & Thurs 8:30 AM - 8:30 PM, Wed, Fri & Sat 8:30 AM - 5:30 PM
Income: Financed by city appropriations, endowment & fines
Purchases: $8,000
Library Holdings: Book Volumes 15,373, Cassettes, Compact Disks 3,197, Framed Reproductions 104, Records, Video Tapes
Exhibitions: Patron's art works, crafts, collectibles

A **MANCHESTER HISTORIC ASSOCIATION,** Millyard Museum, 255 Commercial St, Manchester, NH 03101; 129 Amherst St, Manchester, NH 03101-1809. Tel 603-622-7531; Email history@manchesterhistoric.org; Web: www.manchesterhistoric.org; *Exec Dir* Aurore Eaton; *Mus Educator* Jennifer Yakunovich; *Asst Exec Dir* Jeffrey Barraclough
Open Tues - Sat 10 AM - 4 PM, cl national & state holidays; Admis adults $8, students & seniors $6, children $4, under 12 free; Estab 1896 to collect, preserve & make known Manchester's historical heritage; Permanent exhibit on Manchester history; 12,000 sq ft changing exhibit gallery; Average Annual Attendance: 10,000; Mem: 700; dues $30, individual & up
Library Holdings: Book Volumes, Clipping Files, Fiche, Manuscripts, Maps, Memorabilia, Micro Print, Original Documents, Periodical Subscriptions, Photographs, Video Tapes
Special Subjects: Historical Material
Collections: Amoskeag Manufacturing Company records, artifacts, books, documents, maps & photographs on Manchester History, paintings, sculpture, decorative arts relating to Manchester
Exhibitions: Permanent & changing exhibs reflecting all aspects of Manchester history; 2 -3 changing exhibits per yr
Publications: Annual report; newsletter, calendar of events, books, videos
Activities: Educ prog; classes for adults & children; walking tours; family progs; lects open to pub; concerts; gallery talks; tours; pub & school progs linked to permanent & changing exhibits; outreach progs, research library; ann Historic Preservation awards prog; mus shop sells books, original art, reproductions, gift items

L **Library,** 129 Amherst St, Manchester, NH 03101. Tel 603-622-7531; Email library@manchesterhistoric.org; Web: www.manchesterhistoric.org; *Exec Dir* Aurore Eaton; *Asst Exec Dir* Jeffrey Barraclough; *Mus Educator* Jennifer Yakunovich
Open Sat 10 AM - 4 PM & by appointment; Admis adults $8, students & seniors $6, 6 - 18 yrs $4; Estab as research library open to pub
Library Holdings: Book Volumes 5000, Cassettes, Clipping Files, Manuscripts, Memorabilia, Other Holdings Maps 500, Pamphlets, Periodical Subscriptions 14, Photographs 20,000, Prints, Reproductions
Collections: Amoskeag Manufacturing Company Archives, art, architecture, cloth samples, decorative arts, documents, early textile mill records, manuscripts, 19th century music, photos, publications of local history

M **NEW HAMPSHIRE INSTITUTE OF ART,** (Manchester Institute of Arts & Sciences Gallery), 148 Concord St, Manchester, NH 03104-4858. Tel 603-623-0313; Fax 603-641-1832; Web: www.nhia.edu; *VPres Acad Affairs* Karen Burgess Smith; *Acad Affairs Asst* Christine Fales; *Dir Communs* Linda Seabury; *VPres Operations* Sandra Barry; *Interim Pres* Daniel Lyman; *VPres Finance* Erik Gross
Open Mon - Sat 9:30 AM - 5 PM; No admis fee; Estab 1898, as a pvt nonprofit educational institution in order to promote, encourage & stimulate educ in the arts & sciences; Gallery has limited space which is devoted to a variety of exhibs including historical as well as contemporary themes; Mem: 670; dues family $35, individual $25; ann meeting in June
Income: Financed by endowment, mem, tui & grants
Publications: Exhib catalogs; schedule of courses, exhibs & progs, 2 - 3 times per yr

Activities: Classes for adults & children; competitions with prizes; schols & fels offered; sales shop sells handcrafted items, books & art supplies

M **SAINT ANSELM COLLEGE,** Alva de Mars Megan Chapel Art Center, 100 Saint Anselm Dr #1718, Saint Anselm College Manchester, NH 03102-1308. Tel 603-641-7470; Fax 603-641-7116; Email chapelartcenter@anselm.edu; Web: www.anselm.edu/chapelart; *Dir* Iain MacLellan, OSB; *Asst Cur* Margaret Dimock
Open Tues - Sat 10 AM - 4 PM, Thurs until 7 PM (during exhibs); No admis fee; Estab 1967; Large gallery, formerly college chapel with painted, barrel-vaulted ceiling, stained glass windows; Average Annual Attendance: 5,000
Income: Financed through col
Special Subjects: Antiquities-Egyptian, Architecture, Carpets & Rugs, Ceramics, Collages, Crafts, Decorative Arts, Drawings, Etchings & Engravings, Furniture, Historical Material, Jewelry, Landscapes, Painting-American, Painting-American, Painting-German, Photography, Portraits, Prints, Prints, Sculpture, Religious Art, Stained Glass, Watercolors, Woodcuts
Collections: New England artists & craftsmen, Prints, Paintings, Sculpture
Publications: Exhib catalogues, occasional
Activities: Lect open to pub; 2-4 vis lectrs per yr; gallery talks; concerts; individual paintings lent to faculty & staff of Saint Anselm College; lending coll contains paintings; book traveling exhibs 1-2 per yr

M **SEE SCIENCE CENTER,** 200 Bedford St, Manchester, NH 03101-1132. Tel 603-669-0400; Fax 603-669-0400; Email info@see-sciencecenter.org; Web: www.see-sciencecenter.org; *Dir* Douglas Heuser; *Educ & Mem* Rebecca Mayhew; *Opers & Design* Adele Maurier; *Develop Coord* Peter Gustafson
Open Mon-Fri 10AM-4PM, Sat & Sun 10AM-5PM; Admis $5, mems & children under 1 no admis fee; Estab 1986; A hands-on science ctr estab to promote the understanding & excitement of science for all ages. Pvt nonprofit org; FT paid 4, PT paid 6, PT vols 20; 1st congressional district; Average Annual Attendance: 50,000 - 99,999; Mem: dues Family $60
Publications: SEE News, quarterly newsletter
Activities: Guided tours; traveling exhibs

MERIDEN

M **AIDRON DUCKWORTH ART PRESERVATION TRUST,** Aidron Duckworth Art Museum, 21 Bean Rd, Meriden, NH 03770; PO Box 61, Meriden, NH 03770-0061. Tel 603-469-3444; Email info@aidronduckworthmuseum.org; Web: www.aidronduckworthmuseum.org; *Trustee & Dir* Grace Harde; *Contact Admin* Mary Jane Morse
Open Fri - Sun 10 AM - 5 PM; other times by appointment; No admis fee; donations accepted; Estab May 2002 to preserve & present works by the late Aidron Duckworth; Former school bldg; modern galleries built in 2002; Average Annual Attendance: 1,000
Income: Rental studio income & donations; grants
Library Holdings: Book Volumes
Special Subjects: Painting-American
Collections: Artwork by Aidron Duckworth
Exhibitions: Exhibs of works by regional artists in guest gallery & on grounds
Publications: Aidron Duckworth-Paintings & Drawings (2007)
Activities: Classes for adults; lects open to pub; 1 vis lectr per yr; gallery talks; tours

PETERBOROUGH

M **SHARON ARTS CENTER,** Sharon Arts Center Exhibition Gallery, 30 Grove St, Peterborough, NH 03458-1453. Tel 603-924-7676; Fax 603-924-6795; Email sharonarts@sharonarts.org; Web: www.sharonarts.org; *School Dir* Deb DeCicco; *Exec Dir* Elizabeth Smith; *CEO, Pres* Beth Rank-Beauchamp; *Dir Communs* Lajla LeBlanc; *Asst Gallery Mgr* Laurie Rebac; *Admin Asst* Barbara Nay; *Asst Gallery Mgr* Susan Schaefer; *Financial Admin* Diane Hayden
Open Summer Mon-Thurs 10AM-6PM, Fri & Sat 10AM-8PM, Sun noon-5PM, Winter Mon-Thurs 11AM-6PM, Fri 11AM-7PM, Sat 10AM-6PM, Sun noon-5PM; No admis fee; Estab 1947 to promote the educ, sales & enjoyment of the arts; Center consists of three galleries, store & classroom facility; maintains lending library to mems only; Average Annual Attendance: 32,000; Mem: 1100; dues family $50, individual $35; ann meeting in Sept
Income: Financed by endowment, mem & state appropriation, tuition & sales
Library Holdings: Book Volumes, Exhibition Catalogs
Collections: Bird carvings of Virginia & Robert Warfield, Nora S Unwin Collection of Wood Engravings, Drawings, Watercolors
Exhibitions: Annual members exhib of paintings, drawings & sculpture; 16 exhibits per yr featuring fine artists & craftsmen throughout New England
Publications: Exhibit catalogs
Activities: Classes for adults & children; lect open to pub, 3 vis lectrs per yr; concerts; gallery talks; tours; schols offered; exten dept serves area elementary schools; individual paintings & original objects of art lent to area pvt schools, banks, Town Hall, resorts; lending coll contains 20 original prints, 50 paintings, & assorted crafts (weaving & pottery); originate traveling exhibs; sales shop sells original art, reproductions & fine crafts

PLYMOUTH

M **PLYMOUTH STATE UNIVERSITY,** Karl Drerup Art Gallery, Main St, Fl 1 Draper & Maynard Bldg MSC 21B Plymouth, NH 03264; 17 High St, D & M Bldg, MSC 21 B Plymouth, NH 03264-1595. Tel 603-535-2614; Fax 603-535-2938; Web: www.plymouth.edu/gallery; *Dir* Catherine Amidon; *Asst* Greg Finley
Open Mon -Sat 10AM-4PM, Wed until 8PM; Estab 1871 to serve the acad and personal needs of the col's students & faculty; Maintains exhib space of 1960 sq ft; Average Annual Attendance: 6,000
Income: 40,000
Purchases: $250,000
Library Holdings: Pamphlets
Activities: Lect open to pub; library tours; bibliographic instruction; gallery talks

PORTSMOUTH

A **THE NATIONAL SOCIETY OF THE COLONIAL DAMES OF AMERICA IN THE STATE OF NEW HAMPSHIRE,** Moffatt-Ladd House & Garden, 154 Market St, Portsmouth, NH 03801-3730. Tel 603-436-8221, 430-7968; Fax 603-431-9063; Email moffattladd@gmail.com; Web: www.moffattladd.org; *Dir & Cur* Barbara McLean Ward, Ph.D.; *Progs Coordr* Jennifer Belmont-Earl; *Special Events Coordr* Marsha Gmyrek; *Mus Properties Chmn* Meredith Harding; *Mus Properties VChmn* Cheryl Cullimore
Open June - Oct; Mon - Sat 11 AM - 5 PM, Sun 1 - 5 PM; Admis adults $8, children $2.50; Soc estab 1892, mus estab 1912; Moffatt-Ladd House was completed in 1763; Average Annual Attendance: 6,000; Mem: 140; annual meeting in June; NSCDA-NH mem based on lineage; Friends of Moffatt-Ladd House open to all
Income: $150,000 variable (financed by memberships, rents, donations, grants & investments)
Library Holdings: Manuscripts, Memorabilia, Original Art Works, Original Documents, Photographs, Prints, Slides, Video Tapes
Special Subjects: Architecture, Carpets & Rugs, Ceramics, Costumes, Decorative Arts, Dolls, Embroidery, Furniture, Glass, Historical Material, Jewelry, Leather, Manuscripts, Maps, Marine Painting, Painting-American, Period Rooms, Pewter, Porcelain, Portraits, Pottery, Prints, Sculpture, Silver, Textiles
Collections: Original china & porcelain, furniture, documents, letters & papers, portraits, wallpaper & documented wallpaper, prints, floor cloths (all documented to house), textiles, costumes
Publications: The Moffatt-Ladd House: From Mansion to Museum, The Garden Book of Alexander H Ladd
Activities: Educ progs; school tours; lects open to members only, 4 vis lectrs per year; guided tours open to the public; competitions with awards; concerts; gallery talks; tours; scholarships offered; individual paintings lent to Currier Gallery of Art; mus shop sells books, prints & historic related items

M **NEW HAMPSHIRE ART ASSOCIATION,** 136 State St, Portsmouth, NH 03801-3826. Tel 603-431-4230; Fax 603-431-4230; Email nhartassociation@comcast.net; Web: nhartassociation.org; *Exec Dir* Billie Tooley
Open Wed-Sat 10AM-5PM, Sun noon-4PM; No admis fee; Estab 1940, statewide art assn; Mem: Mem: 425; dues $80; juried mem
Collections: paintings; photographs; sculpture; drawings; graphic arts
Exhibitions: Monthly exhibs with special exhibs; 3-4 juried (open) offsite around state exhibs per yr
Activities: Workshops, lect, demos open to pub; gallery talks

A **NEW HAMPSHIRE ART ASSOCIATION, INC,** 136 State St, Portsmouth, NH 03802. Tel 603-431-4230; Email nhartassociation@gmail.com; Web: www.nhartassociation.org; *Exhibs Mgr* Danielle Antico
Open Tues - Thurs 11 AM - 5 PM, Fri - Sat 11 AM - 8 PM, Sun Noon - 5 PM; Estab 1940, incorporated 1962, as a nonprofit organization, to promote the public's understanding & appreciation of the arts; to provide artists with a forum for their work & ideas. Offers a year-round exhib & sales gallery at its headquarters in Boscawen & Portsmith; an Aug exhib at Sunapee State Park; Mem: 400; dues $60; ann meeting in June
Income: Financed by grants, dues, patrons, rental art & sales
Exhibitions: Annuals at Currier Gallery of Art; Summer Annual combined with New Hampshire League of Arts & Crafts at Mount Sunapee State Park; Summer Annual Juried Exhibition at Prescott Park; Year-Round exhibits at N E Center; Durham NH; various one-person & group shows
Activities: Educ prog for schools; patron prog; lect demonstrations by mem artists; awards; originate traveling exhibs

M **PORTSMOUTH ATHENAEUM,** Joseph Copley Research Library, Peter Randall Gallery, 9 Market Sq, Portsmouth, NH 03801. Tel 603-431-2538; Fax 603-431-7180; Email info@portsmouthathenaeum.org; Web: www.portsmouthathenaeum.org; *Pres* Karen Bouffard; *Treas* William Purinton; *Keeper* Tom Hardiman; *Librn* Robin Silva; *Research Librn* Carolyn Marvin; *Archivist* Susan Kindstedt
Open Tues & Thurs 1 PM - 4 PM, Sat 10 AM - 4 PM and by special appt; No admis fee; Estab 1817 to house mus of historical objects of local, statewide & national interest & is listed on National Register of Historical Sites; Maintains local history research library; Average Annual Attendance: 8,500; Mem: 375; dues $175; annual meeting 2nd Wed in Jan
Income: Financed by endowment & mem
Special Subjects: Painting-American, Architecture, Furniture, Historical Material, Manuscripts, Marine Painting
Collections: American paintings, Colonial & later portraits, ship models & half-models, New England history, maritime history
Exhibitions: Rotating exhibits 3 - 4 times per year
Activities: Lect; gallery talks; concerts; tours

M **PORTSMOUTH HISTORICAL SOCIETY,** John Paul Jones House & Discover Portsmouth, 43 Middle & State St, Portsmouth, NH 03802-0728; PO Box 728, Portsmouth, NH 03801-0728. Tel 603-436-8433; Email info@portsmouthhistory.org; Web: www.portsmouthhistory.org; *Pres* Edward Mallon; *VPres* Martha Fuller Clark; *Secy* Tom McCarron; *Treas* Tim Driscoll; *Exec Dir* Kathleen Soldati; *Cur & Colls* Gerry Ward
Open John Paul Jones House: Memorial Day - Columbus Day, daily 11 AM - 5 PM, Veteran's Day; Discover Porstmouth March - Dec daily 9:30 AM - 5 PM; Admis John Paul Jones House: adults $6, AAA, seniors, retired military & Portsmouth residents $5, children 12 & under free; Estab 1920 to identify & retain local history. The House was built in 1758 by Gregory Purcell, a merchant sea-captain. Purchased & restored in 1920 by the Portsmouth Historical Society; Free changing exhibits; Average Annual Attendance: 15,000; Mem: 450; dues $15; ann meeting Apr
Income: Financed by mem, investment & admis fees

Special Subjects: Afro-American Art, Ceramics, Costumes, Decorative Arts, Embroidery, Furniture, Glass, Historical Material, Maps, Painting-American, Period Rooms, Marine Painting, Military Art
Collections: Guns, books, china, costumes, documents, furniture, glass, portraits and silver pertaining to the early history of Portsmouth
Activities: Lect, 3-4 vis lectrs per year; daily tours; original objects of art lent to other museums; lending coll contains looking glass & furniture; mus shop sells books, prints, slides, cards & jewelry

M **PORTSMOUTH MUSEUM OF FINE ART,** 909 Islington St, Portsmouth, NH 03801. Tel 603-436-0332
Open Mon - Fri 11 AM - 5 PM, Sat - Sun Noon - 6 PM, other times by appt
Collections: paintings; photographs; sculpture

M **WARNER HOUSE ASSOCIATION,** MacPheadris-Warner House, 150 Daniel St, Portsmouth, NH 03801-3831; PO Box 895, Portsmouth, NH 03264-0895. Tel 603-436-5909; Email info@warnerhouse.org; Web: www.warnerhouse.org; *Chair* Carol Seely; *Dir* Jeffrey Hopper
Open June - Oct Wed - Mon 11 AM - 4 PM, cl Tues; Admis adults $8, seniors $4, children 7-12 $4, children under 7 free; Estab 1931; Period rooms from 1717-1930; Average Annual Attendance: 1500; Mem: 200; dues $25 and up; annual meeting in Nov; Scholarships
Income: $50,000 (financed by endowment, mem, admis, grants & fundraising)
Special Subjects: Architecture, Ceramics, Decorative Arts, Furniture, Portraits, Historical Material, Painting-American, Period Rooms, Portraits, Pottery
Collections: Joseph Blackburn Collection: portraits, Portsmouth Furniture, Stair murals (1720), complete set of English Copperplate bed hangings made in America (1780-85), Family Memorabilia
Exhibitions: Joseph Blackburn: Portraits (1761); Archaeological Exhibits
Activities: Lect open to pub, 1-2 vis lectrs per yr; gallery talks; tours; original objects of art lent to museums & other historic houses; Mus shop sells books

WATERVILLE VALLEY

M **THE MARGARET & H A REY CENTER AND CURIOUS GEORGE COTTAGE,** 35 Village Rd (Bldg C), Waterville Valley, NH 03215; PO Box 286, Waterville Valley, NH 03215-0286. Tel 603-236-3308; Email info@thereycenter.org; Web: www.thereycenter.org/welcome.html
Open July - Sept 5: Wed - Sat 10 AM - 5 PM, Sept 6 - June: Sat 10 AM - 5 PM; No admis fee, donations accepted
Activities: Educ progs

NEW JERSEY

ATLANTIC CITY

M **ATLANTIC CITY ARTS COMMISSION,** Garden Pier Art Gallery, New Jersey Ave & Boardwalk, Atlantic City, NJ 08401; PO Box 7536, Atlantic City, NJ 08401. Tel 609-347-5837; Fax 609-347-5844; Email atlanticcityarts@gmail.com; Web: acartcommission.wordpress.com; *Cur & Art Project Mgr* Donna Marie Shea
Open Mon - Sat 10 AM - 5 PM, cl national holidays; No admis fee
Activities: Educ progs

L **PRINCETON ANTIQUES BOOKSERVICE,** Art Marketing Reference Library, 2915-17 Atlantic Ave, Atlantic City, NJ 08401. Tel 609-344-1943; Fax 609-344-1944; Email princetn@earthlink.net; Web: www.princetonantiques.com; *Pres* Robert E Ruffolo Jr; *Secy* Robert A Ruffolo
Open Mon-Fri 8:30AM-5PM, Sat 9AM-2PM; No admis fee; Estab 1974 for pricing documentation of books and antiques; Gallery open by appointment only; maintains art gallery; Average Annual Attendance: 1,000
Library Holdings: Book Volumes 250,000, Framed Reproductions, Maps, Memorabilia, Other Holdings Exhibition catalogs; Original art works & prints, Periodical Subscriptions 20, Photographs, Prints
Special Subjects: Architecture, Art History, Bookplates & Bindings, Carpets & Rugs, Folk Art, Furniture, Glass, Historical Material, Lettering, Marine Painting, Painting-American, Photography, Pottery, Prints, Watercolors, Woodcarvings
Collections: 19th century art, Atlantic City collection of postcards, photographs & memorabilia, 1900-1960: 12,000 postcards, 90,000 photographs
Activities: Mus shop sells books, original art, reproductions, prints & Atlantic City photographs & memorabilia; Sales shop sells books & original art

BAYONNE

L **BAYONNE FREE PUBLIC LIBRARY,** Cultural Center, 697 Ave C, Bayonne, NJ 07002. Tel 201-858-6971; Fax 201-437-6928; Email library@bayonnelibrary.org; Web: www.bayonnelibrary.org; *Library Dir* Sneh Bains
Open Mon - Thurs 9 AM - 9 PM, Fri - Sat 9 AM - 5PM; Estab 1894; Art Gallery has 194 running ft exhib space
Income: Financed by city appropriation & state aid
Library Holdings: Book Volumes 222,000, Clipping Files, Filmstrips, Periodical Subscriptions 517, Slides 736
Activities: Adult & children film progs weekly; concerts

BELMAR

M **OCEANSIDE GALLERY,** 1010 Main St, Belmar, NJ 07719-2726. Tel 732-280-2167; Fax 732-280-2167; Email gallery@oceansidegallery.com; Web: www.oceansidegallery.com
Open Tues & Sat 10 AM - 5 PM, Wed 10 AM - 8:30 PM, Thurs 10 AM - 6 PM, Fri 10 AM - 8 PM

BERKELEY HEIGHTS

L **BERKELEY HEIGHTS FREE PUBLIC LIBRARY,** 290 Plainfield Ave, Berkeley Heights, NJ 07922-1494. Tel 908-464-9333; Fax 908-464-7098; Email reference@bhplnj.org; Web: library.bhpl.nj.org; *Dir* Stephanie Bakos; *Dept. Head* Laura Fuhro
Open Mon - Thurs 9 AM - 9 PM, Fri & Sat 9 AM - 5 PM, Sun 2 - 5 PM, Summer Mon-Tues & Thurs 9AM-9PM, Wed & Fri 9AM-5PM, Sat 9AM-1PM; Estab 1953
Income: $570,000 (financed by city appropriation)
Library Holdings: Audio Tapes, Book Volumes 71,890, Cassettes, Clipping Files, Fiche, Pamphlets, Periodical Subscriptions 32, Reels, Slides, Video Tapes
Special Subjects: Afro-American Art, American Indian Art, Architecture, Art History, Asian Art, Crafts, Decorative Arts, Folk Art, Glass, Landscape Architecture, Painting-American, Painting-British, Painting-European, Painting-Japanese, Photography
Collections: Art & art history prints

BLOOMFIELD

M **HISTORICAL SOCIETY OF BLOOMFIELD,** 90 Broad St, Bloomfield, NJ 07003-2585. Tel 973-743-8844; Fax 201-429-0170; Email info@hsob.org; Web: www.firstbaptistbloomfield.org/hist-society.htm; *Pres* Jean Kuras; *VPres* Joseph Barry Jr; *Treas* Emma-Lou Czarnecki; *Cur* Dorothy Johnson
Open Wed 2 PM - 4:30 PM, Sept-June Sat 10 AM - 12:30 PM, also by appointment; No admis fee; Estab 1966 to collect, preserve & exhibit items which may help to establish or illustrate the history of the area; Mus located in the gallery of the Bloomfield Pub Library; Average Annual Attendance: 1,436; Mem: 115; dues, commercial organization $25, nonprofit organization $10, couple $10, individual $7, student under 18 $3; meeting Sept, Nov, May - 4th Mon of the month
Income: Financed by mem, Ways & Means Comt & bequests
Special Subjects: Ceramics, Costumes, Dioramas, Furniture, Glass
Collections: Miscellaneous items of books, clothing & accessories, deeds & other documents, dioramas, early maps & newspapers, furniture, household articles, letters, memorabilia, paintings, postcards, posters, tools, toys
Exhibitions: Revolving Charles Warren Eaton (items donated by people of Bloomfield and/or heirs)
Activities: Lect open to pub, 3 vis lectrs per yr; tours; sales shop sells books, prints, postcards, mugs, notepaper, medallions

BORDENTOWN

M **THE ARTFUL DEPOSIT, INC,** The Artful Deposit Gallery, 142 Farnsworth Ave, Bordentown, NJ 08505-1345. Tel 609-298-6970; Email artfuldeposit@gmail.com; Web: www.artfuldeposit.com; *Owner* C J Mugavero
Open Wed - Thurs & Sat 1 PM - 6 PM, Fri 4 PM - 9 PM, Sun 1 PM - 5 PM, Mon & Tues by appointment; No admis fee; Estab in 1986 for display & sale of original fine art; Representation in gallery stable for approx 20 artists with local, national & international acclaim. Primary location in Bordentown, NJ. Tel: 609-298-6970
Collections: Representative of original works by Alan Fetterman (1936-2008), Joseph Dawley (Impressionist), Hanneke de Neve (Expressionist), Ken McIndoe (Naturalist), Gennady Spirin (Illustrator), Michael Budden (plein air and studio oil painter), Richard McKinley (Pastel Society of America), Eleinne Basa (plein air award winner); Sarah J. Webber (AZ & WY), AJ Wainright, PSA/ Barbara Jaenicke, PSA, Mike Beeman, PSA
Exhibitions: Louis Russomanno, Cynthia Dawley
Activities: Educ prog; artist run workshops; gallery talks; lect open to pub; sponsor competitions

BRANCHBURG

A **PRINTMAKING CENTER OF NEW JERSEY,** 440 River Rd, Branchburg, NJ 08876-3565. Tel 908-725-2110; Fax 908-725-2484; Email studio@printnj.org; Web: www.printnj.org; *Interim Director* Patricia Franchino
Open Tue - Fri 10 AM - 4 PM, Sat 1 - 4 PM, cl Sun; No admis fee; Estab 1973 to promote & educate the fine art of printmaking, photography & papermaking; Average Annual Attendance: 50,000; Mem: 189; dues $35 & up; ann meeting in January
Income: Financed by mem & individual, foundation & corporate gifts including NJ State Council on the Arts & Somerset County Parks Commission
Exhibitions: 4 exhibs per yr; national juried exhibits
Activities: Classes for adults & children; lect open to pub; competitions with awards; NJSCA Citations of Excellence; Roving Press (traveling print mentoring prog for pub schools), free demos; Organize traveling exhibitions to libraries in the area; sales shop sells original art

BURLINGTON

A **BURLINGTON COUNTY HISTORICAL SOCIETY,** 457 High St, Burlington, NJ 08016-4514. Tel 609-386-4773; Fax 609-386-4828; Email burlcohistsoc@verizon.net; Web: www.burlingtoncountyhistoricalsociety.org; *Pres* Gus Mosca; *VPres* Bernadette Boyle; *Exec Dir* Lisa Fox-Pfeiffer; *Educ Dir* Jeffrey Macechak
Open Tues-Sat 1PM-5PM; Admis $3 for library & mus gallery, $3 guided tour of 3 period houses, $5 combination; Estab 1915 to preserve & interpret Burlington County history; Average Annual Attendance: 5,000; Mem: 1,000; dues $15 & up; ann meeting fourth Thurs in May
Income: Financed by endowment & donations
Special Subjects: Decorative Arts
Collections: Clocks, Decorative Arts, Delaware River Decoys, Quilts, Samplers

Exhibitions: Ingenuity & Craftsmanship
Publications: Quarterly newsletter
Activities: Tours for children; docent training; lect open to pub, several vis lectrs per yr; tours; mus shop sells books, magazines & reproductions

CALDWELL

M **CALDWELL COLLEGE,** The Visceglia Art Gallery, 120 Bloomfield Ave, Caldwell, NJ 07006-5310. Tel 973-618-3457; Web: www.caldwell.edu; *Dir* Kendall Baker
Open Mon - Sat 10 AM - 4 PM; No admis fee; Estab 1970 to provide students & area community with exposure to professional contemporary talent, to afford opportunities for qualified artists to have one-person shows; Scholarships
Income: Financed by col budget
Exhibitions: 3-4 exhibits per yr; Alumni Show
Activities: Educ dept in connection with the col art dept; lect open to pub, 3 vis lectrs per yr; lending coll contains 12,000 Kodachromes, motion pictures

CAMDEN

M **RUTGERS UNIVERSITY,** Stedman Art Gallery, 326 Penn St, Camden, NJ 08102-1410. Tel 856-225-6245, 225-6350; Fax 609-225-6597; Email arts@camdenrutgers.edu; Web: seca.camden.rutgers.edu; Others TTY 609-225-6648; *Dir & Cur* Virginia Oberlin Steel; *Assoc Dir Educ* Noreen Scott Garrity
Open Sept - April Mon - Sat 10 AM - 5 PM, Summer Mon - Fri 10 AM - 5 PM; No admis fee; Estab 1975 to serve educ needs of the campus & to serve community of southern New Jersey; Average Annual Attendance: 14,000
Income: Financed by endowment, state appropriation & gifts from pvt sources
Special Subjects: Etchings & Engravings, Painting-American, Photography, Prints, Sculpture, Watercolors
Collections: Modern & contemporary art, works on paper
Exhibitions: Changing exhibs of visual arts & interdisciplinary exhibs
Publications: Catalog for a major exhibition, yearly
Activities: Vis lectr; symposia, concerts & gallery talks open to pub

CLINTON

A **HUNTERDON ART MUSEUM,** 7 Lower Center St, Clinton, NJ 08809-1303. Tel 908-735-8415; Fax 908-735-8416; Email info@hunterdonmuseumofart.org; Web: www.hunterdonartmuseum.org; *Bd Pres* Elizabeth Matto; *Exec Dir* Marjorie Frankel Nathanson; *Dir Educ* Jennifer Brazel
Open Tues - Sun 11 AM - 5 PM; Admis by requested donation; Estab 1952 as a nonprofit organization to provide arts enrichment through fine & performing arts; The first, second & third fls provide gallery space. The old stone mill has been remodeled retaining the original atmosphere with open broad wooden beams, white walls & plank flooring; Average Annual Attendance: 22,000; Mem: 600; dues patron $500, sponsor $250, contributor $100, family $50, individual $35, senior $25; ann meeting in April; Scholarships
Income: Financed by mem, city, state & county appropriations, donations, tuitions
Purchases: $100
Special Subjects: Prints
Collections: Print collection
Exhibitions: National Print Exhibition
Activities: Classes for adults & children; lect open to pub, 3 vis lectrs per yr; gallery talks; competitions with cash awards; ann juried mems show; works from print coll lent to nearby corporations; lending coll contains 200 original prints; originate traveling exhibs to Newark Museum and corp mem; sales shop sells books, original art, reproductions & crafts

M **REDMILL MUSEUM VILLAGE,** (Hunterdon Historical Museum), 56 Main St, Clinton, NJ 08809-1328. Tel 908-735-4101; Fax 908-735-0914; Email admin@theredmill.org; Web: www.theredmill.org; *Cur Collections* Elizabeth Cole; *Exec Dir* The Hon Paul Muir
Open April - Sept 22 & Nov 7 - Dec Tues - Fri 10 AM - 4 PM, Sat - Sun noon - 6 PM, call for additional hours, Cl Mon, New Year's Eve & Day, Easter, Independence Day, Thanksgiving, Christmas Eve & Day; Admis adults $10, seniors $8, children 6-12 $6, members & children under 6 free; Estab 1960 for the preservation & display of artifacts from the 18th & 19th century & early 20th century for educational & cultural purposes; Four-floor grist mill, blacksmith shop, gen store, schoolhouse, log cabin, herb garden & quarry buildings; Average Annual Attendance: 26,000; Mem: 400; dues $25 - $2500; ann meeting in May
Income: $150,000 (financed by mem & donations)
Special Subjects: Historical Material
Collections: Artifacts pertaining to 18th, 19th & early 20th centuries
Exhibitions: Variety of special events
Activities: Classes for children; docent training; re-enactments; lect; concerts; tours; sales shop sells books & gift items

CLOSTER

M **BELSKIE MUSEUM,** 280 High St, Closter, NJ 07624. Tel 201-768-0286; Fax 201-768-4220; Email contact@belskiemuseum.com; Web: www.belskiemuseum.com; *Pres* Kurt Haiman; *VPres* Tsun Tam
Open Sat & Sun 1 - 5 PM, special hours by appt; No admis fee, donations accepted; Founded 1993 by the Closter Lions Club; The goal of the mus is to preserve & display the work of Abram Belskie & to promote his reputation as a major sculpture, medallic artist & medical instructor of the 20th century; mus also displays works of other local & internat artists with new exhibits monthly. Nonprofit org; Average Annual Attendance: 3,000; Mem: 300; Mem Patron $100 (ann); Supporting $25 (ann)
Special Subjects: Art History, Metalwork, Painting-American, Painting-European, Sculpture, Photography, Pottery
Collections: Drawings, sculpture, medical models, medallic molds & completed medallic pieces created by Abram Belskie (1907-1988), Numerous donated original paintings
Exhibitions: Rotating exhibs of international artists & artists within the tri-state area in all mediums; ann exhibition & sale of paintings from students & teachers from the Art Students League, NY & Vytlacil School of Art; art exhibs by students from Northern Valley Regional High School, Demarest, NJ
Activities: Artist receptions; tours; mus shop sells note cards

CRANFORD

M **CRANFORD HISTORICAL SOCIETY,** The Hanson House, 38 Springfield Ave, Cranford, NJ 07016. Tel 908-276-0489; Email cranfordhistoricalsociety@verizon.net; Web: www.bobdevlin.com/crhis.html
Open Sept - June Sun; No admis fee, donations accepted; Founded 1927 and dedicated to the perpetuation of Cranford's history. Nonprofit org
Special Subjects: Costumes, Photography, Historical Material, Textiles, Restorations
Collections: Crane-Phillips Living Museum, a Victorian cottage built in 1845 that served as honeymoon house for Josiah Crane Jr, great-grandson of the original miller. House depicts life in Cranford in the latter part of the 19th Century, photographs, scrapbooks, glass negatives, books, letters, Indian artifacts, costumes & textiles
Publications: Cranford Home Journal; Image of America: Cranford, by Robert Fridlington & Lawrence Fuhro
Activities: Walking tours; research assistance; educ tours; school & scout progs; Autumn Harvest Festival; Christmas Open House; Victorian Garden Tour; ongoing restoration of the Crane-Phillips House

DENVILLE

A **BLACKWELL STREET CENTER FOR THE ARTS,** PO Box 808, Denville, NJ 07834-0808. Tel 201-337-2143; Fax 201-337-2143; Email eprovost17@earthlink.net; Web: www.blackwell-st-artists.org
Open - varies according to exhibit; No admis fee; Estab 1983; professional gallery for NJ & NY artists to exhibit variety of art work; Initiated in 1998 as a cyber gallery; Average Annual Attendance: 2,100; Mem: 11 artists; qualifications for mem; artists mems juried by credentials commission; dues $50 once a yr; monthly meeting
Income: $2,200 (financed by mem, grants & donations)
Collections: Member artists' works in many pvt colls
Exhibitions: Six or more exhibs scheduled per yr at different sites; Morris County High School Student Art Show with awards
Activities: Educ dept; lect open to pub; gallery talks; competitions & awards; yearly high school juried exhibit with awards

EAST BRUNSWICK

QUIETUDE GARDEN GALLERY, 24 Fern Rd, East Brunswick, NJ 08816-3213. Tel 732-257-4340; Web: www.sculpture.org; *Dir* Sheila Thau; *Dir* Ed Thau
Open Wed - Thurs & Sat - Sun 11 AM - 5 PM; 4 acres of wooded property
Special Subjects: Sculpture
Collections: Contemporary sculpture by international artists
Exhibitions: Temporary exhibits
Activities: Tours

ELIZABETH

L **FREE PUBLIC LIBRARY OF ELIZABETH,** 11 S Broad St, Elizabeth, NJ 07202-3486. Tel 908-354-6060; Fax 908-354-5845; Email elizpublib@gmail.com; Web: www.elizpl.org; *Dir* Mary Faith Chmiel; *Asst Dir* Andy Luck
Open Mon - Thurs 9 AM - 9 PM, Fri 10 AM - 7 PM, Sat 9 AM - 5 PM, cl Sun; No admis fee; Special exhibit area displays paintings & miscellaneous objects d'art; Average Annual Attendance: 450,000
Income: Financed by city and state appropriation
Library Holdings: DVDs 8,300
Collections: Japanese prints by various artists (in storage)
Exhibitions: Works by artists & photographers; other special exhibs from time to time
Activities: Classes for adults; writing group; fall concert series, mems library consortium; lects open to pub, 15 vis lectrs per yr; concerts; awards, Multicultural Heritage award from NJ state library; material available to patrons of Middlesex & Union Counties

ENGLEWOOD

L **ENGLEWOOD LIBRARY,** Fine Arts Dept, 31 Engle St, Englewood, NJ 07631-2903. Tel 201-568-2215; Fax 201-568-6895; Email englref@bccls.org; Web: www.englewoodlibrary.org; *Dir Library* Mary Witherell
Open Mon - Thurs 9 AM - 9 PM, Fri & Sat 9 AM - 5 PM, Sun 1 - 5 PM (Oct- May); No admis fee; Estab 1901 to estab a free pub library for citizens
Income: $510,000 (financed by endowment, city & state appropriation)
Library Holdings: Cassettes, Clipping Files, Filmstrips, Framed Reproductions, Motion Pictures, Original Art Works, Pamphlets, Records, Reels, Slides
Exhibitions: Members of Salute to Women In the Arts; Quilts; Rare Books & Manuscripts; World of Renaissance; rotating exhibits
Activities: Lect open to pub; concerts

EWING

M **COLLEGE OF NEW JERSEY,** Art Gallery, 2000 Pennington Rd, Ewing, NJ 08618-1104; PO Box 7718, Holman Hall CN 4700 Trenton, NJ 08628-0718. Tel 609-771-2615, 771-2633, 771-2198; Email tcag@tcnj.edu; Web: www.tcnj.edu/~tcag/; *Art Dir* Margaret Pezalla-Granlund; *Student Gallery Coordr* Tracy Lee
Open Tues - Thurs noon - 7 PM, Sun 1 - 3 PM; No admis fee; Estab to present students & community with the opportunity to study a wide range of artistic expressions & to exhibit their work; Average Annual Attendance: 2,500
Income: Financed by art dept budget & grants including NJ State Council on the Arts, Mercer County Cultural & Heritage Commission
Special Subjects: Drawings, Prints
Collections: Purchases from National Print & Drawing Show
Exhibitions: Craft Show; Faculty Show; Mercer County Competitive Art; Mercer County Competitive Photography; National Drawing Exhib; National Print Exhib; Selections from the State Mus; Sculpture Shows; Student Show; Contemporary Issues; African Arts
Publications: Catalog for African Arts; Catalog for Contemporary Issues; Catalog for National Drawing Exhibition; Catalog for National Print Exhibition
Activities: Classes for adults & children; lect open to pub, 5 vis lectrs per yr; gallery talks; tours; competitions with awards; individual paintings & original objects of art lent to other offices & depts on campus; lending coll contains original art works; original prints; paintings; originates traveling exhibs to other state cols & art schools

FRANKLIN LAKES

M **THE GALLERY AT THE PRESBYTERIAN CHURCH AT FRANKLIN LAKES,** 730 Old Franklin Lake Rd, The Presbyterian Church at Franklin Lakes Franklin Lakes, NJ 07417-2200. Tel 201-891-0511; Fax 201-891-0517; Email pcflmgr@yahoo.com; Web: pcfl.org
Call for hours; No admis fee
Income: artist donations
Collections: Paintings; photographs; sculpture

GLASSBORO

M **HERITAGE GLASS MUSEUM,** 25 East High St, Glassboro, NJ 08028. Tel 856-881-7468; Email comments@boroughofglassboro.org; Web: www.fieldtrip.com
Open June - Aug Sat 11 AM - 2 PM, 4th Sun each month 1 - 4 PM, Sept - May Wed noon - 3 PM, Sat 11 AM - 2 PM, 4th Sun 1 - 4 PM, call before visiting; No admis fee, donations accepted; Estab 1979; Historical mus with the purpose to preserve & perpetuate the heritage of the glass industries of the region. Mus situated in the former Whitney Brothers Glass Works land; Average Annual Attendance: 1,200; Mem: 150; $25
Library Holdings: Book Volumes, Clipping Files, Maps, Original Documents, Photographs, Slides
Special Subjects: Coins & Medals, Costumes, Flasks & Bottles, Glass, Historical Material, Manuscripts, Maps
Collections: Display of bottles & jars from the Whitney Glass Company, Glass from other Gloucester County glass factories
Publications: Glassboro Briefs, newsletter
Activities: Educ & historic talks; volunteer progs; docent training; tours; originates traveling exhibs; sales shop sells books, glass articles, postcards, note paper, paperweights

HACKENSACK

M **FAIRLEIGH DICKINSON UNIVERSITY,** Edward Williams Gallery, 150 Kotte Pl, Hackensack, NJ 07601-6112. Tel 201-692-2449; Fax 201-692-2503; Email geraghty@fdu.edu; *Dir* Diana Soorikian
Open Mon-Fri 8:30AM-2:30PM, Sat 9:30AM-2:30PM
Collections: works by contemporary artists

HAMILTON

M **GROUNDS FOR SCULPTURE,** 80 Sculptors Way, Hamilton, NJ 08619-3447. Tel 609-586-0616; Fax 609-586-0968; Email info@groundsforsculpture.org; Web: www.groundsforsculpture.org; *Exec Dir* Gary Garrido Schneider; *Mgr Membership* Claire Cossaboon; *Chief Cur & Artistic Dir* Tom Moran
Open Tues - Sun 10 AM - 6 PM, cl Mon, Thanksgiving; Admis adults $10, students 13 and over & seniors $8, children 6-12 $6, members and children under 6 free; Estab 1992 to promote greater understanding & appreciation for contemporary sculpture; Two 10,000 sq ft mus buildings with interior gallery spaces sited in a 22-acre landscaped sculpture park; Average Annual Attendance: 50,000
Income: Financed by pub charitable foundation
Special Subjects: Sculpture
Collections: Includes contemporary sculpture
Exhibitions: 3 yearly; spring, summer & fall/winter
Publications: Exhibition catalogues
Activities: Docent progs, yr round activities include art, poetry, music & dance; lect open to pub, 10 vis lectrs per yr, concerts; sales shop sells books, magazines, posters, postcards& children's art kits; full service restaurant

M **INTERNATIONAL SCULPTURE CENTER,** 19 Fairgrounds Rd Ste B, Hamilton, NJ 08619-3450. Tel 609-689-1051; Fax 609-689-1061; Email ics@sculpture.org; Web: www.sculpture.org; *Chmn Bd* Joshua S Kanter; *Exec Dir* Johannah Hutchison
Open Mon - Fri 9 AM - 5 PM; No admis fee; Estab 1960, dedicated to expand the base of understanding & support of contemporary sculpture through its progs & services. The ISC serves the needs & interests of sculptors, educators, arts supporters & the gen pub; Mem: 8,000; dues $95
Income: Financed by mem dues, pvt donations & grants
Publications: A Sculpture Reader: Contemporary Sculpture Since 1980
Activities: Conferences & lectrs; lifetime achievement award; patron award; outstanding student in contemporary sculpture award; educator award

HOPEWELL

M **HOPEWELL MUSEUM,** 28 E Broad St, Hopewell, NJ 08525-1828. Tel 609-466-0103; *Pres* David Mackey
Open Mon, Wed & Sat 2 - 5 PM, cl national holidays; groups by appointment only; No admis fee, donations suggested; Estab 1922 as a mus of local history from early 1700 to the present day; Research on Mon & Wed only; Average Annual Attendance: 2,000
Income: Financed by endowment, mem & donations
Special Subjects: Period Rooms
Collections: Antique china, glass, silver & pewter, colonial furniture, colonial parlor, early needlework, Indian handicrafts, photograph coll, Victorian parlor
Publications: Hopewell Valley Heritage; Pioneers of Old Hopewell; maps

JERSEY CITY

M **CURIOUS MATTER,** 272 5th St, Jersey City, NJ 07302-2304. Tel 201-659-5771; Email gallery@curiousmatter.org; Web: www.curiousmatter.org; *Dir* Arthur Bruso; *Dir* Raymond E Mingst
Open during exhibitions Sun 12 PM - 3 PM, & by appointment; No admis fee; Exhibs & publs; Contemporary art
Purchases: Ryan Browning, Suzanne Norris
Collections: works by regional & national artists
Activities: Gallery talks; tours

C **FORBES MAGAZINE, INC,** Forbes Collection, 499 Washington Blvd Fl9, Jersey City, NJ 07310-2055. Tel 212-206-5549; Email mkellytrombly@forbes.com; *Dir* Margaret Kelly Trombly
Open Tues - Sat 10 AM - 4 PM, Thurs group tours; No admis fee; Estab 1985
Collections: Antique Toys, Faberge Imperial Eggs Collection, French Military Paintings, Presidential Papers, Toy Soldiers
Activities: Gallery talks; individual paintings & original objects of art lent to museums & galleries

M **MANA CONTEMPORARY,** 888 Newark Ave, Jersey City, NJ 07306. Tel 201-604-2702; Email hello@manacontemporary.com; Web: manacontemporary.com; *Chmn* Moishe Mana; *Artistic Dir* Eugene Lemay; *Curatorial Dir* Ysabel Pinyol; *Creative Dir* Nerissa Cooney
Open Mon - Fri tours 3 PM, Sat & Sun tours 1, 3, & 5 PM; No admis fee; Estab 2011 to unite artist studios, exhibition spaces and art services such as art storage, transportation & management in a single location allowing for the exchange of ideas, experimentation, collaboration and inspiration; Integrated hive structure housed in a former tobacco warehouse encompassing an area of more than 2 million sq ft
Collections: Contemporary art
Exhibitions: Rotating exhibits
Activities: Educ progs; classes for adults; lects open to pub; gallery talks; gallery tours; programming, residencies; ancillary art servs

M **NEW JERSEY CITY UNIVERSITY,** Courtney Art Gallery & Lemmerman Gallery, 2039 John F Kennedy Blvd, Dept of Art Grossnickel Hall, 1st Flr Jersey City, NJ 07305-1596. Tel 201-200-3214; Fax 201-200-3224; Email hbastidas@njcu.edu; *Dir* Midori Yoshimoto
Open Mon - Fri 11 AM - 5 PM, or by appointment; No admis fee; Estab 1969 to bring examples of professional work to the campus in each of the areas in which students are involved: Painting, sculpture, film, photog, textiles, weaving, ceramics, graphic design; Gallery is operated by students & with the Jersey City Mus for a student internship training prog; Average Annual Attendance: 3,000
Income: Financed by city, state appropriation & Art Department
Collections: Small coll of prints & paintings
Exhibitions: Robert Blackburn, Robert Indiana, Jose Morales
Activities: Lect open to pub, 5 vis lectrs per yr; concerts; gallery talks; tours; exten dept serving community organizations; individual paintings & original objects of art lent; lending collection contains color reproductions, film strips, Kodachromes, motion pictures, photographs; originates traveling exhibs

M **Lemmerman Art Gallery**, 2039 John F Kennedy Blvd, Hepburn Hall, 3rd Flr Jersey City, NJ 07305-1596. Tel 201-200-3214; Fax 201-200-3224; Email hbastidas@njcu.edu; *Dir* Midori Yoshimoto
Open Mon - Fri 11 AM - 5PM, or by appointment; Estab 1961 to bridge community (col) to Art of all levels; Gothic structure; Average Annual Attendance: 3,000
Income: Financed by art department, state, city
Activities: Educ dept; lect open to pub; gallery talks; tours; individual paintings lent to galleries & other institutions that have pub access; lending coll contains 31 original art works

M **SAINT PETER'S COLLEGE,** Art Gallery, 2641 Kennedy Blvd, Jersey City, NJ 07306. Tel 201-761-6480; Email fineartsgallery@saintpeters.edu; *Dir* Oscar Magnan
Open Mon, Tues, Fri & Sat 11 AM - 4 PM, Wed & Thurs 11 AM - 9 PM; No admis fee; Estab 1971 to present the different art trends; Gallery is maintained with good space, lighting and alarm systems; Average Annual Attendance: 2,000
Income: Financed by the col
Special Subjects: Anthropology, Antiquities-Byzantine, Antiquities-Egyptian, Antiquities-Greek, Antiquities-Oriental, Antiquities-Persian, Antiquities-Roman, Archaeology, Architecture, Art Education, Art History, Asian Art, Bronzes, Ceramics, Coins & Medals, Collages, Collages, Decorative Arts, Dolls, Drawings, Embroidery, Enamels, Flasks & Bottles, Folk Art, Furniture, Glass, Graphics, History of Art & Archaeology, Interior Design, Jewelry, Landscape Architecture,

Landscapes, Latin American Art, Manuscripts, Metalwork, Metalwork, Mexican Art, Miniatures, Mosaics, Oriental Art, Painting-American, Painting-Australian, Painting-British, Painting-Canadian, Painting-Dutch, Painting-European, Painting-Flemish, Painting-French, Painting-German, Painting-Israeli, Painting-Italian, Painting-Japanese, Painting-New Zealand, Painting-Polish, Painting-Russian, Painting-Scandinavian, Painting-Spanish, Photography, Porcelain, Portraits, Posters, Pre-Columbian Art, Primitive art, Prints, Religious Art, Reproductions, Restorations, Sculpture, Stained Glass, Textiles, African Art, Afro-American Art, American Indian Art, American Western Art, Anthropology, Antiquities-Assyrian, Antiquities-Etruscan, Baroque Art, Bookplates & Bindings, Bronzes, Calligraphy, Carpets & Rugs
Activities: Classes for adults; docent training; lects open to pub, 20 vis lectrs per yr; concerts; gallery talks; tours; extension dept serving students

LAKEWOOD

M **GEORGIAN COURT UNIVERSITY,** (Georgian Court College) M Christina Geis Gallery, 900 Lakewood Ave, Lakewood, NJ 08701-2697. Tel 732-987-2388; Fax 732-987-2010; Email ksettles@georgian.edu; *Dir* Kathleen Settles
Open Mon - Thurs 9 AM - 8 PM, Fri 9 AM - 5 PM; No admis fee; Estab 1964 to offer art students the opportunity to view the works of professional artists & also to exhibit student work; Gallery is one large room with 100 running ft of wall area for flat work; the center area for sculpture; Average Annual Attendance: 1,000
Income: Financed through the col
Special Subjects: Architecture, Calligraphy, Ceramics, Drawings, Photography, Sculpture
Collections: Advertising Design, Art History, Commercial Art, Drafting, Fashion Arts, Graphic Design, Illustration, Lettering, Painting, Printmaking, Teacher Training, Textile Design, Weaving
Exhibitions: Monthly exhibs
Activities: Schols offered

LAWRENCEVILLE

M **RIDER UNIVERSITY,** Art Gallery, 2083 Lawrenceville Rd, Lawrenceville, NJ 08648-3009; PO Box 6400, Lawrenceville, NJ 08648. Tel 609-895-5588; Fax 609-896-5232; Email hnaar@rider.edu; Web: www.rider.edu/artgallery; *Prof Art & Dir* Harry I Naar
Open Tues - Thurs 11 AM - 7 PM, Sun noon - 4 PM (subject to change); No admis fee; Estab 1970 to afford mems of the community & univ the opportunity to expand their knowledge & exposure to art; Gallery has 1,513 sq ft of space divided into two rooms of different height. Collections displayed throughout campus; main collections displayed in Moore Library; Average Annual Attendance: 5,000
Income: $8,000 (univ funded)
Library Holdings: Exhibition Catalogs, Reproductions
Special Subjects: Drawings, Painting-American, Prints, Sculpture, Textiles, Watercolors
Collections: African Art, statues & masks, contemporary art, drawings, paintings, prints, sculpture
Publications: Exhibit catalogs
Activities: Classes for adults; dramatic progs; docent training; internships; gallery management class; lect open to pub, 4 vis lectrs per yr; concerts; gallery talks; tours; individual paintings & original objects of art lent to museums, group shows, one-person shows, major exhibs; book traveling exhibs; exhib catalogues are available for sale

LAYTON

L **PETERS VALLEY SCHOOL OF CRAFT,** 19 Kuhn Rd, Layton, NJ 07851-2004. Tel 973-948-5200, 973-948-5202; Fax 973-948-0011; Email info@petersvalley.org; Web: www.petersvalley.org; *Exec Dir* Kristin Muller; *Gallery Dir* Brienne Rosner; *Educ Dir* Jennifer Apgar; *Devel Dir* Lindsay Gates
Call for hours; Estab 1970 as a nonprofit craft educ center to promote & encourage traditional & contemporary crafts through exhibs, demonstrations, workshops & educational programs; Over 300 artists work exhibited in store, gallery has changing exhibs; Average Annual Attendance: 10,000; Mem: 500; dues $50; ann meeting in Oct
Income: Financed in part by a grant from NJ State Council on the Arts/Department of State, the Geraldine R Dodge Foundation & mems, friends, corporations & local companies
Library Holdings: Book Volumes 500, Exhibition Catalogs, Original Art Works, Pamphlets, Photographs, Slides
Special Subjects: Ceramics, Crafts, Decorative Arts, Handicrafts, Metalwork, Photography, Silversmithing, Textiles, Woodcarvings
Collections: Teaching coll of craft works, art & photographs
Exhibitions: Theme Shows & changing Exhibs
Publications: Summer Workshop Catalog, ann
Activities: Educ dept; classes for adults and children; lect open to pub; gallery talks; tours; schols & residencies; exten dept serves North Jersey; sales shop sells original art

LINCROFT

M **MONMOUTH MUSEUM & CULTURAL CENTER,** PO Box 359, Lincroft, NJ 07738-0359. Tel 732-747-2266; Fax 732-747-8592; Email monmuseum@netlabs.net; Web: www.monmouthmuseum.org; *Chmn* Daniel J Fenski III; *VChmn* Michael Rubin; *VChmn* Marianne Ficarra; *Exec Dir* Avis Henderson
Open Tues - Sat 10 AM - 5 PM, Sun noon - 5 PM; Admis $8, free to Museum mems, children under 2, & Brookdale Community College staff & students; Estab 1963 to advance interest in art, science, nature & cultural history; Mus houses one large gallery, the Becker Children's Wing, & The Wonder Wing for children age 6 & under. Exhibs are changed eight times per yr; also an educ area & a conference area; Average Annual Attendance: 50,000; Mem: 1600; dues family $60, individual $30, seniors $20; ann meeting in Jan
Income: Financed by mem, donations, county funds & benefits
Exhibitions: Annual Monmouth County Arts Council Juried Exhibition; Biannual NJ Watercolor Society Exhibition; All Aboard at the Monmouth Museum
Publications: Calendar of events; catalogues of exhibitions; newsletter
Activities: Classes for adults & children; docent training; lects open to pub; originate traveling trunks for use in schools; mus shop sells books & gift items

LONG BRANCH

L **CITY OF LONG BRANCH,** Long Branch Free Public Library, 328 Broadway, Long Branch, NJ 07740-6938. Tel 732-222-3900; Fax 732-222-3799; Email jbirckheadlbpl@gmail.com; Web: www.longbranchlib.org; *Dir* Tonya Garcia; *Adult Servs Dept Head* Janet Birckhead; *Mktg & Outreach Mgr* Lisa Kelly; *Elberon Branch Head & Children's Dept Head* Linda Wurzel; *Librn* Kate Angelo; *Technical Servs* Thalia Sweet
Open Main Library: Mon - Thurs 10 AM - 8 PM, Fri & Sat 10 AM - 5 PM; Elberon Branch: Tues & Thurs - Fri 9 AM - 5 PM, Wed noon - 8 PM, Sat 9 AM - 1 PM; 66 ft for hanging art, two small flat display cases
Income: $1,602,000
Library Holdings: Audio Tapes 1357, Book Volumes 79528, Motion Pictures 9720, Periodical Subscriptions 100, Photographs, Records 3336, Reels 488
Collections: David H Lilian Alterman Collection, Elwood L Baxter Collection, Dangler Collection, James F Durnell Collection, Daniel J Hennessey Historic Photograph Collection of Long Branch, New Jersey at the Long Branch Free Public Library, Long Branch Free Public Library Archives, Long Branch Library Newspaper Collection, George H Moss Jr Collection, Elsalyn Palmisano Collection for the Local History Room, Robert F Van Benthuysen Monmouth County & New Jersey History Collection, materials on Presidents Grant & Garfield, scrapbook collection, newspaper articles, images and materials of the Long Branch & North Jersey Shore area, local maps
Exhibitions: Eclecticism by Michael Garvey; Anniversary of the Death of President James Garfield

M **LONG BRANCH HISTORICAL ASSOCIATION CHURCH OF THE PRESIDENTS MUSEUM,** 1260 Ocean Ave, Long Branch, NJ 07740-4550; 328 Broadway, Long Branch, NJ 07740. Tel 732-223-0905; Email lbhma1879@gmail.com; Web: www.churchofthepresidents.org; *Pres* Jim Foley
Open by appointment only; No admis fee; Estab 1953 as post Civil War historical mus; Average Annual Attendance: 10,000; Mem: Dues $1
Special Subjects: Historical Material
Collections: Period furniture

LOVELADIES

M **LONG BEACH ISLAND FOUNDATION OF THE ARTS & SCIENCES,** 120 Long Beach Blvd, Loveladies, NJ 08008-6131. Tel 609-494-1241; Fax 609-494-0662; Email office@lbifoundation.org; Web: www.lbifoundation.org; *Exec Dir* Jennifer Begonia
Open Mon - Fri 9 AM - 4 PM, Sat 9 AM - 3 PM, Sun 9 - 11 AM; No admis fee; Estab 1948 to promote understanding of and participation in the arts; Average Annual Attendance: 18,000; Mem: 700 families; dues $165 per yr; all persons welcome; mem provides discounts on classes & purchases
Collections: Works by local & national artists
Exhibitions: Monthly exhibs in various media by local, regional, national, and internationally known artists
Activities: classes for adults & children; Special events; performances; lectrs; workshops; youth progs; films; lects open to pub; concerts; gallery talks; sales shop sells original art & prints

MADISON

M **DREW UNIVERSITY,** Elizabeth P Korn Gallery, 36 Madison Ave, Madison, NJ 07940-1493. Tel 973-408-3758; Fax 973-408-3098; Email korngallery@drew.edu; Web: www.drew.edu/korngallery; *Dean* Chris Taylor
Open Tues - Fri 12:30 - 4 PM & by appointment, selected weekends; No admis fee; Estab 1968 to provide exhibs each school year to augment prog of courses & to serve the community
Income: Financed by Univ instructional budget
Collections: Ancient Near-East archaeological coll, Colonial America, Contemporary abstraction, Native American artifacts, 19th century acad, Oriental art
Activities: Lect open to pub, 3-4 vis lectrs per yr; gallery talks

L **Art Dept Library**, 36 Madison Ave, Madison, NJ 07940-1434. Tel 973-408-3000; Fax 973-408-3770; Email hryan@drew.edu; *Admin Asst to the Arts* Helen Ryan
Library maintained for art history courses
Purchases: $7400 annually (for purchases to support art history courses at the col level)
Library Holdings: Audio Tapes, Book Volumes 350,000, Exhibition Catalogs, Fiche, Filmstrips, Manuscripts, Original Art Works, Pamphlets, Periodical Subscriptions 1900, Photographs, Records, Slides, Video Tapes

M **UNITED METHODIST CHURCH GENERAL COMMISSION ON ARCHIVES & HISTORY,** 36 Madison Ave, PO Box 127 Madison, NJ 07940. Tel 973-408-3189; Email gcah@gcah.org; Web: www.gcah.org; *Gen Sec* Alfred T Day III; *Archivist & Records Admin* L. Dale Patterson
Open Mon - Fri 9 AM - 5 PM; No admis fee; Estab 1885 as a religious history mus; The Archives & History Center is located on Drew University Campus & it contains a mus, a library & a spacious 180,000 cubic ft archival vault. Maintains reference library
Income: Financed by gen church funds
Special Subjects: Historical Material, Religious Art
Collections: Letters, Photographs

Exhibitions: Chinese Missionaries
Publications: Methodist History, quarterly
Activities: Lects open to pub, 1 vis lectrs per yr; tours; sales shop sells books & prints

L **Archives & History Center**, 36 Madison Ave, PO Box 127 Madison, NJ 07940. Tel 973-408-3590; Email methodist@drew.edu; Web: www.drew.edu/library/methodist; *Head Spec Colls, Archives & Methodist Librn* Brian Shetler
Open Mon - Thurs 9 AM - 5 PM, Fri 9 AM - 1 PM; No admis fee; Estab 1983; For reference only; Average Annual Attendance: 580
Library Holdings: Audio Tapes, Book Volumes 70,000, CD-ROMs, Cassettes, Clipping Files, Compact Disks, DVDs, Exhibition Catalogs, Fiche, Filmstrips, Lantern Slides, Manuscripts, Maps, Memorabilia, Motion Pictures, Original Art Works, Original Documents, Pamphlets, Periodical Subscriptions 600, Photographs, Prints, Records, Reels, Slides, Video Tapes
Special Subjects: Ceramics, Drawings, Furniture, Historical Material, Manuscripts, Painting-American, Painting-British, Porcelain, Portraits, Religious Art, Video
Collections: Methodist materials, pamphlets & manuscripts of John Wesley & his assoc, materials pertaining to women & ethnic minorities, Jacob Landou Art Collection, University Art Collection
Activities: Gallery talks & tours

MAHWAH

M **THE ART GALLERIES OF RAMAPO COLLEGE,** 505 Ramapo Valley Rd, Mahwah, NJ 07430-1623. Tel 201-684-7587; *Gallery Dir* Sydney O Jenkins
Open Mon - Fri 11 AM - 2 PM, Wed 5 - 7 PM, cl Sat & Sun; No admis fee; Estab 1979 as outreach for community, faculty, staff & students to support undergrad curriculum; Three galleries: thematic changing exhibs gallery; permanent coll gallery; alternate space gallery; Average Annual Attendance: 5,000; Mem: 300 (friends); dues $15
Income: Financed by state appropriation & grants
Special Subjects: Prints
Collections: Rodman Collection of Popular Art, Art by Haitians, Study Collection of Prints, fine art printmaking from 15th century to present
Publications: Exhibit catalogs
Activities: Classes for adults & children; dramatic progs; docent training; lect open to pub, 10 vis lectrs per yr; competitions; schols & fels offered; individual paintings lent to institutions, cols & museums; book traveling exhibs; originate traveling exhibs

MERCERVILLE

L **JOHNSON ATELIER TECHNICAL INSTITUTE OF SCULPTURE,** Johnson Atelier Library, 60 Sculptors Way, Mercerville, NJ 08619-3428. Tel 609-890-7777; Fax 609-890-1816; Email Info@ atelier.org; Web: www.atelier.org; *Librn* Eden R Bentley; *Dir Gallery* Gyuri Hollosy
Estab 1977 to provide an information center for apprentices, instructors & staff on sculpture, art appreciation & art history; Library provides space for lects, movies, slides & critique sessions; gallery adjacent to library
Income: Financed by appropriation from the Johnson Atelier Technical Institute of Sculpture
Library Holdings: Book Volumes 2670, Clipping Files, Exhibition Catalogs, Periodical Subscriptions 23, Slides
Special Subjects: Bronzes, Sculpture
Collections: Exhibition catalogues on sculptors & group shows, slides of about 50 sculptor's work

MILLVILLE

M **RIVERFRONT RENAISSANCE CENTER FOR THE ARTS,** 22 N High St, Millville, NJ 08332-3830. Tel 856-327-4500; Email rrcarts@yahoo.com; Web: www.rrcarts.com; *Exec Dir* Diane Roberts; *Asst Dir* Lisa Romano
Open Sun - Thurs 11 AM - 5 PM, Fri - Sat 11 AM - 6 PM, 3rd Fri 11 AM - 9 PM; Estab 2001 to serve as a community arts & cultural center; Mem: dues $20-$250
Collections: Features art across all mediums
Exhibitions: Temporary exhibits
Activities: Educ progs; classes for adults & children; workshops

M **WHEATON ARTS & CULTURAL CENTER,** Museum of American Glass, 1000 Village Dr, Millville, NJ 08332; 1501 Glasstown Rd, Millville, NJ 08332-1568. Tel 856-825-6800; Fax 856-825-2410; Email museum@wheatonarts.org; Web: www.wheatonarts.org; *Exec Dir* Kristin Qualls; *Curatorial Asst* Dianne Wood; *Registrar* Elizabeth Wilk
Open Jan - Mar call for hours; Apr - Dec Tues - Sun 10 AM - 5 PM; cl New Year's Day, Easter, Thanksgiving, Christmas; Admis adults $10, seniors (62+) $9, students $7, mems no charge; Estab 1968, a cultural center dedicated to American craft; Average Annual Attendance: 57,000; Mem: dues $20-$55
Library Holdings: Auction Catalogs, Book Volumes, Clipping Files, Exhibition Catalogs, Maps, Original Documents, Photographs, Slides, Video Tapes
Special Subjects: Glass
Collections: American glass
Activities: Educ prog; docent training; tours; mus shop sells books, magazines, original art

MONTCLAIR

M **MONTCLAIR ART MUSEUM,** 3 S Mountain Ave, Montclair, NJ 07042-1747. Tel 973-746-5555; Fax 973-746-9118; Web: www.montclairartmuseum.org; *Dir* Lora Urbanelli; *Chief Cur* Gail Stavitsky; *CFO* Michael Frasco; *Dir Mktg & Commun* Kate Premo; *Cur Native American Art* Pam Jardine; *Dir Develop* Amy Fitzpatrick
Open Wed - Sun Noon - 5 PM, cl Mon, Tues & major holidays; Admis adults $12, seniors & students $10, children under 12 & mems free; 1st Thurs of mon Oct-June 5 PM - 9 PM free; 1st Fri of mon free; Estab 1914; Two galleries of changing exhibs; five galleries of permanent exhibs; student gallery; Average Annual Attendance: 66,000; Mem: 2700; college student $35; individual $50; dual & family $70; friend $165; curator's circle $325; sustaining $750; benefactor $1,500; director's circle $3,000; inness $5,500
Income: Financed by endowment & mems
Special Subjects: Afro-American Art, American Indian Art, Anthropology, Archaeology, Ceramics, Costumes, Drawings, Ethnology, Landscapes, Painting-American, Photography, Portraits, Pottery, Prints, Sculpture, Silver, Pottery
Collections: Rand Collection of American Indian Art, George Inness Collection, Morgan Russell Archive
Exhibitions: 18th Jun, 2017) Janet Taylor Pickerr: The Matisse Services; (5th Feb, 2017-18th Jun, 2017) Matisse and American Art
Publications: Bulletin, 3 times per yr; exhib catalogs; pub progs brochure; Art School Brochure; ann report
Activities: Classes for adults, teens & children; MAM art truck; docent training; workshops coordinated progs with school groups; dramatic progs; family progs; creative aging;; lect open to pub; 10 vis lectrs per yr; concerts; gallery talks every Sunday; tours; sponsoring of competitions; schols; mus shop sells books, notecards, reproductions, slides, Native American jewelry & crafts, jewelry, games/toys for children & diverse art-related items

MOORESTOWN

M **PERKINS CENTER FOR THE ARTS,** 395 Kings Hwy, Moorestown, NJ 08057-2725. Tel 856-235-6488; Fax 856-235-6624; Email create@perkinscenter.org; Web: www.perkinscenter.org; *Exec Dir* Karen Chigounis
Open Thurs - Sun; No admis fee; Estab 1977 as a multi-disciplinary art center; A Tudor mansion built in 1910 on 5-1/2 acre lot. The building is listed on the National Register of Historic Places; Average Annual Attendance: 25,000; Mem: 1200; dues family $50, adult $30, student $20
Income: $1,200,000 (financed by mem, state appropriation, corporate, foundation & earned income)
Exhibitions: Annual Photography Exhib; Annual Pottery Show & Sale; Annual Works on Paper Exhib; Annual Watercolor Exhib; Director's Choice; Mems & Faculty Show
Publications: Perkinsight, quarterly newsletter & class catalog
Activities: Classes for adults & children; docent progs; lect open to pub, 5 vis lectrs per yr; awards given; schols & fels offered

MORRISTOWN

L **COLLEGE OF SAINT ELIZABETH,** Mahoney Library, 2 Convent Rd, Morristown, NJ 07960-6989. Tel 973-290-4237; Fax 973-290-4226; Email pchervenie@liza.st-elizabeth.edu; *Dir Library* Amira Unvir
Open Mon -Thurs 8:30 AM - 10 PM, Fri 8:30 AM - 5 PM, Sat 2 AM - 6 PM, Sun 2 PM - 10 PM; Estab 1899 for acad purposes
Income: Financed by pvt funds
Library Holdings: Book Volumes 140,200, Cassettes, Exhibition Catalogs, Fiche 65,664, Filmstrips 200, Original Art Works, Periodical Subscriptions 848, Photographs, Prints, Records 1800, Reels 4690, Reproductions, Sculpture
Exhibitions: Sculpture, paintings, prints by the Art Dept faculty

M **MORRIS MUSEUM,** 6 Normandy Heights Rd, Morristown, NJ 07960-4627. Tel 973-971-3700; Fax 973-538-0154; Email info@morrismuseum.org; Web: www.morrismuseum.org; *Exec Dir* Dr Cleveland Johnson; *Chair* Gerri Horn; *Coll Mgr* Maria Ribaudo
Open Tues - Sat 11 AM - 5 PM, Sun noon - 5 PM, cl major holidays; Admis adults $10, seniors & children $7; mems free; Estab 1913 to educate diverse pub on topics in art, humanities & the sciences; 12 galleries of changing & permanent exhibs; Average Annual Attendance: 200,000; Mem: 2500; dues $40 - $65; ann meeting in Sept
Income: Mem dues, funds, grants
Special Subjects: African Art, American Indian Art, Anthropology, Archaeology, Asian Art, Bronzes, Carpets & Rugs, Ceramics, Collages, Costumes, Crafts, Decorative Arts, Etchings & Engravings, Glass, Painting-American, Period Rooms, Pottery, Primitive art, Sculpture, Watercolors
Collections: Antique dolls & toys, fine & decorative arts, geology, mineralogy, paleontology, textiles, mechanical musical instruments, automata
Exhibitions: North American Indian & Woodland Indian Galleries; Rock & Mineral Gallery; Gallery; Dinosaur Gallery; Children's Room; Mammal Gallery; Model Train Gallery; juried art exhibitions; Mechanical musical instruments & automata
Publications: Sassona Norton Sculpture; Murtough D Guinness Collection of Mechanical Musical Instruments and Automata; New Jersey Crafts, ann
Activities: Classes for adults & children; dramatic progs; docent training; lect open to pub, 6-10 vis lectrs per yr; concerts; gallery talks for schools; tours; competitions with prizes; Citation of Excellence from NJ State Council on the Arts; exten dept serves north & central NJ schools, sr centers & hospitals; artmobile; individual paintings & original objects of art lent to other local organizations & museums; 250 book traveling exhibs; originate traveling exhibs to mus; mus shop sells books, original art, reproductions, prints, exhibs-related gifts & toys

M **SCHUYLER-HAMILTON HOUSE,** 5 Olyphant Pl, Morristown, NJ 07960-4231. Tel 973-267-4039; Fax 908-852-1361; Email aben85271@aol.com; *Cur* JoAnn Bowman
Open Sun 2 - 4 PM, other times by appointment; Admis adults $4, children under 12 free; Estab 1923 for preservation of historical landmark; House is furnished with 18th Century antiques; five large portraits of General & Mrs Philip Schuyler, their daughter, Betsey Schuyler Hamilton, Alexander Hamilton & Dr Jabez Campfield; old lithographs, silhouette of George Washington, needle & petit point; Average

Annual Attendance: 1,500; Mem: 90; dues $30; ann meeting 1st Thurs in May, Chap meets Oct - May
Income: Financed by mem, Friends of Schuyler-Hamilton, foundations & matching gifts
Special Subjects: Decorative Arts, Period Rooms
Collections: China - Canton, blue willow, Staffordshire, doll china, pewter, brass candlesticks, rugs, tunebooks
Activities: Docent training; lect for mems; tours; competitions with awards; sales shop sells stationery, cards & reproductions

NEW BRUNSWICK

A **MIDDLESEX COUNTY CULTURAL & HERITAGE COMMISSION,** 703 Jersey Ave, New Brunswick, NJ 08901-3651. Tel 732-745-4489; Fax 732-745-4524; Email info@cultureheritage.com; Web: www.co.middlesex.nj.us/culturalheritage; *Exec Dir* Anna M Aschkenes
Open Tues-Friday 8:30AM-4:15PM, Sun 1PM-4PM; No admis fee; Estab 1979 to provide exhib opportunities & information services for mems & educ & cultural opportunities for the gen pub; Slide file of mems' art work is maintained; Mem: 177; dues family or friend $25, mem $15, students & srs $10; monthly board meetings
Income: Financed by mem, state grants, fundraising
Exhibitions: New Brunswick Tomorrow; Annual Statewide Show
Publications: ALCNJ Newsletter, monthly
Activities: Demonstrations open to pub; competitions with awards

M **RUTGERS, THE STATE UNIVERSITY OF NEW JERSEY,** Zimmerli Art Museum at Rutgers University, 71 Hamilton St, New Brunswick, NJ 08901-1248. Tel 848-932-7237; Fax 732-932-8201; Email info@zimmerli.rutgers.edu; Web: www.zimmerlimuseum.rutgers.edu; *Dir* Thomas Sokolowski; *Develop Dir* Whitney Prendergast; *Cur Prints, Drawings & European Art* Christine Giviskos, PhD; *Cur American Art & Mellon Dir Academic Programs* Donna Gustafson, PhD; *Cur Russian & Soviet Nonconformist Art* Julia Tulovsky, PhD; *Registrar* Leslie Kriff
Open Tues - Fri 10 AM - 4:30 PM, first Tues of the month 10 AM - 9 PM, Sat & Sun noon - 5 PM; cl Mon & month of Aug, Memorial Day, Independence Day, Thanksgiving & Fri after, Dec 24 & 25, Jan 1; No admis fee; Estab 1966; 70,000 sq ft facility; Average Annual Attendance: 58,909; Mem: 500 households; dues student $25, individual $50, dual $85, family $100, assoc $250, patron $500, Cur's Circle $1,000, Dir's Gallery $2,500, Hamilton Society $5,000
Income: Ann support from Rutgers, income from the Avenir Foundation & Andrew W Mellon Foundation endowments, ann contributions from individuals, foundations & corps.
Special Subjects: Antiquities-Greek, Antiquities-Roman, Etchings & Engravings, Landscapes, Painting-American, Painting-French, Painting-Russian, Portraits, Prints, Sculpture
Collections: Permanent Collection: 60,000+ works in a wide range of media, incl survey of Western art from 15th c. - present, Russian & Soviet Nonconformist art from the Dodge Collection, American art, with concentrations on prints & original illustrations for children's books, focused presentations of Ancient Greek & Roman art & Pre-Columbian art, always on view at the Zimmerli
Exhibitions: (17th Jan, 2017-28th May, 2017) Innovation and Abstraction: Women Artists and Atelier 17; (17th Jan, 2017-31st Jul, 2017) Reflections: Photographs of Iconic African Americans by Terrence A. Reese; (21st Jan, 2017-31st Jul, 2017) News Fit to Print; (4th Feb, 2017-31st Jul, 2017) Guerrilla Girls: Attitude and Activism; (1st Mar, 2017-31st Jul, 2017) The Ecology of Being: Approaches to Landscape; 25th Jun, 2017) Fletcher and the Knobby Boys: Illustrations by Harry Devlin; 31st Jul, 2017) Three American Painters: David Diao, Sam Gilliam, Sal Sirugo
Publications: Exhib catalogs; Zimmerli Journal; Annual Prog Guide; Gallery Notes; books
Activities: Tours for K-12 students; teacher training in collaboration with the Grad School of Educ at Rutgers; drawing classes for children, teens, & adults; symposia for the acad community; access to the museum's coll of drawings, prints, & photographs at the Zimmerli's Morse Center; Docent Training; lects open to pub, 4-6 vis lectrs per year; concerts; gallery talks; tours; fels available; Dodge Fellows; Dodge Lawrence Fellows; original objects of art lent to art museums nationally & internationally; book traveling exhibs: one every two or three yrs; organize traveling exhibs to other art museums

L **Art Library,** 71 Hamilton St, Voorhees Hall New Brunswick, NJ 08901-1248. Tel 732-932-7739; Fax 732-932-6743; Web: www.libraries.rutgers.edu/rul/libs/art_lib/art_lib.shtml
Open Mon - Thurs 8:30 AM - 10 PM, Fri 8:30 AM - 5 PM, Sat 10 AM - 5 PM, Sun 2 - 10 PM; Estab 1966 for acad research; Circ Non-circulating; For reference only
Library Holdings: Book Volumes 65,000, Clipping Files, Exhibition Catalogs, Fiche, Pamphlets, Periodical Subscriptions 240
Collections: Mary Barlett Cowdrey Collection of American Art, Howard Hibbard Collection, George Raibov Collection of Russian Art, Louis E Stern Collection of Contemporary Art
Activities: Bibliographic instruction; lect; tours

M **Mary H. Dana Women Artists Series, a Partnership of the Center for Women in the Arts & Humanities and Rutgers University Libraries,** 8 Chapel Dr, New Brunswick, NJ 08901; 640 Bartholomew Rd #125A, Piscataway, NJ 08854. Tel 848-932-3726; Fax 732-932-1207; Email womenart@rci.rutgers.edu; Web: cwah.rutgers.edu
Open Mon - Fri 9 AM - 10 PM; No admis fee; Estab 1971 to exhibit the work of emerging & established contemporary women artists; Located in galleries of Mabel Smith Douglass Library on the Douglass college campus of Rutgers University
Income: Financed from gifts from endowment, student groups & departmental funds
Exhibitions: Rotating exhibits each acad yr
Publications: Exhib catalogues
Activities: Lect open to pub; vis lectr; artists selected by jury

L **Mabel Smith Douglass Library,** 8 Chapel Dr, New Brunswick, NJ 08901-8527. Tel 732-932-9407 ext 26; Fax 732-932-6777; Email olin@rci.rutger
Open Mon - Thurs 8 AM - 2 AM, Fri 8 AM - 10 PM, Sat 10 AM - 10 PM, Sun Noon - 2 AM; Estab 1918
Special Subjects: Graphic Arts, Graphic Design, Photography, Theatre Arts

NEWARK

A **ALJIRA CENTER FOR CONTEMPORARY ART,** 591 Broad St, Newark, NJ 07102-4403. Tel 973-622-1600; Fax 973-622-6526; Email info@aljira.org; Web: www.aljira.org; *Exec Dir* Victor Davson; *Dir Exhibs & Progs* Edwin Ramoran; *Mgr Exhibs & Progs* Christine Walia
Open Wed - Fri Noon - 6 PM, Sat 11 AM - 4 PM; call for information; Admis $5 suggested donation, children under 12 no charge; Estab 1983 as a multi-cultural visual art organization
Exhibitions: Various exhibs; call for information

M **NEW JERSEY HISTORICAL SOCIETY,** 52 Park Pl, Newark, NJ 07102-4302. Tel 973-596-8500; Fax 973-596-6957; Web: www.jerseyhistory.org; *Exec Dir* Steven Tettamanti; *Educ Specialist* Maribel Jusino-Iturralde; *Devel Assoc* Melanie McLaurin
Open Tues - Sat 10 AM - 5 PM; No admis fee; Estab 1845 to col, preserve, exhibit & make available to study the materials pertaining to the history of New Jersey & its people; The mus has three changing exhib spaces & special colls library; Average Annual Attendance: 20,000; Mem: 1700; dues adults $30 & up; ann meeting third Wed in Apr
Income: Financed by endowment, mem, gifts, grants & benefits
Special Subjects: Archaeology, Coins & Medals, Costumes, Dolls, Drawings, Embroidery, Flasks & Bottles, Furniture, Glass, Historical Material, Landscapes, Miniatures, Portraits, Posters, Painting-American, Photography
Collections: Ceramics, glassware, furniture, important technical drawings from 1790-1815, New Jersey portraits, landscapes, prints & photographs, sculpture, silhouettes & miniatures, silver, toys, manuscripts, maps, New Jersey history artifacts
Publications: Exhib catalogs; Jersey Journeys; New Jersey History, biannual; New Jersey News, monthly newsletter
Activities: Classes for adults & children; gallery talks; individual paintings & original objects of art lent to established institutions; variable book traveling exhibs; originates traveling exhibs; mus shop sells books, original art, toys

L **Library,** 52 Park Pl, Newark, NJ 07102. Tel 973-596-8500; Fax 973-596-6957; Email library@jerseyhistory.org; Web: www.jerseyhistory.org; *Library Specialist* James Amemasor
Open Wed-Thurs & Sat Noon - 5 PM or by appt; No admis fee; Estab 1845 to preserve the history of NJ; Time changing galleries on historical NJ topics; Mem: 1000; $25, ann Apr meetings
Library Holdings: Audio Tapes 100, Book Volumes 65,000, Cassettes, Clipping Files, Exhibition Catalogs, Fiche 7800, Lantern Slides, Manuscripts, Maps 2000, Memorabilia, Original Art Works, Original Documents, Other Holdings Manuscript Material 2000 linear feet, Pamphlets 12,000, Periodical Subscriptions 300, Photographs 100,000, Prints, Reels 3500 reels of microfilm, Video Tapes 200
Special Subjects: Afro-American Art, American Indian Art, Anthropology, Archaeology, Decorative Arts, Drawings, Etchings & Engravings, Folk Art, Historical Material, History of Art & Archaeology, Illustration, Interior Design, Landscape Architecture, Landscapes, Marine Painting
Collections: Manuscript, Book and Special Collections
Publications: New Jersey History; No Easy Walk Summer-Fall 2004; Resourceful New Jersey 2004-2005
Activities: Classes for children; docent training; teacher workshops; teen parent prog; lect open to pub; gallery talks; tours; mus shop sells books & reproductions

L **NEW JERSEY INSTITUTE OF TECHNOLOGY,** Littman Architecture & Design Library, 323 Martin Luther King Blvd, Newark, NJ 07102-1982. Tel 973-642-4390 (reference); Fax 973-643-5601; Web: archlib.njit.edu; *Dir* Maya Gervits; *Archit Librn* Monica Kenzie
Open Mon - Thurs 8 AM - 8:15 PM, Fri 8AM-5:45PM, Sat noon-5:45PM, Sun 1PM-6:45PM; No admis fee; Estab 1975 to serve the needs of the school of architecture; For lending & reference; Average Annual Attendance: 80,000
Income: Financed by univ
Purchases: $50,000
Library Holdings: Audio Tapes, Book Volumes 20,000, Cassettes, Clipping Files, Compact Disks, DVDs, Exhibition Catalogs, Filmstrips, Maps, Pamphlets, Periodical Subscriptions 80, Slides, Video Tapes
Special Subjects: Architecture, Art History, Constructions, Decorative Arts, Drafting, Drawings, Furniture, Graphic Design, History of Art & Archaeology, Industrial Design, Interior Design, Landscape Architecture, Maps, Period Rooms, Photography, Restoration & Conservation
Activities: Concerts

M **NEWARK MUSEUM ASSOCIATION,** The Newark Museum, 49 Washington St, Newark, NJ 07102-3176. Tel 973-596-6550; Fax 973-642-0459; Web: www.newarkmuseum.org; *Deputy Dir Finance & Admin* Beth Aron; *Interim Co-Dir, Chief Cur & Cur Decorative Arts* Ulysses Grant Dietz; *Interim Co-Dir, Deputy Dir Institutional Advancement* Deborah Kasindorf; *Deputy Dir Design & Exhibition* Timothy Wintemberg
Open Wed - Sun Noon - 5 PM, cl Mon & Tues (except Dr Martin Luther King Jr Day & Presidents Day) & Tues, Christmas, New Year's Day, July 4 & Thanksgiving; Suggested: adults $15, children, seniors & students $8, mems free; Estab 1909 to exhibit articles of art, science & industry & for the study of the arts & sciences; Founded in 1909 in the Newark Pub Library, the bldg was a gift of Louis Bamber, opened in 1926, held in trust by the Newark Museum Assn for the City of Newark. The North and South Wings were acquired in 1937 and 1982. The renovation of the museum was designed by Michael Graves, reopened in 1989, and won the 1992 American Institute of Architects Honor Award. It contains 60,000 sq ft of gallery space, as well as educ facilities and a 300-seat auditorium. The Ballantine House, a 1885 historical mansion, designated a National Historical Landmark in 1985, showcases the decorative arts coll in 8 period rms and 6 thematic galleries; Average Annual Attendance: 500,000; Mem: 4750; dues $50 & up; ann meeting in Feb
Income: $12,000,000 (financed by city & state appropriations, county funds & pvt donations)

Collections: Africa, the Americas (including Pre-Columbian art), and the Pacific; American paintings and sculpture; Asian art, including Japanese, Korean, Chinese, Indian, and Tibetan; the decorative arts; the Classical cultures of Egypt, Greece and Rome, including the Eugene Schaefer Collection of ancient glass; numismatics; as well as the Alice and Leonard Dreyfus Planetarium, and the Natural Science Collection
Publications: Magazine, quarterly; catalogs on major exhibs; New Jersey Arts Annual
Activities: Extensive educ progs including classes for adults & children; docent training; lects open to pub; films; concerts; gallery talks; tours; competitions; exten dept serves community neighborhoods; individual paintings & original objects of art lent to other museums; mus shop sells catalogues, reproductions, prints, original craft items from around the world

M **Junior Museum,** 49 Washington St, Newark, NJ 07102-3176. Tel 973-596-6605; Fax 973-642-0459; Email juniormuseum@newarkmuseum.org; Web: www.newarkmuseum.org/juniormuseum/; *Mgr Family Events* Rob Craig; *Jr Mus Supv* Lynette Diaz
Open Wed - Sun Noon - 5 PM; No admis fee; Estab 1926 to provide art & science progs designed to stimulate the individual child in self-discovery & exploration of the world & to teach effective use of the Mus as a whole, which may lead to valuable lifetime interests; Average Annual Attendance: 17,000; Mem: 3500 active; dues $10 lifetime mem; ann meeting in May
Income: Financed through the Newark Mus
Exhibitions: Changing exhibs of children's artwork; ann spring & summer exhibs in Junior Gallery
Activities: Weekday pre-school & after school; Saturday morning & summer workshops for ages 3-16; parents' workshops; community outreach & school enrichment progs; special events workshops & holiday festivals & hospital outreach; Junior Gallery offering a self-guided gallery game & art activity sessions, weekend Sept-June & weekdays in summer

L **NEWARK PUBLIC LIBRARY,** Reference, 5 Washington St, Newark, NJ 07102-3105; PO Box 630, Newark, NJ 07101-0630. Tel 973-733-7779, 733-7820, 733-7745; Fax 973-733-5648; Email reference@npl.org; Web: www.npl.org; *Supvr* Leslie Kahn; *Supvr* James Capuano; *Prin Librn* Jane Seiden; *Sr Librn* Monica Malinowski; *Librn* Nadine Sergejeff; *Dir* Wilma Grey
Open Sept - June Tues - Thurs 9 AM - 8:30 PM, Mon, Fri & Sat 9 AM - 5:30 PM, July - Aug Mon, Tues, Thurs & Fri 9 AM - 5:30 PM, Wed 9 AM - 8:30 PM, Sat 11 AM - 3 PM; Estab 1888, provides information on all of the visual arts to the NJ Library Network & pub; Maintains an art gallery: a total of 300 running ft
Income: Financed by city & state appropriations, endowment & gift funds
Library Holdings: Auction Catalogs, Book Volumes 75,000, CD-ROMs, Clipping Files, Exhibition Catalogs, Manuscripts 200, Maps 200, Original Art Works 23,000, Original Documents, Periodical Subscriptions 40, Photographs, Prints 20,000
Special Subjects: Afro-American Art, Architecture, Art History, Cartoons, Ceramics, Crafts, Decorative Arts, Drawings, Furniture, Glass, Graphic Arts, Bookplates & Bindings, Calligraphy, Etchings & Engravings, Fashion Arts, Illustration, Interior Design, Latin American Art, Lettering, Manuscripts
Collections: Original Prints (22,000), Historic Posters (5,000), The Richard C Jenkinson Coll of Printing History (2,300), The Wilbur Macy Stone Coll of Historic Books for Children (1,200), Illustrated Book Coll (2,800), Autographs (1,000), The McEwen Christmas Coll (900), Artists Book Coll (600), Pop-Up Book Coll (600), The Rabin & Kreuger Archives (250 folders), Shopping Bags (1,100), Historic Greeting Cards (800)
Exhibitions: Movable Books: A Paradise of Pop-Ups, A Feast of Fold Outs & a Mix of Mechanicals; Prints by Joseph Pennell; Posters & Prints from Puerto Rico, 1950-1990; 20th Century American Illustrations; A Potpourri of Pop (Pop art prints & pop-up books); Over There...1917-1918, A Victory Salute to the USA in World War I; The Essential Calendar: The Art & Design of Calendars; Prints & Posters of the Circus and Vintage Greeting Cards; Travel Posters & Memorable Works on Paper from Africa, China, India & Taiwan; Where, When and Who Took That Photograph?; Nostalgic and Unforgettable Travel Posters from the 20th Century; Robert Sabuda: Travels in Time & Space via Pop-Up Books; Original Prints by African-American Artists; John Cotton Dana: Innovative Librn, Civic Leader, Mus Founder; A Salute to Two Great 20th Century Artists: Picasso & Lichtenstein in prints, posters and rare books; A Contemporary & Historic Survey of Shopping Bags
Activities: Tours; gallery talks; tours; originate traveling exhibs to art institutions

C **PRUDENTIAL ART PROGRAM,** 100 Mulberry St, Gateway Center 2-17th Flr Newark, NJ 07102-4056. Tel 973-367-7151; *Mgr* Carol Skuratofsky
Estab 1969 to enhance the surroundings & living up to social responsibility in supporting art as a genuinely important part of life
Collections: Approx 12,000 holdings of paintings, sculptures & unique works on paper, 2558 signed graphics, 1182 posters, 241 billboards, 200 photographs

NORTH PLAINFIELD

M **FLEETWOOD MUSEUM,** 614 Greenbrook Rd, North Plainfield, NJ 07063-1621; 135 Sandford Ave, North Plainfield, NJ 07060. Tel 908-756-7810; Email nciampa@netscape.net; Web: www.fleetwoodmuseum.com; *Cur* Mr George E. Helmke
Open Sat 10 AM - 4 PM; cl major holidays; No admis fee; Estb 1985 ro promote interest in art, science & techniques of photo imaging; Average Annual Attendance: 1800
Income: $3,500; financed by Fleetwood Fond of Plainfield Foundation
Library Holdings: Book Volumes 800, Original Art Works 20, Photographs 500
Collections: over 800 cameras; oil paintings; art & science of photography
Activities: Concerts

OCEAN CITY

A **OCEAN CITY ARTS CENTER,** 1735 Simpson Ave, Ocean City, NJ 08226-3070. Tel 609-399-7628; Fax 609-399-6145; Email info@oceancityartscenter.org; Web: www.oceamcityartscenter.org; *Bd Pres* Jack Devine; *Exec Dir* Rosalyn Lifshin
Open Mon - Fri 9 AM - 9 PM, Sat 9 AM - 3 PM; No admis fee; Estab 1967 to promote the arts; Teaching studios & a gallery for monthly changing exhibs throughout the yr; Average Annual Attendance: 10,000; Mem: 1200; dues individual $15, family $30; ann meeting in Feb; Scholarships
Income: $70,000 (financed by mem, city appropriation, New Jersey State Council on the Arts Grant 1981)
Collections: Paintings, photog, pottery
Exhibitions: Juried Art Show, Boardwalk Art Show, Juried Photog Show, Craft Show, Monthly Exhibs; Themed Invitational Show
Publications: Newsletters, quarterly
Activities: Classes for adults & children; summer children's art camps; lects open to pub, 12 vis lectrs per yr; concerts; competitions with awards; mus shop sells books, jewelry, prints, original art & crafts

ORADELL

M **BLAUVELT DEMAREST FOUNDATION,** Hiram Blauvelt Art Museum, 705 Kinderkamack Rd, Oradell, NJ 07649-1504. Tel 201-261-0012; Fax 201-391-6418; Email info@blauveltartmuseum.com; Web: www.blauveltartmuseum.com; *Dir* Marijane Singer, PhD
Open Wed - Fri 10 AM - 4 PM, Sat & Sun 2 - 5 PM; No admis fee; Estab 1950; 1893 shingle & turret-style Queen Anne carriage house; Average Annual Attendance: 13,224; Mem: ann meeting in June
Library Holdings: Book Volumes, Compact Disks, Exhibition Catalogs, Original Art Works, Prints, Sculpture, Video Tapes
Special Subjects: African Art, American Western Art, Bronzes, Dioramas, Drawings, Eskimo Art, Ivory, Painting-American, Painting-British, Painting-Canadian, Painting-European, Painting-Scandinavian, Photography, Portraits, Prints, Scrimshaw, Sculpture, Southwestern Art, Watercolors, Woodcarvings
Collections: Audubon folio, Big Game Species, Extinct Birds, Ivory Collection, Master & Contemporary Wildlife & Animal Art Paintings & Sculptures, Animal Art & Wildlife Art
Exhibitions: Art works by Guy Coheleach, Charles Allmond, Mary Taylor, Dwayne Harty, Charles Livingston Bull; The Art of Conservation
Publications: Charles Livingston Bull Catalog; Art & the Animal I; Art & the Animal II
Activities: Classes for adults & children; docent training; lect open to pub; gallery talks; tours; ann Purchase Award - Soc Animal Artists; Artists for Conservation - Blauvelt Purchase Award, Ann Mem of society or animal artist; mus shop sells books, magazines, original art, reproductions, prints & videos

PALISADES PARK

L **PALISADES PARK PUBLIC LIBRARY,** 257 Second St, Palisades Park, NJ 07650. Tel 201-585-4150; Fax 201-585-2151; Email kumar@bccls.org; Web: www.bccls.org/palisadespark; *Dir* Susan Kumar; *Children's Librn* Steven Cavallo
Open Mon - Thurs 10:30 AM - 9 PM, Fri 10:30 AM - 5 PM, Sat. 10:30 AM - 4 PM; Estab 1909; Maintains a community room used for exhibits
Library Holdings: Book Volumes 40,000, Cassettes, Periodical Subscriptions 75, Video Tapes

PARAMUS

M **BUEHLER CHALLENGER & SCIENCE CENTER,** 305 N State Rte 17, Paramus, NJ 07653; PO Box 647, Paramus, NJ 07653-0647. Tel 201-262-0984; Fax 201-251-9049; Email missionservices@bcsc.org (Coordr); Web: www.bcsc.org; *Mission Coordr* Peggy Silverman
Call for hours & further information; Created in 1994 by the Emil Buehler Trust as the 21st center in the Challenger Learning Center network; Dedicated to inspiring students, educators and the community in the pursuit of scientific educ. Mus is child org of the Challenger Center for Space Science Educ, founded in 1986 by the families of the Challenger 51-L astronauts
Activities: Progs & Outreach progs; tours; Mission Simulations; Space Camp; Astro Camp; Family Science Morning

PARSIPPANY

A **NEW JERSEY WATERCOLOR SOCIETY,** 55 Richard St, Parsippany, NJ 07054; 83 Clifford Dr, Wayne, NJ 07470-3501. Tel 873-887-5860; Web: www.njwcs.org; *Pres* Mark de Mos
Estab 1938 to bring to the pub the best in NJ watercolorists - teachers; Mem: 135; dues $25; open to exhibitors in the Annual Open Exhib whose work conforms to standards of the Soc & are legal residents of the State of NJ
Exhibitions: Annual Mems Show in spring; Annual Open Statewide Juried Exhib in fall - alternating between the Ridgewood Art Institute & the Monmouth Museum, Lincroft, NJ
Publications: Illustrated catalogue; newsletter, 3 per yr
Activities: Classes for adults & children; workshops; lect open to pub, 2-4 vis lectrs per yr; competitions with awards; ann dinner; reception for Open & Mems Shows

PATERSON

M **PASSAIC COUNTY COMMUNITY COLLEGE,** Broadway, LRC, and Hamilton Club Galleries, One College Blvd, Paterson, NJ 07505-1179. Tel 973-684-6555; Fax 973-523-6085; Email jhaw@pccc.edu; Web: www.pccc.edu/culturalaffairs; *Young People's Theatre Coordr* Susan Amsterdam; *Exec Dir Cultural Affairs* Maria Mazziotti Gillan; *Gallery Cur* Jane Haw; *Sec* Smita Desai
Open Mon - Fri 9 AM - 9 PM, Sat 9 AM - 5 PM; No admis fee; Changing exhibits of contemporary art & permanent colls of 19th & early 20th century paintings & sculpture & contemporary art

Special Subjects: Painting-American, Painting-British, Painting-European, Painting-Flemish, Painting-French, Painting-German, Painting-Scandinavian, Period Rooms, Prints, Watercolors
Collections: Hamilton Club Art Collections, Federici Studio Collection: sculpture, Contemporary Art Collection
Exhibitions: Monthly & bimonthly exhibits of local & tri-state artists. Works are mostly 2-D; paintings, drawings, mixed media, silkscreens, woodblock prints, photography, textile & some ceramics
Publications: The Hamilton Art Collection; Passaic County Community College Contemporary Art Collections
Activities: Workshops; lects open to pub; gallery talks; tours

M **PASSAIC COUNTY HISTORICAL SOCIETY,** Lambert Castle Museum & Library, 3 Valley Rd, Lambert Castle Paterson, NJ 07503-2932. Tel 973-247-0085; Fax 973-881-9434; Email info@lambertcastle.org; Web: www.lambertcastle.org; *Historic Site Mgr & Cur* Heather Garside
Open Memorial Day to Labor Day Wed - Sun 12 - 4 PM, Sept - May Wed - Sun 1 PM - 4 PM, call for holiday hours; Admis adults $5, seniors $4, children 5-17 $3, under 5 & mems no charge; Estab 1926; Located in Lambert Castle built in 1892; Average Annual Attendance: 25,000; Mem: Dues $10-$150
Income: Financed by donations, gifts, grants, mem dues
Library Holdings: Book Volumes, CD-ROMs, Micro Print, Original Documents, Photographs
Special Subjects: Costumes, Decorative Arts, Folk Art, Furniture, Historical Material, Landscapes, Manuscripts, Maps, Painting-American, Painting-Italian, Period Rooms, Portraits, Prints, Watercolors, Photography, Textiles
Collections: Koempel Spoon Collection, local historical material, paintings
Publications: Historic Passaic County, bimonthly newsletter; pamphlets; exhib catalogues
Activities: Classes for children; lect open to pub, 4-6 vis lectrs per yr; gallery talks; tours; individual paintings & original objects of art lent to qualified museums by written request; mus shop sells books, reproductions, prints, publs, postcards, souvenirs & gifts

PLAINFIELD

L **PLAINFIELD PUBLIC LIBRARY,** 800 Park Ave, Plainfield, NJ 07060-2517. Tel 908-757-1111; Fax 908-754-0063; Web: www.plainfieldlibrary.info; *Dir* Mary Ellen Rogan; *Archivist* Sarah Hull
Open Mon - Thurs 9 AM - 9 PM, Fri & Sat 9 AM - 5 PM, cl Sun; No admis fee; Estab 1881; Maintains an art gallery with original artworks on permanent display, group shows as scheduled; Average Annual Attendance: 200,000
Income: Financed by endowment & city appropriation
Library Holdings: Maps, Original Art Works, Other Holdings Blueprints, Photographs 110000
Special Subjects: Historical Material, Painting-American, Ceramics, Photography, Porcelain
Collections: Winslow Homer Collection, John Carlson; Alonzo Adams; Riva Helfond; Cloisonne Collection, Selections from permanent collection may be viewed at www.plfdpl.info
Activities: Gallery talks

PRINCETON

M **MORVEN MUSEUM & GARDEN,** 55 Stockton St, Princeton, NJ 08540-6812. Tel 609-924-8144; Fax 609-924-8331; Email info@morven.org; Web: www.morven.org; *Exec Dir* Jill Barry; *Cur Colls & Exhibits* Elizabeth Allan
Open Wed - Sun 10 AM - 4 PM; Admis adults $5, seniors & students $4; Built c1758 by Richard Stockton, a signer of the Declaration of Independence & later the residence of NJ Governors; tours & exhibs highlight Stockton Family & architectural preservation
Income: Program of the NJ State Mus; financed by gifts, grants & benefits
Special Subjects: Historical Material, Painting-American, Period Rooms, Decorative Arts
Collections: Material culture relating to the house

M **PRINCETON UNIVERSITY,** Princeton University Art Museum, Princeton, NJ 08544-1018. Tel 609-258-3788; Fax 609-258-3610; Email artmuseum@princeton.edu; Web: artmuseum.princeton.edu; *Dir* James Steward; *Assoc Dir Educ* Caroline Harris; *Assoc Dir Finance & Opers* Karen Ohland; *Assoc Dir Information & Technology* Stephen J. Kim; *Assoc Dir Institutional Advancement* Nancy Stout; *Assoc Dir Publishing & Communs* Curtis Scott; *Research Cur European Painting & Sculpture* Betsy J Rosasco; *Cur American Art* Karl Kusserow; *Cur & Lectr Art of Ancient Americas* Bryan Just; *Cur Ancient Art* J Michael Padgett; *Cur Asian Art* Cary Liu; *Cur Prints & Drawings* Laura Giles; *Assoc Cur Prints & Drawings* Calvin Brown; *Assoc Dir Colls & Exhibs* Bart Thurber; *Peter C. Bumell Cur Photog* Kate Bussard; *Asst Cur Asian Art* Zoe Kwok
Open Tues - Wed & Fri - Sat 10 AM - 5 PM, Thurs 10 AM - 9 PM, Sun 12 PM - 5 PM, cl Mon & holidays; No admis fee; Estab 1882; one of the nation's leading art mus, with coll of some 72,000 works ranging from ancient to contemporary, concentrating on Europe, the Mediterranean, Asia & the Americas. Works to advance Princeton's teaching mission while serving the local, national & international communities through coll, exhib, educ & social activities; About 65,600 sq ft of gallery space for permanent, semi-permanent & changing installations; Average Annual Attendance: 120,000; Mem: 1,000; dues $75 & up
Income: Financed by endowment, univ & by government, corporate & pvt sources
Special Subjects: African Art, American Indian Art, American Western Art, Antiquities-Assyrian, Antiquities-Byzantine, Antiquities-Egyptian, Antiquities-Etruscan, Antiquities-Greek, Antiquities-Oriental, Antiquities-Persian, Archaeology, Asian Art, Baroque Art, Calligraphy, Ceramics, Collages, Decorative Arts, Drawings, Etchings & Engravings, Folk Art, Furniture, Glass, Gold, Graphics, Hispanic Art, Islamic Art, Ivory, Jade, Jewelry, Landscapes, Latin American Art, Marine Painting, Medieval Art, Metalwork, Miniatures, Mosaics, Oriental Art, Painting-American, Painting-British, Painting-Dutch, Painting-European, Painting-Flemish, Painting-French, Painting-German, Painting-Italian, Painting-Japanese, Painting-Russian, Painting-Scandinavian, Painting-Spanish, Photography, Porcelain, Portraits, Posters, Pottery, Pre-Columbian Art, Primitive art, Prints, Religious Art, Renaissance Art, Scrimshaw, Sculpture, Silver, Stained Glass, Watercolors, Woodcarvings
Collections: Art of the Ancient Americas, African Art, American Art, Ancient & Islamic Art, Asian Art, Campus Coll, Contemporary Art, European Art, Modern Art, Prints & Drawings, Photography
Publications: Catalogs, occasionally; Record of the Art Museum, annually; magazine, quarterly
Activities: Classes for adults & children; docent training; lects open to pub; concerts; gallery talks; tours; exten prog serves Trenton, NJ schools & mus around the globe; book traveling exhibs, 2-4 per yr; originates traveling exhibs to interested & selected museums; mus store sells books, reproductions, prints, cards, jewelry, apparel, unique works of art, home decor

L **Index of Christian Art,** A Level McCormick Hall, Dept of Art & Archaeology Princeton, NJ 08544-1018. Tel 609-258-3773; Fax 609-258-0103; Email ppatton@princeton.edu; Web: www.ica.princeton.edu; *Dir* Pamela Patton
Open Mon - Fri 9 AM - 5 PM, cl holidays; No admis fee; Estab 1917 as a division of the Department of Art & Archaeology. It is a research & reference coll of cards & photographs designed to facilitate the study of Christian iconography in works of art before 1400. Duplicate copies exist in Washington, DC in the Dumbarton Oaks Research Center & in Los Angeles in the Getty Research Institute. European copies are in Rome in the Vatican Library & in Utrecht in the Univ; electronic access to files now available on a subscription basis
Library Holdings: Book Volumes, Cards, Exhibition Catalogs, Manuscripts, Photographs, Slides
Special Subjects: Art History
Publications: Studies in Iconography
Activities: Educ prog; lect open to pub, 3-4 vis lectrs per yr; sponsoring of competitions; schols offered

L **Marquand Library of Art & Archaeology,** McCormick Hall, Princeton, NJ 08544-0001; One Washington Rd, Princeton, NJ 08544. Tel 609-258-3783; Fax 609-258-7650; Email marquand@princeton.edu; Web: marquand.princeton.edu/; *Librn* Sandra Ludig Brooke; *Asst Librn* Rebecca K Friedman; *Western Bibliographer* Nicola Shilliam; *Chinese Art Specialist* Kimberly Wishart; *Japanese Art Specialist* Nicole Fabricand-Person
Open to pub for a fee; access for researchers; see: library.princeton.edu/services/privileges; Estab 1908 to serve study & research needs of the students & faculty of Princeton Univ in the History of Art, Architecture & Archaeology; Circ 24,000 (internal only); Adjacent to the art museum; Average Annual Attendance: 150,000
Income: Financed by endowments & gen univ funds
Library Holdings: Auction Catalogs, Book Volumes 450,000, CD-ROMs, DVDs, Exhibition Catalogs, Fiche, Manuscripts, Periodical Subscriptions 600, Reels
Special Subjects: Aesthetics, Afro-American Art, American Indian Art, American Western Art, Antiquities-Assyrian, Antiquities-Byzantine, Antiquities-Egyptian, Antiquities-Etruscan, Antiquities-Greek, Antiquities-Oriental, Antiquities-Persian, Antiquities-Roman, Archaeology, Architecture, Art History, Asian Art, Bronzes, Calligraphy, Carpets & Rugs, Ceramics, Decorative Arts, Etchings & Engravings, Fashion Arts, Folk Art, Furniture, Glass, Historical Material, History of Art & Archaeology, Islamic Art, Landscape Architecture, Latin American Art, Manuscripts, Mexican Art, Oriental Art, Painting-American, Painting-Australian, Painting-British, Painting-Canadian, Painting-Dutch, Painting-European, Painting-Flemish, Painting-French, Painting-German, Painting-Italian, Painting-Japanese, Painting-New Zealand, Painting-Polish, Painting-Russian, Painting-Scandinavian, Painting-Spanish, Photography, Portraits, Posters, Pottery, Pre-Columbian Art, Primitive art, Printmaking, Religious Art, Restoration & Conservation, Sculpture, Silver, Tapestries, Textiles, Video, Woodcuts

RINGWOOD

M **RINGWOOD MANOR HOUSE MUSEUM,** 1304 Sloatsburg Rd, Ringwood, NJ 07456-1706. Tel 973-962-2240; Fax 973-962-2247; Email rspris@verizon.net; Web: www.ringwoodmanor.org; *Historic Site Admin* Sue Shutte; *Supt* Eric Pain
Open Wed - Sun 10 AM - 3 PM, cl all holidays except, Memorial Day, Independence Day & Labor Day; Adults $3, children 6-12 $1, children under 5 no charge; Estab 1938; Average Annual Attendance: 35,000
Income: Financed by state appropriation & funds raised by pvt organization-sponsored spec events
Special Subjects: Decorative Arts, Historical Material, Restorations
Collections: Decorative arts, firearms, furniture, graphics, historical material, New Jersey iron making history, paintings
Activities: Classes for adults & children, docent training; lects open to the pub; guided tours; spec events; sales shop sells books, magazines, reproductions & prints

RIVER EDGE

M **BERGEN COUNTY HISTORICAL SOCIETY,** Steuben House Museum, 1209 Main St, River Edge, NJ 07661-2026; PO Box 55, River Edge, NJ 07661-0055. Tel 201-343-9492, 487-1739 (museum); Fax 201-498-1696; Email contactbchs@bergencountyhistory.org; Web: www.bergencountyhistory.org; *Mus Shop Mgr* Marie Ruggerio
Open Grounds: daily, dawn - dusk; Buildings: for special events; No admis fee; Estab 1902 to collect & preserve historical items of Bergen County; Maintains reference library; Average Annual Attendance: 10,000; Mem: 300; dues $15; ann meeting in June
Income: Financed by mem, grants & corporate support
Collections: Collection of artifacts of the Bergen Dutch 1680-1914, Campbell Christie House (restored 18th century tavern)
Publications: In Bergen's Attic, quarterly newsletter
Activities: Classes for children; docent progs; lect open to pub, 8 vis lectrs per yr; concerts; gallery talks; mus shop sells books & reproductions

SOUTH ORANGE

M **SETON HALL UNIVERSITY,** 400 S Orange Ave, South Orange, NJ 07079-2697. Tel 973-761-9459; Fax 973-275-2368; Web: www.shu.edu; *Dir* Charlotte Nichols
Open Mon - Fri 10 AM - 5 PM; No admis fee; Estab 1963. Troast Memorial Gallery, estab 1974, houses permanent coll of contemporary American art; Wang Fang-Yu Collection of Oriental art was estab in 1977; Average Annual Attendance: 35,000
Collections: Archaeology Colls
Activities: Lect open to pub; gallery talks

M **Walsh Gallery & Library**, 400 S Orange Ave, South Orange, NJ 07079. Tel 973-275-2033; Fax 973-761-9550; Email brasilje@shu.edu; Web: library.shu.edu/gallery; *Gallery Dir* Jeanne Brasile; *Collections Mgr* Romana Schaeffer; *Gallery Asst* Jesse Benicaso
Open Mon - Fri 10:30 AM - 4:30 PM; call to confirm; Estab 1994; 2100 sq ft gallery offers interdisciplinary exhibitions, 6-8 exhibs per yr
Library Holdings: Book Volumes 500,000, Clipping Files, Exhibition Catalogs, Original Art Works, Slides 12,000
Special Subjects: Painting-American, Prints, Religious Art, Reproductions, Sculpture, Textiles, Watercolors
Collections: Paintings; photographs; sculpture
Activities: Classes for adults & children; poetry readings; film screenings; lects open to pub; 1-5 vis lets per yr; gallery talks; tours; symposia; panel discussions; lending of original art to qualified lenders

SPRINGFIELD

L **SPRINGFIELD FREE PUBLIC LIBRARY,** Donald B Palmer Museum, 66 Mountain Ave, Springfield, NJ 07081-1786. Tel 973-376-4930; Fax 973-376-1334; Email questions@sfplnj.org; Web: www.sfplnj.org/joomla; *Dir* Dale Spindel; *Head Adult Svcs* Susan Tegge; *Head Circulation Dept* Karen Gallini; *Head Youth Svcs* Debra Sandford
Open Mon, Wed, Thurs 10 AM - 9 PM, Tues, Fri, & Sat 10 AM - 5 PM, Sun 1 - 4 PM; open Sat July & Aug 10 AM - 1 PM; cl Sun June 1 - Sept 30; No admis fee; Estab 1975 as a mus addition to a pub library established to preserve local history; The library, including a meeting room, serves as a cultural center for exhibits, concerts & lectures; Average Annual Attendance: 113,000; Mem: 11,500
Collections: Permanent coll colonial historical artifacts & other ephemera, Changing art exhibits incl painting, photography, sculpture, etc. Artists submit application to display
Activities: Dramatic progs; 20 vis lectrs; concerts; gallery talks; films; puppet shows; lending coll contains books, photographs, slides, periodicals, videos, DVDs & compact disks; mus shop sells original art by exhibiting artists

STOCKHOLM

A **OIL PASTEL ASSOCIATION,** PO Box 374, Stockholm, NJ 07460-0374. Tel 845-353-2483; Fax 845-358-3821; *Pres* John Elliott; *Exec Dir* Dorothy Coleman
Estab 1983 exhib forum for new & traditional types of pastel paintings; Average Annual Attendance: 2,000; Mem: 350; dues $25 per yr
Income: $4,000 (financed by donations & mem)
Exhibitions: Oil pastels; soft pastels; water-soluble pastels
Publications: Art & Artists, USA
Activities: Classes for adults; workshops; schols offered

SUMMIT

A **VISUAL ARTS CENTER OF NEW JERSEY,** 68 Elm St, Summit, NJ 07901-3472. Tel 908-273-9121; Fax 908-273-1457; Email info@artcenternj.org; Web: www.artcenternj.org; *Exec Dir* Melanie Cohn; *Dir Opers* Ernie Palatucci; *Cur* Mary Birmingham
Open Mon - Thurs 10 AM - 8 PM, Fri 10 AM - 5 PM (includes hours for exhibs & for classes), Sat - Sun 11 AM - 4 PM; Admis adults $5, students & seniors $3; Estab 1933 to educate through gallery exhib & classroom instruction for diverse audience in contemporary arts; Four gallery spaces, containing 5000 ft of exhib space, specializing in contemporary art; Average Annual Attendance: 30,000; Mem: 1300; Individual $50, Dual/Family $75, Friend $125, Contributor $250, Supporter $500, Benefactor $1,000
Income: Membership grant tui (classes), fundraising
Exhibitions: Nine annual exhibs of contemporary visual art
Publications: Exhibition catalogs
Activities: Classes for adults & children; docent training; summer camp for children & teens; lects open to pub & mems; 10 vis lectrs per yr; concerts; gallery talks; tours; members show; awards, NJ State Council of the Arts Award of Excellence; schols; dept serves outreach progs

SUSSEX

M **WARD-NASSE GALLERY,** Home of the Year-Round Salon, 35 Main St, Sussex, NJ 07461. Tel 973-875-1987; Fax 917-974-3602; Email wardnasse@gmail.com; Web: www.wardnasse.com; *Pres* Harry Nasse; *VPres* Mark Herdter; *Outreach* Leda Nasse
Open Tues - Sat 11 AM - 6 PM, Sun 1 - 6 PM; No admis fee; Estab 1969 to provide an artist-run gallery; also serves as resource center for artists & pub; to provide internships for students; First floor, 2,000 sq ft space; Average Annual Attendance: 7,000; Mem: 300; dues $40
Income: Financed by mem
Exhibitions: Seventeen exhibitions per year ranging from 3 person shows, up to large salon shows with 100 artists
Publications: Brochure; gallery catalog, every two years; quarterly newsletter
Activities: Work study progs; lects open to pub; concerts; poetry readings; multi-arts events; sales shop sells original art

TRENTON

A **ARTWORKS TRENTON,** 19 Everett Alley, Trenton, NJ 08611. Tel 609-394-9436; Fax 609-394-9551; Email info@artworkstrenton.org; Web: www.artsworksnj.org; *Bd Chair* Lehze Flax
Open Tues - Wed & Sat 11 AM - 6 PM, Thurs - Fri 11 AM - 8 PM; No admis fee; Estab 1964 to establish & maintain educ & cultural progs devoted to visual arts; Skylit gallery, 2,000 sq ft, in downtown Trenton; Average Annual Attendance: 7,500; Mem: 1,000; dues $40 - $100; ann meeting in May
Income: Financed by friends, class fees, workshops & demonstration fees, trip fees, entry fees, grants, corporate & pvt contributions
Exhibitions: Exhibitions are held at the Trenton Gallery & at various locations throughout the community
Publications: The Artworks Reader, quarterly
Activities: Classes for adults & children; lect open to pub, 3-10 vis lectrs per yr; tours; competitions with awards; schols offered

L **Library**, 19 Everett Alley, Trenton, NJ 08611. Tel 609-394-9436; Fax 609-394-9551; Email info@artworkstrenton.org; Web: www.artworkstrenton.org
Estab 1964, to serve local artists and children and adults in the community; Reference library
Library Holdings: Book Volumes 200, Slides

M **NEW JERSEY STATE MUSEUM,** Fine Art Bureau, 205 W State St, Trenton, NJ 08608-1001; PO Box 530, Trenton, NJ 08625-0530. Tel 609-292-6300; Fax 609-292-7636; Email njsm.info@sos.nj.gov; Web: www.statemuseum.nj.gov; *Exec Dir* Margaret M O'Reilly; *Foundation Exec Dir* Nicole Jannotte
Open Tues -Sun 9 AM - 4:45 PM, cl Mon & all state holidays; Admis $5 suggested admis, children 12 & under & mems free; Estab 1895 by legislation to collect, exhibit & interpret fine arts, cultural history, archaeology-ethnography & natural history; changing exhibit galleries, fine art & NJ history galleries; planetarium; Average Annual Attendance: 158,000; Mem: dues $20-$5,000; ann meeting in June
Income: $2,000,000 (financed by state appropriation)
Library Holdings: Book Volumes 3000+, Exhibition Catalogs
Special Subjects: Afro-American Art, Anthropology, Archaeology, Ceramics, Collages, Costumes, Crafts, Decorative Arts, Dioramas, Drawings, Embroidery, Etchings & Engravings, Flasks & Bottles, Folk Art, Furniture, Glass, Graphics, Historical Material, Ivory, Landscapes, Leather, Maps, Metalwork, Mosaics, Painting-American, Pewter, Photography, Porcelain, Portraits, Posters, Pottery, Prints, Scrimshaw, Sculpture, Silver, Stained Glass, Textiles, Watercolors, Woodcarvings, Woodcuts
Collections: American fine & decorative arts of the 19th, 20th & 21st centuries, American painting with spec emphasis on the Stieglitz Circle, Regionalist, Abstract Artists, NJ fine & decorative arts, Ben Shahn's graphic work; art by African-Americans, NJ History; Archaeology & Ethnography, Natural History
Exhibitions: Changing exhibs focus on American artists, NJ material culture, science, archaeology; long-term exhib galleries on the fine art, NJ history & archaeology
Publications: Annual report (on line); catalogs & irregular serials
Activities: Classes for adults & children; dramatic progs; docent training; lect open to pub; lect for mems; vis lectrs per yr varies; concerts; gallery talks; tours; individual objects, artifacts & specimens lent to other qualified institutions; book traveling exhibs; mus shop sells books

M **OLD BARRACKS MUSEUM,** 101 Barrack St, Trenton, NJ 08608. Tel 609-396-1776; Fax 609-777-4000; Email info@barracks.org; Web: www.barracks.org; *Dir* Richard Patterson; *Tour Coordr* Linda Mathies; *Develop Coordr* Cathleen Crown
Open Mon - Sat 10 AM - 5 PM, cl Sun, New Year's Day, Thanksgiving, Christmas Eve & Day; Admis adults $8, seniors & students $6, children 5 & under free; Built 1758, estab 1902 as mus of history & decorative arts; Located in English barracks that housed Hessian Soldiers Dec 1776 & served as American Military hospital during Revolutionary War; Average Annual Attendance: 30,000; Mem: 460; dues $30, $40, $60 $125 & $200; ann meeting Sep
Income: Financed by mem, state appropriation & donations
Special Subjects: Decorative Arts, Period Rooms, Historical Material
Collections: American decorative arts 1750-1820, archaeological materials, early American tools & household equipment, military artifacts, 19th century New Jersey portraits, patriotic paintings & prints
Publications: The Barracks Parade, quarterly newsletter; The Barracks of Trenton & Princeton, book
Activities: Classes for children; dramatic progs; docent training; lects open to pub, 3 vis lectrs per yr; tours; exten dept serves elementary schools; individual paintings & original objects of art lent to mus; lending collection contains slides & reproduction military objects/costumes; book traveling exhibs; mus shop sells books, reproductions, prints, slides, historical toys & ceramics

M **TRENTON CITY MUSEUM,** Ellarslie in Cadwalader Park, Trenton, NJ 08606; PO Box 1034, Trenton, NJ 08606. Tel 609-989-3632; Fax 609-989-3624; Email info@ellarslie.org; Web: www.ellarslie.org; *Mus Shop Mgr* Mary Kay Girmschied
Open Wed - Sat noon - 4 PM, Sun 1 - 4 PM, cl Mon & Tues, municipal holidays; No admis fee; Estab 1973 to provide a cultural window into the ongoing life of the city & its people; Mus is a historical site, an Italian Revival mansion; only remaining example of John Notman architecture in Trenton & is located in historic Cadwalader Park, designed by Frederick Law Olmstead; Average Annual Attendance: 13,000; Mem: Dues $25 - $1,000
Income: Financed by mem & city appropriation
Special Subjects: Ceramics, Porcelain
Collections: Trenton-made Ceramics, objects made in or pertaining to Trenton, full set of Trenton directories
Exhibitions: Ellarslie Open XXIII
Publications: Biannual newsletter
Activities: Classes for adults & children accompany changing exhibits; lect open to pub, 10 vis lectrs per yr; sales shop sells books, prints, original art, jewelry & toys for children

UNION

M **KEAN UNIVERSITY,** James Howe Gallery, 1000 Morris Ave, Kean University Art Galleries Center for Academic Success Union, NJ 07083-7131. Tel 908-527-2307, 527-2347; Web: www.library.kean.edu; *Dir Gallery* Neil Tetkowski
Open Fall Mon 12:30 PM - 3:30 PM, Tues 10 AM - 3 PM, Wed 10 AM - 4:30 PM, Thurs 1:30 PM - 3:30 PM, Fri 10 AM -1 PM, call for additional hours; No admis fee; Estab 1971 as a forum to present all art forms to students & the community through original exhibitions, catalogues, fine art, by guest cur, art history & mus training students; One gallery 22 x 34 ft plus an alcove 8 x 18 ft on first floor of arts & humanities building; Average Annual Attendance: 3,000
Income: Financed by state appropriation & private grants
Special Subjects: Painting-American
Collections: American painting, prints sculpture by Audobon, L Baskin, Robert Cooke, Max Ernst, Lamar Dodd, W Homer, P Jenkins, J Stella, Tony Smith, Walter Darbby Bannard, Werner Drewes, B J O Norfeldt, James Rosenquist, Robert Rauschenberg, Odilon Redon, photographs, rare books & 1935-50 design & furniture, Ben Yamimoto Art Work
Exhibitions: Rotating exhibits
Publications: Catalogues for exhibitions
Activities: Dramatic progs; lects open to pub; individual paintings lent to colleges, institutions, corporations & departments on the campus

L **Nancy Thompson Library**, 1000 Morris Ave, Union, NJ 07083-7133. Tel 908-737-4618; Fax 908-527-2365; Email library@turbo.kean.edu; Web: www.library.kean.edu; *Univ Librn* Luis Rodriguez
Open Mon - Thurs 8 AM - 12 AM, Fri 8 AM - 5 PM, Sat 9 AM - 4 PM, Sun 1 - 10 PM; Estab 1855 to support instruction
Income: State appropriation & private grants
Purchases: $6,000
Library Holdings: Audio Tapes 150, Book Volumes 265,000, Exhibition Catalogs, Filmstrips, Pamphlets, Periodical Subscriptions 1350, Slides

UPPER MONTCLAIR

M **MONTCLAIR STATE UNIVERSITY,** Art Galleries, 1 Normal Ave, Life Hall Upper Montclair, NJ 07043-1699. Tel 973-655-3382; Fax 973-655-7665; Email artgalleries@mail.montclair.edu; Web: www.montclair.edu/arts/galleries; *Pres* Dr Susan A Cole; *VPres* Richard Lynde; *Dean* Geoffrey Newman; *Dir* M Teresa Lapid Rodriguez; *Chmn Art Dept* Daryl Moore
Open Mon, Wed & Fri 9:30 AM - 4 PM, Tues & Thurs 10 AM - 6 PM; No admis fee; Estab 1973; Circ 100,000; Three galleries with 1,200 sq ft, 600 sq ft & 600 sq ft; Average Annual Attendance: 5,000
Income: Financed by the college
Collections: Cosla Collection of Renaissance Art, Lida Hilton Print Collection, Wingert Collection of African & Oceanic Art, Lucy Lewis Collection of Native American Pottery
Exhibitions: Contemporary East Indian Artists; Japanese Expressions in Paper
Activities: Classes for adults; lect open to public; concerts; gallery talks; scholarships offered

L **Calcia Art and Design Image Library**, 1 Normal Ave, Calcia Art and Design Bldg Rm 214 Montclair, NJ 07043-1699. Tel 973-655-4445; Fax 973-655-7833
Open by appt only
Income: Financed by state funding
Library Holdings: Slides, Video Tapes
Collections: 100,000 35mm art slides

WAYNE

M **WILLIAM PATERSON UNIVERSITY,** University Galleries, 300 Pompton Rd, Wayne, NJ 07470-2152. Tel 973-720-2654; Fax 973-720-3270; Email evangelistak@wpunj.edu; Web: www.wpunj.edu; *Dir* Kristen Evangelista; *Gallery Mgr* Emily Johnsen; *Visual Resources Cur* Heidi Rempel
Open during academic yr: Mon - Fri 10 AM - 5 PM, select Sun noon - 4 PM (see website for details); No admis fee; Estab 1979 to educate students & visitors through exhibits & programs; 5000 sq ft space divided into three gallery rooms specializing in the exhibition of contemporary art; Average Annual Attendance: 10,000
Income: Financed by Univ; New Jersey State Council on the Arts, various grants
Special Subjects: African Art, Landscapes, Painting-American, Photography, Prints, Sculpture
Collections: Permanent collection of 19th century landscapes, paintings & sculptures from 1950's to present, Tobias Collection of African and Oceanic Art and Artifacts, prints, artists books & photography
Exhibitions: Three gallery rooms of rotating exhibits of contemporary art that change twice during each semester
Publications: Exhibition catalogs
Activities: Exhibs; gallery tours; tours of outdoor sculpture; artist talks; panel discussions; arts educ workshops; lects open to public; 10 lectrs per yr; gallery talks; tours

WEST LONG BRANCH

M **800 GALLERY & ROTARY ICE HOUSE GALLERY,** Monmouth University, 400 Cedar Ave West Long Branch, NJ 07764-1804. Tel 732-571-3400
Call for hours
Collections: Paintings; photographs; sculpture; drawing; ceramics
Activities: Special events; receptions; temporary exhibits

WEST WINDSOR

M **MERCER COUNTY COMMUNITY COLLEGE,** The Gallery at Mercer, 1200 Old Trenton Rd, West Windsor, NJ 08550-3407. Tel 609-586-4800, Ext 3589; Email gallery@mccc.edu; Web: www.mccc.edu/community_gallery; *Gallery Dir* Dylan Wolfe
Open Mon - Thurs 11 AM - 3 PM, Wed until 7 PM, check for additional hours; No admis fee; Estab 1971 as an educational resource for students & the community; Gallery of 2,000 sq ft primarily for exhibiting work by New Jersey and other regional artists; Average Annual Attendance: 3,600
Income: Financed by college support, pub funding, M C Cultural & Heritage Commission grant & sales commissions
Purchases: Annual purchases from Mercer county artists and student exhibitions
Special Subjects: Ceramics, Folk Art
Collections: Painting by Wolf Kahn, Sculptures by Salvador Dali & Isaac Whitkin, Paintings by Reginald Neal, Darby Bannard, B J Nordfeldt, NJ artist collection, Art Work by Frank Rivera, Paintings by Mel Leipzig, Cybis Collection
Exhibitions: Rotating exhibs every 6-8 weeks
Publications: Mailing lists for exhibition post cards; occasional catalogue (ex: "Glimpses of America" catalogue)
Activities: Classes for adults & children; dramatic progs; lects open to pub, 12 vis lectrs per yr; concerts; gallery talks; tours; competitions with purchase awards; Mercer County Artist Purchase awards; scholarships offered; individual paintings & original objects of art lent to other galleries & museums; lending collection contains original prints; MCCC at Artworks located in Trenton, NJ; fine arts classes for adults & children in the central NJ/Bucks County, PA region. Warehouse gallery offers 5-7 annual exhibits by local & regional artists

L **Library**, 1200 Old Trenton Rd, West Windsor, NJ 08550-3407. Tel 609-586-4800; Web: www.mccc.edu/students/library; *Library Dir* Pam Price
Open Mon - Thurs 8 AM - 10 PM, Fri 8 AM - 5 PM, Sat 9 AM - 4 PM, cl Sun; Estab 1891 to provide library services for the col; portion of the main floor is devoted to permanent display cabinets. In addition display panels are used for faculty exhibits, community exhibits & traveling exhibits
Library Holdings: Audio Tapes 1460, Book Volumes 64,518, CD-ROMs 200, Filmstrips, Pamphlets 644, Periodical Subscriptions 718, Records 3107, Slides 17, Video Tapes 2878
Publications: Library handbook, annually; Videocassette catalog, annually

WOODBRIDGE

M **WOODBRIDGE TOWNSHIP CULTURAL ARTS COMMISSION,** Barron Arts Center, 582 Rahway Ave, Woodbridge, NJ 07095-3419. Tel 732-634-0413; Fax 732-634-8633; Email barronarts@twp.woodbridge.nj.us; Web: www.woodbridge.nj.us (link then to Barron Arts Center); *Chmn* Dr Dolores Gioffre; *Program Coordr* Brandon Powell; *Dir* Cynthia Knight
Open Mon - Fri 11 AM - 4 PM, Sat & Sun 2 - 4 PM, cl holidays; No admis fee, $5 suggested donation for concerts & lects; Estab 1977 to provide exhibits of nationally recognized artists, craftsmen & photographers, & of outstanding NJ talent; Gallery is housed in an 1877 Richardsonian Romanesque Revival building on the National Register of Historic Places; Average Annual Attendance: 10,000
Income: $71,000 (city appropriation)
Library Holdings: Cards, DVDs, Pamphlets
Exhibitions: Varied exhibits in art, juried shows, historical exhibits, monthly poetry readings
Activities: Classes for adults & children; dramatic progs; docent training; photography; children's summer camp; lects open to pub, 15 vis lectrs per yr; awards; concerts; tours; poetry readings; gallery talks; awards, Best of the Best Readers Choice Winner; sales shop sells original art, postcards, T-shirts, etc

NEW MEXICO

ALBUQUERQUE

M **516 ARTS,** 516 Central Ave SW, Albuquerque, NM 87102. Tel 505-242-1445; Fax 505-244-4101; Email info@516arts.org; Web: www.516arts.org; *Exec Dir* Suzanne Sbarge
Open Tues - Sat Noon - 5 PM; Admis free; 2006; nonprofit exhib space; Independent nonprofit arts & educ organization with a museum-style gallery in downtown Albuquerque; Average Annual Attendance: 35,000; Mem: 300
Income: Financed by grants, business sponsors, membership, art & gift shop sales
Publications: Land/Art New Mexico, art exhib catalogs; Isea2012 Albuquerque: Machine Wilderness; Digital Latin America; Fraction of a Second
Activities: Docent training; tours for students of all ages; performances; collaborations; public art, workshops for kids, teens & adults; lects open to pub; 3 - 10 vis lects per yr; tours; gallery talks; tours;; sales shop sells books, magazines, original art, reproductions, prints & t-shirts

M **ALBUQUERQUE MUSEUM OF ART & HISTORY,** 2000 Mountain Rd NW Albuquerque, NM 87104. Tel 505-243-7255; Fax 505-764-6546; Email albuquerquemuseum@cabq.gov; Web: www.albuquerquemuseum.org; *Dir* Cathy Wright; *Cur Art* Andrew Connors; *Cur History* Deborah Slaney; *Cur Educ* Elizabeth Becker
Open Tues - Sun 9 AM - 5 PM; Admis fee adults $3, seniors $2, children ages 4 - 12 $1; Estab 1967 as a municipal mus. Maintains photo archive & research library. Owns & operates Casa San Ysidro, the Gutierrez/Minge House, a historic site & Heritage Farm in the village of Corrales; Average Annual Attendance: 120,000; Mem: Benefactor $500, supporter $250, friend $100, general $60, senior $40
Income: Financed by city appropriation & Albuquerque Museum Foundation
Library Holdings: Auction Catalogs, Book Volumes, Clipping Files, Exhibition Catalogs, Original Art Works, Original Documents, Photographs, Prints, Sculpture
Special Subjects: American Western Art, Bronzes, Ceramics, Coins & Medals, Collages, Costumes, Crafts, Decorative Arts, Drawings, Embroidery, Etchings & Engravings, Flasks & Bottles, Folk Art, Furniture, Glass, Graphics, Hispanic Art, Historical Material, Jewelry, Landscapes, Latin American Art, Leather, Manuscripts, Maps, Metalwork, Painting-American, Painting-Spanish, Photography, Portraits, Pottery, Sculpture, Southwestern Art, Textiles, Watercolors, Woodcarvings, Woodcuts, Prints, Silver, Stained Glass

Collections: Decorative arts, costumes, fine arts and crafts, objects and artifacts relevant to our cultural history from 20,000 BC to present, photography, permanent coll of Southwest American, Hispanic & Native American art
Exhibitions: Sensory crossovers: Synesthesia in American Art
Publications: Abqmuseum, monthly; Sensory crossovers: Synesthesia in American Art, 2010
Activities: Classes for children; docent training; 10 vis lectrs per yr; concerts; gallery talks; tours; schols avail; original objects of art lent to qualified museums; hosts 1-2 nat & internat traveling exhibs; originate traveling exhibs with select museums; mus shop sells books, original art & prints photo archive

A **INDIAN ARTS & CRAFTS ASSOCIATION,** 4010 Carlisle NE, Ste C Albuquerque, NM 87107-4532. Tel 505-265-9149; Fax 505-265-8251; Email info@iaca.com; Web: www.iaca.com; *Bd Pres* Kathi Ouellet
Office hours vary; Admis varies; Estab 1974 to promote, preserve, protect & enhance the understanding of authentic handmade American Indian arts & crafts; Mem: 882; quarterly meetings in Jan, Apr, July & Oct
Income: Financed by mem dues, markets
Library Holdings: Book Volumes
Special Subjects: American Indian Art
Exhibitions: Annual Indian IACA Artists of the Year; IACA Spring Wholesale Market; IACA Fall Wholesale Market
Publications: Annual directory; brochures on various Indian arts & crafts; newsletter, 6 times per year
Activities: Marketing seminars for Indian artists & crafts persons; lects open to public & mem only, 4-5 vis lectrs per yr; competitions; Artist of the Year Awards

M **INDIAN PUEBLO CULTURAL CENTER,** 2401 12th St NW, Albuquerque, NM 87104-2397. Tel 505-843-7270; Fax 505-842-6959; Email info@indianpueblo.org; Web: www.indianpueblo.org; *Pres & CEO* Michael Canfield; *COO* Dwayne Virgint; *Acting Mus Dir* Monique Fragua
Open 9 AM - 5 PM; Admis adults $8.40, seniors $6.40, children (5-17) & students $5.40, children under 5 free; Estab 1976 to advance understanding & ensure perpetuation of Pueblo culture; Permanent exhibit on Pueblo culture & history & changing gallery on Native artists & issues; Average Annual Attendance: 125,000; Mem: 400; dues individual $80, family $125, students & seniors $20
Library Holdings: Audio Tapes, Book Volumes, Cassettes, Clipping Files, Fiche, Kodachrome Transparencies, Maps, Original Documents, Pamphlets, Periodical Subscriptions, Photographs, Slides, Video Tapes
Special Subjects: American Indian Art, Anthropology, Archaeology, Art History, Southwestern Art
Collections: Jewelry, paintings, photos, pottery, rugs, sculptures, textiles, Archives & library
Publications: Pueblo Horizons, quarterly membership publ
Activities: Educ progs for adults & children; docent training; lects open to pub; lects members only; 10 vis lectrs per yr; summer camp for children in June; quarterly arts markets; weekend Native dances; art demonstrations; mus shop sells books, original art, reproductions, prints, jewelry, pottery, clothing

M **NATIONAL HISPANIC CULTURAL CENTER, ART MUSEUM,** 1701 4th St SW, Albuquerque, NM 87102-4508. Tel 505-246-2261; Fax 505-246-2613; Web: www.nhccnm.org; *Exec Dir* Rebecca L Avitia; *Chmn* Thomas Briones
Open Tues - Sun 10 AM - 5 PM, cl New Year's Day, Easter, Thanksgiving, Christmas; Admis adults $6, senior citizens $5, school groups, children 16 & under, members & Sun free
Library Holdings: Book Volumes 11,000
Collections: contemporary & historic art, period photographs
Publications: quarterly newsletter, Que Pasa
Activities: Educ prog for children & Univ of New Mexico students; docent prog; computer training prog; lects; guided tours; arts festivals; concerts; dance recitals; films; theater; mus shop

A **NEW MEXICO ART LEAGUE,** Gallery & School, PO Box 16554, Albuquerque, NM 87191-6554. Tel 505-293-5034; Web: newmexicoartleague.wildapricot.org; *Pres* Cynthia Rowland; *Sec* Ann Pisto; *Treas* Kate Fry
Open Tues - Sat 10 AM - 4 PM, cl Sun - Mon; No admis fee; Estab 1929 to promote artists of New Mexico; art gallery; Members' works exhibited in space 1400 sq ft; Average Annual Attendance: 5,000; Mem: 325; dues $35; monthly mem meetings
Income: Financed by mem, sales, classes & gallery room rentals
Collections: National Small Paintings Exhibit
Exhibitions: 24th Annual Small Painting Exhibit (national competition)
Publications: Newsletter, monthly
Activities: Classes for adults & children; lects & workshops open to pub; 6 vis lectrs per year; gallery talks; tours; competitions with awards; individual paintings lent to schools & museums; lending collection contains original art works & prints, paintings, sculptures & slides; sales shop sells original art

M **NORTH FOURTH ART CENTER & GALLERY,** 4904 4th St NW, Albuquerque, NM 87107. Tel 505-345-2872; Fax 505-345-2896; Email info@vsartsnm.org; Web: vsartsnm.org/gallery; *Exec Dir* Marjorie Neset; *Deputy Dir* Brynne Badeaux; *Intake Coordr* Tamarah Gonzalez; *Day Arts Dir* Christopher MacQueen; *Exploratory Arts Dir* Tim Psomas; *Community Outreach Dir* Deborah Brink; *Visual Arts Outreach Dir* Susanna Kearny; *Technical Dir, Theatre Mgr & IT Mgr* Josh Bien
Open Mon - Fri 10 AM - 4 PM & by appt; Estab to promote art in a way that benefits the community
Collections: Work by diverse emerging & established artists
Exhibitions: Temporary exhibits
Activities: Educ progs; visual, performing & literary arts instruction; performance & exhib opportunities; Art programming

A **THE SOCIETY OF LAYERISTS IN MULTI-MEDIA (SLMM),** 1408 Georgia NE, Albuquerque, NM 87110; PO Box 897, Guthrie, OK 73044-0897. Tel 405-260-3455; Fax 405-293-6699; Email info@slmm.org; Web: www.slmm.org; *Founder* Mary Carroll Nelson; *Pres* Jaleh A Etemad; *VPres* Lynn C Mikami; *Exec Admin* Karen Van Hooser
Estab 1982; Network for artists; Mem: 400; assoc dues $40; annual meeting
Income: $4000 (financed by mem)
Collections: Mixed Media
Exhibitions: Exhibitions around the country; Calendar of Events on website "slmm.org"
Publications: Bridging Time & Space; newsletter, 2 times per year on web for members; The Art of Layering: Making Connections; Visual Journies
Activities: Art Educ; 3 lectrs per yr open to mems only; gallery talks; national & regional exhibs; ann conferences; mus shop sells books

M **UNIVERSITY OF NEW MEXICO,** University of New Mexico Art Museum, 1 University of New Mexico, MSC04 2570 Albuquerque, NM 87131-0001. Tel 505-277-4001; Fax 505-277-7315; Email artmuse@unm.edu; Web: artmuseum.unm.edu; *Dir* Arif Khan; *Cur Photographs & Prints* Mary Statzer; *Coll Mgr* Stephen Lockwood; *Preparator* Christopher Thobe; *Colls Asst* Mariah Carrillo
Open Tues - Fri 10 AM - 4 PM, Sat 10 AM - 8 PM, cl Sun - Mon & major holidays; No admis fee; Estab 1963; Maintains five galleries; a print & photograph room which is open to the pub at certain hours; Average Annual Attendance: 49,000; Mem: 200; dues $10-$500; annual meeting in May
Income: Financed by university appropriations, grants & donations
Special Subjects: Collages, Drawings, Etchings & Engravings, Graphics, Historical Material, Painting-American, Prints, Sculpture, Southwestern Art, Textiles
Collections: Spanish Colonial art, Tamarind Archive of lithographs, 19th & 20th century American painting & sculpture, drawings, prints by American & European masters, 19th & 20th century lithographs & photography
Publications: Bulletin; exhibition catalogs
Activities: Educ dept; lects open to pub; vis lectrs 6-8 per yr; gallery talks; tours; individual paintings & original objects of art lent to other comparable institutions; originates traveling exhibs

M **Raymond Jonson Collection & Archive,** MSC04 2570, 1 University of New Mexico, Albuquerque, NM 87131-0001. Tel 505-277-4001; Fax 505-277-7315; Web: www.unm.edu/~artmuse
Open by appt; No admis fee; Estab 1950 for the assemblage & preservation of a comprehensive collection of the works of Raymond Jonson; a depository for works of art by other artists & their preservation, with emphasis on the Transcendental Painting Group (1938-42); the exhibition of contemporary works of art; Average Annual Attendance: 4,000-6,000
Income: Financed through University & art museum trust & donations
Library Holdings: Audio Tapes, Book Volumes, CD-ROMs, Cards, Cassettes, Compact Disks, Exhibition Catalogs, Kodachrome Transparencies, Manuscripts, Memorabilia, Original Documents, Pamphlets, Photographs, Prints, Records, Slides, Video Tapes
Collections: Raymond Jonson Reserved Retrospective Collection of Paintings, other artists' works, Jonson Estate
Publications: The Art of Raymond Jonson; The Transcendental Painting Group, New Mexico 1938-1941; To Form From Air: Music & the Art of Raymond Jonson (2010)
Activities: individual paintings & original works of art lent to mus; lending collection contains color reproductions, original prints, slides, sculpture, 1000 books, 2000 original art & 2000 paintings; originate traveling exhibs; books sold by order

L **Fine Arts Library,** Fine Arts Ctr, Albuquerque, NM 87131-0001. Tel 505-277-2357; Fax 505-277-7134; Email falref@unm.edu; Web: www.unm.edu; *Dir* Karl Benedict; *Prin Cataloger* Laura Kohl; *Mgr Library Operations* Anne Schultz; *Library Information Specialist* Kyle Nelson
Open Mon - Thurs 8 AM - 9 PM, Fri 8 AM - 6 PM, Sat 10 AM - 6 PM, Sun Noon - 8 PM fall semester hours; Estab 1963 to provide library assistance, literature, microforms & sound recording materials to support the programs of the university in the areas of art, architecture, music & photography
Library Holdings: Audio Tapes, Book Volumes 120,000, CD-ROMs, Cards, Cassettes, Compact Disks, DVDs, Exhibition Catalogs, Fiche, Other Holdings, Pamphlets, Periodical Subscriptions 237, Records, Reels, Video Tapes
Special Subjects: American Indian Art, American Western Art, Architecture, Art Education, Art History, Ceramics, Conceptual Art, Decorative Arts, Drafting, Drawings, Furniture, Goldsmithing, Graphic Arts, Islamic Art, Jewelry
Collections: Dean Neuforth Landscape 1954, Untitled 1954 Oil on Masonite

ARTESIA

M **ARTESIA HISTORICAL MUSEUM AND ART CENTER,** 505 W Richardson Ave, Artesia, NM 88210-2062. Tel 575-748-2390; Fax 575-748-7345; Email artesiamuseum@artesianm.gov; Web: artesianm.gov (under Departments); *Mus Mgr* Nancy Dunn
Open Tues - Fri 9 AM - Noon & 1 - 5 PM, Sat 1 - 5 PM; No admis fee; Estab 1970 to preserve & make available local history; maintains reference & research library; Gallery showcases local & regional artists, exhibits drawn from permanent art collection, traveling exhibits; Average Annual Attendance: 2,000
Income: Financed by city appropriation
Special Subjects: American Western Art, Architecture, Drawings, Embroidery, Furniture, Historical Material, Laces, Landscapes, Leather, Manuscripts, Maps, Painting-American, Period Rooms, Photography, Pottery, Primitive art, Southwestern Art, Textiles, Watercolors
Collections: Art, Early Area History, Farm, Kitchen, Ranch, Native American Artifacts, Oil & Mineral, WWI & WWII, Genealogy, Native American Artifacts
Exhibitions: Honoring Artesia's Veterans, annual show; Artesia Quilters Guild, annual show; Russell Floore Memorial Student Art Show, annual show
Activities: School & civic club progs; lects open to pub, 1-3 vis lectrs per yr; gallery talks; tours; competitions with awards, Living Treasures (annual); individual paintings & objects of art lent to other mus & organizations; book traveling exhibs 1-2 per yr

CARLSBAD

M **CARLSBAD MUSEUM & ART CENTER,** 418 W Fox St, Carlsbad, NM 88220-5743. Tel 575-887-0276; Email museumstaff@cityofcarlsbadnm.com; Web:

www.cityofcarlsbadnm.com; *Mus Dir* Dave W Morgan; *Cur Colls* Edward Vanscotter
Open Mon - Sat 10 AM - 5 PM, cl New Year's Day, Martin Luther King Jr Day, Memorial Day, Independence Day, Labor Day, Veterans Day, Thanksgiving & day after, Christmas Eve & Day, Good Friday; No admis fee; 1931; interpret & preserve history & art of American Southwest, especially New Mexico; Art history; Average Annual Attendance: 11,000
Income: Financed by municipality
Special Subjects: American Indian Art, American Western Art, Anthropology, Archaeology, Bronzes, Ceramics, Historical Material, History of Art & Archaeology, Painting-American, Photography, Pre-Columbian Art, Sculpture, Southwestern Art, Carpets & Rugs, Dioramas, Leather, Painting-American, Pottery, Watercolors, Woodcarvings
Collections: New Mexico art, Pueblo pottery, Taos Society of Artists
Publications: newsletter, Amigos; exhibition brochures
Activities: Classes for adults & children; Lectures open to the public; Concerts; mus shop sells books, original art

CHURCH ROCK

M **RED ROCK PARK,** Red Rock Park, PO Box 10, Church Rock, NM 87311-0010. Tel 505-722-3829; Fax 505-905-1277; Email redrockpark@ci.gallup.nm.us; Web: www.gallupnm.gov; *Park Dir* Ben Welch; *Park Supv* Pete Becenti; *Park Specialist* Beverly Lovett
Open Mon - Fri 8 AM - 4 PM, cl on holidays; Admis adults $3, children $1.50; Native American art, pottery, rugs, jewelry, Anasazi artifacts; Average Annual Attendance: 10,000
Library Holdings: Book Volumes 350, Cards, Clipping Files, Manuscripts, Pamphlets, Photographs, Prints
Special Subjects: American Indian Art, American Western Art, Anthropology, Archaeology, Costumes, Crafts, Ethnology, Historical Material, Painting-American, Southwestern Art
Collections: Kachina Carving Doll Collection, Anasazi relics, arts & crafts of Navajo, Zuni, Hopi & other Pueblos, specimens of geological, herbarium, archaeological & cultural materials of the Four Corners area
Exhibitions: Permanent exhibits: Navajo Hogan; Pueblo Culture; Elizabeth Andron Houser Collection of Native American Arts; Gallup Intertribal Indian Ceremonial Posters, Jewelry, Basketry, Navajo Rugs; temporary exhibits vary
Publications: Exhibitions catalog; quarterly newsletter
Activities: Lects open to pub; gallery talks; tours; concerts; rodeos; individual paintings & original objects of art lent to other museums; book traveling exhibs 1-4 per yr; originates traveling exhibs to museums & arts & educational organizations; sales shop sells books, reproductions, magazines, prints, sandpaintings, pottery, jewelry & other Native American crafts, cassettes & compact discs of Native American music

CIMARRON

M **PHILMONT SCOUT RANCH,** Philmont Museum - Seton Memorial Library, 17 Deer Run Rd, Cimarron, NM 87714-9638. Tel 575-376-2281; Email philmont.museums@scouting.org; *Dir* David Werhane; *Librn* Robin Taylor; *Cur Villa Philmont* Nancy Klein
Open Mon - Sat 8 AM - 5 PM; No admis fee; Estab 1967 to exhibit art & history of Southwestern United States; 3 galleries (new exhibs ea yr; tours of historic Estate of White Phillips; Average Annual Attendance: 30,000
Income: Financed by endowment & sales desk revenue
Collections: Art by Ernest Thompson Seton, American Indian Art, History of Boy Scouts of America, History of New Mexico
Exhibitions: Ernest Thompson Seton's Collection of Plains Indian Art
Activities: Docent progs; lects open to pub; gallery talks; tours; lending collection contains over 6000 items; BBC, Smithsonian, Seton Centre, The Academy for the Love of Learning; mus shop sells books, original art, reproductions, prints & native American jewelry

CLOVIS

M **EULA MAE EDWARDS MUSEUM & GALLERY,** Clovis Community College, 417 Schepps Blvd Clovis, NM 88101-8345. Tel 505-769-4956; Fax 575-769-4190; Email stephanie.spencer@clouis.edu; Web: www.clouis.edu; *Div Chair Fine Art & Commun* Jan Lloyd
Open upon request
Special Subjects: Mixed Media, Photography, Sculpture, Silversmithing, Watercolors, Woodcarvings, Woodcuts, American Indian Art
Collections: Artwork from local artists, Paintings & photographs
Activities: Lects open to pub, vis lectrs 3-4 per yr; gallery talks

DEMING

M **DEMING-LUNA MIMBRES MUSEUM,** 301 S Silver St, Deming, NM 88030. Tel 575-546-2382; Email dlmm@qwestoffice.net; Web: www.lunacountyhistoricalsociety.com; *Coordr* Katy Hofacket; *Archives* Art Ramon; *Dir* Sharon Lein
Open Mon - Sat 9 AM - 4 PM, cl New Year's Day, Easter, Thanksgiving & Christmas Day; No admis fee with donations; Estab 1957, moved into Old Armory 1978, to preserve Luna County history, historical items & records for reference; Art gallery is in a passageway 50 ft x 10 ft, one full block, no windows; open to local artists for displays; Average Annual Attendance: 21,000; Mem: 200; dues $5 & up; annual meeting in Jan
Income: Financed by donations & endowment earnings
Special Subjects: American Indian Art, Anthropology, Decorative Arts, Dolls, Eskimo Art, Folk Art, Furniture, Glass, Historical Material, Leather, Pottery
Collections: Chuck wagon, vintage clothing, dolls, frontier life objects & other items on the local history, Mimbres Indian artifacts, mine equipment, minerals, paintings & saddles, camera display, phone equipment, quilt room, old lace display, National Guard display, Bataan-Corregidor display & monument, facsimile of front of Harvey House, bell collection, bottle collection, china, ceramics & silver displays, antiques, Military Room
Publications: History of Luna County & Supplement One
Activities: Dramatic progs; docent training; tours; service awards; mus shop sells Indian jewelry, postcards & pottery

LAS CRUCES

M **BRANIGAN CULTURAL CENTER,** 500 N Water St, Las Cruces, NM 88001-1224. Tel 505-541-2155; Fax 505-525-3645; Web: www.las-cruces.org/public-services/museums; *Mgr* Garland Courts; *Cur Educ* Mary Kay Shannon; *Cur Educ* Carol Blue; *Asst Mgr* Rebecca Slaughter
Open Mon - Fri 10 AM - 5 PM, Sat 9 AM - 1 PM, cl New Year's Day, Martin Luther King Jr Day, Presidents' Day, Memorial Day, Independence Day, Labor Day, Thanksgiving & day after, Christmas; No admis fee; Average Annual Attendance: 79,000
Collections: Las Cruces history, 20th century art, Victorian artifacts

M **NEW MEXICO STATE UNIVERSITY,** Art Gallery, PO Box 30001, MSC 3572, Las Cruces, NM 88001. Tel 575-646-2545; Fax 575-646-8036; Email artglry@nmsu.edu; Web: uag.nmsu.edu; *Dir* Marisa Sage; *Gallery Mgr* Jasmine Woodul
Open Tues - Sat 10 AM - 4 PM, Wed noon - 4 PM & 6 PM- 8 PM; No admis fee; Gallery estab in 1973 as an educational resource for the University & southern New Mexico; 5000 sq ft exhibition space; Average Annual Attendance: 23,000; Mem: 200; dues $10 & up; annual meeting in June
Purchases: Eric Avery, Luis Jimenez, Frances Whitehead, Garo Antreasian, Hollis Sigler & Gregory Amenoff
Special Subjects: Ceramics, Crafts, Drawings, Etchings & Engravings, Folk Art, Hispanic Art, Landscapes, Painting-American, Pre-Columbian Art, Prints, Religious Art, Southwestern Art, Woodcuts
Collections: 19th Century Retablos from Mexico, 20th century prints, photographs, works on paper, graphics & paintings
Exhibitions: El Favor De Los Santos; The Retablo Collection of New Mexico State University; Close to the Border VIII
Publications: Visiones, biannual arts newsletter; semiannual exhibit catalogs
Activities: Docent training; school tours & outreach; family day; lects open to public, 12 vis lectrs per year; gallery talks; tours; competitions with awards; individual paintings & original objects of art lent to museums with appropriate security & climate control conditions; lending collection contains original art works, original prints, paintings & photographs; book traveling exhibs up to 5 per year; originates traveling exhibs circulating to art museums

LAS VEGAS

M **NEW MEXICO HIGHLANDS UNIVERSITY,** The Ray Drew Gallery, PO Box 9000, Las Vegas, NM 87701-9000. Tel 505-425-7511, 454-3338; Fax 505-454-0026; Email gallery@nmhu.edu; *Art Dir* Bob Read
Open Mon - Fri 8 AM - 5 PM, Sat & Sun 1 - 5 PM; No admis fee; Estab 1956 to acquaint University & townspeople with art of the past & present; Gallery dimensions approx 20 x 40 ft; Average Annual Attendance: 4,000-5,000
Income: Financed by state appropriation
Library Holdings: Original Art Works, Prints
Collections: Permanent coll, Fine art print coll 1500s to present
Exhibitions: Twelve individual & group shows
Publications: University general catalog, annually
Activities: Classes for adults & children; lects open to pub, 1 vis lectr per yr; concerts; gallery talks; tours; competitions; book traveling exhibs, 1-2 per yr; originate traveling exhibs

A **SURFACE DESIGN ASSOCIATION, INC,** PO Box 4044, Las Vegas, NM 87701-7044. Tel 707-829-3110; Fax 707-829-3285; Email info@surfacesign.org; Web: www.surfacedesign.org; *Pres* Astrid Bennett; *Treas* Sarah Bush; *Ed Surface Design Journal* Marci McDade; *Exec Dir* Danielle Kelly
Open 9 AM - 4 PM; No admis fee; Estab 1976; Mem: 3800; dues students $40, regular $75, digital $60
Income: Financed by mem
Publications: SDA NewBlog, quarterly; Surface Design Journal, quarterly; eNews, monthly
Activities: Classes for adults; national conferences; workshops; seminars; lect open to members only; competitions with cash prizes; scholarships & fels offered; originate traveling exhibs

LORDSBURG

M **SHAKESPEARE GHOST TOWN,** 2 1/2 Mile S of Main St, Lordsburg, NM 88045; PO Box 253, Lordsburg, NM 88045-0253. Tel 505-542-9034; Web: www.shakespeareghostown.com; *Dir & Pres* Emanuel D Hough; *Develop Mem* Jeane La Marca; *Pub Rels* Steve Hill
Open during regularly-scheduled tours or by appt; Admis adults & seniors $4, children 6 - 12 $3, mems & children under 6 no admis fee; Estab 1970; A National Historic Site; pub nonprofit org; FT volunteers 4, PT volunteers 20; handicapped-accessible ramps. Shakespeare Ghost Town is the remains of a pioneer, southwestern town. Walk the streets trod by Billy the Kid, John Ringo, Curley Bill, Russian Bill, The Clantons, Jim Hughes and Sandy King. Emphasis on American SW History 1856 - 1935; Average Annual Attendance: 3000; Mem: dues Life $500, Patron $100, Sponsor or Bus $50, Family $25, Individual $10
Collections: 300-vol library on Southwest History, Blacksmith shop & items, Seven historic buildings including The Grant House, Stratford Hotel, Old Mail Station, among others
Publications: Shakespeare Quarterly, newsletter
Activities: Re-enactments & living history 4 times per yr; guided tours

LOS ALAMOS

M **FULLER LODGE ART CENTER,** 2132 Central Ave Frnt, Los Alamos, NM 87544-4013; PO Box 1295, Espanola, NM 87303-1295. Tel 505-662-1635; Email info@fullerlodgeartcenter.com; Web: www.fullerlodgeartcenter.com; *Dir* Ken Nebel; *Communs Coordr* Nancy Coombs; *Gallery Shop Mgr* Amy Bjarke; *Bookkeeper* Pam Erickson
Open Mon - Sat 10 AM - 4 PM; No admis fee; Estab 1977 to provide an art center to the regional area; to foster the interests of the artists & art interested pub of the Community; Circ 100 books monthly; Located on first floor of historic Fuller Lodge; Average Annual Attendance: 20,000
Income: Financed by county, gallery, gallery shop sales, annual arts & crafts fairs
Library Holdings: Book Volumes, Exhibition Catalogs, Original Art Works
Exhibitions: Rotating exhibits every 6 weeks
Activities: Classes for adults & children; seminars for artists; docent training; lects open to pub; competitions with awards; gallery talks; book traveling exhibs; sales shop sells original art, jewelry, cards & prints, small community art library

M **MESA PUBLIC LIBRARY ART GALLERY,** 2400 Central Ave, Los Alamos, NM 87544-4014. Tel 505-662-8240; Fax 505-662-8245; Web: www.losalamosnm.us; *Dir* Carol Meine; *Dir* Charles Kalogeros-Chattan
Open Mon-Thurs 10AM-9PM, Fri 10AM-6PM, Sat 10AM-5PM, Sun 12PM-5PM
Collections: works by local, regional & nat artists; paintings; prints; drawings; photographs; sculpture; architectural models; digital art; decorative arts

MESILLA

M **GADSDEN MUSEUM,** 1875 Boutz Rd, Mesilla, NM 88046; PO Box 147, Mesilla, NM 88046-0147. Tel 575-526-6293; Web: www.gadsdenmuseum.org; *Owner & Cur* Mary F Bird; *Co-Owner* R Eileen Betzen
Open Summer Mon - Sat 9 - 11 AM & 1 - 5 PM, Winter Mon - Sat, Sun by appt, cl Easter, Thanksgiving, Christmas; Admis $5 per person; Estab 1931 to preserve the history of Mesilla Valley & ancestor Col. Albert Jennings Fountain history of family to the present generation; 1860 structure; Average Annual Attendance: 3,000
Income: $2,000 (financed by donations)
Special Subjects: Dolls, Glass, Military Art, Painting-American, Portraits, Pottery, Religious Art, Southwestern Art, Textiles, Woodcarvings
Collections: Civil War coll, clothing, gun coll, Indian artifacts, including pottery, paintings, Santo coll
Activities: Tours

PORTALES

M **EASTERN NEW MEXICO UNIVERSITY,** Runnels Gallery, Golden Library, 1500 S Ave K, ENMU Station 54 Portales, NM 88130-7400. Tel 575-562-2778; Fax 575-562-2388; Web: www.enmu.edu; *Chair Art, Asst Prof Art & Graphic Design* Brad Hamann; *Gallery Mgr* Bryan Hahn; *Prof Art & Animation* Greg Erf; *Prof Art* Greg Senn; *Prof Art* Mic Muhlbauer; *Asst Prof Art & Graphic Design* David Deal
Open 7 AM - 9 PM; No admis fee; Estab 1935 for exhibiting student & professional artists' artwork; gallery is room converted for revolving shows
Income: Financed by University funds
Collections: Student works in Art Department Collection
Activities: Individual paintings & original objects of art lent to the university

L **Golden Library/Runnels Gallery,** 1500 S Ave K, Station 32, Portales, NM 88130-7400. Tel 575-562-2607; Fax 575-562-2388; Email enmuart@enmu.edu; Web: www.enmu.edu; *Library Dir* Melveta Walker; *Gallery Mgr* Christopher Calderon
Open Mon - Thurs 7 AM - 12 AM, Fri 7 AM - 8 PM, Sat 10 AM - 7 PM, Sun Noon - 12 AM; No admis fee; Estab 1934; Public exhibits & artist presentations
Income: $3000 (financed by University & grants)
Purchases: Some student art is purchased
Library Holdings: Audio Tapes, Book Volumes 10,000, Cards, Cassettes, Exhibition Catalogs, Fiche, Filmstrips, Framed Reproductions, Kodachrome Transparencies, Micro Print, Motion Pictures, Original Art Works, Pamphlets, Periodical Subscriptions 35, Photographs, Prints, Records, Reels, Sculpture, Slides, Video Tapes
Activities: Gallery talks; sponsoring of competitions; 6 vis lectrs per yr

ROSWELL

M **ROSWELL ARTIST-IN-RESIDENCE FOUNDATION,** (Anderson Museum of Contemporary Art) Anderson Museum of Contemporary Art, 409 E College Blvd Roswell, NM 88201-7524. Tel 575-623-5600; Fax 575-623-5603; Email email@roswellamoca.org; Web: www.roswellamoca.org; *CEO & Pres* Donald B Anderson; *Exec Dir* Dameron Midgette; *Mus Co-Dir* Nancy Fleming; *Mus Co-Dir* Susan Wink; *Residency Dir* Stephen Fleming
Open Mon - Fri 9 AM - 4 PM, Sat & Sun 1 - 5 PM, cl New Year's Day, Independence Day, Thanksgiving, Christmas; No admis fee; Estab 1994; 22,000 sq ft; 10 galleries; Average Annual Attendance: 10,000+; Mem: Supporter levels begin at $20
Income: 501c3 non-profit
Library Holdings: CD-ROMs, DVDs, Exhibition Catalogs, Memorabilia, Pamphlets, Slides
Special Subjects: Ceramics, Collages, Dioramas, Drawings, Landscapes, Metalwork, Mosaics, Photography, Sculpture, Textiles, Watercolors, Woodcarvings, Woodcuts
Collections: Collection of works by 200+ former fellows of the Roswell Artist-in-Residence prog
Publications: brochure; newsletter
Activities: Concerts; Tours

M **ROSWELL MUSEUM & ART CENTER,** 100 W 11th St, Roswell, NM 88201-4998. Tel 575-624-6744; Fax 575-624-6765; Email rufe@roswellmuseum.org; Web: www.roswellmuseum.org; *Pres Board Trustees* Robert Phillips; *VPres* Jimi Gadzia; *Treas/Secy* Elly Mulkey; *Asst Dir* Caroline Brooks; *Cur Coll* Andrew John Cecil; *Registrar* Stacie Petersen; *Dir* Laurie Rufe; *Cur Educ* Ellen Moore
Open Mon - Sat 9 AM - 5 PM, Sun & holidays 1 - 5 PM, cl Thanksgiving, Christmas Eve, Christmas & New Year's Day; No admis fee; Estab 1937 to promote & cultivate the fine arts. Purpose: To increase public enjoyment of art, history, and cultural change with particular focus in the Southwest; 16 galleries are maintained for art & historical collections; plus Robert H Goddard rocket collection; 24,000 sq ft of exhibition space. Maintains reference library; Average Annual Attendance: 65,000; Mem: 700; dues $15 & up
Income: $1,036,344 (financed by mem, city & county appropriation)
Library Holdings: Auction Catalogs, Audio Tapes, Book Volumes, CD-ROMs, Cassettes, DVDs, Exhibition Catalogs, Manuscripts, Pamphlets, Periodical Subscriptions, Photographs, Video Tapes
Special Subjects: Afro-American Art, American Indian Art, American Western Art, Anthropology, Archaeology, Bronzes, Ceramics, Collages, Costumes, Crafts, Decorative Arts, Dolls, Drawings, Etchings & Engravings, Ethnology, Folk Art, Graphics, Hispanic Art, Historical Material, Landscapes, Latin American Art, Leather, Mexican Art, Painting-American, Portraits, Pottery, Pre-Columbian Art, Prints, Prints, Sculpture, Sculpture, Southwestern Art, Textiles, Watercolors, Woodcarvings, Woodcuts
Collections: Regional & Native American fine arts & crafts & Western historical artifacts, international graphics coll, 20th century Southwestern paintings & sculpture, drawings, Hispanic art
Exhibitions: Permanent collection plus 10-14 temporary exhibitions annually
Publications: Bulletin, quarterly; Exhibition Catalogs
Activities: Classes for adults & children; docent training; school outreach prog; lects open to pub, 8-10 vis lectrs per yr; concerts; gallery talks; tours; schols for children's classes offered; individual paintings & original art objects lent to qualified mus; book traveling exhibs 3-4 per yr; mus shop sells books, magazines, original art, reproductions & prints

L **Library,** 100 W 11th St, Roswell, NM 88201. Tel 505-624-6744; Fax 505-624-6765; Email jordan@roswellmuseum.org; Web: www.roswellmuseum.org; *Libm & Mus Library Cataloger* Candace Jordan; *Exec Dir* Jeanie Weiffenbach; *Asst Dir* Caroline Knebelsberger
Open Mon - Fri 1 PM - 4:45 PM, cl holidays & vacation; Estab 1937 as a study for reading, research in art, anthropology and later regional history; Circ 1,000 items ann; Reference only; Average Annual Attendance: 500
Income: Endowments, gifts, grants, City of Roswell pays much of operating expense, portion of museum's budget, whether from City of Roswell or Grant is allocated for library purchases
Library Holdings: Audio Tapes 232, Book Volumes 5812, CD-ROMs 7, Cassettes, Clipping Files 1670, Exhibition Catalogs 1500, Filmstrips, Manuscripts 30, Maps 44, Memorabilia 20, Motion Pictures 33, Original Documents 300, Pamphlets 1500, Periodical Subscriptions 33, Photographs 2000, Slides 7000, Video Tapes 425
Special Subjects: American Indian Art, Ceramics, Historical Material, Painting-American, Photography, Printmaking, Southwestern Art, Ethnology, Landscapes, Pottery, Pre-Columbian Art, Religious Art, Sculpture
Collections: Rogers Aston Library Collection, Robert H Goddard Collection & Archives, New Mexico Artists' Files, Artist-in-Residence Files

SANDIA PARK

M **TINKERTOWN MUSEUM,** 121 Sandia Crest Rd, Sandia Park, NM 87047; PO Box 303, Sandia Park, NM 87047-0303. Tel 505-281-5233; Web: www.tinkertown.com; *Dir & Owner* Carla Ward
Open daily Apr 1 - Nov 1 9 AM - 6 PM, cl Nov - Mar; Adults $4; Seniors $3.50; Kids $2; Estab 1983; Folk art mus created over the course of 40 yrs by the late Ross Ward (1940 - 2002); what was once a four-room summer cabin has been transformed into a 22-rm legacy showcasing one man's work of carvings & colls; Average Annual Attendance: 26,000
Income: $160,000 admissions & gift shop sales
Special Subjects: Dioramas, Dolls, Drawings, Folk Art, Miniatures, Painting-American, Sculpture, Woodcarvings
Collections: Over 40 yrs worth of woodcarvings including a 1880s miniature animated western town, three-ring circus, and many handmade dolls & toys, colls assembled by Ross Ward & his wife including a wedding cake couple coll made up of 140 couples, modern day & antique swords, circus banners & memorabilia including a side show giant's shoes & pants, 7 antique mechanical coin-operated arcade machines, several hundred dolls & toys, handmade antique western livery & mining memorabilia
Publications: I Did All This While You Were Watching TV-The Tinkertown Story; Emily Finds a Dog-A Tinkertown Tale
Activities: Festival of Tinkering, in conjunction with local school art classes; mus related items for sale

SANTA FE

M **CARL & MARILYNN THOMA ART FOUNDATION,** Art House Santa Fe, 231 Delgado St, Santa Fe, NM 87501. Tel 505-995-0231; Email info@thomafoundation.org; Web: thomafoundation.org; *Gallery Attendant* Kitty Ballard-Ryan; *Assoc Dir & Cur Contemporary Art* Staci Boris; *Progs Coordr* Helen Colton; *Communs Mgr* Robyn Day; *Cur Digital Art* Jason Foumberg; *Dir Strategic Initiatives* Erin Fowler; *Adminstr* Ashley Klingler; *Exhibs Mgr & Progs Coord* Kathleen Richards; *Colls Mgr & Registrar* Kate Weinstein
Open Thurs - Sat 10 AM - 5 PM; Estab 1986 to support the visual arts, exhib development, fellowships, and curatorial position endowments
Collections: Digital & electronic art, Japanese bamboo, post-war painting & sculpture, Spanish colonial
Exhibitions: Rotating exhibits
Activities: Lects open to pub; tours; art programming; seminars; symposiums

A **THE CENTER FOR CONTEMPORARY ARTS OF SANTA FE,** 1050 Old Pecos Trail, Santa Fe, NM 87505-2688. Tel 505-982-1338; Fax 505-820-0751; Email contact@ccasantafe.org; Web: www.ccasantafe.org; *Cinema Dir* Jason Silverman; *Exec Dir & Chief Cur* Stuart A Ashman; *Asst Cur & Exhibitions Coordr* Shastyn Blomquist
Open Mon - Sat Noon - 5 PM; open evenings for performances or cinema screenings; Admis $5 for gallery; films: mems $8, non mem $10; Estab 1979, as a multidisciplinary contemporary arts organization. Hosts performance art: dance, poetry, musical, mixed media, films; Exhibition space, gallery, cinema (2 theatres), living room, workshop space, Turrell sky space; Average Annual Attendance: 64,000 (all events); Mem: 535
Exhibitions: Visual arts exhibitions
Publications: catalogs for exhibits, public program guide for exhibs
Activities: Classes for adults & youth (middle-HS & college); performing, visual, mixed media, & drawing workshops; cinema progs; lects open to public, 25 vis lectrs per year; concerts, film, theatre; gallery talks; tours

M **GEORGIA O'KEEFFE MUSEUM,** 217 Johnson St, Santa Fe, NM 87501-1826. Tel 505-946-1000; Fax 505-946-1091; Web: www.okeeffemuseum.org; *Dir* Robert A Kret; *Cur* Carolyn Kastner; *Registrar Colls Mgr* Judith Chiba Smith; *Head Conservation* Dale Kronkright; *Communs Mgr* Mara Harris; *Educ* Liz Brindley; *Dir Fin* Rich Murray; *Dir IT & Opers* Ben Finberg; *Sr Director Colls & Interpretation* Cody Hartley; *Director of Research Center* Eumie Imm Stroukoff; *Dir Employee & Organizational Develop* Cathy Ullery; *Director Historic Properties* Agapita Judy Lopez
Open daily 10 AM - 7 PM, Fridays 10 AM - 7 PM; cl Easter Sunday, Thanksgiving Day, Christmas Day & New Year's Day; Admis adults $13, students 18 & up with ID $11, youth under 18; Estab 1997; Average Annual Attendance: 159,000; Mem: 1,800+; dues individual $60, household $80, NM Household $65, Supporter $150, Friend $250, Patron $500, Benefactor $1,000, Director's Circle $2,500
Income: Financed by endowment
Library Holdings: Book Volumes, DVDs, Exhibition Catalogs, Manuscripts, Original Art Works, Original Documents, Periodical Subscriptions, Photographs 1,770, Sculpture
Special Subjects: Drawings, Painting-American, Photography, Sculpture, Watercolors
Collections: 2,989 works: 1,149 by Georgia O'Keeffe & 1,840 by other artists, The Georgia O'Keeffe Foundation Collection, acquired 2006, Georgia O'Keeffe Ghost Ranch home, Abiquiu House & Studio
Activities: Classes for adults & children; docent training; teacher development; school outreach; Art & Leadership Prog; internships; lects open to pub; 10 vis lectrs per yr; concerts; gallery talks; tours; schols; Fellowship program; book prize; library & archives; sales shop sells books, prints, reproductions & home merchandise

L **Research Center**, 135 Grant St, Santa Fe, NM 87501; 217 Johnson St, Santa Fe, NM 87501. Tel 505-946-1011; Email center@okeeffemuseum.org; Email library@okeeffeemuseum.org; Web: www.okeeffemuseum.org; *Dir Research Ctr* Eumie Imm-Stroukoff; *Digital Initiatives Librn* Elizabeth Ehrnst
Open Mon - Tues & Fri 9 AM - Noon, Wed - Thurs 9 AM - 4 PM
Library Holdings: Book Volumes, Clipping Files, DVDs, Exhibition Catalogs, Original Documents, Periodical Subscriptions, Photographs, Video Tapes
Collections: Georgia O'Keeffe's art materials, clothes, & colls of found objects, William Innes Homer Archive, Marie Chabot Archive, Georgia O'Keeffe Foundation Archive; correspondence

M **INSTITUTE OF AMERICAN INDIAN ARTS,** IAIA Museum of Contemporary Native Arts, 108 Cathedral Pl, Santa Fe, NM 87501-2027. Tel 505-983-8900; Fax 505-983-1222; Email pphillips@iaia.edu; Web: iaia.edu; *Dir* Patsy Phillips; *Chief Cur* Manuela Well-Off-Man; *Facilities & Security Mgr* Thomas Atencio; *Security* Maria Favela; *Cur Colls* Tatiana Lomahaftewa-Singer; *Graphic Designer* Sallie Wesaw Sloan; *Mem & Prog Mgr* Andrea R Hanley
Open Mon & Wed - Sat 10 AM - 5 PM, Sun Noon - 5 PM; cl Tues; Admis adults $10, students & seniors $5, children under 16, veterans & mems free, native people & NM residents free on Sun; Estab as the only Mus in the world solely dedicated to advancing the scholarship, discourse & understanding of contemporary Native arts; 2100 sq ft of exhibition galleries, 15,000 sq ft outdoor Art Park Performance Gallery; Average Annual Attendance: 100,000; Mem: Dues $25 - $2,500
Income: $928,000 (financed by Congressional appropriation)
Purchases: $50,000
Library Holdings: Book Volumes, Exhibition Catalogs, Manuscripts, Maps, Original Art Works, Original Documents, Pamphlets, Periodical Subscriptions, Photographs, Prints, Reproductions, Slides, Video Tapes
Special Subjects: American Indian Art, Carpets & Rugs, Ceramics, Jewelry, Metalwork, Painting-American, Photography, Pottery, Prints, Sculpture, Silver, Textiles, Watercolors
Collections: National collection of contemporary Native American, includes paintings, graphics, textiles, ceramics, sculpture, jewelry, photographs, printed textiles, costumes
Exhibitions: 2-3 major exhibs & annual student exhib
Publications: Exhib catalogs; gallery guides; coll catalogs
Activities: Docent training; lectrs open to the public; 6 vis lectrs per yr; gallery talks; tours; schols offered; individual paintings & original objects of art lent to mus, state capital & colleges; originate traveling exhibs; sales shop sells books, magazines, original art, reproductions, prints & jewelry

L **College of Contemporary Native Arts Library and Archives**, 83 Avan Nu Po Rd, Santa Fe, NM 87508-1300. Tel 505-424-5715; Web: www.iaia.edu/academics/library; *Library Specialist* Grace Nuvayestewa; *Library Dir* Valerie Nye; *Librn Public Servs & Catalog* Jessica Mlotkowski; *Archivist* Ryan Flahive
Open Mon - Thurs 8 AM - 9 PM, Fri 8 AM - 5 PM, Sun Noon - 9 PM; Estab 1962 to support col curriculum; Circ 5,500
Income: Financed by congressional appropriation & pvt fund raising
Library Holdings: Book Volumes 40,200, Clipping Files 500, Compact Disks 750, DVDs 1,575, Exhibition Catalogs 3,000, Original Art Works, Original Documents, Other Holdings Artists Files, Oral Histories, IAIA History, Periodical Subscriptions 120, Photographs 25,000, Records 300, Video Tapes 800

LANNAN FOUNDATION
For further information, see National and Regional Organizations

M **MUNOZ WAXMAN GALLERY - CENTER FOR CONTEMPORARY ARTS,** 1050 Old Pecos Trail, Santa Fe, NM 87505. Tel 505-982-1338; Email curator@ccasantafe.org; Web: www.ccasantafe.org; *Exec Dir* Stuart A Ashman
Admin hours Mon - Fri 9:30 AM - 5 PM; Estab 1979 to support emerging & established artists; 3,000 sq ft; Mem: dues $45-$2,500
Collections: works by contemporary artists; paintings; sculptures
Exhibitions: Temporary exhibits
Activities: Educ progs; artist talks

M **MUSEUM OF NEW MEXICO,** Office of Cultural Affairs of New Mexico, The Governor's Gallery, PO Box 2087, State Capitol Santa Fe, NM 87504-2087. Tel 505-827-3089; Fax 505-827-3026; Web: www.governor.state.nm.us; *Cur* Terry Bumpass
Open Mon - Fri 8 AM - 5 PM; No admis fee; Estab 1977 to promote New Mexico artists; Gallery located in Governor's reception area in the State Capitol; Average Annual Attendance: 50,000
Income: Financed by state appropriation & the Mus of New Mexico
Exhibitions: Exhibits of New Mexico Art (all media); New Mexican Governor's Awards Show
Activities: Educ dept; docent training; lects open to pub, 200 vis lectrs per yr; gallery talks; tours; A Governor's Award for Excellence in the Arts; individual paintings & original objects of art lent to other mus; book traveling exhibs 1 per yr; originate traveling exhibs to other pub galleries; mus shop sells books, original art & prints

M **NEW MEXICO DEPARTMENT OF CULTURAL AFFAIRS,** New Mexico Museum of Art, 710 Camino Lejo, Santa Fe, NM 87504-7511; PO Box 2087, Santa Fe, NM 87504-2087. Tel 505-476-1250; Email rebecca.potance@state.nm.us; Web: www.nmartmuseum.org; *Dir* Mary Kershaw; *Head Educ & Visitor Servs* Rebecca Aubin; *Librn, Archivist & Webmaster* Rebecca Potance; *Head Curatorial Affairs, Cur Contemporary Art* Merry Scully
Open Tues - Sun 10 AM - 5 PM, cl January 1, Easter Sunday, Thanksgiving & Christmas; Admis adults $12, New Mexico residents $7, children 16 & under free; Estab 1909. Mus is a state institution & operates in 4 major fields of interest: Anthropology, Archaeology, Native American Art & Culture; 1 permanent & 4 temporary galleries: Southwestern Indian art, anthropology & archaeology; Average Annual Attendance: 65,000
Income: Financed by state appropriation, federal grants & private funds
Collections: Over 10 million objects, artifacts & works of art in the fields of Native American art, archaeology & history
Publications: Exhib catalogs; guides; magazines; monographs; pamphlets
Activities: Classes for adults & children; docent training; lects open to pub; concerts; gallery talks; tours; original objects of art lent to other cultural institutions; mus shop sells books, magazines, prints & original art

L **Fray Angelico Chavez History Library**, 120 Washington Ave, Santa Fe, NM 87501; PO Box 2087, Santa Fe, NM 87504-2087. Tel 505-476-5090; Fax 505-476-5104; Email historylibrary@state.nm.us; Web: www.palaceofthegovernors.org/library.html; *Dir* Andrew J Wulf; *Sr Cataloguer* Patricia Hewitt
Open by appointment only; Mus houses four separate research libraries on folk art, fine arts, history & anthropology
Income: Financed by endowments, grants & state
Library Holdings: Book Volumes 15,000, Other Holdings Journals 40

M **New Mexico Museum of Art, Unit of NM Dept of Cultural Affairs,** 107 W Palace, Santa Fe, NM 87501; PO Box 2087 Santa Fe, NM 87504-2087. Tel 505-476-5072; Fax 505-476-5076; Email mary.jebsen@state.nm.us; Web: www.nmartmuseum.org; *Cur 20th Century Painting* Joseph Traugott; *Cur Contemporary* Laura Addison; *Asst Dir* Mary Jebsen; *Mus Shop Mgr* John Stafford; *Dir* Mary Kershaw; *Librn & Archivist* Devon Skeele; *Cur Photog* Kate Ware; *Chief Registrar* Michelle Roberts; *Registrar* Dan Goodman; *Admin* Laura Kohl
Open Tues - Sun 10 AM - 5 PM, cl Mon; Admis adults $9, 4-day & annual passes available for $20, children free; Estab 1917 to serve as an exhibitions hall, chiefly for New Mexican & Southwestern art; Building is of classic Southwestern design (adobe); attached auditorium used for performing arts presentations; Average Annual Attendance: 290,000; Mem: 7,000
Income: Financed by state appropriation
Library Holdings: Book Volumes, Clipping Files, Compact Disks, Exhibition Catalogs, Periodical Subscriptions, Photographs, Slides, Video Tapes
Special Subjects: American Indian Art, American Western Art, Ceramics, Mexican Art, Photography, Sculpture
Collections: Drawings, paintings, photographs, prints & sculpture with emphasis on New Mexican & regional art, including Native American artists
Publications: Exhibition catalogs; gallery brochures
Activities: Classes for adults & children; dramatic progs; docent training; lects open to pub, 30 vis lectrs per yr; concerts; gallery talks; tours; competitions; individual paintings & original objects of art lent to art mus; lending collection contains original prints, paintings, photographs & sculpture; originate traveling exhibs; mus shop sells books, magazines, original art, reproductions & prints

L **New Mexico Museum of Art**, 107 W Palace Ave, Santa Fe, NM 87501-2014; PO Box 2087, Santa Fe, NM 87504-2087. Tel 505-476-5061; Fax 505-827-5076; Email rebecca.potance@state.nm.org; Web: www.nmartmuseum.org; *Head Educ & Visitor Experience* Rebecca Potance; *Dir* Mary Kershaw
Open daily 10 AM - 5 PM; Admis non-residents $12, state residents $7; Estab 1917 to provide fine arts research materials to mus staff, artists, writers & community; Circ 10,000; Average Annual Attendance: 80,000
Library Holdings: Audio Tapes, Book Volumes 10,000, Cassettes, Clipping Files, DVDs, Exhibition Catalogs, Manuscripts, Motion Pictures, Original Documents, Other Holdings, Pamphlets, Periodical Subscriptions 45, Photographs, Reproductions, Slides
Special Subjects: American Indian Art, American Western Art, Architecture, Art History, Ceramics, Drawings, Etchings & Engravings, Glass, Graphic Arts, History of Art & Archaeology, Illustration, Landscapes, Mexican Art, Painting-American, Photography, Prints, Sculpture, Southwestern Art, Watercolors, Woodcarvings, Woodcuts, Portraits, Printmaking

Collections: Biography files of artists, Archives of artists & galleries assoc with New Mexico, Exhibition catalogs
Activities: Tours for children; docent training; lects open to pub; concerts; gallery talks; tours; sponsor competitions; mus shop sells books, reproductions & prints, slides, jewelry

M **Museum of International Folk Art**, 706 Camino Lejo, Santa Fe, NM 87505; PO Box 2087, Santa Fe, NM 87504-2087. Tel 505-476-1200; Fax 505-476-1300; Email info.moifa@state.nm.us; Web: www.internationalfolkart.org; *Dir* Khristaan Villela; *Cur Latino, Hispano ,Spanish Colonial Colls* Nicolasa Chavez; *Cur Textiles & Dress* Carrie Hertz, PhD; *Registrar* Ruth LaNore; *Dir Colls* Polina J Smutko; *Outreach Educator* Patricia Sigala; *Sr Cur & Cur Asian & Oceanic Folk Art* Felicia Katz-Harris; *Cur Latin American & Caribbean Colls* Amy Groleau
Open daily 10 AM - 5 PM, cl Mon, Labor Day to Memorial Day; Mon open during summer (Memorial Day to Labor Day); Admis adults $7 res, $12 non-res, students (res) $6 (non res) $11, children under 17 & mem free; Estab 1953 to collect, exhibit & preserve worldwide folk art; Average Annual Attendance: 100,000
Income: Financed by endowment, grants & state appropriation
Special Subjects: Costumes, Folk Art, Hispanic Art, Textiles
Collections: Arts of Traditional Peoples, with emphasis on Spanish Colonial & Hispanic-related cultures, costumes & textiles
Exhibitions: (Permanent) Familia y Fe/Family & Faith; Multi-Visions: A Common Bond.
Publications: American Folk Masters, 1992; the Spirit of Folk Art, 1989, Mud, Mirror & Thread: Folk Traditions of Rural India, 1993; Traditional Arts of Spanish New Mexico, 1994; Rio Grande Textiles, 1994; Recycled, Re-Seen; Folk Art from the Global Scrap Heap, 1996, The Extraordinary in the Ordinary, 1998; Masks in Mexico, fall 1999; Maiolica Ole; Village of Painters, Carnaval, Visionaries, Cermicay Cultura, Folk art Journey, Sin Nombre
Activities: Classes for adults & children; docent training; lects open to pub; concerts; gallery talks; tours; original objects of art lent to responsible mus nationwide; originate traveling exhibs; mus shop sells books, original art, reproductions & prints

L **Bartlett Library**, 706 Camino Lejo, Santa Fe, NM 87505-7511; PO Box 2087, Santa Fe, NM 87504-2087. Tel 505-476-1210; Fax 505-476-1300; Email caroline.dechert@state.nm.us; Web: www.internationalfolkart.org/learn/library-and-archives.html; *Librn & Archivist* Caroline Dechert
Open by appointment; No admis fee; Estab 1953 to support museum's research needs; Reference library
Income: Financed by private & state support
Purchases: $5500
Library Holdings: Audio Tapes, Book Volumes 12,500, Cassettes, Clipping Files, Exhibition Catalogs, Manuscripts, Original Art Works, Pamphlets, Periodical Subscriptions 180, Photographs, Records, Slides, Video Tapes
Special Subjects: Afro-American Art, Anthropology, Asian Art, Calligraphy, Carpets & Rugs, Crafts, Decorative Arts, Dolls, Embroidery, Ethnology, Folk Art, Handicrafts, Islamic Art, Jewelry, Latin American Art, Mexican Art
Collections: Folk literature & music of the Spanish Colonist in New Mexico c 1800-1971, International folk arts & crafts
Activities: Mus shop sells books, original art & folk art

M **Palace of Governors**, PO Box 2087, Santa Fe, NM 87504-2087. Tel 505-476-5100 (Palace of Governors), 505-476-5200 (NM History Museum); Web: www.nmhistorymuseum.org, www.palaceofthegovernors.org; *Cur Southwest & Mexican Colonial Art & History Colls* Josef Diaz; *Opers Mgr* Seth McFarland; *Registrar* Deborah King; *Colls & Educ Progs Mgr* Rene Harris; *Librn* Patricia Hewitt; *Photo Archivist* Emily Brock; *Dir Palace Press* Tom Leech; *Admin Asst* Vickie Ortega; *Events Coordr* Tay Balenovic
Open Tues - Sun 10 AM - 5 PM; Memorial Day - Labor Day open daily; Admis $12 out-of-state visitors, $7 NM residents; no admis fee: Sun to NM residents, Wed NM senior citizens, mus mems & children under 17; free Fri eves 5 - 7 PM; Built in 1610 (Palace of the Governors) built in 2009 (NM History Mus); History mus; Average Annual Attendance: 120,000
Income: Financed by state appropriations & donations
Special Subjects: Hispanic Art, Historical Material, Painting-Spanish, Period Rooms, Photography, Southwestern Art
Exhibitions: Society Defined; Another Mexico; Long Term Exhibs: Segesser Hide Paintings, Palace of the Governors, West Wing; Telling NM - Stories from then & now, NM History Mus; Treasures of Devotion/Tesoros de Devocion, Palace of the Governors; Santa Fe Found: Fragments of Time, Palace of the Governors; Telling NM, Sant Fe Found
Activities: Awards: Edward L Hewett Award, 2009; 2 first-place honors from the American Assoc of Mus; 2 first-place honors from the Mountain Plains Assoc of Mus, 2009, 2010; Nonprofit Prog Award, 2009 & numerous other awards

M **Laboratory of Anthropology Library**, 708 Camino Lejo, Santa Fe, NM 87505-7511; PO Box 2087, Santa Fe, NM 87504-2087. Tel 505-476-1269; Fax 505-476-1330; Email miac.info@state.nm.us; Web: indianartsandculture.org; *Librn* Allison Colborne
Open Tues - Sun 10 AM - 5 PM; Admis general $12, NM res & seniors 60+ $7, students (res) $6 (non res) $11, children under 17 & mem free; Estab 1929 as a research laboratory in archaeology & ethnology of the Southwest; Circ 25,000+
Library Holdings: Auction Catalogs, Book Volumes, Exhibition Catalogs, Manuscripts, Maps, Periodical Subscriptions
Special Subjects: American Indian Art, Anthropology, Archaeology, Ethnology, History of Art & Archaeology, Maps, Pre-Columbian Art, Silversmithing, Textiles
Collections: Reference materials on various Indian cultures of the Southwest: jewelry, pottery & textiles

A **PUEBLO OF POJOAQUE,** Poeh Museum, 78 Cities of Gold Rd, Santa Fe, NM 87501-0918. Tel 505-455-5041; 455-1110 (Dir); Fax 505-455-3684; Web: www.poehmuseum.com; *Dir* Vernon Lujan; *Cur* Nadine Ulibarri; *Colls Mgr* Reuben Martinez; *Admin Asst* Lynda Romero; *Gift Shop Mgr* Frances Quintana
Open 9 AM - 5 PM; No admis fee; Estab 1988 & opened 1991 to house & exhibit contemporary arts & crafts by artists of the Northern Pueblos, to facilitate the educ of Native American people & the pub-at-large & to preserve Pueblo culture; Average Annual Attendance: 1,200
Library Holdings: Photographs 10,000
Collections: Drawings, paintings, photography, prints, sculptures & other works on baskets, beadwork, ceramics, costumes, jewelry, paper, pottery & textiles, Photo Archives
Exhibitions: Poeh Arts Program, semi-annual exhibit; Nah Poeh Meng (Permanent); 3 rotating exhibs per yr
Activities: Classes for Native American adults; original objects of art lent to museums

M **PUEBLO OF SAN ILDEFONSO,** Maria Martinez Museum, 02 Tunyo PO, Santa Fe, NM 87506. Tel 505-455-2273 (business office), 455-3549 (visitors' center); Fax 505-455-7351; Web: www.indianpueblo.org, www.sanipueblo.org; *Tourism Dir* Denise Moquino; *Tourism Asst* Harold Torres
Open Mon - Fri 8 AM - 4 PM; Admis to mus incl in $10 entrance fee to the Pueblo; Estab to display pottery: history, artists & methods of pottery making
Collections: Arts & crafts, clothing, painting, pottery

M **SCHOOL FOR ADVANCED RESEARCH (SAR),** (School of American Research) Indian Arts Research Center, 660 Garcia St, Santa Fe, NM 87505; PO Box 2188, Santa Fe, NM 87504-2188. Tel 505-954-7205; Fax 505-989-9809; Email info@sarsf.org; Web: sarweb.org; *Pres & CEO* Michael F Brown; *Dir* Brian Vallo; *Registrar* Jennifer Day; *Admin Asst* Daniel Kurnit; *Cur Educ* Elysia Poon; *Colls Asst* Lilyan Jones
Open with appointment public tours Fri at 2 PM; Admis by tour $15, mem free, reservations req; Estab 1907, collection initially formed in 1922 as the Indian Arts Fund. Dedicated to advance studies in anthropology, support advanced seminars for post-doctoral scholars, archaeological research, anthropological publication & a pub educ program; Southwest Indian Arts Building houses collections for research; open storage facility; Average Annual Attendance: 1,400; Mem: 1,100; dues begin at $50; Scholarships
Income: Financed by endowment, mem, special grants & individuals
Special Subjects: American Indian Art, Jewelry, Pottery, Textiles
Collections: 12,000+ items
Publications: Publications of Advanced Seminar Series
Activities: Docent training; lects open to public; tours; paid & unpaid internships; fels offered; individual paintings & original objects of art lent to other museums; sales shop sells books, note cards, video tapes, posters

M **SITE SANTA FE,** 1606 Paseo de Peralta, Santa Fe, NM 87501. Tel 505-989-1199; Fax 505-989-1188; Email info@sitesantafe.org; Web: sitesantafe.org; *Phillips Dir & Chief Cur* Irene Hofmann
Open Mon - Wed & Sat, 10 AM - 5 PM, Thurs 10 AM - 5 PM, Fri 10 AM - 7 PM, Sun Noon - 5 PM; Admis $10, seniors & students $5, mems & Fri free; Estab 1995; 15,000 sq ft exhibition space available. Interior configurations vary according to exhibition demands; Average Annual Attendance: 20-25,000; Mem: 800; dues $35 & up
Income: Financed by mem & private funds
Library Holdings: Audio Tapes, DVDs, Exhibition Catalogs, Kodachrome Transparencies, Periodical Subscriptions, Photographs, Slides, Video Tapes
Exhibitions: Rotating exhibitions; International Biennial exhibition
Publications: Exhibit catalogs
Activities: Classes for adults & children; siteguides; vol progs; outreach to schools; young curators; progs for youth; site scholars; lects open to public; adult lectures; concerts; gallery talks; tours; biennial book traveling exhibitions; originate traveling exhibs to other contemporary mus; mus shop sells books, original art, prints, t-shirts & hats, limited editions, tightly curated selection of artist made items

M **WHEELWRIGHT MUSEUM OF THE AMERICAN INDIAN,** PO Box 5153, Santa Fe, NM 87502-5153. Tel 505-982-4636; Fax 505-989-7386; Email info@wheelwright.org; Web: www.wheelwright.org; *Cur* Cheri Falkenstien-Doyle; *Dir* Jonathan Batkin
Open Sun - Sat 10 AM - 5 PM; Admis gen $8, children under 12 and students with ID admitted free; Native Americans admitted free; Active military admitted free; Estab 1937 to record & present creative expressions of Native American people; Original gallery is shaped like inside of Navajo Hogan or house. Friends, Slater & info ctr Galleries are smaller exhibit space. The center for the study of southwestern jewelry and Schwartz Gallery.; Average Annual Attendance: 54,000; Mem: 1500; dues $50 - $1200
Income: Financed by endowment & mem
Special Subjects: American Indian Art, Anthropology, Ceramics, Costumes, Crafts, Dolls, Drawings, Embroidery, Ethnology, Folk Art, Historical Material, Jewelry, Leather, Manuscripts, Metalwork, Miniatures, Photography, Pottery, Primitive art, Prints, Religious Art, Sculpture, Silver, Textiles
Collections: American Indian art & ethnographic material of Southwestern US, Navajo, Apache & Pueblo people, Jim & Lauris Phillips Center for the Study of Southwestern Jewelry
Exhibitions: Two exhibitions per yr; please call museum for info; Juarilla: Home Near the Heart of the MacWorld; Eveli: Energy and Significance
Publications: Bulletins & books on Native American culture; exhibition catalogs
Activities: Classes for adults & children; docent training; tours; lect; slide-lect; lects open to pub, 10 vis lectrs per yr; gallery talks; tours; individual paintings & original objects of art lent to mus; lending collection contains books, color reproductions, framed reproductions, Kodachromes, nature artifacts, original art works, original prints, paintings & phono records; mus shop sells books, magazines, original art, reproductions, prints, pottery, jewelry, textiles & beadwork (all original)

L **Mary Cabot Wheelwright Research Library**, 704 Camino Lejo, Santa Fe, NM 87505-7511; PO Box 5153, Santa Fe, NM 87502-5153. Tel 505-982-4636; Fax 505-989-7386; Email wheelwright@wheelwright.org; Web: www.wheelwright.org; *Dir* Jonathan Batkin; *Cur* Cheri Falkenstien-Doyle
Open to researchers for reference
Income: Financed by mem
Library Holdings: Book Volumes 4000, Other Holdings Per Issues 3000, Periodical Subscriptions 3000
Special Subjects: American Indian Art, Anthropology, Archaeology, Architecture, Art History, Carpets & Rugs, Ceramics, Costume Design & Constr, Crafts, Eskimo Art, Ethnology, Folk Art, Historical Material, Jewelry, Painting-American

TAOS

M **BENT MUSEUM & GALLERY,** 117 Bent St, Taos, NM 87571-6075; PO Box 153, Taos, NM 87571-0153. Tel 575-758-2376; Fax 575-758-2376; Email gnideon@laplaza.org; *Owner* Thomas Noeding
Open daily 10 AM - 4 PM; Admis adults $2, children 8 - 15 $1, under 8 free; Estab 1959; Home of the first territorial governor of New Mexico - Site of his death in 1847; Average Annual Attendance: 5,000
Income: Financed from admissions & gift shop
Special Subjects: American Indian Art
Collections: American Indian Art, old Americana, old Taos art
Activities: Mus shop sells books, original art, reproductions, prints, Indian jewelry, pottery & dolls

M **MILLICENT ROGERS MUSEUM,** 1504 Millicent Rogers Rd, Taos, NM 87571; PO Box 1210, Taos, NM 87571-1210. Tel 575-758-2462; Fax 575-758-5751; Email mrm@millicentrogers.org; Web: www.millicentrogers.org; *Cur* Carmela Quinto; *Office Mgr* Kathleen Michaels; *Store Mgr* Nancy Colvert; *Executive Director* Caroline Jean Ferrald
Open Apr-Oct daily 10 AM - 5 PM; Nov-Mar Tues - Sun 10 AM - 5 PM; cl New Year's Day; Easter; San Geronimo Day (Sep 30, Taos Pueblo feast day); Thanksgiving; Christmas; Admis adults $10, seniors $8, students $6, Veterans $6, New Mexican residents $5, children under 16 $2; members free; Estab 1956 the MRM is dedicated to sharing & celebrating the art & culture of the southwest; The museum's permanent home is a traditional adobe building, once the private residence of Claude J K Anderson; Average Annual Attendance: 25,000; Mem: 400
Income: Financed by endowment, mem, donations, admis, grants & revenue from mus store
Special Subjects: American Indian Art, American Western Art, Architecture, Ceramics, Costumes, Crafts, Decorative Arts, Drawings, Embroidery, Folk Art, Furniture, Hispanic Art, Historical Material, Jewelry, Metalwork, Photography, Pottery, Pre-Columbian Art, Religious Art, Sculpture, Silver, Southwestern Art, Textiles, Watercolors
Collections: American Indian Art of Western United States, emphasis on Southwestern groups, paintings by contemporary Native American artists, religious arts and non-religious artifacts of Hispanic cultures, nucleus of coll formed by Millicent Rogers
Exhibitions: Rotating exhibits & from permanent collection
Activities: Classes for adults & children; lects open to pub, 2-3 vis lectrs per yr; gallery talks; docent tours; field trips; seminars; accredited by the American Assn of Mus; Best of Taos award; original works of art lent to similar institutions; mus store sells books, jewelry, original art, prints, art & craft work by contemporary Southwest artisans & artists

M **TAOS ART MUSEUM,** 277 Paseo del Pueblo Norte, Taos, NM 87571-7316; PO Box 1848, Taos, NM 87571-1848. Tel 575-758-2690; Fax 575-758-7320; Email museum@taosartmuseum.org; Web: www.taosartmuseum.org; *Exec Dir* Erion Simpson
Open Tues-Sun 10AM-5PM; Admis $8; Taos County Residents free on Sun
Collections: art exhibits dedicated to the art of early 20th century Taos; paintings by the Taos Society of Artists

A **TAOS CENTER FOR THE ARTS,** Stables Gallery, 133 Paseo de Pueblo Norte, Taos, NM 87571. Tel 575-758-2052; Fax 575-751-3305; Email info@tcataos.org; Web: www.tcataos.org; *Pres* Alford Johnson; *Exec Dir* Ron Usherwood
Open Mon - Fri 10 AM - 5 PM, cl Sat & Sun; No admis fee; Estab Oct 1952 as a nonprofit community art center to promote the arts in Taos for the benefit of the entire community; Average Annual Attendance: 30,000; Mem: 300; annual meeting Jan
Income: Financed by mem, contributions, grants, sales of art works & admissions
Activities: Children's program in music & theater; dramatic progs; concerts; classes for adults & children; concerts

M **TAOS HISTORIC MUSEUMS,** 222 Ledoux St, Taos, NM 87571-5944. Tel 505-758-0505; Fax 505-758-0330; Email thm@taoshistoricmuseums.com; Web: www.taoshistoricmuseums.com; *Dir* Karen S Young
Estab 1949. In 1962 the home of Ernest L Blumenschein was given to the Foundation by Miss Helen C Blumenschein; it is now classified as a Registered National Landmark. In 1967 Mrs Rebecca S James gave the Foundation the Ferdinand Maxwell House & Property. In 1972, acquired the Hacienda de Don Antonio Serverino Martinez, prominent Taos merchant & official during the Spanish Colonial Period; designated a Registered National Historic Landmark; Average Annual Attendance: 60,000; Mem: 280; dues patron $1000, sponsor $500, benefactor $250, sustaining $150, contributing $75, partners $50, individual $25
Income: $300,000 (financed by admis, museum shops, rentals, donations & grants)
Special Subjects: Furniture, Period Rooms
Collections: Historical & Archaeological Collection, Western Americana
Publications: Director's annual report; Taos Lightning Newsletter, quarterly; publications on the historic sites; technical reports
Activities: Classes for adults & children; docent training; lect; gallery talks; mus shop

L **E.L. Blumenschein Home & Museum & La Hacienda de los Martinez**, 222 Ledoux St, Taos, NM 87571-5944. Tel 575-758-0505; Fax 505-758-0330; Email director@taoshistoricmuseum.org; Web: taoshistoricmuseums.org; *Dir* Carmen Zaccerras; *Colls Mgr* Anita McDaniel
Open Mon - Sat 10 AM - 5 PM, Sun noon - 5 PM; Admis adults $8; Museum welcomes visitors
Income: Donations
Library Holdings: Audio Tapes, Book Volumes 5000, Cassettes, Clipping Files, Exhibition Catalogs, Kodachrome Transparencies, Lantern Slides, Manuscripts, Maps, Memorabilia, Original Documents, Other Holdings Maps, Pamphlets, Periodical Subscriptions, Photographs, Reproductions, Slides
Special Subjects: American Western Art, Anthropology, Archaeology, Historical Material, Maps, Southwestern Art
Collections: Photograph archives, Textiles, primary source materials & paintings
Activities: Classes for adults; docent training; gallery talks; tours; museum shop sells books, original art, reproductions, prints & other merchandise

M **Ernest Blumenschein Home & Studio**, 222 Ledoux St, Taos, NM 87571-5944. Tel 505-758-0505; Fax 505-758-0330; Email thm@taohistoricmuseums.com; Web: www.taoshistoricmuseums.com; *Dir* Karen S Young; *Educator* Morris Whitten; *Registrar* Joan A Phillips
Open daily 9 AM - 5 PM, cl Christmas, Thanksgiving & New Year's Day; Admis family rate $10, adults $6, children $3, children under 6 years free with parents, group tour rates available; Home of world renowned artist & co-founder of famous Taos Soc of Artists; Restored original mud plaster adobe dating to 1797 with traditional furnishings of New Mexico & European furnishings; Average Annual Attendance: 17,000; Mem: 280; dues $15-$500
Income: Donations & admissions, shop sales
Special Subjects: American Western Art, Architecture, Carpets & Rugs, Ceramics, Drawings, Furniture, Historical Material, Painting-American, Period Rooms, Portraits, Pottery, Southwestern Art, Tapestries, Textiles
Collections: Taos Society of Artists Collection, fine art paintings, Ernest L Blumenschein & Family Collection
Exhibitions: Temporary exhibits of arts and crafts of the Taos area and of New Mexico
Activities: Classes for adults & children; docent training; lect open to public, 2 vis lectrs per year; tours; annual founder art show; book traveling exhibitions; mus shop sells books, original art, reproductions & prints

M **La Hacienda de Los Martinez**, 222 Ledoux St, Taos, NM 87571-5944. Tel 505-758-1000; Fax 505-758-0330; Email thm@thoshistoricmuseums.com; Web: www.taohistoricmuseums.com; *Dir* Karen S Young; *Educator* Morris Witten; *Registrar* Joan A Phillips
Open daily 9 AM - 5 PM, cl Thanksgiving, Christmas, New Year's Day; Admis family rate $10, adults $6, children $3, children under 6 free with parents, group tour rates; Estab 1972, built & occupied by Don Antonio Severino Martinez 1804-1827. Last remaining hacienda open to pub in northern New Mexico. Martinez, an important trader with Mexico, also served as Alcalde of Northern New Mexico; Spanish Colonial fortress hacienda having 21 rooms & two large patios. Living mus program; Average Annual Attendance: 30,000
Income: Financed by admis, donations, & shop sales
Special Subjects: Embroidery, Furniture, Hispanic Art, Historical Material, Metalwork, Mexican Art, Period Rooms, Religious Art, Textiles, Woodcarvings
Collections: Furniture, tools & articles of Spanish Colonial period & personal family articles, Blacksmithing, Weaving
Exhibitions: Various art & craft exhibits, irregular schedule
Activities: Classes for adults & children; docent training; lect open to public, 6 vis lectrs per year; tours; The Annual Taos Trade Fair; mus shop sells books, original art, reproductions & prints

L **TAOS PUBLIC LIBRARY,** Fine Art Collection, 402 Camino De La Placita, Taos, NM 87571-6071. Tel 575-758-3063; Fax 575-737-2586; Email librarian@taosgov.com; Web: www.taoslibrary.org; *Librn* Laurie Macrae
Open Tues - Thurs 10 AM - 6PM, Mon Noon - 6 PM, Fri 10 AM - 6 PM, Sat 10 AM - 5 PM; No admis fee; Estab 1936; Circ 60,000
Library Holdings: Book Volumes 55,000, CD-ROMs, Clipping Files, Compact Disks, DVDs, Exhibition Catalogs, Original Art Works, Pamphlets, Periodical Subscriptions 60, Photographs, Prints, Reproductions, Video Tapes
Special Subjects: American Indian Art, American Western Art, Archaeology, Art History, Southwestern Art
Activities: Children's summer prog includes arts & crafts; bilingual reading discussion prog; lects

M **UNIVERSITY OF NEW MEXICO,** The Harwood Museum of Art, 238 Ledoux St, Taos, NM 87571-7009. Tel 575-758-9826; Fax 575-758-1475; Email info@harwoodmuseum.org; Web: www.harwoodmuseum.org; *Cur* Jina Brenneman; *Dir* Susan Longhenry; *Cur of Educ* Rebeca Aubin; *Develop Officer* Juniper Manley
Open Tues - Sat 10 AM - 5 PM, Sun Noon - 5 PM; summer hours Mon 10 AM - 5 PM; Admis adults $10, students & seniors $8, children under 18 free; Estab 1923, Buildings & contents given to the University by Elizabeth Case Harwood, 1936, to be maintained as an art, educational & cultural center; maintained by the University with all activities open to the pub; Building was added to the National Register of Historic Places in 1976; major renovation expansion completed in 1997, another completed in 2010; Average Annual Attendance: 24,000; Mem: 700; dues $35 - $1000 per year
Income: Financed by University of New Mexico, private contributions & grants, government grants, endowment income
Special Subjects: American Western Art, Architecture, Ceramics, Decorative Arts, Drawings, Etchings & Engravings, Furniture, Hispanic Art, Historical Material, Landscapes, Painting-American, Photography, Portraits, Pottery, Prints, Religious Art, Southwestern Art, Textiles, Watercolors, Woodcarvings, Sculpture
Collections: Permanent collection of works by Taos artists, Hispanic traditions, bultos & retables of NMex
Exhibitions: Changing exhibits each year
Publications: Exhibit catalogs; e-newsletter, monthly
Activities: Classes for children; docent training; lects open to pub, 10 vis lectrs per yr; concerts; gallery talks; tours; competitions; individual paintings & original objects of art lent to museums; lending collection contains original prints, paintings, photographs & sculpture; 1-2 exhibs per yr; organize traveling exhibs to Albright-Knox Art Gallery & Tacoma Art Mus; 1 nat exhib circulated every 3 yrs; mus shop sells books, original art, crafts, jewelry & postcards

NEW YORK

ALBANY

M **ALBANY INSTITUTE OF HISTORY & ART,** 125 Washington Ave, Albany, NY 12210-2296. Tel 518-463-4478; Fax 518-462-1522; Email information@albanyinstitute.org; Web: www.albanyinstitute.org; *Dir* Christine M Miles; *Deputy Dir Coll & Exhibs* Tammis K Groft; *Dir Educ* Erika Sanger; *Chair Bd Trustees* George R Hearst III; *Dir Facilities* Robert Nilson; *Mus Shop Mgr*

Elizabeth Bechand; *Pub Rels & Mktg Mgr* Steve Ricci; *Dir Finance & Admin* Lori Veshia
Open Wed - Sat 10 AM - 5 PM, Sun 12 PM - 5 PM, Tues groups only, cl Mon; Admis adults $10, seniors & students $8, children 6-12 $6, children under 6 & members free; Estab 1791, inc 1793 as the Society for the Promotion of Agriculture, Arts & Manufactures; 1829 as Albany Institute; 1900 as Albany Institute & Historical & Art Soc. Present name adopted 1926; Average Annual Attendance: 100,000; Mem: 2000; dues $35 & up; annual meeting in May
Income: Financed by endowment, mem, sales, foundation, city, county, state & federal grants & special gifts
Special Subjects: American Indian Art, Antiquities-Egyptian, Ceramics, Coins & Medals, Crafts, Decorative Arts, Drawings, Embroidery, Flasks & Bottles, Folk Art, Furniture, Furniture, Glass, Historical Material, Ivory, Jewelry, Landscapes, Manuscripts, Metalwork, Miniatures, Painting-American, Pewter, Porcelain, Portraits, Pottery, Prints, Sculpture, Silver, Tapestries, Textiles, Woodcarvings, Woodcuts
Collections: Art, decorative arts & historical artifacts related to the art, history & culture of Upper Hudson Valley Region from the 17th century to present, 18th & 19th century paintings, Hudson River School, Ceramics, New York (especially Albany) costumes, furniture, glass, pewter, silver & other regional decorative arts, textiles
Exhibitions: Hudson River School paintings from the Institute's collection; Ancient Egypt; 18th & 19th Century Sculpture & Paintings Colonial Albany
Publications: Catalogues; several books about the history of New York State; Remembrance of Patria: Dutch Arts & Culture in Colonial America; Thomas Cole: Drawn to nature members' newsletter & calendar
Activities: Classes for adults & children; dramatic progs; docent training; lects open to pub, 20 vis lectrs per yr; concerts; gallery talks; tours; individual paintings & original objects of art lent to other mus; book traveling exhibs 4 per yr; mus shop sells books, reproductions, prints, handcrafted items

L **Library**, 125 Washington Ave, Albany, NY 12210. Tel 518-463-4478; Fax 518-463-5506; Email library@albanyinstitute.org; Web: www.albanyinstitute.org
Open Thurs 1:00 PM - 4:30 PM & by appointment; Admis $10; Estab 1791 to collect historical material concerning Albany & the Upper Hudson region, as well as books on fine & decorative art related to the Institute's holdings; For reference only; Average Annual Attendance: 600
Library Holdings: Auction Catalogs, Book Volumes 25,000, Clipping Files, Compact Disks, DVDs, Exhibition Catalogs 50, Kodachrome Transparencies, Lantern Slides, Manuscripts, Maps 350, Memorabilia, Original Documents, Other Holdings Architectural Plans; Deeds; Ephemeral; Posters, Pamphlets, Periodical Subscriptions 60, Photographs, Reels, Slides, Video Tapes
Special Subjects: Antiquities-Egyptian, Architecture, Art Education, Art History, Ceramics, Folk Art, Furniture, Manuscripts, Painting-American, Pewter, Photography, Porcelain, Portraits, Prints, Sculpture, Silver, Silversmithing

M **COLLEGE OF SAINT ROSE,** Art Gallery, 324 State St, Albany, NY 12210-2002. Tel 518-485-3902; Fax 518-485-3920; Email flanagaj@strose.edu; Web: www.strose.edu; *Dir* Jeanne Flanagan
Open Mon - Fri 10 AM - 4:30 PM, Mon - Thurs 6 - 8 PM, Sun Noon - 4 PM, cl Sat; No admis fee; Estab 1969 exhibiting contemporary art not previously seen in Capital Region; Average Annual Attendance: 2,700
Income: Financed by college funds
Special Subjects: Painting-American, Prints, Sculpture
Collections: Paintings, prints
Exhibitions: Rotating exhibits & student shows
Activities: Classes for adults; lect open to public, 6-8 vis lectrs per year; gallery talks; tours; scholarships offered

M **HISTORIC CHERRY HILL,** 523-1/2 S Pearl St, Albany, NY 12202-1111. Tel 518-434-4791; Fax 518-434-4806; Email housemus@knick.net; Web: www.historiccherryhill.org; *Cur* Deborah Emmons; *Educ Dir* Rebecca Watrous; *CEO & Dir* Liselle LaFrance; *VPres* Michael Beiter; *Mus Shop Mgr* Lauren Mastin
Open Apr - June & Oct - Dec Tues - Fri Noon - 3 PM, Sat 10 AM - 3 PM, Sun 1 - 3 PM; July - Sept Tues - Sat 10 AM - 3PM, Sun 1 - 3 PM; Admis adults $5, seniors & students $4, children $2; Estab 1964 to preserve & research the house & contents of Cherry Hill, built for Philip Van Rensselaer in 1787 & lived in by him & four generations of his descendants until 1963; Georgian mansion having 14 rooms of original furniture, ceramics, paintings and other decorative arts spanning all five generations & garden; Average Annual Attendance: 5,000; Mem: 250; dues $15 & up
Income: Financed by endowment fund, admis, mem, program grants, sales shop revenue
Special Subjects: Ceramics, Costumes, Decorative Arts, Dolls, Furniture, Landscapes, Manuscripts, Oriental Art, Painting-American, Period Rooms, Porcelain, Portraits, Pottery, Silver, Textiles
Collections: Catherine Van Rensselaer Bonney Collection of Oriental decorative arts, New York State furniture, textiles and paintings dating from the early 18th thru 20th centuries, Manuscript Collection, Seasonal exhibitions in the period room
Publications: New Gleanings, quarterly newsletter
Activities: Educ dept; docent training; classroom materials; lects open to pub; tours; paintings and art objects are lent to other mus and exhibs; mus shop sells books, postcards & reproductions

A **NEW YORK OFFICE OF PARKS, RECREATION & HISTORIC PRESERVATION,** Natural Heritage Trust, Empire State Plaza, Agency Building 1 Albany, NY 12238. Tel 518-474-0456, 486-1899 (TDD); Web: www.nyparks.state.ny.us; *Chair & NHT Commissioner* Carol Ash; *Commissioner Dept Environmental Conservation* Pete Grannis; *Chair State Council Parks, Recreation & Historic Preservation* Lucy R Waletzky
See website for admis fees; Estab to administer individual gifts & funds; funding appropriated by state legislatures for various purposes
Exhibitions: Letchworth Art & Crafts Show

L **NEW YORK STATE LIBRARY,** Manuscripts & Special Collections, Cultural Educ Center, 222 Madison Ave Albany, NY 12230. Tel 518-474-6282; Fax 518-474-5786; Email mscolls@mail.nysed.gov; Web: www.nysl.nysed.gov; *Assoc Librn* Kathi Stanley
Open Mon - Sat 9:30 AM - 5 PM
Income: Financed by State
Library Holdings: Auction Catalogs, Book Volumes, Manuscripts, Maps, Original Documents
Special Subjects: Art History, Historical Material, Manuscripts, Maps
Collections: Over 50,000 items: black & white original photographs, glass negatives, daguerreotypes, engravings, lithographs, bookplates, postcards, original sketches & drawings, cartoons, stereograms & extra illustrated books depicting view of New York State & Portraits of its citizens past & present
Exhibitions: Exhibit program involves printed & manuscript materials

M **NEW YORK STATE MUSEUM,** Cultural Education Ctr Rm 3023, Empire State Plaza Albany, NY 12230-0001. Tel 518-474-5877; Fax 518-486-3696; Email cryan@mail.nysed.gov; Web: www.nysd.nysed.gov; *Dir & Asst Commissioner* Clifford Siegfried; *Dir Research & Coll* John Hart; *Supvr Exhibit Production* Dave LaPlante; *Dir Exhibits* Mark Schaming; *Chief Geological Survey* Robert Fakundiny; *Dir Commun* Joanne Guilmette; *Head Educ* Jeanine Grinage
Open Mon - Sun 9:30 AM - 5 PM; Admis by donation; Estab 1836 to research, collect, exhibit & educate about the natural & human history of New York State for the people of New York; to function as a cultural center in the Capital District of the Empire State; Museum has 1 1/2 acres of exhibit space; three permanent exhibit halls devoted to people & nature (history & science) themes of Adirondack Wilderness, Metropolitan New York, Upstate New York; three temporary exhibit galleries of art, historical & technological artifacts; Average Annual Attendance: 900,000
Income: $5,700,000 (financed by state appropriation, government & foundation grants & private donations)
Special Subjects: Decorative Arts, Ethnology
Collections: Ethnological artifacts of Iroquois-Algonquian (New York area) Indians, circus posters, costumes, decorative arts, paintings, photographs, postcards, prints, toys, weapons
Activities: Classes for adults & children; lects open to pub; concerts; individual paintings & original objects of art lent to mus; lending collection contains nature artifacts, original art works, original prints, paintings, photographs & slides; book traveling exhibs, 6 per yr; originate traveling exhibs; mus shop sells books, magazines, original art, reproductions, prints, slides, toys, baskets, pottery by local artists, jewelry, stationery & posters

M **SAGE COLLEGE OF ALBANY,** Opalka Gallery, 140 New Scotland Ave, Albany, NY 12208-3491. Tel 518-292-7742; Fax 518-292-1903; Email opalka@sage.edu; Web: www.sage.edu/opalka; *Dir* Elizabeth Greenberg; *Exhib Coordr* Jacqueline Lynch
Open Tues - Fri 10 AM - 8 PM, Sat & Sun noon - 5 PM; Summer: Mon - Fri 10 AM - 4 PM; other times by appointment; Estab 2002
Library Holdings: Exhibition Catalogs
Collections: Paintings; photographs; sculpture
Activities: Poetry readings; recitals; symposia; documentary film screenings; lects open to pub; gallery talks

M **The Little Gallery**, 140 New Scotland Ave, Rathbone Hall Albany, NY 12208-3491. Tel 518-292-8625
Open Wed - Thurs 3 PM - 5 PM; other times by appointment
Collections: Works by faculty & student artists

M **SCHUYLER MANSION STATE HISTORIC SITE,** 32 Catherine St, Albany, NY 12202-1605. Tel 518-434-0834; Fax 518-434-3821; Email marcy.shaffer@oprhp.stat; Web: www.nysparks.com; *Historic Site Mgr* Marcy Schaffer; *Interpreter* Deborah Emmons-Andarawl; *Interpreter* Umber Gold; *Interpretive Program Dir* Darlene Rogers
Open Wed - Sat 10 AM - 5 PM, Sun 1 - 5 PM, Nov - mid Apr; call for winter hours; Admis adults $3, New York seniors $2, children 5-12 $1; Estab 1917 for the preservation and interpretation of the 18th century home of Philip Schuyler, one of the finest examples of Georgian architecture in the country; The house boasts a substantial collection of Schuyler family pieces & fine examples of Chinese export porcelain, delftware & English glassware; Average Annual Attendance: 15,000
Income: Financed by state appropriation
Special Subjects: Historical Material
Collections: American furnishings of the Colonial & Federal Periods, predominantly of New York & New England origins
Publications: Schuyler Genealogy: A Compendium of Sources Pertaining to the Schuyler Families in America Prior to 1800; vol 2 prior to 1900
Activities: Educ dept; lect; tours; special events

M **UNIVERSITY AT ALBANY, STATE UNIVERSITY OF NEW YORK,** University Art Museum, 1400 Washington Ave, Albany, NY 12222-1000. Tel 518-442-4035; Fax 518-442-5075; Email museum@albany.edu; Web: www.albany.edu/museum; *Exhib Designer* Zheng Hu; *Admin Asst* Joanne Lue; *Dir* Janet Riker; *Assoc Dir* Corinna Schaming; *Outreach Coordr* Naomi Lewis; *Registrar* Darcie Abbatiello; *Preparator* Jeffrey Wright-Sedam
Open Tues 10 AM - 8 PM, Wed - Fri 10 AM - 5 PM, Sat Noon - 4 PM; No admis fee; Estab 1968 to advance knowledge & foster understanding in contemporary visual arts, & to provide a forum for art, artists & audiences through collections, progs & publications; Average Annual Attendance: 25,000
Income: Financed by state appropriation
Special Subjects: Drawings, Painting-American, Prints, Sculpture
Collections: Paintings, prints, drawings & sculpture of 20th century contemporary art, photographs
Exhibitions: Rotating exhibition
Publications: Exhibition catalogs
Activities: Lects open to public, 6-10 vis lectrs per yr; gallery talks; tours; competitions with awards; book traveling exhibs; originate traveling exhibs

L **Visual Resources Library**, Fine Arts Bldg, Rm 121, Albany, NY 12222-0001. Tel 518-442-4018; Email cdlewis@albany.edu; Web: www.albany.edu/val; *Visual Resources Cur* Caitlain Devereaux Lewis
Open Tues - Thurs 9 AM - 4:30 PM; Estab 1967 to provide instruction & reference for the university & community; Circ more than 7,000 slides per year
Income: financed by the college

Library Holdings: Book Volumes, CD-ROMs, Kodachrome Transparencies, Pamphlets, Photographs, Slides 90,000
Collections: Approx 90,000 slides of ancient art, medieval art, pre-modern & modern art, architecture & classics; art periodicals and MFA thesis work

ALFRED

L **NEW YORK STATE COLLEGE OF CERAMICS AT ALFRED UNIVERSITY,** Scholes Library of Ceramics, 2 Pine St, Alfred, NY 14802-1214. Tel 607-871-2494; Fax 607-871-2349; Email ccjohnson@alfred.edu; Web: scholes.alfred.edu; *Visual Resources Cur* John Hosford; *Dir* Carla C Johnson
Open acad yr Mon - Thurs 8 AM - 12 AM, Fri 8 AM - 8 PM, Sat 10 AM - 6 PM, Sun noon-midnight, other periods Mon - Fri 8 AM - 4:30 PM; Estab 1947 to service art educ to the Master's level in fine art & the PhD level in engineering & science related to ceramics; Circ Artbooks 5,808; slides 42,859; The College has a 2500 sq ft Art Gallery which is managed by the Art & Design Division; Average Annual Attendance: 80,497
Income: $671,884 (financed by endowment & state appropriation)
Purchases: $55,000
Library Holdings: Audio Tapes 51, Book Volumes 64,495, CD-ROMs 33, Cassettes 643, Clipping Files, Exhibition Catalogs, Fiche, Filmstrips, Lantern Slides 200, Motion Pictures, Original Art Works, Other Holdings Art books 26,188; Audio cassettes 171; College arc, Pamphlets 1408, Periodical Subscriptions 707, Reels, Slides 158,890, Video Tapes 15
Special Subjects: Art History, Asian Art, Bronzes, Ceramics, Commercial Art, Crafts, Decorative Arts, Folk Art, Glass, Graphic Design, History of Art & Archaeology, Painting-American, Painting-European, Photography, Printmaking
Publications: Scholes Library Bulletin, biannual
Activities: Tours

ALMOND

M **ALMOND HISTORICAL SOCIETY, INC,** Hagadorn House, The 1800-37 Museum, 7 Main St, Almond, NY 14804; PO Box 209, Almond, NY 14804-0209. Tel 607-288-2833; Email almondhistoricalsociety@gmail.com; Web: www.usgennet.org/usa/ny/tour/almond; *Pres* Louise Schwartz; *VPres* Helen Spencer; *Treas* Teresa Johnson; *Newsletter Ed/Sec* Donna B Ryan; *Archivist* Doris Montgomery; *Director* Thomas Steere; *Director* Kim Costello; *Director* Bradley Hager; *Director* Michael Baker; *Director* Cindy Banker; *Director* Robert Schwartz
Open Fri 2 - 4 PM & by appointment; Admis free - donations accepted; Estab 1965 to preserve local history, genealogy & artifacts; The Little Gallery 4 ft x 12 ft, burlap covered walls, 4 display cases, 8-track lighting system; Average Annual Attendance: 2,000; Mem: 395; mem open to those interested in local history; life member single $250, couple $500; bus or professional $30, family $20, couple $15, individual $15; annual meeting in Nov
Income: $25,908 (financed by endowment, mem, city appropriations)
Collections: 1513 genealogies of local families, town & village records, slide coll of local houses, 1500 costumes & hats, 50 quilts, toys, school books, maps, cemetery lists, photographs, scrapbooks
Exhibitions: Local architecture: drawings & photographs; history of the local post office
Publications: The Cooking Fireplace in the Hagadorn House; Forgotten Cemeteries of Almond; My Father's Old Fashioned Drug Store; Recollections of Horace Stillman; School Days; 12 page quarterly newsletter mailed to mems & posted on website
Activities: Classes for children; lect open to public, 3 vis lectrs per yr; tours

AMENIA

A **AGES OF MAN FOUNDATION,** 57 Sheffield Rd, Box 5 Amenia, NY 12501-5629. Tel 845-373-9380; *VPres* Andrew Rauhauser; *Pres* Dr Nathan Cabot Hale; *Sub Dir* Dr Niels Berg
Open 10 AM - 5 PM; No admis fee, suggested donation; Estab 1968 for the building & design of a sculpture chapel based on the thematic concepts of the Cycle of Life; Average Annual Attendance: 35; Mem: 20; dues $100; meetings May & Nov
Income: Financed by mem & contributions
Collections: Sculpture & architectural models of the chapel, biological references; forms of nature
Exhibitions: varied sculpture concepts to document historical background & concept of the human form
Publications: Project report, yearly; Abstraction in Art & Nature; Perception of Human Form in Sculpture: A History of Figurative Understanding by NC Hale, PhD
Activities: Art history; apprenticeship & journeyman instruction in Cycle of Life design; lects open to public, 20 vis lectrs per yr; gallery talks; original objects of art lent to museums, art assns, educational institutions; originate traveling exhibs

AMHERST

M **BUFFALO NIAGARA HERITAGE VILLAGE,** (Amherst Museum), 3755 Tonawanda Creek Rd, Amherst, NY 14228-1599. Tel 716-689-1440; Fax 716-689-1409; Email info@bnhv.org; Web: www.bnhv.org; *Cur Educ* Kathy Slade; *Exec Dir* Herb Schmidt; *Cur* Kayla Shypski; *Develop Dir* Spencer Morgan; *Exhib Tech* Lee Leiser; *Facilities Supv* Tim Lewis; *Bookkeeper* Andrew Donohue; *Guest Servs* Rachel Ravago
Open Sept - May Wed - Fri 9:30 AM - 4:30 PM, June - Aug Wed - Fri 9:30 AM - 4:30 PM, Sat 10:30 AM - 4:30PM, Sun 12:30 - 4:30 PM, cl Mon, Tues & Municipal Holidays; Admis summer: adults $8, seniors $6, children $4, winter: adults $6, seniors $4, children $2, members free; Estab 1972 to preserve town of Amherst history; name changed in 2011 to be more inclusive of regional history; Maintains reference library, local history exhibits & temporary art exhibits; Average Annual Attendance: 40,000; Mem: 825; dues family $35, individual $20
Income: $550,000 (financed by mem, town appropriation, earned income)
Library Holdings: Audio Tapes, Book Volumes, Clipping Files, Fiche, Filmstrips, Lantern Slides, Manuscripts, Maps, Memorabilia, Original Documents
Special Subjects: Anthropology, Architecture, Carpets & Rugs, Coins & Medals, Costumes, Crafts, Decorative Arts, Dioramas, Dolls, Embroidery, Flasks & Bottles, Folk Art, Furniture, Glass, Historical Material, Jewelry, Laces, Leather, Maps, Metalwork, Period Rooms, Photography, Portraits, Posters, Prints, Textiles
Collections: American Material Culture, 19th Century Historic Buildings, textiles & costumes
Exhibitions: The Erie Canal, children's exhib; Pioneer Kitchen; Niagara Frontier Wireless Radio Gallery; How They Moved Here from Forest to Front Lawn; Vice & Virtue: The Rise & Fall of Prohibition
Publications: Ephemera, quarterly newsletter; Glancing Back: A Pictorial History of Amherst NY
Activities: Classes for adults & children; docent training; special events; lects open to pub, 2-5 vis lectrs per yr; gallery talks; tours; mus shop sells books, prints, reproductions, folk art & unique gift items, reproduction 19th cent general store hours

L **Niederlander Research Library**, 3755 Tonawanda Creek Rd, Amherst, NY 14228-1599. Tel 716-689-1440; Fax 716-689-1409; Email info@bnhv.org; Web: www.bnhv.org; *Exec Dir* Herb Schmidt III; *Librn* Rachel Ravago
Open Wed-Fri 9:30 AM-4:30 PM, Tue 4:30 8 PM (winter only), Sat - Sun noon - 4:30 PM (summer only); library open by appointment only; Admis summer: adults $8, seniors $6, children $4; winter: adults $6, seniors $4, children $2; For reference only
Library Holdings: Book Volumes 3000, Clipping Files, Fiche, Kodachrome Transparencies, Lantern Slides, Manuscripts, Memorabilia, Pamphlets, Photographs, Prints, Reels, Slides, Video Tapes
Collections: 19th-20th century photographs & archival materials related to Town of Amherst, NY & Village of Williamsville, NY
Publications: Genealogical Society newsletter
Activities: Classes for adults & children; docent training; lects open to pub; tours; mus shop sells books, prints

M **DAEMEN COLLEGE,** Fanette Goldman & Carolyn Greenfield Gallery, 4380 Main St, Duns Scotus Hall Amherst, NY 14226-3544. Tel 716-839-8241; Fax 716-839-8516; Web: www.daemen.edu; *Dir* Kevin Kegler
Open Mon - Fri 9 AM - 4 PM; No admis fee; Estab to add dimension to the art program and afford liberal arts students opportunity to view art made by established artists as well as art students; Gallery area is part of main building (Duns Scotus Hall), recently renovated exterior & entrance; Average Annual Attendance: 1,500
Income: Financed by College Art Department
Activities: Lect open to public, 4 - 5 vis lectrs per year

L **Marian Library**, 4380 Main St, Amherst, NY 14226-3592. Tel 716-839-8243; Fax 716-839-8475; Web: www.daemen.edu; *Reference Librn* Andrea Sullivan; *Ref Librn* Randolph Chojecki; *Asst Head Librn* Frank Carey; *Head Librn* Glenn V Woike; *Circ & ILL Librn* Kara McGuire
Library Holdings: Book Volumes 140,000, DVDs 500, Periodical Subscriptions 940, Slides 4911, Video Tapes 1536
Special Subjects: Art Education, Art History, Calligraphy, Graphic Arts, Graphic Design, Painting-American, Textiles

AMSTERDAM

M **MOHAWK VALLEY HERITAGE ASSOCIATION, INC,** Walter Elwood Museum, 100 Church St, Amsterdam, NY 12010-2236. Tel 518-843-5151; Fax 518-843-6098; Email director@walterelwoodmuseum.org; Web: www.walterelwoodmuseum.org; *Exec Dir* Ann M Peonie; *Brd Treas* Guy Cappuccio; *Brd Pres* Susan Wollman; *Assistant* Chastity George
Open Mon- Fri 9 AM - 2 PM & weekend by appointment; Admis fee adults $3, seniors $2, children free; Estab 1939 to preserve local heritage & natural history; Gallery displays changing exhibits, local & professional collections & museum's works of art; Average Annual Attendance: 5,000; Mem: 560; dues family $40, individual $25, seniors $20
Income: $137,000 (financed by grants, donations & mem)
Library Holdings: Framed Reproductions, Lantern Slides, Manuscripts, Maps, Memorabilia, Original Documents, Pamphlets, Periodical Subscriptions, Photographs, Prints, Records, Reels, Sculpture
Special Subjects: Etchings & Engravings, Historical Material, Military Art, Painting-American, Bronzes, Carpets & Rugs
Collections: Oil paintings by turn of the century local artists, photographs of early Amsterdam & vicinity, steel engravings by turn of the century artists, Victorian; Native American; military, Local Artists
Exhibitions: Rotating exhibitions; Local History
Publications: Annual newsletter in Fall
Activities: Classes for adults & children; lects open to pub; 5 visiting lectures per year; gallery talks; concerts; tours; mus shop sells books, original art; reproductions & prints

ANNANDALE-ON-HUDSON

M **BARD COLLEGE,** Center for Curatorial Studies and the Hessel Museum of Art, 33 Garden Rd, Annandale-on-Hudson, NY 12504-5000; PO Box 5000, Annandale-on-Hudson, NY 12504-5000. Tel 845-758-7598; Fax 845-758-2442; Email ccs@bard.edu; Web: www.bard.edu/ccs; *Dir Exhibs & Opers* Marcia Acita; *Dir Library & Archives* Ann Butler; *Exec Dir* Tom Eccles; *Dir Grad Prog* Paul O'Neill; *Dir Admin & Devel* Tracy Pollock; *Registrar* Amy Linker; *Dir External Affairs* Ramona Rosenberg; *Grad Program Coordr* Sarah Higgins; *Prep* Mark DeLura; *Security Mgr* George Acker; *Admin Asst* Trian Mort; *Admin & Develop Coordr* Karlene King; *Librn* Bronwen Bitetti; *Archivist* Ryan Evans
Open Tues - Sun 11 AM - 6 PM; No admis fee; Estab 1992 for the presentation of contemporary art; Circ Non-circulating, research; 25,000 sq ft of exhibition space, changing exhibitions (temp & coll); Average Annual Attendance: 12,000
Library Holdings: Audio Tapes, Book Volumes, CD-ROMs, Cards, Cassettes, Clipping Files, Compact Disks, DVDs, Exhibition Catalogs, Memorabilia, Original

Documents, Other Holdings, Pamphlets, Periodical Subscriptions, Photographs, Slides, Video Tapes
Special Subjects: Drawings, Painting-American, Painting-British, Painting-European, Painting-German, Photography, Restorations
Collections: contemporary art from 1960s to the present in all media, including installations & video, Contemporary Art, International Art, Marieluise Hessel Collection
Activities: Educ progs; artist's talks; grad prog in curatorial studies; AS-AP or archive project; lects open to pub; concerts; gallery talks; tours; schols; fels; annual award for curatorial excellence; book traveling exhibs 1 per yr; originate traveling exhibs; mus shop sells books

L **Center For Curatorial Studies Library**Tel 914-758-7567; Fax 914-758-2442; Email ccs@bard.edu; *Librn* Susan Leonard
Estab 1990; For reference only; non-circulating research collection supporting the graduate program in Curatorial Studies
Library Holdings: Book Volumes 11,000, Clipping Files 1000, Exhibition Catalogs, Memorabilia, Pamphlets, Periodical Subscriptions 52, Slides 10,000, Video Tapes
Special Subjects: Aesthetics, Art History, Conceptual Art, Mixed Media, Painting-American, Painting-British, Painting-European, Painting-German, Painting-Italian, Photography, Restoration & Conservation, Sculpture, Video

M **BARD COLLEGE,** Fisher Art Center, PO Box 5000, Annandale-on-Hudson, NY 12504-5000. Tel 845-758-7674; Fax 845-758-7683; Email fishercenter@bard.edu; Web: www.fishercenter.bard.edu; *Dir* Tambra Dillon; *Chair* Jeanne Donovan Fisher
Open daily 10 AM - 5 PM; No admis fee; Estab 1964 as an educational center; Art center has a gallery, slide library and uses the college library for its teaching
Exhibitions: Four guest-curated exhibitions of contemporary art & two student exhibitions per year; End of Yr Sr Thesis Exhibit
Publications: Catalogs
Activities: Lects open to public; 10 vis lectrs per yr; gallery talks; tours

ASTORIA

M **AMERICAN MUSEUM OF THE MOVING IMAGE,** 36-01 35th Ave, Astoria, NY 11106-1226. Tel 718-777-6888 Admin Offices, 6820; Fax 718-784-4681; Email education@movingimage.us; Web: www.movingimage.us/; *Dir* Rochelle Slovin, MA; *Chmn Bd Trustees* Herbert S Schlosser
Open Tues - Thurs 10:30 AM - 5 PM, Fri 10:30 AM - 8 PM (free admis 4 - 8 PM), Sat & Sun 10:30 AM - 7 PM; Admis adults $12, seniors & col students with valid ID $9, children 3-18 yrs $6, mems & children under 3 yrs no charge; Estab 1988, devoted to art, history, technique & technology of moving image media; Temporary gallery on first floor, 1800 sq ft; 2nd & 3rd floors 5500 sq ft of permanent exhibition space; Average Annual Attendance: 90,000; Mem: 1500; dues $65-$1000
Special Subjects: Cartoons, Costumes
Collections: The museum has a collection of over 70,000 artifacts relating to the material art form of movies & television, magazines, dolls, costumes, clothing, Cinema Arts, Material Culture, Television
Exhibitions: Behind the Screen; Computer Space; Television Set Design: Late Show with David Letterman
Publications: Behind the Screen; Who Does What in Motion Pictures & Television
Activities: Classes for children; ESL progs; docent training; adult tours; lects open to pub, 50 vis lectrs per yr; gallery talks; tours; originate traveling exhibs; mus shop sells books, magazines, & reproductions

AUBURN

M **CAYUGA MUSEUM OF HISTORY & ART,** 203 Genesee St, Auburn, NY 13021-3380. Tel 315-253-8051; Fax 315-253-9829; Email cayugamuseum@verizon.net; Web: www.cayugamuseum.org; *Dir* Eileen McHugh; *Cur* Kirsten Wise
Open Tues - Sun Noon - 5 PM, cl Mon, Jan & holidays; Admis $5; Estab 1936 for research & Cayuga County history; Average Annual Attendance: 10,000; Mem: 250; dues $25-$250; annual meeting in Sep
Income: Financed by endowment, mem & county
Special Subjects: American Indian Art, American Western Art, Anthropology, Archaeology, Decorative Arts, Folk Art, Historical Material, Landscapes, Maps, Painting-American, Photography, Posters, Scrimshaw, Stained Glass, Watercolors, Portraits
Collections: Fine & Decorative Arts, Native American Collection, Soundfilm, Industrial history
Exhibitions: Ongoing series of changing exhibits; Auburn Prison; TimeClocks; Case Research Lab; Native American Art
Activities: Classes for adults & children; docent training; lects open to pub; 2-6 vis lectrs per yr; concerts; gallery talks; tours; lending collection contains motion pictures & slides; mus shop sells books, reproductions, postcards & small gifts

M **SCHWEINFURTH ART CENTER,** (Schweinfurth Memorial Art Center), 205 Genesee St, Auburn, NY 13021-3304. Tel 315-255-1553; Fax 315-255-0871; Email mail@schweinfurthartcenter.org; Web: www.myartcenter.org; *Dir* Donna Lamb; *Dir Progs & Special Projects* Deidre Aureden; *Prog Coord* Davana Robedee; *Admin Coordr* Lindsey Tidd
Open Tues - Fri 10 AM - 5 PM, Sat 10 AM - 5 PM, Sun 1 - 5 PM; Admis $7; Estab 1981; community art center focusing on fine art, architecture & design; 4,000 sq ft contemporary gallery; Average Annual Attendance: 20,000; Mem: 550; dues $40 - $1,000
Income: $240,000 (financed by endowment, mem, city & state, federal, public & private)
Special Subjects: Carpets & Rugs, Coins & Medals, Collages, Crafts, Decorative Arts, Embroidery, Enamels, Landscapes, Metalwork, Painting-American, Photography, Pottery, Prints, Sculpture, Textiles, Watercolors, Woodcarvings, Woodcuts
Exhibitions: Regional artists, traveling & annual children's exhibit (Feb); annual quilt exhibit (Nov -Jan)
Publications: Monthly calendar
Activities: Classes for adults & children; docent training; lects open to pub; 12 vis lectrs per yr; concerts; gallery talks; tours; scholarships offered; originate traveling exhibs; sales shop sells books, original art & gifts; special events

BALDWIN

M **BALDWIN HISTORICAL SOCIETY MUSEUM,** 1980 Grand Ave, Baldwin, NY 11510; P.O. Box 762, Baldwin, NY 11510. Email baldwinhistoricalsociety@gmail.com; Web: baldwinhistoricalsociety.com; *VPres & Cur* Karen Montalbano; *Pres* Gary Farkash; *Treas* Doris A Lister; *Rec Secy* Francis J Balducci
Open Sun 1 - 4 PM or by appointment; No admis fee; Estab 1971, mus estab 1976 to preserve Baldwin history memorabilia including historical photographs; Average Annual Attendance: 500; Mem: 225; dues family $25, individual $15; monthly meetings except Jan, Feb, July & Aug
Income: $3,000 (financed by mem, fundraising)
Purchases: 1916 brass cash register used by Baldwin's Allen dept store
Special Subjects: Ceramics, Costumes, Etchings & Engravings, Furniture, Glass, Jewelry, Manuscripts, Maps, Painting-American, Photography
Collections: Collection of local history photographs, postal cards, advertising objects, decorative art objects, manuscripts
Exhibitions: Selection of Baldwin's memorabilia
Publications: Newsletter
Activities: Classes for adults & children in local history progs; lects open to pub, 4 vis lectrs per yr

BALLSTON SPA

A **SARATOGA COUNTY HISTORICAL SOCIETY,** Brookside Museum, Six Charlton St, Ballston Spa, NY 12020. Tel 518-885-4000; Fax 518-885-4055; Email info@brooksidemuseum.org; Web: www.brooksidemuseum.org; *Exec Dir* Joy Houle; *Cur* Kathleen Coleman; *Dir Educ* Anne Clothier; *Admin Asst* Samantha Strevy
Open Tues - Fri 10 AM - 4 PM, Sat 10 AM - 2 PM, cl Sun & Mon; Admis family $5, adults $2, seniors, $1.50, children $1; Estab 1965 to inform pub on the history of Saratoga County; 4 small galleries; Average Annual Attendance: 12,000; Mem: 500; dues individual $25
Income: $160, 000 (financed by endowment, mem, city appropriation & grants)
Library Holdings: Audio Tapes, Book Volumes, Clipping Files, Lantern Slides, Manuscripts, Maps, Original Documents, Other Holdings, Photographs
Special Subjects: Historical Material
Collections: History of Saratoga County, books, manuscripts, objects, photographs
Exhibitions: Saratoga County: The Story of Brookside changing exhibitions; Go to the Head of the Class; Taking the Waters
Publications: Gristmill, 1 per year; columns, 6 per year
Activities: Classes for adult & children; lects open to pub; concerts; sponsor competitions; mus shop sells books, original art, reproductions & prints

BAYSIDE

M **QUEENSBOROUGH COMMUNITY COLLEGE,** Art Gallery, 222-05 56th Ave, Bayside, NY 11364-1497. Tel 718-631-6396, 281-5095; Fax 718-631-6620; Email artgallery@qcc.cuny.edu; Web: www.qccartgallery.org; *Executive Director* Faustino Quintanilla; *Asst Dir* Lisa Scandaliato; *Admin Asst* Grace Duran
Open Tues & Fri 10AM-5PM, Wed & Thurs 10AM-7PM, Sat & Sun noon-5PM; No admis fee; Estab 1981 to provide the col & Queens Community with up to date documentation outline on the visual arts; Average Annual Attendance: 12,000; Mem: 500; dues $25
Income: $214,793 (financed by endowment & mem)
Purchases: Ruth Rothschild & Hampton Blake
Library Holdings: Book Volumes, CD-ROMs, Exhibition Catalogs, Original Documents, Slides
Special Subjects: African Art, Archaeology, Architecture, Ceramics, Drawings, Etchings & Engravings, Graphics, Manuscripts, Painting-American, Painting-Australian, Painting-British, Painting-Canadian, Painting-Dutch, Painting-European, Painting-Flemish, Painting-French, Painting-German, Painting-Israeli, Painting-Italian, Painting-Japanese, Painting-New Zealand, Painting-Polish, Painting-Russian, Painting-Scandinavian, Painting-Spanish, Prints, Photography
Collections: Contemporary Art, works on paper, Richard Art Schwager, Roger Indiana, Paul Jenkins, R Dichtenstein, Larry Rives, Frank Stella, Judy Ritka, Alfonso Ossorio, Jules Allen, Jimmy Ernst, Josef Albers, Sirena, Pre-Columbian artifacts, African Art
Exhibitions: Siri Berg-Suzane Winkler; The Priva B Gross International Works On/Of Paper; Permanent Collection: Larry Rives; Picasso: A Perpetual Metamorphosis (2008)
Publications: Signal; Politics & Gender; Romanticism & Classicism; Power of Popular Imagery; Art & Politics
Activities: Lects open to pub, 4-8 vis lectrs per yr; gallery talks; tours; competitions with awards; schols offered; individual paintings & original objects of art lent for exhibit purposes to organizations that follow loan criteria; lending collection contains original art works, photographs, sculptures & videos (art-New York & others); art lent to Seoul Art Gallery Korea; originate traveling exhibs annually; mus & accredited galleries; mus shop sells reproductions, books, prints, jewelry; magazines; original art; slides; junior mus

BEACON

A **DIA ART FOUNDATION DIA: BEACON, RIGGIO GALLERIES,** 3 Beekman St, Beacon, NY 12508; 535 W 22nd St, 4th Fl, New York, NY 10011. Tel 845-440-0100; Fax 845-440-0092; Email info@diacenter.org; Web: www.diaart.org; *Cur* Yasmil Raymond

Open Jan - March Fri - Mon 11 AM - 4 PM, April - Oct Thurs - Mon 11 AM - 6 PM, Nov - Dec Thurs - Mon 11 AM - 4 PM, cl Tues & Wed, Thurs (Jan, Feb & March), Thanksgiving Day, Christmas Eve & Day, New Year's Day; Admis general $15, students & seniors (65+) $12, mems & children under 12 free; Estab 1974 for planning, realization & presentation of important works of contemporary art. Commitment to artist's participation in display of works in long term, carefully maintained installations; Galleries: Dan Flavin Art Institute, Bridgehampton, NY; The Lightning Field, Quemado, NM. In 2003 Dia Art Foundation opened a museum to house its permanent collection comprising major works of art from the 1960's to the present.; Mem: Dues, artist, senior & student $50, individual $75, family $125, supporter $250, patron $500, fellow $1000
Income: Financed by grants
Publications: The Foundation has published collections of poetry & translations of poetry
Activities: Educ dept, classes for children; lects open to pub, 3 vis lectrs per yr, concerts, gallery talks, tours; exhibit catalogues; Series of discussions on contemporary cultural issues; mus shop sells books & original art

BINGHAMTON

M **ROBERSON MUSEUM & SCIENCE CENTER,** 30 Front St, Binghamton, NY 13905-4779. Tel 607-772-0660; Fax 607-771-8905; Email info@roberson.org; Web: www.roberson.org; *Cur & Registrar* Eve Daniels; *Exec Dir* Terry McDonald; *Dir Exhibits* Peter Klosky; *Dir Educ* Katherine Howorth-Bouman
Open Wed, Thurs & Sat - Sun noon - 5 PM, Fri noon - 9 PM, cl Mon & Tues; Admis adults $8, seniors & students $5, children under 4 free; Estab 1954 as a regional museum of art, history & science educ; The Roberson Mus & Science Center, built in 1905-06 contains eight galleries; the Martin Building, built in 1968, designed by Richard Neutra, contains five galleries; the A Ward Ford Wing, completed in 1983 contains the Irma M Ahearn Gallery; Average Annual Attendance: 20,000; Mem: 1600; dues $30-$85
Income: $1,500,000 (financed by endowment, mem, city, county & state appropriations, federal funds & foundations)
Special Subjects: Archaeology, Crafts, Decorative Arts, Drawings, Ethnology, Furniture, Painting-American, Photography, Prints, Historical Material
Collections: Loomis Wildlife Collection: Northeastern Birds & Mammals, natural history specimens, historical archives & photographic collections, Hands-on science displays & interactive art, Link Planetarium
Exhibitions: Voices & Visions; Edwin Link: The Air Age; Local History Gallery; Decker Life Science Learning Center (DNA Lab); Audubon, Masks; Confluence
Activities: Educ prog; classes for adults & children; school progs; pub progs & workshops; dramatic progs; docent training; lects open to pub, 5 vis lectrs per yr; gallery talks; tours; sponsoring of competitions; scholarships offered; progs sent to schools in eleven counties; individual paintings & original objects of art lent; lending collection contains slide tape progs with hands-on-activities for groups; book traveling exhibs 2-3 per yr; originate traveling exhibs to other mus; mus shops sell books, original art, reproductions, prints, contemporary crafts, unique & unusual gifts

M **STATE UNIVERSITY OF NEW YORK AT BINGHAMTON,** Binghamton University Art Museum, 4400 Vestal Pkwy, Binghamton, NY 13902; PO Box 6000, University Art Museum Binghamton, NY 13902-6000. Tel 607-777-2634; Email hogan@bighampton.edu; Web: binghamtonuniversityart museum; *Dir* Diane Butler, PhD; *Registrar & Cur Educ* Silvia Ivanova; *Asst Dir* Jacqueline Hogan; *Technical Support & Installation* Dr Ronald Polesnak; *Cur* Lucie Nelson, PhD; *Staff Asst* Cynthia Riley
Open Tues - Sat Noon - 4 pm, Thurs Noon - 7 PM, cl all holidays; No admis fee; Estab 1967; Eight areas of art; Average Annual Attendance: 4,000
Income: $30,000 (financed by state appropriations)
Library Holdings: CD-ROMs
Special Subjects: African Art, Afro-American Art, Anthropology, Asian Art, Baroque Art, Carpets & Rugs, Ceramics, Decorative Arts, Drawings, Embroidery, Etchings & Engravings, Furniture, Glass, Graphics, Ivory, Jade, Jewelry, Landscapes, Manuscripts, Maps, Medieval Art, Oriental Art, Painting-American, Painting-British, Painting-Dutch, Painting-European, Painting-Flemish, Painting-Italian, Painting-Spanish, Photography, Porcelain, Pre-Columbian Art, Religious Art, Renaissance Art, Restorations, Sculpture, Textiles, Woodcuts, Painting-French, Photography, Posters, Scrimshaw, Tapestries, Watercolors
Collections: Asian coll, Teaching coll from Egyptian to contemporary art, African, Wedgewood, Works on Paper
Publications: Exhibit catalogs; books
Activities: Educ prog; classes for adults & children; tours; lects open to pub; 6 vis lectrs per yr; gallery talks; seminars; tours; internships offered; mus shop sells jewelry, reproductions, handmade jewelry & dyed scarves

BLUE MOUNTAIN LAKE

M **THE ADIRONDACK HISTORICAL ASSOCIATION,** The Adirondack Museum, 9097 State Rte 30, Blue Mountain Lake, NY 12812; PO Box 99, Blue Mountain Lake, NY 12812-0099. Tel 518-352-7311; Fax 518-352-7653; Email info@adirondackmuseum.org; Web: www.adirondackmuseum.org; *Dir* David M Kahn; *Chief Cur* Laura Rice; *Dir Fin & Opers* Todd Friebel; *Dir Mktg* Todd Happer; *Human Resources Mgr* Colleen Sage; *Mgr Retail Operations* Debbie Austin
Open Memorial Day - mid Oct daily 10 AM - 5 PM; Admis Adults 17 & over $18, 13-17 $12, 6-12 $6, 5 & under no charge; Estab 1957 to interpret the history & culture of the Adirondack Park; Museum contains two large galleries for paintings; Average Annual Attendance: 73,000; Mem: 4,000; Individual $40, Family $95
Library Holdings: Audio Tapes 244, Book Volumes 8,809, Manuscripts 650, Maps 1,397, Memorabilia 16,813, Original Art Works, Original Documents, Pamphlets, Periodical Subscriptions, Photographs, Reproductions, Slides, Video Tapes
Special Subjects: Photography, Prints
Collections: Drawings, Paintings, Prints, Photographs
Publications: Newsletters, books
Activities: Classes for adults & children; lects open to pub, 8 vis lectrs per yr; concerts; gallery talks; tours; individual paintings & original objects of art loaned to museums & galleries; mus shop sells books, magazines, reproductions, prints, slides, postcards, clothing, jewelry & toys

L **Library,** PO Box 99, Blue Mountain Lake, NY 12812-0099. Tel 518-352-7311; Fax 518-352-7603; *Library Dir* Jerold L Pepper
Open by appointment; Estab to provide research materials for mus staff (exhibit documentation) & researchers interested in the Adirondack & to preserve written materials relating to the Adirondack; For research only
Library Holdings: Audio Tapes 25, Book Volumes 8000, Cassettes, Clipping Files, Exhibition Catalogs, Fiche, Kodachrome Transparencies, Lantern Slides, Manuscripts, Other Holdings Maps, Periodical Subscriptions 13, Reels, Slides

A **ADIRONDACK LAKES CENTER FOR THE ARTS,** PO Box 205, Blue Mountain Lake, NY 12812-0205. Tel 518-352-7715; Fax 518-352-7333; Email info@adirondackarts.org; Web: www.adirondackarts.org; *Exec Dir* Sarah Reynolds; *Artistic Assoc* Barry Pratt; *Production Mgr* Joseph Perrault
Open Mon - Fri 10 AM - 4 PM, Sat 11 AM - 3 PM; Fall & Spring Thurs - Sat 10 AM - 4 PM; Summer Mon - Sat 10 AM - 4 PM; Admis concerts $20, $15 mem; Estab 1967; this Community Art Center offers both community & artist - craftsmen the opportunity for creative exchange; 7000 sq ft facility with 4 studios & 130 seat theatre & 3 separate galleries; Average Annual Attendance: 30,000; Mem: 600; annual meeting in July
Income: $365,000 (financed by private contributions, county, state & federal assistance, foundations, local bus, government, mem & fundraising events)
Exhibitions: Exhibits change every month
Publications: Newsletter - Program, quarterly
Activities: Classes for adults & children; dramatic programs; concerts; competitions; gallery talks; tours; administers NYSCA Regrant Prog; consignment shop

BOLTON LANDING

A **MARCELLA SEMBRICH MEMORIAL ASSOCIATION INC,** Marcella Sembrich Opera Museum, 4800 Lake Shore Dr, Bolton Landing, NY 12814; PO Box 417, Bolton Landing, NY 12814-0417. Tel 518-644-9839, 644-2431; Fax 518-644-9531; Email office@thesembrich.org; Web: www.thesembrich.org; *Assoc Pres* William Post Hubert; *Artistic Dir* Richard Wargo; *Dir* Elizabeth Barton-Navitsky; *VPres* Lisa H Hall; *Secy* Rebecca Smith; *Treas* Elizabeth Spinelli
Open June 15 - Sept 15 10 AM - 12:30 PM & 2 - 5 PM; Admis free, suggested donation $5; Estab 1937 to exhibit memorabilia of Marcella Sembrich & the Golden Age of Opera; Exhibits in Sembrich's former teaching studio on the shore of Lake George; Average Annual Attendance: 2,500; Mem: 300; dues $35 & $50; annual meeting in June
Income: $70,000 (financed by mem & gifts)
Collections: Memorabilia of the life & career of Marcella Sembrich, opera star of international acclaim (1858 - 1935), paintings, sculpture, furnishings, photographs, costumes, art works, gifts & trophies from colleagues & admirers
Publications: Newsletter, biennial; Recollection of Marcella Sembrich, Biography
Activities: Lect open to pub; 2 vis lectrs per yr; concerts; gallery talks; concerts; tours; mus shop sells books, postcards, recordings, cassettes & Sembrich CD's, jewelry, scarves & handbags

BROCKPORT

M **STATE UNIVERSITY OF NEW YORK, COLLEGE AT BROCKPORT,** Tower Fine Arts Gallery, 350 New Campus Dr, Brockport, NY 14420-2997. Tel 585-395-2805; Fax 585-395-2588; *Dir* Elizabeth McDade
Open Mon-Thurs 10AM-7PM, Fri 10AM-5PM, Sun 1PM-4PM; Estab to present quality exhibitions for purpose of educ; 160 running ft, 1,900 sq ft; Average Annual Attendance: 9,000
Income: Financed by state appropriation & student government
Collections: EE Cummings Collection of Paintings & Drawings
Exhibitions: Alumni Invitational III; The Faculty Selects; Rock, Scissors, Paper; Social Work: Photographs by Vincent Cianni & Jim Tynan
Activities: Lects open to public, 6 vis lectrs per yr; book traveling exhibs 1-2 per yr; originate traveling exhibs

BRONX

M **BARTOW-PELL MANSION MUSEUM & GARDENS,** 895 Shore Rd, Pelham Bay Park Bronx, NY 10464-1030. Tel 718-885-1461; Fax 718-885-9164; Email info@bpmm.org; Web: www.bartowpellmansionmuseum.org; *Exec Dir* Alison McKay; *Mus Admin* Susan M Chesloff
Open Wed, Sat & Sun noon - 4 PM, cl New Year's Eve & Day, Easter, Thanksgiving, weekend, Christmas; Admis adults $8, seniors & students $6, children under 6 & mems no admis fee; Estab 1914; Average Annual Attendance: 15,000; Mem: dues $50-$3,500
Library Holdings: Book Volumes
Special Subjects: Period Rooms
Collections: Greek Revival, period furnishings, paintings, sunken gardens
Activities: Tours for adults & children; lects open to pub; concerts; mus shop sells books

M **BRONX COMMUNITY COLLEGE (CUNY),** Hall of Fame for Great Americans, 2155 University Blvd, Bronx, NY 10453-5100. Tel 718-289-5161; Fax 718-289-6496; Web: www.bcc.cuny.edu/halloffame; *Dir & Historian* Susan Zuckerman; *Historian* Art Zuckerman
Open daily 10 AM - 5 PM; Group tour donation suggested; Estab 1900; Nat landmark; Average Annual Attendance: 30,000
Library Holdings: Clipping Files, Exhibition Catalogs, Pamphlets, Sculpture
Special Subjects: Archaeology, Architecture, Bronzes, Coins & Medals, Historical Material, Miniatures, Sculpture, Stained Glass

Activities: Classes for children; dramatic progs; films; puppet shows; musical events; docent training; lect open to public; concerts; tours; NY Conservancy & Municipal Arts Society

M **BRONX COUNCIL ON THE ARTS,** Longwood Arts Gallery @ Hostos, 450 Grand Concourse, C-190, Art Gallery Bronx, NY 10451. Tel 718-518-6728; Fax 718-518-6690; Email longwood@bronxarts.org; Web: www.bronxarts.org; *Exec Dir* Deirdre Scott; *Develop* Ellen Pollan; *Dir & Cur* Juanita Lanzo; *Gallery Coordr & Technology Adminr* Kimberly Vaquedano; *Gallery Asst* Vanessa Gonzalez
Open Mon - Sat 10 AM - 6 PM (Oct 2011-May 2012); Summer Hours: Mon - Thurs 10 AM - 5 PM; No admis fee; Estab 1985 for exhibits & programming of interest to artists & pub of all ages. Mission is to support the presentation & creation of work from emerging & underrepresented artists, especially women & artists of color.; Gallery organizes 4-6 exhibs per yr that present group & solo exhibs centering on contemporary themes of interest to artists & our audiences. Recent exhibs included collaborative projects between artists & communities & artists working on issues about migration, environment, social justice & national & cultural identity.; Average Annual Attendance: 300
Income: Financed by city, state & federal grants, foundation & corporate support
Exhibitions: Vietnamese Artists; Post-Colonialism; Feminism & the Body; Puerto Rican Taino Imagery in Contemporary Art; Real Life Comics; Like Butter; Maze-phantasm; Mini-Murals; Sovereign State; Here & Now, Now & Then
Activities: Lects open to pub, 3 vis lectrs per yr; fel; originate traveling exhibs 2 per yr

M **BRONX MUSEUM OF THE ARTS,** 1040 Grand Concourse, at 165th St Bronx, NY 10456-3999. Tel 718-681-6000; Fax 718-681-6181; Email info@bronxmuseum.org; Web: www.bronxmuseum.org; *Exec Dir* Holly Block; *Dir Progs* Antonio Sergio Bessa; *Dir Develop* Allison Chernow; *Dir Fin* Alan Highet; *Dir Security* Francisco Rosario
Open Thurs - Sun 11 AM - 6 PM, Fri until 8 PM, cl Mon - Wed, Thanksgiving, Christmas & New Year's Day; No admis fee; Estab 1971 as a 20th century & contemporary arts museum; serves the culturally diverse populations of the Bronx and the greater New York metropolitan area; the Museum has a long-standing commitment to increasing & stimulating audience participation in the visual arts through its Permanent Collection, special exhibitions & educational programs; Mem: 125; sponsor $1000, patron $500, assoc $250, sustaining $100, family/dual $75, individual $50, student, artist & senior $25
Income: Financed by mem, city, state & federal appropriations, foundations & corporations
Collections: Collection of 20th & 21st c works by artists of Latin American, African & Southeast Asian ancestry, File on Bronx artists
Exhibitions: Rotating Exhibits
Publications: Exhibition catalogs; educational workbooks; walking tours of the Bronx
Activities: Classes for adults, children & seniors; lects open to pub; concerts; gallery talks; tours; films; annual arts & crafts festival; originate traveling exhibs; mus shop sells books, posters, catalogs, original art, prints, jewelry, children's & mus gift items

M **BRONX RIVER ART CENTER INC,** 1087 E Tremont Ave, Bronx, NY 10460-2328; PO Box 5002, West Farms Station Bronx, NY 10460-0251. Tel 718-589-5819, 589-6379; Email info@bronxriverart.org; Web: www.bronxriverart.org; *Gallery Mgr* Christie Gonzalez; *Exec Dir* Gail Nathan
Open Mon - Fri 10 AM - 6 PM & Sat 10 AM - 5 PM; No admis fee, nominal fee for classes; Estab 1987 as a professional, multi-cultural art center, 18,000 sq ft w/educ classrooms, artist studios, gallery & multi-purpose space; 2,000 sq ft, handicapped accessible, ground floor gallery. Two main gallery rooms, natural light; Average Annual Attendance: 5,000
Income: $500,000 (Financed by government, foundations, corporations, donations)
Exhibitions: Exhibitions of contemporary artists focusing on innovative multi-cultural, multi-media work; exhib of interdisciplinary art & environmental justice; 5 exhibits 2015: Food Systems, Surroundings & Sensibilities; 5 exhibits 2016: Way Points: Platforms for Renewal
Activities: Fee-based classes for adults & children; lects open to pub, 5*10 vis lectrs per yr; concerts; gallery talks; tours; YC Design Commission Award; schols available; exten prog BRAC on the Block serves the Bronx

M **EN FOCO, INC,** 1738 Hone Ave, Bronx, NY 10461-1403; PO Box 1757, Bronx, NY 10451-1757. Tel 718-731-9311; Fax 718-409-6445; Email info@enfoco.org; Web: www.enfoco.org; *Exec Dir* Miriam Romais; *Prog Dir* Dani Cattan; *Relationship Mktg Coordr* Layza Garcia
Open Mon - Thurs 10 AM - 5 PM, other hours by appt, cl Fri & all major holidays; No admis fee; Estab 1974 to support photographers of Latino, African, Asian, & Native American heritage via exhibits, publications, & workshops; Circ 36,000; Five exhibits per yr in different NY venues; Average Annual Attendance: 40,000; Mem: dues basic $50
Special Subjects: African Art, Afro-American Art, American Indian Art, Asian Art, Hispanic Art, Latin American Art, Mexican Art, Photography
Collections: Photographs by leading photographers of color
Exhibitions: New Works Exhibitions; Touring Gallery Exhibitions; Membership Exhibitions
Publications: Nueva Luz, bilingual photography journal
Activities: lects open to the public; gallery talks; fels; competitions with awards, New Works Photography Awards Fel; honorarium; originates traveling exhibs; mus shop sells prints

A **HOSTOS CENTER FOR THE ARTS & CULTURE,** 450 Grand Concourse & 149th St, Bronx, NY 10451-5323. Tel 718-518-4444; Web: www.nostoscenter.org; *Dir* John MacElwee; *Production Mgr* Jack Jacobs; *Pres* David Gomez; *Office Asst* Katrina Perez; *Performing Arts Mgr* Felix Arocho; *Col Asst* Arlene Ferrer
Open gallery: Mon - Fri noon - 5 PM (except Wed during school yr); No admis fee; Estab 1993 to present artists of national & international renown; presents emerging & estab local artists; offers workshops in drama, folk arts & dance to community residents; serves as a forge for new art, & thus has estab an individual artists' program consisting of commissions & residencies; Center consists of a museum-grade art gallery, 367-seat theater & 907-seat concert hall; Average Annual Attendance: 33,000
Income: Financed by mem, city appropriation, state appropriation, government sources, corporations
Special Subjects: Latin American Art
Activities: Dramatic progs; lects open to pub; 3 lectrs per yr; originate traveling exhibs

M **LEHMAN COLLEGE ART GALLERY,** 250 Bedford Park Blvd W, Bronx, NY 10468-1589. Tel 718-960-8731; Fax 718-960-6991; Email susan@lehman.cuny.edu; Web: www.lehman.edu/gallery, www.lehman.edu/publicart, www.lehman.edu/architecture; *Grants Officer* Mary Ann Siano; *Dir* Susan Hoeltzel; *Asst Cur* Yuneikys Villalonga; *Educ Cur* Hannah Brenner-Leonard
Open Tues - Sat 10 AM - 4 PM; No admis fee; Estab 1984 to exhibit work of contemporary artists; Two galleries housed in Fine Arts building on Lehman College campus, City University NY, designed by Marcel Breuer; Average Annual Attendance: 32,000; Mem: 200; dues $30-$1000
Income: Financed by endowment, mem, city & state appropriation, federal grants, & private foundations
Special Subjects: Afro-American Art, Latin American Art
Exhibitions: Changing Contemporary Exhibs
Publications: Online exhib catalogs
Activities: Classes for children & adults; docent training; lects open to pub, 6 vis lectrs per yr; gallery talks; tours; book traveling exhibs; originate traveling exhibs; other mus

M **VAN CORTLANDT HOUSE MUSEUM,** W 246th & Broadway, Bronx, NY 10471-3431; c/o NSCDNY, 215 E 71st St New York, NY 10021. Tel 718-543-3344; Fax 718-543-3315; Email info@vchm.org; Web: www.vchm.org; *Dir* Laura Carpenter Meyers; *Mus Educator* Michael Grillo; *Mus Mgr* Oneida Vasquez
Open Tues - Fri 10 AM - 4 PM, Sat & Sun 11 AM - 4 PM, cl Mon; Admis adults $5, seniors & students $3, children 12 and under free, free to all on Wed; Estab 1898; Average Annual Attendance: 30,000
Special Subjects: Furniture, Historical Material
Collections: Furniture & objects of the 18th century
Activities: Classes for children; slide progs for visitors

M **WAVE HILL,** W 249th St & Independence Ave, Bronx, NY 10471; 675 W 252 St, Bronx, NY 10471-2840. Tel 718-549-3200, 549-2055; Fax 718-884-8952; Email information@wavehill.org; Web: www.wavehill.org; *Pub Rels Dir* Marty Weitzman; *Pres* Kate Pearson French; *VChmn* David O Beim; *Dir Visitor Svcs* Michael Wiertz; *Dir Horticulture* Scott Canning; *Dir Educ* Margot Perron; *Dir Exec/Pres* Claudia Bonn
Open Tues - Sun 10 AM - 4:30 PM; No admis fee Tues & Sat AM, adults $4, sr citizens & students $2, children under 6 free, no admis fee Nov 15-Mar 14; Estab 1960 as a pub garden & cultural center; Wave Hill House Gallery; Glyndor Gallery; Outdoor Sculpture Garden; Average Annual Attendance: 100,000; Mem: 8000; dues $35
Income: Financed by mem, city & state appropriation, private funding
Exhibitions: 28 Acres of Gardens; Visual exhibitions
Publications: Calendar, 4 per yr; exhibit catalogues, annually
Activities: Classes for adults & children; dramatic progs; natural history/ environmental workshops; lects open to pub, 3 vis lectrs per yr; concerts; originate traveling exhibs; sales shop sells books, magazines, reproductions

BRONXVILLE

L **BRONXVILLE PUBLIC LIBRARY,** 201 Pondfield Rd, Bronxville, NY 10708-4828. Tel 914-337-7680; Fax 914-337-0332; Email brolibrary@westchesterlibraries.org; Web: www.bronxvillelibrary.org; *Dir Library* Laura Eckley; *Head of Reference* Patricia Root; *Head of Circ* Marianne Wingertzahn
Open winter Mon, Wed & Fri 9:30 AM - 5:30 PM, Tues 9:30 AM - 9 PM, Thurs 1 - 9 PM, Sat 9:30 AM - 5 PM, Sun 1 - 5 PM, summer Mon, Wed, Thurs & Fri 1 - 5:30 PM, Sat 9:30 AM - 1 PM; No admis fee; Estab as public library in 1906; Average Annual Attendance: 150,000
Income: Financed by city & state appropriations
Special Subjects: Painting-American, Prints
Collections: American painters: Bruce Crane, Childe Hassam, Winslow Homer, William Henry Howe, Frederick Waugh, Japanese Art Prints, 25 Original Currier and Ives Prints
Exhibitions: Current artists, changed monthly; original paintings and prints
Publications: newsletter, quarterly

L **SARAH LAWRENCE COLLEGE LIBRARY,** Esther Raushenbush Library, 1 Meadway, Bronxville, NY 10708-5999. Tel 914-395-2474; Fax 914-395-2473; Email library@mail@slc.edu; Web: www.slc.edu/library; *Dir Lib & Acad Computing* Sha Fagan; *Asst Dir* Janet Alexander
Open Mon-Thurs 8:30AM-1AM, Fri 8:30AM-midnight, Sat 11AM-midnight, Sun 11AM-1AM; Estab to provide library facilities for students & members of the community with an emphasis on art history; Slide collection cl to the pub; non-circulating reference materials available to the pub; Mem: $45 per year
Library Holdings: Book Volumes 225,000, Periodical Subscriptions 1073, Slides 88,000, Video Tapes
Exhibitions: Changing exhibits
Activities: Lect in connection with exhibits; tours on request

BROOKLYN

M **A.I.R. GALLERY,** 155 Plymouth St, Brooklyn, NY 11201-1150. Tel 212-255-6651; Email info@airgallery.org; Web: www.airgallery.org; *Exec Dir* Roxana Fabius; *Dir Fellowship* Patricia Margarita Hernandez

Open Wed - Sun 12 PM - 6 PM; No admis fee; Estab 1972 as a not-for-profit, artist run gallery; also provides programs & services to women artists; runs fellowship program for emerging women artists; Average Annual Attendance: 10,000; Mem: $500 initiation fee; $240 monthly mem dues; monthly meetings
Income: Financed by mem & grants & donations
Library Holdings: Audio Tapes, CD-ROMs, Clipping Files, DVDs, Exhibition Catalogs, Manuscripts, Memorabilia, Original Art Works, Original Documents, Pamphlets, Photographs, Prints, Slides, Video Tapes
Special Subjects: Painting-American, Photography, Sculpture, Woodcarvings, Woodcuts
Collections: Contemporary Women Artists
Exhibitions: One-woman exhibitions; invitational which can be international, regional and performance or theme shows
Publications: Invitational exhibition catalogues, bi-annually
Activities: Children's art walk; Lect open to public; concerts; gallery talks; competitions with awards; sponsored fellowship award; original prints, paintings, photographs, sculpture, slides & videos; organize traveling exhibitions; Organizes traveling exhibitions to galleries/museums in the USA

AMERICAN ABSTRACT ARTISTS
For further information, see National and Regional Organizations

M **AMOS ENO GALLERY,** 56 Bogart St, Brooklyn, NY 11206-3817. Tel 718-237-3001; Email amosenogallery@gmail.com; Web: www.amoseno.org; *Dir* Mary Gagler
Open Thurs - Sun Noon - 6 PM; No admis fee; Estab 1974 as a nonprofit art gallery; 700 sq ft; Mem: dues $225
Collections: Features work by emerging & mid-career artists; visual, performance, installation, interactive & digital media artists
Exhibitions: Temporary exhibits
Activities: Art programming; performance art; film & music; lectures; panels; workshops

A **ART IN GENERAL,** 145 Plymouth St, Dumbo Brooklyn, NY 11201; 20 Jay St, Ste. 210A Brooklyn, NY 11201-8318. Tel 212-219-0473; Fax 212-219-0681; Email social@artingeneral.org; Web: www.artingeneral.org; *Exec Dir & Cur* Laurel Ptak; *Progs & Opers Mgr* Lina Alfonso; *Asst Cur* Patrick Jaojoco
Open Tues - Sat noon - 6 PM; No admis fee; Estab 1981 as a nonprofit arts organization, which relies on private & public support to meet its expenses; Assists artists with the production & presentation of new work; Average Annual Attendance: 10,000; Mem: 90; dues vary
Income: Financed by state & private funds (foundations, corporations)
Publications: Manual of exhibitions & programs, annual
Activities: Interactive discussions & art workshops; lects open to pub; lects mems only; 5 vis lectrs per yr; gallery talks; tours; originate traveling exhibs; sales shop sells books & limited editions

M **BLACK & WHITE GALLERY,** 56 Bogart St, Brooklyn, NY 11206. Tel 718-599-8775; Fax 347-881-9033; Email info@blackandwhiteartgallery.com; Web: www.blackandwhiteartgallery.com; *Founder & Co Dir* Tatyana Okshteyn; *Co Dir & Cur* Sasha Okshteyn
Open Fri - Sun 1 PM - 6 PM & by appointment; Estab 2002 to foster artists' careers
Collections: works by contemporary artists; paintings; sculpture; drawings
Exhibitions: Temporary exhibits

M **BOSE PACIA,** 163 Plymouth St, Brooklyn, NY 11201. Tel 212-989-7074; Fax 212-989-6982; Email mail@bosepacia.com; Web: www.bosepacia.com; *Dir* Sadia Rehman; *Dir Archives* Anita Sharma
Open Tues - Sat 11 AM - 6 PM by appointment; Estab 1994 to facilitate dialogue between South Asian artists & an international art community
Collections: works by contemporary South Asian artists; paintings; drawings
Exhibitions: Temporary exhibits

M **BRIC - BROOKLYN INFORMATION & CULTURE,** BRIC House, 647 Fulton St, Brooklyn, NY 11217. Tel 718-683-5600; Fax 718-488-0609; Email bric@bricartsmedia.org; Web: bricartsmedia.org; *Pres* Leslie Schultz; *VPres Contemporary Art* Elizabeth Ferrer
Open Tues - Fri 10 AM - 8 PM, Sat & Sun 10 AM - 6 PM; No admis fee; Estab 1979 to exhibit the works of professional Brooklyn affiliated artists; 3,000 sq ft gallery; Average Annual Attendance: 17,500
Income: $250,000 (financed by federal, state & municipal sources, private foundations, corporations & individuals)
Exhibitions: Various exhib
Activities: Classes for adults & children; lects open to public, 6-10 vis lectrs per year; gallery talks; tours; fels; computerized slide registry

A **BROOKLYN ARTS COUNCIL,** BAC Gallery, 111 Front St, Ste 218, Brooklyn, NY 11201; 20 Jay St, Ste 616 Brooklyn, NY 11201-8329. Tel 718-625-0080; Fax 718-625-3294; Email gallery@brooklynartscouncil.org; Web: www.brooklynartscouncil.org
Open Mon - Fri 10 AM - 5:30 PM; No admis fee; Estab 1966 to promote education, excellence & exchange in the visual & performing arts; Average Annual Attendance: 600,000; Mem: Artist Registry 6059 artists, free to artists of all disciplines who live or work in Brooklyn, NY
Income: (financed by government, corporate & foundation support, earned income & educational services)
Exhibitions: Solo exhibitions by Brooklyn-based artists; Artist & Guest-curated group & thematic exhibitions
Activities: Dumbo 1st Thurs Gallery Walks; artist & curatorial talks; screenings; installations; receptions

M **BROOKLYN BOTANIC GARDEN,** Steinhardt Conservatory Gallery, 1000 Washington Ave, Brooklyn, NY 11225-1099. Tel 718-623-7200; Fax 718-622-7839; Email anitajacobs@bbg.org; Web: www.bbg.org; *Dir Pub Progs* Anita Jacobs
Open Tues - Fri 8 AM - 4:30 PM, Sat & Sun 10 AM - 4:30 PM; Admis adult $8, children 15 & under free, free on Tues & Sat AM; Estab 1988 to display works of botanical, floral & landscape art; Multi-use space serves as an art gallery, entryway to conservatory pavilions & seasonal eating area; Average Annual Attendance: 800,000
Special Subjects: Landscapes
Collections: Living plants, Botanical Art, Floral Art
Activities: Classes for adults

A **BROOKLYN HISTORICAL SOCIETY,** 128 Pierrepont St at Clinton St, Brooklyn, NY 11201-2711. Tel 718-222-4111; Fax 718-222-3794; Email mduncan@brooklynhistory.org; Web: www.brooklynhistory.org; *Pres* Deborah Schwartz; *VP Programs & External Affairs* Marcia Ely; *Dir Fin & Opers* Jason Pietrangeli; *Dir Educ* Emily Potter-Ndiaye
Open Wed-Sun Noon-5PM, cl Mon & Tues, July 4, Thanksgiving Day, Christmas Day & New Year's Day; Admis adults $10, seniors, teachers $6, students age 12+ (with id), mems, military & children under 12 free; Estab in 1863 to collect, preserve & interpret documentary & other materials relating to the history of Brooklyn. BHS connects the past to the present for today's diverse audiences.; Gallery used for exhibits on Brooklyn history and culture; Average Annual Attendance: 4,500; Mem: 1,750; dues $35 - $1,250; annual meeting May
Income: $650,000 (financed by grants, endowment & mem)
Library Holdings: Cards, Cassettes, Clipping Files, Filmstrips, Framed Reproductions, Manuscripts, Memorabilia, Micro Print, Motion Pictures, Original Art Works, Original Documents, Periodical Subscriptions, Photographs, Reproductions, Sculpture
Collections: Paintings, drawings, watercolors, prints, sculpture, decorative arts, archeological artifacts relating to Brooklyn's history & key citizens
Exhibitions: 31st Jul, 2017) Truman Capote's Brooklyn: The Lost Photographs of David Attie; 31st Jan, 2018) Brooklyn Abolitionists
Publications: Bimonthly newsletter; Neighborhood History Guides
Activities: Educ dept; docent training, tours for children, after school programs for K-12 students; lects open to pub, 15 vis lectrs per yr; gallery talks, concerts, tours; individual paintings & original objects of art lent to other institutions; lending collection contains 3000 original prints, 275 paintings, sculptures; books, original art, reproductions, jewelry

L **Othmer Library**, 128 Pierrepont St, 2nd Fl Brooklyn, NY 11201-2711. Tel 347-381-3708; Email library@brooklynhistory.org; Web: www.brooklynhistory.org; *Mng Dir Library & Archives* Julie L May; *Reference Libr* Cecily Dyer
Open Library: Wed - Sat 1 - 5 PM, contact before visiting, appt req for Archive & Manuscript Collections; Museum & Mus Store: Wed - Sun 12 - 5 PM; Mus admis req for libr access; Estab 1863 for the purpose of collecting, preserving & interpreting the history of Brooklyn & its varied cultures-housed in registered landmark building in Brooklyn Heights; Open to general pub; Mem: dues $50 & up
Library Holdings: Book Volumes 100,000, Clipping Files, Fiche, Kodachrome Transparencies, Lantern Slides, Manuscripts 2,000, Maps 2,000, Original Art Works, Original Documents, Pamphlets, Periodical Subscriptions, Photographs 90,000, Prints
Special Subjects: Decorative Arts, Drawings, Folk Art, Graphic Arts, Historical Material, Landscapes, Manuscripts, Maps, Painting-American, Photography, Portraits, Watercolors
Collections: Reference Books
Exhibitions: In Pursuit of Freedom, (through winter 2018)
Publications: Neighborhood History Guides; books
Activities: Classes for children; tours; docent training; concerts; dramatic progs; varied school-oriented progs; develop workshops for teachers; lects open to pub; book traveling exhibs; originate traveling exhibs circulating to local Brooklyn sites; mus shop sells books, original art, reproductions, prints

M **BROOKLYN MUSEUM,** 200 Eastern Pkwy, Brooklyn, NY 11238-6052. Tel 718-638-5000; Fax 718-501-6136; Email information@brooklynmuseum.org; Web: www.brooklynmuseum.org; Cable BRKLYN-MUSUNYK; Telex 12-5378; *Dir* Anne Pasternak; *Hagop Kevorkian Assoc Cur Islamic Art* Aysin Yoltar-Yildirim; *Cur European Art* Lisa Small; *Dir Curatorial Affairs* Sharon Matt Atkins; *Assoc Cur Egyptian Art* Yekaterina Barbash; *Sr Cur Egyptian, Classical & Ancient Near Eastern Art* Edward Bleiberg; *Andrew W Mellon Cur American Art* Kimberly Orcutt; *Lisa & Bernard Selz Sr Cur Asian Art* Joan Cummins; *Asst Cur Elizabeth A Sackler Center for Feminist Art* Carmen Hermo; *Cur Decorative Arts* Barry R Harwood; *Cur Elizabeth A Sackler Center for Feminist Art* Catherine J Morris; *Andrew W Mellon Cur of the Arts of the Americas* Nancy Rosoff; *John & Barbara Vogelstein Cur Contemporary Art* Eugenie Tsai
Open Wed & Fri - Sun 11 AM - 6 PM, Thurs 11 AM - 10 PM, cl Mon & Tues; Admis adults $16, students (with ID) and seniors 65 & up $10, under 19 & mem free; Estab 1823 as the Apprentices Library Assoc; Five floors of galleries maintained; Average Annual Attendance: 350,000; Mem: dues benefactor's circle $5,000, curator's circle $2,500, fellow $1,000, donor $600, patron $350, contributor $150, family & friends $85, individual $55, 1stfans $20
Income: $14,374,000 (financed by endowment, mem, city & state appropriation, gifts)
Library Holdings: Audio Tapes, Book Volumes, CD-ROMs, Cards, Clipping Files, Compact Disks, Exhibition Catalogs, Fiche, Manuscripts, Other Holdings, Periodical Subscriptions, Photographs
Collections: Art from the Americas & South Pacific, American period rooms, European & American paintings, sculpture, prints, drawings, costumes, textiles & decorative arts, major colls of Egyptian & Classical, Asian, Middle Eastern & African art, Americas & the Pacific, sculpture garden of ornaments from demolished New York buildings
Exhibitions: (Permanent) The Arts of China; The Arts of the Pacific; European Paintings Reinstallation.
Publications: Newsletter, bimonthly; catalogues of major exhibitions; handbooks
Activities: Classes for adults & children; film; docent training; lects open to pub; gallery talks; tours; concerts; sponsoring of competitions; Augustus Graham medal; schols for student progs; individual paintings & original objects of art lent to other mus; originate traveling exhibs; mus shops sell books, original objects, reproductions, prints, magazines, slides, T-shirts, clothes & bags

L **Libraries Archives**, 200 Eastern Pkwy, Brooklyn, NY 11238-6052. Tel 718-501-6307; Fax 718-501-6125; Email library@brooklynmuseum.org; Web: brooklynmuseum.org; *Prin Librn Libraries & Archives* Deirdre E Lawrence
Open by appointment; Estab 1823 to serve the staff of the mus & pub for reference

Income: Financed by city, state & private appropriation
Purchases: $50,000
Library Holdings: Auction Catalogs, Audio Tapes, Book Volumes 200,000, CD-ROMs, Clipping Files, Exhibition Catalogs, Fiche, Lantern Slides, Original Documents, Pamphlets, Periodical Subscriptions 400, Photographs, Video Tapes
Special Subjects: Afro-American Art, American Indian Art, Anthropology, Antiquities-Assyrian, Antiquities-Egyptian, Antiquities-Greek, Antiquities-Oriental, Antiquities-Persian, Antiquities-Roman, Archaeology, Art History, Asian Art, Ceramics, Costume Design & Constr, Decorative Arts, Drawings, Eskimo Art, Etchings & Engravings, Fashion Arts, Folk Art, History of Art & Archaeology, Interior Design, Islamic Art, Latin American Art, Mexican Art, Oriental Art, Painting-American, Period Rooms, Photography, Pre-Columbian Art, Primitive art, Restoration & Conservation, Sculpture, Silversmithing, Southwestern Art, Crafts
Collections: Fashion plates, original fashion sketches 1900-1950, 19th century documentary photographs
Publications: Newsletter, bi-monthly
Activities: Classes for children; docent training; progs relating to current exhibs; lects open to pub, 30 vis lectrs per yr; gallery talks; tours; originate traveling exhibs to other mus

L **Wilbour Library of Egyptology**, 200 Eastern Pkwy, Brooklyn, NY 11238-6052. Tel 718-501-6219; Fax 718-501-6125; Email library@brooklynmuseum.org; Web: brooklynmuseum.com
Open Wed - Fri 10 AM - noon & 1 PM - 4:30 PM, first Sat of month 1PM-4PM except July-Sep; Estab 1934 for the purpose of the study of Ancient Egypt
Income: Financed by endowment & city, state & private appropriation
Purchases: $30,000 annually
Library Holdings: Auction Catalogs, Book Volumes 37,000, Exhibition Catalogs, Fiche, Other Holdings Original documents, Pamphlets, Periodical Subscriptions 150
Collections: Seyffarth papers
Publications: Wilbour Monographs; general introductory bibliographies on Egyptian art available to visitors

L **BROOKLYN PUBLIC LIBRARY,** Art & Music Division, 10 Grand Army Plaza, Brooklyn, NY 11238-5619. Tel 718-230-2183/4; Fax 718-230-2063; Email k.badalamenti@brooklynpubliclibrary.org; Web: www.brooklynpubliclibrary.org
Open Mon & Fri 9AM-6PM, Tues-Thurs 9AM-9PM, Sat 10AM-6PM, Sun 1PM-6PM; No admis fee; Estab 1892; Lobby Gallery on 1st fl; Average Annual Attendance: 12,000
Income: Financed by city & state appropriation
Library Holdings: Audio Tapes, Book Volumes 260,000, Cards, Cassettes, Exhibition Catalogs, Filmstrips, Micro Print, Motion Pictures, Other Holdings Mounted pictures, Pamphlets, Periodical Subscriptions 420, Records, Reels, Slides, Video Tapes
Collections: Checkers Collection, Chess Collection, Costume Collection, Picture & Art Reproduction File, Song Finding Collection
Exhibitions: lect of writing on arts by Bookforum
Publications: Monthly calendar
Activities: Classes for children; progs; lects open to pub; 1-2 vis lectrs per yr; gallery talks; films; book traveling exhibs Pop Up Books (2000); sales shop sells books, magazines, original art

M **DIEU DONNE PAPERMILL, INC,** Gallery, Bldg 3, Ste 602 Brooklyn, NY 11205. Tel 212-226-0573; Fax 212-226-6088; Email diuedonne@dieudonne.org; Web: www.dieudonne.org; *Exec Dir* Kathleen Flynn; *Artistic Dir* Paul Wong; *Prog & Communs Mgr* Kirsten Flaherty; *Studio Collaborator & Educ Mgr* Amy Jacobs; *Develop Assoc* Stephanie Skaff
Open Mon - Fri 10 - 6 PM, cl Sat - Sun; No admis fee; Estab 1976 to promote the art of hand papermaking; Editions gallery for recent works at Dieu Donne, main gallery works in hand paper; maintains archive & reference library; Mem: Dues artist & friend $50, contributor $125, editions club $500, collectors series $800, publishers support $1500, papermaking patron $3500, corp sponsor $10,000
Collections: Chase Manhattan Banks, Johnson & Johnson, Rutgers University, Zimmerli Art Museum, Metropolitan Museum of Art
Exhibitions: Melvin Edwards Aqua y Acero en Papel
Publications: Pulp, quarterly newsletter; exhib catalogs
Activities: Classes for adults & children; lects open to pub, 5 vis lectrs per yr; gallery talks; tours; competitions; scholarships offered; original objects of art lent to members & institutions; lending collection contains books, slides & works in handmade paper; originate traveling exhibs; sales shop sells books, original art & products in handmade paper, Dieu Donne paper

L **FRANKLIN FURNACE ARCHIVE, INC,** 200 Willoughby Ave, ISC Bldg., Rooms 209-211 Brooklyn, NY 11205-7501. Tel 718-398-7255; Fax 718-398-7256; Email mail@franklinfurnace.org; Web: www.franklinfurnace.org; *Founding Dir* Martha Wilson; *Sr Archivist* Michael Katchen; *Deputy Dir* Harley Spiller; *Prog Coordr* Jenny Korns
Office: Mon - Fri 10 AM - 6 PM; Estab 1976 to champion ephemeral art forms neglected by mainstream art institutions; current mission to present, preserve, interpret, proselytize & advocate on behalf of avant-garde art; Virtual institution, accessible to public by web site only; Mem: 1,000 members; dues $33, $66, $99, $333, $999, & $33,000; benefits increase with dues
Library Holdings: Clipping Files, Exhibition Catalogs, Manuscripts, Memorabilia, Motion Pictures, Original Art Works, Original Documents, Pamphlets, Photographs, Prints, Slides, Video Tapes
Publications: Goings On, weekly e-newsletter
Activities: Classes for children; Sequential Art for Kids; awards, Franklin Furnace Furd; mus shop sells books, magazines, & original art

M **HOLLAND TUNNEL ART PROJECTS,** 61 S Third St, Brooklyn, NY 11211; 63 S 3rd St, Brooklyn, NY 11249-5128. Tel 718-384-5738; Fax 718-384-5738; Email hollandtunnelart@gmail.com; Web: www.hollandtunnelgallery.com; *Dir* Paulien Lethen; *Graphic Designer* Roy Lethen; *Asst Dir* Fran Kornfeld
Open Sat & Sun 1 PM - 5 PM & by appt; No admis fee; Estab 1997 connecting people with art; A prefab shed converted into a small gallery featuring local & international artistic talent; Average Annual Attendance: 2,000
Income: Dir assumes costs with artists
Exhibitions: Holland Tunnel in Paros, Greece; 5; Bound; More Than I Would Say About Most People (Nina Levy)
Publications: Catalogue for "5" (5th anniversary show)
Activities: Concerts; tours; poetry reading & artist talks; films & videos; Holland Tunnel in Paros, Greece, "Inside Harry's House" Holland Tunnel Project in the Netherlands; originate traveling exhibs 3 per yr; mus shop sells original art, flat file in gallery

A **HUDSON VALLEY ART ASSOCIATION,** 8 Everit St, Brooklyn, NY 11201-1321. Tel 917-280-2207; Email info@hudsonart.org; Web: www.hvaaonline.org; *Pres Sculpture* Jacqueline Lorieo; *Pres Oil* Rick Daskam; *Sec* Mary Jay Costello; *Treas* John Belardo
Estab 1928, incorporated 1934 to perpetuate the artistic traditions of American artists such as made famous the Hudson River School of painting through exhibitions of painting & sculpture with pub support; Mem: By invitation; dues sustaining lay $35, patrons $70, underwriters $100
Exhibitions: Annual spring exhibition of oils, aqua media, pastels, graphics & sculpture, open to mem & non-mem
Publications: Exhib catalogs
Activities: Awards totaling $100,000

INTERNATIONAL SOCIETY OF COPIER ARTISTS (ISCA)
For further information, see National and Regional Organizations

M **KINGSBOROUGH COMMUNITY COLLEGE, CUNY,** The Art Gallery at Kingsborough Community College, 2001 Oriental Blvd, Brooklyn, NY 11235-2333. Tel 718-368-5720; Fax 718-368-4872; Email kccgallery@gmail.com; Web: www.kccgallery.org
Open Mon - Fri 10 AM - 3 PM; when classes are in session; No admis fee; Estab 1975 for exhibition of visual art; 42 ft x 42 ft gallery, 42 x 50 ft outdoor sculpture courtyard; Average Annual Attendance: 5,000
Income: Financed by Kingsborough Community College Assn
Activities: Lect open to public, 2 vis lectrs per yr; competitions with awards; gallery talks

M **MOCADA - THE MUSEUM OF CONTEMPORARY AFRICAN DIASPORAN ARTS,** James E Davis Art Bldg, 80 Hanson Place Brooklyn, NY 11217-1506. Tel 718-230-0492; Fax 718-230-0246; *Exec Dir* Laurie Cumbo
Open Mon - Tues 9 AM - 5 PM, Wed & Fri - Sun 11 AM - 6 PM, Thurs 11 AM - 8 PM; No admis fee
Collections: African American history & culture; paintings; sculpture; photographs
Activities: Educ programs; special events; internships; museum-related items for sale

M **MOMENTA ART,** 56 Bogart St, Brooklyn, NY 11206-3817. Tel 718-218-8058; Fax 718-347-448-8268; Email momenta@momentaart.org; Web: www.momentaart.org; *Co Dir* Laura Parnes; *Co Dir* Eric Heist
Open Mon-Thurs Noon- 6PM; No admis fee; Estab 1986 as a not-for-profit exhibition organization promoting the work of under-represented & emerging artists; 1,200 sq ft in Williamsburg, Brooklyn; Average Annual Attendance: 5,000; Mem: 200; dues $30-$500
Income: $105,000 (financed by endowment, mem, city & state appropriation)
Activities: Lects open to pub, 6 vis lectrs per yr; sales shop sells catalogs & artist multiples

L **NEW YORK CITY TECHNICAL COLLEGE,** Ursula C Schwerin Library, 300 Jay St, Brooklyn, NY 11201-1909. Tel 718-260-5470; Fax 718-260-5631; Web: www.library.citytech.cuny.edu; *Admin Svcs Librn* Prof Paul T Sherman; *Chief Cataloguer* Morris Hownion; *Reference Coordr* Joan Grissano
Open Mon - Thurs 9 AM - 10 PM, Fri 9 AM-7 PM, Sat 10AM-4PM; Estab 1947
Library Holdings: Reproductions
Special Subjects: Advertising Design, Graphic Arts
Publications: Library Alert & Library Notes, occasional publications
Activities: Tours; Library Instruction; BRS Data Base Searching

L **NEW YORK FOUNDATION FOR THE ARTS,** 20 Jay St Ste 740, Brooklyn, NY 11201-8352. Tel 212-366-6900; Fax 212-366-1778; Email deleget@nyfa.org; Web: www.nyfa.org; *Exec Dir* Michael Royce
Open Mon - Fri 9:30 AM - 5:30 PM, or by appointment; Estab to make more available research in art hazards; For reference only
Library Holdings: Book Volumes 500
Activities: Adult classes; lects

A **ORGANIZATION OF INDEPENDENT ARTISTS, INC,** 117 Sterling Pl #8, Brooklyn, NY 11217. Tel 347-405-2422; Email oiaonline@yahoo.com; Web: www.oia-ny.org; *Dir* Geraldine Cosentino
Open by appt only; No admis fee at all art spaces used for exhibits; Estab 1976 to facilitate artist-curated group exhibitions in public spaces; Alternative spaces; Average Annual Attendance: 500; Mem: 50+ mems, qualifications practicing artist; dues $60
Income: under $25,000 (financed by mem, private donors
Activities: Group exhibs in 3 venues

L **PRATT INSTITUTE,** Art & Architecture Dept, 200 Willoughby Ave, Brooklyn, NY 11205-3899. Tel 718-636-3714, 636-3685; Web: www.lib.pratt.edu/plice
Open Mon - Thurs 9 AM - 11 PM, Fri 9 AM - 7 PM, Sat & Sun Noon - 6 PM for students, faculty & staff, others by appointment or with METRO or ALB card; Estab 1887 for students, faculty, staff & alumni of Pratt Institute; The school has several galleries, the library has exhibitions in display cases
Library Holdings: Book Volumes 85,000, Clipping Files, Exhibition Catalogs, Fiche, Maps, Motion Pictures, Periodical Subscriptions 150, Prints, Reels, Reproductions, Slides, Video Tapes
Special Subjects: Architecture, Photography, Art History

M **The Rubelle & Norman Schafler Gallery**, 200 Willoughby Ave, Brooklyn, NY 11205. Tel 718-636-3517; Email exhibits@pratt.edu; Web: www.pratt.edu/exhibitions

Open Mon - Fri 9 AM - 5 PM, Sat noon - 5 PM, summer Mon. - Fri. 9 AM - 4 PM; No admis fee; Estab 1960; Contemporary art & design in all media & disciplines; Average Annual Attendance: 4,000
Collections: Permanent collection of fiber art, paintings, pottery, prints, photographs & sculpture

A **PROMOTE ART WORKS INC (PAWI),** Laziza Electrique Dance Co, 123 Smith St, Brooklyn, NY. Tel 718-797-3116; Fax 718-855-4746; Email executive@micromuseum.com; Web: www.micromuseum.com; *Technical Dir* William Laziza; *Technician* Mike MacIvor; *Exec Dir* Kathleen Laziza
Open by appointment; Admis 0-$25; Estab 1980; Gallery includes interactive kinetic sculpture & media installation; Average Annual Attendance: 1,200; Mem: 501(C)3
Income: $65,000 (financed by contributions & earned income)
Library Holdings: CD-ROMs, DVDs, Original Art Works, Photographs, Records, Sculpture, Slides, Video Tapes
Special Subjects: Costumes, Drawings, Folk Art, Glass, Photography
Collections: Electronic & video art
Exhibitions: Micro Museum Dec - June
Activities: Classes for adults & children; internships; archival prog for pub television; lects open to pub, 5 vis lectrs per yr; Art of the Future NY Times selected for new millennium; video traveling exhibs 1 per yr; originate traveling exhibs of videotapes to schools

A **The MicroMuseum,** 123 Smith St, Brooklyn, NY 11201. Tel 718-797-3116; Fax 718-855-1208; Email tech@micromuseum.com; Web: www.micromuseum.com; www.pawi.org; *Tech Dir* William Laziza
Open Sun-Fri by appointment 9 AM - 9 PM & Sat noon-7PM; Admis fee 0 - $25; Estab 1993 as art lab for interdisciplinary work; Gallery features media kinetic installation; Mem: National Artists Assoc Org
Income: 63,000 (financed by contributions & earned income)
Library Holdings: Audio Tapes, Cassettes, Kodachrome Transparencies, Lantern Slides, Manuscripts, Memorabilia, Original Art Works, Photographs, Prints, Records, Reproductions, Sculpture, Slides
Collections: 78 RPM record coll from Metropolitan Museum of Art, Spontaneous Combustion
Activities: Originates traveling exhibs of videotapes to schools

SCULPTORS GUILD, INC
For further information, see National and Regional Organizations

M **SOHO20 GALLERY,** 56 Bogart St, Brooklyn, NY 11206. Tel 718-366-3661; Email info@soho20gallery.com; Web: soho20gallery.com; *Gallery Dir* Rachel Steinberg; *Archivist* Andrew Hottle
Open Thurs - Sun noon - 6 PM; No admis fee; Estab 1973 as a women's nonprofit, artist-run gallery; 1400 sq ft for exhibition. Main gallery 1000 sq ft invitational space; Average Annual Attendance: 50 per day; Mem: 27; dues $1320; meetings first Tues each month
Income: Financed by funding programs, sponsored exhibitions
Activities: Lects open to pub, 52 vis lectrs per yr; gallery talks; tours; individual paintings & original objects of art lent to corporations, universities & other galleries; originate traveling exhibs to other museums

A **URBANGLASS AGNES VARIS ART CENTER,** Robert Lehman Gallery, 647 Fulton St, Brooklyn, NY 11217. Tel 718-625-3685; Fax 718-625-3889; Email info@urbanglass.org; Web: www.urbanglass.org; *Exec Dir* Cybele Maylone; *Dir Develop* Rachel Feinberg; *Dir Opers* Brian Kibler; *Dir Educ* Ben Wright
Open Sun, Wed & Thurs noon - 6 PM, Fri & Sat noon - 7 PM; No admis fee; Estab 1977 to provide facility for artists who work in glass; Average Annual Attendance: 8,000; Scholarships; Fellowships
Income: nonprofit, fund raising
Exhibitions: Rotating-3 per yr
Publications: GLASS: The UrbanGlass Art Quarterly
Activities: Classes for adults; lects open to pub, 7 vis lectrs per yr; gallery talks; tours; competitions; fels; shop sells magazines & original art

M **WATERFRONT MUSEUM,** 290 Conover St, Brooklyn, NY 11231-1020. Tel 718-624-4719; Fax 888-320-2485; Email dsharps@waterfrontmuseum.org; Web: www.waterfrontmuseum.org; *Pres* David Sharps; *Bd Pres* Alison Tocci; *Treas* George Tocci
Open Thurs 4 PM - 8 PM & Sat 1 PM - 5 PM; also by appt; Admis $7, group tours by appt; Estab 1986; The Waterfront Mus & Showboat Barge is housed aboard the 1914 Lehigh Valley Railroad Barge #79 listed on the National Register of Historic Places; mus provides pub access to the NY Harbor's waterfront & progs in maritime & environmental educ. Nonprofit org; congressional district 8; FT paid 1, PT paid 4, PT volunteers 35; floating classroom; ramps to barge; Average Annual Attendance: 10,000 by estimate
Special Subjects: Woodcarvings
Collections: Coll of artifacts from The Lighterage Era (1860 - 1960), a period in which goods traded & consumed in NYC were transferred from port docks to railroad terminals by tug & barge, 1914 LV Barge #79, maritime artifacts
Publications: Transfer Magazine: pub by Railroad Marine Info Group
Activities: Educ progs for adults & children; cultural progs; community meetings; spec events; concerts & various showboat performances; mus shop sells books, prints, juggling balls

M **WILLIAMSBURG ART & HISTORICAL CENTER,** 135 Broadway, Brooklyn, NY 11211-6129. Tel 718-486-6012; Email wahcenter@earthlink.net; Web: www.wahcenter.net; *Founder & Chmn* Yuko Nii; *Pres & Treas* Terrance Lindall
Open Fri - Sun Noon - 6 PM; No admis fee; Estab 1996; First floor is the grand Reception Hall with mahogany interior, information center, gift shop & coffee nook. Gallery on second floor presenting shows of emerging & established artists. Basement facility provides space for artists working in the areas of photography, film, video & computer arts; Average Annual Attendance: 10,000; Mem: dues $35
Income: $150,000 (financed by mem, city & state appropriation & contributions)
Purchases: $5000
Library Holdings: Auction Catalogs, Audio Tapes, Book Volumes, Cassettes, Exhibition Catalogs, Manuscripts, Maps, Original Art Works, Original Documents, Photographs, Prints, Sculpture
Collections: Contemporary art, theater, film, video, music (experimental & other), poetry, any art-related event, symposiums, etc
Exhibitions: The Calculus of Transfiguration: Meaning Form & Process in Late 20th Century Art
Publications: The Williamsburg Papers
Activities: Dramatic progs; lects open to pub, 5 vis lectrs per yr; tours, concerts, gallery talks, sponsoring of competitions; mus shop sells books, mags, original art, prints, reproductions

L **Library,** 135 Broadway, Brooklyn, NY 11211.
Open Sat & Sun Noon to 6 PM, Mon by appointment; 40 ft x 60 ft, 20 ft ceiling in main gallery; for reference use
Income: $150,000 (financed by mem, city & state appropriation)
Purchases: $20,000
Library Holdings: Auction Catalogs, Audio Tapes, Book Volumes 2000, Cassettes, Clipping Files, Compact Disks, Kodachrome Transparencies, Manuscripts, Maps, Memorabilia, Original Art Works, Original Documents, Pamphlets, Photographs, Prints, Records, Reproductions, Sculpture, Slides, Video Tapes

BROOKVILLE

M **C W POST CAMPUS OF LONG ISLAND UNIVERSITY,** Hillwood Art Museum, 720 Northern Blvd, Brookville, NY 11548-1300. Tel 516-299-4073; Fax 516-299-2787; Email museum@cwpost.liu.edu; Web: www.liu.edu/museum; *Mus Educator* Tonito Valderrama; *Dir* Barry Stern; *Cur of Coll* Elizabeth Fleming; *Pub Rels* Rita Langdon
Open Mon - Fri 9:30 AM - 4:30 PM, Thurs 9:30 AM - 8 PM, Sat 11 AM - 3 PM; No admis fee; Estab 1973; Mus is located in the student complex and occupies a space of approx 5000 sq ft; Average Annual Attendance: 25,000
Income: Financed by university budget, grants & donations
Special Subjects: African Art, American Indian Art, Antiquities-Egyptian, Antiquities-Greek, Antiquities-Persian, Antiquities-Roman, Asian Art, Bookplates & Bindings, Drawings, Painting-American, Photography, Posters, Pre-Columbian Art, Prints, Textiles
Collections: Near Eastern antiquities, American abstract painting, contemporary photography, Pre-Columbian & African Art, Chinese paintings 10th - 19th century
Exhibitions: Chinese Silk: Symbols of Rank & Privilege (Garments from the Ch'ing Dynasty); Esphyr Slobodkina Retrospective (Works from the Permanent Collection); Kuba Kingdom Dress: Textiles from the Congo; Obsessive Compulsive Order (Contemporary sculpture including works by Amanda Guest, Jeanne Jaffe, Lesly Dill & Gail Deery); Dennis Oppenheim: Realized/Unrealized (Works from the Permanent Collection); Theodore Roosevelt: Icon of the American Century (Artists include John Singer Sargent, Edward Curtis & Frederic Remington); Threads of Time: African Textiles
Publications: Exhibition catalogs; newsletter; study guides
Activities: Educ dept; classes for children; lects open to pub; 6-8 vis lectrs per yr; concerts; gallery talks; tours; concerts; AAM Publication Award; individual paintings & original objects of art lent; lending collection contains books, cassettes, 3000 prints; originates 1-2 traveling exhibs; mus shop sells books, original art, prints & catalogues

BUFFALO

M **ALBRIGHT-KNOX ART GALLERY,** 1285 Elmwood Ave, Buffalo, NY 14222-1096. Tel 716-882-8700; Email info@albrightknox.org; Web: www.albrightknox.org; *Peggy Pierce Elfvin Dir* Janne Siren; *Chief Cur* Cathleen Chaffee
Open Tues - Sun 10 AM - 5 PM, cl New Year's Day, Independence Day, Thanksgiving, Christmas.; Admis adults $12, students, seniors (62+) & veterans $8, youth 6-18 $6, mems & children 5 & under free; Estab 1862

L **BUFFALO & ERIE COUNTY PUBLIC LIBRARY,** 1 Lafayette Sq, Buffalo, NY 14203-1887. Tel 716-858-8900; Fax 716-858-6211; Web: www.buffalolib.org; *Dir* Bridget Quinn-Cary; *Asst Deputy Dir Pub Svcs* Ruth Collins; *Deputy Dir Finance* Kenneth H Stone
Open Mon - Wed, Fri & Sat 8:30 AM - 6 PM, Thurs 8:30 AM - 8 PM; Estab 1954 through a merger of the Buffalo Pub, Grosvenor & Erie County Pub Libraries
Income: $25,000,000 (financed by county appropriation & state aid)
Library Holdings: Book Volumes 3,000,000, Exhibition Catalogs, Manuscripts 4178, Original Art Works, Periodical Subscriptions 3200, Photographs, Prints, Video Tapes
Special Subjects: Drawings, Etchings & Engravings, Prints, Woodcuts
Collections: J J Lankes Collection, William J Schwanekamp Collection, Niagara Falls Collection, Rare book room with emphasis on fine printing
Publications: Bimonthly library bulletin
Activities: Dramatic progs; consumer progs; gallery talks; tours; concerts; book talks; architectural progs

M **BUFFALO ARTS STUDIO,** Art Gallery, 2495 Main St, Ste 500, Buffalo, NY 14214. Tel 716-833-4450 ext 10; Email cori@buffaloartsstudio.org; Web: www.buffaloartsstudio.org; *Exec /Artistic Dir* Cori Wolff; *Educ Coordr* Jayne Hughes; *Develop Officer* Catherine Willett; *Accounting Asst* Anne Simon
Open Tues - Fri 11 AM - 5 PM, Sat 11 AM - 3 PM; No admis fee; A not-for-profit arts organization which provides regular pub exposure for regional, national & international artists through exhibs. BAS enriches the community with art classes, mural programs & pub art projects & provides studio space for emerging artists; Three galleries, two classrooms, 36 artist studios; Average Annual Attendance: 350,000
Income: Corporations, foundations & individuals
Exhibitions: Regional, national & international artists; annual resident artists exhibit
Publications: Evolution/Revolution: The 20th Anniversary

Activities: Classes for adults & children; lects open to pub; exhibits; gallery talks; tours; pub art projects; city wide mural programs; scholarships; gift shop sells books, original art & prints

M **THE BUFFALO FINE ARTS ACADEMY,** Albright-Knox Art Gallery, 1285 Elmwood Ave, Buffalo, NY 14222-1096. Tel 716-882-8700; Fax 716-882-1958; Email info@albrightknox.org; Web: www.albrightknox.org; *Dir* Louis Grachos; *Chief Cur* Douglas Dreishpoon; *Cur Educ* Mariann Smith; *Cur* Heather Pesanti; *Sr Registrar* Laura Fleischmann; *Deputy Dir* Karen Lee Spaulding; *Interim Head Develop* Jennifer Bayles; *Events Coordr* Caterine Gatewood; *Interim Head Opers* Bryan Gawronski; *Sr Art Preparator* Jody Hanson; *HR Mgr* Andrea Griffa Harden; *Head Publs* Pam Hatley; *COO* Mark Hoffman; *Coll Cur* Holly E Hughes; *Opers Mgr Gallery Shop* Tracey Levy; *Interim Head Mktg, Corp & Pub Rels* Maria Scully-Morreale; *Head Research Resources* Susana Tejada; *Head Bldgs & Grounds* Kenneth D Walker
Open Tues - Sun 10 AM - 5 PM, cl Mon, Independence, Thanksgiving, Christmas & New Year's Day; Admis adults $12, seniors & students 13 & up $8, children 6-12 $5, children 5 & under & mems free; Estab 1862 as The Buffalo Fine Arts Academy. Gallery dedicated in 1905, with a new wing added in 1962; Center of modern and contemporary art, the collection offers a panorama of art through the centuries, dating from 3000 BC; Average Annual Attendance: 150,000; Mem: 9500; dues individual $50; ann meeting in Oct
Income: $4,700,000 (financed by contributions, mem. endowment, county appropriations, individual & corporate grants, earned income & special projects)
Special Subjects: African Art, Antiquities-Byzantine, Antiquities-Egyptian, Antiquities-Etruscan, Antiquities-Greek, Antiquities-Oriental, Antiquities-Persian, Antiquities-Roman, Asian Art, Baroque Art, Etchings & Engravings, Glass, Graphics, Mexican Art, Oriental Art, Painting-American, Painting-British, Painting-European, Painting-French, Painting-German, Painting-Israeli, Painting-Italian, Photography, Posters, Religious Art
Collections: Painting & drawings, prints & sculpture ranging from 3000 BC to the present with special emphasis on American & European contemporary art, sculpture & constructions
Publications: Annual report; calendar (bi-monthly); exhibition catalogs
Activities: Classes for adults & children; docent training; family workshops & progs; progs for the handicapped; outreach progs for inner-city schools; lects open to pub, 12 vis lectrs per yr; concerts; gallery talks; tours; National Award for Museum Service 2000; individual paintings & original objects of art lent to major mus worldwide; lending colls contain paintings, photographs & sculptures; book traveling exhibs; originate traveling exhibs; mus shop sells books, reproductions, slides, jewelry, gift items & toys

L **G Robert Strauss Jr Memorial Library,** 1285 Elmwood Ave, Buffalo, NY 14222. Tel 716-270-8225, 270-8240; Fax 716-882-6213; Email artref@albrightknox.org; Web: www.albrightknox.net/library.html; *Asst Libm* Tara Riese
Open Tues - Sat 1 - 5 PM & Fri 3PM-5PM by appt; Estab 1933 to support the staff research & to document the Gallery collection, also to serve the fine art & art history people doing research in the western New York area; Exhibits are prepared in a small vestibule, rare items in the library collection & print collection are displayed
Library Holdings: Audio Tapes, Book Volumes 31,000, Cassettes, Clipping Files, Exhibition Catalogs, Fiche, Manuscripts, Memorabilia, Original Art Works, Other Holdings Original documents, Pamphlets, Periodical Subscriptions 100, Photographs, Prints, Reproductions, Video Tapes
Special Subjects: History of Art & Archaeology, Painting-American, Photography, Pre-Columbian Art, Printmaking, Prints, Sculpture
Collections: Artists books, Graphic Ephemera, Illustrated books
Exhibitions: Books and Prints of Maillol; Photography in Books; Rare Art Periodicals; Woodcuts from the Library Collection; Artists' Books; Illustrated Books; Derriere Le Miroir; From the Gallery Archives; General Ide; Books with a Difference Circle Press Publications

L **BUFFALO SOCIETY OF NATURAL SCIENCES,** Buffalo Museum of Science, 1020 Humboldt Pkwy, Buffalo, NY 14211-1293. Tel 716-896-5200; Fax 716-897-6723; Email library@sciencebuff.org; Web: www.buffalomuseumofscience.org; *Cur Coll* Kathryn Leacock; *Coll Mgr* Kacey Page; *Pres & CEO* Marisa Wigglesworth; *CFO* Hope Kianka; *Chmn, Buffalo Soc Natural Sci Bd Dirs* Christopher Hogan; *Deputy Director* Karen Wallace
Museum - Mon-Sun 10am-4pm; Library by appointment; $10; Estab 1861 to further the study of natural history among the people of Buffalo; Museum has exhibition space for permanent & temporary exhibitions; Average Annual Attendance: 200,000
Income: Financed by endowment, mem, county & state appropriation, grants, gifts
Library Holdings: Audio Tapes, Book Volumes 40,000, Clipping Files, Exhibition Catalogs, Fiche, Filmstrips, Manuscripts, Pamphlets, Periodical Subscriptions 500, Photographs, Reels, Video Tapes
Special Subjects: Afro-American Art, American Indian Art, Anthropology, Archaeology, Asian Art, Bronzes, Coins & Medals, Dioramas, Eskimo Art, Ethnology, History of Art & Archaeology, Jade, Mexican Art, Oriental Art, Southwestern Art
Collections: African, Asian, American, European, Oceanic & Oriental Art, E W Hamlin Oriental Library of Art & Archaeology
Publications: Bulletin of the Buffalo Society of Natural Sciences, irregular; Collections, quarterly
Activities: Classes for adults & children;; lects open to pub & for mems only, gallery talks; tours;

M **BURCHFIELD PENNEY ART CENTER,** SUNY Buffalo State, 1300 Elmwood Ave Buffalo, NY 14222. Tel 716-878-6011; Fax 716-878-6003; Email burchfld@buffalostate.edu; Web: www.burchfieldpenney.org; *Exec Dir* Anthony L Bannon; *Assoc Dir & Chief Cur* Scott Propeack; *Assoc Dir* Don Metz; *Dir Mktg & Pub Rels* Kathleen Heyworth; *Head Colls & Charles Cary Rumsey Cur* Nancy Weekly; *COO* Carolyn Morris-Hunt; *Sr Preparator* Patrick Robideau; *Cur & Mgr Archives* Tullis Johnson; *Registrar* Robert Cutrona; *Events & Rental Mgr* Allie Brady; *Membership Mgr* Suzanne Belz; *Archivist* Heather Gring
Open Tues - Sat 10 AM - 5 PM, Sun 1 - 5 PM; Thurs until 9PM; Admis adults $10, students $5, mem free; Estab 1966; dedicated to the art & vision of Charles W Burchfield & distinguished artists of Buffalo-Niagara & Western NY State. Through its affiliation with SUNY Buffalo State, it encourages learning & celebrates its community; Museum has thirteen exhibition galleries, archives, collection study area, Museum (TM), auditorium, cafe & store; Average Annual Attendance: 100,000; Mem: 5000; dues Friend $125, Family/Dual $60, Individual $45, Cur Circle $275, Dir Circle $500, Burchfield's Circle $1,000
Income: Financed by grants, endowment, mem, SUNY & other sources
Library Holdings: Auction Catalogs, Audio Tapes, Book Volumes, CD-ROMs, Cards, Cassettes, Clipping Files, Compact Disks, DVDs, Exhibition Catalogs, Kodachrome Transparencies, Lantern Slides, Manuscripts, Memorabilia, Motion Pictures, Original Art Works, Original Documents, Pamphlets, Photographs, Prints, Records, Sculpture, Slides, Video Tapes
Special Subjects: Architecture, Bronzes, Cartoons, Ceramics, Collages, Crafts, Decorative Arts, Drawings, Furniture, Glass, Historical Material, Jewelry, Metalwork, Painting-American, Photography, Prints, Sculpture, Watercolors, Woodcuts
Collections: Charles E Burchfield, Works by contemporary & historical artists of Western New York, Roycroft Artisans Objects, American art contextualizing Burchfield, Art Institute of Buffalo, Buffalo Society of Artists, Patteran Society, Art & Archives of Paul Sharits, Birge Wallpaper Co, Philip C Elliot, Virginia Cuthbert, Martha Visser't Hooft, Charles Cary Rumsey, Milton Rogovin, Marion Faller, Hollis Frampton, David Moog, Andrew Topolski, Burchfield's studio
Exhibitions: Charles E Burchfield (rotating)
Publications: Exhibition catalogues; online pubs; vinyl record
Activities: Classes for adults & children; docent training; dramatic programs; lects open to pub; concerts; symposia; tours; poetry readings; competitions; gallery talks; Sylvia L Rosen Endowment Purchase Award; Langley H Kenzie Award; Charles E Burchfield Award; educ dept serves area schools & community organizations; originates traveling exhibs nationally; mus shop sells books, magazines, catalogues, craft art, reproductions & wallpapers designed by Charles Burchfield, original art, prints

L **Library,** 1300 Elmwood Ave, Buffalo State College Buffalo, NY 14222-1004. Tel 716-878-6011; Fax 716-878-6003; Email burchfld@buffalostate.edu; Web: www.burchfieldpenney.org; *Exec Dir* Anthony Bannon; *Assoc Dir & Chief Cur* Scott Propeack; *COO* Carolyn Morris-Hunt
Open Tues - Wed & Fri - Sat 10 AM -5 PM, Thurs 10 AM - 9 PM, Sun 1 - 5 PM; Admis adults $10, seniors $8. students $5; Estab 1967; Dedicated to the vision of Charles E Burchfield & artists of western New York
Library Holdings: Audio Tapes, Book Volumes 2500, Cassettes, Clipping Files, Exhibition Catalogs, Kodachrome Transparencies, Manuscripts, Memorabilia, Motion Pictures, Other Holdings Monographs; Periodicals, Pamphlets, Photographs, Records, Reels, Slides, Video Tapes
Special Subjects: American Western Art, Architecture, Art Education, Art History, Bookplates & Bindings, Crafts, Decorative Arts, Drawings, Etchings & Engravings, Folk Art, Furniture, Historical Material, Manuscripts, Painting-American, Photography, Portraits, Posters, Pottery, Printmaking, Prints, Sculpture, Textiles, Watercolors, Woodcarvings, Woodcuts
Collections: Charles Rand Penney colls; Archives relating to Charles E Burchfield, Charles Cary Rumsey, Frank K M Rehn Gallery, J J Lankes, Martha Visser't Hooft, Buffalo Society of Artists, Patteran Society, Artpark, Artist Gallery, Paul Sharits Archives, Milton Rogovin Collection & Archives
Exhibitions: See website for past & present exhibs
Activities: Classes for adults & children; docent training; lects open to pub; concerts; gallery talks; tours; schols; fels; organize traveling exhibs; mus shop sells books, original art, reproductions & prints

M **CENTER FOR EXPLORATORY & PERCEPTUAL ART,** CEPA Gallery, 617 Main St, Rm 201, Buffalo, NY 14203-1400. Tel 716-856-2717; Fax 716-270-0184; *interim Exec & Artistic Dir* Sean Donaher; *Educ Dir* Lauren Tent; *Exec Asst* Lynda Kaszubski
Open Mon - Fri 10 AM - 5 PM, Sat Noon - 4 PM; No admis fee; Estab 1974 as a non-profit art center for the advancement of contemporary ideas & issues expressed through photographically related work; Five gallery rooms, 225 running ft of wall space, track light, hardwood floors; Average Annual Attendance: 50,000; Mem: 200; dues $25- $500
Income: $100,000 (financed by mem, city & state appropriation, NY State Council on the arts, National Endowment for the Arts)
Exhibitions: A View from Within; Keepers of the Western Door/Works by Native American Artists; Ritual Social Identity
Publications: CEPA Quarterly; Artist Project Publications, 2 artist books per year
Activities: Adult classes; lect open to public, vis lectr; competitions with awards; book traveling exhibitions 1 per year; shop sells books, original art

L **CEPA Library,** 617 Main St, Rm 201, Buffalo, NY 14203. Tel 716-856-2717; Fax 716-856-2720; Email cepa@aol.com; Email info@cepagallery.com; Web: www.cepagallery.com; *Exec Dir* Lawrence F Brose; *Assoc Dir* Kathleen Kearnan; *Artistic Dir* Sean Donaher; *Educ Coordr* Lauren Tent; *Commun Educ* Crystal Tinch; *Designer & Digital Facility* Kim Meyerer; *Admin Asst* Timothy J Hobin
Open Mon - Fri 10 - 5, Sat Noon - 4; pub galleries daily 9 AM - 9 PM; Estab May 1974; Reference library only
Library Holdings: Clipping Files, Exhibition Catalogs, Lantern Slides, Pamphlets, Records, Slides, Video Tapes
Special Subjects: Photography

M **HALLWALLS CONTEMPORARY ARTS CENTER,** 341 Delaware Ave, Buffalo, NY 14202-1871. Tel 716-854-1694; Fax 716-854-1696; Email john@hallwalls.org; Web: www.hallwalls.org; *Dir* Edmund Cardoni; *Visual Arts Cur* John Massier; *Dir Develop* Polly Little; *Music Dir* Steve Baczkowski; *Tech Dir* Bill Sack; *Media Cur* Carolyn Tennant
Open Tues - Fri 11 AM - 6 PM, Sat 11 AM - 2 PM, cl Sun & Mon; No admis fee; Estab 1974 to provide exhibition space for emerging artists; besides exhibitions, programming includes film, literature, music, performance art & video; The gallery is comprised of 1 large 1400 sq ft room; Average Annual Attendance: 25,000; Mem: 1600; dues $20-$300; annual meeting in Jan
Income: Funded by the National Endowment for the Arts, city, county & state appropriations, New York State Council on the Arts, contributions from private corporations, foundations & individuals
Collections: 400 tape video library

Publications: Consider the Alternatives: 20 Years of Contemporary Art at Hallwalls
Activities: Concerts; gallery talks; tours

CANAJOHARIE

M **CANAJOHARIE LIBRARY & ART GALLERY,** Arkell Museum of Canajoharie, 2 Erie Blvd, Canajoharie, NY 13317-1198. Tel 518-673-2314; Fax 518-673-5243; Email etrahan@sals.edu; Web: www.arkellmuseum.org; *Pres of Board* Oliver Simonsen; *Dir* Eric Trahan; *Chief Cur* Diane Forsberg; *Registrar* Emily Spallina; *Head Librn* Kari Munger
Open Mon - Fri 10AM-5PM, Sat-Sun 12:30PM-5PM; Admis adults $7, seniors & students $5; Estab 1914 as a memorial to Senator James Arkell; Two galleries total area 1500 sq ft exhibit works from permanent collection including major collection of paintings by Winslow Homer; Average Annual Attendance: 50,000; Mem: Annual meeting in Jan
Income: Financed by endowment, grants & fundraising
Library Holdings: Book Volumes, CD-ROMs, Compact Disks, Exhibition Catalogs, Framed Reproductions, Original Art Works, Original Documents, Periodical Subscriptions, Photographs, Prints, Slides, Video Tapes
Special Subjects: American Western Art, Bronzes, Historical Material, Painting-American, Photography, Portraits, Prints, Sculpture, Watercolors
Collections: Archival Materials & Artifacts on Regional History, Paintings by American artists, colonial period-present
Exhibitions: Permanent collection
Publications: Catalog of Permanent Art Collection varies
Activities: Lects provided, 5 vis lectrs per yr; concerts; gallery talks; tours; individual paintings & original objects of art lent to other mus & galleries; lending collection contains 28,617 books, 831 cassettes, color reproductions, paintings, 682 phono records, 376 slides, 523 video cassettes; mus shop sells books, original art, prints & reproductions

L **Library,** 2 Erie Blvd, Canajoharie, NY 13317. Tel 518-673-2314; Fax 518-673-5243; *Pres of Board* Oliver Simonsen; *Cur* James Crawford; *Dir Library* Eric Trahan
Open Mon-Thurs 10AM-7PM, Fri 10AM-5PM, Sat-Sun 12:30PM-5PM; No Admis fee; Estab 1914 to represent American Art
Library Holdings: Audio Tapes, Book Volumes 28,617, Cassettes, Clipping Files, Exhibition Catalogs, Framed Reproductions, Pamphlets, Periodical Subscriptions 146, Photographs, Records, Reels, Slides, Video Tapes
Activities: Lects open to pub, 5 vis lectrs per yr; concerts; gallery talks; tours; lending collection contains 29,022 books, cassettes, framed reproductions & 788 phono records; mus shop sells books, magazines, original art, reproductions, prints, slides, notecards & postcards

CAZENOVIA

M **CAZENOVIA COLLEGE,** Chapman Art Center Gallery, 22 Sullivan St, Cazenovia, NY 13035-1085. Tel 315-655-7162; 655-7138; Fax 315-655-2190; Email jrandall@cazenovia.edu; *Dir* John Aistars
Open Mon - Thurs 1 - 4 PM & 7 - 9 PM, Fri 1 - 4 PM, Sat & Sun 2 - 6 PM; No admis fee; Estab 1977 as a col gallery for students & community; Gallery is 1,084 sq ft with track lighting; Average Annual Attendance: 1,000
Income: Financed by College
Collections: A small permanent coll of work donated to college
Exhibitions: Annual shows of faculty, students & invitational work; Cazenovia Watercolor Society
Activities: Schols offered

M **STONE QUARRY HILL ART PARK,** John & Virginia Winner Memorial Art Gallery, 3883 Stone Quarry Rd, Cazenovia, NY 13035; P.O. Box 251, Cazenovia, NY 13035. Tel 315-655-3196; Fax 315-655-5742; Email office@stonequarryhillartpark.org; Web: www.stonequarryartpark.org; *Mgr* Lesley Owens-Pelton, JD
Open daily sunset-sunrise; gallery Thurs - Sun noon - 5 PM during exhibitions; No admis fee ($5 donation requested); Estab 1991; 4 1/2 miles of maintained walking trails; Average Annual Attendance: 25,000; Mem: 400; dues $35-75; annual meeting Jan
Income: $125,000 (financed by memberships, donations, grants & sponsors)
Collections: Environmental land, outside sculpture, permanent coll of Dorothy Riester, 100 installations of environmental art & sculpture
Activities: Classes for adults & children; docent training; lects open to pub; concerts; gallery talks; tours; ann pottery fair; Finding Nature in Art & Kite Festival; artists in residence prog

M **Winner Gallery,** 3883 Stone Quarry Rd, Cazenovia, NY 13035; PO Box 251, Cazenovia, NY 13035-0251. Tel 315-655-3196; Fax 315-655-5742; Email office@stonequarryhillartpark.org; Web: www.stonequarryartpark.org; *Site Mgr* Dylan Otts; *Art Adminr* Amber Blanding
Open daily 10AM-5PM; Admis suggested donation for non-mem $5; Estab 1991 to address issues of art & environmental preservation; Average Annual Attendance: 47,000; Mem: 250; dues $35-$5000; annual meeting in Jan
Income: $207,000 (financed by endowment, mem & NYSCA)
Library Holdings: Book Volumes, Exhibition Catalogs, Original Art Works, Original Documents, Sculpture, Slides, Video Tapes
Special Subjects: Afro-American Art, Afro-American Art, American Western Art, Archaeology, Architecture, Art Education, Art History, Asian Art, Bronzes, Ceramics, Conceptual Art, Decorative Arts, Drawings, Etchings & Engravings, Ethnology, Folk Art, Furniture, Glass, Historical Material, History of Art & Archaeology, Interior Design, Intermedia, Islamic Art, Landscape Architecture, Landscapes, Latin American Art, Manuscripts, Maps, Mexican Art, Mixed Media, Oriental Art, Sculpture, Porcelain, Portraits, Posters, Pottery, Pre-Columbian Art, Primitive art, Religious Art, Sculpture, Southwestern Art, Textiles, Woodcarvings, Woodcuts
Collections: Tree houses, Dorothy Riester Sculpture, Emilie Brzezinski
Activities: Classes for adults & children; lects open to pub, 2-3 vis lectrs per yr; concerts; gallery talks; tours; fels offered; sales shop sells books, original art, reproductions, magazines, prints

L 3883 Stone Quarry Rd, Cazenovia, NY 13035; PO Box 251, Cazenovia, NY 13035. Tel 315-655-3196; Email Office@stonequarryhillartpark.org; Web: www.sqhap.org; *Exec Dir* Emily Zaengle
Open year-round dawn to dusk; Admis $5 per person, mems & children 16 & under free; Estab 1991; 1200 sq ft indoor gallery
Income: financed by mem & endowment
Library Holdings: Book Volumes 3500, Exhibition Catalogs, Original Art Works, Sculpture, Slides
Special Subjects: Art History, Asian Art, Crafts, Landscape Architecture, Metalwork, Mixed Media, Oriental Art, Painting-American, Photography, Porcelain, Pottery, Printmaking, Sculpture, Theatre Arts, Watercolors
Collections: Dorothy Prester
Publications: Art & the Land-A Narrative History of Stone Quarry Hill Art Park by Dorothy Riester
Activities: classes for children; workshops for adults; active artist in residence prog

CHAUTAUQUA

M **CHAUTAUQUA CENTER FOR THE VISUAL ARTS,** PO Box 28, Chautauqua, NY 14722-0028. Tel 716-357-2771; Email ccva@mainalley.com; Web: www.clweb.org/arts.html; *Pres* Thomas Becker; *Exec & Artistic Dir* Cynnie Gaasch; *Asst Dir* Alissa Shields
Open daily 10 AM - 6 PM July - Sept; No admis fee; Estab 1952 to promote quality art, culture & appreciation of the arts; Main gallery with 3 smaller galleries; Average Annual Attendance: 10,000; Mem: 300; dues $25; one annual meeting
Income: Financed by mem, grants, donations & fundraising activities
Collections: 75 two dimensional purchase prizes
Exhibitions: 15 exhibitions per year including prints, paintings, glass, metals & sculpture; Annual Chautauqua National Exhibition of American Art (entering 44th year)
Publications: Chautauqua National, annual catalog; Calendar of Events, annual; Chautauqua National Prospectus, annual; annual report; promotional materials; exhibition brochures; membership brochures
Activities: Lects open to pub, 17 vis lectrs per yr; concerts; gallery talks; docent tours; competitions with awards; annual juried National Exhibition of American Art award $2500; individual paintings & original objects of art lent to Chautauqua institution, area libraries, exhibition sites, area galleries & theatres; book traveling exhibs annually; originate traveling exhibs; sales shop sells books, original art, reproductions, prints, original jewelry, small gifts & handicraft from around the world

CLINTON

M **HAMILTON COLLEGE,** Emerson Gallery, 198 College Hill Rd, Clinton, NY 13323-1295. Tel 315-859-4396; Fax 315-859-4060; Email emerson@hamilton.edu; Web: www.hamilton.edu/gallery; *Assoc Dir & Cur* Susanna White; *Registrar* Dana Krueger; *Office Asst* Megan Austin; *Consulting Dir* Ian Berry
Open Mon - Fri 10AM - 5 PM, Sat & Sun 1 - 5 PM; No admis fee; Estab 1982; Housed in 1914 building; Average Annual Attendance: 20,000
Income: Financed by Hamilton College appropriations
Purchases: Martin Lewis, Rainy Day on Murray Hill, etching; George Bellows Between Rounds 1916, lithograph; Jefferson David Chalfant Working Sketch for the Chess Players, pencil; Roman, c 2nd Century AD; Two Sarcophagi Fragments, marble
Special Subjects: American Indian Art, Antiquities-Egyptian, Antiquities-Greek, Drawings, Etchings & Engravings, Painting-American, Prints, Watercolors, Photography
Collections: Greek vases, Roman glass, Native American artifacts, 16th-20th century prints, 19th-20th century paintings, Pre-Columbian Art
Publications: Exhibition catalogues
Activities: Lects open to pub, 2-3 various vis lectrs per yr; concerts; gallery talks; tours; individual paintings & original objects of art lent

A **KIRKLAND ART CENTER,** 9-1/2 E Park Row, Clinton, NY 13323-1544; PO Box 213, Clinton, NY 13323-0213. Tel 315-853-8871; Fax 315-853-2076; Email info@kacny.org; Web: www.kacny.org; *Executive Director* Megan Ratcliffe; *Office Assistant* Jessie Caracciolo
Open Tues - Fri 9:30 AM - 4:30 PM; No admis fee; Estab 1960 to promote the arts in the town of Kirkland & surrounding area; The center has a large main gallery, dance studio & studio space for classes; Average Annual Attendance: 15,000 - 17,000; Mem: 700; dues adults $35; annual meeting June
Income: Financed by endowment, mem, state, county & town appropriation, fund raising events, United Way & United Arts Funds
Library Holdings: Book Volumes, Original Art Works, Photographs, Prints
Special Subjects: Ceramics, Crafts, Decorative Arts, Juvenile Art, Sculpture, Painting-American, Photography, Portraits, Prints, Sculpture, Tapestries, Textiles, Watercolors
Exhibitions: Works by contemporary artists
Activities: Classes for adults & children; performances for children; bluegrass & folk music series; film series; dramatic progs; lect open to public; competitions; concerts; tours; Museum Shop sells books, original art & art supplies

COLD SPRING

M **PUTNAM COUNTY HISTORICAL SOCIETY,** Foundry School Museum, 63 Chestnut St, Cold Spring, NY 10516-2613. Tel 845-265-4010; Fax 845-265-2884; Email office@pchs-fsm.org; Web: www.pchs-fsm.org; *Exec Dir* Mindy Krazmien; *Dir Admin* Kara Shier
Open Wed-Sun 11AM-5PM; Admis free; Estab 1906 to present local history & West Point Foundry artifacts; Three exhib galleries; Average Annual Attendance:

1,000; Mem: 1,000; dues family $100 individual $50, seniors & students $30, annual meeting in Mar
Income: financed by endowment, mem & fundraising events
Library Holdings: Auction Catalogs, Book Volumes, Clipping Files, Fiche, Kodachrome Transparencies, Manuscripts, Maps, Memorabilia, Original Documents, Pamphlets, Photographs, Reproductions, Slides, Video Tapes
Special Subjects: Furniture, Historical Material, Painting-American, Period Rooms, Costumes, Decorative Arts, Graphics, Historical Material, Landscapes, Maps, Photography, Portraits, Prints, Watercolors
Collections: 19th Century Country Kitchen, West Point Foundry, 19th Century Prints and Photographs, 19th and Early 20th Century Costumes
Publications: George Pope Morris: Defining American Culture; This Perfect River-View: The Hudson River School & Contemporaries in Pvt Colls in the Highlands; A Ramble Through the Hudson Highlands: A History in Pictures & the Writings of Donald H MacDonald; The Gilded Age: High Fashion & Society in the Hudson Highlands 1865 - 1914; America the Beautiful: Women & the Flag
Activities: School progs; docent training; lects open to pub, 2 vis lectrs per yr; competitions with awards; gallery tours; individual paintings & original objects of art lent; originates traveling exhibitions to museums and libraries; mus shop sells books, reproductions, prints, postcards, pamphlets, children's toys & books

COOPERSTOWN

A **COOPERSTOWN ART ASSOCIATION,** 22 Main St, Cooperstown, NY 13326-1170. Tel 607-547-9777; Fax 607-547-1187; Email gallery@cooperstownart.com; Web: www.cooperstownart.com; *Dir* Janet Erway; *Gallery Mgr* Karl Benner; *Gallery Mgr* Marie DiLorenzo
Open Mon - Sat 11 AM - 4 PM, Sun 1 - 4 PM, cl Tues from Labor Day to Memorial Day; Estab 1928 to provide a cultural program for the central part of New York State; An art gallery is maintained; 3 gallery spaces; Average Annual Attendance: 14,000; Mem: 400; dues $5 & up
Income: Financed by mem
Special Subjects: Bronzes, Ceramics, Collages, Crafts, Etchings & Engravings, Furniture, Glass, Jewelry, Photography, Portraits, Pottery, Textiles, Watercolors, Woodcarvings, Woodcuts
Collections: Crafts, paintings, sculpture
Exhibitions: Annual Regional & National Juried Exhibitions; Solo & Group Shows; Ann NY Craft Invitational
Publications: Annual newsletter
Activities: Classes & workshops for adults & children; monthly exhibits; special events; ann schols; awards; lending collection contains paintings, sculpture, crafts

M **NATIONAL BASEBALL HALL OF FAME & MUSEUM,** 25 Main St, Cooperstown, NY 13326-0590. Tel 607-547-7200; Fax 607-547-2044; Email info@baseballhall.org; Web: baseballhall.org; *Pres* Jeffrey L Idelson; *VPres* Jeff Jones; *Library Dir* James L Gates Jr; *VPres Sponsorship & Develop* Ken Meifert; *VPres Retail Mktg & Licensing* Sean Gahagan; *VPres Exhibs & Colls* Erik Strohl; *Dir Communications* Craig Muder
Open Labor Day - Memorial Day daily 9 AM - 5 PM, May 28 - Sept 3 daily 9 AM - 9 PM; Admis adults $23, seniors $15, children ages 7-12 $12; Estab 1936 to collect, preserve & display memorabilia pertaining to the national game of baseball and honoring those who have made outstanding contributions to our national pastime; Maintains reference library; Average Annual Attendance: 300,000; Mem: 30,000
Income: $1,500,000 (financed by admis & gift shop sales, Hall of Fame Game & contributions)
Library Holdings: Auction Catalogs, Audio Tapes, Book Volumes, CD-ROMs, Cards, Cassettes, Clipping Files, Compact Disks, DVDs, Exhibition Catalogs, Fiche, Lantern Slides, Manuscripts, Memorabilia, Motion Pictures, Original Art Works, Original Documents, Pamphlets, Periodical Subscriptions, Photographs, Prints, Records, Reels, Sculpture, Slides, Video Tapes
Special Subjects: Bronzes, Cartoons, Ceramics, Coins & Medals, Collages, Costumes, Decorative Arts, Drawings, Folk Art, Furniture, Glass, Graphics, Historical Material, Historical Material, Illustration, Jewelry, Leather, Manuscripts, Miniatures, Painting-American, Painting-American, Painting-Japanese, Photography, Porcelain, Portraits, Portraits, Posters, Pottery, Prints, Sculpture, Silver, Textiles, Watercolors, Woodcarvings, Judaica
Collections: Baseball & sport-related art & memorabilia, Library collections
Publications: National Baseball Hall of Fame & Museum Yearbook, annually; bi-monthly newsletter
Activities: Classes for children; educ prog; gallery talks; lects open to public; concerts; gallery talks; tours; lending of original art to AAM accredited museums; book traveling exhib on a case by case basis; originate traveling exhib to museums, baseball clubs; museum shop sells books, reproductions, prints, t-shirts, caps, glassware, postcards, mugs & jackets

M **NEW YORK STATE HISTORICAL ASSOCIATION,** Fenimore Art Museum, 5798 State Hwy 80, Cooperstown, NY 13326; PO Box 800, Cooperstown, NY 13326-0800. Tel 607-547-1400; Fax 607-547-1404; Email info@fenimoreart.org; Web: www.fenimoreartmuseum.org; *Pres & CEO* Dr Paul S D'Anbrosio; *VP Opers* Joseph Siracusa
Open Apr 1 - May 9 Tues - Sun 10 AM - 4 PM, May 10 - Oct 10 daily 10 AM - 5 PM, Oct 11 - Dec 31 Tues - Sun 10 AM - 4 PM, cl Mon Thanksgiving & Christmas; Admis adults & hunior (13-64) $12, seniors 65+$10.50, mem & children 12 & under free; Estab 1899 as a historical soc whose purpose is to promote the study of New York State through a state wide educational program, the operation of two museums & graduate programs offering master's degree in conjunction with the State University of New York at Oneonta; Fenimore Art Museum is an art & history museum with an extensive collection of folk, acad, decorative art & North American Indian Art. Opened a new American Indian Art wing in 1995 to house the Eugene & Clare Thaw Collection of American Indian Art; Mem: 2800; dues $25 & up; annual meeting in July
Library Holdings: Auction Catalogs, Audio Tapes, Book Volumes 90,000, CD-ROMs, Cassettes, Compact Disks, DVDs, Manuscripts, Maps, Memorabilia, Original Documents, Pamphlets, Periodical Subscriptions, Photographs, Records, Video Tapes
Special Subjects: American Indian Art, Architecture, Art History, Carpets & Rugs, Ceramics, Crafts, Decorative Arts, Embroidery, Etchings & Engravings, Folk Art, Furniture, Glass, Graphics, Historical Material, History of Art & Archaeology, Jewelry, Landscape Architecture, Landscapes, Manuscripts, Maps, Painting-American, Photography, Portraits, Pottery, Primitive art, Restorations, Silversmithing, Stained Glass, Textiles, Watercolors, Woodcarvings, Woodcuts, Tapestries
Collections: American folk art, American Indian Art, Browere life masks of famous Americans, James Fenimore Cooper (memorabilia), genre paintings of New York State, landscapes, portraits, Hudson River historic & contemporary school paintings
Publications: Annual Report; New York History, quarterly journal; Heritage, yearly membership magazine, occasional manuscripts, exhibit catalogues
Activities: Classes for adults & children; dramatic progs; docent training; seminars on American culture; junior prog; conferences; lects open to pub; gallery talks; tours; individual paintings & original objects of art lent to selected mus; book traveling exhibs; originate traveling exhibs; mus shop sells books, magazines, original art, reproductions, prints & slides

L **Research Library**, 5798 St Hwy 80, Cooperstown, NY 13326; PO Box 800, Cooperstown, NY 13326-0800. Tel 607-547-1470; Fax 607-547-1405; Email library@nysha.org; Web: www.nysha.org; *Pres* Paul D'Ambrosio; *Dir Colls* Erin Richardson; *Special Colls Librn* Joseph Festa
Open summer Mon-Fri 10 AM - 5 PM, winter, spring & fall Mon - Fri 10 AM - 5 PM, Sat 1 - 5 PM; Admis $5 daily use free for non-mems; free for NYSHA mems, NYSHA vols & students; Estab 1968 as non-circulating research library; Open to public for reference only
Library Holdings: Auction Catalogs, Audio Tapes, Book Volumes 82,000, Cassettes, DVDs, Exhibition Catalogs, Manuscripts, Maps, Original Documents, Pamphlets, Periodical Subscriptions 160, Photographs, Records, Reels
Special Subjects: American Indian Art, Architecture, Art History, Carpets & Rugs, Ceramics, Costume Design & Constr, Crafts, Decorative Arts, Embroidery, Etchings & Engravings, Folk Art, Furniture, Glass, Historical Material, Jewelry, Laces, Landscape Architecture, Landscapes, Manuscripts, Maps, Painting-American, Pewter, Photography, Portraits, Pottery, Printmaking, Restoration & Conservation, Scrimshaw, Silver, Stained Glass, Woodcarvings, Woodcuts

CORNING

A **THE ARTS COUNCIL OF THE SOUTHERN FINGER LAKES,** The Hawkes Building, 79 W Market St Corning, NY 14830. Tel 607-962-1332; Fax 607-962-4128; Email infoarts@earts.org; Web: www.earts.org; *Exec Dir* Constance R Sullivan-Blum; *Special Projects Coord* Tamar Samuel-Siegel; *Community Arts Mgr* Chris Walters; *Devel Asst* Laura Charles
Open Mon - Fri 9 AM - 5 PM; No admis fee; Estab to increase resident participation in the arts; Mem: 34; annual meeting in June
Exhibitions: Artsfest; The Westend Gallery (Local Artists); Easter eggs & paper cuttings (Felicia Dvornicky)
Publications: Artscope, 6 times per year; See, Hear, Do, 12 times per year
Activities: Educ dept; infuses art into education in area schools; lect open to public; partnership awards given; grants to local schools & nonprofit organizations

M **CORNING MUSEUM OF GLASS,** Museum, One Museum Way, Corning, NY 14830-2253. Tel 800-732-6845, 607-937-5371; Fax 607-438-5367; Email info@cmog.org; Web: www.cmog.org; *Pres & Exec Dir* Karol Wight; *Cur European Glass* Christoper Maxwell; *Cur Modern & Contemporary Glass* Susie Silbert; *Cur American Glass* Kelly Conway; *Cur Science & Technology* Marvin Bolt
Open daily 9 AM - 5 PM; Memorial Day - Labor Day 9 AM - 8 PM; cl New Years Day, Thanksgiving Day, Dec 24 & 25; Admis adults $19.50, students $16.60, local res with ID $9.75, children under 18 free; Estab 1951 to collect & exhibit the finest glass from 1500 BC to the present; Art, history, science of glass; Average Annual Attendance: 420,000; Mem: 3,000; dues $60 & up
Purchases: Glass & books
Library Holdings: Auction Catalogs, Audio Tapes, Book Volumes, Cards, Cassettes, Exhibition Catalogs, Fiche, Kodachrome Transparencies, Manuscripts, Memorabilia, Original Art Works, Original Documents, Pamphlets, Periodical Subscriptions, Photographs, Prints, Slides, Video Tapes
Special Subjects: Glass
Collections: over 45,000 objects representing 3,500 yrs of glass history, Origins of Glassmaking Gallery, Glass of the Romans, Glass in the Islamic World, Early European Glass Gallery, Later European Glass Gallery, Asian Glass, Glass in America, Crystal City, Paperweights in the World, Modern Glass Gallery, Glass after 1960, Study Gallery
Exhibitions: 3 exhibitions annually
Publications: Annual catalog for spec exhibs; Journal of Glass Studies, ann; New Glass Review, ann
Activities: Classes for adults & children; docent training; annual seminar on glass; lects open to pub, 30 vis lectrs per yr; film series; gallery talks; tours; competitions; Rakow Award; Rakow Commission; annual student art show awards; schols & fels offered; original art objects lent to the other mus; lending collection contains 50,000 books, 350 lantern slides; originate traveling exhibs; mus shop sells books, postcards, prints, reproductions & slides, glass, hands-on glass activities, story hour for youth, jr cur program, glassworking classes

L **Juliette K and Leonard S Rakow Research Library**, 5 Museum Way, Corning, NY 14830-2253. Tel 607-438-5300; Fax 607-438-5392; Email rakow@cmog.org; Web: www.cmog.org; *Chief Librn* James Galbraith; *Cataloger* Kelly Bliss; *Bibliographer* Peter Bambo-Kocze; *Reference Librn* Gail Bardhan; *Assoc Librn Coll Mgmt* Lori Fuller; *Reference & Emerging Tech Librn* Regan Brumagen; *Reference & Educ Librn* Beth Hylen; *Outreach Librn* Rebecca Hopman; *Special Colls & Archives Librn* Mary Anne Hamblen
Open daily 9 AM - 5 PM; No admis fee; Estab 1951 for the purpose of providing comprehensive coverage of the art, history, & early technology of glass; Circ Non-circulating; The library is a pub facility that welcomes both museum visitors & glass researchers; Average Annual Attendance: 5,000

Library Holdings: Auction Catalogs 27,000, Audio Tapes, Book Volumes 75,000, Cassettes, Clipping Files, Compact Disks, DVDs, Exhibition Catalogs, Fiche 19,000, Framed Reproductions, Manuscripts, Maps, Memorabilia, Micro Print 21,000, Motion Pictures, Original Art Works 25,000, Original Documents 7,500, Other Holdings Monographs: 59,000; Ephemera: 3,000+, Pamphlets, Periodical Subscriptions 550, Photographs, Prints 550, Reels 800, Slides 230,000, Video Tapes 2,600
Special Subjects: Glass
Collections: Chambon (Raymond) Collection, Digital Files: 225,000+, incl 225+ virtual books, Miscellaneous: incl postage stamps, calendars & glass-related resources, 3,500 linear ft of archival colls (200+ archival collections total)
Activities: Docent training; classes for teachers; gallery talks; tours; schols & fels offered; mus shop sells books

M **The Studio**, 1 Museum Way, Corning, NY 14830-2253. Tel 607-974-6467; Email thestudio@cmog.org; Web: www.cmog.org; *Dir Devel, Educ & The Studio* Amy Schwartz; *Educ Progs Mgr* Mary Cheek Mills; *RA* William Gudenrath
Activities: Glassmaking classes held yr-round; Schols available

M **THE ROCKWELL MUSEUM,** 111 Cedar St, Corning, NY 14830-2632. Tel 607-937-5386; Fax 607-974-4536; Email info@rockwellmuseum.org; Web: www.rockwellmuseum.org; *Pub Progs* Brett Smith; *Controller* Andrew Braman; *Dir* Kristin A Swain; *Mktg Dir* Beth Manwaring; *Dir Educ* Gigi Alvare
Open Mon - Sun 9 AM - 5 PM, Sun 9 AM - 8 PM; Admis adults $9, sr citizens $8, students $4, children 19 & under free; Estab 1976 to house & exhibit the collection of the Robert F Rockwell family & to collect & exhibit American Western art; Average Annual Attendance: 35,000; Mem: 300; dues $70 - $1,000; meetings in June & Dec
Income: $$400,000 (financed by a grant from Corning Incorporated)
Purchases: $50,000
Special Subjects: American Indian Art, American Western Art, Bronzes, Carpets & Rugs, Etchings & Engravings, Glass, Painting-American, Pottery, Prints
Collections: 19th & 20th century American Western paintings & illustrations, Robert F Rockwell Foundation Collection
Exhibitions: Celebration of Geniuses: Ansel Adams; Fields & Streams: Hunting & Wildlife
Publications: Exhibition catalog
Activities: Classes for adults & children; docent training; lects open to public; gallery talks; tours; concerts; AAM Accredited; paintings, original objects of art lent to established museums; lending collection contains reproductions, original art works, original prints, Carder Steuben Glass; originate traveling exhibs; shop sells books, magazines, reproductions, prints, Indian jewelry, postcards, crafts from the Southwest, T-shirts, Pueblo pottery, Hopi Kachinas, toys, glass

L **Library**, 111 Cedar St, Corning, NY 14830. Tel 607-937-5386; Fax 607-974-4536; Email rmuseum@stny.lrun.com; *Dir* Richard B Bessey
For reference only
Income: Financed by mem, bequests, grants, corporate donations from Corning Glass Works
Library Holdings: Book Volumes 3000, Cards, Cassettes, Clipping Files, Exhibition Catalogs, Filmstrips, Manuscripts, Original Art Works, Pamphlets, Periodical Subscriptions 40, Photographs, Slides, Video Tapes

CORNWALL ON HUDSON

M **MUSEUM OF THE HUDSON HIGHLANDS,** The Boulevard, Cornwall On Hudson, NY 12520; PO Box 337, Cornwall on Hudson, NY 12520-0337. Tel 845-534-5506; *Dir* Jacqueline Grant; *Admin Dir* Susan Brander; *Pres* Edward Hoyt
Call for hours; Admis $2 suggested donation; Estab 1962; primarily a children's natural history & art mus; A large octagonal gallery & a small gallery; Average Annual Attendance: 33,000; Mem: 450; artists qualify by approval of slides; dues $30 and up
Income: $140,000 (financed by mem, city appropriation & grants)
Special Subjects: Drawings
Collections: Richard McDaniels: Hudson River Drawings
Exhibitions: Rotating exhibitions, six per yr
Activities: Classes for adults & children; lects open to pub, 2 vis lectrs per yr; competitions with awards; lending collection contains nature & history kits; book traveling exhibs, annually; mus shop sells books, magazines, original art, reproductions, prints, toys, pottery, jewelry, batik scarves

CORTLAND

M **1890 HOUSE-MUSEUM & CENTER FOR THE ARTS,** 37 Tompkins St, Cortland, NY 13045-2555. Tel 607-756-7551; Email the1890house@gmail.com; Web: www.1890house.org; *Mus Coordr* Meg Hutchins; *Pres* Joanne Sweeney
Open Thurs - Sat 12 - 4 PM; pvt tours by appt; Admis adults $8, seniors, students & military $5, children 10 & under no charge; Estab 1978
Library Holdings: Book Volumes, Original Art Works, Original Documents, Periodical Subscriptions, Photographs, Reproductions, Slides
Special Subjects: Architecture, Decorative Arts, Painting-American, Period Rooms, Stained Glass
Collections: Decorative arts, Oriental Furnishings, Paintings, 1890 - 1920's Documentary Photographs, Victorian Furniture, Victorian Silver, Industrial Artifacts
Publications: Whispers Near the Inglenook
Activities: Classes for adults & children; docent training; tours

L **Kellogg Library & Reading Room**, 37 Tompkins St, Cortland, NY 13045-2555. Tel 607-756-7551; Fax 607-756-7551; *Admin Asst* Grace Nicholas
Open Tues - Sun 1 - 4 PM; For lending & reference
Library Holdings: Book Volumes 1800, Periodical Subscriptions 12

M **CORTLAND COUNTY HISTORICAL SOCIETY,** Suggett House Museum, 25 Homer Ave, Cortland, NY 13045. Tel 607-756-6071; Email cchs@clarityconnect.com; *Pres* Robert Ferris; *Treas* Christine Buck; *Dir* Mary Ann Kane; *Coll Mgr* Anita Wright
Open Tues - Sat 1 - 4 PM, mornings by appointment; Admis adults (16 & up) $2; Estab 1925 to collect, store & interpret the history of Cortland County through programs, exhibits & records in our 1882 Suggett House; Some art displayed in period settings, 1825-1900; Average Annual Attendance: 2,000; Mem: 800; dues vary; meetings several times during the year
Income: $75,000 (financed by endowment, mem, county appropriations, grants, sales & fundraisers)
Special Subjects: Folk Art, Furniture
Collections: Antique furniture, children's toys, china, folk art, glass, military memorabilia, paintings, textiles & clothing
Publications: 15 books on local history; bulletin, 1-3 times per yr; newsletter, 1-3 times per yr
Activities: Classes for adults & children; docent training; lects open to pub; individual paintings & original objects of art lent to other mus & college galleries; mus shop sells books

L **Kellogg Memorial Research Library**, 25 Homer Ave, Cortland, NY 13045. Tel 607-756-6071; *Dir* Mary Ann Kane
Open Tues - Sat 1 - 5 PM, mornings by appointment; Estab 1976 to collect, preserve & interpret information about the history of Cortland County; For reference only
Purchases: $500
Library Holdings: Book Volumes 5000, Cassettes, Clipping Files, Exhibition Catalogs, Lantern Slides, Manuscripts, Memorabilia, Original Art Works, Other Holdings Microfilm, Pamphlets, Photographs, Prints, Records, Reels, Reproductions, Sculpture, Slides, Video Tapes
Collections: Cortland County & regional genealogical records

L **CORTLAND FREE LIBRARY,** 32 Church St, Cortland, NY 13045-2798. Tel 607-753-1042; Fax 607-758-7329; Web: www.flls.org/cortlandlib; *Dir* Kay Zaharis
Open Mon-Thurs 9:30AM-8PM, Fri 9:30AM-5:30PM, Sat 9:30AM-4:30PM; No admis fee; Estab 1938; Circ 1122; Average Annual Attendance: 1,600
Income: financed by dept of assn library
Purchases: $2100
Library Holdings: Book Volumes 1700, Original Art Works, Periodical Subscriptions 14, Reels
Exhibitions: Occasional monthly exhibitions held

M **STATE UNIVERSITY OF NEW YORK COLLEGE AT CORTLAND,** Dowd Fine Arts Gallery, PO Box 2000, Cortland, NY 13045-0900. Tel 607-753-4216; Fax 607-753-5728; Email mounta@cortland.edu; Web: www.cortland.edu; *Dir* Allison Mount
Open Tues-Sat 10AM-4PM & also by appt; No admis fee; Estab 1967; Three separate spaces, total 2200 sq ft completely secure, full environmental control. Maintains a lending & reference library; wheelchair accessible; Average Annual Attendance: 15,000
Income: $25,000 (financed by state appropriation)
Purchases: $4500
Special Subjects: Ceramics, Collages, Drawings, Etchings & Engravings, Graphics, Historical Material, Landscapes, Latin American Art, Manuscripts, Painting-American, Photography, Portraits, Prints, Sculpture, Textiles, Woodcuts
Collections: Cortland College Permanent Collection
Publications: Exhibit catalogs, 2-3 per year
Activities: Docent training; lects open to pub, 10-12 vis lectrs per yr

L **STATE UNIVERSITY OF NEW YORK COLLEGE AT CORTLAND,** Visual Resources Collection, PO Box 2000, 87 Dowd Bldg Cortland, NY 13045-0900. Tel 607-753-5519; Email joycel@cortland.edu; *Visual Resources Cur* Lisa Joyce
Open Mon - Fri 8:30 AM - 5 PM & by appointment; No admis fee; Estab 1967 to provide visual resources to faculty, students & community
Income: Financed by state appropriation
Library Holdings: Book Volumes 1000, Exhibition Catalogs, Fiche, Filmstrips, Kodachrome Transparencies, Lantern Slides 5000, Periodical Subscriptions 10, Photographs 10,000, Slides 125,000, Video Tapes 100
Special Subjects: Art History

COXSACKIE

M **GREENE COUNTY HISTORICAL SOCIETY,** Bronck Museum, 90 County Rte 42, Coxsackie, NY 12051-3022; PO Box 44, Coxsackie, NY 12051-0044. Tel 518-731-6490; Web: www.gchistory.org; *Pres* Robert Hallock, PhD; *Librn* Steve Pec; *Mus Mgr* Shelby Mattice
Open Memorial Day-Labor Day Wed-Fri noon-4PM, Sat & Mon holidays 10AM-4PM, Sun 1-4PM; Admis adults $5, youth 12-15 $3, children 5-11 $2, children under 5 & members free; Estab 1929 to preserve the history of Greene County & promote the awareness of that history; 20 ft x 20 ft gallery located in the Bronck Mus Visitor Center; maintains also The Vedder Memorial Library, & Bronck Museum, A Historic House Museum; Average Annual Attendance: 1,700; Mem: 900; dues $10 & up; annual meeting in June
Income: $75,000 (financed by endowment, mem, admissions, shop sales)
Special Subjects: Carpets & Rugs, Costumes, Drawings, Folk Art, Furniture, Glass, Historical Material, Landscapes, Painting-American, Period Rooms, Portraits, Pottery, Textiles
Collections: American Art, Ceramics, Costumes, Furniture, Glass, 19th century Agricultural & Handcrafts, Silver, Textiles, Tools
Exhibitions: Local History
Publications: Greene County Historical Journal, quarterly
Activities: Lects open to pub, 3-5 vis lectrs per yr; concerts; tours; individual paintings lent to other mus & occasionally to university galleries; lending collection contains over 50 original prints & over 300 paintings; mus shop sells books, antiques, collectables, memorabilia & old postcards

DOUGLASTON

A **THE NATIONAL ART LEAGUE,** 44-21 Douglaston Pkwy, Douglaston, NY 11363. Tel 718-229-9495, 718-224-3957; Email info@nationalartleague.org; Web:

www.nationalartleague.org; *VPres* Nat Bukar; *Pres* Robert Stefani; *Correspondence Secy* Mary Anne Klein
Open Mon - Thurs & Sat 1:30PM-4PM; No admis fee; Estab 1930 to unite for common interest in the study & practice of art; Mem: 300; dues $25; monthly meetings 1st Fri every month 8 PM; Scholarships
Income: Financed by mem dues & contributions
Exhibitions: Six annual major shows, one national; gallery exhibitions
Publications: Brochures; bulletins; catalogs; Artworks newsletter, monthly
Activities: Art classes for adults & children; demonstrations; monthly lects & short courses; lects open to pub, 10 vis lectrs per yr; gallery talks; competitions with awards

EAST HAMPTON

L **EAST HAMPTON LIBRARY,** Long Island Collection, 159 Main St, East Hampton, NY 11937-2794. Tel 631-324-0222, Ext. 4; Fax 631-329-7184; Email lic@easthamptonlibrary.org; Web: www.easthamptonlibrary.org; *Dir* Dennis Fabiszak; *Dept Head* Gina Piastuck; *Librn & Archivist* Steve Boerner; *Librn* Suzanne Setter
Open Mon -Sat 1PM-4:30PM, cl Wed, mornings by appt; No admis fee; Estab 1930 by Morton Pennypacker; Average Annual Attendance: 400
Income: Financed by donations & fund raisers
Library Holdings: Auction Catalogs, Audio Tapes, Book Volumes, CD-ROMs, Cassettes, Clipping Files, Compact Disks, DVDs, Exhibition Catalogs, Manuscripts, Maps, Original Art Works, Original Documents, Pamphlets, Periodical Subscriptions, Photographs, Prints, Sculpture, Slides, Video Tapes
Special Subjects: American Western Art, Architecture, Drawings, Etchings & Engravings, Historical Material, Landscapes, Manuscripts, Maps, Painting-American, Portraits, Prints, Scrimshaw, Watercolors
Collections: The Long Island Collection contains material relating to the history & people of Long Island, Thomas Moran Biographical Art Collection contains original pen & ink & pencil sketches by Thomas Moran, lithographs, etchings & engravings by Moran & other members of the family, biographical material, exhibit catalogues, books & pamphlets, photographs & postcards
Exhibitions: The Gardiner Family; rotating
Activities: Lect open to public; tours; sales shop sells books, maps, posters

M **GUILD HALL OF EAST HAMPTON, INC,** Guild Hall Museum, 158 Main St, East Hampton, NY 11937-2795. Tel 631-324-0806; Fax 631-329-5043; 324-2722; Email museum@guildhall.org; Web: www.guildhall.org; *Chmn* Martin Cohen; *1st VChmn* Cheryl Minikes; *2nd VChmn* Michael Lynne; *Treas* Jim Peterson; *Mus Dir & Chief Cur* Christina Mossaides Strassfield; *Asst Cur & Registrar* Stephanie de Troy Miller; *Institutional Advancement Assoc* Genevieve Linnehan
Open Winter - Spring Fri-Sat 11 AM - 5 PM, Sun Noon - 5 PM, Summer open 7 days noon-5PM; Free Admission; Estab 1931 as a cultural center for the visual & performing arts with a State Board of Regents Educational Charter. Emphasis in art collection & exhibitions is chiefly on the many artists who live or have lived in the area; Mus has four galleries and sculpture garden; Average Annual Attendance: 80,000; Mem: 4000; dues $45-$2500; annual meeting in May
Income: $1,400,000 (financed by mem, federal, state, county & town appropriations, corporate, foundation, individual contributions, benefits, fund drives & mus shop)
Special Subjects: Painting-American, Photography, Prints, Sculpture
Collections: Focuses on American artists assoc with the region of Eastern Long Island, including James Brooks, Jimmy Ernst, Adolf Gottlieb, Childe Hassam, William de Kooning, Roy Lichtenstein, Thomas Moran, Jackson Pollock, Larry Rivers, as well as contemporary artists such as Eric Fischl, Donald Sultan & Lynda Benglis, paintings, works on paper, prints, photographs, sculpture
Publications: Newsletter, exhibition catalogues, annual report, monthly calendar
Activities: Classes for adults & children; dramatic programs; docent training; cooperative projects with area schools; lects open to pub, 25 vis lectrs per yr; concerts, gallery talks; tours, competitions; Academy of the Arts; original art objects lent to mus, libraries, schools, public building; lending collection contains cassettes, original art works & prints, paintings, photographs, sculpture, slides; book traveling exhibs; originate traveling exhibs to museums & galleries; mus sales shop sells mainly posters created for Guild Hall by artists of region; also gift items and local crafts, books, reproductions & prints

EAST ISLIP

M **ISLIP ART MUSEUM,** 50 Irish Ln, East Islip, NY 11730-2003. Tel 631-224-5402; Fax 631-224-5009; Email info@islipartmuseum.org; Web: www.islipartmuseum.org; *Exec Dir* Lynda A Moran; *Mus Exhibs Dir* Beth Gacummo; *Mus Adminr* Rosa Ramos; *Mus Cur Asst* Jason Schuck
Open Thurs - Fri 10 AM - 4 PM, Sat & Sun Noon - 4 PM; cl New Year's Day; Easter; Memorial Day; Independence Day; Labor Day; Thanksgiving; Christmas; Admis suggested donation $5; Estab 1973 for group showings of contemporary art from local & city based artists; 3000 sq ft of exhibition space divided among 4 rooms & a hallway on the Brookwood Hall estate; Average Annual Attendance: 12,000; Mem: 500; dues mem $25; patron $75; sponsor $125; benefactor $250; special benefactor $500; founder $1,000
Income: $150,000 (financed by mem, city & state appropriation, & National Endowment for the Arts)
Collections: Contemporary & avant-garde art
Exhibitions: Satellite Gallery & a Project Space
Publications: Exhibition brochures; Newsletter
Activities: Classes for adults & children; docent training; lects open to pub, 15 vis lectrs per yr; gallery talks; tours; arts festivals; competitions with awards; mus shop sells books, handmade gifts, jewelry, original art, postcards, posters, reproductions

EAST OTTO

A **ASHFORD HOLLOW FOUNDATION FOR VISUAL & PERFORMING ARTS,** Griffis Sculpture Park & Essex Arts Center, Griffis Sculpture Park, 6902 Mill Valley Rd East Otto, NY 14729-9735; The Essex Arts Center, 28 Essex St Buffalo, NY 14213. Tel 716-667-2808; Email griffispark@aol.com; Web: www.griffispark.org; *Exec Dir* Nila Griffis Lampman; *Griffis Sculpture Park Manager* Damian Gfiffis; *Essex Arts Center Mgr* Tyler Griffis
Open May 1 - Nov 31 8 AM - 8 PM; Admis $5 adults, students & seniors $3, children under 12 no admis fee; Estab 1966 to promote the visual & performing arts by sponsoring exhibitions & performances; Funds for the 400 acre sculpture park donated by Ruth Griffis in memory of her husband, L W Griffis Sr. The original park accommodates the work of Larry Griffis Jr. The expanded areas now include works of numerous other sculptors. Materials include welded steel, wood, aluminum & bronze, most of which has been cast at the Essex St Foundry. Sculpture park festival stage is an open-air platform for regional artist's performance of dance, music, poetry & drama; Average Annual Attendance: 30,000; Mem: 200
Income: $108,000 (financed by admis fees, donations, mem, grants, programs & pub funds
Exhibitions: Twelve distinctly different groups of work by Larry Griffis Jr are displayed
Publications: Brochure; postcards
Activities: Classes for adults & children; concerts; tours; book 4 traveling exhibitions per year; sales shop sells prints, original art, reproductions, metal sculptures; junior mus, Big Orbit, 30 Essex St, Buffalo, NY

ELMIRA

M **ARNOT ART MUSEUM,** 235 Lake St, Elmira, NY 14901-3118. Tel 607-734-3697, ext 120; Fax 607-734-5687; Email mmanly@arnotartmuseum.org; Web: www.arnotartmuseum.org; *Exec Dir* Rick Pirozzolo; *Cur Collections* Laura Wetmore; *Bus Mgr* Lynda Williams; *Cur Educ* Meghan O'Loughlin
Open Tues - Fri 10 AM - 5 PM, Sat 12 noon - 5 PM, cl Sun, Mon & national holidays; Admis Tues - Fri $7 adults, $4 seniors; Estab 1913 with the permanent collection of Matthias H Arnot consisting of 17th to 19th century European art & housed in his 1890's Picture Gallery the collection now includes 19th & 20th century American art & a growing collection of contemporary representational art; Average Annual Attendance: 18,000; Mem: 550; dues $75 & up
Library Holdings: Auction Catalogs, Audio Tapes, Book Volumes, CD-ROMs, Cassettes, Clipping Files, Compact Disks, DVDs, Exhibition Catalogs, Filmstrips, Kodachrome Transparencies, Lantern Slides, Manuscripts, Maps, Memorabilia, Original Documents, Other Holdings, Pamphlets, Periodical Subscriptions, Prints, Records
Special Subjects: American Indian Art, American Western Art, Antiquities-Egyptian, Antiquities-Etruscan, Antiquities-Greek, Antiquities-Oriental, Architecture, Asian Art, Baroque Art, Bronzes, Calligraphy, Ceramics, Collages, Decorative Arts, Drawings, Enamels, Eskimo Art, Etchings & Engravings, Etchings & Engravings, Furniture, Glass, Graphics, Historical Material, Judaica, Landscapes, Latin American Art, Maps, Marine Painting, Medieval Art, Metalwork, Military Art, Oriental Art, Painting-American, Painting-American, Painting-British, Painting-British, Painting-Canadian, Painting-Dutch, Painting-European, Painting-Flemish, Painting-French, Painting-German, Painting-Italian, Painting-Japanese, Painting-Scandinavian, Painting-Spanish, Period Rooms, Photography, Porcelain, Portraits, Pottery, Pre-Columbian Art, Prints, Religious Art, Renaissance Art, Restorations, Sculpture, Silver, Southwestern Art, Tapestries, Textiles, Woodcarvings, Woodcuts
Collections: Matthias H Arnot Collection, Contemporary Realism Collection, Hudson River School Collection
Exhibitions: Annual Regional Art Exhibition with prizes; Representing Representation 8; Art Now group show; Gallery Gala Invitational
Publications: Books; catalogs
Activities: Classes for adults & children, two wk summer adult painting school, docent training, outreach dramatic progs for community groups through educ center; lects & gallery talks open to pub; lects members only; 6 vis lectrs per yr; concerts; tours; gallery talks; competitions; individual paintings lent; one to two book traveling exhibs per yr; originate traveling exhibs to US mus; mus shop sells books, catalogues, original art & craft work, reproductions, slides, prints

M **ELMIRA COLLEGE,** George Waters Gallery, One Park Pl, Elmira, NY 14901. Tel 607-735-1800; Fax 607-735-1723; Web: www.elmira.edu; *Dir* Leslie Kramer
Open Tues - Sat 1 - 5 PM, cl Mon & Sun (varies); No admis fee; The Gallery is located in the Elmira Campus Center; Average Annual Attendance: 1,000
Income: Financed by school budget
Exhibitions: Annual Student Exhibition

FISHKILL

M **FISHKILL HISTORICAL SOCIETY,** Van Wyck Homestead Museum, 504 Route 9, Fishkill, NY 12524-0133; PO Box 133, Fishkill, NY 12524-0133. Tel 845-896-9560; Email vanwyckhomestead@aol.com; Web: www.pojonews.com; *Librn* Roy Jorgensen; *Pres* Steve Lynch; *1st VPres* Jack Hale
Open weekdays by appointment, Weekends 1 - 5 PM (May 30 - Oct 30); No admis fee; Estab 1962; Hudson Valley Portraits, AMMI Phillips Portraits; Average Annual Attendance: 2,000; Mem: 500; dues $10 - $500; meetings yr round
Library Holdings: Book Volumes 800, CD-ROMs, Cassettes 12, Clipping Files, Compact Disks, Maps, Original Documents, Other Holdings, Pamphlets, Photographs, Prints
Special Subjects: Archaeology, Architecture, Costumes, Decorative Arts, Dolls, Embroidery, Folk Art, Furniture, Historical Material, Laces, Miniatures, Painting-American, Porcelain, Portraits, Silver, Drawings, Jewelry, Photography, Textiles
Collections: Hudson Valley Portraits, decorative arts, quilts, Decorative Arts, Local Silver, Forms, Annie Phillips Paintings
Activities: Classes for children; docent training; lect open to public; 3 vis lectrs per year; tours; concerts; sales shop sells books, prints, reproductions

FLUSHING

A **BOWNE HOUSE HISTORICAL SOCIETY,** 37-01 Bowne St, Flushing, NY 11354. Tel 718-359-0528; Email office@bownehouse.org; Web: www.bownehouse.org; *Pres* Rosemary Vieter; *VPres* Barly Grodenchik; *Treas* George Farn III; *Dir* Yvonne Engglezos
Open Tues, Sat & Sun 2:30 - 4:30 PM; Admis adults $2, sr citizens, students & children $1; Estab 1945 for historic preservation, educ, collection of 17th, 18th & 19th century furnishing & decorative & fine art. Examples of colonial life; Average Annual Attendance: 5,000; Mem: 620; dues $250, $100, $50, $25, $10; annual meeting third Tues in May
Income: Financed by mem, private & pub contributions
Collections: Furnishings from the 17th, 18th & early 19th centuries, Furniture, pewter, fabrics, china, portraits, prints & documents
Exhibitions: Photo Documentation of ongoing Restoration
Publications: Booklets regarding John Bowne & the House; quarterly newsletter
Activities: Classes for adults & children; docent training; lects open to pub; mus shop sells books, reproductions, prints, slides, products of herb garden, plates & tiles

M **QUEENS COLLEGE, CITY UNIVERSITY OF NEW YORK,** Godwin-Ternbach Museum, 65-30 Kissena Blvd, 405 Klapper Hall Flushing, NY 11367-1575. Tel 718-997-4747; Fax 718-997-4734; Email amy-winter@qc.edu; Web: www.qc.cuny.edu/godwin_ternbach; *Dir & Cur* Amy Winter; *Research Asst* Brita Helgesen; *Colls Mgr* Allyson Mellone
Open Mon - Thurs 11 AM - 7 PM, Sat 11 AM - 5 PM; No admis fee; Estab 1957 for a study collection for Queens College students & in 1981 independently chartered; Collection located in one large exhibition gallery on Queens College Campus; Average Annual Attendance: 10,000; Mem: 60, dues $25
Income: Financed by state appropriation, Friends of the Mus, federal state & local grants
Special Subjects: African Art, American Indian Art, Antiquities-Byzantine, Antiquities-Egyptian, Antiquities-Etruscan, Antiquities-Greek, Antiquities-Oriental, Antiquities-Roman, Asian Art, Baroque Art, Bronzes, Carpets & Rugs, Cartoons, Ceramics, Coins & Medals, Decorative Arts, Drawings, Embroidery, Eskimo Art, Etchings & Engravings, Folk Art, Furniture, Glass, Graphics, Hispanic Art, Historical Material, Islamic Art, Ivory, Jade, Jewelry, Landscapes, Latin American Art, Leather, Manuscripts, Marine Painting, Medieval Art, Metalwork, Mexican Art, Mosaics, Oriental Art, Painting-American, Painting-British, Painting-Dutch, Painting-European, Painting-Flemish, Painting-German, Painting-Italian, Painting-Russian, Painting-Spanish, Photography, Porcelain, Portraits, Posters, Pottery, Pre-Columbian Art, Primitive art, Prints, Religious Art, Renaissance Art, Reproductions, Restorations, Sculpture, Stained Glass, Textiles, Watercolors, Woodcarvings, Woodcuts
Collections: Ancient & antique glass, Egyptian, Greek, Luristan antiquities, Old Master & WPA prints, Renaissance & later bronzes, 16th - 20th century paintings
Publications: Brochures, exhibition catalogs; newsletter; posters
Activities: Classes for adults & children; docent training; high school creative arts prog; lects open to pub, 20 lectrs per yr; gallery talks; tours; concerts; individual paintings & original objects of art lent to qualified art organizations & mus

M **Queens College Art Center,** 65-30 Kissena Blvd, Flushing, NY 11367. Tel 718-997-3770; Fax 718-997-3753; Email artcenter@qc.cuny.edu; Web: www.qcpages.qc.cuny.edu/art_library; *Cur* Alexandra de Luise; *Dir* Dr Suzanna Simor; *Admin Asst* Mollie Moskowitz; *Asst Cur* Tara Mathison
Open Mon - Thurs 9 AM - 9 PM, Fri Noon - 5 PM (when school is in session); No admis fee; Estab 1937; Gallery presents a variety of exhibitions of modern & contemporary art in diverse media; Average Annual Attendance: 30,000
Income: financed by donations, grants
Collections: modern contemporary art
Publications: exhibition catalogues
Activities: Lects open to pub, 5-10 vis lectrs per yr; gallery talks; tours

L **Art Library,** 65-30 Kissena Blvd, Flushing, NY 11367. Tel 718-997-3770; Fax 718-997-3753; Email artlibrary@qc.cuny.edu; Web: qcpages.qc.cuny.edu/art_library; *Head* Dr Suzanna Simor; *Admin Asst* Frances Chan; *Asst Librn* Paul Remeczki; *Admin Asst* Donna Schultz
Open Mon - Thurs 9 AM - 10 PM, Fri 9 AM - 5 PM, Sat-Sun 11AM-5PM, when school is in session, Mon - Fri 9 AM - 5 PM other times; No admis fee; Estab 1937 to support instruction; Circ 80,000
Library Holdings: Book Volumes 80,000, CD-ROMs, Clipping Files, Compact Disks, DVDs, Exhibition Catalogs 20,000, Fiche 2000, Lantern Slides, Micro Print, Original Art Works CA 100, Original Documents, Other Holdings Exhibition catalogs & pamphlets 50,000, Pamphlets, Periodical Subscriptions 200, Photographs, Reels, Reproductions 60,000, Slides 15,000
Collections: Books, periodicals, pictures, pamphlets, reference, special colls
Activities: Lending coll contains 80,000 books, 60,000 color reproductions, 50,000 exhib catalogs & pamphlets & 15,000 slides

A **QUEENS HISTORICAL SOCIETY,** Kingsland Homestead, 143-35 37th Ave Flushing, NY 11354-5729. Tel 718-939-0647; Fax 718-539-9885; Email info@queenshistoricalsociety.org; Web: www.queenshistoricalsociety.org; *Coll Mgr* Richard Hourahan; *Educ & Outreach Coordinator* Daniela Addamo; *Bd Pres* Patricia B Sherwood; *Executive Director* Branica Dukhic
Open Mon - Fri 9 AM - 4:30 PM (research appts) Museum: Tues, Sat - Sun 2:30 PM - 4:30 PM; Admis adults $5, seniors & students $3, QHS mems free, children under 12 yrs free; Estab 1968 as a historical society to collect Queens history materials; First floor for changing exhibits; second floor permanent Victorian parlor room; Maintains reference library/archives; Average Annual Attendance: 5,000; Mem: 600; dues bus $200-$750, family $45, individual $25, students & seniors $15; annual meeting varies
Income: $75,000 (financed by mem, city & state appropriation)
Library Holdings: Audio Tapes, Book Volumes, CD-ROMs, Cards, Cassettes, Clipping Files, Compact Disks, DVDs, Exhibition Catalogs, Filmstrips, Framed Reproductions, Lantern Slides, Manuscripts, Maps, Memorabilia, Motion Pictures, Original Art Works, Original Documents, Pamphlets, Periodical Subscriptions, Photographs, Prints, Reels, Sculpture, Slides, Video Tapes
Special Subjects: Archaeology, Carpets & Rugs, Ceramics, Coins & Medals, Costumes, Decorative Arts, Dolls, Drawings, Embroidery, Etchings & Engravings, Flasks & Bottles, Folk Art, Furniture, Historical Material, Jewelry, Manuscripts, Maps, Painting-American, Period Rooms, Photography, Porcelain, Portraits, Sculpture, Textiles, Architecture
Collections: photographs, postcards, maps & atlases, personal papers of Margaret Carman, King and Murray families, Doughty, textiles, furniture, decorative arts, ephemera
Exhibitions: Kingsland: From Homestead to House Museum; The Kingsland Victorian Room (permanent exhibit); Aunt Mary's Landing (permanent exhibit)
Publications: Quarterly newsletter; Angels of Deliverance, The Underground Railroad in Queens, Long Island, and Beyond; So this is Flushing, Flushing Freedom Mile; Friends of Freedom: The Underground Railroad in Queens and on Long Island
Activities: Educ prog; classes for adults & children; docent training; lects open to pub; 200 vis lectrs per yr; concerts; gallery talks; tours; sponsoring for competitions; 3rd-5th grade art & history contest/Queensmark prog; 1-2 traveling exhibs per yr; originate traveling exhibs; mus shop sells books, postcards & prints

M **THE QUEENS MUSEUM OF ART,** Flushing Meadows Corona Park, New York City Bldg Flushing, NY 11368-3398. Tel 718-592-9700; Fax 718-592-5778; Email info@queensmuseum.org; Web: www.queensmuseum.org; *Dir Educ* Jason Yoon; *Dir External Affairs* David Strauss; *Dir Fin* Julie Lou; *Dir Devel* Jodi Hanel; *Dir Strategic Partnerships* Debra Wimpfheimer
Open Wed - Sun Noon - 6 PM, cl New Year's Day, Thanksgiving, Christmas Day; Admis by suggested donation, adults $8, seniors & children $5, children under 5 & members free; Estab 1972 to provide a vital cultural center for the more than 2.5 million residents of Queens County; it provides changing, high-quality, fine art exhibitions & a wide-range of educational & public programs; Reopened in 2013 with 105,000 sq ft of exhibit, pub event & studios incl The Panorama of New York City, a 9,335 sq ft architectural scale model of New York City; Average Annual Attendance: 200,000; Mem: 1000; dues family $75, individual $50, seniors & students $35
Income: $5,000,000 (financed by city & state appropriation, corporate & foundation grants, earned income & individual support)
Collections: The Panorama of New York City (world's largest architectural scale model), Small collection of paintings, photographs & prints, Collection of materials from 1939 - 1940 & 1964 - 1965 New York World's Fairs
Exhibitions: Tiffany Glass from the Neustadt Museum of Tiffany Art (permanent display); A Watershed Moment: Celebrating the Homecoming of the Relief Map of the NYC Water Supply System; 1939 & 1964 New York World's Fair Open Storage
Publications: Catalogs; quarterly newsletter
Activities: Guided tours for adults & children; docent training; projects involving elementary school children; films; drop-in arts & crafts workshops on Sun during school year & certain weekdays in summer; lects open to pub, 10 vis lectrs per yr; concerts; gallery talks; tours; competitions; satellite gallery at Bulova Corporate Center in Jackson Heights, NY; mus shop sells books, reproductions, prints, exhibition catalogs, children's items & 1939-40 & 1964-65 World's Fair memorabilia

L **QUEENSBOROUGH COMMUNITY COLLEGE LIBRARY,** Kurt R Schmeller Library, 22205 56th Ave, Flushing, NY 11364-1432. Tel 718-631-6396; Fax 718-631-6620; Web: www.web.acc.qcc.cuny.edu/library; *Coordr Technical Svcs* Prof Sheila Beck; *Chief Librn* Prof Jeanne Galvin
Open Mon - Thurs 8:30 AM - 9 PM, Fri 8:30 AM - 5 PM, Sat 10 AM - 4 PM; No admis fee; Estab 1961 to serve the students and faculty of the col
Income: Financed by city and state appropriation, state and local grants, through the University, Friends of Library and pvt donations
Purchases: $80,000
Collections: Book & periodical coll includes material on painting, sculpture & architecture, print coll, reproductions of famous paintings, reproductions of artifacts & sculpture, vertical file coll
Publications: Library Letter, biannual

FREDONIA

M **STATE UNIVERSITY OF NEW YORK COLLEGE AT FREDONIA,** Cathy and Jesse Marion Art Gallery, 280 Central Ave, Fredonia, NY 14063-1127. Tel 716-673-4897; Fax 716-673-4990; Email tina.hastings@fredonia.edu; Web: www.fredonia.edu; *Dir* Tina Hastings
Open Tues - Thurs & Sun 2 - 6 PM, Fri - Sat 2 - 8 PM; No admis fee; Estab 1963 and relocated in 1969 to new quarters designed by I M Pei and Partners; The gallery serves as a focal point of the campus, uniting the college with the community; Average Annual Attendance: 5,000
Income: Financed by state appropriation and student groups, private endowments
Special Subjects: Architecture, Prints, Sculpture
Collections: Primarily 20th-century American art and architectural archival material, with an emphasis on prints and sculpture
Exhibitions: Graduating Seniors I; Graduating Seniors II; Graduating Seniors III; curated & traveling shows
Activities: Lects open to pub; 2-3 vis lectrs per yr; gallery talks; individual paintings and original objects of art lent to offices and public lobbies on campus

FULTONVILLE

M **THE NATIONAL SHRINE OF THE NORTH AMERICAN MARTYRS,** 136 Shrine Rd, Fultonville, NY 12072. Tel 518-853-3033; Fax 518-853-3051; Email office@martyshrine.org; Web: www.martyrshrine.org; *Dir* Fr Peter J Murray S.J.; *Dir Opers* Thomas F Ralph; *Dir Mktg* Fran Ralph; *Graphics Design & Editor* Dorothy Domkowski; *Martyrs Mus Mgr* Beth Lynch; *Kateria Media Center Mgr* Lily Fiorenza; *Information Systems* Joanne Freeman; *Music Dir* Jenna Poling
Open late Apr-Oct Sun & Weekdays 10AM-5PM, Sat 10AM-5:30PM; No admis fee; Estab 1885 as a religious & historic shrine; Average Annual Attendance: 60,000
Income: Financed by donations

Special Subjects: American Indian Art, Decorative Arts, Folk Art, Historical Material, Manuscripts, Maps, Painting-American, Posters, Religious Art, Tapestries, Textiles, Woodcarvings
Publications: The Pilgrim, quarterly

GARDEN CITY

M **NASSAU COMMUNITY COLLEGE,** Firehouse Art Gallery, 1 Education Dr Garden City, NY 11530. Tel 516-572-7165; Fax 516-572-7302; Email lynn.rozzi@ncc.edu; Web: www.art.sunynassau.edu irehouse; *Dir & Cur* Lynn Rozzi Casey; *Cur* Meg Oliveri
Estab 1964 to exhibit fine art & varied media; Two exhibition spaces, carpeted with track lighting
Income: Financed by state, college & county appropriation
Special Subjects: Prints, Sculpture
Collections: Painting, sculpture, prints, photography
Exhibitions: Invitational exhibits, national or regional competition; faculty & student exhibits per year
Activities: Lect open to public; competitions with awards

GARNERVILLE

M **GARNER ARTS CENTER,** Garnerville Arts & Industrial Ctr, 55 W Railroad Ave Garnerville, NY 10923. Tel 845-947-7108; Email info@garnerartscenter.org; Web: garnerartscenter.org; *Exec Dir* James Tyler; *Prog Dir* Christine Olivier
Call for hours; Estab to promote contemporary art & educate diverse audiences; Repurposed textile mill
Collections: works by estab & emerging artists; paintings; sculpture; photographs; ceramics.
Exhibitions: Temporary exhibits
Activities: Educ prog; classes for adults & children

GARRISON

L **ALICE CURTIS DESMOND & HAMILTON FISH LIBRARY,** Hudson River Reference Collection, Routes 9D & 403, Garrison, NY 10524; PO Box 265, Garrison, NY 10524-0265. Tel 845-424-3020; Fax 845-424-4061; Email desmondfishdirector@gmail.com; Web: desmondfishlibrary.org; *Library Dir* Jen McCreery
Open Mon, Wed, Fri 10 AM - 5 PM, Tues & Thurs 2 - 9 PM, Sat 10 AM - 4 PM, Sun 1 - 5 PM; No admis fee; Estab 1980; Circ 83,000; Average Annual Attendance: 70,000
Library Holdings: Audio Tapes, Book Volumes 30,000, Compact Disks, DVDs, Kodachrome Transparencies 1,000, Periodical Subscriptions 100
Special Subjects: Art Education, Art History, Landscape Architecture, Landscapes, Painting-American
Collections: Slide Archive: Hudson River views in 19th century painting
Exhibitions: Shows annually: Contemporary artists as well as Hudson River School Works
Activities: Lects open to pub; 4 vis lectrs per yr

M **GARRISON ART CENTER,** 23 Garrison's Landing, Garrison, NY 10524; PO Box 4, Garrison, NY 10524-0004. Tel 845-424-3960; Web: www.garrisonartcenter.org; *Pres* Jaynie Crimmins; *VPres* Bill Burback; *Exec Dir* Elizabeth Turnock
Open daily 12 - 5 PM
Collections: works by local artists

GENESEO

M **BERTHA V B LEDERER FINE ARTS GALLERY-SUNY GENESEO,** Bertha V B Lederer Fine Arts Gallery, 1 College Circle, Brodie Hall 232, Geneseo, NY 14454-1401. Tel 585-245-5814; Fax 585-245-5815; Email hawkins@geneseo.edu; Web: www.llbgalleries.geneseo.edu; *Dir Galleries* Cynthia Hawkins; *Secy* Lori Morsch
Open Tues - Thurs 12:30 PM - 3:30 PM, Fri - Sat 1 - 5 PM; No admis fee; Estab 1966 (Fine Arts Bldg); 2,000 sq feet; 2 movable walls; Average Annual Attendance: 1,000
Income: State financed
Special Subjects: Afro-American Art, American Indian Art, Calligraphy, Collages, Drawings, Etchings & Engravings, Furniture, Graphics, Painting-American, Painting-French, Portraits, Pottery, Prints, Stained Glass, Watercolors, Woodcuts, Landscapes, Silver
Collections: Paintings; sculpture; photographs; prints; drawings; furniture
Activities: Lects open to the pub; concerts; gallery talks

M **LIVINGSTON COUNTY HISTORICAL SOCIETY,** Museum, 30 Center St, Geneseo, NY 14454-1204. Tel 716-243-9147; Email lchistory@frontier.com; Web: www.livingstoncountyhistoricalsociety.com; *Mus Admin* Anna Kowalchuk; *Pres* Bill Brummett; *VPres* Liz Porter; *Treas* Jon Perkins; *Research Secy* Sandy Brennan; *Research Sec* Jeanne Galbraith
Open May - Oct Sun & Thurs 2 - 5 PM; No admis fee; Estab 1876 to procure, protect & preserve Livingston County history; Average Annual Attendance: 1,500; Mem: 380; dues $10; meetings first Sun in Nov & May plus monthly programs
Income: Financed by mems, grants, donations
Library Holdings: Book Volumes, Clipping Files, Filmstrips, Framed Reproductions, Manuscripts, Original Documents, Photographs, Records, Video Tapes
Special Subjects: Archaeology, Architecture, Ceramics, Crafts, Dolls, Embroidery, Folk Art, Furniture, Furniture, Glass, Glass, Historical Material, Painting-American, Pewter, Portraits, Posters, Pottery, Silver, Textiles, Landscapes, Painting-American
Collections: China & Silver, Indian Artifacts, primitive tools, Shaker items, toy coll, war items, paintings of local landmarks & personalities, 10-15 paintings of Genesee Valley subjects, Wadsworth coach
Exhibitions: Cobblestone Schoolhouse
Publications: Newsletter, quarterly
Activities: Educ prog for adults & children; work with col students at SUNY Geneseo; docent training; lects open to pub, 6 vis lectrs per yr; concert; sales shop sells books, maps, notepaper, coverlets, big tree pieces, historical society pins & magnets

M **STATE UNIVERSITY OF NEW YORK AT GENESEO,** Bertha V B Lederer Gallery, 1 College Cir, Brodie Hall Geneseo, NY 14454-1492. Tel 585-245-5814; Fax 585-245-5815; Email hawkins@geneseo.edu; Web: www.geneseo.edu/galleries; *Dir of Galleries* Cynthia Hawkins; *Interim Provost* Dave Gordon; *Sec* Lori Morsch
Open Wed-Thurs 1PM - 4PM; Fri & Sat 1 PM - 5 PM; No admis fee; Estab 1967; the gallery serves the col and community; 2,000 sq ft environmentally controlled, lighting system; Average Annual Attendance: 6,000
Income: Financed by state appropriation
Special Subjects: Afro-American Art, American Indian Art, Calligraphy, Carpets & Rugs, Ceramics, Collages, Drawings, Etchings & Engravings, Glass, Graphics, Landscapes, Latin American Art, Painting-American, Pottery, Reproductions, Sculpture, Watercolors, Woodcuts, Silver
Collections: Ceramics, furniture, graphics, paintings, sculpture
Exhibitions: Changing exhibitions; permanent colls
Publications: Catalogs; Photography as Witness
Activities: Lect open to public; lending collection

M **Lockhart Gallery**, 26 Main St, McClellan House Geneseo, NY 14454-1214; Suny Geneseo, 1 College Circle, Brodie Hall 232 Geneseo, NY 14454-1401. Tel 585-245-5813; Fax 585-245-5815; Email hawkins@geneseo.edu; Web: www.llbgalleriesgeneseo.edu; *Dir Galleries* Cynthia Hawkins; *Sec* Lori Morsch
Open Tues-Thurs 12:30PM-3:30PM, Fri & Sat 1PM - 5PM; Estab 2001; 750 sq ft gallery with environmentally controlled lighting; Average Annual Attendance: 1,000
Income: Private & public funding
Special Subjects: Afro-American Art, American Indian Art, American Western Art, Drawings, Etchings & Engravings, Landscapes, Painting-American, Painting-French, Prints, Watercolors, Woodcuts
Collections: Permanent coll & prints (primary)
Activities: Lects open to pub; concerts; gallery talks

GHENT

M **THE FIELDS SCULPTURE PARK AT OMI INTERNATIONAL ARTS CENTER,** 1405 Cty Rte 22, Ghent, NY 12075-3809. Tel 518-392-4747; Fax 518-392-4748; Email bmaynes@artomi.org; Web: www.artomi.org; *Dir* Bill Maynes; *Cur* Nicole Hayes
Open daily dawn to dusk; No admis fee
Collections: paintings; photographs; contemporary sculpture
Activities: Classes for children; lects open to the pub; 5 vis lects per yr; concerts; gallery talks

GLENS FALLS

M **THE HYDE COLLECTION,** 161 Warren St, Glens Falls, NY 12801-4562. Tel 518-792-1761; Fax 518-792-9197; Email adminassist@hydecollection.org; Web: www.hydecollection.org; *Interim Dir* Anne Saile; *Director of Cur Affairs & Programming* Jonathan Canning
Open Tues - Sat 10 AM - 5 PM, Sun Noon - 5 PM; Admis gen admis $12, Seniors (60+) $10, children 12 & under, US military & family, students w/ID, veterans, companions or aides of persons with disabilities & 2nd Sun of month free; Every Wed Seniors are free; Estab 1952 to promote & cultivate the study & improvement of the fine arts; Historic house and modern wing with 4 temporary gallery spaces; Average Annual Attendance: 25,000; Mem: 1,522; dues $60 - $5,000
Income: Financed by endowment, mem, contributions, municipal support & grants
Special Subjects: Furniture, Painting-European, Painting-Italian, Prints, Sculpture, Tapestries, Architecture, Asian Art, Baroque Art, Bronzes, Carpets & Rugs, Decorative Arts, Drawings, Embroidery, Etchings & Engravings, Landscapes, Medieval Art, Painting-American, Painting-British, Painting-Dutch, Painting-Flemish, Painting-French, Painting-German, Period Rooms, Photography, Prints, Religious Art, Renaissance Art, Textiles, Watercolors, Woodcarvings, Woodcuts
Collections: Works by Botticelli, da Vinci, Degas, Eakins, El Greco, Hassam, Homer, Matisse, Picasso, Raphael, Rembrandt, Renoir, Rubens, Ryder, Tintoretto & others, furniture, sculpture, tapestries
Exhibitions: Nine temporary exhibitions throughout the year;
Publications: Exhibit catalogs
Activities: Classes for adults & children; docent training; lects open to pub; concerts; gallery talks upon request; tours; scholarships offered; original objects of art lent to accredited museums; originate traveling exhibs; mus shop sells books, magazines, original art & reproductions

L **Library**, 161 Warren St, Glens Falls, NY 12801. Tel 518-792-1761; Fax 518-792-9197; Web: www.hydeart.museum.org
Open Tues - Fri 10 AM - 5 PM; For reference only
Income: Financed by the Hyde Collection Trust
Library Holdings: Book Volumes 1000, Clipping Files, Exhibition Catalogs, Filmstrips, Memorabilia, Other Holdings Original documents 3000, Periodical Subscriptions 8, Photographs
Collections: Hyde Family Archives

GOSHEN

M **HARNESS RACING MUSEUM & HALL OF FAME,** 240 Main St, Goshen, NY 10924-2157. Tel 845-294-6330; Fax 845-294-3463; Email

Library@harnessmuseum.com; Web: www.harnessmuseum.com; *Dir* Janet T Terhune
Open 7 days a week, 10 AM - 6 PM, holidays 10 AM - 6 PM, cl Christmas & New Years; No admis fee; Estab 1951 to preserve the artifacts of harness racing; There are two galleries, three theaters and a 3-D harness racing simulation; Average Annual Attendance: 20,000; Mem: Dues benefactor $5000, fellow $1000 - $4999, corporate $1000+, family $100 - $999, associate $50, friend $35
Income: Financed by endowment & mem
Library Holdings: Auction Catalogs, Audio Tapes, Book Volumes, CD-ROMs, Cassettes, Clipping Files, DVDs, Fiche, Filmstrips, Manuscripts, Maps, Memorabilia, Motion Pictures, Original Art Works, Original Documents, Pamphlets, Periodical Subscriptions, Photographs, Prints, Reels, Reproductions, Sculpture, Video Tapes
Special Subjects: Painting-American, Portraits, Prints, Sculpture, Textiles
Collections: Historic Coll incl: 1,500+ works of fine art, 5,000 pieces of ephemera, 13,000 photographs, 400 jackets, caps & helmets, 90 sulkies & harnesses
Publications: Catalogs
Activities: Classes for adults & children; workshops; lects open to public; tours; gallery talks; awards, Ross Merrill 2012; mus store sells books, original art, reproductions, prints, related items & catalogs

HAMILTON

M **COLGATE UNIVERSITY,** Picker Art Gallery, Charles A Dana Arts Ctr, Hamilton, NY 13346-1398; 13 Oak Drive, Hamilton, NY 13346. Tel 315-228-7634; Fax 315-228-7932; Email pickerart@colgate.edu; Web: www.pickerartgallery.org; *Dir* Anja Chavez; *Registrar* Sarisha Guarneiri; *Educ* Melissa Davies; *Sr Cur Colls* Jill Shaw; *Curatorial Asst* Sarah Horowitz; *Preparator* Aaron Jakos; *Admin Asst* Jasmine Kellogg; *Information Serv Technologist* Michelle Van Auken
Open Tues - Fri 10 AM - 5 PM, Sat - Sun noon - 5 PM, third Thurs every month 10 Am - 8 PM; No admis fee; Estab 1966, as an educative adjunct to study in the fine arts & liberal arts curriculum; Building designed by architect Paul Rudolph; Average Annual Attendance: 5,000
Income: Financed by the University & Friends of the Picker Art Gallery
Library Holdings: Exhibition Catalogs, Pamphlets, Photographs, Sculpture, Slides, Video Tapes
Special Subjects: Afro-American Art, American Indian Art, Asian Art, Bronzes, Cartoons, Ceramics, Drawings, Etchings & Engravings, Landscapes, Manuscripts, Medieval Art, Painting-American, Painting-British, Painting-European, Painting-French, Painting-Italian, Painting-Scandinavian, Photography, Portraits, Pre-Columbian Art, Primitive art, Prints, Religious Art, Renaissance Art, Sculpture, Watercolors, Woodcuts, Posters
Collections: Herman Collection of Modern Chinese Woodcuts, Gary M Hoffer '74 Memorial Photography Collection, Luis de Hoyos Collection of pre-Columbian Art, Luther W. Brady: 20th-Century Painting & Sculpture, Harry Neigher Collection of Political Cartoons, 1928-1975, photographs by Yergeny Khaldei, Herbert A Mayer: Collection of Artwork
Publications: Exhib catalogs
Activities: Classes for adults & children; high school teaching seminars; docent training; lects open to pub; tours; gallery talks; individual paintings & original objects of art lent; book traveling exhibs; originate traveling exhibs

A **THE EXHIBITION ALLIANCE,** (Gallery Association of New York State), PO Box 345, Hamilton, NY 13346-0345. Tel 315-824-2510; Fax 315-824-1683; Email mail@exhibitionalliance.org; Web: www.exhibitionalliance.org; *Exec Dir* Donna Anderson; *Design Dir* Ted Anderson; *Exhibs Asst* Jessie Schmitt
Estab 1972 to facilitate cooperation among exhibiting institution in state/region; Mem: 200; mem open to exhibiting organization; dues $100-$500

HEMPSTEAD

M **HOFSTRA UNIVERSITY,** Hofstra University Museum, 112 Hofstra University, Hempstead, NY 11549-1120. Tel 516-463-5672; Fax 516-463-4743; Email beth.e.levinthal@hofstra.edu; Web: www.hofstra.edu/museum; *Assoc Dir Exhibs & Coll* Karen Albert; *Exec Dir* Beth E Levinthal; *Communications Director* Charmise Woodside-Desire; *Mus Educ Dir* Nancy Richner; *Colls Mgr* Kristy L Caratzola; *School and Youth Programs* Renee Kurot
Open Tues - Fri, 10 AM - 4 PM, Sat & Sun noon - 4 PM; No admis fee; Estab 1963; a university mus that serves the needs of its student body & the New York Metropolitan region; Mus includes exhibition facilities; Average Annual Attendance: 25,000; Mem: 100; dues $35
Income: Financed by university, mem & grants
Library Holdings: Exhibition Catalogs
Special Subjects: African Art, Antiquities-Oriental, Antiquities-Persian, Asian Art, Bronzes, Ceramics, Collages, Drawings, Etchings & Engravings, Graphics, Hispanic Art, Islamic Art, Landscapes, Oriental Art, Painting-American, Painting-European, Painting-French, Painting-German, Painting-Japanese, Painting-Russian, Photography, Posters, Pre-Columbian Art, Prints, Sculpture, Woodcarvings, Woodcuts, Watercolors, Mexican Art, Painting-Flemish, Portraits
Collections: American paintings & prints, African, Pre-Columbian, Melanesian, 19th & 20th century European painting, contemporary prints, painting & photographs, outdoor sculpture, Asian art
Exhibitions: Mother & Child: the Art of Henry Moore; Shapes of the Mind: African Art from L I Collections; People at Work: 17th Century Dutch Art; Seymour Lipton; 1979 - 1989: American, Italian, Mexican Art for the Collection of Francesco Pellizzi; The Coming of Age of America: The First Decades of the Sculptors Guild; The Transparent Thread: Asian Philosophy in Recent American Art.; Street Scenes: 1930's - '50's; Leonard Bramer's Drawing of the 17th Century Dutch Life; T.V. Sculpture; R.B. Kitaj (Art and Literature); Indian Miniatures; Maelstrom; Preserving Our Heritage: The Realm of the Coin; Money in Contemporary Art; Appeasing the Spirits: Sui and Early Tang Tomb Sculpture from the Schloss Collection; The Butcher, The Baker, The Candlestick Maker; Jan Luyken's Mirrors of 17th Century Dutch Daily Life; Poster: The Art of 10 Masters; Rodin's Gates to Hell; Breaking the Wall of Bias: Art from Survivors; Paul Jenkins: The Early Years in Paris & New York; Moby Dick Art; Euclid to E-Books: Ideal Books Moving Ideas; Voiceless in the Presence of Realities: 9/11/01 Remembrances from the Long Island Studies Institute; Baile y Musica; Am Perspectives: 1907 to 1992; Lawrence Parks Bearden: Artists of Influence; African American Highlights from the Reader's Digest Assn Collection; Twardowicz-Dudson: Artists in Parallel; Photographing Suburbia: Crewdson, Owen, and Weiner; The Greatest of All Time Muhammad Ali; Sacred to the Memory: The Photography of Robert Reinhardt; Ancient Echoes in Contemporary Printmaking; Tranquil Power: The Art of Perle Fine; Out of Africa: Works from the Hofstra University Museum Collection; Burton Morns: Pop!; Indian Art After Independence: Selected works from the colls of Virginia & Ravi Akhoury & Shelley & Donald Rubin; Andy Warhol; The Photographic Legacy Program; Children's Pleasures; American Celebrations of Childhood; Settling into Nature: Photography of Mikael Levin; America's Irreplaceable Dance Treasures: the First 100; Something's Afoot: Small works from the Hofstra Univ Mus Coll; The Humanist Spirit: Burton Silverman; Barbara Roux: Environments; Yonia Fain: Remembrance; The Disappearing Landscape; Opportunity & Impact: Works by Emigre Artists; We Hold These Truths; David Jacobs; Sight & Sound; Don Resnlk: Essence of Nature; Land of the Rising Sun: Art of Japan; Spirit & Identity: Melanesian Art; Past Traditions/New Voices in Asian Art; Exploring the Centuries: 3rd-20th Century Asian Art; From Portraits to Tweets: Imagery, Technology & the US Presidency; Enduring Images; Portfolios I: The 1970s; Doug Hilson: Urbanscapes; Africa: Subsaharan Diversity; In Print; Over the River: Transform Long Island; Political Slant II: Editorial Cartoons
Publications: Exhibition catalogs; catalogs available for all of the above listings
Activities: Classes for children; school program K-12; poetry workshops; lects open to public, 6 vis lectrs per yr; concerts; gallery talks; tours for school groups & community organizations; exhibitions related to scholarly conferences; lending of original objects of art

HEWLETT

L **HEWLETT-WOODMERE PUBLIC LIBRARY,** 1125 Broadway, Hewlett, NY 11557-2336. Tel 516-374-1967; Fax 516-569-1229; Web: www.hwpl.org; *Art Librn* Diana Qureshi; *Dir* William Ferro
Open Mon - Thurs 9 AM - 9 PM, Fri 9 AM - 6 PM, Sat 9 AM - 5 PM, Sun 12:30 - 5 PM (except summer); No admis fee; Estab 1947 as a library for art & music; Gallery maintained
Income: Financed by state appropriation & school district
Library Holdings: Auction Catalogs, Book Volumes 200,000, CD-ROMs, Compact Disks, DVDs, Exhibition Catalogs, Motion Pictures, Pamphlets, Periodical Subscriptions 520, Photographs, Slides
Special Subjects: Architecture, Crafts, Film, Photography
Collections: Art Slides/Vintage Posters
Exhibitions: Hold local exhibits
Publications: Index to Art Reproductions in Books (Scarecrow Press)
Activities: Classes for adults & children; dramatic progs; lects open to pub; 10 vis lectrs per yr; concerts; gallery talks; tours

HOWES CAVE

M **IROQUOIS INDIAN MUSEUM,** 324 Caverns Rd, Howes Cave, NY 12092; PO Box 7, Howes Cave, NY 12092-0007. Tel 518-296-8949; Fax 518-296-8955; Email info@iroquoismuseum.org; Web: www.iroquoismuseum.org; *CEO & Dir* Stephanie Shultes; *Chmn & Pres* Christina Hanks
Open May - Oct Tues - Sat 10 AM - 5 PM, Sun noon - 5 PM; April & Nov Thurs - Sat 10 AM - 4 PM, Sun noon - 4 PM; cl Easter, Thanksgiving & Dec - March; Admis adults $8, sr citizens & students 13 -17 $6.50, children 5 -12 $5; Estab 1980 to teach about Iroquois culture today & in the past; Exhibits follow a time line from the earliest times to present day. Trace the development of native culture from the time of Paleo-Indians (8000 BC) through the 1700s to contemporary art & cultural expression; Average Annual Attendance: 10,000; Mem: 400; dues basic $25; family $35; friend $50; donor $100; sponsor $250; patron $500; benefactor $1,000
Income: $300,000 (financed by mem, admis, sales shop, fundraising & grants)
Library Holdings: Book Volumes, Clipping Files, DVDs, Original Art Works, Photographs, Prints, Sculpture, Video Tapes
Special Subjects: American Indian Art, Anthropology, Archaeology, Ceramics, Crafts, Dolls, Drawings, Ethnology, Folk Art, Furniture, Historical Material, Jewelry, Leather, Photography, Posters, Pottery, Sculpture, Silver, Textiles, Woodcarvings
Collections: Contemporary art & craft work of the Iroquois, prehistoric materials of the Iroquois & their immediate antecedents relating to Schoharie County, color slides; black & white prints; photographic collection of Iroquois arts
Exhibitions: Buckskin to Bikinis: Iroquois Wearable Art (2015)
Publications: Exhibition catalogs; Museum Notes, quarterly
Activities: Family & adult progs; artist demos; social dance demo; story telling; school progs; concerts; gallery talks; tours; internships; mus shop sells books, prints, slides, reproductions & original art; Iroquois Indian Children's Museum, early technology day, Iroquois Arts Festival

HUDSON

M **OLANA STATE HISTORIC SITE,** 5720 State Route 9-G, Hudson, NY 12534. Tel 518-828-0135; Fax 518-828-6742; Email linda.mclean@oprhp.state; Web: www.olana.org; *Historic Site Mgr* Linda McLean; *Head Educ* Carri Manchester; *Chief Cur* Evelyn Trebilcock; *Assoc Cur* Valerie Balint; *Archivist & Librn* Ida Brier; *Mus Shop Mgr* Rachel Patton; *Pres The Olana* Sara Griffen
Call for hours; main fl studio & 2nd fl open Thurs - Sun; Admis adults $9, sr citizens $8, children 12 & under free; main fl studio admis adults $12, sr citizens 10, children 12 & under free; Opened as historic house museum 1966 to promote interest in & disseminate information of life, works & times of Frederic Edwin Church, landscape painter of the Hudson River School; The building is a Persian-style artists residence & studio overlooking the Hudson River; Average Annual Attendance: House 27,000; Grounds 200,000; Mem: 700; dues $25 - $5000; annual meeting June

Income: Financed by NY State appropriation & The Olana Partnership
Special Subjects: Architecture, Ceramics, Decorative Arts, Drawings, Furniture, Metalwork, Oriental Art, Painting-American, Painting-European, Pottery, Prints, Sculpture, Silver, Textiles, Woodcarvings, Photography
Collections: Frederic Edwin Church Collection: oil sketches, drawings, paintings
Exhibitions: Rotating exhibs Maurice & Evelyn Sharp Gallery
Publications: The Crayon, quarterly (journal produced by the Olana Partnership); Catalogs: Glories of the Hudson, Fern Hunting with the artist FEC in Jamaica, Treasures of Olana
Activities: Classes for adults & children; docent training; lects open to pub, 3-4 vis lectrs per yr; concerts; gallery talks; tours; slide programs; summer arts camp; exten dept with outreach programs, individual paintings & original objects of art lent to other museums & galleries; mus shop sells books & reproductions

L **Library**, 5720 State Route 9-G, Hudson, NY 12534. Tel 518-828-0135; Fax 518-828-6742; Web: www.olana.org; *Historic Site Mgr* Kimberly Flook; *Cur* Evelyn Trebilcock; *Pres Olana Partnership* Sara Griffen; *Librn & Archivist* Ida Brier; *Cur* Valerie Balint
Open Apr - Oct 10 AM - 5 PM, Nov - Mar Fri - Sun 11 AM - 3 PM, Dec holiday prog; Admis adults $9, seniors & students $8, children 12 & under free; $5 vehicle fee Apr -Oct weekends; Estab in 1968 as historic house museum; Historic House open to the pub; Average Annual Attendance: 24,611; Mem: 400
Library Holdings: Book Volumes, Clipping Files, Exhibition Catalogs 10, Manuscripts, Memorabilia 200, Original Art Works, Original Documents, Photographs, Prints
Special Subjects: Antiquities-Greek, Antiquities-Persian, Furniture, Landscapes, Mexican Art, Painting-American, Period Rooms, Pre-Columbian Art, Sculpture, Textiles, Woodcarvings, Decorative Arts, Painting-European
Collections: Family papers, photographs, books, correspondence diaries, receipts, Decorative arts, coll of Frederic Edwin Church paintings, American & European Art on Canvas, furnishings
Exhibitions: Ann summer exhibs
Publications: Crayon, twice a year; exhib catalogs
Activities: Classes for adults & children; docent training; lects open to pub; historic house & landscape tours; organize traveling exhibs to mus; mus shops sells books, reproductions, prints, gift items

HUNTINGTON

M **THE HECKSCHER MUSEUM OF ART,** 2 Prime Ave, Huntington, NY 11743-7702. Tel 631-351-3250; Fax 631-423-2145; Email info@heckscher.org; Web: www.heckscher.org; *Exec Dir & CEO* Michael W Schantz, PhD; *Dir Develop* Deborah J Johnson; *Cur* Lisa Chalif; *Dir Educ & Pub Progs* Joy L Weiner; *Dir Finance* Doug Cohen
Open Wed - Fri 10 AM - 5 PM, Sat & Sun 11 AM - 5 PM; Admis adults $8, seniors (62+) $6, students (10+ $5, children under 10, mems & active military personnel free; Huntington residents with proof of residency: adults $6, seniors & students $4, free Wed after 2 PM & Sat before 1 PM; Estab 1957; Five galleries, approx 4,800 sq ft; Average Annual Attendance: 23,000; Mem: Dues Aug Heckscher Society $1,000+; Patron $500; Fellow $175; Family $75; Dual $65; Individual $40; Student/Senior $35
Income: Financed by endowment, mem, town appropriations & grants
Special Subjects: Drawings, Graphics, Landscapes, Marine Painting, Painting-American, Photography, Portraits, Prints, Sculpture
Collections: American & European, works including paintings, sculpture, works on paper & photography, Long Island artists Moran family, George Grosz, Arthur Dove, Helen Torr, Esphry Slobodkina & early American Modernists
Publications: The Guide, quarterly programming guide; Family Gallery Guide; educator resource packets; exhib catalogs
Activities: K-12th grade school progs; family adult & senior progs; curator & docent led tours; art-themed public events; concert series; changing exhibs; mem & major donor activities & events

L **Library**, 2 Prime Ave, Huntington, NY 11743-7702. Tel 631-351-3250; Fax 631-423-2145; Email info@heckscher.org; Web: www.heckscher.org; *Exec Dir* Beth E Levinthal
Open by appointment only; Estab to provide range of research materials & unique resources; Open to researchers & pub. For reference only
Income: $979,735 (financed by endowment, mem, town appropriation & grants)
Library Holdings: Auction Catalogs, Book Volumes 3803, Cards, Clipping Files, Exhibition Catalogs, Memorabilia, Pamphlets, Periodical Subscriptions 2, Reproductions, Slides
Special Subjects: Painting-American, Painting-British, Painting-Dutch, Painting-European, Painting-Flemish, Painting-French, Painting-German, Photography, Prints
Collections: Major works by the Moran family, George Grosz, Lucas Cranach the Elder, R A Blakelock, Arthur Dove, Helen Torr, Thomas Eakins, James M & William Hart, Asher B Durand, Esphyr Slobodkina Research & Study Center, paintings, sculptures, drawings & preparatory sketches
Exhibitions: The Art of Thomas Anshutz; Baudelaire's Voyages: The Poet & His Painters; The Collector's Eye: American Art from Long Island Collections; Coney Island to Caumsett: 50 years of Photography by N Jay Jaffee; Garden of Earthly Delights; Huntington Township Art League Island Artists Exhibition; INSIGHTS Ron Schwerin: Paintings & Studies; Millennium Messages (time capsules by leading artists, architects & designers); Shaping a Generation: The Art & Artists of Betty Parsons; regional artists are featured in contemporary exhibitions
Publications: Bi-monthly newsletter; On Vie, bi-monthly calendar of events; Family Gallery Guides; Educator Resource Packets; Catalog of the collection; exhibition catalogs

HYDE PARK

M **NATIONAL ARCHIVES & RECORDS ADMINISTRATION,** Franklin D Roosevelt Museum, 4079 Albany Post Rd, Hyde Park, NY 12538. Tel 845-229-8114; Fax 845-486-1147; Email library@roosevelt.nara.gov; Web: www.fdrlibrary.marist.edu; *Dir* Cynthia Koch, PhD; *Cur* Herman Eberhardt; *Registrar* Michelle Frauenberger; *Chief Archivist* Bob Clark
Open daily 9 AM - 6 PM, (Nov - Apr), 9 AM - 5 PM (Apr - Oct); Admis adults $14 for combination ticket to the Roosevelt Home & Museum, children under 15 free; Estab 1939; contains displays on President & Mrs Roosevelt's lives, careers & special interests, including personal items, gifts & items collected by President Roosevelt; Average Annual Attendance: 120,000
Income: Financed by congressional appropriation, trust fund
Special Subjects: Historical Material
Collections: Papers of President & Mrs Roosevelt & of various members of his administration, prints, paintings & documents on the Hudson Valley, paintings, prints, ship models, documents & relics of the history of the United States Navy as well as other marine items, early juvenile books
Publications: The Museum of The Franklin D Roosevelt Library; Historical Materials in the Franklin D Roosevelt Library; The Era of Franklin D Roosevelt
Activities: Classes for adults & children; docent training; lects open to pub; gallery talks; tours to school groups competitions with prizes; scholarships & fels offered; individual paintings & original objects of art lent to mus; lending collection contains 23,000 artifacts; originate traveling exhibs to libraries & museums; mus shop sells books & reproductions

L **Franklin D Roosevelt Library**, 4079 Albany Post Rd, Hyde Park, NY 12538. Tel 845-486-7760; Fax 845-486-1147; Email roosevelt.library@nara.gov; Web: www.fdrlibrary.marist.edu; *Dir* Cynthia M Koch, PhD; *Deputy Dir* Lynn Bassanese; *Cur* Herman Eberhardt; *Coll Mgr* Michelle Frauenberger; *Supervisory Archivist* Robert Clark
Open May - Oct 9 AM - 6 PM, Nov - Apr 9 AM - 5 PM, Research room Mon-Fri 8:45AM-5PM, cl Thanksgiving, Christmas & New Year's Day; Combination ticket for FDR Museum and home $14, children under 15 free; Estab 1939 to preserve, interpret & make available for research archives & memorabilia relating to Franklin & Eleanor Roosevelt, their families & assoc; Average Annual Attendance: 120,000
Income: Financed by Federal government & trust fund
Library Holdings: Audio Tapes, Book Volumes, Cassettes, Clipping Files 500, Exhibition Catalogs, Fiche, Filmstrips, Manuscripts, Maps, Memorabilia 300, Motion Pictures, Original Art Works, Original Documents, Other Holdings Broadsides; Newspapers; Maps, Pamphlets, Photographs 200, Prints, Records, Reels, Sculpture, Slides, Video Tapes
Special Subjects: Portraits, Posters, Pre-Columbian Art, Prints, Scrimshaw, Sculpture, Silver, Textiles
Collections: Naval history, Hudson River Valley history, early juvenile books, illustrated ornithology, Eleanor and Franklin Roosevelt, US History: 20th Century
Exhibitions: Permanent exhibitions on lives & times of Franklin & Eleanor Roosevelt; changing exhibitions gallery
Publications: The Era of Franklin D Roosevelt: A Selected Bibliography of Periodicals, Essays & Dissertation Literature, 1945-1971; Franklin D Roosevelt and Foreign Affairs
Activities: Educ prog; lects open to pub; gallery talks; tours; originate traveling exhibitions; mus shop sells books, reproductions, prints, slides, souvenir items

M **ROOSEVELT-VANDERBILT NATIONAL HISTORIC SITES,** 4097 Albany Post Rd, Hyde Park, NY 12538-1997. Tel 845-229-9115; Fax 845-229-0739; Web: www.nps.gov/hofr/home.htm; *Supt* Sarah Olson
Open daily 9 AM - 5 PM Apr - Oct, cl Tues & Wed Nov - Mar, cl Thanksgiving, Christmas & New Year's Day, Eleanor Roosevelt NHS open daily Nov, Dec, Mar & Apr, by appt only Thurs - Sun, Jan - Mar, Groups of 10 or more require reservations; Admis $1.50, under 16, over 62 & school groups free; Vanderbilt Mansion NHS estab 1940; home of Franklin D Roosevelt NHS 1944; Eleanor Roosevelt NHS, 1977; Average Annual Attendance: 330,000
Income: Financed by Federal Government
Special Subjects: Decorative Arts
Collections: Vanderbilt & Home of FDR colls consist of original furnishings, Eleanor Roosevelt site colls are combination of originals, reproductions & like items
Exhibitions: Annual Christmas Exhibition; Antique Car Show
Publications: Vanderbilt Mansion, book; Art in the Home of Franklin D Roosevelt, brochure
Activities: Tours; sales shop sells books, postcards & slides

ITHACA

M **CORNELL UNIVERSITY,** Herbert F Johnson Museum of Art, Central & University Aves, Ithaca, NY 14853-4001. Tel 607-255-6464; Fax 607-255-9940; Email museum@cornell.edu; Web: www.museum.cornell.edu; *Interim Co-Dir, Deputy Dir & Dir Fin & Admin* Peter Gould; *Interim Co-Dir, Chief Cur & Cur Asian Art* Ellen Avril; *Cur European & American Art, Prints & Drawings* Nancy E Green; *Cur Modern & Contemp Art* Andrea Inselmann; *Ames Assoc Dir & Cur Educ* Cathy Rosa Klimaszewski; *Coordr School & Family Progs* Carol Hockett; *Registrar* Matthew Conway; *Chief Security & Special Events Coordr* Holly Fairlie; *Chief Preparator & Bldg Coordr* David Ryan; *Dir Develop* Matt Braun; *Editorial Mgr* Andrea Potochniak; *Cur Earlier Eur & Amer Art* Andrew Weislogel
Open Tues - Sun 10 AM - 5 PM, Thurs until 7:30 PM, cl Mon & Holidays; No admis fee; Estab 1973, replacing the Andrew Dickson White Mus of Art, originally founded in 1953 as Cornell University's Art Mus to serve students, the Tompkins County community & the Finger Lakes region; The collection & galleries are housed in an I M Pei designed building on Cornell University campus overlooking downtown Ithaca & Cayuga Lake; Average Annual Attendance: 89,000; Mem: 700; dues $10 - $1,000
Income: Financed by endowment, mem, grants & university funds
Special Subjects: African Art, Asian Art, Coins & Medals, Drawings, Ethnology, Painting-American, Painting-European, Painting-German, Photography, Pre-Columbian Art, Primitive art, Prints, Sculpture, Watercolors, Woodcuts
Collections: Asian art, European & American paintings, drawings, sculpture, graphic arts, photographs, video, Ethnographic Arts
Publications: Collections handbook; exhibition catalogs; seasonal newsletter; annual report; gallery brochure
Activities: Classes & workshops for adults & children; docent training; lects open to pub; concerts; gallery talks; tours; individual paintings & original objects of art lent to other institutions for special exhibs; originate traveling exhibs; mus shop sells books, exhib catalogs, postcards & notecards

L **Fine Arts Library**, 235 Rand Hall, Ithaca, NY 14853-6701. Tel 607-255-3710; Fax 607-255-6718; Email fineartsart@cornell.edu; Web: www.library.cornell.edu/finearts/; *Collections Librn* Martha Walker; *Art Librarian* Susette Newberry
Open Sat 12 PM - 5 PM, Sun 1 - 11 PM, Mon - Thurs 8AM - 11 PM, Fri 8AM - 5 PM, hours change for University vacation & summer session; No admis fee; Estab 1871 to serve Cornell students; Circ 68,006
Income: Financed through University funds
Purchases: $195,000
Library Holdings: Auction Catalogs, Book Volumes 240,000, CD-ROMs, Clipping Files, DVDs, Exhibition Catalogs, Fiche 5928, Periodical Subscriptions 1400, Reels 424, Video Tapes
Special Subjects: Architecture, Art History, Landscape Architecture

M **THE HISTORY CENTER IN TOMPKINS COUNTY,** 401 E State St, Ithaca, NY 14850. Tel 607-273-8284; Fax 607-273-6107; Email community@thehistorycenter.net; Web: www.thehistorycenter.net; *Exec Dir* Scott Callan
Open Tues, Thurs, & Sat 11 AM - 5 PM; No admis fee; Estab 1935 to collect, preserve & interpret the history of Tompkins County, New York; 10,000 sq ft; Average Annual Attendance: 8,000; Mem: 750; gifts $35 and up; annual meeting in last quarter
Income: $280,000 (financed by endowment, mem, county appropriation, state & federal grants, earned income & foundations)
Library Holdings: Original Documents, Pamphlets, Photographs, Prints, Records, Reproductions
Special Subjects: American Indian Art, Anthropology, Archaeology, Architecture, Carpets & Rugs, Costumes, Crafts, Decorative Arts, Drawings, Ethnology, Flasks & Bottles, Folk Art, Furniture, Furniture, Glass, Glass, Landscapes, Maps, Painting-American, Photography, Portraits, Posters, Stained Glass, Textiles, Watercolors, Reproductions
Collections: Decorative arts, local historical objects, painting & sketches by local artists, portraits, photographers - Louise Boyle, Joseph Burritt, Curt Foerster, Charles Howes, Charles Jones, Henry Head, Robert Head, Verne Morton, Sheldon Smith, John Spires, Trevor Teele, Marion Wesp
Exhibitions: Five to six rotating exhibitions per yr
Publications: History Happenings, monthly e-newsletter
Activities: Classes for adults & children; lects open to pub, 12 vis lectrs per yr; gallery talks; tours; mus shop sells books, reproductions of photographs; gift items, postcards & exhib- related items

M **ITHACA COLLEGE,** Handwerker Gallery of Art, 1170 Gannett Ctr, Ithaca, NY 14850-7276. Tel 607-274-3548; Fax 607-274-1774; Email handwerker@ithaca.edu; Web: www.ithaca.edu/handwerker; *Dir* Jelena Stojanovic; *Chmn Art History* Steven Clancy; *Gallery Dir* Cheryl Kramer
Open Mon - Wed & Fri 10 AM - 6 PM, Thurs 10 AM - 9 PM, Sat-Sun 10AM-5PM; No admis fee; Estab 1978 for display of contemporary art & critical interpretation of image; Average Annual Attendance: 7,500
Collections: African Art, Photographs, Pre-Columbian Art, 20th Century Graphic Art
Publications: Quarterly newsletter
Activities: Critical forum; lects open to pub; 4 vis lectrs per yr

JAMAICA

M **JAMAICA CENTER FOR ARTS & LEARNING (JCAL),** 161-04 Jamaica Ave, Jamaica, NY 11432-6112. Tel 718-658-7400; Fax 718-658-7222; Email info@jcal.org; Web: www.jcal.org; *Interim Exec Dir* Carl Fields Jr; *Dir Finance & Admin* Jennifer Chiang; *Sr Prog & Develop Dir* Akua-Ak Loh Anokye; *Educ Dir* Juan Carlos Salinas; *Gen Mgr, JPAC* Courtney Ffrench
Open Mon - Fri 8:30 AM - 9 PM, Sat 9 AM - 6 PM; No admis fee; Estab 1972 to provide educational opportunity in the visual & performing arts, exhibitions & performances; Five story landmark building; workshop studios for painting, drawing, mask making, ceramics, silkscreen & photography; 3 dance studios; 1650 sq ft art gallery; 99 seat state-of-the-art theatre; 1 multi-purpose space; 1 computer lab; 1 toddler studio; 1 multi-media studio; Average Annual Attendance: 25,000
Income: $1,600,000 (financed by New York City Department of Cultural Affairs, New York State Council on the Arts, Honorable Claire Shulman, Queens Borough President, foundations, corporations & workshop tuitions)
Exhibitions: Up to 12 changing exhibitions annually in three museum quality galleries
Publications: Exhibition catalogs & posters
Activities: Classes for adults & children; dramatic progs; concerts; gallery talks; tours; competitions; schols offered; exten dept serves New York City; photographs & blow ups of original photographs lent; book traveling exhibs annually

L **QUEENS BOROUGH PUBLIC LIBRARY,** Fine Arts & Recreation Division, 89-11 Merrick Blvd, Jamaica, NY 11432. Tel 718-990-0755; Fax 718-658-8342; Email username@queens.lib.ny.us; Web: www.queenslibrary.org; *Div Mgr* Esther Lee; *Asst Mgr* Rebecca Wilkins; *Lib Dir* Thomas Galante
Open Mon - Fri 10 AM - 9 PM, Sat 10 AM - 5:30 PM, Sun, Sept - May, Noon - 5 PM; No admis fee; Estab 1933 to serve the general public in Queens, New York
Income: Financed by city & state appropriations
Library Holdings: Audio Tapes, Book Volumes 150,000, CD-ROMs 270, Cassettes 10,500, Compact Disks 23,000, Pamphlets, Periodical Subscriptions 398, Photographs, Prints, Records 2000, Reels 4100, Reproductions 30,000, Video Tapes 20,000
Collections: The WPA Print Collection
Activities: Concerts

JAMESTOWN

L **JAMES PRENDERGAST LIBRARY ASSOCIATION,** 509 Cherry St, Jamestown, NY 14701-5098. Tel 716-484-7135; Fax 716-483-6880; Email tscott@cclslib.org; Web: www.prendergastlibrary.org; *Gallery Coordr* Anne Plyler; *Exec Dir* Tina Scott
Open Mon - Fri 10 AM - 8:30 PM, Sat 10 AM - 4 PM; No admis fee; Estab 1891 as part of library; Circ 657,000; Maintains art gallery; Average Annual Attendance: 259,000; Mem: 43,375
Income: Financed by state & local funds
Library Holdings: Audio Tapes, Book Volumes 383,160, Cassettes 4,002, Compact Disks 3,203, DVDs 1,221, Maps 652, Micro Print, Original Art Works 60, Periodical Subscriptions 359, Video Tapes
Special Subjects: Prints
Collections: Prendergast paintings, 19th & 20th century paintings, Roger Tory Peterson, limited edition print collection, Alexander Calder mats
Exhibitions: Traveling Exhibitions; local one-person and group shows
Publications: Mirror Up To Nature, collection catalog
Activities: Classes for adults & children; lects open to pub; gallery talks; tours; concerts; competitions; lending collection contains books, cassettes, framed reproductions; books traveling exhibitions

M **JAMESTOWN COMMUNITY COLLEGE,** The Weeks, 525 Falconer St, Jamestown, NY 14701-1999. Tel 716-665-9188; *Dir* James Colby
Open Mon-Wed 11AM-4PM, Fri 11AM-3PM; No admis fee; Estab 1969 to show significant regional, national & international contemporary art; Facility includes 2000 sq ft exhibition area
Income: $93,000 (financed through Faculty Student Assn & private foundation funds)
Exhibitions: PhotoNominal
Publications: Exhibition catalogs, semiannual
Activities: Lects open to pub, 200 vis lectrs per yr

KATONAH

M **CARAMOOR CENTER FOR MUSIC & THE ARTS, INC,** Rosen House at Caramoor, 149 Girdle Ridge Rd Katonah, NY 10536; PO Box 816, Katonah, NY 10536-0816. Tel 914-232-5035, 232-1252 (Box office phone); Fax 914-232-5521; Email info@caramoor.org; Web: www.caramoor.org; *Chmn Bd Trustees* Judy Evnin; *Mng Dir* Paul Rosenblum; *Develop Dir* Gary Himes; *CEO & Gen Dir* Michael Barrett; *Dir Finance* Tammy Belanger-Turner; *Archivist* Hilton Bailey; *Dir Spec Events & Facility Rental* Christine Bosco; *Mgr Annual Giving* Alithia Dutschke; *Mktg Mgr* Sal Vaccaro
Open May - Oct Wed - Sun 1 PM - 4 PM, with last tour at 3 PM; Nov - Apr Mon - Fri by appt; Admis adults $10, children 16 & under free; Estab 1970 to preserve the house & its collections, the legacy of Walter T Rosen & to provide interpretive & educ programs; Period rooms from European palaces are showcase for art collection from Europe & the Orient, spanning 6 centuries; Average Annual Attendance: 60,000
Income: $365,000
Special Subjects: Asian Art, Bronzes, Carpets & Rugs, Ceramics, Costumes, Decorative Arts, Embroidery, Enamels, Furniture, Ivory, Jade, Manuscripts, Medieval Art, Painting-German, Painting-Italian, Period Rooms, Photography, Porcelain, Portraits, Religious Art, Renaissance Art, Sculpture, Stained Glass, Tapestries, Textiles
Collections: Period rooms - Fine & decorative arts from Europe & Asia (1400-1950), Tapestries; paintings; sculpture; Urbino Maiolica; jade & cloisonné
Publications: Guidebook to collection; New book Caramoor
Activities: Classes for children; docent training; concerts; lects open to pub, 4 vis lectrs per yr; tours; mus shop sells books & original art, jewelry & other gift items

M **KATONAH MUSEUM OF ART,** 134 Jay St, Katonah, NY 10536-3737. Tel 914-232-9555; Fax 914-232-3128; Email info@katonahmuseum.org; Web: www.katonahmuseum.org; *Exec Dir* Darsie Alexander; *Dir Devel* Alexis Ferguson DiMarco; *Dir Communications* Sarah S Marshall
Open Tues - Sat 10 AM - 5 PM, Sun noon - 5 PM, cl Mon; Admis Tues - Fri & Sun Noon - 5PM adults $10, seniors & students $5, Sat 10 AM - 5 PM adults $10, seniors & students $5, mems & children under 12 free; Estab 1953 to present exhibitions created with loaned works of art, programs for schools, films, lectures, demonstrations & workshops; The Katonah Museum consists of 3000 sq ft of exhibition space with a sculpture garden and children's learning center; Average Annual Attendance: 50,000; Mem: 1400; dues $50 & up
Income: financed by mem, contributions & grants
Library Holdings: Exhibition Catalogs
Publications: Exhibition catalogues: Dress Codes: Clothing as Metaphor, 2009; Lichtenstein in Process, 2009; Conversations in Clay, 2008; Here's The Thing: Single Object Still Lifes, 2008; Shattering Glass, 2007; Children Should Be Seen: The Image of the Child in American Picture Book Art, 2006; Ancient Art of the Cyclades, 2006; Andromeda Hotel: The Art of Joseph Cornell, 2006
Activities: For adults: guided tours; lects; symposia; films; workshops; concerts; trips; For children: gallery games; book readings; workshops; community festivals; hands-on activities in Learning Ctr; teacher training workshop; lects open to public; concerts; tours; awards given for best local mus (Westchester Magazine); member school: on-site & out-reach progs & servs; originate traveling exhibs for selected institutions

M **NEW YORK STATE OFFICE OF PARKS RECREATION & HISTORIC PRESERVATION,** John Jay Homestead State Historic Site, 400 Rte 22, Katonah, NY 10536; PO Box 832, Katonah, NY 10536-0832. Tel 914-232-5651; Fax 914-232-8085; Web: www.johnjayhomestead.org; *Interpretive Progs Asst* Allan M Weinreb; *Historic Site Mgr* Heather Iannucci; *Mus Educator* Bethany White
Open Tues-Sat 10AM-3PM, Sun 11AM-3PM, Nov-Mar; Tues-Sat 10AM-4M, Sun 11AM-4PM Apr-Oct; Admis adults $7, seniors (62 & older) $5, children up to 12 yrs free; Estab 1958 to inform public on John Jay and his contributions to national, state & local history; Ten restored period rooms reflecting occupancy of the Jay family in the 1820s; art distributed throughout; also on exhibit is the art studio of John Jay's great-great-great granddaughter, Eleanor Iselin Wade; Average Annual Attendance: 30,000; Mem: 1000; Friends of John Jay Homestead, Inc; dues $25 & up; annual meeting in spring
Income: Financed by state appropriation

Library Holdings: Original Documents, Other Holdings, Photographs
Special Subjects: Ceramics, Decorative Arts, Etchings & Engravings, Furniture, Historical Material, Manuscripts, Maps, Metalwork, Painting-American, Period Rooms, Photography, Porcelain, Portraits, Portraits, Reproductions, Restorations, Silver, Textiles, Sculpture
Collections: American art and American decorative arts, John Jay memorabilia and archives, Westchester mansion with estate & out-buildings, artworks & art-making tools of equestrian artist, Eleanor Iselin Mason Wade
Exhibitions: Federal Period Decorations; Period Home, Federal decor including art, decorative arts furnishings & memorabilia; Changing exhibitions in Back Parlor Gallery
Publications: John Jay and the Constitution, a Teacher's Guide; John Jay 1745-1829; The Jays of Bedford
Activities: Classes for adults & children; docent training; call for information; lect open to public; concerts; group tours by advance reservation; school on site and outreach; craft demonstrations; special exhibits; sale of books & prints

KINDERHOOK

M **COLUMBIA COUNTY HISTORICAL SOCIETY,** Columbia County Museum and Library, 5 Albany Ave, Kinderhook, NY 12106; PO Box 311, Kinderhook, NY 12106-0311. Tel 518-758-9265; Fax 518-758-2499; Email cchs@cchsny.org; Web: www.cchsny.org; *Acting Exec Dir* David H. Smith
Open Thurs & Fri 10 AM - 4 PM, Sat & Sun noon - 4 PM; Admis adults $5, mems, children 12 & under free; Estab 1916; County Historical Society Museum Gallery with changing exhibits; 2 historic houses: 1737 Van Alen House & c1820 Vanderpoel House; In large hall, wall space 40 ft x 38 ft; Average Annual Attendance: 6,000; Mem: 500; dues $30-1000; annual meeting Oct
Income: $250,000 (financed by mem, endowment, activities, projects, events, private donations, admis, government & corporate grants)
Special Subjects: Architecture, Ceramics, Costumes, Decorative Arts, Furniture, Historical Material, Manuscripts, Maps, Painting-American, Sculpture
Collections: Historical objects pertaining to history of county, New York regional decorative arts, furniture & costumes, paintings of 18th through 20th centuries
Exhibitions: Local history & cultural exhibits
Publications: Brochures; exhibit catalogs; magazine; books
Activities: Classes for children; docent training; lects open to pub; vis lectrs 5 per yr; concerts; gallery talks; tours; schols; originate traveling exhibs; mus shop sells books, reproductions

M **Luykas Van Alen House**, Rte 9 H, Kinderhook, NY 12106; PO Box 311, Kinderhook, NY 12106-0311. Tel 518-758-9265; Fax 518-758-2499; Email cchs@cchsny.org; Web: www.cchsny.org; *Exec Dir* Ann-Eliza Lewis; *Educator* Ashley Hopkins-Benton; *Cur* Diane Shewchuk
Open Memorial Day weekend - Labor Day weekend, Fri & Sat 10 AM - 4 PM, Sun noon - 4 PM; Admis adults $5, members, seniors & children 12 & under free; Estab 1737; Mem: 700; dues $25-$1,000; annual meeting 3rd Sat of Oct
Special Subjects: Decorative Arts, Architecture, Furniture
Activities: Classes for children; field trips; tours; sells books & reproductions

M **1820 James Vanderpoel House**, Rte 9, Kinderhook, NY 12106; PO Box 311, Kinderhook, NY 12106-0311. Tel 518-758-9265; *Cur* Helen M McLallen; *Exec Dir* Sharon S Palmer
Open Memorial Day weekend - Labor Day weekend Thurs - Sat 11 AM - 5 PM, Sun 1 PM - 5 PM; tours by appt only; Admis adults $3, senior citizens & students $2, children 12 & under free; Federal Period house museum with furnishings of the period; Mem: 700; dues $25-$1000, annual meeting 3rd Sat in Oct

KINGSTON

M **FRIENDS OF HISTORIC KINGSTON,** Fred J Johnston House Museum, Corner of Main & Wall Sts, Kingston, NY 12401; PO Box 3763, Kingston, NY 12402-3763. Tel 845-339-0720; Email twothings@hvc.rr.com; Web: www.fohk.org; *Dir* Jane Kellar; *Pres Bd* Avery Leete Smith; *Pub Rels* Patricia Murphy
Open May - Oct Sat & Sun 1 - 4 PM & by appt; Admis adult $5, children $2; Estab 1965; Gallery of changing exhibs related to the city of Kingston's local history; house mus with period rooms; Average Annual Attendance: 5000 by estimate; Mem: dues Patron $500, Household $50, Student/Senior $10
Library Holdings: Book Volumes, Clipping Files, Kodachrome Transparencies, Manuscripts, Maps, Memorabilia, Original Art Works, Original Documents, Pamphlets, Photographs, Prints
Special Subjects: Ceramics, Decorative Arts, Drawings, Painting-American, Painting-European, Period Rooms, Textiles
Collections: 200 book vols on local history, items of local history for the city of Kingston, NY, 1,400 objects of American decorative arts
Publications: Friends of Historic Kingston, newsletter; Stockade District, walking tour brochure; Kingston New York: The Architectural Guide
Activities: Lects; 1 vis lectr per year; gallery talks; guided tours; temporary exhibs; mus shops sells books, prints

M **NEW YORK STATE OFFICE OF PARKS: RECREATION AND HISTORIC PRESERVATION,** Senate House State Historic Site, 296 Fair St, Kingston, NY; 312 Fair St, Kingston, NY 12401-3836. Tel 914-338-2786; *Historic Site Mgr* Rich Goring
Open Apr - Oct Wed - Sat 10 AM - 5 PM, Sun 1 - 5 PM, Jan - Mar Sat 10 AM - 5 PM, Sun 1 - 5 PM; No admis fee; Estab 1887 as an educational community resource which tells the story of the growth of state government as well as the stories of the lives & works of local 19th century artists; Average Annual Attendance: 20,000
Special Subjects: Decorative Arts
Collections: 18th & 19th century decorative arts, 18th & 19th century paintings & other works of art, particularly those by James Bard, Jervis McEntee, Ammi Phillips, Joseph Tubb & John Vanderlyn
Publications: Exhibition catalogs
Activities: Classes for adults & children; docent training; lects open to pub, 2 vis lectrs per yr; individual paintings & original objects of art lent to well-established institutions; lending coll contains color reproductions, original art works, original prints, paintings & sculptures; book traveling exhibs

L **Reference Library**, 312 Fair St, Kingston, NY 12401. Tel 845-338-2786; *Historic Site Mgr* Rich Goring
Open Mon, Wed, & Sat 10AM-5PM, Sun 11AM-5PM; Admis adults $4, seniors $3, children 11 and under free; Estab 1887; Open by appointment to scholars, students & researchers for reference only
Library Holdings: Book Volumes 10,000, Exhibition Catalogs, Manuscripts, Memorabilia, Pamphlets, Periodical Subscriptions 10
Collections: Collection of letters relating to the artist John Vanderlyn
Publications: Exhibit catalogs

LAKE GEORGE

M **LAKE GEORGE ARTS PROJECT,** Courthouse Gallery, Canada St, Lake George, NY 12845; 1 Amherst St, Lake George, NY 12845. Tel 518-668-2616; Fax 518-668-2616; Email mail@lakegeorgearts.org; Web: www.lakegeorgearts.org; *Gallery Dir* Laura Von Rosk; *Dir* John Strong
Open Tues - Fri Noon - 5 PM, Sat Noon - 4 pm (during exhibitions); no admis fee; Estab 1977, gallery estab 1985 to provide income & exposure for national & regional artists; 26 ft by 30 ft; Average Annual Attendance: 1,000; Mem: 500; dues $20-$100; annual meeting in Dec
Income: $150,000 (financed by mem & by city & state appropriation)
Activities: Lects open to the pub, gallery talks

LEROY

A **LEROY HISTORICAL SOCIETY,** The Jell-O Gallery, 23 E Main St, LeRoy, NY 14482-1209. Tel 585-768-7433; Fax 716-768-7579; Email info@jellogallery.org; Web: www.jellogallery.org; *Dir* Lynne Belluscio
Open Apr-Dec Mon-Sat 10AM-4PM, Sun 1-4PM, Jan-Mar Sat-Sun 10AM-4PM; Admis adults $24 children 6-11 $1.50, children 5 & under free; Estab 1940; Mem: 400; dues $18-$30; annual meeting in May
Income: financed by endowment, mem, city & state appropriations
Special Subjects: Carpets & Rugs, Ceramics, Decorative Arts, Dolls, Drawings, Embroidery, Etchings & Engravings, Flasks & Bottles, Furniture, Glass, Historical Material, Jewelry, Laces, Maps, Metalwork, Painting-American, Period Rooms, Photography, Portraits, Posters, Pottery, Prints, Silver, Textiles, Watercolors
Collections: Decorative Arts, Jell-O Museum, LeRoy related, 19th Century Art, Textiles, Tools, Western NY Redware
Publications: Quarterly newsletter
Activities: Classes for adults & children; docent training; lects open to pub; tours; individual paintings & original objects of art lent to other mus; mus shop sells books & reproductions

LITTLE FALLS

M **MOHAWK VALLEY CENTER FOR THE ARTS INC,** 401 Canal Pl, Little Falls, NY 13365. Tel 315-823-0808; Fax 315-823-0805; Email director@mohawkvalleyarts.org; Web: ww.mohawkvalleyarts.org; *Dir* Barbara Boucher
Open Tues-Sat 11AM-4PM
Collections: works by local artists; paintings

LONG BEACH

L **LONG BEACH ART LEAGUE,** Long Beach Library, PO Box 862, Long Beach, NY 11561-0862. Tel 516-432-0195; Email mjmlido@aol.com; Web: www.longbeachartleague.com; *Treas* Mary Mendoza; *Program Dir* Selma Stern; *Pres* Dina Fine; *VPres* Shoshana Findling
Open Mon - Sat 9 AM - 6 PM, Sun 1 PM - 5 PM; No admis fee; Estab in 1952 by a group of interested resident artists determined to form an organization to promote art activity & appreciation with emphasis on quality & exhibitions, demonstrations; Public galleries in Long Beach Library, Long Beach Community Center; Average Annual Attendance: 500 per week; Mem: 160; dues $25; meetings 1st Wed each month
Income: Member dues, donations, foundation recipient
Purchases: Established gallery at Long Beach Medical Ctr
Exhibitions: 10 monthly exhibits at library; 6 bimonthly exhibits at community center
Publications: Exhibitions brochures; Monthly newsletter; Publicity flyer monthly
Activities: Classes for adults & children; workshops; demonstrations; lect; 4 vis lectrs/demos per year; gallery talks; sponsoring of competitions; 8 cash awards at 4 open exhibs; equal merit awards 4 times per yr; senior community ctr exhibits & classes

L **LONG BEACH PUBLIC LIBRARY,** 111 W Park Ave, Long Beach, NY 11561-3300. Tel 516-432-7201; Fax 516-889-4641; Email lblibrary@hotmail.com; *Asst Dir* Laura Weir; *Bus & Vocations Librn* Theresa Cahill; *Dir* George Trepp
Open Oct - May Mon, Wed, Thurs 9 AM - 9 PM, Tues & Fri 9 AM - 6 PM, Sat 9 AM - 5 PM, Sun 1 - 5 PM; Estab 1928 to serve the community with information & services, including recreational, cultural & informational materials; The Long Beach Art Assn in cooperation with the library presents monthly exhibits of all types of media
Library Holdings: Book Volumes 100,000, Cassettes, Fiche, Filmstrips, Memorabilia, Pamphlets, Periodical Subscriptions 300, Photographs, Records, Reels, Video Tapes
Collections: Local history, 300 photographs of Long Beach
Exhibitions: Local talent; membership shows; juried exhibitions
Publications: Monthly newsletter
Activities: Dramatic progs; lects open to pub, 18-20 vis lectrs per yr; concerts; gallery talks; films; tours

LONG ISLAND CITY

M **DORSKY GALLERY,** Dorsky Gallery Curatorial Programs, 11-03 45th Ave, at the corner of 11th St Long Island City, NY 11101-5109. Tel 718-937-6317; Email info@dorsky.org; Web: www.dorsky.org; *Dir* David Dorsky
Open Thurs-Mon 11AM-6PM; other times by appointment; Free admis; Contemporary art
Collections: works by contemporary artists
Activities: Lects open to pub; gallery talks; tours

M **ISAMU NOGUCHI FOUNDATION,** Isamu Noguchi Garden Museum, 32-37 Vernon Blvd, Long Island City, NY 11106. Tel 718-204-7088; Fax 718-278-2348; Email info@noguchi.org; Web: www.noguchi.org; *Admin Dir* Amy Hau; *Cur* Bonnie Rychlak; *Head Educ* Rebecca Herz; *Exec Dir* Jenny Dixon
Open all yr Wed, Thurs & Fri 10 AM - 5 PM, Sat & Sun 11 AM - 6 PM; Admis suggested contribution $10, sr citizens & students $5, children 11 and under free; Estab 1985 to preserve, protect & exhibit important sculptural, environmental & design work of Isamu Noguchi; 13 galleries & a garden exhibiting over 350 sculptures, models, drawings & photos; 24,000 sq ft factory converted by the artist; Average Annual Attendance: 25,000
Income: $400,000 (financed by Noguchi Foundation, New York City Department of Cultural Affairs & private donations)
Library Holdings: Auction Catalogs, Exhibition Catalogs, Original Documents
Special Subjects: Sculpture
Collections: Sculptures in stone, wood, metal, paper, clay, models and drawings, photos of Noguchi's gardens and plazas, stage sets
Exhibitions: Permanent exhib; temp exhibs that contextualize Noguchi
Publications: Exhib catalogs
Activities: Classes for adults & children; tours; docent training; artist in residence prog; workshops; lects open to pub; gallery talks; tours; concerts; originates traveling exhibs to other mus; mus shop sells books & Noguchis Akari light sculptures

M **NEUSTADT COLLECTION OF TIFFANY GLASS,** 5-26 46th Ave, Administrative Office Long Island City, NY 11101-5229. Tel 718-361-8489; Email info@neustadtcollection.org; Web: www.neustadtcollection.org; *Sec* Elizabeth De Rosa; *Dir & Cur* Lindsy R Parrott; *Conservator* Susan Tomlin; *Bd Pres* Cynthia Williams; *Treas* Patricia Specter
Open Neustadt Gallery at Queens Museum NYC: Wed - Sun noon - 6 PM; Admis suggested donation adults $8, students & seniors $4, children under 12 free; Estab 1969; 1,000 sq ft present rotating shows from permanent coll; Average Annual Attendance: 250,000
Special Subjects: Decorative Arts, Glass, Historical Material, Metalwork, Stained Glass, Mosaics
Collections: Tiffany lamps & windows, Tiffany flat and pressed glass archive, Tiffany metalwork
Publications: The Lamps of Tiffany; Tiffany by Design: An In-Depth Look at Tiffany Lamps
Activities: Educ progs for children & adults; oral history prog; lect; lending of original objects of art to art museums across the USA & Europe & Corning Museum of Glass, New York Historical Soc; organize traveling exhibs to museums (small & mid-size); originate traveling exhibitions to small & mid-size museums across USA; Mus shop sells reproductions & products developed from perm colls & sold at Queens mus shop

M **PS1 CONTEMPORARY ART CENTER,** 22-25 Jackson Ave, Long Island City, NY 11101. Tel 718-784-2084; Fax 718-482-9454; Email mail@ps1.org; Web: www.ps1.org; *Exec Dir* Alanna Heiss; *Dir Operations* Tony Guerrero; *Assoc Dir Press & Mktg* Rachael Dorsey
Open Thurs - Mon Noon - 6 PM; Admis Gen $5, students & seniors $2; Estab 1972 as artist studios & exhibition contemporary & experimental art; Located in a vast renovated 19th century Romanesque schoolhouse, the gallery contains 46,000 sq ft of exhibition space; Average Annual Attendance: 60,000; Mem: 100,000+; Dues leadership council $5,000, patrons council $1,000
Income: Financed by city & state appropriations, corporate & private donations, National Endowment for the Arts
Library Holdings: CD-ROMs, Cards, Compact Disks, Fiche, Kodachrome Transparencies, Pamphlets
Special Subjects: Architecture, Collages, Drawings, Painting-American, Painting-Australian, Painting-Canadian, Painting-Dutch, Painting-French, Painting-German, Painting-Israeli, Painting-Italian, Painting-Japanese, Painting-New Zealand, Painting-Polish, Painting-Russian, Painting-Scandinavian, Painting-Spanish, Photography, Sculpture
Collections: Architecture, fashion, film, painting, photography, sculpture, video
Exhibitions: International Studio Exhibition; Alternating 1-100 & Vice Versa by Alighiero e Boetti; Gilles Peress Farewell to Bosnia; Stalin's Choice Soviet Socialistic Realism; The Winter of Love
Publications: Loop; Short Century; Mexico City; Video Acts
Activities: Classes for adults & children; dance; film; video; photography; fashion; architectural presentations; lects open to pub; concerts; gallery talks; tours; competitions for studio program with awards of studio residency; scholarships offered; original works of art lent to nonprofit institutions with appropriate facilities; book traveling exhibs; originate traveling exhibs; sales shop sells books, catalogues, posters, postcards, clothing

M **SCULPTURECENTER,** 44-19 Purves St, Long Island City, NY 11101. Tel 212-737-9870; Web: www.sculpture-center.org; *Pres* Armand Bartos; *VPres* Edwin Nochberg; *VPres* Jan Abrams; *Treas* Arthur Abelman; *Asst Dir* Elizabeth Eder; *Asst Dir* Jay Gibson; *Exec Dir* Mary Ceruti
Open Tues - Sat 11 AM - 5 PM; No admis fee; Estab 1928 as Clay Club of New York to further the interest of student & professional sculptors. Incorporated in 1944 as the Sculpture Center, a nonprofit organization for the promotion of the art of sculpture & to provide work facilities. Moved into the new building in 1950, when the present name was adopted. Slide file maintained for unaffiliated sculptors for use by consultants, curators, collectors & architects; A gallery is maintained & has represented in it professional sculptors. School & studio space can be provided for beginning, intermediate & advanced students; Average Annual Attendance: 35,000
Income: School tution
Exhibitions: Solo & group exhibitions of emerging & mid-career sculptors; selection from the Sculptor Center Slide File;; Video Installations; ongoing series of installations on AIDS as well as monthly readings by poets & writers
Publications: Announcements (for the gallery and school); brochures; exhibition catalogs
Activities: Classes for adults & children; lects open to public; concerts; gallery talks; tours; scholarships offered; original objects of art lent to private galleries & corporate lobbies; sales shop sells tools & supplies for sculptors

L **Gallery,** 44-19 Purves St, Long Island City, NY 11101-2907. Tel 718-361-1750; Fax 718-786-9336; Email info@sculpture-center.org; Web: www.sculpture-center.org; *Exec Dir* Mary Ceruti; *Assoc Dir* Ben Whine; *Cur* Ruba Katrib; *Develop Dir* Allison Perusha
Open Thurs - Mon 11 AM - 6 PM; Suggested donation $5; Estab 1928; Nonprofit organization that identifies the innovative ideas that define contemporary sculpture; Average Annual Attendance: 14,000; Mem: See website for levels
Income: Nonprofit
Library Holdings: Auction Catalogs, Audio Tapes, Book Volumes 200, CD-ROMs, Cassettes, Clipping Files, Compact Disks, DVDs, Exhibition Catalogs, Filmstrips, Lantern Slides, Memorabilia, Original Art Works, Original Documents, Pamphlets, Periodical Subscriptions 3, Photographs, Sculpture, Slides, Video Tapes
Special Subjects: Sculpture
Exhibitions: 8 exhibs per yr
Publications: Inquiries into Contemporary Sculpture Series; Exhibition Catalogs
Activities: Classes for children; lects open to public; vis lectrs 3 per yr; concerts; gallery talks; tours; museum shop sells books, magazines, original art, limited editions

M **SOCRATES SCULPTURE PARK,** 32-01 Vernon Blvd, Long Island City, NY 11106; P.O. Box 6259, Long Island City, NY 11106. Tel 718-956-1819; Fax 718-626-1533; Email info@socratessculpturepark.org; Web: www.socratessculpturepark.org; *Exec Dir* John Hatfield; *Dir of Pub Progs & Community Rels* Shaun Leonardo; *Dir Develop & Communs* Katie Denny; *Studio Mgr* Lars Fisk; *Events Mgr* Leonard White; *Exhibs Prog Mgr* Elissa Goldstone
Open everyday 10 AM - sunset; No admis fee; Estab 1986; Outdoor sculpture park & artist residency program; Average Annual Attendance: 80,000
Special Subjects: Sculpture
Collections: Changing exhibitions of large scale sculpture & multi media installations
Exhibitions: Annual spring exhibition; Collaborative projects; billboard
Publications: Catalogs
Activities: Classes for adults & children; summer workshops for children; school outreach; fitness progs; family events; internships; concerts; tours; fels

MEDINA

M **MEDINA RAILROAD MUSEUM,** 530A West Ave, Medina, NY 14103-1554. Tel 585-798-6106; Fax 585-798-1086; Email office@railroadmuseum.net; Web: www.medinarailroad.com; *Pres* Rick Henn; *VPres* Janien Klotzbach; *Treas* Hugh James; *Founder & Cur* Martin C Phelps
Open Tues - Sun 11 AM - 5 PM, cl most major holidays; Admis adults $8, seniors $7, children $6, mem adults no admis fee; Estab 1997; Railroad & firefighting mus with displays; largest coll of railroad artifacts & memorabilia known to exist under one roof; Average Annual Attendance: 28,000; Mem: dues Corporate $100, Bus $75, Family $50, Individual $20
Income: $800,000 (Excursion Train Events)
Purchases: Pair of 1948 railroad passenger table cars
Library Holdings: Book Volumes, Maps, Original Documents, Pamphlets, Photographs, Prints, Slides
Special Subjects: Coins & Medals, Dioramas, Flasks & Bottles, Furniture, Historical Material, Maps, Miniatures, Photography, Posters, Reproductions
Collections: Over 6000 items including railroad artifacts & memorabilia; HO-scale model train layout (204 ft x 14 ft); photos; models; toy coll & large firefighting artifact
Activities: Excursion train rides; guided tours; loan exhibs; slide presentations; mus shop sells souvenirs & toys

MOUNT VERNON

L **MOUNT VERNON PUBLIC LIBRARY,** Fine Art Dept, 28 S First Ave, Mount Vernon, NY 10550. Tel 914-668-1840; Fax 914-668-1018; *Dir* Rodney Lee; *Acting Dir* Opal Lindsay
Open Mon - Thurs 10 AM - 9 PM, Fri & Sat 9 AM - 5 PM, Sun 1 - 5 PM, cl Sat & Sun during July and Aug; No admis fee; Estab 1854; Library contains Doric Hall with murals by Edward Gay, NA; Exhibition Room with frescoes by Louise Brann Soverns; & Norman Wells Print Alcove, estab 1941
Income: $2,200,000 (financed by city & other funds)
Library Holdings: Audio Tapes 1,293, Book Volumes 450,000, Cassettes 1,293, Other Holdings Art books 17,000, Periodical Subscriptions 800, Photographs 11,700, Records 12,500
Special Subjects: Architecture, Ceramics, Costume Design & Constr, Decorative Arts, Painting-American, Photography, Prints
Exhibitions: Costume dolls; fans; metalwork; one-man shows of painting, sculpture & photographs; porcelains; silver; woodcarving; jewelry; other exhibits changing monthly cover a wide range of subjects from miniatures to origami
Activities: Lect open to public, 6 vis lectrs per year; concerts; gallery talks; tours; individual paintings & original objects of art lent to library members

MUMFORD

M **GENESEE COUNTRY VILLAGE & MUSEUM,** John L Wehle Art Gallery, 1410 Flint Hill Rd, Mumford, NY 14511-0310; PO Box 310, Mumford, NY

14511-0310. Tel 585-538-6822; Fax 585-538-2887 & 6927; Email email@gcv.org; Web: www.gvc.org; *Chair, Bd Trustees* A Thomas Hildebrandt; *Pres & CEO* Peter Arnold; *CFO* Samantha Nickerson; *Sr Dir Develop* Laura Scala; *Sr Dir Facilities & Grounds* Roger Magrin; *Sr Dir Human Resources* Cheryl Barney; *Sr Dir Progs & Colls* Chuck LeCount; *Sr Dir Guest Relations & Admin* Christine Rovet; *Cur Colls* Peter Wisbey; *Cur John L Wehle Art Gallery* Patricia Tice; *Dir Retail & Vis Servs* Robin Lott; *Dir Interpretation* Brian Nagel; *Dir Educ Servs* Maria Neale
Call for hours; Gallery is currently cl for renovation until May 2012; Admis adults $15, seniors & students $12, children (4-16) years $9; Estab 1976; Gallery has over 600 paintings & sculptures dealing with wildlife, sporting art & western art.; Average Annual Attendance: 130,000; Mem: 2001 John Hamilton Society $5,000+, MICAH Brooks Society $2,500, Julia Hyde Society $1,000; Sylvester Hosmer Society $500, Premier $175, Family & Grandparent $99, Individual + 1 $$80, Individual $60
Income: Financed by admissions, mem, corporate sponsorship, local, state, federal funding, & foundations
Library Holdings: Book Volumes, Periodical Subscriptions
Special Subjects: Architecture, Art Education, Art History, Ceramics, Costumes, Crafts, Decorative Arts, Folk Art, Furniture, Historical Material, Painting-American, Period Rooms, Pottery, Restorations, Sculpture, Textiles, Watercolors
Collections: Decorative arts, restored 19th Century buildings, paintings & sculpture, Sporting Art, Wildlife Art (North American & European), 19th century textiles & clothing
Publications: Booklets; Four Centuries of Sporting Art; Genesee Country Museum; Scenes of Town & Country in the 19th Century; Bi-monthly newsletter; asst brochures
Activities: Classes for adults & children; docent training; lects open to pub; concerts; gallery talks; tours; movable mus serves schools, nursing homes, etc; mus shop sells books, magazines & gifts

NEW CITY

M **HISTORICAL SOCIETY OF ROCKLAND COUNTY,** 20 Zukor Rd, New City, NY 10956-4302. Tel 845-634-9629; Fax 845-634-8690; Email info@rocklandhistory.org; Web: www.rocklandhistory.org; *Cur* Kimberly Kennedy; *Cur Educ* Christopher Kenney; *Publications* Marjorie Bauer; *Exec Dir* Sarah E Henrich; *CEO* Erin L Martin; *VPres* Lawrence Codispot
Open Tues - Fri 9:30 AM - 5 PM, Sat & Sun 1 - 5 PM; Admis adults $5, children $3; Estab 1965 to preserve & interpret history of Rockland County; Average Annual Attendance: 15,000; Mem: 2000; dues $30
Income: $250,000 (financed by endowment, mem & state appropriation)
Special Subjects: Archaeology, Historical Material
Collections: Archaeological Collection, Educational Materials Collection/ Reproductions, General Collections, Historical Structures, Special Archival Collections
Exhibitions: Dollhouse Exhibition; Miniatures Exhibition
Publications: South of the Mountains, quarterly journal; 28 books on local history
Activities: Classes for adults & children; docent training; lects open to pub, 8 vis lectrs per yr; concerts; gallery talks; tours; competitions; History Awards Program for high school seniors; History Preservation Merit Awards; Student History Awards; individual paintings, original objects of art & artifacts lent to other mus; originate traveling exhibs in Rockland County; mus shop sells books & educational gifts

NEW PALTZ

M **HISTORIC HUGUENOT STREET,** (Huguenot Historical Society of New Paltz Galleries), 88 Huguenot Street, New Paltz, NY 12401. Tel 845-255-1660; Fax 845-255-0376; Email info@huguenotstreet.org; Web: www.huguenotstreet.org; *Executive Director* Josephine Bloodgood; *Director of Public Programming* Kara Gaffken; *Sales + Tours Manager* Kristine Gillespie
Open May 1- Oct 31; Open Daily, Closed Wednesdays, 10am - 5:30pm; Guided tours - $15/person, Seniors & Friends of Historic Huguenot Street - 10% off, Children 12 and under - free, Active Military Members and their Families - Free; School Group Tours - $8/student and chaperone (minimum of 15 students), to schedule a school group, contact Jennifer Bruntil (School Programming Coordinator) at educations@huguenotstreet.org; Private Group Tours - Available by Appointment, Contact Kristine Gillespie (Sales & Tours Manager) at kristine@huguenotstreet.org.; Estab 1894 to preserve memory & material culture of Huguenot settlers; Huguenot Street National Historic Landmark District; Maintains reference library; Average Annual Attendance: 18,000
Income: Financed by mem, endowment
Library Holdings: Book Volumes, Manuscripts, Memorabilia, Original Art Works, Original Documents, Other Holdings, Pamphlets, Photographs, Records, Reproductions
Special Subjects: Archaeology, Architecture, Carpets & Rugs, Ceramics, Coins & Medals, Costumes, Decorative Arts, Dolls, Drawings, Embroidery, Folk Art, Furniture, Glass, Historical Material, Manuscripts, Maps, Painting-American, Painting-Dutch, Period Rooms, Pewter, Photography, Porcelain, Portraits, Pottery, Restorations
Collections: American primitive paintings, early 19th century furnishings, paintings, decorative arts & documents
Exhibitions: Revolving in-house displays
Publications: genealogies & histories
Activities: Classes for adults & children, dramatic programs, docent training; lects open to pub, 3 vis lectrs per yr; concerts; tours, gallery talks, scholarships; schols offered; individual paintings are lent to institutions & galleries; mus shop sells books, magazines, original art, reproductions, prints & slides, home furnishings, bed + bath

M **STATE UNIVERSITY OF NEW YORK AT NEW PALTZ,** Samuel Dorsky Museum of Art, 1 Hawk Dr, New Paltz, NY 12561-2447. Tel 845-257-3844; Fax 845-257-3854; Email sdma@newpaltz.edu; Web: www.newpaltz.edu/museum; *Coll Mgr* Wayne Lempka; *Dir* Neil C Trager; *Preparator* Bob Wagner; *Visitor Svcs* Amy Pickering; *Educ Coordr* Judi Esmond; *Assoc Cur of Coll* Dr Jaimee Uhlenbrock; *Cur* Brian Wallace; *Interim Dir* Sara Pasti
Open Tues - Fri 11 AM - 5 PM, Sat-Sun 1 - 5 PM, cl school holidays, cl Mon during legal holidays & intersessions; No admis fee; 2001; With an exhib schedule of 10 exhibitions per year, the Samuel Dorsky Mus of Art provides support for the various art curricula & serves as a major cultural resource for the col & surrounding community; There are two wings comprising 6 galleries, 9,000 sq ft; Average Annual Attendance: 16,000; Mem: 100; $15 - $2,500
Income: Financed by university, grants, endowment & membership
Special Subjects: African Art, Antiquities-Byzantine, Antiquities-Egyptian, Asian Art, Calligraphy, Ceramics, Etchings & Engravings, Graphics, Islamic Art, Landscapes, Painting-American, Painting-German, Painting-Japanese, Photography, Posters, Pottery, Pre-Columbian Art, Prints, Silver, Metalwork
Collections: Artifacts, Folk Art, Asian Prints, Painting, principally 20th century America, Photographs, Posters, Pre-Columbian Art, Prints, African & New Guinea, Sculpture, Hudson Valley Art
Exhibitions: Rotating exhibits every 8 weeks
Publications: Exhibition catalogs, Robert Morris, Lesley Dill, George Bellows, Raoul Hague, Rimer Cardillo, Don Nice, Bolton Coit Brown, Judy Pfaff
Activities: Docent training; lects open to public, 8 per yr; concerts; gallery talks; competitions; tours; individual paintings & original objects of art lent to museums & galleries; lending collection contains artifacts, original prints, paintings, photographs, sculpture, folk art, textiles, drawings & posters

L **Sojourner Truth Library**, 300 Hawk Dr, New Paltz, NY 12561-2452. Tel 845-257-3719; Fax 845-257-3718; Email leec@newpaltz.edu; Web: www.lib.newpaltz.edu; *Information Access* Valerie Mittenberg; *Coll Access* Nancy Nielson; *Team Leader Bibliographic Access* Marjorie Young; *Coll Develop* Gerlinde Barley; *Dir* Chui-Chun Lee
Open Mon - Thurs 8:30 AM -11:30 PM, Fri 8:30 AM - 9 PM, Sat 10 AM - 9PM, Sun 1-11:30 PM; Circ 158,000; For lending & reference; Average Annual Attendance: 343,964
Income: Financed by state appropriation
Library Holdings: Book Volumes 476,000, CD-ROMs, Cassettes, Exhibition Catalogs, Fiche, Micro Print, Pamphlets, Periodical Subscriptions 1,029, Video Tapes
Special Subjects: Anthropology, Art Education, Art History, Drawings, Oriental Art, Painting-American, Painting-European, Painting-Japanese, Photography, Silversmithing, Theatre Arts, Watercolors
Publications: Newsletter, biannual

NEW ROCHELLE

M **COLLEGE OF NEW ROCHELLE,** Castle Gallery, 29 Castle Pl, New Rochelle, NY 10805. Tel 914-654-5423; Fax 914-654-5014; Email krhein@cnr.edu; Web: www.cnr.edu/arts/artsmain; *Dir* Katrina Rhein; *Mgr* Michelle Jammes
Open Tues & Thurs-Fri 10AM-5PM, Wed 10AM-8PM, Sat-Sun noon-4PM; No admis fee; Estab 1979 as a professional art gallery to serve the col, city of New Rochelle & lower Westchester & provide exhib & interpretation of fine arts & material culture; Located in Leland Castle, a gothic revival building, listed in National Register of Historic Places; gallery is modern facility, with flexible space
Publications: Newsletter
Activities: Docent training; lects open to pub, 6 vis lectrs per yr; originate traveling exhibs

L **NEW ROCHELLE PUBLIC LIBRARY,** Art Section, One Library Plaza, New Rochelle, NY 10801. Tel 914-632-7878; Fax 914-632-0262; Web: www.nrpl.org; *Head Reference* Beth Mills; *Dir* Tom Geoffino
Open Mon, Tues & Thurs 9 AM -8 PM, Wed 10 AM - 6 PM, Fri & Sat 9 AM - 5 PM, Sun 1-5PM, July & Aug cl Sat & Sun; Estab 1894
Library Holdings: Book Volumes 8,000, Cassettes, Clipping Files, Exhibition Catalogs, Fiche, Original Art Works, Pamphlets, Photographs, Records, Reels, Slides, Video Tapes
Exhibitions: All shows, displays & exhibits are reviewed & scheduled by professional adv panel
Activities: Lect; demonstrations; lending collection contains framed prints & art slides

A **New Rochelle Art Association**, One Library Plaza, New Rochelle, NY 10801. Tel 914-632-7878; Email info@nraaonline.org; Web: www.nraaonline.org; *Pres* Jesse Sanchez
Open Mon, Tues, Thurs 9AM-8PM, Wed 10AM-6PM, Fri & Sat 9AM-5PM, Sun 1-5PM; Estab 1912 to encourage art in the area; Lumen Winter Gallery 84' x 18' space in lib lobby of New Rochelle Public Lib; Mem: 200; dues $20; monthly meeting
Income: Financed by mem
Exhibitions: Four exhibitions per yr
Activities: Classes for adults; lects open to public, 4 vis lectrs per year; competitions with awards

NEW WINDSOR

M **STORM KING ART CENTER,** 1 Museum Rd, New Windsor, NY 12553-8883. Tel 845-534-3115; Fax 845-534-4457; Email info@stormkingartcenter.org; Web: www.stormking.org; *Chief Cur* David R Collens; *Pres* John P Stern; *Dir Finance* Dwayne Jarvis; *Cur* Nora Lawrence; *Dir Develop* Rachel Coker; *Dir Edu & Pub Progs* Victoria Lichtendorf; *Dir Opers* Anthony Davidowitz
Open Apr 1 - Nov 29 10 AM - 5:30 PM Wed - Sun (hours vary), until 8 PM Summer weekends; Admis adults $15, seniors $12, col students with valid ID & students K-12 $8, children 4 & under & mems free; Estab 1960; Average Annual Attendance: 120,000; Mem: $1,000 patron, $500 sponsor, $250 donor, $100 family, $60 individual, $40 student & senior (with proper ID)
Special Subjects: Sculpture
Collections: 500 acre sculpture park with over 100 large scale 20th century sculptures, including works by Abakanowicz, Aycock, Armajani, Bourgeois, Calder, Caro, di Suvero, Goldsworthy, Grosvenor, Hepworth, Zang Huan, LeWitt,

Liberman, Maya Lin, Moore, Nevelson, Noguchi, Paik, Rickey, Serra, David Smith, Snelson, von Rydingsvard
Publications: Earth, Sky, and Sculpture, Storm King Art Center; Louise Bourgeois; Maya Lin; Mark de Suveso; Sculpture Guide
Activities: Educ dept; classes for children; lects open to pub; lects for mems only; 4 vis lectrs per yr; concerts; guided tours of sculpture park; hikes; outdoor concerts; mus shop sells books, original art & prints; cafe; bike rentals

NEW YORK

A **AESTHETIC REALISM FOUNDATION,** 141 Greene St, New York, NY 10012-3201. Tel 212-777-4490; Fax 212-777-4426; Web: www.aestheticrealism.org; *Chmn Educ* Ellen Reiss; *Exec Dir* Margot Carpenter
Open Wed & Fri 10 AM - 7 PM, Thurs 10 AM - 6 PM, Sat 10 AM - 4 PM; Estab 1973 as a nonprofit educational foundation to teach Aesthetic Realism, the philosophy founded in 1941 by the great American poet & critic Eli Siegel (1902-1978), based on his historic principle - "The world, art, & self explain each other; each is the aesthetic oneness of opposites"
Publications: The Right of Aesthetic Realism to Be Known, bi-weekly periodical
Activities: Monthly public seminars & dramatic presentations; classes in the visual arts, drama, poetry, music, educ, marriage; class for children; individual consultations in person & by telephone worldwide

M **Terrain Gallery**, 141 Greene St, New York, NY 10012. Tel 212-777-4490; Fax 212-777-4426; Web: www.terraingallery.org; *Coordr* Marcia Rackow
Open Wed - Fri Noon - 5 PM, Sat Noon - 4 PM; Estab 1955 with a basis in this principle stated by Eli Siegel: "All beauty is a making one of opposites, and the making one of opposites is what we are going after in ourselves"
Collections: Permanent collection of paintings, prints, drawings & photographs with commentary

L **Eli Siegel Collection**, 141 Greene St, New York, NY 10012-3201. Tel 212-777-4490; Fax 212-777-4426; Web: www.aestheticrealism.org; *Librn* Richita Anderson; *Librn* Leila Rosen; *Librn* Meryl Simon
Open to faculty, students & qualified researchers by appointment; Estab 1982; The Collection houses the books & manuscripts of Eli Siegel
Library Holdings: Audio Tapes, Book Volumes 25,000, Manuscripts
Special Subjects: Aesthetics, Anthropology, Art History, Film, Photography, Sculpture, Theatre Arts

L **Aesthetic Realism Foundation Library**, 141 Greene St, New York, NY 10012-3201. Tel 212-777-4490; Fax 212-777-4426; Web: www.terraingallery.org
Open to faculty, students & qualified researchers by appointment; Estab 1973
Special Subjects: Aesthetics, Anthropology, Architecture, Art Education, Art History, Photography, Theatre Arts
Collections: Published poems & essays by Eli Siegel, published & unpublished lectures by Eli Siegel

M **THE AFRICA CENTER,** (Museum for African Art), 1280 5th Ave, Ste 7H New York, NY 11129-7815. Tel 212-444--9795; Fax 212-722-0219; Email info@theafricacenter.org; Web: theafricacenter.org; *Interim C.E.O.* Dana M Reed; *Exec VPres & CFO* Phil Conte; *VPres Admin* Bridget W Foley; *Controller* Velky Valentin; *Publs Mgr* Carol Braide; *Community Outreach Liaison* Lawrence Ekechi; *Curatorial Fellow* Evelyn Owen
Currently under construction (see website for details); Admis varies with exhib (see website for details); Estab 1984; multidisciplinary institution providing a gateway for engagement with contemporary Africa; Admin offices; Mem: 125; dues vary
Library Holdings: Book Volumes
Special Subjects: African Art
Exhibitions: Rotating exhibitions; Hair in African Art and Culture
Publications: Over 40 scholarly catalogues (see website for a full list of publs)

ALLIED ARTISTS OF AMERICA, INC
For further information, see National and Regional Organizations

AMERICAN ACADEMY OF ARTS & LETTERS
For further information, see National and Regional Organizations

AMERICAN ARTISTS PROFESSIONAL LEAGUE, INC
For further information, see National and Regional Organizations

THE AMERICAN FEDERATION OF ARTS
For further information, see National and Regional Organizations

M **AMERICAN FOLK ART MUSEUM,** 2 Lincoln Sq, New York, NY 10023. Tel 212-595-9533; Email info@folkartmuseum.org; Web: www.folkartmuseum.org; *Exec Dir* Dr Anne-Imelda Radice; *Deputy Dir Admin & CFO* Kathleen Hayes; *Deputy Dir Curatorial Affairs, Chief Cur & Dir Exhibs* Stacy C Hollander; *Cur, Art of the Self-Taught & Art Brut* Dr Valerie Rousseau; *Registrar* Judy Steinberg; *Chmn* Laura Parsons; *Pres* Edward V Blanchard Jr
Open Tues - Thurs 11:30 AM - 7 PM, Fri 12 PM - 7:30 PM, Sat 11:30 AM - 7 PM, Sun 12 PM - 6 PM; No admis fee; Estab 1961 for the collection & exhibition of American folk art in all media, including painting, sculpture, textiles & painted & decorated furniture; Single floor, cruciform shape gallery approx 3,000 sq ft; Average Annual Attendance: 165,000; Mem: 5,000; dues $70 & up
Income: Financed by mem, state appropriation & personal donations
Special Subjects: Afro-American Art, American Indian Art, Carpets & Rugs, Ceramics, Crafts, Decorative Arts, Drawings, Embroidery, Folk Art, Furniture, Landscapes, Metalwork, Painting-American, Pewter, Portraits, Scrimshaw, Textiles, Pottery, Sculpture
Collections: American folk paintings & watercolors, folk sculpture including shop & carousel figures, shiphead figures, decoys, weathervanes, whirligigs, wood carvings & chalkware, painted & decorated furniture, tradesmen's signs, textiles including quilts, coverlets, stenciled fabrics, hooked rugs & samplers, works from 18th, 19th & 20th centuries, paintings, drawings
Activities: Educ dept; classes for adults & children; docent training; lects open to pub; gallery talks; tours; Visionary Award; free music Friday concerts; outreach programs; book traveling exhibs; originate traveling exhibs to qualifying art & educational institutions; mus shop sells books, reproductions & prints

L **Shirley K. Schlafer Library**, 2 Lincoln Sq, New York, NY 10023. Tel 212-265-1040; Fax 212-265-2350; Email library@folkartmuseum.org; Web: www.folkartmuseum.org; *Cur Spec Projects* Lee Kogn; *Dir* Maria Conelli
Open by appointment Wed - Thurs, 10 AM - 12:30 PM & 1:30 PM - 4 PM; No admis fee; Estab 1961; Library open to pub by appointment Wed & Thurs 10 AM - 12:30 PM & 1:30 PM - 4 PM
Library Holdings: Auction Catalogs 2000, Audio Tapes 200, Book Volumes 10,000, Clipping Files, Exhibition Catalogs, Manuscripts, Memorabilia, Pamphlets, Periodical Subscriptions 200, Photographs, Reproductions, Slides, Video Tapes 250
Collections: Archives and manuscripts of American self-taught artist Henry Darger, Archives of Historical Society of Early American Decoration, Library & archives of quilt scholar Cuesta Benberry
Activities: Classes for adults & children; lects; concerts; gallery talks; talks; book traveling exhib annually; originates traveling exhibs; mus shop sells books & mus-related items

AMERICAN INSTITUTE OF GRAPHIC ARTS
For further information, see National and Regional Organizations

A **AMERICAN JEWISH HISTORICAL SOCIETY,** The Center for Jewish History, 15 W 16th St, New York, NY 10011-6301. Tel 212-294-6160; Fax 212-294-6161; Email publicservices@ajhs.org; Web: www.ajhs.org; *Exec Dir* Rachel Lithgow; *Dir Library & Archives* Susan Malbin; *Dir Develop* Jacqueline Leitzes; *Sr Archivist* Tanya Elder; *Asst Processing Archivist* Rachel Lintz
Open Mon & Wed 9:30 AM - 8 PM, Tues & Thurs 9:30 AM - 5 PM, Fri 9:30 AM - 4 PM, Sun 11 AM - 5 PM; Admis varies, call for specific rates; Estab 1892 to collect, preserve, catalog & disseminate information relating to the American Jewish experience; Average Annual Attendance: 5,000; Mem: 3,000; dues $50; annual meeting in May
Income: $500,000 (financed by endowment, mem, Jewish Federation allocations, grants & donations)
Special Subjects: Manuscripts, Portraits
Exhibitions: Gustatory Delights in the New World; German Jews in America; Emma Lazarus, Joseph Pulitzer & The Statue of Liberty; Yiddish Theatre in America; American Jewish Colonial Portraits; Sephardim in America; Machal: American Veterans of Israel's War of Independence
Publications: American Jewish History, quarterly; Heritage; Local Jewish Historical Society News; books; newsletters
Activities: Lects open to public, 10 vis lectrs per yr; tours; individual paintings & original objects of art lent to museums & historical societies; lending collection contains motion pictures, paintings, books, original art works, original prints & photographs

L **Lee M Friedman Memorial Library**, 101 Newbury St, Boston, MA 02116-3062. Tel 617-226-1245; Fax 617-226-1248; Email info@ajhs.org; *Dir* Judy Garner
Open Mon - Thurs 9:30 AM - 4:30 PM, Fri researcher hours only; No admis fee; Estab 1892 to collect, preserve & catalog material relating to Colonial American Jewish history; Open for reference
Income: $514,000 (financed by endowment, mem, contributions, grants, allocations from Jewish welfare funds)
Library Holdings: Book Volumes 95,000, Cassettes, Manuscripts, Memorabilia, Motion Pictures, Other Holdings Archives, Pamphlets, Periodical Subscriptions 120, Photographs, Prints, Records, Slides
Collections: Stephen S Wise Manuscripts Collection, Archives of Major Jewish Organizations
Exhibitions: Colonial American Jewry; 19th Century Jewish Families; On Common Ground: The Boston Jewish Experience, 1649-1980; Statue of Liberty; German American Jewry; Moses Michael Hays & Post- Revolutionary Boston
Publications: American Jewish History, quarterly; Heritage, bi-annually
Activities: Lects open to public, 2-3 vis lectrs per yr; tours; originate traveling exhibs to libraries, museum societies, synagogues

AMERICAN NUMISMATIC SOCIETY
For further information, see National and Regional Organizations

L **AMERICAN UNIVERSITY,** Jack I & Dorothy G Bender Library & Learning Resources Center, 520 W 43rd St, Apt 21E New York, NY 10036-4352. Tel 202-885-3232; Fax 202-885-3226; Email librarymail@american.edu; Web: www.library.american.edu; *University Librn* William A Mayer; *Assoc University Librn* Diana Vogelsong; *Acting Asst University Librn* Janice Flug; *Coll Develop Librn* Martin Shapiro; *Reference Team Leader* Melissa Becher; *Media Librn* Chris Lewis; *Archives & Spec Coll* Susan McElrath
Open 24 hrs starting 9 AM Sun - 9 PM Fri, Sat 9 AM - 9 PM during school yr, see website for hrs during univ holidays; Estab 1893; Circ 315,041 for all disciplines; Mem: Friends of American University Libr, 800 members qualified by donation
Library Holdings: Audio Tapes, Book Volumes 1,112,500, CD-ROMs, Cassettes, Compact Disks, DVDs, Fiche, Filmstrips, Manuscripts, Maps, Memorabilia, Motion Pictures, Original Documents, Other Holdings playbills, Periodical Subscriptions 36,353 electronic, 1,960 print, Photographs, Records, Reels, Video Tapes
Special Subjects: Advertising Design, Aesthetics, Anthropology, Archaeology, Art History, Commercial Art, Costume Design & Constr, Ethnology, Film, Graphic Arts, Graphic Design, Historical Material, History of Art & Archaeology, Judaica, Latin American Art, Mixed Media, Painting-American, Painting-British, Painting-European, Painting-French, Painting-German, Painting-Italian, Painting-Russian, Painting-Spanish, Photography, Pre-Columbian Art, Printmaking, Prints, Sculpture, Stage Design, Theatre Arts, Video, Watercolors, Conceptual Art
Collections: General academic collection supporting all art fields, archives of the Frederick Law Olmsted Documentary editing project, Charles Nelson Spinks Collection of Japanese prints, Watkins Collection of Artist's Books
Activities: Lect open to pub

AMERICAN WATERCOLOR SOCIETY
For further information, see National and Regional Organizations

A **THE AMERICAN-SCANDINAVIAN FOUNDATION,** Scandinavia House: The Nordic Center in America, 58 Park Ave, New York, NY 10016-3007. Tel 212-779-3587; Fax 212-686-1157; Email info@amscan.org; Web: www.scandinaviahouse.org; *Pres & CEO* Edward Gallagher; *Sr Advisor* Lynn

Carter; *Communs & Outreach Asst* Jennifer Hutzel; *Coordr Exhibs & Public Progs* Emily Stoddart
Open Tues - Sat 12 - 6 PM (Wed until 7 PM); Admis varies by exhib; Foundation estab 1910 to promote cultural exchange Scandinavia House opened in 2000 presents best of Nordic culture incl art & design exhibs from Denmark, Finland, Iceland, Norway & Sweden; Exhibs of Scandinavian art & design; Average Annual Attendance: 110,000; Mem: 7,000; dues $60
Library Holdings: Book Volumes, Exhibition Catalogs, Manuscripts, Pamphlets, Periodical Subscriptions
Special Subjects: Architecture, Crafts, Decorative Arts, Drawings, Folk Art, Furniture, Glass, Historical Material, Landscapes, Maps, Metalwork, Painting-Scandinavian, Photography, Prints, Sculpture, Silver, Textiles
Exhibitions: Scandinavian painting, sculpture, design and crafts; artwork is selected for exhibition by a comt of professional art adv
Publications: Scandinavian Review, 3 times a year; SCAN, newsletter 4 times a year
Activities: Classes for adults & children; language classes in conjunction with NYU School of Continuing & Professional Studies; lect open to public; lects for mems only; 5 vis lectrs per yr; concerts; gallery talks; tours; ASF Cultural Award; schols & fels offered; sales shop sells books, design objects, tableware, jewelry, toys, watches, music, Nordic foods & holiday items

AMERICANS FOR THE ARTS
For further information, see National and Regional Organizations

M **AMERICAS SOCIETY ART GALLERY,** 680 Park Ave, New York, NY 10021-5072. Tel 212-249-8950; Fax 212-249-5668; Email grangel@as-coa.org; Web: www.americas-society.org; Telex 42-9169; *Dir Visual Arts* Gabriela Rangel; *Coordr Exhibs & Pub Progs* Veronica Flom; *Assoc Cur Visual Arts* Susanna Temkin
Open Wed - Sat noon - 6 PM; No admis fee; Estab 1967 to broaden understanding & appreciation in the United States of the art & cultural heritage of other countries in the Western Hemisphere; One large gallery with 3-4 exhibitions a year of Latin American, Caribbean & Canadian art; Average Annual Attendance: 25,000; Mem: 900; dues $75
Income: $120,500
Library Holdings: Exhibition Catalogs
Special Subjects: Furniture, Historical Material, Latin American Art, Mexican Art, Painting-Canadian, Photography, Pre-Columbian Art, Prints, Sculpture, Silver, Textiles, Decorative Arts
Publications: Exhibition catalogs
Activities: Classes for adults & children in conjunction with exhibitions; docent training; lects open to public, 12 vis lectrs per yr; gallery talks; concerts; tours; book traveling exhibs 1-2 per yr; originate traveling exhibs & circulate to other galleries within; exhibition catalogues available for purchase at front desk

A **ANDY WARHOL FOUNDATION FOR THE VISUAL ARTS,** 65 Bleecker St, Fl 7 New York, NY 10012-2420. Tel 212-387-7555; Fax 212-387-7560; Email info@warholfoundation.org; Web: www.warholfoundation.org; *Pres* Joel Wachs; *VP & Liaison to Andy Warhol Mus* Donald Warhola; *CFO & Treas* KC Maurer; *Cur Drawings & Photography* Sally King-Nero
Estab 1987 for the advancement of the visual arts
Activities: Grants & fels offered

M **ANTHOLOGY FILM ARCHIVES,** 32 Second Ave, New York, NY 10003. Tel 212-505-5181; Fax 212-477-2714; Email robert@anthologyfilmarchives.org; Web: www.anthologyfilmarchives.org; *Artistic Dir* Jonas Mekas; *Dir* John Mhiripiri; *Publs & Mem* Wendy Dorsett; *Develop Assoc & Mem* Hannah Greenberg; *Dir Emeritus Colls & Spec Projs* Robert A Haller
Open for film screenings Mon - Fri evenings, Sat & Sun afternoon - evenings; check calendar online for time; Admis adults $11, seniors & students $9, spec rates for groups, children under 13 $7, mem free; Estab 1970; mus of the cinema with progs in film & video preservation; Average Annual Attendance: 50,000; Mem: dues Preservation Donor $1000, Donor $300, Dual Adult $125, Individual Adult $70, Senior or Student $50
Library Holdings: Book Volumes 8000, Clipping Files 12,000, Other Holdings, Periodical Subscriptions 42,000, Photographs 1200, Prints
Special Subjects: Photography
Collections: Library coll of over 12,000 films & tapes on avant-garde, classic & documentary cinema, mail-order publ svc, approx 1 million books, photos, documents in a closed-stack facility that services scores of scholars every yr
Publications: quarterly film exhibition schedule; Annual Film Preservation Honors Dinner Journal; catalogs; books
Activities: Research projs on Jim Davis, Storm DeHirsch, Marie Menken; films; Film Preservation Honors Dinner

A **ARCHITECTURAL LEAGUE OF NEW YORK,** 457 Madison Ave, New York, NY 10022-6843; 594 Broadway, Ste 3607 New York, NY 10012-3233. Tel 212-753-1722; Fax 212-486-9173; Email info@archleague.org; Web: www.archleague.org; *Exec Dir* Rosalie Genevro; *Pres* Billie Tsien
Open Mon - Fri 9 AM - 5 PM; Admis seminars $10-$5, mems free; Estab 1881 to promote art & architecture; serves as a forum for new & experimental ideas in the arts; Average Annual Attendance: 7500; Mem: 1,600; dues over 35 years $100, under 35 years $60, students $35; ann meeting in June
Exhibitions: Annual Juried Exhibition of Young Architects Competition; New New York; Toward the Sentient City
Publications: Exhibition catalogs; posters
Activities: Lect; slide lect; gallery talks; tours; competitions; awards for young architects, emerging voices, Deborah J. Norden Fund; urbanomnibus.net; schols offered

ART DEALERS ASSOCIATION OF AMERICA, INC
For further information, see National and Regional Organizations

ART DIRECTORS CLUB
For further information, see National and Regional Organizations

A **ART INFORMATION CENTER, INC,** 100 Cabrini Blvd Apt 31, New York, NY 10033-3413. Tel 212-966-3443; *Pres & Dir* Dan Concholar
Open 10 AM - 6 PM or by appointment; No admis fee; Organized 1959, inc 1963, presently a consulting service for artists; The Center helps to channel the many artists in New York, & those coming to New York, seeking New York outlets for their work. Advise artist seeking galleries in New York City
Income: $15,000 (financed by donations & small grants)

A **ART STUDENTS LEAGUE OF NEW YORK,** 215 W 57th St, New York, NY 10019-2193. Tel 212-247-4510; Fax 212-541-7024; Email info@artstudentsleague.org; Web: www.theartstudentsleague.org; *Pres* Ellen Taylor; *Cur* Jillian Russo; *Archivist* Stephanie Cassidy
Open Mon - Fri 9 AM - 8:30 PM, Sat 9 AM - 4 PM; No admis fee; Estab 1875 to maintain art school & mem activities; Maintains an art gallery open to pub for league exhibits; Average Annual Attendance: 8,000 - 9,000; Mem: 6,000; dues $25; annual meeting in Dec; 3 months full-time study required for mem
Income: Financed by tuitions & investments
Library Holdings: Book Volumes, Clipping Files, Periodical Subscriptions
Collections: Permanent collection of paintings, sculpture & works on paper by former league students & instructors
Exhibitions: Exhibitions by members, students & instructors
Publications: Linea, quarterly newsletter
Activities: Classes for adults & children; lect open to public, 3 vis lectrs per year; sponsoring of competitions; McDowell Travel Grant, Edwards-Gonzalez Travel Grant & Neosa Cohen award; scholarships offered; individual paintings & original objects of art lent to museums

L **Library,** 215 W 57th St, New York, NY 10019. Tel 212-247-4510; Fax 212-541-7024; Email stephanie@artstudentsleague.org
Reference library for students & members & archive of instructors, prominent students & members, past & current
Income: Financed by tuition & endowments
Library Holdings: Auction Catalogs, Audio Tapes, Book Volumes 6,000, Cassettes, Clipping Files, Exhibition Catalogs, Filmstrips, Manuscripts, Pamphlets, Photographs, Reproductions, Slides, Video Tapes
Collections: Paintings, Sculpture & works on paper by instructors & students, past & current
Exhibitions: Exhibitions by instructors & students
Publications: Linea, newsletter of the Art Students League of New York, 3-4 issues per yr
Activities: Classes for adults & children; gallery talks; scholarships offered; sales shop sells art supplies

A **ARTISTS SPACE,** 55 Walker St, New York, NY 10013. Tel 212-226-3970; Fax 212-226-7036; Email info@artistsspace.org; Web: artistsspace.org; *Exec Dir & Chief Cur* Jay Sanders; *Cur* Jamie Stevens
Open Wed - Sun noon - 6 PM; Admis $5 donation; Estab 1972; Artists Space has successfully contributed to changing the institutional & economic landscape for contemporary art in NYC lending support to emerging ideas & emerging artists alike
Activities: Classes for children; presents 4-5 exhibs per yr; pub progs (screenings, talks, etc); sales shop sells books, prints, limited edition artworks

M **Artists Space Gallery,** 55 Walker St, New York, NY 10013. Tel 212-226-3970; Fax 212-226-7036; Email info@artistspace.org; Web: www.artistsspace.org; *Exec Dir & Chief Cur* Jay Sanders
Open Wed - Sun noon - 6 PM; No admis fee for exhibitions, films & events $4; Estab 1973 to assist emerging & unaffiliated artists; Five exhibition rooms & hall gallery; Average Annual Attendance: 20,000
Income: Financed by National Endowment for the Arts, New York State Council, corporate & foundation funds & private contributions
Exhibitions: Five exhibitions of local emerging artists
Activities: Gallery talks by appointment; financial aid to artists for public presentation; book traveling exhibs; originate traveling exhibs; junior mus

L **Irving Sandler Artists File,** 55 Walker St, New York, NY 10013. Web: local-artists.org; *Artists File Coordr* Letha Wilson; *Dir* Barbara Hunt
Open Fri - Sat 10 AM - 6 PM; Slide file of over 2,500 New York state artists; Available to dealers, critics, cur & artists for reference only

A **ARTISTS TALK ON ART (ATOA),** PO Box 1384, Old Chelsea Station New York, NY 10113. Tel 212-475-3424; Email mail@atoa.org; Web: www.atoa.org; *Chmn & Treas* Doug Sheer; *Pres* Lynne Mayocole; *IT Dir* Flash Light
Admis gen $8, students & seniors $5; Estab 1974 to promote dialogue in the arts; Average Annual Attendance: 5,000; Mem: dues season pass $60
Income: $30,000 (financed by mem, state appropriation, admis, contributions & corporate funding)
Library Holdings: Audio Tapes, CD-ROMs, Cassettes, DVDs, Manuscripts, Photographs, Prints, Video Tapes
Publications: Artists Talk on Art Calendar, semi-annually
Activities: Lects open to pub, 6-8 vis lectrs per season; gallery talks; competitions with awards; annual: Curator's Choice contest; book traveling exhibs 1-3 per yr; originate traveling exhibs 1-3 per yr

ARTISTS' FELLOWSHIP, INC
For further information, see National and Regional Organizations

A **ARTS, CRAFT & THEATER SAFETY,** 181 Thompson St #23, New York, NY 10012. Tel 212-777-0062; Email actsnyc@cs.com; Web: www.artscraftstheatersafety.org; *Pres* Monona Rossol
Estab 1986 to provide health & safety services to artists & theatrical professionals. ACTS provides lectures; US & Canadian reg compliance training & inspections; technical assist for bldg planning, renovations & ventilation projects; research & editing of safety publications; books & articles; & newsletter; Not open to off-street traffic, but 6 days/wk e-mails, letters & phone calls are answered or returned. ACTS answers an average of 35 inquiries/day; Mem: Not a membership organization
Income: Nonprofit
Publications: Newsletter
Activities: Outreach activities; safety services on artists procedures, ventilation, OSHA compliance

A **ARTSCONNECTION INC,** 520 8th Ave, Ste 321 New York, NY 10018. Tel 212-302-7433; Fax 212-302-1132; Email coveneyc@artsconnectin.org; Web: www.artsconnection.org; *Exec Dir* Steve Tennen; *Deputy Dir Education* Carol Morgan; *Deputy Dir Fin* Tavia Huggins; *Dir Progs* Rachel Watts; *Communs Mgr* Rina Ortega
Estab 1979 to make the arts an essential part of educ & connect artists with children, families & schools in creative partnerships for teaching & learning
Activities: Educ progs; activities & after-school classes for children; family events; High 5 teen ticket discounts to arts performances, mus & events; teacher & artist professional devel; in-school artist res; school outreach publications; artist grants available

M **ASIA SOCIETY MUSEUM,** 725 Park Ave, New York, NY 10021-5088. Tel 212-288-6400; Fax 212-517-8315; Email info@asiasociety.org; Web: www.asiasociety.org; Cable ASIAHOUSE NEW YORK; *Museum Dir* Boon Hui Tan; *Museum Deputy Director* Marion Kocot; *John H. Foster Senior Curator for Traditional Asian Art* Adriana Proser; *Senior Curator of Modern and Contemporary Art* Michelle Yun
Open Tues - Sun 11 AM - 6 PM, Fri 11 AM - 9 PM; cl Mon & major holidays. Summer hours change; Admis fee $12, seniors $10, students w/id $7, mems & children under 16 free; Estab 1956 as a nonprofit organization to further greater understanding & mutual appreciation between the US & peoples of Asia.; In 1981 the Asia Society came into possession of its permanent collection, the Mr & Mrs John D Rockefeller 3D Collection of Asian Art, which is shown in conjunction with temporary exhibitions of traditional & contemporary Asian art; Average Annual Attendance: 95,000; Mem: dues $75 & up;
Income: Financed by endowment, mem, & grants from foundation, individual, federal & state government
Special Subjects: Asian Art
Collections: The Asia Society Museum Collection includes the masterpiece quality Mr & Mrs John D Rockefeller 3rd Collection of contemporary Asian Art and Asian American art., loans obtained from the US & foreign colls for special exhibs
Exhibitions: Rotating exhibits
Publications: Archives of Asian Art, annually
Activities: Lect by guest specialists in connection with each exhibition & recorded lect by the gallery educ staff available to visitors; concerts; gallery talks; tours; loan exhibitions originated; traveling exhibitions; sales shop sells books, magazines, prints & slides

A **ASIAN AMERICAN ARTS CENTRE,** 111 Norfolk St, Fl 1 New York, NY 10002. Tel 212-233-2154; Email aaacinfo@artspiral.org; Web: www.artspiral.org; *Exec Dir* Robert Lee; *Prog & Web Mgr* Adliana Bahrin; *Archivist & Develop Assoc* Talice Lee
Open Mon - Fri 12:30 - 6:30 PM; No admis fee; Estab 1974 to promote the cultural presence of Asian-American contemporary art in the US; Circ Packet historical materials available; Maintains research library & artist archive; Average Annual Attendance: 12,000
Income: Public & private grants, sponsorships, donations
Library Holdings: Audio Tapes, Book Volumes, Cards, Cassettes, Exhibition Catalogs, Kodachrome Transparencies, Memorabilia, Original Art Works, Original Documents, Pamphlets, Photographs, Slides, Video Tapes
Special Subjects: Folk Art, Asian Art
Collections: Permanent collection of works commemorating Tiananmen Square, China June 4, collection of works by contemporary Asian-American artists (400+), folk arts collection (predominantly Chinese - 150+), Asian American Art, Asian American artist archive, 1,700+ items, Digital Artist Archive, at www. artasiamerica.org
Publications: Out of the Archive catalog
Activities: Lects open to pub, 5 vis lectrs per yr; competitions with awards; originate traveling exhibs

ASSOCIATION OF ART MUSEUM DIRECTORS
For further information, see National and Regional Organizations

M **ATLANTIC GALLERY,** 548 W 28th St, Ste 540 New York, NY 10001. Tel 212-219-3183; Email info@atlanticgallery.org; Web: atlanticgallery.org
Open Tues - Sat noon - 6 PM, Thurs until 8 PM; No admis fee; Estab 1971 as an artist-run gallery presenting the work of member & guest artists in solo exhibitions & group shows; 1 large gallery; Average Annual Attendance: 10,000; Mem: Upon request
Income: Financed by mem & artists of the gallery
Exhibitions: Solo and group show every three weeks
Publications: Periodic flyers
Activities: Lect open to public; life-drawing sessions; concerts; gallery talks; tours; poetry readings; individual paintings & original objects of art lent; sales shop sells original art

M **AUSTRIAN CULTURAL FORUM GALLERY,** 11 E 52nd St, New York, NY 10022-5301. Tel 212-319-5300; Fax 212-644-8660; Email new-york-kf@bmeia.gv.at; Web: www.acfny.org; Cable AUSTRO-CULT; Telex 17-7142; *Dir* Christine Moser; *Deputy Dir* Christian-Joseph Ebner; *Head Admin* Michaela Ebner
Open daily 10 AM - 6 PM; No admis fee; Estab 1962 for presentation of Austrian Art & culture in America; 4 - 10 exhibs per yr, focus on contemporary Austrian art & architecture
Publications: Austria Kultur, bimonthly
Activities: Lect open to public; gallery talks

M **BARUCH COLLEGE OF THE CITY UNIVERSITY OF NEW YORK,** Sidney Mishkin Gallery, 135 E 22nd St, Box D-0100 New York, NY 10010-5505. Tel 646-660-6652; Web: www.baruch.cuny.edu/mishkin; *Dir* Dr Sandra Kraskin, PhD
Open Mon - Fri Noon - 7 PM; No admis fee; Estab 1983; 2,400 sq ft; Average Annual Attendance: 10,000
Income: Financed by the Baruch College Fund & federal, state & private grants
Special Subjects: Afro-American Art, Drawings, Etchings & Engravings, Hispanic Art, Painting-American, Photography, Prints, Prints, Sculpture, Watercolors, Woodcuts
Collections: American & European drawings, paintings, photographs, prints & sculptures
Publications: Exhibition catalogues
Activities: Lect open to public, 3-7 vis lectrs per year; gallery talks; tours; book traveling exhibitions 1-2 per year

M **BLUE MOUNTAIN GALLERY,** 530 W 25th St 4th Fl, New York, NY 10001-5516. Tel 646-486-4730; Email bluemountaingallery@verizon.net; Web: www.bluemountaingallery.org; *Treas* Gulgun Aliriza; *Dir* Marcia Clark; *Secy* Janet Sawyer
Open Tues - Sat 11 AM - 6 PM; No admis fee; Estab 1980, an artist supported co-op gallery exhibiting works of gallery members & guests; 30 ft x 30 ft, white walls, wood floors; Mem: 32; members must be artists willing to exhibit & sell own work & must be chosen by existing members; dues $1800; 8 meetings a yr
Income: Financed through membership
Exhibitions: Change Monthly
Publications: Evolution of a Gallery, 1968-2010
Activities: Lect open to public; 5-8 vis lectrs per yr; concerts; gallery talks; sponsoring competitions, juried show; organize traveling exhibs to universities

A **CARIBBEAN CULTURAL CENTER AFRICAN DIASPORA INSTITUTE,** Cultural Arts Organization & Resource Center, 1825 Park Ave Rm 602, New York, NY 10035-1636. Tel 212-307-7420; Fax 212-315-1086; Email info@cccadi.org; Web: www.cccadi.org; *Communs & Social Media Coordr* Janet L Sackey; *Deputy Dir* Melody Capote; *Founder & Bd Pres* Dr Marta Moreno Vega; *Dir Educ* Dan'etta Jimenez
Open Mon - Fri 11 AM - 6 PM; Admis $2; Estab 1976; Resource center for reference only; Average Annual Attendance: 100,000; Mem: dues $25
Income: Financed by federal, state & city appropriations, mem, foundation & corporate support
Publications: Caribe Magazine, irregular; occasional papers
Activities: Adult & children classes; concerts; conferences; curriculum development; cultural arts progs; lects open to pub, 5-10 vis lectrs per yr; original objects of art lent to nonprofit organizations, universities & colleges; originate traveling exhibs; retail store sells books, reproductions, artifacts from the Caribbean, Latin America & Africa

A **CATHARINE LORILLARD WOLFE ART CLUB, INC,** 802 Broadway, New York, NY 10003-4804. Email info@clwac.org; Web: www.clwac.org; *Pres* Jeanette Dick; *VPres Historian* Sharon Florin; *VPres Painting* Flo Kemp; *VPres Sculpture* Priscilla Heep-Coll; *VPres Catalog* Carlina Valenti; *Treas* Patt Baldino; *Recording Secy* Jeanette Koumijian; *Corresp Secy* Kate Faust
Estab 1896, incorporated in as a nonprofit club to further fine, representational American Art; A club of professional women painters, graphic artists & sculptors; Mem: 325; dues $45 assoc mem $25; monthly meetings; acceptance in 3 annual exhibs in a 10-year period
Income: Financed by mem
Exhibitions: Members Exhibition (spring); Open Annual Exhibition (fall); Occasional mems & assoc shows
Activities: Lects for mems only, 2 vis lectrs per yr; Metropolitan Museum Benefit, annually; lect; demonstration progs; 8 awards approx $10,000 in 2-3 shows per yr

M **CATHEDRAL OF SAINT JOHN THE DIVINE,** 1047 Amsterdam Ave, New York, NY 10025-1798. Tel 212-316-7540, 212-932-7347 (Tours); Email info@stjohndivine.org; Web: www.stjohndivine.org; *Interim Dean* Rev Clifton Daniel III
Open Mon - Sun 7:30 AM - 6 PM; No individual admis fee, donations accepted; groups $1 per person; Estab 1974; The museum building was erected in the 1820's & forms part of the complex of the Cathedral of Saint John the Divine; Average Annual Attendance: 500,000
Income: Financed by federal government appropriations & Cathedral assistance
Special Subjects: Religious Art
Collections: Old Master Paintings, decorative arts, sculptures, silver, tapestries, vestments
Exhibitions: Monthly Photography Exhibitions; annual exhibitions planned to spotlight specific areas of the Cathedral's permanent art collection
Activities: Lect open to public, 10 vis lectrs per year; concerts; gallery talks; tours

L **Library,** 1047 Amsterdam Ave, New York, NY 10025. Tel 212-316-7495; *Librn* Madeleine L'Engle
No admis fee; For reference only
Income: $3,000

M **CENTER FOR BOOK ARTS,** 28 W 27th St 3rd Fl, New York, NY 10001-0000. Tel 212-481-0295; Fax 866-708-8994; Email education@centerforbookarts.org; Web: www.centerforbookarts.org; *Exec Dir & Cur* Alexander Campos; *Educ & Studio Mgr* Anne Muntges; *Outreach Coord* Emilie Ahern; *Develop & Mem* Paul Romaine; *Colls Mgr* Theo Roth
Open Mon - Fri 11 AM - 6 PM, Sat 10 AM - 5 PM, cl Sun; No admis fee; Estab 1974, dedicated to contemporary bookmaking; 1 large gallery; Average Annual Attendance: 21,000; Mem: 800; dues $50 to $5,000
Income: Financed by earned and re-earned income
Library Holdings: Exhibition Catalogs, Original Art Works, Prints
Special Subjects: Etchings & Engravings, Prints
Collections: Book Arts Collection, Reference Library
Exhibitions: Annual Chapbook Poetry Competition, 3-4 changing exhibitions annually; Featured Artist Projects, 6 annually
Publications: Exhibition catalogues
Activities: Educ prog; classes for adults & children; lects open to pub, 15 vis lectrs per yr; gallery talks; tours; competitions with prizes; book travelling exhibs, 2 per yr; sales shop sells books, prints & exhib catalogs

A **CHILDREN'S ART CARNIVAL,** 62 Hamilton Terrace, New York, NY 10031. Tel 212-234-4093; Fax 212-234-4011; *Exec Dir* Pamela Babb; *Prog Dir* Misha McGlown
Open Mon - Thurs 9:30 AM - 6 PM, Sat 10 AM - 4 PM; No admis fee; Estab 1969 as a center for children; Maintains reference library; Average Annual Attendance: 10,000

Activities: Classes for adults & children; awards; scholarships offered; book traveling exhibitions 3 per year

M **CHILDREN'S MUSEUM OF MANHATTAN,** 212 W 83rd St, The Tisch Bldg New York, NY 10024-4901. Tel 212-721-1223; Fax 212-721-1127; Email info@cmom.org; Web: www.cmom.org; *Exec Dir* Andrew Ackerman; *Deputy Dir Educ & Guest Svcs* Leslie Bushara; *Dir Exhibits & Bldg Opers* Thomas G Quaranta; *Deputy Dir Educ & Guest Servs* Leslie Bushara; *Art Dir* Kristin Lilley; *Dir Public Progs* David Rios; *Dir Strategic Communs* Deirdre Lurie
Open Sun - Fri 10 AM - 5 PM, Sat 10 AM - 7 PM; Admis adults $14, seniors 65 & over $11; children under 1 yr & members no admis fee; Estab 1973 as a children's museum & art center featuring participatory art, science & nature exhibits; 38,000 sq ft gallery; Average Annual Attendance: 350,000; Mem: 4,000; dues $225-$325, corp mem $5,000 - $100,000
Income: $4,100,000 (financed by city, state, federal, corporate & foundation support, admis, mem, donations, program fees, tuition & sales shop)
Special Subjects: Asian Art, Anthropology, Cartoons, Collages, Costumes, Crafts, Drawings, Graphics, Historical Material, Islamic Art, Juvenile Art, Mosaics
Collections: Dynamic H2O, America to Zanzibar: Muslim Cultures Near & Far
Publications: Monthly calendars; program brochures
Activities: Educ dept with parent/child workshops, classes for children, toddler progs, summer day camp, outreach, performing artists, volunteer/intern training, teacher training prog; classes for families, guided group visits; lectures open to the public; concerts; gallery talks; tours; book out 2-4 exhibitions annually; originates traveling exhibs to museums and institutions across the US; mus sales shop sells books, games, prints, toys & puzzles

M **CHINA INSTITUTE IN AMERICA,** China Institute Gallery, 100 Washington St, New York, NY 10065-1707. Tel 212-744-8181; Fax 212-628-4159; Web: www.chinainstitute.org; *Dir Galleries* Willow Weilan Hai; *Pres* James Heimowitz; *Office Mgr* Ingrid Mei; *Gallery Coordr* Xenna Goh; *Asst Dir* Insher Pan
Open Mon - Fri 10 AM - 5 PM, Thurs 10 AM - 8 PM, Sat 11 AM - 5 PM, cl Sun & holidays; Admis adult $10, students & seniors $5, children under 16 free; Estab 1966 to promote a knowledge of Chinese culture & art; Two-room gallery; Average Annual Attendance: 12,000; Mem: 950; dues gen $65-$75, dual family $125, family $185
Publications: Exhibition catalogs
Activities: Classes for adults & children; docent training; hands on workshops; lects open to public; concerts; gallery talks; tours; one traveling exhib per yr; originate traveling exhibs; sales shop sells books

A **CHINESE-AMERICAN ARTS COUNCIL,** 456 Broadway, Fl 3 New York, NY 10013. Tel 212-431-9740; Fax 212-431-9789; Email info@caacarts.org; Web: www.caacarts.org; *Exec Dir* Alan Chow
Open Mon - Fri 1 - 6 PM; No admis fee; Estab 1975 to provide exhibition space to Chinese-American artists; Gallery 456 opened 1989; 700 sq ft with track lighting; Average Annual Attendance: 600 - 800; Mem: 300; dues $10 - $100
Income: Financed by endowment, city & state appropriation & private funds
Collections: Slide Registry: biographies of Chinese American artists
Exhibitions: 10 - 12 exhibs annually
Activities: Classes for children; performances; concerts

L **CITY COLLEGE OF THE CITY UNIVERSITY OF NEW YORK,** Morris Raphael Cohen Library, 160 Convent Ave, New York, NY 10031-9198. Tel 212-650-7611; Fax 212-650-7604; Email reference@ccny.cuny.edu; Web: library.ccny.cuny.edu; *Reference Librn* Philip Barnett; *Chief Librn* Sarah Aponte; *Archivist* Sydney C Van Nort; *Architecture Librn* Judy Connorton; *Art/Architecture Visual Resources Librn* Ching-Jung Chen; *Chief of User Servs* Michael Crowley
Open Mon - Fri 7 AM - 12 AM, Sat 9 AM - 6 PM, Sun noon - 5 PM (see website for alternate hours); No admis fee; Estab 1847 to support the educ at the City College; Atrium ca 7,000 sf; archives gallery 1300 sf; Average Annual Attendance: 500,000
Library Holdings: Book Volumes 27,000, Clipping Files, Compact Disks, DVDs, Exhibition Catalogs, Fiche, Memorabilia, Original Art Works 1,300, Other Holdings 1,290,000 Digital Images, Pamphlets, Periodical Subscriptions 60, Photographs 45,000, Prints 500, Sculpture, Slides 135,000
Special Subjects: Afro-American Art, American Indian Art, Anthropology, Antiquities-Greek, Architecture, Art Education, Art History, Ceramics, Conceptual Art, Costume Design & Constr, Decorative Arts, Drawings, Etchings & Engravings, Ethnology, Film, Folk Art, Graphic Arts, Graphic Design, Historical Material, Illustration, Interior Design, Islamic Art, Jewelry, Judaica, Landscape Architecture, Landscapes, Manuscripts, Mosaics, Oriental Art, Painting-American, Painting-British, Painting-European, Painting-French, Painting-Italian, Photography, Portraits, Sculpture, Textiles, Theatre Arts, Video, Watercolors
Collections: History of Costume, Artistic Properties Collection
Exhibitions: 6-10 exhibitions per yr
Publications: CircumSpice newsletter
Activities: Lects open to public; 2-8 vis lectrs per yr; concerts; gallery talks; lending of original objects of art to recognized museums; books traveling exhibs 1 per yr; originates traveling exhibs to institutions in NYC metro area & also upon request; sales shop sells posters from exhibs

L **Architecture Library**, 160 Convent Ave, New York, NY 10031-9101. Tel 212-650-8768; *Librn* Nilda Sanchez-Rodriguez
Mon - Thurs 10 AM - 9 PM, Fri 10 AM - 6 PM, Sat noon - 5 PM, cl Sun; Reference use for public; circulation for patrons with CUNY ID's
Library Holdings: Audio Tapes, Book Volumes 20,500, Clipping Files, Fiche, Periodical Subscriptions 48, Reels
Special Subjects: Architecture, Landscape Architecture

M **CITY OF NEW YORK PARKS & RECREATION,** Arsenal Gallery, 64th St at Fifth Ave, Arsenal Bldg 3rd Fl New York, NY 10021; The Arsenal Central Park, 830 Fifth Ave New York, NY 10065-7095. Tel 212-360-8163; Fax 212-360-1329; Email artandantiquities@parks.nyc.gov; Web: www.nyc.gov/parks; *Cur* Jennifer Lantzas
Open Mon - Fri 9 AM - 5 PM; No admis fee; The purpose is to show art based on natural & urban themes; Large open space in third floor of Arsenal building. Working busy space - work must be hung from monofilament line & molding hooks
Collections: Mixed Media-Park & Nature themes
Exhibitions: Six week shows
Activities: Lects open to pub, 8 vis lectrs per yr

COLLEGE ART ASSOCIATION
For further information, see National and Regional Organizations

COLOR ASSOCIATION OF THE US
For further information, see National and Regional Organizations

L **COLUMBIA UNIVERSITY,** Avery Architectural & Fine Arts Library, 1172 Amsterdam Ave, MC-0301, New York, NY 10027. Tel 212-854-6199; Email avery@library.columbia.edu; Web: www.columbia.edu/cu/web/indiv/avery/index.html; *Dir* Carole Ann Fabian; *Cur Drawings & Archives* Nicole Richard; *Avery Index & Communs Coordr* Ted Goodman; *Fine Arts Librn* Paula Gabbard; *Assoc Dir & Head Access Servs* Kitty Chibnik; *Cur Classics* Teresa Harris; *Cur Art Properties* Roberto Ferrari
Open during Fall & Spring school terms Mon - Thurs 9 AM - 11 PM, Fri 9 AM - 9 PM, Sat 10 AM - 7 PM, Sun noon - 10 PM; Estab 1890; Circ non-circulating; Primarily for reference; Average Annual Attendance: 177,000
Library Holdings: Book Volumes 600,000, CD-ROMs, DVDs, Exhibition Catalogs, Fiche, Manuscripts, Maps, Memorabilia, Other Holdings Original documents, Periodical Subscriptions 1,000, Photographs, Prints, Reels
Special Subjects: Afro-American Art, Antiquities-Assyrian, Antiquities-Byzantine, Antiquities-Egyptian, Antiquities-Etruscan, Antiquities-Greek, Antiquities-Oriental, Antiquities-Persian, Antiquities-Roman, Archaeology, Architecture, Art History, Asian Art, Ceramics, Collages, Conceptual Art, Constructions, Decorative Arts, Drawings, Etchings & Engravings, Folk Art, Furniture, Glass, Graphic Arts, History of Art & Archaeology, Interior Design, Islamic Art, Landscape Architecture, Latin American Art, Mexican Art, Mosaics, Oriental Art
Collections: Over 1.5 million original architectural drawings & manuscripts, mainly American; 600,000 volumes
Publications: Catalog of Avery Memorial Architectural Library; Avery Index to Architectural Periodicals (available as a data base)

L **Dept of Art History & Archaeology**, 826 Schermerhorn Hall, 1190 Amersterdam Ave New York, NY 10027-6900. Tel 212-854-4505; Fax 212-854-7329; Web: www.columbia.edu/cu/arthistory; *Dept Chair* Michael Cole
Library Holdings: Lantern Slides 70,000, Other Holdings Gallery announcements 15,000, Photographs 250,000, Slides 500,000
Collections: Berenson I-Tatti Archive, Dial Iconographic Index, Haseloff Archive, Bartsch Collection, Gaigleres Collection, Arthur Kingsley Porter Collection, Ware Collection, Courtauld Collection, Marburger Index, Windsor Castle, Chatsworth Collection, Millard Meiss Collection

M **Miriam & Ira D Wallach Art Gallery**, 615 W 129th St, New York, NY 10027; 1190 Amsterdam Ave, 926 Schermerhorn Hall New York, NY 10027-7054. Tel 212-854-6800; Fax 212-854-7800; Email wallach@columbia.edu; Web: www.columbia.edu/cu/wallach; *Dir & Chief Cur* Deborah Cullen; *Assoc Dir* Jeanette Silverthorne; *Administrative Assistant* Zachary Valdez
Open Wed - Fri noon - 8 PM, Sat & Sun noon - 6 PM; No admis fee; Estab 1987 to complement the educational goals of Columbia University & to embody the research interests of faculty & graduate students; 5 rooms, 2,300 sq ft, 310 running ft - moving to new space summer 2017; Average Annual Attendance: 4,000
Exhibitions: Temporary exhibitions only;
Publications: Exhibition catalogs
Activities: Lects open to public; 3 - 6 vis lectrs per yr; gallery talks; tours; originate traveling exhibs to public art institutions

M **CONGREGATION EMANU-EL,** Bernard Judaica Museum, One E 65th St, New York, NY 10021-6596. Tel 212-744-1400; Fax 212-570-0826; Email museum@emanuelnyc.org; *Cur* Warren Klein; *Sr Rabbi* Joshua M Davidson; *Pres* John Harrison Streicker
Open Sun - Thurs 10 AM - 4:30 PM; No admis fee; Estab 1997 as a Judaica museum; Building is a landmark & is open for touring
Income: Financed by subvention from congregation
Collections: Congregational Memorabilia, Paintings, Judaica
Exhibitions: Seasonal exhibits; Congregational History; Photographic exhibit of stained glass; A Temple Treasury, The Judaica Collection of Congregation Emanu-El of the City of New York
Activities: Docent training, religious school tours; lects open to public, 2 -4 vis lectrs per year; gallery talks & tours

M **COOPER HEWITT, SMITHSONIAN DESIGN MUSEUM,** Smithsonian Institution, 2 E 91st St, New York, NY 10128-8330. Tel 212-849-8400; Fax 212-849-8401; Email chtours@si.edu; Web: www.cooperhewitt.org; *Dir* Caroline Baumann; *Assoc Dir Communs & Mktg* Laurie Bohlk
Open Mon - Fri & Sun 10 AM - 6 PM, Sat 10 AM - 9 PM, cl Thanksgiving & Christmas; Admis adults $16, seniors $10, students with ID $7, mems & children under 18 free; Founded 1897 as the Cooper Union Museum, to serve the needs of scholars, artisans, students, designers & everyone who deals with the built environment; Museum is based on large & varied collections of historic & contemporary design & a library strong in those fields; changing exhibitions are based on the museum's vast collections or loan shows illustrative of how design affects everyone's daily life; its emphasis on educ is expanded by special courses & seminars related to design in all forms & of all periods; the galleries occupy the first & second floors; exhibitions relate to the collections & other aspects of design. Maintains library (Bureau of the Smithsonian Institution); Average Annual Attendance: 221,000; Mem: Dues $75-$10,000
Income: Financed by private contributions, mem & partly Smithsonian Institution
Special Subjects: Afro-American Art, Architecture, Bookplates & Bindings, Calligraphy, Carpets & Rugs, Cartoons, Ceramics, Crafts, Decorative Arts, Drawings, Embroidery, Etchings & Engravings, Furniture, Glass, Gold, Historical Material, Jewelry, Latin American Art, Leather, Manuscripts, Metalwork, Pewter, Porcelain, Posters, Pottery, Prints, Silver, Textiles, Watercolors
Collections: Drawings including works by Frederic Church, Winslow Homer, Thomas Moran & other 19th century American artists, ceramics, furniture & woodwork, glass, original drawings & designs for architecture & the decorative

arts, 15th-20th century prints, textiles, lace, wallpaper, 200,000 works representing a span of 24 centuries, wall coverings, Contemporary Design, Industrial Design
Publications: Books on decorative arts; collection handbooks; exhibition catalogues; National Design Journal
Activities: Classes for adults & children; performances; docent training; Master's Degree prog in Decorative Arts through Parsons; lects open to pub, 50-100 vis lectrs per yr; concerts; gallery talks; tours; National Design awards; fellowships offered; paintings & original objects of art lent to other mus; lending collection contains original art works, original prints & 40,000 books; book traveling exhibs; originate traveling exhibs; mus shop sells books & objects related to historical & contemporary design

L **Library**, 2 E 91st St, Fl 3 New York, NY 10128-8330. Tel 212-849-8330; Fax 212-849-8339; Email askalibrarian@si.edu; Web: library.si.edu; *Dept Head, Librn* Stephen H Van Dyk; *Ref Librn* Elizabeth Broman; *Librn* Jennifer Cohlman Bracchi
Open Mon - Fri 9:30 AM - 5:30 PM to researchers by appt only; cl Federal holidays; No admis fee; Estab to serve staff of museum & students from Parsons School of Design; Interlibrary lending only (branch of Smithsonian Institution Libraries)
Income: Financed through SIL budgets
Library Holdings: Book Volumes 55,000, Cards, Clipping Files, Exhibition Catalogs, Fiche, Kodachrome Transparencies, Lantern Slides, Manuscripts, Memorabilia, Micro Print, Original Art Works, Other Holdings Original documents; Pictures & photographs 1,500,900, Pamphlets, Periodical Subscriptions 300, Photographs, Prints, Reels, Reproductions, Slides, Video Tapes
Special Subjects: Advertising Design, Decorative Arts, Graphic Design, Industrial Design, Interior Design
Collections: Spec Coll of Industrial & Graphic Designers, Donald Deskey Archive, Henry Dreyfuss Archive, Ladislav Sutnar Archive

A **CREATIVE TIME,** 59 E 4th St, Fl 6 New York, NY 10003-8963. Tel 212-206-6674; Fax 212-255-8467; Email info@creativetime.org; Web: www.creativetime.org; *Acting Exec Dir* Alyssa Nitchun; *Artistic Dir* Nato Thompson; *Sr Cur* Elvira Dyangani Ose; *Acting Deputy Dir Opers & Fin* Cynthia Pringle; *Digital Mktg Mgr* RJ Rushmore
Open Mon - Fri 10 AM - 5 PM, exhibition hours vary depending on site; Admis performances $8, exhibitions usually free; Estab 1974; Venues include a variety of public locations; Average Annual Attendance: 50,000; Mem: 200; members give tax-deductible contributions
Income: $3,000,000 (financed by National Endowment for the Arts, NY State Council of the Arts, NYC Dept of Cultural Affairs, private corporations & foundations)
Library Holdings: Book Volumes, Exhibition Catalogs, Original Art Works, Prints
Exhibitions: Art in the Anchorage
Publications: Creative Time; biannual program/project catalogs
Activities: Multidisciplinary; lects open to pub; Annenberg prize; sales shop sells books

M **DAVID ZWIRNER GALLERY,** 525 W 19th St, New York, NY 10011. Tel 212-727-2070; Email newyork@davidzwirner.com; Web: www.davidzwirner.com; *Owner* David Zwirner
Open Tues - Sat 10 AM - 6 PM, cl Sun - Mon; No admis fee; Estab 1993; Five contemporary galleries, three in New York, one in London and one in Hong Kong for changing exhibs
Collections: Contemporary art
Exhibitions: Temporary exhibits
Activities: Organize traveling exhibs

A **DESIGN COMMISSION OF THE CITY OF NEW YORK,** 1 City Hall, Fl 3 New York, NY 10007-1298. Tel 212-788-3071; Fax 212-788-3086; Email pressoffice@cityhall.nyc.gov; Web: www1.nyc.gov/site/designcommission/about/about.page; *Exec Dir* Justin Garrett Moore; *Pres* Signe Nielsen
Open by appointment only; No admis fee; Estab 1898 to review designs for city buildings, landscape architecture & works of art proposed for city owned property. Portraits are installed in Governors Room and other areas in City Hall; Mem: 11
Income: Financed by city appropriation
Collections: 100 portraits of historic figures, state, city and national
Publications: The Art Commission & Municipal Art Society Guide to Outdoor Sculpture by Margot Gayle & Michele Cohen; Imaginary Cities, European Views from the Collection of the Art Commission; National Directory of Design Review Agencies (1991); New York Re-Viewed, Exhibition Catalogue of 19th & 20th Century Photographs from the Collection of the Art Commission

A **Associates of the Art Commission, Inc**, 1 City Hall, Fl 3 New York, NY 10007-1298. Tel 212-788-3071; Fax 212-788-3086; Web: www1.nyc.gov/site/designcommission/index.page; *Exec Dir* Justin Moore
Estab 1913 to advise and counsel Art Commission as requested; Mem: 35; dues $35; annual meeting in Jan
Income: Financed by mem

A **THE DRAWING CENTER,** 35 Wooster St, New York, NY 10013-5300. Tel 212-219-2166; Fax 888-380-3362; Email info@drawingcenter.org; Web: www.drawingcenter.org; *Exec Dir* Brett Littman; *Co Chmn* Rhiarnon Kubieka; *Co Chmn* Jane Dresner Sadaka; *Exec Ed* Noah Chasin; *Dir Educ & Community Progs* Aimee Good; *Chief Cur* Claire Gilman; *Cur Open Sessions* Lisa Sigal; *Coordr Opers* Dan Gillespie; *Asst Cur* Amber Harper; *Mng Ed* Joanna Ahlberg; *Communs Dir* Molly Gross; *Deputy Dir Admin* Champ Knecht; *Exhib Mgr* Olga Tetkowski; *Develop Dir* Bruno Nouril
Open all year Wed & Fri - Sun noon - 6 PM, Thurs noon - 8 PM; cl Mon - Tues, New Year's Day, Thanksgiving, Christmas; Admis adults $5, student & seniors $3, children under 12 & mem free; free admis Thurs 6 PM - 8 PM; Estab 1977 to express the quality & diversity of drawing through exhib & educ; Main gallery 2,386 sq ft; Drawing Room gallery 709 Sq ft; Lab gallery 904 sq ft; Average Annual Attendance: 55,000
Income: Pvt & pub support
Special Subjects: Drawings
Publications: Exhib catalogs; Drawing Papers publ series
Activities: Classes for children; lects open to pub & for mems only, 20 vis lectrs per yr; concerts; gallery talks; tours; internship program offered; originate traveling exhibs to major national & international museums; mus shop sells books & limited edition prints

M **EARTHFIRE,** Art from Detritus: Recycling with Imagination, Box 1149, New York, NY 10013-0866. Tel 212-925-4419; Email ncognita@earthfire.org; Web: www.ncognita.com; www.artfromdetritus.com; *Founder & Exec Dir* Vernita Nemec
Open by appointment & during exhibit hours; No admis fee; Estab 1993 to raise environmental awareness by organizing exhibits of art made primarily from recycling trash, found objects, throwaways & discarded material that would have otherwise polluted the planet; Circ 4 catalogs available; Exhibition available for travel and adaptable to site; Average Annual Attendance: 5,000
Income: Financed by grants, pub & private contributions incl Puffin Found & Kauffmann Found, nat recycling coalition
Exhibitions: Art From Detritus: Recycling with Imagination; 13 Exhibitions: 1993 - 2015
Publications: Exhibit catalogues (1-4)
Activities: Classes for adults & children; lects open to pub, gallery talks, tours; originates traveling exhibs annually, to universities, conferences, corporate galleries & municipal organizations; mus shop sells catalogs of past exhibitions by mail, original art

M **EL MUSEO DEL BARRIO,** 1230 5th Ave, New York, NY 10029-4401. Tel 212-831-7272; Fax 212-831-7927; Email info@elmuseo.org; Web: www.elmuseo.org; *Exec Dir* Patrick Charpenel; *Registrar* Melisa Lujan; *Permanent Coll Mgr* Noel Valentin; *Exhib Mgr & Asst Cur* Trinidad Fombella; *Assoc Cur, Special Projects* Rocio Aranda-Alvarado; *Curatorial Asst* Stephanie Spahr; *Sr Mgr Pub Rels* Carolina Alvarez-Mathies
Open Wed - Sat 11 AM 6 - PM, Sun noon - 5 PM, cl Mon; Admis adults $9 seniors & students with ID $5, children under 12 when accompanied by adult & mems no charge, seniors no charge on Wed, 3rd Sat of month no charge; Estab 1969 to conserve & display works by Puerto Rican artists & other Hispanic artists; Located on Museum Mile. Gallery space divided into 4 wings: Northwest Wing houses Santos de Palo, East Gallery will house Pre-Columbian installation, F-Stop Gallery devoted to photography & Children's Wing opened fall of 1982; Average Annual Attendance: 21,000; Mem: Mems $50 - $2,500+
Collections: 16mm Films on History, Culture and Art, 300 Paintings and 5000 Works on Paper, by Puerto Rican and other Latin American Artists, Pre-Columbian Caribbean Artifacts, Santos (Folk Religious Carvings)
Activities: Classes for adults & children; dramatic progs; children's workshops; lects open to pub, 25 vis lectrs per yr; concerts; gallery talks; tours; awards; schols; individual & original objects of art lent to other mus & galleries; originate traveling exhibs; Junior Museum; 510 seat theatre

A **ELECTRONIC ARTS INTERMIX (EAI),** 535 W 22nd St 5th Fl, New York, NY 10011-1119. Tel 212-337-0680; Fax 212-337-0679; Email info@eai.org; Web: www.eai.org; *Exec Dir* Lori Zippay; *Distribution Dir* Rebecca Cleman; *Distribution Mgr* Karl McCool
Open Mon - Fri 10 AM - 6 PM; Viewing Room open by appt Mon - Fri 11 AM - 5 PM; No admis fee for individuals; group fee negotiable; Estab 1971 as a nonprofit corporation to assist artists seeking to explore the potentials of the electronic media, particularly television, as a means of personal expression; Viewing Room provides access to EAI coll
Income: Financed by videotape & editing fees & in part by federal & state funds & contributions
Library Holdings: DVDs, Video Tapes
Collections: Over 3,500 works from 200+ artists of video art & digital art projects from mid 1960's-present, A Kinetic History: The EAI Archives Online
Exhibitions: Periodic exhibs
Publications: Electronic Arts Intermix Videocassette Catalog, annual; Online Resource Guide for Exhibiting, Collecting & Preserving Media Art
Activities: Lects open to pub; film screenings; artist talks; panels; performances; internships available; sales shop sells copies of all media in coll in various formats

M **EMEDIALOFT.ORG,** 55 Bethune St Ste 629, New York, NY 10014-2035. Tel 646-368-5623; Email info@emedialoft.org; Web: www.emedialoft.org; *Acting Dir* C T Rhodes; *Dir Emeritus* Bill Creston; *Artist in Residence* Barbara Rosenthal; *Office Asst* Aliza Tuckes; *Creative Projects Resident* Jeffrey Cyhers Wright; *Creative Projects Resident* Prudence Groube
Open by appointment; No admis fee; Estab 1982 for artists in video production, artists' books, photography, performance text art, ideas, philosophy of art, new media; Circ non-circ; Conceptual photography, video, post production area, photo studio, darkroom, performance and avant-garde art & documentation; display walls, book shelves, 950 sq ft; maintains reference library; currently houses 7,000 vols & 1,000 papers Barbara Rosenthal authors archives; Average Annual Attendance: 300
Income: $40,000 (financed by private funds & facility fees)
Purchases: Video & audio equipment, filing & office equipment, computer equipment
Library Holdings: Audio Tapes, Book Volumes, CD-ROMs, Cards, Cassettes, Clipping Files, Compact Disks, DVDs, Exhibition Catalogs, Kodachrome Transparencies, Lantern Slides, Manuscripts, Maps, Memorabilia, Motion Pictures, Original Art Works, Original Documents, Other Holdings, Pamphlets, Periodical Subscriptions, Photographs, Prints, Slides, Video Tapes
Special Subjects: Conceptual Art, Drawings, Photography
Collections: Artists books, art books, classic literature, Leon Rosenthal American Watercolors, Barbara Rosenthal Archive, Bill Creston Archive
Exhibitions: Artists books & photos, videotapes, super 8 film, video, performance, new media online
Publications: Exhibit catalogs
Activities: Educ prog; one-on-one workshops; digital video & photog workshops; individual training in media performance; writing; photog; 2 vis lectrs per yr, screenings open to pub; gallery talks; tours, awards; creative projects grant offered; original objects of art lent to exhibitors; lending collection contains artists' books, videos, photos to galleries & museums; book traveling exhibs; originate traveling exhibs to vis artists & residents; sales shop sells books, original art, reproductions,, prints

M **FASHION INSTITUTE OF TECHNOLOGY - SUNY,** The Museum at FIT, 7th Ave at 27th St, New York, NY 10001-5992. Tel 212-217-4558; Email museuminfo@fitnyc.edu; Web: www.fitnyc.edu/museum; *Dir* Dr Valerie Steele
Open Tues - Fri Noon - 8 PM, Sat 10 AM - 5 PM, cl Sun, Mon & holidays; No admis fee; Estab 1967; 6,000 sq ft of space divided into three galleries; Average Annual Attendance: 100,000
Income: Financed by city, state, endowment & grants
Purchases: fashion, accessories & textile collections
Special Subjects: Textiles, Costumes
Publications: Exhibit catalogs
Activities: Lect open to public, 10 vis lectrs per yr; gallery talks; tours, lects & annual fashion symposium

L **Gladys Marcus Library**, 7th Ave at 27th St, New York, NY 10001-5992. Tel 212-217-4370; Fax 212-217-4371; Web: www.fitnyc.edu/library; *Spec Coll & FIT Archives* Karen Trivette; *Dir & Head Research & Instructional Servs* N J Bradeen; *Assoc Dir* Greta K Earnest; *Evening Access Servs & ILL* Paul Lajoie; *Elec Resources & Serials* Lana Bittman; *Head Acquisitions & Metadata servs* Leslie Preston; *Daytime Access Servs Mgr* Jennifer Mak; *Library Tech Servs* Jana C Duda; *Graphics Lab* Jasper Lin
Open Mon - Thurs 9 AM - 9 PM, Fri 9 AM - 6:30 PM, Sat 10 - 4 PM, Sun noon - 8 PM; Estab 1944 to meet the acad needs of the students & faculty & to serve as a resource for the fashion & related industries; Circ 59,500; For reference only; Average Annual Attendance: 78,000; Mem: SUNY, METRO, NYLINK, NYLA
Income: $3,212,440
Purchases: $317,368
Library Holdings: Auction Catalogs, Audio Tapes, Book Volumes 168,897, CD-ROMs, Cards, Cassettes, Clipping Files, Compact Disks, DVDs, Exhibition Catalogs, Fiche 4712, Memorabilia, Micro Print, Motion Pictures, Original Art Works 184, Original Documents, Other Holdings Artist Books, Online Database, Pamphlets, Periodical Subscriptions 350, Photographs, Prints, Reels, Reproductions, Slides, Video Tapes
Special Subjects: Advertising Design, Art History, Costume Design & Constr, Decorative Arts, Fashion Arts, Graphic Design, Interior Design, Jewelry
Collections: Oral History Project on the Fashion Industry, several sketchbook colls, Fashion Illustration
Activities: Love Your Library program; three vis lectrs per yr

FEDERATION OF MODERN PAINTERS & SCULPTORS
For further information, see National and Regional Organizations

M **FIRST STREET GALLERY,** 526 W 26th St, Rm 209, New York, NY 10001-5518. Tel 646-336-8053; Fax 646-336-8054; Email info@firststreetgallery.org; Web: www.firststreetgallery.org; *Chmn* Rallou Malliarakis; *Pres* Tracy Collamore; *Treas* Suzi Evalenko; *Secy* Jessica McGarry Bartlet; *Gallery Administrator* Alexandra Deters
Open Tues - Sat 11 AM - 6 PM; No admis fee; Estab 1969 to promote artists' creative efforts & exhibit their work & provide a forum for exchange of ideas & the public's understanding & appreciation of contemporary art; Artist-run 501(c)(3) organization; Average Annual Attendance: 5,600; Mem: (please see website for information)
Income: Financed by dues, contributions, grants, juried exhib entry fees, etc.
Exhibitions: (3rd Jan, 2017-28th Jan, 2017) Matthew Dibble; (31st Jan, 2017-25th Feb, 2017) Jessica Bartlet; (28th Feb, 2017-25th Mar, 2017) Marianne Perry Salas; (28th Mar, 2017-21st Apr, 2017) Nicole Santiago; (25th Apr, 2017-20th May, 2017) Kathleen Bennet Bastis; (23rd May, 2017-17th Jun, 2017) Marion Miller; (22nd Jun, 2017-15th Jul, 2017) National Juried Exhibition; (20th Jul, 2017-11th Aug, 2017) MFA National Competition
Publications: 40th Anniversary Exhib Catalog, Dec 2009
Activities: Gallery talks; competitions; outreach exhibs for non-mem artists to engage the pub; sponsoring of competitions; originate traveling exhibs

M **FLAG ART FOUNDATION,** 545 W 25th St, Fl 9 New York, NY 10001. Tel 212-206-0220; Email info@flagartfoundation.org; Web: flagartfoundation.org; *Dir* Stephanie Roach; *Assoc Dir* Jonathan Rider; *Exhibs & Progs Mgr* Risa Daniels
Open Wed - Sat 11 AM - 5 PM; Summer Hours: Tues - Fri 11 AM - 5 PM; No admis fee; Estab 2008 to promote the appreciation of contemporary art
Collections: Contemporary art
Exhibitions: Temporary exhibits
Activities: Artist talks; tours; workshops

M **FRAUNCES TAVERN MUSEUM,** 54 Pearl St, New York, NY 10004-4300. Tel 212-425-1778; Fax 212-509-3467; Email publicity@frauncestavernmuseum.org; Web: www.frauncestavernmuseum.org; *Develop Officer* Diego Foronda; *Mktg Coordr* Amy Kennard; *Exec Dir* Jessica B Phillips; *Asst Bldg Mgr* Eric Sussman
Open Mon - Sat 10 AM - 5 PM; Admis adults $7, students, children & seniors $4, children under 5 & active military free; Estab 1907 for focus on early American history, culture, historic preservation & New York City history; Museum is housed in the site of eighteenth-century Fraunces Tavern and four adjacent nineteenth-century buildings. The museum houses two fully furnished period rooms: the Long Room, site of George Washington's farewell to his officers at the end of the Revolutionary War, and the Clinton Room. a nineteenth-century dining room; Mem: 500; dues $20 - $1000
Collections: 17th, 18th, 19th & 20th century prints, paintings, artifacts & decorative arts relating to early American history, culture & historic preservation, New York City history, George Washington & other historic figures in American history
Exhibitions: Various exhib
Publications: Exhibit catalogs
Activities: Educ dept; docent training; lects open to pub; tours; demonstrations; films; off-site programs; individual paintings lent to qualified mus & historical organizations, lending collection contains 750 original works of art, 150 original prints, & 1,300 decorative art & artifacts; book traveling exhibs; mus shop sells books, reproductions, prints & slides

L **FRENCH INSTITUTE-ALLIANCE FRANCAISE,** Library, 22 E 60th St 2nd Fl, New York, NY 10022-1077. Tel 212-355-6100 (Alliance), 646-388-6655 (Library); Fax 212-935-4119 (Alliance & Library); Email reception@fiaf.org; Web: www.fiaf.org; *Dir* Marie-Catherine Glaser; *VPres Library* Katherine Branning
Open Mon 4 PM - 8 PM, Tues - Thurs 11:30 AM - 8 PM, Fri 11:30 AM - 3 PM, Sat 9:30 AM - 3 PM, cl Sun; No admis fee; Estab 1911 to encourage the study of the French language & culture; Library lends to members, reference only for non-members; maintains art gallery
Income: Financed by endowment & mem, tax deductible contributions & foundation grants
Library Holdings: Audio Tapes, Book Volumes 30,000, CD-ROMs, Cassettes 900, Exhibition Catalogs, Periodical Subscriptions 100, Video Tapes
Special Subjects: Film
Collections: Architecture, costume, decorative arts, paintings, French literature & culture
Exhibitions: Changes monthly; concentrates on up & coming artists
Activities: Classes given; lect open to public

L **THE FRICK COLLECTION,** Frick Art Reference Library, 10 E 71st St, New York, NY 10021-4967. Tel 212-547-0641; Fax 212-879-2091; Email library@frick.org; Web: www.frick.org/library; *Dir Center for the History of Collecting* Inge Reist; *Chief Coll Mgmt & Access* Deborah Kempe; *Chief Coll Preservation & Graphic Designer* Don Swanson; *Chief Pub Servs* Suzannah Massen; *Chief Archives & Records Mgmt* Sally Brazil; *Andrew W Mellon Chief Librn* Stephen Bury
Open (Sept - May) Mon - Fri 10 AM - 5 PM, Sat 10 AM - 2 PM, Mon - Fri 10 AM - 5 PM (June - July), Tues - Thurs 10 AM - 5 PM (August); No admis fee; Estab 1920 as a reference library to serve adults & graduate students interested in the history of European & American painting, drawing, sculpture, illuminated manuscripts; For reference only; Average Annual Attendance: 6,000
Library Holdings: Auction Catalogs 75,000, Book Volumes 300,000, CD-ROMs 87, Compact Disks 100, DVDs 20, Exhibition Catalogs 95,400, Fiche 52,000, Other Holdings Microfiche; Negatives 56,000; Architect, Periodical Subscriptions 700, Photographs 900,000, Reels 233, Video Tapes 13
Special Subjects: Art History, Bronzes, Ceramics, Decorative Arts, Enamels, Furniture, Landscapes, Marine Painting, Miniatures, Painting-American, Painting-Australian, Painting-British, Painting-Canadian, Painting-Dutch, Painting-European, Painting-Flemish, Painting-French, Painting-German, Painting-Italian, Painting-New Zealand, Painting-Polish, Painting-Russian, Painting-Scandinavian, Painting-Spanish, Period Rooms, Porcelain, Portraits, Prints, Religious Art, Restoration & Conservation, Sculpture, Tapestries, Watercolors
Collections: Archives (unrecorded), Helen Clay Frick Family Papers
Publications: Frick Art Reference Library Original Index to Art Periodicals; Frick Art Reference Library Sales Catalogue Index (microform); Spanish Artists from the Fourth to the Twentieth Century (4 vols); The Story of the Frick Art Reference Library: The Early Years, by Katharine McCook Knox; Archives Directory for the History of Collecting in America
Activities: Internships; fellowships; tours; awards, Sotheby's prize for a Distinguished Publication in the History of Collecting in America

M **FRICK COLLECTION,** 1 E 70th St, New York, NY 10021-4981. Tel 212-288-0700; Fax 212-628-4417; Email info@frick.org; Web: www.frick.org; *Dir* Ian Wardropper; *Sr Cur* Susan Grace Galassi; *Chief Registrar & Exhibs Mgr* Diane Farynyk; *Secy* Michael J Horvitz; *Deputy Dir Extern Affairs* Tia Chapman; *Chief Cur* Xavier Salomon; *Chief Librarian* Stephen Bury
Open Tues - Sat 10 AM - 6 PM, Sun 11 AM - 5 PM; cl Mon, Jan 1, July 4, Thanksgiving, Dec 25; Admis adults $22, visitors with disabilities $17, seniors (65 +) $17, students w/ID $12, children under 10 not admitted; Estab 1920; opened to public 1935 as a gallery of art; The Frick Collection is housed in the former residence of Henry Clay Frick (1849-1919), built in 1913-14 & alterations & additions were made 1931-1935 & further extension & garden were completed in 1977. The rooms are in the style of English & French interiors of the 18th century. Maintains art reference library; Average Annual Attendance: 421,800; Mem: 725 Fellows; dues $1,200 minimum contribution; 17,600 friends; dues $75 minimum contribution
Income: $27,800,000 (financed by endowment, mem, bookshop & admis)
Library Holdings: Auction Catalogs, Book Volumes, Exhibition Catalogs, Fiche, Pamphlets, Periodical Subscriptions, Photographs
Special Subjects: Bronzes, Drawings, Furniture, Painting-European, Painting-Italian, Porcelain, Prints, Renaissance Art, Sculpture
Collections: 15th-18th century sculpture, of which Renaissance bronzes are most numerous, 14th-19th century paintings, with fine examples of Western European masters & suites of Boucher & Fragonard decorations, Renaissance & French 18th century furniture, 17th-18th century Chinese & French porcelains, 16th century Limoges enamels, 16th-19th century drawings & prints
Publications: Art in the Frick Collection (paintings, sculpture & decorative arts); exhibition catalogs; The Frick Collection, illustrated catalog; guide to the galleries; handbook of paintings; Ingres & the Comtesse d'Haussonville; paintings from the Frick Collection; Building The Frick Collection
Activities: Docent training; Lects open to pub; concerts; gallery talks; originates traveling exhibs; mus shop sells books, prints, postcards & greeting cards

C **FRIED, FRANK, HARRIS, SHRIVER & JACOBSON,** Art Collection, One New York Plaza, New York, NY 10004. Tel 212-859-8000; Telex 747-1526; *Chmn* Arthur Fleischer Jr; *Preparator* Macyn Bolt
Open by appointment; Estab 1979 intended as a survey
Purchases: Over 1,000 pieces in all offices (NY, DC, LA & London)
Collections: Fried, Frank, Harris, Shriver & Jacobson Art Collection, Contemporary Art, Photography
Exhibitions: Permanent exhibition
Activities: Tours

M **GOETHE-INSTITUT NEW YORK,** 30 Irving Pl, New York, NY 10003-2303. Tel 212-439-8700; Fax 212-439-8705; Email info@newyork.goethe.org; Web: www.goethe.de/newyork; *Dir* George Blochmann; *Prog Cur* Sara Stevenson
Open Mon - Fri 9 AM - 5 PM; No admis fee; 2008; Downtown space for contemporary art of the Goethe-Institut New York with residency prog for young curators from Germany; Average Annual Attendance: 1500

Income: Financed by German government & BMW/Mini
Activities: Lect open to public; gallery talks; tours; exhibs; performances; publications; book sale at library once per yr

A **GRAPHIC ARTISTS GUILD,** 31 W 34th St, Flr 8, New York, NY 10001-3030. Tel 212-791-3400; Fax 212-791-0333; Email admin@graphicartistsguild.org; Web: graphicartistsguild.org; *Exec Dir* Patricia McKiernan; *Pres* Lara Kisielewska; *Fin Secy* Diane Barton; *Rec Secy* Bill Morse
Open 10 AM - 6 PM; Estab 1967 to improve the economic & social condition of graphic artists; to provide legal & cr services to members; to increase pub appreciation of graphic art (including illustration, cartooning & design) as an art form; Mem: 1,300
Income: Financed by mem & publication sales
Publications: Cartooning books; GAG Directory of Illustration, annual; GAG Handbook, Pricing & Ethical Guidelines, biennial; monthly newsletter
Activities: Walter Hortens Memorial Awards for Distinguished Service & Outstanding Client

M **GREENWICH HOUSE POTTERY,** First Floor Gallery, 122 W 27th St, Flr 16, New York, NY 10001-6291. Tel 212-242-4106; Fax 212-645-5486; Email pottery@greenwichhouse.org; Web: www.greenwichhouse.org; *Dir* Adam Welch
Open Mon 4 PM - 10 PM, Tues - Fri 9:30 AM - 10 PM, Sat 9:30 AM - 6 PM; No admis fee; First Floor Gallery displays works of its members
Activities: Classes for adults & children; lects open to pub, 10 vis lectrs per yr; competitions; schols & fellowships offered; mus shop sells original art

M **Jane Hartsook Gallery,** 16 Jones St, New York, NY 10014. Tel 212-242-4106; Fax 212-645-5486; Email pottery@greenwichhouse.org; Web: www.gharts.org; *Dir* Adam Welch; *Educ Coordr* Jenni Lukasiewicz
Open Wed - Sat noon - 6 PM; No admis fee; Estab 1969 as a nonprofit venue for ceramic arts
Exhibitions: Artists on Their Own, annual juried exhibit
Activities: Classes for adults & children; lects open to pub, 10 vis lectrs per yr; competitions; schols offered; mus shop sells original art

L **Library,** 16 Jones St, New York, NY 10014. Tel 212-242-4106; Fax 212-645-5486; Web: www.gharts.org; *Dir* Adam Welch
Estab 1909; For reference only
Library Holdings: Audio Tapes, Book Volumes 700, Exhibition Catalogs, Pamphlets, Periodical Subscriptions 10, Slides, Video Tapes
Special Subjects: Ceramics

L **GROLIER CLUB LIBRARY,** 47 E 60th St, New York, NY 10022-1098. Tel 212-838-6690; Fax 212-838-2445; Email ejh@grolierclub.org; Email mconstantinou@grolierclub.org, jsheehan@grolierclub.org; Web: www.grolierclub.org; *Dir* Eric Holzenberg; *Pres* G Scott Clemons; *Librn* Meghan R Constantinou; *Exhibs Mgr* Jennifer K Sheehan
Open Mon - Fri 10 AM - 5 PM, cl Aug, New Year's Eve, New Year's Day, Presidents' Day, Martin Luther King Day, Memorial Day, Independence Day, Labor Day, Columbus Day, Thanksgiving Day & Fri following, Christmas Eve & Christmas Day; No admis fee; Estab 1884, devoted to the arts of the book; Mem: 800; annual meetings fourth Thurs of Jan
Purchases: $15,000
Library Holdings: Auction Catalogs, Book Volumes 100,000, Exhibition Catalogs, Manuscripts, Original Documents, Periodical Subscriptions 35, Prints
Collections: Bookseller & auction catalogs from 17th-21st centuries; book arts
Activities: Lect for members only

GUILD OF BOOK WORKERS
For further information, see National and Regional Organizations

L **HAMPDEN-BOOTH THEATRE LIBRARY,** 16 Gramercy Park S, New York, NY 10003-1705. Tel 212-228-1861; Web: www.hampdenbooth.org; *Cur & Librn* Raymond Wemmlinger
Open Mon - Fri 9 AM - 5 PM & by appointment; Estab 1957 to provide scholarly & professional research on American & English theater with emphasis on 19th century
Purchases: $10,000
Library Holdings: Audio Tapes, Book Volumes 10,000, Cassettes, Clipping Files, Exhibition Catalogs, Framed Reproductions, Manuscripts, Memorabilia, Original Art Works, Pamphlets, Photographs, Prints, Records, Reels, Reproductions, Sculpture
Special Subjects: Coins & Medals, Costume Design & Constr, Etchings & Engravings, Painting-American, Painting-British, Photography, Portraits, Prints, Sculpture, Stage Design, Reproductions, Theatre Arts
Collections: Documents, letters, photos, paintings, memorabilia, prompt books of Walter Hampden, Edwin Booth, Union Square Theater, English playbill (18th & 19th century)

A **HARVESTWORKS, INC,** 596 Broadway, Ste 602, New York, NY 10012. Tel 212-431-1130; Fax 212-431-8473; Email harvestworks@gmail.com; Web: www.harvestworks.org; *Exec Dir* Carol Parkinson
Open Mon - Fri 11 AM - 6 PM; Estab 1977 to provide support & facilities for audio art & experimental music; Maintains reference library; Average Annual Attendance: 2,000; Mem: 250; dues $75
Income: $150,000 (financed by endowment, mem, city & state appropriations, recording studio)
Purchases: Pro-tools by Digi Design, Digital Audio Editing
Library Holdings: Audio Tapes
Exhibitions: The New York Electronic Art Festival
Publications: TELLUS, the Audio Series, biannual
Activities: Adult classes; artist in residence prog; computer art; lects open to pub, 20 vis lectrs per yr; concerts; gallery talks; competitions with awards; Van Lier Residency Prog; schols offered; lending collections contains 26 cassettes; retail store sells audio art & music cassettes & CDs

A **HATCH-BILLOPS COLLECTION, INC,** 491 Broadway 7th Fl, New York, NY 10012. Tel 212-966-3231; Fax 212-966-3231; Email hatchbillops@yahoo.com; Web: www.hatch-billopsarchive.org; *Pres* Camille Billops; *Mem Bd Dir* James V Hatch; *Mem Bd Dir* John A Williams; *Mem Bd Dir* Cora Myers Mendoza; *Mem Bd Dir* Noriko Sengoku; *Mem Bd Dir* Gordon Davis
Open by appt; No admis fee; Estab 1975 to collect & preserve primary & secondary resource materials in the Black Cultural Arts, to provide tools & access to these materials for artist, scholars & general pub, to develop programs in arts which use resources of Collection; Maintains Oral History Library & Reference Library
Income: Grants and public donations
Library Holdings: Audio Tapes, Book Volumes, CD-ROMs, Clipping Files, Exhibition Catalogs, Kodachrome Transparencies, Lantern Slides, Manuscripts, Memorabilia, Original Art Works, Original Documents, Other Holdings, Pamphlets, Photographs 4,000, Records, Slides 13,200, Video Tapes
Special Subjects: Afro-American Art, Historical Material, Painting-American, Photography, Prints, Sculpture
Collections: Owen & Edith Dodson Memorial Collection, Theodore Ward Collection: play scripts, interviews & letters, Charles & Elease Griffin Collection: lobby cards, interviews & still photos, Arthur Smith Collection: drawings of his jewelry, patterns, photos, interviews & letters, Harlem Renaissance Theatre Bibliography: photocopies of all theatre articles published in major black periodicals, 1917 - 1930, Dorothy & Reuben Silver Collection: plays & programs from early days at Karamu House, Cleveland OH, Bio-Data Archives
Publications: Artist & Influence, annual journal
Activities: Classes for adults & children; dramatic progs; lects open to pub; book traveling exhibs; originate traveling exhibs

M **HEBREW UNION COLLEGE - JEWISH INSTITUTE OF RELIGION MUSEUM,** (Universal Technical Institute) Jewish Institute of Religion, One W Fourth St, New York, NY 10012-1186. Tel 212-824-2218; Fax 212-388-1720; Email museumnyc@huc.edu; Web: www.huc.edu/museums/ny; *Cur* Laura Kruger; *Dir* Jean Bloch Rosensaft
Open Mon - Thurs 9 AM - 5 PM, Fri 9 AM - 3 PM; No admis fee; Estab 1984 to present 4000 years of Jewish art with stress on contemporary art expressing Jewish identity & themes; 2,000 sq ft of space; Average Annual Attendance: 30,000
Income: Financed by annual budget & fundraising
Library Holdings: Original Art Works, Photographs, Prints, Sculpture
Special Subjects: Archaeology, Architecture, Bookplates & Bindings, Bronzes, Calligraphy, Ceramics, Collages, Crafts, Etchings & Engravings, Folk Art, Graphics, Historical Material, Judaica, Juvenile Art, Manuscripts, Maps, Medieval Art, Miniatures, Painting-American, Painting-Israeli, Painting-Russian, Photography, Prints, Religious Art, Sculpture
Collections: Biblical archaeology, contemporary art expressing Jewish identity & themes, Jewish ritual art, Biblical Archaeology Collection, Jewish Ritual Art Collection
Exhibitions: Living in the Moment: Contemporary Artists Celebrate Jewish Time; (See Website)
Publications: Exhibition catalogs & brochures
Activities: Classes for adults & children; dramatic progs; docent training; lects open to pub, 5 vis lectrs per yr; concerts; gallery talks; tours; lending of original objects of art to other mus; book traveling exhibs 3 per yr; originate traveling exhibs to mus & univs throughout North America, 6 per yr; mus shop sells original art

M **HENRY STREET SETTLEMENT,** Abrons Art Center, 265 Henry St, New York, NY 10002-4808. Tel 212-766-9200; Fax 212-505-8329; Email info@henrystreet.org; Web: www.henrystreet.org; *Exec Dir* David Garza; *Dir Engagement & Visual Arts* Carolyn Sickles
Open second Tues of month group tours of agency 10:30 - 11:30 AM; No admis fee; Estab 1975 as a multi discipline community arts center for the performing & visual arts programs; Thematic group exhib of the work of contemporary artists, photo gallery for solo shows; Average Annual Attendance: 100,000
Income: government, foundations, individual support
Exhibitions: Contemporary art by emerging artists, women artists & artists of color, changing thematic exhibitions; rotating
Activities: Classes for adults & children in all arts disciplines; drama, dance and music prog; docent training; gallery educ prog for school and community groups; lects open to pub; 5 vis lectrs per yr; concerts; gallery talks; tours; schol and fels offered

M **THE HISPANIC SOCIETY OF AMERICA,** Hispanic Society Museum & Library, Audubon Terrace, Broadway between 155th & 156th Sts New York, NY 10032; 613 W 155th, New York, NY 10032. Tel 212-926-2234; Fax 212-690-0743; Email info@hispanicsociety.org; Web: www.hispanicsociety.org; *Exec Dir & Pres* Mitchell A Codding; *Asst Dir & Cur Decorative Arts* Margaret Connors McQuade; *Cur Archaeology & Sculpture* Constancio del Alamo; *Cur Prints & Photographs* Patrick Lenaghan; *Cur Emeritus* Priscilla E Muller; *Cur Rare Books* John O'Neill; *Asst Cur Rare Books & US* Vanessa Pintado; *Asst Cur Modern Books (1830-Present)* Edwin Rolon; *Sr Cur Paintings & Metalwork* Marcus Burke; *Develop Officer* Elaine Delgado; *Dir Pub Relations, Progs & Special Events* Mencia Figueroa
Closed until fall 2019, appointment only; No admis fee; Estab 1904 by Archer Milton Huntington as a free public museum and library devoted to the art & culture of the Hispanic world; Average Annual Attendance: 25,000; Mem: Open to the public, basic dues $50; additional group of scholarly members, 400 in 2 categories, by election only
Income: Financed by endowment
Purchases: Hispanic objects in various media
Library Holdings: Audio Tapes, Book Volumes, Exhibition Catalogs, Manuscripts, Maps, Original Documents, Prints
Special Subjects: Antiquities-Greek, Archaeology, Baroque Art, Bookplates & Bindings, Calligraphy, Carpets & Rugs, Ceramics, Ceramics, Coins & Medals, Costumes, Crafts, Decorative Arts, Drawings, Embroidery, Enamels, Etchings & Engravings, Ethnology, Folk Art, Furniture, Graphics, Hispanic Art, Historical Material, Islamic Art, Ivory, Jewelry, Judaica, Laces, Landscapes, Latin American Art, Manuscripts, Maps, Medieval Art, Metalwork, Mexican Art, Painting-American, Painting-European, Painting-Spanish, Photography, Porcelain, Portraits, Posters, Pottery, Primitive art, Prints, Religious Art, Renaissance Art, Sculpture, Silver, Textiles, Watercolors, Woodcuts, Art History, History of Art & Archaeology, Glass

Collections: Hispanic Collection, rare books, photographic reference files, fine & decorative arts from Spain, Portugal & Latin America
Exhibitions: Permanent gallery exhibits are representative of the arts and cultures of Iberian Peninsula from prehistory to the present; Viceregal Latin America
Publications: Works by members of the staff and society on Spanish art, history, literature & bibliography, with spec emphasis on the collections of the society
Activities: Educational progs for adults & children; docent training; lects open to public, 6 vis lectrs per year; concerts; gallery talks; tours; exten prog serves New York area schools; Mus shop sells books, reproductions, prints, jewelry & accessories

M **HUDSON GUILD,** Hudson Guild Gallery, 441 W 26th St, New York, NY 10001-5699. Tel 212-760-9800; Fax 646-599-8784; Email info@hudsonguild.org; Web: hudsonguild.org; *Gallery Dir* Jim Furlong
Open Tues - Fri 10 AM - 7 PM; No admis fee; Estab 1948 for exhibition of contemporary art; A modern facility within the Hudson Guild Building. The Art Gallery is also open for all performances of the Hudson Guild Theatre; Average Annual Attendance: 2,000
Income: Financed by the New York City Department of Cultural Affairs, Avery Foundation, Jolie Stahl
Activities: Educ prog; classes for adults & children; lects open to pub; 10 vis lectrs per year; gallery talks; tours for youth & seniors

A **INDEPENDENT CURATORS INTERNATIONAL,** 799 Broadway #205, New York, NY 10013-3020. Tel 212-254-8200; Fax 212-477-4781; Email info@ici-exhibitions.org; Web: www.ici-exhibitions.org; *Exhib Mgr* Frances Wu Giarratano; *Exec Dir* Kate Fowle; *Develop Mgr* Kristin Nelson
Open 10 AM - 6 PM; Estab 1975 as a nonprofit traveling exhib service specializing in contemporary art
Income: $750,000
Exhibitions: Everything Can Be Different; My Reality: Contemporary Art and Culture of Japanese Animation; The Gift; Thin Skin; Walkways; Beyond Preconceptions; Pictures, Patents and Monkeys; On Collecting; Telematic Connections; Mark Lombard: Global Networks; Beyond Green: Toward a Sustainable Art; High Times, Hard Times: New York Paintings 1967-1975; Jess: To and From the Printed Page; Phantasmagoria: Specters of Absence
Publications: Exhibition catalogs
Activities: Originate traveling contemporary art exhibs; ICI independents; museums; university galleries & art centers

M **INTAR GALLERY,** P.O. Box 756, New York, NY 10108-0025. Tel 212-695-6134; Email intar@intartheatre.org; Web: www.intartheatre.org; *Dir* John McCormack
Open Mon - Fri 10 AM - 6 PM; No admis fee; Estab 1978. Assists & exhibits artists of diverse racial backgrounds. Devoted to artists who inhabit a dimension of their own in which the tension between singularity & universality has been acknowledged successfully; Only Hispanic gallery in area; Average Annual Attendance: 7,000
Income: Financed by endowment
Special Subjects: Afro-American Art, American Indian Art, Latin American Art, Mexican Art, Photography, Sculpture, Southwestern Art
Exhibitions: Rotating exhib
Publications: Exhibition catalogues
Activities: Lect open to public; gallery talks; originates traveling exhibs

M **THE INTERCHURCH CENTER,** Galleries at the Interchurch Center, 475 Riverside Dr Ste 240, New York, NY 10115-0003. Tel 212-870-2200; Fax 212-870-2440; Email admin@interchurch-center.org; Web: www.interchurch-center.org; *Dir & Cur* Dorothy Cochran; *Interim CEO* Gleniss Schonholtz
Open daily 9 AM - 5 PM; No admis fee; Estab 1969; Two exhibit spaces Treasure Room Gallery 2,000 sq ft, Corridor Gallery 20 self-lite cases which line North & South Corridor each approx 36 x 50 ft; Average Annual Attendance: 10,000
Income: Financed by the bldg corporation
Purchases: Substantial sales throughout the yr
Special Subjects: African Art, Afro-American Art, American Indian Art, Asian Art, Bookplates & Bindings, Calligraphy, Ceramics, Collages, Crafts, Decorative Arts, Dolls, Drawings, Embroidery, Enamels, Eskimo Art, Etchings & Engravings, Graphics, Hispanic Art, Jewelry, Landscapes, Latin American Art, Marine Painting, Mexican Art, Mosaics, Oriental Art
Collections: Lenore Tawney tapestry (permanent installation)
Exhibitions: Rotating exhibits, 10 per year
Publications: website newsletter
Activities: Educ Prog; lects open to pub, 2 vis lectrs per yr; concerts; gallery talks

L **Library**, 475 Riverside Dr, New York, NY 10115-0003. Tel 212-870-3804; Fax 212-870-2440; Email tdelduca@interchurch-center.org; Web: interchurch-center.org; *Dir & Cur Galleries* Dorothy Cochran; *Pres & Exec Dir* Mary McNamara
Open Mon - Fri 9 AM - 5 PM; Estab 1959 to enhance the employee environment & be a New York City neighborhood art resources; 2,000 sq ft (Treasure Room Gallery) & twenty (46ft x 36 ft) built in, self-light wall display cases; Average Annual Attendance: 4,000
Income: $6,000,000
Purchases: $6,000
Library Holdings: Book Volumes 14,000, Periodical Subscriptions 95
Exhibitions: Changing exhibitions on a 10 month schedule
Publications: 475 Newsletter, monthly
Activities: Noon time music & arts programming; lects open to pub, 5 vis lectrs per yr; concerts; gallery talks; tours

A **INTERNATIONAL CENTER OF MEDIEVAL ART,** 99 Margaret Corbin Dr, The Cloisters, Fort Tryonn Park New York, NY 10040-1198. Tel 212-928-1146; Fax 212-928-9946; Email icma@medievalart.org; Web: www.medievalart.org; *Pres* Helen C Evans; *VPres* Nina Rowe; *Treas* David Raizman; *Secy* Anne Rudloff Stanton; *Admin* Ryan Frisinger
Open Mon - Tues & Thurs - Fri 9 AM - 5 PM; Estab 1956 to promote greater knowledge of the arts of the Middle Ages working with mus & scholars to contribute & make new research available to the pub; Sponsors many sessions & lects worldwide & expanding; Mem: 900; dues $20-$1,200 (depending on level)
Publications: Gesta (illustrated journal), two issues per year; ICMA Newsletter, 3 issues per year; Romanesque Sculpture in American Collections I, II, III, New England Museums; Gothic Sculpture in American Collections I,II, & III
Activities: Lects open to pub; 1,000 lectrs per yr; awards: Student Travel Awards, Kress Research Award, Kress Travel Awards, & Student Essay Award

M **INTERNATIONAL CENTER OF PHOTOGRAPHY,** Museum, 250 Bowery, New York, NY 10012. Tel 212-857-0000; 857-9725 (Store); Email info@icp.org; Web: www.icp.org; *Exec Dir* Mark Lubell; *COO & CFO* Laurie McLeod; *Controller* Victor Quinones; *Chief Devel Officer* Julie Davidson; *Sr Dir Opers & Vis Engagement* Karen Eckhaus; *Dir Exhibs & Colls* Erin Barnett
Open Tues - Wed & Fri - Sun 10 AM - 6 PM, Thurs 10 AM - 9 PM; Admis adults $14, seniors $12, students $10, mems & children 14 & under free; Estab 1974 to encourage & assist photographers of all ages & nationalities who are vitally concerned with their world & times, to find & help new talents, to uncover & preserve forgotten archives & to present such work to the pub; Maintains five exhibition galleries showing a changing exhibition program of photographic expression & experimentation by over 2,500 photographers; Average Annual Attendance: 100,000; Mem: 4,600; dues $40 & up
Income: Financed by public & private grants, NYC Dept of Cultural Affairs
Library Holdings: Audio Tapes, Book Volumes 15,000, Cassettes, Clipping Files, Exhibition Catalogs, Filmstrips, Kodachrome Transparencies, Original Documents, Pamphlets, Periodical Subscriptions 75, Photographs, Slides, Video Tapes
Special Subjects: Photography
Collections: The core of the collection is 20th century documentary photography, with a companion collection of examples of master photographs of the 20th century. Major holdings incl works from the documentary tradition as well as fashion & other aesthetic genres
Publications: Annual report; monographs; exhibition catalogs; programs guide
Activities: Classes for adults & children; docent training; cert & MFA prog; scholarships; lects open to pub; lects for members only; gallery talks; tours; awards; scholarships; book traveling exhibs; originate traveling exhibs; mus shop sells books, magazines, slides

L **Research Center**, 1114 Ave of the Americas at 43rd St, New York, NY 10036-7703. Tel 212-857-0004 (Library); 857-9733 (Archives); Fax 212-857-0091; 768-4688 (Print Study Rm); Email library@icp.org; collections @ icp.org; Web: www.icp.org; *Librn* Deirdre Donahue
Open Mon - Thurs 10 AM - 7 PM, Fri 10 AM - 6 PM to students, staff & faculty; open to pub by appt only; Comprised of Mus coll, library, archives, reference materials & digital assets; maintains Print Study Room; available to students & scholars; Average Annual Attendance: 5,000
Income: Financed by pub & private grants
Library Holdings: Auction Catalogs, Audio Tapes, Book Volumes 8,000, Cassettes, Clipping Files, DVDs, Exhibition Catalogs, Filmstrips, Kodachrome Transparencies, Pamphlets, Periodical Subscriptions 100, Slides, Video Tapes
Special Subjects: Photography
Collections: Archives contains films, video tapes & audio recordings of programs related to photographs in the colls as well as programs about the subject & history of photography, Work by: Henri Cartier-Bresson, Martin Munkasci, W Eugene Smith, Gerda Taro, Impact Visuals Coll, September 11 Coll, Time-Life Coll, AIDs Graphics Coll, Artists Poster Committee Coll, Photographic Album Coll, African American History Coll, Hiroshima Coll, Cornell Cappa Archives, Robert Cappa Archives, David Seidner Archives, Roman Vishniac Archives, Weegee Archives, Lecture Series Archive, Photomuse online resource, eMuseum database
Publications: ICP/Steidl books

M **Rita K Hillman Education Gallery**, 1114 Ave of the Americas, at 43rd St New York, NY 10036-7703. Tel 212-857-0001; Fax 212-857-0091; Email education@icp.org; Web: www.icp.org; *Facilities Supv* Per Gylfe
Open daily 10 AM - 6 PM; Exhibs the work of students, faculty & staff of the ICP School. See separate listing under US Schools in New York, NY for ICP School
Special Subjects: Photography
Activities: Classes for adults & children; lects open to pub, tours

INTERNATIONAL FOUNDATION FOR ART RESEARCH, INC
For further information, see National and Regional Organizations

M **JAPAN SOCIETY, INC,** Japan Society Gallery, 333 E 47th St, New York, NY 10017-2399. Tel 212-832-1155 (General), 212-715-1258 (Box Office); Fax 212-715-1262; Web: www.japansociety.org; *Pres Japan Society* Motoatsu Sakurai; *Gallery Dir* Yukie Kamiya; *Exhibs Mgr* Rylan Buchholz; *Gallery Assoc* Lia Monti
Open Tues - Thurs noon - 7 PM, Fri noon - 9 PM, Sat & Sun 11 AM - 5 PM, cl Mon & major holidays; Admis non-members $5, seniors & students $3, mems free for summer exhibitions; Estab 1907, bi-cultural membership organizations to deepen understanding and friendship between Japan and the United States; Asian/Japanese Art; Average Annual Attendance: 30,000 gallery exhibitions/80,000 includ other programs; Mem: 2,500 individual; dues $10,000, $5,000, $2,000, $1,000, $500, $250, $150, $100, $60; Friends of Gallery $2000; Qualifications for mem AAM, ICOM, Mus Council NY
Income: Financed by mem, grants & donations
Special Subjects: Asian Art, Decorative Arts, Graphics, Painting-Japanese, Sculpture, Textiles
Collections: Japan Society permanent coll: ceramics, paintings, prints, sculpture & woodblocks
Publications: Japan Society Newsletter, monthly; exhibition catalogs accompanying each exhibition
Activities: Educ dept; classes for adults & children; docent training; lects open to public; concerts, gallery talks; tours, sponsor competitions; fellowships & Japan Society Award; 1-2 per yr; originate traveling exhibs to museums worldwide

L **C.V. Starr Library**, 333 E 47th St, New York, NY 10017. Tel 212-832-1155, Ext 256; Fax 212-715-6752; Email gen@japansociety.org; Web: www.japansociety.org/contentcfn/library; *Dir* Reiko Sassa; *Asst Librn* Rebecca Leonard
Open Mon - Fri Noon - 5 PM; Admis only for members & Toyota language students; Estab 1971; Mem: 3,000; dues $55 - $1500
Income: Financed by mem

Library Holdings: Book Volumes 14,000, Clipping Files, Pamphlets, Periodical Subscriptions 35
Publications: What Shall I Read on Japan

M **THE JEWISH MUSEUM,** 1109 5th Ave at 92nd St, New York, NY 10128. Tel 212-423-3200; Fax 212-423-3232; Email info@thejm.org; Web: www.thejewishmuseum.org; *Dir* Claudia Gould; *Chief of Staff* David Goldberg; *Deputy Dir Fin & Admin* Joseph Rorech; *Deputy Dir Prog Admin* Ruth Beesch; *Deputy Dir Devel* Elyse Buxbaum; *Deputy Dir Mktg & Communs* Sarah Supcoff; *Dir Educ* Nelly Silagy Benedek; *Sr Cur* Susan Braunstein; *Chief Counsel & Talent Officer* Cindy Caplan
Open Fri - Tues, 11 AM - 5:45 PM, Thurs 11 AM - 8 PM; Admis adults $15, seniors $12, students with ID cards $7.50, mems, children 18 & under & Sat free; Estab 1904 to preserve & present the Jewish cultural tradition. Three exhibition floors devoted to the display of ceremonial objects & fine art in the permanent collection, special exhibitions from the permanent collections & photographs & contemporary art on loan; Maintains reference library; Average Annual Attendance: 200,000; Mem: 13,000; dues $65 & up
Income: Financed by mem, grants, individual contributions & organizations
Special Subjects: Archaeology, Architecture, Carpets & Rugs, Cartoons, Ceramics, Coins & Medals, Decorative Arts, Drawings, Embroidery, Etchings & Engravings, Graphics, Textiles, Judaica
Collections: Broadcast media material, Jewish ceremonial objects, comprehensive collection of Jewish ceremonial art, Harry G Friedman Collection of Ceremonial Objects, Samuel Friedenberg Collection of Plaques & Medals, Rose & Benjamin Mintz Collection of Eastern European Art, Harry J Stein-Samuel Friedenberg Collection of Coins from the Holy Land
Exhibitions: Culture & Continuity: The Jewish Journey, Pickles & Pomegranates; Modigliani: Beyond the Myth; Eva Hesse: Sculpture; Action/Abstraction; Pollock, de Kooning & American Art, 1940-1976; Man Ray: The Art of Reinvention; Edouard Vuillard: A Painter and His Muses, 1890-1940; Chagall: Love, War & Exile, other Primary Structures; Helena Rubinstein: Beauty Is Power
Publications: Annual report; exhibition catalogs; newsletter, quarterly; poster & graphics; program brochures
Activities: Classes for adults & children; docent training; dramatic programs; lects open to pub; 20 vis lectrs per yr; concerts; gallery talks; tours; individual paintings lent to other museums; book traveling exhibs 1-2 per yr; originate traveling exhibs circulating to other museums; mus shop sells books, magazines, original art, reproductions, prints, slides, needlecrafts, posters, catalogs & postcards

L **Library,** 1109 Fifth Ave, New York, NY 10128. Tel 212-423-3200; Fax 212-423-3232; *Dir* Claudia Gould
Open Sun - Mon & Wed - Thurs 11 AM - 5:45 PM, Tues 11 AM - 9 PM, Fri 11 AM - 3 PM; Reference library open to the public by appointment only
Income: Financed by Jewish Museum budget & private sources
Library Holdings: Audio Tapes, Book Volumes 8,000, Cassettes, Clipping Files, Exhibition Catalogs, Other Holdings Vertical Files 2,500, Pamphlets, Photographs, Slides, Video Tapes
Special Subjects: Archaeology, Ethnology, Folk Art, Judaica, Painting-American, Painting-European, Painting-Russian, Photography, Posters, Religious Art
Collections: Esther M Rosen Slide Library (contains slides of objects in the museum's coll)

A **JOHN SIMON GUGGENHEIM MEMORIAL FOUNDATION,** 90 Park Ave, New York, NY 10016-1301. Tel 212-687-4470; Fax 212-697-3248; Email fellowships@jsgmf.org; Web: www.gf.org; *Chmn* William P Kelly; *Pres* Edward Hirsch
Open 9 AM - 4:30 PM; Estab & incorporated 1925; offers fellowships to further the development of scholars & artists by assisting them to engage in research in any field of knowledge & creation in any of the arts, under the freest possible conditions & irrespective of race, color or creed; For additional information see section devoted to Scholarships and Fellowships
Activities: Fels offered

C **THE JPMORGAN CHASE,** Art Collection, 270 Park Ave, New York, NY 10017-2014. Tel 212-270-6000; Web: www.jpmorganchase.com; *Exec Dir & Chief Cur* Lisa K Erf
Open during bank hours; artwork displayed during exhibitions offsite, hours vary by location; Estab 1959 to support young & emerging artists & enhance bank offices world-wide; Collection displayed in branches, offices in New York City, state & world-wide
Collections: Largely contemporary American, 30,000 works in all media
Exhibitions: Various exhibitions
Publications: Exhibit catalogs
Activities: Lects for employees; individual objects of art lent to museum & gallery exhibs; originate traveling exhibs

A **KENKELEBA HOUSE, INC,** Kenkeleba Gallery, 214 E Second St, New York, NY 10009-8031. Tel 212-674-3939; Fax 212-505-5080; *Art Dir* Joe Overstreet; *Dir* Corrine Jennings
Open Tues - Sat 11 AM - 6 PM; No admis fee; Estab 1975, Committed to the goals of presenting, preserving & encouraging the development of art excluded from the cultural mainstream. Supports experimental & interdisciplinary approaches. Features exhibitions of contemporary & modern painting, sculpture, experimental media, performance, poetry readings & literary forums
Collections: 20th Century African American Artists
Exhibitions: Eleanor Magid & Tom Kendall; Frank Stewart & Adal (photography)

M **KENNEDY GALLERIES,** Kennedy Galleries, Inc, 730 Fifth Ave, New York, NY 10019. Tel 212-541-9600; Fax 212-977-3833; Email inquiry@kgny.com; Web: www.kgny.com; *Pres* Martha Fleischman
No admis fee; Private dealer of 18th, 19th & 20th century American art
Collections: 18th, 19th & 20th Century American paintings, drawings, prints
Publications: American Art Journal

M **THE KITCHEN,** 512 W 19th St, New York, NY 10011-2899. Tel 212-255-5793; Fax 212-645-4258; Email info@thekitchen.org; Web: www.thekitchen.org; *Exec Dir & Chief Cur* Tim Griffin
Open Tues - Sat 11 AM - 6 PM; No admis fee; Estab 1971 and showing innovative work by emerging & established artists across disciplines
Collections: Video Collection: over 600 titles by almost 300 artists
Exhibitions: Katherine Hubbard: Bring Your Own Lights; Sondra Perry: Resident Evil
Activities: Performances; talks; discussions

M **LA MAMA LA GALLERIA,** 47 Great Jones St, New York, NY 10003. Tel 212-505-2476; Email lamamagalleria@gmail.com; Web: lamama.org/lagalleria; *Gallery Dir* Matt Nasser
Open Wed - Sun 1 - 7 PM; No admis fee; Estab 1984 for exhibition of emerging artists; 2,500 sq ft, bi-level; Average Annual Attendance: 8,000
Income: Financed through grants & donations
Exhibitions: Rotating exhibitions, 14 per yr
Activities: Classes for adults & children; lects open to pub, 6 vis lectrs per yr; concerts; gallery talks

A **LEO BAECK INSTITUTE,** 15 W 16th St, New York, NY 10011-6301. Tel 212-744-6400; Fax 212-988-1305; Email lbi1@lbi.com; Web: www.lbi.org; *Pres* Ronald B Sobel; *Head Archivist* Hermann Teifer; *Exec Dir* Dr William Weitzer
Open Mon - Thurs 9 AM - 5 PM, Fri 9 AM - 3 PM; No admis fee; Estab 1955 to document history of German-Speaking Jews; Center includes library & archives; about 180 running ft, various display cases for books & documents; Average Annual Attendance: 2,000; Mem: 800; dues $200
Library Holdings: Book Volumes, Clipping Files, DVDs, Original Art Works, Original Documents, Photographs, Prints, Video Tapes
Special Subjects: Architecture, Cartoons, Costumes, Drawings, Embroidery, Etchings & Engravings, Graphics, Historical Material, Judaica, Landscapes, Manuscripts, Metalwork, Mosaics, Painting-German, Painting-Israeli, Photography, Porcelain, Posters, Prints, Religious Art, Reproductions, Sculpture, Silver, Textiles, Watercolors
Collections: Drawings, paintings, prints, sculpture, ritual objects, textiles from 15th - 20th centuries, 19th - 20th Century German-Jewish Artists, including Max Liebermann, Lesser Ury, Ludwig Meidner, Hugo Steiner-Prag
Exhibitions: Portraits of German Jews; Special thematic exhibits e.g.: Publishing in Exile (German); Publishers in U.S.; Radical Departure - avant garde Expressionist art 1900-1950 (German)
Publications: Year Book; LBI News, semi-annually
Activities: Lect open to public, 7-8 vis lectrs per year; concerts; gallery talks; tours; annual Leo Baeck Medal; scholarships & fellowships offered; individual paintings & original objects of art lent to cultural art institutions; lending collection contains paintings, sculptures, 50,000 books, 5,000 original art works, 2,500 original prints, 40,000 photographs; sells books

L **Library,** 15 W 16th St, New York, NY 10011-6301. Tel 212-744-6400; Fax 212-988-1305; Email hteifer@lbi.cjh.org; Web: www.lbi.org/; *Head Archivist* Hermann Teifer; *Exec Dir* Dr William Weitzer; *Head Librn* Ginger Barna
Open Mon 9:30 AM - 8 PM, Tues - Thurs 9:30 AM - 5 PM, Fri - 9:30 AM - 3 PM, Sun 11 AM - 5 PM; Estab 1955 to collect & preserve materials by & about history of German-speaking Jews; For reference only; Mem: $200 general, $500 institutional
Income: Financed by endowment & mem
Library Holdings: Book Volumes 80,000, Fiche, Original Art Works 6,300, Original Documents, Pamphlets, Periodical Subscriptions 150, Photographs 30,000, Prints 5,000, Sculpture 30
Special Subjects: Drawings, Folk Art, Historical Material, History of Art & Archaeology, Judaica, Painting-German, Portraits, Prints, Stage Design, Watercolors
Collections: Archival library and art colls relating to German-Jewish life & history
Exhibitions: 3-4 exhibs per year
Publications: LBI yearbook; LBI memorial lect
Activities: Lects open to public; concerts; gallery talks; Fels

C **LOIS WAGNER FINE ARTS,** 15 E 71st St Ste 2A, New York, NY 10021-4171. Tel 212-396-1407; Fax 212-396-1408; Email lwagnerfinearts@gmai.com; Web: www.lwagnerfinearts.com; *Pres* Lois Wagner
Open by appointment only; No admis fee; Estab 1993; 19th & 20th Century American art, 19220 Century European Art
Collections: American Impressionism & Realism Collection (1880-1930), Contemporary Realism Collection, figurative, landscape & still-life paintings, American Impressionism & Realism Collection, Contemporary Photography, Post Impressionism - European

M **M55ART,** 530 W 25th St, Fl 4 New York, NY 10027-6401. Tel 212-467-7063; Email info@m55art.org; Email m55artgallery@gmail.com; Web: www.m55art.org
Open Tues - Sat 11 AM - 6 PM; No admis fee; Estab 1969 to give unaffiliated artists a space to show their work; Gallery is a cooperative gallery; Average Annual Attendance: 8,000; Mem: 22; dues $1,350; meeting every 2 months
Income: Financed by mem dues
Exhibitions: One Person & Group shows including John Bradford, David Woodell, Joe Sandman, Michael Tice, Kye Carbone, Bob Meltzmuff, Sydney Drum, Barry Malloy, Milt Connors, Megan Lipke, Catherine Hall, Joe Smith, Joy Walker, Diane Whitcomb, Ethlin Honig, Cris Blyth, Courtney Cavalieri, Masako Honjo, Annette Morris, Esme Thompson, Steve Ridell, Daniel Heyman, Virginia Vogel, Jonathan Lev, Robert Jessel, Michael Amato, Alexis Kuhr, Bobbi Goldman, Josh Dorman
Activities: Apprenticeship prog; competitions; individual paintings & original objects of art lent to college shows

M **MARYMOUNT MANHATTAN COLLEGE HEWITT GALLERY,** 221 E 71 St, New York, NY 10021. Tel 212-517-0693; Fax 212-517-0413; Email art@mmm.edu; Web: www.mmm.edu/departments/art/the-hewitt-gallery-of-art.php; *Dir* Hallie Cohen
Open daily 9 AM - 9 PM; No admis fee; Estab 1982 as a showcase for unaffiliated artists; Gallery is 30 x 40 ft; Average Annual Attendance: 2,500
Exhibitions: Various exhibitions
Activities: Classes for adults; lect by artist; gallery talks

M **THE METROPOLITAN MUSEUM OF ART,** 1000 5th Ave, Main Bldg New York, NY 10028-0113. Tel 212-535-7710 (General Information), 879-5500 (Museum Offices); Fax 212-570-3879; Email communications@metmuseum.org; Web: www.metmuseum.org; *Acting Dir & CEO* Daniel Weiss; *Interim Deputy Dir Colls & Admin* Andrea Bayer; *Sr Admin Exhibs & International Affairs* Martha Deese; *Publr & Ed in Chief* Mark Polizzotti; *Chief Registrar* Aileen Chuk; *Sr VPres & Chief Investment Officer* Lauren A. Meserve; *Cur in Charge, Arts of Africa, Oceania & the Americas* Alisa LaGamma; *Cur in Charge, American Decorative Arts* Alice Cooney Frelinghuysen; *Cur in Charge, Arms & Armor* Pierre Terjanian; *Chmn Asian Art* Maxwell Hearn; *Cur in Charge, The Costume Inst* Andrew Bolton; *Cur in Charge, Drawings & Prints* Nadine Orenstein; *Cur in Charge, Egyptian Art* Diana Craig Patch; *Chmn, European Paintings* Keith Christiansen; *Chmn, European Sculpture & Decorative Drawings* Luke Syson; *Cur in Charge, Islamic Art* Sheila Canby; *Cur in Charge & Admin, Robert Lehman Coll* Dita Amory; *Cur in Charge, Medieval Art & The Cloisters* C. Griffith Mann; *Chmn, Modern & Contemporary Art* Sheena Wagstaff; *Cur in Charge, Musical Instruments* J. Kenneth Moore; *Cur in Charge, Photographs* Jeff Rosenheim; *Conservator in Charge, Objects* Lisa Pilosi; *Conservator in Charge, Paintings* Michael Gallagher; *Conservator in Charge, Paper* Marjorie Shelley; *Conservator in Charge, Photographs* Jeff L Rosenheim; *Scientist in Charge* Marco Leona; *Conservator in Charge, Textiles* Florence Zaharia; *Chmn, Educ* Sandra Jackson-Dumont; *Mng Archivist* James Moske
Open Sun - Thurs 10 AM - 5:30 PM, Fri & Sat 10 AM - 9 PM, cl Thanksgiving, Christmas Day, New Year's Day & the first Mon in May; Admis suggested for adults $25, seniors $17, students $12, members & children under 12 with adult free; Estab 1870 to encourage & develop the study of the fine arts & the application of arts to life; of advancing the general knowledge of kindred subjects & to that end of furnishing popular instruction & recreation; Average Annual Attendance: 7,000,000; Mem: 97,245; dues patron $4000, sponsor $2000, donor $900, contributing $600, sustaining $300, dual $125, individual $70, student $30, national assoc $35
Income: $78,146,461 (financed by endowment, mem, city & state appropriations & other)
Special Subjects: Antiquities-Assyrian, Antiquities-Byzantine, Antiquities-Egyptian, Antiquities-Etruscan, Antiquities-Greek, Antiquities-Persian, Antiquities-Roman, Costumes, Decorative Arts, Drawings, Medieval Art, Oriental Art, Painting-American, Painting-European, Painting-German, Photography, Primitive art, Sculpture, Asian Art
Collections: Acquisitions-Departments: Africana, Oceanic, American decorative arts, paintings & sculpture, Ancient Near Eastern art, arms & armor, Costume Institute, Egyptian art, European paintings, sculpture & decorative arts, Greek & Roman art, Islamic art, Lehman Collection, medieval art & The Cloisters, musical instruments, prints, photographs, Twentieth Century Art Exhibitions, Charles A Greenfield Collection, Sackler Collection, Leon Spilliaert Collection, Photograph Study Collection
Publications: Bulletin, quarterly; Calendar, bi-monthly; The Journal, annually; exhibition catalogs, scholarly books
Activities: Classes for adults & children; docent training; films; progs for the disabled touch collection; lects open to pub; concerts; gallery talks; tours; outreach; exten dept serves community progs for greater New York City area; color reproductions, individual paintings & original objects of art lent to other institutions; book traveling exhibs; originate traveling exhibs to US mus; mus shop sells books, magazines, original art, reproductions, prints, slides, children's activities, records, postcards & posters

M **The Met Cloisters**, 99 Margaret Corbin Dr, Fort Tryon Park New York, NY 10040. Tel 212-923-3700; Fax 212-795-3640; Email cloisters@metmuseum.org; Web: www.metmuseum.org/cloisters/; *Cur in Charge* Michel David-Weill; *Sr Cur* Barbara Boehm; *Cur Emeritus* Timothy Husband; *Mgr Admin* Christina Alphonso
Open Mar - Oct, daily 10 AM - 5:15 PM; Nov - Feb, daily 10 AM - 4:45 PM, cl New Year's Day, Thanksgiving & Christmas; Admis suggested for adults $25, seniors $17, students $12, mems & children under 12 with adult free; Estab 1938 to display in an appropriate setting works of art & architecture of the Middle Ages; Medieval French cloisters incorporated into the building, as well as the chap house, a chapel & Romanesque apse; also Medieval herb garden. Branch of Metropolitan Museum of Art, New York, NY; Mem: Part of Met Museum
Collections: Frescoes, ivories, precious metalwork, paintings, polychromed statues, stained glass, tapestries, and other French and Spanish architectural elements, gardens
Publications: A Walk Through The Cloisters; exhib catalogs; Medieval Gardens Enclosed, blog
Activities: Dramatic progs; workshops; lects open to pub; concerts; gallery talks; tours; original objects of art lent to other mus; mus shop sells books, reproductions, prints and slides

L **The Cloisters Library & Archives**, 99 Margaret Corbin Dr, Fort Tryon Park New York, NY 10040. Tel 212-396-5319; Fax 212-795-3640; Email cloisters.library@metmuseum.org; Web: www.metmuseum.org/art/libraries-and-research-centers/the-cloisters-library-and-archive; *Assoc Mus Librn* Michael Carr
Open Tues - Fri 10 AM - 4:30 PM by appt only; No admis fee; Estab 1938 to be used as a small highly specialized reference library for the curatorial staff at The Cloisters; scholars & accredited graduate students are welcome & qualified researchers by appointment only
Income: Financed by endowment
Library Holdings: Book Volumes 12,000, Fiche 9,000, Other Holdings Original documents, Periodical Subscriptions 58, Photographs 22,000, Reels, Slides 20,000
Special Subjects: Architecture, Art History, Enamels, Sculpture, Stained Glass, Tapestries
Collections: George Grey Barnard Papers, Harry Bober Papers, Joseph & Ernest Brummer Papers, Summer McKnight Crosby Papers, Demotte Photograph Archive, Archives of the Cloisters

M **The Met Breuer**, 945 Madison Ave, New York, NY 10021. Tel 212-731-1675; Web: www.metmuseum.org/breuer/; *Asst for Admin* Tempris Small; *Mgr Mus Experience* Richard Carroll; *Asst Mgr Mus Experience* Cristina Ambroselli; *Assoc Coordr Mus Experience* Amy Novak; *Assoc Coordr Mus Experience* Cody Barbour
Open Tues - Thurs 10 AM - 5:30 PM, Fri & Sat 10 AM - 9 PM, Sun 10 AM - 5:30 PM; cl Thanksgiving Day, Christmas & New Year's Day; Admis suggested for adults $25, seniors $17, students $12, members & children under 12 with adult free; Modern & contemporary art program incl exhibs, performances, art commissions, residencies and educ initiatives.

L **Museum Libraries**, 1000 5th Ave, New York, NY 10028-0113. Tel 212-650-2225; Fax 212-570-3847; Email watson.library@metmuseum.org; Web: library.metmuseum.org; *Mus Librn, Sherman Fairchild Ctr for Book Conservation* Mindell Dubansky; *Chief Librn, Thomas J. Watson Library* Kenneth Soehner; *Assoc Chief Librn* Tony White; *Assoc Chief Librn* Daniel Starr; *Mgr Library Admin* Dana Hart; *Assoc Mgr Colls* Holly Phillips; *Assoc Mgr Circulation & Tech Servs* Jessica Ranne; *Assoc Library Mgr* Angela Washington; *Asst Mus Librn, Irene Lewisohn Costume Reference Library* Julie Tran Le
Thomas J Watson Library: open Mon - Fri 10 AM - 5:15 AM, Sat 10 AM - 5 PM; No admis fee; Estab 1880; primary mission is to serve museum staff; researchers col age & older may apply for Reader's Card w/ photo ID & are welcome; see library website for details; Circ Collections circulate to Mus research staff, non-circulating for visitors; Incl the Thomas J Watson Library, Nolen Library, Irene Lewisohn Costume Reference Library, Joyce F Menschel Photography Library, Onassis Library for Hellenic & Roman Art, Robert Goldwater Library & Visual Resource Archive, Robert Lehman Collection Library, Antonio Ratti Textile Center & Reference Library; Average Annual Attendance: 30,000
Income: Financed by endowment
Library Holdings: Auction Catalogs, Book Volumes 996,000, Clipping Files, Exhibition Catalogs, Fiche, Micro Print, Other Holdings Ephemera; Monographs, Periodical Subscriptions 2,250
Special Subjects: Art History, Asian Art, Decorative Arts, Drawings, Islamic Art, Painting-American, Painting-European, Prints, Sculpture

L **Dept of Drawings & Prints**, 1000 5th Ave, New York, NY 10028-0113. Tel 212-570-3920 (Print Study Rm); 570-3912 (Drawing Study Rm); Fax 212-570-3921; Web: www.metmuseum.org; *Cur in Charge, Drawings & Prints* Nadine M Orenstein; *Sr Colls Mgr* Mary Zuber
Open Tues - Fri 10 AM - 12:30 PM & 2 - 4:30 PM by appointment; No admis fee; Estab 1917 to collect & preserve prints, illustrated books & drawings for ornament & architecture; dept created 1993; Has 3 exhibition galleries; Average Annual Attendance: 2,600
Income: financed by museum
Library Holdings: Original Art Works, Prints
Special Subjects: Architecture, Art History, Decorative Arts, Drawings, Etchings & Engravings, Illustration, Landscape Architecture, Portraits, Printmaking, Prints, Woodcuts

L **MIDMARCH ASSOCIATES/MIDMARCH ARTS PRESS,** Midmarch Arts Press and Library, 300 Riverside Dr, Apt 8A, New York, NY 10025. Tel 212-666-6990; 212-865-5509; Fax 212-865-5509; Email info@midmarchartsbooks.org; Web: midmarchartsbooks.org; *Exec Dir* Cynthia Navaretta; *Educ* Judy Seigel; *Educ* Sylvia Moore
Open by appointment; No admis fee; Estab 1975 to maintain archival material on women artists world wide & to publish books on 20th century art & artists; 20th C paintings & sculpture; pre-Columbian shards & sculpture
Income: Financed by public funding, contributions & book sales
Library Holdings: Book Volumes, Clipping Files, Exhibition Catalogs, Manuscripts, Memorabilia, Original Art Works, Original Documents, Pamphlets, Photographs, Sculpture, Video Tapes
Special Subjects: Afro-American Art, Architecture, Art History, Ceramics, Conceptual Art, Constructions, Crafts, Drawings, Embroidery, Film, Flasks & Bottles, Latin American Art, Mexican Art, Mixed Media, Painting-American, Painting-British, Painting-European, Painting-Japanese, Photography, Pre-Columbian Art, Sculpture, Theatre Arts, Watercolors, Pottery, Prints
Collections: In-house collection of 20th century art
Publications: Please visit website www.midmarchartspress.org for list of publications or midmarchartsbooks.org
Activities: Educ dept; lect provided

M **THE MORGAN LIBRARY & MUSEUM,** Museum, 225 Madison Ave at 36th St, New York, NY 10016-3405. Tel 212-685-0008; Fax 212-481-3484; Email visitorservices@themorgan.org; Web: www.themorgan.org; *Cur Mary Flagler Cary Music Manuscripts & Dept Head* Frances Barulich; *Astor Cur & Dept Head Printed Books & Bindings* John Bidwell; *Cur & Dept Head Medieval & Renaissance Manuscripts* Roger Wieck; *Eugene & Clare Thaw Cur Drawings & Prints* Jennifer Tonkovich; *Cur & Dept Head Seals & Tablets* Sidney Babcock; *Robert H Taylor Cur & Dept Head* Declan Kiely; *Engelhard Cur & Dept Head* John Marciari
Open Tues - Thurs 10:30 AM - 5 PM, Fri 10:30 AM - 9 PM, Sat 10 AM - 6 PM, Sun 11 AM - 6 PM, cl Mon, Thanksgiving Day, Christmas Day & New Year's Day; Admis adults $20, children under 16, seniors 65+ & students with ID $13, mems & children 12 & under free, Fri 7 - 9 PM free; Estab 1924 for research & exhibition purposes; The Gallery has changing exhibition with Old Master drawings, Medieval & Renaissance illuminated manuscripts, rare printed books & literary, historical, & music manuscripts; Average Annual Attendance: 169,000; Mem: 1,100; dues conservator $1,000, sustainer $500, contributor $250, dual/ family $150, individual $100, intro individual $75
Income: $4,000,000 (financed by endowment & mem)
Purchases: $1,000,000
Special Subjects: Architecture, Bookplates & Bindings, Drawings, Etchings & Engravings, Historical Material, Islamic Art, Manuscripts, Medieval Art, Miniatures, Painting-European, Painting-Italian, Painting-Spanish, Period Rooms, Photography, Portraits, Prints, Religious Art, Renaissance Art
Collections: Ancient written records including seals, cuneiform tablets and papyri, art objects, autograph manuscripts, book bindings, early children's books, Medieval & Renaissance illuminated manuscripts, later printed books, letters and documents, mezzotints, modern calligraphy, music manuscripts, original drawing from 14th-19th centuries, printed books before 1500, Rembrandt prints
Publications: Report to the Fellows, annual; books; catalogs; facsimiles
Activities: Lects open to pub; tours; concerts; readings; video presentations; sales shop sells books, reproductions, prints, slides, cards, calendars, address books and posters

L **Library**, 225 Madison Ave at 36th St, New York, NY 10016-3405. Tel 212-590-0315 (Reading Room); 590-0386 (Photography & Rights); Email readingroom@themorgan.org; Web: www.themorgan.org; *Head Reader Svcs* John Vincler; *Dir Research Servs* V Heidi Haas

Open by appt only; Tues - Thurs 10:30 AM - 5 PM, Fri 10:30 AM - 9 PM, Sat 10 AM - 6 PM, Sun 11 AM - 6 PM, cl Mon; New Year's Day; Thanksgiving Day; & Christmas Day; Admis adults $20 children under 16, seniors 65+ & students with ID $13, mems & children 12 & under free, Fri 7-9 PM free; Circ Non-circulating; Maintains Reading Room & Drawing Study Ctr
Library Holdings: Auction Catalogs, Book Volumes 160,000, Exhibition Catalogs, Kodachrome Transparencies, Manuscripts 70,000, Original Art Works 8,000, Original Documents, Photographs, Prints 13,000, Slides

M **MORRIS-JUMEL MANSION, INC,** 65 Jumel Terr, New York, NY 10032. Tel 212-923-8008; Fax 212-923-8947; Email mjm1765@aol.com; Web: www.morrisjumel.org; *Co Exec Dir* Alexis Marnel; *Co-Exec Dir* Christopher Davalos; *Pres* Pamela Palanque North; *Mgr School & Family Progs* G Romero; *Asst Cur* Vanessa Soto; *Sec* Alexander Campos; *Treas* Robin LeBaron
Open Tues - Fri 10 AM - 4 PM, Sat - Sun 10 AM - 5 PM; Admis adults $10, students & seniors $8, children under 12 free; Estab 1904 as a Historic House Museum; Morris-Jumel Mansion consists of 11 period rooms which are restored to represent the colonial, revolutionary & nineteenth-century history of the mansion, highlighting its owners & inhabitants (the Morris family, George Washington, Eliza Jumel & Aaron Burr); Average Annual Attendance: 30,000; Mem: 200; contributors 500; dues $35-$2500
Income: Financed by mem, contributions, private sources, state & city funds
Special Subjects: Architecture, Ceramics, Costumes, Decorative Arts, Etchings & Engravings, Furniture, Glass, Historical Material, Laces, Painting-American, Painting-Italian, Period Rooms, Portraits, Textiles
Collections: Architecture, decorative art, furniture of the 18th & 19th centuries
Publications: Morris-Jumel News, biannual
Activities: Classes for adults; classes for 4th - 11th grade students, focus on study of historical artifacts, documents & architecture; dramatic progs; docent training; lects open to pub; concerts; tours; originate traveling exhibs; mus shop sells books, reproductions, postcards & CDs

M **MOUNT VERNON HOTEL MUSEUM & GARDEN,** 421 E 61st St, New York, NY 10065-8736. Tel 212-838-6878; Fax 212-838-7390; Email info@mvhm.org; Web: www.mvhm.org; *Dir* Mary Anne Caton; *Cur* Charlotte Trautman; *Educ* Dana Settles; *Pub Rels* Terri Daly
Open Tues - Sun 11 AM - 4 PM, cl Mon; Admis adults $8, seniors (65 & up) & students with ID $7, children under 12 free; Estab 1939, historic site representing early 19th century New York City hotel; Eight period rooms in original 1826 interiors; 1799 Landmark building; Average Annual Attendance: 10,000; Mem: 450; dues $30-$500
Special Subjects: Afro-American Art, Archaeology, Architecture, Carpets & Rugs, Ceramics, Decorative Arts, Furniture, Glass, Historical Material, Landscapes, Manuscripts, Maps, Painting-American, Painting-British, Period Rooms, Porcelain, Portraits, Pottery, Prints, Reproductions, Restorations, Silver, Silver, Textiles, Pewter
Collections: Decorative arts-furniture, ceramics, silver, textiles, documents & manuscripts, Fine Art: paintings/prints, Landscapes, portraits, pewter
Exhibitions: Period rooms in original 1820s interiors; American Decorative Arts
Publications: Newsletter & brochure, quarterly
Activities: Classes for adults & children; dramatic progs; docent progs; musical performances; craft demonstrations; workshops ie (knitting; talking, terrariums); lects open to pub; 10 vis lectrs per yr; awards; concerts; gallery talks; tours; schols & fels offered; mus shop sells books, original art, prints, reproductions, slides, toys, jewelry, garden related items & craft items

A **MUNICIPAL ART SOCIETY OF NEW YORK,** 488 Madison Ave, Ste 1900 New York, NY 10022-5706. Tel 212-935-3960; Fax 212-753-1816; Email info@mas.org; Web: www.mas.org; *Pres* Elizabeth Goldstein; *Dir Public Progs* Stacey Anderson; *VPres Communs & Public Affairs* Meaghan Baron; *Dir Facilities & IT* Al Castricone; *Dir Public Art* Phyllis Samitz Cohen; *Dir Community Engagement & Educ* Joanna Crispe; *Controller* Michele Farina; *Mgr Communs* Laurance Fauconnet; *Dir Tours Prog* Ted Mineau; *Proj Mgr Preservation & Planning* Marcel Negret
Open Mon - Fri 9 AM - 5 PM; No admis fee; Estab 1892, incorporated 1898; The Society is the one organization in New York where the layman, professional & bus firm can work together to encourage high standards for pub art, architecture, planning, landscaping & preservation in the five boroughs; Mem: 4,500; dues $25 & up; annual meeting in June
Income: Financed by members & grants
Collections: Photographs
Exhibitions: Rotating exhibits; Tribute in Light, annual 9/11 commemoration
Publications: The Livable City, quarterly
Activities: Pub progs incl Livable Neighborhoods; lects; architectural walking tours; competitions

L **Greenacre Reference Library**, 488 Madison Ave, Ste 1900 New York, NY 10022. Tel 212-935-3960 x 1274; Fax 212-753-1816; Email ebutler@mas.org; Web: mas.org; *Information Resources* Erin Butler
Open Mon - Fri 10 AM - 5 PM by appointment; No admis fee; Estab 1978; Reference Library & Archives; Mem: Parent inst has a membership program
Income: Library supported by Greenacre Foundation; archives cataloging supported by Fdn
Library Holdings: Audio Tapes off site, Book Volumes 3,200, CD-ROMs, Cassettes off site, Clipping Files 20,000, Clipping Files off site, Compact Disks, Compact Disks off site, DVDs off site, DVDs, Exhibition Catalogs, Fiche (off-site), Filmstrips, Manuscripts 2,000 printed archival pubs & materials, Memorabilia off site, Original Art Works off site, Original Documents, Pamphlets, Periodical Subscriptions 10, Photographs, Photographs off site, Reels off site, Slides off site, Video Tapes off site
Special Subjects: Aesthetics, Architecture, Decorative Arts, Historical Material, Illustration, Industrial Design, Landscape Architecture, Painting-American, Photography, Sculpture, Watercolors, History of Art & Archaeology, Interior Design, Maps, Theatre Arts
Collections: onsite library contains books, archives, reports; Governance records; Presidents' and Executive Directors' Papers; Greenacre Reference Library (Newsclippings, subject files); Planning & Preservation Committees & Projects; Planning Center; The Urban Center & Urban Center Books; Exhibitions & Events; Exhibition Publications; Tours; Major Public Programs (Tribute in Light, Imagine New York, MAS Summit); Awards; Publications; Photographs & Slides; Media (Audio-Visual); Artifacts & Realia;

M **MUSEUM OF ARTS & DESIGN,** 2 Columbus Circle, New York, NY 10019. Tel 212-299-7777; Fax 212-299-7701; Email info@madmuseum.org; Web: www.madmuseum.org; *Dir Communs* Claire Laporte; *Dir Educ & Progs* Cathleen Lewis; *Chief Cur* Shannon R. Stratton; *Chief Devel Officer* Maureen Nash; *Dir Exhibs* Hendrik Gerrits
Open Tues - Wed & Fri - Sun 10 AM - 6 PM, Thurs 10 AM - 9 PM, cl Mon & major holidays; Admis adults $16, seniors $14, students $12, 18 & under free; Estab 1956 by the American Craft Council (see National Organizations); Gallery displays contemporary art, design, craft & jewelry; Average Annual Attendance: 300,000; Mem: 7,500; dues $75, student & out-of-town $50, dual $100, family $125, contributing $250, supporting $500
Income: Financed by mem, government grants, private & corporate donations
Special Subjects: Ceramics, Crafts, Embroidery, Furniture, Glass, Jewelry, Laces, Metalwork, Porcelain, Pottery, Sculpture, Sculpture, Silver, Stained Glass, Tapestries, Textiles, Woodcarvings, Decorative Arts
Collections: 2,000 objects that document the history of craft, art & design from the mid 20th century to present, 500 pieces of contemporary art jewelry
Exhibitions: 6-10 exhibitions per year
Publications: MAD Views, biannual newsletter; exhib catalogs
Activities: Classes for adults & children; docent training; lects open to public; gallery talks; tours; fels; Visionaries award; museum shop sells original art, artists' jewelry, decorative objects & fashion accessories

M **MUSEUM OF CHINESE IN AMERICA,** 215 Centre St, New York, NY 10013-3601. Tel 855-955-6622; Fax 212-619-4720; Email info@mocanyc.org; Web: www.mocanyc.org; *Cur & Dir Exhib* Herb Tam; *Pres* Nancy Yao Maasbach; *Colls Mgr* Kevin Chu; *VPres Progs & Mus Experience* Beatrice Chen; *Dir Colls & Research* Yue Ma
Open Tues - Wed & Fri - Sun 11 AM - 6 PM, Thurs 11 AM - 9 PM, cl Mon; Admis general $10, seniors & students $5, mems & children under 12 in groups less than 10 free, Free admis first Thursday of month; Estab 1980 dedicated to preserving 160 years of Chinese American history; Located in a stunning new site designed by Maya Lin with more than 14,000 sq ft of exhib space, a multipurpose classroom, two galleries, cultural meeting space, gift shop collections & research ctr at 70 Mulberry St; Average Annual Attendance: 30,000; Mem: 350; dues $25 - $5000
Income: Financed by mem, pub & private funds
Library Holdings: Audio Tapes, Book Volumes, CD-ROMs, Cards, Cassettes, Clipping Files, Compact Disks, DVDs, Exhibition Catalogs, Framed Reproductions, Manuscripts, Memorabilia, Motion Pictures, Original Art Works, Original Documents, Other Holdings, Pamphlets, Periodical Subscriptions, Photographs, Records, Reels, Reproductions, Sculpture, Slides, Video Tapes
Special Subjects: Anthropology, Architecture, Asian Art, Cartoons, Costumes, Crafts, Decorative Arts, Drawings, Ethnology, Folk Art, Historical Material, Manuscripts, Maps, Period Rooms, Photography, Reproductions, Restorations, Textiles
Collections: Archives: Chinese American history & culture, including oral histories, photographs, documents, personal & organizational records, sound recordings, textiles, artifacts & a library of over 2,000 volumes covering Asian American topics
Exhibitions: With a Single Step: Stories in the Making of America (core exhib)
Activities: Classes for adults & children; docent training; workshops; lects open to pub & mems only, 12-24 vis lectrs per yr; concerts; gallery talks; walking tours; competitions; family events; legacy awards; mus shop sells books, magazines, original art, souvenirs, apparel, gift items

M **MUSEUM OF MODERN ART,** 11 W 53rd St, New York, NY 10019-5497. Tel 212-708-9400, (Exhibit & Film Info) 708-9480; Fax 212-708-9889; Email info@moma.org; Web: www.moma.org; Cable MODERNART; Telex 6-2370; *Assoc Dir and Cur* Kathy Halbreich; *Hon Chmn* Ronald Lauder; *Chmn Emeritus* Robert B Menschel; *COO & Asst Treas* James Gara
Open Sun - Sat 10:30 AM - 5:30 PM, Fri until 8 PM; Admis adults $25, seniors $18, students with ID $14, guests of mem $5, mem & children under 16 free, Fri 4-8:00 PM free; Estab 1929, the Museum offers an unparalleled overview of modern art; maintains exhibitions of wide range of subject matter, mediums & time periods; Designed in 1939 by Phillip Goodwin & Edward Durell Stone, the building is one of the first examples of the International Style in the US. Subsequent expansions took place in the 1950s & 1960s under the architect Philip Johnson, who also designed the Abby Aldrich Rockefeller Sculpture Garden. A major renovation, completed in 1984, doubled the Museum's gallery space & enhanced visitor facilities; Average Annual Attendance: 1,500,000; Mem: 52,000; dues student $25, others $45 & up
Income: Financed by admis, mem, sales of publications, other services & contributions
Special Subjects: Architecture, Drawings, Graphics, Painting-American, Photography, Posters, Prints, Sculpture
Collections: Painting, sculptures, drawings, prints, photographs, films, videos & other media works, architectural models & Plans, & design objects 200,000, artist books & periodicals 300,000, museum archives hold historical documentation & photographs
Publications: Annual report; books on exhibitions & artists; Members Quarterly; Members Calendar; monographs; catalogs; exhibitions catalogs
Activities: Classes for adults & children; prof develop for teachers & admins; lects open to pub; concerts; gallery talks; tours; film showings, international in scope; virtual visits & audio progs; courses at MoMA; weekend family programs; sales shop sells publications, postcards, note & seasonal cards, posters, slides, calendars, design objects & furniture

L **Library and Museum Archives**, 4520 33rd St, Long Island City, NY 11101-2406; 4 W 54th St, midtown Manhattan New York, NY 10022-4203; 11 W 53rd St, New York, NY 10019-5498. Tel 212-708-9433 (library), 708-9617 (archives); Fax 212-333-1122; Email library@moma.org; archives@moma.org; Web: www.moma.org; *Librn, Collection Develop* Jennifer Tobias; *Chief Library & Mus Archives* Michelle Elligott

Open Manhattan Wed - Fri - 11 AM - 5 PM by appointment, cl Aug; Queens Mon - Tues - 11 AM - 5 PM by appointment, cl Aug; No admis fee; Estab 1929 as a research library; For museum staff, art researchers & the public
Library Holdings: Auction Catalogs, Audio Tapes, Book Volumes 260,000, CD-ROMs, Cassettes, Clipping Files, Exhibition Catalogs, Fiche, Original Documents, Other Holdings Artists files 53,000, Pamphlets, Periodical Subscriptions 300, Records, Reels, Video Tapes
Special Subjects: Architecture, Art History, Collages, Conceptual Art, Drawings, Film, Graphic Design, Industrial Design, Latin American Art, Mixed Media, Photography, Posters, Prints, Sculpture
Collections: Archives of artists' groups, artists' books, avant-garde art, Dada & Surrealism, archive of museum publications, Latin American art, personal papers of artists, writers, dealers, political art documentation archives
Exhibitions: Fluxus: Selections from the Gilbert & Lila Silverman Collection, 1988-89 (catalog)
Publications: Annual Bibliography of Modern Art; Bibliography of Modern Art on Disc; catalog of the Library of the Museum of Modern Art
Activities: Internship prog

M **MUSEUM OF THE CITY OF NEW YORK,** Museum, 1220 5th Ave at 103rd St, New York, NY 10029-9958. Tel 212-534-1672; Fax 212-423-0758; Email info@mcny.org; Web: www.mcny.org; *Dir* Susan Henshaw Jones
Open daily 10 AM - 6 PM, cl New Year's Day, Thanksgiving Day, Christmas Day; Suggested admis adults $18, seniors & students (with ID) $12, mems & children 19 & under free, family & group rates available; Estab 1923 to preserve the cultural accomplishments of New York City & to meet the needs & interests of the community of today; Permanent & temporary exhibition galleries on subjects related to mission; Average Annual Attendance: 350,000; Mem: 2,500; dues $45 & up
Income: $5,000,000 (financed by private & nonprofit institutions, individual contributions, city, state & federal funds)
Special Subjects: Anthropology, Archaeology, Architecture, Cartoons, Ceramics, Coins & Medals, Costumes, Crafts, Decorative Arts, Dioramas, Dolls, Drawings, Embroidery, Etchings & Engravings, Folk Art, Furniture, Glass, Graphics, Historical Material, Jewelry, Landscapes, Manuscripts, Maps, Marine Painting, Metalwork, Painting-American, Photography, Sculpture, Prints
Collections: NY Fashions, Costumes & Textiles Coll, Decorative Arts Coll, Marine Colls, NYC Photography, Prints & Drawings, NYC Theatre & Broadway Coll, NY Toy Coll, NY Paintings & Sculpture
Publications: Annual report; exhibit catalogs; quarterly newsletter; quarterly programs brochure for members
Activities: Classes for adults & children; docent training; History Day for high school & younger students; lects open to pub; gallery talks; concerts; city walking tours; competitions with awards; original objects of art lent to affiliated institutions; lending collection contains sculptures, 40,000 books, 5,000 original art works, 15,000 original prints, 2,000 paintings & 300,000 photographs; book traveling exhibs 1-2 per yr; originate traveling exhibs to other mus; mus shop sells books, reproductions, prints & slides

L **Research Room,** 1220 5th Ave at 103rd St, New York, NY 10029-9958. Tel 212-534-1672; Fax 212-534-5974; Email research@mcny.org; Web: www.mcny.org; *Pres & Dir* Susan Henshaw Jones; *Deputy Dir & Chief Cur* Dr Sarah Henry; *COO* Jerry Gallagher
Open Tues - Sun 10 AM - 6 PM; Suggested admis families (max 2 adults) $20, adults $10, seniors & students $6, mems & children under 12 no admis fee; Museum founded 1923, devoted to the history of New York City; Museum exhib focus on history of NYC and its people; Average Annual Attendance: 150,000; Mem: Various categories of membership
Income: public & private partnership
Library Holdings: Book Volumes 8,000, Clipping Files, Manuscripts, Maps, Memorabilia, Original Art Works, Original Documents, Periodical Subscriptions 25, Photographs, Prints, Reproductions, Sculpture
Special Subjects: Architecture, Cartoons, Ceramics, Coins & Medals, Costume Design & Constr, Decorative Arts, Dioramas, Dolls, Drawings, Etchings & Engravings, Furniture, Glass, Graphic Arts, Historical Material, Jewelry, Landscapes, Leather, Manuscripts, Maps, Marine Painting, Metalwork, Miniatures, Painting-American, Period Rooms, Pewter, Photography, Porcelain, Portraits, Posters, Prints, Sculpture, Silver, Textiles, Watercolors
Collections: Paintings, sculpture, prints, photography, costumes, decorative arts, toys, theater memorabilia, manuscripts & ephemera
Exhibitions: see website www.mcny.org for current schedule
Publications: various
Activities: Classes for adults & children; lects open to pub; museum shop sells books & prints

NATIONAL ANTIQUE & ART DEALERS ASSOCIATION OF AMERICA, INC
For further information, see National and Regional Organizations

NATIONAL ASSOCIATION OF WOMEN ARTISTS, INC
For further information, see National and Regional Organizations

M **NATIONAL MUSEUM OF THE AMERICAN INDIAN,** George Gustav Heye Center, Alexander Hamilton US Custom House, One Bowling Green New York, NY 10004. Tel 212-514-3700; Email nmai-info@si.edu; Web: americanindian.si.edu; *Dir* Kevin Grover
Open daily 10 AM - 5 PM, Thurs until 8 PM, cl Christmas; No admis fee; Estab 1989 to recognize & affirm the historical & contemporary cultures & cultural achievements of the Native peoples of the Western Hemisphere; 20,000 sq ft exhibition galleries. Bureau of the Smithsonian Institution; Average Annual Attendance: 270,000; Mem: dues $25 & up
Income: Financed by trust, endowments & revenues, gifts, grants, contributions, mem & funds appropriated by Congress
Special Subjects: American Indian Art, Anthropology, Archaeology, Ceramics, Coins & Medals, Costumes, Decorative Arts, Eskimo Art, Ethnology, Historical Material, Latin American Art, Manuscripts, Painting-American, Photography, Pottery, Pre-Columbian Art, Sculpture, Textiles
Collections: Native American art & objects
Exhibitions: Rotating exhibits
Publications: Books, occasionally; brochures; catalogs; recordings
Activities: Classes for adults & children; lects open to pub, 3-5 vis lectrs per yr; concerts; gallery talks; tours; guided tours for children; scholarships offered; individual paintings & original objects of art lent to museums, including tribal mus & cultural ctrs, nonprofit institutions & other appropriate sites; originate traveling exhibs; mus shop sells Indian crafts, jewelry, masks, pottery, beadwork, basketry, weavings, carvings, paintings, prints, books, magazines, original art, reproductions, slides, postcards & notepaper

NATIONAL SCULPTURE SOCIETY
For further information, see National and Regional Organizations

NATIONAL SOCIETY OF MURAL PAINTERS, INC
For further information, see National and Regional Organizations

M **NEUE GALERIE NEW YORK,** 1048 5th (at 86th St), New York, NY 10028-0111. Tel 201-628-6200; Fax 212-628-8824; Email museum@neuegalerie.org; Web: neuegalerie.org; WATS www.neueglaerie.org; *Director* Renee Price; *Book Store Dir* Bruno Keusch; *Design Shop Dir* Paul Landy
Open Thurs - Mon 11AM - 6PM; Admis adult $20, students $10, & seniors 65 & up $15; 2001; Museum devoted to early twentieth century German/Austrian art and design; Average Annual Attendance: 120,000
Special Subjects: Ceramics, Decorative Arts, Drawings, Furniture, Jewelry, Metalwork, Painting-German, Photography, Porcelain, Portraits, Posters, Prints, Sculpture, Silver, Textiles, Watercolors, Woodcarvings
Collections: paintings; sculpture; works on paper; decorative arts; photographs

M **NEW MUSEUM OF CONTEMPORARY ART,** New Museum, 235 Bowery, New York, NY 10002. Tel 212-219-1222; Fax 212-431-5328; Email info@newmuseum.org; Web: www.newmuseum.org; *Toby Devan Lewis Dir* Lisa Phillips; *Deputy Dir* Karen Wong; *Artistic Dir* Massimiliano Gioni
Open Tues - Wed & Fri - Sun 11 AM - 6 PM & Thurs 11 AM - 9 PM; cl Mon, Thanksgiving, Christmas & New Year's Days; Admis general $18, seniors $15, students $12, mem & under 18 free, Thurs 7-9 PM (pay-what-you-wish); Estab 1977; New Museum is a leading destination for new art & new ideas; Mem: Dues standard individual mem $70 (see website for other mem options)
Publications: Exhib catalogs
Activities: Family, school & youth progs; lects open to pub; gallery talks; tours; fels; mus shop sells books, limited editions; magazines; original art

L **The Soho Center Library,** 235 Bowery, New York, NY 10002-1218. Tel 212-219-1222; Fax 212-431-5328; Email newmu@newmuseum.org; Web: www.newmuseum.org; *Dir* Lisa Phillips
Open by appointment; Estab 1985; Reference library, cl to pub for renovations
Income: Financed by mem & city appropriation
Library Holdings: Book Volumes 200, Periodical Subscriptions 150
Special Subjects: Architecture, Art History, Conceptual Art, Film, Painting-American, Painting-Australian, Painting-British, Painting-Canadian, Painting-Dutch, Painting-European, Painting-French, Painting-German, Painting-Italian, Painting-Japanese, Painting-New Zealand
Activities: Mus shop sells books, clothing, cd-rom, dvd, video

M **NEW WORLD ART CENTER,** T F Chen Cultural Center, 250 Lafayette St (SoHo), New York, NY 10012. Tel 212-966-4363, 212-941-9296; Fax 212-966-5285; Email chen@tfchen.org; Web: www.tfchen.org; *Dir* Julie Chen; *Pres & Exec Dir* Lucia Chen; *VPres* Ted Chen
Open Tues - Sat 1 PM - 6 PM, appt preferred; No admis fee; Estab 1996 to advance new artistic & cultural ideas & further global harmony; A strikingly redesigned six-story art center that aims to be the hub of a New Renaissance & act as a unifying force to bring together a world family of artists, thinkers, art lovers & visionaries focus on art educ & a global cultural of peace; Average Annual Attendance: 5,000; Mem: Dues $30 & up
Income: Financed by mem & private donations
Library Holdings: Book Volumes, Cards, Clipping Files, Exhibition Catalogs, Framed Reproductions, Original Documents, Pamphlets, Photographs, Records, Reproductions, Slides, Video Tapes
Special Subjects: African Art, American Western Art, Antiquities-Oriental, Asian Art, Calligraphy, Ceramics, Decorative Arts, Drawings, Etchings & Engravings, Ethnology, Folk Art, Graphics, Oriental Art, Painting-American, Painting-European, Painting-Italian, Painting-Japanese, Photography, Portraits, Posters
Collections: African Art, T F Chen, Neo-Iconography paintings, Emerging Artists, all media, Italian Art, Master Artists (Picasso, Miro, Chagall & others), Vietnamese Art & Art Objects
Exhibitions: Post-Van Gogh Retrospective (1954-1998); Art from the Mediterranean; Japanese Art; group shows
Publications: Art Books, 12 & up
Activities: Classes for adults & children; Lects open to pub; gallery talks; concerts; tours; awards: art competitions, essay on Neo-Iconography; lending of original objects of art to Taiwan mus of art; book traveling exhibs, 2 per yr; originates traveling exhibs; mus shop sells books, original art, reproductions & prints

A **NEW YORK ARTISTS EQUITY ASSOCIATION, INC,** 245 Broome St, New York, NY 10002-3839. Tel 646-397-8340; Email info@nyartistsequity.org; Web: www.nyartistsequity.org; *Exec Dir* Regina Stewart
Open Wed - Sat noon - 6 PM; No admis fee; Estab 1947 as a politically non-partisan group to advance the cultural, legislative, economic and professional interest of painters, sculptors, printmakers, and others in the field of visual arts. Various committees concerned with aims. Administrators of the Artists Welfare Fund, Inc; Broome Street Gallery; Mem: Over 3000; dues $30 & up
Income: Financed by dues
Collections: Artbank; NYAEA Collection
Publications: The Artists Proof newsletter, quarterly
Activities: Lect open to public; trips to cultural institutions; advocacy; information services; artists benefits

L **THE NEW YORK PUBLIC LIBRARY,** 476 5th Ave, New York, NY 10018-2788. Tel 212-930-0730& 917-275-6975; Email spev@nypl.org; Email generalresearch@nypl.org; Web: www.nypl.org; *Pres. & CEO* Tony Marxpresident@nypl.org; *Chief Digital Officer* Tony Ageh; *Dir. of the Research Libraries* Andrew W. Mellon; *Vice Pres., Gen. Counsel & Sec.* Michele Coleman Mayes; *Chief Branch Library Officer* Christopher Platt; *Chief Operating Officer, Chief Financial Officer, & Treasurer* Iris Weinshall; *Chief External Relations Officer* Carrie Welch
Open Mon, Thurs - Sat 10 AM - 6 PM, Tues & Wed 10 AM - 8 PM, Sun 1 PM - 5 PM (excluding July & August); No admis fee, exhib pricing may vary; Estab 1895; Entire library contains over 43,000,000 items

L **Print Room,** Fifth Ave & 42nd St, Rm 308 New York, NY 10018. Tel 212-930-0837; Fax 212-930-0530; Email prints@nypl.org; Web: www.nypl.org; *Cur Prints & Photogs* Madeleine Viljoen; *Assoc Chief Librn* Maria Liriano
Open Mon - Sat 1 PM - 6 PM; Estab 1899
Library Holdings: Book Volumes 25,000, Other Holdings Stereographs 72,000, Photographs 15,000, Prints 175,000
Collections: Samuel Putnam Avery Collection (primarily 19th century prints), Radin Collection of Western European bookplates, British & American caricatures, Beverly Chew bequest of Milton & Pope portraits, Eno Collection of New York City Views, McAlpin Collection of George Washington Portraits, Smith Collection of Japanese Prints, Phelps Stokes Collection of American Views, Lewis Wickes Hine Collection, Robert Dennis Collection of Stereoscopic Views, Pageant of America Collection, Romana Javitz Collection, Portrait File, Artists Book Collection, Spencer Collection
Exhibitions: 2 rotating exhibits per year
Activities: Classes for adults; tours; fels available

L **Spencer Collection,** 5th Ave & 42nd St, Third Fl, Rm 308 New York, NY 10018. Tel 212-275-6975; 930-0817; Fax 212-930-0530; Email prints@nypl.org; Web: www.nypl.org
Open Tues - Sat 1 PM - 6 PM by appt only; Available through Prints & Photographs Study Room
Library Holdings: Book Volumes 9000

L **Art & Architecture Collection,** 476 5th Ave, Rm 300, Stephen A Schwarzman Bldg New York, NY 10018-2788. Tel 212-930-0835; Fax 212-930-0530; Email art@nypl.org; Web: www.nypl.org; *Miriam & Ira D Wallach Asst Cur, Prints & Photographs* Elizabeth Cronin; *Librn* Vincenzo Rutigliano; *Librn* Miguel Rosales; *Librn* Lori Salmon
Open Mon, Thurs - Sat 10 AM - 5:45 PM, Tues & Wed 10 AM - 7:45 PM, Sun 1 PM - 4:45 PM (Sept - June); Estab 1895; Circ 105,000
Income: pub/private
Library Holdings: Auction Catalogs, Book Volumes 556,000, Clipping Files, Exhibition Catalogs, Fiche, Other Holdings, Pamphlets, Periodical Subscriptions, Reels
Special Subjects: Aesthetics, American Western Art, Architecture, Art History, Asian Art, Bronzes, Carpets & Rugs, Cartoons, Ceramics, Collages, Conceptual Art, Constructions, Costume Design & Constr, Crafts, Decorative Arts, Drawings, Embroidery, Enamels, Eskimo Art, Fashion Arts, Folk Art, Furniture, Glass, Gold, Goldsmithing, Graphic Arts, Graphic Design, Handicrafts, Illustration, Interior Design, Islamic Art, Ivory, Jade, Jewelry, Laces, Landscapes, Latin American Art, Marine Painting, Metalwork, Mexican Art, Miniatures, Mixed Media, Mosaics, Oriental Art, Painting-American, Painting-Australian, Painting-British, Painting-Canadian, Painting-Dutch, Painting-European, Painting-Flemish, Painting-French, Painting-German, Painting-Israeli, Painting-Italian, Painting-Japanese, Painting-New Zealand, Painting-Polish, Painting-Russian, Painting-Scandinavian, Painting-Spanish, Pewter, Photography, Porcelain, Portraits, Pottery, Sculpture, Silver, Silversmithing, Tapestries, Textiles, Video, Watercolors, Woodcarvings, Southwestern Art, Stained Glass
Activities: Classes for adults; lectrs open to pub; tours

L **Schomburg Center for Research in Black Culture,** 515 Malcolm X Blvd, New York, NY 10037-1801. Tel 212-275-6975; Fax 212-491-6760; Web: www.nypl.org; *Dir* Kevin Young
Open Mon - Sat 10 AM - 6 PM, cl Sun; Estab 1926; Circ 5,607; A reference library devoted to black people throughout the world; two galleries in lobby for rotating exhibition program; comprised of Schomburg Bldg, Langston Hughes Bldg & Landmark Bldg; Average Annual Attendance: 191,266
Library Holdings: Book Volumes 130,000, Clipping Files, Filmstrips, Other Holdings Broadsides; Maps; Playbills; Programs, Photographs, Prints, Records, Reels
Special Subjects: Afro-American Art, Art History, Collages, Commercial Art, Decorative Arts, Drawings, Ethnology, Film, Folk Art, Historical Material, Manuscripts, Maps, Painting-American, Photography, Portraits, Posters, Primitive art, Printmaking, Prints, Sculpture, Tapestries, Textiles, Video, Watercolors, Woodcarvings, Woodcuts
Collections: Books on Black Culture & Art, a research collection containing African Art, American Art by Black artists, Afro-Caribbean art & artifacts, Art & Artifacts Division, Manuscripts, Archives & Rare Books Division, Moving Image & Recorded Sound Division, Photographs & Prints Division
Exhibitions: Rotating exhibits
Activities: Lects open to pub; gallery talks; tours; fellowships offered; originate traveling exhibs; sales shop sells books, reproductions, exhib catalogs & cards

L **Mid-Manhattan Library, Art Collection,** 455 Fifth Ave at 40th St, Fl 3 New York, NY 10016-0119. Tel 970-275-6975 (General), 212-340-0871 (Coll); Email mmart@nypl.org; Web: www.nypl.org
Open Mon - Thurs 8 AM - 8 PM, Fri - Sat 10 AM - 5 PM; No admis fee
Library Holdings: Book Volumes 40,000, Clipping Files, Exhibition Catalogs, Fiche, Other Holdings, Periodical Subscriptions 200, Photographs, Prints, Reels, Video Tapes
Collections: Vertical Files on Artists with brochures & exhib catalogs
Exhibitions: Art Wall on Third Exhib Series; Art in the Window Exhib Series
Activities: Lects open to pub
—Mid-Manhattan Library, Picture Collection, 455 Fifth Ave at 40th St, Fl 3 New York, NY 10016-0119. Tel 917-275-6975 (General), 212-340-0878 (Coll); Email mmpic@nypl.org; Web: www.nypl.org; *Supervising Librn* Constance Novak
Open Mon - Thurs 8 AM - 9 PM, Fri 8 AM - 8 PM, Sat - Sun 10 AM - 6 PM; No admis fee; Estab 1915
Library Holdings: Other Holdings, Photographs, Prints
Collections: Approx 5,000,000 classified images, Original prints, photographs, poster, postcards & illustrations from books, magazines & newspapers classified into 12,000 subject headings, Digital Picture Coll: 38,000+ images in NYPL Digital Gallery

M **The New York Public Library for the Performing Arts,** 40 Lincoln Ctr Plaza, New York, NY 10023-7498. Tel 917-275-6975; Fax 212-870-1860; Web: www.nypl.org; *Dir* Jacqueline Z Davis; *Cur Exhib* Barbara Cohen-Stratyner; *Cur Dance* Jan Schmidt; *Theatre Cur* Doug Reside; *Cur Recordings* Jonathan Hiam; *Chief Librn Circ Coll Mgr* David Callahan; *Deputy Dir* Don Baldini; *Designer* Caitlin Whittington
Open Mon & Thurs 10:30 AM - 8 PM, Tues - Wed 10:30 AM - 6 PM; No admis fee; Estab 1965 to present exhibitions of high quality pertaining directly with the performing arts; Vincent Astor Gallery is 38 x 36 x 16 ft; Oenslager Gallery is 116 x 20-36 x 10 ft + 20 x 40 x 24 ft section. Both galleries have full media playback capability; Average Annual Attendance: 300,000
Income: Financed by endowment & city appropriation
Library Holdings: Audio Tapes, Book Volumes, CD-ROMs, Cassettes, Clipping Files, Compact Disks, DVDs, Exhibition Catalogs, Fiche, Lantern Slides, Manuscripts, Memorabilia, Motion Pictures, Original Art Works, Original Documents, Pamphlets, Periodical Subscriptions, Photographs, Prints, Records, Reels, Slides, Video Tapes
Special Subjects: Interior Design
Collections: Prints, letters, documents, photographs, posters, films, video tapes, memorabilia, dance music, recordings
Activities: Docent training; symposia; lects open to pub, 20 vis lectrs per yr; concerts; gallery talks; tours; awards; lending collection contains books, cassettes, motion picture videos & phono records; book traveling exhibs 1 per yr; originate traveling exhibs 3 per yr to mus, libraries & cultural heritage centers; mus shop sells books, magazines, original art, reproductions & prints

L **NEW YORK SCHOOL OF INTERIOR DESIGN,** New York School of Interior Design Library, 170 E 70th St, New York, NY 10021-5167. Tel 212-452-4160; Fax 212-472-8175; Email libraryinfo@nysid.edu; Web: www.nysid.edu, www.nysid.net/library; *Library Dir* Billy Kwan; *Librn* Meg Donabedian; *Archivist & Asst Librn* Nora Reilly
Open Mon - Thurs 9 AM - 9 PM, Fri 9 AM - 5 PM, Sat 10 AM - 6 PM, Sun noon - 8 PM (reduced hours between sems); Pub admitted with METRO referral card; Estab 1924 to supplement the courses given by the school & to assist students & faculty in their research & information needs; Circ 7000; Average Annual Attendance: 40,000
Income: $195,490 (financed by New York State grant & general operating fund)
Purchases: $44,000
Library Holdings: Auction Catalogs 250, Audio Tapes 35, Book Volumes 15,000, CD-ROMs 100, DVDs, Exhibition Catalogs, Lantern Slides, Other Holdings Product Literature; Samples, Periodical Subscriptions 102, Slides 3,500, Video Tapes 125
Special Subjects: Architecture, Decorative Arts, Interior Design

A **NEW YORK SOCIETY OF ARCHITECTS,** 132 Nassau St, Ste 811 New York, NY 10038. Tel 212-385-8950; Fax 212-385-8961; Email office@nysarch.com; Web: www.nysarch.com; *Pres* Andrew Antoniades; *VPres* Hugh Robotham; *Treas* John Sweeney; *Secy* Adrian Figueroa; *Exec Sec* Nereida Sanchez
Open 9:30 AM - 4:30 PM; Incorporated 1906; Mem: 450; dues $275
Income: $100,000 (financed by dues & sales)
Publications: Bulletin, bi-monthly; New York City Building Code Manual; New York City Fire Prevention Code
Activities: Educ progs; educ seminars; Honorary Membership Certificate to affiliated professions other than architect, Distinguished Service Award to members, Sidney L Strauss Memorial Award to architect or layman, Fred L Liebmann Book Award

M **NEW YORK STUDIO SCHOOL OF DRAWING, PAINTING & SCULPTURE,** Gallery, 8 W Eighth St, New York, NY 10011. Tel 212-673-6466; Fax 212-777-0996; Email info@nyss.org; Web: www.nyss.org; *Dean* Graham Nickson; *Program Coordinator* Kaitlin McDonough; *Gallery Coordinator* Rachel Rickert
Open daily 10 AM - 6 PM; No admis fee; Estab 1964, a nonprofit organization; Gallery is located on ground floor of the Studio School, site of the original Whitney Museum of Art;; Average Annual Attendance: 1,000; Scholarships
Income: Financed by private funding
Library Holdings: Auction Catalogs, Book Volumes, DVDs, Exhibition Catalogs, Periodical Subscriptions, Slides
Special Subjects: Drawings, Etchings & Engravings, Painting-American, Painting-Australian, Painting-British, Painting-European, Painting-French, Sculpture, Watercolors, Aesthetics, Anthropology, Architecture, Art History, Asian Art, Conceptual Art, Decorative Arts, Drafting, Etchings & Engravings, History of Art & Archaeology, Islamic Art, Landscape Architecture, Landscapes, Latin American Art, Oriental Art, Portraits, Pre-Columbian Art, Primitive art, Religious Art
Exhibitions: See website for archive of past exhibs
Publications: Evening lecture schedule, exhibition series
Activities: Classes for adults; MFA, Certificate, Marathons,; Public lectures; gallery receptions; historic tours; scholarships; scholarship & fels offered; exten dept

L **Library,** 8 W Eighth St, New York, NY 10011. Tel 212-673-6466 (Ext 118); Email library@nyss.org; *Dean* Graham Nickson
Open appointments required; No admis fee; Estab 1964 for pedagogical purposes; Open to pub
Library Holdings: Audio Tapes, Book Volumes 4700, Cassettes, Clipping Files, Exhibition Catalogs, Periodical Subscriptions, Reproductions, Slides, Video Tapes
Special Subjects: Drawings, Sculpture
Activities: Lectures open to public

M **NEW YORK UNIVERSITY,** Grey Art Gallery, 100 Washington Sq E, New York, NY 10003-6688. Tel 212-998-6780; Fax 212-995-4024; Email greyartgallery@nyu.edu; Web: www.nyu.edu/greyart; *Dir* Lynn Gumpert; *Assoc Dir & Head Colls & Exhibs* Michele Wong; *Head of Finance & Admin.* Laurie Duke;

Head of Education and Programs Lucy Oakley; *Exhibitions & Publications Mgr.* Ally Mintz; *Chief Preparator* Richard Wager; *Preparator* Noad Landfield; *Asst. to the Dir. & Press Officer* Allegra Favila; *Admin. Asst.* Yilin Chen; *Graduate Curatorial Asst.* J. English Cook
Open Tues, Thurs & Fri 11 AM - 6 PM, Wed 11 AM - 8 PM, Sat 11 AM - 5 PM, cl Sun & Mon; Admis suggested contribution $5; Estab 1975 as university art mus to serve pub as well as university community. The New York University Art Collection of approx 5000 works is now under the Grey Art Gallery; Gallery space of approx 4000 sq ft used for changing exhibitions; Average Annual Attendance: 50,000
Special Subjects: Asian Art, Painting-American, Painting-European, Prints, Watercolors
Collections: New York University Art Collection, Ben & Abby Grey Foundation Collection of Asian & Middle Eastern Art
Publications: Exhibition catalogs
Activities: Lects open to public, 2-3 vis lectrs per yr; individual paintings & original objects of art lent to other cultural institutions & sister organizations for exhibs; originate traveling exhibs; sales shop sells exhibition catalogs

M **Washington Square East Galleries**, 80 Washington Sq E, New York, NY 10003-6697. Tel 212-998-5747; Fax 212-998-5752; Email 80wse@nyu.edu; Web: www.nyu.edupagesgalleries; *Dir* Nicola Lees; *Exhibs Coordr* Ben Hatcher; *Gallery Mgr* Hugh O'Rouke
Open Tues - Sat 11 AM - 6 PM; No admis fee; Estab 1975 for exhibitions of works by graduate student artists; Eight gallery rooms containing solo shows; Average Annual Attendance: 10,000
Exhibitions: 70 group shows annually; Annual Small Works Competition; Thesis Exhibitions
Publications: Press releases
Activities: Annual International Art Competition, Small Works

L **Stephen Chan Library of Fine Arts**, One E 78th St (Duke House), New York, NY 10075. Tel 212-992-5825; Fax 212-992-5807; Email ifa.library@nyu.edu; Web: www.nyu.edu/gsas/dept/fineart; *Head Librn* Amy Lucker; *Ref Libn* Michael Hughes; *Libr Asst* Kimberly Hannah; *Libr Asst* Shirin Khaki
Open Mon & Fri 9 AM - 5 PM, Tues - Thurs 9 AM - 6 PM; Estab to provide scholarly materials for graduate studies in art history, archaeology & conservation of works of art; Circ Non-circulating; Research Library
Library Holdings: Book Volumes 150,000, CD-ROMs, Exhibition Catalogs, Periodical Subscriptions 460
Special Subjects: Antiquities-Assyrian, Antiquities-Byzantine, Antiquities-Egyptian, Antiquities-Etruscan, Antiquities-Greek, Antiquities-Oriental, Antiquities-Persian, Antiquities-Roman, Archaeology, Art History, Asian Art, Painting-European

L **Institute of Fine Arts Visual Resources Collection**, One E 78th St (Duke House), B Level, New York, NY 10075. Tel 212-992-5810; Fax 212-992-5807; Email jenni.rodda@nyu.edu; Web: www.ifa.nyu.edu; *Photographer* Nita Roberts; *Cur* Jenni Rodda; *Information Svc Asst* Michael Konrad; *Circ & Reference Asst* Fatima Tanglao; *Info Serv* Jason Varone
Open Mon - Fri 9 AM - 6 PM by appointment; Circ Non-circulating; Library open to qualified researchers & academia
Library Holdings: Lantern Slides 150,000, Other Holdings B&W photographs, mounted & unmounted 750,000; 35mm slides 350,000
Special Subjects: Archaeology, Art History
Collections: Biblioteca Berenson, Frank Caro Archives (b&w, Oriental), Census, Gertrude Achenbach Coor Archives, D.I.A.L., Walter Friedlaender Archives, Corpus Gernsheim (85,000 pieces, drawings), Henry Russell Hitchcock Archives (B&W), architecture), Richard Offner Archives (b&w, Italian painting), James Stubblebine Archives (b&w, Italian painting), Emile Wolf Archives (b&w, Spanish art), photographs are used for teaching & research purposes only

A **NEW-YORK HISTORICAL SOCIETY,** Museum, 170 Central Park W, New York, NY 10024-5194. Tel 212-873-3400; Fax 212-595-5707; Email info@nyhistory.org; Web: www.nyhistory.org; *Pres & CEO* Louise Mirrer; *Exec VPres & COO* Jennifer Schantz; *VPres & Library Dir* Michael Ryan; *VPres & Mus Dir* Margi Hofer; *VPres Communs* Ines Asian; *VPres Devel* Matt Bregman; *VPres Opers* Andrew Buonpastore; *VPres Educ* Mia Nagawiecki; *VPres Pub Prog* Dale Gregory; *Historian & VPres Scholarly Progs* Valerie Paley; *VPres History Exhibs* Marci Reaven; *CFO* Richard Shein; *Dir DiMenna Children's History Museum* Alice Stevenson; *Dir Opers & Maintenance* Tony Christoforou; *Dir Engineering Svcs* Ron Gilchrist; *Dir IT* Armando Lopez; *Dir Visitor Svcs* Nick Mancini; *Dir Security* Bill Montgomery; *Dir Institutional Giving* Cheryl Morgan; *Dir Library Opers* Nina Nazionale; *Dir Merchandis Opers* Ione Saroyan; *Dir Exhib & Creative Dir* Gerhard Schlanzky; *Dir Spec Events* Anne Vanderwal
Open Tues - Thurs & Sat 10 AM - 6 PM, Fri 10 AM - 8 PM, Sun 11 AM - 5 PM, cl Labor Day, Thanksgiving, Christmas; Admis adults $21, seniors, educators & active military $16, students w/ID $13, children 5 - 13 yrs $6, children 4 & under free. Fri 6 PM - 8 PM pay what you wish; Estab 1804 to collect & preserve material relating to the history of the US through the eyes of New York; Maintains 1st & 2nd Floor Galleries, W 77th St Rotunda Gallery, Henry Luce III Center for the Study of American Culture (temporarily closed for renovations); Average Annual Attendance: 310,000; Mem: 8100; dues senior $75, individual $90, dual $125, family $150, young friend $175, friend $250, patron family $500, benefactor $1,000, Gotham Fellow $2,500
Income: $16,000,000 (financed by endowment, grants, contributions, federal, state & local government, mem, admis)
Library Holdings: Book Volumes, Clipping Files, Exhibition Catalogs, Fiche, Manuscripts, Maps, Memorabilia, Original Art Works, Original Documents, Other Holdings ephemera, Pamphlets, Periodical Subscriptions, Photographs
Special Subjects: Architecture, Ceramics, Decorative Arts, Drawings, Historical Material, Manuscripts, Maps, Painting-American, Photography, Prints, Sculpture, Silver, Watercolors, Landscapes, Portraits
Collections: The Birds of America: Audubon's 433 original watercolors, American paintings from the Colonial period to 20th century, including genre scenes, portraits & landscapes by major artists of this period, 60,000+ objects & works of art relating to the founding of America, history of art in the US, & history of NY & its people, Tiffany Lamp Collection, World Trade Center artifacts, Hudson River landscapes, Gilder Lehrman Collection
Publications: catalogs & compendia of permanent collections; portraits, drawings, Tiffany lamps, Slaver, Grant/Lee; Armory Show at 100; Chinese American: Exclusion/Inclusion
Activities: Classes for adults & children; docent talks; teacher resources; outreach progs; Saturday Academy; lects open to pub & for mems only, 75 vis lectrs per yr; Bernard & Irene Schwartz Distinguished Speakers Series; concerts; gallery talks; tours; symposia; fellowships; individual paintings & original objects of art lent to mus; lending collection contains 2700 paintings, 5000 drawings, 675 sculptures, 800 miniatures; Touch Collection, Web-based training; book traveling exhibs 4 per yr; originate traveling exhibs to other mus; mus shop sells books, reproductions, cards, magazines, slides, history and themed decorative objects; DiMenna Children's History Museum, 170 Central Park West, New York, NY 10024

L **Library**, 2 W 77th St, New York, NY 10024; 170 Central Park West, New York, NY 10024. Tel 212-485-9226; Fax 212-875-1591; Web: www.nyhistory.org; *VPres & Dir of Patricia D Klingstein Library* Michael Ryan
Open Printed & Manuscript Collections: Tues - Sat 10 AM - 5 PM, Summer: Tues - Fri 10 AM - 5 PM; Graphic Collections: Tues - Fri 10 AM - 5 PM by appt only; No admis fee; photocopying fees apply
Library Holdings: Book Volumes 500,000, Cards 10,000, Clipping Files, Exhibition Catalogs, Fiche, Manuscripts, Maps, Memorabilia, Micro Print, Original Art Works, Original Documents, Other Holdings AV maps 15,000, Micro film 50,000, Vertical files 10,000 (including menus), Pamphlets, Periodical Subscriptions 150, Photographs, Prints, Reels, Sculpture
Special Subjects: Architecture, Art History, Historical Material, Manuscripts, Maps, Photography, Posters, Prints, Woodcuts
Collections: American Almanacs, American Art Patronage, American Genealogy, American Indian (accounts of & captivities, Early American Imprints, Early Travels in America, Early American Trials, Civil War Regimental Histories & Muster Rolls, Jenny Lind (Leonidas Westervelt) Maps, Military History (Military Order of the Loyal Legion of the United States, Commander of the State of New York) Military History & Science (Seventh Regiment Military Library), Naval & Marine History (Naval History Society), 18th & 19 Century New York City & New York State Newspapers, Slavery & the Civil War, Spanish American War (Harper), Among the Manuscript Collections, Horatio Gates, Alexander McDougall, Rufus King, American Fur Company, Livingston Family, American Art Union, American Academy of Fine Arts, Broadside Collection, Hotel Files, Arnold Shircliffe Menu Collection, Newspapers Collection, Online Catalog, Manuscript Collections Relating to Slavery (online), Children's Aid Society Images (online), Marion Mahoney Griffin's The Magic of America, typescript & illustrations, Examination Days: The NY African Free School Collection, Alexander Hamilton Digital Project, Witness to the Early American Experience
Exhibitions: Civil War Treasures from the NY Historical Society; Brooklyn Revealed

M **NICHOLAS ROERICH MUSEUM,** 319 W 107th St, New York, NY 10025-2799. Tel 212-864-7752; Fax 212-864-7704; Email director@roerich.org; Web: www.roerich.org; *Pres* Edgar Lansbury; *Exec Dir* Daniel Entin
Open Tues noon - 5 PM, Sat - Sun 2 PM - 5 PM, cl Mon & holidays; No admis fee; donations accepted; Estab 1958 to show a permanent collection of paintings by Nicholas Roerich, internationally known artist, to promote his ideals as a thinker, writer, humanitarian, scientist, and explorer, and to promote his Pact and Banner of Peace; New York brownstone with three exhibit floors; Average Annual Attendance: 20,000; Mem: 800; dues patron $100, contributing $50, assoc $25
Income: Financed by mem & donations
Collections: Permanent collection of paintings by Nicholas Roerich
Publications: Altai-Himalaya, A Travel Diary; Flowers of Morya, The Theme of Spiritual Pilgrimage in the Poetry of Nicholas Roerich; The Invincible; Nicholas Roerich, An Annotated Bibliography; Nicholas Roerich, A Short Biography; Nicholas Roerich 1874-1974 Centenary Monograph; Roerich Pact & Banner of Peace; Shambhala; two books by Nicholas Roerich: On Eastern Crossroads, and Foundations of Buddhism
Activities: Lects open to pub; concerts; tours; mus shop selling books, prints, reproductions and postcards

M **THE NIPPON GALLERY AT THE NIPPON CLUB,** 145 W 57th St, New York, NY 10019-2220. Tel 212-581-2223; Fax 212-581-3332; Email info@nipponclub.org; Web: www.nipponclub.org; *Deputy Pres & Exec Officer* Hiroshi Suehiro
Open Mon - Fri 9 AM - 5 PM, cl Sat, Sun & holidays; No admis fee; Estab 1981 for the purpose of international cultural exchange of arts & crafts from Japan & US; Located in the main lobby of a 7 story club house; gallery space is 1000 sq ft; Mem: 1200; dues $420
Income: Financed by mem
Special Subjects: Crafts
Publications: The Nippon Club Directory, annual; The Nippon Club News, monthly
Activities: Classes for adults; lects for members and the public, various sports activities & cultural events, concerts, gallery talks & tours

A **THE ONE CLUB,** 260 5th Ave, 2nd Fl New York, NY 10001. Tel 212-979-1900; Fax 212-979-5006; Email info@oneclub.org; Web: www.oneclub.com; *CEO* Kevin Swanepoel; *VP, Content and Marketing* Yash Egami
Check website for hrs; Free for members and members of NARM; Estab 1975 to support the craft of advertising, informal interchange among creative people, develop advertising excellence through advertising students who are tomorrow's professionals; Exhibits feature different advertising agencies; Mem: dues individual & faculty $200, junior $150, student $95
Special Subjects: Advertising Design, Art Education, Commercial Art, Graphic Design
Publications: The One Show Annual, Advertising's Best Print, Radio & TV, annually
Activities: Educ dept; lect open to public & some for members only; gallery talks; competitions with awards; scholarships offered; sales shop sells books & DVDs

PASTEL SOCIETY OF AMERICA
For further information, see National and Regional Organizations

A **PEN & BRUSH, INC,** 29 E 22nd St, New York, NY 10010. Tel 212-475-3669; Fax 212-475-6018; Email info@penandbrush.org; Web: www.penandbrush.org; *Exec Dir* Janice Sands; *Assoc Dir* Dawn Delikat; *Pres* Nette Forne Thomas
Open Tues - Sat noon - 6 PM; No Admis fee; Estab 1894, incorporated 1912 for encouragement in the arts; The Clubhouse was purchased in 1923, and contains artists studios, meeting room and 3 exhibition galleries; Average Annual Attendance: 1,000; Mem: 270; dues $250 professional women writers, artists, sculptors, craftsmen, musicians; annual meeting in Apr
Library Holdings: Other Holdings Members' Books
Collections: Collages, crafts, graphics, mixed media, oil, paintings, pastels, sculpture, watercolor
Exhibitions: Ten annual exhibitions of members' work; one man shows; solo winner shows
Publications: Pen & Brush bulletin, monthly
Activities: Dramatic progs; lects open to pub; concerts; scholarships; scholarships offered; sales shop sells original art, paintings, sculpture & craft items

L **Library**, 29 E 22nd St, New York, NY 10010. Tel 212-475-3669; Fax 212-475-6018; *Dir* Janice Sands
For members only
Library Holdings: Book Volumes 1000, Periodical Subscriptions 5
Publications: Bulletin, monthly

M **PERFORMANCE SPACE 122,** 150 First Ave, New York, NY 10009; 67 West St, Ste 315 Brooklyn, NY 11222. Tel 212-477-5829; Fax 212-353-1315; Web: www.ps122.org
Open Mon - Fri 9 AM - 9 PM, Sat - Sun 10 AM - 6 PM; Estab 1980 to show work by emerging artists
Activities: Competitions

M **PHOENIX GALLERY,** 210 11th Ave, (at 25th St) Ste 902 New York, NY 10001-1224. Tel 212-226-8711; Fax 212-343-7307; Email nycphoenixart@gmail.com; Web: www.phoenix-gallery.com; *Pres* Pamela Flynn; *Secy* Harriet Sobie Goldstein; *Treas* Joseph O'Neill
Open Tues - Sat 11:30 AM - 6 PM; No admis fee; Estab 1958; 190 linear ft of exhibition walls. Not for profit artist-member gallery; Average Annual Attendance: 10,000; Mem: 33; dues non-active $2,700, active $2,160; meetings one per month
Income: $64,000 (financed by mem)
Collections: Contemporary Art - 33 members from all over the United States, Paris & Korea, Contemporary Art
Activities: Dramatic progs; poetry & dance progs; lects open to pub, 5 vis lectrs per yr; sponsoring of competitions

M **PRINCE STREET GALLERY,** 530 W 25th St, New York, NY 10001-5516. Tel 646-230-0246; Web: www.princestreetgallery.com; *Co-Dir* Daniel Abrams; *Co-Dir* Arthur Kvarnstrom; *Sec* Ellen Piccolo; *Treas* Arthur Elias
Open Tues - Sat 11 AM - 6 PM; No admis fee; Estab 1970 to provide a showing place for members, mainly figurative art; cooperative artist run gallery; Gallery has about 30 members who have shown in New York as well as throughout the country & internationally; Average Annual Attendance: 8,000; Mem: 30; mem enrollment fees $500, mem $100 per month for 12 months (local), $130 (non-local); 6 meetings per yr
Income: Financed by mem
Exhibitions: Gallery Artists: Barbara Kulicke, Elizabeth Higgins, Marion Lerner-Levine, Gerald Marcus, Mary Salstrom, Gina Werfel, Rani Carson, Arthur Elias, Barbara Tipping Fitzpatrick, Nancy Grilikhes, Arthur Kvarnstrom, Paul Warren; Summer: invitational shows
Publications: Annual catalog
Activities: Lects open to public; gallery talks

C **PRINTED MATTER, INC,** 231 11th Ave, New York, NY 10001-1206. Tel 212-925-0325; Fax 212-925-0464; Email info@printedmatter.org; Web: www.printedmatter.org; *Pres* Philip Aarons; *Exec Dir* Max Schumann; *Assoc Dir* Max Schumann; *Bibliographer & Inventory Mgr* Leslie Lasiter; *Dir Asst & Gen Mgr* Cory Siegler; *Order Fulfillment* Aaron Fisher
Open Mon - Wed & Sat 11 AM - 7 PM, Thurs - Fri 11 AM - 7 PM, Sun noon - 6 PM; Estab 1976 to foster appreciation, dissemination & understanding of artists' publications; Small gallery; Average Annual Attendance: 100,000
Special Subjects: Maps
Exhibitions: Conceptual artists books from the 70's & early 80's
Publications: On-line
Activities: Lect open to pub; concerts; gallery talks; tours; Mus shop sells books, magazines, original art, prints, audio, video

A **PUBLIC ART FUND, INC,** One E 53rd St, New York, NY 10022. Tel 212-223-7800; Fax 212-223-7801; Email info@publicartfund.org; Web: www.publicartfund.org; *Pres* Susan K Freedman; *Dir & Chief Cur* Nicholas Baume; *Finance & HR Mgr* Joni Todd; *Proj Mgr* Seth Cohen; *Communs Mgr* Allegra Thoresen
Open Mon - Fri 9:30 AM - 5:30 PM; No admis fee; Estab 1977 to present artists projects, new commissions, installations & exhibitions in public space
Publications: Catalogues; manuals on public art; newsletter; postcards
Activities: Temporary exhibition program; artist talks; In the Public Realm

L **Visual Archive**, One E 53rd St 11th Floor, New York, NY 10022. Tel 212-980-4575; Fax 212-980-3610; Email info@publicartfund.org; Web: www.publicartfund.org; *Pres* Susan K Freedman; *Dir & Chief Cur* Nicholas Baume; *Project Mgr* Seth Cohen; *Mgr Finance & HR* Joni Todd; *Communs Mgr* Allegra Thoresen
Open by appointment only, other project specific hours; No admis fee; Estab 1977; NYC's leading presenter of artists' projects, new commissions & exhibs in public spaces
Library Holdings: Audio Tapes, Cassettes, Clipping Files, Compact Disks, DVDs, Exhibition Catalogs, Kodachrome Transparencies, Lantern Slides, Manuscripts, Original Art Works, Original Documents, Other Holdings Documentation of public art projects, Pamphlets Brochures on all PAF projects, Photographs, Slides 4000, Video Tapes
Collections: Murals, outdoor sculpture, sponsors temporary installations throughout New York City
Publications: PAFlet; various books; semi-annual magazine
Activities: Lects open to pub; 6 vis lectrs per yr; sales shop sells books

A **QUEEN SOFIA SPANISH INSTITUTE,** 55E 59th St, New York, NY 10022. Tel 212-628-0420; Fax 212-734-4177; Email info@qssi.org; Email pholder@queensofiasi.org; Web: www.qssi.org; *Interim Co-Chmn* David L Askren; *Interim Co-Chmn* Valentin Fuster; *VChmn* Beatrice Santo Domingo; *Secy* Renate Rennie; *Dir Admin* Peggy Holder-Jones
Open Mon - Thurs 10 AM - 6 PM, Fri 10 AM - 8 PM, Sat 10 AM - 5 PM; Admis general $15, mem $10, students & seniors $5; Estab 1954 to promote understanding of Spanish culture, past & present, & current Spanish pub affairs & economic issues in the United States; enhance an understanding of the influence of Spanish culture in Americas; Housed in a McKim, Mead & White landmark building donated by Margaret Rockefeller Strong de Larrin, Marquesa de Cuevas; Mem: Dues individual $60, friend $500, patron $1000+, sponsor $5000+, benefactor $15,000+, golden benefactor $25,000+
Income: Financed by individual & corporate mem fees, donations, foundation grants & endowment
Special Subjects: Latin American Art
Exhibitions: Exhibits of rich & varied traditions of the visual arts of Spain & Latin America
Activities: Spanish language classes; lect open to public; symposia; Queen Sofia Spanish Institute Translation Prize

C **THE READER'S DIGEST ASSOCIATION INC,** 750 Third Ave, New York, NY 10007-2703. Tel 646-293-6000
Art collection located throughout corporate headquarters
Collections: Over 8000 works of art, 19th century American & contemporary American artists & International artists, graphics, decorative arts, sculpture, painting, mixed media, works on paper, Photography, Bloomsbury Group

M **THE RENEE & CHAIM GROSS FOUNDATION,** Chaim Gross Studio, 526 LaGuardia Pl, New York, NY 10012. Tel 212-529-4906; Fax 212-529-1966; Email info@rcgrossfoundation.org; Web: www.rcgrossfoundation.org; *Pres* Mimi Gross; *Cur Colls* Sasha Davis
Open Thurs & Fri 1- 3 PM (guided one-hours tours), cl July & Aug; Admis $15 (online reservations required); Estab 1989 to demonstrate the continuity of Gross's personal vision in sculpture over 70 years of work; Sculpture studio where Gross worked for over 30 years
Library Holdings: Auction Catalogs, Clipping Files, Exhibition Catalogs, Lantern Slides, Memorabilia, Original Documents, Pamphlets, Photographs, Prints, Records, Reels, Reproductions, Sculpture, Slides, Video Tapes
Collections: Permanent collection consists of 70 years of Chaim Gross's (1904-91) sculpture in wood, stone & bronze, drawings, prints & watercolors
Exhibitions: Exhibs, biannual
Activities: Tours for groups; gallery talks; lect open to public

M **RUBIN MUSEUM OF ART,** 150 W 17th St, New York, NY 10011-5402. Tel 212-620-5000; Fax 212-620-0628; Email info@rubinmuseum.org; Web: www.rubinmuseum.org; *Exec Dir* Patrick Sears; *Dir Finance & Admin* Marilena Christodoulou; *Dir Exhibs, Colls & Research* Jorrit Britschgi; *Dir Progs & Engagement* Tim McHenry; *Sr Opers Mgr* Steven Battaglia; *Head Coll Mgmt & Registration* Michelle Bennett Simorella; *Head Major Gifts & Fundraising Events* Nicky Combs; *Head Mktg & Communs* Elke Dehner; *Spec Events Mgr* Olivia Cohen
Open Mon & Thurs 11 AM - 5 PM, Wed 11 AM - 9 PM, Fri 11 AM - 10 PM, Sat - Sun 11 AM - 6 PM, cl Tues, Christmas, Thanksgiving, and New Year's Day; cafe & shop open during museum hours; Admis adults $15, seniors & students with ID $10, children under 12 & Fri 6 PM - 10 PM free; Estab 2004 as a dynamic environment that stimulates learning, promotes understanding, and inspires personal connections to the ideas, cultures and art of Himalayan Asia; Facilities include educ center, photography gallery, classroom, state-of-the-art theater, cafe, shop & space rental; Average Annual Attendance: 200,000; Mem: 4,000
Special Subjects: Asian Art, Carpets & Rugs, Embroidery, Metalwork, Religious Art, Sculpture
Collections: Paintings, sculptures & textiles relating to the Himalayas
Activities: Classes for adults & children; docent training; internships; lectrs open to the public, 30-40 vis lectrs per year; concerts; gallery talks; tours; organize traveling exhibs; mus shop sells books, original art, reproductions, prints, DVDs, film, jewelry, cards, candles

C **RUDER FINN ARTS & COMMUNICATIONS, INC,** 425 E 53rd St, New York, NY 10022-2905. Tel 212-593-6400; Fax 212-715-1507; Email coless@ruderfinn.com; Web: www.ruderfinn.com; *Dir Mktg & Communs* Sarah Coles
Estab to link corporations which support the arts with museum exhibitions and performing arts events, to develop major corporate sponsored exhibitions and special projects created for public spaces. Assistance given for marketing and publicity assignments for cultural institutions and the selection, installation and documentation of corporate art collections
Activities: Originate traveling exhibs to museums nationwide

SALMAGUNDI CLUB
For further information, see National and Regional Organizations

M **SCHOOL OF VISUAL ARTS,** Chelsea Gallery, 601 W 26th St, New York, NY 10001. Tel 212-592-2145; Email gallery@svu.edu; Web: www.sva.edu/exhibitions; *Dir & Cur* Francis DiTommaso
Open Mon - Sat 10 AM - 6 PM; No admis fee; Estab 1961 as SVA's premier exhibition facility; Comprised of four state-of-the-art galleries and large terrace; Average Annual Attendance: 8,000
Special Subjects: Cartoons, Collages, Drawings, Etchings & Engravings, Graphics, Juvenile Art, Painting-American, Posters, Prints, Watercolors, Photography
Exhibitions: New York Digital Salon; The Master's Series; Sculptors Drawings; Ann international traveling exhibition of art made with computers; Ann award exhibition honoring the great visual communicators of our time
Publications: Exhibition catalogs & posters

A **SEGUE FOUNDATION,** Reading Room-Archive, 300 Bowery, Apt. 2, New York, NY 10012-2802. Tel 212-353-0555; Fax 212-254-4145; Email sequefoundation@verizon.net; Web: www.seguefoundation.com; WATS 800-869-7553; *Pres* James Sherry; *Exec Dir* Daniel Machlin
Open by appointment; Estab 1977; For reference only
Library Holdings: Audio Tapes, Cassettes, Manuscripts, Memorabilia, Other Holdings Vols & per subs 2000, Reproductions, Video Tapes
Collections: Language poetry books, periodicals, rare archival materials manuscripts, reading series footage
Publications: Poetry, literary criticism, film & performance texts

SOCIETY OF AMERICAN GRAPHIC ARTISTS
For further information, see National and Regional Organizations

M **SOCIETY OF ILLUSTRATORS,** Museum of American Illustration, 128 E 63rd St, New York, NY 10065-7303. Tel 212-838-2560; Fax 212-838-2561; Email info@societyillustrators.org; Web: www.societyillustrators.org; *Pres* Tim O'Brien; *Dir* Anelle Miller; *Dir Opers* John Capobianco
Open Tues & Thurs 10 AM - 8 PM, Wed & Fri - Sat; Admis fee adults $15, seniors & students $10, children under 11, mem & Tues 5 PM - 8 PM free; Estab 1901; Average Annual Attendance: 30,000
Collections: Original illustrations from 1838 to present, all media
Exhibitions: Student Scholarship competition - May; Children's book illustration exhibit - Oct; Members open - July
Activities: Classes for Adults; Lects open to pub, 18 vis lectrs; sponsor competitions for professional illustrators; awards; individual paintings & original objects of art lent to muse & universities; lending collection contains 1200 art works; originate traveling exhibs to schools; mus shop sells books, prints, t-shirts & gift items

SOCIETY OF ILLUSTRATORS
For further information, see National and Regional Organizations

A **SOCIETY OF SCRIBES, LTD,** PO Box 933 New York, NY 10150-0933. Tel 212-452-0139; Email info@societyofscribes.org; Web: www.societyofscribes.org; *Co-Pres* Chi Nguyen; *Co-Pres* Susan Steele; *VPres* Cynthia Dantzic; *Treas & Acting Secy* Nacy Redgate Favorito; *Recording Secy* Ana Rodriguez; *Corresp Secy* Eva Kokoris; *Advertising & Publicity* Susan Steele
Open Mon - Fri 10 AM - 5 PM (office); calligraphic exhibitions throughout New York City; Estab 1974; Mem: Dues overseas $45, Canada & Mexico $45, USA $40; annual meeting in Feb, annual Fair in Dec; memberships open to all interested in the calligraphic arts.
Exhibitions: Donnell Library
Publications: NewSOS Newsletter publ twice a year; Our journal Letters from New York
Activities: Adult classes in calligraphy & lettering arts & calligraphy in the graphic arts; lects & demonstrations open to public; 4-6 vis lectrs per year; gallery talks; competitions; lects at the Morgan Library, Grolier Club & the Donnell

M **SOLOMON R GUGGENHEIM MUSEUM,** 1071 Fifth Ave, New York, NY 10128-0173. Tel 212-423-3500; Email visitorinfo@guggenheim.org; Web: www.guggenheim.org; *Dir Mus & Foundation* Richard Armstrong; *Artistic Dir & Chief Cur* Nancy Spector; *Deputy Dir & COO* Elizabeth Duggal; *Deputy Dir & Chief Officer Global Strategies* Juan Ignacio Vidarte; *Gen Counsel* Sarah Austrian; *Deputy Dir & Chief Global Commun* Tina Vaz; *Deputy Dir & Chief Conservator* Carol Stringari; *Sr Cur Colls & Exhibs* Susan Davidson; *Cur Asian Art* Alexandra Munroe; *Cur Photography* Jennifer Blessing; *Cur 19th & Early 20th c Art* Vivian Greene; *Cur Colls & Exhibs* Tracy Bashkoff; *Assoc Cur Contemporary Art & Mgr Cur Affairs* Joan Young; *Cur & Mgr Curatorial Affairs* Valerie Hillings; *Cur Performance & Media* Nat Trotman; *Cur Contemporary Art* Katherine Brinson; *Asst Cur Colls* Lauren Hinkson; *Asst Cur Colls* Megan Fontanella; *Conservator Colls & Exhibs* Julie Barten; *Assoc Chief Conservator Colls* Gillian McMillan; *Sr Conservator Objects* Nathan Otterson; *Conservator Paper & Photographs* Jeffrey Warda; *Sr Conservator Time-Based Media* Joanna Phillips; *Dir Educ School & Family Progs* Sharon Vatsky; *Dir Educ Pub Progs* Christina Yang
Open Sun - Wed & Fri 10 AM - 5:45 PM, Sat 10 AM - 7:45 PM, cl Thurs, Thanksgiving, Christmas Eve & Day; Admis general $15, students with valid ID cards & seniors over 65 $10, children under 12 free, Sat 5 - 7:45 PM Pay What You Wish; Estab 1937 as a nonprofit organization which is maintained by the Solomon R Guggenheim Foundation; founded for the promotion, encouragement & educ in art; to foster an appreciation of art by acquainting mus visitors with significant paintings & sculpture of our time; The gallery was designed by architect Frank Lloyd Wright; Average Annual Attendance: 700,000; Mem: 7,000; dues $75 & up
Income: Financed by endowment, mem & state & federal appropriations
Special Subjects: Drawings, Painting-American, Painting-French, Painting-German, Painting-Italian, Painting-Russian, Painting-Spanish, Photography, Sculpture, Watercolors
Collections: Reflects the creative accomplishments in modern art from the time of the Impressionists to the constantly changing experimental art of today. The coll of nearly four thousand works, augmented by the Justin K Thannhauser Collection of 75 Impressionists & Post-Impressionist masterpieces, including the largest group of paintings by Vasily Kandinsky, one of the largest & most comprehensive coll of paintings by Paul Klee, largest number of sculptures by Constantin Brancusi in any New York museum, paintings by Chagall, Delaunay, Lager, Marc, Picasso, Bacon, Bonnard, Braque, Cezanne, Malevitch, Modigliani, Moore, Reusseau & Seurat, with concentration of works by Dubuffet, Miro & Mondrian among the Europeans, Americans such as Davis, de Kooning, Diebenkorn, Gottlieb, Guston, Johns, Lichtenstein, Agnes Martin, Motherwell, Nevelson, Noguchi, Pollack, younger artists include Andre, Flavin, Judd, Christenson, Hamilton, Hesse, Mangold, Nauman, Stella & Serra, paintings, drawings & sculpture colls are being enlarged, Constantin Brancusi Sculpture Collection, Vasily Kandinsky Collection, Paul Klee Collection, Justin K Thannhauser Collection of Impressionist & Post-Impressionist Paintings
Publications: Exhibition catalogs, Guggenheim Museum Magazine (2 times per year)
Activities: Classes & workshops for children, youth, teens & adults; teacher resources & school collaboration progs; professional development progs; Works & Process performances & receptions, artist interaction; lects open to pub; concerts; gallery talks; acoustiguide & docent-led tours; individual paintings & original objects of art lent to other mus & galleries; lending collection contains original art works, original prints, painting, sculpture; originates traveling exhibs; mus shop sells books, jewelry & t-shirts

L **Library & Archives**, 345 Hudson St, Fl12 New York, NY 10014. Tel 212-360-4230; Email library@guggenheim.org; archives @ guggenheim.org; Web: www.guggenheim.org
Open to qualified scholars by appt only on Mon, Tues & Fri 10:30 AM - 5:30 PM; Library estab 1952 to document the Museum's coll of 20th century art; Archives estab 1973 to trace develop of Guggenheim's coll & the Foundation, as well as actively collecting materials on the Museum's history since its inception as the Museum of Non-Objective Painting in 1939; For reference only
Library Holdings: Book Volumes, Cards, Exhibition Catalogs, Kodachrome Transparencies, Other Holdings Artist Files; Early Avant-Garde Periodicals, Pamphlets, Periodical Subscriptions 50, Slides

M **Sackler Education Center**, 1071 5th Ave, New York, NY 10128-0173. Tel 212-423-3500; Email visitorinfo@guggenheim.org; Web: www.guggenheim.org
Estab 2001 as an educ hub & learning laboratory offering pub progs in visual, performing & literary arts; Located below the rotunda of the Guggenheim Museum; Maintains Peter B Lewis Theater, News Corporation New Media Theater, JP Morgan Chase Foundation Exhib Gallery, studio art lab, multimedia lab, computer lab, resource center
Activities: Classes for adults & children; variety of pub progs; film screenings; tours; gallery progs; competitions; awards; internships; fellowships

M **SOUTH STREET SEAPORT MUSEUM,** 12 Fulton St, New York, NY 10038-2109. Tel 212-748-8600; Fax 212-748-8590; Email info@seany.org; Web: www.southstreetseaportmuseum.org; *Exec Dir* Capt Jonathan Boulware
Open Wed - Sun 11 AM - 5 PM (ongoing exhibs & ship tours); Admis gen $12, seniors & students with valid ID $8, children ages 2-17 $6, children under 2 & mems free; Estab 1967 to preserve the maritime history & traditions of the Port of New York; Several gallery spaces: The Seaport Gallery for art exhibits; the printing press gallery at Bowne & Co Stationers; the mus children's center; Average Annual Attendance: 325,000; Mem: 9000; dues family $75, individual $50, seniors & students $40; annual meeting May
Income: Financed by mem & corporate grants
Special Subjects: Archaeology, Architecture, Drawings, Folk Art, Historical Material, Manuscripts, Maps, Marine Painting, Photography, Posters, Prints, Scrimshaw, Woodcarvings
Collections: Restored historic buildings, fleet of historic ships, permanent coll of marine art & artifacts, colls of ship models, archive of ship plans, photos & negatives
Exhibitions: Traveling In Style, ongoing; My Hammer Hand; Mens Lives; New York Trades Transformed; Peking At Sea; Recent Archeology in Lower Manhattan; Titanic; Waterfront Photography
Publications: Seaport Magazine, quarterly
Activities: Educ dept; docent training; lects open to pub; gallery talks; tours; individual paintings and original objects of art lent to institutions; mus shop sells books & prints; junior mus

L **Melville Gallery**, 12 Fulton St, New York, NY 10038. Tel 212-748-8648; Fax 212-748-8610; Email info@seany.org; Web: southstreetseaportmuseum.org; *Exec Dir* Capt. Jonathan Boulware
Open Mon - Fri 11 AM - 5 PM; Exhibition & social gathering space
Income: Mem and corporate grants
Library Holdings: Audio Tapes, Book Volumes 20,000, Clipping Files, Exhibition Catalogs, Kodachrome Transparencies, Manuscripts, Memorabilia, Motion Pictures, Original Art Works, Other Holdings Negatives, Pamphlets, Periodical Subscriptions 30, Photographs, Prints, Reels, Reproductions, Slides
Special Subjects: Archaeology, Folk Art, Historical Material, Industrial Design, Maps, Marine Painting, Painting-American, Painting-British, Scrimshaw, Woodcarvings

M **STOREFRONT FOR ART & ARCHITECTURE,** 97 Kenmare St, New York, NY 10012-4506. Tel 212-431-5795; Fax 212-431-5755; Email info@storefrontnews.org; Web: storefrontnews.org; *Founder* Kyong Park; *Exec Dir & Chief Cur* Eva French; *Gallery Mgr & Progs Producer* Max Lauter; *Pres* Charles Renfro; *Develop & Outreach Assoc* Andrew Emmet
Open Tues - Sat 11 AM - 6 PM, cl Sun & Mon; No admis fee; Estab 1982 to show interdisciplinary & experimental works of art & architecture, often never previously shown in New York. Organizes large events or competitions of an experimental nature; 15 ft x 100 ft x 2 ft, triangle; Average Annual Attendance: 80,000
Income: Financed by grants and contributions
Exhibitions: Ecotec Forum, held in Corsica, France; Future Systems; Gunther Domeney (Austrian architect); Mark West (Canadian artist); Big Soft Orange, Dutch architectural exhibit
Publications: Exhibition catalogs; monthly bulletin; quarterly reports
Activities: Lects open to pub; 20 vis lectrs per yr; mus shop sells books

M **THE STUDIO MUSEUM IN HARLEM,** 144 W 125th St, New York, NY 10027-4423. Tel 212-864-4500; Fax 212-864-4800; Email director@studiomuseum.org; Web: www.studiomuseum.org; *Dir & Chief Cur* Thelma Golden; *Deputy Dir, Finance & Admin* Sheila McDaniel; *Deputy Dir Institutional Advancement* Hallie S Hobson
Open Wed 5 PM - 7 PM (mem only) Thurs - Fri noon - 9 PM, Sat 10 AM - 6 PM, Sun noon - 6 PM, cl Mon - Wed, Jul 4, Thanksgiving, Christmas & New Year's Days; Suggested admis adults $7, students & seniors $3, mems & children under 12 free; Estab 1967 to exhibit the works of contemporary Black American artists, mount historical & informative exhibitions & provide culturally educational programs & activities for the general pub; 10,000 sq ft of exhib & educ space, new exhib space & cafe (spring 2005); Average Annual Attendance: 100,000; Mem: 50,000; dues $15 - $1,000
Income: Financed by mem, city & state appropriation, corporate & foundation funding, federal funding, rental income, gift shop sales & individual contributions
Special Subjects: Afro-American Art, Photography, Sculpture
Collections: James VanDerZee Collection of Photography, over 1500 works of art by African-American artists including sculpture, painting & works on paper

Publications: Freestyle; Challenge of the Modern; Black Belt; Photographs; Africa Comics; Frequency
Activities: Classes for adults & children; docent training; workshops; panel discussions; demonstrations; cooperative school prog; internship prog; lects open to pub, 10 vis lectrs per yr; concerts; gallery talks; tours; schols offered; book traveling exhibs; originate traveling exhibs; mus shop sells books, magazines, original art, reproductions, prints, jewelry, baskets, crafts, pottery & catalogues

M **SWISS INSTITUTE,** 117 2nd Ave, Fl 2 New York, NY 10013. Tel 212-925-2035; Fax 212-925-2040; Email info@swissinstitute.net; Web: www.swissinstitute.net; *Dir* Simon Castets; *Dir Institutional Devel & Opers* Kristin Wawruck; *Gallery Mgr* Scott Kiernan
No admis fee; Estab 1986 to promote artistic dialogue between Switzerland & the United States; 2000 sq ft; Average Annual Attendance: 10,000; Mem: 300; dues $25-$1000; annual meeting in Fall
Income: Financed by mem, corporate contributions, sponsors & foundations
Special Subjects: Painting-European
Collections: Swiss affairs
Exhibitions: Rotating
Publications: Exhibition catalogs, 3 per year
Activities: Educ dept; lects open to pub, 4 vis lectrs per yr; concerts; gallery talks; tours; originate traveling exhibs

L **TAIPEI ECONOMIC & CULTURAL OFFICE,** Chinese Information & Culture Center Library, 1 E 42nd St, Fl 7 New York, NY 10017-6904. Tel 212-697-6188; Fax 212-697-6303; Email tpecc@tpecc.org; Web: www.tpecc.org; *Dir* Jack Lee
Open Mon - Fri 9:30 AM - 5:30 PM by appointment only; Estab 1991
Library Holdings: Book Volumes 42,000, Clipping Files, Motion Pictures, Pamphlets, Periodical Subscriptions 155, Prints, Reels, Reproductions, Video Tapes
Special Subjects: Oriental Art
Publications: CICC Currents, bimonthly

A **UKRAINIAN INSTITUTE OF AMERICA, INC,** 2 E 79th St, New York, NY 10021-0106. Tel 212-288-8660; Email mail@ukrainianinstitute.org; Web: www.ukrainianinstitute.org; *Dir Prog* Dr Walter Hoydysh
Open Tues - Sat noon - 6 PM, Sun by appointment; Admis adults $8, seniors $6, students $4, children under 12 free; Estab 1948 to develop, sponsor & promote educational activities which will acquaint the general public with history, culture & art of Ukrainian people; Ukrainian & East European art; Average Annual Attendance: 8,500; Mem: 480
Income: Financed by endowment, mem & contributions
Purchases: $2,500
Library Holdings: Original Art Works, Sculpture
Collections: Church & religious relics, folk art, ceramic & woodwork, patents of Ukrainian-American engineers, Gritchenko Foundation Collection, sculptures by Archipenko, Kruk, Mol & others, Ukrainian paintings
Publications: UIA Newsletter, irregular; Anniversary of UIA
Activities: Dramatic progs; seminars; symposiums; workshop seminars; literary evenings; lects open to pub, concerts; gallery talks; Awards: Person of the Year; Chicago Ukrainian Museum of Modern Art; mus shop sells books, magazines, original art, reproductions & prints

M **THE UKRAINIAN MUSEUM,** 222 E 6th St between 2nd & 3rd Aves, New York, NY 10003. Tel 212-228-0110; Fax 212-228-1947; Email info@ukrainianmuseum.org; Web: www.ukrainianmuseum.org; *Pres* Chryzanta Hentisz; *Dir* Maria Shust; *Admin Dir* Daria Bajko; *Mktg & Pub Relations* Hanya Krill; *Cur Folk Art* Lubow Wolynetz
Open Wed - Sun 11:30 AM - 5 PM; Admis adults $8, seniors, students $6, children under 12 & mems free; Since 1976, The Ukrainian Museum preserves the cultural heritage of Ukrainian Americans through exhibitions, educational/community oriented programs for adults and children, scholarly research and publications. The museum maintains folk art, fine arts and photographic/documentary collections. Current major projects include computerization of collections data; Average Annual Attendance: 10,500; Mem: 1,450; dues family $125; sustaining family $125; individual $50; sustaining individual $100; senior citizen $20 student $15;
Income: $700,000 (financed by mem, donations & grants)
Special Subjects: Ceramics, Coins & Medals, Costumes, Crafts, Decorative Arts, Drawings, Embroidery, Etchings & Engravings, Ethnology, Folk Art, Graphics, Historical Material, Jewelry, Landscapes, Metalwork, Photography, Pottery, Primitive art, Sculpture, Textiles, Watercolors, Woodcarvings, Woodcuts
Collections: Major crafts in Ukrainian folk art: woven & embroidered textiles (including costumes & kilns), woodwork, ceramics, metalwork, Ukrainian Easter Eggs, fine arts, photographic/documentary archival coll on Ukrainian cultural heritage, among them photographs of individuals in their native dress, architectural landmarks as well as photographic records of historic events, Ukrainian paintings
Exhibitions: Rotating exhibits 3 times yr
Publications: Annual report; bulletins; bilingual exhibition catalogs or brochures
Activities: Classes for adults & children; lects open to pub, 2-3 vis lectrs per yr; gallery talks; tours; concerts; individual paintings & original objects of art lent; lending collection contains 3000 Ukrainian Folk Art, including costumes & textiles, 1000 original prints, 500 paintings, 200 works on paper; originate traveling exhibs; mus shop sells books, magazines, original art & reproductions

L **Library**, 222 E 6th St, New York, NY 10003-8201. Tel 212-228-0110; Fax 212-228-1947; Email info@ukrainianmuseum.org; Web: ukrainianmuseum.org; *Dir* Maria Shust
Open Wed - Sun 11:30 AM - 5 PM; Library for internal use only. For reference by appointment
Library Holdings: Book Volumes 4000, Exhibition Catalogs, Pamphlets, Photographs, Slides 600, Video Tapes
Special Subjects: Archaeology, Architecture, Art History, Crafts, Drawings, Etchings & Engravings, Folk Art, Jewelry, Landscapes, Leather, Portraits, Pottery, Religious Art, Sculpture, Woodcarvings
Collections: Historical photographic documentary archives, Folk Art, Ukrainian Fire
Publications: Extensive catalogues with major exhibitions; Annual reports

L **UNION FOR REFORMED JUDAISM,** Synagogue Art & Architectural Library, 633 Third Ave, 7th Fl, New York, NY 10017. Tel 212-650-4000, 212-249-0100; Fax 212-650-4109; Web: urj.org; *Dir, Synagogue Mgr* Dale Glasser; *Dir Library* John Crotty
Open Mon - Fri 9 AM - 5 PM; cl Sat & Sun & Jewish holidays; Estab 1957; Books for use on premises only
Income: Financed by budgetary allocation plus rental fees for slides
Library Holdings: Book Volumes 350, Slides 3400
Publications: An American Synagogue for Today & Tomorrow (book); Contemporary Synagogue Art (book)
Activities: Slide rental service

L **UNIVERSITY CLUB LIBRARY,** One W 54th St, New York, NY 10019. Tel 212-572-3418; Fax 212-572-3452; *Assoc Dir & Cur* Scott Overall; *Librn* Maureen Manning; *Conservation Librn* Laurie Bolger; *Dir & Cur Collections* Andrew Berner
Open to members & qualified scholars (inquire by letter or telephone first) Mon - Fri 9 AM - 6 PM; No admis fee; Estab 1865 for the promotion of the arts & culture in post-university graduates; Art is displayed in all areas of the building; Average Annual Attendance: 7,000; Mem: 4,250
Income: Financed by endowments & mem
Library Holdings: Book Volumes 90,000, CD-ROMs, Compact Disks, Manuscripts, Original Art Works
Collections: Art, architecture, fine printing, book illustration, works by George Cruikshank
Publications: The Illuminator, occasional

M **VIRIDIAN ARTISTS INC,** 548 W 28th St, Ste 632 New York, NY 10001-5673. Tel 212-414-4040; Email viridianartistsinc@gmail.com; Web: www.viridianartists.com; *Dir* Vernita Nemec; *Asst to Dir* Jenny Belin
Open Tues - Sat noon - 6 PM; No admis fee; Estab 1968 to exhibit work by emerging & established artists; Gallery shows contemporary work by emerging & established artists; Average Annual Attendance: 10,000; Mem: 30; dues $250 per mo; application to current mems see website
Income: Mem; sales; competitions
Special Subjects: Afro-American Art, Collages, Drawings, Landscapes, Painting-American, Painting-Japanese, Photography, Portraits, Prints, Sculpture
Exhibitions: Juried exhibitions every spring, cur from a contemporary museum; Member's exhib changing every 3 weeks; Guest shows; curated shows; theme shows; Director's choice shows
Publications: Gallery Artists; Gallery Catalogue; individual artist books & catalogues
Activities: Docent training; lects open to pub; gallery talks; national juried show annually with cash or exhibs prize; sponsoring of competitions; exten dept lends paintings, sculpture & photographs; book traveling exhibs 1 per yr; originate traveling exhibs 2 per yr

VISUAL ARTISTS & GALLERIES ASSOCIATION (VAGA)
For further information, see National and Regional Organizations

L **VISUAL ARTS LIBRARY,** 380 Second Ave, New York, NY 10010; 209 E 23rd St, New York, NY 10010-3901. Tel 212-592-2660; Fax 212-592-2655; Web: www.sva.edu/library; *Visual Resources Cur* Lorraine Gerety; *Dir Library* Caitlin Kilgallen; *Head Tech Servs* Zimra Panitz; *Assoc Dir Library* Rebecca Clark
Open to students & faculty Mon - Thurs 8:30 AM - 10 PM, Fri 8:30 AM - 7:30 PM, Sat noon - 5:30 PM, Sun Noon - 8 PM; No admis fee; Estab 1962 to serve needs of School of Visual Arts students and faculty; Circ 50,000; Exclusively for student & faculty use, lending to students
Income: Financed by tuition
Purchases: $80,000
Library Holdings: Audio Tapes, Book Volumes 70,000, CD-ROMs, Cassettes, Clipping Files, Compact Disks, Exhibition Catalogs, Filmstrips, Other Holdings Comic books, Periodical Subscriptions 260, Slides, Video Tapes
Special Subjects: Advertising Design, Art History, Commercial Art, Film, Graphic Design, Illustration, Photography
Publications: Library Handbook; accessions lists

M **WHITE COLUMNS,** White Columns Curated Artist Registry, 320 W 13th St, New York, NY 10014-1200. Tel 212-924-4212; Fax 212-645-4764; Email info@whitecolumns.org; Web: www.whitecolumns.org; *Dir & Chief Cur* Matthew Higgs; *Deputy Dir & Cur* Erin Somerville; *Pres* Gregory Miller; *Archivist/Curation Assistant* Christina Leung; *Devel Gallery Mgr* Kerri Ammirata
Open Tues - Sat noon - 6 PM; No admis fee; Estab 1970 to showcase the works of emerging artists; Exhibs, progs, & servs for emerging artists; Average Annual Attendance: 20,000; Mem: No Membership
Exhibitions: Annual benefit auction
Activities: Lects open to pub; concerts; gallery talks; tours

M **WHITNEY MUSEUM OF AMERICAN ART,** 99 Gansevoort St, New York, NY 10014-1404. Tel 212-570-3600; Email info@whitney.org; Web: www.whitney.org; *Dir* Adam D Weinberg; *Deputy Dir International Initiatives & Sr Cur* Donna De Salvo; *Deputy Dir Progs* Scott Rothkopf; *Deputy Dir Advancement* Alexadra Wheeler; *COO* John S Stanley
Open Mon, Wed, & Thurs 10:30 AM - 6 PM, Fri & Sat10:30 - 10PM Sun 10:30AM - 6 PM, cl Tues & national holidays; Admis general $25, seniors & students with ID $18, mems & children 18 & under free; Estab 1930, inc 1931 by Gertrude Vanderbilt Whitney for the advancement of contemporary American art; Museum opened 1931 on Eighth Street & moved to 54th Street in 1954; new building opened in 1966; Average Annual Attendance: 500,000; Mem: 5,000; dues $85 & up
Income: Financed by endowment, admis, grants, mem
Purchases: Numerous annual acquisitions
Library Holdings: Auction Catalogs, Audio Tapes, Book Volumes, Clipping Files, Compact Disks, DVDs, Exhibition Catalogs, Manuscripts, Original Documents, Pamphlets, Periodical Subscriptions, Photographs
Special Subjects: Drawings, Painting-American, Prints, Sculpture
Collections: Over 22,00 works; drawings, paintings, prints, sculpture of mainly 20th & 21st century American artists

Exhibitions: Rotating exhibits every 3-4 months
Publications: Annual report; brochures, cards, posters; calendars; exhibition catalogues; gallery brochures
Activities: Classes for adults, teens, children, students & families; progs for seniors; docent training; symposia & panel discussions; teachers' workshops; school partnerships; Regent Family Residence art progs; access for the disabled; lects open to pub; concerts; gallery talks; tours; independent study; Artreach provides introductory art education to elementary & high school students; individual paintings & original objects of art lent; originate traveling exhibs for mus here & abroad; sales shop sells books, magazines, reproductions, slides, cards & posters

L **Frances Mulhall Achilles Library,** 99 Gansevoort St, New York, NY 10014-1404. Tel 212-570-3648; Email library@whitney.org; Web: www.whitney.org; *Mng Librn* Ivy Blackman; *Dir Research* Farris Wahbeh; *Archives Mgr* Tara Hart; *Research Resources Asst* Monica Crozier
Open by appointment for advanced research; No admis fee; Estab 1931 for encouragement & advancement of American art & art scholarship; Circ Non-Circulating
Library Holdings: Auction Catalogs, Audio Tapes, Book Volumes 50,000, CD-ROMs, Cassettes, Clipping Files, Compact Disks, DVDs, Exhibition Catalogs, Fiche, Manuscripts, Memorabilia, Original Documents, Other Holdings Vertical Files: 450+ linear ft, Pamphlets, Periodical Subscriptions 500, Photographs, Records, Reels, Reproductions, Slides, Video Tapes
Special Subjects: American Western Art, Art History, Drawings, Film, Painting-American, Photography, Printmaking, Prints, Sculpture, Video
Collections: 20th - 21st century & contemporary American art, Special Collections: artists' books, portfolios, photographs, titles in the White Fellows Artist & Writers Series (1982-2001), posters & valuable ephemera related to Museum's permanent coll, Museum Archives: 2,500+ linear ft of historical records documenting the evolution of the Whitney Museum from inception of the Whitney Studio (1914) to present, incl: Whitney Studio Club & Galleries: Administrative & Exhib Records, 1916-1930, Whitney Mus of American Art: Admin Records, 1930 - 1960, Exhib Records 1931-2000 (Ongoing), Curatorial Records, 1935-2000 (Ongoing), Film & Video Artist Files, 1970 - 1998, Film & Video Image Files, Performance Series, 1968-1997, Property Records, 1949-1993, Photograph Coll, Special Coll Artist Files, Arshile Gorky Research Coll 1920s-1990s, Edward Hopper Research Coll 1894-2000, Resources for Rebels on 8th St: Juliana Force & The Whitney Museum of American Art by Avis Berman, Lloyd Goodrich Artists Correspondence, 1917-1978, John Depol Coll, 1953-2004, Francis M Naumann Research Coll for How, When & Why Modern Art Came to New York by Marius de Zayas, 1910-1936, Florence Rubenfeld Coll of Archival Material for Clement Greenberg: A Life, 1988-1998

WOMEN'S CAUCUS FOR ART
For further information, see National and Regional Organizations

M **WOMEN'S INTERART CENTER, INC,** Interart Gallery, 549 W 52 St, New York, NY 10019. Tel 212-246-1050; *VPres* Bill Perlman; *Artistic Dir* Margot Lewitin; *Dir Programming* Ronnie Geist
Open Mon - Fri 1 - 6 PM; No admis fee; Estab 1970 to present to the pub the work of significant, emerging women artists; Average Annual Attendance: 9,000; Mem: Dues $35
Income: Financed by state appropriation, National Endowment for the Arts, private foundations, corporations & individuals
Exhibitions: Community as Planner
Publications: Women's Interart Center Newsletter, quarterly
Activities: Classes for adults; lects open to pub, 2 vis lectrs per yr; originate traveling exhibs

M **YESHIVA UNIVERSITY MUSEUM,** 15 W 16th St, Center for Jewish History New York, NY 10011-6301. Tel 212-294-8330; Fax 212-294-8335; Email info@yum.cjh.org; Web: www.yumuseum.org; *Cur & Registrar* Bonni-Dara Michaels; *Assoc Dir Museum Admin* Jody Heher; *Dir* Jacob Wisse, PhD; *Educator* Ilana Benson
Open Mon 3:30 PM - 8 PM, Tues, Thurs & Sun 11 AM - 5 PM, Wed 11 AM - 8 PM, Fri 11 AM - 2:30 PM; Admis adults $8, students & seniors $6; Mon & Fri free; Estab 1973 to collect, preserve & interpret Jewish art & objects of material culture in the light of Jewish history; 6000 sq ft of galleries; maintains reference library; Average Annual Attendance: 40,000; Mem: 550; dues $50-$1000
Special Subjects: Decorative Arts, Judaica, Manuscripts, Photography, Religious Art, Sculpture, Textiles
Collections: Architectural models, ceremonial objects, documents, ethnographic material, fine & decorative art, manuscripts, photographs, sculpture, textiles, Art history, History of Art & Archaeology, Contemporary art
Exhibitions: Changing exhibs of Contemporary & Historical Fine Arts; Multi-disciplinary exhibs of Jewish history & culture
Publications: Catalogs
Activities: Classes for children; dramatic progs; docent training; craft workshops; lects open to pub; concerts; gallery talks; tours; individual paintings & original objects of art lent for purposes of exhibs to institutions which provide specified levels of care; book traveling exhibs 1 per yr; originate traveling exhibs; sells books

NIAGARA

M **NIAGARA UNIVERSITY,** Castellani Art Museum, 5795 Lewiston Rd, Niagara, NY 14109; PO Box 1938, Niagara University, NY 14109-1938. Tel 716-286-8200; Fax 716-286-8289; Email cam@niagara.edu; Web: www.niagara.edu/cam; *Registrar* Kathleen Fraas; *Gallery Mgr* Kurt VonVoetcsch; *Museum Shop Mgr* Anne LaBarbera; *Asst Mus Shop Mgr* Carla Castellani; *Dir* Kate Koperski; *Cur Colls & Exhibs* Michael J Beam
Open Tues - Sat 11 AM - 5 PM, Sun 1 - 5 PM, cl Mon; No admis fee; Estab 1978; The gallery is a 10,000 sq ft museum that displays the permanent collection of over 3000 works of art encompassing 19th century to present with a concentration on contemporary art; Mem: 300
Income: $120,000
Special Subjects: Afro-American Art, Collages, Graphics, Painting-American, Painting-British, Painting-Canadian, Painting-French, Painting-German, Photography, Pre-Columbian Art, Prints, Sculpture, Watercolors, Woodcuts
Collections: Modern paintings, sculpture & works on paper (19th -20th centuries), Pre-Columbian Pottery
Exhibitions: Glass art: Arnold Mesches; John Moore; Michael Kessler; Arcadia Revisted: Niagara River & Falls from Lake Erie to Lake Ontario, Photographs by John Pfahl
Publications: Exhibition catalogs, 4 per yr
Activities: Classes for adults & children; Public Art Project on Underground Railroad; docent training; learning disabled prog; senior citizen outreach prog; lects open to pub, 1-6 vis lectrs per year; concerts; gallery talks; tours; competitions; awards; scholarships & fels offered; individual paintings & original objects of art lent to qualified museums; originate traveling exhibitions

NORTH SALEM

M **HAMMOND MUSEUM & JAPANESE STROLL GARDEN,** Cross-Cultural Center, 28 Deveau Rd, North Salem, NY 10560; PO Box 326, North Salem, NY 10560-0326. Tel 914-669-5033; Email gardenprogram@yahoo.com; Web: www.hammondmuseum.org; *Dir* Lorraine Laken; *Bus Mgr* Judy Schurmacher
Open Apr - Nov, Wed - Sat Noon - 4 PM; Admis to Museum & Garden, adults $5, seniors $4, mems & children under 12 free; Estab 1957; Exhib provide an East-West cultural experience supplemented by programs of related special events such as the Asian Arts Festival and Moonviewing Concert. The 3.5 acre Japanese Stroll Garden includes a pond, waterfall, Zen garden, bamboo grove, Maple Terrace, etc; Average Annual Attendance: 5,800; Mem: 250; dues $35-$2,500
Income: Financed by mem, matching funds, private foundations & corporations
Special Subjects: Asian Art, Costumes, Decorative Arts, Ethnology, Photography, Photography, Portraits
Collections: Fans, Carl Van Vechten Collection of Photographs
Activities: Classes for adults & children; lect open to public, 5 vis lectrs per year; concerts; gallery talks; tours; individual paintings & original objects of art lent to other museums; lending collection contains photographs & slides; mus shop sells books, original art, prints, jewelry, giftware

NORTH TONAWANDA

M **NORTH TONAWANDA HISTORY MUSEUM,** 54 Webster St, North Tonawanda, NY 14120-5814. Tel 716-213-0554; Email nthistorymuseum@aol.com; Web: www.nthistorymuseum.org; *Dir* Donna Zellner Neal; *Archival Records Coordr & Cur* Jane Garis; *Admin & Colls Asst* Carol Kopczynski; *Research Coordr* Faith Jaskulski; *Events Coord* Danielle Oney
Open Mon & Tues 9 AM - 9 PM, Wed - Fri 9 AM - 5 PM, cl Independence Day, Thanksgiving Day, Christmas Eve & Day, New Year's Eve & Day; Donations accepted; school tours $2 per student, Seaway Trail walks: adults $8, children $4; other history walks: adults $4, children $2; Estab 2004; History mus with emphasis on rich ethnic heritage, Erie Canal/Niagara River Influence as role of lumber & industrial ctr in 19th & 20th centuries. Pvt nonprofit org; FT vols 1, PT vols 4, interns 3; 26th Congressional Dist; Mem: dues Life $250, Contributing $100, Bus/Civic $50, Family of 2 or more $25, Individual $15, Senior $10
Collections: Artifacts, oral histories, photographs, directories & archival materials, 50 vols of city directories & other local history books, 10 high school yearbooks
Publications: Quarterly newsletter; Annual Report
Activities: Formal educ progs for adults & children; research in ethnic, industrial, lumber & Erie Canal heritage; ethnic heritage festivals; historic home tours & tours of other historic venues; garden walks; concerts; virtual mus online

NORTHPORT

L **NORTHPORT-EAST NORTHPORT PUBLIC LIBRARY,** 151 Laurel Ave, Art Dept Northport, NY 11768-3161. Tel 631-261-6930; Fax 631-261-6718; Email nenpl@suffolk.lib.ny.us; Web: www.nenpl.org; *Asst Dir* Eileen Minogue; *Dir* Stephanie Heineman; *Chairperson* Michael L Glennon
Open Mon - Fri 9 AM - 9 PM, Sat 9 AM - 5 PM, Sun 1 - 5 PM (Sep - June only); No admis fee; Estab 1914; Circ 968,285
Library Holdings: Audio Tapes, Book Volumes 215,000, Cassettes, Clipping Files, Exhibition Catalogs, Fiche, Filmstrips, Manuscripts, Other Holdings Compact discs 2250, Pamphlets, Periodical Subscriptions 720, Prints, Records, Reproductions, Sculpture, Video Tapes 7890
Publications: Library, monthly
Activities: Lect open to public, 5 vis lectrs per year; concerts; competitions

NYACK

M **EDWARD HOPPER HOUSE ART CENTER,** 82 N Broadway, Nyack, NY 10960-2628. Tel 845-358-0774; Email info@hopperhouse.org; Web: www.hopperhouse.org; *Exec Dir* Jennifer Paton; *Artistic Dir* Carole Perry
Open Wed - Sun 12 PM - 5 PM; Students $2; Seniors $5; Adults $7; Children free; Estab 1971 to memorialize Edward Hopper & exhibit current regional artists; Four galleries on first floor of historical house and Edward Hopper's bedroom upstairs. Interior of house intact; Average Annual Attendance: 2,200; Mem: 400; dues $25-$250
Income: Financed by mem
Special Subjects: Painting-American, Photography, Posters, Reproductions
Exhibitions: Exhibits by local & national American artists; Edward Harper (loan exhib)
Activities: Adult classes, docent training; lects open to public, 3 vis lectrs per year; juried art competitions, concerts; sales shop sells books & prints

OGDENSBURG

M **FREDERIC REMINGTON ART MUSEUM,** 303 Washington St, Ogdensburg, NY 13669-1517. Tel 315-393-2425; Fax 315-393-4464; Email info@fredericremington.org; Web: www.fredericremington.org; *Dir & Cur* Laura Foster; *Admin Aid* Shannon Ghize; *Project Coordr* Shirley McDonald; *Accnt Mgr* Debbie Ormasen; *Educ Specialist* no replacement yet; *Dir Develop* Melanie Flack
Open May 15 - Oct 15 Mon - Sat 10 AM - 5 PM, Sun 1 - 5 PM, Oct 16 - May 14 Wed - Sat 11 AM - 5 PM, Sun 1 - 5 PM, cl legal holidays; Admis adults $9, seniors & youth $8, mems & 16 & under free; organized tour groups $7 per person; Estab 1923 to house & exhibit works of art of Frederic Remington (1861-1909), a native of northern New York; The mus is in the converted Parish Mansion, built 1809-1810 & the recently constructed Newell Wing.; Average Annual Attendance: 15,000; Mem: 1200; dues family $50
Income: Financed by endowment & city appropriation
Library Holdings: Framed Reproductions, Manuscripts, Original Art Works, Original Documents, Pamphlets, Sculpture
Special Subjects: American Western Art, Bronzes, Furniture, Glass, Painting-American, Painting-European, Porcelain, Prints, Sculpture, Silver, Stained Glass, Watercolors, Painting-American
Collections: Remington paintings, bronzes, watercolors, drawings, photographs, letters & personal art collection, studies in plaster by Edwin Willard Deming, sculpture by Sally James Farnham, Parish Collection of Furniture, Sharp Collection of Period Glass, China, Silver & Cameos
Exhibitions: The Children's Exhibit; The Frederic Remington Exhibit
Activities: Classes for adults & children; docent training; lects open to pub; gallery talks; tours; for anyone; mus shop sells books, reproductions, prints

OLD CHATHAM

M **SHAKER MUSEUM & LIBRARY,** 88 Shaker Museum Rd, Old Chatham, NY 12136-2601. Tel 518-794-9100, ext 218; Fax 518-794-8621; Email contact@shakermuseumandlibrary.org; Web: www.shakermuseumandlibrary.org; *Finance Mgr* Ann Montag; *Dir* Lili Ott; *Cur* Starlyn D'Angelo
Open May - Oct daily 10 AM - 5 PM, cl Tues; Admis adults $8, reduced rates for seniors, children & groups; Estab 1950 to promote interest in & understanding of the Shaker cultural heritage; The exhibits are housed in a complex of eight buildings; Average Annual Attendance: 16,000; Mem: 475; dues $35 - $1000
Income: $700,000 (financed by earned revenue, endowment, contributions, private & public grants)
Purchases: $3000
Library Holdings: Auction Catalogs, Book Volumes, Clipping Files, Manuscripts, Maps, Memorabilia, Slides
Special Subjects: Costumes, Decorative Arts, Dolls, Drawings, Embroidery, Furniture, Glass, Historical Material, Textiles, Watercolors
Collections: 35,000 artifacts & archival material representing 200 years of Shaker history & culture including, baskets, furniture, metal work, personal artifacts, stoves, textiles, tools & equipment, transportation
Exhibitions: Orientation to Shaker History; Shakers in the 20th Century; Shaker Cabinetmakers and Their Tools; study storage related to individual collections
Publications: Members update; The Shaker Adventure; Shaker Seed Industry; pamphlets; booklets; gallery guide; catalogs; postcards, reprints, and broadsides
Activities: Classes for adults & children; docent training; seminars; lects open to pub; concerts; adult tours; symposia; festivals; family events; originate traveling exhibs; mus shop sells Shaker reproduction furniture, craft items & publications

L **Emma B King Library,** 202 Shaker Road, New Lebanon, NY 12125; PO Box 630, New Lebanon, NY 12125. Tel 518-794-9100, Ext 220; Fax 518-794-8621; Email contact@shakerml.org; Web: www.shakerml.org; *Director of Collections and Research* Jerry Grant; *Executive Director* Lacy Schutz; *Programs & Operations Manager* Wyatt Erchak
Seasonally June-Oct, year-round research by appt; $10 for guided tours, all other entry by donation; 1950, to share the story of the American Shakers; Circ non-circulating; For reference only; Average Annual Attendance: 2,000; Mem: Part of museum
Income: financed by museum
Library Holdings: Audio Tapes, Book Volumes 2000, Cassettes, Clipping Files, Filmstrips, Kodachrome Transparencies, Manuscripts, Memorabilia, Motion Pictures, Original Art Works 100, Original Documents, Pamphlets, Photographs 3500, Prints, Records, Reels 189, Slides, Video Tapes
Special Subjects: Archaeology, Architecture, Art History, Crafts, Folk Art, Furniture, Handicrafts, Historical Material, Interior Design
Collections: Manuscripts and records, Photographic and map archive; furniture; textiles; machinery; ephemera; household items
Exhibitions: seasonal, changing and loan
Activities: lects open to the public; gallery talks; tours;; Shop sells books; prints; & Shaker-made items

OLD WESTBURY

M **NEW YORK INSTITUTE OF TECHNOLOGY,** Gallery, PO Box 8000, Old Westbury, NY 11568-8000. Tel 516-686-7542; *Chmn* Peter Voci
Open Mon - Fri 9 AM - 5 PM; Estab 1964; Gallery maintained for the many exhibits held during the year; Average Annual Attendance: 5,000
Exhibitions: Annual faculty & student shows; some traveling exhibitions
Publications: Graphic Guild Newsletter, quarterly
Activities: Classes in custom silk-screen printmaking; gallery talks; awards; scholarships offered; exten Dept serves all areas

L **Art & Architectural Library,** PO Box 8000, Education Hall Old Westbury, NY 11568-8000. Tel 516-686-7579; Fax 516-686-7921; Email lheslin@nyit.edu; Web: www.nyit.edu; *Librn* Karen Cognato; *Branch Dir* Linda Heslin; *Lib Asst* Kim Renskers
Open Mon - Thurs 9 AM - 9 PM, Fri 9 AM - 5 PM, Sat 10 AM - 5 PM; No admis fee; Estab 1976
Library Holdings: Book Volumes 1808, DVDs, Exhibition Catalogs, Motion Pictures 23, Other Holdings CD's, Periodical Subscriptions 258, Video Tapes 80
Special Subjects: Afro-American Art, American Western Art, Antiquities-Egyptian, Architecture, Art Education, Art History, Asian Art, Decorative Arts, Drawings, Etchings & Engravings, Folk Art, Furniture, Graphic Arts, Graphic Design, History of Art & Archaeology, Islamic Art, Mexican Art, Painting-American, Painting-British, Painting-Dutch, Southwestern Art, Painting-European, Painting-Flemish, Painting-French, Painting-German, Painting-Italian
Exhibitions: Architecture dept student projects
Activities: Tours

M **STATE UNIVERSITY OF NEW YORK COLLEGE AT OLD WESTBURY,** Amelie A Wallace Gallery, Rte 107 (Broadway), Old Westbury, NY 11568; PO Box 210, Old Westbury, NY 11568-0210. Tel 516-876-3056; Fax 516-876-4984; Email amelieawallacegallery@gmail.com; Email yih@oldwestbury.edu; Web: www.owestbury.edu; *Gallery Dir* Hyewon Yi; *Chmn Art Dept* Patricia McLaughlin
Open Mon - Thurs; No admis fee; Estab 1976 to serve as a teaching aid & for community enlightenment; 2,000 sq ft on three levels; Average Annual Attendance: 3,000
Income: $4,500 (financed by endowment & HYS)
Collections: none
Exhibitions: 4 annual exhibitions by contemporary artists + 2 student shows
Publications: Exhibit brochures
Activities: Lect open to public, 4 vis lectrs per year; gallery talks

ONEIDA

M **MADISON COUNTY HISTORICAL SOCIETY,** Cottage Lawn, 435 Main St, Oneida, NY 13421-2440. Tel 315-363-4136, 361-9735; Email history@mchs1900.org; Web: www.mchs1900.org; *Exec Dir* Sydney Loftus; *Pres* Mishell Magnusson; *VPres* Barbara Chamberlain; *Treas* Julie Stokes
Open Mon - Fri 10 AM - 4 PM by appointment; Admis adults $5, discounts for school groups, children 12 & under & members free; Estab 1898 to collect, preserve & interpret artifacts indigenous to the history of Madison County; 1849 A J Davis gothic dwelling with period rooms, library & craft archive; Average Annual Attendance: 9,000; Mem: 500; dues $15-$100; annual meeting last Wed in Oct
Income: $100,000 (financed by endowment, mem, county, city & state appropriation, Annual Craft Fair)
Library Holdings: Clipping Files, Fiche, Maps
Special Subjects: Decorative Arts
Collections: Locally produced & or used furnishings, paintings, silver, textiles & ceramics
Exhibitions: Permanent exhibit in the barn; Bittersweet: Hop Culture in Central New York
Publications: Quarterly Newsletter; Madison County Heritage, published annually; Country Roads Revisited
Activities: Educ outreach progs for nursing homes & schools; lects open to pub, 10 vis lectrs per yr; slides, tapes & movies documenting traditional craftsmen at work; individual paintings & original objects of art lent to qualified mus & galleries for special exhibits; sales shop sells books, magazines, prints & slides, reproductions

ONEONTA

M **HARTWICK COLLEGE,** Foreman Gallery, PO Box 4020, Oneonta, NY 13820-4020. Tel 607-431-4575; Fax 607-431-4191; Email goldenn@hartwick.edu; Web: www.hartwick.edu; *Cur* Nancy Golden
Open Tues - Fri Noon - 8 PM, Sat noon - 4 PM or by appointment, cl last half of Dec & summers; No admis fee; Estab 1968, contemporary exhibitions; Open space housed within the Campus Arts Center; Average Annual Attendance: 1,500
Library Holdings: Clipping Files, DVDs, Exhibition Catalogs, Kodachrome Transparencies, Slides
Special Subjects: Baroque Art, Cartoons, Drawings, Painting-American, Prints, Renaissance Art, Sculpture
Exhibitions: Changing exhibitions; student & faculty exhibitions; professional artist exhibs per yr; (as schedule permits)
Activities: Lects open to pub, vis lectrs 3-4 per yr; gallery talks; Occasional booked traveling exhibitions

M **The Yager Museum,** 1 Hartwick Dr, Oneonta, NY 13820-4000; PO Box 4020, Oneonta, NY 13820. Tel 607-431-4299; Fax 607-431-4468; Email salluzzoa@hartwick.edu; Web: www.hartwick.edu/museum.xml; *Cur Anthropology* Dr David Anthony; *Colls Mgr* Whitney Birkett; *Bus Progs Mgr* Anne Sallozzo; *Coordr* Douglas Kendall Dr
Open Tues - Sat noon - 4:30 PM, cl acad holidays; No admis fee; Estab 1928; galleries feature temporary exhibits, anthropology, fine art & Yager collections; Average Annual Attendance: 802
Income: Income from college budget & endowment
Special Subjects: American Indian Art, Anthropology, Archaeology, Cartoons, Drawings, Etchings & Engravings, Ethnology, Graphics, Hispanic Art, Landscapes, Mexican Art, Painting-American, Painting-European, Prints, Renaissance Art, Sculpture, Watercolors, Woodcuts, Baroque Art, Coins & Medals, Decorative Arts, Historical Material
Collections: Coll of North American, Mexican & South American Indian art & artifacts & mask coll, fine arts featuring European and American works from 15th - 20th centuries, Micronesia
Exhibitions: Changing exhibitions.
Publications: The Rüdisühli: A Family of Painters; Oneonta's Native Son: Carleton E. Watkins, photographer

M **STATE UNIVERSITY OF NEW YORK COLLEGE AT ONEONTA,** Martin - Mullen Art Gallery, 108 Ravine Pkwy, 222 Fine Arts Ctr Oneonta, NY 13820-3717. Tel 607-436-3456; Fax 607-436-3466; Email timothy.sheesley@oneonta.edu; Web: www.oneonta.edu/academics/art/gallery.html; *Gallery Dir* Timothy Sheesley
Open Mon - Fri 11 AM - 5 PM; No admis fee; Contemporary fine art/teaching; Art Gallery is a major feature of the Art Wing, separate fine arts & student galleries; Average Annual Attendance: 3,000
Income: Financed by state appropriation

Exhibitions: Annual student art exhibition; 2 exhibs per semester
Activities: Prog for interns; gallery talks; 6 vis lectrs per yr; James Mullen annual student exhib awards

ORIENT

M **OYSTERPONDS HISTORICAL SOCIETY,** Museum, 1555 Village Ln, Orient, NY 11957; PO Box 70, Orient, NY 11957-0070. Tel 631-323-2480; Fax 631-323-3719; Email office@ohsny.org; Web: www.oysterpondshistoricalsociety.org; *Cur* William McNaught; *Colls Mgr* Amy Folk
Open exhibs: June - Sept Thurs, Sat & Sun 2 - 5 PM, archives by appointment only; Free; Estab 1944 to discover, procure, & preserve material related to the history of East Marion & Orient, NY; Average Annual Attendance: 6,000; Mem: 700; dues family $50, individual $30; annual meeting in Nov
Income: $160,000 (financed by endowment, mem, grants & fundraising)
Library Holdings: Audio Tapes, CD-ROMs, Cassettes, DVDs, Exhibition Catalogs, Lantern Slides, Manuscripts, Maps, Memorabilia, Motion Pictures, Original Art Works, Original Documents, Photographs, Prints, Sculpture, Slides, Video Tapes
Special Subjects: Decorative Arts, Furniture, Historical Material, Landscapes, Maps, Marine Painting, Portraits
Collections: Early Native American artifacts, including arrowheads, baskets & clay vessels, 18th century furniture & decorative arts, late 19th century Victorian furniture, marine & portrait paintings, photographs, textile coll, including quilts, scarves, fans, tools, & equipment related to the agricultural & sea-related occupations of this area, manuscript colls relating to local history
Exhibitions: 19th Century Boarding House; 18th Century Period Rooms; Rotating exhibs
Publications: Griffin's Journal, book; Historical Orient Village, book; She Went A'Whaling, book; quarterly newsletter; Captain's Daughter, book; Coasterman's Wife, book; In the Wake of Whales, book; In Her Own Name (book); The Diaries of Augustus Griffin, book;
Activities: Classes for adults & children; docent training; lects open to pub; 4 - 5 vis lectrs per yr; mus shop sells books, magazines, original art, reproductions & prints

OSSINING

M **MUSEUM OF OSSINING HISTORICAL SOCIETY,** 196 Croton Ave, Ossining, NY 10562-4504. Tel 914-941-0001; Email info@ossininghistorical.org; Web: www.ossininghistorical.org; *Dir* Roberta Y Arminio; *Pres* Norman D McDonald
Open Sun - Thurs 1 - 4 PM & by appointment; No admis fee; Estab 1931 to educate the pub in the history & traditions of the vicinity; East Gallery contains changing exhibitions & a portion of the permanent collection; West Gallery contains permanent collection; Average Annual Attendance: 2,500; Mem: 497; dues patron $100, civic, commercial & contributing $25, family $15, individual $10, senior citizens & students $5
Income: Financed by mem & town appropriation
Library Holdings: Video Tapes 32
Special Subjects: Costumes
Collections: Costumes, textiles & quilts, slides & films of old Ossining, old photographs & daguerreotypes, Victorian dollhouse complete in minute detail, contains antique dolls, toys, miniatures, old school books & photographs, oil portraits, fine arts, Italian Art & Architecture
Publications: Monthly brochure
Activities: Educ dept; class visits; special assignment guidance; lect open to public, 4 vis lectrs per year; gallery talks; tours; competitions with awards; individual paintings & original objects of art lent to schools, banks & industry; sales shop sells books, magazines

L **Library,** 196 Croton Ave, Ossining, NY 10562. Tel 914-941-0001; Email ohsm@optimum.net; *President* Joseph Burton; *Curator* Norm MacDonald
By Appointment Only; None; 1931 - Local Museum; Four Galleries, Fine art and Local Artifacts; Average Annual Attendance: 2,000; Mem: 700
Income: Grants, Dues, Donations
Library Holdings: Audio Tapes, Book Volumes 1000, Cassettes, Clipping Files, DVDs, Exhibition Catalogs, Framed Reproductions, Lantern Slides, Memorabilia, Original Art Works, Photographs, Prints, Reels, Reproductions, Slides, Video Tapes 32
Activities: Classes for children; Lectures open to the public; 4 visiting lectures per year; tours; scholarships;; Books;

OSWEGO

M **STATE UNIVERSITY OF NEW YORK AT OSWEGO,** Tyler Art Gallery, 126 Tyler Hall, SUNY Oswego Oswego, NY 13126. Tel 315-312-2113; Fax 315-312-5642; Email lbuckley@oswego.edu; *Asst Dir* Laurene Buckley; *Admin Aide* Lisa M Shortslef; *Asst Dir* Michael Flanagan
Open Mon - Fri 10 AM - 4 PM, Sat & Sun 12:30 PM - 4:30 PM, Sept - May; summer hours as posted; No admis fee; Estab 1969 to provide cultural stimulation & enrichment of art to the col community & to the residents of Oswego County; Two gallery spaces in Tyler Hall, the North Gallery is approx 2400 sq ft & the South Gallery is approx 1300 sq ft; Average Annual Attendance: 20,000
Income: Financed by University funds
Special Subjects: Painting-American, Painting-British, Posters, Pottery, African Art, Sculpture
Collections: Grant Arnold Collection of Fine Prints, Contemporary American Prints & Paintings
Exhibitions: Two galleries show a combined total of 14 exhibitions per school year
Publications: Brochures; occasional catalogs for exhibitions; posters
Activities: Lects open to public, 8-10 vis lectrs per yr; concerts, gallery talks; lending collection contains individual & original objects of art; originates traveling exhibs

L **Penfield Library,** 7060 State Rte 104, Oswego, NY 13126-3501. Tel 315-312-4267; Fax 315-312-3194; Email refdesk@oswego.edu; Web: www.oswego.edu/library; *Dir* Marybeth Bell; *Art Subject Librn* Nedra Peterson
Open Mon - Thurs 8 AM - 11 PM, Fri 8 AM - 9 PM, Sat 10 AM - 9 PM, Sun 11:30 AM - 11 PM; For lending & reference
Income: Financed by univ
Library Holdings: Audio Tapes, Book Volumes 437,000, Cassettes, Fiche, Filmstrips, Framed Reproductions, Motion Pictures, Original Art Works, Pamphlets, Periodical Subscriptions 1469, Records, Reels, Sculpture, Slides, Video Tapes
Special Subjects: Advertising Design, Aesthetics, Art Education, Art History, Costume Design & Constr, Graphic Arts

OYSTER BAY

L **PLANTING FIELDS FOUNDATION,** Coe Hall at Planting Fields Arboretum, 1395 Planting Fields Rd, Oyster Bay, NY 11771-1302; PO Box 660, Oyster Bay, NY 11771-0660. Tel 516-922-9210; Fax 516-922-9226; Email coehall@plantingfields.org; Web: www.plantingfields.org; *Dir* Ellen Cone Busch; *Dir Develop* Cindy Krezel; *Coll Mgr* Marianne Della Croce
Open Apr - Sept Mon - Fri noon - 3:30 PM; Admis adults $6.50, seniors $5, children 7-12 $2; Archives estab 1979 for Coe family papers, architectural drawings, photos, Planting Fields Foundation documents; For reference only. Coe Hall, a Tudor revival mansion being restored to its 1920's appearance, contains 17th-20th century paintings; Mem: $40 & up individual
Income: Financed by endowment
Library Holdings: Audio Tapes, Book Volumes 6000, Cassettes, Clipping Files, Filmstrips, Lantern Slides, Manuscripts, Memorabilia, Motion Pictures, Original Art Works, Pamphlets, Photographs, Prints, Slides, Video Tapes
Special Subjects: American Western Art, Architecture, Decorative Arts, Historical Material, Landscape Architecture, Painting-British, Painting-Dutch, Painting-European, Painting-Italian, Period Rooms, Photography, Porcelain, Portraits, Restoration & Conservation, Stained Glass
Activities: Classes for adults & children; docent training; outdoor science programs grades Pre K - 6; lect open to public, 5 vis lectrs per year; concerts; guided tours of historic house; sales shop sells books & garden related items

SOCIETY OF AMERICAN HISTORICAL ARTISTS
For further information, see National and Regional Organizations

PELHAM

M **PELHAM ART CENTER,** 155 Fifth Ave, Pelham, NY 10803-1503. Tel 914-738-2525; Fax 914-738-2686; Email info@pelhamartcenter.org; Web: www.pelhamartcenter.org; *Exec Dir* Lisa Robb; *Prog Mgr* Jessica Cioffoletti; *Finance Mgr* Bridget Beltke; *Educ & Outreach Mgr* Filomena Iolascon
Open Tues - Fri 10 AM - 5 PM; Sat 10 AM - 4 PM; Sun ((in Dec only) 12 - 4 PM; No admis fee; Estab 1972 as a community art center to give area residents & visitors a place, the opportunity & the resources to see, study & experience the arts in a community setting; Multipurpose space; Gallery A 1120 sq ft; Gallery B 670 sq ft; Average Annual Attendance: 20,000; Mem: 500; dues $25-$1000
Income: $280,000 (financed by mem, tuition, earned income & gift shop sales)
Activities: Classes for adults & children; studio classes; workshops, docent progs; lects open to pub, 7 exhibs annually, 2-3 vis lectrs per yr, gallery talks; schols offered; retail store sells unique gift items

PENN YAN

M **THE AGRICULTURAL MEMORIES MUSEUM,** 1110 Townline Rd, Penn Yan, NY 14527-9002. Tel 315-536-1206; Email jr.jensen@usadatanet.net; Web: www.agriculturalmemoriesmuseum.com; *Owner & Operator* Jennifer R Jensen; *Mus Asst* Hilbert J Jensen
Open June - Oct Sun 1 PM - 4 PM, Mon - Sat by appt, cl Nov - May; Admis adults $4, students & children 2 - 12 $1, children under 5 no admis fee; Estab 1997, dedicated in 1998; Pvt, family-owned org; 6500 sq ft exhib space; over 40-yr coll of horse-drawn carriages/sleighs, antique tractors, gasoline engines, toys, signs & misc. Mus preserves & restores items independently
Library Holdings: Book Volumes, Filmstrips
Collections: Over 45 carriages/sleighs, 50 gasoline engines, 50 antique tractors, pedal tractors & cars, signs & misc toys
Activities: Lects; guided tours & films

PLATTSBURGH

M **CLINTON COUNTY HISTORICAL ASSOCIATION,** Clinton County Historical Museum, 98 Ohio Ave, Plattsburgh, NY 12903-4401. Tel 518-561-0340; Email director@clintoncountyhistorical.org; Web: http://clintoncountyhistorical.org; *Dir & Cur* Carol Blakeslee-Collin; *Pres* Roger Harwood
Open Wed - Sat 10 AM - 3 PM & by appt; Admis adults $4, seniors $3, children ages 12 & under $2, mems & organized school & youth groups free
Special Subjects: Decorative Arts, Furniture, Glass, Maps, Painting-American, Porcelain, Portraits, Textiles, Photography
Exhibitions: Area history from 1600's to present
Activities: mus shop sells books

M **STATE UNIVERSITY OF NEW YORK AT PLATTSBURGH,** Art Museum, 101 Broad St, Plattsburgh, NY 12901-2637. Tel 518-564-2813 Kent, 564-2288 Burke, 564-2474 Main Office; Fax 518-564-2473; Web: www.plattsburgh.edu/museum; *Dir* Cecilia Esposito; *Coll Mgr* David Driver; *Coll Specialist* Eric Ruckler; *Docent Coordr* Marguerite Eisinger
Open daily Noon - 4 PM, cl university holidays; No admis fee; Estab 1978; Kent Gallery & Burke Gallery; Average Annual Attendance: 17,000

Special Subjects: African Art, Asian Art, Bronzes, Eskimo Art, Etchings & Engravings, Painting-American, Painting-Canadian, Porcelain
Collections: Rockwell Kent Collection, paintings, prints, drawings, sketches, proofs & designs, books, Nina Winkle Sculpture Garden, Slathin Collection, Louise Norton Classic Design Collection, Outlook Sculpture Park, Myers Lobby Gallery
Exhibitions: Twelve exhibitions each year; antique & contemporary, all media
Publications: Exhibition catalogs; monthly exhibition announcements; semi-annual calendar of events
Activities: Progs for undergrad students, elementary & secondary schools & community groups in area; docent progs; lects open to pub, 6 vis lectrs per yr; tours; gallery talks; competitions with awards; individual paintings lent

PLEASANTVILLE

M **PACE UNIVERSITY GALLERY,** Art Gallery in Choate House, 861 Bedford Rd, Pleasantville, NY 10570-2799. Tel 914-773-3694; Fax 914-773-3676; Email tromer@pace.edu; Web: www.pace.edu; *Dept Chair* Dr John Mulgrew; *Admin Asst* Teresa Romer
Open Mon - Wed Noon - 4PM, Thurs noon - 6 PM, cl Sat; No admis fee; Estab 1978 to exhibit the works of nationally known professional artists & groups, & to serve as a focal point for artistic activities within the university & surrounding communities; The gallery has a commanding view of the center of campus; it is both spacious & modern
Income: Financed by the university
Activities: Lect open to public, 8-10 vis lectrs per year; gallery talks; tours

POCANTICO HILLS

M **HISTORIC HUDSON VALLEY,** 639 Bedford, Pocantico Hills, NY 10591. Tel 914-631-8200; Fax 914-631-0089; Email info@hudsonvalley.org; Web: www.hudsonvalley.org; *Pres* Waddell Stillman; *Librn* Catalina Hannan; *Dir Finance* David Parsons; *Dir Devel* Peter Pockriss; *Dir Human Resources* Lynda Jones; *Dir Pub Rels* Rob Schweitzer; *Colls Mgr* Jessa J Krick; *Archivist* Karen W Morse
See website for current hours & rates; Chartered 1951 as a nonprofit educational foundation; Owns & operates six historic properties which are Sunnyside in Tarrytown, the home of author Washington Irving; Philipsburg Manor in Sleepy Hollow, A Dutch-American gristmill-farm site of the early 1700s; Van Cortlandt Manor in Croton-on-Hudson, a manorial estate of the Revolutionary War period; Montgomery Place in Annandale-on-Hudson- a 380 acre estate overlooking the Hudson River, Catskill Mountains, and the Union Church of Pocantico Hills, with windows by Matisse & Chagall. Historic Hudson Valley also operates the visitation program of Kykuit, the Rockefeller estate in Sleepy Hollow, NY; Average Annual Attendance: 247,000
Library Holdings: Auction Catalogs, Book Volumes, Clipping Files, Exhibition Catalogs, Lantern Slides, Manuscripts, Maps, Memorabilia, Original Art Works, Original Documents, Pamphlets, Periodical Subscriptions, Photographs, Prints, Reels, Reproductions
Special Subjects: Architecture, Ceramics, Coins & Medals, Costumes, Decorative Arts, Folk Art, Furniture, Maps, Marine Painting, Metalwork, Painting-American, Pewter, Porcelain, Portraits, Pottery, Restorations, Stained Glass, Textiles
Collections: Historic house; memorabilia of Washington Irving, Van Cortlandt and Philipse families, 17th, 18th and 19th century decorative arts; Matisse & Chagall stained glass
Exhibitions: Beauty and the Brick (online); America's River (online); A Garden in Print (online); American Arcadia (online); Pretends to be free (online)
Publications: American Industrialization, Economic Expansion, & the Law; America's Wooden Age; Aspects of Early New York Society & Politics; Bracebridge Hall; Business Enterprise in Early New York; Diedrich Knickerbocker's A History of New York; An Emerging Independent American Economy: 1815-1875; The Family Collections at Van Cortlandt Manor; The Howe Map; The Hudson River 1850-1918, A Photographic Portrait; Life Along the Hudson; Life of George Washington; The Loyalist Americans; Material Culture of the Wooden Age; The Mill at Philipsburg Manor, Upper Mills, & a Brief History of Milling; Old Christmas; Party & Political Guidebook; A Portfolio of Sleepy Hollow Prints; Rip Van Winkle & the Legend of Sleepy Hollow; Six Publications related to Washington Irving; An American Treasure: The Hudson River Valley; Cross Roads and Cross Rivers: Diversity in New York; Beauty and the Brick; The Great Estates regions of the Hudson Valley; Great Houses of the Hudson River
Activities: Classes for adults and children; docent training; school progs; special events including The Great Jack O'Lantern Blaze; demonstrations of 17th and 18th century crafts & tasks lectrs open to pub; guided tours by interpreters in period clothing; candlelight tours; gallery talks; John D Rockefeller Founder's Award (annual); mus shop sells books, original art, reproductions, prints & Hudson Valley memorabilia

PORT CHESTER

L **PORT CHESTER-RYE BROOK PUBLIC LIBRARY,** One Haseco Ave, Port Chester, NY 10573. Tel 914-939-6710; Fax 914-939-4735; Web: www.portchesterlibrary.org; *Dir* Robin Lettieri
Open Mon 9 AM - 9 PM, Tues 9 AM - 8 PM, Wed - Fri 9 AM - 5 PM, Sep - June: Sat 9 AM - 5 PM, July - Aug: 9 AM - noon; No admis fee; Estab 1876 to circulate books, records, magazines, to the general public to provide reference services; Circ 103,598; Maintains a small art gallery, with mostly local artists; Average Annual Attendance: 32,493
Income: $494,600 (financed by endowment, villages & state appropriations)
Purchases: $50,500
Library Holdings: Book Volumes 85,000, Filmstrips, Framed Reproductions, Pamphlets, Periodical Subscriptions 2000, Prints, Records, Reels, Slides
Exhibitions: Water colors, oils, acrylics, photographs
Activities: Educ dept; lect & films open to public; films; career seminars & workshops; individual paintings lent

PORT WASHINGTON

M **THE GRAPHIC EYE GALLERY,** 402 Main St Port Washington, NY 11710. Tel 516-883-9668; Email gallery@graphiceyegallery.com; Web: www.graphiceyegallery.com
Open Thurs - Sun 12 PM - 5 PM; No admis fee; Estab 1974; Works in all mediums
Income: Financed by mem & individual project grants
Special Subjects: Prints
Collections: Slide collection, Private collections
Exhibitions: Annual Winter Show: Journeys-Group Show; Group, individual & juried shows throughout the year
Activities: Educ dept; lect & demonstrations in print & other media open to public, 3-4 vis lectrs per year; Salmagundi Award; Bell Award; competitions with awards; scholarships offered; sales shop sells reproductions, prints, handmade gifts

L **PORT WASHINGTON PUBLIC LIBRARY,** One Library Dr, Port Washington, NY 11050-2794. Tel 516-883-4400; Fax 516-944-6855; Web: www.pwpl.org; *Dir* Nancy Curtin
Open Mon, Tues, Thurs & Fri 9 AM - 9 PM, Wed 11 AM - 9 PM, Sep - June: Sat 9 AM - 5 PM, Sun 1 - 5 PM, July - Aug: 9 AM - 1 PM; No admis fee; Estab 1892; Circ 303,500
Income: Financed by state appropriation & school district
Library Holdings: Audio Tapes, Book Volumes 128,000, Cards, Cassettes, Clipping Files, Filmstrips, Manuscripts, Pamphlets, Periodical Subscriptions 750, Photographs, Prints, Records, Reels, Video Tapes
Special Subjects: Drawings, Illustration, Manuscripts, Photography
Collections: Ernie Simon Collection of Photographs & Newspaper Articles on the History of Port Washington, Sinclair Lewis Collection of books, manuscripts, photographs & ephemera, Mason Photograph Archive of photographic negatives spanning over 75 years of Port Washington social history, P W Play Troupe Archive of memorabilia covering the 60 year history of the oldest theatre group on Long Island, Collection of drawings by children's illustrator Peter Spier
Exhibitions: Lita Kelmenson (drawings & wood sculpture); Hajime Okubo (box constructions); Paul Wood (oil painting & watercolors); Photographers: Dency Ann Kane, Mariou Fuller, Christine Osinski
Publications: Monthly guide catalog

POTSDAM

M **THE STATE UNIVERSITY OF NEW YORK AT POTSDAM,** (Potsdam College of the State University of New York) The Art Museum, 44 Pierrepont Ave, Potsdam, NY 13676-2200. Tel 315-267-3290, 267-2481; Fax 315-267-4884; Email vasherak@potsdam.edu; Web: www.potsdam.edu/museum; *Colls Mgr* Romi Sebald; *Secy* Claudette Fefee; *Dir* April Vasher-Dean
Open Tue-Thur 1-7PM; Fri & Sat 1-5PM; No admis fee; Estab 1967 to serve col & community as a teaching gallery; 4800 square feet of exhibition space on three levels with security & environmental controls; Average Annual Attendance: 18,000
Library Holdings: Compact Disks, DVDs, Exhibition Catalogs, Video Tapes
Special Subjects: Drawings, Painting-American, Painting-Italian, Painting-Japanese, Prints, Sculpture, Ceramics, Eskimo Art, Photography, Portraits, Watercolors, Woodcuts
Collections: Modern Japanese, Italian & American art (painting, sculpture & prints), Modern & contemporary drawing collection, Andy Warhol Polaroids & gelatin silver prints, available for travel: Max Klinger, The Intermezzi Print Cycle; Resounding Spirit: Japanese Contemporary Art of the 1960's; Warhol!
Publications: Exhibition catalogs & posters
Activities: lects open to public, gallery talks; tours; competitions; original objects of art lent to public institutions, art museums; book traveling exhibs 1-3 times per yr; originates traveling exhibs to other mus

M **VILLAGE OF POTSDAM,** Potsdam Public Museum, 2 Park St, Civic Center Potsdam, NY 13676-2099; PO Box 5168, Potsdam, NY 13676-5168. Tel 315-265-6910; Email museum@vl.potsdam.ny.us; Web: www.potsdampublicmuseum.org; *Dir & Cur* Mimi Van Deusen; *Mus Aide* Fred Rollins; *Mus Aide* Tom Dashnaw
Open Tues - Sat 10 AM - 4 PM; Admis $1 suggested donation; Estab 1940; educational, cultural & historical center for the Village of Potsdam & surrounding area with pub research & archives available to the pub; History of Potsdam & rotating exhibits; Average Annual Attendance: 12,000
Income: Village financed by town, state & federal appropriation
Library Holdings: Audio Tapes, Clipping Files, Exhibition Catalogs, Lantern Slides, Maps, Memorabilia, Original Documents, Pamphlets, Periodical Subscriptions, Photographs, Slides
Collections: Burnap Collection of English Pottery, costumes of the 19th & 20th centuries, Mandarin Chinese hangings, china & costumes, photograph coll, artifacts & material on local history, pressed glass & art glass of the 19th & early 20th century, Archives - local family & cemetery records, biblical instrument coll (reproductions), barn looms, & coverlets, early American tools, postcards
Exhibitions: Changing exhibitions
Publications: news website/Facebook; Potsdam Museum & Archives
Activities: Classes for children; progs for schools; Sandstone Festival; lects open to pub; concerts; architectural tours; gallery talks; concerts; mus shop sells books, prints, reproductions, postcards; maps

POUGHKEEPSIE

M **DUTCHESS COUNTY ARTS COUNCIL,** 696 Dutchess Tpke, Poughkeepsie, NY 12603-6445. Tel 845-454-3222; Fax 845-454-6902; Email info@artsmidhudson.org; Web: www.artsmidhudson.org; *Exec Dir* Linda Marston-Reid; *Dir Admin* Lisa Fiorese; *Folk Arts Prog Mgr* Elinor Levy
Open Mon - Fri 9:30 AM - 5:30 PM, Sat 10 AM - 3 PM; Estab to foster arts in the community; Mem: dues $25-$5,000
Collections: Work by Hudson Valley artists
Activities: Mus shop sells glass, jewelry, greeting cards, textiles, ceramics, wood products, prints, paintings & home decorating items

M **VASSAR COLLEGE,** The Frances Lehman Loeb Art Center, 124 Raymond Ave, Box 703 Poughkeepsie, NY 12604. Tel 845-437-5237; Fax 845-437-5955; Web: fllac.vassar.edu; *Dir* James Mundy; *Cur & Asst Dir Strategic Planning* Mary-Kay Lombino; *Cur Prints & Drawings* Patricia Phagan; *Cur Academic Progs* Elizabeth Nogrady; *Cur Public Educ* Margaret Vetare
Open Tues - Wed & Fri - Sat 10 AM - 5 PM, Thurs 10 AM - 9 PM, Sun 1 - 5 PM; cl Mon, Easter, Thanksgiving & Dec 24 - Jan 15; No admis fee; Estab 1864; collects Eastern & Western art of all periods; New mus opened in Nov 1993 in addition designed by Cesar Pelli; Average Annual Attendance: 37,000; Mem: 1100; dues $35 & up; bi-annual meeting fall & spring
Income: Financed by Vassar College, endowment & mem
Special Subjects: Antiquities-Egyptian, Antiquities-Etruscan, Antiquities-Greek, Antiquities-Roman, Archaeology, Architecture, Asian Art, Ceramics, Drawings, Etchings & Engravings, Glass, Graphics, Jade, Medieval Art, Oriental Art, Painting-American, Painting-European, Painting-Italian, Photography, Portraits, Renaissance Art, Sculpture, Watercolors, Jewelry
Collections: Matthew Vassar collection of 19th century American paintings of Hudson River School & 19th century English watercolors, Felix M Warburg Collection of medieval sculpture & graphics including Duerer & Rembrandt, 20th century art of all media including photography, European paintings, sculpture & drawings ranging from the Renaissance to the 20th century, including Bacchiacca, Cezanne, Salvator Rosa, Claesz, Tiepolo, Robert, Corot, Cezanne, Delacroix, Gifford, Van Gogh, Tanner, Munch, Klee, Bourdelle, Laurent, Davidson, Gabo, Calder, Moore, 20th Century American & European paintings including Henri, Hartley, O'Keeffe, Bacon, Nicholson, Rothko, de Kooning, Hartigan, Weber, graphics ranging from Barocci to Rembrandt to Goya to Picasso, Matisse, Braque, Kelly, Grooms & Graves, photography from Anna Atkins, Cameron, Gilpin, Steichen, Abbott, Lange, Lynes & Linda Conner, The Classical Collection includes Greek vases, Egyptian, Etruscan & Mycenaean objects, Roman glass, portrait busts, jewelry, other archaeological finds, Dexter M Ferry Collection, Olga Hasbrouck Collection of Chinese Ceramics, Charles Pratt Collection of Chinese Jades
Publications: Occasional exhibition catalogues & biannual newsletter
Activities: Docent training; lects open to public; gallery talks; tours; exten prog lends original objects of art to other museums; book traveling exhibitions vary; originate traveling exhibs to other museums; sales shop sells books, prints, postcards, notecards, posters & exhib catalogues

L **Art Library**, 124 Raymond Ave, Poughkeepsie, NY 12604-6198; PO Box 512, Poughkeepsie, NY 12604-0001. Tel 914-437-5790; Web: iberia/vassar.edu/art, www.artlibrary.vassar.edu; *Librn* Thomas Hill
Open Mon - Thurs 8:30 AM - 11:30 PM, Fri 8:30 AM - 10 PM, Sat 9 AM - 10 PM, Sun 10 AM - 1:30 AM, cl summer; Estab 1937; Circulation to students & faculty only
Library Holdings: Book Volumes 45,000, Exhibition Catalogs, Fiche, Other Holdings CD-ROMS, Periodical Subscriptions 250, Reels

PURCHASE

M **MANHATTANVILLE COLLEGE,** Brownson Gallery, 2900 Purchase St, Brownson Bldg Purchase, NY 10577-2131. Tel 914-323-5331; Fax 914-323-3131; Email mcgillc@mville.edu; Web: www.mville.edu; www1.mville.edu/gallery/index.htm; *Gallery Dir* Charles McGill; *Faculty Cur* Christine Dehne; *Student Employee* Saul Botier
Open 9:30 AM - 5 PM and by appointment; No admis fee; Estab 1950s to bring artists to col & community; Average Annual Attendance: 6,400
Income: Financed by endowment & tuition
Collections: Sculpture, Photography Collection
Publications: Magazine, bimonthly; catalogs
Activities: Lects open to public, 2 vis lectrs per yr; concerts; gallery talks; scholarships; original objects of art lent; originate traveling exhibs

L **Library**, 2900 Purchase St, Purchase, NY 10577-2132. Tel 914-694-2200, Ext 274, 323-5282; Fax 914-694-6234; Email goodman@mvill.edu; Web: www.mville.edu/library; *Dir* Rhonna Goodman; *Asst Library Dir* Jeff Rosedale; *Archivist, Spec Colls Librn* Lauren Georger
Open Mon - Thurs 8 AM - 8PM, Fri 8 AM - 8 PM, Sat 10 AM - 6 PM, Sun 10 AM - 8 PM
Income: financed by endowment & tuition
Library Holdings: Book Volumes 250,000, Periodical Subscriptions 1100

M **Arthur M Berger Gallery**, 2900 Purchase St, Purchase, NY 10577-2131. Tel 914-323-3190; Email mcgillc@mville.edu; Web: www1.mville.edu/gallery/index.htm; *Gallery Dir* Charles McGill; *Faculty Cur* Christine Dehne; *Student Employee* Saul Botier
Open Mon - Fri 11 AM - 6 PM, Thurs until 7 PM, Sat Noon - 4 PM, cl Sun; Estab 2008

C **PEPSICO INC,** Donald M Kendall Sculpture Garden, 700 Anderson Hill Rd, Purchase, NY 10577-1444. Tel 914-253-2900; Fax 914-253-3553; *Former Chmn & CEO* Donald M Kendall; *Dir Art Prog* Jacqueline R Millan
Open Mon - Sun 9 AM - 5 PM; Estab 1970 to present sculpture of mus quality; Average Annual Attendance: 10,000
Collections: Forty-two large outdoor sculptures, works by Alexander Calder, Henry Moore, Louise Nevelson, David Smith, Arnaldo Pomodoro, Jacques Lipchitz,, Henry Laurens, Auguste Rodin, Miro, Giacometti, Max Ernst, Jean DuBuffet, Tony Smith, George Segal, Claes Oldenburg, George Rickey, Richard Erdman & Barbara Hepworth

M **PURCHASE COLLEGE STATE UNIVERSITY OF NEW YORK,** Neuberger Museum of Art, 735 Anderson Hill Rd, Purchase, NY 10577-1400. Tel 914-251-6100; Fax 914-251-6101; Email neuberger@purchase.edu; Web: www.neuberger.org; *Acting Dir* Lea Emery; *Chief Cur & Deputy Dir Cur Affairs* Helaine Posner; *Chief Preparator* David Bogosian; *Asst Cur* Avis Larson; *Assoc Cur New Media & Digital Mus* Jacqueline Shilkoff; *Cur Art of the Americas* Patrice Giasson; *Cur & Asst Prof Art History* Tracy Fitzpatrick; *Registrar* Patricia Magnani; *Cur Educ* Emily Mello; *Head Mus Educ* Eleanor Brackbill; *Dir Mktg* Kristi McKee
Open Tues - Sun 12 PM - 5 PM; cl Mon & major holidays; Admis adults $5, seniors 62 & over & students $3, mems, college students, faculty, staff & children under 12 free, 1st Sat of month free; Estab 1968, opened May 1974 to serve university & residents of New York State & Connecticut; 78,000 sq ft facility designed by Philip Johnson with nine total galleries, five outside sculpture courts; Average Annual Attendance: 75,000; Mem: Dues dir circle $2500, sustaining $1000, patron $500, donor $250, contributing $100, family-dual $50, individual $35
Income: Financed by State University of New York, endowment fund, government grants, private foundations, donors & mem
Special Subjects: African Art, Drawings, Painting-American, Painting-European, Photography, Prints, Sculpture
Collections: Six thousand objects featuring 20th century European & American paintings, sculpture, drawings, prints, photographs & audio works, African & ancient art
Publications: Exhibition catalogues; brochures; quarterly calendars
Activities: Docent training; internships for Purchase College students; tours for children, adults & citizens with special needs; progs for families & children; lects open to public, vis lectrs; concerts; gallery talks; performances; films; tours; internships offered; original objects of art lent to other museums; book traveling exhibs; originate traveling exhibs to other museums; sales shop sells books, magazines, prints, small gift items & cards

L **Library**, 735 Anderson Hill Rd, Purchase, NY 10577-1402. Tel 914-251-6400; Fax 914-251-6437; Web: www.purchase.edu/departments/library; *Dir* Patrick Callahan; *Art Librn* Heather Kirkwood
Open during school yr Mon - Thurs 8 AM - 2 AM, Fri 8 AM - 10 PM, Sat 11 AM - 8 PM, Sun 12 PM - 2 AM
Income: Financed by univ
Library Holdings: Audio Tapes, Book Volumes 255,000, Cards, Cassettes, Compact Disks, DVDs, Fiche, Motion Pictures, Periodical Subscriptions 1000, Records, Reels, Reproductions, Slides, Video Tapes
Special Subjects: Afro-American Art, Art History, Conceptual Art, Costume Design & Constr, Drawings, Film, Furniture, Graphic Arts, Graphic Design, History of Art & Archaeology, Painting-American, Painting-British, Painting-Dutch, Painting-European, Painting-Flemish, Painting-French, Painting-German, Painting-Italian, Photography, Prints, Printmaking, Sculpture, Stage Design, Theatre Arts, Video

QUEENS

M **SAINT JOHN'S UNIVERSITY,** Dr. M.T. Geoffrey Yeh Art Gallery, 8000 Utopia Pkwy, Sun Yat Sen Hall Queens, NY 11439-9000. Tel 718-990-7476; Fax 718-990-1881; *Dir Gallery* Parvez Mohsin; *Gallery Asst* Aliza Moorji
Open Mon-Fri10 AM - 5 PM, Sat 12 PM- 5 PM; summer hours: Mon - Thurs 10 AM - 5 PM, Sat noon - 5 PM, cl Fri & Sun; No admis fee; Estab 1977 to make available Oriental art objects to the pub & to expose the metropolitan area to the Oriental culture through various exhibits & activities; Gallery displays contemporary as well as ancient objects, mainly Oriental with a few western subjects & newer exhibits; national contemporary American artists; recently hosted Images from the Atomic Front; Average Annual Attendance: 50,000
Income: Financed by the University, endowments & private contributions
Special Subjects: Calligraphy, Ivory, Jade, Oriental Art, Painting-Japanese, Porcelain
Collections: Harry C Goebel Collection: 595 pieces of rare & beautiful art objects dating from the 7th-19th century, incl jades, permanent coll contains 700 pieces of Chinese porcelain, paintings, textiles, calligraphy & paper cuttings dating from 7th-20th century, rare book coll from China
Exhibitions: Two Great Textiles of Modern Chinese Paintings; The Chinese Ancient Coin Exhibit; Images from the Atomic Front; Power Animals: Artwork of Marshall Arisman; From the Inside Art: Feminist Art Then & Now
Publications: Exhibition catalogues
Activities: Lects open to public, 6-10 vis lectrs per yr; concerts; gallery talks; tours; competitions with awards; individual paintings & original objects of art lent; lending collection contains 200 original art works; original prints; 200 paintings; originates traveling exhibs
—**Asian Collection**, 8000 Utopia Pkwy, Sun Yat Sen Hall Queens, NY 11439-9000. Tel 718-990-1526; Fax 718-990-1881; *Librn* Kenji Niki
Open to the pub for reference only
Library Holdings: Book Volumes 50,500, Cards, Exhibition Catalogs, Fiche, Manuscripts, Micro Print, Periodical Subscriptions 90, Reels
Collections: Collected Works of Chinese & Japanese Calligraphy, Japan Foundation Coll includes 200 volumes on various Japanese art subjects, Series of Chinese Arts

RIVERHEAD

A **EAST END ARTS & HUMANITIES COUNCIL,** 133 E Main St, Riverhead, NY 11901-2494. Tel 631-727-0900; Fax 631-727-0966; Email gallery@eastendarts.org; Web: www.eastendarts.org; *Exec Dir* Patricia Snyder; *Gallery Dir* Jane Kirkwood
Open Tues - Sat 10 AM - 4 PM; No admis fee; Estab 1972; Historic building situated in downtown; Average Annual Attendance: 11,000; Mem: 1,200; dues $35-$70
Income: Financed by public & private sector
Exhibitions: Various group shows; Juried shows, national juried show, holiday marketplace
Activities: Classes for adults & children; music & art pre-school-adult; summer camp ages 5-8 & 8-12; wine press concert series; music instruction; lect open to public; competitions with awards, Bank of America Neighborhood Builders award; gallery talks; tours; sales shop sells books, original art & crafts, hand crafted items, art, jewelry

ROCHESTER

M **GEORGE EASTMAN MUSEUM,** (George Eastman House), 900 East Ave, Rochester, NY 14607-2298. Tel 585-327-4800; Web: www.eastman.org; *Bd Chmn* Kevin Gavagan; *Cur Technology Coll* Todd Gustavson; *Operations & Finance* Thomas Combs; *Mgr Publications* Amy Schelemanow; *Dir Communs & Audience*

Develop Eliza Benington-Kozlowski; *House Cur* Kathy Connor; *Cur Motion Picture Coll* Paolo Cherchi Usai; *Pub Rel Mgr* Kellie Fraver; *Dir* Dr Bruce Barnes; *Cur Photog* Lisa Hostetler
Open Tues - Sat 10 AM - 5 PM, Sun 11 AM - 5 PM; Admis adults $15, seniors 65 & over $13, students $5, children 4 & under & mems free; Estab 1949 for photography exhibitions, research & educ; Restored landmark, gardens, photography & film mus; Average Annual Attendance: 150,000; Mem: 4200; individual $65, senior citizens $60, student $25
Income: Financed by corp & individual gifts, foundation & government grants, earned income
Library Holdings: Book Volumes, Exhibition Catalogs, Kodachrome Transparencies, Lantern Slides, Manuscripts, Maps, Memorabilia, Micro Print, Motion Pictures, Original Art Works, Original Documents, Other Holdings, Pamphlets, Periodical Subscriptions, Photographs, Prints, Records, Reels, Reproductions, Sculpture, Slides, Video Tapes
Special Subjects: Landscapes, Photography
Collections: Equipment (photographic), film, 19th, 20th & 21st century photography, George Eastman Legacy Collection
Publications: Image, bi-annual books & catalogs
Activities: Classes for children; docent training; teacher workshops; school exhibs prog; lects open to pub; concerts; gallery talks; tours; fellowships; awards, George Eastman Award, Eastman Honorary Scholar Award; exten dept; lending collection contains photographs & original objects of art; book traveling exhibs; originates traveling exhibs; mus shop sells books, magazines & reproductions

M **LANDMARK SOCIETY OF WESTERN NEW YORK, INC,** The Campbell-Whittlesey House Museum, 133 S Fitzhugh St, Rochester, NY 14608-2204. Tel 585-546-7029 (Ext 10); Fax 585-546-4788; Email mail@landmarksociety.org; Web: www.landmarksociety.org; *Exec Dir* Wayne Goodman; *Dir Public Progs* Cindy Boyer
Open Mon - Fri 9 AM - 3 PM, other times by appointment; Admis adults $3, children under 14 $1; Estab 1937; Mem: dues keystone $500, cornerstone $250, pillar $150, patron $100, family $70
Library Holdings: Book Volumes, Kodachrome Transparencies, Manuscripts, Maps, Memorabilia, Original Art Works, Original Documents, Periodical Subscriptions, Photographs, Prints, Reproductions, Slides, Video Tapes
Special Subjects: Architecture, Decorative Arts, Furniture, Historical Material, Landscapes, Period Rooms, Restorations
Collections: Art, furnishings & decorative arts of the 1830s, furnishings & decorative arts of early 19th century
Publications: Bi-monthly newsletter; booklets; brochures; guides; postcards
Activities: Dramatic progs; docent training; tours

L **Wenrich Memorial Library**, 133 S Fitzhugh St, Rochester, NY 14608-2204. Tel 716-546-7029; Fax 716-546-4788; Email chowk@landmarksociety.org; Web: www.landmarksociety.org; *Res Coordr* Cynthia Howk
Open Tues - Fri 9 AM - 4 PM by appointment only; No admis fee for mem of the Landmark Soc; $10 per hr for all other patrons; Estab 1937 to preserve historic resources & neighborhoods in Western New York; information center containing drawings, photographs, slides, books & periodicals, as well as archives of local architecture & information on preservation & restoration techniques; Mem: 3200
Income: Financed by mem & special grants
Purchases: $1000
Library Holdings: Book Volumes 5000, Clipping Files, Exhibition Catalogs, Kodachrome Transparencies, Manuscripts, Original Art Works, Pamphlets, Periodical Subscriptions 15, Photographs, Prints, Slides, Video Tapes
Special Subjects: Architecture, Decorative Arts, Furniture, Historical Material, Landscape Architecture, Interior Design
Collections: Claude Bragdon Collection of Architectural Drawings, Historic American Buildings: Survey Drawings of Local Architecture, John Wenrich & Walter Cassebeer Collection of Prints & Watercolors, Cobblestone Buildings; Covered Bridges; Erie Canal Photo Surveys
Exhibitions: Adaptive Use: New Uses for Old Buildings; The Architecture of Ward Wellington Ward; Rochester Prints, from the drawings of Walter Cassebeer
Publications: Newsletter, bi-monthly
Activities: Classes for adults & children; docent training; lects open to pub; tours; originate traveling exhibs to area schools, colleges, banks, community centers; mus shop sells books, original art, reproductions, prints, apparel, jewelry & gifts

M **ROCHESTER CONTEMPORARY,** (Pyramid Arts Center) Art Center, 137 East Ave, Rochester, NY 14604-2572. Tel 585-461-2222; Fax 585-461-2223; Email info@rochestercontemporary.org; Web: www.rochestercontemporary.org; *Exec Dir & Cur* Bleu Cease; *Pres* Stewart D Davis; *VPres* Colleen Buzzard
Open Wed - Sun Noon - 5 PM, Fri Noon - 9 PM; Admis general $2, mem free; Estab 1977 to hold exhibitions & performances, nonprofit organization; a venue for the exchange of ideas providing unique encounters for audiences & opportunities for emerging artists; Average Annual Attendance: 16,902; Mem: 500; dues $20 & up
Income: Financed by mems, gifts & donations
Activities: Educ dept; workshops with guest artists; docent training; lect open to public, 10 vis lectrs per year; concerts; gallery talks; new history & bicycle tours; competitions; Best in Show award for members exhib; sales shop sells screenings

A **ROCHESTER HISTORICAL SOCIETY,** 121 Lincoln Ave, Rochester, NY 14611. Tel 585-623-8285; Web: www.rochesterhistory.org; *Admin* Christy Lou Zuhlke; *Librn & Archivist* William Keeler
Open Tues - Thurs 9 AM - 1 PM & by appointment; Estab 1860, refounded 1888, to obtain & preserve relics & documents & publish material relating to Rochester's history; Headquarters at Rundel Library, 2nd floor; Average Annual Attendance: 2,000; Mem: 450; annual meeting in Spring
Income: Financed by mem
Special Subjects: Ceramics, Costumes, Decorative Arts, Drawings, Embroidery, Etchings & Engravings, Furniture, Glass, Graphics, Historical Material, Landscapes, Maps, Painting-American, Pewter, Photography, Portraits, Posters, Pottery, Prints, Sculpture, Textiles, Watercolors
Collections: Rochester costumes, furnishings & portraits, Over 200,000 books, archives & objects
Exhibitions: 3-4 exhibs each yr
Publications: Observer Magazine
Activities: Lects open to public

L **ROCHESTER INSTITUTE OF TECHNOLOGY,** Corporate Education & Training, 67 Lomb Memorial Dr, Rochester, NY 14623-5602. Tel 716-475-2411, Ext 7090; Fax 716-475-7000; Email kavcet@rit.edu; Web: www.rit.edu/corporate/Education-And-Training; WATS 800-724-2536; *Dir* Kitren Van Strander
Center has been a leading provider of professional training for the graphic arts & imaging industries for more than 40 years. The T & E Center provides seminars & hands on workshops in traditional & leading edge technologies for graphic design & publishing software, image editing & compositing, digital photography & electronic prepress & publishing. In addition, introductory & advanced programs are also offered in printing production & technologies, business & production management, & Total Quality. T & E Center programs draw upon resources from RIT's School of Printing Management & Sciences, School of Photographic Arts & Sciences & the Center for Imaging Science as well as from industry to deliver practical training to today's graphic arts professional
Publications: T & E Update, monthly
Activities: Seminars for the graphic arts & imaging industries

M **UNIVERSITY OF ROCHESTER,** Memorial Art Gallery, 500 University Ave, Rochester, NY 14607-1414. Tel 585-276-8900; Fax 585-473-6266; Email maginfo@mag.rochester.edu; Web: mag.rochester.edu; Others TDD 716-473-6152; *Dir* Jonathan P Binstock, PhD; *Sr Dir, Prin & Major Gifts* Joseph T Carney; *Pub Rels Mgr, Social Media & Webmaster* Meg Colombo; *Engagement Specialist* Jessica Gasbarre; *Cur* Jess Marten; *Exhib Coord* Margot Muto; *COO & Deputy Dir* Patti Giordano
Open Wed - Sun 11 AM- 5 PM and Thurs until 9 PM; cl Mon & Tues; Admis adults $15, seniors $12, students & children 6-18 $6, children 5 & under, mems & University of Rochester students free; half price admis fee Thurs 5 - 9 PM; Estab 1913 as a university art mus & pub art mus for the Rochester area; The original building is in an Italian Renaissance style; Average Annual Attendance: 325,000; Mem: 6,000; dues $75 & up
Income: Financed by endowment, mem, grants, earned income & University support
Special Subjects: African Art, Afro-American Art, American Indian Art, Antiquities-Assyrian, Antiquities-Egyptian, Ceramics, Crafts, Decorative Arts, Drawings, Folk Art, Furniture, Hispanic Art, Landscapes, Marine Painting, Medieval Art, Oriental Art, Painting-French, Porcelain, Portraits, Pottery, Primitive art, Prints, Renaissance Art, Sculpture, Watercolors
Collections: Covers all major periods & cultural areas from Assyria & predynastic Egypt to the present, paintings, sculpture, prints, drawings, decorative arts, special strengths are medieval, 17th century Dutch painting, English Portraiture, 19th & early 20th century French painting, American art & American folk art
Publications: Articulate; calendar
Activities: Studio art classes for adults & children; docent training; lects open to public; gallery talks; tours; concerts; exten dept serving Rochester area & surrounding nine counties; lending collection contains slides; book traveling exhibs 4-6 per yr; originate traveling exhibs 10-12 per yr; gallery store sells original art, fine crafts, prints, books & paper products, reproductions, prints

L **Charlotte W Allen Library-Memorial Art Gallery**, 500 University Ave, Rochester, NY 14607-1414. Tel 585-276-8999; Fax 585-473-6266; Email lharper@mag.rochester.edu; Web: mag.rochester.edu/library; *Librn* Lu Harper; *Libr Asst* Kathleen Nicastro
Open Wed - Fri 1 - 5 PM & by appointment, cl Sat - Tues; No admis fee; Estab 1913 as a research library; Circ 3,900
Income: Financed by endowment, mem & grants
Library Holdings: Auction Catalogs, Book Volumes 45,860, CD-ROMs, Clipping Files, Compact Disks, DVDs, Exhibition Catalogs, Manuscripts, Memorabilia, Pamphlets, Periodical Subscriptions 60, Photographs, Reels, Reproductions, Slides, Video Tapes
Special Subjects: Architecture, Art Education, Art History, Decorative Arts, Drawings, Etchings & Engravings, Folk Art, Graphic Arts, History of Art & Archaeology, Laces, Landscapes, Painting-American, Painting-British, Painting-European
Collections: Memorial Art Gallery Archives
Activities: Teacher resource ctr

L **Art/Music Library**, 755 Library Rd, PO Box 270055 Rochester, NY 14627-0055. Tel 585-275-4476; Fax 585-273-1032; Email artlib@library.rochester.edu; Web: www.library.rochester.edu/artmusic/home; *Librn* Stephanie J Frontz; *Library Asst* Marc Bollmann
Open Mon - Thurs 9 AM - midnight, Fri 9 AM - 10 PM, Sat noon - 10 PM, Sun noon - midnight; Estab to support acad progs of Dept of Art & Art History, Music Dept & other acad depts within the University; Small gallery is maintained by Art & Art History Dept & Library
Library Holdings: Auction Catalogs, Audio Tapes 100, Book Volumes 90,000, Compact Disks 3,000, Exhibition Catalogs, Lantern Slides, Periodical Subscriptions 425, Records 850, Slides 125,000

ROME

A **ROME ART & COMMUNITY CENTER,** 308 W Bloomfield St, Rome, NY 13440-4197. Tel 315-336-1040; Fax 315-336-1090; Email executivedirector@romeart.org; Web: www.romeart.org; *Dir* Lauren Marie Getek; *Office Mgr* Dale A Kaier
Open Tues-Thurs 10AM-6PM, Fri & Sat 10AM-2PM; No admis fee; Estab 1967 for art exhibits & classes, community events, educ; Four galleries; Average Annual Attendance: 20,000; Mem: 1000; dues from $5-40
Income: Financed by city appropriation, New York State Council on the Arts, mem, donations & private foundations
Exhibitions: Various art exhibitions every month
Publications: Newsletter, bimonthly; community calendar, quarterly; class brochures, quarterly

Activities: Classes for adults & children; dramatic progs; docent training; lect open to public, 20 vis lectrs per yr; readings; concerts; gallery talks; tours; weekly films; scholarships to gifted children; monetary awards art exhibs

M **ROME HISTORICAL SOCIETY,** Museum & Archives, 200 Church St, Rome, NY 13440-5872. Tel 315-336-5870; Fax 315-336-5912; Email info@romehistoricalsociety.org; Web: www.romehistoricalsociety.org; *Bd Pres* Michael Kohli; *First VPres* Matthew Fadler; *Exec Dir* Arthur L Simmons III
Open Tues - Fri 9 AM - 3 PM, Sat 10 AM - 2 PM; No admis fee; library & archives $20 per hr, non-mem (research fee); Estab 1936 as a historical mus & soc; 2 galleries for temporary exhibitions on specific topics of local interest; Average Annual Attendance: 4,000; Mem: 200; dues $20-$1,000
Income: Financed by mem, city appropriation, private foundations, federal & state grants
Library Holdings: Book Volumes, Filmstrips, Manuscripts, Maps, Memorabilia, Original Art Works, Original Documents, Other Holdings, Pamphlets, Periodical Subscriptions, Photographs, Prints, Reels, Reproductions, Slides, Video Tapes
Special Subjects: Archaeology, Costumes, Crafts, Decorative Arts, Furniture, Glass
Collections: E Buyck, P F Hugunine, Forest Moses, Ann Marriot, Will Moses, Revolutionary War period paintings, Rome Turney Radiator, Griffiss Air Force Base, Joan Evans Doll House Village
Exhibitions: Our Goodly Heritage - movie on Rome NY
Publications: RHS News quarterly; quarterly newsletter
Activities: Classes for children; lects open to pub; 12 visiting lectures per year; gallery talks; tours; medal of the Order of 1777 yearly award; outreach program to schools, sr citizens' homes & community organizations; sales shop sells books; reproductions; prints

L **William E Scripture Memorial Library**, 200 Church St, Rome, NY 13440. Tel 315-336-5870; Fax 315-336-5912; Email info@romehistoricalsociety.org; Web: www.romehistoricalsociety.org; *Exec Dir* Arthur L Simmons III
Open Tues - Fri 9 AM - 3 PM, Sat 10 AM - 2 PM; None; Estab 1936 for historical research of Rome NY & Oneida county; Circ Non-circulating; Reference library; Average Annual Attendance: 4,000; Mem: 200
Income: Financed by mem, city appropriation grants
Library Holdings: Book Volumes 3500, Clipping Files, Manuscripts, Maps, Memorabilia, Original Art Works, Original Documents, Other Holdings, Pamphlets, Photographs, Prints, Reels, Reproductions, Slides
Special Subjects: Archaeology, Architecture, Crafts, Decorative Arts, Folk Art, Furniture, Historical Material, Manuscripts, Maps
Collections: Area paintings from the Revolutionary War period to the present, Frederick Hodges Journals, The Hathaway Papers, Local Militia Records 1830-1840; Griffiss Air Force Base articles & pictures, La Vita: Local newspaper printed in Rome New York 1918-1950
Exhibitions: History of Rome; History of Griffiss Air Force Base
Activities: Lects open to the public; 12 visiting lectures per year; tours; concerts; gallery talks; Medal of the Order of 1777;; museum shop sells books, reproductions, prints

ROSENDALE

A **WOMEN'S STUDIO WORKSHOP, INC,** 722 Binnewater Ln, Rosendale, NY 12472; PO Box 489, Rosendale, NY 12472-0489. Tel 845-658-9133; Fax 845-658-9031; Email info@wsworkshop.org; Web: www.wsworkshop.org; *Artistic Dir* Tana Kellner; *Exec Dir* Ann Kalmbach; *Develop Dir* Julia Hickey; *Studio Mgr* Chris Petrone; *Opers Mgr* Rachel Myers; *Technician* Robert Woodruff; *Clay Prog Coordr* Ruth McKinney Burket; *Deputy Exec Dir* Lauren V Walling; *Web Communs Mgr* Kathryn Scudier
Open Mon - Fri 10 AM - 5 PM; Estab 1974; Mem: 400; dues $50
Income: $625,000 (financed by sales, tuition & grants)
Library Holdings: Book Volumes, Kodachrome Transparencies, Original Art Works, Original Documents, Photographs, Prints, Slides
Collections: Artists' books, Prints (contemporary)
Exhibitions: 12 exhibitions yearly of work by grant recipients; Traveling Exhibs: Hand, Voice, Vision: Artists' Books from Women's Studio Workshops
Publications: Artists' books, 5-7 per yr
Activities: Classes for adults & children; lect open to public, 45 vis lectrs per year; tours; grants offered; exten dept; original objects of art lent; book traveling exhibitions, annually; sales shop sells workshop products, books & handmade paper

ROSLYN

L **BRYANT LIBRARY,** 2 Paper Mill Rd, Roslyn, NY 11576-2193. Tel 516-621-2240; Fax 516-621-7211, 621-5905, 621-2542; Email rnlinfo@lilrc.org; Web: www.nassaulibrary.org/bryant; *Coordr Progs & Pub Rels* Victor Caputo; *Dir* Cathleen Mealing
Open Mon, Tues, Thurs, Fri 9 AM - 9 PM, Wed 10 AM - 9 PM, Sat 9 AM - 5 PM, Sun (Oct - May) 1 - 5 PM; No admis fee; Estab 1878 as a public library; Circ 288,865; Gallery houses monthly exhibits, mostly paintings. Has been renamed the Heckscher Museum of Art at Bryant Library
Income: $3,200,000 (financed by property tax)
Library Holdings: Book Volumes 230,320, Cassettes 25,964, Clipping Files, Fiche, Filmstrips, Manuscripts 11,933, Pamphlets 1866, Periodical Subscriptions 299, Photographs 7697, Reels, Video Tapes 5493
Special Subjects: Architecture, Historical Material
Collections: William Cullen Bryant, Christopher Morley, local history of Roslyn, Long Island, New York
Publications: Bryant Library Calendar of Events, monthly; Bryant Library Newsletter, bi-monthly; The Bryant Library: 100 Years, 1878-1978, exhibit catalogue; W C Bryant in Roslyn, book; exhibit catalog
Activities: Lect open to public, 30-40 vis lectrs per year; concerts

ROSLYN HARBOR

M **NASSAU COUNTY MUSEUM OF ART,** One Museum Dr, Roslyn Harbor, NY 11576. Tel 516-484-9337; Fax 516-484-0710; Email kwillers@nassaumuseum.org; Web: nassaumuseum.org; *Dir* Karl Emil Willers Ph.D.; *Registrar* Fernanda Bennett; *Dir Educ* Laura Lynch; *Office Mgr* Rita Mack; *Dir Develop* Monica Reischmann; *Asst Cur* Rhianna Ellis
Open Tues - Sun 11 AM - 4:45 PM; Admis adults $10, sr citizens $8, children $4; Estab 1989 to exhibit major exhibitions; Art mus housed in c 1900, three story Neo-Georgian brick mansion, former estate of Childs Frick, 9 galleries & 145 acres for sculpture park, formal gardens; hiking trails, pinetum; Average Annual Attendance: 250,000; Mem: 3000; dues $40-$5,000; annual meeting in Jan
Income: $900,000 (financed by mem, county appropriation, corporate & foundation grants, admis & special events)
Library Holdings: Exhibition Catalogs, Sculpture Outdoor
Special Subjects: Collages, Drawings, Hispanic Art, Latin American Art, Painting-American, Painting-European, Painting-French, Painting-German, Painting-Russian, Period Rooms, Renaissance Art, Sculpture, Watercolors, Prints
Collections: 20th century American prints, drawings, outdoor sculpture, architectural blueprints & drawings relating to the museum building & property, major Latin contemporary coll, Pop & Minimalist Prints
Exhibitions: 3 major exhibs per yr
Publications: Catalogs for exhibitions
Activities: Educ prog; classes for adults & children; docent training; lects open to pub; vis lectrs 8 per yr; gallery talks; tours; competition; originates traveling exhibs to the Gallery Assn of New York State; mus shop sells art books, related gifts of mus exhibs; jewelry

SAINT BONAVENTURE

M **SAINT BONAVENTURE UNIVERSITY,** Regina A Quick Center for the Arts, Rte 417 at Constitution Ave, Saint Bonaventure, NY 14778; Drawer BH, Saint Bonaventure, NY 14778. Tel 716-375-2494; Fax 716-375-2690; Email quick@sbu.edu; Web: www.sbu.edu; *Exec Dir* Joseph A LoSchiavo; *Cur* Evelyn Penman; *Asst Dir* Ludwig Brunner
Open Mon - Fri 10 AM - 5 PM, Sat - Sun 12 PM - 4 PM; No admis fee; Estab 1995 to house the University's art coll; 18,000 sq ft of exhib space; Average Annual Attendance: 30,000
Income: Financed by university budget
Special Subjects: Antiquities-Greek, Ceramics, Decorative Arts, Drawings, Etchings & Engravings, Ivory, Jade, Landscapes, Painting-American, Painting-Dutch, Painting-European, Painting-Flemish, Painting-French, Photography, Porcelain, Pottery, Pre-Columbian Art, Prints, Religious Art, Renaissance Art, Sculpture, Watercolors, Woodcuts
Collections: Paintings, sculpture, drawings, prints, decorative arts
Publications: Art Catalog of Collection
Activities: Educ progs for K - 12 children; dramatic progs; lects open to pub; 10 vis lectrs per yr; concerts; gallery talks; tours; sponsoring of competitions & fellowships; artist residencies in schools; lending of original objects of art to other art organizations with appropriate facility report to 6 counties of Southern Tier NY: Allegany, Cattaraugus, Chautauqua & PA: McKean, Potter & Warren; artmobile; originates traveling exhibs to university & art mus; mus shop sells prints & local artisan items

SALAMANCA

M **SENECA-IROQUOIS NATIONAL MUSEUM,** 814 Broad St, Salamanca, NY 14779-1378. Tel 716-945-1760; Fax 716-945-1624; Email dave.shango@sni.org; Web: www.senecamuseum.org; *Dir* David George-Shengo; *Gift Shop Mgr & Fin Advisor* Eva Aidman
Open Mon noon - 5 PM, Tue - Sun 9 AM -5 PM (May-Oct); Sun noon - 5 PM; cl Mon, Tues - Sat 9 AM - 5 PM (Nov-Apr); Admis adult $5, college students & seniors $3, children 7-16 & Military $3, children 6 & under free, bus group discount rates available; Estab 1977 to present historical & contemporary Iroquois arts & culture & ancestral materials; Six exhibit areas, dedicated to various cultural periods up to contemporary & central seating space for video; Average Annual Attendance: 20,000
Income: Seneca Nation of Indians
Purchases: Hodino's Onih artists' items (handmade)
Library Holdings: Book Volumes, Cassettes, Maps, Memorabilia, Original Art Works, Original Documents, Photographs, Reels, Slides, Video Tapes
Special Subjects: American Indian Art, Archaeology, Ceramics, Costumes, Crafts, Decorative Arts, Dioramas, Dolls, Drawings, Ethnology, Furniture, Historical Material, Jewelry, Leather, Maps, Metalwork, Painting-American, Photography, Pottery, Religious Art, Reproductions, Sculpture, Silver, Watercolors, Woodcarvings
Collections: Archeological, anthropological & archival colls, including photography, audio, traditional & contemporary works
Publications: SINM - Collection
Activities: Classes for adults & children; docent training; games demos; interactive children's area; 20 vis lectrs per yr; galley talks; tours; sponsoring competitions; awards; Western New York/Northern Pennsylvania extension progs; lending original artifacts to Iroquois Museum; organize traveling exhibs to fairs & other organizations; mus shop sells books, original art, prints, hand-made Iroquois art, calendars, videos, CDs, games, DVDs

SANBORN

M **NIAGARA COUNTY COMMUNITY COLLEGE,** Art Gallery, 3111 Saunders Settlement Rd, Sanborn, NY 14132-9460. Tel 716-614-5775; Fax 716-614-6826; Web: www.sunyniagara.cc.ny.us; *Dir Gallery* Kathleen Sherin
Open Mon - Tues 10 AM - 5 PM, Wed - Thurs 10 AM - 8 PM, Fri 10 AM - 2 PM; No admis fee; Estab 1973 for varied exhibits that will be of interest to students &

the community; Gallery has 270 sq ft of area & approx 250 running ft; Average Annual Attendance: 9,000
Income: Financed by the college
Exhibitions: African Treasures; Faculty Exhibit; Spring Student Exhibit; Student Art Exhibit; Student Illustration Exhibit/SUNY Buffalo; NCCC Student Exhibition; Runca-NCC Alumni Exhibition (paintings, mixed media)
Publications: Catalogs
Activities: Classes for adults; dramatic progs; lects; 2-3 vis lectrs per yr; gallery talks

SARATOGA SPRINGS

M **NATIONAL MUSEUM OF RACING,** National Museum of Racing & Hall of Fame, 191 Union Ave, Saratoga Springs, NY 12866-3556. Tel 518-584-0400; Fax 518-584-4574; Email nmrinfo@racingmuseum.net; Web: www.racingmuseum.org; *Dir* Joe Aulisi; *Cur Hall of Fame* Kate Cravens; *Cur Coll* Beth Sheffera
Open Jan - Mar: Tues - Sat 10 AM - 4 PM, Sun noon - 4 PM, cl Mon & Tues; Apr - Oct: Mon - Sat 10 AM - 4 PM, Sun Noon - 4 PM; Nov - Dec: Tues - Sat 10 AM - 4 PM, Sun noon - 4 PM cl Mon; Admis adults $7, seniors & students $5, mems & children under 5 free, children under 12 must be accompanied by parents; Estab 1950 as a mus for the collection, preservation & exhibition of all kinds of articles assoc with the origin, history & development of horse racing; There are 10 galleries of sporting art. The handsome Georgian-Colonial design brick structure houses one of the world's greatest collections of equine art along with trophies, sculptures & memorabilia of the sport from its earliest days; Average Annual Attendance: 60,000; Mem: 1950; dues $35-2500
Income: Financed through annual appeal, individual contributions, grants, shop sales & endowment
Library Holdings: Book Volumes, Clipping Files, Manuscripts, Motion Pictures, Original Documents, Periodical Subscriptions, Photographs
Special Subjects: Bronzes, Prints
Collections: Oil paintings of thoroughbred horses, trophies, racing silks, bronzes, prints, racing memorabilia
Activities: Classes for children; gallery talks; tours; art & photography competitions; mus shop sells books, magazines, original art, reproductions, prints, clothing & toys

L **Reference Library**, 191 Union Ave, Saratoga Springs, NY 12866. Tel 518-584-0400; Fax 518-584-4574; Email nmrinfo@racingmuseum.net; Web: www.nationalmuseumofracing.org; *Acting Dir* Joseph E Aulisi; *Cur Coll* Beth Sheffer; *Asst Dir* Catherine Maguire
Open by appointment; Estab 1970 as a reference library on Thoroughbred racing; Open to researchers, students & authors by appointment; Average Annual Attendance: 50; Mem: 2300; dues varies
Library Holdings: Book Volumes 3000, Clipping Files, Exhibition Catalogs, Manuscripts, Memorabilia, Original Art Works, Pamphlets, Photographs
Special Subjects: Painting-American, Painting-British

M **NEW YORK STATE MILITARY MUSEUM AND VETERANS RESEARCH CENTER,** 61 Lake Ave, Saratoga Springs, NY 12866-2315. Tel 518-581-5100; Fax 518-581-5111; Email historians@ny.ngb.army.mil; Web: www.nysmm.org; *CEO & Dir* Michael Aikey; *Registrar* Christopher Morton; *Chief Cur* Courtney Burns; *Archivist* Jim Gandy; *Mus Shop Mgr* Lucille Millarson
Open Tues - Sat 10 - 4, Sun noon - 4; cl all NY state holidays; no admis fee; Estab 1863; 9000 sq ft exhib space; auditorium capacity 70; handicapped-accessible in mus only; FT Paid 10, PT Paid 1, PT Volunteers 50, Interns 3; NY Congressional Dist 20. New York State's military history coll that ranges from colonial times to the present; Average Annual Attendance: 13,000
Library Holdings: Book Volumes, Lantern Slides, Manuscripts, Maps, Memorabilia, Motion Pictures, Original Art Works, Original Documents, Photographs, Prints, Sculpture
Special Subjects: Costumes, Drawings, Furniture, Graphics, Leather, Military Art, Painting-American, Photography, Portraits, Prints, Sculpture, Silver, Textiles, Watercolors
Collections: Coll includes NY state's battle flag coll & the state's Veterans Oral History coll, 3000 vols of books on military history, Military art; military uniforms
Activities: Educ prog for adults & children; ann events: Civil War Weekends; lects open to pub; 5-10 vis lectrs per yr; guided tours; docent prog; mus shop sells books, original art, prints

M **SKIDMORE COLLEGE,** Schick Art Gallery, 815 N Broadway, Saratoga Springs, NY 12866-1632. Tel 518-580-5049; Fax 518-580-5029; Email mjablons@skidmore.edu; Web: www.skidmore.edu/schick; *Asst Dir* Mary Kathryn Jablonski
Open Sept - May Mon - Fri 9 AM - 5 PM, Sat & Sun 1 - 4:30 PM; summer hours variable according to summer class schedules, cl Aug; No admis fee; Estab 1978 for educational enrichment of the col & community. Exhibs are intended to bring awareness of both contemporary & historical trends in art; Average Annual Attendance: 20,080
Income: Financed through College
Exhibitions: Rotating exhibits monthly
Publications: Exhibition catalogs, occasionally
Activities: Lect open to public, vis lectr; gallery talks; originates traveling exhibitions

L **Lucy Scribner Library**, 815 N Broadway, Art Reading Area Saratoga Springs, NY 12866-1632. Tel 518-580-5002; Web: www.skidmore.edu/library; *Visual Resource Assoc* Theresa Somaio; *Supv* Nancy Rudick
Open Mon - Thurs 8 AM - 1 AM, Fri 8 AM - 10 PM, Sat 9 AM - 10 PM, Sun 11 AM - 1 AM; Estab 1925
Income: Financed by col
Library Holdings: Book Volumes 392,014, Cards, Exhibition Catalogs, Filmstrips, Kodachrome Transparencies, Lantern Slides, Memorabilia, Motion Pictures, Original Art Works, Periodical Subscriptions 1653, Photographs, Prints 600, Records, Reproductions, Sculpture, Slides 53,000
Collections: Anita Pohndorff Yates Collection of Saratoga History

SAYVILLE

M **ART WITHOUT WALLS INC,** PO Box 341, Sayville, NY 11782-0341. Tel 631-567-9418; Email artwithoutwalls@outlook.com; *Exec Dir* Sharon Lippman; *Representative* Paula Lippman
Open Sat & Sun 10 AM - 4 PM; No admis fee; Estab 1985 to foster non-traditional public art & the historical, social & aesthetic elements of fine art as well as art therapy programs to exhibit to the public innovative & original public art, non-traditional, Holocaust art, contemporary art & art of the handicapped & terminally ill emerging artists, outsider art, national & international artists - thematic exhibs; Circ 2,000; Average Annual Attendance: 2,000; Mem: 450; dues $75; open membership; for artists resume & annual dues $375 with slides of work; representative & show fee $375; estb professional artists must have exhib resume unless outsider or emerging artist
Income: Grants/donations
Library Holdings: Auction Catalogs, Book Volumes, CD-ROMs, Cards, Clipping Files, DVDs, Exhibition Catalogs, Filmstrips, Framed Reproductions, Kodachrome Transparencies, Manuscripts, Memorabilia, Motion Pictures, Original Art Works, Original Documents, Pamphlets, Periodical Subscriptions, Photographs, Prints, Reproductions, Sculpture, Slides, Video Tapes
Special Subjects: Afro-American Art, American Indian Art, American Western Art, Anthropology, Antiquities-Egyptian, Antiquities-Greek, Antiquities-Oriental, Antiquities-Roman, Archaeology, Architecture, Asian Art, Baroque Art, Cartoons, Collages, Costumes, Dolls, Drawings, Eskimo Art, Ethnology, Folk Art, Graphics, Hispanic Art, Historical Material, Islamic Art, Ivory, Jade, Jewelry, Judaica, Juvenile Art, Laces, Landscapes, Latin American Art, Leather, Manuscripts, Maps, Marine Painting, Medieval Art, Metalwork, Mexican Art, Mosaics, Oriental Art, Painting-American, Painting-Australian, Painting-British, Painting-Canadian, Painting-Dutch, Painting-European, Painting-Flemish, Painting-French, Painting-German, Painting-Israeli, Painting-Italian, Painting-Japanese, Painting-New Zealand, Painting-Polish, Painting-Russian, Painting-Scandinavian, Painting-Spanish, Period Rooms, Photography, Porcelain, Portraits, Posters, Pottery, Pre-Columbian Art, Prints, Renaissance Art, Reproductions, Restorations, Sculpture, Silver, Southwestern Art, Stained Glass, Tapestries, Textiles, Watercolors, Woodcarvings, Woodcuts
Collections: American Contemporary Art, Art Therapy, International Art, Non-Traditional Art, Public Art, American Contemporary Art, Art Therapy, International Art, Holocaust Art, Outsider Art-Emerging Artists, Southwestern Art/ Film/Photography/Fashion Illustration, Design - Architecture
Exhibitions: South Street Seaport-Museum Without Walls; Central Park-Museum Without Walls; Battery Park NYC-Museum Without Walls; Bryant Park-Museum Without Walls; Ellis Island Immigrant Museum, Fort Wadsworth, NY (National Parks Service); Central Park Zoo, NYC; Local Long Island Public Libraries
Activities: Educ prog; classes for adults & children; dramatic progs; art therapy; tours; lects open to pub, 10 vis lectrs per yr; gallery talks; American Artist Award, Newsday; National Women's History Award, National Poetry Press; Suffolk County Legislature Award, LI Hall of Fame, Suffolk County News Inspiration Award; Honorary Bench: "Art Without Walls, Inc, Sharon Lippman-Founder", Bethpage State Park LI, NY for cultural arts; Brooklyn Borough President Proclamation; scholarships; schols; individual paintings & original objects of art lent; terminally ill & disabled individuals; Hospitals - Pediatrics/Geriatric wards; book traveling exhibs 2 per yr; originate traveling exhibs to local libraries & NYC pub spaces 5 per yr; 2 murals donated to National Monument at Fort Wadsworth, NY on NY Waterways and Baymen Homage; mus shop sells original art, reproductions & prints

SCHENECTADY

A **PRINT CLUB OF ALBANY,** 150 Barrett St, Schenectady, NY 12305. Tel 518-399-7231, 518-449-4756; Email semowich@gmail.com; Web: pcaprint.org; *Pres Print Selection Comt Chmn* Thomas Andress; *Curator* Charles Somowich
Open by appointment; No admis fee; Estab 1933 for those interested in all aspects of prints & printmaking; Maintains reference library; permanent collection; temporary exhibs; Average Annual Attendance: 2,000; Mem: 200; dues $95, active mems receive an original print; mem open to artists who have national recognition, non-artists need interest in prints; annual meeting in May; mem application on website
Income: Financed by mem, city & state appropriation, sales, commissions & auction
Purchases: Prints & printmakers' archives
Library Holdings: Auction Catalogs, Book Volumes 150, DVDs, Kodachrome Transparencies, Manuscripts, Original Art Works, Slides, Video Tapes
Special Subjects: Drawings, Etchings & Engravings, Graphics, Prints, Woodcuts, Watercolors
Collections: Drawings, Plates, Prints from all periods & countries concentrating on 20th century America, 18,000 items
Exhibitions: mem exhibs; Nat Open; historical shows
Publications: Exhib catalogues
Activities: Educ dept; workshops; lects open to pub, 1 vis lectrs per yr; talks; competition with prizes; Lathrop; awards, Cogswell, Distinguished Mem; objects of art lent to state capital & county offices; originate traveling exhibs; sales shop sells original art; commissions a print each year for its members;

A **SCHENECTADY COUNTY HISTORICAL SOCIETY,** 32 Washington Ave, Schenectady, NY 12305-1600. Tel 518-374-0263; Fax 518-688-2825; Email office@schenectadyhistorical.org; Web: www.schenectadyhistorical.org; *Pres* Marianne Blanchard; *Librn* Melissa Tacke; *Cur* Mary Zawacki; *Educ & Asst Cur* Jenna Peterson; *Asst Cur* Kaitlin Morton-Bentley; *Preparator* John Ackner
Open Schenectady History Museum & Library: Mon - Fri 9 AM - 5 PM, Sat 10 AM - 2 PM; Mabee Farm: Tues - Sat 10 AM - 4 PM; Admis $5; Estab 1905, for the preservation of local historical materials; History museum, living history farm & research library; Average Annual Attendance: 7,500; Mem: 850; dues sponsor $100, donor $50, family $40, individual $25; annual meeting 2nd Sat of Apr
Income: Financed by mem, grants, donations

Library Holdings: Book Volumes, CD-ROMs, Clipping Files, Manuscripts, Maps, Memorabilia, Original Art Works, Original Documents, Other Holdings, Pamphlets, Periodical Subscriptions, Photographs, Prints
Special Subjects: Archaeology, Architecture, Decorative Arts, Historical Material, Furniture, Painting-American, Period Rooms, Portraits, Textiles
Collections: Decorative & fine arts; 17th. 18th, 19th, 20th century material culture including farm & household implements, textiles, furniture, plus archival materials & photographs
Publications: Bi-monthly newsletter
Activities: classes for adults & children; living history demonstrations, workshops; reenactments; festivals; 6 exhibs each yr; docent training; lects open to public, 12+ vis lectrs per year; concerts; gallery talks; tours; sponsoring competitions; exten dept serves elementary schools; museum shop sells books, reproductions, prints & gifts

L **Grems-Dolittle Library**, 32 Washington Ave, Schenectady, NY 12305. Tel 518-374-0263; Email librarian@schenectadyhistorical.org; Web: www.schenectadyhistorical.org; *Librn/Archivist* Melissa Tacke; *Cur* Mary Zawacki; *Educator* Jenna Peterson Riley; *Librn/Archivist* Michael Maloney
Open Mon - Fri 9 AM - 5 PM, Sat 10 AM - 2 PM; Admis research $5, mus tour $5, mems free; Estab 1905 to promote history & genealogy of the county & nearby counties; Circ Non-circulating; For reference only; Mem: 700; dues $25 & up; annual meeting in Apr
Income: Financed by mem, grants, donations
Library Holdings: Audio Tapes, Book Volumes 6,000, Cassettes, Clipping Files, Fiche, Filmstrips, Manuscripts 16,000, Memorabilia, Motion Pictures, Pamphlets, Photographs, Reels, Reproductions, Slides
Activities: Educ dept; some lect open to public & some to members only; tours; sales shop sells books, reproductions & gifts

SEA CLIFF

M **SEA CLIFF VILLAGE MUSEUM,** 95 Tenth Ave, Sea Cliff, NY 11579; PO Box 72, Sea Cliff, NY 11579-0072. Tel 516-671-0090; Fax 516-671-2530; Email seacliffmuseum@aol.com; *Dir, Treas & Cur* Sara Reres; *Vol Chmn* Patricia F Smith; *Mus Shop Mgr* Kathleen Diresta
Open Sun 2 - 5 PM; cl Jun - Aug; No admis fee, donations accepted; Estab 1979; Housed in former Sea Cliff Methodist Church built in 1913, the mus is made of brick & stucco and is of Tudor style; mus focuses on Sea Cliff history from 1870 - mid 20th c; Average Annual Attendance: 1,000; Mem: dues Family $25, Indiv $10, Senior $10
Income: municipal govt
Library Holdings: Audio Tapes, Book Volumes, Motion Pictures, Original Art Works, Original Documents, Photographs, Prints, Reels, Slides
Special Subjects: Costumes, Dolls, Historical Material, Maps
Collections: Over 3,000 photos, artifacts, documents & costumes that span this time period
Exhibitions: (1st Oct, 2016-30th Jun, 2017) Uncommon collections
Publications: Friends, annual newsletter
Activities: Friends Exhib Opening Reception; two lects per yr; shop sells books, original art, reproductions, prints, posters & postcards

SENECA FALLS

M **SENECA FALLS HISTORICAL SOCIETY MUSEUM,** 55 Cayuga St, Seneca Falls, NY 13148-1222. Tel 315-568-8412; Fax 315-568-8426; Email sfhs@rochester.rr.com; Web: www.sfhistoricalsociety.org; *Exec Dir* Philomena M Cammuso; *Educ Dir* Frances J Barbieri; *Colls Mgr* Kathleen Jans-Duffy
Open Mon - Fri 9 AM - 4 PM; Admis adults $5, children & students $2, AARP & AAA $4; Estab 1896 as an educational institution dedicated to the preservation & interpretation of Seneca County; Victorian 23 room house with decorative arts collection; Average Annual Attendance: 15,000; Mem: 600; dues family $50, single $30; annual meeting in May
Income: $100,000 (financed by endowment, mem, city, state & federal appropriation, United Way)
Library Holdings: Book Volumes, Original Documents
Special Subjects: Architecture, Costumes, Furniture, Historical Material, Period Rooms, Manuscripts, Maps, Photography
Collections: Victoriana, Women's Rights Memorabilia, history of industry, canal, genealogy research
Exhibitions: Civil War
Publications: Reprints of archival material
Activities: Classes for adults & children; docent training; school group progs; lects open to pub, 3-4 vis lectrs per yr; concerts; gallery talks; tours; original objects of art lent to other institutions; mus shop sells books, prints, reproductions & articles published by members

SETAUKET

M **GALLERY NORTH,** 90 N Country Rd, Setauket, NY 11733-1352. Tel 631-751-2676; Fax 631-751-0180; Email gallerynorth@aol.com; Web: www.gallerynorth.org; *Pres & Chmn* Nancy Goroff; *Dir Cur* Judith Levy
Open Tues - Sat 10 AM - 5 PM, Sun 12 - 5 PM, cl Easter, Thanksgiving, Christmas; No admis fee; Estab 1965 to exhibit the work of contemporary Long Island artists & crafts people; Gallery is housed in Victorian building with 3 main exhibition rooms; Average Annual Attendance: 10,000; Mem: 185; dues $50 - $1,000; quarterly meetings
Income: $210,000 (financed by mem, sales & fundraisers)
Library Holdings: Book Volumes, Memorabilia, Periodical Subscriptions
Collections: Long Island Landscapes
Exhibitions: 12 changing exhibitions per yr; annual outdoor art show open to artists & crafts people
Activities: Classes for adults & children; lecta open to public; 12 vis lectrs per year; tours; artist workshops; competitions with awards; 6 vis lectrs per yr; gallery talks; outdoor art show-11 categories; art scholarship - graduating college Senior; sales shop sells crafts from local artists & imported crafts, original art, prints, reproductions & other items

SKANEATELES

M **JOHN D BARROW ART GALLERY,** 49 E Genesee St, Skaneateles, NY 13152-1341. Tel 315-685-5135; Email jdbag1900@aol.com; Web: www.barrowgallery.org; *Dir* Margaret M Whitehouse; *Treas* Elizabeth K Dreyfuss; *Sec* Elizabeth M Sio
Open Memorial Day-Labor Day Mon-Sat 1-4PM, Sept-May Thurs & Fri 11 AM - 4 PM, tours by appt; No admis fee; Estab in 1900 to exhibit paintings of John D Barrow; Single artist mus, second generation Hudson River Sch; Average Annual Attendance: 4,000; Mem: AAM
Income: Financed by donations
Special Subjects: Painting-American
Collections: Paintings of John D Barrow 1824 - 1906
Activities: Classes & hands-on activities for children; docent training; pvt & school children tours; lects open to public, 3 vis lectrs per yr; gallery talks; tours; competitions; John D Barros Scholastic Art Award for young artists; John D Barrow Award for Excellence in Painting through Scholastic Arts of CNY; schols; lending of original objects of art to individuals, area bus, Skaneateles & surrounding communities; sales shop sells postcards, ornaments, reproductions, prints, notecards, tote bags

A **SKANEATELES LIBRARY ASSOCIATION,** 49 E Genesee St, Skaneateles, NY 13152-1396. Tel 315-685-5135; Web: www.skaneateleslibrary.com; *Pres* Meg O'Connell
Open Mon, Wed, Fri 10 AM - 5 PM, Tues & Thurs 10 AM - 8:30 PM, Sat 10 AM - 4 PM and by request; Summer hours: Memorial Day - Labor Day Mon & Wed 9 AM - 5 PM, Tues & Thurs 9 AM - 8 PM, Fri - Sat 9 AM - 4 PM; Library estab 1890; Gallery estab 1900 to display paintings of John D Barrow; Annex of Library, 2 rooms, one with single & one with triple wainscoting of paintings; Mem: Ann meeting
Income: Financed by annual fundraising drive & endowments
Collections: 300 paintings by John D Barrow, 19th century landscapes & portraits
Exhibitions: Occasional special exhibitions
Activities: Annual guided tours for 4th graders; docent training; occasional open lect; gallery talks; tours; paintings lent for one year on the condition that borrower pays for restoration

SOUTH SALEM

A **TEXTILE CONSERVATION WORKSHOP INC,** 3 Main St, South Salem, NY 10590-1413. Tel 914-763-5805; Fax 914-763-5549; Email textile@bestweb.net; Web: www.textileconservationworkshop.org; *Exec Dir* Patsy Orlofsky; *Sr Conservator* Karen Clark; *Sr Conservator* Mary Kaldany; *Conservator* Rebecca Johnson-Dibb; *Field Svcs Dir* Katherine Barker; *Conservator* Barbara Lehrecke
Open Mon - Fri 9:30 AM - 5 PM, visits by appt
Activities: Workshops; lects

STAATSBURG

M **NEW YORK STATE OFFICE OF PARKS, RECREATION & HISTORIC PRESERVATION,** Staatsburgh State Historic Site, 75 Mills Mansion Dr, Staatsburg, NY 12580; PO Box 308, Staatsburg, NY 12580-0308. Tel 845-889-8851; Fax 845-889-8843; Email pam.malcolm@parks.ny.gov; Web: www.nysparks.com; *Historic Site Mgr* Pamela Malcolm
Open Apr - Oct 31, special holiday hrs; Jan-Mar by appointment & for scheduled pub progs; Admis adults $8, seniors, students & groups $6, children under 12 free; Estab 1938 to interpret lifestyle of the very affluent segment of American society during the period 1890-1929; Original furnishings & art left by the Mills family after their gift of the mansion to the state of NY; Average Annual Attendance: 20,000; Mem: Friends of Mills Mansion
Special Subjects: Antiquities-Greek, Architecture, Art Education, Art History, Carpets & Rugs, Ceramics, Decorative Arts, Etchings & Engravings, Furniture, Historical Material, Interior Design, Landscape Architecture, Landscapes, Painting-American, Painting-European, Period Rooms, Portraits, Restorations, Tapestries, Textiles
Collections: Original furnishings, paintings, prints, decorative art objects and tapestries from Mr and Mrs Mills
Activities: Classes for children; docent training; workshops; lects open to pub; concerts; gallery tours; house tours; landscape tours; loans of paintings or original art objects have to be approved by New York State Office of Parks and Recreation, Division of Historic Preservation; mus shop sells books, reproductions, jewelry, scarves, cards, etc

STATEN ISLAND

M **JACQUES MARCHAIS MUSEUM OF TIBETAN ART,** 338 Lighthouse Ave, Staten Island, NY 10306-1217. Tel 718-987-3500; Fax 718-351-0402; Email mventrudo@tibetanmuseum.org; Web: www.tibetanmuseum.org; *CEO* Meg Ventrudo; *Bookkeeper* Jayne Catalfo; *Museum Asst* Alison Baldassano
Open Wed - Sun 1 - 5 PM, other times by appt, cl major holidays; Admis adults $6, seniors & students $4, mems free; Estab 1945 The mission of the Jacques Marchais Museum of Tibetan Art is to foster interest, research, & appreciation of the art and culture of Tibet & other Asian countries through collections, preserving & interpreting art objects & photographs & making them available to the public through exhibitions, programs & publications; The Jacques Marchais Museum of Tibetan Art displays its collection of Tibetan art in two Himalayan-style fieldstone buildings set in a terraced hillside in Staten Island; Average Annual Attendance: 5,200; Mem: dues $25-$75
Income: Financed by membership dues & contributions, city, state & federal appropriations, foundation & corporate grants

Purchases: Art, artifacts & photographs related to Tibet & other Asian countries
Library Holdings: Auction Catalogs, Audio Tapes, Book Volumes, Cassettes, Clipping Files, Compact Disks, DVDs, Exhibition Catalogs, Lantern Slides, Manuscripts, Maps, Memorabilia, Motion Pictures, Original Art Works
Special Subjects: Anthropology, Asian Art, Bronzes, Calligraphy, Carpets & Rugs, Decorative Arts, Ethnology, Furniture, Historical Material, Maps, Metalwork, Miniatures, Oriental Art, Textiles, Period Rooms, Photography, Portraits, Religious Art, Reproductions, Sculpture, Silver
Collections: Tibetan, Mongolian, Nepalese & Chinese art including sculpture, paintings, textiles, furniture, as well as the archive & library of Jacques Marchais
Exhibitions: Freed from the Vault (through 2017)
Publications: Treasures of Tibetan Art: The Collections of the Jacques Marchais Museum of Tibetan Art
Activities: The mus features a diverse range of programming - rotating exhibs, musical concerts, lectures, films, children's workshops, yoga, tai chi, & meditation courses; classes for adults; 4 lects per yr open to pub; concerts, gallery talks, tours; exten servs New York City; individual paintings & original objects of art lent to mus for special exhibs; originate traveling exhibs - 1-2 annually; mus shop sells books, crafts, jewelry, CDs & music tapes, posters, prints, textiles, gift ware & unique items from Tibet & Nepal

M **THE NOBLE MARITIME COLLECTION,** 1000 Richmond Terrace, Staten Island, NY 10301. Tel 718-447-6490; Fax 718-447-6056; Email erinurban@noblemaritime.org; Web: www.noblemaritime.org; *Dir* Erin Urban; *Asst Dir* Ciro Galeno Jr; *Program Director* Dawn Daniels; *Curator* Megan Beck
Open Thurs - Sun 1 - 5 PM; Donations accepted; Estab 1986 to present art & maritime history; Permanent installation of John A Noble's Houseboat Studio; art; gallery for changing exhibitions of prints & maritime history; exhibs about sailors' snug harbor; Average Annual Attendance: 15,000; Mem: 500; dues $25; annual meeting in Apr
Income: $300,000 (financed by mem, state & city appropriation)
Library Holdings: Auction Catalogs, Exhibition Catalogs, Kodachrome Transparencies, Manuscripts, Maps, Motion Pictures, Original Art Works, Original Documents, Periodical Subscriptions, Photographs, Prints, Reproductions, Slides
Special Subjects: Decorative Arts, Drawings, Etchings & Engravings, Folk Art, Furniture, Glass, Graphics, Historical Material, Landscapes, Manuscripts, Manuscripts, Maps, Marine Painting, Painting-American, Prints, Restorations, Watercolors
Collections: Archives, Art, Maritime Artifacts, Coll of the trustees of sailer's Snug Harbor
Exhibitions: Treasures of Sailors' Snug Harbor, Daily Life at Sailors Snug Harbor,; Robbins Reef Lighthouse; A Home in the Harbor
Publications: Hold Fast, quarterly newsletter
Activities: Classes for adults & children; dramatic progs; lects open to public, vis lectrs 2 per yr; concerts; tours; schols; lending collection contains 80 paintings & art objects; mus sales shop sells books, original art, reproductions, prints, crafts, & toys

M **ORDER SONS OF ITALY IN AMERICA,** Garibaldi & Meucci Museum, 420 Tompkins Ave, Staten Island, NY 10305-1704. Tel 718-442-1608; Fax 718-442-8635; Email info@garibaldimeuccimuseum.org; Web: www.garibaldimeuccimuseum.org; *Dir* Michela Traetto; *Publicity Coordr* Bonnie McCourt; *Admin Asst* Stephanie Lundegard; *Educ Dir* Janet Grillo
Open Tues - Sun 1 - 5 PM; Admis $5, children 10 & under free; Estab 1919 to collect, preserve & interpret material pertaining to Italian culture; Circ 12,000; Average Annual Attendance: 70,000; Mem: 400; dues household $50; individual $40; seniors/students $25
Income: $140,000 (financed by endowment, mem, city & state appropriation, Order Sons of Italy in America)
Special Subjects: Bronzes, Coins & Medals, Decorative Arts, Prints, Painting-Italian
Collections: Books, Bronzes, Coins, Decorative Arts, Medals, Paintings, Paper, Photographs, Prints, Stamps, Weapons, Giuseppe Garibaldi's "Red Shirt"
Exhibitions: Historical exhibitions; Antonio Meucci "The True Inventor of the Telephone"
Activities: Italian language classes for adults & children; school programs for children; lect open to pub, many progs per yr; 12 vis lectrs per yr; concerts; gallery talks; tours; schols offered; mus shop sells books & souvenirs

M **SNUG HARBOR CULTURAL CENTER,** Newhouse Center for Contemporary Art, 1000 Richmond Terrace, Staten Island, NY 10301-1114. Tel 718-448-2500; Fax 718-815-0198; Email fverpoorten@snug-harbor.org; Email info@snugharbor.org; Web: www.snug-harbor.org; *Acting Pres & CEO* JoAnn Mardikos; *Chief Financial Officer* Gerard Kelly; *Dir Performing Arts & Pub Progs* Larry Anderson
Open mid-Mar - Nov 6 Tues - Fri 8 AM - 6 PM; Admis adults $5, seniors (65 & over), students (6-17 with valid IDs) $4, children (under 5) & mems no charge; Estab 1977 to provide a forum for regionally & nationally significant visual art; Average Annual Attendance: 50,000; Mem: Dues $35 - $150
Income: Financed by mem, city & state appropriation, corporate funds
Library Holdings: Exhibition Catalogs, Original Documents, Photographs, Prints, Records, Slides, Video Tapes
Publications: Exhibition catalogs
Activities: Classes for adults & children; children's progs; docent progs; lects open to pub; gallery talks; tours; mus shop sells books & reproductions

M **STATEN ISLAND MUSEUM,** Snug Harbor, 1000 Richmond Ter Staten Island, NY 10301; 75 Stuyvesant Pl, Staten Island, NY 10301. Tel 718-727-1135; Fax 718-273-5683; Email info@statenislandmuseum.org; Web: www.statenislandmuseum.org; *Chmn Board* David Businelli; *Pres & CEO* Cheryl Adolph; *VPres Exhibs & Progs* Diane Matyas; *VPres Mktg & External Affairs* Henry K Behnke; *Communs Coordr* Rachel Somma; *Cur Art* Robert Bunkin; *Facilities Mgr* Frank Perkins; *Mgr Exhibs* Donna Pagano; *Community Campaign Coord* Amanda Stranieri; *Visitor Svcs Mgr* Renee Bushelle; *Dir Fin & Admin* Dorothy Pinkston; *Mgr Educ* Christine Szeluga; *Cur History* Cara Delatte
Open Mon - Fri 11 AM - 5 PM, Sat 10 AM - 5 PM, Sun noon - 5 PM; Admis adults $8, seniors & students $5; Estab 1881, inc 1906; Average Annual Attendance: 79,000; Mem: 500; dues $25 & up
Library Holdings: Book Volumes, Clipping Files, Exhibition Catalogs, Fiche, Kodachrome Transparencies, Manuscripts, Maps, Memorabilia, Original Documents, Photographs, Prints, Records, Reproductions
Special Subjects: African Art, Antiquities-Greek, Antiquities-Oriental, Antiquities-Roman, Baroque Art, Bronzes, Ceramics, Coins & Medals, Costumes, Crafts, Decorative Arts, Embroidery, Etchings & Engravings, Ethnology, Flasks & Bottles, Furniture, Glass, Graphics, Historical Material, Ivory, Jade, Jewelry, Laces, Landscapes, Manuscripts, Maps, Marine Painting, Medieval Art, Miniatures, Oriental Art, Painting-American, Painting-American, Painting-Dutch, Painting-European, Photography, Porcelain, Portraits, Posters, Pottery, Pre-Columbian Art, Primitive art, Prints, Religious Art, Renaissance Art, Reproductions, Scrimshaw, Sculpture, Silver, Tapestries, Textiles, Woodcuts
Collections: American paintings of the 19th & 20th centuries, Oriental, Greek, Roman & primitive art objects, prints & small sculptures, science & history publs, history, archives, postcards, Natural Science Coll, Entomology, Botany
Exhibitions: Decorative arts;; design exhibitions in various media; major loan shows of paintings & prints; special exhibitions of graphic arts & of photography; permanent: Staten Island Ferry, The Lenape: The First Staten Islanders, Hall of Natural Science; changing art exhibits
Publications: Annual Reports; catalog; Proceedings (scholarly book), The Cemeteries of Staten Island; The Staten Island Ferry: A History
Activities: Fall & spring terms for adults & children classes; teacher training; docent training; lects on art & science open to pub; complete prog of lectr, art & natural history for school children with annual registration of 30,000; concerts; gallery talks; tours; competitions with awards; mus shop sells books, original art, reproductions, prints, ferry mugs & magnets

L **Archives Library**, 75 Stuyvesant PL, Staten Island, NY 10301. Tel 718-727-1135 (Ext 122); Fax 718-273-5683; Email info@statenislandmuseum.org; Web: www.statenislandmuseum.org; *Archivist* Cara Dellatte; *Dir Exhibs & Programs* Diane Matyas; *CEO & Pres* Elizabeth Egbert; *Mgr Exhibs* Donna Pagano; *Chief Operating Officer* Cheryl Adolph
Open Mon - Fri & Sun 11 AM - 5 PM, Sat 10 AM - 5 PM, Tues, Thurs, Fri 10 AM - 4 PM by appointment only; History Center: Tues - Sat 1 - 4 PM; Admis adults $5, seniors $3, under 12 free; Estab Nov 1881 for research and reference only; History, Arts & Sciences exhibitions; Average Annual Attendance: 80,000; Mem: Dues family $50, indiv $35, others $25
Income: state, city, pvt foundations, pvt citizens & memberships
Library Holdings: Audio Tapes, Book Volumes 30,000, Clipping Files, Exhibition Catalogs, Lantern Slides, Manuscripts, Maps, Memorabilia, Micro Print, Original Art Works, Original Documents, Other Holdings, Pamphlets, Periodical Subscriptions 10, Photographs, Prints, Reproductions, Sculpture, Slides, Video Tapes
Special Subjects: Archaeology, Architecture, Asian Art, Flasks & Bottles, Folk Art, Furniture, Glass, Landscapes, Manuscripts, Maps, Painting-American, Photography, Portraits, Prints, Watercolors
Collections: 30,000 volumes on science, art and history, Staten Island newspapers on microfilm 1834-1934, various letters, documents, journals, clippings and other ephemera relating to the history of Staten Island and the metropolitan region; architecture, environmental and genealogy documents, George W Curtiss collection of books, manuscript & memorabilia, the Staten Island Ferry coll
Publications: The Realms of History: Cemeteries of Staten Island; The Staten Island Ferry: A History
Activities: Classes for adults & children; dramatic progs; summer earth camp; lects open to pub; concerts; gallery talks; tours; sponsoring of competitions; lending of original art objects; book 1-2 traveling exhibs per yr; mus shop sells books, prints & toys

A **WOMEN IN THE ARTS FOUNDATION, INC,** 100 Stuyvesant Pl. #T2, c/o Estelle Levy Staten Island, NY 10301; c/o M Schepis, 149 Marine Ave #6J Brooklyn, NY 11209. Tel 212-749-5492; Email wiafoundationorg@aol.com; Web: www.anny.org/organizations, www.wiaf.org; *Newsletter Ed & Bd Mem* Erin Butler; *Financial Coordr* Diane Waller; *Coordr Bd Mem* Helaine Soller; *Coordr Bd Mem* Pamela Hawkins; *Coordr Bd Mem* Betsy Gross; *Coordr Bd Mem* Marcia Ostwind
Open 3rd Wed 7 - 9 PM for monthly progs & meetings; Admis fee free; Estab 1971 for the purpose of overcoming discrimination against women artists both in government & the private sector; Circ Newsletter circ 150 mem; Sponsors discussions, workshops, panels and exhibits the work of women artists, both established & unknown; Average Annual Attendance: 250; Mem: 75; mems pay dues & be involved in the arts; dues $65; meeting 3rd Wed Sept thru June
Income: $12,000 (financed by endowment & mem)
Library Holdings: CD-ROMs, Cards, Cassettes, Clipping Files, Exhibition Catalogs, Memorabilia, Original Documents, Pamphlets, Periodical Subscriptions, Photographs, Reproductions
Publications: WIA Newsletter, three times a yr (Women in the Arts)
Activities: Public educ as to the problems & discrimination faced by women artists; lects open to public; individual paintings & original objects of art lent to museum & university art galleries for special exhibitions; original art works for exhibitions are obtained from member artists; career edu & encouragement for women artists

STONE RIDGE

M **STATE UNIVERSITY OF NEW YORK AT ULSTER,** Muroff-Kotler Visual Arts Gallery, 491 Cottekill Rd, Stone Ridge, NY 12484. Tel 845-687-5113; Web: www.sunyulster.edu; *Gallery Coordr* Susan Jeffers
Open Mon - Fri 11 AM - 3 PM, fall & spring semesters, cl summer; No admis fee; Estab 1963 as a center for creative activity; Gallery is maintained as an adjunct to the college's cultural & acad prog; John Vanderlyn Hall has 40 x 28 ft enclosed space & is located on the campus; Average Annual Attendance: 3,000
Income: Financed by college funds
Special Subjects: Drawings, Painting-American, Photography, Prints, Sculpture
Collections: Contemporary drawings, paintings, photographs, prints, sculpture, historical works
Exhibitions: 6 exhibitions per year annual student show
Publications: Flyers announcing each exhibit, every four to six weeks
Activities: Lect open to public, 2-3 vis lectrs per year; concerts

STONY BROOK

M **THE LONG ISLAND MUSEUM OF AMERICAN ART, HISTORY & CARRIAGES,** 1200 Rte 25A, Stony Brook, NY 11790. Tel 631-751-0066; Fax 631-751-0353; Email mail@longislandmuseum.org; Web: www.longislandmuseum.org; *Exec Dir* Neil Watson; *Dir Develop* Deirdre Doherty; *Grants & Membership Manager* Lorraine Whiffen; *Dir Pub Rels* Julie Diamond; *Dir Coll & Interpretation* Joshua Ruff; *Coll Mgr* Christine Marzano; *Designer & Preparator* Joe Esser; *Dir Educ* Lisa Unander
Open Thurs - Sat 10 AM - 5 PM, Sun Noon - 5 PM; Admis adults $10, seniors 62 & over $7, students 6-17 $5, under 6 & mems free; Estab 1942 to make Long Island history & American Art available to pub; The Museums' 13 buildings, 9 acre complex include a History Mus, Art Mus, Carriage Mus, various period buildings & the Hawkins-Mount House (currently not open to the pub); Average Annual Attendance: 50,000; Mem: 1,000; dues $25-$5,000
Library Holdings: Auction Catalogs, Book Volumes, CD-ROMs, Clipping Files, Compact Disks, DVDs, Exhibition Catalogs, Kodachrome Transparencies, Manuscripts, Maps, Original Art Works, Original Documents, Pamphlets, Periodical Subscriptions, Photographs, Prints, Records, Sculpture, Slides, Video Tapes
Special Subjects: Carpets & Rugs, Ceramics, Coins & Medals, Collages, Costumes, Crafts, Decorative Arts, Dolls, Drawings, Embroidery, Etchings & Engravings, Flasks & Bottles, Folk Art, Furniture, Glass, Gold, Graphics, Historical Material, Jewelry, Juvenile Art, Laces, Landscapes, Leather, Manuscripts, Maps, Marine Painting, Metalwork, Miniatures, Painting-American, Photography, Porcelain, Portraits, Posters, Pottery, Prints, Prints, Sculpture, Silver, Tapestries, Textiles, Watercolors, Woodcarvings, Woodcuts
Collections: Paintings & drawings by William Sidney Mount & other American Artists including Shepard Alonzo Mount, Henry S Mount, William M Davis, Edward Lange, Charles H Miller
Publications: Annual Report; Quarterly Newsletter; exhibition catalogs; brochures
Activities: Classes for adults & children; docent training; lects open to pub; 12 vis lectrs per yr; concerts; gallery talks; tours sponsoring competitions; lending of original object of art as requested; 1-2 book traveling exhibs per yr; mus shop sells books, original art, reproductions, prints & gift items

L **Library,** 1200 Rte 25A, Stony Brook, NY 11790. Tel 631-751-0066; Fax 631-751-0353; Email mail@longislandmuseum.org; Web: www.longislandmuseum.org; *Exec Dir* Neil Watson; *Dir Colls & Interpretation* Joshua Ruff; *Colls Mgr* Christa Zaros; *Curatorial Asst* Mary McNulty; *Curatorial Asst* Christine Marzanno; *Exhib Designer* Joseph Esser
Open Thurs - Sat 10 AM - 5 PM, Sun Noon - 5 PM; Admis adults $9, seniors 60 & up $7, students 6-17 & college with id $4, children free; Estab 1939; 3 galleries: art, history & carriage; Average Annual Attendance: 50,000
Library Holdings: Auction Catalogs, Book Volumes 2194, Cards, Clipping Files, Exhibition Catalogs, Framed Reproductions, Lantern Slides, Manuscripts, Memorabilia, Motion Pictures, Original Art Works, Other Holdings Trade catalogs, Pamphlets, Periodical Subscriptions 62, Photographs, Prints, Reproductions, Sculpture, Slides, Video Tapes
Special Subjects: Advertising Design, American Western Art, Anthropology, Art Education, Art History, Decorative Arts, Drawings, Embroidery, Fashion Arts, Flasks & Bottles, Folk Art, Graphic Arts, History of Art & Archaeology, Jewelry, Marine Painting
Collections: Artworks & papers of William Sidney Mount, Mount Family Artwork 19th, 20th & 21st century, Long Island artists carriages & horse-drawn vehicles, carriage & caveman artifacts, 18th-20th century costumes, decoys, Long Island artifacts & documents, William Cooper papers, Dominick family papers, Thompson family papers
Activities: Educ program; classes for adults & children; dramatic progs; docent training; lects open to pub, 20 vis lectrs per yr; concerts; gallery talks; tours; average four; originates traveling exhibs; mus shop sells books, reproductions, prints, slides, various jewelry & decorative items

M **STATE UNIVERSITY OF NEW YORK AT STONY BROOK,** University Art Gallery, Stony Brook University, Staller Center for the Arts Stony Brook, NY 11794-5425. Tel 631-632-7240; Web: www.stallercenter.com/gallery; *Dir* Rhonda Cooper
Open Tues - Fri Noon - 4 PM, Sat 7 - 9 PM; No admis fee; Estab 1967 to serve both the campus and the community by exhibiting student and professional artists; One gallery 41 x 73 with 22 ft ceiling; second space 22 x 73 ft with 12 ft ceilings; Average Annual Attendance: 10,000 students & members of the community per yr
Income: Financed by donations
Publications: Catalogues, four times a year

SYRACUSE

M **EVERSON MUSEUM OF ART,** 401 Harrison St, Syracuse, NY 13202-3091. Tel 315-474-6064; Fax 315-474-6943; Email everson@everson.org; Web: www.everson.org; *Director & CEO* Elizabeth Dunbar
Open Sun, Wed & Fri noon - 5 PM, Thurs noon - 8 PM, Sat 10 AM - 5 PM, cl Mon & Tues; Adults $8, Seniors (65+) and students $6, Everson Members, Children 12 and under, military (with ID) Free, Pay what you wish admission every Wednesday; Estab 1896 to present free exhibitions by lending artists, chiefly American to serve as an educational element for the cultural & general community; The Everson's permanent collection primarily focuses on American modern and contemporary art and encompasses approximately 11,000 works, including painting, ceramics, sculpture, videos, photographs, works on paper, and decorative arts. Core collections include ceramics and video art.; Average Annual Attendance: 80,000; Mem: 2000; dues Founders Cir $10,000, Dir Cir $5,000, Everson Cir Gold $2,500, Everson Cir $1,000, patron $500, friend $250, fellow $125, household $75, sr household $60, individual $50
Income: Financed by mem, county & state appropriation, New York Council on the Arts, gifts & grants
Library Holdings: Auction Catalogs, Book Volumes, Clipping Files, Exhibition Catalogs, Periodical Subscriptions
Special Subjects: Ceramics, Decorative Arts, Painting-American, Photography, Porcelain, Portraits, Sculpture
Collections: African Coll, contemporary American ceramics, contemporary American painting & sculpture, 17th, 18th & 19th century English porcelain, traditional American painting & portraiture, video-tape coll, Cloud Wampler Collection of Oriental Art, photographs
Publications: Art books; Quarterly bulletin; Educational materials; exhibition catalogs
Activities: Docent training; classes for adults, teens & children; family progs; educ dept services public schools of Syracuse; lects open to pub; 4-6 vis lectrs per yr; concerts; gallery talks; films; tours; competitions; 1-3 book traveling exhibs per yr; originate traveling exhibs to nat mus; mus shop sells books, magazines, original art

M **LE MOYNE COLLEGE,** Wilson Art Gallery, 1419 Salt Springs Rd, Syracuse, NY 13214-1301. Tel 315-445-4331; Web: www.lemoyne.edu; *Library Dir* Robert C Johnston
Open Mon - Thurs 9 AM - 11 PM, Fri 9 AM - 9 PM, Sat & Sun 9 AM - 5 PM; No admis fee; Estab 1966; Average Annual Attendance: 1,500
Collections: Paintings, etchings, prints & watercolors
Exhibitions: Student, Faculty & outside exhibitions
Activities: Individual painting & original objects of art lent

A **LIGHT WORK,** Robert B Menschel Photography Gallery, 316 Waverly Ave, Syracuse, NY 13244-0001. Tel 315-443-1300, 443-2450; Fax 315-443-9516; Email info@lightwork.org; Web: www.lightwork.org; *Prog Mgr* Mary Lee Hodgens; *Exec Dir* Jeffrey Hoone; *Customer Svcs Mgr* Vernon Burnett; *Digital Lab Mgr* John Mannion; *Dir* Hannah Frieser; *Promotions Coordr* Jessica Reed; *Technical Producer* Anneka Herre
Open Galleries: Sun - Fri 10 AM - 6 PM; Darkrooms: Sun & Mon 10 AM - 10 PM, Tues - Fri 10 AM - 6PM, cl Sat; No admis fee to galleries, darkrooms carry semester lab fee; Estab 1973 to support artists working in the photographic arts; Circ 5,000; Maintains small reference library
Income: Financed by NEA, NYSCA, Institute of Museum & Library Services & private contributions
Library Holdings: Original Art Works
Special Subjects: Photography
Collections: Light Work Collection, photographic prints, Computer Imaging, Permanent collection of over 3,500 photographs
Exhibitions: Temporary exhibs held throughout the yr
Publications: Contact Sheet, 5 per year
Activities: Classes for adults & children; lects open to pub, 4 vis lectrs per yr; gallery talks; competitions with awards; tours; artist residence grants offered; schols & fels; book traveling exhibs occasionally; sales shop sells books & prints

M **SYRACUSE UNIVERSITY,** SUArt Galleries, Shaffer Art Bldg, Sims Hall Syracuse, NY 13244-1230. Tel 315-443-4097; Fax 315-443-9225; Email suart@syr.edu; Web: suart.syr.edu/; *Dir* Domenic J Iacono; *Assoc Dir* David Prince; *Registrar* Laura Wellner; *Asst Dir Mus Opers* Andrew Saluti; *Admin Specialist* Joan Recuparo; *Coll & Exhib Coordr* Emily Dittman; *Secy & Office Coordr* Alex Hahn
Open Tues - Sun 11 AM - 4:30 PM; Thurs until 8PM; No admis fee; Average Annual Attendance: 20,000
Income: Financed through University with additional outside grants
Special Subjects: African Art, Bronzes, Cartoons, Ceramics, Coins & Medals, Decorative Arts, Drawings, Etchings & Engravings, Folk Art, Glass, Laces, Metalwork, Painting-American, Painting-French, Photography, Pre-Columbian Art, Prints, Religious Art, Sculpture, Textiles, Watercolors, Woodcuts
Collections: Encyclopedic from pre-history to contemporary strength in 20th century American art & prints
Exhibitions: Various exhibitions, call for details
Activities: Classes for adults & children; lects open to pub; gallery tours; private tours on request; originate traveling exhibs to small & medium mus & galleries

M **Art Collection,** Sims Hall, Syracuse, NY 13244-1230. Tel 315-443-4097; Fax 315-443-9225; Web: sumweb.syr.edu/suart/; *Dir* Domenic J Iacono; *Cur* David Prince; *Preparator* William Kramer; *Registrar* Laura Wellner
Open Mon - Fri 9 AM - 5 PM; No admis fee; The Art Collection is housed in a temperature & humidity-controlled area of Sims Hall, adjacent to the Art Gallery. Used primarily for exhibition, storage & care of the 35,000 object collection, this facility also includes a teaching display area to accommodate classes & individuals involved in research; Average Annual Attendance: 15,000
Income: Financed by university funds & endowments
Purchases: WPA Federal Art Projects Prints, Contemporary American Prints, 20th Century American Art
Special Subjects: African Art, Bronzes, Cartoons, Ceramics, Decorative Arts, Drawings, Etchings & Engravings, Glass, Graphics, Laces, Landscapes, Oriental Art, Painting-American, Painting-French, Painting-German
Collections: West African tribal art, Korean, Japanese & American ceramics, Indian folk art, Pre-Columbian & contemporary Peruvian ceramics, Scandinavian designs in metal, wood, clay & textiles, 20th century American works with an emphasis on the Depression & War years (prints & paintings), 19th century European Salon paintings, history of printmaking (emphasis on American artists), decorative arts, Mary Petty-Alan Dunn Center for Social Cartooning
Exhibitions: Rembrandt: The Consummate Etcher (subject to change); Thematic Interpretation in Western Art, John R Fox Collection of Korean Ceramics, American Woodblock Prints 1900-1995
Activities: Originate traveling exhibs to small museums, university museums, galleries & libraries

TARRYTOWN

M **THE NATIONAL TRUST FOR HISTORIC PRESERVATION,** Lyndhurst, 635 S Broadway, Tarrytown, NY 10591-6401. Tel 914-631-4481; Fax 914-631-5634; Email info@lyndhurst.org; Web: www.lyndhurst.org
Open mid Apr - Dec Fri - Sun 10 AM- 5 PM; Admis adults $14, seniors & students $13, children 6-16 $10, group rates by arrangement, National Trust mems $7; National Trust Historic site & a National Historic Landmark. Lyndhurst is a Gothic revival mansion designed in 1838 for General William Paulding by Alexander Jackson Davis, one of America's most influential 19th century architects. Commissioned in 1865 by second owner George Merritt to enlarge the house, Davis

continued the Gothic revival style in the additions. It was purchased in 1880 by Jay Gould & willed to his daughter, Helen. Later acquired by another daughter, Anna, Duchess of Talleyrand-Perigord, Lyndhurst was left to the National Trust in 1961; Period rooms with original furnishings owned by Lyndhurst families; Average Annual Attendance: 65,000; Mem: 1100; dues $50-$1000
Income: Financed by admis fees, mem, private contributions & special events
Special Subjects: Furniture, Glass
Collections: Collection of Gothic furniture designed by architect A J Davis in the 1830s & 1860s, Herter Brothers furniture, 19th century furnishings & paintings, Tiffany glass, Jay Gould's Collection of 19th century paintings by Daubigny, Bouguereau, Gerome & others
Publications: Lyndhurst (guide book)
Activities: Classes for adults & children; dramatic progs; lects open to pub; 8 vis lectrs per yr; concerts; tours; mus shop sells books & magazines

TICONDEROGA

M **FORT TICONDEROGA ASSOCIATION,** PO Box 390, Ticonderoga, NY 12883-0390. Tel 518-585-2821; Fax 518-585-2210; Email fort@fort-ticonderoga.org; Web: www.fort-ticonderoga.org; *Chmn* Sanford W Morhouse; *Cur* Christopher D Fox; *Pres & CEO* Beth Hill; *Military Progs Supervisor* Cameron Green; *Accounting Mgr* Sidney Collier; *Dir Develop* Martha Strum; *Dir Interpretation* Stuart Lilie
Open daily early May - late Oct 9:30 AM - 5 PM; Admis adults $17.50, seniors 65 & over $15, children 5-12 $8, children 4 & under no charge; Estab 1909 to preserve & present the Colonial & Revolutionary history of Fort Ticonderoga; The Mus is in the restored barracks of the Colonial fort; Average Annual Attendance: 100,000; Mem: 1000; dues $50 & up
Income: Financed by admis fees, mus shop sales & donations
Library Holdings: Auction Catalogs, Book Volumes 13,000, CD-ROMs, Exhibition Catalogs, Fiche, Manuscripts, Maps, Motion Pictures, Pamphlets, Periodical Subscriptions, Photographs, Prints, Slides, Video Tapes
Special Subjects: Archaeology, Bookplates & Bindings, Costumes, Historical Material, Landscapes, Manuscripts, Maps, Military Art, Painting-American, Photography, Portraits, Decorative Arts, Etchings & Engravings, Prints, Woodcuts
Collections: Artifacts, manuscripts, paintings, prints, rare books
Exhibitions: Held in mid-May - mid-Oct
Activities: Classes for adults & children; dramatic progs; lects open to pub, concerts; tours; original objects of art lent to qualified mus; mus shop sells books, magazines, reproductions, prints, clothing & Souvenirs

TROY

A **THE ARTS CENTER OF THE CAPITAL REGION,** 265 River St, Troy, NY 12180-3215. Tel 518-273-0552; Fax 518-273-4591; Email lauren@artscenteronline.org; Web: www.artscenteronline.org; *Pres* Christopher Marblo; *Dir Performing Arts & Outreach* Jill Rafferty-Weinisch; *Educ & Exhibs Mgr* Caroline Corrigan; *Dir Devel* Beth Schroeder; *Mktg & Develop Mgr* Lauren Hittinger
Open Mon - Thurs 11 AM - 7 PM, Fri - Sat 9 AM - 5 PM, Sun Noon - 4 PM; No admis fee; Estab 1961, a regional center for the advancement of the arts in daily life. Through education, presentation, outreach, service advocacy; The Arts Center promotes a richer community through broad participation in the making & personal experience of art
Activities: Classes for adults, teens & children; family Sundays; dramatic progs; dance; lectures open to pub; films; concerts; performances; grants; gallery talks; sponsoring of competitions; schols

M **RENSSELAER COUNTY HISTORICAL SOCIETY,** Hart-Cluett Mansion, 1827, 59 Second St, Troy, NY 12180. Tel 518-272-7232; Fax 518-273-1264; Email info@rchsonline.org; Web: www.rchsonline.org; *Dir* Karin Krasevac-Lenz; *Cur* Stacy F Pomeroy Draper; *Registrar* Kathryn Sheehan; *Pres* Laudelina Martinez
Open Feb - Dec Tues - Sat 10 AM - 4 PM, call for varying hours; Admis donation for adults $3; Estab 1927 to promote historical research & to collect & exhibit materials of all kinds related to the history of the Rensselaer County area including books, papers, fine & decorative arts. The Hart-Cluett Mansion is an historic house mus with 11 furnished rooms; Average Annual Attendance: 15,000; Mem: 600; dues individual $35, family $50; annual meeting 2nd Mon in Sep
Income: $327,000 (financed by endowment, mem, grants, foundations & other contributions)
Special Subjects: Carpets & Rugs, Ceramics, Costumes, Crafts, Decorative Arts, Dolls, Drawings, Embroidery, Etchings & Engravings, Folk Art, Furniture, Glass, Graphics, Historical Material, Ivory, Jewelry, Laces, Landscapes, Manuscripts, Maps, Pottery, Prints, Sculpture, Silver, Textiles, Portraits
Collections: Three centuries of fine & decorative arts, including ceramics, Elijah Galusha 19th century furniture, paintings by local artists including C G Beauregard, Joseph Hidley & Abel Buel Moore, quilts & coverlets
Publications: Annual report; quarterly newsletter
Activities: Classes for adults & children; docent training; lects open to pub, 3 vis lectrs per yr; concerts; gallery talks; tours; competitions; book traveling exhibs; originates traveling exhibs; mus shop sells books, prints, original art & reproductions

L **Museum & Library**, 57 Second St, Troy, NY 12180. Tel 518-272-7232; Fax 518-273-1264; Email info@rchsonline.org; Web: www.rchsonline.org; *Dir* Karin Krasevac-Lenz; *Cur* Stacy Pomeroy Draper; *Registrar* Kathryn T Sheehan
Open Tues - Sat Noon - 5 PM, cl Dec 24 - Jan 31 & major holidays; Admis adults $5, seniors $4, youth $4, children under 12 free, group rates available; Estab 1927; Circ Non-circulating; Two historic townhouse buildings; Hart-Cluett House(1827); Carr Building; Average Annual Attendance: 10,000; Mem: 550; individual dues $35 & up, family $50; annual meeting in Sep
Income: Financed by endowment, mem, grants & events
Library Holdings: Audio Tapes, Book Volumes 2000, Clipping Files, Filmstrips, Framed Reproductions, Lantern Slides, Manuscripts, Maps, Memorabilia, Motion Pictures, Original Documents, Pamphlets, Periodical Subscriptions 4, Photographs, Prints, Slides
Special Subjects: Architecture, Ceramics, Costume Design & Constr, Crafts, Decorative Arts, Etchings & Engravings, Folk Art, Furniture, Glass, Historical Material, Landscapes, Manuscripts, Maps, Painting-American, Period Rooms, Photography, Porcelain, Portraits, Pottery, Silver, Textiles, Embroidery, Watercolors
Collections: Library & museum collections relating to Rensselaer County history
Publications: Call for information
Activities: Classes for adults & children; docent training; lects open to public; gallery talks; tours; traveling exhibs; museum shop sells books, reproductions & prints

M **RENSSELAER NEWMAN FOUNDATION CHAPEL + CULTURAL CENTER,** The Gallery at the Chapel & Cultural Center, 2125 Burdett Ave, Troy, NY 12180; 10 Tom Phelan Pl, Troy, NY 12180. Tel 518-274-7793; Fax 518-274-5945; Email rnf@rpi.edu; Web: www.chapelandculturalcenter.org; *Pres* Sharon Valiquette; *VPres* Megan Fannon; *Treas* Father Ed Kacerguis; *Secy* Brett Hutton; *C+CC Dir* Tom Mattern
Open 8:30AM - 10PM; No admis fee; Estab 1968 to provide religion and culture for members of the Rensselaer Polytechnic Institute and Troy area, a broadly ecumenical service; Gallery maintained; Average Annual Attendance: 30,000
Income: $150,000 (financed by contributions)
Library Holdings: Audio Tapes, Book Volumes, Cassettes, Compact Disks, Filmstrips, Framed Reproductions, Original Art Works, Photographs, Sculpture, Slides, Video Tapes
Special Subjects: Medieval Art, Religious Art, Sculpture
Collections: Contemporary paintings, sculpture and needlework, liturgical vestments & artifacts, medieval sculpture
Exhibitions: New York State Council on the Arts; National juried individual exhibs; Local artists' shows
Publications: Sun & Balance, three times a year
Activities: Classes for adults & children; dramatic progs; lects open to pub, 10 vis lectrs per yr; concerts; gallery talks; Poetry Series; Peace Fair

UTICA

M **MUNSON-WILLIAMS-PROCTOR ARTS INSTITUTE,** Museum of Art, 310 Genesee St, Utica, NY 13502-4799. Tel 315-797-0000; Fax 315-797-5608; Email info@mwpai.org; Web: www.mwpai.org; *Dir & Chief Cur* Anna T D'Ambrosio; *Librn* Kathryn Corcoran; *Cur Modern & Contemporary Art* Mary E Murray; *Educ Dir* April Oswald; *Registrar & Exhib Mgr* Michael Somple; *Dir Emeritus* Paul D Schweizer
Open Tues - Thurs & Sat 10 AM - 5 PM, Fri 10 AM - 8 PM, Sun 1 - 5 PM, cl Mon & holidays; No admis fee, donations accepted (admis fees for some special exhibs); Estab 1919 to collect, preserve & exhibit art, artifacts & articles of importance; Circ 17,000; The institute became active in 1953 with the purpose of establishing & maintaining a gallery & collection of art to give instruction & to have an auxiliary library. It consists of a School of Art estab 1941; a Mus of Art opened in 1960; Fountain Elms, a house-mus was restored in 1960; a Meetinghouse opened in 1963 & a Performing Arts Division. Maintains reference library; Average Annual Attendance: 182,000; Mem: 3,823; dues individual $50, student $25
Income: Financed by endowment, tuition & private contributions, voluntary donations at entrances, ticketed special exhibs
Purchases: 19th - 21st century American, European paintings, sculpture, graphic & 19th century decorative arts
Library Holdings: Auction Catalogs, Audio Tapes, Book Volumes, CD-ROMs, Cassettes, Clipping Files, Compact Disks, DVDs, Exhibition Catalogs, Fiche, Other Holdings, Periodical Subscriptions, Slides, Video Tapes
Special Subjects: Carpets & Rugs, Decorative Arts, Drawings, Furniture, Landscapes, Marine Painting, Miniatures, Painting-American, Period Rooms, Photography, Portraits, Pottery, Prints, Sculpture, Silver, Watercolors
Collections: Arts of Central New York, 19th & 20th century European paintings & sculpture, 18th - 21st century American paintings, sculpture, 19th century decorative arts
Exhibitions: Rotating exhibits from permanent collection
Publications: Bulletin, monthly; exhibition catalogues
Activities: Classes for adults & children; docent training; workshops, dramatic progs; lects open to pub, lects for mems. only, 5 vis lectrs per yr; gallery talks; tours. N.Y. Upstate Organization award for Advancing Cultural Development, 2002; fellowships; individual paintings & original objects of art lent to members from the Art Lending Library; lending collection contains original prints, paintings, sculpture; book traveling exhibs 2-3 per yr; originate traveling exhibs to mus in other areas including international mus; mus shop sells books, magazines, original art, prints, handmade jewelry, catalogs, children's items, pottery, note cards, greeting cards & crafts, textiles

L **Art Reference Library**, 310 Genesee St, Utica, NY 13502-4799. Tel 315-797-0000, Ext 2123; Fax 315-797-5608; Email library@mwpai.org; *Dir Library Svcs* Kathryn L Corcoran; *Asst Librn* Kathleen Salsbury
Open Mon - Fri 10 Am - 5 PM, Sat Noon - 5 PM, cl Sun; No admis fee; Estab 1940 to support School of Art, Mus of Art staff, Institute Mem & general pub; circulation only to members & staff of the Institute & Pratt MWP students; Circ 5,000
Library Holdings: Auction Catalogs, Book Volumes 29,000, CD-ROMs, Clipping Files, Compact Disks 2,980, DVDs 1,324, Exhibition Catalogs, Manuscripts, Pamphlets, Periodical Subscriptions 60, Slides 20,000, Video Tapes 754
Special Subjects: Aesthetics, Afro-American Art, Architecture, Art Education, Art History, Asian Art, Bookplates & Bindings, Carpets & Rugs, Ceramics, Collages, Commercial Art, Conceptual Art, Constructions, Crafts, Decorative Arts, Drawings, Etchings & Engravings, Folk Art, Furniture, Graphic Arts, Graphic Design, History of Art & Archaeology, Illustration, Jewelry, Landscapes, Latin American Art, Marine Painting, Metalwork, Mixed Media, Painting-American, Painting-British, Painting-Dutch, Painting-European, Painting-Flemish, Painting-French, Painting-German, Painting-Italian, Painting-Japanese, Painting-Spanish, Pewter, Photography, Porcelain, Portraits, Posters, Pottery, Printmaking, Prints, Video, Watercolors, Sculpture, Silver, Silversmithing, Woodcarvings
Collections: Fountain Elms Collection, autographs, rare books & manuscripts, book plates, artists' files; archives

Publications: Bibliographies related to museum exhibitions; bibliographic instructional materials

M **SCULPTURE SPACE, INC,** 12 Gates St, Utica, NY 13502-3414. Tel 315-724-8381; Fax 315-797-6639; Email info@sculpturespace.org; Web: www.sculpturespace.org; *Dir* Tom Montan; *Office Mgr* Holly Flitcroft; *Studio Mgr* George Hendrickson
Open by appointment only; No admis fee; Estab 1976 to provide professional artists with studio space; 5,500 sq ft open studio including 5 private studios; Average Annual Attendance: 1,000
Income: $200,000 (grants, special events, ann appeal)
Library Holdings: Compact Disks, DVDs, Exhibition Catalogs, Original Art Works, Original Documents, Photographs, Slides, Video Tapes
Special Subjects: Sculpture
Publications: Sculpture Space News, semi-annual
Activities: Classes for children; lect open to public; gallery talks; Awards (20 funded residences); tours; fellowships offered; organization also manages commissioned works, sells books, prints, original art & limited edition sculptures

VALLEY COTTAGE

L **VALLEY COTTAGE LIBRARY,** Gallery, 110 Rte 303, Valley Cottage, NY 10989. Tel 845-268-7700; Fax 845-268-7760; Email vclref@rcls.org; Web: www.vclib.org; *Library Dir* Amelia Kalin; *Dir Exhib* Joanne McNally
Open Mon - Thurs 10 AM - 9 PM, Fri & Sat 10 AM - 5 PM; Sep - June Sun noon - 4 PM; Estab 1959; 27 x 7, artificial & natural light
Publications: Focus, quarterly

WATER MILL

M **PARRISH ART MUSEUM,** 279 Montauk Hwy, Water Mill, NY 11976-2639. Tel 631-283-2118; Fax 631-283-7006; Email info@parishart.org; Web: www.parrishart.org; *Dir* Terrie Sultan; *Asst Dir* Anke Jackson; *Lewis B & Dorothy Cullman Chief Cur Art & Educ* Alicia Longwell; *Registrar* Chris McNamara; *Dir Special Events* Nina Madison; *Dir Educ* Cara Conklin-Wingfield; *Cur, Robert Lehman* Klaus Ottmann
Open Mon, Thurs, Fri, Sat 11 AM - 5 PM, Sun 1 - 5 PM; open every day June - mid-Sep, cl Tues & Wed; Admis suggested donation $5, seniors & students $3, children under 18 & mems free; Estab 1898 to exhibit, care for & research permanent collections & loan works of art with emphasis on American 19th, 20th & 21st century art and the art of Eastern Long Island; Three main galleries are maintained; total dimensions 4288 sq ft, 355 running feet; Average Annual Attendance: 40,000; Mem: 1,800; dues $25-$1,000 & up
Income: Financed by contributions & grants
Library Holdings: Book Volumes, Clipping Files, Exhibition Catalogs, Original Documents, Periodical Subscriptions, Photographs, Prints, Slides
Special Subjects: Etchings & Engravings, Oriental Art, Painting-American, Drawings, Photography, Reproductions, Sculpture
Collections: William Merritt Chase Collection, Dunnigan Collection of 19th-century etchings, Samuel Parrish Collection of Italian Renaissance panel, Fairfield Porter Collection, American paintings, 19th, 20th & 21st century, Japanese woodblock prints & stencils
Publications: Fairfield Porter: Raw - The Creative Process of an American Master by Klaus Ottmann; American Landscapes: Treasures from the Parrish Art Museum by Alicia Longwell; First Impressions: 19th C. American Master Prints by Alicia Longwell; Rackstraw Downes: Onsite Paintings, 1972-2008 by Klaus Ottmann; Underground Pop by David Pagel
Activities: Classes for adults & children; dramatic progs; docent training; lects open to pub, special lectrs; concerts; gallery talks; films; tours; individual paintings & original objects of art lent; originates traveling exhibs; mus shops sells books, original art, jewelry, note cards, prints, educational toys; gifts, posters & stationery

WATERFORD

A **NEW YORK STATE OFFICE OF PARKS, RECREATION AND HISTORIC PRESERVATION,** Bureau of Historic Sites, Peebles Island, PO Box 189 Waterford, NY 12188-0219. Tel 518-237-8643; Fax 518-235-4248; Web: www.nysparks.com; *Dir* Mark Peckham; *Supervising Cur* Travis Bowman; *Coll Mgr* Ronna Dixson; *Assoc Cur* Amanda Massie; *Interpretation Supv* Audrey Nieson; *Chief Conservator* Michele Phillips
Open by appointment only; No admis fee; Estab 1974 as a resource center providing technical services to state historic sites & parks in the areas of research, interpretation, collections management, curatorial & conservation services, restoration of historic structures, exhibit design, fabrication & historic archeology; All exhibits are housed at the state historic sites
Income: A branch of state government
Special Subjects: Archaeology, Carpets & Rugs, Ceramics, Coins & Medals, Costumes, Decorative Arts, Dolls, Drawings, Embroidery, Etchings & Engravings, Folk Art, Furniture, Glass, Historical Material, Islamic Art, Landscapes, Manuscripts, Maps, Painting-American, Painting-European, Period Rooms, Porcelain, Portraits, Reproductions, Restorations, Sculpture, Tapestries, Textiles
Collections: Painting collections exist at several sites most notably Olana & Senate House. Artists include Church, Cole, Vanderlyn, Stuart, Pissaro., furniture, decorative arts & textiles at most of the sites includ furniture designed by Frank Lloyd Wright at the Darwin Martin House
Activities: Internships offered

WATERTOWN

M **JEFFERSON COUNTY HISTORICAL SOCIETY,** 228 Washington St, Watertown, NY 13601. Tel 315-782-3491; Fax 315-782-2913; Email curator@jeffersoncountyhistory.org; Web: www.jeffersoncountyhistory.org; *Cur Educ* Melissa Widrick; *Dir* Timothy J Abel; *Pres* Roxanne M Burns; *Progs & Chmn* Judith N George; *Exec Sec* Elaine Bock; *Cur Coll* Elise Chan
Open May-Dec Tues - Fri 10 AM - 5 PM, Sat 10 AM - 4 PM, Jan - Apr Tues - Fri 10 AM - 5 PM; Admis $2 donation; Estab 1886; Average Annual Attendance: 12,000; Mem: 924; annual meeting in May
Income: $142,000 (financed by endowment, mem, county appropriation, grants, private foundations & gifts)
Special Subjects: Costumes, Furniture, Glass, Historical Material, Textiles
Collections: Tyler Coverlet Collection, Costume Collection, Kinne Water Turbine Collection, 19th century Furniture, Prehistoric Indian Arts, Jefferson County
Exhibitions: Fort Drum: A Historical Perspective
Publications: Bulletin, 1-2 times per yr; Museum Musings; 6 times per yr; Abraham Tuthill (catalogue)
Activities: Classes for adults & children; in-school local history progs; docent training; lects open to pub, 2-6 vis lectrs per yr; tours; artmobile; lending collection includes; artifacts, 155 items; book traveling exhibs 1-2 per yr; originate traveling exhibs; mus shop sells books, toys & other souvenir items

L **Library,** 228 Washington St, Watertown, NY 13601. Tel 315-782-3491; Fax 315-782-2913; Web: www.jeffersoncountyhistory.org; *Exec Dir* William G Wood; *Coll Mgr* Lenka Walldroff; *Office Mgr* Lisa C Earp; *Caretaker* David Coleman
Open Tues - Fri 10 AM - 5 PM, Sat 10 AM - 4 PM; Admis adult $6, military & seniors $5, students $4; Estab 1886; Mem: 650
Income: Endowment, county appropriation, grants, pvt foundations
Library Holdings: Book Volumes 2211, Clipping Files, Exhibition Catalogs, Framed Reproductions, Manuscripts, Memorabilia, Original Art Works, Pamphlets, Prints
Special Subjects: American Indian Art, Architecture, Art History, Decorative Arts, Furniture, Glass, Historical Material
Publications: Museum Musings Newsletter, quarterly; Bulletin, annually
Activities: Mus shop sells books, original art, reproductions, prints

M **ROSWELL P FLOWER MEMORIAL LIBRARY,** 229 Washington St, Watertown, NY 13601-3324. Tel 315-788-2352; Fax 315-788-2584; Email ueblertm@northnet.org; Email watlib@nnyln.net; Web: www.flowermemoriallibrary.org; *Dir* Barbara Wheeler; *Reference Librn* Yvonne Reff; *Children's Librn* Ginger Tebo
Open Labor Day - Memorial Day Mon, Tues & Thurs 9 AM - 9 PM, Wed, Fri & Sat 9 AM - 5 PM, cl Sun; No admis fee; Estab 1904; The library contains murals, paintings & sculptures throughout the building
Income: $900,000 (financed by NY State and City of Watertown)
Library Holdings: Audio Tapes, Book Volumes, CD-ROMs, Cassettes, Clipping Files, Compact Disks, DVDs, Fiche, Filmstrips, Maps, Micro Print, Original Art Works, Other Holdings, Pamphlets, Periodical Subscriptions, Prints, Sculpture, Slides, Video Tapes
Collections: New York State material & genealogy, United States military history
Activities: Lects open to pub; tours

WELLSVILLE

M **THE MATHER HOMESTEAD MUSEUM, LIBRARY & MEMORIAL PARK,** 343 N Main St, Wellsville, NY 14895-1016. Tel 585-593-1636; *Dir & Owner* Barbara Williams
Open by appt; No admis fee; Estab 1981; Pvt nonprofit mus; home of Mather family & descendants. House & grounds share a look at lifestyles of different decades and in different parts of the world. Emphasis on pleasures for those who are blind or poorly sighted; Average Annual Attendance: 500 - 999
Income: private
Library Holdings: Audio Tapes, Book Volumes, Cards, Cassettes, Exhibition Catalogs, Kodachrome Transparencies, Memorabilia, Original Art Works, Pamphlets, Periodical Subscriptions, Prints, Sculpture, Video Tapes
Collections: Barn holds coll of artifacts, music, books, games, catalogues & toys of the 1930s, visiting 1937 automobile returned to working condition, antiques; art; arts & crafts; children's mus; historic house/site; library; musical instruments; typography mus; wildlife refuge/bird sanctuary; info sharing about cultural lifestyles; works of area artists; aids for poorly-sighted, coll on British Arts Council's Festival (1951), coll of printed materials, samplers, tools
Publications: The Homestead Hoot, newsletter; An in-house publishing program: Sound Adventures, music and papers
Activities: Lects; concerts; guided tours; ann events: Easter Egg Hunt for ages 6 & under; Halloween Paint-Out; reading of Declaration of Independence

WEST NYACK

M **ROCKLAND CENTER FOR THE ARTS,** 27 S Greenbush Rd, West Nyack, NY 10994-2700. Tel 845-358-0877; Fax 845-358-0971; Email info@rocklandartcenter.org; Web: www.rocklandartcenter.org; *Exec Dir* Julianne Ramos, MFA; *School Dir* Daly Flanagan, MS; *Artistic Dir* Lynn Stein
Open Mon - Fri 9 AM - 5 PM, Sat - Sun 9 AM - 4 PM; No admis fee; Estab 1947 to present excellence in the arts, educ & servs; 40 ft x 70 ft gallery space, 4 acre sculpture park; 5 exhibit areas, Emerson Gallery, Gallery One, Gallery Two Project Media Space & Catherine Konner Sculpture Park; Average Annual Attendance: 25,000; Mem: 1500; dues family $45, singles $25; annual meeting in Oct
Income: $850,000 (financed by mem, state appropriations, corporations, foundations & earned income)
Exhibitions: Sculpture in the Park; 8 curated gallery exhibs annually
Publications: Art school catalogues; exhibition catalogue, Sculpture Park catalogue & Audio Tour
Activities: Classes for adults & children in visual, literary & performing arts; lects open to pub; performances in classical, jazz, folk music; exten prog for Rockland Cty NY schools, Rockland Co Pub Art Prog Admin

WEST POINT

M **UNITED STATES MILITARY ACADEMY,** West Point Museum, Olmsted Hall at Pershing Center, West Point, NY 10996-5000; 2110 S Post Rd, West Point, NY 10996. Tel 845-938-3590; Fax 845-938-7478; Email museum@usma.edu; Web: www.usma.edu/museum/; *Dir* David M Reel; *Cur History* Michael Mcafee; *Cur Weapons* Leslie D Jensen; *Mus Specialist* Paul Ackermann; *Security Chief* Gloria J Johnson; *Exhib Designer* Jose Cartagena; *Cur Art* Marlana L Cook; *Registrar* Brian Rayca; *Admin* Lisa Taylor; *Mus Technician* Christopher Goodrow
Open daily 10:30 AM - 4:15 PM; No admis fee; Estab 1854, supplementing the acad, cultural & military instruction of cadets; also disseminates the history of the US Army, the US Military Academy & the West Point area; Collections open to the pub; Average Annual Attendance: 130,000
Income: Federal Institution
Purchases: $5000
Library Holdings: Book Volumes, Manuscripts, Maps, Memorabilia, Original Art Works, Original Documents, Pamphlets, Periodical Subscriptions, Photographs, Records
Special Subjects: American Indian Art, American Western Art, Bronzes, Cartoons, Coins & Medals, Dioramas, Drawings, Etchings & Engravings, Folk Art, Graphics, Military Art, Painting-American, Portraits, Posters, Prints, Watercolors, Painting-European
Collections: Alexander M Craighead Collection of European & American Military Art, Jonas Lie Collection of Panama Canal Oils, Liedesdorf Collection of European Armor, Peter Rindisbacher Watercolors, Thomas Sully Portrait Collection, cadet drawings from 1820-1940, European & American war posters, extensive holdings from World War I & World War II, military & homefront subjects, military artifacts including weapons, flags, uniforms, medals, etc, military paintings & prints, paintings & prints of West Point, Hudson River School artists
Exhibitions: Cadet Drawings from the 19th Century to World War I; Jonas Lie & the Building of the Panama Canal; The Land of Counterpane: Toy Soldiers; Art of the Panama Canal; Come Join Us Brothers, African Americans in the US Army; Timeless Treasures: 200 Years of West Point Memories (A bicentennial exhibition); Tabletops and Tradition: The Officer's Mess and Cadet Mess at West Point; The West Point Museum: A Museum for the Army (1854-2004); Age of Exploration - Hudson's 400th Anniversary; The Mexican War; Remember Fort Sumter (1861-1865); Dark Blue is the National Color; Straw Blowers & Sheepskin Fiddlers; Appomattox; Pictures of Panama
Publications: The West Point Museum: A Guide to the Collections; Exhibition brochures; West Point Museum Treasure Hunt
Activities: 20th century re-enactment progs and military memorabilia displays from volunteer's collections; lects open to pub; 4 vis lectrs per yr; gallery talks; tours; individual paintings & original objects of art lent to accredited mus; mus shop sells books, original art, reproductions, prints & West Point memorabilia

WESTFIELD

L **PATTERSON LIBRARY & OCTAGON ART GALLERY,** (Patterson Library & Art Gallery), 40 S Portage St, Westfield, NY 14787-1496. Tel 716-326-2154; Fax 716-326-2554; Email octagongallery@gmail.com; Web: www.pattersonlibrary.info; *Dir* Erin Hauenstein; *Arts Specialist* Nancy H Nixon; *Cur* Nancy N Ensign
Open Tues & Thurs 9 AM - 8 PM, Mon, Wed & Fri - Sat 9 AM - 5 PM, cl Sun; No admis fee; Estab 1896 (Octagon Gallery estab 1971) to provide opportunity for educ & recreation through the use of literature, music, films, paintings & other art forms; Circ 72,000; Octagon Gallery is 1115 sq ft with 11 ft ceilings & 100 ft running space, maintains lending/reference library; Average Annual Attendance: 14,000
Income: Financed by endowment & private sources
Library Holdings: Audio Tapes, Book Volumes 45,000, Clipping Files, Compact Disks, Compact Disks, DVDs, Fiche, Filmstrips, Manuscripts, Maps, Memorabilia, Motion Pictures, Original Art Works, Original Documents, Pamphlets, Periodical Subscriptions, Photographs 10,000, Reels, Sculpture, Slides, Video Tapes
Collections: Glass plates of local history, mounted birds, Seashells, WWI posters, photographs, postcards
Exhibitions: Annual Westfield Revisited Exhibition; monthly exhibs with regional artists
Activities: Classes for adults & children; dramatic programs; lects open to pub; concerts; gallery talks; tours; individual paintings

WOODSTOCK

A **CENTER FOR PHOTOGRAPHY AT WOODSTOCK INC,** 59 Tinker St, Woodstock, NY 12498-1236. Tel 845-679-9957; Fax 845-679-6337; Email info@cpw.org; Web: www.cpw.org; *Exec Dir* Ariel Shanberg; *Educ Coordr* Lindsay A Stern; *Opers Mgr* Lawrence R Lewis; *Prog Assoc* Akemi Hiatt; *Digital Lab Mgr* Phil Mansfield
Open gallery Wed - Sun noon - 5 PM, office Mon - Fri 10 AM - 6 PM; No admis fee; Estab 1977, a nonprofit organization, an art & educ center, an artist-centered space; 2 large galleries showcase contemporary photography, hosting workshops, lect & artist residencies; Average Annual Attendance: 50,000; Mem: Open mem
Income: Financed by pub funding, foundations, individuals
Library Holdings: Exhibition Catalogs
Collections: Permanent collection contains 1750 photographic prints & art work which incorporates photography, Maverick Festival Archive
Exhibitions: Ten shows per year
Publications: Photography magazine, quarterly (featuring best of contemporary photography)
Activities: Classes for adults, children, professionals & amateurs; workshops; lects open to pub, 30 vis lectrs per yr; gallery talks; tours; sponsoring of competitions; scholarships; fels; originates traveling exhibs; mus shop sells books, notecards, postcards

A **WOODSTOCK ARTISTS ASSOCIATION & MUSEUM,** 28 Tinker St, Woodstock, NY 12498-1233. Tel 845-679-2940; Fax 845-679-2198; Email info@woodstockart.org; Web: www.woodstockart.org; *Exec Dir & Cur Permanent Coll* Josephine Bloodgood; *Gallery Dir* Carl Van Brunt; *Preparator & Bldg Mgr* Ben Caswell; *Educ Cur* Beth Humphrey; *Archivist* Emily Jones; *Gallery Assoc* Patricia Seminara
Open Sun, Mon & Thurs noon - 5 PM, Fri & Sat noon - 6 PM, cl Tues & Wed; Suggested donation $5; Estab 1919 to exhibit the work of artists of the region; Upstairs Gallery, Members Group Exhibitions; Downstairs Gallery-Solo exhibitions; Phoebe & Belmont Towbin Wing; Exhibitions from the Permanent Collection; exhibiting members must live within 50 miles of Woodstock; Average Annual Attendance: 24,000; Mem: 400; dues (check website for current info)
Income: $90,000 (financed by endowment, mem, city appropriation, donations, earned income)
Special Subjects: Historical Material, Jewelry, Landscapes, Painting-American, Photography, Portraits, Pottery, Sculpture, Watercolors, Woodcuts, Decorative Arts, Drawings, Prints
Collections: Permanent Collection incl oils, prints & sculpture, graphic arts, intermedia, prints, Historic Woodstock Artists
Exhibitions: Rotating juried exhibits for members; solo shows for members
Publications: Woodstock Art Heritage: The Permanent Collection of the Woodstock Artists Assn (1987)
Activities: Classes for adults & children; Lects open to pub, concerts; gallery talks; tours; competitions with multiple monthly & year-end awards; lending collection contains books, color reproductions, original art works, original prints, paintings, sculpture, slides & videos; mus shop sells books, gift items, original art, prints & reproductions

YONKERS

M **THE HUDSON RIVER MUSEUM,** 511 Warburton Ave, Yonkers, NY 10701-1899. Tel 914-963-4550; Fax 914-963-8558; Email visitorserv@hrm.org; Web: www.hrm.org; *Dir* Michael Botwinick; *Dir Pub Rels* Linda Locke; *Dir Community Devel* Richard Halevy; *Chief Cur Collections* Laura Vookles; *Cur Exhibs* Bartholomew Bland; *Planetarium Coordr* Marc Taylor
Open Wed - Sun noon - 5 PM, cl Mon & Tues; Planetarium shows Sat & Sun 12:30 PM, 2 PM & 3:30 PM; Admis museum adults $5, seniors & children $3, mems free; planetarium admis adults $2 + mus admis, seniors & children $1 + mus admis, mems free; Estab 1924 as a general mus of art, history & science; Maintains Planetarium; Average Annual Attendance: 70,000; Mem: 800
Income: $700,000 (financed by mem, city & county appropriation, state arts council, federal grants & donations)
Special Subjects: Architecture, Decorative Arts, Painting-American, Photography, Sculpture
Collections: 19th & 20th century American art, decorative arts, furniture, toys, dolls, costumes, accoutrement, silver, china, paintings, sculpture, photography, Red Grooms: The Bookstore, Nybelwyck Hall
Publications: Tri-annual calendar of events; spec exhibs flyers; ann report
Activities: Classes for children; docent training; teacher resources; family workshops; progs for seniors; community progs & celebrations; holiday progs; lects & special events open to pub; concerts; gallery talks; tours; performances; art lent to other mus for exhib purposes; lending collection contains original art works, paintings, photographs, sculpture; originates traveling exhibs organized and circulated to mus, college galleries - regional & national; mus disciplines, art history & science

M **PHILIPSE MANOR HALL STATE HISTORIC SITE,** 29 Warburton Ave, Yonkers, NY 10701-2721. Tel 914-965-4027; Fax 914-965-6485; Web: www.nystateparks.com; *Historic Site Mgr* Kimberly Flook
Open Apr - Oct Tues - Fri noon - 5 PM, Sat - Sun 11 AM - 5 PM, Nov - Mar Sat - Sun noon - 4 PM, cl holidays; Admis $4, seniors & students $3, children under 12 $1, children under 5 free; Estab 1908 to preserve Georgian manor house owned by the Frederick Philipse family; to interpret Philipse Manor Hall's architecture, its significance as the home of an American Loyalist & its importance as an example of 17th & 18th century Anglo-Dutch patterns in landholding & development; The State Historic Site is part of the New York State Office of Parks & Recreation; the Hall houses contemporary style exhibits of history, art & architecture hung against a backdrop of fine 18th & 19th century architectural carvings; Average Annual Attendance: 29,000
Income: Financed by state appropriation
Library Holdings: Book Volumes, Clipping Files, Kodachrome Transparencies, Maps, Memorabilia, Photographs, Prints, Slides
Special Subjects: Historical Material, Portraits
Collections: Cochran Portrait of Famous Americans, Cochran Collection of Windsor Chairs
Exhibitions: Historic Trail; People's Choice: Presidential Portraits from Washington to FDR
Activities: Docent training; lect open to public, 4 vis lectrs per yr; concerts; tours; demonstrations; films

L **YONKERS PUBLIC LIBRARY,** Fine Arts Dept, 1500 Central Park Ave, Yonkers, NY 10710-6007. Tel 914-337-1500, Ext 311; *Librn* Joanne Roche; *Librn* John Connell
Open Mon - Thurs 10 AM - 9 PM, Fri & Sat 10 AM - 5 PM, Sun Noon - 5 PM, cl Sat & Sun during summer; Estab 1962 to serve the general pub with a special interest in the arts, especially the fine arts, performing arts & the decorative & applied arts; Circ printed material approx 22,000; recorded material approx 66,000
Income: $65,000 (financed by city appropriation & gifts)
Purchases: $65,000
Library Holdings: Audio Tapes 3100, Book Volumes 14,000, Cassettes 1000, Clipping Files, Fiche, Other Holdings Scores 3000, Pamphlets 7000, Periodical Subscriptions 82, Records 15,000, Reels, Video Tapes 200

L **Will Library**, 1500 Central Park Ave, Yonkers, NY 10710. Tel 914-337-1500; *Librn* John Connell; *Librn* Joanne Roche
Library Holdings: Book Volumes 126,000, Periodical Subscriptions 75
Exhibitions: Exhibits work by local artists & craftsmen

YORKTOWN

AMERICAN SOCIETY OF CONTEMPORARY ARTISTS (ASCA)
For further information, see National and Regional Organizations

NORTH CAROLINA

ASHEVILLE

M **ASHEVILLE ART MUSEUM,** 2 S Pack Sq, Asheville, NC 28801-3521; PO Box 1717, Asheville, NC 28802-1717. Tel 828-253-3227; Fax 828-257-4503; Email mailbox@ashevilleart.org; Web: www.ashevilleart.org; *Exec Dir* Pamela L Myers; *Capital Campaign Coordr* Rebecca Lynch-Maas; *Communications Mgr* Jennifer Swanson; *Educ Progs Mgr* Sharon McRorie; *Vis Servs & Mus Shop Mgr* Laura Wheeler; *Grant Mgr* Mark Jackson; *Financial Officer* Lindsay G Rosson; *Mus Preparator* Jay Milner; *Progs Mgr* Kristi McMillan; *Asst Cur* Carolyn Grosch; *Mus Shop* Lauren Bacchus; *Membership & Events* Joanna K Miller
Open year round Tues-Sat10AM - 5 PM, Sun 1 - 5 PM,; Admis adults $8, students & seniors $7, special exhibition fees may apply, free to mems; Estab 1948 to provide art experiences to the Southeast & Western North Carolina area through exhibitions of American 20th & 21st century art; Eight galleries maintained, 8 with changing exhibits; maintains reference library; Average Annual Attendance: 125,000; Mem: 1,300; dues family $75, single $55
Income: Financed by mem, earned income, grants & pvt contributions
Purchases: Romare Bearden, James Chapin, Joseph Fiore, William Wegman, Whitfield Lovell, Willie Cole, Karen Karnes
Library Holdings: Auction Catalogs, Audio Tapes, Book Volumes, CD-ROMs, Clipping Files, DVDs, Exhibition Catalogs, Kodachrome Transparencies, Pamphlets, Periodical Subscriptions, Slides
Special Subjects: Afro-American Art, American Indian Art, Architecture, Ceramics, Crafts, Folk Art, Furniture, Glass, Metalwork, Painting-American, Photography, Portraits, Posters, Pottery, Prints, Watercolors, Etchings & Engravings
Collections: southeast regional, 20th & 21st Century American Art, Studio craft, Black Mountain College Collections
Exhibitions: Sol LeWitt: Creating Place, ongoing; Community: Sharon Louden; Vault Visible
Publications: Quarterly membership; newsletter, catalogues
Activities: Classes for adults & children; docent training; art camp; lects open to pub, 6-10 vis lectrs per yr; concerts; gallery talks; tours; competitions with awards; WNC Regional Scholastic Art Awards; schols offered; individual paintings & original objects of art lent to other mus; books traveling exhibs 1-3 per yr; originates traveling exhibs to other mus venues; mus shop sells books, magazines, original art, reproductions, prints, cards, art supplies, toys & other gift items

A **SOUTHERN HIGHLAND CRAFT GUILD,** Folk Art Center, 382 Blue Ridge Pkwy, Asheville, NC 28805; PO Box 9545, Asheville, NC 28815-0545. Tel 828-298-7928; Fax 828-298-7962; Email shcg@buncombe.main.nc.us; Web: www.Southernhighlandguild.org; *Dir* Ruth Summers; *Archivist* Ginny Daley; *Librn* Deb Schillo; *Mem Adminr* Rebecca Orr
Open Mon - Sun 9 AM - 5 PM, cl Thanksgiving, Christmas & New Year's; No admis fee; Estab 1930 to encourage wider appreciation of mountain crafts; raise & maintain standards of design & craftsmanship & encourage individual expression; Main exhib gallery, a focus gallery & interpretive gallery; Average Annual Attendance: 300,000; Mem: 700; open to eligible craftsmen from Southern Appalachian Mountain Region upon approval of applicant's work by Standards Comt & Board of Trustees; dues group $40, single $20; annual meeting in Apr
Income: Financed by mem & merchandising
Library Holdings: Audio Tapes, Book Volumes, Clipping Files, Exhibition Catalogs, Kodachrome Transparencies, Manuscripts, Maps, Memorabilia, Motion Pictures, Original Documents, Pamphlets, Periodical Subscriptions, Photographs, Records, Reels, Slides, Video Tapes
Special Subjects: American Indian Art, Calligraphy, Ceramics, Crafts, Decorative Arts, Dolls, Embroidery, Enamels, Textiles
Collections: Object coll focused on regional contemporary crafts & historical folk arts, Library & Archives
Publications: Highland Highlights; monthly newsletter
Activities: Workshops for adults & children; lects open to pub & some for mems only; gallery talks; tours; competitions; lending collection contains 2500 objects/ American crafts; originate traveling exhibs to museums & nonprofit galleries

M **YMI CULTURAL CENTER,** 39 S Market St, Asheville, NC 28801-3725; PO Box 7301, Asheville, NC 28802. Tel 848-252-4614; 257-4541; Fax 828-257-4539; Email ymicc1@aol.com; Web: www.ymiculturalcenter.org; *Chair* Stephanie Swepson-Twitty; *Vice Chair* Monique A Taylor; *Secy* Leonard E Jones; *Treas* Macky Bah
Open Tues - Fri 12 PM - 4 PM; Estab 1906; 18,000 sq ft facility; 1,385 sq ft gallery
Exhibitions: Temporary exhibits

BLOWING ROCK

M **BLOWING ROCK ART AND HISTORY MUSEUM,** 159 Chestnut St, Blowing Rock, NC 28605; PO Box 828, Blowing Rock, NC 28605. Tel 828-295-9099; Fax 828-295-9029; Web: www.blowingrockmuseum.org; *Exec Dir* Lee Carol Giduz; *Bus Mgr* David Harwood
Open Tues - Wed & Fri - Sat 10 AM - 5 PM, Thurs 10 AM - 7 PM, Sun 1 PM - 5 PM (June - Oct); Adults $7, children & students $5; children 4 & under, active military & members no charge; Estab 2001; 26,000 sq ft bldg
Special Subjects: Ceramics, Drawings, Landscapes, Painting-American, Pottery, Watercolors
Collections: local visual arts, history & heritage; American paintings; period artifacts; facejug collection
Activities: Classes for adults & children; docent training; lects for mems, concerts, gallery talks, tours

BOONE

M **APPALACHIAN STATE UNIVERSITY,** (Turchin Center for the Visual Arts) Turchin Center for the Visual Arts, 423 W King St, Boone, NC 28608-2139; ASU Box 32139, Boone, NC 28608-2139. Tel 828-262-3017; Fax 828-262-7546; Email turchincenter@appstate.edu; Web: www.tcva.org; *Associate Vice Chancellor for Arts Engagement* Hank T Foreman; *Visitor & Mem Serv* Jackie Garner; *Dir Admin* Sandra Black; *Cur* Mary Anne Redding; *Director of Arts & Cultural Programs* Denise Ringler
Open Tues-Thurs & Sat 10AM-6PM, Fri noon-8PM; No admis fee; Estab 2003; Contemporary art gallery & mus; Average Annual Attendance: 20,000; Mem: 200; dues variable levels
Income: Private & state funding
Library Holdings: Exhibition Catalogs, Framed Reproductions, Original Documents, Photographs, Prints, Reproductions, Sculpture
Collections: Works by regional, national, & international artists
Exhibitions: 16-18 exhibs per yr
Activities: Classes for adults & children; Docent training; community art school; lects open to pub; 8-10 vis lectrs per yr; gallery talks; tours; sponsoring of competitions; 2 competitions (Nat) per yr; lending of original objects of art (Intra Campus Art Loan Prog); Wataugh & surrounding counties; 1-2 book traveling exhibs per yr; traveling exhibs; 1 per year (varies)

BREVARD

M **BREVARD COLLEGE,** Spiers Gallery, 1 Brevard College Dr, Brevard, NC 28712-4283. Tel 828-884-8188, 828-883-8292, ext 2245; Fax 828-884-3790; Email bbyers@brevard.edu; Web: http://www.brevard.edu/library; *Dir* Bill Byers; *Library Dir* Dr Michael M McCabe
Open Mon - Fri 8 AM - 3 PM; No admis fee; Estab 1969 as art dept with gallery; Center has three areas, 160 ft running space, & 1500 sq ft floor space
Income: Financed by departmental appropriation
Library Holdings: Book Volumes 4500, Exhibition Catalogs, Manuscripts, Original Art Works, Original Documents, Periodical Subscriptions 25, Records, Video Tapes 400
Special Subjects: Pottery, Prints, Watercolors
Collections: Contemporary art, 1940-1970 paintings & watercolors, print & pottery coll
Exhibitions: Student & visiting artist exhibitions
Activities: Classes for adults; dramatic progs; college classes & continuing education; lects open to pub, 4 vis lectrs per yr; 4 gallery talks; competitions with cash awards; schols offered; lending collection contains books, cassettes, color reproductions, film strips, photographs, slides

L **James A Jones Library,** One Brevard College Dr, Brevard, NC 28712-4283. Tel 828-884-8268; Email library@brevard.edu; Web: www.brevard.edu/library; *Library Dir* Michael M McCabe; *Chmn Art* Anne Chapin
Open Mon - Fri 8:30 AM - 5 PM; Estab 1934; For reference & circulation for students & faculty
Income: Financed by parent institution
Library Holdings: Book Volumes 4,725, DVDs 85, Exhibition Catalogs, Periodical Subscriptions 20, Records
Special Subjects: Art History, Ceramics, Graphic Arts, Graphic Design, History of Art & Archaeology, Painting-American, Painting-British, Photography, Sculpture
Publications: New book list, bi-monthly

CARRBORO

M **THE ARTSCENTER,** The Nicholson Gallery at the Arts Center, 300-G Main St, Carrboro, NC 27510. Tel 919-929-2787 ext 201; Fax 919-969-8574; Email info@artscenterlive.org; Web: www.artscenterlive.org; *Exec Dir* Daniel Mayer; *Gallery Coordr* Heather Gevni
Open Nicholson Gallery: Mon - Sat 10 AM - 9 PM; No admis fee except for special events; 1974; Atrium Gallery with new exhibit each month; Average Annual Attendance: 89,000; Mem: 640; $95/yr
Collections: Paintings; photographs; sculpture
Exhibitions: Exhibs change ea month
Activities: Classes for adults & children; dramatic progs; lects open to pub; 6 visiting lectrs per yr; concerts; schols; ArtsCenter honors award; extension prog serves rural Orange County; sales shop sells original art & prints

CARY

M **PAGE-WALKER ARTS & HISTORY CENTER,** 119 Ambassador Loop, Cary, NC 27511; PO Box 8005, Cary, NC 27512-8005. Tel 919-460-4963; Fax 919-388-1141; Email kris.carmichael@townofcary.org; *Supv* Kris Carmichael
Open 10AM - 9PM Mon- Thurs, 10AM-5PM Fri, 10AM-1PM Sat; No admis fee; Estab 1992; Galleries housed in renovated historic hotel (c 1868); Average Annual Attendance: 30,000; Mem: 300
Special Subjects: African Art, Afro-American Art, American Indian Art, American Western Art, Architecture, Etchings & Engravings, Folk Art, Furniture, Glass, Historical Material, Jewelry, Latin American Art, Manuscripts, Maps, Painting-American, Photography, Religious Art, Restorations, Sculpture, Textiles
Exhibitions: Monthly changing exhibs
Activities: Classes for adults & children; dramatic progs; docent training; lects open to pub; 30 vis lectrs per yr; concerts; gallery talks; tours; sponsoring competitions; Books 1-2 traveling exhibs per yr; originate traveling exhibs

CHAPEL HILL

M **UNIVERSITY OF NORTH CAROLINA AT CHAPEL HILL,** Ackland Art Museum, 101 S Columbia St, Chapel Hill, NC 27514; Campus Box 3400, Chapel Hill, NC 27599-3400. Tel 919-966-5736; Fax 919-966-1400; Email ackland@email.unc.edu; Web: www.ackland.org; Others TTY 919-962-0837; *Dir* Katie Ziglar; *Deputy Dir Cur Affairs* Peter Nisbet; *Dir Acad Progs* Carolyn Allmendinger; *Asst Cur for the Coll* Lauren Turner; *Dir Communs* Ariel Fielding; *Public Programs Mgr* Allison P Lathrop; *Store Mgr* Keilayn Skutvik
Open Wed - Sat 10 AM - 5 PM, Sun 1 PM - 5 PM, 2nd Fri of month 10 AM - 9 PM, cl Mon & Tues; No admis fee; Estab 1958 as an art mus which serves the members of the university community as well as the public; The mus houses a permanent collection & presents a program of changing exhibitions; Average Annual Attendance: 60,000; Mem: UNC Student $15; Artist & Educator $30; Individual $50; Household $75; Contributor $125; Patron $250; Benefactor $500; Sponsor $1,000; Leadership $2,500 and above
Income: Financed by endowment, mem, donations & state appropriation
Special Subjects: African Art, Antiquities-Byzantine, Antiquities-Greek, Antiquities-Oriental, Asian Art, Baroque Art, Bronzes, Ceramics, Drawings, Etchings & Engravings, Folk Art, Glass, Islamic Art, Landscapes, Manuscripts, Painting-American, Painting-British, Painting-Dutch, Painting-European, Painting-Flemish, Painting-French
Publications: Newsletter, fall, winter, spring & summer
Activities: Classes for adults & children; free family days; docent training; lects open to pub; concerts; gallery talks; tours; musical performances; individual paintings & original objects of art lent to other mus; organize travelling exhibs vary; mus shop sells books, magazines, original art, reproductions, exhib catalogs, household goods, jewelry & accessories

L **Joseph Curtis Sloane Art Library**, 102 Hanes Art Ctr CB# 3405, Univ of North Carolina at Chapel Hill Chapel Hill, NC 27599-3405. Tel 919-962-2397; Fax 919-962-0722; Email hgendron@email.unc.edu; Email hockensm@email.unc.edu; Web: www.lib.unc.edu/art/index.html; *Art Librn* Heather Gendron; *Libr Technical Asst* Josh Hockensmith
Open Mon - Thurs 8 AM - 9 PM, Fri 8 AM - 5 PM, Sat Noon - 5 PM, Sun 3 - 9 PM; 1985; Circ 19,000
Income: Financed by state appropriation
Library Holdings: Auction Catalogs, Book Volumes 105,000, CD-ROMs 64, Clipping Files, DVDs 60, Exhibition Catalogs, Fiche 15,174, Pamphlets, Periodical Subscriptions, Reels 401, Video Tapes 302
Activities: Bibliographic instruction

CHARLOTTE

A **ARTS & SCIENCE COUNCIL,** 227 W Trade St Ste 250, Charlotte, NC 28202. Tel 704-333-2272; Fax 704-332-2720; Email asc@artsandscience.org; Web: www.artsandscience.org; *Pres* Robert Bush; *Sr VP & COO* Susan Gary; *Develop Officer* Nick Stewart; *VPres Mktg & Communs* Krista Terrell; *Sr VP Cultural & Community Investment* Ryan Deal
Estab 1958 to provide planning, oversight & funding required to ensure & support a vibrant, culturally diverse arts & science community in Mecklenburg County
Income: Financed by government appropriations & private fund drive
Activities: Grants offered

M **BECHTLER MUSEUM OF MODERN ART,** 420 S Tryon St, Charlotte, NC 28202-1937. Tel 704-353-9200; Email info@bechtler.org; Web: bechtler.org; *Pres & CEO* John Boyer; *Dir Commun & Mktg* Sharon Holm
Open Mon 10 AM - 5 PM, Wed - Sat 10 AM - 5 PM, Sun Noon - 5 PM, cl Tues & major holidays; Admis fee adults $8, seniors, teachers & students $6, youth 11-8 $4, children, mem & military free; Estab 2010; Mem: dues $50-$10,000
Collections: Modern & contemporary art
Exhibitions: Temporary exhibits
Activities: Educ progs; lects open to pub; concerts; tours; mus shop sells art related items

M **CLAYWORKS GALLERY,** 4506 Monroe Rd, Charlotte, NC 28205. Tel 704-344-0795; Fax 704-344-0795; Email adellinger@clayworksinc.org; Web: clayworksinc.org; *Exec Dir* Adrienne Dellinger; *Studio Mgr* Kimberly Tyrrell
Gallery by appointment only; Estab 1977 to promote ceramic arts & offer workshops & studio space to artists
Special Subjects: Sculpture, Ceramics
Collections: Handmade sculpture & functional pottery
Exhibitions: Temporary exhibits
Activities: Educ progs; classes for adults & children; workshops

M **DISCOVERY PLACE INC,** Nature Museum, 301 N Tryon St, Charlotte, NC 28202-2138. Tel 704-372-6261 ext 605; Fax 704-333-8948; Web: www.discoveryplace.org; *Pres & CEO* Catherine Wilson Horne; *Chief Mktg Officer* Debra Smul
Open Tues 9 AM - 8 PM, Wed - Fri 9 AM - 4 PM, Sat 9 AM - 5 PM, Sun Noon - 5 PM; Admis adults & children $8, mems and children under 2 yrs free; Estab 1981 as a science museum with hands on concept of learning by doing; A small staff reference library is maintained; Average Annual Attendance: 600,000; Mem: 7000; dues family $70, senior $35, student $30
Income: $7,500,000 (financed by city & county appropriations, fees, sales shop & pvt donations)
Special Subjects: Pre-Columbian Art, Primitive art, Eskimo Art
Collections: Arthropods, gems & minerals, Lepidoptera, Pre-Columbian: Mayan, North American, Peruvian, primitive art: African, Alaskan Eskimo, Oceania, South America, reptilia
Publications: Science Magazine, quarterly; activities bulletin, quarterly
Activities: Classes for adults & children; volunteer training prog for demonstrators & guides; major programming for school lects; tours; acceptable for internship from UNCC & Queens College; book traveling exhibs 4 per yr; originate traveling exhibs that circulate to science mus collaborations; mus shop sells books, prints, shells, jewelry, school supplies & souvenirs; junior mus is primarily geared to pre-school and early elementary age children

M **ELDER GALLERY,** 1520 S Tryon St, Charlotte, NC 28203. Tel 704-370-6337; Email info@eldergalleryclt.com; Web: www.elderart.com; *Owner & Creative Dir* Sonya Pfeiffer
Tues - Fri 11 AM - 6 PM, Sat 11 AM - 5 PM; Estab to unite the community through art
Collections: Fine glass art & paintings
Exhibitions: Temporary exhibits

M **HARVEY B GANTT CENTER FOR AFRICAN AMERICAN ARTS + CULTURE,** 551 S Tryon St, Charlotte, NC 28202. Tel 704-547-3700; Email info@ganttcenter.org; Web: www.ganttcenter.org; *Pres & CEO* David Taylor; *COO* Bonita Buford; *Exec Admin Asst* Gloria Leguillow-Torres; *Dir Develop* Witnie A Martinez; *Colls & Exhibs Mgr* Alexys Taylor
Open Tues - Sat 10 AM - 5 PM, Sun 1 PM - 5 PM, cl Mon; Admis adults $9, college students, military, seniors & youth (6-17) $7, youth under 6 & mem free; Estab 1974 to present excellence in the art, history & culture of African-Americans & those of African descent; 46,500 sq ft; architectural references to African & African-American history; Mem: Dues $35 - $10,000
Collections: The John and Vivian Hewitt Collection of African-American Art
Exhibitions: Temporary exhibits
Activities: Educ progs; classes for adults & children; family progs; Artist talks; tours; art programming; symposiums; workshops; film screenings; cultural events

M **JERALD MELBERG GALLERY,** 625 S Sharon Amity Rd, Charlotte, NC 28211-2811. Tel 704-365-3000; Email gallery@jeraldmelberg.com; Web: www.jeraldmelberg.com; *Dir* Jerald Melberg
Open Mon - Fri 10 AM - 6 PM, Sat 10 AM - 4 PM; Estab 1983; Classic contemporary art on two parallel tracks: mid-career & well established living artists, incl Wolf Kahn & Robert Kushner. Also exhib important 20th cen estates, incl Robert Motherwell & Romare Bearden
Special Subjects: Afro-American Art, Drawings, Painting-American, Painting-Spanish, Prints
Publications: Writing catalogue raisome on Romare Bearden graphic works
Activities: Lects open to pub; 5 vis lectrs per yr; gallery talks y artists & Jerald Melberg; Lend art to museums & Art In Embassies; organize traveling exhibs to mus & galleries & other non-profit arts institutions

M **THE LIGHT FACTORY,** 1817 Central Ave, Charlotte, NC 28205. Tel 704-333-9755; Fax 704-333-5910; Email info@lightfactory.org; Web: www.lightfactory.org; *Exec Dir* Kay Tuttle; *Dir Educ* Laurie Schorr
Open Wed - Sat noon - 6 PM; No admis fee, donations accepted; Estab 1972, non-collecting mus presenting the latest in photography, video & the internet. Year-round educ programs, community outreach & special events complement its changing exhibitions; Average Annual Attendance: 30,000; Mem: 400; dues $35 - $100
Income: Financed by grants, NEA, memberships, Arts & Sci Council
Exhibitions: Rotating
Publications: Exhibit catalogs
Activities: Classes for adults & children; lects open to pub, 3 vis lectrs per yr; gallery talks; tours; scholarships offered; originate traveling exhibs to museums & galleries nationally

M **THE MINT MUSEUM,** 2730 Randolph Rd, Charlotte, NC 28207-2012. Tel 704-337-2000, 337-2020; Fax 704-337-2101; Email info@mintmuseum.org; Web: www.mintmuseum.org; *Pres & CEO* Dr. Todd Herman; *COO & CFO* Gary Blankemeyer; *Dir Craft, Design & Fashion* Annie Carlano; *Chief Art Servs & Installation* Ian Larson; *Cur Decorative Arts* Brian Gallagher; *Dir Library & Archives* Joyce Weaver; *Chief Registrar* Katherine Steiner
Open Wed 11 AM - 9 PM, Thurs - Sat 10 AM - 5 PM, Sun 1 PM - 5 PM, cl Mon, Tues & holidays; Admis adults $15, college students & seniors $10, children (5-17) $6, children 4 & under free; Estab 1936 as an art mus in what was the first branch of the US mint erected in 1837; Mus houses seven changing galleries, 16 permanent galleries, Delhom Decorative Arts Gallery; Average Annual Attendance: 135,000; Mem: 5,350; dues Mint Master $1000, benefactor $500, sustainer $250, patron $125, school teacher $45, individual $60, senior citizen or student discounted
Income: Financed by endowment, mem & city appropriation, foundation & corporate giving
Special Subjects: African Art, Afro-American Art, American Indian Art, Antiquities-Assyrian, Antiquities-Byzantine, Antiquities-Oriental, Antiquities-Persian, Antiquities-Roman, Architecture, Asian Art, Baroque Art, Calligraphy, Ceramics, Collages, Costumes, Crafts, Decorative Arts, Drawings, Enamels, Etchings & Engravings, Painting-French, Painting-German, Painting-Italian, Painting-Japanese, Painting-Russian, Painting-Spanish, Period Rooms, Photography, Porcelain, Portraits
Collections: African art, decorative arts, historic pottery, 19th & 20th century European & American paintings, porcelain, pre-Columbian art, sculpture, Spanish Colonial art
Exhibitions: Rotating exhibits
Publications: Mint Museum Newsletter and calendar of events, six times a year
Activities: Classes for adults; docent training; lects open to pub, 25 vis lectrs per yr; concerts; gallery talks; tours; competitions; schols & fels offered; original objects of art lent to other mus; mus shop selling books, original art, prints, gifts, museum replicas, jewelry, cards

L **Art Organization & Library**, 2730 Randolph Rd, Charlotte, NC 28207-2012. Tel 704-337-2000; Fax 704-337-2101; Email info@mintmuseum.org; Web: www.mintmuseum.org; *Interim Pres & CEO* Bruce Larowe; *COO & CFO* Gary Blankenmeyer; *Sr Cur American, Modern & Contemporary Art* Dr Jonathan Stuhlman; *Dir Craft Design* Annie Carlano
Open Tues 10 AM - 9 PM, Wed - Sat 10 AM - 6 PM, Sun 1 -5 PM, cl Mon; Admis members free, adults $10, seniors (65+) $8, college students $8, students (5-17) $5, 4 yr & under free, & free Tues 5 PM - 9 PM; Estab 1936; Mem: dues: teachers & students $45, individuals $60, dual $80, family $100, supporting mems available from $250-$10,000
Library Holdings: Auction Catalogs, Book Volumes 18,000, CD-ROMs, Clipping Files, Exhibition Catalogs, Original Documents, Other Holdings, Periodical Subscriptions 100

Special Subjects: Aesthetics, Afro-American Art, American Indian Art, Art Education, Art History, Ceramics, Coins & Medals, Crafts, Decorative Arts, Fashion Arts, Glass, Jewelry, Metalwork, Painting-American, Photography, Pre-Columbian Art, Prints
Collections: American Art; Contemporary Art; Decorative Arts; Historic Costumes; Ancient American Art; Craft & Design
Activities: Classes for adults & children; dramatic progs; docent training; lects open to pub; concerts; gallery talks; tours; Spirit awards; fels; outreach progs for schools & community; lend original objects of art to other mus; mus shop sells books, magazines, original art, reproductions, prints, jewelry, cards & gifts

M **Mint Museum of Craft & Design**, 2730 Randolph Rd, Charlotte, NC 28202-2137. Tel 704-337-2000; Fax 704-337-2101; Email info@mintmuseum.org; Web: www.mintmuseum.org; *Dir* Annie Carlano; *Asst Cur* Allie Farlowe; *Cur Asst* Emily Pazar
Open Tues, Wed, Thurs, Fri & Sat 10 AM - 5 PM, cl Sun & Mon; Admis adults $10, seniors & students $8, children 5-17 $5, members & children 4 & under free; Estab 1999; 82,000 sq ft total with 16,000 sq ft of gallery space, 26,000 sq ft of commercial rental space & 40,000 sq ft for offices, storage, workshop & museum shop; Average Annual Attendance: 150,000
Purchases: Works by Stanislav Libinsky & Jarsolava Brychtova
Library Holdings: Auction Catalogs, Book Volumes, CD-ROMs, Exhibition Catalogs, Kodachrome Transparencies, Original Documents, Other Holdings, Periodical Subscriptions, Photographs, Records, Slides, Video Tapes
Special Subjects: Ceramics, Crafts, Decorative Arts, Furniture, Glass, Historical Material, Jewelry, Metalwork, Porcelain, Pottery, Sculpture, Woodcarvings, African Art, Costumes, Painting-American
Collections: Bresler Collection of Historic Am Quilts, Allan Chasanoff Ceramic Collection, Jane & Arthur Mason Collection, Founders' Circle Collection, Grice Native American Ceramic Collection
Exhibitions: Turning Wood into Art: The Jane and Arthur Mason Collection; Selections from the Allan Chasanoff Ceramic Collection
Activities: Classes for adults & children; docent training; lects open to pub; lects open to members only; gallery talks; tours; Purchase awards; fels offered; lending of original objects of art to mus; originates traveling exhibs; mus shop sells books, crafts, jewelry, original art, reproductions, prints & posters, clothing items

M **Mint Museum Uptown**, Levine Center for the Arts, 500 S Tryon St Charlotte, NC 28202-1811. Tel 704-337-2000; Web: www.mintmuseum.org
Open Wed 11 AM - 9 PM, Thurs - Sat 11 AM - 6 PM; Sun 1 PM - 5 PM; Admis adults $15, students & seniors $10, children 5-17 $6, children 4 & under free
Collections: American & European contemporary art, craft & design collection

M **NEW GALLERY OF MODERN ART,** 435 S Tryon St, Ste 110 Charlotte, NC 28202. Tel 704-373-1464; Email info@newgalleryofmodernart.com; Web: newgalleryofmodernart.com; *Dir* Irina Toshkova
Open Tues - Fri 10 AM - 6 PM, Sat 11 AM - 5 PM, Sun & Mon by appt only; No admis fee; Estab 2011
Special Subjects: Etchings & Engravings, Woodcuts, Prints, Painting-American
Collections: Paintings
Activities: Art progs; art lects & discussions, book signings; corp art loan/purchase prog

M **PROVIDENCE GALLERY,** 601 A Providence Rd, Charlotte, NC 28207. Tel 704-334-4535; Fax 704-333-3726; Email providenceframes@bellsouth.net; Web: www.providencegallery.net; *Senior Design Consultant* Rod Wimer; *Sales Assoc* Tonya Jay
Open Mon - Fri 9 AM - 6 PM, Sat 10 AM - 2 PM; No admis fee; Estab 1978; Representing 30 local & regional artists
Activities: Four vis lectrs per yr

L **PUBLIC LIBRARY OF CHARLOTTE & MECKLENBURG COUNTY,** 310 N Tryon St, Charlotte, NC 28202-2139. Tel 704-416-0100; Fax 704-336-2677; Email infoserv@plcmc.lib.nc.us; Web: www.plcmc.org; *Dir* David Singleton
Open Mon - Thurs 9 AM - 9 PM, Fri & Sat 9 AM - 6 PM, Sun 1 - 6 PM, cl Sun June - Aug; No admis fee; Estab 1903 to provide free public library service to citizens of Mecklenburg County; Gallery contains 90 linear feet of wall space, often dedicated to children's art; "L" Gallery with quarterly changing exhibits
Income: $10.9 million (financed by state & county appropriations)
Library Holdings: Audio Tapes, Book Volumes 1,615,682, CD-ROMs, Cassettes, Compact Disks, DVDs, Filmstrips, Motion Pictures 2772, Other Holdings Maps 6865, Prints 424, Records 27,869, Sculpture, Slides 9261, Video Tapes
Exhibitions: Theme exhibitions changing quarterly dedicated to children's art
Activities: Computer learning center accessible to people with physical & mental disabilities

M **SHAIN GALLERY,** 2823 Selwyn Ave, Charlotte, NC 28209. Tel 703-334-7744; Fax 704-334-7754; Email shainart@earthlink.net; Web: www.shaingallery.com; *Owner* Gabrielle Shain-Bryson; *Dir* Sybil Godwin
Open Tues - Sat 10 AM - 5 PM or by appointment; No admis fee; Estab 1998; Original fine art

A **SPIRIT SQUARE CENTER FOR ARTS & EDUCATION,** 345 N College St, Charlotte, NC 28202-2113. Tel 704-372-9664; Fax 704-377-9808; *Pres* Tomn Gabbard
Open Mon - Fri, 8 AM - 5 PM; Estab 1983; 5000 sq ft for six art galleries; Average Annual Attendance: 20,000
Income: $3,000,000 (financed by mem, city & state appropriation & local arts drive)
Activities: Classes for adults & children; dramatic progs; docent training; lects open to pub, 18 vis lectrs per yr; concerts; gallery talks; tours; schols; artmobile; mus shop sells books & original art

CONCORD

M **SAM BASS GALLERY,** 6104 Performance Dr, Concord, NC 28207-3435. Tel 704-455-6915; Fax 704-455-6916; Email info@sambass.com; Web: www.sambass.com; *Exec Dir* Carrie Cardinale; *Graphic Arts Designer & PR Mgr* Ashton Starnes
Open Tues - Fri 10 AM - 12:30 & 1:30 PM - 5 PM
Collections: Sam Bass' artwork
Exhibitions: Permanent exhibits

CORNELIUS

M **THE COMMUNITY ARTS PROJECT GALLERY,** 19725 Oak St, Unit 1 Cornelius, NC 28031-5705; PO Box 1166, Davidson, NC 28036-1166. Tel 704-892-7323; Web: www.creativeartexchange.org
Open Mon - Thurs 9 AM - 5 PM, Fri - Sat 9 AM - 12 PM
Exhibitions: Temporary exhibits
Activities: Classes for adults & children; art programming

DALLAS

M **GASTON COUNTY MUSEUM OF ART & HISTORY,** 131 W Main St, Dallas, NC 28034-2021; PO Box 429, Dallas, NC 28034-2021. Tel 704-922-7681; Fax 704-922-7683; Email museum@co-gaston.nc.us; Web: www.gastoncountymuseum.org; *Dir* Elizabeth Dampier; *Progs Coordr* Jeff Pruett; *Registrar* Regan Brooks
Open Tues - Fri 10 AM - 5 PM, Sat 1 - 5 PM, every 4th Sun 2 - 5 PM; No admis fee; Estab 1975, opened 1976 to promote the fine arts & local history in Gaston County, through classes, workshops & exhibitions; to preserve Historic Dallas Square; promote the history of the textile industry; The mus is located in an 1852 Hoffman Hotel; the Hands-On Gallery includes sculpture & weaving which may be touched; the two small galleries are on local history, with three galleries for changing & traveling exhibitions; Average Annual Attendance: 53,000; Mem: 300 households; dues $15-$1000; annual meeting in Oct, with 6 meetings per year
Income: $345,000 (financed by mem & county appropriation)
Purchases: $1000 per yr for regional art
Special Subjects: Painting-American, Sculpture, Textiles
Collections: Period furniture, documents, 19th - 20th century American art, objects of local history, paintings by regional artists, 450,000 documented photographs, textile history
Publications: Patchworks quarterly
Activities: Classes for adults & children; docent training; lect open to public, 2 vis lectrs per year; gallery talks, tours; Getaway Sunday, Blues Outback summer concert series, summer drop in day camp; book traveling exhibitions 2 per year; sales shop sells books, magazines, original art, reproductions, prints, stationery, postcards, gifts & jewelry

DAVIDSON

M **DAVIDSON COLLEGE,** William H Van Every Jr & Edward M Smith Galleries, 315 N Main St, Davidson, NC 28036-9404; PO Box 7117, Davidson, NC 28035-7117. Tel 704-894-2519; Fax 704-894-2691; Email linewman@davidson.edu; Web: www.davidson.edu; *Dir* Lia Newman
Open Mon - Fri 10 AM - 5 PM, Sat & Sun Noon - 4 PM, cl holidays; No admis fee; Estab 1993 to provide exhibitions of educational importance; William H Van Every Jr Gallery-1400 sq ft; Edward M Smith Gallery-400 sq ft; Average Annual Attendance: 10,000
Income: $32,000
Special Subjects: Afro-American Art, Architecture, Asian Art, Ceramics, Collages, Drawings, Embroidery, Etchings & Engravings, Ethnology, Folk Art, Hispanic Art, Historical Material, Latin American Art, Mexican Art, Painting-American, Primitive art, Prints, Sculpture, Textiles, Watercolors, Woodcarvings, Woodcuts
Collections: Over 3,200 works, mainly graphics, from all periods, Contemporary Art, campus sculpture prog
Publications: Exhibition brochures & catalogs, 3-5 per year
Activities: Intern training; lect open to public, 5-7 vis lectrs per year; gallery talks; tours; scholarships offered; individual paintings & original objects of art lent

L **Katherine & Tom Belk Visual Arts Center**, PO Box 7117, Visual Resources Collection Davidson, NC 28035-7117. Tel 704-894-2590; Email jeerickson@davidson.edu; Web: www.davidson.edu/personal/jeerickson/jeerick1.htm; *Visual Resources Cur* Jeffrey Erickson
Estab 1993; Open to students, faculty & staff of the college
Library Holdings: Slides 65,000
Collections: Slide & digital images

DURHAM

M **DUKE UNIVERSITY,** Nasher Museum of Art at Duke University, 2001 Campus Dr, Durham, NC 27705; PO Box 90732, Durham, NC 27708-0732. Tel 919-684-5135; Fax 919-681-8624; Email nasherinfo@duke.edu; Web: www.nasher.duke.edu; *Dir* Sarah Schroth; *Chief Cur& Cur Contemporary Art* Trevor Schoonmaker
Open Tues, Wed, Fri, Sat 10 AM - 5 PM, Thurs 10 AM -10 PM, Sun noon - 5 PM, cl Mon, New Year's Day, Independence Day, Thanksgiving, Christmas Eve, Christmas Day; Admis gen $5, seniors, mems Duke Alumni Assn with mem card $4, non-Duke students with ID $3, children 16 & younger, Duke Univ students, faculty & staff with ID & Durham city residents free; Estab 1969 as a study mus with the collections being used & studied by various university departments, as well as the pub school system & surrounding communities; The museum is located on the East Campus in a renovated two-story neo-Georgian building; gallery space includes part of the first floor & entire second floor with the space divided into eight major gallery areas; Average Annual Attendance: 30,000; Mem: 850; dues $35 - $1000
Income: Financed by University
Special Subjects: African Art, Decorative Arts, Medieval Art, Painting-European, Painting-Russian, Pre-Columbian Art, Renaissance Art, Etchings & Engravings

Collections: African, Contemporary Russian, Greek & Roman, Medieval decorative art & sculpture, paintings, Pre-Columbian, ceramics & textiles, American paintings, Old Masters
Exhibitions: 3-4 temporary exhibitions per year
Publications: Exhibition catalogs 1-2 per year
Activities: Educ dept; docent training; tours; competitions with awards; lects open to pub, 6-8 vis lectrs per yr; concerts; gallery talks; tours; scholarships offered; individual paintings & original objects of art lent to other mus & galleries; lending collection contains paintings & sculpture; book traveling exhibs 1-3 per yr; originate traveling exhibs to other mus 1-2 per yr; mus shop sells books

L **Lilly Art Library**, PO Box 90727, Durham, NC 27708-0727. Tel 919-660-5995; Fax 919-660-5999; Email lilly-requests@duke.edu; Web: www.lib.duke.edu/lilly/artsearch/home.htm; *Art Librn* Lee Sorensen
Open 8 AM - 2 AM; No admis fee; Estab 1930 to support the study of art at Duke University
Income: Financed by budget & endowment
Purchases: $85,000 excluding approval plan expenditure
Library Holdings: Book Volumes 155,000, CD-ROMs, Cards, Clipping Files, Compact Disks, DVDs, Exhibition Catalogs, Fiche, Motion Pictures, Pamphlets 5125, Periodical Subscriptions 416, Reels, Video Tapes
Special Subjects: Afro-American Art, American Western Art, Architecture, Art History, Graphic Arts, History of Art & Archaeology, Judaica, Painting-American, Painting-British, Painting-Dutch, Painting-European, Painting-Flemish, Painting-French, Painting-German, Painting-Italian
Collections: Emphasis on European & American Art, Germanic-Language Historiography
Publications: Duke University Libraries, quarterly

L **DUKE UNIVERSITY LIBRARY,** Hartman Center for Sales, Advertising & Marketing History, Box 90185, Durham, NC 27708-0185. Tel 919-660-5827; Fax 919-660-5934; Email hartman-center@duke.edu; Web: library.duke.edu/specialcollections/hartman; *Reference Archivist* Lynn Eaton; *Dir* Jacqueline Reid
Open Mon - Fri 9 AM - 5 PM, Sat 1 - 5 PM; No admis fee; Estab 1992; Open to acad, bus, general pub, for on-premises use. Fees charged for extended research by staff
Library Holdings: Audio Tapes, Book Volumes 3000, Cassettes, Clipping Files, Filmstrips, Kodachrome Transparencies, Manuscripts, Memorabilia, Motion Pictures, Original Art Works, Original Documents, Other Holdings Advertising Proofs & Tearsheets, Pamphlets, Photographs, Records, Reels, Slides, Video Tapes
Special Subjects: Advertising Design, Commercial Art, Historical Material, Illustration, Manuscripts, Graphic Arts, Graphic Design
Collections: DMB&B Archives, Outdoor Advertising Assn of America (OAAA) Archives, J Walter Thompson Co Archives, billboards, print advertising, TV commercials
Publications: Front & Center, semiannual newsletter

M **DUKE UNIVERSITY UNION,** Louise Jones Brown Gallery, 036 Bryan Center, 125 Science Dr Durham, NC 27708; PO Box 90834, Durham, NC 27708-0834. Tel 919-684-2323, 919-684-2911; Fax 919-684-8395; Email lisa.gao@duke.edu; Web: www.duuvisarts.org, www.union.duke.edu; *Visual Arts Comt Chair* Justin M Sandulli; *Program Coordr & Visual Arts Comt Advisor* Allison Shumar
Open Mon - Fri 9 AM - 9 PM, Sat - Sun 10 AM - 6 PM; No admis fee; Founded in 1968 under the name Graphic Arts, the DUU Visual Arts Comt is dedicated to promoting the presence of the visual arts on the Duke Univ campus; Two 15X15 sq rooms with 7'2" high walls; these two rooms are connected by two bridges. The gallery is situated in the student union of Duke Univ; Average Annual Attendance: 500+; Mem: 30; bi-weekly meetings
Income: Financed by endowment, commission on exhibit works sold & student fees
Exhibitions: Professional & local artists, approx 4 per semester (1 in each gallery); plus Duke student artists in 1 gallery monthly; Occasional collaborations with student organizations, local artists, etc
Activities: Classes for adults; lects open to pub, 1 vis lectr per yr; competitions; gallery talks

M **DURHAM ART GUILD,** 120 Morris St, Durham, NC 27701-3230. Tel 919-560-2713; Fax 919-560-2704; Email director@durhamartguild.org; Web: www.durhamartguild.org; *Dir* Taj Forer
Open Mon - Sat 9 AM - 9 PM, Sun 1 - 6 PM; No admis fee; Estab 1948 to exhibit work of NC artists; 3600 sq ft gallery located in Arts Council Building; Average Annual Attendance: 15,000; Mem: 400; dues $25; annual member show in June
Income: $72,000 (financed by mem, city & state appropriations)
Special Subjects: Crafts, Etchings & Engravings, Furniture, Landscapes, Metalwork, Photography, Portraits, Prints, Sculpture, Textiles
Exhibitions: Exhibitions of work by regional artists, 20+ per year; annual juried art show
Publications: Juried Show Catalogue, annual
Activities: 1 vis lectr per yr; receptions; competitions with awards, special proposals accepted

M **THE HAYTI HERITAGE CENTER,** Lyda Moore Merrick Gallery, 804 Old Fayetteville St, Durham, NC 27701-3958. Tel 919-683-1709; Fax 919-682-5869; Email info@hayti.org; Web: www.hayti.org

M **NORTH CAROLINA CENTRAL UNIVERSITY,** NCCU Art Museum, 1801 Fayetteville St, Durham, NC 27707; PO Box 19555, Durham, NC 27707-0021. Tel 919-530-6211; Fax 919-560-5649; Web: web.nccu.edu/artmuseum/; *Dir* Kenneth G Rodgers
Open winter Tues - Fri 8 AM - 5 PM, Sun 2 - 5 PM, summer Mon - Fri 8:30 AM - 4:30 PM; No admis fee; Estab 1971 in a former black teaching institution with a collection of contemporary art, many Afro-American artists, reflecting diversity in style, technique, medium & subject; Three galleries are maintained; one houses the permanent collection & two are for changing shows; Average Annual Attendance: 10,500
Income: Financed by state appropriation
Special Subjects: African Art, Painting-American, Sculpture
Collections: African & Oceanic, Contemporary American with a focus on minority artists
Exhibitions: Rotating exhibits
Publications: Artis, Bearden & Burke: A Bibliography & Illustrations List; exhibition catalogs
Activities: Lect open to public; gallery talks; tours

FAYETTEVILLE

M **ARTS COUNCIL OF FAYETTEVILLE-CUMBERLAND COUNTY,** The Arts Center, 301 Hay St, Fayetteville, NC 28301-5535; PO Box 318, Fayetteville, NC 28302-0318. Tel 910-323-1776; Fax 910-323-1727; Email admin@theartscouncil.com; Web: www.TheArtsCouncil.com; *Exec Dir* Deborah Mintz; *Exhibits Coordr* Kelvin Culbreth; *Gen Mgr* Nancy Silver
Open Mon - Thurs 8:30 AM - 5 PM, Fri 8:30 AM - Noon, Sat Noon - 4 PM; No admis fee; Estab 1973 to nurture, celebrate & advocate all of the arts in Cumberland County; Main gallery & featured artist gallery; Average Annual Attendance: 60,000; Mem: 575
Income: Financed by contributions, grants & taxes
Special Subjects: African Art, Afro-American Art, American Indian Art, Architecture, Collages, Crafts, Decorative Arts, Dolls, Drawings, Glass, Hispanic Art, Judaica, Juvenile Art, Landscapes, Leather, Manuscripts, Mexican Art, Military Art, Oriental Art, Painting-American, Photography, Portraits, Posters, Pottery, Sculpture
Exhibitions: exhibitions for local and area residents
Publications: monthly newsletter
Activities: Arts educ prog; artists in schools progs; Duke nonprofit management courses; awards for annual juried competitions; local grants offered, grants for artists, workshops, assemblies & residencies; school tours of exhibits; book traveling exhibs

GREENSBORO

M **AFRICAN AMERICAN ATELIER,** 200 N Davis St, Box 14 Greensboro, NC 27401. Tel 336-333-6885; Fax 336-373-4826; Email info@africanamericanatelier.org; Web: www.africanamericanatelier.org
Open Tues - Sat Noon - 7 PM, Sun 2 PM - 5 PM; No admis fee; Estab 1991 to promote awareness, appreciation & sensitivity to the visual arts & culture of African Americans & work in harmony with other ethnic groups
Special Subjects: African Art, Afro-American Art, Ceramics, Collages, Dolls, Drawings, Photography, Portraits, Posters, Prints, Sculpture, Tapestries
Collections: African American history & culture; paintings; photographs
Activities: Classes for adults & children; lects open to pub; gallery talks; tours; mus shop sells books, original art, reproductions & prints

A **THE CENTER FOR VISUAL ARTISTS - GREENSBORO,** 200 N Davie St, Box 13, Greensboro, NC 27401. Tel 336-333-7475 (Office); 333-7485 (Gallery); Fax 336-333-7477; Email info@greensboroart.org; Web: www.greensboroart.org; *Gallery Cur* Kristy Thomas; *Educ Coordr* Sidney Stretz
Open Tues - Fri Noon - 7 PM, Sat Noon - 5 PM, Sun 2 PM - 5 PM, cl Mon; No admis fee; Estab 1956 to encourage local artists to show & sell their works; Exhibitions gallery located in the Greensboro Cultural Center, a nonprofit contemporary art gallery featuring emerging local artists; Average Annual Attendance: 100,000; Mem: 500
Income: $110,000
Exhibitions: All mem exhibs; student art & design exhib; solo exhib; invitational exhib; holiday show; Dirty Fingernails; Trash exhib; photography exhibition; skate art show; typography exhib
Publications: Monthly newsletter
Activities: Classes & workshops for adults & children; summer camps for children ages 3 - 15; afterschool & outreach progs; gallery tours; schols offered; exten dept; originate traveling exhibs 1 per yr

M **GREEN HILL CENTER FOR NORTH CAROLINA ART,** Greenhill, 200 N Davie St, Greensboro, NC 27401-2819. Tel 336-333-7460; Fax 336-333-2612; Email info@greenhillnc.org; Web: www.greenhillnc.org; *Exec Dir* Laura Way; *Dir Curatorial & Artistic Progs* Edie Carpenter; *Dir Educ* Jaymie Meyer; *Mktg & Design Specialist* Lauren Gordon; *Art Educator & Volunteer Coordr* Laura Maruzella; *Shop Mgr & Registrar* Elizabeth Harry; *Curatorial Asst* Rachel Siminoski; *Guest Servs Coordr* Imani Barnes; *Guest Servs Coord* Delois Bynum; *Office Mgr & Bookkeeper* Lisa Bunch
Open Tues - Fri Noon - 7 PM, Sat Noon - 5 PM, Sun 2 - 5 PM, cl Mon & legal holidays; No admis fee, donation suggested; Art Quest $6 per person, members no charge; Estab & incorporated 1974 as a nonprofit institution offering exhibition & educational programming featuring the visual arts of North Carolina; Nonprofit visual arts ctr promoting the visual arts of NC through dynamic exhibs & educ progs; Average Annual Attendance: 40,000; Mem: 500; dues $35-$5000
Income: Financed by mem, Arts Greensboro, North Carolina Arts Council, grants, donations & sales
Publications: Catalogues; quarterly newsletter
Activities: Classes for adults & children; docent training; artists-in-the-schools prog; hands-on studio; lects open to pub; lect for members only; gallery talks; tours; exten prog serves primarily Guilford County, NC; originate traveling exhibs internationally; mus shop sells books & original works of art & craft

M **GREENSBORO COLLEGE,** Irene Cullis Gallery, 815 W Market St, Greensboro, NC 27401-1875. Tel 336-272-7102; Fax 336-271-6634; Email langerj@greensboro.edu; Web: www.art.gborocollege.edu/gallery.html; *Gallery Cur & Chmn Dept Art* James V Langer
Open Mon - Fri 9 AM - 5 PM; Estab to exhibit visual art by visiting professional artists, Greensboro College art students & faculty; College art gallery
Exhibitions: Scholastic High School Competition, February

M **GUILFORD COLLEGE,** Guilford College Art Gallery, 5800 W Friendly Ave, Greensboro, NC 27410-4173. Tel 336-316-2251, 336-316-2438; Fax 336-316-2950;

Email thammond@guilford.edu; Web: www.guilford.edu/artgallery; *Dir & Cur* Theresa Hammond
Open Mon - Fri 9 AM - 5 PM, Sun 2 - 5 PM during acad yr, cl holidays; Atrium areas open during library hrs; No admis fee; Estab 1990; 5000 sq ft of exhibition space located in Hege Library
Special Subjects: Baroque Art, Calligraphy, Coins & Medals, Drawings, Etchings & Engravings, Glass, Painting-American, Painting-Italian, Photography, Prints, Renaissance Art, Religious Art, Sculpture, Watercolors, Woodcuts, African Art, Ceramics, Graphics, Landscapes
Collections: Contemporary American Crafts, Contemporary Polish etching & engraving, Renaissance & Baroque Period Collection, 20th Century American Art, 19th & 20th Century African, Maness Collection of West and Central African Art
Activities: Lect open to public; gallery talks; tours; book traveling exhibitions 1-2 per year

M **UNIVERSITY OF NORTH CAROLINA AT GREENSBORO,** Weatherspoon Art Museum, Spring Garden & Tate St, Greensboro, NC 27402; PO Box 26170, Greensboro, NC 27402-6170. Tel 336-334-5770; Fax 336-334-5907; Email weatherspoon@uncg.edu; Web: weatherspoon.uncg.edu; *Cur Coll* Elaine D Gustafson; *Cur Educ* Ann Grimaldi; *Pub & Community Relations* Loring Mortensen; *Dir* Nancy Doll; *Cur of Exhib* Emily Stamey; *Registrar* Kim Terbush; *Preparator* Susan Taaffe; *Preparator* Shane Carrico; *Accnt* Valerie McConnell; *Chief Security* Brad Young; *Assoc Cur of Educ* Terri Dowell-Dennis; *Security Officer* Kenneth Crane
Open Tues, Wed & Fri 10 AM - 5 PM, Thurs 10 AM - 9 PM, Sat & Sun 1 - 5 PM, cl Mon, university holidays; No admis fee; Estab 1941; Circ Ca 400; The museum collects & presents modern & contemporary art; 6 galleries, 46,271 sq ft; Average Annual Attendance: 36,000; Mem: 600; dues $35 & up; annual meeting in May
Income: State of NC, UNCG, individuals, foundations, government grants & endowment
Purchases: Acquisition endowments
Library Holdings: Auction Catalogs, Exhibition Catalogs, Pamphlets
Special Subjects: Afro-American Art, Asian Art, Drawings, Latin American Art, Painting-American, Photography, Prints, Sculpture
Collections: Modern & Contemporary American paintings, drawings, prints & sculpture, Dillard Collection: Works on Paper, Cone Collection: Matisse prints & bronzes, Lenoir C. Wright Collection of Japanese Woodblock Prints
Publications: Art on Paper Catalogue, biannually; exhibition catalogues, gallery handouts; Matisse brochure; 3 per yr member newsletter; Weatherspoon Art Museum bulletin, biannually
Activities: Classes for adults; docent training; member progs; trips to national art centers; lects open to pub, 50 vis lectrs per yr; concerts; gallery talks; tours; children's programs; exhib related film & video; opening receptions & special events; volunteer opportunities; lend original objects of art nationally & internationally; originate traveling exhibs to mus across the country; mus shop sells books, prints, gifts, exhib related items & jewelry

GREENVILLE

M **EAST CAROLINA UNIVERSITY,** Wellington B Gray Gallery, 1000 E 5th St, Leo Jenkins Fine Arts Center (Rm 200) Greenville, NC 27858-4353. Tel 252-328-6336; Fax 252-328-6441; Email braswellg@ecu.edu; Web: www.ecu.edu/graygallery; *Dir* Tom Braswell; *Admin Asst* Susan Nicholls
Open Mon - Fri 10 AM - 4 PM, Sat 10 AM - 2 PM yr round, cl university holidays; No admis fee; Estab 1977, the Gallery presents 10 exhibitions annually of contemporary art in various media. Understanding of exhibitions is strengthened by educational programs including lectures, workshops, symposia & guided tours; The gallery is a 6000 sq ft facility; Average Annual Attendance: 23,000; Mem: Art Enthusiasts Group $25
Income: Financed by state appropriation, Art Enthusiasts of Eastern Carolina, state & federal grants, corporate & foundation donations
Special Subjects: African Art, Afro-American Art, American Indian Art, American Western Art, Anthropology, Folk Art, Hispanic Art, Latin American Art, Mexican Art, Painting-American
Collections: African art 1000 works, Larry Rivers: The Boston Massacre - Color Lithographs, Baltic States Ceramic Collection
Publications: Anders Knuttson: Light Paintings; The Dream World of Minnie Evans; Jacob Lawrence: An American Master; exhibition catalogs
Activities: Classes for adults & children; lects open to public, 20 vis lectrs per yr; workshops & symposia; gallery talks; sponsoring of competitions; 5 $1,000 awards; photog image exhib; scholarships offered; individual paintings & original objects of art lent; originate traveling exhibs

L **Media Center,** Jenkins Fine Arts Ctr, Rm 2000 Mail Stop 502 Greenville, NC 27858-4353. Tel 252-328-6785; Fax 252-328-6441; Email adamsk@mail.ecu.edu; Web: www.ecu.edu; *Dir* Kelly Adams
Open daily 8 AM - 5 PM; Estab 1977 for Art School study of current & selected periodicals & selected reference books & slides; For lending & reference
Library Holdings: Audio Tapes, Book Volumes 3500, Cards, Cassettes, Exhibition Catalogs, Filmstrips, Manuscripts, Micro Print 30, Motion Pictures, Periodical Subscriptions 62, Prints, Slides 80,000, Video Tapes

A **GREENVILLE MUSEUM OF ART, INC,** 802 S Evans St, Greenville, NC 27834. Tel 252-758-1946; Email info@gmoa.org; Web: www.gmoa.org; *Exec Dir* Ned Puhner; *Colls & Exhibs Mgr* Paige Hackler
Open Tues - Fri 10 AM - 4:30 PM, Sat 1 PM - 4 PM, cl major holidays; No admis fee; donations accepted; Estab 1939, incorporated in 1956, to foster pub interest in art & to form a permanent collection; Six galleries 2000 sq ft including a children's gallery; Average Annual Attendance: 17,000; Mem: 600; dues $45 & higher; annual meeting in Spring
Income: $100,000 (financed by plus Foundation income for acquisition of art, contributions, mem, appropriations & grants)
Collections: 20th century contemporary paintings, drawings, graphics, regional & national, North Carolina artists featured
Exhibitions: Exhibitions featuring work of regional artists; National traveling exhibits; Collection exhibits
Publications: Annual Report; A Visit to GMA, brochure; monthly exhibit announcements; quarterly members' newsletter
Activities: Classes for adults & children; demonstrations; docent training; workshops; lects open to pub, 8 vis lectrs per yr; gallery talks; tours; individual paintings & original objects of art lent to mus & educational institutions; lending collection contains prints, paintings, sculpture & drawings; book traveling exhibs 3-5 per yr; mus shop sells books, catalogues & notecards

L **Reference Library**, 802 S Evans St, Greenville, NC 27834. Tel 252-758-1946; Fax 252-758-1946; *Exec Dir* Barbour Strickland
Open Tues - Fri 10 AM - 4:30 PM, Sat & Sun 1 - 4 PM; No admis fee; Estab as a reference source for staff
Library Holdings: Book Volumes 300, Periodical Subscriptions 150

HICKORY

M **HICKORY MUSEUM OF ART, INC,** 243 Third Ave NE, Hickory, NC 28601. Tel 828-327-8576; Fax 828-327-7281; Email info@hickorymuseumofart.org; Web: www.hickoryart.org; *Exec Dir* Lise C Swensson; *Youth Educator* Ginny Zellmer; *Develop Mgr* Kelly Smith; *Shop HMA/Collections Manager* Clarissa Starnes; *Exhibs Mgr* Kristina Anthony; *Bookkeeper* Mary Johnson
Open Tues - Sat 10 AM - 4 PM, Sun 1 - 4 PM, cl Mon; No admis fee; Estab 1944 to collect, exhibit & foster American art; Located in a renovated 1926 high school building; 10,000 sq ft gallery space for exhibition of permanent collection & traveling shows; Average Annual Attendance: 39,000; Mem: 700; dues $40-$32,500
Income: Financed by mem, donations, local United Arts Fund grants
Library Holdings: Book Volumes, Exhibition Catalogs
Special Subjects: Collages, Drawings, Etchings & Engravings, Folk Art, Glass, Graphics, Landscapes, Marine Painting, Painting-American, Photography, Pottery, Primitive art, Prints, Religious Art, Sculpture, Watercolors, Woodcuts, Portraits
Collections: collection of 19th & 20th century American paintings, NC glass, American art pottery, NC pottery, Southern Contemporary Folk Art
Publications: Quarterly newsletter; calendar; exhibition catalogs
Activities: Classes for adults & children; dramatic progs; docent training; periodic art classes; films; lects open to pub; concerts; gallery talks; tours; competitions with awards; exten dept serves Catawba County & surrounding area; individual paintings & original objects of art lent to other mus & galleries; traveling exhibs; originate traveling exhibs which circulate to qualifying mus & galleries; mus shop sells books, magazines, reproductions, gift items & original artworks

L **Library,** 243 3rd Ave NE, Hickory, NC 28601. Tel 828-327-8576; Fax 828-327-7281
Open Tues - Sat 10 AM - 4 PM; Estab as reference library open to staff & pub; Circ Non-circulating
Library Holdings: Book Volumes 2000, Cassettes 50, Clipping Files, Exhibition Catalogs, Manuscripts, Memorabilia, Motion Pictures, Pamphlets, Periodical Subscriptions 8, Photographs, Reproductions, Slides 500, Video Tapes

HIGH POINT

M **CITY OF HIGH POINT,** High Point Museum, 1859 E Lexington Ave, High Point, NC 27262-3499. Tel 336-885-1859; Fax 336-883-3284; Email hpmuseum@highpointnc.gov; Web: www.highpointmuseum.org; *Exec Dir* Edith Brady; *Registrar* Corinne Midgett; *Community Rels* Teresa Loflin; *Cur Colls* Marian Inabinett; *Cur Educ* Michael Scott; *Mus Store Mgr* Mary Barnett
Open Tues - Sat 10 AM - 4:30 PM; No admis fee; Estab 1971 to preserve the history of High Point; History of High Point, mus displays variety of exhibits interpreting local history; Average Annual Attendance: 16,000; Mem: 300; dues $20 - $2,000; ann meeting 4th Tues in May
Library Holdings: Book Volumes, Clipping Files, Maps, Original Documents
Special Subjects: Coins & Medals, Costumes, Decorative Arts, Dolls, Folk Art, Furniture, Historical Material, Maps, Miniatures, Photography, Pottery, Reproductions, Textiles, Ceramics
Collections: Over 35,000 objects including artifacts, photos & historic documents relating to High Point & inhabitants
Exhibitions: High Point's Furniture Heritage; Meredith's Miniatures
Publications: Quarterly newsletter
Activities: Adult classes; docent training; lects open to pub, 14 vis lectrs per yr; concerts; guided tours; mus shop sells books, magazines, original art, jewelry, toys, CDs

HIGHLANDS

M **THE BASCOMB,** 323 Franklin Rd, Highlands, NC 28741; PO Box 766, Highlands, NC 28741-0766. Tel 828-526-4949; Fax 828-526-0277; Email info@thebascom.org; *Dir* Jane Jery
Open Mon - Sat 10 AM - 5 PM, Sun noon - 5 PM; No admis fee; Estab 1983, Center of Visual Arts
Activities: Classes for adults & children; lects open to the pub; 4 vis lectrs per yr; gallery talks; tours; fells; mus shop sells books, original art

KINSTON

A **COMMUNITY COUNCIL FOR THE ARTS,** 400 N Queen St, Kinston, NC 28501-4328. Tel 252-527-2517; Fax 252-527-8280; Web: www.kinstoncca.com; *Pres* John McPhail; *Exec Dir* Sandy Landis
Open Tues - Fri 10 AM - 6 PM, Sat 10 AM - 2 PM; No admis fee; Estab 1965 to promote the arts in the Kinston-Lenoir County area; Six exhibition galleries & one sales gallery; Average Annual Attendance: 50,000; Mem: 750; dues renaissance $5000, sustainer $1000, patron $500, donor $150, sponsor $250, family $100, individual $50
Income: Financed by local govt appropriations, mem, grants & rentals
Library Holdings: Book Volumes, Cassettes, Clipping Files, Compact Disks, DVDs, Framed Reproductions, Memorabilia, Original Art Works, Original

Documents, Other Holdings, Pamphlets, Photographs, Prints, Sculpture, Video Tapes
Special Subjects: Decorative Arts, Painting-American, Photography, Drawings, Graphics, Prints, Sculpture
Collections: Louis Orr engravings-history of North Carolina, Henry Pearson Collection-donations of works by Henry Pearson & other leading modern artists, permanent coll of over 250 works, Public Art Program
Publications: Kaleidoscope, monthly newsletter
Activities: Classes for adults & children; docent training; dramatic progs; concerts; tours; gallery talks; competitions with awards; sponsorships; individual paintings & original objects of art lent to adjoining counties; lending collection contains original art works, original prints, paintings & sculpture; book traveling exhibs; originates traveling exhibs; gift shop sells books, original art, reproductions, prints & gift items; Art Center Children's Gallery

LEXINGTON

M **ARTS UNITED FOR DAVIDSON COUNTY,** The Arts Center, 220 S Main St, Lexington, NC 27292. Tel 336-249-2742; Fax 336-249-6302; Web: www.co.davidson.nc.us/arts; *Exec Dir* Doris Brown
Open Mon - Fri 10 AM - 4:30 PM, Sat 10 AM - 2 PM; No admis fee; Estab 1968 to expose & to educate the public in different art forms; 2 main galleries in a Greek revival-style building built in 1911; 1986 building was renovated into an arts center; Average Annual Attendance: 20,000; Mem: 575; due $35 - $99 friend, $100 - $249 patron, $250 - $499 sponsor, $500 - $999 producer, $1000 - $1999 dir circle, $2000 - $4999 president's circle, $5000 benefactor
Income: $130,000 (financed by foundations, contributions, sponsorships, local and state appropriation, sales)
Exhibitions: Ann Juried Photography Exhib; Ann Mems Open; Juried Spotlight Exhib
Publications: Ann Guide to the Arts, quarterly
Activities: Adult & children's classes; workshops; demonstrations; museum trips; lect open to public, gallery talks; tours; competitions with awards; celebration series; artist residency in 3 sch systems; sales shop sells books, original art, reproductions, prints, pottery, jewelry & glass

LOUISBURG

M **LOUISBURG COLLEGE,** Art Gallery, 501 N Main St, Louisburg, NC 27549-2399. Tel 919-496-2521, 919-497-3238; Email whinton@louisburg.edu; Web: www.louisburg.edu; *Dir & Cur* William Hinton
Open Jan - Apr, Aug - Dec Mon - Fri 9 AM - 4 PM, cl holidays; No admis fee; Estab 1957
Collections: American Impressionist Art, Primitive Art
Activities: Arts festivals; lect; gallery talks; tours

MONROE

M **UNION COUNTY PUBLIC LIBRARY UNION ROOM,** 316 E Windsor St, Monroe, NC 28112-4842. Tel 704-283-8184; Fax 704-282-0657; Email administration@union.lib.nc.us; Web: www.union.lib.nc.us; Others TDD 704-225-8554; *Dir* Nina Meadows; *Asst Dir* Lindsey Shuford
Open Mon & Tues 9 AM - 7 PM, Wed & Thurs 9 AM - 7 PM, Fri 9 AM - 6 PM, Sat 1 - 5 PM, Sun 2 - 5 PM; Gallery accommodates 25 large paintings & monthly exhibits of local work or traveling exhibitions
Exhibitions: Various local artists exhibitions

MOREHEAD CITY

M **CARTERET COUNTY HISTORICAL SOCIETY,** The History Place, 1008 Arendell St, Morehead City, NC 28557. Tel 252-247-7533; Fax 252-247-2756; Email museumdirector.cchs@gmail.com; Web: www.thehistoryplace.org; *Pres* Jim Buckingham; *VPres* Michelle Powers; *Exec Dir* Steve A Anderson; *Bd Secy* Stacey Veros; *Treas* Pam Janoskey
Open Tues - Fri & 1st Sat of month 10 AM - 4 PM; Admis suggested donation adult $2, child $1; Estab 1985 to promote the heritage of Carteret County; org began 1971; Research library, exhibs & artifacts from 1700, 1800 & art gallery, mus shop & tea room; Average Annual Attendance: 30,000; Mem: 450; dues $25 per month
Income: financed by fundraisers, grants, donations & membership
Library Holdings: Book Volumes, Clipping Files, Compact Disks, DVDs, Manuscripts, Maps, Micro Print, Original Art Works, Original Documents, Periodical Subscriptions, Photographs, Video Tapes
Special Subjects: Afro-American Art, Archaeology, Costumes, Decorative Arts, Dolls, Drawings, Etchings & Engravings, Ethnology, Flasks & Bottles, Folk Art, Furniture, Glass, Historical Material, Military Art, Jewelry, Marine Painting
Collections: Artifacts from early American Indians (8000 BC) to Tuscarora (1400's-1700's) to Civil War, World War I & II, Art, Aviation, Dolls Toys, Genealogy, Medicine, Native American Studies, Victoriana, Women's Studies, Guthrie Photo Collection, Schumacher Photo Coll
Publications: CCHS newsletter, quarterly
Activities: Educ prog; classes for children-preschool, 4th & 5th grades; docent training; history camps; traveling trunks; lects open to pub, 15 vis lectrs per yr; tours; concerts family programs; Albert Ray Newsome Award, Claude Hunter Moore Journal Award, DT Smithwick Newspaper Award, Willie Parker Peace History Book Award, the Garland P Stout Publishers Award, Robert Bruce Cook Family History Book Award, Malcolm Fowler Society Award, Paul Green Multimedia Award, Joe M McLaurin Newsletter Award, Paul Jehu Barringer Award, Evelina Davis Miller Museum Award & the National Certificate of Commendation; mus shop sells books, magazines, original art, reproductions, prints & merchandise

MORGANTON

M **BURKE ARTS COUNCIL,** Jailhouse Galleries, 115 E Meeting St, Morganton, NC 28655-3548. Tel 828-433-7282; Fax 828-433-7282; Email director@burkearts.org; Web: www.burkearts.org; *Exec Dir* Nikki Brant
Open Tues - Fri 9 AM - 5 PM; No admis fee, gifts accepted; Estab 1977 to provide high quality art shows in all media; Circ 200; One large gallery in an old jail; Average Annual Attendance: 2,500; Mem: 500; dues from $35; annual meeting in May
Income: $55,000 (financed by mem, city & state appropriations, foundations & grants)
Library Holdings: Book Volumes, Original Art Works, Records, Sculpture, Slides
Special Subjects: Art Education, Ceramics, Conceptual Art, Drawings, Pottery, Religious Art, Textiles, Watercolors, Painting-American, Pottery, Prints, Sculpture
Collections: Wachovia Permanent Collection
Exhibitions: First frost juried sculpture exhibit & sale (Nov - Dec); Tour d'Art (1st weekend Jun)
Publications: Burke County Artists & Craftsmen, every 3-4 years
Activities: Classes for adults & children; tours; competitions with awards, including Top 20 events of SE - Tour d'Art; fundraisers; concerts; tours; schols; scholarships offered; individual paintings & original objects of art lent to local bus & corporations; lending collection contains books, original art works, original prints, paintings, phonorecords, photographs & sculpture; sales shop sells original art, prints, local & regional crafts, books

NEW BERN

M **TRYON PALACE,** 529 S Front St, New Bern, NC 28562-5614; PO Box 1007, New Bern, NC 28563-1007. Tel 252-639-3500, 800-767-1560; Fax 252-514-4876; Email info@tryonpalace.org; Email lerae.umfiezt@ncdcr.gov; Web: www.tryonpalace.org; *Asst Dir* LeRae Umfleet; *Cur Colls* Alyson Rhodes-Murphy; *Mktg Mgr* Craig Ramey; *Develop Mgr* Anna Shepherd; *Dir Educ* Megan G Raby
Open Mon - Sat 9 AM - 5 PM, Sun 1 - 5 PM; Admis adults $20, children $10; Estab 1945; accredited by American Assn of Museums in 1989, 1998 & 2008; Maintained are the historic house museums & galleries (Tryon Palace, Dixon-George House, Robert Hay House, John Wright Stanly House & New Bern Academy) with 18th & 19th century English & American furniture, paintings, prints, silver, ceramic objects & textiles; Average Annual Attendance: 100,000; Mem: Tyron Palace Foundation, 1200 mem, annual meeting in Apr
Income: Financed by state & private bequests, endowment, furniture, paintings, historic artifacts
Library Holdings: Auction Catalogs, Audio Tapes, Book Volumes, Compact Disks, DVDs, Fiche, Manuscripts, Maps, Memorabilia, Original Documents, Periodical Subscriptions, Reels
Special Subjects: Archaeology, Architecture, Carpets & Rugs, Ceramics, Costumes, Furniture, Glass, Historical Material, Manuscripts, Maps, Period Rooms, Pewter, Porcelain, Portraits, Prints
Collections: Paintings by William Carl Brown, Nathaniel Dance, Gaspard Dughet, Thomas Gainsborough, Daniel Huntington, School of Sir Godfrey Kneller, Claude Lorrain, Paul LaCroix, David Martin, Richard Paton, Matthew William Peters, Charles Willson Peale, Charles Phillips, Alan Ramsay, Jan Siberechts, Edward B Smith, E Van Stuven, Simon Preter Verelst, Richard Wilson, John Wollaston, Graphics
Exhibitions: Temporary exhibitions on history & decorative arts, 3 per yr
Activities: Crafts demonstrations for adults & children; audio-visual orientation prog; annual symposium on 18th & 19th century decorative arts; interpretive drama prog; docent training; educ prog; Fife & Drum Corp, 1st person interpretation; lects open to pub, 25 vis lectrs per yr; concerts; galley talks; tours; scholarships offered; lending of original objects of art to museum organizations that meet requirements; mus shop sells books, magazines, reproductions, prints, slides & ceramics

L **Library & Museum,** 529 S Front St, New Bern, NC 28562-5614; PO Box 1007, New Bern, NC 28563-1007. Tel 252-514-4900; Fax 252-639-3500; Web: www.tryonpalace.org; *Conservation Specialist* Richard Baker
Open Mon - Sat 9 AM - 5 PM, Sun noon - 5 PM; Admis call for current fee; For reference; open for use with permission
Income: Financed by state & private donations
Library Holdings: Book Volumes 8500, Clipping Files, Pamphlets, Periodical Subscriptions 45, Photographs, Slides, Video Tapes
Special Subjects: Archaeology, Architecture, Art History, Costume Design & Constr, Decorative Arts, Historical Material, Interior Design, Landscape Architecture, Painting-American, Painting-British, Period Rooms, Porcelain, Portraits, Prints, Restoration & Conservation
Collections: 18th & early 19th century decorative arts
Publications: Tryon Palace Magazine, The Living History Classroom
Activities: Educ prog; dramatic progs; crafts & special interest; lects open to pub; concerts; tours; museum shop sells books, original art, reproductions & prints

NORTH WILKESBORO

M **WILKES ART GALLERY,** 913 C St, North Wilkesboro, NC 28659-4119. Tel 336-667-2841; Fax 336-667-9264; Email wilkesartgallery@gmail.com; Web: www.wilkesartgallery.org; *Exec Dir* Cindy Pardue; *Bd Pres* Joe Johnston; *Educ Coordr* Kim Reid
Open Tues & Wed - Fri 10 AM - 5 PM, Sat 10 AM - 2 PM, evenings for special events, cl New Year's Day, Easter, Easter Mon, Independence Day, Thanksgiving, Labor Day, Memorial Day & Christmas; No admis fee; Estab 1962 to take art to as many areas as possible; Recently completed renovation of 10,000 sq ft facility in downtown North Wilkesboro. The WAG offers 12 annual exhibits, classes & workshops for all ages; Average Annual Attendance: 10,400; Mem: 400; dues patron & corp $500, donor $250, sponsor $125, family $75; annual meeting in May
Income: Financed by mem, local governments, state arts council & corporations
Purchases: Fundraising events, sponsors & grants
Library Holdings: Book Volumes, Cards, Framed Reproductions, Original Art Works, Pamphlets, Photographs, Prints, Sculpture

Special Subjects: Art Education, Crafts, Decorative Arts, Drawings, Enamels, Folk Art, Glass, Graphics, Jewelry, Landscape Architecture, Landscapes, Metalwork, Painting-American, Painting-American, Photography, Pottery, Pre-Columbian Art, Prints, Sculpture, Silver, Stained Glass, Textiles, Watercolors
Collections: Contemporary paintings, graphics, sculpture, primarily of NC artists, Fiber artwork, photography
Exhibitions: Artist League Juried Competition; Blue Ridge Overview (amateur photography); temporary exhibitions; Northwest Artist League Competition; Youth Art Month in March; Fiber Fantasy, Natives Go Nature
Publications: Title of Exhibition, monthly brochures & catalogues; Wilkes Art Gallery Newsletter, monthly
Activities: Classes for adults & children; docent training; arts festivals; films; art & craft classes; workshops in different media; film camps; lects open to pub, 3 vis lectrs per yr; gallery talks; tours; competitions with awards; concerts; schols; individual paintings lent to medical center; originate traveling exhibs to other mus & galleries; mus shop sells, books, crafts, original art, pottery, prints & reproductions

RALEIGH

A **ARTSPACE INC,** 201 E Davie St, Raleigh, NC 27601-1869. Tel 919-821-2787; Fax 919-821-0383; Email info@artspacenc.org; Web: www.artspacenc.org; *Exec Dir* Mary Poole
Open Tues - Sat 10 AM - 6 PM, Thurs until 7 PM, first Fri 10 AM - 10 PM, office Mon - Fri 9 AM - 5 PM; No admis fee; Estab 1986; Two fls; Average Annual Attendance: 100,000; Mem: Annual meeting in Apr
Income: $400,000 (financed by mem, city & state appropriation, rental income)
Exhibitions: Exhibits rotate every 4 - 8 weeks
Activities: Classes for adults & children; lects open to pub; tours; gallery talks; scholarships; residencies for emerging artists (2 six month residencies per yr) & established artists (summer); book traveling exhibs 2 per yr; originate traveling exhibs annually; sales shop sells original art, prints

M **CAM CONTEMPORARY ART MUSEUM,** 409 W Martin St, Raleigh, NC 27603-1819. Tel 919-261-5920; Email info@camraleigh.org; Web: www.camraleigh.org; *Exec Dir* Gab Smith; *Exhibs Dir* Eric Gaard; *Gallery Educ* Jaclyn Bowie; *Gallery Educ* Jeanny Sandoval; *Prog Coordr* Mollie Earls
Open Tues & Wed by appointment, Thurs - Fri Noon - 6 PM, Sat - Sun Noon - 5 PM, cl Mon; Admis $5; free for CAM Raleigh mems; Estab 1983; CAM provides the platform for enriching community & educational & cultural experiences ignite ideas & connect people to what is now & what is next; Renovated 20,000 sq ft historic warehouse-turned-museum; Average Annual Attendance: 35,000; Mem: 1400
Income: Financed by mem, city & state appropriation, contributions & foundations
Publications: Exhibition catalogues
Activities: Teacher workshops; docent training; lects; lects open to pub; performances; film series; concerts; gallery talks; tours; video programs; internships for college & graduate students; Cam-To-Go (school outreach prog); book traveling exhibs; originate traveling exhibs; sales area sells books, catalogs, posters, postcards, T-shirts, caps, mugs & novelty items

A **CITY OF RALEIGH ARTS COMMISSION,** Miriam Preston Block Gallery, 222 W Hargett St, Raleigh, NC 27601-1479; PO Box 590, Raleigh, NC 27602-0590. Tel 919-996-3610; Fax 919-831-6351; Web: www.raleighnc.gov/arts; *Admin Asst* Carol S Mallette; *Arts Prog Coordr* Beula Parker; *Pub Art Coordr* Kim Curry-Evans
Open Mon - Fri 8:30 AM - 5:15 PM; No admis fee; Estab 1984 to showcase Raleigh-based artists/art collections in the local area; First & second floor lobbies of the Raleigh Municipal Building; Average Annual Attendance: 10-20,000
Income: $4340 (financed by city & state appropriation)

M **MEREDITH COLLEGE,** Frankie G Weems Gallery & Rotunda Gallery, Gaddy-Hamrick Art Ctr, 3800 Hillsborough St Raleigh, NC 27607-5298. Tel 919-760-8600; Fax 919-760-2347; Email gallery@meredith.edu; Web: www.meredith.edu/art; *Dir* Lisa Pearce
Open Mon - Fri 9 AM - 5 PM, Sat & Sun 2 - 5 PM; No admis fee; Rotunda Gallery estab 1970, Weems Gallery 1986; Weems Gallery; 30 ft x 43 ft & dividers, skylights; Rotunda Gallery: 3 story, domed space, located in admin building; Average Annual Attendance: 2,000
Special Subjects: African Art, Afro-American Art, American Indian Art, Architecture, Carpets & Rugs, Ceramics, Collages, Costumes, Crafts, Dolls, Drawings, Enamels, Etchings & Engravings, Furniture, Historical Material, Jewelry, Juvenile Art, Painting-American, Painting-European, Painting-Italian, Painting-Russian, Photography, Posters, Sculpture, Woodcarvings
Exhibitions: Weems Gallery: North Carolina Photographer's Annual Exhibition; Raleigh Fine Arts Society Annual Exhibition; Meredith College Art Faculty Exhibition; Rotunda Gallery: Annual Juried Student Exhibition
Activities: Lect open to public, 3 vis lectrs per year, competitions with awards; lending collection contains paintings & original objects of art; book traveling exhibitions annually

M **NORTH CAROLINA MUSEUM OF ART,** 2110 Blue Ridge Rd, Raleigh, NC 27607-6494; 4630 Mail Service Ctr, Raleigh, NC 27699-4630. Tel 919-839-6262; Fax 919-733-8034; Email markcomm@ncartmuseum.org; Web: www.ncartmuseum.org; *Chief Cur* Linda Dougherty; *Chief Conservator* William Brown; *Registrar* Maggie Gregory; *Librn* Natalia Lonchyna; *Dir, Develop & Mem* Ellen Stone; *Dir* Lawrence J Wheeler; *Dep Dir Art Coll* John Coffey; *Dir Planning & Design* Dan Gottlieb; *Dir Mktg* Jen Bahus; *Dir Exhibs* Tiara L Paris; *Chief Deputy Dir & CFO* Caterri Woodrum; *Dir Opers* John Knox
Open Tues - Thurs 10 AM - 5 PM, Fri until 9 PM, Sat - Sun 10 AM - 5 PM, cl Mon, Thanksgiving, & Christmas Eve & Day; Park open daily dawn - dusk; No admis fee to Museum or Park; fees apply for special exhibs & progs; Estab 1947, open to pub 1956, to acquire, preserve, & exhibit international works of art for the educ & enjoyment of the people of the state & to conduct programs of educ, research & publications designed to encourage interest in & an appreciation of art; European Galleries with Dutch, Flemish, French, Italian, British, Spanish & N European Galleries, Classical, Ancient Egyptian, Jewish Ceremonial, Ancient American, African, American, 20th Century Galleries; Expansion opened 2010 adds 127,000 sq ft of exhib space & transformed East Bldg into ctr for temp exhibs; Average Annual Attendance: 265,000; Mem: 63,000; dues $40 & up
Income: Financed by state appropriations, contributions & grants administered by the NCMA Foundation
Special Subjects: African Art, Afro-American Art, Antiquities-Egyptian, Antiquities-Greek, Antiquities-Roman, Baroque Art, Decorative Arts, Painting-American, Painting-British, Painting-Dutch, Painting-European, Painting-Flemish, Painting-French, Painting-German, Painting-Israeli, Painting-Italian, Painting-Spanish, Pre-Columbian Art, Renaissance Art, Sculpture, Textiles, American Indian Art
Collections: Jewish Ceremonial, 20th century art coll, Samuel H Kress Collection
Exhibitions: North Carolina Artists Exhibitions; wide range of temporary exhibitions
Publications: Preview, bimonthly; exhibition & permanent collection catalogs
Activities: Classes for adults & children; dramatic progs; docent training; lects open to pub; concerts; gallery talks; tours; competitions; outreach dept serving North Carolina; individual paintings & original objects of art lent to state institutions & offices, mus, & national & international exhibits; book traveling exhibs; originate traveling exhibs; mus shop sells books, reproductions, prints, slides, educational gifts for children & adults, jewelry, & other gifts

L **Art Reference Library,** 2110 Blue Ridge Rd, Raleigh, NC 27607; 4630 Mail Service Center, Raleigh, NC 27699-4630. Tel 919-664-6770; Fax 919-733-8034; Email natalia.lonchyna@ncdcr.gov; Web: ncartmuseum.org/art/library; *Librn* Natalia Lonchyna
Open Tues - Fri 10 AM - 4 PM, cl Mon & holidays; Estab 1957 to serve research needs of museum staff, citizens of NC and anyone interested in NCMA; Circ non-circulating; Open to pub for reference
Income: Financed by State and NCMA Foundation
Purchases: $40,000
Library Holdings: Auction Catalogs, Book Volumes 43,000, Clipping Files, Exhibition Catalogs, Pamphlets, Periodical Subscriptions 90
Special Subjects: Afro-American Art, Antiquities-Byzantine, Antiquities-Egyptian, Antiquities-Greek, Antiquities-Roman, Art Education, Art History, Conceptual Art, Folk Art, History of Art & Archaeology, Judaica, Marine Painting, Mosaics, Painting-American, Painting-British, Painting-Dutch, Painting-European, Painting-Flemish, Painting-French, Painting-German, Painting-Israeli, Painting-Italian, Painting-Scandinavian, Painting-Spanish, Photography, Pottery, Pre-Columbian Art

A **NORTH CAROLINA MUSEUMS COUNCIL,** PO Box 2603, Raleigh, NC 27602-2603. Tel 919-832-3775; Fax 919-832-3085; Web: www.ncmuseums.org; *Pres* Peter Koch; *Treas* Christian Edwards; *VPres* Scott Warren
Estab 1963 to stimulate interest, support & understanding of museums; all-vol organization; Mem: 300; dues individual $20; annual meeting in the fall
Income: Financed by mem
Publications: NCMC Newsletter, quarterly; North Carolina Museums Guide
Activities: Awards given

L **NORTH CAROLINA STATE UNIVERSITY,** Harrye Lyons Design Library, Design Library 209 Brooks Hall, Campus Box 7701 Raleigh, NC 27695-7701. Tel 919-515-2207; Fax 919-515-7330; Web: www.lib.ncsu.edu/design; *Head Design Library* Karen DeWitt; *Visual Resources Librn* Barbara Brenny; *Library Asst* Sharon Silcox; *Library Tech* Carmen Spradlin
Open Mon - Thurs 7:30 AM - 10 PM, Fri 7:30 AM - 6 PM, Sat 1 PM - 7 PM, Sun 1 - 10 PM; Estab 1942 to serve the reading, study, reference & research needs of the faculty, students & staff of the School of Design & the University campus, as well as off-campus borrowers; Circ 56,058; Primarily for lending
Income: Financed by state appropriation, private funds & mem
Purchases: $41,450
Library Holdings: Audio Tapes, Book Volumes 40,747, Motion Pictures, Other Holdings Trade literature, Vertical files, Pamphlets, Periodical Subscriptions 210, Slides, Video Tapes
Special Subjects: Advertising Design, Aesthetics, Afro-American Art, Architecture, Art History, Asian Art, Furniture, Graphic Arts, Graphic Design, Illustration, Industrial Design, Landscape Architecture, Landscapes
Collections: File on measured Drawings of North Carolina Historic Sites, 458 maps & plans, 300 bibliographies compiled by the Design Library staff
Publications: Index to the School of Design, student publication book Vols 1-25

M **Gregg Museum of Art & Design,** 1903 Hillsborough St, Campus Box 7330 Raleigh, NC 27607. Tel 919-515-3503; Fax 919-515-6163; Email gregg@ncsu.edu; Web: gregg.arts.ncsu.edu; *Dir* Roger Manley; *Registrar & Assoc Dir* Mary Hauser; *Cur Educ* Zoe Starling; *Opers Mgr* Hilary Kinlaw; *Art Preparator* Matt Gay; *Asst Registrar* Jordan Cao; *Collections Asst* Janine LeBlanc
Open Tues - Wed & Fri - Sat 10 AM - 5 PM, Thurs 10 AM - 9 PM, Sun 1 PM - 5 PM, first Fri until 7 PM, cl Mon & holidays; No admis fee; Estab 1979 to collect, exhibit & provide changing exhibitions in the art & design; In transition period, exhibits being held at other venues; Average Annual Attendance: 20,000; Mem: 200; dues $25-$1500; annual meeting in June
Income: (financed by student fees)
Purchases: $3,000 - $5,000
Library Holdings: Book Volumes, Exhibition Catalogs
Special Subjects: African Art, Afro-American Art, Architecture, Carpets & Rugs, Ceramics, Costumes, Crafts, Decorative Arts, Dolls, Drawings, Embroidery, Folk Art, Furniture, Glass, Jewelry, Laces, Latin American Art, Metalwork, Miniatures, Painting-American, Photography, Photography, Porcelain, Porcelain, Portraits, Pottery, Pottery, Pre-Columbian Art, Pre-Columbian Art, Prints, Religious Art, Reproductions, Sculpture, Southwestern Art, Tapestries, Tapestries, Textiles, Woodcarvings, Woodcuts
Collections: American, Indian, Asian & pre-Columbian textiles, ceramics (fine, ironstone, porcelain, traditional), furniture, product design, photographs, contemp glass
Publications: Exhibition catalogs
Activities: Docent & self-guided tours; lects open to public; gallery talks; tours; competitions; scholarships offered; individual paintings & original objects of art lent to other museums; exten prog serves NC, SC, VA; originate traveling exhibs

A **PORTRAITS SOUTH,** 3901 Computer Dr, Ste 110 Raleigh, NC 27609. Tel 919-833-1630; Fax 919-833-3391; Email info@portraitsouth.com; Web: www.portraitsouth.com; *Owner & CEO* Stephen W ReVille; *Operations Mgr* Beverly Graves; *Accounting Mgr* Karen O'Connell
Open by appointment, Mon - Fri 9 AM - noon; No admis fee; Estab 1980, agent for professional portrait artists; 3,500 sq ft; Mem: 100 represented artists
Income: Pvt income
Publications: Newsletters for artists, twice a year
Activities: Book traveling exhibs 100 per yr; originate traveling exhibs 100 per yr

A **VISUAL ART EXCHANGE,** 309 W Martin St, Raleigh, NC 27601-1352. Tel 919-828-7834; Fax 919-828-7833; Email info@visualartexchange.org; Web: www.visualartexchange.org; *Exec Dir* Brandon Cordrey; *Bus Dir* Erika Corey; *Prog Dir* Rachel Herrick; *Dir Exhibs* Kyle Hazard
Open Tues - Sat 11 AM - 4 PM, 1st Fri of month 6 PM - 10 PM; No admis fee; Estab 1980 to serve emerging & professional artists; Mem: 300; dues $55
Income: Financed by grants & corporate sponsors
Exhibitions: Holiday Show; New Show; Young Artist Show; International Show; Lay of the Land; Salon des Refuses
Publications: Expressions, 10 per year
Activities: Classes for adults & children; lects open to pub, 10 vis lectrs per yr; gallery talks; competitions with prizes; workshops; book traveling exhibs 1 per yr; originate traveling exhibs; sales shop sells original art

ROCKY MOUNT

A **IMPERIAL CENTRE'S MARIA V HOWARD ARTS CENTER,** (Rocky Mount Arts Center), 270 Gay St., Rocky Mount, NC 27804. Tel 252-972-1266 (Front Desk); Fax 252-972-1563; Email alicyn.wiedrich@rockymountnc.gov; Email info@rockymountnc.gov; Web: www.imperialcentre.org/arts; *Cur* Alicyn Wierdrich; *Cur Educ* Leigh White; *Exhibs Cur* Steve Armstrong; *Theatre Mgr* Brooke Edwards; *Prog Supv* Sheila Long; *Educ Coordr* Tracy Grosner
Open Tues - Sat 10 AM - 5 PM, Sun 1 - 5 PM; No admis fee; Estab 1957 to promote the development of the creative arts in the community through educ, participation & appreciation of music, dance, painting, drama, etc; to provide facilities & guidance for developing talents & enriching lives through artistic expression & appreciation; Maintains the Permanent Collection Gallery, 4 Exhibition Galleries; Average Annual Attendance: 25,000
Income: Financed by City Recreation Department with supplemental support by mem
Collections: Regional works
Exhibitions: Permanent collection & traveling shows change every 31/2 months; Sculpture Salmagundi (indoor & outdoor); Handcrafted; National Juried Art Show; Solo + Group Exhibitions
Activities: Conduct art classes; year-round theatre prog; classes for adults & children;; concerts; gallery talks; tours; sponsoring of competitions; gallery shop sells original art, prints, pottery, jewelry

SALISBURY

M **HORIZONS UNLIMITED SUPPLEMENTARY EDUCATIONAL CENTER,** Science Museum, 1636 Parkview Circle, Salisbury, NC 28144. Tel 704-639-3004; Fax 704-639-3015; Web: www.rss.k12.nc.us; *Dir* Lisa Wear
Open to public by appointment; office hours Mon - Fri 7:30 AM - 4 PM; No admis fee; Estab 1968 to exhibit art work of pub schools, supplemented by exhibits of local artists from time to time during the school year; primary purpose is to supplement science educ activities in the pub schools; The center is comprised of two areas, one approx 24 x 65 ft, the other 15 x 70 ft with an adjoining classroom for instruction & demonstrations; Average Annual Attendance: 19,000
Income: Financed by mem, state & county appropriation & from local foundations
Collections: Planetarium, touch tank Rain Forest
Activities: Classes for adults & children; lect open to public, 5 vis lectrs per year; gallery talks; tours; individual & original objects of art lent; summer camps

M **WATERWORKS VISUAL ARTS CENTER,** 123 E Liberty St, Salisbury, NC 28144-5038. Tel 704-636-1882; Fax 704-636-1895; Email admin@waterworks.org; Web: www.waterworks.org; *Exec Dir* Anne Scott Clement
Open Mon - Fri 10 AM - 5 PM, Sat 10 AM - 2 PM; No admis fee; Estab 1977 for exhibition & instruction of visual arts; Four galleries with changing exhibitions. Accredited by the American Alliance of Museums; Average Annual Attendance: 18,334; Mem: 400; dues $75 & up; annual meeting in the spring
Income: $315,605 (financed by mem, city, county, grants & foundations, United Arts Fund, exhibition & educational corporate sponsors)
Library Holdings: Book Volumes 750+
Special Subjects: Afro-American Art, Bronzes, Ceramics, Costumes, Crafts, Decorative Arts, Drawings, Etchings & Engravings, Folk Art, Glass, Graphics, Historical Material, Jewelry, Judaica, Juvenile Art, Landscapes, Mosaics, Painting-American, Painting-British, Painting-European, Photography, Portraits, Posters, Pottery, Prints, Religious Art, Sculpture, Silver, Watercolors, Woodcarvings, Stained Glass, Textiles, Woodcuts
Exhibitions: Rotating exhibs throughout the yr; approx 15 professional exhibs per yr; 5 galley changes per yr; 6 young people's exhibs per yr
Publications: Annual exhibition catalogue
Activities: Classes for adults & children; classes for special populations; classes for children in pub housing; in-school progs; outreach progs; docent training; lects open to pub; 4 vis lectrs per year; gallery talks; tours; competitions & cash awards; annual Dare to Imagine Award given to one talented high school senior in the Rowan-Salisbury school system each yr; scholarships offered; book traveling exhibs; museum shop books, sells original art

SEAGROVE

M **MUSEUM OF NC TRADITIONAL POTTERY,** 127 E Main St, Seagrove, NC 27341-8246; PO Box 500 Seagrove, NC 27341-0500. Tel 336-873-7887; Fax 336-873-7736; Web: www.seagrovepotterymuseum.net
Estab to preserve & promote pottery tradition
Special Subjects: Pottery
Collections: 80 pottery items
Exhibitions: Temporary exhibits

STATESVILLE

M **IREDELL MUSEUMS,** 134 Court St, Statesville, NC 28677; P O Box 223, Statesville, NC 28687. Tel 704-873-7347; Email mherzog@iredellmuseums.org; Web: www.iredellmuseums.org; *Exec Dir* Melinda Herzog; *Program Dir* Angel Johnston; *Program Assistant* Melanie Vaughn
Open Tues - Sat 10 AM - 5 PM; $6 plus tax; Merged with children's museum 12/2004 to preserve, promote & provide learning experiences in culture, heritage, science & the arts; Rotating exhibits in local history, science, and art; Average Annual Attendance: 20,000; Mem: 300; dues based on categories of giving; yearly meetings
Income: Financed by mem, grants & sponsorships
Special Subjects: Afro-American Art, Anthropology, Antiquities-Egyptian, Antiquities-Roman, Carpets & Rugs, Ceramics, Costumes, Decorative Arts, Dolls, Drawings, Embroidery, Etchings & Engravings, Flasks & Bottles, Folk Art, Furniture, Glass, Historical Material, Landscapes, Manuscripts, Maps, Metalwork, Miniatures, Oriental Art, Painting-American, Painting-Australian, Painting-British, Photography, Portraits, Pottery, Pre-Columbian Art, Primitive art, Prints, Sculpture, Stained Glass, Tapestries, Textiles, Watercolors, Woodcarvings, Woodcuts
Collections: Collections entail Ancient Arts, Decorative Arts, Fine Arts, Natural History, Historic Cabins, Mummy (Egyptian), Glassware, Textiles, Military
Exhibitions: 30th Sep, 2017) The Mummy Treasure of Al Faiyum
Activities: classes for children; docent training; Tours, field trips, public programs; sells children's toys

TARBORO

M **EDGECOMBE COUNTY CULTURAL ARTS COUNCIL, INC,** Blount-Bridgers House, Hobson Pittman Memorial Gallery, 130 Bridgers St, Tarboro, NC 27886-3868. Tel 252-823-4159; Fax 252-823-6115; Email edgecombearts@embargmail.com; Web: www.edgecombearts.org; *Mgr* Carol Banks
Open Wed-Sat 10AM-4PM, Sun 2 - 4 PM; Admis $5; Estab 1982, to present local culture as it relates to state & nation; Located in a restored 1810 plantation house, 5 rooms in period interpretation, 3 used as gallery space for 20th century art permanent & traveling exhibits; Average Annual Attendance: 5,000; Mem: 350; dues $50; monthly meeting 4th Thurs
Income: $175,000 (fin by state, local, fed & pvt
Library Holdings: Book Volumes, Cassettes, Clipping Files, DVDs, Manuscripts, Maps, Original Art Works, Pamphlets, Periodical Subscriptions, Photographs, Prints, Records
Special Subjects: Archaeology, Architecture, Ceramics, Decorative Arts, Furniture, Historical Material, Manuscripts, Maps, Period Rooms, Textiles, Reproductions, Restorations
Collections: Pittman Collection of Oil, Watercolors & Drawings, American Collection of oils, watercolor & drawings, Decorative arts 19th century Southern
Exhibitions: Hobson Pittman retrospect; period rooms, 1810-1870
Publications: quarterly newsletter
Activities: Classes for adults & children, docent progs; lects open to pub, 5 vis lectrs per yr; concerts; gallery talks; tours; exten dept lends out paintings; 1 - 2 book traveling exhibs; originate traveling exhibs, once per yr to accredited mus; mus shop sells original art, reproductions, prints

WADESBORO

M **ANSON COUNTY HISTORICAL SOCIETY, INC,** 209 E Wade St, Wadesboro, NC 28170-2228. Tel 704-694-6694; Fax 704-694-3763; Email ansonhistorical@windstream.net; Web: www.ansonhistoricalsociety.org; *Pres* Don Scarborough
Open Mon - Fri 10 AM - 4 PM, other times by appointment; No admis fee; Estab 1960 as a mus of 18th & 19th century furniture; Average Annual Attendance: 1,000; Mem: 240; dues family $15, single $10; annual meeting in Nov
Income: $12,000 (financed by mem)
Special Subjects: Furniture
Collections: Collection of 18th & 19th century furniture
Publications: Cemeteries of Anson County, Volume 1; History of Anson County, 1750 - 1976

WASHINGTON

A **BEAUFORT COUNTY ARTS COUNCIL,** 108 Gladden St, Washington, NC 27889-4910; PO Box 634, Washington, NC 27889-0634. Tel 252-946-2504; *Admin Asst* Eleanor Rollins; *Dir* Wanda Johnson; *Prog Dir* Joey Toler; *Visual Arts Coordr* Sally Hofmann
Open Tues - Fri 9 AM - 4 PM; No admis fee; Estab 1972
Collections: Aslando Suite by Jim Moon, Johannes Oertel Collection
Exhibitions: Rotating multi-media exhibits
Activities: Book traveling exhibs

WILMINGTON

M **CAMERON ART MUSEUM,** 3201 S 17th St, Wilmington, NC 28412-6554. Tel 910-395-5999; Fax 910-395-5030; Web: www.cameronartmuseum.com; *Dir* Deborah Velders; *Cur Pub Programs* Daphne Holmes; *Develop Officer* Heather Wilson; *Registrar* Holly Tripman; *Exhib Mgr* Robert Unchester; *Cur Educ* Georgia Mastroeini; *Chmn Bd* Frances Goodman; *Asst Dir* Anne Brennan
Open Tues - Fri 11 AM - 5 PM, Thurs 11 AM - 9 PM, Sat - Sun 11 AM - 5 PM; Admis non-mems $8, mems & children $5, discounts to NARM members; Estab 1962 to promote the visual arts in southeastern North Carolina; 42,000 sq ft designed by Gwathmey Siegel & Assoc Architects (NYC); Average Annual Attendance: 40,000
Library Holdings: Auction Catalogs, Audio Tapes, Book Volumes, CD-ROMs, Cassettes, Clipping Files, DVDs, Exhibition Catalogs, Original Documents, Pamphlets, Slides, Video Tapes
Special Subjects: Asian Art, Bookplates & Bindings, Ceramics, Collages, Crafts, Decorative Arts, Drawings, Etchings & Engravings, Folk Art, Furniture, Glass, Landscapes, Mosaics, Painting-American, Painting-European, Pewter, Photography, Portraits, Pottery, Prints, Sculpture, Stained Glass, Tapestries, Textiles, Watercolors
Collections: Mary Cassatt's color prints including The Ten, Minnie Evans, Utagawa Hiroshige, Claude Howell, Jugtown Pottery, 17th century - present American, European, Asian Fine Art, crafts, design
Publications: Robert Delford Brown; William Ivey Long; Maud Gatewood & Gwathmey Siegel exhib catalogs
Activities: Classes for adults & children; docent training; lects open to pub; 3+ vis lectrs per yr; concerts; gallery talks; tours; originates traveling exhibs to museums, Montgomery Mus of Fine Arts, Yale Univ Art & Architecture; mus shop sells books, reproductions, prints, crafts & jewelry

M **STATE OF NORTH CAROLINA,** Battleship North Carolina, 1 Battleship Rd, Wilmington, NC 28401; PO Box 480, Wilmington, NC 28402-0480. Tel 910-399-9100; Fax 910-251-5807; Email museum@battleshipnc.com; Web: www.battleshipnc.com; *Exec Dir* Terry A Bragg; *Asst Dir Opers* Chris Vargo; *Comptroller* Elizabeth Haynes; *Dir Promotions* Meaghan Holmes; *Maintenance Dir* Terry Kuhn; *Cur* Kim Robinson Sincox; *Cur* Mary Ames Booker; *Dir Sales* Leesa McFarlane; *Prog Dir* Danielle Wallace
Open daily Labor Day - Memorial Day 8AM - 5PM, Memorial Day weekend - Labor Day 8AM - 8PM; Admis adults $12, children between 6 & 11 $6, under 6 free; 65 & over, active & retired military $10; Estab 1961 as a historic ship museum to memorialize the North Carolinians of all the services that gave their lives in WWII; Average Annual Attendance: 200,000; Mem: 182; $15-$500 memberships; bimonthly meetings
Income: Financed by admis, sales in gift shop & snack bar, rental functions & donations
Special Subjects: Costumes, Folk Art, Historical Material, Manuscripts, Maps, Marine Painting, Military Art, Painting-American, Period Rooms, Photography, Silver, Textiles, Watercolors
Collections: Artifacts, photos & archival materials associated with or appropriate to the ships bearing the name North Carolina: BB-55 (1936-1947), CA-12 (1905-1930) & Ship-of-the-line (1818-1867); SSN777 attack submarine North Carolina (2008), also artifacts assoc with the memorial itself
Publications: Battleship North Carolina; Ship's Data 1; Battleship North Carolina, Capt Ben Blee, USN (Retired)
Activities: Educ progs for schools; progs open to pub; lifelong learning progs; special event progs; sales shop sells books, reproduction prints, slides, souvenirs & post cards

WILSON

M **BARTON COLLEGE,** Barton Museum - Virginia Graves Gallery - Lula E Rackley Gallery, 704A College St, Wilson, NC 27893; PO Box 5000, Wilson, NC 27893-7000. Tel 252-399-6477; Fax 252-399-6571; Email sfecho@barton.edu; Web: www.barton.edu/departmentofart/bartonmus
Open Mon - Fri 10 AM - 3 PM; No admis fee; Estab 1960 to provide art exposure for our students & community; Gallery has 200 linear feet wall space; Average Annual Attendance: 2,000
Income: Financed by endowment income
Library Holdings: Audio Tapes, Book Volumes, DVDs, Original Art Works, Original Documents, Photographs, Prints, Reproductions, Sculpture, Slides
Collections: African masks, various objects of fine and decorative arts, watercolors by Paula W Patterson
Exhibitions: National Scholastic Art Award Competition for Eastern North Carolina; Annual graduating artists exhibitions
Activities: Educ prog; classes for adults; lects open to pub; gallery talks; tours; gallery tours for children; 4 lects per yr open to pub; 2 lects per yr for mems; schols

L **Library,** Whitehead & Gold Sts, College Station Wilson, NC 27893; PO Box 5000, Wilson, NC 27893-7000. Tel 252-399-6500; Fax 252-237-4957; *Dir* Shirley Gregory
For reference only
Library Holdings: Book Volumes 2500, Exhibition Catalogs, Kodachrome Transparencies, Original Art Works, Pamphlets, Periodical Subscriptions 94, Sculpture, Video Tapes 50
Special Subjects: Art History

WINSTON-SALEM

A **THE ARTS COUNCIL OF WINSTON-SALEM & FORSYTH COUNTY,** 305 W Fourth St, Winston-Salem, NC 27101. Tel 336-722-2585; Fax 336-761-8286; Email info@IntoTheArts.org; Web: www.IntoTheArts.org; *Pres & CEO* Milton Rhodes; *Admin Mgr* Mona Campbell
Open Mon - Fri 8:30 AM - 5 PM; Estab 1949, The Arts Council of Winston-Salem and Forsyth County enriches the quality of life for people in Winston-Salem and neighboring communities by strengthening cultural resources, promoting the arts and united arts fundraising. Each year we award more than $1 million in grant support to arts and cultural organizations, arts educ progs and individual artists throughout the community; Facilities include Hanes Community Center: theatre, classroom, & rehearsal rooms; Mem: Annual meeting in the fall
Income: Financed by fund drives, pub & private grants & endowments
Activities: R Philip Hanes Jr Young Leader Recognition award given

A **ASSOCIATED ARTISTS OF WINSTON-SALEM,** 251 N Spruce St, Winston-Salem, NC 27101-2735. Tel 336-722-0340; Fax 336-722-0446; Email staff@associatedartists.org; Web: www.associatedartists.org; *Exec Dir* Sharon Nelson; *Communs Dir* Terri Goff; *Gallery Coordr* Ginger Wiggins
Open Mon - Fri 9 AM - 5 PM, Sat Sept - Thanksgiving 10 AM - 2 PM; No admis fee; Estab 1956 to promote & conduct activities that support the awareness, educ, enjoyment & appreciation of visual fine art; The assn rents the walls of the gallery from the Arts Council; Average Annual Attendance: 75,000; Mem: 500; dues $15-$40; regular programs
Income: $100,000 (financed by mem & Arts Council funds)
Exhibitions: One Southeastern regional show; two national art competitions; professional & assoc invitational shows; various member exhibitions
Publications: Exhibit catalogs; newsletter, quarterly
Activities: Membership progs; workshops; lect; demonstrations; lects open to pub, 8 vis lectrs per yr; gallery talks; tours; opening receptions; competitions with awards; gallery sells original art

M **OLD SALEM MUSEUMS & GARDENS,** Museum of Early Southern Decorative Arts, 924 S Main St, Winston-Salem, NC 27101-5335. Tel 336-721-7360; Fax 336-721-7367; Email mashley@oldsalem.org; Web: www.oldsalem.org; *VPres Publs* Gary J Alpert; *Dir Educ & Spec Progs* Sally Gant; *Librn & Cur Research Coll* June Lucas; *Dir Research Center* Martha Rowe
Open Jan - Feb Tues - Sat 9:30 AM - 4:30 PM, Sun 1 - 5 PM, Mar - Dec Mon - Sat 9:30 AM - 4:30 PM, Sun 1 - 5 PM; Admis adults $14, children ages 5-16 $10; Estab 1965 to bring to light the arts & antiquities produced in Maryland, Virginia, Kentucky, Tennessee, North & South Carolina & Georgia through the first two decades of the 19th century; Three galleries are furnished with Southern decorative arts or imported objects used in the South & fifteen period settings from Southern houses dating from 1690 to 1821; Average Annual Attendance: 25,000; Mem: 1250; dues $25 & up; annual meeting in spring
Income: $225,000 (financed by endowment, mem, state appropriation & other funds)
Purchases: $50,000
Special Subjects: Ceramics, Decorative Arts, Folk Art, Furniture, Glass, Gold, Historical Material, Landscapes, Maps, Metalwork
Collections: Southern decorative arts in general, & specifically furniture, paintings, silver, ceramics, metalwares, & woodwork of southern origin
Exhibitions: Ongoing Research in Southern Decorative Arts
Publications: Journal of Early Southern Decorative Arts, semiannually; catalog of the collection 1991, Museum of Early Southern Decorative Arts; The Luminary, newsletter, semiannually
Activities: Classes for adults & children; graduate Summer Institute; lects open to public, 15 vis lectrs per yr; gallery talks; scholarships offered; exten dept serves eight Southern States; individual paintings & original objects of art lent to museums & cultural institutions & with special permission from staff are available for special exhibs; lending collection contains 2000 original art works, 100 paintings, 18,000 photographs & 30,000 slides; originate traveling exhibs; sales shop sells books, slides

L **Library and Research Center,** 924 S Main St, Winston-Salem, NC 27101-5335. Tel 336-721-7372; Email library@oldsalem.org; *Dir Research* June Lucas; *Librn* Michele Doyle; *Admin Research Assoc* Martha Rowe
Open Thurs - Fri 9:30 AM - 4:30 PM, except holidays; Estab 1965 to display & research early southern decorative arts through 1860
Library Holdings: Auction Catalogs, Audio Tapes, Book Volumes 20,000, CD-ROMs, Cards, Cassettes, Clipping Files, Compact Disks, DVDs, Exhibition Catalogs, Fiche, Manuscripts, Micro Print, Other Holdings Craftsman Database & Object Database, Periodical Subscriptions 125, Photographs, Reels, Slides, Video Tapes
Special Subjects: Archaeology, Architecture, Art History, Ceramics, Furniture
Publications: Journal of Early Southern Decorative Arts, bi-annual magazine for friends & supporters
Activities: Docent training; Lects open to public; concerts; gallery talks; tours; fels offered; furniture & needlework seminars; Mus shop sells books, reproductions & prints

M **REYNOLDA HOUSE MUSEUM OF AMERICAN ART,** 2250 Reynolda Rd, Winston-Salem, NC 27106-5117; PO Box 7287, Winston-Salem, NC 27109-7287. Tel 336-758-5150; Fax 336-758-5670; Email reynolda@reynoldahouse.org; Web: reynoldahouse.org; *Exec Dir* Allison C Perkins; *Dir Educ* Kathleen Hutton; *External Relations* Sarah Smith; *Director of Program & Interpretation* Phil Archer; *Dir Colls Management* Rebecca Eddins; *Dir of Development* Stephan Dragisic
Open Tues - Sat 9:30 AM - 4:30 PM, Sun 1:30 - 4:30 PM, cl Mon; Admis adults $14, students, mems & children free; Estab 1964 to offer a learning experience through a correlation of art, music & literature using the house & the collection of American Art as resources; 2,869 sq ft for changing exhibs; Average Annual Attendance: 55,000; Mem: 1400; board meeting in Sep, Nov, Mar, June
Income: Financed by endowment, annual fund, government & foundation grants, admis & earned income, Wake Forest Univ, donations
Library Holdings: Audio Tapes, Book Volumes, CD-ROMs, Cassettes, Clipping Files, Compact Disks, DVDs, Exhibition Catalogs, Memorabilia, Original Documents, Other Holdings, Photographs
Special Subjects: Architecture, Costumes, Decorative Arts, Furniture, Painting-American, Prints, Sculpture
Collections: Doughty Bird Collection
Exhibitions: changing exhibs featured twice a year; exhibs from the museum's permanent collection offered throughout the year; 31st Dec, 2016) Grant Wood and the American Farm; 4th Jun, 2017) Samuel FB Morsels Gallery of the Louvre and the art of Invention
Publications: Annual Report; Calendar of Events, 2 per year; Reynolda House: An American Country Home becomes a Home for American Art
Activities: Classes for adults and children; dramatic progs; docent training; lects open to pub, concerts; gallery talks; tours; Best Gallery by Winston-Salem Journal;

individual paintings and original objects of art lent to specific mus with reciprocity agreement; lending collection contains original prints, paintings; sales shop sells books, reproductions, gifts for adults & children

L **Library**, PO Box 7287, Winston-Salem, NC 27109-7287. Tel 336-758-3139; Fax 336-758-5704; *Dir Archives & Libr* F Todd Crumby
Open 9:30 AM - 4:30 PM; Circ 2,500; Open to public
Library Holdings: Audio Tapes, Book Volumes 2,500, Clipping Files, Compact Disks, Original Art Works 300, Periodical Subscriptions 30, Records, Video Tapes
Special Subjects: Afro-American Art, Art Education, Art History, Painting-American, Costume Design & Constr
Activities: Classes for adults & children; docent training; concerts; gallery talks; original objects of art lent to mus

M **SOUTHEASTERN CENTER FOR CONTEMPORARY ART,** 750 Marguerite Dr, Winston-Salem, NC 27106-5861. Tel 336-725-1904; Fax 336-722-9142; Email seccainfo@secca.org; Web: www.secca.org; *Exec Dir* Mark R Leach; *Cur Contemporary Art* Steven Matijcio; *Dir Fin & Opers* Karin Burnette; *Mktg & Pub Rels Mgr* Ellen Wallace; *Cur Educ* Deborah Randolph
Open Tues - Sat 10 AM - 5 PM, Thurs until 8 PM, Sun 1-5 PM, cl Mon & major holidays; No admis fee; Estab 1956 to identify & exhibit the world's major contemporary artists of exceptional talent; to present educational programs for children & adults; to bring the viewing public in direct contact with artists & their art. SECCA fosters creative excellence through temporary exhibs; Maintained are three indoor & outdoor exhibition areas; Average Annual Attendance: 34,000
Income: Financed by mem, local & state arts councils, grants, sales commissions & contributions
Library Holdings: Exhibition Catalogs, Periodical Subscriptions
Special Subjects: Afro-American Art, Ceramics, Collages, Crafts, Drawings, Folk Art, Glass, Hispanic Art, Juvenile Art, Landscapes, Latin American Art, Metalwork, Painting-American, Photography, Prints, Sculpture
Collections: Contemporary Art
Publications: Catalogs, 3-4 per yr; newsletter, quarterly
Activities: Classes for adults & children; dramatic progs; docent training; teacher resources; lects open to pub; 10 vis lectrs per yr; concerts; gallery talks; tours; sponsoring of competitions; scholarships; book 2 traveling exhibs per yr; originate traveling exhibs; mus shop sells original art

L **WAKE FOREST UNIVERSITY,** A Lewis Aycock Visual Resource Library, 1834 Reynolda Rd, Winston-Salem, NC 27106-5193; PO Box 7232, 110 Scales Fine Art Ctr Winston-Salem, NC 27109-7232. Tel 336-758-5078; Fax 336-758-6014; Email martine@wfu.edu; Web: www.wfu.edu/art; *Visual Resources Librn* Martine Sherrill; *Visual Libr Tech* Kendra Battle
Open Mon - Fri 9 AM - 5 PM; Estab 1968; Reference and research for students and faculty only
Income: Financed by University
Library Holdings: CD-ROMs, Clipping Files, Compact Disks, DVDs, Exhibition Catalogs, Kodachrome Transparencies, Lantern Slides, Original Art Works, Other Holdings Laserdisks, Pamphlets, Periodical Subscriptions 19, Photographs, Prints, Records 128,088, Slides 136,000, Video Tapes
Special Subjects: Afro-American Art, American Indian Art, Folk Art, History of Art & Archaeology, Islamic Art, Mexican Art, Oriental Art, Period Rooms, Pre-Columbian Art, Prints, Religious Art, Architecture, Art History, Etchings & Engravings, Printmaking, Restoration & Conservation, Woodcuts
Collections: Art Department Slide Collection, University Print Collection

M **Charlotte & Philip Hanes Art Gallery**, PO Box 7232, Reynolds Sta, Scales Fine Arts Ctr Winston-Salem, NC 27109-7232. Tel 336-758-5585; Email faccinto@wfu.edu; Web: www.wfu.edu/art; *Asst Dir* Paul Bright; *Dir* Victor Faccinto
Open Mon - Fri 10 AM - 5 PM, Sat & Sun 1 - 5 PM; No admis fee; Estab 1976 for international contemporary & historical exhibitions; 3,500 sq ft of exhibition space in two separate galleries; Average Annual Attendance: 9,000
Income: Financed by university
Collections: R J Reynolds Collection, Simmons Collection, General Collection, Portrait Collection, Print Collection, Student Union Collection of Contemporary Art
Publications: Exhibit catalog
Activities: Lects open to pub, 6 vis lectrs per yr

M **Museum of Anthropology**, Wingate Dr, Winston-Salem, NC 27109-7267; PO Box 7267, Winston-Salem, NC 27109-7267. Tel 336-758-5282; Fax 336-758-5116; Email moa@wfu.edu; Web: http://moa.wfu.edu; *Museum Educ* Tina Smith; *Asst Dir* Sara Cromwell; *Acad Dir* Andrew Gurstelle
Open Tues - Sat 10 AM - 4:30 PM; No admis fee; Estab 1963; Average Annual Attendance: 15,000; Mem: 70; dues $25 - $1,000
Income: $38,000 (financed by University, educ programs & mem)
Special Subjects: African Art, American Indian Art, Anthropology, Archaeology, Asian Art, Carpets & Rugs, Ceramics, Costumes, Dolls, Eskimo Art, Ethnology, Folk Art, Jewelry, Latin American Art, Mexican Art, Mexican Art, Oriental Art, Pottery, Pottery, Pre-Columbian Art, Pre-Columbian Art, Textiles, Primitive art
Collections: Archaeological & ethnographic objects from the Americas, Africa, Asia & Oceania
Publications: MOA News
Activities: Classes for adults & children; lects open to pub, 2 vis lectrs per yr; gallery talks; tours; awards for AAM Publication Design, SEMC Publication Design, SEMC Exhibition; exten prog: Forsyth County K-12 schools; traveling exhibs 1-2 per yr

M **WINSTON-SALEM STATE UNIVERSITY,** Diggs Gallery, 601 Martin Luther King Jr Dr, Winston-Salem, NC 27110-0003. Tel 336-750-2458; Fax 336-750-2463; Email diggsinfo@wssu.edu; Web: www.wssu.edu; *Gallery Asst* Leon Woods; *Dir, Cur, Develop & Registrar* Belinda Tate
Open Tues - Sat 11 AM - 5 PM; No admis fee; Estab 1990 as a university exhibition space highlighting African & African-American Art; 7000 sq ft, state of the art gallery, flexible space; Average Annual Attendance: 15,000
Income: $150,000-$200,000 (financed by endowment, state appropriation, grants & donations)
Library Holdings: CD-ROMs, DVDs, Exhibition Catalogs
Special Subjects: African Art, Afro-American Art, Painting-American, Photography, Pottery, Primitive art, Prints, Religious Art, Sculpture, Textiles, Watercolors, Woodcarvings, Woodcuts
Collections: African-American Art Collection
Exhibitions: African-American Quilts; Romare Bearden, John Biggers; Memory Juggs; Jacob Lawrence; Juan Logan; Alison Saar; Richmond Barthe; Lloyd Toone
Publications: Ashe Improvisation & Recycling In African-American Art Through African Eyes; Forget-Me-Not: The Art & Mystery of Memory Jugs; Model In The Mind
Activities: Classes for adults & children; lect open to public, 10-15 vis lectrs per year; individual paintings & original objects of art lent; book traveling exhibitions 5 per year

YADKINVILLE

M **CHARLES BRUCE DAVIS MUSEUM OF ART, HISTORY & SCIENCE,** 127 Hemlock St, Yadkinville, NC 27055; PO Box 356, Yadkinville, NC 27055-0356. Tel 910-679-2941
Call for hours
Collections: Local history; paintings; photographs; sculpture

NORTH DAKOTA

BELCOURT

M **TURTLE MOUNTAIN CHIPPEWA HISTORICAL SOCIETY,** Turtle Mountain Heritage Center, PO Box 900, Belcourt, ND 58316. Tel 701-477-2639; *Pres* Les Thomas
Open summer hours Mon - Fri 8 AM - 4:30 PM, Sat & Sun 1 - 5 PM, winter hours Mon - Fri 8 AM - 4:50 PM; No admis fee; Estab 1985 to promote & preserve culture; Small gallery consisting of historical photos, memorabilia, artifacts, art works, beadwork, all pertaining to the Turtle Mountain Chippewa; Mem: 200; dues $10-$500; annual meeting in Aug
Income: $98,496 (financed by mem, sales, bazaars & promotions)
Special Subjects: Archaeology, Architecture, Historical Material, Manuscripts, Maps
Collections: Ancient tools & implements, basketry, beaded artifacts, contemporary Indian crafts, costumes, memorabilia, paintings, pottery, sculpture, stones
Publications: Newsletter, twice a year
Activities: Lects open to pub; competitions with prizes; originate traveling exhibs to high school juried art shows & tri-state museums; sales shop sells books, prints, original art & reproductions

BISMARCK

A **BISMARCK ART & GALLERIES ASSOCIATION,** 422 E Front Ave, Bismarck, ND 58504-5641. Tel 701-223-5986; Fax 701-223-8960; Email baga@midconetwork.com; Web: bismarck-art.org; *Exec Dir* Linda Christman; *Program Dir* Sherry Niesar; *Admin Asst* Kathy Fetig
Open Tues - Fri 10 AM - 5 PM, Sat 1 PM - 3 PM; Mem: Student & Senior $20; Artist $25; Individual $40; Family $50; Contributor $100-$499; Donor $500-$999; Supporter $1,000-$4,499; Sustainer $2,500-$4,999; Benefactor $5,000-$9,999; Patron $10,000 & up.
Collections: Local history & culture; art exhibits

CANDO

M **CANDO ARTS CENTER,** 1115 4th Ave, Cando, ND 58324-6161. Tel 701-968-4501; Email sblordtwo@gondtc.com; *Dir* Shelley Lord
Open Tues - Sun 1 PM - 4 PM
Collections: Paintings; student artwork

DICKINSON

M **DICKINSON STATE UNIVERSITY,** Art Gallery, 291 Campus Dr, Dickinson, ND 58601-4896. Tel 701-483-2312; Fax 701-483-2006; Email carol.eacret-simmons@dickinsonstate.edu; *Assoc Dir* Rhonda Walter-Frojen; *Dir* Carol Eacret-Simmons
Open Mon - Fri 8 AM - 8 PM; No admis fee; Estab 1972 as a visual arts gallery presenting monthly exhibits representing the work of local, national & international artists; Gallery is a secure, large room approx 40 x 30 ft, with a 10 ft ceiling & approx 120 running ft of sheetrock display space; Average Annual Attendance: 6,000; Mem: 38
Income: Financed by North Dakota Council on the Arts, grants, students activities fees & mem
Special Subjects: American Indian Art, Ceramics, Graphics, Painting-American
Collections: Zoe Beiler Paintings Collection
Exhibitions: Student Exhibition; Senior Exhibition; Faculty Show; Jari Chevalier collages; Yellowstone: Then and Now; Brad Bachmeier Raku; Rhonda Walter Frojen: Willowaw Tales; Carol Eacret-Simmons: Anonymous is Another Name for Woman
Publications: Exhibit announcements
Activities: Classes for adults & children; ongoing artist-in-residence prog; lects open to pub, 4 vis lectrs per yr; gallery talks; student competitions; concerts; tours; merit awards; scholarships offered; individual paintings & original objects of art lent to faculty members; lending collection contains 70 original art works, 20 original prints & 10 photographs; book traveling exhibs 4 per yr; originate traveling exhibs

L **Stoxen Library**, 291 Campus Dr, Dickinson, ND 58601-4896. Tel 701-483-2135; Fax 701-483-2006; Email eileen.kopren@dsu.nodak.edu; Web: www.dsu.nodak.edu/library.asp; *Dir Acquisition & Cataloging* Rita Ennen; *Dir Pub Svcs* Eileen Kopren; *Librn Dir* Lillian Crook
Open Mon - Thurs 8 AM -11 PM, Fri 8 AM - 4 PM, Sat 1 - 4 PM, Sun 6 - 11 PM; Open to college students & general pub
Library Holdings: Book Volumes 97,000, Periodical Subscriptions 650

FARGO

M **GALLERY 4, LTD,** 114 Broadway, Fargo, ND 58102-4942. Tel 701-237-6867; Email gallery4ltd@gmail.com; Web: www.gallery4fargo.com; *Artist & Owner* William Damon; *Artist & Owner* Marcy Dronen; *Artist & Owner* Dennis Krull; *Artist & Owner* Kathryn Luther; *Artist & Owner* Barbara Nagle; *Artist & Owner* Jon Offutt; *Artist & Owner* Karman Rheault; *Artist & Owner* Connie Riedman; *Artist & Owner* Elizabeth Schwankl; *Artist & Owner* Scott Seiler; *Artist & Owner* Doug Stuckle
Open Mon - Sat 11 AM - 5 PM; Estab 1975; Mem: 12; dues $65 for artists
Collections: works by local artists including paintings, drawings, & sculpture
Exhibitions: Temporary exhibits

M **NORTH DAKOTA STATE UNIVERSITY,** Memorial Union Gallery, PO Box 6050, Dept 5340, Fargo, ND 58105-6050. Tel 701-231-8239, 231-7900; Fax 701-231-7866; Email ndsu.mugallery@ndsu.edu; Web: mu.ndsu.edu/mu/programs/gallery/; *Dir* Netha Cloeter
Open Tues-Sat 11AM-5PM, Thurs 11AM-8PM; No admis fee; Estab 1975 to educate through exposure to wide variety of visual artwork; 2,000 sq ft of track lighting, glass doors, temperature & in-line humidity control, attendant & security system; Average Annual Attendance: 45,000
Income: $17,000 (financed by student activity fee allocation); grants; & partnerships
Purchases: Master printmakers, original prints, original oils
Library Holdings: Book Volumes, Exhibition Catalogs, Framed Reproductions, Original Art Works
Special Subjects: Ceramics, Collages, Drawings, Etchings & Engravings, Graphics, Landscapes, Painting-European, Photography, Portraits, Posters, Pottery, Prints, Sculpture, Textiles, Watercolors, Woodcarvings, Woodcuts
Collections: Permanent collection of contemporary work by American artists, Contemporary Art, Native America
Exhibitions: Contemporary works by American artists; Regional Artists, NDSU - affiliated Artists
Publications: Roseanne Olson Photography
Activities: Educ dept; lect open to public, 4 vis lectrs per year; concerts; gallery talks; tours; competitions & awards; book traveling exhibitions 4-6 per year to museums & galleries in North Dakota & Minnesota; sales shop sells prints, reproductions & original art

M **PLAINS ART MUSEUM,** 704 First Ave N, Fargo, ND 58102-4904; PO Box 2338, Fargo, ND 58108-2338. Tel 701-551-6100; Fax 701-293-1082; Email museum@plainsart.org; Web: plainsart.org; *Dir & CEO* Andrew J Maus; *Dir Native American Progs* Laura Youngbird; *Assoc Cur Colls & Exhibs* Tasha Kubesh; *Develop Dir* Sandy Thompson; *Develop Coord* Megan Even; *Graphics & Communs Mgr* Cody Jacobson; *Registration & Bldg Opers Mgr* Steve Jacobs; *Mus Preparator* Frank McDaniels; *Dir Educ & Social Engagement* Netha Cloeter; *Exec & Development Asst* Jennifer South
Open Tues - Wed & Fri 11 AM - 5 PM, Thurs 11 AM - 9 PM, Sat 10 AM - 5 PM, cl Sun - Mon; No admis fee; Estab 1975 to bring people & art together.; Former International Harvester Building (1908); 3 galleries for permanent collection & traveling exhibits. Maintains reference library; Average Annual Attendance: 60,000; Mem: 1000; annual meeting in May
Income: Financed by mem, NEH, NEA & foundations grants & charitable gaming, special events, state & bus grants
Library Holdings: Exhibition Catalogs, Periodical Subscriptions
Special Subjects: African Art, American Indian Art, American Western Art, Ceramics, Drawings, Folk Art, Glass, Graphics, Landscapes, Painting-American, Painting-Canadian, Photography, Portraits, Posters, Pottery, Prints, Sculpture, Watercolors, Woodcuts, Woodcarvings
Collections: 4,000 works including national, international, regional fine art & ethnographic objects; Contemporary Painting, Native American Art, West African Art
Publications: Plains Art Museum, quarterly; exhibition checklist & catalogs with each exhibition
Activities: Classes for adults & children; docent training; artist residencies; Native American artists prog; lects open to pub; 6 vis lectrs per yr; concerts; gallery talks; tours; competitions with prizes; family art workshops; exten dept serves North Dakota, Minnesota, Montana, South Dakota & Manitoba; book traveling exhibs; originate traveling exhibs circulated to galleries and mus in a 6 state area: ND, SD, MN, MT, Manitoba, Saskatchewan; mus shop sells books, magazines, original art, posters and prints, reproductions, t-shirts, jewelry, postcards and local craft items

FORT RANSOM

M **SVACA - SHEYENNE VALLEY ARTS & CRAFTS ASSOCIATION,** Bjarne Ness Gallery at Bear Creek Hall, PO Box 21, Fort Ransom, ND 58033-0021. Tel 701-973-4461, 973-4491; *Prog Coordr* Georgia Rusfvold
Open Sat, Sun & holidays 1 - 6 PM, June 1 - Sept 30; No admis fee, donations accepted; Estab 1966 to promote & encourage the arts in a rural setting; The Gallery is the former studio of the late Bjarne Ness; Average Annual Attendance: 2,400; Mem: 180; dues couple $8; annual meeting in Oct
Income: Financed by mem, grants & Annual Festival
Special Subjects: Painting-American, Woodcarvings
Collections: Bjarne Ness Paintings Collection, paintings & wood carvings by area artists in SVACA's Bear Creek Hall
Activities: Classes for adults & children

A **Organization**, Box 21, Fort Ransom, ND 58033. Tel 701-973-4461; Email svaca@drtel.net; Web: www.svaca.org
Open last weekend in Sept 10 AM - 5 PM; Admis $2; Open to members for reference; Average Annual Attendance: 8,000; Mem: dues individual $5, family $10
Income: Proceeds from admis fees & craft show vendors
Library Holdings: Book Volumes 100, Periodical Subscriptions 3
Exhibitions: Fine art show during annual festival

FORT TOTTEN

A **FORT TOTTEN STATE HISTORIC SITE,** Pioneer Daughters Museum, PO Box 224, Fort Totten, ND 58335-0224. Tel 701-766-4441; Email shstotten@nd.gov; *Co-Site Supv* Rhonda Greene; *Co-Site Supvr* John Mattson
Open May 16 - Sept 15 8 AM - 5 PM, Sept 16 - May 15 weekdays by appointment; Admis adults $5, children 6-15 $2, children 5 & under free; Estab 1867 to preserve & display local & state history; Average Annual Attendance: 14,000; Mem: 150; dues $40
Income: Financed by state appropriation, donations
Collections: Buildings of historic site, outdoor museum, Pioneer Artifacts
Activities: Classes for adults & children; guided group tours; lects open to pub; tours; competitions; originate traveling exhibs; mus shop sells books & magazines; junior mus

GRAND FORKS

M **BROWNING ARTS,** 23 S Fourth St, Grand Forks, ND 58201-4733. Tel 701-746-5090
Open Jan- late Nov Mon-Fri 9AM-5:30PM, Thanksgiving-Christmas Mon-Sat 9AM-5:30PM
Collections: ceramics; painting; drawings; photography; computer art; sculpture; jewelry

M **NORTH DAKOTA MUSEUM OF ART,** 261 Centennial Dr, Stop 7305 Grand Forks, ND 58202-6003. Tel 701-777-4195; Fax 701-777-4425; Email ndmoa@ndmoa.com; Web: www.ndmoa.com; *Dir & Chief Cur* Laurel J Reuter; *Exhib Coordr* Greg Vettel; *Dir Educ* Sue Fink; *Bus Mgr* Amy Hovde; *Dir Develop* Bonnie Sobolik; *Asst to Dir* Brian Lofthus; *Asst Dir Educ* Matt Wallace; *Office Mgr* Connie Hulst; *Tech Asst* Justin Dalzell; *Mem Coordr* Stacy Warcup
Open Mon - Fri 9 AM - 5 PM, Sat & Sun 1PM- 5 PM, cl major holidays; No admis fee; Estab 1971 as a contemporary art museum; In 1989 the museum moved into a renovated 1907 campus building/gymnasium after 3 yrs of renovations; Average Annual Attendance: 50,000; Mem: 500; dues individual $35; annual meeting in June
Income: Financed by private endowments, gifts, grants, mem & earned income
Collections: American, Contemporary & International art in all media from 1970s to present, Contemporary Native American Art
Publications: Exhibition catalog with some exhibits
Activities: Dramatic progs; docent training; workshops; annual concert series; readers series; summer art camp; lects open to pub, 25 vis lectrs per yr; gallery talks; tours; originate traveling exhibs for circulation to US mus & abroad; mus shop sells books, magazines, folk & ethnic art

M **UNIVERSITY OF NORTH DAKOTA,** Hughes Fine Arts Center-Col Eugene Myers Art Gallery, Dept of Visual Arts, Rm 127, UND Art Department Grand Forks, ND 58202-7099; 3350 Campus Rd Stop 7099, Grand Forks, ND 58202-7099. Tel 701-777-2257; Fax 701-777-2903; Email art.jones@und.edu; Web: www.und.edu
Open 11:30 AM - 4 PM; No admis fee; Estab 1979 to augment teaching & offer another location to display art; 96 running ft of wall space; Average Annual Attendance: 1,200
Income: Financed through university
Purchases: CE Myers Trust Fund
Special Subjects: Calligraphy, Ceramics, Drawings, Jewelry, Sculpture, Textiles
Collections: Collection chosen from Annual Print & Drawing Juried Exhibit, Myers Foundations
Exhibitions: Rotating exhibitions

MAYVILLE

M **MAYVILLE STATE UNIVERSITY,** Northern Lights Art Gallery, 330 NE 3rd St, Mayville, ND 58257. Email director@northernlightsart.org; Web: www.northernlightsart.org; *Dir* Cynthia Kaldor; *Dir Comm Sch Arts* Mike Bakken
Open Mon - Fri 11 AM - 3 PM; No admis fee; Estab 1999; Gallery in student center bldg 40 'x 40'; Average Annual Attendance: 900; Mem: over 100 mem, $25 fee
Income: mem fees, ann auction
Exhibitions: Contemporary American & North Dakota artists; student exhibitions; visiting collections
Activities: Classes for adults; docent training; January auction; vis artists; gallery tours; sponsoring of competitions

MINOT

M **LILLIAN & COLEMAN TAUBE MUSEUM OF ART,** 2 N Main St, Minot, ND 58703. Tel 701-838-4445; Fax 701-838-6471; Email taube@srt.com; Web: www.taubemuseum.org; *Exec Dir & Cur* Nancy F Brown; *Educ Coordr* Margaret Lee; *Gallery Mgr* Doug Pfliger
Open Jan 1 - Dec 31, Tues - Fri 10:30 AM - 5:30 PM, Sat 11 AM -4 PM; Admis is by suggested contribution; Estab 1970 to promote means & opportunities for the educ of the pub with respect to the study & culture of the fine arts; Renovated bank; Average Annual Attendance: 20,000; Mem: Membership 500; dues $25 - $1000, board meeting 3rd Thurs of month
Income: Financed by endowment, mem, contributions, sales, grants & mem fees

Library Holdings: Compact Disks, Framed Reproductions, Memorabilia, Original Art Works, Pamphlets, Photographs, Prints, Sculpture
Special Subjects: African Art, Afro-American Art, American Indian Art, American Western Art, Asian Art, Ceramics, Glass, Hispanic Art, Jewelry, Juvenile Art, Landscapes, Latin American Art, Metalwork, Mexican Art, Oriental Art, Painting-American, Photography, Porcelain, Portraits, Pottery, Prints, Sculpture, Stained Glass, Textiles, Watercolors, Woodcarvings
Collections: Original art works, paintings, pottery, printmaking, sculpture, all done by local & national artists
Exhibitions: Art competitions; art fests; one-person exhibits; traveling art exhibits; exhibitions change monthly
Publications: Calendar of Exhibits; quarterly newsletter
Activities: Classes for adults & children; dramatic progs; educ prog; gallery talks; concerts; tour; competitions; North Dakota juried student art awards; book traveling exhibs 2-3 per yr; originates traveling exhibs to North Dakota galleries; mus shop sells books, original art, reproductions, prints, cards, & children's art supplies

M **MINOT STATE UNIVERSITY,** Northwest Art Center, 500 University Ave W, Minot, ND 58707-0002. Tel 701-858-3264; Fax 701-858-3894; Email nac@minotstateu.edu; Web: www.minotstateu.edu/nac; *Dir* Avis Veikley
Open Mon - Fri 8 AM - 4:30 PM, cl holidays; No admis fee; Estab 1975 as a supplementary teaching aid, resource for Minot State University, Northwest & Central North Dakota; Two galleries: Hartnett Hall Gallery & Gordon B Olson Library Gallery; 600 sq ft; Average Annual Attendance: 6,000
Income: $25,000 (financed by grants, university, juried show entry fees)
Purchases: $2,500
Library Holdings: Exhibition Catalogs, Original Art Works, Photographs, Prints, Slides
Special Subjects: American Western Art, Ceramics, Drawings, Etchings & Engravings, Graphics, Landscapes, Painting-American, Photography, Portraits, Posters, Pottery, Prints, Watercolors, Woodcuts
Collections: More than 600 works in collection; focus is contemporary 2-D works on paper in all media (printmaking, drawing, painting)
Exhibitions: America's 2000: All Media (Aug-Sept); America's 2000: Paperworks Exhibition (Jan-Feb); 20 exhibitions annually
Publications: Calendar of exhibits, annual; posters
Activities: Classes for adults; artist in residence; lects open to pub, 10-12 vis lectrs per yr; gallery talks; tours; competitions with awards, merit, best of show & purchase; book traveling exhibs 6-10 per yr; originate traveling exhibs to regional venues, galleries in ND

MOTT

M **MOTT GALLERY OF HISTORY & ART,** 202 E 3rd St, PO Box 116 Mott, ND 58646. Tel 701-824-2163; Web: www.discovermott.com/history-art/history-art-gallery.html; *Contact Person* Geno Sloan
Open Thurs & Sat 1 PM - 4 PM
Collections: Banking and railroad history, early business exhibits, military & school displays
Exhibitions: Monthly exhibits
Activities: Tours

OHIO

AKRON

M **AKRON ART MUSEUM,** One South High, Akron, OH 44308-2084. Tel 330-376-9185; Fax 330-376-1180; Email mail@akronartmuseum.org; Web: www.akronartmuseum.org; *Dir & CEO* Mark Masuoka; *Colls Mgr* Arnold Tunstall; *CFO* Sherry Streb; *Dir Educ* Alison Caplan; *Pres (V)* Chris Myeroff; *Mus Shop Mgr* Laura Firestone; *Assoc Educator* Gina Thomas-McGee; *Development Officer* Jenee Garlando; *Dir Design* Joseph Walton; *Development Officer* Eliza Williams; *Chief Cur* Janice Driesbach; *Preparator* Chris Ross; *Design, Marketing & Communications Coordinator* Dominic Caruso; *Library & Archives Manager* Stefanie Hilles; *Special Project Manager* Jennifer Shipman; *Operations Manager* John Kane; *Associate Curator* Theresa Bemonister; *Assistant Curator* Liz Carney; *Educator for Early Childhood, Family & Youth Engagement* Amanda Crow
Open Wed - Sun 11 AM - 5 PM, Thurs 11 AM - 9 PM, cl Mon & Tues, New Year's Day, Memorial Day, Independence Day, Labor Day, Thanksgiving, Christmas Eve & Day; Admis adults $7, students $5, seniors 65 & over $5, children 12 & under & members free; Estab 1922 as a mus to exhibit & collect art; In 1981 opened new Akron Art Mus in restored & reconstructed 1899 National Register Historic Building; Coop Himmelblau's 64,000 sq ft bldg opened in 2007 connected to existing bldg; Average Annual Attendance: 65,000; Mem: 2,300; dues general $45; annual meeting in Sept
Income: $3,600,000 (financed by mem, endowment, corporate, foundation & government grants)
Purchases: Tony Feher, Yinka Shonibare, Barbara Probst, Michalene Thomas
Library Holdings: Auction Catalogs, Audio Tapes, Book Volumes 12,000, Cassettes, Clipping Files, DVDs, Exhibition Catalogs, Kodachrome Transparencies, Pamphlets, Periodical Subscriptions, Photographs, Slides, Video Tapes
Special Subjects: Art History, Decorative Arts, Folk Art, Latin American Art, Painting-American, Painting-European, Photography, Sculpture
Collections: 20th Century American & European painting, photography & sculpture; Late 19th Century American painting
Publications: Biennial report, quarterly magazine, gallery guides & exhib catalogues
Activities: Educ dept; classes for adults & children & babies; docent training; lects open to pub, 8+ vis lectrs per yr; concerts; gallery talks; tours; Knight Purchase Award for Photographic Media; book traveling exhibs 4 per yr; originates traveling exhibs 1 per yr; mus shop sells books, magazines, original art, reproductions, prints, gift items, video CD

L **Martha Stecher Reed Art Library**, One South High, Akron, OH 44308. Tel 330-376-9185; Fax 330-376-1180; Email shilles@akronartmuseum.org; Web: www.akronartmuseum.org; *Librn & Archives Mgr* Stefanie Hilles
Open by appointment; no admis fee; Circ 12,000; Open to pub for reference, non-circulating
Library Holdings: Auction Catalogs, Audio Tapes, Book Volumes 12,000, Cassettes, Clipping Files, DVDs, Exhibition Catalogs, Kodachrome Transparencies, Pamphlets, Periodical Subscriptions, Photographs, Slides, Video Tapes 50
Special Subjects: Afro-American Art, Conceptual Art, Folk Art, Latin American Art, Painting-American, Photography, Sculpture, Art History
Collections: Edwin Shaw Volumes, to accompany coll of American Impressionist Art
Activities: Classes for children; docent training; lects open to pub; gallery talks; concerts; tours

L **AKRON-SUMMIT COUNTY PUBLIC LIBRARY,** Fine Arts Division, 60 S High St, Akron, OH 44326-1000. Tel 330-643-9040; Fax 330-643-9033; Email esdiv@akronlibrary.org; Web: www.akronlibrary.org; *Mgr History & Humanities Div* Bob Ethington; *Dir* David Jennings; *Asst Dir* Pam Hickson-Stevenson; *Main Library Gen Mgr* Rick Ewing; *Mktg Dir* Carla Davis
Open Mon - Thurs 9 AM - 9 PM, Fri 9 AM - 6 PM, Sat 9 AM - 5 PM, Sun 1 - 5 PM; Estab 1904 to serve the educational & recreational needs of the general public of Summit & contiguous counties
Income: $75,000 (financed by state and local taxes)
Library Holdings: Book Volumes 55,000, Clipping Files, Exhibition Catalogs, Fiche, Pamphlets, Periodical Subscriptions 150
Special Subjects: Architecture, Art History, Ceramics, Costume Design & Constr, Decorative Arts, Crafts, Drawings, Embroidery, Folk Art, Graphic Arts, Glass, Illustration, Jewelry, Photography
Activities: Book traveling exhibs 1-3 per year

M **STAN HYWET HALL & GARDENS,** 714 N Portage Path, Akron, OH 44303-1399. Tel 330-836-5533; Fax 330-836-2680; Email info@stanhywet.org; Web: www.stanhywet.org; *Pres & CEO* Linda Conrad; *Dir Mus Services* Julie Frey; *Dir Horticulture* Tom Hrivnak
Open Apr - Dec Tues - Sun 10 AM - 6 PM, last admission at 4:30 PM; Varies by tour, please visit website; Incorporated 1957, Stan Hywet Hall is a house mus & garden, serving as a civic & cultural center. All restoration & preservation work is carefully researched to retain the original concept of the property, which represents a way of life that is gone forever; The mansion, the focal point of the estate, is a 65-room Tudor Revival manor house, furnished with priceless antiques & works of art dating from the 14th century. The property is the former home of Frank A Seiberling, (Akron rubber industrialist & co-founder of Goodyear Tire & Rubber) & was completed in 1915. There are 70 acres of formal gardens, meadow, woods & lagoons; Average Annual Attendance: 200,000; Mem: 3700; dues $55 & up; ann meeting in May
Income: $5,000,000 (financed by endowment, mem, admis, gifts, grants, rentals & special events)
Library Holdings: Audio Tapes, Book Volumes, CD-ROMs, Clipping Files, Compact Disks, DVDs, Framed Reproductions, Manuscripts, Maps, Memorabilia, Motion Pictures, Original Art Works, Original Documents, Pamphlets, Periodical Subscriptions, Photographs, Prints, Records, Reels, Reproductions, Sculpture, Slides, Video Tapes
Special Subjects: Period Rooms
Collections: Antique furniture, china, crystal, paintings, porcelain, rugs, sculpture, silver, tapestries, architectural drawings, manuscripts & photographs
Exhibitions: Permanent & temporary exhibitions through the year
Publications: Stan Hywet Hall and Gardens Annual Report, yearly; Stan Hywet Hall Newsletter, quarterly
Activities: Children's progs; dramatic progs; docent training; classes for adults & children; lects open to pub; lects open to mems only; 6 vis lectrs per yr; yr round special events; concerts; tours; exten dept serves libraries; original objects of art lent to historical societies & mus; mus shop sells books, original art, reproductions, slides & wide variety of gift items

M **THE SUMMIT COUNTY HISTORICAL SOCIETY OF AKRON, OH,** 550 Copley Rd, Akron, OH 44320-2398. Tel 330-535-1120; Fax 330-535-0250; Email schs@summithistory.org; Web: www.summithistory.org/blog; *President & CEO* Leianne Neff Heppner; *Board Chair* Dave Lieberth; *Bus Mgr* Sandy Pecimon; *Educ Coordr* Claire Lucas; *Admin* Mary Conley; *Vol Coordr* Gayle Glanville; *Curator* Theodore Mallison; *Development Director* Bethany Scheffler
Open Office: Tues - Fri 8 AM - 4 PM; Tours: Wed - Sat 1 PM - 4 PM; Admis adults $6, seniors $4, children $2; Estab 1924 for the collection, preservation & display of items of an historical nature from Summit County; mission to preserve, interpret & educate others on the history of Akron; 1837 Perkins Stone Mansion - Greek revival home with period rooms; Average Annual Attendance: 14,000; Mem: 500; dues $40 - $500; annual meeting in spring
Income: $370,000 (financed by endowment, mem & foundations)
Library Holdings: Audio Tapes, Book Volumes, Lantern Slides, Manuscripts, Maps, Memorabilia, Motion Pictures, Original Art Works, Original Documents, Pamphlets, Photographs, Prints, Records, Reels, Reproductions, Slides, Video Tapes
Special Subjects: Architecture, Carpets & Rugs, Ceramics, Costumes, Decorative Arts, Dolls, Embroidery, Etchings & Engravings, Folk Art, Furniture, Glass, Historical Material, Manuscripts, Maps, Military Art, Painting-American, Period Rooms, Photography, Portraits, Pottery, Prints, Silver, Textiles, Tapestries
Collections: 19th & 20th century costumes & accessories, 1810-1900 era furniture, 19th century chinaware, glassware, silverware & pottery, 19th century portraits, 19th & 20th century tools, household items & toys, Native Am material, The John Brown House, Numerous works of art on paper & canvas, Works of art on paper are stored at Akron-Summit County Pub Libr
Exhibitions: Perkins Stone Mansion; Framework of Fashion; Photography: An Invention Without Future; 10 intern-led exhibitions due to grant from the Ohio Humanities Council, a state affiliate of the National Endowment for the Humanities and the Ohio Assn of Historical Societies & Museums; Securing the Shadow: Portrait Photography in Akron, 1850-1900; A Garden Wedding
Publications: Old Portage Trail Review, quarterly

Activities: Educ dept; classes for adults & children; docent training; outreach focused; gallery talks; tours; Stuart B Steiner award for Volunteerism; The Summit Awards to Akron & Summit County residents who have made a national impact; scholarships; lending of original objects of art to city, county, regional & some out-of-state exhib; SCHS books available for purchase about the local history

M **UNIVERSITY OF AKRON,** University Art Galleries, 150 E Exchange St, Akron, OH 44325-7801. Tel 330-972-5950; Fax 330-972-5960; Email bengsto@uakron.edu; Web: art.uakron.edu/university-galleries/
Open Mon, Tues & Fri 10 AM - 5 PM, Wed & Thurs 10 AM - 9 PM; No admis fee; Estab 1974 to exhibit the work of important contemporary artists working in all regions of the United States, as well as to provide a showcase for the work of artists working within the university community; Two galleries: Emily H Davis Art Gallery, 2000 sq ft of floor space; 200 running ft of wall space; Guzzetta Hall Atrium Gallery, 120 running ft of wall space; Average Annual Attendance: 12,000-15,000
Income: Financed by university funds & grants
Collections: Contemporary Art
Exhibitions: Rotating exhibits, call for details
Publications: Catalogs & artists books in conjunction with exhibitions
Activities: Lects open to pub, 5-10 per yr; gallery talks; tours; competitions; awards for Student Show; scholarships & fels offered; book traveling exhibs; originate traveling exhibs, circulation to other university galleries & small museums with contemporary program

ASHLAND

M **ASHLAND COLLEGE ARTS & HUMANITIES GALLERY,** The Coburn Gallery, 401 College Ave, Ashland, OH 44805-3799. Tel 419-289-4142, 419-289-5652; Fax 419-289-5999; *Dir* Larry Schiemann
Open Mon-Fri 10 AM-5PM; No admis fee; Estab 1969; Gallery maintained for continuous exhibitions
Collections: Mostly contemporary works, some historical
Exhibitions: Invitational Printmaking; annual student exhibition; rotating exhibitions
Activities: Classes for children; dramatic progs; lects open to pub; 2-3 gallery talks; tours & regular tours to leading art mus; concerts; schols; original objects of art lent to Akron Art Institute and Cleveland Museum of Art

ASHTABULA

A **ASHTABULA ARTS CENTER,** 2928 W 13th St, Ashtabula, OH 44004-2498. Tel 440-964-3396; Fax 440-964-3396; Email info@ashtabulaartscenter.org; Web: ashtabulaartscenter.org; *Pres* Lauren Hammond; *Exec Dir* Meaghan Humphrey; *Fin Dir* Krist Morris; *Dance Dir* Shelagh Dubsky; *Visual Art Dir* Linda Merchant; *Theater & Music Dir* Kimberly Godfrey; *Tech Dir* Ray Beach; *Mktg & Pub Rels Dir* Amanda Frazier
Open Mon - Thurs 9 AM - 9 PM, Fri 9 AM - 4 PM, Sat 9 AM - 1 PM, cl holidays; No admis fee; Estab 1953 as a nonprofit, tax exempt art organization, to provide high quality instruction; One major gallery area with smaller annex-fixed panels on all walls; Average Annual Attendance: 15,000; Mem: 1000; dues family $50, individual $25
Income: Financed by mem, tui, ticket sales, foundations, OH Arts Council
Collections: Local & regional contemporary work, small international contemporary print collection, regional wood sculpture (major portion of collection represents local & regional talent)
Publications: Ashtabula Arts Center News, 5 per yr; monthly exhibit information
Activities: Classes for adults & children; dramatic prog; lects open to pub, 5-10 vis lectrs per yr; concerts; gallery talks; tours; competitions; cash awards; schols & fels offered

ATHENS

A **THE DAIRY BARN ARTS CENTER,** 8000 Dairy Ln, Athens, OH 45701-9393. Tel 740-592-4981; Fax 740-592-5090; Email artsinfo@dairybarn.org; Web: www.dairybarn.org; *Exec Dir* Andrea Lewis; *Dir Educ* Lyn Smith; *Quilt Natl Dir* Kathleen Dawson; *Facilities Mgr* Reid Secoy; *Gallery Shop Mgr* Claire White; *Dir Exhibs* Deanna Schwartz
Open Tues - Sat Noon - 5 PM, Thurs until 8 PM, Sun 1-5 PM; Admis varies; Estab 1977 to promote art & culture; 7000 sq ft gallery located in historic dairy barn; Average Annual Attendance: 15,000; Mem: 650; dues $50-$100; annual meeting in Jan
Income: Financed by admis, mem, corp sponsorships, grants, exhib tours & art sales
Special Subjects: Ceramics, Collages, Crafts, Decorative Arts, Folk Art, Furniture, Glass, Juvenile Art, Landscapes, Sculpture, Watercolors
Exhibitions: Athens Voices, Quilt National (summer-odd years); OH+5 (winter)
Activities: Educ prog; classes for adults & children; dramatic progs; docent training; summer art camp; lects open to pub; concerts; gallery talks; tours; competitions with awards; exten dept serves area schools; book traveling exhibs nationally; originate traveling exhibs; open to galleries, museums, universities; mus shop sells books, magazines, original art, reproductions & prints

M **OHIO UNIVERSITY,** Kennedy Museum of Art, Ohio University, 1 Lin Hall Athens, OH 45701-2979. Tel 740-593-1304; Fax 740-593-1305; Email kennedymuseum@ohio.edu; Web: www.ohiou.edu/museum; *Registrar* Jeffrey Carr; *Cur Educ* Sally Delgado; *Dir* Edward E Pauley; *Cur* Petra Kralickova; *Admin Assoc* Lori Spencer
Open Tues, Wed, Fri Noon - 5 PM, Thurs Noon - 8 PM, Sat - Sun 1 - 5 PM; No admis fee; 1993; Average Annual Attendance: 10,000; Mem: 220; dues vary; annual meeting in spring
Special Subjects: African Art, American Indian Art, Bronzes, Carpets & Rugs, Ceramics, Drawings, Etchings & Engravings, Graphics, Historical Material, Jewelry, Landscapes, Metalwork, Painting-American, Painting-American, Photography, Prints, Sculpture, Silver, Textiles, Woodcuts, Southwestern Art, Watercolors
Collections: Contemporary prints, paintings, photographs & sculpture, Edwin L & Ruth E Kennedy Southwest Native American Collection, African masks, Southwest Native American jewelry & weavings
Exhibitions: Four rotating exhibits per yr; Permanent exhibit - rotates every 2 yrs
Publications: Exhibition catalogs; Member Newsletter
Activities: Classes for children; lec for members; gallery talks; tours; individual paintings & original objects of art lent for southeastern Ohio; artmobile for K-12 schools; book traveling exhibitions 1 per year

M **Ohio University Art Gallery**, 528 Seigfred Hall, School of Art Athens, OH 45701-2978. Tel 740-593-0796; Fax 740-593-0457; *Dir* David LaPalombara; *Gallery Dir* Courtney Kessel
Open Mon- Sat 10 AM - 4 PM, Thurs 10 AM - 8 PM; No admis fee; Estab 1960; Gallery is used for faculty exhibitions, student exhibitions & vis artist shows; Average Annual Attendance: 15,000
Exhibitions: Rotating exhibits by students & faculty; National & international vis artists

L **Fine Arts Library**, Alden Library, 30 Park Place Athens, OH 45701-2978. Tel 740-593-2663; Fax 740-593-0138; Email ginther@ohio.edu; Web: library.ohio.edu/finearts/index.html; *Art Librn* Gary Ginther; *Library Support Specialist* Nancy Story; *Library Support Specialist* Laura Burns
Open Mon - Thurs 8 AM - 12 AM, Fri 8 AM - 9 PM, Sat 10 AM - 9 PM, Sun Noon - 12 AM; 0; Selective exhibition of student & faculty work
Income: Financed by state appropriation
Library Holdings: Book Volumes 75,000, CD-ROMs, DVDs, Exhibition Catalogs, Fiche, Periodical Subscriptions 300
Special Subjects: Photography
Collections: Research coll in history of photography, small coll of original photographs for study purposes, Yao Research Collection of Vietnamese cultural objects

BAY VILLAGE

A **BAY ARTS, INC,** (Baycrafters, Inc), 28795 Lake Rd, Huntington Metropark Bay Village, OH 44140-1364. Tel 440-871-6543; Fax 440-871-0452; Email info@bayarts.net; Web: www.bayarts.net; *Dir* Nancy Heaton
Open Mon - Sat 12 - 5 PM; No admis fee; Estab 1948 for advancement & enjoyment of arts & crafts in the region; Average Annual Attendance: 30,000; Mem: 1800, dues individuals $25, family $40, students $10, bus people $50
Exhibitions: Christmas Show; Emerald Necklace Juried Art Show; Juried Art Show; Renaissance Faire; student competition; individual gallery shows; floral juried art show; Victoria Garden Party; Heritage Days
Publications: Bulletins & competition notices
Activities: Classes for adults & children; lect open to public, 9-12 vis lectrs per year; gallery talks; tours; tea room for children's birthday parties; monetary prizes awarded; scholarships offered; sales shop sells original art, reproductions, prints, pottery & other crafts work from local & out-of-town artists

BEACHWOOD

M **THE TEMPLE-TIFERETH ISRAEL,** The Temple Museum of Religious Art, 26000 Shaker Blvd, Beachwood, OH 44122-7199. Tel 216-831-3233, ext 108; Email skoletsky@ttti.org; Web: www.ttti.org; *Dir Mus* Susan Koletsky
Open daily 9 AM - 3 PM by appointment only; No admis fee; Estab 1950 for the display & teaching of Judaica; Two galleries, each housed in a national landmark temple; Average Annual Attendance: 10,000; Mem: 15,000; annual meeting
Special Subjects: Archaeology, Costumes, Decorative Arts, Embroidery, Etchings & Engravings, Ethnology, Glass, Graphics, Historical Material, Judaica, Landscapes, Leather, Manuscripts, Maps, Metalwork, Painting-Israeli, Portraits, Pottery, Religious Art, Silver, Stained Glass, Textiles, Watercolors
Collections: Antique Torah hangings, Holy Land pottery, Israel stamps, paintings, sculpture, stained glass, Torah ornaments
Exhibitions: 50 Years of Israel Stamps from the Miriam Leikind Collection & Albert Friedberg Collection
Activities: Classes for adults & children; lects open to pub, 12 vis lectrs per yr; gallery talks; tours; original objects of art lent to other professional institutions; mus shop sells Judaic ritual objects

L **Lee & Dolores Hartzmark Library**, 26000 Shaker Blvd, Beachwood, OH 44122. Tel 216-831-3233, ext 120; Fax 216-831-4216; Web: www.ttti.org; *Dir & Librn* Andrea Davidson; *Asst Librn* Wendy Wasman
Two buildings
Library Holdings: Audio Tapes, Book Volumes 10,000, Cassettes, Exhibition Catalogs, Filmstrips, Framed Reproductions, Manuscripts, Memorabilia, Original Art Works, Other Holdings Audio Books; Computer Software, Pamphlets, Periodical Subscriptions 50, Photographs, Prints, Records, Reproductions, Sculpture, Video Tapes
Special Subjects: Archaeology, Architecture, Art History, Bookplates & Bindings, Calligraphy, Drawings, Embroidery, Ethnology, Folk Art, Handicrafts, Historical Material, Judaica, Painting-European, Painting-Israeli, Religious Art
Collections: Permanent collection of silver, manuscripts & fabrics of Judaica over the last 200 years, pottery from antiquity
Exhibitions: 50 years of Israel Stamps from the Miriam Leikind Collection & Albert Friedberg Collection
Publications: The Loom and the Cloth: an exhibition of the fabrics of Jewish life

BEREA

M **BALDWIN-WALLACE COLLEGE,** Fawick Art Gallery, 275 Eastland Rd, Berea, OH 44017-2088. Tel 440-826-2152; Fax 440-826-3380; Email info@bw.edu; Web: www.bw.edu/academics/art/gallery; *Dir* Prof Paul Jacklitch
Open Mon - Fri 2 - 5 PM; No admis fee; The Art Gallery is considered to be a part of the art prog & the dept of art; its purpose is that of a teaching mus for the students of the col & the general public; Average Annual Attendance: 2,500

Income: Financed through budgetary support of the college
Special Subjects: Drawings, Painting-American, Prints, Sculpture
Collections: Approx 200 paintings and sculptures by Midwest artists of the 20th century, approx 1900 drawings and prints from 16th - 20th century, with a concentration in 19th & 20th century examples
Exhibitions: Annual Spring Student Show & Senior Exhibition
Activities: Lect open to public; gallery talks; tours; competitions; individual paintings lent to schools; book traveling exhibitions

BOWLING GREEN

M **BOWLING GREEN STATE UNIVERSITY,** Fine Arts Center Galleries, Fine Arts Bldg, Bowling Green, OH 43403-0211. Tel 419-372-8525; Fax 419-372-2544; Web: www.digitalarts.bgsu.edu/art/galleries; *Dir Galleries* Jacqueline S Nathan
Open Tues - Sat 11 AM - 4 PM, Thurs 6PM-9PM, Sun 1 - 4 PM, cl holidays; No admis fee; Estab 1964 to contribute to the enrichment of the broader area community while supporting the acad mission of the university; 12-14 exhibits are produced each yr with goals of stimulating and educating artists & art audiences, communicating ideas, and promoting the vitality & significance of the arts; Three galleries located in the Fine Arts bldg have a combined total of approx 8000 sq ft of exhib space; Average Annual Attendance: 9,500
Income: Financed by the University, state grants & donations
Collections: Contemporary prints, Student work
Activities: Lects open to public, 6-8 vis lectrs per yr; book traveling exhibs; originate traveling exhibs

BROOKLYN

M **BROOKLYN HISTORICAL SOCIETY,** 4442 Ridge Rd, Brooklyn, OH 44144-0422; PO Box 44422, Brooklyn, OH 44144-0422. Tel 216-749-2804; Email groundhogsgarden@wowway.com; Web: brooklynohiohistory; *Trustee & Secy* Elaine Schmidt; *VPres* John Geralds; *Pres* Barbara Stepic; *Treas* Thomas Hites; *Trustee* Carole Thomson; *Trustee* Marlene Roschmann
Open Tues 10 AM - 2 PM, tours by appointment; No admis fee; Estab 1970 to preserve history of area; Wheelchair accessible to 1st floor. Maintains reference library; Average Annual Attendance: 1,500; Mem: 150; dues life $100, couple $7, single $5; meetings last Wed of month, except Jan, Feb, July, Aug & Nov
Income: $10,000 (financed by fundraisers)
Library Holdings: Audio Tapes, Clipping Files, Maps, Memorabilia, Original Documents, Other Holdings, Pamphlets, Periodical Subscriptions, Photographs, Records
Special Subjects: Dolls, Furniture, Glass, Historical Material, Laces, Maps, Period Rooms, Textiles
Collections: China, dolls, pre-1900 & 1920's furniture, glass, herb garden, kitchenware, old tools, quilts & linens
Exhibitions: World War I & Brooklyn Airport; Early schools in Brooklyn
Publications: Early Schools in Brooklyn, 2003
Activities: Classes for children; docent training; quilting & rug loom weaving demonstrations; lect open to public, 4 vis lectrs per year; 3rd grade tours every May; mus shop sells handicrafts, rag rugs, quilted items, dried herb products, handmade crafts, jams & jellies

CANTON

M **CANTON MUSEUM OF ART,** 1001 Market Ave N, Canton, OH 44702-1075. Tel 330-453-7666; Fax 330-453-1034; Email al@cantonart.org; Web: www.cantonart.org; *Treas* Lee DeGraaf; *Exec Dir* Manuel J Albacete; *Bus, Admin & Mus Shop Mgr* Kay McAllister; *Pres* David Baker; *Coordr Educ* Lauren Kuntzman; *Cur Coll & Registrar* Lynnda Arrasmith; *Asst Cur & Mus Guild Coordr* Kathy Fleeher
Open Mon-Sat 10 AM-5 PM, Tues, Wed, and Thurs 7PM-9PM, Sun 1PM-5PM; Admis adults $4, seniors & students $2.50, mems & children under 10 free; Estab 1935, incorporated 1941; Nine modern gallery areas of various sizes; Average Annual Attendance: 50,000; Mem: 1200; dues $15 and higher; annual meeting Fall
Special Subjects: Ceramics, Costumes, Decorative Arts, Graphics, Painting-American, Painting-Italian, Painting-Spanish, Portraits, Sculpture, Watercolors
Collections: Collection focus is 19th & 20th century American watercolors and works on paper, also contemporary ceramics
Exhibitions: Approx 25-40 traveling or collected exhibs of commercial & industrial arts; painting; sculpture annually; French Music Hall Posters from 1890 to 1940's.
Activities: Formally organized education progs for adults & children; docent training; lects open to pub, 10 vis lectrs per yr; films; gallery talks; art festivals; competitions with awards; guided tours; scholarships offered; individual and original objects of art lent; book traveling exhibs; originate traveling exhibs; mus shop sells books, original art, prints

L **Art Library,** 1001 Market Ave N, Canton, OH 44702. Tel 330-453-7666; Fax 330-453-1034; Email max@cantonart.org; Web: www.cantonart.org; *Exec Dir* M J Albacete; *Mktg Dir* Max Barton; *Develop Dir* Christine Shearer; *Cur & Registrar* Lynnda Arrasmith
Open Tues & Wed 10 AM - 8 PM, Thurs & Fri 10 AM - 5 PM, Sat 10 AM - 3 PM, Sun 1 PM - 5 PM; Admis adults $6, seniors $4; Estab 1935; National Touring & CMA produced exhibs; Average Annual Attendance: 40,000; Mem: Go to: www.cantonart.org/membership
Income: Local, state & National Grant supported; pub & private donors
Library Holdings: Audio Tapes, Book Volumes 2500, Clipping Files, Exhibition Catalogs, Pamphlets, Periodical Subscriptions 25, Prints, Slides, Video Tapes 120
Special Subjects: Art History, Ceramics
Collections: CMA permanent collection: 19th, 20th & 21st century American Works on Paper; American ceramics
Activities: Classes for adults & children; docent training; in-school & in-museum educ outreach; lects open to pub; gallery talks; tours; sponsor competitions; schols; mus shop sells books, original art, reproductions, jewelry & local art

CHILLICOTHE

M **PUMP HOUSE CENTER FOR THE ARTS,** PO Box 1613, Chillicothe, OH 45601-5613. Tel 740-772-5783; Fax 740-772-5783; Email info@pumphouseartgallery.com; Web: www.pumphouseartgallery.com; *Dir* Charles Wallace
Open Tues - Fri 11 AM - 4 PM, Sat & Sun 1 - 4 PM, Cl. Mon; No admis fee; Estab 1986; Historic Pump House restored for art center, gift shop & gallery. Arts Festival held the last weekend in June; Average Annual Attendance: 20,000; Mem: 350; dues 15-375
Income: $110,000 (financed by mem, sales of artwork & Rio Grande Univ Partnership
Library Holdings: Book Volumes, Periodical Subscriptions
Special Subjects: Afro-American Art, American Indian Art, Painting-American, Painting-Dutch, Pewter, Photography, Porcelain, Portraits, Posters, Pottery, Prints, Reproductions, Scrimshaw, Sculpture, Silver, Stained Glass, Watercolors, Woodcarvings, Woodcuts
Collections: Baskets, fine art, fine designer crafts, glass, prints, quilts, woodcarving, woodworking, All media
Activities: Classes for adults & children; dramatic progs; docent training; lects open to pub, 4 vis lectrs per yr; gallery talks; tours; competitions

CINCINNATI

A **ARTSWAVE,** 20 E Central Pkwy, Cincinnati, OH 45202-7239. Tel 513-871-2787; Fax 513-871-2706; Email info@fineartsfund.org; Web: www.artswave.org; *Pres & CEO* Alecia Kintner; *VPres Opers & CFO* Teri Haught; *Communs Mgr* Zach Moning
Open Mon - Fri 9 AM - 5 PM, cl Sat & Sun; Estab & incorporated in 1927 to provide for the continuance & growth of educ & culture in the various fields of fine arts in the metropolitan community of Cincinnati; Mem: Annual meeting Oct
Income: Financed through endowments by Cincinnati Symphony Orchestra, Cincinnati Art Museum, Cincinnati Opera, Taft Museum, May Festival, Cincinnati Ballet, Contemporary Arts Center, Playhouse in the Park, Special Projects Pool & Annual Community Wide fine Arts Fund Drive
Publications: Quarterly calendar

A **CINCINNATI ART CLUB,** 1021 Parkside Pl, Cincinnati, OH 45202-1550. Tel 513-241-4591; Email info@cincinnatiartclub.com; Web: www.cincinnatiartclub.com; *Pres* Clark Stevens; *VPres* Don Schuster; *Secy* Heidi Hanssen; *Treas* Steve Hart; *Cur Colls* Roger Heuck
See website for show schedule; No admis fee; Estab 1890, incorporated 1923 for purpose of advancing love & knowledge of fine art; Gallery contains a small collection of paintings by American artists; modern building 100 ft x 50 ft; Average Annual Attendance: 3,500; Mem: 340; open to all who show interest & appreciation of art; signature members must be judged by proficiency of works; dues signature $120, assoc $105
Income: Financed by dues, rental of gallery, sales commissions, bequests
Library Holdings: Compact Disks, Exhibition Catalogs, Original Art Works
Collections: Small collection of works by former members, Henry Farney, Frank Duveneck, John Rettig, Herman Wessel, Bessie Wessel
Exhibitions: Exhibition of members' work changed monthly. Annual Club Shows Sept, Feb, Spring (March-Apr) & Christmas Art Bazaar; juried annual national competition in Nov
Publications: Dragonfly Members Newsletter, monthly
Activities: Classes for adults; weekend workshops, monthly; lects open for mems only, 8 vis lectrs demonstrations per year; competitions with awards; schols offered to Cincinnati Art Academy

M **CINCINNATI ART MUSEUM,** Cincinnati Art Museum, 953 Eden Park Dr, Cincinnati, OH 45202-1596. Tel 513-721-2787; Fax 513-721-0129; Email information@cincyart.org; Web: www.cincinnatiartmuseum.org; *Cur South Asian Art* Dr. Ainsley M. Cameron; *Dir* Cameron Kitchin; *Chief Admin Officer* David Linnenberg; *Dir Colls & Exhibitions* Susan Hudson; *Chief Cur & Cur Fashion & Textile* Cynthia Amneus; *Cur Prints* Kristin Spangenberg; *Cur American Painting & Sculpture* Dr Julie Aronson; *Cur Asian Art* Dr Hou-Mei Sung; *Cur Decorative Arts & Design* Amy Dehan; *Dir Learning & Interpretation* Emily Holtrop; *CFO* Carol Edmondson
Open Tues - Sun 11AM - 5 PM, Thurs until 8 PM, cl Mon, Thanksgiving & Christmas; Admis adults (18+) $12, seniors (65+), children (6-17), & college students (with valid ID) $6, children under 5 & Thurs 5 - 8 PM free; Estab 1881 to collect, exhibit, conserve & interpret works of art from all periods & civilizations (range of 6000 years of major cultures of the world); Circ 12,000; Exhibition galleries cover an area of approx 4 acres, occupying three floors, assembly areas & social center on ground level; altogether some 80 galleries given over to permanent collections, with additional galleries set aside for temporary exhibitions; Average Annual Attendance: 200,000; Mem: 6,293; dues $1,500 founder - $30 student
Income: $13,000,000 (financed by endowment, mem, city appropriation, private donations, admis & Cincinnati Fine Arts Fund, mus shop earnings, federal, state, city & private grants)
Library Holdings: Auction Catalogs, Book Volumes, Clipping Files, DVDs, Exhibition Catalogs, Fiche, Lantern Slides, Manuscripts, Memorabilia, Original Documents, Pamphlets, Periodical Subscriptions, Photographs, Prints, Slides, Video Tapes
Special Subjects: African Art, American Indian Art, Antiquities-Assyrian, Antiquities-Byzantine, Antiquities-Egyptian, Antiquities-Etruscan, Antiquities-Greek, Antiquities-Oriental, Antiquities-Persian, Antiquities-Roman, Asian Art, Baroque Art, Bronzes, Calligraphy, Carpets & Rugs, Ceramics, Coins & Medals, Costumes, Decorative Arts, Islamic Art, Landscapes, Medieval Art, Miniatures, Oriental Art, Painting-Flemish, Painting-French, Painting-German, Painting-Italian, Painting-Spanish, Pre-Columbian Art, Prints, Religious Art, Renaissance Art, Sculpture, Silver, Southwestern Art, Textiles, Watercolors, Woodcarvings, Woodcuts
Collections: Artists, art in Cincinnati, Egyptian, Greek, Roman, Near and Far Eastern arts, musical instruments, paintings (European & American), world costumes, textiles, arts of Africa & the Americas, world prints, drawings &

photographs, world sculpture, world decorative arts & period rooms, portrait miniatures, Cincinnati wing, contemporary
Publications: Catalogues for exhibitions & collections
Activities: Classes for adults & children; dramatic progs; docent training; lects open to pub & mem only, 16 vis lectrs per yr; gallery talks; tours; concerts;; book traveling exhibs 4-6 per yr; originate traveling exhibs to other mus, 2 per yr; mus shop sells books, magazines, reproductions, prints, slides, original art

L **Mary R Schiff Library & Archives**, 953 Eden Park Dr, Cincinnati, OH 45202-1596. Tel 513-639-2978; Fax 513-721-0129; Email library@cincyart.org; Web: www.cincinnatiartmuseum.org; *Head Librn* Galina Lewandowicz; *Archivist* Geoffrey Edwards; *Asst Librn* Jennifer Hardin
Open Tues - Fri 11 AM - 5 PM; 2nd Sat (Sep - June); No admis fee; Estab in 1881 to satisfy research needs of museums staff, art academy faculty & students, the public; Reference library; Average Annual Attendance: 5,500
Income: Financed by endowment
Library Holdings: Auction Catalogs 20,000, Book Volumes 85,000, Clipping Files 10,000, Exhibition Catalogs, Fiche, Manuscripts, Memorabilia, Original Documents, Other Holdings, Pamphlets, Periodical Subscriptions 150, Photographs, Prints, Reproductions, Video Tapes 600
Special Subjects: Afro-American Art, American Indian Art, American Western Art, Antiquities-Assyrian, Architecture, Art History, Commercial Art, Costume Design & Constr, Decorative Arts, Drawings, Folk Art, Furniture, History of Art & Archaeology, Oriental Art
Collections: Files on Cincinnati Artists, Art in Cincinnati; Archives of the Cincinnati Art Museum & the Art Academy of Cincinnati, Reference collection covering 6000 yrs of art & art history, rare books
Activities: 15 vis lectrs per yr

M **COLLEGE OF MOUNT SAINT JOSEPH,** Studio San Giuseppe, 5701 Delhi Rd, Art Dept Cincinnati, OH 45233-1669. Tel 513-244-4314; Fax 513-244-4222; Email velma.dailey@msj.edu; Web: www.msj.edu; *Dir* Velma Dailey
Open Mon - Fri 10 AM - 5 PM, Sat & Sun 1 PM - 5 PM, cl holidays; No admis fee; Estab 1962 to exhibit a variety of art forms by professional artists, faculty & students; Average Annual Attendance: 5,000
Activities: Lect open to public; concerts; gallery talks; tours

L **Archbishop Alter Library,** 5701 Delhi Rd, Cincinnati, OH 45233-1670. Tel 513-244-4216; Fax 513-244-4355; Email library@msj.edu; Web: library.msj.edu; *Dir* Scott Lloyd; *Head Pub Svcs* Susan M Falgner
Open Mon - Thurs 7:30 AM - 12 AM, Fri 7:30 AM - 5 PM, Sat 10 AM - 5 PM, Sun 1 PM - 10 PM; Estab 1920 to serve students of art department; Circ 1,200
Library Holdings: Audio Tapes, Book Volumes 97,863, Cassettes, Compact Disks, DVDs, Exhibition Catalogs, Filmstrips, Periodical Subscriptions 706, Prints, Slides, Video Tapes
Collections: Salvador Dali Prints
Exhibitions: Student art exhibit
Activities: Competition with award

M **CONTEMPORARY ARTS CENTER,** 44 E Sixth St, Cincinnati, OH 45202-2518. Tel 513-345-8400; Fax 513-721-7418; Email rplatow@contemporaryartscenter.org; Web: www.contemporary arts center.org; *Dir & Chief Cur* Raphaela Platow; *Chief Preparator* Joe Cintello; *Develop Dir* Susan Berliant; *Finance & HR Manager* Holly Cahill; *Develop Officer Grant Funding* Michael Brown Jr; *Exhib Coordr* David Dillon; *Finance Dir* Craig Lattardo; *Facility Dir* Dave Gearding; *Curator* Steven Matijcio; *Rental Manager* Marty Karp; *IT Mgr* Mark Kamphuis; *Dir Commun & Community Engagement* Regina Russo; *Cur Educ* Jaime Thompson
Open Mon 10 AM - 4 PM, Wed - Fri 10 AM - 9 PM, Sat & Sun 11 AM - 6 PM, cl Tues, Thanksgiving, Christmas & New Year's Day; Free, all times; Estab 1939. The Center is a mus for the presentation of current developments in the visual & related arts. It does not maintain a permanent collection but offers changing exhibitions of international, national & regional focus; Average Annual Attendance: 150,000; Mem: 2200; dues from $45-$5000
Income: $2,595,000 (financed by endowment, fine arts fund drive, city state art council & federal groups, corporate sponsorship)
Exhibitions: Rotating Exhibitions
Publications: Catalogues of exhibitions, 1-2 per year
Activities: Classes for adults & children; docent training; performance progrs; family progs; lects open to pub & mems only, 8-10 vis lectrs per yr; concerts; gallery talks; progs for adults & children; tours; book traveling exhibs 2-5 per yr; originates traveling exhibs; mus shop sells books, cards, reproductions & prints

L **Library,** 44 E 6th St, Cincinnati, OH 45202-2518. Tel 513-345-8400 (admin office); Fax 513-721-7418

M **HEBREW UNION COLLEGE - JEWISH INSTITUTE OF RELIGION,** Skirball Museum Cincinnati, 3101 Clifton Ave, Cincinnati, OH 45220-2488. Tel 513-487-3053; Fax 513-221-0316; Email hucinu@gmail.com; Web: www.huc.edu; *Coordr Outreach Educ* Jen Ladu
Open to groups of 5+ for tours Mon - Thurs 8:30 AM - 3:30 PM, by appointment; No admis fee, donations welcome; Estab 1913 to interpret Judaism to the gel pub through Jewish art & artifacts; also the archaeological work of the col in Israel; 2,450 sq ft of exhibition space; traveling exhibition gallery; Average Annual Attendance: 5,000; Mem: 300; dues $35-$500
Income: Financed by endowment, donations & grants
Special Subjects: Antiquities-Egyptian, Antiquities-Roman, Archaeology, Archaeology, Bronzes, Calligraphy, Carpets & Rugs, Drawings, Folk Art, Folk Art, Furniture, Historical Material, Judaica, Manuscripts, Painting-American, Painting-American, Painting-Israeli, Photography, Prints, Religious Art, Stained Glass, Textiles, Textiles, Woodcuts
Collections: Jewish ceremonial art, archaeology artifacts, paintings, drawings & sculpture by Jewish artists, photography, textiles
Exhibitions: An Eternal People: The Jewish Experience (permanent)
Activities: Docent training; lect open to public, tours

M **HILLEL FOUNDATION,** Hillel Jewish Student Center Gallery, 2615 Clifton Ave, Cincinnati, OH 45220-2822. Tel 513-221-6728; Fax 513-221-7134; Email email@hillelcincinnati.org; Web: hillelcincinnati.org; *Exec Dir* Sharon Stern; *Program Dir* Landon Cohen; *Asst Dir* Anne Weinstein; *Cur* Sandy Spinner
Open Mon - Thurs 9 AM - 5 PM, Fri 9 AM - 3 PM; No admis fee; Estab 1982 to promote Jewish artists & educate students; Jewish artists in various media (exhibit & sale) & collection of antique Judaica from around the world. Listed in AAA guide
Income: Financed by contributions, fundraisers, & The Jewish Federation of Cincinnati
Special Subjects: Architecture, Judaica
Collections: Antique architectural Judaica from synagogues throughout the US, Art in various media by living Jewish artists

M **MANIFEST GALLERY,** 2727 Woodburn Ave, Cincinnati, OH 45206. Tel 513-861-3638; Email info@manifestgallery.org; Web: www.manifestgallery.org; *Founding Exec Dir & Chief Cur* Jason Franz; *Opers Mgr* Erin Corley; *Exhib Coordr* Katie Baker; *Drawing Center Coordr* Adam Mysock; *Proj Mgr* Kelia Hamilton Baker
Open Tues - Fri Noon - 7 PM, Sat Noon - 5 PM, cl Mon; Estab 2004 to revitalize the community culturally & financially; Formerly vacant storefront; Mem: dues $25 - $5,000 & up
Collections: Contemporary art
Exhibitions: Temporary exhibits
Activities: Artist residencies; artist workshops; interactive progs

L **PUBLIC LIBRARY OF CINCINNATI & HAMILTON COUNTY,** Info & Reference Dept, 800 Vine St, Cincinnati, OH 45202-2009. Tel 513-369-6900; Fax 513-665-3388; Web: www.cincinnatilibrary.org; *Dir* Kimber L Fender; *Head Info & Reference* Angela Farmar
Open Mon - Wed 9 AM - 9 AM, Thurs - Sat 9 AM - 6 PM, Sun 1 PM - 5 PM; Estab 1872 to provide the community with both scholarly & recreational materials in area of fine arts; Circ 112,400; Display cases in the department to exhibit collections
Income: $85,000 (financed by taxes, state & county appropriations)
Library Holdings: Audio Tapes, Book Volumes 207,337, Cards, Cassettes, Clipping Files 825,560, Exhibition Catalogs 6,440, Fiche 9375, Filmstrips, Lantern Slides, Memorabilia, Micro Print, Motion Pictures, Original Art Works, Other Holdings Vertical file, Pamphlets, Periodical Subscriptions 60, Photographs, Prints 5,340, Records, Reels 505, Reproductions, Slides, Video Tapes
Special Subjects: Advertising Design, Aesthetics, Afro-American Art, American Indian Art, American Western Art, Antiquities-Assyrian, Archaeology, Art History, Calligraphy, Drawings, Folk Art, History of Art & Archaeology, Landscape Architecture, Mexican Art, Mixed Media, Painting-American, Photography, Pre-Columbian Art, Religious Art, Southwestern Art
Collections: Langstroth Collection of Chromolithographs of the 19th Century, Plaut Collection, 20th century artist's books, slides, audio tapes & DVDs, Valerio Collection of Italian art, Film & recording center coll of videos, slides & audio tapes, Contemporary Artists' Book Coll
Activities: Tours; sales shop sells books, reproductions, prints, tote bags, toys & stationery items

M **TAFT MUSEUM OF ART,** 316 Pike St, Cincinnati, OH 45202-4293. Tel 513-241-0343; Fax 513-241-7762; Email taftmuseum@taftmuseum.org; Web: www.taftmuseum.org; *Pres & CEO* Deborah Emont Scott; *Deputy Dir Curatorial Affairs & Chief Cur* Lynne Ambrosini, PhD; *CFO* Beth Kip Siler, CPA; *Assoc Cur* Tamera Muente
Open Wed -Fri 11 AM - 4 PM, Sat & Sun 11 AM - 5 PM, cl New Year's Day, Thanksgiving & Christmas; Admis adults $12, seniors & students $10, children 18 or younger free; Estab 1927, a gift of Mr and Mrs Charles P Taft's art collection to the Cincinnati Institute of Fine Arts including the house and an endowment fund for maintenance. Active control was taken in 1931; museum opened in 1932; Built in 1820, a National Historic Landmark. The federal period building is home to nearly 730 works of art, including European & American paintings by masters such as Rembrandt, Sargent, Turner, Hals & Whistler; Chinese Porcelains; and European Decorative Arts. Taft Museum reopened in May 2004 after a 2.5 yr renovation and expansion. Renovated museum houses new amenities including parking garage, spec exhib gallery, performance & lecture facility, cafe, expanded museum shop, redesigned garden; Average Annual Attendance: 60,000; Mem: dues $50 & up
Income: Financed by endowment & annual fine arts fund drive
Library Holdings: Book Volumes, Exhibition Catalogs, Original Documents, Photographs, Prints, Slides
Special Subjects: Afro-American Art, Architecture, Asian Art, Ceramics, Decorative Arts, Drawings, Enamels, Furniture, Gold, Ivory, Jade, Medieval Art, Miniatures, Oriental Art, Painting-American, Painting-British, Painting-Dutch, Painting-European, Painting-Flemish, Painting-French, Painting-Spanish, Porcelain, Portraits, Religious Art, Renaissance Art, Jewelry
Collections: Furnishings include antique toiles, satins & a notable coll of Duncan Phyfe furniture, paintings including works by Rembrandt, Hals, Turner, Corot, Gainsborough, Raeburn, Whistler & other Old Masters, 200 notable Chinese Porcelains Kangxi, Yongzheng & Qianlong, 97 French Renaissance enamels, Renaissance jewelry & 16th-18th century watches from Europe
Exhibitions: three to four exhibitions scheduled per year
Publications: The Portico, quarterly
Activities: Educ prog; classes for adults & children; dramatic progs; docent training; lects open to pub, 10-15 vis lectrs per yr; chamber music; concerts; gallery talks; tours; individual paintings & objects of art lent to accredited mus; lending collection contains paintings, sculptures, Chinese ceramics, European decorative arts; book traveling exhibs 2-3 per yr; originate traveling exhibs to accredited mus; mus shop sells books, reproductions, prints, slides, gifts, jewelry, porcelains & art kits

M **UNIVERSITY OF CINCINNATI,** DAAP Galleries-College of Design Architecture, Art & Planning, 5470 Aronoff Bldg, Cincinnati, OH 45221; PO Box 210016, Cincinnati, OH 45221-0016. Tel 513-556-2839; Fax 513-556-3288; Web: daap.uc.edu/galleries.html; *Dir* Aaron J Cowan
Open Sun - Thurs 10 AM - 5 PM; No admis fee; Estab 1967 to preserve & maintain the University's art collection & to present quality contemporary & historical exhibitions of works by artists of local, regional & national reputation. Operates three exhibition facilities: Reed Gallery, Meyers Gallery; Gallery is maintained & presents quality contemporary & historical exhibitions of works by artists of local, regional & national reputation; Average Annual Attendance: 10,000

Income: Financed through university, grants & co-sponsorships
Special Subjects: Antiquities-Greek, Asian Art, Bronzes, Drawings, Etchings & Engravings, Graphics, Landscapes, Painting-American, Painting-German, Painting-Russian, Painting-Scandinavian, Photography, Portraits, Posters, Pre-Columbian Art, Prints, Sculpture, Watercolors
Collections: Art of the United States, Europe, Asia & the Americas, Julius Fleischman Collection
Publications: Fragments, catalogue
Activities: Lects open to public; performances; film & dance; gallery talks; tours; originate small traveling exhibs

L **Robert A. Deshon and Karl J. Schlachter Library for Design, Architecture, Art, and Planning**, 5480 Aronoff Center for Design and Art, Cincinnati, OH 45221-0033. Tel 513-556-1335; Fax 513-556-3006; Email elizabeth.meyer@uc.edu; Web: www.libraries.uc.edu/libraries/daap; *Visual Resources Librn* Elizabeth Meyer; *Circ & Student Supvr* Sara Mihaly
Open Mon - Thurs 8 AM - 10 PM, Fri 8 AM - 5 PM, Sat 1 - 5 PM, Sun 1 - 10 PM, summer hours vary; No admis fee; Estab 1925 to support the programs of the College of Design, Architecture, Art & Planning; Circ 42,000; Rotating exhibits; Average Annual Attendance: 78,000
Library Holdings: Book Volumes 90,000, DVDs, Exhibition Catalogs, Fiche, Filmstrips, Kodachrome Transparencies, Manuscripts, Memorabilia, Motion Pictures, Original Art Works Artist's Books, Pamphlets, Periodical Subscriptions 400, Photographs, Reels 1000, Slides, Video Tapes
Special Subjects: Art Education, Art History, Architecture, Graphic Design, Industrial Design, Interior Design
Collections: architecture, art educ, art history, fashion arts, graphic design, design (interior, landscape), urban planning, industrial
Activities: Classes for adults; docent training; lects open to pub; tours; sponsoring of competitions

L **Visual Resource Center**, PO Box 0016, Aronoff Design & Art, 5480 Cincinnati, OH 45221-0016. Tel 513-556-0279; Fax 513-556-3006; Web: www.libraries.uc.edu; *Vis Reference Librn* Elizabeth Meyer
Open Mon - Thurs 8 AM - 10 PM, Fri 8 AM - 5 PM, Sat 1 - 5 PM, Sun 1 - 10 PM; Library contains 210,000 slides
Library Holdings: Memorabilia, Slides
Special Subjects: Architecture, Drafting

M **XAVIER UNIVERSITY,** Art Gallery, 1658 Herald Ave, Cincinnati, OH 45207-7311; 3800 Victory Pkwy, Cincinnati, OH 45207. Tel 513-745-3811; Fax 513-745-1098; Email uetz@xavier.edu; Web: www.xavier.edu/art; *Dir* M Katherine Uetz; *Publicist* Terri Yontz
Open Mon - Fri 10 AM - 4 PM; No admis fee; Estab 1987 as acad facility for students, faculty & community; Spacious galleries with white walls & hardwood floors; main gallery 21 x 50 ft, adjacent gallery 20 x 20 ft
Income: Privately financed
Special Subjects: Anthropology, Ceramics, Crafts, Drawings, Embroidery, Etchings & Engravings, Graphics
Exhibitions: Professional artists; qualified students of Xavier University; temporary exhibitions only
Activities: Classes for adults; lect open to public, 4-6 vis lectrs per year; gallery talks; give awards; scholarships offered

CLEVELAND

L **CLEVELAND BOTANICAL GARDEN,** Eleanor Squire Library, 11030 East Blvd, Cleveland, OH 44106-1706. Tel 216-721-1600; Fax 216-721-2056; Email info@cbgarden.org; Web: www.cbgarden.org; *Mus Shop Mgr* Kate Fox; *Exec Dir* Natalie Ronayne; *Dir Develop* Sara Stone; *Dir Educ* Geri Unger; *Librn* Gary Esmonde; *CFO* Kenneth Sinchak
Open Mem Day - Labor Day: Tues -Sat 10 AM - 5 PM, Sun Noon - 5PM, Wed until 9 PM; Admis adult $8.50; Estab 1930; Circulation to members only
Income: Financed by endowment
Library Holdings: Audio Tapes, Book Volumes 16,000, Cassettes, Clipping Files, DVDs, Exhibition Catalogs, Original Art Works, Pamphlets, Periodical Subscriptions 120, Photographs, Prints, Sculpture, Slides
Special Subjects: Landscape Architecture, Landscapes
Collections: Rare book coll: 2,000 vols
Publications: The Bulletin, monthly
Activities: Educ prog; classes for adults & children; docent training; lects open to pub, 1 - 3 vis lectrs per yr; mus shop sells books

M **CLEVELAND INSTITUTE OF ART,** Reinberger Galleries, 11141 East Blvd, University Circle Cleveland, OH 44106-1710. Tel 216-421-7407; Fax 216-754-3631; Email reinbergergallery@cia.edu; Web: www.cia.edu; *Pres* Grafton Nunes; *Gallery Dir* Bruce Checefsky
Open Tues-Sat 10 AM - 5 PM, Fri 10 AM - 9 PM, Sun 10 AM - 5 PM; No admis fee; Estab 1882 as a 4 yr, fully accredited professional col of art; Gallery is maintained with extensive exhibitions
Income: Financed by federal, state, local grants & private foundations
Publications: Link (alumni magazine), quarterly; posters to accompany each exhibit
Activities: Classes for adults & children; lects open to pub, 5-10 vis lectrs per yr; gallery talks; tours; book traveling exhibs; originate traveling exhibs

L **Jessica Gund Memorial Library**, 11610 Euclid Ave, Cleveland, OH 44106-4390. Tel 216-421-7440; Email referencehelp@cia.edu; Web: www.cia.edu/library; *Technical Svcs Librn* Dana Bjorklund; *Image & Instruc Srvcs Librn* Laura Ponikvar; *Library Dir* Cristine Rom; *Patron Svcs Librn* Beth Owens
Open Acad Term: Mon - Thurs 8 AM - 9 PM, Fri 8 AM - 5 PM, Sat & Sun noon - 6 PM; Otherwise: Mon - Fri 10 AM - 4 PM; Estab to select, house & distribute library material in all media that will support the Institute's studio & acad areas of instruction; Circ 10,000; Average Annual Attendance: 23,000
Income: Financed by tuition, gift, endowments
Library Holdings: Book Volumes 47,000, CD-ROMs, Clipping Files, Compact Disks, DVDs, Exhibition Catalogs, Fiche, Memorabilia, Micro Print, Original Art Works, Original Documents, Other Holdings Artists' books 1,700, Periodical Subscriptions 130, Video Tapes
Special Subjects: Advertising Design, Ceramics, Commercial Art, Conceptual Art, Crafts, Decorative Arts, Drawings, Enamels, Glass, Goldsmithing, Graphic Arts, Graphic Design, Illustration, Industrial Design, Interior Design, Intermedia, Jewelry, Metalwork, Mixed Media, Photography, Printmaking, Sculpture, Silversmithing, Textiles, Video
Activities: Library tours & library instruction

A **Cleveland Art Association**, 11141 East Blvd, Develop Office-University Circle Cleveland, OH 44106-1710. Tel 216-421-7359; Fax 216-421-7438; Email clevelandartassociatiion@gmail.com; Web: www.clevelandartassociation.org; *Pres* Janer Danforth Belson
Open during gallery hours-varies; Estab & inc 1916, re-incorporated 1950 as a non-profit organization, to unite artists & art lovers of Cleveland into a working body whose purpose it shall be to advance, in the broadest possible way, the art interest of the city; Gallery utilizes space periodically at Reinberger Gallery; Mem: 200; dues $100, active mem
Income: $30,000 (financed through endowment, sales & dues)
Purchases: $12,000
Collections: Collection of art by Cleveland artists which includes ceramics, drawings, glass, paintings, prints & small sculpture
Exhibitions: Lending collection exhibited annually; art auction
Activities: Competitions; awards; scholarships offered; works of art lent to members for one yr period

M **THE CLEVELAND MUSEUM OF ART,** 11150 East Blvd, Cleveland, OH 44106-1796. Tel 216-421-7350, 877-262-4748; Fax 216-421-0411; Email info@clevelandart.org; Web: www.clevelandart.org; *Dir, Pres & CEO* Dr William M Griswold; *Chief Digital Information Officer* Jane Alexander; *Dep Dir & Head of Public and Academic Engagement* Dr Cyra Levenson; *Dep Dir and Chief Curator* Heather Lemonedes; *Dir Design & Architecture* Jeffrey Strean; *Cur Medieval Art* Stephen Fliegel; *Sr Cur Modern Art* Dr William Robinson; *Cur Photog* Dr Barbara Tannenbaum; *Cur Contemporary Art* Dr Reto Thuring; *Assoc Cur European Art* Dr Cory Korkow; *Assoc Cur Contemporary Art* Beau Rutland; *Chief Curator* Dr Heather Lemonedes; *Cur Japanese Art* Dr Sinead Vilbar; *Cur Pre-Columbian & Native North American Art* Dr Susan Bergh; *Assistant Curator of Korean Art* Sooa McCormick; *Dir Exhibitions & Publications* Heidi Stream
Open Tues, Thurs, Sat & Sun 10 AM - 5 PM, Wed & Fri 10 AM - 9 PM, cl Mon; No admis fee; Estab & incorporated 1913; building opened 1916; Circ 12,803; Educ Wing in 1971; East Wing addition 2009; West & North addition 2013; Average Annual Attendance: 300,000; Mem: 19,842; dues $65 & up
Income: $38,000,000 (financed by trust & endowment income, earned revenue, mem, gifts, grants, retail, parking & cafe)
Purchases: $7,500,000
Library Holdings: Auction Catalogs, Book Volumes, CD-ROMs, Clipping Files, Compact Disks, DVDs, Exhibition Catalogs, Fiche, Lantern Slides, Manuscripts, Maps, Memorabilia, Original Documents, Pamphlets, Periodical Subscriptions, Photographs, Prints, Reproductions, Slides, Video Tapes
Special Subjects: Antiquities-Egyptian, Antiquities-Greek, Antiquities-Roman, Ceramics, Decorative Arts, Oriental Art, Painting-American, Painting-European, Painting-Japanese, Sculpture, Textiles
Collections: Ancient Near Eastern, Egyptian, Greek, & Roman art, drawings & prints, European & American paintings, sculpture & decorative arts of all periods, with notable colls of medieval art, 18th-century French decorative arts & 17th-century European painting & 19th-century European & American painting, Islamic art, North American Indian, African & Oceanic art, Oriental art, including important colls of Chinese & Japanese painting & ceramics & Indian sculpture, photographs, Pre-Columbian American art, textiles, especially from Egypt & medieval Persia
Publications: Members magazine, 6 per yr; collection catalogs; exhibition catalogs
Activities: Classes for adults, students & children, studio workshops; teacher resource center; disability access dramatic progs; docent training; lects open to pub, lects for mems; 14 vis lectrs per yr; concerts; gallery talks; tours; originate traveling exhibs; mus shop sells books, reproductions, prints & slides

L **Ingalls Library**, 11150 East Blvd, Cleveland, OH 44106-1797. Tel 216-707-2530; Fax 216-421-0921; Email circulation@clevelandart.org; Web: library.clevelandart.org; *Serials & Electronic Resources Librarian* Jason Shafer; *Head Research Pub Progs* Louis Adrean; *Reference Librn* Christine Edmonson; *Cataloging Librarian* Margaret Castellani; *Head Access Servs* Matthew Gengler; *Digital Projects Librarian* Rachel McPherson; *Interim Director of Library & Museum Archives, Museum Archivist & Records Manager* Leslie Cade; *Digital Archivist & Systems Librn* Susan Hernandez; *Acquisitions & Collection Development Librarian* Anne Trenholme
Open Tues - Fri 10 AM - 5 PM; Estab 1916; Circ 15,267; Open to mus members, vis graduate students, faculty, cur, pub; Average Annual Attendance: 6,209
Library Holdings: Auction Catalogs 93,000, Book Volumes 510,000, CD-ROMs, Clipping Files 24,000, Compact Disks, DVDs, Exhibition Catalogs, Fiche, Lantern Slides, Original Documents Digital Images, 285,000, Other Holdings, Pamphlets, Periodical Subscriptions 1,120, Photographs 388,000, Prints, Reels, Video Tapes 400
Special Subjects: American Indian Art, Antiquities-Assyrian, Antiquities-Egyptian, Antiquities-Greek, Antiquities-Oriental, Antiquities-Persian, Antiquities-Roman, Art History, Asian Art, Bronzes, Calligraphy, Ceramics, Coins & Medals, Collages, Conceptual Art, Drawings, Embroidery, Enamels, Etchings & Engravings, Furniture, Glass, Gold, History of Art & Archaeology, Islamic Art, Ivory, Jade, Jewelry, Laces, Landscapes, Metalwork, Miniatures, Mixed Media, Oriental Art, Painting-American, Painting-British, Painting-Dutch, Painting-European, Painting-Flemish, Painting-French, Painting-German, Painting-Italian, Painting-Japanese, Painting-Spanish, Pewter, Photography, Porcelain, Portraits, Pottery, Pre-Columbian Art, Printmaking, Prints, Religious Art, Restoration & Conservation, Scrimshaw, Sculpture, Silver, Silversmithing, Stained Glass, Tapestries, Textiles, Textiles, Video, Watercolors, Woodcarvings, Woodcuts, Afro-American Art
Activities: Classes for adults & children; docent training; lects open to pub

A **Print Club of Cleveland**, 11150 East Blvd, Cleveland, OH 44106-1797. Tel 216-707-2579; Email printclub@clevelandart.org; info@printclubcleveland.org; Web: www.printclubcleveland.org; *Cur Prints & Mem* Dr Jane Glaubinger

Estab 1919 to stimulate interest in prints & drawings through educ, collecting & commissioning of new works & enhancement of the museum's collection by gifts & purchases; Mem: 250; dues $200 & up; annual meeting in Jan
Income: Financed by endowment, dues, sells prints from club inventory & sponsors annual fine print fair
Publications: The Print Club of Cleveland 1969-1994, Available at Museum Sales Desk, $19.94 plus postage
Activities: Lects open to pub & members, 1 vis lectr per yr; gallery talks; tours; awards; Ralph E King Award

L **CLEVELAND PUBLIC LIBRARY,** Fine Arts & Special Collections Dept, 325 Superior Ave NE, Fl 3 Cleveland, OH 44114-1271. Tel 216-623-2800; 623-2848; Fax 216-623-7015; Email information@cpl.org; Web: www.cpl.org; *Head Spec Colls* Stephen Zietz; *Head Main Library* Joan Clark; *Interim Dir* Holly Carroll; *Library Admin* Cindy Lombardo; *Mgr* Pamela J Eyerdam
Open Mon - Sat 10 AM - 6 PM, cl Sun; No admis fee; Estab 1869; Circ 5,624,099
Income: $34,577,461
Library Holdings: Book Volumes 190,092, Clipping Files, Compact Disks 40,000, Fiche 31,196, Manuscripts, Micro Print, Other Holdings Folklore & Chess Archives; Original Documents; Special Collections-Rare Book vols 178,906 & per sub 425, Pamphlets, Periodical Subscriptions 217, Photographs, Prints, Reels 2008
Special Subjects: Architecture, Art History, Decorative Arts, Oriental Art, Primitive art
Collections: Cleveland Artist Original Graphics, Architecture: plans, blueprints, drawings, monographs, general & professional books, career materials, histories, treatises, Sheet Music: 20,000+ song titles, Music Educ: theory, instruction, history, composition, techniques, educ & info about the industry, Antiques & Collectibles: price guides for items incl furniture, ceramics, glass, jewelry, clocks & toys, Art: instruction guides, dictionaries, biographical listings, international art encyclopedias, monographs, catalogues raisonnes, museum catalogs & handbooks, annual indexes, Lockwood Thompson bequest, Arts Educ: materials to assist teachers, Magazines: circ copies of current & popular magazines on art, architecture, decoration & music
Publications: Descriptive pamphlets of holdings
Activities: Lect & collections open to public; tours available for groups; sales shop sells books, reproductions, prints & gift items

C **FEDERAL RESERVE BANK OF CLEVELAND,** 1455 E 6th St, Cleveland, OH 44114; PO Box 6387, Cleveland, OH 44101-1387. Tel 216-579-2461; Email anne.s.ujczo@clev.frb.org; Web: www.clevelandfed.org; *Consulting Cur* Jane B Tesso; *Facilities Planner* Anne Ujczo
No admis fee; Collection represents fine art and artists who have lived or worked in the 4th District of the Federal Reserve since its institution in 1914
Collections: High quality regional art made after 1910 including painting, sculpture, drawing, prints & photographs

INTERMUSEUM CONSERVATION ASSOCIATION
For further information, see National and Regional Organizations

M **MUSEUM OF CONTEMPORARY ART CLEVELAND,** 11400 Euclid Ave, Ste 100, Cleveland, OH 44106-5923. Tel 216-421-8671; Fax 216-421-0737; Web: www.mocacleveland.org; *Exec Dir* Jill Snyder; *Sr Adjunct Cur* Margo Crutchfield; *Deputy Dir Finance* Grace Garver
Open Tues-Sun 11AM-5PM, Offices Mon-Fri 9AM-5PM; Admis $4 non-members, $3 students & seniors, children under 12 free; Estab 1968 to enrich the cultural life of the community; Five galleries 20,000 sq ft, which change exhibits every 6-8 wks. Located in a renovated building which is part of the Cleveland Playhouse complex. Maintains reference library; Mem: 600; dues center circle $500; sustaining $129; contributing $50; family $35; single $25; student or artist $15
Income: $175,000 (financed by mem, state appropriation, federal & state agencies & local foundations)
Publications: Exhibition catalogues
Activities: Educ dept; docent training; lects open to pub; 20 vis lectrs per yr; gallery talks; tours; individual & original objects of art lent to corporate members; originate traveling exhibs; mus shop sells original art works, books, prints & reproductions

L **Library,** 11400 Euclid Ave, Ste 100, Cleveland, OH 44106-5923. Tel 216-421-8671; Fax 216-421-0737; *Dir* Jill Snyder
Reference Library; Mem: 900; dues $35
Library Holdings: Book Volumes 2000, Clipping Files, Exhibition Catalogs, Periodical Subscriptions 10, Photographs, Slides

L **NORTHEAST OHIO AREAWIDE COORDINATING AGENCY (NOACA),** Information Resource Center, 1299 Superior Ave, Cleveland, OH 44114-3204. Tel 216-241-2414, Ext 240; Fax 216-621-3024; Email kgoldberg@mpo.noaca.org; Web: www.noaca.org; *Librn* Kenneth P Goldberg
Open Mon - Fri 8 AM - 4:30 PM; Estab 1965, staff checkout only, public phone inquiries or browsing welcome; calling for appointment advisable; Transportation, environment-related & archival displays scattered around Agency
Library Holdings: Auction Catalogs, Audio Tapes, Book Volumes 5850, CD-ROMs, Cassettes, Clipping Files, Compact Disks, DVDs, Exhibition Catalogs, Fiche, Filmstrips, Manuscripts, Maps, Memorabilia, Micro Print, Original Art Works, Original Documents, Pamphlets, Periodical Subscriptions 205, Photographs, Prints, Reels, Reproductions, Sculpture, Slides, Video Tapes
Special Subjects: Advertising Design, Ceramics, Display, Furniture, Graphic Design, Industrial Design, Interior Design, Judaica, Maps, Metalwork, Miniatures, Photography, Porcelain, Religious Art, Restoration & Conservation, Graphic Arts, Historical Material, History of Art & Archaeology
Collections: Relative to the arts & art history: Architectural Preservation & Restoration, Land use & sprawl-related issues, Urban Planning & Urban Design, Ohio architecture; Ohio history
Publications: Decision Maker; NOACA News; various reports related to planning, transportation & environmental issues; Seeking Grants in Times of Uncertainty
Activities: Tours; Northeast Ohio, 5 counties+

M **SAINT MARY'S ROMANIAN ORTHODOX CATHEDRAL,** Romanian Ethnic Art Museum, 3256 Warren Rd, Cleveland, OH 44111-1144. Tel 216-941-5550; Fax 216-941-3368; Web: www.smroc.org; *Dir* Rev Remus Gramma; *Secretary* Mihaela Hetruc
Open Mon - Fri 8:30 AM - 4:30 PM, & on request; No admis fee; Estab 1963; Average Annual Attendance: 5,000
Income: Financed by parish appropriation
Special Subjects: Folk Art
Collections: Anisoara Stan Collection, O K Cosla Collection, Gunther Collection, Romanian art, artifacts, costumes, ceramics, painters, rugs, silver & woodwork, Romanian Statues, mosaics, icons on glass & wood, books
Activities: Lect open to public; tours; individual paintings & original objects of art lent to other ethnic museums & faiths for exhibits; lending collection contains 100 original art works, 250 original prints, 50 paintings, sculpture, 2000 costumes, rugs & artifacts

A **SOCIETY FOR PHOTOGRAPHIC EDUCATION (SPE),** SPE Gallery, 2530 Superior Ave E #403, Cleveland, OH 44114-4239. Tel 216-622-2733; Fax 216-622-2712; Email membership@spenational.org; Web: www.spenational.org; *Exec Dir* James Wyman; *Exposure Ed* Stacey McCarroll Cutshaw; *Office & Accts Mgr* Carla Kurtz; *Events & Publs Coordr* Ginenne Clark; *Advertising, Exhibs & Design* Nina Barcellona Kidd; *Exposure Designer* Amy Schelemanow; *Exposure Copyeditor* Robyn Rime; *Registrar* Kayla Milligan
Open Mon - Fri 9 AM - 5 PM, or by request; Estab 1963 to provide a forum for discussion of photog; Circ 2,000; Open to all with an interest in photog; Average Annual Attendance: 1,500; Mem: 2,000; dues $55 - $125; national conference in March
Income: $250,000 (financed by mem & conference registrations)
Publications: Exposure, biannual; mem directory & resource guide; Conference Prog Guide, ann
Activities: Classes for adults; Lect open to pub, 75 vis lectrs per yr; lects for mems; gallery talks; tours; SPE Student Awards; Freestyle Crystal Apple Award; schols offered

M **SPACES,** 2220 Superior Viaduct, Cleveland, OH 44113-2367. Tel 216-621-2314; Fax 216-621-2314; Email contact@spacesgallery.org; Web: wwwspacesgallery.org; *Gallery Mgr* Marilyn Ladd-Simmons; *Develop Dir* Martha Loughridge; *Community Engagement Mgr* Michelle Epps; *Exec Dir* Christina Vassallo; *Residency Coordr* Bruce Edwards
Open Tues - Sun noon - 5 PM, Thurs open until 8 PM, cl Mon; No admis fee; Estab 1978 to show innovative work by living artists; Single room, 6000 sq ft & 12 ft ceiling. Exhibitions, curated & group exhibitions change monthly; Average Annual Attendance: 15,000; Mem: 400
Income: $420,000 (financed by mem, state appropriation & foundations)
Exhibitions: 6 exhibitions annually
Publications: Exhibition catalogs, 3 annually
Activities: Docent training; educator outreach; Lects open to pub, gallery talks, tours

M **WESTERN RESERVE HISTORICAL SOCIETY,** 10825 East Blvd, Cleveland, OH 44106-1788. Tel 216-721-5722; Fax 216-721-8934; Web: www.wrhs.org; *Pres & CEO* Gainor B Davis PhD; *COO* Kermit J Pike; *Vice Pres* Kelly Falcone-Hall
Open Tues 10AM - 4PM, Wed 10AM - 9PM, Fri & Sat 10AM - 4PM, Sun Noon - 4PM, cl Mon; Admis adults $8, seniors $7.50, youth $5, group rates available; Estab 1867 to discover, collect & preserve whatever relates to the history, biography, genealogy & antiquities of Ohio; Average Annual Attendance: 210,000; Mem: 5300; dues from $40 - $500
Income: Operating budget $7.3 million
Special Subjects: Costumes, Historical Material, Period Rooms, Decorative Arts
Exhibitions: People at the Crossroads-Settling the Western Reserve, 1796- 1870; Chisholm Halle Custom Wing; Crawford Auto-Aviation collection
Publications: Books on Regional History; Western Reserve Historical Society News, bi-monthly
Activities: Classes for adults & children; docent training; lects open to public, 25 vis lectrs per yr; tours; gallery talks; awards; individual paintings & objects of art lent to qualified institutions; originate traveling exhibs to children's museums and history museums; sales shop sells books, magazines, reproductions & prints

L **Library,** 10825 East Blvd, Cleveland, OH 44106-1788. Tel 216-721-5722; Fax 216-721-0891; Web: www.wrhs.org; *COO* Kermit J Pike; *Dir Mus Servs* Ed Pershey; *VPres* Patrick H Reymann; *Dir Research* John Grabowski; *Dir Educ* Janice Ziegler; *CFO* John Holtzhauser; *Dir Mktg & Communs* Rita Kueber
Open Mon - Sat 10 AM - 5 PM, Sun Noon - 5 PM; Admis adults $8, seniors $7.50, children ages 3-12 $5; Estab 1867; For reference only
Library Holdings: Audio Tapes, Book Volumes 250,000, Cards 200, Exhibition Catalogs, Fiche 2000, Lantern Slides, Manuscripts 5,000,000, Other Holdings Microfilm 40,000, Pamphlets, Periodical Subscriptions 100, Photographs, Prints, Records, Reels 25,000, Slides
Special Subjects: Architecture, Decorative Arts, Folk Art, Maps, Photography, Prints, Furniture, Glass, Manuscripts, Period Rooms
Collections: Crawford Auto Aviation Mus, Halle Costume Wing, Library Archives, History Museum
Activities: Lects open to pub; mus shop sells books, reproductions, prints & gifts

COLUMBUS

M **CAPITAL UNIVERSITY,** Schumacher Gallery, 1 College & Main, Columbus, OH 43209-2394. Tel 614-236-6319; Fax 614-236-6490; Email dgentili@capital.edu; Web: capital.edu/schumacher; *Dir* David Gentilini
Open Mon - Sat 1 - 5 PM; No admis fee; Estab 1964 to provide the best available visual arts to the students; to serve the entire community with monthly traveling shows, community programming & permanent colls; Gallery is 16,000 sq ft, that includes six display galleries of permanent holdings, gallery area for temporary monthly exhibits, galleries, fabrication room, lect area seating 25
Income: Financed by foundation grants & individual gifts
Special Subjects: African Art, American Indian Art, Asian Art, Eskimo Art, Graphics, Painting-American, Painting-British, Painting-European, Pre-Columbian Art, Primitive art, Sculpture, Watercolors

Collections: Ethnic Arts (including American Indian, African, Inuit, Oceanic), American paintings, sculpture & graphics of 20th century, Period works from 16th - 19th century, Major Ohio Artists, Graphics, Asian Art, Inuit Art
Exhibitions: Seven individual & group visiting shows per yr; individual exhibits include contemporary artists & loans from individuals & other museums
Activities: Lect open to public; gallery talks; competitions; individual paintings & original art objects lent by special request only

L **Art Library**, 1 College & Main, Columbus, OH 43209; 2199 E Main St, Columbus, OH 43209. Tel 614-236-6615; Fax 614-236-6490
Open to students, faculty, staff & for reference only to the pub
Library Holdings: Book Volumes 5300, Periodical Subscriptions 15

L **COLUMBUS COLLEGE OF ART & DESIGN,** Packard Library, 60 Cleveland Ave Columbus, OH 43215-1758. Tel 614-222-3273; Email library@ccad.edu; Web: www.ccad.edu; *Library Dir* Gail Storer; *Visual Resources Librn* Tara Haas; *Tech Svcs Librn* Leslie Jankowski; *Pub Svcs Librn* Christine Mannix; *Dir Library Servs* Leslie Jankowski; *Instruction Librn* Christine Mannix; *Mktg & Outreach Librn* Shiva Shakeri
Open Mon - Thurs 7:30 AM - 9:30 PM, Sat 1 PM - 5 PM during acad yr; Estab 1879 to support the programs of the Columbus Col of Art & Design; Circ 15,400
Income: tuition, grants & gifts
Library Holdings: Book Volumes 82,323, CD-ROMs, DVDs 1,556, Exhibition Catalogs, Fiche, Periodical Subscriptions 300, Video Tapes 208
Special Subjects: Advertising Design, Art History, Asian Art, Ceramics, Commercial Art, Costume Design & Constr, Drawings, Fashion Arts, Film, Glass, Graphic Arts, Graphic Design, Illustration, Industrial Design, Interior Design, Intermedia, Landscape Architecture, Lettering, Mixed Media, Painting-American, Painting-European, Photography, Portraits, Printmaking, Sculpture, Textiles, Video

M **COLUMBUS CULTURAL ARTS CENTER,** 139 W Main St, Columbus, OH 43215-5064. Tel 614-645-7047; Email gamartin@columbus.gov; Web: www.culturalartscenteronline.org; *Arts Adminr* Geoffrey Martin
Open Mon 1 PM - 4 PM & 7 PM - 10 PM, Tues - Thurs 9 AM - 4 PM & 7 PM - 10 PM, Fri - Sat 9 AM - 4 PM, cl Sun; No admis fee; Estab 1978, visual arts facilities & gallery; Maintains small reference library
Income: Financed by city of Columbus gen funds
Library Holdings: Book Volumes
Exhibitions: local, regional, & national artists monthly exhibitions
Publications: Quarterly catalog
Activities: Classes for adults & youth outreach. Studio classes for adults offered in 8-wk terms include painting, drawing, relief printing, sculpture, jewelry, weaving, copper enameling, ceramics, surface design, stone carving & bronze casting; lect open to pub, 58 vis lectrs per yr; gallery talks; tours; festivals

L **COLUMBUS METROPOLITAN LIBRARY,** Arts & Media Division Carnegie Gallery, 96 S Grant Ave, Columbus, OH 43215-4781. Tel 614-645-2275; Fax 614-645-2883; Email artsnmedia@columbuslibrary.org; Web: www.columbuslibrary.org; *CEO* Patrick Losinski; *Chief Info Officer* Carl Powell
Open Mon - Thurs 9 AM - 9 PM, Fri & Sat 9 AM - 6 PM, Sun 1 - 5 PM; No admis fee; Main library estab 1873; Supported by Friends of the Library, the gallery creates unique cultural experiences for library visits by presenting quality art exhibits, featuring emerging & established artists; Average Annual Attendance: 1,000
Income: Financed by state & county appropriation
Library Holdings: Book Volumes 100,000, Compact Disks, DVDs, Exhibition Catalogs, Maps, Original Art Works, Other Holdings Catalogs, Periodical Subscriptions 2181
Special Subjects: Architecture, Art History, Decorative Arts, Film, Photography, Theatre Arts
Exhibitions: OOVAR, Annual; various non-profit art groups
Activities: Classes for adults & children; summer reading for all ages; lects open to pub; 3 vis lectrs per yr; tours; concerts; Celebration of Learning Award; OOVAR People's Choice; OOVAR Jury's Choice; exten prog serves Columbus Metropolitan Area; sales shop sells books & original art

M **COLUMBUS MUSEUM OF ART,** 480 E Broad St, Columbus, OH 43215-3823. Tel 614-221-6801; Fax 614-221-0226; Email info@cmaohio.org; Web: www.columbusmuseum.org; *Exec Dir* Nannette V Maciejunes; *Executive Deputy Dir Oper & Chief Registrar* Rod Bouc; *Cur Contemp Art* Tyler Cann; *Exec Asst Dir & Dir Learning & Experience* Cindy M Foley; *Dir Mktg & Communs* Melissa E Ferguson; *Dir Retail Opers* Pam L Edwards; *Mgr Community Engagement* Lauren R Emond; *Cur-at-Large* Carole Genshaft; *Dir Special Events Sales* Susan Brehm; *Chief Cur* David Stark; *Dir Facilities & Security* David Leach; *Head Exhibs & Assoc Cur Photog* Drew Sawyer
Open Tues - Wed & Fri - Sun 10 AM - 5 PM, Thurs until 9 PM, cl Mon & holidays; Admis adults $14, students 6-17 $5, seniors 60+ & students 18+ with valid ID $8, Sun & children under 5 free; Estab 1931 (chartered 1878); Present main building constructed in 1931 in a Renaissance Revival style; addition built in 1974; Interactive space; Maintains reference library; Euro & American Modernism; Contemporary Art; expansion and Margaret M. Walter wing completed in 2015; Average Annual Attendance: 200,000; Mem: 7000; dues $75 household
Income: Financed by ann contributions, endowment, mem & pub support
Special Subjects: American Western Art, Carpets & Rugs, Decorative Arts, Drawings, Eskimo Art, Etchings & Engravings, Folk Art, Glass, Landscapes, Oriental Art, Painting-American, Painting-British, Painting-European, Painting-Flemish, Painting-French, Painting-German, Painting-Italian, Painting-Japanese, Photography, Porcelain, Portraits, Pottery, Pre-Columbian Art, Prints, Religious Art, Renaissance Art, Sculpture, Textiles
Collections: 16th - 18th century European paintings, Late 19th & early 20th century European and American paintings, sculpture & works on paper, 20th century Folk Art, 19th century American textiles, Schiller Collection of Social Commentary Art 1930-1970, Photo League
Publications: Exhib & permanent coll catalogs; interpretive materials; bimonthly mems' magazine & calendar of events; six-month guide to progs & events; gallery handouts
Activities: Classes for adults & children; docent training; summer arts camp; lectrs open to pub, 12 vis lectrs per yr; concerts; gallery talks; tours; competitions; annual creativity summit; 2015 Expy Award, The Columbus Foundation Award; schols offered; exten dept serves Speaker Bureau & Docents-in-the-Schools; individual paintings & original objects of art lent to other museums & government buildings; lending coll contains 30 color reproductions, 5000 slides & videos; 1-2 book traveling exhibs per yr; originate traveling exhibs; mus shop sells books, reproductions & prints

A **OHIO HISTORY CONNECTION,** 800 E 17 Ave, Columbus, OH 43211-2474. Tel 614-297-2300; Email info@ohiohistory.org; Web: ohiohistory.org; *Sr History Cur* Cliff Eckle; *History Cur* Eric Feingold; *History Cur* Becky Preiss Odom PhD
Open May 1 - Oct 31 Wed - Sat 10 AM - 4 PM, Sun 1 PM - 4 PM, Nov 1 - April 30 by appt only, cl major holidays; Admis adult $10, seniors 60 & over $9, youth 6-12 $5, mems & children 5 & under free; Estab 1885, Ohio Historical Soc was chartered on this date, to promote a knowledge of history, natural history & archaeology, especially of Ohio; to collect & maintain artifacts, books & archives relating to Ohio's history; Main gallery covers over one acre of fl space & includes exhibits on history, natural history, archaeology; also houses a natural history demonstration laboratory & av theatre; Average Annual Attendance: 500,000
Income: Financed by endowment, mem, state appropriation & contributions
Collections: Archaeology, artifacts, ceramics, clothing, furniture, glassware, paintings
Publications: Museum Echoes, newsletter, monthly; Ohio History, scholarly journal, quarterly; Timeline, popular journal, bimonthly
Activities: Classes for adults & children; docent training; lect open to pub; photographic competitions with awards; individual paintings & original art objects lent; lending coll to mus & art galleries; books traveling exhibs; originate traveling exhibs; sales shop sells books, magazines, reproductions, prints, slides and other souvenir items, postcards, jewelry

L **Archives-Library Division**, 800 E 17th Ave, Columbus, OH 43211-2474. Tel 614-297-2510; Fax 614-297-2546; Email reference@ohiohistory.org; Web: www.ohiohistory.org
Open Wed - Sat 10 AM - 5 PM; Admis tours $4; Estab 1885, to collect, preserve & interpret evidences of the past; For reference only; Average Annual Attendance: 13,000
Income: $1,100,000 (financed by state appropriation & pvt revenue)
Purchases: $80,000
Library Holdings: Audio Tapes, Book Volumes 148,600, Cassettes 2500, Exhibition Catalogs, Filmstrips, Kodachrome Transparencies, Lantern Slides, Manuscripts 1000, Memorabilia, Motion Pictures, Other Holdings Maps 5000, Pamphlets, Periodical Subscriptions 300, Photographs 50,000, Prints, Records, Reels 47,500, Reproductions, Slides, Video Tapes
Collections: Broadsides, Ohio government documents, Ohio newspapers, Temperance coll, maps, papers of early Ohio political leaders, posters, rare books, trade catalogs, photographs, manuscripts
Publications: Ohio History (biannual); Timeline (bimonthly)
Activities: Classes for adults & children; docent training

M **OHIO STATE UNIVERSITY,** Wexner Center for the Arts, 1871 N High St, Columbus, OH 43210-1393. Tel 614-292-0330; Fax 614-292-3369; Web: www.wexarts.org; *Dir Exhibs Mgmt* Megan Cavanaugh; *Dir Performing Arts* Lane Czaplinski; *Dir Mktg & Communs* Densil R R Porteous II; *Dir Educ* Shelly Casto; *Dir* Sherri Geldin; *Dir Develop* Christy Schoedinger
Open Sun & Tues - Wed 11 AM - 6 PM, Thurs 11 AM - 8 PM, cl Mon; No admis fee for gallery, performances and screenings vary; Estab 1989 the Wexner Center for the arts is Ohio State University's multidisciplinary, international laboratory for exploration and advancement of contemporary art.; Administers the permanent coll & exhibs in 4 professionally-equipped galleries & is the center for long-range planning in visual arts; Average Annual Attendance: 273,000; Mem: 1,835
Income: $7,623,260 (financed by operating funds from the univ, prog support from the Wexner Center Foundation & government foundation & corporate grants, earned income)
Special Subjects: Painting-American
Collections: Contemporary Collection, Study Collection of graphic arts & manuscripts, Wiant Collection of Chinese art
Exhibitions: Various exhibits
Publications: Exhib catalogs
Activities: Docent training; lect open to pub, 12 vis lectrs per yr; concerts; gallery talks; tours; invitational juried exhibs; Wexner Prize, presented ann; rent traveling exhibs 1-5 per yr; originate traveling exhibs

L **Fine Arts Library**, 1871 N High St, Columbus, OH 43210-1105. Tel 614-292-6184; Fax 614-292-4573; Email franks.157@osu.edu; Web: library.osu.edu; *Head Librn* Tina Franks
Open Mon - Fri 9 AM - 6 PM, Sun 1 PM - 5 PM, cl Sat; No admis fee; Estab during 1930's to support teaching & research in art, art educ, design, history of art & photography; Average Annual Attendance: 200,000
Purchases: $120,000
Library Holdings: Book Volumes 130,000, Cards, Exhibition Catalogs, Fiche, Original Art Works, Periodical Subscriptions 350, Reels, Slides, Video Tapes 250
Special Subjects: Advertising Design, Afro-American Art, Antiquities-Assyrian, Antiquities-Greek, Antiquities-Oriental, Antiquities-Persian, Antiquities-Roman, Archaeology, Architecture, Art Education, Art History, Asian Art, Bronzes, Calligraphy, Carpets & Rugs, Ceramics, Collages, Commercial Art, Conceptual Art, Constructions, Crafts, Decorative Arts, Dioramas, Display, Drafting, Drawings, Embroidery, Enamels, Eskimo Art, Etchings & Engravings, Ethnology, Folk Art, Furniture, Glass, Gold, Goldsmithing, Graphic Arts, Graphic Design, Handicrafts, History of Art & Archaeology, Illustration, Industrial Design, Interior Design, Intermedia, Ivory, Jade, Jewelry, Judaica, Landscapes, Latin American Art, Manuscripts, Maps, Marine Painting, Metalwork, Mexican Art, Miniatures, Mixed Media, Mosaics, Oriental Art, Painting-American, Painting-Australian, Painting-British, Painting-Canadian, Painting-Dutch, Painting-European, Painting-Flemish, Painting-French, Painting-German, Painting-Israeli, Painting-Italian, Painting-Japanese, Painting-New Zealand, Painting-Polish, Painting-Russian, Painting-Scandinavian, Painting-Spanish, Photography, Porcelain, Portraits, Posters, Pottery, Primitive art, Printmaking, Prints, Religious Art, Sculpture, Silver, Silversmithing, Stained Glass, Tapestries, Video, Watercolors, Woodcarvings, Woodcuts

L **Visual Resources Library**, 204 Hayes Hall, Columbus, OH 43210; 108 N Oval Mall, Columbus, OH 43210-1318. Tel 614-292-0520; Fax 614-292-4401; Email maguire.18@osu.edu; Web: history-of-art.osu.edu/vrl; *Cur* Michelle Maguire
Open Mon - Fri 9 AM - 5 PM, summer hours vary; Estab 1925 to provide visual resources for instruction & research in history of art; Teaching - Reference Coll, restricted circulation, staff & students
Income: Financed by state funds through State Univ System
Library Holdings: Audio Tapes 30, Book Volumes 150, Exhibition Catalogs, Framed Reproductions, Original Art Works, Photographs 230,000, Prints, Reproductions, Slides 270,000, Video Tapes 150
Special Subjects: Asian Art, Islamic Art, Architecture
Collections: history of Western art & architecture

L **Billy Ireland Cartoon Library & Museum**, 110 Sullivan Hall, 1813 N High St Columbus, OH 43210. Tel 614-292-0538; Fax 614-292-9101; Email cartoons@osu.edu; Web: cartoons.osu.edu; *Cur* Jenny E Robb
Open Mon - Fri 9 AM - 5 PM (Office); Tues - Sun 1 PM - 5 PM (Museum); Mon - Fri 9 AM - 5 PM, Sun 1 - 5 PM (Library), cl national holidays; No admis fee; Estab 1977, renamed 2009
Income: Financed by state appropriation
Library Holdings: Book Volumes 50,000; serial & comic book titles: 61,000, Cassettes, Clipping Files 2,500,000, DVDs, Exhibition Catalogs, Manuscripts 3,000 ft, Memorabilia, Original Art Works cartoons: 450,000, Other Holdings, Photographs, Records
Special Subjects: Cartoons, Illustration, Manuscripts
Collections: Cartoonist Collection, clippings, proofs & scrapbooks (hundreds of artists represented), editorial cartoons, comic strips, comic books, graphic novels; manga, sports cartoons, magazine cartoons, Nick Anderson Collection, Jim Borgman Collection, Milton Caniff Collection, Eldon Dedini Collection, Edwina Dumm Collection, Will Eisner Collection, Woody Gelman Collection of Winsor McCay cartoons, Walt Kelly Collection, Toni Mendez Collection, Bill Watterson Deposit Collection, International Museum of Cartoon Art Collection: 200,000+ original cartoons, San Francisco Academy of Comic Art Collection, Jay Kennedy Collection: 9,500+ underground comic books, Robert Roy Metz Collection, Archives of professional organizations including: Assoc of American Editorial Cartoonists, National Cartoonists Society, Newspaper Features Council & Cartoonists Guild, biographical registry of cartoonists

A **PEGGY R MCCONNELL ARTS CENTER OF WORTHINGTON,** (Worthington Arts Council), 777 Evening St, Columbus, OH 43085-3048. Tel 614-431-0329; Fax 614-431-2491; Email arts@mcconnellarts.org; Web: www.mcconnellarts.org; *Exec Dir* Jon Cook; *Dir Progs & Outreach* Missy Donovan; *Dir Opers* Andy Herron
Open Tues - Thurs 10 AM - 9 PM, Fri & Sat 10 AM - 5 PM, Sun 12 PM - 5 PM, cl Mon; No amis fee; Estab 1977 to encourage & stimulate the practice & appreciation of the arts by providing opportunities in the community to participate in, experience & enjoy the arts so as to enrich the quality of daily life & further cultural growth of Worthington & to help the art & cultural organizations of the city grow & flourish; Circ 45,000; A 20,000 sq ft bldg, 213 seat theatre, exhib gallery, 4 classrooms, digital imaging studio, dance studio & rotating exhibs; Average Annual Attendance: 50,000; Mem: 256; annual dues $50-$65
Income: $700,000, 65% contributed, 35% earned
Activities: Visual arts series & sculpture on village green; classes for adults & children; dramatic progs; lect open to pub; 12 vis lectrs per yr; performance series; concerts; gallery talks; tours; competitions; schols offered; teacher in-service workshops; one book traveling exhib per yr; sales shop sells original art

COSHOCTON

M **JOHNSON-HUMRICKHOUSE MUSEUM,** 300 N Whitewoman St, Roscoe Village Coshocton, OH 43812-1061. Tel 740-622-8710; Email jhmuseum@jhmuseum.org; Web: www.jmuseum.org; *Dir* Patti Malenke; *Registrar* Jennifer Bush
Open daily Noon - 5 PM May through Oct, 1 - 4:30 PM Nov through Apr, cl Mon, Thanksgiving, Christmas Eve, Christmas, New Year's Day & Easter Sun; Admis family $11, adults $4, children 5-12 $3; Estab 1931, as a gift of two pioneer residents; Five galleries: American Indian, Decorative Arts, Historical Ohio & Special Exhibits; Average Annual Attendance: 16,000; Mem: Dues, indiv $30, family $50, contributing $50, supporting $100, sustaining $200, benefactor $350 & founder $500
Special Subjects: American Indian Art, Decorative Arts, Oriental Art, Pottery, Prints
Collections: American Indian baskets and bead work, Aztec, Toltec and Mayan pottery heads, Chinese and Japanese cloisonne, embroideries, ivory, jade, lacquers, metals, porcelains, prints, samurai armor & swords, wood carvings, European glass, laces, pewter, porcelains, prints, Eskimo artifacts, material from Coshocton County Mound Builders, 19th century furnishings and implements used by Coshocton County pioneer families, Early Americana, Newark holy stones
Exhibitions: Permanent collection exhibitions changed periodically; traveling exhibitions.
Publications: American Indian Basketry; Newark Holy Stones Symposium; Pop-Gosser China; quarterly newsletter
Activities: Educ dept; classes for adults & children; lect open to pub; 4 vis lectrs per yr; tours; mus shop sells books, collection-oriented items & original art

M **POMERENE CENTER FOR THE ARTS,** 317 Mulberry St, Coshocton, OH 43812-2037. Tel 740-622-0326; Email pomerenearts@gmail.com; Web: www.pomerenearts.org; *Artistic Dir & Community Studio Artist* Anne Cornell; *COO* Donovan Rice
Open Tues - Sat 1 - 5 PM; No admis fee; Est. 1984; Circ galleries change monthly; Community art center/venue
Purchases: Art Park, Main St. Coshocton, OH
Collections: works by local, regional & national artists
Activities: Classes for adults & children; concerts; tours; Original art; prints

CUYAHOGA FALLS

M **JACK RICHARD GALLERY, ALMOND TEA MUSEUM & JANE WILLIAMS GALLERIES,** Divisions of Studios of Jack Richard, 2250 Front St, Cuyahoga Falls, OH 44221-2510. Tel 330-929-1575; Email jackrichard@att.net; Web: jackrichard.com; *Agent* Jane Williams; *Chief of Staff* Maric Giangaspero
Open Tues - Fri 11:30 AM - 5 PM, Tues Eve 7 - 10 PM, cl Sun, Mon, & Sat other hours by appointment; No admis fee; Estab 1961, for exhib of local, regional & national works of art; Circ 2,000; 14,400 sq ft; Average Annual Attendance: 12,000
Income: Financed privately
Library Holdings: Auction Catalogs, Audio Tapes 30, Book Volumes 2,000, CD-ROMs 40, Cassettes 60, Clipping Files 1/2 million, DVDs 30+, Framed Reproductions, Kodachrome Transparencies, Original Art Works 400, Pamphlets 30, Photographs, Prints, Reproductions, Sculpture, Slides, Video Tapes
Special Subjects: American Indian Art, American Western Art, Antiquities-Oriental, Art Education, Art History, Asian Art, Cartoons, Conceptual Art, Drawings, History of Art & Archaeology, Illustration, Landscapes, Maps, Marine Painting, Mixed Media, Oriental Art, Painting-American, Painting-Australian, Painting-European, Painting-Flemish, Painting-German, Painting-Italian, Painting-Japanese, Painting-Russian, Painting-Spanish, Photography, Portraits, Posters, Prints, Religious Art, Renaissance Art, Reproductions, Restorations, Sculpture, Watercolors, Woodcuts, Costumes
Collections: Ball, Brackman, Cornwell, Grell, Gleitsmann, Loomis, Oriental, Over 260 additional pieces, Native American: 50 pieces
Exhibitions: 50 Women Plus; student exhibits; Japanese Prints; mems exhibits; 30 one-person exhibits; Pastel Exhibit; Age Old Masters; Brackman Masterpieces; Flowers, Flowers, Flowers; Great American Nude; Progress & Change in Paintings; over 500 exhibs
Publications: Asahi Press, Japan; over 20 other publications
Activities: Classes for adults & children; lect open to pub, lects for mems only, 5 vis lectrs per yr; gallery talks; tours; competitions with awards; over 30 regional, local, & national awards, sponsoring of competitions; schols offered; individual paintings & original objects of art lent; lending coll contains paintings, prints & cassettes; book traveling exhibs; originate traveling exhibs; sales shop sells books, magazines, original art, reproductions, prints & slides; frame shop, sculpture

L **Library**, 2250 Front St, Cuyahoga Falls, OH 44221. Tel 330-929-1575; Email jackrichard@att.net; Web: www.jackrichard.comMobile 330-929-2285
Open Tues, Thurs, Fri 11:30 AM - 5 PM, Tues evening 7 - 10 PM; Sat - Mon by appointment; No admis fee; 1961; For reference & limited lending only; Average Annual Attendance: 16,000
Income: Art sales, restoration, tuition
Library Holdings: Auction Catalogs, Audio Tapes, Book Volumes 2,000+, Cards, Cassettes, Clipping Files Half million, DVDs, Exhibition Catalogs, Framed Reproductions, Kodachrome Transparencies, Motion Pictures, Original Art Works 800+, Other Holdings, Pamphlets 40, Photographs 20,000, Prints 2,000, Records 300, Reproductions, Sculpture 8, Slides 208,000, Video Tapes 400
Special Subjects: Advertising Design, American Indian Art, Antiquities-Oriental, Art Education, Cartoons, Commercial Art, Costume Design & Constr, Decorative Arts, Etchings & Engravings, Landscapes, Marine Painting, Mixed Media, Oriental Art, Painting-American, Painting-Japanese, Painting-Russian, Photography, Portraits, Prints, Religious Art, Restoration & Conservation, Sculpture, Video, Watercolors
Exhibitions: Various year-round exhibs
Publications: Over 30 (various subjects)
Activities: Art classes for adults & children; over 50 special art progs for various groups; lectrs open to the public; gallery talks; tours; sponsoring of competitions; over 100 local & national awards; schols available; mus shop sells books, magazines, original art, reproductions, prints, slides, photographs, sculptures, & art supplies

DAYTON

M **DAYTON ART INSTITUTE,** 456 Belmonte Park N, Dayton, OH 45405-4700. Tel 937-223-5277; Fax 937-223-3140; Email info@daytonart.org; Web: www.daytonartinstitute.org; *Dir & CEO* Michael R Roediger; *Cur Educ* Susan Martis; *Mus Shop Mgr & Facilities Rentals Mgr* Diane Haskel; *Mem Relations Mgr* Heather Leppla; *Chmn* Edward J Blake; *Mktg & Communs Mgr* Eric Brockman; *Chief Cur* Jerry N Smith
Open Wed - Sat 11 AM - 5 PM, Sun noon - 5 PM, cl Mon, Tues & major holidays; Suggested general admis adults $8, seniors 60 & up & military $5, college students, youth under 18 free; some spec exhibs may carry an admis fee; Estab 1919 for the pub benefit; Some of the galleries include: African Gallery, Glass Gallery, Contemporary Gallery, European 16th-18th Century Galleries, Experiencenter Gallery, Regional Artists Gallery, Special Exhibs Gallery & an Asian Wing & an American Wing; Average Annual Attendance: 569,155; Mem: 12,000; dues $35 - $5000+; ann meeting Jan
Income: $1,300,000 (financed by federal, state & local funds, mem dues, endowment & corporate grants)
Special Subjects: Painting-American, Painting-European, Oriental Art
Collections: American Coll, European Art From Medieval Period to Present, Oriental Coll
Publications: Annual report; bulletin; Calendar of Events, monthly; gallery guides & catalogs, periodically
Activities: Classes for adults & children; docent training; lect open to pub, 3-6 per yr; gallery talks; tours; concerts; ann Oktoberfest; Leonardo League Volunteer Organization; schols offered; mus shop sells books, reproductions, original art, toys & jewelry

L **Library**, 456 Belmonte Park N, Dayton, OH 45405-4700. Tel 937-223-5277; Fax 937-223-3140; Email library@daytonartinstitute.org; Web: www.daytonartinstitute.org; *Ref Librn* Alice Saidel; *Librn* Ellen Rohmiller; *Archivist* Kristina Klepacz
By appointment; Estab 1922; Open to the pub for art reference only
Income: Financed by Dayton Art Institute budget
Library Holdings: Book Volumes 25,000, Clipping Files, Exhibition Catalogs, Other Holdings Auction catalogs - from 1975-2007, Periodical Subscriptions 30, Slides

Special Subjects: Carpets & Rugs
Collections: Louis J P Lott & Walter G Schaeffer, architectural libraries, Guy Elbert Alloh & Gwen Jones Allott Collection of Oriental Carpets
Activities: Fiction, Fine Art, and Fun Book Club

M **DAYTON VISUAL ARTS CENTER,** 118 N Jefferson St, Dayton, OH 45402-1708. Tel 937-224-3822; Fax 937-224-4356; Email dvac@daytonvisualarts.org; Web: www.daytonvisualarts.org; *Exec Dir* Eva Buttacavoli; *Gallery Mgr* Patrick Mauk
Open Tues - Sat 11 AM - 6 PM; No admis fee; Estab 1991 to showcase important regional contemporary art; New gallery space located in downtown Dayton; Average Annual Attendance: 15,000; Mem: 700; dues $45 - $1,000
Income: Financed by mem, county appropriation & grants
Collections: Contemporary Art
Publications: exhibit catalogues; e-newsletters
Activities: Classes for adults; 6-8 exhibs annually in gallery; professional develop workshops & critiques for artists; lect, forums & field trips; gallery talks open to pub; 12 vis lectrs per yr; schols offered; sales gallery of original art during Nov-Dec & at off-site locations during the yr; ann art auction in Apr

M **WRIGHT STATE UNIVERSITY,** Robert and Elaine Stein Galleries, 3640 Colonel Glenn Hwy, Dayton, OH 45435-0001. Tel 937-775-2978; Fax 937-775-4082; Email artgalleries@wright.edu; Web: www.wright.edu/artgalleries; *Galleries Coordr* Tess Cortes
Open Tues - Fri 10 AM - 4 PM, Sat & Sun Noon - 4 PM, cl Mon & holidays; No admis fee; Estab 1974, devoted to exhibs of & research in contemporary art; Four galleries; multi-level contemporary building with over 5000 sq ft & over 500 running ft of wall space; Average Annual Attendance: 25,000
Income: Financed through the univ, grants & individual support
Collections: Collection of Contemporary Art
Publications: Artist's books & exhib catalogs, 2 per yr
Activities: Lect open to pub; gallery talks; tours; individual paintings & art objects lent to faculty & admin areas; lending coll contains original art works, original prints, paintings, drawings, photographs & sculpture; originate traveling exhibs; sales desk sells catalogs

L **Visual Resources Center, Department of Art & Art History**, 3640 Colonel Glenn Hwy, Dayton, OH 45435-0001. Tel 937-775-2896; Email shannon.michalak@wright.edu; Web: www.wright.edu/vrc; *Visual Resource Cur* Shannon Michalak
Open Mon - Thurs 9 AM - 2 PM; Estab 1970 to serve instruction at Wright State Univ
Library Holdings: Auction Catalogs, Book Volumes 750, Exhibition Catalogs, Other Holdings Art school catalogs, Periodical Subscriptions 12, Slides 60,000
Special Subjects: Architecture, Art History, Drawings, Etchings & Engravings, History of Art & Archaeology, Painting-American, Painting-British, Painting-Dutch, Painting-European, Painting-Flemish, Painting-French, Painting-German, Painting-Italian, Painting-Polish, Painting-Russian

DELAWARE

M **RICHARD M ROSS ART MUSEUM AT WESLEYAN UNIVERSITY,** 61 S Sandusky St, Delaware, OH 43015-2333; 60 S Sandusky St, Delaware, OH 43015-2333. Tel 740-368-3606; Fax 740-368-3515; Email ramuseum@owu.edu; *Dir* Justin Kronewetter; *Sr Asst* Tammy Wallace; *Gallery Asst* Stephen Perakis
Open Tues - Fri 10 AM - 5 PM, Thurs until 9 PM, Sun 1 PM - 5 PM, cl Mon & Sat; Admis free; Estab 2002 to house permanent art coll, 4 galleries, 1 dedicated to display of objects from mus coll, 3 dedicated to display of temporary exhibs; Average Annual Attendance: 10,000
Income: Income from endowed accounts and donations
Purchases: Purchases made with funds from endowed accounts
Collections: Primarily works on paper; minimal non-paper based works
Exhibitions: 10-12 solo & group shows per school yr; solo & group shows in the 2 off-site galleries
Activities: Artist lectrs open to pub; 15 vis lectrs per yr; gallery talks; tours; venue for various univ & community related events; lend original object of are to other mus; periodic book traveling exhibs

DOVER

M **WARTHER MUSEUM INC,** 331 Karl Ave, Dover, OH 44622-2767; PO Box 686, Dover, OH 44622-0686. Tel 330-343-7513; Email carol@thewarthermuseum.com; Web: www.thewarthermuseum.com; *Pres & Gen Mgr* Carol Warther Moreland
Open daily 9 AM - 5 PM, cl New Year's Day, Easter, Thanksgiving, Christmas; Admis $13.50 adults, students 6 - 17 yrs old $5; Estab 1936 to display carvings; Average Annual Attendance: 100,000
Income: $250,000 (financed by admis)
Special Subjects: Ivory, Woodcarvings
Collections: Carvings of American Railroad History, Carvings of ivory, ebony & walnut depicting the evolution of the steam engine
Exhibitions: Carvings of American Railroads by Ernest Warther
Activities: Lects open to pub; Tours; retail store sells books, souvenirs, gen gifts, handcrafted cutlery

DUBLIN

M **DUBLIN ARTS COUNCIL,** (Bunte Gallery), Dublin Arts Council, 7125 Riverside Dr. Dublin, OH 43016-9586. Tel 614-889-7444; Web: www.dublinarts.org; *Mktg Dir* Janet Cooper; *Exec Dir* David S Guion, Ph.D
Open Tues 10 AM - 7 PM, Wed-Fri 10 AM - 5 PM, Sat 11 AM - 2 PM; Estab 1983
Special Subjects: Art Education, Asian Art, Bronzes, Ceramics, Collages, Dioramas, Glass, Jewelry, Landscapes, Metalwork, Mixed Media, Painting-American, Pewter, Photography, Portraits, Pottery, Prints, Sculpture, Textiles, Watercolors, Woodcarvings
Collections: Artwork of local & regional artists, Dublin Art in Public Places Collection (commissioned, on-loan & gifted)
Activities: Educational workshops; classes; camps; visual arts series; DAC Sundays at Suoto summer concert series; Dublin Art in Public Places prog

ELYRIA

M **SOUTHERN LORAIN COUNTY HISTORICAL SOCIETY,** Spirit of '76 Museum, 509 Washington Ave, Elyria, OH 44035-5128. Tel 216-647-4367; *VPres* Phyllis Perkins; *Cur* Diane Stanley; *Pres* Dick Landis
Open Apr - Oct Sat & Sun 2:30 - 5 PM, groups of ten or more any time by reservation; No admis fee; Estab 1970 to memorialize Archibald M Willard who created the Spirit of '76, nation's most inspirational painting; Average Annual Attendance: 2,000; Mem: 259; dues couple $10, individual $5; ann meeting in Apr
Income: $10,000 (financed by mem, gifts & gift shop)
Purchases: $10,000
Special Subjects: Costumes, Furniture, Historical Material, Painting-American, Portraits
Collections: Archibald M Willard Paintings, artifacts of local interest, memorabilia of Myron T Herrick
Publications: Quarterly newsletters
Activities: Sales shop sells books, reproductions, prints & miscellaneous items

FINDLAY

M **MAZZA MUSEUM,** The University of Findlay, Gardner Arts Pavilion, Findlay, OH 45840-3653; 1000 N Main St, Findlay, OH 45840-3653. Tel 800-472-9502; Fax 419-434-6480; Email sapp@findlay.edu; Web: www.mazzamuseum.org
Open Wed-Fri noon-5PM, Sun1PM-4PM, other times by appointment; cl major holidays; No admis fee; donations accepted; Mus of original art from picture books; Average Annual Attendance: 10,000
Collections: over 3000 works of art; children's picture book art; literacy
Activities: Classes for adults & children, docent training; lects open to pub, 29 vis lectrs per yr, gallery talks, tours; lending coll contains original objects of art; mus shop sells books, autographed books, & other literature related items

M **UNIVERSITY OF FINDLAY,** Dudley & Mary Marks Lea Gallery, 1000 N Main St, Findlay, OH 45840-3653. Tel 419-434-4534; Fax 419-434-4531; *Dir* Ed Corle
Open Mon - Fri 9 AM - 4:30 PM; Estab in 1962 as an auxiliary to the col art department
Income: Financed by endowment & tui
Special Subjects: Prints
Exhibitions: Annual Student Exhibition; Contemporary Art & Crafts; Regional & Nat Faculty & Student Exhibits
Publications: Individual exhib catalogs
Activities: Classes for adults & children; dramatic progs; lect open to pub, 2-3 vis lectrs per yr; gallery talks; tours; competitions with awards; schols; fels; individual paintings & original objects of art lent, primarily to College offices

FOSTORIA

M **FOSTORIA OHIO GLASS ASSOCIATION,** Glass Heritage Gallery, 109 N Main St, Fostoria, OH 44830-2215. Tel 419-435-5077; Email museum@fostoriaglass.com; Web: fostoriaglass.com
Open Mar Thurs-Sat 10AM-4PM, Apr - Dec Tues-Sat 10AM-4PM; No admis fee, donations accepted; Estab 1992 to show glass made in Fostoria, OH 1887-1920; Over 1,200 pieces on display; Mem: annual dues $20
Income: Corporate sponsors & donations, dues
Collections: glassmaking history & industries; local industry glass, 1887-1920; vases; lamps; pitchers, records & glass works
Publications: Victoria Views quarterly newsletter
Activities: Shop sells glass on consignment from mems

GALLIPOLIS

A **FRENCH ART COLONY,** 530 1st Ave, Gallipolis, OH 45631-1245; PO Box 472, Gallipolis, OH 45631-0472. Tel 740-446-3834; Fax 740-446-3834; Email info@frenchartcolony.org; Web: www.frenchartcolony.org; *Bd Mem* Janice M Thaler; *Bd Mem* Peggy Evans; *Exec Dir* Joseph Wright
Open Tues - Fri 10 AM - 5 PM, Sun 1 - 5 PM, Sat 10 AM - 3 PM; No admis fee; Estab 1964 to promote the arts throughout the region; Monthly regional artists & traveling exhibs; Average Annual Attendance: 7,000; Mem: 325; dues $15 & up
Income: Financed by mem & donations
Special Subjects: Ceramics, Collages, Costumes, Crafts, Drawings, Folk Art, Glass, Metalwork, Miniatures, Painting-American, Photography, Portraits, Pottery, Prints, Sculpture, Watercolors, Woodcarvings
Collections: 2D Art coll of various artists & media
Exhibitions: Exhibits change monthly & include: International, Juried Festival, Ceramics, Watercolors, Oils & Mixed-Media; 3D sculpture
Publications: Newsletter, bimonthly "Currents"
Activities: Classes & progs for adults & children in visual & performing art; community progs; creative writing; volunteer progs; juried competitions; historic tours; facility rental; fundraising events; lects open to pub; concerts; book traveling exhibs; mus shop sells prints

L **Library,** 530 First Ave, PO Box 472 Gallipolis, OH 45631. Tel 740-446-3834; Email facart@zoomnet.net; *Dir* Mary Bea McCalla
Open Tues - Fri 10 AM - 3 PM, Sat & Sun 1 - 5 PM; Estab 1972 as small reference library dealing primarily with visual arts
Library Holdings: Book Volumes 2000, Cassettes, Clipping Files, Exhibition Catalogs, Lantern Slides, Memorabilia, Pamphlets, Periodical Subscriptions 5, Photographs, Prints, Reproductions, Slides

GAMBIER

M **KENYON COLLEGE,** Gund Gallery, 101 1/2 College Drive, Gambier, OH 43022. Tel 740-427-5972; Email gundgallery@kenyon.edu; Web: www.thegundgallery.org; *Director* Natalie Marsh; *Assistant Director* Christopher Yates; *Collections Manager and Registrar* Robin Goodman; *Curator of Academic Programs* Jodi Kovach; *Director of Digital Communication and Engagement* Caroline Culbert; *Administrative Assistant* Megan Evans
Monday: closed; Tues, Weds, & Fri: 1-7pm; Thursday: 1-10pm; Sat & Sun 1-5pm; No admis fee; Opened in 2011, the Fund Gallery is part of a larger campus initiative to expand access to art and visual culture for the College's student body, faculty, and staff along with the surrounding community; The Gund Gallery celebrates the power of art as a critical centerpiece of Kenyon's liberal arts mission and our community. We champion the best art and artists of the 20th and 21st centuries via an active exhibition schedule, expanding permanent collection, and formal and informal learning experiences.
Income: Financed by col
Collections: The Gund Gallery Collection is dedicated to 20th and 21st century art. This focus was chosen to expose students and our community to the rich array of material, conceptual techniques and methodologies deployed by artists of the 20th and 21st centuries. The collection fosters opportunities to contribute to Kenyon College1s liberal arts curricula and the community through exhibitions and collections-dependent programs., Distributed across campus, the Kenyon College Collection is a diverse sampling of our long history., Art coll and items of some historical importance
Activities: classes for adults & children; workshops; films; Lect open to pub; gallery talks; tours;; Lending of original objects to students; Book traveling exhibitions; Organize traveling exhibitions

GRANVILLE

M **DENISON UNIVERSITY,** Art Gallery, Burke Hall of Music & Art, Granville, OH 43023; PO Box 810, Granville, OH 43023-0810. Tel 740-587-6255; Fax 740-587-5701; Email harlacher@denison.edu; Web: www.denisonmuseum.org; *Dir* Sherry Harlacher; *Cur Colls* Anna Cannizzo; *Cur Asst* Sarah Baker
Open Mon - Sat noon - 5 PM; extended hrs Thurs 5 - 7 PM; No admis fee; Estab 1943 for educ & exhib purposes; 2 galleries, conservation lab, storage; Average Annual Attendance: 2,000
Income: Financed through Univ
Special Subjects: American Indian Art, Archaeology, Asian Art, Baroque Art, Bronzes, Cartoons, Ceramics, Costumes, Decorative Arts, Etchings & Engravings, Ethnology, Folk Art, Furniture, Manuscripts, Painting-American, Painting-European, Painting-French, Painting-Italian, Photography, Porcelain, Prints, Religious Art, Reproductions, Sculpture, Silver, Textiles, Textiles, Woodcarvings, Woodcuts, Watercolors
Collections: American and European paintings, prints, drawings and sculpture, Burmese textiles, lacquerware and Buddhist sculpture, Chinese bronzes, robes and porcelains, Kuna Indian Molas, Uchus and ceremonial objects, American Indian pottery, baskets and rugs, African sculpture and basketry
Exhibitions: Faculty show; senior student shows; special exhibs from permanent coll; visiting artists exhibs; traveling exhibs
Activities: Book Club; film screenings; family day; lects open to pub, 4-6 vis lectrs per yr; gallery talks; tours; fels offered; exten dept; individual paintings & original objects of art lent to other museums

L **Slide Library,** 400 West Loop, Rm 503 Granville, OH 43023. Tel 740-587-6480; Fax 740-587-5701; Email hout@denison.edu; Web: www.denison.edu; *Art Image Cur & Developer* Jacqueline Pelasky Hout
Open Mon - Fri 9 AM - 4 PM; Open to faculty & to students for reference only
Library Holdings: Slides 200,000

HAMILTON

M **FITTON CENTER FOR CREATIVE ARTS,** 101 S Monument Ave, Hamilton, OH 45011-2833. Tel 513-863-8873 ext 110; Fax 513-863-8865; Email cathy@fittoncenter.org; Web: www.fittoncenter.org; *Exec Dir* Rick H Jones; *Arts in Common Dir* Henry Cepluch; *Exhib* Cathy Mayhugh; *Dir Pub Rel and Mktg* Jodi Fritsch; *Dir Develop* Elaine Hemmelgarn; *Educ Coordr* Jenn Acus-Smith
Open Office: Mon - Thurs 8:30 AM - 8PM, Fri 8:30 AM - 5 PM, Sat 9 AM - Noon, cl Sun; Gallery: Mon - Thurs 9 AM - 8 PM, Fri 10 AM - 5 PM, Sat 9 AM - noon, cl Sun (except for special events); No admis fee; Estab 1992 to build community excellence through the arts & culture; Two large galleries with foyer on second floor. Large lobby display area on ground fl. Student gallery on ground fl; Average Annual Attendance: 100,000; Mem: 300; dues $30 & up
Income: Financed by Ohio Arts Council, corporations, Hamilton Community Foundation & mem, sponsorship & special gifts, ticket sales, & classifieds
Special Subjects: African Art, Afro-American Art, Asian Art, Decorative Arts, Graphics, Hispanic Art, Historical Material, Jewelry, Landscapes, Latin American Art, Leather, Manuscripts, Painting-American, Painting-Japanese, Photography, Portraits, Posters, Pottery, Pre-Columbian Art, Primitive art, Prints, Reproductions, Sculpture, Silver, Textiles
Publications: The Schooled Mind: Spectra+; quarterly newsletter; ann report
Activities: Classes for adults & children; dramatic progs; performing arts series; teacher workshops; lect open to pub; concerts; gallery talks; tours; competitions with prizes; schols offered

M **PYRAMID HILL SCULPTURE PARK & MUSEUM,** 1763 Hamilton-Cleves Rd, Hamilton, OH 45013-9601. Tel 513-868-8336 (office), 887-9514 (park); Fax 513-868-3585; Email pyramid@pyramidhill.org; Web: www.pyramidhill.org; *Bd Pres* William Groth; *Dir Prog & Admin* Jeni Barton; *Dir Park Opers* Shaun Higgins; *Creative Assistant* Elizabeth Eversole; *Event Coordinator* Nikki Koedel
Open daily Mon - Fri 8 AM - 7 PM, Sat & Sun 8 AM - 5 PM; Admis adults $8, children 5-12 $3; Estab 1997; 300+ acres, 7 lakes with fountains, pavilion, amphitheater, 65+ outdoor sculptures & Ancient sculpture mus; Average Annual Attendance: 32,000; Mem: 1183; dues founder's society $5000, ambassador $2500, benefactor $1000, sponsor $500, patron $250, contributor $125, family $45, individual $40
Income: Non-profit
Special Subjects: Antiquities-Byzantine, Antiquities-Egyptian, Antiquities-Etruscan, Antiquities-Greek, Antiquities-Roman, Architecture, Sculpture
Collections: Monumental Sculpture, 65 pieces, Museum of Ancient Sculpture indoor museum, Greek, Egyptian, Etruscan, Roman and Syrian Sculpture from 1550 BC
Publications: Quarterly newsletter
Activities: Classes for adults & children; dramatic progs; music; bus trips (art excursions); summer series for children; docent training; lects for members only; concerts; gallery talks; tours; sponsoring of competitions; 2 vis lectrs per yr; sales shop sells books & original art

KENT

M **KENT STATE UNIVERSITY,** School of Art Galleries, Terrace Dr, Kent, OH 44242-0001; PO Box 5190 Kent, OH 44242-0001. Tel 330-672-7853, 672-2192 (Art Dept); Fax 330-672-4729; Email haturner@kent.edu; Web: www.galleries.kent.edu; *Galleries Dir* Anderson Turner; *School of Art Dir* Christine Havice, PhD
Open School of Art Gallery: Tues - Fri 11 AM - 5 PM; Downtown Gallery: Wed - Fri noon - 5 PM, Sat 10 AM - 4 PM, cl school holidays; No admis fee; Estab 1950 as part of the instructional prog at Kent State; One main gallery 2200 sq ft; two student galleries; Eells Gallery; Blossom Music Center; Downtown Gallery 1200 sq ft; Michener Gallery 1,000 sq ft; Average Annual Attendance: 22,000; Mem: 76; dues $20; ann meeting in June
Income: Financed by Univ, grants & fundraising
Special Subjects: Painting-American, Prints, Sculpture
Collections: Michener Coll, contemporary prints & paintings, permanent coll sculpture, paintings, prints, crafts & photog, textiles
Exhibitions: Annual Invitational; faculty & student one-man & group exhibitions; traveling exhibitions from museums
Publications: Brochures; catalogs, 2-3 per yr
Activities: Classes for students in mus preparation; lect open to pub, 6 vis lectrs per yr; gallery talks; tours; competitions; individual paintings & original objects of art lent to offices on campus; book traveling exhibs 3 per yr; organize 1-2 traveling exhibs to circulate nationally

LAKEWOOD

A **BECK CENTER FOR THE ARTS,** 17801 Detroit Ave, Lakewood, OH 44107-3499. Tel 216-521-2540; Fax 216-228-6050; Email yvette@beckcenter.org; Web: www.lkwdpl.org/beck; *Pres Bd Trustees* Fred Unger; *Dir Develop* John Farina; *Educ & Outreach* Rachel Spence; *Dir Educ* Edward Gallagher; *Exec Dir* Jim Walton; *Dir Mktg* Yvette A Hanzel; *Artistic Dir* Scott Spence
Open Mon - Fri 9 AM - 8 PM, Sat Noon - 6 PM, performance evenings Thurs & Fri 6 - 9 PM, 8 - 10 PM, Sun 2 - 4 PM; No admis fee; Estab 1976 to present a wide variety of the fine & graphic arts; A cooperative art gallery, home to 73 artists, juried art shows & visual art progs; Average Annual Attendance: 50,000
Income: Financed by individual, corporate & foundation donations, box office & class registration revenue
Collections: Contemporary pieces including acrylics, collages, etchings, oils, sculpture & watercolors
Exhibitions: Kwo, Miller, Thurmer (paintings & sculpture); Touching Stories, from Cleveland Mus of Art; Hungarian Art; Krabill (paintings);
Publications: Bulletins; Programs, every five weeks
Activities: Classes for adults & children; dramatic progs; music; dance; visual arts; creative arts therapy; docent training; lects open to pub; 5 vis lectrs per yr; concerts; gallery talks; competitions with awards; exten dept serves youth in schools; sales shop sells original art, prints, jewelry & all art media

LIMA

M **ARTSPACE/LIMA,** 65 Town Sq, Lima, OH 45801-4950. Tel 419-222-1721; Fax 419-222-8439; Email artspacelima@woh.rr.com; Web: www.artspacelima.com; *Mgr Opers* William J Sullivan; *Assoc Mgr* Kay Van Meter
Open Tues - Fri 10 AM - 5 PM, Sat 10 AM - 2 PM, cl Sun & Mon; No admis fee; Estab 1953 for the promotion of visual arts through educ & exhib; Maintains resource center; Average Annual Attendance: 5,000; Mem: 300; dues family $65, individual $40, student & senior $25; ann meeting in Aug
Income: $25,000 (financed by mem, grants & fundraising events)
Library Holdings: Book Volumes, Compact Disks, DVDs, Kodachrome Transparencies, Memorabilia, Original Art Works, Photographs, Prints, Slides, Video Tapes
Special Subjects: Afro-American Art, American Indian Art, American Western Art, Anthropology, Archaeology, Architecture, Asian Art, Bronzes, Calligraphy, Cartoons, Ceramics, Coins & Medals, Collages, Costumes, Crafts, Decorative Arts, Dolls, Drawings, Enamels, Etchings & Engravings, Ethnology, Folk Art, Furniture, Glass, Woodcuts
Exhibitions: 18 exhibits annually; Permanent gallery space at St Rita's hospital with 4 new exhibs annually
Publications: Newsletter
Activities: Classes for adults & children; docent progs; lect open to pub, 6 vis lectrs per yr; gallery talks; tours; competitions with awards; schols offered; individual paintings & original objects of art lent to local bus, pub school classrooms & art teachers; mus shop sells books, original art, reproductions, prints & children's art kits

MANSFIELD

A **MANSFIELD FINE ARTS GUILD,** Mansfield Art Center, 700 Marion Ave, Mansfield, OH 44906-5007. Tel 419-756-1700; Fax 419-756-0860; Web: www.mansfieldartcenter.com; *Dir* H Daniel Butts III
Open Tues - Sat 11 AM - 5 PM, Sun Noon - 5 PM, cl Mon & national holidays; No admis fee; Estab 1945, incorporated 1956 to maintain an art center in which exhibs, lects, gallery talks, spec progs, symposia & series of classes for adults & children are provided for the North Central Ohio area; maintained by mem, commission on sales & classes; Gallery dimensions 5000 sq ft with flexible lighting, movable walls, props, etc to facilitate monthly exhib changes; Average Annual Attendance: 25,000; Mem: 1050; dues $2 5- $1000; ann meeting in Apr
Income: Financed by mem, grants, donations
Exhibitions: Changing exhibs of member artists' work; traveling shows & locally organized one-man, group & theme exhibs changing monthly throughout the yr
Publications: Catalogs; class schedules; monthly newsletter
Activities: Classes for adults & children; lect open to pub, 6 vis lectrs per yr; gallery talks mainly for school groups; competitions; schols offered

L **Library**, 700 Marion Ave, Mansfield, OH 44906-5007. Tel 419-756-1700; Web: www.mansfieldartcenter.com; *Art Dir* H Daniel Butts III
Open by appointment only; Estab 1971; The library is basically a collection of monographs & studies of styles & periods for teacher & student reference
Income: financed by arts center
Library Holdings: Book Volumes 500

MARIETTA

M **MARIETTA COLLEGE,** Grover M Hermann Fine Arts Center, 215 Fifth St, Marietta, OH 45750. Tel 740-376-4696; Fax 740-376-4529; Web: www.marietta.edu; *Chmn* Valdis Garoza
Open Mon - Fri 8 AM - 10:30 PM, Sat & Sun 1 - 10:30 PM; No admis fee; Estab 1965; Gallery maintained; Average Annual Attendance: 20,000
Special Subjects: Painting-American, Sculpture, Crafts, African Art, American Western Art
Collections: Permanent coll of contemporary American paintings, sculpture & crafts, significant coll of African & pre-Columbian art
Activities: Lect open to pub; competitions

M **THE OHIO HISTORICAL SOCIETY, INC,** Campus Martius Museum & Ohio River Museum, 601 Second St, Marietta, OH 45750-2122. Tel 740-373-3750, 800-860-0145; Fax 740-373-3680; Email cmmoriv@ohiohistory.org; Web: www.ohiohistory.org; *Mgr* Andrew J Verhoff; *Secy* Leann Hendershot; *Educational Specialist* Sherry Potochnik
Open Campus Martius Mus: Mar - Oct Wed - Sat 9:30 AM - 5 PM, Sun noon - 5 PM, Memorial Day, July 4, Labor Day noon - 5 PM; Ohio River Mus: Memorial Day Oct Sat 9:30 AM - 5 PM, Sun 1 2 - 5 PM, Memorial Day, July 4, Labor Day 12 - 5 PM; Admis fee adults $7, student $3, mem & children under 6 free; Estab 1929 the Campus Martius Mus is the Ohio Historical Soc's gateway to the settlement of Ohio & the movement of people into & within the state; buildings, artifacts, audio and video exhibits tell the story; estab 1941 the Ohio River Mus is the Ohio Historical Soc's interpretive ctr for river history, especially steamboats; exhibits include a steam towboat, river diorama, small craft, steamboat artifacts, models, paintings & a video history of steamboats; Campus Martius Mus has 12,500 sq ft of exhib space on three floors plus a two-story home, a portion of the original fort of 1790-95 enclosed within the building. The Ohio River Mus has approx 4500 sq ft of exhib space in three separate bldgs connected by walkway; Average Annual Attendance: 18,000
Income: Financed by state appropriation, mem, grants, fundraising, admis & sales
Special Subjects: American Indian Art, Archaeology, Costumes, Crafts, Decorative Arts, Dolls, Drawings, Folk Art, Furniture, Glass, Historical Material, Jewelry, Landscapes, Marine Painting, Painting-American, Period Rooms, Pewter, Photography, Porcelain, Portraits, Pottery, Restorations, Silver, Textiles
Collections: Steamer W P Snyder Jr, Tell City Pilothouse, a replica of the 18th century flatboat, decorative arts from 19th century Ohio, early Ohio paintings, prints, & photographs, items from early Putnam, Blennerhassett & other families, Ohio Company & Marietta materials, Ohio River landscapes
Activities: Classes for adults & children; tours; mus shop sells books & souvenir items

MASSILLON

M **MASSILLON MUSEUM,** 121 Lincoln Way E, Massillon, OH 44646-6633. Tel 330-833-4061; Fax 330-833-2925; Web: www.massillonmuseum.org; *Exec* Alexandra Nicholis Coon; *Archivist* Mandy Pond; *Registrar* Cristina Savu
Open Tues - Sat 9:30 AM - 5 PM, Sun 2 - 5 PM; No admis fee; Estab 1933 as a mus of art & history; The mus places emphasis on the Ohio area by representing the fine arts & crafts & the Massillon area with an historical collections; Average Annual Attendance: 20,000; Mem: 750, dues $25 & higher
Income: Financed by local property tax
Library Holdings: Audio Tapes, CD-ROMs, Cards, Cassettes, Clipping Files, Exhibition Catalogs, Lantern Slides, Manuscripts, Memorabilia, Motion Pictures, Original Art Works, Original Documents, Photographs, Prints, Records, Reels, Sculpture, Video Tapes
Special Subjects: American Indian Art, Archaeology, Carpets & Rugs, Ceramics, Costumes, Decorative Arts, Dolls, Drawings, Ethnology, Furniture, Glass, Landscapes, Military Art, Painting-American, Photography, Photography, Portraits, Pottery, Renaissance Art, Textiles, Watercolors, Antiquities-Roman
Collections: Ceramics, china, costumes, drawings, furniture, glass, jewelry, paintings, prints, photography
Exhibitions: Monthly exhibs; Immel miniature circus diorama; Massillon Tiger Football gallery
Publications: Pamphlet of activities & exhibs, quarterly
Activities: Classes for adults & children; docent training; lect open to pub, 3 vis lectrs per yr; gallery talks; tours; concerts; sponsoring of competitions; exten dept serves pub schools; individual paintings & original objects of art lent to area museums; organize traveling exhibs to accredited mus & galleries; mus shop sells books, original art, reproductions, prints & jewelry

MEDINA

M **PORTHOLES INTO THE PAST,** 4450 Poe Rd, Medina, OH 44256; 2027 Lyndway, Lyndhurst, OH 44121. Tel 330-725-0402; Fax 330-722-2439; *Pres & Dir* Merle Mishne
Open by appointment, cl New Year's Day, Christmas; No admis fee
Collections: over 2,000 images of car art, blue prints & cutaway drawings, over 200 images of Bugatti cars, over 60 c.1910 Montaut-Gamy lithographs, over 500 images of airplanes, impressionist art, models, American Indian artifacts, World War II posters, paintings, drawings, photographs, advertising art
Publications: biannual brochure, Portholes
Activities: Lect, guided tours, films, rental gallery

MIDDLETOWN

A **MIDDLETOWN ARTS CENTER,** 130 N Verity Pkwy, Middletown, OH 45042-1916; PO Box 441, Middletown, OH 45042-0441. Tel 513-424-2417; Fax 513-424-1682; Email contact@middletownartscenter.com; Web: www.middletownartscenter.com; *Dir* Patt Belisle; *Pres* Jackie Phillips
Open Mon 9 AM - 4 PM, Tues - Thurs 9 AM - 9 PM, Sat 9 AM - noon, cl Sun; No admis fee; Estab 1957 to offer exhibits & classes to the pub; Auditorium for large exhibits; gallery for small exhibits; Average Annual Attendance: 7500; Mem: 596; dues minimum $25; ann meeting in July
Income: Funds generated through mem & donations
Exhibitions: 10-12 exhibitions per year including Annual Area Art Show; Annual Student Show; plus one & two-man invitational shows of regional artists; American Watercolor Society & Ohio Watercolor Society
Publications: Brochures publicizing exhibs; e-newsletters; schedule of classes
Activities: Classes for adults, children & the handicapped; workshops with nat artists; lects open to pub, 1-3 vis lectrs per yr; tours; competitions with awards; schols offered; individual paintings & original objects of art lent usually to bus for display; lending coll contains books, original art works & paintings within 50 mile radius of Middletown; book traveling exhibs; sales shop sells pottery, jewelry & paintings produced at Center

L **Library**, 130 N Verity Pkwy, Middletown, OH 45042-1916; PO Box 441, Middletown, OH 45042-0441. Tel 513-424-2417; Fax 513-424--1682; Email mfac@siscom.net; Web: www.middletownfinearts.com; *Adminr* Peggy Davish
Open Mon 9 AM - 4 PM, Tues - Thurs 9 AM - 9 PM, Sat 9 AM - noon, cl Sun; Estab 1963, to provide information and enjoyment for students and instructors; Circ 30; Library open for lending or reference
Income: Financed through ann budget & donations
Purchases: $150
Library Holdings: Book Volumes 1500, Periodical Subscriptions 6, Slides
Special Subjects: Art Education, Art History, Ceramics, Conceptual Art, Crafts, Decorative Arts, Drawings, Folk Art, Historical Material, Illustration, Photography, Portraits, Sculpture, Southwestern Art, Watercolors
Collections: All books pertain only to art subjects: Art history, ceramics, crafts, illustrations, references, techniques, theory
Activities: Classes for adults & children; one vis lectr per yr; sponsoring of competitions; schols

NEWARK

M **LICKING COUNTY ARTS,** Art Gallery, 50 S 2nd St, Ste 2 Newark, OH 43055-5440. Tel 740-349-8031; Email lcagalleryonsecond@gmail.com; Web: www.lickingcountyarts.net; *Pres* Martha Cotton
Open Mon - Sat 11:30 AM - 3:30 PM; Estab 1968 to support art education & exhibitions; Mem: dues $10-$1,000
Collections: Work by local & regional artists
Exhibitions: Temporary exhibits
Activities: Mus shop sells wall art, jewelry, greeting cards, pottery, glass, scarves & purses

NORTH CANTON

L **NORTH CANTON PUBLIC LIBRARY,** The Little Art Gallery, 185 N Main St, North Canton, OH 44720-2595. Tel 330-499-4712, Ext 12; Fax 330-499-7356; Email harberla@oplin.lib.oh.us; Web: www.northcantonlibrary.org/lag; *Chmn Art Comt* David Smetana; *Cur* Laurie G Fife Harbert; *Library Dir* Karen Sonderman; *Asst* Debbie Hansel
Open Mon - Thurs 9 AM - 9 PM, Fri 9 AM - 6 PM, Sat 9 AM - 5 PM, Sun 1 - 5 PM (Labor Day - Memorial Day); No admis fee; Estab 1936 to encourage & promote appreciation & educ of fine art & other related subjects; also recognizes & encourages local artists by promoting exhibs of their work; 600 sq ft; approx 30-50 works on view at a time; Average Annual Attendance: 7,000; Mem: 175; dues $15; meetings in Sept, Nov, Feb, Apr & Jun
Income: Financed by city & state appropriation
Purchases: $500
Library Holdings: Book Volumes 54,014, Original Art Works, Periodical Subscriptions 180, Photographs, Sculpture
Special Subjects: Ceramics, Drawings, Embroidery, Etchings & Engravings, Glass, Jewelry, Landscapes, Painting-American, Photography, Pottery, Prints, Religious Art, Sculpture, Stained Glass, Textiles, Watercolors
Collections: Original works by contemporary artists, religious reproductions, reproductions for juvenile
Exhibitions: Monthly exhibits; Stark County Competitive Artists Show
Activities: Classes for adults & children; classes for home schooled students; gallery talks; tours; competitions with awards; lending of original objects of art to estab art organizations

NORWICH

M **OHIO HISTORY CONNECTION,** National Road-Zane Grey Museum, 8850 East Pike, Norwich, OH 43767. Tel 740-826-3305; 800-752-2602; Email info@johnglennhome.org; Web: www.ohiohistory.org; *Pres* Robert W Lucas
Open May - Oct Wed - Sat 10 AM - 4 PM, Sun 1 PM - 4 PM, Nov - Apr by appt; Admis adults $7 seniors $6, students $3, mems free; Estab 1973; American art pottery
Income: Financed by endowment, mem & state appropriation
Special Subjects: American Indian Art, American Western Art, Ceramics, Dioramas, Pottery, Southwestern Art
Collections: Zanesville Art Pottery & Tile
Exhibitions: Zanesville Art Pottery & Tile
Activities: Lects open to pub, 6 per yr; tours; sales shop sells books, original art, reproductions, prints, souvenirs

OBERLIN

A **FIRELANDS ASSOCIATION FOR THE VISUAL ARTS,** 39 S Main St, Oberlin, OH 44074-1662. Tel 440-774-7158; Fax 440-775-1107; Email favagallery@oberlin.net; Web: www.favagallery.org; *Exec Dir* Elizabeth Manderen; *Dir Gallery* Kyle Michalak; *Educ Coordr* James Peake
Open Tues - Sat 11 AM - 5 PM, Sun 1 - 5 PM; No admis fee; Estab 1979 as a nonprofit community art organization with exhib, educ & outreach programs; Average Annual Attendance: 10,000; Mem: 350; dues basic $25 - $50, contributors up to $1000; ann meeting in May
Income: $205,000 (financed by grants, mem, fees, tui, commissions, contributions fundraisers & the Ohio Arts Council
Exhibitions: Monthly changing exhibits by contemp regional artists; Annual Juried Six-State Photography; Annual FAVA Members' Holiday Show; Biennial national juried Artist as Quiltmaker Exhibition
Activities: Classes for adults, teens & children; family workshops; lect open to pub; gallery talks; tours; competitions with awards; schols for low income children; sales shop sells original art

M **OBERLIN COLLEGE,** Allen Memorial Art Museum, 87 N Main St, Oberlin, OH 44074-1151. Tel 440-775-8665; Fax 440-775-8799; Email sally.moffitt@oberlin.edu; Web: www.oberlin.edu/amam; *Dir* Andria Derstine; *Registrar* Lucille Stiger; *Cur Educ* Jill Greenwood; *Head Preparator* Kendall Christian; *Asst Preparator* Michael Reynolds; *Cur American & European Art* Andaleeb Badiee Banta; *Asst Registrar* Selina Bartlett; *Admin Asst* Sally Moffitt; *Publications, Mem & Media Mgr* Megan Harding; *Cur Acad Progs* Liliana Milkova; *Cur Asian Art* Kevin Greenwood
Open Tues - Sat 10 AM - 5 PM, Sun 1 - 5 PM, cl Mon; No admis fee; Estab 1917 to serve teaching needs of Oberlin Col & provide cultural enrichment for Northern Ohio region; Original building was designed by Cass Gilbert, a new addition opened in 1977 & was designed by Venturi, Rauch & Assoc; Average Annual Attendance: 40,000; Mem: 525; dues Collectors Circle $2,500; Dir Circle $1000; Patrons Circle $500; supporting $150; contributing $100; family/Dual $75; student, Oberlin College student & senior $20; individual $50;
Income: Financed by endowment, mem & Oberlin College gen fund
Library Holdings: Auction Catalogs, Book Volumes, CD-ROMs, Compact Disks, Exhibition Catalogs, Fiche, Lantern Slides, Manuscripts, Maps, Micro Print, Original Documents, Periodical Subscriptions, Slides, Video Tapes
Special Subjects: Asian Art, Painting-American, Painting-Dutch, Painting-Flemish, Sculpture
Collections: The collection which ranges over the entire history of art is particularly strong in the areas of Dutch & Flemish paintings of the 17th century, European Art of the late 19th & early 20th centuries, contemporary American art, old masters & Japanese prints
Exhibitions: 4 -6 exhibs per yr drawn from permanent colls & loan exhibs
Publications: AMAM Newsletter, 2 times per yr; exhib catalogues
Activities: Classes for adults & children; docent training; lect open to pub, 6 vis lectrs per yr; gallery talks; concerts; tours; original objects of art lent to other institutions for spec exhib; art rental coll contains 400 original art works for lending to students on a semester basis; books; cards

L **Clarence Ward Art Library**, 83 N Main St, Allen Art Bldg Oberlin, OH 44074-1151. Tel 440-775-8635; Fax 440-775-5145; Email art.help@oberlin.edu; Web: www.oberlin.edu/library/art; *Art Librn* Barbara Q Prior; *Art Library Asst* Paula Baymiller
Open Mon - Thurs 8:30 AM - 5:30 PM & 7 - 11 PM, Fri 8:30 AM - 5:30 PM, Sat 12:30 - 5:30 PM, Sun 12:30 - 5:30 PM & 7 - 11 PM; No admis fee; Estab 1917 to serve the library needs of the art dept, the Allen Memorial Art Mus & the Oberlin Col community in the visual arts; Circ 22,000; Average Annual Attendance: 35,000
Income: Financed by appropriations from Oberlin Col Libraries
Library Holdings: Auction Catalogs, Book Volumes 100,000, CD-ROMs, Clipping Files, Compact Disks, DVDs, Exhibition Catalogs, Motion Pictures, Other Holdings Auction sales catalogs 10,000, Periodical Subscriptions 250, Video Tapes
Special Subjects: Aesthetics, Afro-American Art, Antiquities-Etruscan, Archaeology, Oriental Art, Antiquities-Greek, Antiquities-Oriental, Painting-European, Art History, Asian Art, Bronzes, Conceptual Art, History of Art & Archaeology, Illustration, Islamic Art, Judaica, Landscape Architecture, Landscapes, Painting-American, Painting-British, Painting-Dutch, Painting-Flemish, Painting-French, Painting-German, Painting-Italian, Painting-Japanese, Painting-Russian, Painting-Spanish, Photography, Portraits, Posters, Printmaking, Prints, Religious Art, Restoration & Conservation, Sculpture, Video, Watercolors, Woodcarvings, Woodcuts
Collections: Thomas Jefferson Collection of American architectural books
Publications: Bibliographies & library guides
Activities: Classes for students; tours

OXFORD

M **HIESTAND GALLERIES,** 124 Art Bldg, Oxford, OH 45056. Tel 513-529-1883; Email taulbeae@miamioh.edu; Web: miamioh.edu/cca/academics/departments/art/galleries/hiestand-galleries/index.html; Telex 513-529-2900; *Dir* Ann Taulbee
Open Mon - Fri 9 AM - 4:30 PM, other times by appointment; Estab to promote and support contemporary art
Collections: paintings; sculpture; drawings
Exhibitions: 20 exhibits annually

M **MIAMI UNIVERSITY,** Art Museum, 801 Patterson Ave, Oxford, OH 45056-3404. Tel 513-529-2232; Fax 513-529-6555; Web: www.muohio.edu/artmuseum/; *Cur Coll* Edna Carter Southard; *Cur Educ* Bonnie C Mason; *Museum Registrar* Beverly Bach; *Preparator* Mark DeGennaro; *Dir* Richard Wicks, PhD
Open Tues - Fri 10 AM - 5 PM, Sat & Sun Noon - 5 PM, cl Mon & university holidays; No admis fee; Estab 1978, Art Mus facility opened Fall 1978, to care for & exhibit Univ art colls, to arrange for a variety of traveling exhibitions & for the educational & cultural enrichment of the University & the region; Mus is maintained with exhib space of 9000 sq ft, consisting of 5 galleries in contemporary building designed by Walter A Netsch, Skidmore, Owing & Merrill, Chicago; operates the McGuffey Mus, home of William Holmes McGuffey, a national historic landmark; accredited by the American Assoc of Museums; Average Annual Attendance: 35,000; Mem: 1000; dues $25 & up
Income: Financed by gift & state appropriation
Special Subjects: Decorative Arts, Folk Art, Painting-American, Photography, Prints, Sculpture, Textiles
Collections: Charles M Messer Leica Camera Collection, Ancient Art, Decorative Arts, International Folk Art, largely Middle European, Middle Eastern, Mexican, Central & South America, European & American paintings, prints & sculpture, African art, Chinese Art, Gandharan art, Native American Art, Oceanic Art, photography, textiles
Exhibitions: Twelve per yr; Looking Back: 20th Century American Art; From Puri to Bombay: Art of India
Publications: Brochures; catalogs, approx 6-8 per year; quarterly newsletter
Activities: Progs for adults & children; docent training; lect open to pub, 5-6 vis lectrs per yr; concerts; gallery talks; tours; individual paintings & original objects of art lent to qualified museums in US; book traveling exhibs 2-3 per yr; originate traveling exhibs; mus shop sells books, magazines, original art, prints, note cards, jewelry & collectibles

L **Wertz Art & Architecture Library**, 501 E High St, Oxford, OH 45056-1846. Tel 513-529-6638; Web: www.lib.muohio.edu; *Librn* Stacy Brinkman; *Library Assoc* Jessica Wray
Open Mon - Thurs 8 AM - 10 PM, Fri 8 AM - 5 PM, Sat 1 - 5 PM, Sun 1 - 10 PM during acad yr; No admis fee; Estab to support the progs of the Schools of Art & Architecture & related disciplines
Income: Part of univ
Library Holdings: Book Volumes 65,000, Exhibition Catalogs, Other Holdings Per & serial subs 400
Special Subjects: Afro-American Art, American Indian Art, American Western Art, Architecture, Art Education, Asian Art, Decorative Arts, Folk Art, History of Art & Archaeology, Islamic Art, Jewelry, Landscape Architecture, Latin American Art, Marine Painting, Mexican Art, Oriental Art, Painting-American, Photography, Southwestern Art, Art History

PARMA

L **CUYAHOGA COUNTY PUBLIC LIBRARY,** 2111 Snow Rd, Parma, OH 44134. Tel 216-398-1800; Fax 216-749-9500; Web: www.cuyahogalibrary.org; *Exec Dir* Sari Feldman; *Deputy Dir* Tracy Strobel
Open Mon - Fri 8 AM - 5 PM; No admis fee; Circ 100,000
Income: Financed by county
Library Holdings: Auction Catalogs, DVDs, Exhibition Catalogs, Original Art Works, Periodical Subscriptions, Video Tapes
Exhibitions: Original art works by local artists; Exhibs on a monthly basis
Activities: Classes for adults; lectr open to pub, concerts, sponsor competitions

PORTSMOUTH

M **SOUTHERN OHIO MUSEUM CORPORATION,** Southern Ohio Museum, 825 Gallia St, Portsmouth, OH 45662-4137; PO Box 990, Portsmouth, OH 45662-0990. Tel 740-354-5629; Fax 740-354-4090; Email mark@somacc.com; Web: www.somacc.com; *Exec Dir* Mark Chepp; *Artistic Dir* Charlotte Gordon
Open Tues - Fri 10 AM - 5 PM, Sat 1 - 5 PM; No admis fee; Estab 1979 to provide exhibs & performances; Mus facility is a renovated & refurbished neoclassical building, 21,000 sq ft, constructed in 1918 as a bank. Facility has three temporary exhibit galleries & a theatre; maintain reference library; permanent colls; Average Annual Attendance: 31,000; Mem: 250; dues $20 - $1,000
Income: $470,000 (financed by endowment, mem & city appropriation, fundraisers & grants)
Library Holdings: Book Volumes, Exhibition Catalogs, Photographs
Special Subjects: Baroque Art, Ceramics, Collages, Dioramas, Dolls, Folk Art, Furniture, Glass, Historical Material, Landscapes, Painting-American, Painting-European, Photography, Porcelain, Prints, Watercolors, Sculpture, Woodcarvings, Woodcuts
Collections: Clarence Carter Paintings, Historic photograph coll, Native American artifacts - Hopewell & Adena cultures of Ohio River Valley, Carl Ackerman Collection of Historic Photographs, Ann Louise Stanton Antique Dollhead Collection
Exhibitions: Contemporary & traditional arts, history, or humanities
Publications: Annual report; exhib catalogs
Activities: Classes for adults & children; dramatic progs; docent training; lect open to pub, 3-4 vis lectrs per yr, concerts, gallery talks, tours, sponsor competitions; exten dept serves county; 1 or 2 book traveling exhibs; originates traveling exhibs periodically to Ohio museums & galleries; mus shop sells books, original art, gift items, jewelry & prints

SPRINGFIELD

M **CLARK COUNTY HISTORICAL SOCIETY,** Heritage Center of Clark County, 117 S Fountain Ave, Springfield, OH 45502. Tel 937-324-0657; Fax 937-324-1992; Web: www.heritagecenter.us; *Dir Colls* Virginia Weygandt; *CEO* Roger Sherrock; *Cur* Kasey Eichensehr; *Asst Cur* Natalie Fritz; *Dir Educ & Progs* Ardath Dellapina; *Dir Develop* Bridget Deane; *Admin Asst* Anna Roberts
Open Tues - Sat 9 AM - 5 PM, cl Mon; No admis fee; suggested donation, $5 person, $10 family; Estab 1897 for coll & preservation of Clark County history & historical artifacts; Average Annual Attendance: 32,000; Mem: 600; dues individual $35, family $50, friend $100, patron $250, student $5; ann meeting Nov
Income: $650,000 (financed by memberships, rentals, grants)
Library Holdings: Clipping Files, Manuscripts, Maps, Memorabilia, Original Art Works, Original Documents, Other Holdings, Periodical Subscriptions, Photographs, Prints, Slides
Special Subjects: Archaeology, Costumes, Crafts, Decorative Arts, Dolls, Drawings, Embroidery, Etchings & Engravings, Flasks & Bottles, Furniture, Glass, Historical Material, Landscapes, Manuscripts, Maps, Painting-American, Photography, Portraits, Textiles
Collections: Oil Paintings, mostly mid-late 19th century, of prominent Springfielders, artifacts
Publications: Newsletter, quarterly
Activities: Classes for adults & children; docent training; lects open to pub; tours; individual paintings & original objects of art lent to museums; lending coll contains 150 original artworks, 50 original prints, 75 paintings & 2000 photographs; sales shop sells books

L **Library**, 117 S Fountain Ave, Springfield, OH 45504-1207. Tel 937-324-0657; Fax 937-324-1992
Open Wed - Sat 10 AM - 5 PM; No admis fee; Estab 1897; For reference only
Library Holdings: Book Volumes 4000, Clipping Files, Manuscripts, Maps, Memorabilia, Original Art Works, Original Documents, Periodical Subscriptions, Photographs, Reels, Slides
Collections: Photograph Collection, Local History Collection
Publications: Chronicles of Clark County
Activities: Classes for adults & children; docent training; Benjamin F Prince Award; mus shop sells books, reproductions & gen merchandise

M **SPRINGFIELD MUSEUM OF ART,** 107 Cliff Park Rd, Springfield, OH 45501-2501. Tel 937-325-4673; Fax 937-325-4674; Email smoa@main-net.com; Web: spfld-museum-of-art.org; *Exec Dir* Ann Fortescue; *Mus Opers Mgr* Eve Reck; *Art Educator* Deb Housh
Open Tues, Thurs, Fri 9 AM - 5 PM; Thurs 9 AM - 9 PM; Sat 9 AM - 5 PM; Sun 12:30 - 4:30 PM; cl Mon; Admis general $5, Sun free; Estab 1951 for educ & cultural purposes, particularly the encouragement of the appreciation, study of, participation in & enjoyment of the fine arts; American Collection; Average Annual Attendance: 30,000; Mem: 1000; dues benefactor $100, sustaining $55, family $35, individual $25; meetings third Tues in June
Income: $250,000 (financed by endowment, mem & tui fees)
Collections: 19th & 20th Century Artists (mostly American, some French)
Exhibitions: Rotating exhibits every 2-3 months
Publications: Newsletter, bimonthly
Activities: Classes for adults & children; docent training; lects open to pub, vis lectrs; tours; gallery talks; competitions; schols offered; individual paintings & original objects of art lent; sales shop selling original art

L **Library**, 107 Cliff Park Rd, Springfield, OH 45501. Tel 937-325-4673; Fax 937-325-4674; Email smoa@main-net.com; Web: www.springfieldart.museum; *Dir* Mark Chepp; *Mus Cur* Thomas Skwerski; *Mus Educ* Deena Pinales; *Develop Dir* Rosemary Navlty
Open Tues, Thurs, Fri 9 AM - 5 PM, Wed 9 AM - 9 PM, Sat 9 AM - 3 PM, Sun 2 - 4 PM; No admis fee; Estab 1973 for art study; For reference only; Average Annual Attendance: 35,000
Income: Financed by endowment & mem
Library Holdings: Book Volumes 4500, Clipping Files, Exhibition Catalogs, Pamphlets, Slides 400
Special Subjects: Art Education, Art History, Photography, Afro-American Art, American Indian Art, American Western Art
Collections: American Art
Activities: Classes for adults & children; docent training; lects open to pub; concerts; gallery talks; tours; sponsoring of competitions; scholarships; schols; book traveling exhibs, 8-10 per yr; mus shop

SYLVANIA

L **LOURDES COLLEGE,** Duns Scotus Library, 6832 Convent Blvd, Sylvania, OH 43560-4805. Tel 419-824-3761; Fax 419-824-3511; Web: www.lourdes.edu/library/; *Dir Libr Svcs* Sr Sandra Rutkowski; *Asst Librn* Sr Karen Mohar
Open to students & guests Mon - Thurs 8:30 AM - 9 PM, Fri - Sat 8:30 AM - 4 PM, Sat 9 AM - 4 PM, cl Sun; Estab 1949; Art pieces exhibited on walls of three acad bldgs; classroom & library; Average Annual Attendance: 600
Income: Financed through col
Library Holdings: Audio Tapes, Book Volumes 67,000, Cassettes, Fiche 13,599, Manuscripts, Memorabilia, Original Art Works, Periodical Subscriptions 420, Prints, Reproductions, Sculpture, Slides, Video Tapes
Special Subjects: Afro-American Art, American Indian Art, American Western Art, Art Education, Art History, Asian Art, Calligraphy, Ceramics, Commercial Art, Crafts, Decorative Arts, Drawings, Enamels, Etchings & Engravings, Graphic Arts
Collections: 350 art pieces in library cataloged
Activities: Lect open to pub; tours; schols & fels offered

TOLEDO

A **SPECTRUM GALLERY,** 5403 Elmer Dr, Toledo Botanical Garden Toledo, OH 43615-2803. Tel 419-531-7769; *Gallery Coordr* Mandi Gorbelt; *Pres* Buzz Meyers; *1st VPres* Mary Jane Erard; *Treas* Millard Stone; *VPres* Marge Cadaret
Open Wed - Sun Noon - 4 PM; No admis fee; Estab 1975 to encourage & support pub appreciation of fine art & to organize & promote related activities; promote mutual understanding & cooperation among artists, artist groups & the pub promote beautification of Toledo through use of art work; Clubhouse (3 galleries, sales room office & working studio) part of Artist Village in Toledo Botanical Garden; large adjacent Art Educ Center; Average Annual Attendance: 15,000-20,000; Mem: 200
Income: $20,000 (financed by mem & fundraising events, sales of art, donations & art classes)
Exhibitions: Juried Membership Show; Crosby Festival of the Arts; Toledo Festival; spot exhibitions
Publications: Spectrum (newsletter), monthly
Activities: Classes for adults & children; lect open to pub, 4-5 vis lectrs per yr; competitions; originates traveling exhibs; sales shop sells original art

A **TOLEDO ARTISTS' CLUB,** Toledo Artists' Club & Gallery, 5403 Elmer Dr, Toledo Botanical Garden Toledo, OH 43615-2803. Tel 419-531-4079; Email toledoartist@sbcglobal.net; Web: toledoartistclub.com; Facebook: Toledo Artists' Club & Gallery; *Pres* Richard Carle; *Office Adminr* Cynthia Hoot; *Secy* Elaine Gregory; *Treas* Faye Edinger
Open May - Sept Tues, Thurs, Sat & Sun 1 - 4 PM; Oct - April Tues, Thurs & Sat 1 - 4 PM; No admis fee; Estab 1943 to promote art in the area; Located on the grounds of the Toledo Botanical Garden's north side; Mem: 200; dues $40; monthly board meetings
Income: Financed by mem & exhibs, sales of paintings, ann art auction, workshop classes
Special Subjects: Drawings, Embroidery, Glass, Graphics, Jewelry, Landscapes, Miniatures, Photography, Portraits, Pottery, Sculpture, Textiles, Watercolors
Exhibitions: Approx 40 pieces of artwork exhibited each month in main gallery; includes paintings, pottery, sculpture, stained glass
Publications: Newsletter, monthly
Activities: Classes for adults & children; workshops; demonstrations; lects open to pub; competitions with awards; juried gallery show each month; member groups meet to paint; Website contains monthly newsletter & activities; sales shop sells original art; all displayed art for sale

M **TOLEDO MUSEUM OF ART,** 2445 Monroe St at Scottwood Ave, Toledo, OH 43620-1517; PO Box 1013, Toledo, OH 43697-1013. Tel 419-255-8000; Fax 419-255-5638; Email information@toledomuseum.org; Web: www.toledomuseum.org; Cable TOLMUSART; *Bd Chmn* Cynthia B. Thompson; *Dir Collections* Andrea Gardner; *Sr Cur* Lawrence Nichols; *Dir Develop* Todd Ahrens; *Communs Dir* Stephanie Elton; *Dir Educ & Engagement* Mike Deetsch; *Pres, Dir & CEO* Brian P Kennedy; *Dir Cur Affairs* Halona Norton-Westbrook; *Chief Revenue Officer* Kris Crystal; *Dep Dir* Adam Levine
Open Tues & Wed 10 AM - 4 PM, Thurs & Fri 10 AM - 9 PM, Sat 10 AM - 5 PM, Sun noon - 5 PM, cl Mon & major holidays; No admis fee; Estab & incorporated 1901; building erected 1912, additions 1926, 1933 & 2006 (Glass Pavilion). Mus contains Canaday Gallery, Print Galleries, School Gallery, Collector's Corner & a museum store; jewelry gallery; glass pavilion erected 2006; Circ 2,092; Average Annual Attendance: 400,000; Mem: 7500; dues $35 & up
Income: Financed by contributed funds & memberships
Library Holdings: Auction Catalogs, Book Volumes, Clipping Files, DVDs, Exhibition Catalogs, Original Documents, Periodical Subscriptions
Special Subjects: Antiquities-Assyrian, Antiquities-Egyptian, Antiquities-Greek, Antiquities-Oriental, Antiquities-Roman, Ceramics, Decorative Arts, Glass, Medieval Art, Painting-American, Painting-European, Prints, Sculpture
Collections: Ancient to modern glass, European paintings, sculpture & decorative arts, American paintings, sculpture & decorative arts, books & manuscripts, Egyptian, Greek, Roman, Near & Far East art, African art, Modern & Contemporary Art, Jewelry
Publications: American Paintings; Ancient Glass; Art in Glass; Corpus Vasorum Antiquorum I & II; European Paintings; Guide to the Colls; Masterworks
Activities: Educ prog; classes for adults & children; docent training; community outreach; lects open to pub; 40 vis lectrs per yr; concerts; gallery talks; tours; awards, Institutional Excellence-Ohio Museums Assn, 2005, 2006 & 2008, 2012 Visual Communications Gold Award & Best Exhib; schols; fels; book traveling exhibs; originate traveling exhibs; mus shop sells books, original art, reproductions, prints, gifts, jewelry

L **Art Reference Library**, 2445 Monroe St, Toledo, OH 43620; PO Box 1013, Toledo, OH 43697-1013. Tel 419-254-5770; Fax 419-255-5638; Email library@toledomuseum.org; Web: www.toledomuseum.org/learn/reference-library; *Head Librn* Alison L Huftalen; *Asst Librn* Teressa Conlan
Open Mon - Thurs 10 AM - 8 PM, Fri 12 PM - 4 PM, Sat Noon - 4 PM during university sessions; Summer: Mon - Thur 10 AM - 5 PM, Fri & Sat noon - 4 PM; Estab 1901 to provide resources for the museum's staff; Circ 1,600; Primarily for reference but does lend to certain groups of users; Average Annual Attendance: 6,500; Mem: 173; dues $10 - $100
Income: Financed by mus & mem
Library Holdings: Auction Catalogs, Book Volumes 90,000, Clipping Files 21,000, Exhibition Catalogs 18,000, Fiche, Periodical Subscriptions 100, Reels 75
Special Subjects: Art Education, Art History, Decorative Arts, Glass, Graphic Arts, Painting-American, Painting-European, Photography

VAN WERT

M **WASSENBERG ART CENTER,** 214 S Washington St, Van Wert, OH 45891-1941. Tel 419-238-6837; Email info@wassenbergartcenter.org; Web: www.wassenberg.org; *Exec Dir* Hope Wallace; *Office Mgr* Matt Temple; *Gallery/ Event Coord* Kendra Bilimek; *Facility & Grounds* Austin Anderson
Open Tues-Sun 1 - 5 PM, cl Mon; No admis fee; Estab 1954 to encourage the arts in the Van Wert area; Two large gallery areas, basement classroom; maximum exhibit 150 pieces; Average Annual Attendance: 1,500; Mem: 490; dues individual $25, various other
Income: $150,000 (financed by endowment, mem, fundraisers)
Library Holdings: Audio Tapes, Book Volumes 250, Cassettes, Filmstrips, Original Art Works, Periodical Subscriptions 6, Prints, Reproductions, Sculpture, Slides, Video Tapes

Collections: Wassenberg Collection, Prints & Original Art, All subjects & media, Faces of Little Bighorn the David Humphreys Miller Collection
Exhibitions: Annual June Art Exhibit; Annual Oct Photography Exhibit; 8 different free exhibits per year
Publications: Gallery Review, quarterly
Activities: Classes for adults & children; docent progs; lects open to pub, some only to mems; competitions; book traveling exhibs 6-8 per yr; Sales shop sells original art, prints, ceramics & jewelry

VERMILION

M **GREAT LAKES HISTORICAL SOCIETY,** Inland Seas Maritime Museum, 480 Main St, Vermilion, OH 44089-1015; PO Box 435, Vermilion, OH 44089-0435. Tel 440-260-0230; Email glhsl@inlandseas.org; Web: www.inlandseas.org; WATS 800-893-1485; *Exec Dir* Christopher Gillcrist
Open daily 10 AM - 5 PM, cl major holidays; Admis adults $5, seniors $4, youth $3, children under 6 free; Estab 1944 to promote interest in discovering and preserving material about the Great Lakes and surrounding areas; Maintains an art gallery as part of the Maritime History Mus; Average Annual Attendance: 20,000+; Mem: 2500; dues family $49; ann meetings in May
Income: $500,000 (financed by endowment, mem, sales from mus store & fundraising)
Special Subjects: Dioramas, Drawings, Historical Material, Maps, Marine Painting, Photography, Prints, Reproductions
Collections: Collection of Ship Models, Marine Relics, Paintings & Photographs dealing with the history of the Great Lakes, paintings by Sprague, Shogren, LaMarre, Nickerson, Forsythe & Huntington
Exhibitions: Annual Antique Boat Show Exhibition
Publications: Chadburn (newsletter), quarterly; Inland Seas, quarterly journal
Activities: Classes for adults & children; dramatic progs; docent training; boat building & lofting classes; lect open to pub, 16 vis lectrs per yr; gallery talks; tours; competitions with prizes; individual painting lent to other museums; book traveling exhibs 1 per yr; originate traveling exhibs; mus shop sells books, reproductions, prints, slides & videotapes

WEST LIBERTY

M **PIATT CASTLES,** 10051 Township Rd, West Liberty, OH 43357; PO Box 497, West Liberty, OH 43357-0497. Tel 937-465-2821; Fax 937-465-7774; Email macochee@logan.net; Web: www.piattcastles.org; *Pres & CEO* Margaret Piatt; *VPres* James White; *Prog Asst* Beverly Lee
Open Apr - May & Sept - Oct Sat-Sun 11 AM - 4 PM, Memorial Day - Labor Day 11 AM - 5 PM; Admis adults $8, students $6, children 5-12 $5; sr & AAA discount; Estab 1912; Paintings & sculptures displayed throughout both homes - room like settings; Average Annual Attendance: 40,000
Special Subjects: American Indian Art, Period Rooms, Architecture, Decorative Arts, Furniture, Restorations
Collections: Early American family furnishings, Native American artifacts, Rare Art, Weapons, European & Asian Furnishings
Publications: Brochures; Don Piatt of Mac-O-Chee, Wit and Wisdom of Donn Piatt
Activities: Dramatic progs; docent training; ann vintage baseball game; storytelling; Christmas prog; musical events; tours; gallery talks; concerts; art festival; mus shop sells books & original art

WESTERVILLE

AMERICAN CERAMIC SOCIETY
For further information, see National and Regional Organizations

WILBERFORCE

M **OHIO HISTORY CONNECTION,** National Afro-American Museum & Cultural Center, 1350 Brush Row Rd, Wilberforce, OH 45384-0578; PO Box 578, Wilberforce, OH 45384-0578. Tel 937-376-4944; Fax 937-376-2007; Email lbuckwalter@ohiohistory.org; Web: www.ohiohistory.org; *Acting Dir* Floyd Thomas Jr, PhD; *Coordr Traveling Exhibs & Registrar* Wendy Felder; *Educ Specialist* Dianne Turner-Ingham; *Archivist* Dr Charles Wash
Open Wed - Sat; Admis adults $4, seniors $3.60, children $1.50; Estab 1987; Maintains staff reference library, archives & 5 exhib spaces totaling 6000 sq ft; Average Annual Attendance: 45,000
Library Holdings: Book Volumes, Clipping Files, Exhibition Catalogs, Records, Sculpture, Slides
Special Subjects: Afro-American Art, Coins & Medals, Crafts, Dolls, Ethnology, Folk Art, Historical Material, Manuscripts, Painting-American, Photography, Sculpture
Collections: African American Art, noted for Black Nationalist/Black Protest art of the 1960s & 70s, African Coll (ethnographic material), Craft
Exhibitions: Dolls; Photography; The Legend of John Brown: prints by Jacob Lawrence; When the Spirit Moves: African American Dance in History & Art; Uncommon Beauty in Common Objects: The Legacy of African American Craft Art; Quilting African American Woman's History
Activities: docent training; Lects open to pub; galley talks; tours; Individual paintings & original objects of art lent to qualified museums; lending coll contains original art works & paintings; book traveling exhibs; originate traveling exhibs from small institutions to the Smithsonian; mus shop sells books, original art, reproductions & prints

WILLOUGHBY

M **ARCHAEOLOGICAL SOCIETY OF OHIO,** Indian Museum of Lake County, Ohio, Technical Center Bldg B, Willoughby, OH 44094; PO Box 883, Willoughby, OH 44096-0883. Tel 440-951-3813; Web: indianmuseumoflakecounty.org; *Dir* Ann Dewald
Open Mon - Fri 10 AM - 4 PM, Sat & Sun 1 - 4 PM, cl major holiday weekends; Admis adults $2, students (K-12) $1, seniors $1.50, preschool children free; Estab 1980 to educate & preserve arts & crafts of all cultures of Native Americans; Average Annual Attendance: 5,000; Mem: 250; dues $20 - $1,000
Income: Financed by mem
Library Holdings: Book Volumes, Clipping Files
Special Subjects: American Indian Art, Archaeology, Eskimo Art
Collections: Crafts & art of all cultures of Native Americans of North America, Prehistoric artifacts from 10,000 BC to 1650 AD of early Ohio & Reeve Village Site, Lake County, Ohio
Activities: Classes for adults & children; docent training; lect open to pub; tours; competitions with awards; mus shop sells books, Native American crafts

L **Indian Museum of Lake County Library**, WE Tech Ctr - Bldg B, 25 Public Sq Willoughby, OH 44094; 25 Public Sq, PO Box 883 Willoughby, OH 44096-0883. Tel 440-951-3813; Web: indianmuseumoflakecounty.org; *Dir* Ann Dewald
Open Mon-Fri 10AM-4PM, June-Aug 10AM-4PM, Sat-Sun 1PM-4PM, cl holidays & winter & spring break; Admis adults $2, seniors $1.50, children grades K-12 $1; Estab 1980; For reference
Income: Financed by mem
Library Holdings: Book Volumes, Periodical Subscriptions 4
Special Subjects: American Indian Art, Archaeology, Eskimo Art
Activities: Classes for adults & children, docent training; mus sales shop sells Native American items

A **FINE ARTS ASSOCIATION,** School of Fine Arts, 38660 Mentor Ave, Willoughby, OH 44094-7797. Tel 440-951-7500; Fax 440-975-4592; Email faa@bbs2.rmrc.net; Web: www.fineartsassociation.org; *Pres* Richard T Spote Jr; *Exec Dir* Charles D Lawrence
Open Mon - Fri 9 AM - 8 PM, Sat 9 AM - 5 PM; No admis fee; Estab 1957 to bring arts educ to all people regardless of their ability to pay, race or social standing; Main floor gallery houses theme, one-man & group monthly exhibs; 2nd floor gallery houses monthly school exhibits; Average Annual Attendance: 70,000; Mem: 500; dues $25 & up; ann meeting in Sept
Income: Financed by class fees and donations
Exhibitions: Monthly exhibs, theme, one man & group; ann juried exhibit for area artists
Activities: Classes for adults & children; dramatic progs; lect open to pub, 10 vis lectrs per yr; gallery talks; tours; concerts; competitions with awards; schols; mus shop sells original art

WOOSTER

M **THE COLLEGE OF WOOSTER,** The College of Wooster Art Museum, 1220 Beall Ave, Ebert Art Center Wooster, OH 44691-2393. Tel 330-263-2388, 330-263-2495; Fax 330-263-2633; Email kzurko@wooster.edu; Web: www.wooster.edu/cwam; *Dir* Kitty McManus Zurko; *Preparator* Douglas McGlumphy; *Art Mus Admin Coordr* Rose Seling
Open Tues - Fri 11 AM - 4 PM, Sat & Sun 1 - 4 PM, cl Mon & during col breaks; No admis fee; Academic Art Museum; Average Annual Attendance: 9,000
Income: Financed by col gen fund & grants
Special Subjects: African Art, American Indian Art, Antiquities-Egyptian, Antiquities-Greek, Antiquities-Oriental, Bronzes, Carpets & Rugs, Ceramics, Coins & Medals, Collages, Decorative Arts, Ethnology, Furniture, Glass, Graphics, Historical Material, Oriental Art, Painting-American, Painting-French, Porcelain, Portraits, Pottery, Pre-Columbian Art, Prints, Tapestries, Textiles, Woodcuts, Asian Art
Collections: John Taylor Arms Print Collection, William C Mithoefer Collection of African Art, ancient & contemporary ceramics, Chinese snuff bottles & bronzes, Cypriote pottery, ethnographic materials, WWII posters, Middle Eastern pottery
Exhibitions: Traveling exhibs & special in-house exhibs. Average six yearly exhibs drawn either from the colls or focusing on the work of contemporary artists
Publications: Exhibition catalogs, brochures
Activities: Lect & receptions open to pub, 4-6 vis lectrs per year; gallery talks; tours; concerts; originates traveling exhibs to other museums, col & univ galleries

M **WAYNE CENTER FOR THE ARTS,** 237 S Walnut St, Wooster, OH 44691-4753. Tel 330-264-2787; Fax 330-264-9314; Email WayneCtr@wayneartscenter.org; Web: www.wayneartscenter.org; *Exec Dir* Robb Hyde; *Educ Coordr* Lisa Zemancik
Open Mon noon - 9 PM, Tues - Thurs 9 AM - 9 PM, Fri 9 AM - 7 PM, Sat 9 AM - 2 PM, cl Sun; No admis fee for exhibs; performances vary; Estab 1973 to strengthen our community by enriching peoples' lives through the arts; The Ctr for the Arts is housed in a former school bldg, offering large & open galleries & studios; Average Annual Attendance: 12,000; Mem: 400+
Income: donations; memberships; ticket fees; grants; sponsorships
Special Subjects: African Art, Bronzes, Ceramics, Oriental Art, Painting-American, Porcelain, Prints, Tapestries
Exhibitions: Monthly showing of local, regional and nationally renowned artists
Publications: ARTtalk newsletter, quarterly
Activities: Classes for adults & children; community outreach progs; lect open to pub, 10-15 vis lectrs per yr; gallery talks; concerts; book traveling exhibs

XENIA

A **GREENE COUNTY HISTORICAL SOCIETY,** 74 W Church St, Xenia, OH 45385-2902. Tel 937-372-4606; Fax 937-376-5660; Email GCHSXO@yahoo.com; Web: www.gchsxo.org; *Exec Dir* Catherine Wilson
Open Tues, Thurs, Fri 9 AM - Noon & 1 - 3:30 PM; Admis adult $3, under 18 $2; Estab 1929 to preserve the history of Greene County, OH; Average Annual Attendance: 2,000; Mem: 450; dues individual $20, seniors $10; monthly meeting 2nd Mon
Income: Financed by mem, county appropriation & various fund raising activities

Library Holdings: Clipping Files, Manuscripts, Memorabilia, Original Documents, Photographs
Collections: Clothing, Medical, Military, Railroad (historic model)
Exhibitions: Conestoga Wagon; Log House & furnishings; Railroad; Victorian House & furnishings
Publications: Historic Greene County
Activities: Lect open to pub, 12 vis lectrs per yr; sales shop sells books, notepaper, materials relating to county

YELLOW SPRINGS

M **ANTIOCH COLLEGE,** Herndon Gallery, South Hall, 1st Fl, One Morgan Pl Yellow Springs, OH 45387-1635. Tel 937-319-0114; Email jwenker@antiochcollege.org; Web: www.antiochcollege.org/campus-life/herndon-gallery; *Creative Dir* Jennifer Wenker, MFA
Open Tues - Sun 1 - 4 PM; No admis fee; Herndon Gallery offers works in many medias, including painting, photography & video
Exhibitions: World Community of Ceramists

YOUNGSTOWN

M **THE BUTLER INSTITUTE OF AMERICAN ART,** Art Museum, 524 Wick Ave, Youngstown, OH 44502-1286. Tel 330-743-1711; Fax 330-743-9567; Email info@butlerart.com; Web: www.butlerart.com; *Exec Dir & Chief Cur* Dr Louis A Zona; *Asst Dir* M Susan Carfano; *Dir Educ* Joyce Mistrovich; *Bus Mgr* Amy Kaufman; *Dir Information* Wendy Swick; *Mus Shop Mgr* Renee Sheakoski
Open Tues - Sat 11 AM - 4 PM; Sun Noon - 4 PM, cl Mon & major holidays; No admis fee; Estab 1919 & is the first mus building to be devoted entirely to American Art; Eighteen galleries containing 11,000 works of American artists; three new galleries containing folk art & American; Average Annual Attendance: 140,000; Mem: 2,500; dues individual $35, household (couple) $45, sustainer $60, sponsor $300, patron $500, collector $1,000, connoisseur $3,000, corporate $5,000; meetings in Sept
Income: Financed by endowment, grants & gifts
Library Holdings: Auction Catalogs, Clipping Files, Exhibition Catalogs, Kodachrome Transparencies, Photographs, Slides
Special Subjects: American Indian Art, Ceramics, Drawings, Marine Painting, Painting-American, Prints, Sculpture, Watercolors
Collections: Comprehensive coll of American art covering three centuries, American Impressionism, The American West & Marine & Sports Art colls, Principle artists: Winslow Homer, Albert Bierstadt, Martin Johnson Heade, Georgia O'Keeffe, Charles Sheeler, Helen Frankenthaler, John S Sargent, J M Whistler, Mary Cassatt, Thomas Cole, Edward Hopper, Romare Bearden, Andy Warhol & Robert Motherwell, American Glass Bells, Miniatures of all the Presidents of the United States (watercolor), Robert Rauschenberg, Americana & Folk Art
Publications: Exhib catalogues; bimonthly newsletter; biennial report
Activities: Classes for adults & children; docent training; films; stroller art; you friends adventure; senior art & learn; lects open to pub; concerts; gallery talks; tours; competitions with awards; objects of art lent to Trumball & Columbiana Counties; book traveling exhibs 2 per yr (varies); originates traveling exhibs to museums; mus shop sells books, original art, prints & reproductions; Trumbell Branch, Salem Branch

L **Hopper Resource Library**, 524 Wick Ave, Youngstown, OH 44502. Tel 330-743-1107, 743-1711
Open Tues & Thurs - Sat 11 AM - 4 PM, Wed 11 AM - 8 PM, Sun Noon - 4 PM; No admis fee; For reference only; Average Annual Attendance: 122,000; Mem: 3090
Income: Financed by endowment, grants & gifts
Library Holdings: Book Volumes 1500, Clipping Files, Exhibition Catalogs, Framed Reproductions, Kodachrome Transparencies, Memorabilia, Pamphlets, Periodical Subscriptions 10, Photographs, Slides

M **YOUNGSTOWN STATE UNIVERSITY,** The John J McDonough Museum of Art, One University Plaza, Youngstown, OH 44555. Tel 330-742-1400; Fax 330-742-1492; Email sbkreism@cc.ysu.edu; Web: www.ysu.edu; *Interim Dir* Angela DeLucia
Open Thurs - Sat 11 AM - 4 PM, Sun Noon - 4 PM; cl Tues; No admis fee; Estab 1991 to serve as a professional exhib facility for all art students & studio art faculty, to present visual arts progs of educ & artistic significance to the community, to exhibit works of established & emerging regional artists & present works from other university & larger mus colls; The purely post-modern structure has 18,000 sq ft & includes two outdoor sculpture terraces. The mus offers a 50-seat seminar auditorium, a two-story raw space installation gallery & two traditional galleries. Maintains lending library; Average Annual Attendance: 20,000
Collections: Contemporary Art
Exhibitions: Exhibs vary; call for details
Publications: Exhib catalogs; gallery guides
Activities: In-service workshops, art workshops; tours; competitions; lending coll contains slides; Contemporary Latino Voices; Aspects of Photography: Work on Loan from Mother Jones Magazine; GNATLAND: An Installation by Kay Willens; Governor's Institute for Gifted & Talented Students; Scholastic Art Awards Exhib

ZANESVILLE

A **ZANESVILLE MUSEUM OF ART,** 620 Military Rd, Zanesville, OH 43701-1533. Tel 740-452-0741; Fax 740-452-0797; Email vanessa@zanesvilleart.org; Web: www.zanesvilleart.org; *Pres Bd Trustees* Richard Duncan; *VPres* Dr Chad Brown; *Office Mgr* Vanessa Brosie; *Opers Tech* Fred Orr; *Temp Opers Mgr* Andrew Near; *Exec Dir* Laine Snyder
Open Wed & Fri 10 AM - 5 PM, Thurs 10 AM - 7:30 PM, Sat 10 AM - 5 PM, cl Sun, Mon, Tues & holidays; Admis adults $6, seniors 60 & over & children 10-18 $4, children under 10 & mems free; Estab 1936 to provide a pub center for the arts, permanent colls & temporary exhibs, classes in arts, library of art volumes & a meeting place for art & civic groups; There are 10 galleries for permanent collection & temporary exhibitions; handicapped facilities; Average Annual Attendance: 25,000; Mem: 250; dues $30 & up
Income: Financed by endowment & mem
Collections: American, European & Oriental paintings, sculptures, ceramics, prints, drawings & crafts, children's art, Midwest & Zanesville ceramics & glass
Exhibitions: Rotating exhibits
Publications: Bulletin, trimonthly
Activities: Classes for adults & children; docent training; lect open to pub; gallery talks; tours; competitions with awards; book 2 traveling exhibs per yr; originate traveling exhibs to Ohio museums; mus shop sells books

OKLAHOMA

ANADARKO

M **NATIONAL HALL OF FAME FOR FAMOUS AMERICAN INDIANS,** PO Box 548, Anadarko, OK 73005-0548. Tel 405-247-5555; *Dir & Exec VPres* Joe McBride; *Treas* George F Moran; *Secy* Carolyn N McBride
Open Mon - Sat 9 AM - 5 PM, Sun 1 - 5 PM; No admis fee; Estab 1952 to honor famous American Indians who have contributed to the culture of America, including statesmen, innovators, sportsmen, warriors; to teach the youth of our country that there is a reward for greatness; An outdoor mus in a landscaped area containing bronze sculptured portraits of honorees; Average Annual Attendance: 23,000; Mem: 250; dues life $100, Individual or Family $25; ann meeting Aug
Income: Finance by mem, city & state appropriation & donation
Purchases: $2500 - $20,000
Special Subjects: Bronzes, American Indian Art
Collections: Bronze sculptured portraits & bronze statues of two animals important to Indian culture
Publications: Brochure
Activities: Dedication ceremonies for honorees in Aug; sales shop sells books & postcards

M **SOUTHERN PLAINS INDIAN MUSEUM,** 801 E Central, Anadarko, OK 73005-4437; PO Box 749, Anadarko, OK 73005-0749. Tel 405-247-6221; Fax 405-247-7593; *Cur* Bambi Allen
Open June - Sept Tues - Sat 9 AM - 5 PM; Oct - April Mon Fri 9 AM - 5 PM; No admis fee; Estab 1947-48 to promote the development of contemporary Native American arts & crafts of the United States. Administered & operated by the Indian Arts & Crafts Board, US Department of the Interior; Average Annual Attendance: 40,000
Income: Financed by federal appropriation
Purchases: Primarily dependent upon gifts
Special Subjects: American Indian Art, Crafts, Dioramas
Collections: Contemporary Native American arts & crafts of the United States, Historic Works by Southern Plains Indian Craftsmen, Historic Southern Plains Indian arts
Exhibitions: Historic Southern Plains Indian Arts; changing exhibs by contemporary native American artists & craftsmen; continuing series of one-person exhibs
Publications: One-person exhib brochure series, quarterly
Activities: Gallery talks

ARDMORE

A **CHARLES B GODDARD CENTER FOR THE VISUAL & PERFORMING ARTS,** 401 First Ave SW, Ardmore, OK 73401; PO Box 1624, Ardmore, OK 73402-1624. Tel 580-226-0909; Fax 580-226-8891; Email ken@goddardcenter.org; Web: www.goddardcenter.org; *Treas* Andy Harlow; *Exec Dir* Dr Kenneth Bohannon; *Admin Asst* Marjorie Dolman; *Chmn* Jan Tindale; *Cur* Cory Blankenship
Open Tues - Fri 9 AM - 5 PM, Sat 1 - 4 PM, cl Sun, Mon & major holidays; No admis fee to art galleries; Estab Mar 1970 to bring fine art progs in the related fields of music, art & theater to local community at minimum cost, gallery to bring traveling exhibits to Ardmore; Four exhibit galleries; maintains lending & reference art library; Average Annual Attendance: 50,000; Mem: 600; dues $25 - $1000
Income: Supported by memberships, sponsorships & grant funding
Library Holdings: Audio Tapes, CD-ROMs, Compact Disks, DVDs, Sculpture
Collections: Western & Contemporary Art, paintings, sculpture, prints, Small coll of Western Art & bronzes, American Graphic Art, photography, lifetime works of watercolor artist Dorothy Bertine
Exhibitions: Ardmore Art Exhibition; exhibits bi-monthly
Publications: Annual season review guide
Activities: Classes for adults & children in art & theatre; docent training; dramatic progs; art studio classes for adults & children; granite carving workshops; concerts; gallery talks; competitions with awards; tours; lects open to the pub; Lawrence London Award; individual paintings & original objects of art lent to qualified institutions & museums; mus shop sells original art; Bedre Chocolate

BARTLESVILLE

M **THE FRANK PHILLIPS FOUNDATION INC,** Woolaroc Museum, 1925 Woolaroc Ranch Rd, Bartlesville, OK 74003; PO Box 1647, Bartlesville, OK 74005-1647. Tel 918-336-0307; Fax 918-336-0084; Email lstone@woolaroc.org; Web: www.woolaroc.org; *Dir* Shiloh Thurman; *Cur Art* Linda Stone; *CEO* Bob Fraser; *Director of Strategic Planning* Kaci Fouts
Open Summer: Memorial Day - Labor Day Tues - Sun 10 AM - 5 PM, Winter: Wed - Sun - 10 AM - 5 PM,; Admis 12 & older $12, 65 & older $10, under 12 free; Estab 1929 to house art & artifacts of the Southwest. Mus dedicated by Frank Phillips; Gallery has two levels, 8 rooms upstairs & 4 rooms downstairs; Average Annual Attendance: 125,000; Mem: 500

Income: Financed by endowment & revenues generated by admis fees & sales
Special Subjects: American Indian Art, Archaeology, American Western Art, Anthropology, Archaeology, Bronzes, Dolls, Drawings, Etchings & Engravings, Ethnology, Graphics, Historical Material, Mosaics, Painting-American, Pottery, Prints, Southwestern Art, Textiles, Watercolors
Collections: American Indian artifacts, prehistoric artifacts, paintings, drawings, graphics, minerals, sculpture, weapons
Exhibitions: various exhibits call for details
Publications: Woolaroc Story; Woolaroc, mus guidebook
Activities: Educ prog; classes for children; docent training; gallery talks; tours; lectures open to the public; lectures for members only; scholarships; lending coll contains transparencies to be used to illustrate educ publs; book traveling exhibs; mus & sales shops sell books, magazines, original art, reproductions, prints, slides, Indian-made jewelry and pottery, postcards

L **Library**, State Hwy 123, Route 3 Box 2100 Bartlesville, OK 74003; PO Box 1647, Bartlesville, OK 74003-1647. Tel 918-336-0307; Fax 918-336-0084; Email lstone@woolaroc.com; *Dir* Robert R Lansdown
Open to employees only; Circ Reference library open to employees only; private facility
Library Holdings: Book Volumes 1000, Clipping Files, Exhibition Catalogs, Kodachrome Transparencies, Pamphlets, Photographs, Slides

CLAREMORE

M **WILL ROGERS MEMORIAL MUSEUM & BIRTHPLACE RANCH,** 1720 W Will Rogers Blvd, Claremore, OK 74018-3208; PO Box 157, Claremore, OK 74018-0157. Tel 918-341-0719; Fax 918-343-8119; Email wrinfo@willrogers.com; Web: willrogers.com; *Cur* Gregory Malak; *Dir* Michelle Lefebvre-Carter; *Library & Colls* Steven Gragert; *Ranch Mgr* Jim Williams
Open daily 8 AM - 5 PM; No admis fee, donations accepted; Estab 1938 to perpetuate the name, works & spirit of Will Rogers; There are nine main galleries, diorama room, foyer & gardens. The large Jo Davidson statue of Will Rogers dominates the foyer; the north gallery includes photographs & paintings of Will Rogers & his ancestors (including a family tree, explaining his Indian heritage) & many other personal items; east gallery has saddle collection & other Western items; Jo Mora dioramas; additional gallery, research library & theatre; children's mus in basement. Maintains reference library; Average Annual Attendance: 202,000
Income: $750,000 (financed by state appropriation & pvt donations)
Library Holdings: Audio Tapes, Book Volumes, CD-ROMs, Clipping Files, Framed Reproductions, Manuscripts, Memorabilia, Motion Pictures, Original Art Works, Original Documents, Photographs, Prints, Records, Sculpture, Slides, Video Tapes
Collections: Colls of Paintings by various artists commissioned by a calendar company with originals donated to Memorial, Count Tamburini Oil of Will Rogers, Jo Mora Dioramas (13), Large Equestrian Statue by Electra Wagoner Biggs, Mural by Ray Piercey, Original of Will Rogers by Leyendecker, Paintings of Will & his parents by local artists, Original of Will Rogers by Charles Banks Wilson, 7-foot oil on canvas by Wayne Cooper of Will Rogers on horseback, Gordon Kuntz Coll (81 original movie poster coll of Will Rogers' movies)
Publications: Brochures and materials for students
Activities: Lect open to pub; tours; assist with publishing project: The Papers of Will Rogers; originate traveling exhibs; sales shop sells VHS tapes, Will Rogers & Oklahoma items; Will Rogers Youth Museum

L **Media Center Library**, 1720 W Will Rogers Blvd, Claremore, OK 74017-3208; PO Box 157, Claremore, OK 74018-3208. Tel 918-341-0719; Fax 918-341-8246; WATS 800-324-9455; *Librn* Patricia Lowe; *Cur* Gregory Malak; *Dir* Joseph Carter
Reference library for research by appointment only
Library Holdings: Audio Tapes, Book Volumes 2500, CD-ROMs, Cassettes, Clipping Files, Exhibition Catalogs, Filmstrips, Framed Reproductions, Kodachrome Transparencies, Manuscripts, Memorabilia, Motion Pictures, Original Art Works, Original Documents, Other Holdings Original writings on CD Rom, Pamphlets, Periodical Subscriptions 15, Photographs 1500, Prints, Records, Reproductions, Sculpture, Slides, Video Tapes
Collections: Will Rogers Collection

CUSHING

L **LACHENMEYER ARTS CENTER,** Art Resource Library, 700 S Little, Cushing, OK 74023; PO Box 586, Cushing, OK 74023-0586. Tel 918-225-7525; Email roblarts@sbcglobal.net; *Dir* Rob Smith
Open Mon, Wed & Fri 9 AM - 5 PM, Tues & Thurs 6 - 9 PM; No admis fee; Estab 1984 to provide art classes & art exhibits to the pub
Income: Financed by endowment
Library Holdings: Book Volumes 125, Periodical Subscriptions, Video Tapes
Exhibitions: Youth Arts Exhibit (March annually); Community Art Show (every other Sept); Tour de Quartz (Dec annually)
Activities: Classes for adults & children

GOODWELL

M **NO MAN'S LAND HISTORICAL SOCIETY,** No Man's Land Museum, 214 E Ave, Goodwell, OK 73939-0278; PO Box 278, Goodwell, OK 73939-0278. Tel 580-349-2670; Fax 580-349-2670; Email mmlhs@outlook.com; Web: www.nmlhs.org; *Pres* Ronald Kincannon; *Dir* Sue Weissinger
Open Tues - Fri 10 AM - noon & 1 PM - 4 PM, Sat 10 AM - 4 PM, cl Sun, Mon & legal holidays; No admis fee; Estab 1934 to procure appropriate mus material with spec regard to portraying the history of No Man's Land (Oklahoma Panhandle) & the immediate adjacent regions; The gallery is 14 ft x 40 ft (560 sq ft); Average Annual Attendance: 4,000; Mem: 307; dues life $200, family $25, individual $15
Income: Financed by donations
Special Subjects: American Indian Art, American Western Art, Anthropology, Archaeology, Dolls, Embroidery, Ethnology, Folk Art, Historical Material, Painting-American, Southwestern Art, Textiles, Watercolors, Sculpture
Collections: Duckett Alabaster Carvings, Oils by Pearl Robison Burrows Burns
Exhibitions: Nine exhibits each yr by regional artists
Activities: Sales shop sells books & prints

LANGSTON

M **LANGSTON UNIVERSITY,** Melvin B Tolson Black Heritage Center, PO Box 1600, Langston, OK 73050-1600. Tel 405-466-3346; Fax 405-466-2979; Email egrady@lunet.edu; *Dir Library* Bettye Black; *Cur Tolson Ctr* Jovani Williams; *Asst Cur Tolson Ctr* Edward Grady
Open Mon, Wed & Fri 8 AM - 5 PM, Tues - Thurs 8 AM - 8 PM; No admis fee; Estab 1959 to exhibit pertinent works of art, both contemporary & traditional; to serve as a teaching tool for students; Library reading room; Average Annual Attendance: 6,000
Income: Financed by state appropriation
Library Holdings: Book Volumes, Cassettes, Clipping Files, Compact Disks, DVDs, Fiche, Filmstrips, Framed Reproductions, Memorabilia, Original Art Works, Original Documents, Periodical Subscriptions, Records, Reels, Sculpture, Slides
Special Subjects: African Art, Afro-American Art, Painting-American, Sculpture
Collections: African American Art & Artifacts, Paintings & Photographs, Books, tapes, video colls
Activities: Classes for adults; lects open to pub, 6-10 vis lectrs per yr; gallery talks; tours

LAWTON

M **CAMERON UNIVERSITY ART GALLERY,** 2800 Gore Blvd, Art Building 205 Lawton, OK 73502-6377. Tel 580-581-2211; Web: www.cameron.edu
No admis fee
Collections: Paintings; photographs; sculpture

M **TRUST AUTHORITY,** Museum of the Great Plains, 601 NW Ferris, Lawton, OK 73507-5443. Tel 580-581-3460; Fax 580-581-3458; Email develop@museumgreatplains.org; Web: www.museumgreatplains.org; *Photo Lab Technician* Brian Smith; *Head Cur* Deborah Baroff; *Exec Dir* John Hernandez; *Dir Develop* Bart McClenny; *Educator Cur* Jana Brown; *Exec Asst* Mary Owensby
Open Mon - Sat 10 AM - 5 PM, Sun 1 - 5 PM; Admis adults 12 & over $6, seniors $5, children between 7 & 11 $2.50, children under 6 free; Estab 1960 to collect, preserve, interpret & exhibit items of the cultural history of man in the Great Plains of North America. Galleries of the Mus of the Great Plains express a regional concept of interpreting the relationship of man to a semi-arid plains environment; 27,000 sq ft; Average Annual Attendance: 25,000; Mem: 700; dues $30 - $200
Income: Financed by endowment, city appropriations & contributions
Library Holdings: Original Documents, Periodical Subscriptions, Photographs
Special Subjects: American Indian Art, American Western Art, Anthropology, Archaeology, Architecture, Costumes, Crafts, Ethnology, Historical Material, Manuscripts, Maps, Period Rooms, Photography, Restorations, Southwestern Art
Collections: Archaeological, ethnological, historical & natural science colls relating to man's inhabitance of the Great Plains, photographs relating to Plains Indians, agriculture, settlement, ranching
Exhibitions: Changing History, archaeology & ethnological exhibits
Publications: Great Plains Journal, ann; Museum Newsletter, quarterly
Activities: Classes for adults & children; dramatic progs; docent training; lects open to pub, 6 vis lectrs per yr; gallery talks; tours; AAM accredited; lending colls contains framed reproductions, Kodachromes, photographs & slides; originate traveling exhibs; mus store sells books, magazines, original art, reproductions, prints, slides, clothing & souvenir items

L **Research Library**, 601 NW Ferris, Lawton, OK 73507-5443. Tel 580-581-3460; Email mgp@sirinet.net; *Cur Spec Coll* Deborah Baroff
Open Tues - Fri 8 AM - 5 PM; Estab 1961 to provide research materials for the 10-state Great Plains region; Lending to staff only
Income: Financed by endowment, city & state appropriations
Library Holdings: Book Volumes 30,000, Clipping Files, Exhibition Catalogs, Filmstrips, Kodachrome Transparencies, Manuscripts, Memorabilia, Motion Pictures, Original Art Works, Other Holdings Documents 300,000, Pamphlets, Periodical Subscriptions 150, Photographs 22,000, Prints, Reels, Slides
Special Subjects: American Indian Art, American Western Art, Anthropology, Archaeology, Coins & Medals, Ethnology, Historical Material, Painting-American, Period Rooms, Photography, Southwestern Art
Collections: Archives, photographic colls
Publications: Great Plains Journal, annual; Museum of the Great Plains Newsletter, irregularly

MUSKOGEE

M **ATALOA LODGE MUSEUM,** 2299 Old Bacone Rd, Muskogee, OK 74403-1568. Tel 918-781-7283; Fax 918-683-4588; Email jtimothy@bacone.edu; Web: www.bacone.edu/ataloa; *Dir* John Timothy
Open Mon - Sat 8 AM - 5 PM, cl noon - 1 PM, Sun 1 - 5 PM; No admis fee, donations accepted; Estab to enhance Indian culture by having a coll of artifacts from various Indian tribes; Three large rooms; Average Annual Attendance: 3,000
Income: Financed through Bacone Col
Special Subjects: American Indian Art
Collections: Indian art, Indian crafts & artifacts, silverwork, weapons, blankets, dolls, beadwork, pottery, weaving & basketry, items of daily use
Exhibitions: Rotating exhibits
Activities: Tours; sales shop sells books, magazines, original art, reproductions, prints, ceramics, beadwork, silversmithing work, baskets & handcrafted items

M **FIVE CIVILIZED TRIBES MUSEUM,** 1101 Honor Heights Dr, Agency Hill Muskogee, OK 74401-1321. Tel 918-683-1701; Fax 918-683-3070; Email 5tribesdirector@sbcglobal.net; Web: www.fivetribes.org; *Executive Director* Sean Barney

Open Mon - Sat 10 AM - 5 PM, Sun 1 - 5 PM; Admis adults $2, seniors $1.75, students $1, children under 6 free; Estab 1966 to exhibit artifacts, relics, history, and traditional Indian art of the Cherokee, Chickasaw, Choctaw, Creek, and Seminole Indian Tribes; Average Annual Attendance: 30,000; Mem: 1000; dues vary; ann meeting in Mar
Income: $48,000 (financed by mem & admis)
Special Subjects: American Indian Art, Bronzes, Maps, Photography, Pottery, Sculpture, Woodcarvings
Collections: Traditional Indian art by known artists of Five Tribes heritage, including original paintings & sculpture, large coll of Jerome Tiger originals
Exhibitions: Four Annual Judged Exhibitions: Competitive Art Show; Students Competitive Show; Craft Competition; Masters' Exhibition
Publications: Quarterly newsletter
Activities: Docent training; lect open to pub; gallery talks; tours; competitions with awards; individual paintings & original objects of art lent to other museums & spec exhibits with board approval; lending coll contains original art works; mus shop selling books, original art, reproductions, prints, beadwork, pottery, basketry & other handmade items

L **Library**, 1101 Honor Heights Dr, Agency Hill Muskogee, OK 74401-1321. Tel 918-683-1701; Fax 918-683-3070; Web: www.fivetribes.com; *Dir* Mary Robinson
Open Mon - Sat 10 AM - 2 PM, cl Sun; Admis adult $3, senior $2, student $1.50; Estab 1966 to preserve history, culture, traditions, legends, etc of Five Civilized Tribes (Cherokee, Creek, Choctaw, Chickasaw, and Seminole tribes); Maintains an art gallery
Income: 501(c)(3)
Library Holdings: Book Volumes 3500, Cassettes, Clipping Files, Exhibition Catalogs, Framed Reproductions, Lantern Slides, Manuscripts, Memorabilia, Original Art Works, Other Holdings Original documents, Pamphlets, Periodical Subscriptions 5, Photographs, Prints, Reproductions, Sculpture
Special Subjects: American Indian Art, Historical Material, Manuscripts, Maps
Exhibitions: Mar - Student Art Show; Apr - Art under the Oaks; July - Competitive Art Show; Nov - Master Art Show
Publications: Newsletter, every three months

NORMAN

M **FIREHOUSE ART CENTER,** 444 S Flood Ave, Norman, OK 73069. Tel 405-329-4523; Fax 405-292-9763; Email info@normanfirehouse.com; Web: www.normanfirehouse.com; *Exec Dir* Douglas Shaw Elder
Open Mon - Fri 9:30 AM - 5:30 PM, Sat 10 AM - 4 PM; No admis fee; Estab 1971; 6 exhibits per year of contemporary work by local, state, regional & national artists; Average Annual Attendance: 10,000; Mem: 300; dues family $100
Income: $485,000 (financed by mem, city & state appropriation, grants, donations, fundraising)
Exhibitions: Annual Holiday Gallery; changing monthly exhibits; children's summer art show
Activities: Classes for adults & children; workshops; lect open to pub, 2 vis lectrs per yr; gallery talks; competitions; awards, 2012 Governor's Award for Art Educ; schols offered; sales store sells original art, prints, pottery, jewelry, wood works & metal works

M **UNIVERSITY OF OKLAHOMA,** Fred Jones Jr Museum of Art, 555 Elm Ave, Norman, OK 73019-3003. Tel 405-325-3272; Fax 405-325-7696; Email museuminfo@ou.edu; Web: www.ou.edu/fjjma; *Dir & Chief Cur* Mark White, PhD; *Chief Preparator* Brad Stevens; *Dir Admin & Operations* Tanya Denton; *Dir Communs* Kaylee Kain
Open Tues - Sat 10 AM -5 PM, Thurs 10 AM - 9 PM, Sun 1 - 5 PM, cl Mon; No admis fee; Estab 1936 to provide cultural enrichment for the people of Oklahoma; to collect, preserve, exhibit & research art of various periods; Approx 15,000 sq ft for permanent & temporary exhibs on two indoor levels; 34,000 sq ft expansion added to existing bldg which totals 29,000 sq ft; Average Annual Attendance: 50,000; Mem: 500; dues $15 - $1000; meetings in Sept & Jan
Income: Financed by state, univ allocation, foundation endowment, Board of Visitors & grants
Purchases: Focus upon French Impressionism, American art, Native American art, contemporary art & photography
Special Subjects: African Art, Painting-European, Photography
Collections: French Impressionism, American art, Native American art, contemporary art, photography, icons
Publications: Calendar of activities; posters; announcements; exhib catalogues
Activities: Docent training; classes for adults & children; dramatic progs; lects open to pub; 5-10 lectrs per yr open to pub; concerts; gallery talks; scheduled tours; family days; student exhibs with awards; 3 per yr; organize traveling exhibs; museum shop sells books, magazines, reproductions, prints, jewelry, notecards, children's toys & other gifts

L **Architecture Library**, 830 Van Vleet Oval, Gould Hall Rm 105 Norman, OK 73019. Tel 405-325-5521; Fax 405-325-6637; Web: libraries.ou.edu/depts/architecture; *Library Technician* Tracy Chapman; *Fine & Applied Arts Librn* Matthew Stock
Open fall Tues - Fri 8 AM - 7 PM, Sun 1 - 5 PM, summer Tues - Fri 8 AM - 7 PM, cl weekends
Library Holdings: Book Volumes 17,000, Periodical Subscriptions 42
Special Subjects: Architecture, Interior Design, Landscape Architecture

L **Fine Arts Library**, 500 W Boyd St, Catlett Music Ctr Norman, OK 73019-3130. Tel 405-325-4243; Fax 405-325-4243; Email drmosser@ou.edu; Web: libraries.ou.edu; *Library Technician III* Dennis Mosser; *Fine & Applied Arts Librn* Matthew Stock
Open fall sem Mon - Thurs 8 AM - 9 PM, Fri 8 AM - 5 PM, Sat 11 AM - 4 PM, Sun 2 - 9 PM; Estab to provide instructional support to the acad community of the univ & gen service to the people of the state; Circ 6900
Income: Financed by state appropriation
Library Holdings: Book Volumes 27,000, CD-ROMs, Fiche, Periodical Subscriptions 50, Reels, Video Tapes

OKLAHOMA CITY

C **AMERICAN HOMING PIGEON MUSEUM & LIBRARY,** (American Homing Pigeon Institute), 2300 NE 63rd St, Oklahoma City, OK 73111-8208. Tel 405-478-5155; Email theamericanpigeonmuseum@gmail.com; Web: theamericanpigeonmuseum.org; *Dir* Jessica Nguyen; *Exec Officer Finance* Jerry Black; *Dir Museum Logistics* Douglas Jones; *Exec Officer Mus Opers* Lorrie Monteiro
Estab 1973 to preserve & display the rich heritage of domestic pigeons & doves & to foster the keeping of registered pigeons as a unique & rewarding hobby; Mem: dues $25 - $250
Income: Financed by mem
Activities: Classes for children; exten dept

M **INDIVIDUAL ARTISTS OF OKLAHOMA,** 706 W Sheridan Ave, Oklahoma City, OK 73102. Tel 405-232-6060; Email info@individualartists.org; Web: www.iaogallery.org; *Exec Dir* Laura Reese
Open Mon - Fri 9 Am - 4 PM; No admis fee; Estab 1979 to promote Oklahoma artists of all disciplines; Average Annual Attendance: 7,000
Income: Financed by mem, fundraising & art sales
Exhibitions: Monthly exhibits of 3 visual artists, including spec photog gallery
Publications: Artzone, monthly newsletter
Activities: Lect open to pub, 1-2 vis lectrs per yr; competitions; concerts, gallery talks; film & video; traveling exhibs 1 per yr; originate traveling exhibs 1 per yr statewide

M **OKLAHOMA CITY MUSEUM OF ART,** 415 Couch Dr, Oklahoma City, OK 73102-2214. Tel 405-236-3100; Fax 405-236-3122; Email info@okcmoa.com; Web: www.okcmoa.com; *Pres & CEO* E Michael Whittingham; *CFO* Rita Craig; *Mus Store Mgr* Richard Bruner; *Mus Cafe Gen Mgr* Ahmad Farnia; *Mgr Tours & Adult Learning* Bryon Chambers; *Registrar* Maury Ford; *Head Design & Installation* Ernesto Sanchez Villarreal; *Facility Opers Dir* Jack Madden; *Projectionist & Film Asst* John Dudley Marshall; *Chief Preparator* Trent Lawson; *Chief Safety & Security* Steve Thompson
Open Wed - Sat 10 AM - 5 PM, Thurs 10 AM - 9 PM, cl Mon, New Year's Day, Independence Day, Thanksgiving & Christmas Day; Admis adults $12, college students, seniors & children 6-18 $10, military w/ID $5, children under 5 & mems free; Estab 1945; Circ Library; 15 galleries, theatre, library, classrooms, store & full service cafe; Average Annual Attendance: 130,000; Mem: 4000; dues $50 - $1000; ann meeting in June
Income: Pvt funded by earned income, corp, foundations & indiv contributions & interest earned on endowments
Library Holdings: Auction Catalogs, Audio Tapes, Book Volumes, DVDs, Exhibition Catalogs, Kodachrome Transparencies, Motion Pictures, Original Art Works, Periodical Subscriptions, Photographs, Prints, Reels, Sculpture, Slides, Video Tapes
Special Subjects: Drawings, Etchings & Engravings, Glass, Landscapes, Latin American Art, Maps, Oriental Art, Painting-American, Painting-British, Painting-European, Painting-French, Painting-German, Painting-Italian, Photography, Portraits, Prints, Sculpture, Watercolors, Woodcuts
Collections: 19th-20th century American paintings including works by Bellows, Tiffany, Chase, Cropsey, Benton, Moran, Hassam, 20th century American paintings & graphics, including Henri, Marin, Kelly, Indiana, Francis, Davis, Warhol, Sculpture by Bertoia, Bontecou, Calder, Henry Moore, Most comprehensive collection of Chihuly glass in world, Washington Gallery of Modern Art collection, RA Young Collection, Westheimer Family Collection
Exhibitions: Dale Chihuly: The Collection
Publications: Coll catalogues; spec exhib catalogs
Activities: Classes for adults & children; docent training; lects open to pub; gallery talks; tours; schol; individual paintings & original objects of art lent to other accredited mus; lending collection contains original art works, original prints, paintings & photographs; book traveling exhibs 1-3 per yr; originate traveling exhibs to other mus nationally; mus shop sells books, magazines & prints

M **OKLAHOMA CITY UNIVERSITY,** Hulsey Gallery-Norick Art Center, 2501 N Blackwelder, Oklahoma City, OK 73106. Tel 405-208-5226; Email hmmoye@okcu.edu; Web: www.okcu.edu; *Dir School Visual Arts* Holly Moye
Open Mon - Fri 9 AM - 5 PM, Summer Mon - Thurs 10 AM - 5 PM, cl major holidays & acad breaks; No admis fee; Estab 1985 to educ in the arts; Gallery is 2,200 sq ft with fabric covered walls & moveable display forms
Income: Financed by endowment & the Univ
Collections: Oklahoma City University Art Coll, Art donated by individuals & organizations from Oklahoma
Exhibitions: Oklahoma City University Student Exhibit; Oklahoma High School Print & Drawing Exhibit; exhibits change monthly
Activities: Classes for adults; lect open to pub, 2-3 vis lectrs per yr; individual paintings & original works of art lent to various departments of the Oklahoma City Univ campus

M **OKLAHOMA CONTEMPORARY ARTS CENTER,** (City Arts Center at Fair Park), 3000 General Pershing Blvd, Oklahoma City, OK 73107-6202. Tel 405-951-0000; Fax 405-951-0003; Web: www.oklahomacontemporary.org; *Exec Dir* Donna Rinehart-Keever; *Artistic Dir* Jeremiah Matthew Davis; *Dir Develop* Jennifer Thurman; *Dir Educ & Public Programming* Erin Oldfield; *Curatorial & Exhibs Dir* Jennifer Scanlan; *Dir Communs* Lori Brooks; *Dir Fin* Salvador Ontiveros; *Exhibits Mgr* Steve Boyd; *Visitor Svcs Facility Mgr* Laura Rice; *Educ Mgr* Christine Gibson; *Staff Accountant* Deepa Ghimire
Open Mon - Thurs 9 AM-10 PM, Fri - Sat 9 AM - 5 PM; cl Sun & major holidays; No admis fee; donations accepted; Estab 1989 to provide the community with quality accessible and affordable arts programming and educaton; Temporary exhibs by contemporary artists; small art library located at satellite facility; Mem: dues $100 & up
Income: $2,400,000 (financed by foundation, individual & corporate donations & prog revenue)
Collections: contemporary works

Activities: Art educ classes for adults & children; artist & cur lects held at the beginning of exhibs; Art for Every 5th Grader Prog, held in conjunction with Oklahoma City Pub Schools

M **OKLAHOMA HISTORICAL SOCIETY,** State Museum of History, 800 Nazih Zuhdi Dr, Oklahoma City, OK 73105. Tel 405-521-2491, 405-522-5248; Email dprovo@okhistory.org; Web: www.okhistory.org; *Dir* Dan Provo; *Deputy Dir* Jeff Briley
Open Mon - Sat 9 AM - 5 PM, cl State holidays; Admis adults $7, seniors 62 & over $5, students $4, children 5 & under, active-duty military, veterans & immediate family & mems free; Estab 1893 to provide an historical overview of the State of OK, from prehistory to the present, through interpretive exhibits, 3-D artifacts, original art & photographs; Average Annual Attendance: 150,000
Income: Financed by state appropriations & mem; soc depends on donations for additions to its colls
Special Subjects: American Indian Art, American Western Art, Anthropology, Archaeology, Decorative Arts, Ethnology, Historical Material, Military Art, Painting-American, Period Rooms
Collections: Anthropology, archaeology, historical artifacts, documents, American Indian art, Oklahoma art, Western art
Exhibitions: Permanent exhibits depicting pre-history, Oklahoma Indian Tribes' history, the Five Civilized Tribes' occupancy of Indian Territory, the land openings of the late 19th and early 20th centuries, statehood, and progress since statehood; spec exhibits 2-3 times per yr
Publications: Mistletoe Leaves, monthly newsletter; The Chronicles of Oklahoma, Society quarterly; various brochures and reprints
Activities: Special presentations & films for children & adults; interpretive progs; self-guided tours; individual paintings & original objects of art lent to qualified museums; lending coll contains paintings, 19th century beadwork & Indian artifacts; originate traveling exhibs; sales shop sells books, magazines

L **Research Center,** 800 Nazih Zuhdi Dr, Oklahoma City, OK 73105. Tel 405-522-5225; Email research@okhistory.org; Web: okhistory.org/research/index; *Exec Dir* Bob Blackburn; *Dir* Chad Williams
Open Tues - Sat 10 AM - 4:45 PM, cl Sun, Mon & all state holidays; No admis fee; Estab 1893 to collect & preserve historical materials & publications on Oklahoma history; For reference only
Income: financed by state appropriations & members
Library Holdings: Book Volumes 65,000, Clipping Files, Fiche, Pamphlets, Periodical Subscriptions 80, Photographs, Reels 12,493
Publications: Chronicles of Oklahoma, quarterly; Mistletoe Leaves, monthly newsletter

M **OMNIPLEX SCIENCE MUSEUM,** 2100 NE 52nd, Oklahoma City, OK 73111. Tel 405-602-6664 (Omniplex), 427-5461; Fax 405-424-5106; Email omnipr@omniplex.org; Web: www.omniplex.org; *Exec Dir* Chuck Schillings
Open Mon - Fri 9 AM - 5 PM, Sat 9 AM - 6 PM, Sun 11 AM - 6 PM; Admis adults $13.95, children & seniors $10.75, one price for entire center; Estab 1958 to focus on the inter-relationships between science, arts & the humanities & to supplement educ facilities offered in the pub schools in the areas of arts & sciences; The Kirkpatrick Center houses Omniplex, a hands-on science mus; mus shop; George Sutton bird paintings; Oklahoma Aviation & Space Hall of Fame & Mus; Center of American Indian Gallery; Sanamu African Gallery; Oriental Art Gallery; International Photography Hall of Fame; Oklahoma Zoological Society Offices; Kirkpatrick Planetarium; miniature Victorian house; antique clocks; US Navy Gallery; retired senior volunteer program; Oklahoma City Zoo offices; Average Annual Attendance: 350,000
Income: Financed by mem, pvt donations, Allied Arts Foundation, admis fees, & class tui
Special Subjects: African Art, Ivory, Painting-American, Prints, Pre-Columbian Art, Oriental Art
Collections: European & Oriental Ivory Sculpture, Japanese Woodblock Prints, Oceanic art, Pre-Columbian & American Indian art, Sutton paintings, Traditional & Contemporary African art, 1,000 photographs in Photography Hall of Fame
Exhibitions: Changing exhibs every 6-10 weeks; Dinosaurs
Publications: Insights, quarterly; Omniplex Newsletter, monthly
Activities: Classes for adults & children; docent training; lect open to pub; tours; book traveling exhibs; mus shop sells books, prints, science-related material, cards & jewelry

OKMULGEE

M **CREEK COUNCIL HOUSE MUSEUM,** 106 W 6th St, Okmulgee, OK 74447-5014; PO Box 918, Okmulgee, OK 74447-0918. Tel 918-756-2324; Fax 918-756-3671; Email creekmuseum@prodigy.n; *Dir* David Anderson; *VPres* Terry Bernis; *Mus Shop Mgr* Becka Hutchinson
Open Tues - Sat 10 AM - 4:30 PM; No admis fee; Estab 1867, first Council House built, present Council House erected in 1878 to collect & preserve artifacts from Creek history; Five rooms downstairs containing artifacts; four rooms upstairs showing art work, early time of Okmulgee; rooms of House of Warriors & House of Kings; Average Annual Attendance: 10,000-12,000
Income: Financed by mem & city appropriation
Special Subjects: Period Rooms
Collections: Creek Artifacts
Exhibitions: Annual Oklahoma Indian Art Market (juried competitions)
Activities: Seminars on Creek Culture & history; Ann Wild Onion Feast (traditional tribal foods); lect open to pub, 5-10 vis lectrs per yr; gallery talks; artmobile; book traveling exhibs; mus shop sells books, original art, reproductions, prints & Native American art & craft items

L **Library,** 106 W 6th St, Okmulgee, OK 74447-5014; PO Box 918, Okmulgee, OK 74447-0918. Tel 918-756-2324; Fax 918-756-3671; *Dir* David Anderson
Open Tues - Sat 10 AM - 4:30 PM & by appointment; Estab 1923 to collect & educate all Native American Tribes with emphasis on Muscogee Creek; For reference only, staff & academia
Library Holdings: Audio Tapes, Book Volumes 250, Clipping Files, Exhibition Catalogs, Framed Reproductions, Manuscripts, Memorabilia, Motion Pictures, Original Art Works, Pamphlets, Periodical Subscriptions 10, Photographs, Prints, Reels, Sculpture, Video Tapes

PARK HILL

A **CHEROKEE HERITAGE CENTER,** 21192 S Keeler Dr, Park Hill, OK 74451; PO Box 515, Tahlequah, OK 74465-0515. Tel 918-456-6007, 888-999-6007; Fax 918-456-6165; Email membership@cherokeeheritage.org; Web: www.CherokeeHeritage.org; *Exec Dir* Carey Tilley; *Cur* Mickel Vantz; *Mktg Dir* Judy Pierce
Open Feb - Dec Mon - Sat 10 AM - 5 PM, Sun 1 - 5 PM, cl Jan; Admis adults $8.50, seniors 55 & over & students with ID $7.50, children $5, 6 & under free; rates vary with each show; Estab 1963 to commemorate & portray the history, traditions & lore of a great Indian tribe & to assist in improving local economic conditions; Maintains an art gallery, primarily Indian art; Average Annual Attendance: 150,000; Mem: 1500; dues $25 & up
Income: Financed by mem, admis & grants
Special Subjects: Archaeology, Historical Material, Manuscripts, Photography, Pottery, Textiles
Collections: Indian artists interpretations of Trails of Tears
Exhibitions: Trail of Tears Art Show, annually; various shows, lectures & classes
Publications: The Columns, quarterly
Activities: Classes for adults; lect open to pub; mus shop sells books, reproductions, prints & slides

L **Library & Archives,** PO Box 515, Tahlequah, OK 74465. Tel 918-456-6007, 888-999-6007; Fax 918-456-6165; Email archives@cherokeeheritage.org; Web: www.CherokeeHeritage.org; *Archivist & Cur* Tom Mooney
Open Mon - Sat 10 AM - 5 PM, Sun 1 - 5 PM; Admis fees vary, call for details; Estab 1976 to preserve remnants of Cherokee history & to educate the general pub about that cultural heritage; a repository of Indian art & documents; Maintains an art gallery with work by artists of several different tribes; heavy emphasis given to the Cherokee experience
Income: Financed by mem, admis & grants
Library Holdings: Audio Tapes, Book Volumes 3000, Cassettes, Clipping Files, Filmstrips, Framed Reproductions, Kodachrome Transparencies, Manuscripts, Memorabilia, Original Art Works, Other Holdings Archival materials in excess of 500 cu ft; Manuscripts, Pamphlets, Periodical Subscriptions 10, Photographs, Prints, Reels 127, Sculpture, Slides
Exhibitions: Annual Trail of Tears Art Show (Indian artists' interpretation of the Trail of Tears theme); Cherokee Artists Exhibition; rotating exhibitions; special exhibitions, periodically (primarily Indian artists)
Publications: Quarterly columns
Activities: Classes for adult; tours

PONCA CITY

A **PONCA CITY ART ASSOCIATION,** 819 E Central Ave, Ponca City, OK 74601-5506. Tel 580-765-9746; Email poncacityartcenter@gmail.com; Web: poncacityartcenter.com; *Dir* Jerry Cathey
Open Wed - Sun 1 - 5 PM; No admis fee; Estab 1947 to encourage creative arts, to furnish place & sponsor art classes, art exhibits & workshops; Historical mansion; Average Annual Attendance: 3,000; Mem: 250; dues $40 family; ann meeting third Tues in Apr
Income: $40,000 (financed by mem, flea market, corporate & pvt)
Collections: Permanent fine arts coll, additions by purchases & donations
Exhibitions: Eight per year
Publications: Assn Bulletin, 6 per yr
Activities: Classes for adults & children; lect open to pub; tours; competitions for mems only with awards; schols offered; individual paintings lent to city-owned buildings; sales shop sells original art, reproductions & prints

M **PONCA CITY CULTURAL CENTER & MUSEUM,** 1000 E Grand Ave, Ponca City, OK 74601-5607. Tel 405-767-0427; *Exec Dir* Kathy Adams
Open Mon, Wed - Sat 10 AM - 5 PM, Sun & holidays 1 - 5 PM; cl Tues, Thanksgiving, Christmas Eve & Christmas Day, New Year's Eve & New Year's Day; Admis adults $1; The Cultural Center & Mus, a National Historic House since 1976, houses the Indian Mus, the Bryant Baker Studio, the 101 Ranch Room, & the DAR Memorial Mus; The Indian Mus, estab in 1936, places an emphasis on materials from the five neighboring tribes (Ponca, Kaw, Otoe, Osage, and Tonkawa) whose artistic use of beading, finger weaving & ribbon-work are displayed throughout the Mus. The Bryant Baker Studio is a replica of the New York Studio of Bryant Baker, sculptor of the Pioneer Woman Statue, a local landmark, & the studio contains original bronze & plaster sculpture. The 101 Ranch Room exhibits memorabilia from the world renowned Miller Brothers' 101 Ranch, located south of Ponca City in the early 1900s. The mus is the former home of Ernest Whitworth Marland, oilman & philanthropist & the tenth governor of Oklahoma; Average Annual Attendance: 35,000; Mem: Dues $10 - $1000
Income: Financed by the City of Ponca City & donations
Special Subjects: American Indian Art, Archaeology, Sculpture
Collections: Bryant Baker Collection: original sculpture, 101 Ranch memorabilia, Indian ethnography & archeology of Indian tribes throughout the United States
Exhibitions: Smithsonian Indian Images; Indian costumes, jewelry, pottery, baskets, musical instruments & tools
Publications: Brochure
Activities: Tours; sales shop sells books, arrowheads, Indian arts & crafts

L **Library,** 1000 E Grand Ave, Ponca City, OK 74601. Tel 405-767-0427; *Exec Dir* Kathy Adams
Open Mon, Wed - Sat 10 AM - 5 PM, Sun 1 - 5 PM, cl Tues; Primarily research library
Income: Financed by Ponca City
Library Holdings: Book Volumes 230, Periodical Subscriptions 13
Special Subjects: Anthropology, Archaeology

L **PONCA CITY LIBRARY,** Art Dept, 515 E Grand, Ponca City, OK 74601. Tel 580-767-0345; Fax 580-767-0377; *Head Technical Svcs* Paula Cain; *Dir* Holly LaBossiere
Open Mon - Thurs 9 AM - 9 PM, Fri 9 AM - 6 PM, Sat 9 AM - 5 PM, Sun 2 - 5 PM, cl Sun in June, July & Aug; Estab 1904 to serve the citizens of Ponca City; Circ 150,000; Gallery maintained
Library Holdings: Book Volumes 75,000, Cassettes, Framed Reproductions, Original Art Works, Pamphlets, Periodical Subscriptions 250, Photographs, Sculpture
Collections: Oriental Art Collection, Sandzen Collection, paintings

SHAWNEE

M **MABEE-GERRER MUSEUM OF ART,** 1900 W MacArthur St, Shawnee, OK 74804-2403. Tel 405-878-5300; Fax 405-878-5133; Email info@mgmoa.org; Web: www.mgmoa.org; *Dir and Chief Cur* Dane Pollei; *Cur Collections* Delaynna Trim; *Cur Educ* Donna Merkt; *Preparator* Daniel Lay; *Dir Develop* Tonya Ricks
Open daily Tues - Sat 10 AM - 5 PM, Sun 1 - 4 PM, cl Mon & holidays; Admis $5; Estab 1915 to contribute to the cultural growth & appreciation of the gen pub of Oklahoma as well as of the student body of Saint Gregory's Univ; A new 16,000 sq ft gallery was completed in 1979. In 1990, 1500 sq ft was added which includes a new gallery, a multi-purpose room & theater. Collections are being enlarged by purchases & by gifts; Average Annual Attendance: 40,000
Income: Financed by endowment, mem & foundation funds & grants
Special Subjects: African Art, American Indian Art, Antiquities-Egyptian, Antiquities-Greek, Antiquities-Oriental, Antiquities-Persian, Antiquities-Roman, Asian Art, Ceramics, Decorative Arts, Drawings, Etchings & Engravings, Ethnology, Hispanic Art, Ivory, Landscapes, Medieval Art, Mexican Art, Military Art, Painting-American, Painting-European, Painting-Italian, Photography, Pre-Columbian Art, Primitive art, Prints, Religious Art, Renaissance Art, Sculpture, Southwestern Art
Collections: Artifacts from ancient civilization, African, Egyptian, Roman, Grecian, Babylonian, Pre-Columbian North, South and Central American Indian, and South Pacific, etchings, engravings, serigraphs and lithographs, oil paintings by American and European artists, Native American, Icons: Greek, Russian & Balkan, Retablos from Mexico & New Mexico
Activities: Classes for adults & children; dramatic programs; docent training, teacher in service; arts integration teacher training; lects open to pub, 5 vis lectrs per yr; gallery talks; tours; individual paintings & original objects of art lent to other museums; books 1-2 traveling exhibs per yr; originates traveling exhibs; mus shop sells books, original art, reproductions

STILLWATER

M **OKLAHOMA STATE UNIVERSITY,** Gardiner Art Gallery, 108 Bartlett Ctr, Dept of Art, Bartlett Ctr for Studio Arts Stillwater, OK 74078-4084. Tel 405-744-6016, 405-744-9086; Fax 405-744-5767; Email nwilkin@okway.okstate.edu; *Dir* B J Smith
Open Mon - Fri 8 AM - 4 PM, Sun 1 - 5 PM; No admis fee; Estab 1970 as a visual & educ exten of the department's classes & as a cultural service to the community & area; One gallery located on the ground fl, Bartlett Center for the Studio Arts; 250 running ft of wall space, 12 ft ceiling; Average Annual Attendance: 5,500
Income: Financed by col
Collections: 7250 drawings, prints, paintings, sculptures & ceramics, mostly mid-late 20th century
Exhibitions: Exhibitions change every 3-4 weeks year round; faculty, student, invitational & traveling shows
Publications: Exhib brochures; exhib schedules
Activities: Book traveling exhibs

L **Architecture Library**, 201A Architecture Bldg, Stillwater, OK 74078-0185. Tel 405-744-6047; Email bobos@okstate.edu; Web: www.library.okstate.edu; *Architecture Librn* Susan Bobo
Open fall & spring semesters Mon - Thurs 9 AM - 9 PM Fri 9 AM - 5:30 PM, Sun 5 - 9 PM, hours may vary; Estab 1976 to meet the needs of the faculty & students of the School of Architecture
Income: financed by college
Purchases: $14,000
Library Holdings: Book Volumes 13,000, Other Holdings Compact discs, Periodical Subscriptions 40, Photographs, Slides, Video Tapes

TULSA

C **BANK OF OKLAHOMA NA,** Art Collection, 1 William Ctr, Tulsa, OK 74172-0172; PO Box 2300, Tulsa, OK 74102-2300. Tel 918-588-6000; Fax 918-588-8692; *VPres Exec Comt* Scott Ellison
Open 8 AM - 5 PM; Estab 1968 to enhance work environment; Coll displayed on 7 floors of the Bank of Oklahoma Tower
Purchases: $15,000
Collections: Modern Art
Activities: Lect; tours; schols offered to University of Tulsa

M **PHILBROOK MUSEUM OF ART,** 2727 S Rockford Rd, Tulsa, OK 74114-4104; PO Box 52510, Tulsa, OK 74152-0510. Tel 918-749-7941; Fax 918-743-4230; Email information@philbrook.org; Web: www.philbrook.org; *Dir Colls & Exhibs* Rachel Keith; *Mus Shop Mgr & Buyer* Susan Shrewder; *Chief Preparator* George Brooks; *Facility & Special Events Coordr* Charisse Cooper; *Cur Native American & Non-Western Art* Christina Burke; *Dir Educ & Pub Prog* Jessimi Jones; *Dir Horticulture* Sheila Kanotz; *Dir & Pres* Scott Stulen; *Cur European Art* Sarah Lees; *Chief Cur & Cur American Art* Catherine Whitney; *Cur Modern & Contemp Art* Sienna Brown
Open Wed - Sun 9 AM - 5 PM, Fri until 9 PM, cl Mon & Tues; Admis adults $9, students, groups of 10 or more & seniors (62+) $7, children 17 & under free; Estab 1939 as a gen art mus in an Italian Renaissance Revival Villa, the former home of philanthropist & oil baron Waite Phillips; Twenty-three acres of formal & natural gardens. Also contains a special exhib gallery; Average Annual Attendance: 148,452; Mem: 5000; dues $50 & up; ann meeting in June
Income: Financed by endowment, mem, earned income, corporate & pvt gifts & pub grants
Library Holdings: Auction Catalogs, Audio Tapes, Book Volumes, CD-ROMs, Clipping Files, Exhibition Catalogs, Pamphlets, Periodical Subscriptions, Photographs, Slides, Video Tapes
Special Subjects: African Art, American Indian Art, American Western Art, Asian Art, Ceramics, Furniture, Glass, Historical Material, Oriental Art, Painting-American, Painting-European, Painting-Italian, Prints, Sculpture, Watercolors
Collections: Laura A Clubb Collection of American & European Paintings, Clark Field Collection of American Indian Baskets & Pottery, Gillert Collection of Southeast Asian Ceramics, Samuel H Kress Collection of Italian Renaissance Paintings & Sculpture, Roberta Campbell Lawson Collection of Indian Artifacts; Tabor Collection of Oriental Art, Gussman Collection of African Sculpture, Eugene B Adkins Collection of Native American & Western Art, George R Kraus II Collection of Modern & Contemporary Design, Tabor Collection of Oriental Art
Publications: Quarterly magazine; exhibition catalogs
Activities: Dramatic progs; classes for adults & children; docent training; lect open to pub, 27 vis lectrs per yr; concerts; gallery talks; tours; scholarships; awards: 2010 Oklahoma Mus Assoc Educ program & conservation project, 2010 Oklahoma Magazine Best Museum; individual & original objects of art lent to museums, schools, corporations & city government; book traveling exhibs 2 - 4 per yr; originate traveling exhibs; mus shop sells books, magazines, original art, reproductions, prints, slides, jewelry, children's toys, garden items & gift items

L **H.A. & Mary K Chapman Library**, 2727 S Rockford Rd, Tulsa, OK 74114-4104; PO Box 52510, Tulsa, OK 74152-0510. Tel 918-748-5306; Fax 918-743-4230; Email tyoung@philbrook.org; Web: www.philbrook.org; *Librarian/Archivist* Thomas E Young
Open Tues 10 AM - Noon, 1 - 5 PM, Wed - Fri 10 AM - noon, Mon by appointment; No admis fee; Estab 1940; Circ 24,000 vol library; Reference-resource center for the curatorial staff, teaching faculty, volunteers & mem
Library Holdings: Auction Catalogs, Book Volumes 24,000, Clipping Files, DVDs, Exhibition Catalogs, Original Documents, Pamphlets, Periodical Subscriptions 135, Photographs, Reproductions, Slides, Video Tapes
Special Subjects: American Western Art, Art History, Decorative Arts, Folk Art, History of Art & Archaeology, Landscape Architecture, Painting-American, Painting-European, Painting-Italian, Photography, Pottery, Pre-Columbian Art, Primitive art, Asian Art
Collections: Oklahoma art & artists, Wade Phillips Collection

L **Eugene B Adkins Study Center**, 116 E Brady St, Tulsa, OK 74107-2014; PO Box 52510, Tulsa, OK 74152-0510. Tel 918-748-5306; Fax 918-743-4239; Email tyoung@philbrook.org; Web: www.philbrook.org; *Librarian/Archivist* Thomas E Young
Open Wed - Fri 1 - 5 PM (or by appointment); No admis fee; Estab 2013; Circ 5,000 vols; Reference & Special Colls with focus on Native American Art
Library Holdings: Auction Catalogs, Audio Tapes, Book Volumes 5,000, Clipping Files, DVDs, Exhibition Catalogs, Manuscripts, Original Documents, Pamphlets 20, Periodical Subscriptions, Photographs 1,000, Records, Slides, Video Tapes
Special Subjects: American Indian Art
Collections: Native American Art, Eugene B Adkins Library & Archives, Roberta Campbell Library & Archives, Nettie Wheeler Collection, Native American artists files, photograph coll of Native Americans

M **THE SHERWIN MILLER MUSEUM OF JEWISH ART,** (Gershon & Rebecca Fenster Museum of Jewish Art), 2021 E 71st St, Tulsa, OK 74136-5408. Tel 918-492-1818; Fax 918-492-1888; Email info@jewishmuseum.net; Web: www.jewishmuseum.net; *Exec Dir* Drew Diamond; *Dir Colls & Exhibs* Mickel Yantz; *Dir Develop & Progs* Tracey Hearst-Woods; *Dir Holocaust Educ* Cassie Nodine; *Vol Tours Coordr* Cathey Wilson; *Preparator* Charles Taylor
Open Mon - Fri 10 AM - 5 PM, Sun 1 - 5 PM; Admis adults $6.50, seniors & groups $5.50, students $3.50, groups of 10+ $3; Estab 1966 to collect, preserve & interpret cultural, historical & aesthetic materials attesting to Jewish cultural history, Jewish history of Oklahoma & the Holocaust; Average Annual Attendance: 14,000; Mem: 300; dues $35 - $2,500, ann meeting in Dec
Income: $450,000 (financed by endowment, mem & special events)
Library Holdings: Audio Tapes, Cassettes, Compact Disks, DVDs, Exhibition Catalogs, Memorabilia, Original Documents, Photographs, Prints, Records, Reels, Reproductions, Sculpture, Slides, Video Tapes
Special Subjects: Judaica
Collections: Anti-semitica, archeology of old world, ethnographic materials, fine art by Jewish artists & on Jewish themes, ritual & ceremonial Judaica, Holocaust, Oklahoma Jewish Archive
Exhibitions: Permanent Jewish History & Practice exhibit; Permanent Holocaust exhibit
Publications: newsletter, monthly by email
Activities: Classes for adults & children, docent training; lect open to pub; gallery talks; tours; awards; individual paintings & original objects of art lent to other museums & religious institutions; mus shop sells books & Judaica

M **UNIVERSITY OF TULSA,** Alexandre Hogue Gallery, 600 S College Ave, Art Dept Tulsa, OK 74104-9700. Tel 918-631-2202; Fax 918-631-3423; Email mark-lewis@utulsa.edu; *Contact* Mark Lewis
Open Mon - Fri 8 - 5 PM; No admis fee; Estab 1966 to display the works of regionally & nationally known artists; 176 running ft; Average Annual Attendance: 1,000
Income: Financed by Univ
Exhibitions: Annual Student Art Competition; National Scholastic Art Awards Scholarships & Competition; various regional & local artists on a rotating basis
Activities: Lect open to pub, 6 vis lectrs per yr; competition with awards; schols offered; individual paintings & original objects of art lent

M **UNIVERSITY OF TULSA,** Gilcrease Museum, 1400 Gilcrease Museum Rd, Tulsa, OK 74127-2100. Tel 918-596-2700, 888-655-2278 (Toll free); Fax

918-596-2770; Email sandi-freeman@utulsa.edu; Web: gilcrease.org; *Exec Dir* Susan Neal; *Dir Opers* Sandi Freeman; *Sr Cur & Cur Art* Laura Fry
Open Tues - Sun 10 AM - 5 PM, cl Mon, Thanksgiving & Christmas Day; Admis adults $8, seniors (62 & older) & active US military $6, groups of 10 or more $6, college students with ID $5, children 18 & under & mems no charge; Estab by the late Thomas Gilcrease as a pvt institution; acquired by the City of Tulsa 1954 (governed by a Board of Dir & City Park Board); building addition completed 1963 & 1987; partner with the University of Tulsa in 2008; Average Annual Attendance: 76,366; Mem: 4500; dues $25 & up
Income: Financed by city funds & the University of Tulsa
Special Subjects: American Indian Art, American Western Art, Anthropology, Bronzes, Drawings, Eskimo Art, Etchings & Engravings, Ethnology, Folk Art, Gold, Hispanic Art, Historical Material, Landscapes, Latin American Art, Leather, Manuscripts, Maps, Mexican Art, Painting-American, Photography, Portraits, Pottery, Pre-Columbian Art, Sculpture, Southwestern Art
Collections: American art from Colonial period to 20th century with emphasis on art of historical significance, sculpture, painting, graphics. Much of the work shown is of documentary nature, with emphasis on the Native American material & the opening of the Trans-Mississippi West. Art Collections include 100,000 books, 10,000 paintings by 400 American artists, artifact collections include 350,000 objects including both prehistoric & historic materials from most of the Native American cultures in Middle & North America
Exhibitions: Special exhibitions periodically; rotating exhibits during fall, winter, spring seasons; Gilcrease Rendezvous; 8000 sq ft permanent exhibit of Art from Mexico
Publications: The Journal, biannual
Activities: Classes for adults & children; docent training; lect open to pub; gallery talks; tours; individual paintings & original objects of art lent to comparable art institutions; book traveling exhibs 3-4 per yr; originate traveling exhibs to other museums; mus shop sells books, magazines, original art, reproductions, prints, slides, pottery & jewelry

L **Library,** 1400 Gilcrease Museum Rd, Tulsa, OK 74127-2100. Tel 918-596-2700; Fax 918-596-2770; *Cur Archival Coll* Sarah Erwin
Open Tues - Sat 9 AM - 5 PM, Sun 11 AM - 5 PM, cl Christmas; No admis fee; donations $3 per person, $5 per family; Library open for research by appointment, contains 90,000 books & documents, many rare books & manuscripts of the American frontier period, as well as materials concerning the Five Civilized Tribes
Income: Financed by city appropriation
Library Holdings: Book Volumes 40,000, Exhibition Catalogs, Manuscripts, Memorabilia, Pamphlets, Periodical Subscriptions 10, Photographs
Special Subjects: American Indian Art, American Western Art, Historical Material, Manuscripts

WOODWARD

M **PLAINS INDIANS & PIONEERS HISTORICAL FOUNDATION,** Museum & Art Center, 2009 Williams Ave, Woodward, OK 73801-5717. Tel 580-256-6136; Fax 580-256-2577; Email pipm@swbell.net; *Dir & Cur* Louise James; *Dir Asst* Robert Roberson
Open Tues - Sat 10 AM - 5 PM, cl Sun & Mon; No admis fee; Estab 1966 to preserve local history & to support visual arts; Average Annual Attendance: 15,000; Mem: 450; dues $25 - $500; ann meeting in Nov
Income: Financed by mem & trust fund
Special Subjects: American Indian Art
Collections: Early day artifacts as well as Indian material
Exhibitions: Juried contests for high school students & photographers; Fine Arts, Creative Crafts (guest artist featured each month in the gallery)
Publications: Below Devil's Gap (historical book); brochures; quarterly newsletter; Oklahoma's Northwest Territory Map; Woodward County Pioneer Families, 1907-57 (2 volumes)
Activities: Classes for adults & children; docent training; lect open to pub; tours; competitions with prizes; book traveling exhibs 3 per yr; mus shop sells books, magazines, original art & prints & Northwest Oklahoma artisans crafts

OREGON

ASHLAND

M **SOUTHERN OREGON UNIVERSITY,** Stevenson Union Gallery, 1250 Siskiyou Blvd, Ashland, OR 97520-5001. Tel 541-552-6465; Fax 541-552-6440; Web: www.sou.edu
Open Mon - Fri 8 AM - 9 PM, Sat 9:30 AM - 2 PM; No admis fee; Estab 1972 to offer col & community high quality arts; Located on the third floor of Stevenson Union, the gallery is about 1200 sq ft; Average Annual Attendance: 20,000
Income: Financed by student fees
Collections: Permanent collection: prints, paintings by local artists & a sculpture by Bruce West
Exhibitions: Ceramics, paintings, photography, prints, sculpture, faculty & student work.; Annual Student Art Show; Installations, Alternative Works
Activities: 3 vis lectrs per yr; competitions

M **Schneider Museum of Art,** 1250 Siskiyou Blvd, Ashland, OR 97520-5001. Tel 541-552-6245; Fax 541-552-8241; Email cranem@sou.edu; Web: sma.sou.edu; *Dir* Scott Malbaurn
Open Mon - Sat 10 AM - 4 PM; Admis: $5 donation suggested; Estab 1986; Univ Art Mus - Contemporary Art Focus; Average Annual Attendance: 20,000; Mem: 350; dues $30 - $250+; ann meeting in Oct
Income: Financed by endowment, mem, state appropriations & federal grants
Special Subjects: African Art, Drawings, Landscapes, Latin American Art, Oriental Art, Painting-American, Prints
Collections: Waldo Peirce-oils, watercolors & lithographs & a diverse collection of contemporary American art, Pre-Columbian work, W Zundel Collection: Oriental Materials
Activities: Classes for adults & children; docent training; free family day;; lect open to public, lects for mem only, 2 lect per yr; concerts; gallery talks; tours; lending original objects of art to other mus; book traveling exhibitions 1 per year; exhibs change every 7-8 wks

ASTORIA

M **COLUMBIA RIVER MARITIME MUSEUM,** 1792 Marine Dr, Astoria, OR 97103-3525. Tel 503-325-2323; Fax 503-325-2331; Email information@crmm.org; Web: www.crmm.org; *CEO & Dir* Sam Johnson; *Cur* Jeff Smith; *Mus Shop Mgr* Blue Anderson; *Educ Dir* Betsey Ellerbroek; *VPres* Roger Qualman; *Deputy Dir* David Pearson
Open daily 9:30 AM - 5 PM, cl on Thanksgiving & Christmas; Admis adults $10, seniors $8, children $5, children under 6 free; Estab 1962 as a maritime mus, to collect, preserve & interpret maritime history of Pacific Northwest; Maintains seven galleries of nautical history including works of art; Average Annual Attendance: 97,000; Mem: 2000; dues 30; ann meeting in Nov
Income: $500,000 (financed by admis, sales, mem & individual & corporate donations
Special Subjects: Marine Painting
Collections: Maritime Paintings, Prints & Photography, Ship Models & nautical artifacts, Lightship Columbia
Exhibitions: Rotating & temporary exhibit space in Great Hall; visiting vessels as available
Publications: The Quarterdeck, quarterly
Activities: Classes for adults; volunteer opportunities; docent training; lect open to pub, 6 vis lectrs per yr; tours; competitions; outreach program to schools; individual paintings & original objects of art lent to accredited museums; mus shop sells books, limited edition prints, posters, reproductions, contemporary scrimshaw & jewelry

L **Library,** 1792 Marine Dr, Astoria, OR 97103-3525. Tel 503-325-2323; Fax 503-325-2331; Web: www.crmm.org; *Dep Dir* David Pearson; *Cur* Jeff Smith
Open by appointment only; Estab as reference library for maritime activities relevant to the Northwest; Circ Non-circulating; Library for use on the premises; majority of contents are not relevant to art; Mem: 2000
Income: Financed by admis, trusts, mem dues & donations
Library Holdings: Book Volumes 6000, Cassettes, Clipping Files, DVDs 200, Exhibition Catalogs, Manuscripts, Maps, Motion Pictures, Original Art Works, Pamphlets, Periodical Subscriptions 196, Photographs, Prints, Reproductions
Special Subjects: Drafting, Historical Material, Maps, Marine Painting, Scrimshaw
Collections: Quivira Collection of maps
Publications: The Quarterdeck, quarterly
Activities: Classes for adults & docent training; lects open to pub

BEND

M **HIGH DESERT MUSEUM,** 59800 S Hwy 97, Bend, OR 97702-7962. Tel 541-382-4754; Fax 541-382-5256; Email info@highdesertmuseum.org; Web: www.highdesertmuseum.org; *Dir Finance* Carmen Melamed; *Exec Dir* Dr Dana Whitelaw; *Dir Progs* Dr Christina Cid; *Dir Communs* Sandy Cummings; *Dir Develop* Heather Vihstadt
Open May - Oct 31: daily 9 AM - 5 PM, Nov - April 30: 10 AM - 4 PM; cl Memorial Day, Independence Day, Labor Day, Thanksgiving Day & Christmas; Admis adults $15, seniors $12, youth 5-12 $9, children 4 & under free; Estab 1982 to bring to life natural & cultural history of region; Brooks Gallery, Spirit of the West Gallery & by hand through Memory Gallery, Donald Kerr Birds of Prey Exhibit; Average Annual Attendance: 169,000; Mem: 5000; dues $60 & up; ann meeting in Sept
Income: Financed by mem, donations, grants, admis & sales
Special Subjects: American Indian Art, American Western Art, Painting-American, Period Rooms, Sculpture, Anthropology, Archaeology, Bronzes, Costumes, Drawings, Ethnology, Folk Art, Historical Material, Photography, Textiles
Collections: Sherry Sander Sculpture Collection, Rod Frederick Collection of Prints, Georgia Gerber Sculpture Collection, Joe Halco Sculpture Collection, Philip Hyde Photography Collection
Exhibitions: Spirit of the West; Raptors of the Desert Sky; By Hand Through Memory; Autzen Otter Exhibit; Wildlife, Miller Ranch
Publications: High Desert Quarterly; biannual exhibit catalogues
Activities: Classes for adults and children; docent progs; teacher in-service training; lect open to publ, 5-8 vis lectrs per yr; gallery talks; tours; awards given; book traveling exhibs 3 per yr; organize traveling exhibs; mus shop sells books, magazines, original art, reproductions, prints, slides, folk art, jewelry, educ games & toys, nature items

COOS BAY

M **COOS ART MUSEUM,** 235 Anderson Ave, Coos Bay, OR 97420-1610. Tel 541-267-3901, 267-4877; Fax 541-267-4877; Email adavenport@coosart.org; Web: www.coosart.org; *Exec Dir* Steven Broocks
Open Tues - Fri 10 AM - 4 PM, Sat 1 - 4 PM, cl Sun & Mon; Admis adults $5, seniors & students $2, members no charge; Estab 1950 (relocated to an historic former Post Office Building in downtown district) to bring contemporary art to Southwestern Oregon through colls, exhibs & educ programming; Six galleries; Average Annual Attendance: 14,017; Mem: 356; dues $15-$2,500; annual meeting first quarter of yr
Income: $240,000 (mem, fundraising, grants, fees, government)
Special Subjects: Painting-American, Prints, Sculpture, Woodcuts
Collections: Contemporary American Printmakers, paintings, photographs, sculpture
Exhibitions: Changing exhibits of painting, print, sculpture
Publications: Exhibit announcements, every 6 wks

Activities: Classes & workshops for adults & children; Artists-in-Educ Program for pub schools; lect open to pub; concerts; gallery talks; tours; schols; lend original objects of art to CAM Business Members; rental & sales

M **COOS COUNTY HISTORICAL SOCIETY MUSEUM,** 1210 N Front St, Coos Bay, OR 97420. Tel 541-756-6320; Fax 541-756-6320; Email info@cooshistory.org; Web: www.cooshistory.org; *Dir* Frank Smoot; *Pres* Joe Slack; *VPres* Bill Mast; *Colls Mgr* Vicki Wiese
Open Tues - Sat 10 AM - 4 PM; Admis $2, children 12 & under $1; Estab 1891 to collect, preserve & interpret history of Coos County; Average Annual Attendance: 7,255; Mem: 450; dues $10-$250; annual meeting in June
Income: $60,000 (financed by endowment, mem, admis, sales & donations)
Collections: Maritime objects, Native American artifacts, photographs, tools/ implements of pioneer lifeways, Native American Artifacts
Exhibitions: Pioneer Kitchen; Formal Parlor (c1900); rotating Exhibits; Maritime
Publications: Coos Historical Journal, annual; trimonthly newsletter
Activities: Lect open to pub, vis lectr; lending coll contains 100 items

COQUILLE

A **COQUILLE VALLEY ART ASSOCIATION,** 10144 Hwy 42, Coquille, OR 97423. Tel 541-396-3294; *Pres* Kathy Phillips; *VPres* Pat Haley; *Treas* Jean Waggoner; *Sec* Nancy Shinn; *Bd Mem (Past Pres)* Anna Crosby; *Bd Mem* Patsy Weaver; *Bd Mem* Leland Simpson; *Bd Mem* Robin Hurston; *Bd Mem* DeAnn Shaw; *Bd Mem* Shirley Lee
Open Mon - Fri 10 AM - 3 PM, cl Sun & holidays; No admis fee; Estab 1950 to teach art & art appreciation; Gallery maintained on main floor of Art Assoc owned old refurbished schoolhouse; Average Annual Attendance: 2,900 including classes, workshops & events; Mem: 140; dues $50, seniors $45; ann meetings first Wed in Apr
Income: Financed by mem, auctions, plant & rummage sales, donations, grants, comm on classes, sales & workshops
Library Holdings: Book Volumes, Clipping Files, Periodical Subscriptions
Collections: Permanent coll of paintings 1950 - 2010, largest coll of J Pajares-Barret Paintings
Exhibitions: Exhibits by local members; monthly shows
Publications: Monthly newsletter
Activities: Classes for adults & children; competitions; Youth Show; awards for Youth Art Show, Best of Show for Youth at the Coos Co Fair; individual paintings lent to banks & lobbies; sells original art, miniatures & handicraft

L **Library**, 10144 Hwy 42, Coquille, OR 97423. Tel 541-396-3294; *Pres* Diana Amling
Open to mems only

CORVALLIS

M **THE ARTS CENTER,** 700 SW Madison Ave, Corvallis, OR 97333-4514. Tel 541-754-1551; Email info@theartscenter.net; Web: theartscenter.net; *Exec Dir* Cynthia Spencer; *Cur* Hester Coucke
Open Tues - Sat noon - 5 PM; No admis fee; Estab 1963; Main Gallery & smaller focus gallery in carpenter gothic building; Average Annual Attendance: 12,000; Mem: 800
Activities: Classes for adults & children; lects open to the pub; ArtsCare in area hospitals; mus shop sells original art

M **OREGON STATE UNIVERSITY,** Fairbanks Gallery, 220 SW 26th St, Corvallis, OR 97331. Tel 541-737-5009; Fax 541-737-8686; Email drussell@oregonstate.edu; *Gallery Dir* Douglas Russell
Open Mon - Fri 8 AM - 5 PM, weekends during special events; No admis fee; Estab 1933 to display work of contemporary artists; 120 linear ft; Average Annual Attendance: 5,000
Income: Financed by state appropriation & grants
Collections: Fine art print coll includes: Goya to Rauschenberg, Japanese Print Coll, German Expressionism, Wendel Black Print Coll
Activities: Lect open to public; 3 vis lectrs per yr; gallery talks; concerts; grad senior awards; schols

M **Memorial Union Art Gallery**, 1500 SW Jefferson Ave, Corvallis, OR 97331-8655. Tel 541-737-6371; Fax 541-737-1565; Email susan.bourque@oregonstate.edu; Web: mu.oregonstate.edu/art-gallery; *Exhibits Coordr* Susan Bourque
Open daily 8 AM - 11 PM; Estab 1928; Average Annual Attendance: 50,000
Income: $70,000
Collections: William Henry Price Memorial Collection of Oil Paintings
Exhibitions: Various exhibs, call for details
Publications: Calendar & exhib pamphlets
Activities: Educ prog; lect; exten dept serving the State; individual paintings lent to schools; material available to responsible galleries for fees

M **Giustina Gallery**, 875 SW 26th St, 100 LaSells Stewart Ctr Corvallis, OR 97331-3301. Tel 541-737-2402; Web: oregonstate.edu/lasells/gallery; *Gallery Cur* Tina Green-Price
Open Mon - Fri 8 AM - 5 PM, additional hrs during special events at LaSells Stewart Ctr; No admis fee; Estab 1981 to display work of contemporary artists in northwest; Gallery is 4,800 sq ft
Income: Financed by grants & state appropriation
Exhibitions: Exhibs changing monthly

DALLAS

A **NORTHWEST PASTEL SOCIETY (NPS),** 1785 SW Woodbridge Ct, Dallas, OR 97338. Web: www.nwps.org
Open by appointment; Estab 1988 to promote, encourage & foster creative painting with pastels, encourage pastel artists in their artistic growth & success, promote a fellowship of pastel artists & to promote public awareness about pastel; Mem: dues $30
Income: Financed by mem, gifts & donations
Exhibitions: Open juried international exhibitions & member exhibitions
Publications: Bimonthly newsletter

EUGENE

M **LANE ARTS COUNCIL,** Jacobs Gallery, 1590 Willamette St #200, Eugene, OR 97401. Tel 541-684-5635; Fax 541-485-2478; *Gallery Dir* Tina Rinaldi
Open Tues - Sat 11 AM - 3 PM and during Hult Ctr performances; No admis fee; Estab 1982 for art appreciation & educ; Gallery in lower level of Hult Center for the Performing Arts. Functions as a meeting & reception area, as well as a gallery; Average Annual Attendance: 10,000
Income: $70,000 (financed by gallery sales commissions & cost reimbursements from artists, fundraising & community donations)
Exhibitions: Exhibits selected rotating jury (3 mems) & scheduled by Jacobs Gallery Exhibition Comt

M **LANE COMMUNITY COLLEGE,** LCC Art Gallery, 4000 E 30th Ave, Eugene, OR 97405-0640. Tel 541-463-3431; Fax 541-744-4185; Web: www.lanecc.edu/artgallery
Open Mon - Fri 8 AM - 5 PM; No admis fee; Estab 1970 as an educational gallery exhibiting works by National & Northwest artists; 1 fl; Average Annual Attendance: 15,000
Income: Financed through county funds & state funds; donations & grants
Collections: Contemporary Art
Exhibitions: 16 exhibs per yr
Activities: Lect open to pub, 9 vis lectrs per yr; gallery talks; competitions; schols offered

M **MAUDE KERNS ART CENTER,** 1910 E 15th Ave, Eugene, OR 97403-2094. Tel 541-345-1571; Fax 541-345-6248; Email mkart@pond.net; Web: www.premierelink.com/clients/mkac, www.mkartcenter.org; *Pres* Bryce Krehbiel; *Exec Dir* Hilary Moster
Open Mon - Fri 10 AM - 5:30 PM, Sat Noon - 4 PM; Admis suggested $2 donation; Estab 1950, the Center is a nonprofit educational organization dedicated to promoting quality in the arts & crafts through classes, exhibs, workshops, community projects & special events; The center houses 3 galleries: Henry Korn Gallery, Brockelbank Gallery & Maude I Kerns Salon Gallery. Features monthly shows of contemporary artists, the work of Maude Kerns, Ceramics Co-op; Average Annual Attendance: 12,000; Mem: 500; dues family $55, individual $35; annual meeting in Jan/Feb
Income: $300,000 (financed by mem, class tui, art sales, contributions, grants, proceeds from ann outdoor fundraising festival)
Special Subjects: Ceramics, Crafts, Drawings, Etchings & Engravings, Furniture, Glass, Graphics, Jewelry
Collections: Maude I Kerns Collection
Exhibitions: Every 6 weeks exhibits featuring individual theme & group shows by Pacific Northwest artists; satellite gallery temporarily at 68 W Broadway downtown Eugene
Publications: Quarterly newsletter
Activities: Classes for adults & children; dramatic progs; volunteer prog; workshops; seminars; lects open to pub; concerts; gallery talks; tours; competitions; schols offered; exten dept

M **NEW ZONE VIRTUAL GALLERY,** 164 W Broadway, Eugene, OR 97401-3004; PO Box 21015, Eugene, OR 97402. Tel 541-683-0759; Email nzonegallery@gmail.com; Web: www.newzonegallery.org; *Pres* Dianne Story Cunningham; *VPres* Andrea Ros; *Sec* Karyn Smith; *Treas & Gallery Coodr* S. LaRiccia
Open Mon - Sat noon - 6 PM; No admis fee; Estab 1984 as a modern experimental gallery; Circ 150 yr; A gallery featuring experimental 2-D & 3-D art; Average Annual Attendance: 7,500; Mem: dues $150
Income: financed by membership & sales
Library Holdings: Cards, DVDs, Exhibition Catalogs, Kodachrome Transparencies, Memorabilia, Original Art Works, Original Documents, Pamphlets, Periodical Subscriptions, Photographs, Prints, Records, Reproductions, Video Tapes
Collections: Mike Randells Collection (abstract figurative), Jerry Ross Collection (oils, landscape, figurative, portraits), Experimental Art, Modern Art, Steve LaRiccia, Bob Devine Collection
Exhibitions: Exhibits by members; invitationals
Publications: Exhibit brochures
Activities: Classes for adults & children; lect open to pub; sponsors competitions; gallery talks; tours; artmobile; book 1-2 traveling exhibs per yr; organizes traveling exhibs; sales shop sells prints, reproductions, original art

SOCIETY OF NORTH AMERICAN GOLDSMITHS
For further information, see National and Regional Organizations

M **UNIVERSITY OF OREGON,** Jordan Schnitzer Museum of Art, 1430 Johnson Ln, Eugene, OR 97403; 1223 University of Oregon, Eugene, OR 97403-1205. Tel 541-346-3027; Fax 541-346-0976; Email jschnitz@uoregon.edu; Web: jsma.uoregon.edu; *Exec Dir* Jill Hartzhartz@uoregon.edu; *Assoc Dir Admin & Exhibitions* Kurt Neugebauerkurtn@uoregon.edu; *Business Mgr* Karri Pargeterpargeter@uoregon.edu; *Comm Mgr* Debbie Williamson Smithdebbiews@uoregon.edu; *Chief Cur of Collections* Anne Rose Kitagawaark@uoregon.edu; *Registrar* Miranda Callandermirandac@uoregon.edu; *Dir Education/Outreach* Lisa Abia-Smith
Open Wed 11 AM - 8 PM, Thurs - Sun 11 AM - 5 PM, cl Mon & university holidays; Admis adults $5, seniors $3, children 13 & under, K-12 students, university students, UO faculty & staff & museum members free; Estab 1932 to promote among university students & faculty & the general pub an active & continuing interest in the cultures around the world; Average Annual Attendance: 50,233; Mem: Individual $45; Family/Dual $55; Contributing Member $100 - $1,000
Income: $1,000,000 (financed by state appropriation, endowment income & private donations)
Special Subjects: Asian Art, Oriental Art, Painting-American, Textiles

Collections: Greater Pacific Basin Collection, Asian Art representing the cultures of China, Japan, Cambodia, Korea, Mongolia, Tibet, Russia, American & British works executed in the traditional Oriental manner, Northwest Art, Contemporary Northwest Collection, Cuban, South America
Exhibitions: Various exhibits
Publications: Exhibition catalog
Activities: Classes for adults & children; docent training; school tours; outreach to k-12; lects open to pub, 20+ vis lectrs per yr; gallery talks; concerts; tours; individual paintings & original objects of art lent to other museums that can provide suitable security & climate control; book traveling exhibs1-2 per yr; originate traveling exhibs to other art museums; mus shop sells books, slides, cards, gifts

M **Aperture Photo Gallery - EMU Art Gallery**, 1228 University of Oregon, L110 Erb Memorial Union Eugene, OR 97403. Tel 541-346-4373; Fax 541-346-4400; Web: www.darkwing.uoregon.edu/cultural; *Office Mgr* Rafael Arroyo; *Prog Coordr* Laura Morris
Open daily 7:30 AM - midnight; No admis fee; Estab 1981 to provide space for the display of art & exhibs; Average Annual Attendance: 5,000
Income: Financed by student fees
Collections: EMU Permanent Art Collection
Exhibitions: Periodic art exhibs on display in the Adell McMillan Gallery, Aperture Gallery & Buz Gallery
Activities: Classes for adults; lects open to pub; 1 vis lectr per yr

L **Architecture & Allied Arts Library**, 200 Lawrence Hall, Eugene, OR 97403; 1299 University of Oregon, Eugene, OR 97403-1299. Tel 541-346-3637; Web: www.uoregon.edu.âaaºme; *Reference Librn* Kara List; *Visual Resources Cur* Christine L Sundt; *Head Librn* Ed Peague
Open Mon - Thurs 8 AM - 11 PM, Fri 8 AM - 7 PM, Sat 11 AM - 7 PM, Sun 11 AM - 11 PM; Estab 1915 to provide resources for the courses, degree programs & research of the departments in the School of Architecture & Allied Arts; Primarily for lending
Income: Financed by state appropriation
Library Holdings: Book Volumes 71,000, Exhibition Catalogs, Fiche, Periodical Subscriptions 400, Photographs 30,000, Slides 275,000
Special Subjects: Aesthetics, Architecture, Art History, Interior Design, Landscape Architecture

FOREST GROVE

M **VALLEY ART GALLERY,** 2202 Main St, Forest Grove, OR 97116; Valley Art Assoc, PO Box 333 Forest Grove, OR 97116. Tel 503-357-3703; Email office@valleyart.org; Web: www.valleyart.org; *Educ* April Hoff
Open Mon - Sat 11 AM - 5:30 PM; Estab 1966
Special Subjects: Jewelry, Sculpture, Pottery, Bookplates & Bindings, Glass
Collections: Painting; jewelry; sculpture; pottery; glass; books; fiber art
Exhibitions: Temporary exhibits
Activities: Classes for adults & children

GRANTS PASS

M **GRANTS PASS MUSEUM OF ART,** 229 SW G St, Grants Pass, OR 97526; PO Box 966, Grants Pass, OR 97528-0081. Tel 541-479-3290; Email museum@gpmuseum.com; Web: www.gpmuseum.com; *Exec Dir* Hyla Lipson; *Pres* Nancy Yonally-Coleman; *Mus Shop Mgr* Cindy Kahoun
Open Tues - Sat 10 AM - 5 PM, cl New Year's Day, Easter, Memorial Day, Independence Day, Labor Day, Thanksgiving, Christmas; No admis fee; Estab 1979 - Art Mus & Educ Center; Circ (art libraries) 2,000 vols; Average Annual Attendance: 21,346; Mem: Student & teacher $20-$29, individual $30-$59, family $60-$99, guild $100-$249, patron $250-$499, benefactor $500 & up
Income: Mems & donations
Library Holdings: Audio Tapes, Book Volumes 1,000, CD-ROMs, DVDs, Exhibition Catalogs, Sculpture
Collections: contemporary regional art
Exhibitions: Exhibs throughout the yr
Activities: Classes for adults & children; watercolor slide prog; educ prog for children; workshops; dramatic progs; lects; 6-12 vis lectrs per yr; guided tours; gallery talks; concerts; schols; sales shop sells original art, prints

M **ROGUE COMMUNITY COLLEGE,** Wiseman Gallery - FireHouse Gallery, 3345 Redwood Hwy, Grants Pass, OR 97527-9298. Tel 541-956-7241; Fax 541-471-3588; Email hgreen@roguecc.edu; Web: www.roguecc.edu/galleries; *Dir* Karl Brake; *Gallery Coordr* Heather Green
Call for hours; No admis fee; Estab 1985 to present exhibits of high artistic content in a range of aesthetics which contribute to the educational environment & serve to inspire the community & to serve our community & students with an additional venue for fine art that will inspire, create & promote understanding of the arts & the part they play in our lives
Special Subjects: Painting-American, Prints, Sculpture
Collections: African tools, Japanese woodblock prints, varied paintings
Publications: Exhibit brochures; quarterly catalogues; monthly postals
Activities: Classes for adults & children; docent training; artist talks; workshops; lect open to pub, 10 vis lectrs per yr; gallery talks; competitions

KLAMATH FALLS

M **FAVELL MUSEUM OF WESTERN ART & INDIAN ARTIFACTS,** 125 W Main St, Klamath Falls, OR 97601-4287. Tel 541-882-9996; Fax 541-850-0125; Email favellmusem@favellmuseum.org; Web: www.favellmuseum.org
Open Tues - Sat 10 AM - 5PM, cl Sun, Mon & all major holidays; Admis adults $7, youth 6 - 16 years $4, children under 6 free; Estab 1972 to preserve Western heritage as represented by Indian artifacts & contemporary Western art; Gallery features contemporary western artists combined with art & artifacts displays; Average Annual Attendance: 20,000; Mem: Patron mem $100 per yr
Income: $250,000 (financed by admis, sales & non-profit)
Purchases: Paintings by: Charles Russell, McCarthy, Arlene Hooker Fay & James Bama; 800 works of art by 300 artists
Library Holdings: Book Volumes, Periodical Subscriptions
Special Subjects: American Indian Art, American Western Art, Miniatures, Pottery, Bronzes, Coins & Medals, Dioramas, Historical Material, Jewelry
Collections: Contemporary western art, Western Indian artifacts: pottery, stonework, baskets, bead and quiltwork, miniature firearms, archeological excavation site displays
Publications: A Treasury of Our Western Heritage (book on cross section of museum collection)
Activities: Tours for groups & children; featured artist each month; lects open to pub, 3 vis lectrs per yr; gallery talks; fels offered; mus shop sells books, original art, prints, jewelry, consigned items, & unique gifts

A **KLAMATH ART ASSOCIATION,** 120 Riverside Dr, Klamath Falls, OR 97601-4250; PO Box 955, Klamath Falls, OR 97601-0051. Tel 541-883-1833; *Pres* Will Dawson; *Co-Pres* Ken Barkee
Open Thurs - Sun Noon - 4 PM; No admis fee; Estab 1948 to provide art training for local residents; Gallery estab 1948 to provide display & teaching space for the Assn's activities; Average Annual Attendance: 5,000; Mem: 150; dues $15 - $20; meetings 7 PM third Wed of month
Income: Financed by mem, gallery sales, tuition
Collections: Ceramics, paintings, weaving (owned by members)
Exhibitions: Twelve annually; one mem show, remainder varies
Activities: Classes in painting, drawing, weaving; children's summer art classes; workshops; lect, vis lectr

M **KLAMATH COUNTY MUSEUM,** 1451 Main St, Klamath Falls, OR 97601-5915. Tel 541-883-4208; Fax 541-884-0666; *Dir* Kim Bellabia
Open all year daily 9 AM - 5 PM Tues - Sat, cl Sun & Mon; Admis 12 & up $12, 62 & up, 5-12 $1, under 5 free; Estab 1957 to tell the story of the Klamath County & to preserve & exhibit related material; Average Annual Attendance: 20,000
Income: Financed by county appropriation
Special Subjects: Historical Material
Collections: Indian & pioneer artifacts, four original Rembrandt etchings, Healey paintings, photograph document files
Exhibitions: Rotating exhibitions
Publications: Museum Research Papers
Activities: Mus shop sells books, reproductions of photos & area souvenirs

L **Research Library**, 1451 Main St, Klamath Falls, OR 97601-5915. Tel 541-883-4208; Fax 541-884-0666; Email tourklco@cdsnet.net; *Dir* Kim Bellabia
Open to the pub for reference Tues - Sat 9 AM - 4:30 PM by appointment; Admis research fee; Estab 1955 to collect, preserve, document & interpret the local history
Income: Financed by County General Fund
Library Holdings: Book Volumes 10,000, Clipping Files, Manuscripts, Motion Pictures, Original Art Works, Pamphlets, Photographs 5000, Reels, Slides
Collections: Modoc Indian Books, Documents & Manuscripts
Activities: Guided tours for 4th grade students; school kits lent to area schools; sales shop sells books, prints, paintings, ceramic & other miscellaneous items

M **Baldwin Hotel Museum Annex**, 31 Main St, Klamath Falls, OR 97601-3174. Tel 503-883-4208; Fax 541-884-0666; *Dir* Kim Bellabia
Open Tues - Sat 10 AM - 4 PM, June - Sept; Admis family $6, adults $3, students & seniors $2, under 3 free; A State & national historic landmark purchased by Klamath County in Jan 1978. Restoration of building began in Feb 1978 & it was dedicated as a mus by Oregon's Governor Robert Straub June 3, 1978. Opened to the pub Aug 19, 1978; May be viewed by tour only; Average Annual Attendance: 20,000
Income: Financed by county appropriations
Activities: Guided tours for 5th grade students; Mus shop sells books & original art

MARYLHURST

M **MARYLHURST UNIVERSITY,** The Art Gym, 17600 Pacific Hwy, Marylhurst, OR 97036-7036. Tel 503-636-8141; Fax 503-636-9526; Email artgym@marylhurst.edu; Web: www.marylhurst.edu; *Dir* Terri M Hopkins
Open Tues - Sun Noon - 4 PM; No admis fee; Estab 1980; 3,000 sq ft; Average Annual Attendance: 5,000; Mem: 150; dues $15 - $500
Income: $100,000 (financed by mem, grants & college budget)
Special Subjects: Cartoons, Ceramics, Collages, Drawings, Etchings & Engravings, Folk Art, Furniture, Graphics, Landscapes, Painting-American, Photography, Portraits, Prints, Sculpture
Collections: Contemporary Northwest Art, Installation Art
Publications: Exhibition catalogs
Activities: Lect open to pub, 5 vis lectrs per yr; gallery talks; tours; schols offered; book traveling exhibs; originate traveling exhibs circulate to col galleries & museums; sales shop sells art gym catalogs & books

MEDFORD

A **ROGUE VALLEY ART ASSOCIATION,** Rogue Gallery & Art Center, 40 S Bartlett, Medford, OR 97501. Tel 541-772-8118; Fax 541-772-0294; Email info@roguegallery.org; Web: www.roguegallery.org
Open Tues - Fri 10 AM - 5 PM, Sat 11 AM - 3 PM, cl Sun & Mon; No admis fee, donations accepted; Estab 1960 to provide a full range of programs, exhibits & classes to the region; Gallery 6000 sq ft, 2200 sq ft, sales & rental space, 2000 sq ft & 200 running ft of sliding panels; Average Annual Attendance: 20,000; Mem: 671; dues $20-$500; annual meeting in Oct
Income: Financed by mem dues, grants, fund raising events
Collections: Contemporary Northwest prints
Publications: Newsletter, 6 per yr
Activities: Classes for adults & children; lect open to pub, 2 vis lectrs per yr; gallery talks; tours; schols & fels offered; individual paintings lent through a rental prog to mems; lending coll contains art works, paintings, photographs & sculpture; book traveling exhibs 2-3 per yr; sales shop sells original art, crafts, books, prints, reproductions, prints, sculpture, pottery, jewelry, greeting cards

MONMOUTH

M **WESTERN OREGON UNIVERSITY,** Dan & Gail Cannon Gallery of Art, 345 N Monmouth Ave, Monmouth, OR 97361. Tel 503-838-8340; Fax 503-838-8128; Email boothp@wou.edu; Web: www.wou.edu; *Head Art Dept* Jodie Garrison; *Dir Gallery* Paula Booth
Open Thurs & Fri 8 AM - 5 PM during scheduled exhibits, Mon - Wed 8 AM - 6 PM; No admis fee; Estab to bring contemporary art work to the community & the col for study & visual understanding; Library located in Art Department, Campbell Hall; Average Annual Attendance: 3,000-4,000
Income: $6,000 (financed by state appropriation & student fees)
Exhibitions: Contemporary Northwest Visual Art; rotating faculty & student exhibits
Activities: Educ prog; lects open to pub, 6 vis lectrs per year; gallery talks; tours; competitions with awards; scholarships offered

NEWPORT

M **NEWPORT VISUAL ARTS CENTER,** 777 NW Beach Dr, Newport, OR 97365-3565. Tel 541-265-6540; Email twebb@coastarts.org; Web: www.coastarts.org; *Dir* Tom Webb
Open Tues - Sun 11 AM - 6 PM; Estab 1983
Exhibitions: Temporary exhibits
Activities: Educ progs; classes for adults & children; workshops; community events

PENDLETON

M **PENDLETON CENTER FOR THE ARTS,** 214 N Main St, Pendleton, OR 97801-1644. Tel 541-278-9201; Email director@pendletonarts.org; Web: www.pendletonarts.org; *Exec Dir* Roberta Lavadour; *Develop Dir* JD Smith; *Coordr Educ & Outreach* Kaisa Hill
Open Tues - Fri 10 AM - 4 PM, Sat Noon - 4 PM; Estab 1974; 1,800 sq ft
Collections: Features work by local artists
Exhibitions: Temporary exhibits
Activities: Classes for adults & children

PORTLAND

L **ART INSTITUTES INTERNATIONAL AT PORTLAND,** 1122 NW Davis St, Portland, OR 97209-2911. Tel 503-228-6528; Fax 503-228-4227; Email aipdadm@aii.edu; Web: www.artinstitutes.edu/portland; *Pres* Dr Gregg Crowe; *Dean Educ* Dr Robert Ridel; *Librn* Jennifer Cox
Open daily 7:30 AM - 6 PM, open some evenings, Sat 10 AM - 4:30 PM; No admis fee; Estab 1964 to provide practical instruction in retail merchandising, interior design, display, fashion design, advertising & promotion, fashion history & textiles, industrial design; Average Annual Attendance: 200
Library Holdings: Book Volumes 14,000, Clipping Files, Periodical Subscriptions 120, Slides, Video Tapes 300
Special Subjects: Art History, Costume Design & Constr, Fashion Arts, Furniture, Industrial Design, Interior Design, Textiles
Collections: Collection of Fashion & Costume History Books, Collection in Furniture & Interior Decoration Fields, Collection of Graphic Design & Muffimedia
Exhibitions: Rotating exhib
Activities: Schols offered

M **BLUE SKY GALLERY,** Oregon Center for the Photographic Arts, 122 NW 8th Ave, Portland, OR 97209-3502. Tel 503-225-0210; Fax 503-225-2990; Email bluesky@blueskygallery.org; Web: www.blueskygallery.org; *Exec Dir* Lisa DeGrace; *Mem & Gallery Mgr* Amanda Clem; *Exhibs Mgr* Zemie Barr
Open Tues - Sun Noon - 5 PM, 1st Thurs 6 - 9 PM, New Year's Eve & Christmas Eve noon - 3 PM, cl New Year's Day, Independence Day, Thanksgiving Day, Christmas Day; No admis fee; Estab 1975; Average Annual Attendance: 22,000; Mem: Dues $40 - $1000
Income: 501(c)3 - mems, grants, sales
Library Holdings: Book Volumes
Special Subjects: Photography
Exhibitions: Monthly rotating exhibits
Publications: ann exhib catalog
Activities: Lect open to pub; 12 vis lectrs per yr; gallery talks; mus sells books & prints

L **MULTNOMAH COUNTY LIBRARY,** Henry Failing Art & Music Dept, PO Box 6997, Portland, OR 97228-6997. Tel 503-988-5234 (reference line); Web: www.multcolib.org; *Multnomah County Libr Dir* Vailey Oehlke
Open Mon & Thurs - Sat 10 AM - 6 PM, Tues & Wed 10 AM - 8 PM, Sun noon - 5 PM; No admis fee; Estab 1864 as a pub library service to Multnomah County; Collins Gallery - rotating exhibs of fine & decorative arts, book arts
Library Holdings: Book Volumes over 60,000, Clipping Files 800,000
Special Subjects: Architecture, Art History, Asian Art, Ceramics, Crafts, Decorative Arts, History of Art & Archaeology, Latin American Art, Oriental Art, Painting-American, Painting-European, Painting-French, Painting-Italian, Photography, Pottery, Prints, Sculpture, Watercolors
Exhibitions: Rotating exhibits in the Collins Gallery
Activities: Concerts; gallery talks; tours

L **OREGON COLLEGE OF ART & CRAFT,** (Oregon College of Art Craft) Hoffman Gallery, 8245 SW Barnes Rd, Portland, OR 97225-6349. Tel 503-297-5544; Fax 503-297-9651; Email hoffmangallery@ocac.edu; Web: ocac.edu/galleries/hoffman-gallery; *Pres* Denise Mullen; *Advancement Officer* Heather Ohta; *Communs Mgr* Beth Fridh; *Art Prog Mgr* Shirod Younker
Open daily 10 AM - 5 PM, cl holidays; No admis fee, except for special events & classes; Estab 1907 to teach seven disciplines in the arts & crafts; Hoffman Exhibition Gallery features national & international craftspeople. Maintains library; Average Annual Attendance: 30,000; Mem: 600; dues $35 - $1000; annual meeting in June
Income: Financed by tui, endowment, mem, state appropriation & National Endowments of the Arts, Washington, DC
Library Holdings: Book Volumes, Exhibition Catalogs, Periodical Subscriptions, Slides
Special Subjects: Art History, Asian Art, Bookplates & Bindings, Calligraphy, Carpets & Rugs, Ceramics, Collages, Costume Design & Constr, Crafts, Decorative Arts, Embroidery, Enamels, Etchings & Engravings, Folk Art, Furniture, Glass
Collections: Permanent collection of historic, traditional craftwork
Exhibitions: Annual Juried Student Show; Thesis Show; Craft Biennial; Biennial faculty show
Publications: Course schedules, quarterly; gallery announcements, 12 per yr; newsletter to mems, 2 per yr; 2 yr catalog; 2 yr viewbook
Activities: Classes & workshops for adults; classes for children; BFA & cert prog in crafts; lects open to pub; 10-12 vis lectrs per yr; concerts; gallery talks; tours; schols offered; exten prog serves fine craft: book arts, ceramics, drawing, fibers, metals, photography, wood; mus shop sells books, magazines, original art, prints & crafts

L **Library**, 8245 SW Barnes Rd, Portland, OR 97225-6349. Tel 503-297-5544; Fax 503-297-9651; Web: library.ocac.edu; *Dir Library Servs* Elsa Loftis
Open Mon - Fri 9 AM - 5 PM (during acad terms); Estab 1979; Craft reference library for students & faculty & others interested in crafts
Library Holdings: Book Volumes 5500, DVDs, Exhibition Catalogs, Original Art Works, Pamphlets, Periodical Subscriptions 90, Photographs, Prints, Slides, Video Tapes
Special Subjects: Architecture, Art History, Bookplates & Bindings, Ceramics, Crafts, Decorative Arts, Drawings, Embroidery, Folk Art, Furniture, Glass, Metalwork, Painting-American, Photography, Printmaking, Textiles, Textiles, Handicrafts, Jewelry
Activities: Interlibrary loan services available

A **OREGON HISTORICAL SOCIETY,** Oregon History Museum, 1200 SW Park Ave, Portland, OR 97205-2483. Tel 503-222-1741; Fax 503-221-2035; Email orhist@ohs.org; Web: www.ohs.org; *Exec Dir* Kerry Tymchuk; *Dir Develop* Sue Metzler; *CFO* Sheri Neal; *Dir Information Technology* Dwight Peterson; *Library Dir* Shawna Gandy; *Ed* Eliza Canty-Jones
Open Mon - Sat 10 AM - 5 PM, Sun Noon - 5 PM; Admis adults $11, students seniors $9, children (6-18) $5, children under 6 & mem free; Estab 1873, incorporated 1898, to collect, preserve, exhibit & publish materials pertaining to the Oregon country; Average Annual Attendance: 200,000; Mem: 5,000; dues individual & family $60 - $80, student $25; 10% senior & teacher mem discount; annual meeting Apr
Income: $4,000,000 biennially (financed by state appropriation, mem, grants, gifts & donations)
Library Holdings: Book Volumes, Manuscripts, Maps, Motion Pictures, Original Documents, Photographs, Video Tapes
Special Subjects: Historical Material
Collections: Artifacts, Manuscripts, paintings, photographs, coll by Oregon Country & Oregon State artists
Publications: Oregon Historical Quarterly
Activities: Programming for adults & children; docent training; lects open to the pub; gallery talks; Fellowships; ALA Cleo Award AAM; book traveling exhibs; organize traveling exhibs; mus shop sells books, reproductions & prints

L **Research Library**, 1200 SW Park Ave, Portland, OR 97205. Tel 503-306-5240; Fax 503-219-2040; Email libreference@ohs.org; Web: www.ohs.org; *Library Dir* Shawna Gandy
Open Tues 1 - 5 PM, Wed - Sat 10 AM - 5 PM; See Website; Estab 1898; For reference only
Income: Dept within Oregon Hist Soc
Library Holdings: Audio Tapes, Book Volumes, Cards, Cassettes, Clipping Files, DVDs, Exhibition Catalogs, Fiche, Filmstrips, Kodachrome Transparencies, Lantern Slides, Manuscripts, Maps, Memorabilia, Micro Print, Motion Pictures, Original Art Works, Original Documents, Pamphlets, Periodical Subscriptions, Photographs, Prints, Records, Reels, Slides, Video Tapes
Special Subjects: Architecture, Film, Historical Material, Maps, Manuscripts, Painting-American, Art History, Cartoons, Commercial Art, Drawings, Etchings & Engravings, Ethnology, Graphic Arts, Graphic Design, Illustration, Industrial Design, Interior Design, Landscape Architecture, Landscapes, Photography, Posters, Printmaking, Prints, Stage Design, Theatre Arts, Watercolors
Collections: manuscript colls, Historic photographs & negatives, maps, Oral history, Microfilm, Film, Sound recordings
Activities: Geneology & archives workshops; public programs; exhibits; Books; Prints

M **PORTLAND ART MUSEUM,** 1219 SW Park Ave, Portland, OR 97205-2430. Tel 503-226-2811; Fax 503-226-4842; Email info@pam.org; Web: portlandartmuseum.org; *Dir & Chief Cur* Brian Ferriso; *Arlene & Harold Schnitzer Cur Asian Art* Maribeth Graybill; *Cur Prints & Drawings* Mary Weaver Chapin; *Dir Educ & Pub Rels* Michael Muirawski
Open Tues - Sun 10 AM - 5 PM, Thurs & Fri until 8 PM, cl most holidays; Admis adults $20, adult groups $16, seniors & students 18+ $17, mems, school groups & children under 18 free; Estab 1892 to serve the pub by providing access to art of enduring quality, by educating a diverse audience about art & by collecting & preserving a wide range of art for the enrichment of present & future generations; The mus campus consists of two buildings. The main building, designed by Pietro Belluschi, was built in three stages. The Ayer (1932) & Hirsch (1939) wings comprise the museum's current 19 galleries (26,942 sq ft). The Hoffman wing (1968) is undergoing renovation. Maintains reference library, Jubitz Ctr for Modern & Contemporary Art, Gilkey Ctr fror Graphic Arts & Northwest Film Ctr; Average Annual Attendance: 350,000; Mem: 23,000 households; dues $35 & up; ann meeting in Sept
Income: Financed by admis, endowment, grants, contributions & mem
Library Holdings: Auction Catalogs, Audio Tapes, Book Volumes, Clipping Files, DVDs, Exhibition Catalogs, Other Holdings, Periodical Subscriptions
Special Subjects: African Art, American Indian Art, Antiquities-Greek, Antiquities-Oriental, Asian Art, Bronzes, Calligraphy, Carpets & Rugs, Ceramics,

Coins & Medals, Decorative Arts, Drawings, Eskimo Art, Etchings & Engravings, Graphics, Laces, Miniatures, Oriental Art, Painting-American, Painting-European, Photography, Pre-Columbian Art, Prints, Renaissance Art, Sculpture, Silver
Collections: Alice B Nunn Collection of English Silver, Rasmussen Collection of Northwest Coast Indian & Eskimo Arts, Evan H Roberts Memorial 19th & 20th Century Sculpture Collection, Elizabeth Cole Butler Collection of Native American Art, Gebauer Collection of Cameroon Art, Vivian & Gordon Gilkey Graphics Art Collection, Samuel H Kress Collection of Renaissance Painting & Sculpture, Mary Andrews Ladd Collection of Japanese Prints, Lewis Collection of Classical Antiquities, Hirsh Collection of Oriental Rugs, Lawther Collection of Ethiopian Crosses, William S Ladd Collection of Pre-Columbian Art, Clement Greenberg Collection
Exhibitions: Contemporary Northwest Art Awards
Publications: Annual report; exhibition catalogs; collection catalogs
Activities: Educ dept; workshops for students & adults; docent training; lects open to pub, 20-25 vis lectrs per yr; concerts; gallery talks; tours; competition; individual paintings & original objects of art lent to mus & art galleries; book traveling exhibs 4-5 per yr; originate traveling exhibs; mus shop sells books, reproductions, cards, unique items, handbags, jewelry

L **Crumpacker Family Library**, 1219 SW Park Ave, Portland, OR 97205-2430. Tel 503-276-4215; Fax 503-226-4842; Email library@pam.org; Web: www.pam.org
Open by appointment; Estab 1892 to provide reference for pub & Portland Art Assn members, mus staff; Circ Non-circulating; Located on 2nd Fl of Mark Bldg, maintains reading room
Library Holdings: Auction Catalogs, Audio Tapes, Book Volumes 35,000, CD-ROMs, Cassettes, Clipping Files, DVDs, Exhibition Catalogs, Lantern Slides, Motion Pictures, Original Documents Portland Art Assn Archive, Other Holdings Northwest artist archive, Pamphlets, Periodical Subscriptions 75, Photographs, Records, Slides 5000, Video Tapes 300
Collections: Portland Art Museum Archive, The Portland Center for the Visual Arts (PCVA) Archive, NW Artists Archive, Art Museum Collection Artists File, Contemporary Artists & Photographers Files, Art Subject Files, 300+ videos & DVDs about art

A **Northwest Film Center**, 934 SW Salmon St, Portland, OR 97205-2431; 1219 SW Park Ave, Portland, OR 97205-2430. Tel 503-221-1156 ext 10; Fax 503-294-0874; Email info@nwfilm.org; Web: www.nwfilm.org; *Dir* Bill Foster; *Mem & Develop Assoc* Meg Cook; *PR & Mktg* Benna Gottfried; *Exhib Prog Mgr* Morgen Ruff
Open Tues - Sun 10 AM - 5 PM; Admis gen $9, mem, students & seniors $8, children under 12 $6; Estab 1972 as a regional media arts center; Maintains film archive, circ film library, film & video exhib prog & classes; Average Annual Attendance: 60,000
Income: financed by admissions, grants, contributions, mems, endowments
Library Holdings: Filmstrips, Other Holdings
Exhibitions: Portland International Film Festival; Northwest Film & Video Festival; Jewish Film Festival; Reel Music; Young People's Film & Video Festival; Northwest Tracking
Activities: Film screening prog; courses in film and video; video/ filmmaker-in-schools prog; lects open to pub, 24 vis lectrs per yr; competitions with awards; scholarships & fels offered; exten dept; originate traveling exhibs

M **PORTLAND CHILDREN'S MUSEUM,** 4015 SW Canyon Rd, Portland, OR 97221. Tel 503-233-6500; Fax 503-223-6600; Email info@portlandcm.org; Web: www.portlandcm.org; *Exec Dir* Ruth Shelly; *Dir Teaching & Learning* Susan Harris MacKay; *Dir External Relations* Stephanie Tolk; *Dir Exhibs* Somya Singh
Open daily 9 AM - 5 PM; Admis general $10.75, ages 65+ & military $9.75, mems & infants under 1 free; Estab 1946; mission is to inspire imagination, creativity & the wonder of learning in children & adults by inviting moments of shared discovery. Mus includes Opal School & Mus School as resources for early childhood development & research; Mus has 3 art studios, 3 party rooms, cafe & mus store; Average Annual Attendance: 300,000; Mem: 6,500; dues premier plus $250, premier $135, family plus $100, family & grandparent $85, 1 + 1 $65
Income: Financed 85% by earned income & 15% contribution
Collections: Children's art, natural history, toys, dollhouses, miniatures, multicultural artifacts relating to children's culture, teaching coll
Exhibitions: Water Works; Vroom Room; Baby's Garden; The Pet Hospital; Grasshopper Grocery & Butterfly Bistro; The Clay Studio; The Garage; Dig Pit; Play It Again Theatre; Wonder Corner; Treehouse Adventure; Building Bridgetown; Twilight Trail & more
Activities: Classes for adults & children; hands-on art activity for children; mus shop sells educ books & toys for children, creative teaching material for teachers, parents & caregivers

M **PORTLAND COMMUNITY COLLEGE,** North View Gallery, 12000 SW 49th Ave, Portland, OR 97219-7199. Tel 503-977-4269; Fax 503-977-4874; Web: www.pcc.edu; *Dir* Mark Smith
Open Mon - Fri 8 AM - 4 PM, Sat 11 AM - 4 PM; No admis fee; Estab 1970; Gallery's primary focus on contemporary Northwest artists, through solo shows, group invitations, installations & new genres; Average Annual Attendance: Over 20,000 in the Portland Metro area
Income: Financed by the college
Exhibitions: Contemporary art of the Northwest
Activities: Lect open to pub; 4-6 vis lectrs per yr; schols & fels offered

M **PORTLAND STATE UNIVERSITY,** Littman Gallery, 1825 SW Broadway, Rm 250 Portland, OR 97201-3256; PO Box 751, Portland, OR 97207-0751. Tel 503-725-5656; Email littmanandwhite@gmail.com; Web: littmanwhite.tumblr.com; *Admin Coordr* Sasha Jones; *Preparator* Holly Richwine; *Visual Arts Cur* Carlin Brown; *Visual Arts Cur* Paul Maziar; *Publicity Coordinator* Andrew Jankowski
Open Mon - Weds 12 PM - 5 PM; Thurs/Fri 12 - 6 PM; No admis fee; Estab 1969, seeks to cultivate artistic experience and educ on campus and in community & provide a platform for contemporary work; Gallery space has 1500 sq ft; Average Annual Attendance: 8,386
Income: Financed by PSU; non-profit
Library Holdings: Book Volumes, CD-ROMs, DVDs, Exhibition Catalogs, Maps, Original Art Works, Original Documents, Pamphlets, Photographs
Exhibitions: 10-11 exhibs annually
Publications: OCCSNL readings & performances & artist talks
Activities: Lect open to pub; 5 vis lectrs per yr; gallery talks

M **White Gallery**, 1825 SW Broadway, Room 289 Portland, OR 97201-3256; PO Box 751, Smith Ctr Portland, OR 97207-1751. Tel 503-725-5656; Fax 503-725-5080; Email littmanandwhite@gmail.com; Web: littmanwhite.tumblr.com; *Gallery Dir* Sasha Jones; *Co-Curator* Carlin Brown; *Co-Curator* Paul Maziar; *Publicity Coordinator* Andrew Jankawski
Open Mon - Fri 8 AM - 10 PM, Sat 9 AM - 7 PM; No admis fee; Estab 1970 as a student operated gallery exhibiting works by professional artists representing primarily photog; Average Annual Attendance: 44,000
Income: Financed by PSU
Collections: Permanent collection contains work by local professional artists with a few nationally recognized artists
Exhibitions: 11 exhibitions annually
Activities: Lect open to pub; gallery talks; individual paintings & original objects of art lent to other schools or museums; lending coll contains original prints, paintings & sculpture

M **REED COLLEGE,** Douglas F Cooley Memorial Art Gallery, 3203 SE Woodstock Blvd Portland, OR 97202-8199. Tel 503-777-7251; Fax 503-788-6691; Web: www.reed.edu; *Dir* Stephanie Snyder
Open Tues - Sun Noon - 5 PM, Drawings Room open by appointment for study of works on paper; No admis fee; Estab 1989 to enhance the teaching of art, art history & the humanities. The prog brings to the col & the community exhibs of art from a variety of periods & traditions as well as significant contemporary art not otherwise available in the Northwest
Special Subjects: Prints
Collections: Pre-20th century prints, 20th century prints, drawings, paintings, photographs & sculptures
Publications: Brochures; catalogues
Activities: Pub openings; lects; gallery talks

A **REGIONAL ARTS & CULTURE COUNCIL,** Metropolitan Center for Public Arts, 1120 SW 5th Ave, Portland, OR 97209; 411 NW Park, Ste 101, Portland, OR 97209-3318. Tel 503-823-5111; Fax 503-823-5432; Email info@racc.org; Web: www.racc.org; Others 503-823-6868; *Interim Exec Dir* Jeff Hawthorne; *Dir Opers* Cynthia Knapp; *Communs Assoc* Jeff Hawthorne; *Chmn* Mike Golub
Open Mon - Fri 8:30 AM - 5 PM; No admis fee; Estab 1973, to promote and encourage progs to further the development and pub awareness of and interest in the visual and performing arts
Income: Financed by city & county appropriation
Purchases: Visual Chronicle of Portland, 2 percent for Public Art projects, Portable Works Coll
Collections: Works by local artists
Publications: Newsletter, bimonthly
Activities: Artist in Residence Program for elementary schools; competitions with awards; schols offered; individual paintings & original objects of art lent

M **RONNA AND ERIC HOFFMAN GALLERY OF CONTEMPORARY ART,** 0615 SW Palatine Hill Rd, MSC 95 Portland, OR 97219. Tel 503-768-7687; Fax 503-768-7682; Email gallery@lclark.edu; Web: www.lclark.edu/hoffman_gallery; *Dir* Linda Tesner
Open Tues - Sun 11 AM - 4 PM; Circ No admis fees
Collections: works by contemporary artists; paintings; sculpture; drawings

M **UNIVERSITY OF PORTLAND,** Buckley Center Gallery, 5000 N Willamette Blvd, Portland, OR 97203-5798. Tel 503-943-7792; Fax 503-943-7805; Email bognar@up.edu; *Dir* Pat Bognar
Open Mon - Fri 8:30 AM - 8 PM, Sat - Sun 8:30 AM - 4 PM; Estab 1977
Exhibitions: Noel Thomas; Terry Waldron; Martha Wehrle

L **UNIVERSITY OF PORTLAND,** Wilson W Clark Memorial Library, 5000 N Willamette Blvd, Portland, OR 97203-5743. Tel 503-943-7111; Fax 503-943-7491; Email library@up.edu; *Dean* Xan Arch; *Reference Librn* Heidi Senior; *Head Colls Servs* Susan Hinken
Open Mon - Thurs 7 AM - 2 AM, Fri 7 AM - 9 PM, Sat 10 AM - 9 PM, Sun 10 AM - 2 AM; Estab 1901 to support the university curriculum; Circ 50,000; Maintains an art gallery with a rotating exhibit
Income: Financed through the univ
Library Holdings: Book Volumes over 121,000, Compact Disks, Fiche, Filmstrips, Manuscripts, Maps, Original Art Works, Original Documents, Periodical Subscriptions, Records, Sculpture, Slides, Video Tapes over 4000
Exhibitions: Rotating exhibs

M **UPFOR GALLERY,** 929 NW Flanders St, Portland, OR 97209. Tel 503-227-5111; Email welcome@upforgallery.com; *Prin* Theo Downes-Le Guin; *Dir* Melissa Soltesz; *Gallery Mgr* Heather Lee Birdsong; *Registrar* Caitlin Motley; *Preparator* Daniel Williams
Tues - Sat 11 AM - 6 PM & by appointment; Estab 2013 to present artists' works which examine contemporary issues & challenge traditional practices
Exhibitions: Temporary exhibits

A **WEST HILLS UNITARIAN FELLOWSHIP,** The Doll Gardner Art Gallery, 8470 SW Oleson Rd, Portland, OR 97223-6977. Tel 503-246-3351 ext 4; Email arts@whuuf.org; Web: www.whuuf.net
Open (check website for hours or call); No admis fee; Estab 1970 gallery has exhibited work of a wide range of artists& organizations from the celebrated to the emerging; The entire sanctuary wall space a large gallery & the building is light, airy with a woodsy backdrop
Income: $30,000 (financed by mem)
Collections: Paintings, wall sculptures by local artists
Publications: Bulletin, weekly; newsletter, monthly
Activities: Classes for adults & children; dramatic progs; lect open to pub, 8 vis lectrs per yr; concerts

ROSEBURG

PASTEL SOCIETY OF OREGON
For further information, see National and Regional Organizations

SAINT BENEDICT

L **MOUNT ANGEL ABBEY LIBRARY,** 1 Abbey Dr, Saint Benedict, OR 97373; PO Box 497, Saint Benedict, OR 97373-0497. Tel 503-845-3102; Email victoria.ertelt@mtangel.edu; Web: www.mountangelabbey.org/abbey-library; *Admin* Victoria Ertelt
Open Sun 1 - 4 PM, Mon - Thurs 8:30 AM - 5 PM & 6:30 - 9:30 PM, Fri 8:30 AM - 5 PM, Sat 10 AM - 4 PM; No admis fee; Estab 1882; The library serves Mount Angel Abbey and Seminary & the pub. It sponsors art exhibits in the foyer designed for this purpose & makes the auditorium available for concerts
Library Holdings: Book Volumes 275,000, Fiche 10, Framed Reproductions 30, Manuscripts, Original Art Works 100, Periodical Subscriptions 1000, Prints 30
Exhibitions: Local artists; changes monthly
Publications: Angelus, quarterly
Activities: Classes for adults

SALEM

A **SALEM ART ASSOCIATION,** 600 Mission St SE, Salem, OR 97302-6203. Tel 503-581-2228; Web: www.salemart.org; *Exec Dir* Debby Leahy
Open Tues - Fri 10 AM - 5 PM, Sat & Sun Noon - 5 PM; No admis fee; Estab 1919 to collect, preserve & interpret history & art; Sales gallery & exhib galleries featuring contemporary art; Average Annual Attendance: 125,000; Mem: 1500; dues $25; ann meeting in Sept
Income: $900,000 (financed by sales, Salem Art Fair & Festival special fundraisers, admis, mem & donations)
Exhibitions: 10 exhibits yearly in 2 galleries
Publications: Art Matters newsletter, 3 per year; class schedule, 5 per year
Activities: Classes for adults & children; lect open to pub; gallery talks; sales shop sells original art

M **Bush Barn Art Center**, 600 Mission St SE, Salem, OR 97302-6203. Tel 503-581-2228; Web: www.salemart.org; *Exec Dir* Sandra Burnett; *Gallery Dir* Catherine Alexander
Open Tues - Fri 10 AM - 5 PM, Sat & Sun Noon - 5 PM; No admis fee; Estab 1965 to exhibit & interpret works of 20th & 21st century fine art & crafts; Houses the A N Bush Gallery, Focus Gallery & Camas Gallery which features 24 exhibs ea yr & a gift gallery of Northwest art & crafts; Average Annual Attendance: 31,000
Activities: Docent training; lects open to pub; concerts; gallery talks; awards; individual paintings rented to mems only (2-D work only); sales shop sells original art, reproductions & prints

M **Bush House Museum**, 600 Mission St SE, Salem, OR 97302-6203. Tel 503-363-4714; Email bushhouse@salemart.org; Web: www.salemart.org; *Bush House Mus Dir* Ross Sutherland
Open visit website; Admis visit website; Estab 1953, illuminating Oregon history & culture associated with the lives & legacy of Salem's Bush family; 100 acre gentleman farm now furnished house mus (1878); art center & city park; cultural heritage & bus history of Salem; Average Annual Attendance: 5,000
Collections: Original furnishings, decorative arts, fine arts & wallpapers
Activities: Educ progs; special events & contemporary exhibs; guided tours

L **Archives**, 600 Mission St SE, Salem, OR 97302-6203. Tel 503-363-4714; Web: www.salemart.org; *Bush House Coordr* Patricia Narcum-Perez
Open Tues - Sun Noon - 4 PM by appointment only; No admis fee; Estab 1953; Circ Non-circulating; For reference only
Library Holdings: Audio Tapes, Book Volumes 150, Cassettes, Clipping Files, Manuscripts, Memorabilia, Motion Pictures, Photographs, Video Tapes
Collections: Bush family papers 1840-1950
Exhibitions: Victorian Historic House with furniture

M **WILLAMETTE UNIVERSITY,** Hallie Ford Museum of Art, 700 State St, Salem, OR 97301; 900 State St, Salem, OR 97301-3931. Tel 503-370-6855; Fax 503-375-5458; Email museum-art@willamette.edu; Web: www.willamette.edu/arts/hfma; *Dir* John Olbrantz; *Asst to Dir* Carolyn Harcourt; *Coll Cur* Jonathan Bucci; *Educ Cur* Elizabeth Garrison; *Designer/Preparator* David Andersen; *Mem/Pub Rels Mgr* Andrea Foust
Open Tues - Sat 10 AM - 5 PM; Sun 1 PM - 5PM; General: $6; Seniors (55+) $4; student (18+ with ID) $3; $4 per person school groups (with reservation); Tuesdays free; Estab 1998 to support the liberal arts curriculum of Willamette Univ & to serve as an intellectual & cultural resource for the campus, the City of Salem & surrounding area; The Hallie Ford Mus of Art maintains a 27,000 sq ft facility which includes permanent galleries devoted to colls of regional art, Native American Art, & Asian, European & American Art; Average Annual Attendance: 30,000; Mem: 625 mem; Dues $25 - $1,000
Income: Financed by endowment, mem, admissions, grants, sales
Collections: Regional art; Native American art; American, European, Asian art; American, European, Asian works on paper; African and Oceanic art; Meso-American Art
Exhibitions: Temporary exhibs devoted to historic & contemporary art
Publications: Newsletter - Brushstrokes; Collection Guides; Exhibition Catalogues
Activities: Docent training; lect; gallery talks; films; workshops; artist demonstrations; symposia; poetry readings; concerts; originates traveling exhibs to regional & nat museums; mus shop sells books

SPRINGFIELD

A **EMERALD EMPIRE ART ASSOCIATION,** Emerald Art Center, 500 Main St, Springfield, OR 97477-5469. Tel 541-726-8595; Fax 541-726-2954; Email admin@emeraldartcenter.org; Web: www.emeraldartcenter.org; *Pres (2013)* Chris Mackay; *Gallery Dir* Paula Goodbar
Open Tues - Sat 11 AM - 4 PM; No admis fee; Estab 1957 to promote cultural arts in Springfield & surrounding areas; Downtown area is 12,000 sq ft; Average Annual Attendance: 10,800; Mem: 220; dues assoc mem $175, contributing mems $75; monthly meetings 3rd Tues every other month
Income: Financed by mem dues, commission on sales, fundraisers, revenue from workshops
Library Holdings: Book Volumes, Exhibition Catalogs, Periodical Subscriptions
Special Subjects: African Art, Afro-American Art, American Indian Art, American Western Art, Asian Art, Bronzes, Calligraphy, Ceramics, Collages, Crafts, Decorative Arts, Drawings, Folk Art, Glass, Graphics, Hispanic Art, Landscapes, Latin American Art, Metalwork, Mexican Art, Miniatures, Oriental Art, Photography, Porcelain, Pottery, Prints, Sculpture, Southwestern Art, Stained Glass, Textiles, Watercolors, Woodcarvings
Collections: Paintings donated by workshop teachers & guest artists
Exhibitions: Exhibs bimonthly at local shopping malls & convention centers; Host to Springfield Mayor Annual Art Show; Emerald Spring Exhibition (nat juried show); Photo Zone Annual Juried Show; Photography at Oregon Photographic Auction
Publications: Monthly newsletter
Activities: Classes for adults & children, material available to anyone; lect open to pub, 2 vis lectrs per year; gallery talks; tours; picture of the month award; competitions; awards; schols offered; individual paintings & original objects of art lent; originates traveling exhibs; gift shop sells original art, reproductions, prints, jewelry

THE DALLES

A **THE DALLES ART ASSOCIATION,** The Dalles Art Center, 220 E 4th St, The Dalles Art Ctr & Gallery The Dalles, OR 97058-2206; PO Box 1026, The Dalles, OR 97058-9026. Tel 541-296-4759; Email thedallesart@embarqmail.com; Web: www.thedallesartcenter.org; *Exec Dir* Carmen Toll
Open Tues - Sat 11 AM - 5 PM; No admis fee; Estab 1959 for presentation of community arts activities; Gallery maintained; Average Annual Attendance: 5,000 +; Mem: 250; dues corporate $250, sponsor $100, bus $75, family $45, individual $35, senior $25; meeting held second Tues of each month
Income: Financed by dues, fundraising events, grants, sponsorships & sales
Exhibitions: Member & guest exhibits; state services exhibits
Publications: Bimonthly newsletter
Activities: Art classes for adults & children; docent training; lect open to pub; competitions; cash for awards; 2 open judged & juried shows per yr; gallery shop sells original art, jewelry, pottery, basketry, glass

TOLEDO

M **YAQUINA RIVER MUSEUM OF ART,** 151 NE Alder St, Toledo, OR 97391-1521. Tel 541-336-1907; Fax 541-336-1907; Email yrartmuseum@charter.net; Web: www.michaelgibbons.net/museum.htm; *Cur* Michael Gibbons
Open Fri-Sun 11AM-6PM
Collections: artwork by Michael Gibbons & other local artists

WOODBURN

M **WOODBURN ART CENTER,** Glatt House Gallery, 2251 N Boones Ferry Rd, Woodburn, OR 97071-9669. Tel 503-982-6450; Email woodburnartcenter@live.com; Web: woodburnartcenter.com; *Bd Pres* Colleen Vancil; *VPres* Judy Massaia; *Treas* Jacque Buchanan; *Secy* Linda Reeves
Open Mon 10 AM - 3 PM, Tues - Sat Noon - 3 PM, cl Sun; Estab 1966 to promote art appreciation and development in the community; Mem: dues $10-$750
Special Subjects: Sculpture
Exhibitions: Temporary exhibits
Activities: Classes for adults & children

PENNSYLVANIA

ALLENTOWN

M **ALLENTOWN ART MUSEUM,** 31 N 5th St, Allentown, PA 18101-1605. Tel 610-432-4333; Fax 610-434-7409; Email askus@allentownartmuseum.org; Web: www.allentownartmuseum.org; *Pres & CEO* David Mickenberg; *Mus Store Mgr* Sharon Yurkanin; *Bldg Operations Mgr* Tom Edge; *Chmn* Dolores A Laputka Esq; *VPres Curatorial Affairs* Elaine Mehalakes, PhD; *Mgr Mktg & PR* Chris Potash; *Acting Registrar* Christopher Berner
Open Wed - Sat 11 AM - 4 PM, Sun noon - 4 PM, every 3rd Thurs 11 AM - 8 PM, cl holidays; Admis adults $12, seniors 60 & up, students, children 6 & up $10, children 5 & under free,; Estab 1939 to acquire, protect, display & interpret the visual arts from the past & present, world wide; Building & land cover a 17,000 sq ft gallery space; Mem: 2,550; see website for dues info
Income: $850,000 (financed by endowment, mem, city, county & state appropriation & contributions)
Special Subjects: Architecture, Baroque Art, Bronzes, Ceramics, Decorative Arts, Drawings, Embroidery, Etchings & Engravings, Folk Art, Furniture, Historical Material, Jade, Jewelry, Laces, Landscapes, Oriental Art, Painting-American, Painting-Dutch, Painting-European, Painting-Flemish, Painting-German, Painting-Italian, Period Rooms, Pewter, Photography, Porcelain, Prints, Silver, Sculpture
Collections: Samuel H Kress Collection of European Paintings & Sculpture, c 1350-1750 (Bugiardini, Lotto, de Heem, Rembrandt, Ruisdael, Steen & others), textile study room, Frank Lloyd Wright period room, 1912, American paintings & sculpture

Publications: Calendar of events, quarterly; catalogs of major exhibitions; descriptive gallery handouts
Activities: Classes for adults & children; docent training; 3 family events each yr; lects open to pub; gallery talks; tours; competitions; concerts; mus shop sells books, jewelry & other art related games & stationery; Art Ways, interactive children's gallery

M **LEHIGH VALLEY HERITAGE CENTER,** 432 W Walnut St, Allentown, PA 18102-5428. Tel 610-435-1074; Fax 610-435-9812; Email lchs@voicenet.com; Web: www.lchs.museum; *Exec Dir* Joseph Garrera; *Cur Coll* Andree Mey; *Coll Mgr* Morgan McMillan; *Archivist* Jan Ballard; *Cur Educ* Sarah Nelson; *Dir Develop* David Voellinger; *Mem Coordr* Linda Buesgen; *Research Librn* Carol Herrity; *Bookkeeper* Elaine Johaneman; *Educ Asst* Lorinda Macaulay; *Properties Mgr* Beverly Renaldi; *Office Mgr* Pat Arnold; *VPres* Raymond Holland; *VChmn* Robert M McGovern
Open George Taylor House: by appointment only; Trout Hall: June - Oct Tues - Sun 1 - 4 PM, Apr - May & Sept - Nov Sat & Sun 1 - 4 PM; Troxell-Stickel House: June - Oct Sat & Sun 1 - 4 PM; Lehigh County Mus: Mon - Fri 9 AM - 4 PM, Sat & Sun 1 - 4 PM; Claussville School, Lock Ridge Furnace, Saylor Cement Kilns, Haines Mill & Frank Buchman House: May - Sept Sat & Sun 1 - 4 PM; Admis $2 for non-mems at Taylor House, Trout Hall, Troxell-Steckel House, Claussville School; others free; Estab 1904 for coll, preservation & exhib of Lehigh County history; Lock Ridge Furnace Mus 1868, Frank Buchman House 1894, Haines Mill Mus 1760 & 1909, Lehigh County Mus 1814-1914, Trout Hall 1770, George Taylor House 1768, Saylor Cement Industry Mus 1868, Troxell-Steckel House 1756, Claussville One-Room Schoolhouse 1893; Average Annual Attendance: 36,000; Mem: 1,300; dues $15 - $1,000; ann meeting 3rd Wed in Apr
Income: $900,000 (financed by endowment, mem, tax-based support, foundations, corporate & bus support)
Special Subjects: Anthropology, Archaeology, Architecture, Costumes, Crafts, Decorative Arts, Dioramas, Drawings, Embroidery, Ethnology, Folk Art, Furniture, Glass, Historical Material, Leather, Manuscripts, Maps, Painting-American, Period Rooms, Pewter, Photography, Porcelain, Portraits, Textiles, Watercolors
Collections: Extensive regional history archives, 10,000 books, 65,000 photographs & negatives, 1600 linear feet of pamphlets, documents, newspapers, maps, microfilm, 32,000 objects related to social history, daily life, agriculture & industry, textiles, fine & folk art, architectural elements, bus, American Indians, decorative arts, furniture, historic structures & elements of historic structures
Publications: Proceedings, biennial; Town Crier, quarterly newsletter; occasional books & monographs
Activities: Workshops; lects open to pub, 15 vis lectrs per yr; concerts; tours; mus shop sells books, pamphlets & local souvenirs

L **Scott Andrew Trexler II Library**, Old Court House, Hamilton at Fifth, Allentown, PA; 432 W Walnut St, Allentown, PA 18102. Tel 610-435-1074; Fax 610-435-9812; Web: www.voicenet.com/~lchs; *Librn & Archivist* Jan Ballard; *Reference Librn* Carol M Herrity
Open Mon - Sat 10 AM - 4 PM; No admis fee for mems, $5 for non-mems; Estab 1974; For reference only; Average Annual Attendance: 2,000
Income: $45,000
Purchases: $14,000
Library Holdings: Audio Tapes 10, Book Volumes 10,000, Cassettes 200, Framed Reproductions, Lantern Slides 1000, Manuscripts 1000, Memorabilia 1000, Original Art Works, Pamphlets 200, Periodical Subscriptions 20, Photographs 50,000, Prints, Reels 400
Collections: Allentown imprints, broadsides, Civil War, early German newspapers, fraktur, Native American materials, photographs
Publications: Proceedings, semi-annual; Town Crier

M **MUHLENBERG COLLEGE,** Martin Art Gallery, 2400 Chew St, Allentown, PA 18104-5586. Tel 484-664-3467; Fax 484-664-3113; Email pnicholson@muhlenberg.edu; Web: www.muhlenberg.edu; *Dir* Paul Nicholson
Open Tues - Sat 12 PM - 8PM; No admis fee; Estab 1976; The building was designed by architect Philip Johnson; the focal point of its design & function is a 220 ft glass-covered galleria which bisects the structure; Average Annual Attendance: 7,000
Income: Financed by the col
Special Subjects: American Western Art, Drawings, Etchings & Engravings, Painting-American, Photography, Prints, Religious Art, Sculpture, Woodcuts
Collections: Master prints, Rembrandt, Durer, Whistler, Goya, 20th century American & contemporary art, Edward S Curtis Photogravures of the North American Indian
Exhibitions: Year round schedule of 6 to 8 exhibitions
Publications: Exhibition catalogs
Activities: Lect open to pub; films; gallery talks

AUDUBON

M **NATIONAL AUDUBON SOCIETY,** John James Audubon Center at Mill Grove, 1201 Pawlings Rd Audubon, PA 19403. Tel 610-666-5593; Fax 484-831-5305; Email millgrove@audubon.org; Web: pa.audubon.org/centers-mill-grove.html; *Dir* Jean Bochnowski; *Senior Cur* Nancy Powell; *Facilities Coordr* Susannah Conard; *Admin Coordr* Linda Ridgway; *Educ Coordr* Carrie Ashley
Open Tues - Sat 10 AM - 4 PM, Sun 1 - 4 PM, cl Mon & major holidays; Admis adults $4, seniors (60 & over) $3, children $2; Estab 1951 to display the major artwork of John James Audubon, artist-naturalist, who made Mill Grove his first home in America 1803-06; This is a National Historic Landmark & features original artworks by Audubon, plus examples of all his major publs; Average Annual Attendance: 20,000
Library Holdings: Auction Catalogs, Book Volumes, Manuscripts, Original Art Works
Special Subjects: Painting-American, Period Rooms, Prints
Collections: Birds of America (double elephant folio, 4 vols, Audubon & Havell), Birds of America (first ed Octavo, 7 vols, Audubon, Lithos by Bowen), Quadrupeds of North America (Imperial size, 2 vols, Audubon & Bachmann), Quadrupeds of North America (Octavo, 3 vols, Audubon, Lithos by Bowen), Birds of America, Art, work, and life of artist John James Audubon, 19th Century American Art, Ornithological Art of the 20th Century
Exhibitions: Annual Juried Art Show in April
Activities: Classes for adults & children; docent training; lects open to pub; gallery talks, tours; ann award Friends of A Feather: for art in serv of nature/wildlife conservation; mus shop sells books, prints, original art, reproductions, bird related items, work by local artists & artisans

BETHLEHEM

M **ARTSQUEST,** (Banana Factory), Banana Factory, 25 W Third St Bethlehem, PA 18015-1238; ArtsQuest Center at SteelStacks, 101 Founders Way Bethlehem, PA 18015. Tel 610-332-1300; Web: www.bananafactory.org, www.steelstacks.org; *Dir Visual Art & Educ* Debra Miller
Open Gallery 11AM-4PM, Building Mon-Fri 8AM-9:30PM, Sat-Sun 8:30AM-5PM Call to verify; No admis fee; Making the arts accessible to the community; Two gallery spaces: Banana Factory & SteelStacks; Average Annual Attendance: 12,000
Special Subjects: Glass, Jewelry, Photography
Collections: paintings; photographs; sculpture
Exhibitions: 22 exhibs per yr
Activities: Classes for adults & children; Olympus InVision Photo Festival; lects open to pub; gallery talks; tours; sponsoring of competitions; schols

M **LEHIGH UNIVERSITY ART GALLERIES,** Museum Operation, 420 E Packer Ave, Zoellner Arts Ctr Bethlehem, PA 18015-3010. Tel 610-758-3615; Fax 610-758-4580; Email rv02@lehigh.edu; Web: www.luag.org; *Dir Exhib & Coll* Ricardo Viera; *Asst to Dir* Denise Stangl; *Ed* Patricia Kandianis; *Coll Mgr* Mark Wonsidler; *Coll Asst* Vasti DeEsch; *Preparator* Jeffrey Ludwig; *Asst Preparator* Khalil Allaik
Open Mon - Fri 9 AM - 10 PM, Sat 9 AM - Noon, cl Sun (DuBois Gallery), Wed - Sat 11 AM - 5 PM, Sun 1 - 5 PM (Zoellner Gallery); Mon - Thurs 9 AM - 10 PM, Fri 9 AM - 5 PM (Siegel Gallery Iacocca Hall); No admis fee; Estab to bring diverse media & understanding to the Lehigh students & general pub of the Lehigh Valley area; Collection is maintained in three galleries; DuBois Gallery has four floors of approx 250 running ft of wall hanging space per floor; Zoellner Gallery has two floors of exhibition space; Average Annual Attendance: 25,000 (per all galleries)
Income: Financed by endowment & gifts
Special Subjects: African Art, Afro-American Art, Antiquities-Byzantine, Antiquities-Etruscan, Antiquities-Oriental, Antiquities-Roman, Architecture, Bronzes, Coins & Medals, Etchings & Engravings, Folk Art, Graphics, Hispanic Art, Landscapes, Latin American Art, Painting-American, Painting-British, Painting-European, Painting-French, Painting-Japanese, Painting-Spanish, Photography, Photography, Porcelain, Portraits, Portraits, Posters, Pre-Columbian Art, Pre-Columbian Art, Primitive art, Prints, Sculpture, Textiles, Watercolors, Woodcuts, Prints
Collections: Baker Collection of Chinese Porcelain, Phillip & Muriel Berman Collection of Japanese prints, Paintings & Outdoor Sculpture, Dreyfus Collection of French Paintings. Folk & Outsider Art, Grace Collection of Paintings, Ralph Wilson Collection of American Paintings & Graphics, Prasse Collection of Prints, Fearnside Collection of European Old Master Prints & Drawings, Langermann Collection of Pre-Columbian & Ethnographic Sculpture, Mr & Mrs Franklin H Williams Collection of African Art, Photography Collection, Latin American Collection, Contemporary Prints & Drawings Collection
Publications: Calendar, twice per year; exhibition catalogs
Activities: University classes & workshops for children; docent training; lects open to pub, 4 vis lectrs per yr; gallery talks; tours; individual paintings & original objects of art lent to other schools & galleries; originate traveling exhibs; gallery shop sells books, original art, prints, handcrafted ceramics & jewelry

M **MORAVIAN COLLEGE,** Payne Gallery, Hurd Campus, 99 W Church St Bethlehem, PA 18018; 1200 Main St, Bethlehem, PA 18018-6650. Tel 610-861-1675, 861-1680 (office); Fax 610-861-1682; Email medjr01@moravian.edu; dradycki@moravian.edu; Web: www.moravian.edu; *Dir* Dr Diane Radycki; *Asst to Dir* David Leidich; *Chmn Art Dept* Angela Fraleigh
Open Tues - Sun noon - 4 PM; No admis fee; Estab 1982 to present historic & contemporary art to a diverse audience; Main floor & mezzanine have a combined total of 200 running ft; Average Annual Attendance: 15,000
Income: Financed by endowment & through the col
Purchases: Coll of paintings by W Elmer Schofield, Susan Eakins, John Marin, Albert Bierstadt, Cecilia Beaux, Reginald Marsh & Gustavus Grunewald acquired
Special Subjects: Drawings, Painting-American, Photography, Prints, Watercolors, Woodcuts
Collections: American Impressionists of the New Hope Circle, Collection of 19th & 20th century landscape paintings of Eastern Pennsylvania, Previously Underrecognized Women of the Philadelphia School, Collection of contemporary paintings & prints, Nineteenth & Twentieth Century American Landscape Art, Paintings - Susan Eakins, Gustavus Grunewald, Antonio Martino, Elmer Schofield, Twentieth Century Paintings
Publications: Exhib catalogues
Activities: Lects open to pub; 6 vis lectrs per yr; concerts; gallery talks; schols offered; lending of original objects of art to other museums & galleries; book 1-2 traveling exhibs per yr; originate traveling exhibitions to other museums & galleries

BLOOMSBURG

M **BLOOMSBURG UNIVERSITY OF PENNSYLVANIA,** Haas Gallery of Art, 400 E Second St, Dept of Art & Art History Bloomsburg, PA 17815-1301. Tel 570-389-4708; Fax 570-389-4459; Email lmillard@bloomu.edu; Web: departments.bloomu.edu/haasgallery; *Chmn Dept of Art* Dr Christine Sperling; *Gallery Assoc* Lee S Millard
Open Mon - Fri 9 AM - 4 PM; No admis fee; Estab 1966 as an educational & cultural exten of the College's Dept of Art; Gallery covers 875 sq ft with approx 90 ft of running wall space & track lighting; Average Annual Attendance: 16,000
Income: Financed by community activities & grants

Collections: Permanent Collection
Exhibitions: 8 - 10 spring exhibs annually in a variety of media by established, emerging & student artists
Activities: Lect open to public, 5 vis lectrs per yr; gallery talks

BOALSBURG

M **COLUMBUS CHAPEL & BOAL MANSION MUSEUM,** 163 Boal Estate Dr, Boalsburg, PA 16827; PO Box 116, Boalsburg, PA 16827-0116. Tel 814-466-6210; Email office@boalmuseum.com; Web: www.boalmuseum.com; *CEO* Christopher Lee
Open June - Labor Day daily (except Mon) 10 AM - 5 PM, May, Sept & Oct 1:30 - 5 PM; Admis adults $10, children $6; Estab 1952 as a nonprofit educational organization devoted to preservation of this unique American & international heritage & collection; Christopher Columbus relics imported from Spain in 1909 to the 1789 Boal Family Mansion; Average Annual Attendance: 25,000
Income: Financed by admis
Library Holdings: Book Volumes, Manuscripts, Memorabilia, Original Art Works, Original Documents, Photographs, Prints, Sculpture
Special Subjects: Furniture, Glass, Painting-American, Painting-Flemish, Painting-German, Painting-Italian, Painting-Spanish
Collections: Chapel contains 16th & 17th century Spanish, Italian & Flemish art, furniture, china & glassware, mansion contains 18th & 19th century French, Spanish, Italian, Flemish & American art, weapons: American, French & German (1780-1920)
Activities: Classes for adults & children, docent training, experimental action learning for grade 5; lects open to public, 2 lects per year; concerts; gallery talks; tours; three ann awards for educ, preservation & community svcs; mus shop or sales shop sells books, prints

BRYN ATHYN

M **ACADEMY OF THE NEW CHURCH,** Glencairn Museum, 1001 Cathedral Rd, Bryn Athyn, PA 19009; 1001 Cathedral Rd, PO Box 757 Bryn Athyn, PA 19009-0757. Tel 267-502-2600; Fax 267-502-2686; Email info@glencairnmuseum.org; Web: www.glencairnmuseum.org; *Dir* Brian Henderson; *Educ Coordr* Christine McDonald; *Tour Coordr* Leah Smith; *Cur* C Edward Gyllenhaal; *Colls Mgr* Bret Bostock; *Mktg & Pub Rels Coordr* Joralyn Glenn; *Concert Coordr & Oper Mgr* Peter Childs; *Dir Emeritus* Stephen Morley; *Asst Colls Mgr & Office Mgr* Glenn Greer; *Archivist* Greg Jackson
Tours Tues - Fri 2:30 PM, Sat & Sun 1 PM, 1:45 PM, 2:30 PM, 3 PM or by appointment; Admis adults $10, seniors & students $8, children under 4 free, discounts for mems; Estab 1878 to display, study & teach about works of art & artifacts which illustrate the history of world religions; Museum housed in family crafted Romanesque style building (1939), former home of Raymond & Mildred Pitcairn; Average Annual Attendance: 19,500; Mem: 582; dues Individual $30; Family $60; Gold Individual $100; Gold Family & Friends $200, Patron $500
Income: Financed by endowment
Library Holdings: Book Volumes, Exhibition Catalogs
Special Subjects: African Art, American Indian Art, Antiquities-Assyrian, Antiquities-Egyptian, Antiquities-Etruscan, Antiquities-Greek, Antiquities-Oriental, Antiquities-Roman, Archaeology, Architecture, Asian Art, Calligraphy, Carpets & Rugs, Ceramics, Coins & Medals, Costumes, Decorative Arts, Dioramas, Drawings, Embroidery, Enamels, Furniture, Glass, Historical Material, Islamic Art, Ivory, Jewelry, Landscapes, Manuscripts, Maps, Medieval Art, Metalwork, Mosaics, Oriental Art, Painting-American, Period Rooms, Photography, Portraits, Pottery, Primitive art, Religious Art, Sculpture, Scrimshaw, Stained Glass, Tapestries, Textiles, Watercolors, Woodcarvings
Collections: American Indian, Ancient Near East, Egypt, Greece & Rome, Medieval sculpture, stained glass & treasury objects, 19th & 20th Century art by Swedenborgian artists, oriental rugs, Asian, African Beads
Publications: Monthly e-newsletter
Activities: Progs for school groups; college internship prog; lects open to publ; lects for mems only; concerts; gallery talks; tours; individual paintings & original art objects are lent to mus & institutions which provide satisfactory evidence of adequate security, insurance, fire protection; mus shop sells books, original art, prints, jewelry, postcards, CDs, DVDs, hand blown glass decorations & souvenirs

BRYN MAWR

L **BRYN MAWR COLLEGE,** Rhys Carpenter Library for Art, Archaeology, Classics & Cities, 101 N Merion Ave, Bryn Mawr, PA 19010-2899. Tel 610-526-5271; Fax 610-526-7911; Email cmackay@brynmawr.edu or jblatchl@brynmawr.edu; Web: www.brynmawr.edu/Library; *Head Librn* Camilla MacKay; *Reference Librn* Jeremy Blatchley; *Library Asst* Christine Purkiss
Open during acad yr Mon - Thurs 8 AM - midnight, Fri 8 AM - 8 PM, Sat 10 AM - 7 PM, Sun noon - midnight, summer Mon - Fri 9 AM - 9 PM (hours vary); No admis fee; Estab 1931 to serve the needs of the general col prog, the undergraduate majors & graduate students through the PhD degree in History of Art; Classical & Near Eastern archaeology, classics & the undergraduate prog in Growth & Structure of Cities
Income: Financed by college funds
Library Holdings: Auction Catalogs, Book Volumes 100,000, Compact Disks, Exhibition Catalogs, Fiche, Framed Reproductions, Kodachrome Transparencies, Lantern Slides, Original Art Works, Pamphlets, Periodical Subscriptions 400, Photographs, Prints, Reels, Reproductions, Sculpture, Slides, Video Tapes
Special Subjects: Antiquities-Assyrian, Antiquities-Byzantine, Antiquities-Egyptian, Antiquities-Greek, Archaeology, Architecture, Art History, Asian Art, Carpets & Rugs, Coins & Medals, Furniture, Islamic Art, Landscape Architecture, Manuscripts, Antiquities-Persian, Latin American Art, Painting-American, Painting-British, Painting-Dutch, Painting-European, Painting-Flemish, Painting-French, Painting-German, Painting-Italian, Painting-Japanese, Painting-Russian, Painting-Spanish
Exhibitions: Changing exhibitions curated by college collections

CARLISLE

M **DICKINSON COLLEGE,** The Trout Gallery, 240 W High St, Carlisle, PA 17013; PO Box 1773, Carlisle, PA 17013-2896. Tel 717-245-1344; Fax 717-254-8929; Email trout@dickinson.edu; Web: www.dickinson.edu/trout; *Registrar & Exhib Preparator* James Bowman; *Cur Educ* Wendy Pires; *Dir* Phillip Earenfight; *Admin Asst* Stephanie Keifer
Open Tues - Sat 10 AM - 4 PM; No admis fee; Estab 1983 as display & care facilities for col's art coll, serves col & community; Two floors with exhib & permanent coll space; Average Annual Attendance: 9,000
Income: $325,000 (financed by endowment, college & special grants)
Purchases: Auguste Rodin's St John the Baptist; Joseph Stella's Bold Flowers; African Art; Baselitz's Madchen mit Harmonika IV; Thomas Sully's Portrait of Benjamin Rush; Fabio Mauroner's etchings
Library Holdings: Auction Catalogs, Book Volumes, Exhibition Catalogs
Special Subjects: African Art, American Indian Art, Antiquities-Egyptian, Antiquities-Roman, Asian Art, Baroque Art, Calligraphy, Ceramics, Decorative Arts, Drawings, Etchings & Engravings, Graphics, Historical Material, Islamic Art, Landscapes, Oriental Art, Painting-American, Painting-French, Painting-Spanish, Photography, Portraits, Posters, Pottery, Pre-Columbian Art, Primitive art, Prints, Religious Art, Renaissance Art, Southwestern Art, Woodcuts
Collections: Carnegie Collection of Prints, Old Master & modern prints, photographs, Cole Collection of Oriental & Decorative Arts, Gerofsky Collection of African Art, Potamkin Collection of 19th & 20th Century Work
Publications: Exhibition catalogues, 3 - 5 per year
Activities: Classes for adults & children by appointment only; lects open to pub, 1 - 2 vis lectrs per yr, awards given; book traveling exhibs 2 - 4 per yr; originate traveling exhibs

CHADDS FORD

M **BRANDYWINE CONSERVANCY,** Brandywine River Museum, 1 Hoffman's Mill Rd Chadds Ford, PA 19317; PO Box 141, Chadds Ford, PA 19317-0141. Tel 610-388-2700; Fax 610-388-1197; Email inquiries@brandywine.org; Web: www.brandywinemuseum.org; *Dir Fin & Admin* Joel E. Necowitz; *Cur Collections* Virginia O'Hara; *Dir Pub Rels* Hillary Holland; *Registrar* Jean A Gilmore; *Supv Educ* Mary W Cronin; *Brandywine Conservancy Exec Dir* Virginia A Logan; *Vol Coordr* Donna M Gormel; *Chmn (V)* George A Weymouth; *Chief Security* Robert Booker; *VPres* Wendell Fenton; *Assoc Cur NC Wyeth Collections* Christine B Podmaniczky; *Mus Shop Mgr* Erika G Bucino; *Dir Develop* Suzanne M Regnier; *Asst Educ* Jane V Flitner; *Assoc Cur* Audrey Lewis; *Brandywine River Mus Dir* Thomas Padon
Open daily 9:30 AM - 4:30 PM, cl Christmas; Admis adults $10, seniors & students (6 - 12) $6, mems and children under 6 free; Estab 1971, devoted to the preservation, documentation & interpretation of art history in the Brandywine Valley, the history of American illustration, American still-life paintings & the relationship of regional art to the natural environment; Six galleries of permanent colls & special exhibs, changing approx 5 times per yr; Average Annual Attendance: 115,655; Mem: 4600; dues vary
Library Holdings: Book Volumes, Clipping Files, Exhibition Catalogs, Manuscripts, Maps, Memorabilia, Original Documents
Special Subjects: Drawings, Etchings & Engravings, Landscapes, Painting-American, Prints, Sculpture, Watercolors
Collections: American illustration, American still-life painting, drawing & sculpture, including a major Wyeth Family Collection, art of the Brandywine Valley from early 19th century, regional artists of the 20th century, Nineteenth Century Landscapes
Publications: The Catalyst, quarterly; Catalogue of the Collection; exhibition catalogs
Activities: Classes for adults & children; docent training; family progs; school progs; lects for mems & open to pub; 1 vis lectr per yr; guided tours; volunteer activities; individual paintings & original objects of art lent to other mus for exhib purposes; book traveling exhibs; originates traveling exhibs to other mus; mus shop sells books, magazines, reproductions, prints, gifts, jewelry, children's items & cards

L **Library**, PO Box 141, Chadds Ford, PA 19317. Tel 610-388-2700; Fax 610-388-1197; *Librn* Ruth Bassett; *Coll Librn* Gail Stanislow
Open daily 9:30 AM - 4:30 PM; For reference to staff & volunteers; by appointment to the pub
Purchases: $4000
Library Holdings: Book Volumes 6500, Clipping Files, Exhibition Catalogs, Manuscripts, Other Holdings Artist memorabilia; Posters, Pamphlets, Periodical Subscriptions 20, Photographs, Reproductions, Video Tapes 25
Special Subjects: Art History, Illustration, Painting-American
Collections: Howard Pyle's published work, Other collections related to American illustration & American art history, Wyeth family memorabilia

CHESTER

M **WIDENER UNIVERSITY,** Art Collection & Gallery, 1 University Center, Fl 1 Chester, PA 19013-5700. Tel 610-499-1189, 499-4000; Fax 610-499-4425; Email rmwarda@widener.edu; Web: www.widener.edu; *Coll Mgr* Rebecca Warda
Open Tues 10 AM - 7 PM, Wed - Sat 10 AM - 4:30 PM; call for summer hours; Estab 1970
Income: Financed by endowment & univ funding
Special Subjects: Oriental Art, Painting-American, Painting-European, Pre-Columbian Art, Sculpture
Collections: 18th & 19th century Oriental art objects, 19th century European landscape & genre pictures, 20th century American paintings & sculpture
Exhibitions: Contemporary exhibs, 6-7per yr
Publications: Exhib catalog
Activities: Lect; guided tours

CLARION

M **CLARION UNIVERSITY,** Hazel Sandford Gallery, Merick-Boyd Bldg, Clarion, PA 16214; 840 Word St, Clarion, PA 16214. Tel 814-226-2412, 393-2000, 393-2412 (gallery); Fax 814-226-2723; Web: www.clarion.edu; WATS 800-669-2000; *Chmn* Joe Thomas; *Dir* Diane Malley
Open Mon - Fri 11 AM - 4:30 PM; No admis fee; Estab 1970 for aesthetic enjoyment & artistic educ of students; Gallery is 66 ft long, 17ft 3 inches wide; lit by some 50 adjustable spotlights; one side of gallery is glassed in; other side is fabric-covered panels & a dozen free-standing panels, available for hanging; Average Annual Attendance: 4,000; Mem: 95
Income: Financed by univ & mem
Collections: Original paintings, drawings & prints, purchased from selected artists who have shown at gallery, sculpture & ceramics, photographs
Exhibitions: Rotating Exhibits
Publications: Monthly announcements of shows
Activities: Lect open to pub, 2-3 vis lectrs per yr; concerts; gallery talks; tours; competitions; individual paintings & original objects of art lent to departments on campus & other state colleges; lending collection contains original art works, original prints, paintings, photographs & sculpture; book traveling exhibs

COLLEGEVILLE

M **URSINUS COLLEGE,** Philip & Muriel Berman Museum of Art, 601 E Main St, Collegeville, PA 19426; PO Box 1000, Collegeville, PA 19426-1000. Tel 610-409-3500; Fax 610-409-3664; Email lhanover@ursinus.edu; Web: www.ursinus.edu/berman; *Assoc Dir Educ* Susan Shifrin; *Admin Asst* Suzanne Calvin; *Coll Mgr* Julie Choma
Open Tues - Fri 10 AM - 4 PM, Sat & Sun Noon - 4:30 PM; No admis fee; Estab 1987 to support the educational goals of Ursinus College & to contribute to the cultural life of the campus & regional community; Main gallery: 3200 sq ft; sculpture ct; upper gallery 800 sq ft; Average Annual Attendance: 32,000; Mem: 250; dues minimum $50; ann meeting in June
Income: $150,000 (financed by endowment, mem, Ursinus College, government, foundation & corporate grants)
Purchases: $25,000
Special Subjects: Drawings, Etchings & Engravings, Folk Art, Furniture, Landscapes, Latin American Art, Marine Painting, Painting-American, Painting-British, Painting-Dutch, Painting-European, Painting-Flemish, Painting-French, Painting-German, Painting-Israeli, Painting-Italian, Painting-Japanese, Painting-Russian, Painting-Spanish, Portraits, Posters, Pottery, Prints, Religious Art, Sculpture, Tapestries, Textiles, Watercolors, Woodcuts
Collections: Philip & Muriel Berman Collection, Lynn Chadwick Sculpture Collection, 18th, 19th & 20th century European & American Art (drawings, paintings, prints & sculpture), Japanese Prints & Scrolls
Exhibitions: Temporary exhibitions, 10 per year; selections from permanent collections on continuous view
Publications: Quarterly exhib calendar; exhibs catalogues; museum newsletter, 3 times per year
Activities: Lect open to pub, 6 vis lectrs per yr; concerts; gallery talks; tours; individual paintings & original objects of art lent to museums & galleries for exhib; book traveling exhibs 4-6 per yr; originate traveling exhibs; sales shop sells books & prints

DOYLESTOWN

M **BUCKS COUNTY HISTORICAL SOCIETY,** Mercer Museum, 84 S Pine, Doylestown, PA 18901. Tel 215-345-0210; Fax 215-230-0823; Email info@mercermuseum.org; Web: www.mercermuseum.org; *Exec Dir* Douglas Dolan; *Cur Coll* Cory Amsler; *Chmn* William Maeglin
Open Mon-Sat 10AM-5PM, Sun noon-5PM; Admis adults $12, seniors $10, children 5-17 $6, mems and children under 5 free; Estab 1880; Inside this poured, reinforced concrete castle, four galleries wrap around a towering central court where early American hand crafts are exhibited inside small cubicles. Additional artifacts hang from ceilings, walls and railings. Changing exhibitions & an audio tour complete a visit.; Average Annual Attendance: 55,000; Mem: 2400; dues $40 & up
Income: Contributions, grants, earned income-admis & mem
Special Subjects: Crafts, Folk Art
Collections: Over 50,000 artifacts representing more than 60 early American crafts, their tools and finished products, large American folk art coll, the history and growth of our country as seen through the work of the human hand
Exhibitions: Continuous changing exhibits.
Publications: Newsletter, twice annually
Activities: Classes for adults & children; lect open to pub; individual paintings & original objects of art lent to other mus; 3-5 per yr; mus shop sells books & hand crafts

L **Mercer Museum Research Library**, 84 S Pine, Doylestown, PA 18901. Tel 215-345-0210; Fax 215-230-0823; Email mmlib@mercermuseum.org; Web: www.mercermuseum.org; *Colls Mgr* Sara C Good
Open Tues - Thurs 1 PM - 5 PM, Fri & Sat 10 AM - 5 PM, cl July 4th, Thanksgiving, Christmas & New Year's Day; No admis fee for BCHS members only; fee for museum & Research Library; Circ Non-circulating; Open to the pub for reference only; Bucks County history, Delaware Valley; Average Annual Attendance: 60,000; Mem: 2,500
Library Holdings: Auction Catalogs, Audio Tapes, Book Volumes 20,000, Clipping Files, Exhibition Catalogs, Fiche, Lantern Slides, Manuscripts, Maps, Original Art Works, Original Documents, Other Holdings Archives, Pamphlets, Periodical Subscriptions 100, Photographs, Prints, Reels, Slides, Video Tapes
Special Subjects: American Indian Art, Anthropology, Antiquities-Greek, Costume Design & Constr, Archaeology, Architecture, Art Education, Art History, Ceramics, Commercial Art, Decorative Arts, Dolls, Drawings, Embroidery, Etchings & Engravings, Folk Art, Furniture, Glass, Gold, Goldsmithing, Historical Material, History of Art & Archaeology, Manuscripts, Maps, Painting-American, Painting-European, Pewter, Photography, Porcelain, Portraits, Posters, Pottery, Pre-Columbian Art, Primitive art, Prints, Scrimshaw, Sculpture, Silver, Silversmithing, Tapestries, Textiles, Woodcuts
Collections: Life of Henry Mercer, papers
Activities: Classes for adults & children held through historical society; lects open to pub; 5-10 vis lectrs per yr; gallery talks; tours; lending of original objects of art; 3-5 book traveling exhibs per yr; mus shop sells books, original art, reproductions & prints

M **JAMES A MICHENER ART MUSEUM,** 138 S Pine St, Doylestown, PA 18901-4931. Tel 215-340-9800; Fax 215-340-9807; Web: www.michenerartmuseum.org; *Registrar* Sara Beuhler; *Mem Coordr* Louise Beder; *Cur Exhib & Sr Cur* Brian Peterson; *Cur Pub Progs* Zorianne Siokalo; *Dir* Lisa Tremper Hanover; *Dir Mktg* Ilene Dube; *Comm Coord* Keri Smotrich; *Dir Advanc* Laurie McGahey; *Deputy Dir* Candace Clarke; *Exec Asst* Kip Malloy; *Information Mgmt Specialist* Alyson Avery
Open Tues-Sun 11AM-5PM, Sat 11AM-6PM; Admis $15, seniors $13, children 6-18 $7.50, children under 6 & mems free; Estab 1987; Circ Reference only; Average Annual Attendance: 300,000; Mem: 5000; dues $40 - $1000
Library Holdings: Audio Tapes, Book Volumes 1400, CD-ROMs, Cassettes, Clipping Files 1500, Compact Disks, DVDs, Exhibition Catalogs, Lantern Slides, Manuscripts, Memorabilia, Original Documents, Pamphlets, Periodical Subscriptions, Photographs, Slides, Video Tapes
Special Subjects: Drawings, Painting-American, Photography, Prints, Sculpture, Watercolors
Collections: American Art Collection, special focus on the arts in Bucks County, Pennsylvania, 20th Century American Sculpture Collection, American Art Collection
Activities: Classes for adults & children; docent training; mus trips; walking tours; lects open to pub, 15-20 vis lectrs per yr; concerts; gallery talks; tours; schols offered; individual paintings & original objects of art lent to mus & cultural institutions; originate traveling exhibs; mus shop sells books, magazines, original art, reproductions, prints, pottery, crafts, toys, stationery, tiles & jewelry

DUBOIS

M **WINKLER GALLERY OF FINE ART,** 36 N Brady St, DuBois, PA 15801-2256. Tel 814-375-5834; Email winklergallery@gmail.com; Web: www.winklergallery.org
Open Tues-Thurs 11AM-5PM, Fri-Sat 11AM-8PM; No admis fee
Special Subjects: Photography, Mosaics, Glass, Sculpture
Collections: paintings; photography; mosaics; blown glass; sculpture
Exhibitions: Temporary exhibits
Activities: Educ progs; classes for adults & children

EASTON

M **LAFAYETTE COLLEGE,** Lafayette College Art Galleries, 317 Hamilton St, Williams Center for the Arts Easton, PA 18042-1768. Tel 610-330-5361, 330-5010; Fax 610-330-5642; Email artgallery@lafayette.edu; Web: artgalleries.lafayette.edu; *Dir Gallery* Michiko Okaya; *Registrar* Ellen Sapienza
Open Mon - Fri 11 AM -5 PM, Sat & Sun noon - 5 PM, performance nights 7:30 PM - 9:30 PM; No admis fee; Estab 1983 to present a variety of exhibs for enrichment of campus & community's exposure to visual arts; Versatile space with movable panels & 160 running ft of wall space, climate control & track lighting; Average Annual Attendance: 6,000
Income: Financed by endowment, prog subsidy, government grants
Special Subjects: Cartoons, Ceramics, Decorative Arts, Drawings, Etchings & Engravings, Graphics, Landscapes, Painting-American, Painting-British, Painting-European, Painting-French, Photography, Portraits, Pottery, Prints, Sculpture, Textiles, Watercolors, Woodcuts
Collections: 19th & 20th century American painting, prints, photographs & sculpture, Nineteenth & Twentieth Century American Painting, Prints & Photographs Collection
Exhibitions: Past/Present: Selections from the Lafayette Art Collection; In the Line of Duty: Collecting African American Art; Gail Skudera/In Time, Out of Time: Woven Photo Collages; Tiffany Glass: Painting with Color and Light
Publications: Annual exhibit catalogue; brochures; exhibit handouts
Activities: Lects open to pub, 8 - 10 vis lectrs per yr; gallery talks; lending of original art varies; book traveling exhibitions; organize traveling exhibitions varies; mus shop sells slides, catalogues, license art collection images

EPHRATA

A **HISTORICAL SOCIETY OF THE COCALICO VALLEY,** 249 W Main St, Ephrata, PA 17522-2016; PO Box 193, Ephrata, PA 17522-0193. Tel 717-733-1616; Web: www.cocalicovalleyhs.org; *Librn* Cynthia Marquet
Open Mon, Wed & Thurs 9:30 AM - 6 PM, Sat 8:30 AM - 5 PM; No admis fee; Estab 1957; Average Annual Attendance: 1,200; Mem: 585; dues family $25, individual $18
Income: Endowment, mem, publs
Special Subjects: Folk Art, Furniture, Historical Material
Collections: Pennsylvania German Folk Art
Publications: Journal of the Historical Society of the Cocalico Valley, annual
Activities: Classes for children; lect open to pub, 10 vis lectrs per yr

ERIE

M **ERIE ART MUSEUM,** 411 State St, Erie, PA 16501-1106. Tel 814-459-5477; Fax 814-452-1744; Web: www.erieartmuseum.org; *Exec Dir* Susan Black; *Cur* Susan Barnett; *Dir Develop* Christine Eddy; *Dir Fin* Mary Pruchniewski; *Dir Devel* Chrisine Eddy; *Devel Asst* Laura Paris; *Dir Educ & Folk Art* Kelly Armor; *Frame Shop Mgr* James Pearson; *Sr Designer* Andrea Krivak; *Educ Coordr* Ally Thomas; *Facility Opers & Event Mgr* Tavon Markov; *Registrar* Vance Lupher

Open Tues - Sat 11 AM - 5 PM, Sun 1 - 5 PM, cl New Year's Day, Easter, Independence Day, Thanksgiving, Christmas; Admis adults $9; seniors & students $7; children under 5, AAM, ICOM & mus mems free; Estab 1898 for the advancement of visual arts; Galleries are located in historic buildings connected with a new (2010) structure that also houses galleries & other pub facilities; Average Annual Attendance: 42,300; Mem: Dues family $75, individual $50
Income: $1,100,000 (financed through pvt donations, fundraising, mem & grants)
Library Holdings: Auction Catalogs 13, Book Volumes 2,023
Special Subjects: Antiquities-Oriental, Asian Art, Bronzes, Cartoons, Ceramics, Collages, Crafts, Decorative Arts, Dolls, Drawings, Embroidery, Etchings & Engravings, Folk Art, Graphics, Jade, Juvenile Art, Landscapes, Oriental Art, Painting-American, Painting-American, Photography, Photography, Porcelain, Pottery, Pottery, Pre-Columbian Art, Prints, Sculpture, Silver, Southwestern Art, Textiles, Textiles
Collections: Indian Bronze & Stone Sculpture, Chinese Porcelains, Jades, Textiles, American Ceramics (historical & contemporary), Graphics (European, American & Oriental), Photography, Paintings & Drawings (predominately 20th century), Contemporary Baskets
Exhibitions: (23rd Jun, 2017-28th Jan, 2018) Ancient Ink: Mark Perrott
Publications: Four exhibition catalogues
Activities: Classes for adults & children; docent training; lect open to pub, 3-5 vis lectrs per yr; concerts; gallery talks; tours; competitions; Leed Gold certification 2015; individual paintings & original objects of art lent to pub buildings, colleges & universities, galleries & museums; originates traveling exhibs; mus shop sells books, postcards, pencils, t-shirts & mugs. Frame shop offers retail framing

M **ERIE COUNTY HISTORICAL SOCIETY,** 356 W 6th St, Erie, PA 16507-1245. Tel 814-454-1813 x26; Fax 814-454-6890; Email aandrick@eriecountyhistory.org; Web: www.eriecountyhistory.org; *Dir Library & Archives* Annita Andrick; *Dir Visitor & Mem Svcs* Melanie Kuebel-Stanky; *Educ & Events Dir* Andrew Adams; *Exec Dir* Alyson Amendola Cummings
Open Watson-Curtze Mansion & Erie Co History Ctr: Sept - May Wed - Sat 11 AM - 4 PM, June - Aug Tues - Sat 11 AM - 4 PM, hours subject to change; Libr in HQ History Ctr: Tues - Sat, 11 AM - 4 PM; Admis adults $5, students with ID & seniors $4, children $3; Research Library: day pass or mem $7; Estab 1903 to collect & preserve Erie County history; Mus has exhibits on all 3 properties it owns. Maintains Victorian Watson - Curtze Mansion & Planetarium, built in 1891-1892 & designed by Green & Wicks of Buffalo, NY; Cashier's House; Erie Co History Ctr features formal galleries, exhibs and research libr & archives; Battles Mus of Rural Life with 2 c. 1860 historic houses; Average Annual Attendance: 24,500; Mem: 600; dues corporate $500, couple $45, individual $45, student $15, family $60, grandparent $60, patron $75, sustaining $100, sponsor $250
Income: Financed by soc, grants
Library Holdings: Book Volumes, CD-ROMs, Cassettes, Manuscripts, Maps, Memorabilia, Original Art Works, Original Documents, Photographs, Prints, Reels, Video Tapes
Special Subjects: American Indian Art, Asian Art, Bronzes, Carpets & Rugs, Ceramics, Costumes, Crafts, Dolls, Drawings, Embroidery, Folk Art, Furniture, Historical Material, Jewelry, Manuscripts, Maps, Marine Painting, Period Rooms, Photography, Portraits, Posters, Pottery, Prints, Silver, Stained Glass, Textiles, Watercolors, Decorative Arts
Collections: Moses Billings (paintings), George Ericson-Eugene Iverd (paintings), genre paintings, Native American pottery, Southwest & Northwest Coast baskets, Victorian decorative arts, Local history & maritime, Robert J MacDonald Great Lakes Maritime Coll, Erie Art Mus Archives, Erie Art Center Archives, Erie Art Club Archives, Battles Family coll; FJ Bassett coll; CB Hall coll; Ottomar Jarecki coll; Ossowski coll; Sanford-Spencer coll
Activities: Classes for adults & children; docent tours; lesson tours for students; concerts; lects open to pub; local history & preservation awards prog; lending coll serves Erie Maritime Mus; mus shop sells books, magazines, original art, reproductions, prints, photographs

FARMINGTON

A **TOUCHSTONE CENTER FOR CRAFTS,** Hart Moore Museum, 1049 Wharton Furnace Rd, Farmington, PA 15437-1195. Tel 724-329-1370; Fax 724-329-1371; Email info@touchstonecrafts.org; Web: www.touchstonecrafts.org; *Admin Asst* Meghan Feather; *Exec Dir* Scott Hilliard; *Opers Dir* Stephanie Glover; *External Relations & Events Coordr* Kari Garber; *Campus Mgr* Matt DiNardo; *Accnt* Sue Cromwell
Open Mon - Fri 9 AM - 5 PM; Tuition & materials fees; Estab 1972 to promote excellence in art & craft educ; Average Annual Attendance: 1200; Mem: 400
Income: $690,000 (financed by opers, grants & donations)
Special Subjects: Ceramics, Glass, Jewelry, Sculpture
Exhibitions: 3 to 5 per yr
Activities: Classes for adults, children, college credit & continuing educ reqs; lect & demos open to pub; concerts; tours; schols offered; outreach programs; field trips; artist-in-residency projects; sales shop sells books, magazines, original art, reproductions, prints, ceramics, jewelry, t-shirts, sweatshirts, hats, iron works & glass art

GETTYSBURG

M **ADAMS COUNTY HISTORICAL SOCIETY,** 111 Seminary Ridge, Gettysburg, PA 17325; PO Box 4325, Gettysburg, PA 17325-4325. Tel 717-334-4723; Fax 717-334-0722; Email info@achs-pa.org; Web: www.achs-pa.org; *Exec Dir* Wayne E Motts; *Coll Mgr* Benjamin F Nelly; *Admin Asst* Sheryl Snyder; *Research Asst* Timothy H Smith
Open Research Libr: Wed - Sat 9 AM - noon & 1 PM - 4 PM, Thurs 6 PM - 9 PM; Mus: by appt only; Admis $3 museum, non-member researcher $5; Historical Soc estab 1939, mus estab 1987; Museum of local history; Average Annual Attendance: 5,750; Mem: 1,100; dues family $50, supporting $35; meetings Jan - June & Sept - Dec
Income: $200,000 (financed by mem, appeal, grants, sale of publs)
Special Subjects: Costumes, Historical Material, American Indian Art, Coins & Medals, Dolls, Flasks & Bottles, Folk Art, Furniture, Glass, Historical Material, Manuscripts, Maps, Military Art, Period Rooms, Portraits, Religious Art, Silver, Stained Glass, Textiles
Collections: Blacksmith Shop/Earth Science, Barber Shop Equipment, 1940's Doll House, Uniforms, Spanish & American/WW I & WW II, 1930 Conoco Gas Station, Agriculture, Art History
Publications: Annual journal; 6 newsletters per year
Activities: Classes for adults; lect open to pub; tours; lending coll consists of lantern slides; originate traveling exhibs; mus shop sells books & maps

GLENSIDE

M **ARCADIA UNIVERSITY ART GALLERY,** (Beaver College Art Gallery) Spruance Fine Arts Center, 450 S Easton Rd, Glenside, PA 19038-3215. Tel 215-572-2131; Fax 215-881-8774; Email gallery@arcadia.edu; Web: www.arcadia.edu/gallery; *Gallery Dir* Richard Torchia; *Cur Asst* Jamar Nicholas
Open Tues-Wed & Fri 10AM-5PM, Thurs 10AM-8PM; No admis fee; Estab 1974 to show contemporary art generally; Gallery dimensions 20 x 50 ft; Average Annual Attendance: 6,500; Mem: 150; dues $35
Income: College & board funding
Collections: Benton Spruance Print Collection
Exhibitions: Contemporary artist solo & thematic exhibitions
Publications: Brochures for major exhibitions
Activities: Lect open to pub, 4 vis lectrs per yr; gallery talks; competitions with awards

GREENSBURG

L **SETON HILL COLLEGE,** Reeves Memorial Library, 1 Seton Hill Dr, Reeves Memorial Library, Seton Hill University Greensburg, PA 15601-1548. Tel 724-838-4291; Fax 724-834-4611; *Reference & Pub Servs Librn* Denise Sticha
Open Mon-Thurs 8AM-10:50PM, Fri 8AM-4:50PM, Sat, 9AM-4:50PM, Sun 1PM-10:50PM; For lending & reference; Circ 40,000
Library Holdings: Audio Tapes, Book Volumes 101,000, Cards, Cassettes, Filmstrips, Motion Pictures, Original Art Works, Pamphlets, Periodical Subscriptions 500, Records, Sculpture, Slides, Video Tapes

M **WESTMORELAND MUSEUM OF AMERICAN ART,** 221 N Main St, Greensburg, PA 15601-1808. Tel 724-837-1500; Email info@thewestmoreland.org; Web: www.thewestmoreland.org; *CEO & The Richard H Scaife Dir* Judith H O'Toole; *Chief Cur* Barbara L Jones; *Deputy Dir & Dir Devel* Catena Bergerin; *Dir Budget & Fin* Suzanne Wright; *Dir Educ & Vis Svcs* Joan McGarry; *Dir Mktg & Pub Rels* Claire Erbl; *Mgr Colls* Douglas W Evans; *Mus Shop Mgr* Carol Sullivan
Open Tues & Thurs - Sun 11 AM - 5 PM, Wed 11 AM - 7 PM, cl New Year's Day, Easter, Thanksgiving, Christmas; Admis suggested donation: adults $15, Seniors 65 & over $10, members, children 18 & under, students, veterans & their families free; Estab 1949 to operate & maintain a free pub art mus; The mus houses three galleries for changing exhibs; eight galleries for permanent coll; Average Annual Attendance: 23,300; Mem: dues $75 - $2000
Income: Financed by endowment, grants & gifts
Special Subjects: Decorative Arts, Dolls, Drawings, Etchings & Engravings, Folk Art, Furniture, Glass, Painting-American, Photography, Portraits, Pottery, Sculpture, Silver, Textiles, Watercolors
Collections: Extensive toy coll, Furniture, paintings, sculpture & works on paper, 19th & early 20th century Southwestern Pennsylvania paintings, American Art, 1750-Present
Publications: quarterly newsletter; exhibition catalogs
Activities: Educ prog; classes for adults and children; docent training; lects open to pub, 20-24 vis lectrs per yr; gallery talks; tours; Westmoreland Society Gold Medal (annually); concerts; individual paintings & original objects of art lent to other mus & institutions accredited by AAM; lending collection contains original art works & paintings; book traveling exhibs 1-2 per yr; originate traveling exhibs to other museums; mus shop sells books, reproductions, postcards & notepaper, jewelry, and giftware

L **Art Reference Library**, 221 N Main St, Greensburg, PA 15601-1808. Tel 724-837-1500; Fax 724-837-2921; Email info@wmuseumaa.org; Web: www.wmuseumaa.org; *Dir & CEO* Judith H O'Toole; *Preparator* PJ Zimmerlink; *Cur Educ* Katie Barnard; *Dir Mktg & Pub Rels* Judy Linz Ross; *Cur* Barbara L Jones; *Asst Pub & Finance* Pat Erdelsky; *Registrar* Douglas R Evans; *VPres* Jack Smith; *Asst to Dir* Janet Carns; *Mus Shop Mgr* Virginia Leiner; *Dir Develop & Finance* Amy Baldonieri
Open Tues - Sat 10 AM - 5 PM, Sun 1 - 5 PM, cl Mon & holidays; Estab 1949 for art reference; For reference only; Average Annual Attendance: 20,000
Income: Financed by endowment, grants & gifts
Purchases: $1200
Library Holdings: Book Volumes 8000, Clipping Files, Exhibition Catalogs, Pamphlets, Periodical Subscriptions 15

GREENVILLE

M **THIEL COLLEGE,** Weyers-Sampson Art Gallery, 75 College Ave, Greenville, PA 16125-2181. Tel 724-589-2095; Fax 724-589-2021; *Dir Spec Events* Marianne Colenda; *Dir Permanent Coll* Sean McConnor
No admis fee; Estab 1971 to provide students, faculty, col staff & the community with a gallery featuring a variety of exhibs & give students an opportunity to show their work; Two galleries 20' x 38' & 20' x 31', grey carpeted walls & track lighting; Average Annual Attendance: 1,000
Income: $1,000 (financed by college budget)
Collections: 18th & 19th century paintings & prints
Exhibitions: Monthly exhibs by students & faculty
Activities: Lect open to pub; gallery talks

HARRISBURG

M **ART ASSOCIATION OF HARRISBURG,** School & Galleries, 21 N Front St, Harrisburg, PA 17101-1625. Tel 717-236-1432; Fax 717-236-6631; Email carrie@artassocofhbg.com; Web: www.artassocofhbg.com; *Cur* Terrie Hosey; *Asst Cur* Rachel O'Connor; *Pres* Carrie Wissler-Thomas; *Webmaster* Randall Miller III; *Gallery Asst* Bryan Molloy; *Gallery Asst* Mark Bradshaw
Open Mon - Thurs 9:30 AM - 9 PM, Fri 9:30 AM - 4 PM, Sat 10 AM - 4 PM, Sun 2 - 5 PM; No admis fee; Estab 1926 to act as showcase for mem artists and other professionals; community services offered; Building is historic Brownstone Building, former Governor's mansion (1817) & holds 4 floors of galleries, classrooms & a garden; Average Annual Attendance: 20,000; Mem: 600, dues $40 - $1000; ann meeting in May
Income: Financed by mem, tuitions, contributions, grants
Collections: Old area masters, member's work, Lavery & Lebret
Exhibitions: Annual International Juried Exhibition; Art School Annual; invitational shows; mem shows, 2 times per yr; community shows in 14 locations - 90 total per yr
Publications: Monthly exhibition announcements; newsletter, quarterly newsletter with class schedule
Activities: Classes for adults and children; lect open to pub; competitions open to all states; monetary awards; concerts; gallery talks; tours; schols offered; sales shop sells original art & prints by mem artists

A **CITIZENS FOR THE ARTS IN PENNSYLVANIA,** 100 N Cameron St, Ste 108A Harrisburg, PA 17101-2424. Tel 717-234-0959; Fax 717-234-1501; Email info@citizensfortheartsinpa.org; Web: www.citizensfortheartsinpa.org; *Mng Dir* Jenny Hershour; *Chair* Robert Lettieri
Estab 1986 to develop & strengthen Pennsylvania arts at the local, state & federal levels by networking arts admin, arts organizations, artists & volunteers & by providing technical assistance & professional training programs & services
Publications: eNewsletter
Activities: Conferences & educational workshops

A **PENNSYLVANIA DEPARTMENT OF EDUCATION,** Arts in Education Program, 333 Market St, Fl 8 Harrisburg, PA 17126-0333. Tel 717-525-5058; Fax 717-783-3946; Email jakasper@state.pa.us; Web: www.pde.state.pa.us; *State Advisor* Jamie Kasper; *Exhibs Coordr* Wendy Sweigart
The Arts in Educ Prog provides leadership & consultative & evaluative servs to all Pennsylvania schools & arts educ agencies in arts prog develop & instructional practices. Infusion of arts processes into differentiated curriculums for all students is a particular thrust. The prog offers assistance in designing aesthetic learning environments & consultation in identifying & employing regional & community resources for arts educ
Exhibitions: rotating exhibs and permanent collections of student work
Activities: Arts educ program

A **PENNSYLVANIA HISTORICAL & MUSEUM COMMISSION,** The State Museum of Pennsylvania, 300 North St, Harrisburg, PA 17120-0024. Tel 717-787-4980; Fax 717-783-4558; Web: www.statemuseumpa.org; *Cur Adminr* Bradley K Smith; *Mus Dir* David W Dunn; *PHMC Exec Dir* James M Vaughan; *Colls Mgr* Mary Jane Miller; *Dir External Affairs* Howard Pollman; *PHMC Chmn* Andrew Masich
Open Wed - Sat 9 AM - 5 PM, Sun Noon - 5 PM, cl Mon & Tues to pub; Admis adult $5, children 12 & under & seniors $4; Estab 1945 to interpret the history & heritage of Pennsylvania; Mem: 3000; dues vary; ann meeting second Wed in Apr
Income: $18,000,000 for entire commission
Exhibitions: Art of the State, ann spring-summer juried statewide exhib; Contemporary Artists Series; changing history exhibits
Publications: Pennsylvania Heritage, quarterly
Activities: Classes for adults & children; docent training; lects open to pub; concerts; tours; exhibits; special events

M **The State Museum of Pennsylvania**, 300 North St, Harrisburg, PA 17120-0024. Tel 717-783-9911; Fax 717-783-4558; Email hpollman@state.pa.us; Web: www.statemuseumpa.org; *Sr Cur Art* N Lee Stevens; *Acting Cur* Dr Curt Miner; *Acting Registrar* Mary Jane Miller; *Mus Dir* David Dunn
Open Wed - Sat 9 AM - 5 PM, Sun Noon - 5 PM; offices Mon - Fri 8:30 AM - 5 PM; Admis adults $5, seniors, children, & groups $4, free every third Sat; Mus estab 1905; Three floors of permanent & changing exhibs, including art; Average Annual Attendance: 350,000
Income: Financed by state & pvt funds minimal, rely on donations
Special Subjects: Anthropology, Archaeology, Decorative Arts, Historical Material
Collections: Anthropology, archaeology, art photography, ceramics, decorative arts, folk art, glass, Indian artifacts, paintings & sculpture, paleontology & geology, silver, textiles, works on paper, 2 million objects in all disciplines relating to Pennsylvania
Publications: Books, brochures, quarterly calendar, quarterly newsletter
Activities: Classes for adults & children; docent training; dramatic progs; lects open to pub; concerts; gallery talks; tours; awards; individual paintings & original objects of art lent to accredited mus, history orgs; book traveling exhibs 1-2 per yr; originate traveling exhibs; mus shop sells books, reproductions, prints & gift items
—Brandywine Battlefield Park, Box 202, Chadds Ford, PA 19317-0202. Tel 610-459-3342; Fax 610-459-9586; *Mus Educ* Helen Mahnke; *Educ Coordr* Richard Wolfe; *Adminr* Toni Collins
Open 9 AM - 5 PM; Estab 1947 to commemorate Battle of the Brandywine, Sept 11, 1777; 2 historic Quaker farmhouses; Average Annual Attendance: 90,000; Mem: 95; dues $35; ann meeting in summer
Income: $295,000 (financed by endowment, mem & state appropriation)
Activities: Classes for children

L **State Archives Div**, 350 North St, Harrisburg, PA 17120-0150. Tel 717-783-3281; Email ra-statearchives@state.pa.us; Web: www.portal.state.pa.us/portal/server.pt/community/state_archives/2887; *Educ* Robert McFadden
Open Wed - Fri 9 AM - 4 PM, Sat for microfilm only 9 AM - Noon & 1-4 PM; cl Mon, Tues & major holidays

M **Railroad Museum of Pennsylvania**, 300 Gap Rd, Strasburg, PA 17579; PO Box 15, Strasburg, PA 17579-0015. Tel 717-687-8628; Fax 717-687-0876; Email info@rrmuseumpa.org; Web: www.rrmuseumpa.org; *Cur* Bradley Smith; *Office Mgr* Cindy Adair; *Librn & Archivist* Kurt Bell; *Asst Educ* Troy Grubb; *Dir* David W Dunn; *Restoration Mgr* Allan Martin; *Educ* Patrick Morrison; *Dir Mus Advancement* Deborah Reddig
Open Mon - Sat 9 AM - 5 PM, Sun Noon - 5 PM, cl Mon Nov - Apr; Admis adults $8, seniors $7, children 6-17 $6; Estab 1975 for preservation of significant artifacts appropriate to railroading; Maintains reference library & railroad art gallery; Average Annual Attendance: 150,000; Mem: 1,900; dues $35; ann meeting in the fall
Income: $1,800,000 (financed by state appropriation & pvt fundraising)
Library Holdings: Auction Catalogs, Book Volumes, Cards, Filmstrips, Kodachrome Transparencies, Lantern Slides, Manuscripts, Maps, Memorabilia, Motion Pictures, Original Art Works, Original Documents, Pamphlets, Periodical Subscriptions, Photographs, Prints, Records, Reels, Slides, Video Tapes
Special Subjects: Dioramas, Historical Material, Manuscripts, Maps, Painting-American, Painting-American, Photography, Portraits, Posters, Prints, Restorations, Sculpture, Textiles, Watercolors
Collections: Railroad Rolling Stock, locomotives & related artifacts including tools, maps, manuals, timetables, passes, uniforms, silverware & lanterns, Transportation History (Railroad Locomotives & Train Cars), Railroad art & photographs
Publications: Milepost, 5 times annually
Activities: Children progs; docent progs; lects open to pub, 5-10 vis lectrs per yr; concerts; gallery talks; tours; schols offered; individual paintings & original objects of art lent; lending coll includes paintings & art objects; mus shop sells books, magazines, original art, reproductions, prints & slides

M **ROSE LEHRMAN ART GALLERY,** Harrisburg Area Community College, One HACC Dr Harrisburg, PA 17110-2903. Tel 717-780-2478; Email smwillia@hacc.edu; Web: www.hacc.edu; *Cur* Kim Banister
Mon - Fri 11 AM - 3 PM; Tues & Thurs 5 PM - 7 PM; small gallery, 7 exhibs per yr, contemporary art; Average Annual Attendance: 5,000
Special Subjects: Ceramics, Crafts, Drawings, Etchings & Engravings, Glass, Graphics, Landscapes
Collections: Painting & photographs; art exhibitions

A **SUSQUEHANNA ART MUSEUM,** 1401 N 3rd St, Harrisburg, PA 17102. Tel 717-233-8668; Email info@sqart.org; Web: www.sqart.org; *Exec Dir* Alice Anne Schwab; *Dir Exhibs* Lauren Nye; *Dir Educ* Tina Sell; *Events & Van Go* Ross Tyger; *Develop Mgr* Rick Stevens; *Office Mgr* Tasha James
Open Tues - Sat 10 AM - 5PM, Sun noon - 5 PM; Admis adults $8; Estab 1989 as a nonprofit; 20,000 sq ft museum & education center that hosts large scale regional & International exhibs; Average Annual Attendance: 12,000; Mem: 400
Exhibitions: 3 exhibs per yr
Activities: Classes for adults & children; student internships; docent training; lects open to pub; lects for mems only; 4 vis lectrs per yr; gallery talks; tours; exten prog serves central PA, schools & communities; artmobile; organize traveling exhibs to schools, festivals & communities; mus shop sells books, prints & jewelry

HAVERFORD

A **MAIN LINE ART CENTER,** 746 Panmure Rd, Haverford, PA 19041-1218. Tel 610-525-0272; Fax 610-525-5036; Email jherman@mainlineart.org; info@mainlineart.org; Web: www.mainlineart.org; *Exec Dir* Judy Herman
Open Mon - Thurs 9 AM - 9 PM, Fri 9 AM - 5 PM, Sat & Sun 9 AM - 5 PM; No admis fee; Estab 1937 to develop and encourage the fine arts; Three large, well-lit galleries, completely modernized to accommodate exhibits including sculptures, ceramics, paintings, crafts; Average Annual Attendance: 1,200; Mem: 800; dues family $75; individual $50; children $35
Income: Financed by mem, tui, fundraising, & sponsors
Exhibitions: Ann mem exhib
Publications: Brochures, five times per yr
Activities: Classes for adults, teens & children; lect open to pub; gallery talks; trips; tours; member exhibitions juried; competitions with awards; curated exhibitions

HERSHEY

M **HERSHEY MUSEUM,** 111 W Chocolate Ave, Hershey, PA 17033-1558. Tel 717-520-5722; Fax 717-534-8940; Email info@hersheymuseum.org; Web: www.hersheystory.org; *Exec Dir* Marta Howell; *Interim Dir* Don Papson; *Dir Educ* Mariella Trosko; *Pub Programs Mgr* Lois Miklas; *Coll Mgr* Valerie Seiber
Open Memorial Day - Labor Day daily 10 AM - 8 PM, Sept - May daily 10 AM - 5 PM, cl New Year's Day, Thanksgiving, Christmas Eve & Day; Admis adults $10, seniors $9 children 3-12 $7.50, 2 & under free; Estab 1933 to preserve & collect history of Hershey, Central Pennsylvania heritage (Pennsylvania Germans); Average Annual Attendance: 90,215; Mem: 2600; dues individual $35, household $60, inventor $150, industrialist $250, entrepreneur $500, philanthropist $1,000
Special Subjects: Crafts, Decorative Arts, Furniture, Porcelain, Pottery, Textiles, Woodcarvings, American Indian Art, Ceramics, Folk Art, Historical Material, Glass, Painting-American
Collections: History of Hershey (the town, the bus, & M S Hershey), 19th century Pennsylvania German Life American Indian
Publications: Quarterly newsletter
Activities: Classes for adults & children; docent training; family progs; progs in schools; lect open to pub; concerts; gallery talks; tours; mus shop sells books & craft items relating to mus colls; childrens' discovery room

HONESDALE

M **WAYNE COUNTY HISTORICAL SOCIETY,** Museum, 810 Main St, Honesdale, PA 18431-1847; PO Box 446, Honesdale, PA 18431-0446. Tel 570-253-3240; Fax 570-253-5204; Email wchs@ptd.net; Web:

www.waynehistorypa.org; *Pres* Elaine Herzog; *Dir* Sally Talaga; *Librn* Gloria McCullough; *Shop Mgr* Kay Stephenson; *VPres* Lars Hanson; *Treas* Tom Colbert
Open Wed - Sat 10 AM - 4 PM (Apr - Dec), cl Jan - mid-Apr; Admis adults $5, children 6-18 $3, children under 5 free; Estab 1924 as a repository of artifacts, publs, archival & other items relating to Wayne County; Historic building; Average Annual Attendance: 19,750; Mem: 750; dues $35 - $50; 12 meetings per yr
Income: $82,000 (financed by dues, donations, sales & grants)
Special Subjects: American Indian Art, Archaeology, Furniture, Glass, Historical Material, Manuscripts, Maps, Painting-American, Photography, Portraits
Collections: Artifacts of Wayne County History, Jennie Brownscombe (paintings), Native American Archaeology Coll, Costume Coll, Cut Glass Coll, Early Glass Coll, Stourbridge Lion (first locomotive to run in America)
Exhibitions: Wayne County Glass, Window Pane to White House Crystal; Datt Canal Company permanent exhibit
Publications: Quarterly newsletter
Activities: School group tours; docent training; lect open to public, 4 vis lectrs per year; tours; ann historic preservation awards; sales shop sells books, maps, t-shirts, train memorabilia & art reproductions

HUNTINGDON

M **JUNIATA COLLEGE MUSEUM OF ART,** 1700 Moore St, Huntingdon, PA 16652-2119. Tel 814-641-3505; Fax 814-641-3607; Email maloney@juniata.edu; Web: www.juniata.edu/museum; *Dir* Judy Maloney
Open May - Aug Wed - Fri noon - 4 PM; Sept - Apr Mon - Fri 10 AM - 4 PM, Sat noon-4PM; cl major holidays & col holidays; No admis fee; Estab 1998 to serve the Pennsylvania & mid-Atlantic arts community; 2 galleries, 1,000 sq ft each, 1 permanent coll & 1 temporary exhib; Average Annual Attendance: 2,000; Mem: 35; dues student & sr citizen $15; family $35; contributor $100; supporter $250; patron $500
Income: Financed by parent institution (Juniata College) & endowments
Purchases: W B Stottlemyer Coll of Art
Special Subjects: American Indian Art, Decorative Arts, Drawings, Etchings & Engravings, Graphics, Landscapes, Painting-American, Painting-British, Painting-Dutch, Painting-French, Painting-German, Painting-Italian, Photography, Posters, Prints, Watercolors, Woodcuts
Collections: American Portrait miniatures, Contemporary works on paper, Hudson River School paintings, Navajo weavings, Old Master prints & paintings, 19th century Japanese prints
Publications: Exhib publs
Activities: Mus studies prog; lect open to pub; book traveling exhibs 4 per yr

HUNTINGDON VALLEY

AMERICAN COLOR PRINT SOCIETY
For further information, see National and Regional Organizations

INDIANA

M **INDIANA UNIVERSITY OF PENNSYLVANIA,** Kipp Gallery, 470 Sprowls Hall, 11th St Indiana, PA 15705-0001. Tel 724-357-6495; Fax 724-357-7778; Email field27@hotmail.com; Web: www.iup.edu; *Dir Gallery* Dr Richard Field
Open Tues - Wed & Fri-Sat noon-5PM, Thurs noon-9PM; No admis fee; Estab 1970 to make available a professional gallery prog to Western Pennsylvania & to the university community; Versatile space with portable wall system, track lighting, secure, humidity controlled; Average Annual Attendance: 12,000
Income: Financed by Student Coop Assoc
Exhibitions: Student Honors Show; National Metal & Clay Invitational; rotating exhibits
Activities: Lect open to pub, 3-5 vis lectrs per yr; gallery talks; tours; book traveling exhibs; originates traveling exhibs

JENKINTOWN

M **ABINGTON ART CENTER,** 515 Meetinghouse Rd, Jenkintown, PA 19046-2964. Tel 215-887-4882; Fax 215-887-5789; Email info@abingtonartcenter.org; Web: abingtonartcenter.org; *Exec Dir* Laura E Burnham; *Chmn* Eric Weckel; *Educ Dir* Marge Horner; *Develop Dir* Betsy Weand-Kilkenny
Open Wed - Fri 10 AM - 5 PM, Thurs 10 AM - 7 PM, Sat - Sun 10 AM - 3 PM, cl New Year's Eve & Day, Presidents Day, Passover, Good Friday, Memorial Day, Independence Day, Labor Day, Rosh Hashanah, Yom Kippur, Thanksgiving & Christmas week; No admis fee, donations accepted; Estab 1939; Average Annual Attendance: 34,500; Mem: 649; dues individual $50, dual/family $65, mem plus $75, patron mem $125 & up
Income: Financed by mem, donations, earned income
Special Subjects: Costumes, Textiles, Decorative Arts, Painting-American, Photography, Prints, Drawings, Graphics, Sculpture
Exhibitions: Sculpture park; semi-permanent installations; Exhibs feature work by regional contemporary artists
Publications: Exhibit catalogs
Activities: Classes for adults & children; lect open to the pub; 2-6 vis lectrs per yr; concerts; gallery talks; tours; sponsoring of competitions; schols; ann juried show awards for best of show & other outstanding work; sales shop sells original art, eco-themed merchandise

KING OF PRUSSIA

M **MONTGOMERY COUNTY GUILD OF PROFESSIONAL ARTISTS,** PO Box 60736, King of Prussia, PA 19406. Tel 610-265-6963; Email mcgopa_art@yahoo.com; Web: www.mcgopa.org; *Gallery Dir* Pam McLean-Parker
Estab 1998
Collections: paintings; sculpture; drawings

KUTZTOWN

M **KUTZTOWN UNIVERSITY,** The Martin & Regina Miller Gallery, College Blvd & Main St, Kutztown, PA 19530-0730; PO Box 730, Kutztown, PA 19530-0730. Tel 646-484-5803, 610-683-1575; Fax 610-683-4547; Email stanford@kutztown.edu; Web: www.kutztown.edu/acad/artgallery; *Dir Univ Galleries & Community Outreach* Karen Stanford
Open Tues - Fri 10 AM - 4 PM; Sat Noon - 4 PM, Sun 2 - 4 PM; No admis fee; Estab 1956 to make high quality contemporary art available to the college, community & region; 2400 sq ft facility that presents contemporary art, design & crafts; Average Annual Attendance: 6,000
Income: Financed by state & pvt appropriations
Special Subjects: Ceramics, Collages, Crafts, Decorative Arts, Drawings, Folk Art, Graphics, Hispanic Art, Jewelry, Landscapes, Latin American Art, Painting-American, Portraits, Posters, Prints, Sculpture, Silver, Textiles, Watercolors, Woodcarvings, Woodcuts
Collections: Approx 1,000 works in prints, drawings & paintings
Exhibitions: 7 temporary exhibs per year
Publications: Brochure listing gallery shows; ann catalog
Activities: Artist-in-residence series; lectr progs; lects open to pub

L **Rohrbach Library**, 15200 Kutztown Rd, Bldg 5 Kutztown, PA 19530-9335. Tel 610-683-4480; Fax 610-683-4747; Web: www.kutztown.edu/library; *Reference Librn* Janet Bond; *Dean Library Serv* Barbara Simpson Darden
Open Mon - Thurs 7:45 AM - 12 AM, Fri 7:45 AM - 5 PM, Sat 9 AM - 5 PM, Sun 2 PM - 12 AM during school; Estab 1866; Circ 118,592
Library Holdings: Audio Tapes, Book Volumes 414,000, Cards 17,331, Cassettes, Exhibition Catalogs, Fiche 1,201,000, Filmstrips, Micro Print 212,908, Motion Pictures, Pamphlets, Periodical Subscriptions 1926, Records, Reels 35,000, Slides
Special Subjects: Art Education, Art History
Collections: Curriculum Materials, maps, Russian Culture

M **NEW ARTS PROGRAM, INC,** NAP Museum, NAP Main Gallery, William Zimmer Reference Library, 173 W Main St, Kutztown, PA 19530-1742; PO Box 82, Kutztown, PA 19530-0082. Tel 610-683-6440; Fax 610-683-6440; Email napconn@aol.com; Web: www.newartsprogram.org; *Dir* James F L Carroll; *Admin Asst* Joanne Carroll; *Vice Pres* Ted Ormai
Open Fri - Sun 11 AM - 3 PM or by appointment; No admis fee; min fee for performances & concerts, $5-$10, Performance Concerts $35-$40; Estab 1974 for each artist to have pub one to one conversation residencies, exhibs, and/or performance & presentations; Circ For reference libraries 150; 325 sq ft, 65 linear ft; Average Annual Attendance: 3,500; Mem: 250 supporting members, dues $30
Income: $55,000 (financed by mem, state appropriation, foundations, sales, supporting individuals & bus)
Library Holdings: Audio Tapes 100, Book Volumes 3,500, CD-ROMs 400, Cassettes 100, DVDs 4,500, Exhibition Catalogs 1,800, Kodachrome Transparencies 50,000 (slides), Original Art Works 350, Original Documents, Other Holdings 400, Pamphlets 100, Periodical Subscriptions 35, Photographs 200, Prints 1200, Records 200, Reels 100, Slides 40,000, Video Tapes 2,000
Collections: Prints, paintings, drawings, 50,000 slides, Booklets, 500 DVDs, 400 CDs, William Zimmer Art Reference Library, book from includes: periodicals, Catalogues, Slikes, ED.s DVD's and books with extensive information on the business of art, studio materials, color, grant, art law and safety + archives of 600 artists since 1974.
Exhibitions: International Salon Invitational (small works) exhib; one juried solo residency & exhibition & 3 invitation solo residency & exhibition, performances, each year; Exhibition Main Gallery Space, since 1984. Three invited Artists Solo Conversation Residencies + annually Exhibition or performance. Annual International Invitational Salon Exhibition of Small Works, since 1990. Annual National Juried Solosss Conversation Residency since 1997.; Artists and Writers Group Forum, monthly meetings since 2002; Workshops: "Paint & Conservation" by Mark Golden of Golden Artist Colors, 2003; "Varnishes & Conservation" by Mark Golden, 2004, "On Being Archival" by Mark Golden, 2010"; Forum on Writing and Understanding Art Criticism, with William Zimmer, art critic, 2004 and 2005; The Project Wall, for 12 weeks includes a booklet at Closing Reception, since 2012; Acrylic Clinic by Roy Kinzer from Golden Artist Colors, 2013
Publications: In & Out of Kutztown; NAP Text(s), International video festival booklets; NAP Preview and annual fan fold cards, DVDs CDs; Books and Catalogues: In and Out of New York catalogue, 1980; In and Out of Kutztown: The First Seven Years, 1981; Ideas from Individual Impressions and Marks: Prints of non-printmakers catalogue (17 artists), 1988, with Lehigh University Art Galleries, Bethlehem PA; Patricia Johnson: Public Landscape, catalogue, 1991; Julius Tobias: Works, 1965-92, catalogue, 1992; Dance on Paper, dancers and choreographers who have participated in the NAP Residency program for the past 27 years, catalogue, 2001, with Lehigh University Art Galleries, Bethlehem, PA; NAP Text (s), literary art journal, (seven volumes), since 1994; NAP International Traveling Video Festival, five screenings throughout the US from 1996-2003; CD Connection, the first 10 musicians/composers from 1975-1982, released 1996; Booklets, over 90 artists in conversations about their work have been recorded and transcribe (20-40 pages) since 1996; NAP: Crating, Packing and Shipping Art, released 1999, a professionally directed and produced, instructional 80-minute DVD with transcript; Keith Haring Video, released 2001, presentation, exhibition, and drawings at the New Arts Program in 1982 & 1987, an 86-minute DVD with transcript, since 2001
Activities: Two one hour TV progs monthly; Fanfold Cards for yearly activities; preview for yearly activities; Dance on Paper; ideas from individual impressions & marks; Prints of non-printmakers; In & Out of New York; First 10 Composers & Musicians through 1974; Keith Haring DVD; individual consultations (one-to-one) 2 day residency for each artist; presentations open to pub; 4 vis presentations per yr; concerts; gallery talks & presentations; sponsoring of competitions; exhibition residency and consultation; lects open to pub; solo exhibition competition; residency and consultation; Lehigh Valley, Phil, Berks, Lancaster Counties; Television Programs, two one hour cable programs live each month on BCTV.org New Arts Alive, since 1987, and NAP Connection since 1992 both rebroadcast in Philadelphia and New York City since 1996; sales shop sells original art, prints, and NAP publications, CDs, DVDs, VHS, catalogues, posters, T-shirts; new/used donated art materials; Limited Print editions, 69+ editions, since 1979; Poster by Robert Stanley, 1985, signed and unsigned; Posters by Keith Haring, 1984 and

1990, unsigned; Live On Paper: book form, an ongoing project of literary, visual and performing artists making a book form with handmade paper, edition of ten, in collaboration with White Crow Paper Mill, since 1997; T-shirts designs by Keith Haring and Lawrence Weiner, since 1998

L **PENNSYLVANIA GERMAN CULTURAL HERITAGE CENTER AT KUTZTOWN UNIVERSITY,** 22 Luckenbill Rd, Kutztown, PA 19530-9203. Tel 610-683-1589; Email heritage@kutztown.edu; Web: www.kutztown.edu/community/pgchc
Open Mon - Fri 10 AM - Noon and 1 - 4 PM, cl holidays; tours by appt; Admis non-mems $5, mems free; Estab 1992 to preserve the Pennsylvania German Culture; Reference library for genealogy, history & folk art, mus tours & pub events; Mem: Dues $25
Income: Financed by donations & mems
Library Holdings: Audio Tapes, Book Volumes 1500, CD-ROMs, Cassettes, Clipping Files, Filmstrips, Manuscripts, Maps, Memorabilia, Pamphlets, Periodical Subscriptions 4, Photographs, Prints, Records, Reels 27, Slides, Video Tapes
Special Subjects: Architecture, Carpets & Rugs, Crafts, Decorative Arts, Folk Art, Handicrafts, Historical Material, Maps, Textiles, Ethnology
Collections: Approx 10,000 items relating to 18th & 19th century homelife, farmlife & schooling
Publications: Review
Activities: Classes for adults & children; Easter on the Farm; Children's Cultural Camp; Christmas on the Farm; lects open to pub; school tours

LANCASTER

M **LANCASTER MUSEUM OF ART,** 135 N Lime St, Lancaster, PA 17602-2952. Tel 717-394-3497; Fax 717-394-0101; Email info@lmapa.org; Web: www.lmapa.org; *Dir* Stanley I Grand PhD
Open Tues - Sat 10 AM - 4 PM, Sun Noon - 4 PM; Admis by donation; Estab 1965 to present contemporary art exhibits; 4,000 sq ft facility in historic 1845; Grubb mansion; Average Annual Attendance: 35,000; Mem: 1,000; dues, various categories
Income: $750,000 (financed by mem, local foundations, corporations
Collections: Permanent collection focusing on works by regional artists
Exhibitions: Exhibition schedule includes 15 exhibits per year
Publications: Quarterly newsletter
Activities: Classes for adults & children; lect open to pub, vis lectrs; gallery talks; tours; competition with awards; mus shop sells original art & prints

M **LANDIS VALLEY VILLAGE AND FARM MUSEUM, PA HISTORICAL & MUSEUM COMMISSION,** 2451 Kissel Hill Rd, Lancaster, PA 17601-4809. Tel 717-569-0401; Fax 717-560-2147; Email bbomberger@pa.gov; Web: www.landisvalleymuseum.org; *Dir* Stephen S Miller; *Cur* Bruce Bomberger; *Cur Community Life* Susan Messimer; *Events Coordr* Susan Kelleher; *Mus Shop Mgr* Shelby Chunko; *Farm & Garden Mgr* Joseph Meyer; *Heirloom Seed Project* Joseph Schott; *Bus Mgr* Judy Weese; *Board Pres* Peter Barber; *Interpretation Supvr* April Frantz; *Mktg & Develop* Marilyn Monath
Open Mon - Sat 9 AM - 5 PM, Sun Noon - 5 PM, cl some holidays; Admis adults $10, seniors $8, children 6-17 $7, children under 6 free, group rates available; Estab 1925 to collect, preserve & interpret Pennsylvania rural life & Pennsylvania German culture, c 1750 to 1940; farm implements, crafts, tools, domestic furnishings & folk art; The outdoor mus has 25 exhibit buildings, including restored 18th & 19th century structures & historical garden landscapes, as well as historical animal breeds; Average Annual Attendance: 57,000; Mem: 480; dues information upon request
Income: Financed by state appropriation & local support group
Special Subjects: Architecture, Calligraphy, Crafts, Decorative Arts, Folk Art, Furniture, Glass
Collections: Baskets, books, ceramics & glass, farm equipment, Fraktur, ironware, musical instruments, Pennsylvania German furniture, textiles, toys & weapons, tools, vehicles
Exhibitions: Dreamers and Visionaries: Focusing on the Landis Valley Legacy
Publications: Newsletter, 4 times per yr; Valley Gazette; spec exhibit catalogs
Activities: Classes for children; tours; research coll contains ceramics & glass, textiles, tools & equipment; mus shop sells books, original art, prints, craft items and period reproductions

L **Landis Collections Gallery**, 2451 Kissel Hill Rd, Lancaster, PA 17601-4809. Tel 717-569-0401; Fax 717-560-2147; Email bbomberger@pa.gov; Web: www.landisvalleymuseum.org; *Dir* James Lewars; *Cur* Dr Bruce D Bomberger; *Cur* Mrs Jennifer Royer
Open Mon - Sat 9 AM - 5 PM, Sun noon - 5 PM; Admis adults $12; estab 1925; Open to staff, scholars by appointment for reference only; Average Annual Attendance: 65,000; Mem: 2,500
Income: Financed by state appropriations & Landis Valley Assoc support group
Library Holdings: Book Volumes 12,000, Exhibition Catalogs, Manuscripts, Maps, Original Art Works, Original Documents, Periodical Subscriptions 25, Photographs
Special Subjects: Decorative Arts, Folk Art, Furniture, Historical Material, Tapestries
Collections: Approx 100,000 objects, most representing PA German & rural PA heritage
Exhibitions: Changing annually
Activities: Classes for adults & children; Lects open to pub; 6 vis lects per yr; gallery talks; tours; concerts; mus shop sells books, magazines, reproductions & prints

M **ROCK FORD FOUNDATION, INC,** Rock Ford Plantation, 881 Rock Ford Rd, Lancaster, PA 17602-1225. Tel 717-392-7223; Fax 717-392-7283; Email rockfordmail@yahoo.com; Web: www.rockfordplantation.org; *Pres Bd* Ray Bradley; *Exec Dir* Samuel C Slaymaker; *Cur, Educ Prog Coordr & Vol Coordr* Sarah Alberico; *Asst to Dir* Nancy Bradley
Open Apr - Oct Tues - Sun 11 AM - 3 PM, Nov - March by appt; Admis adult $8, senior $7, children 6 - 12 $6; Estab 1958 for preservation of General Edward Hand Mansion; Late 18th century & American furnishing & decor; Average Annual Attendance: 3,000; Mem: 600; dues $50 - $10,000; ann meeting first Fri in Dec
Income: $278,000 (financed by mem, endowment, shop sales & special events)
Library Holdings: Book Volumes, CD-ROMs, Compact Disks, Exhibition Catalogs, Manuscripts, Memorabilia, Original Art Works, Original Documents, Photographs, Reproductions
Special Subjects: Decorative Arts, Furniture, Period Rooms
Collections: American furniture & decorative arts 1780 - 1802, Portraits of General Hand & Family Members
Publications: Newsletter
Activities: Classes for children & adults; docent progs; Revolutionary War encampment; Colonial Tavern Nights Yuletide tours; Haunted History Prog; lects open to pub; tours; concerts; TripAdvisor, Certificate of Excellence, 2016; serves Lancaster, PA region; mus shop sells books, magazines, original art, prints & reproductions

M **WOLF MUSEUM OF MUSIC AND ART,** 423 W Chestnut Ave, Lancaster, PA 17603; PO Box 701, Lancaster, PA 17608-0701. Tel 717-392-6382; Web: wolfmuseum.org
Open by appointment & for public recitals
Collections: Family history; period furnishings; personal artifacts; two 1915 Knabe concert grand pianos; paintings
Activities: Public recitals

LEWISBURG

M **BUCKNELL UNIVERSITY,** Edward & Marthann Samek Art Gallery, 701 Moore Ave, Elaine Langone Ctr Fl 3 Lewisburg, PA 17837-2010. Tel 570-577-3792; Fax 570-577-3215; Email peltier@bucknell.edu; Web: www.departments.bucknell.edu/samek; *Operations Mgr* Cynthia Peltier; *Asst Registrar* Tracy Graham
Open Mon - Wed & Fri 11 AM - 5 PM, Thurs 11 AM - 8 PM, Sat & Sun 1 - 5 PM; No admis fee; Estab 1983; Gallery contains a permanent display of 20 Baroque & Renaissance paintings and 1 sculpture of the Renaissance given by the Samuel H Kress Foundation; Average Annual Attendance: 24,853
Income: Financed by endowment, tui, gifts, & grants
Library Holdings: DVDs, Exhibition Catalogs, Original Art Works, Photographs, Prints, Sculpture, Video Tapes
Special Subjects: African Art, Antiquities-Egyptian, Antiquities-Etruscan, Antiquities-Greek, Antiquities-Oriental, Antiquities-Persian, Antiquities-Roman, Asian Art, Baroque Art, Bronzes, Calligraphy, Carpets & Rugs, Ceramics, Collages, Decorative Arts, Drawings, Etchings & Engravings, Graphics, Hispanic Art, Historical Material, Landscapes, Latin American Art, Manuscripts, Mexican Art, Oriental Art, Painting-American, Painting-British, Painting-Canadian, Painting-Dutch, Painting-European, Painting-Flemish, Painting-French, Painting-German, Painting-Italian, Painting-Japanese, Painting-Russian, Photography, Portraits, Posters, Prints, Religious Art, Renaissance Art, Sculpture, Tapestries, Watercolors, Woodcarvings, Woodcuts, Painting-Polish, Painting-Scandinavian, Painting-Spanish
Collections: The permanent coll contains over 5,000 objects from many cultures & all over the globe
Exhibitions: Rotating exhibits 5 times per yr
Publications: see catalogue & brochure section on website-www.bucknell.edu/samek
Activities: Lect open to pub, 1-5 vis lectrs per yr; concert; gallery talks; tours; competitions; individual paintings & original objects of art lent to mus & acad inst; occasionally 1-2 book traveling exhibs per yr; originate traveling exhibs to Univ galleries & museums; mus shop sells books

M **FETHERSTON FOUNDATION,** Packwood House Museum, 15 N Water St, Lewisburg, PA 17837-1531. Tel 570-524-0323; Fax 570-524-0548; Email info@packwoodhousemuseum.com; Web: www.Packwoodhousemuseum.com; *Admin* Jennifer Snyder
Open Tues - Sat 10 AM - 5 PM; mus tours by appt only; Admis adults $10, seniors $7, students $7, under 12 free; Estab 1976 to serve the community as an educational institution; Historic house with decorative arts, 18th-20th century & changing exhibits galleries; Average Annual Attendance: 4,500; Mem: 300; dues life-time $2,500, benefactor $500, patron $250, sponsor $125, family $45, individual $30, student $5
Income: Financed by endowment, admis, mem, mus shop & grants
Library Holdings: Auction Catalogs, Book Volumes, Exhibition Catalogs, Lantern Slides, Manuscripts, Maps, Original Documents, Pamphlets, Photographs, Slides
Special Subjects: American Indian Art, Antiquities-Assyrian, Antiquities-Byzantine, Antiquities-Egyptian, Antiquities-Etruscan, Antiquities-Greek, Antiquities-Oriental, Antiquities-Persian, Antiquities-Roman, Archaeology, Art History, Asian Art, Bronzes, Carpets & Rugs, Ceramics, Coins & Medals, Costumes, Crafts, Decorative Arts, Dioramas, Dolls, Embroidery, Etchings & Engravings, Ethnology, Flasks & Bottles, Folk Art, Furniture, Glass, Historical Material, History of Art & Archaeology, Islamic Art, Ivory, Jade, Jewelry, Landscapes, Manuscripts, Maps, Metalwork, Oriental Art, Painting-American, Photography, Porcelain, Portraits, Pottery, Sculpture, Silver, Stained Glass, Textiles, Watercolors, Woodcarvings, Pre-Columbian Art
Collections: American Fine Arts, Central Pennsylvania artifacts, Fine Period Clothing ranging from 1890s to 1960s, 1780-1940 decorative arts: ceramics, furniture, glass, metalwork, textiles, Fetherston Family Archives, Edith H K Fetherston Collection, Pennsylvania German decorative arts
Exhibitions: Packwood House; annual summer exhibit (June-Sept); annual scholastic Art Exhibit (Apr-May); one-person art exhibits
Publications: Chanticleer, three times yearly, newsletter for members
Activities: Classes for adults & children; docent training; lect open to pub; 3 vis lectrs per year; tours; gallery talks; Scholastic Arts Exhibit; mus shop sells books, original art, prints, slides, reproductions & local handcrafted items

LORETTO

M **SOUTHERN ALLEGHENIES MUSEUM OF ART,** Loretto Facility, St Francis University Mall, 112 Franciscan Way Loretto, PA 15940; PO Box 9, Loretto, PA 15940-0009. Tel 814-472-3920; Fax 814-472-4131; Email loretto@sama-art.org; Web: www.sama-art.org; *Exec Dir* G Gary Moyer; *Cur Visual Arts* Dr V Scott Dimond; *Educ Coordr* Jessica Campbell; *Coll Mgr* Bobby J Moore; *Facilities Mgr* Lee Rummel; *Bookkeeper* Sandra Hampton
Open Tues - Fri 10 AM - 5 PM, Sat 1 - 5 PM, cl Sun, Mon & holidays; No admis fee; fees for special exhibs & progs apply; Estab & dedicated June 1975 to facilitate interest, understanding & the appreciation of the visual arts of the past, present & future through the exhibition of our permanent as well as temporary colls; Large open main gallery with flexible space, second floor graphics gallery; Average Annual Attendance: 75,000; Mem: 1000
Income: Financed by mem, bus, corporate & foundation grants
Purchases: Contemporary American Art especially by living Pennsylvania artists are purchased for the permanent collection
Special Subjects: Ceramics, Drawings, Graphics, Painting-American, Prints, Sculpture, Crafts
Collections: Frank & Margaret Sullivan Collection, Nicholas Unkovic Collection, Charles M Schwab Collection, Mark Del Costello Collection, Rezk Collection
Publications: Online catalogs; newsletters; exhib & events brochures
Activities: Classes for adults & children; intern prog in cooperation with area colleges; school progs; workshops; family activities; artist-in-res progs; lects open to pub, 8 vis lectrs per yr; gallery talks; tours; film series; exten dept serves Altoona, Johnstown & Ligonier; individual paintings & original objects of art lent to other institutions on request for special exhibs; lending collection contains 2000 lantern slides; book traveling exhibs 1-3 per yr; originate traveling exhibs to art galleries

M **Johnstown Gallery**, 450 Schoolhouse Rd, Pasquerilla Performing Arts Center at University of Pittsburgh Johnstown, PA 15904-2912; PO Box 9, Loretto, PA 15940. Tel 814-269-7234; Fax 814-269-7240; Email loretto@sama-art.org; Web: www.sama-art.org; *Exec Dir* G Gary Moyer; *Johnstown Coordr* Tina Lehman
Open Mon - Fri 9:30 AM - 4:30 PM, before & during all performing arts events, cl holidays; No admis fee; fees for special exhibs & progs apply; Estab 1982 to bring regional art to a wider audience & provide educational opportunities; Gallery 135 running ft; Average Annual Attendance: 38,500
Income: Financed by mem, city appropriation, private & foundation support, state & federal art agency funding
Special Subjects: Asian Art, Ceramics, Collages, Drawings, Etchings & Engravings, Folk Art, Landscapes, Painting-American, Photography, Portraits, Posters, Prints, Sculpture, Textiles, Watercolors, Woodcuts
Publications: Online catalogs; newsletters; exhib & events brochures
Activities: Classes for adults & children; docent progs; film series; workshops; family progs; artist-in-res progs; lects open to pub, 8 vis lectrs per yr; gallery talks; tours; book traveling exhibs 1 per yr; originate traveling exhibs nationally to other mus

M **Altoona Facility**, 1210 11th Ave, Altoona, PA 16601; PO Box 9, Loretto, PA 15940-0009. Tel 814-946-4464; Fax 814-946-3131; Email loretto@sama-art.org; Web: www.sama-art.org; *Exec Dir* G Gary Moyer; *Altoona Coordr* Barbara J Hollander
Open Tues - Fri 10 AM - 5 PM, Sat 1-5 PM, cl Sun, Mon & holidays; No admis fee; special progs & exhib fees apply; State of the art exhib space, storage space
Special Subjects: Photography
Collections: Shirley & Fred A Pechter Gallery, Wolf Gallery, William H Rau Collection: albumen photographic prints c1900
Exhibitions: Quarterly exhibs
Publications: Online catalogs; newsletters; exhib & events brochures
Activities: Classes for adults & children; family progs; workshops; artist-in-res progs; lects open to pub; film series; tours

M **Ligonier Valley Facility**, 1 Boucher Ln, Rte 711 Ligonier, PA 15658; PO Box 9, Loretto, PA 15940-0009. Tel 724-238-6015; Fax 724-238-6281; Email loretto@sama-art.org; Web: www.sama-art.org; *Exec Dir* G Gary Moyer; *Ligonier Valley Coordr* Sommer Toffle; *Pub Rels Coordr* Travis Mearns
Open Tues - Fri 10 AM - 5 PM, Sat & Sun 1-5 PM, cl Mon & holidays; No admis fee; fees for special exhibs & progs apply; Modeled on an authentic log cabin design that reflects the historic community, & surrounded by gardens
Special Subjects: Glass
Collections: Walter Carlyle Shaw Paperweight Collection
Publications: Online catalogs; newsletters; exhib & event brochures
Activities: Classes for adults & children; family progs; workshops; artist-in-res progs; lects open to pub; film series; tours

MEADVILLE

M **ALLEGHENY COLLEGE,** Bowman, Megahan & Penelec Galleries, 520 N Main St, Campus Box 23 Meadville, PA 16335-3903. Tel 814-332-4365; Fax 814-332-6238; Email damiller@allegheny.edu; Web: www.allegheny.edu/artgalleries; *Gallery Dir* Darren Lee Miller; *Bldg Coordr* Sherry Vardaro
Open Tues - Fri 12:30 - 5 PM, Sat 1:30 - 5 PM, Sun 2 - 4 PM, cl Mon; No admis fee; Estab 1971 as one of the major exhibition spaces in northwest Pennsylvania; the galleries present exhibits ranging from works of contemporary artists to displays relevant to other fields of study; Galleries are housed in three spacious rooms, white walls, terrazzo floor, 10 ft ceilings; Average Annual Attendance: 5,000
Income: Financed by college funds & grants
Collections: Allegheny College Permanent Collection
Activities: Lects open to pub, 8-10 vis lectrs per yr; gallery talks; tours; student awards; individual paintings & original objects of art lent to art galleries & museums; book traveling exhibitions, 1 every 1-2 yrs

M **CRAWFORD COUNTY HISTORICAL SOCIETY,** Baldwin-Reynolds House Museum, 411 Chestnut St, Meadville, PA 16335-2902. Tel 814-333-9882 (Mus, seasonal); 724-6080 (Historical Society, yr round); Email museum@baldwinreynolds.org; crawfordhistorical@zoominternet.net; Web: www.baldwinreynolds.org; www.crawfordhistorical.org
Open mid-May - Aug Wed - Sun Noon - 4 PM; tours at Noon, 1, 2 & 3 PM; Admis adults $5, children ages 6 - 18 $3, children under 6 with adult free; group rates available

A **MEADVILLE COUNCIL ON THE ARTS,** PO Box 337, Meadville, PA 16335-0337. Tel 814-336-5051; Fax 814-336-5051; Email artscouncil@zoominternet.net; Web: www.meadvillecouncilonthearts.com
Open Wed & Fri Noon - 4 PM; Sat 10 AM - 2 PM; No admis fee; Estab 1975 for local arts information & programming; to create community arts center; Gallery has 50 ft of wall space; Average Annual Attendance: 8,000; Mem: benefactor $500, partner $200-499, sustaining $100-199, family $70, individual $40, student/senior $20
Income: $60,000 (financed by mem & state appropriation)
Purchases: Yearly piece for permanent collection
Exhibitions: Annual October Evenings Exhibition; annual county wide exhibits; monthly gallery shows for local artists and crafters exhibits; Annual juried member exhib; annual photo juried exhib
Publications: Quarterly newsletter
Activities: Classes for adults & children; dramatic progs; special populations; lects open to pub; concerts; $1100 visual arts awards, annual juried show; gallery talks; plays & shows in theatre; schols offered; exten prog serving Meadville & surrounding area; Taste of Arts Prog for nursing homes & senior ctrs; collaborate with Meadville Housing Authority - art related progs for children

MERION

M **BARNES FOUNDATION,** 300 N Latch's Ln, Merion, PA 19066-1729; 2025 Benjamin Franklin Pkwy, Philadelphia, PA 19130. Tel 215-278-7000; Fax 215-278-7017; Email info@barnesfoundation.org; Web: www.barnesfoundation.org; *Chair* Joseph Neubauer; *Exec Dir* Thomas Collins; *Deputy Dir Research, Interpretation & Educ* Martha Lucy; *Dir Living Collections & Horticulture Progs* Jacob Thomas, PhD
Open Wed - Mon 11 AM - 5 PM, cl Tues; Admis general $25, seniors $23, college students & youth (13-18) $5, mems & children under 3 free; Estab 1922 to promote the advancement of educ & the appreciation of fine art & horticulture; Maintains Gallery & Arboretum, & owns Ker-Feal farmhouse; Average Annual Attendance: 65,000; Mem: 600; dues $90
Income: Grants, individual contributions & earned income
Library Holdings: Auction Catalogs, Book Volumes 5,000, Exhibition Catalogs, Lantern Slides, Manuscripts, Maps, Original Documents, Other Holdings Correspondence; Publications, Photographs, Video Tapes
Special Subjects: African Art, Antiquities-Egyptian, Antiquities-Oriental, Asian Art, Carpets & Rugs, Ceramics, Decorative Arts, Drawings, Furniture, Painting-American, Painting-Dutch, Painting-European, Painting-Flemish, Painting-French, Painting-German, Pottery, Southwestern Art, Tapestries, Textiles, Watercolors
Collections: Permanent coll of post-impressionism & early French modern art. Includes works by Cezanne, Matisse & Renoir, 18th century American decorative art, Native American decorative art, African Art, Greek, Roman & Egyptian antiquities, Botanical coll featuring magnolias, fern, stewartia
Activities: Classes for adults; docent training, K-12 teacher training & ACE evaluation for undergraduate cr; lects for mems only, 3-4 vis lectrs per yr, tours; mus shop sells books, reproductions & prints

MILL RUN

M **WESTERN PENNSYLVANIA CONSERVANCY,** Fallingwater, PO Box R, Mill Run, PA 15464-0167. Tel 724-329-8501; Fax 724-329-0881; Email fallingwater@paconserve.org; Web: www.fallingwater.org; *Mus Prog Asst* Clinton Piper; *Dir* Lynda Waggoner; *VPres Institutional Advancement* Genny McIntyre; *Dir Communs* Carmen Bray; *Cur Educ* Roy Young; *Dir Preservation* Scott Perkins
Open daily 10 AM - 4 PM, Mid-Mar - Nov, cl Wed; Admis $25 advance, $27 purchase on site; Estab 1963 to preserve, maintain & make available for public educ & appreciation Frank Lloyd Wright's Fallingwater; 1935 Frank Lloyd Wright weekend house for Edgar J Kaufmann family of Pittsburgh built between 1936-1939; Average Annual Attendance: 167,270; Mem: 1,574 members; dues $20-$40
Income: $2,800,000 (financed by mem, grants, admis, sales & royalties)
Library Holdings: Audio Tapes, Original Art Works
Special Subjects: Architecture
Collections: Ceramics, Decorative Arts, including furniture by Frank Lloyd Wright, Glass, Paintings & Graphic Works by Picasso, Diego Rivera, 19th century Japanese Prints, Sculptures by Lipschitz, Arp & Voulkos, Textiles
Activities: Educ prog; classes for adults & children; docent training; lect open to pub; tours; mus shop sells books, reproductions, prints, original art & slides

NAZARETH

M **MORAVIAN HISTORICAL SOCIETY,** 214 E Center St, Nazareth, PA 18064-2209. Tel 610-759-5070; Email info@moravianhistoricalsociety.org; Web: www.moravianhistoricalsociety.org; *Dir* Megan van Rarenswaay; *Shop Mgr* Colleen McMahon
Open daily 1 PM - 4 PM, cl major holidays; Admis $5, members & children under 5 free; Established in 1857, the Moravian Historical Society preserves and presents Moravian contributions toNorth American art, history, and culture. Housed in the 1740/1743 Whitefield House on the historicEphrata Tract, site of the first successful Moravian settlement in North America and home to thecontinent's oldest remaining Moravian structure. Museum collections include rare musical instruments, books, furniture, and art from three centuries of Moravian history.; Average Annual Attendance: 8,000; Mem: 500; dues $15 & up; ann meeting in Oct
Income: Financed by endowment, men, admissions & grants
Library Holdings: Audio Tapes, Book Volumes, Clipping Files, Compact Disks, DVDs, Framed Reproductions, Lantern Slides, Manuscripts, Maps, Original Art

Works, Original Documents, Pamphlets, Periodical Subscriptions, Photographs, Prints, Records, Reels, Reproductions, Slides, Video Tapes
Special Subjects: Decorative Arts, Eskimo Art, Etchings & Engravings, Folk Art, Furniture, Glass, Historical Material, Manuscripts, Maps, Painting-American, Portraits, Pottery, Religious Art, Textiles, Watercolors
Collections: John Valentine Haidt Collection of Religious Paintings
Exhibitions: 31st Dec, 2017) "Diverse Voices: Three Perspectives of Early Bethlehem"
Publications: Transactions, biennial; Journal of Moravian History - biannual
Activities: Classes for adults & children; docent training; internship opportunities; history camp for children; annual arts& crafts and christmas festivals; lects open to pub, 7 vis lectrs per yr; concerts; gallery talks; library tours; original objects or art lent to recognized & approved museums & historical societies; lending coll contains individual & original objects of art; mus shop sells books, original art, reproductions, prints, handmade crafts, German Moravian Stars

NEW BRIGHTON

M **MERRICK ART GALLERY,** 1100 5th Ave, New Brighton, PA 15066; PO Box 312, New Brighton, PA 15066-0312. Tel 724-846-1130; Email merrickartgallery@verizon.net; Web: www.merrickartgallery.org; *Dir & Educ Dir* Cynthia A Kundar; *Trustee* Karen Capper
Open Tues - Sat 10 AM - 4 PM; Sun 1 - 4 PM, Summer Wed-Sat 10AM-4PM cl Mon & holidays; No admis fee; charge for docent tour; Estab 1880 to preserve & interpret the collection of paintings & other objects owned by Edward Dempster Merrick, the founder. Also to foster local art through classes & one-man shows; All galleries are on the second floors of two parallel buildings with a connecting bridge; there are three small rooms & one large one. Three rooms have skylight monitors overhead; Average Annual Attendance: 6,000; Mem: 243; dues $25, $15 & $10; ann meeting Jan or Feb
Income: Financed by endowment & mem
Library Holdings: Memorabilia, Original Art Works, Original Documents, Photographs, Records, Sculpture, Slides
Special Subjects: Painting-American, Painting-European
Collections: Most paintings date from the 18th & 19th century. American artists Emil Bott, Birge Harrison, Thomas Hill, A F King, Edward and Thomas Moran, E Poole, F K M Rehn, W T Richards, W L Sonntag, Thomas Sully, Charles Curran, John F Kensett, Andrew Melrose, Ralph A Blackelock, Asher B Durand, Worthington Whittredge. European artists Gustave Courbet, Hans Makart, Pierre Paul Prud'hon, Richard Westall, Franz Xavier, Winterhalter, Peter Baumgartner, Leon Herbo, Jaques Bertrand, Rocks & minerals, Zoological
Publications: Newsletter, bimonthly
Activities: Classes for adults & children; docent training; dramatic progs; lects open to public; 2 vis lectrs per yr; concerts; gallery talks; tours; sponsoring of competitions; scholarships; ann student award; mus shop sells books

NEW CASTLE

M **HOYT CENTER FOR THE ARTS,** Arts & Education of the Hoyt, 124 E Leasure Ave, New Castle, PA 16101-2398. Tel 724-652-2882; Fax 724-657-8786; Email hoyt@hoytartcenter.org; Web: www.hoytartcenter.org; *Pres* Maria McKee; *Exec Dir* Kimberly Koller Jones; *Prog Dir* Robert Presnar; *Exhib Coordr* Patricia McLatchy; *Mktg Dir* Melissa Maiella
Open Tues, Weds & Thurs 11AM - 8 PM, Fri & Sat 11AM-4PM; No admis fee; Estab 1965 to encourage the development of the arts within the community; Maintains reference library; Average Annual Attendance: 74,000; Mem: 400; dues $30 - $2,500
Income: Classes, commissions, events, rentals, competitions, sponsorship, grants, membership
Library Holdings: Auction Catalogs, Book Volumes, Exhibition Catalogs, Maps, Memorabilia, Original Art Works, Original Documents, Periodical Subscriptions, Reproductions, Sculpture, Video Tapes
Special Subjects: American Western Art, Architecture, Carpets & Rugs, Ceramics, Collages, Costumes, Crafts, Decorative Arts, Dolls, Drawings, Embroidery, Enamels, Etchings & Engravings, Folk Art, Furniture, Glass, Graphics, Historical Material, Jewelry, Landscapes, Maps, Metalwork, Painting-American, Period Rooms, Pewter, Photography, Porcelain, Portraits, Posters, Pottery, Prints, Sculpture, Silver, Stained Glass, Textiles, Textiles, Watercolors, Woodcuts
Collections: Historic & contemporary works of national & regional artists, 19th Century Antiquities & Decorative Arts, WPA Posters; Shenango Chu-ina
Exhibitions: Hoyt Regional Art Show; Juried Art Shows
Publications: Quarterly newsletter
Activities: Classes for adults & children; dramatic progs; concerts; gallery talks; tours; sponsoring of competitions; lect open to pub, lects year-round; concerts; gallery talks; tours; competitions; festivals;; schols awarded; multiple venues; 1-2 traveling exhibs per yr; mus shop sells books; original art; reproductions; prints; jewelry & other items

NEW WILMINGTON

M **WESTMINSTER COLLEGE,** Art Gallery, Market St, New Wilmington, PA 16172-0001. Tel 724-946-7266; Fax 724-946-7256; Web: www.westminster.edu; *Dir* Kathy Koop
Open Mon - Sat 9 AM - 9 PM, Sun 1 - 9 PM; No admis fee; Estab 1854 to organize & present 7 exhibs per season, to organize traveling exhibs, publish art catalogs of national interest & to conduct visiting artists program; Average Annual Attendance: 15,000
Income: Financed by endowment, state & local grants
Special Subjects: Drawings, Painting-American, Prints
Collections: 19th & 20th century paintings, 20th century drawings & prints
Exhibitions: Seven exhibs annually by regional & national artists
Publications: Catalogs; Westminster College Art Gallery, annually
Activities: Lect open to pub, 4 vis lectrs per yr; gallery talks; originates traveling exhibs

NEWTOWN

M **BUCKS COUNTY COMMUNITY COLLEGE,** Hicks Art Center, 275 Swamp Rd, Fine Arts Dept Newtown, PA 18940-1524. Tel 215-968-8425; Fax 215-504-8530; *Dir Exhib* Fran Orlando; *Chmn* Frank Dominguez
Open Mon & Fri 9 AM - 4 PM, Tues - Thurs 9 AM - 8 PM, Sat 9 AM - Noon; No admis fee; Estab 1970 to bring outside artists to the community; Gallery covers 960 sq ft; Average Annual Attendance: 5,000
Income: Financed by county and state appropriation
Exhibitions: Six exhibits each acad yr, ending with student ann exhibit
Activities: Lect open to pub, 4 vis lectrs per yr; competitions; gallery talks; artmobile; 1 book traveling exhib per yr

PAOLI

M **WHARTON ESHERICK MUSEUM,** PO Box 595, Paoli, PA 19301-0595. Tel 610-644-5822; Fax 610-644-2244; Email information@whartonesherickmuseum.org; Web: www.whartonesherickmuseum.org; *Exec Dir & Cur* Paul Eisenhauer; *Pres* Laurence A Liss
Open Sat 10 AM - 5 PM, Sun 1 - 5 PM, weekdays groups only Mon - Fri 10 AM - 4 PM, cl Jan - Feb & major holidays; Admis adults $10, children under 12 $5; Estab 1971 for the preservation and exhib of the Studio and coll of sculptor Wharton Esherick (1887-1970), one of America's foremost artist/craftsmen. Esherick worked mostly in wood and is best known for his sculptural furniture; Studio is set high on hillside overlooking the Great Valley & is one of Wharton Esherick's monumental achievements. He worked forty years building, enlarging & altering it. A National Historic Landmark; Average Annual Attendance: 5,000; Mem: 450; dues family $75, individual $40
Income: $220,600 (financed by mem, endowment, admis, sales & grants)
Library Holdings: Audio Tapes, Clipping Files, Compact Disks, DVDs, Exhibition Catalogs, Original Documents, Photographs, Prints, Records
Special Subjects: Furniture, Ceramics, Crafts, Decorative Arts, Furniture, Painting-American, Sculpture, Woodcarvings, Woodcuts, Watercolors
Collections: 200 pieces of the artist's work, including furniture, paintings, prints, sculpture in wood, stone and ceramic, utensils and woodcuts
Exhibitions: Annual Thematic Woodworking Competition/Exhibition; Annual Woodworking Competition
Publications: Brochures; coll & exhibit catalogues
Activities: Lects open to pub; 6 vis lectrs per yr; tours; competitions with awards: PMA Craft Show - Excellence in Wood, Woodcut Award - Pennsylvania Academy of the Fine Arts; individual paintings & original objects of art lent to mus or exhibs; lending coll contains original art works & sculptures; originate traveling exhibs to colleges, galleries & mus; mus shop sells books, magazines, reproductions; slides, videos, posters, notecards, postcards & T-shirts

PHILADELPHIA

M **AFRICAN AMERICAN MUSEUM IN PHILADELPHIA,** 701 Arch St, Philadelphia, PA 19106-1504. Tel 215-574-0380; Fax 215-574-3110; Email programs@aampmuseum.org; Web: www.aampmuseum.org; *Pres & CEO* Patricia Wilson Aden; *Exhibs Mgr & Artist in Res* Richard Watson; *Devel Coordr* Margaret Smyth; *Dir Curatorial Svcs* Dejay Duckett; *Admin Mgr & Asst to Pres* Amber Mays
Open Wed - Sat 10 AM - 5 PM, Sun Noon - 5 PM, cl New Years, Memorial Day, Labor Day, Thanksgiving & Christmas; Admis adults $14, students, seniors & children (4-12) $10; group rates adults; Estab 1976; Gallery has 2 changing exhibits & 1 perm exhibit; Average Annual Attendance: 67,000; Mem: 1,000; Leon Sullivan Soc $1,000, Alain Locke Soc $500, small bus & organization $400, Sadie Alexander Soc $250, Marian Anderson Soc $150, family $75, individual $50, students & seniors $30
Special Subjects: Afro-American Art, Costumes, Crafts, Dolls, Drawings, Furniture, Graphics, Historical Material, Military Art, Painting-American, Photography, Portraits, Posters, Prints, Sculpture, Textiles, Watercolors, Woodcarvings, Archaeology, Coins & Medals, Collages, Etchings & Engravings, Religious Art, Woodcuts
Collections: Negro Baseball Leagues Collection of photographs & documents, Chief Justice Robert N C Nix Sr Collection, legal writings & memorabilia, Afro-American, artifacts relating to African American contributions to political, religions & family life, Civil Rights Movement, arts & entertainment, sports, medicine, law & technology, paintings, prints & sculpture by African American artist, archival documents, Joseph E Coleman Collection, Jack T Franklin Photographic Collection, Dr Ruth Wright Hayre Collection, Anna Russell Jones Collection
Exhibitions: Audacious Freedom-Permanent
Publications: Annual report; brochure; exhib catalog
Activities: Classes for adults & children; docent training; lect open to pub; concerts; gallery talks; tours; awards; fels; individual paintings & original objects of art lent to other museums & institutions which conform to our security & climatic specifications; book traveling exhibs 2 per yr; originate traveling exhibs; mus sales shop sells books, magazines, original art, reproductions, prints, jewelry, memorabilia & novelties

M **ALLENS LANE ART CENTER,** Carolyn-Fielder-Alber Gallery, 601 W Allens Ln, Philadelphia, PA 19119. Tel 215-248-0546; Fax 215-248-0559; Email info@allenslane.org; Web: www.allenslane.org; *Exec Dir* Craig Stover; *Admin Coord* Laurie Lundin; *Develop Mgr* Kelly Kuwabara
Open Mon - Fri 10 AM - 5 PM, evenings & weekends by appt; Estab 1953
Special Subjects: Drawings, Printmaking, Sculpture, Photography, Bookplates & Bindings, Jewelry, Crafts, Ceramics
Collections: Painting; drawing; printmaking; sculpture; photography; woodworking; book arts; jewelry; crafts; ceramics
Exhibitions: Temporary exhibits

M **AMERICAN SWEDISH HISTORICAL FOUNDATION & MUSEUM,** American Swedish Historical Museum, 1900 Pattison Ave, Philadelphia, PA

19145-5999. Tel 215-389-1776; Fax 215-389-7701; Email info@americanswedish.org; Web: www.americanswedish.org; *Exec Dir* Tracey Beck; *Cur* Trevor Brandt; *Mktg Asst* Emma Ronn; *Facility Mgr* Frank Sanders; *Educ & Public Progs Mgr* Lauren Burnham; *Board Chmn* Erik Muther
Open Tues - Fri 10 AM - 4 PM, Sat & Sun Noon - 4 PM, cl Mon & holidays; Admis adults $6, seniors & students $5, children under 12 free; Estab 1926 to create an awareness & understanding of the contributions of Swedish-American people & of Sweden; 14 galleries containing materials interpreting over 300 years of Swedish influence on American life; Average Annual Attendance: 12,000; Mem: 750; dues family $65, individual $50; ann meeting in Sept
Library Holdings: Book Volumes
Special Subjects: Architecture, Coins & Medals, Costumes, Crafts, Decorative Arts, Drawings, Embroidery, Etchings & Engravings, Folk Art, Furniture, Glass, Painting-Scandinavian
Collections: History and culture of Americans of Swedish descent
Exhibitions: Scandinavian history & culture; temporary exhibitions of paintings, arts & crafts by Scandinavian & Swedish-American artists
Publications: Newsletter, quarterly
Activities: Classes for adults & children; lects open to pub, 1-3 vis lectrs per yr; concerts; gallery talks; tours; Spirit of Raoul Wallenberg Humanitarian Award; individual paintings & original objects of art lent to other mus & cultural attractions; book traveling exhibs 1 per yr; exten dept serves history & Swedish museums & historical societies; mus shop sells books & prints

L **Nord Library**, 1900 Pattison Ave, Philadelphia, PA 19145-5999. Tel 215-389-1776; Fax 215-389-7701; Email info@americanswedish.org; Web: www.americanswedish.org; *Exec Dir* Tracey Beck; *Cur* Trevor Brandt; *Educ & Public Progs Mgr* Lauren Burnham
Open Tues - Fri 10 AM - 4 PM, Sat & Sun Noon - 4 PM; Admis adults $8, seniors & students $6, children 5-12 $4, children under 5 free; Estab 1926 to create an awareness of Swedish & Swedish-American contribution to the US; Library is for research & reference only; Average Annual Attendance: 20,000; Mem: 750; dues $35 to $75; ann meeting in Sept
Library Holdings: Book Volumes 15,000, Clipping Files, Exhibition Catalogs, Memorabilia, Periodical Subscriptions 5, Records, Reels, Slides
Special Subjects: Painting-Scandinavian
Collections: Patent models & papers of John Ericsson
Publications: Elin's America by Marguerite DeAngeli
Activities: Classes for adults & children; lects open to pub; 1-3 vis lectrs per yr; concerts; gallery talks; tours; Outstanding Achievement Award (given annually to notable Swedes & Swedish Americans); The Spirir of Raoul Wallenberg Award; traveling exhibs to other Scandinavian mus & organizations; mus shop sells books & prints

L **ART INSTITUTE OF PHILADELPHIA LIBRARY,** 1622 Chestnut St, Philadelphia, PA 19103-5198. Tel 215-405-6402; Fax 215-405-6378; Web: www.artinstitutes.edu/philadelphia; *Libr Dir* Ruth Schachter
Open Mon - Thurs 7:50AM-10PM, Fri 7:50AM-9PM, Sat 11AM-5PM; Estab 1966; Reference library for students & staff only
Library Holdings: Book Volumes 21,500, Exhibition Catalogs, Periodical Subscriptions 200, Video Tapes
Special Subjects: Advertising Design, Architecture, Art History, Cartoons, Commercial Art, Decorative Arts, Fashion Arts, Film, Graphic Arts, Graphic Design, Illustration, Industrial Design, Interior Design, Lettering, Painting-American

A **ASSOCIATION FOR PUBLIC ART,** 1528 Walnut St, Ste 1000, Philadelphia, PA 19102-3627. Tel 215-546-7550; Fax 215-546-2363; Email apa@associationforpublicart.org; Web: www.fpaa.org; *Pres* Barbara B Aronson; *VPres* Suzanne Sheehan Becker; *Exec Dir* Penny Balkin Bach; *Asst Dir* Laura S Griffith; *Treas* William D McCall; *Office Mgr* Ginger Osbourne; *Asst Cur & Project Mgr* Susan Myers; *Develop Mgr* Nora Banks Sutherland; *Media & Communs Mgr* Caitlin Martin
Open by appointment only (not open to pub); Estab 1872 to promote integration of art & urban planning & to promote appreciation of pub art through progs & advocacy efforts; Mem: 350; dues $15 - $500; ann meeting May
Income: Financed by mem, grants & endowment
Special Subjects: Sculpture
Exhibitions: New-Land-Marks: Public Art, Community & the Meaning of Place
Publications: New Land Marks
Activities: Children's progs; lects open to pub, lects for mems only; 1 vis lectr per yr, tours

M **ATHENAEUM OF PHILADELPHIA,** 219 S 6th St, E Washington Sq Philadelphia, PA 19106-3794. Tel 215-925-2688; Fax 215-925-3755; Email conn@philaathenaeum.org; Web: www.philaathenaeum.org; *Exec Dir* Peter Conn PhD; *Cur Architecture* Bruce Laverty; *Librn* Jill L Lee; *Dir Regional Digital Imaging Ctr* Michael Seneca
Open Mon - Fri 9 AM - 5 PM, cl bank holidays; No admis fee; Estab 1814 to collect, preserve & make available original sources on American cultural history, 1814-1914; 1899 to circulate books; Haas gallery: 4 exhibs ann; Average Annual Attendance: 20,000; Mem: 1375; ann meeting in Apr; dues $200 per yr
Income: $1,000,000 (financed by endowments, dues & fees)
Library Holdings: Audio Tapes, Book Volumes, CD-ROMs, DVDs, Manuscripts, Maps, Memorabilia, Original Art Works, Original Documents, Pamphlets, Periodical Subscriptions, Photographs, Prints, Sculpture
Special Subjects: Architecture, Bookplates & Bindings, Decorative Arts, Furniture, Historical Material, Painting-American, History of Art & Archaeology, Landscape Architecture, Maps, Architecture
Collections: Permanent study collection of American decorative arts, 1810-1850, 19th & 20th century architectural books, architectural drawings, trade catalogues, rare books - 19th century, Joseph Bonaparte Collection
Publications: Monthly e-newsletter; Archive; Annual Report; Bookshelf, 6 per yr
Activities: Classes for adults & children; lect open to pub, 10 vis lectrs per yr; concerts; gallery talks; tours; competitions with awards, Annual Literary Award; Charles E Peterson Research Fellowships; architectural research; originate traveling exhibs to small historic site museums; sells books, prints & slides

L **Library**, 219 S Sixth St, Philadelphia, PA 19106. Tel 215-925-2688; Fax 215-925-3755; Email laverty@philaathenaeum.org; Web: www.philaathenaeum.org; *Cur Architecture* Bruce Laverty; *Circ Librn* Ellen Rose
Open Mon - Fri 9 AM - 5 PM by appointment for reference only; No admis fee; Estab 1814; Haas Gallery; Mem: 1300
Library Holdings: Book Volumes 75,000, Cards, Cassettes, Fiche, Manuscripts, Original Art Works, Other Holdings Architectural drawings & related materials, Periodical Subscriptions 50, Reels
Special Subjects: Architecture, Asian Art, Bookplates & Bindings, Decorative Arts, Furniture, Illustration, Painting-American
Collections: Nineteenth century fiction and literary periodicals, trade materials relating to the building arts, architectural drawings; manuscripts; photographs
Publications: Biographical dictionary of Philadelphia Architects, monograph
Activities: Tours of National Historic Landmark library building; symposia; lects open to pub, lects for mems only; gallery talks; tours; fels offered; sales shop sells books

A **BRANDYWINE WORKSHOP,** Center for the Visual Arts, 730 S Broad St, Philadelphia, PA 19146-2203; Brandywine Workshop & Archives, 728 S Broad St Philadelphia, PA 19146. Tel 215-546-3675; Email prints@brandywineworkshop.com; Web: www.brandywineworkshopand archives.org; *Pres & Exec Dir* Allan L Edmunds; *Assoc Dir* Gustavo Garcia
Open Mon - Fri 10 AM - 5 PM, Sat & Sun by appointment only; No admis fee; Estab 1972 to develop interest & talent in printmaking & other fine visual arts; Over 10,000 sq ft with 2 buildings in downtown Philadelphia. Facilities include offset lithography presses, screen printing & computer/video technology lab & classrooms. Printed Image Gallery for professional exhibits of works on paper by contemporary artists & archives of prints, books, artist videos & other research materials; Average Annual Attendance: 2,600 - 10,000; Mem: 300; dues $30 & up
Income: Financed by mem, city & state appropriations, pvt corporations & foundations
Library Holdings: Audio Tapes, Book Volumes, CD-ROMs, Cassettes, DVDs, Exhibition Catalogs, Kodachrome Transparencies, Manuscripts, Original Art Works, Original Documents, Periodical Subscriptions, Photographs, Slides, Video Tapes
Special Subjects: African Art, Afro-American Art, American Indian Art, Asian Art, Etchings & Engravings, Latin American Art, Mexican Art, Painting-Japanese, Painting-Russian, Prints, Woodcuts, Photography
Collections: Contemporary fine art prints, including etchings, woodblocks, offset lithographs, silkscreens
Exhibitions: USA Artworks; Contemporary Print Images; Rotating exhibits
Publications: Three Decades of American Printmaking (2004)
Activities: Intern training in archival colls management; computer/video for high school & college students; free online educ services; lects open to pub, 6 vis lectrs per yr; gallery talks; tours; schols, Joyce de Guatemala fel; fels offered; original objects of art donated to historically black colleges, major mus collections, centers for research & Library of Congress; lending coll contains original prints; organize traveling exhibs to colleges, universities, art mus; originate traveling exhibs; mus shop sells books, prints, note cards, calendars, t-shirts, caps, tote bags, brand items & mugs

M **THE CLAY STUDIO,** 139 N Second St, Philadelphia, PA 19106. Tel 215-925-3453; Fax 215-925-7774; Email info@theclaystudio.org; Web: www.theclaystudio.org; *Pres* Christopher Taylor; *VPres* Jennifer Martin; *Dir Devel U Cur Artistic Progs* Jennifer Zwilling; *Events & Mktg Coord* Eva Piatek; *Dir Educ* Josie Bockelman
Open Mon - Sat 11 AM - 6 PM, Sun Noon - 6 PM; No admis fee; Estab 1974; Three galleries with exhibits changing monthly of various ceramic artwork of solo, group & historical shows; Average Annual Attendance: 33,000; Mem: Dues $50 & up
Income: Financed through mem, donations & grants, tui, host fees
Special Subjects: Ceramics
Collections: Ceramic Arts
Exhibitions: Annual Resident Artist Solo Show; The Clay Studio National Small Favors Spec Exhibs
Activities: Classes for adults & children; lect open to pub, 4 - 8 vis artists per yr; gallery talks; tours; spring jurying for group & solo exhibition & residency program; awards, Zeldin Fellowship; fels offered; sales shop sells original functional art

M **CLIVEDEN,** 6401 Germantown Ave, Philadelphia, PA 19144-1925. Tel 215-848-1777; Fax 215-438-2892; Email info@cliveden.org; Web: www.cliveden.org; *Exec Dir* David Young; *Preservation Dir* Libbie Hawes; *Educ Dir* Carolyn Wallace; *Communs Coordr* Jocelyn Rouse; *Develop Coordr* Mackenzie Warren
Open April 1 - Dec 29 Thurs - Sun Noon - 4 PM, cl Thanksgiving, Christmas & New Year's; Admis adults $10, students $8, mems AAA & the National Trust $5, children 6 & under free; Estab 1971 in celebration of American Revolutionary War History; 18th Century house mus; Average Annual Attendance: 14,000; Mem: 250,000
Special Subjects: Historical Material, Period Rooms
Collections: 18th Century house museum with decorative arts, furniture, paintings, colls site related only, no acquisitions
Activities: Classes for children; docent training; guided tours for individuals & groups; mus shop sells books, reproductions, prints, gift items

A **THE COMMUNITY EDUCATION CENTER,** 3500 Lancaster Ave, Philadelphia, PA 19104-4916. Tel 215-387-1911; Fax 215-387-3701; Email cec@cecarts.org; Web: www.cecarts.org; *Exec Dir* Theresa Shockley
Open Mon - Fri 9 AM - 5 PM; No admis fee; Estab 1973 to support emerging talent; 35 ft x 60 ft room, 14 ft ceilings; Average Annual Attendance: 1,500
Income: $180,000 (financed by mem, city & state appropriation, foundation, corporate & pvt donors)
Activities: Classes for adults & children; lect open to pub, 4 vis lectrs per yr

A **CONSERVATION CENTER FOR ART & HISTORIC ARTIFACTS,** 264 South 23rd St, Philadelphia, PA 19103. Tel 215-545-0613; Fax 215-735-9313;

Email ccaha@ccaha.org; Web: www.ccaha.org; *Exec Dir* Laura Hortz Stanton; *Deputy Dir* Michelle Eisenberg
Open Mon - Fri 9 AM - 5 PM; Estab 1977 as a nonprofit regional conservation laboratory serving cultural, educational & research institutions as well as private individuals & organizations throughout the United States; Maintains small reference library; Mem: Dues $250
Income: $3,000,000 (financed by earned income & grants)
Activities: Workshops & conferences; Fels offered

M **DREXEL UNIVERSITY,** Drexel Collection, 3141 Chestnut St, Rm 304 Philadelphia, PA 19104-2816. Tel 215-895-2414; Fax 215-895-6157; Email lcc48@drexel.edu; Web: www.drexel.edu/drexelcollection; *Dir* Lynn C Clouser
Open Mon - Fri 3:30 PM - 5 PM, cl Sat, Sun & holidays; No admis fee; Estab 1891; Anthony J Drexel Picture Gallery 1902; Main Gallery contains the John D Lankenau & the Anthony J Drexel Collections of German & French paintings, sculpture & decorative arts of the 19th century & a changing exhib gallery; Average Annual Attendance: 10,000
Income: Financed by Drexel University
Special Subjects: Asian Art, Ceramics, Decorative Arts, Oriental Art, Painting-French, Painting-German, Sculpture, Textiles
Collections: 19th century sculpture, acad European painting, decorative arts & costumes, ceramics, Anthony J Drexel Collection of 19th Century Paintings & Sculptures, John D Lankenau Collection of 19th Century Paintings & Sculptures
Exhibitions: Regional Artists; Rotating exhibitions of permanent collection objects

M **THE FABRIC WORKSHOP & MUSEUM,** 1214 Arch St, Philadelphia, PA 19107-2800. Tel 215-561-8888; Fax 215-561-8887; Email info@fabricworkshopandmuseum.org; Web: www.fabricworkshopandmuseum.org; *Exec Dir* Susan Lubowsky Talbott
Open Mon - Fri 10 AM - 6 PM, Sat - Sun Noon - 5 PM; No admis fee; Estab 1977 devoted to experimental fabric design & silkscreen printing by nationally recognized & emerging artists representing all mediums, incl painting, sculpture, ceramics, architecture & theater. Invites artists to collaboratively explore new directions for their work, while furthering the use of fabric as an integral medium for contemporary art
Collections: Extensive permanent coll of unique contemporary art (over 6,000 artworks)
Exhibitions: Ongoing series of exhibs including print multiples, monoprints, sculptural objects, installation pieces, performance costumes, furniture & functional objects, along with preliminary objects & paintings for artists projects & related sculptures & ceramics
Publications: An Industrious Art; exhibit catalogs; New Materials as New Media; Cai Guo-Qiang: Fallen Blossoms, Sarah Sze; Carrie Mae Weems; Comfort Zone: Doug Aitken A-Z Book (fractals); Ed Ruscha: Industrial Strength; Jorge Pardo & The Fabric Workshop & Museum; New American Voices; Senga Nengudi
Activities: Classes for adults & children; high school & college apprentice training progs; workshops; lect open to pub, study tours; print demonstrations; gallery talks; tours; mus sales shop sells unique, artist-designed functional objects & workshop publs, books, original art, artist multiples

L **FREE LIBRARY OF PHILADELPHIA,** Art Dept, 1901 Vine St, Philadelphia, PA 19003-1189. Tel 215-686-5403; Email erefart@freelibrary.org; Web: www.freelibrary.org; *Library Pres & Dir* Siobhan A Reardon; *Head Librn Art, Dept* Karen Lightner; *Asst Head, Art* David DuPuy
Open Mon - Thurs 9 AM - 9 PM, Fri 9 AM - 6 PM, Sat 9 AM - 5 PM, Sun 1 PM - 5 PM; Estab 1891, art department estab 1896, to serve the citizens of the City of Philadelphia; Circ 16,000; Reference & research coll
Income: Financed by endowment, city & state appropriations
Purchases: $12,000
Library Holdings: Book Volumes 60,000, Clipping Files, Exhibition Catalogs, Fiche, Other Holdings Vertical files 40,000, Pamphlets, Periodical Subscriptions 150
Collections: 18th & 19th century architectural pattern books, John Frederick Lewis Collection of books on fine prints & printmaking, 368 original measured drawings of colonial Philadelphia buildings, Philadelphia Chap, American Institute of Architects
Exhibitions: Rotating exhibs

L **Print & Picture Collection**, 1901 Vine St, Philadelphia, PA 19103-1189. Tel 215-686-5405; Email erefpix@freelibrary.org; Web: www.freelibrary.org; *Acting Head* Karen Lightner
Open Mon - Fri 9 AM - 5 PM; Estab 1954 by combining the Print Department (estab 1927) & the Picture Coll
Income: Financed by endowment & city appropriations
Purchases: $5,000
Library Holdings: Original Art Works, Photographs, Prints
Special Subjects: Drawings, Etchings & Engravings, Photography, Portraits, Printmaking
Collections: (non-circulating) Americana (1200), Hampton L Carson Collection of Napoleonic prints (3400), Fine Art Prints (8000), Fine Art Photographs (3000), graphic arts (2000), greeting & tradesmen cards (27,000), John Frederick Lewis Collection of portrait prints (211,000), Philadelphiana (15,000), Rosenthal Collection of American Drawings (900), Benton Spruance lithographs (450), (circulating) coll of pictures in all media and universal in subject coverage (1,000,000), Artists books (200)
Activities: Friends of the Print & Picture Collection, meets 4 times per yr; lects open to pub, 1 vis lectr per yr; lending collection of original objects of art extended to mus

L **Rare Book Dept**, 1901 Vine St, Philadelphia, PA 19103-1189. Tel 215-686-5416; Fax 215-563-3628; Email refrbd@library_phila.gov; *Head* James D DeWalt; *Asst Head* Janine Pollock
Open Mon - Fri 9 AM - 5 PM; No admis fee; Estab 1949; Average Annual Attendance: 3,000
Special Subjects: Illustration, Manuscripts
Collections: American Sunday-School Union, Early American children's books including Rosenbach Collection of Early American Children's books (1682-1836), Elisabeth Ball Collection of Horn books, Borneman & Yoder Collection of Pennsylvania German Fraktur, Hampton L Carson Collection of legal prints, Frederick R Gardner Collection of Robert Lawson original drawings, Kate Greenaway, Grace Clark Haskell Collection of Arthur Rackham, John Frederick Lewis Collection of cuneiform tablets & seals, Medieval & Renaissance manuscripts & miniatures, Oriental manuscripts & miniatures (mostly Mughal, Rajput & Persian), Thornton Oakley Collection of Howard Pyle & His School, books & original drawings, Beatrix Potter, including H Bacon Collamore Collection of original art, Evan Randolph Collection consisting of angling prints from the 17th to the 20th century & prints of Philadelphia from 1800-1950, original drawings, paintings, prints & other illustrative material relating to the works of Dickens, Goldsmith, Poe & Thackeray
Activities: Individual paintings & original objects of art lent to other institutions for exhib not to exceed 3 months; lending coll contains books, original artworks & paintings

M **GERMANTOWN HISTORICAL SOCIETY,** 5501 Germantown Ave, Philadelphia, PA 19144-2225. Tel 215-844-1683; Fax 215-844-2831; Email programs@germantownhistory.org; Web: www.germantownhistory.org; *Exec Dir* Trapeta Mayson; *Librn & Archivist* Alex Bartlett
Open Tues 9 AM - 1 PM, Thurs 1 PM - 5 PM; Admis Museum $3, seniors & students $2, children under 10 & mem free; Estab 1900 as an historical society; Maintains reference library & mus galleries; Average Annual Attendance: 1,000; Mem: 250; dues $35
Income: $200,000 (financed by endowment, mem, city & state appropriations, foundations & corporations)
Library Holdings: Audio Tapes, Book Volumes, Cassettes, Clipping Files, Compact Disks, Exhibition Catalogs, Lantern Slides, Manuscripts, Maps, Memorabilia, Micro Print, Motion Pictures, Original Documents, Pamphlets, Photographs, Prints, Slides, Video Tapes
Special Subjects: Architecture, Bookplates & Bindings, Costumes, Decorative Arts, Dolls, Drawings, Furniture, Historical Material, Landscape Architecture, Landscapes, Manuscripts, Maps, Painting-American, Photography, Portraits, Posters, Prints, Flasks & Bottles, Metalwork, Silver, Textiles
Collections: African-American history, costume, family papers, furniture, genealogy, German immigration, glass negatives, industrial heritage, local bus archives, local history, photographs, textiles, toys & dolls, Wissahickon natural area
Publications: The Germantown Crier, semiannual
Activities: Classes for adults & children; lects open to pub & mems only, 2 vis lectrs per yr; individual paintings & original objects of art lent to institutions meeting professional standards; shop sells books, magazines & original art

M **GIRARD COLLEGE,** Stephen Girard Collection, 2101 S College Ave, #116, Philadelphia, PA 19121-4857. Tel 215-787-4434; Fax 215-787-4404; Email khaas@girardcollege.edu; Web: www.girardcollege.edu; *Dir Historical Resources* Kathy Haas; *Pres* Clarence D Armbrister
Open Thurs 9 AM - 2 PM; Admis free Thurs; reserved group tours other days of wk fee charged; Estab 1848; The art and historical colls of Girard Col are housed on the second fl of Founder's Hall. Of white marble and monumental scale, the bldg is generally regarded the finest example of Greek Revival architecture in America. Designed by Thomas U Walter in 1832 and constructed 1833-1848, Founder's Hall was the school's original classroom bldg; Average Annual Attendance: 2,300
Income: Financed by endowment, grant support & donations
Library Holdings: Manuscripts, Maps, Memorabilia, Original Art Works, Original Documents, Pamphlets, Photographs, Prints, Sculpture
Special Subjects: Architecture, Ceramics, Costumes, Decorative Arts, Furniture, Glass, Graphics, Historical Material, Manuscripts, Metalwork, Painting-American, Painting-American, Period Rooms, Photography, Porcelain, Portraits, Prints, Sculpture, Silver, Watercolors, Textiles
Collections: Furniture, silver, porcelain, paintings, marble busts & statues which belonged to Stephen Girard (1750 - 1831) founder of Girard College, Philadelphia's finest single-owner coll from the early national period
Exhibitions: Continuous display in room settings
Publications: Monument to Philanthropy: The Design and Construction of Girard College 1833-47; Girard College a Living History; The Stephen Girard Collection
Activities: Classes for children

L **HISTORICAL SOCIETY OF PENNSYLVANIA,** 1300 Locust St, Philadelphia, PA 19107-5699. Tel 215-732-6200; Fax 215-732-2680; Email hsppr@hsp.org; Web: www.hsp.org; *Pres & CEO* Charles T Cullen; *Dir Library & Colls & COO* Lee Arnold; *Ed* Rachel Moloshok; *Dir Archives* Cary Hutto; *Dir Institutional Develop & Grants Mgmt* Jon-Chris Hatalski; *Dir Progs & Servs* Beth Twiss-Houting; *Dir Research* David Haugaard; *Dir Conservation* Tara O'Brien; *Chief Info Officer* John Houser; *Dir Public Progs* Christopher Damiani; *Vis Servs Coordr* Kate Devlin; *Digital Servs Mgr* Caroline Hayden
Open Tues & Thurs 12:30 - 5:30 PM, Wed 12:30 - 8:30 PM, Fri 10 AM - 5:30 PM; Admis $8, students no admis fee; Estab 1824, the library collects & preserves documentary records relating primarily to 18th century national US history, 19th century regional Pennsylvania & 20th century Delaware Valley history, ethnic, immigration & family history; Average Annual Attendance: 11,000; Mem: 1200; dues $75; meetings once per yr
Income: (financed by endowment, mem dues & contributions)
Purchases: $49,204
Library Holdings: Auction Catalogs, Book Volumes, Clipping Files, Exhibition Catalogs, Manuscripts, Maps, Memorabilia, Original Art Works, Original Documents, Pamphlets, Periodical Subscriptions, Photographs, Prints
Special Subjects: Architecture, Cartoons, Drawings, Etchings & Engravings, Graphic Arts, Historical Material, Landscape Architecture, Landscapes, Manuscripts, Maps, Miniatures, Photography, Portraits, Posters, Prints, Reproductions, Watercolors, Woodcuts, Bookplates & Bindings
Collections: Collection of 19 million+ manuscripts, archives, graphics from pre-Revolution through the present, Balch Institute holdings document ethnic & immigrant experience in the USA since 1877
Publications: Guide to the Manuscript Collections of the Historical Society of Pennsylvania; The Historical Society of Pennsylvania in the Twentieth Century; Index to the Pennsylvania Magazine of History and Biography (vols 76-123, 1952-99); Pennsylvania Legacies, semi-annually
Activities: Lects open to the public; lects for mems; 1,000 vis lectrs per year; tours; workshops for adults; conferences on history & historical research; orientations to

documentary colls; 2 exhibits per yr; Founder's Award; fels offered; sales shop sells books & magazines

M **INDEPENDENCE NATIONAL HISTORICAL PARK,** 143 S 3rd St, Philadelphia, PA 19106-2818. Tel 215-597-8787; Fax 215-597-5556; Web: www.nps.gov/inde; *Chief Mus Branch* Karie Diethorn; *Superintendent* Cynthia Machead; *Deputy Superintendent* BJ Dunn; *Chief, Division of Cultural Resources Management* Doris Fanelli
Open daily 9 AM - 5 PM; No admis fee; Estab 1948 to preserve & protect for the American people, historical structures, properties & other resources of outstanding national significance & assoc with the Revolution & growth of the Nation; Seventeen pub buildings with 54 period rooms & 38 on-site exhibits. Maintains reference library; Average Annual Attendance: 4,500,000
Income: Financed by federal agency
Library Holdings: Auction Catalogs, Manuscripts, Original Art Works, Periodical Subscriptions
Special Subjects: Decorative Arts, Period Rooms, Portraits, Archaeology, Painting-American
Collections: 18th century American period furnishings, decorative arts, American portraits from 1740-1840, Architectural fragments collection, archaeology collection
Exhibitions: Rotating exhibs
Activities: Classes for adults & children; docent training; lect open to pub, 6 vis lectrs per yr; tours; individual paintings & original objects of art lent to qualified professional institutions; mus shop sells books, magazines, reproductions, prints & slides

L **Library**, 313 Walnut St, Philadelphia, PA 19106-2705. Tel 215-597-8787; Fax 215-597-5556; Email thadius_love@nps.gov; Web: www.nps.gov/inde; *Archivist* Tyler Love; *Librn Technician* Andrea Ashby; *Chief Cur* Karie Diethorn; *Pub Affairs Officer* Gina Gilliam; *Chief Historian* Jed Levin; *Chief Cultural Resources* Doris Fanelli; *Supt* Cynthia Machead; *Chief Interpretation* Pat James
Open to pub Mon - Fri 9:30 AM - 4:30 PM by appointment only (archives & library); No admis fee; Circ 300
Income: financed by federal funds
Library Holdings: Audio Tapes, Book Volumes 9500, Cassettes, Clipping Files, Exhibition Catalogs, Fiche, Kodachrome Transparencies, Manuscripts, Motion Pictures, Other Holdings Research notecard file, Pamphlets, Periodical Subscriptions 12, Photographs, Records, Reels, Slides, Video Tapes
Collections: Decorative arts of Philadelphia & Pennsylvania from the 18th century

M **INDEPENDENCE SEAPORT MUSEUM,** 211 S Columbus Blvd, Penn's Landing Philadelphia, PA 19106-3100. Tel 215-925-5439; Fax 215-925-6713; Email seaport@phillyseaport.org; Web: phillyseaport.org; *VPres Interpretation & Visitor Experience* Michael J Flynn; *CEO & Pres* John Brady; *Chief Cur* Craig Bruns; *Exhib & Graphic Design Mgr* Dan Kennedy; *Controller* Debralynn Murdock
Open Mon - Sun 10 AM - 5 PM; Admis adults $16, seniors, students, military, & children 3-12 $12, children 2 & under free; Estab 1960 to preserve & interpret the maritime heritage of the Bay & River Delaware & the Ports of Philadelphia; Gallery 1, The Sea Around Us, general maritime history; Gallery 3, changing exhibits; Gallery 4 changing exhibits; Average Annual Attendance: 80,000; Mem: 700; dues $35 minimum
Income: Financed by endowment, mem & federal, pvt & corporate gifts
Library Holdings: Audio Tapes, Book Volumes, CD-ROMs, Cassettes, Clipping Files, DVDs, Exhibition Catalogs, Fiche, Filmstrips, Kodachrome Transparencies, Lantern Slides, Manuscripts, Maps, Memorabilia, Micro Print, Motion Pictures, Original Art Works, Original Documents, Other Holdings, Pamphlets, Periodical Subscriptions, Photographs, Prints, Records, Reels, Reproductions, Slides, Video Tapes
Special Subjects: Archaeology, Bookplates & Bindings, Ceramics, Coins & Medals, Costumes, Crafts, Decorative Arts, Dioramas, Drawings, Embroidery, Etchings & Engravings, Folk Art, Furniture, Glass, Graphics, Historical Material, Landscapes, Manuscripts, Maps, Marine Painting, Painting-American, Photography, Porcelain, Posters, Prints, Scrimshaw, Silver, Textiles, Watercolors, Woodcarvings, Woodcuts
Collections: Paintings by major American marine artists, Philadelphia Views, 19th-20th century maritime prints
Publications: Annual Report; books & catalogs, intermittently; Masthead, quarterly newsletter
Activities: Classes for adults & children; docent training; lects open to pub, lects for mems only; concerts; gallery talks; tours; competitions; individual paintings & original objects of art lent to recognized nonprofit museums with adequate facilities & pertinent need, six months only; mus shop sells books, reproductions & maritime related gifts

L **Library**, 211 S Columbus Blvd, ISM Archives and Library Philadelphia, PA 19106-3100. Tel 215-925-5439; Fax 215-925-6713; Email library@phillyseaport.org; Web: www.phillyseaport.org; *Library Dir* Terry Potter; *Chief Cur* Craig Burns Fox
Open by appointment only; Mus admis required; Estab 1960; Open to members & scholars, for reference only
Income: Financed by federal funding, donations
Library Holdings: Auction Catalogs, Book Volumes 15,000, Cassettes 150, Clipping Files, Exhibition Catalogs, Fiche, Kodachrome Transparencies, Lantern Slides, Manuscripts, Memorabilia, Motion Pictures, Original Art Works, Original Documents, Other Holdings Boat plans 9000, Rare books & maps, Pamphlets, Periodical Subscriptions 100, Photographs 25,000, Prints, Reels, Slides 2000
Special Subjects: Archaeology, Asian Art, Commercial Art, Constructions, Drafting, Drawings, Etchings & Engravings, Film, Historical Material, Industrial Design, Manuscripts, Maps, Marine Painting, Painting-American, Photography, Portraits, Posters, Prints, Scrimshaw, Silver, Textiles, Watercolors, Woodcarvings
Collections: Photographic file of Birch prints, photographic file of ships built by New York Shipbuilding Corp, art reference books on marine artists
Activities: Mus shop sells books, original art, reproductions, prints

M **LA SALLE UNIVERSITY ART MUSEUM,** 20th & Olney Ave, Philadelphia, PA 19141; 1900 W Olney Ave, Philadelphia, PA 19141-1199. Tel 215-951-1221; Fax 215-951-5096; Email artmuseum@lasalle.edu; Web: www.lasalle.edu/museum; *Dir & Chief Cur* Klare Scarborough; *Cur Educ & Public Progs* Miranda Clark-Binder; *Colls Mgr & Registrar* Rebecca Oviedo
Open Mon - Fri 10 AM - 4 PM; cl Sat & Sun; No admis fee; Estab 1975 for educ purposes and to house the coll begun in 1965, also as support for the art history prog and as a service to the community; a collection of European & American art from the Renaissance to the present, plus special coll of non-west; Average Annual Attendance: 7,000; Mem: 150; dues $25 - $5000
Income: Financed by endowment, univ budget, grants, pub & pvt donations
Special Subjects: African Art, Antiquities-Greek, Asian Art, Baroque Art, Ceramics, Collages, Drawings, Etchings & Engravings, Graphics, Landscapes, Painting-American, Painting-British, Painting-Dutch, Painting-European, Painting-Flemish, Painting-French, Painting-German, Painting-Italian, Period Rooms, Photography, Portraits, Pottery, Pre-Columbian Art, Prints, Religious Art, Renaissance Art, Sculpture, Watercolors, Woodcuts
Collections: 15th - 21st century paintings, drawings & prints, Western, European & American art, with a few pieces of sculpture & decorative art, Japanese prints, Indian miniatures, African art, Pre-Colombian artifacts, Chinese ceramics
Exhibitions: Five special exhibs are held each year; Additional exhibitions of art produced by students & the community are held in the community gallery
Publications: La Salle Art Museum Guide to the Collection
Activities: Educ prog; classes for children; internships; lects open to pub, 3 vis lectrs per yr; gallery talks; tours; individual paintings & original objects of art lent to museums; mus shop sells reproductions

L **LIBRARY COMPANY OF PHILADELPHIA,** 1314 Locust St, Philadelphia, PA 19107-5679. Tel 215-546-3181; Fax 215-546-5167; Email cking@librarycompany.org; Web: www.librarycompany.org; *Librn* James N Green; *Cur Prints & Photogs* Sarah Weatherwax; *Cur African American History* Krystal Appiah; *Chief Conservation* Jennifer Woods Rosner; *Chief Cataloguer* Holly Phelps; *Chief Ref & Cur Women's History* Cornelia S King; *Cur Printed Books* Rachel D'Agostino
Open Mon - Fri 9 AM - 4:45 PM; No admis fee; Estab 1731 for the purpose of scholarly research; Revolving exhibits that highlight colls; Average Annual Attendance: 6.000; Mem: 750; dues $100; ann meeting in May
Income: Financed by endowment, mem, city appropriation, state & federal grants
Library Holdings: Auction Catalogs, Book Volumes 500,000, Cards, Exhibition Catalogs, Filmstrips, Framed Reproductions, Maps, Memorabilia, Original Art Works, Pamphlets, Periodical Subscriptions 60, Photographs, Prints, Sculpture
Special Subjects: Afro-American Art, Architecture, Art History, Bookplates & Bindings, Cartoons, Coins & Medals, Drawings, Etchings & Engravings, Fashion Arts, Historical Material, History of Art & Archaeology, Judaica, Landscape Architecture, Landscapes, Manuscripts
Collections: American Printing, Philadelphia prints, watercolors, drawings and photography, collection of Americana, paintings, sculpture, decorative arts
Publications: Annual Report; Occasional Miscellany, 2 times per year; exhibition catalogs
Activities: Lect open to pub; 10 vis lectrs per yr; gallery talks; tours; fel; individual & original objects of art lent to museums, libraries & cultural institutions; sale of books & publs

L **LUTHERAN THEOLOGICAL SEMINARY,** Krauth Memorial Library, 7301 Germantown Ave, Philadelphia, PA 19119-1794. Tel 215-248-6329; Fax 215-248-4577; Email sbaker@ltsp.edu; Web: ltsp.edu/academics/library; *Pub Servs Asst* Sharon Baker; *Acquisitions Asst* Ron Townsend
Open Mon - Fri 9 AM - 5 PM, during acad sessions, Mon - Thurs 5 PM - 10 PM, summer Mon - Fri 8:30 AM - 5 PM, June intensive Tues & Thurs 6:30 PM - 9:30 PM; Estab 1906
Library Holdings: Audio Tapes, Book Volumes 185,000, Cassettes, Filmstrips, Kodachrome Transparencies, Lantern Slides, Manuscripts, Memorabilia, Original Art Works, Periodical Subscriptions 570, Records, Reproductions, Slides, Video Tapes
Special Subjects: Architecture, Religious Art
Collections: Liturgical arts, Modern Prints, Rentschler Collection of Last Supper Art, Schreiber Collection of Numismatic Art on Martin Luther & the Reformation
Exhibitions: 20 Religious Artists

M **MOORE COLLEGE OF ART & DESIGN,** The Galleries at Moore, 20th & The Parkway, Philadelphia, PA 19103. Tel 215-965-4027; Fax 215-568-5921; Email galleries@moore.edu; Web: thegalleriesatmoore.org; *Gallery Dir* Gabrielle Lavin; *Educ & Pub Engagement Coordr* Matt Kalasky
Open Mon - Sat 11 AM - 5 PM, cl Sun, acad & legal holidays; No admis fee; Estab 1984 to display contemporary art, photog, design & works by Moore's faculty & students; Gallery is housed in moderate exhib space with flexible panels to accommodate current exhibit; Average Annual Attendance: 35,000
Income: Financed by endowment, government & foundation grants, individual & corporate donation
Special Subjects: Architecture, Ceramics, Crafts, Drawings, Folk Art, Photography, Portraits, Sculpture, Textiles, Watercolors
Exhibitions: William Daley; Hanne Darboven; Marlene Dumas, Terry Fox; Valie Export; Dan Graham; Benedetta Cappa Marmetti; Jean-Frederic Schnyder; Pat Ward Williams; Rosamond Purcell; Mary Cassatt; Alice Neel; Karen Kilimnik; Faith Ringgold; Lisa Kereszi; Anthony Campuzano; Artur Barrio; Andrea Baldeck; Mary McFadden; Sarah McEneaney; Deb Sokolow
Publications: Catalogs for major exhibitions; exhibition brochures & gallery notes
Activities: lect open to pub, 6 vis lectrs per yr; gallery talks; tours; book signings; films; performances; symposia; originate traveling exhibs to other univ galleries & small exhib spaces in large museums throughout US & Canada

L **Library**, 20th & The Parkway, Philadelphia, PA 19103. Tel 215-965-4054; Fax 215-965-8544; Email amacrina@moore.edu; Web: library.moore.edu; *Slide Cur* Helen F McGinnis; *AV Specialist* Chuck Duguense; *Archivist* Annabelle Curran; *Cataloging Librn* Elisa Graydon; *Lib Dir* Sharon Watson-Mauro
Open Mon - Thurs 8 AM - 10 PM, Fri 8 AM - 5 PM, Sat 8:30 AM - 5 PM, for student use; pub use Mon - Fri 8:30 - 10 PM & by appointment; Circ privileges $15/yr, alumni only; Estab to serve Moore staff & students; Circ 17,752; For lending & reference; Average Annual Attendance: 30,000
Purchases: $37,000

Library Holdings: Audio Tapes, Book Volumes 40,000, Cassettes, Clipping Files, DVDs, Exhibition Catalogs, Filmstrips, Lantern Slides, Manuscripts, Memorabilia, Motion Pictures, Original Art Works In archives, Original Documents In archives, Other Holdings Picture files, Periodical Subscriptions 230, Photographs, Prints, Records, Reproductions, Slides 117,000, Video Tapes
Collections: Sartain Family Collection, Bookworks Artists Books Collection
Activities: Classes for adults and children; lect open to pub; gallery talks; tours

M **MUSE ART GALLERY,** 52 N Second St, Philadelphia, PA 19106. Tel 215-627-5310; Email arts@musegalleryphilly.com; Web: www.musegalleryphiladelphia.com; *Dir* Nancy Neill
Open Wed - Sun noon- 5 PM; Estab 1970 as an art cooperative exhibiting members works; Gallery is a co-op; Average Annual Attendance: 2,500; Mem: 20; qualifications: professional exhibiting or emerging artist; dues $1,440; monthly meetings
Income: Financed by mem, sales commissions, Pennsylvania State Council of the Arts & pvt contributions
Exhibitions: Mems & community-oriented exhibs
Publications: Catalogues; MUSE Gallery and Her Own Space
Activities: Art consultant prog; lects open to pub, 2 vis lectrs per yr; poetry readings; competitions; originate international traveling exhibs; original art for sale

M **PAINTED BRIDE ART CENTER GALLERY,** 230 Vine St, Philadelphia, PA 19106-1293. Tel 215-925-9914; Fax 215-925-7402; Email info@paintedbride.org; Web: www.paintedbride.org; *Exec Dir* Laurel Raczka; *Audience Serv Mgr* Kyle Jackson; *Music Cur* Lenny Seidman; *Dir Develop* Celeste DiNucci
Open Tues - Sat noon - 6 PM; No admis fee; Estab 1968, forum for work outside traditional channels to present interdisciplinary work; Average Annual Attendance: 27,000; Mem: 350
Collections: Contemporary Art & Theater, Contemporary Art, Theater
Activities: Educ workshops for all ages; lects open to pub; concerts; gallery talks; tours; exten prog serves Philadelphia & suburbs; sales shop sells books & original art

M **PENNSYLVANIA ACADEMY OF THE FINE ARTS,** 118 N Broad St, Philadelphia, PA 19102. Tel 215-972-7600; Fax 215-569-0153; Web: www.pafa.org; *Pres & CEO* David Brigham; *Dir* Brooke Davis Anderson
Open Tues - Fri 10 AM - 5 PM, Sat & Sun 11 AM - 5 PM, cl Mon & holidays; Admis adults $15, seniors & students $12, youth 13-18 $8, child 12 & under no admis fee; Estab 1805 by Charles Willson Peale to cultivate collecting, training & development of the fine arts in America; The Academy Building, opened in 1876, was restored for the American Bicentennial. Considered the masterpiece of its architect, Philadelphian Frank Furness, its style is called, alternatively, polychrome picturesque & High or Gothic Victorian. It was designated a Registered National Historic Landmark in 1975. The School Gallery features faculty & student exhibs; Average Annual Attendance: 75,000; Mem: 3000; dues $35 & up
Income: Financed by endowment, mem, city & state appropriations, contributions & federal grants
Special Subjects: Afro-American Art, Architecture, Bronzes, Coins & Medals, Collages, Etchings & Engravings, Graphics, Historical Material, Landscapes, Marine Painting, Painting-American, Portraits, Posters, Prints, Sculpture, Tapestries, Woodcarvings, Woodcuts
Collections: American contemporary works, 18th, 19th & early 20th century American paintings, sculpture, drawings & prints, including Allston, West, the Peale Family, Stuart, Sully, Rush, Neagle, Mount, Eakins, Cassatt, Homer, Hopper, Hassam, Carles, Bellows, Henri, Beaux, Pippin
Publications: Annual report; Calendar of Events; exhibition & school catalogues; quarterly newsletter
Activities: Classes for adults & children; docent training; lect open to pub, 50 vis lectrs per yr; concerts; gallery talks; tours; competitions with awards; schols offered; exten dept serves senior citizens; original objects of art lent to other institutions, the White House, the Governor of Pennsylvania & embassies abroad; book traveling exhibs 2-3 per yr; originate traveling exhibs; mus shop sells books, magazines, reproductions, prints, slides, ceramics, games, stationery, jewelry, toys & pottery

L **Library,** 1301 Cherry St, Philadelphia, PA 19107; 118 North Broad St, Philadelphia, PA 19107. Tel 215-972-2030; Fax 215-569-0153; Email library@pafa.org; Web: www.pafa.org/library; *Dir Library & Info Servs* Brian Duffy
Open Mon - Thurs 8 AM - 9 PM, Fri 8 AM - 4:30 PM, Sat 10 AM - 4 PM, cl Sun; Admis by appointment; Estab 1805, the library serves students of painting, sculpture, printmaking & research in American Art; Open to pub for reference
Income: Financed by school funds
Library Holdings: Book Volumes 13,500, Clipping Files, Exhibition Catalogs, Periodical Subscriptions 82, Slides, Video Tapes

L **The Dorothy and Kenneth Woodcock Archive,** 118 N Broad St, Philadelphia, PA 19102-1598. Tel 215-972-2066; Email archives@pafa.org; Web: www.pafa.org; *Director of Archives* Hoang Tran
Open weekdays 9:30 AM - 4:30 PM by appointment only for researchers; No admis fee
Library Holdings: Audio Tapes, Cassettes, Clipping Files, Compact Disks, DVDs, Exhibition Catalogs, Filmstrips, Kodachrome Transparencies, Lantern Slides, Manuscripts, Memorabilia, Original Documents, Other Holdings Artifacts, Pamphlets, Photographs, Reels, Slides, Video Tapes
Collections: Charles Bregler's Thomas Eakins Collection, consisting of more than 1000 art objects & documents
Publications: Brochure about the archives; Index to Annual Exhibitions, 3 vols

A **Fellowship of the Pennsylvania Academy of the Fine Arts,** 118 N Broad St, New Philadelphia, PA 19102. Tel 610-520-9286; Email fellowshippafa@gmail.com; Web: www.fellowshippafa.org; *Pres* Maureen Drdak
Estab 1897 to provide opportunities for creative incentive & sharing in responsibilities for the development of facilities & activities in the field of art for its members & to maintain relations with the students of the Pennsylvania Academy of the Fine Arts; Mem: 200; dues $35
Income: $20,000 (financed by mem & investments)
Purchases: $1000 (art collection & operating expenses)
Special Subjects: Sculpture
Exhibitions: Annual Fellowship Show; Juried Members Exhibition
Publications: Perspective magazine, 3 times yr
Activities: lect; awards; juried student exhibs; individual paintings & original objects of art lent to schools, library & other pub institutions; lending coll contains original art works, original prints, paintings, photographs, sculpture

A **PHILADELPHIA ART ALLIANCE,** 251 S 18th St, Philadelphia, PA 19103-6168. Tel 215-545-4302; Fax 215-545-4302; Email info@philartalliance.org; Web: www.philartalliance.org; *Pres & Brd Chmn Emeritas* Carole Price Shanis; *Chief Cur* Melissa Caldwell; *Exec Dir* Thora Jacobson
Open Tues - Sun Noon - 6 PM, cl Mon; Suggested donation $5 adults, $3 seniors & students; Contemporary craft design; 3 fls of exhib space; Average Annual Attendance: 20,000; Mem: 300; both artist & non-artist categories are available; dues $75-$5000
Income: Financed by mem, board & corporate, foundation & pvt contributions
Library Holdings: Auction Catalogs, Cards, Exhibition Catalogs
Special Subjects: Ceramics, Crafts, Glass, Jewelry, Metalwork, Porcelain, Pottery, Textiles
Collections: Collection of archives to 1980 are located at Univ of Pa Library
Exhibitions: 3 exhibs annually
Publications: Exhib catalogs
Activities: Classes for children; lects open to pub; concerts; gallery talks; 10 vis lectrs per yr

A **PHILADELPHIA ART COMMISSION,** 1515 Arch St, 13th Floor Philadelphia, PA 19102. Tel 215-683-2095; Fax 215-683-2105; Email artcommission@phila.gov; Web: www.phila.gov/artcommission; *Exec Dir* William J Burke
Open 8:30 AM - 5 PM; No admis fee; Estab 1911 under Philadelphia Home Rule Charter as the Art Jury, later retitled Art Commission. An Art Ordinance passed in 1959 provides for art work in city buildings and on city owned property; The Art Commission reviews architectural designs and art work covering all media for municipal locations or other locations in which municipal funds are expended. The Art Commission's files are open to inspection by anyone since the information contained therein qualifies as public information. As indicated, the material deals solely with art proposals and architectural designs. Designs cover all buildings, major highways, and bridges; Mem: 9; between 20 and 24 meetings annually
Income: Financed by city appropriation

M **PHILADELPHIA HISTORY MUSEUM,** (Atwater Kent Museum of Philadelphia), 15 S Seventh St, Philadelphia, PA 19106. Tel 215-685-4830; Fax 215-685-4837; Email info@philadelphiahistory.org; Web: www.philadelphiahistory.org; *Exec Dir & CEO* Charles Croce; *Dir Colls & Exhibs* Kristen Froehlich; *Historian* Cynthia Little; *Dir External Relations & Special Events* Kelly Murphy; *Admin Asst* Alexandria Lang; *Vis Servs & Mem Mgr* Joanne Gasiowski
Open Tues - Sat 10:30 AM - 4:30 PM; Admis fee adults $10, seniors $8, students & youth $6, children under 12 free; Estab 1938. The mus is dedicated to the history of Philadelphia; Renovations in 2009 - 2010 made room for additional gallery space for exhibition of 100,000+ item coll; Average Annual Attendance: 25,000; Mem: dues $25 - $1000
Income: $1.2 million (financed by grants, contributions, earned revenue & city support
Special Subjects: Ceramics, Coins & Medals, Costumes, Decorative Arts, Dolls, Drawings, Embroidery, Etchings & Engravings, Flasks & Bottles, Folk Art, Furniture, Glass, Graphics, Historical Material, Maps, Metalwork, Painting-American, Photography, Porcelain, Portraits, Sculpture, Silver, Textiles, Watercolors
Collections: Artifacts of the colonial city, costumes, print & painting coll, manufactured & trade goods, maritime artifacts, toys & dolls, ceramics & glassware, urban archaeology, Art & Artifact Coll of the Historical Society of PA
Exhibitions: Permanent exhibs include, City Stories
Publications: Historically Speaking; Newsletter, The Ordinary, The Extraordinary & The Unknown: The Power of Objects
Activities: Classes for children; dramatic progs; after-school prog; lect open to pub; 5-10 vis lectrs per yr; gallery talks; media events; tours; fels; 1500 original art works, 2500 original prints, 100 paintings available on loan to museums with adequate security systems; originates traveling exhibs to community organizations & schools; mus shop sells books, prints & Philadelphia products

M **PHILADELPHIA MUSEUM OF ART,** Main Building, 26th & Benjamin Franklin Pkwy, Philadelphia, PA 19130; PO Box 7646, Philadelphia, PA 19101-7646. Tel 215-763-8100; Fax 215-236-4465; Email visitorservices@philamuseum.org; Web: www.philamuseum.org; *The George D Widener Dir & CEO* Timothy Rub; *Pres & COO* Gail Harrity
Open Tues -Sun 10 AM - 5 PM, Wed & Fri until 8:45 PM, cl Mon, July 4, Thanksgiving Day & Christmas Day; Admis adults $20, seniors $18, students & children 13-18 $14, mems & children 12 & under free; special exhib fees apply; Estab 1876 as an art mus & for art educ; known as Pennsylvania Mus of Art until the present name was adopted in 1938; Museum founded in 1876; buildings owned by the City, opened 1928; wings 1931 & 1940; fashion galleries 1949, 1951 & 1953; Gallatin & Arensberg Collections 1954; Far Eastern Wing 1957; decorative arts galleries 1958; Charles Patterson Van Pelt Auditorium 1959; Nepalese-Tibetan Gallery 1960; new galleries of Italian & French Renaissance Art 1960; American Wing, galleries of contemporary painting, sculpture & decorative arts & special exhibs galleries 1976; Alfred Stieglitz Center of Photography 1978; print & drawing gallery 1979; 19th century decorative arts galleries 1980 & 1981. Mus contains 200 galleries; Average Annual Attendance: 800,000; Mem: 50,000; dues $40 & up
Income: $46,000,000 (financed by endowment, mem, city & state appropriations, grants, bequests & auxiliary activities)
Special Subjects: Architecture, Asian Art, Folk Art, Furniture, Glass, Oriental Art, Painting-American, Painting-European, Period Rooms, Porcelain
Collections: Indian sculpture & miniature painting & the installation of 16th century South Indian temple, Chinese & Southwest Asian sculpture, ceramics & decorative arts from the Crozier, Crofts, Williams, McIlhenny, Thompson & other colls, with installations of a Ming period Chinese palace hall & temple & a Ch'ing scholar's study, Japanese scroll paintings, prints & decorative arts, with installations of a tea house & a 14th century temple, Himalayan sculpture & painting, Middle

Eastern tile, miniatures & decorative arts from the White & other colls, Oriental carpets from the McIlhenny, Williams & other colls, Pre-Columbian sculpture & artifacts from the Arensberg Colls, Medieval & Renaissance sculpture, painting & decorative arts from the Foulc, Barnard & other colls, installations of a Gothic chapel, Romanesque cloister, French Renaissance choir screen & period rooms, Kienbusch Collection of Arms & Armor, French, Dutch, English & Italian painting & decorative arts of the 14th-19th centuries, from the Wilstach, Elkins, McFadden, Tyson, John G Johnson, McIlhenny, Coxe-Wright & other colls, Italian, Dutch & French drawings from the Clark & other colls, French & English 17th & 18th century decorative arts from the Rice, Bloomfield-Moore & other colls, with period rooms, French & English art-nouveau decorative arts, costume & textiles from all periods of western & eastern art, including the Whitman sampler coll, American colls include painting, sculpture & decorative arts from the colonial era to the present, with period rooms, Philadelphia furniture & silver, Tucker porcelain, Lorimer Glass Collection & the Geesey Collection of Pennsylvania German folk art, 20th century painting, sculpture & works on paper from the Gallatin, Arensberg, Tyson, White, Stern, Stieglitz, Zigrosser, Greenfield, Woodward & other colls, Ars Medica Collection of prints on the subject of sickness & healing from all periods of western art, Alfred Stieglitz Center Collection of Photography, 20th century decorative arts, Stiegal Glass
Publications: Bulletin, quarterly; exhibs catalogs; members' magazine, semi-annually; monthly calendar
Activities: Classes for adults, children & families; guide & docent training; symposia; concerts; lect open to pub; concerts; gallery talks, films; tours; originates traveling exhibs; mus shops sells books, magazines, reproductions, prints, slides, jewelry, needlework & postcards; art sales & rental gallery

M **Rodin Museum of Philadelphia**, 2151 Benjamin Franklin Pkwy, Philadelphia, PA 19130; PO Box 7646, Philadelphia, PA 19101-7646. Tel 215-763-8100; Fax 215-763-8955; Email epartinfo@philamuseum.org; Web: www.rodinmuseum.org; *The Gloria and Jack Drosdick Curator of European Painting and Sculpture and Curator of the John G Johnson Collection* Jennifer Thompson
Open Wed - Mon 10 AM - 5 PM, cl Tues & holidays; Admis suggested admis: adults $10, seniors $8, students (with ID) $7, children 12 & under free; Opened 1929; Rodin Mus of Philadelphia houses one of the largest colls outside of Paris of works by the major late 19th Century French sculptor, Auguste Rodin; Average Annual Attendance: 60,000
Special Subjects: Sculpture
Collections: Coll includes many of the most famous sculptures created by Rodin, as well as drawings, prints, letters, books & a variety of documentary material, The Thinker, The Gates of Hell, The Burghers of Calais, Eternal Springtime, Apotheosis of Victor Hugo
Exhibitions: Rotating exhibits
Activities: Classes for adults & children; docent training; concerts; gallery talks; tours; lending of original objects of art to other museums for exhibs; mus shop sells books, reproductions, slides, cards & memorabilia; audio tour, prints

M **Ruth & Raymond G Perelman Building**, Fairmount & Pennsylvania Aves, Philadelphia, PA 19130; PO Box 7646, Philadelphia, PA 19101-7646. Tel 215-763-8100; Email visitorservices@philamuseum.org; Web: www.philamuseum.org
Open Tues - Sun 10 AM - 5 PM; Admis adults $8, seniors $7, students & children 13-18 $6, mems & children 12 & under free; special exhib fees apply; Newly renovated & expanded, bldg is the first phase of enhancement & modernization of Philadelphia Mus of Art

M **Mount Pleasant**, Fairmount Park, Philadelphia, PA 19101; PO Box 7646, Philadelphia, PA 19101-7646; Mount Pleasant, 3800 Mt Pleasant Dr Philadelphia, PA 19121. Tel 215-763-8100; Email visitorservices@philamuseum.org; Web: www.philamuseum.org; *Site Mgr Historic Houses* Justina Barrett
Open April - Dec Thurs - Sun: tours at 1 & 2:30 PM; Admis adults $8, children under 12 free; Historic house built in 1761; an outstanding example of the Georgian style in 18th century building & woodcarving; installed with period furnishings
Collections: Period furnishings from the mus represent the elegant way of life in Philadelphia in the 1760s
Activities: Tours

M **Cedar Grove**, Cedar Grove Mansion Fairmount Park, Lansdowne Dr Philadelphia, PA 19101; PO Box 7646, Philadelphia, PA 19101-7646; Cedar Grove, 1 Cedar Grove Dr Philadelphia, PA 19131. Tel 215-763-8100; Email visitorservices@philamuseum.org; Web: www.philamuseum.org; *Site Mgr Historic Houses & Educ* Justina Barrett
Open April - Dec Thurs - Sun tours 11 AM, 1 PM & 2:30 PM; first Sun of month tours 10 AM - 4 PM; Admis adults $8, children under 12 free; This Quaker farmhouse built as a country retreat in 1748 was moved stone by stone to Fairmount Park in 1928 & restored with the furnishings of the five generations of Quakers who lived in it
Collections: The furniture was given with the house & reflects changes in styles through the 17th, 18th & 19th centuries
Activities: Tours

M **John G Johnson Collection**, 2600 Benjamin Franklin Pkwy, Philadelphia, PA 19130; PO Box 7646, Philadelphia, PA 19101-7646. Tel 215-763-8100; Fax 215-763-8955; Email epartinfo@philamuseum.org; Web: www.philamuseum.org; *The Gloria and Jack Drosdick Curator of European Painting & Sculpture & Curator of the John G Johnson Collection* Jennifer Thompson; *The Agnes and Jack Mulroney Associate Curator of European Painting and Sculpture before 1900* Christopher Atkins; *Curator Emeritus* Joseph Rishel; *Curator Emeritus* Carl Strehlke
Open Tues - Sun 10 AM - 5 PM; Wed & Fri until 8:45 PM; Admis to Philadelphia Mus of Art adult $20, senior $18, student (with ID) $14, children under 12 free; Upon his death in 1917, prominent Philadelphia lawyer, John Graver Johnson left his extensive coll intact to the city of Philadelphia; since 1933 the coll has been housed in the Philadelphia Mus of Art; admin & trusteeship of the coll is maintained separately from the other colls in the mus
Income: Financed by trust, contributions city of Philadelphia & Philadelphia Mus of Art
Special Subjects: Painting-British, Painting-Dutch, Painting-European, Painting-Flemish, Painting-German, Painting-Italian, Portraits, Religious Art, Renaissance Art, Painting-French
Collections: Early & later Italian Renaissance paintings, French 19th century paintings, northern European schools of Flanders, Holland & Germany in the 15th, 16th & 17th centuries
Exhibitions: In house exhibs featuring works from permanent coll
Publications: Several catalogs for various parts of the collection including Catalog of Italian Paintings & Catalog of Flemish & Dutch Paintings
Activities: Special lect & related activities; occasional lending of collection to significant exhibitions; lending of original objects of art to other museums; mus shop sells books, reproductions

M **Samuel S Fleisher Art Memorial**, 719 Catharine St, Philadelphia, PA 19147-2811. Tel 215-922-3456 ext 300; Fax 215-922-5327; Email info@fleisher.org; Web: fleisher.org; *Exec Dir* Elizabeth Grimaldi; *Dir Progs* Magda Martinez; *Dir Develop* Melissa Phegley; *Exhib Mgr* Jose Ortiz; *Mgr Adult Progs* Vita Litvak; *Youth Progs Coordr* Rebecca Franco; *Mgr Audience Engagement & Rentals* Adrianne Waxman; *Dir Communs* Dominic Mercier
Open Mon - Thurs 9 AM - 9 PM, Fri 9 AM - 5 PM, Sat 9 AM - 4 PM; No admis fee; Estab 1898 as a free art school & sanctuary (Mus of Religious Art); Comprised of 4 bldgs: the Sanctuary, the St Martin's College bldg, & 2 three-story row houses. Permanent colls are housed in the Sanctuary, an Italian Romanesque Revival building designed by Louis C Baker & E James Dallett of Furness & Evans; Maintains Dene M Louchheim Galleries & Suzanne Leisher & Ralph Joel Roberts Gallery. Administered by Philadelphia Museum of Art; Average Annual Attendance: 8,000; Mem: 2,800; mem contribution $25 per term
Income: $650,000 (financed by estate income, mem, materials fees, grants & gifts)
Collections: Medieval & Renaissance religious paintings & sculpture, 18th-19th century Portuguese liturgical objects, 17th-20th century Russian icons, some sculpture
Exhibitions: Challenge Series, ann schedule of four exhibs featuring work by Philadelphia area artists; annual student, faculty, adult & children's exhibs; occasional special subject exhibs
Activities: Classes for adults & children; workshops; lect open to pub, 4 vis lectrs per yr; concerts; gallery talks; tours; competitions; sales shop sells art materials & books

L **Library & Archives**, 2525 Pennsylvania Ave, Perelman Bldg Philadelphia, PA 19130; PO Box 7646, Philadelphia, PA 19101-7646. Tel 215-684-7650; Fax 215-236-0534; Email library@philamuseum.org; Web: www.philamuseum.org/library; *Arcadia Dir Libr & Archives* Kristen Regina; *Librn Collection Develop* Mary S Wassermann; *Archivist* Susan K Anderson; *Reader Svc Librn* Richard Sieber
Open Tues - Fri 10 AM - 5 PM; No admis fee.; Estab 1876 as research library for mus staff, members & scholars (appointments recommended); Circ 10,282; For reference only
Library Holdings: Auction Catalogs, Book Volumes 220,000, Clipping Files, Exhibition Catalogs, Fiche, Manuscripts, Original Documents, Other Holdings Digital Images, Pamphlets, Periodical Subscriptions 450, Photographs, Reels, Slides
Special Subjects: Art History, Asian Art, Ceramics, Conceptual Art, Costume Design & Constr, Decorative Arts, Drawings, Enamels, Etchings & Engravings, Fashion Arts, Glass, Gold, Jewelry, Latin American Art, Miniatures, Painting-American, Painting-European, Photography, Prints, Silver, Textiles, Period Rooms
Collections: Albert M Greenfield Visual & Digital Resources Ctr: 200,000+ digital images & slides
Activities: Lect open to pub; one vis lectr per yr

A **Women's Committee**, PO Box 7646, Philadelphia, PA 19101-7646. Tel 215-684-7931; Fax 215-236-8320; Email info@twcpma.org; twcpma@philamuseum.org; Web: twcpma.org; *Exec Dir* Nancy G O'Meara; *Pres* Judy Pote
Open Mon - Fri 9 AM - 5 PM; Estab 1883, inc 1915; takes an active interest in the mus; Organization sponsors Art Sales & Rental Gallery, park houses & mus guides, The Philadelphia Mus of Art Craft Show, classes for blind artists & tours for the deaf; Mem: 45
Income: Financed by fund raising events

A **PHILADELPHIA SKETCH CLUB,** 235 S Camac St, Philadelphia, PA 19107-5609. Tel 215-545-9298; Email info@sketchclub.org; Web: www.sketchclub.org; *Pres* William C Patterson; *VPres* Richard A Harrington; *Treas* William C Patterson; *Secy* Frances Carter; *Gallery Mgr* Michelle Lockamy
Open Mon & Wed and Fri-Sun 1PM-5PM; No admis fee; Estab 1860 to promote the creation & appreciation of the visual arts; 30 ft X 40 ft with skylight & spotlights; Average Annual Attendance: 19,000; Mem: 225; applicants must be proposed by two mems & show portfolio of their artwork to Board of Dir; dues $150; monthly meetings 2nd Fri of each month
Income: Financed by mem, grants & fundraising activities
Special Subjects: Bronzes, Cartoons, Drawings, Etchings & Engravings, Graphics, Painting-American, Prints, Sculpture, Watercolors, Woodcuts, Coins & Medals, Landscapes, Marine Painting, Metalwork, Photography, Portraits, Posters, Stained Glass, Woodcarvings
Collections: Permanent collection is from past & present members, oils, watercolors, etchings, forty-four Thomas Anshutz Portraits, J Pennell Lithographs
Exhibitions: Approximately 15 exhibs per yr
Publications: The Portfolio, (bulletin), monthly
Activities: Classes for adults; life classes; 5 art workshops per wk; lect open to pub, 9 vis lectrs per yr; gallery talks; tours; competitions with cash awards; individual paintings & original objects of art lent to art museums who have exhibs of PSC past mems; lending coll contains original prints, paintings & sculptures

M **PHILADELPHIA UNIVERSITY,** Paley Design Center, 4201 Henry Ave, Philadelphia, PA 19144-5497. Tel 215-951-2722; Fax 215-951-2662; Email thedesigncenter@philau.edu; Web: www.philadelphia.edu; *Cur Textile & Costume Coll* Marcella Milio
Open Tues - Fri 10:30 AM - 4:30 PM; No admis fee; free guided tour by reservation; Estab 1978 to promote knowledge & appreciation of textiles & their design; Three galleries; small library of textile & costume subjects available to scholars & mems
Income: Financed by PU&S & grants from the PCA, pvt & individual foundations
Special Subjects: Costumes, Textiles

Collections: Costumes - 18th to 20th centuries, historic & contemporary textiles 1st - 20th centuries, International, Manufacturers' fabric swatches 19th & 20th centuries, American & Western European, manuscripts, records, textile fibers, tools & related materials
Publications: The Art of the Textile Blockmaker; Floribunda: The Evolution of Floral Design on Fabrics; Flowers of the Yayla, Yoruk Weaving of the Toros Mountains; The Philadelphia System of Textile Manufacture 1884 - 1984
Activities: Mus shop sells unique works by craft artists in jewelry, pottery, glass, wood, paper & textiles; ann holiday crafts market

A **PLASTIC CLUB,** Art Club, 247 S Camac St, Philadelphia, PA 19107-5609. Tel 215-545-9324; Email plasticclub@att.net; Web: plasticclub.org; *Pres* Rick Wright; *1st VPres* Cynthia Arkin; *Treas* Jane J Wilkie; *Corresp Secy* Eileen Eckstein; *Recording Secy* Janice Moore; *2nd VPres* Alan J Klawans; *Exhib Chair* Susan Stromquist; *3rd VPres* Michael Guinn; *Communications* Roberta Gross; *Publicity* Bob Moore; *Finance* Bonnie Schorske
Open Tues 9:30 AM - 12:30 PM, Wed - Thurs 10 AM - 1 PM, Thurs evening 6:30 PM - 9:30 PM, Fri evening 6:30 PM - 9:30 PM, Sat 1 PM - 4 PM & by appointment; No admis fee; Estab 1897 to promote wider knowledge of art and to advance its interest among artists; Two historic homes provide space for exhibits & a studio; Average Annual Attendance: 3,000; Mem: 215; must qualify for mem by submitting three framed paintings or other works of art to be juried; dues $60; assn mems (non-exhibiting) $40; ann meeting in May; work juried by board of dir for active membership; no jurying for assoc
Income: Financed by mem, donations, gifts & money-making projects
Library Holdings: Book Volumes, Exhibition Catalogs, Manuscripts, Memorabilia, Original Art Works, Original Documents, Pamphlets, Photographs, Records
Special Subjects: Drawings, Historical Material, Landscapes, Painting-American, Portraits, Posters, Watercolors
Collections: American Women artists, Art History, Printmaking, paintings & posters
Exhibitions: Monthly exhibs of paintings by mems & invited artists; Open Works on Paper; Open Show All Media; workshop & various theme exhibs
Publications: Calendar of Events, 3 times a year; newsletter, 4 times per yr
Activities: Classes for adults; workshops open to mems & pub; art salons; lects open to pub; 4-5 vis lectrs per yr; competitions with awards; exhib prizes; ann Plastic Club Gold & Silver medals; concerts; gallery talks; 1st, 2nd & 3rd prizes and honorable mention at each juried show; contains original art works, original prints, paintings

M **PLEASE TOUCH MUSEUM,** 4231 Ave of the Republic, Memorial Hall & Fairmount Park Philadelphia, PA 19103-3719. Tel 215-581-3181; Fax 215-581-3182; Email info@pleasetouchmuseum.org; Web: www.pleasetouchmuseum.org; *Pres & CEO* Patricia Wellenbach; *Chief Staff* Barry Becker; *Chief Develop Officer* Nancy Green; *Dir Opers* David Pritchard; *Dir Educ* Jennifer Kalter; *CFO* Geoff Lapres
Open Mon - Sat 9 AM - 5PM, Sun 11 AM - 5 PM, cl Thanksgiving, Christmas & New Year's Day; Admis fee $19; Estab 1976 & accredited by American Assoc of Museums (1986) to provide a developmentally appropriate mus for young children, their parents & teachers; Gallery spaces are small-scaled, objects are accessible; two-tiered interpretation for adults coming with children (arts, crafts, ethnic materials & childlife exhibits); Average Annual Attendance: 600,000; Mem: 14,000; family of 4 $150, family of 6 $180, family of 6 with extra benefits $220
Income: $1,600,000 (financed by earned income: admis, store receipts, program fees; contributions, mem, governmental appropriations, foundations, corporate support & individuals)
Special Subjects: Costumes, Crafts, Dolls, Restorations, Maps
Collections: Contemporary American toys, artifacts & archives documenting American childhood, art works by contemporary artists, sculpture, environmental, paintings & crafts, cultural artifacts from around the world: costumes, playthings, musical instruments, objects from daily life: Materials from the natural sciences
Exhibitions: Wonderland; City Capers; Flight Fantasy; Roadside Attractions; Centennial Exploration; Liberty Arm & Torch; River Adventures; Woodside Park: Dentzel Carousel
Publications: Annual report; The Please Touch Museum Cookbook; quarterly newsletter; thematic exhib catalog, biannual
Activities: Workshops for adults & children; theater progs; docent training; work with area colleges, universities & art schools; coop progs; lect open to pub, 3 vis lectrs per yr; concerts; tours; competitions with awards; original objects of art lent; lending coll contains art works, sculpture & artifacts concerning childhood; originate traveling exhibs; mus shop sells books, toys, arts & crafts kits, souvenirs

THE PRINT CENTER
For further information, see National and Regional Organizations

M **THE ROSENBACH MUSEUM & LIBRARY,** 2008-2010 DeLancey Pl, Rosenbach Foundation Philadelphia, PA 19103-6510. Tel 215-732-1600; Fax 215-545-7529; Email info@rosenbach.org; Web: www.rosenbach.org; *Dir* Derick Dreher; *Librn* Elizabeth E Fuller
Open Tues & Fri 12 PM - 5 PM, Wed - Thurs 12 PM - 8 PM, Sat & Sun 12 PM - 6 PM; Open for research: Wed & Thurs 10:30 AM - 6 PM, Fri 10:30 AM - 4:30 PM; Admis adults $10, seniors $8, students & children $5, children 5 and under no charge; Estab 1953 as a nonprofit corporation; Changing exhibitions based on collections; Average Annual Attendance: 80,000; Mem: approx. 600 members
Library Holdings: Book Volumes, Exhibition Catalogs, Manuscripts, Maps, Memorabilia, Original Art Works, Photographs, Prints, Sculpture
Special Subjects: Carpets & Rugs, Drawings, Judaica, Manuscripts, Painting-British, Photography, Porcelain, Prints, Silver, Antiquities-Egyptian, Miniatures
Collections: 18th & 19th century English & American antiques & silver, paintings, prints & drawings, porcelain, rugs & objets d'art, rare books & manuscripts, consisting of British & American literature, Americana, & book illustrations, 300,000 manuscripts, 30,000 books, Marianne Moore Archive, Maurice Sendak Archive
Publications: A Selection from Our Shelves; Fantasy Sketches; The Rosenbach Newsletter; exhib catalogs
Activities: Classes for adults & children; dramatic progs; docent training; lect open to pub, 3 vis lectrs per yr; gallery talks; tours; individual paintings & original objects of art lent to mus & libraries with proper environmental & security systems; originate traveling exhibs; mus shop sells books, prints & reproductions

M **RYERSS VICTORIAN MUSEUM & LIBRARY,** 7370 Central Ave, Philadelphia, PA 19111-3059. Tel 215-685-0544, 685-0599; Email ryerssmuseum@gmail.com; Web: ryerssmuseum.org; *Site Supvr* Theresa Stuhlman; *Site Supvr* Martha Moffat; *Librn* Beth Atkinson; *Librn* Harry Kyriakodis
Open Mus & Library Fri - Sun 10 AM - 4 PM; No admis fee; Estab 1910; House (Historic Register) left to City complete with contents in 1905; three period rooms; three other mus rooms with art objects - eclectic coll from around the world; fine Asian gallery; Average Annual Attendance: 6,000; Mem: 75; dues $5; meeting first Mon every month
Income: Financed by endowment, city appropriation, volunteer fundraising & trust fund
Library Holdings: Book Volumes, Manuscripts, Original Documents, Photographs
Special Subjects: American Indian Art, Architecture, Asian Art, Ceramics, Decorative Arts, Furniture, Glass, Ivory, Jewelry, Landscapes, Painting-American, Painting-American, Painting-French, Period Rooms, Porcelain, Porcelain, Portraits, Prints, Religious Art, Sculpture, Sculpture
Collections: Static collection, export china, ivory, paintings, period rooms, prints, sculpture, weapons, natural history Asian artifacts
Activities: Educ prog; children's craft activities; Lects open to pub; 15 vis lectr per yr; tours; lending coll contains 12,000 books; Mus shop sells T-shirts; greeting cards; local history publs

A **TALLER PUERTORRIQUENO INC,** Lorenzo Homar Gallery, 2721 N 5th St, Philadelphia, PA 19133. Tel 215-426-3311; Fax 215-426-5682; Email cfebo@tallerpr.org; Web: www.tallerpr.org; *Exec Dir* Carmen Febo San Miguel; *Exhibs Prog Mgr & Cur* Rafael Damast
Open Mon - Sat 10 AM - 6 PM; No admis fee; Estab 1974 to develop, educate & promote Puerto Rican arts & cultural traditions while exploring common Latin American roots; Contemporary Latin American art with social relevance to Latino culture; Average Annual Attendance: 5,000; Mem: 450; dues $15 & up
Income: Financed by gov, federal, corp & pvt foundations
Purchases: Permanent coll of prints & works on paper
Library Holdings: Audio Tapes, Book Volumes, Exhibition Catalogs, Maps, Original Art Works, Original Documents, Other Holdings, Pamphlets, Periodical Subscriptions, Photographs, Prints, Records, Slides, Video Tapes
Special Subjects: Latin American Art, Pre-Columbian Art, Religious Art, Prints
Collections: Permanent coll includes silk prints, lithographs & woodcuts
Exhibitions: Five exhibs annually
Publications: 25 Years - 25 Prints: catalogue documenting permanent collection & history of the organization
Activities: Classes for adults & children; summer arts prog; lect open to pub, 2-3 vis lectrs per yr; concerts; gallery talks; tours; schols or fels offered; originate traveling exhibs; galleries, pvt & pub orgs; sales shop sells books, crafts, original art; reproductions & prints

M **TEMPLE UNIVERSITY TYLER SCHOOL OF ART,** Temple Contemporary, 2001 N 13th St, Philadelphia, PA 19122-6016. Tel 215-777-9139; Fax 215-777-9143; Email exhibitions@temple.edu; Web: www.templecontemporary.org; *Dean* Robert Stroker; *Dir Exhibs* Robert Blackson; *Exhibs Technician* Adam Blumberg
Open Wed - Sat 11 AM - 6 PM; No admis fee; Average Annual Attendance: 15,000
Income: Financed by state appropriation & grants
Exhibitions: Peter Eiseman: Tow Projects; Martin Poryear: The Cave Project
Publications: Brochures, posters, announcements or exhibitions catalogs for major shows
Activities: Classes for adults; lects open to pub, 8 vis lectrs per yr; concerts; gallery talks; tours; special events; concerts

L **Tyler School of Art Library,** 2001 N 13th St, Philadelphia, PA 19122-6016. Tel 215-782-2849; Fax 215-782-2799; Web: library.temple.edu; *Librn* Jill Luedke
Open Mon - Thurs 8:30 AM - 9 PM, Fri 8:30 AM - 4:30 PM, Sat 9 AM - 5 PM, Sun 1 - 9 PM; Estab 1935 to provide library services to students & faculty; Circ 27,254
Income: $118,368 (financed by appropriation from Central University Library)
Purchases: $32,600
Library Holdings: Book Volumes 38,000, Cassettes, Exhibition Catalogs, Fiche, Other Holdings Auction sale catalogs, Pamphlets, Periodical Subscriptions 100, Prints, Reels, Video Tapes
—**Slide Library,** Beech & Penrose Aves, Elkins, PA 19027; 2001 N 13th St., Philadelphia, PA 19122-6016. Tel 215-782-2848; Fax 215-782-2848; Email slidelib@unix.temple.edu; Email sliderm@vm.temple.edu; *Asst Cur* Beth Peckman; *Slide Cur* Kathleen Szpila
Library Holdings: Slides 390,000
Special Subjects: Art History, Ceramics, Decorative Arts, Graphic Design, Photography

A **UNIVERSITY OF PENNSYLVANIA,** Institute of Contemporary Art, 118 S 36th St, Philadelphia, PA 19104-3211. Tel 215-898-7108; Fax 215-898-5050; Email hello@ica.upenn.edu; Web: www.icaphila.org; *Chief Cur* Anthony Elms; *Asst Cur* Meg Onli; *Dir Mktg & Communs* Jill Katz; *Visitor Servs Coordr* Jessica L Johnson; *Digital Ed & Communs* Heather Holmes; *Asst to Dir* Catzie Vilayphonh; *Dir Cur Affairs* Robert Chaney
Open Wed 11 AM - 8 PM, Thurs & Fri 11 AM - 6 PM, Sat & Sun 11 AM - 5 PM, cl Mon. & Tues; No admis fee; Estab 1963 to provide a continuing forum for the active presentation of advanced development in the visual arts; Gallery space devoted to exhibiting contemporary art in all media; Average Annual Attendance: 25,000; Mem: 218; dues $25, $50, $100, $250, $500 & up
Income: financed by endowment, mem & grants
Library Holdings: Audio Tapes, Cards, Cassettes, Clipping Files, DVDs, Exhibition Catalogs, Fiche, Kodachrome Transparencies, Original Art Works, Original Documents, Pamphlets, Periodical Subscriptions, Photographs, Prints, Records, Slides, Video Tapes
Special Subjects: Architecture, Drawings, Photography, Prints, Sculpture
Publications: Annual newsletter; calendar of events; exhibition catalogs

Activities: School groups; teacher training; lect open to pub, vis lectrs; concerts; gallery talks; tours; fellowships; originates 1-2 traveling exhibs; sales shop sells original art, catalogs & Cereal Art

M **UNIVERSITY OF PENNSYLVANIA,** Arthur Ross Gallery, 220 S 34th St, Philadelphia, PA 19104-3808; Box 5 College Hall, University of Pennsylvania Philadelphia, PA 19104-6303. Tel 215-898-2083; Fax 215-573-2045; Email arg@pobox.upenn.edu; Web: www.arthurrossgallery.org; *Dir & Univ Cur* Lynn Marsden-Atlass; *Asst Dir & Assoc Cur* Heather Gibson Moqtaderi; *Asst Dir Develop & Mktg* Sara Stewart; *Admin Asst* Meg Pendoley
Open Tues - Fri 10 AM - 5 PM, Weds 10 AM - 7 PM, Sat & Sun noon - 5 PM; No Admis fee; Estab 1983 to make art accessible to campus community & the general pub; One large high-ceilinged room & an entrance room with approx 1700 sq ft of exhibition space; Average Annual Attendance: 12,000; Mem: 54; dues $50; ann meeting
Income: $400,000 (financed by endowment, grants, gifts, in-kind contributions)
Special Subjects: African Art, Afro-American Art, Carpets & Rugs, Drawings, Etchings & Engravings, Painting-American, Painting-French, Photography, Prints, Sculpture, Stained Glass
Collections: University art collection of paintings, prints, photographs, books, manuscripts, textiles & sculpture, Irish paintings
Exhibitions: Four - six rotating per yr
Publications: Exhibition catalogues
Activities: Classes for children; lects open to pub, 2-3 vis lectrs per yr; concerts; gallery talks; tours; book traveling exhibs 1 per yr; originate traveling exhibs to other univ galleries & museums

L **UNIVERSITY OF PENNSYLVANIA,** Fisher Fine Arts Library, 220 S 34th St, Philadelphia, PA 19104-6308. Tel 215-898-8325; Fax 215-573-2066; Email hbennett@upenn.edu; Web: www.library.upenn.edu/finearts; *Dir Fine Arts & Museum Librares* Hannah Bennett
Open Mon - Fri 8:30 AM - 6 PM; Research library
Library Holdings: Book Volumes 150,000, CD-ROMs, Cassettes, Exhibition Catalogs, Fiche, Kodachrome Transparencies, Lantern Slides, Maps, Pamphlets, Periodical Subscriptions 800, Photographs, Reels, Slides, Video Tapes
Special Subjects: Architecture, Art History, Landscapes, Religious Art

M **Museum of Archaeology & Anthropology,** 3260 South St, Philadelphia, PA 19104-6324. Tel 215-898-4000; Fax 215-898-7961; Email info@pennmuseum.org; Web: www.penn.museum; *Dir* Julian Siggers; *Deputy Dir & Chief Cur* Dr Stephen J Tinney; *Historical Arch Assoc Cur* Dr Robert L Schuyler; *Cur in Charge* Clark L Erickson; *Assoc Cur in Charge* Dr Richard L Zettler; *Egyptian Section Cur* Dr David Silverman; *Mediterranean Section Cur* Dr C Brian Rose; *Physical Anthropology Cur* Dr Janet Monge
Open Tues - Sun 10 AM - 5 PM, cl Mon, holidays, summer Suns & Memorial Day thru Labor Day; Admis adults $15, seniors $13, children 6 - 17 & students $10, members, University of Pennsylvania faculty, staff & students with Penn card free; Estab 1887 to investigate the origins & varied developments of human cultural achievements in all times & places; to preserve & maintain colls to document these achievements & to present to the pub the results of these investigations by means of permanent exhibits, temporary exhibs & special events; Average Annual Attendance: 150,000; Mem: 2000; dues individual $55, Loren Eiseley Assoc $1000
Income: $5,000,000 (financed by endowment, mem, state appropriation & univ)
Special Subjects: African Art, American Indian Art, Anthropology, Antiquities-Egyptian, Antiquities-Etruscan, Antiquities-Greek, Antiquities-Oriental, Antiquities-Roman, Archaeology, Asian Art, Bronzes, Ceramics, Coins & Medals, Costumes, Crafts, Eskimo Art, Ethnology, Flasks & Bottles, Folk Art, Glass, Gold, Hispanic Art, Historical Material, Islamic Art, Ivory, Jade, Jewelry, Latin American Art, Metalwork, Mexican Art, Mosaics, Oriental Art, Photography, Pottery, Pre-Columbian Art, Sculpture, Southwestern Art, Tapestries, Textiles, Woodcarvings
Collections: Archaeological & ethnographic artifacts relating to the Old & New World, the classical civilization of the Mediterranean, Egypt, Mesopotamia, Iran & the Far East, North & Middle America, Oceania, Africa
Exhibitions: Ancient Greek World. Living in Balance: The Universe of The Hopi, Zuni, Navajo & Apache
Publications: Expedition Magazine, quarterly; Museum Applied Science Center for Archaeology Journal; Museum Monographs; exhib catalogues
Activities: Classes for adults & children; docent training; family day; lect open to pub, 20 vis lectrs per yr; concerts; gallery talks; tours; 5 or more book traveling exhib; exten dept servs Pennsylvania Commonwealth; objects of art lent to libraries & instructional centers in the state; lending coll contains motion pictures, original art works & slides; originates traveling exhibs; mus shop sells books, magazines, reproductions, slides, jewelry & craft items

L **Museum Library,** 3260 South St, Philadelphia, PA 19104-6324. Tel 215-898-7840; Fax 215-573-2008; Email library@pobox.upenn.edu; Web: www.library.upenn.edu/museum; *Dir* Dr John Weeks
Open Mon & Fri-Sat 9 AM - 5 PM, Tues & Thurs 9 AM - 9 PM, Sun 1 PM - 5 PM; For reference & research only
Library Holdings: Book Volumes 110,000, Fiche, Filmstrips, Other Holdings Microforms 70,000, Pamphlets, Periodical Subscriptions 800, Reels
Special Subjects: Anthropology, Archaeology
Collections: Univ Anthropology Collection

M **THE UNIVERSITY OF THE ARTS,** Rosenwald-Wolf Gallery, 333 South Broad St, Philadelphia, PA 19107-5839; 320 South Broad St, Philadelphia, PA 19102. Tel 215-717-6480; Fax 215-717-6468; Email ssachs@uarts.edu; Web: www.uarts.edu/about/rosenwald-wolf-gallery; *Provost* Patricia Kucker; *Pres & CEO* David Yager; *Dir Exhibs* Sid Sachs
Open Mon - Fri 10 AM - 5 PM, Sat 12 noon - 5 PM; No admis fee; College contains two galleries; Rosenwald-Wolf Gallery & Hamilton Hall Building Galleries; Temporary exhibs which relate to the University's diverse instruction. The galleries present high quality contemporary exhibs which attract national & international artists to the campus. Major exhibs are accompanied by catalogs, symposia & lects; Average Annual Attendance: 4,000
Income: Financed by city, state & federal appropriations, pvt & corporate support
Exhibitions: Contemporary & 20th century work in visual arts & design
Publications: Catalogs & brochures accompany major gallery exhibs
Activities: Lect open to pub; gallery talks; 2-4 vis lectrs per yr; originates traveling exhibs for museums, univ galleries

L **University Libraries,** 333 South Broad St Philadelphia, PA 19102; 320 South Broad St, Philadelphia, PA 19102-4901. Tel 215-717-6280; Fax 215-717-6287; Email libraries@uarts.edu; Web: library.uarts.edu; *Visual Resources & Special Colls Librn* Laura Grutzeck; *Pub Services Librn* Sara MacDonald; *Library Dir* Carol H Graney; *Reference Librn* Mary Louise Castaldi; *Technical Svcs* Kathryn Coyle; *Digital Initiatives & Systems Librn* Joshua Roberts; *Access Servs Librn* Kimberly Lesley; *Cataloger/Processing Archivist* Phoebe Kowalewski; *Music Reference Librn* James Cowen
Open Mon - Fri 9 AM - 5 PM by appointment; Estab 1876 to support the acad progs of the School; Circ 30,000; Lending to univ patrons only & mem holders; Average Annual Attendance: 91.072; Mem: Dues general pub $50
Library Holdings: Audio Tapes 538, Book Volumes 127,600, CD-ROMs 350, Cassettes 538, Clipping Files, Compact Disks 10,476, DVDs 2,804, Exhibition Catalogs, Fiche, Kodachrome Transparencies, Micro Print, Other Holdings Picture files 114,830; Laserdiscs 6; Textiles, Periodical Subscriptions 314, Photographs, Prints, Records 9,834, Reels 450, Reproductions, Slides 61,576, Video Tapes 1,112
Special Subjects: Art Education, Ceramics, Crafts, Decorative Arts, Film, Graphic Arts, Graphic Design, History of Art & Archaeology, Illustration, Industrial Design, Jewelry, Mixed Media, Photography, Printmaking, Sculpture, Stage Design, Textiles, Theatre Arts

M **WOODMERE ART MUSEUM INC,** 9201 Germantown Ave, Philadelphia, PA 19118. Tel 215-247-0476; Fax 215-247-2387; Email info@woodmereartmuseum.org; Web: woodmereartmuseum.org; *Dir & CEO* William Valerio
Open Tues - Thurs & Sun 10 AM - 5 PM, Fri 10 AM - 8:45 PM, Sat 10 AM - 6 PM; Admis for spec exhibs adults $10, seniors $7, children & students free; Estab 1940; founded by Charles Knox Smith, in trust for benefit of the pub; A large addition in 1965 provides additional gallery & studio space; Mem: 2500; dues $35 & higher; annual meeting in Dec
Income: Financed by endowments, gifts, grants & mem fees
Purchases: Philadelphia art, past & present
Library Holdings: Cards, Clipping Files, Exhibition Catalogs
Special Subjects: Antiquities-Oriental, Antiquities-Persian, Architecture, Asian Art, Carpets & Rugs, Ceramics, Decorative Arts, Drawings, Embroidery, Etchings & Engravings, Folk Art, Furniture, Graphics, Juvenile Art, Laces, Landscapes, Oriental Art, Painting-American, Painting-European, Period Rooms, Photography, Porcelain, Portraits, Prints, Renaissance Art, Sculpture, Afro-American Art, Bookplates & Bindings, Watercolors
Collections: Contemporary Philadelphia paintings, sculpture & graphics, European porcelains & furniture, European & American sculpture, Oriental rugs, furniture, porcelains, Smith Collection of European & American paintings
Exhibitions: 12 changing exhibitions annually; prizes awarded in winter Juried Annual & Special Exhibitions
Publications: Selections from the permanent coll of the Woodmere Art Museum
Activities: Classes for adults & children; docent training; lect open to pub; concerts; gallery talks; tours; competitions with prizes; 10 visiting lectures per year; individual paintings & original objects of art lent to other museums & galleries; mus shop sells books, gifts, jewelry & original art, prints; Helen Millard Children's Gallery

L **Library,** 9201 Germantown Ave, Philadelphia, PA 19118. Tel 215-247-0948; Fax 215-247-2387; Email phoffman@woodmereartmuseum.com; Web: www.woodmereartmuseum.org
Open Tues - Fri 10 AM - 4 PM; Reference only
Library Holdings: Cards, Clipping Files, Exhibition Catalogs, Slides

PITTSBURGH

M **THE ANDY WARHOL MUSEUM,** 117 Sandusky St, Pittsburgh, PA 15212-5890. Tel 412-237-8300; Fax 412-237-8340; Email information@warhol.org; Web: www.warhol.org; *Dir* Patrick Moore; *Deputy Dir* Rachel Baron-Horn; *Admin & Fin Coord* Lena Tavoletti; *Dir Exhibs* Keny Marshall; *Dir Colls & Registration* Amber Morgan; *Milton Fine Cur of Art* Jessica Beck; *Chief Cur* Jose Diaz
Open Tues - Sun 10 AM - 5 PM, Fri 10 AM - 10 PM, cl Mon & major holidays; Admis adults $20, students with ID, seniors & children ages 3-18 $10, children under 3 & mem free; Estab 1994; Mem: Carnegie Mus of Pittsburgh; dues $50 - $250
Special Subjects: Costumes, Graphics, Manuscripts, Photography, Portraits, Posters, Painting-American
Collections: Film & Video (permanent), Over 4,000 art works in all media, sketchbook drawings, hand-painted images, self-portraits
Exhibitions: Rotating exhibs featuring 500 items from permanent collection; special exhibs on specific areas of Warhols work & work of related artists
Activities: Weekend Factory hands-on art prog; lects open to pub; concerts; film screenings; parties; exhib openings; mus shop sells accessories, books, calendars, magnets, posters, prints, stationery, videos

L **Archives,** 117 Sandusky St, Pittsburgh, PA 15212-5890.
Open to researchers by appt, cl to gen pub
Library Holdings: Audio Tapes 4,000, Book Volumes, Clipping Files, Filmstrips 273, Other Holdings Source Material, Periodical Subscriptions, Photographs, Records, Sculpture, Video Tapes
Special Subjects: Decorative Arts, Film, Graphic Arts, Manuscripts, Photography, Sculpture, Posters
Collections: Over 8,000 cubic ft of material, Time Capsules, scrapbooks, art supplies & material, run of Interview magazine

M **ART INSTITUTE OF PITTSBURGH,** John P. Barclay Memorial Gallery, 420 Blvd of the Allies, Pittsburgh, PA 15219-1328. Tel 412-263-6600; Fax 412-263-6667; Web: www.artinstitutes.edu/pittsburgh; *Dir Resource Center* Susan Moran; *Dir* Nancy Ruttner
Open Mon, Tues & Thurs 9 AM - 8 PM, Wed & Fri 9 AM - 5 PM, Sat 9 AM - 4 PM; No admis fee; Estab 1921 as an art school & proprietary trade school

Exhibitions: Local art group shows; local artists; loan exhibs; student and faculty mems; technical art exhibits
Publications: Brochures; Catalog; School Newspaper
Activities: Classes for adults & teens; lect open to pub, 2-4 vis lectrs per yr; schols offered

L **Resource Center**, 420 Blvd of the Allies, Pittsburgh, PA 15219-1328. Tel 412-291-6357; Email aiplibrary@aii.edu; Web: www.aiplib.aiiresources.com; www.artinstitutes.edu/pittsburgh; *Dir Libr Svcs* Kathy Ober
Open Mon - Thurs 7:30 AM - 9:30 PM, Fri 7:30 AM - 5 PM, Sat 9 AM - 4 PM
Library Holdings: Book Volumes 5674, Cassettes, Clipping Files, Exhibition Catalogs, Fiche, Filmstrips, Framed Reproductions, Memorabilia, Pamphlets, Periodical Subscriptions 208, Records, Slides

A **ASSOCIATED ARTISTS OF PITTSBURGH,** 100 43rd St, Ste 102 Pittsburgh, PA 15201-3101. Tel 412-361-1370; Fax 412-471-1765; Email aapgh1@verizon.net; Web: www.aapgh.org; *Exec Dir* Juliana Morris
Open Tues - Fri 11 AM - 4 PM, Sat 11 AM - 3 PM; No admis fee; Estab 1910 to give exposure to mem artists & for educ of the area in the field of art; 2 fls of galleries with changing exhibits; Average Annual Attendance: 15,000; Mem: 500 (must be juried into the group) & live within 150 miles of Pittsburgh; dues $80
Income: Financed by mem; donations from foundations, corporations & individuals
Exhibitions: Annual Exhibition at Carnegie Museum of art open to all regional artists; Changing exhibs, 10 per yr
Publications: The First 75 Years
Activities: Special progs linking students & artists; classes for adults & children; workshops for professional artists; lect open to pub; competitions with awards; individual paintings & original objects of art lent to interested individuals & bus; sells mems artwork

C **BANK OF NY MELLON CORPORATION,** 500 Grant St, One Mellon Financial Ctr Pittsburgh, PA 15219-2502. Tel 412-234-4775; Fax 412-234-0831; *Art Dir* Brian J Lang
Collections: 18th & 19th century British drawings & paintings, American historical prints, 19th century American & Pennsylvanian paintings, contemporary American & British paintings, contemporary works on paper, textiles, contemporary photography

M **CARNEGIE MELLON UNIVERSITY,** The Frame, 5200 Forbes Ave, Pittsburgh, PA 15213-3890. Tel 412-268-2000 (main), 268-2409 (art dept); Web: www.cmu.edu, www.art.cfa.cmu.edu; *Co-Dir* Jamie Walters
Open Wed 3 - 6 & 7 - 9 PM, Thurs & Fri Noon - 6 PM & Thurs evening 7 - 9 PM, Sat Noon - 6 PM, Sun Noon - 3 PM; Estab 1969 to offer exhib space to students, & an opportunity to learn about gallery management through practice; Gallery is approx 20 x 40 ft plus small back room space; Average Annual Attendance: 750
Income: $5000 (financed by univ funding)
Exhibitions: Weekly senior art student exhibs

L **Hunt Library**, 4909 Frew St, 5th Fl Pittsburgh, PA 15213-3890. Tel 412-268-7272; Fax 412-268-7148; Email artsref@andrew.cmu.edu; Web: www.library.cmu.edu; *Head of Access Services* Joan Stein; *Head of Hunt Reference* Jean Alexander
Open Mon-Thurs 8AM-Midnight, Fri 8AM-0PM, Sat 10AM-9PM, Sun noon-Midnight; Estab 1912; The Arts Library is on the 4th fl of the Hunt Library, supports College of Fine Arts prog & is open to the pub
Income: Financed by Univ Libraries operating funds & endowments
Library Holdings: Audio Tapes, Book Volumes 80,000, CD-ROMs, Cassettes, Clipping Files, Compact Disks, DVDs, Exhibition Catalogs, Fiche, Manuscripts, Memorabilia, Original Art Works, Original Documents, Other Holdings Architectural drawings; electronic data files, Pamphlets, Periodical Subscriptions 350, Photographs, Prints, Records, Reels, Reproductions, Sculpture, Slides 120,700, Video Tapes
Special Subjects: Architecture
Collections: Architecture Archives, Swiss Poster Coll, Thomas Gonda design coll, artists books

M **Hunt Institute for Botanical Documentation**, Frew St, Pittsburgh, PA 15213-3890; 5000 Forbes Ave, Pittsburgh, PA 15213-3890. Tel 412-268-2434; Fax 412-268-5677; Email huntinst@andrew.cmu.edu; Web: huntbot.andrew.cmu.edu; *Dir* Terry D Jacobsen; *Cur Art* Lugene Bruno; *Librn* Charlotte Tancin; *Archivist* J Dustin Williams; *Bibliographer* Donald W Brown; *Asst Librn* Jeannette McDevitt; *Asst Cur Art* Carolina Roy
Open Mon - Fri 9 AM - Noon & 1 - 5 PM, Sun 1 - 4 PM during exhibs; No admis fee; Estab 1961 for the study of botany, history of botany, botanical art & illustration; Two exhibs per yr
Special Subjects: Drawings, Etchings & Engravings, Prints, Watercolors, Woodcuts
Collections: Botanical Art Collection, Archives
Publications: Huntia, irregular; Bulletin, semi-annually; exhib catalogues, reference works, monographs
Activities: Gallery talks; tours; traveling exhibs to mus, galleries, botanical gardens; Retail store sells books, posters & cards

M **CARNEGIE MUSEUMS OF PITTSBURGH,** Carnegie Museum of Art, 4400 Forbes Ave, Pittsburgh, PA 15213-4080. Tel 412-622-3131; Fax 412-622-3112; Email membership@carnegiemuseums.org; Web: www.cmoa.org; *Deputy Dir* Sarah Minnaert; *CMOA Bd* Martin McGuinn; *Cur Decorative Arts* Rachel Delphia; *Cur Educ* Marilyn M Russell; *Cur Fine Art* Louise W Lippincott; *Chief Conservator* Ellen Baxter; *Dir Colls & Registration* Orian Neumann; *Media Rel Mgr* Jonathan Gaugler; *Cur Architecture* Raymond Ryan; *Chief Cur* Catherine Evans; *Chief Preparator* Kurt Christian; *Cur Contemp Art* Eric Crosby; *Cur Photography* Don Leers; *Dir Mktg* Brad Stephenson
Open Mon, Wed, Fri - Sun 10 AM - 5 PM, Thurs 10 AM - 8 PM, cl Tues New Year's Day, Easter, Thanksgiving & Christmas; Admis adults $19.95, seniors (65+) $14.95, children (3-18) & students with ID $11.95, mems & children under 2 free; discounts to mems with ACCESS/EBT card; 50% discount to military personnel & teachers; Estab 1895, incorporated 1926. Original building 1896-1907; Scaife Wing 1974; Most coll & special exhibs are on view in 50,000 sq ft Scaife Wing designed by Edward Larrabee Barnes in 1974; Average Annual Attendance: 330,000; Mem: 27,400; dues $50 & up
Income: Financed by endowment, mem, city, county & state appropriation & other funds
Library Holdings: Auction Catalogs, Fiche
Special Subjects: Decorative Arts, Dolls, Drawings, Furniture, Oriental Art, Painting-American, Painting-European, Photography, Prints, Sculpture, Woodcuts
Collections: American & European paintings & sculpture, especially Impressionist & Post-Impressionist, Contemporary International Art, Japanese woodblock prints, American & European decorative arts, Antiquities, Asian Art, African Art, Films, Video tapes, Photographs, Prints & Drawings
Exhibitions: See website
Publications: Carnegie Magazine, four times per yr; catalogue of permanent coll; exhib catalogs; quarterly newsletter, email newsletters to members & non-members
Activities: Classes for adults & children; docent training; lect open to pub, concerts; gallery talks; tours incl free audio guide; Carnegie award; inter-museum loans; originate traveling exhibs; mus shop sells books, periodicals, original art, posters, reproductions, textiles, jewelry, ceramics, postcards, designer household objects: furniture, lighting, tableware

L **Carnegie Library of Pittsburgh**, 4400 Forbes Ave, Pittsburgh, PA 15213. Tel 412-622-3131; Fax 412-578-2561; Email info@carnegielibrary.org; Web: www.clpgh.org; *Pres & Dir* Barbara K Mistick
Open Mon-Thurs 10AM-8PM, Fri & Sat 9AM-5:30 PM, Sun noon-5PM; Open to staff & mus docents for reference only
Library Holdings: Book Volumes 2,000,000, CD-ROMs, Cassettes, Fiche, Filmstrips, Memorabilia, Periodical Subscriptions, Photographs, Prints, Video Tapes

M **CHATHAM COLLEGE,** Art Gallery, Woodland Rd, Art & Design Center Pittsburgh, PA 15232. Tel 412-365-1100; Fax 412-365-1505; Web: www.chatham.edu; *Dir* Michael Pestel; *Dir Fine & Performing Arts* William Lenz
Open Mon - Fri 11 AM - 5 PM; No admis fee; Estab 1960 as an art gallery in a small liberal arts col, serving both the col & community by mounting exhibs of high quality; Gallery is 100 running ft, is located in Jennie King Mellon Library & is fitted with track lighting; Average Annual Attendance: 1,500
Income: Financed by col
Exhibitions: Linda Benglis; Don Reitz; Idelle Weber; Jerry L Caplan
Activities: Lect open to pub, 2 vis lectrs per yr; gallery talks; schols offered; individual paintings & original objects of art lent

M **THE FRICK ART & HISTORICAL CENTER, INC,** Frick Art Museum, 7227 Reynolds St, Pittsburgh, PA 15208-2923. Tel 412-371-0600; Fax 412-241-5393; Email info@thefrickpittsburgh.org; Web: www.thefrickpittsburgh.org; *Dir* William Bodine Jr; *Dir Cur Affairs* Sarah Hall; *Dir Fin & Admin* Christine D Chambers; *Dir Educ* Pam St John; *Dir External Affairs* Susan Neszpaul; *Dir Opers & Vis Servs* Bill Nichols
Open Tues - Sun 10AM-5PM; Admis to Clayton Mansion $12 non-mem; $10 seniors & students; mem free; art mus free; Estab 1970 as an art mus for pub enjoyment & educ; Average Annual Attendance: 132,000; Mem: 3,200
Income: Financed by endowment
Special Subjects: Bronzes, Ceramics, Decorative Arts, Drawings, Furniture, Furniture, Glass, Medieval Art, Painting-American, Painting-British, Painting-Dutch, Painting-Flemish, Painting-French, Painting-Italian, Period Rooms, Porcelain, Portraits, Religious Art, Renaissance Art, Sculpture, Silver, Tapestries, Tapestries, Watercolors
Collections: Italian, French Renaissance, bronzes, Chinese porcelains, furniture, sculpture, tapestries, antique cars
Publications: Exhibit catalogs
Activities: Classes for adults & children; dramatic progs; docent training; studio workshops; family progs; lect open to pub, 10 vis lectrs per yr; concerts; gallery talks; tours; competitions with awards; schols & fels offered; original objects of art lent to museums; book traveling exhibs 3 per yr; originate traveling exhibs to museums; mus shop sells books, catalogues, color reproductions, photographs, posters, post cards & gifts, clothing

M **MANCHESTER BIDWELL CORPORATION,** Manchester Craftsmen's Guild Youth & Arts Program, 1815 Metropolitan St, Pittsburgh, PA 15233-2233. Tel 412-322-1773; Fax 412-321-2120; Email rmgubser@mcg-btc.org; Web: http://mcgyouthandarts.org; *Exec Asst* Rose Mary Gubser; *VPres MCG Youth & Arts* Dave Deily; *Dir MCG Youth & Arts* Justin Mazzei
Open Mon-Fri 9AM-5:30PM; Estab 1968 to present photog & ceramic art of regional & nationally recognized artists; Connie Kerr Gallery; Average Annual Attendance: 2,500-5,000
Special Subjects: African Art, Afro-American Art, Cartoons, Ceramics, Crafts, Drawings, Jewelry, Juvenile Art, Landscapes, Leather, Metalwork, Mosaics, Photography, Sculpture, Textiles, Watercolors
Collections: Martin Luther King permanent exhib of photographs
Activities: Art classes for adults & children; MCG Invitational Art Show; lects free open to pub, 4-6 vis lectrs per yr; gallery talks; tours; scholarships; cash prizes for high school students; sales shop sells original art, reproductions, & prints

M **THE MATTRESS FACTORY,** 500 Sampsonia Way, Pittsburgh, PA 15212-4444. Tel 412-231-3169; Fax 412-322-2231; Email info@mattress.org; Web: www.mattress.org; *Bd Mem, Co-Dir* Michael Olijnyk; *Bd Mem, Co-Dir* Barbara Luderowski; *Bd Chmn* Michael White
Open Tues - Sat 10 AM - 5 PM, Sun 1 - 5 PM, cl Mon, New Year's Day, Easter, Memorial Day, Independence Day, Thanksgiving & Christmas; Admis fee Adults $20, students & seniors $15, children under 6 & mems free; Estab 1977 as a research & development residency program featuring site-specific installations; Average Annual Attendance: 75,000
Collections: Permanent collection of William Anastasi, Jene Highstein, Rolf Julius, Yayoi Kusama, Winifred Lutz, James Turrell, Allan Wexler & Bill Woodrow
Activities: Classes for adults, children & teachers; lectures open to the public; concerts, gallery talks & tours; mus shop sells books, magazines, original art & prints

A **PITTSBURGH CENTER FOR THE ARTS,** 6300 5th Ave, Pittsburgh, PA 15232-2922. Tel 412-361-0873; Fax 412-361-8338; Email info@pittsburgharts.org; Web: www.pittsburgharts.org/index.php; *Exec Dir* Charlie Humphrey; *Dir* Laura Domencil; *Cur* Adam Welch
Open Tues- Wed & Mon in Dec, 10 AM - 5 PM, Thurs 10 AM - 9 PM, Fri - Sat 10 AM 7 PM, Sun Noon - 5 PM, cl Mon, New Year's Day, Thanksgiving, Christmas; No admis fee, suggested donation $5, mems no charge; Estab 1945 by artists; Non-profit community arts ctr that offers arts educ programs & contemporary art exhibits & provides services & resources for artists throughout western PA; Average Annual Attendance: 150,000; Mem: 6500; dues vary; patron mems
Income: Financed by school tui, mem, commission on art sales & contributions
Publications: Artists directory; class schedule; exhib catalogs; monthly calendar
Activities: Arts & crafts classes for adults and children; workshops; summer art camps; lect open to pub; concerts; gallery talks; tours; ann holiday art sales; awards: Artist of the Year, Emerging Artist of the Year, Service to the Arts Award & Lifetime Achievement Award; schols & fels offered; exten dept serves western Pennsylvania; originate traveling exhibs; sales shop sells books & original art

L **PITTSBURGH HISTORY & LANDMARKS FOUNDATION,** James D Van Trump Library, 100 W Station Sq Dr, Ste 450, Pittsburgh, PA 15219-1134. Tel 412-471-5808; Fax 412-471-1633; Email info@phlf.org; Web: www.phlf.org; *Pres* Arthur P Ziegler Jr; *Exec Dir* Louise Sturgess
Open Mon - Fri 9 AM - 5 PM; Estab 1964 to preserve the architectural legacy & historic neighborhoods of Allegheny County; Reference for mems only; Mem: 2200; dues $15 or more
Library Holdings: Book Volumes 4700, Clipping Files, Original Art Works, Other Holdings Architectural & engineering drawings, Periodical Subscriptions 17, Photographs, Prints
Special Subjects: Architecture, Drawings, Landscape Architecture
Collections: Paintings: Aaron Gorson, Otto Kuhler, Edward B Lee, William C Wall
Activities: Classes for adults & children; dramatic progs; docent training; lect open to pub, 2 vis lectrs per yr; tours; competitions with prizes; mus shop sells books, reproductions, prints & slides

A **SILVER EYE CENTER FOR PHOTOGRAPHY,** 1015 E Carson St, Pittsburgh, PA 15203-1109. Tel 412-431-1810; Fax 412-431-5777; Email info@silvereye.org; Web: www.silvereye.org; *Exec Dir* Ellen Fleurov
Open Tues - Sat Noon-6PM; No admis fee; Mem: dues $35 - $750
Income: Financed by government, corporations, foundations & individuals
Special Subjects: Photography
Exhibitions: Rotating exhibits of national & international photography, 2 national photo competitions per yr
Activities: Classes for children; outreach pub school prog; lects open to pub, 1-5 vis lectrs per yr; gallery talks; fels available

M **SOCIETY FOR CONTEMPORARY CRAFT,** 2100 Smallman St, Pittsburgh, PA 15222-4440. Tel 412-261-7003; Fax 412-261-1941; Email info@contemporarycraft.org; Web: www.contemporarycraft.org; *Dir Exhibs* Kate Lydon; *Exec Dir* Janet McCall; *Sales Mgr* Megan Crowell; *Dir Develop* Loretta Stanish; *Studio Prog Coordr* Rachel Saul; *Finance Mgr* Yu-San Cheng; *Marketing Mgr* Norah Guigmon
Open Mon - Fri 10 AM - 5 PM, Sat 10 AM - 5 PM; No admis fee; Estab 1971 to engage pub in the creative experience through contemporary craft; Gallery features contemporary crafts by nationally & internationally recognized artists in thematic shows; educ & outreach progs; retail store; Average Annual Attendance: 40,000; Mem: No mem prog
Income: Financed by donations, grants & earned revenue
Library Holdings: Exhibition Catalogs, Original Art Works, Periodical Subscriptions
Special Subjects: Ceramics, Crafts, Enamels, Furniture, Glass, Jewelry, Metalwork, Mixed Media, Mosaics, Pewter, Pottery, Textiles, Silversmithing
Collections: Ceramics, contemporary crafts, fiber, furniture, glass, jewelry, metals, mixed media
Publications: Exhibit catalogs
Activities: Classes for adults & children;; lect open to pub, competitions with cash awards, Leap Award, Raphael Founder's Prize; gallery talks; tours;; schols; lends original objects of art to educational insts; originate traveling exhibs 4 per yr to museums and university art galleries; museum shop sells books, magazines, original art, crafts

M **UNIVERSITY OF PITTSBURGH,** University Art Gallery, 650 Schenley Dr, Frick Fine Arts Bldg Pittsburgh, PA 15260. Tel 412-648-2423; Fax 412-648-2792; Email uag@pitt.edu; Web: www.haa.pitt.edu; *Cur* Isabelle Chartier; *Dir* Barbara McClsokey
Open Mon - Fri 10 AM - 4 PM; No admis fee; Estab 1965 to provide exhibs for the univ community & the community at large & to provide students with gallery experience; Gallery comprised of 350 running ft in five areas; Average Annual Attendance: 4,000
Income: Financed through the univ
Special Subjects: Antiquities-Oriental, Antiquities-Roman, Archaeology, Architecture, Asian Art, Baroque Art, Bronzes, Calligraphy, Ceramics, Drawings, Eskimo Art, Etchings & Engravings, Flasks & Bottles, Glass, Historical Material, Landscapes, Oriental Art, Painting-American, Painting-British, Painting-European, Painting-French, Painting-Italian, Painting-Japanese, Photography, Portraits, Pottery, Prints, Reproductions, Sculpture, Sculpture, Stained Glass, Tapestries, Watercolors, Woodcuts
Collections: Drawings, paintings, prints & sculpture, European, Western Pennsylvania, Asian, Inuit
Exhibitions: Mus studies exhib, studio arts faculty & student show
Activities: Educ prog; guided tours; lects open to pub; gallery talks; tours; Original objects of art lent; lending to art institutions; coll contains original art works, original prints, paintings, photographs, sculptures & drawings; originate traveling exhibs

L **Henry Clay Frick Fine Arts Library,** 650 Schenley Dr, Frick Fine Arts Bldg, first fl Pittsburgh, PA 15260. Tel 412-648-2410; Fax 412-648-7568; Email uls-fineartslibrary@mail.pitt.edu; Web: www.library.pitt.edu/libraries/frick/fine_arts; *Head Librn* James P Cassaro; *Bibliographer & Pub Svcs Librn* Ray Anne Lockard
Open Mon - Thurs 9 AM - 9 PM, Fri 9 AM - 5 PM, Sat & Sun noon-5PM; Estab 1928 to support the teaching activities of the Departments of History Art & Architecture & Studio Arts; For reference only
Library Holdings: Book Volumes 82,000, CD-ROMs 20, Exhibition Catalogs, Fiche 20,000, Pamphlets, Periodical Subscriptions 250, Reels
Special Subjects: Archaeology, Architecture, Decorative Arts, Graphic Arts, History of Art & Archaeology, Islamic Art, Landscape Architecture, Landscapes, Oriental Art, Religious Art, Tapestries, Sculpture
Collections: Facsimile mss, small coll of rare books & artists book

READING

M **ALBRIGHT COLLEGE,** Freedman Gallery, 13th & Bern Sts, Reading, PA 19612-5234; PO Box 15234, Reading, PA 19612-5234. Tel 610-921-7541; Fax 610-921-7768; Web: www.albright.edu/freedman; *Dir* Michael Howell
Open Tues, Noon - 8 PM, Wed - Fri Noon - 6 PM, Sat & Sun Noon - 4 PM, also by appointment; No admis fee; Estab 1976 to present primarily contemporary art in a context of teaching; Large Gallery: 40 ft x 50 ft; Small Gallery: 20 ft x 24 ft; Average Annual Attendance: 18,000; Mem: 220; dues Dir Circle $1000, supporter $500, contributor $100, family $50, individual $25
Income: $150,000 (financed by endowment, college, mem & grants)
Special Subjects: Painting-American, Photography, Prints, Sculpture
Collections: Contemporary Painting, Prints, Sculpture, Photography
Publications: Exhibit catalogues & brochures available
Activities: Classes for children; workshops & tours; ann student juried exhibs; lect open to pub, 4 vis lectrs per yr; gallery talks; tours; Freedman Gallery Student Award; produce video-tapes on exhibs, these include interviews with artists & commentary, tapes are available for rent; film series; individual paintings & original objects of art lent to galleries & museums; originate traveling exhibs; sales shop sells catalogues, prints, t-shirts

A **BERKS ART ALLIANCE,** 1100 Belmont Ave, Institute of the Arts Reading, PA 19610-2004. Tel 610-376-1576, 775-9444; *Pres* Diana Kleiner; *VPres Prog* Elaine Reinert; *Mem* Joanne Dietz; *Rec Secy* Jane Debauchy; *Treas* Brian Gallagher; *Corresp Secy* Carol Sumner; *Publicity* Jay Ressler; *Newsletter Ed* Amanda Condict; *Pres Elect* Frances Parzanese
Estab 1941 to maintain active art center in Reading & Berks county; Mem: 305; dues $25; ann meetings 2nd Tues of odd months: Sept, Nov, Jan, Mar, May; mems must be 18 or older interested in the purpose of the Alliance
Income: Financed by dues; commissions from mems shows, including ann juried show at Reading Public Museum, Jul & Aug, or other venue
Library Holdings: Book Volumes 250, Video Tapes 50
Exhibitions: Two annual membership shows, plus solo or two-persons shows of a two week period each; juried show at Reading Public Museum or Goggle Works, Jul & Aug
Publications: Palette, every other month Aug - Apr
Activities: Life or costume drawing workshop Thurs morning, Sept - Aug; open painting workshop Thurs afternoon; life drawing workshop Thurs evening; three day seminars by professional artists; 5 vis lectrs per yr; sponsors ann trip to American Watercolor Society Show in New York and other bus trips to Baltimore & Washington, DC

M **READING PUBLIC MUSEUM,** 500 Museum Rd, Reading, PA 19611-1425. Tel 610-371-5850; Fax 610-371-5632; Email museum@readingpublicmuseum.org; Web: www.readingpublicmuseum.org; *Chmn* Kathleen Kleppinger; *1st VChmn* Richard Zuidema; *Sec* Leigh Rye; *Treas* Socrates J Georgeadis Esq; *Cur Arts & Civilization* Scott A Schweigert; *Dir Educ* Anne Corso; *CFO* Jennifer Wilson; *Asst Secy* Judith Phelps; *Immediate Past Chair* Rolf D Schmidt; *Dir & CEO* John Graydon Smith
Open Tues - Sat 11 AM - 5 PM, Sun Noon - 5PM; Admis adults $8, children $6, students, seniors; Estab 1904; Gen-art to nat history; Average Annual Attendance: 60,000; Mem: 2,800; $60, AAM accredited
Income: donations, admis, grant
Library Holdings: Auction Catalogs, Book Volumes, Exhibition Catalogs
Special Subjects: African Art, American Indian Art, Anthropology, Antiquities-Egyptian, Antiquities-Etruscan, Antiquities-Greek, Antiquities-Oriental, Antiquities-Persian, Antiquities-Roman, Asian Art, Baroque Art, Bronzes, Ceramics, Coins & Medals, Decorative Arts, Dioramas, Dolls, Drawings, Enamels, Eskimo Art, Etchings & Engravings, Flasks & Bottles, Folk Art, Furniture, Glass, Islamic Art, Ivory, Jade, Jewelry, Judaica, Landscapes, Latin American Art, Manuscripts, Marine Painting, Medieval Art, Metalwork, Mexican Art, Oriental Art, Painting-American, Painting-British, Painting-European, Painting-Flemish, Painting-French, Painting-German, Painting-Italian, Painting-Japanese, Painting-Polish, Painting-Russian, Painting-Scandinavian, Painting-Spanish, Photography, Portraits, Pottery, Religious Art, Renaissance Art, Scrimshaw, Sculpture, Silver, Stained Glass, Tapestries, Textiles, Watercolors, Woodcarvings, Woodcuts
Collections: American & European paintings, Natural Science, 19th Century Paintings, Old Masters Gallery, Pennsylvania-German Gallery, Ancient Civilizations, North American Indian Arms & Armor, Pre-Colombian Latin American
Exhibitions: Rotating & permanent exhibs
Publications: Catalog of selections from Permanent Collection & Exhibits
Activities: Classes for adults & children; lects open to pub, 6 vis lectrs per yr; concerts, gallery talks, tours; lending of original objects of art to international mus; books traveling exhibs 1 per yr; mus shop sells books, original art, reproductions & novelties

SCRANTON

M **EVERHART MUSEUM,** 1901 Mulberry St, Scranton, PA 18510-2390. Tel 570-346-7186; Fax 570-346-0652; Email general.information@everhart-museum.org; Web: www.everhart-museum.org; *Cur* Nezka Pfeifer; *Exec Dir* Aurore Enguet; *Dir Progs* Stefanie Colarusso; *Dir Development* Amy Everetts

Open Mon, Thurs - Fri Noon - 4 PM, Sat 10 AM - 5 PM, Sun Noon - 5 PM cl Tues, Wed, January, Easter, July 4, Thanksgiving & Christmas; Admis adults $7, seniors & students $5, children 6 - 12 $3, under 6 no charge; Estab & incorporated 1908, a gift to the city by Dr Isaiah F Everhart; building enlarged 1928-29; Average Annual Attendance: 20,000; Mem: 1400; dues $25 & up
Income: Financed by endowment, city, state & county appropriations & mem
Library Holdings: Book Volumes, Exhibition Catalogs, Memorabilia, Pamphlets, Periodical Subscriptions, Reels
Special Subjects: African Art, Anthropology, Antiquities-Egyptian, Antiquities-Greek, Antiquities-Roman, Archaeology, Asian Art, Ceramics, Coins & Medals, Decorative Arts, Dioramas, Dolls, Drawings, Ethnology, Folk Art, Glass, Oriental Art, Painting-American, Photography, Porcelain, Portraits, Pre-Columbian Art, Prints, Sculpture, Tapestries, Watercolors, Woodcuts, Miniatures
Collections: American Folk Art; Ethnographic and Natural history Collections
Exhibitions: permanent exhibitions; highlight collections; 2-3 temporary shows yrly
Publications: Newsletter; brochures; rack cards; e-news, weekly
Activities: Classes for adults & children; docent training; gallery talks; tours; educ progs for schools & other groups by appointment; book traveling exhibs; sales shop

SELINSGROVE

M **SUSQUEHANNA UNIVERSITY,** Lore Degenstein Gallery, 514 University Ave, Selinsgrove, PA 17870-1164. Tel 570-372-4385; Fax 570-372-2729; Email gallery@susqu.edu; Web: www.susqu.edu/art_gallery/; *Dir* Dr Daniel Olivette; *Registrar* Judy Marvin; *Coll Mgr* Sara Herlinger
Open daily noon-4PM; No admis fee; Estab 1993 to exhibit, interpret, collect & preserve objects of art & material culture through a rich & diverse exhibition program of inquiry supporting acad investigations & contributing to the cultural life of central Pennsylvania; Gallery offers a schedule of changing exhibs focusing its program on historic, contemporary, regional, national & decorative art. Sponsors lects & opening receptions; Average Annual Attendance: 4,000
Special Subjects: Decorative Arts, Drawings, Etchings & Engravings, Furniture, Glass, Historical Material, Landscapes, Manuscripts, Painting-American
Collections: American Painting
Activities: Docent training; lect open to pub, gallery talks, 3-4 vis lectrs per yr; book traveling exhibs 2-3 per yr; traveling exhibs

SHIPPENSBURG

M **SHIPPENSBURG UNIVERSITY,** Kauffman Gallery, 1871 Old Main Dr, Shippensburg, PA 17257-2299. Tel 717-477-1530; Fax 717-477-4049; Email clgrah@ship.edu; Web: www.ship.edu; *Secy* Cathy Graham; *Dir* Steve Dolbin
Open Mon - Thurs 9 AM - 4 PM, Wed 7 PM - 9 PM, Fri 9 AM - noon; No admis fee; Estab 1972 to bring art to the col community; Average Annual Attendance: 1,500
Income: Financed by Student Assn funds & univ
Exhibitions: Scholastic Art Awards - Area 6; Faculty Exhibits; Student Art Exhibits; changing exhibs every month; Senior Art Exhibits
Activities: Lects open to pub, 4 vis lectrs per yr; gallery talks

SOMERSET

M **LAUREL ARTS,** 214 S Harrison Ave, Somerset, PA 15501; PO Box 414, Somerset, PA 15501-0414. Tel 814-443-2433; Fax 814-443-3870; Web: www.laurelarts.org; *Dir* Michael S Knecht
Open Mon - Thurs 10 AM - 8 PM, Fri 10 AM - 4 PM, Sat Noon - 4 PM; No admis fee; Estab 1975; Average Annual Attendance: 51,015; Mem: dues $25-$125
Collections: Rural arts
Exhibitions: 8 exhibits annually; Rotating exhibits
Activities: Classes for adults & children

STRASBURG

A **LANCASTER COUNTY ART ASSOCIATION, INC,** 149 Precision Ave, Strasburg, PA 17579-9608. Tel 717-687-7061; Email icaanews@yahoo.com; Web: www.lcaaonline.org; *VPres* Bradley Gebhart; *Pres* Henrietta Holton-Thomas; *Gallery Dir* Carol Herr
Open Wed - Sat 11 AM - 4 PM, Sun 1 - 4 PM; No admis fee; Estab 1936, inc 1950, to increase appreciation of & participation in the fine arts; Average Annual Attendance: 10,000; Mem: 300; dues $40
Income: Financed by dues, classes, contributions & volunteer service
Exhibitions: Monthly exhibs for professional & non-professional mems; National juried exhib
Publications: Quarterly newsletter
Activities: Classes for adults & children; lect open to pub, 2-3 vis lectrs per yr; gallery talks; competitions with awards; Myrtle Tremblay Watercolor Award; schols offered

STROUDSBURG

M **MONROE COUNTY HISTORICAL ASSOCIATION,** Elizabeth D Walters Library, 900 Main St, Stroudsburg, PA 18360-1604. Tel 570-421-7703; Fax 570-421-9199; Email mcha@ptd.net; Web: www.monroe.historical.org; *Exec Dir* Amy Leiser
Open Tues - Fri 9 AM - 4 PM, 1st & 3rd Sat 10 AM - 4 PM, cl Sun & Mon; Admis adults $8, seniors $6, children $4; Estab 1921 for research; Average Annual Attendance: 5,000; Mem: 550; dues $20; ann meeting 4th Sun in Feb
Income: $116,000 (financed by endowment, mem, state appropriation & county)
Special Subjects: Collages, Decorative Arts, Embroidery, Furniture, Historical Material, Painting-American, Period Rooms, Textiles
Collections: Decorative Arts, Furniture, Indian Artifacts, Textiles
Exhibitions: Period Room; Toy Room; Rotate 4 per yr
Publications: Fanlight Newsletter, six times per year
Activities: Lect open to pub, 5 vis lectrs per yr; Historic Preservation Awards; mus shop sells books

SWARTHMORE

L **SWARTHMORE COLLEGE,** Friends Historical Library of Swarthmore College, 500 College Ave, Swarthmore, PA 19081-1306. Tel 610-328-8496; Fax 610-690-5728; Email friends@swarthmore.edu; Web: www.swarthmore.edu/library/friends; *Cur* Christopher Densmore; *Cur Peace Coll* Wendy Chmielewski
Open Mon - Fri 8:30 AM - 4:30 PM, Sat 10 AM - 1 PM; cl Sat when col not in session; No admis fee; Estab 1871 to preserve & make available to the pub material by & about Quakers & their concerns, records of non-sectarian peace organizations & papers of peace movement leaders; Gallery housed in McCabe Library
Income: financed by endowment & col
Library Holdings: Audio Tapes, Book Volumes 55,000, Cassettes, Clipping Files, Kodachrome Transparencies, Lantern Slides, Manuscripts, Memorabilia, Motion Pictures, Original Art Works, Original Documents, Other Holdings charts; Maps; Posters, Pamphlets, Periodical Subscriptions 584, Photographs, Prints, Records, Reels, Sculpture, Slides, Video Tapes
Special Subjects: Historical Material, Painting-American, Painting-British, Photography, Portraits, Posters, Religious Art
Collections: Quaker paintings, Quakers as subject in art, Meeting House Picture Collection, portraits, group pictures, residence pictures, silhouettes & sketches of individual Friends, Swarthmore College pictures, Swarthmore College Peace Collection: primarily archival material, records of non-sectarian peace organizations in the United States and 59 foreign countries, papers of peace leaders including Jean Addams, Emily Greene Balch, Elihu Burritt, A J Muste,Wilhelm Sollmann and others, 6000 peace posters and war posters, Benjamin West sketches, Edward Hicks journals

UNION DALE

A **SUSQUEHANNA STUDIO,** 16 Lewis Lake Rd, Union Dale, PA 18470-0021. Tel 570-972-2662; Email susquehannastudio@gmail.com; Web: susquehannastudio.blogspot.com; *Dir* Robert Stark
Open by appointment Sat - Sun; No admis fee; Estab 1970 to provide opportunities for community participation in the creative voices & forms of expression within the region, to bring to the community the art forms of other cultures & people, to support local & regional artists in the documentation & exhib of their work; & to be a vigorous advocate for the development of the visual, verbal, performing, & craft arts within the community & region; Maintains reference library; Average Annual Attendance: 500
Activities: Sales shop sells original art, reproductions & prints

UNIVERSITY PARK

M **THE PENNSYLVANIA STATE UNIVERSITY,** Palmer Museum of Art, Curtin Rd, University Park, PA 16802-2507. Tel 814-865-7672; Fax 814-863-8608; Email jkm11@psu.edu; Web: www.palmermuseum.psu.edu; *Dir* Jan Keene Muhlert; *Registrar* Beverly Sutley; *Cur* Dr Patrick J McGrady; *Cur* Dr Joyce Henri Robinson; *Sr Preparator* Richard Hall; *Cur Educ* Dana Carlisle Kletchka; *Coordr Mem & Pub Rels* Jennifer Cozad Feehan; *Mus Store Mgr* Steve Artz; *Mus Security & Facility Mgr* Jeremy Warner; *Preparator* Craig Witter; *Asst Security & Facility Mgr* Dan Esposito; *Cur American Art* Adam Thomas
Open Tues - Sat 10 AM - 4:30 PM, Sun Noon - 4 PM, cl Mon & major holidays; No admis fee; Estab 1972 to promote a program of changing exhibs; a window to the world for the university & surrounding communities; The mus expanded in 1993 and again in 2002, has eleven galleries which accommodate continuous display of the permanent coll as well as changing exhibs that are national & international in scope; Average Annual Attendance: 42,000; Mem: 434; students $10 - $34, individual $35 - $59, family/household $60 - $99, sustaining $100 - $299, benefactor $300 - $599, sponsor $600 - $999, dir's cir $1000 & more
Income: Financed by state appropriation & donations
Purchases: American & European paintings, prints, drawings, & photographs
Library Holdings: Auction Catalogs, Book Volumes, Clipping Files, Exhibition Catalogs, Periodical Subscriptions, Slides
Special Subjects: African Art, Afro-American Art, Asian Art, Baroque Art, Bronzes, Ceramics, Coins & Medals, Collages, Decorative Arts, Drawings, Etchings & Engravings, Furniture, Glass, Graphics, Historical Material, Jade, Judaica, Landscapes, Manuscripts, Marine Painting, Medieval Art, Metalwork, Miniatures, Oriental Art, Painting-American, Painting-European, Painting-Flemish, Painting-French, Painting-German, Painting-Italian, Painting-Japanese, Painting-Scandinavian, Painting-Spanish, Photography, Porcelain, Portraits, Posters, Pre-Columbian Art, Prints, Renaissance Art, Sculpture, Watercolors, Woodcuts
Collections: American & European paintings, drawings, sculpture, prints & photographs, 19th & 20th Centuries, Asian paintings, sculpture, prints & decorative art (ceramics, jade & cloisonne), British, Japanese, Scandinavian & American Contemporary ceramics, Pennsylvania Prints from the late 18th to the early 20th Century, Tonkin Collection of Chinese export porcelain, Chinese jade carvings, paintings & watercolors related to the Oriental Trade, Baroque paintings; Japanese prints; ancient coins & ancient Peruvian ceramics, Adolf Austrian Academic Painting Collection, Markley Ancient Peruvian Ceramic Collection
Publications: Brochures; exhibition catalogs; newsletter, triannual
Activities: Educ prog; classes for adults with Osher Lifelong Learning Institute; summer workshops; docent training; print study club; lects open to pub; concerts; gallery talks; tours; symposia; book & originate traveling exhibits to other art mus; mus store sells books, original art & reproductions, paper products

L **Arts & Humanities Library,** 510 Paterno Library, University Park, PA 16802-1812. Tel 814-865-3616; Email henryp@psu.edu; Web: www.libraries.psu.edu; *Head Arts & Humanities Library* Amanda Maple; *Arts & Architecture Librn* Henry Pisciotta

Open Mon - Thurs 7:45 AM - 2 AM, Fri 7:45 AM - 7 PM, Sat 10 AM - 7PM, Sun 10AM - 2 AM; Estab 1957 to support the acad progs of the College of Arts & Architecture & the Division of Art & Music Educ; to provide information on the arts to members of the univ & community; reestablished in 1998 to support arts & humanities programs at Penn State and its community
Income: Financed through University Library, operating expenses & endowments
Library Holdings: Book Volumes 1,000,000, CD-ROMs 50, Compact Disks 22,000, DVDs 7,000, Exhibition Catalogs, Other Holdings Electronic texts; Image databases, Periodical Subscriptions 2300, Prints 250, Records 20,000, Video Tapes 2,600
Special Subjects: Art Education, Prints, Antiquities-Byzantine
Collections: Prints Collection (original prints), Faculty works on paper

M **HUB Robeson Galleries**, 241 HUB Robeson Ctr, University Park, PA 16802-6601. Tel 814-865-2563; Fax 814-865-6034; Email studentaffairs@pennstate/hub-robesongalleries; Web: www.sa.psu.edu/usa/galleries; *Dir* Ann Shields
Open Tues-Thurs noon-6PM, Fri & Sat noon-4PM; No admis fee; Estab 1976 to provide life-enriching visual arts experiences to the University & community; HUB Gallery; Robeson Gallery; Art Alley Exhibit Areas & Cases; Average Annual Attendance: 55,000
Income: financed by Pennsylvania State University
Collections: John Biggers and murals
Exhibitions: Central Penn Arts Exhibit; variety of contemporary exhibits
Publications: art brochure
Activities: Educ program; classes for college students; book traveling exhibs 7 per yr; sales shop

L **Architecture & Landscape Architecture Library**, 111 Stuckeman Family Bldg, University Park, PA 16802-1901. Tel 814-865-3614; Fax 814-865-5073; Email arch@psulias.psu.edu; Web: www.libraries.psu.edu; *Library Supv* Stephanie Movahedi-Lankarani; *Arts & Architecture Librn* Henry Pisciotta
Open Mon - Thurs 7:45 AM - 11 PM, Fri 7:45 AM - 7 PM, Sat Noon - 5 PM, Sun Noon - 11 PM; Estab 1978 to support the acad progs of the Dept of Architecture & Dept of Landscape Architecture to provide information on architecture & landscape architecture to members of the university & community
Income: Financed through university libraries, operating expenses & endowments
Library Holdings: Book Volumes 29,500, CD-ROMs, DVDs, Exhibition Catalogs, Other Holdings, Periodical Subscriptions 150, Video Tapes Digital Images
Special Subjects: Architecture, Landscape Architecture

VILLANOVA

M **VILLANOVA UNIVERSITY ART GALLERY,** The Art Gallery, Connelly Ctr, 800 Lancaster Ave Villanova, PA 19085. Tel 610-519-4612; Fax 610-519-6046; Email annetta.stowman@villanova.edu; Web: www.artgallery.villanova.edu; *Asst Dir* Annetta T Stowman; *Dir* Richard Cannuli O.S.A.
Open Mon - Fri 9 AM - 5 PM, call for weekend hours; No admis fee; Estab 1979 to enrich the learning experience of Villanova University Students & the surrounding community through its programs of study & presentations of works of art in the gallery & throughout the campus; Average Annual Attendance: 2,500
Income: Financed by gifts & university budget
Collections: Abstract Art 20th century, African & Oceanic Art, Philadelphia Artists 19th & 20th century, Southeast Asian Antiquities
Activities: Classes for children; lect open to pub; lending coll contains over 4000 items

WARREN

M **CRARY ART GALLERY,** 511 Market St, Warren, PA 16365-1765. Tel 814-723-4523; Email crarygallery@gmail.com; Web: www.crarygallery.org; *Pres* Barbara Kersey; *VPres* Bonnie Anderson; *Treas* Leyna Bimber; *Sec* Rebecca Yeager
Open Thurs - Sun during special exhibs; No fee; Estab 1977 for art appreciation & educ & to exhibit the work of Clare J Crary, Gene Alden Walker & guest artists; The gallery was constructed in 1962 as a private dwelling on the general plan of a Roman Villa. There are 6 gallery rooms, one housing a permanent exhibit of Crary photographs. The others accommodate other permanent-collection art & traveling shows.; Average Annual Attendance: 1500; Mem: 150 mems; $50 annual dues
Income: financed by endowment
Special Subjects: Painting-American, Photography, Prints, Watercolors, Woodcuts
Collections: Photographs by Clare J Crary, Oils by Gene Alden Walker, drawings, etchings, oils, acrylics by various artists, 19th Century Japanese wood-block prints, Edward Curtis
Activities: Class for adults; Lects open to pub; 12 vis lectrs per yr; gallery talks; tours; 1 traveling book exhib per yr; Mus shop sells original art & reproductions

WASHINGTON

M **WASHINGTON & JEFFERSON COLLEGE,** Olin Fine Arts Center Gallery, 60 S Lincoln St, Washington &Jefferson College Art Dept Washington, PA 15301-4812. Tel 724-503-1001 ext 6043; Fax 724-250-3319; Email dmcglumphy@washjeff.edu; Web: www.washjeff.edu/olin.uspx
Open daily noon-7PM; No admis fee; Estab 1980 to provide col & community with art shows; Flexible lighting, air conditioned gallery; Average Annual Attendance: 6,000
Income: Financed by college
Purchases: Over $3,000 annually during National Painting Show
Collections: Art dept coll, college historical coll, National Painting Show coll
Exhibitions: Monthly exhibits
Publications: Exhibition catalogs
Activities: Lects open to pub; 2-3 vis lectrs per yr; concerts; gallery talks; tours; competitions with awards; individual paintings & original objects of art lent to students, faculty & staff; lending coll contains 200 original art works, 100 original prints, 300 paintings, 200 photographs & 4 sculpture; book traveling exhibs 1 - 2 per yr

WAYNE

A **WAYNE ART CENTER,** 413 Maplewood Ave, Wayne, PA 19087-4792. Tel 610-688-3553; Fax 610-995-0478; Email info@wayneart.org; Web: www.wayneart.com; *Dir* Nancy Campbell
Open Mon - Fri 9 AM - 5 PM, Sat 10 AM - 4 PM; No admis fee; Estab 1930 as a community art center; Two galleries offer rotating exhibits of work by local artists; Average Annual Attendance: 2,000; Mem: 400; dues $20; annual meeting May
Income: $60,000 (financed by mem, grants, corporations & Pennsylvania Council on the Arts)
Exhibitions: 10-12 changing exhibs per yr
Publications: promotional catalogs
Activities: Classes for adults & children; workshops; gallery talks; competitions

WEST CHESTER

A **CHESTER COUNTY HISTORICAL SOCIETY,** 225 N High St, West Chester, PA 19380-2658. Tel 610-692-4800; Fax 610-692-4357; Email cchs@chestercohistorical.org; Web: www.chestercohistorical.org; *Pres* Elizabeth Laurent; *Dir Coll & Cur* Ellen Endslow; *Photo Archivist* Pamela C Powell; *Libr* Jasmine Smith
Open Tues - Sat 9:30 AM - 4:30 PM; Admis adults $6, seniors 65 & over $5, children 6-17 & students with ID $3.50, children under 6 & CCHS mems free; Estab 1893 for the acquisition & preservation of art and information historically significant to Chester County; A historical center encompassing a reference library, historical archives, photo archives, a collection of Chester County materials covering 300 years and the County archives; Average Annual Attendance: 33,000; Mem: dues $45-$500
Income: Financed by membership, sponsorship, grants and endowment
Library Holdings: Audio Tapes, Book Volumes, CD-ROMs, Clipping Files, Exhibition Catalogs, Fiche, Kodachrome Transparencies, Manuscripts, Maps, Original Art Works, Original Documents, Pamphlets, Periodical Subscriptions, Photographs, Prints, Records, Reproductions, Slides, Video Tapes
Special Subjects: Ceramics, Costumes, Decorative Arts, Dolls, Folk Art, Furniture, Glass, Painting-American, Period Rooms, Pewter, Photography, Porcelain, Portraits, Pottery, Silver, Textiles
Collections: Museum houses regional collections of furniture, from 1690 to early 20th century through Victorian, ceramics, needlework, glassware, pewter, textiles, clocks, iron, dolls & costumes
Publications: Chester County History, occasionally; Newsletter, 3 times per yr for mems
Activities: Docent training, educational progs for children, Nat History Day for middle & HS students; traveling trunks; monthly lect series & conferences, 20-80 lectrs per yr; tours, concerts, gallery talks & sponsoring competitions; fels; individual paintings and original objects of art lent to other museums; mus shop sells books, reproductions, prints, ceramics, toys, magazines, original art, crafts & other gifts with historical significance to Chester County and the surrounding region

WHITEHALL

NATIONAL SOCIETY OF PAINTERS IN CASEIN & ACRYLIC, INC
For further information, see National and Regional Organizations

WILKES-BARRE

M **WILKES UNIVERSITY,** Sordoni Art Gallery, 141 S. Main St, Wilkes-Barre, PA 18702. Tel 507-408-4325; Fax 507-408-7733; Email heather.sincavage@wilkes.edu; Web: www.wilkes.edu/sordoniartgallery; *Dir* Heather Sincavage
Open Tues - Wed & Fri 10 AM - 5 PM, Thurs 10 AM - 7 PM, Sat - Sun noon - 4:30 PM, cl major holidays; No admis fee; Estab 1973 to encourage the fine arts in the Wilkes-Barre & the northeastern Pennsylvania areas; The Gallery has one exhib space, 1,500 sq ft; Average Annual Attendance: 5,000; Mem: dues $10 & up
Income: Financed by mem, foundation endowment & Wilkes University
Library Holdings: Exhibition Catalogs, Original Documents, Periodical Subscriptions
Special Subjects: Painting-American, Painting-European, Sculpture
Collections: 20th century American paintings & prints, European prints
Exhibitions: Consists of loan exhibs from other col galleries, independent galleries, major museums & loan services; group & one-person exhibits feature estab modern masters & contemporary artists; curriculum-based exhibs
Publications: Calendar of Events, bimonthly; scholarly catalogs; illustrated brochures; posters
Activities: Lects open to pub; 2 vis lectrs per yr; gallery talks; tours; loans to other universities & museums; book traveling exhibs 1 per yr; originate traveling exhibs to schools & museums

WILLIAMSPORT

M **LYCOMING COLLEGE GALLERY,** 700 College Pl, Lycoming College Art Dept Williamsport, PA 17701-5157. Tel 570-321-4002; Fax 570-321-4090; *Dir* Rose Dirocco
Open Mon - Thurs 8 AM - 11 PM, Fri 8 AM - 4:30 PM, Sat 10 AM - 5 PM, Sun 1 - 11 PM; No admis fee; Estab 1980 to bring quality art work to the students & faculty as well as to the interested community; The new gallery, 30 x 60 ft, is located in the College Library; Average Annual Attendance: 5,000
Income: Financed by school budget & local & state grants
Special Subjects: Painting-American, Prints
Collections: Paintings & prints of 19th & 20th century artists
Exhibitions: One-man shows of regional artists & alumni of the Department
Activities: Gallery talks; tours; individual paintings lent; book traveling exhibs; originate traveling exhibs

YORK

HISTORICAL SOCIETY OF YORK COUNTY
For further information, see The York County Heritage Trust

L **MARTIN MEMORIAL LIBRARY,** 159 E Market St, York, PA 17401-1269. Tel 717-846-5300; Fax 717-848-1496 (ref dept); Web: www.yorklibraries.org; *Dir* William H Schell; *Dir Operations* Paula Gilbert
Open Mon - Thurs 9 AM - 8 PM, Fri & Sat 9 AM - 5:30 PM, Sun 1 PM - 5 PM; No admis fee; Estab 1935
Library Holdings: Book Volumes 100,000, Cassettes, Motion Pictures, Other Holdings Mounted pictures, Pamphlets, Periodical Subscriptions 200, Records
Publications: Ann Reports; Bulletin, monthly; Martin Memorial Library Historical Series; occasional bibliographies of spec colls
Activities: Programs for adults and children; lect; concerts

M **YORK COLLEGE GALLERIES,** MAC, Wolf Hall, 1 Country Club Rd York, PA 17405-3643. Tel 717-815-1354 & 1528
Open Mon - Tues & Thurs - Fri 10 AM - 5 PM, Wed 10 AM - 9 PM, Sat - Sun 12 PM - 5 PM; No admis fee
Collections: Works by local & national artists
Activities: Lectures & workshops

A **YORK COUNTY HERITAGE TRUST,** 250 E Market St, York, PA 17403-2013. Tel 717-848-1587; Fax 717-812-1204; Email info@yorkheritage.org; Web: www.yorkheritage.org; *Pres & CEO* Joan J Mummert; *Dir Libr & Archives* Lila Fourhman-Shaull; *Dir Educ* Daniel Roe; *Colls Mgr* Janie Carscallen
Open Tues - Sat 9 AM - 4 PM; Historic Houses call for times, cl Sun, Mon & all major holidays; Admis adults $15, children 6-18 $7; children 5 & under free; Estab 1895 to record, preserve, collect & interpret the history of York County, PA; Colonial Complex: General Gates House (1751); Golden Plough Tavern (1741) & Colonial Courthouse, 157 W Market; Bonham House (1875),152 E Market. Maintains reference library, 250 E. Market St, Historical Society Museum, 250 E Market St, Fire Museum 757 W Market St & Agricultural & Industrial Museum, 217 W Princess St; Average Annual Attendance: 30,000; Mem: 1400; dues $40 & up; annual meeting in Sept
Income: $1,200,000 (financed by endowment, gifts & mem)
Library Holdings: Auction Catalogs, Audio Tapes, Book Volumes 35,000, Cards, Cassettes, Clipping Files, Exhibition Catalogs, Filmstrips, Manuscripts, Maps, Memorabilia, Motion Pictures, Other Holdings, Pamphlets, Periodical Subscriptions 30, Photographs, Prints, Records, Reels, Slides, Video Tapes
Special Subjects: Architecture, Calligraphy, Cartoons, Ceramics, Coins & Medals, Costumes, Crafts, Decorative Arts, Dioramas, Dolls, Drawings, Embroidery, Etchings & Engravings, Flasks & Bottles, Folk Art, Furniture, Glass, Historical Material, Jewelry, Landscapes, Metalwork, Painting-American, Painting-German, Period Rooms, Pewter, Porcelain, Portraits, Pottery, Prints, Religious Art, Silver, Textiles, Watercolors, Woodcarvings, Woodcuts, Reproductions, Sculpture, Stained Glass
Collections: Fraktur & other Pennsylvania German decorative arts & furnishings, Works by Lewis Miller & other local artists, James Shettel Collection of theater & circus material, Horace Bonham artworks, Pfaltzgraff Collection of pottery
Exhibitions: Six galleries at the Historical Society Museums featuring various subjects of regional interest; historic houses; numerous galleries at the Agricultural and Industrial Museum, Fire Museum & Colonial Complex
Publications: The Kentucky Rifle; Lewis Miller Sketches & Chronicles; monthly newsletter; The Philadelphia Chair, 1685-1785; William Wagner-Views of York in 1830; J W Gitt & His Legendary Newspaper; York Co Journal; Lewis Miller's People
Activities: Educ prog; classes for adults & children; docent training; lects open to pub; lects for members only; concerts; gallery talks; tours; mus shop sells books, reproductions & prints

L **Library and Archives**, 250 E Market St, York, PA 17403. Tel 717-848-1587; Fax 717-812-1204; Email lfourhman-shaull@yorkhistorycenter.org; Web: www.yorkhistorycenter.org; *Librn* Lila Fourhman-Shaull; *Asst Librn* Amanda Eveler
Open to the public 9 AM - 5 PM, cl Sun & Mon; Admis $8; Estab 1895 to collect, preserve & interpret the history, people & culture of York county, Pennsylvania; For reference only; Average Annual Attendance: 2400; Mem: 1,500
Library Holdings: Auction Catalogs, Book Volumes 35,000, Clipping Files, Manuscripts, Maps, Memorabilia, Motion Pictures, Original Art Works, Original Documents, Photographs, Slides
Special Subjects: Advertising Design, Archaeology, Architecture, Art History, Commercial Art, Costume Design & Constr, Crafts, Decorative Arts, Dolls, Drafting, Drawings, Embroidery, Etchings & Engravings, Ethnology, Flasks & Bottles, Folk Art, Furniture, Glass, Gold, Goldsmithing, Historical Material, History of Art & Archaeology, Industrial Design, Jewelry, Landscapes, Manuscripts, Maps, Metalwork, Painting-American, Pewter, Photography, Porcelain, Portraits, Pottery, Printmaking, Prints, Reproductions, Restoration & Conservation, Sculpture, Silver, Silversmithing, Tapestries, Textiles, Theatre Arts, Woodcarvings, Woodcuts, Film, Handicrafts, Illustration, Interior Design
Collections: Fraktur & other Pennsylvania German decorative arts; material about Lewis Miller, Horace Bonham, William Wagner & other local artists, James Shettle coll of circus/entertainment photos, posters ephemera, advertising & industrial/ commercial design, John Durang Memoir; movie film coll; extensive photograph coll; poster coll; rare books, architectural drawings - commercial, residential, civil
Exhibitions: Lewis Miller drawings: ongoing, rotated ann; Horace Bonham Paintings (ongoing); Pennsylvania German decorative arts (ongoing)
Activities: Classes for adults & children; docent training; lects open to pub; lects for members only; concerts; tours; annual awards for contributions to local history; mus shop sells books, reproductions & prints

RHODE ISLAND

BRISTOL

L **ROGER WILLIAMS UNIVERSITY,** Architecture Library, One Old Ferry Rd, Bristol, RI 02809-2921. Tel 401-254-3833; Fax 401-254-3565; Email jschlinke@rwu.edu; *Circ Supv* Claudia DeAlmeida; *Architecture Art Librn* John Schlinke
Open during acad semester Mon-Thurs 8AM-12AM; Fri 8AM-6PM; Sat 1PM-5PM; Sun noon-12AM; No admis fee; Estab 1987
Library Holdings: Book Volumes 22,000, Maps 150, Pamphlets, Periodical Subscriptions 200, Slides 80,000
Special Subjects: Architecture, Drafting, Furniture, Historical Material, Industrial Design, Interior Design, Landscape Architecture, Maps, Restoration & Conservation, Art History
Collections: Architecture, historic preservation

KINGSTON

A **SOUTH COUNTY ART ASSOCIATION,** Helme House, 2587 Kingstown Rd, Kingston, RI 02881. Tel 401-783-2195; Web: www.southcountyart.org; *Pres* Alan Wynne; *1st VPres* Mary Papenfoth; *Recording Secy* Judith Kaplin; *Treas* Peter Anderson; *Cur & Caretaker* Jim Duffy; *Dir* Rhonda Shumaker; *2nd VPres* Stephen Palmer
Open Wed - Sun 1 - 5 PM during exhibs; No admis fee; Estab 1929 to promote an interest in art & to encourage artists & to support, in every way, the aesthetic interests of the community; 1802 building, modern gallery space, 900 sq ft; Average Annual Attendance: 800; applicants for membership must submit three paintings and be accepted by a comt; dues lay member & artist $50; annual meeting Oct; artist must be accepted in juried show
Collections: No large permanent coll, paintings by early mems, usually not on display
Exhibitions: 13 varied exhibs per year
Publications: Newsletter, 6 issues
Activities: Classes for adults & children; lect open to pub, 4 vis lectrs per yr; gallery talks; competitions with awards; schols; original objects of art lent to other art assns; lending coll contains books, lantern slides, sculpture, original art works & slides

M **UNIVERSITY OF RHODE ISLAND,** Fine Arts Center Galleries, 105 Upper College Rd Kingston, RI 02881-0820. Tel 401-874-2775/2627; Fax 401-874-2007; Email shar@uri.edu; Web: www.uri.edu/artgalleries; *Galleries Dir* Judith Tolnick; *Asst to Dir* Sharon Clark; *Interim Chair Art & Art History* Prof Robert Dilworth
Open Main Gallery Tues - Fri Noon - 4 PM & 7:30 - 9:30 PM, Sat 1 - 4 PM, Photography Gallery Tues - Fri Noon - 9 PM, Sat 1 - 4 PM, Corridor Gallery, Mon - Fri 9 AM - 5 PM; No admis fee; Estab 1970 to expose university & Southern New England communities to contemporary & historical art; Average Annual Attendance: 20,000
Income: Financed through university & outside grants
Special Subjects: Afro-American Art, American Indian Art, American Western Art, Architecture, Collages, Drawings, Painting-American, Photography, Prints, Sculpture
Exhibitions: 18-20 ongoing exhibs per yr
Publications: Exhibition catalogues
Activities: Educ dept; classes for adults; lect open to public, 5-10 vis lectrs per yr; concerts; gallery talks; sponsor competitions; originate traveling exhibs to university museums & galleries nationally

NEWPORT

M **AMERICAN CIVILIZATION FOUNDATION,** National Museum of American Illustration, Vernon Court, 492 Bellevue Ave Newport, RI 02840-4127. Tel 401-851-8949; Fax 401-851-8974; Email art@americanillustration.org; Web: www.americanillustration.org; *Dir* Judy AG Cutler; *Chmn* Laurence S Cutler; *Interiors Admin* Jill Perkins; *Caretaker Bldgs & Grounds* Craig Knowles; *Asst to Dir* Sara Bliss
Open off season by appointment, in season Thurs - Sun 11 AM - 5 PM, other times by reservation; Admis adults $18, seniors $16, discounts to military, groups & gratis to AAM, NEMA; 1998 to present the American Imagist Collection to the public in perpetuity; Golden Age American illustration art exhibited in Gilded Age architecture. Named by TripAdvisor and Flipkey as the 2016 Museum most worthwhile to travel to visit for this year - NMAI also named by the State of Rhode Island an Arboretum making Rhode Island the only state with four Arboretums. Visitors in 2016 from New Zealand, Australia, Italy, UK, Ireland, England, Brazil, Germany, Russia, France, Holland, Venezuela, Panamas, Scotland, Switzerland, India, Mexico, Iceland, Hawaii, Nigeria, Israel, Egypt, Iraq, Panama, Canada; Average Annual Attendance: 50,000
Income: Attendees + gifts
Purchases: Sculpture: The Vigil of Rizpah by Joseph Mozier, 1869, Rome
Library Holdings: Auction Catalogs, Book Volumes 2,000, CD-ROMs, Cards, Clipping Files, Compact Disks, DVDs, Exhibition Catalogs, Framed Reproductions, Memorabilia, Original Art Works, Original Documents, Photographs, Prints, Reproductions, Sculpture, Slides
Special Subjects: American Western Art, Architecture, Art Education, Art History, Bookplates & Bindings, Bronzes, Carpets & Rugs, Cartoons, Decorative Arts, Drawings, Etchings & Engravings, Furniture, Graphics, Historical Material, History of Art & Archaeology, Illustration, Landscape Architecture, Landscapes, Marine Painting, Painting-American, Painting-American, Painting-British, Period Rooms, Portraits, Posters, Prints, Reproductions, Sculpture, Photography, Restorations
Collections: works by illustrators including Norman Rockwell, Maxfield Parrish, Howard Pyle, NC Wyeth, JC Leyendecker & 150 other luminaries, John Rogers sculpture collection, 19th century American/European Sculpture, Illustration Art (American) collection of 150 different Artist-illustrators from The Golden Age of

American Illustration in Gilded Age Architecture, The American Imagist Collection of Illustration Art
Exhibitions: current - Norman Rockwell: American Imagist; Norman Rockwell & his mentor JC Leyendecker; Maxfield Parrish: The Retrospective; Howard Pyle & the Brandywine; author Tom Wolfe's 'In Our Time'; N.C. Wyeth & Howard Pyle; The American Muse; Norman Rockwell's America & others; Norman Rockwell & His Contemporaries; Paul Szep: Famous Faces; Mary Jane Begins Under the Sparkling Sea; Secrets Behind the Wall - Donald Tracte Jr. Lectures
Publications: newsletter; guidebook, The Grand Tour; MuseNews; YouTube; Twitter; Facebook; Norman Rockwell and his mentor JC Leyendecker exhib catalog; Norman Rockwell's America in England; Norman Rockwell's America in Birmingham; Norman Rockwell and His Contemporaries
Activities: Docent training; providing art books authored by our founders to schools & to heads of state of 150 nations via the United Nations; lecs open to pub; 3 vis lectrts per yr; intern prog; gallery talks; tours; American Civilization Foundation Awards for contributors to popular culture, NMAI Laureates include: Whoopi Goldberg, Tom Wolfe, Nat Arts Club, Matt Lauer, Evangeline Lilly, & Paul Szep; 7 concerts per year;; lend original objects of art to Birmingham Art Mus, Naples Art Mus, Dulwich Picture Gallery - London; Shanghai Art Mus; 2 traveling exhibs per yr; organize traveling exhibs 2-5 ann globally; Birmingham AL Art Mus, Nassau County Mus, Dulwich Picture Gallery, London; circulated globally - Italy, England, Asia, Japan, China, USA; mus shop sells books, magazines, original art, reproductions & prints, stained glass products, floor tiles with illustration images, CDs, Tru-chrome prints, videos, lamps, pens & other items

M **NAVAL WAR COLLEGE MUSEUM,** 686 Cushing Rd, Newport, RI 02841-1207. Tel 401-841-4052; Fax 401-841-7074; Email museum@usnwc.edu; Web: usnwc.edu/NWC-Museum; *Cur* Robert Cembrola; *Dir* John B. Hattendorf
Open Mon - Fri 10 AM - 4 PM, Sat Noon - 4:30 PM; No admis fee; Estab 1978, Themes: history of naval warfare, history of Navy in Narragansett Bay; 7000 sq ft on two floors of Founder Hall, a National Historic Landmark; Average Annual Attendance: 39,000
Income: Financed by Federal Navy & Naval War College Foundation, Inc
Special Subjects: Costumes, Historical Material, Manuscripts, Maps, Marine Painting, Military Art, Miniatures
Collections: Paintings, Sculpture (statuary, busts), Prints, Ship models
Publications: Exhibition catalogs - Faces of the Naval War College (2009)
Activities: Staff talks on themes & exhibits; lect open to pub, 2 vis lectrs per yr; gallery talks; tours; retail store sells books, reproductions, prints, clothing, & costume jewelry

M **NEWPORT ART MUSEUM AND ASSOCIATION,** 76 Bellevue Ave, Newport, RI 02840-7411. Tel 401-848-8200; Fax 401-848-8205; Email info@newportartmuseum.edu; Web: www.newportartmuseum.org; *Dir Educ* Judy Hambleton; *Grants* Judy Blake; *Cur* Nancy Grinnell; *Vol Coordr* Suzanne Hauerstein; *Dir Opers* John Schneider; *Exec Dir* Elizabeth Goddard; *Mem* Larry Bacon; *Office Mgr* Diane Montenegro; *Dir Finance & Admin* Jim Hockhousen
Open summer Tues - Sat 10 AM - 5 PM, Sun & most holidays Noon - 5 PM, winter Tues - Sat 11 AM - 4 PM, Sun & most holidays Noon - 4 PM, cl Christmas, New Year's Day, Thanksgiving, & July 4th; Admis adults $10, seniors & students $8, children 12 & under, mems free, students and military $6; Estab 1912, Collects, preserves, exhibits, and interprets contemporary and historic visual arts with an emphasis on the rich heritage of the Newport region, and integrates appreciation for the arts and art-making into all programs. The Griswold House is a National Historic Landmark; Buildings contain 16 galleries in 2 bldgs exhibiting contemporary visual arts, historic & regional exhibits; Average Annual Attendance: 25,000; Mem: 1850; dues $25 & up; annual meeting in Fall
Income: Financed by donations, endowment, mem, classes & admis
Special Subjects: Drawings, Etchings & Engravings, Painting-American, Period Rooms, Photography, Prints, Sculpture, Watercolors, Woodcuts
Collections: Drawings, Paintings, Photographs, Prints, Sculpture
Exhibitions: Changing & permanent exhibs, all media
Publications: Members' newsletters, quarterly; school class brochure
Activities: Day & evening classes for adults & children; docent training; outreach programs in house & off site; lect open to pub & some for mems only, 6-20 vis lectrs per yr; concerts; gallery talks; tours; awards; competitions; annual juried mems show awards in 6 categories; awards in 6 categories for annual school exhibs; schols offered; outreach dept serves area schools & underserved populations; individual paintings & original objects of art lent to other museums; originate traveling exhibs; sales shop sells books, original art, reproductions, and consignment antiques and collectibles, jewelry

A **NEWPORT HISTORICAL SOCIETY & MUSEUM OF NEWPORT HISTORY,** 82 Touro St, Newport, RI 02840-2978. Tel 401-846-0813; Fax 401-846-1853; Email info@newporthistorical.org; Web: www.newporthistorical.org; *Pres* John J Salesses; *1st VPres* Dennis McCoy; *2nd VPres* Richard Burnham; *Secy* Hope P Alexander; *Treas* Paul Steinbrenner; *Pres Emeritus* Bradford A Brecken; *Pres Emeritus* Kenneth H Lyons; *Financial Adminr* Janet W Boyes; *Dir Mktg* Leslie Lindeman; *Registrar* Kim A Krazer; *Reference Librn & Genealogist* Bert Lippincott III, C.G.; *Mem Secy* Judy Kelley; *Historic Sites & Colls Mgr* Adams Taylor; *Newsletter Ed* James Yarnall; *Admin Asst* Cheryl Carvalho
Open May 5 - June 12 Thurs - Sat, 10 AM - 4 PM, Sun 1 - 4 PM; June 15 - Sept 5 daily 10 AM - 4 PM; call for other hours; Suggested mus admis adults $4, children over age 5 $2; Estab 1853 to collect & preserve items of historical interest pertaining to the city; Maintains gallery & also owns & exhibits the first Seventh Day Baptist Church in America (1729); the Wanton-Lyman-Hazard House (1675), the first home to be restored in Newport; the Friends Meeting House (1699), site of the annual New England Quakers Meeting for over 200 years & mus of Newport History. Maintains reference library; Average Annual Attendance: 20,000; Mem: 1250; dues 1854 Society $1,000; Sponsor $500; Contributor $100; Indiv $50; Library/Mus $35; Student $25
Income: Financed by endowment, mem, state appropriation & other contributions
Special Subjects: Architecture, Costumes, Decorative Arts, Dolls, Drawings, Furniture, Glass, Graphics, Historical Material, Jewelry, Landscapes, Manuscripts, Maps, Marine Painting, Painting-American, Period Rooms, Photography, Sculpture, Silver, Textiles
Collections: Artifacts, china, Colonial silver, dolls, glass, furniture, Newport scenes & portraits, pewter & toys, photographs, ship models, paintings, printing press used by James Franklin, ball gown worn by a member of the Summer Colony, figurehead from the yacht Aloha, 18th century women's shoe exhibit
Exhibitions: Numerous changing exhibits
Publications: Newport History, quarterly; Newport Historical Society Newsletter, 6 times per yr
Activities: Educ dept; lect open to pub, 12 vis lectrs per yr; gallery talks; tours; audio-visual progs; competitions with awards; mus shop sells books & prints

L **Library,** 82 Touro St, Newport, RI 02840. Tel 401-846-0813; *Librn* Bertram Lippincott III
Open Tues - Fri 9:30 AM - 4:30 PM, Sat 9 AM - Noon, summers, Sat 9:30 AM - 4:30 PM; Estab 1853 to provide resource materials; For reference only
Library Holdings: Audio Tapes, Book Volumes 9000, Clipping Files, Exhibition Catalogs, Fiche, Kodachrome Transparencies, Manuscripts, Memorabilia, Original Art Works, Pamphlets, Periodical Subscriptions 10, Photographs, Prints, Reels, Sculpture, Slides, Video Tapes
Special Subjects: Architecture, Art History, Ceramics, Costume Design & Constr, Decorative Arts, Dolls, Furniture, Historical Material, Landscape Architecture, Maps, Painting-American, Period Rooms, Pewter, Restoration & Conservation, Silver, Silversmithing, Stained Glass, Textiles
Activities: Walking tour; school progs; Explore the Newport National Historic Landmark District through interactive computer progs; video tour of Bellevue Ave

L **REDWOOD LIBRARY & ATHENAEUM,** 50 Bellevue Ave, Newport, RI 02840-3292. Tel 401-847-0292; Fax 401-841-5680; Email redwood@redwoodlibrary.org; Web: www.redwoodlibrary.org; *Dir* Ken Brockway; *Spec Coll Librn* Whitney Pape; *Dir Develop* Beth Watson; *Coll Develop* Robert E Kelly; *Technical Servs* Lori Brosrven
Open Mon - Wed, Fri & Sat 9:30 AM - 5:30 PM, Thurs 9:30 AM - 8 PM, Sun (summer only) 1-5 PM; No admis fee; Estab 1747 as a general library; Average Annual Attendance: 20,000; 13,000 vis per yr; Mem: 1400; dues $100; annual meeting in Aug
Income: Financed by endowment, mem, ann giving, grants
Library Holdings: Auction Catalogs, Audio Tapes 300, Book Volumes 172,000, Clipping Files, Compact Disks 2,000, DVDs 300, Exhibition Catalogs, Manuscripts, Maps, Memorabilia, Original Art Works, Original Documents, Periodical Subscriptions 95, Photographs, Sculpture 40, Slides, Video Tapes
Special Subjects: Sculpture, Decorative Arts
Collections: 150 paintings, largely portraits, 40 sculptures, 50 pieces of furniture & other decorative arts items, those on display include portraits by Washington Allston, Robert Feke, G P A Healy, Charles Willson Peale, Rembrandt Peale, John Smibert, Gilbert Stuart, Thomas Sully, many paintings by Charles Bird King, historical & classical busts, & early Newport furniture
Exhibitions: rotating exhibs
Publications: To Preserve Hidden Treasures: From the Scrapbooks of Charles Bird King; Vitruvius Americanus
Activities: Classes for children; dramatic progs; lects open to pub; 10 vis lectrs per yr; concerts; gallery talks; group tours by prior arrangement; individual paintings & original objects of art lent to Preservation Society of Newport County & other mus; sales shop sells books, slides, cards & bookbags

M **ROYAL ARTS FOUNDATION,** Belcourt Castle, 657 Bellevue Ave, Newport, RI 02840-4280. Tel 401-846-0669, 849-1566; Fax 401-846-5345; Email belcourtcastle@aol.com; Email royalarts@aol.com; Web: www.belcourtcastle.com; *Exec Dir* Harle Tinney; *Pres* Mark P Malkovich III
Open Mar - Jun, & Nov - Dec, Thurs - Mon Noon to 4 PM (5 PM summers); Jul - Oct, Wed - Mon Noon - 4 PM; Dec holiday prog Sun 1 - 4 PM; Feb weekends & daily during Newport Winter Festival; cl Tues, Thanksgiving Day & Christmas; Admis adult $12, seniors 65+ & college student $8, student (ages 13-18) $7, child (ages 6-12) $5, children under 5 free; Estab 1957; 60-room private residence of the Tinney family open to visitors under the auspices of the Royal Arts Foundation; Average Annual Attendance: 30,000; Mem: annual meeting in Jan
Income: $300,000 (financed by admis fees)
Special Subjects: Antiquities-Byzantine, Antiquities-Egyptian, Antiquities-Oriental, Antiquities-Persian, Architecture, Asian Art, Ceramics, Costumes, Embroidery, Furniture, Gold, Historical Material, Jewelry, Oriental Art, Painting-American, Painting-British, Painting-European, Period Rooms, Porcelain, Renaissance Art, Sculpture, Silver, Stained Glass, Tapestries, Textiles
Activities: Lect open to pub, 4 vis lectrs per yr; guided & specialty tours (reservations by phone or web); mus shop sells books & magazines

M **UNITED STATES NAVY SUPPLY CORPS SCHOOL,** US Navy Supply Corps Museum, 1378 Porter Ave, Newport, RI 02841-1208. Email dan.roth@cnet.navy.mil; Web: www.nscs.snet.navy.mil; *Cur & Dir* Dan Roth
Open Mon - Fri 9 AM - 5:15 PM, cl federal holidays; No admis fee; Estab 1974. Exhibits depict the history & activities of US Navy Supply Corps & commemorate noteworthy individuals assoc with the Corps; Mus housed in National Register Carnegie Library building (c1910); Average Annual Attendance: 2,000
Income: Financed by federal appropriation
Special Subjects: Historical Material, Military Art
Collections: Nautical paintings, ship models, gallery gear, navigational equipment, uniforms, personal memorabilia, Archives: official records, manuals, photographs, yearbooks, scrap books, newsletter, directories
Publications: Base guide; museum brochure
Activities: Sales shop operates out of Navy Supply Corps Foundation Office

PAWTUCKET

A **RHODE ISLAND WATERCOLOR SOCIETY,** Armistice Blvd, Slater Memorial Park Pawtucket, RI 02861. Tel 401-726-1876; Email riwsgallery@gmail.com; Web: www.riws.org; *Pres* Jacqueline Canna; *Treas* Dennis Finlay; *Gallery Dir* Lori Estrella; *Gallery Asst* Nicole Monfils
Open Tues - Sat 10 AM - 4 PM, Sun 12 - 4 PM; cl Jan & every Mon; No admis fee; Estab 1896 to encourage & promote the advancement of watercolor painting; Large

carpeted upper & lower tiled gallery. Lower level gallery open for classes & exhibs; Mem: 350; dues $60 - $75; annual meeting Apr; assoc mem open to all
Income: Financed by dues, commissions, contributions & progs
Exhibitions: Annual Exhibition of Member's work; Annual Christmas Exhibition; Annual National Open Juried Watermedia Show; Annual New Members Show; 12 or more mem exhibs per yr
Publications: Member newsletter
Activities: Classes for adults; workshops; lect & demonstrations, open to members & guests; competitions with prizes; sales shop sells wrapped matted paintings from bins, reproductions, original art & prints, gift cards & postcards

M **SLATER MILL,** Old Slater Mill Association, 67 Roosevelt Ave, Pawtucket, RI 02860-2127; PO Box 696, Pawtucket, RI 02862-0696. Tel 401-725-8638; Fax 401-722-3040; Email info@slatermill.org; Web: www.slatermill.org; *Exec Dir* Lori Urso; *Dir Events & Progs* Eleanor Langham; *Educ Coordr* Marina Flannery
Open Mar & Apr: Sat - Sun 11 AM - 3 PM, May - Oct: Tues - Sun 10 AM - 4 PM; July 4 - Labor Day daily 10 AM - 4 PM; Nov - Feb group tours by appointment; Admis adults (13-64) $12, seniors & students with ID $10, children (6-12) $8.50, children under 6 free; Estab 1921; Three permanent galleries in historic buildings; Average Annual Attendance: 30,000; Mem: Annual meeting in June; approx 500 mems; dues Sponsor $250, Friend $100, Family $50, Individual $35
Income: $500,000 (financed by endowment, mem & city appropriation)
Library Holdings: Book Volumes, Clipping Files, Photographs
Special Subjects: Archaeology, Costumes, Decorative Arts, Furniture, Historical Material, Laces, Manuscripts, Painting-American, Textiles
Collections: Machine tools, manuscripts, photographs, textiles, textile machinery
Publications: Quarterly, print newsletter; monthly, e-newsletter
Activities: Classes for adults & children; traditional arts classes & workshops; docent progs; lects open to pub; 3-5 vis lectrs per yr; tours; concerts; gallery talks; traveling educ progs; originate traveling exhibs; museum shop sells books, magazines, original art, prints, slides, photographs & local artists works

PROVIDENCE

M **AS220,** Main Gallery, 115 Empire St, Providence, RI 02903; 95 Mathewson St, Unit 204 Providence, RI 02903. Tel 401-831-9327; Email info@as220.org; Web: as220.org; *Artistic Dir, Co-Dir* Shey Rivera; *Mng Dir, Co-Dir* Shauna Duffy; *Develop Dir* Ruth Harvey; *Communs Dir* David Dvorchak; *Gallery Dir* Neal Walsh
Open (office) Mon - Fri 10 AM - 6 PM; Estab 1985 to create performance & exhib opportunities for artists across genres
Collections: Media arts; performing arts
Exhibitions: Rotating exhibits
Activities: Educ progs; classes for adults; Artist talks; art programming; workshops; events

ASSOCIATION OF INDEPENDENT COLLEGES OF ART & DESIGN
For further information, see National and Regional Organizations

M **BERT GALLERY,** 540 S Water St, Providence, RI 02903-4322. Tel 401-751-2628; Email info@bertgallery.com; Web: www.bertgallery.com
Open by appointment only
Collections: paintings; drawings; woodcuts; sculpture

M **BROWN UNIVERSITY,** David Winton Bell Gallery, 64 College St, Providence, RI 02912. Tel 401-863-2932; Fax 401-863-9323; Web: www.brown.edu/bellgallery; *Dir* Jo-Ann Conklin; *Adminr* Terrence Abbott; *Preparator* Ian Budish; *Cur* Ian Alden Russell
Open Mon - Wed & Fri 11 AM - 4 PM, Thurs 1 PM - 9 PM, Sat & Sun 1 PM - 4 PM; No admis fee; Estab 1971 to present exhibs of interest to the univ & community; The gallery is modern, covers 2625 sq ft, 14 ft ceilings & has track lighting; Average Annual Attendance: 8,000
Income: Financed by endowment & univ funds
Special Subjects: Painting-American, Photography, Prints, Woodcuts
Collections: Print & photography collection of historical & modern masters, selected color field paintings & modern sculpture
Exhibitions: Mall media juried student & faculty exhibs; International contemporary art
Publications: Exhibition catalogs
Activities: Lects open to pub; art work lent to exhibs mounted by museums & galleries; permanent coll contains 5000 original prints & photographs, over 100 modern paintings & sculptures; originates traveling exhibs

M **Annmary Brown Memorial**, 21 Brown St, Box A Providence, RI 02912-9005. Tel 401-863-2942; Email barbara_schulz@brown.edu; *Univ Cur* Robert Emlen; *Bldg Contact* Barbara Schulz
Open Mon - Fri 1 PM - 5 PM; No admis fee; Estab 1905 to offer representatives of schools of European & American painting; There are three galleries which house the art collection of the founder & his wife, & portraits of the Brown family & Mazansky collection of British swords; Average Annual Attendance: 3,000

M **Haffenreffer Museum of Anthropology**, 21 Prospect St, Box 1965 Providence, RI 02912; 300 Taver St., Bristol, RI 02809. Tel 401-863-2065; Fax 401-253-1198; Email haffenreffermuseum@brown.edu; Web: www.brown.edu/Facilities/Haffenreffer/index.html; *Deputy Dir & Cur* Kevin P Smith; *Cur* Thierry Gentis; *Dir* Robert Preucel; *Dir Educ & Public Progs* Geralyn Ducady; *Exhib Designer & Photo Archivist* Rip Gerry; *Mus Opers & Communs Coord* Emily Jackson
Open Tues - Sun 10 AM - 4 PM, cl federal holidays & univ breaks; No admis fee; Estab 1956 to educate Brown Univ Students & the general pub through anthropological research on humankind, about cultural differences & human similarities & to serve its constituencies with excellence; Average Annual Attendance: 17,000; Mem: Dues: Student $15, Individual $25, Dual & Couple $30, Family $35, Contributing $50-$99, Saville Society $100-$249, Giddings Society $250-$499, Mount Hope Society $500-$999, Haffenreffer Society $1,000 & up
Special Subjects: African Art, American Indian Art, Anthropology, Antiquities-Egyptian, Antiquities-Etruscan, Antiquities-Greek, Archaeology, Asian Art, Ceramics, Costumes, Eskimo Art, Ethnology, Ivory, Mexican Art, Pottery, Primitive art, Sculpture, Southwestern Art, Textiles
Exhibitions: Various exhibs, call for details
Activities: Classes for adults & children; docent training; lect open to pub, 8-10 vis lectrs per yr; gallery talks; tours; fels; artmobile; book traveling exhibs 1 per yr; originate traveling exhibs; mus shop sells books, magazines, original art, reproductions, prints, slides & objects related to the colls

M **CITY OF PROVIDENCE PARKS DEPARTMENT,** Roger Williams Park Museum of Natural History, 1000 Elmwood Ave, Providence, RI 02907-3655. Tel 401-680-7201; Email mmassaro@musnathist.com; Web: www.providenceri.gov/parks-recreation; *Cur* Marilyn R Massaro; *Dir* Tracey Keough; *Asst Cur* Shara Chase
Open daily 10 AM - 5 PM; Admis adult $2, children $1; Estab 1896; 5 exhibit galleries (one rotates); Average Annual Attendance: 15,000
Income: Financed by state appropriations, admis & donations
Library Holdings: Auction Catalogs, Book Volumes, Exhibition Catalogs, Kodachrome Transparencies, Lantern Slides, Original Documents, Photographs, Slides
Special Subjects: Anthropology, Archaeology, Ethnology, Folk Art
Collections: Natural history, Native American, Oceanic, African ethnography
Exhibitions: All Things Connected (Native American Collection); Natural Selections (Victorian Natural History); Circle of the Sea (Oceana); rotating exhibit
Publications: Exhibit catalogs (Native American, Oceana)
Activities: Children's classes; lect open to pub; mus shop sells books, children's items, exhibit-related

L **Library**
Estab 1896
Library Holdings: Book Volumes 10,000, Clipping Files, Exhibition Catalogs, Kodachrome Transparencies, Lantern Slides, Photographs, Slides

A **PROVIDENCE ART CLUB,** 11 Thomas St, Providence, RI 02903-1314. Tel 401-331-1114; Fax 401-521-0195; Email info@providenceartclub.org; Web: www.providenceartclub.org; *Pres* Kelly Milukas; *Gallery Mgr* Michael Rose; *Gen Mgr* Seb Borges; *Events Planning & Mem Servs* Angel Dean
Open Mon - Fri 12 PM - 4 PM, Sat & Sun 2 - 4 PM; No admis fee; Estab 1880 for art culture & to provide exhibition space for artists; Galleries maintained in two 18th century buildings on historic Thomas Street in Providence; Average Annual Attendance: 12,000; Mem: 650; to qualify, artists' work must pass a board of artists; personal qualifications for non-artists; dues non-artist $948, artist $720; initiation fee: artist $1,600, non-artist $2,000; ann meeting first Wed in June
Income: Financed by endowment & mem
Collections: Small permanent collection of paintings & sculpture by Club members since 1880
Exhibitions: Forty shows a season of which one is a juried open shows
Publications: Newsletter for members, monthly
Activities: Studio art classes & workshops provided regularly for members; Lect for mems & guests; gallery talks; competitions with awards; tours; schols offered

M **PROVIDENCE ATHENAEUM,** 251 Benefit St, Providence, RI 02903-2799. Tel 401-421-6970; Fax 401-421-2860; Email info@providenceathenaeum.org; Web: www.providenceathenaeum.org; *Exec Dir* Matt Burriesci; *Dir Admin & Fin* Ken Garrepy
Open Mon - Thurs 9 AM - 7 PM, Fri - Sat 9 AM - 5 PM, Sun 1 - 5 PM; No admis fee; Estab 1753 to provide cultural services, information, rare & current materials in an historic setting; Maintains a rare book library; Mem: Estab 1367; dues $25 - $150 annual meeting in the Fall
Income: $303,544 (financed by endowment & mem)
Purchases: $40,000
Collections: Strength in the 19th century
Exhibitions: Exhibs vary each month; local artists' works shown
Publications: The Athenaeum Bulletin, summer; Annual Report, Fall
Activities: Dramatic progs; film progs; lects open to pub; tours; festivals; concerts; day trips; original objects of art lent to bona fide institutions, libraries or societies; lending coll contains books, periodicals, records, videotapes, cassettes; sales shop sells Audubon prints in limited editions, stationery, t-shirts & Athenaeum cookbooks

L **Library**, 251 Benefit St, Providence, RI 02903. Tel 401-421-6970; Fax 401-421-2860; Email info@providenceathenaeum.org; Web: www.providenceathenaeum.org; *Dir Colls & Library Servs* Kate Wodehouse; *Reference & Special Colls* Stephanie Knott
Open Mon - Thurs 9 AM - 7 PM, Fri & Sat 9 AM - 5 PM, Sun 1 - 5 PM, cl Sun in summer, July & Aug; No admis fee; Estab 1753 to provide cultural services, information rare & current materials in a historic setting; Circ 106,000; Mem: Dues $35 - $185; annual meeting in spring
Income: endowment, mem fees, ann appeal
Library Holdings: Audio Tapes, Book Volumes 161,486, Cassettes, Exhibition Catalogs, Manuscripts, Memorabilia, Original Art Works, Other Holdings Posters, Pamphlets, Periodical Subscriptions 133, Prints, Records, Sculpture, Video Tapes
Special Subjects: Art History
Collections: 19th century Robert Burns coll, 19th century library - rare book library, Audubon, Old Fiction, Holder Borde Bowen coll
Activities: Children's progs; film progs; festivals; readings & lects; tours; trips

L **PROVIDENCE PUBLIC LIBRARY,** Art & Music Services, 150 Empire St, Providence, RI 02903-3219. Tel 401-455-8000; Fax 401-455-8013; Email pplref@provlib.org; Web: www.provlib.org; *Exec Dir* Jack Martin; *Assoc Dir* Aaron Peterman
Open Mon & Wed 12:30 PM - 8:30 PM, Tues 9:30 AM - 5:30 PM, Thurs - Fri 12:30 PM - 5:30 PM, Sat 9:30 AM - 2:30 PM, Sun 1 PM - 5 PM; Estab 1875 to serve needs of the public
Income: financed by endowment, city and state appropriations and federal funds
Library Holdings: Book Volumes 43,000, Clipping Files, Compact Disks, DVDs, Framed Reproductions, Original Art Works, Other Holdings Posters, Periodical Subscriptions 85, Photographs, Prints, Records, Video Tapes
Special Subjects: Advertising Design, Architecture, Cartoons, Ceramics, Commercial Art, Costume Design & Constr, Crafts, Decorative Arts, Drawings, Furniture, Graphic Design, Handicrafts, Illustration, Interior Design, Landscape

Architecture, Painting-American, Painting-British, Photography, Pottery, Sculpture, Silversmithing
Collections: Nickerson Architectural Collection, art & music books

M **RHODE ISLAND COLLEGE,** Edward M Bannister Gallery, 600 Mount Pleasant Ave, Providence, RI 02908-1940. Tel 401-456-9765; Fax 401-456-8269; Email bannistergallery@ric.edu; Web: www.ric.edu/bannister; *Gallery Dir* James Montford
Open Tues - Fri Noon - 8 PM, cl Sat - Mon & holidays; No admis fee; Estab 1978 to provide the Rhode Island community with a varied & progressive exposure to the visual arts, to offer to the col community, with its liberal arts perspective, access to top quality exhibits, artists & workshops; View map on web site; Average Annual Attendance: 5,000
Income: Financed by state appropriation, student organizations & RIC Foundation
Collections: Teaching collection of works purchased from exhibiting artists
Publications: Brochures; semiannual calendars; monthly exhibit announcements
Activities: Lects open to pub; average of 12 vis lectrs per yr; gallery talks

A **RHODE ISLAND HISTORICAL SOCIETY,** 110 Benevolent St, Providence, RI 02906-3103. Tel 401-331-8575; Fax 401-351-0127; Web: www.rihs.org; *Exec Dir* C Morgan Grefe; *Deputy Dir Fin & Admin* Charmyne Goodfellow
Open Aldrich House Offices: Mon - Fri 9 AM - 5 PM; John Brown House Museum: Tues - Sat 10 AM - 4 PM, winter hours Fri & Sat 10 AM - 4 PM; Library: Wed - Fri 10 AM - 5 PM, 2nd Sat of mo 12 - 5 PM; Museum of Work & Culture: Tues - Sat 10 AM - 5 PM, Sun 1 - 4 PM; Admis $7; Estab 1822 to preserve, collect & interpret Rhode Island historical materials, including books, manuscripts, graphics, films, furniture & decorative arts; Art exhibits at John Brown House Mus, Mus of Work & Culture; Average Annual Attendance: 30,000; Mem: 1,500; dues $40; annual meeting in Nov
Income: Financed by endowment, mem, city & state appropriation, earned income
Library Holdings: Auction Catalogs, Audio Tapes, Book Volumes, CD-ROMs, Cards, Cassettes, Clipping Files, Compact Disks, DVDs, Exhibition Catalogs, Fiche, Filmstrips, Kodachrome Transparencies, Lantern Slides, Manuscripts, Maps, Memorabilia, Micro Print, Motion Pictures, Original Art Works, Original Documents, Other Holdings, Pamphlets, Periodical Subscriptions, Photographs, Prints, Records, Reels, Reproductions, Sculpture, Slides, Video Tapes
Special Subjects: African Art, American Indian Art, Archaeology, Architecture, Carpets & Rugs, Ceramics, Coins & Medals, Costumes, Crafts, Decorative Arts, Dioramas, Dolls, Drawings, Embroidery, Etchings & Engravings, Ethnology, Flasks & Bottles, Folk Art, Furniture, Glass, Graphics, Hispanic Art, Historical Material, Islamic Art, Jewelry, Laces, Landscapes, Manuscripts, Maps, Marine Painting, Painting-American, Painting-British, Painting-European, Period Rooms, Pewter, Photography, Porcelain, Portraits, Pottery, Prints, Religious Art, Sculpture, Silver, Textiles, Watercolors
Exhibitions: Changing exhibitions on Rhode Island history & decorative & graphic arts
Publications: American Paintings in the Rhode Island Historical Society, (catalogue); The John Brown House Loan Exhibition of Rhode Island Furniture; Nathanael Greene Papers; Rhode Island History, bi-annual; Roger Williams Correspondence; occasional monographs; newsletter
Activities: Classes for adults & children; teacher education; exhibits; children's tours; film progs; lects open to pub, 8-10 vis lectrs per yr; concerts; gallery talks; tours; lending coll contains 10,000 prints for reference and copying; originates traveling exhibs; museum shop sells books, magazines & original art

M **John Brown House**, 110 Benevolent St, Providence, RI 02906. Tel 401-273-7507; Fax 401-351-0127; Web: www.rihs.org; *Exec Dir* C Morgan Grefe; *Dir Goff Center* Geralyn Ducady; *Educ & Outreach Mgr* Rachel Brask Hutchinson
Open (April - Nov) Tues - Fri 1 PM - 4 PM, Sat 10 AM - 4 PM, (Dec - March) Sat 10 AM - 4 PM; Admis adults $10, seniors & mems $8, children 7-17 $6, mem free; Estab 1942, the 1786 house carefully restored & furnished with fine examples of RI & period materials; Average Annual Attendance: 9,000; Mem: 1,700; basic mem $40
Income: RIHS Institutional budget, $2.2 million (2006)
Purchases: RIHS does purchase material related to history of John Brown House & important RI archives & objects
Library Holdings: Auction Catalogs, Audio Tapes, Book Volumes, CD-ROMs, Cards, Cassettes, Clipping Files, Compact Disks, DVDs, Exhibition Catalogs, Filmstrips, Lantern Slides, Manuscripts, Maps, Memorabilia, Motion Pictures, Original Art Works, Original Documents, Other Holdings, Pamphlets, Periodical Subscriptions, Photographs, Prints, Records, Reels, Sculpture, Slides, Video Tapes
Special Subjects: Carpets & Rugs, Ceramics, Coins & Medals, Costumes, Crafts, Decorative Arts, Dolls, Embroidery, Etchings & Engravings, Furniture, Glass, Historical Material, Jewelry, Landscapes, Maps, Marine Painting, Miniatures, Painting-American, Period Rooms, Pewter, Porcelain, Portraits, Silver, Textiles, Watercolors
Collections: Carrington Collection of Chinese export objects, McCrillis Collection of Antique Dolls, furniture by Rhode Island cabinetmakers, some original to the house, major archival colls on Rhode Island subjects
Exhibitions: A Passion for the Past (by C Morgan Grefe, B Fishman & J K Hammerstrom)
Publications: Rhode Island History, Papers of Nathanael Greene
Activities: Educ prog; classes for adults; concerts; gallery talks; tours; schols; history makers awards; lending of original objects of art to qualified non-profit educational institutions; mus shop sells books, magazines, prints

M **Aldrich House**, 110 Benevolent St, Providence, RI 02906. Tel 401-331-8575
Open Tues - Fri 7:30 AM - 4 PM, cl Sun & Mon; Estab 1974; Galleries for changing exhibs of RI artists & history
Income: Financed by endowment, state & local funds, grants (state & federal) & admis rates

L **Library**, 121 Hope St, Providence, RI 02906-2098. Tel 401-273-8107; Fax 401-751-7930; Email reference@rihs.org; Web: www.rihs.org; *Librn* Phoebe Bean; *Registrar* Dana Signe K Munroe; *Research Assoc* Jennifer Galpern; *Library Asst* Owen Gibbs
Open Wed - Fri & second Sat of month 10 AM - 5 PM; Admis to out of state non-mems $5 per day; Estab 1822 to collect, preserve & make available materials relating to state's history & development; Galleries at John Brown & Aldrich Houses; Average Annual Attendance: 4,000; Mem: 1,400; dues individual $40; ann meetings in Sept
Income: $700,000 (financed by endowment, mem & state appropriation)
Library Holdings: Book Volumes 88,000, Manuscripts 6,696, Maps 200, Memorabilia 866, Motion Pictures 9,000,000 ft, Periodical Subscriptions 2600, Photographs 100,000
Special Subjects: Architecture, Historical Material, Manuscripts, Maps
Collections: 5000 manuscripts colls dating from 17th century, Rhode Island Imprints, 1727-1800, Rhode Island Broadsides, Providence Postmaster Provisional Stamps, Rhode Island Post Office Covers, genealogical sources, all state newspapers, maps, films, TV news films and movies, graphics, architectural drawings, 150,000 reference volumes, 200,000 photographs, bus archives, oral history tapes
Publications: Rhode Island History, twice yearly
Activities: Workshops for adults; lects open to pub; vis lectrs 6 per yr; tours; mus shop sells books, magazines, prints, genealogical charts

M **RHODE ISLAND SCHOOL OF DESIGN,** Museum of Art, 224 Benefit St, Providence, RI 02903-2723. Tel 401-454-6500; Fax 401-454-6556; Email museum@risd.edu; Web: www.risdmuseum.org; *Dir* John W Smith; *Cur Ancient Art* Gina Borromeo; *Cur Contemporary Art* Dominic Molon; *Cur Costumes & Textiles* Kate Irvin; *Assoc Cur Costumes & Textiles* Laurie Brewer; *Deputy Dir Exhibs, Educ & Progs* Sarah Ganz; *Cur Painting & Sculpture* Maureen O'Brien; *Cur Prints, Drawings & Photos* Jan Howard; *Mktg & PR Assoc* Matthew Berry; *Pres* Roseanne Somerson
Open Tues - Sun 10 AM - 5 PM, 3rd Thurs of month until 9 PM, cl Mon, Aug, & holidays; Admis adults $15, seniors 62+ $12, college students w/ID $8, youth 5-, mems, RISD & Brown students, faculty, staff, children under 5 and active-duty U.S. military personnel and their families free; pay what you wish every Sun 10 AM - 5 PM,; Estab 1877 to collect & exhibit art for general educ of RISD students & the pub; Present buildings opened in 1897, 1906, 1926 & 1990, 2008; Average Annual Attendance: 100,000; Mem: 3500
Income: Financed by endowment, mem, state & federal appropriation, pvt & corporate contributions
Special Subjects: Antiquities-Greek, Antiquities-Roman, Asian Art, Bronzes, Carpets & Rugs, Ceramics, Coins & Medals, Costumes, Decorative Arts, Drawings, Embroidery, Furniture, Furniture, Glass, Graphics, Ivory, Jade, Jewelry, Metalwork, Mixed Media, Mosaics, Oriental Art, Painting-American, Painting-European, Painting-French, Photography, Porcelain, Pre-Columbian Art, Prints, Renaissance Art, Sculpture, Silver, Tapestries, Textiles, Watercolors, Woodcarvings, Painting-British
Collections: Lucy Truman Aldrich Collection of European porcelains & Oriental textiles, Ancient Oriental & ethnographic art, American painting, contemporary graphic arts, Nancy Sayles Day Collection of modern Latin American art, English watercolors, 15th - 18th century European art, 19th & 20th century French art from Romanticism through Surrealism, Albert Pilavin Collection of 20th century American Art, Pendleton House collection of 18th century American furniture & decorative arts, Abby Aldrich Rockefeller coll of Japanese prints
Publications: Gallery guides for select exhibits; catalogs
Activities: Classes for adults & children; docent training; lect open to pub; lects for mems only; gallery talks; concerts; tours; fels; competitions with awards; outreach programs serve schools, nursing homes & hospital children's ward in the area; books traveling exhibs 1 per yr; originates traveling exhibs nationally & internationally; mus shop sells books, original art, reproductions, prints, jewelry, posters & postcards

L **Fleet Library at RISD**, 15 Westminster St, Providence, RI 02903-2784; 2 College St, Providence, RI 02903-2784. Tel 401-709-5900; Fax 401-709-5903; Email risdlib@risd.edu; Web: library.risd.edu; *Spec Coll Librn* Claudia Covert; *Archivist* Andrew Martinez; *Visual & Material Resource Librn* Mark Pompelia; *Technical Servs Librn* Robert Garzillo; *Research & Instruction Librn* Ellen Petraits; *Access Servs Mgr* Gail Geisser; *Catalog/Reference Librn* Marc Calhoun
Open Mon - Thurs 8:30 AM - 11 PM, Fri 8:30 AM - 8 PM, Sat 10 AM - 6 PM, Sun noon - 11 PM; summer and holiday hours vary; Circ 46,000; Open to the pub for reference & research (appointment recommended); Average Annual Attendance: 53,000; Mem: Dues $100
Library Holdings: Auction Catalogs 19,000, Book Volumes 167,500, CD-ROMs, Clipping Files 490,000, Compact Disks, DVDs, Exhibition Catalogs, Fiche, Lantern Slides 22,000, Motion Pictures, Other Holdings Artists' books; Postcards; Posters, Periodical Subscriptions 330, Photographs, Reproductions 19,000, Video Tapes 5,000
Special Subjects: Architecture
Collections: Artists' books, Lowthorpe coll on landscape, Architecture, Gorham Design Library, miniature books, Walter Lorraine Coll of Children's Books

M **RHODE ISLAND SCHOOL OF DESIGN,** Bayard Ewing Building Gallery, 231 S Main St, Providence, RI 02903; 2 College St, Providence, RI 02903-2717. Tel 401-454-6281; Fax 401-465-6299; Web: www.risd.edu; *Gallery Dir* James Barnes
Call for hours; No admis fee; Estab 1979 to show rotating exhibs & student work; Single space; Average Annual Attendance: 2,000
Income: Financed via school budget
Collections: paintings; photographs; sculpture
Activities: Lects open to pub; gallery talks; originates traveling exhibs

SAUNDERSTOWN

M **GILBERT STUART MEMORIAL ASSOCIATION, INC,** Gilbert Stuart Birthplace & Museum, 815 Gilbert Stuart Rd, Saunderstown, RI 02874-2911. Tel 401-294-3001; Fax 401-294-3869; Email info@gilbertstuartmuseum.org; Web: www.gilbertstuartmuseum.org; *Exec Dir* Margaret O'Connor; *Pres* Margaret Todd
May - June 14 & Sept Thurs - Mon, cl Tues & Wed; June 15 - Aug 31 open daily; Oct limited hours, check website; Admis adults $10, children 6 - 12 $6, children under 6 no admis fee; Designated 1966 as a national historic landmark, the furnished birthplace of America's foremost portrait painter; the home was built 1751; Restored home with grist mill & snuff mill; Average Annual Attendance: 4,500; Mem: 425; dues $60 family, $40 individuals; ann meeting in May
Income: Financed by endowment, admis fees, grants, mem

Library Holdings: Clipping Files, Compact Disks, Memorabilia, Photographs, Prints
Special Subjects: Portraits
Collections: Collections of artifacts, period tools & prints, Artifacts, Period Tools, Prints
Exhibitions: Artist in residence
Activities: Classes for adults; docent training, children trained as jr docents who give weekend tours and hold spec events; dress in colonial costume ages 8-20; guided tours of the home; sales of books, reproductions, prints, cards

WAKEFIELD

M **HERA EDUCATIONAL FOUNDATION,** Hera Gallery, 10 High St, Wakefield, RI 02879-7403; PO Box 336, Wakefield, RI 02880-0336. Tel 401-789-1488; Email info@heragallery.org; Web: www.heragallery.org; *Pres* Mara Trachtenberg; *Gallery Dir* Abigael McGuire; *Gallery Director* Adrien Merger; *President* Barbara Pugh
Open Wed - Fri 1 - 5 PM, Sat 10 AM - 4 PM, or by appointment; No admis fee; Estab 1974 as a women's cooperative gallery exhibiting the work of mems & non-mems; 30 ft x 40 ft in dimension with 9 ft ceiling; Average Annual Attendance: 1,500; Mem: Dues $185 - $480; monthly meetings second Wed; reduced fees for bd mems; membership based on artistic merit
Income: Financed by mem, contributions, grants & schols
Library Holdings: Slides of mems
Special Subjects: Collages, Drawings, Jewelry, Painting-American, Photography, Prints, Sculpture, Textiles
Exhibitions: 10 - 11 exhibs per yr; Curated, juried & member exhibitions
Activities: Classes for children; readings; critiques, film festivals; lect open to pub on contemporary culture, 2-3 vis lectrs per yr; gallery talks by artists; juried competition with cash award; symposia; critique group, concerts; exten prog serves Rhode Island; artmobile; sales shop sells reproductions, prints

WARWICK

M **COMMUNITY COLLEGE OF RHODE ISLAND,** Knight Campus Art Gallery, 400 East Ave, Knight Campus Warwick, RI 02886-1805. Tel 401-825-2220; Fax 401-825-1148; Email knightgallery@ccri.edu; Web: www.ccri.edu/art/galleries.shtml; *Dir* Viera Levitt
Open Mon & Sat 11 AM - 4 PM, Tues, Wed, Fri 10 AM - 4 PM, Thurs 10 AM - 7 PM; No admis fee; Estab 1972; Maintains reference library; Average Annual Attendance: 1,000
Exhibitions: Exhibs are changed monthly
Activities: Lects open to public, 10 vis lectrs per yr; concerts; gallery talks; tours; competitions with awards; exten dept; individual paintings & original objects of art lent; lending collection contains 300 color reproductions, 20 filmstrips, 10,000 Kodachromes, motion pictures & clippings & small prints; originate traveling exhibs

M **Flanagan Valley Campus Art Gallery,** 1762 Louisquisset Pike, Lincoln, RI 02865-4585. Tel 401-333-7000; Fax 401-825-2265; Email flanagangallery@ccri.edu; Web: www.ccri.edu/art/galleries2.html; *Dir & Librn* Tom Morrissey
Open Mon - Fri 10 AM - 2 PM; No admis fee; Estab 1974; 26 sq ft space with track lighting; Average Annual Attendance: Over 5,000
Exhibitions: Exhibitions are changed bi-monthly
Activities: Lects open to pub, 10 vis lectrs per yr; concerts; gallery talks; tours; competitions with awards; exten dept; individual paintings & original objects of art lent; originate traveling exhibs

M **WARWICK MUSEUM OF ART,** 3259 Post Rd, Warwick, RI 02886-7145. Tel 401-737-0010; Email taylor@warwickmuseum.org; Web: www.warwickmuseum.org; *Pres* Deborah O Mercer; *VPres* Pam Unwin-Barkley; *2nd VPres* Diane Newman-Goins; *Treas* Teresa Hamel; *Secy* Michelle Place-Gleason; *Office Mgr* Taylor Terreri
Open Wed, Fri & Sat 12:30 PM - 4:30 PM, Tues & Thurs 12:30 PM - 7:30 PM; Estab 1976 to promote a dynamic resource for all aspects of the cultural arts; Small gallery, formerly the Kentish Artillery built in 1912; Average Annual Attendance: 3,000
Income: $40,000 (financed by mem & city & state appropriation)
Exhibitions: Rhode Island Open Juried Exhibit (all media); RI State Council on the Arts Exhibits; Spring Juried Exhibit (themes change); Group shows
Activities: Art classes for adults & children; art exhibits that change every 6-8 wks; children's summer art camp; gallery talks; special events; comedy performances wkly; excellence awards for RI Open Juried exhib

WESTERLY

M **WESTERLY PUBLIC LIBRARY,** Hoxie Gallery, 44 Broad St, Westerly, RI 02891-6009. Tel 401-596-2877; Fax 401-596-5600; Email ktaylor@westerlylibrary.org; Web: www.westerlylibrary.org; *Dir* Kathryn T Taylor; *Community Svcs* Jane Johnson
Open Mon - Wed 9 AM - 9 PM, Thurs & Fri 9 AM - 6 PM, Sat 9 AM - 4 PM, Sun Oct - May Noon - 4 PM; No admis fee; Estab 1892 as a memorial to soldiers of the Civil War & to provide a library & activities center for the community; Art gallery maintained, 30 x 54 ft, 16 ft ceiling, with incandescent track lighting; Average Annual Attendance: 5,000
Income: Financed by endowment, city & state appropriation
Collections: Margaret Wise Brown Archive, Children's Book Week Posters
Exhibitions: Ten - twelve exhibs scheduled per yr; local artists exhib
Activities: Lect open to pub; library tours

SOUTH CAROLINA

AIKEN

M **AIKEN COUNTY HISTORICAL MUSEUM,** 433 Newberry St SW, Aiken, SC 29801-4844. Tel 803-642-2015; Fax 803-642-2016; Email bbaratto@aikencountysc.gov; Web: www.aikencountyhistoricalmuseum.org; *Dir* Brenda Baratto; *Commission Chair* Owen Clary; *Site & Event Mgr* Leah Walker; *Colls Mgr* Lauren Virgo; *Mus Shop Mgr* Nancy Goetz
Open Tues - Sat 10 AM - 5 PM, Sun 2 - 5 PM; No admis fee; Open 1970 to document local history; Average Annual Attendance: 20,778; Mem: 450; mem open to residents; dues $10 & up; ann meeting in Oct
Income: $71,000 (financed by endowment, mem, county subsidiary)
Special Subjects: Historical Material
Collections: Agricultural-implements, Dairy-implements, log cabins, military, Savannah River Site (nuclear), Schools-furniture & winter items, Winter Colony-furniture, county history, Edgefield pottery
Exhibitions: Selections from permanent collection
Activities: Children's classes; docent progs & training; 10 vis lectrs per yr; tours; book traveling exhibs 10 per yr; retail store sells books & prints

ANDERSON

A **ANDERSON COUNTY ARTS COUNCIL,** Anderson Arts Center, 110 W Federal St, Anderson, SC 29625. Tel 864-222-2787; Fax 864-716-3840; Web: www.andersonarts.org; *Exec Dir* Kimberly Spears; *Prog Dir* Sydney Berkeley
Open Tues - Fri 9:30 AM - 5:30 PM, cl Sat - Mon & holidays; No admis fee; Estab 1972 as a nonprofit institution, encouraging & stimulating the practice & appreciation of the arts among the people living in the County of Anderson & the State of South Carolina; Bay 3 Artisan Gallery rotates exhibits monthly, featuring locally, regionally & nationally known artists; Average Annual Attendance: 10,000; Mem: 692; dues $1000, $500, $300, $150, $50, $35, $25; annual meeting last Tues of Sept
Income: Financed by mem, foundations, donations, county appropriation & grants
Exhibitions: Anderson Artist Guild Members Show; Soiree Clay Invitational; Youth Art Month; Changes; annual juried show; Art on the Town
Publications: Calendar of events; newsletter; annual report
Activities: Classes for adults & children; make & takes; gallery talks; tours; youth volunteer of the year, business of the year; shop sells original art

BEAUFORT

M **UNIVERSITY OF SOUTH CAROLINA BEAUFORT ART GALLERY,** Univ S Carolina, 801 Carteret St Beaufort, SC 29902. Tel 843-521-4145; Email info@beaufortarts.com; Web: www.beaufortarts.com; *Prog Coordr* Sarah Van Winkle; *Exec Dir* Eric V Holowacz
Open daily 9 AM - 5 PM; No admis fee; Estab 1990; Two-room community art gallery in Performing Arts Center at the University of South Carolina Beaufort; Average Annual Attendance: 10,000; Mem: 700; dues $10-$1000; ann meeting in May
Income: $150,000 (financed by mem, city & state appropriations)
Activities: Classes for adults; dramatic progs; lects open to pub, 1 - 4 vis lectrs per yr; book traveling exhibs 2-4 per yr

BELTON

M **BELTON CENTER FOR THE ARTS,** 306 City Sq, Belton, SC 29627; PO Box 368, Belton, SC 29627-0368. Tel 864-338-8556; Fax 864-338-0280; Email betsy@beltonarts.org; Web: www.beltoncenterforthearts.org; *Exec Dir* Betsy Chapman; *Admin Asst, Graphic Designer & Instructor* Kendell Lusk
Open Tues - Fri 10 AM - 5:30 PM, Sat 10 AM - 2 PM, cl Sun - Mon; Estab 1999; Mem: dues $20-$1,000
Collections: Features work by local artists
Exhibitions: Temporary exhibits
Activities: Classes for adults & children

CHARLESTON

M **CAROLINA ART ASSOCIATION,** Gibbes Museum of Art, 135 Meeting St, Charleston, SC 29401-2217. Tel 843-722-2706; Fax 843-720-1682; Web: www.gibbesmuseum.org; *Exec Dir & Chief Cur* Angela D Mack; *Dir Colls & Opers* Zinnia Willits; *Develop & Visitor Servs Mgr & Bd Liason* Wendi Ammons; *Media & PR* Lou Hammond Group; *Dir Finance & Admi* Courtney Soler
Open Tues & Thurs - Sat 10 AM - 5 PM, Wed 10 AM - 8 PM, Sun 1 PM - 5 PM cl Mon; Admis adults $15; seniors & military $13; college students $10, children (4-17) $6; children under 4 free; Estab 1858 as an art gallery & mus; Circ non-circulation; Beau-Arts style building erected in 1905, renovated in 1978; gallery is 31,000 sq ft; Average Annual Attendance: 60,000; Mem: 4,000; dues $30 & up; annual meeting 3rd Mon in Oct
Income: $1,300,000 (financed by endowment, mem, city & county appropriation, grants & contributions)
Purchases: Contemporary & historical paintings, sculpture, prints, drawings & photographs
Library Holdings: Book Volumes, Clipping Files, Exhibition Catalogs, Lantern Slides, Manuscripts, Maps, Memorabilia, Original Art Works, Original Documents, Other Holdings, Pamphlets, Photographs, Slides
Special Subjects: Miniatures, Oriental Art, Painting-American, Portraits, Prints, Woodcuts
Collections: American Colonial, Federal & Contemporary Paintings & Prints, Miniature Portraits, American art related to Charleston, Japanese Woodblock prints
Exhibitions: Approx 14 per yr

Publications: Bulletins, quarterly; books; exhibit catalogs & brochures
Activities: Docent training; lects open to pub, 2 vis lectrs per yr; gallery talks; tours; exten dept serves tri-county area; individual paintings & original objects of art lent to museums; 8 per yr; originate traveling exhibs, regional & national venues to mus; mus store sells books, magazines, original art, reproductions, prints, original crafts, jewelry & various mus related products

L **Library**, 135 Meeting St, Charleston, SC 29401. Tel 843-722-2706; Email research@gibbesmuseum.org; *Dir* Angela Mack
Open Tues - Sat 10 AM - 5 PM, Sun 1 PM - 5 PM; Admis adults $9, seniors, students & military $7, children ages 6-12 $5; 1858; Open to scholars for reference only, by appointment; Average Annual Attendance: 25,000
Income: Financed by pub & pvt support
Library Holdings: Book Volumes 3709, Clipping Files, Exhibition Catalogs, Kodachrome Transparencies, Manuscripts, Original Art Works, Pamphlets, Periodical Subscriptions 26, Photographs, Records, Sculpture, Video Tapes
Collections: Painting, Sculpture, Works on paper, Miniature portraits
Activities: Classes for adults & children; Lect open to public, 4 vis lectrs per year, gallery talks, tours; Originate Traveling Exhibs to Mus; Mus shop sells books, reproductions, prints

M **CHARLESTON MUSEUM,** 360 Meeting St, Charleston, SC 29403-6297. Tel 843-722-2996; Fax 843-722-1784; Email cborick@charlestonmuseum.com; Web: www.charlestonmuseum.org; *Dir & CEO* Carl P Borick; *CFO* Marc Meech; *Cur Historical Archaeology* Martha Zierden; *Cur History* J Grahame Long; *Chief Educ & Interpretation* Stephanie Thomas; *Cur Textiles* Jan Z Hiester; *Archivist & Colls Mgr* Jennifer McCormick; *Chief Mus Opers* Susan McKellar; *Bldg Maintenance Supvr* Marty Durham; *Pub Rels & Events Coordr* Suzanne Dibella-Olson
Open daily Mon - Sat 9 AM - 5 PM, Sun 1 - 5 PM, cl Easter, Thanksgiving, Christmas; Admis adults $12, children $5, mem free; Estab 1773 as a mus & library to diffuse knowledge of history, decorative arts, art, natural history, anthropology & technology; also to preserve houses & monuments; It is the oldest mus in the United States; Average Annual Attendance: 108,657; Mem: dues $50 & up; annual meeting in Feb
Income: Financed by mem, city & county appropriations, admis & sales
Special Subjects: Ceramics, Decorative Arts, Furniture, Glass, Textiles
Collections: Ceramics, decorative arts, furniture, glass, maps, photos, prints & textiles, art of northern BC
Publications: Bimonthly newsletter
Activities: Tours for adults & children; docent training; 8 lects per yr; concerts; sales shop sells books, magazines & prints related to collections

L **Library & Archives**, 360 Meeting St, Charleston, SC 29403-6297. Tel 843-722-2996; Fax 843-722-1784; Email info@charlestonmuseum.org; Web: www.charlestonmuseum.org; *Colls Mgr* Jennifer McCormick
Open Mus: Mon - Sat 9 AM - 5 PM, Sun 1 - 5 PM; Mon - Fri Archives & Library by appointment only; Admis $12; Estab 1773 as an educational institution, collects, preserves & uses artifacts of natural history, history, anthropology & decorative arts for staff & scholarly research; Mem: Dues $40
Library Holdings: Book Volumes 5000, Clipping Files, Exhibition Catalogs, Manuscripts, Maps, Memorabilia, Original Art Works, Original Documents, Other Holdings Maps, Pamphlets, Periodical Subscriptions 120, Photographs, Prints, Records, Reproductions
Special Subjects: Anthropology, Archaeology, Drawings, Etchings & Engravings, Furniture, Historical Material, Manuscripts, Maps, Photography, Pottery, Silver, Textiles, Prints
Collections: Artwork of: Alice Ravenel Huger Smith; Maria Martin Bachman; Charles Fraser; Mary Wilson Ball; Gabriel Manigault & Anna Heyward Taylor
Activities: Classes for adults & children; lect open to the pub; gallery talks; tours; mus shop

M **Heyward-Washington House**, 360 Meeting St, Charleston, SC 29403-6235. Tel 843-722-0354; Fax 843-722-1784; Email info@charlestonmuseum.org; Web: www.charlestonmuseum.org; *Historic House Admin* Katrina P Lawrimore
Open daily 10 AM - 5 PM; Sun 1 - 5 PM; Admis adults $12, youth $10, children $5; Built 1772; home of Thomas Heyward, Jr; purchased by the Mus in 1929; Mus is furnished with Charleston-made furniture of the period; a National Historic Landmark
Special Subjects: Architecture, Decorative Arts, Etchings & Engravings, Furniture, Glass, Painting-American, Period Rooms, Porcelain
Collections: House furnishings, 18th century Chippendale & Charleston made furniture
Activities: Classes for children; docent training; lects open to pub; daily tours

M **Joseph Manigault House**, 360 Meeting St, Charleston, SC 29403-6235. Tel 843-722-2996; Fax 843-722-1784; Email info@charlestonmuseum.org; Web: www.CharlestonMuseum.org; *Historic House Admin* Katrina P Lawrimore
Open Mon - Sat 10 AM - 5 PM, Sun 1 - 5 PM; Admis adults $12, youth $10, children $5; Estab 1773 to preserve & interpret Charleston natural & social history; This house was built in 1803 & is a premier example of Adam style, or Federal architecture; Average Annual Attendance: 50,000; Mem: 2200; dues varies
Special Subjects: Architecture, Decorative Arts, Glass, Painting-American, Period Rooms, Porcelain, Silver
Collections: American, English, French furnishings of the period capture the lifestyle of the wealthy rice-planting Manigault family
Activities: Classes for children; docent training; gallery talks; Tours; mus shop sells books, reproductions, prints & other local crafts in neighboring (patron) mus

M **CITY OF CHARLESTON,** City Hall Council Chamber Gallery, 80 Broad St, Charleston, SC 29401-2225. Tel 843-724-3799; Fax 843-720-3827; *Cur* Carol Ezell-Gilson
Open Mon - Fri 9 AM - 5 PM, cl major holidays; No admis fee; Estab 1818 to preserve for the citizens of Charleston a portrait coll of the city's history; A unique collection of American portraits housed in the 2nd oldest city council chamber in continuous use in the US; Average Annual Attendance: 20,000
Income: Financed by city
Collections: Washington Trumbull, 1791, J Monroe Samuel Morse, 1819, A Jackson John Vanderlyn, 1824, Zachary Taylor James Beard, 1848, Marquis de Lafayette Charles Fraser, 1825, Pierre Beauregard George Healy, 1861, C Gaddsen-R Peale, portraits by Jarvis, Savage, John Blake White, James Earle, G Whiting Flagg

Publications: Catalog of paintings & sculpture
Activities: Lect open to pub; tours

M **COLLEGE OF CHARLESTON SCHOOL OF ARTS,** Halsey Institute of Contemporary Art, 161 Calhoun St, Charleston, SC 29401. Tel 843-953-4422; Fax 843-953-7890; Email halsey@cofc.edu; Web: www.halsey.cofc.edu; *Dir* Mark Sloan; *Mgr Exhibs & Public Programs* Bryan Granger
Open Mon - Sat 11 AM - 4 PM, Thurs until 7 PM; No admis fee; Estab 1978 as a col gallery with focus on contemporary art; New & improved facilities with two inter-linked galleries as well as a lib resource room, media room, offices & storage; Average Annual Attendance: 26,000
Income: $770,000 (financed by state appropriation, earned income, grants & contributions
Library Holdings: Auction Catalogs, Book Volumes, Exhibition Catalogs, Periodical Subscriptions
Publications: Periodic catalogs & gallery guides; Evon Streetman in Retrospect; Hung Liu: Washington Blues; The Right to Assemble; With Beauty Before Us: The Navajo of Chil Chin Beto; Appropriate to the Moment: Michael Tyzack; Cheryl Goldsleger: Improvisations; Force of Nature: Site Installations by Ten Japanese Artists; Alive Inside: The Lure & Lore of the Sideshow; Aldwyth: work v./work n. -Collage & Assemblage 1991-2009; Palmetto Portraits Project; Renee Stout: Tales of the Conjure Woman; Reform to the Sea: Saltworks by Motoi Yamamoto; Aggie Zed: Keepers Keep; Something to Take My Place: The Art of Lonnie Holley
Activities: Docent training; lect open to pub; lects for mems; 8-10 vis lectrs per yr; gallery talks; tours; concerts; juried student competitions; contemporary, emerging, & mid-career artists from all over the world, film series; artist in residence; AAM Design Publication Award 2010; book traveling exhibs 0-2 per yr; originate traveling exhibs to nationwide

M **PRINCIPLE GALLERY,** Charleston, 125 Meeting st, Charleston, SC 29401. Tel 843-727-4500; Email art@principlecharleston.com; Web: www.principlegallery.com/charleston; *Owner* Michele Ward; *Dir* Frank Conrad Russen; *Asst Dir* Thomas Provost; *Key Mktg & Event Planner* Liz Platanis
Open Mon - Wed 10 AM - 6 PM, Thurs - Sat 10 AM - 9 PM, Sun 11 AM - 6 PM; Estab 1994 to represent contemporary realism & its artists
Collections: Contemporary & classical realism, oil paintings, bronze sculpture
Exhibitions: Temporary exhibits
Activities: Events

CLEMSON

M **CLEMSON UNIVERSITY,** Rudolph E Lee Gallery, Lee Hall, Clemson, SC 29634-0001. Tel 843-656-3883; Fax 843-864-656-7523; Email woodwaw@exchange.clemspm/edi; *Dir* Denise Woodward-Detrich
Open Mon - Fri 9 AM - 4:30 PM, Sun 2 - 5 PM, cl Sat; No admis fee; Estab 1956 to provide cultural & educational resources; to collect, preserve, interpret & display items of historical, educational & cultural significance; Average Annual Attendance: 20,000
Income: Financed by state appropriation
Special Subjects: Architecture, Graphics, Painting-American
Collections: Clemson Architectural Foundation Collection, Contemporary American Paintings & Graphics
Publications: Exhibition Bulletin, annually; Posters on Exhibits, monthly
Activities: Lect open to pub, 3-5 vis lectrs per yr; gallery talks; tours; exten dept servs Southeast United States; individual paintings & original objects of art lent to museums, universities; lending collection contains original prints, paintings, sculpture; originate traveling exhibs

L **Emery A Gunnin Architectural Library**, Lee Hall, Clemson, SC 29634-0001. Tel 864-656-3933; Fax 864-656-3932; Web: www.clemson.edu/gunnin/; *Media Resources Cur* Christopher Chapman; *Branch Head* Gypsey Teague; *Ref Librn* Kathy Edwards
Open during school yr Sun 2 -10PM, Mon - Thurs 7:30AM - 10PM, Fri 7:30AM - 5PM; No admis fee; For reference only for univ & pub use; Average Annual Attendance: 91,000
Library Holdings: Audio Tapes, Book Volumes 45,000, CD-ROMs, Exhibition Catalogs, Pamphlets, Periodical Subscriptions 212, Slides 150,000, Video Tapes
Special Subjects: Aesthetics, Archaeology, Architecture, Art History, Ceramics, Commercial Art, Conceptual Art, Constructions, Crafts, Decorative Arts, Drafting, Drawings, Landscape Architecture, Photography, Pottery, Sculpture
Collections: Rare Book Collection, South Carolina City & Regional Planning Documents

M **Fort Hill Plantation**, Fort Hill St, Clemson, SC 29634-5605; 109 Daniel Dr, Clemson Univ Visitor Center Clemson, SC 29631-3006. Tel 864-656-3311, 656-2475; Fax 864-656-1026; *Dir Historic Houses & Cur* Will Hiott; *Dir Visitor Services* Helen Adams
Open Mon - Fri 10 AM - 5 PM, Sat 10 AM - 5 PM, Sun 2 - 5 PM, cl holidays & Christmas week; Admis by donation; A historic house mus located in the home of John C Calhoun. Restoration of the house & furnishings are an on-going project of the John C Calhoun Chap of the United Daughters of the Confederacy & Clemson University
Income: Financed by Clemson University
Special Subjects: Painting-Flemish, Period Rooms, Portraits, Decorative Arts, Furniture
Publications: Fort Hill, brochure
Activities: Lect; guided tours

COLUMBIA

M **COLUMBIA MUSEUM OF ART,** 1515 Main St, Columbia, SC 29201; PO Box 2068, Columbia, SC 29202-2068. Tel 803-799-2810; Fax 803-343-2150; Email info@columbiamuseum.org; Web: www.columbiamuseum.org; *Exec Dir* Della Watkins; *Deputy Dir & Dir External Affairs* Joelle Ryan-Cook; *Facility Project Advisor* Michael Roh; *Dir Educ & Engagement* Jackie Adams; *Chief Develop Officer* Angi Fuller Wildt

Open Tues - Fri 11 AM - 5 PM, Sat 10 AM - 5 PM, Sun noon - 5 PM, 1st Thurs of month until 8 PM; Admis adults $12, military & seniors $10, students $5, children under 5 & mem free; Estab 1950 to extend & increase art understanding, to assist in the conservation of a valuable cultural heritage & to recognize & assist contemporary art expression; Tues-Fri 11 AM - 5 PM, Sat 10 AM -5 PM, Sun noon - 5 PM, 1st Thurs each month 11 AM - 8 PM. Adults $6, senior citizen & military $5, students $2.50; children 6 & under no charge.; Average Annual Attendance: 120,000; Mem: 3,500; dues individual $45, dual $65, household $75, patron $200, Premier Society $500 & above; annual meeting in May
Income: $2,572,500 supported by citizens and corporations of the Midlands, City of Columbia, Richland County, SC Arts Commission, Cultural Council of Richland & Lexington Counties
Purchases: Works of art on paper, Southeastern artists, textiles, paintings & decorative arts
Library Holdings: Auction Catalogs, Book Volumes, Clipping Files, Exhibition Catalogs, Original Documents, Periodical Subscriptions
Special Subjects: Decorative Arts, Furniture, Graphics, Painting-American, Painting-European, Painting-Italian, Renaissance Art, Textiles
Collections: Kress Collection of Renaissance Paintings, International coll of fine & decorative arts from Medieval to present included Renaissance & Baroque Old Masters, Seibels Collection of Renaissance Art, Scotese Collection of Graphics, Turner Collection of Asian Art
Publications: Annual report; Collections Magazine, bimonthly; exhibition brochures
Activities: Educ progs for adults & children; docent training; lects open to pub, 6 vis lectrs per yr; concerts; gallery talks; tours; schols offered; lending coll of original art objects; mus shop sells books, reproductions, prints, ceramics, glass, jewelry, original art & other items

L **Lee Alexander Lorick Library**, PO Box 2068, Columbia, SC 29202. Tel 803-799-2810, 343-2155, 343-2156; Fax 803-343-2219; Email nrice@columbiamuseum.org; Web: www.colubiamuseum.org; *Curatorial Asst* Noelle Rice
Open by appointment only; Admis adults $10, military & seniors 65+ $8, students $5; under 5 yrs no admis fee; Estab 1950; Open to by appointment to mems & pub for reference only; Average Annual Attendance: 119,552; Mem: Various mem levels & meetings
Income: $10,000 (financed by mus)
Library Holdings: Audio Tapes, Book Volumes 14,000, Cassettes, Clipping Files, Exhibition Catalogs, Memorabilia, Other Holdings Vertical files, Pamphlets, Periodical Subscriptions 50, Video Tapes
Special Subjects: American Indian Art, American Western Art, Antiquities-Egyptian, Antiquities-Greek, Antiquities-Roman, Architecture, Art Education, Art History, Asian Art, Bronzes, Ceramics, Collages, Conceptual Art, Crafts, Decorative Arts, Drawings, Enamels, Etchings & Engravings, Folk Art, Furniture, Glass, Historical Material, History of Art & Archaeology, Illustration, Islamic Art, Ivory, Jade, Landscapes, Latin American Art, Manuscripts, Maps, Oriental Art, Painting-American, Painting-British, Painting-Dutch, Painting-Flemish, Painting-French, Painting-Italian, Photography, Porcelain, Portraits, Pottery, Pre-Columbian Art, Religious Art, Sculpture, Silver, Southwestern Art, Stained Glass, Textiles, Watercolors, Woodcarvings, Woodcuts
Activities: Ten visiting lectrs per year; concerts; gallery talks; tours; sponsoring of competitions; extension progs serve boys & girls clubs of the Midlands; lending of original art to various mus at various times; mus shop sells books, original art, jewelry, stationary, organizers etc

M **PONDER FINE ARTS GALLERY-BENEDICT COLLEGE,** 1600 Harden St, Columbia, SC 29204. Tel 803-253-5000; Web: www.ponderartgallerybc.com
Open Mon - Fri 10 AM - 5 PM; No admis fee
Collections: African & African-American work, especially contemporary art on paper
Exhibitions: Temporary exhibits

A **SOUTH CAROLINA ARTS COMMISSION,** 1026 Sumter St Rm 102, Columbia, SC 29201-3746. Tel 803-734-8696; Fax 803-734-8526; Email info@arts.sc.gov; Web: www.southcarolinaarts.com; *Exec Dir* Ken May; *Dir Visual Arts* Harriett Green; *Dir Literary Arts* Sara June Goldstein; *Mgr Grants & Communications* Laurel Posey
Open Mon - Fri 8:30 AM - 5 PM; No admis fee; State Agency estab 1967 to promote & develop the arts in South Carolina
Income: $1.8M (financed primarily by state & federal income)
Collections: State Art Collection
Activities: Educ programming; lect open to pub, gallery talks; competitions with awards, Folk Heritage Award, Verner Award; artists' workshops; grants-in-aid & fels offered; exten dept serves state; individual paintings & original objects of art lent to other galleries & museums; lending coll contains 446 original art works, paintings, photographs, sculpture, slides; originate traveling exhibs, circulates to 6 sites in South Carolina

L **Media Center**, 1026 Sumter St Rm 102, Columbia, SC 29201-3746. Tel 803-734-8696; Fax 803-734-8526; Email sleonard@arts.state.sc.us; *Dir* Susan Leonard
Open Mon - Fri 8:30 AM - 5 PM
Income: Financed by state & federal income
Library Holdings: Audio Tapes, Cassettes, Motion Pictures, Slides, Video Tapes
Special Subjects: Film

M **SOUTH CAROLINA STATE MUSEUM,** 301 Gervais St, Columbia, SC 29201-3041. Tel 803-898-4921; Fax 803-898-4969; Web: www.museum.state.sc.us; *Exec Dir* William Calloway; *Dir Admin* Bonnie Moffatt; *Dir Mktg* Merritt McNeely; *Dir Educ* Tom Falvey; *Dir Collections* Paul Matheny; *Dir Exhibits* Huck Behrends; *Dir Operations* Doug Beerman
Open Tues - Sat 10 AM - 5 PM, Sun 1 - 5 PM; Estab 1973; Four large floors in a renovated textile mill with exhibits in art, history, natural history & science & technology; Average Annual Attendance: 250,000; Mem: 6500; ann meeting in June
Income: Financed by admis, state appropriations, store revenue & supplement state money
Special Subjects: Afro-American Art, Crafts, Decorative Arts, Folk Art, Hispanic Art, Juvenile Art, Miniatures, Painting-American, Photography, Sculpture, Textiles
Collections: Art - all media, Cultural History, Natural History, Science & Technology
Exhibitions: Art - South Carolina/Kentucky Exchange; History - The Palmetto State Goes Tower: WW II & South Carolina; Natural History - Fossil Collectors & Collections; 100 Years/100 Artists: A View of 20th Century South Carolina Art
Publications: Annual report; Images, quarterly
Activities: Docent progs; lect open to pub; lending coll contains 500 paintings; book traveling exhibs 10 per yr; originate traveling exhibs 4 per yr; retail store sells books & slides

M **UNIVERSITY OF SOUTH CAROLINA,** McKissick Museum, 816 Bull St, Columbia, SC 29208-0001. Tel 803-777-7251; Fax 803-777-2829; Email mcksmail@sc.edu; Web: www.cla.sc.edu/mcks, www.cas.sc.edu/mcks/; *Exec Dir* Jane Przybysz; *Cur Folk Art & Research* Saddler Taylor
Open Mon - Fri 8:30 AM - 5 PM, Sat 11 AM - 3 PM, cl July 4th, Labor Day, Thanksgiving & day after, Dec 25, Jan 1; No admis fee; Estab 1976 to centralize the university's mus colls; Contains 4 major gallery areas for temporary & changing exhibs in art, science & history; Average Annual Attendance: 70,000
Income: Financed by state appropriation & donations
Purchases: Southern Folk Art
Special Subjects: Silver
Collections: Bernard Baruch Collection of 18th Century Silver, Movietonews News Reels, James F Byrnes Collection, Howard Gemstone Collection, Richard Mandell: Art Nouveau Collection, Colburn Gemstone Collection, university memorabilia, southeastern folk art, minerals, fossils, rocks & meteorites, contemporary art works
Exhibitions: A Portion of the People: Three Hundred Years of Jewish Life in South Carolina; student & faculty art
Publications: Exhibition catalogs; Calendar of events (quarterly)
Activities: Docent training; lect open to pub, 4-5 vis lectrs per yr; concerts; gallery talks; tours; competitions; slide-tape progs & classes for students & senior citizens; community outreach to senior citizen groups & children's hospital wards; originate traveling exhibs

DUE WEST

M **BOWIE ARTS CENTER,** 2 Washington St, Erskine College Due West, SC 29639. Tel 864-379-8867; Fax 864-379-2167
Open Mon - Thurs 1 PM - 4 PM, Sun 2 PM - 4 PM, cl Fri - Sat; No admis fee; 14,000 sq ft
Collections: Antique mechanical musical instruments; clocks; decorative arts; glass & porcelain; furnishings from the 19th & early 20th centuries; photographs, Regional works by contemporary artists
Exhibitions: Travelling exhibit

FLORENCE

M **FLORENCE COUNTY MUSEUM,** 111 W Cheves St, Florence, SC 29501-4401. Tel 843-662-3351; Email contact@florencemuseum.org; Web: florencemuseum.org; *VChmn* Hunter Stokes; *VPres* Vicki Stokes; *Dir* Andrew R Stout; *Cur Coll* Stephen Motte; *Cur Educ* Heather Dillon
Open Tues - Sat 10 AM - 5 PM, Sun 2 - 5 PM, cl Mon & major holidays; Admis general $1, mems free; Estab 1924 (incorporated in 1936) as a general mus of art, natural science & history of South Carolina, with emphasis on the region known as the Pee Dee to acquaint the pub with fine art; Changing art exhibs, main galleries; Average Annual Attendance: 25,000; Mem: 450; dues benefactor $1000, patron $500, donor $250, sustaining $100, sponsor $50, family $30, individual $15
Income: $200,000 (financed by mem, county & city appropriation & donations)
Library Holdings: Auction Catalogs, Book Volumes, Clipping Files, Exhibition Catalogs, Manuscripts, Maps, Memorabilia, Original Art Works, Photographs, Prints, Reels, Reproductions, Slides, Video Tapes
Special Subjects: Afro-American Art, American Indian Art, Antiquities-Byzantine, Antiquities-Egyptian, Antiquities-Etruscan, Antiquities-Greek, Antiquities-Oriental, Antiquities-Persian, Antiquities-Roman, Archaeology, Architecture, Asian Art, Carpets & Rugs, Ceramics, Coins & Medals, Collages, Decorative Arts, Drawings, Embroidery, Etchings & Engravings, Furniture, Glass, Graphics, Historical Material, Islamic Art, Ivory, Jade, Jewelry, Judaica, Landscapes, Manuscripts, Military Art, Miniatures, Oriental Art, Painting-American, Painting-British, Painting-European, Painting-Flemish, Painting-French, Painting-Japanese, Portraits, Pottery, Pre-Columbian Art, Pre-Columbian Art, Primitive art, Prints, Religious Art, Renaissance Art, Restorations, Textiles, Watercolors, Woodcarvings, Woodcuts, Tapestries, Southwestern Art, Silver
Collections: Permanent Collection includes: African, Asian, Southwestern American Indians, Catawba Indian Collections, Greek & Roman Archaeological material, historical artifacts, works of local Black artist William H Johnson, works of local & regional artists, Museum Permanent Collection, Regional Artists, Native American Art
Exhibitions: PeeDee Regional Art Competition
Publications: Florence Museum magazine, biannual
Activities: Classes for adults & children; docent training; lects open to pub, 4 vis lectrs per yr; gallery talks; self-guided tours; art competitions with prizes; schols; book traveling exhibs; original art

GREENVILLE

M **BOB JONES UNIVERSITY MUSEUM & GALLERY INC,** 1700 Wade Hampton Blvd, Greenville, SC 29614-0001. Tel 864-770-1331; Fax 864-770-1306; Email contact@bjumg.org; Web: www.bjumg.org; *Chmn Bd* Bob Jones III; *Dir* Erin Jones; *Dir Educ* Donnalynn Hess; *Registrar* Barbara Sicko; *Dir Security & Plant Operations* James Jackson; *Events Coordr* Amy Basinger; *Guest Svcs* Rebekah Cobb
Open Tues - Sat 2 - 5 PM, cl Mon, mid-Dec - mid-Jan, New Year's Day, July 4, Thanksgiving weekend & Commencement weekend in May. Satellite location open

Tues - Sat 10 AM - 5 PM, cl Mon, Dec 24 - 25, Jan 1, July 4 & Thanksgiving Day; Admis Adults $7; Seniors (60+) $6; Students $5; Children 12 & under & members free; Estab 1951 to show the development of 14th - 19th century Old Masters paintings; 30 elegant galleries filled with art; tapestries, furniture, sculpture, & architectural motifs from the 13th through 19th centuries. Satellite location has rotating Old Masters exhibit & Learning Ctr with hands-on interactive displays; Average Annual Attendance: 22,000; Mem: Dues; mem levels - family/dual $150, individual $65
Income: Gifts from mems, donations, grants & admissions, gift shop sales
Library Holdings: Auction Catalogs, Book Volumes, Exhibition Catalogs
Special Subjects: Painting-European, Religious Art, Antiquities-Assyrian, Antiquities-Egyptian, Antiquities-Greek, Antiquities-Persian, Antiquities-Roman, Archaeology, Baroque Art, Bronzes, Ceramics, Coins & Medals, Decorative Arts, Embroidery, Enamels, Etchings & Engravings, Furniture, Ivory, Medieval Art, Mosaics, Oriental Art, Painting-American, Painting-British, Painting-Dutch, Painting-Flemish, Painting-French, Painting-German, Painting-Italian, Painting-Russian, Period Rooms, Porcelain, Portraits, Renaissance Art, Sculpture, Silver, Stained Glass, Tapestries, Textiles, Woodcarvings
Collections: Religious art by the Old Masters from the 14th-19th centuries including Botticelli, Cranach the Elder, G David, Murillo, Ribera, Rubens, Tintoretto, Veronese, Zurbaran, Revealed Religion by Benjamin West, 7 paintings, Bowen Collection of biblical antiquities & illustrative material from the Holy Land
Exhibitions: The Art of Sleuthing (Oct 23, 2015 opening)
Publications: Catalogs; illustrated booklets; gallery newsletter, calendar of events
Activities: Classes for children; educator seminars; dramatic progs; docent training; lectrs open to pub; concerts; gallery talks; tours for school & adult groups by appointment; awards, Certificate of Excellence 2012 Exhib Competition; Certificate of Excellence 2013, 2014, 2015 & 2016 Trip Advisor; individual paintings lent to other galleries in the US & abroad; progs for pub & pvt local schools; gift shop sells books, reproductions, prints, postcards, gift items & educational products

M **GREENVILLE COUNTY MUSEUM OF ART,** 420 College St, Greenville, SC 29601-2099. Tel 864-271-7570; Fax 864-271-7579; Email info@greenvillemuseum.org; Web: www.greenvillemuseum.org; *Registrar Pub Rels* Claudia Beckwith; *Dir* Thomas W Styron; *Develop* Mary Lawson; *Pub Rels* Mary McCarthy; *Comptroller* Jeanne Marsh
Open Tues - Sat 11 AM - 5 PM, Sun 1 - 5 PM, cl Mon & major holidays; No admis fee, donations accepted; Estab 1958 for the coll & preservation of American Art; Seven major galleries devoted to permanent collections of American art from the colonial to the contemporary, changing & traveling exhibitions. Colls featuring Andrew Wyeth, Jasper Johns; Average Annual Attendance: 123,000; Mem: 1250; dues $50 - $10,000
Income: Financed by mem, donations & county appropriation
Special Subjects: Afro-American Art, Painting-American, Portraits
Collections: Pre World War II Southern Art, Andrew Wyeth, Watercolors, contemporary art
Exhibitions: Andrew Wyeth: Friends & Family; Southern Scenes; local artists
Publications: Exhibit catalogs
Activities: Classes for adults & children; docent training; Museum School of Art; lect open to pub, 6-10 vis lectrs per yr; gallery talks; tours; exten dept serves Greenville County schools; lending coll contains slides; mus shop sells books, original art, slides, prints, children's educ toys, regional crafts & cards

C **LIBERTY LIFE INSURANCE COMPANY,** 2000 Wade Hampton Blvd, Greenville, SC 29615-1036; PO Box 789, Greenville, SC 29602-0789. Tel 864-609-8111; *Pres* Francis M Hipp
Open during normal bus hours by appointment; Estab 1978 to collect textile art selections from various cultures & historical periods; Collection displayed throughout corporate headquarters
Collections: Limited edition prints, graphics & silkscreens, textile art works from around the world
Publications: The Liberty Textile Collection
Activities: Individual paintings & original objects of art lent to regional & national museums & galleries

GREENWOOD

M **THE MUSEUM,** 106 Main St, Greenwood, SC 29646-2763; PO Box 3131, Greenwood, SC 29648-3131. Tel 864-229-7093; Fax 864-229-9317; Email greenwoodmuseumdirector@gmail.com; Web: www.greenwoodmuseum.org; *Exec Dir* Stacey Thompson; *Progs Dir* Bethany Wade; *Exec Asst* Jalissa Adger
Open Wed - Sat 10 AM - 5 PM, cl Mon & Tues; Admis free; Estab 1967 for educ purposes; Three floors of interactive exhibits focusing on history, nat history & science; Average Annual Attendance: 10,000; Mem: 400; dues $35 & up
Income: Financed by mem, contributions & grants
Library Holdings: Audio Tapes, Book Volumes, Cassettes, DVDs, Manuscripts, Memorabilia, Periodical Subscriptions, Photographs
Special Subjects: African Art, Anthropology, Antiquities-Egyptian, Antiquities-Greek, Antiquities-Oriental, Antiquities-Roman, Archaeology, Art Education, Asian Art, Carpets & Rugs, Ceramics, Coins & Medals, Costumes, Crafts, Dioramas, Dolls, Drawings, Embroidery, Ethnology, Folk Art, Furniture, Glass, Historical Material, Historical Material, Ivory, Laces, Mexican Art, Painting-American, Period Rooms, Pewter, Photography, Porcelain, Pottery, Primitive art, Scrimshaw, Sculpture, Textiles, Woodcarvings, Flasks & Bottles
Collections: Main Street Timeline 1800s-1950, Carriages and Coaches, Coll of over 45,000 objects, 7 historic railcars
Exhibitions: Traveling exhibs, regional & international; History, Natural History & Science
Publications: Newsletter, quarterly
Activities: Classes for adults & children; lect open to pub, tours; traveling exhibs 2 major show per yr; sales shop sells books, prints & Greenwood items

HARTSVILLE

M **COKER COLLEGE,** Cecelia Coker Bell Gallery, Coker College, Gladys C Fort Art Bldg Hartsville, SC 29550; 300 E College Ave, Hartsville, SC 29550-3797. Tel 843-383-8156; Fax 843-383-8048; Email artgallery@coker.edu; Web: www.ceceliacokerbellgallery.com; *Dir* Ashley Gillespie
Open Mon - Fri 10 AM - 4 PM (when classes are in session); No admis fee; Estab 1983 to serve campus & community; 30 ft x 40 ft self-contained, movable partitions, track light, security system; Average Annual Attendance: 5,000
Exhibitions: Area artists; annual student juried show; senior students show; vis artists; 5 solo national & international exhibitions
Publications: Collection catalog
Activities: Lect open to public, 3 - 5 vis lectrs per yr; gallery talks; student juried competitions with awards

MURRELLS INLET

M **BROOKGREEN GARDENS,** 1931 Brookgreen Gardens Dr, Murrells Inlet, SC 29576; P. O. Box 3368, Pawleys Island, SC 29585-3368. Tel 843-235-6000, 800-849-1931 (Toll Free); Fax 843-235-6039; Email info@brookgreen.org; Web: www.brookgreen.org; *CEO & Pres* Robert Jewell; *CFO & VPres Fin* Kathleen Zeiss; *VPres Horticulture & Conservation* Sara Millar; *VPres Pub Opers* Phillip A Tukey; *VPres Mktg* Helen Benso; *Vol Mgr* Jay Rowe; *Mus Shop Mgr* Ashley Gray
Open daily 9:30 AM - 5 PM, cl Christmas; Admis adults $14, seniors $12, children 4-12 $7, children 3 & under & members free; Estab 1931 to exhibit the flora & fauna of South Carolina & to exhibit objects of art; The outdoor mus exhibits American sculpture & has changing sculpture exhibitions in indoor galleries; Average Annual Attendance: 275,000; Mem: 6000; dues individual $65, family $100, President's Council $275, Chairman's Council $1,000, Huntington Society $2,500, Atalay Society $5,000
Income: Financed by endowment, mem, gifts, grants & admis
Special Subjects: American Western Art, Bronzes, Coins & Medals, Historical Material, Sculpture
Collections: Collection of American figurative, sculpture, pieces by sculptors, Art Education, Art History, Landscape Architecture, Exploring American Sculpture
Publications: Brookgreen Journal, biannual; The Garden Path, biannual; exhibition catalogues
Activities: Classes for adults & children; docent training; workshops; dramatic progs; lects open to public; gallery talks; tours; concerts; People's Choice Award; awards; lends original objects of art to museums; originate traveling exhibs; mus shop sells books, magazines, original art, reproductions, prints, postcards, pamphlets, sculpture, jewelry & gifts

L **Library,** 1931 Brookgreen Garden Dr, Murrells Inlet, SC 29576; PO Box 3368, Pawleys Island, SC 29585-3368. Tel 843-235-6012; Fax 843-235-6003; Email rsalmon@brookgreen.org; Web: www.brookgreen.org
Open Tues 10 AM - 1 PM; Thurs 1 PM - 5 PM; No admis fee; Estab 1931; For reference only to staff & vol
Income: financed by Brookgreen Gardens
Library Holdings: Auction Catalogs, Audio Tapes, Book Volumes 2200, CD-ROMs, Cassettes, Clipping Files, Exhibition Catalogs, Filmstrips, Framed Reproductions, Kodachrome Transparencies, Manuscripts, Maps, Memorabilia, Motion Pictures, Other Holdings Architectural & engineering drawings & prints; Maps, Pamphlets, Periodical Subscriptions 50, Photographs, Prints, Reels, Slides, Video Tapes
Special Subjects: American Western Art, Art History, Coins & Medals, Drawings, Historical Material, History of Art & Archaeology, Landscape Architecture, Maps, Restoration & Conservation, Sculpture, Woodcarvings

PICKENS

M **PICKENS COUNTY MUSEUM OF ART & HISTORY,** 307 Johnson St, Pickens, SC 29671-2463. Tel 864-898-5963; Fax 864-898-5580; Email picmus@co.pickens.sc.us; Web: www.co.pickens.sc.us/culturalcommission; *Exec Dir* C Allen Coleman; *Chmn* Susan Benjamin; *Cur* Helen Hockwelt; *Mill Site Mgr* Ed Bolt; *Mus Shop Mgr* Den Keys
Open Tues - Wed & Fri 9 AM - 5 PM, Thurs 9 AM - 7:30 PM, Sat 9 AM - 4:30 PM; No admis fee; Estab 1975 as a general mus; Average Annual Attendance: 35,000
Collections: regional 20th & 21st century art, photographs
Publications: newsletter, Old Gaol Gazette
Activities: Educ progs; workshops; classes; guided tours; lect; gallery talks; concerts

ROCK HILL

M **MUSEUM OF YORK COUNTY,** 4621 Mount Gallant Blvd, Rock Hill, SC 29732-9905. Tel 803-329-2121; Fax 803-329-5249; Email information@chmuseum.org; Web: http://chmuseums.org/myco/; *Exec Dir* Van W Shields
Open Mon - Sat 10 AM - 5 PM, Sun 1 - 5 PM; Admis $5, seniors $4, youth $3, children under 3 & mems free, no admis fee Sun; Estab 1948; Spring, Alternative & Lobby galleries (changing art exhibits); Average Annual Attendance: 50,000; Mem: 1248; dues vary
Income: $1,383,225 (financed by mem, admis & county appropriation)
Special Subjects: African Art, Anthropology, Archaeology, Ceramics, Costumes, Decorative Arts, Dioramas, Ethnology, Historical Material, Painting-American, Posters, Sculpture, Textiles, Woodcarvings
Collections: African animals - mounted specimens, African art & ethnography, local art, local history & archaeology, local natural history specimens
Publications: Quarterly, bi-monthly; Teacher's Guide, annual
Activities: Classes for adults & children; docent progs; lect open to pub, 10 vis lectrs per yr; competitions with purchase awards; exten dept servs county; book traveling exhibs 5 per yr; retail store sells books & prints

L **Staff Research Library**, 4621 Mount Gallant Rd, Rock Hill, SC 29732-9637. Tel 803-329-2121; Fax 803-329-5249; *Cur Coll* Anne Lane
For research
Income: Financed by departmental budgets
Library Holdings: Audio Tapes, Cassettes, Exhibition Catalogs, Pamphlets, Video Tapes
Special Subjects: American Indian Art, Anthropology, Archaeology, Art Education, Crafts, Ethnology, Photography, Primitive art, Restoration & Conservation

M **WINTHROP UNIVERSITY GALLERIES,** 126 McLaurin Hall, Rock Hill, SC 29730. Tel 803-323-2493; Fax 803-323-2333; Email derksenk@winthrop.edu; Web: www.winthrop.edu/galleries; *Dir* Karen Derksen
Open Mon - Fri 9 AM - 5 PM; No admis fee; Housed within Rutledge Bldg, the Col of Visual & Performing Arts at Winthrop University. Presents temporary visual art & design exhibs for the enhancement of acad achievement & understanding within the col community; Gallery is 3500 sq ft; Average Annual Attendance: 15,000
Income: Financed by state appropriation
Collections: Paintings & photographs; art exhibitions
Exhibitions: Student Exhibs; South Carolina State Art Collection; one-person shows; invitational exhibs in photo, drawing, painting, printmaking, textiles, design, ceramics & glass
Activities: lect open to pub; concerts; gallery talks; schols & fels offered; originate traveling exhibs

SPARTANBURG

A **ARTS PARTNERSHIP OF GREATER SPARTANBURG, INC,** Chapman Cultural Center, 200 E St John St, Spartanburg, SC 29306. Tel 864-583-2776; Fax 864-948-5353; Email info@spartanarts.org; Web: www.chapmanculturalcenter.org; *Pres & COO* Jennifer Evins; *Dir Arts Educ* Ava Hughes; *Mktg Dir* Steve Wong
Open Tues - Sat 10 AM - 5 PM, Sun 1 - 5 PM; No admis fee; Estab 1993 to coordinate & develop all cultural activities in the area; Three mus: contemporary art, local art & local history; Average Annual Attendance: 250,000
Special Subjects: Decorative Arts, Historical Material, Sculpture, Textiles, Watercolors
Exhibitions: Changing exhibits
Publications: Membership Brochure, ann; Spartanburg Arts Calendar, monthly
Activities: Classes for adults & children; artist residences in schools; performances in school; docent training; lects open to pub; 20 lectrs per yr; concerts; gallery talks; tours; sponsoring competitions; schols

M **CONVERSE COLLEGE,** Milliken Art Gallery, 580 E Main, Spartanburg, SC 29302. Tel 864-596-9177; Fax 864-596-9606; Email artdesign@converse.edu; Web: www.converse.edu; *Dir* Kathryn Boucher
Open Mon - Fri 9 AM - 5 PM, Sun 2 - 5 PM, cl holidays; No admis fee; Estab 1971 for educational purposes; A brick & glass structure of 40 x 60 ft; movable panels 4 x 6 ft for exhibition of work, 16 panels, 12 sculpture stands; Average Annual Attendance: 2,400
Income: Financed by endowment
Exhibitions: Invitational exhibits of regional artists; annual juried student show; senior exhibit
Activities: Educ dept; lect open to public, 5-6 vis lectrs per year; gallery talks; tours

M **SPARTANBURG ART MUSEUM,** 200 E St John St, Spartanburg, SC 29306. Tel 864-582-7616; Fax 864-948-5353; Email museum@spartanarts.org; Web: www.spartanburgartmuseum.org; *Exhibs Coordr* Ashleigh Payne; *Art School Dir* Kathleen Digney; *Colors Coordr* Kathy Wofford; *Exec Dir* Elizabeth Goddard; *PR & Mktg Coordr* Sara Shealy
Open Tues - Sat 10 AM - 5 PM, Sun 1 - 5 PM; No admis fee; Estab 1969 to promote the works of contemporary artists in the southeastern United States; Gallery is located in the Chapman Cultural Center & contains both a permanent coll & temporary exhibs; Average Annual Attendance: 10,000; Mem: 500; dues $25 - $200
Income: Financed by endowment & mem, art school revenue
Library Holdings: Clipping Files, Exhibition Catalogs, Memorabilia
Special Subjects: Ceramics, Folk Art, Juvenile Art, Landscapes, Painting-American, Photography, Portraits, Pottery, Prints, Sculpture, Textiles, Watercolors, Woodcarvings
Collections: Permanent coll of over 1,000 works of art predominantly created by Contemporary Southeastern Artists
Exhibitions: 15 exhibs per yr
Publications: weekly & monthly electronic newsletters; 1 catalog per yr
Activities: Classes for adults & children; docent training; community exhibs & collaborations; lect open to pub, gallery talks; tours; schols; Colors-a free afterschool art studio for at-risk youth-Mon-Thurs 3-6pm

M **UNIVERSITY OF SOUTH CAROLINA AT SPARTANBURG,** Art Gallery, 800 University Way, Division of Fine Arts, Languages & Literature Spartanburg, SC 29303-4932. Tel 864-503-5689; Fax 864-503-5835; *Dir Gallery* Jane Nodine
Open daily 10 AM - 4 PM; No admis fee; Estab 1982, primarily as a teaching gallery. Contemporary art displayed; 800 sq ft of carpeted wall space with windows along one wall, located across from Performing Art Center
Income: $1200 (financed by Student Affairs Office of University)
Exhibitions: Annual Student Art Exhib; Exhibs of Regional Artists
Publications: Exhibition announcements
Activities: Lect open to pub, 4-6 vis lectrs per yr; competitions; book traveling exhibs 5 per yr; originate traveling exhibs 1 per yr

M **WOFFORD COLLEGE,** Sandor Teszler Library Gallery, 429 N Church St, Spartanburg, SC 29303-3663. Tel 864-597-4300; Fax 864-597-4329; Web: www.wofford.edu; *Dir* Oakley H Coburn
Open during school yr Mon-Thurs 8 AM - 12 AM, Fri 8 AM - 7 PM, Sat 10 AM - 5 PM, Sun 1 PM - 12 AM; Estab 1969 to support educ & cultural activities of the col; Gallery located within col library; Average Annual Attendance: 100,000
Collections: Hungarian Impressionist
Exhibitions: Various exhib
Activities: Book traveling exhibs, 1-2 per yr

SUMTER

M **SUMTER GALLERY OF ART,** 200 Hasel St, Sumter, SC 29150-4506; PO Box 1316, Sumter, SC 29151-1316. Tel 803-775-0543; Fax 803-778-2787; Email director@sumtergallery.org; Web: www.sumtergallery.org; *Exec Dir* Karen Watson; *Asst Dir & Cur* Frank McCauley; *Art Educ Dir* Amanda Cox
Open Tues - Fri 11 AM - 5 PM, Sat 1:30 - 5 PM, cl Easter, Thanksgiving, Christmas & month of July; No admis fee; Estab 1970 to bring to area exhibits of works of recognized artists, to provide an outlet for local artists for showing & sale of their work & to serve as a facility where visual art may become a part of life & educ of the people, particularly children of this community; The Gallery is the 1850 home of the late Miss Elizabeth White, well-known artist of Sumter, which was deeded to the gallery in 1977 under the terms of her will. Presently using hall, four downstairs rooms, back studio & rooms upstairs; Average Annual Attendance: 8,500; Mem: 460; dues commercial patron & patron $100, family $40, individual $25; annual meeting in May
Income: $100,000 (financed by mem, earned income, exhibit sponsors, donations, County Council)
Collections: 62 paintings, etchings & drawings of Elizabeth White given to the gallery by trustees of her estate
Exhibitions: Annual Young People's Exhibit; Individual & group exhibits of paintings, sculpture, collages, photography & crafts by recognized artists primarily from Southeast; Touchable exhibit for the blind & visually impaired; Sumter Artist Guild Exhibit; Annual Sumter Teacher Exhibit
Publications: Newsletter, 2 times per year
Activities: Classes & workshops for adults & children; docent training; lect open to pub; competitions, awards given; gallery talks; tours; schols; gallery gift shop primarily sells works by South Carolinian artists. Also on sale art to wear including jewelry; reproductions; prints

WALTERBORO

M **SOUTH CAROLINA ARTISANS CENTER,** 318 Wichman St, Walterboro, SC 29488-2921. Tel 843-549-0011; Fax 843-549-7433; Email artisan@lowcountry.com; Email info@scartisanscenter.com; Web: www.scartisanscenter.com
Open Mon - Sat 10 AM - 6 PM, Sun 1 - 6 PM; No admis fee; Estab 1994 to provide a showcase & market for the handcrafted work of the state's leading artisans; Housed in restored nine-room Victorian cottage; 2800 sq ft retail facility; Average Annual Attendance: 26,000
Special Subjects: Afro-American Art, American Indian Art, Bookplates & Bindings, Carpets & Rugs, Ceramics, Collages, Crafts, Decorative Arts, Dolls, Drawings, Folk Art, Furniture, Glass, Jewelry, Leather, Metalwork, Painting-American, Pewter, Photography, Porcelain, Pottery, Prints, Reproductions, Sculpture, Stained Glass, Textiles, Watercolors, Woodcarvings, Woodcuts
Exhibitions: Sweetgrass Baskets; Live demonstrations (3rd Sat. every month); Mary Whyte author/artist - Life of Alfreda
Publications: Hands On, newsletter monthly
Activities: Classes for adults & children; demonstrations; workshops; classes for artists; summer art camp; lects open to pub; 4 vis lectrs per yr; tours; sponsoring of competitions; schols; Made in SC: standardized curriculum; rural SC communities; sales shop sells books, original art & original crafts; magazines; reproductions; prints; SC food products

SOUTH DAKOTA

ABERDEEN

M **DACOTAH PRAIRIE MUSEUM,** Lamont Art Gallery, 21 S Main St, Aberdeen, SD 57402-4218. Tel 605-626-7117; Fax 605-626-4026; Email dpm@brown.sd.us; Web: www.dacotahprairiemuseum.com; *Cur Educ* Sherri Rawstern; *Cur Exhib* Lora Schaunam; *Dir* Sue Gates; *VPres* Kim Lien
Open Tues - Fri 9 AM - 5 PM, Sat & Sun 1 - 4 PM; No admis fee; Estab 1969 to preserve the heritage of the peoples of the Dakotas; Average Annual Attendance: 60,000; Mem: 300 foundation mems
Income: Financed by county funds
Special Subjects: American Indian Art, Historical Material
Collections: Sioux & Arikara Indian artifacts, local & regional artists, photography
Publications: Annual Report; Dacotah Prairie Times, 3 per yr
Activities: Classes for adults & children; gallery talks; tours; individual paintings & original objects of art lent to museums, art centers & some materials to schools; book traveling exhibs 12 per yr; mus shop sells books, magazines, prints, original art & reproductions

L **Ruth Bunker Memorial Library**, 21 S Main St, Aberdeen, SD 57401-4218. Tel 605-626-7117; Fax 605-626-4026; Web: www.brown.sd.us/museum; *Cur Coll* Michele Porter; *Dir* Sue Gates
Open Tues - Fri 9 AM - 5 PM, Sat & Sun 1 - 4 PM, cl national holidays; Estab 1980 to store books, archives, maps, blueprints, etc; Circ Non-circulating; Reference for staff & academia only
Income: Financed by county funds
Library Holdings: Audio Tapes, Book Volumes 2800, Clipping Files, Exhibition Catalogs, Manuscripts, Original Art Works, Pamphlets, Photographs, Prints, Reproductions, Sculpture, Slides
Activities: Special classes; lect open to pub; gallery talks; tours; book traveling exhibs; originate traveling exhibs in midwest

M **NORTHERN STATE UNIVERSITY,** Northern Galleries, 1200 S Jay St, Aberdeen, SD 57401-7198. Tel 605-626-7766; Fax 605-626-2263; Email

hoarw@northern.edu; Web: www.northern.edu/galleries; *Dir Gallery* Rebecca Mulvaney
Open 8 AM - 5 PM; No admis fee; Estab 1902 to support Univ program; Four galleries: Lincoln professional secure setting, Union - student area, two hallway locations; Average Annual Attendance: 3,000
Income: $6,000 (financed by state appropriation)
Collections: Drawings, painting, photography, prints, sculpture
Exhibitions: Rotating exhibits
Activities: Educ dept; lect open to pub, 3 vis lectrs per yr; gallery talks; tours; competitions with prizes; individual paintings & original objects of art lent to regional locations; lending coll contains framed reproductions, original prints, paintings, photographs; book traveling exhibs 2 per yr

M **WEIN GALLERY,** Presentation College, 1500 N Main St Aberdeen, SD 57401-1280. Tel 605-229-8577; Fax 605-229-8518; Email brad.tennant@presentation.edu; Web: www.presentation.edu/weingallery; *Dir* Brad Tennant
Open Mon - Fri 8 AM - 8 PM, Sat 1 PM - 7 PM; No admis fee; Estab 1971
Collections: Artwork by local artists.

BROOKINGS

M **SOUTH DAKOTA STATE UNIVERSITY,** South Dakota Art Museum, 936 Medary Ave at Harvey Dunn St, Brookings, SD 57007-0999; PO Box 2250, Brookings, SD 57007. Tel 605-688-5423; 866-805-7590; Fax 605-688-4445; Email sdsu.sdam@sdstate.edu; Web: www.southdakotaartmuseum.com; *Cur Coll* Lisa Scholten; *Cur Exhibs* Jodi Lundgren; *Dir* Lynn Verschoor; *Marketing & Develop* Stacy Aesoph; *Store Mgr* Pam Adler
Open Mon - Fri 10 AM - 5 PM, Sat 10 AM - 4 PM, Sun Noon - 4 PM; No admis fee; Estab 1970 as the state center for visual arts with various programs; The facility was designed by Howard Parezo, AIA, Sioux Falls, & occupies 112 x 90 ft site. There are seven galleries & a 147-seat auditorium; Average Annual Attendance: 150,000; Mem: 850, dues $30
Income: Financed by state appropriation, endowment, gifts & grants
Special Subjects: Afro-American Art, American Indian Art, American Western Art, Art Education, Carpets & Rugs, Ceramics, Decorative Arts, Drawings, Embroidery, Eskimo Art, Folk Art, Furniture, Glass, Graphics, Historical Material, Jewelry, Landscapes, Mixed Media, Mosaics, Painting-American, Photography, Porcelain, Portraits, Posters, Pottery, Pottery, Prints, Reproductions, Sculpture, Southwestern Art, Stained Glass, Tapestries, Textiles, Textiles, Watercolors, Woodcarvings, Woodcuts
Collections: American Art, Harvey Dunn Paintings, Oscar Howe Paintings, Marghab Linens, Native American Art, Native American Tribal Art
Publications: Exhibition catalogs; newsletter; brochures
Activities: Classes for adults & children; docent training; lect open to pub, 2-4 vis lectrs per yr; gallery talks; tours; individual paintings & original objects of art lent to professionally run museums with excellent facilities; originates traveling exhibs to other art galleries & mus; mus shop sales shop sells books, magazines, original art, reproductions, prints, jewelry, international items, pottery, Native American art, Christmas, textiles, fiber arts, CDs, cards & stationery

L **Hilton M. Briggs Library**, Box 2115, Brookings, SD 57007. Tel 605-688-5106; Fax 605-688-6133; Email kristi.tornquist@sdstate.edu; Web: www.sdstate.edu/hiton-m-briggs-library; *Chief Univ Librn* Kristi Tornquist; *Head of Pub Servs* Jeanne Davidson; *Univ Archivist* Michele Christian; *Library Operations Manager* Emmeline Elliott
Open Mon - Thurs 7:45 AM - Midnight, Fri 7:45 AM - 9 PM, Sat 10 AM- 9 PM, Sun 1 PM - Midnight; Open to the pub for lending through the main library; Average Annual Attendance: 265,000
Income: Financed by state appropriation, endowment, gifts & grants
Library Holdings: Book Volumes 4,500, Exhibition Catalogs, Original Art Works, Photographs, Slides, Video Tapes
Special Subjects: Advertising Design, Aesthetics, American Indian Art, Architecture, Art Education, Art History, Decorative Arts, Fashion Arts, Film, Furniture, Graphic Arts, Graphic Design, Interior Design, Landscape Architecture, Landscapes, Maps, Painting-American, Painting-Flemish, Painting-French, Pottery, Sculpture, Stage Design, Textiles, Theatre Arts
Collections: Daschle Career Papers
Publications: Open Prairie (Public Research Access Institutional Repository and Information Exchange - openkrairie.sdstate.edu)

CRAZY HORSE

M **CRAZY HORSE MEMORIAL,** Indian Museum of North America, Native American Educational & Cultural Center & Crazy Horse Memorial Library (Reference), 12151 Ave of the Chiefs, Crazy Horse, SD 57730-8900. Tel 605-673-4681; Fax 605-673-2185; Email memorial@crazyhorsememorial.org; Web: www.crazyhorse.org; *CEO & Pres* Ruth Ziolkowski; *Mus Registrar* Janeen Melmer; *Head Librn* Marguerite Cullum
Open 8 AM - dark; Admis memorial $27 per car, $10 per person, under 6 free, mus & center free; Memorial estab 1947, mus estab 1974, Center estab 1995, for preservation of the culture of the North American Indian; Three wings; Average Annual Attendance: 1,100,000
Income: Financed by Crazy Horse Memorial Foundation
Library Holdings: Auction Catalogs, Audio Tapes, Book Volumes, CD-ROMs, Cassettes, Clipping Files, Framed Reproductions, Memorabilia, Original Art Works, Photographs, Prints, Sculpture
Special Subjects: Painting-American, Sculpture
Collections: North American Indian Artifacts, Mountain Sculpture/Carving Displays, Pioneer memorabilia, Paintings & Sculptures, North American Artifacts, Mountain Sculpture-Carving
Exhibitions: Gift from Mother Earth Art Show (ann, second weekend in June)
Publications: Memorial: Progress; Mus: Indian Museum of North America; Crazy Horse Coloring Book
Activities: Classes for adults; lect open to pub; 2-3 vis lectr; concerts; schols offered; book traveling exhibs; mus shop sells books, prints, original art, reproductions

CUSTER

M **GLORIDALE PARTNERSHIP,** National Museum of Woodcarving, Hwy 16 W, Custer, SD 57730; PO Box 747, Custer, SD 57730-0747. Tel 605-673-4404; Web: www.blackhills.com/woodcarving; *Owner* Dale E Schaffer
Open May - Oct, daily 9 AM -7PM, cl Nov - May; Admis adults $9.99, seniors $9.49, children 5 - 14 $7.99, group rates available; Estab 1972 in order to elevate the art of woodcarving; Average Annual Attendance: 70,000
Income: $250,000 (financed by mus admis)
Purchases: $100,000 for gallery & gift shop
Library Holdings: Cards, DVDs, Framed Reproductions, Original Art Works, Prints, Reproductions, Sculpture, Video Tapes
Special Subjects: American Indian Art, American Western Art, Historical Material, Painting-American, Religious Art, Reproductions, Sculpture, Woodcarvings, Furniture
Collections: Wooden Nickel Theater, 36 scenes by original animator of Disneyland, carving studio
Exhibitions: Area woodcarvers & artists
Activities: Classes for adults; lects open to pub; tours; schols & fels offered; exten dept serves Custer Community School; mus shop sells books, magazines, original art, reproductions, prints & USA made products

FLANDREAU

M **MOODY COUNTY HISTORICAL SOCIETY,** Moody County Museum, 706 E Pipestone Ave, Flandreau, SD 57028-1523. Tel 605-997-3191; Email mchsmus1@vastbb.net; Web: www.moodycountymuseum.com; *Dir* Steve Stunes
Open Tues - Thurs & Sat 9 AM - 2 PM, cl New Year's Eve & Day, Memorial Day, Thanksgiving weekend, Christmas Eve & Day; No admis fee; Estab 1964 to promote understanding of history of Moody County, South Dakota; Jones' one-room school; 1880 depot; 1871 Santee Sioux Riverbend Meeting House, historic first frame building in Flandreau, Moody County; Average Annual Attendance: 1,500; Mem: dues $20
Income: $17,000 (financed by county & city appropriation, donations, memorials & mem)
Library Holdings: Book Volumes, CD-ROMs, DVDs, Maps, Memorabilia, Original Documents, Pamphlets, Photographs, Video Tapes
Special Subjects: Carpets & Rugs, Costumes, Crafts, Dolls, Furniture, Glass, Historical Material, Laces, Landscapes, Leather, Manuscripts, Maps, Period Rooms, Photography, Portraits, Pottery, Religious Art, Textiles, Military Art
Collections: County artifacts, census records on microfilm, newspapers, photographs (available for reproduction), postcards, Indian Artifacts (1890-1927)
Exhibitions: Fourth of July Festival; Christmas Tree Festival-Thanksgiving to New Year
Publications: Trekking thru Trent newsletter, quarterly; Trent Moody County, SD, book; Echoes of Egan, Egan, Moody Co, SD; Annual of the Ages, Flandreau SD 2009 All-School Reunion
Activities: Classes for adults & children; Brown Bag luncheons from Sept - May; lect open to pub, 2 vis lectrs per yr; gallery talks; bus tours; competitions with prizes; contests; sales shop sells note papers; 1896, 1908 & 1915 Plat Books; histories of county communities, prints & collages of Flandreau, SD history

HOT SPRINGS

M **PIONEER HISTORICAL MUSEUM OF SOUTH DAKOTA,** 300 N Chicago, Hot Springs, SD 57747; PO Box 361, Hot Springs, SD 57747. Tel 605-745-5147; Email pioneer@pioneer-museum.com; Web: www.pioneer-museum.com; *Pres* Carol Sides; *Treas* Robert Phares; *Secy* Joan Howard
Open May 15 - Oct 1 Mon - Sat 9 AM - 5 PM; Admis discount to families; Built in 1893 & used as a school until 1961, this historic sandstone bldg now houses a coll which includes 25 exhibit areas showcasing pioneer life in Hot Springs/Fall River County. handicapped-accessible with elevator to 25 exhibit areas; Average Annual Attendance: 3,000; Mem: Dues Lifetime $150; Bus $25 (ann); Family $20 (ann); Individual $15 (ann)
Special Subjects: Dolls, Flasks & Bottles, Folk Art, Furniture, Glass, Historical Material, Maps, Miniatures, Period Rooms, Photography, Portraits, Pottery, Stained Glass, Tapestries, Watercolors
Collections: over 600 historical pieces of original artwork, tapestries, famous prints & photos, authentic 19th century classroom, recreated doctor's office, old washing machines, wood cook stoves, kerosene lamp & many other historical items
Activities: Ann Mem Drive; Pioneer Days & Mus Tour; history conference; mus related books & gift items for sale

LEMMON

M **GRAND RIVER MUSEUM,** 114 10th St W, Lemmon, SD 57638-2202. Tel 605-374-7574, 605-374-3911; Email grmuseum@sdplains.com; Web: www.thegrandrivermuseum.com; *Bd Dir* Edward Schmidt; *Bd Dir* Phyllis Schmidt; *Pres, Bd Dir* Stuart Schmidt; *Bd Dir* Lisa Schmidt; *Bd Dir* John Lopez; *Bd Dir* Kim Petik; *Bd Dir* Jim Petik
Open May - Sep, Mon - Sat 9AM-6PM, Sun Noon - 5PM; Admis by suggested donations; Founded 1998 to establish a forum with topics devoted to culture & paleontology, with an emphasis on the Grand River area. Nonprofit org; Large display of dinosaur fossils & displays of cowboy, ranching & Native Am artifacts from the local area; Average Annual Attendance: 4,500; Mem: Donor levels Bus 250 & over; Sponsor $100; Family $35
Library Holdings: Photographs, Prints
Special Subjects: American Indian Art, Ethnology, Historical Material, Photography, Historical Material

Collections: Dinosaur & fossil room, Native American room, Early ranching room, exhibs on creation science, Homestead Room
Exhibitions: John Lopez Art Show-periodically
Publications: newsletter, quarterly
Activities: School & teacher progs, cultural exchange, community involvement & cooperation with other similar institutions; one vis lectr per yr; tours; sales shop sells books; clothing-memorabilia

MITCHELL

M **MIDDLE BORDER MUSEUM & OSCAR HOWE ART CENTER,** 1300 McGovern Ave, Mitchell, SD 57301-7901; PO Box 1071, Mitchell, SD 57301-7071. Tel 605-996-2122; Fax 605-996-0323; Email history@dakotadiscovery.com; Web: www.dakotadiscovery.com; *Museum Manager* Roderick R Brown
Open Summer: May-Oct 1 Mon-Fri 9-6, Sat 10-4; Winter Oct 1 - Apr 30 Mon-Fri 9-5; No admis fee; Estab 1939 for historical preservation of pioneer & Native American way of life & to promote local and regional artists as well as the Mitchell community; Housed in 4 historic buildings on grounds of Dakota Wesleyan University campus; handicapped accessible; Average Annual Attendance: 4,800; Mem: 300; dues $25 & up
Income: Financed by pvt & pub funds
Special Subjects: American Indian Art, American Western Art, Architecture, Bronzes, Dolls, Embroidery, Etchings & Engravings, Furniture, Glass, Historical Material, Maps, Painting-American, Period Rooms, Photography, Porcelain, Pottery, Prints, Sculpture, Textiles, Watercolors
Collections: Paintings by Sioux artist & South Dakota artist laureate, Oscar Howe, Charles Hargens Western art, Harvey Dunn
Exhibitions: Youth Art Exhibit (March)
Publications: The Case Quarterly - quarterly newsletter
Activities: Classes for adults & children; lects open to pub, 2-4 vis lectrs per yr; gallery talks; tours; awards (Youth Art); concerts; individual paintings & original objects of art lent to other galleries; lending coll contains paintings; book traveling exhibs; mus shop sells books, original art, reproductions, prints, jewelry, pottery Native American crafts & quilts

MOBRIDGE

M **KLEIN MUSEUM,** 1820 W Grand Crossing, Mobridge, SD 57601-1114. Tel 605-845-7243; Email kleinmuseum@westriv.com; Web: www.mobridgekleinmuseum.com; *Cur & Mus Shop Mgr* Diane Kindt; *Pres* Judy Curran; *VPres* Jane Leibel; *Treas* Dr Leonard Linde
Open Mon & Wed - Fri 9 AM - Noon & 1 - 5 PM, Sat & Sun 1 - 4 PM; cl Tues; Admis adults $4, students $3; Estab 1975; Average Annual Attendance: 4,500; Mem: 225; dues bus $45, family $35; ann meeting in Apr
Income: $55,000 (financed by mem & donations)
Special Subjects: American Indian Art, American Western Art, Archaeology, Dolls, Drawings, Embroidery, Glass, Furniture, Jewelry, Period Rooms, Photography, Pottery
Collections: Native American, Pioneer, Native American Artifacts, Arikara Earth Lodge
Exhibitions: Native American Beadwork; Sitting Bull Pictorial Display; Prairie Period Rooms
Activities: Living history school tours; Best Museum in SD, 2013; Sales shop sells books, prints, SD pottery, locally made Native American jewelry & t-shirts

PIERRE

M **SOUTH DAKOTA NATIONAL GUARD MUSEUM,** 301 E Dakota Ave, Pierre, SD 57501-3225. Tel 605-224-9991; Web: ngmuseum.sd.gov; *Dir* Robert L Kusser; *Cur* Seb Axtman
Open Mon - Fri 9 AM - 4 PM; cl weekends & holidays; group tours avail other times by appt; No admis fee, donations accepted; Originated as the 147th Field Artillery Historical Society in 1975; Mus estab 1983 to provide a facility for memorabilia & historical documents pertaining to the SD National Guard. The mus is a repository of historical info for both the Army & Air National Guard; Nonprofit org; ADA accessible; Mem: dues Adjutants Gen Club $500 & up, Charter Life $100, Sustaining Org $1 per mem per yr, Indiv Sustaining $10 per yr
Collections: Historical documents; military equipment; records; relics & memorabilia from Civil War, Spanish American War, WWI & WWII, Korean War, Desert Storm & Bosnian Peace-Keeping Mission, Sherman Tank, Armored Personnel Carrier, 75mm cannon, 105mm Howitzer, anti-aircraft guns, A-7-D Jet

PINE RIDGE

M **HERITAGE CENTER, INC,** 100 Mission Dr, Red Cloud Indian School Pine Ridge, SD 57770-2100. Tel 605-867-8257, 867-5491 (218); Fax 605-867-1291; Email heritagecenter@redcloudschool.org; Web: www.redcloudschool.org/museum; *Pres* Peter J Klink; *VPres* Alvin Tibbitts; *Dir* Peter Strong; *Cur* Mary Bordeaux
Open Winter Mon - Fri 8 AM - 5 PM; Summer Mon - Fri 8 AM - 6 PM, Sat - Sun 8 AM - 5 PM; No admis fee; Estab 1974 to exhibit Indian art & culture; Mus has four changing galleries of American & Canadian Native American art. Mainly paintings & sculpture; Average Annual Attendance: 11,000
Income: Financed by donations & grants
Special Subjects: American Indian Art, Anthropology, Ceramics, Collages, Decorative Arts, Dolls, Drawings, Eskimo Art, Etchings & Engravings, Ethnology, Folk Art, Graphics, Historical Material, Jewelry, Landscapes, Leather, Painting-American, Painting-Canadian, Southwestern Art, Portraits, Pottery, Prints, Sculpture, Silver, Textiles, Watercolors, Woodcarvings
Collections: Native American paintings & prints, Native American sculpture, star quilts & tribal arts
Exhibitions: Selections from permanent collection; Eskimo prints; Northwest coast prints; Annual Red Cloud Indian Art Show

Activities: Docent training; tours; awards; individual paintings & original objects of art are lent to other museums & art centers; book traveling exhibs 4-6 per yr; originate traveling exhibs; mus shop sells books, original art, reproductions & prints

RAPID CITY

M **INDIAN ARTS & CRAFTS BOARD, US DEPT OF THE INTERIOR,** Sioux Indian Museum, 222 New York St, Rapid City, SD 57701-1199. Tel 605-394-2381; Fax 605-348-6182; Web: www.iacb.doi.gov; *Mus Aid* Marshall Burnette; *Interim Cur* Paulette Montileaux
Open 9 AM - 6 PM daily (Memorial Day - Labor Day), Mon - Sat 10 AM - 5 PM, Sun 1 - 5 PM (Labor Day - Memorial Day); Admis adults (18-61) $8, seniors (62+) $6.90, children (11-17) $5.75, children 10 & under free; Estab 1939 to promote the development of contemporary Native American arts & crafts of the United States; Average Annual Attendance: 45,000; Mem: (see www.journeymuseum.org)
Income: Financed by federal appropriation
Special Subjects: American Indian Art, Crafts
Collections: Contemporary Native American arts & crafts of the United States, Historic works by Sioux craftsmen
Exhibitions: Continuing series of one-person exhibitions
Publications: One-person exhibition brochure series, bimonthly
Activities: Lect; tours; sales shop sells original arts & crafts

M **RAPID CITY ARTS COUNCIL,** Dahl Arts Center, 713 Seventh St, Rapid City, SD 57701. Tel 605-394-4101; Fax 605-394-6121; Email contact@thedahl.org; Web: www.thedahl.org; *Cur* Mary Maxon; *Exec Dir* Linda Anderson; *Visual Art Educ* Victoria Ledford; *Community Serv Dir* Barbara Evanson
Open Tues, Wed &- Fri. 10 AM - 6 PM, Thurs 10 AM - 8 PM, Sat & Sun 1 - 5 PM, cl Mon; Admis $2.50; Estab 1974 to promote & nourish creativity through the arts; The art center contains 3 galleries: Cyclorama Gallery, a 200 ft oil mural of American history; Central Gallery, touring & invitational exhibitions; Ruth Brennan Gallery, the main educ gallery; Average Annual Attendance: 60,000; Mem: Ann meeting fourth Mon in July
Income: $4,280,000 (financed by earned income, city appropriation, rentals, grants & contributions)
Special Subjects: Painting-American, Prints, Watercolors
Collections: Grace & Abigail French Collection, oils & watercolors, Hazel Schwentker Collection, watercolors, inks & washes, contemporary original work by regional artists
Activities: Classes for adults & children; dramatic progs; docent training; lect open to pub, 3 lect per yr; concerts; gallery talks; tours; sponsoring of competitions; schols offered; individual paintings & original objects of art lent; originate traveling exhibs to museums, galleries, colleges & art centers

SIOUX FALLS

M **AUGUSTANA UNIVERSITY,** (Augustana College) Eide-Dalrymple Gallery, 30th St & Grange Ave, Center for Visual Arts, Augustana College Sioux Falls, SD 57197; Eide-Dalrymple Gallery, 2120 S Grange Ave Sioux Falls, SD 57197. Tel 605-274-4609; Email lindsay.twa@augie.edu; Web: www.augie.edu/eidedalrymple-gallery; *Dir* Lindsay Twa PhD; *Gallery Coordr* John Peters
Open Mon - Fri 10 AM - 5 PM, Sat 1 - 4 PM; No admis fee; Estab 1960 to serve as active force in art educ by presenting art within a cross-cultural perspective; Located on campus, featuring changing exhibits of works by professional artists in the region as well as occasional ethnographic shows, houses permanent coll of signed original prints
Income: Financed by College appropriation & gifts
Purchases: Japanese woodcuts, European signed prints, New Guinea masks & objects
Special Subjects: Archaeology, Drawings, Etchings & Engravings, Primitive art, Prints, Painting-American
Collections: Ethnographic & primitive art, original prints of European & American artists, Andy Warhol photographs
Exhibitions: Monthly changing exhibitions of contemporary, ethnographic, student art
Activities: Art & mus classes; lects open to pub, 6 vis lectrs per yr; concerts; gallery talks; tours; sponsoring of competitions; scholarships; mus shop sells original art

A **AUGUSTANA UNIVERSITY,** (Augustana College) Center for Western Studies, 2121 S Summit Ave, Sioux Falls, SD 57197; 2001 S. Summit Ave, Sioux Falls, SD 57197. Tel 605-274-4007; Fax 605-274-4999; Email cws@augie.edu; Web: augie.edu/center-for-western-studies; *Exec Dir* Harry F Thompson, PhD; *Colls Asst* Liz Cisar; *Educ Asst* Kristi Thomas; *Office Coordr* Kari Mahowald
Open Mon - Fri 8 AM - 5 PM; 1st Sat 10 AM - 2 PM; No admis fee; Estab 1970 for coll & preservation of historic & cultural material for understanding of Northern Plains region; Artists of the Plains Gallery, original oils, watercolors, bronzes & prints by regional artists
Income: Financed by endowment, mem, gifts, grants & book sales
Purchases: Four Feathers by Richard Red Owl
Library Holdings: Audio Tapes, Book Volumes, CD-ROMs, Cassettes, Compact Disks, DVDs, Exhibition Catalogs, Manuscripts, Maps, Memorabilia, Original Art Works, Original Documents, Periodical Subscriptions, Photographs, Prints, Sculpture, Slides, Video Tapes
Special Subjects: American Indian Art, American Western Art, Manuscripts, Photography
Collections: South Dakota & Northern Plains Art, historical manuscripts, photos, art by regional artists, Blue Cloud Abbey
Exhibitions: 3-4 exhibits per year featuring South Dakota & Northern Plains Artists
Publications: An Illustrated History of the Arts in South Dakota; Poems & Essays of Herbert Krause; Lewis & Clark Then and Now: A New South Dakota History; A Harvest of Words: Contemporary South Dakota Poetry; Little Business on the Prairie

Activities: Boe Forum on Public Affairs; lect open to pub, Dakota Conference on the Northern Plains; gallery talks; tours; competitions with awards; individual paintings & original objects of art lent to other offices on campus; book traveling exhibs 1-2 per yr; mus shop sells books, original art, prints, reproductions

M **WASHINGTON PAVILION OF ARTS & SCIENCE,** Visual Arts Center, 301 S Main Ave, Sioux Falls, SD 57106. Tel 605-367-6000; Email info@washingtonpavilion.org; Web: www.washingtonpavilion.org; *Pres & CEO* Darrin Smith; *COO* John Seitz; *CFO* Jane Hathaway; *Community Learning Center Dir* Rose Ann Holland; *Visual Arts Center Dir* Jason Folkerts; *Husby Performing Arts Center Dir* Regina Ruhberg; *Dir Patron Svcs* Nick Suridis; *Dir Mktg & Pub Rels* Rebecca Sevening; *Dir Develop* Ann Parker
Visit website for hours; Admis adults $7, seniors $5, mems, youth 3-17, students with student ID, active military, 1st Fri 5 PM - 8 PM & mems free; Estab 1961 as a contemporary mus; Seven galleries
Income: Financed by state appropriations, mem, gifts, contributions
Collections: Historical & contemporary interest, monthly 2-D work, National Printmakers collection
Activities: Classes for adults & children; docent training; lect open to pub, receptions; concerts; gallery talks; tours; individual paintings & original art lent; mus shop sells books, magazines, original art, prints, reproductions, pottery, cards & craft pieces; children's studio on site

L **Library**, 301 S Main Ave, Sioux Falls, SD 57104. Tel 605-367-7397; Web: www.washingtonpavilion.org
Call for hours; Open to mems only
Income: Financed by state appropriations, mem, gifts, contributions
Library Holdings: Book Volumes 320
Publications: Art News

SPEARFISH

M **BLACK HILLS STATE UNIVERSITY,** Ruddell Gallery, Student Union, Fl 2, Spearfish, SD 57799-0002; 1200 University St, Unit 9573, Spearfish, SD 57799. Tel 605-642-6275; Fax 605-642-6105; Email ann.porter@bhsu.edu; Web: www.bhsu.edu; *Prof* Ann Porter; *Asst Prof* Desy Schoenweis
Open Mon - Thurs 7 AM - 10 PM, Fri 7 AM - 6 PM, Sat noon - 5 PM, Sun 2 PM - 10 PM; Estab 1936 to encourage art expression & greater appreciation in the Black Hills area. Work of the art center is promoted jointly by Black Hills State College Art Department & the Student Union; Average Annual Attendance: 2,000; Mem: 500; dues $5 & up
Exhibitions: Photography, regional & vis artists
Activities: Lect open to pub, 3 vis lectrs per yr; competitions with awards; individual paintings & original objects of art lent to other colleges & universities; sales shop sells original art

L **Library**, 1200 University, Spearfish, SD 57799. Tel 605-642-6833; Fax 605-642-6105; *Dir Library* Edmund Erickson
Open Mon - Thurs 7:30 AM - 11:30 PM, Fri 7:30 AM - 5 PM, Sat 10 AM - 5 PM, Sun 2 PM - 11 PM
Library Holdings: Book Volumes 300, Motion Pictures, Reproductions
Collections: Carnegie gift library containing 1000 prints and 150 books

VERMILLION

M **UNIVERSITY OF SOUTH DAKOTA,** University Art Galleries, W M Lee Ctr for the Fine Arts, Vermillion, SD 57069; 414 E Clark St, Vermillion, SD 57069-2390. Tel 605-677-3177; Email alison.erazmus@usd.edu; Web: www.edu/fine-arts/university-art-galleries/index.cfm; *Dir* Alison Erazmus
Open Mon - Fri 8 AM - 5 PM; No admis fee; Estab 1976. Primary mission is educational, serving specifically the needs of the col & augmenting the university curriculum as a whole; There are three galleries. The John A. Day Gallery has rotating contemporary art exhibs, retrospectives, & student art exhibs. 50' x 50' located in the Fine Arts Center. The second houses the university collection of works by Oscar Howe, a Native American painter. This facility is approx 30' x 20'. The third is a small changing gallery approx 18' x 20'; Average Annual Attendance: 15,000
Income: $110,000 (financed by state appropriation & student fee allotment)
Purchases: $5,000
Special Subjects: American Indian Art
Collections: 60 Works by Oscar Howe, variety of media by contemporary artists, Northern Plains Native American Fine Arts, faculty & student colls, African masks & sculptures, German Expressionist
Exhibitions: Varied by year
Publications: Catalogues for major exhibs
Activities: Educ prog; docent training; lect open to pub; 2 lectrs per year; exten dept serves 300 miles in general region; individual paintings & original objects of art lent to professional museums & galleries; book traveling exhibs 2 per yr; organize traveling exhibs to regional art mus focusing on Regionalist & Native American Art; mus shop sells reproductions, prints, Oscar Howe

WALL

M **WOUNDED KNEE MUSEUM,** 217 10th Ave, Wall, SD 57790. Tel 605-279-2573 (Seasonal), 970-226-3218 (Admin office); Email info@woundedkneemuseum.org; Web: www.woundedkneemuseum.org
Open seasonally to Oct 12: daily 8:30 AM - 5:30 PM; call for extended hours; Admis adults $5, seniors 60 & over $4, children under 12 no admis fee; tour groups please call or email for more info; Mus tells the story of a small band of Lakota families who became the focus of the last major military operation of the US Army in its centuries-long effort to subdue the Native American tribes. Handicapped-accessible
Special Subjects: Historical Material, American Indian Art, Photography
Collections: Exhibs & photos surrounding the Wounded Knee Massacre, trading post
Exhibitions: Smothering the Seven Fires; Wovoka's Ghost Dance; Words That Killed; Big Foot's Trail; The Adaptable Lakota; Treaty of 1868
Publications: A Sioux Chronicle, by George E Hyde; The Ghost Dance Religion and the Sioux Outbreak of 1890, by James Mooney; Bury My Heart at Wounded Knee, by Dee Brown; Lost Bird of Wounded Knee, by Renee Samsom Flood
Activities: Group tours & self-guided tours; educ progs; memorial movie on the Lakota people; books & mus related items for sale

YANKTON

M **BEDE ART GALLERY,** Mount Mary College, Art Office, 1105 W 8th St Yankton, SD 57078-3725. Tel 605-668-1574; Email dkahle@mtmc.edu; Web: www.mtmc.edu; *Dir* David Kahle
Open Mon - Fri 8 AM - 8 PM; No admis fee
Collections: Student artwork

M **YANKTON COUNTY HISTORICAL SOCIETY,** Dakota Territorial Museum, 610 Summit St, Yankton, SD 57078-3858. Tel 605-665-3898; Web: dakotaterritorialmuseum.org; *Dir & Cur* Crystal Nelson; *Pres* Joan Neubauer
Open Mon - Fri 10 AM - 5 PM; Sun Noon - 4 PM (May - Sep 30); Mon - Sun noon - 4 PM (Oct - Apr 30); No admis fee; Estab 1961 as an historical museum; Average Annual Attendance: 6,000; Mem: 250; dues vary; annual meeting in Oct
Income: $20,000 (financed by city & county appropriation)
Special Subjects: Dolls, Furniture, Historical Material
Collections: Paintings by Louis Janousek, sculptures by Frank Yaggie, historic photographs
Exhibitions: Rotating
Activities: Educ progs; riverboats; roads; & rails in June; lects open to pub; free monthly brown bag; gift shop sells books, reproductions, prints, jewelry, kids items & t-shirts

TENNESSEE

CHATTANOOGA

L **CHATTANOOGA-HAMILTON COUNTY BICENTENNIAL LIBRARY,** Fine Arts Dept, 1001 Broad St, Chattanooga, TN 37402-2620. Tel 423-757-5310; Email library@lib.chattanooga.gov; Web: www.lib.chattanooga.gov/finearts.html; *Head of Dept* Barry Bradford
Open Mon - Thurs 9 AM - 9 PM, Fri - Sat 9 AM - 6 PM, Sept - May; No admis fee; Estab 1888, dept estab 1976
Income: Financed by city, county & state appropriation
Library Holdings: Audio Tapes, Cassettes, Clipping Files, DVDs, Motion Pictures, Periodical Subscriptions 63, Video Tapes
Special Subjects: Art History, Film, Furniture, Historical Material, Painting-American, Painting-British, Pre-Columbian Art
Collections: Collection of books, cassette tapes, compact discs, music books, phono records, 16mm film & video VHS tapes

M **HOUSTON MUSEUM OF DECORATIVE ARTS,** 201 High St, Chattanooga, TN 37403-1185. Tel 423-267-7176; Email houstonmuseumchattanooga@gmail.com; Web: www.thehoustonmuseum.org; *Mus Exec Dir* Amy Autenreith
Open Wed - Sat Noon - 4 PM & 1st Sun of the month; Admis adults $9, students $5, children 4-17 $3.50; discount to AAA members; Estab 1961, incorporated 1949; Average Annual Attendance: 20,000; Mem: 500; dues $50-$1,000; ann meeting in May
Income: Financed by mem dues, foundation cook book sales, profits from antiques show, parking lot & admis fees, gift shop profits, individual & corporate donations
Special Subjects: Decorative Arts, Dolls, Furniture, Glass, Illustration
Collections: Coverlet coll, Early American furniture, rare coll of pressed glass (5,000 pitchers, 600 patterns of pressed glass, all types of art glass, steins & Tiffany glass), ceramics, dolls, porcelains, music boxes; Indian artifacts
Publications: Always Paddle Your Own Canoe: The Life, Legend & Legacy of Ann Safley Houston; Fabulous Houston; Houston Museum of Decorative Arts Coverlet Collection
Activities: Classes for children; docent training; classes for adults; lect open to pub, 3 - 4 vis lectrs per yr; tours; lend original objects of art to Hunter Mus, Chattanooga; mus shop sells books, reproductions, prints, decorative art objects & items reflective of pieces in permanent coll

M **HUNTER MUSEUM OF AMERICAN ART,** 10 Bluff View, Chattanooga, TN 37403-1197. Tel 423-267-0968; Fax 423-267-9844; Web: www.huntermuseum.org; *Mem & Donor Coordr* Alyson Haughland; *Dir Mktg & Communs* Cara McGowan; *Cur Educ* Adera Causey; *Chief Cur* Nandini Makrandi; *Exec Dir* Virginia Anne Sharber
Open Mon - Tues & Fri - Sat 10 AM - 5 PM, Wed & Sun noon - 5 PM, Thurs 10 AM - 8 PM; Admis adults $15, mems & children 17 & under free; Estab 1952 to present a visual arts program of high quality, maintain a fine coll of American art & to carry out a vigorous educational program in the community & the schools; The permanent coll of American art is housed in the George Thomas Hunter Mansion constructed in 1904, an addition was opened in 1975, and a second addition was opened in 2005; designed by Randall Stout; Average Annual Attendance: 65,000; Mem: 1800; dues individual $50, sponsor $250, patron $500; Chairman's Circle Member $1,000,
Library Holdings: Cards, Cassettes, Clipping Files, Memorabilia, Original Documents, Pamphlets, Periodical Subscriptions, Photographs
Special Subjects: Glass, Painting-American, Photography, Portraits, Posters, Pottery, Prints, Sculpture, Silver, Stained Glass, Tapestries, Textiles, Watercolors, Woodcarvings
Collections: American paintings, later 18th century to present, including works by Bierstadt, Benton, Burchfield, Cassatt, Durand, Hassam, Henri, Inness, Marsh, Miller, Twachtman, Whistler & others, contemporary works including Beal,

Bechtle, Fish, Frankenthaler, Golub, Goodman, Johns, LeWitt, Park, Pearlstein, Rauschenberg, Schapiro, Stackhouse, Wesselman, Wonner & Youngerman, contemporary American prints, sculpture by Calder, Hunt, Nevelson, Segal, Snelson & others, glass by Chihuly, Littleton, Morris, Zinsky
Publications: Brochures & announcements; bulletin, quarterly; A Catalogue of the American Collection, Hunter Museum of Art, 1985, 300-page illustrated focus on pieces in the permanent collection
Activities: Classes for adults, teens & children; docent training; internships; Designing Innovation prog; community partnerships; student gallery; lect open to pub; gallery talks; concerts; tours; book traveling exhibs 6-8 per yr; originate traveling exhibs which circulate to qualified galleries & art museums; mus shop sells books, reproductions, prints, gift items, jewelry

L **Reference Library**, 10 Bluff View, Chattanooga, TN 37403. Tel 423-267-0968; Fax 423-267-9844; Web: www.huntermuseum.org; *Dir* Virginia Anne Sharber; *Chief Cur* Nandini Makrandi; *Cur Educ* Adera Causey; *Assoc Cur* Miranda Hofelt; *Asst Cur Educ* Rachel White
Open daily; Admis fee; Estab 1958 as reference source for staff only; Circ Non-circulating; Average Annual Attendance: 60,000; Mem: 2,500
Library Holdings: Book Volumes 1500, Cards, Cassettes, Clipping Files, Exhibition Catalogs, Memorabilia, Motion Pictures, Original Art Works, Pamphlets, Periodical Subscriptions 8, Photographs, Prints, Sculpture, Slides
Special Subjects: Afro-American Art, American Western Art, Architecture, Art History, Decorative Arts, Drawings, Etchings & Engravings, Furniture, Glass, Painting-American, Photography, Portraits, Prints, Sculpture, Silver, Stained Glass, Watercolors, Woodcuts
Collections: American Art 1735 - present
Activities: Classes for adults & children; docent training; lects open to pub; 4-6 vis lectrs per yr; concerts; gallery talks; tours; lending of original objects of art to other accredited mus; 2-3 book traveling exhibs; organize traveling exhibs to other accredited mus; mus shop sells books

M **SWINE GALLERY,** 100 W Main St, Chattanooga, TN 37408. Tel 423-521-1716; Web: thecinerama.org; *Cur* Matthew Dutton; *Cur* Aaron Cowan; *Cur* Adam Kirby
Open during exhibits; Estab to expand the public's appreciation for artistic innovation in Chattanooga
Collections: paintings; sculpture

M **UNIVERSITY OF TENNESSEE AT CHATTANOOGA,** Cress Gallery of Art, Fine Arts Ctr, 752 Vine St Chattanooga, TN 37043; 615 McCallie Ave, Dept of Art # 1301 Chattanooga, TN 37403-2504. Tel 423-304-9789; Fax 423-425-2101; Email ruth-grover@utc.edu; Web: www.cressgallery.org; *Dir & Cur* Ruth Grover
Open Mon - Fri 9:30 AM - 7:30 PM, Sat & Sun 1 - 4 PM; No admis fee; Estab 1980 as an academic gallery serving the art department, campus & community; 2-room gallery, main 116+ running ft, auxiliary 54 running ft; Average Annual Attendance: 8,000
Income: School funding, grants and gifts
Library Holdings: Exhibition Catalogs, Kodachrome Transparencies, Lantern Slides, Original Art Works, Other Holdings teaching collection with Western art & archit, Prints, Sculpture, Slides, Video Tapes
Collections: Graphics, paintings, sculpture, photographs
Exhibitions: 6 - 7 temporary exhibitions per year
Activities: Diane Marek vis artist series in association with exhibs; lects open to pub; 4 vis lectrs per yr; gallery talks; tours on request; individual paintings & original objects of art lent to various campus areas; lending coll contains original prints & paintings; temporary and traveling exhibs

CLARKSVILLE

M **AUSTIN PEAY STATE UNIVERSITY,** Margaret Fort Trahern Gallery, Trahern Bldg, College & 8th St Clarksville, TN 37044; PO Box 4677 Clarksville, TN 37044. Tel 931-221-6519; Fax 931-221-7432; Email holteb@apsu02.edu; Web: www.apsu.edu/art/gallery/trahern.html; *Dir* Michael Dickins
Open Mon - Fri 9 AM - 4 PM; No admis fee; Estab 1962 as a univ community service to exhibit a variety of visual media; Average Annual Attendance: 8,000
Income: Financed by univ appropriations
Exhibitions: Average 6-8 per yr
Publications: Announcements of shows & artist biographies
Activities: Lect open to pub, 6-8 vis lectrs per yr; gallery talks; tours; competitions with awards; schols offered

L **Art Dept Library**, 601 College St, Dept of Art Austin Peay State University Clarksville, TN 37044. Tel 931-221-7333; Web: www.apsu.edu; *Dean College Arts & Letters* Dixie Webb; *Gallery Dir* Warren Greene
Collections: Larson Drawing Collection

M **Mabel Larsen Fine Arts Gallery**, PO Box 4677, Clarksville, TN 37044-0001. Tel 931-221-7334; Fax 931-221-7432; Email holteb@apsuoz.edu; *Dir* Bettye S Holte
Open Mon - Fri 8 AM - 4 PM, cl holidays; No admis fee; Estab 1994 to house Austin Peay State Univ permanent art colls; Average Annual Attendance: 5,000
Income: Financed by state funds
Library Holdings: Original Art Works
Collections: Larson Drawing Collection, Hazel Smith Collection, Center of Excellence Student Collection
Exhibitions: Changing exhibits of the University permanent collection
Activities: Gallery talks; competitions

COOKEVILLE

A **CUMBERLAND ART SOCIETY INC,** Cookeville Art Gallery, 186A S Walnut, Cookeville, TN 38501. Tel 931-526-2424; Email cumberlandartsociety@yahoo.com; Web: cumberlandartsociety.com; *Past Pres* Adele Seitzinger; *1st Vice Pres* Chuck Becker; *2nd Vice Pres* Colleen Hughes; *Treas* Rose Dahms; *Sec* Bonnie Masters; *Pres* Gail Cicutto
Open Mon - Fri 12-4 PM & Sun 1 - 4 PM; No admis fee; Estab 1961 to promote arts in the community & area; A new building with adequate gallery & studio space. The gallery is carpeted & walls are finished with wallscape & track lighting; Average Annual Attendance: 3,000; Mem: 125; dues $35, renewal $35; meeting quarterly
Income: Financed by mem, city & state appropriations
Exhibitions: Changing exhibits, monthly
Activities: Classes for children & adults; art educ for elementary school age children; lect open to pub, 6 vis lectrs per yr; gallery talks; tours; competitions with awards

HENDERSONVILLE

A **HENDERSONVILLE ARTS COUNCIL,** Monthaven Mansion, 1154 W Main St, Hendersonville, TN 37077-2823; PO Box 64, Hendersonville, TN 37077-2823. Tel 615-822-0789; Email artscouncil@monthaven.org; Web: www.hendersonvillearts.org; *Interim Exec Dir* Jerry Tachora
Open 9 AM - 3 PM; No admis fee; Estab 1975 to promote & educate through the arts; Galleries are located in 200 yr old home; Average Annual Attendance: 10,000
Income: non-profit, funding through grants/fundraisers
Exhibitions: Monthly changing exhibits
Publications: News d'Art, quarterly
Activities: Classes for adults & children; dramatic progs; concerts; gallery talks; gift shop sells local crafts & prints

JOHNSON CITY

M **EAST TENNESSEE STATE UNIVERSITY,** The Reece Museum, 363 Stout Dr, Johnson City, TN 37614. Tel 423-439-4392; Fax 423-439-4283; Email sandersr@etsu.edu; Web: www.etsu.edu/reece; *Dir* Randy Sanders
Open Mon - Fri 9 AM - 4:30 PM, cl major holidays; Admis suggested donation $5; Estab 1965 to enhance the cultural & educational advantages of the University & the people of upper East Tennessee; 3 galleries host rotating exhibs & events; Average Annual Attendance: 7,089
Income: Financed through the state of TN
Special Subjects: Drawings, Etchings & Engravings, Furniture, Woodcarvings, Woodcuts
Collections: Southern Appalachian Art, historical Appalachian artifacts from frontier settlement to present day, pre-historic and archaeological artifacts, East Tennessee politics, Appalachian music and crafts, East Tennessee State University coll, paintings and prints by national and international artists
Exhibitions: Rotating exhibs
Publications: CRM Calendar; quarterly, gallery guides with exhibs; exhib catalogs
Activities: Lects open to pub; 10 vis lectrs per yr; concerts; progs for student & community; gallery talks; tours; schols

KINGSPORT

A **ARTS COUNCIL OF GREATER KINGSPORT,** Renaissance Center Main Gallery, 1200 E Center St, Kingsport, TN 37660-4958. Tel 423-392-8420; Fax 423-392-8422; Email info@kingsportarts.org; Web: www.kingsportarts.org; *Pres* Bob Lawrence; *Pres Elect* Elaine Barker
Open Mon - Fri 8 AM - 5 PM; No admis fee, charge for special events; Estab 1968 to promote & present all the arts to all the people in area; this includes performing arts, visual arts & classes; One gallery with monthly shows; Average Annual Attendance: 20,000; Mem: 400; dues $20 - $500
Income: Financed by mem & grants
Activities: Classes for adults & children; lect open to pub, 3 vis lectrs per yr; concerts; competitions with awards; schols; originate traveling exhibs through Southern Arts Federation

KNOXVILLE

M **BECK CULTURAL EXCHANGE CENTER, INC,** 1927 Dandridge Ave, Knoxville, TN 37915-1909. Tel 865-524-8461; Fax 865-524-8462; Email beckcenter@beckcenter.net; Web: www.beckcenter.net
Open Tues - Sat 10 AM - 6 PM; No admis fee, donations accepted; Estab 1975 to encourage, collect, preserve & display local, regional, & national Black history; Average Annual Attendance: 35,000; Mem: 1,000; annual meeting in Sept
Income: $90,000 (financed by mem, city, county & state appropriations)
Library Holdings: Audio Tapes, Cassettes, Clipping Files, Compact Disks, Original Art Works, Original Documents, Records, Sculpture, Slides, Video Tapes
Special Subjects: African Art, Afro-American Art, Cartoons
Exhibitions: Federal Judge William H Hastie Room; Library of Books & Recordings; oral histories; weekly newspapers of the local Black experience; Senior Citizens Story Writing Contest
Publications: 200 Year History of Knoxville & 125 Year History of Knoxville College; State of Black Economy in Tennessee
Activities: Classes for adults & children; school & community presentations; docent progs; lects open to pub; competitions with cash awards; traveling slide presentations; mus shop sells books, prints, music & clothing

M **KNOXVILLE MUSEUM OF ART,** 1050 World's Fair Park Dr, Knoxville, TN 37916-1653. Tel 865-525-6101; Fax 865-546-3635; Email info@knoxart.org; Web: www.knoxart.org; *Exec Dir* David Butler; *Cur* Stephen Wicks; *Asst Cur* Clark Gillespie; *Dir Develop* Mary Walker; *Dir Mktg* Angela Thomas; *Dir Finance & Opers* Joyce Jones
Open Tues - Sat 10 AM - 5 PM, Sun 1 PM - 5 PM; No admis fee; Estab 1961 as a nonprofit private corporation. Grand opening was held in 1990. Located on the former World's Fair site downtown; New state-of-the-art 53,000 sq ft facility. Maintains reference library; Average Annual Attendance: 117,000; Mem: 4300; dues $40 - $1000
Income: Financed by mems, contributions, sponsorships, foundations & local, state & federal grants
Purchases: Therman Statom's 'Antartica'; John Wilson's 'Martin Luther King, Jr'; Warrington Colescott's 'Jazz Piano'

Library Holdings: Auction Catalogs, Book Volumes, CD-ROMs, Exhibition Catalogs, Original Documents, Pamphlets, Periodical Subscriptions, Slides, Video Tapes
Special Subjects: Afro-American Art, American Indian Art, American Western Art, Bronzes, Decorative Arts, Drawings, Etchings & Engravings, Folk Art, Hispanic Art, Landscapes, Latin American Art, Medieval Art, Mexican Art, Miniatures, Painting-American, Painting-European, Period Rooms, Photography, Porcelain, Portraits, Prints, Sculpture, Watercolors, Woodcuts
Collections: Modern & contemporary art in all media, Works by artists who worked during & after the 20th century in painting, photography, sculpture & works on paper
Publications: Bi-monthly calendar; exhibition catalogs; newsletter
Activities: Classes for adults & children; docent preparation; artists in the classrooms; school outreach; lects open to pub, 5-8 vis lectrs per yr; concerts; gallery talks; tours; competitions with awards; scholarships & fels offered; exten dept serves 9 county region; lending collection contains books, cassettes, color reproductions & slides; Art2Go: suitcases for classroom use; originate traveling exhibs; mus shop sells books, original art, reproductions, prints, jewelry, accessories (apparel), greeting cards, calendars, toys, t-shirts & art-related gifts; Exploratory Gallery on-site for students & families

M **UNIVERSITY OF TENNESSEE,** McClung Museum of Natural History & Culture, 1327 Circle Park Dr, Knoxville, TN 37996-3200. Tel 865-974-2144; Fax 865-974-3827; Email museum@utk.edu; Web: mcclungmuseum.utk.edu; *Dir* Jefferson Chapman; *Asst Dir, Cur Art & Cultural Colls, Head of Web & Media* Catherine Shteynberg; *Assoc Dir External Relations* Stacy Palado; *Cur Paleoethnobotany* Gary Crites; *Cur Archaeology* Dr Timothy Baumann; *Coordr Academic Progs* Lindsey Wainwright; *Cur Malacology* Gerald Dinkins; *Registrar & Colls Mgr* Adriane Tafoya; *Media Productions Coordr* Lindsay Kromer; *Exhib Preparator & Coordr* Chris Weddig; *Cur Educ* Leslie Chang Jantz; *Asst Mus Educ* Callie Bennett; *Coordr Academic Progs* Lindsey Wainwright; *Mus Shop Mgr* Lecy Campbell
Open Mon - Sat 9 AM - 5 PM, Sun 1 - 5 PM, cl New Year's Day, Easter, Memorial Day, Independence Day, Labor Day, Thanksgiving, Christmas Eve & Day; No admis fee; Estab 1961 to collect, maintain & interpret paintings, works of art, items of natural history & historical objects with emphasis placed on the Tennessee area. A major purpose is to provide research materials for students & faculty of the university; Average Annual Attendance: 63,460; Mem: 520; dues $30-2,500
Income: Financed by state appropriations & private contributions
Library Holdings: Auction Catalogs, Maps, Photographs, Slides
Special Subjects: American Indian Art, Anthropology, Antiquities-Egyptian, Archaeology, Asian Art, Decorative Arts, Etchings & Engravings, Historical Material, Maps, Oriental Art, Porcelain, Pottery, Prints, Photography
Collections: Eleanor Deane Audigier Art Collection, Frederick T Bonham Collection (18th - 20th Century furniture, art objects), Lewis-Kneberg Collection (Tennessee archaeology), Malacology Collection (marine species & fresh water North American mollusks)
Exhibitions: The Decorative Experience; Ancient Egypt: The Eternal Voice; Archaeology & the Native Peoples of Tennessee; Geology and the Fossil History of Tennessee; Human Origins; Battle of Ft Sanders; Freshwater Mussels
Publications: Museum member newsletter; occasional papers
Activities: Classes for children; docent training; lects open to pub, 3-5 vis lectrs per yr; individual paintings & original objects of art lent; book traveling exhibs, 1-3 per yr; mus shop sells books, original art, reproductions & slides

M **Ewing Gallery of Art and Architecture**, 1715 Volunteer Blvd, Knoxville, TN 37996-0001. Tel 865-974-3200; Fax 865-974-3198; Email ewing@utk.edu; Web: www.ewing-gallery.utk.edu; *Dir & Cur* Sam Yates; *Colls Mgr* Sarah McFalls; *Registrar & Exhibs Coordr* Eric Cagley
Open Mon - Wed 10 AM - 5 PM, Thurs 10 AM - 7:30 PM, Fri 10 AM - 5 PM, Sun 1 PM - 4 PM; No admis fee; Estab 1981 to provide quality exhibitions focusing on contemporary art & architecture; Gallery consists of 3,500 sq ft exhibition space; Average Annual Attendance: 6,000
Collections: Contemporary American prints, paintings & drawings, Japanese prints, Joseph Delaney
Activities: Lects open to pub, 12 vis lectrs per yr; gallery talks; tours; sponsor competitions; scholarships offered; lending collection contains individual & original objects of art; originate traveling exhibs

A **Visual Arts Committee**, 305 University Center, Knoxville, TN 37996-4800. Tel 423-974-5455; Fax 423-974-9252; Email vac@utk.edu; Web: www.activities.utk.edu; *Prog Dir* Ashleigh Moyer; *Asst Dir* Philip Smith; *Grad Advisor* Meghan Terry
Open Mon - Fri 7:30 AM - 10:30 PM, Sat 7 AM - 10 PM, Sun 1 - 6 PM; No admis fee; Estab to provide visual arts for the students of the univ & vis artist lectr series; Two major galleries: Gallery Concourse has 300 running ft; Average Annual Attendance: 20,000
Income: Financed by student activities fees
Exhibitions: 8 exhibits per year; student shows
Publications: Visual Arts Comt Ann Catalog
Activities: Lects open to pub; 6 vis lectrs per yr; competitions

MARYVILLE

M **MARYVILLE COLLEGE,** Fine Arts Center Gallery, 502 E Lamar Alexander Pkwy, Maryville, TN 37804-5907. Tel 865-981-8150, 981-8000; Fax 865-273-8873; Email sowders@maryvillecollege.edu; Web: www.maryvillecollege.edu; *Chmn* Mark Hall
Open Mon - Fri during school year 9 AM - 5 PM; No admis fee; Located in fine arts center
Income: School funding
Exhibitions: Monthly rotating exhibitions
Activities: Gallery programs in connection with circulating exhibitions; art movies, four times a year

MC MINNVILLE

M **SOUTHERN MUSEUM & GALLERIES OF PHOTOGRAPHY,** 210 E Main St, Mc Minnville, TN 37111-2508. Tel 931-507-8102; *Southern Standard Staff Reporter* Monty Wanamaker
Open Wed & Fri - Sat 10 AM - 4 PM
Collections: Photographs

MEMPHIS

M **BELZ MUSEUM OF ASIAN & JUDAIC ART,** 119 S Main St, Concourse Level Memphis, TN 38103. Tel 901-523-2787; Fax 901-523-8603; Email info@belzmuseum.org; Web: www.belzmuseum.org; *Dir & Educ Coordr* Belinda D Fish; *Guest Servs Admin* Wesley Morgan Paraham; *Guest Svcs Asst* Victoria Martin
Open Tues - Fri 10 AM - 5:30 PM, Sat - Sun noon - 5 PM; cl New Year's Day, Easter, Independence Day, Thanksgiving, Christmas; Admis adults $6, seniors $5, students $4
Collections: Asian art pertaining to China's Quing Dynasty, including works in jade and ivory; Chinese puppets; historic and literal pieces relating to Judaism

A **CENTER FOR SOUTHERN FOLKLORE,** 119 S. Main St, Peabody Place Trolley Shop Memphis, TN 38103-3647. Tel 901-525-3655; Fax 901-525-3945; Email info@southernfolklore.com; Web: www.southernfolklore.com; *Exec Dir* Judy Peiser
Open Mon - Fri 11 AM - 6 PM, Sat 2 PM - 11 PM, Sun 2 PM - 8 PM; Estab 1972 as a nonprofit organization which archives, documents & presents folk art, culture & music through film, photography, exhibits & lectures; Mem: 800; dues $25
Income: $350,000 (financed by mem, state appropriation & national endowment)
Collections: African - American Quilt, Contemporary Slides - Folk Art & Culture, Folk Art, Historical & Contemporary Photographs
Activities: Classes for adults & children; cultural tourism; lect open to public; lending collection contains 50 paintings & art objects; retail store sells books, magazines & original art

M **THE DIXON GALLERY & GARDENS,** 4339 Park Ave, Memphis, TN 38117-4698. Tel 901-761-5250; Fax 901-682-0943; Email ntrenthem@dixon.org; Web: www.dixon.org; *Dir* Kevin Sharp; *Cur* Julie Pierotti; *Dir Horticulture* Dale Skaggs; *Dir Communs* Chantal Drake; *Dir Devel* Elise Piper; *Registrar* Kristen Kimberling; *Dir Planned Giving* Susan Johnson; *Cur Educ* Margarita Sandino; *Controller* Gail Hopper
Open Tues - Sat 10 AM - 5 PM, Sun 1 PM - 5 PM, 3rd Thurs 10 AM - 8 PM, cl Mon, New Year's Day, July 4, Thanksgiving, Christmas; Admis adults $7, students 18 & older w/ID & seniors $5, children 7-17 yrs $3, mems, children 6 & under free & Sat 10 AM - Noon free;; Estab 1976 as a bequest to the pub from the late Margaret & Hugo Dixon. Their Impressionist Art Collection & their Georgian-style home & gardens, situated on 17 acres of landscaped woodland, serve as the museum's foundation; Two wings added in 1977 & 1986 house the developing permanent collection & accommodate loan exhibitions. Formal & informal gardens, conservatory & greenhouses are located on the site; Average Annual Attendance: 103,294; Mem: dues $45-$25,000
Income: Financed by endowment, contributions, mem, & corporate sponsorships
Library Holdings: Auction Catalogs, Book Volumes, DVDs, Exhibition Catalogs, Kodachrome Transparencies, Original Documents, Photographs, Video Tapes
Special Subjects: Decorative Arts, Painting-American, Painting-British, Painting-French, Pewter, Porcelain, Prints, Watercolors, Ceramics
Collections: French Impressionist painting, Barbizon, Post-Impressionist & related schools, 18th century British paintings, Warda Stevens Stout Collection of 18th century German porcelain, 18th & 19th centuries works by Jaques-Emile Blanche, Pierre Bonnard, Eugene Boudin, Georges Braque, Theodore Earl Butler, A F Cals, Jean-Baptiste Carpeaux, Mary Cassatt, Paul Cezanne, Marc Chagall, William Merritt Chase, John Constable, J B C Corot, Kenyon Cox, Henri-Edmond Cross, Charles Francois Daubigny, Edgar Degas, Raoul Dufy, Julien Dupre, Sir Jacob Epstein, Henri Fantin-Latour, Thomas Gainsborough, Paul Gauguin, Edmond Grandjean, Francesco Guardi, Paul Guigou, Armand Guillaumin, Henri Joseph Harpignies, L G E Isabey, William James, Johan Jongkind, Gaston La Touche, S V E Lepine, Maximilien Luce, Albert Marquet, Paul Mathey, Henri Matisse, Claude Monet, Berthe Morisot, Henriette A Oberteuffer, Ludovic Piette, Camille Pissarro, Maurice Prendergast, Sir Henry Raeburn, J F Raffaelli, Auguste Renoir, Sir Joshua Reynolds, Henri Rowart, John Singer Sargent, Georges Seurat, Paul Signac, Alfred Sisley, Allen Tucker, J M W Turner, Horatio Walker and Richard Wilson, Gardens & Gardening, The Adler Pewter Collection, Jean-Louis Forain Collection, The Charlotte Stuart Hooker Collection of English Ceramics, The Noufflard Collection
Publications: Exhibition catalogs; quarterly newsletter
Activities: Classes for adults; workshops; progs for children; docent training; mobile art educ in Art-to-Grow van; teacher resources; internships; 4 - 6 lects open to pub; concerts; gallery talks; tours; film series; individual paintings & original objects of art lent to mus & galleries; lending collection contains original paintings, prints, sculpture & porcelain, Artmobile; originate 1-3 book traveling exhibs per yr; originate traveling exhibs to mus; mus shop sells art & garden books, prints, jewelry, notecards & garden items

L **Library**, 4339 Park Ave, Memphis, TN 38117. Tel 901-761-5250; Fax 901-682-0943; Email info@dixon.org; Web: www.dixon.org; *Colls & Exhibs Asst* Katie Kizer
Open Tues - Sat 10 AM - 5 PM, Sun 1 - 5 PM; Admis adults $5, seniors $4, students & children free; Circ 3500; Open to members during mus hours, for reference only; Average Annual Attendance: 50,000
Income: $10,000 (financed by mem, corporate & private sponsorship & the Hugo Dixon Foundation)
Library Holdings: Auction Catalogs, Book Volumes, Cards, Clipping Files, DVDs, Exhibition Catalogs, Manuscripts, Pamphlets, Periodical Subscriptions 15, Photographs, Slides, Video Tapes
Special Subjects: Ceramics, Decorative Arts, Painting-French, Pewter
Collections: French and American Art in the 19th and 20th centuries
Activities: Classes for adults & children; dramatic progs; docent training; concerts; gallery talks; exten dept serves school outreach, 18,000 students per yr; originate traveling exhibs; mus shops sells books, reproductions, & prints

C **FIRST HORIZON NATIONAL CORP,** First Tennessee Heritage Collection, 165 Madison Ave, Memphis, TN 38103-2723. Tel 901-523-4291; Fax 901-523-4354; *CEO* Bryan Jordan; *Tours* Lizzy Haymond
Open Mon - Fri 8:30 AM - 6 PM, Sat 9 AM - Noon; Estab 1979 to depict Tennessee's heritage & history through art; Gallery, with over 150 original works, is located in First Tennessee's corporate headquarters; Average Annual Attendance: 5,000
Income: Financed by corporation
Special Subjects: Etchings & Engravings, Painting-American, Prints, Sculpture, Watercolors
Collections: Engravings, etchings, lithographs, murals, paintings, sculpture, watercolors
Exhibitions: Permanent collection
Activities: Educ dept

C **FIRST TENNESSEE BANK,** 165 Madison Ave, Memphis, TN 38103. Tel 901-523-4352 (Communs Dept); Fax 901-523-4354 (Communs Dept); *In Charge Art Coll* Kathy Alexander; *Office Mgr* Nancy Bradfield
Estab to provide community interest in the arts; to aid participating artists; to enhance lobby; Supports local artists & art forms on display that lend an interest to the community
Collections: Paintings by local artists in a variety of media
Activities: Sponsors Wildlife Artist Guy Coheleach

M **MEMPHIS BROOKS MUSEUM OF ART,** 1934 Poplar Ave, Memphis, TN 38104-2765. Tel 901-544-6200; Fax 901-725-4071; Email pr@brooksmuseum.org; Web: www.brooksmuseum.org; *Dir* Dr Emily Ballew Neff
Open Wed 10 AM - 8 PM, Thurs - Fri 10AM - 4 PM, Sat 10 AM - 5 PM, Sun 11 AM - 5PM; Admis adults $7, seniors $6, youth & students $3, children under 6 free; Estab 1912 to exhibit, preserve & elucidate works of art; The original building was opened in 1916 with additions in 1955 and 1973. Maintained by the city of Memphis, Public Service Department; Average Annual Attendance: 125,000; Mem: 3156; dues $35 & up
Income: $1,000,000 (financed by city appropriation & Friend's Foundation)
Special Subjects: Asian Art, Glass, Oriental Art, Painting-American, Painting-Dutch, Painting-Flemish, Painting-Italian, Porcelain, Renaissance Art, Sculpture, Textiles, Painting-British, Painting-French
Collections: American Paintings & Sculpture, 18th-20th centuries, Dutch & Flemish Paintings, 16th-18th centuries: Eastern & Near-Eastern Decorative Arts Collection (Han, Tang & Ching Dynasty), English Paintings, 17th-19th centuries, French Paintings, 16th-19th centuries, International Collection of Paintings & Sculpture, 19th & 20th centuries, Kress Collection of Italian Paintings & Sculptures, 13th-18th centuries, Mid-south Collection of 20th century paintings & sculptures, glass, textile & porcelain collection, Dr Louis Levy Collection of American Prints
Exhibitions: 4 rotating exhibitions per year
Publications: Bimonthly newsletter
Activities: Classes for adults & children; docent training; outreach prog & studio art activities for student groups; lects open to pub, 9 vis lectrs per yr; concerts; gallery talks; tours; competitions; awards; individual paintings & original objects of art lent; book traveling exhibs 7-10 per yr; originate traveling exhibs; mus shop sells books, reproductions, prints, slides, mus replicas, jewelry & regional pottery

L **Library,** 1934 Poplar Ave, Overton Park Memphis, TN 38104-2765. Tel 901-544-6200; Fax 901-725-4071; Email karen.brunsting@brooksmuseum.org; Web: www.brooksmuseum.org; *Librarian* Karen Brunsting; *Executive Director* Emily Ballew Neff
By appointment only; No admis fee; Estab 1912; Circ Reference Only; Reference only; Average Annual Attendance: varies; Mem: Part of museum
Income: financed by city appropriations, memberships
Library Holdings: Book Volumes 6134, Clipping Files 4223, Exhibition Catalogs 2367, Periodical Subscriptions 24
Activities: Docent training; lects open to the public

L **MEMPHIS COLLEGE OF ART,** G Pillow Lewis Memorial Library, 1930 Poplar Ave, Memphis, TN 38104-2764. Tel 901-272-5131; Fax 901-272-5104; Email library@mca.edu; Web: www.mca.edu; *Head Librn* Sylvia Page
Open Mon - Wed 8 AM - 8 PM, Thurs - Fri 8 AM - 5 PM, Sat 11 AM - 4 PM, Sun 3 PM - 7 PM, summer hours Mon - Fri 8 AM - 5 PM; No admis fee; Estab 1936 as an adjunct educational program; The Standing Committee on Exhibitions arranges visiting shows
Library Holdings: Auction Catalogs, Book Volumes 17,000, Clipping Files, Exhibition Catalogs, Periodical Subscriptions 110, Prints, Reproductions, Slides
Special Subjects: Art Education, Art History, Bookplates & Bindings, Calligraphy, Drawings, Graphic Arts, Graphic Design, History of Art & Archaeology, Illustration, Jewelry, Metalwork, Mixed Media, Photography, Pottery, Printmaking
Collections: Jacob Marks Memorial Collection, works by college graduates & faculty, Dennis Sexsmith Visual Resources Collection
Exhibitions: Juried student shows; one & two-person faculty shows; senior exhibition; summer student show; traveling exhibitions
Publications: Exhibition catalogs
Activities: Classes for adults, children, undergraduate & graduate college students; lect; guided tours; films; competitions; book traveling exhibitions

L **MEMPHIS-SHELBY COUNTY PUBLIC LIBRARY & INFORMATION CENTER,** Humanities Department, 3030 Poplar Ave, Memphis, TN 38111-3527. Tel 901-415-2726; Fax 901-323-7206; Email kennon.mccloy@memphista.gov; Web: www.memphislibrary.org; *Dir Libraries* Keenon McCloy
Open Mon - Thurs 9 AM - 9 PM, Fri & Sat 9 AM - 6 PM, Sun 1 - 5 PM; Estab 1895 to serve the reference, informational, cultural & recreational needs of residents of Memphis-Shelby County; Goodwyn Gallery exhibits promising & established local & regional artists of various media
Income: Financed by city appropriation
Library Holdings: Book Volumes 63,000, Cassettes 800, Compact Disks, DVDs, Fiche, Motion Pictures 3000, Periodical Subscriptions 245, Records 35,000, Video Tapes 3000

M **MISSISSIPPI RIVER MUSEUM AT MUD-ISLAND RIVER PARK,** 125 N Front St, Memphis, TN 38103-1713; 22 N Front St, Ste 960 Memphis, TN 38103. Tel 901-576-7241; Fax 901-576-6666; Web: www.mudisland.com; *Gen Mgr* Trey Giuntini; *Mus & Park Opers Mgr* Alisa Bradley
Open Apr 8 - Oct 31 10 AM - 5 PM; cl Mon; No admiss fee; mus package adults $10, seniors $9, youth 5-11 $7, children under 5 free; Estab 1978 to interpret the natural & cultural history of the Mississippi River Valley; Maintains reference library; Average Annual Attendance: 150,000
Income: $350,000 (financed by city appropriation)
Special Subjects: Afro-American Art, American Indian Art, Anthropology, Archaeology, Architecture, Carpets & Rugs, Coins & Medals, Costumes, Dioramas, Folk Art, Furniture, Glass, Graphics, Historical Material, Jewelry, Laces, Manuscripts, Maps, Period Rooms, Pottery
Collections: 2-D & 3-D pieces that interpret the natural & cultural history of the lower Mississippi River
Activities: Classes for children; dramatic prog; docent training; lects open to pub; gallery talks; tours; competitions with prizes; book traveling exhibs 3-5 per yr; originate traveling exhibs; mus shop sells books, magazines, reproductions & prints

M **RHODES COLLEGE,** Clough-Hanson Gallery, 2000 N Parkway, Clough Hall Memphis, TN 38112-1624. Tel 901-843-3442; Fax 901-843-3727; Email parsonsj@rhodes.edu; Web: www.rhodes.edu/content/clough-hanson-gallery; *Gallery Dir* Joel Parsons
Open Tues - Sat 11 AM - 5 PM, cl Sun - Mon; Estab 1970 to exhibit local, regional & national artists & mount student exhibitions; Average Annual Attendance: 2,200
Special Subjects: Textiles, Woodcarvings
Collections: Jessie L Clough Art Memorial for Teaching, Asian & European textiles, Japanese & woodblock prints, 20th Century American Prints
Exhibitions: Changing exhibitions
Publications: Annual exhibit catalog
Activities: Lect open to public; gallery talks; 1 book traveling exhibition per year

M **UNIVERSITY OF MEMPHIS,** Art Museum, 3750 Norriswood, 142 Communication & Fine Arts Bldg Memphis, TN 38152-3200. Tel 901-678-2224; Fax 901-678-5118; Email artmuseum@memphis.edu; Web: www.memphis.edu/amum; *Dir* Leslie L Luebbers, PhD; *Asst Dir* Edmund Warren Perry; *Mus Media Specialist* Jason N Miller; *Admin Asst* Anita Huggins; *Exhib Specialist & Preparator* Neil O'Brien
Open Mon - Sat 9 AM - 5 PM year round except between changing exhibits; closed Univ Holidays; No admis fee; Estab 1981 to sponsor programs & mount temporary exhibitions to expand knowledge about all periods of art with a special emphasis on contemporary art; Mus has 7000 sq ft of exhibition space including one permanent exhibit of ancient Egyptian art; Average Annual Attendance: 9,500; Mem: 200
Income: Financed by state appropriation, pub & private support
Special Subjects: Anthropology, Antiquities-Egyptian, Archaeology, Architecture, Drawings, Etchings & Engravings, Folk Art, Graphics, Painting-American, Period Rooms, Photography, Prints, Sculpture, Woodcarvings, Woodcuts
Collections: Egyptian Hall: antiquities from 3500 BC - 7th century AD, Print Collection: contemporary prints, collection of over 250 prints, an overview, African Art Coll from Martha & Robert Fogelman coll
Exhibitions: Changing contemporary shows
Activities: Lects open to pub, 5 vis lectrs per yr; tours; competitions with awards; schols offered; permanent collections lent to other institutions with proper facilities; originate traveling exhibs

L **Visual Resource Collection**, 220 Jones Hall, Memphis, TN 38152-3306. Tel 901-678-2938; Fax 901-678-2735; Email bbilledx@memphis.edu; Web: www.uom.edu; *Special Colls Librarian & Archivist* Brigitte Billeaudeaux
Open Mon - Sat 9 AM - 6 PM except when exhibitions are being changed; No admis fee; Estab 1967 to provide slides for Art Faculty, University Faculty, & some outside organizations; Circ 160,000; Maintains Egyptian Museum, the Gallery Museum & a student-run museum
Income: Financed by the university
Library Holdings: Audio Tapes, Book Volumes 218, CD-ROMs, Cassettes, Clipping Files, Compact Disks, DVDs, Exhibition Catalogs, Filmstrips, Original Art Works, Periodical Subscriptions 160, Prints, Records, Reproductions, Sculpture, Slides, Video Tapes
Special Subjects: Afro-American Art, American Indian Art, American Western Art, Antiquities-Assyrian, Antiquities-Byzantine, Antiquities-Egyptian, Antiquities-Etruscan, Antiquities-Greek, Antiquities-Oriental, Antiquities-Persian, Antiquities-Roman, Archaeology, Architecture, Art Education, Art History
Collections: 35 mm slides of history of Western art, photography, non-Western art, Western Art, African Art, Native American Art, Murname Collection of Egyptian Slides, Collection of 17th-19th century American Architecture
Activities: Educ program; lects open to pub; 10-15 vis. lectrs per yr; concerts; gallery talks; tours; competitions; schols offered; exten prog includes Family Day prog

MORRISTOWN

A **ROSE CENTER & COUNCIL FOR THE ARTS,** 442 W Second North St, Morristown, TN 37814-4026; PO Box 1976, Morristown, TN 37816-1976. Tel 423-581-4330; Fax 423-581-4307; Email info@rosecenter.org; Web: www.rosecenter.org; *Exec Dir* Drew Ogle; *Operations Mgr* Patty Gracey; *Educ & Special Events* Beccy Hamm; *Facilities Mgr* Ray James
Open Mon - Wed & Fri 9 AM - 5 PM, Thurs 9 AM - 7 PM; No admis fee; Estab 1975 to promote, implement, & sustain historical, educational & cultural activities & projects of both local & national importance; to preserve & maintain Rose School as a museum & cultural center; Circ 1,000; Art gallery, historic gallery, children's touch mus, historical classroom; Average Annual Attendance: 75,000; Mem: 450
Income: Financed by endowment, mem, city, county & state appropriation, class instruction
Library Holdings: Book Volumes, Original Art Works, Other Holdings, Photographs, Slides
Special Subjects: Crafts, Decorative Arts, Folk Art, Historical Material, Painting-American, Photography, Textiles
Collections: Local historical material, crafts & art, clothing

Publications: Monthly newsletter; Qtr calendar
Activities: Classes for adults & children; dramatic progs; art camps; lects open to pub; 5 vis lectrs per yr; concerts; gallery talks; tours; school progs; competition sponsoring; schols; Rose Art award; book traveling exhibs 1 per yr; originates traveling exhibs of various fine art; mus shop sells books & crafts, books & reproductions

MURFREESBORO

M **MIDDLE TENNESSEE STATE UNIVERSITY,** Baldwin Photographic Gallery, PO Box 305, Murfreesboro, TN 37132-0001. Tel 615-898-2300; Fax 615-898-5682; Email tjimison@mtsu.edu; *Cur* Tom Jimison
Open Mon - Fri 8 AM - 4:30 PM, Sat 8 AM - Noon, Sun 6 - 10 PM; No admis fee; Estab 1970 for the exhibition of outstanding photographers; Gallery has 193 running ft of display area; Average Annual Attendance: 30,000
Income: Financed by the university
Purchases: Purchase work from exhibiting photographers
Special Subjects: Photography
Collections: Ansel Adams, Shelby Lee Adams, Richard Avedon, Harold Baldwin, Harry Callahan, Marrie Camhi, Geri Della Rocea de Candal, Barbara Crane, Jim Ferguson, Dore Gardner, Philip Gould, Tom Jimison, Builder Levy, Minor White & others, Jim Norton, April Ottey, John Pfahl, Walter Rosenblum, John Schulze, Aaron Sisking, Marianne Skogh, H H Smith, Michael P Smith, Jerry Velsman, Ed Weston by Cole, Jack Wilgus, Sean Wilkinson, Kelly Wise
Publications: Lightyear, annually
Activities: Lects open to pub; 4 vis lectrs per yr; original objects of art lent to responsible organizations; lending collection contains photographs; book traveling exhibs 3 per yr; originate traveling exhibs to university galleries

NASHVILLE

M **BOARD OF PARKS & RECREATION,** The Parthenon, Centennial Park, 2500 West End Ave Nashville, TN 37203. Tel 615-862-8431; Fax 615-880-2265; Email info@pantheon.org; Web: www.parthenon.org; *Dir* Wesley M Paine
Open Tues - Sat 9 AM - 4:30 PM, Sun 12:30 -4:30 PM; Admis adults $6.00, children 4-17 & seniors 62 & over $4; Estab 1897 to offer Nashville residents & tourists quality art for viewing in a Historical setting of significance & beauty; 2 changing exhibit galleries & James M Cowan Gallery of American Art; Mem: dues $25 & up
Income: Financed by city & county taxes, donations & memberships
Special Subjects: Architecture, Painting-American, Sculpture
Collections: Cowan Collection, sixty three paintings by 19th & 20th century American artists, donated by James M Cowan, Century III Collection, sixty two art works, purchased from area artists, juried by John Canaday in celebration of Nashville's bicentennial
Exhibitions: Exhibitions change every 4 months
Publications: Century III Catalog; The Cowan Catalog; A Tale of Two Parthenons; Winslow Homer: An American Genius at the Parthenon; Carlton Wilkinson-Coming Home: A Retrospective
Activities: Docent training; lect open to public, 9 vis lectrs per year; concerts; gallery talks; guided tours; lending of original objects of art to Farnsworth Museum, ME; Berry-Hill Galleries, NY; book traveling exhibitions 1-2 per yr; sales shop sells books, souvenirs, prints & slides

M **CHEEKWOOD-TENNESSEE BOTANICAL GARDEN & MUSEUM OF ART,** 1200 Forrest Park Dr, Nashville, TN 37205-4242. Tel 615-356-8000; Email info@cheekwood.org; Web: www.cheekwood.org; *Pres & CEO* Jane O MacLeod; *CFO* Cassie Fahrney; *CAO* Elizabeth Epley Sheets; *VPres Museum Affairs & Cur Decorative Arts* Leslie B Jones; *VPres Gardens and Horticulture* Peter Grimaldi
Open Tues - Sun 9 AM - 5 PM, cl Mondays, New Year's Day, Memorial Day, Labor Day, Thanksgiving, Christmas; Admis adults $20, seniors 65 & over $18, college students with ID $16, youth 3-17 $13, children 2 & under free; Estab 1957 to collect, preserve & interpret American art. Mus opened to pub in 1960 in a Georgian-style mansion built in 1929 by Mr & Mrs Leslie Cheek. The site underwent further renovation & adaptation in 1980 & 1998; Circ Non-circulating; Galleries contain 12,000 sq ft of exhibition space, divided almost equally between installation of permanent collection & traveling exhibitions. Permanent exhibitions include the American Experience fine art from the collection, Worcester porcelain collection, American and European silver and snuff bottle collection. Separate facility for modern and contemporary art. Outdoor sculpture trail (approx 1 mile) contains regional, national and international sculpture from the collection; Average Annual Attendance: 225,000; Mem: 12,500; dues $55 - $750
Income: Financed by mem, admis, corporate & foundation grants, private gifts, several fundraising events
Library Holdings: Auction Catalogs, Audio Tapes, Book Volumes, CD-ROMs, Exhibition Catalogs, Pamphlets, Periodical Subscriptions, Video Tapes
Special Subjects: American Western Art, Decorative Arts, Graphics, Painting-American, Porcelain
Collections: American paintings, contemporary art, European & American decorative arts, William Edmondson Collection
Exhibitions: Andrew Wyeth Helga Pictures; A Century of Progress: 20th Century Painting in Tennessee; Glass of the Avant-Garde from Vienna Secession to Bauhaus; Young America from the National Museum of American Art
Publications: Brochures, catalogues, checklists, monographs, monthly newsletter, posters
Activities: Classes for adults & children; docent training; lects open to pub; concerts; tours; workshops; individual paintings & original objects of art lent to other mus; book traveling exhibs 5-6 per yr; originate traveling exhibs; mus shop sell books, prints & posters; junior mus

L **Museum of Art,** 1200 Forrest Park Dr, Nashville, TN 37205-4242. Tel 615-356-8000; Email museum@cheekwood.org; Web: www.cheekwood.org; *Pres & CEO* Jane O MacLeod; *CFO* Cassie Fahrney; *COO* Elizabeth A Murdock; *CAO* Elizabeth Epley Sheets; *VPres Museum Affairs & Cur Decorative Arts* Leslie B Jones; *VPres Gardens & Horticulture* Peter Grimaldi
Tues-Sun 9-5; Admis adults $20, seniors 65 & over $18, college students with ID $16, youth 3-17 $13, children 2 & under free; Estab 1960; Historic House; Galleries; Outdoor Installations; Sculpture Trail;; Average Annual Attendance: 250,000
Special Subjects: American Western Art, Architecture, Art History, Decorative Arts, Graphic Arts, Painting-American, Photography, Printmaking, Prints, Restoration & Conservation, Sculpture, Asian Art, Ceramics, Costumes, Drawings, Etchings & Engravings, Flasks & Bottles, Furniture, Glass, Graphics, Historical Material, Landscapes, Miniatures, Porcelain, Pottery, Portraits, Silver, Tapestries, Textiles, Watercolors, Woodcuts
Collections: Mainly American Art (paintings, drawings & sculpture); Outdoor Contemporary Sculpture, American & European decorative arts
Exhibitions: See Website
Activities: Classes for adults & children; dramatic progs; docent training; lects open to pub; 2 vis lectrs per yr; concerts; gallery talks; tours; sponsoring of competitions; Martin Schallenburger Artist-in-Residence Program; lending of original objects of art to other mus; mus shop: books, magazines; reproductions; prints

L **Botanic Hall Library**, 1200 Forrest Park Dr, Nashville, TN 37205-4242. Tel 615-356-8000
Library Holdings: Book Volumes 5000

M **FISK UNIVERSITY,** Carl Van Vechten Gallery, 1000 17th Ave N, Nashville, TN 37208-3051. Tel 615-329-8720; Email galleries@fisk.edu; Web: www.fisk.edu/services-resources/fisk-university-galleries/the-carl-van-vechten-gallery; *Dir & Cur Fisk Univ Galleries* Jamaal Sheats
Open during acad yr Mon - Wed & Sat 10 AM - 4 PM, Thurs - Fri 10 AM - 7 PM, cl Sun & univ holidays; Call for admis; Estab 1949 as an educ resource center for the Fisk & Nashville communities & for the promotion of the visual arts; Neo-Romanesqu structure built 1888 as a church, served as univ gym 1903-1949, converted to art gallery & opened 1949, renovated early 1980's & rededicated 1984; Gallery 1 features rotating traveling exhibs & Gallery 2 houses the permanent Stieglitz Collection; Average Annual Attendance: 24,000
Income: Financed through the university, state appropriations, grants & private donations
Special Subjects: African Art, Drawings, Folk Art, Painting-American, Painting-French, Photography, Prints, Afro-American Art
Collections: African-American Collection, European & American prints & drawings, Traditional & Contemporary African Art Collection, Carl Van Vechten Collection of Photographs, Alfred Stieglitz Collection of Modern American & European Art, Cyrus Baldridge Drawings
Publications: Fisk Art Report, annually
Activities: Lects open to public, 4-6 vis lectrs per yr; gallery talks; tours; book traveling exhibs; originates traveling exhibs; sales shop sells books & reproductions

M **Aaron Douglas Gallery**, 1000 17th Ave N, Nashville, TN 37208. Tel 615-329-8544; Email galleries@fisk.edu; Web: www.fisk.edu/services-resources/fisk-university-galleries/the-aaron-douglas-gallery; *Dir & Cur Fisk Univ Galleries* Jamaal Sheats
Open Mon - Wed & Sat 10 AM - 4 PM, Thurs - Fri 10 AM - 7 PM, cl Sun & university holidays; Admis free; Estab 1949; Located in John Hope & Aurelia E Franklin Univ Library, 3rd fl; Special Collections located on 2nd fl
Special Subjects: African Art, Afro-American Art, Drawings, Folk Art, Painting-American, Painting-European, Photography, Prints, Sculpture
Exhibitions: Changing exhibs from the permanent collection of classical & contemporary African art, modern & contemporary African-American art, & American & European art

L **Library**, 17 Ave N, North Nashville, TN 37208; 1000 17th Ave, North Nashville, TN 37208. Tel 615-329-8720; Email jcsmith@fisk.edu; Web: www.fisk.edu; *Dir* Jessie Carney Smith; *Info Literacy Librn* Cheryl Jones Hamberg; *Reference Librn Spec Colls* DeLisa Minor Harris; *Archivist* Mattie McHollin
Open Mon - Thurs 7:45 AM - 10 PM, Fri 7:45 AM - 5 PM, Sun 2-10 PM; hours subject to change during exam periods & univ holidays; No admis fee; Estab 1949; Publications are used by students & instructors for research
Library Holdings: Audio Tapes, Book Volumes 1100, Clipping Files, Exhibition Catalogs, Filmstrips, Kodachrome Transparencies, Lantern Slides, Manuscripts, Motion Pictures, Original Art Works, Original Documents, Pamphlets, Photographs, Reproductions, Slides
Collections: Multiple collections consisting of primary & secondary materials on African-American themes, Aaron Douglas Collection: general & personal correspondence (1921-1974) with the Metropolitan Mus of Art & the Harmon Foundation, early drawings, sketches & watercolors, lectures, speeches, programs, photographs, newspaper clippings (1930-1973)

M **GENERAL BOARD OF DISCIPLESHIP, THE UNITED METHODIST CHURCH,** The Upper Room Chapel & Museum, 1908 Grand Ave, Nashville, TN 37212-2129. Tel 877-899-2780, ext 7207; Email kkimball@upperroom.org; Web: chapel.upperroom.org; *Upper Room Cur* Kathryn Kimball
Open Mon - Fri 8 AM - 4:30 PM; Suggested donation: $5; Estab 1953 as a religious mus reflecting universal Christianity
Income: Self supporting
Library Holdings: Book Volumes, Fiche, Periodical Subscriptions
Special Subjects: African Art, Afro-American Art, American Indian Art, Antiquities-Byzantine, Art History, Asian Art, Bronzes, Calligraphy, Carpets & Rugs, Ceramics, Coins & Medals, Decorative Arts, Embroidery, Folk Art, Furniture, Hispanic Art, Historical Material, Judaica, Manuscripts, Mexican Art, Painting-American, Painting-British, Painting-European, Painting-Flemish, Painting-Italian, Painting-Japanese, Painting-Russian, Painting-Spanish, Porcelain, Religious Art, Renaissance Art, Reproductions, Sculpture, Stained Glass, Tapestries, Textiles, Woodcarvings, Painting-Dutch, Painting-French
Collections: Bibles from 1577, 2/3 Lifesize Woodcarving of da Vinci's Last Supper, Nativity Scenes, Ukrainian Eggs, furniture, illuminated manuscripts, oriental rugs, porcelain, Nativity Scenes (over 100 sets)
Exhibitions: Woodcarving; Porcelains; Furniture; Manuscripts from 1300-1800s; Paintings-copies from several masterworks of Raphael, da Vinci, Ruebens
Publications: Upper Room Devotional Guide, every 2 months; books; magazines
Activities: Docent training; gallery talks; tours; sales shop sells books, magazines, slides, postcards of woodcarving, original art, reproductions, prints

A **TENNESSEE HISTORICAL SOCIETY,** 305 Sixth Ave N, Nashville, TN 37243. Tel 615-741-8934; Web: www.tennesseehistory.org; *Exec Dir* Ann Toplovich; *Dir Mem* Jennifer C Core; *Editor, TN Historical Quarterly* Kristofer Ray
Open Mon - Fri 8 AM - 4:30 PM, cl national holidays; No admis fee; Estab 1849 to preserve & interpret the history of all Tennesseans; Average Annual Attendance: dues $35 - $250; Mem: dues $35 - $250
Income: Financed by mem dues, grants & gifts
Collections: Art, decorative art & artifacts related to Tennessee culture, history & pre-history.
Publications: Tennessee Historical Quarterly
Activities: Lect provided, 7 vis lectrs per year

M **TENNESSEE STATE MUSEUM,** 505 Deaderick St, Polk Cultural Ctr Nashville, TN 37243-1120. Tel 615-741-2692, 800-407-4324; Email museuminfo@tnmuseum.org; Web: www.tnmuseum.org; *Exec Dir* Ashley Howell; *Deputy Dir* Mary Jane Crockett-Green; *Dir Spec Projects* Tammi Edwards; *Dir Pub Rels* Paulette Fox; *Chief Cur & Dir Colls* Dan Pomeroy
Open Sun 1 - 5 PM, Tues - Sat 10 AM - 5 PM, cl Mon, New Year's Day, Easter, Thanksgiving, Christmas; No admis fee; Estab 1937 to preserve & interpret the historical artifacts of Tennessee through mus exhibits & statewide outreach & educational programs; A military history mus in the War Memorial Building depicts Tennessee's involvement in modern wars (Spanish-American to World War II). Exhibits highlight life in Tennessee from early man through 1920. Gallery houses changing art & history exhibits. Maintains small reference library; Mem: dues $25 - $500
Income: Financed by state appropriation
Purchases: Tennessee related early 19th century paintings & prints; 19th century Tennessee made silver; 19th century Tennessee made firearms
Special Subjects: Historical Material
Collections: Objects relating to Tennessee history from pre-historic times to the present, Tennessee Historical Society, portraits & paintings of & by prominent Tennesseans, contemporary Tennessee related artists' works
Publications: Exhibition catalogs; quarterly newsletter
Activities: Docent training, dramatic progs; lects open to pub, gallery talks, tours, sponsors competitions; exten dept serving statewide; individual paintings & original objects of art; book traveling exhibs; originate traveling exhibs; mus shop sells books, Tennessee crafts, items relating to the collection; junior mus

M **VANDERBILT UNIVERSITY,** Vanderbilt University Fine Arts Gallery, Cohen Memorial Hall, 1220 21st Ave S Nashville, TN 37203; 230 Appleton Pl, PMB 0273 Nashville, TN 37203-5721. Tel 615-322-0605; Web: www.vanderbilt.edu/gallery; *Dir* Joseph S Mella; *Art Cur Asst* Margaret F.M. Walker
Open Sept - April Mon - Fri 11 - 4 PM, Sat & Sun 1 - 5 PM; May - August Tues - Fri noon - 4 PM, Sat 1 PM - 5 PM, cl July 4, univ breaks & installations; No admis fee; Estab collection 1956, gallery 1961, to provide exhibitions for the university & Nashville communities, & original art works for study by Vanderbilt students & gen pub; The gallery is housed in the historic Cohen Memorial Hall built in 1928
Income: Financed by university resources
Special Subjects: Drawings, Painting-American, Painting-European, Painting-Italian, Prints, Renaissance Art, Photography
Collections: Herman D Doochin Collection of Asian Art, Anna C Hoyt Collection of Old Master Prints, former Peabody College Art Collection including Kress Study Collection of Italian Renaissance Paintings, Harold P Stern Collection of Oriental Art & Rare Books, Contemporary Works on Paper and other Multiples, Samuel H Kress Collection
Exhibitions: Rotating exhibits every 2-4 months
Publications: Far From the Sea: October Foundation 1998-2003; Of Rage And Redemption: The Art of Oswaldo Guayasamín; Reflections of the Dutch Golden Age Etchings by Adriaen van Ostade; Reading Pictures: Text & Contemporary Art; Maria Magdalena Campos-Pons: Mama/Reciprocal Energy; I Am Unbeatable - Documenting & Celebrating Stories of Empowerment -Photographs by Donna Ferrato
Activities: Lects open to public; gallery talks; tours; individual paintings & original objects of art lent to museums & galleries; book traveling exhibs 2-3 per yr; originate traveling exhibits

A **WATKINS COLLEGE OF ART, DESIGN & FILM,** Brownlee O Currey Gallery, 2298 Rosa L Parks Blvd Nashville, TN 37228-1306. Tel 615-383-4848; Email info@watkins.edu; Web: www.watkins.edu; *Pres* J Kline
Open Mon-Fri 9 AM - 8 PM, Sat 10 AM - 4 PM, Sun 2 Pm - 4 PM; No admis fee; Estab 1885 as an adult educ center for art, interior design, adult evening high school & courses of a gen nature; currently a 4 yr undergrad BFA col of visual arts
Income: Financed by rent from bus property
Collections: All-State Artist Coll (oldest coll of Tennessee art in the state), this is a purchase-award coll of oil, pastels, watercolors, graphics and sculpture, several other colls of lesser value
Exhibitions: Ten exhibitions per year
Publications: Art brochure; qtr catalogue listing courses
Activities: Classes for adults & children; lects open to pub, 6-8 vis lectrs per yr; competitions; Student Exhib Awards; individual paintings lent to schools; original objects of art lent; originates traveling exhibs

L **Library,** 2298 Rosa L Parks Blvd, Nashville, TN 37228. Tel 615-277-7426; Email librarian@watkins.edu; Web: www.watkins.edu; *Librn* Amy Kammerman
Open Mon - Thurs 9 AM - 6 PM, Fri 9 AM - 4 PM; Estab 1885
Library Holdings: Book Volumes 12,000, Filmstrips, Periodical Subscriptions 15, Slides, Video Tapes

OAK RIDGE

A **OAK RIDGE ART CENTER,** 201 Badger Rd, Oak Ridge, TN 37830-6216. Tel 423-482-1441; *Dir* Leah Marcum-Estes; *Pres* William Capshaw
Open Tues - Fri 9 AM - 5 PM, Sat - Mon 1 - 4 PM; No admis fee; Estab 1952 to encourage the appreciation & creation of the visual arts; Two galleries house temporary exhibitions & permanent collection exhibitions, one rental gallery, classrooms & library; Average Annual Attendance: 20,000; Mem: 450; dues $35; meetings 2nd Mon of month
Income: $130,000 (financed by mem & grants)
Collections: The Mary & Alden Gomez Collection, Contemporary Regional Works, European Post World War II
Exhibitions: Open Show, Juried Competition (all media); monthly exhibit
Publications: Art Matters, monthly bulletin
Activities: Classes for adults & children; docent training; forums; workshops; lect open to public, 6-8 vis lectrs per year; gallery talks; tours; competitions with awards; individual paintings & original objects of art rented to individuals & bus on semi-annual basis; lending collection contains original art works, VCR tapes, 2000 books & 1000 slides

L **Library,** 201 Badger Rd, Oak Ridge, TN 37830-6216. Tel 423-482-1441; *Dir* Leah Marcum-Estes
Open Tues - Fri 9 AM - 5 PM; Open to members for lending & reference
Income: financed by members & grants
Library Holdings: Audio Tapes, Book Volumes 2000, Exhibition Catalogs, Filmstrips, Memorabilia, Original Art Works, Slides, Video Tapes
Special Subjects: Pottery
Publications: Monthly newsletter

PURYEAR

A **INTERNATIONAL SOCIETY OF MARINE PAINTERS,** 1800 Goldston Springs Rd, Puryear, TN 38251-3711. Tel 406-293-8447; Email dlarge@schoonerlinks.com; Web: www.ismpart.com; *Pres* David Large; *VPres* Richard Levesque
Estab 1984; Mem: mem $15 - $25
Income: Financed by dues & contributions
Special Subjects: Marine Painting
Exhibitions: Annual Marine Artist Breakfast in Gloucester, MA & Bradenton, FL
Publications: Seascaped, every 3 months
Activities: Originate traveling exhibs to major art galleries, art centers & marine museums

SEWANEE

L **UNIVERSITY OF THE SOUTH,** Jessie Ball duPont Library, 29 Alabama Ave, Sewanee, TN 37383-0001. Tel 931-598-1664; Fax 931-598-1145; Email cpfeiff@sewanee.edu; *Dir* Cheryl Pfeiffer
Open Mon - Thurs 7:45 AM - 1 AM, Fri 7:45 AM - 9 PM, Sat 9 AM - 6 PM, Sun 10 AM - 1 AM; Estab 1863
Special Subjects: Bronzes, Carpets & Rugs, Coins & Medals, Collages, Drawings, Embroidery, Enamels, Etchings & Engravings, Furniture, Glass, Gold, Ivory, Jewelry, Landscapes, Manuscripts

M **UNIVERSITY OF THE SOUTH,** University Art Gallery, 68 Georgia Ave Sewanee, TN 37383. Tel 931-598-1223; Fax 931-598-3335; Email sjmaclar@sewanee.edu; Web: www.sewanee.edu/gallery/; *Gallery Dir* Shelly MacLaren
Open Tues - Fri 10 AM - 5 PM, Sat & Sun Noon - 4 PM, holidays & acad holidays by appointment; No admis fee; Estab 1938 to provide exhibits of interest to students & local & regional audiences; One large space with balcony, one main entry door, carpeted walls, track lighting; Average Annual Attendance: 3,000-5,000
Income: Financed by college funds, contributions & gifts
Library Holdings: CD-ROMs, Compact Disks, DVDs, Lantern Slides, Original Art Works, Photographs, Prints, Sculpture, Slides, Video Tapes
Special Subjects: Drawings, Etchings & Engravings, Furniture, Graphics, Historical Material, Manuscripts, Painting-American, Photography, Silver, Stained Glass, Watercolors, Prints, Sculpture
Exhibitions: 5 exhibitions during school year
Activities: Lects open to public; concerts; gallery talks; sponsor competitions; original objects of art lent to qualified venues; book traveling exhibs (occasional)

TRENTON

M **PORCELAIN VEILLEUSES-THEIERES MUSEUM,** 309 S College St, Trenton City Hall Trenton, TN 38382-2171. Tel 731-855-2013; Fax 731-855-1091; Web: www.teapotcollection.com

TULLAHOMA

M **TULLAHOMA FINE ARTS CENTER REGIONAL MUSEUM OF ART,** 401 S Jackson St, Tullahoma, TN 37388-3469. Tel 931-455-1234; Fax 931-455-1234; Email lucy@tullahomafinearts.org; Web: www.tullahomafinearts.org; *Dir* Lucy Hollis
Exhibitions: Temporary exhibits

TEXAS

ABILENE

M **CENTER FOR CONTEMPORARY ARTS,** 220 Cypress St, Abilene, TX 79601. Tel 925-677-8389; Fax 925-677-1171; Email info@center-arts.com; Web: www.center-arts.com; *Exec Dir* Darla Harmon; *Gallery Mgr* Trudy Six
Open Tues - Sat 11 AM - 5 PM; Estab 1989; Mem: dues $50-$1,000
Collections: works by contemporary artists; paintings; sculpture; photographs
Exhibitions: Temporary exhibits

M **GRACE MUSEUM, INC,** The Grace Museum, 102 Cypress St, Abilene, TX 79601-5817. Tel 325-673-4587; Fax 325-675-5993; Email

info@thegracemuseum.org; Web: www.thegracemuseum.org; *Cur Educ* Kathryn Mitchell; *Pres & CEO* Laura Moore; *Chief Cur* Judy Denton; *Dir Finance* Vicki Butts; *Dir Mktg & Pub Rels* Emerald Cassidy
Open Tues - Sat 10 AM - 5 PM, Thurs 10 AM - 8 PM, cl Sun & Mon; Admis adults $6, children $3, active duty military free; Estab 1937 as an art & history educ institution; Contemporary, neutral spaces; Average Annual Attendance: 80,000; Mem: 600; dues $45 & up
Income: Financed by mem, grants, fund-raising events, sponsors & endowment
Special Subjects: Painting-American, Prints
Collections: American Paintings & Prints, Local History, T&P Railway Collection, Texas Heritage: Peter Searcy, Allen Houser, Fidencio Duran, Maxine Rerini, Photography Collection by Bill Wright
Exhibitions: Regular schedule of temporary & long-term exhibitions, including contemporary art
Publications: Brochures; biannual newsletter
Activities: Classes for adults & children; docent training; lects open to public, 2-5 vis lectrs per year; gallery talks; tours; individual paintings & original works of art lent to other museums; lending collection contains original art works, original prints, paintings, photographs, sculptures, slides; book traveling exhibitions 2-3 per year; museum shop sells books, magazines, reproductions, prints, slides, games, toys, crafts, note cards & decorative arts

M **MCMURRY UNIVERSITY,** Ryan Fine Arts Center, 514th & Sayles Blvd, Abilene, TX 79697; PO Box 8, Abilene, TX 79697-0001. Tel 915-793-3823; Fax 915-793-4662; Web: www.mcm.edu
Open Mon - Fri 8 AM - 5 PM, cl Sat & Sun; No admis fee; Estab 1970 when building was completed; Large room overlooking larger sculpture garden; Average Annual Attendance: 2,500
Income: Financed by college art budget
Exhibitions: Varied exhibitions, changing monthly, of national, regional & area artists
Activities: Classes for adults in photography; lect open to public; gallery talks; competitions; individual paintings & original objects of art lent to college offices

ALBANY

M **THE OLD JAIL ART CENTER,** 201 S Second St, Albany, TX 76430. Tel 325-762-2269; Fax 325-762-2260; Email info@theojac.org; Web: www.theojac.org; *Exec Dir* Patrick Kelly; *Registrar* Amy Kelly; *Dir Educ* Erin Whitmore; *Archivist & Librn* Molly Sauder
Open Tues - Sat 10 AM - 5 PM; No admis fee; Estab 1980 to collect & display art of US & Europe, Asian & Pre-Columbian art; Four galleries in old 1877 jail. 9 additional galleries plus Stasney Center for Educ. Marshall R Young Courtyard for outdoor sculpture; Average Annual Attendance: 12,000; Mem: 800; dues $25
Library Holdings: Book Volumes, Exhibition Catalogs, Periodical Subscriptions, Video Tapes
Special Subjects: Antiquities-Oriental, Architecture, Bronzes, Ceramics, Drawings, Furniture, Historical Material, Manuscripts, Maps, Painting-American, Painting-French, Painting-German, Painting-Italian, Painting-Spanish, Photography, Pre-Columbian Art, Prints, Sculpture, Watercolors, Woodcuts, Asian Art, Landscapes, Pottery
Collections: Pre-Columbian, Sculpture, Paintings & drawings, Photography, Asian pottery & Chinese tomb figures, Contemporary
Publications: Exhibit catalogs; newsletter, semi-annual
Activities: Classes for adults & children; dramatic progs; docent training; distance learning making classrooms nationally & internationally; lects for members only, 2 vis lectrs per yr; gallery talks; tours; schols offered; individual paintings & original objects of art lent; lending collection contains 2,400 paintings & some sculpture; book traveling exhibs annually; originate traveling exhibs; mus shop sells books, reproductions, notecards, plus other items

L **Green Research Library**, 201 S 2nd St, Albany, TX 76430. Tel 325-762-2269; Fax 325-762-2260; Email archivist@theoldjailartcenter.org; Web: www.theoldjailartcenter.org; *Registrar* Amy Kelly; *Exec Dir* James Peck; *Archivist/ Librn* Molly Sauder; *Cur Exhibs* Patrick Kelly
Open Tues - Sat 10 AM - 5 PM, Sun 2 - 5 PM; No admis fee; Estab 1984; For reference only; Average Annual Attendance: 15,000; Mem: 608
Library Holdings: Book Volumes 2000, Periodical Subscriptions 4
Special Subjects: American Indian Art, American Western Art, Antiquities-Egyptian, Antiquities-Greek, Architecture, Art Education, Art History, Bronzes, Drawings, Etchings & Engravings, Furniture, Historical Material, History of Art & Archaeology, Illustration, Mexican Art, Oriental Art, Painting-American, Painting-European, Photography, Pre-Columbian Art, Sculpture, Prints
Collections: Pre-Columbian, Asian, 20th Century, Fort Worth Circle, Contemporary & Emerging Texas
Activities: Classes for adults & children; docent training; lects open to pub; concerts; gallery talks; sponsoring of competitions; schols; lending of original art to museums; museum shop sells books

AMARILLO

A **AMARILLO ART ASSOCIATION,** Amarillo Museum of Art, 2200 S Van Buren St, Amarillo, TX 79109-2407; PO Box 447, Amarillo, TX 79105-0447. Tel 806-371-5050; Fax 806-373-9235; Web: www.amarilloart.org; *Dir & Cur* Patrick McCracken; *Cur Educ* Mark Morey; *Admin Asst* Liz Seliger; *Admin Asst* Cindy Mote; *Coll Mgr* Reba Jones
Open Tues - Fri 10 AM - 5 PM, Sat & Sun 1 - 5 PM; No admis fee; Estab 1972 for visual arts; Gallery 100, 90 x 30 ft, atrium area 45 ft; Gallery 200 & 203, 90 x 32 ft, 11 ft ceiling; Gallery 305 & 307, each 32 x 28 ft, 10 ft ceiling; Average Annual Attendance: 60,000; Mem: 1800; dues $50-$500
Income: Financed by mem, college, endowment sponsorship program & exhibition underwriting
Collections: Contemporary American drawings, paintings, prints & sculpture, Asian Art Collection
Publications: Annual Report; brochures, as needed; Calendar of Events, bimonthly; catalogs on exhibits
Activities: Classes for adults & children; docent training; lectrs open to pub, 2 vis lectrs per yr; gallery talks; tours; individual paintings & original objects of art lent to qualified institutions; originate traveling exhibs; mus shop sells books, original art, reproductions, prints, posters, crafts

L **Library**, 2200 S Van Buren St, Amarillo, TX 79109-2407; PO Box 447, Amarillo, TX 79105-0447. Tel 806-371-5050; Fax 806-373-9235; Web: www.amarilloart.org; *Librn* Dru Scamahorn
Open Tues-Fri 10AM-5PM, Sat & Sun 1-5PM; Circ Non-circulating; For reference only
Library Holdings: Book Volumes 1500, Periodical Subscriptions 18

ARLINGTON

M **ARLINGTON MUSEUM OF ART,** 201 W Main St, Arlington, TX 76010. Tel 817-275-4600; Fax 817-345-3567; Email arlingtonmuseum@gmail.com; Web: arlingtonmuseum.org; *Dir* Chris Hightower
Open Tues - Sat 10 AM - 5 PM, Sun 1 - 5 PM; Adults $8, seniors & students $5; Estab 1989 to provide access to art for the cultural enrichment and development of the community; Large converted J C Penney's with Mezzanine galleries; Average Annual Attendance: 18,000; Mem: 400; dues $25-$10,000
Income: Financed by endowment, mem, city appropriation & reception rental
Collections: Texas Contemporary Art
Publications: Artifaces, quarterly; AMA News, biannual; exhib catalogs
Activities: Classes for adults & children; docent training; lects series open to pub; gallery talks; tours; originate traveling exhibs

M **UNIVERSITY OF TEXAS AT ARLINGTON,** Gallery at UTA, 502 S Cooper St, Fine Arts Bldg Arlington, TX 76010. Tel 817-272-3110; Fax 817-272-2805; Email bhuerta@uta.edu; Web: www.uta.edu/gallery; *Dir & Cur* Benito Huerta; *Asst Cur* Patricia Healy
Open Mon-Fri 10 AM - 5 PM, Sat Noon - 5 PM, cl acad holidays & summers; No admis fee; Estab 1975 on completion of Fine Arts Complex. The Gallery serves the entire university; exhibitions are contemporary; Main Gallery is air-cooled, 4000 sq ft with incandescent light; Average Annual Attendance: 15,000
Income: $25,000 (financed by state appropriation, private gifts & grants)
Special Subjects: Painting-American
Publications: Tri-fold color brochures on exhibs from past 5 years; exhib catalog; Celia Muñoz: Stories Your Mother Never Told You
Activities: Undergraduate course on museum techniques; lect open to public, 6 vis lectrs per year; gallery talks; catalogs on sale

AUSTIN

M **CITY OF AUSTIN PARKS & RECREATION,** O Henry Museum, 409 E Fifth St, Austin, TX 78701. Tel 512-974-1398; Fax 512-472-7102; Email ohenrymuseum@austintexas.gov; Web: www.ohenrymuseum.org; *Educ Coordr* Michael Hoinski; *Asst Cur* Quinn Argall
Open Wed - Sun Noon - 5 PM; No admis fee, donations accepted; Estab 1934 to preserve O Henry's works; The 1891 historic home of the famous short story writer. The home exhibits artifacts & memorabilia relating to the author; Average Annual Attendance: 10,000; Mem: 30; dues $25; annual meeting in Jan
Income: $112,000 (financed by mem, city appropriations & programs)
Special Subjects: Decorative Arts, Furniture, Historical Material, Manuscripts, Period Rooms, Porcelain, Pottery, Restorations, Textiles
Exhibitions: Annual O Henry PUN-OFF Festival of Wit & Puns; O Henry Writing Club
Activities: Classes for adults & children; lects open both to mems & pub, 1 vis lectr per yr; book traveling exhibs 1 per yr; originate traveling exhibs 1 per yr; mus shop sells books

M **CITY OF AUSTIN PARKS & RECREATION DEPARTMENT,** Julia C Butridge Gallery, Dougherty Arts Ctr, 1110 Barton Springs Rd Austin, TX 78704-1150. Tel 512-974-4000; Fax 512-974-4039; Email megan.weiler@ci.austin.tx.us; Web: www.ci.austin.tx.us/dougherty/butridge.htm; *Art in Pub Places Mgr* Martha Peters; *Art in Pub Places Coordr* Megan Weiler
Open Mon - Thurs 10 AM - 10 PM, Fri 10 AM - 6 PM, Sat 10 AM - 4 PM, cl Sun; No admis fee; Estab to preserve & enrich the cultural life of the city; 1800 sq ft of space in a multi-use arts facility available to organizations & artists in the Austin area
Income: Financed by city appropriation
Exhibitions: Rotating schedule presented by local artists & art organizations (all media & subject matter)
Activities: Gallery talks

M **THE CONTEMPORARY AUSTIN,** Laguna Gloria, 3809 W 35th St Austin, TX 78703-1001; Jones Center, 700 Congress Ave Austin, TX 78701. Tel 512-453-5312 (Jones Center), 512-458-8191 (Laguna Gloria); Email info@thecontemporaryaustin.org; Web: thecontemporaryaustin.org; *Dir* Judith Smith; *Assoc Dir* Matt Hoggle; *Assoc Dir* Kelcie Tisher; *Registration Coord* Maggie McGrath; *Ceramics Coord* James Tisdale
Open Tues - Sat 11 AM - 7 PM, Sun Noon - 5 PM (Jones Center); Tues - Sun 10 AM - 4 PM (Laguna Gloria); Admis adults $5, seniors & students $3, under 18, military, mems & Tues free; Estab 1911 to reflect the spectrum of contemporary art through exhibs, commissions, educ & colls; 9000 sq ft (Jones Center) 2200 sq ft (Laguna Gloria); Average Annual Attendance: 125,000; Mem: Dues $35 - $5,000
Income: Financed by corporate & individual donations, special events, grants, ann fund, mem, City of Austin
Library Holdings: Auction Catalogs, Audio Tapes, Book Volumes, CD-ROMs, Cassettes, Exhibition Catalogs, Kodachrome Transparencies, Periodical Subscriptions, Slides, Video Tapes
Special Subjects: Afro-American Art, Latin American Art, Mexican Art, Photography
Collections: 20th century painting, sculpture, photographs, prints & drawings, contemporary art
Exhibitions: Changing exhibitions of contemporary art from throughout the world

Publications: Monthly newsletter & exhib catalogues
Activities: Art School classes for adults & children; cultural & educational progs in conjunction with exhibs, docent tours; lects open to pub, 12 vis lectrs per yr; gallery talks; tours; awards, Texas prize; schols offered; individual paintings & original objects of art lent to mus; book traveling exhibs 3-4 per yr; originate traveling exhibs

M **ELISABET NEY MUSEUM,** 304 E 44th St, Austin, TX 78751-3813. Tel 512-974-1625; Email enm@ci.austin.tx.us; Web: www.ci.austin.tx.us/elisabetney; *Dir* Mary Collins Blackmon
Open Wed - Sun Noon - 5 PM, cl Mon & Tues; No admis fee, donations accepted; Estab 1911 to preserve the memory and legacy of 19th C. portrait sculptor, Elisabet Ney (1833-1907). Elisabet Ney portraits and personal memorabilia displayed in the artists 1892 Austin, TX studio; One of five 19th-century American sculpture studios to survive with its contents, the museum is a national, state & historic landmark comprised of artists former studio bldg, 2.5 acres of original 6 acre site & 508 piece coll on permanent loan from Harry Ransom Humanities Research Ctr of Univ TX at Austin; Average Annual Attendance: 10,000
Income: $100,000 (financed by city appropriation, grants & donations)
Special Subjects: Sculpture, American Western Art, Architecture, Historical Material, Portraits, Restorations
Collections: Portrait sculptures of 19th-century European & Texas notables by Elisabet Ney in plaster & marble, tools, furnishings & personal memorabilia
Activities: Summer progs for children; school outreach progs; progs for at-risk children & youth; concerts; gallery talks; tours

L **Library**, 304 E 44th, Austin, TX 78751. Tel 512-458-2255; Fax 512-453-0638; *Dir* Mary Collins Blackmon
Open Wed - Sat 10 AM - 5 PM, Sun Noon - 5 PM; Estab 1908 to collect background material on subjects relevant to the museum's history & period; For reference only
Library Holdings: Book Volumes 330, Clipping Files, Exhibition Catalogs, Manuscripts, Memorabilia, Original Art Works, Other Holdings Letters, Pamphlets, Periodical Subscriptions 7, Photographs, Slides
Special Subjects: Art Education, Art History, Bronzes, Furniture, Historical Material, Manuscripts, Portraits, Sculpture
Exhibitions: A Life in Art; Elisabet Ney in Austin
Publications: SURSUM, collected letters of Elisabet Ney
Activities: Classes for adults & children; dramatic progs; docent training; AV programs; lects open to pub, 3-5 vis lectrs per yr; concerts; gallery talks; tours; exten dept serves Austin area school systems

A **MEXIC-ARTE MUSEUM,** 419 Congress Ave, Austin, TX 78768; PO Box 2273, Austin, TX 78768-2273. Tel 512-480-9373; Fax 512-480-8626; Email info@mexic-artemuseum.org; Web: www.mexic-artemuseum.org; *Exec Dir* Sylvia Orozco; *Pres* George Elliman; *VPres Public Affairs* Laura Granado; *VPres Develop* Kim Vincent; *VPres Mem* Laurel Prats
Open Mon - Thurs 10 AM - 6 PM; Fri & Sat 10 - 5 PM; Sun noon - 5 PM; Admis adults $5, seniors & students $4, children 12 & under $1, mems no charge; Estab 1984; dedicated to cultural enrichment & educ through the presentation & promotion of traditional & contemporary Mexican, Latino American art and Culture; 4500 sq ft; Average Annual Attendance: 100,000; Mem: 400
Income: 600,000
Library Holdings: Audio Tapes, Book Volumes, Cassettes, Exhibition Catalogs, Records, Video Tapes
Special Subjects: Hispanic Art, Latin American Art, Mexican Art, Prints, Woodcuts
Collections: Graphic prints from workshop of popular graphics from Mexico, Contemporary art work in all disciplines with a focus on Mexican & Latino art, Masks from the State of Guerrero, The Serie Print Project, The Ernest De Soto Collection
Activities: Classes for children; children's hands-on activities; panel discussions; docent training; lect open to public; gallery talks; awards; tours; three vis lectrs; original objects of art lent to other arts facilities; lending collection; museums; mus shop sells books, magazines, reproductions, folk art

M **SAINT EDWARD'S UNIVERSITY,** Fine Arts Gallery, 3001 S Congress Ave, Austin, TX 78704-6489. Tel 512-428-1360; Fax 512-448-8492; Email alexan@stedwards.edu; Web: www.stedwards.edu/fine-arts-gallery; *Contact* Alex Robinson
Open Mon - Fri 9 AM - 5 PM; No admis fee; Estab 1961 to present for the university population & general pub a monthly schedule of exhibits in the visual arts, as a means of orientation toward established & current trends in art styles in terms of their historical-cultural significance & aesthetic value, through teaching exhibitions, pub & private collections from distributing & compiling agencies, museums, galleries, artists & exhibs by regional, nat & international artists; Average Annual Attendance: 10,000
Income: Financed by the college
Exhibitions: Annual student & faculty exhibitions; Fall term exhibits by vis artists; local, nat & international
Activities: Classes; lects, 3-5 vis lectrs per yr; gallery talks; tours; literature

M **THINKERY,** (Austin Children's Museum), 1830 Simond Ave, Austin, TX 78723-4603. Tel 512-469-6200; Email info@thinkeryaustin.org; Web: www.thinkeryaustin.org; *CEO* Patricia Young Brown; *Dir Educ* Dr Robin Gose
Open Mon 9 AM - noon (children under 3 yrs only), Tues - Fri 10 AM - 5 PM, Wed 10 - 8 PM (4 PM - 8 PM community night), Sat & Sun 10 AM - 6 PM (4 - 5 PM no charge), cl New Year's Day, Easter, Memorial Day, Independence Day, Thanksgiving Day & Christmas Day; Admis gen $12, children under 2 & mem free; Estab 1983 to create innovative learning experiences for children & families that equip & inspire the next generation of creative problem solvers; Offers a variety of hands-on exhibits for children of all ages; Average Annual Attendance: 600,000; Mem: 14,500; dues $75 & up
Income: Financed through mem, donations & grants
Exhibitions: Light Lab, Currents, Junk City, Kitchen Lab, Innovators' Workshop, Let's Grow & Spark Shop
Activities: Workshops; birthday parties; camps; ed exchange; Spark Club; early learners

M **UMLAUF SCULPTURE GARDEN & MUSEUM,** 605 Robert E Lee Rd, Austin, TX 78704-1453. Tel 512-445-5582; Fax 512-445-5583; Email info@umlaufsculpture.org; Web: www.umlaufsculpture.org; *Exec Dir* Nina Seely; *Cur* Katie Edwards; *Dir Progs* Diane Sikes; *Develop Mgr* Lilly Davis; *Venue & Event Mgr* Ally Boyd Hinojosa; *Volunteer & Outreach Coord* Nohemi Rodriguez
Open Tues - Fri 10 AM - 4 PM, Sat & Sun Noon - 4 PM, cl Mon; Admis general $5, seniors $3, student $1, children under 13 & active military free; Estab 1991 to provide educational programs & experiences that encourage the appreciation of sculpture; Average Annual Attendance: 27,000; Mem: Friends of the UMLAUF Sculpture Garden
Income: Financed by endowment, garden rentals for weddings, receptions & parties, fundraiser The Garden Party
Library Holdings: Auction Catalogs, Audio Tapes, Book Volumes, Clipping Files, DVDs, Exhibition Catalogs, Filmstrips, Kodachrome Transparencies, Manuscripts, Memorabilia, Motion Pictures, Original Art Works, Original Documents, Photographs, Prints, Sculpture
Special Subjects: Bronzes, Ceramics, Drawings, Painting-American, Religious Art, Sculpture, Watercolors, Woodcarvings
Collections: Charles Umlauf Collection: sculptures & drawings, original drawings & paintings, sculptures in exotic woods, terra cotta, cast stone, bronze, alabaster & marble in detailed realism & abstractions
Publications: Garden Grapevine, Newsletter biannual
Activities: Docent training; sculpture tours & workshops for students; lects open to pub, 6-8 vis lectrs per yr; gallery talks; original objects of art lent to other mus that fit borrowing criteria; mus shop sells books, postcards, notecards, mugs & t-shirts

L **UNIVERSITY OF TEXAS AT AUSTIN,** Fine Arts Library, Doty Fine Arts Bldg 3-200, 2306 Trinity Stop 55437 Austin, TX 78712-1478. Tel 512-495-4481; Fax 512-495-4490; Email lschwartz@austin.utexas.edu; Web: www.lib.utexas.edu/fal; *Head Librn & Music Librn* David Hunter; *Theatre & Dance Librn* Beth Kerr; *Media Coordr, Audio Visual* Gary Lay; *Media Coordr, Images* Sydney Kilgore; *Art Librarian* Vacant
Open Mon - Thurs 8 AM - 10 PM; Fri 8 AM - 5 PM; Sat noon - 5 PM; Sun noon - 10 PM; Estab 1948 to support teaching & research in Fine Arts fields including PhD level in art history & to the master's level in art educ & studio art; Circ 100,000; For lending; Average Annual Attendance: 100,000
Income: Financed by student tuition
Library Holdings: Auction Catalogs, Audio Tapes, Book Volumes 300,000, CD-ROMs, Cassettes, Compact Disks 100,000, DVDs 15,000, Exhibition Catalogs, Fiche 24,000, Other Holdings 17,000, Periodical Subscriptions 400, Records 100,000, Reels 4500, Slides 550,000, Video Tapes 16,000
Special Subjects: Art Education, Art History, Textiles, Theatre Arts, Advertising Design, Aesthetics, Afro-American Art, American Indian Art, American Western Art, Anthropology, Antiquities-Assyrian, Antiquities-Byzantine, Antiquities-Egyptian, Antiquities-Etruscan, Antiquities-Greek, Antiquities-Oriental, Antiquities-Persian, Antiquities-Roman, Asian Art, Bronzes, Calligraphy, Collages, Commercial Art, Conceptual Art, Constructions, Costume Design & Constr, Crafts, Decorative Arts, Drafting, Drawings, Embroidery, Etchings & Engravings, Ethnology, Fashion Arts, Folk Art, Glass, Gold, Goldsmithing, Graphic Arts, Graphic Design, Handicrafts, Historical Material, History of Art & Archaeology, Illustration, Intermedia, Interior Design, Islamic Art, Judaica, Landscape Architecture, Landscapes, Latin American Art, Manuscripts, Metalwork, Mexican Art, Miniatures, Mixed Media, Mosaics, Oriental Art, Painting-American, Painting-Australian, Painting-British, Painting-Canadian, Painting-Dutch, Painting-European, Painting-Flemish, Painting-French, Painting-German, Painting-Israeli, Painting-Italian, Painting-Japanese, Painting-New Zealand, Painting-Polish, Painting-Russian, Painting-Scandinavian, Painting-Spanish, Photography, Portraits, Posters, Pottery, Pre-Columbian Art, Primitive art, Printmaking, Prints, Religious Art, Reproductions, Restoration & Conservation, Sculpture, Silver, Silversmithing, Southwestern Art, Stage Design, Stained Glass, Tapestries, Video, Watercolors, Woodcarvings, Woodcuts
Activities: classes for adults; Lects open to pub; concerts; tours

M **Blanton Museum of Art**, 1 University Station D1303, Austin, TX 78712. Tel 512-471-5482; Fax 512-471-7023; Email info@blantonmuseum.org; Web: www.blantonmuseum.org; *Dir* Simone J Wicha; *Deputy Dir Curatorial Affairs & Cur Prints & Drawings* Carter Foster; *Dir Mktg & Comms* Carlotta Stankiewicz
Open Tues - Fri 10 AM - 5 PM, Sat 11 AM - 5 PM, Sun 1 PM - 5 PM, cl Mon; Admis Adults $9, seniors (65 & over) $7, college students & youth (13-21) $5, current faculty, students, staff & children under 12, active military free; Estab 1963 to serve the students & faculty of the university & the general pub; 57 Renamed the Jack S Blanton Museum of Art in 98; Average Annual Attendance: 240,000; Mem: 7253; dues $45 & up
Special Subjects: Afro-American Art, American Western Art, Antiquities-Greek, Baroque Art, Drawings, Etchings & Engravings, Hispanic Art, Latin American Art, Mexican Art, Painting-American, Painting-European, Portraits, Prints, Religious Art, Renaissance Art, Reproductions, Sculpture, Southwestern Art, Textiles, Watercolors, Woodcarvings, Woodcuts
Collections: Suida-Manning Collection, 19th & 20th Century American paintings, including Mari & James A Michener Collection of 20th Century American Art & the C R Smith Collection of Art of the American West, Leo Steinberg Collection
Exhibitions: Masterpieces of European Painting - Permanent Installation
Publications: Exhibition catalogues
Activities: Classes for adults & children; docent training; lects open to public, 5-15 vis lectrs per yr; concerts; gallery talks; tours; school tours K - 12; symposia; vis artists; film & video series; exten dept serves Texas & the region; individual paintings & original objects of art lent to educational exhibiting organizations (universities & college museums); originate traveling exhibs to other university art museums & city museums; mus shop sells books, magazines, original art, reproductions & prints

L **Harry Ransom Humanities Research Center**, 21st & Guadalupe Sts, Austin, TX 78712; PO Box 7219, Austin, TX 78713-7219. Tel 512-471-8944; Fax 512-471-9646; Web: www.hrc.utexas.edu; *Dir* Stephen Enniss PhD; *Assoc Dir* Megan Barnard, PhD; *Assoc Dir* Danielle Brune Sigler; *Assoc Dir* Cathy Henderson, MLS; *Assoc Dir* Ellen Cunningham-Kruppa
Open Mon, Tues, Wed & Fri 10 AM - 5 PM, Thurs 10 AM - 7 PM, Sat - Sun 12 PM - 5 PM; No admis fee; Library estab 1957; Circ Non-circulating; Feature rotating

exhibitions drawn from the Center's collection; Average Annual Attendance: 75,000; Mem: 900; dues $50 - $1,000
Income: Financed by endowment, mem & state appropriation
Library Holdings: Book Volumes 1,000,000, Manuscripts, Maps, Memorabilia, Original Art Works, Original Documents, Other Holdings, Photographs, Prints, Sculpture
Special Subjects: Bookplates & Bindings, Costume Design & Constr, Drawings, Film, Industrial Design, Latin American Art, Manuscripts
Collections: manuscripts, rare books, photography, film, performing arts
Activities: Research library docent training; lects open to public, 12 vis lectrs per yr; gallery talks; tours; fels offered; individual paintings & original objects of art lent

L **Architecture & Planning Library**, Battle Hall 200, Austin, TX 78713-8916; PO Box P, Austin, TX 78713-8916. Tel 512-495-4620; Email apl@lib.utexas.edu; Web: www.lib.utexas.edu/apl; *Head Libn & Cur Alexander Architectural Archive* Beth Dodd; *Archit & Planning Librn* Katie Pierce Meyer
Open fall & spring semesters Mon -Thurs 9 AM - 10 PM, Fri 9 AM - 7 PM, Sat Noon - 6 PM, Sun 1 PM - 10 PM, reduced hours during summer sessions & intersessions; Estab 1925; Circ 172,700; Average Annual Attendance: 97,500
Library Holdings: Auction Catalogs, Audio Tapes 31, Book Volumes 96,000, CD-ROMs 33, Cards, Cassettes, Clipping Files, Exhibition Catalogs, Fiche 25,042, Filmstrips 1, Kodachrome Transparencies, Lantern Slides, Manuscripts 1,600 linear ft, Maps 160, Memorabilia, Motion Pictures 1, Original Art Works, Original Documents, Other Holdings, Pamphlets, Periodical Subscriptions 240, Photographs, Prints, Reels 499, Reproductions, Sculpture, Slides 155,311, Video Tapes
Special Subjects: Architecture, Carpets & Rugs, Constructions, Decorative Arts, Drafting, Furniture, Historical Material, Interior Design, Landscape Architecture, Period Rooms, Restoration & Conservation, Stained Glass, Tapestries
Collections: Alexander Architectural Archive
Exhibitions: Blake's Choice web exhibit (ongoing); Texas Architecture: A Visual History from the Marian Davis & Doug Blakeley Alexander Collections; Spanish Colonial Architecture in the Alexander Architectural Archive; The Architectural Legacy of Herbert Miller Greene
Activities: Classes for adults & children; tours; lending of original objects of art for exhibs

A **WOMEN & THEIR WORK,** 1710 Lavaca, Austin, TX 78701-1316. Tel 512-477-1064; Fax 512-477-1090; Email info@womenandtheirwork.org; Web: www.womenandtheirwork.org; *Exec Dir* Chris Cowden; *Prog Dir* Diane Sikes; *Gallery Dir* Rachel Stuckey
Open Mon - Fri 10 AM - 6 PM, Sat 12 - 6 PM, cl Sun; No admis fee, donations appreciated; Estab 1978 to promote recognition & appreciation of women's art; 2000 sq ft of exhib space & a gallery gift shop; Average Annual Attendance: 25,000; Mem: 1000; dues $50
Income: $500,000 (financed by endowment, mem, city & state appropriation, private foundations, corporations & gallery gift shop)
Exhibitions: Visual Arts Exhibs - Juried and curated exhibs of Tex artists & touring exhibs from outside the region; Gallery Artist Sers - Solo exhibs showcasing emerging & mid-career visual artists selected from an ann selection panel; Artist Commissions & Fees - Direct financial support for visual & performing artists through honoraria & grants; Dance, Music & Theater Performances - A member of the National Performance Network, Women & Their Work produces events featuring local, regional, and national performing artists, often in collaborative venues
Publications: Artists Brochures every 7 wks
Activities: Classes for adults & children; docent training; workshops & symposia for teachers; lects open to pub, 4 vis lectrs per yr; gallery talks; tours; originate traveling exhibs all over Texas & other sites outside the state; mus shop sells books, original art, reproductions, prints, craft items, jewelry

BANDERA

M **FRONTIER TIMES MUSEUM,** 510 13th St, Bandera, TX 78003; PO Box 1918, Bandera, TX 78003-1918. Tel 830-796-3864; Email information@frontiertimesmuseum.org; Web: www.frontiertimesmuseum.org; *Exec Dir* Rebecca Huffstutler Norton; *Pres* Kirk McMullan; *Secy* Dr William Pannebaker; *Treas* Carol Anne Boyle; *Admin Asst* Kim Miles
Open Mon - Sat 10 AM - 4:30 PM; Admis adults $5, seniors $3, children under 12 years $2; Estab 1933 to preserve records, photographs & artifacts of the American West with emphasis on the local Texas hill country area; Doane Gallery - Western & Tex regional art; Average Annual Attendance: 12,000; Mem: 25; Board of Dir meets 11 times a yr
Income: Earned income; $10,000 from F B Doane Foundation)
Special Subjects: American Western Art, Anthropology, Coins & Medals, Dolls, Drawings, Etchings & Engravings, Flasks & Bottles, Folk Art, Furniture, Historical Material, Photography, Portraits, Pottery, Prints, Textiles, Decorative Arts
Collections: F B Doane Collection of Western Paintings, Louisa Gordon Collection of Antiques, including bells from around the world, J Marvin Hunter Collection of Photographs, Artifacts, Memorabilia of American West and the Texas Hill Country, Western Hat Collection
Exhibitions: Texas Heroes Hall of Honor
Publications: Bandera County: Images of America
Activities: Group rates for educational groups; classes for children; ann Nation Day of the American Cowboy celebration in July; lects open to pub; mus shop sells books, magazines, reproductions & prints, jewelry, decorative arts

BEAUMONT

M **ART MUSEUM OF SOUTHEAST TEXAS,** 500 Main St, Beaumont, TX 77701; PO Box 3703, Beaumont, TX 77704-3703. Tel 409-832-3432; Fax 409-832-8508; Email info@amset.org; Web: www.amset.org; *Registrar* Tim Robtoy; *Cur Educ* Sandra Laurette; *Events Coordr* Christle Fengin; *Pub Rels* Menique Sennett; *Exec Dir* Lynn Castle; *Cur Art* Caitlin Williams
Open Mon - Fri 9 AM - 5 PM, Sat 10 AM - 5 PM, Sun Noon - 5 PM, cl major holidays; No admis fee; Estab 1950 as a non-profit institution to serve the community-through the visual experience & its interpretation as an instrument for educ, cultural enrichment & aesthetic enjoyment; The mus has 2400 sq ft of exhibition space, four galleries; Average Annual Attendance: 65,000; Mem: 850; dues individual $30; annual meeting in Sept
Income: Financed by endowment, mem, city appropriation, fund raisers, grants, mus shop & contributions
Purchases: Regional contemporary art
Library Holdings: Auction Catalogs, Audio Tapes, Book Volumes, Exhibition Catalogs, Periodical Subscriptions, Slides, Video Tapes
Special Subjects: Decorative Arts, Drawings, Etchings & Engravings, Folk Art, Graphics, Landscapes, Painting-American, Painting-American, Photography, Prints, Sculpture, Sculpture, Photography
Collections: 19th & 20th century American folk art, painting, sculpture, graphics & photography, James Whistler etchings & engravings
Publications: Qtr newsletter; see website for listing of other publications www. amset.org
Activities: Educ prog; classes for adults & children; docent training; lects open to pub, 9 vis lectrs per yr; Power Point lect; gallery talks; tours; sponsors competitions with awards; scholarships offered; individual paintings & original objects of art lent to other institutions; originates traveling exhibs; mus shop sells books, original art & reproductions

A **THE ART STUDIO INC,** 720 Franklin, Beaumont, TX 77701. Tel 409-838-5393; Fax 409-838-4695; Email Info@artstudio.org; Web: www.artstudio.org; *Dir* Greg Busceme; *Admin Asst* Elizabeth French
Open Tues - Sat 2 PM - 5 PM; No admis fee; Estab 1983 to provide workspace for area artist/community outreach; One gallery 60 x 30 for exhibitions; one sales gallery; 2-D & 3-D work specializing in ceramics; Average Annual Attendance: 8,000; Mem: 1700; dues minimum $35
Income: $70,000 (financed by mem, individual contributions & private foundations)
Library Holdings: Book Volumes, Exhibition Catalogs, Manuscripts, Memorabilia, Original Art Works, Original Documents, Periodical Subscriptions
Special Subjects: Afro-American Art, American Indian Art, American Western Art, Architecture, Asian Art, Bronzes, Calligraphy, Ceramics, Collages, Crafts, Decorative Arts, Drawings, Enamels, Etchings & Engravings, Folk Art, Furniture, Glass, Historical Material, Jewelry, Metalwork, Photography, Porcelain, Pottery, Pre-Columbian Art, Primitive art, Sculpture, Stained Glass, Watercolors, Woodcuts
Collections: Permanent ceramic collection of local & international artists' work
Exhibitions: 9 per yr, Feb - June & Sept - Dec, opening first Sat evening featuring local artists
Publications: Issue
Activities: Classes for adults & children; juvenile & adult probation progs; dramatic progs; lects open to pub; concerts; gallery talks; tours; low income, fixed income

M **BEAUMONT ART LEAGUE,** 2675 Gulf St, Beaumont, TX 77703-4417. Tel 409-833-4179; Email bal-dana@gtbizclass.com; Web: www.beaumontartleague.org; *Pres* Sue Bard; *Dir* Dana Dorman
Open Tues - Fri 10 AM - 4 PM, Sat 10 AM - 2 PM by appointment, cl New Year's Day, Independence Day, Thanksgiving & Christmas; No admis fee, donations accepted; Estab 1943 to promote fine art through exhibitions & art educ; Two spacious galleries with color corrected lighting & spot lights; Average Annual Attendance: 1,000; Mem: 325; dues student $20, individual $35, family $45, friend $50, patron $100, benefactor $500, lifetime $1,000; annual meeting in May
Income: $26,000 (financed by mem, donations & fundraising), grants
Purchases: Five paintings through purchase awards from juried competition
Library Holdings: Book Volumes 500, Video Tapes 20
Special Subjects: Collages, Painting-American, Sculpture, Woodcarvings
Collections: Permanent collection of paintings, photography & sculpture (93 pieces)
Exhibitions: Portrait Show; 3-D Show; Neches River Festival Exhibition; Gulf Coast Educators; Photography; Beaumont National Juried Exhibition, Membership Show; Tri-State Plus
Publications: Newsletters, 12 per year; class schedules, 4 per year; show entry forms & invitations
Activities: Classes for adults; lects open to pub, 1-2 vis lectrs per yr; gallery talks; competitions with awards; BAL National Purchase Award; Frank Gerrietts Purchase Award; lending collection contains books; mus shop sells original art

M **LAMAR UNIVERSITY,** Dishman Art Museum, 1030 E Lavaca, Beaumont, TX 77705; PO Box 10027, Beaumont, TX 77710-0027. Tel 409-880-8959; Fax 409-880-1799; Web: www.lamar.edu/dishman; *Dir* Dennis Kiel; *Mus Asst* Alyssabeth Guerra
Open Mon - Fri 10 AM - 5 PM, cl New Year's Day, Good Friday, Memorial Day, Labor Day, Thanksgiving & Christmas Day; No admis fee; Estab 1983; 6,000 sq ft exhibition space; Average Annual Attendance: 4,000
Library Holdings: Book Volumes 500
Special Subjects: African Art, Carpets & Rugs, Ceramics, Decorative Arts, Painting-American, Primitive art, Prints, Tapestries, Watercolors, Woodcarvings, Woodcuts
Collections: African & New Guinea masks & shields, 19th century painting, 19th-century porcelain, contemporary painting, prints & ceramics, Eisenstadt Collection, Robert Willis Print Collection
Activities: Lects open to pub; gallery talks; tours; schols

M **MAMIE MCFADDIN WARD HERITAGE HISTORIC FOUNDATION INC,** 725 Third St, Beaumont, TX 77701; 1906 McFaddin Ave, Beaumont, TX 77701. Tel 409-832-1906; Fax 409-832-3483; Email info@mcfaddin-ward.org; Web: www.mcfaddin-ward.org; *Cur Coll* Sherri Birdsong; *Buildings & Grounds Supv* Felix McFarland; *Dir* Matthew White; *Admin/Deputy Dir* William Stark Jr; *Educ Coordr* Janis Becker; *Mgr Visitor Center* Becky Fertitta
Open Tues - Sat 10 AM - 4 PM, Sun 1 - 4 PM, cl Mon; Admis adults $3, seniors $1.50, children under 8 not admitted; Estab 1982 to preserve, publish, exhibit & present knowledge of the period; Historic house mus with original collections of decorative arts of the period 1890-1950 as left by original owners; 17 rooms, 12,800

sq ft wood frame Beaux Arts Colonial Home with carriage house; Average Annual Attendance: 10,000
Income: $950,000 (financed by endowment)
Special Subjects: Decorative Arts, Period Rooms
Collections: American-made furniture, Continental European ceramics, Oriental rugs, period glass, period silver & porcelain
Publications: Brochure; souvenir booklet; Viewpoints, quarterly
Activities: Classes for children; docent training; family open house; lects open to pub, 4-6 vis lectrs per yr; mus shop sells books, magazines, prints & slides

L **McFaddin-Ward House**, 1906 McFaddin Ave, Beaumont, TX 77701. Tel 409-832-1906; Fax 409-832-3483; Email info@mcfaddin-ward.org; *Dir* Matthew White
Open Tues - Sat 10 AM - 4 PM, Sun 1 - 4 PM; Admis adults $3; Estab 1982 for staff & docent study; For reference only; Average Annual Attendance: 10,000
Income: Foundation funded
Library Holdings: Audio Tapes, Book Volumes 700, Clipping Files, Memorabilia, Pamphlets, Periodical Subscriptions 100, Photographs, Slides, Video Tapes
Collections: Decorative arts
Activities: Classes for adults & children; docent training; lects open to pub, 3 vis lectrs per yr; mus shop sells books, magazines, slides

BROWNSVILLE

M **BROWNSVILLE ART LEAGUE,** Brownsville Museum of Fine Art, 660 E Ringgold St, Brownsville, TX 78520-7974. Tel 956-542-0941; Fax 956-542-6931; Email rene.vanhaaften@brownsvillemfa.org; Web: www.brownsvillemfa.org; *Exec Dir* Rene Van Haaften; *Pres* Gerardo Gonzalez; *Artist Dir* Marcela Hinojosa; *Bookkeeper* Dee Ramirez; *Rentals* Dora Duarte; *Mktg & Develop Dir* Corie Olivares
Open Mon & Tues, Thurs - Sat 10 AM - 4 PM, Wed 10 AM - 8 PM, cl New Years, Easter, Labor Day, Thanksgiving & Christmas; Admis adults $10, children 6-12 $5, children under 6 no charge; Estab 1935, mus opened 1957 to offer cultural advantages to lower Rio Grande Valley; Permanent collection on rotating basis housed in the Brownsville Mus of Fine Art; Average Annual Attendance: 15,000; Mem: 300; dues Individual $60; artist $120;
Income: Financed by donations, fundraisers, mem dues
Library Holdings: Audio Tapes, Book Volumes, CD-ROMs, Cards, Clipping Files, Lantern Slides, Original Art Works, Records, Slides
Collections: Paintings by Marc Chagall, H A DeYoung, M Enagnit, William Hogarth, Augustus John, Dale Nichols, Jose Salazar, Ben Stahl, Fredric Taubes, Hauward Veal, James McNeil Whistler, N C Wyeth, Milford Zornes
Exhibitions: International Art Show
Publications: Brush Strokes, six per year
Activities: Classes for adults & children; workshops by vis artists; docent training; music classes; painting classes; lects open to pub; 4 vis lectrs per yr; concerts; gallery talks; tours; sponsoring of competitions; schols; awards: $5,000 Int Art Show, $400 Student Art Show; individual paintings lent to schools; originate traveling exhibs; mus shop sells books, original art, reproductions, prints, jewelry, pillows, notecards, pencils & other items

CANYON

M **PANHANDLE-PLAINS HISTORICAL MUSEUM,** 2503 4th Ave, WTAMU Box 60967, Canyon, TX 79015. Tel 806-651-2244; Fax 806-651-2250; Email museum@pphm.wtamu.edu; Web: www.panhandleplains.org; *Dir* Guy C Vanderpool; *Art Cur* Michael R Grauer; *Mktg Mgr* Stephanie Price
Open June - Aug, Mon - Sat 9 AM - 6 PM, Sun 1 PM - 6 PM; Sept - May, Mon - Sat 9 AM - 5 PM, Sun 1 PM - 6 PM; cl New Year's Day, Thanksgiving, Christmas Eve & Day; Admis adults $10, seniors $9, children 4-12 $5, under 4 yrs free; Estab 1933 to preserve history of the region, including all phases of history, fine arts & natural sciences; Five galleries for American, European, Texas & Frank Reaugh art & changing exhibitions; 22 galleries for art, archaeology, petroleum, textiles, western heritage, paleontology & transportation; Average Annual Attendance: 75,000; Mem: 1000; dues Goodnight Circle $1000, patron $500, supporter $250, contributor $100, family $75, friend $50
Income: $1,800,000 (financed by state, endowment & membership)
Library Holdings: Audio Tapes, Book Volumes, Cards, Clipping Files, DVDs, Fiche, Filmstrips, Manuscripts, Maps, Memorabilia, Original Documents, Periodical Subscriptions, Photographs, Prints, Records, Slides
Special Subjects: Afro-American Art, American Indian Art, American Western Art, Anthropology, Antiquities-Egyptian, Antiquities-Roman, Archaeology, Architecture, Asian Art, Baroque Art, Bookplates & Bindings, Bronzes, Calligraphy, Carpets & Rugs, Cartoons, Ceramics, Coins & Medals, Costumes, Crafts, Decorative Arts, Dioramas, Dolls, Drawings, Embroidery, Enamels, Eskimo Art, Etchings & Engravings, Ethnology, Flasks & Bottles, Folk Art, Furniture, Glass, Gold, Graphics, Hispanic Art, Historical Material, Islamic Art, Ivory, Jade, Jewelry, Landscapes, Latin American Art, Leather, Manuscripts, Maps, Marine Painting, Medieval Art, Metalwork, Mexican Art, Military Art, Miniatures, Mosaics, Oriental Art, Painting-American, Painting-British, Painting-Dutch, Painting-European, Painting-Flemish, Painting-French, Painting-German, Painting-Italian, Painting-Japanese, Painting-Polish, Painting-Russian, Painting-Scandinavian, Painting-Spanish, Period Rooms, Pewter, Photography, Porcelain, Portraits, Posters, Pottery, Pre-Columbian Art, Primitive art, Prints, Religious Art, Renaissance Art, Reproductions, Restorations, Sculpture, Silver, Southwestern Art, Stained Glass, Tapestries, Textiles, Watercolors, Woodcarvings, Woodcuts
Collections: Over 1300 paintings by 19th & early 20th century American Painters, 16th-19th century European painters
Exhibitions: Exhibitions rotate & change
Publications: Panhandle-Plains Historical Review, annually
Activities: Events for adults & children; docent training; outreach progs for pub schools; podcasts; lects open to pub; 5-6 vis lectrs per yr; gallery talks, tours; Pioneer Spirit Award; originate traveling exhibs to mus with Texas & Southwestern art interest; mus shop sells books, mag, & gifts; Panhandle-Plains Western Art Show & Sale, Summer Institute

L **Research Center**, 2401 Fourth Ave, Canyon, TX 79015. Tel 806-651-2261; Fax 806-651-2250; Web: panhandleplains.org; *Archivist & Librn* Warren Stricker; *Research Assistant* Millie Vanover
Open June - Aug Mon - Fri 12 PM - 5 PM; Sept - May Tues - Fri 12 PM - 5 PM; Circ non-circulating; For reference only
Library Holdings: Audio Tapes, Book Volumes 2000, Cards, Cassettes, Clipping Files, Compact Disks, DVDs, Exhibition Catalogs, Fiche, Framed Reproductions, Kodachrome Transparencies, Lantern Slides, Manuscripts, Maps, Memorabilia, Micro Print, Motion Pictures, Original Documents, Pamphlets, Periodical Subscriptions 40, Photographs, Records, Reels, Reproductions, Slides, Video Tapes
Special Subjects: Ethnology, Fashion Arts, History of Art & Archaeology, Illustration, Manuscripts, Maps, Painting-American, Photography, Porcelain, American Indian Art, Restoration & Conservation, Southwestern Art, Textiles, American Western Art, Anthropology, Archaeology, Architecture, Art Education, Art History, Carpets & Rugs, Cartoons, Ceramics, Commercial Art, Crafts, Decorative Arts

COLLEGE STATION

M **TEXAS A&M UNIVERSITY,** J Wayne Stark University Center Galleries, 4229 Tamu, College Station, TX 77843-0001. Tel 979-845-6081; Fax 979-862-3381; Email uart@stark.tamu.edu; Web: stark.tamu.edu; *Dir* Catherine A Hastedt; *Admin Secy* Beverly Wagner
Open Tues - Fri 9 AM - 8 PM, Sat - Sun Noon - 6 PM; No admis fee; Estab 1974 to bring art exhibits of state & national significance to Texas A & M University; Average Annual Attendance: 45,000
Income: Financed by university funds
Special Subjects: Painting-American, Art Education, Art History
Collections: Paintings by Texas artists
Activities: Classes for adults & children; docent training; lects open to pub; gallery talks; tours; book traveling exhibs; organize traveling exhibs; mus shop sells books & prints

A **MSC Visual Arts Committee**, 1237 TAMU, Memorial Student Ctr College Station, TX 77843-1237. Tel 979-845-1515; Fax 979-845-5117; Email mcompton@msc.tamu.edu; Web: www.vac.tamu.edu
Open Tues - Fri 9 AM - 8 PM, Sat & Sun Noon to 6 PM, cl Mon; No admis fee; Estab 1989; Gallery is 16 x 60 ft with lighting; windows to interior hallway for partial viewing after hours; Average Annual Attendance: 8,000; Mem: 30
Income: Financed by student service fees allotment, donations & art sales
Exhibitions: Annual Juried Student Competition
Publications: Exhibition brochures
Activities: Lects open to pub, 2 or more vis lectrs per yr; gallery talks; tours; juried competitions, 6 - 7 exhibs per yr, receptions, workshops; 1 book traveling exhib per yr

COLORADO CITY

M **HEART OF WEST TEXAS MUSEUM,** 340 E 3rd St, Colorado City, TX 79512-6408. Tel 325-728-8285; Fax 325-728-8944; Email museum@cityofcoloradocity.org; Web: www.coloradocitytexas.org; *Pres* Gay Houston; *Dir* Patty Pharis
Open Tues - Fri noon - 5 PM, cl Sat, Sun & Mon; No admis fee
Income: Financed by city appropriation
Library Holdings: Clipping Files, Maps, Memorabilia, Original Documents, Photographs, Prints, Records, Slides
Special Subjects: Anthropology, Archaeology, Dolls, Furniture, Glass, Historical Material, Period Rooms
Exhibitions: Mammoth exhibit (found nearby); Antiquus Bison exhibit (found nearby)

COMMERCE

M **TEXAS A&M UNIVERSITY - COMMERCE,** University Gallery, PO Box 3011, Commerce, TX 75429-3011. Tel 903-886-5208; Fax 903-886-5987; Email barbara_frey@tamu-commerce.edu; *Dir* Barbara Frey
Open Mon - Fri 1 PM - 5 PM; No admis fee; Estab 1979 to provide exhibitions of interest to the University & local community; Gallery 37 x 30 ft; running ft 206, sq ft 1460; track lighting; floor electrical outlets, climate control, security system; Average Annual Attendance: 3,000
Income: Financed by state appropriation
Collections: Collection of Student Work
Exhibitions: New American Talent 23rd Exhibition; Michael Peven: Good Dog/ Bon Chien; Ann Holiday Art Sale; MFA Thesis Exhibition; A&M Corpus Christi Art Faculty Exhibition; Piero Fenci & Elizabeth Alcamatsu; Graduating Senior show
Activities: Lect open to public; 4 vis lectrs per yr; gallery talks; tours; ann juried student art exhib award; assistantships offered; individual paintings & original objects of art lent to regional citizens & University facilities; originate book traveling exhib

CORPUS CHRISTI

M **ART COMMUNITY CENTER,** Art Center of Corpus Christi, 100 Shoreline, Corpus Christi, TX 78401. Tel 361-884-6406; Fax 361-884-8836; Email info@artcentercc.org; Web: artcentercc.org; *Dir* Bob Baker; *Admin Asst* Malissa Kay Baker; *Rental Coordr* Sarah Norris
Open Tues - Sun 10 AM - 4 PM; No admis fee; Estab 1972 to promote & support local artists; 5 galleries, all media; Average Annual Attendance: 7,500; Mem: 700; dues $30-$50
Special Subjects: Ceramics, Drawings, Etchings & Engravings, Glass, Graphics, Hispanic Art, Juvenile Art, Landscapes, Latin American Art, Marine Painting, Metalwork, Mexican Art, Mosaics, Painting-American, Photography, Porcelain, Portraits, Pottery, Sculpture, Stained Glass, Watercolors

Exhibitions: Monthly exhibits by member groups; Annual Dimension Show
Publications: Artbeat, bimonthly newsletter
Activities: Classes for adults & children; gallery talks; tours; lect open to public; Dimension, all-mem awards; sales gift shop sells books, original art, prints, clay & jewelry

M **BILLIE TRIMBLE CHANDLER ARTS FOUNDATION,** Texas State Museum of Asian Cultures, 1809 N Chaparral St, Corpus Christi, TX 78401-1111. Tel 361-882-2641; Fax 361-882-5718; Email asiancm@yahoo.com; Web: www.geocities.com/asiancm; *Mng Dir* Joye LaBarrett; *Admin Asst* Nozomi Lundberg
Open Tues - Sat 10 AM - 4 PM, cl New Years, Easter, Memorial Day, July 4, Labor Day, Thanksgiving & Christmas; Admis adults $6, students, seniors & military $4, children (3-12) $3, children under 3 yrs no admis fee; Estab 1973; Exhibits artifacts from Asian countries. Asian gift shop on site, gallery rental space for exhibits & events
Income: Financed by private donations, grants & memberships
Library Holdings: Framed Reproductions, Original Art Works, Periodical Subscriptions, Photographs, Reproductions, Slides, Video Tapes
Special Subjects: Antiquities-Oriental, Asian Art, Bronzes, Calligraphy, Ceramics, Costumes, Dioramas, Dolls, Embroidery, Ivory, Jade, Jewelry, Oriental Art, Painting-Japanese, Pottery, Watercolors, Woodcarvings, Woodcuts
Collections: Buddhist decorative arts, Asian & decorative arts including Hakata dolls, porcelains, metal ware, cloisonne & lacquerware, oriental fan coll, jade & ivory
Activities: Educ dept; classes for adults & children; docent training; special events monthly, Asia After Five each first Fri of month; lects open to pub; gallery talks; tours; sponsoring of competitions; sales shop sells general gift items Asian influenced, books, magazines, original art, reproductions, prints, toys & games

M **DEL MAR COLLEGE,** Joseph A Cain Memorial Art Gallery, 101 Baldwin, Corpus Christi, TX 78404-3897. Tel 361-698-1216; Fax 361-698-1511; Email krosier@delmar.edu; Web: www.delmar.edu; *Chair Art & Drama Dept* Ken Rosier; *Gallery Dir* Randy Flowers
Open Mon - Thurs 9 AM - 4 PM, Fri 9 AM - Noon; No admis fee; Estab 1932 to teach art & provide exhib showcase for col & community; Gallery consists of 1750 sq ft plus other smaller areas; Average Annual Attendance: 3,300
Income: Financed by state appropriation & private donations
Special Subjects: Drawings, Sculpture
Collections: Purchases from Annual National Drawings and Small Sculpture Show
Exhibitions: Annual Juried Exhibition open to any U.S. artist
Publications: Exhibition mailer & catalog

M **SOUTH TEXAS INSTITUTE FOR THE ARTS AFFILIATED WITH TEXAS A&M UNIVERSITY - CORPUS CHRISTI,** (South Texas Institute for the Arts) Art Museum of South Texas, 1902 N Shoreline Blvd, Corpus Christi, TX 78401-1138. Tel 361-825-3500; Fax 361-825-3520; Email artmuseum@tamucc.edu; Web: www.artmuseumofsouthtexas.org; *Assoc Dir* Sara Morgan; *Cur* Deborah Fullerton; *Dir* Joe Schenk; *Cur Educ* Linda Rodriguez; *Mktg Dir* Karol Stewart
Open Tues - Sat 10 AM - 5 PM; Sun 1 PM - 5 PM, Thurs 10 AM - 9 PM, cl Mon, New Year's, Christmas, Thanksgiving; Admis fee adults $8, seniors, students and military $6, 12 & under free; Estab 1960 as a nonprofit organization to stimulate & encourage the fullest possible understanding & appreciation of the fine arts in all forms with particular interest in the region; Average Annual Attendance: 125,000; Mem: 1,000; dues $50-$5,000
Income: $1.25 million (financed by mem, city & state appropriations, school district)
Special Subjects: American Western Art, Architecture, Ceramics, Collages, Crafts, Drawings, Etchings & Engravings, Folk Art, Furniture, Glass, Graphics, Hispanic Art, Juvenile Art, Landscapes, Latin American Art, Marine Painting, Mexican Art, Painting-American, Painting-Canadian, Pre-Columbian Art, Prints, Prints, Sculpture, Southwestern Art, Watercolors, Woodcarvings, Woodcuts
Collections: 2,000 piece permanent coll
Exhibitions: Varies, call for details
Publications: Exhibition catalogs
Activities: Classes for adults & children; docent training; filmstrips; lects open to pub, 10 vis lectrs per yr; concerts; gallery talks; tours; competitions; schols; extension prog serves South Texas; 3-5 book traveling exhibs; organize traveling exhibs (call for details; mus shop sells books, magazines, original art & artifacts related to exhibits, reproductions, prints

L **Library**, 1902 N Shoreline Blvd, Corpus Christi, TX 78401. Tel 361-825-3500; Fax 361-825-3520; Email deborah.fullerton@tamucc.edu; Web: www.artmuseumofsouthtexas.org; *Cur Exhibs* Deborah Fullerton; *Dir* Joe Schenk
Open Tues - Fri 10 AM - 5 PM; Admis fee adults $8, seniors, students & military $4, 12 & under free; Estab 1965, to provide reference information for visitors to mus & docent students; For reference only; Average Annual Attendance: 75,000; Mem: 1,200
Income: $2723
Library Holdings: Audio Tapes, Book Volumes 8000, Cassettes, Clipping Files, Exhibition Catalogs, Kodachrome Transparencies, Pamphlets, Periodical Subscriptions 40, Photographs, Reproductions, Slides, Video Tapes
Special Subjects: American Western Art, Historical Material, Landscapes, Painting-American, Photography, Pottery, Pre-Columbian Art, Prints, Sculpture, Southwestern Art, Watercolors, Woodcarvings, Woodcuts

M **TEXAS A&M UNIVERSITY-CORPUS CHRISTI,** Weil Art Gallery, 6300 Ocean Dr, Ctr for the Arts Corpus Christi, TX 78412-5815. Tel 361-825-2752; Fax 361-825-6097; Email laura.petican@tamucc.edu; Web: www.cla.tamucc.edu/art/; *Galleries Dir* Dr Laura Petican
Open Mon - Fri, 10 AM - 5 PM (different times for each exhibit), cl school holidays; No admis fee; Estab 1979 to provide high quality art exhibitions to the university & the pub; Average Annual Attendance: 10,000
Income: Financed by private & state funding
Collections: The Lee Goodman Collection
Exhibitions: Contemporary, National, International & Local Artists
Publications: Exhibition catalogs
Activities: Classes for adults & children; dramatic progs; docent training; lects open to pub; gallery talks; tours; schols offered; exten dept serves regional & local communities

CORSICANA

L **NAVARRO COLLEGE,** Gaston T Gooch Library & Learning Resource Center, 3200 W Seventh Ave, Corsicana, TX 75110-4818. Tel 903-874-6501; Fax 903-874-4636; Email dbeau@nav.cc.tx.us; Web: www.nab.cc.ts.us.org
Open Mon - Thurs 8 AM - 9 PM, Fri 8 AM - 5 PM, Sun 5 - 8 PM; No admis fee; Estab 1996 to inform & educate regarding the US Civil War; Open viewing of documents in cases
Income: Financed by endowment
Purchases: $1,000,000
Special Subjects: Advertising Design, American Indian Art, Art History, Commercial Art, Drafting, Historical Material, Intermedia, Woodcarvings
Collections: Samuels Hobbitt Collection, woodcarvings, Pearce Civil War Documents Collection, Pearce Western Art Collection, Reading Indian Artifacts Collection, Roe & Ralston Law Library, documents
Exhibitions: Civil War Documents & Memorabilia; Native American Artifacts; Woodcarvings of Artist Ludwig Kieninger

DALLAS

M **AFRICAN AMERICAN MUSEUM,** 3536 Grand Ave, Dallas, TX 75315-0157; PO Box 150157, Dallas, TX 75315-0157. Tel 214-565-9026; Fax 214-421-8204; Email info@aamdallas.org; Web: www.aamdallas.org; *Pres & CEO* Dr Harry Robinson Jr; *VPres* Jane Jones; *Exec Asst* Daphne Stephenson Baty; *Mgr Finance & Admin* Khaliq Bryant; *Mgr Progs & Graphic Design* Patrick Finnell
Open Tues - Fri 11 AM - 5 PM, Sat 10 AM - 5 PM, cl Sun - Mon; Admis for groups of 10 or more, adults $5, children & youth 4-17 $3; Average Annual Attendance: 201,000
Library Holdings: Book Volumes 1,500
Collections: African American fine art & folk art, Texas Black history
Publications: Quarterly newsletter
Activities: Educ prog; docent prog; lects; book traveling exhibs

M **DALLAS CONTEMPORARY,** Dallas Visual Art Center, 161 Glass St, Dallas, TX 75207-6903. Tel 214-821-2522; Fax 214-821-9103; Email info@dallascontemporary.org; Web: www.dallascontemporary.org; *Exec Dir* Peter Dirishenko; *Adjunct Cur* Pedro Alonzo; *Visitor Servs & Learning Assoc* Amy Dierdorf; *Develop Asst* Amy Dierdorf
Open Tues - Sat, 11 AM - 6 PM, Sun noon - 5 PM; No admis fee; Estab 1981 to provide exhibition, educ & information opportunities for visual artists & art appreciators in North Texas; 5 galleries totaling 12,000 sq ft, natural light; track lighting; Average Annual Attendance: 15,000; Mem: 800; dues $50-$2500; mem open to artists & art appreciators
Income: Financed by donations, grants, facility use fees, mem & fundraising
Exhibitions: Theme & solo exhibitions open to the public with both private & public openings; Annual Membership Exhibition
Publications: Exhibition programs & catalogs; newsletter, monthly
Activities: Tours for adults & children; self guided tours; drawing classes; off-site progs for students; classes for adults; tours & classes for children; gallery talks; Legends, in it's 12th yr, honors the artist, professional, patron; traveling exhibs: galleries, mus in Texas & in the Southwest

A **DALLAS HISTORICAL SOCIETY,** Hall of State, 3939 Grand Ave, Dallas, TX 75315; PO Box 150038, Fair Park Dallas, TX 75315-0038. Tel 214-421-4500; Fax 214-421-7500; Email amy@dallashistory.org; Web: www.dallashistory.org; *Exec Dir* Amy Alderedge; *Dir Colls* Alan Olson
Open Tues - Sat 10 AM - 5 PM, Sun 1 - 5 PM, cl Mon; No admis fee; Estab 1922 to collect & preserve materials relative to the history of Texas & Dallas; The Hall of State is an example of Art-Deco architecture; exhibition space totals 5000 sq ft; Average Annual Attendance: 130,000; Mem: dues $25 & up; annual meeting in Apr
Income: Financed by mem & city appropriation, private donations
Library Holdings: Auction Catalogs, Audio Tapes, Book Volumes, Cards, Cassettes, Clipping Files, Exhibition Catalogs, Fiche, Filmstrips, Framed Reproductions, Kodachrome Transparencies, Lantern Slides, Manuscripts, Maps, Memorabilia, Micro Print, Motion Pictures, Original Art Works, Original Documents, Other Holdings, Pamphlets, Periodical Subscriptions, Photographs, Prints, Records, Reels, Reproductions, Sculpture, Slides, Video Tapes
Collections: Texas/Dallas Gallery, Frank Reaugh, Bound for Texas, White House in Miniature
Publications: Dallas Historical Society Register, newsletter biannual; Dallas Rediscovered: A Photographic Chronicle of Urban Expansion; When Dallas Became a City: Letters of John Milton McCoy, 1870-1881; A Guide to Fair Park, Dallas
Activities: In-class progs; classes for adults & children; dramatic progs; docent training; summer children's workshops; lects open to pub, 2 vis lectrs per yr; gallery talks; tours; awards; book signings; historic & current affairs open forums; sponsor local Awards for Excellence; Stanley Marcus Gale for fashion design achievement; exten dept; individual & original objects of art lent to local school & Houston Museum of Fine Arts; book traveling exhibs 6 per yr; originate traveling exhibs; sales shops sells books, magazines, reproductions, prints, slides, photos

L **Research Center Library**, Hall of State, Fair Park, PO Box 150038 Dallas, TX 75315-0038. Tel 214-421-4500; Fax 214-421-7500; Email alan@dallashistory.org; Web: www.dallashistory.org; *Dir Colls* Alan Olson
Open Tues - Sat 10 AM - 5 PM, Sun 1 PM - 5 PM; For reference only
Library Holdings: Book Volumes 1600, Cards, Cassettes, Clipping Files, Exhibition Catalogs, Filmstrips, Framed Reproductions, Lantern Slides, Manuscripts, Maps, Memorabilia, Motion Pictures, Original Art Works, Other Holdings Archives, pages 2,000,000, Pamphlets, Periodical Subscriptions 20, Photographs, Prints, Records, Reels, Reproductions, Sculpture, Slides, Video Tapes
Special Subjects: Manuscripts, Maps, Historical Material

Collections: R M Hayes Photographic Collection of Texas Historic Sites, J J Johnson & C E Arnold Photographs of Turn-of-the-Century Dallas, Frank Reaugh Paintings, Allie Tennant Papers, Texas Centennial Papers, WWI & WWII posters
Exhibitions: All Together; WWI Posters of the Allied Nations; Fair Park Moderne: Art & Architecture of the 1936 Texas Centennial Exposition
Publications: Exhibit catalogs
Activities: Activities for school children; docent training; city tours

M **DALLAS MUSEUM OF ART,** 1717 N Harwood St, Dallas, TX 75201-2315. Tel 214-922-1200; Fax 214-922-1350; Email members@dma.org; Web: www.dma.org; *Dir* Agustin Arteaga; *Dir Mktg & Commun* K.C. Hurst; *Cir Collections Mgmt* Gabriella Truly; *Dep Dir* Tamara Wootton-Forsyth; *Assoc Cur Contemporary Art* Suzanne Weaver; *Sr Cur Arts of Africa, Pacific & Americas* Dr Roslyn A Walker; *Cur Contemporary Art* Charles Wylie; *Dir Communs & Pub Affairs* Jill Bernstein
Open Tues - Sun 11 AM - 5 PM, Thurs until 9 PM, Late Night Fridays on 3rd Fri of all months (except Dec) open until Midnight, cl Mon, New Year's Day, July 4, Thanksgiving & Christmas; No gen admis fee, special exhib admis adults $16, seniors & military $14, students $12, mems & children under 12 free; Estab 1903 to purchase and borrow works of art from all periods for the aesthetic enjoyment and educ of the pub; Fifteen galleries for permanent collection; 14,000 sq ft for temporary exhibition; Average Annual Attendance: 550,000; Mem: 22,000 dues $50 & up; annual meeting May
Income: $8,900,000 (financed by endowment, mem & city appropriation)
Purchases: $1,000,000
Special Subjects: African Art, Afro-American Art, American Indian Art, American Western Art, Antiquities-Assyrian, Antiquities-Byzantine, Antiquities-Egyptian, Antiquities-Etruscan, Antiquities-Greek, Antiquities-Oriental, Antiquities-Persian, Antiquities-Roman, Archaeology, Architecture, Asian Art, Baroque Art, Bronzes, Calligraphy, Carpets & Rugs, Ceramics, Coins & Medals, Collages, Crafts, Decorative Arts, Drawings
Collections: European & American painting & sculpture, ancient Mediterranean & Pre-Columbian art, African, Oceanic & Japanese art, drawings, prints, American & European decorative arts, Audio-Visual Installations, Texas Regional Art
Publications: Annual report; exhibition catalogs; President's newsletter; quarterly newsletter
Activities: Classes for adults & children; workshops; Family Celebrations; weekends at the Museum; Late Nights; summer camps; school outreach; docent training; lects open to pub, 50 vis lectrs per yr; concerts; Jazz series Thursday Night Live; film series; gallery talks; tours; exten dept serving Dallas County; artmobile; individual paintings & original objects of art lent to other mus; book traveling exhibs 3-4 per yr; originate traveling exhibs; mus shop sells books, magazines, original art, prints, slides, jewelry, toys, cards & puzzles

L **Mildred R & Frederick M Mayer Library,** 1717 N Harwood St, Dallas, TX 75201-2398. Tel 214-922-1277 (Library), 214-922-1367 (Archives); Email archives@dma.org; Email library@dma.org; Web: www.dma.org/research/library; *Dir Libraries* Jacqueline Allen; *Librn* Jenny Stone; *Asst Librn* Kellye Hallmark; *Cataloger* Cathy Zisk
Open Tues - Fri 11 AM - 4:30 PM, Sat noon - 4:30 PM; For reference and research use by staff & pub
Income: Financed by city & private endowment
Library Holdings: Auction Catalogs, Book Volumes 100,000, Clipping Files, Exhibition Catalogs, Original Documents, Other Holdings Artist File, Periodical Subscriptions 105
Special Subjects: Art History, Decorative Arts

L **J ERIC JOHNSON LIBRARY,** Fine Arts Division, 1515 Young St, Dallas, TX 75201-5411. Tel 214-670-1700; Fax 214-670-1646; Email askalibrarian@dallaslibrary.org; Web: www.dallaslibrary.org; *Mgr Fine Art Div* Victor Kralisz; *Art Librn* Gwen Dixie; *Theater/Film Librn* Cathy Ritchie
Open Mon & Fri - Sat 10 AM - 6 PM, Tues -Thurs 10 AM - 8 PM; Sun 1 PM - 5 PM; No admis fee; Estab 1901 to furnish the citizens of Dallas with materials and information concerning the arts; 42 ft x 32 ft; Average Annual Attendance: 1,500
Income: Financed by city appropriation, federal & state aid, Friends of the Library, endowment
Library Holdings: Auction Catalogs, Audio Tapes, Book Volumes 88,000, Clipping Files 81 drawers, Compact Disks 11,500, DVDs 2,900, Exhibition Catalogs 750, Fiche, Memorabilia, Other Holdings 19,000 Music Scores, Periodical Subscriptions 375, Photographs, Prints, Records 39,000, Video Tapes 4,500
Collections: W E Hill Collection (history of American theater), Lawrence Kelly Collection of Dallas Civic Opera Set & Costume Designs, Manuscript Archives (music), Margo Jones Theater Collection, original fine print coll, John Rosenfield Collection (art and music critic), Interstate Theatre Collection, USA Film Festival Files, Local Archival Material in Film, Dance, Theatre & Music, Dallas Theater Archives, Dallas Theater Center & other local theater colls, Undermain Theater
Exhibitions: "First Timers": Students, Schools, Less Established Artists
Activities: Dramatic progs, dance progs; concerts; sales shop sells books & magazines

M **THE MCKINNEY AVENUE CONTEMPORARY (THE MAC),** 1601 S Ervay St, Dallas, TX 75215; PO Box 600272, Dallas, TX 75360-0272. Tel 214-953-1212; Fax 214-953-1873; Email rachel@the-mac.org; Web: the-mac.org; *Dir* Rachel Rogerson
Closed for renovations; No admis fee, suggested donation $5; Estab 1994; non-profit supporting emerging & established artists; Average Annual Attendance: 11,000
Income: (financed by mem, sponsorships, donations & grants)
Exhibitions: Annual Membership Exhib
Activities: Lects open to pub; concerts; gallery talks; art talks; community events; mus shop sells books, magazines, original art & prints

M **MIRACLE AT PENTECOST FOUNDATION,** Biblical Arts Center, 7500 Park Ln, Dallas, TX 75225-2025; PO Box 12727, Dallas, TX 75225-0727. Tel 214-691-4661; Fax 214-691-4752; Web: www.biblicalarts.org; *Dir* Ronnie L Roese; *Cur* Susan E Metcalf
Open Tues - Sat 10 AM - 5 PM, Thurs evenings by appointment, Sun 1 - 5 PM, cl New Year's Day, Thanksgiving, Christmas Eve & Christmas Day; Admis adults $4, seniors $3.50, students 13-18 $3, children 6-12 $2.50, exhibition galleries free; Estab 1966 to provide a place where people of all faiths may have the opportunity to witness the Bible as it inspires mankind in the arts; Average Annual Attendance: 45,000
Income: Financed by private foundation
Special Subjects: Religious Art
Collections: Joseph Boggs Beale's Biblical Illustrations, founder's collection of oriental art, Torger Thompson's Miracle at Pentecost painting & Miracle at Pentecost pilot painting, Biblical art
Exhibitions: Annual Children's Juried Art Show
Publications: Books, Creation of a Masterpiece, Videotape, Pentecost: Gift from God, Christianity and the Arts Magazine
Activities: Educ progs; docent training; gallery talks; competitions; individual paintings & original objects of art lent; book traveling exhibs 8-12 per yr; originate traveling exhibs to other mus; mus shop sells books, reproductions, prints, slides

L **SOUTHERN METHODIST UNIVERSITY,** Hamon Arts Library, 6100 Hillcrest Ave, Dallas, TX 75275-0356; PO Box 750356, Dallas, TX 75275-0356. Tel 214-768-2894; Fax 214-768-1800; Email bmitchel@smu.edu; Web: www.smu.edu/cul/hamon; *Dir & Head Reserach Servs* Jolene de Verges; *Art Librn* Beverly Mitchell; *Head Bywaters Spec Coll* Ellen Buie Niewyk; *Cur Asst* Scott Martin
Open Mon - Thurs 8 AM - 12 AM, Fri 8 AM - 6 PM, Sat 12 PM - 5 PM, Sun 2 PM - 12 AM; No admis fee; Estab to support educational curriculum of art & art history department of university; Circ 42,500; Average Annual Attendance: 150,000
Library Holdings: Audio Tapes, Book Volumes 152,000, Cassettes, Compact Disks 10,000, DVDs 200, Exhibition Catalogs, Fiche, Original Art Works, Other Holdings Music scores, Pamphlets, Periodical Subscriptions 269, Reels, Video Tapes 1,100
Special Subjects: Antiquities-Byzantine, Antiquities-Egyptian, Antiquities-Etruscan, Antiquities-Greek, Antiquities-Roman, Architecture, Art History, Ceramics, Coins & Medals, Costume Design & Constr, Etchings & Engravings, Film, Painting-American, Painting-British, Painting-Spanish, Painting-European
Activities: Lects open to pub

M **Meadows Museum,** 5900 Bishop Blvd, Dallas, TX 75205; PO Box 750357, Dallas, TX 75275-0357. Tel 214-768-2516; Fax 214-768-1688; Email meadowsmuseuminfo@smu.edu; Web: meadowsmuseumdallas.org; *Dir* Mark Roglan; *Mus Accnt* Roni Arifin; *Mktg & Pub Rels Mgr* Carrie Sanger; *Asst to Dir* Irene Davies; *Mus Servs & Opers Mgr* Jennifer Aprea; *Assoc Dir & Cur Exhibs* Bridget Marx; *Security Supv* Brenda Laury; *Dir Educ* Scott Winterrowd; *Educ Coordr* Kayle Patton; *Cur* Nicole Atzbach; *Curatorial Asst* Shelley DeMaria; *Collections Mgr* Anne Lenhart; *Special Events Mgr* Robin Benson Linek; *Exhibitions Coordinator* Julie Herrick; *Publications Coord* Anne Keefe
Open Tues-Sat 10AM-5PM, Thurs until 9PM, Sun 1PM-5PM; Admis $12 adults, $10 seniors (65+), $4 students; Estab 1965 to preserve & study the art of Spain; Average Annual Attendance: 50,000; Mem: Approx 2,000, dues $60 & up
Income: 3 million; financed by endowment, gifts, tuition allocation, and museum revenue
Special Subjects: Baroque Art, Etchings & Engravings, Landscapes, Medieval Art, Painting-Spanish, Religious Art, Sculpture, Hispanic Art, Portraits, Prints, Renaissance Art
Collections: Paintings: Fernando Yanez de la Almedina (active 1505-1531), Saint Sebastian (1506), Juan de Borgona (active 1508-1514), Juan Carreno de Miranda (1614-1685), The Flaying of Saint Bartholomew (1666), Bartolome Esteban Murillo (1618-1682), The Immaculate Conception (ca 1655), Jacob Laying the Peeled Rods Before the Flocks of Laban (ca 1665), Jusepe de Ribera (1591-1652), Portrait of a Knight of Santiago (ca 1630-40), Diego Rodriguez de Silva y Velazquez (1599-1660), Sibyl With Tabula Rasa (ca 1644-1648), Francisco de Goya (1746-1828), The Madhouse at Saragossa (1794), Joan Miro (1893-1983), Queen Louise of Prussia (1929), Pablo Picasso (1881-1973), Still Life in a Landscape (1915), Antoni Tapies Grand Noir (Great Black Relief) (1973), Sculpture: Alejo de Vahia (active ca 1480-1510), Pieta (1490-1510), Juan Martinez Montanes (1568-1649), Saint John the Baptist (ca 1630-1635), Anonymous (Follower of Pedro de Mena), Saint Anthony of Padua Holding the Christ Child (ca 1700), El Grecco: St Francis Kneeling in Meditation, Elizabeth Meadows Sculpture Collection, University Art Collection
Publications: Exhibition Catalogues; Bi-annual Members Magazine at the Meadows
Activities: Classes for adults & children; docent training; outreach prog, university initiatives; lects open to pub; lects for mems only; vis lectrs 25 per yr; concerts; tours; gallery talks; Moss/Chumley Award; competitions with awards, family days; internships & fellowships offered; individual paintings & original objects of art lent to other museums & galleries in US & Europe for scholarly exhibs, SMU continuing studies; originates traveling exhibs; mus shop sells books, reproductions, prints, catalogs, jewelry, and various items

DENTON

M **TEXAS WOMAN'S UNIVERSITY ART GALLERY,** PO Box 425469, Denton, TX 76204-5469. Tel 817-898-2530; Fax 817-898-2496; Email visualarts@twu.edu; Web: www.twu.edu/as/va/gallery.html; *Dir* Corky Stuckenbruck; *Chair* John L Weinkein
Open Mon - Fri 9 AM - 4 PM, Sat 1 - 4 PM & Sun upon request; No admis fee; Fine Arts Building consists of two galleries, each consisting of 3000 sq ft; Average Annual Attendance: 4,000
Income: Financed by Art Department & student activities fees
Exhibitions: Departmental galleries have approx twelve exhibits per school yr
Activities: Concerts; gallery talks; tours; competitions with awards; scholarships offered

M **UNIVERSITY OF NORTH TEXAS,** Art Gallery, 1155 Union Circle # 305100, College of Visual Arts and Design Arts Bldg Room 17 Denton, TX 76203-5100. Tel 940-565-2000, 565-4316; Fax 940-565-4717; *Gallery Dir* Diana Block
Open Mon & Tues Noon - 8 PM, Wed - Sat Noon - 5 PM, cl Thanksgiving; No admis fee; Estab 1960 as a teaching gallery directed to students of University of North Texas, the Denton Community & Dallas/Fort Worth area; The gallery covers

193 running ft of exhibition wall space, approx 10 ft high, which may be divided into smaller spaces by the use of semi-permanent portable walls; the floor is carpeted-terrazzo; Average Annual Attendance: 10,000
Income: Financed by state appropriation
Collections: Voertman Collection (student purchases), permanent coll
Publications: Exhibition announcements
Activities: Lects open to public, 4-8 vis lectrs per yr; tours; competitions; individual paintings & original objects of art lent to the university offices; originate traveling exhibs to other universities & museums

L **Visual Resources Collection**, 1155 Union Circle #305100, College of Visual Arts and Design Arts Bldg Room 107 Denton, TX 76203-5100. Tel 940-565-4019; Fax 940-565-4717; Email graham@unt.edu; *Visual Resources Cur* Ann Graham, MFA; *Asst Cur* Jennifer Richmond, MA
Estab to provide art images for instruction; For reference only
Purchases: $6000
Library Holdings: DVDs 500, Lantern Slides, Other Holdings Interactive CD 50; Laserdiscs 10, Image Database, Video Tapes 700

L **Libraries**, 1155 Union Circle #305190, Denton, TX 76203-5017. Tel 940-565-2413, 565-3025, 565-2696; Fax 940-369-8760; Email dgrose@library.unt.edu; Web: www.library.unt.edu; *Dean* Donald Grose; *Asst Dean* Sandra Atchison
Open Mon - Thurs 7:30 AM - 2 AM; Fri 7:30 AM - 12 AM; Sat 9 AM - 12 AM, Sun 1 PM - 2 AM; Estab 1903 to support the acad progs & faculty & student research
Income: Financed by state appropriation
Library Holdings: Audio Tapes, Book Volumes 50,000, Cassettes, Exhibition Catalogs, Fiche, Filmstrips, Motion Pictures, Original Art Works, Periodical Subscriptions 186, Prints, Records, Reels, Reproductions, Slides, Video Tapes
Special Subjects: Advertising Design, Art Education, Art History, Ceramics, Photography, Printmaking, Sculpture, Textiles
Collections: Art auction sales catalogs & information

EDINBURG

M **HIDALGO COUNTY HISTORICAL MUSEUM,** 121 E McIntyre St, Edinburg, TX 78541-3537. Tel 956-383-6911; Fax 956-381-6911; Email hchm@hiline.net; Web: www.riograndeborderlands.org; *Exec Dir* Mrs Shan Rankin; *Asst Dir & Cur Exhibits* Thomas A Fort; *Cur Archives & Coll* David J Mycue; *Develop Officer* Lynne Beeching; *Educ* Rachel Brown; *Pub Rels Officer* Jim McKone; *Coll & Exhib* Robert Garcia; *Programming Officer* Mia Marisol Buentello; *Archival Asst* Esteban Lomas; *Maintenance* Nazario Reyna; *Chmn Board Trustees* Danny Gurwitz; *Admin Asst* Marisela Saenz; *Receptionist* Sandra Luna
Open Tues - Fri 9 AM - 5 PM, Sat 10 AM - 5 PM, Sun 1 - 5 PM; Admis adults $2, seniors $1.50, students $1, children $.50; Estab 1967 to preserve & present the borderland heritage of south Texas & northeastern Mexico; Maintains reference library; Average Annual Attendance: 25,000; Mem: 800; dues $25-$1000
Income: $800,000 (financed by endowment, mem, county & city appropriation, fundraising)
Special Subjects: American Indian Art, American Western Art, Anthropology, Graphics, Hispanic Art, Latin American Art, Manuscripts, Maps, Mexican Art, Photography, Portraits, Posters
Collections: Historic Artifacts of Region
Exhibitions: Regional Emphasis: Early Spanish Settlement; Mexican American War; Civil War; Ranching; Steamboat Era; Hanging Tower; Early Agriculture; Revolution on the Rio Grande
Publications: Exhibition catalogs
Activities: Classes for adults & children; dramatic progs; docent training; lects open to pub, 15-20 vis lectrs per yr; tours; mus shop sells books, gifts & toys

M **UNIVERSITY OF TEXAS PAN AMERICAN,** Charles & Dorothy Clark Gallery; University Gallery, Fine Arts Complex, 1201 W University Dr Edinburg, TX 78539. Tel 956-381-2655; Fax 956-384-5072; Email galleries@utpa.edu; Web: www.utpa.edu/dept/art/pages/artgall.html; *Gallery Dir* Patricia Ballinger
Open Mon - Fri 9 AM-5 PM, nights and weekends for theater performances; No admis fee; To serve our growing students body & community-at-large; 2 art galleries on campus of University of Texas Pan-American; Average Annual Attendance: 10,000
Income: University funding
Special Subjects: Ceramics, Posters, Prints, Sculpture
Collections: Coll includes pieces by: Josef Albers, Salvador Dali, Honore Daumier, Francisco Goya, Rudolf Hausner, Roy Lichtenstein, Georges Rouault, permanent coll of ceramics, modern sculpture, paintings, posters, pre-Columbian artifacts, prints
Exhibitions: Temporary exhibitions by contemporary artists from around the United States & Mexico; BFA student shows; MFA shows
Activities: Lects open to pub; gallery talks; tours; sponsoring of competitions; Ann Student Art Show awards; lending of original objects of art to Univ offices and buildings

M **UTPA Art Galleries**, Communications Arts & Sciences Bldg, 1201 W University Dr Edinburg, TX 78539-2970. Tel 956-381-2655; Fax 956-384-5072; Email galleries@utpa.edu; Web: www.utpa.edu/dept/art/pages/artgall.html; *Gallery Dir* Patricia Ballinger
Open Mon - Thurs 10 AM - Noon, Tues & Thurs 1 - 3 PM; No admis fee; Estab 1986 to serve the university student body as well as the community at large; Average Annual Attendance: over 10,000 per yr
Income: Univ funding
Special Subjects: Ceramics, Posters, Prints, Sculpture
Collections: Coll includes pieces by: Joseph Albers, Salvador Dali, Honore Daumier, Francisco Goya, Rudolf Hausner, Roy Lichtenstein, Georges Rouault, permanent coll of ceramics, modern sculpture, paintings, posters, pre-Columbian artifacts, prints
Exhibitions: Temporary exhibitions by contemporary artists from around the United States & Mexico; BFA student shows; Masters Fine Arts Exhibitions
Activities: Lects open to pub; gallery tours; student competitions

EL PASO

M **CITY OF EL PASO,** One Arts Festival Plaza, El Paso, TX 79901-1135. Tel 915-532-1707; Fax 915-532-1010; Email tomormx@elpasotexas.gov; Web: www.elpasoartmuseum.org; *Dir* Michael A Tomor Ph.D.; *Cur of Coll* William R Thompson; *Registrar* Elizabeth A Schorr; *Asst Cur* Jerry Medrano; *Asst Cur Educ* Ann Camp
Open Tues - Sat 9 AM - 5 PM, Sun noon - 5 PM, cl Mon; Admis general $1, students & children $.50, free on Sun; Estab 1960 as a cultural & educational institution; Tom Lea Gallery, De Wetter Gallery, Contemporary Gallery, Samuel H. Kress Gallery; Average Annual Attendance: 80,000; Mem: 750; dues $15-$5000
Income: Financed by mem & city appropriation
Library Holdings: Auction Catalogs, Exhibition Catalogs, Pamphlets, Periodical Subscriptions
Special Subjects: Afro-American Art, American Western Art, Baroque Art, Graphics, Hispanic Art, Latin American Art, Mexican Art, Painting-American, Painting-European, Painting-Flemish, Painting-French, Painting-Italian, Painting-Spanish, Photography, Pre-Columbian Art, Renaissance Art, Southwestern Art, Watercolors, Woodcuts
Collections: Kress Collection of Renaissance & Baroque Periods, 19th & 20th century American painting, contemporary American & Mexican, Mexican Colonial paintings, works on paper, American & European, Samuel H Kress Collection
Publications: Members' newsletter, teacher newsletter
Activities: Classes for adults & children; docent training; lects open to pub, concerts; gallery talks; tours; individual paintings & original objects of art lent to other mus & institutions on request; originate traveling exhibs to accredited mus & university galleries; mus shop sells unique gifts, mus catalogs, souvenirs, books, reproductions, slides, jewelry, toys, home & office products

L **El Paso Museum of Art**, One Arts Festival Plaza, El Paso, TX 79901-1135. Tel 915-532-1707; Fax 915-532-1010; Web: www.elpasoartmuseum.org; *Dir* Victoria Ramirez PhD; *Cur* Kate Green; *Preparator* Nick Munoz; *Registrar* Michelle Villa
Open Tues, Wed, Fri & Sat 9 AM - 5 PM, Thurs 9 AM - 9 PM, Sun noon - 5 PM, cl Mon & city holidays; No admis fee; Estab 1947; Open to the pub & mem for reference only; Average Annual Attendance: 100,000; Mem: 900
Library Holdings: Auction Catalogs, Book Volumes 1500, Cards, Exhibition Catalogs, Kodachrome Transparencies, Periodical Subscriptions 8, Slides
Special Subjects: Aesthetics, Afro-American Art, American Indian Art, American Western Art, Art History, Latin American Art, Mexican Art, Painting-American, Painting-European, Painting-Flemish, Painting-French, Painting-German, Painting-Italian, Painting-Spanish, Photography, Prints
Collections: 19th- & 20th-century American Art, Colonial Mexican Art, Samuel H Kress Collection
Publications: James Surls: Walking with Diamonds, 99; Eugene Thurston: The Majesty of the Southwestern Landscape, 2000
Activities: Classes for adults & children; dramatic progs; docent training; lects open to pub, 25 vis lectrs per yr; concerts; gallery talks; tours; Design Awards, TX Assoc Museums; exten prog lends original objects of art to mus; book traveling exhibs; originate traveling exhibs to regional mus; mus shop sells books, slides & original art

M **El Paso Museum of Archaeology**, 4301 Transmountain Rd, El Paso, TX 79924. Tel 915-755-4332; Fax 915-759-6824; Email archaeologymuseum@elpasotexas.gov; Web: archaeology.elpasotexas.gov; *Dir* Jeff Romney; *Cur* George Maloof; *Community Engagement Manager* Brittany Hutchinson
Open Tues - Sat 9 AM - 5 PM,; No admis fee; Estab 1977 as an archaeological mus to show human adaptation to a desert environment; Mus contains replica of Olla Cave, a Mogollon cliff dwelling & four other prehistoric dioramas & artifacts from the US Southwest & Mexico; Average Annual Attendance: 15,000; Mem: Student $15, individual $25, family $40
Income: Financed by city appropriation
Special Subjects: American Indian Art, Archaeology
Collections: Five dioramas depict life styles & climate changes of Paleo Indians including the hunting & gathering area & the Hueco Tanks site, Pre-Columbian (Casas Grandos) & Mogollon archaeological artifacts, Apache, Tarahumara artifact colls
Activities: Classes for children; slide lect demonstrations at schools & civic organizations; docent training; lects open to pub; tours, sponsor competitions; 24 visiting lects per year;; book traveling exhibs annually; sales shop sells books, reproductions, original art & prints

M **INTERNATIONAL MUSEUM OF ART,** 1211 Montana Ave, El Paso, TX 79902-5511. Tel 915-543-6747; Fax 915-543-9222; Email iavatx@aol.com; Web: www.internationalmuseumofart.net; *Dir* Mitzi Quirarte; *Asst to Dir* Louie Garcia
Open Wed - Fri 10 PM - 5 PM, Sat & Sun 1 - 5 PM; No admis fee; Estab 1991; Historical Trost Building, home of Mr & Mrs William Turney; permanent & rotating exhibs; Average Annual Attendance: 3,000; Mem: 250; dues $50
Income: Contributions, rental fees, gift shop sales
Special Subjects: African Art, Architecture, Asian Art, Bronzes, Carpets & Rugs, Coins & Medals, Costumes, Decorative Arts, Dolls, Drawings, Etchings & Engravings, Furniture, Glass, Hispanic Art, Landscapes, Latin American Art, Mexican Art, Oriental Art, Porcelain, Portraits, Religious Art, Reproductions, Sculpture, Southwestern Art, Stained Glass, Tapestries, Watercolors, Woodcarvings, Painting-American, Painting-Japanese, Painting-Polish, Painting-Russian, Painting-Spanish
Collections: collections from Asia & Africa; Mexican Revolution collection including a replica of Pancho Villa's death mask & a replica of a Mexican casita, dolls, sculptures, antiques
Activities: Classes for adults & children; art classes; docent training; lects open to pub; concerts; gallery talks; tours; sponsored competitions; mus shop sells reproductions, prints, books, magazines, original art, jewelry, sculpture, consignment artwork

M **UNIVERSITY OF TEXAS AT EL PASO,** Stanlee & Gerald Rubin Center for the Visual Arts, 500 W University Ave, Department of Art El Paso, TX 79902-5816. Tel 915-747-6151; Fax 915-747-6067; Email rubincenter@utep.edu; Web: www.rubincenter.utep.edu; *Dir* Kerry Doyle; *Asst Dir* Melissa Barba; *Graphic/ Production Mgr* Victoria Aviles; *Preparator* Daniel Szwaczkowski

Open Tues, Wed, & Fri 10AM-5PM, Thurs 10AM-7PM, Sat Noon-5PM; No admis fee; University estab 1914, Department of Art established 1940, Rubin Center est 2004; 3 galleries: 1900, 1100, and 550 sq ft; Average Annual Attendance: 50,000
Income: Public and private gifts and grants
Special Subjects: Crafts, Painting-American, Prints
Exhibitions: Contra Flujo: Independence & Revolution; Fernando Llanos: Revolutionary Imaginary; Zeke Pena: Reclaim; Feral: Federation by Agency
Publications: Exhibition catalogs
Activities: Classes for adults & children; lect open to public; 10 vis lectrs per yr; 2-4 gallery talks per year; tours; competitions; gallery tours; exten work offered through university exten service to anyone over high school age; fees vary; 1 book traveling exhib per yr; Originates traveling exhibitions that circulate to other museums and galleries

FORT WORTH

M **AMON CARTER MUSEUM OF AMERICAN ART,** 3501 Camp Bowie Blvd, Fort Worth, TX 76107-2695. Tel 817-738-1933; Fax 817-989-5099; Email visitors@cartermuseum.org; Web: www.cartermuseum.org; *Head of Collections & Registrar* Marci Driggers; *Cur Paintings & Sculpture* Shirley Reece-Hughes; *Sr Cur Photographs* John Rohrbach; *Head of Library* Samuel Duncan; *Head of Publications* Will Gillham; *Public Relations Mgr* Stefanie Ball; *COO* Scott Wilcox; *Director* Andrew Walker; *Conservator of Photography* Fernanda Valverde; *Exhibs Mgr* Alessandra Guzman; *Conservator, Works on Paper* Jodie Utter; *Director of Development & Communications* Guy C Vanderpool
Open Tues - Wed & Fri - Sat 10 AM - 5 PM, Thurs 10 AM - 8 PM, Sun 12 PM - 5 PM, cl Mon & major holidays; No admis fee; Estab 1961 for the study & documentation of American art through permanent collections, exhibitions & publications; Twenty one small galleries, special Exhib galleries, atrium; Average Annual Attendance: 105,000; Mem: 1,500; dues $65 - $500
Income: Financed by endowment, grants & contributions
Special Subjects: Afro-American Art, American Indian Art, American Western Art, Art History, Bronzes, Drawings, Etchings & Engravings, Folk Art, Historical Material, Landscapes, Landscapes, Maps, Painting-American, Photography, Photography, Prints, Prints, Reproductions, Restorations, Sculpture, Southwestern Art, Watercolors, Woodcuts, Portraits
Collections: American paintings & sculpture, print coll, photographs, illustrated books, works on paper, Remington & Russell, Artists archives (include photographic holdings of Eliot Porter, Laura Gilpin, Karl Struss, Clara Sippell, Nell Dorr, Carlotta Corpron, Helen Post & Erwin E Smith
Publications: Monthly Calendar of Events, bi-annual Program & active publication program in American art & history
Activities: Programs for adults & children; docent training; lects open to public, gallery talks; tours; Davidson Family Fellowship; individual paintings & original objects of art lent to national art mus; lending collection contains original art works, paintings, photographs, sculpture, ephemera material; fels; book traveling exhibs 2-3 per yr; originate traveling exhibs 2-3 to national art mus; mus shop sells books, prints & gift items

L **Research Library**, 3501 Camp Bowie Blvd, Fort Worth, TX 76107-2062. Tel 817-989-5040; Fax 817-989-5032; Email library@cartermuseum.org; Web: www.cartermuseum.org/library; library.tcu.edu/cdlccat (catalog); *Head of Library & Archives* Samuel Duncan; *Archivist & reference Servs Mgr* Jon Frembling; *Technical Services Librarian & Archivist* Rachel Panella
Open Wed & Fri - Sat 11 AM - 4 PM, Thurs 11 AM - 7 PM; Estab 1961
Library Holdings: Auction Catalogs, Book Volumes 55,000, Clipping Files, Exhibition Catalogs, Fiche 60,000, Maps, Original Art Works, Original Documents Archives of American Art, Pamphlets, Periodical Subscriptions, Photographs, Prints, Reels 7000, Reproductions
Special Subjects: Afro-American Art, American Indian Art, American Western Art, Architecture, Art History, Bookplates & Bindings, Bronzes, Drawings, Etchings & Engravings, Ethnology, Folk Art, Graphic Arts, Historical Material, History of Art & Archaeology, Illustration, Landscapes, Maps, Painting-American, Photography, Printmaking, Prints, Reproductions, Restoration & Conservation, Sculpture, Watercolors, Woodcuts, Southwestern Art, Woodcarvings
Collections: 1,500 item collection including: exhibition catalogs, monographs, catalogues raisonnes, reference material, periodicals, auction catalogs, ephemera, and electronic resources on American art, history, and photography, with emphasis on the history and visual record of the Western US, Microform holdings include large nineteenth-century U.S. newspaper coll, city directories, Western Americana: Frontier History of the Trans-Mississippi West, 1550-1900, New York Public Library artists and print files, History of Photography periodicals, Knoedler Library, and Archives of American Art, fine examples of rare and illustrated books, archival holdings include museum institutional records and artist archives, including Laura Gilpin, Eliot Porter, Karl Struss, and the records of the Roman Bronze Works

C **BANK ONE FORT WORTH,** 500 Throckmorton, Fort Worth, TX 76102-3708; PO Box 2050, Fort Worth, TX 76113-2050. Tel 817-884-4000; Fax 817-870-2454; *Property Mgr* Lew Massey
Estab 1974 to enhance the pub areas of bank lobby & building; to provide art for offices of individual bank officers; Collection displayed throughout bank building, offices & public space
Collections: Alexander Calder sculpture, more than 400 pieces of drawings, graphics, paintings, prints, sculpture & tapestries, focusing on art of the Southwest, including artists throughout the nation & abroad
Activities: Tours for special groups only; sponsor two art shows annually; provide cash prizes; scholarships offered

L **FORT WORTH PUBLIC LIBRARY ARTS & HUMANITIES,** Fine Arts Section, 500 W 3rd, Fort Worth, TX 76102. Tel 817-871-7737; Fax 817-871-7734; Email tstone@fortworthlibrary.org; Web: www.fortworthgov.org/library; *Unit Mgr* Thelma Stone; *Librn* Elmer Sackman; *Libr Asst* Gayle Mays; *Librn Asst* D Metcalf
Open Mon - Thurs 9 AM - 9 PM, Sat 10 AM - 6 PM, Sun Noon - 6 PM; No admis fee; Estab 1902
Income: Financed by appropriation
Library Holdings: Cassettes, Clipping Files, Fiche, Original Art Works, Other Holdings Articles, Books, Music scores, Pamphlets & programs, Sheet music, Special clipped picture files, Pamphlets, Photographs, Prints, Records, Video Tapes
Special Subjects: Bookplates & Bindings, Cartoons
Collections: Hal Coffman Collection of original political cartoon art, Nancy Taylor Collection of bookplates, historic picture & photograph collection autographed by various celebrities, rare books
Exhibitions: Antiques, crafts, prints, original photographs & original works; also art gallery exhibs of paintings, sculpture, photographs, folk crafts
Publications: Bibliographies; catalogs; monthly Focus
Activities: Tours

M **KIMBELL ART FOUNDATION,** Kimbell Art Museum, 3333 Camp Bowie Blvd, Fort Worth, TX 76107-2792. Tel 817-332-8451; Fax 817-877-1264; Email pr@kimbellmuseum.org; Web: www.kimbellart.org; *Dir* Eric M Lee; *Deputy Dir* George TM Shackelford; *Cur European Art & Head Acad Svcs* Nancy Edwards; *Dir Conservation* Claire M Barry; *Librn* Chia-Chun Shih; *Deputy Dir Finance & Admin* Susan R Drake; *Head Mktg & Pub Rels* Jessica Brandrup; *Cur of Asian & non-Western Art* Jennifer Casler Price; *Mgr Publications* Megan Smyth; *Mem & Spec Events Mgr* Robert McAn; *Opers Mgr* Larry Eubank; *Security Mgr* David McMillan; *Head Develop* Angie Bulaich
Open Tues - Thurs & Sat 10 AM - 5 PM, Fri Noon - 8 PM, Sun Noon - 5 PM, cl Mon, July 4, Thanksgiving, Christmas & New Year's; No admis fee to permanent coll; fees apply to special exhibs, half-price offered Tues all day & Fri 5-8 PM; Open to public 1972 for the collection, preservation, research, publication & public exhibition of art of all periods; Average Annual Attendance: 261,688; Mem: 18,800; dues $75-$25,000
Income: Financed by foundation
Library Holdings: Auction Catalogs 14,000, Book Volumes 47,300, Exhibition Catalogs, Fiche, Periodical Subscriptions 103
Special Subjects: African Art, Antiquities-Assyrian, Antiquities-Byzantine, Antiquities-Egyptian, Antiquities-Etruscan, Antiquities-Greek, Antiquities-Persian, Antiquities-Roman, Architecture, Asian Art, Baroque Art, Bronzes, Calligraphy, Ceramics, Drawings, Enamels, Etchings & Engravings, Flasks & Bottles, Glass, Gold, Ivory, Jade, Jewelry, Landscapes, Medieval Art, Mosaics, Oriental Art, Painting-British, Painting-Dutch, Painting-European, Painting-Flemish, Painting-French, Painting-German, Painting-Italian, Painting-Japanese, Porcelain, Portraits, Pre-Columbian Art, Religious Art, Renaissance Art, Sculpture, Silver, Watercolors, Woodcarvings
Collections: Artworks from antiquity to 20th century including western European paintings & sculptures, Egyptian, Near Eastern, Greek & Roman antiquities, Asian, Precolumbian & African art, Displayed in two mus bldgs: 1972 original bldg designed by Louis I Kahn & 2013 bldg designed by Renzo Piano
Exhibitions: (16th Oct, 2016-29th Jan, 2017) Monet: The Early Years; (26th Mar, 2017-25th Jun, 2017) Louis Kahn: The Power of Architecture; (14th May, 2017-13th Aug, 2017) A Modern Vision: European Masterworks from the Phillips Collection
Publications: Exhibition catalogues: Kimbell Art Museum Guide; Kimbell Masterpiece Series; Light is the Theme: Louis I Kahn & the Kimbell Art Museum; The Kimbell Cookbook; biannual mem's Calendar magazine; brochures; art prints
Activities: Docent training; summer camps; family festivals & gallery guides; studio workshops for adults, teens & families; teacher training; lects open to the pub; 20 vis lectrs per yr; symposia; colls open to pub; gallery talks; tours; films; book discussion club; concerts; schls; original objects of art & individual paintings lent to other mus organizing important international loan exhibs; book 2 traveling exhibs per yr; originate traveling exhibs to parterning mus nationally & internationally; travel prog for mus mems; mus shop sells books, magazines, art prints, reproductions, postcards, gifts, jewelry, fashion accessories, home decorations, toys & posters

M **MODERN ART MUSEUM,** (Fort Worth Art Association), 3200 Darnell St, Fort Worth, TX 76107-2872. Tel 817-738-9215, 866-824-5566; Fax 817-735-1161; Email info@themodern.org; Web: www.themodern.org; *Cur Educ* Terri Thornton; *Mem & Spec Events* Suzanne Woo; *Pub Information Officer* Kendal Smith Lake; *Head Design & Installation* Tony Wright; *Museum Store Mgr* Lorri Wright; *Dir* Marla Price; *Cur* Andrea Karnes
Open Tues - Sun 10 AM - 5 PM, Fri until 8 PM, cl Mon & holidays; Admis general (18-adult) $16, seniors (60+) $12, students w/ID $10, children under 18 free; Modern & contemporary art; Average Annual Attendance: 200,000; Mem: 5,500; Benefactor $25,000, Chmn's Cir $10,000 President's Cir $5,000; Patron $1,200; Contributor $550; Sustainer $225; Family $150; Assoc $150; Basic $75
Special Subjects: African Art, Afro-American Art, Architecture, Ceramics, Collages, Furniture, Glass, Hispanic Art, Landscapes, Latin American Art, Metalwork, Mexican Art, Painting-American, Painting-Australian, Painting-British, Painting-Canadian, Painting-Dutch, Painting-European, Painting-Flemish, Painting-French, Painting-German, Painting-Israeli, Painting-Italian, Painting-Japanese, Painting-New Zealand
Collections: Works by modern & contemporary masters, notably Picasso, Kandinsky, Still, Rothko, Judd, Marden, Dine, Rauschenberg, Oldenburg, Lichtenstein, Warhol, Hodgkin, Avery, Scully & Motherwell, Post 1940's art from all countries, paintings, sculpture, drawings, prints & gifts, Photography by Cindy Sherman, Carrie May Williams, Bill Viola
Publications: Biannual calendar; Art the Modern (Magazine)
Activities: Classes for adults, teens & children; teacher workshops; internships; lects open to pub & for members only, 20 vis lectrs per yr; gallery talks; tours; concerts; scholarships; originate traveling exhibs; mus shop sells books, magazines & reproductions

M **SID W RICHARDSON FOUNDATION,** Sid Richardson Museum, 309 Main St, Fort Worth, TX 76102-4006. Tel 817-332-6554; Email info@sidrichardsonmuseum.org; Web: www.sidrichardsonmuseum.org; *Dir* Mary Burke; *Dir Tour Progs* Andrea Hassenteuffel; *Dir Adult Progs* Leslie Thompson
Open Mon - Thurs 9 AM - 5 PM, Fri - Sat 9 AM - 8 PM, Sun 12 AM - 5 PM, cl major holidays; No admis fee; Estab 1982; totally renovated in 2006, the museum exhibits paintings by Frederic Remington & Charles M. Russell. Educ programs & museum store; Average Annual Attendance: 42,000
Income: Financed by the Sid W Richardson Foundation

Library Holdings: Book Volumes
Special Subjects: American Western Art, Bronzes, Painting-American, Watercolors
Collections: Frederic Remington Collection, Charles M Russell Collection, Peter Hurd, William R Leigh, Frank Tenney Johnson, Oscar Berninghaus
Exhibitions: Permanent exhibit of paintings by Frederic Remington, Charles M Russell & other Western artists; (1st Jan, 2017-1st Sep, 2017) Legacy
Publications: Remington & Russell, The Sid Richardson Collection
Activities: Classes for adults & children; docent training; summer camp; lects open to pub; gallery talks; tours; mus shop sells books, prints, postcards, note cards, posters, reproduction bronzes & prints on canvas

M **TEXAS CHRISTIAN UNIVERSITY,** Fort Worth Contemporary Art, TCU Box 298000, Dept of Art & Art History Fort Worth, TX 76129. Tel 817-257-2588; Email theartgalleries@tcu.edu; Web: www.theartgalleries.tcu.edu; *Dir School of Art* Sally Packard; *Cur* Sara-Jayne Parsons
Open Wed - Sat 12 noon - 5 PM & by appointment; No admis fee; Exhibs, residences & projects by contemporary national & international artists; over 2,000 sq ft with some natural light; Average Annual Attendance: 10,000
Income: Financed by college funds & charitable sources
Special Subjects: Drawings, Photography, Prints, Sculpture
Collections: University Permanent Art Collection
Publications: Exhibition catalogues & artist books
Activities: Classes for adults; lects open to public; vis lects; gallery talks; tours;; traveling exhibs regionally & nationally

M **Moudy Gallery,** Moudy Bldg N, 2805 S University Dr Fort Worth, TX 76129. Tel 817-257-2588; Email theartgalleries@tcu.edu; Web: www.theartgalleries.tcu.edu; *Dir* Devon Nowlin; *Cur* Sara-Jayne Parsons
Open acad yr Mon 11AM-6PM, Tues-Fri 10AM-4PM, Sat 1PM-4PM; No admis fee
Collections: works by students & professional artists

M **UNIVERSITY OF NORTH TEXAS HEALTH SCIENCE CENTER FORT WORTH,** Atrium Gallery, 3500 Camp Bowie Blvd, Fort Worth, TX 76109-2644. Tel 817-735-0301; Email shea.pattersonyoung@unthsc.edu; Web: www.hsc.unt.edu/atriumgallery/; *Cur* Shea Patterson Young
Open Mon - Fri 8 AM - 5 PM; No admis fee; Estab 1986 as a nonprofit, pub service gallery; Three-story pub service gallery in North Texas featuring international groups like The SFA & SWA, PSH works in all media by a variety of artists; Average Annual Attendance: 2,000
Income: Financed by state appropriation
Collections: Permanent Collection of the Society of Watercolor Artists
Exhibitions: Annual 12-County High School Art Competition; changing monthly exhibits; Colored Pencil Society of America
Activities: Teacher workshops; competitions with prizes; 12 vis lectrs per yr; sponsoring of competitions; scholarships

FREDERICKSBURG

M **JOE GISH'S OLD WEST MUSEUM,** 502 N Miliam St, Fredericksburg, TX 78624. Tel 940-872-9698; 830-997-2794; Fax 940-872-8504; Email sunsettradingpost@earthlink.net; Web: www.cowboymuseum.net; *Owner & Cur* Jack Glover; *Co-Owner* Cherie Glover; *Owner* Joe Gish
Open by appointment; Admis no charge; Estab 1987; 2 room log building 2 1/2 blocks off Main St in St. Fredericksburg Texas; Average Annual Attendance: 67,000; Mem: 300; dues $35
Income: Financed by endowment & mem
Special Subjects: American Western Art, Architecture, Costumes, Painting-American, Photography, Posters, Prints, Restorations, Sculpture, Textiles
Collections: Historic clothing, sculpture, western art
Exhibitions: Western Art Show & Sale; Western Spirit Art Show
Publications: Stageline, quarterly
Activities: Classes for adults & children; docent training; lects open to pub, 10 vis lectrs per yr; competitions; book traveling exhibs, 2 per yr; sales shop sells books, reproductions, prints

GAINESVILLE

L **NORTH CENTRAL TEXAS COLLEGE,** Library, 1525 W California St, Gainesville, TX 76240-4636. Tel 940-668-7731, Ext 338; Fax 940-668-6049; *Dir Library Svcs* Dana Pearson
Open Mon - Thurs 8 AM - 9:30 PM, Fri 8 AM - 4:30 PM, Sun 2 - 5 PM; Estab 1924 to serve the needs of the admin, faculty & students; Circ 500
Purchases: $1500
Library Holdings: Audio Tapes, Book Volumes 50,000, Cards, Cassettes, Clipping Files, Fiche, Filmstrips, Lantern Slides, Motion Pictures, Pamphlets, Periodical Subscriptions 175, Prints, Records, Reproductions, Slides, Video Tapes
Activities: Brownbook reviews

GALVESTON

L **ROSENBERG LIBRARY,** 2310 Sealy Ave, Galveston, TX 77550. Tel 409-763-8854; Fax 409-763-0275; Email jaugelli@rosenberg-library.org; Web: www.rosenberg-library.org; *Head Spec Coll* Casey Greene; *Museum Cur* Eleanor Clark; *CEO, Exec Dir* John Augelli; *Pres* Jan Coggeshall
Open Mon - Sat 9 AM - 5 PM; cl Sun & national holidays; No admis fee; Estab 1904 to provide library services to the people of Galveston, together with lectures, concerts, exhibitions; Library includes the Harris Art Gallery, The James M Lykes Maritime Gallery, The Hutchings Gallery, together with miscellaneous art & historical exhibit galleries & halls
Income: $55,000,100 (financed by endowment, city & state appropriation)
Library Holdings: Book Volumes 250,000, Compact Disks, DVDs, Fiche, Manuscripts, Maps, Memorabilia, Motion Pictures, Original Art Works, Original Documents, Periodical Subscriptions 500, Photographs, Prints, Sculpture
Collections: Historical objects relating to Galveston & Texas, photographic & manuscript colls, historic maps & architectural drawings, large coll of paintings with a focus on regional artists & maritime subjects, large colls of American & European decorative glass, textiles, silver & Native American crafts
Exhibitions: Permanent exhibit of Galveston maritime history; rotating exhibits of framed art, decorative arts, photographs & other historic objects
Activities: Historical lect & presentations; book signings; public prog; gallery tours; joint exhibs with other local mus; active loan prog

GLEN ROSE

M **BARNARD'S MILL ART MUSEUM,** 307 SW Barnard St, Glen Rose, TX 76043; PO Box 2537, Glen Rose, TX 76043-2537. Tel 254-897-7494; *Dir* Richard Moore; *Chmn* SC Coconaur; *Treas* David Morrow; *Cur* Hollis Taylor
Open Sat 10 AM - 5 PM, Sun 1 - 5 PM; No admis fee; Average Annual Attendance: 650
Library Holdings: Book Volumes
Collections: 200 paintings, bronzes & etchings
Activities: Educ prog for college students affiliated with Tarleton State Univ; guided tours

HOUSTON

A **ART LEAGUE OF HOUSTON,** 1953 Montrose Blvd, Houston, TX 77006-1243. Tel 713-523-9530; Fax 713-523-4053; Email alh@artleaguehouston.org; Web: www.hfac.uh.edu/freeland/ALH; *Pres (V)* Kristen Johnson; *Exec Dir* Khell R. Willetts Ph.D.
Open Tues - Fri 9 AM - 5 PM, Sat noon - 5 PM, cl Sun. & Mon; No admis fee; Estab 1948 to promote pub interest in art & the achievements of Houston area artists; Gallery maintained for monthly exhibits; Average Annual Attendance: 20,000; Mem: 1500; dues $25-$1000; annual meeting in May/June
Income: $300,000 (financed by grants, mem & fundraising functions)
Exhibitions: Monthly exhibits; Regional exhibitions; The Gala, Sharon Koprova
Publications: Exhibition catalogs; newsletter, monthly
Activities: Classes for adults & children; Cameron Foundation Artpresence docent Program; HIV & Art Outreach Program; Multiple Sclerosis Outreach Program; lect open to public; competitions with prizes; workshops, gallery talks; tours; sales shop sells calendars, craft items, original art, print reproductions

M **CONTEMPORARY ARTS MUSEUM HOUSTON,** 5216 Montrose Blvd, Houston, TX 77006. Tel 713-284-8250; Fax 713-284-8275; Email info@camh.org; Web: www.camh.org; *Dir* Bill Arning; *Asst Dir Facilities & Risk Management* Mike Reed; *Registrar* Tim Barkley; *Cur* Dean Daderko; *Educ & Pub Progs Mgr* Felice Cleveland; *Retail Operations Dir* Sue Pruden; *Dir Develop* Libby Conine; *Preparator* Jeff Shore; *Gallery Supervisor* Kenya Evans
Open Tues, Wed & Fri 10 AM - 7 PM, Thurs 10 AM - 9 PM, Sat 10 AM - 6 PM, Sun noon - 6 PM, cl Mon, Thanksgiving & Christmas Days; No admis fee; Estab 1948 to provide a forum for art with an emphasis on the visual arts of the present & recent past, to document new directions in art through changing exhibitions & publications, to engage the public in a lively dialogue with today's art & to encourage a greater understanding of contemporary art through educational programs; the mus is a non-collecting institution; Current bldg was designed by Gunnar Birkerts & opened in 1972; comprises one large gallery of 10,500 sq ft and a smaller gallery of 1500 sq ft; Average Annual Attendance: 91,000; Mem: 700; dues $35 & up
Activities: Progs for families; teacher resources; Teen Council; lects open to pub, 6-12 vis lectrs per yr; concerts; gallery talks; tours; originate traveling exhibs to other art mus; mus shop sells books & gifts

M **DIVERSE WORKS,** 3400 Main St, Ste 292 Houston, TX 77002-9516. Tel 713-223-8346; Email info@diverseworks.org; Web: www.diverseworks.org; *Exec Dir & Chief Cur* Xandra Eden; *Deputy Dir* Jennifer Gardner; *Cur* Rachel Cook; *Exhibition & Prog Coord* Taylor Hoblitzell; *Finance Mgr* Stephanie Atwood
Open Wed - Thurs Noon - 6 PM, Fri - Sat noon - 8 PM; No admis fee; Estab 1983 to present work by contemporary artists working in all arts media & residencies; Approx 3,000 sq ft; Average Annual Attendance: 30,000
Income: $500,000 (financed by individual & foundation contributions, federal & city funds, earned income)
Exhibitions: 10-15 exhibitions a year of National International Artists; 25 exhibitions per year of dance, music, performance & theatre
Activities: Classes for adults; Lect open to public, 20 vis lectrs per year; concerts; tours

A **FOTO FEST INTERNATIONAL,** 2000 Edwards St, Building C Ste 2 Houston, TX 77007. Tel 713-223-5522; Fax 713-223-4411; Email info@fotofest.org; Web: www.fotofest.org; *Chmn & Co-Founder* Fred Baldwin; *Artistic Dir & Co-Founder* Wendy Watriss; *Exec Dir* Steven Evans; *Assoc Cur & Exhib Coordr* Jennifer Ward
Open Wed - Sat 11 AM - 5 PM (during exhibs); No admis fee; Estab to promote public appreciation for photographic art, international & cross-cultural exchange & literacy through photography
Special Subjects: Photography
Exhibitions: All exhibs held at FotoFest HQ, Houston unless indicated otherwise
Activities: Educ prog; gallery talks; tours; sales shop sells books

M **HOUSTON BAPTIST UNIVERSITY,** Museum of American Architecture and Decorative Arts, 7502 Fondren Rd, Houston, TX 77074-3298. Tel 281-649-3997; *Dir* Suzie Snoddy
Open Mon - Sat 10 AM - 4 PM, cl holidays & Sun; Admis adults $6, seniors $5, children $4; Estab 1969 to depict social history of Americans & diverse ethnic groups who settled in Texas; Average Annual Attendance: 9,000; Mem: 125; dues $25
Income: Financed by mem & donations
Special Subjects: Architecture, Decorative Arts, Dolls, Furniture, Miniatures, Period Rooms, Portraits, Maps

Collections: Theo Redwood Blank Doll Collection, Schissler Antique Miniature Furniture Collection, Dolls; European Decorative Miniature Furniture; Dog-Trot Log Cabin
Activities: Docent training; lect open to public, 2-4 vis lectrs per year; tours

A **HOUSTON CENTER FOR PHOTOGRAPHY,** 1441 W Alabama, Houston, TX 77006-4103. Tel 713-529-4755; Fax 713-529-9248; Email info@hcponline.org; Web: www.hcponline.org; *Executive Director* Ashlyn Davis; *Dir Devel* James Hays, PhD; *Finance Mgr* Monica Jaster; *Exhibitions Coord* Jessi Bowman; *Access & Community Educ Coord* Natalie Rodgers; *Educ Asst* Hallie Gluk; *Gallery Assoc* Martin Ivy
Open Wed - Thurs 11 AM - 9 PM, Fri 11 AM - 5 PM, Sat & Sun 11 AM - 7 PM; No admis fee; Estab 1981; Maintains reference library; Average Annual Attendance: 22,000; Mem: 1,400; dues $35 & up
Income: $850,000 (financed by foundations, private gifts, earned income, mem, city & state government)
Special Subjects: Photography
Exhibitions: Membership & Fellowship exhibitions
Publications: Spot, bi-annual
Activities: Classes for adults & children; outreach prog; lects open to pub; gallery talks; tours; competitions; scholarships; fels; book traveling exhibs; originate traveling exhibs to mus & non-profit galleries

L **HOUSTON PUBLIC LIBRARY,** 500 McKinney St, Fine Arts & Recreation Dept Houston, TX 77002-2530. Tel 832-393-1313; Email jharvath@hpl.lib.tx.us; Web: www.houstonlibrary.org; *Mgr Fine Arts & Recreation* John Harvath
Open Mon - Wed 9 AM - 7 PM, Thurs 9 AM - 8 PM, Fri - Sat 10 AM - 5 PM, cl Sun; Estab 1848 as a private library for the Houston Lyceum & opened to the pub in 1895; Circ 142,651; Monthly exhibits, including art shows are spread throughout the Central Library Building
Income: Financed by endowment, city appropriation & Friends of the Library
Library Holdings: Book Volumes 160,110, Clipping Files 24,131, Exhibition Catalogs, Other Holdings Auction Catalogs 6742; Compact Discs 9500; Sheet Music 15,325, Pamphlets, Periodical Subscriptions 400, Records
Special Subjects: Decorative Arts, Oriental Art
Activities: Lect open to public; tours; lending collection contains 9500 compact discs

M **LAWNDALE ART CENTER,** 4912 Main St, Houston, TX 77002. Tel 713-528-5858; Fax 713-528-4140; Email askus@lawndaleartcenter.org; Web: www.lawndaleartcenter.org; *Exec Dir* Stephanie Schumann Mitchell; *Controller* Lauren Lohman; *Gallery Attendant* Emily Fens
Open Wed & Fri noon - 6 PM, Thurs noon - 8 PM, Sat - Sun noon - 5 PM; No admis fee; Estab 1979; Develops local contemporary artists & the audience for their art; Average Annual Attendance: 18,000
Exhibitions: Over 20 exhibs ann by local & regional artists

M **MENIL FOUNDATION, INC,** The Menil Collection, 1533 Sul Ross, Houston, TX 77006-4729; 1511 Branard St, Houston, TX 77006-4797. Tel 713-525-9400; Fax 713-525-9444; Email info@menil.org; Web: www.menil.org; *Chmn* Louisa S Sarofim; *Dir* Rebecca Rabinow; *Information Technology* Buck Bakke; *Cur* Michelle White; *Chief Conservator* Brad Epley; *Librn* Lauren Gottlieb-Miller; *Colls Registrar* David Aylsworth; *CFO* Michael Nicknish
Open Wed - Sun 11 AM - 7 PM, cl Mon & Tues, New Year's Day, Easter, Independence Day, Thanksgiving Day, Christmas Day; No admis fee; Opened in 1987, estab to organize & present art exhibitions & progs; two landmark bldgs designed by Renzo Piano; Average Annual Attendance: 175,000; Mem: 1500; dues $100 - $10,000
Income: Financed by pvt foundation and pvt endowment & mems
Library Holdings: Auction Catalogs, Book Volumes, Clipping Files, Photographs, Prints
Special Subjects: African Art, Afro-American Art, Antiquities-Assyrian, Antiquities-Byzantine, Antiquities-Egyptian, Antiquities-Etruscan, Antiquities-Greek, Antiquities-Oriental, Antiquities-Persian, Antiquities-Roman, Drawings, Medieval Art, Painting-American, Photography, Pre-Columbian Art, Primitive art, Prints, Religious Art, Renaissance Art
Collections: Antiquities from the Paleolithic to the pre-Christian eras, Art of Africa, Medieval & Byzantine art, Oceanic & Pacific Northwest tribal cultures, 20th century drawings, paintings, photographs, prints & sculpture, Permanent collection at 16,000
Publications: Exhibition catalogs
Activities: Classes for children; lects open to pub, lects for mems only; concerts; gallery talks; tours; Walter Hopps Award for Curatorial Achievement; fels; originate traveling exhibs; mus shop sells books, magazines & original art

M **MIDTOWN ART CENTER,** 3414 La Branch St, Houston, TX 77004-3841. Tel 713-521-8803; Fax 713-521-9003; Email midtownartcenter@hotmail.com; Web: www.midtownartcenter.com
Call for hours; No admis fee; Estab 1982 as a multi-cultural, multi-disciplinary art center serving grassroots artists
Income: Financed by mem & donations
Exhibitions: Local artist exhibitions throughout the year
Activities: Classes for adults & children

M **MUSEUM OF FINE ARTS HOUSTON,** Bayou Bend Collection & Gardens, 6003 Memorial Dr, Houston, TX 77007; PO Box 6826, Houston, TX 77265-6826. Tel 713-639-7750; Fax 713-639-7770; Email bayoubend@mfah.org; Web: www.mfah.org/bayoubend; *Dir Educ* Jennifer Hammond; *Conservator* Steven Pine; *Cur Gardens* Bart Brechter; *Exec Asst* Caryn Fulda; *Admin Asst, BB* Janet Marshall; *Dir BB Library* Margaret Culbertson; *Prog Mgr* Joey Milillu; *Visitor Servs Mgr* Lavinia Ignat; *Shop Supervisor* Lisa Sugita; *Hill Archive Proj Mgr* Marie Wise
Temporarily closed, call for updated information; Admis gen admis $12.50 -$15, students & seniors (ID required) $11-$13.50, children 10-17 $6.25-7.50, gardens only $5, children under 9 no charge; Estab 1957 dedicated to serving all people by pursuing excellence in art & horticulture through collection, exhibition & education; Twenty-eight room settings that trace the evolution of American style from 1620's to 1870's & an area focused on 19th century Texas furniture, pottery & decorative arts. Affiliate of Museum of Fine Arts, Houston; Average Annual Attendance: 100,000; Mem: Board meetings Sep - Nov & Jan - May
Library Holdings: Auction Catalogs, Book Volumes, Exhibition Catalogs
Special Subjects: American Western Art, Carpets & Rugs, Ceramics, Decorative Arts, Drawings, Embroidery, Etchings & Engravings, Flasks & Bottles, Folk Art, Furniture, Glass, Historical Material, Jewelry, Landscapes, Maps, Metalwork, Painting-American, Period Rooms, Pewter, Porcelain, Portraits, Pottery, Prints, Silver, Textiles, Sculpture, Watercolors, Woodcarvings
Collections: Bayou Bend Collection of American decorative arts & paintings
Publications: Bayou Bend Gardens: A Southern Oasis; America's Treasures at Bayou Bend: Celebrating Fifty Years; American Material Culture and the Texas Experience: The David B. Warren Symposium
Activities: lects open to pub, 2 vis lectrs per yr; concerts; gallery talks; tours; schols & fels offered; mus shops sells books & gifts

M **MUSEUM OF FINE ARTS, HOUSTON,** 1001 Bissonnet St, Houston, TX 77005-1803; PO Box 6826, Houston, TX 77265-6826. Tel 713-639-7300; Fax 713-639-7399; Email guestservices@mfah.org; Web: www.mfah.org; *Dir* Gary Tinterow; *COO* Willard Holmes; *Chief Develop Officer* Amy Purvis; *CFO* Eric Anyah; *Asst Dir Exhibs* Deborah Roldan
Open Tues - Wed 10 AM - 5 PM, Thurs 10 AM - 9 PM, Fri & Sat 10 AM - 7 PM, Sun 12:15 - 7 PM, cl Mon, except Mon holidays, Thanksgiving & Christmas Days; Admis adults $15, seniors $10, military $10, students & youth $7.50, 12 & younger free, mems free & Thurs free, group rates available; Estab 1900 as an art mus containing works from prehistoric times to the present; Exhibition space totals 325,000 sq ft; Average Annual Attendance: 900,000; Mem: 35,000; dues $60-$1,500
Library Holdings: Auction Catalogs, Book Volumes, CD-ROMs, Clipping Files, DVDs, Exhibition Catalogs, Fiche, Other Holdings, Pamphlets, Periodical Subscriptions
Special Subjects: African Art, Asian Art, Baroque Art, Decorative Arts, Drawings, Embroidery, Flasks & Bottles, Islamic Art, Latin American Art, Photography, Prints, Renaissance Art
Collections: Coll of world art in all media, spanning 5,000 years, 2 house museums, Bayou Bend Collection & Gardens, Rienzi Center for European Decorative Arts
Publications: Annual report; calendar of events, bimonthly; catalogs of exhibitions
Activities: Classes for adults & children; docent training; progs specifically for educators; lects open to pub, 100 vis lectrs per yr; concerts; gallery talks; tours; internships available; individual paintings & objects lent to other art institutions; originate traveling exhibs to qualified mus; mus shop sells books, magazines, prints

L **Hirsch Library**, 1001 Bissonnet St, Houston, TX 77005-1803; PO Box 6826, Houston, TX 77265-6826. Tel 713-639-7325; Fax 713-639-7399; Email hirsch@mfah.org; Web: www.mfah.org/library/home.asp; *Chief Dir* Jon Evans; *Catalog Librn* Sunyoung Park; *Ref Librn* Lynn Wexler; *Tech Svcs Librn* Cheryl Payne
Open to researchers Tues - Wed & Fri 10 AM - 5 PM, Thurs 10 AM - 9 PM, Sat Noon - 5 PM, cl Sun - Mon; No admis fee; Estab 1900; For reference only
Income: Financed by Hirsch Endowment
Library Holdings: Book Volumes 100,000, Clipping Files, Compact Disks, DVDs, Exhibition Catalogs, Fiche, Other Holdings Archival Records; Artists' Ephemera Files; Museum Files, Pamphlets, Periodical Subscriptions 250, Prints, Reels, Slides, Video Tapes
Special Subjects: Afro-American Art, American Indian Art, Art Education, Art History, Asian Art, Costume Design & Constr, Decorative Arts, Fashion Arts, Film, Furniture, Glass, Gold, History of Art & Archaeology, Jewelry, Latin American Art
Collections: Collection of world art in all media, spanning 5000 years, 2 house museums for American decorative arts & European decorative arts
Publications: MFAH Houston Visitor Guide; numerous exhibition catalogs; MFAH Today, bimonthly member publication

—Bayou Bend Collection & Gardens
See separate listing in Houston, Tx

—Glassell School of Art
See separate listing under US Art Schools in Houston, TX

—Rienzi Center for European Decorative Arts
Tours: Wed - Sat 10 AM - 5 PM, Sun 1 PM - 5 PM by appointment; Admis adults $8, seniors, students & youth 13-18 $5. children 12 & under free; See separate listing in Houston, TX

M **MUSEUM OF FINE ARTS, HOUSTON,** Rienzi Center for European Decorative Arts, 1406 Kirby Dr, Houston, TX 77019-1412; Rienzi MFAH, PO Box 6826 Houston, TX 77265-6826. Tel 713-639-7800; Fax 713-639-7810; Email rienzi@mfah.org; Web: www.mfah.org/rienzi; *Dir* Katherine S Howe; *Assoc Cur Decorative Arts* Christine Gervais; *Curatorial Asst* Caroline Cole; *Docent Prog Mgr* Stephanie Niemeyer; *Pub Progs Mgr* Sara Foley Edwards; *Exec Asst* Adriana Rubio; *Educ Asst* Casey Monahan; *Facilities Coordr* Juan Alonzo
Open Center: Wed - Fri 10 AM - 5 PM, Sat 10 AM - 4 PM, Sun 1-5 PM; Gardens: Wed - Sun 10 AM - 4:30 PM; cl Aug & most natl holidays; Admis to Ctr, advance ticket purchase req: adults $8, seniors & students with ID $5, MFAH mem $4, group rates available, admis to Gardens free; Affiliate of Museum of Fine Arts, Houston; Average Annual Attendance: 20,000
Special Subjects: Baroque Art, Ceramics, Decorative Arts, Drawings, Furniture, Glass, Hispanic Art, Metalwork, Miniatures, Painting-British, Porcelain, Portraits, Sculpture, Silver, Textiles, Painting-European, Painting-Spanish
Collections: Rienzi Collection of European Decorative Arts & Paintings, Portrait Miniatures from the Caroline A Ross Collection
Exhibitions: The Wedding Dress; Rienzi Begins: John F Staub & the Mastersons
Publications: Rienzi: European Decorative Arts & Paintings, Katherine S. Howe et al
Activities: Docent training; family art workshops; sketching; tea & tour events; salons; concerts; gallery talks, tours; lects open to pub; book club; story time; family days/ 4 vix lects per yr

M **MUSEUM OF SOUTHERN HISTORY,** Joella & Stewart Morris Cultural Arts Center, 7502 Fondren Rd, Houston, TX 77074. Tel 281-649-3997; Email ssnoddy@hbu.edu; Web: www.hbu.edu; *Cur* Maggie Brown; *Dir* Suzie Snoddy

Open Mon - Sat 10 AM - 4 PM, cl univ holidays & holiday weekends; Admis adults $6, seniors $5, children $4; Estab 1978; Average Annual Attendance: 5,000; Mem: 300; $25, $50, $75 & $100
Income: nonprofit donations
Special Subjects: Costumes, Decorative Arts, Furniture, Historical Material, Jewelry, Maps, Military Art, Painting-American, Period Rooms, Photography, Portraits, Silver, Tapestries, Watercolors, Prints
Collections: Antique handguns, Confederacy-money & uniforms, Medical exhibit, late 1800's, quilts, Sharecropper's Cabin, Terry's Texas Rangers, various oils, historic paintings
Publications: Quarterly newsletter
Activities: Docent training; lects open to pub; 5 vis lectrs per yr; book traveling exhibs; mus shop sells books

L **RICE UNIVERSITY,** Brown Fine Arts Library, 6100 Main St, Rice Univ Houston, TX 77005; PO Box 1892, Brown Fine Arts Library Fondren Library MS 44 Houston, TX 77005-1892. Tel 713-348-5113; Email ask@rice.libanswers.com; Web: library.rice.edu; *Art & Architecture Librn* Jet M Prendeville; *Music Librn* Mary Brower
Open acad yr 24 hrs starting noon Sun & closing 10 PM Fri, Sat 9 AM - 6 PM, holiday hrs vary; Estab 1964 combined art, architecture, music collections in the Alice Pratt Brown Library estab 1986; Located in Fondren Library, 3rd fl
Income: Financed by Rice Univ
Library Holdings: Book Volumes 190,000, Cassettes, DVDs, Exhibition Catalogs 6000, Other Holdings Scores, Periodical Subscriptions 493, Records
Special Subjects: Architecture, Art History, Film, Photography
Collections: Brown Fine Arts Collection

M **Rice Gallery**, 6100 Main St, 352 Sewall Hall Houston, TX 77005; PO Box 1892, Rice Univ Art Gallery MS-59 Houston, TX 77251-1892. Tel 713-348-6069; Fax 713-348-5980; Email ruag@rice.edu; Web: www.ricegallery.org; *Asst Cur* Joshua Fischer; *Preparator* David Krueger; *Designer* Antonio Manega; *Photographer* Nash Baker
Open Tues - Sat 11 AM - 5 PM & Thurs 11 AM - 7 PM, Sun Noon - 5 PM, cl Mon; No admis fee; Support the education & research mission of Rice Univ & serve as an artistic resource for the Rice & Houston communities by commissioning & presenting site-specific installations & related programming; 40 x 44 ft white box with one glass wall; Average Annual Attendance: 25,000; Mem: 150; dues student, artist & educator $25, catalyst $50, friend $100, advocate $250, assoc $500, partner $1000, patrons $3000+
Income: Rice University, Rice Patrons & Members, The Brown Foundation Inc, the City of Houston, the Robert J Card, M.D. & Karol Kreymer Catalogue Endowment, & the Leslie & Brad Bucher Artist Residency Endowment
Purchases: $450,000; non-collecting institution
Publications: Exhibit catalogs
Activities: Opportunity to work with artists during their residencies; lect & panel discussions, 5+ vis lectrs per yr; symposia & performances are free & open to public; gallery talks; tours; gallery store sells publications, clothing, accessories, stationery, posters

M **UNIVERSITY OF HOUSTON,** Blaffer Art Museum, 120 Fine Arts Bldg, University of Houston Houston, TX 77204-4018; 4173 Elgin St, Houston, TX 77004. Tel 713-743-9521; Fax 713-743-9525; Web: www.class.uh.edu/blaffer/; *Dir & Chief Cur* Toby Kamps; *Cur Educ* Katherine Veneman; *Registrar* Youngmin Chung
Open Tues - Sat 10 AM - 5 PM; cl Sun, Mon, univ & major holidays; No admis fee; Estab 1973 to present a broad spectrum of visual arts, utilizing the interdisciplinary framework of the University, to the acad community and to the rapidly increasing diverse population of greater Houston; Main gallery is 3,760 sq ft, ceiling height varies from 10-25 ft; Second floor gallery is 2,980 sq ft; Average Annual Attendance: 45,000
Income: Financed by state appropriation, university, local funds, grants, gifts
Special Subjects: Afro-American Art, Asian Art, Decorative Arts, Graphics, Latin American Art, Mexican Art, Painting-American, Painting-Australian, Painting-British, Painting-French, Painting-German, Painting-Italian, Painting-Japanese, Painting-Spanish, Photography
Exhibitions: Exhibitions change quarterly, call for details
Publications: Exhibition catalogs on originating shows
Activities: Outreach school progs; workshops; videos; docent training; lects open to pub, 6-10 vis lectrs per yr; concerts; gallery talks; tours; competitions with awards; book traveling exhibs 3-4 per yr; originate traveling exhibs 1 per yr to various contemporary art mus; mus shop sells books & gift items

L **William R Jenkins Architecture & Art Library**, 114 University Libraries, Houston, TX 77004-2000. Tel 713-743-2340; Email archlib@mail.uh.edu; Web: info.lib.uh.edu/aa; *Libr Coordr* Catherine Essinger; *Sr. Libr Specialist* Danny Fuller; *Libr Specialist* Julia Kress
Open Mon - Thurs 8 AM - 8 PM, Fri 8 AM - 5 PM, Sat 10 AM - 5 PM, cl Sun; No admis fee; For reference only, students & faculty
Income: Financed by state appropriation
Library Holdings: Book Volumes 70,000, Fiche 15,683, Pamphlets, Periodical Subscriptions 230, Reels 182
Special Subjects: Architecture, Art History, Photography

INGRAM

A **HILL COUNTRY ARTS FOUNDATION,** Duncan-McAshan Visual Arts Center, 120 Point Theater Rd S, Ingram, TX 78025; PO Box 1169, Ingram, TX 78025-1169. Tel 830-367-5121, 367-5120; Fax 830-367-4332; Email visualarts@hcaf.com; Web: www.hcaf.com; *Art Dir* Rosanne Thrall; *Visual Arts Coordr* Phyllis Garey
Open Mon - Fri 10 AM - 4 PM, Sat 10 - 2 PM; No admis fee except for special events; Estab 1958 to provide a place for creative activities in the area of visual arts & performing arts; also to provide classes in arts, crafts & drama; 1800 sq ft; Average Annual Attendance: 35,000; Mem: 600; dues $50 & up; annual meeting first Sat in Dec
Income: Financed by endowment, mem, benefit activities, donations & earned income
Library Holdings: Auction Catalogs, Audio Tapes, Filmstrips, Motion Pictures, Original Art Works, Original Documents, Other Holdings, Sculpture, Slides, Video Tapes
Collections: 50+ pieces - contemporary paintings, prints, photographs & sculpture
Exhibitions: 8 rotating exhibits per yr; Regional Christmas Show
Publications: Spotlight, quarterly newsletter
Activities: Classes for adults & children; dramatic progs; lects open to pub, 2 vis lectrs per yr; concerts; tours; national juried competitions with awards; scholarships offered; mus shop sells books, magazines, original art, prints & gift items

IRVING

M **IRVING ARTS CENTER,** Galleries & Sculpture Garden, 3333 N MacArthur Blvd, Irving, TX 75062-8026; City of Irving, 825 W Irving Blvd Irving, TX 75060. Tel 972-252-7558; Fax 972-570-4962; Email boxoffice@cityofirving.org; Web: www.irvingartscenter.com; *Exec Dir* Todd Eric Hawkins; *Dir Exhibs & Educ Progs* Marcie J Inman
Open Mon - Wed & Fri 9 AM - 5 PM, Thurs 9 AM - 8 PM, Sat 10 AM - 5 PM, Sun 1 - 5 PM; No admis fee; Estab 1990
Income: Financed by hotel/motel occupancy tax
Special Subjects: Painting-American, Photography, Pottery, Sculpture, Watercolors, Woodcuts
Collections: Permanent installations by James Surls, Jesus Moroles & Michael Manjarris in Sculpture Garden
Activities: Classes for children; dramatic progs; docent training; lect open to public, 2-3 vis lectrs per yr; concerts; gallery talks; tours; sponsor competitions; book traveling exhibitions 4-6 per yr

JOHNSON CITY

M **THE BENINI FOUNDATION & SCULPTURE RANCH,** 377 Shiloh Rd, Johnson City, TX 78636-4584. Tel 830-868-5244; Web: www.sculptureranch.com; *Pres* Lorraine Benini
No admis fee; Estab 1984
Special Subjects: Sculpture
Collections: Contemporary Italian paintings & sculpture

KERRVILLE

M **L D BRINKMAN FOUNDATION,** 444 Sidney Baker S, Kerrville, TX 78028. Tel 830-257-2000; Fax 830-257-2030; *Cur* Mel Vick-Knueiper; *Trustee* Charles Thomas; *Trustee* Don Brinkman; *Trustee* Pam Stone
Open weekdays by appointment; No Admis fee; Estab 1985 to promote western art; Average Annual Attendance: 900
Special Subjects: American Indian Art, American Western Art, Bronzes, Painting-American, Southwestern Art, Watercolors
Collections: American Western Art (1870's - Present): works on paper, paintings & sculpture, including Cowboy Artists of America
Activities: Individual paintings & original objects of art lent

M **THE MUSEUM OF WESTERN ART,** 1550 Bandera Hwy, Kerrville, TX 78028-9547; PO Box 294300, Kerrville, TX 78029-4300. Tel 830-896-2553; Fax 830-257-5206; Email sturnham@mowatx.com; Web: www.museumofwesternart.org; *Exec Dir* Stephanie Turnham; *Opers Mgr* Gladys Simon
Open Tues - Sat 10 AM - 4 PM; Admis adults $7, seniors $6, children adolescents 9-17, col students with ID & adult groups 15 or more $5, children 8 & under & school tours k-12 with reservations free; Estab 1983 to display contemporary art of American West; Average Annual Attendance: 20,000; Mem: dues $35-$10,000
Income: Financed by mem dues, contributions, entrance fees, sales in mus shop & grants
Library Holdings: Auction Catalogs, Book Volumes, Clipping Files, Exhibition Catalogs, Memorabilia, Original Art Works, Pamphlets, Photographs, Prints, Reels, Sculpture, Slides, Video Tapes
Special Subjects: American Western Art, Architecture, Bronzes, Cartoons, Decorative Arts, Drawings, Landscapes, Painting-American, Prints
Collections: Permanent coll of Western American Realism from mid 20th c to present
Publications: Visions West: History of the Cowboy Artists Museum
Activities: Classes for adults & children; lect talks; tours; gallery talks; competitions; schols offered; original objects of art lent to other mus; book traveling exhibs 2 per yr; originate traveling exhibs; mus shop sells books, reproductions, original art & prints

L **Museum of Western Art & Research Library**, 1550 Bandera Hwy, Kerrville, TX 78028; PO Box 294300, Kerrville, TX 78029-4300. Tel 830-896-2553, Ext. 226; Fax 830-896-2556; Email library3@mowatx.com; Web: www.museumofwesternart.org; *Librn* Dee Putnam
Open by appointment during museum hours Tues - Sat 10 AM - 4 PM; Admis $7; 1983; For reference only; Average Annual Attendance: 25,000
Income: Financed by donations & mem
Library Holdings: Book Volumes 4,000, Cards, Clipping Files, Exhibition Catalogs, Framed Reproductions, Manuscripts, Memorabilia, Original Art Works, Pamphlets, Periodical Subscriptions 10, Photographs, Prints, Slides
Special Subjects: American Indian Art, American Western Art, Art Education, Art History, Bronzes, Historical Material, History of Art & Archaeology, Illustration, Painting-American, Printmaking, Prints, Sculpture, Southwestern Art
Activities: Classes for adults & children; Western Art Academy; vis lectrs 2 per yr; gallery talks; tours; sales shop sells books, magazines, reproductions, prints, gifts, original art; Journey West Gallery

KINGSVILLE

M **TEXAS A&M UNIVERSITY,** Art Gallery, 700 University Blvd, Art Dept Kingsville, TX 78363-8203. Tel 361-593-2619, 593-2111; *Dir* Santa Barraza
Open Mon - Fri 9 AM - 4 PM; No admis fee; Estab to exhibit art work of students, as well as visitors; Average Annual Attendance: 3,000
Income: Financed by state appropriations
Exhibitions: Student Art Exhibits

LAREDO

M **LAREDO CENTER FOR THE ARTS,** 500 San Agustin, Laredo, TX 78040. Tel 956-725-1715; Fax 956-725-1741; Email info@laredoartcenter.org; Web: www.laredoartcenter.org
Open call for hours
Collections: works by local & international artists
Activities: Workshops

LONGVIEW

M **LONGVIEW MUSEUM OF FINE ART,** 215 E Tyler St, Longview, TX 75601; PO Box 3484, Longview, TX 75606-3484. Tel 903-753-8103; Fax 903-753-8217; Email fineart@lmfa.org; Web: www.lmfa.org; *Exec Director* Tiffany Nolan Jehorek; *Events Coordr* Jack Barkley; *Admin Asst* Christopher Manley; *Art Education Director* Paula Davis
Open Tues - Fri 10 AM - 4 PM, Sat 10 AM - 2 PM; Admis $5 non-mems, Free on Fridays; Estab 1958 by Junior Service League for the purpose of having a contemporary art museum in the community; Circ 1000; East Gallery 15, 000 sq ft in 3 open rooms; Average Annual Attendance: 20,000; Mem: 500; $10 - $5000, $50 family; Board of Trustees monthly meetings
Income: Financed by mem & guild projects, donations, grants & fundraisers
Library Holdings: Book Volumes
Special Subjects: Afro-American Art, Ceramics, Collages, Etchings & Engravings, Landscapes, Painting-American, Painting-Australian, Photography, Portraits, Posters, Prints, Sculpture, Watercolors, Woodcuts
Collections: Regional Artists Collection formed by purchases from Annual Invitational Exhibitions over the past 57 years, work by contemporary Texas artists
Exhibitions: (Mar) Annual Student Art; (2nd & 4th quarters) Open to Artists; (3rd quarter) East Texas Regional Artists Invitational; Jan-Feb Daniel Hays Its Not About Me/Aboriginal Collection; March - student show; April-June Oscar Qursoda O the Clouds/ Art Wells Elegance w/Stone; July-Sept East TX Collects; Oct-Dec 17 Mallory Page/ Renart Collection
Publications: Newsletter
Activities: Classes for adults & children; docent training; artworks creative learning center; 4 - 6 vis lectrs per yr; talks; competitions with cash awards; individual paintings & original objects of art lent to City Hall, East Texas Regional Airport, Sysco, Convention Center, Student Center; originate traveling exhibs; mus shop sells prints, mus quality crafts & gifts, glasswork & jewelry; books; original art

LUBBOCK

M **CITY OF LUBBOCK,** Buddy Holly Center, 1801 Crickets Ave, Lubbock, TX 79401-5128. Tel 806-775-3560; Fax 806-767-0732; Email bwitcher@mylubbock.us; Web: www.buddyhollycenter.org; *Sales & Mktg* Vassandra Okoruwa; *Educ Coordr* Sebastian Forbush; *Asst Dir* Eddy Grigsby; *Gift Shop Mgr* David Seitz; *Cur* Jacqueline Bober
Open Tues - Fri 10 AM - 5 PM, Sat 10 AM - 5 PM, Sun 1 PM - 5 PM; Estab 1984; Fine Art Gallery; Foyer Gallery; Buddy Holly Gallery
Collections: Buddy Holly memorabilia, Contemporary art
Exhibitions: Buddy Holly; Illuminance; Celebration; crafts
Activities: Classes for adults & children; docent training; dramatic progs; lects open to pub; concerts; gallery talks; tours; sponsoring of competitions; organize traveling exhibs to mus & univ; mus shop sells books, magazines, original art, reproductions

M **LOUISE HOPKINS UNDERWOOD CENTER FOR THE ARTS,** 511 Ave K, Lubbock, TX 79401. Tel 806-762-8606; Email contact@lhuca.org; Web: www.lhuca.org; *Exec Dir* Jean Caslin
Open Tues - Sat 11 AM - 5 PM; No admis fee; Estab 1997; to inspire & enrich the community by being a catalyst for the arts; 4 galleries with nearly 5,000 sq ft of exhib space; Average Annual Attendance: 45,000
Special Subjects: Afro-American Art, American Indian Art, American Western Art, Asian Art, Bronzes, Carpets & Rugs, Ceramics, Collages, Costumes, Dolls, Drawings, Embroidery, Enamels, Etchings & Engravings, Folk Art, Furniture, Glass, Hispanic Art, Historical Material, Islamic Art, Jewelry, Juvenile Art, Landscapes, Latin American Art, Metalwork, Mexican Art, Military Art, Miniatures, Mosaics, Painting-American, Photography, Porcelain, Posters, Pottery, Prints, Sculpture, Southwestern Art, Stained Glass, Tapestries, Textiles, Watercolors, Woodcarvings, Woodcuts
Collections: works by contemporary artists; sculpture; paintings
Exhibitions: 45 exhibs per yr
Activities: Classes for adults & children; workshops; concerts; gallery talks; tours

M **TEXAS TECH UNIVERSITY,** Museum of Texas Tech University, PO Box 43191, Lubbock, TX 79409-3191; 3301 4th St, Lubbock, TX 79415. Tel 806-742-2490; Fax 806-742-1136; Email museum.texastech@ttu.edu; Web: www.museum.ttu.edu; *Cur Art* Dr Peter S Briggs; *Exec Dir* Eileen Johnson
Open Main Building Tues - Sat 10 AM - 5 PM, Sun 1 - 5 PM, cl Mon; No admis fee for Museum & Lubbock Lake Landmark; Moody Planetarium adults $5, student & senior $3, children under 5 free; Estab 1929 for pub service, research & teaching. Mus mission: collect, preserve & interpret knowledge about Texas, the Southwest & other regions as related by natural history, heritage & climate; 12 permanent galleries for art; 5 temporary galleries in Main Building, 1 gallery at Landmark; Average Annual Attendance: 150,000; Mem: 1,000; dues MTTUA $50, $75 & $1.50; annual meetings MTTUA in July & Nov
Income: Financed by state appropriations, Museum of Texas Tech University Assn, private donations, local, regional, national research grants
Library Holdings: Auction Catalogs, Book Volumes, Exhibition Catalogs, Original Documents, Pamphlets, Periodical Subscriptions
Special Subjects: Anthropology, Archaeology, Bronzes, Ceramics, Costumes, Crafts, Dolls, Drawings, Embroidery, Etchings & Engravings, Ethnology, Flasks & Bottles, Folk Art, Furniture, Glass, Hispanic Art, Historical Material, Ivory, Jade, Laces, Landscapes, Leather, Photography, Pre-Columbian Art, Prints, Sculpture, Southwestern Art, Textiles, Watercolors
Collections: Archaeology, ethnology, history, sciences, paleontology, 19th-21st century American Art
Exhibitions: Changing exhibitions of art, sciences, & history; permanent exhibitions of art, anthropology, archaeology & history; Paleo/Indian archaeological site, Lubbock Lake Landmark
Publications: MuseNews e-newsletter, monthly; Museum Journal, annually; occasional papers
Activities: Classes for adults & children; docent training; lects open to pub, 8-9 vis lectrs per yr; concerts; gallery talks; tours; sponsoring of competitions; scholarships offered; individual paintings & original objects of art lent to other mus; exten program serves local school districts, hostels, MHMR; book traveling exhibs 8-10 per yr; originate traveling exhibs usually within Texas; two mus shops sell books, magazines, reproductions, prints & slides

L **School of Art Visual Resource Center**, Box 42081, Lubbock, TX 79408-2081. Tel 806-742-3825 exten 261; Email paula.l.yeager@ttu.edu; Web: www.depts.ttu.edu/ART/SOA/nav/resources/vrc/vrc.php; *Cur* Paula Yeager
Open Mon - Fri 8:30 AM - 5:30 PM; Reference & teaching library
Income: $10,000 (financed by state legislature appropriation, private donations & grants)
Library Holdings: Book Volumes 4000, Compact Disks, DVDs, Other Holdings CD-Roms, Periodical Subscriptions 50, Slides 110,000, Video Tapes 190
Special Subjects: Advertising Design, Aesthetics, American Indian Art, Antiquities-Assyrian, Antiquities-Byzantine, Antiquities-Egyptian, Antiquities-Etruscan, Antiquities-Greek, Antiquities-Oriental, Antiquities-Persian, Antiquities-Roman, Art Education, Art History, Asian Art, Calligraphy

LUFKIN

A **MUSEUM OF EAST TEXAS,** 503 N Second St, Lufkin, TX 75901. Tel 409-639-4434; Fax 936-639-4435; Email jmcdonald@metlufkin.org; *Exec Dir* J P McDonald; *Admin Asst* Claudine Lovejoy; *Cur Coll* Kyley Cantwell; *Cur Educ* Ann N Reyes
Open Tues - Fri 10 AM - 5 PM, Sat - Sun 1 - 5 PM, cl Independence Day, Thanksgiving & Christmas; No admis fee; Estab 1975 by the Lufkin Service League to bring the fine arts to East Texas & to cultivate an interest in regional history; Average Annual Attendance: 12,000; Mem: 500; dues President's Circle $1000, patron $500, sustainer $250, sponsor $150, contributor $100, family $50, individual $25
Income: financed by mem & grants
Exhibitions: East Texas Art; Exhib change every 4 months
Publications: Bi-monthly newsletter
Activities: Classes for adults & children; docent training; trips; lect open to public; gallery talks; tours; competitions with awards; traveling trunks; mus shop sells books, prints & various items

MARFA

M **CHINATI FOUNDATION,** One Cavalry Row, Marfa, TX 79843; PO Box 1135, Marfa, TX 79843-1135. Tel 432-729-4362; Fax 432-729-4597; Email information@chinati.org; Web: www.chinati.org; *Dir* Jenny Moore, PhD; *Pres* Andrew Cogan
Open Wed - Sun first 1/2 of tour 10 AM, 2nd 1/2 of tour 2 PM; Admis adults $10, seniors & students $5, members free; Estab 1986; Non profit pub foundation, permanent installations by limited number of artists; Average Annual Attendance: 10,000; Mem: 1,200
Income: financed by mem, grants & donations
Library Holdings: Cards, Exhibition Catalogs, Slides
Special Subjects: Architecture, Sculpture
Collections: Carl Andre Collection of Poems, John Chamberlain Collection: 23 sculptures, Donald Judd Collection: 100 mill aluminum sculptures & 15 concrete outdoor works, Ilya Kabakov Collection: mixed media installation, Claes Oldenburg Collection: aluminum/fiberglass outdoor work, Dan Flavin works in fluorescent light
Exhibitions: Permanent installation: six buildings of work in fluorescent light by Dan Flavin
Publications: Art in the Landscape, 1997; Chinati Foundation Newsletter, annual
Activities: Classes for adults & children; docent training; artist residencies; intern training; lect open to public, 7 per biennial symposium, tours; museum shop sells books; prints; reproductions; t-shirts & caps

M **JUDD FOUNDATION,** 104 S Highland Ave, PO Box 218 Marfa, TX 79843. Tel 432-729-4406; Fax 432-729-4614; Email info@juddfoundation.org; Web: juddfoundation.org; *Artistic Dir* Flavin Judd; *Pres* Rainer Judd; *Dir Develop* Hannah Parker; *Progs & Communs Mgr* Elizabeth Abrahamson
Advance reservation for guided visits; Admis general $25, students & seniors with valid ID $12.50; Estab 1996 to preserve Donald Judd's installed living & working spaces, libraries & archives; Judd's formerly private living & working spaces that make up 126,000 sq ft across Texas & New York
Collections: Judd's furniture, paintings from the 1950s and 1960s, modernist & period furniture, works by prominent twentieth-century artists & designers
Activities: Gallery talks; guided visits; drawing sessions; events

MARSHALL

M **HARRISON COUNTY HISTORICAL MUSEUM,** 707 N Washington, Marshall, TX 75670; PO Box 1987, Marshall, TX 75671-1987. Tel 903-938-2680; Fax 903-927-2534; Email museum@shreve.net; Web: www.cets.sfasu.edu/Harrison/; *Pres* Alex Liebling; *CEO* Carrol Fletcher; *Mus Shop Mgr* Gwen Nolan Warren
Open Tues - Sat 10 AM - 4 PM, cl Sun & Mon; Estab 1965, history preservation; Gallery is housed in 1901 Harrison county courthouse; Average Annual Attendance: 2,000; Mem: 375; dues family $35, individual $25, students $10
Income: Financed by mem, donations, admis & endowment
Special Subjects: Ceramics, Historical Material
Collections: Cut & Pressed Glass, 400 BC - 1977 Ceramics, Hand-painted China, Historical Material, Religious Artifacts, etchings, jewelry, paintings, porcelains, portraits, Pioneer implements, transportation
Publications: Historical Newsletter, quarterly
Activities: Classes for adults & children; guided tours; genealogical records researched; mus shop sells books, original art, reproductions

M **MICHELSON MUSEUM OF ART,** 216 N Bolivar, Marshall, TX 75670; PO Box 8290, Marshall, TX 75671-8290. Tel 903-935-9480; Fax 903-935-1974; Email leomich@sbcglobal.net; Web: www.michelsonmuseum.org; *Educ Dir* Bonnie Strauss; *Dir* Susan Spears
Open Tues - Fri 10 AM - 4 PM, Sat 1 - 4 PM, cl holidays; No admis fee; Estab 1985 to exhibit works of Leo Michelson & special exhibits; Three galleries, one exhibits permanent collection of works by Leo Michelson & other American artists; Average Annual Attendance: 8,000; Mem: 400; dues $35 & up
Income: $360,000 (financed by mem, city & state appropriations)
Library Holdings: Book Volumes, Prints
Special Subjects: African Art, American Indian Art, American Western Art, Drawings, Eskimo Art, Painting-American, Painting-French, Painting-German, Painting-Russian, Portraits, Prints, Watercolors, Woodcuts
Exhibitions: Leo Michelson (1887 - 1978 Russian/American); Selections from the permanent collection
Activities: Classes for adults & children; docent training; lects open to pub; vis lectrs 1 per yr; gallery talks; tours; concerts; book traveling exhibs 4 per yr; mus shop sells books, original art, reproductions & prints

MCALLEN

M **INTERNATIONAL MUSEUM OF ART & SCIENCE,** 1900 Nolana, McAllen, TX 78504. Tel 956-682-1564; Fax 956-686-1813; Email infor@imasonline.org; Web: www.mcallenmuseum.org; *Exec Dir* Joseph Bravo; *Cur* Maria Elena Macias
Open Tues, Wed, Fri & Sat 9 AM - 5 PM, Thurs 9 AM - 8 PM, Sun 1 PM - 5 PM; Admis adults $7, seniors & students $5, children 4-12 $4, children 3 & under free; Estab 1967; Open to staff, volunteers & researchers for reference only; Average Annual Attendance: 80,000; Mem: Mem start at $42
Special Subjects: Art Education, Art History, Folk Art, Painting-American, Painting-European, Photography, Prints, Textiles, Watercolors, Woodcarvings, Woodcuts
Collections: Local, state & regional artists, Mexican folk art, Mexican Prints, US & European paintings
Exhibitions: Abstract Works from the MIM Collection; Christmas Tree Forest; Nightscapes; Arte Rio Grande, Francis Valesco
Publications: Bulletins & brochures periodically; Newsletter, monthly
Activities: Classes for adults & children; lects open to pub, gallery talks; tours; mus shop sells books, original art, prints

MIAMI

M **ROBERTS COUNTY MUSEUM,** PO Box 306, Miami, TX 79059-0306; 120 E Commercial St, Miami, TX 79059. Tel 806-868-3291; Fax 806-868-3381; Email robertscomuseum@amaonline.com; Web: www.robertscountymuseum.org; *Dir* Emma Bowers; *Exec Dir* Cecil Gill
Open Tues - Fri 10 AM - 5 PM, weekends by appointment, cl Mon & holidays; No admis fee; Estab 1979; Average Annual Attendance: 3,000
Library Holdings: Book Volumes, Maps, Original Art Works, Original Documents, Other Holdings, Pamphlets, Periodical Subscriptions, Photographs, Prints, Records
Special Subjects: American Indian Art, Anthropology, Archaeology, Furniture
Collections: Locke Collection of Indian artifacts, Mead Collection of mammoth bones & fossils, Historical Museum of early Miami, Native American Art Collection, Miami Mammoth Kill Site
Exhibitions: Annual Nat Cow-Calling Contest with Art Show first Sat in June
Activities: Classes for children; quilting demonstrations daily; lects open to pub; tours; mus shop sells books, T-shirts, jewelry & keychains, traveling exhibs

MIDLAND

M **MUSEUM OF THE SOUTHWEST,** 1705 W Missouri, Midland, TX 79701-6516. Tel 432-683-2882; Fax 432-684-9151; Email info@museumsw.org; Web: www.museumsw.org; *Exec Dir* Brian Lee Whisenhunt
Open Tues - Sat 10 AM - 5 PM, Sun 2 - 5 PM, cl Mon; No admis fee; $3 Children's Mus & $3 planetarium, additional cost for shows; Incorporated 1965 as an art & history mus with a separate planetarium providing various science exhibits; children's mus; Six galleries exhibiting traveling exhibits & permanent colls; Average Annual Attendance: 100,000; Mem: 800; dues $40-$1200; board meeting third Wed monthly
Income: Financed by mem, contributions & grants
Special Subjects: American Indian Art, American Western Art, Ceramics, Drawings, Etchings & Engravings, Landscapes, Painting-American, Photography, Pre-Columbian Art, Prints, Sculpture, Southwestern Art, Watercolors, Archaeology, Bronzes, Historical Material, Pottery, Textiles
Collections: Art & archaeological materials of the Southwest, Indian art coll, permanent art coll
Publications: Annual Report; Intersections, twice yearly
Activities: Classes for adults & children; docent training; arts & crafts classes; video showings; lects open to pub & for members only, 204 vis lectrs per yr; concerts; gallery talks; tours; individual paintings lent to other mus; book traveling exhibs 6-8 per yr; mus shop sells books, jewelry, gifts & original clothing

NACOGDOCHES

M **STEPHEN F AUSTIN STATE UNIVERSITY,** SFA Galleries, 208 Griffith Fine Arts Bldg, Stephen F Austin State University Nacogdoches, TX 75962. Tel 936-468-1131; Fax 936-468-2938; Email baileysl@sfasu.edu; *Dir* Shannon Bailey
Open Tues - Sun 12:30 - 5 PM; No admis fee; Estab as a teaching gallery & to bring in art from outside this area for our students & the East Texas community; One room approx 56 x 22 ft, plus storage; Average Annual Attendance: 5,000
Income: Financed by state educ funds & private contributions
Activities: Classes for children; docent training; workshops; lect open to public; gallery talks; tours; museum trips; competitions with awards

ODESSA

M **ELLEN NOEL ART MUSEUM OF THE PERMIAN BASIN,** 4909 E University Blvd, Odessa, TX 79762-8144. Tel 432-550-9696; Fax 432-550-9226; Web: www.noelartmuseum.org; *Collection Mgr* Letha Hooper; *Dir* George Jacob; *Develop Officer* Judith Motyka; *Publicity* Jessica Smith; *Admin* Stacy Benavides; *Security/ Facilities Technician* Willie Sturgeon; *Cur Educ* Doylene Land; *Educ Coordr* Annie Stanley; *Vis Servs Coordr* Daniel Zies
Open Tues - Sat 10 AM - 5 PM, Sun 2 - 5 PM, cl Mon; No admis fee; Estab 1985 to increase public awareness & appreciation of art through exposure & education; Accessible galleries & sculpture garden; Average Annual Attendance: 20,000; Mem: 475; dues $30 & up; annual meeting in May
Income: $210,000 (financed by mem, grants, donations & fund raisers)
Library Holdings: Book Volumes, Clipping Files, Exhibition Catalogs, Original Documents, Pamphlets, Periodical Subscriptions, Prints, Records
Special Subjects: American Western Art, Bronzes, Ceramics, Collages, Drawings, Embroidery, Etchings & Engravings, Folk Art, Hispanic Art, Jewelry, Juvenile Art, Landscapes, Mexican Art, Photography, Porcelain, Portraits, Posters, Prints, Religious Art, Renaissance Art, Sculpture, Silver, Southwestern Art, Watercolors, Woodcarvings
Collections: Permanent collection of American art since 1860
Exhibitions: Rotating exhibitions, 20 per yr
Activities: Classes for adults & children; workshops; demonstrations; videos; community art days; lects open to pub, lects for mems; gallery talks; tours; schols offered; exten dept; lending collection, contains paintings; internships, related course at Univ of Texas of the Permian Basin; mus shop sells art related books, magazines, original art, Smithsonian merchandise, children's art activities

M **PRESIDENTIAL MUSEUM & LEADERSHIP LIBRARY,** 4919 E University Blvd, Odessa, TX 79762-8144. Tel 432-363-7737; Email president.museum@att.net; Web: www.thepresidentialmuseum.com; *Adminr* Charles Cotten; *Assoc Adminr* Gail Barnes
Open Tues - Sat 10 AM - 5 PM; Donations accepted; Estab 1965 & dedicated to the office of the Pres, electoral process & pub serv; Average Annual Attendance: 5,000
Income: Financed by grants and donations
Library Holdings: Audio Tapes, Book Volumes 5,000, Cassettes, Clipping Files, Exhibition Catalogs, Memorabilia, Pamphlets, Periodical Subscriptions 15, Records, Reproductions, Sculpture, Slides, Video Tapes
Special Subjects: Dolls, Portraits
Collections: Campaign memorabilia, original signatures, portraits, First lady inaugural gowns coll
Exhibitions: Long-term exhibitions on the presidency & first ladies; special temporary exhibitions
Activities: Present a brief history of the United States as seen through the presidency

ORANGE

M **NELDA C & H J LUTCHER STARK FOUNDATION,** Stark Museum of Art, 712 Green Ave, Orange, TX 77630-5721. Tel 409-886-2787; Fax 409-883-6361; Email info@starkmuseum.org; Web: www.starkmuseum.org; *Pres & CEO Stark Foundation* Walter Riedel; *Exhibs Designer & Mgr* Terri Fox; *Chief Security Officer* Jimmy Porterfield; *Library and Archive Mgr* Jenniffer Hudson-Connors; *Collections Mgr & Registrar* Allison Evans; *Dir Stark Art & History Venues* Trina Nelson Thomas; *Cur* Sarah E Boehine, PhD; *Cur Educ* Jennifer Restauri
Open Tues - Sat 9 AM - 5 PM; No admis fee except for special exhibs; Estab 1978 to preserve & display the Stark collection of art & promote interests in subjects relative to the same through exhibitions, publications & educational programs; Five galleries & lobby, 18,000 sq ft of total exhibition area; Average Annual Attendance: 14,000
Income: Financed by endowment
Library Holdings: Auction Catalogs, Audio Tapes, Book Volumes, CD-ROMs, Clipping Files, DVDs, Exhibition Catalogs, Kodachrome Transparencies, Manuscripts, Original Art Works, Original Documents, Periodical Subscriptions, Photographs, Prints, Sculpture, Video Tapes
Special Subjects: American Indian Art, American Western Art, Bronzes, Carpets & Rugs, Decorative Arts, Drawings, Etchings & Engravings, Furniture, Glass, Manuscripts, Painting-American, Porcelain, Prints, Restorations, Southwestern Art
Collections: Art relating to American West 1830-1965, special emphasis on artist explorers, illustrators & New Mexico artists, Native American Art (Plains, Southwest Northwest Coast, decorative arts, glass), rare books & manuscripts
Publications: Exhibition catalogs; Stark Museum of Art: A Guide to the Galleries, Orange, TX, David C. Hunt; Stark Foundation 1998, Nelda C & HJ Lutcher; Stark

Museum of Art: Taos Portfolio, Orange, TX, David C Hunt; Stark Foundation 2001, Nelda C & HJ Lutcher
Activities: Classes for adults & children; dramatic progs; docent training; tours for school children and adults; lect open to public; gallery talks; tours; 1-2 book traveling exhibs per yr; mus shop sells books, prints & Christmas ornaments based on colls

PANHANDLE

M **CARSON COUNTY SQUARE HOUSE MUSEUM,** Fifth & Elsie Sts, PO Box 276 Panhandle, TX 79068; PO Box 276, Panhandle, TX 79068-0276. Tel 806-537-3524; Fax 806-537-5628; Email shm@squarehousemuseum.org; Web: www.squarehousemuseum.org; *Interim Dir* Dr Bill Green; *Admin Asst & Mus Store Mgr* Janie Plumlee; *Bus Mgr* Shirlyn Grantham
Open Mon - Sat 9 AM - 5 PM, Sun 1 - 5 PM, cl Thanksgiving, Christmas Eve, Christmas, New Year's Day & Easter; No admis fee; Estab 1965 as a general mus with art galleries, area & State & National historical displays; Wildlife building & displays; Historic house, listed in National Register of Historic Places; Two enclosed security controlled art galleries, an educ center & art gallery; Average Annual Attendance: 30,000
Income: Financed by endowments, income & pub contributions
Special Subjects: American Indian Art, Anthropology, Archaeology, Bronzes, Carpets & Rugs, Costumes, Crafts, Decorative Arts, Dioramas, Dolls, Drawings, Etchings & Engravings, Ethnology, Folk Art, Furniture, Historical Material, Laces, Leather, Manuscripts, Maps, Painting-American, Period Rooms, Photography, Primitive art, Prints
Collections: Paintings of area pioneers by Marlin Adams, sculpture & bronze by Jim Thomas, Grant Speed & Keith Christi, Kenneth Wyatt paintings, Ben Carlton Mead & Harold Bugbee paintings, contemporary Native American art, Native American beadwork, Acoma pottery, costumes, antiques, Native American Art
Publications: A Time To Purpose, county history book; Land of Coronado, coloring book; The Square House Cook Book; Voices of the Square House, poems
Activities: Classes for adults & children; dramatic progs; docent training; lects open to pub, 1 vis lectrs per yr; concerts; gallery talks; tours; mus shop sells books, reproductions, prints & mus related gift items

PARIS

M **HAYDEN MUSEUM OF AMERICAN ART,** 930 Cardinal Lane, Paris, TX 75460. Tel 903-785-1925; Fax 903-784-7631; *Dir & Pres* William Hayden, MD
Open by appointment; No admis fee; Average Annual Attendance: 2,500
Library Holdings: Book Volumes
Collections: paintings, decorative arts, prints, photographs, sculpture, American art history
Activities: Seminars; lect

ROUND TOP

M **JAMES DICK FOUNDATION,** Festival - Institute, PO Box 89, 248 Jaster Rd Round Top, TX 78954-0089. Tel 979-249-3129; Fax 979-249-5078; Email lamarl@festivalhill.org; Web: www.festivahill.org; *Founder & Dir* James Dick; *Managing Dir* Richard R Royall; *Dir Library & Mus* Lamar Lentz
Open by appointment; Tours $5, summer concerts $20 per person, chamber music $10 per person; Estab 1971 as a center for music, the arts & humanities; Guion Room, Oxehufwud Room, Historic House Collection. Maintains reference library; Average Annual Attendance: 40,000-50,000
Income: Financed through ticket sales & donations
Library Holdings: Auction Catalogs, Book Volumes, Clipping Files, Compact Disks, DVDs, Exhibition Catalogs, Manuscripts, Memorabilia, Motion Pictures, Original Art Works, Photographs, Prints, Records, Reels
Special Subjects: American Western Art, Architecture, Art History, Carpets & Rugs, Ceramics, Coins & Medals, Costumes, Crafts, Decorative Arts, Folk Art, Furniture, Furniture, Glass, Graphics, Historical Material, History of Art & Archaeology, Interior Design, Jewelry, Laces, Landscape Architecture, Landscapes, Manuscripts, Maps, Painting-American, Painting-Russian, Painting-Scandinavian, Period Rooms, Pewter, Photography, Porcelain, Southwestern Art
Collections: British Country Houses, Decorative Arts, Historic House Collection, Music Instruments, Painting, Swedish Decorative Arts - 16th century to present, Texas History, 20th-century photography
Activities: Classes for students; docent training; lect open to public; 16 vis lectrs per yr; concerts; gallery talks; tours; scholarships offered to music students; sales shop

SAN ANGELO

M **ANGELO STATE UNIVERSITY,** Houston Harte University Center, PO Box 11027, San Angelo, TX 76909-0001. Tel 915-942-2062; Fax 915-942-2354; *Dir Prog* Rick E Greig
Open Mon - Fri 8 AM - 10:30 PM, Sat 9 AM - 10:30 PM, cl Sun; No admis fee; Estab 1970 to provide entertainment & informal educ for the students, faculty & staff; Gallery is maintained
Income: $3000 (financed by city & state appropriations)
Collections: Wax drawings done by Guy Rowe for illustration of the book In Our Image by Houston Harte
Exhibitions: Historical artifacts; modern drawings; photography; pottery; weaving; children, students and faculty exhibitions
Activities: Lects open to public, 2 vis lectrs per yr; gallery talks; tours; concerts; dramatic progs; competitions

M **SAN ANGELO ART CLUB,** Helen King Kendall Memorial Art Gallery, 119 W First St, San Angelo, TX 76903. Tel 915-653-4405; *Pres* Mary Taylor; *1st VPres* Mary Kollmeyer; *Secy* Sue Meacham; *Treas* Patty Towler
Open Wed 9 AM - 2 PM, Sat & Sun 1 - 4 PM; No admis fee; Club estab 1928 & gallery estab 1948 to promote the visual fine arts in San Angelo; Average Annual Attendance: 1,500; Mem: 90; dues $30; meeting first Mon each month
Income: $8,000 (financed by Memorial Endowment Fund)
Collections: Paintings by George Biddle, Gladys Rockmore Davis, Xavier Gonzales, Iver Rose & Frederick Waugh, Hazel Janick, Karl Albert, Joseph Sharp, Willard Metcalf, Robert Woods, Dwight Holmes
Exhibitions: Monthly exhibits from area artists; The Gallery supports the local art community with exhibs including an annual HS art show and an annual exhibit which supports the Concho Valley Assn for the blind
Publications: Splashes, monthly newsletter
Activities: Classes for adults & children & dramatic progs; tours; competitions with awards; individual paintings & original objects of art lent to libraries, churches & bus

M **SAN ANGELO MUSEUM OF FINE ARTS,** One Love St, San Angelo, TX 76903. Tel 325-653-3333; Fax 325-658-6800; Email museum@samfa.org; Web: www.samfa.org; *Pres* Rodney Mayberry; *VPres* John Klingemann; *Dir* Howard J Taylor; *Coll Mgr* Laura Romer Huckaby; *Exec* Tracy Hedges; *Preparator* Shaydee Watson; *Cur Educ* Rebekah Coleman; *Gift Shop Mgr* Martha McCloskey; *Maintenance Chief/Security* Joel Quintella; *Office Mgr* Jan Mulkey; *Facilities Mgr* Brandon Mansell
Open Tues - Sat 10 AM - 4 PM, Sun 1 - 4 PM, art walk (every 3rd Thurs) until 9 PM; cl Mon & major holidays; Admis adults $2, sr citizens $1, members, local students, military & children & adults with children free; Estab 1981 to provide quality visual arts exhibits & stimulating programs for educational & cultural growth; 30,000 sq ft bldg designed by architect Malcolm Holzman & contains three gallery spaces; Average Annual Attendance: 65,000; Mem: Dues $10 and up
Income: 1.2 million (financed by endowment, sales, admis & grants
Library Holdings: Auction Catalogs, Audio Tapes, Book Volumes, CD-ROMs, Clipping Files, Compact Disks, DVDs, Exhibition Catalogs, Kodachrome Transparencies, Original Documents, Other Holdings, Periodical Subscriptions, Slides, Video Tapes
Special Subjects: Baroque Art, Ceramics, Decorative Arts, Glass, Gold, Mexican Art, Latin American Art, Painting-American, Prints, Sculpture
Collections: Texas art; American crafts (1945-present), particularly ceramics, American paintings & sculpture of all eras, Mexican & Mexican-American art of all eras, Selected European, Oriental & African art, Spanish Colonial Art, American Manufactured Glass
Exhibitions: (Biennial) San Angelo National Ceramic Competition
Publications: Exhibit catalogs
Activities: Classes for adults & children; outreach progs; docent training; concerts; gallery talks; tours; lects open to pub, 15 vis lectrs per yr; sponsoring competitions with awards; National Museum Service Award; exten dept serves 17 counties in W Texas; book traveling exhibs, 2 - 3 per yr; originate traveling exhibs to mus; mus shop sells books, magazines, original art, reproductions, prints, educational toys, paper goods, jewelry & ceramics & other gift items

SAN ANTONIO

M **BISCOE WESTERN ART MUSEUM,** 210 W Market St, San Antonio, TX 78205. Tel 210-299-4499; Fax 210-299-4118; Email info@briscoemuseum.org; Web: www.birscoemuseum.org; *Exec. Dir* Thomas A Livesay
Open Tues - Thurs 10 AM - 4 PM, Fri - Sun 10 AM - 5 PM, first Tues of the month 10 AM - 9 PM; cl Mon, New Year's Day, Battle of the Flowers Fiesta Parade, Thanksgiving, Christmas; Admis adults $10, seniors 65 & over, students & retired military $8; children 12 & under, active military & family, members no admis fee; Estab 2013; Mem: $35 - $10,000
Special Subjects: Painting-American, Sculpture
Activities: Tours; films series; mus shop sells books, arts & crafts, handmade jewelry

M **BLUE STAR CONTEMPORARY ART CENTER,** 116 Blue Star, San Antonio, TX 78204-1713. Tel 210-227-6960; Fax 210-229-9412; Email bluestarart@bluestarart.org; Web: www.bluestarart.org; *Exec Dir* Mary Heathcott; *Exhib & Prog Mgr* Jacqueline McGilvray; *MOSAIC Artist-in-Res* Alex Rubio; *Develop Mgr* Elaine Leahy
Open Thurs - Fri 10 AM - 8 PM, Sat - Sun 10 AM - 6 PM, first Fri 10 AM - 6 PM; Admis general $5, seniors $3, mem, military, educ & students free; Estab 1986 to advance contemporary art by presenting culturally diverse exhibitions and programs to broaden San Antonio's local contemporary art experience by nurturing and showcasing local talent and participating in a diverse exchange on regional, nat & international levels; 13,000 sq ft warehouse; Average Annual Attendance: 125,000; Mem: 65; contemporary $250, individual $40, family $60
Income: Financed by an oper endowment, mem, community educational prog & activities, Board dues, city & state grants, grants from pub & private foundations & trusts
Collections: Contemporary multimedia painting, prints, sculpture, photographs
Publications: BS, Blue Star mem quarterly newsletter; small exhib pamphlets & catalogues
Activities: Educ prog for adults & school children; docent training; lects open to pub; 4-5 vis lectrs per yr; gallery talks; tours; concerts; awards for supporting SA Express-News Literacy Prog; consistently recognized by local journals at best contemp art gallery in town; schols offered; satellite exhib sites; senior art classes at satellite & other venues; book traveling exhibs 1-2 per yr to local & regional art & educ organizations; mus shop sells books, original art, reproductions, prints, T-shirts, posters; on-line purchasing
Open Tues - Sat noon - 6 PM, Thurs noon - 8 PM

L **CENTRAL LIBRARY,** Dept of Fine Arts, 600 Soledad St, San Antonio, TX 78205-1208. Tel 210-207-2500; Fax 210-207-2552; *Dir* Ramiro S Salazar; *Asst Dir* Nancy Gandara
Open Mon - Fri 9 AM - 9 PM, Sat 9 AM - 5 PM, Sun 11 AM - 5 PM; Estab to provide art reference & lending materials to the residents of Bexar County; Art gallery is maintained. Also serves as a major resource center to regional libraries in South Texas

Income: Financed by city, state & federal appropriation
Purchases: $250,000
Library Holdings: Audio Tapes, Cassettes, Clipping Files, Compact Disks, Exhibition Catalogs, Fiche, Filmstrips, Memorabilia, Motion Pictures, Pamphlets, Photographs, Records, Reels, Reproductions, Video Tapes
Exhibitions: Regular Exhibition of local & National artists
Activities: Classes for children; dramatic progs; lects open to pub, 2 vis lectrs per yr; concerts; gallery talks; tours; competitions with awards; exten dept; lending collection contains 320,000 books, 400 video cassettes, 10,000 audio cassettes, 15,000 motion pictures; book traveling exhibs

A **CENTRO CULTURAL AZTLAN,** 1800 Fredericksburg Rd, Deco Bldg, Ste 103 San Antonio, TX 78201. Tel 210-432-1896; Fax 210-432-1983; Email centroaztlan@sbcglobal.net; Web: www.centroaztlan.org; *Exec Dir* Malena Gonzalez-Cid; *Arts Prog Dir* Ruth M. Guajardo
Open Mon - Fri 9 AM - 5 PM; No admis fee; Estab 1977 to support & strengthen Chicano/Latino culture & identity; Expression Fine Art Gallery mounts 10 art exhibits per year to showcase visual artists; Average Annual Attendance: 62,000
Special Subjects: Ceramics, Folk Art, Hispanic Art, Jewelry, Metalwork
Exhibitions: Annual Lowrider Car Exhibition, held annually 1st Sun in Apr
Publications: ViAztlan, quarterly journal of contemporary arts & letters
Activities: Classes for children; gallery talks; guest lectr; reading recitals; mus shop sells original art, prints

M **CITY OF SAN ANTONIO,** Spanish Governor's Palace, 105 Plaza de Armas, San Antonio, TX 78205-2412. Tel 210-224-0601; Fax 210-223-5562; Email spanishgovpalace@sanantonio.gov; *Mus Supv* Charlotte Boord
Open Tues - Sat 9 AM - 5 PM, Sun 10 AM - 5 PM, cl Mon; Admis adults $4, children under 14 $2, military & seniors $3, children 6 & under free; Estab 1749; Historic site with period furnishings; Average Annual Attendance: 25,000
Income: $65,000 (financed by city appropriation)
Special Subjects: Architecture, Folk Art, Furniture, Hispanic Art, Historical Material, Maps, Period Rooms, Pottery, Religious Art, Restorations, Textiles
Collections: Spanish-colonial furnishings, paintings, earthenware, brass & copper pieces from 16th - 17th century
Publications: Spanish Governor's Palace brochure
Activities: Mus shop sells notecards, key chains, histories, courtyard sketches, postcards

A **COPPINI ACADEMY OF FINE ARTS,** Elizabeth di Barbieri, 115 Melrose Pl, San Antonio, TX 78212-1924. Tel 210-824-8502; Email webmaster@coppini.us; Web: www.coppini-us; *Pres* Janice Yow
Open by appointment; No admis fee; Estab 1945 to promote classic & representational art; to encourage worthy accomplishment in the field of art & to serve as a means of public exhibition for the work of active members & guests; Hosted & mem exhibits; Average Annual Attendance: 1,000; Mem: dues per annum; ann meeting third Sun of Nov
Income: Membership & trust
Collections: Oil paintings by Rolla Taylor, sculpture & paintings by Waldine Tauch & Pompeo Coppini
Exhibitions: Annual May Garden Show. Monthly changing exhibits in upper gallery by members; (exhibs listed on website)
Publications: Coppini News Bulletin, monthly newsletter distributed to members
Activities: Classes for adults & children; lects open to pub, 6 vis lectrs per yr; gallery talks; tours; competitions; Artist of the Year award; scholarships offered; individual paintings & original objects of art lent; originate traveling exhibs; mus shop sell reproductions

L **Library,** 115 Melrose Pl, San Antonio, TX 78212. Tel 210-824-8502; Email coppini1@sbcglobal.net; Web: www.coppiniacademy.org; *Pres* Dr Hal Martin; *1st VPres* Donna Bland; *Secy* Sussanne Clark; *Treas* Ron Watkins; *Art Dir* Louis Mar
Estab 1945 to promote classical art; Circ 1500; Monthly exhibits of membership & museum coll; Average Annual Attendance: 1,000; Mem: dues $35; monthly meeting 3rd Sun
Income: Trust & fund raising
Library Holdings: Book Volumes 200, Clipping Files, Original Art Works, Periodical Subscriptions 50, Photographs, Sculpture, Slides, Video Tapes
Special Subjects: Sculpture
Activities: Classes for adults & children; lects open to pub; Awards - Artist of the Year; ann Schols $3000, HS Sr Art Major, 1 year

A **GUADALUPE CULTURAL ARTS CENTER,** 723 S Brazos St, Ste 1 San Antonio, TX 78207-5578. Tel 210-271-3151; Email info@guadalupeculturalarts.org; Web: www.guadalupeculturalarts.org; *Exec Dir* Cristina Balli; *Communs & Special Projects Dir* Yadhira Lozano; *Educ Dir* Belinda Menchaca; *Opers Dir* Loretta Zevallos
Open Mon - Fri 9 AM - 5 PM & spec events as scheduled; Admis fee varies; Estab 1979, non-profit, multi-disciplinary arts organization dedicated to the development, preservation & promotion of Latino arts & to facilitating a deeper understanding & appreciation of Chicano/Latino & Native American cultures; Center manages the beautifully restored, historic Guadalupe Theatre, a 410 seat, handicapped accessible, multi-purpose facility that houses the Theater Gallery, a large auditorium, a proscenium stage & equipment for theatrical & cinematic presentations; maintains Guadalupe Gallery & Cesar Chavez Project Space; Average Annual Attendance: 150,000
Income: $1,700,000
Exhibitions: Annual Tejano Conjunto Festival; Annual San Antonio Inter-Americas Bookfair; Annual Juried Women's Art Exhibit; Annual Student Exhibit; Hecho a Mano/Made by Hand (annual fine arts & crafts market)
Activities: Visual arts prog; classes & workshops; creative dramatics classes; dance prog; media prog; classes for adults & children; 4-6 vis lectrs per yr; fels & schols available; sales shop

M **MCNAY ART MUSEUM,** 6000 N New Braunfels Ave, San Antonio, TX 78209-4618. Tel 210-824-5368; Email info@mcnayart.org; Web: www.mcnayart.org; *Pres* Toby Calvert; *Dir* Richard Aste; *Head Educ* Katherine E Carey; *Coll Mgr* Heather Lammers; *Librn* Ann Jones; *Museum Store Mgr* Janet D Goddard; *Cur Prints & Drawings* Lyle Williams; *Head Cur Affairs* Rene Paul Barilleaux
Open Wed & Fri 10 AM - 6 PM, Thurs 10 AM - 9 PM, Sat 10 AM - 5 PM, Sun Noon - 5 PM, cl Mon, Tues (except for tours), Jan 1, July 4, Thanksgiving & Christmas; Admis adults $20, students with ID, seniors 65 & over & active military $15, children 12 & under & mems free; extra admis during special exhibs; Estab 1954 for the encouragement & development of modern art; 30,000 vol art history reference library; Robert L B Tobin Theatre Arts Library; 23 acres of gardens; 300-seat auditorium; McNay Mus Store; handicap accessibility, 200 seat lect hall, 45,000 sq ft new exhib hall, Jane & Arthur Stieren Ctr for Exhibs; Average Annual Attendance: 125,000; Mem: Dues assoc sustaining $550, contributing $275, supporting $150, family/dual $85, individual $55
Income: Financed by endowment, mem & private gifts
Special Subjects: American Indian Art, Decorative Arts, Graphics, Medieval Art, Painting-American, Painting-European, Sculpture
Collections: Oppenheimer Collection of late medieval & early Renaissance sculpture & paintings, Tobin Theatre Arts Collection related to opera, ballet & musical stage
Publications: Annual report; exhibition catalogues & brochures; Impressions, quarterly newsletter
Activities: Teen workshops; family activities; teacher resources; docent training; lects open to pub, 8 vis lectrs per yr; concerts; gallery talks; tours; individual paintings & original objects of art lent to other mus; book traveling exhibs 2 per yr; originates traveling exhibs; mus shop sells books & original art

L **McNay Art Museum Library & Archives,** 6000 N New Braunfels St, San Antonio, TX 78209; PO Box 6069, San Antonio, TX 78209. Tel 210-805-1727; Fax 210-805-1760; Email library@mcnayart.org; Web: www.mcnayart.org; *Librn* Ann Jones
Open to the pub Tues - Wed 10 AM - 3:45 PM, Thurs 10 AM - 4:45 PM, Fri 10 AM - 3:45 PM, cl Sat - Mon; Estab 1954 as an adjunct to the mus; Circ non-circulating
Income: Financed by endowment & gifts
Library Holdings: Auction Catalogs, Book Volumes 30,000, CD-ROMs, Clipping Files, Compact Disks, DVDs, Exhibition Catalogs, Fiche, Original Documents, Other Holdings Vertical Files: 27,000, Pamphlets, Periodical Subscriptions, Photographs, Records, Video Tapes
Special Subjects: Art History, Collages, Costume Design & Constr, Decorative Arts, Drawings, Etchings & Engravings, Glass, Graphic Arts, Handicrafts, Latin American Art, Mexican Art, Oriental Art, Painting-European, Painting-French, Painting-German, Painting-Russian, Photography, Printmaking, Prints, Sculpture, Southwestern Art, Stage Design, Theatre Arts, Watercolors, Woodcuts
Collections: Monographs, museum publications, magazines & periodicals, indexes, catalogues raisonnes, Rare Book Collection, Archives incl: admin records, McNay publications, catalogs of visiting exhibs, images, papers & records of Marion Koogler McNay, papers & records of museum affiliated persons & organizations

A **SAN ANTONIO ART LEAGUE,** San Antonio Art League Museum, 130 King Williams St, San Antonio, TX 78204. Tel 210-223-1140; Fax 210-223-2826; Web: www.saalm.org; *Pres* Lyn Belisle Kurtin
Open Tues - Sat 10 AM - 3 PM, cl Sun - Mon; No admis fee; Estab 1912 as a pub art gallery for San Antonio & for the promotion of a knowledge & interest in art by means of exhibitions; 4 rooms & large hall capable of hanging 150 paintings; Mem: 820; dues $15-$500; meetings monthly Oct - May
Income: Financed by mem & fundraising projects
Special Subjects: Crafts, Prints, Sculpture
Collections: Davis Collection, 1920 American Art, focus on San Antonio & Texas artist
Exhibitions: Rotating exhibits
Publications: Exhibition catalogs; monthly calendar of events
Activities: Educ dept; lects open to public, 3 vis lectrs per year; gallery talks; tours; paintings & original art objects lent

L **Library,** 130 King Williams St, San Antonio, TX 78204. Tel 210-223-1140; Email saalm@idworld.net; Web: www.saalm.org; *Pres* Louise Cantwell
Open Tues - Sat 12 PM - 6 PM; For reference only
Income: Financed by mem & fundraising
Library Holdings: Book Volumes 350

M **SAN ANTONIO MUSEUM OF ART,** 200 W Jones Ave, San Antonio, TX 78215-1406. Tel 210-978-8100; Fax 210-978-8182; Email info@samuseum.org; Web: www.samuseum.org; *Dir* Katherine Luber, PhD; *Cur Emeritus Latin American Art* Marion Oettinger Jr, PhD; *Cur Ancient Mediterranean Art* Jessica Powers, PhD; *Cur Asian Art* Emily Sano; *Chief Cur* William Keyse Rudolph, PhD; *Cur Contemporary Art* Suzanne Weaver
Open Tues & Fri 10 AM - 9 PM, Wed - Thurs & Sat - Sun 10 AM - 5 PM, cl Mon; Admis adult $20, sr citizen $17, students $12, children 12 & under free; Estab 1981; a renovation project, the Brewery was originally chartered in 1883; Anheuser-Busch Brewing Assoc of St Louis, during the early 1900's replaced the original wooden structures with a castle-like brick complex. 70,959 sq ft of exhibition pace; Average Annual Attendance: 160,000; Mem: 6,000; dues $55 & up
Library Holdings: Auction Catalogs, Book Volumes, Exhibition Catalogs, Periodical Subscriptions
Special Subjects: Afro-American Art, American Western Art, Antiquities-Egyptian, Antiquities-Greek, Antiquities-Oriental, Antiquities-Roman, Archaeology, Art Education, Art History, Asian Art, Baroque Art, Bronzes, Calligraphy, Ceramics, Coins & Medals, Conceptual Art, Decorative Arts, Dolls, Drawings, Embroidery, Enamels, Etchings & Engravings, Ethnology, Flasks & Bottles, Folk Art, Folk Art, Furniture, Glass, Gold, Hispanic Art, History of Art & Archaeology, Islamic Art, Ivory, Jade, Jewelry, Judaica, Juvenile Art, Laces, Landscapes, Latin American Art, Leather, Marine Painting, Medieval Art, Metalwork, Mexican Art, Mexican Art, Miniatures, Mixed Media, Mosaics, Oriental Art, Painting-American, Painting-Australian, Painting-British, Painting-Dutch, Painting-European, Painting-Flemish, Painting-French, Painting-Italian, Painting-Japanese, Painting-Russian, Painting-Spanish, Photography, Porcelain, Portraits, Pottery, Pre-Columbian Art, Pre-Columbian Art, Prints, Religious Art, Silver, Renaissance Art, Reproductions, Sculpture, Southwestern Art, Textiles, Watercolors, Woodcarvings
Collections: American photography since 1920, contemporary & modern art, 18th-20th century paintings & sculpture, European & American paintings &

decorative art, Greek & Roman antiquities, Mexican folk art, Pre-Columbian art, Spanish colonial art, Asian art; Islamic art; Oceanic art
Publications: Exhibition catalogues
Activities: Classes for adults & children; docent training; teacher workshops; parent-child classes; lects open to pub, 10-20 vis lectrs per yr; concerts; gallery talks; tours; individual paintings & original objects of art lent to other art institutions for special exhibitions; originate traveling exhibs to other art mus; mus shop sells books, reproductions prints, general art-interest merchandise, t-shirts, jewelry

A **SOUTHWEST SCHOOL OF ART,** 300 Augusta St, San Antonio, TX 78205-1216. Tel 210-224-1848; Fax 210-224-9337; Email information@swschool.org; Web: www.swschool.org; *Chair* Elise Boyan; *Exhibs Admin Assit* Teri Hatch Aguilar
Open Mon - Sat 9 AM - 5 PM; gallery shop open Mon - Sat 10 AM - 5 PM; No admis fee; Estab 1965; non-profit/community-based art school for all ages & skill levels; Russell Hill Rogers Galleries Constitute 3,500 sq ft of Exhib space for contemporary art. The Ursuline Gallery displays local & regional artists; Average Annual Attendance: 250,000; Mem: 700; dues $45 & up
Income: Financed by pvt donors, earned income from art school & City of San Antonio Office of Cultural Affairs
Exhibitions: 12 changing exhibs per year-contemporary art and craft
Publications: Opening Invitations; handouts for all exhibitions including photo of artists, cur essay, exhibition checklist; catalogues of classes
Activities: Classes for adults & children; arts workshop progs with vis artists; lects open to pub, 10 vis lectrs per yr; tours; gallery talks; schols offered; gallery shop sells original art, etc

M **THE UNIVERSITY OF TEXAS AT SAN ANTONIO,** Institute of Texan Cultures, 801 E Durango Blvd, San Antonio, TX 78205-3209. Tel 210-458-2300; Fax 210-458-2380; Email itcweb@utsa.edu; Web: www.texancultures.com; *Lead Curatorial Research* Dr Sarah Gould; *Cur Colls* Kathryn S McCloud; *Dir Educ & Interpretation* Christian D Clark; *Interpretive Mgr* Lynn Yakubik
Open Mon - Sat 9 AM - 5 PM, Sun 12 PM - 5 PM; Admis adults $10, seniors 65 & older, children 6-17 & military with ID $8, children under 6 free; Estab 1968; Maintains reference library; Average Annual Attendance: 200,000; Mem: See website for mem info
Income: $4,500,000 (financed by endowment, mem, state appropriation, gifts & sales)
Library Holdings: Audio Tapes, Fiche, Photographs
Special Subjects: Afro-American Art, Anthropology, Ethnology, Folk Art
Collections: Ethnic culture including Anglo, Belgian, Black, Chinese, Czech, Danish, Dutch, English, Filipino, French, German, Greek, Hungarian, Indian, Irish Italian, Japanese, Jewish, Lebanese, Mexican, Norwegian, Polish, Scottish, Spanish & Swedish (all Texans), one room school house, barn, windmill, fort & log house
Activities: Classes for adults & children; dramatic progs; docent progs; oral histories; lects open to pub; concerts; gallery talks; tours; festivals; traveling exhibs 2-3 per yr; sales shop sells books, prints, original art, reproductions & international gift items

M **WITTE MUSEUM,** 3801 Broadway, San Antonio, TX 78209. Tel 210-357-1900; Fax 210-357-1882; Email witte@wittemuseum.org; Web: www.wittemuseum.org; *Pres & CEO* Marise McDermott; *Chief Admin Officer* Bea Abercrombie; *Dir Communs* Katye Brought; *VChmn* J J Feik; *Dir Retail Svcs* Linda Gerber
Open Mon, Wed - Sat 10 AM - 5 PM, Tues 10 AM - 8 PM, Sun Noon - 5 PM; summer until 6 PM; Admis adults $12, seniors 65 & older $11, children 4-11 $9, children 3 & under free; group discount rates; Tues free from 3 - 9 PM; Estab 1926 by Ellen Schulz (later Quillin); Historical building located on the edge of the 450 acre Brackenridge Park on the banks of the San Antonio River & ancient Indian encampment area. Three restored historic homes on the grounds-the Ruiz, Navarro & Twohig houses; Average Annual Attendance: Over 250,000; Mem: 3000; dues family $95, individual $50
Special Subjects: American Indian Art, Anthropology, Costumes, Decorative Arts, Dolls, Embroidery, Folk Art, Furniture, Historical Material, Laces, Painting-American, Silver, Textiles
Exhibitions: Various exhibitions; call for details
Activities: Classes for adults & children; dramatic progs; docent training; lects open to pub; concerts; gallery talks; tours; camp-ins; family days; hands-on activities; behind-the-scenes tours; book traveling exhibs

SHERMAN

M **AUSTIN COLLEGE,** Ida Green Gallery, 900 N Grand Ave, Sherman, TX 75090-4400. Tel 903-813-2251; Fax 903-813-2273; Web: www.dustincollege.edu; *Chair* Mark Monroe
Open 9 AM - 5 PM weekdays; No admis fee; Estab 1972 to serve campus and community needs; Selected exhibitions of contemporary art by regional & national artists; Average Annual Attendance: 7,000
Income: Financed by endowment
Purchases: Occasional purchases of outdoor sculpture
Special Subjects: Prints
Collections: Prints
Exhibitions: Monthly, except summer
Activities: Classes for adults & children; lect open to public, 20 vis lectrs per year; gallery talks; tours; competitions; scholarships offered

SPRING

M **PEARL FINCHER MUSEUM OF FINE ARTS,** 6815 Cyrpresswood Dr, Spring, TX 77379-7705. Tel 281-376-6322; Fax 281-376-2944; Web: www.pearlmfa.org; *Dir* Ani Boyajian; *Opers Mgr* Kayla Osby; *Community Engagement Dir* Emily Guerra; *Admin Asst* Shannon Jacobson; *Dir Develop* Clara Lewis; *Facilities Mgr* Henry Griffin; *Museum Opers Asst* David Remley; *Cur* Terry Capps
Open Tues - Sat 10 AM - 5 PM, cl Sun - Mon; Suggested donation $5; Mem: dues $25-$5,000
Collections: paintings, drawings, sculptures
Exhibitions: Temporary exhibits
Activities: Educ progs; classes for adults & children

TYLER

M **TYLER MUSEUM OF ART,** 1300 S Mahon Ave, Tyler, TX 75701-3438. Tel 903-595-1001; Fax 903-595-1055; Email info@tylermuseum.org; Web: www.tylermuseum.org; *Head Educ Cur* Ken Tomio; *Facilities & Spec Events* Robert Owen; *Dir* Kimberley Bush Tomio; *Pres* Verna Hall; *Pub Rels & Mktg* Caleb Bell; *Accnt & HR Mgr* Kerry Moses
Open Tues - Sat 10 AM - 5 PM, Sun 1 - 5 PM; No admis fee, donations accepted; some special exhibs ticketed; Estab 1971 as a museum of art from 19th century to the present & specializing in early to contemp Texas art; Two galleries are 40 x 60 ft with 20 ft ceilings; Average Annual Attendance: 26,000; Mem: 700; dues $10 - $25,000
Income: $1.1 million (financed by endowment, memberships & donations)
Library Holdings: Auction Catalogs, Book Volumes, DVDs, Exhibition Catalogs, Kodachrome Transparencies, Other Holdings Harry Worthman Archives, Periodical Subscriptions, Photographs, Slides, Video Tapes
Special Subjects: Asian Art, Mexican Art, Painting-American, Photography, Sculpture
Collections: 1,700 works: special focus on early to contemporary Texas art, artists represented: Keith Carter, Joseph Glaso, Al Souza, Porfirio Salinas, Clyde Connell, Vernon Fisher, Terry Allen, Graydon Parrish & Norman Rockwell, contemporary Mexican folk art
Publications: Harry Worthman: A Life in Art, 2005; L O Griffith: Painting the Texas Landscape (2010); The Wyeths Across Texas (2012)
Activities: Classes for children; docent training; lects open to pub, 4 vis lectrs per yr; gallery talks; tours; high school student annual art exhib awards; exten prog serves local school district (elementary school); originate traveling exhibs to regional mus; mus shop sells books, assoc items, notecards, gift items relating to Texas & special exhib

L **Reference Library,** 1300 S Mahon Ave, Tyler, TX 75701. Tel 903-595-1001; Fax 903-595-1055; Email info@tylermuseum.org; Web: www.tylermuseum.org; *Dir* Kimberley Bush Tomio; *Spec Events & Facilities Mgr* Robert Owen; *Cur & Head Educ* Ken Tomio; *Develop Officer* Caroline Wylie; *Registrar* Toni Lee Kraft
Open Tues - Sat 10 AM - 5 PM, Sun 1 - 5 PM; No admis fee for most exhibitions; Estab 1971 as an educational & cultural center to enrich the lives of East Texas citizens & visitors through the collection, preservation, study, exhibition, interpretation & celebration of the visual arts; Circ Non-circulating; 2 galleries; Average Annual Attendance: 30,000; Mem: 800
Income: $750,000 (financed by memberships, private donations, grants & city appropriation)
Library Holdings: Book Volumes 2,000, Clipping Files, Exhibition Catalogs, Kodachrome Transparencies, Periodical Subscriptions 6, Photographs, Slides, Video Tapes
Special Subjects: Bronzes, Ceramics, Drawings, Folk Art, Landscapes, Painting-American, Painting-French, Painting-German, Photography, Porcelain, Portraits, Prints, Sculpture, Watercolors, Woodcuts
Collections: 19th, 20th & 21st century Contemporary art
Publications: The Preview mag semi-annually
Activities: Classes for adults & children; docent training; summer art camp for children; school tours; family days; lects open to pub; 7-8 vis lectrs per yr; gallery talks; tours; performances; artist demonstrations; mus shop sells books, original art, reproductions, prints, postcards & other cards

VAN HORN

M **CULBERSON COUNTY HISTORICAL MUSEUM,** Clark Hotel Historical Museum, PO Box 231, Van Horn, TX 79855-0231. Tel 915-283-8028; Email clarkhotelmuseum.vh@gmail.com; Web: clarkhotelmiseum.squarespace.com; *Secy* Ellen Lipsey; *Pres* Larry Simpson; *Dir* Patricia Golden
Open Mon - Fri 8 AM - 5 PM, Sat by appointment; No admis fee, donations accepted; Estab 1972; history of Culberson County & original settlers
Income: Donations
Library Holdings: Book Volumes, CD-ROMs, Maps, Original Art Works, Pamphlets, Photographs
Special Subjects: American Indian Art, American Western Art, Archaeology, Costumes, Dolls, Drawings, Folk Art, Furniture, Leather, Manuscripts, Maps, Period Rooms, Restorations, Southwestern Art
Collections: Collections from old ranch families of Culberson County
Exhibitions: 1890s saloon, saddles & cowboy gear; Native American artifacts; Frontier Day; local rocks & minerals, as well as mining
Activities: School tours; mus shop sells post cards

VERNON

M **RED RIVER VALLEY MUSEUM,** 4600 College Dr W, Vernon, TX 76385-4052; PO Box 2004, Vernon, TX 76385-2004. Tel 817-553-1848; Fax 817-553-1849; Email director@redrivervalleymuseum.org; Web: www.redrivervalleymuseum.org; *Exec Dir* Sherillyn Yoakum; *Asst Dir* Carolyn Trafton; *Pres Bd Dirs* Stanley Heatly; *VPres* Bobby Burrus
Open Tues - Sun 1 - 5 PM; No admis fee, donations accepted (large groups $2 per person); Estab 1963 to provide for & preserve local heritage while maintaining national exhibits in the arts, history & science programs; Two galleries with one hundred linear ft of hanging space; Average Annual Attendance: 8,000
Income: Financed by contributions, hotel/motel tax & donations
Special Subjects: American Indian Art, Dolls, Historical Material, Reproductions, Sculpture
Collections: Electra Waggoner Biggs Sculpture Collection, J Henry Ray American Indian Artifacts Collection, Taylor Dabney Gems, Rocks & Minerals Collection, Bill Bond Wild Game Trophies, Western Cattle Trail, annual Quilt Show - Oct/Nov, Red River Valley International Juried Art Exhibition - May/June

Publications: Museum Newsletter, quarterly
Activities: Classes for children, docent training; lects open to pub; 1-2 vis lectrs; gallery talks; tours; volunteer of the year award; book traveling exhibs; mus shop sells books, magazines, brochures, prints, collector's items, reproductions

WACO

M **THE ART CENTER OF WACO,** 1300 College Dr, Waco, TX 76708-1497. Tel 254-752-4371; Email artcenterwaco1300@gmail.com; Web: www.artcenterwaco.org; *Exec Dir* Meg Gilbert; *Prog Coordr* Megan Legband; *Educ Coordr* Karen Alleman
Open Tues - Sat 10 AM - 5 PM; Suggested donation $5; Estab 1972 to provide a variety of exhibitions for appreciation & classes for participation; Former residence of William Cameron, now renovated & contains one large main gallery & a small adjacent gallery,; Average Annual Attendance: 8,000; Mem: 250; dues $25 - $1,000;
Income: $80,000 (financed by endowment, mem & grants)
Special Subjects: Drawings, Graphics, Jewelry, Juvenile Art, Landscapes, Photography, Porcelain, Pottery, Sculpture, Stained Glass, Watercolors
Exhibitions: Exhibitions vary, call for details
Publications: Catalogs; exhibit brochures; newsletter; press releases
Activities: Classes for adults & children; gallery talks; tours; competitions; exten dept serves ethnic minorities & low socio-economic groups; mus shop sells books, glass, gift items, original art; prints

L **Library**, 1300 College Dr, Waco, TX 76708. Tel 254-752-4371; Fax 254-752-3506; Email info@artcenterwaco.org; Web: www.artcenterwaco.org; *Exec Dir* Mark Arnold; *Bus Office Mgr* Jennifer Warren
Open Tues - Sat 10 AM - 5 PM, Sun 1 - 5 PM; Admis $2 suggested donation; Estab 1976 as a source for staff, faculty, patrons of the Art Center & children to enhance artistic creativity through instruction & research; Former residence of William Cameron; Average Annual Attendance: 120,000; Mem: 900; dues $20 - $1,000
Income: Financed by mem, class fees, grants etc.
Library Holdings: Book Volumes 1,000, Exhibition Catalogs, Periodical Subscriptions 18
Special Subjects: Afro-American Art, American Indian Art, American Western Art, Art Education, Art History, Asian Art, Calligraphy, Ceramics, Commercial Art, Drawings, Etchings & Engravings, Folk Art, History of Art & Archaeology, Landscapes, Latin American Art
Exhibitions: Rotating exhibitions
Activities: Classes for adults & children; docent training; lects open to the public; lects for mems; gallery talks; tours; schols awarded

M **BAYLOR UNIVERSITY,** Martin Museum of Art, 1401 S University Parks Dr, Waco, TX 76798-7263; 1 Bear Pl, #97344 Waco, TX 76798-7344. Tel 254-710-1867; Fax 254-710-1566; Email heidihornik@baylor.edu; Web: www.baylor.edu/art; *Dir* Dr Heidi Hornik
Open Tues - Fri 10 AM - 5 PM, Sat Noon - 5 PM, cl Sun & Mon; No admis fee; Estab 1967 as a teaching arm of the university to serve the area; Gallery contains one large room with storage & preparation room; Average Annual Attendance: 7,000
Income: Financed through the art dept
Purchases: Contemporary American Art
Special Subjects: African Art, Drawings, Glass, Graphics, Painting-American, Prints, Sculpture, Watercolors
Collections: Contemporary painting & sculpture, graphics, local artists, prints, sculpture from Sepik River area, New Guinea, Africa
Activities: Lects open to pub, 4 vis lectrs per yr; gallery talks

L **Armstrong Browning Library**, Eighth & Speight Sts, Waco, TX 76798-7152; One Bear Place #97152, Waco, TX 76798-7152. Tel 254-710-3566; Fax 254-710-3552; Email abloffice@baylor.edu; Web: www.browninglibrary.org; *Dir & Cur Manuscripts* Rita S Patteson; *Cur Books & Printed Material* Cynthia A Burgess; *Access & Outreach Librn* Jennifer Borderud
Open to visitors Mon - Fri 9 AM - 5 PM, Sat 10 AM - 2 PM; open for research Mon - Fri 9 AM - 5 PM, Sat by appointment; No admis fee; Estab 1918 to provide a setting for the personal possessions of the Brownings' & to have as complete as is possible a collection for the use of Browning scholars; Gallery is maintained; Average Annual Attendance: 30,000; Mem: dues individual $50
Income: Financed by endowment & private university
Library Holdings: Auction Catalogs, Audio Tapes, Book Volumes 27,000, Cassettes, Clipping Files, Filmstrips, Manuscripts 10,000, Memorabilia, Motion Pictures, Original Art Works, Original Documents, Other Holdings, Pamphlets, Periodical Subscriptions, Photographs, Prints, Records, Reels, Reproductions, Sculpture, Slides, Video Tapes
Collections: Kress Foundation Study Collection, Pen Browning Paintings, portraits of Robert Browning & Elizabeth Barrett Browning, portraits of donors, Julia Margaret Cameron, photographs, Wedgwood, Dresden, Joseph Milsand Collection
Publications: Armstrong Browning Library Newsletter, semi-annual; Baylor Browning Interests, irregular; Studies in Browning & His Circle, annual; More Than Friend, The Letters of Robert Browning to Katharine DeKay Bronson; Elizabeth Barrett Browning: Life in a New Rhythm, An exhibition held at the Grolier Club, 15 Dec 1993 through 19 February 1994; The Pied Piper: A Tale of Two Ditties; Armstrong Browning Library Souvenir booklet; Boundless Life: A Biography of Andrew Joseph Armstrong
Activities: Lects open to pub, concerts; tours; fels offered; sales shop sells books, postcards, Victorian style mementoes

MIDWEST ART HISTORY SOCIETY
For further information, see National and Regional Organizations

M **TEXAS RANGER HALL OF FAME & MUSEUM,** 100 Texas Ranger Trl, Waco, TX 76706; PO Box 2570, Waco, TX 76702-2570. Tel 254-750-8631; Fax 254-750-8629; Email info@texasranger.org; Web: www.texasranger.org; *Exec Dir* Byron Johnson; *Deputy Dir Opers* Christina Stopka; *Colls Asst* Tina Brumm; *Colls Mgr* Shelly Crittendon
Open daily 9 AM - 5 PM, cl Thanksgiving, Christmas, New Year's Day; Admis adults $7, children (6 & up) $3; 1968; Average Annual Attendance: 50,000; Mem: Dues individual, student & senior $35
Income: Financed by contributions, gifts, grants, mem & state appropriations
Special Subjects: American Indian Art, American Western Art, Painting-American, Photography, Sculpture, Southwestern Art
Collections: Texas Ranger items, Western history, paintings & sculpture
Publications: The Texas Ranger Dispatch; The Online Journal of Texas Ranger History
Activities: Educ prog; Lect; research on Texas Rangers; mus shop

L **Texas Ranger Research Center**, PO Box 2570, Waco, TX 76702-2570. Tel 254-750-8631; Fax 254-750-8629; Email trhf@eramp.net; Web: www.texasranger.org; *Head* Christina Stopka
Open Mon - Sat 9 AM - Noon, 1-3 PM; Estab 1976; For reference only
Income: Financed by City of Waco
Library Holdings: Book Volumes 1,600, Cassettes, Clipping Files, Manuscripts, Memorabilia, Photographs, Reels, Video Tapes
Activities: Mus shop

WAXAHACHIE

M **ELLIS COUNTY MUSEUM INC,** 201 S College St, Waxahachie, TX 75165-3711; PO Box 706, Waxahachie, TX 75168-0706. Tel 972-937-0681; Fax 972-937-0681; Email ecmuseum@sbcglobal.net; Web: www.elliscountymuseum.org; *Cur* Shannon Simpson
Open Mon-Sat 10 AM - 5 PM, cl Sun; No admis fee, donations accepted; Estab 1969 to collect & maintain artifacts relating to county's history; Average Annual Attendance: 10,000-12,000; Mem: 275; dues benefactor $1000, sponsor $200, patron $100, bus $50, family $25 individual $15
Income: $70,000 (financed by annual fundraiser)
Special Subjects: Decorative Arts, Furniture
Collections: Decorative Arts, Clothing, Furniture, Folding Fans, Photographs, Memorabilia, Technological Implements, Weaponry
Exhibitions: Artifacts relating to county's history
Activities: Retail store sells books, reproductions, prints

WICHITA FALLS

M **KEMP CENTER FOR THE ARTS,** 1300 Lamar, Wichita Falls, TX 76301. Tel 940-767-2787; Fax 940-767-3956; Email info@kempcenter.org; Web: www.kempcenter.org; *Dir* Carlana Fitch; *Pres* Michael Koen; *Mus Shop Mgr* Pat Wearth
Open Mon - Fri 9 AM - 5 PM, cl New Year's Day, Independence Day, Labor Day, Christmas; No admis fee; Average Annual Attendance: 32,000
Collections: works by regional artists
Publications: quarterly newsletter; annual sculpture catalogue
Activities: classes; mus shop

M **WICHITA FALLS MUSEUM & ART CENTER,** Two Eureka Circle, Wichita Falls, TX 76308. Tel 940-692-0923; Fax 940-696-5358; Email wfma@mwsu.edu; Web: www.mwsu.edu/wfma; *Cur Coll & Exhib* Danny Bills; *Dir* Cohn Drennan
Open Tues - Fri 9:30 AM - 5 PM, Thurs until 7PM, Sat 10:30 AM - 5 PM, cl Sun & Mon; Admis fee varies with exhibits; Estab 1964 for the purpose of serving the community; Three galleries house art exhibits, two galleries house science exhibits; Average Annual Attendance: 50,000; Mem: 800; dues $30 - $1,000
Income: Financed by endowment, mem & city appropriation
Special Subjects: Prints
Collections: American prints, Photography/Lester Jones; Caldecott Collection of children's book illustrations
Publications: Events calendar, Sept, Jan, May
Activities: Classes for adults & children; dramatic progs; docent training; lects open to pub, concerts; tours, competitions; lending collection of original prints to Midwestern State University; originate traveling exhibs

WIMBERLEY

M **PIONEER TOWN,** Pioneer Museum of Western Art, 333 Wayside Dr, Wimberley, TX 78676-5117. Tel 512-847-3289; Fax 512-847-6705; *Dir* Raymond L Czichos; *Secy* Kasia Zinz; *Dir Video* C L Czichos; *Secy & Treas* John D White
Open Memorial Day - Labor Day by appointment only (512-847-3289); Estab 1956 as a village & art museum
Income: Financed by donations
Special Subjects: American Western Art, Architecture, Bronzes, Crafts, Decorative Arts, Metalwork, Sculpture
Collections: Remington Bronze Collection, Jack Woods Collection

UTAH

BLANDING

M **THE DINOSAUR MUSEUM,** 754 S 200 W, Blanding, UT 84511-3909. Tel 435-678-3454; Email dinos@dinosaur-museum.org; Web: www.dinosaur-museum.org
Open Apr 15 - Oct 15 Mon - Sat 9 AM - 5 PM; cl Sun; Admis adults $3.50, seniors $2.50, children $2; 1992; Mus covers history of the world of dinosaurs, complete with skeletons, fossilized skin, eggs, footprints, feathered dinosaurs & dinosaurs in the movies, state-of-the-art graphics and realistic. sculptures. Nonprofit org
Special Subjects: Historical Material, Sculpture
Collections: Herrerasaurus from Argentina, Plateosaurus from Germany, life-size dinosaur sculptures, Tarbosaurus from Mongolia, Permian logs from Utah,

mummified Edmontosaurus from Wyoming, Feathered Dinosaurs Hall, original dinosaur movie posters & memorabilia
Exhibitions: The Art and Science of Dinosaurs in Movies: traces the changing image of the motion picture dinosaur from the silent 1919 Ghost of Slumber Mountain to present day blockbusters; Feathered Dinosaurs
Publications: Feathered Dinosaurs and the Origin of Flight, edited by Sylvia J Czerkas; Cine-Saurus the History of Dinosaurs in the Movies, Stephen Czerkas author 2006
Activities: Guided tours by appt; research projects; originates traveling exhibs to mus in USA & Canada; mus shop sells books, magazines, reproductions; toys

BRIGHAM CITY

M **BRIGHAM CITY CORPORATION,** Brigham City Museum of Art & History, 24 N 300 W, Brigham City, UT 84302-2030; PO Box 583, Brigham City, UT 84302-0583. Tel 435-226-1439; Email bcmuseum@brighamcity.utah.gov; Web: www.brighamcitymuseum.org; *Dir* Kaia Landon; *Publicity & Heritage Writer* Mary Alice Hobbs
Open Tues - Fri 11 AM - 6 PM, Sat 1 - 5 PM, cl Sun & Mon; No admis fee; Estab 1970 to document local history & host traveling exhibitions; Rotating gallery 2,500 sq ft, History Area 1,700 sq ft; Average Annual Attendance: 13,000
Income: Financed by Brigham City Corporation
Special Subjects: American Indian Art, American Western Art, Anthropology, Ceramics, Decorative Arts, Drawings, Folk Art, Furniture, Glass, Historical Material, Landscapes, Painting-American, Photography, Portraits, Prints, Pottery, Southwestern Art
Collections: Ceramics, crystal & glass, fibers, folk art, 19th century clothing, artifacts & furniture, painting, printmaking, pioneer furniture of Brigham City, art quilts, fine art by artists from western US
Publications: Historic Tour of Brigham City; Mayors of Brigham City
Activities: Educ dept for research, & oral histories; lects open to public; gallery talks; tours; competitions; awards; 1-2 book travelling exhibs per yr; monthly rotating exhibs of art & varied collections; mus shop sells books

CEDAR CITY

M **SOUTHERN UTAH UNIVERSITY,** Braithwaite Fine Arts Gallery, 351 W Center St, Cedar City, UT 84720-2470. Tel 435-586-5432; Fax 435-865-8012; Email museums@suu.edu; Web: www.suu.edu/pva/artgallery; *Dir* Lydia Johnson
Open Tues-Sat Noon - 7 PM; No admis fee; Estab 1976 to provide a quality visual arts forum for artists' work and the viewing public; The gallery has 2,500 sq ft of space with 300 linear ft of display surface; it is equipped with facilities for two & three-dimensional media with electronic security system; Average Annual Attendance: 10,000; Mem: 100; dues $50 - $500
Income: Financed by city and state appropriations and private donations
Special Subjects: Painting-American
Collections: 18th, 19th & 20th century American art
Publications: Exhibition announcements, quarterly; newsletter, quarterly
Activities: Gallery talks; tours; competitions; book traveling exhibitions 6 per year

EPHRAIM

M **SNOW COLLEGE ART GALLERY,** 150 E College Ave, Ephraim, UT 84627-1550. Tel 435-283-7416; Email adam.larsen@snow.edu; Web: www.snow.edu/art/gallery/index.html; *Dir* Adam Larsen
Open Mon-Fri 9AM-5PM, other times by appointment
Collections: student & faculty artwork

FILLMORE

M **UTAH DEPARTMENT OF NATURAL RESOURCES, DIVISION OF PARKS & RECREATION,** Territorial Statehouse State Park Museum, 50 W Capitol Ave, Territorial Statehouse State Park Museum Fillmore, UT 84631-5556. Tel 435-743-5316; Fax 801-435-743-4723; Email parkcomment@utah.gov; Web: stateparks.utah.gov; *Cur* Carl Camp
Open Mon - Sat 9 AM - 5 PM, cl Sun, Thanksgiving, Christmas & New Year's Day; Admis $2 per person, children 6 - 11 $1; Estab 1930, as a museum for pioneer relics; Restored by the state & local Daughters of Utah Pioneers; owned & operated by Utah State Division of Parks & Recreation; Average Annual Attendance: 35,000
Income: Financed by state appropriations
Library Holdings: Book Volumes, Manuscripts, Original Documents
Special Subjects: Ceramics, Furniture, Historical Material, Manuscripts, Painting-American, Period Rooms, Photography, Porcelain, Portraits, Posters, Pottery, Prints, Textiles, American Western Art
Collections: Charcoal & pencil sketches, paintings by Utah artists, photograph prints coll, pioneer portraits in antique frames, silk screen prints, rooms arranged in period settings
Exhibitions: Rotating exhibits
Activities: Educ dept; 3 day youth camps with pioneer activities; 1 day family reunion activities; lect; gallery talks; tours; Arts & Living History Festival; mus shop sells books, postcards, kids' toys, old time toys & candy

KANAB

M **KANAB HERITAGE MUSEUM & JUNIPER FINE ARTS GALLERY,** 13 S 100 E, Kanab, UT 84741. Tel 435-644-3966, 435-644-3898; *Cur* Deanna Tait Glover; *Cur* Win Barney
Open Summer: Mon - Fri 1 PM - 5 PM; No admis fee
Collections: Local history & culture; period furnishings; photographs; personal artifacts; works by local artists, William Cody "Buffalo Bill" camp table
Exhibitions: John Wesley Powell artifacts; Maynard Dixon & Milford Zornes exhibits
Activities: Western Legends Roundup award; mus shop sells books & prints

LOGAN

M **UTAH STATE UNIVERSITY,** Nora Eccles Harrison Museum of Art, 650 N 1100 E, Logan, UT 84322-4020; 4020 Old Main Hill, Utah State Univ Logan, UT 84322-4020. Tel 435-797-0163; Fax 435-797-3423; Email NEHMA@usu.edu; Web: artmuseum.usu.edu; *Exec Dir & Chief Cur* Katie Lee Koven; *Educ Cur* Nadra E Haffar; *Bus Mgr* Adam Rounds; *Registrar* Casey Allen; *Cur of Collections & Exhibitions* Rebecca Dunham; *Admin Coordr* Andrea DeHaan; *Coordinator of Exhibitions* Zaira Arredondo
Open Tues - Sat 10 AM - 5 PM, cl Mon, most Sun & major holidays; $5 suggested donation; Estab 1982; Over 10,000 sq ft of exhibition area; Average Annual Attendance: 13,000; Mem: 100; dues $10 - $500
Purchases: $300,000
Library Holdings: Clipping Files, Compact Disks, DVDs, Exhibition Catalogs, Memorabilia, Original Documents, Pamphlets, Periodical Subscriptions, Photographs, Slides, Video Tapes
Special Subjects: American Western Art, Ceramics
Collections: 20th century American art, with emphasis on Western US artists, 20th century American ceramics
Publications: Exhibition catalogs; newsletter, monthly
Activities: Educ prog; lects open to pub, lects for mems, 2-4 vis lectrs per yr; gallery talks; tours; concerts; schols & fels offered; lending original objects of art to community and other VSV campuses; 2-3 book traveling exhibs per yr; sales shop sells books, DVDs & CDs

MOUNT CARMEL

M **THUNDERBIRD FOUNDATION FOR THE ARTS,** 2002 State St, Mount Carmel, UT 84755; Maynard Dixon Home & Studio, Hwy 89-mile Marker 84 Mount Carmel, UT 84755. Tel 435-648-2653, 801-533-5330; Web: www.thunderbirdfoundation.com; *Dir* Susan Bingham
Open May - Oct Mon - Sun 10 AM - 4 PM, and by appointment; Estab 2001; Average Annual Attendance: 3,000

OGDEN

A **ECCLES COMMUNITY ART CENTER,** 2580 Jefferson Ave, Ogden, UT 84401-2411. Tel 801-392-6935; Fax 801-392-5295; Email eccles@ogden4arts.org; Web: www.ogden4arts.org; *Dir* Patrick E Poce; *Cur of Educ* MandiAnne Poll; *Asst Dir* Debra Muller
Open Mon - Fri 9 AM - 5 PM, Sat 9 AM - 3 PM, cl Sun & holidays; No admis fee; Estab 1959 to serve as focal point for community cultural activities & to promote cultural growth; Maintains an art gallery with monthly exhibits; Average Annual Attendance: 25,000; Mem: 600; dues $25 - $100; annual meeting in Nov
Income: $100,000 (financed by mem, state appropriation & fund raising)
Special Subjects: Architecture, Ceramics, Collages, Crafts, Drawings, Glass, Jewelry, Landscapes, Painting-American, Textiles, Watercolors, Woodcuts
Collections: Utah Artists (historic & contemporaries)
Exhibitions: Local artists open monthly with art show first Fri of each month
Publications: Newsletter, quarterly
Activities: Classes for adults & children; docent training; dramatic progs; lects open to pub, 6 vis lectrs per yr; concerts; gallery talks; tours; competition with awards; schols offered; book traveling exhibs; sales shop sells original art, reproductions, prints, ceramics, jewelry & artist produced cards

M **OGDEN UNION STATION,** Myra Powell Art Gallery & Gallery at the Station, 2501 Wall Ave, Ogden, UT 84401-1359. Tel 801-393-9880; Fax 801-621-0230; Email rebeverlyous@msn.com; Web: www.theunionstation.org/galleries.html; *Exec Dir* Roberta Beverly
Open Mon - Sat 10 AM - 5 PM; No admis fee; Estab 1979 to acquaint more people with the visual arts & to heighten awareness of art; 12.5 ft x 113 ft; 39 panels 6 ft x 4 ft; Average Annual Attendance: 2,500; Mem: Practicing Artists
Income: Financed by endowment & donations
Collections: Non-objective painting, Indian Design, Landscape, Navajo Sand Painting, Aluminum Sculpture
Exhibitions: Exhibs change monthly
Activities: Lects open to public; 6 vis lectrs per yr; competitions with awards; schols & fellowships offered; individual paintings & original objects of art lent

M **Union Station Museums**, 2501 Wall Ave, Ogden, UT 84401. Tel 801-393-9886; Web: www.theunionstation.org; *Exec Dir* Roberta Beverly; *Mus Mgr* Amanda Felix
Open Mon - Sat 10 AM - 5 PM; Admis adults $5, sr citizens $4, children under 12 $3; Estab 1976 to serve as a cultural & civic center for Ogden, Utah; Average Annual Attendance: 40,000; Mem: Dues $50
Income: 501 (c) (3) non-profit
Library Holdings: Audio Tapes, Book Volumes, CD-ROMs, Cassettes, DVDs, Framed Reproductions, Manuscripts, Maps, Memorabilia, Original Documents, Other Holdings, Periodical Subscriptions, Photographs, Prints, Reproductions
Special Subjects: American Western Art, Dioramas, Furniture, Historical Material, Maps
Collections: Railroad memorabilia
Exhibitions: Browning Firearms; Classic Cars; Wattis-Dumke Model Railroad; Myra Powell Gallery; Utah State Railroad Museum; Utah Cowboy & Western Heritage Museum
Publications: Union Station-monthly via e-mail; Union Station Annual Publication
Activities: Concerts; gallery strolls; mus shop sells books, reproductions, prints, gifts

OREM

M **UTAH VALLEY UNIVERSITY,** Woodbury Art Museum, 575 E University Pkwy, #250, Orem, UT 84097-7400. Tel 801-863-4200; Email

uvmuseum@uvu.edu; Web: www.uvu.edu/museum; *Interim Dir* Melissa Hempel; *Admin* Katherine Hall; *Graphic Designer* Amanda Luker; *Registrar* Rebekah Monahan
Open Wed - Sat 11 AM - 5 PM, Tues 11 AM - 8 PM; No admis fee
Collections: artwork
Activities: Museum studies class through UVU

PARK CITY

A **KIMBALL ART CENTER,** 638 Park Ave, Park City, UT 84060-5106; PO Box 1478, Park City, UT 84060-1478. Tel 435-649-8882; Fax 435-649-8889; Web: www.kimball-art.org; *Dir* Robin Rankin; *Art Educ Coordr* Jenny Diersen; *Develop Dir* Konstantine Deslis; *Exhib Coordr* Erin Linder; *Pub Rels* Corinne Humphrey
Open weekdays 10 AM - 5 PM, Sat noon - 7 PM, Sun noon - 5 PM; No admis fee; Estab 1976 for monthly gallery shows & workshops in arts & crafts, fine arts; Main gallery has movable walls & is 80 x 180 ft, Badami gallery measures 17 x 20 ft; Average Annual Attendance: 250,000; Mem: 600; dues individual $40, family $70
Income: $700,000 (financed by endowment, mem & contributions)
Exhibitions: Twenty four exhibits annually in various styles & mediums
Activities: Classes for adults & children; docent training; lects open to public, 6 vis lectrs per year; gallery talks; tours; competitions; opening receptions with exhibiting artists; ann art festival; awards, 2013 P/A (Progressive Architecture) Award for new building design; book traveling exhibitions; sales shop sells original art, reproductions & prints

PRICE

M **COLLEGE OF EASTERN UTAH,** Gallery East, 451 E Fourth N, Price, UT 84501. Tel 435-637-2120; Fax 435-637-4102; Web: www.ceu.edu; *Gallery Coordr* Karen Green
Open Mon - Fri 8:30 AM - 5 PM; No admis fee; Estab 1976 to provide an educational & aesthetic tool within the community; 2,300 sq ft; maintains reference library; Average Annual Attendance: 15,000
Income: $1,600 (financed by school appropriation)
Special Subjects: Prints, Painting-American
Exhibitions: Changing exhibits
Activities: Classes for adults; docent training; lects open to pub, 4-5 vis lectrs per yr; gallery talks; tours; competitions with awards; scholarships offered; originates traveling exhibs to colleges

PROVO

M **BRIGHAM YOUNG UNIVERSITY,** B F Larsen Gallery, A-41 ASB, Provo, UT 84602. Tel 801-378-2881; Fax 801-378-5964; Email gallery303@byu.edu; Web: visualarts.byu.edu; *Gallery Dir* Todd Frye
Open 9 AM - 5 PM; No admis fee; Estab 1965 to bring to the University students & faculty a wide range of new experiences in the visual arts; B F Larsen Gallery is a three story atrium shaped gallery with exhibition areas in center floor & upper levels; Gallery 303 is large room with foyer & single entrance-exit; total exhibition space 15,260 sq ft; Average Annual Attendance: 55,000 Gallery 303; 100,000 Larsen
Income: Financed by university
Special Subjects: American Western Art, Drawings, Manuscripts, Painting-American, Prints, Sculpture
Collections: Maynard Dixon Collection, Mahonri Young Collection of Manuscripts, J Alden Weir Collection
Exhibitions: Invitational exhibits; exhibits by students & faculty, curated exhibits of contemporary artists & circulating exhibits
Activities: Lects open to pub; competitions; monetary & cert awards; individual paintings & original objects of art lent to university executive, faculty & university library; book traveling exhibs monthly

L **Harold B Lee Library,** PO Box 26800, Provo, UT 84602-6800. Tel 801-422-6731; Web: www.lib.byu.edu; *Dir Libraries* Jennifer Paustenbaugh; *Fine Arts Librn* Christiane Erbolato-Ramsey; *Special Collections* Gordon Dawes III; *Photo Archivist* Tom Wells; *Cur European Books* Maggie Kopp; *Cur Arts, Communs & Film* James D'Arc
Open Mon - Sat 7 AM - Midnight; No admis fee; Estab 1875 to support the university curriculum
Income: Financed by endowment, mem & the Church of Latter-Day Saints
Library Holdings: Audio Tapes, Book Volumes 3,677,805, CD-ROMs, Cassettes, Compact Disks, Exhibition Catalogs, Fiche, Filmstrips, Memorabilia, Motion Pictures, Pamphlets, Periodical Subscriptions 16,487, Photographs 12,000, Prints, Reels, Slides, Video Tapes
Special Subjects: American Western Art, Graphic Arts, Photography
Collections: 15th & 16th century graphic art coll, George Anderson Collection of Early Utah Photographs, C R Savage Collection, George Beard Photograph Collection; William Henry Jackson Art and Photographs; Huntington-Bagley Photograph Collection.
Activities: Tours

M **Museum of Art,** North Campus Dr, Provo, UT 84602-1400. Tel 801-422-8287; Email moa@byu.edu; Web: moa.byu.edu; *Dir* Mark Magleby; *Head Cur* Ashlee Whitaker
Mon, Thurs, Fri 10 AM - 9 PM; Tues, Wed, Sat 10 AM - 6 PM; cl Sun & major holidays; No admis fee, special exhibs may require tickets; Estab 1993 to educate patrons & community; 11 galleries; study & general purpose sculpture garden; Average Annual Attendance: 135,000+
Special Subjects: American Western Art, Bronzes, Carpets & Rugs, Cartoons, Ceramics, Drawings, Etchings & Engravings, Landscapes, Marine Painting, Painting-American, Painting-French, Portraits, Posters, Pottery, Prints, Religious Art, Renaissance Art, Sculpture, Watercolors, Woodcarvings, Woodcuts
Collections: American Art-Hudson River School of American Impressionism, Collections include: Maynard Dixon, Mahonri Young, J. Alden Weir
Publications: InSite, Biannual online magazine
Activities: Classes for adults & children; docent progs; acad & pub progs; lects open to pub, 5-6 vis lectrs per yr; concerts; gallery talks; tours; lending collection contains 17,000 items, including individual paintings & original objects of art; book traveling exhibs 2-3 per yr; mus shop sells books, magazines, prints, reproductions & slides

SAINT GEORGE

M **DIXIE STATE UNIVERSITY,** Sears Art Museum Gallery, 155 S University Ave, Saint George, UT 84770. Tel 435-652-7500; Web: dixieculturalarts.com; dixie.com; *VPres Cultural Affairs & Develop* Christina Schultz; *Cur & Collections Mgr* Kathy C Cieslewicz
Open Mon - Fri 9 AM - 5 PM, cl school holidays; No admis fee; Estab 1960 to serve southwestern Utah as a visual arts exhibit center; Gallery is located in the Eccles Fine Art Center; Average Annual Attendance: 10,000-15,000
Income: Financed by state appropriation & 35% of sales from monthly shows
Special Subjects: Painting-American, American Indian Art, American Western Art, Bronzes, Carpets & Rugs, Ceramics, Drawings, Etchings & Engravings, Landscapes, Photography, Portraits, Pottery, Prints, Sculpture, Watercolors, Woodcuts
Collections: Early & contemporary Utah painters, Ceramics, Artifacts, Contemporary Native American
Exhibitions: Dixie State University, Sears Invitational Art Show & Sale; Art Dept Showcase, plus 3 curated exhibs
Activities: Classes for adults; dramatic progs; lects open to pub, vis lectrs; concerts; gallery talks

M **ST GEORGE ART MUSEUM,** 47 E 200 N, Saint George, UT 84770-2845. Tel 435-627-4525; Fax 435-627-4526; Email museum@sgcity.org; Web: www.sgartmuseum.org; *Dir* Deborah Reeder
Open Mon-Sat 10AM-5PM, 3rd Thurs of month 10AM-9PM with art conversations at 7PM; Admis adults $3, children 3 - 11 $1, children under 3 & mems no admis fee; Estab 1991; Mus houses work of Utah artists; mus is located in a fully-restored sugar beet storage structure that is part of the St George's historic district; Average Annual Attendance: 10,000; Mem: Dues Pres Circle/Corporate Sponsor $1000; Benefactor $750; Friend $500; Patron $250; Contributor $100; Indiv $50
Income: City of St. George municipal, non-profit
Library Holdings: Audio Tapes, Book Volumes, Cassettes, Exhibition Catalogs, Periodical Subscriptions, Video Tapes
Special Subjects: Painting-American, Historical Material
Collections: Permanent collection available online
Publications: A Century of Sanctuary, the Art of Zion National Park
Activities: Art Festival; 3rd Thurs Conversations at 7 PM; docent training; family discovery center; lects open to pub; 10 vis lectrs per yr; tours, gallery talks; sponsoring of competitions; books traveling exhibs varies per yr; mus shop sells books, magazines, prints & related merchandise

SALT LAKE CITY

M **CHURCH OF JESUS CHRIST OF LATTER-DAY SAINTS,** Church History Museum, 45 N West Temple St, Salt Lake City, UT 84150-0902. Tel 801-240-3310; Fax 801-240-5342; Email churchmuseum@ldschurch.org; Web: history.lds.org/museum; *Dir* Alan Johnson
Open Mon - Fri 9 AM - 9 PM, Sat 10 AM - 5 PM, cl Sun, New Year's Eve, New Year's Day, Easter, Independence Day, Thanksgiving, Christmas; No admis fee; Estab 1869 to disseminate information & display historical memorabilia, artifacts & art to the vis pub; Exhibs focused on church history & art; Average Annual Attendance: 250,000
Income: Financed by Church
Special Subjects: American Indian Art, American Western Art, Architecture, Costumes, Decorative Arts, Folk Art, Furniture, Historical Material, Landscapes, Painting-American, Photography, Portraits, Pottery, Primitive art, Religious Art, Sculpture, Southwestern Art, Stained Glass, Textiles, Watercolors, Woodcarvings, Bronzes
Collections: Mostly 19th & 20th century Mormon art & historical artifacts: portraits, paintings, drawings, sculpture, prints, American furniture, china, pottery, glass, Mormon quilts & handwork, decorative arts, clothing & textiles, architectural elements & hardware, Oceanic & American Indian pottery, basketry & textiles, Mormon Collection
Publications: Exhibition catalogs; brochures; Image of Faith: Art of the Latter-day Saints (1995)
Activities: Docent training; seminars; gallery demonstrations; school outreach; lects open to pub; gallery talks tours; International Art Competition; individual paintings & original objects of art lent; mus shop sells books, prints, slides & postcards

A **SALT LAKE ART CENTER,** Utah Museum of Contemporary Art, 20 S W Temple, Salt Lake City, UT 84101. Tel 801-328-4201; Fax 801-322-4323; Email info@utahmoca.org; Web: www.utahmoca.org; *Exec Dir* Kristian Anderson; *Mktg & Communs Dir* Christie Marcy; *Cur Exhibs* Jared Steffensen
Open Tues - Thurs 11 AM - 6 PM, Fri 11 AM - 9 PM, Sat 11 AM - 6 PM; Admis suggested $5; Estab 1931 to educate the community in the contemporary visual arts through exhibitions & classes; UMOCA has five exhib spaces; Average Annual Attendance: 48,000; Mem: 1,560; dues Basic $40, Deluxe $150, annual meeting in June
Income: Financed by mem, city & state appropriation, earned income, gifts, private & corporate contributions
Collections: Utah artists (1930-Present), contemporary art
Activities: Classes for adults & children; docent training; studio & lect courses; lects open to pub, 10 vis lectrs per yr; gallery talks; tours; 2 - 3 book traveling exhibs per yr; mus shop sells books, jewelry, ceramics, cards, journals, magazines, original art, prints & textiles

L **SALT LAKE CITY PUBLIC LIBRARY,** Nonfiction & Audiovisual Dept & Gallery at Library Square, 210 E 400 St S, Salt Lake City, UT 84111-2849. Tel

801-524-8200; Fax 801-322-8194; Web: www.slcpl.org; *Dir* Peter Bromberg; *Deputy Dir* Deborah Ehrman; *Mgr Communs* Andrew Shaw
Open Mon - Thurs 9 AM - 9 PM, Fri - Sat 9 AM - 6 PM, Sun 1 - 5 PM; No admis fee; Estab 1898; Maintains an art gallery with monthly exhibitions; Average Annual Attendance: 300
Income: Financed by city appropriation
Library Holdings: Book Volumes 400,000, DVDs, Exhibition Catalogs, Original Art Works, Reproductions
Special Subjects: Film
Collections: Art of Western United States, Utah Artists, American & European Works on Paper
Publications: Brochures accompanying individual exhibitions; Permanent Art Collection Catalogue
Activities: Films; gallery talks; tours; demonstrations; slide presentations; individual paintings & original objects of art lent to museums & non-profit galleries

M **UNIVERSITY OF UTAH,** Utah Museum of Fine Arts, 410 Campus Center Dr, Marcia & John Price Museum Bldg Salt Lake City, UT 84112-0350. Tel 801-581-7332; Fax 801-585-5198; Email emma.ryder@umfa.utah.edu; Web: www.umfa.utah.edu; *Exec Dir* Gretchen Dietrich; *Cur Educ, Family Progs, Visitor Experience & Community Outreach* Virginia Catherall; *Sr Cur* Whitney Tassie; *Dir Coll & Exhibs* David Carroll; *Deputy Dir Finance & Opers* George Lindsey
Open Tues, Thurs, Fri 10 AM - 5 PM, Wed 10 AM - 9 PM, Sat & Sun 11 AM - 5 PM, cl Mon & holidays; Admis adults $12.95, seniors & youth $9.95, UFA mems & children under 6 free; Estab to engage visitors in discovering meaningful connections with the artistic expressions of the world's cultures; Average Annual Attendance: 110,000; Mem: 2,500; dues individual $49, family $99, patron $150
Income: Financed by university & private gifts
Special Subjects: African Art, American Indian Art, Antiquities-Egyptian, Antiquities-Greek, Asian Art, Baroque Art, Bronzes, Carpets & Rugs, Ceramics, Costumes, Drawings, Embroidery, Flasks & Bottles, Furniture, Furniture, Glass, Graphics, Hispanic Art, Ivory, Jade, Jewelry, Juvenile Art, Landscapes, Latin American Art, Medieval Art, Mexican Art, Mosaics, Oriental Art, Painting-American, Painting-British, Painting-Dutch, Painting-European, Painting-Flemish, Painting-French, Painting-German, Painting-Italian, Painting-Japanese, Painting-Spanish, Photography, Porcelain, Portraits, Pre-Columbian Art, Primitive art, Religious Art, Renaissance Art, Sculpture, Silver, Silver, Southwestern Art, Tapestries, Textiles, Watercolors, Woodcarvings, Woodcuts
Collections: Winifred Kimball Hudnut Collection, Natacha Rambova Egyptian Collection, Marion Sharp Robinson Collection, Bartlett Wicks Collection
Activities: Classes for children & adults; docent training; lect open to public, some for mem only; concerts; gallery talks; tours; organize traveling exhibs to BBHC in Cody WY; Missouri History Mus; museum shop sells reproductions, prints, jewelry & apparel, films, & books, cafe

L **Katherine W Dumke Architecture Library, Marriott Library,** 295 S 1500 E, Salt Lake City, UT 84112-0860. Tel 801-581-8558; Fax 801-585-3464; Web: www.lib.utah.edu/fa; *Head Fine Arts* Greg Hatch; *Fine Arts Librn* Luke Leither
Open Mon - Thurs 7 AM - 1 AM, Fri 7 AM - 8 PM, Sat 9 AM - 8 PM, Sun noon - 1 AM; Estab 1967 to serve the students & faculty of the University with research materials & specialized services; For lending & reference
Income: Financed by state appropriation
Purchases: $60,000 per yr for fine arts books
Library Holdings: Auction Catalogs, Audio Tapes, Book Volumes 2,000,000, CD-ROMs, Cassettes, Clipping Files, Compact Disks, DVDs, Exhibition Catalogs, Fiche, Manuscripts, Memorabilia, Motion Pictures, Original Art Works, Original Documents, Other Holdings, Periodical Subscriptions 17,000, Photographs, Prints, Reproductions, Slides, Video Tapes
Special Subjects: Advertising Design, Aesthetics, Afro-American Art, American Western Art, Architecture, Art Education, Art History, Asian Art, Bookplates & Bindings, Folk Art, Folk Art, Furniture, Glass, Graphic Arts, Graphic Design, Painting-American, Painting-British, Painting-Dutch, Painting-European, Painting-Flemish, Photography, Southwestern Art
Activities: Library supports in-house traveling exhibits & research & curriculum needs of the Univ; lects open to pub; book traveling exhibs; organize traveling exhibs

M **UTAH ARTS COUNCIL,** Chase Home Museum of Utah Folk Arts, 600 E. 1100 S. in Salt Lake City's Liberty Park, Salt Lake City, UT 84105; 617 E South Temple, Salt Lake City, UT 84102-1177. Tel 801-533-5760; Fax 801-533-4202; Email cedison@utah.gov; Web: arts.utah.gov; *Dir* Victoria Panella Bourns; *Asst Dir* Natalie Petersen; *Visual Arts Mgr* Jim Glenn; *Mktg & Communs Mgr* Sarina Ehrgott; *Folk Arts Specialist* Adrienne Decker; *Pub Arts & Design Arts Mgr* Jim Glenn; *Community Outreach Mgr* Anna Boulton; *Arts Educ Mgr* Jean Tokuda Irwin
Open (winter) Tues - Fri 10 AM - 4 PM, (summer) Tues & Thurs - Sat 11 AM - 4 PM, Wed 11 AM - 8 PM, cl Sun & Mon; No admis fee; Estab 1986 to showcase folk art in the State Art Collection; Four small galleries, one small reception area & two hallways for display in a 19th century two-story farmhouse; Average Annual Attendance: 25,000
Income: Financed by state & federal appropriations
Library Holdings: Audio Tapes, Book Volumes 600, Cassettes, Clipping Files, Motion Pictures, Pamphlets, Periodical Subscriptions 5, Photographs, Prints, Records, Slides
Special Subjects: Crafts, Photography, Sculpture, Folk Art
Collections: Ethnic, Familial, Occupational, Religious, Regional with an emphasis on traditional work by living folk artists, Native American
Exhibitions: Annual exhibit of Utah folk art; rotating exhibits
Publications: Publications & recordings featuring old-time social dance, Navajo baskets, Hispanic traditions
Activities: Lects open to pub; concerts; group tours; originates traveling exhibs; mus shop sells books & folk art music

A **UTAH LAWYERS FOR THE ARTS,** 170 S Main St, Ste 1500, Salt Lake City, UT 84101-1644. Tel 801-521-3200; Fax 801-328-0537; Email info@utahlawyersforthearts.org; Web: www.utahlawyersforthearts.org; *Bd Mem* Nicholas Wells; *Bd Mem* Heather Sneddon; *Bd Mem* Randy Wood; *Bd Mem* Aaron Garrett; *Bd Mem* Jeffrey J Hunt; *Bd Mem* Matt Tenney
Estab 1983 to provide pro bono legal services; Mem: 36; mem open to attorneys & law students; $30 annual fee, $15 student fee
Income: Financed by mem
Publications: Art/Law News, quarterly newsletter

SANDY

M **HILL GALLERY AND SCULPTURE PARK,** Canyon Ridge Center, 9045 South 1300 East Sandy, UT 84094; 8847 South 360 East, Sandy, UT 84070. Tel 801-562-9242; Email dchill35@outlook.com; Web: www.danhillsculpture.com; *Dir* Dan C Hill
Open Tues-Fri noon-5PM, other times by appointment
Collections: life-size monumental outdoor sculptures, carvings, paintings, giclee prints, photographs, kaleidoscopes, lamps, baskets, cards & books by local and regional artists

SPRINGVILLE

M **SPRINGVILLE MUSEUM OF ART,** 126 E 400 South, Springville, UT 84663. Tel 801-489-2727; Fax 801-489-2739; Email npetersen@springville.org; Web: www.smofa.org; *Assoc Dir* Natalie Petersen; *Head of Programs & Education* Jessica Weiss; *Dir* Dr. Rita R Wright
Open Tues - Sat 10 AM - 5 PM, Wed 10 AM - 9 PM, cl Sun, Mon & Holidays; No admis fee; Estab 1903 for the collection & exhibition of Utah fine arts & as educational resource; Built in Spanish Colonial style in 1937 with 28 galleries and sculpture garden; Average Annual Attendance: 120,000; Mem: 200; membership starts as low as $25
Income: $1,000,000 (financed by donations, bookstore, mem, city & state appropriations)
Purchases: varies
Library Holdings: Exhibition Catalogs, Original Documents, Pamphlets, Photographs
Special Subjects: American Western Art, Bronzes, Carpets & Rugs, Painting-American, Painting-British, Painting-Russian, Period Rooms, Photography, Portraits, Pottery, Religious Art, Reproductions, Southwestern Art, Watercolors
Collections: Artwork by Cyrus Dallin & John Hafen, 20th Century American Realism, Soviet Realism, Utah artists from 1850 to present of all styles
Exhibitions: Annual Spring Salon; High Schools of Utah Show; Annual Spiritual & Religious Art of Utah; Annual Quilt Show
Publications: Annual exhibition catalogues
Activities: Educ prog; docent progs; children's progs; art teacher in-service progs earn cr toward teaching cert; classes for children; lects open to pub; concerts; gallery talks; tours; competitions with awards; Best of Utah 2015&2016; Best of Utah Valley 2016; individual paintings & original objects of art lent to professional, governmental & educational institutions & mus; lending collection contains paintings & sculpture; originate traveling exhibs to Utah Arts Council, other mus & to schools; mus shop sells books, magazines, reproductions, prints & catalogues

VERMONT

BARRE

M **STUDIO PLACE ARTS,** 201 N Main St, Barre, VT 05641-4125. Tel 802-479-7069; Email info@studioplacearts.com; Web: www.studioplacearts.com; *Exec Dir* Sue Higby; *Gallery Assoc* James Secor
Open Tues - Fri 11 AM - 5 PM, Sat noon - 4 PM; No admis fee; Estab 2000; non-profit, visual arts center; Three gallery exhibits that change every six weeks yr round; Average Annual Attendance: 12,000; Mem: 1,800; dues $35 yr
Income: $160,000 (private donations)
Collections: paintings; photographs; sculpture
Exhibitions: See website for archive of exhibs
Activities: Classes for adults & children; lects open to pub; 5-8 vis lectrs per yr; gallery talks

BENNINGTON

M **BENNINGTON MUSEUM,** 75 Main St, Bennington, VT 05201-2885. Tel 802-447-1571; Fax 802-442-8305; Email info@benningtonmuseum.org; Web: www.benningtonmuseum.org; *Exec Dir* Robert Wolterstorff; *Cur* Jamie Franklin; *Colls Mgr* Callie Stewart; *Dir Pub & Educ Progs, Vol* Deana Mallory; *Dir Mktg & Pub Rels, Space Rentals & Grp Tours* Susan Strano; *Dir Develop* Jeanne Conner
Open daily 10AM - 5PM, open seven days a week in June thru Oct, cl Wed; cl Jan & Feb; Admis adults $10, students over 18 & senior citizens $9, students under 12 free; Estab 1875 as resource for history and fine and decorative arts of New England; Mus of art, history & innovation with 14 galleries, Grandma Moses Schoolhouse; Average Annual Attendance: 35,000; Mem: 500; dues $50 - $600; annual meeting in Oct
Income: Financed by dues, donations, admissions & grants
Special Subjects: Ceramics, Coins & Medals, Costumes, Decorative Arts, Dolls, Drawings, Embroidery, Etchings & Engravings, Folk Art, Furniture, Glass, Historical Material, Landscapes, Manuscripts, Maps, Military Art, Painting-American, Photography, Portraits, Pottery, Pottery, Prints, Sculpture, Textiles, Watercolors
Collections: Bennington pottery, Bennington Flag, Grandma Moses Paintings, rare documents
Publications: Exhibition catalogs; Milton Avery's Vermont
Activities: Classes for adults; docent training; lects open to pub, 10 vis lectrs per yr; gallery talks; tours; Yankee Magazine Best of New England Editors' Choice 2015; Best Museum Makeover; individual paintings & original objects of art lent to other

qualifying organizations; book traveling exhibs; originate traveling exhibs to other northern New England mus; mus shop sells books, magazines, original art, reproductions, prints & decorative arts

BRATTLEBORO

M **BRATTLEBORO MUSEUM & ART CENTER,** 10 Vernon St Brattleboro, VT 05301-3623. Tel 802-257-0124; Email info@brattleboromuseum.org; Web: www.brattleboromuseum.org; *Dir* Danny Lichtenfeld; *Museum Educator* Linda Wheihan; *Chief Cur* Mara Williams; *Opers Mgr* Erin Jenkins; *Exhibitions Mgr* Sarah Freeman
Open 11AM-5PM daily, closed Tuesdays; Admis adults $8, seniors $6, students $4, children under 18 & members free; Estab 1972 to present art & ideas in ways that inspire, educate & engage people of all ages; The museum is located in a railroad station built in 1915, now a registered historic site. Six galleries with changing exhibitions & museum gift shop; Average Annual Attendance: 20,000; Mem: 800; dues family $80, individual $45, senior $40; annual meeting in May
Income: $400,000 (financed by mem, donations, town, state, federal grants, corporate sponsorships, program fees & gift shop sales)
Exhibitions: Approx 15 exhibits annually
Publications: Built Landscapes Gardens of the Northeast; Seeing Japan; The Art of Frank Stout; Artful Jesters; Wolf Kahn Landscape of Light; From Street to Studio; Call & Response: Cecily Kahn; Sleight of Hand: Eric Sealine; Brattleboro: Past, Present, Future; Jules Olitski: An Inside View
Activities: Classes for adults; docent training; progs for school groups; family workshops; lects open to pub, 12 vis lectrs per yr; concerts; gallery talks; tours; Scholastic Arts Writing Awards exhib (Vermont); organize traveling exhibs for museums & galleries; mus shop sells books, notecards, postcards

M **VERMONT CENTER FOR PHOTOGRAPHY,** 49 Flat St, Brattleboro, VT 05301. Tel 802-251-6051; Email info@vcphoto.org; Web: vcphoto.org; *Exec Dir* Joshua Farr
Open Thurs - Sun Noon - 5 PM, first Fri of month 5:30 PM - 8:30 PM; 750 sq ft; handicap accessible; Mem: dues $25 - $115
Collections: Photography
Exhibitions: Temporary exhibits
Activities: Artist lects open to pub; workshops; film screenings; events; photography books, small prints, postcards & used camera & lenses

BURLINGTON

M **UNIVERSITY OF VERMONT,** Robert Hull Fleming Museum, 61 Colchester Ave, Burlington, VT 05405-0001. Tel 802-656-0750; Fax 802-656-8059; Email fleming@uvm.edu; Web: www.flemingmuseum.org; *Dir* Janie Cohen; *Cur* Andrea P Rosen
Open Labor Day - May 22 Tues & Thurs - Fri 10 AM - 4 PM, Wed 10 AM - 7 PM, Sat - Sun Noon - 4 PM; Admis family $10, adults $5, senior & students $3; Estab 1931; contains 20,000 objects; Average Annual Attendance: 14,000; Mem: 400; dues director's circle $1,000, patron $250, contributing $100, family $45, individual $30
Income: Financed by mem, university appropriations & grants, private gifts
Special Subjects: Oriental Art, Medieval Art, Costumes, Ethnology, Drawings, Prints, Antiquities-Greek, Antiquities-Roman
Collections: over 20,000 objects
Exhibitions: American historic & contemporary; Asian; Ethnographic; Medieval & Ancient; European; Egyptian
Publications: Exhibition catalogs; newsletter-calendar, 3 per yr
Activities: Classes for adults & children; docent training; lects open to pub, 12 vis lectrs per yr; concerts; gallery talks; tours; community outreach serves all Vermont; individual paintings & original objects of art lent to mus community; annual family day; annual heirloom appraisal day; book traveling exhibs; originate traveling exhibs; mus shop sells books, magazines, reproductions, prints, publications, kids merchandise, & Vermont crafts

M **Francis Colburn Gallery**, Williams Hall, Burlington, VT 05405-0001. Tel 802-656-2014; Fax 802-656-2064
Open Mon - Fri 9 AM - 4 PM; No admis fee; Estab 1975
Exhibitions: Student, faculty & visiting artist works

M **VERMONT STATE CRAFT CENTER AT FROG HOLLOW,** 85 Church St, Burlington, VT 05401-4420. Tel 802-863-6458; Fax 802-860-6506; Email info@froghollow.org; Web: www.froghollow.org; *Exec Dir* Rob Hunter
Open Jan 10 - April 15 Mon - Sat 10 AM - 6 PM, Sun Noon - 5 PM; Summer & Fall April 16 - Nov 27 Mon - Tues 10 AM - 6 PM, Wed - Sat 10 AM - 8 PM, Sun 11 AM - 7 PM; No admis fee; Estab 1971 to provide craft educational, informational & marketing services to school children, adults & professionals; Sales gallery exhibits the work of over 250 juried Vermont crafts people, also hosts yearly exhibition schedule featuring the work of noted crafts people world wide; Average Annual Attendance: 200,000; Mem: 1,200; dues $50 & up; annual meeting in Nov; exhibiting members are juried into the gallery
Income: Financed by mem, federal & state grants, fundraising activities, consignment receipts & tuition
Special Subjects: Crafts
Collections: Vermont Crafts
Publications: Information services bulletin; calendar; show announcements; course brochures
Activities: Classes for adults & children; craft demonstrations; professional workshops for crafts people; pottery facility; resident potter studios; lects open to public, 4 vis lectrs per yr; tours; original objects of fine craft lent to Vermont State Senate office in Washington; originates traveling exhibs; gallery shop sells books & Vermont crafts

CAMBRIDGE

M **BRYAN MEMORIAL GALLERY,** 180 Main St, Cambridge, VT 05444; PO Box 340, Jeffersonville, VT 05464-0340. Tel 802-644-5100; Email info@bryangallery.org; Web: www.bryangallery.org; *Exec Dir* Mickey Myers; *Gallery Manager* Tom Waters; *Graphics & Data Manager* Marcie Vallette
Open Feb-Mar, Oct-Dec Thurs - Sun 11AM - 4 PM; July-Oct daily 11 AM to 5 PM; No Fee; Estab 1984; preserving & exhibiting New England landscape painting; Building designed by the gallery's founder, Alden Bryan.; Average Annual Attendance: 5,000; Mem: 500; Mem dues $40 per yr
Special Subjects: Landscapes, Painting-American
Collections: Paintings
Exhibitions: 12 Exhibitions per year
Activities: Classes for adults; workshops; educational progs; gallery talks; competitions; Alden Bryan medal for landscape painting; Organizes Traveling Exhibitions of Works by Alden and Mary Bryan; sales hop sells books & cards

COLCHESTER

M **MCCARTHY GALLERY,** McCarthy Arts Center, 1 Winooski Park Colchester, VT 05439-1000. Tel 802-654-2851; Email bcollier@smcvt.edu; Web: knightsite.smcvt.edu/mccarthygallery; *Dir & Assoc Prof Fine Arts* Brian D Collier
Open Mon - Sat 9 AM - 5 PM & by appointment
Collections: paintings; photographs; sculpture
Exhibitions: Temporary exhibits

FERRISBURGH

A **ROKEBY MUSEUM,** 4334 Route 7, Ferrisburgh, VT 05456-9779. Tel 802-877-3406; Fax 802-877-3406; Email rokeby@comcast.net; Web: www.rokeby.org; *Dir* Jane Williamson
Open May - Oct daily 10 AM - 5 PM, open by appointment only remainder of yr; Admis fees Adult $10, seniors $9, students $8, children under 5 free; Estab 1963 to exhibit & interpret lives & works of the Robinson family; Robinson family (prolific artists) art is displayed throughout the house. Work of Rachael Robinson Elmer (1878 - 1919), student at Art Students League, is most prominent. She & her father, Rowland E Robinson (1833 - 1900), were published artists; Average Annual Attendance: 2,400; Mem: 250; dues life $500, family $40, individual $25, student $10
Income: Financed by mem, contributions & grants
Special Subjects: Costumes, Furniture, Hispanic Art, Manuscripts, Textiles, Watercolors, Period Rooms
Collections: Art, oils & watercolor sketches, books & manuscripts, 17th - 20th century furnishings, textiles & costumes
Publications: Messenger
Activities: Classes for children; docent training; lects open to pub; gallery talks; tours; mus shop sells books, reproductions & prints

GLOVER

M **BREAD & PUPPET THEATER,** Bread & Puppet Museum, 753 Heights Rd, Rt 122 Glover, VT 05839-9637. Tel 802-525-6972/3031; Web: www.breadandpuppet.org; *Artist* Peter Schumann; *Mgr* Elka Schumann
Open June - Oct daily 10 AM - 6 PM; No admis fee, donations welcome; Estab 1975 to exhibit & promote the art of puppetry; 100 ft long, 2-storied former dairy barn; Average Annual Attendance: 20,000
Income: $10,000 (financed by donations, sales of publications & art & by the Bread & Puppet Theater)
Special Subjects: Decorative Arts, Drawings, Graphics, Manuscripts, Posters, Prints, Woodcuts, Costumes
Collections: giant puppets, masks, graphics of The Bread and Puppet Theater, paintings; reliefs
Exhibitions: Woodshed gallery for small temporary exhibits
Publications: The Radicality of Puppet Theater; Bread & Puppet Museum catalog
Activities: Sacred Harp/Shap Note sings July & Aug; tours; free mus tour, Sun 1 PM July - Aug; lends art to various exhibits; mus shop sells books, original art, prints, reproductions & DVDs

HARDWICK

M **GRASS ROOTS ART & COMMUNITY EFFORT (GRACE),** Firehouse Gallery, 59 Mill St, Hardwick, VT 05843; PO Box 960, Hardwick, VT 05843-0960. Tel 802-472-6857; Fax 802-472-9578; Email grace@vtlink.net; Web: www.graceart.org; *Mng Dir* Carol Putnam; *Exhib Dir* Kathy Stark; *Develop Coordr* Mimi Smyth
Open Tues - Thurs 10 AM - 4 PM; No admis fee; 1975; Average Annual Attendance: 500
Special Subjects: Folk Art, Painting-American, Watercolors
Collections: Estate of Gayleen Aiken
Publications: States of Grace; Moonlight & Music: The Enchanted World of Gayleen Aiken
Activities: Classes for adults & children; sales shop sells books, original art & prints

JERICHO

M **EMILE A GRUPPE GALLERY,** 22 Barber Farm Rd, Jericho, VT 05465-9795. Tel 802-899-3211; Web: www.emilegruppegallery.com
Open Thurs - Sun 10 AM - 3 PM & by appointment; Estab 2003; Renovated 1860s sheep barn
Collections: paintings; photographs

Exhibitions: Temporary exhibits

A **JERICHO HISTORICAL SOCIETY,** 4A Red Mill Dr, Jericho, VT 05465; PO Box 35, Jericho, VT 05465-0035. Tel 802-899-3225; Web: www.jerichohistoricalsociety.org; *Pres* Ann Squires; *Sales Shop Mgr* Gail Prior
Open Apr - Dec Mon - Sat 10 AM - 5 PM, Sun 11:30 AM - 4 PM, Jan - Mar Wed & Sat 10 AM - 5 PM, Sun 11:30 AM -4 PM; cl Sun July & Aug; No admis fee; Estab 1978
Income: Financed by mem & contributions
Collections: Milling Machinery, Slides of Snow Flakes & Ice Crystals (video tape)
Exhibitions: Machinery, permanent exhibit; Snowflake Bentley Exhib, permanent

JOHNSON

M **JULIAN SCOTT MEMORIAL GALLERY,** 337 College Hill, Johnson State College, Dibden Center Johnson, VT 06565. Tel 800-635-1481; Email phillip.robertson@jsc.edu; Web: www.jsc.edu; *Dir* Phillip Robertson
Open Tues - Fri 10 AM - 6 PM, Sat 10 AM - 4 PM; No admis fee
Collections: paintings; drawings; sculptures
Exhibitions: Temporary exhibits

M **VERMONT STUDIO CENTER,** The Red Mill, 80 Pearl St, Johnson, VT 05656; PO Box 613, Johnson, VT 05656-0613. Tel 802-635-2727; Email info@vermontstudiocenter.org; Web: vermontstudiocenter.org; *Pres* Gary Clark; *Prog Dir* Kathy Black; *Visual Arts Dir* Tara Thacker; *Devel & Writing Dir* Ryan Walsh
Space contains admin offices, dining hall, resident lounge, two galleries & art book library

LUDLOW

M **BLACK RIVER ACADEMY MUSEUM & HISTORICAL SOCIETY,** Black River Academy Museum, High St, Ludlow, VT 05149-1091; PO Box 73, Ludlow, VT 05149-0073. Tel 802-228-5050; Email glbrehm@tds.net; Web: bramvt.org; *Dir* Georgia L Brehm; *Asst* Linda L Tucker
Open Noon - 4 PM, summer only; Admis $2; Estab 1972; 3-story brick building built in 1889; Average Annual Attendance: 1,200; Mem: 200; dues family $45, single $25
Income: $25,000 (financed by endowment)
Library Holdings: Manuscripts, Maps, Memorabilia, Original Documents, Pamphlets, Photographs
Special Subjects: Furniture, Glass, Maps
Collections: School memorabilia, farming implements, domestic items - 19th century, furnishings, clothing, Calvin Coolidge School Days Memorabilia, Fiber-R Arts Spinning Wheels/Weaving Looms, Barns of Ludlow
Publications: History of Ludlow, VT, J Harris (monograph); Black River Academy Booklet; Village Walking Tour Booklet
Activities: Dramatic progs; classes for adults & children; docent training; lects open to pub, 5 vis lectrs per yr; concerts; tours on holidays; VT Historical Society Educational Awards; schols; traveling exhibs 2 per yr; sales shop sells books, reproductions

LYNDON CENTER

M **SHORES MEMORIAL MUSEUM,** Main St, Lyndon Center, VT 05850; PO Box 85, Lyndon Center, VT 05850-0085. Tel 802-626-3265; Web: www.shoresmuseum.org; *Cur* Christopher Raymond; *Pres* Eric Paris; *Secy* Linda Toborg; *Treas* Patricia Jauch; *Historian* Bonnie Paris Ott
Open in summer by appt; No admis fee, donations accepted; Mus portrays a working man's home of the late Victorian era. Completed in 1896, this Queen Anne-style house was home to the Shores family of Lyndon Center, VT; Mem: 230; dues $5 ann
Library Holdings: Clipping Files, Memorabilia, Original Documents, Photographs
Special Subjects: Costumes, Dolls, Furniture, Historical Material, Period Rooms, Photography
Collections: Photographs, organs, kitchen & pantry exhib which demonstrates the time in which food preparation meant hours of hand labor. Coll includes wooden plates & bowls, a mortar & pestle, wire basket for egg collecting, long-handled bedwarmer, and a sadiron for pressing clothes, upstairs room features period clothing, exhib of war memorabilia & a doll exhib
Publications: Mr. Vail Comes to Town (Biog of Theodore N Vail)
Activities: Resource room for historical research; classes for children; tours

MANCHESTER

A **SOUTHERN VERMONT ART CENTER,** 2522 West Rd, Manchester, VT 05254; PO Box 617, Manchester, VT 05254-0617. Tel 802-362-1405; Fax 802-362-3279; Email info@svac.org; Web: www.svac.org; *Pres* Charles M Ams III; *Dir* Christopher Madkour; *Dir Pub Rels* Margaret Donovan
Open Tues - Sat 10 AM - 5 PM, Sun Noon - 5 PM, cl July 4th; Admis adults $8, students $3, free admis Sun; members and children under 13 free; Estab 1929 to promote educ in the arts & to hold exhibitions of art in its various forms; 10 galleries; sculpture garden; Average Annual Attendance: 25,000; Mem: Dues $55 - $75; annual meeting in Sept
Income: Financed by mem & contributions
Collections: Contemporary American sculptors & painters, loan coll
Exhibitions: Annual exhibitions for members; Fall Show; one-man & special exhibitions
Publications: Annual catalog & brochures
Activities: Classes for adults & children in painting, drawing, graphic arts, photography, sculpture & pottery; concerts; scholarship & fels offered

L **Gallery,** PO Box 617, West Rd, Manchester, VT 05254. Tel 802-362-1405; Email info@svac.org; Web: www.svac.org; *Exec Dir* Jennifer Weinstein; *Bus Mgr* Deedee Goebel
Open Tues - Sat 10 AM - 5 PM, Sun noon - 5 PM; Estab 1922 to further art in all aspects - primarily exhibition & educ; 1917 retrofitted mansion; 2,000 sq ft climate controlled contemporary space
Income: Income from contributions
Library Holdings: Book Volumes 500
Activities: Classes for adults & children; lects open to pub; lects for mems only; concerts; gallery talks; sponsoring competitions; schols; lending original art to other mus; sales shop sells original art, prints

MIDDLEBURY

M **HENRY SHELDON MUSEUM OF VERMONT HISTORY AND RESEARCH CENTER,** One Park St, Middlebury, VT 05753. Tel 802-388-2117; Email info@henrysheldonmuseum.org; Web: www.henrysheldonmuseum.org; *Exec Dir* William F Brooks Jr; *Archivist* Eva Garcelon-Hart; *Assoc Dir* Mary Manley
Open Mon - Sat 10 AM - 5 PM; Admis family $12, adults $5, seniors & students $4.50, youth $3; Estab 1882 for the preservation of furniture, portraits, decorative arts, artifacts & archival material of Middlebury & Addison County, VT; Museum housed in 1829 marble merchants home and with a gallery; Average Annual Attendance: 7,500; Mem: 650; dues $35 & up
Library Holdings: Book Volumes, Lantern Slides, Manuscripts, Maps, Memorabilia, Original Art Works, Original Documents, Pamphlets, Photographs, Prints, Slides
Special Subjects: Architecture, Ceramics, Coins & Medals, Costumes, Crafts, Decorative Arts, Dolls, Drawings, Embroidery, Etchings & Engravings, Flasks & Bottles, Folk Art, Furniture, Glass, Graphics, Hispanic Art, Historical Material, Ivory, Jewelry, Juvenile Art, Landscapes, Leather, Manuscripts, Maps, Metalwork, Miniatures, Painting-American, Period Rooms, Pewter, Photography, Porcelain, Portraits, Posters, Pottery, Prints, Scrimshaw, Sculpture, Silver, Tapestries, Textiles, Watercolors, Woodcarvings
Collections: China, furniture, glass, historical material, landscapes, pewter, portraits, prints
Exhibitions: Changing art and history exhibits in the Cerf Gallery; permanent exhibits of 19th Century home & furnishings
Publications: Marble in Middlebury; Walking History of Middlebury; annual report; newsletter
Activities: Traditional craft classes for adults and workshops for children; docent training; learning kits & resource material; lects open to pub; 6 vis lectrs per yr; guided tours; gallery talks; tours; one concert annually; out-reach program to county schools; mus shop sells gifts, original art, prints, home accessories, jewelry, toys, games, reproductions, prints & books on Vermont history

M **MIDDLEBURY COLLEGE,** Museum of Art, Rte 30, Mahaney Center for the Arts Middlebury, VT 05753-6177. Tel 802-443-5007, 443-5235; Fax 802-443-2069; Email deperkin@middlebury.edu; Web: museum.middlebury.edu; *Chief Cur* Emmie Donadio; *Cur Educ* Jason Vrooman; *Dir* Richard Saunders; *Registrar* Margaret Wallace; *Designer* Ken Pohlman; *Admin Opers Mgr* Douglas Perkins; *Events Outreach Coordr* Mikki Lane
Open Tues - Fri 10 AM - 5 PM, Sat & Sun Noon - 5 PM, cl Mon & holidays; No admis fee; Estab 1968 as a teaching collection. Now also presents loan exhibitions, work by individuals & groups, student exhibits; In 1992 moved to new Middlebury College Center for the Arts, designed by Malcolm Holzman of Hardy, Holzman & Pfeiffer Assoc; Average Annual Attendance: 15,000 - 17,000; Mem: 350; dues vary on 7 levels; annual meeting in Apr, triannual board meetings
Income: Financed through College, Friends of Art & grants
Special Subjects: American Western Art, Antiquities-Assyrian, Antiquities-Greek, Antiquities-Oriental, Antiquities-Roman, Asian Art, Bronzes, Calligraphy, Coins & Medals, Decorative Arts, Drawings, Etchings & Engravings, Painting-American, Painting-European, Period Rooms, Photography, Portraits, Prints, Sculpture, Watercolors, Woodcarvings
Collections: Asian art, drawings, paintings, photographs, prints, sculpture, antiquities
Publications: Gallery brochure; exhibition catalogues & brochures; exhibitions & events calendars
Activities: Classes for children; docent training; family workshops; teacher workshops; lects open to pub, 2-3 vis lectrs per yr; gallery talks; Friends of Art sponsor Annual Arts Awards given to members of the local community; book traveling exhibs 6-7 per yr; originate traveling exhibs; mus shop sells books, prints, notecards, postcards, posters

MONTPELIER

M **T W WOOD GALLERY,** 46 Barre St, Montpelier, VT 05602-3508. Tel 802-262-6035; Email twwoodgallery@gmail.com; Web: twwoodgallery.org; *Exec Dir* Ginny Callan; *Educ Dir* Binta Colley
Open Tues - Sat Noon - 4 PM & by appointments; Admis by donation; Estab 1895 by 19th century genre & portrait artist T W Wood to house & exhibit a portion of his works. Gallery acts as archive for information about T W Wood; 4 gallery spaces at 46 Barre St in Montpelier, VT at the Center for Arts & Learning; Average Annual Attendance: 10,000; Mem: 200; dues $40 - $1,000
Income: Financed by endowment, city appropriation, grants & mem
Special Subjects: Painting-American, Prints, Woodcuts
Collections: Oil paintings, watercolors, prints by T W Wood, A B Durand, J G Brown, A Wyant, Edward Gay, 100 works from the 1920s & 30s, some by WPA painters Reginald Marsh, Louis Boucher, Paul Sample, Joseph Stella, early 19th century American portraits
Exhibitions: Contemporary Vermont Artwork
Publications: Monograph on the Wood Collection
Activities: Classes for adults & children; docent training; children's art camp; after school arts programs & classes; lects open to pub; concerts; gallery talks; tours; individual paintings & original objects of art lent to local organizations, bus & other

mus with appropriate security systems; lending collection includes original prints & photographs

M **VERMONT HISTORICAL SOCIETY,** Museum, 109 State St, Montpelier, VT 05609-0901. Tel 802-828-2291; Fax 802-828-1415; Email info@vermonthistory.org; Web: www.vermonthistory.org; *Registrar* Mary Labate Rogstad; *Public Prog Mgr* Amanda Gustin
Open Tues - Sat 10 AM - 4 PM, cl state and federal holidays; Admis adults $7, students, children (6-17) & seniors $5, mem & children under 6 free; Estab 1838 to collect, preserve and make available for study items from Vermont's past; Average Annual Attendance: 22,000; Mem: 2,600; dues $25 - $600; annual meeting in Aug or Sept
Income: Financed by endowment, mem, state appropriation & contributions
Collections: Collection of fine arts, decorative arts, tools & equipment and work of Vermont artists, genealogy
Exhibitions: Generation of Change; Vermont, 1820-1850; All the Precious Past; Baseball in VT
Publications: Vermont History, 2 times per year; Vermont History News, bi-monthly
Activities: Lects open to pub; fellowships offered; mus shop sells books, prints, gifts & postcards

L **Library**, 109 State St, Montpelier, VT 05609-0901. Tel 802-479-8509; Fax 802-479-8510; Email library@vermonthistory.org; Web: vermonthistory.org; *Asst Librn* Marjorie Strong; *Library Asst* Claire Gilbertson; *Library Asst* Bernadette Harrington
Open Tues & Thurs - Fri 9 AM - 4 PM, Wed 9 AM - 8 PM, second Saturdays 9 AM - 4 PM; Admis user fee $7; Estab 1838; Reference Library
Income: Financed by endowment, mem, state & contributions
Purchases: $4900
Library Holdings: Audio Tapes, Book Volumes 150,000, Cassettes, Manuscripts, Motion Pictures, Pamphlets, Photographs, Reels, Video Tapes
Special Subjects: Advertising Design, Archaeology, Architecture, Bookplates & Bindings, Ceramics, Coins & Medals, Costume Design & Constr, Crafts, Decorative Arts, Dolls, Embroidery, Flasks & Bottles, Folk Art, Furniture, Glass, Handicrafts, Historical Material, Interior Design, Landscape Architecture, Landscapes, Manuscripts

MOSCOW

M **LITTLE RIVER HOTGLASS STUDIO & GALLERY,** 593 Moscow Rd, Moscow, VT 05662; PO Box 1504, Stowe, VT 05672-1504. Tel 802-253-0889; Fax 802-253-4128; Email info@littleriverhotglass.com; Web: www.littleriverhotglass.com; *Owner* Michael Trimpol; *Business Mgr* Monique LaJeunesse
Open Mon & Thurs - Sun 10 AM - 5 PM, cl Tues - Wed; No admis fee; Estab 1995
Collections: blown glass sculptures
Exhibitions: Temporary exhibits
Activities: Mus shop sells bowls, vases, perfume bottles, paperweights, ornaments, tableware, sculpture

PITTSFORD

M **NEW ENGLAND MAPLE MUSEUM,** Rte 7, Pittsford, VT 05763; PO Box 131, Pittsford, VT 05763-0131. Tel 802-483-9414; Fax 802-483-2101; Email newenglandmaplemuseum@yahoo.com; Web: www.maplemuseum.com; *Pres* Michael Blanchard; *Cur, Mgr & Purchasing* Mary Blanchard; *Asst Mgr* Laura Goodrich
Open daily 9:30 AM - 5:30 PM (May 20 - Oct 31), 10 AM - 4 PM (Nov 1 - Dec 23 & mid-Mar - May 19); Admis adults $5, seniors $4, children between 6 - 12 $1, children under 6 free; Estab 1977 to present the complete history of maple sugaring; Photographs, paintings, carvings, dioramas; Average Annual Attendance: 35,000
Income: $400,000 (financed by gift shop sales & admis)
Purchases: $2,000 per yr, mainly maple sugaring antiques
Library Holdings: Photographs, Slides, Video Tapes
Special Subjects: Ceramics, Crafts, Dioramas, Drawings, Folk Art, Historical Material, Painting-American, Photography, Woodcarvings
Collections: Oil paintings on maple sugaring by Paul Winter, oil murals on early maple sugaring by Vermont artist Grace Brigham, Photo Collection 1900-1938 Maple sugaring in Vermont
Exhibitions: Permanent collection
Activities: Tours; Mus shop sells books, magazines, original art, reproductions, prints, slides, travel videos, pottery, jewelry, Vermont crafts & specialty foods

READING

M **HALL ART FOUNDATION,** 544 VT Route 106, PO Box 127 Reading, VT 05062. Tel 802-952-1056; Email info@hallartfoundation.org; Web: www.hallartfoundation.org; *Owner* Andrew Hall; *Owner* Christine Hall
Open May - Nov, Wed & Sat - Sun 11 AM, 1 PM & 3 PM by appointment; first Friday of every month 5 PM - 8 PM; No admis fee; Estab 2007 to make postwar & contemporary artwork available to the public; collaborates globally with public institutions to organize exhibs & educate audiences; Converted 19th-century dairy farm; stone farmhouse & three barns
Collections: Contemporary & postwar art coll comprised of more than 5,000 works
Exhibitions: Rotating exhibits; temporary exhibits
Activities: Lects open to pub; tours; art programming; workshops; film screenings; organize traveling exhibs

RUTLAND

M **NORMAN ROCKWELL MUSEUM OF VERMONT,** 654 Route 4 E, Rutland, VT 05701. Tel 877-773-6095; Fax 802-775-2440; Email sales@normanrockwellvt.com; Web: www.normanrockwellvt.com
Open every day 9 AM - 5 PM; Admis adults $6.50, seniors $6, children $2.50; Estab in 1976 to commemorate Norman Rockwell's Vermont years & the entire span & diversity of the artist's career which ran from 1911-1978; Located in Rutland, near the corners of Rt 4 and Rt 7, two miles east on Rte 4
Special Subjects: Painting-American, Posters, Prints, Folk Art
Collections: Chronological display of more than 2,500 Rockwell magazine covers, advertisements, calendars & other publ works which shows his develop as an illustrator & links his works to the political, economic & cultural history of the US, featured works of artist Robert Duncan, member of the Cowboy Artists of America
Activities: mus shop sells books, magazines, reproductions, prints, figurines, plates, puzzles & mugs

A **RUTLAND AREA ART ASSOCIATION,** Chaffee Art Center & Chaffee Downtown Galleries, 75 Merchants Row, Rutland, VT 05701; 16 S Main St, Rutland, VT 05701-4136. Tel 802-775-0356, 802-775-0062; Fax 802-775-6242; Email mbarros@chaffeeartcenter.org; Web: www.chaffeeartcenter.org; *Exec Dir* Margaret Creed Barros; *Gallery & Educ Coord* Richelle Franzoni
Open Chafee Art Center Gallery: Thurs - Fri noon - 6 PM, Sat noon - 4 PM, cl Sun - Wed; Chafee Downtown Gallery: Wed - Fri noon - 6 PM, Sat 10 AM - 4 PM, cl Sun & Tues; No admis fee; donations accepted; Estab & incorporated 1961 to promote & maintain an educational & cultural center in the central Vermont region for the area artists, all artistic mediums presented; 1896 Queen Anne Victorian mansion listed on state & national register; Average Annual Attendance: 30,000; Mem: 400; juried artists; dues $75; annual meeting in Sep
Income: Financed by mem, special funding, contributions, grants, foundations, activities & spec events
Exhibitions: Annual Members Exhibit, juried; Art-in-the-Park outdoor festivals; group & invitational exhibits; featured artists exhib; (visit website for complete listing)
Publications: Calendar of events, annually; exhibition posters
Activities: Classes for adults & children; docent training; lects open to pub, 6-8 vis lectrs per yr; concerts; gallery talks; tours; competition with awards; schols offered; individual printings lent to local banks, corporations & other area cultural organizations; sales shop sells all original artwork, prints & reproductions; Chaffee downtown gallery year round exhibits

SAINT JOHNSBURY

M **FAIRBANKS MUSEUM & PLANETARIUM,** 1302 Main St, Saint Johnsbury, VT 05819-2224. Tel 802-748-2372; Fax 802-748-1893; Email info@fairbanksmuseum.org; Web: www.fairbanksmuseum.org; *Exec Dir* Adam Kane
Open 9 AM - 5 PM, 7 days per wk; Admis families $20, adults $8, sr citizens & children $6, group rates available; Estab 1889 as a center for exhibits, special exhibitions & programs on science, technology, the arts & the humanities; Average Annual Attendance: 40,000; Mem: 700; indiv $50
Income: $1,000,000 (financed by admis income, grants, endowment, mem & municipal appropriations)
Special Subjects: African Art, American Indian Art, Anthropology, Antiquities-Egyptian, Antiquities-Oriental, Archaeology, Architecture, Asian Art, Ceramics, Coins & Medals, Collages, Costumes, Dioramas, Dolls, Eskimo Art, Ethnology, Folk Art, Historical Material, Islamic Art, Ivory, Manuscripts, Maps, Military Art, Mosaics, Oriental Art, Pewter, Photography, Textiles, Watercolors, Pre-Columbian Art, Sculpture, Stained Glass
Collections: natural science, history & anthropology colls, Oceanic Art
Publications: Quarterly newsletter
Activities: Classes for adults & children; docent training; lects open to pub, concerts; gallery talks; tours; Franklin Fairbank Award; exten dept serving Northeast Vermont; individual paintings & original objects of art lent to other accredited mus; lending collection contains 500 nature artifacts, 50 original art works, 10 paintings & 500 photographs; book traveling exhibs one per yr; mus shop sells books, magazines, original art, reproductions, prints & science-related items; junior mus

M **NORTHEAST KINGDOM ARTISANS GUILD,** 430 Railroad St, Number 2 Saint Johnsbury, VT 05819-1727. Tel 802-748-0158; Email nekguild@kingcon.com; Web: www.nekartisansguild.com
Open Mon-Sat 10:30AM-5:30PM; Estab in 1997 featuring a variety of fine traditional & contemporary craft by Vermont artisans
Collections: handmade crafts & fine arts including baskets, clay, fiber, glass, metal, paper, & wood; prints; watercolors; oils; photographs

M **SAINT JOHNSBURY ATHENAEUM,** 1171 Main St Saint Johnsbury, VT 05819. Tel 802-748-8291; Fax 802-748-8086; Email inform@stjathenaeum.org; Web: www.stjathenaeum.org; *Library Dir* Lisa Von Kann; *Exec Dir* Mathew Powers
Open Mon-Fri 10 AM - 5:30 PM, Sat 9:30 AM - 4PM; Admis $5 to gallery for non-residents; donations accepted; Estab 1873 & maintained as a 19th century gallery; given to the townspeople by Horace Fairbanks; It is the oldest art gallery still in its original form in the United States; the only art-related nat historic landmark in the state of Vermont; Average Annual Attendance: 10,000
Income: Financed by endowment, town appropriation & annual giving
Special Subjects: Architecture, Landscapes, Manuscripts, Maps, Painting-American, Painting-European, Period Rooms, Portraits, Religious Art, Sculpture
Collections: 19th century American landscape paintings of the Hudson River School (Bierstadt, Colman, Whittredge, Cropsey, Gifford, Hart brothers), copies of masterpieces, sculpture
Exhibitions: Permanent Collection
Publications: Art Gallery Catalogue
Activities: Docent training; youth progs; lect open to public; gallery talks; tours; concerts; mus shop sells books, reproductions, art card-reproductions, prints & posters

M **STEPHEN HUNECK GALLERY AT DOG MOUNTAIN,** 143 Parks Rd, Saint Johnsbury, VT 05819-8907. Tel 800-449-2580; 802-748-2700; Fax 802-748-3075;

Email info@dogmt.com; Web: www.dogmt.com; *Gallery Mgr* Amanda McDermott; *Art Dir* Gwendolyn Huneck; *Sales Mgr* Jill Brown
Open Mon-Sat 10AM-5PM, Sun 11AM-4PM; No admis fee; Estab 2000; Gallery is the home of the artwork of the late Stephen Huneck & the only Dog Chapel in the world; Average Annual Attendance: 5,000+
Collections: sculptures; paintings; photographs
Activities: Hiking trails; dog ponds; dog chapel; sales shop sells books, original art, reproductions, prints, sculptures, dog toys, clothing

SHELBURNE

M **SHELBURNE MUSEUM,** Museum, 6000 Shelburne Rd, Shelburne, VT 05482; PO Box 10, Shelburne, VT 05482-0010. Tel 802-985-3346; Fax 802-985-2231; Email info@shelburnemuseum.org; Web: www.shelburnemuseum.org; *Dir* Tom Denenberg
Open Mon-Sat 9 AM - 5PM, Sun 1 PM - 5PM; Adults $25, seniors (AAA Member) $23, college students $15, youth (13-17) $14, child (5-12) $12, active military & children under 5 free; Estab 1947 exhibits American fine, decorative & utilitarian arts, particular emphasis on Vermont and New England heritage; 37 buildings on 45 acres; Average Annual Attendance: 160,000; Mem: Dues $35 - $1000
Income: Financed primarily by admissions & fundraising from members
Special Subjects: Ceramics, Decorative Arts, Dolls, Ethnology, Folk Art, Painting-American, Painting-European, Period Rooms, Textiles
Collections: American paintings, folk art, decoys, architecture, furniture, quilts & textiles, dolls, sporting art & sculpture, ceramics, tools, sleighs & carriages, toys, farm & home implements, seven period houses, European material: Impressionist & Old Master paintings, English furniture & architectural elements, Native American ethnographic artifacts, Sidewheeler Ticonderoga, railroad memorabilia including steam train, circus material & carousel animals
Activities: Classes for children; docent training; lect open to public, 5 vis lectrs per year; concerts; gallery talks; tours; exten dept serves Vermont; book traveling exhibitions annually; mus shop sells books, reproductions, prints, slides & original art

L **Library**, PO Box 10, Shelburne, VT 05482-0010. Tel 802-985-3346; Fax 802-985-2331; Email info@shelburnemuseum.org; Web: www.shellburnemuseum.org; *Archives & Library Manager* Allison Gillette
Open May - Oct 10 AM - 5 PM; Admis Adults $18, children $9; Estab 1947, art & Americana; Open to pub by appointment; Average Annual Attendance: 120,000; Mem: 5,500 members
Income: Financed by grants & contributions, admissions & earned income
Library Holdings: Audio Tapes, Book Volumes 6,000, Cassettes, Clipping Files, DVDs, Exhibition Catalogs, Filmstrips, Kodachrome Transparencies, Manuscripts, Memorabilia, Motion Pictures, Original Documents, Pamphlets, Periodical Subscriptions 66, Photographs, Prints, Records, Reels, Slides, Video Tapes
Special Subjects: American Indian Art, American Western Art, Architecture, Art History, Asian Art, Carpets & Rugs, Ceramics, Decorative Arts, Dolls, Drawings, Embroidery, Etchings & Engravings, Flasks & Bottles, Folk Art, Furniture, Glass, Handicrafts, Historical Material, Laces, Landscapes, Marine Painting, Miniatures, Painting-American, Painting-European, Painting-French, Period Rooms, Pewter, Porcelain, Pottery, Scrimshaw, Textiles, Woodcarvings
Collections: Art & Americana from the 17th - 20th centuries
Activities: Classes for adults & children; docent training; lects open to pub; concerts; gallery talks; tours; fellowships; mus shop sells books, magazines, reproductions, prints

SPRINGFIELD

A **SPRINGFIELD ART & HISTORICAL SOCIETY,** 65 Route 106, Springfield, VT 05156; PO Box 313, Springfield, VT 05156-0313. Tel 802-886-7935; Email putnams@vermontel.net; *Pres* Rosane Putnam; *Treas* Betty Kinsman; *Secy* Kathi Byam; *VPres* David Byam
Open new gallery space to open Fall 2016; by appointment; Admis by donation; Estab 1956 for the purpose of presenting history, arts & sciences of Springfield & environs; Average Annual Attendance: 1,200; Mem: 150; dues $50, $35 & $20; ann meeting in Fall
Income: $25,000 (financed by endowment & mem)
Library Holdings: Audio Tapes, Book Volumes, CD-ROMs, Cassettes, Clipping Files, Manuscripts, Maps, Memorabilia, Original Art Works, Original Documents, Photographs, Prints, Sculpture, Slides, Video Tapes
Special Subjects: Architecture, Costumes, Decorative Arts, Dolls, Drawings, Historical Material, Landscapes, Manuscripts, Maps, Miniatures, Painting-American, Period Rooms, Pewter, Photography, Portraits, Pottery, Prints, Sculpture, Textiles, Watercolors, Folk Art, Furniture, Porcelain, Posters
Collections: Primitive portraits by H Bundy, Aaron D Fletcher & Asahel Powers, Richard Lee, pewter, Bennington pottery, paintings by local artists, toys, costumes, sculpture, crafts, machine tool industry
Exhibitions: Historical exhibits: costumes; toys; photography; fine arts; student & mem art exhibs
Publications: Annual schedule of events & monthly notices; members quarterly newsletter
Activities: Classes for adults & children; civil war living history group; lects open to pub, 4 vis lectrs per yr; concerts; gallery talks; tours; individual paintings & objects of art lent to local galleries; lending collection contains original art work, paintings, photographs, sculpture, slides; living history - Sanitary Commission - Civil War group presentations; 2 book traveling exhibs per yr; organize traveling exhibs to VT History Expo; mus shop temporarily closed due to move

STOWE

M **CLARKE GALLERIES,** 51 S Main St, PO Box 777 Stowe, VT 05672-0777. Tel 917-454-8779; Email clarkegalleries@gmail.com
Call for hours
Collections: American & European paintings and sculpture from 1800s to present; photographs; prints

M **GREEN MOUNTAIN FINE ART GALLERY,** 64 S Main St, Stowe, VT 05672; PO Box 1384, Stowe, VT 05672-1384. Tel 802-253-1818; Fax 802-253-6837; Email scott@greenmountainfineart.com; Web: www.greenmountainfineart.com; *Owner* Scott Noble; *Owner & Mgr* Sandra Noble
Open Mon & Thurs - Sun 11 AM - 6 PM, cl Tues & Wed; Estab 2001
Collections: watercolors; oils; pastels; prints; mixed media; photography
Exhibitions: Temporary exhibits

M **ROBERT PAUL GALLERY,** 394 Mountain Rd, Stowe, VT 05672; PO Box 1413, Stowe, VT 05672-1413. Tel 800-873-3791
Open Mon-Sat 10AM-6PM, Sun 10AM-5PM
Collections: paintings; sculpture; photography

M **WEST BRANCH GALLERY & SCULPTURE PARK,** 17 Towne Farm Ln, Stowe, VT 05672-4138; PO Box 250, Stowe, VT 05672-0250. Tel 802-253-8943; Web: www.westbranchgallery.com
Open Wed-Sun 11AM-6PM, other times by appt; No admis fee; Estab 2004; Contemporary paintings & sculpture
Collections: paintings, sculptures

WEST RUTLAND

M **CARVING STUDIO AND SCULPTURE CENTER,** 636 Marble St, West Rutland, VT 05777; PO Box 495, West Rutland, VT 05777-0495. Tel 802-438-2097; Fax 802-438-2020; Email info@carvingstudio.org; Web: www.carvingstudio.org
Call for hours
Collections: sculptures

WHITE RIVER JUNCTION

M **MAIN STREET MUSEUM,** 58 Bridge St, White River Junction, VT 05001-7040. Tel 802-356-2776; Email info@mainstreetmuseum.org; Web: www.mainstreetmuseum.org
Open Tues - Wed 4 PM - 7 PM; Estab 1992
Collections: local history & culture; photographs; sculptures; paintings
Exhibitions: Temporary exhibits
Activities: Educ progs; classes for adults & children

VIRGINIA

ALEXANDRIA

A **THE ART LEAGUE GALLERY & SCHOOL,** 105 N Union St, Alexandria, VA 22314-3217. Tel 703-683-2323, 683-1780; Fax 703-683-0167; Email info@theartleague.org; Web: www.theartleague.org; *Pres* Nancy Pane Fortwengler; *Exec Dir* Suzanne Bethel; *Treas* David Dullum; *VPres* Cindi Lewis; *Gallery Dir* Whitney Staiger; *Dir School* Kathi Cohen
Open Mon - Sat 10 AM - 6PM, Thurs until 9 PM, Sun Noon - 6 PM; No admis fee; Estab 1954 to promote & maintain standards of art through mem juried exhibs & a large school which teaches all facets of the fine arts & some high skill crafts; Sixteen classrooms total; three classrooms in the Torpedo Factory Art Center in Old Town Alexandria, Virginia; three gallery rooms & thirteen classrooms in two annexes; Average Annual Attendance: 500,000; Mem: 1,200; dues $70; annual meeting in June; open to all
Income: program income, grants & contributions, member dues
Library Holdings: Book Volumes 1665, Periodical Subscriptions
Exhibitions: Monthly juried shows for members; solo shows monthly; Annual Student Faculty Show; Art in City Hall
Activities: Classes for adults & children; foreign & domestic art-travel workshops; lect open to public; gallery talks; tours; sponsors competitions with monthly Best in Show cash awards & other recognition awards; sales shop sells art supplies

ART SERVICES INTERNATIONAL
For further information, see National and Regional Organizations

M **FRANK LLOYD WRIGHT'S POPE-LEIGHEY HOUSE,** 9000 Richmond Hwy, Alexandria, VA 22309; PO Box 15097, Alexandria, VA 22309-0097. Tel 703-780-4000; Fax 703-780-8509; Email woodlawn@savingplaces.org; Web: www.woodlawnpopeleighey.org; *Dir Site Interpretation & Partnerships* Amanda Phillips
Open April - Dec, Fri - Mon 11 AM - 4 PM, cl Tues, Wed, Thurs; Admis adults $15, seniors/active military with ID $12, students K-12 $7.50; combination tickets with Woodlawn: adults $20, seniors/active military with ID $18, students K-12 $11; Estab 1964 (built 1940); Frank Lloyd Wright's Pope-Leighey House is a property of the National Trust for Historic Preservation, located on the grounds of Woodlawn Plantation. This residence was designed in 1939 by Frank Lloyd Wright for his clients, the Loren Pope Family. Built of cypress, brick and glass, the Usonian structure contains such features as a flat roof, radiant heat, indirect lighting, carport & custom furniture, all designed by Frank Lloyd Wright, as an example of architecture for the average-income family. Threatened by construction of an interstate highway in 1964, Mrs Marjorie Folsom Leighey, second owner, presented the property to the National Trust for Historic Preservation. It was then moved to the Woodlawn grounds; Average Annual Attendance: 15,000; Mem: dues family $30 (through National Trust for Historic Preservation)
Income: Non-profit; through town admissions & donations
Special Subjects: Architecture
Collections: Pope & Leighey Family Collections, Original furniture & textiles
Publications: Brochure and hardcover history of house
Activities: Classes for adults & children; docent training; lects open to pub; tours daily; sales shop sells books, reproductions, prints, ornaments, postcards, etc

M **THE GEORGE WASHINGTON MASONIC NATIONAL MEMORIAL ASSOCIATION,** The George Washington Masonic National Memorial, 101 Callahan Dr, Alexandria, VA 22301-2751. Tel 703-683-2007; Fax 703-519-9270; Email gseghers@gwmemorial.org; Web: www.gwmemorial.org; *Executive Director* George D Seghers; *Director Mus & Library Collections* Mark A Tabbert; *Dir Communs & Develop* Shawn E Eyer
Open daily 9 AM - 5 PM; Admis fee $15, children 12 & under free; Estab 1932; Maintains a reference library;; Average Annual Attendance: 60,000 - 70,000; Mem: 1.8 million; voluntary contributions; annual meeting Feb 22
Income: Privately funded charitable organization
Library Holdings: Book Volumes, Compact Disks, DVDs, Fiche, Framed Reproductions, Maps, Memorabilia, Original Documents, Pamphlets, Periodical Subscriptions, Photographs, Prints, Reproductions
Special Subjects: Coins & Medals, Dioramas, Furniture, Painting-American, Portraits, Stained Glass
Collections: George Washington Portraits & Relics, Masonic & related artifacts
Exhibitions: Relics & portraits of George Washington, murals, Lafayette & Intimates of Washington; Art & Architecture 1900 - 1930
Publications: Light, quarterly
Activities: Dramatic programs; lects open to pub, 3 vis lectrs per yr; concerts; tours; George Washington Memorial Award; mus shop sells books, reproductions, prints, original art

A **NORTHERN VIRGINIA FINE ARTS ASSOCIATION,** The Athenaeum, 201 Prince St, Alexandria, VA 22314-3313. Tel 703-548-0035; Fax 703-948-0456; Email admin@nvfaa.org; Web: www.nvfaa.org; *Exec Dir* Veronica Szalus; *Events Coordr* Richard Webber
Open Thurs, Fri & Sun 12 noon - 4 PM, Sat 1 PM - 4 PM, cl Mon, Tues, Wed & holidays; No admis fee; Estab 1964 to promote education, appreciation, participation & pursuit of excellence in all forms of art & crafts; to enrich the cultural life of the metropolitan area & Northern Virginia; Main gallery space on main floor, with additional area available; Average Annual Attendance: 10,000; Mem: 70; dues $100-$1000
Income: Financed by mem, fundraisers & grants
Exhibitions: Annual Joint Art League/Athenaeum Multi-media Juried show; Five Virginia Photographers: Sally Mann, E Gowen & Others; Thomas Hart Benton; Washington Color School: Stars & Stripes; Kathleen Ewing's Dog Days Dog Show; Portent curated by Richard Dana; Networked curated by J. T.Kirtland; Waxworks curated by Ellen Weiss; Hair Apparent curated by Twig Murray
Publications: Quarterly newsletter
Activities: Dance classes for adults & children; dramatic progs; docent training; lects open to pub, gallery talks; tours; sponsoring of competitions; schols offered; exten prog serving Northern Virginia

SPECIAL LIBRARIES ASSOCIATION
For further information, see National and Regional Organizations

M **WOODLAWN/THE POPE-LEIGHEY,** PO Box 15097, Alexandria, VA 22309-0097; 9000 Richmond Hwy, Alexandria, VA 22309. Tel 703-780-4000; Fax 703-780-8509; *Asst Dir* Gail Donahue; *Dir* Ross Randall
Open 10 AM - 5 PM, cl New Years; Admis adults $6, seniors & students $5, group rates by arrangement; Estab 1805; Land originally part of Mount Vernon. Built in 1800-05 for George Washington's granddaughter upon her marriage to Lawrence Lewis, Washington's nephew. It was designed with central pavilion & flanking wings by Dr William Thornton, winner of the architectural competition for the design of the United States Capitol. A group of Quakers, a pioneer anthropologist, a playwright & Senator Oscar W Underwood of Alabama were among Woodlawn's residents after the Lewis'. In 1951 the foundation's trustees decided that the visiting public would be better served if Woodlawn was administered by the National Trust. The mansion furnishings are largely from the Federal & early Empire periods & include Lewis family furniture; Average Annual Attendance: 60,000; Mem: 350; dues family $40
Special Subjects: Archaeology, Architecture, Carpets & Rugs, Ceramics, Coins & Medals, Costumes, Decorative Arts, Drawings, Embroidery, Etchings & Engravings, Furniture, Glass, Historical Material, Jewelry, Leather, Maps, Miniatures, Painting-American, Painting-British, Period Rooms, Pewter, Porcelain, Portraits, Restorations, Sculpture, Silver, Textiles, Watercolors
Exhibitions: Needlework Exhibit; A Woodlawn Christmas in Dec; Haunted History Tours
Publications: Friends of Woodlawn Newsletter, quarterly; Welcome to Woodlawn, booklet
Activities: Classes for adults & children; dramatic progs; docent training; special events; lects open to pub; tours; individual paintings & original objects of art lent to qualified mus; lending collection consists of original prints, paintings, furnishings & textiles; mus shop sells books, reproductions, prints, antiques, foods, toys

ARLINGTON

M **ARLINGTON ARTS CENTER (AAC),** 3550 Wilson Blvd, Arlington, VA 22201-2348. Tel 703-248-6800; Fax 703-248-6849; Email information@arlingtonartscenter.org; Web: www.arlingtonartscenter.org; *Exec Dir* Stefanie Fedor
Open Wed - Fri 12-7 PM, Sat & Sun Noon - 5 PM; No admis fee; Estab to present new work by emerging & established artists from the region (Virginia, Maryland, Washington DC, West Virginia, Pennsylvania & Delaware); 17,000 sq ft venue for contemporary art; Average Annual Attendance: 11,000
Special Subjects: Calligraphy
Activities: Classes for adults, teens & children; studio res prog; workshops; lects open to pub; gallery talks; tours; vis artist prog; juried exhibs

L **ARLINGTON COUNTY DEPARTMENT OF PUBLIC LIBRARIES,** Fine Arts Section, 1015 N Quincy St, Arlington, VA 22201-4603. Tel 703-228-5990; 228-5996; Fax 703-228-5692; Email ikauff@arlingtonva.us; Web: www.arlingtonva.us/library; *Branch Librn* Margaret Brown; *Head Art Prog* Ingrid Kauffman
Open Mon - Thurs 10 AM - 9 PM, Fri & Sat 10 AM - 5 PM, Sun 1 - 9 PM; No admis fee; Estab 1935 to serve needs of an urban-suburban population in all general subjects; Juried shows of 4-5 artists change monthly
Income: Financed by county & state appropriations
Purchases: Jeff Wilson - Blue Lids
Library Holdings: Book Volumes 3,000, Other Holdings Total holdings: 323,000, Periodical Subscriptions 15
Exhibitions: Local artists, crafts people & photographers have exhibitions at the central library each month; additional exhibs at Shirlington Branch library; see website for addition exhib info
Activities: Lects open to pub, 10 vis lectrs per yr; workshops; film shows; extended learning institute video tapes from Northern Virginia Community Col available

M **BLUEMONT HISTORICAL RAILROAD JUNCTION,** Blueprint Junction Park, 801 N Manchester St Arlington, VA 22205. Tel 703-228-6523; Email lcore@arlingtonva.us; *Mgr* Lyndell Core
Open sunrise to sunset; No admis fee, donations accepted; Estab 1992; Arlington & Alexandria's only railway mus interprets the history of these communities that grew up around the lines; housed on former southern railway caboose X-441, built in 1972; Average Annual Attendance: 2,500
Income: A feature of Arlington County parks and recreation
Collections: Photos & objects from local railway history
Activities: Guided tours

M **LEE ARTS CENTER,** 5722 Lee Hwy, Arlington, VA 22207. Tel 703-228-0560; Fax 703-228-0559; Email leearts@arlingtonva.us; Web: www.arlingtonarts.org; *Dir* Steven Munoz; *Asst Dir* Darlene Tsukamoto
Open Mon & Fri 9:30 AM - 6 PM; Tues - Thurs 9:30 AM - 9 PM, Sat 9:30 AM - 5 PM, cl Sun
Collections: painting; sculpture
Exhibitions: 12 exhibits annually
Activities: Workshops; open studios; artist residencies

ASHLAND

M **RANDOLPH MACON COLLEGE,** Flipp Gallery, 211 N Center St, Randolph Macon College, Pace-Armistead Hall Ashland, VA 23005. Tel 804-752-7337
Open Mon - Fri 10 AM - 4 PM, Sat - Sun by appointment; 0; College gallery showing contemporary art from southeastern and local artists; Average Annual Attendance: 500-700; Mem: 0
Collections: Student & faculty artwork; exhibits by national & state artists
Exhibitions: 4-5 exhibitions per year

BLACKSBURG

A **BLACKSBURG REGIONAL ART ASSOCIATION,** PO Box 525, Blacksburg, VA 24063-0525. Email braa-info@bev.net; Web: www.braa.arts.bev.net; *Pres* Roberta Sallee; *Mem Chmn* Tom Barnhart; *Treas* Jeanette Bowker; *VPres* Nancy Norton; *VPres* Danie Janov
No admis fee; contributions; Estab 1950, affiliated with the Virginia Museum of Fine Arts, dedicated to the encouragement & enjoyment of the arts; 11 galleries in merchant venues; Mem: 130; dues individual $20, family $25; annual meeting in Apr
Income: Financed by mem & patron contributions
Library Holdings: DVDs
Exhibitions: 11 rotating exhibitions per yr & juried exhibits
Publications: BRAA newsletter, monthly
Activities: Art classes for pub & members only; lects open to pub & members only, 3 vis lectrs per yr; competitions; sponsored shows; art sales events

M **VIRGINIA POLYTECHNIC INSTITUTE & STATE UNIVERSITY,** Armory Art Gallery, 201 Drapper Rd, Blacksburg, VA 24061-0103. Tel 540-231-4859, 231-5547; Fax 540-231-7826; *Art Chair & Interim Staff Dir* Bailey Van Hook; *Gallery Coordr* Francis Thompson
Open Mon - Fri Noon - 5 PM, Sat Noon - 4 PM; No admis fee; Estab 1969 to serve needs of art department as a teaching gallery as well as to meet community needs in an area where there are few large art centers & museums; Gallery is located in same building as Art Department; exhibition area is approx 16 x 40 ft; Average Annual Attendance: 2,000 plus student use
Income: Financed through special university budget
Exhibitions: Special invited exhibitions & exhibitions by Virginia artists, students & visiting artists
Publications: Exhibition calendar; gallery announcements
Activities: Docent training to college students; lects open to public, 3 vis lectrs per yr; gallery talks; individual paintings & original objects of art lent to faculty & staff offices on campus, as well as library & continuing educ center; originate traveling exhibs

M **Perspective Gallery**, 118 N Main St, Squires Student Ctr Blacksburg, VA 24060-3939. Tel 540-231-5431; Fax 540-231-5430; *Art Dir* Tom Butterfield
Open Tues - Fri Noon - 10 PM, Sat & Sun 2 - 10 PM, cl Mon; No admis fee; Estab 1969 to provide a broad arts experience for the students, faculty & the university community; Average Annual Attendance: 50,000
Income: Financed by university unions & student activities

L **Art & Architecture Library**, 302 Cowgill Hall, Blacksburg, VA 24062; PO Box 90001, Blacksburg, VA 24062-9001. Tel 540-231-9271; Email h.ball@vt.edu; Web: www.lib.vt.edu; *Librn* Heather Ball; *Visual Resources Cur* Brian Shelburne
Open Mon - Thurs 8 AM - 11 PM, Fri 8 AM - 5 PM, Sat 1 - 5 PM, Sun 2 - 11 PM; Estab 1928 to provide service to the College of Architecture & Urban Studies & the other divisions of the university; Circ 60,000
Income: Financed by state appropriation & gifts
Purchases: $69,500
Library Holdings: Book Volumes 65,000, CD-ROMs, Cassettes, Clipping Files, DVDs, Exhibition Catalogs, Fiche, Pamphlets, Periodical Subscriptions 300, Reels, Slides 70,000, Video Tapes
Special Subjects: Architecture, Landscape Architecture

BROOKNEAL

M **PATRICK HENRY MEMORIAL FOUNDATION,** Red Hill National Memorial, 1250 Red Hill Rd, Brookneal, VA 24528-3302. Tel 804-376-2044; Fax 804-376-2647; Web: www.redhill.org; *Admin Asst* Lynn Davis; *Exec Dir* Dr Jon Kukla; *Cur* Edith Poindexter; *Assoc Cur* Karen Gorham-Smith
Open 9 AM - 5 PM, winter, 9 AM - 4 PM; Admis fee $6; Estab 1944 to preserve & develop a memorial to Patrick Henry; One room with Rothermel painting as focal point; Average Annual Attendance: 11,000; Mem: dues $25 & up; annual meeting in May
Income: $250,000 (financed by endowment, mem, county & state appropriation)
Library Holdings: Audio Tapes, Clipping Files, Framed Reproductions, Manuscripts, Maps, Memorabilia, Motion Pictures, Original Art Works, Original Documents, Pamphlets, Photographs, Sculpture, Video Tapes
Special Subjects: Architecture, Landscape Architecture, Furniture, Photography, Portraits, Sculpture, Silver
Collections: Patrick Henry images; decorative arts; furniture & memorabilia
Exhibitions: Patrick Henry Before the Virginia House of Burgesses by P F Rothermel; Patrick Henry Memorabilia
Publications: Quarterly newsletter
Activities: Classes for adults & children; docent progs; lects open to pub; 2 vis lectrs per yr; tours; schols offered; National Forensic League Annual Competition; mus shop sells reproductions

CHANTILLY

M **NATIONAL AIR AND SPACE MUSEUM,** Steven F Udvar-Hazy Center, 14390 Air & Space Museum Pkwy, Chantilly, VA 20151-3002. Tel 703-572-4118; Email NASM-VisitorServices@si.edu; Web: airandspace.si.edu/udvar-hazy-center; *John & Adrienne Mars Dir* Ellen R Stofan, PhD; *Deputy Dir* Christopher Browne
Open daily 10 AM - 5:30 PM, cl Dec 25; extended summer hrs until 7 PM; No admis fee; pub parking $15, free after 4 PM; Bldg opened 2003 to provide extra exhib space unavailable to National Air & Space Mus on National Mall; James S. McDonnell Space Hangar opened 2004; Comprised of Boeing Aviation Hangar, James S McDonnell Space Hangar, Donald D Engen Observation Tower & Airbus IMAX Theater. Bureau of the Smithsonian Institution in Washington, DC; Average Annual Attendance: 1,100,000; Mem: Dues $35 - $10,000
Collections: National Aviation & Space Exploration Wall of Honor, Aircraft & Engines, Aerial Cameras, International Space, Awards & Insignia, Propulsion, Rocketry
Exhibitions: Applications Satellites; Human Spaceflight; Rockets & Missiles; Space Science; Flight Simulator; Aerobatic Flight; Business Aviation; Cold War Aviation; Commercial Aviation; General Aviation; Korea & Vietnam Aviation; Modern Military Aviation; Pre-1920 Aviation; Sport Aviation; Ultralight Aircraft; Vertical Flight; World War II Aviation; World War II German Aviation
Activities: Educ progs; school group activities; tours; mus store

M **Donald D Engen Observation Tower**, 14390 Air & Space Museum Pkwy, Chantilly, VA 20151-3002. Tel 703-572-4118; Email NASM-VisitorServices@si.edu; Web: airandspace.si.edu
Open 10 AM - 4:30 PM; No admis fee; Exhibs on two levels; observation tower accessible by elevator
Exhibitions: Lower Level Exhib: air traffic control workstation, equipment, & artifacts; Observation Level Exhib: explains basic features of an airport

CHARLES CITY

M **SHIRLEY PLANTATION FOUNDATION,** 501 Shirley Plantation Rd, Charles City, VA 23030-2907. Tel 804-829-5121; Fax 804-829-6322; Email info@shirleyplantation.com; Web: www.shirleyplantation.com; *Owner* Charles Hill Carter Jr; *Dir* Janet L Appel; *Deputy Dir* Randy Carter
Open daily 9:30 AM - 4:30 PM; cl Thanksgiving and Christmas; Admis adults $11, discounts for AAA, military & seniors 60 & up, & youth; Estab 1613 to share the history of one distinguished family from colonial times to the present; oldest family-owned bus in North America; Oldest Virginia Plantation continuous home to the Hill Carter Family, currently 10th & 11th generations; maintains 8 original colonial outbuildings circa 1730's & 1750's; Average Annual Attendance: 45,000
Special Subjects: Anthropology, Antiquities-Oriental, Archaeology, Architecture, Bookplates & Bindings, Ceramics, Coins & Medals, Decorative Arts, Drawings, Etchings & Engravings, Furniture, Glass, Historical Material, Landscapes, Manuscripts, Maps, Metalwork, Painting-American, Painting-British, Painting-European, Painting-Flemish, Painting-French, Period Rooms, Pewter, Porcelain, Portraits, Pottery, Prints, Reproductions, Restorations, Silver, Textiles, Woodcarvings, Woodcuts
Collections: 18th century English silver & oil portraits, 18th & 19th century furniture & handcarved woodwork, Civil War, culinary, gardens, genealogy, trees
Exhibitions: Timeline, permanent exhib
Publications: Shirley Plantation booklet
Activities: Classes for adults & children; dramatic progs, thematic seasonal progs; tours; lending collections contain books, original art works, original prints, photographs & over 18,000 documents on permanent loan to Colonial Williamsburg Foundation; mus shop sells books, reproductions, prints, silver & porcelain

M **WESTOVER PLANTATION,** 7000 Westover Rd, Charles City, VA 23030-3329. Tel 804-829-2882; Fax 804-829-5528; Email info@westover-plantation.com; Web: westover-plantation.com; *Mgr* Andrea F Erda
Open daily 10 AM - 5 PM; Admis $5, children $3; house interior open by appointment; Built about 1730 by William Byrd II, Founder of Richmond, the house is considered one of the finest example of Georgian architecture in America, with steeply sloping roof, tall chimneys in pairs at both ends, elaborate Westover doorway, a three story central structure with two end wings. The path from the Caretakers House to the house is lined with tulip poplars over 100 years old; former kitchen is a separate small brick building. East of the house (open to visitors) is the Necessary House, an old icehouse & a dry well with supposed passageways leading under the house to the river. The Westover gates of delicate ironwork incorporate initials WEB; lead eagles on the gateposts, fence column topped with stone finials cut to resemble pineapples, beehives, & other symbolic designs. Long estab boxwood garden with tomb of William Byrd II. Members of his family, & Captain William Perry, who died Aug 1637, are buried in old church cemetery one-fourth mile west of house
Special Subjects: Architecture

CHARLOTTESVILLE

M **SECOND STREET GALLERY,** 115 Second St SE, Charlottesville, VA 22902. Tel 434-977-7284; Fax 434-979-9793; Email ssg@secondstreetgallery.org; Web: www.secondstreetgallery.org; *Pres* Steve Taylor; *VPres* Steve Delgado; *Treas* Ryan Ford; *Secy* Mary M Murray; *Exec Dir* Rebecca Young Schoenthal; *Gallery Opers & Outreach* Andrew M Greeley; *Mem & Develop Assoc* Amanda Currie Jones
Open Tues - Sat 11 AM - 6 PM; No admis fee; Estab 1973 as an alternative arts space to present emerging & accomplished contemporary artists from regional & national localities and to promote an appreciation of contemporary art and culture by educating the public; Two galleries: main gallery 1520 sq ft, Dove gallery 360 sq ft; Average Annual Attendance: 15,000; Mem: 375; dues benefactor $1,000, Patron $500, sponsor $250, friend $100, individual $35
Income: Financed by individual, corporate & foundation contributions & grants from the Virginia Commission for the Arts & fundraising activities
Publications: The Second Glance, quarterly newsletter; exhibit catalogs
Activities: Adult educ; Lect; tours; literary readings; in-school workshops; grant support from the Andy Warhol Foundation for the Visual Arts

M **THOMAS JEFFERSON FOUNDATION, INC,** Monticello, PO Box 316, Charlottesville, VA 22902-0316. Tel 434-984-9801, 434-984-9822; Fax 434-977-7757; Email administration@monticello.org; Web: www.monticello.org; *Pres* Leslie Greene Bowman
Open Mar - Oct Mon - Sun 8 AM - 5 PM, Nov - Feb Mon - Sun 9 AM - 4:30 PM, cl Christmas; Admis adults $17 Nov-Feb $22 March-Oct, children 6-11 $8; Estab 1923 to preserve education; Monticello is owned & maintained by the Thomas Jefferson Foundation, a nonprofit organization founded in 1923. The home of Thomas Jefferson, designed by him & built 1769-1809, contains many original furnishings & art objects; Average Annual Attendance: 525,000
Income: Pvt
Library Holdings: Audio Tapes, Book Volumes, CD-ROMs, Cards, Cassettes, Clipping Files, Compact Disks, DVDs, Exhibition Catalogs, Fiche, Filmstrips, Manuscripts, Maps, Memorabilia, Original Documents, Other Holdings, Pamphlets, Periodical Subscriptions, Photographs, Prints, Reproductions, Slides, Video Tapes
Special Subjects: Afro-American Art, American Indian Art, Archaeology, Architecture, Ceramics, Decorative Arts, Drawings, Etchings & Engravings, Furniture, Historical Material, Landscapes, Manuscripts, Maps, Painting-American, Portraits, Religious Art, Reproductions, Restorations, Sculpture
Activities: Classes for children; lects open to pub; concerts; talks, fels; mus shop sells books, reproductions & prints

M **UNIVERSITY OF VIRGINIA,** The Fralin Museum of Art at the University of Virginia, 155 Rugby Rd, Charlottesville, VA 22904-4119; PO Box 400119, Charlottesville, VA 22904-4119. Tel 434-924-3592, 434-243-2050 (tours); Fax 434-924-6321; Web: www.virginia.edu/artmuseum; *COO* Hunter Hollins; *Dir Develop* Elizabeth Wright; *Family Dir* Matthew McLendon; *Exhibs Coordr* Patrick Burton; *Acad Cur* M Jordan Love; *Docent Coordr* Emily Lazaro; *Dir Annual Giving* Sarah Althoff; *Mktg Mgr* Rhonda Deck; *Asst to Dir* Lisa Jevack; *Assoc Acad Cur* Aimee Hunt
Open Tues - Wed & Fri - Sat 10 AM - 5 PM, Thurs 10 AM - 7 PM, Sun noon - 5 PM, cl Mon; No admis fee, donations accepted; Estab 1935 to make original works of art available to the university community & to the general pub; Perm coll & temp exhibitions; teaching museum; more than 12,000 works; Average Annual Attendance: 28,000; Mem: 2,200; dues dir circle $5,000, cur circle $2,500, benefactor $1,000, patron $500, sponsor $200, basic $75, seniors $40, student free
Income: Financed by mem, state appropriation & gifts
Special Subjects: African Art, American Indian Art, American Western Art, Antiquities-Byzantine, Antiquities-Etruscan, Antiquities-Greek, Antiquities-Oriental, Antiquities-Roman, Asian Art, Baroque Art, Ceramics, Coins & Medals, Etchings & Engravings, Landscapes, Painting-Flemish, Painting-French, Painting-German, Painting-Italian, Painting-Japanese, Photography, Porcelain, Portraits, Posters, Pottery, Pre-Columbian Art
Collections: American art, European & American Art in the age of Jefferson, Old Master prints, East Asian art, contemporary art, American Indian art, Oceanic Art, prints, drawings, photographs, Roman Coins, Ancient Mediterranean
Exhibitions: Various rotating exhibitions, call for schedule
Publications: exhibition brochures; calendar
Activities: Educ progs for adults, students, children; docent training; lects open to pub, 5+ vis lectrs per yr; gallery talks; tours; fels & internships offered; original works of art lent; book traveling exhibs 1-3 per yr; mus shop sells books & cards

L **Fiske Kimball Fine Arts Library**, Bayly Dr, Charlottesville, VA 22903; PO Box 400131, Charlottesville, VA 22904-4131. Tel 804-924-7024; Fax 804-982-2678; Email jsr8s@virginia.edu; Web: www.lib.virginia.edu/fine-arts/index.htm/; *Asst Librn & Pub Services* Barbara Jackson
Open school year Mon - Thurs 8 AM - Midnight, Fri 8 AM - 8 PM, Sat 10 AM - 8 PM, Sun Noon-Midnight; Estab 1970; combination of existing art & architecture libraries to provide a research facility providing printed, microform, audio visual & electronic materials for the art, architecture & drama curriculum; Circ 115,000; Fifty percent of collection is non-circulating
Income: $212,000
Library Holdings: Audio Tapes, Book Volumes 127,000, Cassettes, Exhibition Catalogs, Fiche, Filmstrips, Kodachrome Transparencies, Manuscripts, Periodical Subscriptions 285, Photographs, Reels, Slides 171,000
Special Subjects: Archaeology, Architecture, Art History, Film, Photography
Collections: Francis Benjamin Johnson Photographs of Virginia Architecture, Rare books
Publications: Bibliography of the Arts: Including Fine & Decorative Arts, Architecture, Design & the Performing Arts, updated quarterly; Guide To Sources, irregular serial; Notable Additions to the library collection, quarterly

CHESAPEAKE

M **PORTLOCK GALLERIES AT SONO,** 3815 Bainbridge Blvd, Chesapeake, VA 23324-1607. Tel 727-502-4901; Email nbenson@cityofchesapeake.net; Web: www.portlockgalleries.com; *Gallery Dir* Nicole Benson
Open Tues - Fri 10 AM - 5 PM, Sat - Sun 1 PM - 5 PM; cl holidays; No admis fee
Collections: Paintings & photographs; art exhibitions

CHRISTIANBURG

M **MONTGOMERY MUSEUM & LEWIS MILLER REGIONAL ART CENTER,** 300 S Pepper St, Christianburg, VA 24073. Tel 540-382-5644; Fax 540-382-9127; Email info@montgomerymuseum.org; Web: www.montgomerymuseum.org; *Dir* Shearon Campbell; *Pres (Vol)* Robert L Puff
Open Mon - Sat 10:30 AM - 4:30 PM, Sun 1:30 - 4:30 PM; Admis adult $1, children $.50; Estab 1983; Average Annual Attendance: 3,500
Income: Financed by grants, gifts & members
Library Holdings: Book Volumes, Clipping Files, Memorabilia, Original Art Works, Pamphlets, Photographs, Prints, Slides
Collections: Lewis Miller Art, clothing, family genealogy, photographs, dolls, local history books, old photo albums, household items, bus machines, weaving loom
Exhibitions: Rotating exhibits
Publications: Quarterly newsletter; Montgomery Museum newsletter; booklets

L **Library,** 300 S Pepper St, Christianburg, VA 24073. Email info@montgomerymuseum.org; Web: www.montgomerymuseum.org; *Dir* Linda L Martin
Open Mon - Sat 10:30 AM - 4:30 PM, Sun 1:30 - 4:30 PM; Admis adult $2, children 12 & under $1, free to members; Reference
Library Holdings: Book Volumes 300, Clipping Files, Memorabilia, Original Art Works, Other Holdings, Pamphlets, Photographs, Prints, Slides
Special Subjects: Crafts, Dolls, Folk Art, Historical Material, Photography, Prints

COURTLAND

M **RAWLS MUSEUM ARTS,** 22376 Linden St Courtland, VA 23837. Tel 757-653-0754; Fax 757-653-0341; Email rma@beldar.com; Web: www.rawlsarts.cjb.net; *Exec Dir* Barbara Easton-Moore; *Educational Outreach Coordr* Elizabeth Fox; *VPres* Dorothy Council
Open Tues - Fri 10 AM - 4 PM, Sat Noon - 4 PM; No admis fee; Estab 1958 to promote the arts in the city of Franklin & the counties of Isle of Wight, Southampton, Surry & Sussex; Main gallery is 45 ft x 50 ft, 12 ft high with track lighting, adjunct Francis Gallery also has track lighting; Average Annual Attendance: 7,500; Mem: 248; dues $15 - $42, annual meeting in June, Board of Dir meet monthly
Income: $40,000 (financed by endowment, mem & grants)
Special Subjects: Crafts, Drawings, Glass, Painting-American, Photography, Silver, Watercolors, Portraits, Posters, Pottery
Collections: Antique glass & silver, Southeastern Virginia Artists, drawings, paintings, lithographs
Exhibitions: Annual Regional Photography Exhibition; two Annual Student Art Shows; regular group exhibitions by area artists; Virginia Museum of Fine Arts Traveling Exhibitions; annual regional exhibition
Publications: R M A Bulletin
Activities: Classes for adults & children; family fun events; intensive 4-6 hour educ outreach classes addressing SOL's for four school systems; lects open to pub, 4 vis lectrs per yr; concerts; gallery talks; tours; sponsoring of competitions; schols offered; paintings & art objects lent to mus & libraries; mus shop sells books, original art & prints

DANVILLE

M **DANVILLE MUSEUM OF FINE ARTS & HISTORY,** 975 Main St, Danville, VA 24541-1822. Tel 434-793-5644; Email mfo@danvillemuseum.org; Web: www.danvillemuseum.org; *Pres* Kristen Houser Barker; *Exec Dir* Richard A Loveland; *Museum Shop Mgr* CB Maddox
Open Tues - Sat 10 AM - 5 PM, Sun 2 - 5 PM; Admis adult $10; Estab 1974; Museum has two galleries: 27 x 35 ft with track lighting; one smaller gallery 24 x 17 ft with track lighting; Average Annual Attendance: 20,000; Mem: 400; dues $20 - $1,000
Income: Financed by mem, grants, fundraisers, class fees
Library Holdings: Auction Catalogs, Audio Tapes, Book Volumes, CD-ROMs, Exhibition Catalogs, Periodical Subscriptions
Special Subjects: Afro-American Art, Architecture, Art History, Carpets & Rugs, Coins & Medals, Costumes, Drawings, Embroidery, Etchings & Engravings, Folk Art, Furniture, Graphics, Historical Material, Laces, Landscapes, Maps, Medieval Art, Military Art, Painting-American, Painting-European, Period Rooms, Period Rooms, Portraits, Portraits, Prints, Sculpture, Tapestries, Textiles, Watercolors, Woodcarvings, Woodcuts, Textiles
Collections: American Costume Collection including 2 locally made crazy quilts, Civil War, emphasis on works by contemporary Southern & Mid-Atlantic Artists, historic artifacts & documents pertaining to the history of Danville, 19th & 20th century decorative arts including furniture, silver, porcelain, Victorian American paintings & works on paper 1932 - present
Exhibitions: Rotating schedule of art & history exhibitions; Survey shows highlighting historic & modern artists in movement; Historic exhibit includes restored period rooms, a Victorian parlor, bedroom & library; Between the Lines: 1861-1865
Publications: Last Capital of the Confederacy, book; Activities Report, quarterly newsletter
Activities: Classes for adults & children; Story Telling Festival (Feb); History on the Lawn (April) Art'Wine Show (May); Historical Halloween (Oct); season play series; lects open to pub, tours; awards, Danville Hall of Fame; lending of original objects of art to mus; mus shop sells books, original art, prints & souvenirs

FAIRFAX

L **PROVISIONS LIBRARY,** Provisions Research Center for Arts & Social Change, Art & Design Bldg Ste L002, George Mason University Fairfax, VA 22030. Tel 202-670-7768; Email provisionslibrary@gmail.com; Web: www.provisionslibrary.org; *Pres* Ethelbert Miller; *Dir & Cur* Donald Russell; *Dir Arts & Media* Niel Van Tomme
Open Tues - Fri noon - 5 PM; No admis fee, donations accepted; Estab 1993; Circ Non-circulating; Library, exhibs & educ progs linking contemporary global arts with social change issues; Average Annual Attendance: 10,000 - 49,999 by estimate
Library Holdings: Audio Tapes 300, Book Volumes 5000, Compact Disks 200, DVDs 200, Other Holdings 400 DVDs, Periodical Subscriptions 200, Video Tapes 200
Special Subjects: Afro-American Art, Art Education, Cartoons, Conceptual Art, Graphic Arts, Intermedia, Latin American Art, Photography, Video
Collections: Books, periodicals, audiovisuals & films on global social issues
Exhibitions: Close Encounters: Acts of Social Imagination; Revisiting Histories
Publications: Exhib catalogs
Activities: Research on global social change; formal educ progs for adults & col students; training progs for professional mus workers; guided tours; hobby workshops; participatory exhibs; study clubs; lects open to pub; 15 vis lectrs per yr; films; arts festivals; floating mus project; originate traveling exhibs to museums, universities & art centers

FARMVILLE

A **LONGWOOD CENTER FOR THE VISUAL ARTS,** 129 N Main St, Farmville, VA 23901-1305. Tel 804-395-2206; Fax 804-392-6441; Web: www.longwood.edu/lcva/; *Dir* Kay Johnson Bowles; *Prog Mgr* Beth Cheuk; *Colls Mgr* Ashley Webb; *Cur Educ* Emily Greshem; *Exhib Mgr* Alex Grabiec; *Mus Registrar* Robin Sedgwick; *Preparator* Brian Carley
Open Mon - Sat 11 AM - 5 PM; Admin offices open Mon - Fri 8:30 AM - 5 PM; No admis fee; Estab 1978; 27,000 sq ft facility incl the Miller Gallery, Bishop Gallery, Sully Gallery, & Main St Gallery as well as a Kids Activity room, classroom & multi-purpose room; Mem: Dues friend $1 - $99, advocate $100 - $249, fellow $250 - $499, collector $500 - $749, connoisseur $750 - $1249, benefactor $1250 - $2499, champion $2500 - 4999, patron $5000+
Special Subjects: African Art, Decorative Arts, Drawings, Folk Art, Glass, Painting-American, Photography, Porcelain, Pottery, Prints, Sculpture, Woodcarvings, Asian Art
Collections: Virginia Artists Collection: incl work by Theresa Pollak, Gene Davis, Nell Blaine, Sally Mann, Willie Ann Wright, Nancy Witt, Miles Carpenter, Marion Line & Kent Ipson, African Art Collection: incl statues, masks, drums, baskets & garments, American Art Collection: 400+ works by Thomas Sully, James McNeill Whistler, Robert Raushenberg, Gene Davis, Anna Hyatt Huntingdon, Lilly Martin Spencer, Sam Maloof, John Garland Brown, Albert Pinkham Ryder, Homer Martin Dodge, John Neagle & Eastman Johnson, Jackson L Blanton Collection: 450+ works by a variety of VA artists, Waverly Manson Cole Collection of 19th c Decorative Arts, William & Ann Oppenheimer Collection of Folk Art, Rowe Collection of Chinese Art
Activities: Classes for adults & children; lects open to pub; gallery talks; tours; slide presentation; originate traveling exhibs to rural communities in Southside Virginia

FREDERICKSBURG

M **JAMES MONROE MUSEUM,** 908 Charles St, Fredericksburg, VA 22401-5810. Tel 540-654-1043; Fax 540-654-1106; Web: www.jamesmonroemuseum.mwc.edu; *Dir* Scott Harris; *Cur* Jarod Kearney
Open Mar 1 - Nov 30 daily 10 AM - 5 PM, Dec 1 - Feb 28 daily 10 AM - 4 PM, cl Thanksgiving, Dec 24, 25, 31 & Jan 1; Admis adults $5, children 6-18 $1, children under 5 free; Estab 1927 to keep in memory the life & service of James Monroe & of his contribution to the principles of government, to preserve his treasured possessions for present & future generations; Open to the pub in 1928; owned by Commonwealth of Virginia & under the control of Univ of Mary Washington; a National Historic Landmark; Average Annual Attendance: 12,000; Mem: $25 & up
Income: financed by state funds
Special Subjects: Ceramics, Furniture, Jewelry, Portraits, Sculpture, Silver
Collections: Louis XVI furniture purchased by the Monroes in France in 1794 & later used by them in the White House, portraits, sculpture, silver, china, jewelry, books, documents
Exhibitions: Rotating exhibs
Publications: Images of a President: Portraits of James Monroe, catalog Library of James Monroe; catalog; A Presidential Legacy
Activities: Classes for children; docent training; workshops; lects open to pub; 2-4 vis lectrs per yr; gallery talks; tours; scholarships offered; exten dept serves Mary Washington College University of VA area; mus shop sells books, magazines, reproductions, prints, slides, history related objects & exclusive items from local crafts people

L **James Monroe Memorial Library,** 908 Charles St, Fredericksburg, VA 22401. Tel 540-654-1043; Fax 540-654-1106; Web: www.jamesmonroemuseum.mwc.edu; *Dir* John N Pearce; *Cur* David Voelkel
Open by appointment only; Admis adults $5, children 6-18 $1, children under 5 free; Estab 1927 as a presidential mus & library; Open to pub; archival resources available by appointment only; Average Annual Attendance: 12,000
Income: Financed by state allocations & revenues
Library Holdings: Book Volumes 10,000, Manuscripts 27,000, Other Holdings Documents; Letters

M **UNIVERSITY OF MARY WASHINGTON,** Gari Melchers Home and Studio, 224 Washington St, Fredericksburg, VA 22405-2360. Tel 540-654-1015; Fax 540-654-1785; Email garimelchers@umw.edu; Web: www.garimelchers.org; *Cur* Joanna D Catron; *Dir* David Berreth
Open daily 10 AM - 5 PM; Admis adults $10, seniors $9, adult groups $8, children between 6 & 18 $5; Estab 1975 to exhibit, preserve & interpret the works of art &

memorabilia of the late American artist Gari Melchers, in his former estate & studio; Studio consists of four gallery rooms, a work room & storage rooms; Average Annual Attendance: 13,000
Income: $800,000 (financed by endowment & state appropriation)
Library Holdings: Auction Catalogs, Exhibition Catalogs, Manuscripts, Memorabilia, Original Documents, Photographs
Special Subjects: Decorative Arts, Drawings, Furniture, Landscapes, Painting-American, Painting-Dutch, Painting-German, Painting-Italian, Period Rooms, Photography, Porcelain, Sculpture, Watercolors
Collections: Over six hundred works of art, paintings, drawings & etchings by Gari Melchers, Over 1,000 sketches & studies by Gari Melchers, Paintings & drawings by Berthe Morisot, Franz Snyders, Puvis de Chavannes & others, Furnishings from Europe & America
Publications: Exhibition catalogs
Activities: Docent training; educ prog; classes for adults & children; aesthetics tours for school groups; outreach progs for school & nursing homes; lects open to pub; 3 vis lectrs per year; gallery talks; tours; individual paintings & original objects of art lent; mus shop sells books, reproductions & prints

M **University of Mary Washington Galleries,** 1301 College Ave, at Seacobeck St Fredericksburg, VA 22401-5300. Tel 540-654-1013; Fax 540-654-1171; Web: www.umw.edu/umw-galleries; *Office Mgr* Angela Whitley; *Dir* Anne Timpano; *Asst Cur & Registrar* Kyra Swanson; *Vis Svcs Coordr* Justin Geiger
Open Mon, Wed & Fri 10 AM - 4 PM, Sat & Sun 1 - 4 PM; No admis fee; Estab 1956 for educ in art history & cultural history; Average Annual Attendance: 5,000
Special Subjects: Asian Art, Drawings, Etchings & Engravings, Landscapes, Painting-American, Photography, Portraits, Watercolors, Prints, Woodcuts
Collections: 19th & 20th Century American art, Asian Art
Exhibitions: Contemporary art; exhibs from permanent collection; faculty & student
Publications: Booklets; catalogs
Activities: Lects open to pub; 5 vis lectrs per yr; concerts; gallery talks; tours

GLEN ALLEN

M **COUNTY OF HENRICO,** Meadow Farm Museum, 3400 Mountain Rd, Glen Allen, VA; PO Box 27032, Richmond, VA 23273-7032. Tel 804-501-5520; Fax 804-501-5284; Web: www.co.henrico.va.us\rec; *Historic Preservation Supv* Chris Gregson; *Coll Mgr* Kimberly Sicola; *Asst Site Mgr* Linda Eikmeier
Open Tues - Sun Noon - 4 PM; No admis fee; Estab 1981 to exhibit works of 20th century American folk artists; 20 ft x 20 ft, AV room; Average Annual Attendance: 50,000
Income: Financed by Henrico County
Special Subjects: Afro-American Art, Archaeology, Architecture, Carpets & Rugs, Ceramics, Crafts, Decorative Arts, Embroidery, Folk Art, Furniture
Collections: 19th & 20th Century folk art
Exhibitions: Annual Folk-Art Exhibit
Publications: Exhibition flyers, annually
Activities: Children's classes; lect open to public, 4 vis lectrs per year; tours; individual paintings & original objects of art lent to Virginia Beach Art Center; lending collection contains original art works, paintings & sculptures; sales shop sells books & reproductions

L **Library,** 3400 Mountain Rd, Glen Allen, VA 23060; PO Box 27032, Richmond, VA 23273. Tel 804-501-5520; Fax 804-501-5284; *Site Mgr* Anna Beegles
Open by appointment only; For reference only
Library Holdings: Audio Tapes, Book Volumes 100, Clipping Files, Exhibition Catalogs, Kodachrome Transparencies, Periodical Subscriptions 10, Photographs, Slides, Video Tapes

M **THE CULTURAL ARTS CENTER AT GLEN ALLEN,** 2880 Mountain Rd, Glen Allen, VA 23060; PO Box 1249, Glen Allen, VA 23060-1249. Tel 804-261-2787; Fax 804-261-6217; Email info@glenallen.com; Web: www.artsglenallen.com; *Pres & Dir Programming* K Alferio; *Performing Arts Mgr & Technical Dir* Richard Koch; *Visual Arts Mgr* Lauren Hall; *Dir Develop* Molly Kaufman; *Dir Mktg & Pub Rels* Christopher Murphy; *Outreach Progs* Mackenzie Zahler
Call for hours; No admis fee with some ticketed events; Estab 1999; Two galleries feature regional, national, & international artists; Average Annual Attendance: 100,000
Collections: Paintings & photographs; art exhibitions
Activities: Classes for adults & children; dramatic program; sales shop sells books, original art, reproductions, prints, jewelry, apparel, home decor

L **ENVIRONIC FOUNDATION INTERNATIONAL LIBRARY,** 12035 Stonewick Pl, Glen Allen, VA 23059. Tel 804-360-9130; Email info@environicfoundation.org; Web: www.environicfoundation.org; *Pres* William R Godfrey; *Research Dir* Hannah Fuerhoff
Estab 1970 to provide educ that fosters sustainable innovation
Library Holdings: Clipping Files, Original Art Works, Slides, Video Tapes
Special Subjects: Advertising Design, Aesthetics, Anthropology, Archaeology, Architecture, Furniture, Graphic Design, Interior Design, Landscape Architecture, Landscapes, Lettering, Painting-British, Period Rooms, Stained Glass, Watercolors

HAMPTON

A **CITY OF HAMPTON,** Hampton Arts Commission, 4205 Victoria Blvd, Hampton, VA 23669; 125 E Mellen St, Hampton, VA 23663-1711. Tel 757-722-2787; 757-727-1621; Fax 757-727-1167; Email amtheater@city.hampton.va.us; Web: www.amtheatre.com; *Dir* Michael P Curry; *Arts Coordr* Debra Burrell; *Production Mgr* Mary Blackwell; *Box Office Mgr* Mildred Williams
Open Art Center: year round Tues - Fri 10 AM - 6 PM, Sat - Sun 1 - 5 PM, cl major holidays; Theatre: Mon - Fri 9 AM - 5:30 PM; No admis fee; Created in Dec, 1987, housed in the Charles H Taylor Arts Center
Income: Financed by municipal funds & contributions
Library Holdings: Cards
Exhibitions: Regional artists presented at Charles H Taylor Arts Center, monthly; special events art shows; performances by international artists presented at the American Theatre
Activities: Classes for adults & children; master classes in drama & music; dramatic progs; workshops; demonstrations; lects open to pub; lects for mem only; 12 vis lectrs per yr; concerts; gallery talks; tours; competitions with awards; lending to selected bus; 1 - 2 book traveling exhibs

M **HAMPTON UNIVERSITY,** University Museum, 11 Frissell Ave, Hampton, VA 23663-2340. Tel 757-727-5308; Fax 757-727-5170; Email museum@hamptonu.edu; Web: www.hamptonu.edu/museum; *Dir* Dr Nashid Madyun; *Cur Colls* Dr Vanessa Thaxton-Ward
Open Mon - Fri 8 AM - 5 PM, Sat & Sun Noon - 4 PM, cl Sun; No admis fee; Estab 1868 as a museum of traditional art & artifacts from African, Asian, Oceanic & American Indian cultures & contemporary & traditional African-American Art; Average Annual Attendance: 60,000; Mem: Dues start at $25, students $15
Income: Financed by college funds
Special Subjects: African Art, Afro-American Art, American Indian Art
Collections: African, Asian, Oceanic & American Indian Art, Contemporary & traditional African-American Art, artwork & objects relating to history of university, university archives
Publications: The International Journal of African American Art
Activities: Educ dept; lects open to pub; gallery talks; group tours by appointment; Governor's Award for Artistic Org 2008-2009; individual paintings & original objects of art lent to other mus & art galleries with appropriate security; sales shop sells books, magazines & prints

M **HEADQUARTERS FORT MONROE, DEPT OF ARMY,** Casemate Museum, 20 Bernard Rd, Hampton, VA 23651-1004; PO Box 51341, Hampton, VA 23663-0341. Tel 757-788-3935; Fax 757-788-3886; Email claire.samuelson@us.army.mil; *Cur* Claire Samuelson; *Mus Specialist* David J Johnson
Open daily 10:30 AM - 4:30 PM; No admis fee; Estab 1951 to depict history of Fort Monroe; Average Annual Attendance: 40,000; Mem: 250; dues one-time-only fee based on plateaus: annual meeting in mid-Jan
Income: Financed by federal & state appropriation
Library Holdings: Micro Print, Motion Pictures, Original Art Works, Photographs, Prints, Sculpture, Slides
Special Subjects: Architecture, Cartoons, Ceramics, Coins & Medals, Decorative Arts, Drawings, Etchings & Engravings, Furniture, Glass, Graphics, Historical Material, Leather, Manuscripts, Maps, Military Art, Painting-American, Period Rooms, Photography, Porcelain, Posters, Pottery, Prints, Reproductions, Silver, Stained Glass, Watercolors
Collections: Military Posters, Jack Clifton Paintings Collection
Exhibitions: Civil War Artifacts; Coast Artillery Guns in Action; Glass Bottles
Publications: Exhibition catalogs
Activities: Docent training; lects provided upon request to local organizations; tours; originate traveling exhibs 3 per yr; mus shop sells books, reproductions, prints

HARRISONBURG

M **JAMES MADISON UNIVERSITY,** Duke Hall Gallery of Fine Art, MSC 7101, 820 S Main St, Duke Hall, Rm 101 Harrisonburg, VA 22807. Tel 540-568-6407; Fax 540-568-5862; Email freebugl@jmu.edu; Web: www.jmu.edu/artandarthistory; *Gallery Dir* Gary Freeburg
Open Sept - Apr, Mon - Fri 10 AM -5PM, Sat noon - 5PM, May - Aug call for summer schedule & hours; No admis fee; Estab 1967 to schedule changing exhibitions for the benefit of students and citizens of this area; One-room gallery of 3,000 sq ft with movable panels; Average Annual Attendance: 10,000 - 12,000
Income: Financed by state appropriation, and is part of operation in Art Dept budget
Special Subjects: Antiquities-Greek, Antiquities-Roman, Asian Art
Collections: Sawhill Collection, mainly artifacts from classical civilizations, Staples Collection of Indonesian Art
Exhibitions: Rotating exhibitions
Activities: Lects open to pub; competitions; concerts; gallery talks; tours

VIRGINIA QUILT MUSEUM, 301 S Main St, Harrisonburg, VA 22801-2606. Tel 540-433-3818; Fax 540-433-3818
Open Feb-Dec Tues-Sat 10AM-4PM; cl major holidays; Admis adults $5, students 12-18 $3, youth 5-11 $2, children under 5 free
Collections: early & contemporary quilts; quilting; sewing machines

HERNDON

INDUSTRIAL DESIGNERS SOCIETY OF AMERICA
For further information, see National and Regional Organizations

LEESBURG

M **OATLANDS PLANTATION,** 20850 Oatlands Plantation Lane, Leesburg, VA 20175. Tel 703-777-3174; Fax 703-777-4427; *Events Coordr* Jeannie Whitty; *Mgr* David Boyce
Open Apr - Dec, Mon - Fri 10 AM - 5 PM, Sat 9:30 AM - 5 PM, Sun 1 - 5 PM, cl Thanksgiving Day, Christmas, New Year's; Admis adults $8, seniors & youths (7-18) $7, children (5-11) $1; special events at special rates, group rates by arrangement, free to National Trust members & friends except for special events; Oatlands is a Classical Revival Mansion constructed by George Carter, son of Robert (Councillor) Carter (c 1800-06). It was partially remodeled in 1827 when the front portico with hand carved Corinthian capitals was added. Confederate troops were billeted here during part of the Civil War. The home remained in possession of the Carters until 1897. In 1903 Mr & Mrs William Corcoran Eustis, of Washington DC, bought Oatlands. Their daughters gave the property to the National Trust for

Historic Preservation; the property is protected by preservation easements which help ensure the estates continuing role as a center for equestrian sports & cultural events which are produced by Oatlands & various groups
Income: $600,000 (financed by grants, endowments, admis, fundraising events & shop sales)
Special Subjects: Furniture, Period Rooms
Collections: Greek-Revival ornaments adorn interior, Carter & Eustis Collection of Furniture
Exhibitions: Annual needlework Show; Christmas at Oatlands; semi annual Antique Show
Publications: Oatlands Column, quarterly newsletter
Activities: Special events

LEXINGTON

M **WASHINGTON & LEE UNIVERSITY,** Gallery of DuPont Hall, 204 W Washington St, Lexington, VA 24450-2116. Tel 540-463-8861; Fax 540-463-8104; Web: www.wlu.edu; *Dir* Kathleen Olsen; *Chmn Dept Art* Pamela Simpson
Open Mon - Fri 9 AM - 5 PM, Sat 11 AM - 3 PM, Sun 2 - 4 PM; No admis fee; Estab 1929 in separate gallery as teaching resource of art; One room, 30 x 60 ft, is maintained for temporary exhibits; also maintained one storeroom; Average Annual Attendance: 40,000
Income: Financed through the university
Exhibitions: Annual faculty show; annual student show; monthly exhibitions; traveling exhibitions
Publications: Exhibition catalogs
Activities: Lect open to public, 5 vis lectrs per year; gallery talks; tours; book traveling exhibitions 3 per year

L **Leyburn Library,** 204 W Washington St, Lexington, VA 24450-2116. Tel 540-458-8644; Fax 540-458-8964; Email merrilly@wlu.edu; Web: www.library.wlu.edu; *Art Librn* Yolanda Merrill; *Head Librn* John Tombarge; *Sr Reference Librn* Dick Grefe
Open 24 hours a day during school yr, summer Mon - Fri 8:30 AM - 4:30 PM; Open for reference to students, scholars, public; this library is part of the main university library
Collections: Rare books, 17th - early 20th centuries

M **Lee Chapel & Museum,** 204 W Washington St, Lexington, VA 24450-2116. Tel 540-463-8768; Web: www.leechapel.wlu.edu; *Dir* Patricia Hobbs
Open Apr 1- Oct 31 Mon - Sat 9 AM - 5 PM, Sun 1 - 5 PM, Nov 1-Mar 31 Mon - Sat 9 AM - 4 PM, Sun 1 PM - 4 PM; No admis fee; Estab 1868 as a part of the university. It is used for concerts, speeches & other events; Museum relates the history of the university and its ties to its namesakes and is used also to display the paintings, collections & personal items of the Washington & Lee families. The Lee Chapel is a National Historic Landmark; Average Annual Attendance: 55,000
Income: Financed through the university
Special Subjects: Historical Material, Painting-American, Period Rooms, Portraits
Collections: Washington-Custis-Lee Art Collection, Lee archives, Lee family crypt, Lee's office, recumbent statute of General Lee by Valentine
Publications: Brochure
Activities: Mus shop sells books, reproductions, prints & related merchandise

LORTON

M **LORTON ARTS FOUNDATION,** (Workhouse Arts Center) Workhouse Arts Center, 9601 Ox Rd, Lorton, VA 22079. Tel 703-584-2900; Fax 703-690-1880; Email info@workhousearts.org; Web: www.workhousearts.org; *Pres & CEO* John Mason; *Dir Visual Arts* Brett John Johnson
Open Wed - Sat 11 AM - 6 PM, Sun noon - 5 PM; No admis fee; Estab 2008; cultural arts center; A unique arts center that provides visual & performing arts, arts educ & entertainment; Average Annual Attendance: 173,000
Exhibitions: Ongoing monthly exhibs
Activities: Classes for adults & children; dramatic progs; docent training; lects open to pub; 6-10 vis lectrs per yr; concerts; gallery talks; tours; sponsoring of competitions; schols; extension prog to northern VA & DC; sales shop sells original art, reproductions & prints

LYNCHBURG

A **ACADEMY OF FINE ARTS,** (Lynchburg Fine Arts Center Inc), 600 Main St, Lynchburg, VA 24504-1322. Tel 434-528-3256; Fax 434-528-5841; Email Info@AcademyFineArts.com; Web: www.AcademyFinearts.com; *Exec Dir* Richard S Kordos; *Dir Educ* Kelly Allen; *Exhib Cur* Ted Batt
Open Mon - Fri 9 AM - 5 PM, Sat by appt; Estab 2003 through merger of Lynchburg Fine Arts Ctr & Academy of Music; Maintains Academy Gallery & Art UpFront at 600 Main St, & mixed media exhibits in the lobby of The Arts and Education Bldg at Commerce & 5th Streets in historic Downtown Lynchburg

L **JONES MEMORIAL LIBRARY,** 2311 Memorial Ave, Lynchburg, VA 24501-2648. Tel 804-846-0501; *Dir* Edward Gibson
No admis fee; Estab 1907; For reference
Income: $180,000 (financed by endowment & donations)
Purchases: $5,000
Library Holdings: Book Volumes 20,000, Clipping Files, Exhibition Catalogs, Manuscripts, Memorabilia, Original Art Works, Other Holdings Architectural drawings, Periodical Subscriptions 45, Photographs, Sculpture
Special Subjects: Architecture, Drawings, Historical Material
Collections: Lynchburg Architectural Archives

M **LYNCHBURG COLLEGE,** Daura Gallery, 1501 Lakeside Dr, Lynchburg, VA 24501-3113. Tel 804-544-8343; Fax 804-544-8277; Email rothermel@lynchburg.edu; Web: www.lynchburg.edu/daura; *Dir* Barbara Rothermel, PhD; *Asst Dir* Steve Riffee, MFA; *Admin Asst* Laurie Cassidy
Open Mon - Fri 9 AM - 4 PM, (acad yr) or by appointment; No admis fee; Estab 1974 to supplement & support the acad curriculum of Lynchburg College; Average Annual Attendance: 5,000; Mem: 200
Income: Financed by endowment & Lynchburg College
Library Holdings: Book Volumes, Exhibition Catalogs
Special Subjects: Drawings, Etchings & Engravings, Painting-American, Painting-Spanish, Sculpture
Collections: American & Virginia Art, Pierre Daura (paintings, sculpture, works on paper), Works on Paper, African art
Publications: Exhibit brochures, 3-4 per year
Activities: Lects open to pub, 6 vis lectrs per yr; gallery talks; tours; book traveling exhibs, 1 per yr; circulate through Virginia Museum of Fine Arts, Statewide Exhibits Prog, AAMG, VAM, all others by request

M **RANDOLPH COLLEGE,** Maier Museum of Art, 1 Quinlan St, Lynchburg, VA 24503-1526; 2500 Rivermont Ave, Lynchburg, VA 24503-1526. Tel 434-947-8136; Fax 434-947-8726; Email museum@randolphcollege.edu; Web: www.maiermuseum.org; *Dir* Martha K Johnson; *Registrar* Deborah Spanich; *Mus Preparator* John Spanich; *Gallery Monitor* Anne McDaniel; *Curator of Education* Laura McManus
Open Sept - May Tues - Sun 1 - 5 PM, cl Mon; open Jun - Aug Wed - Sun 1 - 4 PM; No admis fee; American Art Collection estab 1920 to promote scholarship through temporary exhibitions & collection; Building currently housing collection built in 1952. 5 galleries contain more than 75 paintings from the permanent collection by American artists. One gallery is used for the 4 to 6 temporary exhibitions displayed each acad yr; Average Annual Attendance: 7,400; Mem: 160; dues $35+
Income: Financed by endowment
Purchases: Joseph Cornell (collage); Jamie Wyeth (watercolor); John Frederick Peto (oil); Jennifer Bartlett (work on paper)
Special Subjects: Ceramics, Collages, Drawings, Etchings & Engravings, Folk Art, Landscapes, Marine Painting, Painting-American, Photography, Portraits, Prints, Religious Art, Textiles, Woodcarvings
Collections: collection of 19th, 20th & 21st Century American paintings, European & American graphics
Exhibitions: Rotating exhibits, exhibit featuring pieces from collection; Annual exhib of contemporary art, Sept-Dec
Publications: Annual exhibition catalogue; biannual newsletter
Activities: Classes for children; docent training; lects open to pub, 3-5 vis lectrs per yr; concerts; gallery talks; tours; Calvert Writing Award; objects of art lent to other mus; originate traveling exhibs; mus shop sells books, exhib catalogs, stationary & reproductions

MARTINSVILLE

M **PIEDMONT ARTS ASSOCIATION,** 215 Starling Ave, Martinsville, VA 24112-3832. Tel 276-632-3221; Fax 276-638-3963; Email paa@piedmontarts.org; Web: www.piedmontarts.org; *Dir Finance & Facility* Pam Allen; *Admin Asst* Barbara Bradshaw; *Asst Dir & Dir Exhib* Branden Adams; *Exec Dir* Kathy Rogers; *Dir Mktg* Bernadette Moore; *Dir Programs* Barbara Parker; *Educ Coordr* Heidi Pinkston
Open Mon - Fri 10 AM - 5 PM, Sat 10 AM - 3 PM, Sun 1:30 - 4:30 PM, cl Mon; No admis fee; Estab 1961 to encourage & develop awareness & appreciation of the arts & provide an opportunity for participation in the arts; Five professionally furnished galleries: two feature artists with extensive show experience & reputation, one features work by both established & emerging artists, one features work by students from local schools & one features small exhibitions of local interest; Average Annual Attendance: 35,000; Mem: 1,000; dues patrons $150 & up, family $50, single $35, senior & student $25
Income: $350,000 (financed by endowment, mem, city & state appropriations, federal government & grants from foundations)
Special Subjects: African Art, Afro-American Art, American Indian Art, American Western Art, Painting-American, Painting-British, Painting-European, Painting-Flemish, Painting-French, Painting-German, Painting-Israeli, Photography, Porcelain, Portraits, Posters, Pottery, Prints, Religious Art, Reproductions, Sculpture, Silver, Southwestern Art, Stained Glass, Textiles, Watercolors
Exhibitions: Rotating exhibits
Publications: The Arts & You, bi-monthly newsletter
Activities: Classes for adults & children; dramatic progs; docent training; performing arts series; lects open to pub, 1 vis lectrs per yr; concerts; gallery talks; tours; sponsoring of competitions with awards; schols offered; book traveling exhibs 5-6 per yr

MASON NECK

M **GUNSTON HALL PLANTATION,** 10709 Gunston Rd, Mason Neck, VA 22079-3901. Tel 703-550-9220; Fax 703-550-9480; Email historic@gunstonhall.org; Web: www.gunstonhall.org; *Asst Dir* Susan A Borchardt; *Dir* Thomas A Lainhoff
Open daily 9:30 AM - 5 PM, cl Thanksgiving, Christmas, New Years Day; Admis adults $7, seniors/groups $6, students (6-18) $3; Estab 1950 to acquaint the pub with George Mason, colonial patriot & his 18th century house & gardens, covering 555 acres; Owned & operated by the Commonwealth of Virginia; Average Annual Attendance: 50,000; Mem: 2,200
Income: Financed by state appropriation & admis fee
Special Subjects: Decorative Arts, Furniture, Historical Material, Painting-American, Restorations, Painting-British
Collections: 18th & 19th century family pieces
Activities: Classes for children; docent training; lect open to public, 8-12 vis lectrs per year; tours; individual paintings & original objects of art lent to other museums; sales shop sells books, reproductions; Children's Touch Museum located in basement

L **Library,** 10709 Gunston Rd, Mason Neck, VA 22079. Tel 703-550-9220; Fax 703-550-9480; Email library@gunstonhall.org; Web: www.gunstonhall.org; *Dir* David Reese; *Cur* Susan Borchardt; *Librn* Mark Whatford; *Cur* Caroline Riley

Open Mon - Fri 9:30 AM - 5 PM & by appointment, cl Thanksgiving, Christmas & New Year's Day; Estab 1950 to recreate the 18th Century home of George Mason IV as a research source plus acquiring a working reference collection on George Mason, early Virginia history & the decorative arts; Average Annual Attendance: 50,000
Income: Financed by endowment
Library Holdings: Auction Catalogs, Book Volumes 11,000, Cassettes, Exhibition Catalogs, Fiche, Filmstrips, Manuscripts, Memorabilia, Motion Pictures, Other Holdings Original documents, Pamphlets, Periodical Subscriptions 50, Photographs, Reels, Reproductions
Special Subjects: Archaeology, Architecture, Decorative Arts, Furniture, Historical Material, Manuscripts, Period Rooms, Pewter, Porcelain, Portraits, Prints, Restoration & Conservation, Silver, Textiles
Collections: Robert Carter Collection, Pamela C Copeland Collection, Elizabeth L Frelinghuysen Collection, Mason-Mercer Rare Book Collection

MIDDLETOWN

M **BELLE GROVE INC,** Belle Grove Plantation, 336 Belle Grove Rd, Middletown, VA 22645; PO Box 537, Middletown, VA 22645-0537. Tel 540-869-2028; Fax 540-869-9638; Email info@bellegrove.org; Web: www.bellegrove.org; *Exec Dir* Kristen Laise; *Outreach & Vol Coordr* Karen Haizlett; *Bldg & Grounds Supv* Dennis Campbell; *Mus Shop Mgr* Karen Schmedding
Open Mar - Oct Mon - Sat 10 AM - 4 PM, Sun 1 - 5 PM; Admis adults $12, seniors $11, student $6, special rates for groups; Open to the pub in 1967, it is preserved as a historic house & is the property of the National Trust for Historic Preservation & managed by Belle Grove, Inc, an independent local nonprofit organization. It serves as a local preservation center & resource for the interpretation of regional culture in the Shenandoah Valley; Built in 1797 for Major Isaac Hite, Jr, a Revolutionary War officer & bro-in-law of James Madison, Belle Grove was designed with the help of Thomas Jefferson. During the Battle of Cedar Creek in 1864, the house served as headquarters to General Phillip Sheridan. The property is a working farm & has an active schedule of annual special events; Average Annual Attendance: 15,000
Library Holdings: Book Volumes, Cassettes, Clipping Files, Maps, Memorabilia, Original Art Works, Original Documents, Pamphlets, Periodical Subscriptions, Photographs, Prints, Reproductions, Video Tapes
Special Subjects: Architecture, Decorative Arts, Furniture, Painting-American, Period Rooms, Portraits, Restorations
Collections: Antique collectibles
Exhibitions: Four Portraits by Charles Peale Polk: Colonel James Madison, Nelly Conway Madison-Hite, Major Isaac Hite, Mrs James Madison
Publications: The Women of Belle Grove; Belle Grove in The Civil War
Activities: Docent training; lect open to public; 1-2 vis lectrs per year; tours; mus shop sells books, reproductions, prints, gifts; Original art; local artisans

MOUNT VERNON

M **GEORGE WASHINGTON'S MOUNT VERNON,** PO Box 110, George Washington's Mt Vernon Estate & Gardens Mount Vernon, VA 22121-0110. Tel 703-780-2000; Fax 703-799-8698; Web: www.mountvernon.org; *Regent* Barbara Lucas; *Cur* Susan Schoelwer; *Pres & CEO* Curt Viebranz; *Sr Cur & VPres* Carol Cadou
Open daily 8 AM - 5 PM: entrance gate closes Mar 1 - Oct 1 at 5 PM, Oct 2 - Mar 2 at 4 PM; Admis annual pass $25, adults $15, $7.50 for groups of 12 or more children or groups of 20 or more adults, student groups $4.50, adults over 62 $14, children 6-11 $7, children under 6 free; Estab 1853; The home of George Washington, purchased in 1858 from his great-grand-nephew by the Mount Vernon Ladies Assoc of the Union, which maintains it. The estate includes Washington'&s private residence, restored flower & kitchen gardens, the tombs of George & Martha Washington, a four acre farm site with a reconstruction of Washington's sixteen sided treading barn & a new state-of-the-art Ford Orientation Center & Donald W Reynolds Mus & Educ Center. Mount Vernon also maintains Washington'&s Gristmill & Distillery & library for the study of George Washington; Average Annual Attendance: 1,000,000; Mem: Semi-annual meeting Oct & Apr
Income: Financed by admis fees & donations
Library Holdings: Auction Catalogs, Book Volumes, Clipping Files, DVDs, Exhibition Catalogs, Fiche, Lantern Slides, Manuscripts, Maps, Memorabilia, Motion Pictures, Original Documents, Pamphlets, Periodical Subscriptions, Photographs, Slides, Video Tapes
Special Subjects: Furniture, Period Rooms
Collections: Mansion is fully furnished with original & period furniture, silver, portraits & prints, large coll of original Washington memorabilia, manuscripts & books, George Washington Memorabilia
Publications: Annual Report; The Gardens & Grounds at Mount Vernon; George Washington, A Brief Biography; The Last Will & Testament of George Washington; The Maxims of Washington; Mount Vernon; The Mount Vernon Coloring Book; The Mount Vernon Cookbook; The Mount Vernon Gardens; Mount Vernon Handbook; Nothing More Agreeable: Music in George Washington's Family; George Washington: Citizen - Soldier
Activities: Educ prog; teacher Institute; lects open to pub; lects for mems only; 3 vis lectrs per yr; concerts; tours; awards include Washington Book Prize; Mount Vernon History Teacher of the Year Award; Fred W Smith National Library Fellowship; book traveling exhibs; Sales shop sells books, reproductions, prints, coloring books, t-shirts, food & Christmas items

L **The Fred W Smith National Library for the Study of George Washington**, 3600 Mt Vernon Memorial Hwy, Mount Vernon, VA 22121. Tel 703-780-3600; Email fwslibrary@mountvernon.org; Web: www.mountvernon.org; *Libr Dir* Douglas Bradburn; *Chief Librn & Archivist* Mark Santangelo; *Pres & CEO* Curt Viebranz
Open library Mon - Fri 9 AM - 5 PM, appt required; estate & mus April - Aug Mon - Fri 8 AM - 5 PM; Mar, Sept, Oct 9 AM - 5 PM; Nov - Feb 9 AM - 4 PM
Library Holdings: Auction Catalogs, Book Volumes, Clipping Files, DVDs, Exhibition Catalogs, Fiche, Filmstrips, Lantern Slides, Manuscripts, Maps, Memorabilia, Motion Pictures, Original Art Works, Original Documents, Other Holdings, Pamphlets, Periodical Subscriptions, Photographs, Prints, Reproductions, Sculpture, Slides, Video Tapes
Special Subjects: Archaeology, Decorative Arts, Furniture, Historical Material, Landscape Architecture, Manuscripts, Maps, Painting-American
Collections: George & Martha Washington's home objects, books manuscripts, Library, archives of the Mount Vernon Ladies Assoc, mus, Washington family, agriculture, Mount Vernon, 18th century life
Activities: Classes for children; training for educators; lects open to pub; 12-15 vis lects; gallery talks; tours; awards; leadership prog; fels; mus shop sells books, magazines, original art, reproductions, prints & other items; jr mus, educ center

NEWPORT NEWS

M **THE MARINERS' MUSEUM,** 100 Museum Dr, Newport News, VA 23606-3759. Tel 757-596-2222; Fax 757-591-7311; Email info@mariner.org; Web: www.mariner.org; WATS 800-581-7245; *VPres Develop & External Relations* Anna Norville; *Pres* Howard Hoege III; *Chmn* Anne C H Conner; *VPres Colls & Chief Cur* Lyles Forbes
Open Mon - Sat 9 AM - 5 PM, Sun 11 AM - 5 PM, cl Thanksgiving & Christmas; Admis adults $13.95, seniors & military $12.95, children (4-12) $8.95, mem & children ages 5 & under free, discounts offered for active duty military, AAA members & sr citizens, group rate for party of 10 or more; Estab 1930 as an educational, nonprofit institution accredited by the American Assoc of Museums, preserves & interprets maritime history & other maritime artifacts. Costumed interpreters & film Mariner, help maritime history come alive; Located in a 550 acre park which features the 5 mile Noland Trail. Museum has twelve permanent galleries, including Age of Exploration & Chesapeake galleries; paintings & decorative arts; Crabtree Collection of miniature ships; collection of International Small Craft; Great Hall of Steam; William F Gibbs: Naval Architect Gallery. Maintains reference library; Average Annual Attendance: 100,000; Mem: 2,500
Special Subjects: Anthropology, Bookplates & Bindings, Ceramics, Coins & Medals, Crafts, Decorative Arts, Dioramas, Drawings, Etchings & Engravings, Ethnology, Folk Art, Graphics, Historical Material, Ivory, Manuscripts, Maps, Marine Painting, Military Art, Painting-American, Painting-Dutch, Painting-French, Painting-Japanese, Photography, Portraits, Posters, Pottery, Pre-Columbian Art, Primitive art, Prints, Scrimshaw, Sculpture, Stained Glass, Watercolors, Woodcarvings, Woodcuts
Collections: Crabtree Collection of miniature ships, thousands of marine artifacts, over 1,000 paintings, over 1,000 ship models
Publications: Mariners' Museum Pipe, quarterly newsletter; Mariners' Museum Annual, annual journal
Activities: Classes for adults & children; docent training; lects open to members, 6 vis lectrs per yr; concerts; gallery talks; tours; competitions with awards; schols & fellowships offered; individual paintings & original objects of art lent to mus; collection contains 120 motion pictures, 2,000 original art works, 8,000 original prints, 1,300 paintings; mus shop sells books, magazines, reproductions, prints, slides, jewelry & other maritime related items

L **Library**, 100 Museum Dr, Newport News, VA 23606-3759. Tel 757-591-7782; Fax 757-591-7310; Email library@marinersmuseum.org; Web: www.marinersmuseum.org/library; *Librn, Tech Svcs* Jennifer Anielski; *Asst Archivist* Bill Barker
Temporarily closed to the public; No admis fee; Estab 1930; For reference only
Income: Financed by endowment
Library Holdings: Auction Catalogs, Book Volumes 75,000, Clipping Files, Exhibition Catalogs, Manuscripts, Memorabilia, Other Holdings Original documents, Pamphlets, Periodical Subscriptions 150, Photographs 350,000, Prints
Special Subjects: Anthropology, Art History, Crafts, Decorative Arts, Drafting, Eskimo Art, Flasks & Bottles, Handicrafts, History of Art & Archaeology, Manuscripts, Maps, Marine Painting, Painting-American, Painting-British, Painting-Dutch, Archaeology, Scrimshaw

A **PENINSULA FINE ARTS CENTER,** 101 Museum Dr, Newport News, VA 23606-3758. Tel 757-596-8175; Fax 757-596-0807; Email info@pfac.va.org; Web: www.pfac-va.org; *Exec Dir* Courtney Gardner; *Cur* Diana Blanchard Gross; *Dir Mktg & Community Engagement* Janelle Burchfield
Open Tues - Sat 10 AM - 5 PM, Sun 1 - 5 PM; Admis adults $7.50, students, seniors, & AAA $6, children 6-12 $4, children 5 & under free; Estab 1962 to promote an appreciation of the fine arts through changing exhibitions with works from the Virginia Mus, other institutions & outstanding artists, both emerging & estab; Three galleries maintained with changing exhibitions; Average Annual Attendance: 40,000; Mem: 1,200+; dues family (incl mem) $60, individual $40
Income: Financed by mem
Library Holdings: DVDs, Exhibition Catalogs, Photographs, Records, Slides
Exhibitions: local, regional, & international art; Diverse rotating exhibition schedule that includes works ranging from historic to contemporary in a range of media
Publications: Art class schedules; e-newsletter to members, monthly; notification of spec events
Activities: Classes for adults & children; lects open to public, lects for mems only, 4 vis lectrs per year; concerts, gallery talks, tours; competitions with awards; cash awards & cert of distinction for college & high school art; originates traveling exhibs to schools, libraries & other art organizations; mus shop sells books, original art, prints, jewelry, accessories & crafts

NORFOLK

M **CHRYSLER MUSEUM OF ART,** 245 W Olney Rd, Norfolk, VA 23510-1587; One Memorial Place, Norfolk, VA 23510. Tel 757-664-6200; Fax 757-664-6201; Email info@chrysler.org; Web: www.chrysler.org; *Dir* Erik H Neil; *Dir Devel* Kate Wilson; *Dir Opers & CFO* Dana Fuqua; *Deputy Dir Colls & Exhibs* Susan Leidy; *Chief Cur* Lloyd DeWitt; *Acting Mgr Glass Studio* Robin Rogers; *Director of Communs* Meredith Gray; *Dir Visitor Servs* Colleen Higginbotham; *Dir Educ & Pub Progs* Anne Corso
Open Tues - Sat 10 AM -5 PM, Sun noon - 5 PM, cl Mon; No admis fee for permanent coll, donations accepted; fees apply to special exhibs; Mus originates

from a memorial assoc estab in 1901 to house a coll of tapestries & paintings donated in memory of & by Irene Leache. The Norfolk Society of Arts was founded in 1917, which raised funds throughout the 1920s to erect a building to permanently hold the collection. Norfolk Museum of Arts & Sciences opened in 1933. After a large donation by Walter Chrysler, Jr, the museum became the Chrysler Museum of Art in 1971.; A Florentine Renaissance style building, named the Norfolk Museum of Arts & Sciences, opened to the pub in 1933. The Houston Wing, housing the Museum Theatre & Lounge, was added in 1956, the Centennial Wing in 1976 & another wing to house the library & additional galleries was opened in 1989. The building has been designated the Chrysler Museum since 1971, when a large portion of the collection of Walter P Chrysler, Jr was given to Norfolk. Mus contains 140,000 sq ft; Average Annual Attendance: 200,000; Mem: 4,500; dues Masterpiece Society Benefactor $10,000; Masterpiece Society Patron $5,000; Masterpiece Society Sponsor $2,500; Dir Circle $1,000; Patron $500; Assoc $100; Household $60 (seniors 65 & up, students, teachers & active-duty military $50); Individual $45 (seniors age 65 & up, students, teachers and active-duty military $35); Corporate memberships available
Income: Financed by municipal appropriation & state appropriations as well as federal grants
Library Holdings: Auction Catalogs, Book Volumes, Clipping Files, Exhibition Catalogs, Framed Reproductions, Manuscripts, Memorabilia, Original Documents, Pamphlets, Periodical Subscriptions, Reproductions, Video Tapes
Special Subjects: Antiquities-Greek, Antiquities-Roman, Decorative Arts, Glass, Oriental Art, Painting-American, Painting-Dutch, Painting-Flemish, Painting-French, Painting-Italian, Sculpture, Photography
Collections: African artists, American art from 18th century primitives - 20th century Pop Art, incl painting & sculpture, Bernini's Bust of the Savior, Francoise Boucher, The Vegetable Vendor, Mary Cassatt, The Family, Thomas Cole, The Angel Appearing to the Shepherds, Decorative arts including furniture, silver, gold, enameled objects & Worcester porcelain, 18th century English paintings, 14th-18th century Italian paintings, 15th-18th century Netherlandish & German works, Gaugin's Loss of Virginity, Bernice Chrysler Garbisch & Edgar William Garbish Native American paintings, Institute of Glass, Matisse, Bowl of Apples on a Table, Near & Far East Artists, Oriental artists, photography coll including Alexander Gardner, Lewis W Hine, Walker Evans, Ansel Adams, W Eugene Smith & contemporaries Joel Meyerowitz & Sheila Metzner, Pre-Columbian artists, Reni, The Meeting of David & Abigail, 16th - 20th century French paintings, works from Spanish school, 8,000 object glass coll including Tiffany glass, English cameo glass & contemporary glass sculpture
Publications: Monthly members' newsletter; exhibition catalogues; Annual Report; quarterly magazine
Activities: Educ prog; family progs; classes for adults & children; docent training; teacher workshops; outreach information packages; lects open to pub, 15 vis lectrs per yr; concerts; gallery talks; tours; competitions (juried); exten dept operates three historic homes; individual paintings & original objects of art lent to accredited mus; Hampton Roads; book traveling exhibs; originates traveling exhibs; mus shop sells books, prints; reproductions; original art

L **Jean Outland Chrysler Library**, One Memorial Place, Norfolk, VA 23510-1587. Tel 757-965-2035; Fax 757-664-6291; Email library@chrysler.org; Web: www.chrysler.org; *Dickson Librn* Allison Termine
Open Tues - Thurs 10:30 AM - 3:30 PM; No admis fee; Estab 1933 to collect materials in support of the collections of the Chrysler Mus; Circ Non-circulating; Open to the pub for reference only; Average Annual Attendance: 2,000
Income: Financed partially by endowment
Library Holdings: Auction Catalogs, Audio Tapes, Book Volumes 100,000, CD-ROMs, Clipping Files, DVDs, Exhibition Catalogs, Fiche, Manuscripts, Maps, Original Documents, Other Holdings, Pamphlets, Periodical Subscriptions 200, Photographs, Video Tapes
Special Subjects: Aesthetics, Afro-American Art, American Indian Art, Anthropology, Antiquities-Byzantine, Archaeology, Art Education, Art History, Asian Art, Bookplates & Bindings, Bronzes, Calligraphy, Carpets & Rugs, Cartoons, Ceramics, Coins & Medals, Collages, Commercial Art, Conceptual Art, Costume Design & Constr, Crafts, Decorative Arts, Dioramas, Display, Dolls, Drafting, Drawings, Embroidery, Enamels, Eskimo Art, Etchings & Engravings, Ethnology, Fashion Arts, Film, Flasks & Bottles, Folk Art, Furniture, Glass, Handicrafts, Historical Material, History of Art & Archaeology, Illustration, Industrial Design, Interior Design, Islamic Art, Jewelry, Landscapes, Latin American Art, Lettering, Manuscripts, Maps, Metalwork, Mexican Art, Miniatures, Mixed Media, Painting-American, Painting-British, Painting-Dutch, Painting-European, Painting-Flemish, Painting-French, Painting-German, Painting-Italian, Painting-Japanese, Painting-Polish, Painting-Russian, Painting-Scandinavian, Painting-Spanish, Period Rooms, Pewter, Photography, Porcelain, Portraits, Posters, Pottery, Pre-Columbian Art, Primitive art, Printmaking, Prints, Religious Art, Reproductions, Restoration & Conservation, Scrimshaw, Sculpture, Silver, Silversmithing, Southwestern Art, Stage Design, Stained Glass, Tapestries, Textiles, Theatre Arts, Video, Watercolors, Woodcarvings, Woodcuts
Collections: 300,000 Volumes

M **HERMITAGE MUSEUM & GARDENS,** (Hermitage Foundation Museum), 7637 N Shore Rd, Norfolk, VA 23505-1730. Tel 757-423-2052; Fax 757-423-1604; Email info@hermitagefoundation.org; Web: thehermitagemuseum.org; *Chmn Bd* Olin Walden; *Cur Colls* Lindsay Neal; *Exec Dir* Jen Duncan
Open daily 10 AM - 5 PM (cl Wed), Sun 1 - 5 PM, cl New Year's Day, Thanksgiving Day, Christmas Day; Admis adults $15, mem, military, students & children (5-12) $12, children under 5 free; Estab 1937 to disseminate information concerning arts & maintain a collection of fine art materials; Large Tudor-style historic house on 12-acre estate houses major collections as well as two small changing exhibition galleries; Average Annual Attendance: 20,000; Mem: 400; dues $50 & up; meeting four times per yr
Special Subjects: Antiquities-Assyrian, Antiquities-Byzantine, Antiquities-Egyptian, Antiquities-Oriental, Antiquities-Persian, Antiquities-Roman, Bronzes, Carpets & Rugs, Ceramics, Coins & Medals, Costumes, Crafts, Decorative Arts, Drawings, Embroidery, Enamels, Furniture, Jade, Landscapes, Maps, Mexican Art, Oriental Art, Painting-American, Painting-European, Painting-French, Photography, Pottery, Primitive art, Prints, Religious Art, Reproductions, Sculpture, Southwestern Art, Stained Glass, Tapestries, Textiles, Woodcarvings, Glass
Collections: English oak & teakwood woodcarvings, Major coll of decorative arts from various periods & countries, Oriental coll of Chinese bronzes & ceramic tomb figures, lacquer ware, jades & Persian rugs, Spanish & English furniture, individual paintings & original objects of art lent to institutions, lending coll contains original art works, paintings, records & sculpture
Exhibitions: American Illustrator; Art on Paper; Isabel Bishop; Bernard Chaet (paintings); Contemporary American Graphics; Currier & Ives; Export Porcelain from a Private Collection; Freshwork (Virginia photographers); Alexandra Georges (photographs); The Photographs of Wright Morris; Henry Pitz (one man show); student exhibitions from summer workshops
Activities: Classes for adults & children; dramatic progs; lects open to pub & auxiliary lects for members only, 10-12 vis lectrs per yr; concerts; tours; Best of Norfolk awards; individual paintings & original objects of art lent to institutions; lending collection contains 750 original art works, 300 paintings, 150 records & 50 sculpture; book traveling exhibs; originate traveling exhibs; mus shop sells original art, t-shirts & umbrellas
—**Museum**, 7637 N Shore Rd, Norfolk, VA 23505. Tel 757-423-2052; Fax 757-423-1604; Email info@thehermitagemuseum.org; Web: www.thehermitagemuseum.org; *Cur Colls* Lindsay Neal; *Exec Dir* Jen Duncan; *Mem & Develop Mgr* Julie Morgan; *Mktg Mgr* Jennifer Luay; *Pub Progs Mgr* Melissa Ball
Open Tues - Sun 10 AM - 5 PM (tours) 11 AM & 2 PM; Admis adults $15, mem, military, students & children (5-12) $12, children under 5 free; Estab 1937 to promote art & culture regionally; Open to students and staff for reference only; Average Annual Attendance: 80,000+; Mem: Dues household $75; individual $50
Library Holdings: Auction Catalogs, Book Volumes 800, Exhibition Catalogs, Original Documents, Periodical Subscriptions, Photographs
Special Subjects: American Indian Art, Antiquities-Byzantine, Antiquities-Egyptian, Antiquities-Greek, Antiquities-Oriental, Antiquities-Persian, Architecture, Art Education, Art History, Bronzes, Carpets & Rugs, Ceramics, Coins & Medals, Crafts, Decorative Arts, Embroidery, Folk Art, Furniture, Glass, Historical Material, Islamic Art, Ivory, Jade, Laces, Oriental Art, Painting-American, Pewter, Porcelain, Pottery, Primitive art, Religious Art, Restoration & Conservation, Sculpture, Silver, Tapestries, Textiles, Woodcarvings
Collections: Personal letters & information on Douglas Volk, Helen M Turner, Harriet W Frishmuth, C T Loo, D Kelekian, Charles Woodsend & Karl von Rydingsvard
Exhibitions: (changing exhibs)
Publications: Hermitage Museum & Gardens by Colin Brady
Activities: Classes for adults & children; docent training; outdoor films; oyster roast; holiday party; concerts; tours; mus shop sells books, reproductions

M **MACARTHUR MEMORIAL,** MacArthur Sq, Norfolk, VA 23510. Tel 757-441-2965; Fax 757-441-5389; Email macarthurmemorial@norfolk.gov; Web: www.macarthurmemorial.org; *Dir* William J Davis; *Cur* Corey Thornton; *Admin Asst* Janice Stafford Dudley; *Archivist* James W Zobel
Open Tues - Sat 10 AM - 5 PM, Sun 11 AM - 5 PM, cl Mon, Thanksgiving, Christmas, New Year's Day; No admis fee; Estab 1964 to memorialize General Douglas MacArthur; Located in the 1850 Court House which was rebuilt in 1962; nine galleries contain memorabilia; Average Annual Attendance: 51,074
Income: $563,312 (financed by city appropriation & the General Douglas MacArthur Foundation)
Special Subjects: Photography, Portraits
Exhibitions: 1-2 rotating exhibitions per year
Activities: Concerts; gallery talks; tours; research assistance grants & fellowships offered; individual paintings and original objects of art lent to mus; mus shop sells books, reproductions, prints, slides

L **Library & Archives**, 1 MacArthur Sq, Norfolk, VA 23510-2382. Tel 757-441-2965; Fax 757-441-5389; Web: www.macarthurmemorial.org; *Archivist* James W Zobel
Open 8:30 AM - 5 PM; No admis fee; Estab 1964; Research library; Average Annual Attendance: 1,000
Income: Financed by the City of Norfolk & the General Douglas MacArthur Foundation as part of the MacArthur Memorial Museum
Library Holdings: Audio Tapes, Book Volumes 6000, Cassettes, Clipping Files, Fiche, Framed Reproductions, Manuscripts, Motion Pictures 130, Other Holdings Original documents 2,000,000, Photographs 80,000, Records, Reels, Slides, Video Tapes 120
Collections: Brigadier General Bonner F Fellers Collection: papers, Major General Courtney Whitney Collection: papers
Activities: Classes for adults & children; lects open to pub, 2-3 vis lectrs per yr; tours; competitions with prizes; schols offered

M **OLD DOMINION UNIVERSITY,** The College of Arts and Letters, Baron and Ellin Gordon Art Galleries, 4509 Monarch Way Norfolk, VA 23508. Tel 757-683-6271; Fax 757-451-1011; Email raustin@odu.edu; Web: www.odu.edu/life/culture/arts/galleries; *Senior Curator* Ramona Austin; *Collections Manager, Registrar, Preparator* Chris Norton
Open Tues - Sat 11 AM - 5 PM, Sun 1 PM - 5 PM; No admis fee; Estab 1972 for the exhibition of contemporary work; also estab as a pub forum for contemporary artists, with student exposure; Average Annual Attendance: 8,000; Mem: no membership required
Income: Financed by endowment & city appropriation
Library Holdings: Book Volumes 7000, Periodical Subscriptions 40
Collections: The Old Dominion University Collection of Contemporary Self-taught Art, The Old Dominion University Collection of Modern and Contemporary Fine Art
Exhibitions: 2nd Apr, 2017) Landscapes of the Collector: The Best of the Baron and Ellin Gordon Collection of Self-taught Art
Publications: Landscapes of the Collector: The Baron and Ellin Gordon Self-Taught Art Collection at Old Dominion University by Ramona Austin; Fire: The Resurrection of Mr. Imagination by Ramona Austin
Activities: Lect open to public, 10 vis lectrs per year; gallery talks; tours; competitions; exten dept

L **Elise N Hofheimer Art Library**, Diehn Fine & Performing Arts Ctr, Rm 109 Norfolk, VA 23529. Tel 757-683-4059; Email gacompan@odu.edu; Web: www.odu.edu/library/art; *Art Library Supervisor* Gay Acompanado

Open Sat - Sun 1 PM - 5 PM; Mon - Thurs 8 AM - 9 PM; Fri 8 AM - 5 PM; Estab 1963; Circ 15,930; Open to students & faculty; open to the public for reference; Average Annual Attendance: 22,000
Income: Financed by state, gifts & grants
Library Holdings: Auction Catalogs, Book Volumes 15,930, CD-ROMs, DVDs, Exhibition Catalogs, Periodical Subscriptions 36, Video Tapes
Special Subjects: Aesthetics, Afro-American Art, Antiquities-Byzantine, Antiquities-Greek, Antiquities-Oriental, Antiquities-Roman, Architecture, Art History, Calligraphy, Cartoons, Ceramics, Collages, Conceptual Art, Decorative Arts, Etchings & Engravings
Activities: Library instruction/orientation sessions; tours

ORANGE

M **ARTS CENTER IN ORANGE,** 129 E Main St, Orange, VA; 129 E Main St, PO Box 13 Orange, VA 22960-0011. Tel 540-672-7311; Web: www.artscenterorange.org; *Exec Dir* Laura Thompson
Open call for hours
Collections: works by emerging artists
Activities: classes; mus shop

PETERSBURG

M **THE CITY OF PETERSBURG MUSEUMS,** 15 W Bank St, Petersburg, VA 23803-3213. Tel 804-733-2404; Fax 804-863-0837; Email petgtourism@earthlink.net; Web: www.petersburg.va.org/tourism; *Coll Cur* Laura Willoughby; *Educ Coordr* Martha Atkinson
Hours seasonal. See website or call for hours; Admis adults $5, seniors, children & groups $4; Estab 1972 as a system of city museums; Three historic sites dating from 1735-1839. Maintains reference library; Average Annual Attendance: 25,000
Income: City of Petersburg, grants
Library Holdings: Auction Catalogs, Book Volumes, Clipping Files, Exhibition Catalogs, Lantern Slides, Manuscripts, Maps, Memorabilia, Original Art Works, Original Documents, Periodical Subscriptions, Photographs, Prints, Reproductions, Slides
Special Subjects: Archaeology, Architecture, Ceramics, Costumes, Decorative Arts, Embroidery, Furniture, Glass, Painting-American, Period Rooms, Photography, Portraits, Prints, Sculpture, Silver, Stained Glass, Watercolors, Manuscripts, Maps
Collections: City of Petersburg photographs & manuscripts, Military-Civil War, 19th century decorative arts, 15 Tiffany stained glass windows by Louis Comfort Tiffany Studio-Blandford Church, Period rooms 19th & early 20th century - Centre Hill Museum
Publications: Petersburg: Images of America Series; Petersburg: Postcard History Series
Activities: Docent training; lects open to pub; 4 vis lectrs per yr; tours; individual paintings & original objects of art lent to other mus; one book traveling exhib per yr, organized for libraries, schools, non-profits; mus shop sells books, postcards & children's merchandise

PORTSMOUTH

M **PORTSMOUTH MUSEUMS,** Courthouse Galleries, 400 High St, Portsmouth, VA 23704-3622; 521 Middle St, Portsmouth, VA 23704-3708. Tel 757-393-8543; Fax 757-393-5228; Email perryn@portsmouthva.gov; Web: www.courthousegalleries.com; *Dir* Nancy S Perry; *Cur* Gayle Paul
Open Tues - Sat 10 AM - 5 PM, Sun 1 - 5 PM, cl Mon; Admis $9 to tour four municipal museums, general fee $3; mems free; Estab 1974 to offer a wide variety of the visual arts to the citizens of Tidewater area & beyond; Average Annual Attendance: 25,000; Mem: 1200; dues mus contributor $1,000, Andalo's clubhouse $500, patron $250, conductor $100, planetarium (military, grandparent, sr couples) $45, passenger $30
Income: $53,000
Exhibitions: Up to 8 changing exhibitions per year; Ceramics, photography, sculpture, drawings/paintings
Publications: Quarterly newsletter
Activities: Classes for adults & children; workshops; school progs; family events & outreach; after school art progs in collaboration with Portsmouth pub schools; art camps; awards related to Outdoor Sculpture exhib; mus shop sells books, prints & gifts related to exhibs & holidays

PULASKI

M **FINE ARTS CENTER FOR THE NEW RIVER VALLEY,** 21 W Main St, Pulaski, VA 24301-5015; PO Box 309, Pulaski, VA 24301-0309. Tel 540-980-7363; Email info@facnrv.org; Web: www.facnrv.org
Open 10 AM - 4:30 PM; No admis fee; Estab 1978 to foster & furnish activities, programs & facilities to increase understanding of the arts; Gallery area 1,800 sq ft, classroom area 1800 sq ft; Average Annual Attendance: 36,000; Mem: 400; dues $10-$1000; annual meeting in the fall
Income: $129,000 (financed by mem, city & state appropriation & bus sponsorship)
Library Holdings: Cards, Clipping Files, DVDs, Memorabilia, Original Art Works, Original Art Works, Prints, Sculpture, Video Tapes
Special Subjects: Asian Art, Baroque Art, Calligraphy, Ceramics, Collages, Crafts, Etchings & Engravings, Folk Art, Glass, Jewelry, Landscapes, Miniatures, Painting-American, Painting-Australian, Painting-British, Painting-Dutch, Painting-European, Painting-Flemish, Painting-French, Painting-German, Painting-Italian, Painting-Japanese, Painting-Polish, Painting-Russian, Painting-Scandinavian
Collections: Permanent collection established by donated pieces of art, sculpture & original paintings from the New River Valley Region
Exhibitions: Biennial Juried competition for artists living within a 100 mile radius; Rotating exhibits
Activities: Classes for adults & children; dramatic progs; docent progs; lects open to pub; concerts; gallery talks; tours; competition with cash awards; Scholastic Awards; Biennial Juried Competition; schols & fels offered; artmobile serves New River Valley; lending collection; sales shop sells books, prints, original art, local craft items, reproductions, jewelry; dvd's

RESTON

INTER-SOCIETY COLOR COUNCIL
For further information, see National and Regional Organizations

NATIONAL ART EDUCATION ASSOCIATION
For further information, see National and Regional Organizations

NATIONAL ASSOCIATION OF SCHOOLS OF ART & DESIGN
For further information, see National and Regional Organizations

RICHMOND

M **1708 GALLERY,** 319 W Broad St, Richmond, VA 23220; PO Box 12520, Richmond, VA 23241-0520. Tel 804-643-1708; Fax 804-643-7839; Email info@1708gallery.org; Web: www.1708gallery.org; *Exec Dir* Emily Smith; *Gallery Coordr & Opers Mgr* Erin Willett
Open Tues - Fri 11 AM - 5 PM, Sat 11 AM - 4 PM, other times by appointment; No admis fee; Estab 1978 to offer an alternative presentation space to emerging & professional artists; Gallery is devoted to the presentation of contemporary art; Average Annual Attendance: 10,000
Library Holdings: Exhibition Catalogs
Special Subjects: Drawings, Etchings & Engravings, Painting-American, Photography, Prints, Sculpture
Publications: Ext. 1708
Activities: Educ dept; internship prog, juried exhibs; Monster Drawing Rally; Assembler; lects, gallery talks; schols; annual auction; books, catalogues (Inlight Richmond)

A **AGECROFT ASSOCIATION,** Agecroft Hall, 4305 Sulgrave Rd, Richmond, VA 23221-3256. Tel 804-353-4241; Fax 804-353-2151; Email kreynolds@agecrofthall.com; Web: www.agecrofthall.com; *Cur Educ* Jill Pesesky; *Exec Dir* Anne Kenny-Urban
Open Tues - Sat 10 AM - 4 PM, Sun 12:30 PM - 5 PM; Admis adults $8, seniors $7, students $5, children under 6 & active military free' group rates by prior arrangements; Estab 1969 to exhibit 15th century Tudor Manor house brought over from Lancashire, England in 1926 & rebuilt in Richmond. Furnished with period objects of art; Average Annual Attendance: 20,000
Income: Financed by endowment & admis
Purchases: 1,560 portrait of William Dauntesey
Collections: 16th & early 17th century furniture & objects of art depicting Elizabethan lifestyle, when Agecroft Hall was at its pinnacle
Exhibitions: Permanent exhibit of British memorabilia 1890 - present
Activities: Classes for adults; docent training; lects open to pub; concerts; gallery talks; specialized tours; mus shop sells books & reproductions

M **Museum,** 4305 Sulgrave Rd, Agecroft Hall Richmond, VA 23221-3256. Tel 804-353-4241; Fax 804-353-2151; Email kreynolds@agecrofthall.com; Web: www.agecrofthall.com; *Cur Educ* Jill Pesesky; *Coll Mgr* Libby Howlett; *Exec Dir* Anne Kenny-Urban; *Mgr Tour Svcs* Katie Reynolds
Open Tues - Sat 10 AM - 4 PM, Sun 12:30 - 5 PM; Admis adults $8, seniors $7, students $5, children under 6 & active military free; Estab 1969 to interpret the material culture & social history of England (1485-1660); Rebuilt from 15th century English house, 7 period rooms & 2 exhibit galleries. Maintains reference library; Average Annual Attendance: 20,000
Special Subjects: Architecture, Bookplates & Bindings, Carpets & Rugs, Ceramics, Costumes, Historical Material, Leather, Manuscripts, Maps, Metalwork, Painting-British, Painting-European, Painting-Flemish, Period Rooms, Pewter, Porcelain, Portraits, Pottery, Renaissance Art, Restorations, Silver, Stained Glass, Tapestries, Textiles, Woodcarvings
Collections: Bone & Ivory, Clocks, English Silver
Activities: Classes for adults & children; dramatic progs; quarterly living history events; workshops; summer Shakespeare festival; lects open to pub, 10-12 vis lectrs per yr; concerts; gallery talks; tours; original objects of art lent to Folger Shakespeare Library in Washington, DC; lending collection contains 3000 books, paintings, photographs & 500 decorative art holdings; mus shop sells books, reproductions, textiles, games, jewelry

M **ARTSPACE,** 31 E 3rd St, Richmond, VA 23224; Zero E 4th St, Richmond, VA 23224-4202. Tel 804-232-6464; Email artspaceorg@gmail.com; Web: www.artspacegallery.org; *Pres* Dana Frostick; *Treas* Martin McFadden; *Secy* Michelle McGrath; *VPres Mem* Michael A Pierce; *Pres-Elect* Paul Terrell; *Admin* Tegan Stephen
Open Tues - Sun Noon - 4 PM; No admis fee; Estab 1988 as an assn of artists interested in exhibiting their own work & providing a space for other artists to reach a wider audience in the greater Richmond area; Three medium rooms, one large room, one small room, office, gallery shop; Average Annual Attendance: 19,000; Mem: 27; artists, photographers, sculptors must submit work to mem for admittance; dues $420; accepts proposal for anyone who wants to exhibit; monthly meetings
Income: $80,000 (financed by mem, fund raising, donations, city & state grants, art auction, art sales)
Special Subjects: Bookplates & Bindings, Drawings, Etchings & Engravings, Painting-American, Photography, Prints, Mixed Media
Exhibitions: Open new exhibit 4th Fri of every month
Publications: online publications on website
Activities: Classes for adults; dramatic progs; lects open to pub, 3-4 per yr; annual support from local arts foundations; concerts; gallery talks; lending contains 30-40 items to VA area; book traveling exhibs 2 per yr; originate traveling exhibs 2 per yr; sales shop sells original art & prints

M **CHASEN GALLERIES OF FINE ART,** 3554 W Cary St, Richmond, VA 23221-2729. Tel 804-204-1048, 800-524-2736; Fax 804-204-1049; Email art@chasengalleries.com; Web: www.chasengalleries.com; *Pres* Andrew Chasen
Open Mon - Sat 10 AM - 6 PM; No admis fee; Estab 1999; Large varied selection of artists, sculptors & glass artists from around the world

M **CROSSROADS ART CENTER GALLERY,** 2016 Staples Mill Rd, Richmond, VA 23230-3109. Tel 804-278-8950; Web: www.crossroadsartcenter.com; *Owner & Exhibs Dir* Jennifer Kirby; *Office Mgr* Kay Goldsby
Open Mon - Sat 10 AM - 6 PM, Sun Noon - 4 PM; Mem: dues $45
Collections: painting; sculpture
Exhibitions: Temporary exhibits
Activities: Educ progs; classes for adults & children; artist residencies

A **CULTUREWORKS,** (Art Council of Richmond, Inc), 1906 A N Hamilton St, Richmond, VA 23230-4113. Tel 804-340-5280; Fax 804-340-5285; Email leslie@richmondarts.org; Web: www.richmondcultureworks.org; *Pres* Scott Garka; *Prog Assoc* Terry Menefee Gau; *Admin Mgr* Leslie Huffman; *Develop & Mktg Assoc* Caron Sterling
Open (office) Mon - Fri 9 AM - 5 PM; No admis fee; Estab 1949 to promote & support the arts & to provide arts programs & services to enhance the quality of city living
Income: Financed by grants, contributions & city appropriation
Publications: Arts Spectrum Directory, annually

M **FOLK ART SOCIETY OF AMERICA,** 1506 Willow Lawn Dr., #209 Richmond, VA 23230; PO Box 17041, Richmond, VA 23226-7041. Tel 804-355-6709; Email fasa@folkart.org; Web: www.folkart.org; *Pres* James Sellman; *Dir* Ann Oppenhimer; *VPres* Mary K McDonald Jr; *C.F.O.* William Oppenhimer; *Board Member* Barbara Sellman; *Board Member* John Willett; *Board Member* Brian Sievelaing
Open by appointment; No admis fee; Estab 1987; Circ non-circulating; Maintains reference library & archives; Average Annual Attendance: 200; Mem: Dues $35 contribution minimum; annual conference in various locations
Library Holdings: Auction Catalogs, Audio Tapes, Book Volumes, CD-ROMs, Clipping Files, Compact Disks, DVDs, Exhibition Catalogs, Kodachrome Transparencies, Manuscripts, Memorabilia, Original Documents, Periodical Subscriptions, Photographs, Slides, Video Tapes
Special Subjects: American Indian Art, Architecture, Art History, Asian Art, Costumes, Crafts, Drawings, Eskimo Art, Ethnology, Folk Art, Historical Material, Latin American Art, Mexican Art, Painting-American, Painting-French, Painting-Japanese, Photography, Portraits, Religious Art, Southwestern Art, Woodcarvings, Pottery, Posters, Primitive art, Afro-American Art, Ceramics, Collages, Furniture, Handicrafts, Sculpture, Textiles, Woodcarvings
Collections: Books, files, magazines, videos, Photographs
Exhibitions: One exhib per yr
Publications: Folk Art Messenger, 3 times a yr
Activities: Lects open to pub, 1 vis lectr per yr; Awards of Distinction for Scholars & Artist; tours; scholarships

M **NATIONAL SOCIETY OF THE COLONIAL DAMES OF AMERICA IN THE COMMONWEALTH OF VIRGINIA,** Wilton House Museum, 215 S Wilton Rd, Richmond, VA 23226-2212. Tel 804-282-5936; Fax 804-288-9805; Email wiltonhouse@mindspring.com; Web: www.wiltonhousemuseum.org; *Exec Dir* Keith MacKay; *Opers & Rental Mgr* Elizabeth Gosack Fleming; *Colls Mgr* Erica Borey; *Visitor Servs* Bailey Hughes
Open Tues - Sat 10 AM - 4:30 PM, Sun 1 PM - 4:30 PM, cl Mon; Admis general $10, seniors $8, students $6, teachers, press, mem, military & children under 7 free; Estab 1935; 18th Century Georgian Mansion with period furnishings; Average Annual Attendance: 3,500
Income: Endowment, grants
Special Subjects: Architecture, Ceramics, Decorative Arts, Furniture, Glass, Maps, Painting-American, Period Rooms, Portraits, Silver, Textiles
Collections: 18th & 19th century furniture, 18th century decorative arts, porcelain, silver, textiles
Activities: Classes for adults & children; docent training; summer camps; lect open to pub, 5-7 vis lectrs per yr; school tours; mus shop sells books & reproductions

M **PAGE BOND GALLERY,** 1625 W Main St, Richmond, VA 23220. Tel 804-359-3633; Email page@pagebondgallery.com; Web: www.pagebondgallery.com; *Dir* Kimberly Burgess; *Registrar & Social Media Mgr* Cidney Blaine-Cher
Open Tues - Sat 10 AM - 5 PM & by appointment; Estab 1999 to create awareness & appreciation of contemporary art
Collections: Contemporary art
Exhibitions: Temporary exhibits
Activities: Artist talks; educational presentations; lects

A **PRESERVATION VIRGINIA,** (Association for the Preservation of Virginia Antiquities), 204 W Franklin St, Richmond, VA 23220. Tel 804-648-1889; Fax 804-775-0802; Email info@preservationvirginia.org; Web: www.preservationvirginia.org; *CEO* Elizabeth S Kostelny; *Develop Coordr* Alexis Feria; *Dir Mus Opers & Educ* Jennifer Hurst Wender
Call for hours; Estab 1889 to acquire & preserve historic buildings, grounds & monuments in Virginia; Preservation VA owns & administers properties in Virginia. Among the properties: Historic Jamestown; Bacon's Castle & Smith's Fort Plantation, Surry County; John Marshall House, Richmond; Scotchtown, Hanover County; Farmers Bank, Petersburg; Cape Henry Lighthouse, Virginia Beach; Hours & admis vary according to location; Average Annual Attendance: 650,000; Mem: 6,000; dues individual $40
Income: Financed by mem, endowment fund donations & grants
Special Subjects: Decorative Arts, Furniture, Historical Material, Period Rooms, Portraits
Collections: Decorative arts, 17th - 19th century furniture, glass, ceramics, metalwork & textiles
Publications: Ventures, biannually
Activities: Classes for adults & children; docent training; lect open to public; preservation awards; endangered sites list; individual paintings & objects of art lent to other nonprofit preservation organizations' exhibits; mus shop sells books, reproductions, prints, gifts, Virginia handicrafts

L **Library,** 204 W Franklin St, Richmond, VA 23220-5012. Tel 804-648-1889; Fax 804-648-1889; Email info@preservationvirginia.org; Web: preservationvirginia.org
Open by appointment only; For reference use only
Library Holdings: Book Volumes 3000, Clipping Files, Exhibition Catalogs, Pamphlets, Periodical Subscriptions 12, Photographs, Slides
Special Subjects: Architecture, Decorative Arts, Historical Material

M **John Marshall House,** 818 E Marshall St, Richmond, VA 23219-1917; PO Box 1098, Richmond, VA 23218. Tel 804-648-7998; Email johnmarshallhouse@preservationvirginia.org; Web: www.preservationvirginia.org/marshall; *Site Coordr* Ashley Ramey; *CEO* Elizabeth S Kostelny; *Dir Mus Operations & Educ* Jennifer Hurst-Wender
Open March - Dec Fri & Sat 10 AM - 5 PM, Sun Noon - 5 PM; Admis general $10, mem, military & seniors $9, students $7, children under 7 free; Estab. 1911; Historical house mus built in 1790. Portrays John Marshall's life (1790-1835) in this historic Richmond home & his contribution to the nation; Average Annual Attendance: 5,000
Special Subjects: Archaeology, Architecture, Ceramics, Costumes, Decorative Arts, Embroidery, Furniture, Glass, Historical Material, Laces, Manuscripts, Painting-American, Period Rooms, Photography, Porcelain, Portraits, Restorations, Sculpture, Textiles
Collections: Decorative arts, period furniture 1790-1835, Marshall memorabilia
Activities: Classes for children; docent training; presentations for groups; lect open to public, some for members only; tours; mus shop sells books, reproductions, prints & Marshall items

M **UNIVERSITY OF RICHMOND,** University Museums, University of Richmond Museums, Richmond, VA 23173-0001. Tel 804-289-8276; Fax 804-287-1894; Email museums@richmond.edu; Email rwaller@richmond.edu; Web: museums.richmond.edu; *Dir* Richard Waller; *Deputy Dir* Elizabeth Schlatter; *Mus Preparator* Steve Duggins; *Mus Preparator* Henley Guild; *Asst Coll Mgr* David Hershey; *Cur Mus Coll* Matthew Houle; *Cur Mus Progs* Heather Campbell; *Coordr Mus Visitor & Tour Servs* Martha Wright; *Opers Mgr* Katreena Clark
Open Sun - Fri 1 - 5 PM, cl fall break, Thanksgiving wk, semester break, spring break & summer break; No admis fee; Estab 1968; 3 Mus: Joel & Lila Harnett Museum of Art; Joel & Lila Harnett Print Study Center; Lora Robins Gallery of Design from Nature; Average Annual Attendance: 12,000
Library Holdings: Exhibition Catalogs
Special Subjects: African Art, Afro-American Art, Antiquities-Byzantine, Antiquities-Egyptian, Antiquities-Greek, Antiquities-Oriental, Asian Art, Baroque Art, Bronzes, Calligraphy, Ceramics, Coins & Medals, Collages, Decorative Arts, Drawings, Embroidery, Eskimo Art, Etchings & Engravings, Folk Art, Glass, Graphics, Ivory, Landscapes, Maps, Marine Painting, Oriental Art, Painting-American, Photography, Porcelain, Portraits, Pottery, Pre-Columbian Art, Primitive art, Prints, Sculpture, Silver, Watercolors, Woodcuts
Collections: I Webb Surratt Jr Print Collection, Center Street Studio Archives, Carver Chinese Ceramics Collection
Publications: Exhibition catalogs
Activities: Classes for adults & children; docent training; lects open to pub; 10 vis lectrs per yr; concerts; gallery talks; tours; sponsoring of competitions; mus; lending of original art; originate book traveling exhibs; originate traveling exhibs to other mus; mus shop sells books

M **THE VALENTINE,** 1015 E Clay St, Richmond, VA 23219-1527. Tel 804-649-0711; Fax 804-643-3510; Email info@thevalentine.org; Web: www.thevalentine.org; *Dir* William J Martin; *Deputy Dir* Sarah M Kim; *Cur Archives* Meg Hughes
Open Tues - Sun 10 AM - 5 PM, cl Mon; Admis adults $10, seniors & students with ID $8, children under 18, military & mem free; Estab 1892 as a mus of the life & history of Richmond; Average Annual Attendance: 90,000; Mem: 1,000; dues individual $30
Income: Financed by endowment, mem, city & state appropriation & gifts
Special Subjects: Ceramics, Costumes, Decorative Arts, Glass, Jewelry, Laces, Painting-American, Photography, Prints, Sculpture, Silver, Watercolors
Collections: Conrad Wise Chapman Collection: oils, almost entire life works, William James Hubard Collection: drawings & oils, William Ludwell Sheppard Collection: drawings & watercolors, Edward Virginius Valentine Collection: sculpture, outstanding coll of Southern photographs, neo classical wall paintings
Exhibitions: Rotating exhibits
Publications: Valentine Newsletter, quarterly
Activities: Classes for adults & children; docent training; dramatic progs; lects open to pub; concerts; tours; exten dept serving city & area counties; originate traveling exhibs; mus & sales shops sell books, original art, reproductions, prints, slides & silver; Family Activity Center

L **Archives,** 1015 E Clay St, Richmond, VA 23219-1590. Tel 804-649-0711; Fax 804-643-3510; Email archives@thevalentine.org; Web: www.thevalentine.org
Open to researchers Tues - Fri noon - 4 PM; Contact for applicable fees; Open to the pub by appointment only; non-lending, reference library
Income: Financed by gifts, mem, endowment
Library Holdings: Audio Tapes, Book Volumes 10,000, Clipping Files, Compact Disks, DVDs, Exhibition Catalogs, Lantern Slides, Manuscripts, Maps, Memorabilia, Original Art Works, Original Documents, Pamphlets, Periodical Subscriptions 20, Photographs 50,000, Prints 600, Reels, Reproductions, Slides, Video Tapes
Special Subjects: Photography
Activities: mus shop sells books

M **VIRGINIA COMMONWEALTH UNIVERSITY,** Anderson Gallery, 907 1/2 W Franklin St, Richmond, VA 23824-2514. Tel 804-828-1522; Fax 804-828-8585; Email arts@vcu.edu; Web: www.vcu.edu/arts/gallery; *Dir* Chase Westfall; *Exhib Mgr* Michael Lease; *Gallery Coordr* Traci Horne Garland
Open Tues - Fri Noon - 7 PM, Sat & Sun noon - 5 PM; No admis fee; Estab 1930, re-opened 1970 as the showcase for the contemporary arts in Richmond; to expose the university & community to a wide variety of current artistic ideas &

expressions; Circ 2-4 exhib books publ yr; Gallery is situated on campus in a four-story converted stable. There are seven galleries with a variety of exhib spaces; Average Annual Attendance: 40,000; Mem: 275
Collections: Contemporary prints & paintings, cross section of prints from the 15th to 20th century covering most periods, vintage & contemporary photography
Publications: Catalogs; newsletters; posters & brochures
Activities: Lects open to pub, 4 vis lectrs per yr; concerts; gallery talks; tours; competitions; lending collection contains original art works, original paintings & photographs; originate traveling exhibs to other univ galleries, mus & non-profit art spaces; mus shop sells books

L **VIRGINIA DEPT HISTORIC RESOURCES,** Research Library, 2801 Kensington Ave, Richmond, VA 23221-2470. Tel 804-367-2323; Fax 804-367-2391; Email hhubbard@dhr.state.va.us; Web: www.dhr.virginia.gov; *Archivist* Quatro Hubbard
Open Tues - Thurs 9 - 5 , cl Fri - Mon & state holidays; Estab 1966; For reference only
Library Holdings: Book Volumes 4500, Clipping Files, Kodachrome Transparencies, Manuscripts, Maps, Periodical Subscriptions 75, Photographs, Slides, Video Tapes
Special Subjects: Anthropology, Archaeology, Architecture, Decorative Arts, Historical Material, History of Art & Archaeology, Maps
Collections: Archaeology, Architecture, Ethnography, History
Publications: Notes on Virginia; Preservation in Progress

A **VIRGINIA HISTORICAL SOCIETY,** PO Box 7311, Richmond, VA 23221-3307. Tel 804-358-4901; Fax 804-355-2399; Email jbosket@vahistorical.org; Web: www.vahistorical.org; *COO, Assoc Dir* Robert Strohm; *Dir Mus Colls & Registration* Rebecca A Rose; *Pres & CEO* Jamie O Bosket; *Cur of Virginia Art* Dr William Rasmussen
Open daily 10 AM - 5 PM; No admis fee; Estab 1831 for collecting, preserving & making available to scholars research material relating to the history of Virginia, its colls include extensive holdings of historical portraiture; Ten galleries feature changing & permanent exhibits drawn from pub & pvt colls throughout Virginia; Average Annual Attendance: 60,000; Mem: 8000; dues $38 & up
Income: Financed by endowment & mem
Library Holdings: Auction Catalogs, Clipping Files, Exhibition Catalogs, Fiche, Kodachrome Transparencies, Lantern Slides, Manuscripts, Maps, Memorabilia, Micro Print, Motion Pictures, Original Art Works, Original Documents, Pamphlets, Periodical Subscriptions, Photographs, Prints, Records, Sculpture, Slides, Video Tapes
Collections: Books, Manuscripts, Museum Collection, Portraits
Exhibitions: The Story of Virginia, an American Experience (permanent); Virginians at Work (permanent); Silver in Virginia (permanent); The Virginia Manufactory of Arms (permanent); Arming the Confederacy (permanent)
Publications: Bulletin, quarterly; Virginia Magazine of History & Biography, quarterly
Activities: Classes for adults & children; docent training; teacher recertification; lects open to pub, 10 vis lectrs per yr; gallery talks; tours; William Rachel Award; fels offered; exten dept; individual paintings & original objects of art lent; lending collection contains paintings, original prints; book traveling exhibs 2-3 per yr; originates traveling exhibs 1-2 per yr in Virginia; mus shop sells books, prints, reproductions

L **Library,** 428 North Blvd, Richmond, VA 23221-0311; PO Box 7311, Richmond, VA 23221-0311. Tel 804-358-4901; Fax 804-342-9647; Email jguild@vahistorical.org; Web: www.vahistorical.org; *Interim CEO* John R Nelson; *Sr Vice Pres Advancement* Pamela R Seay; *CFO* Richard SV Heiman; *Dir Lib Services* John McClure; *VPres Prog* Andrew Talkov; *VPres Coll* Lee Shepard; *Dir Educ* William Obrochta; *Dir Tech Services* Paulette Schwarting; *Cur Art* William Rasmussen; *Mktg & Pub Rels* Cynthia Moore; *Media Rel Spec* Lizzie Oglesby; *Mus Shop Mgr* Jessica Deruosi; *Va House Site Mgr* Katherine Lewis; *Dir of Facilities* Tracy Bryan
Open daily 10 AM - 5PM; Free admission to permanent exhibitions; Estab 1831 for the study of Virginia history; Circ Non-circulating; 7 permanent exhibit galleries, 3 changing exhibit galleries; Average Annual Attendance: 60000; Mem: 8,000
Income: 5.7 million annual budget, endowment, membership, gifts, earned income, grants, admissions
Library Holdings: Book Volumes 150000, CD-ROMs, Clipping Files, Compact Disks, DVDs, Exhibition Catalogs, Fiche, Filmstrips, Manuscripts, Maps, Memorabilia, Original Art Works, Original Documents, Pamphlets, Periodical Subscriptions 300, Photographs 100,000, Prints, Reels, Reproductions, Sculpture, Slides, Video Tapes
Special Subjects: Architecture, Historical Material, Landscape Architecture, Manuscripts, Maps, Painting-American, Bookplates & Bindings, Decorative Arts, Photography, Portraits, Prints, Silver
Collections: 150000 Volumes, 200,000 Photographs, 25000 Mus Paintings
Exhibitions: Story of Virginians Permanent Exhibit
Publications: History Notes, quarterly; Virginia Magazine of History & Biography, quarterly
Activities: Lects open to pub, 12 vis lectrs per yr; gallery talks; tours; fel; awards given, Brenton S. Halory Teaching Award, Bobby Chandler Student Award, W.M. M.E Rachel Award, President's Award for Excellence, Dist History Service Award; originates traveling exhibits to US and Canada; Mus shop sells books, magazines, reproductions, prints

M **VIRGINIA MUSEUM OF FINE ARTS,** 200 N Blvd, Richmond, VA 23220-4007. Tel 804-340-1400; Fax 804-340-1548; Email info@vmfa.museum; Web: www.vmfa.museum; *Pres* Dr. Monroe E. Harris; *Dir & CEO* Alex Nyerges; *Asst Cur American Art* Christopher C Oliver; *Cur East Asian Art* Li Jian; *Cur South Asian & Islamic Art* Dr John Henry Rice; *Cur African Art* Richard B Woodward; *Ancient American Art* Dr Lee Anne Hurt Chesterfield; *Cur Ancient Art* Dr Peter Justin Moon Schertz; *Cur American Painting & Decorative Art* Dr Susan J Rawles; *Cur Decorative Arts After 1890* Barry Shifman; *Paul Mellon Cur & Head Dept European Art* Dr Mitchell Merling; *Cur Modern & Contemporary Art* Emily Smith
Open daily 10 AM- 5 PM, Thurs & Fri until 9 PM; No admis fee; Estab 1934; Participating in the museum's progs are the Fellows of the Virginia Mus, who meet yearly to counsel the mus on its future plans; The Council, which sponsors & originates special progs; the Collector's Circle, a group of Virginia art lovers which meets four times per yr to discuss various aspects of coll; the Corporate Patrons, state & local bus firms who lend financial support to mus progs. Maintains reference library, Pauley Ctr & studio school; Average Annual Attendance: 300,000; Mem: 20,000; dues $15 & up; annual meeting in May
Income: Financed by Commonwealth of VA
Special Subjects: Antiquities-Greek, Asian Art, Bronzes, Decorative Arts, Drawings, Enamels, Etchings & Engravings, Furniture, Glass, Gold, Graphics, Islamic Art, Jade, Jewelry, Painting-European, Painting-Flemish, Painting-Italian, Porcelain, Pottery, Renaissance Art, Sculpture, Silver, Tapestries, Antiquities-Egyptian
Collections: Lady Nancy Astor Collection of English China, Branch Collection of Italian Renaissance Paintings, Sculpture & Furniture, Ailsa Mellon Bruce Collection of 18th Century Furniture & Decorative Arts, Mrs Arthur Kelly Evans Collection of Pottery & Porcelain, Arthur & Margaret Glasgow Collection of Flemish & Italian Renaissance Paintings, Sculpture & Decorative Arts, Nasli & Alice Heeramaneck Collection of Art of India, Nepal, Kashmir & Tibet, T Catesby Jones Collection of 20th Century European Paintings & Drawings, Dr & Mrs Arthur Mourot Collection of Meissen Porcelain, The John Barton Payne Collection of Paintings, Prints & Portuguese Furniture, Lillian Thomas Pratt Collection of Czarist Jewels by Peter Carl Faberge, Adolph D & Wilkins C Williams Collection of Paintings, Tapestries, China & Silver, British Sporting Art, Art Deco Collection, Jerome & Rita Collection of English Silver, Cochrane Collection of American Art, Fischer Collection of Expressionism
Publications: The Arts of India; Dr Joseph M Dye III; James McNeil Whistler: Uneasy Pieces; Virginia Museum Calendar, bi-monthly; brochures; catalogs for spec exhibs & collections; programs
Activities: Classes for adults, teens & children; family progs; teacher workshops; docent training; lects open to pub, concerts; gallery talks; tours; fels offered 10 - 15 per yr to Virginia artists; internships; exten prog; statewide outreach across state of VA; book traveling exhibs, 67 go out to statewide partners; originate traveling exhibs throughout the state of Virginia; mus shop sells books, magazines, original art, reproductions, prints, toys, gifts, notecards, jewelry, apparel

L **Margaret R & Robert M Freeman Library**, 200 N Blvd, Richmond, VA 23220-4007. Tel 804-340-1495; Fax 804-340-1548; Email library@vmfa.museum; Web: www.pandora.vmfa.museum; *Head Fine Arts Librn* Suzanne H Freeman; *Asst Librn* Courtney C Yevich; *Reference Librn* Lee B Viverette
Open Mon - Fri Noon - 5 PM, cl state holidays; Estab 1935 for art history research for gen pub, academia & staff; Circ Non-circulating; For reference only; Average Annual Attendance: 1,500
Income: Financed by private funds
Library Holdings: Auction Catalogs 45,000, Book Volumes 143,000, CD-ROMs 22, Clipping Files, Exhibition Catalogs, Manuscripts, Memorabilia, Original Documents, Other Holdings Monographs: 82,000; Vertical Files: 40,000, Pamphlets, Periodical Subscriptions 234, Reels
Special Subjects: Art History, Crafts, Decorative Arts, Sculpture
Collections: Weedon Collection, Hayes Collection, Maxwell Collection of East Asian Art, McGlothlin Collection of American Art, Tucker Numismatics Collections, Lewis Decorative Art Collection, Pinkney Near West European Collection, Coopersmith Collection, Rare Books Coll, Archives
Exhibitions: Rotating exhibs of rare books & archival material located in libr atrium
Activities: Classes for adults; book club; docent training; internships

A **VISUAL ARTS CENTER OF RICHMOND,** 1812 W Main St, Richmond, VA 23220-4520. Tel 804-353-0094; Fax 804-353-8018; Email info@visarts.org; Web: www.visarts.org; *Exec Dir* Stefanie Fedor; *Dir Opers* Rachel Beanland; *Mktg & Communs Coordr* Kate Garber
Open Mon - Fri 9 AM - 9 PM, Sat - Sun 10 AM - 5 PM; No admis fee; Estab 1963 as a nonprofit center for the visual arts committed to promoting artistic excellence through educational programs, gallery exhibs & artists services; Average Annual Attendance: 5,000; Mem: 750 mem, ann dues vary by category
Publications: Exhibition catalogs
Activities: Classes for adults & children; lect open to pub; gallery talks; tours; competitions with awards; schols offered for children only; originates traveling exhibs; sales shop sells magazines

ROANOKE

M **TAUBMAN MUSEUM OF ART,** 110 Salem Ave SE, Roanoke, VA 24011-1410. Tel 540-342-5760; Fax 540-342-5798; Email info@taubmanmuseum.org; Web: www.taubmanmuseum.org; *Exec Dir* David Mickenberg; *Pres Bd Trustees* Dr Paul Frantz; *COO* Jim Becker; *Dir External Affairs* Kimberly Templeton; *Mus Shop Mgr* Marie Napoli; *Controller* Sheri Rock
Open Tues - Sat 10 AM - 5 PM, Thurs until 8 PM, Sun Noon - 5 PM; Admis adults $10.50, members no charge, Free Thurs 5PM - 8 PM; Estab 1951 as a general art mus with a focus on American art; 81,000 sq ft bldg houses 4 special exhib & 5 permanent coll galleries, educ spaces incl studio classroom & library, multipurpose auditorium, theatre, interactive gallery for children, museum shop & cafe; Average Annual Attendance: 85,000; Mem: 3,000; dues senior & student $35, individual $45, family $70, friend $100, sustainer $250, patron $500, benefactor $1,000
Income: Financed by mem earned income, donations & endowment
Collections: 19th & 20th c. American art, modern & contemporary art, Folk Art, Japanese Prints, Decorative Arts, Regional Art, Photography
Publications: Annual Report; Volunteer newsletter; exhib catalogs; quarterly newsletter
Activities: Classes for adults & children; docent training; art venture family interactive center; lects open to pub, 8-10 vis lectrs per yr; concerts; gallery talks; tours; artmobile; individual paintings & objects of art lent to qualified mus; book traveling exhibs 1-3 per yr; originate traveling exhibs; mus store selling books, original art, prints, reproductions, handmade crafts including jewelry & children's items; junior mus

SPRINGFIELD

L **VICANA (VIETNAMESE CULTURAL ASSOCIATION IN NORTH AMERICA) LIBRARY,** 6433 Northanna Dr, Springfield, VA 22150-1335. Tel 703-971-9178; Fax 703-719-5764; Email 37nnb726@gmail.com; *Pres* Nguyen Ngoc Bich; *Librn* Dao Thi Hoi, Ed.D
Open by special arrangement; No admis fee; Estab 1982; Average Annual Attendance: 100
Income: Gifts, donations, exchanges
Purchases: $2,000 per yr
Library Holdings: Audio Tapes, Book Volumes 30000, CD-ROMs, Cassettes 250, Clipping Files, Compact Disks 200, DVDs 150, Exhibition Catalogs, Filmstrips, Framed Reproductions, Manuscripts 30, Original Documents, Pamphlets, Photographs, Records 100, Video Tapes 100
Special Subjects: Aesthetics, Art Education, Art History, Asian Art, Ceramics, Crafts, Ethnology, Folk Art, Handicrafts, Historical Material, History of Art & Archaeology, Oriental Art
Collections: Historical coll: Vietnamese, English, French, Russian, German, Japanese, slides of Vietnamese life, Vietnamese cultural artifacts
Publications: Tet the Vietnamese New Year
Activities: Lects by invitation; 2-3 book traveling exhibs per yr

STAUNTON

A **STAUTON AUGUSTA ART CENTER,** 20 S New St, Staunton, VA 24401-4308. Tel 540-885-2028; Email info@saartcenter.org; Web: www.saartcenter.org; *Exec Dir* Beth Hodge
Open Mon - Fri 10AM - 5 PM, Sat 10 AM - 4 PM, Sun 1 - 4 PM; No admis fee; Estab 1961 for art exposure & educ to area residents & visitors; state of the art exhibition galleries in a rehabilitated former hotel C 1895; Average Annual Attendance: 12,000; Mem: 550; dues $60 family, $40 individual
Income: $166,000 (financed by mem, city & state appropriations), gallery sales
Exhibitions: Annual Art in the Park; Christmas Art for Gifts; Art & fine craft exhibits change every six weeks
Activities: Classes for adults & children; lect open to public; gallery talks; vis lectrs 6 per yr; Art in the Park art award $1,500; schols; mus shop sells books, original art, reproductions, prints

M **WOODROW WILSON BIRTHPLACE FOUNDATION,** 20 N Coalter St, Staunton, VA 24402; PO Box 24, Staunton, VA 24402-0024. Tel 540-885-0897; Fax 540-886-9874; Web: www.woodrowwilson.org; *Dir Coll* Edmund Potter
Open daily 9 AM - 5 PM Mar - Nov, 10 AM - 4 PM Dec - Feb, cl Thanksgiving, Christmas & New Year's Day; Admis adults $6, AAA discount & seniors $5.50, students age 13 & up or with ID $4, children 6-12 $2, children under 6 free; Estab 1938 for the interpretation & collection of life & times of Woodrow Wilson. Collection is housed in the 1846 Presbyterian Manse which was the birthplace of Woodrow Wilson; Mem: 700; dues $25 & up
Special Subjects: Decorative Arts, Historical Material, Painting-American, Period Rooms
Collections: Historical Material pertinent to the Wilson family, decorative arts, furniture, manuscripts, musical instruments, paintings, photographs, prints & drawings, rare books, textiles
Publications: Brochures; guides; newsletter, quarterly; pamphlets
Activities: Classes for children; lect open to public; tours; internships offered; original objects of art lent to museums & libraries; lending collection contains original art work & sculpture; sales shop sells books, magazines, reproductions, prints & slides

L **Woodrow Wilson Presidential Library**, 20 N Coalter St, Staunton, VA 24402; PO Box 24, Staunton, VA 24402-0024. Tel 540-885-0897; Fax 540-886-9874; Email woodrow@cfw.com; Web: www.woodrowwilson.org; *Dir Coll* Edmund Potter; *Bus Mgr* Janet Campbell
Open daily 10 AM - 5 PM Mar - Nov, 10 AM - 4 PM Dec - Feb, cl Thanksgiving, Christmas & New Year's Day; Admis adults $7, AAA discount $6.25, students age 13 & up or with ID $4, children 6-12 $2, children under 6 free; Estab 1938 for the interpretation & collection of life & times of Woodrow Wilson. Collection is housed in the 1846 Presbyterian Manse which was the birthplace of Woodrow Wilson; Average Annual Attendance: 22,000; Mem: 700; dues $25 & up
Income: Financed by endowment, admis & grants
Library Holdings: Book Volumes 2000, Pamphlets, Photographs
Exhibitions: Women's History; Black History; Wedding Customs
Publications: Wilson Newsletters, quarterly
Activities: Mus shop sells books, original art, reproductions, prints

STRASBURG

M **STRASBURG MUSEUM,** 440 E King St, Strasburg, VA 22657-2433; P.O. Box 333, Strasburg, VA 22657. Tel 540-465-3175; *Pres* Gloria Stickley; *VPres* John Adamson; *Gift Shop Mgr* Margo Hammock
Open May to Oct, daily 10 AM - 4 PM; Admis adults $3, children $.50; Estab 1970 to present the past of a Shenandoah Valley community & to preserve the pottery-making tradition of Strasburg; The mus is housed in the former Southern Railway Depot, which was originally built as a steam pottery; Average Annual Attendance: 2,500; Mem: 160; dues $10; annual meeting in Mar
Income: Financed by mem, admis fees & gifts
Special Subjects: American Indian Art, Ceramics, Costumes, Crafts, Flasks & Bottles, Period Rooms, Pottery, Stained Glass
Collections: Artifacts & exhibits, farm & railroad crafts, pottery (local), WWI & WWII uniforms; colonial rooms;
Exhibitions: Model Train in Southern RR Baggage Car
Activities: Classes for adults & children in pottery making; docent training; open house (free admission) on holidays; mus shop selling books original art, pottery & other local crafts; souvenirs

SWEET BRIAR

L **SWEET BRIAR COLLEGE,** Mary Helen Cochran Library, 134 Chapel Rd, Sweet Briar, VA 24595-5001. Tel 804-381-6138; Fax 804-381-6173; Email lnjohnston@sbc.edu; Web: www.cochran.sbc.edu; *Technical Svcs* Julie Kane; *Pub Svcs* Lisa N Johnston; *Bibliographic Instruction & Branch Librn* Joe Malloy; *Serials Librn* Liz Kent; *Dir* John G Jaffe
Open Mon - Thurs 8 AM - 1 AM, Fri 8 AM - 6 PM, Sat 10 AM - 6 PM, Sun 8 AM - 1 AM; Estab 1961, when it was separated from the main library, the library serves an undergraduate community; The Art Library is now located in the Mary Helen Cochran Library
Income: Financed by college funds
Library Holdings: Book Volumes 12,500, Cassettes, Exhibition Catalogs, Fiche, Kodachrome Transparencies, Lantern Slides, Original Art Works, Pamphlets, Periodical Subscriptions 60, Prints, Video Tapes
Special Subjects: Aesthetics, Afro-American Art, American Indian Art, American Western Art, Antiquities-Assyrian, Folk Art, Furniture, Glass, Gold, Graphic Arts, Painting-American, Painting-Australian, Painting-British, Painting-Canadian, Painting-Dutch

M **Art Collection & Galleries**, 134 Chapel Rd, Anne Gary Pannell Ctr Sweet Briar, VA 24595-5001. Tel 434-381-6248; Email klawson@sbc.edu; Web: www.sbc.edu/art-galleries; *Dir* Karol Lawson; *Registrarial Asst* Nancy McDearmon
Open Mon-Thurs 10AM-5PM, Fri 10AM-2PM, Sun 1-4PM, cl Sat & col breaks; No admis fee; Estab 1985 to support the educational mission at Sweet Briar College through its exhibits, collections & educational programs; Average Annual Attendance: 4,000; Mem: 200; dues $25; annual meeting in Apr
Special Subjects: African Art, Afro-American Art, Antiquities-Greek, Antiquities-Roman, Asian Art, Collages, Drawings, Etchings & Engravings, Graphics, Landscapes, Manuscripts, Painting-American, Photography, Posters, Prints, Watercolors, Woodcuts
Collections: American & European drawings & prints & photographs, Japanese woodblock prints, 18th & 19th century paintings, Works on paper by female artists of the 20th & 21st centuries
Exhibitions: Rotating exhibits from permanent collection plus traveling exhibits; average 12 exhibs per yr
Publications: Visions: News from the Friends of Art newsletter-1 issues per yr; Women Artists of the Twentieth Century: Sweet Briar College Anne Gary Pannell Art Gallery Collection catalog
Activities: Tours for children; lects open to pub; 4 vis lectrs per yr; concerts; gallery talks; music; theater; dance performances in conjunction with exhibs

TRIANGLE

M **MARINE CORPS UNIVERSITY,** National Museum of the Marine Corps, 18900 Jefferson Davis Hwy, Triangle, VA 22172-1938; 2014 Anderson Ave, Quantico, VA 22134-5100. Tel 703-499-3185/ 898-8855; Fax 703-784-5856; Email info@usmcmuseum.org; Web: www.usmcmuseum.com; *Mus Dir* Liz Ezell; *Dep Dir* Charlie Grow; *Senior Cur Art* Joan Thomas; *Art Cur* Vickie Stuart-Hill
Open daily 9 AM - 5 PM; cl Christmas Day; No admis fee; Estab 2006; Average Annual Attendance: 504,000
Library Holdings: CD-ROMs, Clipping Files, DVDs, Framed Reproductions, Kodachrome Transparencies, Manuscripts, Original Art Works, Original Documents, Other Holdings, Photographs, Sculpture
Special Subjects: Bronzes, Cartoons, Drawings, Etchings & Engravings, Historical Material, Military Art, Painting-American, Sculpture, Portraits, Posters, Prints, Reproductions, Watercolors, Woodcarvings, Woodcuts
Publications: Exhibit publications
Activities: Docent training; gallery talks; lend art to other museums; traveling exhibs to other art mus & USMC commands

VIRGINIA BEACH

A **VIRGINIA MUSEUM OF CONTEMPORARY ART,** (Virginia Beach Center for the Arts), 2200 Parks Ave, Virginia Beach, VA 23451-4062. Tel 757-425-0000; Fax 757-425-8186; Email info@virginiamoca.org; Web: www.virginiamoca.org; *Exec Dir* Debi Gray; *Bd Chmn* Andrew Hodge; *Accounting & HR* Joy Blake; *Dir Develop* Emily Barnhill; *Develop Coordr* Ashley Lambert; *Dir Opers & Facility Mgmt* Andrew Coulomb; *Secy* Sue Grube; *Dir Exhibs & Educ* Alison Byrne; *Cur Educ* Alison Byrne; *Registrar & Prep* Monee Marie Bengston; *Cur* Heather Hakimzadeh
Open Tues - Fri 10 AM - 5 PM, Sat 10 AM - 4 PM, Sun Noon - 4 PM, cl Mon, New Year's Day, Thanksgiving & Christmas Day; Admis adults $7, students, seniors & military $2, members & children under 4 free; Estab 1952, as a nonprofit organization serving citizens of the greater Hampton Roads area with exhibits & programming in the visual arts; Exhibition space 5600 sq ft; Average Annual Attendance: 517,000; Mem: 3000, dues standard individual $50, student, senior, military, teacher & individual $30, standard household $65, student, senior, military, teacher household $55, assoc $125, patron $250, donor $500, Collector's Circle $1,250, Chairman's Circle $2,500; annual meeting in Sept
Income: Financed by mem, pub grants, private donations, various fundraising events
Collections: Best-in-Show winners from Boardwalk Art Show
Exhibitions: 10 exhibitions per year of contemporary art
Publications: ArtLetter, monthly; exhibition catalogues
Activities: Classes & workshops for adults & children; dramatic progs; docent training; film series; performing arts; lects open to pub; 15 vis lectrs per yr; concerts; gallery talks; tours; schols & fels offered; exten dept serves municipal employees; mus shop sells books, original art, reproductions, prints, crafts, jewelry, wearable art

WAVERLY

M **MILES B CARPENTER FOLK ART MUSEUM,** 201 Hunter St, Waverly, VA 23890-2631; PO Box 1376, Waverly, VA 23890-1376. Tel 804-834-3327, 804-834-2151; *Secy* Doretha Smith; *Treas* Thelma W Wyatt; *Pres* Shirley Eley; *Pub Relations* Carolyn Cooper Wright
Open Thurs - Mon 2 - 5 PM, other times by appointment; Admis by donation; Estab 1986 to maintain a museum in the home of nationally known folk artist Miles Burkholder Carpenter & to encourage art; Two-floor gallery; Average Annual Attendance: 6,000; Mem: 25 members; no dues; annual meeting last Sat in Jan
Income: $25,000 (financed by state grants & donations)
Special Subjects: Folk Art, Sculpture, Woodcarvings
Collections: Miles B Carpenter Permanent Collection of woodcarvings, tools & memorabilia
Exhibitions: Miles B Carpenter (woodcarvings, tools & memorabilia); Folk Art Paintings; Seven visiting exhibits
Publications: Cutting the Mustard
Activities: Classes for adults & children; dramatic progs; docent training; lects open to pub, 4 vis lectrs per yr; tours; schols

WILLIAMSBURG

M **COLLEGE OF WILLIAM & MARY,** Muscarelle Museum of Art, P.O. Box 8795, Williamsburg, VA 23187-8795. Tel 757-221-2700; Fax 757-221-2711; Email museum@wm.edu; Web: www.wm.edu/muscarelle; *Dir* Aaron H De Groft, PhD; *Asst Dir & Chief Cur* John T Spike PhD; *Head Colls & Exhibs* Melissa Parris; *Asst to Dir* Cindy Lucas
Temporarily Closed; Admis fee $5, additional fee for special exhibs, free to mems, William & Mary students, faculty, staff, & children under 12; Estab 1983; Average Annual Attendance: 65,000; Mem: 1,400; dues $40 & up
Income: Financed by endowments, state appropriations & donations
Special Subjects: Afro-American Art, American Indian Art, Anthropology, Asian Art, Baroque Art, Bookplates & Bindings, Bronzes, Calligraphy, Ceramics, Coins & Medals, Collages, Drawings, Enamels, Eskimo Art, Etchings & Engravings, Furniture, Glass, Gold, Graphics, Historical Material, Islamic Art, Jade, Jewelry, Landscapes, Landscapes, Manuscripts, Maps, Marine Painting, Medieval Art, Metalwork, Metalwork, Oriental Art, Painting-American, Painting-American, Painting-Australian, Painting-British, Painting-Dutch, Painting-European, Painting-Flemish, Painting-French, Painting-French, Painting-German, Painting-Italian, Painting-Polish, Painting-Russian, Painting-Spanish, Pewter, Photography, Porcelain, Portraits, Posters, Pottery, Prints, Religious Art, Renaissance Art, Sculpture, Silver, Southwestern Art, Woodcuts, Watercolors
Collections: African Art, Asian Art, Native American Art, paintings & sculpture, Sixteenth-Twentieth Century American & European Works
Exhibitions: See www.wm.edu/muscarelle/exhibitions for current, upcoming & past exhibs
Publications: Newsletter, two times a year; exhibition catalogues
Activities: Classes for adults & children; docent training; school field trips; lect open to pub; lectrs for mems only; 5 vis lectrs per year; gallery talks; concerts; tours; Cheek Medal (for outstanding contributions in mus, performing or visual arts); sponsoring of competitions; schols; fels; individual paintings & original objects of art lent to special exhibs organized by other museums; book traveling exhibs, 2-9 per yr; originate traveling exhibs that circulate to other mus, art centers, colleges; national & international mus; mus shop sells books, original art, reproductions, notecards, T-shirts, prints

M **COLONIAL WILLIAMSBURG FOUNDATION,** 101 Visitor Center Dr., Williamsburg, VA 23185; PO Box 1776, Williamsburg, VA 23187-1776. Tel 757-229-1000 & 888-965-7254; Fax 757-220-7286; Email cwres@cwf.org; Web: www.colonialwilliamsburg.com/; *Pres & CEO* Michell B Reiss; *Chm. of the Board* Henry C. Wolf
Open 9 AM - 5 PM; Single-Day: Adult $40.99, Youth $20.49; Multiday: Adult $50.99, Youth $25.49; Annual: Adult $66.99, Youth $33.49; Estab 1927 the worlds largest outdoor mus, providing first hand history of 18th-century English colony during period of subjects becoming Americans; The colonial area of this 18th century capital of Virginia, encompassing 300 acres with nearly 500 homes, shops, taverns, dependencies, has been carefully restored to its original appearance. Included are 90 acres of gardens & greens. The work was initiated by John D Rockefeller, Jr. There are more than 40 exhibition homes, public buildings & craft shops where guides & craftsmen in colonial costumes show visitors the way of life of pre-Revolutionary Virginia. Incl are the historic Burton Parish Church, the Governor's Palace, Capitol, the Courthouse of 1770, Bassett Hall (local residence of the Rockefellers), the DeWitt Wallace Dec. Arts Mus & Abby Aldrich Rockefeller Folk Art Mus. The exhibition properties include 225 furnished rooms; Average Annual Attendance: 1,000,000
Income: Financed by admis, gifts & grants, real estate, products, restaurants & hotels
Collections: 18th-Century British & American Painting, English Pottery & Porcelains, Silver; Furniture, with frequent additions, include representative pieces, rare English pieces in the palace, exceptionally fine textiles & rugs, extensive collection of primary & secondary materials relating to British North America, the Colonial Period & the early National Period & American folk art.
Publications: The foundation publishes many books on a wide range of subjects; Colonial Williamsburg, quarterly journal
Activities: Classes & tours for adults & children; lects open to pub, 30 vis lectrs per yr; concerts; gallery talks; special focus tours; individual paintings & original objects of art lent; mus shop sells books, magazines, original art, reproductions, prints & slides

A **Visitor Center**, PO Box 1776, Williamsburg, VA 23187-1776. Tel 757-220-7645; Web: www.history.org; *Dir* William Pfeifer
Open daily 8:30 AM - 8:30 PM; Estab 1927; Outside the historic area this modern center houses graphic exhibits of the restoration & colonial life. Continuous showings of a full-color, vista vision film, Williamsburg: The Story of a Patriot
Publications: Books & brochures on Williamsburg & colonial life; gallery book of the Folk Art Collection
Activities: Limited grant-in-aid prog for researchers; slide lect; annual events including Antiques Forum; Garden Symposium; regular performance of 18th century dramas, organ recitals & concerts

L **John D Rockefeller, Jr Library**, 313 First St, Williamsburg, VA 23185; PO Box 1776, Williamsburg, VA 23187-1776. Tel 757-565-8500; Email jclark@cwf.org; Web: www.research.history.org/library; *Office Mgr* Inge Flester; *Decorative Arts Librn* Susan Shames; *Access Services* Allison Heinbaugh; *Circ Library Asst* Joann Proper; *Special Collections* Doug Mayo; *Pub Svcs Librn* Juleigh Clark; *Tech Svcs Librarian* Melissa Schutt.; *Acquisitions Librn* Annette Parham; *Visual Resources Editorial Librn* Marianne Martin; *Dir* Edward Maris-Wolf; *Deputy Director* Carl Childs
Open Mon - Fri 9 AM - 5 PM, cl major holidays; No admis fee; Circ 10,000; Average Annual Attendance: 21,000
Library Holdings: Auction Catalogs 20,000, Book Volumes 76,053, Cards 800, Clipping Files, Compact Disks, DVDs, Fiche, Manuscripts 50,000, Maps 2,500, Other Holdings Architectural drawings 65,000; Compact discs-Music; Negatives 250,000, Periodical Subscriptions 203, Photographs 250,000, Reels 6000, Slides 250,000, Video Tapes 1000
Special Subjects: Archaeology, Architecture, Folk Art, Furniture, Painting-American, Painting-British
Collections: 18th Century Arts & Trades, Historical Preservation in America, History of the Restoration of Colonial Williamsburg, Decorative Arts, Folk Art, Architecture, Auction Catalogs
Exhibitions: 31st Dec, 2016) Albert Durant: A Lens Focused on African American History
Publications: Exhibit catalogs

M **Abby Aldrich Rockefeller Folk Art Museum**, 326 W Francis St, Williamsburg, VA 21385; PO Box 1776, Williamsburg, VA 21387-1776. Tel 757-220-7724; Fax 757-565-8804; Email mcottrill@cwf.org; Web: www.colonialwilliamsburg.com/do/artmuseums/; *VPres Colls, Conservation & Museums* Ronald Hurst; *Dir Mus Exhibs & Operations* Richard Hadley; *Mgr Mus Operations & Hennage Auditorium* Mary Cottrill; *Mgr Mus Educ* Patricia Balderson; *Mgr Exhibit Planning* Jan Gilliam
Open Jan - Mar daily 10 AM- 5 PM, April - Dec: daily 10 AM - 7 PM; Admis adults $13, youth 6-17 $7, children under 6 free; ann mus pass: adults $23, youth $12; Estab 1957; Colonial & contemporary artists & craftspeople working outside the mainstream of academic art to record aspects of everyday life, making novel & effective use of the materials at hand. Bold colors, simplified shapes, & patterns can be seen in the variety of paintings, carvings, toys, & needleworks. Offers changing exhibs of American folk art from its permanent holdings and mus loan shows; Average Annual Attendance: 200,000
Income: part of Colonial Williamsburg Foundation
Special Subjects: Ceramics, Folk Art, Furniture, Period Rooms, Pottery, Primitive art, Sculpture, Textiles, Watercolors
Collections: 18th to 21st century folk art including painted furniture, toys, dollhouses, paintings, sculptures, signs, textiles, quilts, iron work
Exhibitions: The World Made Small: American's Folk Art; Cross Rhythms; Sidewalks to Rooftops: Outdoor Folk Art; American Ship Paintings; Down on the Farm; German Toys in America; From Forge and Furnace: A Celebration of Early American Iron; The Carolina Room; We The People: American Folk Portraits; A Century of African-American Quilts; Color and Shape: The Art of the American Theorem
Publications: The Art-Full Tree - Jan Gilliam and Christina Westenburger
Activities: Classes for adults & children; dramatic programs; docent & teacher training; lects open to pub, 12 vis lectrs per yr; gallery talks; concerts; tours; special lects & events for the 60th Anniversary of the Folk Art Museum in 2017; paintings & sculpture lent to other mus; book traveling exhibs, 1 per yr; originate traveling exhibs; mus shop sells books, reproductions, magazines, original art, prints, CDs music

M **DeWitt Wallace Decorative Arts Museum**, 326 W Francis St, Williamsburg, VA 23185; PO Box 1776, Williamsburg, VA 23187-1776. Tel 757-220-7724; Fax 757-565-8804; Email mcottnill@cwf.org; Web: www.colonialwilliamsburg.com/do/art-museums/; *Mgr Mus Opers & Hennage Auditorium* Mary Cottrill; *Mgr Mus Security* Ray Armstead; *Mgr Mus Design* James Armbruster
Open Jan - mid-Mar 10 AM - 5 PM daily, mid-Mar - Dec 10 AM - 7 PM daily; Admis adults $12.99, children 6-17 yrs old $6.49, under 6 free; annual museum pass adults $22.99, children 6-17 $11.49, under 6 free; Estab 1985; Extensive collections of American & British antiques; artists & craftspeople from 18th-21st century, working outside the mainstream; Average Annual Attendance: 200,000
Income: part of the Colonial Williamsburg Foundation, DeWitt Wallace Fund for Colonial Williamsburg
Special Subjects: Furniture, Period Rooms, Pottery, Sculpture, Tapestries, Watercolors
Collections: English & American decorative arts from 1600-1830, furniture, metals, ceramics, glass, paintings, prints, firearms, kitchen equipment, textiles, 18th - 21st century folk art
Exhibitions: Silver from Mine to Masterpiece; Birds, Bugs & Blooms: Observing the Natural World in the 18th Century; A Rich and Varied Culture: The Material World of the Early South; Changing Keys: Keyboard Instruments for America 1700-1830; We Are One: Mapping America's Road from Revolution to Independence (opens Mar 5, 2016); Color and Shape: The Art of the American Theorem; American Ship Paintings; Conserving the Carolina Room; Cross Rhythms: Folk Musical Instruments; A Century of African-American Quilts (opens Jan 20, 2016)
Publications: Exhibition catalogues; Painters & Paintings in the Early American South - March 2013; Four Centuries of Quilts - Baumgarten & Ivey; Early Seating Upholstery: Reading the Evidence Leroy Graves
Activities: Educ dept; classes for adults & children, dramatic programs; docent & teacher training; workshops; lects open to pub, 12 vis lectrs per yr; concerts; gallery talks; tours; slide & video presentations; musical events; book traveling exhibs 1 per yr; mus shop sells books, reproductions, magazines, original art, DVDs, CDs, prints & slides

M **JAMESTOWN-YORKTOWN FOUNDATION,** Jamestown Settlement, PO Box 1607, Williamsburg, VA 23187-1607; Rte 31 S, Williamsburg, VA 23185. Tel 757-253-4838; Fax 757-253-5299; Web:

www.historyisfun.org; www.shophistoryisfun.org; *Capital Projects Admin* Michael S Shuflat; *Human Resources Mgr* Patrick G Teague; *Facilities Mgr* Douglas P Duval; *Dir Finance* Jean L Puckett; *Deputy Dir Admin* John J Lunsford; *Chief Develop Officer* Carter S Sonders; *Senior Develop Officer* Julie W Basic; *Exec Asst to Boards* Laura W Bailey; *Exec Dir* Philip G Emerson; *Media Relations Mgr* Deborah L Padgett; *Sr Sales & Promotions Mgr* Joan A Heikens; *Sr Retail Opers Mgr* Gary T Joyner; *Sr Dir Mktg & Retail Opers* Susan K Bak; *OESS Dir Educ* Pamela J Pettengel; *Exhib & Design Mgr* Rhonda R Tyson; *Dir Mus Educ* James S Holloway; *Curatorial Servs Mgr* Thomas E Davidson
Open daily 9 AM - 5 PM, cl Christmas & New Year's; Admis adults $15.50, children 6-12 $7.25 comb ticket adults $20, children 6-12 $10, American Heritage ann pass adults $35, children 6-12 $17.50; Estab 1957 as Jamestown Festival Park, renamed in 1990; Museum consists of indoor theater & gallery exhibs & outdoor living history prog; Average Annual Attendance: 90,639; Mem: 260; dues $25-$5000; annual meeting in Apr
Purchases: $20,000
Library Holdings: Auction Catalogs, Book Volumes, CD-ROMs, Fiche
Special Subjects: African Art, Anthropology, Archaeology, Ceramics, Coins & Medals, Etchings & Engravings, Folk Art, Furniture, Glass, Historical Material, Manuscripts, Maps, Metalwork, Period Rooms, Pewter, Porcelain, Portraits, Prints, Pottery, Reproductions, Silver, Textiles
Collections: 1,430 non-archaeological & approx 179,000 archaeological objects reflecting Jamestown's English origins, 16th & 17th century portraits, documents, furnishings, toys, ceremonial & decorative objects, tools & weapons
Publications: Series of biographies of Revolutionary Virginia leaders; brochures
Activities: Classes for adults & children; docent training; lects open to pub, 8 vis lectrs per yr; tours; outreach educ progs in 118 Virginia school districts; sales shop sells books, original art, reproductions

M **Yorktown-Victory Center,** 200 Water St, Yorktown, VA 23690; PO Box 1607, Williamsburg, VA 23187-1607. Tel 757-887-7116; Fax 757-887-1306; Web: www.historyisfun.org; www.shophistoryisfun.org
Open daily 9 AM - 5 PM, cl Christmas Day & New Year's Day; Admis adults $9.75, children 6-12 $5.50, comb ticket adults $20, children 6-12 $10, American Heritage ann pass adults $35, children 6-12 $17.50; Estab 1976, renovated in 1990's with new gallery exhibs; currently under renovation to become American Revolutionary Museum at Yorktown; Mus consists of timeline, exhib galleries & outdoor living history to recreate the history of the American Revolution
Collections: Approx 1,300 artifacts of 18th century, including documents, paintings, engravings, military equipment, nautical objects, medical tools, clothing, personal effects & household objects

M **WILLIAMSBURG CONTEMPORARY ART CENTER,** (This Century Art Gallery), 219 N Boundary St, Williamsburg, VA 23187; PO Box 388, Williamsburg, VA 23187-0388. Tel 757-229-4949; Web: www.visitWCAC.org; *Pres* Janis Wood; *VPres & Artistic Dir* Apryl Miller Altman; *Art Center Coordinator* Andrea Lemieux
Open Tues - Sat 11 AM - 3 PM, Sun 1 - 4 PM; cl Mon; Thanksgiving; Christmas; No admis fee; Estab 1959; Non-profit, volunteer run organization; Average Annual Attendance: 4,800; Mem: Dues Individual $45; family $65
Income: grants, donations, memberships, fundraisers
Collections: arts & crafts of contemporary artists
Publications: annual brochure; quarterly newsletter
Activities: Educ prog; classes for adults & children; workshops; lect open to the public; gallery talks; tours; sponsoring of competitions; scholarships; high school show; Annual members show awards; Sales shop; Original Art; Reproductions; Prints

WASHINGTON

BAINBRIDGE ISLAND

M **BAINBRIDGE ARTS & CRAFTS GALLERY,** 151 Winslow Way E, Bainbridge Island, WA 98110. Tel 206-842-3132; Fax 206-780-8149; Email gallery@bacart.org; Web: bacart.org; *Exec Dir* Lindsay Masters; *Prog & Outreach Dir* Georgia Browne; *Business Mgr* John Donbeck; *Registrar & Curatorial Team* Anne Gendreau; *Mktg & Curatorial Coordr* Savannah Newton; *Retail Mgr & Art Rental Mgr, Curatorial Team* Sara Papajani; *Chief Storyteller* Alex Sanso; *Dir Exhibs, Curatorial Team* David Sessions; *Educ Coordr, Shipping Assoc & Art Rental* Susan Wiersema
Open Mon - Sat 10 AM - 6 PM, Sun 11 AM - 5 PM; No admis fee; Estab 1948; Non-profit art gallery & education center; Average Annual Attendance: 41,000; Mem: dues $50-$1,000
Special Subjects: Sculpture, Glass, Photography, Printmaking, Ceramics, Jewelry
Collections: sculpture; painting; fiber; glass; photography; printmaking; ceramics; jewelry
Exhibitions: 18 special exhibitions annually
Activities: Classes for adults; lects open to the pub; 12 vis lects per year; gallery talks; Schols available; sales shop sells original art

A **BAINBRIDGE ISLAND ARTS COUNCIL,** 221 Winslow Way W, Ste 201, Bainbridge Island, WA 98110. Tel 206-842-7901; Fax 206-842-8825; Email admin@artshum.org; Web: www.artshum.org; *Exec Dir* Morgan Smith; *Prog Dir* Devon Zotovich Phillips; *Prog Dir* Lindsay Latimore
Open Mon-Thurs 9 AM - 4 PM; Estab 1986
Income: Financed by city & state appropriations & donations
Activities: Artist grants offered

BELLEVUE

M **BELLEVUE ARTS MUSEUM,** 510 Bellevue Way NE, Bellevue, WA 98004-5014. Tel 425-519-0770; Fax 425-637-1799; Email info@bellevuearts.org; Web: www.bellevuearts.org; *Director of Development* Sonia Doughty; *Dir Mktg & Communs* Karin Kidder; *Exec Dir* Linda Pawson
Open Office: Mon - Fri 9 AM - 5 PM; Mus: Tues - Sun 11 AM - 6 PM, free first Fri 11 AM - 8 PM; Admis adults $12, seniors & students $10, children under 6 & mems no admis fee; family ticket (up to 2 adults & 4 children under 18) $30; Estab 1975 to be the Pacific Northwest's center for the exploration of art, craft & design; Maintains 6000 sq ft for changing & temporary exhibs; Average Annual Attendance: 75,000; Mem: 1,800; annual mem fee
Income: $2,900,000 (financed by mem, pvt contributions, store sales, grants, fundraising events, arts & crafts fair)
Special Subjects: Ceramics, Crafts, Decorative Arts, Drawings, Embroidery, Enamels, Folk Art, Furniture, Furniture, Gold, Jewelry, Porcelain, Pottery, Sculpture, Textiles, Woodcarvings, Glass, Metalwork, Prints
Exhibitions: Quarterly rotating exhibs
Publications: Member newsletters; exhibition catalogs; posters; program brochures
Activities: Classes for adults & children; docent training; lects open to pub, 2-4 vis lectrs per yr; films; talks; tours; symposia; hands-on activities for children; awards through art & craft juries; competitions; originates traveling exhibs; mus store sells books, prints, jewelry, reproductions, cards & papers, original art & gifts

M **LEGACY LTD,** 11217 NE 15th St, Bellevue, WA 98004-3720. Tel 206-624-6350; Fax 206-624-4108; Email legacy@drizzle.com; Web: www.thelegacyltd.com; *Pres* Helen Carlson; *VPres* Paul Nicholson
Open Mon - Sat 10 AM - 6 PM; No admis fee; Estab 1933 for the coll & sale of Northwest Coast Indian contemporary & historic material
Exhibitions: Annual in-house special exhibits of historic contemporary Northwest Coast Indian & Eskimo art, ongoing exhibits of same
Activities: Sales shop sells books, magazines, original art & prints

BELLINGHAM

M **WESTERN WASHINGTON UNIVERSITY,** Viking Union Gallery, 516 High St, VU Room 422 Bellingham, WA 98225-5946. Tel 360-650-6534, Exten 6534; Fax 360-650-7736; Email as.gallery@wwwu.edu; Web: www.gallery.as.wwu.edu; *Dir* Hannah Fenske; *Adv* Casey Hayden
Open Mon - Fri 11 AM 5 PM; No admis fee; Estab 1969 to provide a wide variety of gallery exhibits for western students and the community; The gallery is a student run venue that strives to support local, student, and national artists; Average Annual Attendance: 5,000
Income: $8,500 (financed by student activity fees)
Collections: Matthew Curry
Exhibitions: Exhibitions change every month; Annual Beyond Borders International; Undergraduate Fine Art Competition; Annual Labyrinth Women's Exhibition & Literary Journal
Activities: Lects open to pub; sponsoring of competitions; awards to top 3 winners in Beyond Borders

M **Western Gallery,** Fine Arts Complex, WWU Bellingham, WA 98225-9068; 516 High St, MS9068, Western Washington University Bellingham, WA 98225. Tel 360-650-3900; Fax 360-650-6878; Email sarah.clarklangager@wwu.edu; Web: www.westerngallery.wwu.edu; *Mus Spec* Paul Brower
Open Mon, Tues, Thurs & Fri 10 AM - 4 PM, Wed 10 AM - 8 PM, Sat Noon - 4 PM when university is in session; No admis fee; Old gallery estab 1950, new gallery estab 1989 to exhibit contemporary art; Washington Art Consortium office & collections based at Western Gallery. Rotating exhibitions on contemporary art, 3-4 per yr; Average Annual Attendance: 15,000
Income: Financed by state appropriation & endowment for exhibs
Special Subjects: Graphics, Sculpture
Collections: Outdoor Sculpture Collection WWU (contemporary sculpture since 1960), American drawings & prints, 20th Century Chair Collection
Exhibitions: Rotating exhibits every 6-8 weeks
Publications: Outdoor Sculpture Collection brochures; "Sculpture in Place: A Campus as Site" published by Western Washington University
Activities: Lects open to pub, 3 vis lectrs per year; gallery talks; tours of outdoor sculpture collection; Wed noon hour & evening discussions

M **WHATCOM MUSEUM,** 121 Prospect St, Bellingham, WA 98225-4497. Tel 360-778-8930; Fax 360-778-8931; Email info@whatcommuseum.org; Web: www.whatcommuseum.org; *Dir* Patricia Leach; *Cur Art* Barbara Matilsky; *Educ* Mary Jo Maute; *Cur Colls* Rebecca Hutchins; *Dir Learning Innovation* Susanna Brooks; *Develop & Membership Mgr* Althea Harris; *Exhib Designer* Scott Wallin; *Photo Archives Historian* Jeff Jewell; *Mktg & PR Mgr* Christina Claassen
Open Wed - Sun noon - 5 PM, cl Mon, Tues & holidays; Admis adults $10, seniors, youth/students & military $8, children $5; Estab 1941 to collect, preserve & use, through exhibits, interpretation & research, objects of historic or artistic value & to act as a multi-purpose cultural center for the Northwest Washington area providing presentations in all aspects of the arts and history; Three galleries (9,000 sq ft) in the new Leed Silver Lightcatcher bldg; permanent & rotating historical exhib spaces in the 1892 City Hall mus; Average Annual Attendance: 100,000; Mem: 1650; dues family $75, individual $50
Income: Financed by pvt & pub funds
Library Holdings: Exhibition Catalogs, Kodachrome Transparencies, Manuscripts, Maps, Original Art Works, Original Documents, Photographs, Prints, Records, Sculpture, Slides, Video Tapes
Special Subjects: Crafts, Dioramas, Dolls, Drawings, Ethnology, Folk Art, Historical Material, Landscapes, Painting-American, Period Rooms, Photography, Portraits, Sculpture, Textiles, Watercolors, Woodcarvings
Collections: Modern & Contemporary Northwest Art, Darius Kinsey, J Wilbur Sandison, Bert W Huntoon, Jack Carver & Galen Biary Historic Photographic Collections, Northwest Native American Artifacts, Regional Historic Photographs & Artifacts, H C Hanson Naval Architecture Collection, Edson-Edson-Booth Bird Collection
Exhibitions: Rotating exhibits every 4-6 months
Publications: Art & Events Calendar, quarterly; Exhibit catalogs; History texts
Activities: Classes for adults & children; docent training; lects open to pub, 60 vis lectrs per yr; concerts; gallery talks; tours; exten dept serves public school outreach & community outreach; 2-3 book traveling exhibs per year; originate traveling exhibs; mus shop sells books, original art & reproductions; Artifacts Cafe

CLARKSTON

A **VALLEY ART CENTER INC,** 842 Sixth St, Clarkston, WA 99403. Tel 509-758-8331; Email artcenter@cableone.net; *Dir* Robin Harvey; *Treas* Ivy Breen; *VPres* Judy Fairley; *Bd Mbr* Vikki Wayne; *Bd Mbr* Donna Baker
Open Tues - Thurs 9 AM - 3 PM, Fri noon - 6 PM, Sat 11 AM - 3 PM & by appointment; No admis fee, donations accepted; Estab 1968 to encourage & instruct in all forms of the visual arts & to promote the cause of art in the community; A portion of the center serves as the gallery; wall space for display of paintings or other art; showcases for colls & artifacts; Average Annual Attendance: 5,000-7,000; Mem: 200; dues $40; annual meeting in Jan
Income: Financed by mem & class fees
Purchases: Utilities; advertising; supplies
Library Holdings: Book Volumes, Original Art Works, Video Tapes
Publications: Exhibit calendar
Activities: Classes for seniors, adults & children; lect open to public, 4 vis lectrs per year; gallery talks; tours; competitions with awards; scholarships offered; individual paintings & original objects of art lent to local bus & individuals, including artists; lending collection contains books, original prints, paintings, records & photographs; sales shop sells books, original art, sculpture, prints, pottery & soft goods

COUPEVILLE

A **PACIFIC NORTHWEST ART SCHOOL,** Gallery at the Wharf, 15 NW Birch St, Coupeville, WA 98239-3103. Tel 360-678-3396, 866-678-3396; Fax 360-678-7420; Email info@pacificnorthwestartschool.org; Web: www.pacificnorthwestartschool.com; *Exec Dir* Judy G Lynn; *Educ Dir* Soledad Sahdana-Melber; *Reg & Prog Dir* Jan Graham; *Prog Mgr* Cis Branaff
Open Mon - Fri 9 AM - 4 PM; No admis fee; Estab 1989 for arts educ; Average Annual Attendance: 1,400; Mem: 450; dues vary; annual meeting in Jan
Library Holdings: Auction Catalogs, Audio Tapes, Book Volumes, Cassettes, Exhibition Catalogs, Memorabilia
Collections: Paintings & photography donated by NFS faculty & students
Publications: Biannual catalog of visual arts workshops
Activities: Classes for adults & children; lects open to pub 3-4 times per year, scholarships offered; serves Whidbey Island and lends original objects of art to bus and libraries; sales shop sells prints and original art

ELLENSBURG

M **CENTRAL WASHINGTON UNIVERSITY,** Sarah Spurgeon Gallery, 400 E University Way, Ellensburg, WA 98926-7564. Tel 509-963-2665; Fax 509-963-1918; Email art.dept@cwu.edu; Web: www.cwu.edu/art; *Dir Art Gallery* Heather Horn Johnson
Open Mon - Fri 10 AM - 3 PM, Sat & Sun 1 PM -4 PM; No admis fee; Estab 1970 to serve as university gallery & hold regional & national exhibits; The gallery is a large, single unit; Average Annual Attendance: 20,000
Income: Financed by state appropriations
Exhibitions: Rotating exhibits
Publications: Catalogs for all National shows
Activities: Lect open to public; competitions

M **CLYMER MUSEUM OF ART,** The Clymer Museum & Gallery, 416 N Pearl St, Ellensburg, WA 98926-3112. Tel 509-962-6416; Email director@clymermuseum.org; Web: www.clymermuseum.org; *Dir* Jami-Lynn Tate; *Cur* Lucas Orthmann; *Buyer/Merchandiser* Edie Rouleau
Open Mon - Fri 10 AM - 5 PM, Sat 10 AM - 3 PM, cl Sun, major holidays; No admis fee, donations accepted; Estab 1985 to preserve & promote the works of John F. Clymer; Two rooms with art from visiting artists; Average Annual Attendance: 25,000; Mem: 300; dues $35-$1000
Income: Financed by mem, gift shop sales & fund raisers
Library Holdings: Auction Catalogs, Audio Tapes, Cards, Cassettes, Clipping Files, DVDs, Exhibition Catalogs, Framed Reproductions, Memorabilia, Original Art Works, Original Documents, Other Holdings, Pamphlets, Periodical Subscriptions, Photographs, Prints, Reproductions, Sculpture, Slides, Video Tapes
Special Subjects: Bronzes, Drawings, Landscapes, Military Art, Painting-American, Photography, Portraits, Posters, Prints, Reproductions, Restorations, Sculpture, Southwestern Art
Collections: John Ford Clymer's Works of Art, illustration, historical, outdoor
Exhibitions: Life & Art of John F Clymer; exhibits of visiting artists change every two months
Publications: newsletter
Activities: Classes for children; docent training; lects open to pub, 6 vis lectrs per yr; concerts; awards, Juried Art Show; book traveling exhibs 1 per yr; mus shop sells books, original art, reproductions & prints

M **GALLERY ONE VISUAL ARTS CENTER,** 408 N Pearl St, Ellensburg, WA 98926-3112. Tel 509-925-2670; Email director@gallery-one.org; Web: www.gallery-one.org; *Exec Dir* Carol Hassen; *Asst Dir* Monica Miller; *Arts Programmer* Renee Adams; *Retail Mgr* Sarah Haven; *Educ Coordr* Becky Parmenter
Open Mon - Fri 11 AM - 5 PM, Sat & Sun noon - 4 PM; No admis fee; Estab 1968 to offer quality artistic & educational experience to all ages; 3 exhib galleries, gift gallery, 4 ed rooms, ceramics studio, 7 artists studios; Average Annual Attendance: 100,000; Mem: 350; dues $200-$500; meeting 3rd Mon each month
Income: $200,000 (financed by sales, mem & fundraisers)
Special Subjects: Bronzes, Ceramics, Collages, Crafts, Decorative Arts, Dolls, Drawings, Enamels, Etchings & Engravings, Glass, Graphics, Jewelry, Landscapes, Marine Painting, Metalwork, Painting-American, Pewter, Photography, Porcelain, Pottery, Prints, Scrimshaw, Sculpture, Silver, Stained Glass
Exhibitions: See website
Activities: Occasional classes for adults & children; lect open to public, 10 vis lectrs per yr; competitions with awards; gallery talks; tours; juried exhibs $2500 in awards; individual paintings are lent; lending collection contains original artworks, paintings & sculptures; sales shop sells books, original art, reproductions, prints, arts & crafts

A **WESTERN ART ASSOCIATION,** 309 N Pearl St, Ellensburg, WA 98926-3995. Tel 509-962-2934; Fax 509-962-8515; Email waa@elltel.net; Web: www.westernartassoc.org; *Pres* Bill Phillip; *VPres* Larry MacGuffie; *Secy* Sandy Elliot; *Treas & Exec Dir* JoAnn Wise
Open third weekend in May Fri - Sat 10 AM - 10 PM, Sun 10 AM - 3 PM; Estab 1972 to promote western art, artifacts & heritage; Annual art show, sale & auction; Average Annual Attendance: 3,000 - 8,000; Mem: 275; dues family $50, individual $25; annual meeting in Aug
Income: $125,000 (financed by mem, Annual National Ellensburg Art Show & Auction, grants & sponsors)
Special Subjects: American Western Art
Activities: Lect open to pub; competitions with prizes; Best of Show; People's Choice; other media; schols offered; individual paintings & original objects of art lent; originate traveling exhibs 1 per yr; sales shop sells prints & original art

EVERETT

M **RUSSELL DAY GALLERY,** Parks Student Union Bldg, Rm 219, 2000 Tower St Everett, WA 98201-1352. Tel 435-388-9036; Email slepper@everettcc.edu; Web: www.everettcc.edu/russelldaygallery; *Dir* Sandra Lepper
Open Mon - Wed 8 AM - 7 PM, Thurs - Fri 8 AM - 4 PM
Collections: Paintings

FRIDAY HARBOR

M **WESTCOTT BAY INSTITUTE,** Island Museum of Art & Westcott Bay Sculpture Park, 314 Spring St, Friday Harbor, WA 98250; PO Box 339, Friday Harbor, WA 98250-0339. Tel 360-370-5050; Fax 360-370-5805; Email kay@wbay.org; Web: www.wbay.org; *Dir* Kay Kammerzell
Open Island Museum of Art: Tues - Sat 11 AM - 5 PM with extended summer hours, Westcott Bay Sculpture Park: daily dawn - dusk year-round; No admis fee for Island Museum of Art, Westcott Bay Sculpture Park: adults $5, children free; Estab 2000; Exhib of 2 & 3 dimensional art focusing on northwest & west coast contemp art; Average Annual Attendance: 50,000; Mem: 300
Income: Financed by grants & membership
Special Subjects: Bronzes, Glass, Metalwork, Sculpture, Woodcarvings
Activities: Classes for adults & children; tours; exhibitions; mus shop sells books & original art

GOLDENDALE

M **MARYHILL MUSEUM OF ART,** 35 Maryhill Museum Dr, Goldendale, WA 98620-4601. Tel 509-773-3733; Fax 509-773-6138; Email maryhill@maryhillmuseum.org; Web: www.maryhillmuseum.org; *Dir* Colleen Schafroth; *CFO* Leslie Wetherell; *Cur Art* Steven L. Grafe; *Cur Educ* Louise Palermo; *Coll Mgr* Anna Goodwin
Open daily 10 AM - 5 PM Mar 15 - Nov 15; Admis adults $9, seniors $8, students 7-18 $3, under 6 free; Opened 1940 as a museum of art; Chateau-style mansion with 4 stories of galleries on 26 acres of parklands plus full scale Stonehenge nearby; cafe & museum shop; Average Annual Attendance: 45,000; Mem: 450; dues $50 individual, $75 family
Special Subjects: American Indian Art, Antiquities-Greek, Decorative Arts, Drawings, Etchings & Engravings, Ethnology, Furniture, Glass, Historical Material, Painting-American, Painting-British, Prints, Religious Art, Sculpture, Textiles
Collections: American Indian Art, antique & modern chess sets, European & American paintings, Queen of Romania furniture & memorabilia, regional historic photographs, Rodin sculpture & watercolors, Russian icons, 1946 costumed French fashion mannequins, decorative arts, art nouveau glass, Romanian Folk textiles, contemporary sculpture
Exhibitions: Plein air painting event (annually in Aug)
Publications: Brochure, souvenir & exhibition booklets
Activities: Classes for adults & children, performing arts progs, docent training; lects open to pub, 4 vis lectrs per yr; gallery talks; tours; lending collection contains individual paintings & original objects of art; book traveling exhibs, 1 - 2 annually; mus shop sells gift items & publications on collections

GREENBANK

M **ROB SCHOUTEN GALLERY,** 765 Wonn Rd, Greenbank Farm, C103 Greenbank, WA 98253. Tel 360-222-3070; Email rob@robschoutengallery.com; Web: www.robschoutengallery.com
Open Summer daily 10AM-5PM, Winter daily 11AM-4PM
Collections: works by Rob Schouten including oil paintings, etchings, & Giclee prints; works by other artists include paintings, drawings, printmaking, & sculpture

KENNEWICK

A **ARTS COUNCIL OF THE MID-COLUMBIA REGION,** 5 N Morain, Kennewick, WA. Tel 509-943-6702; Fax 509-943-6164; Email arts council@tcfn.org; Web: www.owt.com/arts/artscouncil; *Exec Dir* Beth Perry
Open Mon - Fri 10 AM - 5 PM, Sat 11 AM - 3 PM; Estab Apr 1968 to advocate the arts in the Mid-Columbia Region; Average Annual Attendance: 17,000; Mem: 300; dues $35
Income: $130,000 (financed by city, corporate & private mem)
Publications: Calendar, weekly
Activities: Educ progs; lects open to pub, 5 vis lectrs per yr; gallery talks; tours; book traveling exhibs 1 per yr

KIRKLAND

M **KIRKLAND ARTS CENTER,** KAC Gallery, 620 Market St, Kirkland, WA 98033-5421. Tel 425-822-7161; Email info@kirklandartscenter.org; Web: www.kirklandartscenter.org; *Exec Dir* Pamela Rembold; *Exhib Prog Mgr* Colleen Lenahan; *Educ Dir* Sarah Beggs; *Develop Dir* Jennifer Gill; *Educ Project Mgr* Liz VanBemmel; *Develop Mktg Mgr* Jenny Lee; *Sr Ceramics Technician* Pat Colyar
Open Mon - Fri 11 AM - 6 PM,Sat 11 AM - 5 PM; gallery cl Mon; No admis fee; Estab 1962; Contemporary art gallery; Average Annual Attendance: 10,000
Collections: paintings; sculpture; ceramics; prints
Activities: Classes for adults & children; lects open to pub; 16 vis lectrs per yr; gallery talks; awards: ParentMap Golden Teddy; extension prog to Seattle's eastside; lending of original art to Kirkland pub library

LA CONNER

M **MUSEUM OF NORTHWEST ART,** 121 S First St, La Conner, WA 98257; PO Box 969, La Conner, WA 98257-0969. Tel 360-466-4446; Email christyl@museumofnwart.org; Web: www.monamuseum.org; *Exec Dir* Christopher Shainin; *Mktg Mgr* Christy Lyman; *Educ Dir* Jasmine Valandani; *Finance Dir* Tessa Rose Peterson; *Store Mgr* Keshema May; *Devel Dir* Liz Theaker; *Cur* Kathleen Moles; *Assoc Cur* Chloe Dye Sherpe
Open Sun & Mon noon - 5 PM, Tues - Sat 10 AM - 5 PM; No admis fee; Estab 1981 to preserve, protect & interpret the fine visual art of the Pacific Northwest; Average Annual Attendance: 15,000; Mem: 1000; dues $35-$1000
Income: $700,000 (financed by mem, admis, grants, donations & special events)
Special Subjects: Ceramics, Collages, Drawings, Etchings & Engravings, Glass, Graphics, Historical Material, Jewelry, Landscapes, Landscapes, Latin American Art, Marine Painting, Metalwork, Oriental Art, Painting-American, Painting-American, Photography, Photography, Porcelain, Portraits, Pottery, Prints, Prints, Sculpture, Watercolors, Woodcarvings, Woodcuts, Textiles
Collections: Northwest painting, drawing, sculpture & prints, studio glass
Publications: Catalogs; quarterly newsletter
Activities: Classes for adults & children; docent training; lects open to pub; 15 vis lectrs per yr; gallery talks; tours; Governor's Arts Award; book traveling exhibs 1 per yr; originate traveling exhibs 1 per yr; mus shop sells books, original art, reproductions, prints, jewelry, paper products, fiber art & sculpture

OLYMPIA

M **EVERGREEN STATE COLLEGE,** Evergreen Gallery, 2700 Evergreen Pkwy NW, Olympia, WA 98505. Tel 360-867-5125; Fax 360-867-6794; Email friedma@evergreen.edu; Web: www.evergreen.edu/gallery; *Dir* Ann Friedman
Open Mon - Thurs Noon - 4 PM; No admis fee; Contemporary Gallery; Average Annual Attendance: 4,000
Income: grants, fellowship, donations
Special Subjects: American Indian Art, Ceramics, Drawings, Etchings & Engravings, Painting-American, Photography, Pottery, Prints, Sculpture, Woodcuts, Textiles
Collections: Evergreen State College Art Collection, black & white photography, prints, ceramics, paintings
Exhibitions: Contemporary West Coast & US art; Native American Art
Activities: Lects open to pub; concerts; gallery talks; tours; book traveling exhib 1 or 2 per yr

M **MONARCH CONTEMPORARY ART CENTER & SCULPTURE PARK,** 8431 Waldrick Rd SE, Olympia, WA 98501; 7332 Churchill Rd, Tenino, WA 98589. Tel 360-264-7777; Fax 360-264-4646; Email heernett@aol.com; Web: www.monarchartcenter.org; *Contact* Chanelle Holbrook-Shaw
Open dawn to dusk; Admis donation; Estab 1998; showcasing art work; 1,200 sq ft with reception kitchen attached; Average Annual Attendance: 1,800
Income: Donations & grants, $15,000-$20,000 per yr
Collections: Valentine Wellman paintings & sculptures

M **STATE CAPITAL MUSEUM,** 211 21st Ave W, Olympia, WA 98501. Tel 360-753-2580; Fax 360-586-8322; Email dvalley@wshs.wa.gov; Web: www.wshs.org; *Cur Exhib* Redmond Barnett; *Dir* Derek R Valley; *Cur Educ* Susan Rohrer
Open Tues - Fri 10 AM - 4 PM, Sat Noon - 4 PM, cl Sun & Mon; Admis family $5, adults $2, seniors $1.75, children $1; Estab 1941 to interpret history of the State of Washington & of the capital city; The one-room gallery presents changing monthly shows; Average Annual Attendance: 40,000; Mem: 400; dues family $12, individual $6; annual meeting in June
Income: Financed by city & state appropriation & local funds
Special Subjects: American Indian Art, Etchings & Engravings, Woodcuts
Collections: Etchings by Thomas Handforth, Winslow Homer Woodcuts, Northwest Indian serigraphs
Exhibitions: Rotating exhibits
Publications: Museum Newsletter, bi-monthly; Museum Calendar; every other month: lists all scheduled events; Columbia, The Magazine of Northwest History
Activities: Classes for adults & children; dramatic progs; docent training; lects open to pub; concerts; gallery talks; tours; individual paintings & original objects of art lent to State offices; lending collection contains original prints, paintings; originate traveling exhibs; sales shop sells books & slides

PORT ANGELES

M **CITY OF PORT ANGELES,** Port Angeles Fine Arts Center & Webster Woods Art Park, 1203 E Lauridsen Blvd, Port Angeles, WA 98362-6630; PO Box 1695, Port Angeles, WA 98362. Tel 360-457-3532; Email pafac@olypen.com; Web: www.pafac.org; *Board President* Phillis Olson; *Administrative Director* Jessica Elliott; *Gallery and Program Manager* Laura Alisanne
Check website for hours; No admis fee, donations accepted; Estab 1986; 1950's NW contemporary semi-circular home designed by Paul Hayden Kirk, converted to gallery. Changing shows of contemporary art in all media. Panoramic views & integration of natural surroundings in gallery space via many glass walls. Five acre Webster Woods Art Park with over 125 works; Average Annual Attendance: 18,000; Mem: 300; dues $35 & up
Income: $175,000 (financed by endowment, mem, grants & corporate gifts)
Library Holdings: Exhibition Catalogs, Kodachrome Transparencies, Original Art Works, Photographs, Prints, Sculpture, Slides, Video Tapes
Special Subjects: Ceramics, Collages, Drawings, Glass, Landscapes, Painting-American, Painting-Canadian, Photography, Posters, Sculpture, Watercolors, Woodcuts
Collections: Esther Webster Art Collection, miscellaneous donated works, Art Park has numerous gifted & donated works
Exhibitions: Art outside - year round sculpture park; 4 original exhibits
Activities: Classes for adults and children; docent progs; dramatic programs;; lects open to pub, 4 vis lectrs per yr; concerts; readings; gallery talks; tours; scholarships; fellowships; sales shop sells books, handicrafts, magazines, original art, reproductions & prints

PORT TOWNSEND

A **CENTRUM ARTS & CREATIVE EDUCATION,** Fort Worden State Park, PO Box 1158 Port Townsend, WA 98368-0958. Tel 360-385-3102; Fax 360-385-2470; Email jmacelwee@centrum.org; Web: www.centrum.org; WATS 800-733-3608; *Exec Dir* John A MacElwee; *Young Artist Proj Prog Mgr* Martha Worthley; *Dir Progs* Jodan Hartt; *Dir Opers* Lisa Werner
Open Mon - Fri 8:30 AM - 5 PM; Estab 1973 to assist those who seek creative & intellectual growth & to present visual, literary & performing arts to the pub; Average Annual Attendance: 38,500; Mem: 800; dues $25 & up
Income: Financed by donations, fees & grants
Collections: Collection of prints from artists in residence
Activities: Resident workshops for children; dramatic progs; lects open to pub, 20 vis lectrs per yr; concerts; awards; gallery talks; scholarships; artist in residence prog

M **NORTHWIND ARTS CENTER,** 701 Water St, Port Townsend, WA 98368-5728. Tel 360-379-1086; Email info@northwindarts.org; Web: northwindarts.org; TWX 360-379-1086; *Exec Dir* Michael D'Alessandro; *Gallery Mgr* Jay Haskins
Open Wed - Mon 11:30 AM - 5:30 PM, cl Tues; Estab to foster visual, literary & performing arts
Collections: painting; sculpture
Exhibitions: Monthly exhibits
Activities: Artist talks; workshops

PULLMAN

M **WASHINGTON STATE UNIVERSITY,** Museum of Art, PO Box 647460, Pullman, WA 99164-7460. Tel 509-335-1910 (office); Fax 509-335-1908; Email artmuse@wsu.edu; Web: www.museum.wsu.edu; *Dir* Chris Bruce; *Assoc. Dir* Anna-Maria Shannon; *Cur* Keith Wells; *Asst Cur* Zachary Mazur; *Dir Develop* Jill Aesoph; *Media/PR Mgr* Debby Stinson
Open Mon - Fri 10 AM - 4 PM, Thurs 10 AM - 7 PM, Sat & Sun 1 - 5 PM, cl Sun; No admis fee; Estab 1973 to contribute to the humanistic & artistic educational purpose & goal of the university for the direct benefit of the students, faculty & surrounding communities; Gallery covers 5000 sq ft & is centrally located on campus; Average Annual Attendance: 28,000; Mem: 400; dues $50-$1000; annual meeting in the spring
Income: Financed by the state of Washington, private & pub grants & contributions
Library Holdings: Audio Tapes, Book Volumes, Exhibition Catalogs, Kodachrome Transparencies, Memorabilia, Pamphlets, Slides, Video Tapes
Special Subjects: Painting-American, Photography, Prints
Collections: Late 19th century to present-day American art, with particular strength in the areas of the Ash Can School & Northwest regional art, contemporary American & British prints
Exhibitions: Annual; fine arts faculty & the master of fine arts thesis; permanent collection, rental/traveling
Activities: Classes for children and adults; docent training; lect open to public, 2-5 vis lectrs per year; concerts, gallery talks; tours; competitions; 2-4 book traveling exhibitions per year

RICHLAND

A **ALLIED ARTS ASSOCIATION,** Allied Arts Center & Gallery, 89 Lee Blvd, Richland, WA 99352-4222. Tel 509-943-9815; Fax 509-943-4068; Email info@galleryatthepark.org; Web: www.galleryatthepark.org; *Gallery Adminr* Bethany Beard; *Pres* Bob Allen
Open Tues - Sat 11 AM - 5 PM; No admis fee; Estab 1947 to stimulate interest in various forms of visual art; 4532 sq ft. Consists of the Townside Gallery, Motyka Room, Parkside Gallery & an Educational Wing; Mem: 400; dues $20; annual meeting in Nov
Income: $80,000
Library Holdings: Book Volumes 500
Exhibitions: Monthly Exhibitions; Annual Sidewalk Show
Activities: Classes for adults & children; docent progs; conferences; lects open to pub; Szulinski Award; schols & fels offered; sales shop sells original art, prints, pottery & fine crafts

SEATTLE

A **4 CULTURE,** (King County Arts Commission), 101 Prefontaine Pl S, Seattle, WA 98104-2672. Tel 206-296-7580; Fax 206-296-8629; Email hello@4culture.org; Web: www.4culture.org; *Exec Dir* Jim Kelly

Open Mon - Fri 9 AM - 5 PM, first Thurs of month 6 PM - 8 PM; Estab 1967 to provide cultural arts opportunities to the citizens of King County; 4Culture purchases & commissions many works of art for public buildings; annual grant program for organizations & artists in all artistic disciplines, also multi-cultural & disabled arts population; operates touring program of performing arts events in county locations; Mem: 16; 1 meeting per month
Income: $1,300,000 million (financed by county government, plus one percent for commissioned art in county construction projects)
Purchases: Occasional works commissioned for public art
Exhibitions: Rotating exhibits
Publications: The ARTS, bimonthly newsletter; The Touring Arts Booklet biennially; public art brochure; guide to programs, annually
Activities: Workshops; performances

A **911 MEDIA ARTS CENTER,** 909 NE 43rd St, Ste 206 Seattle, WA 98105-6020. Tel 206-682-6552; Email info@911media.org; Web: www.911media.org; *Exec Dir* Steven Michael Vroom; *Commun Dir* Nichole Rathburn
Open Mon - Fri Noon - 6 PM; No admis fee; Estab 1981 as a film & video post-production center; Exhibition space; Average Annual Attendance: 15,000; Mem: 500; dues $50
Income: Financed by earned income, grants including McArthur Foundation, NEA, WASAC, SAC, KCAC, 4 Culture, Andy Warhol Foundation
Collections: Artists' video tapes
Publications: Film & video calendar, bimonthly
Activities: Workshops in film video making, video editing, grant writing & internet; educ prog; classes for adults & children; lects open to pub, 3 vis lectrs per yr; gallery talks; tours; awards Anne Focke Arts Leadership Award; schols & fel awarded

A **ALLIED ARTS OF SEATTLE,** PO Box 4426, Seattle, WA 98194. Tel 206-696-0414; Email info@alliedartsofseattle.org; Web: alliedartsofseattle.org; *Pres* Laine Ross; *VPres* David Allen
Open Mon - Fri 9 AM - 4:30 PM; No admis fee; Estab 1954 to promote & support the arts & artists of the Northwest & to help create the kind of city that will attract the kind of people who support the arts; Mem: 500; dues $35 - $250 depending on category; annual meeting Jan
Income: $70,000 (financed by mem & fundraising events)
Publications: Access: The Lively Arts, directory of arts organizations in Puget Sound, biannual; Art Deco Seattle; Image of Imagination: Terra-Cotta Seattle

A **COCA CENTER ON CONTEMPORARY ART,** Seattle Design Center Ste 258, 5701 6th Ave S Seattle, WA 98108-2521. Tel 206-728-1980; Email info@cocaseattle.org; Web: www.cocaseattle.org; *Exec Dir* Nichole DeMent; *Project Mgr* Andrea Lim; *Develop & Progs* Megan Glasscock
Open Thurs - Sat 11 AM - 6 PM; No admis fee; Estab 1980 to serve as a catalyst & forum for the advancement & understanding of contemporary art; Average Annual Attendance: 40,000; Mem: 1000; dues $15-$100
Exhibitions: Nirvana: Capitalism & the Consumed Image; Square Painting
Publications: Bimonthly newsletter
Activities: Lects open to pub, 3 vis lectrs per yr; concerts; gallery talks; competitions with awards, five $1000 for new annual artist; book traveling exhibs; mus shop sells items depending on exhib

M **CORNISH COLLEGE OF THE ARTS,** Fisher Gallery, 1000 Lenora St, Seattle, WA 98121-2707. Tel 206-726-5151; Email artdept@cornish.edu; Web: www.cornish.edu/art/; *Dept Chair* Kent Devereaux; *Exhibition Cur* Jess Van Nostrand; *Production Coordr* Megan Campbell-Miller

L **Cornish Library**, 1000 Lenora St, Seattle, WA 98121. Tel 206-726-5145; Fax 206-315-5811; Email libraryref@cornish.edu; Web: www.cornish.edu/library; *Dir Library Svcs* Hollis Near; *Visual Arts Librn* Bridget Nowlin; *Reference & Instruction Librn* Megan Smithling; *Circulation Supervisor* Nicholas Triggs; *Library Specialist* Pamela Naylor
Open Mon - Thurs 8 AM - 9 PM, Fri 8 AM - 6 PM, Sat - Sun 1 PM - 5 PM, cl Veteran's Day & Thanksgiving; Estab 1914; Circ 15,000; Open to students, staff & faculty; open to public for reference only
Library Holdings: Auction Catalogs 600, Book Volumes 26,900, DVDs 1,511, Exhibition Catalogs 1000, Other Holdings CDs: 5,200, Periodical Subscriptions 184, Records 1,000, Slides 44,000, Video Tapes 768
Activities: Four yr visual & performing arts col

A **CORPORATE COUNCIL FOR THE ARTS/ARTS FUND,** 10 Harrison St, Ste 200, Seattle, WA 98109. Tel 206-281-9050; Fax 206-281-9175; Email info@artsfund.org; Web: www.cca-artsfund.org; *Pres & CEO* Mari R Horita; *Dir of Finance & Operations* Bradford Parker; *Develop & Engagement Mgr* Chantilly Chiles; *Program, Advocacy & Opers Mgr* Andrew Golden; *Develop Coord* Mike Myers
Open 8:30 AM - 5:30 PM; Estab 1968 as a clearinghouse for corporate contributions to the arts, to monitor budgeting of art agencies & assess ability of bus to provide funding assistance; Gallery not maintained; Mem: 304 corporate mem & 1697 individual mem; ann meeting in Oct
Income: $2,885,897 (financed by mem)
Publications: Annual Report; brochures; periodic membership reports
Activities: Annual fundraising event & campaign

M **FRYE ART MUSEUM,** 704 Terry Ave, Seattle, WA 98104-2019. Tel 206-622-9250; Fax 206-223-1707; Email info@fryemuseum.org; Web: www.fryemuseum.org; *Dir* Joseph Rosa
Open Tues - Sun - 11 AM - 5 PM, Thurs 11 AM - 7 PM, cl Mon; No admis fee; Estab 1952; Average Annual Attendance: 100,000
Income: pvt financed
Purchases: American paintings, contemporary, German & Austrian 19th & 20th century
Library Holdings: Book Volumes, DVDs, Exhibition Catalogs, Pamphlets, Periodical Subscriptions, Video Tapes
Special Subjects: Etchings & Engravings, Painting-American, Painting-Canadian, Painting-Dutch, Painting-French, Painting-German, Painting-Italian, Painting-Japanese, Painting-Polish, Painting-Russian, Painting-Scandinavian, Painting-Spanish, Prints, Watercolors
Collections: American masters from the Colonial period to painters of today, 19th & 20th century American, German & French paintings, Bordin, Kaulbach, Koester, Lenbach, Leibl, Liebermann, Lhermitte, Max, Monticelli, Stuck, Winterhalter, Zugel, Zumbusch, American paintings by Pendergast, Hassam, Cassatt, Henri, Sargent, Wyeth, Homer, Eakins, Copley, Stuart
Publications: Frye magazine, 3 times per yr
Activities: Classes for adults & children; docent training; films; lects open to pub; 25 vis lectrs per yr; concerts; gallery talks; tours; individual paintings & objects of art lent to mus exhibs; 2 book traveling exhibs per yr; originate traveling exhibs; mus shop sells books, reproductions, prints, original art, posters, slides, videos, art catalogs, toys, jewelry & other gift items

A **GLASS ART SOCIETY,** 6512 23rd Ave NW Ste 329, Seattle, WA 98117-5728. Tel 206-382-1305; Fax 206-382-2630; Email info@glassart.org; Web: www.glassart.org; *Exec Dir* Pamela Figenshow Koss
Open (office) Mon - Fri 9 AM - 5 PM; Estab 1971; Mem: dues $40-$1,000
Special Subjects: Glass
Collections: glass art
Exhibitions: Temporary exhibits

M **HENRY GALLERY ASSOCIATION,** Henry Art Gallery, 15th Ave NE & NE 41st St, Seattle, WA 98195. Tel 206-543-2280; Fax 206-685-3123; Email info@u.washington.edu; Web: www.henryart.org; *Dir* Sylvia Wolf; *Cur Coll* Judy Sourakli; *Communs* Dana Van Nest; *Dir Finance* Daren Hecker; *Foundation & Corp Giving Mgr* Angela Lindou; *Develop Assoc* Ashraf Harham; *Opers* Eric Canson; *Deputy Dir External Rels* Nan Garrison; *HR* Lisa Anderson; *Exec Asst* Dustin Engstrom
Open Sat, Sun & Wed 11 AM - 4 PM, Thurs & Fri 11 AM - 9 PM, cl Mon & Tues; Admis general $10, seniors $6, mems & student w/ID free; Estab 1927 for contemporary art; The Northwest's leading center for contemporary art; Average Annual Attendance: 70,000; Mem: 2500; dues $10 & up; ann meeting in the summer
Income: $3,800,000 (financed by endowment, mem, state appropriation & grants)
Library Holdings: Auction Catalogs, Book Volumes 2761, CD-ROMs 16, Cassettes, Clipping Files, Exhibition Catalogs, Video Tapes 101
Special Subjects: Ceramics, Costumes, Decorative Arts, Drawings, Embroidery, Etchings & Engravings, Graphics, Landscapes, Painting-American, Painting-Canadian, Painting-French, Photography, Porcelain, Posters, Pottery, Prints, Sculpture, Textiles, Watercolors, Woodcuts, Tapestries
Collections: Mixed Media, paintings, prints, photography, sculpture, textiles & costumes
Publications: Exhibition Catalogs
Activities: Classes for adults & children; docent training; film series; lects open to pub; 10 - 15 vis lectrs per yr; gallery talks; tours; sponsoring of competitions; fels; book traveling exhibs 1-2 per yr; originate traveling exhibs to other mus nationally & internationally; mus shop sells books, magazines, reproductions, jewelry, gifts, cards

M **PHOTO CENTER NW,** 900 12th Ave, Seattle, WA 98122. Tel 206-720-7222; Fax 206-720-0306; Email pcnw@pcnw.org; Web: pcnw.org/gallery; *Exec Dir & Cur* Michelle Dunn Marsh
Open Mon - Thurs Noon -9 PM, Sat - Sun Noon - 6 PM, cl Fri; No admis, gallery open to pub; Estab mid 1980's; gallery, school, rental dark rooms; A renowned showcase of photography, exhibiting both contemporary & historic works from photographers around the world. The gallery exhibits photography & related media & operates in an educational institution; Average Annual Attendance: 1500; Mem: 400+; $75 basic
Special Subjects: Photography

A **PRATT FINE ARTS CENTER,** Gallery, 1902 S Main St, Seattle, WA 98144-2206. Tel 206-328-2200; Fax 206-328-1260; Email info@pratt.org; Web: www.pratt.org; *Exec Dir* Steve Galatro
Open daily 8:30 AM - 10 PM; No admis fee; admis fee for art classes; Estab 1976; Average Annual Attendance: 3,500
Exhibitions: Rotating monthly exhibits (glass, jewelry, painting, prints, metal, mixed media, sculpture)
Publications: Quarterly class schedule
Activities: Classes for adults & children; educ prog; lect open to public, 10 vis lectrs per year

M **SCIENCE FICTION AND FANTASY HALL OF FAME,** 325 5th Ave, Seattle, WA 98109-4630. Tel 206-724-3428; Fax 206-770-2727; Email info@mopop.org; Web: www.mopop.org; *Dir* Donna Shirley
Open daily 10 AM - 5 PM; Admis adults $28, seniors $25, military $22, youth 5-17 $19, children 4 & under and mems free; 13,000 sq ft exhib space; Mem: dues $69 & up
Activities: Lects; workshops; educ progs

M **SEATTLE ART MUSEUM,** 1300 1st Ave, Seattle, WA 98101. Tel 206-654-3100; Fax 206-654-3135; Email webmaster@seattleartmuseum.org; Web: www.seattleartmuseum.org; *Cur Modern & Contemporary Art* Catharina Manchanda; *Pres Bd* Winnie Stratton; *COO* Richard Beckerman; *Cur African Art* Pamela McClusky; *Conservator* Nicholas Dorman; *Deputy Dir Art Admin* Zora Hutlova-Foy; *Chmn Bd* Stewart Landefeld; *Controller* Dawn Beck; *Deputy Dir Educ* Regan Pro; *Pub Relations Mgr* Rachel Eggers; *Dir & CEO, Illsley Ball Nordstrom* Kimberly Rorschach; *Dir, Gardner Center Asian Art & Ideas* Sarah Loudon; *Cur, Ann M. Barwick American Art* Patti Junker; *Cur, Japanese & Korean Art* Xiaojin Wu
Open Wed - Sun 10 AM - 5 PM, Thurs until 9 PM, cl Mon, Tues & most major holidays; Admis adults $19.95, military & seniors 65 & up $17.95, students & children 3-17 $12.95, mems & children 12 & under free, 1st Thurs of month free, 1st Fri free to seniors, 2nd Fri 5-9 PM free to teens ages 13-19; group rates available; Estab 1906, incorporated 1917, building opened 1933; gift to the city from Mrs Eugene Fuller & Richard Eugene Fuller, for recreation, educ & inspiration of its citizens; Average Annual Attendance: 400,000; Mem: 30,000

Income: Financed by state appropriations, grants, mem
Library Holdings: Auction Catalogs, Book Volumes, Clipping Files
Special Subjects: Antiquities-Greek, Antiquities-Roman, Primitive art, Asian Art, Oriental Art, Painting-Japanese, Jade, Painting-American, Painting-European, Porcelain, Prints
Collections: LeRoy M Backus Collection of Drawings & Paintings, Manson F Backus Collection of Prints, Norman Davis Collection of Classical Art, Eugene Fuller Memorial Collection: special emphasis on Japan, China, India, & including Egypt, Ancient Greece & Rome, European, Near Eastern, primitive & contemporary Northwest art, & Chinese Jades from Archaic - 18th century, Alice Heeramaneck Collection of Primitive Art, Henry & Martha Isaacson Collection of 18th Century European Porcelain, H Kress Collection of 14th - 18th Century European Paintings, Thomas D Stimson Memorial Collection (with special emphasis on Far Eastern art), Chinese & Indian Collection, 18th Century Drawing Room (furnished by the National Society of Colonial Dames of American in the State of Washington), major holdings in Northwest art, including Tobey, Callahan, Graves as well as all contemporary art, especially American artists Gorky, Pollock, Warhol & Lichtenstein, selected highlights on Asian coll on permanent display (with special emphasis on Japanese screens, paintings, sculpture and lacquers), Katherine C White Collection of African Art
Publications: Quarterly Newsletter; Art from Africa: Long Steps Never Broke a Back; Neri di Bicci and Devotional Painting in Italy; Spain in the Age of Exploration 1492-1819
Activities: Docent training; film progs; double lect course under the Museum Guild; adult art history classes; classes for children; lects open to pub & for mems only, 12 vis lectrs per yr; tours; program for senior citizens; concerts; gallery talks; mus shop sells books, gifts & jewelry

L **Dorothy Stimson Bullitt Library**, 1300 First Ave, Seattle, WA 98101-2003. Tel 206-625-3220; Email libraries@seattleartmuseum.org; Web: www.seattleartmuseum.org; *Librn* Elizabeth de Fato; *Mgr Retail Opers* Brad Bigelow; *Mus Photography* Paul Macapia; *Cur African Art* Pamela McClusky; *Conservator* Nicholas Dorman; *Mgr Exhibitions* Zora Hutlova-Foy; *Dir Garden Center Asian Art & Ideas* Sarah Loudon; *Cur European Painting* Chiyo Ishikawa; *Sr Deputy Dir* Gail Joice
Open Mon - Fri 10 AM - 4 PM; Archives of the Seattle Art Museum's records are held in the Special Collections of the University of Washington Libraries (for reference only)
Income: Financed by state appropriation, grants, mem
Library Holdings: Audio Tapes, Book Volumes 19,000, Exhibition Catalogs, Periodical Subscriptions 50, Slides 75,000, Video Tapes
Special Subjects: Historical Material
Collections: Books, catalogs, journals, videos & ephemera on Northwest Artists, Art of Africa, Oceana & the Americas, Decorative Arts, European Painting & Sculpture, Modern & Contemporary Art, American Art & Native American (Northwest Coast) Art, art reference coll, Northwest Artist Files: 6,000+ local & regional artists, publications & object files on objects in Mus permanent coll, resources for current exhibs, worldwide mus publications, vertical files on the history of the Seattle Art Mus, local arts organizations, galleries, museums & public art

M **Olympic Sculpture Park**, 2901 Western Ave, Seattle, WA 98121; 1300 First Ave, Seattle, WA 98101-2003. Tel 206-332-1377; Fax 206-654-3135; Email webmaster@seattleartmuseum.org; Web: www.seattleartmuseum.org; *Dir* Kimberly Rorschach
Open daily yr round from 30 min before sunrise to 30 min after sunset; PACCAR Pavilion open Nov - Feb Sat - Sun 10 AM - 4PM, March - October Tues - Sun 10 AM - 5 PM, cl Mon; see website for Pavilion holiday closings; No admis fee; PACCAR Pavilion Garage parking fees apply; Purchased 1999, opened 2007; 9 acre former industrial area now a sculpture park and green space on Seattle's waterfront
Income: Financed by Seattle Art Museum
Special Subjects: Sculpture
Collections: PACCAR Pavilion, Gates Amphitheater, The Valley, Henry & William Ketcham Families Grove, Barry Ackerly Family East Meadow, Kreielsheimer North Meadow, The Shore
Activities: Tours

M **Seattle Asian Art Museum**, 1400 E Prospect St, Volunteer Park Seattle, WA 98112-3303. Tel 206-654-3100; Fax 206-324-2828; Email webmaster@seattleartmuseum.org; Web: www.seattleartmuseum.org; *Dir* Kimberly Rorschach; *Foster Foundation Curator of Chinese Art* Ping Fuong; *Cur Japanese & Korean Art* Xiaojin Wu
Open Wed - Sun 10 AM - 5 PM, Thurs 10 AM - 9 PM, cl Mon, Tues & most major holidays; closed for renovation: spring 2017-spring 2018; Admis adult $7, students w/ID, seniors & teens $5, mems & children 12 & under free, 1st Thurs of month free, 2nd Thurs of month 5-9 PM free, 1st Fri free to seniors, 1st Sat free for families; Opened 1994 in former location of Seattle Art Museum as a showcase for the Museum's Asian Art Collection & community hub for Asian culture; Maintains Gardner Center for Asian Art & Ideas
Special Subjects: Asian Art, Historical Material
Exhibitions: (Ongoing) Chinese Art: A Seattle Perspective; (Ongoing) Live Long & Prosper: Auspicious Motifs in East Asian Art; (Ongoing) Looking West, Finding East; 26th Feb, 2017) Tabaimo: Utsutsushi Utsushi (temporary)
Activities: Lects open to pub; Gardner Ctr lect series; tours

L **McCaw Foundation Asian Art Library**, 1400 E Prospect St, Volunteer Park Seattle, WA 98112-3303. Tel 206-654-3210; Fax 206-654-3191; Email libraries@seattleartmuseum.org; Web: www.seattleartmuseum.org; *Dir* Kimberly Rorschach
cl during renovation; reopening 2019; No admis fee; Located on the Lower Level of the Seattle Asian Art Museum (For reference only)
Library Holdings: Auction Catalogs, Book Volumes, Other Holdings
Special Subjects: Asian Art, Historical Material
Collections: Books, catalogs & journals on Chinese, Japanese, Korean, Indian & Southeast Asian Art, art reference coll, publications & object files on objects in Seattle Asian Art Museum's permanent coll, resources for current exhibs

L **Ann P Wyckoff Teacher Resource Center**, 1400 E Prospect St, Volunteer Park Seattle, WA 98112-3303. Tel 206-654-3186; Fax 206-654-3191; Email trc@seattleartmuseum.org; Web: www.seattleartmuseum.org; *Dir* Kimberly Rorschach
Open Thurs & Fri 2-5 Pm, Sat 10 AM - 5 PM, or by appt during mus hrs; No admis fee; Lending libr available to educators. Located on the Lower Level of the Seattle Asian Art Museum
Library Holdings: Book Volumes, Compact Disks, DVDs, Video Tapes
Collections: 4,000+ art & culture related educational resources, curriculum guides, online art-information storage databases

L **SEATTLE PUBLIC LIBRARY,** Arts, Recreation & Literature Dept, 1000 Fourth Ave, Seattle, WA 98104. Tel 206-386-4636; Email arl@spl.org; Web: www.spl.org; *Exec Dir & Chief Librn* Marcellus Turner
Estab 1889; Circ 181,772; Lending & reference library
Income: Financed by city tax dollars & foundation grants
Purchases: $26,000
Library Holdings: Audio Tapes, Book Volumes 147,202, Cassettes, Clipping Files, Exhibition Catalogs, Fiche, Framed Reproductions, Lantern Slides, Manuscripts, Original Art Works, Pamphlets, Periodical Subscriptions 310, Photographs, Prints, Records, Reproductions, Slides, Video Tapes
Special Subjects: Advertising Design, Aesthetics, Afro-American Art, American Indian Art, American Western Art, Antiquities-Assyrian, Antiquities-Byzantine, Antiquities-Egyptian, Antiquities-Etruscan, Antiquities-Greek, Antiquities-Oriental, Antiquities-Persian, Antiquities-Roman, Architecture, Art History

M **UNITED INDIANS OF ALL TRIBES FOUNDATION,** Daybreak Star Center Gallery, 3801 W Government Way, Discovery Park Seattle, WA 98199-1014; PO Box 99100, Seattle, WA 98199-0100. Tel 206-285-4425; Fax 206-282-3640; Email info@unitedindians.org; Web: www.unitedindians.org; *Exec Dir* Mike Tulee; *Finance Mgr* Chelsea Jamison
Open Tues - Fri 10 AM - 5 PM; No admis fee; Estab 1977 to present contemporary American Indian fine art; Average Annual Attendance: 30,000
Collections: Collections of international American Indian tribes & cultures
Exhibitions: Permanent exhibit of different American Indian tribes & cultures as well as changing exhibitions of contemporary native art

M **UNIVERSITY OF WASHINGTON,** Henry Art Gallery, 15th Ave NE & NE 41st St, Seattle, WA 98195; PO Box 351410, Seattle, WA 98195-0001. Tel 206-543-2280; Fax 206-685-3123; Email info@henryart.org; Web: www.henryart.org; *Deputy Dir External Relations* Jill Leininger; *Cur Colls* Judy Sourakli; *Dir* Sylvia Wolf; *Develop & Special Events Mgr* Allie Picha; *Dir Finance & Admin* Daren Hecker; *Human Resources* Lisa Anderson
Open Wed & Fri - Sun 11 AM - 4 PM, Thurs 11 AM - 9 PM, cl Mon - Tues, Independence Day, Veteran's Day, Thanksgiving, Christmas Day & New Year's Day; Admis adults $10, seniors $6, free Sun & every 1st Thurs; Estab 1927; 8 galleries, 6000 sq ft of exhibition space; Average Annual Attendance: 800,000; Mem: 3500; dues $25 & up
Special Subjects: Carpets & Rugs, Ceramics, Costumes, Crafts, Drawings, Embroidery, Photography, Pottery, Prints, Sculpture, Textiles
Collections: 19th century American landscape painting, contemporary West Coast ceramics, works on paper, prints, drawings & photographs, 20th century Japanese folk pottery, Elizabeth Bayley Willis Collection of Textiles from India, western & ethnic textiles, 19th & 20th century western dress (formerly Costume & Textile Study Center)
Exhibitions: Masters of Fine Arts; 12-15 exhibs per yr focused on contemporary art
Publications: Books, exhibition catalogues
Activities: Educ programs; lects open to pub; gallery talks; tours; book traveling exhibs circulating in the US & abroad; originate traveling exhibs to mus in the United States & abroad; mus shop sells books & prints

L **Architecture-Urban Planning Library**, 334 Gould Hall, Seattle, WA 98195; PO Box 355730, Seattle, WA 98195-5730. Tel 206-543-4067; Web: www.lib.washington.edu/aup; *Librn* Alan Michaelson
Open Mon - Thurs 8 AM - 8 PM, Fri 8 AM - 5 PM, Sat - Sun 1 PM - 5 PM; Estab 1923
Library Holdings: Book Volumes 45,000, CD-ROMs, Compact Disks, Exhibition Catalogs, Fiche 5246, Memorabilia, Pamphlets 1684, Periodical Subscriptions 300, Video Tapes
Special Subjects: Architecture, Landscape Architecture
Collections: Carl Gould Portrait

L **Univ of Washington Libraries, Special Collections**, PO Box 352900, Seattle, WA 98195-2900. Tel 206-543-1929; Fax 206-543-1931; Email speccoll@u.washington.edu; Web: www.lib.washington.edu/specialcoll/; *Cur Visual Materials* Nicolette Bromberg; *Book Arts & Rare Books Cur* Sandra Kroupa; *Univ Archivist* John Bolcer; *Pacific Northwest Cur* Anne Jenner
Open while classes in session, Mon - Tues 10 AM - 4:45 PM, Wed 10 AM - 7:45 PM, Thurs - Fri 10 AM - 4:45 PM, cl Sat - Sun; No admis fee; Average Annual Attendance: 5,199
Library Holdings: Maps, Other Holdings Architectural plans, drawings & renderings 63,137, Pamphlets, Photographs, Prints
Special Subjects: Manuscripts, Photography, Bookplates & Bindings
Collections: Book arts coll, Northwest American Indian Art
Exhibitions: Best Western Books
Activities: Classes for adults; book traveling exhib 1 per yr

L **Art Library**, 101 Art Bldg, Seattle, WA 98195; PO Box 353440, Seattle, WA 98195-3440. Tel 206-543-0648; Email art@lib.washington.edu; Web: www.lib.washington.edu/art; *Librn* Angela Weaver
Open Mon - Thurs 8 AM - 7 PM, Fri 8 AM - 5 PM, Sun 1 - 5 PM, cl Sat; Estab 1940 to provide resources for the instructional & research programs of the School of Art & serves as the Art Library for the university community
Income: Financed by state appropriation
Library Holdings: Book Volumes 44,000, Clipping Files, Exhibition Catalogs, Fiche, Periodical Subscriptions 200, Reproductions
Special Subjects: Art History, Ceramics, Industrial Design, Photography, Printmaking, Sculpture
—**Art Slide Library**, 120 Art Bldg, Seattle, WA 98195; PO Box 353440, Seattle, WA 98195-3440. Tel 206-543-0648; Fax 206-685-1657; Email aw6@u.washington.edu; *Head Librn* Angela Weaver; *Library Tech Head* Wade Haddaway
Slide library is a teaching collection that is only available to University of Washington faculty, staff & students

Library Holdings: Slides 330,000
Collections: 35 mm art slides: Western, Asian, Tribal

M **Burke Museum of Natural History and Culture**, University of Washington Campus, Seattle, WA 98195; PO Box 353010, Burke Museum of Natural History & Culture Seattle, WA 98195-3010. Tel 206-616-3962; Fax 206-685-3039; Email theburke@u.washington.edu; Web: www.burkemuseum.org; *Cur Native American Art* Robin Wright; *Cur Paleobotany* Caroline Stromberg; *Cur Invertebrate Paleontology* Elizabeth Nesbitt; *Cur Archaeology* Peter Lape; *Cur Genetic Resources* Adam Leache; *Cur Native Amer Ethnology* Sven Haakanson; *Cur Fishes* Luke Tornabene; *Exec Dir* Julie Stein; *Cur Herbarium* Richard Olmstead; *Cur Vertebrate Paleontology* Christian Sidor; *Cur Birds* John Klicka; *Cur Mammals* Sharlene Santana
Open daily 10 AM - 5 PM, First Thurs of the month 10 AM - 8 PM; Admis general $10, seniors $8, students & youth 5-18 $7.50, children under 5 free; call for spec admis fees; Estab 1885 for research & exhibs; 2 permanent exhibs & 1 temp exhib gallery; Average Annual Attendance: 105,000; Mem: 3,000; dues $25 - $1,000
Income: Financed by state, endowment, gifts, self-generated revenues
Special Subjects: American Indian Art, Anthropology, Archaeology, Asian Art, Eskimo Art, Ethnology, Folk Art, Latin American Art, Mexican Art, Oriental Art, Woodcarvings
Collections: Natural & cultural history of Washington State, the Pacific Northwest & the Pacific Rim
Exhibitions: Life & Times of Washington; Pacific Voices; 3-6 temp exhibs ann
Activities: Classes for adults & children; docent training; lects open to pub & mem only, 8 vis lectrs per yr; gallery talks; tours; exten prog circulates study collection & serves Washington state schools, mus, community ctrs; Burkemobile; Burke in a Box; book traveling exhibs, 1-2 per yr; originates traveling exhibs nationally & statewide to mus; mus store sells books, magazines, reproductions, exhib merchandise & NW-themed gifts

M **WESTERN BRIDGE,** 3412 4th Ave S, Seattle, WA 98134-1905. Tel 206-838-7444; Email info@westernbridge.org; Web: www.westernbridge.org

M **WING LUKE ASIAN MUSEUM,** 719 S King St, Seattle, WA 98104-3035. Tel 206-623-5124, 623-5190 (tour desk); Fax 206-623-4559; Email visit@wingluke.org; Web: www.wingluke.org; *Exec Dir* Margaret Su
Open Tues - Sun 10 AM - 5 PM, 1st Thurs of month 10 AM - 8 PM, cl Mon & holidays; Admis adults $4, students & seniors $3, children $2; Estab 1966 to preserve & present the history, art & culture of Asian Pacific Americans & to bridge Asians, Asian Pacific Americans & Americans of other backgrounds; Changing exhib area; permanent exhib; Average Annual Attendance: 70,000; Mem: 1000; dues $30; annual meeting in Jan
Income: $500,000 (financed by endowment, mem, annual art auction, local & state commissions & grants for exhibits)
Special Subjects: Asian Art
Collections: Asian American Art; Historical Artifacts & Photos
Publications: Publishes exhibit catalogs
Activities: Classes for adults & children; lect open to public, 4 vis lectrs per year; tours

L **Governor Gary Locke Library and Community Heritage Center**, 719 S King St, Seattle, WA 98104. Tel 206-623-5124 ext 117; Fax 206-623-4559; Email library@wingluke.org; Web: www.wingluke.org; *Exec Dir* Beth Takekawa; *Deputy Exec Dir* Cassie Chinn; *Coll Mgr* Robert Fisher
Open by appt; No admis fee; Estab 1967
Income: Financed by contributions, endowment, grants & mem
Library Holdings: Book Volumes 5000, Clipping Files, Photographs, Slides 150, Video Tapes
Exhibitions: One Song, Many Voices: The Asian Pacific American Experience; The Densho: Japanese American Legacy Project; rotating exhibits

SHORELINE

M **SHORELINE HISTORICAL MUSEUM,** 18501 Linden Ave N, Shoreline, WA 98133-4801; PO Box 55594, Shoreline, WA 98155-0594. Tel 206-542-7111; Email shorelinehistorical@juno.com; Web: www.shorelinehistoricalmuseum.org; *Cur* Leah Pepin
Open Tues - Sat 10 AM - 4 PM; Admis by donation; Estab 1976 to preserve local history; Average Annual Attendance: 5,000; Mem: 360; dues family $25, annual $10, pioneer $5; annual meeting 2nd Sat in Nov
Income: $35,000 (financed by mem, donations, room rentals & fundraising)
Special Subjects: Historical Material, Period Rooms
Collections: Historical Artifacts, Ephemera, NW local artists
Exhibitions: School room, home room; transportation exhibit; country store; other rotating exhibits
Publications: Newsletter, 4 times a year
Activities: Classes for children; docent training; hands on days; lect open to public; 3vis lectrs per yr; tours; Trillium Heritage Award for Preservation; original objects of art lent; sales shop sells books, prints, postcards & area photo cards

SPOKANE

A **CORBIN ART CENTER,** 507 W 7th Ave, Spokane, WA 99204-2709. Tel 509-625-6677; Web: www.spokaneparks.org/corbin
Open Mon - Thurs 9 AM - 4 PM; No admis fee
Collections: paintings
Activities: Classes for adults & children; camps

M **EASTERN WASHINGTON STATE HISTORICAL SOCIETY,** Northwest Museum of Arts & Culture, 2316 W First Ave, Spokane, WA 99201. Tel 509-456-3931; Fax 509-363-5303; Email themac@northwestmuseum.org; Web: www.northwestmuseum.org; *Exec Dir* John Meredo-Burich; *Cur History* Marsha Rooney; *Collection Mgr* Valerie Wahl; *Plateau Curator* Tisa Mattleson; *Art at Work* Tammy Gabbert
Open Tues-Sun 10AM - 5PM; Wed 10AM-8PM; $10 Adults; $7 Sr; $5 youth; Estab 1916 to collect & preserve Pacific Northwest History, art & American Indian materials; 5 galleries of 15,000 sq ft, auditorium, library & archives, outdoor amphitheater; Average Annual Attendance: 120,000; Mem: 2500; dues $25-5,000
Income: Financed by mem, state appropriations, fundraising, endowment & contributions
Library Holdings: Audio Tapes, CD-ROMs, Cassettes, Clipping Files, Exhibition Catalogs, Fiche, Filmstrips, Kodachrome Transparencies, Lantern Slides, Manuscripts, Maps, Memorabilia, Motion Pictures, Original Documents, Other Holdings, Pamphlets, Periodical Subscriptions, Photographs, Slides, Video Tapes
Special Subjects: American Indian Art, Architecture, Historical Material, Manuscripts, Maps, Painting-American, Photography, Prints, Woodcarvings
Collections: American Indian, regional history, Northwest modern contemporary art, Historic house of 1898 by architect Kirtland K Cutter, interior designed & decorated with period furnishings, 19th & 20th century American & European art, representative works of Pacific Northwest artists
Exhibitions: Exhibits change regularly
Activities: Classes for adults & children; docent training; lects open to pub; gallery talks; tours; concerts; sponsoring of competitions;; individual paintings & original objects of art lent to professional nonprofit institutions nationally; lending collection contains books, original art works; original prints, paintings, sculptures & 135,000 photographs; book 3 traveling exhibs per year; originates traveling exhibs; mus shop sells books, & gift items

M **GONZAGA UNIVERSITY,** Jundt Art Museum, Gonzaga Univ, 502 East Boone Ave Spokane, WA 99258-0001. Tel 509-313-6843; Email jundtartmuseum@gonzaga.edu; Web: www.gonzaga.edu/jundt; *Dir & Cur* Dr Paul Manoguerra; *Cur Educ* Karen Kaiser
Open Mon - Sat 10 AM - 4 PM, cl Sun & univ holidays; No admis fee; Estab 1995, museum of art; Average Annual Attendance: 25,000
Library Holdings: Book Volumes, Clipping Files, Exhibition Catalogs
Collections: student prints, Old Master's prints, photography prints, contemporary prints, Auguste Rodin sculptures, Chihuly glass, Northwest paintings & sculpture
Activities: Docent training; lect; gallery talks

L **SPOKANE PUBLIC LIBRARY,** 906 W Main St, Spokane, WA 99201. Tel 509-444-5300; *Dir* Pat Partovi
Open Tues - Wed 10 AM - 8 PM, Thurs - Sat 10 AM - 6 PM; No admis fee; Estab 1894 basically to meet citizens educ, information, recreation & cultural lifelong learning needs through a variety of programs & facilities; Gallery maintained for special exhibitions
Library Holdings: Audio Tapes, Cassettes, Clipping Files, Compact Disks, DVDs, Exhibition Catalogs, Fiche, Filmstrips, Kodachrome Transparencies, Manuscripts, Maps, Micro Print, Motion Pictures, Original Art Works, Other Holdings Original documents, Pamphlets, Periodical Subscriptions, Photographs, Records, Reels, Slides, Video Tapes
Collections: AV, children's & young adult, fiction, genealogy, non-fiction, northwest, periodicals, rare books
Publications: Previews, monthly
Activities: Classes for adults & children; dramatic progs; lects open to pub; concerts

TACOMA

M **TACOMA ART MUSEUM,** 1701 Pacific Ave, Tacoma, WA 98402-3214. Tel 253-272-4258; Fax 253-627-1898; Email info@tacomaartmuseum.org; Web: www.tacomaartmuseum.org; *Interim Exec Dir* Mark Holcomb; *Deputy Dir & Chief Cur* Rock Hushka; *Dir Educ* Samantha Kelly; *Deputy Dir & Chief Cur* Rock Hushka; *Dir Mktg & Communs* Adrienne Edmonson
Open Tues - Sun 10 AM - 5 PM, cl Mon, Tues, Thanksgiving, Christmas, New Years, MLK Jr Day & Jul 4; Admis adults $15, seniors 65+, students & military $13, mems & children under 5 free, 3rd Thurs of month 5-8 PM free; group & family rates available; Founded 1935; 12,000 sq ft of galleries are open and airy, highlighting the work on view; eight exhibs spaces; maintains art reference library. Member of the Washington Art Consortium; Average Annual Attendance: 80,000; Mem: 1900; dues $50-$800
Income: $1,000,000 (financed by contributions, grants, mem & carried income)
Library Holdings: Book Volumes 6000, Clipping Files 4000, DVDs 36, Exhibition Catalogs, Pamphlets, Periodical Subscriptions 12, Video Tapes 40
Special Subjects: American Indian Art, Architecture, Asian Art, Ceramics, Etchings & Engravings, Glass, Jewelry, Landscapes, Painting-American, Painting-British, Painting-European, Painting-French, Painting-Japanese, Photography, Portraits, Prints, Prints, Reproductions, Sculpture, Sculpture, Woodcarvings, Woodcuts
Collections: American & French paintings, American sculpture, Chinese Textiles, 19th & 20th Century American Art, European & Asian Works of art, European Impressionism, Japanese Woodblock prints, Dale Chihuly Glass, Northwest Art, Studio Art Jewelry, Works on Paper
Publications: Museum Notes, quarterly to mems; exhib catalogs; Northwest Biennial, catalog
Activities: Educ prog; classes for adults & children; youth summer camp; docent training; lects open to pub, 20 vis lectrs per yr; gallery talks; tours; concerts; performances; film screenings; poetry & book readings; biennial competition with awards; individual paintings & original objects of art lent to other professional mus; mus shop sells books, original art, reproductions, prints, cards, jewelry, concerts & films

L **TACOMA PUBLIC LIBRARY,** Handforth Gallery, 1102 Tacoma Ave S, Tacoma, WA 98402-2098. Tel 253-292-2001; Email info@tacomalibrary.org; Web: www.tacomalibrary.org/handforth-gallery/; *Library Dir* Susan Odencrantz
Open Tues - Wed 11 AM - 8 PM, Thurs - Sat 9 AM - 6 PM, cl Sun - Mon; Estab 1952 to extend library services to include exhibits in all media in the Thomas S Handforth Gallery; Circ 1,237,000; Average Annual Attendance: 20,000
Income: Financed by city appropriation
Library Holdings: Audio Tapes, Book Volumes 800,000, Cassettes, Clipping Files, Exhibition Catalogs, Framed Reproductions, Memorabilia, Motion Pictures, Original Art Works, Other Holdings Audio compact discs, Pamphlets, Periodical Subscriptions 1600, Photographs, Prints, Records, Reels, Video Tapes

Special Subjects: Manuscripts, Photography
Collections: Art book, city, county, federal & state documents, rare books
Exhibitions: 8 monthly changing exhibits; exhibits featuring local & regional artists; educ & historic exhibits
Activities: Classes for children; dramatic progs; lects open to pub, 3-4 vis lectrs per yr; originate traveling exhibs

M **UNIVERSITY OF PUGET SOUND,** Kittredge Art Gallery, 1500 N Warner, CM 1072 Tacoma, WA 98416-0005. Tel 253-879-3701; Fax 253-879-3500; Web: www.pugetsound.edu/kittredge; *Gallery Mgr* Peter Stanley
Open Mon - Fri 10 AM - 5 PM, Sat noon - 5 PM; No admis fee; Estab 1961 for showing of student & professional works; Exhibition space consists of 2 galleries: Small Gallery with 80 ft of running wall space & Kittredge Gallery with 160 ft of running wall space; track lighting; security alarms; Average Annual Attendance: 3,900
Collections: Abby Williams Hill, painter of Northwest scenes from 1880s to 1930s, contemporary west coast ceramics, Northwest paintings, American prints
Activities: Lect open to pub, 20 vis lectrs per yr; gallery talks; individual paintings & original works of art lent to professional art museums & historical museums; lending coll contains original prints, paintings & ceramic works

M **WASHINGTON STATE HISTORICAL SOCIETY,** Washington History Museum, 1911 Pacific Ave, Tacoma, WA 98402-3109. Tel 253-272-3500; Fax 253-272-9518; Web: www.washingtonhistory.org; *Dir* Jennifer Kilmer
Open Tues - Thurs 10 AM - 5 PM, Fri - Sun 10 AM - 5 PM, 3rd Thurs until 8 PM; Admis adults $14, seniors & students $11, members & children under 5 free; Estab 1891 to research, preserve & display the heritage of Washington State; Soc owns three buildings; art gallery under the direction of the Soc; two floors of exhibits (Washington State, Native American Artifacts, temporary special exhibits); Average Annual Attendance: 125,000; Mem: 3000; dues $50 & up; annual meeting in Aug
Income: Financed by mem, state appropriations & gifts
Library Holdings: Audio Tapes, Book Volumes, Clipping Files, Compact Disks, DVDs, Lantern Slides, Manuscripts, Maps, Original Art Works, Original Documents, Pamphlets, Photographs, Prints, Records, Sculpture
Special Subjects: Historical Material, Manuscripts, Maps, Photography, Posters
Collections: Pre-historic artifacts, Indian & Eskimo artifacts, baskets, clothing, utensils, Oriental items, Washington-Northwest pioneer artifacts, archives; photographs; maps
Exhibitions: Train Exhibit (permanent); rotating exhibits
Publications: Explore (newsletter), quarterly; Columbia (popular historical journal), quarterly
Activities: Classes for adults & children; docent training; school tours; lects open to pub, 12-15 vis lectrs per yr; gallery talks; tours; interpretative programs; concerts; dramatic programs with awards; schols offered; individual paintings & original objects of art lent to comparable mus & cultural institutions; lending collection contains natural artifacts, photographs & sculpture; one book traveling exhib per yr; originates traveling exhibs; mus shop sells books, magazines, reproductions, prints, postcards, stationery, original art

L **Research Center,** 315 Stadium Way, Tacoma, WA 98403. Tel 253-798-5914; Fax 253-597-4186; Email lmiller@wshs.wa.gov; Web: www.washingtonhistory.org; *Cur Art* Lynette Miller
Open Tues, Wed & Thurs 12:30 - 4:30 PM by appointment; No admis fee; Estab 1941 for research in Pacific Northwest history; For reference only
Income: Financed by mem, state appropriations & gifts
Library Holdings: Book Volumes 12,000, Clipping Files, Manuscripts 4,500,000, Maps 3,200, Memorabilia, Original Art Works 3,800, Pamphlets, Photographs 500,000, Prints 30,000, Reels, Sculpture 350
Special Subjects: American Indian Art, Anthropology, Archaeology, Asian Art, Bronzes, Ceramics, Coins & Medals, Collages, Crafts, Decorative Arts, Dolls, Drawings, Embroidery, Eskimo Art, Etchings & Engravings, Ethnology, Furniture, Glass, Historical Material, Jewelry, Landscapes, Manuscripts, Maps, Painting-American, Photography, Portraits, Posters, Pottery, Sculpture, Silver, Textiles, Watercolors, Woodcarvings, Cartoons, Dioramas
Collections: Asahel Curtis Photograph Collection, Paintings, prints, drawings by Washington State & NW artists
Publications: Columbia Magazine, quarterly

VANCOUVER

M **CLARK COLLEGE,** Archer Gallery/Gaiser Hall, 1933 Fort Vancouver Way, Vancouver, WA 98663-3598. Tel 360-992-2246; Fax 360-992-2888; Email mhirsch@clark.edu; Web: www.clark.edu; *Dir* Marjorie Hirsch
Open Tues - Thurs 9 AM - 8 PM, Fri 9 AM - 4 PM, Sat & Sun 1 - 5 PM; No admis fee; Gallery has 2,000 sq ft; Average Annual Attendance: 5,000
Exhibitions: Six exhibs during acad yr
Activities: Gallery talks; Lect open to public, 3 - 4 vis lectrs per year

WENATCHEE

M **CHELAN COUNTY PUBLIC UTILITY DISTRICT,** Rocky Reach Dam, 5161 Hwy 97A, Wenatchee, WA 98801; PO Box 1231, Wenatchee, WA 98807-1231. Tel 509-Visitor Center: 663-7522; Fax 509-661-8149; Email debbie.gallaher@chelanpud.org; Web: www.chelanpud.org/visitor-center.html; *Gen Mgr* Steve Wright; *Vis Servs Mgr* Debbie Gallaher
Open Mon - Sun 9 AM - 4 PM; No admis fee; Estab 1961 as a landscape ground & exhibit galleries; Museum of the Columbia Edisonia, Geology, Anthropology - first people & Pioneer History; Average Annual Attendance: 60,000
Income: Financed by hydroelectric revenue
Special Subjects: American Indian Art, Anthropology, Archaeology, Graphics, Historical Material, Portraits
Collections: Electrical artifacts, Indian Artifacts (Central Columbia River Region), Nez Perce Indian Portraits, Edisonia Collection
Exhibitions: Monthly art exhibits
Activities: Educ dept; teacher seminars; classes for children; docent training; seasonal tours; science camp; sponsoring competitions

M **NORTH CENTRAL WASHINGTON MUSEUM,** Wenatchee Valley Museum & Cultural Center, 127 S Mission, Wenatchee, WA 98801. Tel 509-888-6240; Email info@wvmcc.org; Web: www.wenatcheevalleymuseum.com; *CollectionsCur* Melanie Wachholder; *Dir Pub Rels* Lyn Kelly; *Exhibits Curator* Kasey Koski; *Dir* Sandy Cohen; *Education Dir* Selina Danko; *Deputy Dir* Marriah Thornock
Open Tues - Sat 10 AM - 4 PM, cl Sun & major holidays; Admis adults $5, students & seniors $4, youth $2; Estab 1939 to preserve & present history & the arts. Gallery program offers exhibits of regional, national & international importance; 4500 sq ft changing exhibition gallery features 6-8 shows per yr; Average Annual Attendance: 36,000; Mem: 700; dues $25 & up; annual meeting & monthly board meetings
Income: Financed by public-private partnership with city of Wenatchee & non-profit museum assn
Library Holdings: Audio Tapes, Book Volumes, CD-ROMs, Cassettes, Clipping Files, Compact Disks, DVDs, Filmstrips, Kodachrome Transparencies, Manuscripts, Maps, Memorabilia, Original Documents, Photographs, Prints, Records, Reels, Sculpture, Slides, Video Tapes
Special Subjects: Ceramics, Historical Material, Prints
Collections: Archaeological Coll, Archival Colls, Ethnographic coll, Natural History, Sister City colls
Exhibitions: Rotating art exhibits; rotating historical exhibits; permanent history exhibits, Our People Our Place & Apple Industry Exhibit
Publications: The Confluence, quarterly; Museum News, quarterly; books, River of Memory: The Everlasting Columbia by William Layman
Activities: Classes for adults & children; educational kits available on variety of subjects; lects open to pub; 20 vis lectrs per yr; concerts; gallery talks; tours; 2 book traveling exhibs per yr; originates traveling exhibs to Pacific NW & Canada; mus shop sells books, original art, prints, original Apple Box Labels, stationery, jewelry & toys

M **WENATCHEE VALLEY COLLEGE,** Robert Graves Gallery, 1300 Fifth St, Wenatchee, WA 98801. Tel 509-682-6776; Email robertgravesgallery@wvc.edu; Web: www.ctc.edu (select Wenatchee Campus); *Pres* John Crew
Open Mon 8 AM - noon, Tues - Thurs 9 AM - 1 PM, Fri 5 - 7 PM, & week-ends by appointment; No admis fee, donations accepted; Estab 1976 to serve a rural, scattered population in North Central Washington State, which without Robert Graves Gallery, would not have access to a non-sales gallery; Non-profit community art gallery housed in Sexton Hall on Wenatchee Valley College Campus; Average Annual Attendance: 4,000; Mem: 150; dues $20-$100
Income: $20,000 (financed by mem, grants, donations, fundraising events & art classes/workshops)
Library Holdings: Book Volumes, Original Art Works
Collections: Paintings, prints & sculpture (32 pieces total)
Activities: docent training; poetry slam; lect open to public, gallery talks; tours; Invitational Exhibit for member artists; awarded People's Choice at Members Exhibit

WOODINVILLE

A **NORTHWEST WATERCOLOR SOCIETY,** 14519 NE 174th St, Woodinville, WA 98072; PO Box 50387, Bellevue, WA 98015-0387. Tel 425-822-6552; Email molly@mollymurrah.com; Web: www.nwws.org; *VPres* Shirley Jordan; *Treas* Peggy Meyers; *Pres* Molly Murrah; *Rec Secy* Wanda Hickman; *Corresp Secy* Seiko Konya
Open Mon - Fri 9 AM - 5 PM at Seattle Design Ctr; Admis free; Estab 1939 to promote interest in & appreciation for watercolor as an artistic medium; Average Annual Attendance: 1,000; Mem: 900; dues $40; Assoc Mems $40 per yr; Signature mems must exhibit in Juried open & waterworks shows (2 open or 1 open plus 2 waterworks shows) & be current on dues; monthly meetings Sept-May
Income: Financed by members
Library Holdings: CD-ROMs, DVDs, Exhibition Catalogs
Collections: Fred Hutchison Cancer Hospital - permanent coll
Exhibitions: Annual International Juried Show; Waterworks-Juried Members Show; Signature Show
Publications: Hot Press Newsletter, bimonthly
Activities: Educ dept; workshops; lect/demos open to public; free exhibs open to pub; 8 vis lectrs per yr; competitions with awards - Open $10,000, Waterworks $4,000; scholarships offered, funded by the Northwest Watercolor Foundation Charitable Fund; lending collection contains over 50 videos

YAKIMA

M **YAKIMA VALLEY COMMUNITY COLLEGE,** Larson Gallery, PO Box 22520, Yakima, WA 98907-2520; 16th & Nob Hill Blvd, Yakima, WA 98902. Tel 509-574-4875; Fax 509-574-6826; Email gallery@yvcc.edu; Web: www.larsongallery.org; *Dir* David Lynx; *Program Manager* Randy La Pierre; *Registrar* Haylee Olsen
Open Tues - Fri 10 AM - 5 PM, Sat 1 PM - 5 PM; cl Sun & Mon, July & Aug; No admis fee; Estab 1949; Fine arts gallery; Average Annual Attendance: 15,000; Mem: 360; dues $20-$1,000
Income: $180,000 (financed by endowment, fundraising & college support)
Collections: Contemporary art, primarily 2-D
Exhibitions: Rotating exhibitions
Publications: Central Washington Artists 2007-2010; Visual Voices: Women Painters of Washington; The Golden Spiral: Fibonacci, Sacred Geometry, and Divine proportion
Activities: Classes for adults; docent progs; workshops June & July; lects open to pub, 1 vis lectrs per yr; tours; gallery talks; Central Washington Artist Exhibition (5,000 awards annually); Photo Exhibition (5,000 awards biennially); Fiber Exhibition (2,000 awards biennially); 2 juried exhibs with awards; book 1 traveling exhib per yr; sales shop sells books, original art & notecards

WEST VIRGINIA

CHARLESTON

M **AVAMPATO DISCOVERY MUSEUM,** (Sunrise Museum, Inc) The Clay Center for Arts & Sciences, 300 Leon Sullivan Way, Charleston, WV 25301; 1 Clay Sq, Charleston, WV 25301-2424. Tel 304-561-3500; Fax 304-561-3552; Web: www.theclaycenter.org; *CEO/Pres* Dr Al Najjar; *VPres Devel* Kathy Bush; *Dir Educ* Kayte Kincaid
Open Wed - Sat 10 AM - 5 PM, Sun Noon - 5 PM, cl Mon, Tues & national holidays; Admis adults $6.50, students, teachers & seniors $5, children under 3 free; Estab 1960; Circ 3,000; Formerly Sunrise Museum moving to new location in 2003. The museum will house performing arts theatre & symphony; Dual Focus in arts & science. Merged with the Clay Center, July 2006; Average Annual Attendance: 120,000; Mem: dues Benefactors' Circle $1000, patron $500, supporting $250, contributing $100, participating $75 & individual $45
Income: $5.5M (financed by endowment, mem, earned income, corporate & bus contributions)
Library Holdings: Book Volumes, Exhibition Catalogs
Special Subjects: Decorative Arts, Painting-American, Sculpture
Collections: 17th through 20th century American paintings, prints & sculpture, works on paper: emphasis on 20th & 21st century American art
Exhibitions: Numerous regional & international exhibits held throughout the year
Publications: quarterly newsletter
Activities: Classes for adults & children; dramatic progs; docent training; lects open to pub; 6 vis lectrs per yr; guided tours; planetarium & film programs; concerts; gallery talks; STARLAB portable planetarium; individual & original objects of art lent to other mus & pub institutions; 2 or more book traveling exhibs per yr; mus shop sells books, prints & variety of scientific, educational & decorative gift items including jewelry

HUNTINGTON

M **HUNTINGTON MUSEUM OF ART,** 2033 McCoy Rd, Huntington, WV 25701-4999. Tel 304-529-2701; Fax 304-529-7447; Email ltipton@hmoa.org; Web: www.hmoa.org; *Sr Cur* Jenine Culligan; *Dir Educ* Lisa Geelhood; *Pub Rels* John Gillispie; *Comp* Kathy Saunders; *Dir* Margaret A Skove; *Dir Develop* Margaret Mary Layne
Open Tues - Sat 10 AM - 5 PM, Sun Noon - 5 PM; cl Mon; No admis fee; Estab 1952 to own, operate & maintain an art museum for the collection of paintings, prints, bronzes, porcelains & all kinds of art & utility objects; to permit the study of arts & crafts & to foster an interest in the arts; Three building complex on 52-acre site includes ten galleries, two sculpture courts, seven studio workshops, a 10,000 volume capacity library, 300 seat auditorium, two & one-half miles of nature trails & an amphitheatre; Average Annual Attendance: 75,000; Mem: dues vary; annual meeting in June
Income: Financed by endowment, mem, city, state & county appropriations
Special Subjects: Afro-American Art, American Western Art, Antiquities-Assyrian, Antiquities-Byzantine, Antiquities-Persian, Carpets & Rugs, Ceramics, Coins & Medals, Collages, Crafts, Decorative Arts, Ethnology, Folk Art, Furniture, Glass, Graphics, Military Art, Painting-American, Painting-British, Painting-Canadian, Painting-Dutch, Painting-Russian, Painting-Scandinavian, Painting-Spanish, Period Rooms, Photography
Collections: American & European Paintings & Prints, American Decorative Arts, Georgian silver, firearms, historical and contemporary glass, Turkish prayer rugs, Georgian Silver Collection
Publications: Exhibit catalogs; quarterly newsletter
Activities: Classes & workshops for adults & children; docent training; pub lectrs; concerts; theatre productions; gallery talks; tours; individual paintings & original objects of art lent to mus; tri-state area of Ohio, Kentucky, West Virginia in 75-mile radius; originates traveling exhibs; mus shop sells books, original art, reproductions, prints & crafts; Junior Art Mus

MARTINSBURG

M **ASSOCIATES FOR COMMUNITY DEVELOPMENT,** The Arts Center, Inc, 300 W King St, Martinsburg, WV 25401-3202. Tel 304-263-0224; *VPres Bd Dir* Mary Boyd Kearse; *Pres Bd & Dir* Barbara Gibson
Open Mon - Fri 10 AM - 4 PM; No admis fee; Estab 1987 to exhibit the work of local & regional artists & craftsmen; Mem: 200; dues $20-$1,000; quarterly meetings
Income: $88,000 (financed by mem, city appropriation, state appropriation & exhibit sponsors)
Special Subjects: Crafts, Photography, Sculpture
Exhibitions: Changing exhibits featuring a variety of arts & crafts including photography, sculpture, oil, acrylic, watercolor by local artisans; Youth Art Month Exhibit
Publications: Boarman Newsletter, quarterly; annual brochure; show invitations, 7 per year
Activities: Classes for adults & children; artist-in-residence young artists summer workshop; Christmas Show & Sale; lect open to public, 4 vis lectrs per year; competitions with awards; schols & fels offered; book traveling exhibitions 1 per year; sales shop sells books, prints, original art & handcrafts

MORGANTOWN

L **WEST VIRGINIA UNIVERSITY,** Evansdale Library, PO Box 6105, Morgantown, WV 26506-6105. Tel 304-293-5039; Fax 304-293-7330; Web: www.libraries.wvu.edu; *Head Librn* Jo Ann Calzonetti
Open Mon - Thurs 8 AM - 12 AM, Fri 8 AM - 5 PM, Sat 9 AM - 5 PM, Sun 6 - 10 PM
Library Holdings: Book Volumes 260,000, Periodical Subscriptions 2250
Special Subjects: Art Education, Art History, Landscape Architecture

M **Laura & Paul Mesaros Galleries,** PO Box 6111, Creative Arts Ctr Morgantown, WV 26506-6111. Tel 304-293-4841, ext 3210; Fax 304-293-5731; Email kolson@wvu.edu; Web: www.wvu.edu; *Cur* Kristina Olson
Open during acad yr Mon - Sat Noon - 9:30 PM, cl Sun & university holidays; No admis fee; Estab 1867
Collections: Costumes, music, paintings, theatre
Exhibitions: Call for exhibit information
Activities: Lect; gallery talks; tours; concerts; drama; competitions; temporary traveling exhibitions

PARKERSBURG

A **THE CULTURAL CENTER OF FINE ARTS,** Art Gallery, 725 Market St, Parkersburg, WV 26101-4628. Tel 304-485-3859; Fax 304-485-3850; Email ekge@earthlink.net; Web: www.wvfinearts.com; *CEO & Exec Dir* Ed Pauley; *Pres (V)* Harry Schranom
Open Tues - Sat 10 AM - 5 PM, Sun 1 - 5 PM; No admis fee for members, non-members $2, cl nat holidays; Estab 1938 for the operation & maintenance of an art center & mus facility for the appreciation & enjoyment of art, both visual & decorative, as well as art history, crafts & other related educational or cultural activities; Main gallery 7,500 sq ft & upper gallery 3,000 sq ft, completely carpeted, air conditioned & climate controlled; Average Annual Attendance: 25,000; Mem: 500; dues corporate or patron $250, sustaining $100, family $30, individual $20; annual meeting in June; rate schedule upon request
Income: $160,000 (financed by endowment, mem & state appropriation)
Library Holdings: Book Volumes, Clipping Files, Exhibition Catalogs, Framed Reproductions, Memorabilia, Periodical Subscriptions, Reproductions, Slides, Video Tapes
Collections: Advice of Dreams (oil by Beveridge Moore), Amish & African Artifacts, The Hinge (watercolor by Rudolph Ohrning), Parmenides (sculpture by Beverly Pepper), Permanent collection of over 200 2D & 3D works
Exhibitions: Six exhibs per yr
Publications: Calendar of events, bimonthly; annual report; exhibition catalogs
Activities: Classes for adults & children; docent training; workshops; outreach prog, Arts-in-the-Parks; 3 major fundraisers; educational programming; lects open to pub, 6 vis lectrs per yr; concerts; gallery talks; tours; competition with awards; $8,000 for Realism competition, others vary by exhibit; book traveling exhibs; originate traveling exhibs; mus shop sells books, original art, prints, local art, jewelry, Don Whitlatch "Spring Break" print

ROMNEY

L **HAMPSHIRE COUNTY PUBLIC LIBRARY,** 153 W Main St, Romney, WV 26757-1694. Tel 304-822-3185; Fax 304-822-3955; Web: www.wvculture.org; *Librn* Brenda Riffle
Open Mon & Fri 10 AM - 8 PM, Tues - Thurs 10 AM - 6 PM, Sat 10 AM - 4 PM; No admis fee; Estab 1942; 7 Display cases changed every month; Average Annual Attendance: 45,000; Mem: 11,000
Income: $128,000 financed by state, donations, mem
Purchases: $32,000
Library Holdings: Audio Tapes, Book Volumes 38,000, Cassettes, Clipping Files, Maps, Original Documents, Pamphlets, Periodical Subscriptions 96, Photographs, Prints, Records, Reels, Video Tapes
Collections: books
Exhibitions: Children's art; private collections of rocks, antiques, displays of items of other countries; various local artists collection; weaving
Activities: Classes for adults & children; lect open to public; concerts; tours; plays; antique show; competitions with awards; individual paintings lent

WESTON

M **MUSEUM OF AMERICAN GLASS IN WV,** 230 Main Ave, Weston, WV 26452-2044; PO Box 574, Weston, WV 26452-0574. Tel 304-269-5006; Email wvmag@ma.rr.com; Web: www.magwv.com; *Exec Dir* Dean Six; *Archivist* Tom Felt
Open winter hours: Mon - Tues & Thurs - Sat 12 PM - 4 PM; Memorial Day to Labor Day open daily noon - 4 PM; No admis fee, donations accepted; Estab 1993; Located on Main Ave in downtown Weston, WV. Mus has the mission of sharing the diverse & rich heritage of glass as a product & historical object telling of the lives of glass workers, their families & communities, and of the tools & machines they used in glass houses; Average Annual Attendance: 2,500; Mem: Dues Benefactor $500 & up; Patron $100; Sustaining $50; Supporting $35; Ann $25
Special Subjects: Glass, Prints, Historical Material
Collections: Diverse & beautiful glass objects produced by factories during this century, five large covered jars designed by Fritz Driesbach and executed by the Blenko Glass Co, Milton, WV, three Tiffany decorative glass tiles (one signed), hand-painted Top Hat tumbler, a product of the WV Glass Specialty Co, Weston WV, signed by the artist, Al Erbe, commemorative glass bust of M J Owens, a native of WV and inventor of the automatic bottle-making machine, national marble museum, studio art glass by Kelsey Murphy, Roberto Moretti, Dominick Labino & other artists
Publications: Black Glass Book, published by WVMAG; All About Glass, quarterly magazine for mems
Activities: Research library; events such as The Marble Festival; educational interactive displays for children; annual glass gathering; mus shop sells books, magazines & glassware

WHEELING

A **OGLEBAY INSTITUTE,** Stifel Fine Arts Center, 1330 National Rd, Wheeling, WV 26003-5706. Tel 304-242-7700; Email inspire@oionline.com; Web:

www.oionline.com/arts; *Dir* Rick Morgan; *Exhibs Dir* Brad Johnson; *Educ Dir* Jessica Leach
Open Mon - Fri 9 AM - 5 PM, Sat 10 AM - 4 PM; No admis fee; Estab 1930 to present art exhibitions & to provide the opportunity for life-long learning in the fine arts fields; Circ 8; Three galleries located in the Stifel Mansion occupy the center of the facility on both floors.; Average Annual Attendance: 6,000; Mem: 1450; dues $15 & up
Activities: Classes for adults & children; dramatic progs; docent training; school progs; lect open to public; concerts; gallery talks; tours; schols

M **Mansion Museum**, 1330 National Rd, Oglebay Park Wheeling, WV 26003-5706. Tel 304-242-7272; Fax 304-242-4203; Web: www.oionline.com/museum; *Dir* Holly McCluskey
Open Mon - Sat 9:30 AM - 5 PM, Sun & holidays Noon - 5 PM; Admis $5, 55 & over $4.25, students $2, children under 12 free with paying adults; Estab & incorporated 1930 to promote educational, cultural & recreational activities in Wheeling Tri-State area; Building & ground are the property of the city; an exhibition wing adjoins the main house; annual Christmas decorations; Average Annual Attendance: 83,394; Mem: 1450; dues $15 & up
Special Subjects: Glass, Period Rooms, Pewter, Porcelain
Collections: Early 19th century china, early glass made in Wheeling & the Midwest
Exhibitions: Current exhibits of art & other allied subjects change periodically; decorative arts
Activities: Antique show & sales; antique classes; gallery talks; self-guided & prearranged group tours

L **Library**, 1330 National Rd, Oglebay Park Wheeling, WV 26003-5706. Tel 304-242-7272; Fax 304-242-4203
Open by appointment only; Founded 1934; Highly specialized on the early history of the area
Library Holdings: Book Volumes 800, Micro Print 20, Other Holdings Documents bound 100, Maps, VF 4, Slides
Special Subjects: Decorative Arts, Historical Material
Collections: Brown Collection of Wheeling History, photographs, Wheeling City Directories, Wheeling & Belmont Bridge Company Papers
Activities: Classes for adults & children; docent training; 2 vis lectrs per yr; exten prog, 75 mile radius of Wheeling

WISCONSIN

APPLETON

M **LAWRENCE UNIVERSITY,** Wriston Art Center Galleries, 711 E Boldt Way, Appleton, WI 54911-5690. Tel 920-832-6621; Fax 920-832-7362; Email odonnelp@lawrence.edu; Web: www.lawrence.edu; *Cur & Dir* Frank Lewis
Open Tues - Fri 10 AM - 4 PM, Sat & Sun Noon - 4 PM, cl Mon; No admis fee; Estab 1950 for teaching & community exhibitions. Wriston Art Center opened Spring 1989; Three exhibitions galleries for changing exhibits of contemporary & historical shows; Average Annual Attendance: 5,000
Special Subjects: Graphics, Drawings, Prints, Asian Art, Oriental Art
Collections: American regionalist art, Japanese prints & drawings, Ottilia Buerger Collection of Ancient Coins, Pohl Collection-German Expressionism
Exhibitions: Various exhib
Activities: Lect open to public, 3-6 vis lectrs per year; individual paintings & original works of art lent for exhibitions in other museums

BELOIT

M **BELOIT COLLEGE,** Wright Museum of Art, 700 College St, Beloit, WI 53511-5595. Tel 608-363-2677; Fax 608-363-2718; Web: www.beloit.edu/wright; *Dir* Joy Beckman; *Coll Mgr* James Pearson; *Asst* Aaron Wilson
Open Tues - Sun 11 AM - 4 PM; No admis fee; Estab 1893; Wright Art Hall built 1930 to house the coll for the enrichment of the col & community through exhib of permanent coll & traveling & temporary art exhibs of cultural & aesthetic value; A Georgian building architecturally styled after the Fogg Mus in Cambridge, Massachusetts. Three galleries on main floor, on a large center ct; Art Department shares other floors in which two student galleries are included; Average Annual Attendance: 20,000
Purchases: 17th - 20th century graphics; Asian decorative arts
Special Subjects: Anthropology, Antiquities-Egyptian, Antiquities-Greek, Antiquities-Oriental, Antiquities-Roman, Archaeology, Architecture, Asian Art, Baroque Art, Bookplates & Bindings, Calligraphy, Decorative Arts, Gold, Graphics, Ivory, Jade, Jewelry, Latin American Art, Medieval Art, Metalwork, Oriental Art, Painting-American, Painting-British, Painting-European, Photography, Porcelain, Portraits, Sculpture, Painting-German
Collections: European & American (paintings, sculpture & decorative arts), Fisher Memorial Collection of Greek Casts, graphics, emphasis on German Expressionist & contemporary works, Gurley Collection of Korean Pottery, Japanese Sword Guards, Chinese Snuff Bottles & Jades, Morse Collection of Paintings & Other Art Objects, Neese Fund Collection of Contemporary Art, Prints by Durer, Rembrandt, Whistler & others, 19th century photographs, Pitkin Asian Art Collection
Publications: Exhibition catalogs
Activities: Classes; supportive progs; docent training; lects open to pub; gallery talks; tours; originates traveling exhibs; mus shop sells books, original art & reproductions

BROOKFIELD

M **SHARON LYNNE WILSON CENTER FOR THE ARTS,** Ploch Art Gallery, 19805 W Capitol Dr, Brookfield's Mitchell Park Brookfield, WI 53045-2722. Tel 262-781-9470; Fax 262-781-9798; Email rsvp@wilson-center.com; Web: www.wilson-center.com; *Pres & CEO* Jonathan Winkle; *Visual Art Mgr* Jim Charles
Open Mon - Sat 9 AM - 5 PM; No adms fee; Gallery located in the upper level of the Wilson Center's Kettemperoor Grand Hall displays the work of Wisconsin artists
Special Subjects: Ceramics, Crafts, Decorative Arts, Drawings, Enamels, Etchings & Engravings, Furniture, Glass, Jewelry, Landscapes, Metalwork, Photography, Pottery, Prints, Sculpture, Watercolors
Activities: Classes for adults & children

CEDARBURG

A **WISCONSIN FINE ARTS ASSOCIATION, INC,** Ozaukee Art Center, W62 N718 Riveredge Dr, Cedarburg, WI 53012. Tel 262-377-8290; *Art Dir* Paul Yank
Open Wed - Sun 1 - 4 PM, or by appointment; No admis fee; Estab 1971; Historical landmark with cathedral ceiling; Average Annual Attendance: 10,000; Mem: 600; dues bus patron $500, patron $200, sustaining $100, assoc sustaining $50, family $30, individual $22, student $10; annual meeting in Oct
Income: Mem contributions, state appropriations
Collections: Paintings, sculpture, prints, ceramics
Exhibitions: Ozaukee County Show; Harvest Festival of Arts
Publications: Monthly newsletter
Activities: Classes for adults and children; docent training; lects open to public, 2 vis lectrs per year; concerts; gallery talks; tours; competitions with awards; arts festivals

EAU CLAIRE

M **UNIVERSITY OF WISCONSIN-EAU CLAIRE,** Foster Gallery, 121 Water St, Eau Claire, WI 54701-4811; PO Box 4004, Eau Claire, WI 54702-4004. Tel 715-836-2328; Fax 715-836-4882; Email wagenetk@uwec.edu; Web: www.uwec.edu/art/foster; *Dir* Thomas Wagener
Open Foster Gallery: Mon - Fri 10 AM - 4:30 PM, Thurs 6 PM - 8 PM, Sat & Sun 1 - 4:30 PM; No admis fee; Estab 1970 to show finest contemporary art in all media; State University Gallery in Fine Arts Center; Average Annual Attendance: 24,000
Income: Funded by state appropriation
Special Subjects: Ceramics, Collages, Drawings, Etchings & Engravings, Graphics, Painting-American, Photography, Prints, Sculpture, Watercolors, Woodcuts
Collections: Eau Claire Permanent Art Collection, 20th Century Artists
Activities: Lect open to public, 4-5 vis lectrs per year; competition with awards; gallery talks; book traveling exhibitions 3-4 per year

FISH CREEK

M **FRANCIS HARDY GALLERY,** 3038 Anderson Ln, Fish Creek, WI 54212; PO Box 394, Ephraim, WI 54211-0394. Tel 920-854-2210; Email info@thehardy.org; Web: thehardy.org; *Exec Dir* Sarah Zamecnik; *Prog Coordr* Ann Soderlund
Open mid-May through mid-Oct; Mon - Sat 10 AM - 5 PM, Sun Noon - 5 PM; Estab 1962; Mem: dues $35-$250
Collections: acrylic; drawing; fiber; sculpture; ink; mixed media; pastel; photography; oil; watercolor
Exhibitions: Temporary exhibits
Activities: Art programming

FOND DU LAC

M **THELMA SADOFF CENTER FOR THE ARTS,** (Windhover Center for the Arts), 51 Sheboygan St, Fond Du Lac, WI 54935-4219. Tel 920-921-5410; Email info@thelmaarts.org; Web: wwwthelmaarts.org; *Exec Dir* Kevin Miller
Open Wed - Sun 11 AM - 4 PM; No admis fee; Estab 2013, to provide access to the arts for community; 2 floors, 1,600 sq ft each floor

GREEN BAY

M **NEVILLE PUBLIC MUSEUM OF BROWN COUNTY,** 210 Museum Pl, Green Bay, WI 54303-2780. Tel 920-448-7842; Fax 920-448-4458; Email bc_museum@co.brown.wi.us; Web: www.nevillepublicmuseum.org; *Mus Dir* Beth A Lemke; *Colls Mgr* Louise Pfotenhauer; *AV Technician* Dennis Roslonic; *Office Mgr* Kathy Rosera; *Exhib Technician* Maggie Dernehl; *Guest Svcs Coordr* Jessica Day; *Dir Develop Mktg* Rachel Ott; *Mktg Asst* Jenny Seim; *Deputy Dir* Kevin M Cullen; *Educ Specialist* Ryan Swadley; *Cur* Lisa Kain
Open Mon, Tues, Thurs, Fri, Sat 9 AM - 5 PM, Wed 9 AM - 8 PM, Sun Noon - 5 PM; Admis adult $5, children ages 5 & under free; special rates for school & youth groups available; Estab 1915 as Green Bay Pub Mus; names changed 1926, estab to interpret the collections & educate through exhibits, educational programming, research & publications; Art gallery presently in use, largest 3000 sq ft. Maintains reference library; Average Annual Attendance: 66,000; Mem: 800; dues Individual $40, Family $65
Income: Financed by county appropriation & private donations
Special Subjects: Costumes, Dolls, Drawings, Embroidery, Etchings & Engravings, Folk Art, Furniture, Glass, Painting-American, Photography, Porcelain, Prints, Sculpture, Watercolors
Collections: Victoriana, antique furniture, china, glass, costumes, accessories, contemporary & historical paintings, drawings, prints & sculpture, archeology, geology, photographs, news film from local TV stations, David Belasco Collection
Publications: Musepaper, 4 times per yr
Activities: Classes for adults & children; docent training; dramatic progs; lects open to pub, vis lectrs; concerts; gallery talks; tours; juried competitions with awards; schols offered; individual paintings & original objects of art lent to other mus; summer outreach; book traveling exhibs; mus shop sells books, magazines, original art, reproductions, prints, gifts & cards

L **Research Library, Photo & Film Collection**, 210 Museum Pl, Green Bay, WI 54303. Tel 920-448-4460; Fax 920-448-4458; Email mean_jm@co.brown.wi.us; Web: www.nevillepublicmuseum.org; *Colls Mgr* Louise Pfotenhauer
Open by appointment; Open to the public for reference by appt only
Library Holdings: Audio Tapes, Book Volumes 5000, Clipping Files, Exhibition Catalogs, Fiche, Kodachrome Transparencies, Memorabilia, Motion Pictures, Pamphlets, Periodical Subscriptions 20, Photographs, Reels, Slides, Video Tapes
Activities: Lects open to the pub; mus shop sells books & original art

M **UNIVERSITY OF WISCONSIN, GREEN BAY,** Lawton Gallery, 2420 Nicolet Dr, Green Bay, WI 54311-7001. Tel 920-465-2271, 465-2916; Fax 920-465-2890; Email perkinss@uwgb.edu; Web: www.uwgb.edu/lawton; *Acad Cur Art* Dr Stephen Perkins; *Asst Cur* Erin Rose
Open Tues - Sat 10 - 3 PM, cl Sun & Mon; No admis fee; Estab 1974 to show changing exhibs of contemporary & 20th century art, student & faculty work; Gallery is 2,000 sq ft; Average Annual Attendance: 3,000
Income: $5,000
Purchases: Limited purchases & donations to Univ Wisc-Green Bay permanent coll
Collections: Contemporary art & prints, student & faculty work; Native American coll, 160 Andy Warhol Photographs
Exhibitions: Graduating Seniors Exhibition
Publications: Exhibition catalogs
Activities: Gallery & museum practices minor for undergraduates; workshops related to exhibs; lects open to pub; 2-3 vis lectrs per semester; competitions; gallery talks; assorted awards for student juried art exhibition; Lawton Gallery Award for excellence 2D & 3D; schols; exten prog loaned to university departments & offices; learning in retirement; originates traveling exhibs to other university galleries

GREENBUSH

M **WADE HOUSE HISTORIC SITE-WISCONSIN HISTORICAL SOCIETY,** Wesley W. Jung Carriage Museum, W 7824 Center St, Greenbush, WI 53026; PO Box 34, Greenbush, WI 53026-0034. Tel 920-526-3271; Fax 920-526-3626; Email wadehouse@wisconsinhistory.org; Web: www.wadehouse.org; *Dir* David Warner; *Cur Interpretation* James W. Willaert; *Educ Specialist* Bridgitt Zielke
Open mid-May - mid-Oct 10 AM -5 PM; Admis family rate $30, adults $11, seniors $9.25, child $5.50 (includes carriage ride); Estab 1953 to educate public concerning 1860s Wisconsin Yankee town life; Average Annual Attendance: 23,000
Income: $500,000 (financed by state appropriation, admis fees)
Special Subjects: Archaeology, Architecture, Ceramics, Crafts, Decorative Arts, Furniture, Historical Material, Period Rooms
Collections: Wisconsin made Carriages, 1860s Household Furnishings
Exhibitions: 1860s Historic Stagecoach Inn Tour; Working Water-powered Sawmill; Blacksmith Shop
Activities: Classes for adults & children; docent training; spec events; lects open to pub, vis lectrs; tours; mus shop sells books, reproductions, original art & prints

HUDSON

M **THE PHIPPS CENTER FOR THE ARTS,** Galleries, 109 Locust St, Hudson, WI 54016-1518. Tel 715-386-8409; Email info@thephipps.org; Web: www.thephipps.org; *Bd Pres* Chuck Koosmann; *Bd VPres* Roger Olson; *Bd Secy* Monica Weekes; *Bd Treas* Jim Lutiger
Galleries open Mon - Sat 9 AM - 4:30 PM, Sun noon - 4:30 PM & one hour preceding performances; Mem: dues $40-$1,250
Collections: painting; sculpture
Exhibitions: Temporary exhibits
Activities: Classes for adults & children

KENOSHA

M **KENOSHA PUBLIC MUSEUMS,** 5500 1st Ave, Kenosha, WI 53140-3778. Tel 262-653-4140; Fax 262-653-4437; Email djoyce@kenosha.org; Web: www.kenoshapublicmuseum.org; *Dir* Daniel Joyce; *Vol Pres* Cameron Olson; *Deputy Dir* Peggy Gregorski; *Cur Exhibits* Rachel Klees Andersen; *Cur Collections* Gina Radandt; *Sr Cur Educ* Nancy Matthews; *Coordr Opers* Ken Ade
Open Sun noon - 5 PM, Mon - Sat 10 AM - 5 PM; cl New Year's Eve & Day; Martin Luther King Jr Day; Good Friday; Memorial Day; Independence Day; Labor Day; Thanksgiving; Christmas Eve & Day; No admis fee; Estab 1935 to promote interest in general natural history & regional art; The gallery has 8,000 sq ft of permanent exhib space & 8,000 sq ft for temporary exhibits; Average Annual Attendance: 132,839; Mem: 1,500 households, $25 individuals, $40 family
Income: $1,500,000 (financed by city appropriation)
Purchases: $2200
Library Holdings: Book Volumes 5,000, Original Documents, Prints
Special Subjects: African Art, American Indian Art, Anthropology, Antiquities-Greek, Antiquities-Roman, Archaeology, Asian Art, Bronzes, Calligraphy, Carpets & Rugs, Ceramics, Coins & Medals, Costumes, Crafts, Decorative Arts, Dioramas, Dolls, Drawings, Enamels, Eskimo Art, Etchings & Engravings, Ethnology, Flasks & Bottles, Folk Art, Furniture, Glass, Graphics, Hispanic Art, Historical Material, Islamic Art, Ivory, Jade, Jewelry, Juvenile Art, Landscapes, Latin American Art, Leather, Manuscripts, Maps, Metalwork, Mexican Art, Military Art, Miniatures, Mosaics, Oriental Art, Painting-American, Painting-European, Painting-Japanese, Photography, Porcelain, Portraits, Posters, Pottery, Pre-Columbian Art, Primitive art, Prints, Religious Art, Reproductions, Sculpture, Silver, Southwestern Art, Stained Glass, Textiles, Watercolors, Woodcarvings, Woodcuts
Collections: Civil War, Paleontology; Natural History; Art
Publications: Newsletter, bimonthly; Wisconsin Folk Pottery Book
Activities: Classes for adults & children; dramatic progs; docent training; lect open to pub, 20 vis lectrs per yr; concerts; gallery talks; tours; competitions; films; lending collection contains color reproductions, 30 framed reproductions, 280 motion pictures, nature artifacts & slides; originate traveling exhibs; sales shop sells books, crafts, ethnic jewelry, earrings, magazines, original art, reproductions, prints, toys & collectibles

LA CROSSE

M **VITERBO UNIVERSITY,** Art Gallery, 815 S Ninth St, La Crosse, WI 54601. Tel 608-796-3000 (Main), 796-3757; Fax 608-796-3736; *Dir* Joseph E Miller
Open Mon - Fri 10 AM - 5 PM; No admis fee; Estab 1964 to exhibit arts & crafts which will be a valuable supplement to courses offered; Gallery is located in the center of the Art Department; 100 running feet; soft walls; good light
Income: Financed by school appropriation
Collections: Mrs Lynn Anna Louise Miller, Collection of the contemporary United States primitive, Peter Whitebird Collection of WPA project paintings
Activities: Classes for adults & children; dramatic progs; lects open to pub; gallery talks; 2-5 vis lectrs per yr; schols

LAC DU FLAMBEAU

A **DILLMAN'S CREATIVE ARTS FOUNDATION,** 3305 Sand Lake Lodge Ln, Lac Du Flambeau, WI 54538; PO Box 98, Lac Du Flambeau, WI 54538-0098. Tel 715-588-3143; Fax 715-588-3110; Email dillmans@newnorth.net; Email vacations@dillmans.com; Web: www.vacationscdillmans.com; *VPres* Sue Robertson; *Pres* Dennis Robertson; *Marketing* Stephanie Shablerut; *Treasurer* Todd Shablerut; *Website/Brochure* Scott Robertson
Open 24 hours May - Oct; Admis varies, see website; Estab 1987 to offer educational experience; Display on Dillman Lodge walls, hallway, studios & rack in gift shop; Average Annual Attendance: 500
Income: Grant, Wisconsin Art Board; Revenue from workshops
Library Holdings: Audio Tapes, Book Volumes, Compact Disks, DVDs, Framed Reproductions, Original Art Works, Photographs
Exhibitions: Please view our website for 2016-2017-2018 list of workshops and details; (22nd Jan, 2017)Festival of the Artists - Marco Island, Florida; (19th Mar, 2017)Festival of the Artists - Lakes Regional Watercolor Guild - McHenry, Illinois; (25th Mar, 2017)Festival of the Artists - Madison, Wisconsin; (26th Mar, 2017) Festival of the Artists - Hopkins, Minnesota; (20th May, 2017)Open House - Lac du Flambeau; (20th May, 2017)Arrival (Week 1) - Laura Lein-Scencner - Abstract Mixed Media Collage and Composition (5 Teaching Days), Sterling Edwards - Creating Expressive & Dynamic Watercolors (5 Teaching Days), Pam Luer - Nature Sketchbook (4 Teaching Days); (28th May, 2017)Week 2 - Joyce Kicks - Use Shapes and Symbols to Create Beautiful Watercolor Landscapes; (4th Jun, 2017)Week 3 - Frank Webb - Toward Mastery in Watercolor; David Kessler - Bigger, Faster, Fresher, Looser Abstract Painting; Linda Kemp - Transforming Imagery - Negative Painting with Acrylics; Mark Russell - Abstract Landscapes Oil and Cold Wax; (11th Jun, 2017)Week 4 - Susan Lingg - Exploring Watercolor for Beginners and Intermediates; Bonnie Paruch - Plein Air and Studio Oil and Pastel; David R. Becker - The Most Important Watercolor Workshop, Spring Edition; Jan Sitts - Texture, Color, Feeling - Mixed Media; (18th Jun, 2017)Week 5 - John Salminen - Watercolor Through Design (Five Teaching Days); Laurie Goldstein Warren - Simplified Approach Painting Glass Reflections in Watercolor; Nancy Akerly - Marbeling Outside the Box; (25th Jun, 2017)Week 6- Bob Burridge - Loosen Up - Entry Level; Karen Ragus - Loosie-Goosie Abstract Acrylic Painting; Alexis Lavine;; (8th Jul, 2017)Week 7 - Arieta Pech - Pet Portraits in Watercolor (5 Teaching Days); Tom Lynch - Watercolor Secrets Revealed;; (20th Aug, 2017) Week 8 - Janet Rogers - Watercolor Impressions - Faces & Figures - from Life & Photos (4); Steve Rogers - Painting Color, Light and Reflections (4); Walter Porter - Composition, Color and More in Oil/Acrylic/Pastel; (27th Aug, 2017)Week 9 - Mark Nutt - Printmaking Fun; (3rd Sep, 2017)Week 10 - Arieta Pech - Realism in Oil (4 Teaching Days); Alan Lace - Wood Turning Fundamentals; Tony Couch - Watercolor: You Can Do It!; (10th Sep, 2017)Week 11 - Carol Schulz - Engle Impressions... Beauty by the Seasons; Mary Mendia - Opening to Abstraction: An Art Retreat in Acrylic and Mixed Media; Caroline Jasper - Head & Heart Plein Air Painting; Sharon Reilly - Oriental Watercolor - Expressions of the Northwoods; (17th Sep, 2017)Week 12 - David R. Becker - The Most Important Watercolor Workshop, Fall Edition; Jane Barnard - Watercolor on Your Creative Path; Hannah Ineson - The Art of Watercolor Journaling; Dan Mondloch - Bold Undercoatings that Glow;; (24th Sep, 2017)Week 13 - Kath Macaulay - Pocket Sketching and John Singer Sargent; Frank La Lumia - Plein Air Oil Painting; 2017 Dates to be Announced: Margaret (Peggy) Carter Baumgaertner - Mentoring Workshop: A Directed Critique; Mary Bauschelt - Drawing and Painting Botanicals; Greg Disch - Photography; Andy Evansen - Simplifying Watercolor; Joan Fullerton - Contemporary Approaches to Mixed Media Collage; Kami Mendlik; (21st May, 2018-25th May, 2018) Sterling Edwards - Creating Expressive & Dynamic Watercolors; (15th Jun, 2018-20th Jun, 2018) Karen Knuston; 2018 - Carol Nelson - Experimental Acrylics and Mixed Media; Rose Edin; Barbara Jaenicke; Jane Davies; John Lovett;
Publications: Annual brochure
Activities: Classes for adults & children; lects open to pub, 50 vis lectrs per yr; schols & fels offered; exten dept serves England; lending collection contains books; off premises: Green Costa Rica 2016; book traveling exhibs 12-15 per yr; originate traveling exhibs 12-15 per yr; sales shop sells books, original art & prints

L **Tom Lynch Resource Center**, 3305 Sand Lake Lodge Ln, Box 98, Lac du Flambeau, WI 54538. Tel 715-588-3143; Fax 715-588-3110; Email dillmans@newnorth.net; Web: www.dillmans.com; *Pres* Dennis Robertson; *VPres* Sue Robertson; *Secy* Betsy Behnke
Open May - Oct; Admis fees vary by workshop; Estab 1977 for education; Lends books and tapes; sale of art works; Average Annual Attendance: 500
Income: Income from workshop fees
Library Holdings: Audio Tapes 20, Book Volumes 500, Exhibition Catalogs, Framed Reproductions 20, Original Art Works 100, Prints 4000, Reproductions 100, Video Tapes 20
Activities: Classes for adults & children; awards from Midwest Watercolor Soc & Oil Painters of Am; schols offered; workshops in Europe; mus shop sells books, original art, reproductions & prints

M **LAC DU FLAMBEAU BAND OF LAKE SUPERIOR CHIPPEWA INDIANS,** George W Brown Jr Ojibwe Museum & Cultural Center, 603 Peace Pipe, Lac Du Flambeau, WI 54538; PO Box 804, Lac du Flambeau, WI 54538-0804. Tel 715-588-3333, 588-2139; Fax 715-588-2355; Email bearpawn@hotmail.com; *Mus Dir* Christina Breault; *Mus Mgr* Teresa Mitchell; *Colls Technician* Nina Isham
Open May - Oct Mon - Sat 10 AM - 4 PM & Nov - Apr Mon - Fri 10 AM - 2 PM; Admis adult $3, children $2, seniors $2, tour group $4 per person; Estab 1988 to collect, preserve, protect & promote the cultural history of the Lac du Flambeau Ojibwe; Main floor: Four seasons exhibit featuring the harvesting cycle of the traditional ways of the Ojibwe Indian people plus numerous objects of the Ojibwe; Average Annual Attendance: 6,500
Income: $100,000 (financed by Tribal appropriation)
Purchases: Various historical, cultural objects, photos & documents
Library Holdings: Auction Catalogs, Audio Tapes, Cards, Cassettes, Compact Disks, Kodachrome Transparencies, Manuscripts, Maps, Memorabilia, Original Art Works, Photographs, Prints, Reproductions, Slides, Video Tapes
Special Subjects: American Indian Art, Archaeology, Carpets & Rugs, Costumes, Crafts, Decorative Arts, Dioramas, Dolls, Drawings, Embroidery, Etchings & Engravings, Ethnology, Folk Art, Historical Material, Jewelry, Leather, Manuscripts, Maps, Photography, Posters, Textiles, Woodcarvings
Collections: Manuscripts, documents & photography of the Lac du Flambeau Band of the Lake Superior Ojibwe, Objects of the cultural history of The Lake Superior Ojibwe, Lake Superior Ojibwe Collection
Exhibitions: Various exhibits of the cultural ways of the Lac du Flambeau Ojibwe
Activities: Classes for adults & children; interactive TV progs area schools; dramatic progs; lects open to pub, 3 vis lectrs per yr; cultural sharing prog; community art display; history topics; individual paintings lent throughout Wisconsin; mus shop sells books, magazines, original art, reproductions, prints, Ojibwe arts & crafts & food

MADISON

M **EDGEWOOD COLLEGE,** DeRicci Gallery, 1000 Edgewood College Dr, Madison, WI 53711-1997. Tel 608-663-3252; Email davidwells@edgewood.edu; Web: finearts.edgewood.edu; *Dir* David Wells
Open Wed - Fri 11 AM - 4 PM, Sat & Sun 12 PM - 4 PM & by appt

M **MADISON MUSEUM OF CONTEMPORARY ART,** 227 State St, Madison, WI 53703-2214. Tel 608-257-0158; Fax 608-257-5722; Email info@mmoca.org; Web: www.mmoca.org; *Head Registrar* Marilyn Sohi; *Bus Mgr* Michael Paggie; *Dir Installations & Facilities* Brian Bartlett; *Dir Retail Opers* Leslie Genszler; *Cur Educ* Sheri Castelnuovo; *Assoc Dir Mem Engagement* Kaitlin Kropp; *Dir* Stephen Fleischman; *Cur Exhibs* Leah Kolb; *Dir Communs* Erika Monroe-Kane; *Dir Develop* Elizabeth Tucker; *Dir Events & Vols* Annik Depaty; *Director of Public Operations* Bob Sylvester
Open Tues - Thurs & Sun Noon- 5 PM, Fri Noon - 8 PM, Sat 10 AM- 8 PM, cl Mon; No admis fee, donations accepted; Estab 1901 to exhibit and collect modern & contemporary art; Circ non-circulating; 51,500 sq ft of space for the study, presentation & conservation of modern & contemporary art; 7,100 sq ft rooftop sculpture garden; pub amenities include spacious galleries, 230 seat lect hall, children's classroom, media gallery & study center; Average Annual Attendance: 180,000; Mem: 2000; dues $40 & up; annual meeting in May
Income: $2,220,000 (financed by mem, grants, gifts & earned revenue)
Library Holdings: Book Volumes, Clipping Files, Exhibition Catalogs, Original Documents, Periodical Subscriptions
Special Subjects: Drawings, Mexican Art, Painting-American, Photography, Prints, Sculpture
Collections: Emphasis on contemporary America, large print & drawing coll (Japanese, European, Mexican & American), paintings, photographs
Exhibitions: (24th Sep, 2016-8th Jan, 2017) 2016 Wisconsin Triennial; 12th Nov, 2017) Reconfigured Reality: Contemporary Photography from the Permanent Collection; (11th Feb, 2017-31st May, 2017) Do Ho Suh; (11th Feb, 2017-23rd Apr, 2017) Young at Art; (6th May, 2017-30th Jul, 2017) Kambui Olujimi: Trace; (1st Aug, 2017-12th Nov, 2017) Chele Issac: One Possibility
Publications: Catalogs & announcements usually accompany each exhibition; quarterly newsletter
Activities: Classes for adults & children; docent training; youth progs; teaching & learning resources for schools & families; lects open to public, film series; gallery talks; tours; extension prog serves Dane County; artmobile & lending of original objects of art to pub schools; originate traveling exhibs; mus store sells books, jewelry & other artist-made arts & crafts

M **UNIVERSITY OF WISCONSIN-MADISON,** Wisconsin Union Galleries, 800 Langdon St, Madison, WI 53706-1419; 1308 W Dayton St, Rm 235, Madison, WI 53715. Tel 608-262-7592 (committee); 890-4432 (advisor); Fax 608-890-4411; Email art@union.wisc.edu; Email robin.schmoldt@wisc.edu; Web: www.union.wisc.edu/art; *Union Dir* Mark Guthier; *Art Advisor & Art Coll Mgr* Robin Schmoldt
Open 10 AM - 8 PM; No admis fee; Estab 1907 to provide a cultural program for the members of the university community; Owns two fireproof buildings with four separate galleries 1700 sq ft: Memorial Union, 800 Langdon; Union South, 1308 W Dayton St; Average Annual Attendance: 320,000; Mem: 50,000 faculty, alumni & townspeople, plus 45,000 students; dues $50
Special Subjects: Ceramics, Collages, Decorative Arts, Drawings, Etchings & Engravings, Folk Art, Glass, Graphics, Landscapes, Metalwork, Painting-American, Photography, Portraits, Pottery, Prints, Watercolors, Woodcarvings, Woodcuts
Collections: Oil & watercolor paintings, photographs, drawings, prints & sculptures, mostly by Wisconsin artists
Publications: A Reflection of Time: The WI Union Art Collection
Activities: Informal classes in arts & crafts; dramatic progs; lects open to pub; 10-12 vis lectrs per yr; films; gallery talks; competitions with prizes; annual student art show, Purchase Awards; book traveling occasionally

M **Chazen Museum of Art,** 750 University Ave, Madison, WI 53706-1479. Tel 608-263-2246; Fax 608-263-8188; Web: www.chazen.wisc.edu; *Dir* Amy Gilman; *Cur Paintings, Sculpture & Decorative Arts* Maria Saffiotti Dale; *Cur Prints, Drawings & Photos* Andrew Stevens; *Cur Educ* Candie Waterloo; *Registrar* Andrea Selbig; *Registrar* Ann Sinfield; *Preparator* Kate Wanberg; *Develop Specialist* Amy Guthier; *Visitor Services Associate* Adrienne Rich; *Preparator* Brett Stageman; *Editor* Kristin Pires; *Communications Specialist* Jeff Weyer; *Admin Asst* Connie Diring
Open Tues, Wed & Fri 9 AM - 5 PM, Thurs 9 AM - 9 PM, Sat - Sun 11 AM - 5 PM, cl Mon; No admis fee; Estab 1970 as a cultural resource for the state & region & to support the educ & serv mission of the Univ of Wisconsin-Madison; 20 permanent galleries, 16 display niches & 3 temporary exhib halls present over 2,000 objects in over 42,000 sq ft of exhibit space; Average Annual Attendance: 140,000; Mem: 1,300; dues $25-$1000
Income: Financed by endowment, mem, state appropriation & private sources
Purchases: $500,000
Special Subjects: African Art, Afro-American Art, American Indian Art, Antiquities-Byzantine, Antiquities-Etruscan, Antiquities-Greek, Antiquities-Oriental, Antiquities-Roman, Archaeology, Architecture, Asian Art, Baroque Art, Bronzes, Calligraphy, Ceramics, Coins & Medals, Decorative Arts, Drawings, Enamels, Eskimo Art, Etchings & Engravings, Furniture, Glass, Graphics, Hispanic Art, Islamic Art, Ivory, Jade, Jewelry, Landscapes, Latin American Art, Manuscripts, Marine Painting, Medieval Art, Metalwork, Metalwork, Mexican Art, Miniatures, Mosaics, Oriental Art, Painting-American, Painting-Australian, Painting-British, Painting-Dutch, Painting-European, Painting-Flemish, Painting-French, Painting-German, Painting-Italian, Painting-Japanese, Painting-Polish, Painting-Russian, Painting-Scandinavian, Painting-Spanish, Photography, Porcelain, Portraits, Posters, Pottery, Pre-Columbian Art, Primitive art, Prints, Religious Art, Renaissance Art, Sculpture, Silver, Southwestern Art, Textiles, Watercolors, Stained Glass
Collections: Joseph E Davies Collection of Russian Icons, Russian & Soviet Paintings, Vernon Hall Collection of European Medals, Edward Burr Van Vleck Collection of Japanese Prints, Ernest C & Jane Werner Watson Collection of Indian Miniatures, Samuel & Rosemary Chen Coll Chinese paintings, Terese & Alvin Lane Coll Modern Sculpture & Drawings, Andrew Laurie Stengel Coll European Medals, Alexander & Henrietta W Hollaender Coll Contemporary art, Janice & Jean-Pierre Golay Coll Contemporary Art
Exhibitions: 4-6 major temp exhibs, 8-10 rotating exhibits per yr
Publications: Biennial bulletin; calendar, bimonthly; spec exhibition catalogs; newsletter
Activities: Classes for adults & children; docent training; lects open to pub; 10-15 vis lectrs per yr; concerts; gallery talks; tours; ann outstanding MFA student award; individual paintings & original objects of art lent to other mus; book traveling exhibs 2-4 per yr; originate traveling exhibs; sales shop sells books, magazines, original art, prints, reproductions & toys

L **Kohler Art Library**, 160 Conrad A Elvehjem Bldg, Univ Wisconsin Madison Madison, WI 53706; 800 University Ave, Madison, WI 53706-1414. Tel 608-263-2258; Fax 608-263-2255; Email lyn.korenic@wisc.edu; Web: library.wisc.edu/art; *Dir* Lyn Korenic; *Reference Librn* Linda Duychak; *Circ/ Reserves* Soren Schoff; *Tech Svcs* Kelly Tourdot
Open hrs vary seasonally, see website; Estab 1970 to support the teaching & research needs of the Art & Art History Departments & the Chazen Mus of Art; Circ 35,000; Average Annual Attendance: 40,000
Income: Financed by state appropriation & private funding
Library Holdings: Auction Catalogs, Book Volumes 190,000, CD-ROMs, Cassettes 50, Clipping Files, Compact Disks, DVDs, Exhibition Catalogs, Fiche 21,000, Micro Print, Pamphlets, Periodical Subscriptions 200, Reels 400, Video Tapes
Special Subjects: Decorative Arts
Exhibitions: Regular exhibs of materials from library collections
Activities: Tours; lects open to the public; 1 visiting lecture per year

M **WISCONSIN ACADEMY OF SCIENCES, ARTS & LETTERS,** Steenbock Gallery, 1922 University Ave, Madison, WI 53726-4013. Tel 608-263-1692; Fax 608-265-3039; Web: www.wisconsinacademy.org
Open (office) Mon - Fri 8:30 AM - 4:30 PM

M **James Watrous Gallery**, 201 State St Fl 3, Overture Ctr for the Arts Madison, WI 53703-2214. Tel 608-265-2500; Fax 608-265-3039; Email ajohnson@wisconsinacademy.org; Web: www.wisconsinacademy.org; *Dir* Jody Clowes; *Exhibitions Coordinator* Angela Johnson
Open Sun & Wed - Thurs, Fri - Sat noon - 8 PM; No admis fee; Dedicated to Wisconsin artists; Contemporary Wisconsin artists; exhibs that bridge the sciences, arts & letters; Average Annual Attendance: 9,000
Activities: Lects open to pub; gallery talks

M **WISCONSIN HISTORICAL SOCIETY, WISCONSIN HISTORICAL MUSEUM,** 30 N Carroll St, Madison, WI 53703-2707. Tel 608-264-6555; Fax 608-264-6575; Web: www.wisconsinhistory.org/museum; *Dir* Ellsworth Brown; *Cur Art Coll* Joseph Kapler; *Cur Visual Materials* Andy Kraushaar; *Deputy Division Admin* Jennifer Kolb; *Cur Social History* Leslie Bellais; *Cur Economic History* David Driscoll; *Lab Coordr* Denise Wiggins
Open Tues - Sat 9 AM - 4 PM, cl Sun - Mon; Admis adults $5, children (5-17) $3, children under 5 free; Estab 1846, mus added 1854; organized to promote a wider appreciation of the American heritage, with particular emphasis on the collection, advancement & dissemination of knowledge of the history of Wisconsin & of the Middle West; Average Annual Attendance: 71,600; Mem: 12,000; dues $30 & up
Income: Financed by state appropriation, earnings, gifts & federal grants
Special Subjects: American Indian Art, American Western Art, Anthropology, Archaeology, Architecture, Carpets & Rugs, Cartoons, Ceramics, Coins & Medals, Costumes, Crafts, Drawings, Etchings & Engravings, Folk Art, Furniture, Graphics, Jewelry, Leather, Military Art, Painting-American, Pewter, Portraits, Prints, Silver, Woodcarvings
Collections: American Historical & Native American material, iconographic coll, ceramics, coins, costumes, dolls, furniture, paintings, prints, photographs, & slides
Exhibitions: Special case and gallery exhib
Publications: Wisconsin Magazine of History, quarterly
Activities: Educ prog; classes for children; docent training; lect open to public; concerts; tours; gallery talks; individual paintings & original objects of art lent to other museums & individuals for educational purposes; book traveling exhibitions; mus shop sells books, magazines, original art, reproductions, prints, clothing, toys, cards, CDs & DVDs

L **Archives,** 816 State St, Madison, WI 53706-1482. Tel 608-264-6460; Fax 608-264-6472; Email asklibrary@wisconsinhistory.org; Web: www.wisconsinhistory.org
Open Mon - Fri 8 AM - 5 PM, Sat 9 AM - 4 PM, cl Sun & Major Holidays; Average Annual Attendance: 1,846
Income: Financed by state
Library Holdings: Book Volumes, Cassettes, Fiche, Kodachrome Transparencies, Lantern Slides, Manuscripts, Maps, Memorabilia, Motion Pictures, Original Art Works, Original Documents, Other Holdings Original documents; Maps, Photographs, Prints, Records, Reels, Reproductions, Slides, Video Tapes

MANITOWOC

M **RAHR-WEST ART MUSEUM,** 610 N 8th St, Manitowoc, WI 54220-3998. Tel 920-683-3090; Fax 920-683-5047; Email rahrwest@manitowoc.org; Web: rahrwestartmuseum.org; *Asst Dir* Daniel Juchniewich; *Dir* Barbara Bundy-Jost; *Admin Asst* Elaine Schroeder
Open Mon, Tues, Thurs & Fri 10 AM - 4 PM, Wed 10 AM - 8 PM, Sat & Sun 11 AM - 4 PM, cl holidays; No admis fee; Estab 1950 as city art museum and civic center to serve the city of Manitowoc. Transitional gallery in new wing built 1975; period rooms in Victorian Rahr Mansion built c 1991; a Registered Historic home; American art wing built in 1986; Ruth West Gallery 48' x 63'; Corridor Gallery, for changing exhibits; Permanent Collections Gallery; Average Annual Attendance: 22,000; Mem: 600; dues $40 individual
Income: $250,000 (financed by mem & city appropriation)
Library Holdings: Book Volumes 1500, Exhibition Catalogs, Periodical Subscriptions, Video Tapes
Special Subjects: Drawings, Furniture, Glass, Graphics, Ivory, Painting-American, Period Rooms, Prints, Watercolors, Porcelain
Collections: 19th & 20th Century American Paintings & Prints, Schwartz Collection of Chinese Ivories, contemporary art glass, works by Francis, Johns Lichtenstein & O'Keeffe, Schuette Woodland Indian Collection
Exhibitions: Monthly changing exhibitions; Annual exhibitions of community generated art; Traveling exhibitions of a changing schedule each yr
Publications: Catalogues of collections & exhibitions
Activities: Classes for adults & children; docent training; family activities; lects open to pub, concerts; gallery talks; tours; scholarships offered

MARSHFIELD

M **NEW VISIONS GALLERY, INC,** 1000 N Oak Ave, Marshfield Clinic Marshfield, WI 54449-5703. Tel 715-387-5562; Fax 715-387-5506; Email info@newvisionsgallery.org; Web: newvisionsgallery.org; Facebook - @newvisionsgallery; *Dir* Bobbie Erwin; *Asst Dir* James Machtan
Open Mon - Fri 9 AM - 4 PM; No admis fee; Estab 1975 for the education, awareness & appreciation of visual arts; 1500 sq ft exhib space, track lighting, moveable display panels, sculpture stands; Average Annual Attendance: 75,000; Mem: 375; dues $25 - $1000 & up
Income: $150,000 (financed by mem, earned income, fundraising & gifts)
Library Holdings: Auction Catalogs, Book Volumes, Exhibition Catalogs, Video Tapes
Special Subjects: African Art, American Indian Art, Asian Art, Carpets & Rugs, Ceramics, Crafts, Decorative Arts, Drawings, Etchings & Engravings, Glass, Graphics, Juvenile Art, Oriental Art, Painting-American, Painting-Australian, Painting-Japanese, Photography, Porcelain, Posters, Pottery, Prints, Sculpture, Southwestern Art, Watercolors, Woodcuts
Collections: Australian Aboriginal Art Collection, Haitian Painting Collection, West African Art Collection, original prints
Exhibitions: Emerging Talents; New Visions' Culture & Agriculture; Annual Marshfield Art Fair; Rotating exhibs of professional artists & permanent collections
Publications: Brochures, every 6 wks; catalogs
Activities: Classes for adults; docent training; lects open to pub, gallery talks; tours; competitions with awards; concerts; lending collection contains books; book traveling exhibs 2 annually; mus shop sells gifts produced by artists or craft studios, jewelry, pottery, card, reproduction & prints

MENOMONIE

M **UNIVERSITY OF WISCONSIN-STOUT,** J Furlong Gallery, 410A 10th Ave, Dept of Art & Design, Micheels Hall Menomonie, WI 54751-2506. Tel 715-232-2261; Email furlong@uwstout.edu; *Cur* Chris Zerendow
Open Mon - Fri 10 AM - 4 PM, Tues 6 - 9 PM, Sat Noon - 3PM; No admis fee; Estab 1966 to serve university & local community with exhibits of art; A single room gallery; track lighting; Average Annual Attendance: 1,500
Income: Financed by state appropriation
Special Subjects: African Art, Drawings, Painting-American, Prints, Sculpture
Collections: African Art, paintings including works by Warrington Colescott, Roy Deforest, Walter Quirt, George Roualt & Raphael Soyer, drawings, prints, sculpture
Exhibitions: Changing exhibits
Activities: Classes for children; gallery talks; individual paintings & original objects of art lent to faculty, staff & campus offices

MEQUON

M **CONCORDIA UNIVERSITY WISCONSIN,** Fine Art Gallery, 12800 N Lake Shore Dr, Mequon, WI 53092-2418. Tel 262-243-5700; Fax 262-243-4351; Web: www.cuw.edu; *Acad Dean* Dr David Eggebrecht; *Gallery Dir* Prof Jeffrey Shawhan
Open Sun, Tues, Wed & Fri 1 - 4 PM, Thurs 5 - 7 PM; No admis fee; Estab 1972 to exhibit work of area & national artists as an educational arm of the col; Average Annual Attendance: 1,000
Income: Financed through college budget
Special Subjects: Bronzes, Graphics, Painting-Russian
Collections: Graphics include Roualt, Altman & local artists, American landscape, religious art, Russian bronzes & paintings, John Doyle Lithographs, John Wiley Collection
Publications: Annual schedule
Activities: Classes for adults & children; lects for members only, 2-3 vis lectrs per year; gallery talks

MILWAUKEE

M **ALVERNO COLLEGE GALLERY,** Alverno Art and Cultures Gallery, 3441 S 39th St, Milwaukee, WI 53215-4020; PO Box 343922, Milwaukee, WI 53234-3922. Tel 414-382-6142; Fax 414-382-6354; Email linda.sommers@alverno.edu; Web: www.alverno.edu; *Dir Gallery* Lynda J Sommers
Open Mon - Sat 10 AM - 4 PM, Thurs 10 AM - 7 PM, cl Sun; No admis fee; Estab 1954 for the aesthetic enrichment of community & the aesthetic educ of students; Average Annual Attendance: 1,500
Income: $2000
Exhibitions: Senior Show; Juried Student Exhibition; community exhibs; emerging artist; established artists
Activities: Docent training; lects open to pub, 4 vis lectrs per yr; concerts; gallery talks; tours; competitions with awards: Best of Exhibit; book traveling exhibs 1-2 per yr

L **ASCENSION LUTHERAN CHURCH LIBRARY,** 1236 S Layton Blvd, Milwaukee, WI 53215-1694. Tel 414-645-2933; Fax 414-645-0218; *Opers Mgr* Heidi Barret
Open Sun 8:30 AM - 11 AM & upon request; No admis fee; Estab 1954
Income: Financed by church budget, donations & bequests
Library Holdings: Audio Tapes, Book Volumes 13,000, Cassettes, Filmstrips, Framed Reproductions, Periodical Subscriptions 30, Video Tapes 40
Special Subjects: Crafts, Decorative Arts, Embroidery, Religious Art
Collections: Classic Art, framed pictures, organ music

C **BANK ONE WISCONSIN,** 111 E Wisconsin Ave, Milwaukee, WI 53202-4815. Tel 414-765-3000; *Facilities Mgr* Cheri Eddy
Estab to encourage Wisconsin art & artists; Collection displayed in offices, conference rooms & corridors within Bank One Plaza
Collections: Acrylics, batik, bronze sculpture, lithographs, oils, wall sculpture, watercolors by Wisconsin artists

M **CARDINAL STRITCH UNIVERSITY,** Northwestern Mutual Gallery, 6801 N Yates Rd, Milwaukee, WI 53217-3985. Tel 414-414-4107; Web: www.stritch.edu; *Chmn Art Dept* Timothy Abler; *Gallery Dir* Shana McCaw
Open Mon - Fri noon - 4 PM, cl Sat - Sun; No admis fee; Estab 1947 to encourage creative art in each individual; educ gallery featuring student work & local & nat artists; Housed within the Stein Center for Communications/Fine Arts
Income: Financed by endowment, city & state appropriations & tuition
Activities: Lects open to pub; 2-3 vis lectrs per yr; gallery talks

M **CHARLES ALLIS ART MUSEUM,** 1801 N Prospect Ave, Milwaukee, WI 53202; 1630 E Royal Pl, Milwaukee, WI 53202. Tel 414-278-8295; Fax 414-278-0335; Email info@cavtmuseums.org; Web: www.cavtmuseums.org; *Exec Dir* John Sterr; *Sr Cur* Shana McCaw; *Events Mgr* Michael Keiley; *Mgr Mktg* Kayle Karbowski
Open Wed - Sun 1 - 5 PM; Admis general pub $7, seniors & students $5, members & children under 12 free; Estab 1947 as a house-mus with 850 art objects from around the world & spanning 2500 years, collected by Charles Allis, first president of the Allis-Chalmers Company & bequeathed to the people of Milwaukee. The mus is part of the Milwaukee County War Memorial Complex; Average Annual Attendance: 30,000; Mem: 500; dues student $25, senior individual $35, individual $45, senior couple $55, family $60, sustainer $75-$124, patron $125-$249, sponsor $250-$499, benefactor $500-$999, philanthropist $1,000 & up ; ann meetings in Oct
Income: $575,000 (combined budget) financed by endowment, private & public contributions & rental revenue
Special Subjects: Ceramics, Painting-American, Painting-French, Renaissance Art
Collections: Chinese, Japanese & Persian ceramics, Greek & Roman antiquities, 19th century French & American paintings, Renaissance bronzes
Publications: Exhibition catalogs; quarterly newsletter
Activities: Docent training; lects open to pub, 10 vis lectrs per yr; concerts; gallery talks; tours; film series; sponsoring of competitions

M **GROHMANN MUSEUM,** 1000 N Broadway, Milwaukee, WI 53202-3110; 1025 N Broadway, Milwaukee, WI 53202-3109. Tel 414-277-2300; Email grohmannmuseum@msoe.edu; Web: www.msoe.edu/about-msoe/grohmann-museum/; *Dir* James Kieselburg
Open Mon - Fri 9 AM - 5 PM, Sat Noon - 6 PM, Sun 1 - 4 PM; Admis gen $5, students & seniors $3, children under 12 free; 38,000 sq ft; Mem: dues $25-$250
Collections: 1,000 paintings & sculptures
Exhibitions: Temporary exhibits
Activities: Mus shop sells books, clothing & gifts

M **MARQUETTE UNIVERSITY,** Haggerty Museum of Art, 530 N 13th St, Milwaukee, WI 53233-2205; PO Box 1881, Milwaukee, WI 53201-1881. Tel 414-288-1669; Fax 414-288-5415; Email haggertym@marquette.edu; Web: www.marquette.edu/haggerty; *Registrar* Michelle Burton; *Admin Asst* Mary Wagner; *Communs Asst* Mary Dornfeld; *Head Designer & Preparator* Daniel Herro; *Cur Educ* Lynne Shumow; *Dir & Chief Cur* Susan Longhenry
Open Mon - Wed & Fri - Sat 10 AM - 4:30 PM, Thurs 10 AM - 8 PM, Sun Noon - 5 PM; No admis fee; Estab 1984 to provide exhibitions of art from Old Masters to the present; 20,000 sq ft. A modern free standing building with security & climate control. Maintains reference library; Average Annual Attendance: 40,000; Mem: 500; dues $50-$5000; annual meeting in Sept
Income: Financed through private contributions & the university
Library Holdings: Auction Catalogs, Book Volumes, Clipping Files, Exhibition Catalogs

Special Subjects: African Art, American Indian Art, Carpets & Rugs, Decorative Arts, Dolls, Drawings, Etchings & Engravings, Furniture, Glass, Landscapes, Latin American Art, Painting-American, Painting-British, Painting-Dutch, Painting-European, Painting-Flemish, Painting-French, Painting-German, Painting-Italian, Painting-Spanish, Porcelain, Posters, Prints, Religious Art, Renaissance Art
Collections: Old Master, Modern, Contemporary paintings, prints, photography, decorative arts, tribal arts, German art, 1920s - 1930s
Publications: Exhibit catalogs; Italian Renaissance Masters
Activities: Educ dept; docent training; lects & workshops open to pub, 15-20 vis lectrs per yr; gallery talks; tours; awards; concerts; individual paintings & original objects of art lent to mus; originate traveling exhibs; mus shop sells books, reproductions, merchandise cards

M **MILWAUKEE ART MUSEUM,** 700 N Art Museum Dr, Milwaukee, WI 53202-4007. Tel 414-224-3200; Fax 414-271-7588; Email mam@mam.org; Web: www.mam.org; *Pres Bd Trustees* Donald W Layden Jr; *Exec Dir* Marcelle Polednik; *Chief Educ* Barbara Brown Lee; *Sr Dir Devel* Mary Albrecht; *Dir Human Resources* Jan Schmidt; *Sr Conservator* Jim De Young; *Object Conservator* Terri White; *Librn & Archivist* Heather Winter
Open Tues - Sun, 10 AM - 5 PM, Thurs until 8 PM, cl Mon, Thanksgiving Day, Christmas Day; Admis adults $17, seniors & students w/ID $15, mems & children under 12 free, 1st Thurs of month free; Estab 1888 to create an environment for the arts that will serve the people of the greater Milwaukee community; Large flexible galleries, including a sculpture ct & outdoor display areas. Fine arts & decorative arts are mixed to create an overview of a period, especially in the fine American Wings; small galleries provided for specific or unique collections; Average Annual Attendance: 150,000; Mem: 11,000; dues $95 & up
Income: Financed by endowment, mem, county & state appropriations & fund drive
Special Subjects: Antiquities-Egyptian, Antiquities-Greek, Antiquities-Roman, Architecture, Painting-American, Painting-European, Painting-German
Collections: 19th & 20th Century American & European Art, including the Bradley & Layton Collections: The American Ash Can School & German Expressionism are emphasized, All media from Ancient Egypt to Modern America, The Flagg Collection of Haitian Art, Michael & Julie Hall Collection of American Folk Art, a study collection of Midwest Architecture - The Prairie Archives, Layton Collection, Rene Von Schleinitz Collection, Mrs Harry L Bradley Collection, American Decorative Arts & the Chipstone Foundation, Marcia & Granvil Specks Collection, Floyd & Josephine Segel Collection of Photography, Maurice & Esther Leah Ritz Collection
Exhibitions: Rotating exhibits & exhibits from permanent collection
Publications: Exhibs & program brochure, 3 per yr; numbers calendar, bimonthly
Activities: Classes for adults & children; docent training; lects open to pub, 4-6 vis lectrs per yr; concerts; gallery talks; tours; competitions; films; scholastic art prog; originate traveling exhibs; mus shop sells books & magazines

L **George Peckham Miller Art Research Library,** 700 N Art Museum Dr, Milwaukee, WI 53202-4007. Tel 414-224-3270; Email library@mam.org; Web: www.mam.org/collection/library.php; *Archivist & Librn* Heather Winter; *Audio Visual Librn* Beret Balestrieri Kohn
Currently closed; will reopen in fall 2018; No admis fee; photocopying fees apply; Estab 1916; Circ Non-circulating
Library Holdings: Auction Catalogs, Book Volumes 20,000, Clipping Files, Exhibition Catalogs, Original Documents, Other Holdings, Pamphlets, Periodical Subscriptions 60
Collections: National & international museum & gallery publications, incl Milwaukee Art Mus publications, monographs on art & artists, catalogue raisonnes, auction sales catalogues, artist files, Rare Books Collection
Activities: Classes for adults & children; docent training; lects open to the pub; gallery talks; tours; mus shop sells books, prints

L **MILWAUKEE INSTITUTE OF ART & DESIGN,** Library, 273 E Erie St, Milwaukee, WI 53202-6003. Tel 414-847-3342; Fax 414-291-8077; Web: www.miad.edu/; *Asst Dir, Library Serv* Nancy Siker; *Circ Coordr* Cathryn Wilson
Open Mon - Fri 8 AM - 5 PM; Estab 1974 as an Art & Design Library for the art school
Income: Financed by institution & private grants
Library Holdings: Book Volumes 26,000, DVDs 250, Other Holdings Postcards 2,440, Pamphlets, Periodical Subscriptions 125, Slides 32,000, Video Tapes 500
Special Subjects: Advertising Design, Decorative Arts, Graphic Design, Industrial Design, Interior Design, Photography
Collections: Member of Switch Consortium

L **MILWAUKEE PUBLIC LIBRARY,** Art, Music & Recreation Dept, 814 W Wisconsin Ave, Milwaukee, WI 53233-2385. Tel 414-286-3011; Fax 414-286-2137; Web: www.mpl.org; *Library Dir* Paula Kiely; *Dir Central Library Svcs* Joan Johnson
Open Mon noon - 8 PM, Tues - Sat 9 AM - 4 PM, Sun 1 PM - 5 PM; No admis fee; Estab 1878
Income: Financed by budgeted funds & endowments
Library Holdings: Auction Catalogs, Audio Tapes, Book Volumes 2,400,000, CD-ROMs, Cassettes, Clipping Files, Compact Disks, DVDs, Exhibition Catalogs, Fiche, Manuscripts, Maps, Original Documents, Pamphlets, Periodical Subscriptions, Photographs, Records, Video Tapes
Special Subjects: Architecture, Art History, Coins & Medals, Crafts, Decorative Arts, Landscape Architecture, Posters
Collections: Auction catalogs, Audubon Prints - complete
Activities: Lects open to pub; 5-10 visiting lects per year

M **MILWAUKEE PUBLIC MUSEUM,** 800 W Wells St, Milwaukee, WI 53233-1404. Tel 414-278-2702; Fax 414-278-6100; Email smedley@mpm.edu; Web: www.mpm.edu; *Dir Mktg & Communs* Jennifer Tetzlaff; *Sr VPres & Academic Dean* Ellen Censky; *Dir Information Servs & Electronic Systems* Greg Post; *Communs Coordr* Natalie Fairbanks; *VPres Finance & Opers* Patti Dew; *Dir Human Resources* Lisa DeMartino; *Pres & CEO* Dennis Kois
Open Mon - Fri 10 AM - 5 PM, Sat 9 AM - 5 PM, Sun 11 AM - 5 PM; Admis adults $18, seniors(65 & over), students & active military $14, youth (5-13) free; Estab 1883 as a natural history mus; Steigledor-special exhibits gallery, Erwin C Uihlern-smaller exhibits, Clinton B Rose exhibit case; Average Annual Attendance: 413,000; Mem: 7400
Special Subjects: Anthropology, Decorative Arts, Folk Art, Photography
Collections: All major sub-disciplines of anthropology, botany, ethnology, natural history outreach, geology-paleontology, invertebrate & vertebrate zoology, decorative, fine & folk arts, film, photographs & specimen collection
Activities: Classes for children (school groups only), spec events, workshops, summer camps, IMAX dome theatre; lects open to pub & mems; vis lectrs ann; sales shop sells pottery, jewelry, stationery, ornaments, models, games, dolls

M **MOUNT MARY COLLEGE,** Marian Gallery, 2900 Menomonee River Pkwy, Milwaukee, WI 53222. Tel 414-258-4810; Fax 414-256-1224; Email andersojo@mtmary.edu; Web: www.mtmary.edu; *Dir Gallery* Josh Anderson; *Prog Dir Fine Art* Debra Heermans
Open Mon - Fri 9 AM - 7 PM, Sat - Sun 1 - 4 PM; No admis fee; Estab 1940 to provide both students & local community with exposure to art experiences & to provide artists, both estab professionals & aspirants with a showplace for their work; Average Annual Attendance: 1,000
Income: Financed by private funds
Special Subjects: Costumes, Etchings & Engravings, Furniture, Prints
Collections: Antique furniture, 16th Century & Victorian period, contemporary print collection, historic costume collection, watercolors by Wisconsin artists
Activities: Classes for adults & children; lects open to pub, 6 vis lectrs per yr; concerts; gallery talks; tours; competitions & awards; schols offered

M **UNIVERSITY OF WISCONSIN,** Arts Center Gallery, Peck School of Arts, Arts Bldg, 2nd Fl, 2400 E Kenwood Blvd Milwaukee, WI 53202. Tel 414-229-4771; Email art-info@uwm.edu; Web: uwm.edu/arts; *Dir Mktg & Communs* Rebecca Ottman
Open Wed - Thurs 10 AM - 6 PM, Fri 11 AM - 4 PM, cl holidays; No admis fee; Estab as a year round setting for the exhibition of work by students, alumni, special guests, thesis exhibitions, faculty exhibitions & scholarship competitions; 3,516 sq ft split into four adjoining exhibition spaces
Income: Financed by state appropriation
Special Subjects: Graphics, Painting-American, Photography, Prints, Sculpture
Exhibitions: Monthly rotating exhibs
Activities: Lects open to public, gallery talks; tours

M **Union Art Gallery**, 2200 E Kenwood Blvd, Rm W199, Campus Level Milwaukee, WI 53211. Tel 414-229-6310; Fax 414-229-6709; Email agallery@uwm.edu; Web: uwm.edu/studentinvolvement/arts-and-entertainment; *Gallery Mgr* Selena Erdman; *Asst Gallery Mgr* Madison Auten
Open Mon, Tues, Wed & Fri Noon - 5 PM, Thurs Noon - 7 PM, cl Sat & Sun; No admis fee; Estab 1972 to provide space for local & regional artists, along with student art, primarily undergraduate, to be shown in group exhibits established by peer selection and apart from faculty selection; 2500 sq ft, two stories high with more than 250 running feet of exhibit wall space; Average Annual Attendance: 16,500
Income: Union programming budget
Collections: Contemporary art
Activities: Classes for adults; lects open to pub; concerts; competitions with awards; gallery talks; sale shop sells original art

M **VILLA TERRACE DECORATIVE ARTS MUSEUM,** 2220 N Terrace Ave, Milwaukee, WI 53202-1216. Tel 414-271-3656; Email jjunco@cavtmuseums.org; Web: www.villaterracemuseum.org; *Exec Dir* John Sterr; *Asst Cur & Colls Mgr* Jenille Junco; *Rentals Mgr* Robyn Erickson; *Mem Mgr* Matthew Pappas; *Events Mgr* Michael Keiley
Open Wed - Sun 1 - 5 PM; Admis $7 seniors (over 62) & students $5, members & children under 12 free; Estab 1967; Art mus & formal gardens; Average Annual Attendance: 30,000; Mem: 500; dues Student $25, Senior $35, individual $45, Family $60
Income: $575,000 financed through pvt & pub contributions and rental revenue
Library Holdings: Auction Catalogs, Book Volumes
Special Subjects: Architecture, Asian Art, Bronzes, Ceramics, Decorative Arts, Enamels, Furniture, Glass, Ivory, Jade, Maps, Metalwork, Oriental Art, Period Rooms, Porcelain, Pottery, Renaissance Art, Restorations, Sculpture, Silver, Stained Glass, Landscape Architecture
Collections: Decorative arts, furniture, glassware, paintings, wrought iron, Cyril Colnik Archive
Publications: Exhibition catalogs
Activities: Classes for adults & children; docent training; lects open to public; 3-6 vis lectrs per year; concerts; gallery talks; tours; ongoing temporary exhibitions; garden tours; Mayor's Landscape award; lending original objects of art to Museum of Wisconsin Art; mus shop sells books

A **WALKER'S POINT ARTISTS ASSOC INC,** Gallery 218, 207 E Buffalo St, Ste 218, Milwaukee, WI 53202. Tel 414-643-1732; Email director@gallery218.com; Web: www.gallery218.com; *Artist & Pres* Judith Hooks; *Artist* Bernie Newman; *Artist* Joanne O'Hare; *Artist* Rande Barke; *Artist* Natalie Brey; *Artist* Alex Block; *Artist* Tara Keefe; *Artist* Harry Wirth
Open Sat & Sun noon - 5 PM; open late for special events & by appt; Estab 1991 to provide opportunities for artists; Multidisciplinary cooperative gallery presenting contemporary works by members & guest artists; Average Annual Attendance: 19,000; Mem: Qualifications: resume, work samples, artist statement
Income: Financed by membership dues, individual donations, & commissions from sales
Library Holdings: Clipping Files, Kodachrome Transparencies, Pamphlets, Periodical Subscriptions, Photographs, Prints, Sculpture, Slides
Special Subjects: Calligraphy, Collages, Drawings, Etchings & Engravings, Latin American Art, Medieval Art, Painting-American, Painting-European, Painting-Japanese, Photography, Prints, Sculpture, Watercolors
Exhibitions: Eight exhibs per yr - group; The Big Blue Shirt Show; Our Water Our World, After Duchamp
Activities: Lects open to pub & mems, 1 vis lectr per yr; competitions with prizes; poetry readings; concerts; gallery talks; tours; sponsoring of competitions; gallery

nights; film screenings; live music; sales shop sells books, prints, magazines, original art

M **WALKER'S POINT CENTER FOR THE ARTS,** 839 S 5th St, Milwaukee, WI 53204-1730. Tel 414-672-2787; Email xela@wpca-milwaukee.org; Web: wpca-milwaukee.org; *Exec Dir* Marcela Garcia
Open Tues - Sat, Noon - 5 PM; Estab 1987; Mem: dues $60-$2,500
Collections: painting; sculpture; photography
Exhibitions: Temporary exhibits
Activities: Educ progs; classes children; artist residencies

MONROE

M **MONROE ARTS CENTER,** 1315 11th St, Monroe, WI 53566-1744; PO Box 472, Monroe, WI 53566-0472. Tel 608-325-5700; Fax 608-325-5701; Email info@monroeartscenter.com; Web: monroeartscenter.com; *Bd Dir* Don Amphlett; *Bd Dir* Sue Barrett
Open Tues - Sat, 10 AM - 5 PM, cl Sun - Mon; Estab to foster art appreciation & promote creative development
Collections: painting; sculpture; photography
Exhibitions: Temporary exhibits
Activities: Classes for children; community events

NEENAH

M **BERGSTROM-MAHLER MUSEUM OF GLASS,** 165 N Park Ave, Neenah, WI 54956-2956. Tel 920-751-4658; Fax 920-451-4755; Email info@paperweightmuseum.com; Web: www.bergstrom-mahlermuseum.com; *Exec Dir* Alex Vance; *Cur* Jami Severstad; *Mgr Communs* Wendy Lloyd
Open Tues-Fri 10AM-4:30PM, Sat 9AM-4:30PM, Sun 1-4:30PM; No admis fee; Estab 1959 to provide cultural & educational benefits to the pub; Average Annual Attendance: 29,000
Income: $200,000 (financed by endowment, state & county appropriations & gifts)
Special Subjects: Glass, Painting-American, Sculpture
Collections: Over 1900 contemporary & antique paperweights, Victorian Glass Baskets, Germanic Glass, paintings, Ernst Mahler Collection of Germanic Glass
Exhibitions: Monthly exhibitions in varied media
Publications: Museum Quarterly; Glass Paperweights of Bergstrom - Mahler Museum Collection Catalogue; Paul J Stankard: Poetry in Glass
Activities: Classes for adults & children; docent training; lects open to pub; gallery talks; tours; individual paintings & original objects of art lent to mus; mus shop sells glass paperweights & glass items, original art

L **Library,** 165 N Park Ave, Neenah, WI 54956-2956. Tel 920-751-4658; Fax 920-751-4755; Email answers@bmmglass.com; Web: bmmglass.com; *Exec Dir* Jan Mirenda Smith; *Bus Dir* Ben Fauske; *Shop Mgr* Laureen Endter
Open Tues - Sat 10 AM - 4:30 PM, Sun 1 PM - 4:30 PM; No admis fee, donations accepted; 1959-Visual Arts Based Educ Org; Glass mus; paperweights; contemporary studio glass; Average Annual Attendance: 20000; Mem: 400
Income: Endowed
Library Holdings: Book Volumes 2000, Memorabilia, Periodical Subscriptions 10, Slides
Special Subjects: Art History, Decorative Arts, Etchings & Engravings, Glass, Historical Material, Painting-German, Sculpture
Collections: Antique Paperweights and Germanic Contemporary Glass, Drinking Vessels, Victorian Glass Baskets, Studio glass
Activities: Classes for adults & children; arts festival on the 3rd Sun in July; Lect open to the public; gallery talks, sponsoring of competitions; Mus shop sells original art

NEW GLARUS

M **CHALET OF THE GOLDEN FLEECE,** 618 2nd St, New Glarus, WI 53574-9626. Tel 800-527-6838, 608-527-2614; *Cur* Helen Altmann
Open May - Oct Fri - Mon 10 AM - 4 PM; groups with advanced reservations; Admis adults $5, students 6-17 $2; Estab 1955; Authentic Swiss style chalet which was once a private residence; collection from around the world; Average Annual Attendance: 5,000
Income: Financed by admis fees & village of New Glarus
Collections: Swiss wood carvings & furniture, antique silver & pewter samplers, prints, exceptional glass & china, coins, stamps, paintings, etchings, Swiss dolls
Activities: Lect open to public; tours

OSHKOSH

M **OSHKOSH PUBLIC MUSEUM & LIBRARY,** 1331 Algoma Blvd, Oshkosh, WI 54901-2799. Tel 920-236-5799 (museum); 236-5762 (library); Email info@ci.oshkosh.wi.us; Web: www.oshkoshmuseum.org; *Dir* Bradley Larson; *Registrar* Joan Lloyd; *Cur* Debra Daubert; *Staff Artist* Daniel Fiser; *Asst Dir* Michael Breza; *Archivist* Scott Cross
Open Tues - Sat 10 AM - 4:30 PM, Sun 1 - 4:30 PM, cl Mon & major holidays; Admis adults $7, seniors 62 & over $5, children 6-16 $3.50, children 5 & under no admis fee; Estab 1924 to collect & exhibit historical, Indian & natural history material relating to the area & fine & decorative & folk arts. 1908 converted home with new wing, Steiger Memorial Wing, opened in 1983 for additional exhibition space; Mus housed in city owned mansion near university campus; Average Annual Attendance: 35,000; Mem: 550; see website for dues
Income: Financed by city appropriation
Library Holdings: Audio Tapes, Book Volumes, Manuscripts, Maps, Motion Pictures
Special Subjects: Photography, Textiles, Tapestries, Stained Glass, Restorations, Porcelain, Watercolors, Pewter, Period Rooms, Dolls, Dioramas, Architecture, Anthropology, American Indian Art, Woodcarvings, Archaeology, Ceramics, Coins & Medals, Decorative Arts, Glass, Manuscripts, Maps, Portraits, Pottery, Sculpture
Collections: American Artists: archeology, firearms, Indian Artifacts, Local & Wisconsin History, Natural History, Pressed Glass, period textiles
Exhibitions: Monthly changing exhibits; permanent exhibits
Publications: Like A Deer Chased by the Dogs, The Life of Chief Oshkosh; Voices of History, 1941-1945
Activities: Classes for adults & children; lects open to pub; individual paintings & original objects of art lent to mus; book traveling exhibs 1 per yr; organizes traveling exhibs to museums & libraries; mus shop sells books, reproductions, prints & gifts

A **PAINE ART CENTER & GARDENS,** 1410 Algoma Blvd, Oshkosh, WI 54901-7708. Tel 920-235-6903; Fax 920-235-6303; Email mmueller@paineartcenter.com; Web: www.paine.artcenter.com; *Financial Bus Mgr* Doris Peitz; *Cur Horticulture* Sheila Glaske; *Exec Dir* Barbara Hirschfeld; *Cur Coll & Educ* Laurel Spencer Forsythe; *Vol/Educ* Bobbie Scott; *Mus Serv Coordr* Mitzi Mueller
Open Tues - Sun 11 AM - 4 PM, cl Mon & national holidays; Admis adults $5, students with ID $2, seniors $2.50, children & members free; Estab 1947 as a nonprofit corporation to serve the needs of the upper Midwest by showing fine & decorative arts & horticulture; Average Annual Attendance: 30,000; Mem: 900; dues contributing $50, general $35, senior citizens $15
Income: Financed by endowment, mem & donations
Collections: American glass, decorative arts, icons, 19th & 20th century American paintings & sculpture, 19th century English & French paintings, period rooms, oriental rugs, American silver, arboretum contains displays of native & exotic trees, shrubs & herbaceous plants
Exhibitions: Temporary exhibitions drawn from sources, coast to coast
Publications: Exhib catalogues; bimonthly newsletter; class schedules
Activities: Classes for adults & children; docent training; lects open to pub, 3-6 vis lectrs per yr; concerts; gallery talks; tours; individual paintings & original objects of art lent to other mus & institutions; originates traveling exhibs; sales shop sells books, reproductions & jewelry

L **George P Nevitt Library,** 1410 Algoma Blvd, Oshkosh, WI 54901. Tel 920-235-6903; Fax 920-235-6303; Web: www.thepaine.org; *Exec Dir* Aaron Sherer
Open Tues - Sun 11 AM - 4 PM, cl Mon; No admis fee for members, family $18, adults $7, seniors $6, students $5, children 5-12 $4, children under 5; Estab primarily for staff use as an art reference but also open to pub by appointment; Circ 3,000; For reference only; Average Annual Attendance: 30,000; Mem: 542; dues $40 & up; annual meeting in Apr
Library Holdings: Book Volumes 5,200, Cassettes, Clipping Files, Exhibition Catalogs, Kodachrome Transparencies, Memorabilia, Original Art Works, Pamphlets, Photographs, Slides
Special Subjects: Architecture, Art History, Asian Art, Ceramics, Decorative Arts, Drawings, Etchings & Engravings, Goldsmithing, History of Art & Archaeology, Interior Design, Oriental Art, Painting-American, Period Rooms, Photography, Sculpture
Collections: French Barbizon and American landscape paintings
Activities: Classes for adults and children; docent training; horticultural progs; 2-3 vis lectrs per yr; gallery talks; tours; mus shop sells books, original art

M **UNIVERSITY OF WISCONSIN OSHKOSH,** Allen Priebe Gallery, 800 Algoma Blvd, Arts & Communication Bldg Oshkosh, WI 54901-3551. Tel 920-424-2235; Fax 920-424-1738; Web: www.uwosh.edu/apgallery; *Dir* Gail Panske
Open Mon - Fri 10:30 AM - 3 PM, Mon - Thurs 7 - 9 PM, Sat & Sun 1 - 4 PM, Sept thru May; No admis fee; Estab 1971 for the purpose of offering exhibits which appeal to a wide range of people; Gallery is 60 x 40 with additional wall space added with partitions, a skylight along back ceiling; Average Annual Attendance: 15,000
Income: Financed by student allocated monies & Dept of Art
Purchases: $1500
Special Subjects: Drawings, Prints
Exhibitions: Various exhib
Activities: Lects open to pub, 2-4 vis lectrs per yr; gallery talks; tours; competitions with awards; individual paintings & original objects of art lent to Univ staff & area mus

PLATTEVILLE

M **UNIVERSITY OF WISCONSIN - PLATTEVILLE,** Harry & Laura Nohr Gallery, One University Plaza, Platteville, WI 53818. Tel 608-342-2787; Fax 608-342-1737; Email nohr_galalery@uwplatt.edu; Web: www.uwplatt.edu/gallery; *Dir* Michael Breitner; *Cur* Thomas Cabezas
Open Mon - Fri 9 AM - 6 PM, Sat 10 AM - 2 PM; No admis fee; Estab 1978; Average Annual Attendance: 9,000
Income: Financed by student fees & state funds
Collections: Pottery, paintings, sculptures, prints, drawings
Activities: Lects open to pub, 4 vis lectrs per yr; gallery talks; tours; competitions with awards; book traveling exhibs

RACINE

RACINE ART MUSEUM, 441 Main St, Racine, WI 53403; PO Box 187, Racine, WI 53401-0187. Tel 262-638-8300; Fax 262-898-1045; *CEO* Bruce Pepich; *Pres* Bruce Bernberg; *Dir Develop* Laura D'Amato
Open Tues - Sat 10 AM - 5 PM, Sun 10 AM - 5 PM, cl federal holidays; Admis adults $5, discounts to AAM members, members free
Library Holdings: Book Volumes 3,500
Collections: American contemporary art, 20th century American crafts
Publications: exhibition brochures & catalogues
Activities: Educ prog; hobby workshops; guided tours; lects; gallery talks; mus shop

A **WUSTUM MUSEUM ART ASSOCIATION,** 2519 Northwestern Ave, Racine, WI 53404-2242. Tel 262-636-9177; Fax 262-636-9231; *Dir* Bruce W Pepich

Open daily 1 - 5 PM, Mon & Thurs 1 - 9 PM; No admis fee; Estab 1941 to foster & aid the estab & development to pub art galleries & museums, progs of educ & training in the fine arts & to develop pub appreciation & enjoyment of the fine arts; Estab 1846 Italianate farmhouse, 2 stories, 6-room classroom addition, 13 acres of parkland, Boerner-designed formal gardens. Maintains library; Average Annual Attendance: 50,000; Mem: 650; dues $20 & up; ann meeting in May
Income: $500,000 (financed by mem, grants & fundraising)
Special Subjects: African Art, Eskimo Art, Furniture, Glass
Collections: 300 works WPA, 20th century works on paper, studio glass, ceramics, fibers, 19th century African jewelry, metals, artists books, paintings
Exhibitions: Watercolor Wisconsin (annual); Wisconsin Photography (triennial); Annual Nationwide Thematic Show (summer); Area Arts
Publications: Exhibit brochures & catalogs; Vue, quarterly newsletter
Activities: Classes for adults & children; docent training; outreach for local school children; gang intervention progs; lects open to pub, 6-10 vis lectrs per yr; gallery talks; tours; competitions with awards; individual paintings & original art objects lent to mus; lending collection contains books, nature artifacts, original art works; original prints & paintings; book traveling exhibs; originate traveling exhibs; mus shop sells books & original art, gifts & collectibles

M **Charles A Wustum Museum of Fine Arts,** 2519 Northwestern Ave, Racine, WI 53404. Tel 262-636-9177; Fax 262-636-9231; Web: www.wustum.org; *Dir* Bruce W Pepich
Open Tues - Sat 10 AM - 5 PM, cl Sun, Mon, Federal holidays & Easter; No admis fee; Estab 1940 to serve as cultural center for greater Racine community; Mus contains six galleries located in 1856 Wustum homestead & 1996 addition; Average Annual Attendance: 45,000
Income: $500,000 (financed by endowment, city & county appropriations, private gifts & programs)
Purchases: $500-$1000
Special Subjects: Painting-American, Prints, Watercolors
Collections: Contemporary Wisconsin Watercolors, WPA Project paintings & prints, contemporary graphics, works on paper, ceramic sculpture, glass sculpture, all post-1850 & primarily American
Exhibitions: Rotating exhibits
Activities: Classes for adults & children; docent training; lects open to pub, 2-3 vis lectrs per yr; gallery talks; tours; competitions with awards; film progs; individual paintings & original objects of art lent to other institutions; lending collection contains 2500 original art works, 700 original prints, 400 paintings, 200 photographs, 250 sculptures, 700 crafts & artist-made books; book traveling exhibs; originate traveling exhibs; mus shop sells books, original art, stationery, arts & crafts

L **Wustum Art Library,** 2519 Northwestern Ave, Racine, WI 53404. Tel 262-636-9177; Fax 262-636-9231; Web: www.wustum.org; *Librn* Nancy Elsmo; *Dir* Bruce W Pepich
Open Sun - Sat 1 - 5 PM, Mon & Thurs 1 - 9 PM; Estab 1941 to provide mus visitors & students with exposure to art history & instructional books; For reference only to pub, members may check out books
Income: $2500
Library Holdings: Book Volumes 1500, Exhibition Catalogs, Pamphlets, Periodical Subscriptions 12, Video Tapes
Special Subjects: Photography, Porcelain, Pottery, Printmaking, Prints, Sculpture, Textiles, Watercolors, Woodcarvings
Publications: Quarterly catalogues

RHINELANDER

L **RHINELANDER DISTRICT LIBRARY,** 106 N Stevens St, Rhinelander, WI 54501-3158. Tel 715-365-1070; Fax 715-365-1076; *Dir* Virginia Roberts
No admis fee; Estab 1903
Income: financed by endowment
Library Holdings: Book Volumes 1500, DVDs, Exhibition Catalogs, Photographs, Sculpture
Special Subjects: American Western Art, Architecture, Art History, Asian Art, Calligraphy, Etchings & Engravings, Folk Art, Painting-American, Painting-Dutch, Painting-European, Painting-Flemish, Painting-French, Painting-German, Painting-Italian, Photography, Sculpture
Collections: Architecture, arts & crafts, books & videos, Bump Art Collection, European & American Artists, photography

RICHLAND CENTER

M **FRANK LLOYD WRIGHT MUSEUM,** AD German Warehouse, 300 S Church St, Richland Center, WI 53581; PO Box 6339, Madison, WI 53716-0339. Tel 608-647-2808; *Co-Owner, Mgr & Dir* Harvey W Glanzer; *Co-Owner & Creative Dir* Beth Caulkins
Open by request May - Nov, call ahead; Admis adult $10, children $5, group rates by arrangement; Estab 1915; Warehouse is a red brick structure topped by a Mayan concrete frieze. It employs a structural concept known as the Barton Spider-web system. Interior grid of massive concrete columns provide structural support for floors & roof. Elimination of interior walls allows maximum freedom of interior space. Gift shop on first & lower level, mus & gallery on second floor
Exhibitions: Large 8 ft x 8 ft Photographic Murals of Wright's Work; Engineering scale model of Monona Terrace in Madison

RIPON

M **RIPON COLLEGE CAESTECKER ART GALLERY,** 300 Seward St, PO Box 248 Ripon, WI 54971. Tel 920-748-8110, 748-8115; Email kaineu@ripon.edu; *Dir* Rafael Salas
Open Tues - Fri 1 - 4 PM & 7 - 9PM, Sat - Sun 2 - 6 {; No admis fee; Average Annual Attendance: 4,000
Income: Financed by the college
Collections: Paintings, print, sculpture, multi-media
Exhibitions: Rotating exhibits
Activities: Individual paintings lent to schools

RIVER FALLS

M **UNIVERSITY OF WISCONSIN,** Gallery 101, 410 S Third St, Art Dept, Office 172KFA River Falls, WI 54022-5010. Tel 715-425-3266, 425-3911 (main); Email michael.a.padgett@uwrf.edu; Web: www.uwrs.edu; *Dir Gallery* Michael Padgett
Open Mon - Fri 9 AM - 5 PM & 7 - 9 PM, Sun 2 - 4 PM; No admis fee; Estab 1973 to exhibit artists of regional & national prominence & for educational purposes; Maintains one gallery; Average Annual Attendance: 21,000
Income: Financed by state appropriation & student activities funds
Collections: National & International Artists, Regional Artists, WPA Artists
Exhibitions: Rotating exhibits
Activities: Lects open to public; gallery talks; originate traveling exhibs

SHEBOYGAN

C **KOHLER CO,** John Michael Kohler Arts Center - Arts/Industry Program, 608 New York Ave, Sheboygan, WI 53081-4507. Tel 920-458-6144; Fax 920-458-4473; Web: www.jmkac.org; *Dir* Ruth Kohler; *Coordr* Michael Ogilvie
Open Mon, Wed, Fri 10 AM - 5 PM, Tues & Thurs 10 AM - 8 PM, Sat & Sun 10 AM - 4 PM; No admis fee, donations accepted; Estab 1973; Exhibition of collections made by artists in residence; Average Annual Attendance: 200,000
Income: Financed by Kohler Co
Library Holdings: Other Holdings Metalwork, Sculpture
Special Subjects: Ceramics, Sculpture
Collections: Original art pieces created in Kohler Co facilities by resident artists in the Art Industry Program
Activities: Lectrs open to the public; 6 vis lectrs per year

A **SHEBOYGAN ARTS FOUNDATION, INC,** John Michael Kohler Arts Center, 608 New York Ave, Sheboygan, WI 53081-4507. Tel 920-458-6144; Fax 920-458-4473; Web: www.jmkac.com; *Exec Dir* Ruth DeYoung Kohler; *Cur* Alison Ferris; *Assoc Cur* Karen Patterson; *Asst Cur* Emily Schlemowitz
Open Mon, Wed & Fri 10 AM - 5 PM, Tues & Thurs 10 AM - 8 Sat & Sun Noon - 4 PM; No admis fee, donations accepted; Estab 1967 as a visual & performing arts center focusing on contemporary American crafts & works which break barriers between art forms; Contains ten exhibition galleries, the largest being 60 ft x 45 ft, theatre, four studio-classrooms, library, sales gallery; Average Annual Attendance: 135,000; Mem: 1600; dues family /oval $60, individual $48, senior $40; student $30;
Income: Financed by mem, grants, corporate-foundation donations, sales gallery, ticket sales
Library Holdings: Book Volumes, Clipping Files, DVDs, Exhibition Catalogs, Kodachrome Transparencies, Lantern Slides, Manuscripts, Memorabilia, Original Documents, Pamphlets, Periodical Subscriptions, Photographs, Slides, Video Tapes
Collections: Contemporary Ceramics, Self-taught Art, Historical Decorative Arts; Vernacular Art Environments; Contemporary Art
Publications: Biennial Report; Exhibition Checklist 6-10 annually; Exhibition Catalogues, 2-4 annually; Newsletter, bimonthly
Activities: Classes for adults & children; dramatic progs; docent training; artists-in-residence progs; demonstrations; lects open to pub, 18-20 vis lectrs per yr; concerts; gallery talks; tours; competitions with awards; scholarships & fels offered; individual paintings & original objects of art lent to other arts institutions which meet the loan requirements, lending collection includes 6000 original art works & 100 paintings; book traveling exhibs; originates traveling exhibs which circulate to mus & artists organizations; sales shop sells magazines, original art, slides, postcards & notecards

STEVENS POINT

M **UNIVERSITY OF WISCONSIN-STEVENS POINT,** Carlsten Art Gallery, 1800 Portage St, Noel Fine Arts Center Stevens Point, WI 54481-1925. Tel 715-346-4797; Email cheft@uwsp.edu; Web: www.uwsp.edu/art-design/carlsten; *Dir* Caren Heft
Open Mon - Fri 10 AM - 4 PM, Sat & Sun 1 - 4 PM, Thurs 7 - 9 PM; No admis fee; Estab 1971; 2,000 sq ft; Average Annual Attendance: 12,000
Income: Financed through university
Exhibitions: Tom Bamberger; Juried Student Exhibition; Drawing on the Figure; BFA Exhibition; Exhibitions rotate every three weeks

STURGEON BAY

M **MILLER ART CENTER FOUNDATION INC,** Miller Art Museum, 107 S Fourth Ave, Sturgeon Bay, WI 54235. Tel 920-746-0707 (office), 743-6578 (gallery); Email emam@dcwis.com; Web: www.millerartmuseum.org; *Cur* Deborah Rosenthal; *Dir* Elizabeth Meissner-Gigstead; *Mus Asst* Michael Nitsch
Open Mon - Sat 10 AM - 5 PM, Mon evenings until 8 PM; No admis fee; Estab 1975; Gallery is 5000 sq ft; 4 galleries; Average Annual Attendance: 18,000; Mem: 168; dues sustaining mem $50+; vol assoc $20, annual meeting second Thurs in Nov
Income: Financed by endowment, mem, county funds, sustaining, mem & grants
Special Subjects: Collages, Drawings, Etchings & Engravings, Landscapes, Painting-American, Painting-American, Photography, Photography, Portraits, Prints, Watercolors, Woodcuts, Portraits
Collections: permanent coll contains over 800 paintings, emphasis on paintings, prints & drawings by 20th century Wisconsin artists
Exhibitions: See website
Activities: Classes for adults & children; docent training; art library for mems & vols; lects open to pub, 7 vis lectrs per yr; concerts; gallery talks; tours; competitions with awards; individual paintings lent to other mus & art centers; lending coll contains 600 original art works; exten prog serves Master Artists K-5th

gr; museum shop sells books, original art, prints, reproductions, jewelry, cards & pottery

WAUSAU

M **CENTER FOR THE VISUAL ARTS,** Gallery, 427 N 4th St, Wausau, WI 54403-5420. Tel 715-842-4545; Email cva@cvawausau.org; Web: www.cvawausau.org; *Contact* Katie Crotteau; *Exec Dir* Rose DeHut
Open Tues - Fri 10 AM - 5 PM, Sat 10 AM - 4 PM; No admis fee
Activities: Classes for adults & children; lects open to public; gallery talks; tours

M **LEIGH YAWKEY WOODSON ART MUSEUM,** 700 N 12th St, Wausau, WI 54403-5007. Tel 715-845-7010; Fax 715-845-7103; Email museum@lywam.org; Web: www.lywam.org; *Cur Educ* Lisa Hoffman; *Cur Educ* Catie Anderson; *Dir* Kathy Kelsey Foley; *Registrar & Cur Colls* Jane Weinke; *Cur Exhibs* Andy McGivern; *Mktg & Communs Mgr* Amy Beck; *Admin Mgr* Shari Schroeder; *Bus Mgr* Diane Wendt; *Project Mgr* Matt Foss
Open Tues - Fri 9 AM - 4 PM, Sat & Sun Noon - 5 PM; first Thurs every month 9 AM - 7:30PM; No admis fee; Estab 1976; Average Annual Attendance: 60,000
Special Subjects: Bronzes, Decorative Arts, Landscapes, Prints, Sculpture, Watercolors, Woodcarvings, Woodcuts
Collections: Contemporary & historic paintings, drawings & sculptures with birds as the main subject
Publications: Birds in Art, annual exhibition catalog
Activities: Docent progs; classes for adults, children; lects open to pub; gallery talks; tours; 2016 Wisconsin Governor's Arts, Culture, and Heritage Tourism Award; book traveling exhibs 3-4 per yr; originate traveling exhibs to art, natural history & science mus

WEST ALLIS

M **INTERNATIONAL CLOWN HALL OF FAME & RESEARCH CENTER, INC,** State Fair Park, 640 S 84th St #526 West Allis, WI 53214-1438. Tel 414-290-0105; Fax 414-290-0106; Email mirthcon@juno.com; Web: www.theclownmuseum.org; *Exec Dir* James D Mejchar
Open Mon - Fri 10 AM - 4 PM; No admis fee; donations accepted; Estab 1986 to promote & advance the art of clowning through preservation & education; Average Annual Attendance: 15,000; Mem: 500; dues $35-$1000; annual meeting 1st weekend in Aug
Income: $150,000 (financed by endowment, mem, gift shop & admis)
Library Holdings: Cassettes, Clipping Files, DVDs, Kodachrome Transparencies, Memorabilia, Original Art Works, Photographs, Records, Slides, Video Tapes
Special Subjects: Costumes, Crafts, Dolls, Historical Material, Miniatures, Posters, Prints
Publications: Let the Laughter Loose, quarterly newsletter
Activities: Classes for adults & children; dramatic progs; docent training; lects open to pub, 25 vis lectrs per yr, gallery talks, tours; sales shop sells books, magazines, prints, reproductions & clown novelties

WEST BEND

M **MUSEUM OF WISCONSIN ART,** 205 Veterans Ave, West Bend, WI 53095-3312. Tel 262-334-9638; Fax 262-334-8080; Email info@wisconsinart.org; Web: www.wisconsinart.org; *Exec Dir & CEO* Laurie Winters; *Director of Collections and Exhibitions* Graeme Reid; *Director of Development* Heidi Winter; *Director of Public Relations and Social Media* Christina Wright; *Director of Cultural Relations* Miranda Levy; *Director of Finance* Dan Corry; *Graphic Designer* Amy Hafermann; *Building Operations* Ed Geidel; *MOWA Shop Manager* Julia Jackson; *Facilities Rental Manager* Kerry Conway; *Membership Coordinator* Liz Knopke; *Youth Program Coordinator* Jenifer Koebel; *Preparator & Exhibit Director* August Peter; *Associate Curator* Erika Petterson; *Registrar* Andrea Waala; *Director of Member Services* Julia Gray; *Executive Assistant* Pam Schweiger
Open Tues - Sun 10 AM - 5 PM, Thurs 10 AM - 8 PM, cl Mon; Free to MOWA mems; Estab 1961; one of America's great regional art museums; state of the art bldg contains nine galleries featuring the work of today's hottest Wisconsin artists, as well as Wisconsin art from the ages including Carl von Marr's masterpiece The Flagellants; The modern & contemporary new bldg includes nearly 12,000 sq ft of gallery space, approx 7,000 sq ft of facility rental space for special events, a unique gift shop with Wisconsin-made items, two education studios & an outdoor sculpture garden; Average Annual Attendance: 40,000; Mem: 5,000; dues individual $12, 2 people $24, household 3 or more with children 17 & under $50
Income: Financed by endowment, mem & donations
Library Holdings: Audio Tapes, Book Volumes, Cassettes, Clipping Files, Compact Disks, DVDs, Original Art Works, Original Documents, Photographs, Records, Reproductions
Special Subjects: Drawings, Painting-American, Decorative Arts, Etchings & Engravings, Furniture, Sculpture, Watercolors
Collections: Carl von Marr Collection, Wisconsin Art History 1850-1960, 1800-2000 Contemporary Wisconsin Art
Publications: Carl Von Marr, American-German Artist (1858-1936); quarterly printed newsletter; monthly e-newsletter
Activities: Classes for adults and children; docent training; lects open to public; lects for mems only; 12 vis lectrs per yr; tours; gallery talks; sponsored competitions; Educational programs for schools through the region; MOWA On the Lake - serving Saint John's On The Lake in Milwaukee, WI; originate traveling exhibs; mus shop sells books, reproductions, prints and collection; and handmade exhibits by Wisconsin Artists

WHITEWATER

M **UNIVERSITY OF WISCONSIN-WHITEWATER,** Crossman Gallery, 800 W Main St, Whitewater, WI 53190-1705. Tel 262-472-1207, 472-5708; Fax 262-472-2808; Email flanagam@mail.uww.edu; Web: blogs.uww.edu/crossman/; *Dir* Michael Flanagan
Open Mon - Fri 10 AM - 5PM & 6 - 8 PM, Sat 1 - 4 PM, cl Sun; No admis fee; Estab 1965 to provide professional exhibits; 47 ft x 51 ft, secure alarmed facility; Average Annual Attendance: 10,000
Income: $7000 (financed by segregated student fee appropriation)
Collections: American Folk Art Collection, Regional Art Collection, Early 20th century German works on paper
Exhibitions: Ceramic Invitational; Artassa Collaboration; Chronicles of Latin America; Contemporary sculpture
Activities: Classes for adults & children; student training in gallery management; lects open to public, 3 vis lectrs per year; concerts; gallery talks; tours; student juried show

WYOMING

BIG HORN

M **THE NEW MUSEUM AT THE BRADFORD BRINTON RANCH,** (Bradford Brinton) The Brinton Museum, 239 Brinton Rd, Big Horn, WY 82833; PO Box 460, Big Horn, WY 82833-0460. Tel 307-672-3173; Email kschuster@thebrintonmuseum.org; Web: www.thebrintonmuseum.org; *Dir & Chief Cur* Kenneth L Schuster; *Asst Dir & develop* Barbara R Schuster; *Curator of Exhibitions* Barbara McNab; *Chief Registrar & Cur History* Cynthia Clark; *Facilities Mgr* Joel Wardell; *Accountant & Human Resources* Emily Wardell; *Curator of Museum Education* Ariel Downing
Open Mar 15 - Dec 23 7 days a week 9:30am-5pm; Admis adults $10, students over 13 & sr citizens over 62 $8; Estab 1961 to show a typical Gentleman's working ranch of the 1920s complete with Western art & original furnishings; Forrest E Mars, Jr Building at The Brinton Mus with changing exhibs; Ranch House with original displays (art by Russell, Remington, Borein, F T Johnson); Average Annual Attendance: 22,000; Mem: 650; dues $30 & up
Special Subjects: Ceramics, Crafts, Decorative Arts, Furniture, Hispanic Art, Jewelry, Painting-American, Painting-British, Period Rooms, Porcelain, Prints, Sculpture, Silver, Southwestern Art, American Western Art
Collections: Plains Indians Artifacts, Western American Art by Frederic Remington & Charles M Russell, American art & a few pieces of European art, largely of the 19th & 20th century
Exhibitions: (9th Feb, 2017-17th Feb, 2017) All-Schools 5th Grade Student Art Show; (15th Mar, 2017-30th Apr, 2017) 12th Illustrator Show - The Art of John Potter; (15th Mar, 2017-27th Apr, 2017) Pushing the Boundaries - National Basketry Invitational; (7th May, 2017-30th Jun, 2017) David Plowden's High Plains: Sixty Years of Photographs; 16th Jul, 2017) Traditional Cowboy Arts Association; (4th Aug, 2017-4th Sep, 2017) Bighorn Rendezvous Art Show and Sale; (16th Sep, 2017-30th Nov, 2017) Gary Erbe: 50 Year Retrospective; (10th Sep, 2017-15th Oct, 2017) 5th Annual Brinton's Small Works Show - The Brinton 100; (21st Oct, 2017-12th Nov, 2017) Spear-O at The Brinton Museum; (26th Nov, 2017-17th Dec, 2017) 27th Annual Holiday Show, featuring: Dan Young, Lorenzo Chavez, Skip Whitcomb, Kathy Wipfler
Publications: Monographs on artists in the collection from time to time, on exhibitions curated
Activities: Educ dept; art workshops; docent training; lects open to pub, 4-6 vis lectrs per yr; gallery talks; tours; mus shop sells books, magazines, original art, reproductions, prints, American Indian jewelry, crafts, gift merchandise, pillows, baskets, rugs

CASPER

M **NICOLAYSEN ART MUSEUM & DISCOVERY CENTER,** Children's Discovery Center, 400 E Collins Dr, Casper, WY 82601-2815. Tel 307-235-5247; Fax 307-235-0923; Web: www.thenic.org; *Exec Dir* Marie Koernig; *Vol Coordr* Lori Klatt; *Deputy Dir* Jan DeBeer
Open Tues - Sat 10 AM - 5 PM, Sun Noon-4 PM; Admis non mems $5, children $3; Estab 1967 to exhibit permanent collection, nationwide traveling exhibits & provide school tours, art classes & workshops; Two galleries, 2500 sq ft and 500 sq ft; Average Annual Attendance: 40,000; Mem: 1,500; dues individual $35, family $60, annual meeting last Wed of Mar
Income: $900,000 (financed by mem, grants & fundraising events)
Collections: Carl Link Drawings, Artists of the Region, Conrad Schwiering Studio
Exhibitions: Twenty per year.
Publications: Historic Ranches of Wyoming
Activities: Classes for adults & children; docent training; lects open to pub, 5-10 vis lectrs per yr; concerts; gallery talks; competitions with cash awards; individual paintings & original objects of art lent to qualified exhibiting institutions; lending collection contains 2500 original art works; book traveling exhibs; originate traveling exhibs; mus shop sells books, original art & gifts; children's mus

L **Museum,** 400 E Collins Dr, Casper, WY 82601. Tel 307-235-5247; Fax 307-235-0923; *Discovery Center Coordr* Val Martinez; *Registrar* Debbie Oliver; *Dir* Joe Ellis
Open Tues - Sat 10 AM - 5 PM, Thurs 10 AM-8 PM, Sun Noon-4 PM; Admis adults $2, children under 12 $1, free Thurs, Sat & Sun; Estab 1967 to collect & exhibit regional contemporary art; 8000 sq ft including 6 small and 1 large gallery. Computer controlled temperature & humidity. Hands on discovery center for children; Average Annual Attendance: 60,000; Mem: 700; dues $50; annual meeting 3rd Tues May
Income: $235,000 (financed by donations & fundraising events)
Library Holdings: Book Volumes 66, Exhibition Catalogs, Pamphlets, Periodical Subscriptions 8, Slides
Collections: Carl Link Collection, Regional Contemporary Pottery
Activities: Classes for children; dramatic progs; lects open to pub, 2000 lectrs per yr; gallery talks; tours; juried regional competitions; book traveling exhibs 1-2 per yr; mus shop sells books, original art, prints, pottery, glass, jewelry & cards

CHEYENNE

M **DEPARTMENT OF COMMERCE,** Wyoming Arts Council Gallery, 2320 Capitol Ave, Cheyenne, WY 82002-0001. Tel 307-777-7742; Fax 307-777-5499; Web: www.wyoarts.state.wy.us; *Exec Dir* Michael Lange
Open Mon - Fri 8 AM - 5 PM, cl holidays; Estab 1990 to exhibit work of artists living & working in Wyoming; Average Annual Attendance: 1,200
Exhibitions: 4-5 exhibits annually, work of Wyoming artists in all media
Activities: Lects open to pub, gallery talks; originates traveling exhibs to state of Wyo non-profit organizations

M **WYOMING STATE MUSEUM,** 2301 Central Ave, Cheyenne, WY 82002-0001. Tel 307-777-7022 (museum), 7021 (tours), 5320 (store), 5427 (collections); Fax 307-777-5375; Web: www.wyomuseum.state.wy.us; *Dir* Mark Brammer
Open Mon - Sat 9 AM - 4:30 PM; cl Sun & Holidays; No admis fee; Estab 1895 to collect, preserve & to exhibit the work of Wyoming & Western artists; Average Annual Attendance: 34,000
Income: Financed by state appropriation
Special Subjects: American Indian Art, American Western Art, Ceramics, Collages, Costumes, Decorative Arts, Dioramas, Dolls, Drawings, Ethnology, Furniture, Landscapes, Painting-American, Photography, Portraits, Primitive art, Sculpture, Textiles, Watercolors
Collections: Wyoming artists, historical & contemporary including Historical Hans Kleiber, William Gollings, M D Houghton, Cyrenius Hall, William H Jackson, J H Sharp
Exhibitions: Regional & Wyoming contemporary art, western art; Governor's Annual Art Exhibition, Jan - Mar ann
Activities: Classes for children; lects open to pub, 9 vis lectrs per yr; gallery talks; tours; purchase awards, Governor's Capitol Art Exhib; individual paintings & original objects of art lent to institutions belonging to AAM, Colo-Wyo Assn of Museums (CWAM) & Mount Plains Museums Assn; mus shop sells books, original art, reproductions, prints

CLEARMONT

M **UCROSS FOUNDATION,** Big Red Barn Gallery, 30 Big Red Ln, Clearmont, WY 82835-9723. Tel 307-737-2291; Fax 307-737-2322; Email ucross@wyoming.com; *Pres* Elizabeth Guheen; *Exec Dir* Sharon Dynak
Open Mon - Fri 9 AM - 4 PM; No admis fee; Estab 1981; Gallery is located in a renovated barn on the grounds of an artists' & writers' residency program
Special Subjects: Painting-American, Sculpture, Textiles, Watercolors
Exhibitions: Quilts by Linda Behar; 4-6 group & solo shows a year; 4 exhibits annually in winter, spring, summer & fall
Publications: Ucross newsletter, annually
Activities: Sales shop sells books, postcards & gifts

CODY

M **BIG HORN GALLERIES,** 1167 Sheridan Ave, Cody, WY 82414-3627. Tel 307-527-7587; Fax 307-527-7586; Email bhgcody@bighorngalleries.com; Web: www.bighorngalleries.com
Call for hours; Estab 1982
Collections: Western & wildlife art and landscapes
Exhibitions: Temporary exhibits
Activities: Mus shop sells graphics, jewelry, giclee, prints, posters, books & gifts

A **BUFFALO BILL MEMORIAL ASSOCIATION,** Buffalo Bill Historical Center, 720 Sheridan Ave, Cody, WY 82414-3428. Tel 307-587-4771; Fax 307-587-5714; Email leeh@bbhc.org; Web: www.bbhc.org; *Chmn* Alan Simpson; *Exec Dir* Robert Price Shimp; *Cur Plains Indian Museum* Emma Hanson; *Dir Educ* Maryanne Andrus; *Registrar* Elizabeth Holmes; *Assoc Dir* Wally Reber; *Cur Buffalo Bill Mus* Juti Winchester; *Cur Draper Mus of Natural History* Charles Preston; *Librn* Mary Robinson; *Dir Pub Rels* Lee Haines; *Cur McCracken Research Library* Kurt Graham
Open Apr 10 AM - 5 PM, May 8 AM - 8 PM, June - Sept 15 8 AM - 8 PM, Sept 16 - Oct 8 AM - 5 PM, Nov - Mar 10 AM - 3 PM, cl Mon; Admis Adults $15, sr citizens $13 & special group rate; Estab 1917 to preserve & exhibit art, artifacts & memorabilia of the Old West; to operate Buffalo Bill Mus, Plains Indian Mus, Whitney Gallery of Western Art & Cody Firearms Mus & Draper Mus of Natural History; Average Annual Attendance: 250,000; Mem: Dues $38 & up
Income: Financed by admis & private funds
Publications: Annual exhibition catalogues; quarterly newsletter
Activities: Classes for adults & children; docent training; lects open to pub; gallery talks; tours; schols offered; individual paintings & original objects of art lent to other institutions; book traveling exhibs; originate traveling exhibs around the US; mus shop sells books, original art, reproductions, prints, slides, jewelry, collectible items, Indian crafts & Kachina dolls

L **Harold McCracken Research Library**, 720 Sheridan Ave, Cody, WY 82414. Tel 307-587-4771; Fax 307-587-5714, 307-527-6042; Web: www.bbhc.org; *House Cur* Nathan Bender; *Librn* Frances Clymer
Open Mon - Fri 8 AM - 5 PM (summer), Tues, Fri 10 AM - 3 PM (winter); Estab 1980 for research in Western history & art; Circ non circulating; Open to the pub for reference only; Average Annual Attendance: 250,000
Library Holdings: Audio Tapes 1500, Book Volumes 15,000, Cassettes, Clipping Files, Exhibition Catalogs, Fiche, Filmstrips 1300, Kodachrome Transparencies, Lantern Slides, Manuscripts, Memorabilia 300, Motion Pictures, Other Holdings Engraving & Architectural Drawings 200, Pamphlets, Periodical Subscriptions 86, Photographs, Prints, Records, Reels 7000, Reproductions, Slides 6500, Video Tapes
Special Subjects: American Indian Art, American Western Art, Anthropology, Archaeology, Art Education, Art History, Commercial Art, Etchings & Engravings, Ethnology, Folk Art, Landscapes, Manuscripts, Maps, Painting-American, Photography
Collections: WHD Koerner Archives, Buffalo Bill Cody Archives, Photo Collections, Rare Books
Activities: Classes for adults & children; dramatic progs; docent training; lects open to pub, 20 vis lectrs per yr; concerts; gallery talks; tours; mus shop sells books, magazines, original art, reproductions & prints

A **CODY COUNTRY ART LEAGUE,** 836 Sheridan Ave, Cody, WY 82414-3411. Tel 307-587-3597; Email office@codycountryartleague; Web: www.codycountryartleague.com; *Pres* Shirley Barhaug; *Treas* Lynn Mowery
Open summer: Mon - Sat 9 AM -5 PM, Sun 10 AM - 3 PM, winter: Mon - Fri 9 AM - 5 PM; No admis fee; Estab 1964 for promotion of artistic endeavor among local & area artists; also established for exhibits, displays & sales; Average Annual Attendance: 25,000; Mem: 250; dues $40 (artist), annual meeting in Jan; must be juried in
Income: Financed by mem dues, yearly auction, sponsors & events
Special Subjects: American Western Art, Bronzes, Ceramics, Drawings, Furniture, Glass, Landscapes, Metalwork, Mosaics, Photography, Pottery, Stained Glass, Watercolors, Woodcarvings
Exhibitions: Ann Art Show June-July; Ann Garden Tour July
Activities: Classes for adults & children; dramatic progs; films; workshops; community events; lects open to pub, 2-3 vis lectrs per yr; competitions; sales shop sells books, original art,& prints

M **SIMPSON GALLAGHER GALLERY,** 1161 Sheridan Ave, Cody, WY 82414-3627. Tel 307-587-4022; Email sue@simpsongallaghergallery.com; Web: www.simpsongallaghergallery.com
Call for hours
Collections: Paintings; wildlife sculpture; western intaglios

JACKSON

M **NATIONAL MUSEUM OF WILDLIFE ART OF THE UNITES STATES,** 2820 Rungius Rd, Jackson, WY 83001; PO Box 6825, Jackson, WY 83002-6825. Tel 307-733-5771; Fax 307-733-5787; Email info@wildlifeart.org; Web: www.wildlifeart.org; *Dir* Steve Seamons, PhD; *Cur Art & Reserach* Adam D Harris, PhD; *Cur Educ & Exhibs* Jane Lavino; *CFO* Lisa Holmes; *Dir Facility & Security* Joe Bishop; *Dir Opers* Mike Hofhiens; *Mktg Coord* Debbie Phillips
Open May - Oct 9 AM - 5 PM; Nov - April Tues - Sat 9 AM - 5 PM, Sun 11 AM - 5 PM, cl Mon; Admis $14 adults, seniors $12, children 5-18 $6, children under 5 free; Estab 1987 devoted to Fine Wildlife Art; collection includes work from 2500 BC to present; Circ Non-circulating; Facility has 14 galleries, cafe, museum shop, 2 classrooms, 200 seat auditorium & library; galleries house traveling exhibits & permanent colls; Average Annual Attendance: 77,000; Mem: Annual dues $45 individual
Income: Financed by endowment, mem & admis
Library Holdings: Auction Catalogs, Book Volumes, Clipping Files, Compact Disks, DVDs, Memorabilia, Motion Pictures, Periodical Subscriptions, Photographs, Slides, Video Tapes
Special Subjects: American Indian Art, American Western Art, Anthropology, Bronzes, Drawings, Etchings & Engravings, Folk Art, Historical Material, Landscapes, Manuscripts, Maps, Medieval Art, Miniatures, Painting-American, Painting-British, Painting-Canadian, Painting-Dutch, Painting-European, Painting-French, Painting-Scandinavian, Photography, Pre-Columbian Art, Prints, Sculpture, Southwestern Art, Watercolors
Collections: Wildlife Art Collection
Exhibitions: Special Grand Opening exhibits;
Publications: Call of the Wild magazine, annual; eNews
Activities: Classes for adults & children; dramatic progs; docent training; paid internships; lects open to pub, 10 vis lectrs per yr; tours; competitions; awards: Rungius Medal, Bull-Bransom Award, Western Visions People's Choice Award, Western Visions Red Smith Award, Western Visions Trustees Purchase Award, Western Visions Robert Kuhn Award; schols available; lend orig objects of art to other museums; book traveling exhibs 1-2 per yr; originates traveling exhibs; mus shop sells books, prints, magazines, reproductions, gifts, housewares, apparel & jewelry

L **Library**, 2820 Rungius Rd, PO Box 6825 Jackson, WY 83002-6825. Tel 307-733-5771, 800-313-9553; Fax 307-733-5787; Email info@wildlifeart.org; Web: www.wildlifeart.org; *Dir* Francine Carraro
Open Mon - Fri 9 AM - 5 PM (Summer & Winter), Mon-Fri 9 AM - 5 PM, Sat 1 - 5 PM (Spring & Fall); Admis family $16, adults $8, seniors & students $7; Estab 1987 to enrich & inspire pub appreciation & knowledge of fine art & to explore humanity's relationship with nature by collecting fine art focused on wildlife & presenting exceptional exhibs & educational progs; 12 galleries including 6 changing exhib galleries; Mem: dues $35 - $2500
Library Holdings: Auction Catalogs, Audio Tapes, Book Volumes 1000, Clipping Files, Exhibition Catalogs, Motion Pictures, Pamphlets, Slides, Video Tapes
Special Subjects: American Indian Art, American Western Art, Architecture, Art Education, Art History, Bronzes, Drawings, Etchings & Engravings, Film, Folk Art, Landscapes, Miniatures, Painting-American, Painting-British, Painting-Canadian, Painting-European, Painting-German, Photography, Printmaking, Sculpture, Southwestern Art, Watercolors, Woodcuts, Illustration, Maps, Metalwork, Restoration & Conservation
Collections: JKM Collection, American Bison Collection, John Clymer Studio Collection, Carl Rungius Collection, Over 300 works of art by over 200 artists
Publications: Call of the Wild triannual newsletter & spec exhib catalogs
Activities: Classes for adults & children; docent training; lects open to pub; concerts, gallery talks; tours; Rungius Award; Red Smith Award; book traveling exhibs, 6 per yr; mus shop sells books, magazines, reproductions & prints

LARAMIE

M **UNIVERSITY OF WYOMING,** University of Wyoming Art Museum, 2111 Willett Dr, Laramie, WY 82071-2000; 1000 E University Ave, Dept 3807 Laramie, WY 82071-2000. Tel 307-766-6622; Fax 307-766-3520; Email uwartmus@uwyo.edu; Web: www.uwyo.edu/artmuseum; *Dir & Chief Cur* Susan Moldenhauer; *Cur Educ* Katie Christensen; *Cur Coll* Nicole Crawford; *Reg* Sarah Gadd; *Master Teacher* Heather Bender; *Mktg Assoc* Molly Dunnell; *Chief Prep*

Sterling Smith; *Prep* Conor Mullen; *Visitor Serv Assoc* Cherie Kelley; *Admin Asst* Janine Reinhardt
Open Mon - Sat 10 AM - 5 PM; Mon until 7 PM Sept - Nov, Feb -Apr; No admis fee; Estab 1972 to serve as an art resource center for faculty, students & the general public; Exhibition space consists of 9 galleries & outdoor sculpture terrace; Average Annual Attendance: 90,000; Mem: 500; dues $40 & up
Income: Financed by state appropriation, friends organization, individual and corporate gifts & grants
Special Subjects: African Art, Afro-American Art, American Indian Art, American Western Art, Bronzes, Ceramics, Drawings, Etchings & Engravings, Graphics, Latin American Art, Painting-American, Painting-American, Painting-British, Painting-European, Painting-French, Photography, Portraits, Primitive art, Prints, Prints, Sculpture, Sculpture, Woodcuts, Landscapes
Collections: Collection of 8,000 paintings, sculptures, works on paper, photographs, crafts & ethnographic materials, primary 17th to 20th century
Publications: Exhibition catalogs
Activities: Classes for adults & children; docent training; Summer Teaching Institute; lects open to pub, 4 vis lectrs per yr; concerts; gallery talks; tours; student exhib awards; individual paintings and original objects of art lent to other museums regionally and nationally; artmobile; collection contains 8,000 original art works; originates traveling exhibs; mus shop sells logo items, mus publs

MOOSE

A **GRAND TETON NATIONAL PARK SERVICE,** PO Drawer 170, Moose, WY 83012. Tel 307-739-3494; *Cur* Bridgette Guild; *Naturalist* Laine Thom
Open May 8 AM - 5 PM, June - Sept 8 AM - 8 PM, cl Oct - Apr; No admis fee; Estab 1972; Average Annual Attendance: 300,000
Special Subjects: American Indian Art
Collections: David T Vernon Indian Arts Collection
Exhibitions: Native American Guest Artist's Demonstration Program; David T Vernon Indian Arts Collection
Activities: Tours open to public; sales shop sells books & prints

ROCK SPRINGS

A **SWEETWATER COUNTY LIBRARY SYSTEM AND SCHOOL DISTRICT #1,** Community Fine Arts Center, 400 C St, Rock Springs, WY 82901-6225. Tel 307-362-6212; Fax 307-352-6657; Email cfac@sweetwaterlibraries.com; Web: www.cfac4art.com; *Asst to Dir* Jennifer Messer; *Dir* Debora Thaxton Soule; *Receptionist* Doris Christofferson
Open Mon - Thurs 10 AM - 6 PM, Fri & Sat Noon - 5 PM; No admis fee; Estab 1966 to house permanent art collection and hold various exhibits during the year; Halseth Gallery houses permanent art coll owned by local school dist; Circ 200+; 19th - 21st century American art - collection owned by local school district; Average Annual Attendance: 8,000
Income: Financed by grants, city appropriation, county funds & school district No 1
Library Holdings: Book Volumes, DVDs, Periodical Subscriptions, Video Tapes
Special Subjects: American Indian Art, American Western Art, Ceramics, Collages, Drawings, Etchings & Engravings, Folk Art, Landscapes, Mosaics, Painting-American, Photography, Pottery, Prints, Watercolors, Woodcarvings, Woodcuts
Collections: Over 550 pieces of original art including Norman Rockwell, Grandma Moses, Raphael Soyer among others
Publications: Calendar of events; catalogue brochure
Activities: Classes for adults & children; art workshops for children & students; dramatic progs; lectrs open to pub; 3-4 concerts per yr; 1-2 gallery talks per yr, large tours by appointment; competitions; high school awards; book 1-2 traveling exhibs per yr

M **WESTERN WYOMING COMMUNITY COLLEGE ART GALLERY,** 2500 College Dr, Rock Springs, WY 82902; PO Box 428, Rock Springs, WY 82902. Tel 307-382-1723; Email fmcewin@westernwyoming.edu; Web: www.westernwyoming.edu; *Dir* Florence McEwin
Call for hours
Collections: Paintings; sculpture; photographs
Exhibitions: Temporary exhibits

SUNDANCE

M **CROOK COUNTY MUSEUM & ART GALLERY,** PO Box 63, Sundance, WY 82729-0063. Tel 307-283-3666; Fax 307-283-1192; Email ccmuseum@rangeweb.net; Web: www.crookcountymuseum.com; *Dir* Rocky Courchaine
Open Mon - Fri 8 AM - 5 PM, cl holidays; No admis fee; Estab 1971 to preserve & display Crook County history, display County artists & provide a showcase for county residents' collections; Local art; Average Annual Attendance: 6,000; Mem: 60; corporate $500, bus $150, family $75, couple $40, individual $25
Income: Financed by County appropriation
Special Subjects: American Western Art, Anthropology, Archaeology, Bronzes, Coins & Medals, Crafts, Dioramas, Dolls, Drawings, Embroidery, Flasks & Bottles, Folk Art, Furniture, Glass, Historical Material, Jewelry, Laces, Leather, Manuscripts, Maps, Painting-American, Period Rooms, Posters, Textiles, Watercolors, Woodcarvings
Collections: Furniture, pictures, Western historical items
Publications: Brochure
Activities: Docent training; tours for school children; gallery talks; originates traveling exhibs; mus shop sells books

WHEATLAND

M **WYOMING TRAILS GALLERY,** 1004 16th St, Wheatland, WY 82201-2530. Tel 307-322-3300; Email barbaraschaffnerfineart@wyomingwisp.com; Web: www.wyomingtrailsgallery.com
Open Tues - Fri 9 AM - 4 PM, Sat 9 AM - noon; other times by appointment; No admis fee; Barbara Schaffner's studio, gallery of 20 artists; fine art paintings; woodcarvings; pottery & jewelry
Special Subjects: American Western Art, Bronzes, Drawings, Historical Material, Jade, Jewelry, Landscapes, Miniatures, Painting-American, Portraits, Pottery, Reproductions, Silversmithing, Watercolors, Woodcarvings
Collections: Paintings; bronze; pottery; jewelry; folk arts; woodcarving
Publications: Historic Paintings
Activities: Oil & watercolor workshops for adults

PACIFIC ISLANDS

PAGO PAGO, AMERICAN SAMOA

M **JEAN P HAYDON MUSEUM,** PO Box 1540, Pago Pago, American Samoa, PI 96799-1540. Tel 684-633-4347; Fax 684-633-2059; *Chmn Board Trustees* Lauti Simona; *Exec Dir & Cur* Leala E Pili
Open Mon-Fri 7:30AM-4PM; No admis fee; Estab 1971 to establish, maintain, acquire & supervise the collection, study preservation, interpretation & exhibition of fine arts objects & such relics, documents, paintings, artifacts & other historical & related materials as well as evidence that illustrate the history of the Samoan Islands & the culture of their inhabitants, particularly of American Samoa; new extension of the mus is an art gallery displaying local artists work & student arts; Average Annual Attendance: 74,000
Income: Financed by city or state appropriations and grants from NEA
Collections: Natural Sciences, Polynesian Artifacts, Samoan Village Life, US Navy History, paintings, drawings, slides, photographs, artifacts
Exhibitions: Various
Activities: Classes for adults & children; dramatic progs; lects open to pub, 3 vis lectrs per yr; artmobile; duplicate but not original objects of art lent to schools & individuals; lending collection contains books, paintings & photographs; mus & sales shop sells books, reproductions, prints, handicrafts & postcards

PUERTO RICO

OLD SAN JUAN

L **CENTRO DE ESTUDIOS AVANZADOS,** Art Library, Calle Cristo # 52, Old San Juan, PR 00902; Apartado 9023970, San Juan, PR 00902-3970. Tel 787-723-4481 (Gen), 787-723-4481 x 24 (Library); Fax 787-723-4810; Email centro@ceaprc.org; Web: www.ceaprc.edu; *Dir* Prof Francis J Mojica
Open Mon, Wed, Thurs 9 AM - 10 PM, Tues 9 AM - 5:30 PM, Sat 7 AM - 4 PM, cl Fri & Sun; No admis fee; small photocopying fees apply
Library Holdings: Book Volumes 15,000, Compact Disks, Other Holdings, Slides, Video Tapes
Special Subjects: Anthropology, Archaeology

PONCE

M **MUSEO DE ARTE DE PONCE,** The Luis A Ferre Foundation Inc, 2325 Blvd Luis A Ferre-Aguayo, Ponce, PR 00717-0776; PO Box 9027, Ponce, PR 00732. Tel 787-840-1510; Fax 787-841-7309; Email info@museoarteponce.org; Web: www.museoarteponce.org; *Exec Dir* Alejandra Pena; *Conservator of Paintings* Lidia Aravena; *Chief Educ* Ana M Hernandez; *Dir Finance & Admin* Floribeth Anciani CPA; *Librn* Sofia Canepa; *Human Resources Manager* Nancy Colon; *European Art Asst Cur* Pablo Perez
Open Wed - Mon 10 AM - 5 PM, Sun noon - 5 PM, cl Tues; Admis adults $6, children under 12 & students with ID $3, seniors (60+) $3; Estab 1959 to exhibit a representative collection of European paintings & sculpture; Puerto Rican & Latin American art; Fourteen galleries on two floors, present works from permanent collection & a wide variety of temporary exhibitions; Average Annual Attendance: 80,000; Mem: 1000; dues family $75, individual $40
Income: Financed by endowment, mem & government
Library Holdings: Auction Catalogs, Book Volumes, CD-ROMs, Cassettes, DVDs, Exhibition Catalogs, Manuscripts, Original Documents, Periodical Subscriptions, Photographs, Records, Video Tapes
Special Subjects: Archaeology, Decorative Arts, Drawings, Graphics, Painting-American, Painting-British, Painting-Dutch, Painting-Flemish, Painting-French, Painting-Italian, Painting-Spanish, Photography, Prints, Sculpture
Collections: Pre-Raphaelite painting & drawings, Art Nouveau Glass, African, Latin American, Pre-Columbian & Puerto Rican Santos Art, 19th century art, contemporary art, 14th-18th century paintings & sculpture
Exhibitions: Rotating exhibits
Publications: Coincide with large exhibs
Activities: Educ dept, classes for adults and children; docent training, family days, teacher training, student programs; Lects open to pub; 3 vis lectrs per year; concerts, gallery talks, tours; individual paintings & original objects of art lent to other mus; mus shops sells books, prints, reproductions, & various gift items

L **Library,** 2325 Blvd Luis A Ferre, Ponce, PR 00717-0776; PO Box 9027, Ponce, PR 00732-9027. Tel 787-840-1510; Fax 787-841-7309; Email biblioteca@museoarteponce.org; Web: www.museoarteponce.org; *Exec Dir* Alejandra Pena; *Chief Librn* Sofia Canepa
Open daily 10 AM - 5 PM; No admis fee; Estab 1959; Cl for reference with the exception of special permission; Average Annual Attendance: 2,000

Income: financed by mus budget & proposals
Library Holdings: Auction Catalogs 1000, Book Volumes 8,000, DVDs 10, Exhibition Catalogs, Periodical Subscriptions 6
Special Subjects: American Western Art, Art Education, Art History, Conceptual Art, Latin American Art, Painting-American, Painting-British, Painting-Dutch, Painting-Flemish, Painting-French, Painting-Italian, Painting-Spanish, Photography, Religious Art, Restoration & Conservation, Mexican Art, Baroque Art, Pre-Columbian Art
Activities: Classes for Adults; Docent training;; Concerts; Shop sells Books, Original Art, Reproductions & Prints

RIO PIEDRAS

M **UNIVERSITY OF PUERTO RICO,** Museum of Anthropology, History & Art, Ponce de Leon Ave, Rio Piedras, PR 00931; PO Box 21908, San Juan, PR 00931-1908. Tel 787-763-3939; 787-764-000 ext 83083; Fax 787-763-4799; Email museo.universidad@upr.edu; Web: www.facebook.com/museouprrp; *Dir* Flavia Marichal; *Archaeologist* Luis A Chanlatte; *Edu* Lisa Ortega; *Colls Registrar* Chakira Santiago; *Designer* Lionel Ortiz; *Librn* Jessica Valiente; *Archaeologist* Yvonne Norganes; *Admin Asst* Yoland Vazquez
Open Mon, Tues Thurs, Fri 9 AM - 4:30 PM, Wed 9 AM - 9 PM, Sun 12 PM - 5 PM, cl national holidays; No admis fee; Estab 1940; Maintains reference library; Average Annual Attendance: 16,000
Income: Financed by government grants & pub institutions
Purchases: Puerto Rican prints & drawings; paintings of past & contemporary Puerto Rican artists
Library Holdings: Clipping Files, DVDs, Exhibition Catalogs, Manuscripts, Memorabilia, Original Documents, Prints
Special Subjects: Antiquities-Egyptian
Collections: Archaeology, Puerto Rican paintings of the past & present, sculpture & folk art, prints & drawings
Exhibitions: Temporary exhibitions from the collection & from museum loans; Contemporary Puerto Rican art
Activities: Workshops for schools & families; lects open to pub; provide concerts; gallery talks; tours; individual paintings & original objects of art lent to organizations & mus; mus shop sells slides & exhib catalogues

SAN JUAN

M **ATENEO PUERTORRIQUENO,** Ateneo Gallery, PO Box 1180, San Juan, PR 00902-1180. Tel 809-722-4839, 787-202-7425; Fax 809-725-3873, 787-432-8209; Email info@ateneopuertorriquenosanjan.com; Web: www.ateneopr.com; *Pres* Eduardo Morales-Coll
Open Mon - Fri 9 AM - 5 PM, cl Sun & holidays; No admis fee; Estab 1876 & is the oldest cultural institution in Puerto Rico; Puerto Rican Art Collection; Mem: dues $25; annual meeting in June
Library Holdings: Audio Tapes, Book Volumes, CD-ROMs, Exhibition Catalogs, Maps, Memorabilia, Motion Pictures, Original Art Works, Photographs, Sculpture, Video Tapes
Special Subjects: Historical Material
Collections: Decorative arts, drawings, historical material, prints, Puerto Rican paintings, sculpture
Exhibitions: Temporary exhibitions, monthly
Publications: Cuadernos (publications on general topics); Revista Ateneo, every 4 months
Activities: Classes for adults; dramatic progs; lects open to pub; gallery talks; guided tours; films; concerts; recitals; competitions with prizes; dramas; Ateneo Medal; individual paintings & original objects of art lent to other cultural institutions; book traveling exhibs 1 per yr; sales shop sells books & reproductions

L **Library,** Avenido Ponce de Leon, Parada 2 San Juan, PR 00902; PO Box 9021180, San Juan, PR 00902-1180. Tel 787-722-4839; Fax 787-725-3873; *Pres* Eduardo Morales-Coll
Library Holdings: Book Volumes 15,000

M **INSTITUTE OF PUERTO RICAN CULTURE,** Instituto de Cultura Puertorriquena, PO Box 9024184, San Juan, PR 00902-4184. Tel 787-724-0700; Fax 787-724-8993; *Dir* Mercedes Gomez
Open Mon - Fri 8 AM - 12 PM, 1 PM - 4:30 PM; No admis fee; Estab 1955 to stimulate, promote, divulge & enrich Puerto Rico's cultural & historical heritage; The institute has created 19 museums around the island, including museums of historical collections, art museums & archaeological museums
Income: Financed by endowment & state appropriation
Collections: Puerto Rican art, archaeology & historical collections
Publications: Revista del Instituto de Cultura Puertorriquena, quarterly
Activities: Educ dept; lects open to pub, gallery talks; concerts; tours; competitions; exten dept serves cultural centers around the island; artmobile; individual paintings & original objects of art lent to government agencies, universities & cultural centers; lending collection contains motion pictures, original art works; original prints, paintings, photographs; originates traveling exhibs; sales shop sells books, records & craft items; junior mus

M **Museo de Arte Religioso Porta Coeli,** Plaza Porta Coeli, San German, PR 00683; Apartado 9024184, San Juan, PR 00902-4184. Tel 787-892-5845; Fax 787-725-5608; Email museosyparques@icp.gobierno.pr; *Exec Dir ICP* Jorge Irizarry Vizcarrondo
Open Wed -Sun 8 AM - noon, 1 - 4:30 PM; Admis adults $3, children (under 11) & seniors (over 65) $2; Estab 1960 to preserve & expose religious art to our culture; 17th century restored chapel built by Dominican monks in the town of San German; Mem: 15,000
Income: Financed by state appropriations
Special Subjects: Religious Art
Collections: Paintings & sculptures from between the 11th & 19th century obtained from different churches in the island, wood & metal religious artifacts
Activities: Conferences; cultural & craft workshops; 4 vis lectrs per yr; concerts; tours; mus shop sells books, magazines & original art

M **Museo del Grabado Latinoamericano,** Calle San Sebastian, Plaza San Jose Viejo San Juan, PR 00901. Tel 809-724-1844, 724-0700
Open 8:30 AM - 4:30 PM; No admis fee; Houses representative samples of graphic art of past & contemporary Puerto Rican artists along with outstanding works of Latin American graphic engravers. Collection of prized works from the San Juan Biennial of Latin American Graphics
Income: Financed by state appropriations
Collections: Grafics, works from Orozco, Matta, Tamayo, Martorell, Alicea, Cardillo, Nevarez, Hernandez Acevedo

M **Museo y Parque Historico Ruinas de Caparra,** Carretera 2, PR-2 Km .6.4 Guaynabo, PR 00968; Instituto de Cultura Puertorriquena, Apartado 9024184 San Juan, PR 00902-4184. Tel 787-781-4795; 977-2702; Fax 787-724-8393; Email museosyparques@icp.gobierno.pr; Web: www.icp.gobierno.pr/myp; *Dir* Samuel D Febo-Cotto; *Exec Dir* Ora Ramos
Open Mon - Fri 8 AM - 12 noon, 1 PM - 4:30 PM; No admis fee; Contains ruins of Caparra, first nucleus of colonization in Puerto Rico, founded by Ponce de Leon in 1508 & 1509, now excavated & transformed into a park with memorial plaques indicating the historic significance. While the restoration & excavation was being conducted, numerous objects related to the period were discovered, which are now on exhibit; Average Annual Attendance: 1,500
Income: Financed by state appropriations
Special Subjects: Archaeology, Historical Material
Collections: Cannons, flags, pistols, ceramics

L **Library,** Avenida Ponce de Leon 500, Puerta de Tierra San Juan, PR 00901; PO Box 9024184, San Juan, PR 00902-4184. Tel 787-725-7405; Fax 787-722-9097
Open for reference to pub, investigators & students
Library Holdings: Audio Tapes, Book Volumes 120,000, Cassettes, Clipping Files, Exhibition Catalogs, Filmstrips, Framed Reproductions, Kodachrome Transparencies, Lantern Slides, Manuscripts, Memorabilia, Motion Pictures, Original Art Works, Pamphlets, Photographs, Prints, Reproductions, Sculpture, Slides, Video Tapes
Collections: Pre-Columbian Archaeological Collection

A **National Gallery,** Apartado 9024184, San Juan, PR 00902-4184. Tel 787-725-2670; Fax 787-723-7837; Email galerianacional@icp.gobierno.pr; Web: www.ipc.gobierno.pr; *Exec Dir Institute of Culture* Mercedes Gomez Marrero; *Dir Visual Arts & National Gallery* Marilu Purcell
Open Tues - Sat 9:30 AM - Noon & 1 - 5 PM; No admis fee; Estab 2007 to exhibit iconic artworks from the Institute of Puerto Rican Culture's collection that reflect diverse aspects of a vibrant culture; The institute has created 16 museums around the island & has five more in preparation, including museums of historical collections, art museums & archaeological museums; Average Annual Attendance: 24,000
Income: Financed by endowment & state appropriation
Collections: Puerto Rican art
Exhibitions: Exhibs vary
Publications: Revista del Institute de Cultura Puertorriquena, quarterly
Activities: Educ dept; classes for adults & children; lects open to pub, 10 vis lectrs per yr; gallery talks; concerts; tours; competitions sponsored; exten dept serves cultural centers around the Island; artmobile; individual paintings & original objects of art lent to government agencies, universities, museums & cultural centers; lending collection contains motion pictures, original art works, original prints, paintings, photographs; originates traveling exhibs; sales shop sells books, magazines, original art, reproductions, records & craft items; junior mus

M **Dr Jose C Barbosa Museum,** 35 Barbosa St, Bayamon, PR 00961-6351; PO Box 9024184, San Juan, PR 00902-4184. Tel 787-977-2702, 787-786-8670; Fax 787-723-7837; Email museosyparques@icp.gobierno.pr; Web: www.icp.golairno.pr; *Dir* Samuel Febo; *Exec Dir* Liliane Ramos
Open Mon - Fri 8 AM - 12 noon, 1 PM - 4 PM; No admis fee; The house where patriot Jose Celso Barbosa was born & raised, restored to its original status as representative of a typical Puerto Rican family home of the 19th century; Average Annual Attendance: 1,200
Income: Financed by state appropriations
Special Subjects: Historical Material
Collections: Furniture, personal objects & documents belonging to Dr Barbosa, including medical instruments, manuscripts & books

M **Parque Ceremonial Indigena de Caguana,** Rt 111 Km 12 4, Utuado, PR 00641; Apartado 9024184, San Juan, PR 00902-4184. Tel 787-894-7325; Fax 787-894-7310; *Dir* Milagros Castro
Open daily 8:00 AM - 4:30 PM; Admis adults $2, minors $1; Caguana Indian Ceremonial Park & Mus includes the ceremonial center of the Taino Indians in Caguana, Utuado, a small town in the center of the Island, constituting the archeological find of the Caribbean & exposition of Indian primitive engineering. The plazas & walks where the Indians held their ceremonies, celebrations & games were restored & excavated to form an archeological park. Numerous petroglyphs are exhibited in the monoliths bordering the plazas & a mus exhibits Indian objects found during the excavations at the site
Income: Financed by state appropriations

M **LA CASA DEL LIBRO MUSEUM,** 255 Calle Cristo, San Juan, PR 00901. Tel 787-723-0354; Fax 787-723-0354; Email lcdl@prw.net; Web: www.lacasadellibro.org; *Pres* Ingrid M Jiminez; *VPres* Gloria A Vega Vega
Open Tues - Sat 11 AM - 4:30 PM; No admis fee; Estab 1955 as a mus-library devoted to the history & arts of the book & related graphic arts; Maintains reference library; Average Annual Attendance: 14,000; Mem: 350; dues $35 & up
Income: Financed by donations & state appropriation
Special Subjects: Bookplates & Bindings, Manuscripts, Maps, Posters
Collections: Bibliography of graphic arts, binding, book illustration, calligraphy, early printing, especially 15th & 16th Century Spanish, modern fine printing, papermaking, Incunabula, Sixteenth-Twentieth Century Books
Exhibitions: Gallery has displays on the first floor relating to printing and other arts of the book, such as: Editions of the Quixote, Spanish Incunables, Sevilla y El Libro Sevillano, Espana 1492, Homenajea Nebrija, Conversosy Sefarditas
Publications: La Imprenta Sevillana; Libros Espanoles; Libros Venecianos
Activities: Classes for adults & children; visits from school groups; students of library science & workers in graphic arts; material available, no fees; book arts workshops; lect open to pub; gallery talks; tours; original objects of printing arts,

material must be used on premises; originate traveling exhibs; mus shop sells books, posters & cards

M **MUSEO DE ARTE DE PUERTO RICO,** 299 De Diego Ave, Stop 22, Santurce San Juan, PR 00909; PO Box 41209, Santurce San Juan, PR 00940-1209. Tel 787-977-6277; Fax 787-977-4446; Email info@mapr.org; Web: www.mapr.org; *Dir* Lourdes Ramos-Rivas, PhD; *Develop Mem* Myrna Z Perez; *Educ* Doreen Colon; *Vol Pres Bd Trustees* Arturo Garcia-Sola Esq; *Pub Rels Mgr* Yetzenia Alvarez; *Exhibs Mgr* Jacquelina Rodriguez-Mont PhD
Open Tues & Thurs - Sat 10 AM - 5 PM, Wed 10 AM - 8 PM, Sun 11 AM - 6 PM; cl New Year's Day, Good Friday, Election Day, Thanksgiving Day, Christmas Day; Admis adults $6.69, seniors, students & children $3.35, mems no admis fee; Incorporated in 1996 & open to pub in 2000 with the mission to enrich the lives of its diverse audiences by making accessible & promoting the knowledge, appreciation & enjoyment of visual arts from Puerto Rico & the world. Pvt nonprofit org; 41,962 sq ft exhib space; 400-seat theater; sculpture botanical garden; conservation lab; 2 classrooms; 4 workshops; computer lab; seminar rm; mus equipped with elevators & ramps; restaurant & cafe on-site; Average Annual Attendance: 140,000; Mem: dues Exec $1000, Collaborator $500, Friend $250, Family $100, Indiv $50, Students, Teachers, Physically-Impaired & Srs $25
Library Holdings: Auction Catalogs, Audio Tapes, Book Volumes, CD-ROMs, Exhibition Catalogs, Other Holdings, Pamphlets, Periodical Subscriptions, Video Tapes
Special Subjects: Latin American Art
Collections: 17th - 21st c Puerto Rican paintings, sculpture, prints & drawings, photos, installations, conceptual art & multi-media art, Master painters Jose Campeche, Francisco Oller, Rafael Tufino, Augusto Marin, Myrna Baez, Rafael Ferrer, Francisco Rodon, etc, sculpture garden, silkscreens from 1940 to the present
Publications: MAPR, quarterly newsletter; Report, annually; exhib catalogs & brochures
Activities: Docent prog; formal educ progs for adults & children; mus training for professional mus workers; lects open to pub; guided tours; arts festivals; concerts; films; loan exhibs, temporary exhibs & traveling exhibs; ann events: MAPR Ann Gala; mus shop sells books, magazines, prints & miscellaneous merchandise

VIEJO SAN JUAN

M **MUSEO DE LAS AMERICAS,** Cuartel de Ballajá, 2nd piso, Viejo San Juan, PR 00902; Apartado 9023634, San Juan, PR 00902-3634. Tel 787-724-5052; Fax 787-722-2848; Web: www.museolasamerias.org; *Exhib Designer* Marlene Hernandez Casillas; *Exec Dir* Maria Angela Lopez Vilella; *Reg* Ileamarie Vazquez Contreras; *Educ Coordr* Shirley Padilla Virola; *Coll Supvr* Maria del Carmen Rodriguez; *Supvr Educ Guides* Pavlova Mezguida
Open Tues-Sat 9 AM - 12 PM & 1 PM - 4 PM, Sun 12 PM - 5 PM; Admis adults $3, students & senior citizens $2; Estab 1992 - to offer a synoptic vision of the history, art & culture of the Americas; Four permanent exhibs; Average Annual Attendance: 30,000
Activities: Classes for adults & children; concerts; gallery talks; tours

VIEQUES

M **INSTITUTE OF PUERTO RICAN CULTURE,** Museo Fuerte Conde de Mirasol, PO Box 71, Vieques, PR 00765; Magnolia 471, Vieques, PR 00765. Tel 787-741-1717; Fax 787-741-1717; Email bieke@prdigital.com; Web: enchanted-isle.com/elfortin/; *Dir* Robert L Rabin Siegal
Open Wed - Sun 10 AM - 4 PM; Admis adult $2, children $1, in excursions $1; Estab 1989 for the preservation of local culture; Two galleries for itinerant exhibits, 20 x 50 ft; Average Annual Attendance: 15,000
Special Subjects: Anthropology, Archaeology, Architecture, Ceramics, Coins & Medals, Crafts, Decorative Arts, Folk Art, Graphics, Hispanic Art, Historical Material, Latin American Art, Manuscripts, Maps, Photography, Posters, Pre-Columbian Art, Prints, Sculpture, Watercolors
Collections: Archaeology, architecture, history, silkscreens & photography of Vieques; other art of Puerto Rico & Vieques
Exhibitions: La Naturaleza de Vieques: 100 Millones de Anos de Historia (The Nature of Vieques: One Hundred Million Years of History) Flora, Fauna, Geologic Formation
Activities: Classes for adults & children; docent training; student guide prog; school conferences; lects open to pub, 10 vis lectrs per yr; concerts; tours; book traveling exhibs 6 per yr; originate traveling exhibs 6 per yr; sales shop sells books, original art, prints, crafts & t-shirts

National & Regional Organizations in Canada

O **ART DEALERS ASSOCIATION OF CANADA,** 401 Richmond St W, Unit 393 Toronto, ON M5V 3A8 Canada. Tel 416-934-1583; Fax 866-280-9432; Email info@ad-ac.ca; Web: www.ad-ac.ca; *Exec Dir* Elizabeth Edwards; *Appraisal Coordr* Melissa LaVallee
Open Mon - Fri 9 AM - 5 PM; Estab 1966 for the promotion of art & artists of merit in Canada; Mem: 70, mems must have five yrs in operation plus approved reputation, financial integrity; dues vary; ann meeting by board
Income: Financed by mem & appraisal fees
Publications: Benefits of donation brochure; gen information brochure; mem directory; print brochure
Activities: Schols offered

O **ASTED INC,** 2065 rue Parthenais, bureau 387, Montreal, QC H2K 3T1 Canada. Tel 514-281-5012; Fax 514-281-8219; Email info@asted.org; Web: www.asted.org; *Dir Gen* Lionel Villalonga
Estab 1974 for the professional development of French-speaking information & documentation specialists nationwide. Open Mon - Thurs 9 AM - 5 PM; Fri 9 AM - noon; Mem: 500; varies; Oct meetings
Income: financed by government assistance
Exhibitions: Ann exhibits
Publications: Dewey Decimal Classification, 21st French edition; Documentation et Bibliotheques, 4 times per yr
Activities: Schols offered; originate traveling exhibs

O **CANADIAN ART FOUNDATION,** 215 Spadina Ave, Ste 320 Toronto, ON M5T 2C7 Canada. Tel 416-368-8854; Fax 416-368-6135; Email info@canadianart.ca; Web: canadianart.ca; *Ed-in-Chf & Co-Publr* David Balzer; *Art Dir* Barbara Solowan; *Finance Dir* Alex Ivankine; *Assoc Ed* Leah Sandals; *Mng Ed* Bryne McLaughlin
Open Mon - Fri 9 AM - 5 PM; Estab 1984 as a charitable organization that fosters and supports the visual arts in Canada; Circ 22,000
Publications: Canadian Art, quarterly
Activities: Educ prog; school hop; lects open to pub 2-3 per yr, gallery talks, tours, sponsoring competitions; awards, writing prize

O **CANADIAN CONFERENCE OF THE ARTS,** 406-130 Slater St, Ottawa, ON K1P 6E2 Canada. Tel 613-238-3561; Fax 613-238-4849; Email info@ccarts.ca; Web: ccarts.ca; *Nat Dir* Alain Pineau; *Assoc Dir & Sr Policy Advisor* Anne-Marie Des Roches
Open 9 AM - 5 PM; No admis fee; Estab 1945 as a national nonprofit assoc to strengthen pub & pvt support to the arts & enhance the awareness of the role & value of the arts; Mem: 850; dues affiliate mem $2,205; patron $200; individual mem $50; friend $20; ann meeting June
Income: Financed by mem, grants & contracts
Publications: Blizzart, quarterly; Handbook Series: Directory of the Arts; Who Teaches What; policy papers & reports
Activities: Awards-Diplome d'Honneur to persons who have contributed outstanding service to the arts in Canada; Financial Post Awards: in collaboration with The Council for Business & the Arts in Canada, encourages the corporate sector's involvement with the visual & performing arts in Canada & recognizes those corporations whose involvement is already at a high & productive level; Rogers Communications Inc Media Award; Keith Kelly Award for Cultural Leadership; Diplôme d'honneur; Rogers Communications Inc Media Award for Coverage

O **CANADIAN MUSEUMS ASSOCIATION,** Association des Musees Canadiens, 280 Metcalfe St, Ste 400, Ottawa, ON K2P 1R7 Canada. Tel 613-567-0099; Fax 613-233-5438; Email info@museums.ca; Web: www.museums.ca; *Exec Dir & CEO* John G McAvity; *Finance Dir* Sue Lamothe; *Pres* Manon Blanchette
Estab 1947 to advance pub mus services in Canada, to promote the welfare & better admin of museums & to foster a continuing improvement in the qualifications & practices of mus professions; Mem: 2000; dues voting individual $85, senior $50; non-voting affiliate & foreign $100, corporate $250; ann meeting in Apr
Income: Financed by mem & government grants
Publications: Muse, bimonthly
Activities: Educ prog; professional develop activities; CMA Awards; bursary program; travel grants

O **CANADIAN SOCIETY FOR EDUCATION THROUGH ART,** National Office-University of Victoria, Faculty of Education, Dept of Curriculum & Instruction, PO Box 1700 STN CSC Victoria, BC V8W 2Y2 Canada. Tel 250-721-7896; Fax 250-721-7598; Email office.csea@gmail.com; Web: www.csea-scea.ca; *Secy Gen* Mary-Jane Emme; *Pres* Peter Vietgen
Estab 1955; voluntary assn founded in Quebec City. Mems dedicated to the advancement of art educ, the publication of current thinking & action in art educ & the promotion of higher standards in the teaching of art; Average Annual Attendance: 400; Mem: 700; dues professional $65 (CN); student/retired $30 (CN)
Income: Financed by mem
Collections: Historical Canadian Art, Children's Art
Publications: Canadian Review of Art Education, 1-2 times per ye; Journal, 1-2 times per yr; newsletter, quarterly; spec publs
Activities: Workshops; research; lect open to public; gallery talks; tours; awards; scholarships offered

O **CANADIAN SOCIETY OF PAINTERS IN WATERCOLOUR,** 80 Birmingham St, Unit B3, Toronto, ON M8V 3W6 Canada. Tel 416-533-5100; Email info@cspwc.com; Web: www.cspwc.com; *CSPWC Adminr* Anita Cotter
Admis assoc mem $35 ann; Estab 1925 to promote watercolour painting in Canada; AIRD Gallery, MacDonald Block, Queen's Park - shared on a rotating basis with five other societies; monthly exhibs; Mem: 260 & 175 assoc; dues $125; ann meeting in May. Mem qualifications: digital images sent to national mem comt (details listed on website)
Income: financed by mems dues, assoc, commissions on sale of work & book sales
Library Holdings: Clipping Files, Exhibition Catalogs, Memorabilia, Original Art Works, Photographs, Slides
Collections: Dipl Collection at Art Gallery of Peel, Brampton, Ontario, Portfolio of 75 works in collection of Her Majesty the Queen at Windsor Castle
Exhibitions: Annual Open Juried Exhibition; Members' Exhibitions; International Exchanges; International Waters with AWS & RWS
Publications: Aquarelle; Quarterly newsletter (quarterly)
Activities: Classes for adults; lect open to mems; competitions with awards; awards at ann open juried exhib, Open Water; originates traveling exhibs across Canada to galleries; internationally to fellow arts organizations; national watercolor weekend of demonstrations & discussions

O **ORGANIZATION OF SASKATCHEWAN ARTS COUNCILS (OSAC),** 1102 Eighth Ave, Regina, SK S4R 1C9 Canada. Tel 306-586-1250; Fax 306-586-1550; Email info@osac.sk.ca; Web: www.osac.sk.ca; *Exec Dir* Kevin Korchinski; *Visual & Media Arts Coordr* Zoe Schneider; *Opers Coodr* Catherine Tomczak; *Performing Arts Coordr* Skip Taylor; *Coordr Jr Concerts & Mem Liaison* Marinanne Woods
Open Mon - Fri 8:30 AM - 5 PM; Estab 1969 to tour exhibs of Saskatchewan artists work & tour performers from across Canada, US & of international stature; Organization that enables community arts councils & schools to tour & hold live musical & theatre performances, visual art exhibs, workshops & special events across Saskatchewan; Mem: 50 Arts Councils, 100 School Center members, ann conference in Oct
Library Holdings: Audio Tapes, Book Volumes 175, CD-ROMs, Cassettes, Clipping Files, Compact Disks, DVDs, Exhibition Catalogs, Kodachrome Transparencies, Manuscripts, Pamphlets, Periodical Subscriptions 10, Records, Reproductions, Slides, Video Tapes
Activities: Classes for adults & children; dramatic progs; docent training; lects open to pub; exten dept serves lending coll

O **QUICKDRAW ANIMATION SOCIETY,** 351 11th Ave SW, Ste 201, Calgary, AB T2R 0C7 Canada. Tel 403-261-5767; Fax 403-261-5644; Email info@quickdrawanimation.ca; Web: www.quickdrawanimation.ca; *Exec Dir* Pete Hemminger; *Programming Dir* Laura Leif; *Production Coordr* Tyler Klein Longmire; *Educ Coordr* Tanya Freed; *Librn* Jean-Francois Cote
Open Wed & Fri- Sat 10 AM - 5 PM; Wed & Thurs 10 AM - 7 PM; Estab 1984 to promote study of animation & provide equipment for the production of independent animated film; Mem: 150; dues subscription $15, assoc $25, Quick Kid $30, producing $50; ann meeting in Apr
Income: $150,000 from Federal, Provincial, municipal funding, mem fees, courses & workshop fees
Library Holdings: Book Volumes, Video Tapes
Exhibitions: Animated film festivals
Publications: Quickdraw Quarterly
Activities: Classes for adults; lects open to pub; Artist in Residence award; schols; lending coll contains books, videotapes, equipment for use in animated film production

O **ROYAL ARCHITECTURAL INSTITUTE OF CANADA,** 55 rue Murray St, Ste 330, Ottawa, ON K1N 5M3 Canada. Tel 613-241-3600; Fax 613-241-5750; Email info@raic.org; Web: www.raic.org; *Exec Dir* Jody Ciufo; *Dir Finance & Admin* Jonathan Ouellette
Open daily 8:30 AM - 5 PM, summer hours Fri 8:30 AM-12:30 PM; Estab 1908 to promote a knowledge & appreciation of architecture & of the architectural profession in Canada & to represent the interests of Canadian architects; Mem: 3800; mem open to architectural grads; dues $220
Publications: RAIC Directory, annually
Activities: Lect open to pub; awards given; schols offered

L **Library,** 55 Murray St, Ottawa, ON K1N 5M3 Canada. Tel 613-241-3600; Email info@raic.org; Web: www.raic.org; *Exec Asst* Judy Scott
Open daily 8:30 AM - 5 PM, summer hours Fri 8:30 AM - 12:30 PM; Estab for archival info only; Circ Non-circulating
Library Holdings: Book Volumes 200

Special Subjects: Architecture

O **ROYAL CANADIAN ACADEMY OF ARTS,** 401 Richmond St W, Ste 375, Toronto, ON M5V 3A8 Canada. Tel 416-408-2718; Fax 416-408-2286; Email rcaarts@interlog.com; Web: www.rca-arc.ca; *Exec Dir* Lina Jabra
Estab 1880 to better the visual arts field in Canada through exhibs, assistance to young artists & to museums; Mem: 700; honor soc; mem open to visual artists who demonstrated excellence in their own medium; dues $200; AGA ann meeting in May
Income: Nonprofit assoc financed by mem & donations
Exhibitions: Special exhibs of the History of the Royal Canadian Academy 1880-1980; national, multi-disciplined, juried exhib
Publications: Passionate Spirits: A History of the Royal Canadian Academy of Arts 1880-1980; Self Portrait Project
Activities: Originate traveling exhibs

O **SASKATCHEWAN ARTS BOARD,** 1355 Broad St, Regina, SK S4R 7V1 Canada. Tel 306-787-4056; Fax 306-787-4199; Email info@saskartsboard.sk.ca; Web: www.saskartsboard.sk.ca; *CEO* Michael Jones
Open Mon - Fri 8 AM - 4:30 PM; Estab 1948, the Arts Board is an arms-length agency of govt with a mandate to promote, support & facilitate public understanding, access to and participation in the arts, and to support the development of the Saskatchewan arts community and individual artists
Income: Financed by ann provincial government grant
Collections: Permanent Collection containing over 2500 works by Saskatchewan artists & artisans only, dating from 1950 to present
Exhibitions: Clearing a Path: An Exhibition of Traditional Indigenous Art
Publications: Ann Report; website; Business Development Plan; Saskatchewan... Our Place poster kit & teacher's guide
Activities: Grants are provided to individual artists, organizations, galleries and in support of project-based activity in Saskatchewan. The Arts Board is a critical advocacy organization for arts in the Saskatchewan; provides awards for outstanding achievement in the arts

O **SCULPTOR'S SOCIETY OF CANADA,** Canadian Sculpture Centre, 500 Church St, Toronto, ON M4Y 2C8 Canada. Tel 647-435-5858; Email gallery@cansculpt.org; Web: cansculpt.org; *Pres* Judi Michelle Young; *VPres & Gallery Co Dir* Richard McNeill; *Treas* J Young; *Secy* Marlene Kawalez
Open Tues - Fri noon - 6 PM, Sat 11 AM - 4 PM, cl holiday weekends; No admis fee; Estab 1928 to promote the art of sculpture, to present exhibs (some to travel internationally), to educate the pub about sculpture; 1000 sq ft exhib space; Average Annual Attendance: 2,500; Mem: 150; to qualify for mem, sculptors must submit CD of work for jury approval; dues $150; 2 general meetings per yr, exec comt meetings, 12 per yr
Income: Financed by mem & sales commission
Purchases: Ann selection comt (deadline Sep 15)
Library Holdings: CD-ROMs, Exhibition Catalogs, Pamphlets, Periodical Subscriptions
Exhibitions: Annual Graduating Students Juried Exhibition; Canadian National Exhibition; McMichael Canadian Collection; Member Show; Sculptures for the Eighties; 70th Anniversary Exhibition; Annual Emerging Artist Exhibition; Art of Collecting Exhibition
Publications: Exhibition catalogues
Activities: Workshops; lects open to pub; gallery talks; tours; 4-6 vis lectrs per yr; competitions with awards of student exhibs, A&M Green FDN Award, Artcast Inc Award, & MST Bronze LTD Award; originate traveling exhibs to international cultural centres, embassy galleries; sculpture gallery sells books & original art

O **SOCIETY OF CANADIAN ARTISTS,** c/o 24 Lorindale Ave Toronto, ON M5M 3C2 Canada. Email info@societyofcanadianartists.com; Web: www.societyofcanadianartists.com; *Pres* Ortansa Moraru
Estab in 1957 as the Soc of Cooperative Artists & operated the first cooperative gallery in Toronto. In 1967 the name was changed to the Soc of Canadian Artists, registered as a nonprofit organization in 2007; Mem: 270, elected mem by jury, assoc mem open to artists throughout Canada
Income: Financed by mem & commissions on sale
Exhibitions: 2 shows per yr, open juried & mem only
Publications: Quarterly newsletter, exhib catalogues
Activities: Sponsorship of art conferences & workshops; promotion of Canadian artists

Canadian Museums, Libraries & Associations

ALBERTA

BANFF

M **BANFF CENTRE,** Walter Phillips Gallery, 107 Tunnel Mountain Dr, Banff, AB T1L 1H5 Canada; PO Box 1020, Banff, AB T1L 1H5 Canada. Tel 403-762-6100; Fax 403-762-6659; Email walter_phillipsgallery@banffcentre.ca; Web: www.banffcentre.ca/wpg; *Pres & CEO* Janice Price; *VPres Admin & CFO* Bruce Byford
Open Wed - Sun 12:30 PM - 5 PM; No admis fee; Estab 1977 to serve the community & artists in the visual arts prog at The Banff Centre, School of Fine Arts. Contemporary exhibits are presented; Gallery is 15.24 x 21.34 m with 325.5 sq m of running space; Average Annual Attendance: 20,000
Income: Financed by provincial & pub funding
Collections: Walter J Phillips Collection
Publications: Exhib catalogs
Activities: Lect open to pub; concerts; gallery talks; tours; original objects of art lent to other galleries & museums; book traveling exhibs 1 per yr; originate traveling exhibs to Canadian & international galleries; mus shop sells books & original art

L **Paul D Fleck Library & Archives**, 107 Tunnel Mountain Dr, Box 1020, Sta 43 Banff, AB T1L 1H5 Canada. Tel 403-762-6265; Fax 403-762-6266; Email library@banffcentre.ca; *Prog Mgr* Laurie Edward
Open Mon - Thurs 9 AM - 8 PM, Sun 11 AM - 7 PM; Estab 1979; For reference only
Library Holdings: Book Volumes 32,000, CD-ROMs, Cassettes, Compact Disks, DVDs, Exhibition Catalogs, Fiche, Motion Pictures, Periodical Subscriptions 125, Records 12,000, Slides 27,000, Video Tapes 1100
Special Subjects: Aesthetics, Architecture, Art Education, Conceptual Art, Costume Design & Constr, Film, Furniture, Intermedia, Painting-American, Painting-Canadian, Photography, Pottery, Primitive art

M **PETER & CATHARINE WHYTE FOUNDATION,** Whyte Museum of the Canadian Rockies, PO Box 160, 111 Bear St Banff, AB T1L 1A3 Canada. Tel 403-762-2291; Fax 403-762-8919; Email info@whyte.org; Web: www.whyte.org; *Treas* Dan Marinangeli; *Cur Art & Heritage* Anne Ewen
Open daily 10 AM - 5 PM, cl Christmas & New Year's Day; Admis adult $8, students & locals $4, children under 12 & mus mems free; Acquires, preserves, interprets & makes accessible the history & culture of the Rocky Mountains of Canada inspiring & cultivating the exchange of knowledge & ideas through our collections, programs & exhibitions; Gallery consists of the Main Gallery, Rummel Room & Swiss Guides Room; Average Annual Attendance: 50,000; Mem: 600; dues $30
Income: Financed by endowment, federal & provincial special activities grants, pvt funding, admis & sales
Special Subjects: Historical Material, Manuscripts, Maps, Photography, Painting-Canadian, Prints, Sculpture, Textiles, Watercolors, Woodcuts
Collections: Historical & contemporary art by artists of the Canadian Rockies, Cultural history colls of Canadian Rockies
Exhibitions: Visit www.whyte.org for upcoming exhibs
Publications: The Cairn, biannually; Calendar of Events
Activities: Classes for adults & children; lects open to pub, 20 vis lectrs per yr; concerts; gallery talks; tours; films; individual paintings & original objects of art lent to cert mus & art galleries; book traveling exhibs; originate traveling exhibs to other cert mus & art galleries; mus shop sells books, original art, reproductions & prints

CALGARY

M **ALBERTA COLLEGE OF ART & DESIGN,** Illingworth Kerr Gallery, 1407 14th Ave NW, Calgary, AB T2N 4R3 Canada. Tel 403-284-7633; Fax 403-289-6682; Email admissions@acad.ca; Web: www.acad.ca; *Acad Admin Coord* Cassandra Paul; *Technician* Ann Thrale
Open Tues Weds Fri 12 PM - 6 PM, Thurs 12 PM - 8 PM, Sat 12 PM - 4 PM; No admis fee; Estab 1958 as an acad didactic function plus general visual art exhib service to pub; Two galleries: 425 sq meters of floor space; 125 meters running wall space; full atmospheric & security controls; Average Annual Attendance: 20,000
Library Holdings: Book Volumes 35,645, Clipping Files, DVDs 1,052, Other Holdings Digital Images 40,000
Special Subjects: Ceramics, Graphics, Jewelry, Photography, Sculpture
Collections: Permanent collection of ceramics, graphics, paintings, photography, student honors work
Exhibitions: Contemporary art in all media by regional, national & international artists
Publications: Exhib catalogs; posters
Activities: Lects open to pub, 20 vis lectrs per yr; gallery talks; individual paintings & objects of art lent to other galleries; lending coll contains original art works; book traveling exhibs 3-4 per yr

L **Luke Lindoe Library**, 1407 14th Ave NW, Calgary, AB T2N 4R3 Canada. Tel 403-284-7667; Fax 403-289-6682; Email library@acad.ca; Web: www.acad.ab.ca; *Librn* Rene Martin
Open Mon - Thurs 8:30 AM - 8 PM, Fri 8:30 AM - 4:30 PM, Sat 11 AM - 5 PM; Estab 1926; Circ 27,836; Average Annual Attendance: 57,646; Mem: $25 ann fee for community borrowers
Purchases: $85,000
Library Holdings: Book Volumes 35,645, Clipping Files, DVDs 1,052, Exhibition Catalogs, Other Holdings Digital Images: 40,000, Periodical Subscriptions 111
Special Subjects: Advertising Design, Aesthetics, Antiquities-Assyrian, Architecture, Art Education, Art History, Commercial Art, Drawings, Etchings & Engravings, Glass, Goldsmithing, Illustration, Metalwork, Painting-American, Photography

A **ALBERTA SOCIETY OF ARTISTS,** #305-1235 26th Ave SE, Calgary, AB T2G 1R7 Canada. Tel 403-265-0012; Fax 403-263-4610; Email coordinator@albertasocietyofartists.com; Web: www.albertasocietyofartists.com; *Pres* Mali Docktorpresident@albertasocietyofartists.com
Estab 1926 as an assn of professional artists designed to foster and promote the development of visual and plastic fine arts primarily within the province; Mem: Approx 250; dues $60 each yr; AGM: Apr. New members are juried in annually based on slides or digital images of artwork
Exhibitions: Exhib organized annually by provincial & the Calgary & Edmonton branch
Publications: Highlights (newsletter), bimonthly
Activities: Through exhib, educ & commun, the ASA strives to increase pub awareness & appreciation of the visual arts in Alberta; classes for adults; lects open to pub 8 vis lectrs per yr; scholarships; originates traveling exhibs to art galleries in Alberta & other regions of Canada

L **CALGARY PUBLIC LIBRARY,** Arts & Recreation Dept, 616 Macleod Trail SE, Calgary, AB T2G 2M2 Canada. Tel 403-260-2600; Fax 403-262-5929; Email arts&rec@calgarypubliclibrary.com; Web: www.calgarylibrary.ca; *CEO* Bill Ptacek
Open Mon - Thurs 9AM - 8PM, Fri 9 AM - 5 PM, Sat 10 - 5 PM, Sun cl; No admis fee; Estab to provide information & recreational materials for the gen pub
Purchases: $70,000 Canadian
Library Holdings: Book Volumes 85,000, Clipping Files, Compact Disks, DVDs, Exhibition Catalogs, Periodical Subscriptions 250, Records, Video Tapes
Special Subjects: American Indian Art, American Western Art, Architecture, Art History, Crafts, Fashion Arts, Film, Graphic Arts, Painting-Canadian, Photography, Theatre Arts, Video
Collections: Clipping files on local artists
Exhibitions: Rotating exhibit cases

M **CONTEMPORARY CALGARY,** 117 8th Ave SW, Calgary, AB T2P 1B4 Canada. Tel 403-770-1350; Fax 403-264-8077; Email info@contemporarycalgary.com; Web: www.contemporarycalgary.com; *Dir & CEO* Pierre Arpin; *Sr Cur* Lisa Baldissera
Open Weds - Sun noon - 6 PM; cl Mon - Tues; Admis adults $5, student, youth & senior $2.50, under 12 free; Estab 1978 to exhibit the works of emerging & estab western Canadian artists; Top floor of the restored Memorial Park Library (old Carnegie Library); Average Annual Attendance: 90,000; Mem: 500; dues family $30, individual $20, students & srs $15; ann meeting in Apr
Income: $550,000 (financed by mem, city & provincial appropriation, grants, pvt donations & corporate funds)
Special Subjects: Architecture, Carpets & Rugs, Ceramics, Collages, Drawings, Etchings & Engravings, Folk Art, Furniture, Glass, Gold, Graphics, Jewelry, Juvenile Art, Landscapes, Metalwork
Publications: Quarterly exhibit catalogues; quarterly newsletter; semiannual exhibition brochures
Activities: Classes for adults & children; professional develop; lects open to pub, 10 vis lectrs per yr; gallery talks; tours; family days; art appreciation club; exten dept serves city of Calgary; book traveling exhibs 6 per yr; originate traveling exhibs to Southern Alberta; sales shop sells books, t-shirts & cards

M **GLENBOW MUSEUM,** 130 Ninth Ave SE, Calgary, AB T2G 0P3 Canada. Tel 403-268-4100; Fax 403-265-9769; Email glenbow@glenbow.org; Web: www.glenbow.org; *Pres & CEO* Donna Livingstone
Open Tues - Sat 9 AM - 5 PM, Sun noon - 5 PM, Cl Mon; Admis family $40, adults $16, senior & students (with ID) $11, youth (7-17) $10, under 6 & mems free; Estab 1966 for art, books, documents, Indian & pioneer artifacts that lead to the preservation & better understanding of the history of western Canada; Circ 90; Mus has three exhib floors; 93,000 sq ft of exhib space; Average Annual Attendance: 200,000; Mem: 5000; dues family $90, $160/2 yrs, individual $55, $100/2 yrs, student $35, $60/2 yrs

Income: $10,300 (financed by endowment, provincial & federal appropriation, self-generated revenue)
Purchases: $100,000
Special Subjects: Historical Material
Collections: Art: Representative colls of Canadian historical & contemporary art, Indian & Inuit, & works of art on paper, Ethnology: Large coll of material relating to Plains Indians, representative holdings from Africa, Australia, Oceania, Central & South America, Inuit & Northwest Coast, Library & Archives: Western Canadian historical books, manuscripts & photographs, Military history, Cultural History
Publications: Chautauqua in Canada; Max Ernst; Four Modern Masters; exhib catalogs
Activities: Classes for adults & children; dramatic progs; docent training; lect open to pub; gallery talks; tours; exten dept; individual paintings & original objects of art lent to pub museums & galleries; lending coll contains 15,000 works on paper, 5000 paintings, sculpture & 5000 items of decorative art; book traveling exhibs 25 per yr; originate traveling exhibs; mus shop sells books, magazines, reproductions & prints

L **Library**, 130 - 9 Ninth Ave SE, Calgary, AB T2G 0P3 Canada. Tel 403-268-4197; Fax 403-232-6569; Email library@glenbow.org; Web: www.glenbow.org; *Librn* Lindsay Moir; *Archivist* Doug Cass
Open Tues - Thurs 10 AM - 4:30 PM; cl Fri - Mon; Circ Non-circulating; Open for reference
Income: Financed by endowment & government of Alberta
Library Holdings: Auction Catalogs, Book Volumes 90,000, CD-ROMs, Cards, Clipping Files, Exhibition Catalogs, Fiche, Manuscripts, Maps, Pamphlets, Periodical Subscriptions 100, Photographs, Reels
Special Subjects: Illustration, Manuscripts, Maps, Painting-British, Painting-Canadian, Printmaking, Prints, Textiles
Collections: Western Canadian Art, Historic Canadian Art

M **MOUNT ROYAL COLLEGE GALLERY,** 4825 Mount Royal Gate SW, Calgary, AB T3E 6K6 Canada. Tel 403-440-6111

QUICKDRAW ANIMATION SOCIETY
For further information, see National and Regional Organizations

A **TRUCK CONTEMPORARY ART IN CALGARY,** 2009 10th Ave SW, Calgary, AB T3C 0K4 Canada. Tel 403-261-7702; Fax 403-264-7737; Email info@truck.ca; Web: www.truck.ca; *Exec Dir* Ginger Carlson; *Prog Coordr* Brian Wennerstrom
Open Tues - Fri 11 AM - 5 PM, Sat noon - 5 PM, Sun - Mon cl; No admis fee

M **UNIVERSITY OF CALGARY,** Nickle Galleries, 2500 University Dr NW, Calgary, AB T2N 1N4 Canada. Tel 403-210-6201; Fax 403-282-4742; Email nickle@ucalgary.ca; Web: nickle.ucalgary.ca; *Cur* Michele Hardy; *Chief Cur* Christine Sowiak; *Registrar* Lisa Tillotson
Sept - April: Open Mon - Fri 10 AM - 5 PM, Thurs 10 AM - 8 PM, Sat 11 AM - 4 PM, Sun cl May - Aug: Mon - Fri 10 AM - 5 PM Sat - Sun cl; No admis fee; Estab 1970, an Alberta pioneer, Samuel C Nickle, gave the University a gift of one million dollars & the mus was opened in 1979. His son, Carl O Nickle, presented the University with an immensely valuable coll of some 10,000 ancient coins, covering over 2500 yrs of human history which is housed in the Numismatics dept of the mus; Circ yes; Mus houses the permanent collection of the University; exhibs of art, numismatics and textiles are presented on a temporary basis in 3 galleries.; Average Annual Attendance: 15,000; Mem: 250; dues $10 - $40
Income: Financed by state appropriation through the University, donations, earned income & grants
Purchases: $100,000
Library Holdings: Book Volumes 200
Special Subjects: Carpets & Rugs, Coins & Medals, Drawings, Painting-Canadian, Photography, Prints, Sculpture, Textiles, Watercolors, Ceramics
Collections: Coins & bills covering 2500 years of Human History, Jean & Marie Erikson Rug & Textile Collection, Modern Contemporary Western Canadian Art
Exhibitions: Local, national & international exhibs are presented on a continuous basis
Publications: Exhib catalogs
Activities: Liaise with faculties at universities; lects open to pub, 10-20 vis lectrs per yr; gallery talks; tours; individual paintings & original objects of art lent to other museums & art galleries; book traveling exhibs 2 per yr; originate traveling exhibs to Canadian mus; mus shop sells books, jewelry & other gift items

L **Faculty of Environmental Design**, 2500 University Dr NW, Rm 2182 Calgary, AB T2N 1N4 Canada. Tel 403-220-6601; Fax 403-284-4399; Email evdsinfo@ucalgary.ca; Web: evds.ucalgary.ca; *Interim Dean* John Brown, PhD
Open Mon - Fri 9:30 AM - 4:30 PM; No admis fee; Estab 1973 as a resource facility for students & faculty in 5 prog areas: architecture, urban planning, industrial design, environmental science & environmental design; Small gallery for display of student works & traveling exhibs; workshop; photo lab facilities
Library Holdings: Audio Tapes, Book Volumes 500, Cassettes, Manuscripts, Memorabilia, Other Holdings Drawings; Models, Periodical Subscriptions 30, Slides, Video Tapes
Special Subjects: Architecture, Interior Design, Industrial Design

CZAR

M **SHORNCLIFFE PARK IMPROVEMENT ASSOC,** Prairie Panorama Museum, PO Box 60, Czar, AB T0B 0Z0 Canada. Tel 780-857-2435; Email caretaker@shorncliffepark.com; Web: www.shorncliffepark.com
Open Sun 2 - 6 PM, other days by appointment; No admis fee; Estab 1963 for the enjoyment of the pub; Average Annual Attendance: 580
Income: Finances by government grant & donations
Collections: Indian artifacts, clothing, tools, dolls, books, Salt & Pepper Coll, Two 1926 coffeemakers, homemade snowshoes (1920), Cajun accordion
Activities: Classes for children

EDMONTON

A **ALBERTA CRAFT COUNCIL,** 10186 106th St, Edmonton, AB T5J 1H4 Canada. Tel 780-488-6611; Fax 780-488-8855; Email acc@albertacraft.ab.ca; Web: www.albertacraft.ab.ca; *Exec Dir* Barry Moss
Open Mon - Sat 10 AM - 5 PM, Thurs 10 AM - 6 PM; cl Sun & holidays; No admis fee; Estab 1980 to promote craft; Gallery exhibits 12 shows per yr of craft in these 5 media: clay, glass, wood, metal & fiber; Mem: Dues vary
Income: Financed by mem
Exhibitions: 12 shows per yr
Publications: Alberta Craft Magazine, 4 per year
Activities: Annual Alberta Craft Council Awards; book traveling exhibs 1 per yr; originate traveling exhibs 1 every 4 yrs circulating nationally & internationally; sales shop sells crafts

A **ALBERTA FOUNDATION FOR THE ARTS,** 10708 105 Ave, Edmonton, AB T5H 0A1 Canada. Tel 780-427-9968; Email afacontact@gov.ab.ca; Web: www.affta.ab.ca; *Dir Arts Servs* Paul Pearson; *Exec Dir* Jeff Brinton
Open Mon - Fri 8:15 AM - 4:30 PM; No admis fee; Estab 1972 to collect & to exhibit art works produced by Alberta artists; to provide financial assistance to Alberta pub, institutional & commercial art galleries, art groups & organizations for progs & special projects; to assist other galleries in Edmonton
Income: Financed by Alberta Lotteries
Collections: Alberta Foundation for the Arts Collection
Exhibitions: Exhibits are provided through a consortium of Alberta pub galleries. The progs vary from yr to yr & from region to region; Spaces & Places; Little by Little
Publications: Ann Report; exhib catalogs
Activities: Acquisition of art works by Alberta artists; exhib prog in and outside Canada; Jon Whyte Memorial Prize, Tommy Banks Award; scholarships & fels offered; individual paintings & original objects of art lent to pub government buildings; book traveling exhibs; sales shop sells books

M **ART GALLERY OF ALBERTA,** 2 Sir Winston Churchill Sq, Edmonton, AB T5J 2C1 Canada. Tel 780-425-5379; Email info@youraga.ca; Web: www.youraga.ca; *Exec Dir & Chief Cur* Catherine Crowston; *Exec Admin* Gianmarco Visconti; *Curatorial Admin & Interpretation* Leonore-Namkha Beschi; *Head Preparator* Dani Rice; *Dep Dir & Head Finance & Admin* Pedro Carriel
Open Tues - Wed 11 AM - 8 PM, Thurs - Fri 11 AM - 5 PM, Sat - Sun 10 AM - 5 PM, cl Mon; Admis adults $12.50, seniors (65+) & students $8.50, mems & youth (0-17) free; Estab 1924 to collect & exhibit paintings, sculptures, photographs & other works of visual art & to teach art appreciation; Gallery covers 80,000 sq ft; exhibition area 30,000 sq ft; Average Annual Attendance: 100,000 (est)
Special Subjects: Painting-American, Painting-Canadian, Painting-European, Photography, Portraits, Religious Art, Sculpture, Watercolors, Woodcuts
Collections: Contemporary Canadian art, contemporary & historical photography, contemporary international art, historical Canadian art, historical European & American art
Exhibitions: 29 in-house exhibitions & 23 extension shows
Publications: Take part magazine, 3 times per yr; exhibition catalogues
Activities: Classes for adults & children; lects open to pub; lects for mems only; gallery talks & tours; 8 vis lectrs per yr; concerts; book traveling exhibs; originate traveling exhibs; mus shop; junior mus called The Children's Gallery

A **LATITUDE 53 CONTEMPORARY VISUAL CULTURE,** 10248 106th St, Edmonton, AB T5J 1H7 Canada. Tel 780-423-5353; Fax 780-424-9117; Email info@latitude53.org; Web: www.latitude53.org; *Exec Dir* Todd Janes; *Develop Coordr* Sarah Edwards
Open Tues - Fri 11 AM - 7 PM, Sat 11 AM - 5 PM, cl Sun & Mon; No admis fee; Estab 1973 to encourage & promote the artistic endeavours of contemporary artists & to build a pub awareness of current & experimental cultural developments; Visual, installations, performance & video. Resource center for grants & contracts; Average Annual Attendance: 26,000; Mem: 300; dues $25; ann meeting third Mon in Oct
Income: $300,000 (financed by grants, donations, pub & pvt funding, mem & fundraising events)
Library Holdings: Cassettes, Clipping Files, Exhibition Catalogs, Periodical Subscriptions
Publications: Exhib catalogues
Activities: Lects open to pub, 9 vis lectrs per yr; concerts; gallery talks & tours; discussion groups; performance art festival; pub art projects; book traveling exhibs 10 per yr; originate traveling exhibs for other art centers; sales shop sells books, magazines

M **ROYAL ALBERTA MUSEUM,** Royal Alberta Museum, 12845 102nd Ave, Edmonton, AB T5N 0M6 Canada. Tel 780-453-9100; Fax 780-454-6629; Web: www.royalalbertamuseum.ca; *Exec Dir* Chris Robinson; *Dir Coll Servs* Michael Luchanski; *Dir Visitor Experience* Karen Jensen; *Dir Bus Opers* Jayne Custance; *Dir Capital Devel* Tom Thurston
Open daily 9 AM - 5 PM; Admis families $30, adults $11, sr 65+ $8, student with ID $7, youth (7-17) $5, under 6 free; Estab 1967 to preserve & interpret the human & natural history of the Alberta region; Four major exhibit areas divided equally into human & natural history under broad themes of settlement history, archaeology & anthropology, natural history & habitats; Average Annual Attendance: 200,000 - 250,000; Mem: 1200; dues $12 - $19; ann meeting in June
Income: $5,154,000 (financed by provincial government, mus shop, facility rentals, progs, special exhibits & admis)
Library Holdings: Auction Catalogs, Audio Tapes, Book Volumes, CD-ROMs, Cassettes, Clipping Files, Compact Disks, DVDs, Exhibition Catalogs, Fiche, Framed Reproductions, Lantern Slides, Maps, Memorabilia, Original Art Works, Original Documents, Pamphlets, Periodical Subscriptions, Photographs, Prints, Records, Reels, Reproductions, Sculpture, Slides, Video Tapes
Special Subjects: Archaeology, Coins & Medals, Decorative Arts, Dioramas, Dolls, Embroidery, Eskimo Art, Ethnology, Folk Art, Furniture, Historical Material, Jewelry
Collections: Archaeological, ethnographical, fine & decorative arts, folk life, geology, historical, invertebrate zoology, mammalogy, palaeontology, ornithology:

vascular & non vascular plants, ichthyology & herpetology, military & political history, pollen & seeds, numismatics
Exhibitions: Approx 10 feature exhibits
Publications: Occasional papers; occasional series; publ series; exhibit catalogs; teacher guides
Activities: Classes for children; dramatic progs; docent training; lects open to pub, 6-20 vis lectrs per yr; gallery talks; tours; concerts; schols offered; exten dept serves western Canada; individual paintings & original objects of art lent to other museums; outreach sr program; loans artifacts & specimens to pub & educational facilities; book traveling exhibs 5 times per yr; originate traveling exhibs to mems of Alberta Exhibit Network; other museums in Canada; mus shop sells books, children's articles, jewelry, logo pins, original art, reproductions, prints, slides & t-shirts

L **Provincial Archives of Alberta**, 8555 Roper Rd, Edmonton, AB T6E 5W1 Canada. Tel 780-427-1750; Fax 780-427-4646; Email paa@gov.ab.ca; Web: www.culture.alberta.ca/paa/; *Pres* Lauren Wheeler; *FOIP Officer* Laurette Miller; *Team Leader Private Records* Tom Anderson; *Team Leader Government Records* Glynys Hohmann
Open Tues - Sat 9 AM - 4:30 PM, Wed evening until 9 PM, cl Sun - Mon; Estab 1967 to identify, evaluate, acquire, preserve, arrange & describe & subsequently make available for pub research, reference & display those diversified primary & secondary sources that document & relate to the overall history & develop of Alberta; Small gallery which rotates 3-4 exhibs per yr; Average Annual Attendance: 8,000
Income: Financed by provincial appropriation
Library Holdings: Audio Tapes, Book Volumes 10,000, Cassettes, Clipping Files, Fiche, Manuscripts, Motion Pictures, Original Art Works, Other Holdings Original documents, Pamphlets, Periodical Subscriptions 100, Photographs, Prints, Records, Reels, Slides
Collections: Includes: government & private textual records; maps, plans & drawings; photographs; audiovisual images; 14,000+ vol reference library
Exhibitions: Several small displays each year highlighting recent accessions or historical themes; periodic major exhibs
Publications: Exhib catalogues; guides to colls; information leaflets; occasional papers
Activities: Lects open to pub; organize traveling exhibs via the Alberta Trex travelling exhibs prog to schools, libraries & other small venues throughout the province; sales shop sells books, reproductions, prints & archival presentation products

M **UKRAINIAN CANADIAN ARCHIVES & MUSEUM OF ALBERTA,** 9543 110th Ave, Edmonton, AB T5H 1H3 Canada. Tel 780-424-7580; Fax 780-420-5062; Email ucama@shaw.ca; Web: www.ucama.com; *Pres* Paul Teterenko; *1st VP* Nestor Makuch; *2nd VP* Khrystia Kohut
Open Tues - Fri 10 AM - 5 PM, Sat Noon - 5 PM, cl Sun & Mon; Admis $5; Estab 1972; 3 stories, library & mus; Mem: Dues family $40, individual $25
Income: Financed by mem, donations & casinos
Special Subjects: Crafts, Historical Material, Carpets & Rugs, Ceramics, Costumes, Decorative Arts, Dolls, Embroidery, Folk Art, Furniture, Landscapes, Photography, Portraits, Posters, Pottery, Prints, Religious Art, Textiles, Watercolors, Woodcuts
Collections: Drawings, historical material, national costumes, paintings, prints, sculpture & textiles
Activities: Guided tours; displays

M **WHERE EDMONTON COMMUNITY ARTISTS NETWORK SOCIETY,** Harcourt House Arts Centre, 10215 112 St, 3rd Fl Edmonton, AB T5K 1M7 Canada. Tel 780-426-4180; Fax 780-425-5523; Email harcourt@telusplanet.net; Web: www.harcourthouse.ab.ca; *Exec Dir* Jacek Malec; *Gallery Servs Adminr* Hadeel Othman
Open Tues - Sat 10 AM - 5 PM, cl Sun & Mon; No admis fee; Estab 1988; A not-for-profit arts center which includes a pub gallery, art educ prog, & artists' studios. Two gallery spaces include the main space local, national, international (828.5 sq ft) & front room space (536.5 sq ft) for mems & local artists to display their work, open to Alberta, Canada venues only; Average Annual Attendance: 8,000; Mem: 300; dues $25; ann meeting in Apr
Income: Financed by mem, city & state appropriations
Exhibitions: Rotating exhibits
Publications: Harcourt Expressed, quarterly
Activities: Classes for adults & children; lects open to pub, 6 vis lectrs per yr; originate traveling exhibs 8 per yr

GRANDE PRAIRIE

M **THE ART GALLERY OF GRAND PRAIRIE,** 9839-103 Ave, Grande Prairie, AB T8V 6M7 Canada. Tel 780-532-8111; Fax 780-539-9522; Email info@aggp.ca; Web: www.aggp.ca; *Exec Dir* Jeff Erbach; *Mgr & Cur Traveling Exhibs* Todd Schaber; *Cur Learning* Sabine Schneider
Open Mon - Wed 10 AM - 6 PM, Thurs 10 AM - 9 PM, Fri & Sat 10 AM - 5 PM, Sun 1 - 5 PM; No admis fee; Estab 1975 as a pub art mus; Maintains reference library; Average Annual Attendance: 54,000; Mem: 300; dues $40
Income: $700,000 (financed by mem, city appropriation, provincial & federal government grants)
Special Subjects: Cartoons, Decorative Arts, Folk Art, Historical Material, Painting-American, Painting-Canadian, Painting-Dutch, Painting-European, Painting-Flemish, Painting-French, Painting-German, Painting-New Zealand, Painting-Spanish
Collections: Alberta Art, Contemporary Western Canadian Art
Exhibitions: 6 - 8 per yr
Publications: 3-6 per yr
Activities: Classes for adults & children; lects open to pub, 3-6 vis lectrs per yr; tours; Euphemia McNaught Award; Evy McBryan Award; schols offered; extension prog serves Northwestern Alberta; book traveling exhibs 1-2 per yr; originate traveling exhibs to remote & rural communities in Northwestern Alberta

LETHBRIDGE

A **ALLIED ARTS COUNCIL OF LETHBRIDGE,** Bowman Arts Center, 318 7 St S, Lethbridge, AB T1J 2G2 Canada. Tel 403-320-0555; Fax 403-320-2450; Email info@artslethbridge.org; Web: www.artslethbridge.org; *Exec Dir* Suzanne Lint; *Gallery Svcs Coordr* Darcy Logan; *Asst to Dir* Dawn Leite
Open Mon - Fri 9 AM - 5 PM; No admis fee; Estab 1958 to encourage & foster cultural activities in Lethbridge, to provide facilities for such cultural activities & to promote the work of Alberta & western Canadian artists; Average Annual Attendance: 20,000; Mem: 300; dues $25, ann meeting in Feb
Income: $67,000 (financed by mem & city appropriation, Alberta Culture granting & fundraising)
Exhibitions: Local & regional exhibs: Children's art, fabric makers, painters, potters; one-man shows: Paintings, photography, prints, sculpture, silversmithing; provincial government traveling exhibits
Publications: Calendar of Arts, weekly
Activities: Classes for adults & children; dramatic progs; concerts; competitions; schols offered; originates traveling exhibs; sales shop sells original art

M **CITY OF LETHBRIDGE,** Sir Alexander Galt Museum, 502 First St S, Lethbridge, AB T1J 0P6 Canada; 910 Fourth Ave S, Lethbridge, AB T1J 0P6 Canada. Tel 403-320-3898 (mus), 329-7302 (archives); Email info@galtmuseum.com; Web: www.galtmuseum.com; *Exhibit Designer* Brad Brown; *Exec Dir & CEO* Susan Burrows-Johnson; *Cur* Aimee Benoit; *Archivist* Andrew Chemevych; *Media & Communs* Dana Inkster; *Opers Mgr & Finance* Evelyn Yackulic; *Visitor Svcs Coord* Michelle Christensen
Open Mon - Sat 10 AM - 5 PM, Thurs 10 AM - 9 PM, Sun & holidays 1 - 5 PM; Admis families $15, adults $6, seniors & groups of 10+ $5 per person, youth (7-17) $3, children under 6 free; Estab 1964 to promote the study of human history in southern Alberta; Five Galleries; One gallery is for community use; 800 sq ft & 100 ft running wall space; Average Annual Attendance: 25,000
Income: $247,000
Collections: Historical artifact coll, Archives Coll: photos, manuscripts, books, tapes, films
Exhibitions: Rotate 6-8 exhibits per yr
Activities: Children's classes; docent progs; lects open to pub, 10 vis lectrs per yr; tours; book traveling exhibs 8 per yr; originate traveling exhibs to area schools, institutions, fairs; mus shop sells books & locally handcrafted items

L **LETHBRIDGE PUBLIC LIBRARY,** Art Gallery, 810 Fifth Ave S, Lethbridge, AB T1J 4C4 Canada. Tel 403-380-7310; Fax 403-329-1478; Email questions@lethlib.ca; Web: www.lethbridgepubliclibrary.ca; *Dir* Liz Rossnagel
Open Wed 9:30 AM - 9 PM; hours vary other days see website; No admis fee; Estab 1974 to expand human experience, to encourage people to look at art as well as read & attend library progs; Gallery 900 sq ft wall space for each exhibit, 110 linear ft wall space; Average Annual Attendance: 8,000
Income: Financed by city appropriations
Library Holdings: Book Volumes 193,243, Periodical Subscriptions 500
Activities: Lects open to pub, 8-10 vis lectrs per yr; tours; lending coll contains 250,000 books, 250,000 cassettes, CDs & talking books; book traveling exhibs 6 per yr; originate traveling exhibs

M **SOUTHERN ALBERTA ART GALLERY,** 601 Third Ave S, Lethbridge, AB T1J 0H4 Canada. Tel 403-327-8770; Fax 403-328-3913; Email info@saag.ca; Web: www.saag.ca; *Assoc Dir* Danielle Tait; *Admin Coordr* Jessica Humphries; *Communs Coordr* Nicole Hembroff; *Dir & Cur* Ryan Doherty
Open Tues & Weds 10 AM - 5 PM, Thurs, 10 AM - 7 PM, Fri & Sat 10 AM - 5 PM, Sun 1 - 5 PM, cl Mon; Admis adults $5, student & senior $4, under 12, mem & Sun free; Estab 1976 to present historical & contemporary art programs designed to further the process of art appreciation; Three gallery spaces contained in historical Lethbridge building remodeled as art gallery; Average Annual Attendance: 30,000; Mem: 325; dues family $35, single $20, artist & student $10; ann meeting in Feb
Income: Financed by mem, city, provincial & federal appropriation
Collections: Donald Buchanan Art Collection of City of Lethbridge containing mid-20th Century Canadian work & various international pieces
Exhibitions: Historical and contemporary art changing monthly
Publications: Exhib catalogues; quarterly newsletter
Activities: Classes for children; docent training; professional development series; lects open to pub, numerous vis lectrs per yr; gallery talks; tours; artmobile; originate traveling exhibs; sales shop sells magazines & reproductions

L **Library**, 601 Third Ave S, Lethbridge, AB T1J 0H4 Canada. Tel 403-327-8770; Fax 403-328-3913; Web: www.saag.ca; *Librn* Joseph Anderson; *Asst Cur* David Diviney; *Dir* Marilyn Smith; *Cur* Joan Stebbins; *Head Pub Rels* Anine Vonkeman; *Develop Mgr* Karin Champion; *Educ Coordr* Marsha Reich; *Visitors Svcs Mgr* Sue Black; *Librn* Elspeth Nickle
Open Tues - Sat 10 AM - 5 PM, Sun 1 - 5 PM; No admis fee; Estab 1976; Contemporary pub art gallery; Average Annual Attendance: 32,000; Mem: 400+ mem
Library Holdings: Audio Tapes, Book Volumes 4000, Cassettes, Clipping Files, Exhibition Catalogs, Filmstrips, Manuscripts, Pamphlets 3200, Periodical Subscriptions 12, Reproductions, Slides, Video Tapes
Exhibitions: 15 exhibs annually
Publications: 6-8 publs annually
Activities: Classes for adults & children; lects open to pub, 25 - 30 vis lectrs per yr; concerts; gallery talks; tours; video competitions; exten dept serves southern & central Alberta; lending collection contains 520 books, 22 cassettes, 56 videos (in house viewing only); book traveling exhibs; originate traveling exhibs; sales shop sells books, magazines, original art, prints & reproductions

M **UNIVERSITY OF LETHBRIDGE,** Art Gallery, 4401 University Dr, W600, Centre for the Arts Lethbridge, AB T1K 3M4 Canada. Tel 403-329-2666; Fax 403-382-7115; Email josephine.mills@uleth.ca; Web: www.uleth.ca/artgallery; *Preparator & Asst Cur* David Smith; *Registrar* Juliet Graham; *Dir & Cur* Josephine Mills; *Admin Mgr* Jon Oxley; *Cur Asst* Andrea Kremenik
Open daily 9 AM - 4:30 PM, Thurs until 8:30 PM; No admis fee; Estab 1968 for pub service & the teaching mechanism; 29 ft x 42 ft gallery; Visual Arts Study

Centre, 8:30 - 4:30 PM Mon - Fri, where any work from the coll will be made available for viewing, Helen Christou Gallery, Project channel Video Gallery
Income: Financed by univ & government appropriations
Collections: Permanent Coll consists of 19th century art (primarily Canadian), 20th century international art, Inuit
Exhibitions: Exhibs with exception of the Annual BFA show are curated from the permanent collection; approx 10 shows per yr
Activities: Lects open to pub, 10-15 vis lectrs per yr; gallery talks; tours; individual paintings & original objects of art lent to pub & commercial galleries & corporations; organize traveling exhibs nationally & internationally

MEDICINE HAT

M **ESPLANADE ARTS & HERITAGE CENTRE,** 401 First St SE, Medicine Hat, AB T1A 8W2 Canada. Tel 403-502-8580 (main), 502-8583 (gallery); Fax 403-502-8589; Email esplanade@medicinehat.ca; Web: www.esplanade.ca; *Cur Art* Joanne Marion
Open Mon - Fri 9 AM - 5 PM, Sat & Sun noon - 5 PM, cl holidays; Admis family (up to 5) $19.00, adults $6, school tours/field trips $40.00, under 5 free; Estab 1951; Circ 85; Gallery has 3,000 sq ft on main floor; Average Annual Attendance: 18,500; Mem: 250; dues supporting $50, bus $50, family $20, individual $10
Income: Financed by memberships, donations, fund raising & federal appropriation
Collections: Pioneer artifacts of city & the district, Indian artifacts, Regional, Canadian Modern & Contemporary art
Exhibitions: Rotate 12 per yr
Publications: exhib catalogues, several ann
Activities: Classes for children; docent training; films; gallery talks tours; exten prog serves southeastern Alberta; lending of original objects of art to pub galleries in Canada; organize traveling exhibs to pub galleries in Canada; mus shop sells books, magazines, original art, reproductions, prints

L **MEDICINE HAT PUBLIC LIBRARY,** 414 First St SE, Medicine Hat, AB T1A 0A8 Canada. Tel 403-502-8525; Fax 403-502-8529; Email library@city.medicine-hat.ab.ca; Web: mhpl.shortgrass.ca; *Chief Librn* Shelley Ross
Open Mon - Thurs 10 AM - 9 PM, Fri & Sat 10 AM - 5:30 PM, Sun 1 - 5:30 PM; Library has a display area for traveling and local art shows; 600 sq ft room with track lighting and alarm system
Library Holdings: Book Volumes 165,589, CD-ROMs 30, Cassettes 3224, Clipping Files, Compact Disks 3393, Motion Pictures 50, Original Art Works 30, Other Holdings Talking Books 1904, Pamphlets 3317, Periodical Subscriptions 243, Prints, Records, Reels 50, Sculpture, Video Tapes 2437
Exhibitions: Art loans from Alberta Foundation for the Arts; Exhibits of local artists
Activities: Dramatic progs; lects open to pub, 10 vis lectrs per yr; concerts

RED DEER

M **RED DEER & DISTRICT MUSEUM & ARCHIVES,** 4525 47A Ave, Red Deer, AB T4N 6Z6 Canada. Tel 403-309-8405; Fax 403-342-6644; Email museum@reddeer.ca; Web: www.reddeermuseum.com; *Exec Dir* Lorna Johnson; *Cur of Colls* Valerie Miller
Open Mon - Fri 10 PM - 4:30 PM, Sat & Sun noon - 4:30 PM; Admis by donation; Estab 1978 to present the human history of the region through an on-going series of exhibs & interpretive progs; Stewart Room has 64 running ft of exhib space; Volunteer's Gallery has 124 running ft of exhibition space; Donor's Gallery has 160 running ft of exhib space; 2500 sq ft total area of circulating exhib space; 4100 sq ft of permanent exhib space; Average Annual Attendance: 60,000; Mem: 1000; dues family $15, individual $10
Income: Financed by municipal, provincial & federal grants
Special Subjects: Painting-Canadian, Period Rooms, Photography, Porcelain, Primitive art, Restorations, Textiles
Collections: Bower Collection of archaeological specimens from Central Alberta, Central Alberta human history, Inuit carving, prints & related material, Swallow Collection of Inuit & Indian Art, permanent art coll, clothing & textiles
Exhibitions: Programs featuring local, international, national & provincial artists; Alberta Community Art Clubs Assoc; Alberta Wide Juried Exhibition; Central Alberta Photographic Society Annual Exhibit; Red Deer College Student Show
Publications: Quarterly newsletter, Inventive Spirit (compendium & database of Alberta inventions)
Activities: Classes for children; mus-kits; lect open to pub; concerts; gallery talks; tours; originate traveling exhibs provincially, nationally to museums & art galleries; mus shop sells books, magazines, original art, prints, coloring books, learning tools, souvenirs, postcards, stationery & gifts; children's discovery zone

STONY PLAIN

M **MULTICULTURAL HERITAGE CENTRE,** Public Art Gallery, 5411 51st St, Box 2188 Stony Plain, AB T7Z 1X7 Canada. Tel 780-963-2777; Fax 780-963-0233; Email info@multicentre.org; Web: www.multicentre.org; *Managing Dir* Melissa Hartley
Open Tues - Sat 10 AM - 4 PM; No admis fee; Estab 1974 to provide exposure to high quality art with priority given to local Alberta artists, to develop an appreciation for good art, to provide exposure for upcoming artists; Gallery has 2000 sq ft of exhib space; Multicultural Heritage Centre also consists of Oppertshauser House on same site; maintains reference library; Average Annual Attendance: 85,000; Mem: 100; dues $20, ann meeting Jan
Income: Financed by government grants, free for children & adult program, commissions from store sales, Homesteaders Kitchen revenue & fundraising
Special Subjects: Historical Material
Collections: Area history, family histories, photographs
Exhibitions: 20 exhibs per year
Publications: Monthly newsletter
Activities: Classes adults & children, dramatic progs; lects open to pub, 10 vis lectrs per yr, concerts; sales shop sells books, original art, reproductions & prints

BRITISH COLUMBIA

BURNABY

M **BURNABY ART GALLERY,** 6344 Deer Lake Ave, Burnaby, BC V5G 2J3 Canada. Tel 604-297-4422; Fax 604-205-7339; Email gallery@burnaby.ca; Web: www.burnabyartgallery.ca; *Dir & Cur* Ellen van Eijnsbergen
Open Tues - Fri 10 AM - 4:30 PM, Sat - Sun 12 PM - 5 PM, cl Mon; No admis fee, donations accepted; Estab 1967 to collect & exhibit Canadian art, with continually changing exhibs of prints & works of art on paper; Gallery is housed in Ceperley Mansion in Deer Lake Park; Average Annual Attendance: 25,000
Income: Financed by municipal, provincial & federal grants, pub & pvt donations
Library Holdings: Clipping Files, Exhibition Catalogs, Pamphlets
Special Subjects: Prints
Collections: 20th Century prints including contemporary artists, Works on paper, Contemporary Art
Exhibitions: Tracing Culture IV; Day Without Art (video)
Publications: Catalogues & brochures to accompany exhibs
Activities: Classes for adults & children; docent training; workshops for schools; lects open to pub; 4-6 lectrs per yr; gallery talks; tours; exten dept serves BC; Metro Vancouver; individual paintings & original objects of art lent to other exhib centers pub & corp; lending collection contains 600 original prints & drawings; organize traveling exhibs to Canadian institutions

M **SIMON FRASER UNIVERSITY,** Simon Fraser University Gallery, 8888 University Dr, AQ3004 Burnaby, BC V5A 1S6 Canada. Tel 778-782-4266; Fax 778-782-3029; Email gallery@sfu.ca; Web: www.sfu.ca/galleries; *Dir & Cur* Melanie O'Brian
Open Tues, Weds, Sat noon - 5 PM, Thurs & Fri noon - 8 PM; No admis fee; Estab 1971 to collect, conserve & display original works of art, principally contemporary Canadian; Gallery is 150 to 310 running ft, 1200 sq ft. Permanent works are installed throughout the univ campus; Average Annual Attendance: 10,000
Income: Financed by pub univ appropriations, government grants & corporate donations
Special Subjects: Graphics
Collections: Simon Fraser Collection, including contemporary & Inuit graphics, international graphics
Publications: Biannual report
Activities: Lects open to public; gallery talks; tours; individual paintings & original objects of art loaned to art galleries

L **W A C Bennett Library**, 8888 University Dr, Burnaby, BC V5A 1S6 Canada. Tel 778-782-3253; Fax 778-782-4521; Email sf-general@sfu.ca; Web: www.lib.sfu.ca; *Univ Librn & Dean of Libraries* Gwen Bird
Open Mon-Thurs 8 - 11:45 AM, Fri 8 AM - 10 PM, Sat & Sun 10 AM - 10 PM; Reference material available in library & University Archives
Library Holdings: Audio Tapes, Book Volumes 1,000,000, DVDs, Exhibition Catalogs, Fiche, Filmstrips, Manuscripts, Motion Pictures, Other Holdings CD-ROM; Compact discs, Pamphlets, Periodical Subscriptions 11,500, Records, Reels, Slides, Video Tapes

CHILLIWACK

A **CHILLIWACK COMMUNITY ARTS COUNCIL,** Community Arts Centre, 20 - 5725 Vedder Rd, Chilliwack, BC V2R 3N4 Canada. Tel 604-769-2787; Fax 604-769-2788; Email info@chilliwackculturalcentre.ca; Web: www.chilliwackartscouncil.com
Open Mon - Fri 9 AM - 5 PM, Sat during scheduled class times, cl Sun & some holidays; No admis fee; Estab 1959 as Arts Council, Arts Centre estab 1973 to encourage all forms of art in the community; 1 large gallery; Average Annual Attendance: 10,000; Mem: 5000; dues group & family $25, organizational $15, individual $15; annual meeting Sept
Income: Financed by endowment, mem & grants
Exhibitions: Christmas Craft Market
Publications: Arts Council Newsletter, 11 per yr
Activities: Classes for adults & children; dramatic progs; concerts; schols offered

COQUITLAM

A **PLACE DES ARTS AT HERITAGE SQUARE,** 1120 Brunette Ave, Coquitlam, BC V3K 1G2 Canada. Tel 604-664-1636; Fax 604-664-1658; Email info@placedesarts.ca; Web: www.placedesarts.ca; *Exec Dir* Joan McCauley; *Communs Coordr* Kate Lancaster; *Fine & Performing Arts Prog* Oliver McTavish-Wisden
Open Mon - Fri 9 AM - 9 PM, Sat 9 AM - 5 PM, Sun 1 PM - 5 PM; see website for summer hours; No admis fee; Estab 1972 as a cultural, community crafts & resource center, an art centre & music school; 3 galleries - 3 shows monthly; Average Annual Attendance: 58,000
Income: Financed by municipal grant
Exhibitions: Monthly shows of emerging artists, artists & craftsmen throughout the year
Publications: Prog Sept - June; summer prog Jul - Aug
Activities: Satellite courses for school children; classes for adults & children; visual arts, music, drama, dance; lect open to pub; concerts; gallery talks; schols offered

COURTENAY

M **COMOX VALLEY ART GALLERY,** 580 Duncan Ave, Courtenay, BC V9N 2M7 Canada. Tel 250-338-6211; Fax 250-338-6287; Email gallery@comoxvalleyartgallery.com; Web: www.comoxvalleyartgallery.com; *Exec Dir* Sharon Karsten; *Cur* Angela Somerset; *Shop Mgr* Rhonda Burden

Open Tues - Sat 10 AM - 5 PM; Estab 1974; contemporary art/feature local artists; Contemporary & community galleries; Average Annual Attendance: 22,000; Mem: 288; dues $25 per yr
Income: Financed through grants, fundraisers & gift shop sales
Exhibitions: See website
Activities: Art educ progs; pub outreach; classes for adults & children; youth media workshops; lects open to pub; approx 8 vis lectrs per yr; concerts; gallery talks; tours; Nonny Milne schol for youth; sales shop sells books, magazines, original art, reproductions, prints, pottery, jewelry, glass

DAWSON CREEK

M **SOUTH PEACE ART SOCIETY,** Dawson Creek Art Gallery, 101-816 Alaska Ave, Dawson Creek, BC V1G 4T6 Canada. Tel 250-782-2601; Fax 250-782-8801; Email curator@dcartgallery.ca; Web: www.dcartgallery.ca; *Dir* Ellen Corea; *Treas* Barbara Swail; *Pres* Barb Handysides; *Gift Shop Mgr & Admin Asst* Alana Hall
Open June 15 - Aug 31 daily 8 AM - 5 PM; Sep - June 14 Tues - Fri 10 AM - 5 PM; Sat noon - 4 PM; Admis by donation; Estab 1961 to promote art appreciation in community; Art Gallery in elevator annex in NAR Park. NAR Park includes mus & Tourist Information Office; Average Annual Attendance: 65,000; Mem: 100; dues $35; ann meeting third Thurs of Mar
Income: $130,000 (financed by municipal building & ann sponsorship, commission from sales, provincial cultural grant, federal grant Canada council)
Library Holdings: Book Volumes, Exhibition Catalogs, Original Art Works
Exhibitions: Approx 13 per yr, local & traveling
Publications: Newsletter, quarterly
Activities: Classes for adults & children; lects open to pub, 3 vis lectrs per yr; gallery talks; individual paintings lent to mems, bus, pvt homes; lending coll contains color reproductions, slides, 145 books & 350 original prints; book traveling exhibs 4-6 per yr; circulate to galleries in British Columbia; sales shop sells original art, pottery, metal, woodwork, jewelry, stained glass, oils, soaps, weaving, cards & other items

KAMLOOPS

M **KAMLOOPS ART GALLERY,** 101 - 465 Victoria St, Kamloops, BC V2C 2A9 Canada. Tel 250-377-2400; Fax 250-828-0662; Email kamloopsartgallery@kag.bc.ca; Web: www.kag.bc.ca; *Exec Dir* Margaret Chrumka
Open Mon - Sat 10 AM - 5 PM, Thurs 10 AM - 9 PM; cl Sun & holidays; Adults $5; Families $10; Seniors (ages 62+) & Groups of 10 or More $3; Gallery Members, Children and Students (with ID) Free; Estab 1978; pub art mus; Exhib gallery, 4400 running ft, total area of gallery 14,225 ft; Average Annual Attendance: 30,000; Mem: 600; dues family $45, individual $30, senior citizens, artists & students $15, child $10; ann meeting in Apr
Income: $1,400,000 (operating & prog grants, fundraising, sponsorships & donations)
Library Holdings: Auction Catalogs, Clipping Files, Exhibition Catalogs
Special Subjects: Drawings, Etchings & Engravings, Painting-Canadian, Photography, Prints, Sculpture, Watercolors
Collections: Contemporary Canadian Art, Canadian Prints & Drawings, photography, sculpture, Contemporary Canadian Art Collection
Exhibitions: Monthly National & International Exhibs
Publications: Newsletter, 4 times per yr; exhib catalogs
Activities: Classes for adults & children; lects open to pub, 10-12 vis lectrs per yr; concerts; gallery talks; tours; book traveling exhibs; originate traveling exhibs; mus shop sells books, magazines, original crafts, reproductions, prints & gifts

KELOWNA

M **OKANAGAN HERITAGE MUSEUM,** (Kelowna Museum), 470 Queensway Ave, Kelowna, BC V1Y 6S7 Canada. Tel 250-763-2417; Fax 250-763-5722; Email info@kelownamuseum.ca; Web: www.kelownamuseums.ca; *Exec Dir* Linda Digby; *Opers Mgr* Christopher Butt; *Curatorial Mgr* Amanda Snyder; *Mus Servs Coordr* Dana Hopkinson
Open Mon - Sat 10 AM - 5 PM, cl Sun; Admis by donation; Estab 1936 as a community mus where traveling exhibits are received & circulated; 12,000 sq ft of display plus storage, workshop & archives; permanent galleries: Natural History, Local History, Ethnography, two exhibit galleries; Average Annual Attendance: 35,000; Mem: 200; dues $25; ann meeting in Mar
Income: Financed by mem, city & state appropriation
Special Subjects: African Art, American Indian Art, Antiquities-Egyptian, Antiquities-Greek, Antiquities-Roman, Archaeology, Asian Art, Bronzes, Ceramics, Costumes, Crafts, Decorative Arts, Drawings, Eskimo Art, Ethnology, Folk Art, Furniture, Glass, Jewelry, Latin American Art, Metalwork, Miniatures, Painting-American, Silver, Textiles
Collections: Coins & medals, decorative arts, ethnography, general history, Kelowna History, natural history
Exhibitions: Changing exhibs every 3 months
Publications: The Games Grandpa Played, Early Sports in BC; Nan, A Childs Eye View of Okanagan; Lak-La-Hai-Ee Volume III Fishing; A Short History of Early Fruit Ranching Kelowna; Sunshine & Butterflies
Activities: Classes for adults & children; lects open to pub, 6 vis lectrs per yr; tours; gallery talks; individual paintings & original objects of art lent to qualified mus; book traveling exhibs 7-8 per yr; originate traveling exhibs; mus shop sells books, original art, reproductions, prints

L **Kelowna Public Archives,** 470 Queensway Ave, Kelowna, BC V1Y 6S7 Canada. Tel 250-763-2417; Fax 250-763-5722; Email info@kelownamuseums.ca; Web: www.kelownamuseums.ca; *Community Archivist* Tara Hurley
Open by appointment only; Circ Non-circulating
Library Holdings: Cassettes, Clipping Files, Fiche, Manuscripts, Maps, Micro Print, Motion Pictures, Original Art Works, Original Documents, Periodical Subscriptions, Photographs, Prints, Slides, Video Tapes
Collections: Photograph Collection, reference library, reference files, maps
Activities: Classes for adults & children, docent training; lectrs open to pub, gallery talks, tours; Museum shop, books, reproductions, gift items; junior museums located at 1304 Ellis St, 1424 Ellis St

NANAIMO

M **NANAIMO ART GALLERY,** 150 Commercial St, Nanaimo, BC V9R 5G6 Canada. Tel 250-754-1750; Fax 250-741-2214; Email info@nanaimogallery.ca; Web: www.nanaimoartgallery.com; *Pres* Deborah Giunio-Zorkin; *Cur* Jesse Birch; *Admin Dir* Chris Kuderle; *Visitor Servs Coordr* Dawn Marusin; *Exec Dir* Julie Bevan; *Gallery Asst & Cur Tech* Stephen Laidlaw; *Art Educ Coordr* Yvonne Vander Kool
Open Tues - Sat 10 AM - 5 PM, Sun noon - 5 PM; Admis by donation; Estab 1976 to exhibit the works of contemporary visual artists; Two Galleries: gallery I is 1300 sq ft with 11 ft ceilings; gallery II is 775 sq ft with 10 ft ceilings; Average Annual Attendance: 20,000; Mem: 386; dues $10 & up; ann meeting in Apr
Income: Financed by mem, earned gallery shop, city & state appropriations; schools & school districts
Collections: Works by contemporary artists primarily regional but some national & international, Contemporary Art
Exhibitions: Contemporary Art, Historical & Scientific exhibits; Street Banner Painting Competition; rotate 9 exhibs per yr on campus, 12 per yr downtown facility
Publications: Nanaimo Art Gallery newsletter, 3 per yr
Activities: Classes for adults & children; docent training; lects open to pub, 6-8 vis lectrs per yr; gallery talks; tours; competitions with awards; exten dept serves local elementary schools; individual paintings & original objects of art lent; lending coll contains original art work, original prints, paintings & sculpture; book traveling exhibs 1-2 per yr; mus shop sells books, original art & local crafts

PENTICTON

M **THE PENTICTON ART GALLERY,** (Art Gallery of South Okanagan), 199 Marina Way, Penticton, BC V2A 1H5 Canada. Tel 250-493-2928; Email info@pentictonartgallery.com; Web: www.pentictonartgallery.com; *Dir & Cur* Paul Crawford
Open Tues - Fri 10 AM - 5 PM, Sat & Sun 11 AM - 4 PM, cl Mon & Statutory Holidays; Admis adults & non-members $2, members, students & children free, free on weekends

PRINCE GEORGE

M **TWO RIVERS ART GALLERY,** 725 Canada Games Way, Prince George, BC V2L ST1 Canada. Tel 250-614-7800; Fax 250-563-3211; Email art@tworiversartgallery.com; Web: www.tworiversartgallery.com; *Cur* George Harris; *Admin Asst* Jeanne Hodges; *Mng Dir* Carolyn Holmes
Open Mon - Sat 10 AM - 5 PM, Thurs 10 AM - 9 PM, Sun 12 PM - 5 PM; Admis family $15, adults $7.50, sr citizens & students $6, children 5-12 $3, under 5 free; Estab 1970 to foster development of arts & crafts in the community; to foster & promote artists; New Building, 2 floors, art rental section, two sq ft galleries, offices, storage, gift shop, large foyer & sculpture ct; Average Annual Attendance: 26,000; Mem: 382; dues family $43, individual $27, sr citizens & students $22; ann meeting in Feb
Income: Financed by provincial & municipal grants, pvt donations
Special Subjects: Painting-Canadian, Sculpture
Collections: Original paintings by British Columbia artists
Exhibitions: Exhibitions held every 10-12 weeks, primarily Canadian Artists; three ann fundraisers
Publications: Quarterly newsletter
Activities: Classes for adults & children; docent training; lects open to pub, 6-10 vis lectrs per yr; gallery talks; tours; exten dept serves regional district; individual paintings & original objects of art rented to mems; book traveling exhibs 2 per yr; sales shop sells original paintings, drawings, pottery, handicrafts, prints, cards

PRINCE RUPERT

M **MUSEUM OF NORTHERN BRITISH COLUMBIA,** Ruth Harvey Art Gallery, 100 First Ave W, PO Box 669 Prince Rupert, BC V8J 3S1 Canada; 100-1st Ave West, Prince Rupert, BC V8J 1A8 Canada. Tel 250-624-3207; Fax 250-627-8009; Web: www.museumofnorthernbc.com; *Cur* Susan Marsden; *Gift Shop Mgr* Irene Fernandes; *Colls Mgr* Erin Alger; *Performance Coordr* Sampson Bryant
Open Oct-May Tues-Sat 9 AM-5 PM, June-Sep 9 AM -5 PM; Admis adults $6, Teens 13-19 $3, Child 6-12 $2, Young Child under 5 $1; Estab 1924, new building opened 1958, to collect, maintain & display the history of the peoples of the north coast, particularly of the Prince Rupert area; especially the Tsimshian, the First Nations group in this area who have occupied the northwest coast for approx 10,000 yrs; Large main gallery, Treasures Gallery, Hallway of Nations, Monumental Gallery, Ruth Harvey Art Gallery; Average Annual Attendance: 80,000; Mem: 280; dues corporate $75, family $20, individual $15, sr citizen & student $10; ann meeting in May
Income: $250,000 (financed primarily by municipality & province)
Library Holdings: Clipping Files, Manuscripts, Maps, Memorabilia, Original Documents, Pamphlets, Photographs, Reproductions
Special Subjects: Anthropology, Archaeology, Ceramics, Coins & Medals, Crafts, Ethnology, Gold, Graphics, Historical Material, Jewelry, Maps, Painting-Canadian, Porcelain, Portraits, Primitive art, Textiles, Woodcarvings, Photography, Prints
Collections: Contemporary North Coast First Nations, historical colls, native First Nations colls, natural history, photographs
Exhibitions: A continually changing display prog; fine arts exhibs from large galleries; local artists exhibs
Publications: Library contains 800 vols, 50 rare

Activities: Classes for adults & children; dramatic progs; lects open to pub, 3-4 vis lectrs per yr; gallery talks; tours; competitions; book traveling exhibs; mus shop sells books, native art, original art, reproductions, prints & souvenirs

L **Library**, 100 First Ave W, Prince Rupert, BC V8J 1A8 Canada. Tel 250-624-3207; Fax 250-627-8009; Web: www.museumofnorthernbc.com; *Colls Mgr* Erin Alger; *Performance Coordr* Sampson Bryant; *Dir* Robin Weber; *Cur* Susan Marsden
Open June - Aug daily - 9 AM - 5 PM, Sept daily 9 AM - 5 PM, Oct - May Tues - Sat 9 AM - 5 PM, cl Sun, Mon, & holidays; No admis fee for use of reference library; appointments required; Small reference library for staff & researchers
Income: $280,000 (financed by city, province, donations & gift shop)
Library Holdings: Audio Tapes, Book Volumes 1000, Clipping Files, Exhibition Catalogs, Manuscripts, Other Holdings Archival materials, Pamphlets, Periodical Subscriptions 10, Photographs, Video Tapes
Special Subjects: Anthropology, Archaeology, Ceramics, Coins & Medals, Eskimo Art, Ethnology, Historical Material, Painting-Canadian, Porcelain, Primitive art, Prints, Restoration & Conservation, Tapestries, Textiles
Publications: Library contains 800 vols, 50 rare
Activities: Educ dept; lects open to pub; mus shop sells books, original art, reproductions & prints

REVELSTOKE

A **REVELSTOKE VISUAL ARTS CENTRE,** 320 Wilson St, PO Box 2655 Revelstoke, BC V0E 2S0 Canada. Tel 250-814-0261; Email info@revelstokevisualarts.com; Web: www.revelstokevisualarts.com; *Chmn* Joanne Stacey; *Treas* Margaret Pacaud
Admis by donation; Estab 1949 to promote & stimulate interest in art by studying art, artistic methods & artists works, developing local interest & interchanging ideas; Average Annual Attendance: 500; Mem: 45; dues $10; ann meeting in Apr
Income: Grants, sales & donations
Collections: Centennial coll contains 10 watercolors, acrylics & oils by Sophie Atkinson
Exhibitions: Weaving & Pottery by Local Artisans; Sr Citizens' Paintings; Snowflake Porcelain Painters; Works by members of the Revelstoke Art Group - summer
Activities: Classes for adults & children

RICHMOND

A **RICHMOND ARTS CENTRE,** 180-7700 Minoru Gate, Richmond, BC V6Y 1R9 Canada. Tel 604-247-8326; Email camyar.chaichian@richmond.ca; Web: www.richmond.ca/culture/centre/about.htm; *Arts Coordr* Camyar Chaichian
Open Mon - Fri 9 AM - 9:30 PM, Sat & Sun 10 AM - 5 PM; No admis fee; Estab 1967 to provide stimulation & nourishment to the arts in the community
Income: Financed by city appropriation
Activities: Classes for adults & children in visual & dramatic arts, ballet & jazz; concerts; special events & festivals; art truck, takes the arts out to the community; sales shop sells original art & music CDs

SOOKE

M **SOOKE REGION MUSEUM & ART GALLERY,** 2070 Phillips Rd, Sooke, BC V9Z 0Y3 Canada; PO Box 774, Sooke, BC V9Z 1H7 Canada. Tel 250-642-6351; Email info@sookeregionmuseum.com; Web: www.sookeregionmuseum.com; *Exec Dir* Lee Boyko
Open daily 9 AM - 5 PM, Thurs 9 AM - 8 PM; Admis donation; Estab 1977 to advance local history & art; Exhibit changes monthly featuring a different local artist or artist group, or segment of mus coll; Average Annual Attendance: 30,000
Income: Financed by donations
Special Subjects: American Indian Art, Archaeology, Costumes, Crafts, Dolls, Ethnology, Period Rooms
Collections: Fishing, Logging & Mining Artifacts, Native Indian Crafts (post & pre-contact), Pioneer Implements
Exhibitions: Polemaker's Shack; Moss Cottage; Wreck of Lord Western
Activities: Children classes; docent training; lects open to pub, 4 vis lectrs per yr; tours; competitions with awards; retail store sells books & original art

SURREY

M **ARNOLD MIKELSON MIND & MATTER ART GALLERY,** 13743 16th Ave, Surrey, BC V4A 1P7 Canada. Tel 604-536-6460; Email mary@mindandmatterart.com; Web: www.mindandmatterart.com; *Pres* Mary Mikelson; *Asst Dir* Myra Mikelson; *Mgr* Arnold Mikelson; *Asst Mgr* Sapphire Mikelson
Open Noon - 6 PM or by appointment; No admis fee; Estab 1965; 2000 sq ft gallery on three acres, upper flr mus, main flr continues exhibs of Canadian artists; Average Annual Attendance: 15,000
Income: Funded by the Mikelson Family
Special Subjects: Folk Art, Jewelry, Landscapes, Marine Painting, Pottery, Sculpture, Woodcarvings, Watercolors
Collections: Showcase wood sculpture by the late Arnold Mikelson, Arnold Mikelson Wood Sculpture
Exhibitions: Metal art, modern landscape, painting, stone sculpture, wildlife, wood sculpture; Nov-Dec, Annual Art for X-mas; July, Arnold Mikelson Festival of Arts
Activities: Classes for children; lects open to pub, 25-30 lectrs per yr; gallery talks; schols; mus shop sells original art

M **SURREY ART GALLERY,** 13750 88th Ave, Surrey, BC V3W 3L1 Canada. Tel 604-501-5566; Fax 604-501-5581; Email artgallery@surrey.ca; Web: www.arts.surrey.ca, www.surreytechlab.ca; *Dir* Liane Davison; *Cur* Jordan Strom
Open Mon & Fri 9 AM - 5 PM, Tues - Thurs 9 AM - 9 PM, Sat 10 AM - 5 PM, cl Sun; Admis by donation; Estab 1975; Contemporary art; Average Annual Attendance: 50,000
Income: Financed by city & provincial appropriation, special private foundations grants & federal grants per project application
Purchases: $10,000
Library Holdings: Book Volumes, Clipping Files, Exhibition Catalogs, Manuscripts, Original Documents, Periodical Subscriptions
Special Subjects: Painting-Canadian, Photography, Prints, Sculpture
Collections: Contemporary Canadian Art
Publications: Exhib catalogues; Surrey Arts Center Calendar, bimonthly
Activities: Classes for adults & children; docent training; lects open to pub, 10 vis lectrs per yr; concerts; gallery talks; tours; individual paintings & original objects of art lent to other institutions; book traveling exhibs 1 or more per yr; originates traveling exhibs; sales shop sells original art, locally made jewelry, arts & crafts, glasswork, woodwork & cards

L **Library**, 13750 88th Ave, Surrey, BC V3W 3L1 Canada. Tel 604-501-5566; Fax 604-501-5581; Email artgallery@surrey.ca; Web: www.surrey.ca/culture-recreation/1537.aspx; *Dir* Liane Davison; *Cur Prog* Ingrid Kolt; *Cur Exhib & Coll* Jordan Strom; *Chief Librn* Surinder Bhogal; *Asst Cur* Brian Foreman
Open Mon - Fri 9 AM - 5 PM, Sat 10 AM - 5 PM, Sun Noon - 5 PM, Thurs evenings 5 - 9 PM, cl statutory holidays; Admis by donation; Estab 1975 for exhibs & educ in contemporary art. Reference library for staff & docents only; Contemporary art museum; Average Annual Attendance: 50,000
Income: Financed by municipal
Purchases: $1000
Library Holdings: Book Volumes 550, Cards, Clipping Files, Exhibition Catalogs, Periodical Subscriptions 20, Slides
Collections: Contemporary art
Activities: Docent training; lects open to pub; tours; exten prog serves Surrey & region; lending original objects of art to mus

VANCOUVER

M **BILL REID GALLERY OF NORTHWEST COAST ART,** 639 Hornby St, Vancouver, BC V6C 2G3 Canada. Tel 604-682-3455; Fax 604-682-3310; Email info@billreidgallery.ca; Web: www.billreidgallery.ca; *Dir & CEO* Alexandra Montgomery; *Dir Mktg* Paula Fairweather; *Cur* Beth Carter
Open Wed - Sun 11 AM - 5 PM, cl Mon & Tues; Admis adult $10, senior & student (18+ with valid ID) $7, children (5-17) $5; Estab 2008 as a public gallery for contemporary aboriginal art of the northwest coast; Home to the Bill Reid coll & changing exhibs of contemporary Aboriginal Art of the northwest coast; Mem: Dues seniors & students $20, adults $30, couple $40, family $45
Income: Nonprofit
Collections: Bill Reid Collection
Exhibitions: Permanent exhib, Restoring Enchantment: Gold & Silver Masterworks by Bill Reid; Core exhibs & up to 3 temporary exhibs per yr
Publications: Bill Reid & the Haida Canoe & Camping or Irregardless: Humor in Contemporary Northwest Coast Art
Activities: Educ prog; docent training; pub progs associated with exhibs; lects open to pub, 3-4 vis lectrs per yr; gallery talks; tours; originate traveling exhibs; gallery shop sells books, original art, reproductions, prints, jewelry, accessories

A **COMMUNITY ARTS COUNCIL OF VANCOUVER,** 440-111 W Hasting St, Vancouver, BC V6B 1H4 Canada. Tel 604-682-0010; Email info@cacv.bc.ca; Web: www.cacv.ca
Open 9 AM - 5 PM; No admis fee; Estab 1946 as a soc dedicated to the support of arts, with a wide range of interest in the arts; to promote standards in all art fields including civic arts; also serves as a liaison centre; Exhib Gallery shows works of semi-professional & emerging artists; 2200 sq ft on two levels, street level entrance; Average Annual Attendance: 40,000; Mem: 500; dues $15; ann meeting in Sept
Income: Financed by British Columbia Cultural & Lotteries Fund, City of Vancouver, mem & donations
Exhibitions: Two shows per month
Publications: Arts Vancouver Magazine, 4 issues per year
Activities: Lect open to pub; performances; workshops; concerts; gallery talks; competitions; schols & fels offered

M **CONTEMPORARY ART GALLERY,** 555 Nelson St, Vancouver, BC V6B 6R5 Canada. Tel 604-681-2700; Fax 604-683-2710; Email cagart@rogerg.com; Web: www.contemporaryartgallery.ca; *Exec Dir* Nigel Prince; *Cur* Kimberly Phillips
Open Tues - Sun noon - 6 PM; cl BC statutory holidays; No admis fee; Estab 1969
Collections: Permanent collections of contemporary art in Toronto's public schools, Contemporary Art
Exhibitions: Rotating exhibits monthly

M **CONTEMPORARY ART GALLERY SOCIETY OF BRITISH COLUMBIA,** 555 Nelson St, Vancouver, BC V6B 6R5 Canada. Tel 604-681-2700; Fax 604-683-2710; Email info@contemporaryartgallery.ca; Web: www.contemporaryartgallery.ca; *Exec Dir* Nigel Prince; *Cur* Jenifer Papararo; *Prog Coordr* Lisa Fedorak; *Head Develop & Communs* Susan Lavitt; *Gallery Coordr* Jill Henderson; *Bookkeeper* Uli Hobruecker; *Preparator* Phil Dion
Open Tues - Sun noon - 6 PM; No admis fee; Estab 1971 as an exhib space for regional, national & international contemporary art; The Gallery has 1,700 sq ft exhib area; Average Annual Attendance: 16,000; Mem: 300; dues $39
Income: Financed by Federal Government, British Columbia Arts Council, City of Vancouver, mem fees & fundraising
Library Holdings: Auction Catalogs, CD-ROMs, Clipping Files, Compact Disks, DVDs, Exhibition Catalogs, Pamphlets, Periodical Subscriptions, Slides
Collections: City of Vancouver Art Collection, Contemporary Gallery Society of B C Art Collection
Publications: Exhibition brochure & catalogs
Activities: Classes for children; educ prog; docent training; online teaching resources; lects open to pub, 6 vis lectrs per yr; gallery talks; tours; Visual Arts Develop Award; individual paintings & original objects of art lent to civic agencies; lending coll contains 3400 works; organize traveling exhibs to mus & galleries nat & international; mus shop sells books, prints, original art

M **EMILY CARR INSTITUTE OF ART & DESIGN CHARLES H SCOTT GALLERY,** The Charles H Scott Gallery, 520 East 1st Ave, Vancouver, BC V5T 0H2 Canada. Tel 604-844-3809; Fax 604-844-3801; Email libby@ecuad.ca; Web: http://libby.ecuad.ca; *Cur* Cate Rimmer
Open daily 12 PM - 5 PM; No admis fee; Estab 1980 to provide mus quality exhibs & publs of critically significant visual art; 3000 sq ft gallery with all environmental & security safeguards; Average Annual Attendance: 30,000
Income: $95,000 (financed by provincial appropriation)
Exhibitions: Social Process - Collective Action, Mary Kelly 1970-75
Publications: Exhib catalogues
Activities: Tours upon request; book traveling exhibs 1-2 per yr; originate traveling exhibs; sales shop sells exhib catalogues

L **Library**, 520 East 1st Ave, Vancouver, BC BC V5T 0H2 Canada. Tel 604-844-3840; Fax 604-844-3801; *Librn* Donna Zwierciadlowski; *Library Dir* Sheila Wallace
Open May - Aug Mon - Fri 8:30 AM - 5 PM, Sept - Apr Mon - Thurs 8:30 AM - 9 PM, Fri & Sat 8:30 AM - 5 PM; Circ 65,000
Income: Financed by government funding
Library Holdings: Audio Tapes, Book Volumes 18,000, Clipping Files, Exhibition Catalogs, Fiche, Periodical Subscriptions 165, Records, Slides 134,000, Video Tapes 1900
Special Subjects: Film, Painting-American, Painting-Canadian, Painting-European, Photography, Posters, Pottery, Pre-Columbian Art, Primitive art, Printmaking, Prints, Sculpture, Video, Woodcarvings, Graphic Design, Industrial Design

M **MUSEUM OF VANCOUVER,** 1100 Chestnut St, Vanier Park Vancouver, BC V6J 3J9 Canada. Tel 604-736-4431; Fax 604-736-5417; Email guestservices@museumofvancouver.ca; Web: www.museumofvancouver.ca; *Acting CEO* Mike Mallen
Open Mon - Sun 10 AM - 5 PM, Thurs 10 AM - 8 PM, Fri & Sat 10 AM - 9 PM; Admis families $40, adults $19, students & seniors $16, youth (5-18) $9, children under 4 free; Estab 1894 to collect, preserve & interpret natural & cultural history of Vancouver area; Permanent exhibs tell Vancouver's stories from the early 1900s to the late 70s complimented by contemporary ground breaking feature exhibs; Average Annual Attendance: 70,000; Mem: 500
Income: Financed by city of Vancouver, government grants, fundraising & gift shop sales
Special Subjects: African Art, American Indian Art, Anthropology, Antiquities-Egyptian, Antiquities-Greek, Antiquities-Oriental, Antiquities-Roman, Archaeology, Asian Art, Ceramics, Coins & Medals, Costumes, Decorative Arts, Dolls, Drawings, Eskimo Art, Etchings & Engravings, Ethnology, Folk Art, Furniture, Glass, Historical Material, Ivory, Jade, Jewelry
Collections: Vancouver Stories, Anthropology, Asian Studies, History and Natural History Colls
Exhibitions: Vancouver history exhibs; changing temporary exhibs
Publications: Occasional exhib catalogues
Activities: Classes for adults & children; docent progs; lects open to pub; gallery talks; tours; competitions; originate traveling exhibs to mus; mus shop sells books, original art, reproductions & prints

L **Museum of Vancouver Library**, 1100 Chestnut St, Vancouver, BC V6J 3J9 Canada. Tel 604-736-4431; Fax 604-736-5417; Web: www.museumofvancouver.ca; *Acting CEO* Mike Mallen
Open by appointment only; Circ Non-circulating; For reference
Library Holdings: Audio Tapes, Book Volumes 9000, Cassettes, Clipping Files, Exhibition Catalogs, Pamphlets, Periodical Subscriptions 30, Video Tapes
Special Subjects: American Indian Art, Anthropology, Archaeology, Asian Art, Decorative Arts, Eskimo Art, Folk Art, Historical Material, Mexican Art, Oriental Art, Painting-Canadian, Porcelain, Stained Glass
Collections: Vancouver history & culture, Northwest Coast First Nations
Activities: Classes for adults & children; Lects open to pub

M **UNIVERSITY OF BRITISH COLUMBIA,** Morris & Helen Belkin Art Gallery, 1825 Main Mall, Vancouver, BC V6T 1Z2 Canada. Tel 604-822-2759; Fax 604-822-6689; Email belkin.gallery@ubc.ca; Web: www.belkin.ubc.ca; *Dir & Cur* Lorna Brown; *Adminr* Annette Wooff; *Mgr Pub Progs* Naomi Sawada; *Mgr Technical & Design Servs* Owen Sopotiuk
Open Tues - Fri 10 AM - 5 PM, Sat & Sun Noon - 5 PM, cl Mon & statutory holidays; No admis fee; Estab 1948, The gallery has a mandate to encourage projects conceived for its special content. Our programming emphasizes contemporary art & also projects which serve to further understanding of the history of Avant-Garde; Gallery covers 27,000 sq ft; Average Annual Attendance: 15,000; Mem: No mem prog
Income: Financed by departmental funds
Publications: Announcements; exhib catalogues

L **Art & Architecture Planning, UBC Library**, 1961 East Mall, Irving K. Barber Learning Centre Vancouver, BC V6T 1Z1 Canada. Tel 604-822-6375; Fax 604-822-3893; Web: www.library.ubc.ca/aarp; *Univ Librn* Susan Parker; *Deputy Univ Librn* Melody Burton
Open Mon - Thurs 8 AM - 10 P, Fri 8 AM - 6 PM, Sat 10 AM - 6 PM, Sun Noon - 8 PM; No admis fee; Estab 1948 to serve students & faculty in all courses related to fine arts, architecture & planning
Library Holdings: Auction Catalogs, Book Volumes 230,000, CD-ROMs, Clipping Files, Exhibition Catalogs, Pamphlets, Periodical Subscriptions, Reproductions
Special Subjects: Antiquities-Byzantine, Antiquities-Roman, Architecture, Art History, Asian Art, Conceptual Art, Costume Design & Constr, Decorative Arts, Drawings, Etchings & Engravings, Furniture, Graphic Arts, Historical Material, History of Art & Archaeology, Illustration, Interior Design, Landscape Architecture, Latin American Art, Painting-American, Painting-British, Painting-Canadian, Painting-European, Painting-French, Photography, Posters, Pre-Columbian Art, Printmaking, Prints, Reproductions, Restoration & Conservation, Sculpture, Watercolors, Woodcarvings, Woodcuts
Activities: Library instruction, reference servs

M **Museum of Anthropology**, 6393 NW Marine Dr, Vancouver, BC V6T 1Z2 Canada. Tel 604-822-5087; Email info@moa.ubc.ca; Web: www.moa.ubc.ca; *Dir* Anthony Shelton; *Cur of Educ & Pub Prog* Jill Baird; *Cur Pacific Northwest* Pam Brown; *Cur Africa Pacific* Carol Mayer; *Sr Conservator* Heidi Swierenga; *Assoc Dir* Moya Waters; *Asst Dir* Anna Pappalardo; *Mgr Admin/Shop Wholesale* Salma Mawani; *Shop Mgr Retail* Sharon Haswell; *Information Mgr Audrey Harry Hawthorn Libr & Archives* Ann Stevenson; *Coll Mgr* Nancy Bruegeman; *Sr Mktg & Commun Mgr* Bonnie Sun; *Exhib Designer* Skooker Broome; *Pub Servs Mgr* Gwilyn Timmers
Open daily 10 AM - 5 PM, Thurs 10 AM - 9 PM, cl Mondays from Oct 15 - May 15; Admis family $47, adults $18, seniors & students $16, UBC students, staff & faculty, children 6 & under and MOA members free; Estab 1947 to develop a high quality institution that maximizes pub access & involvement while also conducting active progs of teaching, research & experimentation; Average Annual Attendance: 170,000; Mem: Dues family $75, couple $65, student & sr citizens $55, adult & student/sr couple $45
Library Holdings: Auction Catalogs, Book Volumes, Exhibition Catalogs, Pamphlets, Periodical Subscriptions
Special Subjects: American Indian Art, American Western Art, Anthropology, Antiquities-Etruscan, Antiquities-Greek, Antiquities-Oriental, Archaeology, Architecture, Asian Art, Ceramics, Coins & Medals, Crafts, Decorative Arts, Ethnology, Folk Art, Historical Material, Oriental Art, Textiles, Woodcarvings
Collections: Ethnographic areas around the world, especially the northwest coast of British Columbia, European ceramics, mus journals, oriental art & history
Activities: Classes for adults & children; volunteer training; lects open to pub, 20-30 vis lectrs per yr; gallery talks; tours; competitions with awards; exten dept; original objects of art lent to institutions for special exhibs; book traveling exhibs; originate traveling exhibs; mus shop sells books, original art, jewelry, reproductions, prints, slides, postcards, note cards & t-shirts

M **VANCOUVER ART GALLERY,** 750 Hornby St, Vancouver, BC V6Z 2H7 Canada. Tel 604-662-4719; Email customerservice@vanartgallery.bc.ca; Web: www.vanartgallery.bc.ca; *Chair* David Calabrigo; *Dir* Kathleen Bartels; *Assoc Dir & Chief Cur* Rochelle Steiner; *COO* Marie Dickens; *Assoc Dir & Chief Fin Officer* Beth McInnis; *Assoc Dir & Dir Opers & Mus Svcs* Tom Meighan; *Assoc Dir Engagement & Strategic Initiaves* Ann Webb; *Dir Mktg, Communs & Pub Affairs* Johanie Marcoux
Open daily 10 AM - 5 PM; Tues & Fri until 9 PM; Admis adults $24, sr citizens $20, students (with valid ID) $18, children (6-12) $6.50, children 5 & under & gallery members free; Estab 1931 to foster the cultural development of the community & a pub interest in the arts; Gallery moved in 1983 into a reconstructed 1907 classical courthouse which had been designed by Francis Rattenbury. The building contains 41,400 net sq ft of gallery space. Complex contains a total gross area of 164,805 sq ft; Average Annual Attendance: 300,000; Mem: 40,000; dues family $120, individual $75
Income: Financed by city, provincial & federal government grants, pvt & corporate donations, endowment
Library Holdings: Auction Catalogs 500, Audio Tapes 400, Book Volumes 46,000, CD-ROMs, Clipping Files 6,000, Exhibition Catalogs, Periodical Subscriptions 150, Slides 30,000
Special Subjects: Architecture, Asian Art, Drawings, Landscapes, Painting-American, Painting-British, Painting-Canadian, Painting-Dutch, Photography, Portraits, Prints, Sculpture, Textiles
Collections: 11,000 works, including drawings, film, objects, paintings, photographs
Publications: Ann Report; Calendar, 5 times per annum; Exhib Catalogues; biannual mems newsletter
Activities: Classes for adults & children; docent training; lect open to pub, 10 vis lectrs per yr; gallery talks; tours; concerts; individual paintings & original objects of art lent to museums who comply with security & climate control standards; originate traveling exhibs to major art mus across Canada & internationally; mus shop sells books, magazines, reproductions, postcards, posters, prints, native Indian art, jewelry, goods in leather, paper & wood by local artisans, non-circulating reference library open to the public

L **Library**, 750 Hornby St, Vancouver, BC V6Z 2H7 Canada. Tel 604-662-4709; Fax 604-682-1086; Email library@vanartgallery.bc.ca; Web: www.vanartgallery.bc.ca; *Chief Librn* Jane Devine Mejia; *Librn* Lynn Brockington
Open Mon - Thurs 11 AM - 5 PM; Estab 1931 to serve staff, docents, students & the public; For reference only; Average Annual Attendance: 3,000
Library Holdings: Auction Catalogs 500, Audio Tapes 400, Book Volumes 42,000, Clipping Files 6,000, Memorabilia, Pamphlets, Periodical Subscriptions 150, Photographs
Collections: Fine arts specializing in Canadian & contemporary art

L **VANCOUVER CITY ARCHIVES,** 1150 Chestnut St, Vancouver, BC V6J 3J9 Canada. Tel 604-736-8561; Fax 604-736-0626; Email archives@vancouver.ca; Web: vancouver.ca/archives; *Dir* Leslie Mobbs; *City Archivist* Heather M Gordon
Open Mon - Fri 9 AM - 5 PM; No admis fee; Estab 1933
Income: Financed by city appropriation
Library Holdings: Clipping Files, Fiche, Kodachrome Transparencies, Lantern Slides, Manuscripts, Maps, Memorabilia, Motion Pictures, Original Art Works, Original Documents, Other Holdings Charts; Civic Records; Drawings; Maps; Paintings, Pamphlets, Photographs, Slides, Video Tapes
Special Subjects: Maps, Painting-Canadian, Photography
Exhibitions: Temporary exhibs
Activities: Lect open to pub; tours

M **VANCOUVER PUBLIC LIBRARY,** Public Art Program, 350 W Georgia St, Vancouver, BC V6B 6B1 Canada. Tel 604-331-3603; Fax 604-331-3701; Email info@vpl.ca; Web: www.vpl.ca; *Head Librarian* Sandra Singh
Open Sun 11 AM - 6 PM, Mon - Thurs, 10 AM - 9 PM, Fri & Sat 10 AM - 6PM; Library estab 1887 as Vancouver Reading Room. Fine Arts coll estab 1930; Circ 255,900; Mem: 274,700; members free to those living in the region
Library Holdings: Auction Catalogs, Book Volumes 115,400 & 14,300 song books & performance scores, CD-ROMs 90, Compact Disks 17,900, DVDs 9,800, Exhibition Catalogs, Other Holdings Documentation files for British Columbia artists, Periodical Subscriptions 225
Special Subjects: Costumes, Decorative Arts, Painting-Canadian, Porcelain, Silver, Silversmithing, Furniture, Jewelry, Textiles
Activities: Educ progs; ebook, email & internet training for adults; author readings; progs co-sponsored with community groups

VERNON

M **VERNON PUBLIC ART GALLERY,** 3228 31st Ave, Vernon, BC V1T 2H3 Canada. Tel 250-545-3173; Fax 250-545-9096; Email info@vernonpublicartgallery.com; Web: www.vernonpublicartgallery.com; *Exec Dir* Dauna Kennedy Grant; *Curator* Lubos Culen
Open Mon - Fri 10 AM - 5 PM, Sat 11 AM - 4 pm, cl Sun; No admis fee, donations accepted; Estab 1967 for the coll & exhib of art work by Okanagan, national & international artists; Three gallery spaces professionally designed & measure 5500 sq ft, also reception area, gift shop & admin & kitchen area; Average Annual Attendance: 27,000; Mem: 420; dues family $40, individual $31.50, sr citizens & students $10, corporation $50
Income: Financed by mem, regional district & grants
Library Holdings: Exhibition Catalogs
Collections: Permanent coll consists of ceramics, paintings, prints, sculpture and serigraphs
Exhibitions: 20 exhibits ann
Publications: Art Quarterly
Activities: Classes for adults & children; lects, 3 vis lectrs per yr; gallery talks; concerts; tours; performances; competitions; book traveling exhibs 1 per yr; originate traveling exhibs; mus shop sells books, magazines, original art, reproductions & local handmade art crafts

VICTORIA

M **ART GALLERY OF GREATER VICTORIA,** 1040 Moss St, Victoria, BC V8V 4P1 Canada. Tel 250-384-4101, 250-384-4171 (Admin); Fax 250-361-3995; Email mloria@aggv.bc.ca; Web: https://aggv.ca/; *Dir* Jon Tupper; *Cur Asian Art* Barry Till; *Dir Finance & Admin* Barb Lucas; *Coll Mgr* Stephen Topfer; *Chief Cur* Michelle Jacques
Open Mon - Sun 10 AM - 5 PM, Thurs - 10 AM - 9 PM; winter Tues - Sat 10 AM - 5 PM, Thurs 10 AM - 9 PM, Sun 12 PM - 5 PM, cl Mon; Admis adults $13, seniors & students $11, children (6-17) $2.50, under 5 & members free;; Estab 1947; Six modern galleries adjoin 19th Century Spencer Mansion-Japanese Garden; Average Annual Attendance: 56,500; Mem: 1950; dues family $70, individual $50, student & non-resident $25; ann meeting 2nd wk of June
Income: $2,000,000 (financed by mem, city, federal & provincial grants)
Special Subjects: Asian Art, Decorative Arts, Oriental Art, Painting-European, Primitive art, Painting-British, Painting-Canadian
Collections: Chinese, Indian, Persian & Tibetan Art, Contemporary Canadian, American & European, European Painting & Decorative Arts from 16th-19th centuries, Japanese Art from Kamakura to Contemporary, Primitive Arts
Exhibitions: Approx 35 exhibs in 6 exhib halls, changing every 6 wks
Publications: Mem newsletter, 4 times per yr
Activities: Classes for adults & children; docent training; gallery in the schools prog; workshops; lects open to pub, 12 vis lectrs per yr; concerts; tours; gallery talks; exten dept serves BC; individual paintings & original objects of art lent to mus & local pub bldgs; lending colls contains cassettes, original art works, sculpture, scrolls, 4800 books, 5000 original prints, 2000 slides; book traveling exhibs 5-20 per yr; originate traveling exhibs; sales shop sells books, magazines, reproductions, stationery, jewelry, pottery, ornaments, glass & prints

L **Library,** 1040 Moss St, Victoria, BC V8V 4P1 Canada. Tel 250-384-4171; Fax 250-361-3995; Email library@aggv.ca; Web: https://aggv.ca; *Dir* Jon Tupper
Open 10 AM - 5 PM, Thurs 10 AM - 9 PM, Sun 12 - 5 PM; Adult $13; Estab 1951; Circ Non-circulating
Library Holdings: Book Volumes 7,000, Cassettes 25, Clipping Files 1,000, Compact Disks 50, DVDs 20, Exhibition Catalogs 2,500, Photographs 200, Slides 300, Video Tapes 50
Special Subjects: Antiquities-Assyrian, Antiquities-Byzantine, Antiquities-Egyptian, Antiquities-Etruscan, Antiquities-Greek, Antiquities-Oriental, Antiquities-Persian, Antiquities-Roman, Architecture, Art Education, Art History, Asian Art, Ceramics, Decorative Arts, Drawings, Embroidery, Etchings & Engravings, Folk Art, Glass, Graphic Arts, History of Art & Archaeology, Interior Design, Jade, Landscape Architecture, Mixed Media, Oriental Art, Painting-American, Painting-British, Painting-Canadian, Painting-Dutch, Painting-European, Painting-French, Painting-German, Painting-Italian, Painting-Japanese, Photography, Porcelain, Pottery, Prints, Sculpture, Silver, Silversmithing, Textiles, Watercolors, Woodcuts, Tapestries, Woodcarvings

A **BRITISH COLUMBIA MUSEUMS ASSOCIATION,** 675 Belleville St, Victoria, BC V8W 9W2 Canada. Tel 250-356-5700; Fax 250-387-1251; Email bcma@museumsassn.bc.ca; Web: www.museumsassn.bc.ca; *Interim Exec Dir* Alyssa Polinsky; *Pres* David Alexander

CANADIAN SOCIETY FOR EDUCATION THROUGH ART
For further information, see National and Regional Organizations

M **CRAIGDARROCH CASTLE HISTORICAL MUSEUM SOCIETY,** 1050 Joan Crescent, Victoria, BC V8S 3L5 Canada. Tel 250-592-5323; Fax 250-592-1099; Email info@thecastle.ca; Web: www.thecastle.ca; *Exec Dir* John Hughes
Open 10 AM - 4:30 PM; June 15 - Sept 6, 9 AM - 7 PM; Admis adults $14.25, senior $13.25, students $9.25, children 6 to 12 $5, 5 and under free; Estab 1959 for conservation & restoration of house; Average Annual Attendance: 150,000; Mem: 500; dues $25; ann meeting in the spring
Income: $1.4 mil (financed by progs & visitation)
Library Holdings: Auction Catalogs, Audio Tapes, Exhibition Catalogs, Kodachrome Transparencies, Photographs
Special Subjects: Architecture, Carpets & Rugs, Ceramics, Dolls, Embroidery, Furniture, Historical Material, Painting-American, Painting-Canadian, Period Rooms, Restorations, Stained Glass, Textiles
Collections: Historical objects pertaining to the years 1890-1908, 5000 objects used to furnish an historical turn of the century mansion
Publications: Castle Quarterly, newsletter, annual report
Activities: Classes for children; dramatic progs; docent training; lects open to pub, 2 vis lectrs per yr; gallery talks; tours; individual paintings & original objects of art lent to other qualified cultural institutions; lending coll contains books, original art works, prints & paintings; mus shop sells books & souvenirs

A **OPEN SPACE,** 510 Fort St, Fl 2 Victoria, BC V8W 1E6 Canada. Tel 250-383-8833; Email openspace@openspace.ca; Web: www.openspace.ca; *Exec Dir* Helen Marzolf; *New Music Coordr* Christopher Reiche; *Guest Cur* Doug Jarvis; *Technician* Miles Geisbrecht
Open Tues - Sat Noon - 5 PM, cl Mon & Sun; Admis by donation; Estab 1972, open space is dedicated to contemporary art through visual art, new music, performance, literature & new media; Circ 20,000; Gallery has 3000 sq ft, 220 running ft with full light grid controlled to level for works of art & for performance progs; Average Annual Attendance: 25,000; Mem: 150; dues $15 - $30
Income: $400,000 (financed by federal & provincial appropriations, city grants, donations, mem fees & self-generated revenue)
Library Holdings: Audio Tapes, Book Volumes, CD-ROMs, Exhibition Catalogs, Memorabilia, Original Art Works, Original Documents, Other Holdings, Periodical Subscriptions, Photographs, Slides, Video Tapes
Exhibitions: 10-12 contemporary visual art exhibs per yr
Publications: catalogues & monographs published for all exhibs (list available on request)
Activities: Teacher-in-residence prog; Lects open to pub, 8 vis lectrs per yr; concerts; gallery talks; tours; awards for music composers of international stature; visual art lects, new music, performance, new medium, interarts, readings; artist residencies; organize traveling exhibs as requested; mus shop sells books

M **ROYAL BC MUSEUM,** 675 Belleville St, Victoria, BC V8W 9W2 Canada. Tel 250-356-7226; Email reception@royalbcmuseum.bc.ca; Web: www.royalbcmuseum.bc.ca; *CEO* Prof Jack Lohman, CBE; *COO & Dep CEO Archives & Mus Opers* Angela Williams; *Exec Financial Officer* Melissa Sands
May 18 - Oct 6: Sun - Thur 10 AM - 5 PM, Fri & Sat 10 AM - 10 PM; Oct 7 - May 16: daily 10 AM - 5 PM; cl Dec 25 & Jan 1; Admis adults $26.95, senior (65 and over) & student (19 and over with ID) $18.95, youth (6-18) $16.95, children (3-5) free; Estab 1886 as British Columbia's provincial museum & archives, collecting artifacts & specimens of British Columbia's natural & human history; Average Annual Attendance: 880,000

L **ROYAL BRITISH COLUMBIA MUSEUM,** BC Archives, 675 Belleville St, Victoria, BC V8W 9W2 Canada. Tel 250-356-7226; Fax 250-387-2072; Email access@bcarchives.bc.ca; Web: https://www.royalbcmuseum.bc.ca; *Archives Mgr* Claire Gilbert
Open Mon - Fri 10 AM - 5 PM; Admis Adults (19+) $22, seniors (65+) , children (6-18) & students (19 + with ID) $16, children (3-5) free; Estab 1893 to collect & preserve all records relating to the historical development of British Columbia; Archival coll; 10,000 historical works documenting British Columbia
Income: Financed by provincial appropriation
Library Holdings: Audio Tapes, Book Volumes 70,380, Clipping Files, Exhibition Catalogs, Manuscripts, Original Art Works, Other Holdings Original documents; Maps, Pamphlets, Periodical Subscriptions 100, Photographs, Reels
Publications: Art reproductions

M **UNIVERSITY OF VICTORIA,** The Legacy Art Gallery, 630 Yates St, Victoria, BC V8W 1K9 Canada. Tel 250-721-6562; Fax 250-721-6607; Email curator@uvic.ca; Web: www.uvac.uvic.ca; *Dir* Mary Jo Hughes; *Cur* Caroline Reidel
Open Wed - Sat 10 AM - 4 PM; No admis fee; Estab 1963 to collect, preserve & exhibit the decorative arts, maintain teaching colls for the univ; Gallery has 3000 sq ft of environmentally controlled exhib space, three galleries programmed, loan exhibits & from coll permanent exhibit. Maintains reference library; Average Annual Attendance: 100,000
Income: $200,000 (financed by endowment & state appropriation)
Purchases: $500
Special Subjects: American Indian Art, American Western Art, Anthropology, Archaeology, Architecture, Asian Art, Ceramics, Costumes, Crafts, Decorative Arts, Drawings, Etchings & Engravings, Ethnology, Folk Art, Graphics, Islamic Art, Ivory, Jewelry, Medieval Art, Oriental Art, Photography, Porcelain, Portraits, Primitive art, Renaissance Art
Collections: Maltwood Collection of Decorative Art, contemporary art (Canadian), Ethnographic & design art, Pacific Northwest modern & contemporary
Exhibitions: Permanent collections, continuing and rotating
Publications: Collections related exhib catalogues
Activities: Lects open to pub, 10 vis lectrs per yr; gallery talks; tours; individual paintings lent to offices & pub spaces on campus; lending coll contains 3000 original prints, 1000 paintings & sculpture; lend original art objects to on & off campus borrowers; book traveling exhibs 5 per yr; originate traveling exhibs to local mus; mus shop sells books, original art, reproductions & prints

MANITOBA

BOISSEVAIN

M **MONCUR GALLERY,** 298 Mountain St, Boissevain, MB R0K 0E0 Canada; PO Box 1241, Boissevain, MB R0K 0E0 Canada. Tel 204-534-6662; Email info@moncurgallery.org; Web: www.moncurgallery.org; *Chmn* Shannon Moncur; *Secy* Phyllis Hallett; *Treas* Audrey Hicks
Open Tues - Sat 9 AM - 5 PM; Admis adults $5, children (6 to 10) $3, pre school (5 & under) free, tour rate (10 + people) $2 ea; Estab 1986; Native History; Average Annual Attendance: 500-1,000
Income: $8,000 (financed by city & state appropriation)
Special Subjects: Archaeology
Collections: Aboriginal artifacts dating back 10,000 years collected in the Turtle Mountain area, Aboriginal Artifacts

BRANDON

A **THE ART GALLERY OF SOUTHWESTERN MANITOBA,** 710 Rosser Ave Unit 2, Brandon, MB R7A 0K9 Canada. Tel 204-727-1036; Fax 204-726-8139; Email info@agsm.ca; Web: http://agsm.ca/; *Exec Dir* John Hampton
Open Tues, Wed, Fri 10 AM - 5 PM, Thurs 10 AM - 9 PM, Sat noon - 5 PM; No admis fee; Estab 1960 to promote & foster cultural activities in western Manitoba; Average Annual Attendance: 2,400; Mem: 400; dues $6 - $20; ann meeting May
Income: Financed by mem, city & provincial appropriations & federal grants
Exhibitions: Exhibitions of regional, national & international significance
Publications: Bulletin, every 2 months
Activities: Classes for adults & children; lects open to pub, 2 vis lectrs per yr; gallery talks; tours; competitions; individual paintings & original objects of art lent to mems; lending coll contains original art works, original prints, paintings, weaving

L **Brandon Public Library,** 710 Rosser Ave Unit 1, Brandon, MB R7A 0K9 Canada. Tel 204-727-6648; Email info@wmrl.ca; Web: https://www.wmrl.ca/brandon; *Chief Librn* Shelley Mortensen
Open Mon & Thurs 10 AM - 9 PM, Tues, Wed, Fri & Sat 10 AM - 6 PM, cl Sun; Circ Non-circulating; Open to mems
Library Holdings: Book Volumes 78,000

CHURCHILL

M **ESKIMO MUSEUM,** 242 LaVerendrye, Churchill, MB R0B 0E0 Canada. Tel 204-675-2030; Fax 204-675-2140; *Cur* Lorraine Brandson
Open Tues - Sat 9 AM - 5 PM, Mon 1 PM - 5 PM, cl Sun; No admis fee; Estab 1944 to depict the Eskimo way of life through the display of artifacts; Mus has large single display room; Average Annual Attendance: 10,500
Income: Administered & funded by the Roman Catholic Episcopal Corporation of Churchill Hudson Bay
Special Subjects: Eskimo Art, Ethnology, Sculpture
Collections: Contemporary Inuit carvings, ethnographic collections, prehistoric artifacts, wildlife specimens
Publications: Carved From the Land by Lorraine Brandson 1994
Activities: Films & slide shows for school groups upon request; tours upon request; original objects of art lent to special exhibs & galleries; mus shop sells books, original art, art cards, postcards & northern theme clothing (t-shirts, sweatshirts & caps)

L **Library,** 242 La Verendrye, PO Box 10 Churchill, MB R0B 0E0 Canada. Tel 204-675-2030; Fax 204-675-2140; Email chhbay@mts.net; *Cur* Lorraine Brandson; *Asst Cur* Diann Elliott
Open by appointment only; Circ Non-circulating; Estab mainly for Arctic Canada material
Purchases: $1,000
Library Holdings: Book Volumes 500, Clipping Files, Exhibition Catalogs, Maps, Photographs, Video Tapes
Special Subjects: Archaeology, Crafts, Eskimo Art, Ethnology, Handicrafts, Restoration & Conservation

DAUPHIN

M **DAUPHIN & DISTRICT ALLIED ARTS COUNCIL,** Watson Art Centre, 104 First Ave NW, Dauphin, MB R7N 1G9 Canada. Tel 204-638-6231; Fax 204-638-6231; Email info@watsonartcentre.com; Web: www.watsonartcentre.com; *Adminr* Cheryl Nicholson; *Pres* Michelle NyQuist; *Treas* Mark Tiefenbach
Open Mon - Fri Noon - 5 PM; No admis fee; Estab 1973 to provide a home for the arts in the Dauphin District; 1 large gallery; Average Annual Attendance: 20,000; Mem: Dues assoc $100, family $20, individual $15; ann meeting in Mar
Income: $100,000 (financed by mem, town appropriation, provincial appropriation, donations)
Exhibitions: Rotate several exhibits per month
Publications: Arts council newsletter, quarterly
Activities: Classes for adults & children; dramatic progs; concerts; gallery talks; tours; lending coll contains paintings & art objects; book traveling exhibs 1 or 2 per yr; originate traveling exhibs; mus shop sells books & original art

PORTAGE LA PRAIRIE

A **PORTAGE AND DISTRICT ARTS COUNCIL,** Portage Arts Centre, 11-2nd St NE, Portage la Prairie, MB R1N 1R8 Canada. Tel 204-239-6029; Fax 204-239-1472; Email pdac@mts.net; Web: www.portageartscentre.ca; *Exec Dir* Margaret Bernhardt-Lowdon
Open Tues - Sat 11 AM - 5 PM; 200 ft running wall space & 1,700 sq ft floor space; classroom; pottery studio; dance studio; library; Mem: dues students $20, adult $25, family $45, group $75
Activities: Classes; workshops; gift shop sells art supplies, original art

WINNIPEG

L **ARCHIVES OF MANITOBA,** 130-200 Vaughan St, Winnipeg, MB R3C 1T5 Canada. Tel 204-945-3971; Fax 204-948-2672; Email archives@gov.mb.ca; Web: www.gov.mb.ca/chc/index.html
Open Mon - Fri 9 AM - 4 PM; No admis fee; Estab 1952 to gain access to Manitoba's documentary heritage; to preserve the recorded memory of Manitoba
Income: Financed by provincial appropriation through the Minister of Culture, Heritage & Tourism
Collections: Hudson's Bay Company Archives, Documentary & archival paintings, drawings, prints & photographs relating to Manitoba
Activities: Individual paintings & original objects of art lent to pub institutions with proper security; book traveling exhibs

M **CANADIAN MUSEUM FOR HUMAN RIGHTS,** 85 Israel Asper Way, Winnipeg, MB R3C 0L5 Canada. Tel 204-289-2000; Fax 204-289-2001; Email info@humanrights.ca; Web: humanrights.ca; *Pres & CEO* John Young; *CFO* Susanne Robertson; *VPres Exhibs, Research & Design* Corey Timpson; *VPres Visitor Experience & Engagement* Jacques Lavergne; *VPres Pub Affairs & Progs* Angela Cassie; *Head Colls* Heather Bidzinski; *Finance Mgr* Lynn-Joy Slater; *Human Resources Dir* Lorraine Farmer; *VPres* John Kozlowski
Open Tues & Thur - Sun 10 AM - 5 PM, Wed 10 AM - 9 PM, cl Mon; Admis family $52, adults $21, seniors (65 & up) & students w/ID $17, youth (7-17) $10, members & under 7 free; Estab 2008 as a national museum dedicated to the evolution, celebration & future of human rights.; 11 exhibition galleries, a boutique & a research centre; exhibitions change quarterly
Income: Financed by Government of Canada under the Canadian Heritage Portfolio
Special Subjects: Photography, Portraits, Prints
Collections: archival documents, artifacts, art, rare books, film, scholarly articles, published works & oral histories
Activities: Family progs; teacher workshops; educational exhibitions; interpreter training; didactic printed materials; evaluation studies; lects open to pub, vis lectrs; gallery talks; tours for adults & children; original objects of art lent to other mus & galleries for use in exhibs; originate traveling exhibs to other mus, art galleries or spaces that meet conservation requirements across Canada & abroad; mus shop sells books, prints, photo related jewelry, children's gifts & postcards

M **DALNAVERT MUSEUM,** 61 Carlton St, Winnipeg, MB R3C 1N9 Canada. Tel 204-943-2835; Fax 204-943-2565; Email info@dalnavertmuseum.ca; Web: www.friendsofdalnavert.ca; *Pres* Dr Harry W Duckworth; *Chief Admin Officer* Jacqueline Frieseu; *Chief Prog Officer & Cur* Jennifer Bisch
Open Wed - Fri 12 - 4 PM, Sat - Sun 10 AM - 4 PM, cl Mon & Tues; Admis family $12, adults $6, sr citizens & students $5, youth $4; Estab 1975 to preserve & display the way of life of the 1895 well-to-do family; Average Annual Attendance: 2,000
Income: $200,000 (financed by municipal, provincial & federal funding, admissions, programming & donations)
Special Subjects: Architecture, Art History, Carpets & Rugs, Ceramics, Coins & Medals, Costumes, Crafts, Decorative Arts, Dolls, Drawings, Embroidery, Etchings & Engravings, Furniture, Glass, Historical Material, Ivory, Jewelry, Laces, Leather, Metalwork, Painting-Canadian
Collections: Home furnishings of the 1895 period: clothing, decorative arts material, furniture, household items, paintings & original family memorabilia
Activities: Educ prog; classes for adults & children; dramatic progs; docent training; lect open to pub; concerts; tours; mus shop sells books, magazines, original art, heritage seeds & work by local artisans

A **MANITOBA ASSOCIATION OF ARCHITECTS,** 137 Bannatyne Ave, 2nd Flr, Winnipeg, MB R3B 0R3 Canada. Tel 204-925-4620; Fax 204-925-4624; Email info@mbarchitects.org; Web: www.mbarchitects.org; *Exec Dir* Judy Pestrak; *Admin Asst* Taeng Phounsavat
Open Mon - Fri 9 AM - 5 PM; Estab 1906 as a Provincial Architectural Registration Board & professional governing body; Mem: 350; dues $375; ann meeting in Mar
Income: Financed by ann mem dues
Publications: Columns, quarterly

A **MANITOBA SOCIETY OF ARTISTS,** PO Box 21056, Winnipeg, MB R3R 3R2 Canada. Tel 204-832-3045; Email president@mbsa.ca; Web: www.mbsa.ca; *Pres* Bonnie Taylor; *VPres* Danielle King; *Treas* Allyson Watts; *Secy* Ruth Kamenev
Estab 1901 to further the work of the artist at the local & community levels; Mem: 105; dues $50; ann meeting Oct
Income: Financed by mem & commission on sales, donations
Special Subjects: Afro-American Art, Calligraphy, Crafts, Dioramas, Drawings, Etchings & Engravings, Landscapes, Miniatures, Oriental Art, Portraits, Posters, Prints, Sculpture, Watercolors, Woodcuts, Pottery
Exhibitions: Annual competition & exhibition open to all residents of Manitoba; Fresh Paint! annual mems exhib & sale; (mem only)
Publications: Newsletter
Activities: Educ aspects include teaching by mems in rural areas & artist-in-residence work in pub schools; workshops; how to hang exhibs; annual art history conference; lect open to pub; gallery talks; tours; competitions with awards; awards in memory of deceased mems; Bursary to post secondary students in fine arts or graphics; schols offered; originate traveling exhibs

M **PLUG IN,** Institute of Contemporary Art, 460 Portage Ave, Unit 1 Winnipeg, MB R3C 0E8 Canada. Tel 204-942-1043; Fax 204-944-8663; Email info@plugin.org; Web: www.plugin.org; *Pres* Sotirios Kotoulas; *Exec Dir* Jenifer Papararo; *Preparator* Theo Sims
Open Tues Wed Fri noon - 6 PM, Thurs noon - 8 PM, Sat & Sun noon - 5 PM; No admis fee; Estab 1974; 5,000 sq ft; 200 linear ft of gallery wall; renovated street-level gallery in historic Exchange District; Average Annual Attendance: 30,000; Mem: 350; dues $50 regular, $25 artists
Income: $650,000 (financed by mem, federal, city & state appropriation)
Library Holdings: Book Volumes, Exhibition Catalogs, Pamphlets, Periodical Subscriptions
Publications: Memories of Overdevelopment: The Philippine Diaspora in Contemporary Art (1998); Marcel Dzama: More Famous Drawings, Beck & Al Hanson: Playing with Matches, The Paradise Institute - Janet Cardiff & George Bures-Miller, Shaan Syed: Crowds & Constellations, Micah Lexier: David Then & Now, Mitch Robertson: 567 Economies of Good & Evil
Activities: Classes for children; lects open to pub, 10-20 vis lectrs per yr; gallery talks; tours; book traveling exhibs 4 per yr; originate traveling exhibs 4 per yr to galleries & artist-run centers; circulating internationally; mus shop sells books, magazines, original art & prints

M **UKRAINIAN CULTURAL & EDUCATIONAL CENTRE,** 184 Alexander Ave E, Winnipeg, MB R3B 0L6 Canada. Tel 204-942-0218; Fax 204-943-2857; *Pres Brd Dirs* Paul Stanicky
Open Mon - Sat 10 AM - 4 PM; No admis fee; Estab as the largest Ukrainian cultural resource centre & repository of Ukrainian historical & cultural artifacts in North America; Mem: 2000; dues $15, ann meeting June

Income: $216,328 (financed by province of Manitoba, federal government, donations, mem, trust fund, fundraising events)
Collections: Ukrainian Folk Art, folk costumes, embroidery, weaving, pysanky (Easter eggs), woodcarving, ceramics, coins, postage stamps and documents of the Ukrainian National Republic of 1918-1921, works of art by Ukrainian, Ukrainian-Canadian and Ukrainian-American artists: prints, paintings, sculpture, archives: Ukrainian immigration to Canada, music colls
Publications: Visti Oseredok/News from Oseredok, members' bulletin, 2-3 times per yr
Activities: Lect open to pub; gallery talks; tours; competitions; schols offered; individual paintings & original objects of art lent to educ institutions, galleries & museums; lending coll contains color reproductions, framed reproductions, motion pictures, phonorecords, 40,000 photographs, 2000 slides; book traveling exhibs ann; originate traveling exhibs; sales shop sells books, original art, reproductions, prints, folk art, phonorecords, cassettes

M **Gallery**, 184 Alexander Ave E, Winnipeg, MB R3B 0L6 Canada. Tel 204-942-0218; Fax 204-943-2857; Email ucec@mts.net; Web: www.oseredok.org; *Brd Dirs* Paul Stanicky
Open Mon - Sat 10 AM - 4 PM, Sun 1 PM - 4 PM (July - Aug); No admis fee; Mem: Dues family & organization $25, individual $15, student & sr citizen $5
Collections: 18th Century Icons, Contemporary Graphics (Archipenko, Gritchenko, Trutoffsky, Krycevsky, Hluschenko, Pavlos, Kholodny, Hnizdovsky, Mol, Levytsky, Shostak, Kuch), Contemporary Ukrainian, Canadian Coll

L **Library & Archives**, 184 Alexander Ave E, Winnipeg, MB R3B 0L6 Canada. Tel 204-942-0218; Fax 204-943-2857; *Pres Board Dirs* Paul Stanicky
Open Tues & Thurs 10 AM - 11 AM; For reference only; lending to mems
Library Holdings: Book Volumes 30,000, Cassettes, Clipping Files, Exhibition Catalogs, Motion Pictures, Other Holdings Ukrainian newspapers & periodicals, Pamphlets, Photographs, Records, Slides, Video Tapes
Publications: Visti, ann newsletter

M **UNIVERSITY OF MANITOBA,** School of Art Gallery, School of Art, 255 Art Lab, 180 Defoe Rd Winnipeg, MB R3T 2N2 Canada. Tel 204-474-8980; Fax 204-474-7605; Email donna.jones@umanitoba.ca; Web: www.umanitoba.ca/schools/art; *Gallery Dir* Mary Reid; *School of Art Dir* Paul Hess; *Gallery Admin Asst* Donna Jones
Open Mon - Fri 10 AM - 4 PM; No admis fee; Estab 1965; Circ 95; School of art gallery estab 1965 to provide exhibs of contemporary art & activities on the univ campus; exhibitions open to the pub; Average Annual Attendance: 20,000
Collections: Contemporary Canadian & American painting, prints & sculpture, L L Fitzgerald Study Collection
Exhibitions: Exhibs of Canadian, European & American Art, both contemporary & historical; special exhibs from other categories; ann exhibs by the graduating students of the School of Art
Publications: Exhib catalogues
Activities: Discussion groups; workshops; lects open to pub, 3-6 vis lectrs per yr; gallery talks; individual paintings & original objects of art lent; book traveling exhibs, 2-4 per yr; originate traveling exhibs

M **Faculty of Architecture Exhibition Centre**, 215 Architecture, 2 Bldg Winnipeg, MB R3T 2N2 Canada; 201 Russell Bldg, Winnipeg, MB R3T 2N2 Canada. Tel 204-474-9558; Fax 204-474-7532; Web: www.umanitoba.ca; *Co-Dir* Prof Michael Cox; *Co-Dir & Prof* Patrick Harrop
Open Mon - Fri 8:30 AM - 4:30 PM, weekend by special arrangements; Estab 1959 with the opening of the new Faculty of Architecture Building to provide architectural & related exhibs for students & faculty on the univ campus; 760 sq ft, secured climate controlled; over 900 linear ft of hanging space; Average Annual Attendance: 7,500
Income: Financed by endowments, grants & pvt sponsorships
Special Subjects: Antiquities-Greek, Antiquities-Roman, Archaeology, Architecture, Ceramics, Decorative Arts, Drawings, Etchings & Engravings, Furniture, Historical Material, Manuscripts, Mosaics, Painting-American, Painting-Canadian, Painting-French, Painting-German, Photography, Portraits, Pottery, Prints, Reproductions, Sculpture, Tapestries, Textiles, Watercolors
Collections: An extensive coll of drawings, prints, paintings, sculpture, ceramics, furniture & textiles (tapestries)
Exhibitions: Exhibs from a diversity of pvt & pub sources; annual exhibs by the students in the Faculty of Architecture
Activities: Lects open to pub, 6 vis lectrs per yr; gallery talks; symposia; individual paintings & original objects of art lent to recognized institutions; lending coll contains original art works, original prints, paintings, photographs, sculptures, furniture, textiles & ceramics

L **Architecture & Fine Arts Library**, 206 Russell Bldg, Univ Manitoba Winnipeg, MB R3T 2N2 Canada. Tel 204-474-9216; Fax 204-474-7539; Email mary_lochhead@umanitoba.ca; Web: http://libguides.lib.umanitoba.ca/architecture; *Art Librn* Liv Valmestad
Open Mon - Thurs 8:30 AM - 8 PM, Fri 8:30 AM - 4:30 PM, Sun noon - 8 PM, cl Sat; Estab 1916 to serve the needs of students & faculty in the areas of architecture, fine arts, landscape architecture, environmental design, city & regional planning, graphic design, interior design & photography; Circ 100,000; Average Annual Attendance: 68,645
Income: Financed primarily by provincial government
Library Holdings: Audio Tapes 75, Book Volumes 87,395, CD-ROMs 94, Cassettes 88, Clipping Files, Fiche 560, Lantern Slides 13,000, Maps 200, Other Holdings, Pamphlets, Periodical Subscriptions 250, Photographs, Reels 210, Slides 123,000, Video Tapes 294
Special Subjects: Architecture, Interior Design, Landscape Architecture, Photography

M **THE WINNIPEG ART GALLERY,** 300 Memorial Blvd, Winnipeg, MB R3C 1V1 Canada. Tel 204-786-6641; Fax 204-788-4998; Email inquiries@wag.ca; Web: www.wag.ca; *Dir & CEO* Stephen D Borys, PhD, MBA; *Chief Cur* Andrew Kear; *Cur Inuit Art* Darlene Coward Wight; *Head Educ* Rachel Baerg; *Head Mus Servs* Radovan Radulovlic; *Colls Mgr* Karen Kisiow; *Colls Mgr* Nicole Fletcher; *Mgr Media & Mktg* Catherine Maksymiuk; *Deputy Dir Fin & Admin* Bill Elliott; *Human Resources Mgr* Mike Malyk; *Accounting Mgr* Hugh Hansen; *Mgr Events & Rentals* Doren Roberts
Open Tues - Sun 11 AM - 5 PM, Fri 11 AM - 9 PM, cl Mon; Admis family $28, adults $12, sr citizens & students $10, children under 6 free; Estab 1912, incorporated 1963. Rebuilt & relocated 1968, opened 1972, to present a diversified, quality level prog of art in all media, representing various cultures, past & present; Circ Reference only; Building includes 9 galleries as well as displays on mezzanine level, sculpture ct & main foyer; Average Annual Attendance: 142,000; Mem: 4400; dues student $30, senior $50, individual $60, senior citizen couples $75, couple $85, family $95, Preferred $150-$2,500; annual meeting in Aug
Income: $3,500,000 (financed by endowment, mem, city, state & federal appropriation)
Special Subjects: Decorative Arts, Eskimo Art, Painting-American, Painting-Canadian, Photography, Sculpture, Drawings, Prints
Collections: Contemporary Canada, Contemporary Manitoba, Gort Collection, Master Prints & Drawings
Exhibitions: The changing exhibition includes contemporary & historical works of art by Canadian, European & American artists
Publications: Tableau (calendar of events), monthly; exhibition catalogs
Activities: Classes for adults & children; docent training; lects open to pub, 10 vis lectrs per yr; concerts; gallery talks; tours; exten dept serves Manitoba, Canada, United States & Europe; individual paintings & original objects of art lent to centres & mus; book traveling exhibs 4 per yr; originate traveling exhibs; mus shop sells books, magazines, original art, reproductions & prints

L **Clara Lander Library & Archives**, 300 Memorial Blvd, Winnipeg, MB R3C 1V1 Canada. Tel 204-786-6641, Ext 237; Fax 204-788-4998; Email librarian@wag.ca; Web: wag.ca; *Librn* Kenlyn Collins
Open by appt Thurs & Fri 1 - 4:30 PM; Estab 1954 to serve as a source of informational & general interest materials for members & staff of the Winnipeg Art Gallery & to art history students; Circ Reference only
Income: Financed by mem, city & provincial appropriations
Purchases: $10,000
Library Holdings: Auction Catalogs, Audio Tapes, Book Volumes 30,000, CD-ROMs, Clipping Files 10,000, Exhibition Catalogs, Lantern Slides, Manuscripts, Memorabilia, Original Documents, Pamphlets, Periodical Subscriptions 60, Photographs, Reels, Slides
Special Subjects: American Western Art, Art History, Ceramics, Decorative Arts, Photography
Collections: Archival material pertaining to Winnipeg Art Gallery, Rare Books on Canadian & European Art, George Swinton Collection on Eskimo & North American Indian Art & Culture, Artists' Files Collection, special collections

NEW BRUNSWICK

CAMPBELLTON

M **RESTIGOUCHE GALLERY,** 39 Andrew St, Campbellton, NB E3H 3H1 Canada. Tel 506-753-5750; Fax 506-759-9601; Email rgaleri@nbnet.nb.ca; *Pres* Brian Clark
Open Tues - Sat 10AM-4PM Sept to June, Summer 9AM-5PM, cl Sun & Mon; No admis fee; exhibitions in Jeanette MacDonald Room $3.00, Guided tour of Athol House Museum $6.00; Estab 1975 for exhibitions & activities; Building has 4800 sq ft; Exhibition hall is 1500 sq ft, small gallery 400 sq ft; 230 running feet; Average Annual Attendance: 25,000; Mem: 185; dues $20 single membership, $30 family, $50 assoc
Income: $60,000 (financed by provincial & city appropriations & private donations)
Collections: Athol House Museum Collection in Three Show Cases
Exhibitions: Hands on Signs
Publications: Exhibitions catalogues; Restigouche Gallery brochure
Activities: Classes for adults & children; art & craft workshops; lects open to public, 10 vis lectrs per yr; concerts; gallery talks; tours; book and cd launches; artists days; cultural center as well; traveling exhibs exten service; originate traveling exhibs; mus shop sells books, original art, reproductions, prints, cards, tourist items

FREDERICTON

M **BEAVERBROOK ART GALLERY,** 703 Queen St, Fredericton, NB E3B 1C4 Canada; PO Box 605, Fredericton, NB E3B 5A6 Canada. Tel 506-458-8545, 458-2028; Fax 506-459-7450; Email emailbag@beaverbrookartgallery.org; Email lglenn@beaverbrookartgallery.org; Web: www.beaverbrookartgallery.org; *Dir Emeritus* Bernard Riordon; *Dir & CEO* Terry Graff; *Finance Mgr* Jason Fitzgerald
Open Mon - Wed & Fri - Sat 10 AM - 5 PM, Thurs 10 AM - 9 PM, Sat 10 AM - 5 PM, Sun noon - 5 PM; Admis family $20, adults $10, seniors $8, students $5, children under 6 free; Estab 1959 to foster & promote the study & the pub enjoyment & appreciation of the arts; Major galleries upstairs; British, Canadian, High Galleries & Marion McCain Atlantic Gallery. East wing galleries: Hosmer, Pillow-Vaughan Gallery, Sir Max Aitken Gallery & Vaulted Corridor Gallery. Downstairs galleries: Joseph & Fanry Oppenheimer Gallery & Foyer Gallery; Average Annual Attendance: 45,000; Mem: 1000; dues family $60, individual $50
Library Holdings: Auction Catalogs, Book Volumes, Exhibition Catalogs, Pamphlets, Periodical Subscriptions, Video Tapes
Special Subjects: Decorative Arts, Furniture, Medieval Art, Painting-British, Painting-Canadian, Painting-European, Painting-Flemish, Painting-Spanish, Porcelain, Portraits, Religious Art, Renaissance Art, Tapestries
Collections: Hosmer-Pillow-Vaughan coll of continental European fine & decorative arts from the 14th & 19th century, Works by Dali, Constable, Gainsbourough, Hogarth, Cornelius Krieghoff, Reynolds, Sutherland & Turner, 16th-20th century English paintings, 18th & early 19th century English porcelain, 19th & 20th century Canadian & New Brunswick paintings, Contemporary modern & historical Canadian & British art
Publications: Tableau; The magazine of the Beaverbrook Art Gallery ann report, exhib catalogues

Activities: Classes for adults & children; lects open to pub; approx 12 vis lectrs per yr; gallery talks; tours; films; exten dept serving New Brunswick & Atlantic region; individual paintings lent to recognized art galleries; collection contains 3000 original art works, sculpture; 8-10 book traveling exhibs per yr; originate traveling exhibs throughout Canada & within N America; sales shop sells books, magazines & prints

L **Library**, 703 Queen St, Fredericton, NB E3B 5A6 Canada; PO Box 605, Fredericton, NB E3B 5A6 Canada. Tel 506-458-8545; Fax 506-459-7450; Web: www.beaverbrookartgallery.org; *Librn* Barry Henderson
Open to gallery personnel only, for reference
Library Holdings: Exhibition Catalogs, Video Tapes
Special Subjects: Decorative Arts, Furniture, Painting-British, Painting-Canadian, Painting-European, Painting-Flemish, Painting-Spanish, Porcelain, Portraits, Religious Art, Tapestries
Publications: Auction Catalogs

M **NEW BRUNSWICK COLLEGE OF CRAFT & DESIGN,** Gallery, 457 Queen St, Fredericton, NB E3B 5H1 Canada; PO Box 6000, Fredericton, NB E3B 5H1 Canada. Tel 506-453-2305; Fax 506-457-7352; Email nbccdrecruiting@gnb.ca; Web: www.nbccd.ca; *Gallery Coord* Karen Ruet
Open Sept - May, Mon - Fri 9AM - 4:30 PM; No admis fee; Estab 1938 to educate students as professional crafts people & designers; Maintains reference library
Income: Financed by provincial government
Exhibitions: Student & staff juried shows; periodic vis exhibitions
Activities: Classes for adults & children; lects open to pub, 10 vis lectrs per yr; awards; lending coll contains original art works, video tapes, slides & 3000 books

L **Library**, 457 Queen St, PO Box 6000 Fredericton, NB E3B 5H1 Canada; PO Box 6000, Fredericton, NB E3B 5H1 Canada. Tel 506-453-5938; Email julie.mcdonald@gnb.ca; *Library Coordr* Julie McDonald; *Dir Admin* Keith McAlpine
Open Mon - Fri, 8:15 AM - 4:30 PM; A very small but growing library which is primarily for students & craftsmen
Income: Financed by government & book donations
Library Holdings: Book Volumes 3000, Clipping Files, Exhibition Catalogs, Filmstrips, Pamphlets, Periodical Subscriptions 60, Slides, Video Tapes 300
Special Subjects: Advertising Design, Aesthetics, Afro-American Art, American Indian Art, American Western Art, Antiquities-Egyptian, Antiquities-Greek, Antiquities-Oriental, Antiquities-Roman, Architecture, Art Education, Art History, Asian Art, Calligraphy, Carpets & Rugs, Cartoons, Ceramics, Collages, Commercial Art, Conceptual Art, Costume Design & Constr, Decorative Arts, Display, Drawings, Fashion Arts, Film, Folk Art, Goldsmithing, Graphic Arts, Graphic Design, Handicrafts, Illustration, Interior Design, Jewelry, Latin American Art, Lettering, Metalwork, Mexican Art, Mixed Media, Oriental Art, Photography, Portraits, Posters, Pottery, Primitive art, Printmaking, Prints, Religious Art, Sculpture, Silversmithing, Tapestries, Textiles, Watercolors
Publications: Computerized catalogue

M **ORGANIZATION FOR THE DEVELOPMENT OF ARTISTS,** Gallery Connexion, 732 Charlotte St, Fredericton, NB E3B 1M7 Canada; PO Box 696, Fredericton, NB E3B 5B4 Canada. Tel 506-454-1433; Fax 506-454-1401; Email info@connexionarc.org; *Exec Dir* John Edward Cushnie; *Pres* Brendan Doyle
Open Fri & Sat noon - 6 PM; No admis fee; Estab 1984 to show contemporary experimental work; Maintains a reference library; Average Annual Attendance: 2,600; Mem: 110; dues full mem $30, assoc $20, students $15; ann meeting in March
Income: $50,000 (financed by mem, provincial appropriation & Canada Council)
Library Holdings: Exhibition Catalogs, Periodical Subscriptions, Video Tapes
Exhibitions: 6 shows per yr
Publications: Connexionews, monthly
Activities: Classes for adults; lects open to pub; 6-10 vis lectrs per yr; concerts; book traveling exhibs 6-10 per yr; originate traveling exhibs 1 per yr

M **UNIVERSITY OF NEW BRUNSWICK,** Art Centre, Memorial Hall, 3 Bailey Dr, PO Box 4400 Fredericton, NB E3B 5A3 Canada. Tel 506-453-4623; Fax 506-453-5012; Email artists@unb.ca; Web: www.unb.ca; *Dir* Marie Maltais
Open winter Mon - Fri 9 AM - 4:30 PM; summer Mon - Fri 9 AM - 4 PM; No admis fee; Estab 1940 to broaden the experience of the univ students & serve the city & province; Two galleries, each with approx 100 running ft of wall space; display case; Average Annual Attendance: 5,000
Income: Financed by provincial univ & grants for special projects
Purchases: $7,000
Library Holdings: Original Art Works, Photographs, Prints, Sculpture
Special Subjects: Etchings & Engravings, Painting-Canadian, Photography, Portraits, Pottery, Prints, Prints, Sculpture, Stained Glass, Textiles, Watercolors, Woodcuts
Collections: Chiefly New Brunswick Artists, some Canadian (chiefly printmakers)
Publications: Chiefly New Brunswick Artists; Canadian artists
Activities: Classes for adults & children; lects open to pub, 4 vis lectrs per yr; gallery talks; tours; individual paintings & original objects of art lent to pub but secure areas on this campus & the univ campus in Saint John & reproductions to students; lending coll contains framed reproductions, original prints, paintings, photographs, sculptures & slides; book traveling exhibs 4 per yr; originate traveling exhibs provincially to nationally

HAMPTON

M **KINGS COUNTY HISTORICAL SOCIETY & MUSEUM,** 27 Centennial Rd, Box 1813 Hampton, NB E5N 6N3 Canada. Tel 506-832-6009; Email kingscountymuseumnb@gmail.com; Web: www.kingscountymuseum.com; *Pres* Doug Crowell; *Cur* Bria Stokesbury; *Office Mgr* Kate MacInnes-Adams
Open Mon - Fri 9 AM - 4 PM; Admis adults $3, children $1; Estab 1968 to preserve loyalist history & artifacts; Maintains small reference library & research archives; Average Annual Attendance: 1,400; Mem: 300; dues society $20 & $ 25; ann meeting in Nov
Income: $2,250 (financed by provincial & student grants, dues, fairs & book sales)
Library Holdings: Fiche, Maps, Original Documents, Photographs
Special Subjects: Carpets & Rugs, Ceramics, Coins & Medals, Costumes, Decorative Arts, Dolls, Embroidery, Ethnology, Flasks & Bottles, Folk Art, Furniture, Glass, Historical Material, Ivory, Jewelry, Manuscripts, Maps, Metalwork, Painting-Canadian, Period Rooms, Pewter, Photography, Porcelain, Portraits, Pottery, Prints, Scrimshaw, Sculpture, Silver, Tapestries, Textiles, Watercolors, Woodcuts
Collections: Coin, dairy, glass, jewelry, quilts, Brass Measures (1854), tools; furniture; pottery, textiles; military
Exhibitions: The Mysterious Stranger, static display; The Home Children; Crime & Punishment: 200 Years in the Kings County Gaol
Publications: Memories newsletter, 7 per yr
Activities: Classes for adults & children; docent training; lects open to pub, 7 vis lectrs per yr; tours; life memberships; appreciation cert; mus shop sells books

MONCTON

M **GALERIE D'ART DE L'UNIVERSITE DE MONCTON,** 18 Avenue Antonne-Mallet, Moncton, NB E1A 3E9 Canada. Tel 506-858-4121; Fax 506-858-4043; Web: www.umoncton.ca; *Secy* Necol LaBlanc; *Technician* Paul Bourque; *Dir* Luc Charette
Open summer Mon - Fri 10 AM - 5 PM, Sat & Sun 1 - 5 PM; winter Tues - Sat 1 - 4:30 PM, Sat & Sun 1 - 4 PM; No admis fee; Estab 1965 to offer outstanding shows to the univ students & to the pub; 400 linear ft wall space, 3500 sq ft vinyl plywood walls, controlled light, temperature, humidity systems, security system; Average Annual Attendance: 13,000
Income: $100,000 (financed through univ)
Collections: Artists represented in permanent coll: Bruno Bobak, Alex Colville, Francis Coutellier, Tom Forrestall, Georges Goguen, Hurtubise, Hilda Lavoie, Fernand Leduc, Rita Letendre, Toni Onley, Claude Roussel, Romeo Savoie, Pavel Skalnik, Gordon Smith
Exhibitions: Rotating exhibits
Activities: Classes for children; dramatic progs; lects open to pub, 10 vis lectrs per yr; concerts; gallery talks; tours; individual paintings & original objects of art lent to univ personnel & art galleries & mus; lending coll contains 500 reproductions, 300 original art works, 180 original prints, 30 paintings, 20 sculpture

M **RADIO-CANADA SRC CBC,** Georges Goguen CBC Art Gallery, CBC, 250 University Ave, Moncton, NB E1A 3E9 Canada. Tel 506-858-4088; Fax 506-858-4043; Email ghg@nbnet.nb.ca; Web: www.radio-canada.ca/atlantique; *Dir* George Goguen
Open Mon - Fri 9 AM - 5 PM, Sat 9 AM - 1 PM; No admis fee; Estab 1972 for maritime artists; Gallery size 15 x 25, track lighting; Average Annual Attendance: 500
Library Holdings: CD-ROMs, Cassettes, Video Tapes
Special Subjects: Painting-American, Painting-Canadian, Painting-European, Painting-French, Photography, Posters, Prints, Religious Art, Sculpture, Watercolors, Woodcarvings, Woodcuts
Activities: Classes for children; 500 vis lectrs per yr; gallery talks; tours

SACKVILLE

M **MOUNT ALLISON UNIVERSITY,** Owens Art Gallery, 61 York St, Sackville, NB E4L 1E1 Canada. Tel 506-364-2574; Fax 506-364-2575; Email owens@mta.ca; Web: www.mta.ca/owens; Telex 014-2266; *Fine Art Conservator* Jane Tisdale; *Registrar/Preparator* Roxie Ibbitson; *Dir & Cur* Gemey Kelly; *Cur Educ* Lucy MacDonald
Open Mon - Fri 10 AM - 5 PM, Sat - Sun 1 PM - 5 PM; No admis fee; Estab 1895, rebuilt 1972; Building includes five gallery areas; conservation laboratory; Average Annual Attendance: 13,000
Income: Financed by Mount Allison University, government, corporate & pvt assistance
Special Subjects: Graphics, Painting-American, Sculpture
Collections: Broad coll of graphics, paintings, works on paper, 19th & 20th century Canadian, European & American Art, Contemporary Canadian
Publications: Exhib catalogs
Activities: Family Sundays; lects open to pub, 15 vis lectrs per yr; gallery talks; tours; individual paintings lent to other galleries & museums; book traveling exhibs 5 per yr; originate national traveling exhibs

M **STRUTS GALLERY,** 7 Lorne St, Sackville, NB E4L 3Z6 Canada. Tel 506-536-1211; Fax 506-536-4565; Email info@strutsgallery.ca; Web: www.strutsgallery.ca; *Prog Mgr* Amanda Fauteux; *Media Arts Mgr* Ryan Suter
Open 1 PM - 5 PM daily; No admis fee; Estab 1982; 1,000 sq ft; Average Annual Attendance: 1,500; Mem: Open to professional artist, assoc or student; dues professional $35, assoc & student $15; ann meeting in Oct
Income: $100,000 (financed by mem, Canada Council, Province of New Brunswick)
Exhibitions: Show work by contemporary living artists & a broad range of experimental art works
Activities: Lects open to pub, 2-5 vis lectrs per yr

SAINT ANDREWS

M **ROSS MEMORIAL MUSEUM,** 188 Montague St, Saint Andrews, NB E5B 1J2 Canada. Tel 506-529-5124; Fax 506-529-5183; Email rossmuse@nb.aibn.com; Web: www.rossmemorialmuseum.ca; *Dir* Margot Magee Sackett
Open early June to Thanksgiving Mon - Sat 10 AM - 4:30 PM; Admis by donation in season ($3 off-season); Estab 1980; One decorative arts collection in historic house; Average Annual Attendance: 8,000
Special Subjects: American Western Art, Architecture, Bronzes, Carpets & Rugs, Ceramics, Decorative Arts, Furniture, Landscapes, Painting-American, Painting-Canadian, Portraits, Watercolors
Collections: New Brunswick Furniture Collection, Ross Decorative Art Collection
Exhibitions: Special summer exhibit

Activities: Classes for children; lect open to pub

A **SUNBURY SHORES ARTS & NATURE CENTRE, INC,** Gallery, 139 Water St, Saint Andrews, NB E5B 1A7 Canada. Tel 506-529-3386; Fax 506-529-4779; Email info@sunburyshores.org; Web: www.sunburyshores.org; *Pres* Caroline Davies; *Exec Dir* Claire Shiplett
Open Mon - Sat - 10 AM - 4 PM; cl Sun; No admis fee; Estab 1964, to function as a link for & harmonize views of scientists, artists & industrialists; Gallery maintained, 200 running ft, fire & burglar protection, security during hours, controllable lighting & street frontage; Average Annual Attendance: 5,000; Mem: 400; dues family $50, individual, students & sr citizens $30; ann meeting in June/July
Income: Financed by endowment, mem, grants, revenue from courses & activities, including special projects
Collections: Instructor Artwork
Exhibitions: Exhibits change frequently throughout the yr
Publications: Brochure, summer annually; Sunbury Notes, quarterly; weekly newspaper column
Activities: Courses in fine arts & nature; lects open to pub, 10-15 vis lectrs per yr; concerts; gallery talks; Sunbury Shores Awards of Excellence; schols offered; mus shop sells books, original art, reproductions & prints

L **Library,** 139 Water St, Saint Andrews, NB E5B 1A7 Canada. Tel 506-529-3386; Fax 506-529-4779; Email sunshore@nbnet.nb.ca; Web: www.sunburyshores.org; *Dir* Lois Fenety
Open Mon-Fri 9 AM - 4:30 PM, cl Sat & Sun; No admis fee; Circ Non-circulating; Open to pub; primarily for reference
Income: Financed by mem
Library Holdings: Book Volumes 600, Exhibition Catalogs, Periodical Subscriptions 10

SAINT JOHN

M **NEW BRUNSWICK MUSEUM,** 1 Market Sq, Saint John, NB E2L 4Z6 Canada; 277 Douglas Ave, Saint John, NB E2K 1E5 Canada. Tel 506-643-2300, 888-268-9595; Fax 506-643-6081; Email nbmuseum@nbm-mnb.ca; Web: www.nbm-mnb.ca; *CEO* Bill Hicks; *Controller* Lane Atkinson; *Devel Mgr* Gary Chouinard; *Chmn Dept Natural Science, Head Zoology Sect & Research Cur* Dr Donald McAlpine; *Cur New Brunswick Cultural History & Art* Peter Larocque; *Head Botany & Mycology Sect & Research Cur* Dr Stephen Clayden; *History & Technology Cur* Gary Hughes; *Conservator* Dee Stubbs-Lee; *Communs & Mktg* Caitlin Griffiths
Open Mon, Tues, Wed, Fri 9 AM - 5 PM, Thurs 9 AM - 9 PM, Sat 10 AM - 5 PM, Sun Noon - 5 PM; Admis families $22, adults $10, seniors $8, students (18 & up) $7, children/students (17 & under) $6; Estab 1842 to collect, conserve, exhibit & interpret the Human & Natural history of New Brunswick in relation to itself & to the outside world; Twelve major galleries for permanent exhibits, three galleries for changing temporary exhibits; 62,000 sq ft gallery space; Average Annual Attendance: 75,000; Mem: 500; dues $32 - $1,000
Income: $1,600,000 (financed by municipal, federal & provincial appropriations)
Special Subjects: African Art, American Indian Art, Antiquities-Greek, Antiquities-Roman, Carpets & Rugs, Ceramics, Coins & Medals, Collages, Costumes, Crafts, Decorative Arts, Dolls, Drawings, Embroidery, Enamels, Eskimo Art, Etchings & Engravings, Ethnology, Flasks & Bottles, Folk Art, Furniture, Glass, Gold, Historical Material, Jewelry, Judaica, Laces, Landscapes, Leather, Manuscripts, Maps, Marine Painting, Metalwork, Military Art, Miniatures, Painting-American, Painting-British, Painting-Canadian, Period Rooms, Pewter, Prints, Sculpture, Tapestries, Textiles, Watercolors, Woodcarvings, Woodcuts
Collections: 3 galleries: Canadian Art, International Art, New Brunswick Art, Decorative Arts
Exhibitions: Various exhibitions
Activities: Educ prog; classes for adults & children; docent training; lects open to pub; 6-8 vis lectrs per yr; gallery talks; tours; competitions sponsored in schools; schols & fels offered; individual paintings & original objects of art lent to mus & galleries; book traveling exhibs 4-6 per yr; originate traveling exhibs nationally & internationally; mus shop sells books, original art & reproductions

L **Archives & Research Library,** 277 Douglas Ave, Saint John, NB E2K 1E5 Canada. Tel 506-643-2322; Fax 506-643-2360; Email archives@nbm-mnb.ca; Web: www.nbm-mnb.ca; *Head, Archives & Research Library* Felicity Osepchook
Open Tues - Fri 10 AM - 4:30 PM; Circ Non-circulating; Open to the pub for reference only
Income: nonprofit, government funded
Library Holdings: Auction Catalogs, Book Volumes 20,000, Clipping Files, Exhibition Catalogs, Fiche, Manuscripts, Original Documents, Periodical Subscriptions 75, Photographs, Reels
Special Subjects: Aesthetics, Afro-American Art, American Indian Art, American Western Art, Anthropology, Antiquities-Assyrian, Archaeology, Architecture, Art Education, Art History, Bookplates & Bindings, Bronzes, Calligraphy, Carpets & Rugs, Cartoons, Ceramics, Costume Design & Constr, Decorative Arts, Eskimo Art, Etchings & Engravings, Marine Painting, Oriental Art, Asian Art, Crafts, Folk Art, Furniture, Gold, Goldsmithing, Jewelry, Maps, Metalwork, Miniatures, Painting-American, Painting-British, Painting-Canadian, Photography, Porcelain, Portraits, Pottery, Printmaking, Prints, Restoration & Conservation, Scrimshaw, Silver, Silversmithing, Textiles, Watercolors

NEWFOUNDLAND

CORNER BROOK

M **MEMORIAL UNIVERSITY OF NEWFOUNDLAND,** Sir Wilfred Grenfell College Art Gallery, Fine Arts Bldg, 20 University Dr Corner Brook, NF A2H 5G4 Canada; Grenfell Campus Memorial University, PO Box 2000 Corner Brook, NF A2H 6P9 Canada. Tel 709-637-6209; Fax 709-637-6203; Email cjones@grenfell.mun.ca; Web: www.mun.ca; *Visual Arts* Kent Jones; *Head Div Arts* Ken Jacobson
Open Wed 12 PM - 5 PM, Fri 12 PM - 4 PM, Sat 12 PM - 4 PM; No admis fee; Estab 1988; 2,000 sq ft, 324.2 running ft, white walls, neutral carpet; Average Annual Attendance: 6,000; Mem: 300
Income: $100,000 (financed by univ & Canada Council)
Collections: Drawings, paintings, photography & prints (mainly contemporary Canadian)
Exhibitions: Changing contemporary exhibs every 7 wks
Publications: Exhibition catalogues
Activities: Docent progs; lects open to pub, 8 vis lectrs per yr; lending coll; book traveling exhibs 3 per yr; originate traveling exhibs 1 per yr; sales shop sells catalogues

SAINT JOHN'S

A **CRAFT COUNCIL OF NEWFOUNDLAND & LABRADOR,** Devon House, 59 Duckworth St Saint John's, NF A1C 1E6 Canada. Tel 709-753-2749; Fax 709-753-2766; Email info@crafcouncil.nl.ca; Web: www.craftcouncil.nl.ca; *Gallery Dir* Kailey Bryan; *Shop Mgr* Shannon Reid; *Exec Dir* Rowena House
Open Tues - Sat 10 AM - 5 PM; No admis fee; Estab 1991 to promote innovation & excellence in craft; The only gallery in Newfoundland & Labrador dedicated to the promotion & sale of fine craft. It encourages excellence & innovation & promotes craft as a valuable part of our cultural heritage. Maintains lending & reference library; Average Annual Attendance: 50,000; Mem: 300
Income: $80,000 (financed by federal government, foundations, fund raising & earned revenue)
Special Subjects: Ceramics, Crafts, Dolls, Embroidery, Enamels, Furniture, Jewelry, Leather, Metalwork, Pewter, Pottery, Scrimshaw, Stained Glass, Tapestries, Textiles
Collections: Craft Collection
Exhibitions: Revolving theme & solo exhibitions, 6-8 per year
Publications: Newsletter, 6 per yr
Activities: Classes for adults & children; lect open to pub; ann awards of excellence; juried; schols offered; sales shop sells high quality craft

M **THE ROOMS PROVINCIAL ART GALLERY,** 9 Bonaventure Ave, PO Box 1800, Station C Saint John's, NF A1C 5P9 Canada. Tel 709-757-8000; Fax 709-757-8017; Email information@therooms.ca; Web: www.therooms.ca; *Chair* Margaret Allan; *CEO* Dean Brinton
Open Spring/Summer: Mon - Tues, Thur, Sat 10 AM - 5 PM, Wed 10 AM - 9 PM, Sun noon - 5 PM; Fall/Winter: Tues, Thur, Sat 10 AM - 5 PM, Wed 10 AM - 9 PM, Fri 10 AM - 10 PM, Sun noon - 5 PM, cl Mon; Admis family $26, adults $10, seniors & students $6.50, youth (6-16) $5, under 5 free; Estab 1961 to display contemporary Canadian art, with an emphasis on Newfoundland work & provide visual art educ progs; Four galleries with 130 running ft each; Average Annual Attendance: 30,000; Mem: Dues household $75, adult & senior couple $45, student & senior $35
Income: Financed through the univ, federal funding & revenue generation
Collections: Newfoundland Contemporary, Folk & Historic Art, Post 1960 Canadian Art
Exhibitions: Contemporary art rotating exhibit
Publications: Catalogs of in-house exhibitions
Activities: Educ dept; docent training; lects open to pub, 10-12 vis lectrs per yr; concerts; gallery talks; tours; exten dept serves east coast of province; book traveling exhibs 8-10 per yr; originate traveling exhibs to Canadian & international pub art mus; sales shop sells books, art coll products, t-shirts, bags & cards

NOVA SCOTIA

CHERRY BROOK

L **SOCIETY FOR THE PROTECTION & PRESERVATION OF BLACK CULTURE IN NOVA SCOTIA,** Black Cultural Center for Nova Scotia, 10 Cherry Brook Rd, Cherry Brook, NS B2Z 1A8 Canada. Tel 902-434-6223; Fax 902-434-2306; Email contact@bccns.com; Web: www.bccns.com; *Exec Dir* Russell Grosse
Open Sept 1 - May 31, Mon - Fri 9 AM - 5 PM; June 1 - Sept 1, Mon - Fri 9:30 AM - 4:30 PM, noon - 3 PM; Admis families $20, adults $6, students & seniors $4, under 5 free; Estab 1984; For reference only; Average Annual Attendance: 10,000; Mem: Dues $15 & up
Income: Financed by provincial & federal government
Library Holdings: Audio Tapes, Book Volumes 3000, Cassettes, Clipping Files, Framed Reproductions, Lantern Slides, Manuscripts, Memorabilia, Original Art Works, Pamphlets, Prints, Records, Reproductions, Slides, Video Tapes
Collections: African Nova Scotians
Exhibitions: African Canadians
Publications: Newsletter Preserver
Activities: Lect open to public; school tours; presentations; sales shop sells books

DARTMOUTH

M **DARTMOUTH HERITAGE MUSEUM,** (Regional Museum of Cultural History), 26 Newcastle St, Evergreen House Dartmouth, NS B2Y 3M5 Canada. Tel 902-464-2300; Fax 902-464-8210; Email info@dartmouthmuseum.ca; Web: www.dartmouthheritagemuseum.ns.ca; *Dir* Beth Vallis; *Dir* Susan Merchant; *Dir* Marilyn More; *Dir* David Jones; *Dir* Anita Campbell
Open June to Aug Tues - Fri 10 AM - 5 PM, Sat & Sun 10 AM - 1 PM & 2 PM - 5 PM, Sept to May, Tues - Fri 10 AM - 5 PM, Sat 10 AM - 1 PM & 2 PM - 5 PM; Admis adults $5, under 12 free; Estab 1967 to collect & preserve the history &

heritage of the Dartmouth & area; Average Annual Attendance: 15,000; Mem: 110 mems, $20 yr dues Aug-June
Income: Financed by city appropriation, provincial funds & fundraising
Special Subjects: Ceramics, Costumes, Dolls, Embroidery, Furniture, Glass, Graphics, Painting-Canadian, Painting-European, Photography, Porcelain, Portraits, Posters, Pottery, Prints, Scrimshaw, Textiles, Watercolors
Collections: Local history collection including art, archival, textile/costume & general social history material
Exhibitions: Four exhibitions scheduled per year
Activities: Classes for adults & children; gallery talks; tours; exten dept serves historic houses; mus shop sells CDs, calendars & note cards

HALIFAX

M **ART GALLERY OF NOVA SCOTIA,** 1723 Hollis St, Halifax, NS B3J 1V9 Canada; PO Box 2262, Halifax, NS B3J 3C8 Canada. Tel 902-424-7542; Fax 902-424-7359; Web: www.ednet.ns.ca/educ/heritage/agns; *Dir & CEO* Nancy Noble; *Cur Colls* Shannon Parker
Open Mon - Sun 10 AM - 5 PM, Thurs 10 AM - 9 PM; Admis family $25, adults $12, seniors $10, students with valid ID $7, youth (6-17) $5, children 5 & under & members free; Estab 1975 to replace the Nova Scotia Mus of Fine Arts, dedicated to serving the pub by bringing the visual arts & people together in an environment which encourages exploration, dialogue & enjoyment; Thirty-five galleries, for permanent collection & temporary exhibitions; Average Annual Attendance: 85,000; Mem: 3500; dues life members $2000, family $75, individual $50, senior couple $55, senior individual $35, young member/student $20
Income: Financed by Nova Scotia Dept of Tourism, Culture & Heritage, Dept of Canadian Heritage, The Canada Council, municipal governments, private foundations & individual & corporate supporters
Purchases: $150,000
Special Subjects: Ceramics, Crafts, Decorative Arts, Drawings, Embroidery, Eskimo Art, Etchings & Engravings, Folk Art, Graphics, Historical Material, Illustration, Landscapes, Maps, Marine Painting, Medieval Art, Oriental Art, Painting-American, Painting-British, Painting-Canadian, Painting-European, Photography, Porcelain, Portraits, Pottery, Prints, Religious Art, Renaissance Art, Reproductions, Sculpture, Tapestries, Textiles, Watercolors, Woodcarvings, Woodcuts
Collections: Canadian Historical & Contemporary Art Collection drawings, paintings, prints, sculpture, ceramics & international art, Nova Scotia Folk Art Collection, Nova Scotian Collection
Exhibitions: Rotating exhibits
Activities: Classes for adults & children; docent training; outreach; lects open to pub, 5-10 vis lectrs per yr; gallery talks; tours, family Sundays, family weekends; Black Tie Gala; Pick of the Month; Sobey Art Award; exten dept serves Province of Nova Scotia; artmobile; individual paintings & original objects of art lent to Province & Government House; lending collection contains original art works, framed reproductions, original prints, paintings & sculpture; book traveling exhibs 2-3 per yr; originate traveling exhibs 10-15 per yr; mus & sales shop sells books, jewelry, magazines, original art, pottery, prints, reproductions, slides, crafts & also rental service

M **DALHOUSIE UNIVERSITY,** Dalhousie Art Gallery, 6101 University Ave, PO Box 15000 Halifax, NS B3H 4R2 Canada. Tel 902-494-2403; Fax 902-423-0591; Email art.gallery@dal.ca; Web: artgallery.dal.ca; *Registrar & Preparator* Michele Gallant; *Dir & Cur* Peter Dykhuis
Open Tues - Fri 11 AM - 5 PM, Sat & Sun noon - 5 PM; No admis fee; Estab 1943 to collect, preserve, interpret & display works of art, primarily of Canadian origin; Dalhousie Art Gallery is located in the Dalhousie Arts Centre and open to university community and local area; it contains 4 galleries, 400 running ft of wall space & 4000 sq ft floor space; Average Annual Attendance: 12,000
Income: Financed by university supplemented by government grants
Collections: Canadian works on paper, Atlantic Canadian artists all media
Exhibitions: Contemporary & historical exhibitions
Publications: Annual Report; Calendar of Events, 3 times per yr, exhibition catalogues & brochures
Activities: Classes for children; docent training; lects open to pub, 12 vis lectrs per yr; concerts; gallery talks; tours; exten dept serves regional & national area; individual paintings & original objects of art lent to professional galleries & campus areas; book traveling exhibs; originate traveling exhibs; sales shop sells gallery publications

M **EYE LEVEL GALLERY,** 5663 Cornwallis St, Ste 101 Halifax, NS B3K 1B6 Canada. Tel 902-425-6412; Fax 902-425-0019; Email director@eyelevelgallery.ca; Web: www.eyelevelgallery.ca; *Artistic Dir* Julie McMillan
Open Tues - Fri Noon - 5 PM; No admis fee; Estab 1974 to exhibit contemporary art in a non-museum setting; Ten 25 x 40 ft windows on one end; white, grey floor, 2 small pillars. Exhibiting every 4 wks (Sept-Apr) & every 2 wks during the summer; Average Annual Attendance: 10,000; Mem: 150; dues $6 & up; meetings in Feb, Mar, Apr, June, Aug & Nov
Income: $65,000 (financed by mem, Canada Council, Nova Scotia Arts Council)
Collections: Art Poster, 1974-Present, Artist Books Collection
Exhibitions: Cultural Competition; rotating exhibits
Publications: Exhibition catalogues
Activities: Lects open to pub, 5 vis lectrs per yr; competition with awards; sales shop sells books

M **MOUNT SAINT VINCENT UNIVERSITY,** MSVU Art Gallery, 166 Bedford Hwy, Halifax, NS B3M 2J6 Canada. Tel 902-457-6291, 457-6160; Fax 902-457-2447; Email art.gallery@msvu.ca; Web: www.msvuart.ca; *Admin Asst & Website Mgr* Traci Steylen; *Dir Art Gallery* Ingrid Jenkner; *Gallery Technician* David Dahms; *Prog Coordr* Claire Dykuis
Open Tues - Fri 11 AM - 5 PM, Sat, Sun 1 - 5 PM, cl Mon & holidays; No admis fee; Estab 1970 & operating throughout the year with continuously-changing exhibitions of local, regional, national & international origin in the area of visual culture; Gallery situated on the main floor & mezzanine; Average Annual Attendance: 15,000
Income: Financed by university funds & Canada Council for the Arts
Special Subjects: Ceramics, Collages, Decorative Arts, Embroidery, Etchings & Engravings, Graphics, Landscape Architecture, Painting-Canadian, Photography, Porcelain, Pottery, Prints, Sculpture, Tapestries, Textiles, Watercolors, Woodcuts
Collections: The Art Gallery is custodian of a collection of pictures, ceramics & pottery of the late Alice Egan Hagen of Mahone Bay, noted Nova Scotia potter & ceramist, works by Atlantic region artists; contemporary Canadian art, women artists
Publications: Gallery News, biannual; exhib catalogs
Activities: Lects open to public, 4 vis lectrs per yr; gallery talks; tours; book traveling exhibs 2 per yr; originate traveling exhibs to Canadian art galleries

A **NOVA SCOTIA ASSOCIATION OF ARCHITECTS,** 1361 Barrington St, Halifax, NS B3J 1Y9 Canada. Tel 902-423-7607; Fax 902-425-7024; Email info@nsaa.ns.ca; Web: nsaa.ns.ca; *Exec Dir* Margo Dauphinee
Open Mon - Fri 9 AM - 5 PM; Estab 1932 to license & regulate architects of Nova Scotia; Mem: 200; annual meeting in Apr
Income: Financed by memberships
Publications: Newsletter, monthly

M **NOVA SCOTIA CENTRE FOR CRAFT & DESIGN,** Mary E Black Gallery, 1061 Marginal Rd, Ste 140 Halifax, NS B3H 4P7 Canada. Tel 902-492-2522; Fax 902-492-2526; Email info@craft-design.ns.ca; Web: www.craft-design.ns.ca; *Dir* Susan Charles; *Studio Coordr* Alexis Vessey
Open Tues - Fri 9 AM - 5 PM, Sat & Sun 11 AM - 4 PM; cl Mon & holidays; No admis fee; Estab 1990; 900 sq ft in Halifax's seawall develop area near Pier 21 national site. Meets Canadian Conservation Institute Standards for temporary exhibitions; Average Annual Attendance: 15,000
Collections: Permanent collection of crafts
Exhibitions: 6 contemporary, temporary shows of craft & design annually
Publications: Exhibition catalogues
Activities: Classes for adults; lects open to pub, 51 vis lectrs per yr; gallery talks; tours

M **NOVA SCOTIA COLLEGE OF ART AND DESIGN,** Anna Leonowens Gallery, 1891 Granville St, Halifax, NS B3J 3J6 Canada; 5163 Duke St, Halifax, NS B3J 3J6 Canada. Tel 902-494-8223; Fax 902-425-3997; Email annaleonowens@nscad.ca; Web: www.nscad.ca; *Gallery Dir* Melanie Colosimo; *Exhibs Coord* Kate Walchuk
Open Tues - Fri 11 AM - 5 PM, Mon evenings 5:30 - 7:30 PM, Sat Noon - 4 PM; No admis fee; Estab 1968 for educational purposes; 3 exhibition spaces; Average Annual Attendance: 20,000
Income: Financed by state appropriations & tuition
Special Subjects: Ceramics, Collages, Crafts, Drawings, Etchings & Engravings, Graphics, Jewelry, Metalwork, Prints, Sculpture, Textiles
Collections: NSCAD permanent coll, prints from NSCAD lithography workshop
Exhibitions: 120 exhibitions per yr
Publications: Ten books; exhibition catalogs, occasionally
Activities: Lects open to pub; 2 vis lectrs per yr; gallery talks

L **Library,** 5163 Duke St, Halifax, NS B3J 3J6 Canada. Tel 902-494-8196; Fax 902-425-2420; Email library@nscad.ca; Web: www.nscad.ca; *Dir Library Servs* Rebecca Young
Open Mon - Fri 9 AM - 5 PM, Sat Noon - 4 PM; No admis fee; Estab 1887; Circ 30,000
Income: Financed by state appropriation & student fees
Purchases: $120,000
Library Holdings: Book Volumes 50,000, CD-ROMs, Cassettes, Compact Disks, DVDs, Exhibition Catalogs, Fiche, Motion Pictures, Pamphlets, Periodical Subscriptions 250, Records, Reels, Slides, Video Tapes

M **NOVA SCOTIA MUSEUM,** Maritime Museum of the Atlantic, 1675 Lower Water St, Halifax, NS B3J 1S3 Canada. Tel 902-424-7490; Fax 902-424-0612; Web: https://maritimemuseum.novascotia.ca; *Cur Marine History* Rogers Marsters; *Registrar* Lynn-Marie Richard; *Lead Vis Svcs* Krista Jordan; *Mktg & Events Officer* Jenny Nodelman; *Sr Preparator* Corey Mullins; *Gen Mgr* Kim Reinhardt
Open May - Oct: Tues 9:30 AM - 8 PM, Mon & Wed - Sun 9:30 AM - 5:30 PM; Nov - April 30: Tues 9:30 AM - 8 PM, Wed - Sat 9:30 AM - 5 PM, Sun 1 - 5 PM; Admis May - Oct: family $24.75, adult $9.55, senior 65+ $8.50, youth 6-17 $5.15, child 5 & under free; Nov - April: family $11.85, adult $5.15, senior $4.40, youth $3.10, child 5 and under free; Estab 1948 to interpret maritime history of eastern coast of Canada; Gallery exhibits items from Days of Sail, Age of Steam, Navy, Small Craft, Shipwrecks, Underwater Archaeology, Titanic & Halifax Explosion; Average Annual Attendance: 175,000
Income: Financed by province of Nova Scotia Dept Tourism & Culture
Library Holdings: Book Volumes, Clipping Files, Photographs, Slides
Special Subjects: Crafts, Marine Painting
Collections: Halifax Explosion, Historical Marine Painting display, small craft, ship models, ship portraits, uniforms, marine artifacts, Titanic artifacts, WWII Atlantic convoys, Sable Island Canadian Navy
Exhibitions: Rotate 6-8 per yr
Activities: School progs; interpretive progs & tours; lects open to pub; gallery talks; concerts (sea shanties); tours; individual paintings & original objects of art lent to other institutions; mus shop sells books, reproductions, clothing, marine memorabilia & toys

M **ST MARY'S UNIVERSITY,** Art Gallery, 5865 Gorsebrook Ave, Loyola Bldg 1st Fl Halifax, NS B3H 1G3 Canada; 923 Robie St, Halifax, NS B3H 3C3 Canada. Tel 902-420-5445; Fax 902-420-5060; Email gallery@smu.ca; Web: www.smuartgallery.ca; *Dir & Cur* Robin Metcalfe; *Admin Asst* Sara Benini; *Asst Cur* Pam Corell
Open Tues - Fri 11 AM - 5 PM, Sat - Sun Noon - 5 PM; No admis fee; Estab 1970 to present a variety of exhibitions & performances of both regional & national interest & by contemporary artists; Average Annual Attendance: 12,000
Income: Financed by provincial appropriation
Collections: Works on paper by contemporary Canadian artists
Publications: Exhibit catalogues, 1-2 times per year
Activities: Adult drawing classes; lects open to public, 3-4 vis lectrs per year; concerts; gallery talks; tours; individual paintings & original objects of art lent;

exten dept serves university; book traveling exhibs 1-2 per yr; originate 1 traveling exhib; circulated to the Atlantic Provinces of Canada; sales shop sells catalogs

A **VISUAL ARTS NOVA SCOTIA,** 1113 Marginal Rd Halifax, NS B3H 4P7 Canada. Tel 902-423-4694, 866-225-8267 (toll free); Fax 902-422-0881; Email vans@visualarts.ns.ca; Web: visualarts.ns.ca; *Exec Dir* Briony Carros; *Paints Coordr* Andrea Ritchie; *Prog Coordr* Carrie MacKay
Open Mon - Fri 9:30 AM - 5 PM; No admis fee; Estab 1976 as a non-profit arts service organization to foster the development, awareness & understanding of the visual arts in Nova Scotia. Encourages the production, exhibition & appreciation of works by Nova Scotia's visual artists; 1 small gallery maintains slide registry, video library & archives & off-site exhib space - 5 small vitrines; Average Annual Attendance: 1,000; Mem: Over 600; dues corporate $65, couple/group/gallery $45, individual $35, senior $30, student $25
Income: $170,000 (financed by fund raising, mem & provincial appropriation)
Library Holdings: Audio Tapes, Book Volumes, Exhibition Catalogs, Pamphlets, Slides, Video Tapes
Exhibitions: Far & Wide: third biennial exhibition; biennial juried exhibitions, annual open exhibitions & occasional regional exhibitions
Publications: Visual Arts News, 3 times per yr
Activities: PAINTS (Professional Artists in the Schools); classes for adults; workshop prog; mentorship prog; educ prog; internships offered

LUNENBURG

M **LUNENBURG ART GALLERY SOCIETY,** 79-81 Pelham (corner Pelham & Duke), PO Box 1418 Lunenburg, NS B0J 2C0 Canada. Tel 902-640-4044; Fax 902-640-3035; Email lag@eastlink.ca; Web: www.lunenburgartgallery.com; *Pres* Mike Dobson
Open Tues - Sat 10 AM-5 PM, Sun 1-5 PM, cl Mon; No admis fee; Estab 1977 to provide art appreciation to community & venue for artists; 1 exhib gallery & 1 members' gallery; Average Annual Attendance: 4,000; Mem: 150; dues supporters $20; exhibiting artists $30
Income: $30,000 (financed by mem & fundraising)
Purchases: Collection of Earl Bailly Paintings, Lunenburg Mouth Painter
Library Holdings: Cards, Clipping Files, Exhibition Catalogs, Framed Reproductions, Memorabilia, Original Art Works, Original Documents, Pamphlets, Periodical Subscriptions, Photographs, Prints, Reproductions, Sculpture
Collections: Meldrum Collection by Earl Bailly
Exhibitions: Exhibits rotate once per month with "opening receptions" on a Tues - 5 PM every month
Activities: Classes for children; art workshops, school progs; competitions; sales shop sell books, original art, reproductions, prints, cards & notes

WOLFVILLE

M **ACADIA UNIVERSITY ART GALLERY,** 10 Highland Ave, Beveridge Arts Centre Wolfville, NS B4P 2R6 Canada; c/o Beveridge Arts Centre, Rm 129 Wolfville, NS B4P 2R6 Canada. Tel 902-585-1373; Email artgallery@acadiau.ca; Web: gallery.acadiau.ca; *Dir/Cur* Dr Laurie Dalton
Open Tues - Sun noon - 4 PM, Weds 12 PM - 7 PM, cl Mon; No admis fee; Estab 1978, art dept 1928, to exhibit contemporary & historical art particularly from the Atlantic region; Average Annual Attendance: 15,000; Mem: $10 membership
Income: $65,000 (financed by endowment & University funds)
Purchases: $15,000 (works by Atlantic region artists)
Collections: Contemporary & Historical Paintings, Drawings & Prints
Activities: Lects open to pub; 4 vis lectrs per yr; book traveling exhibs 8 per yr; originate traveling exhibs 4 per yr

YARMOUTH

M **YARMOUTH COUNTY HISTORICAL SOCIETY,** Yarmouth County Museum & Archives, 22 Collins St, Yarmouth, NS B5A 3C8 Canada. Tel 902-742-5539; Fax 902-749-1120; Email ycmuseum@eastlink.ca; Web: www.yarmouthcountymuseum.ca; *Cur/Dir* Nadine Gates; *Archivist* Lisette Gaudet
Open June 1 - Sept 30 Mon - Sat 9 AM - 5 PM, Oct 1 - May 30 Tues - Sat 2 PM - 5 PM, cl Sun; Admis adults $3, students $1, seniors (60+) $2.50, children (6-14) $.50, family $6, children under 6 & members free; Estab 1958 to display artifacts & paintings relating to Yarmouth's past; Located in former Congregational Church built in 1893; Average Annual Attendance: 14,000; Mem: 400; dues $25; meetings first Thurs each month
Income: $170,000 (financed by mem, admis & state appropriation)
Purchases: $500
Library Holdings: Audio Tapes, Book Volumes, CD-ROMs, Cassettes, Clipping Files, Compact Disks, DVDs, Exhibition Catalogs, Fiche, Manuscripts, Maps, Memorabilia, Original Art Works, Original Documents, Other Holdings, Pamphlets, Photographs, Prints
Special Subjects: Coins & Medals, Costumes, Crafts, Decorative Arts, Dolls, Drawings, Embroidery, Etchings & Engravings, Ethnology, Flasks & Bottles, Folk Art, Folk Art, Furniture, Glass, Graphics, Historical Material, Ivory, Laces, Landscapes, Manuscripts, Marine Painting, Military Art, Painting-Canadian, Period Rooms, Pewter, Photography, Porcelain, Portraits, Restorations, Textiles
Collections: Gen historical coll, paintings of & by Yarmouthians, coll of ship portraits of Yarmouth vessels & vessels commanded by Yarmouthians, gen & marine artifacts, marine drawings & portraits
Exhibitions: Various local exhibits
Publications: Monthly newsletter
Activities: Classes for children; lects open to pub, 12 vis lectrs per yr; concerts; gallery talks; tours; Heritage Awards; books traveling exhibs 1 per yr; mus shop sells books, prints, reproductions, local handicrafts, pewter jewelry

ONTARIO

ALMONTE

M **MISSISSIPPI VALLEY CONSERVATION AUTHORITY,** R Tait McKenzie Memorial Museum, 2854 Ramsay Concession 8, Mill of Kintail Conservation Area Almonte, ON K0A 1A0 Canada; 10970 Hwy 7, Carleton Place, ON K7C 3P1 Canada. Tel 613-253-0006; Fax 613-253-0122; Email info@mvc.on.ca; Web: www.mvc.on.ca; *Gen Mgr* Paul Lehman; *Cur* Stephanie Kolsters; *Educ Coordr* Sarah O'Grady
Open Mon - Fri 9 AM - 3:30 PM, Sat & Sun 10:30 AM - 4:30 PM; Admis $6 per vehicle, $3 per pers for buses & tour groups; Estab 1952 as a private mus, publicly owned since 1973 by Mississippi Valley Conservation Authority as a memorial to Dr R Tait McKenzie, Canadian sculptor, physical educator, surgeon & humanitarian. Home to Dr James Naismith, inventor of basketball, museum; Average Annual Attendance: 7,500
Income: Financed by provincial government grant
Library Holdings: Exhibition Catalogs, Manuscripts, Memorabilia, Original Art Works, Original Documents, Photographs, Sculpture
Special Subjects: Sculpture, Carpets & Rugs, Furniture, Photography
Collections: 70 Original Athletic, Memorial & Monumental Sculptures, nearly all in plaster, 600 Pioneer Artifacts, mostly collected by Dr McKenzie, Life & Times of Dr James Naismith, basketball artifacts
Exhibitions: Monthly art installations, local artists
Activities: Educ prog; classes for children; tours; gallery talks; scholarships offered; sales shop sells books, reproductions, postcards, gift notes, original art & prints

ATIKOKAN

L **QUETICO PARK,** John B Ridley Research Library, Quetico Park, 108 Saturn Ave Atikokan, ON P0T 1C0 Canada. Tel 807-929-2571 ext 224; Fax 807-929-2123; Email andrea.allison@mnr.gov.on.ca; Web: http://catalogue.legacyforest.ca; *Librn* Andrea Allison
Open Mon - Fri 8 AM - 8PM, Sat - Sun & Holidays 9 AM 6 PM (excluding Dec 25 & Jan 1; Estab 1986; For reference only
Income: Financed by Ontario Parks
Purchases: $1500
Library Holdings: Book Volumes 4,800, Cassettes 380, Periodical Subscriptions 20, Photographs 8000, Slides 18,000, Video Tapes 100
Special Subjects: Archaeology
Collections: Natural history & cultural history displays on Quetico Park including archaeology, fur trade & voyageur history
Activities: Lect open to pub July - Aug

BANCROFT

M **ART GALLERY OF BANCROFT INC,** 10 Flint Ave, Bancroft, ON K0L 1C0 Canada; PO Box 398, Bancroft, ON K0L 1C0 Canada. Tel 613-332-1542; Email agb@nexicom.net; Web: www.artgallerybancroft.ca; *Pres* David Ferguson; *Treas* Carol Kirby
Open Summer: Mon - Sat 10 AM - 4 PM; Winter: Tues - Sat 10 AM - 4 PM; Admis by donation; Estab 1980 to foster the fine arts in the area; Gallery & gift shop in a new location; Average Annual Attendance: 9,000; Mem: 155; dues $20; annual meeting in Sept
Income: Financed by corporate sponsorships, donations, gallery & gift shop sales
Special Subjects: Painting-Canadian, Photography, Pottery, Stained Glass, Textiles, Watercolors, Jewelry, Sculpture
Collections: Murray Schafer: Sound Sculptures, miscellaneous glass, fabric, paintings
Exhibitions: 12 exhibitions per year
Activities: Classes for children; gallery talks; competition with awards; annual juried & student exhib awards; shop sells original art, prints, crafts of all nature, pottery, stained glass, wood carvings & photographs

BELLEVILLE

M **GLANMORE NATIONAL HISTORIC SITE OF CANADA,** 257 Bridge St E, Belleville, ON K8N 1P4 Canada. Tel 613-962-2329; Fax 613-962-6340; Email rrustige@city.belleville.on.ca; Web: www.glanmore.ca; *Educ* Melissa Wakeling; *Cur* Rona Rustige; *Secy* Darlene Rodgers; *Custodian* Mac Ellis; *Weekend Receptionist* Mary Jane Throop; *Database Coordr* Jen Gibson
Open June - Aug Tues - Sun 10 AM - 4:30 PM, Sept - May Tues - Sun 1 - 4:30 PM; Admis adults $6, seniors & students $5, children 5-12 $3.50, children under 5 free; Estab 1973 to collect & interpret history of Belleville & 1880s nat historic site; Historic House with extensive collection of Victorian paintings, notably Horatio Henry Couldery, Bertram & Cecelia Couldery, copies of Gainsborough, Constable, Uens, Wilkie & Rembrandt; Average Annual Attendance: 8,000; Mem: 40; Friends of Glanmore; dues $10 per yr; meeting 1st Tues of month Sept - June
Income: Financed by corporation of City of Belleville & Ontario Ministry of Culture
Library Holdings: Book Volumes, Clipping Files, Lantern Slides, Maps, Original Art Works, Original Documents, Other Holdings, Pamphlets
Special Subjects: Architecture, Asian Art, Bronzes, Carpets & Rugs, Ceramics, Coins & Medals, Decorative Arts, Dolls, Drawings, Embroidery, Enamels, Etchings & Engravings, Furniture, Glass, Gold, Historical Material, Ivory, Jewelry, Landscapes, Leather, Manuscripts, Maps, Miniatures, Oriental Art, Painting-British, Painting-Canadian, Painting-French, Period Rooms, Pewter, Photography, Porcelain, Portraits, Restorations, Sculpture, Silver, Textiles, Watercolors
Collections: Couldery European Art Collection: (Cloisonne, paintings & furniture, typical of upper class turn of the century taste), Phillips-Burrows-Faulkner Collection, Regional History Collection, Manly McDonald Originals, Sir

Mackenzie Bowell Collection, William Sawyer Collection, Dr Paul Lamp Collection
Publications: Exhibit catalog
Activities: Classes for adults & children; docent training; internships; student placements; education kits lent to schools & groups; lects open to pub; tours; gallery talks; sponsoring of competitions; individual paintings & original objects of art lent to mus, galleries; book traveling exhibs, annually; mus shop sells books, reproductions, artifacts, prints, & gift items related to Victoriana

BRACEBRIDGE

M **MUSKOKA ARTS & CRAFTS INC,** Chapel Gallery, 15 King St, PO Box 376 Bracebridge, ON P1L 1T7 Canada. Tel 705-645-5501; Fax 705-645-0385; Email info@muskokaartsandcrafts.com; Web: www.muskokaartsandcrafts.com; *Exec Dir* Elene J Freer
Open Tues - Sat 10 AM-1 PM & 2-5 PM; Admis donations accepted; Estab 1963, museum estab 1989; Average Annual Attendance: 10,000; Mem: 340; dues $20-$30; annual meeting in Oct
Income: Financed by mem & donations
Publications: Newsletter, 12 per year
Activities: Classes for adults & children; lects for mems only, 1-5 vis lectrs per yr; schols offered

BRAMPTON

M **ART GALLERY OF PEEL,** Peel Heritage Complex, 9 Wellington St E, Brampton, ON L6W 1Y1 Canada. Tel 905-791-4055; Fax 905-451-4931; Email HCResearch@peelregion.ca; Web: www.region.peel.on.ca/heritage; *Cur & Supv Mus Servs* Annemarie Hagen; *Colls Registrar, Mus Colls* David Farrell
Open Mon - Wed, Fri 10 AM - 4:30 PM, Thurs 10 AM - 9 PM, Sat 10 AM - 5 PM, Sun 1 - 5 PM; Admis family $12, adults $5, students & seniors 60+ $4, children 5 & under & mems free; Estab 1968 to promote & collect art & artifacts on regional & provincial level; Average Annual Attendance: 20,000; Mem: 200; dues corporate $150, family $45, individual $30; annual meeting in Feb
Collections: Permanent Collection of Canadian Artists, special focus on Peel Region, Works on paper, Caroline & Frank Armington Print Collection
Exhibitions: Eight exhibits per year (all mediums); Annual Open Juried Show; Regional Artists
Publications: Carolina & Frank Armington; Canadian Painter -Etchers in Paris; exhib catalogs
Activities: Classes for adults & children; docent training; lects open to pub, 2-3 vis lectrs per yr; gallery talks; tours, competitions with prizes; exten dept serves Southern Ontario; individual paintings & original objects of art lent to public buildings & other institutions; book traveling exhibs 1 per yr; originate traveling exhibs to libraries & other galleries; sales shop sells books, reproductions & prints

L **Archives,** 9 Wellington St E, Brampton, ON L6W 1Y1 Canada. Tel 905-791-4055; Fax 905-451-4931; Web: www.region.peel.on.ca/heritage; *Archivist* Diane Kuster; *Cur* David Somers
Open Tues, Wed & Fri 10 AM - 4:30 PM, Thurs 10 AM - 8:30 PM; Circ Non-circulating; Reference only
Library Holdings: Book Volumes 550, Clipping Files, Exhibition Catalogs, Memorabilia, Periodical Subscriptions 3

BRANTFORD

M **BRANT HISTORICAL SOCIETY,** Brant Museum & Archives, 57 Charlotte St, Brantford, ON N3T 2W6 Canada. Tel 519-752-2483; Fax 519-752-1931; Email information@brantmuseums.ca; Web: www.brantmuseums.ca; *Prog & Community Coordr* Nathan Etherington
Open Mon - Fri 10 AM - 4 PM; Admis by donation; Estab 1908 to preserve, interpret & display Brant County history; Average Annual Attendance: 9,200; Mem: 200; dues family $40, individual $25, student $20
Income: Financed by mem, provincial, county & city grants & fundraising
Library Holdings: Book Volumes, Clipping Files, Fiche, Filmstrips, Manuscripts, Maps, Original Art Works, Original Documents, Photographs, Prints, Slides
Special Subjects: Historical Material
Collections: Early Indian history, historical figures, portraits & paintings, Brant County history, Old maps & photographs of Brant County
Publications: Annual brochure; Brant County, the Story of its People, vol I & II; Grand River Navigation Company Newsletter, quarterly
Activities: Classes for children; docent training & Kids' camps; lectrs open to pub; tours; mus shop sells books, reproductions & prints

L **Library,** 57 Charlotte St, Brantford, ON N3T 2W6 Canada. Tel 519-752-2483; Fax 519-752-1931; Web: www.brantmuseums.ca
Open Tues - Sat 10 AM - 4PM; Admis $8 (research fees); Estab for research only; Circ Non-circulating
Library Holdings: Book Volumes 500, Maps, Photographs
Special Subjects: Religious Art
Collections: First editions of history & archaeology, old Bibles available for research on premises under supervision of cur, rare books, Photographs of Brant County & old maps
Activities: Classes for adults & children; 8 vis lectrs per yr; mus shop sells books

M **GLENHYRST ART GALLERY OF BRANT,** 20 Ava Rd, Brantford, ON N3T 5G9 Canada. Tel 519-756-5932; Fax 519-756-5910; Email info@glenhyrst.ca; Web: www.glenhyrst.ca; *Dir* Ana Olson
Open Tues - Fri 10 AM - 5 PM, Sat & Sun 11 AM - 4 PM; No admis fee; Estab 1957 as a nonprofit pub arts center serving the citizens of Brantford & Brant County; Situated on 16 picturesque acres, the gallery offers rotating exhib of contemporary art; Average Annual Attendance: 19,000; Mem: 425; dues family $40, individual $30, student & senior citizen $20; annual meeting in Feb
Income: Financed by mem, municipal, provincial & federal appropriations & local foundations
Library Holdings: Book Volumes 140, CD-ROMs, Clipping Files 200, Exhibition Catalogs 200, Periodical Subscriptions 10
Special Subjects: Painting-Canadian, Prints
Collections: Contemporary Canadian graphics/works on paper, historical works by R R Whale & descendants, outdoor sculpture
Exhibitions: Biennial juried exhib
Activities: Classes for adults & children; lect open to pub; tours; gallery talks; individual paintings lent to public art galleries & museums/Brantford and Brant

BURLINGTON

M **ART GALLERY OF BURLINGTON,** 1333 Lakeshore Rd at Brock, Burlington, ON L7S 1A9 Canada. Tel 905-632-7796; Fax 905-632-0278; Email info@BurlingtonArtCentre.on.ca; Web: https://artgalleryofburlington.com; *Pres & CEO* Robert Steven; *Artistic Dir & Chief Cur* Denis Longchamps
Open Mon -Fri 9 AM - 9 PM, Sat & Sun 10 AM - 5 PM; No admis fee, donations appreciated; Estab 1978; Maintains reference library, main gallery, F R Perry Gallery; permanent collection corridor courtyard; Average Annual Attendance: 90,000; Mem: 1200; dues $30-$65; annual meeting in Mar
Income: $1,150,000 (financed by mem, city appropriation, province appropriation, earned revenues, fund raising, donations & sponsorship)
Purchases: $10,000
Collections: Contemporary Canadian Ceramic Art
Activities: Classes for adults & children; docent training; hands-on progs; lects open to pub, 2 vis lectrs per yr; tours; exten dept; original objects of art lent; book traveling exhibs 1 per yr; originate traveling exhibs 20 per yr; mus shop sells original art & jewelry

CAMBRIDGE

L **CAMBRIDGE PUBLIC LIBRARY AND GALLERY,** Idea Exchange, 1 North Sq, Cambridge, ON N1S 2K6 Canada. Tel 519-621-0460; Fax 519-621-2080; Email galleriesinfo@cambridgegalleries.ca; Web: www.cambridgelibraries.ca/main.cfm; *Chair* Gary Price
Open Mon - Thurs 9:30 AM - 8:30 PM, Fri & Sat 9:30 AM - 5:30 PM; Sun 1 - 5 PM; cl Sun May 21 - Sep 3; No admis fee; Estab 1969; Gallery on second floor with 2000 sq ft, 250 linear ft; Average Annual Attendance: 25,000
Income: Financed by provincial appropriation, federal & private
Library Holdings: Book Volumes 150,000, Periodical Subscriptions 100
Collections: Regional Artists
Exhibitions: Rotate 6 - 8 per yr
Publications: Bi-monthly newsletter
Activities: Classes for adults & children; lects open to pub, 10 vis lectrs per yr; concerts; gallery talks; tours; competitions with awards; individual paintings & original objects of art lent; originate traveling exhibs

CHATHAM

A **THAMES ART GALLERY,** 75 William St N, Chatham, ON N7M 4L4 Canada. Tel 519-354-8338; Fax 519-354-4170; Email ckartgallery@chatham-kent.ca; Web: www.chatham-kent.ca/ThamesArtGallery; *Dir & Cur* Carl Lavoy; *Cur Asst* Sonya Blazek
Open daily 1 PM - 5 PM; No admis fee; Estab 1963 to operate as a regional arts centre, to advance knowledge & appreciation of & to encourage, stimulate & promote interest in the study of culture & the visual arts; Gallery maintained; designated National Exhibition Centre for the presentation of visual art works & museum related works, to the public of this country; Average Annual Attendance: 15,000; Mem: $50 Culture Vulture mem
Income: Financed by mem, municipal, & federal governments; Ontario Arts Council, & the Canada Council for the Arts
Library Holdings: Book Volumes, CD-ROMs, Exhibition Catalogs, Original Art Works, Periodical Subscriptions, Photographs, Prints, Sculpture, Slides, Video Tapes
Collections: Local Artists, regional contemporary artists
Exhibitions: Ten various historical and contemporary exhibs per yr
Publications: At the Centre, 10 per yr
Activities: Classes for adults & children; docent training; lects open to public, 9 vis lectrs per yr; concerts; gallery talks; tours; juried fine art shows; individual & original objects of art lent to accredited galleries & museums; lending collection contains 2100 slides; serves Chatham-Kent; 1-2 book traveling exhibs; originate traveling exhibs to other accredited galleries

CORNWALL

M **THE ART GALLERY OF CORNWALL,** 168 Pitt St Promenade, Cornwall, ON K6J 3P4 Canada. Tel 613-938-7387; Fax 613-938-9619; Email info@cornwallregionalartgallery.ca; Web: cornwallregionalartgallery.ca; *Exec Dir* Sylvie Lizotte
Open Tues - Sat 10 AM - 5 PM, cl Sun & Mon; No admis fee; Estab 1982 to promote interest in & study of visual arts; Main gallery has 3 display walls measuring 44.5 ft, 30 ft & 10 ft 9 inches; walls 12 ft; Gallery Shoppe where local art is sold; Average Annual Attendance: 15,000; Mem: 200; dues $20 & up; annual meeting in June
Income: $90,000 - $100,000 (financed by mem & city appropriation)
Special Subjects: Ceramics, Crafts, Decorative Arts, Drawings, Embroidery, Folk Art, Laces, Painting-Canadian, Photography, Porcelain, Portraits, Pottery, Prints, Religious Art, Sculpture, Watercolors
Collections: Contemporary Canadian Art
Exhibitions: Annual Juried Exhibition; rotate exhibits from Canadian artists once per month
Publications: Newsletter, tri-annually
Activities: Classes for adults & children; individual paintings lent; mus shop sells original art

DON MILLS

C **ROTHMANS, BENSON & HEDGES,** Art Collection, 1500 Don Mills Rd, Don Mills, ON M3B 3L1 Canada. Tel 416-449-5525; Fax 416-449-4486; *Mgr Gen Servs* John Bird
Open to public; Estab 1967; Collection displayed at head office
Special Subjects: Eskimo Art
Collections: Contemporary Canadian art from last decade
Activities: Awards for Toronto Outdoor Art Exhibition each yr; individual objects of art lent to traveling or special exhibs; originate traveling exhibs to all major public galleries in Canada

DURHAM

M **DURHAM ART GALLERY,** 251 George St E, PO Box 1021 Durham, ON N0G 1R0 Canada. Tel 519-369-3692; Email info@durhamart.on.ca; Web: www.durhamart.on.ca; *Pres* David Sugarman
Open Tues - Fri 10 AM - 5 PM, Sat - Sun & holidays 1 PM - 4 PM; Estab 1978

GUELPH

M **ART GALLERY OF GUELPH,** 358 Gordon St, Guelph, ON N1G 1Y1 Canada. Tel 519-837-0010; Fax 519-767-2661; Email info@artgalleryofguelph.ca; Web: http://artgalleryofguelph.ca; *Sr Cur* Andrew Hunter; *Admin Asst* Nina Berry; *Gallery Coordr* Verne Harrison
Open Tues - Sun Noon - 5 PM; cl holidays & Aug; Admis by donation; Estab 1978 by University of Guelph, city, county & board of educ to collect & exhibit works of art; maintain & operate a gallery & related facilities for this purpose fulfilling a pub role in city & county; 30,000 sq ft building comprising galleries, lecture room, studio, meeting rooms, resource centre, gift shop & rental service. Restored & renovated in 1980; Average Annual Attendance: 25,000; Mem: 600; dues family $30, individual $20, senior & student $10; annual meeting Sept-Oct
Income: Financed by university, city, county, board of educ, provincial & federal grants, mem & donations
Purchases: Canadian art
Special Subjects: Decorative Arts, Eskimo Art, Prints
Collections: Historical & contemporary Canadian art, historical & contemporary international prints, Inuit Collection, contemporary sculpture, outdoor sculpture (Donald Forster Sculpture Park)
Publications: Catalogue of permanent collection of University of Guelph 1980; exhibition catalogues, 6 per yr; quarterly newsletter
Activities: Classes for children; docent training; workshops; lects open to pub; gallery talks; school & group tours; concerts; tours; exten dept serves Wellington County & other Canadian public galleries, also have circulated in US & Europe; individual paintings lent to institutions & public galleries; art rental to gallery members; lending collection contains 500 original paintings, 400 prints, photographs & 50 sculptures; book traveling exhibs 4-6 per yr; originate traveling exhibs 1 -2 per yr for museums in Canada & abroad; sales shop sells books, magazines, reproductions, toys, pottery, textiles, jewelry & catalogues

HAILEYBURY

M **TEMISKAMING ART GALLERY,** 325 Farr Dr, Haileybury, ON P0J 1K0 Canada; PO Box 1090, Haileybury, ON P0J 1K0 Canada. Tel 705-672-3706; Fax 705-672-5966; Email temiskamingartgallery@gmail.com; Web: www.temiskamingartgallery.ca; *Exec Dir & Cur* Maureen Steward
Open all year Mon - Fri 10 AM - 4 PM; No admis fee; Estab 1980 to educate; 1 large gallery; Mem: Dues $15 & up; Annual meeting May
Income: Financed by mem & city appropriation &Ontario Arts Council
Special Subjects: Ceramics, Collages, Drawings, Etchings & Engravings, Landscapes, Painting-Canadian, Painting-Japanese, Photography, Portraits, Pottery, Sculpture, Watercolors
Collections: North Ontario Collection
Exhibitions: Rotating exhibits
Activities: Classes for adults & children; lects open to pub, 5 vis lectrs per yr; gallery talks; Artmobile; lending of original art to city hall staff

HAMILTON

M **ART GALLERY OF HAMILTON,** 123 King St W, Hamilton, ON L8P 4S8 Canada. Tel 905-527-6610; Fax 905-577-6940; Email info@artgalleryofhamilton.com; Web: www.artgalleryofhamilton.com; *Pres & CEO* Shelley Falconer; *Dir Exhib & Coll & Sr Cur* Tobi Bruce
Open Wed & Fri 11 AM - 6:00 PM, Thurs 11 AM - 8 PM, Sat & Sun noon - 5 PM, cl Mon & Tues; Admis family $25, adults $10, students & seniors $8, children 6-17 $4, children under 5 free; Estab Jan 1914 to develop & maintain a centre for the study & enjoyment of the visual arts; new gallery opened Oct 1977; renovated & reopened May 2005; Building is 76,000 sq ft, 24,000 sq ft of exhibition space; Average Annual Attendance: 150,000+; Mem: 2000; dues family $90, single $55; annual meeting in June
Income: Earned revenue endowment, mem, city & provincial appropriation & federal grants
Special Subjects: American Western Art, Baroque Art, Eskimo Art, Etchings & Engravings, Graphics, Painting-American, Painting-British, Painting-European, Photography, Religious Art, Woodcarvings
Collections: Complete graphics of Karel Appel, Canadian fine arts, American, British & European fine arts, historical, modern & contemporary coll, Joey and Toby Tanenbaum Collection (19th century European)
Exhibitions: Twenty-nine exhibitions scheduled per yr
Publications: Insights, 3 times per yr
Activities: Educ prog; classes for adults & children; docent training; lects open to pub, 10-20 per yr; concerts; gallery talks; tours; 2000 Lieutenant Governor's Award for the Arts; individual paintings & original objects of art lent to other galleries & mus; lending collection contains 7800 art works; book traveling exhibs; originate traveling exhibs to provincial galleries & art ctrs; international art galleries; mus shop sells books, magazines, original art, reproductions & giftware

L **Muriel Isabel Bostwick Library**, 123 King St W, Hamilton, ON L8P 4S8 Canada. Tel 905-527-6610 ext 230; Fax 905-577-6940; Web: www.artgalleryofhamilton.on.ca; *Librn* Helen Hadden
Open Tues - Sun 11 AM - 5PM, Thurs 11 AM - 9 PM; Open to gallery members & researchers for reference
Library Holdings: Book Volumes 4800, Clipping Files, Exhibition Catalogs, Periodical Subscriptions 14, Photographs
Special Subjects: Art History, Mixed Media, Oriental Art, Painting-American, Painting-European, Portraits, Printmaking, Prints, Restoration & Conservation, Sculpture
Collections: References on Canadian art history, exhibition catalogues

M **DUNDURN NATIONAL HISTORIC SITE,** Dundurn Castle, 610 York Blvd Hamilton, ON L8R 3H1 Canada. Tel 905-546-2872; Email dundurn@hamilton.ca; *Cur Asst* Elizabeth Wakeford; *Cur* Bill Nesbitt
Open year-round Tues - Sun noon 4 PM; cl Mon & holidays; Admis family $30, adults 18-59 $11.50, sr citizens 60+ & students 13-17 $9.50, children 6-12 $6, children under 5 free, discounts on group rates for over 20 people; Dundurn, the home of Sir Allan Napier MacNab; Hamilton's Centennial Project was the restoration of this historic house; built in 1832-35, it was tenured by MacNab until his death in 1862. The terminal date of the furnishings is 1855; Approx 43 rooms are shown; two-room on-site exhibit area; Average Annual Attendance: 70,000
Income: Financed by city of Hamilton, owner & operator
Special Subjects: Archaeology, Architecture, Calligraphy, Carpets & Rugs, Coins & Medals, Etchings & Engravings, Furniture, Glass, Painting-Canadian, Period Rooms, Pewter, Photography, Porcelain, Portraits, Pottery, Prints, Religious Art, Reproductions, Restorations, Silver, Stained Glass, Tapestries, Textiles, Watercolors, Woodcarvings
Collections: Regency & mid-Victorian furnishings depicting the lifestyle of an upper class gentleman living in upper Canada in the 1850s, restored servants quarters
Exhibitions: Historical Crafts Fair, Harvest Home-baking & preserving competitions; Victorian Christmas
Activities: Classes for adults & children; docent training; lects open to pub; concerts; gallery talks, tours; individual paintings & original objects of art lent; mus shop sells books, reproductions, prints & slides, tea room & food service facilities

M **MCMASTER UNIVERSITY,** McMaster Museum of Art, Alvin A Lee Bldg, 1280 Main St W Hamilton, ON L8S 4L6 Canada. Tel 905-525-9140, Ext 23081; Fax 905-527-4548; Email museum@mcmaster.ca; Web: museum.mcmaster.ca; *Dir & Chief Cur* Carol Podedworny; *Collections Admin* Julie Bronson; *Installation & Preservation Officer* Jennifer Petteplace; *Communs Officer* Rose Anne Prevec; *Sr Educ Officer* Nicole Knibb; *Educ Officer* Teresa Gregorio; *Cur Indigenous Art* Rheanne Chartrand; *Installation & Preservation Officer* Jennifer Petteplace
Open Tues, Wed & Fri 11 AM - 5 PM, Thurs 11 AM - 7 PM, Sat Noon - 5 PM, cl Mon, Sun & holidays; Admis suggested donation $2; Estab 1967 to provide the university & pub with exhibitions of historical & contemporary art from Canada & other countries; Houses the University's collection of 6000 works of art and present exhibs; Average Annual Attendance: 25,000
Income: $1,000,000 (financed by university & private endowment, corporate & individual support)
Library Holdings: Auction Catalogs, Book Volumes, CD-ROMs, Clipping Files, Exhibition Catalogs, Manuscripts, Maps, Memorabilia, Original Art Works, Original Documents, Pamphlets, Periodical Subscriptions, Photographs, Prints, Sculpture, Slides, Video Tapes
Special Subjects: American Indian Art, Antiquities-Egyptian, Antiquities-Roman, Asian Art, Bronzes, Coins & Medals, Drawings, Etchings & Engravings, Flasks & Bottles, Glass, Landscapes, Maps, Painting-American, Painting-British, Painting-Canadian, Painting-Dutch, Painting-European, Painting-Flemish, Painting-French, Painting-German, Prints, Painting-Italian, Painting-Russian, Photography, Religious Art, Sculpture, Watercolors, Woodcuts
Collections: Levy Collection, impressionist & post-impressionist, paintings & early Dutch panels, American & Canadian Art, European paintings, prints & drawings, Expressionist Prints
Exhibitions: Presents 12-15 exhibitions ann
Publications: The Art Collection of McMaster University; Levy legacy and various exhibition catalogues
Activities: Classes for adults & children; classroom facilities; docent training; lects open to pub; concerts; gallery talks; artist talks; 7 vis lectrs per yr; tours; receptions; individual paintings and original objects of art lent to National Gallery of Canada, Art Gallery of Ontario & other Canadian institutions; originates 5 book traveling exhibs per yr; originate traveling exhibs to other univs or public galleries

JORDAN

M **JORDAN HISTORICAL MUSEUM OF THE TWENTY,** 3800 Main St, Jordan, ON L0R 1S0 Canada. Tel 905-562-5242; Fax 905-562-7786; Email museum@lincoln.ca; Web: www.lincoln.ca; *Mus Dir* Helen Booth; *Asst Mus Dir* Sylvia Beben
Open May - Aug: Tues - Sat 10 AM - 5 PM; Sept - May: Mon - Fri 8:30 AM - 4:30 PM, Sat 1 - 4PM; Admis $3 suggested donation; Estab 1953 to preserve the material & folklore of the area known as The Twenty, Mile Creek vicinity; Average Annual Attendance: 10,000; Mem: 100; dues corp with over 15 employees $50, under 15 $35, family $25, individual $15
Income: Financed by admis, provincial grants, municipal grants, internal fund raising activities & donations
Special Subjects: Historical Material, Period Rooms
Collections: Archives, furniture, historical material & textiles
Exhibitions: Special annual exhibits; Pioneer Day
Activities: Classes for children; special displays as requested by the community; Pioneer Day first Sat after Canadian Thanksgiving holiday; lects open to pub, 1 vis

lectr per yr; individual paintings & original objects of art lent; sales shop sells books, original art, prints, pottery, textiles & local craft items

KINGSTON

M **QUEEN'S UNIVERSITY,** Agnes Etherington Art Centre, 36 University Ave, Bader Ln Kingston, ON K7L 3N6 Canada. Tel 613-533-2190; Fax 613-533-6765; Email aeac@queensu.ca; Web: www.agnes.queensu.ca; *Dir* Jan Allen; *Preparator* Scott Wallis; *Financial Coordr* Barry Fagan; *Bader Cur European Art* Jacquelyn N. Coutre; *Admin Coordr* Kate Yuksel; *Coll Mgr & Exhib Coordr* Jennifer Nicoll
Open Tues - Fri 10 AM - 4:30 PM, Thurs until 9 PM, Sat - Sun 1 PM - 5 PM; Free admis; Estab 1957 to provide the services of a pub art gallery & mus for the community & region; Gallery has approx 8000 sq ft of display space, in eight galleries showing a balanced program of exhibitions of contemporary & historical, national, international & regional art; Average Annual Attendance: 30,000; Mem: 900; dues $15-$200; annual meeting in Sept (Gallery Assn)
Income: $1,000,000 (financed by endowment, city & provincial appropriation, University & Canada Council funds)
Purchases: $100,000
Special Subjects: Antiquities-Greek, Antiquities-Roman, Ethnology, Graphics, Prints, Sculpture
Collections: African Art, Canadian Dress Collection, Canadian Paintings, Prints, Sculpture, Historical & Contemporary, Decorative Objects, Ethnological Collection, European Graphics, European 17th Century, Old Master Paintings, Quilts, Silver
Exhibitions: About 30 exhibitions mounted each year
Publications: Currents, quarterly; annual report; exhibition publications & catalogues; studies
Activities: Docent training regarding tours for school & other groups; lects open to public, 10 vis lectrs per yr; gallery talks; tours; artwork rented by Gallery Assn Art Rental to private individuals & bus; originate traveling exhibs to other cultural institutions; museum shop sells books, reproductions, prints & gift items including ceramics, jewelry, glassware

L **Stauffer Library Art Collection**, 101 Union St, Kingston, ON K7L 5C4 Canada. Tel 613-533-2524; Email lucinda.walls@queensu.ca; Web: http://library.queensu.ca; *Librn* Lucinda Walls
Open (see website); Estab 2003; Open to students, faculty & staff; open to public for reference only
Library Holdings: Book Volumes 50,000, Exhibition Catalogs 14,000, Fiche 1400, Other Holdings Reference bks, Periodical Subscriptions 140, Photographs, Reels 300, Video Tapes 215
Special Subjects: Art History

M **ST LAWRENCE COLLEGE,** Art Gallery, 100 Portsmouth Ave, PO Box 6000 Kingston, ON K7L 5A6 Canada. Tel 613-544-5400, Ext 1283; Fax 613-545-3923; Email gallery@sl.on.ca; Web: www.sl.on.ca; *Cur* Christina Chrysler
Open Tues - Fri 10 AM - 8 PM, Mon & Sat 10 AM - 4 PM; No admis fee; College estab 1968, mus estab 1973 to augment the creative art program with shows, visiting artists; Average Annual Attendance: 4,000

KITCHENER

M **HOMER WATSON HOUSE & GALLERY,** 1754 Old Mill Rd, Kitchener, ON N2P 1H7 Canada. Tel 519-748-4377; Fax 519-748-6808; Web: www.homerwatson.on.ca; *Exec Cur* Faith Hieblinger; *Dir Mktg & Fundraising* Kate Macpherson; *Exec Dir* Helena Ball; *Front End Develop* Laura Mabee; *Dir Educ & Pub Progs* Paige Downey
Open Tues - Sun Noon - 4:30 PM; Admis $5, children 12 and under free; Estab 1981 as Homer Watson Memorial; Three studios for contemporary art - total of 155 running ft; Average Annual Attendance: 6,000; Mem: 250; dues family $30, individual $18; annual meeting 2nd Tues in June
Income: $500,000 (financed by mem, city appropriation, workshops & classes)
Purchases: $6,000
Collections: Watson Family Artifacts, Homer Watson Paintings
Exhibitions: Contemporary art-regional & provincial artists
Activities: Classes for adults & children; lects open to pub; 4 vis lectrs per year; concerts; gallery talks; tours; mus shop sells books, original art, reproductions, prints, confectionery, t-shirts

M **KITCHENER-WATERLOO ART GALLERY,** 101 Queen St N, Kitchener, ON N2H 6P7 Canada. Tel 519-579-5860; Fax 519-578-0740; Email mail@kwag.on.ca; Web: www.kwag.ca; *Exec Dir* Shirley Madill
Open Tues & Thurs 9:30 AM - 9 PM, Wed 9:30 AM - 7 PM, Fri 9:30 AM - 8 PM, Sat 10 AM - 7:30 PM, Sun 1 - 5 PM, cl Mon; No admis fee; Estab 1956, the Kitchener-Waterloo Art Gallery is a pub institution interested in stimulating an appreciation of the visual arts & dedicated to bringing to the community exhibitions, art classes, lectures, workshops & special events; Average Annual Attendance: 40,000; Mem: 820; dues bus $100, family $40, individual $30, senior citizens & students $15
Income: Financed by government grants, foundation grants, corporate & individual donations, special events, mem dues, voluntary admis & sales of publication
Library Holdings: Exhibition Catalogs, Original Art Works
Special Subjects: Drawings, Painting-Canadian, Painting-European, Prints, Painting-German, Photography, Prints, Sculpture, Watercolors
Collections: Homer Watson Collection
Publications: Calendar, quarterly; exhibition catalogs, quarterly
Activities: Art classes for adults & children; docent training; lects open to public; lects for mems only; gallery talks; tours; art travel tours; schol progs

KLEINBURG

M **MCMICHAEL CANADIAN ART COLLECTION,** 10365 Islington Ave, Kleinburg, ON L0J 1C0 Canada. Tel 905-893-1121; Fax 905-893-0692; Email info@mcmichael.com; Web: www.mcmichael.com; *Exec Dir* Ian Dejardin; *Chair* Andrew Dunn
Open Tues - Sun 10 AM - 5 PM; cl Mon; Admis family $36, adults $18, students & sr citizens $15, members & children under 5 free; Estab 1965
Collections: Focus of the coll is the works of art created by Indian, Inuit & Metis artists, the artists of the Group of Seven & their contemporaries & other artists who have made or make a contribution to the development of Canadian Art
Exhibitions: Temporary exhibitions lasting from 1 to 3 months
Publications: Permanent collection catalogue; exhibition catalogues; quarterly newsletters
Activities: Comprehensive educ progs at the elementary & secondary school levels; guided group tours by appointment; exten progs & temporary exhibition progs; progs for kindergarten & special interest groups

L **Library & Archives**, 10365 Islington Ave, Kleinburg, ON L0J 1C0 Canada. Tel 905-893-1121; Fax 905-893-2588; Email library@mcmichael.com; Web: www.mcmichael.com; *Librn & Archivist* Linda Morita
Open by appointment
Library Holdings: Auction Catalogs, Audio Tapes, Book Volumes 5000, Cassettes, Clipping Files, Exhibition Catalogs, Fiche, Manuscripts, Memorabilia, Original Art Works, Original Documents, Other Holdings Archival material, Pamphlets, Periodical Subscriptions 30, Photographs, Reproductions, Slides, Video Tapes
Special Subjects: Art History, Landscapes, Painting-Canadian, Printmaking, Prints, Eskimo Art

LINDSAY

M **THE LINDSAY GALLERY INC,** 190 Kent St W, Fl 2 Lindsay, ON K9V 2Y6 Canada. Tel 705-324-1780; Email art@kawarthagallery.com; Web: www.kawarthagallery.com; *Pres* Susan Taylor
Open Tues - Sat 10 AM - 4 PM; No admis fee; Estab 1976; half of 2d floor of library, Lindsay branch; Average Annual Attendance: 6,000; Mem: 300; family $40, individual $25, senior citizens & student $20
Income: $76,000 (financed by mem, fund raising, & corporate sponsorship)
Special Subjects: Painting-Canadian, Sculpture
Collections: Historical & contemporary Canadian
Publications: Bimonthly Newsletter
Activities: Art classes for adults & children; lects open to pub, 2 vis lectrs per yr; Awards, art student bursary, memorial award to a secondary school student at juried show; book traveling exhibs 1-2 times per yr; 12 Exhibs per yr; Summer Art in the Park; sales shop sells original art, prints, original crafts & artists jewelry

LONDON

M **MUSEUM LONDON,** 421 Ridout St N, London, ON N6A 5H4 Canada. Tel 519-661-0333; Email omercer@museumlondon.ca; Web: www.museumlondon.ca; *Cur Educ* Steve Mavers; *Head Exhibitions & Collections* Melanie Townsend; *Exec Dir* Brian Meehan; *Head Admin* Cydna Mercer; *Registrar* Janette Cousins Ewan; *Cur Art* Cassandra Getty
Open Tues - Sun 12 - 5 PM, Thurs 12 - 9 PM; cl Mon; Admis by donation; Estab 1940; New bldg open 1980 containing 26,500 sq ft of exhibition space, 150 seat auditorium; maintains reference library; Average Annual Attendance: 125,000; Mem: 600; family $65, individual $40, senior citizens & students $20; annual meeting in Apr
Income: $2,992,285 (financed municipal, provincial & fed govts, donations, memberships, sponsorships & fundraising)
Collections: Permanent Collection stresses regional & local artists, who have become internationally & nationally recognized such as Jamelie Hassan, Paterson Ewan, Jack Chambers, Greg Curnoe & Paul Peel, The Moore Collection, a collection of historical art & artifacts, primarily of London & region, Hamilton King Meek Memorial Collection, F B Housser Memorial Collection
Exhibitions: Works of art - international, national & regional; programs of multi-media nature, including performing arts, exhibitions of historical artifacts & art
Publications: Exhibition catalogues; Quarterly magazine
Activities: Classes for adults & children; docent training; workshops; lects open to pub; 40 vis lectrs per yr concerts; gallery talks; tours; individual paintings & original objects of art lent to other art institutions; originate traveling exhibs; mus shop sells books, original art, reproductions, prints & jewelry

M **UNIVERSITY OF WESTERN ONTARIO,** McIntosh Gallery, Western University, London, ON N6A 3K7 Canada. Tel 519-661-3181; Fax 519-661-3059; Email mcintoshgallery@uwo.ca; Web: mcintoshgallery.ca; *Dir & Chief Cur* James Patten; *Cur* Catherine Elliot Shaw; *Collections Mgr* Brian Lambert
Open Mon - Fri 10 AM - 5 PM, Sat noon - 4 PM; cl Sun; No admis fee; Estab 1942; Three galleries with a total of 2960 sq ft; Average Annual Attendance: 14,000; Mem: 155
Income: Financed by endowment, mem, provincial appropriation, special grants & University funds
Collections: Canadian Art
Exhibitions: 12 to 14 exhibitions per year
Publications: Newsletter, 3 times a yr; exhibition catalogues
Activities: Docent training; lects open to public, 6-10 vis lectrs per yr; gallery talks; tours; individual paintings & original objects of art lent to galleries; lending collection contains books, cassettes, framed reproductions, original art works & prints, paintings, photographs & sculpture; book traveling exhibs 1-3 per yr; originate traveling exhibs

L **The D B Weldon Library**, 1151 Richmond St, Ste 2, London, ON N6A 3K7 Canada. Tel 519-661-2111; Fax 519-661-3911; Web: www.lib.uwo.ca; *Res & Instr Srvcs Lib* Peggy Ellis
Open Mon - Fri 8 AM - 11 PM, Sat & Sun 10:30 AM - 11 PM; Open to all university staff, faculty & students for research & borrowing. Open to the public for in-house research; Average Annual Attendance: 1,700,000
Library Holdings: Book Volumes 1,439,855, Clipping Files, Exhibition Catalogs, Fiche, Pamphlets, Periodical Subscriptions 4,956, Reels

Special Subjects: American Western Art, Antiquities-Byzantine, Antiquities-Etruscan, Antiquities-Greek, Antiquities-Roman, Archaeology, Art History, Carpets & Rugs, Decorative Arts, Eskimo Art, History of Art & Archaeology, Maps, Metalwork, Painting-American, Painting-Canadian

MIDLAND

M **HURONIA MUSEUM,** Gallery of Historic Huronia, 549 Little Lake Park, PO Box 638 Midland, ON L4R 4P4 Canada. Tel 705-526-2844; Fax 705-527-6622; Email info@huroniamuseum.com; Web: www.huroniamuseum.com; *Chair* John French; *V-Chair* Rene Hackstatter; *Secy* Tom Barber
Open Victoria Day - Thanksgiving: Mon - Sat 9 AM - 5 PM; cl Sun; Admis adult (18-64) $12, sr citizens (65+) $8.50, children (5-17) $7.25; Estab 1947 to collect art of Historic Huronia; Several large galleries dealing with local contemporary artists, historical regional artists, design exhibit on Thor Hansen & other designers; Average Annual Attendance: 20,000; Mem: Dues family $30, individual $20; annual meeting last Thurs in May
Income: $400,000 (financed by endowment, mem, admis, sales, fundraising, grants)
Purchases: $10,000 (Ted Lord Art Collection); $400,000 (Cultural Properties Donation; Ferguson Collection)
Library Holdings: Auction Catalogs, Book Volumes, Clipping Files, DVDs, Exhibition Catalogs, Kodachrome Transparencies, Lantern Slides, Manuscripts, Maps, Memorabilia, Original Art Works, Original Documents, Pamphlets, Periodical Subscriptions, Photographs, Records, Reproductions, Sculpture, Slides
Special Subjects: American Indian Art, Archaeology, Bookplates & Bindings, Ceramics, Coins & Medals, Costumes, Crafts, Decorative Arts, Dolls, Drawings, Eskimo Art, Etchings & Engravings, Ethnology, Folk Art, Furniture, Glass, Historical Material, Painting-Canadian, Photography
Collections: Mary Hallen Collection (watercolors), Frans Johnston Collection (oils, watercolors), Ted Lord Collection (paintings, prints, watercolors), Bill Wood Collection (etchings, oils, watercolors), General Collection (carvings, oil, watercolors), Lucille Oille Wells, Alex Jackson Collection, Norval Morrisseau Native Art Collection
Exhibitions: A Photographic History of the Georgian Bay Lumber Co 1871-1942; art shows once a month
Publications: Exhibition catalogues, ann report on activities
Activities: Classes for adults & children; educ prog; docent training; lects for Mems only, 6 vis lectrs per yr; concerts; gallery talks; tours; fels; Huronia Heritage Award ann award; lending collection contains paintings to other institutions who put together exhibs; originate traveling circulating to other local mus & galleries; mus shop sells books, original art, magazines, reproductions & prints

MISSISSAUGA

M **ART GALLERY OF MISSISSAUGA,** 300 City Centre Dr, Mississauga, ON L5B 3C1 Canada. Tel 905-896-5088; Fax 905-615-4167; Email robert.freeman@mississauga.ca; Web: www.artgalleryofmississauga.com; *Dir & Cur* Mandy Salter; *Curatorial & Coll Coordr* Laura Carusi; *Bus Opers Mgr* Sadaf Zuberi
Open Mon - Fri 10 AM - 5 PM, Thurs until 8 PM, Sat & Sun Noon - 4 PM; No admis fee; Estab 1987 to promote awareness and the appreciation of the visual arts through the operation, development and growth of a public, not-for-profit art gallery; 3000 sq ft divided into four galleries: Main, Community, Member's & Chapel; Average Annual Attendance: 20,000; Mem: 400; dues $40-$5,000; annual meeting in Apr
Income: Financed by mem, city appropriation, federal & provincial government
Collections: Permanent collection
Exhibitions: 11 exhibitions per year, 6 week average per exhibition
Publications: Brush Up
Activities: Lects open to pub, 5 vis lectrs per yr; 10-15 outreach programs per yr; gallery talks; tours; individual paintings & original objects of art lent to other public art galleries; exten prog serving Mississauga; book traveling exhibs 1-2 per yr; originate traveling exhibitions to Ontario

L **MISSISSAUGA LIBRARY SYSTEM,** 301 Burnhamthorpe Rd W, Mississauga, ON L5B 3Y3 Canada. Tel 905-615-3500; Fax 905-615-3625; Web: www.city.mississauga.on.ca/library; *Mgr* Amanda French
Open: Hours vary according to branch; No admis fee; Outlet for local artists at branch galleries; present more widely recognized artists at Central & Burnhamthorpe Galleries; Total of eleven galleries in system, 90 running ft each, often multi-purpose rooms
Collections: Permanent collection of 135 paintings and prints by Canadian artists, emphasis on prints (all framed)
Publications: Link News Tabloid Format, quarterly
Activities: Lect open to public; competitions with cash prizes; lending collection contains books & motion pictures; book traveling exhibitions

L **Central Library, Arts Dept**, 301 Burnhamthorpe Rd W, Mississauga, ON L5B 3Y3 Canada. Tel 905-615-3500; Fax 905-615-3625; Email library.info@mississauga.ca.; Web: www.mississauga.ca/portal/residents/centrallibrary; *Mgr* Amanda French
Open Mon - Fri 9 AM - 9 PM, Sat 9 AM - 5 PM, Sun 1 - 5 PM
Income: $7,000,000 (financed by Municipal & Provincial funds)
Library Holdings: Book Volumes 38,000, Cassettes, Exhibition Catalogs, Filmstrips, Other Holdings Compact Discs, Periodical Subscriptions 29, Video Tapes

M **UNIVERSITY OF TORONTO AT MISSISSAUGA,** Blackwood Gallery, 3359 Mississauga Rd N, Mississauga, ON L5L 1C6 Canada. Tel 905-828-3789; Fax 905-569-4262; Email blackwood.gallery@utoronto.ca; Web: http://blackwoodgallery.ca; *Dir & Cur* Christine Shaw; *Exhib Coordr* Petrina Ng
Open Mon - Fri noon - 5 PM, Wed until 9 PM, Sat & Sun noon - 3 PM; civic holidays; No admis fee; Estab 1969 to educate the public & present contemporary art; Gallery has four walls with various dividers & floor space of 36 x 30 ft; Average Annual Attendance: 5,000
Collections: Acrylics, drawings, oils, pen sketches & prints, sculpture, water colour, multiples
Publications: exhib catalogs
Activities: Classes for children; lect open to public; presentation of 6-8 exhibs of contemporary art per year; gallery talks; tours; competitions with awards, Blackwood Gallery Award; individual paints & original objects of art lent in house & to public art galleries; book 1 traveling exhib per yr; originates traveling exhibs for small to medium sized galleries & museums; mus shop sells exhibs catalogue

OAKVILLE

M **OAKVILLE GALLERIES,** Centennial Square and Gairloch Gardens, 1306 Lakeshore Rd E, Oakville, ON L6J 1L6 Canada. Tel 905-844-4402; Fax 905-844-7968; Email info@oakvillegalleries.com; Web: www.oakvillegalleries.com; *Dir* Matthew Hyland; *Communs Coordr* Victoria Borg; *Office & Facilities Mgr* Maria Zanetti; *Cur* Frances Loeffler
Open Centennial Square: Tues - Thurs 11 AM - 9 PM, Fri Noon - 5 PM, Sat 10 AM - 5 PM, Sun 1 - 5 PM; Gairloch Garden Tues - Sun 1 - 5 PM; Admis by donation; Estab Centennial 1967, Gairloch 1972, to exhibit contemporary visual arts; Oakville Galleries is a not-for-profit public art gallery committed to contemporary art; Average Annual Attendance: 48,000; Mem: 500
Collections: Contemporary Canadian painting, sculpture, photographs, drawing & prints, contemporary outdoor sculpture
Publications: Exhibition catalogues
Activities: Art classes for adults & children; lects series open to pub; tours; gallery talks; 12 vis lectrs per yr; originate various traveling exhibs; mus shop sells original art and crafts

L **SHERIDAN COLLEGE OF APPLIED ARTS AND TECHNOLOGY,** Trafalgar Campus Library, 1430 Trafalgar Rd, Oakville, ON L6H 2L1 Canada. Tel 905-845-9430, Ext 2482; Fax 905-815-4123; Web: www1.sheridaninstitute.ca; *Dir Library & Learning Svcs* Joan Sweeney Marsh; *Mgr Library User Servs* Marian Traynor; *Mgr Collections & Technical Servs* Jennifer Hance; *Mgr Tutoring Centres* Shelley Woods
Open Mon - Fri 8:30 AM - 4:30 PM, Sat - Sun 11 AM - 4 PM; cl Sat & Sun July & Aug; Estab 1970 to serve the students & faculty of School of Animation, Art & Design; Circ 23,000
Income: Financed by the college
Library Holdings: Book Volumes, Clipping Files, Exhibition Catalogs, Periodical Subscriptions 96, Slides 27,809, Video Tapes 50
Special Subjects: Art History, Crafts, Graphic Design, Illustration, Photography

ORILLIA

M **ORILLIA MUSEUM OF ART & HISTORY,** 30 Peter St S, Orillia, ON L3V 5A9 Canada. Tel 705-326-2159; Email inspire@orilliamuseum.org; Web: www.orilliamuseum.org; *Exec Dir* Ninette Gyorody; *Registrar* Hope McGilly Mitchell; *Communs Coordr* Shannon Hawke
Open Mon - Sat 10 AM - 4 PM, Sun 1 - 4 PM; Admis $5; Estab 1999 to share art & history of region; Art & history mus; Average Annual Attendance: 11,000; Mem: 500 mems
Collections: Art; local artifacts
Exhibitions: See website
Activities: Classes for adults & children; lects open to pub; schols; mus shop sells books, reproductions, prints, original one of a kind art

OSHAWA

M **THE ROBERT MCLAUGHLIN GALLERY,** 72 Queen St, Civic Centre Oshawa, ON L1H 3Z3 Canada. Tel 905-576-3000; Email communications@rmg.on.ca; Web: www.rmg.on.ca; *CEO* Donna Raetsen-Kemp; *Mgr Protection Servs* Stephen Dick; *Mem Coordr* Elsy Gould; *Preparator* Jason Dankel
Open Mon - Fri 10 AM - 5 PM, Thurs 10 AM - 9 PM, Sat 10 AM - 4 PM, Sun Noon - 4 PM; No admis fee; Estab Feb 1967 as The Art Gallery of Oshawa, in May 1969 as the Robert McLaughlin Gallery; R S McLaughlin Gallery 77 x 38 x 15 ft; Isabel McLaughlin Gallery 77 x 38 x 13 ft; Alexandra Luke Gallery (no 1) 62 x 48 x 9 1/2 ft; Alexandra Luke Gallery (no 2) 46 x 27 x 13 ft; E P Taylor Gallery 23 x 37 x 9 ft; General Motors Gallery 25 x 37 x 9 ft; Corridor Ramp (Isabel McLaughlin Gallery) 48 x 8 x 10 ft; Corridor (Alexandra Luke) 68 x 5 1/2 x 8 ft with Foyer & Dir Office; Average Annual Attendance: 40,000; Mem: 500; dues family $45, single $35, student $20; annual meeting in May
Income: Financed by membership, city appropriation, Canada Council, Ministry Culture & Recreation & Ontario Arts Council
Special Subjects: Painting-Canadian, Photography, Portraits, Prints, Sculpture, Watercolors, Woodcuts
Collections: Canadian 19th & 20th century drawings, paintings, prints & sculpture, major coll of works by Painters Eleven
Publications: Annual Report; bi-monthly bulletin; Calendar of Events, annually; exhibition catalogs
Activities: Classes for adults and children; docent training; lects open to pub, 6 vis lectrs per yr; gallery talks; tours; schols & fels offered; original objects of art lent to schools, institutions & industries; lending coll contains cassettes, 300 color reproductions, framed reproductions, original art works, 10,000 slides & 5100 books; sales shop sells books, reproductions, prints & local crafts

L **Library**, 72 Queen St, Civic Centre Oshawa, ON L1H 3Z3 Canada. Tel 905-576-3000; Fax 905-576-9774; Email bduff@rmg.on.ca; Web: www.rmg.on.ca; *Coordr Library Svcs* Barb Duff; *Asst Curator* Sonja Jones
Open to public for in-library use by appointment only; Admis donations accepted; Open to pub, mem available
Library Holdings: Auction Catalogs, Audio Tapes, Book Volumes 8000, Cassettes, Clipping Files, Exhibition Catalogs, Manuscripts, Original Documents, Pamphlets, Periodical Subscriptions, Photographs, Slides, Video Tapes
Collections: Canadian contemporary art books

Activities: Classes for adults & children; docent training; mus shop sells books & original art

OTTAWA

A **CANADA COUNCIL FOR THE ARTS,** Conseil des Arts du Canada, 150 Elgin St, PO Box 1047 Ottawa, ON K1P 5V8 Canada. Tel 613-566-4414; Fax 613-566-4390; Email info@canadacouncil.ca; Web: www.canadacouncil.ca; WATS 800-263-5588; *Dir & CEO* Simon Brault
Open daily 8:45 AM - 5 PM, cl Sat & Sun; Estab 1957 to foster & promote the arts. The Council provides a wide range of grants & services to professional Canadian artists & art organizations in dance, media arts, music, opera, theatre, writing, publishing & the visual arts. Also Art Bank; Estab 1957, the Council is a national arm's-length agency which provides grants & services to professional Canadian artists & arts organizations in dance, media arts, music, theatre, writing & publishing, interdisciplinary work & performance art, & the visual arts. The Art Bank of the Canada Council rents contemporary Canadian art to the pub & private sectors across Canada. The Council also maintains the secretariat for the Canadian Commission for UNESCO, administers the Killam Program of scholarly awards & prizes, & offers a number of other prestigious awards. The Public Lending Right (PLR) Commission, which is operated by the Canada Council, administers a program of payments to Canadian authors for their eligible books catalogued in libraries across Canada. The Canada Council for the Arts is funded by & reports to Parliament through the Minister of Canadian Heritage
Income: Financed by Parliament of Canada, endowment fund & private individuals
Activities: Prizes awarded; grants & fels offered

M **CANADA SCIENCE & TECHNOLOGY MUSEUMS CORPORATION,** Canada Aviation Museum, 11 Aviation Pkwy, Ottawa, ON K1K 4Y5 Canada; PO Box 9724, Station T Ottawa, ON K1G 5A3 Canada. Tel 613-991-3044; Fax 613-993-7923; Email contact@techno-science.ca; Web: www.casmuseum.techno-science.ca/en/index.php; *Dir* Francine Poirier; *Cur* A J (Fred) Shortt
Open May 1 - Sep 5 daily 9 AM - 5 PM; Sep 5 - May 1 10 AM - 5 PM, cl Tues; Admis families $38 adults $15, seniors & students $15, youth 3-17 $10, members, veterans & children 2 and under free; Estab 1960 to illustrate the evolution of the flying machine & the important role aircraft played in Canada's development; Average Annual Attendance: 250,000; Mem: 2000; dues $20-$80
Collections: More than 120 aircraft plus thousands of aviation related artifacts
Activities: Classes for adults & children; lect open to public; tours; sales shop sells books, magazines & prints

CANADIAN CONFERENCE OF THE ARTS
For further information, see National and Regional Organizations

M **CANADIAN MUSEUM OF NATURE,** Musee Canadien de la Nature, 240 McLeod St, Ottawa, ON K2P 2R1 Canada; PO Box 3443, Station D Ottawa, ON K1P 6P4 Canada. Tel 613-566-4770; Fax 613-364-4021; Email questions@mus-nature.ca; Web: nature.ca; *Pres & CEO* Meg Beckel; *VP Corp Svcs* Charles Bloom; *VPres Experience & Engagement* Alisa Barry; *VPres Research & Collections* Mark Graham, Ph D; *CFO & Dir Finance* Ikram Zouari; *Dir Advancement* Laura Evans; *Dir Mktg* John Swettenham; *Dir Content, Experience & Engagement* Stacy Wakeford; *Dir Visitor Experience* Angeline Laffin
Open Sept - May: Tues, Wed & Fri - Sun 9 AM - 5 PM, Thurs 9 AM - 8 PM, cl Mon; June - Sept: Sat - Wed & Fri 9 AM - 6 PM, Thurs 9 AM - 8 PM; Admis adults $14.50, senior (65 & up) & students $12.50, children (3-12) $10.50, children under 3 free; Estab 1856 to disseminate knowledge about the natural sciences, with particular but not exclusive reference to Canada; Canada's national museum of natural history & natural sciences; Average Annual Attendance: 450,000; Mem: Dues family & grandparents $129; daycare $109, adult $69; senior & student $40
Income: Financed by donations, government & self generated revenue
Library Holdings: Audio Tapes, Book Volumes, CD-ROMs, Cards, Cassettes, DVDs, Original Art Works, Periodical Subscriptions, Sculpture
Special Subjects: Ceramics, Dioramas, Drawings, Painting-Canadian, Photography, Posters, Prints, Watercolors, Woodcarvings, Costumes, Crafts
Collections: Prints, Paintings, Sculpture, over ten million specimens
Exhibitions: Talisman Energy Fossil Gallery; Mammal Gallery; Bird Gallery; RBC Blue Water Gallery; Vale Earth Gallery; Animalium
Activities: Classes for children; school progs (primary & secondary); volunteer training; lects, film series; demonstrations & workshops dealing with natural history subjects

CANADIAN MUSEUMS ASSOCIATION
For further information, see National and Regional Organizations

M **CANADIAN WAR MUSEUM,** 1 Vimy Pl, Ottawa, ON K1A 0M8 Canada. Tel 819-776-7000; Email information@warmuseum.ca; Web: www.warmuseum.ca; *Pres & CEO* Mark O'Neill
Open Mon - Wed & Fri - Sun 9:30 AM - 5 PM, Thurs 9:30 AM - 8 PM; Admis family $43, adult $17, senior $15, student $13, child (3-12) $11, mem no charge; Estab 1880 to collect, preserve & display objects relevant to Canadian military history. Promote public understanding of Canada's military history in its personal, national and international dimensions; Average Annual Attendance: 500,000; Mem: Dues ambassador $250, family $125, adult $50, sr citizen, student or child $40
Income: Financed by government funds
Library Holdings: Auction Catalogs, Audio Tapes, Book Volumes, CD-ROMs, Cassettes, Clipping Files, Compact Disks, DVDs, Exhibition Catalogs, Framed Reproductions, Kodachrome Transparencies, Lantern Slides, Manuscripts, Maps, Motion Pictures, Original Documents, Pamphlets, Periodical Subscriptions, Photographs, Prints, Records, Slides, Video Tapes
Special Subjects: Coins & Medals, Historical Material, Painting-Canadian
Collections: Uniforms & accoutrements, medals & insignia, equipment, vehicles, art, archives, photographs, weapons
Exhibitions: Canadian Experience Galleries-permanent exhibition
Activities: Educ dept & prog; classes for adults & children; lect presentations open to pub; tours; gallery talks; concerts; fels offered; lending collection contains 13,000 books; artwork lent to other mus & galleries, educational institutions, national exhib centers; originate traveling exhibs to mus & galleries; mus shop sells books, reproductions, prints, slides, shirts & models

M **CANADIAN WILDLIFE & WILDERNESS ART MUSEUM,** PO Box 98, Sta B, Ottawa, ON K1P 6C3 Canada. Tel 613-237-1581; Fax 613-237-1581; Email cawa@magma.ca; *Co-Dir* Cody Sadler; *Dir* Gary Slimon
Open Mon - Sun 10 AM - 5 PM; Admis $3; Estab 1987; Museum exhibits paintings, sculptures & carvings of wildlife themes; Mem: Dues $50-$1000; annual meeting in Jan
Income: Financed by endowment, mem, state appropriation, mus proceeds
Special Subjects: Painting-American, Sculpture
Collections: Wildlife & wilderness paintings, sculpture, carvings & decoys
Publications: Brochure; newsletter
Activities: Classes for children; 'how-to' seminars; lects open to pub, 4 vis lectrs per yr; individual paintings & original objects of art lent to mus with similar mandates; lending collection contains original art work paintings & sculpture; book traveling exhibs 1 per yr; originate traveling exhibs; mus shop sells books, magazines, prints, slides

L **Library,** PO Box 98, Sta B, Ottawa, ON K1P 6C3 Canada. Tel 613-237-1581 (and fax); Email cawa@bell.net; *Co-Dir* Cody Sadler; *Dir* Gary Slimon
Library mainly for research for member artists
Library Holdings: Exhibition Catalogs, Other Holdings Magazines, Slides
Special Subjects: American Indian Art, American Western Art, Art Education, Commercial Art, Eskimo Art, Ethnology, Graphic Arts, Historical Material, Landscapes, Latin American Art, Mexican Art, Painting-American, Painting-Canadian, Painting-European, Painting-French, Portraits, Pre-Columbian Art, Printmaking, Prints, Reproductions, Sculpture, Southwestern Art, Video, Watercolors, Woodcarvings

A **DEPARTMENT OF CANADIAN HERITAGE,** Canadian Conservation Institute, 1030 Innes Rd, Ottawa, ON K1A 0M5 Canada. Tel 613-998-3721; Fax 613-998-4721; Email pch.ICCservices-CCIServices.pch@canada.ca; Web: www.cci-icc.gc.ca; *Dir Gen & COO* Patricia Kell
Open Tues - Fri 9 AM - 4 PM; No admis fee; Estab 1972; Delivers wide range of services and products, research & preservation
Income: Financed by state appropriation
Library Holdings: Audio Tapes 17, Book Volumes 10,000, Clipping Files, Fiche 139, Pamphlets, Periodical Subscriptions 300, Video Tapes 175
Collections: Conservation of cultural property, conservation research
Publications: CCI Newsletter, biannual; CCI Notes, irregular; CCI Technical Bulletins, irregular

M **ENVIRONMENT CANADA - PARKS CANADA,** Laurier House, National Historic Site, 335 Laurier Ave E, Ottawa, ON K1N 6R4 Canada. Tel 613-992-8142; Fax 613-947-4851; Email laurier.house@pc.gc.ca; Web: www.pc.gc.ca/lhn-nhs/on/laurier; *Visitor Experience Mgr* Anne-Marie Johnson
Open May 1 - June 30 Thurs - Mon 10 AM - 5 PM, July 1 - Sept 5 daily 10 AM - 5 PM, Sept 6 - Oct 10 Thurs - Mon 10 AM - 5 PM; Admis family $9.80, adults $3.90, sr citizens $3.40, youth $1.90, under 6 free; Estab 1951; This is a historic house & former residence of Two Prime Ministers, Sir Wilfrid Laurier & the Rt Honorable William Lyon Mackenzie King containing furniture & memorabilia. The house is primarily furnished in the style of its last occupant, the Rt Honorable William Lyon Mackenzie King, with space given to the Laurier Collection; Average Annual Attendance: 8,014
Income: Financed by federal government & trust fund
Special Subjects: Decorative Arts, Drawings, Furniture, Glass, Jewelry, Landscapes, Painting-Canadian, Painting-Dutch, Painting-Italian, Painting-Japanese, Period Rooms, Portraits, Religious Art, Reproductions, Sculpture, Silver, Textiles
Exhibitions: Visitor Centre Exhibit
Publications: Main Park Brochure provided to visitors
Activities: Guided tours

L **NATIONAL ARCHIVES OF CANADA,** Art & Photography Archives, 395 Wellington St, Ottawa, ON K1A 0N4 Canada. Tel 613-996-7766; Fax 613-995-6575; Web: www.collectionscanada.gc.ca; *Librn & Archivist* Guy Berthiaume; *Dir & Custodian Holdings* Elizabeth Moxley; *Chief Coll Consultation* Robert Grandmaitre; *Documentary Art & Photo Acquisition* Jim Barant; *Descriptive Servs Section* Jennifer Svarckopf
Open daily 9 AM - 4:45 PM; No admis fee; Estab 1905 to acquire & preserve significant Canadian archival material in the area of visual media, including paintings, watercolours, drawings, prints, medals, heraldry, posters & photography relating to all aspects of Canadian life, to the development of the country, to provide suitable research services, facilities to make this documentation available to the pub by means of exhibitions, publications & pub catalogue
Income: Financed by federal appropriation
Purchases: $80,000
Library Holdings: Auction Catalogs, Book Volumes 4000
Special Subjects: American Indian Art, Coins & Medals, Drawings, Etchings & Engravings, Landscapes, Miniatures, Painting-British, Painting-Canadian, Painting-Italian, Photography, Portraits, Posters, Prints, Reproductions, Watercolors
Collections: 1800 paintings, 22,000 watercolours & drawings, 90,000 prints, 30,000 posters, 16,000 medals, 7000 heraldic design & seals, 80,000 caricatures, 22 million photographs
Publications: Catalog of publications available on request
Activities: Lect open to pub; Tours; original art lent to mus & galleries; sales shop sells reproductions & slides

M **NATIONAL GALLERY OF CANADA,** 380 Sussex Dr, Ottawa, ON K1N 9N4 Canada. Tel 613-990-1985; Fax 613-990-8075; Email info@gallery.ca; Web: www.gallery.ca; *Dir & CEO* Marc Mayer; *Deputy Dir Admin & CFO* Julie Peckham; *Deputy Dir Colls & Research & Chief Cur* Ann Thomas; *Deputy Dir Advancement & Pub Engagement* Jean-Francois Bilodeau; *Deputy Dir Exhibs & Outreach* Anne Eschapasse; *Dir Corporate Secretariat & Ministerial Liaison* Matthew Symonds

Open May - Sept daily 10 AM - 6 PM, Thurs 10 AM - 8 PM; Oct - Apr Tues - Sun 10 AM - 5 PM, Thurs 10 AM - 8 PM, cl Mon; Admis family $30, adults $15, seniors (65 & up) $13, students (24 & under) $7, children (11 & under) free; Founded 1880 under the patronage of the Governor-General, the Marquess of Lorne & his wife the Princess Louise; first inc 1913 to develop, maintain, and promote works of contemporary & modern art with special, but not exclusive, reference to Canada; On May 21 1988, the first permanent home of National Gallery of Canada opened to the pub & to critical & popular acclaim. Overlooking the Ottawa river & steps away from Parliament Hill, the gallery is a landmark in the Capital's skyline. Light, spacious galleries & quiet courtyards lead the visitors on a voyage of discovery of Canada's exceptional art coll; Average Annual Attendance: 500,000; Mem: 10,000 - 12,000; dues student $35, senior $55, individual $75, family & duo $105, Privilege $300, Circle Plus $1,000 & up
Purchases: $3,000,000
Library Holdings: Audio Tapes, Book Volumes, CD-ROMs, Cards, Cassettes, Clipping Files, Exhibition Catalogs, Fiche, Filmstrips, Framed Reproductions, Kodachrome Transparencies, Manuscripts, Original Documents, Other Holdings, Periodical Subscriptions, Photographs, Prints, Records, Slides, Video Tapes
Special Subjects: Asian Art, Baroque Art, Bookplates & Bindings, Bronzes, Collages, Decorative Arts, Drawings, Etchings & Engravings, Furniture, Graphics, Landscapes, Medieval Art, Painting-American, Painting-British, Painting-Canadian, Painting-Dutch, Painting-European, Painting-Flemish, Painting-French, Painting-German, Painting-Italian, Painting-Russian, Painting-Spanish, Photography, Portraits
Collections: Over 45,000 works in entire coll, over 1200 on display in permanent coll galleries, contemporary Inuit artists work, historical & contemporary Canadian art, media arts in the world over 600 titles, totaling more than 10,000 hours of video & film, 19,000 photography works, 20th century American art, western European art 14th-20th centuries, Inuit Art, Indigenous Art
Exhibitions: Exhibitions from permanent coll, private & pub sources are organized & circulated in Canada & abroad
Publications: Annual report (incorporating annual review, with current acquisition lists); catalogues of permanent coll; CD-ROM on the Canadian coll; documents in the history of Canadian Art; exhibition books & catalogues; masterpieces in the National Gallery of Canada
Activities: Classes for adults & children; docent training; dramatic progs; film series; workshops for physically & mentally challenged, teen council; lects open to pub, 20 vis lectrs per yr; concerts; gallery talks; tours; schols & fels offered; individual paintings & original objects of art lent to art museums & galleries in Canada & abroad, subject to the same environmental conditions (other conditions apply); book traveling exhibs 25 per yr; originate traveling exhibs to Canadian & international venues; mus shop sells books, magazines, reproductions, prints, jewelry; affiliate Canadian Museum of Contemporary Photography

L **Library**, 380 Sussex Dr, PO Box 427, Sta A Ottawa, ON K1N 9N4 Canada. Tel 613-998-8949; Fax 613-990-9818; Email erefel@gallery.ca; Web: www.gallery.ca; *Library, Archives & Research Fels Prog* Cyndie Campbell
Open May - Sept Mon - Fri 1 - 5 PM, Oct - April Tues - Fri 1 - 5 PM, cl Aug & holidays; No admis fee; Estab 1918 to support the research & information requirements of gallery personnel; to make its collections of resource materials in the fine arts available to Canadian libraries & scholars; to serve as a source of information about art & art activities in Canada; Circ 35,000; For reference only; Average Annual Attendance: 9,000
Library Holdings: Auction Catalogs, Audio Tapes, Book Volumes 300,000, CD-ROMs, Cards, Cassettes, Clipping Files, Compact Disks, Exhibition Catalogs, Fiche, Filmstrips, Kodachrome Transparencies, Lantern Slides, Manuscripts, Memorabilia, Motion Pictures, Original Documents, Other Holdings Auction catalogues; Illustrated books; Rare books, Pamphlets, Periodical Subscriptions 1100, Photographs, Records, Reels, Slides, Video Tapes
Special Subjects: Aesthetics, Architecture, Art History, Drawings, Eskimo Art, Film, Graphic Arts, Painting-Canadian, Printmaking, Video, Conceptual Art
Collections: Art Documentation, Canadiana, Art Metropole
Exhibitions: Various, see website
Publications: Artists in Canada; Reference Database (CHIN); Library and Archives, occasional paper series 1-8; library and archives, exhibition 1-42
Activities: Library tours, exhibs

L **OTTAWA PUBLIC LIBRARY,** Fine Arts Dept, 120 Metcalfe St, Ottawa, ON K1P 5M2 Canada. Tel 613-580-2940; Email InfoService@BiblioOttawaLibrary.ca; Web: www.biblioottawalibrary.ca; *CEO* Danielle McDonald; *Deputy CEO* Monique Desormeaux
Open Mon - Thurs 10 AM - 9 PM, Fri 10 AM - 6 PM, Sat & Sun 10 AM - 5 PM; No admis fee; Estab 1906 to serve the community as a centre for general & reliable information; to select, preserve & administer books & related materials in organized collections; to provide opportunity for citizens of all ages to educate themselves continuously
Income: $8,808,600 (financed by city, province, other)
Library Holdings: Book Volumes 12,000, Cassettes, Clipping Files, Fiche, Filmstrips, Pamphlets, Periodical Subscriptions 85, Reels
Exhibitions: Monthly exhibits highlighting local artists, craftsmen, photographers & collectors
Activities: Lect open to public; library tours

OWEN SOUND

M **OWEN SOUND HISTORICAL SOCIETY,** Marine & Rail Heritage Museum, 1155 First Ave W, Owen Sound, ON N4K 4K8 Canada. Tel 519-371-3333; Email info@waterfrontheritage.ca; Web: www.marinerail.ca; *Pres* Jim Henderson; *Cur* Neil Garneau
Open Sept - May Tues - Fri 10 AM - 4 PM; Sept - Nov Sat 11:30 AM - 3:30 PM, cl Sun; Jun, July & Aug Mon - Sun 10 AM - 4 PM; Admis adults $5, children $2, seniors $4, family $15; Estab 1985 for the preservation of Owen Sound's marine, rail & industrial history; Mem: Dues $10 & up
Income: Financed by mem, donations & government grant
Special Subjects: Historical Material
Collections: Charts, timetables, railway artifacts & models, Corvette HMCS Owen Sound artifacts, Dug-out & Birch-bark canoes, house flags of Marine Transport Coys, lifeboat from the Paul Evans, marine & railway uniforms, patterns from local foundry in production of propellers & shipbuilding, scale models of ships that sailed the Great Lakes
Activities: Lects open to pub, 6 vis lectrs per yr; children's competition with prizes; lending coll contains books

M **TOM THOMSON MEMORIAL ART GALLERY,** 840 First Ave W, Owen Sound, ON N4K 4K4 Canada. Tel 519-376-1932; Fax 519-376-3037; Email ttag@owensound.ca; Web: www.tomthomson.org; *Dir & Chief Cur* Virginia Eichhorn
Open Sept - June Tues - Fri 11 AM - 5 PM, Sat & Sun Noon - 5 PM; June - Aug Mon - Fri 10 AM - 6 PM, Sat 10 AM - 5 PM, Sun 12 PM - 5 PM; No admis fee; Estab 1967 to collect & display paintings by Tom Thomson, a native son & Canada's foremost landscape artist; to educate the public; Paintings by Tom Thomson on permanent display, plus 2 galleries of changing exhibitions; Average Annual Attendance: 30,000; Mem: 300; dues family $25, individual $15, senior citizens & students $10
Income: Financed by city appropriation & provincial grants & fundraising
Collections: Tom Thomson, Historic & Contemporary Canadian Artists, Group of Seven
Publications: Bulletin, six per year; exhibition catalogs 3 per year
Activities: Classes for adults & children; docent training; lects open to pub; gallery talks; tours; films; competitions with awards; concerts; exten dept serves city bldgs; mus shop sells books, reproductions, prints & postcards

L **Library/Archives**, 840 First Ave W, Owen Sound, ON N4K 4K4 Canada. Tel 519-376-1932; Fax 519-376-3037; Web: www.tomthomson.org; *Dir* Stuart Reid; *Educ* David Huff
Open by appointment only; Circ Non-circulating; Open for reference of Tom Thomson files
Library Holdings: Book Volumes 400, Exhibition Catalogs, Periodical Subscriptions 6
Collections: Files on Tom Thomson

PETERBOROUGH

M **ART GALLERY OF PETERBOROUGH,** 250 Crescent St, Peterborough, ON K9J 2G1 Canada. Tel 705-743-9179; Fax 705-743-8168; Email gallery@agp.on.ca; Web: www.agp.on.ca; *Cur* Flynn Leitch; *Gallery Opers Asst* Janice Fortune; *Dir* Celeste Scopelites; *Educ & Prog Coordr* Jane Wild
Open Tues - Sun 11 AM - 5 PM; No admis fee; Estab 1974; Gallery situated along a lake & in a park; new extension added & completed June 1979; Average Annual Attendance: 16,000; Mem: 700; dues family $35, individual $25, sr citizens $20, student $15; annual meeting June
Income: Financed by mem, fundraising & provincial, federal, municipal grants
Library Holdings: Book Volumes, Exhibition Catalogs
Collections: European and Canadian works of art
Publications: Catalogues on some exhibitions; pamphlets on artists in exhibitions
Activities: Classes for adults & children; docent training; workshops; art prog to pub schools; lects open to pub; 6 vis lectrs per yr; gallery talks; tours; individual paintings & original objects of art lent to other galleries; 1 to 2 book travelling exhibs per yr; organize travelling exhibs to public galleries across Canada; sales shop sells books, crafts & fine art

SAINT CATHARINES

M **NIAGARA ARTISTS CENTRE,** 354 St Paul St, Saint Catharines, ON L2R 3N2 Canada. Tel 905-641-0331; Fax 905-641-4970; Email artists@nac.org; Web: www.nac.org; *Minister of Energy, Minds & Resources* Stephen Remus
Open Wed 10 AM - 5 PM, Thurs & Fri noon - 9 PM, Sat noon - 5 PM; No admis fee; Estab 1969; Main gallery has 2400 sq ft, 2nd gallery has 500 sq ft; Average Annual Attendance: 6,100; Mem: 135; mem open to volunteers for exhibits & fundraisers; dues $15-$50; annual meeting mid-July
Income: $120,000 (financed by mem, Ontario government, federal government & sponsorship)
Exhibitions: rotate 6-8 exhibits per yr
Publications: NAC News, monthly
Activities: Lect open to public

A **RODMAN HALL ARTS CENTRE,** 109 St Paul Crescent, Saint Catharines, ON L2S 1M3 Canada. Tel 905-684-2925; Fax 905-682-4733; Email rodmanhall@brocku.ca; Web: www.brocku.ca/rodman-hall; *Dir* Marcie Bronson; *Preparator* Matthew Tegel
Open summer Tues, Wed & Fri 10 AM - 5 PM, Thurs 10 AM - 9 PM, Sat & Sun noon - 5 PM; Admis by donation (suggested $5); Estab 1960, art gallery, cultural centre & visual arts exhibitions; Four galleries in an 1853, 1960 & 1975 addition. 1975 - A1 - National Museums of Canada. Maintains reference library; Average Annual Attendance: 45,000; Mem: 800; dues tax receipt $75 or more, family $40, individual $25; annual meeting in Sept
Income: Financed by mem, city, province & government of Canada
Collections: American graphics & drawings, Canadian drawings, paintings, sculpture & watercolours, international graphics & sculpture
Exhibitions: Monthly exhibitions featuring painting, photographs, sculpture & other art
Publications: Catalogue - Lord and Lady Head Watercolours; monthly calendar; Rodmon Hall Arts Center (1960-1981)
Activities: Classes for adults & children; dramatic progs; docent training; workshops; films; lects open to pub, 6 vis lectrs per yr; concerts; gallery talks; tours; individual paintings & original objects of art lent to city hall & other art galleries; book traveling exhibs 16 per yr; book traveling exhibs 5 per yr; mus shop sells books, original art, gifts, pottery, glassware & jewelry

L **Library**, 109 St Paul Crescent, Saint Catharines, ON L2S 1M3 Canada. Tel 905-684-2925; Fax 905-682-4733; *Librn* Debra Attenborough
Open Tues - Fri 9 AM - 5 PM; Estab 1960; Reference library

Library Holdings: Book Volumes 3500, Cards, Cassettes, Clipping Files, Exhibition Catalogs, Pamphlets, Periodical Subscriptions 7, Photographs, Reproductions, Slides, Video Tapes

SAINT THOMAS

M **ST THOMAS-ELGIN PUBLIC ART CENTRE,** 301 Talbot St, Saint Thomas, ON N5P 1B5 Canada. Tel 519-631-4040; Fax 519-631-4057; Email info@stepac.ca; Web: www.stepac.ca; *Exec Dir & Cur* Laura Woermke
Open Sun 12 PM - 3 PM, Tues - Wed 10 AM - 4 PM, Thurs - Fri 10 AM - 9 PM, Sat 12 PM - 4 PM; No admis fee; Estab 1969; Pub gallery; Average Annual Attendance: 10,000; Mem: 658; dues senior citizens $15, family $30, single $20; annual meeting in March
Income: $150,000 (financed by endowment, mem, municipality, donations, & earned revenues)
Library Holdings: Book Volumes, Exhibition Catalogs, Original Art Works, Photographs, Slides, Video Tapes
Collections: Fine Art Works by Canadian Artists
Publications: Info brochures; gallery newsletter 3 per year
Activities: Educ prog in art for all adults & children; lects open to pub; tours, sponsor competitions; schols offered; lending of original art to other galleries; originate traveling exhibs; gift shop sells original art & promotional items

SCARBOROUGH

M **CITY OF SCARBOROUGH,** Cedar Ridge Creative Centre, 225 Confederation Dr, Scarborough, ON M1G 1B2 Canada. Tel 416-396-4026; Fax 416-396-7044; Email crcc@toronto.ca; *Coordr Cultural Progs* Ann Christian
Open Mon - Thurs 9 AM - 10 PM, Fri - Sun 9 AM - 4 PM; No admis fee; Estab 1985 as a gallery & teaching studio; 3-interconnecting rooms & solarium with oak paneling, 18' x 22', 18' x 28', 16' x 26'; Average Annual Attendance: 1,300; Mem: Annual dues $10 (it entitles member to rent gallery for one week for $39)
Exhibitions: Contemporary Art Show
Activities: Classes for adults & children; one day workshops in arts & crafts; lects open to pub, 2 vis lectrs per yr

SIMCOE

A **LYNNWOOD ARTS CENTRE,** 21 Lynnwood Ave, PO Box 67 Simcoe, ON N3Y 2V7 Canada. Tel 519-428-0540; Fax 519-428-0549; Email lynnwood@kwic.com; Web: www.norfolkartscentre.ca; *Dir & Cur* Deirdre Chisholm
Open Mon - Sat 10 AM - 4 PM; No admis fee; Estab 1973 to provide a focal point for the visual arts in the community; Built in 1851 - Greek Revival Architecture; orange brick with ionic columns & is a National Historic Site; Average Annual Attendance: 8,800; Mem: 300; dues family $30, individual $25, student & senior citizen $20; annual meeting in Mar
Income: $140,000 (financed by mem, patrons-private & commercial, Ontario Arts Council)
Collections: Contemporary Canadian Art
Exhibitions: Exhibitions of contemporary art & permanent collection works; Local artists
Publications: Quarterly newsletter
Activities: Classes for adults & children; docent training; lects open to pub, 15 lectrs per yr; concerts; gallery talks; tours; seminars; juried art exhibs (every two years) with purchase awards; sales shop sells books & hand-crafted items

STRATFORD

M **GALLERY STRATFORD,** 54 Romeo St S, Stratford, ON N5A 4S9 Canada. Tel 519-271-5271; Fax 519-271-1642; Email info@gallerystratford.on.ca; Web: www.gallerystratford.on.ca; *Dir & Cur* Angela Brayham
Open daily 10 AM - 5 PM, Thurs & Fri 10 AM - 7 PM; Estab 1967 as a nonprofit permanent establishment open to the pub & administered in the pub interest for the purpose of studying, interpreting, assembling & exhibiting to the pub; public art gallery; Average Annual Attendance: 25,000; Mem: 400; annual meeting in Mar
Income: $348,743 (financed by mem, city appropriation, provincial & federal grants & fundraising)
Collections: Works of art on paper
Exhibitions: Changing exhibits, geared to create interest for visitors to Stratford Shakespearean Festival; during winter months geared to local municipality
Publications: Catalogs; calendar of events
Activities: Classes for adults & children; docent training; lects open to pub; gallery talks; tours; visual art award for grade 12; scholarships offered; originates traveling exhibs; gift shop sells Canadian craft, glass, jewelry, pottery, silk scarves & cards

SUDBURY

M **LAURENTIAN UNIVERSITY,** Museum & Art Centre, 251 rue John St, Sudbury, ON P3E 1P9 Canada. Tel 705-675-4871; Fax 705-674-3065; Web: www.artsudbury.org; *Dir & Cur* Demetra Christakos
Open Tues - Sat 10 AM - 5 PM, Sun noon - 5PM; Admis fee voluntary; Estab 1968 to present a continuous program of exhibitions, concerts & events for the people of Sudbury & the district; Gallery has two floors of space: 124 running ft in one & 131 running ft in the second gallery & 68.5 running ft in third gallery; Average Annual Attendance: 30,000; Mem: 400; dues family $26.75, single $16.05, student & senior citizen $8.56; annual meeting in June
Income: Financed by endowment, mem, city & provincial appropriations, government & local organizations
Special Subjects: Painting-American, Painting-Canadian, Painting-Polish
Collections: Canadian coll dating from the late 1800s & early 1900s to contemporary. The Group of Seven, Eskimo sculptures & prints as well as works of historical Canadian artists comprise the coll, Indian works from northern Ontario
Publications: Communique, every eight weeks
Activities: Lects open to pub, 10 vis lectrs per yr; concerts; gallery talks; tours; lending collection contains 1300 original art works & 8300 slides; book traveling exhibs 2-4 per yr; mus shop sells magazines, catalogues, postcards, posters, prints & gift items

L **Art Centre Library,** 251 rue John St, Sudbury, ON P3E 2Z7 Canada. Tel 705-675-4871; Fax 705-674-3065; Email gallery@artsudbury.org; Web: www.artsudbury.org; *Dir & Cur* Demetra Christakos
Open Tues, Wed, Sat & Sun Noon-5PM, Thurs & Fri Noon-9PM; Admis $2 donation; Estab 1977; For reference only; Average Annual Attendance: 25,000
Purchases: Contemporary Canadian, new media
Library Holdings: Book Volumes 5000, Cards, Cassettes, Clipping Files, Exhibition Catalogs, Lantern Slides, Pamphlets, Periodical Subscriptions 78, Photographs, Slides 8300, Video Tapes
Activities: Classes for adults & children; lects open to pub; concerts; gallery talks; tours; exten prog serves area schools; artmobile; lending of original objects of art; originate 2 traveling exhibs per yr; mus shop sells books & magazines

TORONTO

M **A SPACE,** 401 Richmond St W, Ste 110, Toronto, ON M5V 3A8 Canada. Tel 416-979-9633; Fax 416-979-9683; Email info@aspacegallery.org; Web: www.aspacegallery.org; *Exec Dir* Rebecca McGowan
Open Tues - Fri 11 AM - 5 PM, Sat Noon - 5 PM, cl Sun & Mon; No admis fee; Estab 1971; 1,000 sq ft of gallery space & hardwood floors. Maintains reference library; Average Annual Attendance: 15,000; Mem: 150; dues $15; 4 meetings yearly
Income: $171,000 (financed by endowment, mem, city & state appropriation)
Collections: Contemporary Visual Art
Exhibitions: Artists' submissions to gallery
Publications: Addendum-A Space Community Newsletter, quarterly
Activities: Lects open to pub, 5 vis lectrs per yr; concerts; gallery talks; tours; book traveling exhibs; originate traveling exhibs; mus shop sells books

M **ART GALLERY OF ONTARIO,** 317 Dundas St W, Toronto, ON M5T 1G4 Canada. Tel 416-979-6648; Web: ago.ca; *Michael & Sonja Koerner Dir & CEO* Stephan Jost; *Chief Communs & Brand* Lisa Clements; *Deputy Dir & Chief Cur* Julian Cox; *Exec Dir Corp Spec Projects & Dir Opers* Mike Mahoney; *Chief of Staff & Corp Secy* Erin Prendergast; *CFO Fin & Info Tech* Rocco Saverino; *Chief Exhibs & Colls* Christy Thompson; *Deputy Dir & Chief Advancement Officer* Alicia Vandermeer
Open Tues & Thurs - 10:30 AM - 5 PM, Wed & Fri 10:30 AM - 9 PM; Sat - Sun 10:30 PM - 5:30 PM; cl Mon; Admis family $49, adults $19.50, seniors (65 & up) $16, students (w/ID) & youth (6-17) $11, children 5 and under free; Estab 1900 to cultivate & advance the cause of the visual arts in Ontario; to conduct programmes of educ in the origin, development, appreciation & techniques of the visual arts; to collect & exhibit works of art & displays & to maintain & operate a gallery & related facilities as required for this purpose; to stimulate the interest of the pub in matters undertaken by the Gallery; 583,000 sq ft facility; Average Annual Attendance: 965,000; Mem: dues student $45, long-distance $90, individual $110, family 7 dual $145, Contributing $205 - $349, Supporting $350 - $674, Sustaining $675 - $1,099, Fellow $1,100 - $1,999
Income: Financed by mem, provincial, city & federal appropriations & earned income
Library Holdings: Auction Catalogs, Audio Tapes, Book Volumes, CD-ROMs, Cards, Clipping Files, DVDs
Special Subjects: Painting-American, Painting-European, Sculpture, African Art
Collections: American & European Art (16th century to present), Canadian Historical & Contemporary Art, Henry Moore Sculpture Center, Prints & Drawings, Henry Moore Sculpture Collection
Exhibitions: Swing Space: Wallworks-Contemporary Art in Unexpected Places
Publications: Art Matters Journal, eleven times per year; annual report; exhibition catalogs
Activities: Classes for adults & children; docent training; lect open to public; gallery talks; tours; individual paintings & original objects of art loaned; sales shop sells books, reproductions, prints & jewelry; art rental shop for members to rent original works of art; Teens Behind the Scenes

M **ART METROPOLE,** 1490 Dundas St W, Toronto, ON M6K 1T5 Canada. Tel 416-703-4400; Fax 416-703-4404; Email info@artmetropole.org; Web: www.artmetropole.com; *Cur* Nasrin Himada; *Exec Dir* Danielle St-Amour; *Registrar* Hanna Myall
Open Wed - Sat 12 AM - 7 PM; No admis fee; Estab 1974 to document work by artists internationally working in non-traditional & multiple media; 900 sq ft
Income: Financed by sales & government funding
Special Subjects: Conceptual Art, Costumes
Exhibitions: Exhibits rotate every 2 months
Activities: Gallery talks; Mus shop sells books, magazines, original art, artists' books & multiples

A **ARTS AND LETTERS CLUB OF TORONTO,** 14 Elm St, Toronto, ON M5G 1G7 Canada. Tel 416-597-0223; Fax 416-597-9544; Email info@artsandlettersclub.ca; Web: www.artsandlettersclub.ca; *Mgr* Fiona McKeown
Open by appointment; Estab 1908 to foster arts & letters in Toronto; Mem: 580; annual meeting May
Library Holdings: Book Volumes, Exhibition Catalogs
Special Subjects: Painting-Canadian
Collections: Club Collection - art by members & others, Heritage Collection - art by members now deceased
Activities: Arts & Letters Award

L **Library,** 14 Elm St, Toronto, ON M5G 1G7 Canada. Tel 416-597-0223; *Librn* Margaret Spence; *Gen Mgr* Jason Clarke
Open by appointment; Open to club members & researchers for reference
Library Holdings: Audio Tapes, Book Volumes 2500, Cassettes, Clipping Files, Exhibition Catalogs, Kodachrome Transparencies, Manuscripts, Memorabilia,

Motion Pictures, Original Art Works, Periodical Subscriptions 40, Prints, Sculpture, Slides, Video Tapes
Special Subjects: Architecture, Sculpture, Theatre Arts

M **BAU-XI GALLERY,** 340 Dundas St W, Toronto, ON M5T 1G5 Canada. Tel 416-977-0600; Fax 416-977-0625; Email toronto@bau-xi.com; Web: www.bau-xi.com; *Dir* Tien Huang
Open Mon - Sun 10 AM - 5:30 PM; No admis fee; Estab 1965; Locations in Toronto & Vancouver, representing a broad spectrum of artists; three floors of artwork
Income: Financed by pvt funding
Collections: Contemporary Canadian Art
Exhibitions: Changing exhibition schedule showcasing gallery artists including: estate of Alistair Bell, Tom Burrows, Tom Campbell, Robert Cadotte, Darlene Cole, Jamie Evrard, Ted Fullerton, Ted Godwin, Fred Hagan, Don Jarvis, Brian Kipping, Ken Lochhead, Hugh Mackenzie, Casey McGlynn, Robert Marchessault, Pat O'Hara, Andre Petterson, Joseph Plaskett, Jack Shadbolt, Shi Le, Stuart Slind, Alex Cameron, Steven Nederveen; rotate 14 - 15 per yr
Activities: Art sales

M **BAYCREST CENTRE FOR GERIATRIC CARE,** The Morris & Sally Justein of Baycrest Heritage Museum, 3560 Bathurst St, Toronto, ON M6A 2E1 Canada. Tel 416-785-2500, Ext 2802, Ext 2645 (pub affairs); Fax 416-785-2464; Email pdickinson@baycrest.org; Web: www.baycrest.org; *Coordr* Pat Dickinson
Open Sun - Fri 8:30 AM - 4:30 PM; No admis fee; Estab 1972; Displays permanent coll of Judaica or temporary exhibs on Jewish themes
Special Subjects: Judaica, Historical Material
Collections: Judaica: ceremonial objects, domestic artifacts, memorabilia, books, photos, documents & works on paper
Exhibitions: Regular temporary exhibs. Contact museum or visit website for current exhibs

CANADIAN ART FOUNDATION
For further information, see National and Regional Organizations

CANADIAN SOCIETY OF PAINTERS IN WATERCOLOUR
For further information, see National and Regional Organizations

M **CITY OF TORONTO CULTURE,** The Market Gallery, 95 Front St E, Toronto, ON M5E 1C2 Canada. Tel 416-392-7604; Fax 416-392-0572; Web: www1.toronto.ca; *Cur* Pamela Wachna; *Exhib & Outreach Technician* Michael Dowbenka; *Gallery Clerk* Jacquie Gardner
Open Tues - Fri 10 AM - 4 PM, Sat 9 AM - 4 PM, cl Sun & Mon; No admis fee; Estab 1979 to bring the art & history of Toronto to the public; Located in original 19th century Toronto City Hall; Average Annual Attendance: 25,000; Mem: Municipal Government
Library Holdings: Exhibition Catalogs, Kodachrome Transparencies, Original Documents
Special Subjects: Historical Material, Landscapes, Marine Painting, Painting-Canadian, Portraits, Prints, Watercolors
Collections: City of Toronto Fine Art Collection (oil, watercolor, prints & sculpture)
Exhibitions: Various exhibitions on Toronto's art, culture & history presented on an on-going basis
Publications: Exhibit catalogs
Activities: Classes for adults & children; lect open to public; gallery talks; paintings lent

A **CITY OF TORONTO MUSEUM SERVICES,** Historic Fort York, 250 Fort York Blvd, Toronto, ON M5V 3K9 Canada; 55 John St, 8th Fl Toronto, ON M5V 3C6 Canada. Tel 416-392-6907; Fax 416-392-1150; Email fortyork@toronto.ca; Web: www.fortyork.ca; *Chair* Donald Cranston
Open Mon - Fri 10 AM - 4 PM, Sat & Sun 10 AM - 5 PM; Admis family $35, adults $14.01, seniors (65+) $10, youth (13-18) $8.02, children (6-12) $5.99, children 5 and under free; Estab 1934 to tell the story of the founding of Toronto & the British Army in the 19th century; All buildings have permanent or temporary exhibits & period - room settings; maintains reference library; Average Annual Attendance: 55,000
Income: Financed by city appropriation
Special Subjects: Historical Material
Collections: 19th century Military, Original War of 1812 Buildings, Original War of 1812 Uniforms, Original War of 1812 Weapons
Activities: Classes for adults & children; lect open to public; sales shop sells books, prints & reproductions

M **DELEON WHITE GALLERY,** 1096 Queen St W, Toronto, ON M6J 1H9 Canada; PO Box 41120, 4141 Dixie Rd Mississauga, ON L4W 1V5 Canada. Tel 905-319-6384; Email info@deleonwhitevintageimages.ca; *Founder* Stephen White
Open Thurs - Fri 2 PM - 8 PM, Sat - Sun 12 PM - 6 PM; No admis fee; Estab 1995
Special Subjects: Architecture, Bronzes, Collages, Drawings, Landscapes, Mexican Art, Painting-American, Painting-Canadian, Painting-French, Painting-German, Painting-Japanese, Photography, Prints, Sculpture, Watercolors, Woodcuts
Collections: Contemporary Ecological Art, Outdoor Environmental Art
Exhibitions: Alan Sonfist, Ian Lazarus
Publications: DeLeon White Gallery News, quarterly
Activities: Lects open to pub; book traveling exhibs 2 per yr; originate traveling exhibs 2 per yr; sales shop sells books, magazines, original art, prints & slides

A **FUSION: THE ONTARIO CLAY & GLASS ASSOCIATION,** Fusion Clay & Glass Association, 1444 Queen St E, Toronto, ON M4L 1E1 Canada. Tel 416-438-8946; Fax 416-438-0192; Email fusion@clayandglass.on.ca; Web: www.clayandglass.on.ca; *Pres* Vickie Salinas; *Office Adminr* Jenanne Longman; *Finance* Deborah Freeman
Open Mon - Fri 10 AM - 5 PM; No admis fee; Estab 1975; Ashbridge House; Mem: Dues $60 per yr
Income: Financed by mem
Special Subjects: Ceramics, Crafts, Decorative Arts, Glass
Collections: Permanent collection housed at Burlington Art Ctr
Exhibitions: Fireworks (biennial juried traveling exhib); Silent Auction (biennial fundraiser)
Publications: Fusion Magazine, 3 per year; Fusion News Magazine, 3 per year
Activities: Classes for adults; workshops; lects open to pub; schols; awards (student exhibs, design awards); originates traveling exhibs to galleries within Ont

M **GALLERY MOOS LTD,** 305-722 College St, Toronto, ON M6G 1C4 Canada. Tel 416-504-5445; Fax 416-504-5446; Email info@gallerymoos.com; Web: www.gallerymoos.com; *Pres* Walter A Moos; *Adminr* Svetlana Novikova; *Asst* Bryan Almas
Open Tues - Sat 11 AM - 6 PM; No admis fee; Estab 1959; Maintains reference library, contemporary art gallery
Income: Financed by pvt funding
Library Holdings: Auction Catalogs
Special Subjects: Painting-American, Painting-Canadian, Prints, Sculpture
Collections: Contemporary Canadian & international art artists include: Karel Appel, Ken Danby, Sorel Etrog, Gershon Iskowitz, Jean-Paul Riopelle, Antoni Tapies, Lester Johnson, WIlliam Scott, Robert Hedrick, Mark Ash, Josue Demarche, Evan Levy, Dennis Geden, Leonidas Correa, Rose Lindzon, Sandra Manzi, Burton Kramer, Scott Ellis, David Urban, Burton Kramer

M **GEORGE R GARDINER MUSEUM OF CERAMIC ART,** 111 Queen's Park, Toronto, ON M5S 2C7 Canada. Tel 416-586-8080; Fax 416-586-8085; Email mail@gardinermuseum.com; Web: www.gardinermuseum.on.ca; *Exec Dir* Kelvin Browne; *Chief Cur* Meredith Chilton
Open Mon - Thurs 10 AM - 6 PM, Fri 10 AM - 9 PM, Sat & Sun 10 AM-5 PM; Admis adults $15, sr citizens $11, students $9, youth & children free; Estab 1984 as the only specialized museum of ceramics in Canada; Museum houses one of the world's greatest collections of ceramic art from the early 15th century to the 20th century; Average Annual Attendance: 60,000; Mem: 1145
Income: Endowment
Library Holdings: Auction Catalogs, Audio Tapes, Clipping Files, Exhibition Catalogs, Periodical Subscriptions
Special Subjects: Ceramics
Collections: English delftware, European porcelain, Italian majolica, Ancient Americas pottery, Chinese porcelain, Minton contemporary ceramics, Japanese porcelain
Activities: Clay classes for adults & children; school prog; docent progs; lects open to pub; gallery talks; tours; RBC Emerging Artist Award ($10,00 Can); book traveling exhibs 3 per yr; retail store sells books, original art, ceramics & artist design objects

M **HARBOURFRONT CENTRE,** The Power Plant Contemporary Art Gallery, 231 Queens Quay W, Toronto, ON M5J 2G8 Canada. Tel 416-973-4949; Email info@thepowerplant.org; Web: www.thepowerplant.org; *Dir* Gaetane Verna
Open Tues, Wed 10 AM - 5 PM; Fri, Sat & Sun -10 AM - 5 PM, Thurs 10 AM- 8 PM; Free admis; Estab 1987; Pub gallery devoted to contemporary visual art; Average Annual Attendance: 70,000
Activities: Classes for children; lects open to pub; gallery talks; tours; mus shop sells books, original art

M **JOHN B AIRD GALLERY,** 900 Bay St, 1st Fl, Macdonald Block Toronto, ON M7A 1C2 Canada. Tel 416-928-6772; Email director@airdgallery.org; Web: http://www.airdgallery.org/; *Exec Dir & Cur* Carla Garnett
Open Mon - Fri 10 AM - 6 PM; Nonprofit, non-collecting exhib ctr
Special Subjects: Photography, Pottery, Sculpture, Silver, Stained Glass, Tapestries, Textiles, Watercolors, Woodcarvings, Woodcuts
Collections: Printmaking, Silversmithing
Exhibitions: 12 ann exhibs

M **KOFFLER CENTRE OF THE ARTS,** (Bathurst Jewish Community Centre) Koffler Gallery, 180 Shaw St, Suite 104-105, Toronto, ON M6J 2W5 Canada. Tel 647-925-0643; Email lstarr@kofflerarts.org; Web: www.kofflerarts.org; *Exec Dir* Cathy Jonasson; *Dir & Cur* Mona Filip
Open Tues - Fri noon - 6 PM, Sat & Sun 11 AM - 5 PM; No admis fee; Estab 1976; 4,000 sq ft, contemporary program; 40,000 sq ft in new ctr under construction; Average Annual Attendance: 100,000
Income: $400,000 (financed by government grants, pvt donations & various institutions)
Library Holdings: CD-ROMs, Clipping Files, DVDs, Exhibition Catalogs, Slides
Special Subjects: Manuscripts
Publications: Catalogues & exhibitions brochures
Activities: Classes for adults & children; dramatic progs; school workshops; docent training; lects open to pub; 20 artist talks per yr; concerts; gallery talks; tours; sponsoring of competitions; visiting artists; schols available; book traveling exhibs, 2 per yr; originate traveling exhibs 1 per yr

M **MERCER UNION,** A Centre for Contemporary Art, 1286 Bloor St W, Toronto, ON M6H 1N9 Canada. Tel 416-536-1519; Fax 416-536-2955; Email office@mercerunion.org; Web: www.mercerunion.org; *Exec Dir* York Lethbridge; *Dir Exhibs & Progs* Julia Paoli
Open Tues - Sat 11 AM - 6 PM; No admis fee; Estab 1979 is an artist-run centre committed to the presentation & examination of Canadian & international contemporary Visual art & related cultural practices; 1500 sq ft; Average Annual Attendance: 15,000; Mem: 200; dues arts supporter $500-$1000, sustaining $100, supporting $50, educational $30, assoc $25, students $15; monthly board meetings
Income: $280,000 (financed by endowment, mem, city & state appropriations, Canada Council, Ontario Arts Council & Toronto Arts Council)
Library Holdings: Exhibition Catalogs
Collections: Michael Buchanan, Patricia Galimente, Gretchen Sankey, Contemporary Art
Exhibitions: rotate every 6 wks
Publications: Exhibition catalogues
Activities: Lects open to pub,10 vis lectrs per yr; gallery talks; sales shop sells books & catalogues, multiples

M **MUSEUM OF CONTEMPORARY CANADIAN ART,** (Art Gallery of North York), 80 Ward Street, Unit 99, Toronto, ON M6H 4A6 Canada. Tel 416-395-0067; Email info@museumofcontemporaryart.ca; Web: www.museumofcontemporaryart.ca; *Exec Dir & Cur* Heidi Reitmaier; *Chair* Julia Ouellette
Open Tues - Sun 11 AM - 6 PM; No admis fee; Estab 1994 to collect & exhibit Canadian contemporary art from 1985 - present; One floor, 6000 sq ft with 6 exhibitions per year of some of the most challenging art being produced in Canada today; Average Annual Attendance: 65,000
Special Subjects: Painting-Canadian, Sculpture
Collections: Contemporary Canadian Art
Activities: Lects open to pub

M **OCAD UNIVERSITY,** Ignite Gallery, 165 Augusta Ave, Toronto, ON M5T 2L4 Canada. Tel 416-977-6000, Ext 262; Email mmavis@ocadu.ca; Web: www.ocadu.ca/gallery; *Comm Coord* Morgan Mavis
Open Wed - Sun 1 - 6 PM; No admis fee; Estab 1970 as a space for OCAD University students & recent graduates to celebrate creativity, enhance professional development & promote the sale of exhibitors work to the public; Average Annual Attendance: 15,000
Income: Financed by College
Exhibitions: Exhibiting student works, rotate every 3 weeks
Publications: Invitations; small scale catalogs

L **Dorothy H Hoover Library,** 113 McCaul St, 2nd Fl Toronto, ON M5T 1W1 Canada. Tel 416-977-6000, ext 334; Fax 416-977-6006; Email jpatrick@ocadu.ca; Web: www.ocadu.ca/services/library; *Dir Library Svcs* Jill Patrick; *Head Coll Devel & Access Svcs* Manda Plavsa; *Head E-Reserves & E-Learning Support* Alex Homanchuk; *Head Instructional Svcs* Daniel Payne; *Head Visual Resources & Spec Colls* Victoria Sigurdson
Open Mon - Thurs 8 AM - 8:45 PM, Fri 8 AM - 6:45 PM, Sat 11 AM - 5:45 PM; Library formed in 1922, estab to support the curriculum; Circ 116,212; Average Annual Attendance: 400,000
Income: Financed through the College
Purchases: $250,000
Library Holdings: Book Volumes 30,000, Cassettes 620, Clipping Files, Exhibition Catalogs, Fiche, Filmstrips, Kodachrome Transparencies, Lantern Slides, Motion Pictures 75, Other Holdings Pictures 40,000; Vertical files 43,000, Pamphlets, Periodical Subscriptions 225, Records, Reels, Slides 85,000, Video Tapes 1000
Special Subjects: Advertising Design, American Indian Art, Art History, Ceramics, Commercial Art, Conceptual Art, Decorative Arts, Drawings, Film, Graphic Arts, Graphic Design, Illustration, Industrial Design, Jewelry, Mixed Media, Aesthetics, Afro-American Art, American Western Art, Anthropology, Archaeology, Architecture, Art Education

A **ONTARIO ASSOCIATION OF ART GALLERIES,** 401 Richmond St W, Ste 395 Toronto, ON M5V 3A8 Canada. Tel 416-598-0714; Fax 416-598-4128; Email oaag@oaag.org; Web: www.oaag.org; *Exec Dir* Zainub Verjee
Open 9 AM - 5 PM; Estab in 1968 as the provincial nonprofit organization representing pub art galleries in the province of Ontario. Institutional mem includes approx 84 pub art galleries, exhibition spaces & arts related organizations. Mem is also available to individuals; Gallery not maintained; Mem: 83; annual meeting in June
Income: Financed by mem, Ontario Arts Council, Ontario Ministry of Culture, Tourism & Recreation, Department of Canadian Heritage
Publications: Context, bimonthly newsletter
Activities: Professional development seminars & workshops; awards; active job file & job hot-line

M **ONTARIO CRAFTS COUNCIL,** OCC Gallery, 1106 Queen St W, Toronto, ON M6J 1H9 Canada. Tel 416-925-4222; Fax 416-925-4223; Email info@craftontario.com; Web: www.craftontario.com; *Interim CEO & Cur* Janna Hiemstra
Open Mon - Sat 11 AM - 6 PM; No admis fee; Estab 1976 to foster crafts & crafts people in Ontario; Maintains an art gallery; Average Annual Attendance: 8,000; Mem: 1,500; dues $130; annual meeting in June; see website for additional information
Income: Financed by mem & provincial appropriation, The Guild Shop, fundraising & publications
Exhibitions: Ontario Crafts Regional Juried Exhibition; bimonthly exhibitions in craft gallery
Publications: Studio magazine
Activities: Lects open to pub; gallery talks; tours; Sales shop sells books, original craft, Inuit art, sculpture & prints

L **Craft Resource Centre,** 990 Queen St W, Toronto, ON M6J 1H1 Canada. Tel 416-925-4222; Fax 416-925-4223; Email info@craft.on.ca; Web: www.craftontario.com; *Portfolio of Makers Mgr* Carol Ann Casselman; *Outreach Coordr* Rommy Rodriguez A
Open Wed - Fri Noon - 5 PM; No admis fee; Estab 1976. A comprehensive, special library devoted exclusively to the field of crafts. It is a primarily mem-funded not-for-profit organization & is available as an information service to the general pub & Ontario crafts Council members. Has an extensive portfolio registry featuring Canadian craftspeople; For reference only; Average Annual Attendance: 6,000; Mem: 3,000; dues $40; annual meeting in June
Library Holdings: Book Volumes 3000, Clipping Files, Exhibition Catalogs, Manuscripts, Other Holdings Portfolios of craftspeople 530, Periodical Subscriptions 350, Slides 100,000, Video Tapes
Special Subjects: Enamels, Glass, Metalwork, Pottery
Activities: Educ dept; tours; schols & fels offered; slide rental; publishing; Portfolio Makers Prog; Sales shop sells books, magazines, contemporary Canadian crafts

A **Artists in Stained Glass,** 121 Bloor St E, 7th Fl Toronto, ON M4W 3M5 Canada. Tel 416-961-1660; Email info@arts.on.ca; Web: www.arts.on.ca; *Dir & CEO* Peter Caldwell
Estab 1974 to encourage the development of stained glass as a contemporary art form in Canada; Maintains slide file library through the Ontario Crafts Council; Mem: 130; dues $25-$70; annual meeting in Nov
Income: $6,000 (financed by mem & state appropriation)
Publications: Flat Glass Journal, quarterly; Leadline, occasionally
Activities: Classes for adults; lects open to pub, 5 vis lectrs per yr

M **REDHEAD GALLERY,** 401 Richmond St W, Ground Fl Ste 115 Toronto, ON M5V 3A8 Canada. Tel 416-504-5654; Email info@redheadgallery.org; *Gallery Adminr* Jennifer Vong
Open Wed - Sat Noon - 5 PM; No admis fee; Estab 1990 as an artist run culture; There are 2 exhibition spaces. One main space is primarily reserved for mem. Annual programming will include exhibitions by visiting artists. Two window spaces are rented on a monthly basis to emerging artists. Also hold poetry reading, exhibits permitting; Average Annual Attendance: 5,400; Mem: 19; dues $1,320
Income: financed by mem
Collections: Contemporary Art
Exhibitions: Contemporary Art; rotating exhibits

M **ROYAL ONTARIO MUSEUM,** 100 Queen's Park, Toronto, ON M5S 2C6 Canada. Tel 416-586-8000; Email info@rom.on.ca; Web: www.rom.on.ca; *Dir & CEO* Josh Basseches; *Deputy Dir Opers & CFO* Niclk Bobrow; *Deputy Dir Colls & Research* Mark Engstrom; *Chief Mktg & Communs Officer* Sandy Bourne; *VPres Natural History* Doug Currie; *VPres Exhib Devel & Project Mgmqt* Lory Drusian; *VPres Programs Events & Comml Svcs* Connie MacDonald; *VPres World Cultures* Chen Shen; *VPres Finance* Dave Tymchuk; *Chief Facilities Officer, Capital Devel & Facilities* Brian McCrady; *VPres Finance* Dave Tymchuk
Open daily 10 AM - 5:30 PM, cl Dec 25; Admis adults $20, senior $17, youth (15-19) & student (w/ID) $16.50, child (4-14) $14, under 3 free; Estab 1912 & includes 20 curatorial departments in the fields of fine & decorative arts, archaeology & the natural & earth sciences; Average Annual Attendance: 1,000,000; Mem: 42,000; dues student $54, individual $112, non-resident $117, senior family $157, family/dual $161
Income: $25,000,000 (financed by federal grants, provincial grants, mus income, mem, bequests, grants & donations)
Special Subjects: African Art, Anthropology, Archaeology, Architecture, Asian Art, Hispanic Art, Historical Material, Medieval Art, Pre-Columbian Art, Primitive art, Southwestern Art
Collections: Far Eastern coll
Publications: Rotunda, quarterly magazine; numerous acad publications; gallery guides; exhibition catalogs; publications in print
Activities: Classes for adults & children; throughout the school yr, prebooked classes receive lessons in the mus; non-conducted classes can also be arranged with the mus at a cost of $3 per student; lects open to pub with vis lectrs, special lects for members only; concerts; gallery talks; tours; competitions; outreach dept serves Ontario; individual paintings & original objects of art lent to mus & galleries; originate traveling exhibs; mus shop sells books, magazines, reproductions, prints & slides

L **Library & Archives,** 100 Queen's Park, Toronto, ON M5S 2C6 Canada. Tel 416-586-5595; Fax 416-586-5519; Email library@rom.on.ca; Web: www.rom.on.ca; *Head Library & Archives* Brendan Edwards; *Archivist & Records Mgr* Charlotte Chaffey; *Librarian, H.H. Mu Far Eastern Library* Max Dionisio
Open Mon - Fri 10 AM - 5 PM; No admis fee; Estab 1960 for curatorial research; Circ Non-circulating; Average Annual Attendance: 5,000
Income: $600,000 (operating grant)
Purchases: $95,000
Library Holdings: Book Volumes 156,769, Compact Disks 48, DVDs, Exhibition Catalogs, Fiche 531, Manuscripts, Memorabilia, Original Art Works, Original Documents, Pamphlets, Periodical Subscriptions 363, Photographs, Sculpture, Video Tapes 15
Special Subjects: American Indian Art, Anthropology, Antiquities-Assyrian, Antiquities-Byzantine, Antiquities-Egyptian, Antiquities-Etruscan, Antiquities-Greek, Antiquities-Oriental, Antiquities-Persian, Antiquities-Roman, Archaeology, Architecture, Art History, Asian Art, Carpets & Rugs, Ceramics, Coins & Medals, Costume Design & Constr, Crafts, Decorative Arts, Dioramas, Embroidery, Enamels, Eskimo Art, Etchings & Engravings, Ethnology, Fashion Arts, Illustration, Glass, Gold, Goldsmithing, Graphic Arts, Handicrafts, Historical Material, History of Art & Archaeology, Islamic Art, Ivory, Jade, Jewelry, Judaica, Laces, Metalwork, Miniatures, Mosaics, Oriental Art, Painting-American, Painting-British, Painting-Canadian, Painting-European, Period Rooms, Pewter, Photography, Porcelain, Portraits, Pottery, Pre-Columbian Art, Primitive art, Printmaking, Prints, Religious Art, Restoration & Conservation, Scrimshaw, Sculpture, Silver, Silversmithing, Stained Glass, Tapestries, Textiles, Watercolors, Woodcarvings, Woodcuts
Collections: Rare book coll, far eastern coll, J H Fleming Collection, Charles Rennie MacKintosh Collection
Activities: Classes for adults; dramatic progs; lects open to pub; concerts

M **Dept of Western Art & Culture,** 100 Queen's Park, Toronto, ON M5S 2C6 Canada. Tel 416-586-5718; *Asst Cur* Paul Denis
Open Mon - Thurs & Sat 10 AM - 6 PM, Fri 9 AM - 9:30 PM, Sun 11 AM - 6 PM; No admis fee; Estab 1951 to collect, exhibit & publish material on Canadian historical paintings & Canadian decorative arts; Canadian Gallery has three galleries: first gallery has six rooms showing English Colonial, French, Maritime, Ontario & German-Ontario furniture, also silver, glass, woodenware; second gallery has ceramics, toys, weathervanes, religious carving, early 19th century Quebec paneled room; third is a picture gallery for changing exhibitions; Average Annual Attendance: 45,000; Mem: 42,000
Special Subjects: Coins & Medals, Decorative Arts, Portraits
Collections: Canadian 18th & 19th centuries decorative arts - ceramics, coins & medals books, furniture, glass, guns, silver, woodenware, 16th-18th centuries exploration, portraits of Canadians & military & administrative people connected with Canada, 18th & 19th centuries topographic & historical Canadian views, 19th century travels
Exhibitions: Various exhibitions
Publications: William Berczy; D B Webster Brantford Pottery; Canadian Watercolors & Drawings; The William Eby Pottery, Conestogo, Ontario 1855 - 1970; English Canadian Furniture of the Georgian Period; An Engraver's Pilgrimage: James Smillie Jr in Quebec, 1821-1830; Georgian Canada: Conflict & Culture, 1745 - 1820; Printmaking in Canada: The Earliest Views & Portraits

L **RYERSON UNIVERSITY,** Ryerson University Library, 350 Victoria St, Toronto, ON M5B 2K3 Canada. Tel 416-979-5055; Fax 416-979-5215; Email refdesk@ryerson.ca; Web: www.library.ryerson.ca; *Chief Librn* Carol Shepstone
Open Mon - Fri 7 AM - 1 AM, Sat - Sun 10 AM - 1 AM; No admis fee; Estab 1948
Income: Financed by provincial appropriation & student fees
Library Holdings: Audio Tapes, Book Volumes 403,897, Cassettes, Fiche, Filmstrips, Micro Print, Motion Pictures, Pamphlets, Periodical Subscriptions 3888, Records, Reels, Slides, Video Tapes
Special Subjects: Architecture, Fashion Arts, Interior Design, Photography, Film, Theatre Arts, Graphic Arts
Collections: Kodak Canada Collection, Camera Collection, Historical Photograph Collection
Exhibitions: Rotate periodically

M **STEPHEN BULGER GALLERY,** 1356 Dundas St W, Toronto, ON M6J 1Y2 Canada. Tel 416-504-0575; Fax 416-504-8929; Email info@bulgergallery.com; Web: www.bulgergallery.com; *Pres* Stephen Bulger; *Gallery Dir* Sarah Burtscher
Open Tues - Sat 11 AM - 6 PM; No admis fee; Estab 1995; Gallery displays historical & contemporary photography; Average Annual Attendance: 20,000
Income: pvt
Special Subjects: Photography
Collections: Canadian & International Photography Collection
Exhibitions: Month-long exhibitions, either solo or thematic group shows
Publications: World's Greatest, Pete Doherty
Activities: Lects open to pub; classes for adults; 6 vis lectrs per yr; occasional gallery talks; free film screenings on Sat afternoons; original objects of art lent; lending coll contains 2000 books & 15,000 photographs; book traveling exhibs; originates traveling exhibs to pub and commercial galleries; sales shop sells books

M **TEXTILE MUSEUM OF CANADA,** 55 Centre Ave, Toronto, ON M5G 2H5 Canada. Tel 416-599-5321; Fax 416-599-2911; Email info@textilemuseum.ca; Web: www.textilemuseum.ca; *Exec Dir* Emma Quin; *Cur Dir* Sarah Quinton; *Opers Mgr* Pat Neal; *Librn* Zachary Osborne
Open daily 11 AM - 5 PM, Wed until 8 PM; Admis family $30, general $15, seniors $10, youth & student $6, children under 5 free; Estab 1975; 15,000 sq ft of gallery space where 6-8 exhibitions are mounted each yr. Maintains reference library; Average Annual Attendance: 36,000; Mem: 1200; dues $65; annual meeting in May
Income: $400,000 (financed by mem, corporate & private sponsorship, fund raising, shop & attendance revenues)
Library Holdings: Exhibition Catalogs, Pamphlets, Periodical Subscriptions, Video Tapes
Special Subjects: Carpets & Rugs, Laces, Textiles
Collections: Artifacts Collection, 12000 textiles from all over the world
Exhibitions: Rotating exhibitions
Publications: Exhibition catalogues, 2-3 per year
Activities: Classes for adults & children; docent training; workshops; symposia; lects open to pub; gallery talks; tours; original objects of art lent; lending collections contains 12000 art objects; sales shop sells books, magazines, original art, reproductions, vintage & contemporary ethnographic textiles, gifts

C **TORONTO DOMINION BANK,** Toronto Dominion Ctr, 79 Wellington St Toronto, ON M5J 2Z9 Canada. Tel 416-982-8473; Fax 416-982-6335; *Sr Cur* Pamela Meredith
Open Contemporary Art Collection: by appointment only; The Inuit Gallery: Mon - Fri 8 AM - 6 PM, Sat & Sun 10 AM - 4 PM; No admis fee; The Contemporary Art Collection is shown throughout branch offices in Canada & internationally; the Inuit Art Collection has its own gallery in the Toronto-Dominion Centre
Collections: Inuit Collection: a selection of prints, as well as stone, bone & ivory carvings, the Contemporary Collection: an ongoing project focusing on the art of emerging & mature Canadian artists, including original prints, paintings, sculpture & works on paper

L **TORONTO PUBLIC LIBRARY BOARD,** Library, 789 Yonge St, Toronto, ON M4W 2G8 Canada. Tel 416-393-7131; Fax 416-393-7030; Web: www.torontopubliclibrary.ca; *City Librn* Vickery Bowles
Open Mon - Fri 9:30 AM - 8:30 PM, Sat 9 AM - 5 PM, Sun Telephone Only 1:30 - 5 PM; Estab 1959 for public reference
Income: Financed by city appropriation
Library Holdings: Auction Catalogs, Book Volumes 66,000, Clipping Files, DVDs, Exhibition Catalogs, Fiche, Periodical Subscriptions 315, Photographs, Prints, Reels, Reproductions, Video Tapes
Special Subjects: Decorative Arts
Collections: Postcards, scenic & greeting, printed ephemera, private presses with emphasis on Canadian, 1,000,000 picture clippings, theatre arts & stage design

M **TORONTO SCULPTURE GARDEN,** 115 King St E, Toronto, ON M4T 2L7 Canada; PO Box 65, Station Q Toronto, ON M4T 2L7 Canada. Tel 416-515-9658; Email info@torontosculpturegarden.com
Open 8 AM - dusk; No admis fee; Estab 1981; Outdoor park featuring exhibitions of site-specific work commissioned for the site
Exhibitions: 2-3 exhibits per yr
Publications: Toronto Sculpture Garden; exhibition brochures

M **UNIVERSITY OF TORONTO,** Art Centre, 15 King's College Circle, Toronto, ON M5S 3H7 Canada. Tel 416-978-1838; Fax 416-971-2059; Email liz.wylie@utoronto.ca; Web: www.utac.utoronto.ca; *Exec Dir & Chief Cur* Barbara Fischer; *Bus & Progs Coordr* Maureen Smith; *Coll Mgr* Heather Darling Pigat; *Cur* Sarah Robayo Sheridan
Open Tues - Sat noon - 5 PM, Wed until 8 PM, cl Sun & Mon; No admis fee; Estab 1996; There are nine galleries each displaying selections from the three collections. Maintains reference library; Average Annual Attendance: 15,000; Mem: 200; dues $50 & up
Income: $260,000 (financed by endowment, mem & the University
Special Subjects: Antiquities-Byzantine, Antiquities-Egyptian, Antiquities-Greek, Antiquities-Oriental, Antiquities-Roman, Asian Art, Bronzes, Carpets & Rugs, Ceramics, Collages, Drawings, Embroidery, Eskimo Art, Etchings & Engravings, Furniture, Graphics, Ivory, Landscapes, Manuscripts, Marine Painting, Medieval Art, Metalwork, Oriental Art, Painting-American, Painting-British
Collections: Malcove Collection, University College Collection, University of Toronto Collection
Exhibitions: Selections from the Malcove Collection, University College Collection & the University of Toronto Collection
Publications: Partners Newsletter, biannual
Activities: Docent training; lects open to pub, 2 vis lectrs per yr; concerts; gallery talks; tours; individual paintings & original objects of art lent to other institutions/ galleries; 2-3 book traveling exhibs per yr; sales shop sells books, reproductions & cards

M **UNIVERSITY OF TORONTO,** Justina M Barnicke Gallery, 7 Hart House Circle, Toronto, ON M5S 3H3 Canada. Tel 416-978-8398; Fax 416-978-8387; Email jmb.gallery@utoronto.ca; Web: www.jmbgallery.ca; *Exec Dir & Chief Cur* Barbara Fischer; *Cur* Sarah Robayo Sheridan
Open Tues - Sat 12 - 5 PM, Wed 12 - 8 PM; No admis fee; Estab 1919 to present contemporary art in Canada; Gallery 2,000 sq ft & total wall space of 350 running ft; produces offsite events; Average Annual Attendance: 12,000
Income: Financed by Hart House
Purchases: Canadian art
Collections: Canadian Art (historical & contemporary)
Exhibitions: Temporary exhibitions of historical & contemporary Canadian art
Activities: Classes for adults; docent training; university students/outreach progs; lects open to pub, 5-10 vis lectrs per yr; concerts; gallery talks; tours; writing award for art criticism; individual paintings & original objects of art lent; book traveling exhibs, 1-2 per yr; originate traveling exhibs; mus shop sells prints & slides & catalogues

L **Fine Art Library**, Sidney Smith Hall, 100 St George St Toronto, ON M5S 3G3 Canada. Tel 416-978-7892; Fax 416-978-1491; Web: www.art.utoronto.ca
Open Mon, Tues, Fri 9:30 AM - 5 PM, Wed - Thurs 9:30 AM - 8 PM; No admis fee; Estab 1936 for reference only
Income: Financed by state appropriation & Department of Fine Art
Library Holdings: Book Volumes 5,000, Exhibition Catalogs 30,000, Photographs 90,000
Special Subjects: Archaeology, Art History
Collections: Catalog materials including temporary, permanent, dealer catalogs, photographic archives in various fields of Western art
Publications: Canadian Illustrated News (Montreal); Index to Illustrations, quarterly

A **WOMEN'S ART ASSOCIATION OF CANADA,** Dignam Gallery, 23 Prince Arthur Ave, Toronto, ON M5R 1B2 Canada. Tel 416-922-2060; Email administration@womensartofcanada.ca; Web: www.womensartofcanada.ca; *Pres* Dale Butterill; *Accnt* Marina Bushuev; *Office Mgr* Cal Lorimer; *Treas* Helga Scott; *Secy* Cindy Clarke
Open Mon - Thurs 9 AM - 4 PM; Estab 1886 to encourage women in the arts; branches in Toronto, Hamilton, St Thomas & Peterborough; Victorian House Gallery & Studios; Average Annual Attendance: 5,000+; Mem: 180; dues $250, qualifications: interest in the arts, nominated & seconded by members; annual meeting in Apr
Income: Donations
Library Holdings: Book Volumes, Clipping Files, DVDs, Framed Reproductions, Manuscripts, Memorabilia, Original Art Works, Original Documents, Other Holdings, Photographs, Prints, Reproductions, Sculpture, Video Tapes
Collections: Canadian Art Collection
Exhibitions: Throughout yr
Activities: Classes for adults; lects open to pub, 25+ vis lectrs per yr; concerts; gallery talks; tours; competitions with awards; schols given to Ontario College of Art, Royal Conservatory of Music, Nat Ballet School, Univ of Toronto Faculty of Music, Unwers Hy of Toronto, George Brown Theatre School; Sheridan Art & Design; individual paintings & original objects of art lent

L **Library**, 23 Prince Arthur Ave, Toronto, ON M5R 1B2 Canada. Tel 416-922-2060; Fax 416-922-4657; *Librn* Isabelle Johnson
Open during exhibs & lects only; Circ Non-circulating
Library Holdings: Book Volumes 1000

M **WYNICK TUCK GALLERY,** 401 Richmond St W, Studio S27 Toronto, ON M5V 3A8 Canada. Tel 416-504-8716; Fax 416-504-8699; Email wtg@wynicktuckgallery.ca; Web: www.wynicktuckgallery.ca; *Co-Dir* David Tuck; *Co-Dir* Lynne Wynick
Open Tues - Sat 11 AM - 5 PM, cl Sun & Mon; No admis fee; Estab 1968 to represent contemporary Canadian artists as well as some international artists featuring paintings, sculptures, works on paper & photos; 4000 sq ft
Income: Financed by pvt funding
Exhibitions: Exhibitions rotate monthly
Activities: Sales shop sells original art

M **YORK UNIVERSITY,** Glendon Gallery, Glendon Hall, Glendon Col, York Univ, 2275 Bayview Ave Toronto, ON M4N 3M6 Canada. Tel 647-785-1012; Email gallery@glendon.yorku.ca; Web: www.glendon.yorku.ca/gallery; *Dir* Elaine Gold
Open Tues - Fri Noon-3 PM, Sat 1-4 PM; No admis fee; Estab 1977, focus on contemporary visual arts; 107.2 ft of running wall space, dark hardwood flooring, natural sunlight & halogen track lighting; ground floor of Glendon Hall; Average Annual Attendance: 2,000
Income: $141,868 (financed by mem, York University & granting agencies)
Publications: Bilingual exhibition catalogue
Activities: Classes for children; lects open to pub, 5 vis lectrs per yr; concerts; gallery talks; tours; book traveling exhibs

M **YORK UNIVERSITY,** Art Gallery of York University, 4700 Keele St, Ross Bldg N145 Toronto, ON M3J 1P3 Canada; 4700 Keele St, Accolade East Bldg Toronto, ON M3J 1P3 Canada. Tel 416-736-5169; Email agyu@yorku.ca; Web: www.yorku.ca/agyu; *Dir & Cur* Philip Monk; *Asst Dir & Cur* Emelie Chhangur; *Asst Cur* Michael Maranda; *Coll & Educ Asst* Allyson Adley; *Asst Cur* Suzanne Carte

Open Mon - Fri 10 AM - 4 PM, Wed 10 AM - 8 PM, Sun noon - 5 PM, cl Sat; Admis donations welcomed; Estab 1970 to maintain a program of exhibitions covering a broad spectrum of the contemporary visual arts; Gallery is 3600 sq ft, exhibition space 2800 sq ft, including program space & support space 750 sq ft; Average Annual Attendance: 15,000
Income: Financed by university, federal, provincial & municipal grants & private donations
Special Subjects: Eskimo Art, Painting-American, Painting-Canadian, Sculpture
Collections: Approx 750 works including ethnographical items & artifacts, approx 550 of the works are by Canadian artists. Current emphasis & expansion of outdoor sculpture coll
Publications: Exhibit catalogs
Activities: Lects open to pub, 3-4 vis lectrs per yr; gallery talks; tours; sponsoring of competitions; Critical Writing award; individual paintings & original objects of art lent for major shows or retrospectives to other members of the University & faculty for their offices; book traveling exhibs; originate traveling exhibs; mus shop sells books

L **Fine Arts Phase II Slide Library**, 4700 Keele St, Rm 274, North York, ON M3J 1P3 Canada. Tel 416-736-5150; Fax 416-736-5447; Web: www.library.yorku.ca; *Librn* Joy Kirchner
Open 8 AM - 4:30 PM daily; cl weekends; Estab for reference only, students & faculty; Circ Slides circulate for staff & faculty
Income: Financed through university
Library Holdings: Periodical Subscriptions, Slides 250,000

M **YYZ ARTISTS' OUTLET,** 140-401 Richmond St W No 140, Toronto, ON M5V 3A8 Canada. Tel 416-598-4546; Fax 416-598-2282; Web: www.yyzartistsoutlet.org; *Dir* Ana Barajas
Open Tues-Sat 11 AM - 5 PM; No admis fee; Estab 1979; Exhibs and pubs books on contemporary art; Average Annual Attendance: 3,000
Library Holdings: Exhibition Catalogs, Memorabilia, Original Documents, Pamphlets
Collections: Contemporary Art
Activities: Lects open to public, 5 vis lectrs per year; sales shop sells books, magazines, original art, multiples

WATERLOO

M **CANADIAN CLAY AND GLASS GALLERY,** 25 Caroline St N, Waterloo, ON N2L 2Y5 Canada. Tel 519-746-1882; Fax 519-746-6396; Email info@canadianclayandglass.ca; Web: www.theclayandglass.ca; *Exec Dir* William D Poole; *Bookkeeper* Charmayne Greig; *Pub Rels* William Hlowatzki; *Cur* Sheila McMath; *Dir Develop* Lynda Abshoff; *Retail Mgr* Linda Brine; *Mgr Pub Progs* Nadine Badran; *Admin, Mktg & Develop Asst* Katherine Ronzio; *Cur Asst* Andrew Bucsis
Open Mon - Fri 11 AM - 6 PM, Sat 10 am - 5 PM, Sun 1-5 PM, cl Mon; No admis fee; Estab 1993; 4 galleries; Average Annual Attendance: 25,000; Mem: 450; dues family dual $45, adults, $35, artist, seniors, students (18+) $25
Income: Grants retail sales, donations, facility rental, fundraising, education progs, admis, exhibs, mems
Library Holdings: Audio Tapes, Book Volumes, CD-ROMs, Clipping Files, Compact Disks, DVDs, Exhibition Catalogs, Kodachrome Transparencies, Original Art Works, Original Documents, Other Holdings, Pamphlets, Periodical Subscriptions, Photographs, Prints, Records, Sculpture, Slides, Video Tapes
Special Subjects: Architecture, Asian Art, Baroque Art, Bronzes, Ceramics, Collages, Conceptual Art, Crafts, Decorative Arts, Dioramas, Drawings, Enamels, Eskimo Art, Etchings & Engravings, Flasks & Bottles, Glass, Historical Material, Porcelain, Pottery, Sculpture, Stained Glass, Folk Art
Collections: Contemporary Canadian & International clay, glass, stained glass & enamel. Holdings include: Paul Stankard, John Khun, William Morris, Marilyn Levine, Joe Fafard, Ruth McKinley, Richard Gomez. Paperweights by Bacarat, Banford, Clichy, St Louis, Whitefriars, Ysart, Heilman, Perthshire & Trabucco, Carl Beam, Julie Oakes, Tim Whiten, Aganetha Dyck
Exhibitions: Rotating every three months, presenting contemporary clay & glass, Artist include: Mary Anne Barkhouse, Christian Bernard Singer, Sarah Saunders, Ruth Chambers, Maurice Savoie, Judy Chicago, Donald Maynard, Yuichiro Komatsu, Julie Oakes, Bruce Taylor, Alfred Engerer, Andre Fournelle, Sadashi Inuzuka, Joan Brigham, Ann Roberts
Publications: Aspects & Excess: Shary Boyle; Boreal Baroque: Mary Anne Barkhouse; Ceramic Work from Rankin Inlet: Roger Aksadjuak, Pierre Aupilardjuk, John Kurok, Yvo Samgushak, Lucy Sanertanut, Jack Nuviak & Leo Napayok; Chicago in Glass: Judy Chicago; It's All Relative: Carl Beam, Ann Beam & Anong Migwans Beam; Ornamenta: Lyndal Osborne; Broken but Still Standing, Louise Pentz; Lucid Dreaming, Bruce Taylor; Glass Factor: Luminaries in the Canadian Art Glass Scene; Swounds: Julie Oakes
Activities: Classes & tours for adults, youth & children; art talks; docent training; play with clay Sundays; lects open to pub, 1 vis lectrs per yr; gallery talks; tours; sponsoring of competitions, Winifred Shantz award for ceramists; Royal Bank Canada (RBC), Award for Glass; fels available; lending of original objects of art to Canadian pub galleries & mus; book traveling exhibs, never more than 1; organize traveling exhibs to other Canadian pub galleries & mus; mus shop sells books, original art, & other decorative ceramic & glass art objects

M **WILFRID LAURIER UNIVERSITY,** Robert Langen Art Gallery, 75 University Ave W, Waterloo, ON N2L 3C5 Canada. Tel 519-884-0710, Ext 3801; Fax 519-886-9721; Email sluke@wlu.ca; Web: www.wlu.ca; *Cur* Suzanne Luke
Open Sep - Apr, Wed - Sat 12 PM - 5 PM; No admis fee; Estab 1969 to exhibit for the students, staff & faculty; The gallery has its own space in the John Aird Building & has 18 x 50 ft rectangular space incl various modular mounts; Average Annual Attendance: 50,000
Income: Financed by the university
Purchases: $16,000
Special Subjects: Drawings, Eskimo Art, Etchings & Engravings, Historical Material, Landscapes, Marine Painting, Metalwork, Oriental Art, Painting-American, Painting-British, Painting-Canadian, Painting-European, Photography, Portraits, Prints, Restorations, Sculpture, Tapestries, Textiles, Watercolors, Woodcarvings, Woodcuts
Collections: 2000 pieces of original art works & prints
Exhibitions: Student, staff & faculty show; the gallery mounts 10 exhibitions each year, mostly shows by artists in local area
Publications: Buried Treasure (75th Anniversary of WLU 1986)
Activities: Classes for adults; docent training; lects open to pub, 1-5 vis lectrs per yr; gallery talks; competitions; individual paintings & original works of art lent to campus offices & public areas; originate traveling exhibs

WINDSOR

M **ART GALLERY OF WINDSOR,** 401 Riverside Dr W, Windsor, ON N9A 7J1 Canada. Tel 519-977-0013; Fax 519-977-0776; Web: www.agw.ca; *Dir* Catherine M. Mastin; *Cur Contemporary Art* Jaclyn Meloche; *Pres* Jim Marsh
Open Wed - Sun 11 AM - 5 PM; cl Mon & Tues; Admis adult $10, youth (6-17) & students with valid ID $5; Estab 1943 for collection & exhibition of works of art, primarily Canadian, for the study & enjoyment of the Windsor-Detroit area; Average Annual Attendance: 50,000; Mem: Gallery family $90, friend $65; seniors & students $30; annual meeting in March
Income: $1,300,000 (financed by mem, city appropriation & federal & provincial grants)
Collections: Primarily Canadian drawings, paintings, prints & sculpture 18th century to present, Inuit prints & sculpture, non-Canadian paintings & sculpture
Exhibitions: Approx 20 exhibitions a year, besides installation of permanent collection, of mostly Canadian historic & contemporary art works, paintings & graphics
Publications: Quarterly bulletin & catalogues for exhibitions organized by this gallery, 4 times a year
Activities: Docent training; educ prog; classes for adults & children; lects open to pub, 20 vis lectrs per yr; gallery talks; tours; book traveling exhibs approx 20 per yr; originate traveling exhibs; Education Gallery

L **Reference Library**, 401 Riverside Dr West, Windsor, ON N9 A 7J1 Canada. Tel 519-977-0013; Fax 519-977-0776; Email agw@mnsi.net; *Librn* Janine Butler
Open Mon-Fri 9 AM - 5 PM; Estab 1966; Circ Non-circulating; Reference for staff, members & public
Income: Financed by mem
Library Holdings: Book Volumes 2500, Clipping Files, Exhibition Catalogs, Other Holdings Catalogs & museum bulletins, Pamphlets, Periodical Subscriptions 30, Video Tapes

WOODSTOCK

M **CITY OF WOODSTOCK,** Woodstock Art Gallery, 449 Dundas St, Woodstock, ON N4S 1C2 Canada; PO Box 1539, Woodstock, ON N4S 0A7 Canada. Tel 519-539-6761 ext 2801; Fax 519-539-2564; Email waginfo@cityofwoodstock.ca; Web: www.woodstockartgallery.ca; *Cur/Dir* Mary Reid; *Educ Officer* Stephanie Porter; *Registrar* Roberta Grosland; *Vis Serv* Sara Cuthbert
Open Tues - Sat 10 AM - 5 PM; cl Sun & Mon; No admis fee; Estab 1967 as a community art gallery; Moved into circa 1913 neo-Georgian building in 1983. Four gallery spaces: Carlyle Gallery (313 sq ft); Verne T Ross Gallery (464 sq ft); Nancy Rowell Jackman Gallery (323 sq ft): East Gallery (1303.75 sq ft); Average Annual Attendance: 18,500; Mem: 400; dues, life member $300, corporate $50, family $30, individual $20, senior citizen, $15, children $10
Income: Financed by City of Woodstock, Ministry of Citizenship & Culture, Ontario Arts Council, mem & donations
Collections: 290 works coll of Canadian Art, concentrating on Florence Carlyle contemporary Canadian regional artists
Publications: Newsletter 4 times per year; educational handouts on current exhibitions; monthly bulletin
Activities: Educ prog, classes for adults & children; dramatic progs, open studio evenings (family), junior cur group, teen film group; lects open to pub, 6-7 vis lectrs per yr; concerts; gallery talks; tours; competitions with awards; schols offered; art rental paintings are leased to residents of Oxford County & bus firms; lending collection contains paintings; lending of original objects of art to other galleries upon request & completion of stand facilities report; originate traveling exhibs to circulate southwestern Ontario & Toronto vicinities; gift shop sells cards, wrapping & writing paper, pottery, jewelry, weaving

PRINCE EDWARD ISLAND

CHARLOTTETOWN

M **CONFEDERATION CENTRE ART GALLERY AND MUSEUM,** 145 Richmond St, Charlottetown, PE C1A 1J1 Canada. Tel 902-628-1864; Fax 902-566-4648; Email info@confederationcentre.com; Web: www.confederationcentre.com/artgallery; *CEO* Jessie Inman; *Dir* Kevin Rice; *Cur* Pan Wendt; *Preparator* Ben Kinder; *Registrar* Paige Matthie; *CFO* Nancy MacRae; *COO* Mike Cochrane
Open Oct 11 - May 21: Wed - Sat 11 AM - 5 PM, Sun 1 PM - 5 PM, May 23 - Oct 8: daily 9 AM - 5 PM; Admis donation; Estab 1964 as a nat coll devoted to Canadian art & fine crafts; Average Annual Attendance: 90,000; Mem: 200; group $20, family $5, individual $3
Income: Financed by federal, provincial, city & private sector
Special Subjects: Crafts, Painting-Canadian, Prints, Decorative Arts, Drawings
Collections: 19th & 20th century Canadian paintings, drawings & decorative arts, paintings & drawings by Robert Harris
Exhibitions: Twenty-five exhibitions
Activities: Classes for adults & children, 6 vis lectr per year; gallery talks; tours; concerts; lects open to pub; tours; concerts; originate traveling exhibs; junior mus

L **Library,** 145 Richmond St, Charlottetown, PE C1A 1J1 Canada; Queen Street at Richmond, Box 7000 Charlottetown, PE C1A 8G8 Canada. Tel 902-368-4642; Fax 902-368-4652; Web: www.library.pe.ca
Open Tues-Thurs 10 AM - 9 PM, Fri & Sat 10 AM - 5 PM, Sun 1 - 5 PM, cl Mon; Open for reference
Library Holdings: Audio Tapes 30, Book Volumes 3500, Filmstrips 60, Periodical Subscriptions 35, Photographs, Slides 5000, Video Tapes

A **PRINCE EDWARD ISLAND MUSEUM & HERITAGE FOUNDATION,** 2 Kent St, Charlottetown, PE C1A 1M6 Canada. Tel 902-368-6600; Fax 902-368-6608; Email mhpei@gov.pe.ca; Web: www.peimuseum.com; *Exec Dir* Dr David Keenlyside; *Cur Colls* Linda Berko; *Cur History* Boyde Beck
Open June - Sep at four of seven sites; call for hours after Aug; Admis family $14.25, adult $5.25, groups $4.50, student $3.50, school groups $3; Estab 1970 for the human & natural history of Prince Edward Island; Seven sites, 3 open yr round; Average Annual Attendance: 120,000; Mem: 500, dues family $40, individual $25
Income: Financed by mem, provincial & federal appropriations
Special Subjects: Carpets & Rugs, Etchings & Engravings, Coins & Medals, Costumes, Crafts, Decorative Arts, Dolls, Embroidery, Furniture, Glass, Historical Material, Maps, Period Rooms
Collections: Provincial coll, 90,000 artifacts
Exhibitions: Rotate 4-5 exhibits per yr
Publications: The Island Magazine, semi-annual
Activities: Lects open to pub; gallery talks; awards: Pet Heritage Awards every Feb; mus shop sells books, magazines, original art, reproductions, prints & other gift items

QUEBEC

DORVAL

A **PETER B. YEOMANS CULTURAL CENTER,** 1401 Lakeshore Dr, Dorval, QC H9S 2E5 Canada. Tel 514-633-4170; Fax 514-633-4177; Web: www.ville.dorval.qc.ca
Open June 30 - Sep 5 Wed & Thurs 1 PM - 9 PM, Fri 1 PM - 5 PM, cl Sat - Tues; No admis fee; Estab 1967 to promote culture and art; Maintains an art gallery
Income: Financed by city appropriation
Publications: Calendar, biannually
Activities: Classes for adults and children; dramatic progs; lects open to pub; gallery talks; tours; concerts

GATINEAU

M **CANADIAN MUSEUM OF HISTORY,** 100 Laurier St, Gatineau, QC K1A 0M8 Canada. Tel 819-776-7000; Fax 819-776-8300; Email web@historymuseum.ca; Web: www.historymuseum.ca; *Pres & CEO* Mark O'Neill
Open Mon - Wed & Fri - Sun 9:30 AM - 5 PM, Thurs 9:30 AM - 8 PM; Admis family $50, adults $20, seniors $18, students $16, children (3 - 12) $12; Estab 1856 to promote the advancement of historical & intercultural understanding & make known the cultural legacy with special, but not exclusive, reference to Canada; The Canadian Mus History was formerly known as the National Mus of Man & the Canadian Mus of Civilization. It is located on a 24-acre site in Gatineau, Quebec, on the Ottawa River, directly opposite Parliament Hill. The building has 1,076,430 sq ft & designed in two distinct structures: the mus bldg, the pub exhibition wing with over 177,611 sq ft of display space children's mus; Imax 295 seat theatre & the curatorial bldg, housing the collections (3 million artifacts), plus conservation labs & admin. Canadian War Mus is part of corp group; Average Annual Attendance: 1,300,000; Mem: Dues ambassador $250, family $125, adult $50, senior, child & student $40
Income: The mus generates $12,000,000 a yr & receives over $50,000,000 a yr from the federal government
Library Holdings: Audio Tapes, Book Volumes 70,000, CD-ROMs, Cards, Cassettes, Compact Disks, DVDs, Exhibition Catalogs, Fiche, Filmstrips, Manuscripts, Maps, Memorabilia, Micro Print, Motion Pictures, Original Art Works, Original Documents, Photographs, Prints, Records, Reels, Sculpture, Slides, Video Tapes
Special Subjects: Anthropology, Archaeology, Bookplates & Bindings, Bronzes, Calligraphy, Carpets & Rugs, Ceramics, Coins & Medals, Collages, Costumes, Decorative Arts, Dioramas, Dolls, Drawings, Embroidery, Enamels, Eskimo Art, Etchings & Engravings, Ethnology, Flasks & Bottles, Folk Art, Folk Art, Furniture, Glass, Gold, Graphics, Historical Material, Historical Material, Ivory, Jewelry, Juvenile Art, Laces, Landscapes, Leather, Manuscripts, Maps, Marine Painting, Metalwork, Military Art, Mosaics, Painting-Canadian, Period Rooms, Pewter, Photography, Porcelain, Portraits, Posters, Pottery, Primitive art, Prints, Religious Art, Reproductions, Restorations, Sculpture, Silver, Stained Glass, Tapestries, Textiles, Watercolors, Woodcarvings, Woodcuts
Collections: Archaeological Collection, Ethnographic Collection, Folk Culture Collections, Historical Collection, Military History Collection, Canadian Children's Mus Coll, Canadian Postal Mus Coll
Exhibitions: Permanent exhibitions: Grand Hall, First Peoples Hall; Face to Face: The Canadian Personalities Hall; Canada History Hall, The Canadian Experience Galleries at the War Mus; Approximately 14 temporary exhibs ann
Publications: Several series of publications & periodicals, 102 titles published in-house in last six years
Activities: Classes for adults & children; dramatic progs; docent training; lects open to pub, several vis lectrs per yr; concerts; gallery talks; tours; sponsoring of competitions; exten dept; original artifacts lent to mus & other institutions meeting specifications regarding security, environment, etc in Canadian Museums; awards, the William E Taylor Research Award Fund; 10 book traveling exhibs per yr; originate traveling exhibs to Mus across Canada & internationally; the boutiques stock a vast range of gift & educational articles; Kidshoppe; Bookstore/Collector's shop offers selection of books & fine crafts including folk art pieces & Native artwork; Canadian Children's Museum 100 Laurier St, PO Box 3100, Sta B Gatineau, QC J8X 4H2 Canada

M **GALERIE MONTCALM,** 25 Laurier St Fl 1, PO Box 1970, Stn Hull Gatineau, QC J8X 3Y9 Canada. Tel 819-595-7488; Fax 819-595-7492; Email galeriemontcalm1@gatineau.ca; *Exec Dir* Jill Birch; *Develop Dir* Adria Miller; *Art Dir* Barbara Solowan
Open Mon-Fri 9 AM-4 PM, Thurs 9 AM-8 PM, Sun Noon-5 PM, cl Sat; No admis fee; Estab 1980, to present the art of local artists & national exhibitions, multi-disciplinary; One gallery, 2505 sq ft; Average Annual Attendance: 8,000
Income: $145,500 (financed by City of Gatineau)
Library Holdings: Book Volumes, Cards, Exhibition Catalogs, Original Art Works, Pamphlets, Reproductions, Sculpture
Special Subjects: Bronzes, Cartoons, Collages, Crafts, Decorative Arts, Drawings, Graphics, Landscapes, Latin American Art, Metalwork, Miniatures, Painting-American, Painting-Canadian, Painting-French, Painting-Japanese, Painting-Polish, Painting-Scandinavian, Porcelain, Portraits, Posters, Pottery, Primitive art, Prints, Sculpture, Textiles, Watercolors, Woodcarvings, Woodcuts
Collections: City of Gatineau (permanent coll), heritage artifacts, paintings, photographs, prints, sculpture, public art
Publications: Exhibition catalogs
Activities: Classes for children; workshops; lects open to pub, 1560 vis lectrs per yr; concerts; gallery talks; tours of the permanent coll; competitions with awards; retail store sells books, prints, original art

JOLIETTE

M **MUSEE D'ART DE JOLIETTE,** 145 rue Pere-Wilfrid-Corbeil, Joliette, QC J6E 4T4 Canada. Tel 450-756-0311; Email info@museejoliette.org; Web: www.museejoliette.org; *Exec Dir & Cur* Jean-Francois Belisle
Open Tues - Fri noon - 5 PM, Thurs - Fri noon - 9 PM, Sat & Sun 10 AM - 5 PM; cl Mon; Admis family $25, adults $15, sr citizens 65+ $12, youth 30 & under $10; Estab 1967 for educational purposes; preservation of the collections; save local patrimony; Circ 75,000; 5 rooms of temporary exhibitions; permanent exhib room: 14th century to present; Average Annual Attendance: 14,000; Mem: 600; dues family $80, individual $50; annual meeting in Sep
Income: Financed by government grants, pvt funds & revenues
Library Holdings: Book Volumes, Exhibition Catalogs, Kodachrome Transparencies, Photographs, Slides
Special Subjects: Painting-European, Pre-Columbian Art, Religious Art
Collections: Canadian art, European art, sacred art of Quebec, painting & sculpture
Exhibitions: 12 exhibitions per year
Publications: Catalog & pamphlet entitled Le Musee d'art de Joliette; catalogs of temporary exhibits
Activities: Classes for adults & children; docent training; educ program; lects open to pub, 6 vis lectrs per yr; concerts; gallery talks; tours; films; book traveling exhibs, 2 per yr; originate traveling exhibs 2 per yr to museums & libraries; sales shop sells books, magazines, original art, postcards, reproductions & prints

JONQUIERE

M **INSTITUT DES ARTS AU SAGUENAY,** Centre National D'Exposition a Jonquiere, 4160 du Vieux Pont (Mont Jacob), CP 605, Ville de Saguenay Jonquiere, QC G7X 7W4 Canada. Tel 418-546-2177; Fax 418-546-2180; Email info@centrenationalexposition.com; Web: www.centrenationalexposition.com; *Pres* Lionel Brassard; *VPres* Therese Ouellet; *Treas* Sylvie Bergeron; *Secy* Claire Simard; *Dir* Manon Guerin
Open Sep - June, Mon - Fri 9 AM - 5 PM, Sat - Sun 12 AM - 5 PM; July - Aug, 10 AM - 6 PM; No admis fee; Estab 1979 as an art exposition; 3 galleries; Average Annual Attendance: 20,000; Mem: 150; open to all interested in Au Milieu Des Arts; dues $25; annual meeting in June
Income: $350,000 (financed by endowment, mem, city & state appropriation)
Activities: Classes for adults & children; gallery talks; tours; fellowships offered; book traveling exhibitions 3-4 per year

KAHNAWAKE

M **KATERI TEKAKWITHA SHRINE/ST. FRANCIS XAVIER MISSION,** PO Box 70, Mission St.Francis Xavier Kahnawake, QC J0L 1B0 Canada. Tel 450-633-6030; Fax 450-632-6031; Email katericausecenter@gmail.com; Email saintkaterishrine@yahoo.com; Web: www.kateritekakwitha.net, www.katericenter.com; *Dir* Deacon Ron Boyer
Open May - Sep: Mon - Thurs 9 AM - 4 PM, Fri, Sat & Sun 9 AM - 3 PM; Sep 5 - April 30 Mon - Fri 9 AM - 4 PM; Sat by appointment only, Sun after 10:45 mass until 1 PM; No admis fee; Estab as a mission in 1667; Large mission & fort with tomb of Kateri Tekakwitha, museum & gift shop; Average Annual Attendance: 5,000
Income: Financed by donations
Special Subjects: Religious Art, American Indian Art, Painting-French, Period Rooms
Collections: Archives, French & Canadian church silver, historic church, rectory & fort, old paintings, religious artifacts, Shrine of Saint Kateri Tekakwitha, Mohawk woman on threshold of becoming a saint, relics are in tomb in church, old known painting of Kateri (1690)
Publications: Kateri, quarterly
Activities: Concerts; tours; individual paintings & original objects of art lent; containing Kodachromes & sculptures; originate traveling exhibs; sales shop sells books, reproductions, religious & Kateri Tekakwitha articles & relic medals

MONTREAL

L **ARTEXTE INFORMATION CENTRE,** Documentation Centre, 2 Sainte Catherine East, Rm 301, Montreal, QC H2X 1K4 Canada. Tel 514-874-0049; Email info@artexte.ca; Web: www.artexte.ca; *Gen Dir* Sarah Watson; *Cur* Zoë Tousignant
Open Wed - Fri noon - 7 PM, Sat noon - 5 PM; No admis fee; Institution estab 1980, libr estab 1982; Documentation of contemporary visual arts, from 1965 - present with particular emphasis on Canadian art, consultation only; Average Annual Attendance: 1,500
Income: $350,000 (financed by city & state grants, donations)
Purchases: $15,500
Library Holdings: Book Volumes 2000, CD-ROMs, Cassettes, Clipping Files 8700, Compact Disks, DVDs, Exhibition Catalogs 10,500, Memorabilia, Pamphlets, Periodical Subscriptions 100, Photographs, Slides, Video Tapes
Publications: Artextes editions; Artexte info

A **ASSOCIATION PROFESSIONNELLE DES DESIGNERS D'INTERIEUR DU QUEBEC,** 420 McGill St, Ste 406 Montreal, QC H2Y 2G1 Canada. Tel 514-284-6263; Email info@apdiq.com; Web: www.apdiq.com; *Exec Dir* Marie-Claude Parenteau-Lebeuf
Open Mon - Thurs 9 AM - 5PM, Fri 9 AM - 12 PM; Estab 2003 as a nonprofit professional assn; Mem: 500 (approx)
Exhibitions: Traveling exhibitions in the Province of Quebec
Publications: Journal magazine, monthly; News Bulletin, 5 issues per year
Activities: Educ Comt to improve the level of teaching in interior design; lects for mems only, 5-8 vis lectrs per yr; book traveling exhibs

ASTED INC
For further information, see National and Regional Organizations

L **CANADIAN CENTRE FOR ARCHITECTURE,** Library, 1920 Baile St, Montreal, QC H3H 2S6 Canada. Tel 514-939-7026; Fax 514-939-7020; Email ref@cca.qc.ca; Web: www.cca.qc.ca; *Dir Emeritus* Phyllis Lambert
Open Wed, Fri - Sun: 11 AM - 6 PM, Thurs 11 AM - 9 PM, Sat & Sun 11 AM - 6 PM, cl Mon & Tues; Admis adults $10, seniors 65+ $7, students, children & friends of the CCA free, Thurs after 6:30 PM free; Estab 1979; Circ 15,000 vols per yr; Estab 1979; on-site & remote research; library catalog available via website; surrogates provided when possible
Library Holdings: Auction Catalogs, Audio Tapes, Book Volumes 200,400, CD-ROMs, Cards, Cassettes, Clipping Files, Compact Disks, DVDs, Exhibition Catalogs, Fiche, Filmstrips, Manuscripts, Maps, Memorabilia, Motion Pictures, Original Documents, Other Holdings 3-D Artifacts including architectural toys, Pamphlets, Periodical Subscriptions 700, Photographs, Prints, Records, Reels, Reproductions, Slides, Video Tapes
Special Subjects: Architecture, Archaeology, Decorative Arts, Furniture, Industrial Design, Interior Design, Landscape Architecture, Photography, Stage Design
Collections: 200,000 printed vols
Activities: Educ prog; lects open to pub; gallery talks; tours; sponsored competitions; fel offered; mus shop sells books

M **CHATEAU RAMEZAY MUSEUM,** 280 rue Notre-Dame E, Montreal, QC H2Y 1C5 Canada. Tel 514-861-3708; Fax 514-861-8317; Email info@chateauramezay.qc.ca; Web: www.chateauramezay.qc.ca; *Exec Dir & Cur* Andre Delisle
Open Jun 1 - Thanksgiving Day 9:30 AM - 6 PM, Nov 1 - May 31 Tues - Sun 10 AM - 4:30 PM, Thanksgiving - Oct 31 daily 10 AM - 5:30 PM; Admis families $26.50, adults $11, seniors $10, students $8.75, children (5-17) $5.75, 4 and under free; Estab 1895 in residence of Claude de Ramezay (1705), governor of Montreal; Average Annual Attendance: 60,000; Mem: 200; dues life $1000, individual $40
Special Subjects: Period Rooms
Collections: Canadian drawings, furniture, paintings, prints & sculptures, 18th, 19th & 20th century colls, Indian colls, Period Rooms to Victorian Era
Activities: Classes for children; docent training; lects open to pub & some for mems only, 6 vis lectrs per yr; gallery talks; tours; sales shop sells books, reproductions, prints & slides

L **Library,** 280 Notre-Dame E, Montreal, QC H2Y 1C5 Canada. Tel 514-861-3708; Fax 514-861-8317; Web: www.chateauramezay.qc.ca; *Librn* Judith Berlyn
Open by appointment only; Estab for research & reference only; Circ Non-circulating
Library Holdings: Book Volumes 2200, Original Documents

M **CONCORDIA UNIVERSITY,** Leonard & Bina Ellen Art Gallery, 1400 Blvd de Maisonneuve W, LB-165 Montreal, QC H3G 1M8 Canada. Tel 514-848-2424 ext 4750; Fax 514-848-4751; Email ellen.artgallery@concordia.ca; Web: ellengallery.concordia.ca; *Dir* Michele Theriault
Open Tues - Fri noon - 6 PM, Sat noon - 5 PM; No admis fee; Estab 1962 for exhibitions of Canadian art, to provide a venue for a variety of significant touring exhibitions chosen from within the region & across Canada; to display the permanent collection, all with the idea of providing an important cultural arena both for the university & public alike; Five interconnected exhibition spaces with a total 3115.81 sq ft; Average Annual Attendance: 66,000
Income: Financed by university & governmental funds
Purchases: Historic, modern & contemporary Canadian art
Special Subjects: Drawings, Etchings & Engravings, Landscapes, Painting-Canadian, Pre-Columbian Art, Prints, Sculpture
Collections: Modern & Contemporary Canadian Art Collection
Exhibitions: Edge & Image; ChromaZone; John MacGregor: A Survey; The Photographs of Professor Oliver Buell (1844-1910); Goodridge Roberts: The Figure Works; Figure Painting in Montreal 1935-1955; Sickert, Orpen, John & their Contemporaries at the New English Art Club; Robert Bordo: New York + Montreal; Conservation: To Care for Art; Undergraduate Student Exhibition; Recent Acquisitions to the Collection: Selections from the Concordia Collection of Art; Michael Jolliffe: Paintings; Phillip Guston: Prints; John Arthur Fraser: Watercolours; Brian Wood: Drawings & Photographs; Barbara Astman: Floor Pieces; K M Graham: Paintings & Drawings 1971-1984; Robert Flaherty: Photographs; Work by Selected Fine Art Graduates: A 10th Anniversary Celebration; Joyce Wieland: A Decade of Painting; Francois Baillarge (1759-1830): A Portfolio of Acad Drawings; Faculty of Fine Arts Biennial; Murray MacDonald & R Holland Murray: Recent Sculptures; Jean Paul Lemieux: Honoured by the University; The Figurative Tradition In Quebec; Contemporary Works on Paper; Undergraduate Student Exhibition; Selections from the Concordia Collection of Art; Canadian Pacific Poster Art 1881-1955; Shelagh Keeley: Drawings; Bernard Gamoy: Paintings; Harold Klunder: Paintings; Marcel Bovis: Photographs; Neerland Art Quebec: an exhibition by artists of Dutch descent in Quebec; Canada in the Nineteenth Century: The Bert & Barbara Stitt Family Collection; Posters from Nicaragua; Betty Goodwin: Passages; Ron Shuebrook: Recent Work; Louis Muhlstock: New Themes & Variations 1980-1985; John Herbert Caddy 1801-1887; Expressions of Will: The Art of Prudence Heward; Riduan Tomkins: Recent Paintings; Undergraduate Student Exhibition; Selections from the Concordia Collection of Art; Concordia: The Early Years of Loyola & Sir George Williams; Porcelain: Traditions of Excellence; Francois Houde: Glass Work; Shelley Reeves: Relics; Pre-Columbian Art from the Permanent Collection: Josef Albers: Interaction of Color; Brian McNeil: Ironworks; Robert Ayre: The Critic & the Collection; Claude-Philippe Benoit: Interieur, Jour; A Decade of Collecting: A Selection of Recent Acquisitions; Contemporary Montreal Sculpture & Installation from the Canada Council Art Bank: A Twentieth Anniversary Celebration; First Impressions: Views of the Natural History of Canada 1550-1850; Local Developments: 20th century Montreal Area Art from the Collection of the Universite de Montreal; Montreal Photo Album: Photographs from Montreal Archives; Joanne Tod: The (Dis) Order of Things; Undergraduate Student Exhibition; Temporal Borders: Image & Site; Faculty Exhibition; Alex Colville: Selected Drawings; Selections from the Permanent Collection; From the Permanent Collection: A Selection of Recent Acquisitions; Chris Cran; Tom Dean; Undergraduate Student Exhibition; Nina M Owens (1869-1959); In Habitable Places
Publications: Exhibition catalogues
Activities: Lects open to public, 3 vis lectrs per yr; originate traveling exhibs

L **CONSEIL DES ARTS DU QUEBEC (CATQ),** Diagonale, Centre des arts et des fibres du Quebec, 500 place d'Armes, etage 15e Montreal, QC H2Y 2W2 Canada. Tel 514-864-3350; Email coordination@artdiagonale.org; Web: www.calq.gouv.qc.ca; *Exec Dir* Anne-Marie Jean
Open Wed - Sat 8:30 AM - 12 PM and 1 - 5 PM; Estab 1980; Specialized in contemporary fiber art exhibits; Average Annual Attendance: 1,000
Income: $60,000 (financed by endowment & mem)
Purchases: $1100
Library Holdings: Book Volumes 800, Cassettes 10, Other Holdings Artist CV (textile), Periodical Subscriptions 17, Slides 1000, Video Tapes 13
Exhibitions: 4 - 6 exhibits a yr
Publications: Diagonale 01; Diagonale 02
Activities: Artist talks; conferences; artists residencies; Artist exchanges; Quebec Univ programs; originates traveling exhibs to other nonprofit galleries across Canada, Quebec

A **GUILDE CANADIENNE DES METIERS D'ART,** Canadian Guild of Crafts, 1356 Sherbrooke St W, Montreal, QC H3G 1J1 Canada. Tel 514-849-6091; Fax 514-849-7351; Email info@laguilde.com; Web: www.theguild-laguilde.com; *Exec Dir* Michelle Joannette; *Programming & Communs Coordr* Karine Gaucher
Open Tues - Fri 10 AM - 6 PM, Wed until 9 PM, Sat & Sun 10 AM - 5 PM; No admis fee; Estab 1906 to promote, encourage & preserve arts & crafts of Canada; Permanent Collection Gallery of Inuit & First Nations Art; Exhibition Gallery; Average Annual Attendance: 30,000; Mem: 107; dues $30 & up; annual meeting in Mar/Apr
Income: Income from retail sales & donations
Library Holdings: Exhibition Catalogs, Periodical Subscriptions, Prints
Collections: Permanent collection of Inuit & First Nations Arts and Crafts, Audio Video tapes
Exhibitions: Fine craft exhibitions every 5 weeks except Jan & Feb; Inuit & First Nations Art (contemporary) twice a yr
Activities: Educ dept; lects open to public, 6-8 vis lectrs per yr; gallery talks; tours; awards; individual paintings & original objects of art lent to accredited institutions; lending collection includes prints; sales shop sells books, original art, reproductions, prints & Canadian crafts

L **JARDIN BOTANIQUE DE MONTREAL,** Bibliotheque, 4101 Sherbrooke St E, Montreal, QC H1X 2B2 Canada. Tel 514-872-1824; Fax 514-872-5167; Email jardin_botanique@ville.montreal.qc.ca; Web: www2.ville.montreal.qc.ca/jardin; *Botanist & Librn* Frederic Pitre; *Information Specialist* Steluta Ovesia; *Cur Slide Library* Lise Servant
Open Tues - Sun 9 AM - 5 PM; No admis fee; Estab 1931; For reference; Average Annual Attendance: 10,000
Income: Financed by city & donations
Library Holdings: Book Volumes 30,000, Cassettes 100, DVDs 50, Other Holdings Posters 300, Periodical Subscriptions 495, Photographs, Slides 100,000, Video Tapes 400
Special Subjects: Asian Art, Landscape Architecture
Exhibitions: Rotate exhibitions once per yr

M **LA CENTRALE POWERHOUSE GALLERY,** 4296 Blvd Saint-Laurent, Montreal, QC H2W 1Z3 Canada. Tel 514-871-0268; Fax 514-871-9830; Email galerie@lacentrale.org; Web: www.lacentrale.org; *Exhib Coordr* Orianne Asselin Van Coppenolle
Open Tues - Fri 11 AM - 7 PM, Sat noon - 5 PM; No admis fee; Estab 1973 to promote & broadcast the work of women artists in all domains; Gallery has 1500 sq ft; Average Annual Attendance: 6,000; Mem: 35; dues subscribers $20, active $10; annual meeting in Sep
Income: $120,000 (financed by mem, grants from federal, provincial & city governments, corporate & private donations)
Collections: Women Artists
Exhibitions: 7 exhibitions per year; a mixture of local & other parts of the country, occasionally American
Publications: Exhibit catalogues
Activities: Lects open to pub, 2-3 vis lectrs per yr; concerts; gallery talks; originate traveling exhibs to Canadian Art Centers; sales shop sells catalogues & t-shirts

M **MAISON SAINT-GABRIEL MUSEUM,** 2146 Dublin Pl, Pointe-Saint-Charles Montreal, QC H3K 2A2 Canada. Tel 514-935-8136; Fax 514-935-5692; Email mjrcip@globetrotter.net; Web: www.maisonsaint-gabriel.qc.ca; *Exec Dir* Madeleine Juneau; *Asst & Cur* Manon Roch
Open June 18 - Sep 3 guided tours Tues - Sun 11 AM - 6 PM; Sep 5 to Dec 22 guided tours Tues - Sun 1 - 5 PM; Admis families $25, adult $15, seniors (65+) $10, students $5, children (6+) $5; Estab 1966
Special Subjects: Crafts, Embroidery, Furniture, Sculpture
Collections: Antique Tools, Embroidery, Paintings & Sculpture, Furniture, Crafts & Upholstery of 18th & 19th centuries located in a 17th century house
Exhibitions: From Root Cellar to Attic; Laces & Embroideries

M **MCCORD MUSEUM OF CANADIAN HISTORY,** 690 Sherbrooke St W, Montreal, QC H3A 1E9 Canada. Tel 514-398-7100; Fax 514-398-5045; Email info.mccord@mccord-stewart.ca; Web: www.mccord-museum.qc.ca; *Pres & CEO* Suzanne Sauvage; *Sr Officer, Government & Institutional Relations* Martine Couillard
Open Tues - Fri 10 AM - 6 PM, Wed until 9 PM, Sat & Sun 10 AM - 5 PM, cl Mon; Admis family $40, adults $20, sr citizens (65+) $17, students (18-30) $14, students (13-17) $13, child, mus mems & Wed evening free; Estab 1919 as a museum of Canadian Ethnology & Social History; Average Annual Attendance: 100,000; Mem: 1600
Income: Financed by mems, government & donations
Special Subjects: Cartoons, Ceramics, Costumes, Decorative Arts, Dolls, Drawings, Embroidery, Eskimo Art, Etchings & Engravings, Ethnology, Folk Art, Furniture, Glass, Graphics, Historical Material, Jewelry, Laces, Landscapes, Manuscripts, Maps, Metalwork, Miniatures, Painting-British, Painting-Canadian, Painting-French
Publications: Exhibition catalogs & monographs; guides to collections for children
Activities: Classes for adults & children; docent training; lects open to pub, 2-3 vis lectrs per yr; concerts; gallery talks; tours; competitions; schols offered; individual paintings & original works of art lent to other mus; book traveling exhibs 3 per yr; originate traveling exhibs to other museological institutions in Canada; mus shop sells books, original art, reproductions, prints & giftware

L **MCGILL UNIVERSITY,** Blackader-Lauterman Library of Architecture and Art, 3459 McTavish St, Redpath Library Bldg, 3rd Fl Montreal, QC H3A 0C9 Canada. Tel 514-398-4742; Fax 514-398-6695; Email marilyn.berger@mcgill.ca; Web: www.mcgill.ca; *Head Librn* Robin Canuel
Open winter & summer Mon - Fri 9 AM - 5 PM; Estab 1922 to establish a special collection of architectural material
Library Holdings: Book Volumes 100,00, CD-ROMs 70, DVDs 50, Exhibition Catalogs, Other Holdings Drawings 250,000, Pamphlets, Periodical Subscriptions 317, Photographs 25,000
Collections: Canadian Architecture Collection
Publications: The Libraries of Edward & W S Maxwell in the Collection of the Blacker-Lauterman; Moshe Safdie: Buildings & Projects, 1967-1992; Sources in Iconography: An Annotated Bibliography

M **MONTREAL MUSEUM OF FINE ARTS,** 1380 Sherbrooke St W, Jean-Noel Desmarais Pavilion Montreal, QC H3G 1J5 Canada; The Montreal Museum of Fine Arts, P.O. Box 3000, Station "H" Montreal, PQ H3G 2T9 Canada. Tel 514-285-2000; Email education@mbamtl.org; Web: www.mbam.qc.ca; *Dir, Chief Cur & Cur European Art* Nathalie Bondil; *Chief Cur & Cur European Art* Nathalie Bondil; *Sr Cur Colls & Old Masters* Hilliard T Goldfarb; *Head Exhibs Mgmnt* Pascal Normandin
Open Tues & Thur - Sun 10 AM - 5 PM, Wed 10 AM - 9 PM, cl Mon; Admis ages 31 & up $23, ages 13-30 $15, ages 12 & under (accompanied by an adult) free; Estab 1860 as an art assoc for the exhibition of paintings; mus estab 1916; Average Annual Attendance: 1,000,000; Mem: 107,000 (VIP mems); dues $35 - $600 (1 yr), $61 - $1,200 (2 yr)
Income: Financed by endowment, mem & provincial appropriation
Library Holdings: Exhibition Catalogs
Special Subjects: African Art, American Western Art, Antiquities-Assyrian, Antiquities-Byzantine, Antiquities-Egyptian, Antiquities-Etruscan, Antiquities-Greek, Antiquities-Oriental, Antiquities-Persian, Antiquities-Roman, Archaeology, Asian Art, Baroque Art, Bronzes, Carpets & Rugs, Ceramics, Decorative Arts, Drawings, Embroidery, Enamels, Eskimo Art, Etchings & Engravings, Furniture, Glass, Gold
Collections: Collection of African art by Fr Gagnon, Chinese, Near Eastern, Peruvian, Inuit primitive art, European decorative arts, French, Spanish, Dutch, British, Canadian and other schools, Japanese incense boxes, The Parker Lace Collection, Harry T Norton Collection of ancient glass, Lucile Pillow Porcelain Collection, decorative arts, painting, sculpture from 3000 BC to the present, Saidye and Samuel Bronfman Collection of Contemporary Canadian Art
Exhibitions: Rotating exhibitions
Publications: Collage (a calendar of events)
Activities: Classes for adults & children; lects open to pub; mus shop sells books, magazines, original art, reproductions, prints

L **Library,** PO Box 3000, Station H Montreal, QC H3G 2T9 Canada. Tel 514-285-1600, ext 160; Fax 514-285-5655; Email biblio@mbamtl.org; Web: www.mbam.qc.ca/en/documentary-resources; *Library Dept Head* Joanne Dery; *Tech Svcs Librarian* Therese Bourgault; *Library Tech Acquisitions* Manon Tremblay
Not open to the pub; Estab 1882 for a reference & research centre for art students, specialists & visitors
Library Holdings: Auction Catalogs 68,000, Audio Tapes, Book Volumes 90,000, CD-ROMs, Cassettes, Clipping Files, Compact Disks, DVDs, Exhibition Catalogs, Fiche, Manuscripts, Other Holdings Vertical files 17,069, Pamphlets, Periodical Subscriptions 930, Video Tapes
Special Subjects: Art History, Decorative Arts, Drawings, Painting-Canadian, Sculpture
Collections: Canadiana, decorative art

M **MUSEE D'ART CONTEMPORAIN DE MONTREAL,** 185 rue Sainte-Catherine Ouest, Montreal, QC H2X 3X5 Canada. Tel 514-847-6226; Email info@macm.org; Web: macm.org; *Dir & Chief Cur* John Zeppetelli; *Cur & Head Exhibs & Educ* Lesley Johnstone; *Cur of the Coll* Marie-Eve Beaupre; *Cur* Marc Lanctot; *Assoc Cur* Francois LeTourneux; *Dir Communs, Mktg & Foundation* Anne-Marie Barnard; *Coordr Vis* Chantal St-Cyr; *Dir Opers & Admin* Yves Theoret; *Chief Finance* Luc Perron; *Colls & Info Resources Mgr* Anne-Marie Zeppetelli
Open Tues 11 AM - 6 PM, Wed - Fri 11 AM - 9 PM, Sat- Sun 10 AM - 6 PM; Admis family $34, adults $17, seniors (60 & up) $12, students (w/ID) $10, teenagers (13-17) $6, 12 & under free, half-price admis Wed 5 - 9 PM; Estab 1964. Conservation & information about contemporary art are the most important aspects of the mus; also to present contemporary artists to the general pub; Circ 26,315; Building is a medium-sized four-story, art mus, with an exhibition area of 2800 sq meters divided in eight galleries & a Multimedia room; Average Annual Attendance: 247,700
Income: Financed by provincial grants
Library Holdings: Auction Catalogs, Audio Tapes, Book Volumes, CD-ROMs, Cards, Cassettes, Clipping Files, Compact Disks, DVDs, Exhibition Catalogs, Fiche, Filmstrips, Periodical Subscriptions
Collections: Contemporary Art - Canadian, international & Quebecois: drawings, engravings, installations, paintings, photographs, sculptures, videos
Publications: Catalogs of exhibitions
Activities: Classes for adults & children; summer camp for children; lects open to pub, 15 vis lectrs per yr; concerts; gallery talks; tours; competitions; exten dept serving Quebec province; originate traveling exhibs circulating Canada, internationally; mus shop sells design accessories

L **Mediatheque/ Media Centre, Centre for Research & Documentation on Contemporary Art,** 185 Saint Catherine St W, Montreal, QC H2X 1Z8 Canada. Tel 514-847-6906; Fax 514-847-6916; Web: media.macm.org; *Librn* Sylvie Alix
Open Tues - Fri 11 AM - 4:30 PM, Wed 11 AM - 8:30 PM; Estab 1965; Circ Non-circulating; For reference only; Average Annual Attendance: 1,700
Income: Partially financed by Quebec Government
Purchases: $22,000
Library Holdings: Audio Tapes 250, Book Volumes 30,015, CD-ROMs, Cassettes, Clipping Files 10,000, DVDs, Exhibition Catalogs 25,644, Framed Reproductions, Kodachrome Transparencies, Motion Pictures, Other Holdings Artists Books: 300, Periodical Subscriptions 359, Photographs, Records, Slides 40,000, Video Tapes 325
Special Subjects: Art Education, Art History, Conceptual Art, Crafts, Drawings, Etchings & Engravings, Film, Graphic Arts, Graphic Design, Metalwork, Mixed Media, Photography, Printmaking, Prints, Sculpture, Textiles, Video
Collections: Archives of Paul-Emile Borduas (Painter 1905-1960), about 12,500 items including writings, correspondence, exhibition catalogs, etc

M **MUSEE DES MAITRES ET ARTISANS DU QUEBEC,** 615 Sainte Croix Ave, Montreal, QC H4L 3X6 Canada. Tel 514-747-7367; Fax 514-747-8892; Email accueil@mmaq.qc.ca; Web: www.mmaq.qc.ca; *Admin Asst* Manon Dube; *Dir* Pierre Wilson; *Cur* Élisabeth Meunier
Open Wed -Sun 12 PM - 5 PM, June 21 - Sept 4: Tues - Thurs noon - 5 PM, Fri - Sun 10 AM - 5 PM; Admis family $14, adults $7, sr citizen (65+) $5, students & children (6+) $4; Estab 1962 to didactic exhibitions of traditional arts & crafts of Quebec; Mus situated in a Gothic chapel of the Victorian period, built in 1867 in Montreal & moved to Saint-Laurent in 1930. Besides its permanent collection, the mus presents periodical exhibitions illustrating various aspects of the Quebec cultural heritage; Average Annual Attendance: 15,000; Mem: 100
Income: Financed by memberships, provincial and municipal appropriations, fund raising
Library Holdings: Book Volumes, Exhibition Catalogs
Special Subjects: American Indian Art, Ceramics, Folk Art, Furniture, Metalwork, Silver, Textiles, Woodcarvings, Crafts
Collections: Traditional & folk art of French Canada from 17th - 19th century: ceramics, crafts, furniture, metalworks, paintings, sculpture, religious art, silver, textiles, tools & wood-carving
Exhibitions: Album: Email au Quebec: 1949 - 1989; La dentelle au fil des ans; Album: Un musee dans une eglise; Rotate every 3 months
Publications: Album: Images Taillees du Quebec; Album: Les eglises et le tresor de Saint Laurent; Album: Les cahiers du musee: Hommage a Jean Palardy; Les cahiers du musee: Premiere biennale de la reliure du Quebec; La main et l'outil; Tapis Crochetes; Tissus conjonctifs, Regards sur le Mobilier laurentien, Rencontres ceramiques; Elibekian: un nom, trois generations; Maurice Savoie, art, architecture, industry; Emergences Alger Montreal; Biou et modernite artistique; chaud devant! Naissance du verre d'art; Fibres Boreales: Cultures en Partage; Expo 6+1, Art contemporain chinois: Chicago; Les artisans d'autrefois: Les objects d'autrefois; Ivar Mendez: deux mondes, un esprit; Maitres ceramistes formes a l'ecole du meuble; Decouvrir le passe au present: au coeur du vieux-Saint-Laurent; L'immigrant, Stella Pace; Reflexion 10e anniversaire, Les artistes canadiennes asiatiques; Violette Dionne, Figures anciennes et nouvelles; Enid Kaplan, Retrospective; Les artistes de la ligne orange; Projets carre rouge: Savoir refaire un printemps; Les legendes d'autrefois; La vie d'autrefois; Les chaussures d'autrefois
Activities: Classes for adults & children; lects open to public; concerts; gallery talks; tours; mus shop sells books, original art & reproductions

M **SAINT JOSEPH'S ORATORY,** Museum, 3800 Queen Mary Rd, Montreal, QC H3V 1H6 Canada. Tel 514-733-8211; Fax 514-733-9735; Email pastorale@saint-joseph.org; Web: www.saint-joseph.org; *Museum Cur* Chantal Turbide, PhD; *Oratory Rector* Claude Grou, CSC
Open daily 10 AM - 4:30PM (museum); Admis adults $4, student & seniors $3, youth (6-17) $2, under 6 free; Shrine founded 1904, estab 1955 as art mus; St Joseph's Oratory is also a Montreal landmark, the highest point in this city (856 ft above sea level), a piece of art - architecture - with a history, style, etc of its own
Library Holdings: Cards, Pamphlets
Special Subjects: African Art, Bronzes, Coins & Medals, Decorative Arts, Drawings, Embroidery, Eskimo Art, Graphics, Ivory, Miniatures, Mosaics, Painting-Canadian, Painting-French, Painting-German, Photography, Porcelain, Posters, Religious Art, Sculpture, Silver, Textiles
Collections: Ancient & Contemporary Art, Nativity Scenes from around the world
Exhibitions: Brother Andre - The Saint of Mount Royal; Nativity Scenes
Publications: 290 Nativity Scenes from 110 Countries
Activities: Concerts; films, tours; mus shop sells books, reproductions, prints & DVDs

L **Centre d'archives et de Documentation Roland-Guthier,** 3800 Queen Mary Rd, Montreal, QC H3V 1H6 Canada. Tel 514-733-8211, Ext 2341; Fax 514-733-9735; Email hleblond@osj.qc.ca; Web: www.saint-joseph.org; *Archiviste* Helene Leblond
Open Mon - Fri 9 AM - 4 PM by appointment; By appointment
Library Holdings: Book Volumes 15,000, Photographs

A **SOCIETE DES MUSEES QUEBECOIS,** 209 rue Sainte-Catherine E, Pavillon Sainte-Catherine, 5th Floor, V5205 Montreal, QC H2X 1L2 Canada; CP 8888, Succursale Centre-Ville - UQAM Montreal, QC H3C 3P8 Canada. Tel 514-987-3264; Fax 514-987-3379; Email info@smq.qc.ca; Web: www.musees.qc.ca; *Exec Dir* Stéphane Chagnon
Open daily 9 AM - Noon & 1 - 5 PM; Estab 1958; Mem: 300; Annual meeting in Oct
Income: $1,300,000 (financed by pub grants & sponsorships)
Publications: Musees, once a year; Bulletin, 2 times a year; Museums to Discover, Quebec & Series of Electronic Guides / Museum Guide (2006); Enjeux
Activities: Classes for mus works; mus shop sells books & magazines

M **THE STEWART MUSEUM,** 20 chemin du Tour de I'Isle, The Fort, St Helen's Island Montreal, QC H3C 0K7 Canada. Tel 514-861-6701; Fax 514-861-2211; Email info@stewart-museum.org; Web: www.stewart-museum.org; *Pres & CEO* Suzanne Sauvage; *Head Opers* Daniel Dupere; *Cur, Head of Colls* Sylvie Dauphin
Open Wed- Sun 10 AM - 5 PM; Admis adults $10, students, seniors, children (13-17), & students (18-25) $8, children 12 & under free; Estab 1955 to exhibit artifacts relating to Canada's history; located in an old British Arsenal, built between 1820-24; galleries cover theme chronologically & by collection; Average Annual Attendance: 75,000; Mem: annual meeting in June
Income: $2,000,000 (financed by grants & self generated sources)
Library Holdings: Book Volumes 8156, Maps 704, Original Art Works, Original Documents 407, Pamphlets 62, Periodical Subscriptions 50, Photographs, Prints, Reproductions, Slides, Video Tapes 97
Special Subjects: Decorative Arts, Drawings, Etchings & Engravings, Ethnology, Glass, Historical Material, Marine Painting, Metalwork, Military Art, Miniatures, Pewter, Portraits
Collections: Firearms, Kitchen & Fireplace, dating from 16th century, prints, maps, navigation & scientific instruments
Publications: Exhibition catalogs
Activities: Classes for children; during summer months 18th century military parades by La Compagnie Franche de la Marine & the 78th Fraser Highlanders; concerts; tours; originate traveling exhibs to interested museums; Mus shop sells books, reproductions, prints & slides

L **Library,** 20 chemin du Tour-de-l'Isle, Montreal, QC H3C QK7 Canada. Tel 514-861-6701; Fax 514-861-2211; Email info.stewart@mccord-stewart.ca; Web: www.stewart-museum.org; *Cur, Head of Colls* Sylvie Dauphin; *Colls Asst* Khan Rooney
Open Library on appointment: Mon - Thurs 9 AM - 5 PM; Museum: Wed - Sun 11 AM - 5 PM; Admis adults $13, senior, student, children $10; Estab 1955 as an 18th century gentleman's library; pvt mus; Library of rare books & rare maps open to researchers & members for reference on appointment
Library Holdings: Book Volumes 8156, CD-ROMs, DVDs, Manuscripts, Maps 704, Original Art Works, Original Documents, Pamphlets, Periodical Subscriptions 50, Photographs, Prints 3501, Reproductions, Slides, Video Tapes
Special Subjects: Maps
Collections: Coll of rare books, maps, documents & prints, artworks, household objects, scientific objects, weaponry & militaria
Publications: Exhibition catalogs
Activities: Educ progs; mus shop sells books & reproductions

L **UNIVERSITE DE MONTREAL,** Bibliotheque d'Amenagement, Pavillon de la Faculte de l'amenagement, 2940 chemin de la Cote Ste-Catherine, Salle 1162 Montreal, QC H3C 3J7 Canada; CP 6128 succursale Centre-ville, Montreal, QC H3C 3J7 Canada. Tel 514-343-7177; Web: www.bib.umontreal.ca/AM; *Chief Librn* Lyne Belanger
Open acad yr: Mon - Thurs 8:30 AM - 9 PM, Fri 8:30 AM - 5 PM, Sat - Sun noon - 5 PM; Admis Universite de Montreal users free; Estab 1964
Purchases: $100,000
Library Holdings: Audio Tapes, Book Volumes 53,679, DVDs, Exhibition Catalogs, Periodical Subscriptions 300, Photographs, Slides 81,000, Video Tapes
Special Subjects: Architecture, Industrial Design, Landscape Architecture
Collections: History of Landscape Architecture, urban planning, design

L **UNIVERSITE DU QUEBEC,** Bibliotheque des Arts, Pavillon Hubert-Aquin, local A-1200, 400 rue Sainte-Catherine E Montreal, QC H3C 3P3 Canada; CP 8889, Succursale Centre-ville, Montreal, QC H3C 3P3 Canada. Tel 514-987-6134; Fax 514-987-0262; Web: www.bibliotheques.uqam.ca; *Librn* Marie-Christine Beaudry; *Librn* Gisele Guay; *Librn* Lucie Seguin
Open Mon - Fri 8:30 AM - 10 PM, Sat 11 AM - 5 PM
Library Holdings: Book Volumes 65,000, CD-ROMs, Clipping Files, Exhibition Catalogs, Periodical Subscriptions 500, Slides
Special Subjects: Advertising Design, Architecture, Art Education, Eskimo Art, Painting-American, Pre-Columbian Art, Primitive art, Religious Art, Restoration & Conservation, Sculpture, Silver, Video, Watercolors, Woodcarvings, Woodcuts

POINTE CLAIRE

A **POINTE CLAIRE CULTURAL CENTRE,** Stewart Hall Art Gallery, Stewart Hall, 176 Bord du Lac Pointe Claire, QC H9S 4J7 Canada. Tel 514-630-1220; Fax 514-630-1259; Email stewarthall@pointe-claire.ca; Web: www.pointe-claire.ca/en/stewart-hall-cultural-centre/cultural-centre.html; *Dir Art Gallery* Joyce Millar; *Gallery Asst* Amanda Johnston; *Gallery Asst* Manel Benchabane
Open Mon - Fri 8:30 AM - 9 PM, Sat 9:30 AM - 5 PM, Sun 1 PM -5 PM; No admis fee; Estab 1963; Gallery is 25 x 120 ft; Average Annual Attendance: 11,000; Mem: Policy & Planning Board meets 6 times per year
Income: Financed by city
Purchases: Contemporary Canadian Art for city of Pointe Claire permanent collection
Collections: Permanent collection of contemporary Canadian art
Exhibitions: Approx eight per yr, local, provincial, national and international content
Publications: Bulletins; schedules of classes, study series, social events, approx 30 per yr
Activities: Classes for children; docent training; lects open to pub, 8-10 vis lectrs per year; concerts, gallery talks, tours; lending collection contains original prints, paintings & crafts to pvt and corporate clients; mus shop sells original art, art objects

QUEBEC

M **L'UNIVERSITE LAVAL,** Ecole des Arts Visuels, Edifice La Fabrique, 295 Charest Blvd E, Bureau 090 Quebec, QC G1K 7P4 Canada. Tel 418-656-7631; Fax 418-656-7678; Email accueil@arv.ulaval.ca; Web: www.arv.ulaval.ca; *Dir* Georges Azzaria
Open Mon - Fri 8:30 AM - 7 PM; No admis fee; Estab 1970; Average Annual Attendance: 800
Library Holdings: Audio Tapes, Book Volumes, CD-ROMs, Compact Disks
Special Subjects: Graphics, Sculpture
Collections: Art color slides, decorative arts, graphics, paintings, sculpture
Exhibitions: Temporary exhibitions, changing monthly
Activities: Classes for adults & children; originates traveling exhibs

L **Library,** Cite' Universitaire, Quebec, QC G1K 7P4 Canada. Tel 418-656-2131, Ext 3451; Fax 418-656-7897; Web: www.art.ulaval.ca; *Dir Art* Madeleine Robin; *Dir Gen Library System* Claude Bonnelly
Open Mon-Fri 8:30 - noon, 1:30 - 5 PM; Open to the pub for use on the premises; original prints & works of art available for study
Library Holdings: Book Volumes 25,000

M **LA CHAMBRE BLANCHE,** 185 Christophe-Colomb E, Quebec, QC G1K 3S6 Canada. Tel 418-529-2715; Fax 418-529-0048; Email info@chambreblanche.qc.ca; Web: www.chambreblanche.qc.ca; *VP* Jacques Blanchet; *Coordr* Francois Vallee
Open Wed - Sun 1-5 PM; No admis fee; Estab 1978 for diffusion of installation & in situation art, web art lab; Mem: 125
Income: Financed by Canada Art Council, Quebec Art Council & Town of Quebec City
Library Holdings: Audio Tapes, Book Volumes, CD-ROMs, DVDs, Exhibition Catalogs, Periodical Subscriptions
Publications: Annual bulletin; Lani Maestro; Residence 1982-1993; Temporalité; Jamelie Hassan; Sur les toits; Largus; Le performatif du Web
Activities: Lects open to pub, 4-5 vis lectrs per yr; L@ Ch@mbre Bl@nche Prize; fels available; mus shop sells books and mus publs

L **LES EDITIONS INTERVENTION, INTER-LE LIEU,** Documentation Center, 345 Du Pont, Quebec, QC G1K 6M4 Canada. Tel 418-529-9680; Fax 418-529-6933; Email infos@inter-lelieu.org; Web: www.inter-lelieu.org; *Dir* Richard Martel
Open Mon - Fri 8 AM - 5 PM; Estab 1978; For reference, possible lending & magazine exchanges; Average Annual Attendance: 10,000; Mem: Dues $20 & up
Income: Financed by pub funds, donations & mem
Special Subjects: American Indian Art, Architecture, Conceptual Art, Constructions, Mixed Media, Photography, Video
Exhibitions: Rotate 8 per yr
Publications: Inter, Art Actuel, 3 per year
Activities: Lects open to public, 3 vis lectrs per yr

M **MUSEE DE L'AMERIQUE FRANCOPHONE,** 2 Cote de la Fabrique, Quebec, QC G1R 3V6 Canada; PO Box 155, Sta B, 85 rue Dalhousie Quebec, QC G1K 7A6 Canada. Tel 418-643-2158; Fax 418-646-9705; Email mcq@mcq.org; Web: www.mcq.org; *Exec Dir* Stephan La Roche
Open Tues - Sun 10 AM - 5 PM, cl Mon; Admis adults (31+) $16, adults (18-30) $10, children (12-17) $5, under 11 free; The Musee de l'Amerique francaise has been integrated to the Musee de la civilisation since 1995. The Musee de la civilisation is subsidized by the ministere de la Culture et des Communications, Gouvernement du Quebec; Average Annual Attendance: 100,000; Mem: dues $25
Income: Financed by Ministere, Gouvernement du Quebec, Gouvernement Federal
Collections: 18th & 19th centuries Canadian paintings, 17th & 18th centuries European paintings, Ethnology, Gold & Silver Objects, Scientific Instruments, Sketches & Prints, Sculpture, Coins & Medals, Zoology
Exhibitions: L'oeuvre du Seminaire de Quebec (Seminaire de Quebec: Widsom and Works); Partir sur la route des francophones (On the road: The Francophone Odyssey)
Activities: Lects open to public; concerts; gallery talks; tours; sales shop sells books, magazines, prints & slides

M **MUSEE DES AUGUSTINES DE L'HOTEL DIEU DE QUEBEC,** 32 rue Charlevoix, Quebec, QC G1R 5C4 Canada. Tel 418-692-2492; Fax 418-692-2668; Email mahdq@augustines.ca; *Dir Mus* Sr Nicole Perron; *Guide* Jacques St-Arnaud
Open Tues - Sat 9:30 AM - Noon & 1:30 - 5 PM, Sun 1:30 - 5 PM; No admis fee, donations appreciated; Estab 1958 in the Monastere des Augustines (1695); The Hotel Dieu relives three centuries of history of the French Canadian people; Average Annual Attendance: 11,000
Special Subjects: African Art, American Indian Art, Calligraphy, Ceramics, Coins & Medals, Dolls, Drawings, Embroidery, Furniture, Glass, Leather, Manuscripts, Painting-European, Painting-Flemish, Painting-French, Painting-Italian, Painting-Spanish, Period Rooms, Photography, Porcelain, Portraits, Pottery, Religious Art
Collections: Antique furniture, embroideries, medical instruments 17th-20th century, objects from everyday life, models & several other unique works, paintings, silver & pewter artifacts
Activities: Original objects of art lent to museums

L **Archive**, 32 rue Charlevoix, Convent Office Quebec, QC G1R 5C4 Canada. Tel 418-692-2492, Ext 247; Fax 418-692-2668; *Archivist* Sr Marie-Paule Couchon; *Dir Mus* Sr Nicole Perron
Open by appointment only; Religious & medical books available for research upon special request
Library Holdings: Book Volumes 4000

M **MUSEE NATIONAL DES BEAUX ARTS DU QUEBEC,** 179 Grand Allee Ouest, Quebec, QC G1R 2H1 Canada. Tel 418-643-2150; Email info@mnbaq.org; Web: www.mnbaq.org; *Gen Dir* Jean-Francois Fusey; *Dir Collections & Research* Annie Gauthier; *Dir Exhibitions & Mediation* Christine Conciatori; *Dir Mktg & Communs* Jean Francois Lippe
Open Tues - Sun 10 AM - 5 PM, Wed 10 AM - 9 PM; cl Mon, Labor Day, Thanksgiving, New Year's Eve, Easter Monday & National Patriot Day; Admis adults $20, seniors (65+) $18, young adults (18-30) $11, youth (13-17) $6, children 12 & under free; Estab 1933 under Government of Province of Quebec; 12 galleries, 1 restaurant, 1 theatre, cafe; Average Annual Attendance: 300,000
Income: Financed by Quebec government appropriation
Library Holdings: Auction Catalogs, Audio Tapes, Book Volumes, CD-ROMs, Cards, Cassettes, Clipping Files, Compact Disks, DVDs, Exhibition Catalogs, Fiche, Filmstrips, Framed Reproductions, Prints
Special Subjects: Bronzes, Decorative Arts, Drawings, Painting-American, Painting-Canadian, Photography, Portraits, Sculpture, Woodcarvings
Collections: Quebec art from 18th century to present, Design, drawings, goldsmith's work, paintings, photography, sculpture, tapestry works, European art
Exhibitions: Rotating exhibitions
Publications: Exhibit catalogs
Activities: Classes for adults & children; lects open to pub; concerts; gallery talks; tours; schol offered; exten dept serves province of Quebec; individual paintings lent to government; originates traveling exhibs; mus shop sells books, magazines, original art, reproductions, prints & postcards; junior mus

L **Bibliotheque**, Parc des Champs-de-Bataille, Quebec, QC G1R 5H3 Canada. Tel 418-644-6460 ext 3341; Fax 418-643-2478; Email bibliom@mnba.qc.ca; Web: mnba.qc.ca; *Dir Colls Mngmt & Info* Pierre Landry; *Documentary & Archives Mngmt* Nathalie Thibault; *Documentation Tech* Lina Doyon; *Documentation Tech* Nicole Gastonguay; *Documentation Tech* Caroline Gauthier; *Reference Agent* Helene Godbout
Open only by appointment; Estab 1933
Income: $100,000 (financed by Quebec government appropriation)
Purchases: $36,000
Library Holdings: Auction Catalogs, Audio Tapes 144, Book Volumes 40,000, CD-ROMs 52, Clipping Files 13,000, Compact Disks 23, DVDs, Exhibition Catalogs, Fiche, Other Holdings CD-ROM, Periodical Subscriptions 123, Photographs, Reels, Slides 58,000, Video Tapes 423
Special Subjects: Art Education, Art History, Decorative Arts, Painting-Canadian, Photography

M **VU CENTRE DE DIFFUSION ET DE PRODUCTION DE LA PHOTOGRAPHIE,** 550 cote d'Abraham, Quebec, QC G1K 3P9 Canada. Tel 418-640-2585; Fax 218-640-2586; Email info@vuphoto.org; Web: www.vuphoto.org; *Pres* Annie Baillargeon; *Co-Dir* Anne-Marie Proulx; *Co-Dir* Jacynthe Carrier
Open Wed - Sun Noon - 5 PM; No admis fee; Estab 1981; Gallery contains exhibition area, digital printing lab & darkrooms; Average Annual Attendance: 15,000; Mem: 200
Income: Financed by endowment, mem, city appropriation & special events
Library Holdings: Book Volumes, CD-ROMs, DVDs, Exhibition Catalogs, Pamphlets, Periodical Subscriptions
Special Subjects: American Western Art, Art History, Photography, Conceptual Art
Collections: Artist Residencies Program Collection
Publications: Complete catalog at website
Activities: Educ prog; exhibs; production facilities in digital & analog photography; publication of books on contemporary photography; lects open to pub, 3 vis lectrs per yr; gallery talks; commented visits on exhibs; mus shop sells books

RIMOUSKI

M **LE MUSEE REGIONAL DE RIMOUSKI,** Centre National d'Exposition, 35 St Germain W, Rimouski, QC G5L 4B4 Canada. Tel 418-724-2272; Fax 418-725-4433; Email info@museerimouski.qu.ca; Web: www.museerimouski.qc.ca; *Gen Mgr* Francine Périnet; *Cur Contemporary Art* Ève De Garie-Lamanque; *Educ & Culture* Brigitte Lacasse; *Material Resources Tech* Gervais Belzile; *Coll Archivist* Nathalie Langelier
Open Sep - Jun Wed - Sun noon - 5 PM, Thurs until 8 PM; June - Sep daily 9:30 AM - 6 PM; Admis family $14, adults $6, students, seniors & children (5-17) $4, children 5 & under free; Estab 1972 for the diffusion of contemporary art, historic & scientific exhibitions; to present local, national & international exhibitions & organize itinerant exhibitions; An old church, built in 1823, now historical monument, completely restored inside with three floors of exhibitions; Average Annual Attendance: 15,000; Mem: 400; dues $40; annual meeting in May or June
Income: $237,000 (financed by federal, provincial & municipal appropriation)
Exhibitions: Scientific Exploration of the Sea
Publications: L'Esprit des lieux; L'Artiste au jardin; Messac; Opera, Les Nuits de Vitre; Cozic; exhibit catalogs
Activities: Classes for children; school progs; lects open to pub, 5 vis lectrs per yr; concerts; gallery talks; tours; originate traveling exhibs; mus shop sells magazines

L **Library**, 35 W St Germain, Rimouski, QC G5L 4B4 Canada. Tel 418-724-2272; Fax 418-725-4433; Web: http://museerimouski.qc.ca
Circ Non-circulating; Open to pub for reference, call for seasonal hours, cl statutory holidays
Library Holdings: Book Volumes 2500, Exhibition Catalogs, Other Holdings Documents 800, Pamphlets, Reproductions, Sculpture

SEPT-ILES

M **MUSEE REGIONAL DE LU COTE-NORD,** 500 blvd Laure, Sept-Iles, QC G4R 1X7 Canada. Tel 418-968-2070; Fax 418-968-8323; Email mrcn@mrcn.qc.ca; Web: www.mrcn.qc.ca; *Conservateur* Steve Dubreuil; *Dir* Christian Marcotte; *Boutique Mgr* Sophie Levesque
Open winter Tues - Fri 10 AM - 5 PM, Sat & Sun 1-5 PM, cl Mon; summer daily 9 AM - 5 PM; Admis adult $7, sr citizens & students $6, children under 12 free; Estab 1975. Protects, preserves, studies & exhibits the heritage of the Cote-Nord region, with particular emphasis on fishing, hunting, mining & archaeological activity; Contemporary art from province of Quebec; Average Annual Attendance: 22,000; Mem: 150; annual meeting in June
Income: Financed by mem, city & state appropriation
Library Holdings: Audio Tapes, Book Volumes, Cards, Compact Disks, DVDs, Exhibition Catalogs, Framed Reproductions, Maps, Memorabilia, Original Art Works, Photographs, Prints, Reproductions
Special Subjects: Archaeology, Ceramics, Drawings, Eskimo Art, Ethnology, Furniture, Historical Material, Juvenile Art, Landscapes, Metalwork, Painting-Canadian, Photography, Porcelain, Portraits, Posters, Pottery, Sculpture, Textiles, Watercolors, Woodcarvings, Woodcuts
Collections: Archaeology, art, ethnology, history
Activities: Classes for adults & children; docent progs; lects open to pub; book traveling exhibs 2 per yr; mus shop sells books, magazines, reproductions, prints, artcraft & regional foodies

SHAWINIGAN

A **SHAWINIGAN ART CENTER,** 2100 blvd des Hetres, Shawinigan, QC G9N 8R8 Canada. Tel 819-539-1888; Fax 819-539-2400; Email corporationculturelle@shawinigan.ca; Web: www.cultureshawinigan.ca; *Gen Dir* Bryan Perreault
Open Mon & Fri 9 AM - noon & 1 PM - 4:30 PM; No admis fee; Estab 1967; Gallery is maintained; Average Annual Attendance: 36,000
Income: Financed by city appropriation & cultural ministry
Collections: Oils, pastels, watercolors, polyesters, reproductions, copper enameling, inks, sculpture, tapestries
Activities: Classes for adults & children; dramatic progs; concerts; lending collection contains original art works, original prints, paintings, sculpture, slides; sales shop sells original art

SHERBROOKE

M **BISHOP'S UNIVERSITY,** Foreman Art Gallery, 2600 College St, Sherbrooke, QC J1M 1Z7 Canada. Tel 819-822-9600 ext 2260/2279; Fax 819-822-9703; Email gallery@ubishops.ca; Web: www.foreman.ubishops.ca; *Dir & Cur* Gentiane Belanger
Open Sep - July Tues - Sat noon - 5PM; No admis fee; Estab 1992 to serve the University Community & the entire Eastern Townships by displaying regional, national & international art work; 154.5 sq m/1667sq ft exhib space located adjacent to the Foyer of Centennial Theatre; Average Annual Attendance: 5,200
Income: Bishop's Univ
Collections: paintings, prints, & sculptures
Publications: catalog of exhibs, yearly
Activities: Docent training; work study prog; workshops; lects open to pub, 5 vis lectrs per yr; gallery talks, sponsoring of competitions; graduating student exhib 3 awards per yr

M **UNIVERSITY OF SHERBROOKE,** Art Gallery, 2500 blvd de l'Universite, Sherbrooke, QC J1K 2R1 Canada. Tel 819-820-1000; Email galerie@usherbrooke.ca; *CEO* Mario Trépanier
Open Tues - Sat 1 - 4 PM; No admis fee; Estab 1964 to introduce pub to the best art work being done in Canada & to place this work in a historical (European) & geographical (American) context; Gallery has three exhibition areas totaling 12,800 sq ft on university campus & serves the community; Average Annual Attendance: 30,000
Income: $300,000 (financed by state & city appropriation & university funds)
Special Subjects: Graphics
Collections: 90 per cent Contemporary Graphics & Paintings Quebec & 10 per cent international
Publications: Monthly bulletin; catalogue
Activities: Lects open to public, 20 vis lectrs per year; gallery talks; lending collection contains books, cassettes, color reproductions, Kodachromes, original prints, paintings, photographs, sculpture, slides & videos

SUTTON

M **COMMUNICATIONS AND HISTORY MUSEUM OF SUTTON,** (Eberdt Museum of Communications), 32 Principal South St, Sutton, QC J0E 2K0 Canada. Tel 450-538-2883
Open Mon - Fri 10 AM - 5 PM; Admis adults $7, 12-17 & 60-80 4$, families 15$; Mem: 160; dues $10
Income: (financed by mem, city & state appropriation)
Special Subjects: Historical Material
Collections: History, art & communs coll, 2300 historic objects
Activities: Lects open to pub; mus shop sells books

TROIS RIVIERES

M **FORGES DU SAINT-MAURICE NATIONAL HISTORIC SITE,** 10000 Blvd des Forges, Trois Rivieres, QC G9C 1B1 Canada. Tel 819-378-5116; Fax 819-378-0887; Email parkscanada-que@pc.gc.ca; Web: www.pc.gc.ca/lhn-nhs/qc/saintmaurice; *Supt* Thierry Bouin

Open May 10 - Sep 1 10 AM - 5:00 PM; Sept 2 - Oct 13, 9:30 AM - 4:30 PM; Admis family $9.80, adult $3.90, senior $3.40, youth $1.90; Estab 1973 as the first iron & steel industry in Canada 1729-1883; 50 acres of land-2 main exhibition centers, the ironmaster's house & the blast furnace; Average Annual Attendance: 50,000
Special Subjects: Archaeology, Metalwork
Collections: Cast Iron Stoves from the 18th & 19th century, Metal objects found between 1973-1980
Exhibitions: Blast Furnace Permanent Exhibition

M **GALERIE D'ART DU PARC-MANOIR DE TONNANCOUR,** Manoir de Tonnancour, 864 rue des Ursulines, CP 871 Trois Rivieres, QC G9A 5J9 Canada. Tel 819-374-2355; Fax 819-374-1758; Email galerie@galeriedart.duparc.qc.ca; Web: www.galeriedartduparc.qc.ca; *Exec Dir* Christiane Simoneau
Open Tues - Fri 10 AM-Noon & 1:30-5 PM, Sat & Sun 1-5 PM, cl Mon; No admis fee; Estab 1972 to promote visual arts; Nonprofit organization; 10-12 exhibitions in visual arts per year & permanent history exhibition; Average Annual Attendance: 19,000
Income: Financed by city appropriation & government
Exhibitions: Rotating exhibitions
Activities: Classes for adults & children; book traveling exhibs 1 per yr; originate traveling exhibs; mus shop sells original art & reproductions

A **MAISON DE LA CULTURE,** (Centre Culturel de Trois Rivieres) Centre d'exposition Raymond-Lasnier, 1425 Place de l'Hotel-de-Ville, CP 368 Trois Rivieres, QC G9A 5H3 Canada. Tel 819-372-4611; Fax 819-372-4632; Email cerl@v3r.net; Web: www.cer-l.ca; *Dir* Marie-Andree Levasseur
Open Tues - Sun noon - 5 PM; No admis fee; Estab 1967 to promote visual art; Gallery features 275 sq meters total area; Average Annual Attendance: 12,000
Income: Financed by city appropriation & a corporation
Purchases: regular contacts with visual arts
Collections: 700 pieces
Publications: Exhib catalogues
Activities: Classes for adults & children; guided group visits; educ prog; tours

VAUDREUIL-DORION

M **MUSEE REGIONAL DE VAUDREUIL-SOULANGES,** 431 Ave St Charles, Vaudreuil-Dorion, QC J7V 2N3 Canada. Tel 450-424-5627; Fax 450-424-5675; Email info@mrvs.qc.ca; Web: www.chlapresquile.qc.ca; *Dir* Daniel Bissonnette
Open Tues - Fri 8:30 AM - 12 PM & 1 PM - 4:30 PM; Admis family $25, adults $7, students $5, children (7-12) $2; Estab 1953, nonprofit organization subsidized by the Direction des Musees et Centres d'Exposition of the Ministere des Affaires culturelles du Quebec. The collection consists of artifacts & artists production that have & still illustrate the traditional way of life in the counties of Vaudreuil & Soulanges, the surroundings & the Province of Quebec; Mus has four rooms for permanent collection & one for temporary & traveling exhibitions. A documentation centre is open for searchers & students & an animator will receive groups on reservation for a commented tour; Average Annual Attendance: 13,000; Mem: 300; dues $20; annual meeting in Apr
Income: Financed by endowment
Special Subjects: Furniture, Painting-American, Portraits, Pottery, Sculpture
Collections: Edison Gramophone 1915, antique pottery, historic documents & material, farming, furniture, paintings, portraits, sculpture & woodworking
Exhibitions: Various exhibitions
Publications: Musee de Vaudreuil Catalog (selectif); Vaudreuil Soulanges, Western Gateway of Quebec
Activities: Classes for children; concerts; original objects of art lent

L **Centre d'Histoire d'la Presqu'ile**, 431 Ave Chaud, Vaudreuil, QC J7V 2N3 Canada. Tel 450-455-2092; Fax 450-455-6782; Web: www.mrds.qu.ca; *Dir* Daniel Bissonnette
Open Mon-Fri 9:30 AM - 4:30 PM, cl Sat & Sun; Circ Non-circulating; Reference only
Library Holdings: Book Volumes 5200, Other Holdings AV cylinders 600, Photographs

SASKATCHEWAN

ESTEVAN

M **ESTEVAN NATIONAL EXHIBITION CENTRE INC,** Estevan Art Gallery & Museum, 118 Fourth St, Estevan, SK S4A 0T4 Canada. Tel 306-634-7644; Fax 306-634-2940; Email eagm@sasktel.net; Web: www.eagm.ca; *Cur* Amber Andersen; *Gallery Educator* Martina Veneziano
Open June - Aug: Mon - Wed & Fri 10 AM - 6 PM, Thurs 10 AM - 9 PM, Sat 10 AM - 4 PM, cl Sun; Sep - May: Mon - Wed & Fri 10 AM - 6 PM, Thurs 10 AM - 9 PM, Sat 1 - 4 PM, cl Sun; No admis fee; Estab 1978 to receive, display & interpret objects & collections, that would increase the communities access to culture; Two galleries; one 16 x 30 ft, the other 26 x 65 ft; North West Mounted Police Museum; Average Annual Attendance: 22,000; Mem: Board of Dir meet first Thurs each month at 6 PM, Ann Gen meeting May
Income: $260,000 (financed by provincial & city appropriation & private sector fundraising)
Purchases: Andrew King Block Printing Coll valued at $120,000
Library Holdings: Audio Tapes, Exhibition Catalogs, Kodachrome Transparencies, Memorabilia, Original Art Works, Original Documents, Photographs, Prints, Sculpture, Slides, Video Tapes
Special Subjects: Painting-Canadian, Prints
Collections: Saskatchewan artists print series, Saskatchewan painting collection, Two ceramic wall murals valued at 18,000
Exhibitions: Rotating exhibs every 6 wks - 2 months
Publications: Annual Report; newsletter, quarterly
Activities: Educ prog; classes for adults, children & seniors; lects open to pub, 4 vis lectrs per yr; gallery talks; tours; children's & regional art show competitions; awards of merit; exten dept serves southeast Saskatchewan; lending of original objects of art to local bus; book traveling exhibs 13-18 per yr; originate traveling exhibs through Canada; sales shop sells books, original art & souvenirs

LLOYDMINSTER

A **LLOYDMINSTER CULTURAL & SCIENCE CENTRE,** (Barr Colony Heritage Cultural Centre), Hwy 16 E & 45 Ave, Lloydminster, SK S9V 0T8 Canada; 4420 50th Ave, Lloydminster, SK T9V 0U2 Canada. Tel 780-874-3720; Fax 780-874-3721; Web: www.lloydminster.ca/lcsc; *Mgr* Kyra Stefanuk
Open Mon - Sat 9 AM - 4:30 PM, Thurs 9 AM - 9 PM, Sun 10 AM - 6 PM; Admis family $5.75, adults $2.75, sr citizens & students $2, children 12 & under $1.50, school tours $.50; Estab 1963 to promote & support appreciation for & educ about local history & the arts; The center is comprised of 4 exhibit galleries (1000 sq ft), a mus bldg (24,000 sq ft) & classroom teaching space
Income: Financed by donations & city appropriations
Collections: Antique Museum, Fuchs' Wildlife, Imhoff Paintings, Berghammer Art Collection, over 5000 artifacts related to the Barr Colonists, the first settlers of the area
Exhibitions: Exhibits rotate 6-8 per yr
Activities: Gallery talks; tours; traveling exhibitions

MOOSE JAW

M **MOOSE JAW ART MUSEUM, INC,** Art & History Museum, 461 Langton Crescent, Moose Jaw, SK S6H 0X6 Canada. Tel 306-692-4471; Fax 306-694-8016; Email mjamchin@sasktel.net; Web: www.mjmag.ca; *Cur Dir* Jennifer McRorie; *Admin Dir* Joan Maier; *Educ Coordr* Christy Schweiger
Open Tues - Sun noon - 5 PM; cl Mon; admis by donation; Estab 1966 for preservation, educ, collection & exhibitions; Gallery has 4304 sq ft with movable walls, Mus has 3970 sq ft, Discovery Centre has 1010 sq ft; Average Annual Attendance: 30,000; Mem: 190; dues family $25, individual $15
Income: $260,000 (financed by city, province & national appropriations & self-generated revenues)
Purchases: $260,000
Special Subjects: American Indian Art, Costumes, Ethnology, Folk Art, Painting-Canadian
Collections: 723 Canadian Historical & Contemporary Art Collection, 4,700 Human History Artifacts Collection, Canadian Historical & Contemporary Art Collection, Human History Artifacts Collection
Exhibitions: Heritage Gallery has permanent exhibits; art gallery rotates exhibits every 6 wks
Publications: Annual catalogs; bi-annual newsletter
Activities: Classes for adults & children; docent training; school tours; Discovery Centre mini science ctr; lects open to pub, 10-15 vis lectrs per yr; gallery talks; tours; individual paintings & original objects of art lent to other professional public institutions that meet appropriate environmental standards; book traveling exhibs 5-10 per yr; originate traveling exhibs; mus shop sells books, original works of art, educational toys

NORTH BATTLEFORD

M **ALLEN SAPP GALLERY,** One Railway Ave E, PO Box 460 North Battleford, SK S9A 2Y6 Canada. Tel 306-445-1760; Fax 306-445-1694; Email sapp@accesscomm.ca; Web: www.allensapp.com; *Cur & Mgr* Leah Garven
Open fall & winter Wed - Sun 1 - 5 PM; spring & summer daily 11 AM - 5 PM; No admis fee; Estab 1989; 8,000 sq ft gallery built in 1916 contains state of the art equipment incl high tech av presentation equipment; Average Annual Attendance: 9,000; Mem: 200; dues $10
Income: $100,000 (financed by municipal & provincial grants & gift shop revenues)
Library Holdings: Auction Catalogs, Book Volumes, CD-ROMs, Cards, Clipping Files, Compact Disks, Exhibition Catalogs, Kodachrome Transparencies, Manuscripts, Memorabilia, Motion Pictures, Original Documents, Pamphlets, Periodical Subscriptions, Photographs, Prints, Records, Slides, Video Tapes
Collections: The Gonor Collection, paintings, photos, slides of art by renowned Cree artist Allen Sapp plus the work of other Canadian 1st Nations artist
Exhibitions: Rotate 2 exhibits per yr featuring powerful and sensitive images of the Northern Plains Cree
Publications: gallery catalog, biennial
Activities: Classes for adults & children; Native studies; lects open to pub, 4 vis lectrs per yr; 1999 & 2002 Attractions Canadian award; circulate exhibs to credited mus; mus shop sells books, reproductions, prints

PRINCE ALBERT

M **JOHN M CUELENAERE PUBLIC LIBRARY,** Grace Campbell Gallery, 125 12th St E, Prince Albert, SK S6V 1B7 Canada. Tel 306-763-8496; Fax 306-763-3816; Email library@jmcpl.ca; Web: www.jmcpl.ca; *Dir* Alex Juorio
Open Mon - Thurs 9 AM - 9 PM, Fri & Sat 9 AM - 5:00 PM, Sun (Sept - May) 1 PM - 5PM; No admis fee; Estab 1973; Gallery is 100 linear ft
Income: Financed by city appropriation
Activities: Tours; one traveling exhib per yr

REGINA

A **MUSEUMS ASSOCIATION OF SASKATCHEWAN,** MAS Office, 424 McDonald St Regina, SK S4N 6E1 Canada. Tel 306-780-9279; Fax 306-780-9463; Email mas@saskmuseums.org; Web: www.saskmuseums.org; *Exec Dir* Wendy Fitch; *Professional Develop Coordr* Dan Holbrow; *Dir Finance* Brenda Herman

Open daily 8 AM-4 PM, cl Sat & Sun; Estab 1967; Mem: 450; dues vary with budget $40 - $410
Income: Financed by lotteries & mem
Publications: Bi-monthly newsletter

ORGANIZATION OF SASKATCHEWAN ARTS COUNCILS (OSAC)
For further information, see National and Regional Organizations

L **REGINA PUBLIC LIBRARY,** Art Dept, PO Box 2311, Regina, SK S4P 3Z5 Canada. Tel 306-777-6070; Fax 306-949-7260; Web: www.rpl.regina.sk.ca; *Acting Dir & Librn* Sandy Cameron
Open Mon - Thurs 9:30 AM - 9 PM, Fri 9:30 AM - 6 PM, Sat 9:30 AM - 5 PM, Sun 1:30 - 5 PM, cl holidays; No admis fee; Estab 1947; Also operates Sherwood Village Branch Gallery
Library Holdings: Audio Tapes, Book Volumes 10,230, Cassettes, Clipping Files, Exhibition Catalogs 4000, Fiche, Filmstrips, Motion Pictures, Original Art Works, Pamphlets, Periodical Subscriptions 60, Photographs, Prints, Slides, Video Tapes

M **Dunlop Art Gallery**, 2311 12th Ave, Regina, SK S4P 3Z5 Canada; PO Box 2311, Regina, SK S4P 3Z5 Canada. Tel 306-777-6040; Fax 306-949-7264; Email dunlop@rpl.regina.sk.ca; Web: www.dunlopartgallery.org; *Dir & Cur* Jennifer Matotek; *Cur Asst* Blair Fornwald; *Registrar* Eric Hill
Open Mon - Thurs 9:30 AM - 9 PM, Fri 9:30 AM - 6 PM, Sat 9:30 AM - 5 PM, Sun 1:30 - 5 PM, cl holidays; No admis fee; Estab 1949 to research practices & histories with visual culture, with emphasis on relationships between cultural production & social context; to present results of research in an informative & publicly accessible format including exhibitions, screenings, lectures, programs, publications & extension programs; to promote the Gallery's purpose scope & programs to the public; to communicate, consult & cooperate with individuals, groups & organizations having similar objectives; to collect research catalog & preserve works of contemporary & historical significance for the people of Regina & Saskatchewan; to acquire & maintain works of contemporary art for circulation through art rental service; Circ 110,897; 122 seat film theater with stage, preview room, meeting rooms, library van, woodworking shop, collections & services of the Regina library. Maintains art research resource centre; Average Annual Attendance: 100,000
Income: Financed by city appropriation, provincial & federal grants
Purchases: $10,000
Library Holdings: Book Volumes, Exhibition Catalogs, Original Documents, Pamphlets, Periodical Subscriptions, Slides, Video Tapes
Special Subjects: American Indian Art, Crafts, Folk Art, Landscapes, Painting-Canadian, Photography, Sculpture
Collections: Permanent collection of Saskatchewan art, Inglis Sheldon-Williams Collection, 205 works of historical & contemporary art including paintings, sculpture & graphic art by Saskatchewan artists, Feminism & Contemporary Visual Art, Popular Culture & Contemporary Visual Art, Art Rental Collection: 226 works of historical & contemporary paintings & graphic art by Canadian artists
Exhibitions: 15 exhibitions per year
Publications: At the Dunlop Newsletter, quarterly; brochures; exhibition catalogs
Activities: Docent training; gallery facilitators available to discuss exhibitions with members of public individually; lects open to pub, 6 vis lectrs per yr; gallery talks; tours; competitions; individual paintings & original objects of art lent to Regina Pub Library card holders through an art rental coll available to the pub & works from permanent coll lent to other galleries; lending coll contains original art works, original prints & drawings; book traveling exhibs; originate traveling exhibs to galleries & museums with acceptable museum standards; sales shop sells books, magazines, cards, catalogues, posters & exhibition catalogues

M **UNIVERSITY OF REGINA,** MacKenzie Art Gallery, 3475 Albert St, Regina, SK S4S 6X6 Canada. Tel 306-584-4250; Fax 306-569-8191; Email info@mackenzieartgallery.ca; Web: www.mackenzieartgallery.ca; *Head Cur* TImothy Long; *Dir Finance & Opers* Jackie Lindenbach
Open Mon Wed Fri & Sat 10 AM - 5:30 PM, Thurs - Fri 10 AM - 9 PM, Sun 12 - 5:30 PM; No admis fee; Estab 1953 to preserve & expand the coll left to the gallery by Norman MacKenzie & to offer exhibs to the city of Regina; to offer works of art to rural areas through the Outreach Prog; Eight discreet galleries totaling approx 1500 running ft of exhibition space; Average Annual Attendance: 100,000; Mem: 1079; dues $35; annual meeting in June
Income: $1,000,000 (financed by federal & provincial governments, University of Regina & city of Regina & private funds)
Special Subjects: Oriental Art
Collections: Contemporary Canadian & American work, contemporary Saskatchewan work, 19th & early 20th century works on paper, a part of the collection is early 20th century replicas of Eastern & Oriental artifacts & art
Exhibitions: Changing exhibitions from the permanent collection & traveling exhibitions
Publications: Exhibition catalogues; staff publications of a professional nature; Vista, quarterly
Activities: Docent training; community prog of touring exhibs in Saskatchewan; interpretive progs; school tours; lects open to pub, 8-10 vis lectrs per yr; concerts; gallery talks; tours; films; exten dept serves entire province of Saskatchewan; originate traveling exhibs nation-wide; gallery shop sells books, magazines, reproductions, cards & catalogues

L **MacKenzie Art Gallery Resource Centre**, 3475 Albert St, Regina, SK S4S 6X6 Canada. Tel 306-522-4242; Fax 306-569-8191
Open Mon, Tues, Fri, Sat & Sun 11 AM - 7 PM, Wed & Thurs 11 AM - 10 PM; Estab 1970 to offer the community a resource for art information, both historical & current; For reference only
Collections: Regional press clippings from 1925
Exhibitions: Between Abstraction & Representation, George Glenn; Jana Sterbak; Jan Gerrit Wyels 1888-1973; The Asymmetric Vision; Philosophical Intuition & Original Experience in the Art of Yves Gaucher; Peace Able Kingdom, Jack Severson; Artists With Their Work; Ryan Arnott; Grant McConnell; Memory in Place
Publications: Exhibition catalog
Activities: Film program, twice a month

L **Visual Resource Center**, Fine Arts Dept, Regina, SK S4S 0A2 Canada. Tel 306-585-5579; Fax 306-585-5744; Email finearts@max.cc.uregina.ca; *Cur* Pat Matheson
Estab for the instruction of art history
Library Holdings: Audio Tapes, Slides 90,000, Video Tapes
Collections: Prehistoric - contemporary, eastern & western art

L **Education/Fine Arts Library**, Univ of Regina Library, Regina, SK S4S 0A2 Canada; 3737 Wascana Pkwy, Regina, SK S45 OA2 Canada. Tel 306-585-5123; Fax 306-585-5115; *Vis Arts Librn* Donna Bowman; *Music Librn & Film Librn* Gillian Nowlan; *Theatre Librn* Larry McDonald
Open (semester) Mon - Thurs 8 AM - 11 PM, Fri & Sat 8 AM - 7:30 PM, Sun 8 AM - 11 PM; Education and Fine Arts Library amalgamated with main library in 2005; For both lending & reference
Library Holdings: Audio Tapes, Book Volumes 18,000, Cassettes, Clipping Files, Compact Disks, Exhibition Catalogs, Fiche, Pamphlets, Periodical Subscriptions 55, Records, Reels, Video Tapes

SASKATOON

M **AKA ARTIST RUN CENTRE,** 424 20th St W, Saskatoon, SK S7M OX4 Canada. Tel 306-652-0044; Fax 306-652-0534; Email gallerycoordinator@akaartistrun.com; Web: www.akaartistrun.com; *Exec Dir* Tarin Hughes; *Gallery Coord* Derek Sandbeck
Open Tues - Fri Noon - 6 PM, Sat noon - 4 PM; No admis fee; Estab 1970, incorporated 1973 to encourage the development of photography as a creative visual art; Main gallery is 650 sq ft, & workshop gallery is 250 sq ft; Average Annual Attendance: 8,000; Mem: 100; dues $25; annual meeting first Sun in May
Income: $196,000 (financed by mem, province appropriation, federal grants & fundraising)
Special Subjects: Photography
Collections: Permanent Collection of 901 Contemporary Canadian photographs
Exhibitions: 7 main gallery exhibitions per year; 7 workshop gallery exhibitions per year
Publications: Backflash, quarterly magazine; members monthly newsletter
Activities: Classes for adults; lects open to pub, 12 vis lectrs per yr; tours; exten dept; workshops throughout the province; portable darkrooms travel with instructors; book traveling exhibs; originate traveling exhibs to pub galleries in Canada; sales shop sells books, postcards, t-shirts

L **Library**, 424 20th St W, Saskatoon, SK S7M 0X4 Canada. Tel 306-244-8018; Fax 306-665-6568; *Program Coordr* Cindy Baker; *Admin Coordr* Troy Gronsdahl
Open Mon - Sat Noon - 5 PM; No admis fee; Estab 1970; Circ Non-circulating; For references mem only
Library Holdings: Audio Tapes, Book Volumes 1500, Cassettes, Clipping Files, Exhibition Catalogs, Manuscripts, Pamphlets, Periodical Subscriptions 10, Reproductions, Slides

M **REMAI MODERN,** 950 Spadina Crescent E, Saskatoon, SK S7K 3L Canada; PO Box 569, Saskatoon, SK S7K 3L6 Canada. Tel 306-975-7610; Fax 306-975-7670; Email info@remaimodern.org; Web: remaimodern.org; *Exec Dir & CEO* Gregory Burke; *Chief Cur* Sandra Guimaraes; *Cur Colls* Sandra Fraser
Open daily 9 AM - 9 PM, cl Christmas Day; No admis fee; Estab 1964 to exhibit, preserve, collect & interpret works of art; to encourage the development of the visual arts in Saskatoon; to provide the opportunity for citizens to enjoy & understand & to gain a greater appreciation of the fine arts; Average Annual Attendance: 200,000; Mem: 700; dues Artist $25; Student $25; Senior $30; Individual $50; Family $60; Not-for-Profit $75; Corporate $500
Income: $2,000,000 (financed by grants, gift shop, mem, donations & other sources)
Special Subjects: Painting-American, Painting-Canadian, Photography, Portraits, Prints, Religious Art
Collections: Regional, National and International Art
Publications: Exhibition catalogues; Folio, gallery newsmagazine
Activities: Classes for adults & children; gallery theatre; dramatic progs; lects open to pub; gallery talks; tours; exten dept; individual paintings & original objects of art lent to other galleries; lending collection contains 7000 artworks; originate traveling exhibs; gallery shop sells books, magazines, original Inuit art, reproductions, prints & craft items, all with an emphasis on Canadian handcrafts

A **SASKATCHEWAN ASSOCIATION OF ARCHITECTS,** 200-642 Broadway Ave, Saskatoon, SK S7N 1A9 Canada. Tel 306-242-0733; Fax 306-664-2598; Email saskarchitects@sasktel.net; Web: www.saskarchitects.com; *Exec Dir* Janelle Unrau; *Mem Services Coordr* Annette Horvath
Open 9 AM - 5 PM weekdays; Estab 1911 to support member architects; Average Annual Attendance: 300; Mem: 111; dues $670; annual meeting in Feb-May; must be registered architect
Income: Financed by mem
Library Holdings: Book Volumes, CD-ROMs
Collections: Books 40's - 70's
Publications: E-newsletter
Activities: Docent training; continuing educ for members; prize given to architectural technology student at Saskatchewan Technical Institute, Moose Jaw (4 twice a year)

M **SASKATCHEWAN CRAFT COUNCIL & AFFINITY GALLERY,** 813 Broadway Ave, Saskatoon, SK S7N 1B5 Canada. Tel 306-653-3616; Fax 306-244-2711; Email saskcraftcouncil@sasktel.net; Web: www.saskcraftcouncil.org; *Exec Dir* Sherry Luther; *Mem Svcs Coordr* Amanda Bosiak; *Exhib & Educ Coordr* Leslie Potter; *Exhib & Educ Coordr* Stephanie Canning; *Admin Asst* Donna Potter; *Communs Coordr* Vivian Orr; *Bookkeeper* Lesley Sutherland
Open Mon-Sat 10 AM - 5 PM, late Thurs until 8 PM; No admis fee; Estab 1975 to support, promote, exhibit & develop excellence in Saskatchewan craft; 900 sq ft; Average Annual Attendance: 25,000; Mem: 420; dues $100; annual meeting in May
Income: $429,000 (financed by mem, city appropriation, provincial grants)
Exhibitions: 8 exhibitions yearly

Activities: Lects open to pub, 8 vis lectrs per yr; gallery talks; tours; open juried competition with award for Saskatchewan residents; book traveling exhibs 2 per yr; originate traveling exhibs to provincial galleries; sales shop sells original fine craft art

M **UNIVERSITY OF SASKATCHEWAN,** Gordon Snelgrove Art Gallery, 3 Campus Dr, Rm 191, Murray Bldg Saskatoon, SK S7N 5A4 Canada. Tel 306-966-4208; Fax 306-966-4266; Email gordon.snelgrove@usask.ca; Web: www.usask.ca/snelgrove; *Dir* Marcus Miller
Open Mon - Fri 9:30 AM - 4:30 PM; No admis fee; Estab approx 1960 for the educ of students & local pub; Gallery covers approx 3000 sq ft of floor space, 300 running ft of wall space; Average Annual Attendance: 12,000
Income: Financed by provincial & federal government appropriations & university funds
Collections: Contemporary art from western & midwestern Canada
Exhibitions: Constantly changing exhibitions of art works; internationally organized & traveling shows
Publications: Show announcements, every three weeks; catalogues for selected exhibits
Activities: Lects open to pub, 10 vis lectrs per yr; gallery talks; tours; individual paintings & original objects of art lent to recognized regional exhibs centres for one time presentation or tour; lending collection contains 150 original art works

M **Diefenbaker Canada Centre**, 101 Diefenbaker Pl, Saskatoon, SK S7N 5B8 Canada. Tel 306-966-8384; Fax 306-966-1967; Email dief.centre@usask.ca; Web: www.usask.ca/diefenbaker; *Archivist* Rob Paul; *Office & Progs Mgr* Temesa Ann DeMong; *Acting Dir* M Teresa Carlson
Open Mon - Wed & Fri, 9:30 AM - 4:30 PM, Thurs 9:30 AM - 8 PM, Sat - Sun & Holidays 12 PM 4:30 PM; Admis adults $5, students, seniors & children $3, family $12.50; Estab 1980 to explore Canada's evolution with its citizens & their visitors. Its focus is Canada's citizenship, leadership & the country's international role; 2,000 sq ft gallery with complete environmental controls; Average Annual Attendance: 15,000
Income: Financed by pub foundations, donations & endowments
Library Holdings: Audio Tapes, Book Volumes, Cards, Cassettes, Clipping Files, Fiche, Framed Reproductions, Manuscripts, Maps, Memorabilia, Original Art Works, Original Documents, Pamphlets, Periodical Subscriptions, Photographs, Prints, Records, Reels, Reproductions, Sculpture, Slides, Video Tapes
Special Subjects: Coins & Medals, Costumes, Crafts, Decorative Arts, Dioramas, Dolls, Drawings, Eskimo Art, Etchings & Engravings, Furniture, Glass, Historical Material, Jewelry, Landscapes, Leather, Manuscripts, Maps, Painting-Canadian, Period Rooms, Pewter, Photography, Portraits, Posters, Prints, Reproductions, Sculpture, Silver, Textiles, Watercolors
Collections: Priministal papers of the Right Honourable J G Diefenbaker & related papers, John G Diefenbaker Memorabilia & Archives
Exhibitions: Canadian Politics focuses upon the country during the 10th decade of the Confederacy; international & national regional travel exhibits; Prime Ministers office & the Canadian Cabinet room
Publications: The Diefenbaker Legacy, 1998
Activities: Study of modern Canadian history; reference service; classes for children; curriculum-based programs on Canadian law, politics & government; Conferences; seminars; pub events; 5 vis lectrs per yr; gallery talks; tours; book traveling exhibs, 30 plus per yr; originate traveling exhibs provincially; retail store sells books, prints, slides, jewelry, scarves, gifts, souvenirs

ST. WALBURG

M **IMHOFF ART GALLERY,** 8km S of St. Walburg off Hwy 26 (E entry) St. Walburg, SK S0M 2T0 Canada; P O Box 313 St. Walburg, SK S0M 2T0 Canada. Tel 306-248-3812; Fax 306-825-9070; Email imhoffstudio@littleloon.ca; *Cur* Barbara McKeand
Open June - Sep daily 10 AM - 5 PM; Admis adults $8 (18+), students $5, children under 5 no charge; Estab to exhibit 200 paintings done by Berthold Imhoff, who died in 1939; 1 large gallery
Income: Financed by municipal and provincial appropriations
Exhibitions: Rotating exhibits

SWIFT CURRENT

M **ART GALLERY OF SWIFT CURRENT,** 411 Herbert St E, Swift Current, SK S9H 1M5 Canada. Tel 306-778-2736; Fax 306-773-8769; Web: www.artgalleryofswiftcurrent.org; *Dir & Cur* Kim Houghtaling
Open Mon - Wed 1 PM - 5 PM & 7 PM - 9 PM, Thur - Sun 1 PM - 5 PM; No admis fee; Estab 1974 to exhibit temporary art exhibitions; 1876 sq ft; Average Annual Attendance: 18,000
Income: $120,000 (financed by city & provincial appropriation & federal grant)
Special Subjects: Painting-Canadian
Exhibitions: Nine temporary exhibitions per year featuring Provincial, national & international artists
Activities: Classes for adults & children; gallery talks; art classes - various mediums; book traveling exhibs occasionally 1 per yr; originate traveling exhibs

WEYBURN

M **WEYBURN ARTS COUNCIL,** Allie Griffin Art Gallery, 45 Bison Ave, Weyburn, SK S4H 0H9 Canada; 424 10th Ave SE, Weyburn, SK S4H 2AI Canada. Tel 306-848-3922; Fax 306-848-3271; Email weyburnartscouncil@weyburn.ca; Web: www.weyburnartscouncil.ca; *Cur* Regan Lanning
Open Mon - Thurs 9:30 AM - 8:30 PM, Fri & Sat 9:30 AM - 6 PM, Sun (Oct - May) 1 PM - 5 PM (cl Sun July thru Aug); No admis fee; Estab 1964 to showcase art & craft work by Weyburn artists, Saskatchewan artists from various large & small communities, nationally known artists & artisans as well as international exhibitions on tour from lending galleries; Public art gallery displaying Saskatchewan art; Average Annual Attendance: 5,000
Collections: City of Weyburn Permanent Collection, incl Courtney Milne: Visions of the Goddess
Exhibitions: Exhibits works from the Weyburn permanent collection at regular intervals throughout each year; Exhibs supplied by lending galleries from across Saskatchewan
Activities: James Weir People's Choice Award given annually; ann adjudicated exhib; book 6 traveling exhibs; originates traveling exhibs to Saskatchewan OSAC mems

YUKON

DAWSON CITY

M **DAWSON CITY MUSEUM,** 595 Fifth Ave, Dawson City, YT Y0B 1G0 Canada; PO Box 303, Dawson City, YT Y0B 1G0 Canada. Tel 867-993-5291; Fax 867-993-5839; Email info@dawsonmuseum.ca; Web: www.dawsonmuseum.ca; *Exec Dir* Alex Somerville; *Admissions & Gift Shop Mgr* Linda Thompson; *Project Cur* Angharad Wenz
Open May - Labour Day daily 10 AM - 6 PM; Labour Day - Sept 30 Tues - Sat 10 AM - 2 PM, Oct - Mid May by appointment; Admis families $18, adult $9, sr citizens & students $7, pre-booked tours $5 per person; Estab 1959 to collect, preserve & interpret the history of the Dawson City area; Two long term, two changing exhibition spaces featuring Dawson & Klondike gold fields; Average Annual Attendance: 20,000; Mem: 170; dues $30-$1000; annual meeting in Apr
Income: $300,000 (financed by mem, state appropriation, grants)
Special Subjects: Coins & Medals, Ethnology, Furniture, Glass, Scrimshaw
Collections: 30,000 piece coll including archives, cultural, ethnographic, household, industrial, paleontology, photographs, Industrial & Domestic Artifacts, Local history of Klondike region art & exhibits
Exhibitions: Gold Rush; Railway; natural history; mining; Han People
Publications: Newsletter, quarterly
Activities: Docent progs; lects open to pub, 10 vis lectrs per yr; book traveling exhibs; originate traveling exhibs 2 per yr; mus shop sells books, original art, jewelry & souvenirs

L **Klondike History Library**, PO Box 303, Dawson City, YT Y0B 1G0 Canada; 595 Fifth Ave, Dawson City, YT Y0B 1G0 Canada. Tel 867-993-5291; Fax 867-993-5839; Email info@dawsonmuseum.ca; Web: www.dawsonmuseum.ca
Open Mid - May to Mid - Sept 10 AM - 6 PM, other by appointment only; Admis family $18, adults $9, seniors & students $7, pre-booked tours $5 per person; Estab 1959; Museum; Average Annual Attendance: 20,000; Mem: 145
Income: Financed by earned income & government grants
Library Holdings: Book Volumes 3500, Cassettes, Clipping Files, Lantern Slides, Photographs, Slides
Special Subjects: Furniture, Glass, Gold, Historical Material, Industrial Design, Manuscripts, Maps, Mixed Media, Photography, Restoration & Conservation, Scrimshaw
Collections: Klondike & Gold Rush History
Activities: Docent training; 7 lects per yr; tours; mus shop sells work of Yukon artisans, books & souvenirs

WHITEHORSE

M **YUKON ARTS CENTRE GALLERY,** 300 College Dr, Whitehorse, YT Y1A 5X9 Canada; PO 16, Whitehorse, YT Y1A 5X9 Canada. Tel 867-667-8575; Web: www.yukonartscentre.com; *Chief Exec Officer* Al Cushing
Open year round, weekdays: 10 AM - 5 PM, Weekends: Sep -May 12 - 5 PM, June - Aug noon - 5 PM, third Thurs of month 11 AM - 9 PM, cl Statutory Holidays during winter; No admis fee, donations accepted; Gallery is comprised of a 4200 square foot exhibition space, focusing on Contemporary Canadian Art

A **YUKON HISTORICAL & MUSEUMS ASSOCIATION,** 3126 3rd Ave, Whitehorse, YT Y1A 1E7 Canada. Tel 867-667-4704; Email info@heritageyukon.ca; Web: heritageyukon.ca; *Pres* Sally Robinson
Open Mon - Fri 9AM - 5 PM; No admis fee; Estab 1977 as a national organization to preserve & interpret history; Mem: 100; dues individual $25, annual meeting in May
Income: Financed by mem, donations & fundraising
Special Subjects: Historical Material, Maps
Publications: Newsletters, tour booklet, Yukon Exploration by G Dawson
Activities: Lects open to pub, 4 or more vis lectrs per yr; tours; competitions with awards; lending collection contains books, photographs, audio equipment (oral history taping); originate traveling photo exhibs to Yukon communities; sales shop sells books, t-shirts, prints, heritage pins & reproductions of old Canadian expedition maps

II ART SCHOOLS

Arrangement and Abbreviations
Key to Art Schools

ARRANGEMENT OF DATA

Name and Address of institution; telephone number, including area code.
Names and titles of key personnel.
Hours open; admission fees; date established and purpose; average annual attendance; membership.
Annual figures on income and purchases.
Collections with enlarging collections indicated.
Exhibitions.
Activities sponsored, including classes for adults and children, dramatic programs and docent training; lectures, concerts, gallery talks and tours; competitions, awards, scholarships and fellowships; lending programs; museum or sales shops.
Libraries also list number of book volumes, periodical subscriptions, and audiovisual and micro holdings; subject covered by name of special collections.

ABBREVIATIONS AND SYMBOLS

Acad—Academic
Admin—Administration, Administrative
Adminr—Administrator
Admis—Admission
A-tapes—Audio-tapes
Adv—Advisory
AM—Morning
Ann—Annual
Approx—Approximate, Approximately
Asn—Association
Assoc—Associate
Asst—Assistant
AV—Audiovisual
Ave—Avenue
Bldg—Building
Blvd—Boulevard
Bro—Brother
C—circa
Cert—Certificate
Chap—Chapter
Chmn—Chairman
Circ—Circulation
Cl—Closed
Col— College
Coll—Collection
Comt—Committee
Coordr—Coordinator
Corresp—Corresponding
Cr—Credit
Cur—Curator
D—Day
Den—Denominational
Dept—Department
Develop—Development
Dipl—Diploma
Dir—Director
Dist—District
Div—Division
Dorm—Dormitory
Dr—Doctor, Drive
E—East, Evening
Ed—Editor
Educ—Education
Elec Mail—Electronic Mail
Enrol—Enrollment
Ent—Entrance
Ent Req—Entrance Requirements
Est, Estab—Established
Exec—Executive
Exhib—Exhibition
Exten—Extension
Fel(s)—Fellowships
Fri—Friday
Fs—Filmstrips
Ft—Feet
FT—Full Time Instructor
GC—Graduate Course
Gen—General
Grad—Graduate
Hon—Honorary
Hr—Hour
HS—High School
Hwy—Highway
Inc—Incorporated
Incl—Including
Jr—Junior
Lect—Lecture(s)
Lectr—Lecturer
Librn—Librarian
M—Men
Maj—Major in Art
Mem—Membership
Mgr—Manager
Mon—Monday
Mss—Manuscripts
Mus—Museums
N—North
Nat—National
Nonres—Nonresident
Per subs—Periodical subscriptions
PM—Afternoon
Pres—President
Prin—Principal
Prof—Professor
Prog—Program
PT—Part Time Instructor
Pts—Points
Pub—Public
Publ—Publication
Publr—Publisher
Pvt—Private
Qtr—Quarter
Rd—Road
Rec—Records
Reg—Registration
Req—Requirements
Res—Residence, Resident
S—South
Sat—Saturday
Schol—Scholarship
Secy—Secretary
Sem—Semeseter
Soc—Society
Sq—Square
Sr—Senior, Sister
St—Street
Ste—Suite
Sun—Sunday
Supt—Superintendent
Supv—Supervisor
Thurs—Thursday
Treas—Treasurer
Tues—Tuesday
Tui—Tuition
TV—Television
Undergrad—Undergraduate
Univ—University
Vis—Visiting
Vol—Volunteer
Vols—Volumes
VPres—Vice President
V-tapes—Videotapes
Vols—Volumes
W—West, Women
Wed—Wednesday
Wk—Week
Yr—Year(s)

† Major offered
A Association
C Corporate Art Holding
L Library
M Museum
O Organization

U.S. Art Schools

ALABAMA

AUBURN

AUBURN UNIVERSITY, Dept of Art & Art History, 108 Biggin Hall, Auburn, AL 36849-5125. Tel 334-844-4373; Fax 334-844-4024; Email art@auburn.edu; Web: www.auburn.edu/art; *Chair & Prof* Allyson Comstock
Estab 1928; Maintain nonprofit art gallery; Biggin Gallery, 101 Biggin Hall, Auburn; Fieldwork Projects, 420 S. Gray St, Auburn; pub; D & E; Scholarships; 457 maj & non-maj
Ent Req: HS dipl, ACT, SAT
Degrees: BFA 4 yr, BA 4 yr
Courses: †Art History, †Ceramics, †Drawing, †Illustration, †Painting, †Printmaking, †Sculpture
Summer School: Complete 10 wk program

BAY MINETTE

JAMES H FAULKNER COMMUNITY COLLEGE, Art Dept, 1900 US Hwy 31 S, Bay Minette, AL 36507. Tel 334-937-9581; Web: www.faulkner.cc.ai.us; *Div Chmn of Art* Walter Allen, MFA
Estab 1965; FT 2; pub; D & E; Scholarships; SC 4, LC 3; D 35, E 40, non-maj 57, maj 18
Ent Req: HS dipl
Degrees: AA 2 yrs
Tuition: Res—undergrad $63 per cr hr; nonres $115 per cr hr; campus res—room & board $1428
Courses: †Art History, †Commercial Design, †Drawing, History of Art & Architecture, †Painting, †Printmaking, †Sculpture
Summer School: Dir, Milton Jackson. Courses—Art Appreciation

BIRMINGHAM

BIRMINGHAM-SOUTHERN COLLEGE, Art & Art History, 900 Arkadelphia Rd, Birmingham, AL 35254-0002; PO Box 549021, Birmingham, AL 35254-0002. Tel 205-226-4928; Fax 205-226-3044; Email jpandeli@bsc.edu; Web: www.bsc.edu; *Art Chair Prof* Pamela Venz; *Prof* Steve Cole; *Art Chair Prof* Jim Neel; *Assoc Prof* Kathleen Spies; *Asst Prof* Timothy B Smith; *Asst Prof* Kevin Shook; *Art Instr* Cooper Spivey; *Office Mgr* Judy E Pandelis
Estab 1946; Art supplies may be purchased at BSC bookstore; FT 5; pvt; D, E; Scholarships; Financial aid; SC 22, LC 8, interim term courses of 4 or 8 wk, 4 req of each student in 4 yr period; 500, maj 50
Ent Req: HS dipl, ACT, SAT scores, C average
Degrees: AB, BS, BFA, BM and BME 4 yr
Courses: Aesthetics, Art Appreciation, Art Education, Art History, Collage, Constructions, Design, Drawing, Film, Graphic Design, History of Art & Architecture, Mixed Media, Painting, Photography, Printmaking, Sculpture, Video
Adult Hobby Classes: Enrl 30; 8 wk term. Courses—Art History, Basic Drawing, Basic Painting
Children's Classes: Enrl approx 20. Laboratory for training teachers
Summer School: Enrl 100; 8 wk beginning June 11 & Aug 10. Courses—Art History, Design, Drawing, Painting, Sculpture

SAMFORD UNIVERSITY, Art Dept, 800 Lakeshore Dr, Birmingham, AL 35229-0002. Tel 205-726-2840; Email lcvann@samford.edu; Web: www.samford.edu; *Chmn* Dr Robin D Snyder
Estab 1841; maintain nonprofit art gallery; FT 4, PT 11; pvt; D; Scholarships; SC 24, LC 4
Ent Req: HS dipl, ent exam, ACT, SAT
Degrees: BA & BS 4 yrs
Courses: Advertising Design, Ceramics, Commercial Art, Costume Design & Construction, Drawing, †Fine Arts, Graphic Arts, †Graphic Design, Handicrafts, History of Art & Architecture, Interior Design, Painting, Photography, Sculpture, Stage Design, Teacher Training, Theatre Arts
Summer School: Dir, Lowell Vann. Enrl 30, 2 five week terms. Courses—Appreciation, Studio Arts

UNIVERSITY OF ALABAMA AT BIRMINGHAM, Dept of Art & Art History, Abroms-Engel Institute for the Arts, 1121 10th Ave S Birmingham, AL 35228; AEIVA 211, 1720 2nd Ave S Birmingham, AL 35294-1264. Tel 205-975-6267; Fax 205-975-2836; Web: www.uab.edu/art, www.uab.edu/aeiva; *Prof* Sonja Rieger, MFA; *Prof* James Alexander, MFA; *Prof* Heather McPherson, MFA, PhD; *Prof* Gary Chapman, MFA; *Asst Prof* Noa Turel, PhD; *Assoc Prof & Chmn* Lauren Lake, MFA; *Assoc Prof* Derek Cracco, MFA; *Assoc Prof* Jessica Dallow, PhD; *Prof* Erin Wright, MFA; *Asst* Doug Baulos, MFA; *Asst Prof* Elisabeth Pellathy; *Asst Prof* Doug Barrett; *Assoc Prof* Cathleen Cummings
Estab 1966, dept estab 1974; Maintain nonprofit art gallery, Abroms-Engel Inst for the Visual Arts, Birmingham, AL; pub; D & E; Scholarships; Fellowships; SC 35, LC 16, GC; D 500, E 300, non-maj 250, maj 210, grad 12
Ent Req: HS dipl, ACT, SAT
Degrees: BA, BFA, MA Art History
Courses: Aesthetics, Art Appreciation, Art Education, Art History, †Art Studio, Ceramics, Conceptual Art, Design, Drawing, Film, Graphic Arts, Graphic Design, Illustration, Mixed Media, Painting, Photography, Printmaking, Sculpture, Video
Summer School: Courses—Range over all fields & are about one half regular offerings

BREWTON

JEFFERSON DAVIS COMMUNITY COLLEGE, Art Dept, PO Box 958, Brewton, AL 36427; 220 Alco Dr, Brewton, AL 36426-2716. Tel 334-867-4832; Fax 334-867-7399; Email slaing@acet.net; Web: www.jeffdavis.cc.al.us/; *Instr* Sue Laing
Estab 1965; pub; D & E; SC 10, LC 1; D 700, E 332, maj 20
Ent Req: HS dipl or equiv
Degrees: AA & AS
Courses: Art Appreciation, Art History, Basic Design, Ceramics, Drawing, Introduction to Art, Painting, Photography
Summer School: Dir, Sue Laing. Enrl 200. Courses—Ceramics, Drawing, Introduction to Art, Art Appreciation

FLORENCE

UNIVERSITY OF NORTH ALABAMA, Dept of Art, UNA Box 5006, Florence, AL 35632-0001. Tel 256-765-4384; Fax 256-765-4511; Email cchen@una.edu; Web: www.una.edu; *Prof* Fred Owen Hensley, MFA; *Assoc Prof* Dr Suzanne D Zurinsky, PhD; *Prof* John D Turner, MFA; *Prof* Ronald L Shady, MFA; *Prof* Wayne Sides, MFA; *Prof* Chiong-Yiao Chen, MFA; *Asst Prof* Lisa Kirch, PhD; *Asst Prof* Nanhee Kim, MFA
Estab 1830, dept estab approx 1930; Maintain nonprofit art gallery; Univ Art Gallery, Box 5006, Univ N Ala; on-campus shop sells art supplies; FT 8; pub; D; Scholarships; SC 34, LC 10, GC 1; D 7250, non-maj 500, maj 150
Ent Req: HS dipl, or GED, ACT
Degrees: BFA, BS & BA 4 yr
Courses: Art Appreciation, Art Education, Art History, †Ceramics, Design, †Digital Media, Drawing, †Painting, †Photography, Printmaking, †Sculpture
Summer School: Dir, Chiong-Yiao Chen. Enrl 90; tuition $1764 for 8 wk term beginning June 8. Courses—Art Appreciation, Digital Media, Painting, Ceramics, Photography, Art History

HUNTSVILLE

UNIVERSITY OF ALABAMA IN HUNTSVILLE, Dept of Art and Art History, Roberts Hall, Rm 313, Huntsville, AL 35899. Tel 256-824-6114; Fax 256-824-6438; Email art@email.uah.edu; Web: uah.edu/html/academics/libarts/art; *Prof* David Stewart, MFA, PhD; *Asst Prof* Lillian Joyce, PhD; *Asst Prof* Keith Jones, MFA; *Temp Asst Prof* Susan Truman-McGlohon, MFA; *Chmn Art & Art History Dept* Michael Crouse, MFA; *Prof* Glenn Dasher, MFA
Estab 1969 (as independent, autonomous campus), dept estab 1965; pub; D & E; Scholarships; SC 46, LC 14; D 150
Ent Req: HS dipl, ACT
Degrees: BA 4 yr
Courses: †Art History, †Art Studio, Graphic Design, Painting, Photography, Sculpture
Adult Hobby Classes: Tuition $411 per 3 hr course. Courses—Computer Graphics, other miscellaneous workshops offered through Div of Continuous Educ
Summer School: Limited number of courses offered in a two 6 wk mini-terms

JACKSONVILLE

JACKSONVILLE STATE UNIVERSITY, Art Dept, 700 Pelham Rd N, Jacksonville, AL 36265-1623. Tel 256-782-5626; Fax 256-782-5419; Email art@jsucc.jsu.edu; *Head* Charles Groover, MFA
Estab 1883; pub; D & E; Scholarships; SC 22, LC 8, GC 4; D 8000, E 24, non-maj 70, maj 170, grad 11, others 15
Ent Req: HS dipl, ACT
Degrees: BFA, BA 4 yr

Courses: Art Appreciation, Art History, Calligraphy, Ceramics, Commercial Art, Drawing, Graphic Arts, Graphic Design, History of Art & Architecture, Painting, Photography, Printmaking, Sculpture

LIVINGSTON

UNIVERSITY OF WEST ALABAMA, Division of Fine Arts, Sta 10, Livingston, AL 35470. Tel 205-652-3400 (main), 652-3510 (arts); Fax 205-652-3405; Web: www.uwa.edu; *Chmn* Jason Guynes
Estab 1835; Maintain nonprofit gallery; pub; D; Scholarships; 1800
Degrees: BA, BS, BMus, MEd, MSc
Courses: Art Appreciation, †Ceramics, †Design, Design, Drawing, †Introduction to Art
Summer School: Chmn, Jason Guynes. Courses—Introduction to Art

MARION

JUDSON COLLEGE, Division of Fine and Performing Arts, 302 Bibb St, Marion, AL 36756. Tel 800-447-9472; Fax 334-683-5147; Email twhisenhunt@judson.edu; Web: www.judson.edu; *Dept Head* Jamie Adams
Estab 1838; Maintain nonprofit art gallery; pvt, den, W; D & E; Scholarships; Grants; Loans; SC 23, LC 6; 450
Ent Req: HS grad, adequate HS grades & ACT scores
Degrees: BA 3-4 yr
Tuition: $3500 per sem
Courses: Commercial Art, Design, Drawing, Elementary Art, Painting, Perspective Drafting, Pottery, Sculpture, Special Courses
Adult Hobby Classes: Enrl 5. Courses—Painting, Studio Drawing
Children's Classes: Drawing, Painting
Summer School: Head Art Dept, Ted Whisenhunt. Courses vary

MOBILE

SPRING HILL COLLEGE, Department of Fine & Performing Arts, 4000 Dauphin St, Mobile, AL 36608-1780. Tel 251-380-3861; Fax 334-460-2110; Web: www.shc.edu; *Chmn* Stephen Campbell, SJ; *Prof, Chmn Communs Div* Thomas Loehr, MFA; *Prof* Ruth Belasco, MFA
Estab 1830, dept estab 1965; den; D & E; SC 21, LC 3; D 163, non-maj 128, maj 35
Ent Req: HS dipl, ACT, CEEB, SAT
Degrees: BA
Courses: Advertising Design, Aesthetics, Art Appreciation, †Art Business, Art Education, Art History, Ceramics, Commercial Art, Costume Design & Construction, Design, Drawing, †Studio Art, Textile Printing, †Therapy
Adult Hobby Classes: Enrl 15. Courses—wide variety
Summer School: Enrl 15. Courses—wide variety

UNIVERSITY OF SOUTH ALABAMA, Dept of Art & Art History, 172 Visual Arts Bldg, Mobile, AL 36688-0002. Tel 334-460-6335; Fax 334-414-8294; Web: www.southalabama.edu/art/; *Chmn & Graphic Design* Larry Simpson; *Printmaker* Sumi Putman; *Art Historian* Robert Bantens; *Art Historian* Janice Gandy; *Art Historian* Philippe Oszuscik; *Sculptor* Pieter Favier; *Graphic Design* Patrick Miller
Estab 1963, dept estab 1964; pub; D & E; SC 32, LC 25; maj & 150
Ent Req: HS dipl, ACT
Degrees: BA, BFA and BA(Art History) 4 yrs
Courses: Art Appreciation, †Art History, †Ceramics, Design, Drawing, †Graphic Design, History of Art & Architecture, Illustration, Mixed Media, †Painting, Photography, †Printmaking, †Sculpture
Summer School: Chmn, Larry Simpson. Courses—Art Appreciation, Art History, Ceramics, Drawing, Graphic Design, Painting

MONROEVILLE

ALABAMA SOUTHERN COMMUNITY COLLEGE, Art Dept, PO Box 2000, Monroeville, AL 36461-2000. Tel 334-575-3156; Email sbrown@ascc.edu; Web: www.ascc.edu; *Chmn* Dr Margaret H Murphy
Sch estab 1965, dept estab 1971; pub; D & E; SC 6, LC 1; D 25, E 8, non-maj 23, maj 3
Ent Req: HS dipl, GED
Degrees: AA & AS 2 yrs
Tuition: In state—$60 per cr; out of state—$104
Courses: Art Appreciation, Drafting, †Drawing, †Painting, Stage Design, Theatre Arts

MONTEVALLO

UNIVERSITY OF MONTEVALLO, College of Fine Arts, Station 6400, Dept of Art Montevallo, AL 35115. Tel 205-665-6400; Fax 205-665-6383; Email stephens@montevallo.edu; Web: www.montevallo.edu; *Dean* Steven Peters; *Chmn* Scott Stephens
Estab 1896; Maintain nonprofit art gallery, Bloch Hall Gallery, Station 6400, University of Montevallo, Montevallo, AL 35115; pub; D & E; Scholarships; Work study; SC 25, LC 5; Maj 260, others 3300
Ent Req: ACT
Degrees: BA, BS, BFA
Courses: Advertising Design, Art Appreciation, Art Education, Ceramics, Design, Drawing, Graphic Design, Mixed Media, †New Media Art, Painting, Photography, Printmaking, Sculpture
Summer School: Chmn, Scott Stephens

MONTGOMERY

ALABAMA STATE UNIVERSITY, Dept of Visual Arts, 915 S Jackson, Montgomery, AL 36101; PO Box 271, Montgomery, AL 36101. Tel 334-229-4474; Fax 334-229-4920; Web: www.ASU.edu; *Chmn* Stephen Cappelli; *Asst Prof* Nathaniel Allen; *Assoc Prof* Charmagne Andrews; *Assoc Prof* Christopher Greenman; *Assoc Prof* Frederick Pellum III; *Instr* Gwen Scherer; *Assoc Prof* Cleve Webber
maintains Warren/Britt Galleries; FT 10, PT 4; pub; D&E; Scholarships; SC, LC
Degrees: BA
Tuition: Res—undergrad $1260 per sem; nonres—undergrad $2520 per sem
Courses: Advertising Design, Art Appreciation, Art Education, Art History, Ceramics, †Computer Graphics, Design, Digital Photography, Drawing, Graphics, Painting, Photography, Printmaking

AUBURN UNIVERSITY MONTGOMERY, Dept of Fine Arts, 7061 Senators Dr, 105 Goodwyn Hall Montgomery, AL 36117; PO Box 244023, Montgomery, AL 36124-4023. Tel 334-244-3377; Fax 334-244-3740; Email ashughes@aum.edu; Web: www.aum.edu/indexm_ektid1090.aspx; *Dept Head* Dr Mark Benson

HUNTINGDON COLLEGE, Dept of Art, 1500 E Fairview Ave, Montgomery, AL 36106-2148. Tel 334-833-4536, 4497; *Chmn* Christopher Payne, MFA
Estab 1973; E; 119
Degrees: AA
Courses: Art Appreciation, Art Education, Art History, Art in Religion, Ceramics, Design, Drawing, Graphic Design, Painting, Photography, Printmaking, Teacher Training, Theatre Arts
Adult Hobby Classes: Enrl 119; tuition $80 per hr. Courses—Art Appreciation, Beginning Drawing, Ceramics, Painting
Summer School: Enrl 329; tuition $800 per term for 6 hrs in Art. Courses—Ceramics, Drawing, Painting, Photography

NORMAL

ALABAMA A & M UNIVERSITY, Dept of Visual Performing & Communication Arts, 4900 Meridian St N, 109 Morrison Fine Arts Bldg Normal, AL 35762. Tel 256-372-5512; Web: www.alabamaa&muniversity.edu; *Chmn* Hoarce Carney; *Secy* Benita Chears
Estab 1875, dept estab 1966; pub; D & E; Scholarships; SC 18, LC 3; non-maj 430, maj 35, grad 10
Ent Req: HS dipl
Degrees: BS (Commercial Art & Art Education), MS, MEd (Art Educ)
Tuition: Res—undergrad $1388 per sem, grad $221 per sem; nonres—undergrad $2981 per sem, grad $375 per sem
Courses: †Advertising Design, Art Appreciation, †Art Education, †Commercial Art, Drawing, Fibers, Glass Blowing, Graphic Arts, Jewelry, Painting, Photography, Printmaking, Sculpture, Weaving
Adult Hobby Classes: Enrl 10 - 15; tuition $89 per sem. Courses offered in all areas
Children's Classes: Enrl 15 - 20; tuition $89 per sem. Courses offered in all areas
Summer School: Dir, Dr Clifton Pearson. Enrl 50; tuition $426 for 8 wk sem. Courses—Art Education, Art History, Ceramics

TANNER

JOHN C CALHOUN STATE COMMUNITY COLLEGE, Department of Fine Arts, 6250 US Hwy 31N, Tanner, AL 35671-4028; PO Box 2216, Decatur, AL 35609-2216. Tel 256-306-2500; Fax 205-306-2925; Web: www.calhoun.cc.al; *Instr* William Godsey, MA; *Instr* Jimmy Cantrell, EDS; *Instr* William Provine, MBA; *Dept Chmn* John T Colagross, MBA, EdD; *Instr* Kristine Beadle, BFA; *Instr* Stephanie Furry, DMA; *Instr* Samuel Timberlake, MM
Estab 1963; pub; D, E & Weekend; Scholarships; SC 30, LC 8; D 80, E 22, non-maj 29, maj 70, others 3
Ent Req: HS dipl, GED
Degrees: AS, AA and AAS 2 yrs
Courses: †Art Appreciation, Art Education, Art History, †Ceramics, †Commercial Art, †Drawing, †Film, †Graphic Design, Illustration, Lettering, †Painting, †Photography, Printmaking, †Sculpture, †Video
Summer School: Courses are selected from regular course offerings

TROY

TROY STATE UNIVERSITY, Dept of Art & Classics, Malone Hall of Fine Arts, Rm 132 Troy, AL 36082. Tel 334-670-3391; Fax 334-670-3390; Email egreen@tsogan.troyst.edu; Web: www.troyst.edu; *Asst Prof* Pamela Allen; *Asst Prof* S L Shillabeer; *Prof* Ed Noriega; *Prof* A J Olson; *Chmn* Jessy John
Estab 1957. University has 2 other campuses; FT 5; pub; Scholarships; SC 23, LC 11
Ent Req: HS grad, ent exam
Degrees: BA and BS (Arts & Sciences), MS
Courses: Art Education, †Art History, Commercial Art, Drawing, Graphic Arts, Handicrafts, Jewelry, Lettering, Museology, Painting, Photography, Pottery, Silversmithing, Teacher Training
Adult Hobby Classes: Courses—Basketry, Crafts, Matting & Framing
Children's Classes: Enrl 30. Courses—Summer Workshop
Summer School: Dir, Robert Stampfli. Enrl 100; tuition $600 for June 12-Aug 11 term. Courses—Art Appreciation, Art Education, Art History, Drawing, Painting

TUSCALOOSA

STILLMAN COLLEGE, Stillman Art Gallery & Art Dept, 3601 15th St, Tuscaloosa, AL 35401-2601. Tel 205-349-4240, Ext 8860; Web: www.stillman.edu; *Asst Prof* Keyser Wilson, MFA; *Prof* R L Guffin, MFA
Estab 1876, dept estab 1951; pvt den; D; SC 8, LC 2; D 73, non-maj 73
Ent Req: HS dipl, ent exam
Courses: Afro-American Art History, Art Education, Art History, Ceramics, Commercial Art, Design, Drawing, Mixed Media, Painting, Sculpture

UNIVERSITY OF ALABAMA, Dept of Art, 103 Garland Hall, Box 870270 Tuscaloosa, AL 35487-0270. Tel 205-348-5967; Fax 205-348-0287; Email cpagani@as.ua.edu; Web: www.ua.edu; *Chair* Dr Catherine Pagani; *Dir Grad Studies Studio Art* Craig Wedderspoon; *Dir Grad Studies Art History* Mindy Nancarrow
Estab 1831, dept estab 1919; Maintains a nonprofit art gallery, Sarah Moody Gallery of Art at University of Alabama; on-campus shop where art supplies may be purchased; pub; D & E; Scholarships; SC 50, LC 20, GC 20; D & E 1500, maj 270, grad 18
Ent Req: HS dipl, ACT
Degrees: BA and BFA 4 yr, MFA 3 yr, MA (art) 2 yr
Tuition: Res—undergrad & grad $2640 per sem; nonres - $8260
Courses: Advertising Design, †Art History, †Ceramics, Constructions, Design, Drafting, Drawing, †Graphic Design, History of Art & Architecture, Intermedia, Mixed Media, Museum Staff Training, †Painting, †Photography, †Printmaking, †Sculpture
Summer School: Enrl 375; tuition $1500 per sem. Courses—Art History, Ceramics, Drawing, Design, Graphic Design, Painting, Photography, Sculpture

TUSKEGEE

TUSKEGEE UNIVERSITY, Liberal Arts & Education, 1470 S Robertson Blvd, # 125 Tuskegee, AL 90035-3402. Tel 334-727-8913, 8011; Fax 334-724-4196; Web: www.tusk.edu; *Instr* Carla Jackson-Reese; *Head Dept Art* Uthman Abdur-Rahman; *Chmn Fine & Performing Arts* Warren Duncan; *Dean Liberal Arts* Benjamin Benford, Dr
Estab 1881; pvt
Courses: Art Appreciation, Art Education, Design Foundation

ALASKA

ANCHORAGE

UNIVERSITY OF ALASKA ANCHORAGE, Dept of Art, 3211 Providence Dr, College of Arts and Sciences Anchorage, AK 99508-4614. Tel 907-786-1783; Fax 907-786-1799; Web: www.uaa.alaska.edu; *Chmn* Sean Licka
FT 11, PT 15; Pub; D & E; Scholarships; SC 43, LC 7-9; College of Arts & Sciences FT 1310
Ent Req: open enrl
Degrees: BA in art, BFA 4 yr
Courses: †Art Education, †Ceramics, †Drawing, Graphic Design, Illustration, †Painting, †Photography, †Printmaking, †Sculpture
Adult Hobby Classes: Same as regular prog
Summer School: Dir, Dennis Edwards. One term of 10 wks beginning May or two 5 wk sessions. Courses—Art Appreciation, Art Education, Native Art History, Photography & various studio courses

FAIRBANKS

UNIVERSITY OF ALASKA FAIRBANKS, Art Department, 310 Fine Arts Complex, Fairbanks, AK 99775; PO Box 755640, Fairbanks, AK 99775-5640. Tel 907-474-7530; Fax 907-474-5853; Email uaf-art@alaska.edu; Web: www.uaf.edu/art/; *Prof* Wendy Ernst Croskrey; *Prof* Todd Sherman; *Prof* Jim Brashear; *Assoc Prof* Michael Nakoneczny; *Dept Chmn & Assoc Prof* David Mollett; *Assoc Prof* Miho Aoki; *Asst Prof* Da-ka-xeen Mehner; *Asst Prof* Mareca Guthrie
Estab 1963; Maintains nonprofit gallery - UAF Art Dept Gallery, PO Box 5640, Fairbanks, AK 99775; pub; D & E; Scholarships; SC 43, LC 6, GC 9; D 312, E 60, maj 133, 7 graduate students
Purchases: On-campus shop with limited amt art supplies
Activities: Schols offered to MFA students
Ent Req: HS dipl
Degrees: BA, BFA, MFA
Tuition: Res—$112 per cr hour (lower dist); nonres $343 per r hour; grad level $222/non-res $453
Courses: Art Appreciation, Art History, †Ceramics, Computer Art, †Drawing, Metalsmithing, Native Art, †Painting, Photography, †Printmaking, †Sculpture, Textile Design
Children's Classes: Enrl 50. Courses—Ceramics, Drawing, Design, Metalsmithing, Painting, Sculpture. Visual Art Academy under supervision of summer session
Summer School: Dir, Michelle Bartlett. Enrl 119; 6 wk term. Courses—Ceramics, Drawing, Printmaking, Sculpture, Native Art, Painting, Art History

ARIZONA

DOUGLAS

COCHISE COLLEGE, Art Dept, 4190 W Hwy 80, Douglas, AZ 85607-9724. Tel 520-364-7943, Ext 225; Web: www.cochise.org; *Instr Dept Head* Monte Surratt; *Instr* Manual Martinez
Estab 1965, department estab 1965; PT 7; pub; D & E; Scholarships; SC 12, LC 2; D 280, E 225, maj 20
Ent Req: HS dipl, GED
Degrees: AA 2 yrs (Painting & Sculpture)
Courses: Appreciation, Art, Art History, Ceramics, Color & Design, Commercial Design, Drawing, Jewelry, Painting, Photography, Printmaking, Sculpture, Special Topics in Art
Adult Hobby Classes: Courses—Painting

FLAGSTAFF

NORTHERN ARIZONA UNIVERSITY, College of Arts & Letters, South San Francisco St, Flagstaff, AZ 86011; PO Box 4094, College of Arts & Letters Flagstaff, AZ 86011-4094. Tel 928-523-2395; Web: www.nau.edu/cal; *Dean* Michael Vincent; *Assoc Dean* Jean Boreen
Estab 1899; pub; D & E; Scholarships; SC 56, LC 19, GC 8-10; D 400, E 100, non-maj 342, maj 300, grad 30
Ent Req: HS dipl, ACT, Sat I
Degrees: BA & BS 4 yr, MA(Art Educ)
Tuition: Res—undergrad $1078 per sem; nonres—undergrad $368 per cr hr, $4416 per sem (12 cr hr); campus res available
Courses: Art Education, Art History, Ceramics, Drawing, †Fine Arts, Interior Design, Jewelry, †Metalsmithing, Painting, Printmaking, Sculpture
Adult Hobby Classes: Most of the above studio areas
Children's Classes: Enrl 80; tuition $5 for 5 Sat. Courses—Ceramics, Drawing, Painting, Puppetry
Summer School: Dir, Richard Beasley. Enrl 150; tuition $46 per cr. Courses—Most regular courses

MESA

MESA COMMUNITY COLLEGE, Dept of Art, 1833 W Southern Ave, Mesa, AZ 85202-4866. Tel 480-461-7524, 461-7000 (main); Fax 480-461-7350; Email gingher@mesacc.edu; Web: www.mc.maricopa.edu; *Chair* Gingher Leyendecker, MFA; *Instr* Kai Kim, MFA; *Instr* Dan Fogel, MFA; *Instr* Linda Speranza, MA; *Instr* Chris Todd, MFA; *Instr* Robert Galloway, MFA; *Instr* Tom Klare, MFA; *Instr* Lindsey Pederson, MA
Estab 1965; Maintains a non-profit art gallery: MCC Art Gallery, 1815 W. Southern Ave, Mesa, AZ 85202; pub; D & E; Scholarships; SC 10, LC 8, Hybrid; D 667, E 394
Ent Req: HS dipl or GED
Degrees: AA 2 yrs, Fine Art, Digital Art
Courses: †Advertising Design, Art Appreciation, †Art History, †Ceramics, †Drawing, Graphic Design, †Painting, †Photography

PHOENIX

GRAND CANYON UNIVERSITY, Art Dept, 3300 W Camelback Rd, Phoenix, AZ 85017-1097. Tel 602-249-3300, Ext 2840, 800-800-9776 Ext 2840; Fax 602-589-2459; Email imorrison@gcu.edu; Web: www.grand-canyon.edu; *Asst Prof Art* Esmeralda Delaney, MFA; *Assoc Prof Art* Gaylen Stewart, MFA; *Asst Prof Art, Chair* Ian Morrison, MA; *Asst Prof Art* Sheila Schumacher, BFA; *Art Instr* Lynn Karns, MA; *Art Hist Instr* Judy Moffit, PhD
Estab 1949; maintains an on-campus gallery - A. P. Tell Gallery; prv; D & E; Scholarships; SC 52, LC 9 (Art Dept); D 106, E 25, non-maj 75, maj 30 (Art Dept)
Ent Req: HS dipl
Degrees: (art) BA & other university colleges/majors/degrees
Courses: †Advertising Design, Aesthetics, †Art Appreciation, †Art Education, Art History, Ceramics, †Collage, †Commercial Art, †Conceptual Art, †Constructions, †Costume Design & Construction, †Design, †Drawing, †Goldsmithing, †Graphic Arts, †Graphic Design, †Jewelry, †Mixed Media, †Painting, †Photography, †Printmaking, Professional Artist Workshop, †Sculpture, †Silversmithing, †Stage Design, †Teacher Training, †Theatre Arts
Adult Hobby Classes: Watercolor, Printmaking
Children's Classes: Enrl 31; tuition $25. Courses—Ceramics, Composition, Drawing, Sculpture

PHOENIX COLLEGE, Dept of Art & Photography, 1202 W Thomas Rd, Phoenix, AZ 85013-4234. Tel 602-264-2492; Fax 602-285-7276; Web: www.pc.maricopa.edu; *Coordr, Photograph Dept* John Mercer; *Chmn* Roman Reyes; *Coordr Computer Graphics* Virginia Brouch, Dr; *Art History* Pamela Reed
Estab 1920; FT 5, PT 22; pub; Scholarships
Ent Req: HS dipl
Degrees: AA & AG 2 yrs
Courses: Art Education, Basic Design, Ceramics, Commercial Art, Computer Design, Computer Graphics, Drawing, Painting, Photography, Sculpture
Adult Hobby Classes: Enrl 500; tuition $22.50 for 16 wks. Courses—Full range incl Computer Art
Summer School: Dir, John Mercer. Enrl 100; two 5 wk sessions. Courses—Intro to Art, Western Art

PRESCOTT

YAVAPAI COLLEGE, Visual & Performing Arts Div, 1100 E Sheldon, Prescott, AZ 86301. Tel 520-445-7300, 776-2035; Fax 520-776-2036; Web: www.yavapai.cc.az.us; *Instr* Glen L Peterson, EdD; *Instr* Dr Will Fisher, MA; *Instr* Roy Breiling, MA
Estab 1966, dept estab 1969; pub; D & E; Scholarships; SC 50, LC 50; D 1650, E 1563
Ent Req: HS dipl
Degrees: AA 2 yr
Courses: Art History, Calligraphy, Ceramics, Collage, Commercial Art, Design, Drawing, Film, Goldsmithing, †Graphic Arts, Illustration, Jewelry, Lathe Turning, Metalsmithing & Jewelry, Painting, †Papermaking, Photography, †Printmaking, Sculpture, Silversmithing, Theatre Arts, Weaving, †Web Page Design, Wood
Adult Hobby Classes: Enrl open; tuition per course. Courses offered through Retirement College
Children's Classes: Enrl open. Courses—Ceramics, Drawing, Painting
Summer School: Dir, Donald D Hiserodt. Enrl open. Courses—Ceramics, Drawing, Jewelry, Painting, Photography, Printmaking

SCOTTSDALE

SCOTTSDALE ARTISTS' SCHOOL, 3720 N Marshall Way, Scottsdale, AZ 85251-5559. Tel 480-990-1422; Fax 480-990-0652; Email info@scottsdaleartschool.org; Web: www.scottsdaleartschool.org; *Program Coordinator* Trudy Hays; *Bus Mgr* Wanda Stillions
Open Mon-Thurs 8:30 AM- 9:30 PM, Fri 8:30 AM - 5 PM, Sat 8:30 AM - 4 PM; Estab 1983; Maintains an art supply shop and an art library; Pub; D & E; Scholarships; SC 100+; 2500
Collections: Paintings, Prints, Sculpture, Drawing
Exhibitions: Best and Brightest Juried Student Show and Sale
Activities: Classes for adults & children
Degrees: No (non-accredited)
Courses: Drawing, Painting, Sculpture

SHOW LOW

NORTHLAND PIONEER COLLEGE, Art Dept, 1001 W Deuce of Clubs, Show Low, AZ 85901; PO Box 610, Holbrook, AZ 86025-0610. Tel 928-532-6176; Email magda.gluszek@npc.edu; Web: npc.edu/fine-arts; *Faculty & Gallery Director* Magda Gluszek; *Faculty* Peterson Yazzie
Estab 1974; FT 2; pub; D & E; SC 28, LC 2
Degrees: AA, Assoc of Applied Sci 2 yr
Courses: Art Appreciation, Art History, Calligraphy, Ceramics, Commercial Art, Crafts, Design, Drawing, Graphic Arts, Lettering, Painting, Photography, Printmaking, Sculpture, Textile Design, Weaving
Adult Hobby Classes: Courses—Same as above
Summer School: 4 wk session in June

TEMPE

ARIZONA STATE UNIVERSITY, Herberger Institute for Design and the Arts, Dixie Gammage Hall, 1001 S Forest Mall, PO Box 872102 Tempe, AZ 85287-2102. Tel 480-965-6536; Fax 480-727-6529; Email herbergeradmissions@asu.edu; Web: herbergerinstitute.asu.edu; *Dean & Prof* Steven J Tepper; *Sr Assoc Dean & Prof* Sandra Stauffer; *Assoc Dean Policy & Initiatives & Assoc Prof* Jacob Pinholster; *Assoc Dean & Prof* Kathryn Maxwell
Estab 1885; maintain nonprofit ASU Art Museum; 400; pub; D & E; Scholarships; Fellowships; SC 88, LC 70, GC 116; 5,000
Ent Req: HS dipl, ACT
Degrees: BA & BFA 4 yrs, MFA 3 yrs, MA 2 yrs, EdD 3 yrs
Tuition: Undergrad (res) $9,834, (nonres) $27,618
Courses: Art Appreciation, †Art Education, †Art History, †Ceramics, Computer Art, †Drawing, Fibers, †Intermedia, †Jewelry, †Painting, †Photography, †Printmaking, †Sculpture, Small Metals, †Textile Design, Video Art, †Weaving
Children's Classes: Courses—Studio
Summer School: Courses—Vary
—**The Design School**, 810 S Forest Ave, Design N Rm 162 Tempe, AZ 85287-1605. Tel 480-965-3536; Fax 480-965-0968; Email designmail@asu.edu; Web: design.asu.edu; *Dir* Jason Schupbach; *Assoc Dir* Catherine Spellman
Estab 1885, col estab 1949; pub; D & E
Ent Req: HS dipl, SAT
Degrees: BA, MA
Tuition: Undergrad (res) $9,834, (nonres) $27,618
Courses: Architecture, Environmental Design, Graphics, History of Art & Architecture, Industrial Design, Interior Design, Landscape Architecture, Urban Design
Summer School: Courses—lower & upper div courses primarily in Design, Graphics, History, Sketching and Rendering

THATCHER

EASTERN ARIZONA COLLEGE, Art Dept, 600 Church St, Thatcher, AZ 85552. Tel 520-428-8233, 428-8460; Fax 520-428-8462; Email wilson@eac.cc.az.us; Web: www.eac.cc.az.us; *Instr* Richard Green PhD; *Instr* James Gentry, MA
Estab 1888, dept estab 1946; PT 14; pub; D & E; Scholarships; SC 25, LC 3; D 105, E 202, maj 30
Ent Req: HS dipl or GED
Degrees: AA & AAS 2 yrs
Courses: Advertising Design, Airbrush, Art Appreciation, Art History, Calligraphy, Ceramics, Design, Drawing, Fibers, Gem Faceting, Lapidary, Life Drawing, Photography, Printmaking, Sculpture, Silversmithing, Stage Design, Stained Glass, Weaving, Wood Carving

TUCSON

UNIVERSITY OF ARIZONA, Dept of Art, 1031 N Olive Rd, J Gross Gallery Rm 101D Tucson, AZ 85721; PO Box 210002, Tucson, AZ 85721-0002. Tel 520-621-7570; Fax 520-621-2955; Email artinfo@cfa.arizona.edu; Web: art.arizona.edu; *Dir* Dennis Jones
Estab 1891, dept estab 1893; pub; D; Scholarships; SC 30, LC 21, GC 32; D 3094, maj 600, grad 100
Ent Req: Res—undergrad $919 per 7 units; grad $942 per 7 units per sem; campus res available
Degrees: BFA(Studio), BFA(Art Educ) and BA(Art History) 4 yrs, MFA(Studio) and MA(Art History or Art Educ) 2-3 yrs
Tuition: Res—undergrad $1174 per 7 units, grad $1132 per 7 units per yr; campus res—available
Courses: Advertising Design, †Art Education, †Art History, †Ceramics, †Drawing, Fibers, †Graphic Design, †Illustration, New Genre, †Painting, †Photography, †Printmaking, †Sculpture, Teacher Training, Video, Weaving
Summer School: Presession & two sessions offered. Request catalog (available in Apr) by writing to: Summer Session Office, Univ of Arizona, Tucson, AZ 85721

ARKANSAS

ARKADELPHIA

OUACHITA BAPTIST UNIVERSITY, Dept of Visual Art, OBU Box 3665, Arkadelphia, AR 71998-0001. Tel 870-245-5559; Fax 870-245-5500; Email thompsonl@obu.edu; *Dean School Fine Arts* Charles Fuller; *Prof* Dr Raouf Halaby; *Chmn* Larry Thompson; *Instr* Stephanie Smith; *Instr* Becky Spradun
Estab 1886, dept estab 1934; Maintain nonprofit art gallery; Mabee Fine Arts Gallery, Box 3633 OBU, Arkadelphia, AR 71998; Pvt; D&E; Scholarships; SC 15, LC 2; D 72, non-maj 130, maj 72
Ent Req: HS dipl, ACT
Degrees: BA, BSE, BS and BME 4 yr
Courses: Art Appreciation, Art Education, Art History, Ceramics, Commercial Art, Conceptual Art, Design, Drawing, Graphic Design, History of Art & Architecture, Illustration, Jewelry, Mixed Media, Painting, Photography, Public School Arts, Sculpture, Teacher Training, †Theatre Arts

CLARKSVILLE

UNIVERSITY OF THE OZARKS, Dept of Art, 415 College Ave, Clarksville, AR 72830. Tel 501-754-3839; Fax 501-979-1349; Web: www.ozarks.edu; *Prof* Blaine Caldwell; *Chmn* David Strain
Estab 1836, dept estab 1952; den; D; Scholarships; SC 9, LC 2; D 83, non-maj 8, maj 17
Ent Req: HS dipl, ACT
Degrees: BA & BS 4 yr
Courses: Art Appreciation, Design, Sculpture
Summer School: Drawing, History of Contemporary Art, Sculpture, Watercolor

CONWAY

UNIVERSITY OF CENTRAL ARKANSAS, Department of Art, McAlister Hall, Rm 101, Conway, AR 72035; 201 Donaghey Ave, McAlister Hall 101 Conway, AR 72035. Tel 501-450-3113; Fax 501-450-5788; Email jyoung@uca.edu; Web: www.uca.edu/cfac/art; *Prof* Dr Gayle Seymour; *Prof* Bryan Massey; *Chair, Prof* Dr Jeff Young; *Prof* Dr Kenneth Burchett; *Assoc Prof* Liz Smith; *Prof* Deborah Kuster; *Prof* Donna Pinckley; *Assoc Prof* Reinaldo Morales; *Asst Prof* Jennifer Rospert; *Assoc Prof* Ray Ogar; *Asst Prof* Sandra Luckett; *Assoc Prof* Holly Laws; *Asst Prof* Li Zeng; *Asst Prof* Jessie Hornbrook; *Lectr* Brian Young
Estab 1908; Maintain nonprofit gallery, Baum Gallery of Art, McCastlain Hall, UCA, 201 Donaghey, Conway, AR 72035, Black Box Student Gallery, Schichtl Hall; FT 15, PT 6; pub; D; Scholarships; SC 26, LC 16; non-maj 700, maj 190
Activities: Schols offered
Ent Req: HS dipl
Degrees: BFA, BA
Courses: Advanced Studio, Art Appreciation, †Art Education, †Art History, †Ceramics, Color, Design, Drawing, Figure, †Graphic Design, Mixed Media, †Painting, †Photography, †Printmaking, †Sculpture
Summer School: 80 students; drawing, design, 3-D design, watercolor I, art appreciation, art history

FAYETTEVILLE

UNIVERSITY OF ARKANSAS, Art Dept, 116 Fine Arts Ctr, Fayetteville, AR 72701-1201. Tel 479-575-5202; Fax 479-575-2062; Email artinfo@uark.edu; Web: http://art.uark.edu/; *Prof* Lynn Jacobs, MFA, PhD; *Dept Chair & Assoc Prof* Jeannie Hulen, MFA; *Assoc Prof* John Newman, MFA; *Prof Emeritus* Robert Ross, MFA; *Assoc Prof* Angela M LaPorte, PhD; *Instr* Joanne Jones, MFA; *Assoc Prof* Marilyn Nelson, MFA; *Assoc Prof* Jacqueline Golden, MFA; *Prof* Michael Peven, MFA; *Asst Prof* Larry Swartwood, MFA; *Instr* Shannon Mitchell; *Assoc Prof* Kristin Musgnug, MFA; *Assoc Prof* Leo Mazow, MA, PhD; *Asst Prof* Bethany Springer, MFA; *Asst Prof* Thomas Hapgood, MFA; *Asst Prof* Alissa Mazow, MA, PhD
Estab 1871; Dept maintains Fine Arts Center Gallery, sUgAR: Student Gallery University of Arkansas & Library; Pub; D, E & Online at Global Campus in

Rogers, AR; Scholarships; Fellowships; SC 40, LC 16, GC 20; Non-maj 50, maj 370, grad 16
Ent Req: HS dipl, portfolio for MFA
Degrees: MFA 60 cr hours & BA & BFA 4 yrs
Tuition: Res-$4,344 per yr; non-res-$10,290; room & board $5000
Courses: Art Appreciation, †Art Education, †Art History, †Ceramics, †Design, †Drawing, †Graphic Design, †Painting, †Photography, †Printmaking, †Sculpture
Adult Hobby Classes: Enrl 10; tuition $620 per sem; Courses—Ceramics
Summer School: Dir, Jeannie Hulen. Enrl 150; 6 wk session. Courses—Ceramics, Drawing, Painting, Photography, 2-D Design, 3-D Design

HARRISON

NORTH ARKANSAS COMMUNITY-TECHNICAL COLLEGE, Art Dept, 1515 Pioneer Ridge, Harrison, AR 72601. Tel 870-391-3000; Fax 870-391-3250; Email sdomino@northark.edu; Web: www.northark.edu; *Chmn Div of Communs & Arts* Bill Skinner; *Dir Art Dept* Dusty Domino
Estab 1974, dept estab 1975; pub; D & E; SC 7, LC 1; in art dept D 80, E 30-40, non-maj 45, maj 35
Ent Req: HS dipl
Degrees: AA 2 yrs, AFA 2 yrs
Courses: Art Appreciation, Ceramics, Commercial Art, Costume Design & Construction, Design, Drafting, Drawing, Elementary Art Education, Graphic Design, Painting, Theatre Arts, Video
Adult Hobby Classes: Various courses offered each sem through Continuing Education Program
Summer School: Enrl 20-30; tuition $30-$35 for term of 6-8 wks beginning June 1. Courses—open; Art Workshop on Buffalo National River

HELENA

PHILLIPS COMMUNITY COLLEGE AT THE UNIVERSITY OF ARKANSAS, Dept of English & Fine Arts, 1000 Campus Dr, Helena, AR 72342; PO Box 785, Helena, AR 72342-0785. Tel 870-338-6474; Fax 870-338-7542; Web: www.pccua.cc.ar.us; *Art Instr* Susan Worrington; *Chmn Visual & Performing Arts* Kirk Whiteside
Estab 1966; Maintain nonprofit art gallery; pub; D & E; Scholarships; SC 8, LC 1; 55
Ent Req: HS dipl, ent exam, GED
Degrees: AA and AAS 2 yr
Courses: Drawing, Pottery, Sculpture

LITTLE ROCK

ARKANSAS ARTS CENTER, 501 E 9th St, Little Rock, AR 72202; PO Box 2137, Little Rock, AR 72203-2137. Tel 501-372-4000; Fax 501-375-8053; Web: www.arkansasartscenter.org; *Dir Educ* Lou Palermo; *Dir Mktg* Angel Galloway; *Registrar* Katie Hall; *Dept Dir & CFO* Laine Harber; *State Svcs* Jessica Wright; *Mgr Mem* Spencer Jansen; *Shop Mgr* Kim White; *Children's Theatre* Bradley Anderson; *Pres* J Shepherd Russell; *Develop Dir* Kelly Fleming; *Mus School Mgr* Andi Tompkins; *Exec Dir* Todd A Herman, PhD; *Chief Cur* Brian Land; *Cur Drawings* Ann P Wagner, PhD
Estab 1960; Maintains non-profit art gallery & art/architecture library - Elizabeth Prewitt Taylor Library; pub; D & E; Scholarships; SC 62, LC 3; D 350, E 300 children & adults
Activities: Schols offered
Ent Req: open to anyone age 4 through adult
Courses: Aesthetics, Art Appreciation, Art History, Ceramics, Drawing, †Fashion Arts, Jewelry, Mixed Media, Painting, Photography, Printmaking, Sculpture, Teacher Training, †Theatre Arts, Woodworking
Adult Hobby Classes: Enrl 1265; tuition $95-$125 for 10 wk term
Children's Classes: Enrl 1373; tuition $65-$75 for 10 wk term. Courses—Theater Arts, Visual Arts
Summer School: Same as above

UNIVERSITY OF ARKANSAS AT LITTLE ROCK, Dept of Art & Design, 2801 S University Ave, Little Rock, AR 72204-1099. Tel 501-569-3182; Fax 501-569-8775; Web: www.ulr.edu/artdept; *Chmn* Mia Hall, MFA
Estab 1928; FT 12, PT 5; pub; D & E; Scholarships; SC, LC; Univ sem 10,200, dept sem 1200
Ent Req: HS grad
Degrees: BA Studio Art, Art History, Art Education, BFA Studio, MA Art History, Art Education, Studio
Tuition: Res—undergrad $1054, grad $1441; non-res— undergrad $2557, grad $2971
Courses: Art Appreciation, Art Education, Art History, Ceramics, Design, Drawing, Graphic Design, Illustration, Painting, Photography, Pottery, Printmaking, Sculpture, Silversmithing
Summer School: Dean, Tom Clifton. Enrl 250; Courses—Art Appreciation, Art Education, Art History, Studio Art

MAGNOLIA

SOUTHERN ARKANSAS UNIVERSITY AT MAGNOLIA, Dept of Art & Design, 100 E University, Magnolia, AR 71753-5000. Tel 870-235-4000; Fax 870-235-5005; Email rsstout@saumag.edu; Web: www.saumag.edu/art; *Prof* Steven Ochs, MFA; *Assoc Prof* Scotland Stout, MFA; *Chair* Dan May, MFA; *Asst Prof* Rebecca Glenn; *Instr* Ann Bittick
Estab 1909; Maintain nonprofit art gallery; on-campus shop where art supplies may be purchased; pub; D & E; Scholarships; SC 18, LC 4; D 240, non-maj 260, maj 40
Ent Req: HS dipl
Degrees: BA, BSE 4 yr, BFA
Tuition: $3,500 per yr
Courses: Advertising Design, †Animation, Art Appreciation, Art Education, Art History, †Calligraphy, †Ceramics, Commercial Art, †Conceptual Art, Design, Drafting, Drawing, †Film, Graphic Arts, †Graphic Design, †Lettering, †Mixed Media, †Motion Gaming Web, †Painting, †Photography, †Printmaking, †Sculpture, †Video
Adult Hobby Classes: Classes & courses open to all at regular tuition rates
Children's Classes: Enrl 30; tuition $30. Courses—Kinder Art
Summer School: Dir, Jerry Johnson. Enrl 60. Courses—Art, Fine Arts

MONTICELLO

UNIVERSITY OF ARKANSAS AT MONTICELLO, Fine Arts Dept, PO Box 3460, Monticello, AR 71656-3460. Tel 870-460-1078; Web: www.cotton.uamont.edu/~richardt/art_index.html; *Chmn* Tom Richard
Dept estab 1909; Scholarships
Ent Req: HS dipl
Degrees: BA
Tuition: Res—undergrad $2680 per sem; waiver from MI, LA, TX
Courses: Art Appreciation, †Art Education, Ceramics, Design, Drawing, Graphic Arts, History of Art & Architecture, Mixed Media, Painting, Printmaking
Summer School: Enrl 25; tuition $65 per cr hr for June-July. Courses—Art Appreciation, Art Education

PINE BLUFF

UNIVERSITY OF ARKANSAS AT PINE BLUFF, Art Dept, 1200 N University Dr, Pine Bluff, AR 71601. Tel 870-575-8326, 575-8328; Email lintonhl@uapb.edu; Web: www.uapb.edu; *Dept Chmn* Henri Linton
Leedell Morehead-Graham Gallery (nonprofit) on campus; pub; D & E; Scholarships
Ent Req: HS dipl
Degrees: BS
Courses: Art Appreciation, Art Education, Art History, Calligraphy, Ceramics, Design, Drawing, Handicrafts, Painting, Photography, Printmaking, Sculpture, Textile Design, Weaving

RUSSELLVILLE

ARKANSAS TECH UNIVERSITY, Dept of Art, 203 W Q St, Russellville, AR 72801-8800. Tel 479-968-0244; Fax 479-498-6002; Email dward23@atu.edu; Web: www.atu.edu/art; *Head Prof* Dawn Ward, PhD; *Prof* David Mudrinich, MFA; *Assoc Prof* Lyn Brands; *Assoc Prof* Neal Harrington; *Assoc Prof* Ty Brunson; *Asst Prof* Joshua Fisher; *Asst Prof* Jasmine Greer
Estab 1909; pub; D & E; Scholarships; SC 25, LC 10, GC 2; D 200, non-maj 130, maj 155
Ent Req: ent req HS dipl, ACT, SAT
Degrees: BA 4 yr; Fine Art; Graphic Design; Art Education
Courses: Animation, Art Education, Art History, Ceramics, †Commercial Art, Digital Illustration, Digital Photography, Display, Drawing, †Fine Arts, †Graphic Design, Illustration, Intro to Art, Packaging Design, Painting, Printmaking, †Sculpture, Teacher Training
Summer School: Courses—Art Education, Art History, Ceramics, Design, Drawing, Painting

SEARCY

HARDING UNIVERSITY, Dept of Art & Design, 915 E Market Ave, Searcy, AR 72149-0001; PO Box 12253, Searcy, AR 72149-0001. Tel 501-279-4426; Fax 501-279-4717; Email art@harding.edu; Web: www.harding.edu; *Chmn Dept* Daniel Adams, MFA; *Prof* Faye Doran, EdD; *Prof* Paul Pitt, MFA; *Prof* John Keller, PhD; *Asst Prof* Beverly Austin, MA; *Assoc Prof Art* Steven B Choate, Ph.D; *Dir Interior Design & Assoc Prof* Amy Cox, MBA; *Prof* Stacy Gibson, MFA; *Assoc Prof Art* Greg Clayton, MFA; *Asst Prof* Sarah Wilhoit, Ph.D
Estab 1924; Maintains nonprofit Stevens Art Center Galleries, 915 E Market, PO Box 12253, Searcy, AR 72149, art/architecture library, & on-campus store for sale of art supplies; pvt; D; Scholarships; SC 44, LC 14, GC 11; D 138, non-maj 19, maj 138
Ent Req: HS dipl, ACT
Degrees: BA and BFA 4 yrs, MEd 5-6 yrs
Tuition: $472 per sem hr; campus res—room & board $6,000 per yr
Courses: 2-D Design, Aesthetics, Architecture, Art Appreciation, Art Education, Art History, Ceramics, Color Theory, Computer Graphics, †Design, Drafting, Drawing, †Graphic Design, †Interior Design, †Painting, Photography, Printmaking, Sculpture, Silversmithing, †Teacher Training, Weaving
Summer School: Dean, Travis Thompson. Tuition per sem hr for two 16 wk sessions beginning Aug Courses—Vary depending upon the demand, usually Art Education, Art History, Ceramics, Drawing, Painting, Watercolor

SILOAM SPRINGS

JOHN BROWN UNIVERSITY, Art Dept, 2000 W University, Siloam Springs, AR 72761. Tel 501-524-3131, Ext 182; Fax 501-524-9548; Web: www.jbu.edu; *Asst Prof* Peter Pohle; *Head Dept* Charles Peer
Estab 1919; FT 2; pvt; D; Scholarships; SC 9, LC 3
Ent Req: HS grad
Degrees: AS(Art)
Courses: Art Appreciation, Art Education, Composition, Crafts (copper tooling, Design & Color, Drawing, enameling, jewelry, macrame, mosaic, Painting, pottery, weaving)

STATE UNIVERSITY

ARKANSAS STATE UNIVERSITY, Dept of Art, PO Box 1630, State University, AR 72467-1630. Tel 870-972-3050; Fax 870-972-3932; Email csteele@aztec.astate.edu; Web: www.astate.edu/; *Prof* Evan Lindquist, MFA; *Prof* William Allen, MFA, PhD; *Prof* Steven L Mayes, MFA; *Prof* Tom Chaffee, MFA; *Prof* John Keech, MFA; *Assoc Prof* Roger Carlisle, MFA; *Assoc Prof* Curtis Steele, MFA; *Assoc Prof* Debra Satterfield, MFA; *Assoc Prof* John J Salvest, MFA; *Asst Prof* Dr Paul Hickman, MFA, PhD; *Instr* Jean Flint; *Instr* Nadine Hawke; *Instr* Gayle Pendergrass, MFA; *Instr* William H Rowe, MFA
Estab 1909, dept estab 1938; FT 13; pub; D & E; Scholarships; SC 33, LC 10, GC 34; D 300, E 100, non-maj 800, maj 132, grad 10
Ent Req: HS dipl
Degrees: BFA, BSE 4 yr, MA
Courses: Art Appreciation, †Art Education, †Art History, Ceramics, Drawing, †Graphic Design, Illustration, Intermedia, Painting, Photography, †Studio Art
Adult Hobby Classes: 20; tuition $82 per sem hr. Courses—Art History, Ceramics, Drawing, Painting
Summer School: Dir, Curtis Steele. Enrl 100; tuition res—$490; nonres—$1260 per 5 wk term. Courses—Art History, Drawing, Painting, Photography, Sculpture

WALNUT RIDGE

WILLIAMS BAPTIST COLLEGE, Dept of Art, 60 W Fulbright, Walnut Ridge, AR 72476. Tel 870-886-6741; Fax 870-886-3924; Web: www.wbeoll.edu/infranetstart.htm; *Instr* Melissa Christiano; *Instr* Jima Mickie; *Chmn* Dr David Midkiff
den; D & E; Scholarships
Degrees: BS (Art Educ) & BA
Courses: Art Education, Ceramics, Conceptual Art, Drawing, Painting, Theatre Arts
Summer School: Dir, Dr Jerrol Swaim. Tuition $925 for 12-16 hrs, &75 per hr

CALIFORNIA

ANGWIN

PACIFIC UNION COLLEGE, Art Dept, 100 Howell Mountain Rd Angwin, CA 94508; One Angwin Ave Angwin, CA 94508. Tel 707-965-6311; Email ctturner@pcu.edu; Web: puc.edu; *Chmn* Tom Turner
Dept estab 1882; pvt; D&E; Scholarships
Degrees: AS, BA, BS
Tuition: $470 per unit, $5445 per qtr
Courses: Art History, Ceramics, †Collage, Design, Drawing, Graphic Design, Illustration, Painting, Photography, Printmaking, Sculpture, Stained Glass
Summer School: Dir, Gary Gifford. Courses—Art History, Photography

APTOS

CABRILLO COLLEGE, Visual & Performing Arts Division, 6500 Soquel Dr, Aptos, CA 95003-3198. Tel 831-479-6464; Fax 831-479-5095; Web: www.cabrillo.cc.ca.us; *Chmn* Dan Martinez
Estab 1959; FT 12, PT 22; pub; D & E; Scholarships; SC 46, LC 7
Ent Req: HS dipl
Degrees: AA 2 yr
Courses: Art History, Ceramics, Color, Design, Drawing, Handicrafts, Jewelry, Painting, Photography, Printmaking, Sculpture, Textile Design

ARCATA

HUMBOLDT STATE UNIVERSITY, College of Arts & Humanities, Art Dept, 1 Harpst St, Arcata, CA 95521-8299. Tel 707-826-3624; Fax 707-826-3628; Email arts@humboldt.edu; Web: www.humboldt.edu; *Chmn* Teresa Stanley; *Assoc Prof* Julia Alderson; *Prof* Don Anton; *Prof* Joanne Berke; *Assoc Prof* Nicole Jean Hill; *Assoc Prof* Heather Madar; *Prof* Kris Patzlaff; *Prof* Keith Schneider; *Assoc Prof* Sondra Schwetman; *Assoc Prof* Sarah Whorf; *Asst Prof* Ricardo Febre; *Lectr* Lien Truong; *Lectr* Denton Crawford; *Lectr* Nancy Frazier; *Lectr* Mimi Djoka; *Lectr* Lisa Rosenstveicht
Estab 1913; Maintains nonprofit First St Gallery, 422 1st St, Eureka, CA 95501 & Reese Bullen Gallery on campus. Art supplies sold at on-campus store; pub; D & E; Scholarships; SC 50, LC 11, Seminar; Maj 450
Degrees: BA 4 yr, BA with credential 5 yr
Tuition: Res—$4500 per yr; campus res available
Courses: Art Education, Art History, Ceramics, Display, Drawing, Graphic Design, Jewelry, †Museum & Gallery Practices, Painting, Photography, Printmaking, Sculpture, Teacher Training
Children's Classes: Children's Art Academy
Summer School: Chair, Teresa Stanley. Summer Prog in Afissos, Greece; tuition $200 per unit & prog costs

AZUSA

AZUSA PACIFIC UNIVERSITY, College of Music & the Arts, Dept of Art & Design, 901 E Alosta, Azusa, CA 91702-2701; PO Box 7000, Azusa, CA 91702-7000. Tel 626-387-5726; Fax 626-387-5727; Email artdesign@apu.edu; Web: www.apu.edu; *Dept Chair, Prof* William Catling, MFA; *Prof* Kent Anderson Butler, MFA; *Prof* J David Carlson, MFA; *Asst Prof* Stephen Childs, MFA; *Assoc Prof* Amy Daly, MFA; *Asst Prof* Brent Everett Dickinson, MFA; *Asst Prof* Terry Dobson, MFA; *Prof* David McGill, MFA; *Assoc Prof* Beck Roe, MFA; *Asst Prof* Lyrica Taylor, PhD; *Prof* James Thompson, EdD
Estab 1899, dept estab 1974; Azusa Pacific Art Gallery; dean; pvt; D & E; Scholarships; SC 54, LC 7; maj 190, non-maj 250, GS 105
Ent Req: HS dipl, state test
Degrees: BFA(visual art) 4 yrs, BA(graphic design) 4 yrs, MA 2 yrs
Courses: Art Appreciation, Art Education, Art History, Ceramics, †Design, Drawing, Graphic Arts, Graphic Design, †Mixed Media, Painting, Photography, Printmaking, Sculpture, Textile Design, Video
Summer School: Dir, W Catling; Enrl varies; Courses—varies

BAKERSFIELD

BAKERSFIELD COLLEGE, Art Dept, 1801 Panorama Dr, Bakersfield, CA 93305-1299. Tel 661-395-4674; Email dkoeth@bakersfieldcollege.edu; Web: www2.bakersfieldcollege.edu/art; *Chair, Prof Art* David M Koeth; *Prof Art* Nancy Magner; *Cur Jones Gallery* Tom Betthauser; *Prof Art* Adel Shafik; *Assoc Prof Art* Kristopher Stallworth; *Instr* Cameron Brian; *Instr* Cecilia Noyes; *Instr* Debora Rodenhauser; *Instr* Kelly McLane; *Instr* Chris Lessley; *Instr* Gina Herrera; *Instr* Armando Rubio; *Instr* Diego Gutierrez; *Instr* Andrew Borrego; *Instr* Penelope Young; *Instr* Emily Maddigan; *Instr* Jared Pankin
Estab 1913; Maintains a nonprofit art gallery, Jones Gallery, 1801 Panorama Dr, Bakersfield, CA 93305; art supplies sold at on-campus store; pub; D, E & online; Scholarships; Fellowships; SC 22, LC 4; D 860, E 330, maj 300
Activities: Schols offered
Ent Req: ent exam, open door policy
Degrees: AA 2 yr
Courses: Advertising Design, Art Appreciation, Art History, Ceramics, Design, †Digital Illustration, †Digital Photography, Drawing, Glassblowing, †Graphic Design, Jewelry, Painting, Photography, Printmaking, Sculpture, †Teacher Training, †Typography
Summer School: Courses—Art Appreciation, Drawing

CALIFORNIA STATE UNIVERSITY, BAKERSFIELD, Dept of Art, 9001 Stockdale Hwy, Bakersfield, CA 93311-1022. Tel 661-664-3031; Fax 661-664-6555; Web: www.csub.edu; *Chair & Assoc Prof* Sarah Vanderup
Estab 1965; Maintains non-profit art gallery, The Todd Madigan Galleries & Walter Stiern Library; FT 9; pub; D&E; Scholarships; SC, LC
Ent Req: HS diploma
Degrees: BA
Courses: Art Education, Art History, Ceramics, Design, Drawing, Painting, Photography, Printmaking, Sculpture

BELMONT

NOTRE DAME DE NAMUR UNIVERSITY, Wiegand Gallery, 1500 Ralston Ave, Belmont, CA 94002-1997. Tel 650-508-3595; Fax 650-508-3488; Web: www.ndnu.edu; *Art Dept Chair* Betty Friedman; *Gallery Dir* Robert Poplack
Estab 1951; Maintains nonprofit art gallery; FT 2, PT 6; pvt; D & E; weekends; Scholarships; SC 20, LC 8; D 200, E 100, maj 35
Ent Req: HS dipl, ent exam
Degrees: BA 3 1/2 - 4 yrs, BFA
Courses: 2-D & 3-D Design, Advertising Design, Art Education, Art History, Color, Commercial Art, Composition, Conceptual Art, Constructions, Costume Design & Construction, Design, Display, Drawing, Etching, Film, Gallery Techniques, Graphic Arts, Graphic Design, History of Art & Architecture, Interior Design, Lettering, Lithography, Mixed Media, Museum Staff Training, Painting, Photography, Printmaking, Sculpture, Stage Design, Teacher Training, Theatre Arts

BERKELEY

UNIVERSITY OF CALIFORNIA, BERKELEY, College of Letters & Sciences-Art Practice Dept, 345 Kroeber Hall, Mail Code 3750 Berkeley, CA 94720-3750. Tel 510-642-2582; Fax 510-643-0884; Email love2jr@uclink4.berkeley.edu; Web: art.berkeley.edu; *Dept Mgr* Margaret Thalhuber, MFA; *Chair* Mary Lovelace O'Neil, MFA; *Chair* Shawn Brixey, MS; *Undergrad faculty adv* Squeak Carnwath, MS; *Undergrad faculty adv* Anne Healy, BA; *Grad & undergrad faculty adv* Richard Shaw, MA; *Grad & undergrad faculty adv* Katherine Sherwood, MFA; *Grad & undergrad faculty adv* Wendy Sussman, MFA; *Grad & undergrad advising asst* Delores Levister, MFA; *Admin Asst* Jude Bell
Estab 1915; pub; D; Scholarships
Degrees: BA, MFA (sculpture & painting)
Courses: Art Theory, Drawing, Painting, Sculpture
—**College of Environmental Design**, Hearst Field Annex, Bldg B, Landscape Archit & Environ Planning Dept Berkeley, CA 94720-2000; 202 Wurster Hall, Landscape Archit & Environ Berkeley, CA 94720-2000. Tel 510-643-9335; Fax 510-643-6166; Email maclark@vclink4.berkeley.edu; Web: www.laep.ced.berkeley.edu/laep/index; *Chmn City & Regional Planning* Michael Southworth PhD; *Chair* Walter J Hood, MLA & MArch; *Prof Urban Design in Architecture, Head Grad Adviser & Head Master Urban Design Prog* Peter Bosselmann, MArch; *Chair, Dept Landscape Architecture & Environmental Planning & Prof Landscape Architecture & Urban Design* Linda Jewell, MLA
pub; D & E; Scholarships
Degrees: BA, MA, MSC, PhD
Tuition: Res—undergrad $2023.25 per sem, grad $2134.25 per sem; nonres—undergrad $7330.25 per sem, grad $7351.25 per sem
Courses: Computer-Aided Design, Drawing, Landscape Architecture

BURBANK

WOODBURY UNIVERSITY, School of Media, Culture & Design, School of Media, Culture & Design, 7500 Glenoaks Blvd Burbank, CA 91504-1052. Tel

818-767-0888; Fax 818-394-3305; Email info@woodbury.edu; Web: med.woodbury.edu; *Chair Animation* Dori Littell-Herrick; *Chmn Fashion Design* Anna Weiker; *Chmn Graphic Design* Behnoush McKay; *Chmn Filmmaking* David Collins; *Chmn Graphic Arts & Design* William Novak
Estab 1884; Maintain art/architecture library; art supplies available on-campus; Maintains a non-profit art gallery: Nam Rae Gallery, 7500 Glenoaks Blvd, Burbank, CA 91504; pvt; D & E; Scholarships; SC 56, LC 18
Ent Req: HS dipl
Degrees: BFA 4 yrs, MRA 2 yrs, BArc 5 yrs
Courses: Advertising Design, Art History, Costume Design & Construction, Design, Display, Drawing, Fashion Arts, †Fashion Design, Film, Graphic Arts, Graphic Design, Illustration, †Interior Architecture, Photography, Textile Design
Summer School: Regular session

CARSON

CALIFORNIA STATE UNIVERSITY, DOMINGUEZ HILLS, Art & Design Dept, 1000 E Victoria St, LCH-A111 Carson, CA 90747-0001. Tel 310-243-3310; Email jkeville@csudh.edu; Web: www.csudh.edu; *Assoc Prof* Jim Keville; *Prof Emeritus* John Goders; *Prof Emeritus* Bernard Baker; *Prof & Chair* Michele Buizy; *Instr* David Parsons; *Prof Emeritus* Dr Louise Ivers; *Asst Prof* Ellie Zenhari; *Instr* Elaine Brandt; *Asst Prof* Devon Tsuno; *Prof* Gilah Yelin Hirsch
Estab 1960; Maintain nonprofit Univ Art Gallery (same address); on-campus bookstore where art supplies may be purchased; pub; D & E; Scholarships; SC 35, LC 25; maj 130
Ent Req: 2.0 GPA
Degrees: BA 4 yr
Courses: †Advertising Design, Aesthetics, Art Appreciation, †Art History, Ceramics, Collage, Design, Drawing, †Graphic Design, History of Art & Architecture, Mixed Media, Painting, Sculpture, Studio Art
Children's Classes: Tuition $36 - $55 per unit for 4 - 8 wk term. Courses—Crafts
Summer School: Dir, Jim Keville. Enrl 40; tuition $36 - $55 per unit for 4 - 8 wk term. Courses—Crafts, Experiencing Creative Art, Ceramics

CHICO

CALIFORNIA STATE UNIVERSITY, CHICO, Department of Art & Art History, First & Normal, Chico, CA 95929-0820. Tel 530-898-5331; Fax 530-898-4171; Email tlcotner@csuchico.edu; Web: www.csuchico.edu/art; *Chmn & Assoc Prof* Teresa Cotner, PhD; *Grad Adv & Prof* Cameron Crawford, MFA; *Prof* Sheri Simons, MFA; *Prof Emeritus* David Hoppe, MFA; *Prof* James Kuiper, MFA; *Prof Emeritus* Yoshio Kusaba PhD; *Prof Emeritus* Sharon Smith, EdD; *Instr* Jason Tannen, MFA; *Prof* Jean Gallagher, MFA; *Prof Emeritus* Michael Simmons, EdD; *Prof Emeritus* Karen VanDerpool, MFA; *Assoc Prof* Nanette Wylde, MFA; *Assoc Prof* Sue Whitmore, MFA; *Assoc Prof* Eileen Macdonald, MFA; *Assoc Prof* Robert Herhusky, MFA; *Prof* Matt Looper, PhD; *Asst Prof* Elise Archias, PhD; *Prof* Kijeong Jeon Mirch; *Prof* Michael Bishop, MFA; *Prof* Tom Patton, MFA; *Prof* Masami Toku, PhD; *Prof Emeritus* James McManus, MFA; *Prof Emeritus* Vernon Patrick, MFA; *Instr* J Pouwels, MFA; *Instr* Nancy Meyer, MA; *Asst Prof* Rouben Mohivddin; *Assoc Prof* Asa Mittman, PhD; *Instr* Michael Murphy, MFA; *Vis Resource Specialist* Erin Herzog, MFA, MLIS; *Technician* David Barta
Estab 1887; maintains nonprofit gallery, Dept of Art, CSU, Chico, Chico, CA 95928; pub; D & E; SC 39, LC 29, GC 29; non-maj & maj 1900, grad 59
Ent Req: Ent exam and test scores
Degrees: BA 4 yr, BFA 5 yr, MFA 3 yr, MA 1 1/2 yr minimum
Courses: Aesthetics, Art Appreciation, Art Education, †Art History, †Ceramics, Design, Display, †Drawing, Glass, †History of Art & Architecture, †Interior Design, Intermedia, Mixed Media, Museum Staff Training, †Painting, Photography, †Printmaking, †Sculpture, Teacher Training, †Weaving
Summer School: Chmn, Vernon Patrick. Enrl 50. Courses—Varies

CLAREMONT

CLAREMONT GRADUATE UNIVERSITY, Art Department, 251 E Tenth St, Claremont, CA 91711. Tel 909-621-8071; Fax 909-607-1276; Email art@cgu.edu; Web: www.cgu.edu/art; *Chair* David Pagel
Estab 1925; maintain nonprofit art gallery; Claremont Graduate University/Art Galleries & Special Exhibs Progs, 251 East Tenth St, Claremont, CA 91711-3913; FT 4, PT 9; priv; D; Scholarships; non-maj 1, grad 60
Ent Req: BA, BFA or Equivalent
Degrees: MA 1 yr, MFA 2 yr
Tuition: 2011-2012 $18,187 per semester
Courses: Art History, †Studio Art

PITZER COLLEGE, Dept of Art, 1050 N Mills Ave, Claremont, CA 91711-6101. Tel 909-621-8217; Fax 909-621-8481; Web: www.pitzer.edu; *Photog* Stephen Cahill; *Drawing* Kathryn Miller; *Prof Ceramics* David Furman; *Photog* Michael Honer
Estab 1963; pvt; D&E; Scholarships; Fellowships; SC 10, LC 6
Ent Req: HS dipl, various criteria, apply Dir of Admis
Degrees: BA 4 yr
Courses: Art History, Ceramics, Constructions, Drawing, Environments, Film, History of Art & Architecture, Mixed Media, Photography, Sculpture, Video
—**Pitzer Art Galleries,** Pitzer College, 1050 N Mills Ave Claremont, CA 91711-6101. Tel 909-607-3143; Email pitzer_galleries@pitzer.edu; Web: www.pitzer.edu/galleries; *Dir* Ciara Ennis
Open Tues-Fri 12PM-5PM, other times by appointment
Collections: Nichols Gallery: works by nat & international artists; Lenzner Family Gallery: works by emerging artists

POMONA COLLEGE, Dept of Art History, 145 E Bonita Ave, Claremont, CA 91711-4426. Tel 909-607-2221; Fax 909-621-8892; Web: www.pomona.edu/academics/departments/art-history; *Prof* George Gorse, PhD; *Chmn & Prof* Frances Pohl, PhD; *Assoc Prof* Phyllis Jackson, PhD
Estab 1889; Maintain library, The Visual Resources Collection of the Dept of Art History at Pomona College (same address); pvt; D; Scholarships; LC 25; D 330 maj 37
Ent Req: HS dipl
Degrees: BA 4 yrs
Courses: †Art History, Art Studio

SCRIPPS COLLEGE, Millard Sheets Art Center-Williamson Gallery, 1030 Columbia Ave, Claremont, CA 91711-3948. Tel 909-621-8000; Fax 909-607-7576; Web: www.scrippscollege.edu; *Chmn Dept* Nancy Macko
Estab 1928, dept estab 1933; pub; D; Scholarships; D 580, non-maj 480, maj 100
Ent Req: HS dipl
Degrees: BA
Courses: Architecture, Art History, Ceramics, Drawing, Fiber Arts, Film, Mixed Media, Painting, Printmaking, †Sculpture, Typography

COALINGA

WEST HILLS COMMUNITY COLLEGE, Fine Arts Dept, 300 Cherry Lane, Coalinga, CA 93210. Tel 559-935-0801, Ext 328; Fax 559-935-5655; Web: www.westhillscollege.com; *Instr* Marilyn Trouse
Estab 1935; pub; D & E; SC 15, LC 2; D 625, E 1250, non-maj 25, maj 10
Ent Req: HS dipl or equivalent
Degrees: AA 2 yrs
Tuition: $11 per unit in-state; $139 out-of-state
Courses: Art History, †Ceramics, Design, †Drawing, Fashion Arts, †Illustration, Lettering, †Museum Staff Training, †Painting, Printmaking, Sculpture

COMPTON

COMPTON COMMUNITY COLLEGE, Art Dept, 1111 E Artesia Blvd, Room E-26 Compton, CA 90221-5393. Tel 310-637-2660; Web: www.compton.cc.ca.us; *Prof* Verneal De Silvo; *Dr* Cornelia Lyles
Estab 1929; FT 1; pub; D & E; Scholarships; SC 16, LC 6; D 3500, E 2000, maj 18
Ent Req: HS dipl, 18 yrs of age
Degrees: AA 2 yr
Courses: Advertising Design, Afro-American Art, Art Appreciation, Drafting, Drawing, History of Art & Architecture, Lettering, Painting, Photography, Show Card Writing, Theatre Arts
Summer School: Courses—Art Appreciation

COSTA MESA

ORANGE COAST COLLEGE, Visual & Performing Arts Division, 2701 Fairview, Costa Mesa, CA 92628. Tel 714-432-5629; Fax 714-432-5075; Web: www.orangecoastcollege.com; *Div Dean* Joe Poshek; *Instr Life Draw* Holly Topping; *Prof Drawing & Painting* Roger Whitridge; *Prof Drawing & Painting* Tom Dowling; *Prof Ceramics* Kevin Myers; *Sculpture* Leland Means; *Art History* Irini Rickerson; *Foundations* Joan Sallinger
Estab 1946; Maintains nonprofit art gallery, Frank M Doyle Arts Pavilion & library, Orange Coast Col Learning Resource Center 2701 Fairview Rd, Costa Mesa, CA 92626; on-campus limited art supply store; FT 30, Adjunct 80; pub; D & E; Scholarships; SC 225, LC 25; D 4500, E 3500, maj 825
Ent Req: ent exam
Degrees: AA 2 yr
Tuition: $46 per unit
Courses: Advertising Design, Advertising Design, †Art, Art Appreciation, Art History, Ceramics, Commercial Art, †Computer Graphics, Design, Display, †Display & Visual Presentation, Drawing, Film, Graphic Arts, Graphic Design, Illustration, Interior Design, Jewelry, Lettering, Mixed Media, †Music, Painting, Photography, Printmaking, Sculpture, Stage Design, Theatre Arts, Video
Summer School: Dir Joe Poshek. Six & eight wk sessions. Courses—same as regular session

CUPERTINO

DE ANZA COLLEGE, Creative Arts Division, 21250 Stevens Creek Blvd, Cupertino, CA 95014-5797. Tel 408-864-8832; Web: www.deanza.fhda.edu; *Instr* William Geisinger; *Instr* Michael Cole; *Instr* Lee Tacang; *Instr* Michael Cooper; *Dean Creative Arts* Dr Nancy Canter
Estab 1967, dept estab 1967; pub; D & E; Scholarships
Ent Req: 16 yrs of age
Degrees: Certificates of Proficiency, AA 2 yrs
Courses: Aesthetics, Art History, Ceramics, Drafting, Drawing, Film, Graphic Arts, Graphic Design, Lettering, Painting, Photography, Printmaking, Sculpture, Stage Design, Theatre Arts, Video
Adult Hobby Classes: Tuition varies per class. Courses—Bronze Casting, Calligraphy, Museum Tours,
Children's Classes: Computer art camp
Summer School: Courses—Drawing, Painting, Printmaking

CYPRESS

CYPRESS COLLEGE, 9200 Valley View St, Fine Arts Division Cypress, CA 90630-5805. Tel 714-484-7000, Ext. 47139; *Fine Arts Mgr* Barbara Russo; *Chairperson* Charlene Felos
Estab 1966; pub; D & E, Sat; Scholarships; SC, LC; D 13,200
Ent Req: HS dipl
Degrees: AA 2 yrs
Courses: Advertising Design, Art Appreciation, Art History, Ceramics, Commercial Art, Design, †Display, Drawing, †Gallery Design, Graphic Arts, Graphic Design, †Metalsmithing, †Painting, †Printmaking

Adult Hobby Classes: Adults may take any classes offered both day & extended; also offer adult education classes
Summer School: Extended Day Coordr, Dr Evelyn Maddox

DAVIS

UNIVERSITY OF CALIFORNIA, DAVIS, Dept of Art & Art History, One Shields Ave, Davis, CA 95616-8528. Tel 530-752-0105; Fax 530-752-0795; Email lcday@ucdavis.edu; Web: www.ucdavis.edu; *Chmn Art Studio* Gina Werfel, MFA; *Dir Art History* Jeffrey Ruda; *Prof Painting & Mixed Media* Conrad Atkinson; *Prof Painting* Mike Henderson, MFA; *Prof Electronic & Digital Arts* Lynn Hershman, MA; *Prof Painting & Drawing* David Hollowell, MFA; *Cooperating Faculty Dept of Art* Malaquias Montoya, BA; *Prof Painting* Pardee Hearne, MFA; *Prof Sculpture* Lucy Puls, MFA; *Prof* Annabeth Rosen, MFA; *Prof Painting* Cornelia Schulz, MFA
Estab 1952; FT 16; pub; D; Scholarships; SC 28, LC 35; maj 130, others 900
Degrees: BA 4 yrs, MA(Art History), MFA(Art Studio)
Courses: Art Appreciation, †Art History, Ceramic Sculpture, Ceramics, Conceptual Art, Constructions, Drawing, Graphic Arts, History of Art & Architecture, Mixed Media, Painting, Photography, Sculpture

EL CAJON

GROSSMONT COLLEGE, Art Dept, 8800 Grossmont College Dr, El Cajon, CA 92020-1765. Tel 619-644-7000; Web: www.grossmont.edu/art/
Courses: Art History, Photography, Sculpture, Video

EUREKA

COLLEGE OF THE REDWOODS, Arts & Languages Dept Division, 7351 Tompkins Hill Rd, Eureka, CA 95501-9300. Tel 707-445-6700, 476-4302 (Art Dept); Fax 707-441-5916; *Dean* Lea Mills
Estab 1964; FT 4, PT 8; pub; D & E; Scholarships; SC 15, LC 3 per sem; 8330, maj 160
Ent Req: HS grad
Degrees: AA & AS 2 yrs
Tuition: Nonres—$148 per unit plus $15 enrollment fee per unit
Courses: Art Fundamentals, Ceramics, Drawing, Fabrics, Jewelry Making, Photography, Weaving

FAIRFIELD

SOLANO COMMUNITY COLLEGE, Division of Fine & Applied Art & Behavioral Science, 4000 Suisun Valley Rd, Fairfield, CA 94534-4017. Tel 707-864-7000; Web: www.solano.edu; *Instr* Jan Eldridge; *Instr* Kate Delos; *Instr* Marc Lancet; *Instr* Marilyn Tannenbaum; *Instr* Ray Salmon; *Instr* Rod Guyer; *Instr* Marc Pondone; *Instr* Debra Bloomfield; *Instr* Vera Grosowsky; *Instr* Christine Rydell; *Instr* Al Zidek; *Instr* Bruce Blondin; *Div Dean* Richard Ida
Estab 1945; pub; D & E; SC 16, LC 5; D 255, E 174, maj 429
Ent Req: HS dipl
Degrees: AA 2 yrs
Courses: †3-D Art, Art History, Ceramics, Commercial Art, Drawing, Fashion Illustration, Form & Composition, Fundamentals of Art, Illustration, Lettering, Painting, Papermaking, Photography, Printmaking, Raku, Sculpture, Silkscreen, Survey of Modern Art
Adult Hobby Classes: Tuition varies per class. Courses—Cartooning, Jewelry Design, Stained Glass
Summer School: Dean summer session, Dr Don Kirkorian

FRESNO

CALIFORNIA STATE UNIVERSITY, FRESNO, Art & Design, 5225 N Backer Ave, Mail-Stop No 65 Fresno, CA 93740-0001. Tel 559-278-4240, 278-2516; Fax 559-278-4706; Email info@csufresno.edu; Web: www.csufresno.edu/art and design; *Chmn* Nancy K Brian
Estab 1911, dept estab 1915; FT 15; pub; E; Scholarships; SC 45, LC 9, GC 4; 1000
Ent Req: HS dipl, SAT or ACT
Degrees: BA 4 yrs, MA 2 yrs
Courses: Art Education, Art History, Ceramics, Crafts, Drawing, Film, †Graphic Design, †Interior Design, Metalsmithing, Painting, Photography, Printmaking, Sculpture, Teacher Training
Adult Hobby Classes: Tuition $35 unit. Courses—various
Summer School: Courses—Ceramics

FRESNO CITY COLLEGE, Art Dept, 1101 E University Ave, Fresno, CA 93741-0002. Tel 559-442-4600; Fax 559-485-3367; Web: www.fcc.cc.ca.us; *Dean* Anthony Cantu
Estab 1910, dept estab 1955; pub; D & E; SC 13, LC 3; D 14,000, E 2000
Ent Req: none, open door policy
Degrees: AA 2 yrs
Courses: Art Appreciation, Art History, Ceramics, Drawing, Fiber Art, Gallery Practices, Interaction of Color, Painting, Printmaking, Sculpture
Adult Hobby Classes: Ceramics, Design, Drawing, Painting, Sculpture
Summer School: Art Appreciation, Art History, Ceramics

FULLERTON

CALIFORNIA STATE UNIVERSITY, FULLERTON, Art Dept, PO Box 6850, Fullerton, CA 92834-6850. Tel 714-278-3471; Fax 714-278-2390; Web: www.art.fullerton.edu; *Dean School of Arts* Jerry Samuelson, MA; *Chmn Dept* Larry Johnson, MA
Estab 1957, dept estab 1959; Art supplies available on-campus; pub; D & E; Scholarships; SC 62, LC 27, GC 12; grad 110, undergrad 1200
Ent Req: HS dipl, SAT or ACT
Degrees: BA, BFA, MA, MFA
Courses: †Art Education, †Art History, †Ceramics, Collage, Conceptual Art, Constructions, Design, Display, †Drawing, Glass, †Graphic Design, †Illustration, Intermedia, †Jewelry, Museum Studies, †Painting, †Photography, †Printmaking, †Sculpture, Silversmithing, Video, Wood
Summer School: Enrl 100; tuition $145 per unit. Courses—Art History

FULLERTON COLLEGE, Division of Fine Arts, 321 E Chapman Ave, Art Dept Fullerton, CA 92832-2011. Tel 714-992-7116; Fax 714-992-9904; Web: www.fullcoll.edu; *Art Dept Chair* Jamie Perez; *Gallery Director* Carol Henke
Estab 1913; Maintains a non-profit art gallery; pub; D & E & Online; Scholarships; SC, LC
Ent Req: HS dipl, ent exam
Degrees: AA 2 yr
Courses: Advertising Design, Art History, Ceramics, Computer Graphics, Desktop publishing, 3D animation, Studio Arts, Drawing, Gallery Design & Exhibition, Graphic Arts, Graphic Design, Illustration, Jewelry, LetteringTypography, Museum Staff Training, Painting, Photography, Printmaking, Sculpture, Textile Design, Weaving

GILROY

GAVILAN COLLEGE, Art Dept, 5055 Santa Teresa, Gilroy, CA 95020. Tel 408-846-4946; Fax 408-848-4801; Email jedberg@gavilan.edu; Web: www.gavilan.cc.ca.us; *Instr* Jane Rekedal; *Chmn & Prof* Jane Edberg
Estab 1919; Maintain nonprofit art gallery; art supplies available on-campus; FT 2, PT 3; pub; D & E, Weekends, Long Distance Learning; SC 12, LC 2; D 450, E 75, maj 30
Ent Req: HS dipl or 18 yrs of age
Degrees: AA 2 yrs
Courses: Aesthetics, Art Appreciation, Art History, Art of the Americans, Ceramics, Design, Drawing, Graphic Design, History of Art & Architecture, Painting, Sculpture, Teacher Training, Theatre Arts
Summer School: Dir Jane Edberg. Courses—Ceramics, Drawing, Painting, Photo, Art Appreciation, Art History

GLENDALE

GLENDALE COMMUNITY COLLEGE, Visual & Performing Arts Div, 1500 N Verdugo Rd, Glendale, CA 91208-2894. Tel 818-240-1000; Fax 818-549-9436; Web: www.glendale.edu; *Prof of Art* Robert Kibler, MA; *Prof of Photog* Joan Watanabe, MFA; *Instr* Susan Sing, MA; *Instr* Annabelle Aylmer, MFA; *Instr* Caryl St Ama, MFA; *MFA* Rodger Dickes; *Assoc Prof of Media Art* Michael Petros, MA; *Instr Art History* Trudi Abram, PhD; *Instr Dance* Dora Krannig; *Instr Music* Peter Green, DMA; *Assoc Prof Music* Beth Pflueger, MM; *Prof Music* Ted Stern, PhD; *Instr* David Attyah, MFA; *Instr* Jayne Campbell, DMA; *Instr* Richard Coleman, MA; *Instr* Byron Delto, MM; *Instr* Jeanette Farr, MFA; *Instr* Rebecca Hillquist, MFA; *Instr* Mark Poore; *Instr* Melissa Randel, MA
Estab 1927; Maintain nonprofit art gallery; pub; D & E; SC 25, LC 7; D 4100, E 3900, nonmaj 800, maj 200
Ent Req: HS dipl, ent exam
Degrees: AA 2 yrs
Courses: †2-D & 3-D Art, †Advertising Design, †Art History, Ceramics, Costume Design & Construction, Design, Drawing, Film, †Graphic Design, Illustration, Lettering, †Media Arts Animation, Music, Painting, †Photography, Printmaking, Sculpture, Stage Design, Theatre Arts
Summer School: Supt, Dr Audrey Levy

GLENDORA

CITRUS COLLEGE, Art Dept, 1000 W Foothill, Glendora, CA 91740. Tel 626-914-8062, 914-8581; Email bbollinger@citrus.cc.ca.us; Web: www.citrus.cc.ca.us; *Dean of Faculty* Ben Bollinger
Estab 1915; pub; D & E; Scholarships; SC 26, LC 7; D 400, E 175, non-maj 400, maj 175
Ent Req: HS dipl
Degrees: AA and AS 2 yrs
Courses: Advertising Design, Art Appreciation, Art History, Ceramics, Commercial Art, Computer Art, Design, Drafting, Drawing, Graphic Design, Illustration, Painting, Photography, Sculpture
Children's Classes: Animation, Art Appreciation, Art History, Clay Sculpture, Computer Art, Design, Figure Drawing, Graphic Design, Watercolor
Summer School: Dir, Tom Tefft. Courses—Art History, Ceramics

HAYWARD

CALIFORNIA STATE UNIVERSITY, HAYWARD, Art Dept, 25800 Carlos Bee Blvd, Hayward, CA 94542-3000. Tel 510-885-3111; Fax 510-885-2281; Web: www.csuhayward.edu; *Interim Chmn* Michael Henninger
Estab 1957; Maintain nonprofit art gallery; University Art Gallery; pub; D & E; Scholarships; SC 30, LC 12; 9900
Ent Req: HS dipl, ent exam, ACT
Degrees: BA 4 yr
Courses: Art Appreciation, Art History, Ceramics, Computer Graphics, Design, Drawing, Electronic Arts, History of Art & Architecture, Intermedia, Painting, Photography, Printmaking, Sculpture
Adult Hobby Classes: Courses offered through Continuing Education Dept

CHABOT COLLEGE, Humanities Division, 25555 Hesperian Blvd, Hayward, CA 94545-2447. Tel 510-723-6600; Web: www.chabot.org; *Chmn* Dr Sally Fitzgerald
Estab 1961; FT 21, PT 50; pub; D & E; Scholarships; SC 27, LC 5
Ent Req: HS dipl
Degrees: AA 2 yr
Courses: Advertising Design, Cartooning, Ceramics, Costume Design & Construction, Drafting, Drawing, History of Art & Architecture, Illustration, Lettering, Painting, Sculpture, Stage Design, Theatre Arts
Summer School: Dir, Robert Hunter. Enrl 72-100; tuition $2-$100 per 6 wks. Courses—Art History, Drawing, Introduction to Art, Sculpture, Watercolor

HUNTINGTON BEACH

GOLDEN WEST COLLEGE, Visual Art Dept, 15744 Golden West St, Huntington Beach, CA 92647. Tel 714-895-8358; Fax 714-895-8784; *Dean* David Anthony; *Chmn & Instr* Roger Camp, MA, MFA; *Instr* P Donaldson, MFA; *Instr* D Ebert, MA; *Instr* C Glassford, MA; *Instr* N Tornheim, MA; *Instr* B Conley; *Instr* S Lee-Warren
Estab 1966; pub; D & E, weekends; Scholarships; SC 12, LC 6; D 13,820, E 9339
Ent Req: HS dipl
Degrees: AA 2 yrs
Courses: †Advertising Design, Art History, Calligraphy, Ceramics, Display, †Drafting, Drawing, Illustration, Interior Design, Jewelry, Lettering, Mixed Media, Painting, Photography, Printmaking, Sculpture, Silversmithing, Stage Design, †Theatre Arts, Video
Summer School: Dir, Dave Anthony. Enrl 250-300; classes vary

IDYLLWILD

IDYLLWILD ARTS ACADEMY, 52500 Temecula Dr, Idyllwild, CA 92549; PO Box 38, Idyllwild, CA 52549-0038. Tel 909-659-2171; Fax 909-659-5463; *Chmn Dance* Jean-Marie Martz; *Chmn Theater* William Scott; *Visual Arts Chmn* Greg Kennedy; *Humanities Chmn* Ned Barrett; *Chmn Math & Science* Jerry McCampbell; *Chmn Music* Laura Melton
Estab 1950; pvt; Idyllwild Arts Academy is a 14 wk summer program beginning in mid-June with courses in the arts for all ages; Scholarships
Degrees: not granted by the Idyllwild Campus, university cr earned through USC-LA Campus; documentation provided to high schools for cr
Tuition: Boarding students $25,000 per yr; day students $12,700 per yr
Courses: Ceramics, Fiber, Painting, Papermaking, Photography, Printmaking, Sculpture
Adult Hobby Classes: Enrl open; tuition $165 per wk
Children's Classes: Enrl open; tuition $90-$120 per wk, $65 for half day program. Day & Residential Children's Arts Program; also Youth Ceramics

IMPERIAL

IMPERIAL VALLEY COLLEGE, Humanities Department, 380 E. Alen Road, Imperial, CA 92251-0158. Tel 760-355-6198; Email carol.hegarty@inperial.edu; Web: www.imperialcc.ca.us; *Chmn Dept Humanities* Carol Hegarty; *Prof Art* Dr. Nannette Kelly
Maintains a non-profit art gallery: Juanita Salazar Lowe Art Gallery, 380 E Atem Rd, Imperial, CA 92231; Pub; D, E, & Online; Scholarships; SC, LC, Online
Degrees: AA
Tuition: $13 per unit
Courses: Art History, Design, Drawing, Graphic Design, Painting, Photography
Summer School: art history

IRVINE

CITY OF IRVINE, Irvine Fine Arts Center, 14321 Yale Ave, Irvine, CA 92604-1901. Tel 949-724-6880; Fax 949-552-2137; *Educ Coordr* Tim Jahns, MA; *Cur* Dori Rawlins, MA
Estab 1980; FT 3; pub; D & E; SC 35; D 600, E 600
Courses: Art Appreciation, Calligraphy, Ceramics, Drawing, Handicrafts, Jewelry, Mixed Media, Painting, Sculpture, Teacher Training
Children's Classes: Enrl 400. Tuition varies. Courses—Arts
Summer School: Enrl 40. Tuition varies. Courses—Arts

UNIVERSITY OF CALIFORNIA, IRVINE, Studio Art Dept, Claire Trevor School of the Arts, 3229 Art Culture & Technology Bldg Irvine, CA 92697-2775; 400 Mesa Rd, Claire Trevor School of the Arts Irvine, CA 92697-2775. Tel 949-824-6648; Fax 949-824-5297; Email stuart@uci.edu; Web: www.arts.uci.edustudioart; *Prof Painting* Kevin Appel; *Assoc Prof Art History & Cur Studies* Juli Carson; *Chair & Assoc Prof Photog* Miles Coolidge; *Assoc Prof Interactive Installation, & Programming* Beatriz da Costa; *Assoc Prof Media Histories* Martha Gever; *Assoc Prof Video, African American Studies* Ulysses Jenkins Jr; *Assoc Prof Digital Media* Antoinette LaFarge; *Assoc Prof Contemporary Art History* Simon Leung; *Prof Critical Theory, Feminism, Photog* Catherine Lord; *Assoc Prof Painting* Monica Majoli; *Prof Pub Art, Sculpture* Daniel Martinez; *Prof Asian American Studies* Yong Soon Min; *Prof Ceramic Sculpture* Gifford C Meyers; *Prof Elec Intermedia, Tech & Culture* Robert Nideffer; *Prof Robotic Sculpture, Critical Theory* Simon Penny; *Prof & Bren Chair* Yvonne Rainer; *Prof Photog & Media Theory* Connie Samaras; *Prof Visual Studies, Culture* David Trend; *Prof Video, Film Theory, Exper Media* Bruce Yonemoto
Estab 1965; pub; D; Scholarships; SC 25, LC 5, GC 4
Ent Req: HS dipl
Degrees: BA(Studio Art) 4 yr, MFA(Art) 3 yr
Courses: Ceramics, Digital Imaging, Drawing, History of Art & Architecture, Installation, Painting, Photography, Sculpture, Video
Summer School: Ceramics, Drawing, Painting

KENTFIELD

COLLEGE OF MARIN, Dept of Art, 835 College Ave, Kentfield, CA 94904-2590. Tel 415-485-9480; *Chmn* Chester Arnold
Estab 1926; pub; D & E; SC 48, LC 8; D 5000
Ent Req: HS dipl, ent exam
Degrees: AA, AS 2 yrs
Courses: Architectural Design, Architecture, Art Gallery Design Management, Art History, Ceramics, Color Theory, Drawing, History of Art & Architecture, Interior Design, Jewelry, Painting, Photography, Printmaking, Sculpture, Textile Design
Adult Hobby Classes: Enrl 400. Courses—Calligraphy, Drawing, Illustration, Jewelry, Painting, Printing
Children's Classes: College for Kids
Summer School: Ceramics, Drawing, Painting, Sculpture

LA JOLLA

UNIVERSITY OF CALIFORNIA, SAN DIEGO, Dept of Visual Arts, 9500 Gilman Dr, La Jolla, CA 92093-0327. Tel 858-534-2860; Fax 858-534-0091; Email jrgriffin@ucsd.edu; Web: visarts.ucsd.edu; *Prof & Chair* Amy Adler; *Chief Admin Officer* Jacqueline Griffin
Estab 1967; FT 29; pub; D & E; Scholarships
Ent Req: HS dipl
Degrees: BA, MFA, PhD
Tuition: Undergrad (res) $14,199 per yr, (nonres) $28,992 per yr; Grad (res) $17,007, (nonres) $15,102
Courses: Art History, Art History, Theory & Criticism, Film, Interdisciplinary Computing and the Arts (ICAM), Media, Photography, Speculative Design, Studio, Video

LA MIRADA

BIOLA UNIVERSITY, Department of Art, 13800 Biola Ave, La Mirada, CA 90639-0001. Tel 562-903-4807; Fax 562-903-4748; Email art@biola.edu; Web: www.biolart.org; *Interim Chair* Jonathan Puls, MFA; *Prof* Barry Krammes, MA; *Assoc Prof* Kurt Simonson, MFA; *Assoc Prof* Daniel Callis, MFA; *Assoc Prof* Jonathan Anderson, MFA
Estab 1908, dept estab 1971; Maintain nonprofit art gallery on-campus; art library; limited art supplies available on-campus; pvt; D & E; Scholarships; SC 28, LC 4; D 120, maj 120
Ent Req: HS dipl, SAT or ACT; portfolio
Degrees: BFA 4 yrs
Courses: 2-D Design, 3-D Design, 4-D Design, Aesthetics, Animation, Art Appreciation, Art History, Ceramics, Critical Thought, Culmination, Design, Drawing, Figure Studies, Graphic Arts, Graphic Design, Illustration, Installation & Performance, Lettering, Mixed Media, Painting, Photography, Sculpture, Video
Summer School: Dir, Barry A Krammes. six week courses. Courses—vary

LA VERNE

UNIVERSITY OF LA VERNE, Dept of Art, 1950 Third St, La Verne, CA 91750. Tel 909-593-3511, Ext 4273, 4763; Email johnson@ulv.edu; Web: www.ulv.edu; *Prof Photog* Gary Colby; *Asst Prof Art* Keith Lord; *Asst Prof Art History* Andres Zervigon; *Dept Chmn, Prof Art* Ruth Trotter
Estab 1891; Maintain nonprofit art gallery; Harris Art Gallery; pvt; D & E; Scholarships; SC 12, LC 10; D 125, E 60, maj 12
Ent Req: HS dipl
Degrees: BA(Art) 4 yrs
Courses: †Advertising Design, †Art Appreciation, †Art Education, †Art History, †Conceptual Art, Contemporary Art Seminar, Drawing, †History of Art, Painting, Photography, Sculpture, †Teacher Training, Theatre Arts
Summer School: Terms of 3 and 4 wks

LAGUNA BEACH

ART INSTITUTE OF SOUTHERN CALIFORNIA, 2222 Laguna Canyon Rd, Laguna Beach, CA 92651-1136. Tel 949-376-6000; Fax 949-376-6009; Email admissions@aisc.edu; Web: www.aisc.edu; *Dean Visual Commun* Jonathan Burke; *Dean Fine Arts* Betty Shelton; *Dean Liberal Arts* Helen Garrison; *Instr* Stephanie Taugner; *Instr* George Zebot; *Instr* Kim Owinell
Estab 1961; pvt; D & E; Scholarships; SC 81, LC 48; D 280, maj 4
Ent Req: SATI or ACT, 3.0 GPA, portfolio, letter reg, personal, state
Degrees: BFA
Courses: Animation, Art History, Drawing, Fine Arts, Graphic Arts, Graphic Design, Painting, Photography, Visual Communication
Adult Hobby Classes: 15 wk semesters. Courses—Studio & Lecture courses
Children's Classes: 15 wk semesters. Courses—Studio & Lecture courses
Summer School: Pres, Patricia Caldwell. Two 5 wk sessions. Courses—Studio & Lecture courses

LANCASTER

ANTELOPE VALLEY COLLEGE, Art Dept, Division of Fine Arts, 3041 W Ave K, Lancaster, CA 93536-5426. Tel 661-722-6300; Fax 661-722-6390; Web: www.avc.edu; *Dean Fine & Performing Arts Div* Dr Dennis White, MFA; *Prof* Robert McMahan, MFA; *Prof* Richard Sim, MFA; *Prof* Patricia Crosby-Hinds, MFA; *Asst Prof* Cynthia Minet, MFA
Estab 1929; pub; D & E
Degrees: AA 2 yrs
Courses: Art History, Ceramics, Color & Design, Computer Graphics, Drawing, Graphic Arts, Jewelry, Painting, Photography, Sculpture

LONG BEACH

CALIFORNIA STATE UNIVERSITY, LONG BEACH, Art Dept, 1250 Bellflower Blvd, Long Beach, CA 90840-0004. Tel 562-985-4376; Fax 562-985-1650; *Chmn* Jay Kvapi
Estab 1949; FT 40, PT 57; pub; D & E; Scholarships; Fellowships; SC 164, LC 26, GC 23, for both locations; 5356 for both locations
Ent Req: HS grad, ent exam, SAT
Degrees: BA, BFA, MA, MFA
Courses: Art Education, Art History, Bio Medical Art, Ceramics, †Digital Media, Drawing, †Fiber Art, †Intermedia, †Metals, Museum Studies, Painting, Photography, Printmaking, Sculpture, †Studio Art, †Wood
Children's Classes: Ceramics, Drawing, Painting
Summer School: Dean, Dr Robert Behm. Tuition $150 per unit. Courses—Art Education, Art History, Ceramics, Drawing, Fiber, Graphic Design, Illustration, Painting, Special Topics, Photography
—**Design Dept**, 1250 Bellflower Blvd, Long Beach, CA 90840. Tel 562-985-5089; Fax 562-985-2284; *Dean* Wade Hobgood; *Chmn* Charles Leinbach
Estab 1949; FT 10, PT 9; pub; SC 164, LC 26, GC 23 for both locations; 5356 for both locations
Ent Req: HS grad, ent exam
Degrees: BF, BFA, BS, MA, MFA
Courses: Design, Industrial Design, Interior Design, Perspective, Rapid Visualization
Summer School: Dean, Dr Donna George

LONG BEACH CITY COLLEGE, Art & Photography Dept, 4901 E Carson St, Long Beach, CA 90808-1780. Tel 562-938-4319; Web: www.art.lbcc.edu; *Instr* Larry White; *Instr* Linda King, MFA; *Instr* Rodney Tsukashima, MA; *Instr* Mike Daniel, MFA; *Instr* Stas Orlovski; *Dept Chmn* Ann Mitchell; *Instr* Colleen Sterritt; *Assoc Prof Jewelry & Metalwork, Program Coordr Applied Design* Kristin Beeler, MFA
Pub; D, E & W; Scholarships; SC 65, LC 26
Ent Req: HS dipl, ent exam
Degrees: AA & cert 2 yrs
Courses: Art History, Ceramics, Commercial Art, Computer Art & Design, Drawing, Illustration, Jewelry, Lettering, Mixed Media, Painting, Photography, Printmaking, Sculpture, Studio Crafts
Adult Hobby Classes: Enrl 1500; tuition $13 per unit sem. Courses—Art History, Ceramics, Computer Graphics, Drawing, Jewelry, Painting, Photography, Printmaking, Sculpture
Summer School: Tuition $13 for 4-8 wk sem. Courses—same as above

LOS ALTOS HILLS

FOOTHILL COLLEGE, Fine Arts & Communications Div, 12345 El Monte Rd, Los Altos Hills, CA 94022. Tel 650-949-7325; Web: www.foothillcollege.edu; *Dean* Alan Harvey
College has three campuses; D; Scholarships
Degrees: AA, cert
Tuition: Res—undergrad & grad $30 per unit; nonres—grad $102 per unit
Courses: Advertising Design, Art Appreciation, Art History, Ceramics, Computer Graphics, Design, Drawing, Film, Illustration, Painting, Photography, Printmaking, Sculpture, Stage Design, Textile Design

LOS ANGELES

ACE GALLERY, 5514 Wilshire Blvd, Los Angeles, CA 90046-3829. Tel 323-935-4411; Fax 323-202-1082; Email acelosa@aol.com; *Dir* Douglas Chrismas
Estab 1955; pvt; D; Scholarships; SC 4, LC 4, GC 4; D 6, E 7, non-maj 2, maj 8, grad 3
Ent Req: art school dipl, ent exam
Courses: Architecture, Calligraphy, Collage, Design, Drafting, Drawing, Graphic Arts, History of Art & Architecture, †History of Art in Architecture, Intermedia, Lettering, Mixed Media, Painting, Photography, Printmaking, Sculpture, Stage Design

AMERICAN FILM INSTITUTE (AFI), 2021 N Western Ave, Los Angeles, CA 90027-1625. Tel 323-856-7600; Fax 323-467-4578; Web: www.afi.com; *Pres & CEO* Bob Gazzole; *COO* Nancy Harris; *Chmn Bd Trustees* Sir Howard Stringer; *Chmn Bd Dirs* Robert A. Daly; *Conservatory Dean* Jan Schuette
Estab 1969; preserves, honors & educates; pvt; D&E; Scholarships
Degrees: MFA
Courses: †Cinematography, †Directing, †Editing, †Film, †Producing, †Production Design & Screen Writing, Screenwriting
Adult Hobby Classes: Non degree evening & weekend classes

BRENTWOOD ART CENTER, 13031 Montana Ave, Los Angeles, CA 90049-4891. Tel 310-451-5657; Fax 310-395-5403; Web: www.brentwoodart.com; *Dir* Edward Buttwinick, BA
Estab 1971; 25; pub & pvt; D & E; SC 40; D 400, E 100
Courses: Design, Drawing, Mixed Media, Painting, Sculpture
Adult Hobby Classes: Enrl 300; tuition $175-$225 per month. Courses—Basic Drawing, Design, Life Drawing, Mixed Media, Painting, Sculpture
Children's Classes: Enrl 300; tuition $100-$180 per month. Courses—Cartooning, Drawing, Mixed Media, Painting, Sculpture
Summer School: Dir, Ed Buttwinick. Enrl 400; tuition $300-$500 for nine wk prog. Courses—Drawing, Mixed Media, Painting, Sculpture

CALIFORNIA STATE UNIVERSITY, LOS ANGELES, Art Dept, 5151 State University Dr, Los Angeles, CA 90032-4226. Tel 323-343-4010; Fax 323-343-4045; Email eforde@calstatela.edu; Web: www.calstatela.edu/
Estab 1947; Maintains fine arts gallery; art supplies available on-campus; pub; D & E; Scholarships; SC 85, LC 12, GC 9; D 2500 (Art), non-maj 150, maj 324, grad 47 (per quarter)
Ent Req: HS dipl, ent exam
Degrees: BA(Art), MA(Art), MFA(Art)
Courses: Advertising Design, Architecture, Art Education, Art History, †Ceramics, †Commercial Art, †Computer Graphics, Costume Design, Costume Design & Construction, Design, †Design Theory, †Drawing, Fashion Illustration, Graphic Arts, History of Art & Architecture, †Illustration, Painting, †Photography, Printmaking, Sculpture, †Teacher Training, †Textile Design, Textiles

INNER-CITY ARTS, 720 Kohler St, Los Angeles, CA 90021-1518. Tel 213-627-9621; Fax 213-627-6469; Email info@inner-cityarts.org; Web: www.inner-cityarts.org; *Co-Founder & Artistic Dir* Bob Bates; *Dir Opers* Susie Goliti; *Deputy Dir* Sharyn L Church; *Chief Financial Officer* Ofelia De Los Santos
Estab to enrich the lives of inner city children, through a total arts program; 4; pub; D

LOS ANGELES CITY COLLEGE, School of Visual & Media Arts, 855 N Vermont Ave, Los Angeles, CA 90029-3588. Tel 323-953-4000; Email wiesena@lacitycollege.edu; Web: www.lacc.cc.ca.us; *Professor of Art* Alexandra Wiesenfeud; *Professor of Art* Laurel Paley; *Professor of Media Arts* Daniel Marios; *Professor of Journalism* Rhonda Guess; *Professor of Media Arts* Nicole Bell; *Professor of Art History* Elizabeth Lopez; *Professor of Media Arts* Linda Okamura
Estab 1929; PT 18; pub; D & E; Scholarships; SC 48, LC 8; D 450, E 150, non-maj approx 2/3, maj approx 1/3
Ent Req: HS dipl & over 18 yrs of age
Degrees: AA 2 yr, ADT in Studio Art, Certificate of Graphic Arts Communicaitons
Courses: †Advertising Design, †Art History, Ceramics, †Commercial Art, Display, Drawing, †Graphic Design, Life Drawing, †Painting, Printmaking, Sculpture
Adult Hobby Classes: Enrl 2090; tuition approx $20 per class of 8 wks. Courses—Ceramics, Design, Drawing, Painting, Perspective, Printmaking, Sculpture
Summer School: Chmn, Phyllis Muldavin. Enrl 250; tuition $50 for term of 6 wks beginning July. Courses—basic courses only

LOYOLA MARYMOUNT UNIVERSITY, Dept of Art & Art History, 1 LMU Dr, MS 8346 Los Angeles, CA 90045-2659. Tel 310-338-7424, 338-5189; Fax 310-338-1948; Email mtang@imu.edu; Web: www.lmu.edu; *Prof* Rudolf Fleck, MFA; *Prof* Terresa Munoz, MFA; *Assoc Prof* Katherine Harper, PhD; *Prof* Jane Brucker, MFA; *Prof* Michael Brodsky, MFA; *Asst Prof* Dmitry Kmelnitsky, MFA; *Asst Prof* Teresa Lenihan, MFA; *Asst Prof* Damon Willick, PhD; *Assoc Prof* Dr Kirstin Noreen, PhD; *Asst Prof* Garland Kirkpatrick, MFA; *Asst Prof* Diane Meyer, MFA; *Asst Prof* Han Dai-Yu, MFA
Estab as Marymount Col in 1940, merged with Loyola Univ 1968; Maintains nonprofit art gallery, Laband Art Gallery; FT 13, PT 24; pvt & den; D & E; Scholarships; SC 65, LC 20; Maj 200
Ent Req: HS dipl
Degrees: BA 4 yrs
Courses: Advertising Design, Aesthetics, Art Appreciation, †Art Education, Art History, Ceramics, Computer Animation, Computer Graphics, †Conceptual Art, Design, Drawing, Graphic Arts, Graphic Design, Illustration, Jewelry, Lettering, †Mixed Media, †Museum Staff Training, Painting, Photography, Printmaking, Sculpture, Silversmithing
Adult Hobby Classes: Ceramics, Jewelry
Summer School: Dir, Chris Chapple, PhD. Courses— Ceramics, Computer Graphics, Jewelry, Art History, Water Color
—**Laband Art Gallery**, One LMU Dr MS 8346, Los Angeles, CA 90045-2659.
—**Von Der Ahe Library**, One LMU Dr MS 8203, Los Angeles, CA 90045-2659.

MOUNT SAINT MARY'S COLLEGE, Art Dept, 12001 Chalon Rd, Los Angeles, CA 90049-1599. Tel 310-954-4000, 954-4361 (art); Email adm@mscm.la.edu; Web: www.msmc.la.edu; *Chmn & Prof* Jody Baral
Estab as Chalon Campus in 1925, also maintains Doheny Campus estab 1962; den; D & E; Scholarships; D 60, non-maj 31, maj 29
Ent Req: HS dipl
Degrees: BA and BFA 4 yrs
Courses: †Art Education, †Art History, Ceramics, †Collage, †Conceptual Art, †Constructions, Drawing, Fiber Design, †Graphic Arts, †Graphic Design, †Illustration, †Intermedia, †Mixed Media, Painting, Photography, †Printmaking, Sculpture, †Textile Design

OCCIDENTAL COLLEGE, Dept of Art History & Visual Arts, 1600 Campus Rd M-2, Los Angeles, CA 90041-3314. Tel 323-259-2749; Fax 323-259-2930; Email admissions@oxy.com; Web: www.oxy.edu; *Chmn* Louise Yuhas, PhD; *Prof* Eric Frank, PhD; *Prof* Amy Lyford, PhD; *Prof* Esther Yau, PhD; *Prof* Broderick Fox, MFA, PhD; *Prof* Linda Besemer, MFA; *Prof* Linda Lyke, MFA; *Prof* Mary Beth Heffernan, MFA
Estab 1887; FT 7, PT 2; pvt; D & E; Scholarships; Grants; SC 19, LC 25, GC 5; maj 40, others 300
Ent Req: HS dipl, col transcript, SAT, recommendations
Degrees: BA 4 yr
Courses: Aesthetics, †Art History, Ceramics, †Drawing, †Film, †Film & Media Studies, †Graphics, Mixed Media, †Painting, †Printmaking, †Sculpture
Adult Hobby Classes: Fundamentals

OTIS COLLEGE OF ART & DESIGN, Fine Arts, 9045 Lincoln Blvd, Los Angeles, CA 90045-3505. Tel 310-665-6885; Fax 310-665--6821; Email finearts@otis.edu; Web: www.otis.edu; *Chmn* Meg Cranston; *Asst Chmn* Alex Slade; *Prog Dir Painting* Scott Grieger; *Prog Dir Photog* Soo Kim; *Prog Dir Sculpture/New Genres* Jacci den Hartog
Estab 1918; Maintains nonprofit art gallery & Millard Sheets Library; Pvt; D & E; Scholarships; SC 276, LC 117, GC 31; D 1,043, E 550, maj 1,043, grad 46
Degrees: BFA 4 yrs, MFA 2 yrs
Tuition: $14,473 per sem
Courses: Architecture/Landscapes/Interiors, Art Education, Communication Design, Digital Media, Environmental Arts, †Fashion Design, Fine Arts, Graphic Design, Illustration, Interactive Product Design, Photography, Toy Design
Adult Hobby Classes: Enrl 2,400; tuition varies
Children's Classes: Enrl 300. Tuition & courses vary
Summer School: Coordr K-12 Prog, Rosina Catalano. Tuition & courses vary

SOUTHERN CALIFORNIA INSTITUTE OF ARCHITECTURE, 960 E 3rd St, Los Angeles, CA 90013-1822. Tel 213-613-2200; Fax 213-613-2260; Email admissions@sciarc.edu; Web: www.sciarc.edu; *Dir* Eric Owen Moss; *Dir Asst* Bijal Shah; *Acad Prog Asst* Paul Holliday; *Undergrad Dir* Chris Genik; *Grad Dir* Ming Fung
Estab 1972; Maintain a nonprofit art gallery, SCI-Arc Gallery, 960 E 3rd St, Los Angeles, CA 90013; pvt; D & E
Degrees: BArch, MArch
Courses: Architecture
Summer School: Summer Foundation Program in Architecture: Making & Meaning, $2,840

UNIVERSITY OF CALIFORNIA, LOS ANGELES, Dept of Art, Broad Art Center, Ste 2275, 240 Charles E Young Dr N Los Angeles, CA 90095; Box 951615, Los Angeles, CA 90095-1615. Tel 310-825-3281; Fax 310-206-6676; Email artinfo@arts.ucla.edu; Web: www.arts.ucla.edu; *Dept Chair* Andrea Fraser
Scholarships; Fellowships
Degrees: BA, MA, MFA
Tuition: CA Resident $13,225; Nonresident $28.992
Courses: Ceramics, Critical & Curatorial Studies, Drawing, Interdisciplinary Studio, New Genres, Painting, Photography, Sculpture
—Dept of Design Media Arts, PO Box 951456, Broad Art Center Ste 2275 Los Angeles, CA 90095-1615. Tel 310-825-9007; Fax 310-206-6676; Email dmainfo@arts.ucla.edu; Web: dma.ucla.edu; *Dept Chmn* Christian Moeller
pub; D; SC, LC, GC
Ent Req: Dept and UCLA Application
Degrees: BA, MA, MFA
Tuition: CA Resident $13,225; Nonresident $28.992
Courses: Art Education, Ceramics, Computer Imagery, Design, Fiber Textile, Graphic Design, Industrial Design, Interior Design, Video
—Dept of Art History, PO Box 9511417, 100 Dodd Hall Los Angeles, CA 90095-1417. Tel 310-206-6905; Fax 310-206-1903; Email arthistory@humnet.ucla.edu; Web: arthistory.ucla.edu; *Dept Chair* Miwon Kwon
Scholarships; Fellowships
Degrees: BA, MA, PhD
Tuition: CA Resident $13,225; Nonresident $28.992
Courses: †Art History

UNIVERSITY OF JUDAISM, Dept of Continuing Education, 15600 Mulholland Dr, Los Angeles, CA 90077-1599. Tel 310-476-9777; Fax 310-471-1278; Web: www.uj.edu; *Dir* Gady Levy
Estab 1947; den; SC 14, LC 6
Degrees: units in continuing education only
Courses: Art History, Book Illustration, Calligraphy, Drawing, History of Jewish Art, Interior Design, Painting, Photography, Picture Book Making for Children, Sculpture, Tile Painting
Adult Hobby Classes: Enrl 8; tuition $127 per sem
Summer School: Courses offered

UNIVERSITY OF SOUTHERN CALIFORNIA, College of Letters, Arts & Sciences, Von KleinSmid Center-VKC 351, University of Southern California Los Angeles, CA 90089-0047. Tel 213-740-4552; Fax 213-740-8971; Email arthist@college.usc.edu; Web: http://college.usc.edu/ahis/home/; *Chair* Carolyn Malone
Estab 1887, school estab 1979
Courses: †Art History

MALIBU

PEPPERDINE UNIVERSITY, SEAVER COLLEGE, Dept of Art, 24255 Pacific Coast Hwy, Malibu, CA 90263-3999. Tel 310-506-4000; Fax 310-506-7403; Email admission-seaver@pepperdine.edu; Web: seavers.pepperdine.edu/finearts; *Prof* Avery Falkner; *Prof* Joe Piasentin; *Asst Prof* K Genevieve Freeman; *Assoc Prof* Cynthia Colburn; *Assoc Prof* Sonia Sorrell; *Chmn Fine Art* Gary Cobb
Estab 1937; Maintain nonprofit art gallery, Weisman Art Museum, Cultural Arts Center, Pepperdine University, Malibu, CA 90263; Church of Christ, pvt; D; Scholarships; SC & LC
Degrees: BA in Art
Tuition: Apartment $26,100; campus res—room & board $25,850 per yr
Courses: Art Appreciation, Art Education, Art History, Ceramics, Design, Drawing, Graphic Arts, Jewelry, Monotypes, Painting, Sculpture
Children's Classes: Children's classes are offered thru Weisman Museum (on campus), Dir Dr. Michael Zahian, Cultural Arts Center, Pepperdine Univ, Malibu, CA 90263
Summer School: Enrl 20; tuition $235 per unit. Courses—Jewelry, Mixed Media, Monotypes, Painting

MARYSVILLE

YUBA COLLEGE, Fine Arts Division, 2088 N Beale Rd, Marysville, CA 95901-7699. Tel 530-741-6700; Web: www.yuba.cc.ca.us; *Assoc Dean* Michael Moyers
Estab 1927; FT 2; pub; D & E; Scholarships; SC 23, LC 2; total 1437, maj 493
Ent Req: HS grad or 18 yrs of age
Degrees: AA 2 yr
Summer School: Dean & Assoc Dean Community Educ, Cal Gower. Courses—Ceramics, Drawing

MENDOCINO

MENDOCINO ART CENTER, 45200 Little Lake St, Mendocino, CA 95460; PO Box 765, Mendocino, CA 95460-0765. Tel 707-937-5818; WATS 800-653-3328; *Exec Dir* Peggy Templer
Estab 1959; pvt; D & E; SC 24, LC 6; D 24
Publications: A&E Magazine, monthly
Ent Req: mutual interview, ceramics ROP 2 yr prog
Degrees: program in ceramics, sculpture, jewelry, textiles, computer arts, & fine arts
Courses: Calligraphy, †Ceramics, Drawing, Graphic Design, Jewelry, Lettering, Painting, Printmaking, Sculpture, Silkscreen, Silversmithing, Textile Design, Weaving
Summer School: Dir, Elaine Beldin-Reed. Enrl 6-15; tuition $175-$250 for 1 wk term. Courses—Acting, Ceramics, Fine Art, Jewelry, Weaving

MERCED

MERCED COLLEGE, Arts Division, 3600 M St - Stop 32, Merced, CA 95348-2898. Tel 209-384-6000; Fax 209-381-6469; Email lisa.givens@mccd.edu; Web: www.merced.cc.ca.us; *Gallery Dir* Susanne French; *Dean* John Albano; *Prof 3-D Prog* Cheryl Barnett; *Prof 2-D Prog* Louisa Benhisen; *Digital Media Prof* Alana Perlin; *Arts Secy* Lisa Givens
Estab 1964; Maintain a non-profit art gallery; Library, Learning Resource Center; on-campus bookstore; pub; D & E; Scholarships; SC 50, LC 10; D 4741, E 3187, non-maj 3700, maj 4228
Activities: Schols offered
Ent Req: 18 yrs & older
Degrees: AA & AS 2 yr
Courses: †Art Education, Art History, Ceramics, Costume Design & Construction, Design, †Digital Media, Drafting, Drawing, †Fine Art, Graphic Design, History of Art & Architecture, †Music, Painting, †Photography, Printmaking, Sculpture, Stage Design, †Theatre Arts
Children's Classes: Col for kids, summer session only

MODESTO

MODESTO JUNIOR COLLEGE, Arts Humanities & Communications Division, 435 College Ave, Modesto, CA 95350-5800. Tel 209-575-6081; Fax 209-575-6086; Web: www.gomjc.org; *Dean Div* Jim Johnson; *Instr* Richard Serroes; *Instr* Doug Smith; *Instr* Terry L Hartman, MA; *Instr* Gui Todd, MA; *Instr* Jerry M Reilly, MFA
Estab 1921, div estab 1964; pub; D & E; Scholarships; 16,024 total
Ent Req: grad of accredited high school, minor with California High School Proficiency Cert & parental permission, 11th & 12th graders with principal's permission, persons 18 or older who are able to profit from the instruction
Degrees: AA and AS 2 yrs
Courses: Advertising Design, Architecture, Art History, Ceramics, Display, Drafting, Drawing, Enameling, Film, Jewelry, Lapidary, Lettering, Painting, †Photography, Printmaking, Sculpture, Silversmithing, Theatre Arts
Adult Hobby Classes: Courses—Arts & Crafts, Lapidary
Summer School: Dir, Dudley Roach. Tuition $6 health fee. Courses—a wide variety offered

MONTEREY

MONTEREY PENINSULA COLLEGE, Art Dept/Art Gallery, 980 Fremont St, Div of Creative Arts Monterey, CA 93940-4704. Tel 831-646-4200; Fax 831-646-3005; Web: www.mpc.edu; *Painting Instr* Robynn Smith; *Art Hist Instr* Richard Janick; *Jewelry & Metals Instr* Theresa Lovering-Brown; *Sculpture Instr* Gary Quinonez; *Graphics Instr* Darien Payne; *Adjunct* Skip Kadish; *Adjunct* Carol Holoday; *Graphics Instr* Jamie Dagdigian; *Ceramics Instr* Diane Eisenbach; *Photog Instr* Kevin Bransfield; *Art Gallery Dir* Melissa Pickford
Estab 1947; Monterey Peninsula College Art Gallery, nonprofit; Adjunct 20; pub; D & E; Scholarships; SC 17, LC 8; D 1,343, E 623, maj 160
Activities: Bookstore
Ent Req: HS dipl, 18 yrs or older
Degrees: AA & AS 2 yrs
Courses: †Architecture, Art Appreciation, Art History, †Ceramics, Collage, †Commercial Graphics, Costume Design & Construction, Design, Drafting, †Drawing, Film, Graphic Arts, Illustration, Intermedia, †Jewelry, Mixed Media, Museum Staff Training, †Painting, †Photography, Printmaking, †Sculpture, Silversmithing, †Studio Art, Video, Weaving
Summer School: Dir, Thorne Hacker. Term of 6 wks beginning June. Courses are limited

MONTEREY PARK

EAST LOS ANGELES COLLEGE, Art Dept, 1301 Avenida Cesar Chavez, Monterey Park, CA 91754-6001. Tel 323-265-8842; Fax 323-780-6847; Email kallanlp@elac.edu; *Dept Chmn* Linda Kallan; *Prof* Mike Owens; *Prof* Marie Alanen; *Assoc Prof* Surana Singh-Bischofberger; *Prof* Jim Uyekawa; *Assoc Prof* Steve Monau; *Prof* Christopher Turk
Estab 1949; Maintain nonprofit art gallery, Vincent Price Art Museum; FT 7; pub; D & E; Scholarships; SC 43, LC 10; D 486, E 160, maj 646
Degrees: AA 2 yr
Courses: †Advertising Design, †Art Fundamentals, †Art Graphic Communications, †Art History, †Ceramics, †Computer Graphics, Design, Display, †Drawing, †Electronic Publishing, Graphic Arts, Graphic Design, Lettering, †Life Drawing, Mixed Media, †Painting
Children's Classes: Enrl 60. Courses—Ceramics, Direct Printing Methods, Drawing, Painting
Summer School: Dir, Carson Scott. Enrl 50; tuition $13 per unit for 6 wk term. Courses—Art 201, Beginning Drawing, Beginning 2-D Design

NAPA

NAPA VALLEY COLLEGE, Art Dept, 2277 Napa Vallejo Hwy, Napa, CA 94558-7555. Tel 707-253-3000; Web: www.nvc.cc.ca.us; *Chmn & Dir* Jan Molen; *Prof* Jay Golik; *Prof* Carolyn Broodwell
Degrees: AA & AS
Tuition: $11 per unit up to 5 units
Courses: Art Appreciation, Art History, Ceramics, Design, Drawing, Painting, Photography, Printmaking, Sculpture
Adult Hobby Classes: Courses offered
Children's Classes: Courses offered
Summer School: Courses—Painting, Ceramics, Drawing

NORTHRIDGE

CALIFORNIA STATE UNIVERSITY, NORTHRIDGE, Dept of Art, 18111 Nordhoff St, College of Arts, Media & Communication Northridge, CA 91330-0001. Tel 818-677-2242; Fax 818-677-3046; Email art.dept@csun.edu; Web: www.csun.edu/artdep; *Dept Chmn* Joe Lewis
Estab 1956; 48; pub; D & E; Scholarships; SC 13, GC 5; D & E 2231, grad 101
Ent Req: HS dipl, GRE, SAT
Degrees: BA 4-5 yrs, MA
Courses: †Animation, †Art Education, †Art History, †Ceramics, †Drawing, †Graphic Design, †Illustration, †Painting, †Photography, †Printmaking, Public Art, †Sculpture, †Textile Design, †Video
Summer School: Dir, Joe Lewis. Enrl 100; tuition $136 per unit for 6 wks beginning June 1. Courses—Art History, Graphic Design

NORWALK

CERRITOS COMMUNITY COLLEGE, Fine Arts & Communication Div, 11110 Alondra Blvd, Norwalk, CA 90650-6298. Tel 562-860-2451; Fax 562-653-7807; Email info@cerritos.edu; Web: www.cerritos.edu/fac; *Instr Dean Fine Arts* Dr Barry Russell
Estab 1956; pub; D & E; SC 36, LC 12
Ent Req: HS dipl or 18 yrs of age
Degrees: AA 2 yrs
Courses: 2-D & 3-D Design, †Acting, Calligraphy, Ceramics, Commercial Art, †Communications, †Directing, Display, Drawing, Graphic Arts, Graphic Design, History of Art & Architecture, Jewelry, †Journalism, Museum Staff Training, †Photography, Printmaking, Sculpture, †Theater
Summer School: Dir Dr Barry Russell. 6 wks per session. Drawing, Painting, History, Design, Ceramics, Calligraphy

OAKLAND

HOLY NAMES COLLEGE, Art Dept, 3500 Mountain Blvd, Oakland, CA 94619-1699. Tel 510-436-1000, Ext 1458; Fax 510-436-1199; Web: www.hnc.edu; *Chmn Dept* Robert Simon
Estab 1917; FT 2, PT 4; pvt; D & E; Scholarships; SC 24, LC 4
Ent Req: HS dipl
Degrees: BA and BFA 4 yrs
Courses: Art History, Calligraphy, Ceramics, Drawing, Jewelry, Painting, Photography, Printmaking, Sculpture

LANEY COLLEGE, Art Dept, 900 Fallon St, Oakland, CA 94607-4893. Tel 510-834-5740; Fax 510-464-3231; *Asst Dean* Carlos McLean; *Chmn* Carol Joy
Estab 1962; FT 8, PT 9; pub; D & E; SC 52, LC 8; D 1400, E 450
Ent Req: HS dipl
Degrees: AA 2 yrs
Courses: Advertising Design and Architectural Design Courses available through the Architectural Design Dept; Photography Courses available through the Photography Dept, Cartooning, †Ceramics, Color & Design, †Commercial Art, Design, Drawing, Etching, †Graphic Arts, Graphic Design, Handicrafts, History of Art & Architecture, Illustration, Lettering, Lithography, †Painting, Portraiture, Relief Printing, †Sculpture, Silkscreen
Summer School: Chmn, David Bradford. Enrl 250; tuition $10 per unit for 6 wk term

MERRITT COLLEGE, Art Dept, 12500 Campus Dr, Oakland, CA 94619-3196. Tel 510-531-4911; Web: www.peralta.cc.ca.us; *Dir* Helmut Schmitt
Estab 1970; FT 2 PT 8; D & E
Degrees: AA
Tuition: Undergrad—$11 per unit
Courses: Art History, Ceramics, Design, Illustration, Life Drawing, Painting, Sculpture
Adult Hobby Classes: Dir, Helmut Schmitt
Summer School: Dir, Helmut Schmitt. Enrol 120; tuition $5 per unit; six week courses. Courses—Life Drawing, Painting

MILLS COLLEGE, Art Dept, 5000 MacArthur Blvd, Oakland, CA 94613-1301. Tel 510-430-2117; Fax 510-430-3148; Email studio_art@mills.edu; Web: www.mills.edu; *Prof* Hung Liu, MFA; *Prof* Anna Valentina Murch; *Prof* Catherine F Wagner; *Prof* Ken Burke; *Prof* Mary-Ann Milford; *Prof* Moira Roth
Estab 1852; Maintain nonprofit art gallery, Mills College, 5000 MacArthur Blvd Oakland, CA 94613; pvt, MFA coed, undergraduate women only; grad, coed; D & E; Scholarships; SC 23, LC 22, GC 20; grad 24
Ent Req: HS dipl, SAT, Advanced Placement Exam for undergrads
Degrees: BA 4 yrs, MFA 2 yrs
Tuition: $35,000 per yr; MFA $30,072 per yr; campus res—room & board $5,000 - $7,000 depending on type of room
Courses: 3-D Design, Aesthetics, †Art Education, Art History, Ceramics, †Conceptual Art, Drawing, †Electronic Arts, †History of Art & Architecture, Mixed Media, †Museum Staff Training, Painting, Photography, †Restoration & Conservation, Sculpture, Video

OCEANSIDE

MIRACOSTA COLLEGE, Art Dept, 1 Barnard Dr, Oceanside, CA 92056-3899. Tel 760-757-2121; Fax 760-795-6817; Web: www.miracosta.cc.ca.us; *Instr* Erik Growborg, MA; *Instr Digital Art* Peggy Jones; *Art History Instr* Susan Delaney
Estab 1934; pub; D & E; Scholarships; SC 12, LC 4; maj 200
Ent Req: HS dipl
Degrees: AA and AS normally 2 yrs
Courses: Aesthetics, †Architecture, Art Appreciation, Art Education, †Art History, Ceramics, Collage, Computer Art, Conceptual Art, Constructions, †Costume Design & Construction, Design, †Drafting, Drawing, Figure Drawing, Figure Painting, Figure Sculpture, Film, †Graphic Design, History of Art & Architecture, Interior Design, Landscape Architecture, Mixed Media, †Painting, †Photography, †Printmaking, †Sculpture, †Stage Design, Teacher Training, †Theatre Arts
Children's Classes: Enrl 200; tuition small fees. Courses—Art, Theater
Summer School: Enrl 2000; tuition $15. Courses—Various subjects

ORANGE

CHAPMAN UNIVERSITY, Art Dept, 333 N Glassell, Orange, CA 92666. Tel 714-997-6729; Fax 714-997-6744; Web: www.chapman.edu; *Chmn* David Kiddie, MFA; *Prof* Jane Sinclair, MFA; *Prof* Richard Turner, MFA; *Prof* Sharon Corey, MFA; *Prof* Denise Weyhrich, MFA; *Prof* Stephen Berens, MFA; *Prof* Wendy Salmond, PhD, MFA
Estab 1918, branch estab 1954; den; D & E; Scholarships; SC 20, LC 15; D 275, non-maj 75
Ent Req: HS dipl, ACT, SAT or CLEP
Courses: Advertising Design, Art Appreciation, Art Education, Art History, Ceramics, Computer Graphics, Design, Drawing, Film, Graphic Arts, Graphic Design, Illustration, Lettering, Painting, Photography, Sculpture, Stage Design, Theatre Arts, Video
Children's Classes: Courses—workshops in connection with art education classes
Summer School: Courses—Ceramics

ORANGE CITY

NORTHWESTERN COLLEGE, Art Dept, 101 7th St SW, Orange City, CA 51041. Tel 712-737-7003, 737-7004; *Chmn, Prof* Phil Scorza, MFA
Estab 1882, dept estab 1965; pvt, affil Reformed Ch Am; D & E; Scholarships; SC 25, LC 3-4; D 200, non-maj 250, maj -25
Ent Req: HS dipl
Degrees: BA 4 yr
Tuition: Campus residency available
Courses: †Art Education, Art History, Ceramics, †Computer Design, Design, †Directed Studies, Drawing, Painting, Photography, Printmaking, Sculpture, †Student Initiated Majors

OROVILLE

BUTTE COLLEGE, Dept of Fine Arts and Communication Tech, 3536 Butte Campus Dr, Oroville, CA 95965-8399. Tel 530-895-2404; Fax 530-895-2346; Web: www.butte.cc.ca.us; *Chmn & Ceramic Coordr* Idie Adams; *Dean Instruction* Dan Walker; *Instr* Will Stull; *Instr* Geoff Fricker; *Instr* Adrian Carrasco-Zanini; *Instr* David Cooper; *Instr* Mark Hall; *Instr* Simone Senat
Estab 1968; pub; D & E; Scholarships; SC 21, LC 4; D 3988, E 4194
Ent Req: HS dipl or 18 yrs or older
Degrees: AA
Courses: Ceramics, Commercial Photography, Fine Arts, Graphic Arts
—**Dept of Performing Arts,** 3536 Butte Campus Dr, Oroville, CA 95965. Tel 530-895-2581; Fax 530-895-2532; Web: www.butte.cc.ca.us; *Head Dept* Margaret Hughes
Degrees: transfer major
Tuition: Res—$12 per unit; nonres—$208 per unit
Courses: Acting, Adaptive Dramatics, Set Design & Construction, Theater Arts Appreciation, Theater for Children

PALM DESERT

COLLEGE OF THE DESERT, Art Dept, 43-500 Monterey Ave, Palm Desert, CA 92260. Tel 760-773-2574; Fax 760-776-7310; Web: www.collegeofthedesert.edu; *Chmn* Doug Walker
Estab 1962; College also has High Desert Campus; FT 3, PT 5; pub; D & E; Scholarships; SC 10, LC 3; D 150, E 150, maj 15
Ent Req: HS dipl, ent exam
Degrees: AA 2 yrs
Courses: Advertising Art, Art History, Ceramics, Design, Drawing, Introduction to Art, Oriental Brush Painting, Painting, Photography, Printmaking, Sculpture
Summer School: Six wk session. Courses—Art History, Ceramics, Painting, Sculpture

PASADENA

ARTCENTER COLLEGE OF DESIGN, 1700 Lida St, Pasadena, CA 91103-1924. Tel 626-396-2200; Fax 626-405-9104; Email frontdesk@artcenter.edu; Web: www.artcenter.edu; *Pres* Lorne M Buchman; *Dean Students* Ray Quirolgico; *Assoc Provost, Faculty Affairs* Ted Young; *Vice Pres, Profl Develop & Industry Engagement* Kristine Bowne; *Dir Alyce de Roulet*

Williamson Gallery Stephen Nowlin; *Exec Dir, Hoffmitz Milken Center for Typography* Gloria Kondrup; *College Libr and Mng Dir, ArtCenter Library* Mario A Ascencio; *Dir, Rapid Prototyping & Model Shops* David Cawley; *Registrar & Dir, Enrollment Svcs* William G Gartrell
Estab 1930; pvt; D & E; Scholarships; SC 168, LC 82, GC 22
Library Holdings: Book Volumes 40,000
Ent Req: HS dipl, ACT, SAT if no col background, portfolio required, at least 12 samples of work in proposed maj
Degrees: BFA, BS, MFA, MS
Tuition: Undergrad $21,408 per term; grad $22,625 per term
Courses: †Advertising Design, †Advertising Illustration, Aesthetics, Architecture, Art History, Calligraphy, Collage, Commercial Art, Conceptual Art, †Critical Theory, Design, Drafting, Drawing, †Environmental Design, Fashion Arts, †Fashion Illustration, †Film, Graphic Arts, †Graphic Design, †Graphic Packaging, History of Art & Architecture, †Illustration, Interior Design, Intermedia, Mixed Media, New Media, †Painting, †Photography, Printmaking, †Product Design, †Transportation Design, Video
Adult Hobby Classes: 14 wk term. Courses—Advertising, Computer Graphics, Film, Fine Arts, Graphics, Illustration, Industrial Design, Liberal Arts & Sciences, Photography
Children's Classes: ArtCenter for Teens (grades 9-12); ArtCenter for Kids (grades 4-8)

PASADENA CITY COLLEGE, Visual Arts and Media Studies Division, 1570 E Colorado Blvd, Rm 118 Pasadena, CA 91106-2003. Tel 626-585-7238; Fax 626-585-7914; Email ajkritselis@pasadena.edu; Web: http://www.pasadena.edu/; *Acting Area Head Design* Jerrold Graves, BA; *Acting Area Head Photog* Victoria Martin, MFA; *Acting Area Head History* Sandra Haynes, MA; *Acting Area Head Jewelry* Kay Yee, MFA; *Acting Area Head Ceramics* Alfred James Gonzalez, MA; *Div Dean* Alexander Kritselis, MFA; *Acting Area Head History* Joseph Futtner, MA
Estab 1902, dept estab 1916; Maintain a nonprofit art gallery; on-campus shop where art supplies may be purchased; pub; D & E; Scholarships; SC 159; D 2000, E 1200, non-maj 3200, maj 400
Ent Req: HS dipl
Degrees: AA 2 yrs, cert
Courses: Advertising Design, Art History, Ceramics, Commercial Art, Drawing, Film Art, Filmmaking, Graphic Arts, Graphic Design, Illustration, Jewelry, Lettering, Painting, Photography, Printmaking, Product Design, Sculpture
Summer School: Alexander Kritselis, Dean. Enrl 500; tuition $26 per unit for 6 wk sessions. Courses—Art History, Ceramics, Cinema, Design, Jewelry, Photography, Studio Arts, Film making

PLEASANT HILL

JOHN F KENNEDY UNIVERSITY, Department of Arts & Consciousness, 100 Ellinwood Way, Pleasant Hill, CA 94523-4817. Tel 510-647-2042; Email ksjoholm@jfku.edu; Web: www.jfku.edu; *Chair* Karen Sjoholm; *Faculty* Robbyn Alexander

POMONA

CALIFORNIA STATE POLYTECHNIC UNIVERSITY, POMONA, Department of Art, 3801 W Temple Blvd, College of Environmental Design Pomona, CA 91768-2557. Tel 909-869-3508; Fax 909-869-4939; Email pmartinez@cpp.edu; Web: www.cpp.edu; *Prof Emer* Dr Maren Henderson PhD; *Prof Emer* Charles Fredrick, MFA; *Prof* Joe Hannibal, MFA; *Prof Emeritus* Babette Mayor, MFA; *Prof* Sarah Meyer, MFA; *Prof* David Hylton, MA; *Lectr* Joyce Hesselgrave, MFA; *Lectr* Ann Phong, MFA; *Lectr* Wendy E Slatkin, PhD; *Lectr* Karen Sullivan, MFA; *Lectr* Deane Swick, MFA; *Prof* Yachin Crystal Lee, MFA; *Prof* Alison Pearlman, PhD; *Assoc Prof* Chari Pradel, PhD; *Assoc Prof* Melissa Flicker, MFA; *Lectr* Barbara Thomason, MFA; *Chair/Assoc Prof* Ray Kampf, MFA; *Assoc Chair/Assoc Prof* Alyssa Lang, MFA; *Asst Prof* Anthony Acock, MFA; *Asst Prof* Sooyum Im, MFA; *Asst Prof* Karlyn Griffith
Estab 1966; Maintains nonprofit Kellogg Univ Art Gallery; art/architecture library; on campus shop to purchase art supplies; pub; D & E; SC 66, LC 15; enrl D 350, E 50, non-Maj 470, maj 350
Ent Req: HS dipl, plus testing
Degrees: BA & BFA, 4 yrs
Courses: †Advertising Design, †Art Appreciation, †Art Education, †Art History, †Ceramics, Design, †Drafting, †Drawing, †Fine Arts, †Graphic Arts, †Graphic Design, †History of Art & Architecture, †Illustration, †Lettering, †Painting, Photography, †Printmaking, †Sculpture, †Studio Crafts, †Teacher Training
Adult Hobby Classes: Courses offered through Office of Continuing Education
Summer School: Courses—usually lower division, 10 & 5 wk quarter offerings

PORTERVILLE

PORTERVILLE COLLEGE, Dept of Fine Arts, 100 E College, Porterville, CA 93257. Tel 559-791-2200; Fax 559-784-4779; Email Thowell@pc.cc.ca.us; Web: www.pc.cc.ca.us; *Chmn* Tom Howell
Estab 1927; FT 2, PT 6; pub; D & E; SC 18, LC 3; D 300, E 78, non-maj 320, maj 58
Ent Req: HS dipl or over 18 yrs of age
Degrees: AA & AS 2 yrs
Courses: Airbrush, Art History, Ceramics, color, Design, Drawing, Handicrafts, Jewelry, Painting, Photography, Sculpture, Textile Design, Theatre Arts, weaving
Adult Hobby Classes: Courses—Jewelry, Weaving
Summer School: Dir, Nero Pruitt. Enrl 700 Term of 6 wks beginning June 13. Courses—Ceramics, Jewelry, Weaving

QUINCY

FEATHER RIVER COMMUNITY COLLEGE, Art Dept, 570 Golden Eagle Ave, Quincy, CA 95971-9124. Tel 530-283-0202; Web: www.frcc.cc.ca.us; *Chmn* Diane Lipscomb; *Adjunct* Linda Hale; *Instr* Roxanne Valladao; *Adjunct* Russ Flint; *Adjunct* Allen Stentzel; *Adjunct* Lance Barker; *Adjunct* Maureen McPhee
FT 25 PT 65; pub; D&E; Scholarships; SC 25, LC 3; 200; non-maj, maj
Ent Req: HS GED
Degrees: AS, AA
Tuition: Res—$22 per unit; nonres—$195 per unit
Courses: Art Appreciation, Art History, Business of Art, Ceramics, Color Theory, Design, Drawing, †History of Art & Architecture, Painting, †Photography, †Printmaking, Sculpture, Textile Design, Weaving
Adult Hobby Classes: spinning & weaving

RANCHO CUCAMONGA

CHAFFEY COMMUNITY COLLEGE, Art Dept, 5885 Haven Ave, Rancho Cucamonga, CA 91737-9400. Tel 909-987-1737; Web: www.chaffey.edu/; *Dept Chmn* Jan Raithel
E; Scholarships
Ent Req: HS dipl or equivalent
Degrees: AA
Tuition: Res—$11 per unit; non res— $155 per unit
Courses: Art History, Ceramics, Design, Drawing, Graphic Arts, Graphic Design, Illustration, Interior Design, Mixed Media, Museum Staff Training, Painting, Photography, Sculpture, Theatre Arts
Summer School: Dir, Byron Wilding. Enrl 200; tuition $13 for 6 wk courses. Courses—Art History, Ceramics, Design, Drawing, Graphic Computer Design

REDDING

SHASTA COLLEGE, Arts, Communications & Social Sciences Division, 11555 Old Oregon Trail, Redding, CA 96003; PO Box 496006, Redding, CA 96049-6006. Tel 530-242-7730; Fax 530-225-4763; Web: www.shastacollege.edu; *Dean Div Arts, Commun & Soc Sciences* Ralph W Perrin, DrPH; *Instr & Gallery Dir* Susan Schimke; *Instr & Gallery Dir* David Gentry; *Admin Asst* Terri Casolary; *Instr* Andrew Patterson-Tutschka
Estab 1950; Maintains a nonprofit art gallery on campus; 2; pub; D & E; Scholarships; SC 28, LC 5
Ent Req: HS dipl
Degrees: AA 2 yr
Courses: Art Appreciation, Art Education, Art History, Ceramics, †Design, Drawing, Glass, Graphic Arts, Graphic Design, Mixed Media, Painting, Photography, Printmaking, Sculpture, †Stage Design, †Theatre Arts
Summer School: Dir, Dean Summer Prog. Enrl 150; tuition same as regular sem

REDLANDS

UNIVERSITY OF REDLANDS, Dept of Art, 1200 E Colton Ave, Redlands, CA 92373-3720. Tel 909-793-2121, Ext 3663; Email brownfie@uor.edu; Web: www.redlands.edu; *Chmn* John Brownfield
Estab 1909; pvt; D & E; Scholarships; Fellowships; SC 18, LC 12; 1500
Ent Req: HS grad, ent exam
Degrees: BA and BS 4 yr, MA, ME, MAT
Courses: Art History, Ceramics, Drawing, Ethnic Art, Graphic Arts, Painting, Teacher Training

RIVERSIDE

CALIFORNIA BAPTIST UNIVERSITY, Art Dept, 8432 Magnolia Ave, Riverside, CA 92504-3297. Tel 909-689-5771, Ext 270; Web: www.calbaptist.edu; *Chmn* Mack Branden
Scholarships
Degrees: BA
Tuition: $420 per unit
Courses: Art Appreciation, Art History, Ceramics, Design, Drawing, Painting, Printmaking, Sculpture

LA SIERRA UNIVERSITY, Art Dept, 4700 Pierce, Riverside, CA 92515. Tel 909-785-2170; Web: www.lasierra.cc.ca.us; *Chmn* Prof Susan Patt; *Instr* Jan Inman; *Prof* Peter Erhard; *Prof* Beatriz Mejia-Krumbein; *Instr* Katrin Weise; *Instr* Donna Adrian; *Instr* Stephne Patt
Estab 1905; den; D & E; SC 29, LC 8, GC 1; D 2354
Ent Req: HS dipl, SAT
Degrees: BA, BS 4 yrs
Courses: Art History, Calligraphy, †Ceramics, Computer Graphics, Drawing, †Graphic Design, Illustration, Lettering, Occupational Therapy, †Painting, †Photography, †Printmaking, †Sculpture
Adult Hobby Classes: Enrl 35 per wk; tuition $330 per wk for 4 wk term. Courses—Watercolor Workshop
Summer School: Chmn, Roger Churches. 6 wk, 2-4 units. Courses—Art in the Elementary & Secondary School

RIVERSIDE COMMUNITY COLLEGE, Dept of Art & Mass Media, 4800 Magnolia Ave, Riverside, CA 92506-1201. Tel 909-222-8000; Fax 909-222-8740; Web: www.rccd.cc.ca.us; *Dance Chmn* Jo Dierdorff; *Media Chmn* Charles Richard; *Chmn Performing Arts & Media* Kevin Mayse; *Chmn Art Dept* Dayna Peterson Mason
Estab 1917; FT8; pub; D & E; 37; D 910, E 175
Ent Req: HS dipl or over 18 yrs of age
Degrees: AA 2 yrs & Certs

Courses: 3-D Design, Advertising Design, Art Appreciation, Art History, Ceramics, †Computer Art, Design, Drawing, †Gallery-Exhib Design & Animation, Painting, Printmaking, Sculpture, Teacher Training
Summer School: Dir Dayna Peterson Mason. Courses—Art for Elementary Teachers, Art History, Ceramics, Drawing, Painting, Sculpture

UNIVERSITY OF CALIFORNIA, RIVERSIDE, Dept of the History of Art, 900 University Ave, Riverside, CA 92507-4600. Tel 951-827-4634; Fax 951-827-2331; Email arthist@ucr.edu; Web: http://arthistory.ucr.edu; *Prof* Jonathan W Green, MA; *Prof Emeriti* Francoise Forster-Hahn, PhD, MA; *Prof Emeriti* Dericksen M Brinkerhoff, PhD, MA; *Prof* Conrad Rudolph, PhD, MA; *Chmn & Assoc Prof* Patricia M Morton, PhD, MA; *Asst Prof* JP Park, PhD, MA; *Asst Prof* Kristoffer Neville, PhD, MA; *Assoc Prof* Jeanette Kohl, PhD, MA; *Assoc Prof* Liz Kotz, PhD, MA; *Asst Prof* Susan Laxton, PhD, MA; *Prof* Malcolm Baker, PhD, MA; *Asst Prof* Jason Weems, PhD, MA
Estab 1968; Maintains a non-profit art gallery, Sweeney Gallery, 3824 Main St, Riverside, CA 92501; pub; D; LC 18, GC 5; maj 62, grad 26
Activities: Fels offered
Ent Req: HS dipl, res grad-point average 3.1, nonres grade-point average 3.4
Degrees: BA, MA, PhD
Tuition: Res—undergrad $6684, grad $8145; nonres—undergrad $23,640, grad $23,085
Courses: Art History, History of Art & Architecture, History of Photography
—**Dept of Art**, 1107 Olmsted Hall, Riverside, CA 92521. Tel 909-787-4634; Email jdivola@earthlink.net; *Prof* John Divola; *Chmn* Erika Suderburg; *Prof* Uta Barth; *Prof* James S Strombotne, MFA; *Lectr* Gordon L Thorpe, MA
Estab 1954; maintain nonprofit art gallery, Sweeny Art Gallery, UC Riverside, UCR California Museum of Photography, 3824 Main St, Riverside, CA 92507; pub; D; SC 14, LC 2; maj 58
Ent Req: HS dipl
Degrees: BA
Tuition: Res—undergrad $1500 per qtr, grad $1603; nonres—undergrad $3930 per qtr, grad $4163
Courses: Drawing, Painting, Photography, Printmaking, Video

ROCKLIN

SIERRA COMMUNITY COLLEGE, Art Dept, 5000 Rocklin Rd, Liberal Arts Division Rocklin, CA 95677-3337. Tel 916-624-3333, 789-2866 (Art Dept); Fax 916-789-2854; Web: www.sierracollege.org; *Dean Humanities* Bill Tsuji; *Instr* Pam Johnson, MA; *Instr* Dottie Brown, MA; *Instr* Rebecca Gregg; *Instr* Tom Fillebrown; *Instr* Randy Snook; *Dept Tech Dir* Anthony Gilo
Estab 1914; pub; D & E; SC 18, LC 4; D & E approx 9000
Ent Req: English Placement Test
Degrees: AA
Courses: Art Education, Art History, Ceramics, Drawing, Painting, Photography, Printmaking, Sculpture
Summer School: Ceramics, Painting

ROHNERT PARK

SONOMA STATE UNIVERSITY, Art & Art History Dept, 1801 E Cotati Ave, Rohnert Park, CA 94928-3609. Tel 707-664-2364, 664-2365; Fax 707-664-4333; Web: www.sonoma.edu/art; *Art Chmn* Michael Schwager
Estab 1961, dept estab 1961; pub; D & E; SC 38, LC 17; D 6000
Ent Req: HS dipl, SAT, eligibility req must be met
Degrees: BA & BFA
Courses: Art Education, Art History, Ceramics, Drawing, Painting, Papermaking, Photography, Printmaking, Sculpture, Teacher Training
Adult Hobby Classes: Various classes offered through Extended Educ
Summer School: Various classes offered through Extended Educ

SACRAMENTO

AMERICAN RIVER COLLEGE, Dept of Art/Art New Media, 4700 College Oak Dr, Sacramento, CA 95841-4286. Tel 916-484-8433; *Instr* Ken Magri, MA; *Spokesperson* Pam Maddock, MFA; *Instr* Tom J Brozovich, MA; *Instr* Gary Pruner, MFA; *Instr* Craig Smith, MFA; *Instr* Laura Parker, MAT; *Instr* Diane Richey-Ward, MFA; *Instr* Judy Hiramoto, MFA
Estab 1954; pub; D & E; Scholarships; SC 65, LC 12; D 10,000, E 10,000, non-maj 5000, maj 5000
Ent Req: HS dipl
Degrees: AA 2 yrs or more
Courses: Art Appreciation, Art History, Ceramics, Commercial Art, Design, Drawing, Film, Gallery Management, Graphic Arts, Graphic Design, Illustration, Interior Design, Jewelry, Lettering, Painting, Photography, Printmaking, Sculpture
Summer School: Area Dean, Sheryl Gessford. Enrl 120; tuition $11 per unit June-Aug. Courses—Ceramics, Design, Drawing, Introduction to Art, Photography

CALIFORNIA STATE UNIVERSITY, SACRAMENTO, Dept of Art, 6000 J St, Sacramento, CA 95819-6000. Tel 916-278-6166; Fax 916-278-7287; Web: www.csus.edu/art; *Chmn* Catherine Turrill
Estab 1950; FT 20; pub; D; Scholarships; SC 40, LC 18, GC 12; maj 585
Ent Req: HS dipl, ent exam
Degrees: BA 4 yr, MA
Courses: Art Education, Art History, Arts with Metals, Ceramics, Computer Art, Drawing, Jewelry, Painting, Printmaking, Sculpture
Summer School: Enrl 225; 3 & 6 wk sessions

SACRAMENTO CITY COLLEGE, Art Dept, 3835 Freeport Blvd, Sacramento, CA 95822-1386. Tel 916-558-2551; Fax 916-558-2190; Web: www.scc.losrios.cc.ca.us; *Dir Humanities & Fine Arts* Chris Iwata; *Instr* Laureen Landau, MFA; *Instr* F Dalkey, MFA; *Instr* Darrell Forney, MFA; *Instr* George A Esquibel, MA; *Instr* B Palisin, MA; *Instr* Mimi Fong; *Instr* Jennifer Griffin; *Instr* Robert Leach; *Instr* Christine Reading; *Instr* Teiko Sasser; *Instr* Isabel Shaskan; *Instr* Frank Zamora
Estab 1916; pub; D & E; Scholarships; SC 17, LC 9; D 880, E 389
Ent Req: HS dipl
Degrees: AA 2 yr
Courses: Ceramics, Commercial Art, Drawing, Jewelry, Modern Art, Painting, Photography, Sculpture, Technology, Theatre Arts
Summer School: Chmn, George A Esquibel. Courses—Art History, Design, Drawing, Oil-Acrylic, Watercolor

SALINAS

HARTNELL COLLEGE, Art & Photography Dept, 156 Homestead Ave, Salinas, CA 93901. Tel 831-755-6905; Fax 831-759-6052; Web: www.hartnell.cc.ca.us; *Dean Fine Arts* Dr Daniel A Ipson
Estab 1922; FT 5, PT 18; pub; D & E; Scholarships; SC 14, LC 3; D 350 E 160, major 30
Ent Req: HS dipl
Degrees: AA 2 yr
Courses: †Calligraphy, Ceramics, Drafting, Drawing, Foundry, Gallery Management, Graphic Arts, History of Art & Architecture, †Jewelry, Metalsmithing, Painting, Photography, Sculpture, Stage Design, Theatre Arts, Video, Weaving
Summer School: Courses—Art Appreciation, Ceramics, Drawing, Film Making, Photography

SAN BERNARDINO

CALIFORNIA STATE UNIVERSITY, SAN BERNARDINO, Dept of Art, 5500 University Pkwy, Visual Arts Center San Bernardino, CA 92407-2393. Tel 909-880-5802; Fax 909-880-7068; Web: www.csusb.edu; *Chmn Dept & Instr* Joe Moran, MFA; *Dir Mus* Eva Kirsch; *Instr* Leo Doyle, MFA; *Instr* Don Woodford, MFA; *Instr* Billie Sessions, MFA; *Instr* Julius Kaplan, MFA, PhD; *Instr* George McGinnis, MFA; *Instr* Sant Khalsa, MFA; *Instr* Kurt Collins, MS; *Instr* Susan Beiner; *Instr* Thomas McGovern
Estab 1965; pub; D & E; Scholarships; D 13,500, maj 220
Ent Req: HS dipl, SAT
Degrees: BA 4 yr, MA 2 yr
Courses: Advertising Design, Art Education, †Art History, Ceramics, Drawing, †Furniture Design, Glassblowing, Glasscasting, †Graphic Design, Painting, Photography, Printmaking, Sculpture, Woodworking

SAN BERNARDINO VALLEY COLLEGE, Art Dept, 701 S Mount Vernon Ave, San Bernardino, CA 92410-2798. Tel 909-888-6511; Web: www.sbccd.cc.ca.us; *Head Dept* David Lawrence
Estab 1926; FT 5, PT 7; pub; D & E; Scholarships; D 750, E 400, maj 230
Ent Req: HS dipl or 18 yrs of age
Degrees: AA and AS 2 yrs
Courses: Advertising Art, Architecture, Art History, Basic Design, Ceramics, Commercial Art, Computer Graphics, Designs in Glass, Drafting, Drawing, Film, Glass Blowing, Lettering, Life Drawing, Painting, Photography, Sculpture, Theatre Arts

SAN DIEGO

SAN DIEGO MESA COLLEGE, Fine Arts Dept, 7250 Mesa College Dr, San Diego, CA 92111-4999. Tel 619-388-2829; Web: www.sdccd.net; *Chmn* Richard Lou; *Instr* Barbara Blackmun PhD; *Instr* Ross Stockwell, MA; *Instr* Anita Brynolf, MA; *Instr* Jeorgia Laris, MA; *Instr* John Conrad, MA
Estab 1964; pub; D & E; Scholarships; SC 20, LC 7; D 15,000, E 8,000, maj 300
Ent Req: HS dipl or age 18
Degrees: AA 2 yrs
Courses: Art Appreciation, Art Education, Art History, Book Arts, Ceramics, Design, Drawing, Gallery Studies, Painting, Photography, Printmaking, Sculpture, Studio Arts
Summer School: Enrl 200; tuition & courses same as regular sem

SAN DIEGO STATE UNIVERSITY, School of Art, Design & Art History, 5500 Campanile Dr, San Diego, CA 92182-4805. Tel 619-594-6511; Fax 619-594-1217; Email artinfo@mail.sdsu.edu; Web: www.sdsu.edu/art; *Studio Grad Coordr* David Hewitt; *Art History Grad Coordr* Jo-Anne Berelowitz, PhD; *Dir* Arthur Ollman, MFA
Estab 1897; Maintains University Art Gallery on campus, & SDSU Downtown Gallery, 725 W Broadway, San Diego, CA 92101; art supplies sold at on-campus store; pub; D & E; Scholarships; SC 140, LC 35, GC 30; maj 982
Ent Req: HS dipl
Degrees: BA 4 yrs, MA, MFA
Courses: Art Education, †Art History, †Ceramics, †Drawing, †Furniture Design, †Gallery Design, †Graphic Design, History of Art & Architecture, Illustration, †Interior Design, Intermedia, †Jewelry, Mixed Media, †Painting, Photography, †Printmaking, †Sculpture, †Silversmithing, †Textile Design

UNIVERSITY OF SAN DIEGO, Art Dept, 5998 Alcala Park, San Diego, CA 92110-2492. Tel 619-260-4600; Fax 619-260-4619, Ext 4486; Web: www.usd.ca.ca.us; *Chmn* Patricia Drinan
Estab 1952; FT 4; pvt; D & E; Scholarships; SC 19, LC 7; univ 5300, maj 50
Ent Req: HS dipl, SAT
Degrees: BA 4 yrs
Courses: †Art History, †Art in Elementary Education, †Art Management, †Ceramics, †Design, †Drawing, †Enameling, †Exhibition Design, †Museum Internship, †Painting, †Photography, †Printmaking, †Sculpture, †Weaving

SAN FRANCISCO

ACADEMY OF ART UNIVERSITY, Fine Arts Dept, 625 Sutter, San Francisco, CA 94102-1017. Tel 415-274-2200, 800-544-2787; Fax 415-618-6287; Web: www.academyart.edu; *Dir Liberal Arts & Grad Studies* Eileen Everett
Estab 1929; FT 2, PT 8; pvt; D & E; Scholarships; SC 200, LC 100; D 2000, E 150, grad 20
Ent Req: HS dipl
Degrees: BFA 4 yrs, MFA 2 yrs
Tuition: Res—undergrad $12,300 per yr, grad $14,200 per yr; campus res available
Courses: Advertising Design, Aesthetics, Architecture, Art History, Ceramics, Collage, Commercial Art, Design, Drawing, Fashion Arts, Film, Graphic Arts, Graphic Design, Illustration, Industrial Design, Interior Design, Jewelry, Mixed Media, Painting, Photography, Printmaking, Sculpture, Video
Adult Hobby Classes: Enrl 75; tuition $350 per unit. Courses—Basic Painting, Ceramics, Portrait Painting, Pottery
Summer School: Term of 6 wks beginning June 23. Courses—Commercial & Fine Art

CALIFORNIA COLLEGE OF THE ARTS, 1111 8th St, San Francisco, CA 94107-2247. Tel 415-703-9500; Fax 415-703-9539; Email info@cca.edu; Web: www.cca.edu; *Pres* Stephen Beal
Estab 1907; Maintains non-profit art gallery: Wattis Institute for Contemporary Arts; FT/PT 190; pvt; D & E; Scholarships; Undergrad 1,515; Grad 455
Ent Req: HS dipl, Portfolio, SAT or ACT recommended, C grade-point average, 2 letters of recommendation
Degrees: BArch 4 yrs, BFA 4 yrs, BA 4 yrs, MFA 2 yrs, MA 2 yrs, MBA 2 yrs & MArch 3 yrs
Tuition: Undergrad $48,648; Grad $51,210
Courses: †Animation, †Architecture, †Ceramics, †Comics, †Community Arts, †Curatorial Practice, †Design Strategy (MBA), †Fashion Arts, †Fashion Design, †Fashion Design, †Film, †Fine Arts, †Glass, Graphic Arts, †Graphic Design, Illustration, †Industrial Design, †Interaction Design, †Interior Architectural Design, †Interior Design, †Jewelry, †Metal Arts, †Metal Arts, Mixed Media, †Painting, †Photography, †Printmaking, †Sculpture, †Textiles, †Video, †Visual Criticism, †Visual Studies, †Woodwork & Furniture Design, †Writing & Literature
Adult Hobby Classes: Courses—Vary
Children's Classes: Courses—Architecture, Creative Writing, Drawing, Fashion Design, Graphic Design, Illustration, Industrial Design, Jewelry/Metal Arts, Painting, Photography (Black & White, Digital), Printmaking, Sculpture, Animation, Film
Summer School: Courses—Animation, Architecture, Computer Graphic, Graphic Design, Drawing, Hat Design, Jewelry Design, Mosaic Design, Painting, Photography, Printmaking, Sculpture, Woodworking; Dir, Nina Sadek. Enrl 300; tuition $1,453 per unit. Courses - Vary

CITY COLLEGE OF SAN FRANCISCO, Art Dept, 50 Phelan Ave, 118 Visual Arts Building San Francisco, CA 94112. Tel 415-239-3157; Fax 415-239-3131; Email mchereme@ccsf.edu; Web: www.ccsf.edu/Departments/Art/; *Dept Chair* Anna Asebedo
Estab 1935

SAN FRANCISCO ART INSTITUTE, 800 Chestnut St, Admissions Office San Francisco, CA 94133-2206. Tel 415-749-4500; Fax 415-749-4592; Email admissions@sfai.edu; Web: www.sfai.edu; *Dir Admissions* Renee Talmon
Estab 1871; Maintain nonprofit art gallery; Walter & McBean Galleries, 800 Chestnut St, San Francisco, CA 94133; pvt; D & E; Scholarships; SC 80, LC 22, GC 11; maj 466 grad 208
Ent Req: HS dipl or GED
Degrees: BFA 4 yrs, MFA 2 yrs
Courses: Art History, †Ceramics, †Conceptual Art, †Digital Media, †Drawing, †Film, †Painting, †Performance/Video, †Photography, †Printmaking, †Sculpture
Adult Hobby Classes: Tuition $290 for 4-11 wk session (per course). Courses—Variety of studio courses year round
Children's Classes: Enrl 40; tuition 8 wk session. Courses—Variety of studio courses, summers only
Summer School: Dir, Kate Eilertsen. Tuition 2-8 wk sessions $1800 course. Courses—Variety of studio courses

SAN FRANCISCO STATE UNIVERSITY, Art Dept, 1600 Holloway, San Francisco, CA 94132. Tel 415-338-2176; Fax 415-338-6537; Email artdept@sfsu.edu; Web: www.sfsu.edu; *Dean* Morrison Keith; *Chmn* Candace Crockett
Estab 1899; Maintains nonprofit gallery, San Francisco State Univ Art Dept Gallery, 1600 Holloway Ave, San Francisco, CA 94132; art supplies available at on-campus shop; FT 23, PT 10; pub; D & E; Scholarships; SC 80, LC 20, GC 15; D 450, maj 600, grad 30
Ent Req: HS dipl
Degrees: BA 4 yrs, MFA 3 yrs, MA 2 yrs
Courses: Art Education, Art History, Ceramics, Conceptual/Information Arts, Mixed Emphasis, Painting, Photography, Printmaking, Sculpture, Textile
Summer School: Not regular session. Self-supporting classes in Art History, Ceramics, Drawing & Painting, Art Educ

SAN JACINTO

MT SAN JACINTO COLLEGE, Art Dept, 1499 N State St, San Jacinto, CA 92583-2399. Tel 951-487-3580; Email srobinso@msjc.cc.ca.us; Web: www.msjc.edu; *Dept Chair* Eileen Doktorski; *Dept Chair* John Seed; *Dept Chair* Jason Bader; *Gallery Dir* Brandelyn Dillaway
Estab 1964; Maintains nonprofit art gallery: Mt San Jacinto College Art Gallery; art supplies sold at on-campus shop; pub; D & E; SC 8, LC 2; D 250, E 420, non-maj 400, maj 50
Ent Req: HS dipl
Degrees: AA & AS
Courses: Art History, Basic Design, Ceramics, †Graphic Design, Painting, Sculpture
Adult Hobby Classes: Courses—Community Educ Ceramics
Children's Classes: Studio courses
Summer School: Courses—Drawing

SAN JOSE

SAN JOSE CITY COLLEGE, School of Fine Arts, 2100 Moorpark Ave, San Jose, CA 95128-2799. Tel 408-298-2181; Fax 408-298-1935; Web: www.sjcc.edu; *Dean Humanities & Social Science* Dr Patrick Gierster; *Instr* Judith Bell; *Interim Pres* Chui L Tsang; *Coordr Fine Arts* Eve Page Mathias; *Instr* Ciaran Maegowan
Estab 1921; pub; D & E; SC 7, LC 2; D 320, E 65
Ent Req: HS dipl or 18 yrs of age or older
Degrees: AA 2 yrs
Courses: 2-D & 3-D Design, Art History, Ceramics, Color, Drawing, Expressive & Representational Drawing, Life Drawing, Painting, Photography, Theatre Arts

SAN JOSE STATE UNIVERSITY, Dept of Art & Art History, One Washington Sq, San Jose, CA 95192-0089. Tel 408-924-4320; Fax 408-924-4326; Web: www.sjsu.edu/art; *Chmn Dept of Art* Brian Taylor
Estab 1857, dept estab 1911; Maintains Natalie and James Thompson Art Gallery, School of Art & Design SJSU, One Washington Square, San Jose, CA 95192-0089; pub; D & E; Scholarships; Fellowships; SC 200+, LC 30+, GC 10+; D 4529, maj 1800, grad 100
Activities: Schols offered
Ent Req: ACT & grade point average, SAT
Degrees: BA(Art), BA(Art History) 4 yrs, BFA(Graphic Design), BS(Industrial Design), BFA(Interior Design) & BFA(Art-Animation, Illustration, Digital Media, Pictorial Art, Spatial Art, Photography) 4 1/2 yrs, MA(Art History), 1 yr, MFA (Pictorial Arts), MFA(Photography), MFA(Spatial Arts) & MFA(Digital Media Arts) 3 yrs
Tuition: Res—(undergrad) $899 - $1328 per sem; nonres—$899 - $1328 plus $282/unit/per sem (non-res undergrad)
Courses: †Animation, †Art Education, †Art History, Ceramics, †Crafts (Jewelry, †Digital Media Art, Drawing, †Graphic Design, Illustration, †Industrial Design, †Interior Design, Jewelry, †Photography, Printmaking, †Sculpture, Teacher Training, Textiles)
Summer School: Dean Continuing Educ, Mark Novak. Tuition $160 per unit for three summer sessions of 3 & 6 wks; 3 wk Jan session. Courses—Vary according to professors available & projected demand

SAN LUIS OBISPO

CALIFORNIA POLYTECHNIC STATE UNIVERSITY AT SAN LUIS OBISPO, Dept of Art & Design, 1 Grand Ave, San Luis Obispo, CA 93407-9000. Tel 805-756-1111; Web: www.artdesign.libart.calpoly.edu; *Asst Prof Art History* Elizabeth Adan; *Dept Chmn, Prof Photog* Sky Bergman; *Asst Prof Digital Media* Enrica Lovaglio Costello; *Asst Prof Studio Art* Daniel Dove; *Asst Prof Art History* Giancarlo Fiorenza; *Asst Prof Studio Art* Tera Galanti; *Prof Photog* Robert Howell; *Asst Prof* Joseph Coates; *Prof* Keith Dills; *Prof Studio Art* George Jercich; *Prof Photog* Eric Johnson; *Prof Graphic Design* Mary LaPorte; *Asst Prof Graphic Design* Charmaine Martinez; *Asst Prof Graphic Design* Kathryn McCormick; *Prof Studio Art* Michael Barton Miller; *Lectr Studio Art* Brian James Priest; *Assoc Prof Art History* Jean Wetzel
Estab 1901, dept estab 1969; FT 12; pub; D & E; SC 40, LC 12; D 1000, E 100, non-maj 1100, maj 220
Ent Req: HS dipl, portfolio review
Degrees: BS (Art & Design) 4 yrs
Tuition: Res—undergrad $3640 per yr; nonres—undergrad $5893 per yr; campus res—room & board $4366 per yr
Courses: Advertising Design, Art History, Ceramics, Design History, Drawing, Glass, Graphic Arts, Graphic Design, Metalsmithing, Painting, Photography, Printmaking, Sculpture
Summer School: Chair, Chuck Jennings. Enrl 215; tuition $740 for term June 20-Sept 2. Courses—Basic b/w Photography, Ceramics, Fundamentals of Drawing, Intermediate Drawing

CUESTA COLLEGE, Art Dept, PO Box 8106, San Luis Obispo, CA 93403-8106. Tel 805-546-3201; Fax 805-546-3995; *Chmn Fine Arts Div & Instr* Bob Pelfrey; *Instr* Guyla Amyx; *Instr* Barry Frantz; *Instr* Marian Galczenski; *Instr* David Prochaska
Estab 1964; pub; D & E; Scholarships
Ent Req: HS dipl or Calif HS Proficiency Exam
Degrees: AA and AS
Courses: Art Appreciation, Art History, Camera Art, Ceramics, Design, Display, Drawing, Graphic Design, Painting, Printmaking, Sculpture, Video
Summer School: Chmn Div Fine Arts, Bob Pelfrey. Courses—Drawing, Art History, Ceramics

SAN MARCOS

PALOMAR COMMUNITY COLLEGE, Art Dept, 1140 W Mission Rd, San Marcos, CA 92069-1487. Tel 760-744-1150, Ext 2302; Fax 760-744-8123; Web: www.palomar.cc.ca.us; *Assoc Prof & Dir* Harry E Bliss, MFA; *Assoc Prof* Jay Shultz, MA; *Assoc Prof* James T Saw, MA; *Assoc Prof* Michael Steirnagle, MA; *Assoc Prof* Steve Miller, MA; *Chmn* Doug Durrant
Estab 1950; pub; D & E; Scholarships; SC 31, LC 4; D 775, E 200
Ent Req: ent exam
Degrees: AA 2 yr
Courses: †Animation, Art History, †Ceramics, Collage, †Commercial Art, Design Composition, †Drawing, Glassblowing, Graphic Arts, Graphic Design, Handicrafts, Illustration, †Jewelry, Lettering, Life Drawing, †Painting, †Printmaking, Sculpture, †Silversmithing, Stained Glass

Summer School: Courses—basic courses except commercial art and graphic design

SAN MATEO

COLLEGE OF SAN MATEO, Creative Arts Dept, 1700 W Hillsdale Blvd, San Mateo, CA 94402-3784. Tel 650-574-6161; Web: www.gocsm.net; *Prof, Art History* Janet Black; *Pres* Michael Claire; *Prof 2D Art* Jude Pittman; *Prof 3D Sculpture & Ceramics* Rory Nakata; *Prof Photog* Lyle Gomes
Pub; D & E
Degrees: AA 2 yr
Tuition: Res—$11 per unit, nonres—$130 per unit; no campus res
Courses: †Architecture, Art History, Ceramics, †Commercial Art, Design, Drafting, Drawing, †Film, †General Art, Graphic Arts, Graphic Design, Painting, Photography, Printmaking, Sculpture, Video

SAN PABLO

CONTRA COSTA COMMUNITY COLLEGE, Dept of Art, 2600 Mission Bell Dr, San Pablo, CA 94806-3195. Tel 510-235-7800, Ext 4261; Fax 510-236-6768; Web: www.contracosta.cc.ca.us; *Dept Head* Rich Akers
Estab 1950; pub; D & E; SC 10, LC 16; D 468, E 200
Ent Req: HS dipl or 18 yrs old
Degrees: Cert of Achievement 1 yr, AA and AS 2 yrs
Courses: Art History, Ceramics, Drawing, Painting, Photography, Sculpture, Silkscreen
Summer School: Assoc Dean Continuing Educ, William Vega. Enrl 50; tuition free for term of 8 wks beginning June 26. Courses—Art, Art Appreciation

SAN RAFAEL

DOMINICAN COLLEGE OF SAN RAFAEL, Art Dept, 50 Acacia Ave, San Rafael, CA 94901-2230. Tel 415-457-4440; Fax 415-485-3205; Web: www.dominican.edu; *Chmn* Edith Bresnahan
Estab 1890; Scholarships
Degrees: BA, MA 4 yr
Tuition: Undergrad—$8628 per sem
Courses: Advertising Design, Art Appreciation, Art Education, Art History, Calligraphy, Ceramics, Design, Drawing, Handicrafts, Painting, Photography, Pottery, Printmaking, Sculpture, Stage Design, Textile Design, Theatre Arts, Weaving

SANTA ANA

RANCHO SANTIAGO COLLEGE
For further information, see Santa Ana College

SANTA ANA COLLEGE, (Rancho Santiago College) Art Dept, 1530 W 17th St, Santa Ana, CA 92706-3398. Tel 714-564-5600; Web: www.sac.edu/academic_progs/art/; *Dean of Fine & Performing Arts* Sylvia Turner; *Co-Chair* Sharon Brown; *Co-Chair* Irene Soriano; *Ceramics* Patrick S Crabb, MA; *Painting* Estelle Orr, MA; *3D Animation & Modeling* Patricia Waterman
Estab 1915, dept estab 1960; pub; D & E; Scholarships; SC 21, LC 5; D 280, E 160, maj 57
Ent Req: HS dipl
Degrees: AA 2 yrs
Tuition: Res—$11 per unit; nonres—$138 per unit
Courses: Advertising Design, Architecture, Art History, Ceramics, Commercial Art, Computer Graphics, Display, Drawing, Glass Blowing, Graphic Arts, Graphic Design, Handicrafts, Interior Design, Jewelry, Museum Staff Training, Painting, Sculpture
Adult Hobby Classes: Ceramics, Stained Glass
Summer School: Dir, Dean Thom Hill. Enrl 3000; tuition free for term of 6-8 wks beginning early June. Courses—Art Concepts, Ceramics, Design, Drawing, Painting

SANTA BARBARA

SANTA BARBARA CITY COLLEGE, Fine Arts Dept, 721 Cliff Dr, Santa Barbara, CA 93109-2394. Tel 805-965-0581; Fax 805-963-7222; Web: www.sbcc.net; *Chmn* Diane Handsloser
Pub; D&E; Scholarships
Degrees: AA
Tuition: In-state—$12 per unit
Courses: Advertising Design, Architecture, Art Appreciation, Art History, Calligraphy, Cartooning, Ceramics, Design, Drawing, Fashion Arts, Film, Glassblowing, Handicrafts, Industrial Design, Interior Design, Jewelry, Painting, Printmaking, Sculpture, Stage Design, Textile Design, Weaving

UNIVERSITY OF CALIFORNIA, SANTA BARBARA, Dept of Art Studio, 552 University Rd, Ellison Hall, Rm 2838 Santa Barbara, CA 93106-0002. Tel 805-893-3138; Fax 805-893-7206; Web: www.arts.ucsb.edu; *Chmn Dept* Kim Yasuda
Estab 1868, dept estab 1950; pub; D&E; Scholarships; SC 30, LC 7, GC 7; D 479, grad 60
Ent Req: HS dipl
Degrees: BA 4 yrs, MFA 2 yrs, PhD 7 yrs
Courses: †Art Theory, Ceramics, Drawing, Painting, †Performance Art, Photography, Printmaking, Sculpture
Summer School: Dir Loy Lytle

SANTA CLARA

SANTA CLARA UNIVERSITY, Dept of Art & Art History, 500 El Camino Real, Santa Clara, CA 95053-0264. Tel 408-554-4594; Fax 408-554-4809; Email artinfo@scu.edu; Web: www.scu.edu/art; *Prof Emeritus* Sam Hernandez, MFA; *Assoc Prof* Kathleen Maxwell PhD; *Assoc Prof* Andrea Pappas, PhD; *Sr Lectr* Pancho Jimenez, MFA; *Chair, Assoc Prof* Blake de Maria, PhD; *Assoc Prof* Katherine Aoki, MFA; *Assoc Prof* Katherine Morris, PhD; *Asst Prof* Ryan Reynolds, MFA; *Assoc Prof* Don Fritz, MFA; *Prof* Kelly Detweiler, MFA; *Asst Prof* Karen Fraser, PhD; *Lectr* Renee Billingslea, MFA; *Lectr* Julie Hughes, MFA; *Asst Prof* Tobias Woffard, PhD; *Asst Prof* Takeshi Moro, MFA
Estab 1851, dept estab 1972; Maintains The Fine Arts Gallery, Fine Arts Bldg, SCU, 500 El Camino Real Santa Clara, CA 95053; Pvt; D, E; Scholarships; SC 60, LC 47; maj 43, minors 56
Ent Req: HS dipl
Degrees: BA Art, Art History
Tuition: $43,812 per yr; campus res—rm & bd $12,921 per yr
Courses: †Art History, Ceramics, Computer Imaging, Drawing, †Graphic Arts, †Graphic Design, †History of Art & Architecture, Mixed Media, Painting, Photography, Printmaking, Sculpture, †Web Design
Summer School: Dir, Rafael Ulate. Enrl 15 per class; 5 wk term; $586 per unit. Courses—Ceramics, Intro to Art History, Painting, Drawing, Photography, Graphic Design, Computer Imaging

SANTA CLARITA

COLLEGE OF THE CANYONS, Art Dept, 26455 Rockwell Canyon Rd, Santa Clarita, CA 91355-1899. Tel 661-259-7800; Fax 661-259-8362; Email lorigan-j@mail.coc.cc.ca.us; Web: www.coc.cc.ca.us; *Instr* Robert Walker, MFA; *Chair* Jim Lorigan, MFA; *Adjunct* Larry Arbino; *Adjunct* Denise Delavaux; *Adjunct* Rebecca Edwards; *Adjunct* Amy Green; *Adjunct* Mercedes McDonald; *Adjunct* Ron Petrosky; *Adjunct* Laura Shurley-Olivas; *Adjunct* Larry Hurst; *Adjunct* Joy Von Wolffersdorff
Estab 1970, dept estab 1974; Maintain nonprofit art gallery at Col of Canyons, Santa Clarita, CA; art supplies available on-campus; pub; D & E, Sat; Scholarships; SC 11, LC 4; D 300, E 300, maj 50
Ent Req: must be 18 yrs of age
Degrees: AA & AS 2 yrs
Courses: 2-D Design, 3-D Design, Advertising Design, Art Appreciation, Art History, Computer Graphics, Drawing, Gallery Practices, Illustration, Painting, Photography, Printmaking, Sculpture, Watercolor
Adult Hobby Classes: Tuition $10 plus lab fees usually another $10 per sem
Children's Classes: Classes offered in continuing educ under child development
Summer School: Dir Carole Long

SANTA CRUZ

UNIVERSITY OF CALIFORNIA, SANTA CRUZ, Art Dept, 1156 High St, E104 Baskin Visual Arts Santa Cruz, CA 95064-1077. Tel 831-459-2272; Fax 831-459-3793; Web: www.arts.ucsc.edu; *Chmn* Norman Locks
Pub; D; SC per quarter 11, LC per quarter 3; D approx 7000, maj 80
Ent Req: HS dipl
Degrees: BA 4 yrs
Courses: Aesthetics, Book Arts, Drawing, Electronic Art, Intaglio Printmaking, Intermedia, Lithography, Metal Sculpture, Painting, Photography, Sculpture

SANTA MARIA

ALLAN HANCOCK COLLEGE, Fine Arts Dept, 800 S College Dr, Santa Maria, CA 93454-6399. Tel 805-922-6966, Ext 3252; Fax 805-928-7905; Web: www.hancock.cc.ca.us; *Head* Steve Lewis
Estab 1920. College has three other locations; FT 10, PT 20; pub; D & E; Scholarships; SC 24, LC 4; D 800, E 220, maj 115
Ent Req: HS dipl, over 18 and educable
Degrees: AA 2 yrs
Courses: Art Appreciation, Art Appreciation, Art History, Ceramics, Costume Design & Construction, Dance, Design, Drawing, †Film, †Graphic Arts, Graphic Design, History of Art & Architecture, Life Drawing, Music, Painting, †Photography, Sculpture, Silk Screen, †Theatre Arts, †Video, Video Production
Adult Hobby Classes: Enrl 100. Courses—Drawing, Watercolor
Children's Classes: Enrl 20. Courses—Drawing
Summer School: Enrl 230; term of 6-8 wks beginning June. Courses—Animation, Art, Computer Graphics, Dance, Drama, Electronic Music, Film, Video, Graphics, Music, Photography

SANTA ROSA

SANTA ROSA JUNIOR COLLEGE, Art Dept, 1501 Mendocino Ave, Santa Rosa, CA 95401-4395. Tel 707-527-4259; Fax 707-527-8416; Web: www.santarosa.edu; *Chmn* Stephanie Sanchez
Estab 1918, dept estab 1935; pub; D & E; Scholarships; SC 40, LC 8; D approx 800, E approx 1000
Ent Req: HS dipl
Degrees: AA 2 yrs
Courses: 3-D Design, Art Appreciation, Art History, Ceramics, Computer Graphics, Drawing, Etching, Graphic Design, Jewelry, Layout, Lettering, Painting, Photography, Poster Design, Pottery, Principles of Color, Printmaking, Sculpture, Silkscreen, Watercolor
Summer School: Chmn, Stephanie Sanchez. Courses—Art History, Ceramics, Design, Drawing, Painting, Printmaking, Sculpture, Watercolor

SARATOGA

WEST VALLEY COLLEGE, Art Dept, 14000 Fruitvale Ave, Saratoga, CA 95070-5698. Tel 408-741-2014; Fax 408-741-2059; *Prof & Dept Chair* Kathy Arnold
Estab 1964; Maintain nonprofit art gallery; Viking Art Gallery; FT 5, PT 8; pub; D & E; SC 51, LC 12; D 1260, E 801
Ent Req: HS dipl or 18 yrs of age
Degrees: AA, 2 yrs
Courses: Aesthetics, †Ceramics, Costume Design & Construction, †Design, Digital Graphics & Animation, †Drawing, †Etching, †Graphic Arts, †History of Art & Architecture, †Jewelry, †Lithography, †Metal Casting, Museum Staff Training, †Occupational Work Experience, †Painting, †Papermaking, †Sculpture, Stage Design, Stained Glass, Theatre Arts
Adult Hobby Classes: Tuition varies. Courses—many classes offered by Community Development Dept
Summer School: Dir, Moises Roizen. Enrl 200-250; tuition $35-$50. Courses—Art Appreciation, Art History, Ceramics, Drawing, Painting

SONORA

COLUMBIA COLLEGE, Fine Arts, 11600 Columbia College Dr, Sonora, CA 95370-8560. Tel 209-588-5100, 588-5150; Fax 209-588-5104; Web: columbia.yosemite.cc.ca.us; *Instr* Li Ching Accurso; *Instr* Laurie Sylwester
Estab 1968; pub; D & E; Scholarships; SC 50, LC 4; D 100, E 75, non-maj 90, maj 10
Ent Req: HS dipl or over 18 yrs old
Degrees: AA 2 yrs
Courses: Art History, Ceramics, †Design, Drafting, Drawing, Film, History of Art & Architecture, Painting, Photography, Sculpture, Theatre Arts, Video
Adult Hobby Classes: Quilting; Watercolor (variable or no fee)
Summer School: Courses—Ceramics, Drawing

SOUTH LAKE TAHOE

LAKE TAHOE COMMUNITY COLLEGE, Art Dept, One College Dr South Lake Tahoe, CA 96150. Tel 530-541-4660, Ext 228; Fax 530-541-7852; Email foster@ltcc.edu; Web: www.ltcc.ca.us; *Painting Instr* Phyllis Shafer, MFA; *Chmn Art Dept* David Foster, MA; *Instr* Ellen Manaffey
Estab 1975; Maintain nonprofit art galleries: Foyer Gallery, Fine Arts Bldg, Lake Tahoe Community Ctr; Main Gallery, Main Bldg. Art supplies available for purchase on campus; pub; D, E & weekends; Scholarships; SC 22, LC 6; D 375, E 150, non-maj 300, maj 75
Ent Req: HS dipl
Degrees: AA 2 yrs
Courses: Art Appreciation, Art History, Bronze Casting, Ceramics, Color, Design, Design, Digital Art, Drawing, Painting, Photography, Printmaking, Sculpture, Theatre Arts
Summer School: Dean Humanities Mrs Diane Rosner. Enrl 100; tuition undergrad $7 per unit, grad $33 per unit. Courses—Art History, Bronze Casting, Ceramics, Design, Intro to Art, Landscape Drawing, Life Drawing, Painting, Photography, Raku Pottery, Sculpture, Watercolor

STANFORD

STANFORD UNIVERSITY, Dept of Art & Art History, McMurtry Bldg, 355 Roth Way Stanford, CA 94305. Tel 650-723-3404; Fax 650-725-0140; Email artdepartment@stanford.edu; Web: art.stanford.edu; *Prof, Dept Chmn & Dir Art History* Alexander Nemerov; *Assoc Prof & Dir Art Practice* Gail Wight; *Assoc Prof & Dir Film/Media Studies* Pavle Levi; *Dir Opers* Elis Imboden
Estab 1891; FT 27; pvt; D; Scholarships; SC 48, LC 63, GC 37 (seminars)
Ent Req: HS dipl
Degrees: BA 4 yrs, MA 1 yr, MFA 2 yrs, PhD 5 yrs
Tuition: $50,703 per yr
Courses: Art History, Drawing, Painting, Photography, Printmaking, Sculpture
Adult Hobby Classes: Offered through Stanford Continuing Education
Children's Classes: Courses—Offered through Museum
Summer School: Courses—Art History, Drawing, Painting, Photography, Printmaking

STOCKTON

SAN JOAQUIN DELTA COLLEGE, Arts & Communication, 5151 Pacific Ave, Stockton, CA 95207-6370. Tel 209-954-5209; Fax 209-954-3747; Email mwamhoff@deltacollege.edu; Web: www.deltacollege.edu; *Fine Arts Div Dean* Dr Meryl Wamhoff; *Instr* Jennifer Barrows; *Instr* Gary Carlos; *Instr* Joe Mariscal; *Instr* Mario Moreno; *Instr* Ruth Santee
Estab 1935; Maintains nonprofit art gallery, L H Horton, Jr. Art Gallery San Joaquin Delta College 515 Pacific Ave Stockton CA 92507; maintains on-campus supplies shop; Pub; D & E; SC 12, LC 2; D 7,000, E 6,000, Maj 100
Ent Req: HS dipl
Degrees: AA 2 yrs
Courses: Advertising Design, †Architecture, Art Appreciation, Art History, Calligraphy, Ceramics, Collage, Commercial Art, Costume Design & Construction, Design, Drafting, Drawing, Fashion Arts, Film, Graphic Arts, Graphic Design, History of Art & Architecture, Interior Design, Landscape Architecture, Lettering, Painting, Photography, Printmaking, Sculpture, Stage Design, Textile Design, Theatre Arts, Video
Summer School: MJ Wamhoff, Dean. Enrl 8,000; Six week session. Courses—Same as regular sessions

UNIVERSITY OF THE PACIFIC, College of the Pacific, Dept of Art & Art History, 3601 Pacific Ave, Stockton, CA 95211-0197. Tel 209-946-2241; Fax 209-946-2518; Web: www.uop.edu; *Chmn* Barbara Flaherty
Estab 1851; FT 9; pvt; Scholarships; 37 (3 unit) courses & 14 (4 unit) courses available over 4 yrs, independent study; maj 55-70
Ent Req: HS grad with 20 sem grades of recommending quality earned in the 10th, 11th and 12th years in traditional subjects, twelve of these grades must be in acad subj
Degrees: BA & BFA
Courses: Art Education, †Art History, †Arts Administration, Ceramics, Commercial Design, Computer Art, Design, Drawing, Graphic Arts, †Graphic Design, Illustration, Lettering, Painting, Photography, Printmaking, Sculpture, †Studio Art
Summer School: Two 5 wk sessions

TAFT

TAFT COLLEGE, Art Department, 29 Emmons Park Dr, Taft, CA 93268-2317. Tel 661-763-4282; Fax 661-763-7705; Web: www.tafp.cc.ca.uf; *Chmn* Sonja Swenson-Wolsey
Estab 1922; pub; D & E; Scholarships; SC 67, LC 6; 1500 total
Ent Req: HS grad or 18 yrs old
Degrees: AA 2 yrs
Courses: Architecture, †Art History, Basic Design, Ceramics, Commercial Art, Conceptual Art, †Drafting, Drawing, Graphic Arts, Graphic Design, †History of Art & Architecture, Illustration, Painting, †Photography, Sculpture
Adult Hobby Classes: Courses—Ceramics, Graphic Arts, Jewelry, Painting, Photography
Summer School: Dean, Don Zumbro. Term of 6-8 wks. Courses—vary

TEMECULA

DORLAND MOUNTAIN ARTS COLONY, Art Residency Program, PO Box 6, Temecula, CA 92593-0006. Tel 951-302-3837; Email info@dorlandartscolony.org; Web: www.dorlandartscolony.org; *Exec Dir* Janice Cipriani-Willis
Estab 1979; non-profit; Grants
Activities: Schols offered
Tuition: $300 per week, $1,000 4 weeks; residency prog
Courses: Architecture & Design, dance, Mixed Media, Music, Performance, Photography, Sculpture, Theatre Arts, Visual Arts, Weaving, Writing

THOUSAND OAKS

CALIFORNIA LUTHERAN UNIVERSITY, Art Dept, 60 W Olson Rd, Thousand Oaks, CA 91360. Tel 805-493-3450; Fax 805-493-3479; Web: www.callutheran.edu; *Prof* Larkin Higgins; *Chmn* Nathan Tierney, PhD; *Asst Prof* Christine Sellin, PhD; *Asst Prof* Michael Pearce; *Asst Prof* Barry Burns; *Asst Prof* Brian Sethem
Estab 1961; maintains a nonprofit art gallery; Kwan Fong Art Gallery, Thousand Oaks, Calif; pvt; D & E; Scholarships; SC 12, LC 7; D 110, non-maj 46, maj 40
Ent Req: HS dipl, SAT or ACT, portfolio suggested
Degrees: BA 4 yr; MA 1 - 2 yr; EdD 3 yr
Courses: Art Education, Art History, Ceramics, †Commercial Art, Design, †Display, Drawing, †Graphic Arts, Graphic Design, Medical Illustration, †Mixed Media, Painting, Photography, Printmaking, Sculpture, Stage Design, Teacher Training, Theatre Arts
Summer School: Asst Prof, Michael Pearce. Tuition $800 per unit for term June-July, July-Aug. Courses—Art Education, Design, Drawing, Painting, Pottery, Sculpture

TORRANCE

EL CAMINO COLLEGE, Division of Fine Arts, 16007 Crenshaw Blvd, Torrance, CA 90506-0003. Tel 310-660-3715; Fax 310-660-3792; Email cfitzsimons@elcamino.edu; Web: www.elcamino.edu; *Dean Div* Constance Fitzsimons
Estab 1947; FT 35, PT 61; pub; D & E; Scholarships; SC 46, LC 6; D 1700, E 900, non-maj 2378, maj 222
Ent Req: HS dipl
Degrees: AA 2 yrs
Courses: †Advertising Design, †Art Appreciation, †Art History, †Ceramics, Drawing, Graphic Arts, Jewelry, †Lettering, Museum Staff Training, Painting, Photography, Printmaking, Sculpture
Children's Classes: Enrl 30. Courses—Exploration of Children's Art
Summer School: Enrl 400; tuition $11 per unit. Courses—Art Appreciation, Drawing, Painting

TUJUNGA

MCGROARTY CULTURAL ART CENTER, 7570 McGroarty Terrace, Tujunga, CA 91042. Tel 818-352-5285, 352-0865; Email director@mcgroartyartscenter.org; Web: www.mcgroartyartscenter.org; *Director* Joe Aguirre
Estab 1982; PT 24; pub, private; D & E; Scholarships; SC 40, LC 1; D 600, E 200
Ent Req: None
Degrees: None
Tuition: $100-200
Courses: Cartooning, Ceramics, Dance, Drawing, Life Drawing, Painting, Piano, Tai Chi Chuan, †Violin, †Yoga
Adult Hobby Classes: Enrl 10; $100; Courses—Ceramics & Painting
Children's Classes: Courses—Ceramics, Creative Drama, Dance, Music for Little People, Painting, Piano, Visual Arts, Violin

TURLOCK

CALIFORNIA STATE UNIVERSITY, Art Dept, 801 W Monte Vista Ave, Turlock, CA 95382. Tel 209-667-3431; Fax 209-667-3871; Email gsenior@csustan.edu; Web: csustan.edu; *Chmn Dept* Gordon Senior, MFA; *Prof* John Barnett, MFA; *Prof* C Roxanne Robbin, PhD; *Prof* David Olivant, MFA; *Prof* Richard Savini, MFA; *Prof* Hope Werness, PhD; *Prof* Dean DeCoker, MFA; *Prof* Jessica Gomula, MFA
Estab 1963, dept estab 1967; Maintain nonprofit art gallery; Univ Art Gallery, 801 University Ave, Bldg D, Turlock, CA 95382; pub; D & E; Scholarships; SC 27, LC 6, GC 4; D 700, E 300, non-maj 350, maj 125, grad 20
Ent Req: HS dipl
Degrees: BA 4 yrs; Printmaking Cert Prog; BFA 5 yrs
Courses: Art History, †Drawing, †Gallery Management, Painting, †Printmaking, †Sculpture, Teacher Training
Summer School: Summer semester offered

VALENCIA

CALIFORNIA INSTITUTE OF THE ARTS, School of Art, 24700 McBean Pkwy, Rm A211C Valencia, CA 91355. Tel 661-253-7801; Fax 661-259-5871; Web: calarts.edu; *Dean* Thomas S Lawson; *Assoc Dean* Darcy Huebler; *Assoc Dean* Andrew Freeman; *Asst Dean* Tom Bland; *Studio & Gallery Mgr* John Hogan; *Dir Opers* Joann Govlya
Estab 1970; maintains art library & nonprofit gallery; FT 30; pvt; D & E; Scholarships; SC, LC, GC; D 285, maj 211, grad 90
Ent Req: portfolio
Degrees: BFA 4 yrs, MFA
Tuition: $48,660 per yr
Courses: Aesthetics, Art History, Collage, Conceptual Art, Constructions, Critical Theory, Drawing, Film, Graphic Arts, †Graphic Design, †Integrated Media, Intermedia, †Mixed Media, †Painting, †Photography, †Post Studio, †Printmaking, †Sculpture, †Video, Visual Communication

VAN NUYS

LOS ANGELES VALLEY COLLEGE, Art Dept, 5800 Fulton Ave, Van Nuys, CA 91401-4062. Tel 818-781-1200; Fax 818-785-4672; Web: www.lavalleycollege.com; *Chmn* Dennis Reed
Degrees: AA, cert
Courses: Advertising Design, Art History, Ceramics, Design, Drawing, Painting, Photography, Printmaking, Sculpture
Summer School: Beginning Design I, Drawing

VENTURA

BROOKS INSTITUTE OF PHOTOGRAPHY, 5301 N Ventura Ave, Ventura, CA 93001-1023. Tel 805-966-3888; Fax 805-564-1475; Email library@brooks.edu; *Librn* Susan Shiras
Open Mon - Fri 8 AM - 5 PM; Lend to students only, reference to non-students
Income: Financed by school tuition
Library Holdings: Book Volumes 7367, CD-ROMs 28, Filmstrips, Periodical Subscriptions 91, Video Tapes 234
Special Subjects: Architecture, Film, Illustration, Mixed Media, Photography
Exhibitions: Various student exhib
Activities: Online instruction for cyber libraries, research instruction

VENTURA COLLEGE, Fine Arts Dept, 4667 Telegraph Rd, Ventura, CA 93003-3899. Tel 805-654-6400 ext 1280; Web: www.vccca.net; *Chmn* Myra Toth
Estab 1925; FT 7, PT 26; pub; D & E; Scholarships; SC 50, LC 15; D 500, E 500, maj 300
Ent Req: HS dipl or 18 yrs of age
Degrees: AA and AS
Courses: Advertising Design, †Art, Art Appreciation, †Art History, †Ceramics, Collage, †Commercial Art, Costume Design & Construction, Design, Display, Drafting, Drawing, Fashion Arts, †Graphic Arts, Graphic Design, History of Art & Architecture, Illustration, Intermedia, Landscape Architecture, Mixed Media, Museum Staff Training, †Painting, †Photography, †Printmaking, †Sculpture, Stage Design, Textile Design, †Theatre Arts
Adult Hobby Classes: Enrl 500; Courses—Art
Summer School: Dir, Gary Johnson. Enrl 325; tuition same as regular courses. 4-8 wk term. Courses—Ceramics, Color & Design, Computer Graphics, Drawing, Photography

VICTORVILLE

VICTOR VALLEY COMMUNITY COLLEGE, Art Dept, 18422 Bear Valley Rd, Victorville, CA 92392-5849. Tel 935-245-4271; Fax 935-245-9745; Web: www.vcconline.com; *Instructional Aide* Richard Ripley; *Chmn* Frank Foster
Estab 1961, dept estab 1971; pub; D & E; Scholarships; SC 20, LC 5; D 125, E 125, non-maj 200, maj 50
Ent Req: HS dipl
Degrees: AA 2 yrs
Courses: Art History, Commercial Art, Design, Drawing, Graphic Design, History of Art & Architecture, Painting, Photography
Adult Hobby Classes: Enrl 100; tuition $10 per 6 wks
Summer School: Dir, John F Foster. Enrl 75; tuition $13 per cr hr. Courses—Art Concepts, Art History, Design, Drawing, Photography

VISALIA

COLLEGE OF THE SEQUOIAS, Art Dept, 915 S Mooney Blvd, Fine Arts Division Visalia, CA 93277-2214. Tel 559-730-3700; Fax 559-730-3894; Web: www.sequoias.cc.ca.us; *Instr* Richard Flores; *Instr* Gene Maddox; *Instr* Barbara Strong
Estab 1925, dept estab 1940; PT 12; pub; D & E; Scholarships; SC 12, LC 4; D 60, E37, maj 10
Ent Req: HS dipl, must be 18 yr of age
Degrees: AA 2 yr
Courses: Art Appreciation, Art History, Calligraphy, Ceramics, Commercial Art, Display, Drawing, Gallery Staff Training, Graphic Arts, Graphic Design, History of Art & Architecture, Illustration, Lettering, Painting, Photography, Printmaking, Sculpture, Stage Design, Textile Design, Theatre Arts, Video
Adult Hobby Classes: Ceramics, Painting, Photography
Summer School: Dir, Marlene Taber. Courses—Drawing, Painting

WALNUT

MOUNT SAN ANTONIO COLLEGE, Art Dept, 1100 N Grand Ave, Walnut, CA 91789-1399. Tel 909-594-5611; Fax 909-468-3954; Web: www.mtsac.edu; *Chmn Art* Carolyn Alexander; *Chmn Art* Craig Deines; *Chmn Art* Kirk Peterson; *Chmn Animation* Don Shore
Estab 1945; FT 14, PT 10; pub; D & E; SC 24, LC 5; D 2254, E 852, maj 500
Ent Req: over 18 yrs of age
Degrees: AA and AS 2 yrs
Courses: Advertising Design, Art History, Ceramics, Commercial Art, Drafting, Drawing, Fibers, Graphic Arts, Illustration, Lettering, Life Drawing, Metals & Enamels, Painting, Photography, Printmaking, Sculpture, Theatre Arts, Woodworking
Summer School: Courses—Ceramics, Drawing

WEED

COLLEGE OF THE SISKIYOUS, Theatre Dept, 800 College Ave, Weed, CA 96094-2899. Tel 530-938-5257; Fax 530-938-5227; Web: www.siskiyous.edu; *Area Dir* Dennis Weathers
Estab 1957; pub; D & E; Scholarships; SC 15, LC 2; D 1200, maj 20
Ent Req: HS dipl
Degrees: AA 2 yrs
Courses: Art History, Ceramics, Computer Graphics, Drafting, Drawing, Graphic Arts, History of Art & Architecture, Life Drawing, Painting, Photography, Printmaking, Sculpture

WHITTIER

RIO HONDO COLLEGE, Arts & Cultural Programs Dept, 3600 Workman Mill Rd, Whittier, CA 90601-1699. Tel 562-908-3471; Fax 562-908-3446; Email cguptill@riohondo.edu; Web: www.riohondo.edu; *Dean* Chris Guptill; *Assoc Prof Painting & Drawing* Ada Pullini Brown; *Prof Photog* Chris Acuna-Hansen; *Asst Prof Painting & Drawing* Margaret Griffith; *Asst Prof 3D & 2D Design* Ron Reeder; *Instr Ceramics & Gallery Dir* Robert Miller; *Asst Prof Art History* Cynthia Lewis; *Prof Art* Dale Harvey; *Prof Art & Art History* Shelia Lynch; *Instr Animation* David Dawson
Estab 1962; On campus shop, Follett Bookstore where art supplies may be purchased; FT 8, PT 14; pub; D & E; SC 18, LC 3; D & E 19,000, non-maj 2100, maj 200
Ent Req: HS dipl
Degrees: AA 2 yrs
Courses: Advertising Design, Art Appreciation, Art History, Ceramics, Commercial Art, Conceptual Art, Design, Display, Drafting, Drawing, Graphic Arts, Graphic Design, History of Art & Architecture, Illustration, Lettering, Painting, Photography, Theatre Arts
Summer School: Enrl 3468

WHITTIER COLLEGE, Dept of Art, 13406 Philadelphia St, Whittier, CA 90608-4413. Tel 562-693-0771, ext 4686; Fax 562-698-4067; Email dsloan@whittier.edu; Web: www.whittier.edu/academic/art/arthome; *Chmn* Dr David Sloan
Estab 1901; pvt; D & E; Scholarships; Fellowships; SC 12, LC 12; 552-560 per sem
Ent Req: HS dipl, accept cr by exam CLEP, CEEBA
Degrees: BA 4 yrs
Courses: Art Education, Art History, Ceramics, Drawing, Painting, Printmaking
Adult Hobby Classes: Tuition $5. Courses—Classes for special students
Children's Classes: Tuition $5. Courses—Classes for special students
Summer School: Dir, Robert W Speier. Enrl 25; tui $140 per cr 1-7 cr, $125 per cr 7-up cr, May 31-June 17, June 20-July 29, Aug 1-Aug 19. Courses—Water Soluble Painting, Color & Basic Drawing

WILMINGTON

LOS ANGELES HARBOR COLLEGE, Art Dept, 1111 Figueroa Pl, Wilmington, CA 90744-2311. Tel 310-522-8200; Fax 310-834-1882; Web: www.lahc.cc.ca.us; *Assoc Prof* John Cassone, MA; *Asst Prof* Nancy E Webber, MFA; *Instr* DeAnn Jennings, MA; *Instr* Jay McCafferty, MA; *Chmn* David O'Shaughnessy
Estab 1949; pub; D & E; SC 48, LC 11; D 10,000, E 4,200
Ent Req: HS dipl
Degrees: AA 2 yrs
Courses: Architecture, Art History, Ceramics, Drawing, Fashion Arts, Painting, Photography, Printmaking, Stage Design, Theatre Arts

Summer School: Art Dept Chmn, DeAnn Jennings. Courses—Art Fundamentals, Art History and Photography

WOODLAND HILLS

PIERCE COLLEGE, Art Dept, 6201 Winnetka, Woodland Hills, CA 91371-0002. Tel 818-710-4366, 719-6475; Fax 818-710-2907; Email oshimad@pierce.laccd.edu; Web: www.piercecollege.com/usr/art/; *Art Dept Chmn* David Oshima; *Prof* Constance Moffat, PhD; *Instr* Angelo Allen; *Instr* Larissa Bank; *Instr* Amy Blount; *Instr* Joane Byce; *Instr* Alex Carrillo; *Instr* Melody Cooper; *Instr* Camille Cornelius; *Instr* Greg Gilbertson; *Instr* David Glover; *Instr* Robert Kingston; *Instr* Lori Koefoed; *Instr* Eduardo Navas; *Instr* Brian Peshek; *Instr* Howell Pinkston; *Instr* Jill Poyourow; *Instr* Nancy Rizzardi; *Instr* Gerald Vicich; *Instr* Constance Kocs
Estab 1947, dept estab 1956; Maintains nonprofit art gallery, 6201 Winnetka Ave, Woodland Hills, CA 91371; pub; D & E; SC 20, LC 8; D & E 23,000
Ent Req: HS dipl 18 yrs and over
Degrees: AA 60 units
Courses: Advertising Design, Architecture, Art Appreciation, Art History, Ceramics, Design, Drawing, Fine Art, Graphic Arts, Graphic Design, Jewelry
Adult Hobby Classes: Offered through Community Services Dept
Children's Classes: Offered through Community Services Dept
Summer School: Dir, Paul Whelan

COLORADO

ALAMOSA

ADAMS STATE COLLEGE, Dept of Visual Arts, 208 Edgemont Blvd, Alamosa, CO 81102-0001. Tel 719-587-7823; Fax 719-587-7330; Email caravens@adams.edu; Web: www.art.adams.edu; *Head Chair & Prof Art* Margaret Doell, MFA; *Prof Art* Eugene Schilling, MFA; *Asst Prof Art* Claire van der Plas, MFA; *Prof Art* Dana Provence, MFA; *Assoc Prof Art* Roger Eriksen, MFA; *PT Instr* Kris Gosar; *PT Instr* Laura Murphy, MA; *Asst Prof* Jenny Gawronski, MFA; *PT Instr* Linda Relyea, MA
Estab 1924; Nonprofit galleries: Cloyde Snook Gallery, Hatfield Gallery, 208 Edgemont Blvd, Alamosa, CO 81101; schols offered annually to undergrads & grads; On-campus shop where art supplies may be purchased; pub; D & E; Scholarships; SC 46, LC 6, GC 11; D 450, non-maj 200, maj 85, grad 15
Ent Req: HS dipl, ACT & SAT
Degrees: BA & BFA 4 yrs, MA 1-1/2 yrs
Tuition: Res—undergrad $3,724 per sem, grad $3,015 per sem; nonres—$9,040 per sem, grad $5,958 per sem; campus res—room & board $4,250
Courses: Art Appreciation, Art Education, Art History, Ceramics, Design, Drawing, Graphic Design, †Lettering, Metalsmithing, Painting, Photography, Printmaking, Sculpture, Weaving
Summer School: Tuition res—$306 per cr hr, nonres—$749 per cr hr. Courses—Art History, Ceramics, Drawing, Metals, Painting, Photography, Sculpture, Printmaking

BOULDER

UNIVERSITY OF COLORADO, BOULDER, Dept of Art & Art History, Visual Arts Complex, 1085 18th St Boulder, CO 80309-0459; 318 CUB, Boulder, CO 80309-0318. Tel 303-492-3580; Fax 303-492-4886; Email finearts@colorado.edu; Web: cuart.colorado.edu; *Chmn* Kirk Ambrose
Estab 1861; FT 27, PT 10; pub; D & E; Scholarships; SC 63, LC 44, GC 31, internships 2; D 800, grad 50, others 100
Ent Req: HS dipl
Degrees: BA or BFA (Art History & Studio Arts) 4 yrs, MA (Art History) 2 yrs, MFA (Studio Arts) 3 yrs
Courses: Art History, Ceramics, †Digital Arts, Drawing, Painting, Photography, Printmaking, Sculpture, Video
Summer School: Dir, James Johnson. Enrl 20-25 per course. Courses—Art History, Drawing, Painting, Photography, Printmaking, Sculpture, Special Topics, Watermedia, Digital Arts, Video

COLORADO SPRINGS

COLORADO COLLEGE, Dept of Art, 14 E Cache la Poudre St, Colorado Springs, CO 80903-3243. Tel 719-389-6366; Fax 719-389-6882; Web: www.coloradocollege.edu; *Chmn* Carl Reed, MFA; *Prof* James Trissel, MFA; *Assoc Prof* Gale Murray, MFA, PhD; *Prof* Bougdon Swider, MFA; *Assoc Prof* Edith Kirsch, MFA, PhD
Estab 1874; pvt; D; Scholarships; SC 20, LC 20; D 1800, maj 40
Ent Req: HS dipl or equivalent & selection by admis comt
Degrees: BA & MAT 4 yr
Courses: 3-D Design, Art History, Art Studio, Drawing, Graphic Design, Painting, Photography, Printmaking, Sculpture
Summer School: Dean, Elmer R Peterson. Courses—Architecture, Art Education, Photography

UNIVERSITY OF COLORADO-COLORADO SPRINGS, Visual & Performing Arts Dept (VAPA), 1420 Austin Bluffs Pkwy, Colorado Springs, CO 80918-3733. Tel 719-255-4065; Fax 719-255-4066; Email bkiselic@uccs.edu; Web: http://web.uccs.edu/vapa/index.shtml, www.galleryuccs.org; *Prof & Dir Film Studies* Robert von Dassanowsky, PhD; *Assoc Prof, Film Studies & Visual & Performing Arts* Teresa Meadows, PhD; *Instr Theater* Murray Ross; *Instr Music* Curtis Smith; *Chair, Visual & Performing Arts* Suzanne MacAulay, PhD; *Asst Prof & Dir, Music* Glen Whitehead, MDA; *Assoc Prof Visual Arts* Elissa Auther, PhD; *Assoc Prof Visual Arts & Dir* Valerie Brodar, MFA; *Asst Prof & Dir Theatre* Kevin Landis, MFA; *Asst Prof Visual Arts* Matt Barton, MFA; *Asst Prof Visual Arts* Corey Dreith, MFA; *Instr Theatre* Leah Chandler-Mills, MA; *Instr Visual Arts* Carol Dass, MA; *Instr Visual Arts* Pauline Foss, MA
Estab 1965, dept estab 1970; Maintain nonprofit gallery, Gallery of Contemporary Art (GOCA) same address as campus & 2nd gallery GOCA located at, 121 S Tejon, Colorado Springs. Maintain art library, VAPA-Visual Resource Center, COH 2012 (same address as campus); FT 5 PT 15; pub; D & E; SC 18 LC 16; maj 100
Ent Req: HS dipl, res-ACT 23 SAT 1000, nonres ACT 24 SAT 1050
Degrees: BA (Studio) 4 yr, BA (Art History) 4 Yr, BA (Visual & Performing Arts) 4 yr, (Concentrations in music, art history, film studies, theatre, visual art
Courses: Aesthetics, †Art, Art Appreciation, Art History, Collage, Computer Art, †Costume Design & Construction, Drawing, †Film Studies, †History of Art & Architecture, Mixed Media, Painting, Photography, Sculpture, †Stage Design, †Theatre Arts
Summer School: Chair & Assoc Prof, Suzanne MacAulay

DENVER

ART INSTITUTE OF COLORADO, 1200 Lincoln St, Denver, CO 80203-2172. Tel 303-837-0825; Fax 303-860-8520; Email alcadm@aii.edu; Web: www.aii.edu; *Dean Acad Affairs* Mitra Watts; *Pres* David Zorn
Estab 1952; Maintain nonprofit gallery; pvt; D & E; Scholarships; SC all; D1,800
Ent Req: HS dipl
Degrees: Assoc 2 yr, BA 4 yr
Courses: Advertising Design, Commercial Art, Computer Animation, Costume Design & Construction, Culinary Arts, Design, Drafting, Fashion Arts, Graphic Arts, Graphic Design, Industrial Design, Interior Design, Multimedia, Video, Website Administration
Adult Hobby Classes: Part time prog available, nights & weekends
Summer School: Summer studio prog for HS Srs

METROPOLITAN STATE UNIVERSITY OF DENVER, Art Dept, PO Box 173362, Campus Box 59 Denver, CO 80204-3936. Tel 303-556-3090; Fax 303-556-4094; Web: www.mscd.art.edu; *Chmn* Greg Watts
Estab 1963, dept estab 1963; Maintains a non-profit art gallery Center for Visual Art, 965 Santa Fe Dr, Denver, CO 80204; pub; D & E & F; Scholarships; SC 52, LC 8; D 650, E 325, maj 500
Ent Req: HS dipl or GED
Degrees: BFA 4 yrs
Courses: †Advertising Design, Aesthetics, Art Appreciation, Art Education, †Art History, †Ceramics, †Design, †Drawing, Electronic Media, Graphic Arts, Graphic Design, Illustration, †Jewelry, †Painting, Photography, Printmaking, Sculpture
Summer School: Same as regular session

REGIS UNIVERSITY, Fine Arts Dept, 3333 Regis Blvd, Denver, CO 80221-1099. Tel 303-458-3576, 458-4286; Web: www.regis.edu; *Dept Chair* Gene Stewart
Estab 1880; FT 3, PT 6; pvt; D & E
Ent Req: HS dipl, ent exam
Degrees: BA, BS & BFA 4 yrs
Courses: Aesthetics, Art Appreciation, Art History, Design, Drawing, Film, Graphic Arts, Graphic Design, Painting, Photography, Sculpture, †Visual Arts

UNIVERSITY OF COLORADO AT DENVER, College of Arts & Media Visual Arts Dept, PO Box 173364, Campus Box 162 Denver, CO 80217-3364. Tel 303-556-4891; Fax 303-556-2355; Web: www.cudenver.edu©AM\visual\; *Prof* Ernest O Porps, MFA; *Asst Prof* Karen Mathews, MFA, PhD; *Chmn* John Hull, MFA; *Painting & Drawing* Quinton Gonzales; *Painting & Drawing* James Elhenny; *Photo* Joan Brennan; *Sculpture* Scott Massey; *Multi-Media Study* Kent Homchick
Estab 1876, dept estab 1955; pub; D & E; Scholarships; SC 21, LC 13, GC 11; maj 168
Ent Req: HS dipl, ACT or SAT, previous acad ability and accomplishment
Degrees: BA and BFA 4 yrs
Courses: †Art History, †Creative Arts, †Drawing, †Painting, †Photography, †Sculpture, †Studio Arts
Summer School: Courses—Art History, Studio Workshops

UNIVERSITY OF DENVER, School of Art & Art History, 2121 E Asbury, Denver, CO 80208-0001. Tel 303-871-2846; Fax 303-871-4112; Email saah-interest@du.edu; Web: www.du.edu/art; WATS 800-876-3323; *Prof Art History* Annette Stott; *Prof Sculpture* Lawrence Argent; *Sr Lectr Art History & Dir Mus Studies* Gwen Chanzit; *Assoc Prof Art History* Annabeth Headrick; *Assoc Prof Drawing & Painting* Deborah Howard; *Assoc Prof Drawing & Printmaking* Catherine Chauvin; *Prof Art History* M E Warlick; *Dir, Assoc Prof Foundations* Sarah Gjertson; *Assoc Prof Electronic Media Arts & Design* Rafael Fajardo; *Assoc Prof Electronic Media Arts & Design* Timothy Weaver; *Assoc Prof Photog* Roddy MacInnes; *Assoc Prof Art History* Scott Montgomery; *Assoc Prof* Mia Fetterman-Mulvey; *Adj Faculty Conservation* Carl Patterson; *Adj Faculty Conservation* Sarah Melching; *Adjunct Faculty Mus Studies* Timothy Standring; *Adj Faculty Art History* Ron Otsuka; *Dir Gallery* Dan Jacobs; *Assoc Prof Electronic Media Arts & Design* Laleh Mehran; *Lectr Foundations* Susan Meyer
Estab 1864; Maintain nonprofit art gallery; Victoria H Myhren Gallery, 2121 East Asbury Ave, Denver, CO 80208 & Penrose Libr. Schol & fel offered in variable amounts to all qualified candidates for 1 yr annually; contact Dr M. E. Warlick; Pvt; D&E; Scholarships; Fellowships; SC 44, LC 34, GC 38; D 450, non-maj 170-200, maj 170, grad 50
Ent Req: HS dipl, ent exam, portfolio
Degrees: BA & BFA 4 yrs, MA & MFA 3 yrs; combined BA/MA 5 yrs
Tuition: $1,064 per qtr hr; campus res available
Courses: Art Appreciation, Art Education, Art History, Ceramics, Design, Digital Media, Drawing, History of Art & Architecture, Museum Studies, Painting, Photography, †Pre-Art Conservation, Printmaking, Restoration & Conservation, Sculpture, †Studio Art

DURANGO

FORT LEWIS COLLEGE, Art Dept, 1000 Rim Dr, Durango, CO 81301-3999. Tel 970-247-7167; Fax 970-247-7520; Web: www.fortlewis.edu; *Asst Prof* Paul Booth; *Assoc Prof* Chad Colby; *Asst Prof* Jay Dougan; *Asst Prof* Anthony Holmquist; *Prof, chmn dept* Susan Moss; *Assoc Prof* Amy K Wendland
Estab 1956; 5 FT; pub; D & E; Scholarships; SC 30, LC 6; D 600, non-maj 450, maj 150
Ent Req: HS dipl, SAT
Degrees: BA & BS
Tuition: $1105 per sem; campus res available—$2528 room & board per sem
Courses: Aesthetics, Art History, Ceramics, Drawing, Handicrafts, Illustration, Industrial Design, Intermedia, Jewelry, Southwest Art
Summer School: Dean, Ed Angus. Enrl 1000. Courses—Art Education, Ceramics, Drawing, Mural Design, Painting

FORT COLLINS

COLORADO STATE UNIVERSITY, Dept of Art, G100 Visual Art Bldg, Fort Collins, CO 80523-9001. Tel 970-491-6774; Fax 970-491-0505; Web: www.colostate.edu/depts/art; *Chmn* Phil Risbeck
Estab 1870, dept estab 1956; 34; pub; D; Scholarships; SC 55, LC 13, GC 5; D 547, non-maj 860, maj 547, grad 22
Ent Req: HS dipl, portfolio if by transfer
Degrees: BA(Art History & Art Education) and BFA 4 yr, MFA 60 hrs
Courses: Advertising Design, Aesthetics, Art Appreciation, †Art Education, †Art History, †Ceramics, †Drawing, †Fibers, Goldsmithing, Graphic Arts, †Graphic Design, History of Art & Architecture, Illustration, Jewelry, †Metalsmithing, †Painting, †Photography, †Pottery, †Printmaking, †Sculpture, Silversmithing, Teacher Training, Textile Design, Weaving
Children's Classes: Continuing education art offerings not on regular basis
Summer School: Dir, James T Dormer. Enrl 700. Courses—most regular session courses

GRAND JUNCTION

COLORADO MESA UNIVERSITY, Art Dept, 1100 North Ave, Grand Junction, CO 81501-3122. Tel 970-248-1833; Fax 970-248-1834; Email sgarner@coloradomesa.edu; Web: coloradomesa.edu; *Dept Head* Teresa S Garner; *Prof* Carolyn I Quinn-Hensley; *Assoc Prof* Joshua Butler; *Asst Prof* Eli M Hall; *Asst Prof* Araan Schmidt; *Asst Prof* Alison Harris; *Asst Prof* Eric Elliott
Estab 1925; Maintain nonprofit art gallery, Johnson Gallery, Mesa State College, 1100 North Ave, Grand Junction, CO 81501; pub; D & E; Scholarships; SC 88, LC 14, Other 4
Ent Req: HS dipl, GED
Degrees: BFA
Courses: †Advertising Design, †Art Appreciation, †Art Education, Art History, Ceramics, Design, Drawing, Exhibitions & Management, Film, †Graphic Design, History of Art & Architecture, Lettering, Mixed Media, Painting, Photography, Printmaking, Sculpture

GREELEY

AIMS COMMUNITY COLLEGE, Visual & Performing Arts, PO Box 69, Greeley, CO 80632-0069. Tel 970-330-8008; Fax 970-330-5705; Web: www.aims.edu; *Dir Visual & Performing Arts* Alysan Broda; *Acad Dean Communs & Humanities* Susan Cribelli
Estab 1967; pub; D & E
Ent Req: HS dipl, equivalent
Degrees: AA
Courses: Art Appreciation, Art History, Ceramics, Design, Drawing, Fashion Arts, Interior Design, Jewelry, Painting, Photography, Sculpture, Textile Design, Weaving
Children's Classes: Courses offered
Summer School: Courses offered

UNIVERSITY OF NORTHERN COLORADO, School of Art & Design, 501 20th St, Greeley, CO 80639-6900. Tel 970-351-2143; Fax 970-351-2299; Web: www.unco.edu; *Dir* Andrew Liccardo
Estab 1889; Maintains nonprofit art gallery: Mariani Gallery; FT 10; pub; D & E; Scholarships; SC 72, LC 20, GC 18; non-maj 75, maj 361, grad 20
Ent Req: HS dipl, Portfolio
Degrees: BA 4 yr, MA
Courses: Art Education, Art History, Ceramics, †Computer Graphics, Drawing, Fiber Art, Graphic Design, Jewelry, Painting, Papermaking, Photographic Imaging, Photography, Printmaking, Sculpture
Summer School: Courses—Comparative Arts Program in Florence, Italy, Study of the Indian Arts of Mesa Verde, Mesa Verde workshop & on campus courses, Workshops in Weaving & Ceramics in Steamboat Springs, Colorado

GUNNISON

WESTERN STATE COLLEGE OF COLORADO, Dept of Art & Industrial Technology, 600 N Adam, Gunnison, CO 81231; Quigley Hall, Gunnison, CO 81231. Tel 970-943-0120, Ext 3090; Web: www.western.edu; *Dept Chair* Heather Orr
Estab 1911; FT 40, PT 10-20; pub; D & E; Scholarships; SC 29, LC 7; 2550
Ent Req: HS dipl, special exam
Degrees: BA & BFA, 4 yr
Courses: Art Appreciation, Art Education, Art History, Calligraphy, Ceramics, Commercial Art, Conceptual Art, Design, Drawing, Graphic Arts, Graphic Design, History of Art & Architecture, Indian Art, Introduction to Art, Jewelry, Mixed Media, Painting, Photography, Printmaking, Sculpture, Silversmithing, Studio Art, Textile Design, Weaving, Weaving
Summer School: 4 & 8 wk courses. Courses—Drawing, Painting, Photography

LA JUNTA

OTERO JUNIOR COLLEGE, Dept of Arts, 1802 Colorado Ave, La Junta, CO 81050-3346. Tel 719-384-8721; Fax 719-384-6880; Web: www.ojc.cccoes.edu; *Head Dept* Timothy F Walsh
Estab 1941; pub; D & E; Scholarships; SC 12, LC 3; 850
Ent Req: HS grad
Degrees: AA & AAS 2 yr
Courses: Art History, Creative Design, Drawing, Painting
Adult Hobby Classes: Enrl 60; tuition $47.50 per cr, non-credit courses vary. Courses—Art, Drawing, Painting

LAKEWOOD

RED ROCKS COMMUNITY COLLEGE, Arts Dept, 13300 W Sixth Ave, Lakewood, CO 80228. Tel 303-914-6563; Fax 303-914-6666; Email deborah.dell@rrcc.edu; Web: www.rrcc/cccoes.edu; *Asst Ceramics Instr* Deborah Dell; *Assoc Prof* Berndt Savig
Estab 1965; Maintain non-profit art gallery, Susan K Arndt Gallery (same address); on-campus shop where art supplies may be purchased; pub; Weekend; Scholarships; SC 38, LC 14; D 423, E 115
Activities: Schols offered
Ent Req: HS dipl, equivalent
Degrees: AA
Tuition: Resident $5,000 per yr; non-resident $12,500 per yr
Courses: Art Appreciation, Art History, Ceramics, Design, Drawing, Electronic Studio, Graphic Arts, Graphic Design, Painting, Printmaking, Sculpture, Stage Design, †Textile Design, Theatre Arts
Summer School: Enrl 80; tuition $99 per 3 cr course per 10 wks. Courses—Ceramics, Drawing, Design, Watercolor

ROCKY MOUNTAIN COLLEGE OF ART & DESIGN, 1600 Pierce St, Lakewood, CO 80214-1897. Tel 303-753-6046; Fax 303-759-4970; Email admissions@rmcad.edu; Web: www.rmcad.edu; WATS 800-888-2787; *Pres & Provost* Dr Maria Puzziferro; *Financial Aid* Tammy Dybdahl; *VPres Admis* John Meurer; *Dean Design & Communs Art* Lauren Pillote; *VPres Mktg* Rebecca Newman; *Dean Fine & Liberal Arts* Dan James
Estab 1963; Maintain nonprofit art gallery, Phillip J. Steele Gallery, Mary K Harris Bldg, 1600 Pierce St, Lakewood, CO 80214. Art supplies sold at on-campus store; FT 19, PT 41; pvt; D & E; Scholarships; SC 68%, LC 32%; D 610
Ent Req: HS grad or GED, portfolio, essay, GEST scores
Degrees: BFA
Tuition: $13,416 fulltime, $1,118 per cr hr incoming freshmen
Courses: †Animation, Art Education, Art History, Ceramics, Character Design, Design, Drafting, Drawing, Film, Game Art, Graphic Arts, †Graphic Design, †Illustration, †Interior Design, Mixed Media, †Painting, Photography, Printmaking, †Sculpture, Teacher Training, Video
Summer School: Enrl 276; tuition $13176 for full term. Courses—Same as regular term

PUEBLO

UNIVERSITY OF SOUTHERN COLORADO, Dept of Art, 2200 Bonforte Blvd, Pueblo, CO 81001-4990. Tel 719-549-2835; Fax 719-549-2120; *Asst Prof* Carl Jensen, MFA; *Chmn* Roy Sonnema, PhD; *Asst Prof* Maya Avina, MFA; *Asst Prof* Dennis Dalton, MFA; *Assoc Prof* Richard Hansen, MFA; *Assoc Prof* Victoria Hansen, MFA
Estab 1933; pub; D & E; Scholarships; SC 50, LC 18; D 700, E 50, non-maj 600, maj 175
Ent Req: HS dipl, GED, Open Door Policy
Degrees: BA and BS 4 yrs
Courses: Art History, Ceramics, Collage, Commercial Art, Computer Animation, Computer Imaging, Drawing, Exhibition Design, Graphic Design, Illustration, Painting, Photography, Printmaking, Sculpture, Teacher Training, Video
Summer School: Dir, Ed Sajbel. Enrl 125. Courses—Art Education, Art History, Ceramics, Introduction to Art, Painting

RANGELY

COLORADO NORTHWESTERN COMMUNITY COLLEGE, Art Dept, 500 Kennedy Dr, Rangely, CO 82648-3502. Tel 800-562-1105; Web: www.cncc.edu; *Chair* Mary Karen Solomon

SALIDA

DUNCONOR WORKSHOPS, PO Box 416, Salida, CO 81201-0416. Tel 719-539-7519; *Head* Harold O'Connor
Estab 1976; pvt; D; SC; D 34
Ent Req: professional experience
Tuition: Varies by course
Courses: Design, Goldsmithing, Jewelry, Silversmithing
Adult Hobby Classes: Enrl 24; tuition $450 per wk. Courses—Jewelry Making
Summer School: Enrl 34; tuition $450 per wk. Courses—Jewelry Making

STERLING

NORTHEASTERN JUNIOR COLLEGE, Art Department, 100 College Ave, Sterling, CO 80751-2345. Tel 970-522-6600, Ext 6701, 521-6701; Email jaci.mathis@njc.edu; Email larry.prestwich@njc.edu; *Prof* Larry B Prestwich, MA; *Instr* Peter L Youngers; *Instr* Joyce May; *Instr* Jaci Mathis, BA
Estab 1941; Maintain nonprofit art gallery on-campus, Peter L Youngers Fine Arts Gallery; art supplies available on-campus; pub; D & E; Scholarships; SC 16, LC 2; D 100, E 24, non-maj 80, maj 20, others 10
Ent Req: HS dipl, GED
Degrees: AA 2 yr
Courses: Advertising Design, Art Appreciation, Art Education, Art History, Ceramics, Commercial Art, Design, Drawing, Graphic Design, Lettering, Mixed Media, Painting, Photography, Printmaking, Sculpture, Teacher Training
Adult Hobby Classes: Enrl 100. Courses—Basic Crafts, Ceramics, Drawing, Macrame, Painting, Stained Glass

CONNECTICUT

BRIDGEPORT

HOUSATONIC COMMUNITY COLLEGE, Art Dept, 900 Lafayette Blvd, Bridgeport, CT 06604-4704. Tel 203-332-5000; Fax 203-332-5123; Web: www.hcc.commnet.edu; *Faculty* Michael Stein, MFA; *Prog Coordr* Ronald Abbe, MFA; *Faculty* John Favret, MFA
Estab 1967, dept estab 1968; maintains nonprofit gallery, Burt Chernow Gallery & Housatonic Museum of Art; on-campus shop where art supplies may be purchased; pub; D & E; Scholarships; SC 20, LC 5; D 200, E 170, maj 75
Ent Req: HS dipl
Degrees: AA Fine Art 2 yr, AA Graphic Design, AA Graphic Design Computer Graphic Option
Courses: †Art History, †Ceramics, Computer Graphics, †Constructions, †Design, †Drawing, †Film, †Graphic Arts, †Graphic Design, Mixed Media, †Painting, †Photography, †Sculpture, †Stage Design, †Theatre Arts
Summer School: Dir, William Griffin. Courses—Same as regular session

UNIVERSITY OF BRIDGEPORT, Shintaro Akatsu School of Design, 84 Iranistan Ave, Bridgeport, CT 06604. Tel 203-576-4239, 576-4709; Fax 203-576-4653; *Dir* Thomas Julius Burger; *Assoc Prof* Donald McIntyre, MFA; *Assoc Prof* Jim Lesko, MFA; *Assoc Prof* Sean Nixon, MFA; *Asst Prof* Ketti Kupper, MFA
Estab 1927, dept estab 1947; pvt; D & E; Scholarships; SC 38, LC 24, GC 15; D 1150, E 200, non-maj 1070, maj 260, GS 22
Ent Req: portfolio for BFA candidates only, college boards
Degrees: BA, BS & BFA 4 yr
Courses: Advertising Design, Art History, Ceramics, †Graphic Design, †Illustration, †Industrial Design, †Interior Design, Painting, Photography, Printmaking, Sculpture, Theatre Arts, Weaving
Adult Hobby Classes: Enrl open; Courses—most crafts
Summer School: Chmn, Sean Nixon. Details from chairperson (203-576-4177)

DANBURY

WESTERN CONNECTICUT STATE UNIVERSITY, School of Visual & Performing Arts, Visual & Performing Arts Center, 43 Lake Ave Ext Danbury, CT 06811; 181 White St, Danbury, CT 06810-6855. Tel 203-837-3222; Fax 203-837-3233; Web: www.wcsu.ctstateu.edu/svpa; *Dean* Dr Dan Groble; *Chmn Art Dept* Cathy Vanaria; *MFA Coordr* Darby Cardonsky
Estab 1903; Maintains nonprofit art gallery; 43 Lake Ave Ext, Danbury, CT 06811; Haas Library Midtown Campus, 181 White St; art supplies available at book & art store Midtown & Westside campus; FT 7; pub; D & E; Scholarships; SC 30, LC 3-6, GC 5; D 155, grad 11
Ent Req: HS dipl
Degrees: BA Art in Graphic Design, Illustration, Photog or Studio Art 4 yr, MFA (painting & illustration) 2 yr
Courses: Animation Production, Ceramics, Design, Drawing, Graphic Arts, †Graphic Design, History of Art & Architecture, †Illustration, Lettering, †Museology, Painting, †Photography, Printmaking, Sculpture, Stage Design, †Studio Art

FAIRFIELD

FAIRFIELD UNIVERSITY, Visual & Performing Arts, 1073 N Benson Rd, Fairfield, CT 06824-5171. Tel 203-254-4000; Fax 203-254-4119; Web: www.fairfield.edu; *Prof, Chmn* Kathryn Jo Yarrington; *Acting Dean* Dr Beverly Khan
Estab 1951; Priv; D & E, summer; Scholarships
Degrees: BA, Masters
Courses: Art History, Art of Film, Design, Drawing, Film Production, History of Film, Painting, Photography, Printmaking, Sculpture, Video, Visual Design
Adult Hobby Classes: Enrl 2000; tuition $330 per 3 cr. Courses—Full Fine Arts curriculum
Summer School: Dir, Dr Vilma Allen. Enrl 2000. Semester June - Aug

SACRED HEART UNIVERSITY, Dept of Art, 5151 Park Ave, Fairfield, CT 06432-1000. Tel 203-371-7737; Web: www.sacredheart.edu; *Prof* Virginia F Zic, MFA
Estab 1963, dept estab 1977; 8; pvt; D & E; Scholarships; SC 26, LC 5; D 300, E 100, non-maj 225, maj 70
Ent Req: HS dipl
Degrees: BA 4 yrs
Tuition: Campus res—available
Courses: Advertising Design, Art History, Computer Design, Design, Drawing, †Graphic Design, History of Art & Architecture, †Illustration, †Painting
Summer School: Prof, Virginia Zic. Courses—Art History

FARMINGTON

TUNXIS COMMUNITY TECHNICAL COLLEGE, Graphic Design Dept, 271 Scott Swamp Rd, Farmington, CT 06032-3187. Tel 860-677-7701; Web: www.tunxis.commnet.edu; *Acad Dean* Sharon LeSuer; *Graphic Design Coordr* Stephen A Klema, MFA; *Assoc Prof* William Kluba, MFA
Estab 1970, dept estab 1973; pub; D & E; SC 15, LC 4; non-maj 40, maj 90
Ent Req: HS dipl
Degrees: AS, AA(Graphic Design, Visual Fine Arts)
Courses: 2-D & 3-D Design, Color, Computer Graphics, Drawing, Graphic Design, Illustration, Painting, Photography, Typography
Summer School: Dir Community Services, Dr Kyle. Courses—Computer Graphics, Drawing, Painting, Photography

HAMDEN

PAIER COLLEGE OF ART, INC, 20 Gorham Ave, Hamden, CT 06514-3902. Tel 203-287-3030; Fax 203-287-3021; Web: www.paiercollegeofart.edu; *Pres* Jonathan E Paier
Estab 1946; FT 36, PT 11; pvt; D & E; Scholarships; SC 10, LC 6 GC 1; D 185, E 130
Ent Req: HS grad, presentation of portfolio, transcript of records, recommendation
Degrees: BFA & AFA programs offered
Courses: Advertising Design, Architecture, Art Education, Art History, Calligraphy, Conceptual Art, Design, Drafting, Drawing, Fine Arts, Graphic Arts, †Graphic Design, History of Art & Architecture, †Illustration, †Interior Design, Lettering, †Painting, †Photography, Printmaking, Textile Design
Summer School: Dir, Dan Paier. Enrl 50. Courses—CADD, Fine Arts, Graphic Design, Illustration, Interior Design, Photography

HARTFORD

CAPITOL COMMUNITY TECHNICAL COLLEGE, Humanities Division & Art Dept, 61 Woodland St, Hartford, CT 06105-2345. Tel 860-520-7800; Fax 860-520-7906; Web: www.commnet.edu; *Chmn* John Christi; *Prof* Thomas Werle
Estab 1967; FT 1, PT 2; D & E
Ent Req: HS dipl or equivalent
Degrees: AA & AS 2 yr
Courses: Art History, Ceramics, Design, Drawing, Figure Drawing, Painting, Printmaking, Sculpture
Summer School: Courses offered

TRINITY COLLEGE, Dept of Studio Arts, 300 Summit St, Hartford, CT 06106-3186. Tel 860-297-2208; Fax 860-297-5349; Email Joseph.Byrne@trincoll.edu; Web: www.trincoll.edu/depts/star; *Prof Fine Arts* Robert Kirschbaum, MFA; *Asst Prof* Pablo Delano, MFA; *Vis Assoc Prof* Nathan Margalit, MFA; *Asst Prof* Patricia Tillman, MFA; *Chmn, Prof Fine Arts* Joseph Byrne
Estab 1823, dept estab 1939; pvt; D; Scholarships; SC 20, LC 22; D 400, non-maj 350, major 50
Ent Req: HS dipl
Degrees: MA
Courses: Design, Drawing, History of Art & Architecture, Painting, Photography, Printmaking, Sculpture, †Studio Arts

MANCHESTER

MANCHESTER COMMUNITY COLLEGE, Visual Fine Art Dept, 60 Bidwell St, Manchester, CT 06040-6449; PO Box 1046, Mail Sta 19 Manchester, CT 06045-1046. Tel 860-512-2697; Email dlong@manchestercc.edu; Web: www.mcc.commnet.edu; *Prof Drawing* Patricia Carrigan; *Prof Art History* Olivia Chiang; *Prof Photog* Daniel Mosher Long; *Prof Painting* Richard Harden; *Prof Sculpture* Timothy Kussow
Estab 1963, dept estab 1968; FT 6; pub; D & E; Scholarships; SC 26, LC 5-10; D 650, E 70, non-maj 600, maj 120
Ent Req: HS dipl
Degrees: AA & AS 2 yrs
Tuition: $2,026 FT per sem
Courses: Aesthetics, Art Appreciation, †Art History, †Basic Design, Calligraphy, †Ceramics, Conceptual Art, Design, †Drawing, †Film, †Graphic Arts, †Graphic Design, History of Art & Architecture, History of Film, Lettering, †Painting, †Photography, †Printmaking, †Sculpture, Sign Painting, Video

MIDDLETOWN

MIDDLESEX COMMUNITY COLLEGE, Fine Arts Div, 100 Training Hill Rd, Middletown, CT 06457-4889. Tel 860-343-5800; Web: www.mxcc.commnet.edu; *Head Dept, Prof* Judith DeGraffenried; *Instr* Matthew Weber
Estab 1966; Maintain a nonprofit art gallery, Pegasus Gallery, Chapman Hall, Niche, Founders Hall; pvt; D & E
Degrees: AS
Courses: †Art Appreciation, Art History, Ceramics, Design, Drawing, †Graphic Arts, †History of Art & Architecture, Painting, †Photography, Sculpture, †Silversmithing

WESLEYAN UNIVERSITY, Dept of Art & Art History, Wesleyan Station, Middletown, CT 06459. Tel 800-685-2682, 860-685-2000; Fax 860-685-2061;

Web: www.wesleyan.edu/art/; *Prof* David Schorr, MFA; *Prof* Jonathan W Best, PhD; *Prof* Clark Maines, MFA, PhD; *Prof* Peter Mark, MFA, PhD; *Assoc Prof* Jeffrey Schiff, MFA; *Assoc Prof, Dir* Tula Telfair, MFA; *Assoc Prof, Dir* Elizabeth Milroy, MFA, PhD; *Assoc Prof* Phillip Wagoner, MFA, PhD; *Chair* Joseph Siry
Estab 1831, dept estab 1928; pvt; D; SC 30, LC 25; in school D 3604, maj 94, undergrad 2667
Ent Req: HS dipl, SAT
Degrees: BA 4 yrs
Tuition: Campus res available
Courses: Architecture, Art History, Film, Film History, Film Production, Graphic Arts, History of Art & Architecture, History of Prints, Painting, Photography, Printmaking, Printroom Methods & Techniques, Sculpture, Theatre Arts, Typography
Summer School: Dir, Barbara MacEachern. Enrl 576; Term of 6 wks beginning July 5. Courses—grad courses in all areas

NEW BRITAIN

CENTRAL CONNECTICUT STATE UNIVERSITY, Dept of Art, 1615 Stanley St, New Britain, CT 06050-2439. Tel 860-832-3200; Fax 860-832-2634; Web: www.ccsu.edu; *Chmn Dept* Dr M Cipriano
Estab 1849; FT 14, PT 15; pub; D & E; SC 36, LC 8, GC 20; D 200, E 150, non-maj 1000, maj 200, grad 200
Ent Req: HS dipl
Degrees: BA(Graphic Design), BA(Fine Arts) & BS(Art Educ) 4 yrs
Courses: Art Education, Art History, Ceramic Sculpture, Ceramics, Color Theory, Curatorship, Display, Drawing, Fibre Sculpture, Fine Arts, Gallery Management, Graphic Arts, Graphic Design, Handicrafts, Jewelry, Lettering, Painting, Photography, Printmaking, Sculpture, Serigraphy (Silk Screen), Stained Glass, Teacher Training
Children's Classes: Enrl 30, 5-17 yr olds. Courses—Crafts, Fine Arts
Summer School: Dean Continuing Educ, P Schubert. Enrl 200. Courses—Crafts, Design, Drawing, Fine Arts

NEW CANAAN

SILVERMINE ARTS CENTER, School of Art, 1037 Silvermine Rd, New Canaan, CT 06840-4337. Tel 203-966-6668 ext 2; Fax 203-966-2763; Email school@silvermineart.org; Web: www.silvermineart.org; *Dir School* Anne Connell
Estab 1949; Maintain nonprofit art gallery, Florence Schick School Exhib Gallery, for student work & the Silvermine Guild Gallery for Silvermine Guild Artists; pvt; D & E; Scholarships; SC 60, LC 1; 2,000
Ent Req: none
Degrees: none
Courses: Art History, bronze jewelry, Ceramics, Computer Graphics, Drawing, Goldsmithing, History of Art & Archeology, Illustration, Mixed Media, Painting, Photography, Printmaking, Sculpture, Silversmithing, Sogetsu Ikebana, Woodworking, Youth Programs in Art
Adult Hobby Classes: Enrl 550-600. Courses offered
Children's Classes: Enrl 80-100. Courses offered
Summer School: Dir, Anne Connell. Courses—Same as above

NEW HAVEN

ALBERTUS MAGNUS COLLEGE, Visual and Performing Arts, 700 Prospect St, New Haven, CT 06511-1189. Tel 203-773-8546, 773-8550; Fax 203-773-3117; Web: www.albertus.edu; *Prof Art* Jerome Nevins, MFA; *Chmn & Assoc Prof Art* Beverly Chieffo, MA; *Asst Prof Art Therapy* Marian Towne, MA
Estab 1925, dept estab 1970; pvt; D & E; Scholarships; SC 20, LC 9; D 120, non-maj 60, maj 40
Ent Req: HS dipl, SAT, CEEB
Degrees: BA, BFA 8 sem
Tuition: Campus res available
Courses: Aesthetics, Art Education, Art History, Art Therapy, Ceramics, Collage, Design, Drawing, Fabric Design & Construction, History of Art & Architecture, Mixed Media, Painting, Photography, Printmaking, Sculpture, Teacher Training, Weaving
Adult Hobby Classes: Courses offered
Summer School: Dir, Elaine Lewis. Courses—vary

SOUTHERN CONNECTICUT STATE UNIVERSITY, Dept of Art, 501 Crescent St, New Haven, CT 06515-1355. Tel 203-392-6653; Fax 203-392-6658; Web: www.southernct.edu/undergrad/schas/ART/index; *Dept Head* Cort Sierpinski
Estab 1893; pub; D & E; SC 40, LC 18, GC 20; D 315, GS 100
Ent Req: HS dipl, SAT
Degrees: BS, MS(Art Educ), BA(Art History) & BA, BS(Studio Art) 4 yrs
Courses: Art Education, Art History, Ceramics, Graphic Design, Jewelry, Metalsmithing, Painting, Photography, Printmaking, Stained Glass, Teacher Training
Summer School: Dir, Keith Hatcher. Enrl 320. Courses—Art History, Crafts, Drawing, Graphic Design, Painting, Photography, Printmaking, Sculpture, Stained Glass

YALE UNIVERSITY, School of Art, 1156 Chapel St, PO Box 208339 New Haven, CT 06520-8339. Tel 203-432-2600; Fax 203-436-4947; Email artschool.info@yale.edu; Web: art.yale.edu; *Dean* Marta Kuzma; *Dir Graduate Studies Graphic Design* Sheila Levrant-Bretteville, MFA; *Dir Graduate Studies in Painting & Printmaking* Anoka Farugee; *Dir Graduate Studies in Photog* Gregory Crewdson; *Dir Graduate Studies in Sculpture* Martin Kersels; *Dir Undergraduate Studies in Art* Lisa Kereszi
Estab 1869; pvt; D; Scholarships; GC118
Ent Req: BFA, BA, BS or dipl from four year professional art school & portfolio
Degrees: MFA 2 yrs
Tuition: $38,761 per yr
Courses: Drawing, Graphic Design, Painting, Photography, Printmaking, Sculpture
Summer School: 8 wk undergrad courses in New Haven, 3 cr each; 5 wk Graphic Design Prog in Brissago, Switzerland; 8 wk Fel Prog in Norfolk
—**Dept of the History of Art**, 56 High St Rm 103, New Haven, CT 06520-8272; PO Box 208272, New Haven, CT 06520-8272. Tel 203-432-2667; Fax 203-432-7462; Web: arthistory.yale.edu; *Chmn & Dir Grad Studies* Tim Barringer; *Dir Undergrad Studies* Marisa Bass
Estab 1940; FT 27, PT 2; pvt; D; Scholarships; Fellowships; Assistantships
Ent Req: for grad prog—BA & foreign language
Degrees: PhD(Art History) 6 yr
Tuition: $26,770 per yr
Courses: †Art History
—**School of Architecture**, 180 York St, New Haven, CT 06520-8924. Tel 203-432-2296, 432-2288; Fax 203-432-7175; Web: www.architecture.yale.edu; *Dean* Deborah Berke
Estab 1869; pvt; Scholarships; 142 maximum
Ent Req: Bachelor's degree, grad record exam
Degrees: MEd 2 yr, MArchit 3 yr
Tuition: $24,500 per yr
Courses: Aesthetics, Architecture, Art History, Design, Drawing, Landscape Architecture, Photography

NEW LONDON

CONNECTICUT COLLEGE, Dept of Art, 270 Mohegan Ave, New London, CT 06320-4125; PO Box 5206, New London, CT 06320-4196. Tel 860-439-2740; Fax 860-439-5339; Web: www.conncoll.edu/departments/art; *Prof* Peter Leibert; *Prof* David Smalley; *Prof* Barkley L Hendricks; *Prof* Maureen McCabe; *Assoc Prof* Pamela Marks; *Assoc Prof* Andrea Wollensak; *Assoc Prof* Ted Hendrickson; *Prof* Tim McDowell; *Vis Asst Prof* Matt Harle; *Vis Asst Prof* Denise Pelletier; *Acad Dept Asst* Heidi Shepard
Estab 1911; pvt; D & E; Scholarships; SC 25; D 1600, maj approx 20
Ent Req: HS dipl, ent exam
Degrees: BA 4 yrs
Tuition: $15,175 per yr; campus res—room & board $4800
Courses: Architecture, Arts & Technology, Ceramics, Collage, Computer Art, Design, Drawing, †Graphic Arts, Graphic Design, Mixed Media, Painting, Photography, Printmaking, Silversmithing, Video
Summer School: Acting Dir, Ann Whitlach. Courses—Vary
—**Dept of Art History, Architectural Studies & Museum Studies**, 270 Mohegan Ave, Box: Art New London, CT 06320. Tel 860-439-2740; Fax 860-439-5339; Web: www.conncoll.edu; *Prof* Andrea Wollensak

OLD LYME

LYME ACADEMY COLLEGE OF FINE ARTS, 84 Lyme St, Old Lyme, CT 06371-2333. Tel 860-434-5232; Fax 860-434-8725; Email admission@lymeacademy.edu; Web: www.lymeacademy.edu; *Campus Dean* Todd Jokl; *Registrar* Patty DeVoe; *Dean* Sally Seaman
Estab 1976; Maintain nonprofit art gallery, The Chauncey Stillman Gallery, 84 Lyme St, Old Lyme, CT 06371; maintains art/architecture library, The Krieble Library, 84 Lyme St, Old Lyme, CT 06371; on-campus shop where art supplies may be purchased; pvt; D & E; Scholarships; Fellowships; SC 83 LC 6; 97
Ent Req: HS dipl, portfolio
Degrees: Cert 3 yr, BFA 4 yr
Courses: Art History, †Drawing, †Illustration, †Painting, Printmaking, †Sculpture
Adult Hobby Classes: Visit website for details
Summer School: Varies, see website for details

STORRS

UNIVERSITY OF CONNECTICUT, Dept of Art & Art History, 830 Bolton Rd, Unit 1099 Storrs, CT 06269-1099. Tel 860-486-3930; Fax 860-486-3869; Email cora-lynn.deibler@uconn.edu; Web: www.art.uconn.edu; *Head Dept* Cora-Lynn Deibler; *Assoc Head* Laurie Sloan
Estab 1882, dept estab 1950; Dept has nonprofit Contemporary Art Galleries, 830 Bolton Rd Storrs CT 06269; on-campus UConn Co-op Bookstore sells art supplies; FT 23, PT 14; pub; D, E, online; Scholarships; SC 43, LC 32, GC 15; D 1600, maj 280, grad 10
Ent Req: HS dipl, SAT, Portfolio Review
Degrees: BA (Art History), BFA (Studio) 4 yrs, MFA 2 yrs
Courses: †Animation, Art Appreciation, †Art History, Ceramics, Drawing, †Graphic Design, †Illustration, †Painting, †Photography, †Printmaking, †Sculpture, †Video

WEST HARTFORD

UNIVERSITY OF HARTFORD, Hartford Art School, 200 Bloomfield Ave, West Hartford, CT 06117-1599. Tel 860-768-4393, 768-4827; Fax 860-768-5296; Email calafiore@mail.hartford.edu; Web: www.hartfordartschool.org; *Assoc Dean* Thomas Bradley, MA; *Asst Dean* Robert Calafiore, MFA; *Prof* Lloyd Glasson, MFA; *Prof* Frederick Wessel, MFA; *Assoc Prof* Gilles Giuntini, MFA; *Assoc Prof* Christopher Horton, MAT; *Assoc Prof* Jim Lee, MFA; *Assoc Prof* Patricia Lipsky, MFA; *Assoc Prof* Ellen Carey, MFA; *Assoc Prof* Walter Hall, MFA; *Assoc Prof* Mary Frey, MFA; *Assoc Prof* Stephen Brown, MFA; *Asst Prof* Douglas Andersen, MA; *Asst Prof* Mark Snyder, MFA; *Asst Prof* Hirokazu Fukawa, MFA; *Asst Prof* Susan Wilmarth-Rabineau, MFA; *Asst Prof* Gene Gort, MFA; *Asst Prof* Matthew Towers, MFA; *Dean* Stuart Schar, PhD; *Asst Prof* Bill Thomson; *Asst Prof* John Nordyke; *Asst Prof* Nancy Wynn; *Asst Prof* Jeremiah Patterson
Estab 1877; pvt; D & E; Scholarships; SC 70, LC 5, GC 32; D 375, E 100, non-maj 125, maj 375, grad 20
Ent Req: HS dipl, SAT, portfolio review
Degrees: BFA 4 yr, MFA 2 yr

Courses: Architecture, †Art History, †Ceramics, Glass, Illustration, Media Arts, †Painting & Drawing, †Photography, †Printmaking, †Sculpture, †Video, †Visual Communication Design
Summer School: Dir, Tom Bradley. Enrl 50-75. Courses—Ceramics, Drawing, Visual Comm Design, Photography, Printmaking, Sculpture

UNIVERSITY OF SAINT JOSEPH, CONNECTICUT, Dept of Fine Arts, 1678 Asylum Ave, West Hartford, CT 06117-2791. Tel 860-232-4571; Fax 860-233-5695; Email dkeller@usj.edu; Web: www.usj.edu; *Chmn Dept* Dorothy Bosch Keller; *Adj* Patricia Weise
Estab 1932; Maintains University of Saint Joseph Art Gallery, 1678 Asylum Ave, West Hartford, CT 06117; on-campus shop sells art supplies; FT 1, PT 2; pvt, W; also weekend prog for adult learner (co-ed); D & E; weekend; summer; Scholarships; SC 5, LC 7; D 104
Activities: Schols offered
Ent Req: HS dipl, CEEB
Degrees: BA, BS and MA 4 yr (except for Art History or Studio Art), PhD (Pharmacy)
Tuition: $27,580 (24-36 cr) incoming freshman
Courses: †African American Art, American Architecture, Architecture, Art Appreciation, †Art History, †Design, Drawing, Egyptian Art, Fundamental of Design, Greek Art, History of American Antiques, History of American Art, History of Art & Architecture, History of Women Artists, Impressionism, †Latin American Art, †Museum Staff Training, Painting, †Pastel Drawing, †Printmaking, Renaissance, †Watercolor
Summer School: Assoc Dean & Dir Professional Studies, Dr Rayne Wayne. Enrl 400; tuition $250 per cr hr. Maj in art history offered

WEST HAVEN

UNIVERSITY OF NEW HAVEN, Dept of Visual & Performing Arts & Philosophy, 300 Boston Post Rd, West Haven, CT 06516-1916. Tel 203-932-7101; Web: www.newhaven.edu; *Coordr of Arts* Christie Summerville; *Chmn* Michael G Kaloyanides
Estab 1927, dept estab 1972; FT 2, PT 8; pvt; D & E; SC 30, LC 5; D 350, E 110
Ent Req: HS dipl
Degrees: BA & BS 4 yrs, AS 2 yrs
Courses: †Advertising Design, Art History, Calligraphy, Ceramics, Commercial Art, Constructions, Dimensional Design, Drawing, Film Animation, Graphic Arts, Graphic Design, History of Art & Architecture, Illustration, Interaction of Color, Interior Design, Mixed Media, Painting, Photography, Printmaking, Sculpture
Summer School: Courses—Ceramics, Drawing, History of Art, Painting, Photography, Sculpture

WILLIMANTIC

EASTERN CONNECTICUT STATE UNIVERSITY, Fine Arts Dept, 83 Windham St, Willimantic, CT 06226-2211. Tel 860-465-5000; Fax 860-456-5508; Web: www.ecsu.ctstate.edu; *Chmn* Lulu Blocton
Estab 1881; FT 4, PT 4; pub; D & E; Scholarships; D 300, E 75, maj 40
Ent Req: HS dipl
Degrees: BA(Fine Arts) & BS(Art) 4 yrs
Courses: Art History, Ceramics, Drawing, Enameling, Graphic Arts, Interior Design, Jewelry, Painting, Sculpture, Weaving
Summer School: Dir, Owen Peagler. Courses—Art & Craft Workshop

WINSTED

NORTHWESTERN CONNECTICUT COMMUNITY COLLEGE, Fine Arts Dept, 2 Park Pl, Winsted, CT 06098-1706. Tel 860-738-6300; Fax 860-379-4995; Web: www.commnet.edu/nwctc; *Prof* Charles Dmytriw; *Prof* Janet Nesteruk; *Prof* Richard Fineman
Dept estab 1965; FT 3; D & E
Ent Req: HS dipl or equivalent
Degrees: AA (Arts)
Courses: Advertising Design, Art Appreciation, Art History, Ceramics, Design, Drawing, Graphic Arts, Painting, Photography, Printmaking, Sculpture, Video

DELAWARE

DOVER

DELAWARE STATE COLLEGE, Dept of Art & Art Education, 1200 N Dupont Hwy, Dover, DE 19901-2276. Tel 302-857-6000, 302-857-6290; Fax 302-739-5182; *Art Dept Chmn* Arturo Bassolos
Estab 1960; FT 4; pub; D & E; Scholarships; SC 13, LC 9; 50-60 maj
Ent Req: HS dipl or GED, SAT or ACT
Degrees: BS(Art Educ), BS(General Art) & BS(Art Business)
Courses: Art Appreciation, †Art Education, Art History, Ceramics, Commercial Art, Design, Drawing, Fibers, Independent Study, Interior Design, Jewelry, Lettering, Painting, Photography, Printmaking, Sculpture, Senior Exhibition (one man show & research), Teacher Training
Adult Hobby Classes: Courses—same as above
Summer School: Courses—same as above

NEWARK

UNIVERSITY OF DELAWARE, Dept of Art, 104 Recitation Hall, Newark, DE 19716; 210 S College Ave, Newark, DE 19716-5200. Tel 302-831-2244; Email artdepartment@udel.edu; Web: www.udel.edu/art/; *Chair* Janet Hethorn
Estab 1833

REHOBOTH BEACH

REHOBOTH ART LEAGUE, INC, 12 Dodds Lane, Rehoboth Beach, DE 19971. Tel 302-227-8408; Fax 302-227-4121; Web: www.rehobothartleague.org; *Chief Operating Officer* Dr Sara Ganter; *Artistic Director* Jay Pastore
Estab 1938; Maintain a non-profit art gallery; pvt; D & E; Scholarships; SC 7; D 400, others 400
Ent Req: interest in art
Courses: Art Appreciation, Calligraphy, Ceramics, Collage, Drawing, Painting, Photography
Adult Hobby Classes: Enrl 150. Courses—Ceramics, Drawing, Painting, Pottery
Children's Classes: Courses—Art Forms

DISTRICT OF COLUMBIA

WASHINGTON

CATHOLIC UNIVERSITY OF AMERICA, School of Architecture & Planning, 620 Michigan Ave NE, Washington, DC 20064. Tel 202-319-5188; Fax 202-319-5728; Email arch@cua.edu; Web: architecture.cua.edu/; *Dean* Gregory K Hunt; *Prof* Stanley I Hallet FAIA; *Prof* Ernest Forest Wilson PhD, MArchit; *Prof* W Dodd Ramberg, BArchit; *Assoc Prof* Julius S Levine, MCP; *Prof* George T Marcou, MArchit; *Prof* Theodore Naos, MArchit; *Assoc Prof* Thomas Walton, PhD; *Prof* John V Yanik, MArchit; *Asst Prof* Ann Cederna, MArchit; *Asst Prof* Jill St Clair Riley RA; *Asst Prof* J Ronald Kabriel, MArchit; *Asst Prof* Lavinia Pasquina; *Assoc Prof* Terrence Williams AIA; *Asst Dean/Asst Prof* Erik Jenkins; *Assoc Prof* Vytenis A Gureckas RA; *Assoc Prof* Barry D Yatt AIA, CSI
Estab 1887, dept estab 1930; den; D & E; SC 6, LC 4 per sem, GC 15 per sem; D 240, maj 240, grad 95
Ent Req: HS dipl and SAT for undergrad, BS or BA in Archit or equivalent plus GPA of 2.5 in undergrad studies for grad
Degrees: BArchit & BS(Archit) 4 yr, MArchit 4 yr
Tuition: $10,110 per sem
Courses: Architecture, Drafting, Graphics, History and Theory of Architecture, Landscape Architecture, Photography, Planning, Practice, Technology, Urban Design
Children's Classes: Session of 3 wks. Courses—High School Program
Summer School: Dir, Richard Loosle. Enrl 100, term of 5-9 wks May-Aug. Courses—Computers, Construction & Documents, Design Studio, Environmental Systems, Graphic, History & Theory of Architecture, Photography, Structures
—**Dept of Art,** 620 Michigan Ave NE, Salve Regina Hall Washington, DC 20064-0001. Tel 202-319-5282; Web: arts-sciences.cua.edu/art/; *Prof* Thomas Nakashima; *Chmn Dept* John Winslow; *Asst Prof* Nora Heimann
Estab 1930; den; D & E; Scholarships; SC 19, LC 9, GC 4; D 412, E 101, non-maj 449, maj 32, grad 4
Ent Req: HS dipl and SAT for undergrad, BA-BFA; MAT, GRE for grad
Degrees: BA (Studio Art, Art History, Studio Art for Secondary Educ)
Tuition: FT $9550 per sem; PT $735 per cr hr
Courses: †Art Education, †Art History, †Ceramics, Design, †Digital Arts, †History of Art & Archeology, †Painting, Photography, Printmaking, †Sculpture
Summer School: Chmn, John Winslow. Term of 4-5 wks beginning June. Courses—Drawing, Ceramics, Painting, Special Independent Courses, Digital Arts

CORCORAN SCHOOL OF ART, 500 17th St NW, Washington, DC 20006-4899. Tel 202-639-1800; Fax 202-639-1768; Web: www.corcoran.edu; *Dir Art & The Book* Kerry McAleer-Keeler MFA; *Assoc Chair* Lorraine Schmidt; *Interim Chair, Undergrad Design* Francheska Guerrero; *Chair Fine Art Photog* Muriel Hasbun; *Interim Chair, Arts & Humanities* Lisa Lipinski; *Interim Chair, Fine Art* Lynn Sures; *Chair, Foundation* Rick Wall
Estab 1890; pvt; D & E; Scholarships; SC 84, LC 42; D 300 maj, E 750 non-maj
Ent Req: HS dipl, SAT or ACT, portfolio & interview
Degrees: BFA 4 yrs
Tuition: $16,970 per yr
Courses: Animation, Art Appreciation, Art History, Business & Law for the Artist, Ceramics, Computer Art, Design, Drawing, Fine Arts, Furniture, History of Photography, Illustration, Interior Design, Painting, Philosophy, Photography, Printmaking, Sculpture, Typography, Video
Adult Hobby Classes: Enrl 1000 per sem; tuition $380-$1060 for 13-15 wks. Courses—Art History, Ceramics, Color & Design, Computer Graphics, Drawing, Furniture, Interior Design, Landscape Design, Painting, Photography, Printmaking, Sculpture
Children's Classes: Enrl 70, tuition $127 per 5 wk session, Saturday ages 6-10; $380 per 13 wk session, Saturday ages 10-15. Courses—General Studio ages 15-18. Courses—Ceramics, Computer Art, Drawing, Painting, Photography, Portfolio Prep Workshop, Screen printing
Summer School: Dean, Samuel Hoi. Enrl 400; Adult—tuition $350-$960 for 6 wks beginning June. Courses—Art History, Ceramics, Computer Graphics, Drawing, Illustration, Interior Design, Landscape Design, Painting, Photography, Printmaking, Sculpture, Watercolor. HS (ages 15-18)—tuition $390-$690 for 5 wks beginning June. Courses—Ceramics, Drawing, Painting, Photography, Portfolio Prep, Pre-College. Children's Workshops (ages 6-10)—tuition $10 for 5 day session beginning June

GEORGE WASHINGTON UNIVERSITY, Dept of Art of Fine Arts & Art History, 801 22nd St NW, Smith Hall of Art Rm 101 Washington, DC 20052-0058.

Tel 202-994-6085; Fax 202-994-8657; Email art@gwu.edu; Web: www.art.gwu.edu; *Prof* David Bjelajac PhD; *Prof* Barbara Von Barghahn PhD; *Prof* J Franklin Wright Jr, MFA; *Prof* Turker Ozdogan, MFA; *Assoc Prof* Philip Jacks, PhD; *Assoc Prof* Dean Kessmann, MFA; *Asst Prof* Alexander Dumbadze, PhD; *Asst Prof* Siobhan Rigg, MFA; *Asst Prof* Bibiana Obler, PhD; *Asst Prof* Julia Brown, MFA; *Asst Prof* James Sham, MFA; *Asst Prof* Mika Natif, PhD
Estab 1821, dept estab 1893; Maintains nonprofit art gallery located at Gallery 102 Smith Hall of Art, maintains art/architecture library; on-campus shop for purchase of supplies; pvt; D & E; Scholarships; SC 103, LC 74, GC 68; D 1350, GS 196
Ent Req: HS dipl, ent exam
Degrees: BA 4 yr, MA 2-2 1/2 yr, MFA 2 yr
Courses: American Art, †Art History, †Ceramics, Classical Art & Archaeology, Commercial Art, Contemporary Art, †Design, †Drawing, †Graphic Arts, History of Art & Architecture, Medieval Art, Mixed Media, †Painting, †Photography, †Printmaking, Renaissance & Baroque Art, Restoration & Conservation, †Sculpture, †Video, †Visual Communications
Summer School: Tuition $680 per cr hr for two 6 wk sessions. Courses—Art History, Ceramics, Drawing, Painting, Photography, Sculpture, Visual Communications

GEORGE WASHINGTON UNIVERSITY, School of Interior Design, 2100 Foxhall Rd NW, Washington, DC 20007-1150. Tel 202-242-6700, 625-4551; Email nblossom@gwu.edu; Web: www.gwu.edu/; *Dept Chmn* Erin Speck
Estab 1875; maintains non profit art gallery, The Dimock Gallery, Lisner auditorium, 730 21st St NW, Washington DC; pvt; D & E; Scholarships; SC 16
Degrees: AA, BA & BFA
Courses: Aesthetics, Art History, Arts & Humanities, Ceramics, Design, Drafting, Drawing, Graphic Arts, †Graphic Design, Historical Preservation, †History of Decorative Art, †Interior Design, Painting, Photography, Printmaking, Sculpture, †Studio Art, Textile Design, Theatre Arts
Adult Hobby Classes: Graphic Design, History of Decorative Art, Interior Design, Studio Art
Summer School: Dir, Dr Sharon Fechter. Enrl 40, 8 wks, June-July. Courses—History of Decorative Art, Interior Design, Studio Arts

GEORGETOWN UNIVERSITY, Dept of Art & Art History, Walsh 102, Washington, DC 20057; Walsh Bldg Rm 102, 1221 36th St NW Washington, DC 20057-0001. Tel 202-687-7010; Fax 202-687-3048; Web: www.georgetown.edu/departments/amth; *Prof* Elizabeth Prelinger PhD; *Chmn & Prof* Alison Hilton PhD; *Prof* Peter Charles, MFA; *Assoc Prof* B G Muhn, MFA; *Asst Prof* John Morrell, MFA; *Prof* Roberto Bocci; *Asst Prof* L Collier Hyams, MFA; *Asst Prof* Al Acres, PhD; *Dir Gallery* Evan Reed, MFA
Estab 1789, dept estab 1967; Maintain nonprofit art gallery, 1221 36th St, NW, Washington, DC 20057; FT 15; pvt; Jesuit/Catholic; D & E; SC 20, LC 15; D 1000 (includes non-maj), maj 20 studio & 15 art history per yr
Ent Req: HS dipl
Degrees: BA 4 yrs
Tuition: campus res available
Courses: †Art History, †Design, Digital Art, †Drawing, †Mixed Media, †Painting, †Photography, †Printmaking, †Sculpture
Adult Hobby Classes: Continuing Studies Dean Robert Manuel
Summer School: Assoc Dean, Ester Rider. Courses offered

TRINITY COLLEGE, Fine Arts Program, 125 Michigan Ave NE, Washington, DC 20017-1090. Tel 202-884-9280, 884-9000; Fax 202-884-9229; Email easbyr@trinitydc.edu; Web: www.trinitydc.edu/academics/depts/finearts/index; *Chmn & Assoc Prof* Dr Rebecca Easby; *Lectr* Eugene D Markowski; *Prof* Dr Yvonne Dixon
Estab 1897; den; D & E; Scholarships; SC 8, LC 2-3; D 120, maj 12
Ent Req: HS dipl, SAT or ACT, recommendation
Degrees: BA 4 yr
Courses: Art History, Design, Documentary, Drawing, Film, Graphic Design, History of Art & Architecture, Lettering, Painting, Photography, Photography, Photojournalism, Printmaking, Sculpture
Summer School: Dir, Susan Ikerd. Courses—Vary

UNIVERSITY OF THE DISTRICT OF COLUMBIA, Dept of Mass Media, Visual & Performing Arts, 4200 Connecticut Ave NW, MB46 A03 Washington, DC 20008-1122. Tel 202-274-7402; Fax 202-274-5817; Web: www.udc.edu; *Prof* Meredith Rode, PhD; *Prof* Manon Cleary, MFA; *Chairperson & Prof* Yvonne Pickering-Carter, MFA; *Asst Prof* George Smith, MS
Estab 1969; pub; D & E; SC 65, LC 21; D 616, E 99, non-maj 405, maj 112
Ent Req: HS dipl, GED
Degrees: AA(Advertising Design) 2 yrs, BA(Studio Art) and BA(Art Educ) 4 yrs
Tuition: Res—undergrad $360 per sem; non-res—undergrad $1320 per sem; no campus res
Courses: †Advertising Design, †Art Education, Art History, Ceramics, Conceptual Art, Drawing, Graphic Arts, Graphic Design, Handicrafts, Illustration, Lettering, Mixed Media, Museum Staff Training, †Painting, Photography, †Printmaking, Sculpture
Summer School: C A Young. Enrl 200. Courses—Art History, Ceramics, Drawings, Painting, Photography

FLORIDA

BOCA RATON

FLORIDA ATLANTIC UNIVERSITY, D F Schmidt College of Arts & Letters Dept of Visual Arts & Art History, 777 Glades Rd, AH52 Room 118 Boca Raton, FL 33431-6424. Tel 561-297-3870; Fax 561-297-3078; Email art@fau.edu; Web: www.fau.edu/vaah; *Chair, Prof Art, Graphic Design* Linda Johnson; *Prof Art, Graphic Design* Stephanie Cunningham; *Asst Prof Art & Photography* Sharon Hart; *Assoc Prof Art, Foundations, Drawing & Painting* Amy Broderick; *Chair, Prof Art, Graphic Design* Eric Landes; *Prof Art, Ceramics* Angela DiCosola; *Assoc Prof Art History* Karen Leader, Ph.D; *Assoc Prof Art History & Classical Archaeology* Brian McConnell, Ph.D; *Assoc Prof Art, Graphic Design* Tammy Knipp; *Prof Art, Painting/Drawing* Carol Prusa; *Vis Instr Graphic Design* Annette Piskel; *Vis Instr Art History* Roger Hurlburt; *Asst Prof Sculpture* Julie Ward; *Asst Prof Printmaking* Joseph Velasquez; *Asst Prof Ceramics* Thomas Stollar; *Asst Prof Painting* Corey Lamb; *Asst Prof Art History* Emily Fenichel, PhD
Estab 1964; Maintains a non-profit art gallery & on-campus art supply shop.; pub; D & E; Scholarships; Fellowships; SC 36, LC 10, GC 12; D 1600, maj 600+, grad 7, gs 16, special students 7
Degrees: BFA & BA 4 yrs, MFA
Tuition: Res—$199.54 per cr hr; nonres—$718.09 per cr hr; grad res—$369.82 per cr hr; nonres—$1,024.81 per cr hr
Courses: Aesthetics, Art Appreciation, †Art Education, †Art History, Ceramics, Design, †Drawing, †Graphic Design, †History of Art & Architecture, Mixed Media, Museum Studies, Painting, Photography, Printmaking, Sculpture, Silkscreen & Etching, †Studio Arts, Web Design
Adult Hobby Classes: Courses offered through continuing education
Summer School: Courses offered

LYNN UNIVERSITY, Art & Design Dept, 3601 N Military Trail, Boca Raton, FL 33431-5507. Tel 561-237-7000; Web: www.lynn.edu; *Prof* Tuscano
Estab 1962; Scholarships
Degrees: AA, BFA, BS & Design
Courses: Advertising Design, Art Appreciation, Art History, Corporate Identity Rendering Techniques, Design, Drawing, Environmental Design, Graphics, Painting, Photography, Portfolio & Exhibition, Textile Design

BRADENTON

STATE COLLEGE OF FLORIDA MANATEE - SARASOTA, Art, Design, Humanities, PO Box 1849, Bradenton, FL 34206-7046. Tel 941-752-5251; Fax 941-727-6088; Web: www.scf.edu; *Prof, Graphic Design* Sherri Hill, MA; *Prof, Film* Del Jacobs, MA; *Prof, Photog* Drew Webster, MFA; *Prof* Sue Wyar, BA; *Prof, Studio Art* Jamie Tracy, MFA; *Prof* Katherine Bzura, MA; *Prod, Humanities* Brandon Montgomery; *Prof, Religion & Philosophy* Kim Hyun
Estab 1958; Maintain a non-profit art gallery, State College of Flroida Fine Art Gallery; on-campus shop where art supplies may be purchased; FT 8, PT 14; pub; D, E, online; Scholarships; SC 30, LC 15; D 525, E 120, maj 100
Activities: Schols offered
Ent Req: HS dipl, SAT
Degrees: AA & AS 2 yrs
Courses: 2-D & 3-D Design, †Advertising Design, Art Appreciation, Art Appreciation, Art History, Ceramics, Color Fundamentals, Commercial Art, Costume Design & Construction, Design, †Digital Photography, Drawing, Figure Drawing, Film, Graphic Arts, Graphic Design, †Graphic Design Technology, History of Art & Architecture, Interior Design, Lettering, Mixed Media, Painting, Photography, †Portfolio Preparation, Printmaking, Sculpture, Stage Design, †Studio Art, Theatre Arts, Video, †Wheel Throwing

CLEARWATER

SAINT PETERSBURG COLLEGE, Fine & Applied Arts at Clearwater Campus, 2465 Drew St, Clearwater, FL 33765; PO Box 13489, Saint Petersburg, FL 33733-3489. Tel 727-341-3600, 341-4360, 791-2611; Fax 727-791-2605; Web: www.spcollege.edu; Telex
727-791-2548; *Assoc Prof* Kevin Grass; *Asst Prof* Kim Kirchman; *Instr* Marjorie Greene; *Asst Prof* Barton Gilmore; *Dean* Dr Jonathan Steele; *Dept Chmn* Jonathan Barnes
Estab 1927. College has eight campuses; Maintain nonprofit art gallery; Muse Gallery, 2465 Drew St Clearwater FL 33765; art library; FT6; pub; D & E; Scholarships; SC 125 LC 5; D 160, E 400, maj 20-25
Ent Req: HS dipl
Degrees: AA & AS 2 yr, BS 4 yr
Courses: †2-D & 3-D, Architecture, Art Appreciation, Art History Survey, Ceramics, Costume Design & Construction, Design, Drawing, Graphic Arts, Painting, Photography, †Printmaking, Sculpture, Stage Design, †Studio Lighting, Theatre Arts
Summer School: Dept Chair, Jonathan Barnes. Courses—Same as regular session; 10 wk session.

CORAL GABLES

UNIVERSITY OF MIAMI, Dept of Art & Art History, PO Box 248106, Coral Gables, FL 33124-8106. Tel 305-284-2542; Fax 305-284-2115; Email art-arh@miami.edu; Web: www.miami.edu/art; *Asst Prof* Ivan Albrecht, MFA; *Prof* Darby Bannard, BA; *Asst Prof* Carsten Meier, MFA; *Assoc Prof* Paula Harper, MFA, PhD; *Prof* Perri Lee Roberts, MFA, PhD; *Assoc Prof* Carlos Aquirre, MFA; *Prof* J Tomas Lopez, MFA; *Asst Prof* William Betsch, MFA, PhD; *Chair, Assoc Prof* Lise Drost, MFA; *Assoc Prof* Brian Curtis, MFA; *Instr* Kyle Trowbridge, MFA; *Instr* Joel Hollander, PhD; *Asst Prof* Billie G Lynn, MFA; *Instr* Mariah Hausman, MFA; *Prof* William D. Carlson, MFA
Estab 1925, dept estab 1960; On-campus shop where art supplies may be purchased; pvt; D&E; Scholarships; SC 71, LC 16, GC 50; D 1100, non-maj 870, maj 230, grad 20, other 5
Ent Req: HS dipl, SAT
Degrees: BA & BFA 4 yrs, MA(Art History) 2 yrs & MFA 3 yrs
Tuition: Res & nonres—undergrad $27,384 per yr, $13,692 per sem, $1,140 per cr hr
Courses: †Art History, †Ceramics, Design, Digital Imaging, Drawing, †Glassblowing, †Graphic Design, †Illustration, †Multimedia, †Painting, †Photography, †Printmaking, †Sculpture
Summer School: Tuition $790 per cr for two 6 wk terms. Courses—Limited regular courses, special workshops, travel

DAYTONA BEACH

DAYTONA BEACH COMMUNITY COLLEGE, Dept of Fine Arts & Visual Arts, PO Box 2811, Daytona Beach, FL 32120-2811. Tel 904-255-8131; Fax 904-947-3134; *Dean* Dr Frank Wetta; *Prof* Denis Deegan, MFA; *Prof* Pamela Griesinger, MFA; *Prof* Gary Monroe, MFA; *Prof* Eric Breitenbach, MS; *Prof* Patrick Van Duesen, BS; *Prof* Dan Biferie, MFA; *Prof* Bobbie Clementi, MFA; *Prof* Jacques A Dellavalle, MFA; *Prof* John Wilton, MFA; *Prof* Patricia Thompson, MA
Estab 1958; pub; D & E; Scholarships; SC 15, LC 3; D 250, E 50, maj 30
Ent Req: HS dipl or GED
Degrees: 2 year program offered
Tuition: Res—$45 per sem hr; nonres—$143.25 per sem hr
Courses: Advertising Design, Art Appreciation, †Art Education, Art History, Ceramics, Cinematography, Constructions, Design, Digital Imaging, Drafting, Drawing, Film, Fine Arts, Graphic Arts, †Graphic Design, History of Art & Architecture, Illustration, Interior Design, Museum Staff Training, Painting, †Photography, Printmaking, Sculpture, Teacher Training, †Theatre Arts, Video
Summer School: Enrl 15; tuition $35 per cr hr for 3 cr. Courses—Painting I & II

DELAND

STETSON UNIVERSITY, Department of Creative Arts, 421 N Woodland Blvd, Unit 8252 Deland, FL 32723-0001. Tel 386-822-7266; Email cnelson@stetson.edu; Web: www.stetson.edu/departments/art; *Dept Chmn* Nathan Wolek; *Prof* Dan Gunderson; *Assoc Prof* Matt Roberts; *Asst Prof* Ekaterina Kudryavtseva; *Prof* Gary Bolding; *Prof* Joseph Witek; *Asst Prof* Julia Schmitt
Estab 1880; Maintains nonprofit art gallery: Hand Art Center, 139 E Michigan Ave, Deland, FL 32724; FT 6; pvt; D&E; Scholarships; SC 7, LC 3 per sem
Ent Req: col boards
Degrees: 4 yr
Courses: Art History, Ceramics, Design, Digital Art, Drawing, Mixed Media, Painting, Photography, Sculpture, Video

DUNEDIN

DUNEDIN FINE ART CENTER, 1143 Michigan Blvd, Dunedin, FL 34698-2712. Tel 727-298-3322; Fax 727-298-3326; Email gabissett@dfac.org; Web: www.dfac.org; *Pres & CEO* George Ann Bissett; *Dir of Youth* Todd Still; *Dir Adult Educ* Christine Renc-Carter; *Admin Asst* Barbara Ferguson; *VPres & COO* Ken Hannon; *Develop Dir* Linda Hamilton; *Finance Dir* Dave Barton
Estab 1975; 501c3 org; continuing education classes; maintains 3 nonprofit art gallery, art library; FT & PT 84; pvt; D & E & weekends; Scholarships; SC 20-25, LC 5-10; approx 900 D, E, non-majors
Activities: gallery store sells art supplies
Ent Req: none
Degrees: none
Tuition: no campus res
Courses: Art Appreciation, Art Education, Art History, Arts for the Handicapped, Batik, Calligraphy, Ceramics, Children's Art, Clay, Collage, †Continuing Studio Arts Education, Design, Drawing, Fashion Arts, Film, Fine Crafts, Graphic Arts, Graphic Design, Handicrafts, History of Art & Architecture, Jewelry, Lettering, Mixed Media, Painting, Pastel, Photography, Pottery, Printmaking, Sculpture, Silversmithing, Studio Visual Arts, Textile Design, Video, Weaving
Children's Classes: Courses—Fine Arts, Drama
Summer School: Dir, Todd Still. Enrl 150 per wk for 10 wks

FORT LAUDERDALE

ART INSTITUTE OF FORT LAUDERDALE, 1799 SE 17th St, Fort Lauderdale, FL 33316-3000. Tel 954-527-1799; Fax 305-728-8637; Web: www.aifl.edu; WATS 800-275-7603; *Dir Admis* Eileen Northrop; *Dir Educ* Steve Schwab; *Dir Visual Communs* Rosanne Giuel; *Dir Photo* Ed Williams; *Dir Interior Design* Bill Kobrynich, AA; *Asst Chmn Advertising Design* Lorna Hernandez, AA; *Dir Music & Video Bus* Ed Galizia, AA; *Dir Fashion Design* June Fisher, AA
Estab 1968; pvt; D & E; Scholarships; D 1900, maj 1900
Ent Req: HS dipl
Degrees: AS(technology), BA
Courses: Advertising Design, Art History, Computer Animation, Conceptual Art, Display, Drafting, Drawing, †Fashion Arts, Fashion Design, Graphic Arts, Graphic Design, Illustration, Industrial Design, †Interior Design, Lettering, Mixed Media, Multimedia, Painting, †Photography, Video
Summer School: Same as regular semester

FORT MYERS

EDISON COMMUNITY COLLEGE, Gallery of Fine Arts, 8099 College Pkwy SW, Fort Myers, FL 33919-5566. Tel 941-489-9313; Web: www.edison.edu; *Instr of Art* Robert York; *Music Instr* Dr Dennis Hill; *Music Instr* Dr Glenn Cornish; *Music Instr* Dr T Defoor; *Theatre Arts Instr* Richard Westlake; *Head Dept Fine & Performing Arts* Edith Pendleton
Estab 1962; FT 1, PT 5; pub; D & E; Scholarships
Ent Req: HS dipl
Degrees: AA & AS 2 yrs
Courses: 3-D Design, Art Appreciation, Art History, Ceramics, Design, Drawing, Intro to Computer Imaging, Jewelry, Painting, Photography, Printmaking, Sculpture
Adult Hobby Classes: Enrl 20. Courses—any non-cr activity of interest for which a teacher is available

FORT PIERCE

INDIAN RIVER COMMUNITY COLLEGE, Fine Arts Dept, 3209 Virginia Ave, Fort Pierce, FL 34981-5596. Tel 772-462-7824; *Asst Dean Arts & Sciences* Raymond Considine; *Chmn Fine Arts* David Moberg; *Vis Arts Dir* Linda Waugaman; *Instr* Francis Sprout; *Instr* Cira Cosentino
Estab 1960; pub; D & E; Scholarships; SC 10, LC 4; D 45, E 18, Maj 25, Non-Maj 10, Other 10
Ent Req: HS dipl
Degrees: AA & AS 2 yrs
Tuition: Res—$48 per unit; nonres—$48 per unit
Courses: Acting, Advertising Design, Art History, Design, Drawing, General Art, Graphic Arts, Intro to Drama, Landscape, Music Theory, Painting, Portrait, Printmaking, Vocal Ensemble
Summer School: Dir, Linda Waugaman. Enrl 80. Courses—Theater & Music

GAINESVILLE

UNIVERSITY OF FLORIDA, School of Art & Art History, 101, FAC Complex, Gainesville, FL 32611-5800; PO Box 115801, Gainesville, FL 32611-5801. Tel 352-392-0201 (Dept); 273-3000 (Univ Galleries); 273-2805 (Libr); Fax 352-392-8453 (Dept); 846-0266 (Univ Galleries); 846-2747 (Libr); Email heipp@ufl.edu; Web: www.arts.ufl.edu/art; *Prof* Anna Calluori Holcombe, MFA; *Prof* Sergio Vega, PhD; *Prof* Barbara Barletta, PhD, MFA; *Prof & Dir* Richard Heipp, MFA; *Prof* Robin Poynor, PhD; *Prof* Nan Smith, MFA; *Prof* Craig Roland, PhD; *Assoc Prof* Robert Mueller, MFA; *Assoc Prof* Brian Slawson, MFA; *Prof* Celeste Rogerge, MFA; *Prof* Linda Arbuckle, MFA; *Assoc Prof* Maria Rogal, MFA; *Prof* Melissa Hyde, PhD; *Assoc Prof* Ron Janowich, MFA; *Prof* Glenn Willumson, PhD; *Assoc Prof* Jack Stenner, PhD; *Asst Prof* Michelle Tillander, PhD, MFA; *Assoc Prof* Guolong Lai, PhD; *Assoc Prof* Julia Morrisroe, MFA; *Assoc Prof* Katerie Gladdys, MFA; *Assoc Prof* Elizabeth Ross, PhD; *Assoc Prof* Ellen Knudson, MFA; *Asst Prof* Sean Miller, MFA; *Assoc Prof* Craig Smith, PhD, MFA; *Asst Prof* Maya Stanfield-Mazzi, Phd; *Asst Prof* Bethany Taylor, MFA; *Asst Prof* Joyce Tsai, PhD; *Assoc Instr* Amy Vigilante, PhD, MFA; *Vis Asst Prof* Amy Freeman, MFA; *Asst Prof* Anthea Behm, MFA; *Asst Prof* Lisa Iglesias, MFA; *Vis Asst Prof* Ashley Jones, PhD; *Vis Asst Prof* Rotem Tamir, MFA
Estab 1925; Maintains nonprofit University Galleries, 400 SW 13th St, Fine Arts Bldg B, Gainesville, FL 32611; Architecture & Fine Arts Library, 201 Fine Arts Bldg A PO Box 117017, Univ FL, Gainesville, FL 32611; FT 33; pub; D & E; Scholarships; Fellowships; SC 40, LC 26, GC 11; maj 400 upper div, grad 160
Activities: Schols & fels offered
Ent Req: HS dipl, SAT, ACT, TOEFL, SCAT or AA degree (transfers must have 2.0 average) GRE
Degrees: BAA & BFA 4 yrs, MA 2 yrs, MFA 3 yrs, PhD
Tuition: Res—undergrad $5700, grad $11,950; nonres—undergrad $29,344, grad $17,150 per cr hr; undergrad room—$5250
Courses: †Art & Technology, †Art Education, †Art History, †Ceramics, †Creative Photography, †Drawing, †Graphic Design, †Museum Studies, †Painting, †Printmaking, †Sculpture
Summer School: Limited classes

JACKSONVILLE

FLORIDA COMMUNITY COLLEGE AT JACKSONVILLE, SOUTH CAMPUS, Art Dept, 11901 Beach Blvd, Jacksonville, FL 32246-6624. Tel 904-646-2031; Fax 904-646-2396; Web: www.fccj.org; *Gallery Coordr* Elizabeth Louis; *Prof* Derby Ulloa; *Prof* Mark Sablow; *Prof* Mary Joan Hinson; *Prof* Stephen Heywood; *Faculty Coordr Fine Arts* Larry Davis
Estab 1966; Maintain nonprofit art gallery; FT 5; pub; D & E; Scholarships; SC 14, LC 6; D 150, E 75
Ent Req: HS dipl
Degrees: AA & AS 2 yrs
Tuition: no campus res
Courses: Batik, Blockprinting, Ceramics, Computer Graphics, Drawing, Experimentations, Graphic Design, History of Art & Architecture, Painting, Photography, Sculpture, Serigraphy
Adult Hobby Classes: Enrl 75-80. Courses—Art Appreciation, Crafts, Drawing, Painting, Photography
Summer School: Courses—Ceramics, Design, Drawing, Painting, Printmaking, Sculpture

JACKSONVILLE UNIVERSITY, 2800 University Blvd N, College of Fine Arts Jacksonville, FL 32211-3321. Tel 904-256-7374; Fax 904-256-7375; Email dchapma@ju.edu; Web: www.ju.edu; *Div Chair & Prof* Dana Tupa; *Dean* Henry Rine; *Vis Asst Prof of Glass* Brian Frus; *Assoc Prof Art Hist* Cheryl Sowder; *Assoc Prof Photog* Ginger Sheridan; *Assoc Prof of Animation* Eric Kunzendorf; *Asst Prof Art & Foundations Coordr* Lily Kuonen; *Asst Prof Sculpture* Jim Benedict; *Assoc Prof Electronic Art* Bill Hill; *Asst Prof Graphic Design* David Smith; *Asst Prof Ceramics* Tiffany Leach
Estab 1932; Maintains nonprofit art gallery, Alexander Brest Museum; on- campus shop for art supplies; pvt; D & E; Scholarships; SC 60, LC 13; D 403, maj 85
Activities: Schols offered
Ent Req: HS dipl, ent exam, portfolio review (for visual arts)
Degrees: BFA, BA, BS & BAEd, 4 yr; MAT, MFA (Visual Arts)
Tuition: Tuition: $16,310 per semester
Courses: Advertising Design, Art Appreciation, Art Education, Art History, Ceramics, Commercial Art, †Computer Art & Design, Conceptual Art, Costume Design & Construction, Design, Drawing, †Film, †Graphic Arts, †Graphic Design, Hot Glass, Lettering, Mixed Media, Painting, Photography, Printmaking, Stage Design, †Studio Art, †Theatre Arts, Video, †Visual Communication

UNIVERSITY OF NORTH FLORIDA, Dept of Communications & Visual Arts, 4567 St Johns Bluff Rd S, Jacksonville, FL 32224. Tel 904-620-2650, 904-620-2624 (admis); Web: www.unf.edu; *Chmn* Oscar Patterson; *Prof* Louise Freshman Brown, MFA; *Assoc Prof* David S Porter, MFA; *Assoc Prof* Robert L

Cocanougher, MFA; *Assoc Prof* Paul Ladnier, MFA; *Asst Prof* Debra E Murphy, MFA
Estab 1970; pub; D & E; Scholarships; maj 385
Ent Req: AA
Degrees: BA 2 yr, BFA
Courses: Advertising Design, Aesthetics, Art Appreciation, Art History, Broadcasting, †Ceramics, Commercial Art, Computer Images, Conceptual Art, Design, Digital Photography, †Drawing, Electronic Multi-Media, Graphic Arts, Graphic Design, †History of Art & Architecture, Illustration, Lettering, Mixed Media, †Painting, †Photography, Printmaking, †Sculpture, †Video
Summer School: Various courses offered on demand

KEY WEST

FLORIDA KEYS COMMUNITY COLLEGE, Fine Arts Div, 5901 College Rd, Key West, FL 33040-4397. Tel 305-296-9081, 296-1520 (Box Office); Fax 305-292-5155; *Chmn Fine Arts Div* G Gerald Cash
Scholarships
Degrees: AA, AS
Tuition: Res—$42 per cr hr; nonres—$158 per cr hr
Courses: Art Appreciation, Art Education, Art History, Calligraphy, †Ceramics, Commercial Art, Costume Design & Construction, Design, Display, Drafting, Drawing, Film, †Fine Arts, Graphic Arts, Graphic Design, Handicrafts, Jewelry, Jewelry Making, Mixed Media, Painting, †Photography, Printmaking, Sculpture, Stage Design, †Theatre Arts, Voice
Adult Hobby Classes: Enrl 150; Sept-Apr. Courses—Acting, Costume Design, Theatre Production (Lighting, Stagecraft, Design)

LAKE CITY

FLORIDA GATEWAY COLLEGE, Liberal Art Dept, 149 SE College Place, Lake City, FL 32025-2006. Tel 386-752-1822; Fax 386-754-4594; Web: www.fgc.edu
Estab 1962
Ent Req: HS dipl
Degrees: AA 2 yrs

LAKE WORTH

PALM BEACH COMMUNITY COLLEGE, Dept of Art, 4200 S Congress Ave, Lake Worth, FL 33461-4796. Tel 561-439-8142; Fax 561-439-8384; Email slateryp@pbcc.cc.fl.us; Cable FLASUNCOM; *Art Dept Chmn* W Patrick Slatery; *Architecture & Interior Design Chmn* Zenida Young; *Graphic Design Chmn* Timothy Eichner
Estab 1933; Maintain nonprofit art gallery; Pub; D & E; Scholarships; SC 20, LC 5; D 15,000 maj 400
Ent Req: HS dipl or over 25
Degrees: AA and AS 2 yr, cert
Courses: Advertising Design, Architectural Drawing, Architecture, Art Appreciation, Art History, †Basic Design, Ceramics, Commercial Art, Design, Drawing, Enameling, †Etching, Graphic Arts, Graphic Arts, Graphic Design, Handicrafts, History of Art & Architecture, Illustration, Interior Design, Intermedia, Jewelry, Lithography, Painting, Photography, Printmaking, Screen Printing, Stage Design, Technical Photo Courses, Theatre Arts, Typography, Weaving
Summer School: Assoc Dean Humanities, Richard Holcomb. Enrl 300; tuition $36.50 per cr hr. Courses—Art Appreciation, Ceramics, Crafts, Design, Drawing, History of Art, Photography

LAKELAND

FLORIDA SOUTHERN COLLEGE, Department of Art & Art History, 111 Lake Hollingsworth Dr, Lakeland, FL 33801-5698. Tel 863-680-4743, 680-4111; Fax 863-680-4147; Email art@flsouthern.edu; Web: www.flsouthern.edu; *Div Fine & Performing Arts Chair, Prof Art History* James Rogers, PhD; *Assoc Prof Art, Dept Art & Art History Chair, Dir Studio Programming* William Otremsky, MFA; *Asst Prof Art & Dir Foundation Prog* Kelly Sturhahn, MFA; *Asst Prof Art & Dir Graphic Design Prog* Samuel Romero, MFA; *Adjunct Asst Prof Art History* Nadine Pantano, PhD; *Adjunct Prof Art* Joseph Mitchell, MFA; *Adjunct Instr Art* Eric Blackmore, BFA; *Adjunct Asst Prof Art Educ* Jacquelyn Hanson, MFA; *Prof Emerita* Beth Ford, MA; *Sec* Katie Imeson, BFA
Estab 1885; Maintains nonprofit art gallery, Melvin Art Gallery, art/architecture library & Roux Library (same address); campus store for purchasing art supplies; den; private; D & E; Scholarships; SC 34, LC 10, maj 34; enrl 100
Activities: Melvin Art Gallery
Ent Req: HS dipl
Degrees: BA/BFA Studio Art, Graphic Design, BA Art History; BA/BS Art Ed, BFA Graphic Design
Courses: †Art Education, †Art History, Ceramics, Conceptual Art, Design, †Drawing, Graphic Design, History of Art & Architecture, †Painting, Photography, Printmaking, †Restoration & Conservation, Sculpture, †Studio Art, †Teacher Training, Video
Summer School: Craig Story. Courses—see summer schedule

MADISON

NORTH FLORIDA COMMUNITY COLLEGE, Dept Humanities & Art, 325 NW Turner Davis Dr, Madison, FL 32340-1611. Tel 850-973-9481; *Chmn* Dr Barbara McCauley; *Instr* Dr William F Gardner Jr
Estab 1958; pub; Scholarships
Degrees: AA
Tuition: Res—$47 per sem hr; nonres—$169.15 per sem hr
Courses: Art History, Ceramics, Design, Drawing, Painting, Sculpture

MARIANNA

CHIPOLA COLLEGE, Dept of Fine & Performing Arts, 3094 Indian Circle, Marianna, FL 32446. Tel 850-718-2301; Fax 850-718-2206; Email stadsklevj@chipola.edu; Web: www.chipola.edu; *VPres Instr* Sarah Clemmons; *Dir Fine & Performing Arts* Daniel Powell
Estab 1947; pub; D & E; Scholarships; SC 8, LC 2; D 60
Ent Req: HS dipl
Degrees: AA 2 yr
Tuition: Res—$59 per sem hr; nonres—$180 per sem hr
Courses: 2-D & 3-D Design, Art History, Ceramics, Color Picture Comp, Crafts, Drawing, Graphic Arts, Painting, Purpose of Arts, Sculpture, Stage Design, Theatre Arts
Summer School: Courses—varied

MIAMI

FLORIDA INTERNATIONAL UNIVERSITY, School of Art & Art History, University Park Campus Bldg VH 216, Miami, FL 33199; Art & Art History Dept, 11200 SW 8 St, VH216 Miami, FL 33199. Tel 305-348-2897; Fax 305-348-0513; Email art@fiu.edu; Web: art.fiu.edu; *Prof* William Maguire; *Prof* William J Burke; *Prof* R F Buckley; *Prof Emeritus* Manuel Torres; *Prof* Ed del Valle; *Prof* Mirta Gomez; *Assoc Prof* Barbara Watts; *Prof Emeritus* Juan Martinez; *Prof Dir, Mus Studies* Carol Damian; *Assoc Prof* Dan Guernsey; *Assoc Prof* Pip Brant; *Assoc Prof* Tori Arpad; *Assoc Prof, Dept Chair* Jacek Kolasinski; *Asst Prof* Michael Namkung; *Asst Prof, Grad Dir* Alpesh Kantilal Patel; *Asst Prof* Lidu Yi; *Asst Prof* Benjamin Zellmer
Estab 1972, dept estab 1972; Maintain non-profit art gallery, Miami Beach Urban Studio, 420 Lincoln Rd, #440, Miami Beach FL 33139; on-campus shop for art supplies; pub; D & E, online; Scholarships; SC 170, LC 27, GC 14; D 900, E 150, non-maj 250, maj 265, grad 25
Activities: Schols offered
Ent Req: 1000 on SAT, 3.0 HS grade point average
Degrees: BFA, BA, MFA, Museum Studies Grad Cert, MFA Curatorial Practice Track
Courses: Art Appreciation, Art History, Ceramics, Drawing, †Electronic Art, Graphic Arts, Graphic Design, Jewelry, Mixed Media, Museum Staff Training, Painting, Photography, Printmaking, Sculpture, Video
Summer School: Dir, Clive King. Enrl 160; tuition $55 per sem hr for term of 6.5 wks beginning May 13 & June 28

INTERNATIONAL FINE ARTS COLLEGE, 1501 Biscayne Blvd (Ste 100) Miami, FL 33132-1459. Tel 305-373-4684; Fax 305-374-7936; *Pres College* Erika Fleming; *Dean Acad Affairs* Deborah Mas; *Pub Rels Media Contact* Kim Resnik
Estab 1965, dept estab 1966; Maintain nonprofit art gallery; pvt; D; SC 6; D 180, maj 110
Ent Req: HS dipl
Degrees: AA
Courses: Accessory Design, Computer Animation, Fashion Design and Merchandising, Film and Digital Production, Graphic Design, Interior Design, Motion Graphics, Visual Effects

MIAMI-DADE COMMUNITY COLLEGE, Arts & Philosophy Dept, 11011 SW 104th St, Miami, FL 33176-3393. Tel 305-237-2281; Fax 305-237-2871; *Chmn* Robert Huff; *Prof* Charles Dolgos; *Prof* Charles Fink; *Prof* Robert Krantzler; *Prof* Peter Kuentzel; *Prof* Alberto Meza; *Prof* Wade Semerena; *Prof* Wickie Whalen; *Prof* Richard Williams; *Instr* Jennifer Basile; *Assoc Prof Sr* Annette Wells
Estab 1960, dept estab 1967; Nonprofit - Kendall Campus Art Gallery, M123, 11011 SW 104th St, Miami, FL 33176; Pub; D & E; Scholarships; SC 14, LC 4; E 300, non-maj 150, maj 150
Ent Req: open door
Degrees: AA & AS 2 yr
Courses: Art Appreciation, Art History, Ceramics, Commercial Art, †Computer Art, Design, Drawing, Jewelry, Metals, Painting, Photography, Printmaking, Sculpture
Adult Hobby Classes: Courses by demand
Summer School: Dir, Robert Huff. Courses vary

NEW WORLD SCHOOL OF THE ARTS, 25 NE Second St, Miami, FL; 300 NE Second Ave, Miami, FL 33132-2297. Tel 305-237-3620; Fax 305-237-3794; Email hgershfe@mdcc.edu; Web: www.mdcc.edu/nwsa/horizons; *Provost* Jeffrey Hodgson
Estab 1987; A Cooperative venture of University of Florida & Miami-Dade Community College; pub; D; SC 43, LC 6; D 249, maj 249
Publications: Art in Ecological Perspective
Ent Req: HS dipl, entrance exam, portfolio review
Degrees: AA 2 yr, BFA 4 yr
Courses: Advertising Design, Art Education, Art History, †Ceramics, Collage, Conceptual Art, Cyberarts, Design, †Drawing, †Graphic Design, †Illustration, Intermedia, Mixed Media, †Painting, †Photography, †Printmaking, Restoration & Conservation, †Sculpture, Theatre Arts
Summer School: scholarships

MIAMI SHORES

BARRY UNIVERSITY, Dept of Fine Arts, 11300 NE Second Ave, Miami Shores, FL 33161. Tel 305-899-3421 (chair), 899-4923 (asst to chmn - Iris Vendetholi); Fax 305-899-2972; Web: www.barry.edu/finearts; *Dean* Dr Karen Callaghan; *Chair Fine Arts Dept* Dr Silvia Lizama
Estab 1940; Maintain nonprofit art gallery, Andy Gato Gallery (same address); on-campus art shop where art supplies may be purchased; FT 8; pvt; D & E; Scholarships; SC 63, LC 15; D 300, E 60, maj 80
Activities: Schols offered
Ent Req: HS dipl
Degrees: BA, BFA, MA (Photo), MFA (Photo), BA/BFA in art with specialization in Art History, Studio Art, Graphic Design, and Photography

Tuition: Undergrad $14,080 per semester; grad $960 per cr hr
Courses: Art Appreciation, Art History, Ceramics, Collage, Design, Drawing, Graphic Design, History of Art & Architecture, Mixed Media, Painting, †Photography, Sculpture, typography
Summer School: Dr Karen Callaghan, Dean, Col of Arts & Sciences. Courses—Ceramics, Drawing, Photography, Graphic Design, Art History

NICEVILLE

NORTHWEST FLORIDA STATE COLLEGE, (Okaloosa-Walton Community College) Mattie Kelly Arts Center Galleries, 100 College Blvd, Niceville, FL 32578. Tel 850-729-6044; Fax 850-729-5286; Email artgalleries@nwfsc.edu; *Dir* Jeanette Shires; *Gallery Dir* KC Williams
Estab 1964, dept estab 1964; Maintain nonprofit art gallery & library; Pub; D & E; Scholarships; SC 26, LC 3; D 2,000, E 1,000, maj 80
Ent Req: HS dipl
Degrees: AA 2 yrs
Courses: 2-D & 3-D Design, Acting, Art Appreciation, Art History, Ceramics, Costume Design & Construction, Design, Drafting, Drawing, Ethics, Graphic Arts, Graphic Design, Handicrafts, History of Art & Architecture, Humanities, Interior Design, Jewelry, Museum Staff Training, Painting, Philosophy, Photography, Printmaking, Religion, Sculpture, Silversmithing, Stage Design, Teacher Training, Theatre Arts, Weaving
Adult Hobby Classes: Enrl 15 per class. Courses—Antiques, Interior Decorating, Painting, Photography, Pottery, Vase Painting, others as needed

OCALA

CENTRAL FLORIDA COMMUNITY COLLEGE, Humanities Dept, 3001 SW College Rd, Ocala, FL 34474-4415. Tel 352-237-2111, Ext 293; Fax 352-231-0510; Web: www.cfcc.cc.fl.us; *Prog Facilitator* Carolyn West
Estab 1957; pub; D & E; SC 5, LC 1; 3500, non-maj 85, maj 15
Ent Req: HS dipl
Degrees: AA & AS 2 yr
Courses: Art History, Ceramics, Design, Drawing, Painting, Printmaking, Sculpture
Adult Hobby Classes: Ceramics, Commercial Art; Design, Drawing, Painting
Summer School: Two 6 wk terms

ORLANDO

UNIVERSITY OF CENTRAL FLORIDA, Art Dept, 4000 Central Florida Blvd, Orlando, FL 32816-8005; PO Box 161342, Orlando, FL 32816-1342. Tel 407-823-2676; Fax 407-823-6470; Web: www.pegasus.cc.ucs.edu/~art; *Dept Adv* Jagdish Chauda
Estab 1963; pub; Scholarships
Degrees: BA, BFA, cert
Courses: Art History, Ceramics, Design, Drawing, Fibers & Fabrics, Graphic Design, Painting, Photography, Printmaking, Sculpture
Summer School: Tuition same as above. Courses—vary

VALENCIA COMMUNITY COLLEGE - EAST CAMPUS, Art Dept, 701 N Econlochachee Trail, Room 3-112 Orlando, FL 32825; PO Box 3028, Orlando, FL 32802-3028. Tel 407-299-5000, Ext 2270; Fax 407-293-8839; Web: www.valencia.cc.fl.us; *Chmn* Rickard Rietveld; *Dir* Jackie Otto-Miller
Estab 1967, dept estab 1974; pub; D & E; Scholarships; SC 16, LC 5; D 6858
Ent Req: HS dipl
Degrees: AA and AS 2 yrs
Courses: Ceramics, Drafting, Drawing, Film, †Graphic Design, History of Art & Architecture, Illustration, Intermedia, Lettering, Painting, Photography, Printmaking, Sculpture, Stage Design, †Theatre Arts, Visual Arts Today
Summer School: Same as for regular acad yr

PALATKA

FLORIDA SCHOOL OF THE ARTS, Visual Arts, 5001 Saint Johns Ave, Palatka, FL 32177-3807. Tel 386-312-4300; Fax 386-312-4306; Email alainhentschel@sjrstate.edu; Web: www.floarts.org; *Dean* Alain Hentschel, MFA; *New Media Design* Aaron Alexander, MFA; *Studio Art* Charles Marsh, MFA; *Studio Art* Dan Askew, MFA
Estab 1974, dept estab 1974; Maintains a non-profit art gallery at school; pub; D & E; Scholarships; SC 35, LC 10; D 85, maj 85
Ent Req: HS dipl, recommendation, review, interview
Degrees: AS 2 yrs, AA 2 1/2 yrs
Tuition: $108 per credit hour
Courses: †Advertising Design, Art Education, †Art History, Ceramics, †Commercial Art, Costume Design & Construction, Design, †Display, †Drafting, †Drawing, †Graphic Arts, †Graphic Design, †Illustration, †Lettering, †Mixed Media, †Painting, †Photography, †Printmaking, Sculpture, †Stage Design, †Theatre Arts

PANAMA CITY

GULF COAST COMMUNITY COLLEGE, Division of Visual & Performing Arts, 5230 W Hwy 98, Panama City, FL 32401-1058. Tel 850-769-1551, ext 3886; Fax 850-873-3520; Email robourke@gulfcoast.edu; Web: www.gc.cc.fl.us; *Dir* Rosemarie O'Bourke, MS; *Assoc Prof* Sharron Barnes, MA; *Assoc Prof* Roland L Hockett, MS
Estab 1957; pub; D & E; SC 5, LC 2; D 300, E 70, non-maj 330, maj 40
Ent Req: HS dipl
Degrees: AA 2 yrs
Courses: Art History, Ceramics, Design, Drawing, Illustration, Lettering, Photography
Adult Hobby Classes: Macrame, Painting, Weaving
—**Art Gallery**, 5230 W Hwy 98, Panama City, FL 32401. Tel 850-872-3887; Fax 850-872-3836
Open Mon - Fri 8 AM - 4 PM; No admis fee
Collections: Paintings; sculpture; photographs

PENSACOLA

PENSACOLA STATE COLLEGE, Visual Arts Dept, 1000 College Blvd, Pensacola, FL 32504-8998. Tel 850-484-2550; Fax 850-484-2564; Email klien@pensacolastate.edu; Web: www.pensacolastate.edu; *Head Dept* Krist Lien
Estab 1948; Maintains nonprofit Anna Lamar Switzer Center for Visual Arts; art supplies sold at on-campus store; FT 9, PT 11; pub; D & E; Scholarships; SC 43, LC 7, GC 7, Other 2; maj 446
Ent Req: HS dipl
Degrees: AS & AA 2 yrs, BAS 4 yrs
Tuition: no campus res
Courses: Advertising Design, †Art, Art History, †Art Studio, Ceramics, Design, Drawing, †Graphic Design, Mixed Media, Painting, †Photography, Pottery, Sculpture, Typography
Adult Hobby Classes: Courses—Ceramics
Summer School: Dir, Krist Lien. Enrl 300. Courses—same as regular session

UNIVERSITY OF WEST FLORIDA, Dept of Art, 11000 University Pkwy, Pensacola, FL 32514-5732. Tel 850-474-2045; Fax 850-474-2043; Email art@uwf.edu; Web: www.uwf.edu/art; *Assoc Prof* Suzette J Doyon, PhD, MFA; *Assoc Prof* Jim Jipson, MFA; *Asst Prof* Joseph Herring, MFA; *Asst Prof* Valerie George, MFA; *Gallery Dir* Nicholas Croghan, MFA, MA; *Program Dir* John Markowitz, MFA; *Asst Prof* Thomas Asmuth, MFA; *Assoc Prof* Barbara Larson, PhD, MA; *Adj Instr* Amy Bowman; *Adj Instr* Dale Castellucci; *Adj Instr* Gina Cestaro; *Adj Instr* Sara Gevurtz; *Adj Instr* Donna Harper; *Adj Instr* Joy Holland; *Adj Instr* Sally Miller; *Adj Instr* Quintin Owens; *Adj Instr* Elizabeth Petersen; *Adj Instr* Rachael Pongetti; *Adj Instr* Marzia Ransom; *Adj Instr* Gregory Saumders; *Adj Instr* Lyda Toy; *Adj Instr* Suzanne Tuzzeo
Estab 1967; Maintain nonprofit art gallery; University Art Gallery, 1000 University Pkwy, Pensacola, FL 32514; Pub; D & E; Scholarships; SC 20, LC 10; non-maj 100, maj 350
Activities: Schls offered
Degrees: BA & BFA 4 yr
Courses: Aesthetics, †Art Education, †Art History, †BFA, Calligraphy, Ceramics, Design, Drawing, †Graphic Design, Handicrafts, †History of Art & Architecture, Illustration, Intermedia, †Jewelry, Mixed Media, Museum Staff Training, Painting, Photography, Printmaking, Sculpture, †Studio Art, Teacher Training, Video
Summer School: Dir, Jim Jipson. Enrl 400; 2 sessions. Courses—Ceramics, Drawing, Painting, Photography, Printmaking, Sculpture

SAINT AUGUSTINE

FLAGLER COLLEGE, Visual Arts Dept, 74 King St, Saint Augustine, FL 32084; PO Box 1027, Saint Augustine, FL 32085-1027. Tel 904-829-6481; Web: www.flagler.edu; *Chmn* Don Martin; *Prof* Enzo Torcoletti, MFA; *Asst Prof* Kerry Tustin, MFA; *Instr* Maureen O'Neil, MFA
Estab 1968; pvt; D & E; Scholarships; SC 29, LC 7; 1000, maj 100
Ent Req: HS dipl
Degrees: BA 4 yr
Courses: Advertising Design, Air Brush, †Art Education, Art History, Drawing, †Graphic Design, Illustration, Painting, Photography, Sculpture, Visual Arts, Visual Communications
Summer School: Acad Affairs, William Abare. Tuition $180 per hr for terms of 7 wks beginning May. Courses—Airbrush, Ceramics, Computer Illustration, Painting

SAINT PETERSBURG

ECKERD COLLEGE, Art Dept, 4200 54th Ave S, Saint Petersburg, FL 33711-4700. Tel 727-864-8340; Fax 727-864-7890; *Prof* Kirk Wang; *Prof* Arthur Skinner; *Prof* Brian Ransom
Estab 1958; Pvt; Scholarships
Degrees: BA, BF
Courses: Art Education, Art History, Calligraphy, Ceramics, Design, Drawing, †Film, Painting, Photography, Printmaking, †Sculpture, †Theatre Arts, †Video
Adult Hobby Classes: Enrl 25. Courses—Ceramics, Drawing, Painting
Summer School: Dir, Cheryl Gold. Enrl 150

SARASOTA

ART CENTER SARASOTA, 707 N Tamiami Trail, Sarasota, FL 34236-4050. Tel 941-365-2032; Fax 941-366-0585; Email visualartcenter@aol.com; Web: www.artsarasota.org; *Exec Dir* Lisa-Marie Confessore; *Educ Coordr* Jill Kowal; *Pres* William van Osnabrugge; *Instr* Barbara Nechis; *Instr* Peter Spataro; *Instr* Edward Minchin; *Instr* Charles Meyrick; *Instr* Win Jones; *Instr* Frank Webb; *Instr* Bill Buchman; *Instr* Joseph Melancon; *Instr* Pat Deadman
Estab 1926; Maintain nonprofit art gallery & library; Art Ctr Sarasota, 707 N Tamiami Trail, Sarasota, FL 34236-4050; Not-for-profit; D&E; SC 32, LC 6, other 5, workshops; D 200, E 10
Ent Req: Varied
Degrees: Cert of Completion
Courses: Art Appreciation, Art Education, Art History, Calligraphy, Ceramics, Collage, Drawing, Mixed Media, Painting, Photography, Sculpture, Watercolor
Adult Hobby Classes: 200. Courses—Drawing, Painting
Children's Classes: 20 per class maximum
Summer School: Educ Coordr Jill Kowal. Enrl 80. Courses—Watercolor

NEW COLLEGE OF THE UNIVERSITY OF SOUTH FLORIDA, Fine Arts Dept, Humanities Division, 5700 N Tamiami Trail, Sarasota, FL 34243. Tel 941-359-4360, 359-5605; Web: www.newcollege.usf.edu
Estab 1963; FT 4; pub; D; SC 6, LC 5; D 150-200, maj 15
Ent Req: ent exam, SAT
Degrees: BA(Fine Arts) 3 yrs
Courses: †Aesthetics, †Art History, Ceramics, †Color Theory, Design, †Drawing, Life Drawing, †Painting, †Printmaking, †Sculpture, Stained Glass

RINGLING SCHOOL OF ART & DESIGN, 2700 N Tamiami Trail, Sarasota, FL 34234. Tel 941-351-5100; Fax 941-359-7517; *Pres* Thomas E Linehan; *Dean Admis* Jim Dean
Estab 1931; 31; pvt; Scholarships; 830
Ent Req: HS dipl or equivalency, portfolio
Degrees: BFA, 4 yrs
Courses: †Computer Animation, †Fine Arts, †Graphic Design, †Illustration, †Interior Design, Painting, †Photography, Sculpture
Adult Hobby Classes: Enrl 150

TALLAHASSEE

FLORIDA A & M UNIVERSITY, Dept of Visual Arts, Humanities & Theatre, 515 Orr Dr, 208 Tucker Hall Tallahassee, FL 32307. Tel 850-599-3831; Fax 850-599-8417; Web: www.famu.edu; *Chmn* Luther D Wells
Estab 1887; pub; D & E; Scholarships; D 5887, non-maj 5800, maj 87
Ent Req: HS dipl, ent exam
Degrees: BS & BA with Fine Arts Cert
Tuition: Res—$62.10 per sem hr; nonres—$236.94 per sem hr
Courses: Art Education, Art History, Ceramics, Design, Drawing, Metals, Plastic, Textile Design, Wood
Summer School: Enrl 125; tuition same as regular session for term of 9 & 7 wks beginning June. Courses—Arts, Ceramics, Design, Drawing, Metal & Plastics, Textile Design, Wood

FLORIDA STATE UNIVERSITY, Art Dept, 220 Fine Arts Bldg, Tallahassee, FL 32306-1150. Tel 850-644-6474; Fax 850-644-8977; Email hdstripl@mailer.fsu.edu; Web: www.fsu.edu/~svad; *Chmn Studio Art* Roald Nasgaard, PhD; *Prof* James Roche, MFA; *Prof Emeritus* Ed Love, MFA; *Prof* George Blakely, MFA; *Prof* Robert Fichter, MFA; *Prof Emeritus* Trevor Bell, MFA; *Prof Emeritus* William Walmsley, MFA; *Assoc Prof* George Bocz, MEd; *Assoc Prof* Janice E Hartwell, MFA; *Assoc Prof* Charles E Hook, MFA; *Assoc Prof* Gail Rubini, MFA; *Prof* Mark Messersmith, MFA; *Assoc Prof* Paul Rutkovsky, MFA; *Assoc Prof* Terri Lindbloom, MFA; *Assoc Prof* Kasuya Bowen, MFA; *Assoc Prof* Keith Roberson, MFA; *Prof & Assoc Chair* Ray Burggraf; *Assoc Prof* Donald Odita; *Prof* Pat Ward Williams; *Assoc Prof* Lilian Garcia-Roil; *Asst Prof* Scott Groeninger; *Asst Prof* Steve Jones
Estab 1857, dept estab 1911; maintains nonprofit gallery; Cate Wyatt-Magalian, Daniel Kariko & John Raulerson; pub; D & E; Scholarships; SC 45, LC. 2, GC 22; non-maj 400, maj 488, grad 35
Ent Req: HS dipl, B average & test scores of at least 24 (composite) on the ACT or 1100 (verbal plus math) on the SAT I
Degrees: BA, BFA, BS, MFA
Tuition: Res--undergrad $73.19 per cr hr, grad $146.01 per cr hr; nonres--undergrad $306.14 per cr hr, grad $506.74 per cr hr
Courses: Ceramics, Drawing, Graphic Arts, Painting, Photography, Printmaking, Sculpture
Summer School: Term of 13 wks; two terms of six & a half wks
—Art Education Dept, 028 WJB, Tallahassee, FL 32306-1232; 301 Francis Eppes Bldg, Tallahassee, FL 32306. Tel 850-644-2926; 850-644-5473; Fax 850-644-5067; Email mrosal@fsu.edu; Web: www.fsu.edu/~are; *Prof* Tom Anderson PhD; *Chmn Art Educ Dept* David Gussak PhD; *Assoc Prof* Pat Villeneuve PhD; *Prof* Marcia L Rosal PhD; *Prof* Anniina Suominen Guyas
Estab 1857, dept estab 1948; Maintain an art/architecture library, Mary Mooty Library, Florida State Univ, 028WJB, Tallahassee, FL 37306-1232; on-campus art supplies shop; pub; D & E; Scholarships; LC, GC; 80 maj, 85 GS
Ent Req: HS dipl
Degrees: BA(Art Educ) 4 yr, MS(Art Edu & Art Therapy) & MA(Arts Admin). 1-2 yr, EDS degree, PhD
Tuition: Res—$2,379; nonres—$9, 716
Courses: †Art Education, Art Therapy, Arts Administration, Special Population, Teacher Training
Summer School: Studio Art & Art History Emphasis
—Art History Dept, PO Box 3061151, Tallahassee, FL 32306-1151; 530 W Call St, Tallahassee, FL 32306. Tel 850-644-1250; Fax 850-644-7065; Email arh@www.fsu.edu; Web: www.fsu.edu/~arh; *Dean School Visual Arts* Jerry L Draper PhD; *Prof* Robert M Neuman PhD; *Prof* Jehnne Teilhet-Fisk; *Prof* Cynthia J Hahn PhD; *Assoc Prof* Lauren Weingarden PhD; *Assoc Prof* Karen Bearor PhD; *Asst Prof* Jack Freiberg PhD; *Asst Prof* Brenda Jordan, PhD; *Chmn* Paula Gerson
Estab 1857, dept estab 1948; Maintain nonprofit art gallery, Fine Art Museum; pub; D & E; Scholarships
Ent Req: HS dipl
Degrees: MA(Art History) 2 1/2 yr, PhD(Art History) 3 yr
Tuition: Res—$59.93 per cr hr; nonres—$223.34 per cr hr
Courses: Art Appreciation, †Art History, Arts Administration, History of Art & Archeology

TALLAHASSEE COMMUNITY COLLEGE, Art Dept, 444 Appleyard Dr, Tallahassee, FL 32304-2895. Tel 850-201-8713; Email baroodyj@tcc.fl.edu; Web: www.tcc.fl.edu; *Art Coordr* Julie Baroody; *Dean* Dr Marge Banocy-Payne
Estab 1966; Maintain nonprofit art gallery; TC Art Gallery, 444 Appleyard Dr, Tallahassee FL 32304; art supplies available on-campus; PT 4; pub; D & E; Scholarships; SC 13, LC 3; D 350 per sem, E 150 per sem
Ent Req: HS dipl
Degrees: AA 2 yrs
Courses: Art Appreciation, Art History, Color Theory, Design, Drawing, †Graphic Design, History & Appreciation of Cinema, Painting, Photography, Printmaking, Silkscreen, Silversmithing, Watercolor
Summer School: Dean, Dr Marge Benocy-Payne. Courses—Basic Photo, Methods/Concepts

TAMPA

HILLSBOROUGH COMMUNITY COLLEGE, Fine Arts Dept, 2112 N 15th St, Tampa, FL 33605-3648. Tel 813-253-7000 ext 7674; Fax 813-259-6425; Web: www.hccfl.edu, www.hccfl.edu/4c; *Dir* Suzanne Crosby; *Assoc Prof* Tracy Reller; *Assoc Prof* Katherine Moyse; *Assoc Prof* Christopher W Weeks; *Gallery Dir* Carolyn Kossar
Estab 1967; Maintains ACC Ybor Campus Art Gallery; pub; D, E & weekends; Scholarships; SC 10, LC 10
Degrees: AA, AS
Tuition: Res—$48.06 per cr hr; nonres—$177.61 per cr hr
Courses: Art Appreciation, Art History, Ceramics, Conceptual Art, Costume Design & Construction, Design, Drawing, †Film, Graphic Arts, Graphic Design, Mixed Media, Painting, Photography, Printmaking, Sculpture, Stage Design, Theatre Arts
Summer School: Summer I & II sems

UNIVERSITY OF SOUTH FLORIDA, School of Art & Art History, 4202 E Fowler Ave, FAH 110, College of the Arts Tampa, FL 33620-7350. Tel 813-974-2360; Fax 813-974-9226; Email jherrin@usf.edu; Web: www.art.usf.edu; *Dir* Wallace Wilson; *Prof* Louis Marcus; *Prof* Elisabeth Fraser; *Assoc Prof* Wendy Babcox; *Assoc Prof* Neil Bender; *Assoc Prof* John Byrd; *Assoc Prof* Gregory Green; *Assoc Prof* Robert Lawrence; *Assoc Prof* Riccardo Marchi; *Assoc Prof* Anat Pollack; *Assoc Prof* Bradlee Shanks; *Assoc Prof* Helena Szepe; *Asst Prof* Cesar Cornejo; *Asst Prof* McArthur Freeman; *Asst Prof* Ezra Johnson; *Asst Prof* Esra Akin-Kivanc; *Assoc Prof* Noelle Mason; *Asst Prof* Allison Moore; *Asst Prof* Sue Havens; *Asst Prof* Joo Woo; *Asst Prof* Jason Lazarus
Estab 1956; Maintain nonprofit library, Visual Resource Library, same address; maintain nonprofit art gallery, Oliver Gallery; FT 4; pub; D&E; online; Scholarships; Fellowships; SC 100, LC 125, GC 20, other 50; D 625, E 50, non-maj 400, maj 350, grad 50
Ent Req: HS grad, 14 units cert by HS, ent exam
Degrees: BA (Art) minimum 120 sem hrs, BFA 120 sem hrs, MFA 60 sem hrs & MA(Art History) 40 sem hrs
Tuition: Undergraduate in State: $211/cr; Out of state $575/cr; Graduate in State $431/cr; Out of state $877/cr
Courses: animation, †Art Appreciation, Art History, Ceramics, Collage, Drawing, Electronic Media, Mixed Media, Museum Staff Training, Painting, Photography, Printmaking, Sculpture, Video
Summer School: Dir Wallace Wilson. Enrol 150

UNIVERSITY OF TAMPA, College of Arts & Letters, 401 W Kennedy Blvd, Tampa, FL 33606-1450. Tel 813-258-7495; Email lrothe@ut.edu; Web: www.utarts.com; *Prof* Lew Harris; *Prof* Catherine Chastain-Elliott; *Dir Gallery* Dorothy Cowden; *Prof* Santiago Echevery; *Prof* Doug Sutherland; *Prof* Kendra Frorup; *Prof* Jack King; *Prof* Ina Kaur; *Prof* Brooke Scherer; *Prof* Chris Valle
Estab 1930; Maintains nonprofit art gallery, University of Tampa, Scarfone/Hartley Gallery; 9; pvt; D & E; Scholarships; SC 17, LC 8; non-maj 100, maj 170
Ent Req: Admis to Univ of Tampa
Degrees: 4 yrs
Tuition: Info on website
Courses: †Animation, †Art Appreciation, Art Education, Art History, Arts Management, Ceramics, Computer Graphics, Design, †Digital Arts, Drawing, Graphic Design, Painting, Photography, Printmaking, Sculpture
Summer School: Art courses offered

TEMPLE TERRACE

FLORIDA COLLEGE, Division of Art, 119 N Glen Arven Ave, Temple Terrace, FL 33617-5578. Tel 813-988-5131; Fax 813-899-6772; Web: www.flcoll.edu; *Faculty* Julia Gibson
Estab 1947; FT 1; pvt; D&E; Scholarships
Degrees: AA
Courses: †Design I, †Design II

WINTER HAVEN

POLK COMMUNITY COLLEGE, Art, Letters & Social Sciences, 999 Ave H NE, Winter Haven, FL 33881-4299. Tel 863-297-1025; Fax 863-297-1037; Web: www.polk.cc.fl.us; *Prof* Gary Baker, MFA; *Prof* Bob Morrisey, MFA; *Dean of Arts* Hugh B Anderson, MFA
Estab 1964; pub; D & E; Scholarships; SC 10, LC 1; D 175, E 50
Ent Req: HS dipl
Degrees: AA & AS 2 yrs
Courses: Advertising Design, Art Appreciation, Ceramics, Design, Drawing, Film, Interior Design, Painting, Photography, Printmaking, Sculpture, Theatre Arts
Adult Hobby Classes: Enrl 60. Courses—Calligraphy, Ceramics, Christmas Crafts, Drawing, Interior Design, Jewelry, Painting

WINTER PARK

ROLLINS COLLEGE, Dept of Art, Main Campus, 1000 Holt Ave, Winter Park, FL 32789-4409. Tel 407-646-2498; Fax 407-628-6395; Web: www.rollins.edu; *Chmn* Ron Larned
Estab 1885; pvt; D & E; Scholarships; SC 11, LC 10; D & E 250
Degrees: BA 4 yr

Courses: Aesthetics, Art History, Art History Survey, Design, Drawing, Humanities Foundation, Painting, Principles of Art, Sculpture
Adult Hobby Classes: Selected Studio & History courses
Summer School: Selected Art History & Appreciation courses

GEORGIA

AMERICUS

GEORGIA SOUTHWESTERN STATE UNIVERSITY, Dept of Fine Arts, 800 Gsw State University Dr, Americus, GA 31709-4376. Tel 912-931-2204; Fax 912-931-2927; *Chmn* Dr Duke Jackson
Scholarships
Degrees: BA, BSEd, BSA, cert
Tuition: Res—$1099 per sem; nonres—$2610 per sem
Courses: Ceramics, Drawing, Glassblowing, Graphic Design, Jewelry, Painting, Photography, Printmaking, Sculpture, Textile Design

ATHENS

UNIVERSITY OF GEORGIA, FRANKLIN COLLEGE OF ARTS & SCIENCES, Lamar Dodd School of Art, 270 River Rd, Athens, GA 30602-7676. Tel 706-542-1511; Fax 706-542-0226; Email artinfo@uga.edu; Web: www.uga.edu; *Dean* Wyatt Anderson; *Dir* Carmon Colangelo; *Assoc Dir* Richard Johnson; *Grad Coordr* Andy Nasisse; *Assoc Dir* Shelley Zuraw; *Assoc Prof Ceramics* Ted Saupe; *Prof Drawing & Painting* Judy McWillie; *Prof Fabric Design* Glen Kaufman; *Prof Graphic Design* Lanny Webb; *Assoc Prof Interior Design* Thom Houser; *Asst Prof Jewelry & Metalwork* Robert Jackson; *Asst Prof Scientific Illustration* Gene Wright; *Prof Sculpture* Larry Millard; *Assoc Prof Printmaking* Melissa Harshman; *Assoc Prof Photog* Stephen Scheer; *Franklin Prof Art History* Andrew Ladis; *Wheatley Prof Drawing & Painting* Arthur Rosenbaum; *Distinguished Research Prof Drawing & Painting* James Herbert; *Gallery Coordr* Robin Dana; *Assoc Prof Art Educ* Dr Carole Henry; *Asst Prof Art Educ* Dr Pam Taylor; *Asst Prof Art Educ* Dr Richard Siegesmund; *Franklin Fellow Asst Prof* Dr Jessie Whitehead; *Prof Art History* Evan Firestone; *Asst Prof Art History* Asen Kirin; *Asst Prof Art History* Alisa Luxenberg; *Assoc Prof Art History* Tom Polk; *Assoc Prof Art History* Janice Simon; *Prof Art History* Francis Van Keuren; *Asst Prof Digital Media* Michael Oliveri; *Asst Prof Drawing & Painting* Radcliffe Bailey; *Asst Prof Drawing & Painting* Jim Barsness; *Assoc Prof Drawing & Painting* Scott Belville; *Assoc Prof Drawing & Painting* Diane Edison; *Assoc Prof Drawing & Painting* Stefanie Jackson; *Assoc Prof Drawing & Painting* Bill Marriott; *Assoc Prof Drawing & Painting* Joe Norman; *Prof Fabric Design* Ed Lambert; *Assoc Prof Foundations* Christopher Hocking; *Asst Prof Foundations* Gretchen Hupfel; *Prof Graphic Design* Ron Arnholm; *Acad Professional Graphic Design* Joey Hannaford; *Asst Prof Graphic Design* Alex Murawski; *Prof Graphic Design* Susan Roberts; *Prof Graphic Design* Ken Williams; *Asst Prof Interior Design* Jane Lily; *Asst Prof Interior Design* Welynda Wright; *Asst Prof Photog* Michael Marshall; *Lectr Photog* Mary Ruth Moore; *Acad Professional Photog* Ben Reynolds; *Assoc Prof Printmaking* Joe Sanders; *Assoc Prof Sculpture* Jim Buonaccorsi; *Assoc Prof Sculpture* Imi Hwangho; *Assoc Prof Sculpture* Rocky Sapp
Opened 1801, chartered 1875; Maintain art library & nonprofit art gallery; Pub; D; Scholarships; Fellowships; Assistantships; SC 145, LC 60, GC 99; non-maj 50, maj 950, grad 80
Ent Req: HS dipl, SAT
Degrees: BA, BFA, BSEd, MA, MFA, MAE, EdS, EdD, PhD
Tuition: Res—undergrad $1,517 per sem, grad $1,888 per sem; nonres—undergrad $5,138 per sem, grad $6,397 per sem
Courses: Art Appreciation, †Art Education, †Art History, †Ceramics, Digital Media, Drawing, †Graphic Arts, †Graphic Design, Illustration, †Interior Design, †Jewelry, Lettering, Mixed Media, †Painting, †Photography, †Printmaking, †Scientific Illustration, †Sculpture, Silversmithing, †Textile Design, Weaving
Summer School: Dir, Carmen Colangelo, Assoc Dir Rick Johnson; Enrl 600, 35 courses

ATLANTA

ART INSTITUTE OF ATLANTA, 6600 Peachtree-Dunwoody, 100 Embassy Row Atlanta, GA 30328-6773. Tel 770-394-8300; Fax 770-394-0008; Web: www.aia.artinstitute.edu; *Pres* Janet Day; *Dean* Larry Stulpz
The Institute has the following departments: Graphic Design, Photography, Interior Design, Culinary Arts, Computer Animation, Multi Media Web Design; Scholarships
Degrees: AA
Courses: Advertising Design, Cartooning, Commercial Art, Design, Display, Drawing, Fashion, Graphic Arts, Interior Design, Lettering, Mixed Media, Painting, Photo Design, Photography, Portrait, Video

ATLANTA TECHNICAL INSTITUTE, Visual Communications Class, 1560 Metropolitan Pkwy, Atlanta, GA 30310. Tel 404-756-3700; Fax 404-756-0932; Web: www.atlantatech.org; *Head Dept* Eric Jefferies
Estab 1967; pub; D; SC 13; D 25, E 25
Ent Req: HS dipl, ent exam
Degrees: AA in conjunction with the Atlanta Metro Col
Courses: Advertising Design, Commercial Art, Graphic Arts, Photography, Print Production Art, Video

CLARK-ATLANTA UNIVERSITY, School of Arts & Sciences, 223 James P Brawley Dr SW, Atlanta, GA 30314-4358. Tel 404-880-8000; Web: www.cau.edu; *Assoc Prof* Christopher Hickey; *Chmn Dept* Belinda A Peters; *Prof* Emmanuel Asihene; *Asst Prof* Dorothy Batey; *Instr* Javier Tolbert; *Instr* Constance Boothe; *Instr* Norman Meyer
Estab 1869, dept estab 1964; pvt; D; Scholarships; SC 8, LC 8; D 198, non-maj 120, maj 85
Ent Req: HS dipl
Degrees: BA (Art, Fashion Design) 4 yrs, Honors Program
Courses: Art Education, Art History, Design, Drawing, Fashion Design, Graphic Design, Illustration, Painting, Photography, Printmaking, Sculpture
Summer School: Summer school program offered.

EMORY UNIVERSITY, Art History Dept, 571 Kilgo Cir, 133 Carlos Hall Atlanta, GA 30322-1120. Tel 404-727-6282; Fax 404-727-2358; Email grobins@emory.edu; Web: arthistory.emory.edu/home/index.html; *Prof* C Jean Campbell PhD; *Asst Prof* Todd Cronan PhD; *Dir Undergrad Studies & Sr Lectr* Dorothy Fletcher MA; *Prof* Sidney L Kasfir PhD; *Prof* Sarah Collyer McPhee, PhD; *Assoc Prof* Judith C Rohrer, PhD; *Assoc Prof* Eric Varner, PhD; *Prof* Walter S Melion; *Assoc Prof* Elizabeth Carson Pastan; *Prof* Gay Robbins; *Assoc Prof* Rebecca R Stone; *Assoc Prof* Bonna Daix Westcoat
Estab 1847; pvt; D; Scholarships; SC 27, LC 26, GC 18; non-maj 240, maj 80, grad 41
Ent Req: HS dipl, ent exam, SAT
Degrees: BA(Art History) & PhD(Art History)
Courses: †Art History, Ceramics, Drawing, Film, History of Art & Architecture, Museum Staff Training, Painting, Photography, Sculpture, Video
Summer School: Dir, Elizabeth Pastan. Enrl 51; tuition $621 per cr hr, 2 six wk sessions. Courses—Drawing, History of Art Abroad, Photography, Video, Sculpture, Studio Art, Various seminars in Europe (variable 8 cr hr)

GEORGIA INSTITUTE OF TECHNOLOGY, College of Architecture, 247 Fourth St, Atlanta, GA 30332-0155. Tel 404-894-3880; Fax 404-894-2678; Email tom.galloway@coa.gatech.edu; Web: arch.gatech.edu; *Dean* Thomas D Galloway PhD; *Assoc Dean* Douglas Allen; *Assoc Dean* Sabir Khan
Estab 1885, dept estab 1908; Maintain nonprofit art gallery, Atlanta Contemporary Art Center; pub; D & E; Scholarships; SC 31, LC 86, GC 109; D 639, maj 731, grad 275
Ent Req: HS dipl, SAT
Degrees: BS(Architecture), BS(Building Construction), BS(Industrial Design) & M (Architecture) 2 yr & 3 1/2 yrs (for students w/out degree in Architecture), PhD MCRP 2 yr, PhD MS (Building Construction & Integrated Facility Management) 2 yr, MS (undesignated) 1-2 yr, MS (Advanced Architectural Design) 1yr, MID 2yr & 3yr (for students w/out degree in Industrial Design), MS (Music Technology) 2 yr
Courses: Aesthetics, †Architecture, Art Appreciation, Art History, †Building Construction, †City & Regl Planning, Conceptual Art, Constructions, Design, Drafting, Drawing, †Facility Management, Graphic Arts, Graphic Design, History of Art & Architecture, †Industrial Design, Intermedia, Music, Painting, Photography, Printmaking, Teacher Training
Summer School: Dir, Ellen Dunham-Jones. Enrl 50; tuition same. Courses—vary

GEORGIA STATE UNIVERSITY, Ernest G Welch School of Art & Design, PO Box 4107, Atlanta, GA 30302-4107. Tel 404-413-5221; Fax 404-413-5261; Email artundergrad@gsu.edu; grad@gsu.edu; Web: www.gsu.edu; *Dir* Michael White; *Assoc Dir* Maria Gindhart; *Grad Dir* John Decker
Estab 1913; Maintain non-profit art gallery, Ernest G Welch School of Art & Design Galleries, 10 Peachtree Ctr Ave, Atlanta, GA 30303; FT 35; pub; D & E; Scholarships; SC 80, LC 16; maj 450, others 300
Activities: Schols, fels offered
Ent Req: HS dipl, ent exam, college board, interview
Degrees: BFA, BA(Art) and BA(Art History) 4 yrs, MA(Art History), MAEd (Art Education), MFA (Studio), MFA
Courses: Art Education, Art History, Ceramics, Drawing, Graphic Design, Interior Design, Painting, Photography, Printmaking, Sculpture, Textile Design
Children's Classes: Enrl 10-15, 8-10 wk term
Summer School: Enrl 350-400. Courses—Art Education, Art History, Studio

AUGUSTA

AUGUSTA STATE UNIVERSITY, Dept of Art, 2500 Walton Way, Augusta, GA 30904-2200. Tel 706-667-4888; Fax 706-729-2429; Email cjunod@aug.edu; Web: www.aug.edu; *Assoc Prof* Kristin Casaletto, MFA; *Prof* Janice Whiting, MFA; *Prof* Michael Schwartz, PhD; *Prof* Brian Rust, MFA; *Morris Eminent Scholar in Art* William Willis, MFA; *Prof* Priscilla Hollingsworth, MFA; *Prof* Jennifer Onofrio, MFA; *Prof* Raoul Pacheco; *Chair* Alan MacTaggart
Estab 1925, dept estab 1965; independent dept estab 2006; Maintains nonprofit art gallery: Mary S Byrd Gallery of Art, Washington Hall, Augusta State University, 2500 Walton Way, Augusta, GA 30904; art supplies may be purchased at bookstore; pub; D & E; Scholarships; SC 46, LC 4; D 300, E 45, non-maj 80, maj 100
Ent Req: HS dipl, SAT
Degrees: BA & BFA
Courses: Aesthetics, Art History, †Ceramics, Design, †Drawing, Mixed Media, †Painting, Photography, Printmaking, †Sculpture
Adult Hobby Classes: Contact Continuing Education Dept for info

BARNESVILLE

GORDON COLLEGE, Dept of Fine Arts, 419 College Dr, Barnesville, GA 30204-1762. Tel 770-358-5118; Fax 770-358-3031; *Instr* Marlin Adams; *Dir* Jason Horn
Scholarships
Degrees: AA
Tuition: Res—$627 per sem; nonres—$2694 per sem
Courses: Art Appreciation, Ceramics, Design, Drawing, Graphic Design, Illustration, Introduction to Art, Painting, Photography, Printmaking, Survey Art History

CARROLLTON

STATE UNIVERSITY OF WEST GEORGIA, Art Dept, 1601 Maple St, Carrollton, GA 30118-0002. Tel 770-836-6521; Fax 770-836-4392; Web: www.westga.edu/~artdept; *Chmn* Bruce Bobick
Estab 1906; Maintain nonprofit art gallery - Department of Art Gallery, State U of West Georgia; Pub; D&E; Scholarships; SC 39, LC 16, GC 2, Other 9; maj 230, grad 15
Ent Req: HS dipl, ent exam
Degrees: BFA, AB(Studio, Pre-Medical Illustration, Art History), MEd 1 yr full-time
Courses: Art Appreciation, †Art Education, Art History, †Ceramics, Design, Drawing, †Graphic Design, †Interior Design, †Painting, Papermaking, †Photography, †Printmaking, †Sculpture
Summer School: Dir, B Bobick, 8 wk sem in Carrollton, summer study abroad program in Bayeux, France. Courses—Art Appreciation, Art Education, Art History, Ceramics, Design, Drawing, Painting, Printmaking, Sculpture, Photography

CLEVELAND

TRUETT-MCCONNELL COLLEGE, Fine Arts Dept & Arts Dept, 100 Alumni Dr, Cleveland, GA 30528-1264. Tel 706-865-2134; Fax 706-865-0975; Web: www.truett.cc.ga.us; *Instr* Susan Chapman; *Prof* Dr David N George; *Chmn* Dr Edwin Calloway
Estab 1946; den; D & E; SC 10, LC 2; D 700, non-maj 98, maj 15
Ent Req: HS dipl, SAT
Degrees: AA and AS 2 yr
Courses: 3-D Design, Aesthetics, Art History, Ceramics, Drawing, Graphic Design, Handicrafts, Painting, Sculpture

COCHRAN

MIDDLE GEORGIA STATE UNIVERSITY, College of Arts & Sciences, Media, Culture & the Arts, 1100 2nd St SE, Cochran, GA 31014-1564. Tel 478-934-3085; Fax 478-934-3517; Email charlie.agnew@mga.edu; Web: www.mga.edu; *Interim Chmn* Dr Robert McTyre; *Assoc Prof of Art, Art Prog Coordr, Gallery Dir Peacock Gallery* Charlie Agnew; *Asst Prof Art* Donald Simmons; *PT Instr* Kay Hutcheson; *Lectr* Shannon Riddle; *PT Instr* Blair Davis
Estab 1884 as Junior College Unit of University of Georgia, now a university; Maintains a nonprofit art gallery, Peacock Gallery, Cochran Campus same address; Campus bookstore; FT 2; Pub; D, E & online AM; Scholarships; SC 15, LC 4, online-Art Apprec, Art History I & II; D 270, E 10, non-maj 169, maj 41, grad online 30
Activities: Schols offered
Ent Req: HS dipl, GED
Degrees: AA 2 yr
Tuition: Total in-state tuition & fees 12 hrs $1,936.04. Total out of state tuition & fees 12 hrs $5,450.36
Courses: Art Appreciation, Art History, Ceramics, Design, Drawing, Graphic Arts, Graphic Design, †Occupational Therapy, Painting, †Perspectives in Art, Photography, Printmaking, Sculpture
Summer School: Enrl 90-120, Art Apprec (multiple campuses); Dr. Martha Venn, VPres Academic Affairs

COLUMBUS

COLUMBUS STATE UNIVERSITY, Dept of Art, Fine Arts Hall, 4225 University Ave, Columbus, GA 31907-5679. Tel 706-568-2047; Fax 706-568-2093; Web: www.colstate.edu; *Chmn* Jeff Burden
Estab 1958; pub; D & E; Scholarships; SC 30, LC 7, GC 28; D 300, E 50, maj 130, grad 20
Ent Req: HS dipl, ent exam
Degrees: BS(Art Educ), BFA(Art) & MEd(Art Educ) 4 yr
Courses: Art Appreciation, Art Education, Art History, Ceramics, Critical Analysis, Design, Drawing, Graphic Arts, Graphic Design, Painting, Photography, Printmaking, Sculpture, Textile Design
Summer School: Enrl 200; term of one quarter. Courses—various

DAHLONEGA

NORTH GEORGIA COLLEGE & STATE UNIVERSITY, Fine Arts Dept, 322 Georgia Cir Dahlonega, GA 30597. Tel 706-864-1423; Fax 706-864-1429; Web: www.ngcsu.edu; *Dept Head* Dr Lee Barrow; *Assoc Prof* CM Chastain; *Asst Prof* Hank Margeson; *Asst Prof* Michael Marling de Cuellar
Estab 1873; pub; D & E; Scholarships
Degrees: BA, BS, MEd
Tuition: Res—undergrad $2954 per yr, grad $2918 per yr; nonres—undergrad $3991per sem, grad $3200 per sem; campus res available
Courses: Art Appreciation, †Art Education, Art History, †Ceramics, Computer Graphics, Design, †Drawing, Painting, †Photography, Printmaking, Scientific Illustration, †Sculpture, Textile Design, Weaving
Children's Classes: Enrl 10; tuition $30. Courses—Children's Art
Summer School: Dir, Lee Barrow. Courses—Art Appreciation, Drawing, Painting, Photography, Pottery

DECATUR

AGNES SCOTT COLLEGE, Dept of Art, 141 E College Ave, Decatur, GA 30030-3797. Tel 404-471-6000; Fax 404-638-5369; Web: www.agnesscott.edu; *Chmn* Anne Beidler
Estab 1889; pvt; D; Scholarships; SC 13, LC 15; non-maj 200, maj 23
Degrees: BA 4 yr
Courses: Aesthetics, Art History, Drawing, Graphic Arts, Painting, Printmaking, Sculpture

DEMOREST

PIEDMONT COLLEGE, Art Dept, PO Box 10, Demorest, GA 30535-0010. Tel 706-778-3000; Fax 706-778-2811; Web: www.piedmont.edu; *Dept Head* Cheryl Goldsleger
Estab 1897; Pvt; Scholarships
Degrees: BA
Courses: Art Appreciation, Art Education, Art History, Ceramics, Drawing, Graphic Design, Painting, Photography, Printmaking, Sculpture

GAINESVILLE

BRENAU UNIVERSITY, Art & Design Dept, 500 Washington St SE, Gainesville, GA 30501. Tel 770-534-6240; Fax 770-538-4599; Email lgann-smith@brenau.edu; Web: www.brenau.edu; *Art & Design Chair* Lori Gann-Smith, MFA; *Fashion Merchandising Prog Dir* Karen Garbow, MFA; *Studio Arts Prog Dir* Claudia Wilburn, MFA; *Gallery Dir* Nichole Rawlings; *Affiliate Faculty* Kasie Alt, PhD
Estab 1878; Maintain nonprofit galleries, 3 galleries on main campus; on-campus shop where art supplies may be purchased; Pvt; D & E; weekends; Scholarships; SC, LC; 100; D, 75; E, 25
Activities: Schols offered
Ent Req: HS dipl
Degrees: BFA, BA, BS 4 yr
Tuition: Varies with program
Courses: Aesthetics, †Art Appreciation, †Art Education, Art History, †Ceramics, †Design, Drafting, †Drawing, †Fashion Design, †Fashion Merchandising, Graphic Design, Mixed Media, Museum Staff Training, Museum Studies, †Painting, Photography, †Sculpture, Textile Design

LAGRANGE

LAGRANGE COLLEGE, Lamar Dodd Art Center Museum, 601 Broad St, LaGrange, GA 30240-2999. Tel 706-812-7211; Fax 706-812-7212; Web: www.lgc.peachnet.edu; *Dept Head* John D Lawrence
Estab 1831; FT 3, PT 1; pvt; D & E; Scholarships; SC 11, LC 2; maj 40
Ent Req: HS dipl, ent exam
Degrees: BA 4 yr
Courses: Art Education, Art History, Art History Survey, Batik, Ceramics, Drawing, Graphic Design, Painting, Photography, Printmaking, Sculpture, Textile Design
Summer School: Dir, Luke Gill. Enrl 200. Courses—Art History, Ceramics, Drawing, Photography

MACON

MERCER UNIVERSITY, Art Dept, 1400 Coleman Ave, Macon, GA 31207-0003. Tel 478-301-2591; Fax 478-301-2171; *Assoc Prof* Gary L Blackburn
Estab 1945; FT 4; den; D; SC 9, LC 7, GC 2; maj 25
Ent Req: HS dipl
Degrees: BA 4 yr
Courses: Art Education, Art History, Ceramics, Drawing, Photography, Printmaking, Sculpture
Adult Hobby Classes: Evening classes
Summer School: Dir, JoAnna Watson. 2 terms, 5 wks. Courses—Art Education, Ceramics, Crafts, Drawing, Painting, Photography, Sculpture

WESLEYAN COLLEGE, Art Dept, 4760 Forsyth Rd, Macon, GA 31210-4462. Tel 478-477-1110; Fax 478-757-2469; Web: www.wesleyancollege.edu; *Asst Prof* Lebe Bailey, MFA; *Asst Prof* Francise de La Rosa, MFA
Estab 1836; den; D & E; Scholarships; SC 38, LC 10; D 159, non-maj 13, maj 45, others 12
Ent Req: HS dipl, SAT, GPA
Degrees: BFA 4 yrs, BA
Courses: Advertising Design, Art Education, Art History, Ceramics, Commercial Art, Drawing, Elementary School Arts & Crafts, Graphic Arts, Graphic Design, Illustration, Painting, Photography, Printmaking, Sculpture, Special Topics in Art, Stage Design, Teacher Training, Theatre Arts, Visual Arts
Summer School: Art History Survey, Ceramics, Graphic Design, Illustration, Painting, Photography, Printmaking, Sculpture

MILLEDGEVILLE

GEORGIA COLLEGE & STATE UNIVERSITY, Art Dept, 231 W Hancock St, Milledgeville, GA 31061. Tel 478-445-4572; Fax 478-445-6088; Web: www.gscu.edu; *Chmn* Dorothy D Brown
Scholarships
Courses: Art Appreciation, †Art Education, Art History, Ceramics, Design, Drawing, Handicrafts, Jewelry, Painting, Printmaking, Sculpture, Textile Design, Weaving
Adult Hobby Classes: Courses offered
Summer School: Courses offered

MOUNT BERRY

BERRY COLLEGE, Art Dept, 2277 Martha Berry Hwy NW, Box 299 Mount Berry, GA 30149-9707. Tel 706-236-2289; Fax 706-238-7835; Web: www.berry.edu; *Assoc Prof* Jere Lykins, MEd; *Assoc Prof* V Troy PhD; *Assoc Prof* Brad Adams, MFA
Estab 1902, dept estab 1942; Maintain nonprofit art gallery; Moon Gallery, Moon Bldg, Berry College Campus, Mt Berry, GA 30149; pvt; D & E; Scholarships; SC 24, LC 9; D 122, non-maj 38, maj 84, others 7
Ent Req: HS dipl, SAT, CEEB, ACT
Degrees: BA, BS 4 yrs
Courses: Aesthetics, †Art Appreciation, Art Education, Art History, Calligraphy, †Ceramics, Collage, Conceptual Art, Constructions, Design, Drawing, Ecological Art, Film, Graphic Arts, †Graphic Design, History of Art & Architecture, †Painting, †Photography, Printmaking, Sculpture, Teacher Training, Video
Summer School: Chair, Art Dept, Dr T J Mew III. Courses—Same as above

MOUNT VERNON

BREWTON-PARKER COLLEGE, Visual Arts, Hwy 280, Mount Vernon, GA 30445; PO Box 197, Mount Vernon, GA 30445-0197. Tel 912-583-2241, Ext 306; Fax 912-583-4498; Web: www.bpc.edu; *Dir* E W Addison, MFA; *Pres* David Smith
Estab 1906, dept re-estab 1976; pvt, den; D & E; SC 10, LC 4; in dept D 19, non-maj 4, maj 15
Ent Req: HS dipl
Degrees: AA(Visual Arts) 2 yrs
Courses: 2-D & 3-D Design, Art for Teachers, Art History, Art Media & Theory, Drawing, Painting, Photography, Printmaking, Sculpture
Adult Hobby Classes: Same courses as above, on and off campus classes
Summer School: Same courses as above

ROME

SHORTER COLLEGE, Art Dept, 315 Shorter Ave, Rome, GA 30165-4267. Tel 706-291-2121; Fax 706-236-1515; Web: www.shorter.edu; *Co-Chair* Brian Taylor; *Prof* Christine Colley
Estab 1873, dept estab 1900; pvt; D; Scholarships; SC 40, LC 7; non-maj 15, maj 20
Ent Req: HS dipl
Degrees: BA(Art) and BFA(Art Ed) 4 yr
Courses: Art Appreciation, Art Education, Art History, †Ceramics, Color Theory, Commercial Art, Design, †Drawing, Graphic Arts, Graphic Design, Illustration, †Mixed Media, †Painting, Photography, Printmaking, †Sculpture, Theatre Arts
Children's Classes: Enrl 20; tuition varies

SAVANNAH

ARMSTRONG ATLANTIC STATE UNIVERSITY, Department of Art, Music & Theatre, 11935 Abercorn St, Savannah, GA 31419-1997. Tel 912-344-2556; Fax 912-344-3419; Web: www.finearts.armstrong.edu; *Chmn* Dr Tom Cato
Maintain nonprofit art gallery; FT 8, PT varies per sem; pub; D&E; Scholarships; SC 35, LC 12, GC 6; Maj 240
Ent Req: Admis to Univ
Degrees: BA, BFA, BS Art Educ
Tuition: $143 per cr hr in-state; $530 per cr hr out-of-state
Courses: †Advertising Design, Art Appreciation, Art Education, Art History, Ceramics, Design, Drawing, Handicrafts, Jewelry, †Mixed Media, Painting, Photography, Printmaking, Sculpture, †Visual Arts, Weaving
Children's Classes: Printing, Sculpture

SAVANNAH COLLEGE OF ART & DESIGN, (SCAD), 342 Bull St, Savannah, GA 31401. Tel 800-869-7223; Email contact@scad.edu; Web: www.scad.edu; *Pres* Paula Wallace
Estab 1978; pvt; D & E
Degrees: BFA, BS, BA, MFA, MS, MA
Tuition: Res—undergrad $35,910, grad $36,765
Courses: Advertising Design, Architecture, Art History, Design, Fashion Arts, Film, Graphic Design, History of Art & Archeology, Illustration, Industrial Design, Intermedia, Jewelry, Mixed Media, Museum Staff Training, Painting, Photography, Printmaking, Sculpture, Stage Design, Textile Design, Theatre Arts

SAVANNAH STATE UNIVERSITY, Dept of Fine Arts, PO Box 20512, Savannah, GA 31404-9708. Tel 912-358-3370; Fax 912-353-3159; *Dir* Dr Peggy Blood, MFA, MA, PhD; *Asst Prof* Nicholas Silberg; *Lectr* Brandon Williams
Estab 1880s, dept estab 1950s; Maintain nonprofit art gallery; pub; D & E; SC 13, LC 3
Ent Req: HS dipl
Degrees: BFA
Tuition: Res—$1700 per sem, nonres—$3800 per sem; campus res available
Courses: Advertising & Editorial Illustration, Art History, Basic Design, Calligraphy, Ceramics, Color Theory, Computer Design, Graphic Design, Interior Design, Painting, Photography, Sculpture, Textile Design, Weaving
Summer School: Dir, Dr Luetta Milledge. Enrl 60; tuition $180. Courses—on demand

STATESBORO

GEORGIA SOUTHERN UNIVERSITY, Betty Foy Sanders Dept of Art, PO Box 8032, Statesboro, GA 30460-1000. Tel 912-478-5358; Fax 912-478-5104; Email art@georgiasouthern.edu; Web: georgiasouthern.edu/art; *Prod* Don Armel, PhD; *Asst Prod* Sarah Bielski, MFA; *Asst Prod* Jessica Burke, MFA; *Prod* Patricia Carter, MFA; *Lectr* Jessica Clevenger, MFA; *Head Dept Prod* Robert Farber, MFA; *Asst Prod* Anthony Faris, MFA; *Asst Prod* Elsie Taliaferro Hill, MFA; *Prof* Jessica Hines, MFA; *Asst Prof* Derek Larson, MFA; *Prod* Christina Lemon, MFA; *Asst Prod* Santanu Majumdar, MFA; *Asst Prod* Hans Mortensen, MS; *Asst Prod* Marc Moulton, MFA; *Prod* Onyile B Onyile, PhD; *Temp Asst Prof* Kimberly Riner, MFA; *Assoc Prod* Edward Rushton, MFA; *Asst Prod* Jeff Schmuki, MFA; *Assoc Prof* Tiffanie Townsend, PhD; *Prod* Patricia Walker, MFA
Estab 1906; maintain a non-profit art gallery, Center for Art & Theatre: Betty Foy Sanders Georgia Artists Coll, Smith Callaway Banks Southern Folk Art Coll, Contemporary Gallery, University Gallery located at 233 Pittman Dr, Statesboro, GA 30460; maintain art/architecture library, Zach S Henderson Library located at 1400 Southern Dr, Statesboro, GA 30460; on-campus shop where art supplies may be purchased; pub; D & E; Scholarships; SC 69, LC 24, GC 37
Activities: Schols offered to dept majors
Ent Req: HS dipl
Degrees: BA, BFA, BS, MFA
Tuition: $3,086 per 12 hour semester
Courses: †Animation, Art History, Ceramics, Commercial Art, †Conceptual Art, Constructions, Drawing, Graphic Arts, †Graphic Communication Management, Graphic Design, †History of Art & Architecture, Lettering, Mixed Media, †New Media, Painting, Photography, Printmaking, Sculpture, †Silversmithing, †Video
Children's Classes: Offered in Laboratory School & Sat Program

THOMASVILLE

THOMAS UNIVERSITY, Humanities Division, 1501 Mill Pond Rd, Thomasville, GA 31792. Tel 229-226-1621, Ext 142; Fax 229-226-1653; Web: www.thomas.edu; *Asst Prof of Art* James Adams; *Div Chmn* Ann Landis
Scholarships
Degrees: AA
Tuition: $250 per cr hr
Courses: Art Appreciation, Art Education, Drawing, Painting
Adult Hobby Classes: Enrl 30; 2 terms (quarters) per yr. Courses—Art Structure
Children's Classes: Courses offered on demand
Summer School: Enrl 60; summer quarter. Courses—same as regular yr

TIFTON

ABRAHAM BALDWIN AGRICULTURAL COLLEGE, Art & Humanities Dept, 2802 Moore Hwy, ABAC Sta Tifton, GA 31794-5698. Tel 912-386-3236, 386-3250; Web: www.abac.peachnet.edu; *Pres* Homer Day
Degrees: Cert AA
Tuition: Res $832 per sem; nonres $2572 per sem
Courses: Art Appreciation, Art History, Design, Drawing, Painting

VALDOSTA

VALDOSTA STATE UNIVERSITY, Dept of Art, 1500 N Patterson St, Valdosta, GA 31698-0001. Tel 229-333-5835; Fax 229-259-5121; Email apearce@valdosta.edu; *Dept Head* A Blake Pearce
Estab 1906; Maintains nonprofit gallery, Valdosta State University Art Gallery; FT 17; pub; D&E; Scholarships; SC 25, LC 10; maj 310, total 11,800
Ent Req: SAT or ACT
Degrees: BA, BFA (Int Des), BFA (Art Ed) & BFA (Art) 4 yr
Courses: Advertising Design, Aesthetics, Art Appreciation, †Art Education, Art History, Ceramics, Collage, Commercial Art, Computer Graphics, Constructions, Design, Drawing, Graphic Arts, Graphic Design, History of Art & Architecture, Illustration, †Interior Design, Intermedia, Lettering, Mixed Media, Painting, Photography, Portfolio Preparation, Printmaking, Sculpture, Teacher Training
Summer School: Tuition res—$155 per qtr hr for 4 or 8 wk term. Courses—Art Appreciation, Computer Graphics, Design, Studio

YOUNG HARRIS

YOUNG HARRIS COLLEGE, Dept of Art, 1 College St, Young Harris, GA 30582-4137; PO Box 68, Young Harris, GA 30582-0068. Tel 706-379-3111; Fax 706-379-4306; Web: www.yhc.edu; *Chmn* Richard Aunspaugh
Estab 1886; Maintain nonprofit art gallery; Clegg Art Gallery, PO Box 236, Young Harris, GA 30582; FT 2; pvt; D; Scholarships; SC 5, LC 1; D 450, maj 25
Ent Req: HS dipl
Degrees: AFA 2 yr
Courses: Art Appreciation, Art History, Design, Drawing, Painting, Sculpture, Stage Design, Theatre Arts

HAWAII

HAIKU

THE ASHLAND ACADEMY OF ART, 222 Laniloa Way, Haiku, HI 96708-5381. Tel 541-482-3567; Fax 541-482-0994; Email info@ashlandacademyofart.com; Web: www.ashlandacademyofart.com

HONOLULU

HONOLULU COMMUNITY COLLEGE, Commercial Art Dept, 874 Dillingham Blvd, Honolulu, HI 96817-4598. Tel 808-845-9211; Fax 808-845-9173; Web: www.hcc.hawaii.edu; *Dept Head* Sandra Sanpei; *Instr Commercial Art* Michel Kaiser; *Instr Graphic Arts* Romolo Valencia, BA

College maintains three art departments: Commercial Art, Art & Graphic Arts; pub; D & E; SC 20, LC 2; D 150 majors
Ent Req: 18 yrs of age, English & math requirements, motivation, interest in learning, willingness to work
Degrees: AS 2 yr
Courses: Advertising Design, Commercial Art, Drafting, Drawing, Graphic Arts, Graphic Design, Illustration, Lettering, Painting, Photography, Printmaking, Textile Design

UNIVERSITY OF HAWAII, Kapiolani Community College, 4303 Diamond Head Rd, Honolulu, HI 96816-4421. Tel 808-734-9282; Fax 808-734-9151; *Chmn* Kauka de Silva
Estab 1965; FT 8, PT 7; pub; D & E; Scholarships; SC 11, LC 5; D 4800, E 500
Ent Req: ent exam
Degrees: AA and AS 1-2 yr
Tuition: No campus res
Courses: Art Appreciation, Art History, Ceramics, Computer Graphics, Conceptual Art, Design, Drawing, History of Art & Architecture, Painting, Photography, Sculpture
Adult Hobby Classes: Enrl 15 per class; tuition depends on number of units. Courses—Art Appreciation, Art History, Ceramics, Color Theory, Computer Graphics, Conceptual Art, Design

UNIVERSITY OF HAWAII AT MANOA, Dept of Art, 2535 McCarthy Mall, Honolulu, HI 96822-2233. Tel 808-956-8251; Fax 808-956-9043; Email uhart@hawaii.edu; Web: www.hawaii.edu/art; *Dept Chair* Gaye Chan; *Assoc Chair* Frank Beaver; *Dir Gallery* Tom Klobe
Estab 1907; FT 26, PT 25; pub; D; Scholarships; SC 64, LC 34; maj 450, grad 40
Ent Req: HS dipl or GED and SAT or ACT
Degrees: BA(Art History), BA(Studio), BFA 4 yr, MA & MFA
Courses: Aesthetics, Art Appreciation, †Art History, Calligraphy, †Ceramics, Design, †Drawing, †Fiber Arts, †Glass, Graphic Arts, †Graphic Design, †Intermedia, Mixed Media, Museum Staff Training, †Painting, †Photography, †Printmaking, Sculpture, Textile Design, Video
Adult Hobby Classes: Drawing, Painting, Sculpture
Summer School: Dean, Victor Kobayashi. Tuition $123 per cr hr, non res $130 per cr hr, plus fees. Courses—Art History (Western, Asian & Pacific), Ceramics, Drawing, Design, Fiber, Glass, Painting, Photography, Printmaking, Sculpture

KAHULUI

MAUI COMMUNITY COLLEGE, Art Program, 310 Kaahumanu Ave, Kahului, HI 96732-1644. Tel 808-244-9181; Web: mauicc.hawaii.edu; *Div Chmn* Dorothy Pyle
Estab 1967; FT 1, PT 3; pub; D & E; Scholarships; SC 8, LC 2; 2600
Ent Req: ent exam
Degrees: AA, AAF, AS, 2 yr Cert (ACH)
Courses: Advertising Design, Architecture, †Batik, †Ceramics, Copper Enameling, Display, †Drawing, Graphic Arts, Graphic Design, History of Architecture, †History of Art & Architecture, Jewelry, †Painting, †Photography, Sculpture, †Textile Design, †Weaving, Welding
Adult Hobby Classes: Enrl 200. Courses—Art, Art History, Ceramics, Drawing, Intro to Visual Art, Painting

LAIE

BRIGHAM YOUNG UNIVERSITY, HAWAII CAMPUS, Division of Fine Arts, 55-220 Kulanui St, Laie, HI 96762-1294. Tel 808-293-3211; Fax 808-293-3645, 293-3900; *Chmn* Dr Jeffrey Belnap
Scholarships
Degrees: BA
Tuition: Church mem $2035 per sem; non church mem $1837 per sem
Courses: †Ceramics, †Painting, Polynesian Handicrafts, †Printmaking, †Sculpture
Summer School: Dir, V Napua Tengaio. Tuition $60 per cr, 2 four wk blocks. Courses—Ceramics, Polynesian Handicrafts

LIHUE

KAUAI COMMUNITY COLLEGE, Dept of Art, 3-1901 Kaumualii, Lihue, HI 96766. Tel 808-245-8284, 245-8226; Fax 808-245-8220; *Faculty* Wayne A Miyata, MFA; *Faculty* Waihang Lai, MA
Estab 1965; FT 2, PT 1; pub; D & E; Scholarships; SC 6, LC 2; D 965, E 468
Ent Req: HS dipl
Degrees: AA and AS 2 yr
Courses: Art History, Ceramics, Drawing, Oriental Brush Painting, Painting, Photography
Summer School: Term of 6 wk beginning June and July

PEARL CITY

LEEWARD COMMUNITY COLLEGE, Arts & Humanities Division, 96-045 Ala Ike, Pearl City, HI 96782. Tel 808-455-0228; Fax 808-455-0638; Web: www.lcc.hawaii.edu; *Dean* Dr Mark Silliman
Estab 1968; pub; D & E; Scholarships; SC 11, LC 3; D 400, E 100
Ent Req: over 18 yrs of age
Degrees: AA & AS 2 yrs
Tuition: Res—$32 per cr hr; nonres—$213 per cr hr
Courses: 2-D Design, 3-D Design, Art History, Aspects of Asian Art, Ceramics, Costume Design & Construction, Drawing, Graphic Arts, Painting, Photography, Printmaking, Sculpture, Theatre Arts
Summer School: Enrl 100; Term of 7 wks beginning June 12th. Courses—vary

IDAHO

BOISE

BOISE STATE UNIVERSITY, Art Dept, 1910 University Dr, Boise, ID 83725-1510. Tel 208-426-1230; Fax 208-426-1243; Email artdept@boisestate.edu; Web: www.boisestate.edu/art; *Chmn* Dr Lee Ann Turner; *Chmn* Kathleen Keys
Estab 1932; maintains visual arts center; on-campus shop sells art supplies; pub; D & E; Scholarships; SC 51, LC 8, GC 4; D 2539, maj 550, GS 14
Ent Req: HS dipl; portfolio admis
Degrees: BA, BFA, BFA(Art Educ), BFA(Graphic Design), BA (History of Art & Visual Culture), BFA(Illustration), BFA(Visual Arts), BFA(Graphic Design) 4 yr, MFA(Visual Arts), MA(Art Educ) 4 yr
Courses: †Art Education, Art History, †Art Metals, Ceramics, Design, Drawing, †Graphic Design, †Illustration, Painting, Photography, Printmaking, Sculpture

COEUR D'ALENE

NORTH IDAHO COLLEGE, Art Dept, 1000 W Garden Ave, Coeur D'Alene, ID 83814-2199. Tel 208-769-3300; Fax 208-769-7880; Web: www.nic.edu; *Dept Chmn* Allie Vogt, MA; *Instr* Lisa Lynes, MA
Degrees: BA, AA
Tuition: Res—in county $564 per sem, $79 per cr hr, $69 each additional cr hr; nonres—$1942 per sem, $251 per cr hr,$241 each additional cr hr
Courses: Art Appreciation, Art History, Ceramics, Design, Drawing, Graphic Design, Illustration, Letter Form, Life Drawing, Painting, Photography, Portfolio, Professional Advertising, Sculpture, Stage Design, Weaving

LEWISTON

LEWIS-CLARK STATE COLLEGE, Art Dept, 500 Eighth Ave, Lewiston, ID 83501-2691. Tel 208-746-2341; Web: www.lcsc.edu; *Prof* Lawrence Haapanen
Estab 1893; Maintains reference library; FT 1; pub; D & E; Scholarships; SC 10, LC 1; D 89, E 43
Ent Req: HS dipl or GED, ACT
Degrees: BA and BS 4 yrs
Courses: Art Education, Composition, Drawing, Graphic Arts, Independent Study, Painting, Stage Design, Teacher Training, Theatre Arts, Video
Adult Hobby Classes: Discipline Coordr, Robert Almquist, MFA

MOSCOW

UNIVERSITY OF IDAHO COLLEGE OF ART & ARCHITECTURE, Dept of Art & Design, 875 Perimeter Dr, MS 2471 Moscow, ID 83844-2471. Tel 208-885-6851; Fax 208-885-9428; Email artdesign@uidaho.edu; Web: www.uidaho.edu/caa/artdesign; *Prof & Dept Chair* Prof Sally Machlis; *Sr Instr* Val Carter; *Asst Prof* Marco Deyasi; *Asst Prof* Casey Doyle; *Asst Prof* Stacy Isenbarger; *Asst Prof* Dave Gottwald; *Asst Prof* Mike Sonnichsen; *Asst Prof* Nishiki Sugawara-Beda; *Assoc Prof* Delphine Keim; *Assoc Prof* Greg Turner-Rahman
Estab 1889; Supplies may be purchased on campus; maintains a non-profit art gallery, U of I Prichard Art Gallery, 414 S. Main St., Moscow, ID 83843; Pub; D & E; Scholarships; SC 35, LC 17, GC 14
Ent Req: HS dipl or equivalent
Degrees: BA, BFA, MFA
Courses: †Art Appreciation, †Art Education, Art History, Ceramics, †Drawing, Graphic Design, Interaction Design, †Mixed Media, Painting, Photography, Printmaking, Sculpture, Visual Communication
Summer School: Courses—vary

NAMPA

NORTHWEST NAZARENE COLLEGE, Art Dept, 623 Holly St, Nampa, ID 83686-5855. Tel 208-467-8011; Web: www.nnu.edu; *Art Head* Jim Willis
FT 3; Den; D & E; Scholarships; SC 12, LC 5; D 200, E 40, maj 24
Ent Req: HS dipl
Degrees: BA & BS 4 yr
Courses: Art Education, Ceramics, Crafts for Teachers, Drawing, Graphic Design, History of Art & Architecture, Illustration, Painting, Printmaking, Sculpture, Teacher Training
Adult Hobby Classes: Crafts, Painting
Summer School: Courses—Art Education

POCATELLO

IDAHO STATE UNIVERSITY, Dept of Art, 921 S 8th Ave, Stop 8004 Pocatello, ID 83209. Tel 208-282-2361, 282-2488; Fax 208-282-4741; Email adamjef2@isu.edu; Web: www.isu.edu; *Chmn* Jeffrey Adams, MFA; *Faculty* Doug Warnock, MFA; *Faculty* Scott Evans, MFA; *Faculty* Naomi Adams, MFA; *Faculty* Dr Andrea Ferber, PhD; *Assoc Lectr* Amy Jo Popa, MFA; *Faculty* Laura Ahola-Young; *Asst Lectr* Ryan Babcock, MFA; *Adjunct* Juliet Feige, MFA; *Asst Lectr* Paul Dodez, MFA; *Affiliate Faculty* Linda Leeuwrik, PhD; *Adjunct* Lynne Parker; *Adjunct* Kirk Young
Estab 1901; Maintains nonprofit John B Davis Gallery of Art & Compartment Gallery, Eli Obler Library; ISU Craft Shop sells art supplies; pub; D & E; Scholarships; Fellowships; SC 32, LC 6, GS 22; maj 75, GS 15, total 500
Ent Req: HS dipl, GED, ACT
Degrees: BA, BFA and MFA 4 yr
Courses: 3D Design, Art Education, Art History, Ceramics, Design, Drawing, Fiber Media, Metals, Painting, Papermaking, Printmaking, Sculpture, Silversmithing, Textile Design, Weaving

Adult Hobby Classes: Enrl 20; tuition $45 for 6 wk term. Courses—Drawing, Landscape Painting
Children's Classes: Enrl 20; tuition $40 for 8 wk term. Courses—Vary
Summer School: Dir/Chair, Anthony Martin & Dean, Kandi Turley-Ames. Enrl 75. Courses—Art History, Ceramics

REXBURG

RICKS COLLEGE, Dept of Art, 16 E Main St, Rexburg, ID 83460-9514. Tel 208-356-2913, 356-4871; *Instr* Scott Franson; *Instr* Vince Bodily; *Instr* Gerald Griffin; *Instr* Mathew Geddes; *Instr* Leon Parson; *Instr* Gary Pearson; *Chmn* Kelly Burgner
Estab 1888; pvt; D & E; Scholarships; SC 23, LC 1; D 123, maj 123
Ent Req: HS dipl
Degrees: AAS, AAdv Design and AFA 2 yrs
Courses: Art Appreciation, Art Education, Art History, Ceramics, Drawing, †Fine Art, †Graphic Design, Illustration, Painting, †Photography, Typography
Adult Hobby Classes: Enrl 150. Courses—Art History, Introduction to Visual Arts
Summer School: Dir, Jim Gee. Enrl 370; tuition $60 per cr hr. Courses—Art History, Ceramics, Drawing, Graphic Design, Illustration, Photography

SUN VALLEY

SUN VALLEY CENTER FOR THE ARTS, Dept of Fine Art, PO Box 656, Sun Valley, ID 83353-0656. Tel 208-726-9491; Fax 208-726-2344; Web: www.sunvalleycenter.org; *Artistic Dir* Kristin Poole; *Dir Educ* Britt Udesen; *Exec Dir* Sam Gappmayer; *Cur Visual Arts* Courtney Gilbert
Estab 1971; Maintain a nonprofit art gallery; D, E & weekends; SC
Ent Req: Some dance require prior exp
Courses: †Calligraphy, †Ceramics, †Collage, †Drafting, †Lettering, †Mixed Media, †Painting, †Photography, †Printmaking, †Sculpture
Adult Hobby Classes: Calligraphy, Ceramics, UFE Drawing
Children's Classes: Enrl vary per sem. Courses—Ceramics
Summer School: Dir, Britt Udesen. Courses—Ceramics, Mixed Media, Painting from Nature, Photography, Watercolor

TWIN FALLS

COLLEGE OF SOUTHERN IDAHO, Art Dept, PO Box 1238, Twin Falls, ID 83303-1238. Tel 208-733-9554, Ext 344; Fax 208-736-3014; Web: www.csi.cc.id.us; WATS 800-680-0274; *Assoc Prof* Russell Hepworth, MFA; *Chmn* Mike Green, MFA
Estab 1965; pub; D & E; Scholarships; SC 26, LC 2; D 3000, E 2000, non-maj 50, maj 45
Ent Req: HS dipl, ACT
Degrees: dipl or AA
Tuition: campus res—room & board
Courses: Art History, Ceramics, Design, Drawing, Lettering, Mixed Media, Painting, Papermaking, Photography, Printmaking, Sculpture, Theatre Arts
Children's Classes: Enrl 50; tuition $20 per class. Courses—Crafts, Drawing, Photography, Pottery
Summer School: Dir Jerry Beck. Courses—Art General, Crafts, Drawing, Papermaking, Pottery

ILLINOIS

AURORA

AURORA UNIVERSITY, Art Dept, 347 S Gladstone Ave, Aurora, IL 60506-4892. Tel 630-844-5519; Email jkao@aurora.edu; Web: www.aurora.edu; *Asst Prof of Art* James Kao
Estab 1893, dept estab 1979; Maintain nonprofit art gallery; Downstairs Dunham Gallery, Dunham Hall; pvt; D; SC 7, LC 1; D 102, E 96, non-maj 171
Ent Req: HS dipl
Degrees: BA 4 yrs
Courses: 2-D Design, 3-D Design, Art Appreciation, Drawing, Media Technology, Painting, Photography, Sculpture
Summer School: Courses—Photography, Media Technology

BELLEVILLE

SOUTHWESTERN ILLINOIS COLLEGE, (Belleville Area College) Art Dept, 2500 Carlyle Ave, Belleville, IL 62221-5899. Tel 618-235-2700; Web: www.southwestern.cc.il.us; *Dept Head* Jerry Bolen
Estab 1948; pub; D & E; Scholarships; SC 36, LC 9; D 4000, E 3500, maj 200
Ent Req: HS dipl
Degrees: AA and AS 2 yrs
Courses: Advertising Design, Art Appreciation, Art Education, Art History, Calligraphy, Ceramics, Commercial Art, Design, Drawing, Film, Graphic Arts, Graphic Design, History of Art & Architecture, Jewelry, Lettering, Painting, Photography, Printmaking, Sculpture, Theatre Arts, Video
Summer School: Dept Head, Jerry Bolen. Tuition $30 per hr for 8 wks. Courses—Art History, Ceramics, Drawing, Photography

BLOOMINGTON

ILLINOIS WESLEYAN UNIVERSITY, School of Art, PO Box 2900, Bloomington, IL 61702-2900. Tel 309-556-1000 (information), 556-3077 (school of art), 556-2993 (Dir); Web: www.iwu.edu; *Instr* Connie Estep, MFA; *Instr* Kristine Nielsen, PhD, MFA; *Instr* Kevin Strandberg, MFA; *Director/Interim & Instr* Julie Johnson, MFA; *Adjunct Instr* Carmen Lozar
Estab 1855, school estab 1946; pvt; D & E; Scholarships; SC, LC; non-maj 150, maj 60
Ent Req: HS dipl, SAT or ACT
Degrees: BA, BFA
Courses: Art History, Ceramics, Digital Photography, Drawing, Graphic Design, Painting, Photography, Printmaking, Sculpture

BOURBONNAIS

OLIVET NAZARENE UNIVERSITY, Dept of Art, 1 University Ave, Bourbonnais, IL 60915-2345. Tel 815-939-5229, 939-5172; Fax 815-939-5112; Email bgreiner@olivet.edu; Web: www.olivet.edu; *Prof & Chair* William Greiner
Estab 1907, dept estab 1953; Maintain a nonprofit art gallery: Brandenburg Gallery, Larsen Fine Arts Bldg; FT 3, PT 3; den; D & E; Scholarships; SC 14, LC 4; D 100, non-maj 80, maj 21
Ent Req: HS dipl
Degrees: MBA, BS & BA 4 yrs, MEd & MTheol 2 yrs
Courses: †Art Education, Art History, †Ceramics, Drawing, Film, Graphic Arts, Graphic Design, Lettering, †Painting, Photography, Printmaking, Sculpture, Teacher Training, Textile Design

CANTON

SPOON RIVER COLLEGE, Art Dept, 23235 N County Hwy 22, Canton, IL 61520. Tel 309-647-4645; Fax 309-647-6498; Web: www.src.edu; *Instr* Tracy Snowman; *Dir* Dr Sue Spencer
College maintains three campuses; Scholarships
Degrees: AA
Tuition: $42 per cr hr
Courses: Ceramics, Design, Drawing, Painting, Sculpture

CARBONDALE

SOUTHERN ILLINOIS UNIVERSITY, School of Art & Design, 1100 S Normal Ave, Mail Code 4301 Carbondale, IL 62901-4301. Tel 618-453-4315; Fax 618-453-7710; Web: www.artanddesign.siuc.edu; *Prof* Harris Deller, MFA; *Undergrad Acad Adv* Valerie Brooks, MS Ed; *Prof, Head Grad Studies & Studio Area Head* Jerry Monteith, MFA; *Asst Dir & Prof* Kay M Zivkovich, MFA; *Assoc Prof* Erin Palmer, MFA; *Prof & Studio Area Head* Richard E Smith, MFA; *Assoc Prof & Acad Area Head* Carma Gorman PhD; *Dir & Prof* Peter Chametzky, PhD; *Assoc Prof* Jiyong Lee, MFA; *Assoc Prof & Head Undergrad Studies* Najjar Abdul-Musawwir, MFA; *Prof & Design Area Head* Steve Belletire, BFA; *Prof* Xuhong Shang, MFA; *Asst Prof* Pattie Chalmers, MFA; *Assoc Prof* Stacey Sloboda, PhD; *Asst Prof* Alex Lopez, MFA; *Assoc Prof* Sally Gradle, PhD; *Coordr Visual Resources/Facilitator Web Enhanced Curriculum* Eric Peterson, BA; *Asst Prof* Barbara Bickel, PhD; *Asst Prof* Sun Kyoung Kim, MFA; *Asst Prof* Robert A Lopez, MFA; *Asst Prof* Aaron Scott, MFA; *Asst Prof* Mark Pease, MFA
Estab 1874; Maintain nonprofit art library - School of Art & Design Surplus Gallery at the Glove Factory, 432 S Washington, SIUC, Carbondale, IL 62901, School of Art Design, Vergette Gallery, located on the first floor of the Allyn Bldg, in room 107; art supplies available on-campus; pub; D & E; Scholarships; SC 100, LC 24, GC 28; D 1304, E 338, non-maj 400, maj 400, grad 60, others 400
Ent Req: HS dipl, upper 50 percent of class, ACT
Degrees: BA, BFA 4 yrs, MFA 3 yrs
Tuition: Res—undergrad $4,740, grad $5,826, undergrad $260 per cr hr, grad $351 per cr hr; nonres—undergrad $9,416, grad $12,137 per sem, undergrad $650 per cr hr, grad $877 per cr hr; campus res—available
Courses: Advertising Design, Aesthetics, †Art Education, Art for Elementary Education, †Art History, †Blacksmithing, †Ceramics, Collage, Commercial Art, †Communication Design, Conceptual Art, Constructions, †Design, Drafting, †Drawing, †Foundry, †Glassblowing, Goldsmithing, Graphic Arts, †Graphic Design, †History of Art & Architecture, †Industrial Design, †Jewelry, Lettering, Mixed Media, Museum Staff Training, †Painting, †Printmaking, †Sculpture, Silversmithing, †Teacher Training, Web Design
Adult Hobby Classes: Drawing, Jewelry, Painting
Children's Classes: Enrl 150; tuition $30 per 4-6 wk term. Courses—Ceramics, Drawing, Fibers, Jewelry, Mask-Making, Painting, Papermaking, Printing, Sculpture, 3-D Design
Summer School: 500; tuition undergrad res $243 per hr, grad res $328 for term of 2-8 wks beginning May. Courses—selection from regular courses
—**Applied Arts,** 1365 Douglas Dr, Mail Code 6604 Carbondale, IL 62901-2583. Tel 618-453-8863; *Prog Rep* David White
Art Dept estab 1960; 5; pub; D; D 65, maj 65
Ent Req: HS dipl, ent exam
Degrees: AAS 2 yr, BS 4 yr
Tuition: Res—undergrad $75.00 per cr hr; nonres—undergrad $225.00 per cr hr
Courses: Air Brush & Photo Retouching, Drawing, Graphic Design

CARLINVILLE

BLACKBURN COLLEGE, Dept of Art, 700 College Ave, Carlinville, IL 62626-1401. Tel 217-854-3231, Ext 235; Fax 217-854-3713; Web: www.blackburn.edu/; *Prof* James M Clark, MFA; *Chmn* Melba Buxbaum
Estab 1837; FT 2, PT 2; pvt; D & E; Scholarships; SC 14, LC 7; maj 15
Ent Req: HS grad
Degrees: BA 4 yrs
Courses: †Art History, Ceramics, Drawing, Painting, Printmaking, Sculpture, Studio Art, †Teacher Training, Theatre Arts

CHAMPAIGN

UNIVERSITY OF ILLINOIS, URBANA-CHAMPAIGN, College of Fine & Applied Arts, 608 E Lorado Taft Dr, 100 Architecture Bldg Champaign, IL 61820-6922. Tel 217-333-1660; Email FAA@illinois.edu; Web: faa.illinois.edu; *Dean* Edward Feser; *Exec Asst Dean* Paul Redman; *Assoc Dean* Linda Robbennolt; *Assoc Dean* Mary Edwards; *Assoc Dean* Kevin Hamilton
Estab 1931; FT 268, PT 150; pub; D; Fellowships; undergrad 2000, grad 750
Ent Req: HS grad, ent exam
Degrees: bachelors 4 yrs, Masters, Doctorate
Adult Hobby Classes: Scheduled through University Extension
Children's Classes: Sat; summer youth classes
Summer School: courses offered
—**School of Art & Design**, 408 E Peabody Dr, 143 Art & Design Bldg Champaign, IL 61820-6924. Tel 217-333-0855; Fax 217-244-7688; Web: www.art.illinois.edu; *Dir, Prof* Nan Goggin, MFA; *Exec Assoc Dir, Prof* Alan T Mette, MFA; *Assoc Dir, Prof* Joseph Squier, MFA; *Asst Dir Grad Studies, Assoc Prof* Conrad Bakker, MFA
Estab 1867, dept estab 1877; pub; D & E; Scholarships; SC 119, LC 72, GC 77; maj 521, grad 100, others 10
Ent Req: HS dipl, ACT, SAT, CLEP
Degrees: BFA 4 yrs, MA 2 yrs, MFA 2-3 yrs, EdD & PhD 5 yrs
Tuition: Res—undergrad $8542 per yr, $4271 per sem; res—grad $8358 per yr, $4179 per sem; nonres—undergrad $22,628 per yr, $11,314 per sem, nonres—grad $21,168 per yr, $10,584 per sem; campus res—room & board $7716 for double
Courses: Art Education, Art History, Drawing, Graphic Design, Industrial Design, Metals, Mixed Media, Painting, Photography, Printmaking, Sculpture, †Video
Adult Hobby Classes: Enrl 150; tuition varies. Courses—Art History, Art Education, Studio
Children's Classes: 220; tuition $75 per sem. Courses—Creative Arts for Children
Summer School: Courses—foundation & lower division courses with some limited offerings & independent study at upper division & graduate levels

CHARLESTON

EASTERN ILLINOIS UNIVERSITY, Art Dept, 600 Lincoln Ave Charleston, IL 61920. Tel 217-581-3410; Fax 217-581-6199; Email artdept@eiu.edu; Web: www.eiu.edu/~artdept; *Dept Chmn* Glenn Hild, MFA; *Prof* Denise Rehm-Mott, MFA; *Prof* Charles Nivens, MFA; *Prof* Janet Marquardt-Cherry, PhD; *Prof* Mary Leonard-Cravens, MFA; *Prof* Jeff Boshart, MFA; *Prof* David Griffin, MFA; *Prof* Eugene Harrison; *Prof* Dwain Naragon, MFA; *Prof* Stephen Eskilson, PhD; *Prof* Patricia Belleville; *Prof* Chris Kahler, MFA; *Assoc Prof* Ke-Hsin Chi, MFA; *Assoc Prof* Ann Coddington Rast, MFA; *Assoc Prof* Robert Petersen, PhD; *Asst Prof* Dave Richardson, MFA; *Asst Prof* Mary Simpson, PhD
Estab 1895, dept estab 1930; Maintain nonprofit art gallery, Tarble Arts Center, 600 Lincoln Ave, Charleston, IL 61920; FT 18, PT 1; pub; D & E; Scholarships; SC 60, LC 27, GC 25; non-maj 724, maj 219, grad 11
Ent Req: HS dipl, ACT
Degrees: BA 4 yrs, MA 1 yr, Specialist Educ 2 yrs
Tuition: AY13 for IL & bordering state residents $279 per credit hr
Courses: Art Appreciation, †Art Education, Art History, Ceramics, Drawing, †Graphic Design, Jewelry, Painting, Printmaking, Sculpture, Studio Art
Summer School: Enrl 95; tuition varies depending on faculty teaching; AY13 for IL & bordering state residents $279 per credit hr Courses—Same as regular session

CHICAGO

AMERICAN ACADEMY OF ART, 332 S Michigan Ave, Chicago, IL 60604-4434. Tel 312-461-0600; Fax 312-294-9570; Email info@aaart.edu; Web: www.aaart.edu; *Dir Educ* Duncan J Webb; *Pres* Richard H Otto
Estab 1923; Maintain nonprofit gallery, Bill L Parks Gallery, on-site; Art & Architecture Library: Irving Shapiro Library, on-site; FT 17, PT 22; pvt; D & E; Scholarships; SC 13, LC; D 406
Ent Req: HS dipl, portfolio
Degrees: BFA
Courses: †3-D Animation, †Advertising Design, Art History, Commercial Art, Design, †Drawing, †Electronic Design, Graphic Arts, †Graphic Design, History of Art & Architecture, †Illustration, †Multimedia/Web Design, †Painting, †Photography, †Sculpture, †Video

CITY COLLEGES OF CHICAGO, Daley College, 7500 S Pulaski Rd, Art & Architecture Dept Chicago, IL 60652-1369. Tel 773-838-7721; Web: www.cc.edu/daley/; *Prof* A Lerner; *Prof* T Palazzolo; *Prof* C Grenda; *Prof* M Rosen; *Prof* D Wiedemann; *Chmn* David Riter
Estab 1960; 5500
Degrees: AA
Tuition: In-county res— $47.50 per cr hr; out-of-county res—$140.36 per cr hr; out-of-state res—$210.45 per cr hr
Courses: Architecture, Art Appreciation, Art History, Ceramics, Design, Drawing, Handicrafts, Painting, Photography, Weaving
—**Kennedy-King College**, 6800 S Wentworth Ave, Art & Humanities Dept Chicago, IL 60621-3733. Tel 773-291-6518; Web: www.ccc.edu/kennedyking/; *Chmn* Dr Thomas Roby
Estab 1935; Enrl 9010
Degrees: AA, AS
Tuition: In-county res—$47.50 per cr hr; out-of-county res—$92.86 per cr hr; out-of-state res—$162.85 per cr hr
Courses: Art Appreciation, Ceramics, Humanities, Painting, Photography
—**Harold Washington College**, 30 E Lake St, Art & Humanities Dept, Rm 406 Chicago, IL 60601-2408. Tel 773-553-6065; 5600; Web: www.ccc.edu/hwashington/; *Chmn Humanities* Paul Urbanick
Estab 1962; Enrl 8000
Degrees: AA, AS
Tuition: In-county res—$47.50 per cr hr; out-of-county res—$145.48 per cr hr; out-of-state res—$204.34 per cr hr
Courses: Art Appreciation, Ceramics, Commercial Art, Humanities, Painting, Photography, Printmaking, Sculpture
—**Malcolm X College**, 1900 W Van Buren St, Art and Humanities Dept Chicago, IL 60612-3145. Tel 312-850-7324; Fax 773-850-3323; Web: www.cc.edu/malcolmx/; *Asst Prof* Barbara J Hogu; *Chmn Humanities* Mark Schwertley
Estab 1911; Enrl 5000
Degrees: AA
Tuition: In-county res—$47.50 per cr hr; out-of-county res—$92.86 per cr hr
Courses: Art Appreciation, Drawing, Freehand Drawing, Individual Projects
—**Olive-Harvey College**, 10001 S Woodlawn Ave, Art and Humanities Dept Chicago, IL 60628-1645. Tel 773-291-6530; 6534; Web: www.ccc.edu/oliveharvey/acaddep/humani/index; *Chmn Humanities* Richard Reed
Estab 1957; Enrl 4700
Degrees: AA, Liberal Arts
Tuition: In-county res—$47.50 per cr hr; out-of-county res—$98.86 per cr hr; out-of-state res—$162.85 per cr hr
Courses: Art Appreciation, Arts & Crafts, Ceramics, Color Photography, Painting, Photography, Visual Arts Photography
—**Truman College**, 1145 W Wilson Ave, Art & Humanities Dept Chicago, IL 60640-6063. Tel 773-907-4062; Fax 773-907-4464; Web: www.ccc.edu/truman; *Chmn Humanities* Dr Michael Swisher
Estab 1956; Enrl 3800
Degrees: AA, AAS
Tuition: In-county res—$47.50 per cr hr; out-of-county res—$92.86 per cr hr; out-of-state res—$162.85 per cr hr
Courses: Ceramics, Painting, Photography
—**Wright College**, 3400 N Austin Ave, Art Dept Chicago, IL 60634-4229. Tel 773-481-8365; Web: www.ccc.edu/wright/; *Chmn* James Mack
Estab 1934; FT 3; pub; D & E; SC 15, LC 8; D 3000, E 2500
Ent Req: HS dipl
Degrees: AA, AS
Tuition: In-county res— $47.50 per cr hr; out-of-county res—$92.86 per cr hr; out-of-state res—$162.85 per cr hr
Courses: Arts & Crafts, Ceramics, Drawing, Lettering, Painting, Photography, Sculpture, Visual Arts
Adult Hobby Classes: Enrl 400; tuition $15 per course for 6 or 7 wks. Courses—Drawing, Fashion, Painting, Watercolor
Summer School: Dir, Roy LeFevour. Enrl 24; 8 wk session. Courses—Vary

COLUMBIA COLLEGE, Art Dept, 600 S Michigan Ave, Chicago, IL 60605-1900. Tel 312-663-1600; Fax 312-987-9893; *Coordr Graphics* Marlene Lipinski, MFA; *Architectural-Grad Studies & Coordr Interior Design* Joclyn Oats, BFA; *Coordr Fine Arts* Tom Taylor, BFA; *Coordr Illustration* Fred Nelson, BFA; *Coordr Fashion Design* Dennis Brozynski, BFA; *Coordr Pkg Designs* Kevin Henry, BFA
Estab 1893; pvt; D & E; Scholarships; SC 43, LC 17
Ent Req: HS dipl
Degrees: BA 4 yrs, MFA
Tuition: Res—undergrad $5800 per sem, $396 per cr hr; no campus res
Courses: Advertising Design, Architecture, Art Education, Art History, Calligraphy, Ceramics, Commercial Art, Drafting, Drawing, Fashion Arts, Film, Graphic Arts, Graphic Design, Handicrafts, Illustration, Industrial Design, Interior Design, Jewelry, Mixed Media, Painting, Printmaking, Sculpture, Silk Screen, Typography

DEPAUL UNIVERSITY, Dept of Art, 1150 W Fullerton Ave, College of Liberal Arts & Sciences Chicago, IL 60614-8160. Tel 312-362-8194; Fax 312-362-5684; Web: www.depaul.edu; *Gallery Dir* Robert Tavani, MFA; *Prof* Robert Donley, MFA; *Assoc Prof* Simone Zurawski, PhD, MFA; *Assoc Prof* Elizabeth Lillehoj, PhD, MFA; *Assoc Prof* Bibiana Swarez, MFA; *Asst Prof* Jenny Morlan, MFA; *Asst Prof* Paul Jaskot, PhD, MFA; *Asst Prof* Mark Pohlad PhD, MFA; *Chmn Dept* Stephen Luecking, MFA
Estab 1897, dept estab 1965; pvt; D; Scholarships; SC 20, LC 12; D 150 art maj
Ent Req: HS dipl, SAT or ACT
Degrees: BA(Art) 4 yrs
Tuition: All tuition fees are subject to change, contact admissions office for current fees; campus res available
Courses: †Advertising Design, Aesthetics, Architecture, Art Appreciation, †Art History, Ceramics, Computer Graphics, Design, †Drawing, Film, Graphic Arts, †Graphic Design, Illustration, Intermedia, Mixed Media, †Painting, †Photography, †Printmaking, †Sculpture, Studio Art, †Video
Summer School: Chmn, Stephen Luecking

HARRINGTON COLLEGE OF DESIGN, 200 W Madison St, Chicago, IL 60606. Tel 312-939-4975; Fax 312-939-8005; Web: www.harrington.edu; *Pres* Max S Shangle
Open Mon - Thurs 8 AM - 7 PM, Fri 8 AM - 5 PM, Sat 8 AM - 3 PM, cl Sun; Estab 1931; pvt; D & E; Scholarships; D 220, E 209
Ent Req: HS dipl, interview
Degrees: AA & BA(interior design)
Courses: Interior Design
Adult Hobby Classes: Courses—Interior Design

THE ILLINOIS INSTITUTE OF ART - CHICAGO, 350 N Orleans St, Ste 136-L Chicago, IL 60654-1510. Tel 312-280-3500; Fax 312-280-8562; Web: www.ilic.artinstitutes.edu; *Pres* John Jenkins; *Dir Admis* Janis K Anton; *Dean Acad Affairs* Sandra Graham; *Dir Financial Services* Robert Smetak; *Dean Student Affairs* Betty Kourasis; *Dir Housing* Valerie Rand; *Librn* Juliet S Teipel; *Registrar* Luciana Stabila
Estab 1916; Maintain art & architecture libr; pvt; D & E, yr-round; Scholarships; SC 7, LC, GC; 2170 total
Ent Req: HS dipl, portfolio review
Degrees: BA, AAS, BFA
Courses: Advertising, Culinary Arts, Culinary Management, Digital Filmmaking & Video Production, Fashion Design, Fashion Marketing & Management, Fashion Merchandising, Fashion Production, Game Art & Design, General Education,

Graphic Design, Interactive Media Design, Interactive Media Production, Interior Design, Media Arts & Animation, Visual Communications, Visual Effects of Motion Graphics

ILLINOIS INSTITUTE OF TECHNOLOGY, College of Architecture, 3360 S State St, S R Crown Hall Chicago, IL 60616-3850. Tel 312-567-3262; Fax 312-567-8871; Email arch@iit.edu; Web: www.arch.iit.edu; *Assoc Prof* Peter Beltemacchi; *Studio Prof* Dirk Denison; *Dean* Donna Robertson; *Assoc Prof* Paul Thomas; *Prof* Mahjoub Elnimeiri; *Prof* Peter Land; *Assoc Prof* David Hovey; *Assoc Prof* George Schipporeit; *Assoc Prof* David Sharpe; *Assoc Prof* Arthur Takeuchi; *Asst Dean Student Affairs* Dr Lee W Waldrep
Estab 1895 as Armour Institute, consolidated with Lewis Institute of Arts & Sciences 1940; FT 23; pvt; 345
Degrees: BA 5 yr, MA 3 yr
Tuition: $15,000 per yr
Courses: Architecture
Summer School: Term June 15 through August 8
—Institute of Design, 350 N La Salle St, 4th Fl Chicago, IL 60654. Tel 312-595-4900; Fax 312-595-4901; Email whitney@id.iit.edu; Web: www.id.iit.edu/; *Dir* Patrick Whitney
Estab 1937; FT 10, PT 29; pvt; D; Scholarships; D 150
Degrees: BS 4 yr, MD, PhD(Design)
Tuition: Undergrad $9300per sem, grad $11,315 per sem
Courses: Industrial Design, Photography, Visual Communications

LOYOLA UNIVERSITY OF CHICAGO, Dept of Fine and Performing Arts, Mundelein Center, Ste 1200, 1020 W Sheridan Rd Chicago, IL 60626-5761. Tel 773-508-7510; Fax 773-508-7515; Email dfpa@luc.edu; Web: luc.edu/finearts; *Chair* Sarah Gabel, PhD; *Dir, Dance* Sandra Kauffman; *Dir, Fine Arts* Matthew Groves, MA; *Dir, Music* Anthony Molinaro, MM; *Dir, Theatre* Mark E Lococo, PhD
Estab 1870, dept estab 1970; FT/PT 76; pvt; D & E; Scholarships
Degrees: BA 4 yr
Tuition: Undergrad $21,360 per sem; Grad $1,033 per cr hr
Courses: Advertising Design, Aesthetics, Art Appreciation, †Art History, †Ceramics, Commercial Art, Dance, †Design, †Drawing, Graphic Design, History of Art & Architecture, Jewelry, Music, †Painting, †Photography, †Printmaking, Sculpture, Theatre Arts
Summer School: Courses—Art Appreciation, Art History, Ceramics, Drawing, Painting, Photography

NORTH PARK UNIVERSITY, (North Park College) Art Dept, 2543 W Cullom Ave, Chicago, IL 60618-1501. Tel 773-244-5637, 6200; Fax 773-583-0858; Email nmurray@northpark.edu; Web: www.northpark.edu; *Chmn Dept* Neale Murray, MA; *Asst Prof* Kelly Vanderbrug; *Asst Prof* David Johanson
Estab 1957; PT2; den; D & E; Scholarships; SC 18, LC 5; D 40
Ent Req: HS dipl
Degrees: BA 4 yrs
Courses: Advertising Design, Aesthetics, Art Education, Art History, Calligraphy, Ceramics, Commercial Art, Drawing, Illustration, Painting, Photography, Printmaking, Sculpture, Teacher Training
Summer School: Enrl 25. Courses—Ceramics, Drawing, Painting, Sculpture

NORTHEASTERN ILLINOIS UNIVERSITY, Art Dept, 5500 N St Louis, Chicago, IL 60625. Tel 773-442-4910; Fax 773-442-4920; Web: www.neiu.edu; *Chmn* Mark P McKernin
Estab 1969; Maintain nonprofit art gallery, Fine Arts Gallery, 550 N St Louis Ave, Chicago, IL 60625; Pub; D & E; Scholarships; SC 44, LC 22; total 10,200, maj 175, grad 1,583, others 798
Ent Req: HS dipl, GED, upper half high school class or higher ACT
Degrees: BA 4 yrs
Courses: Art Education, Art History, Ceramics, Commercial Art, Computer Graphics, Drawing, Graphic Arts, Jewelry, Painting, Photography, Printmaking, Sculpture

SAINT XAVIER UNIVERSITY, Dept of Art & Design, 3700 W 103rd St, Chicago, IL 60655-3199. Tel 773-779-3300; Fax 773-779-9061; Web: www.sxu.edu; *Assoc Prof* Mary Ann Bergfeld, MFA; *Assoc Prof* Brent Wall, MFA; *Assoc Prof* Michael Rabe, PhD, MFA; *Assoc Prof* Cathie Ruggie Saunders, MFA; *Assoc Prof* Monte Gerlach, MS; *Chmn* Jayne Hileman, MFA; *Instr* Nathan Peck
Estab 1847, dept estab 1917; Nonprofit gallery - Gallery/Art & Design, Saint Xavier Un, 3700 W 103rd St, Chicago, Il 60655; FT6; pvt; D & E; Scholarships; SC 35, LC 15; D 50, E 5, maj 75, others 250
Ent Req: HS dipl
Degrees: BA & BS 4 yrs
Courses: Art Business, Art Education, Art History, Ceramics, †Collage, Drawing, Film, Graphic Design, †History of Art & Architecture, Illustration, Painting, Photography, Printmaking, Sculpture, Teacher Training, Video
Adult Hobby Classes: Enrl 15-20; tuition $20-$40 per course. Courses—Drawing, Calligraphy, Painting, Photography
Summer School: Dir, Richard Venneri. Courses—Various studio courses

SCHOOL OF THE ART INSTITUTE OF CHICAGO, 36 S Wabash Ave, Chicago, IL 60603. Tel 312-629-6100; Fax 312-629-6101; Email admiss@saic.edu; Web: www.saic.edu; *Pres* Elissa Tenny; *Dean of Faculty* Lisa Wainwright; *Chancellor* Walter Massey
Estab 1866; FT 173, PT 630; pvt; D & E; Scholarships; 3,650
Ent Req: portfolio; recommendations
Degrees: BFA 4 yrs, MFA 2 yrs; Post-Baccalaureate & Profl certs; Study-Abroad
Tuition: Undergrad & Post-Bac cert $1613 per cr; grad $1665 per cr
Courses: †Art Education, †Art History, Art Therapy, Book Arts, †Ceramics, †Drawing, †Fashion Arts, †Fiber, †Film, †Graphic Arts, Interior Architecture, †Painting, †Performance, †Photography, †Printmaking, †Sculpture, †Sound, †Textile Design, †Video, †Visual Communications, †Weaving

UNIVERSITY OF CHICAGO, Dept of Art History, 5540 S Greenwood, Chicago, IL 60637. Tel 773-702-0278; Fax 773-702-5901; Email arthistory@uchicago.edu; Web: arthistory.uchicago.edu; *Chair* Christine Mehnng; *Dir Grad Studies* Aden Kumle
Estab 1892; Maintains Visual Resource Center; five yr duration fels open to all; art supplies sold at on-campus store; pvt; D; SC, LC and GC vary
Ent Req: Through Humanities Div of students office
Degrees: BA 4 yrs, PhD
Courses: Art History

UNIVERSITY OF ILLINOIS AT CHICAGO, College of Architecture, 929 W Harrison St, M/C 030, Rm 3100, Jefferson Hall Chicago, IL 60607-7076. Tel 312-996-3351, Art & Design 996-3337; Fax 312-996-5378; Web: http://adweb.aa.uic.edu; *Dir School Archit* Katerina Ruedi; *Chmn Dept Art & Art History* David Sokol; *Dean* Judith Russi Kirshner
Estab 1946; FT 80, PT 28; pub; D; Scholarships; SC 79, LC 10, GC 3; D 579, non-maj 325, maj 579, grad 17
Ent Req: 3 units of English plus 13 additional units, rank in top one-half of HS class for beginning freshman, transfer students 3.25 GPA
Degrees: BA(Design), BA(Studio Arts), BA(Art Educ), BA(History of Archit & Art), BA(Music), BA(Theatre), BArchit, MFA(Studio Art or Design), MArchit, MA (Theatre)
Courses: †Architecture, †Art Education, †Art History, Ceramics, †Communications Design, †Comprehensive Design, Drawing, †Film, †Industrial Design, †Painting, †Photography, †Printmaking, †Sculpture, †Studio Arts, †Urban Planning & Policy, †Video
Children's Classes: Enrl 50; tuition $5. Courses—Saturday school in connection with art education classes
Summer School: Dir, Morris Barazani. Tuition res undergrad $229, nonres undergrad $547 for term of 8 wks beginning June

UNIVERSITY OF ILLINOIS AT CHICAGO, Biomedical Visualization, 1919 W Taylor St, Rm 211, College of Health & Human Development Science Chicago, IL 60612-7246. Tel 312-996-7337; Email sbarrows@uic.edu; Web: www.sbhis.uic.edu; *Clinical Asst Prof* Raymond Evenhouse; *Res Asst Prof* Mary Rasmussen; *Clinical Asst Prof* John Daugherty; *Prog Coordr* Scott Barrows CMI, FAMI; *Clinical Asst Prof* Gregory Blew
Estab 1923; pub; D; Scholarships; SC, LC. GC; D 24, grad 24
Ent Req: Bachelor's degree
Degrees: Master of Assoc Medical Sciences in Biomedical Visualization
Courses: 3-D Modeling, †Advertising Design, Computer Animation, †Conceptual Art, Design, Drawing, Graphic Design, Illustration, Instructional, Multimedia, Prosthetics, Sculpture, Surgical Illustration

CHICAGO HEIGHTS

PRAIRIE STATE COLLEGE, Art Dept, 202 S Halsted, Chicago Heights, IL 60411. Tel 708-709-3500, 709-3671; Fax 708-755-2587; Web: www.prairie.cc.il.us; *Dept Chmn* Don Kouba
Estab 1958; FT 4, PT 30; pub; D & E; SC 24, LC 6; dept 600, maj 200
Ent Req: HS dipl, ACT
Degrees: AAF 2 yrs Cert 1 yr
Courses: Advertising Design, Airbrush, Art Appreciation, Art Education, Commercial Art, Computer Graphics, Design, †Drawing, †Graphic Design, Illustration, †Interior Design, Jewelry, Life Drawing, Materials Workshop, Package Design, Painting, †Photography, Production Processes, Sign Painting, Stained Glass, Typography, Video Graphics
Summer School: Dir, John Bowman. Tuition $48 per cr hr for term of 8 wks. Courses—Art History, Drawing, Graphic Design, Interior Design, Painting, Photography

DEKALB

NORTHERN ILLINOIS UNIVERSITY, School of Art & Design, 1425 W Lincoln Hwy, DeKalb, IL 60115-2828. Tel 815-753-1473; Fax 815-753-7701; Email ssailer1@niu.edu; Web: www.niu.edu/art; *Dir School of Art* John Siblik, MFA; *Grad Coordr* Kurt Schultz, MFA; *Div Head FA Studio* Christine LoFaso, MFA; *Div Head Art History* Ann van Dijk, PhD; *Div Head Art Educ* Douglas Boughton, PhD; *Div Head Design* Kurt Schultz, MFA; *Foundations Coordr* Ben Stone, MFA; *Recruiter* Stephanie Sailer, MFA; *Div Head Art History* Helen Nagata, PhD
Estab 1895; Maintain nonprofit art gallery; Jack Olson Memorial Gallery, Rm 200, School of Art; Pub; D & E; Scholarships; Fellowships; SC 127, LC 59, GC 98, other 15; Maj 400, grad 55, Minors 110
Ent Req: HS dipl, ACT, SAT
Degrees: BA, BFA, BSEd 4 yrs, MA, MS 2 yrs, MFA 3 yrs, Phd 3 yrs
Tuition: Res—$9,465 per yr; Midwest nones $13,250, nonres—$18,930 per yr; campus res available
Courses: Advertising Design, Art Appreciation, †Art Education - includes initial cert, †Art History, †Ceramics, †Computer Graphics/Design, †Drawing, Goldsmithing, †Graphic Design, History of Art & Architecture, †Illustration, †Intermedia, †Jewelry/Metalwork, Mixed Media, Museum Staff Training, †Painting, †Photography, †Printmaking, †Sculpture, Silversmithing, Teacher Training, Textile Design, Video, †Visual Communications, Weaving, Web Page Design
Summer School: Tuition res—$348.84 per cr hr, nonres—$697.68 per cr hr.; midwest nones $488.38 per cr hr Courses—Vary

DECATUR

MILLIKIN UNIVERSITY, Art Dept, 1184 W Main St, Decatur, IL 62522-2084. Tel 217-424-6227; Fax 217-424-3993; Email lsalmi@millikin.edu; Web: www.millikin.edu; *Chmn Art Dept* Lyle Salmi
Estab 1901, dept estab 1904; Maintain nonprofit art gallery; Perkinson Gallery, 1184 W Main St, Decatur IL 62522; FT 5, PT 3; pvt; D & E; Scholarships; SC 47, LC 3; D 1,700, non-maj 25, maj 110

Ent Req: HS dipl, ACT
Degrees: BA & BFA 4 yrs
Courses: Art Education, Art History, Ceramics, Commercial Art, Computer Graphics, Design, Drawing, Graphic Arts, Graphic Design, Illustration, Painting, Photography, Printmaking, Sculpture, Teacher Training
Summer School: Dean of Arts & Sciences. Enrl 400; tuition $225 per cr hr for 7 wk term beginning June 13. Courses—Ceramics, Drawing, Painting, Photography

DES PLAINES

OAKTON COMMUNITY COLLEGE, Language Humanities & Art Divisions, 1600 E Golf Rd, Des Plaines, IL 60016-1256. Tel 847-635-1600; Fax 847-376-7094; Email lpierozz@oakton.edu; *Chmn & Prof* James A Krauss Retired, MA; *Assoc Prof* Peter Hessemer Retired, MFA; *Assoc Prof* Bernard K Krule Retired, MS; *Asst Prof* Mark Palmeri, MFA; *Cur Gallery* Nathan Harpaz; *Coord & Asst Prof* Judy Langston; *Asst Prof* Kathryn Howard-Rogers Retired; *Chmn & Prof* Lou Pierozzi; *Prof* Moritz Kellerman; *Asst Prof* Erick Rohn
Estab 1970; Maintain nonprofit art gallery; Koehnline Art Gallery 1600 E Golf Rd, Des Plaines IL 60016; libr resources available as part of general college libr; art supplies sold at on-campus store; Pub; D & E, Weekends; Scholarships; SC 9, LC 4; Enrl 1,000
Degrees: AA, AFA
Courses: Architecture, Art Appreciation, Art History, Ceramics, Design, Drawing, Graphic Arts, Graphic Design, History of Art & Architecture, Museum Staff Training, Painting, Photography, Printmaking, Sculpture
Summer School: Dir, Prof Art James A Krauss. Enrl 90; tuition $91 cr for 8 wk term. Courses—Design I, Photography, Ceramics, Field Study, Painting, Drawing

EAST PEORIA

ILLINOIS CENTRAL COLLEGE, Arts & Communication Dept, One College Dr, East Peoria, IL 61635. Tel 309-694-5113; Fax 309-694-8095; Web: www.icc.edu; *Assoc Dean* Chris Gray, MA; *Prof, Dept Chair & Cur* Jennifer Costa, MFA; *Prof* John Tuccillo, MFA; *Prof* Janet Newton, MFA; *Prof* Roger Bean, MA; *Assoc Prof* Eli Davis, MFA; *Assoc Prof* David Smit, BFA; *Asst Prof* Anita Tuccillo, MFA; *Asst Prof* Megan Foster-Campbell, PhD; *Asst Prof* Anastasia Samoylova, MFA
Estab 1967, dept estab 1967; Maintains nonprofit art gallery, Performing Art Center Gallery 305A; art supplies available on-campus; pub; D & E; SC 27, LC 3; D 1,000, E 500, maj 322
Ent Req: HS dipl
Degrees: Assoc(Arts & Sciences) 2 yrs, Assoc(Applied Science)
Tuition: $93 per sem hr; no campus res
Courses: Advertising Design, †Architecture, Art Education, Art History, Ceramics, Color, Commercial Art, Design, Drawing, Graphic Design, Illustration, Interior Design, Painting, Photography, Printmaking, Sculpture, Typography
Adult Hobby Classes: Tuition $75 per cr hr. Courses—Drawing, Painting, Ceramics
Summer School: See website

EDWARDSVILLE

SOUTHERN ILLINOIS UNIVERSITY AT EDWARDSVILLE, Dept of Art & Design, PO Box 1608, Edwardsville, IL 62026-0001. Tel 618-650-5044; Fax 618-650-5050; Email igausep@siue.edu; Web: www.siue.edu/ART/; *Chmn Dept* Ivy Schroeder, PhD; *Head Art History* Pamela Decoteau; *Head Printmaking* Robert R Malone, MFA; *Head Drawing* Dennis L Ringering, MFA; *Head Fiber & Fabric* Laura Strand, MFA; *Head Ceramic* Daniel J Anderson, MFA; *Art Educ* Joseph A Weber, PhD, MFA; *Photog & Graphic Design* Steven Brown, MFA; *Head Painting* Jane Barrow, MFA; *Head Sculpture* Thomas D Gipe, MFA
Estab 1869, dept estab 1959; pub; D & E; Scholarships; SC 65, LC 26, GC 45; D 250, E 75, maj 200, grad 50
Ent Req: HS dipl, ACT, portfolio req for BFA & MFA
Degrees: BA, BS & BFA 4 yrs NFA 3 yrs, MS 2 yrs
Courses: Aesthetics, †Art Education, Art History, †Ceramics, †Drawing, †Graphic Design, History of Art & Architecture, Jewelry, Metalsmithing, Mixed Media, †Painting, Photography, †Printmaking, †Sculpture, †Teacher Training, Textile Arts
Children's Classes: Enrl 250; Summer classes. Courses—Ceramics, Drawing, Painting, Photography
Summer School: Chmn, Joe Weber. Courses—Ceramics, Drawing, Painting, Photography

ELGIN

ELGIN COMMUNITY COLLEGE, Fine Arts Dept, 1700 Spartan Dr, Elgin, IL 60123-7193. Tel 847-697-1000; *Instr* Roger Gustafson; *Instr* John Grady; *Instr* Howard Russo; *Dean* Dr David Broad
Scholarships
Degrees: AA
Tuition: In district—$52.50 per cr hr; res—$230.26 per cr hr; nonres—$278.70 per cr hr
Courses: Art Appreciation, Art History, Ceramics, Design, Drawing, Jewelry, Painting, Photography, Printmaking, Sculpture

JUDSON UNIVERSITY, School of Art, Design & Architecture, 1151 N State St, Elgin, IL 60123-1498. Tel 847-628-2500, Ext 1030; Fax 847-628-1008; Web: www.judsonu.edu; *Chmn Dept Art & Design & Gallery Dir* Jeffery Carl; *Chmn Dept Architecture* Ian Hoffman; *Grad Coordr* Royce Earnest; *Interim Dean* Dr Jhennifer Amundson; *Asst Prof* David M Ogoli; *Assoc Prof* Dr Chris Miller; *Instr* David Amundson; *Instr* August Domel; *Instr* Craig Farnsworth; *Instr* Tom Jaeger; *Instr* Mark Taxgenson; *Instr* Jeremy Lindsey; *Instr* Ian Hoffman; *Instr* Sean Gallagher; *Instr* Lauren Meranda; *Instr* Anna Filbert; *Instr* Curtis Sartor; *Instr* Jae Cha; *Instr* Alan Frost; *Instr* Keelan Kaiser; *Instr* GE Colpitts; *Instr* Terrence Wandtke
Estab 1964; Maintains nonprofit gallery, Draewell Gallery; maintains Benjamin P Browne Library; Pvt; D, E; Scholarships; SC 15, LC 10, GC 10 (Arch only); D 738, E 376, M 231 (incl arch), GS 63, O 59
Ent Req: HS dipl, ACT, or SAT
Degrees: BA 4 yrs, MArch 6 yrs
Courses: †Architecture, Art Appreciation, Ceramics, Design, Design History, Drawing, Film, †Fine Arts, †Graphic Design, History of Art & Architecture, Painting, Photography, Printmaking, Sculpture, Video, †Visual Communications

ELMHURST

ELMHURST COLLEGE, Art Dept, 190 Prospect, Elmhurst, IL 60126. Tel 630-617-3542; Fax 630-279-4100; Web: www.elmhurst.edu; *Chmn* Richard Paulsen, MFA; *Prof* John Weber, MFA; *Asst Prof* Lynn Hill, MFA; *Asst Prof* Mary Lou Stewart, MFA
Estab 1871; Pvt; D & E; Scholarships; SC 13, LC 8; D 1927, E 1500, maj 33
Ent Req: HS dipl, ACT or SAT
Degrees: BS, BA & BM 4 yrs
Courses: †Art Business, †Art Education, Design, †Electronic Imaging, †Painting, †Photography, †Printmaking, †Sculpture
Summer School: Dir, Dr Marie Baehr. Enrl 1379; tuition $375 per cr hr for courses of 4, 6 & 8 wks. Courses in selected programs

EVANSTON

NORTHWESTERN UNIVERSITY, EVANSTON, Dept of Art Theory & Practice, 1859 Sheridan Rd, Rm 244, Evanston, IL 60208-2207. Tel 847-491-7346; Fax 847-467-1487; Email art-theory@northwestern.edu; Web: www.art.northwestern.edu; *Prof* William Conger; *Prof* Ed Paschke; *Prof* James Valerio; *Assoc Prof* Judy Ledgerwood; *Lectr* James Yood; *Lectr* Charlie Cho; *Assoc Prof* Jeanne Dunning; *Asst Prof* Lane Relyea; *Lectr* William Cass; *Lectr* Dan Devening; *Lectr* Pamela Bannos
Estab 1851; FT 11, PT 3; pvt; D & E; Scholarships; Fellowships; SC 40, LC 6, GC 6, seminars; D 800, E 40, non-maj 750, maj 50, grad 12
Ent Req: requirements set by university admissions; for MFA prog a distinctive record and portfolio is required
Degrees: AB 4 yrs, MFA 2+
Tuition: $27,000
Courses: Conceptual Art, Drawing, †Painting, Photography, †Practice of Art, †Printmaking, Sculpture
Summer School: Courses—Introductory
—**Dept of Art History**, 1880 Campus Dr, 3-400 Kresge Hall Evanston, IL 60208-0888. Tel 847-491-7077; Fax 847-467-1035; Email art-history@northwestern.edu; Web: www.arthistory.northwestern.edu; *Prof* Stephen Eisenman, PhD; *Prof* Hollis Clayson, PhD; *Chmn, Assoc Prof* Claudia Swan, PhD; *Prof* David Van Zanten, PhD; *Chmn & Assoc Prof* Sarah E Fraser, PhD; *Asst Prof* Huey Copeland, PhD; *Asst Prof* Hannah Feldman, PhD; *Asst Prof* Cecily J Hilsdale, PhD; *Assoc Prof* Christina Kiaer, PhD; *Asst Prof* Krista Thompson, PhD; *Adjunct Prof* Hamid Naficy, PhD; *Adjunct Prof* Marco Ruffini, PhD; *Adjunct Prof* Bernadette Fort, PhD; *Assoc Prof* Jesus Escobar; *Lectr* Christine Bell
Estab 1851; Maintains art library, Deering Library, Northwester U, Evanston Il, 60208; pvt; D & E; Scholarships; LC 36, GC 15; maj 60, grad 40
Ent Req: HS dipl, SAT or ACT
Degrees: PhD, MA, BA
Tuition: $5,468 per qtr
Courses: 20th Century Art, Architecture, Architecture of Ancient Rome, †Art History, †Handicrafts, History of Art & Architecture, Introduction to African Art, Medieval Art, Renaissance Art
Summer School: Courses—vary in Art History

FREEPORT

HIGHLAND COMMUNITY COLLEGE, Art Dept, 2998 W Pearl City Rd, Freeport, IL 61032-9341. Tel 815-235-6121; Fax 815-235-6130; Web: www.highland.cc.il.us; *Dir* Thomas Brandt
Estab 1962; FT 1, PT 5; pub; D & E; Scholarships; SC 6, LC 1; 126
Ent Req: HS dipl, ent exam
Degrees: AS, AA, ABA, AAS 2 yrs
Courses: Art History, Art Materials & Processes, Design, Drawing, Fabrics, Graphic Design, History of Modern Art, Introduction to Art, Metals & Jewelry, Painting, Pottery, Printmaking, Sculpture
Adult Hobby Classes: Enrl 278. Courses—Basic Drawing, Oil, Charcoal, Printmaking, Sculpture, Pottery, Handweaving & Related Crafts, Rosemaking, Macrame, Needlepoint
Children's Classes: Occasional summer workshops for high school and elementary school students
Summer School: Courses same as above

GALESBURG

CARL SANDBURG COLLEGE, 2400 Tom L Wilson Blvd, Galesburg, IL 61401. Tel 309-344-2518; Fax 309-341-5471; Email lmohr@sandburg.edu; Web: www.sandburg.edu; *Art Coordr & Instr* Lisa Mohr
Maintains nonprofit art gallery
Courses: Art Appreciation, Art History, Ceramics, Drawing, Graphic Design, Painting, Photography, Printmaking, Theatre Arts

KNOX COLLEGE, Dept of Art, 2 E South St, Galesburg, IL 61401-4999. Tel 309-341-7000, 341-7423 (Art Dept Chmn); *Asst Prof* Lynette Lombard; *Chmn* Frederick Ortner
Scholarships

Degrees: BA 4yrs
Tuition: $28,230 per yr, room & board $5630 per yr
Courses: Art History, Ceramics, Design, Drawing, History of Art & Architecture, Painting, Photography, Printmaking, Sculpture

GODFREY

LEWIS & CLARK COMMUNITY COLLEGE, Art Dept, 5800 Godfrey Rd, Godfrey, IL 62035-2466. Tel 618-468-4669; Web: www.lc.edu; *Asst Prof* Chris Brennan; *Assoc Prof* Joe McFarlane; *Assoc Prof* Jeff Vaughn
Estab 1970, formerly Monticello College; All supplies are provided by art dept.; FT 3, PT 9; pub; D & E; Scholarships; SC 27, LC 6; D 1800, E 600, maj 24
Ent Req: HS dipl, ent exam, open door policy
Degrees: AA & AFA 2 yrs
Courses: Advanced Drawing, †Art Appreciation, Art History, Basic Design, Ceramics, Drawing, †Film, †Graphic Design, Painting, †Photography, Printmaking, Sculpture
Summer School: Enrl 80; 12 wks. Courses—Introduction to Visual Arts, Art History, Drawing, Painting

GRAYSLAKE

COLLEGE OF LAKE COUNTY, Art Dept, 19351 W Washington St, Grayslake, IL 60030-1198. Tel 847-543-2040; Fax 847-543-3040; Web: www.clcillinois.edu; *VPres Educ Affairs* Rich Haney; *Ceramics* David Bolton; *Photog* Roland Miller; *Computer Art* Terry Dixon; *Drawing & Design* Hans Habeger; *Painting & Watercolor* Robert Lossmann
Estab 1969, dept estab 1969; Maintains nonprofit art gallery, Robert T. Wright Community Gallery of Art, 19351 W Washington St, Grayslake, IL, 60030; pub; D & E; SC 22, LC 5; D 250, E 250, non-maj 500, maj 100
Ent Req: HS dipl, SAT, GED
Degrees: AA & AS 2 yrs
Courses: 2-D & 3-D Design, Art Appreciation, Art Education, Art History, Ceramics, Drawing, Graphic Arts, Graphic Design, Jewelry, Mixed Media, Painting, Photography, Sculpture, Watercolor
Adult Hobby Classes: Advertising, Ceramics, Drawing, Lettering, Mixed Media, Portrait, Stained Glass
Summer School: Courses—same as above

GREENVILLE

GREENVILLE COLLEGE, Art Dept, 315 E College Ave, Dept of Art Greenville, IL 62246-1145. Tel 618-664-2800, 664-7119; Fax 618-664-1373; Email steve.heilmer@greenville.edu; Web: www.greenville.edu/academics/departments/art; *Dept Head* Steve Heilmer, MFA; *Asst Prof* Jacob Amundson; *Asst Prof* Jessa Wilcoxen; *Dir* Dr Sharon Grimes
Estab 1892, dept estab 1965; Maintains a nonprofit art gallery - Rowland Art Gallery, Maves Art Center; John Hubbell, Adj; pvt; D & E; Scholarships; SC 20, LC 6; D 135, non-maj 105, maj 30
Activities: Schols offered
Ent Req: HS dipl
Degrees: BA 4 yrs, BS 4 1/2 yrs
Tuition: $15,000per yr; campus—room & board $7,000 per yr
Courses: Advertising Design, Art Education, Art History, †Ceramics, Design, Digital Media, †Drawing, Film, †Graphic Arts, †Graphic Design, Handicrafts, History of Art & Architecture, Mixed Media, †Painting, Photography, †Sculpture, †Teacher Training, Video
Summer School: Intro to Fine Arts - Dr. Sharon Grimes, Dir

JACKSONVILLE

MACMURRAY COLLEGE, Art Dept, 447 E College Ave, Jacksonville, IL 62650-2590. Tel 217-479-7000; Fax 217-479-7086; Web: www.mac.edu; *Chmn Art Dept* Raymond Yeager
Estab 1846; den; Scholarships; SC 29, LC 6
Degrees: BA 4 yr
Courses: Advertising Design, Ceramics, Drawing, Painting, Photography, Sculpture, Teacher Training

JOLIET

JOLIET JUNIOR COLLEGE, Fine Arts Dept, 1215 Houbolt Rd, Joliet, IL 60431-8800. Tel 815-729-9020, Ext 2232; Fax 815-744-5507; Web: www.jjc.cc.il.us; *Chmn Dept* Jerry Lewis, MM; *Instr* James Dugdale, MA; *Instr* Joe Milosevich, MFA; *Instr* Steve Sherrell, MFA
Estab 1901, dept estab 1920; pub; D & E; Scholarships; SC 15, LC 4; D 10,000, maj 120
Ent Req: HS dipl, ent exam
Degrees: AA 2 yrs
Courses: 2-D & 3-D Design, Art Appreciation, Art History, Ceramics, Drawing, Graphic Arts, Interior Design, Jewelry, Painting, Silversmithing, Weaving
Summer School: Dir, Jerry Lewis, MM. Courses—Same as winter school

UNIVERSITY OF SAINT FRANCIS, Fine Arts Dept, 500 N Wilcox St, Division of Humanities & Fine Arts Joliet, IL 60435-6169. Tel 815-740-3360; Fax 815-740-4285; Web: www.stfrancis.edu; *Dept Head* Dr Patrick Brannon
Estab 1950; Maintain nonprofit art gallery; Moser Performing Arts Gallery Center; Pvt; D & E; SC 6, LC 3; D 150, maj 25
Ent Req: HS grad, ent exam
Degrees: BA(Creative Arts with Art Specialization or Art Educ)
Courses: Advanced Drawing & Painting, Applied Studio, Basic Design, Ceramics, Fabrics, Photography, Silversmithing, Special Topics, Textiles
Children's Classes: Courses—Art in variety of media
Summer School: Term of 6 wks beginning June

LAKE FOREST

LAKE FOREST COLLEGE, Dept of Art, 555 N Sheridan Rd, Lake Forest, IL 60045-2399. Tel 847-234-3100; Fax 847-735-6291; Web: www.lfc.edu; *Lectr* Mary Lawton PhD; *Chmn* Anne Roberts
Estab 1857; pvt; D & E; Scholarships; SC 8, LC 21; D 1050 (sch total), maj 38
Ent Req: HS dipl, SAT, CEEB or ACT
Degrees: BA 4 yrs
Courses: Aesthetics, Architecture, Art Appreciation, Art Education, Art History, Computer Assisted Design, Drawing, Film, Graphic Design, History of Art & Architecture, Painting, Photography
Adult Hobby Classes: Enrl 5-15. Courses—Photography
Summer School: Dir, Arthur Zilversmit. Enrl 200; tuition $990 per 4 sem hrs for 7 wks. Courses—Photography

LINCOLN

LINCOLN COLLEGE, Art Dept, 300 Keokuk St, Lincoln, IL 62656-1699. Tel 217-732-3155; Fax 217-732-8859; Web: www.lincolncollege.com; *Assoc Prof* Bob Stefl; *Chmn* E J Miley; *Instr Painting & Design* Karen Miley
Estab 1865; pvt; D & E; Scholarships; SC 35, LC 5; maj 200
Ent Req: HS dipl
Degrees: AA
Courses: Art Appreciation, Art History, Ceramics, Design, Drawing, Graphic Design, Illustration, Mixed Media, Painting, Photography, Stage Design, Theatre Arts
Children's Classes: Courses offered through summer
Summer School: Dir, EJ Miley Jr. Courses—Art of France & Italy

LISLE

ILLINOIS BENEDICTINE UNIVERSITY, Department of Fine Arts, 5700 College Rd, Scholl #105 Lisle, IL 60532-2851. Tel 630-829-6320; Fax 630-960-4805; Email pseely@ben.edu; Web: www.ben.edu/finearts; *Chair* Peter Seely, MA; *Cur* Teresa J Parker; *Prof* William Scarlato; *Instr* Jennifer Scavone; *Instr* David Marcet; *Instr* Vincent Lucarelli
Estab 1887, dept estab 1978; Maintains campus-wide display of permanent coll & 3 areas for rotating exhibs. Scholarships offered annually to all students for one yr; pvt & den & Benedictine Catholic; D & E; Scholarships; SC 10, LC 7; Full time 1150, grad 915
Library Holdings: Slides
Ent Req: HS dipl, ACT, SAT
Degrees: BA, BS, MS & MBA 4 yrs
Tuition: Undergrad $15,220 per yr; campus res available
Courses: Art Appreciation, Art History, Calligraphy, Design, Drawing, Graphic Arts, Lettering, Painting, Photography, Printmaking

MACOMB

WESTERN ILLINOIS UNIVERSITY, Department of Art, 1 University Cir, 32 Garwood Hall Macomb, IL 61455-1390. Tel 309-298-1549; Fax 309-298-2605; Email ca-wright@wiu.edu; Web: www.wiu.edu/art/; *Interim Dean Fine Arts & Commun* Sharon Evans; *Prof* Julie Mahoney, MFA; *Asst Prof* Susan Czechowski, MFA; *Asst Prof* Dr Keith Holz, PhD; *Asst Prof* William Howard, MFA; *Prof* Jenny Knavel, MFA; *Asst Prof* Damon McArthur, MFA; *Asst Prof* Terry Rathje, MA; *Asst Prof* Tim Waldrop, MFA; *Prof* Bruce Walters, MFA; *Assoc Prof* Kat Myers, MFA; *Prof* Jan Clough, MFA; *Chair Dept of Art & Prof* Charles Wright, MFA; *Asst Prof Art* Maile Hutterer, PhD; *Asst Prof Art* Henry Charles Oursler, MFA; *Assoc Prof Art* Brett Eberhardt, MFA; *Asst Prof Art* Shawn Spangler, MFA
Estab 1900, dept estab 1968; Maintains a nonprofit art gallery, Univ Art Gallery, Western Illinois Univ, Macomb, IL, 61455. Tuition Waivers/Talent Grants $500-$2,000 open to all students, renewable 4 yrs; Pub; D & E; SC 49, LC 18, GC 9; non-maj 250, maj 130, gs 40
Ent Req: HS dipl
Degrees: BA 4 yrs, BFA, MA - Museum Studies
Tuition: Res—undergrad $7,200 per yr
Courses: Art Appreciation, Art Education, Art History, Ceramics, Conceptual Art, Design, Drawing, Foundry Casting, Goldsmithing, Graphic Arts, Graphic Design, History of Art & Architecture, Illustration, Jewelry, Metal Working, Mixed Media, Museum Staff Training, Museum Studies, Painting, Printmaking, Sculpture
Summer School: Chair, Charles Wright. Enrl 103; 8 wk session. Courses—Art Appreciation, Studio

MALTA

KISHWAUKEE COLLEGE, Art Dept, 21193 Malta Rd, Malta, IL 60150-9600. Tel 815-825-2086; Fax 815-825-2072; Email arr@kishwaukeecollege.edu; Web: www.kishwaukeecollege.edu; *Pres* Thomas L Choice; *Dean, Arts, Communs & Social Sciences* Tara Y Carter
Courses: †Drawing, †Jewelry, †Metalsmithing, †Painting, †Printmaking

MOLINE

BLACK HAWK COLLEGE, Art Dept, 6600 34th Ave, Moline, IL 61265-5899. Tel 309-796-5469; Fax 309-792-3418; Email thorsonz@bhc.edu; Web: www.bhc.edu; *Assoc Prof* David Murray; *Asst Prof & Co Chair Commun & Fine Arts* Zaiga Thorson; *Instr* Melissa Hebert

Estab 1962; maintain a nonprofit art gallery, Artspace; pub; D & E; Scholarships; SC 17, LC 4; D 300, E 100, non-maj 300, maj 60
Ent Req: HS dipl
Degrees: AA & AAS(Commercial Art) 2 yrs
Courses: Art Appreciation, Art History, Ceramics, Commercial Art, Computer Graphics, Design, Drawing, Graphic Design, Illustrator, Jewelry, Life Drawing, Painting, Photography, Photoshop
Adult Hobby Classes: Calligraphy, Drawing, Painting, Stained Glass, Photography
Summer School: Chmn, Jonathan Palumaki. Enrl 30; tuition $48 per cr hr for term of 6 wks beginning in June. Courses—Art Appreciation

MONMOUTH

MONMOUTH COLLEGE, Dept of Art, 700 E Broadway, McMichael Academic Hall Monmouth, IL 61462-1963. Tel 309-457-2311; Fax 309-734-7500; Web: www.monm.edu; *Dept Chair & Assoc Prof Art* Stacy Lotz; *Prof Art* Cheryl Meeker; *Asst Prof Art* Brian Baugh; *Lectr* Tyler Hennings
College estab 1853; Maintains nonprofit art gallery, Len G. Everett Gallery; FT 3, PT 3; pvt; D&E; Scholarships; Grants; SC 16, LC 4
Ent Req: 15 units incl English, history, social science, foreign language, mathematics & science, SAT or ACT
Degrees: BA 4 yr
Courses: Advanced Special Topics, †Art Education, Art History, Ceramics, Contemporary Art, Drawing, †Graphic Design, Independent Study, Open Studio, Painting, Photography, Printmaking, Sculpture, Secondary Art Methods, Senior Art Seminar
Adult Hobby Classes: 10; ceramics

MOUNT CARROLL

INTERNATIONAL PRESERVATION STUDIES CENTER, 203 E Seminary St, Mount Carroll, IL 61053-1361. Tel 815-244-1173; Fax 815-244-1619; Email brinkmeier@preservationcenter.org; Web: www.preservationcenter.org; *Exec Dir* Matthew Toland; *Asst Dir* Sarah Connors
Estab 1979; Maintains Campbell Memorial Research Library & Campbell Ctr for Historic Preservation Studies, 203 E Seminary, Mt Carroll, Ill; on campus shop where art supplies may be purchased; PT 45; pvt; year round; Scholarships; 85
Activities: schols offered
Ent Req: none
Degrees: Collection Care Certificate, Historic Preservation Certificate, Emerging Museum Professional (EMP) Certificate
Tuition: $550-$1650 fee per course, 2-6 days; campus res available Mid-May through October
Courses: Collections Care, Conservation, Historic Preservation, Museum Staff Training, †Restoration & Conservation

NAPERVILLE

NORTH CENTRAL COLLEGE, Dept of Art, 30 N Brainard St, Naperville, IL 60566-4690. Tel 630-637-5542; Fax 630-637-5691; *Assoc Prof* Barry Skurkis, MA; *Asst Prof Art* Christine Rabenold, MFA
Estab 1861; Maintains nonprofit art gallery & library; on-campus shop sells art supplies; pvt; D & E; Scholarships; SC 30, LC 15; non-maj 3000, maj 50
Ent Req: HS dipl, SAT or ACT
Degrees: BA 4 yrs
Tuition: Res & nonres—undergrad $23,115 per yr, $7705 per term, $570-$1,710 part time per term; non-degree—$135-$2394 per term; campus res—room & board $7440 per yr
Courses: Advanced Studio, Aesthetics, Art Education, Art History, Ceramics, Design, Drawing, Figure Drawing, Handicrafts, History of Art & Architecture, Painting, Photography, Printmaking, Sculpture, Teacher Training, Theatre Arts
Adult Hobby Classes: Enrl 3800. Tuition $50 for 6 wks. Courses offered through Continuing Education
Summer School: Dir, Peter Barger. Enrl 1000; tuition $1440 per course. Courses—Ceramics, Drawing, Painting

NORMAL

ILLINOIS STATE UNIVERSITY, College of Fine Arts, Campus Box 5600, Normal, IL 61790-5600. Tel 309-438-8321; Fax 309-438-8318; Email FineArts@IllinoisState.edu; Web: www.cfa.ilstu.edu; *Dean* James Major
Estab 1857; FT 40; 6 vis profs per yr; pub; D & E; Scholarships; Fellowships; SC 50, LC 35, GC 40; D 20,000, non-maj 100, maj 500, grad 40
Ent Req: HS dipl, SAT or ACT
Degrees: BA & BS 4 yrs, BFA 5 yrs, MA, MS, MFA
Tuition: Res—undergrad & grad $2430 per yr, $1215 per sem, $75 per hr; nonres—undergrad $6030 per yr, $3015 per sem, $225 per hr, grad $2454 per yr, $1227 per sem
Courses: †Art Education, Art Foundations, †Art History, †Art Therapy, †Ceramics, †Drawing, †Fibers, †Glass, †Graphic Design, †Intaglio, Jewelry Design, †Lithography, †Metalwork, Mixed Media, †Painting, †Photography, †Sculpture, Video Art
Summer School: 8 wk term beginning in June

OGLESBY

ILLINOIS VALLEY COMMUNITY COLLEGE, Division of Humanities & Fine Arts, 815 N Orlando Smith Ave, Oglesby, IL 61348-9691. Tel 815-224-2720, Ext 491; *Instr* David Bergsieker, MFA; *Instr* Dana Collins, MFA
Estab 1924; pub; D & E; Scholarships; SC 14, LC 2; D 120, E 44, non-maj 156, maj 8
Degrees: AA 2 yrs
Tuition: $50 per sem hr
Courses: Art Education, Art History, Ceramics, Drawing, Graphic Design, Painting, Photography, Sculpture, Weaving
Summer School: Tuition $50 per sem

PEORIA

BRADLEY UNIVERSITY, Dept of Art, 1501 W Bradley Ave, Heuser Art Ctr Peoria, IL 61606-1048. Tel 309-677-2967; Fax 309-677-3642; Web: www.bradley.edu; *Chair* Gary Will
FT 10, PT 4; Pvt; Scholarships; Assistantships; maj 121, others 500
Ent Req: HS grad
Degrees: BA, BS, BFA 4 yrs, MA, MFA 3 yrs
Courses: Art History, Ceramics, Drawing, Graphic Arts, Graphic Design, Illustration, Painting, Photography, Printmaking, Sculpture

QUINCY

QUINCY UNIVERSITY, Dept of Art, 1800 College Ave, Quincy, IL 62301-2699. Tel 217-228-5200, Ext 5371; Fax 217-228-5354; Web: www.quincy.edu; *Prof Art* Robert Lee Mejer
Estab 1860, dept estab 1953; FT 3, PT 2; pub; D & E; SC 21, LC 13; maj 25, total enrl 1715, E 150
Ent Req: HS grad, ACT or SAT ent exam
Degrees: BA, BS & BFA 4 yrs
Courses: 2-D & 3-D Design, Aesthetics, Art Appreciation, Art Education, Art History, Art Seminars, Ceramics, Commercial Art, Design, Drawing, Illustration, Jewelry, Mixed Media, Modern Art, Non-Western Art, Painting, Photography, Printmaking, Sculpture, Teacher Training, Weaving, Weaving
Summer School: Dir, Robert Lee Mejer. Tuition $190 per sem hr, optional jr yr abroad

RIVER GROVE

TRITON COLLEGE, School of Arts & Sciences, 2000 N Fifth Ave, River Grove, IL 60171. Tel 708-456-0300; Web: www.triton.cc.il.us; *Chmn* Norman Weigo
Estab 1965; FT 5, PT 6; pub; D & E; SC 17, LC 3; D 650, E 150, maj 138, adults and non-cr courses
Ent Req: HS dipl, some adult students are admitted without HS dipl, but with test scores indicating promise
Degrees: AA 2 yrs
Courses: Advertising Design, Art History, Ceramics, Commercial Art, Drawing, Graphic Arts, Graphic Design, Illustration, Lettering, Painting, Printmaking, Recreational Arts & Crafts, Sculpture, Theatre Arts
Adult Hobby Classes: Enrl 550. Courses—Candle Making, Continuing Education Classes, Crafts, Drawing, Ceramics, Jewelry, Quilting, Painting, Plastics, Stained Glass, Sculpture, Theatre Arts
Summer School: Dir, Norm Wiegel. Enrl 100; tuition $27 per cr hr. Courses—Selection from regular classes offered

RIVERSIDE

RIVERSIDE ARTS CENTER, 32 E Quincy Rd, Riverside, IL 60546-2129. Tel 708-442-6400; Email rivarts@sbcglobal.net; Web: riversideartscenter.com; *Financial Dir* Tami Gagne; *Gallery Cur* Garry Henderson

ROCK ISLAND

AUGUSTANA COLLEGE, Art Dept, 639 38th St, Rock Island, IL 61201-2210. Tel 309-794-7729; Fax 309-794-7659; Email arschussheim@augustana.edu; Web: www.augustana.edu; *Prof* Peter Xiao; *Prof* Megan Quinn; *Assoc Prof* Kelvin Mason; *Adj Prof* Christian Mortenson; *Adj Prof* Corrine Smith; *Chair* Rowen Schussheim-Anderson; *Asst Prof* Vickie Phipps
Estab 1860; Maintain nonprofit art gallery, Augustana Art Museum, same location; on-campus shop where art supplies may be purchased; FT 5, PT 1, Adj 2; pvt; D; Scholarships; Fellowships; SC 8, LC 9, LabC 3; Enrol 2200
Activities: Schols offered
Ent Req: HS grad plus exam
Degrees: BA 4 yr
Tuition: Undergrad $35,835
Courses: †Art Education, †Art History, Ceramics, Design, †Drawing, Graphic Arts, †Graphic Design, Painting, Photography, Printmaking, Sculpture, †Studio Art, Teacher Training, Textile Design, Weaving
Children's Classes: Enrl 175; tuition $38 for 4wk term. Courses—Calligraphy, Clay, Drawing, Mixed Media, Painting, Sculpture, Weaving
Summer School: Prof Jeffrey Ratliff-Crane, Assoc Dean. Enrl 100; tuition $513 per sem hr for 5 wk term. Courses—Drawing, Fabric Design, Painting, Photography, Weaving

ROCKFORD

ROCK VALLEY COLLEGE, Humanities and Fine Arts Division, 3301 N Mulford Rd, Rockford, IL 61114-5699. Tel 815-654-4410; Fax 815-654-5359; Email faco1dr@rvc.cc.il.us; Web: www.rvc.cc.il.us; *Prof* Cherri Rittenhouse; *Prof* Lester Salberg; *Prof* Lynn Fischer-Carlson; *Div Chmn* Dave Ross
Estab 1964, dept estab 1965; FT 2, PT 3; pub; D & E; SC 10, LC 4; D 158, non-maj 70, maj 27
Degrees: AA, AS & AAS 2 yrs
Courses: Art Education, Art History, Color Theory, Commercial Art, Design, Drawing, Painting, Printmaking

ROCKFORD UNIVERSITY, Dept of Fine Arts, 5050 E State St, Clark Arts Ctr Rockford, IL 61108-2311. Tel 815-226-4000; Fax 815-394-5167; Web: www.rockford.edu; *Chmn Dept Fine Arts* Robert N McCauley
Estab 1847, dept estab 1848; FT 4, PT 2; pvt; D & E; Scholarships; SC 20, LC 3-4; D 750, E 700, non-maj 135, maj 45
Ent Req: HS dipl, SAT or ACT
Degrees: BA, BFA and BS 4 yrs, MAT 2 yrs
Courses: Art History, Ceramics, Drawing, Painting, Papermaking, Photography, Printmaking, Sculpture
Summer School: Dir, Dr Winston McKean. Courses—Art History, Fine Arts (Studio), Stage Design

SOUTH HOLLAND

SOUTH SUBURBAN COLLEGE, Art Dept, 15800 S State St, South Holland, IL 60473. Tel 708-596-2000; *Chmn* Joe Rejholec
Degrees: AA, AAS
Tuition: $53 per cr hr
Courses: †Advertising Design, Art Appreciation, Art History, Calligraphy, Ceramics, Design, Drawing, Illustration, Jewelry, Painting, Printmaking, Sculpture
Summer School: Dir, Dr Fred Hanzelin. Enrl 65. Courses - Art History, Ceramics, Design, Drawing, Nature of Art

SPRINGFIELD

SPRINGFIELD COLLEGE IN ILLINOIS, Dept of Art, 1500 N Fifth, Springfield, IL 62702. Tel 217-525-1420 ext 518; Email admissions@sci.edu; Web: www.sci.edu; *Head Dept* Jeff Garland; *Instr* Marianne Stremsterfer, BA; *Instr* John Seiz, MA; *Instr* Jim Allen, MA; *Instr* Lisa Manuele, BA
Estab 1929, dept estab 1968; pvt; D & E; SC 12, LC 4; D 27, E 6, non-maj 11, maj 16
Ent Req: HS dipl, ACT
Degrees: AA 2 yrs
Courses: 2-D & 3-D Design, Art History, Ceramics, Design, Drawing, History of Art & Architecture, Painting, Photography, Printmaking, Weaving
Adult Hobby Classes: Enrl 125; tuition $125 per cr hr. Courses—Art History, Ceramics, Design, Drawing, Photography
Children's Classes: Enrl 20; tuition $30 for 2 wks in summer. Courses—Art for Children 6 - 9 yrs, 10 - 14 yrs
Summer School: Dir, Dorothy Shiffer. Tuition $125 per cr hr

UNIVERSITY OF ILLINOIS AT SPRINGFIELD, Visual Arts Program, 1 University Plaza, Springfield, IL 62703-5407. Tel 217-206-6790; Fax 217-206-7280; Email bdixo2@uis.edu; Web: www.uis.edu; *Assoc Prof* Bob Dixon, MFA & MS; *Asst Prof* Barbara Bolser
Estab 1969, dept estab 1974; pub; D & E; Scholarships; SC 24, LC 10
Ent Req: 2 yrs col educ
Degrees: BA(Creative Arts) 2 yrs
Courses: Aesthetics, Art History, †Ceramics, Conceptual Art, Constructions, Design, Drawing, †Graphic Arts, Graphic Design, †Mixed Media, †Painting, †Photography, †Printmaking, †Sculpture, †Video

SUGAR GROVE

WAUBONSEE COMMUNITY COLLEGE, Art Dept, Rte 47 at Waubonsee Dr, Von Ohlen Hall (VON 209), Sugar Grove Campus Sugar Grove, IL 60554-9454. Tel 630-466-4811; Fax 630-466-9102; Web: www.waubonsee.edu; *Chmn* Stephanie Decicco
Estab 1967; pub; D & E; Scholarships; SC 8, LC 3; D approx 275, E approx 200, maj 25
Ent Req: HS dipl, open door policy for adults without HS dipl
Degrees: AA, AS and AAS 2 yrs
Courses: Art Education, Art History, Ceramics, Drawing, Painting, Teacher Training, Theatre Arts
Adult Hobby Classes: Enrl 250; Courses—Ceramics, Interior Design, Painting, Graphic Arts
Children's Classes: Enrl 50. Courses—Dramatics, Experience in Art.
Summer School: Courses— as per regular session

UNIVERSITY PARK

GOVERNORS STATE UNIVERSITY, College of Arts & Science, Art Dept, 1 University Pkwy, University Park, IL 60466-0975. Tel 708-534-5000; Fax 708-534-7895; Web: www.govst.edu; *Div Chmn* Dr Joyce Kennedy
Scholarships; 175
Degrees: BA, MA
Tuition: Undergrad $95 per cr hr, grad $101 per cr hr
Courses: Art History, Art Studio, Ceramics, Drawing, Electronic Arts, History of Art & Architecture, Jewelry, Mixed Media, Painting, Photography, Printmaking, Sculpture
Summer School: Dir, Mary Bookwalter. Enrl 150; tuition $79.25 per cr hr for May-Aug term. Courses—Art History, Art Studio

WHEATON

WHEATON COLLEGE, Dept of Art, 501 E College, Wheaton, IL 60187. Tel 630-752-5050, 752-5000; Web: www.wheaton.edu/homeArt; *Chmn* Dr E John Walford
Estab 1861; FT 4; pvt; D & E; Scholarships; SC 32, LC 16; 2350, maj 38, grad 450
Ent Req: HS dipl
Degrees: BA 4 yrs
Courses: Aesthetics, Art Education, Ceramics, Creativity Practicum, Drawing, Film, Graphic Arts, Graphic Design, History of Art & Architecture, Painting, Philosophy of Art, Photography, Printmaking, Sculpture, Television Production, Theory & Techniques, Video

WINNETKA

NORTH SHORE ART LEAGUE, 620 Lincoln, Winnetka, IL 60093. Tel 847-446-2870; Fax 847-446-4306; Email nsal@sbcglobal.net; Web: www.northshoreartleague.org; *Bd Pres* Cindy Fuller
Estab 1924; pvt; D & E; Scholarships; SC 20; D 200, E 150
Ent Req: adults must be art league mem
Degrees: continuing educ cr
Tuition: Classes meet once per week for a 12-14 week period; no campus res
Courses: Ceramics, Children's Film, Costume Design & Construction, Critique, Drawing, Fashion Arts, Graphic Arts, Mixed Media, Painting, Printmaking
Children's Classes: various classes
Summer School: Arts Educ Mgr, Josh Barney & Exec Dir, Linda Nelson; six week sessions; art camp

INDIANA

ANDERSON

ANDERSON UNIVERSITY, Art Dept, 1100 E Fifth St, Anderson, IN 46012-3462. Tel 765-641-4320; Fax 765-641-4328; *Chmn* M Jason Knapp
Estab 1928; pvt; D & E; Scholarships; SC 30, LC 3; non-maj 15, maj 60
Ent Req: HS dipl, ent exam plus recommendation
Degrees: BA 4 yrs
Courses: Advertising Design, Art Education, †Art History, Ceramics, Commercial Art, Drawing, Glass, †Graphic Arts, Graphic Design, History of Art & Architecture, Illustration, Jewelry, Lettering, Museum Staff Training, †Painting, †Photography, Printmaking, Sculpture, †Stage Design, Teacher Training
Summer School: Dir, Robert Smith

BLOOMINGTON

INDIANA UNIVERSITY, BLOOMINGTON, Henry Radford Hope School of Fine Arts, 1201 E 7th St, Rm 123 Bloomington, IN 47405-5501. Tel 812-855-7766; Fax 812-855-7498; Email faoffice@indiana.edu; Web: www.indiana.edu/~finaweb; *Dir, Assoc Prof* Tim Mather; *Assoc Prof* Malcolm Smith; *Asst Prof* Christyl Boger
Estab 1911; pub; D; Scholarships; SC 55, LC 100, GC 110; maj undergrad 300, grad 135 (45 Art History, 90 Studio), others 5600
Ent Req: admis to the Univ
Degrees: BA, BFA, 4 yrs, MA, MFA, PhD
Tuition: Res—undergrad $4,412 per yr, grad $168.60 per cr hr; nonres—undergrad $13,416 per yr, grad $491.15 per cr hr, room & board avg $5,608 per yr
Courses: Art History, Ceramics, Graphic Design, Jewelry, Painting & Drawing, Photography, Printed Textiles, Printmaking, Sculpture, Woven Textiles
Summer School: Dir, John Goodheart. Tuition res—undergrad $71 per cr hr, grad $93 per cr hr; nonres—undergrad $222.15 per cr hr, grad $266.60 per cr hr. Courses—Art History, Ceramics, Drawing, Painting, Photography

CRAWFORDSVILLE

WABASH COLLEGE, Art Dept, 301 W Wabash Ave, Crawfordsville, IN 47933-2417. Tel 765-361-6386; Fax 765-361-6341; Email huebnerg@wabash.edu; Web: www.wabash.edu; *Chmn* Gregory Huebner; *Prof* Doug Calisch; *Gallery Dir* Lali Hess; *Asst Prof Art History* Elizabeth Morton
Estab 1832, dept estab 1950; Maintain nonprofit art gallery; Eric Dean Gallery, Randolph Deer Art Wing, Fine Arts Ctr, Wabash College, 301 W Wabash Ave, Crawfordsville, IN 47933; Pvt, men only; D; Scholarships; Fellowships; SC 16, LC 7; D 100, non-maj 80, maj 20
Ent Req: HS dipl, SAT
Degrees: BA 4 yrs
Courses: 2-D & 3-D Design, Aesthetics, Architecture, Art History, †Ceramics, Design, †Drawing, †History of Art & Architecture, †Painting, †Photography, †Sculpture

DONALDSON

ANCILLA COLLEGE, Art Dept, PO Box 1, Donaldson, IN 46513-0001. Tel 574-936-8898, 866-262-4552 (toll free); Fax 574-935-1773; *Act Dept Head* Charles Duff
Estab 1936, dept estab 1965; pvt; D & E; SC 9-12, LC 2
Ent Req: HS dipl
Degrees: AA, AAA(Applied Arts) 2 yrs
Tuition: Undergrad $145 per cr hr
Courses: Aesthetics, Art Appreciation, Calligraphy, Ceramics, Design, Drawing, Enameling, Graphic Design, Lettering, Photography
Children's Classes: Enrl 12; tuition $40 for 6 sessions; Courses—Crafts for Children, Drawing and Painting for Children. Classes on Saturday

EVANSVILLE

UNIVERSITY OF EVANSVILLE, Art Dept, 1800 Lincoln Ave, Evansville, IN 47722-0001. Tel 812-488-2043; Fax 812-488-2101; Email bb32@evansville.edu; *Dept Head, Prof* William Brown, MFA; *Assoc Prof* Ralph Larmann, MFA; *Assoc*

Prof Stephanie Frasier, MFA; *Instr* Tracy Maurer, MA; *Instr* Mark Schoenbaum, MFA; *Instr* Evan Crowley, MFA; *Instr* Francis Cadora, BS; *Instr* Valerie Milholland, MA; *Instr* Jesika Ellis, MA
Estab 1854; Maintains nonprofit Mel Peterson Gallery & Krannert Gallery; Pvt; D & E; Scholarships; SC 20, LC 10; D 2,600, maj 70
Ent Req: HS dipl
Degrees: BA(Art History), BS(Art Educ, Art & Assoc Studies), BFA, BA(Art) 4 yrs, pre-BS(Art Theory)
Courses: †Art & Assoc Studies, Art Appreciation, †Art Education, †Art History, †Ceramics, Design, Drawing, †Graphic Design, Jewelry, Life (figure) Drawing, †Painting, Photography, Printmaking, †Sculpture, †Visual Communication
Summer School: Tuition $210 5 wk sessions. Courses—Art Appreciation, Ceramics, Photography

UNIVERSITY OF SOUTHERN INDIANA, Art & Design Dept, 8600 University Blvd, Evansville, IN 47712-3590. Tel 812-465-7047; Fax 812-465-1263; Email vthomas@usi.edu; Web: www.usi.edu; *Prof* Hilary Braysmith, PhD; *Prof Emeritus* Leonard Dowhie, Jr, MFA; *Prof Emeritus* Margaret Skoglund, PhD; *Prof* Kathryn Waters, MFA; *Prof Emeritus* John McNaughton, MFA; *Assoc Prof* Joseph Uduehi, Ed D; *Assoc Prof* Joan Kempf de Jong, MFA; *Prof Emeritus* Michael Aakhus, MFA; *Instr* Virginia Poston, MA; *Assoc Prof* Xinran Hu, MFA; *Assoc Prof* Robert Millard-Mendez, MFA; *Asst Prof Art* Brett Anderson, MFA; *Asst Prof Art* Alisa Holen, MFA; *Instr* Nancy Raen-Mendez, MFA; *Asst Prof* Kristen Wilkins, MFA; *Asst Prof* Shannon Pritchard, PhD; *Instr* James Stanley
Estab 1969; maintains nonprofit art galleries, McCutchan Art Center/Pace Galleries on campus; on-campus shop for purchase of art supplies; FT 13, PT 13; pub; D & E; Scholarships; Fellowships; SC 27, LC 4; D 220, E 32, maj 208, non maj 12
Ent Req: HS dipl
Degrees: BA & BS (Art Educ), BA & BS (Art) 4 yrs
Tuition: Res—$234.82 per cr hr; nonres—$576.22 per cr hr
Courses: Art Appreciation, †Art Education, Art History, Ceramics, Contemporary Art, †Design, †Drawing, †Film, †Graphic Arts, †Graphic Design, Painting, Photography, Printmaking, Sculpture
Adult Hobby Classes: Enrl 25. Courses—Silkscreen
Children's Classes: Enrl 80, Sat am, 3 age groups
Summer School: Summer sessions offered

FORT WAYNE

INDIANA-PURDUE UNIVERSITY, Dept of Fine Arts, 2101 E Coliseum Blvd, Fort Wayne, IN 46805-1499. Tel 260-481-6705; Fax 260-481-6707; Email webers@ipfw.edu; Web: new.ipfw.edu/fine-arts/; *Chmn* Dana Goodman; *Asst Prof* Kirsten Ataoguz; *Asst Prof* Laurel Campbell; *Assoc Prof* Christopher Ganz; *Prof* John Hrehov; *Assoc Prof* Nancy McCroskey; *Prof* Audrey Ushenko
Estab 1920, dept estab 1976; pub; D & E; Scholarships; SC 96, LC 5; non-maj 60, maj 235
Degrees: AB, AS, BFA 4 yrs
Tuition: Res—$122.75 per cr hr; nonres—$213.95 per cr hr; no campus res
Courses: Art History, †Ceramics, †Computer Design, †Crafts, †Drawing, †Graphic Arts, Illustration, †Metalsmithing, †Painting, †Photography, †Printmaking, †Sculpture
Children's Classes: Enrl 75; tuition $60 for 11 wks. Courses—Ceramics, Drawing, Painting, Sculpture

UNIVERSITY OF SAINT FRANCIS, School of Creative Arts, 2701 Spring St, Fort Wayne, IN 46808-3994. Tel 260-399-7700; Fax 260-399-8171; Email rcartwright@sf.edu; Web: www.sf.edu/art; *Dean* Rick Cartwright, MFA; *Asst Dean* Colleen Huddleson, MBA; *Assoc Prof* Mary Klopfer, MFA; *Assoc Prof* Jane Martin, MFA; *Asst Prof* Tim Parsley, MFA; *Asst Prof* Cara Wade, MFA; *Asst Prof* Esperanca Camara, PhD; *Asst Prof* Eric Carlson, MFA; *Asst Prof* Beth Kuebler-Wolf, PhD; *Asst Prof* Jody Nix, MA; *Asst Prof* Matt White, MFA; *Instr* Tom Keesee, MFA; *Instr* Alan Nauts, BA; *Instr* Jared Applegate, MFA; *Instr* Ron O Lewis, BA
Estab 1890; Maintains nonprofit art galleries, Weatherhead Gallery & Lupke Gallery, 2701 Spring St, Fort Wayne, IN 46808; also maintains an art/architecture library, Lee & Jim Vann Library, 2701 Spring St. Ft Wayne, IN 46808; Pvt; D, E, & summer; Scholarships; SC 22, LC 6, GC 14, workshops; D 260, maj 260
Ent Req: HS dipl, class rank in HS, SAT
Degrees: MA (Studio Art), BA (Communication, Museum Studies, Graphic Design, Animation, Studio Art), BS (Education, Visual Art All Grade Major, Grades K-12); AA (Studio Art, Graphic Design); Minors: Art, Art History, Communication, Speech
Tuition: $25000 per year
Courses: †2D Composition, †3D Composition, Advertising Design, Animation, Animation, †Art Education, Art History, Ceramics, †Commercial Art, Computer Graphics, Design, †Design, †Desktop Publishing, Drawing, Fashion Arts, Film, Graphic Arts, Graphic Design, Metal Craft, Museum Staff Training, Painting, Photography, Printmaking, †Sculpture, Silversmithing, †Teacher Training, †Theatre Arts
Children's Classes: Enrl 60; tuition $85 per sem. Courses - Grades K-8 General Art Instruction
Summer School: Dir, Dean Rick Cartwright; two 8 wk sessions. Courses - Art Appreciation, Computer Graphics, Drawing, Painting, Animation

FRANKLIN

FRANKLIN COLLEGE, Art Dept, 101 Branigin Blvd, Franklin, IN 46131-2598. Tel 317-738-8279; Fax 317-736-6030; Web: www.franklincoll.edu; *Chmn Dept* Michael Swanson
Estab 1834; FT 2, PT 2; den; D; Scholarships; SC 9, LC 4; 900
Ent Req: HS grad
Degrees: BA 4 yrs
Courses: Art History, Basic Design, Design, Drawing, Painting, Sculpture

GOSHEN

GOSHEN COLLEGE, Art Dept, 1700 S Main St, Goshen, IN 46526-4794. Tel 219-535-7595; Fax 219-535-7660; Web: www.goshen.edu; WATS 800-348-7422; *Prof* Abner Hershberger, MFA; *Asst Prof* John Mishler, MFA; *Chmn* John Blosser
Estab 1950; den; D & E; Scholarships; D 145, E 25, non-maj 60, maj 50
Ent Req: HS dipl, top half of class
Degrees: BA(Art) with Indiana Teaching Cert
Courses: Aesthetics, Architectural Drawing, Architecture, Art Appreciation, †Art Education, Art History, †Ceramics, Commercial Art, Design, Drafting, Drawing, Graphic Design, †Jewelry, †Painting, Photography, †Printmaking, Sculpture, Stage Design, †Teacher Training, †Theatre Arts, Video

GREENCASTLE

DEPAUW UNIVERSITY, Art Dept, PO Box 37, Greencastle, IN 46135-0037. Tel 765-658-4340, 4800; Fax 765-658-6552; Web: www.depauwuniversity.edu; *Prof Chmn* Mitch Murback; *Prof* David Herrold
Estab 1837, dept estab 1877; pvt den; D; SC 14, LC 9, GC 18; D 300, E 20 (Art Dept), non-maj 25%, maj 75%, grad 20
Ent Req: HS dipl, upper half of high school graduating class
Degrees: BA & BM 4 yrs
Courses: Art Education, Art History, Ceramics, Drawing, Painting, Photography, Printmaking, Studio Arts

HAMMOND

PURDUE UNIVERSITY CALUMET, Dept of Communication & Creative Arts, 2200 169th St, Hammond, IN 46323-2094. Tel 219-989-2393; Fax 219-989-2008; Web: www.calumet.purdue.edu; *Head* Yahya R Kamalipour
Estab 1946; pub; D & E; Scholarships; SC 1-4, LC 1-2, GC 1
Ent Req: HS dipl
Courses: Architecture, Art Education, Ceramics, Drawing, Film, Painting, Photography, Teacher Training, Theatre Arts, Video

HANOVER

HANOVER COLLEGE, Dept of Art, 359 Lagrange Rd, Hanover, IN 47243; PO Box 108, Hanover, IN 47243-0108. Tel 812-866-7000; Fax 812-866-7114; Web: www.hanover.edu; *Interim Chmn Dept* Debbie Whistler
Estab 1827, dept estab 1967; pvt; D & E; Scholarships; SC 16, LC 4; D 1142
Ent Req: HS dipl
Degrees: BS and BA 4 yrs
Courses: Advertising Design, Aesthetics, Art Education, Art History, Ceramics, Collage, Commercial Art, Constructions, Drawing, Fiber, Film, Glass Blowing, Graphic Arts, Graphic Design, Jewelry, Painting, Photography, Printmaking, Sculpture, Stage Design, Stained Glass, Teacher Training, Theatre Arts, Video

HUNTINGTON

HUNTINGTON COLLEGE, Art Dept, 2303 College Ave, Huntington, IN 46750-1299. Tel 219-356-6000; Fax 219-356-9448; *Asst Prof* W Kenneth Hopper; *Asst Prof* Rebecca L Coffman; *Dean* Ron Webb
Estab 1897; den; D & E; SC 5, LC 3
Ent Req: HS dipl, SAT & two recommendations
Degrees: BA 4 yr
Courses: Art Appreciation, †Art Education, Art History, Arts & Crafts, Ceramics, Computer Graphics, Drawing, Fine Arts, †Graphic Design, Painting, Photography
Summer School: Dean, Ron Webb.

INDIANAPOLIS

INDIANA UNIVERSITY-PURDUE UNIVERSITY, INDIANAPOLIS, Herron School of Art & Design, 735 W New York St, Indianapolis, IN 46202-5222. Tel 317-278-9400; Fax 317-278-9471; Web: herron.iupui.edu; *Dean* Valerie Eickmeier; *Asst Prof, Dir Foundation* Reagan Furqueron; *Assoc Prof, Chair Fine Arts* Cory Robinson; *Asst Prof, Dir Art Therapy* Juliet King; *Prof, Visual Communication Design* Eva Roberts; *Prof, Dir Grad Progs* Andrew Winship; *Gallery Dir* Colin Tuis Nesbit
Estab 1902; Non-profit art gallery - Herron Gallery, 735 W New York St, Indianapolis, IN 46202; Herron Library (see above); pub; D & E; Scholarships; SC 115, LC 14, GC 10; D 800, non-maj 400, grad 60
Degrees: BFA and BAE 4 yrs, MAE 5 yrs
Courses: †Art Education, †Art History, †Ceramics, Computer Graphics, Drawing, †Fine Arts, Furniture Design, Graphic Arts, Graphic Design, Illustration, Mixed Media, Painting, †Photography, †Printmaking, †Visual Communications
Adult Hobby Classes: Sat school $225.00
Children's Classes: Enrl 225; tuition $200 (partial scholarships) for 10 wk term, Saturday art classes for jr & sr HS students. Youth Art Day Camp $200 per wk
Summer School: 2 two-week sessions of Honors Art $400/ses

MARIAN UNIVERSITY, Visual Arts Dept, 3200 Cold Spring Rd, Indianapolis, IN 46222-1997. Tel 317-955-6000; Fax 317-955-0263; Web: www.marian.edu; *Instr* Roberta Williams, MA; *Chmn* Jamie Higgs, PhD; *Assoc Prof Art* Megan Wright, MFA; *Asst Prof Art* Brian Crain, MFA; *Asst Prof Art* William Foley, BA; *Asst Prof Art History* Jenny Pauckner, MFA
Estab 1851, dept estab 1938; Maintains nonprofit Marian University Art Gallery (same address); schols open to fine arts students; Annie Loechle, PhD; Pvt; D & E; Scholarships; SC 36, LC 15; D 59, Maj 59
Special Subjects: Art History, Graphic Design
Ent Req: HS dipl, SAT

Degrees: AA 2 yrs, BA 4 yrs
Tuition: Res—undergrad incl room & board $21,172 per yr; nonres—$21,720, room & board incl
Courses: Art Appreciation, †Art Education, †Art History, Art Therapy, †Arts Administration, Ceramics, Crafts, Design, Drawing, †Graphic Design, History of Art & Architecture, Interior Design, Painting, †Photography, Printmaking, Sculpture, Stage Design, Teacher Training, Theatre Arts

UNIVERSITY OF INDIANAPOLIS, Dept Art & Design, 1400 E Hanna Ave, Christel de Haan Fine Arts Ctr Indianapolis, IN 46227-3630. Tel 317-788-3253; Email dschaad@uindy.edu; Web: www.uindy.edu; *Chair* Dee Schaad, MFA; *Assoc Prof* James Vuwigh; *Assoc Prof* Donna Adams; *Asst Prof* Julia Taugner; *Asst Prof* Christine Bently; *Instr* Carolyn Springer; *Instr* Marilyn McEiwan; *Asst Prof* Nelson Weitan
Estab 1902; Christel DeHaan Fine Arts Ctr Gallery; pvt, den; D & E; Scholarships; SC 40, LC 5, GC 8; D 400, E 160, maj 100, grad 20
Ent Req: HS dipl, SAT, upper half of HS class
Degrees: BA, BS 4 yrs & BFA
Courses: Advertising Design, Art Appreciation, Art Education, Art History, Ceramics, Commercial Art, Design, Drawing, Graphic Arts, History of Art & Architecture, Jewelry, Lettering, Occupational Therapy, Painting, Photography, †Pre-Art Therapy, †Pre-Medical Illustration, Printmaking, Sculpture, Teacher Training, †Visual Communications Design
Children's Classes: Enrl 20; free for 10 wk session. Courses—Drawing
Summer School: Dir, Dee Schaad. Enrl 60; $330 per cr hr. Courses—Art Appreciation, Ceramics, Computer, Photography, Printmaking

MARION

INDIANA WESLEYAN UNIVERSITY, School of Arts & Humanities, Division of Art, 4201 S Washington St, Marion, IN 46953-4974. Tel 765-677-2711; Fax 765-677-1042; Web: www.indwes.edu; *Chair, Prof* Rodney Crossman, MFA; *Prof* Ron Mazellen, MFA; *Prof* Dallas Walters, MFA; *Asst Prof* Daniel Hall, MA; *Assoc Prof* William Carpenter, MFA; *Asst Prof* Wendy Puffer, MA; *Asst Prof* Carl Rudy, MFA; *Asst Prof* Anne Greeley, MSt; *Asst Prof* Herb Peterson, MFA; *Asst Prof* Henrik Soderstrom, MFA
Estab 1890, dept estab 1969; Maintains Beards Art Center Galleries, 4200 John Wesley Ct, Marion, IN 46953. Art supplies sold at on-campus store; pvt, den; D & E; Scholarships; SC & LC; Maj 200
Ent Req: HS dipl
Degrees: BS: art educ, graphic design, illustration, media design, photography, pre-art therapy, studio art
Courses: †Animation, Art Appreciation, Art Education, Art History, Ceramics, Commercial Art, Drawing, Graphic Arts, Graphic Design, Illustration, Jewelry, Painting, Photography, Pre-Art Therapy, Printmaking, Sculpture, Silversmithing, Stained Glass, †Teacher Training, †Visual Arts Education, †Web Design
Summer School: Dir, Robert Curfman. Enrl 20

MUNCIE

BALL STATE UNIVERSITY, Dept of Art, 217 Riverside Ave, Muncie, IN 47306-0001. Tel 765-285-5838; Fax 765-285-5275; Web: www.bsu.edu; *Chmn* Thomas Spoerner, EdD
Estab 1918; FT 21; pub; D & E; Scholarships; SC 82, LC 25, GC 30; non-maj 386, maj 341, grad 15
Ent Req: HS dipl
Degrees: BS & BFA 4 yrs, MA 1 yr
Courses: Art Appreciation, †Art Education, Art History, †Ceramics, †Drawing, †Graphic Design, Jewelry, †Metals, †Painting, †Photography, †Printmaking, †Sculpture, Silversmithing
Summer School: Enrl 5000; tuition $1090 for term of 5 wks beginning May

NEW ALBANY

INDIANA UNIVERSITY-SOUTHEAST, Fine Arts Dept, 4201 Grant Line Rd, New Albany, IN 47150-6405. Tel 812-941-2342; Fax 812-941-2529; Web: www.ius.edu; *Coordr of Fine Arts* Anne Allen; *Assoc Prof* John R Guenthler, MFA; *Assoc Prof* Debra Clem, MFA; *Asst Prof* Marilyn Whitesell
Estab 1945, dept estab 1966; pub; D & E; SC 25, LC 2; D 150, E 35, non-maj 100, maj 50
Ent Req: HS dipl
Degrees: BA 4 yrs
Courses: Advertising Design, Art Appreciation, Art Education, Art History, Ceramics, Drawing, Painting, Printmaking
Adult Hobby Classes: Courses—Crafts, Watercolor
Summer School: Courses—Same as above

NORTH MANCHESTER

MANCHESTER COLLEGE, Dept of Art, 604 College Ave, North Manchester, IN 46962. Tel 260-982-5000, Ext 5327; Fax 260-982-5043; Web: www.manchester.edu; *Chmn Dept* Thelma S Rohrer, MA; *Assoc Prof* Ejenobo Oke, MFA
Estab 1889; Maintains nonprofit Gallery G & Link Gallery on campus; campus store for purchase of art supplies; pvt, den; D & E; Scholarships; SC 15, LC 5; D 45, maj 15
Ent Req: HS dipl
Degrees: BA & BS 4 yrs
Courses: Art Appreciation, Art Education, †Art History, Camera Techniques, Ceramics, Drawing, Graphic Design, Handicrafts, History of Art & Architecture, Painting, Photography, Sculpture, Teacher Training, Textile Design

NOTRE DAME

SAINT MARY'S COLLEGE, Dept of Art, Moreau Center for the Arts, Notre Dame, IN 46556. Tel 574-284-4631; Fax 219-284-4716; Email jtourtil@saintmarys.edu; Web: www3.saintmarys.edu; *Chmn* Julie Tourtillotte
Estab 1844; Maintains nonprofit gallery (same address); on-campus shop sells art supplies; Pvt, W; D & E; Scholarships; Fellowships; SC 21, LC 10; maj 50
Ent Req: CEEB, standing, recommendations, others
Degrees: BA and BFA 4 yrs
Tuition: $31,020 per yr
Courses: Art Appreciation, Art Education, Art History, Ceramics, Computer Media, †Costume Design & Construction, †Design, Drawing, Fibers, Holography, Mixed Media, Painting, Photo Silkscreen, Photography, Printmaking, Sculpture, Stage Design, †Video
Children's Classes: Summer fine art camps
Summer School: Dir Registrar. Courses vary. Enrollment up to 15.

UNIVERSITY OF NOTRE DAME, Dept of Art, Art History & Design, 132 O'Shaughnessy Hall, Notre Dame, IN 46556. Tel 219-631-7602; Fax 219-631-6312; Email art.art.1@nd.edu; *Chmn* Austin Collins, CSC; *Grad Dir* Richard Gray; *Office Coordr* Mary Foster
Estab 1855; FT 15, PT 8; pvt; D; Scholarships; SC 38, LC 8, GC 20; maj 100
Ent Req: upper third HS class, ent exam
Degrees: BA, BFA 4 yrs, MA, MFA
Courses: †Art History, †Ceramics, Drawing, Fibers, †Graphic Design, †Industrial Design, †Painting, †Photography, †Printmaking, †Sculpture
Summer School: Enrl 30-50; $93 per cr hr plus general fee for 7 wk term. Courses—Art History, Ceramics, Photography, Studio Workshops

OAKLAND CITY

OAKLAND CITY UNIVERSITY, Division of Fine Arts, 143 N Lucretia St, Oakland City, IN 47660-1037. Tel 812-749-4781, Ext 274; Email dhazelwo@oak.edu; Web: www.oak.edu; *Prof* Donna Hazelwood, PhD; *Prof* Joseph E Smith, MFA; *Assoc Prof* Carol Spitler, MA; *Asst Prof* Brenda Graham, DME
Maintain nonprofit art gallery; J Michael Dunn Gallery; art supplies available on-campus; FT 4, PT 1; pvt, den; D & E; Scholarships; SC 15, LC 5; maj 35
Ent Req: HS dipl, SAT or ACT
Degrees: AA 2 yrs, BA & BS 4 yrs
Courses: Advertising Design, Art Appreciation, †Art Education, Art History, Ceramics, Commercial Art, Conceptual Art, Design, Drawing, Graphic Arts, †Graphic Design, History of Art & Architecture, Painting, Photography, Printmaking, Sculpture, Teacher Training
Summer School: Courses vary

RICHMOND

EARLHAM COLLEGE, Art Dept, 801 National Rd W, Drawer 48 Richmond, IN 47374-4021. Tel 765-983-1200, 983-1410; Fax 765-983-1247; Web: www.earlham.edu; *Convener* Kristin Fedders
Estab 1847; den; D; Scholarships; SC 10, LC 7; maj 12-18
Ent Req: HS dipl
Degrees: BA 4 yrs
Courses: Art History, Ceramics, Drawing, Film, Painting, Photography, Printmaking, Theatre Arts

INDIANA UNIVERSITY-EAST, Humanities Dept, 2325 Chester Blvd, Richmond, IN 47374-1289. Tel 765-973-8200; Fax 765-973-8485; Web: www.indiana.edu; *Chmn* Dr TJ Rivard
Tuition: Res—$108.40 per cr hr; nonres—$267.40 per cr hr
Courses: Art Appreciation, Art Education, Art History, Drawing, Handicrafts, Painting, Photography, Sculpture

SAINT MARY OF THE WOODS

SAINT MARY-OF-THE-WOODS COLLEGE, Art Dept, 1 Saint Mary-of-the-Woods College, Hulman Hall Saint Mary of the Woods, IN 47876. Tel 812-535-5151, 535-5141; Fax 812-535-4613; Web: www.smwc.edu; *Area Coordr* Donna Dene English; *Gallery Dir* Sheila Genteman; *Assoc Prof* Thomas Swopes; *Asst Prof* Pat Jancosek
Estab 1840; FT 2, PT 1; den(W); D; Scholarships; SC 15, LC 4; maj 14
Ent Req: HS dipl, SAT or ACT
Degrees: BA & BS 4 yrs, MAAT
Courses: †Art Education, Art History, †Ceramics, Design, Drawing, †Graphic Design, †Painting, Photography, Teacher Training

SOUTH BEND

INDIANA UNIVERSITY SOUTH BEND, Fine Arts Dept, Ernestine M Raclin School of the Arts, 1700 Mishawaka Ave South Bend, IN 46615-1400. Tel 219-237-4134; Fax 219-237-4317; Web: www.iusb.edu; *Dean* Marvin Curtis; *Assoc Prof, Chair* Susan L More; *Assoc Prof* Dora Natella; *Assoc Prof* Ron Morusma
Estab 1964; Maintain art gallery (same as school); pub; D & E; SC 18, LC 6; non-maj 380, maj 48
Activities: Schols offered
Ent Req: HS dipl
Degrees: BA & BFA(Fine Arts) 4 yr
Courses: Art Education, Art History, Ceramics, Design, Drawing, †Graphic Arts, Graphic Design, History of Art & Architecture, Painting, Photography, Printmaking, Sculpture, Teacher Training, Theatre Arts, Video
Summer School: Chmn, Anthony Droege. Tuition same as regular session; two 6 wk summer sessions. Courses—Art Appreciation, Drawing, Painting

TERRE HAUTE

INDIANA STATE UNIVERSITY, Dept of Art, Fine Arts 108, Terre Haute, IN 47809. Tel 812-237-3697; Fax 812-237-4369; Email artdept@indstate.edu; Web: www.indstate.edu/art-dept/; *Chmn* Alden Cavanaugh
Estab 1870; Maintains nonprofit University Art Gallery, Center for Fine & Performing Arts, Terre Haute, IN 47809; art supplies sold at on-campus store; pub; D & E; Scholarships; SC 66, LC 45, GC 61; D 2432, E 311, maj 180, grad 40
Ent Req: HS dipl, top 50% of class with C average
Degrees: BA(Art History), BS(Studio Art), BSed(Art Education), BFA(Studio Art) 4 yr, MA(Studio Art) 1 yr & MFA(Studio Art) 2 yr
Tuition: Res—undergrad $262 per cr hr, (18 hr) grad $328 per cr hr; nonres—undergrad $558 per cr hr (9 hr), grad $645 per cr hr
Courses: Aesthetics, Art Appreciation, †Art Education, †Art History, †Ceramics, †Drawing, †Graphic Design, †Painting, Papermaking, †Photography, †Printmaking, †Sculpture, Studio Furniture, Teacher Training, Wood Sculpture
Summer School: Dir, Dr Louis Jensen. Tuition res—undergrad $262, grad $328 per cr hr; nonres—undergrad $558, grad $645 per cr hr for term of two 5 wks beginning June. Courses—variety of studio & lecture courses

UPLAND

TAYLOR UNIVERSITY, Visual Art Dept, 236 W Reade Ave, Upland, IN 46989-1002. Tel 765-998-2751, Ext 5322; Fax 765-998-4680; Email visualarts@taylor.edu; Web: www.taylor.edu; *Assoc Prof, Gilkison Family Chair in Art History* Rachel Smith; *Asst Prof* Larry Blakely; *Assoc Prof* Craig Moore; *Asst Prof* Kathy Hermann; *Instr* Shawn Casbarro; *Asst Prof* Robert Alsobrook; *Assoc Prof* Jonathan Bouw
Estab 1846, dept estab 1968; Maintain nonprofit art gallery, Metcalf Gallery; art library, Zondervan Library, Taylor Univ, 236 W Reade Ave Upland IN 46989; FT 7, PT 4; pvt; D; Scholarships; SC 18, LC 7; D 200, non-maj 250, maj 94
Ent Req: HS dipl, SAT, recommendations
Degrees: BA and BS 4 yrs
Courses: Art History, †Art Studio, Ceramics, †Design, Drawing, Graphic Arts, †Graphic Design, †History of Art & Architecture, Metals, Mixed Media, †New Media, Painting, Photography, Printmaking, Sculpture, †Silversmithing, †Video

VINCENNES

VINCENNES UNIVERSITY JUNIOR COLLEGE, Humanities Art Dept, 1002 N First St, Vincennes, IN 47591. Tel 812-888-5110; Fax 812-888-5531; Email ajendrzejewski@indian.vinu.edu; Web: www.vinu.edu; *Prof* Amy DeLap; *Prof* Jim Pearson; *Assoc Prof* Steve Black; *Assoc Prof* Deborah Hagedorn; *Assoc Prof* John Puffer; *Assoc Prof* Bernard Hagedorn; *Chmn* Andrew Jendrzejewski
Estab 1971; Maintain a nonprofit art gallery: Shircliff Gallery of Art, 1002 1st St, Vincennes University, Vincennes, IN 47591; Pub; D&E; Scholarships; SC 14, LC 2, Other Course 2; non-maj 80, maj 80
Ent Req: HS dipl
Degrees: AA, AS
Courses: Art Appreciation, †Art Education, Art History, Ceramics, †Commercial Art, †Design, Drawing, Fine Art, Graphic Arts, †Graphic Design, †Occupational Therapy, Painting, Photography, Printmaking, Sculpture, †Teacher Training

WEST LAFAYETTE

PURDUE UNIVERSITY, WEST LAFAYETTE, Patti and Rusty Rueff School of Visual & Performing Arts, Art & Design Dept, 552 W Wood St, West Lafayette, IN 47907-2002. Tel 765-494-3058; Fax 765-496-2076; Email adinfo@purdue.edu; Web: www.cla.purdue.edu/vpa/vpa; *Dept Chair (art & design)* David L Sigman, PhD; *Head of School (upa)* Harry Bulow, PhD
Estab 1869; Maintain a nonprofit art gallery (same address); FT 32; pub; D & E; Scholarships; SC 39, LC 14, GC 16; Undergrad 465, Grad 36
Ent Req: (see Purdue's admis website)
Degrees: BA 4 yrs, MFA
Tuition: Res—$5,601 per sem; nonres—$14,402 per sem
Courses: †Advertising Design, Aesthetics, Art Appreciation, Art Education, Art History, Ceramics, †Conceptual Art, Costume Design & Construction, Design, †Drawing, †Graphic Arts, †Graphic Design, History of Art & Architecture, Illustration, †Industrial Design, †Interior Design, †Jewelry, †Metals, †New Media, †Painting, †Photography, †Printmaking, †Sculpture, †Silversmithing, Stage Design, Teacher Training, †Textile Design, †Textiles, Theatre Arts, †Video, †Visual Communications Design, †Weaving

WINONA LAKE

GRACE COLLEGE, Dept of Art, 200 Seminary Dr, Winona Lake, IN 46590-1224. Tel 574-372-6021; Fax 574-372-5152; Email davisaw@grace.edu; Web: www.grace.edu; *Assoc Prof* Gary Nietcr, MA; *Assoc Prof* Timothy Young, MFA; *Head Dept* Art Davis, MA
Estab 1952, dept estab 1971; maintain nonprofit art gallery, Mount Memorial Art Gallery; pvt; D & E; Scholarships; SC 12, LC 3; maj 80, non-maj 200
Ent Req: HS dipl, SAT
Degrees: 4 yr Art Major, 4 yr Educ Major, 4 yr Graphic Art, 4 yr Illustration, 4 yr Drawing/Painting
Courses: 2-D Design, 3-D Design, Art Appreciation, †Art Education, Art History, Ceramics, †Drawing, †Graphic Design, †Illustration, Painting, Photography, Printmaking, Teacher Training, Typography
Children's Classes: Children's Art Encounters, 6th - 12th grade, $50

IOWA

AMES

IOWA STATE UNIVERSITY, Dept of Art & Design, 158 College of Design Bldg, Ames, IA 50011-3092. Tel 515-294-6724; Fax 515-294-2725; Web: www.iastate.edu; *Coordr Graphic Design* Sung Yung Kang; *Coordr Graphic Design* Debra Satterfield; *Coordr Integrated Arts* Arthur Croyle; *Coordr Interior Design* Fred Malvern; *Coordr Core Prog* Ann Sobiech-Munson; *Assoc Chair* Steve Herrnstadt
Estab 1858, dept estab 1920; Maintain nonprofit art gallery, Gallery 181, 134 College of Design, Iowa State Univ, Ames IA 50011; pub; D; Scholarships; SC 45, LC 15, GC 15; D 1,000, maj 960, grad 40
Ent Req: HS dipl
Degrees: BA, BFA(Graphic Design, Integrated Studio Arts, Interior Design), MFA (Graphic & Interior Design, Integrated Studio Arts); MA First Professional Degree Interior Design, Graphic Design; MA Environmental Graphic Design
Courses: Art History, †Graphic Design, Integrated Arts: Ceramics, Drawing, Illustration, Digital Design, Metals, Wood, Painting, Photography, Printmaking, Fibers, †Interior Design
Summer School: Dir, Chair Dept Roger Baer. Term of 8 wks. Courses—Art Education, Art History, Design, Drawing, Painting

BOONE

DES MOINES AREA COMMUNITY COLLEGE, Art Dept, 1125 Hancock Dr, Boone Campus Boone, IA 50036-5326. Tel 515-432-7203; Fax 515-433-5033; Web: www.demac.cc.ia.us; *Art Adjunct* Dr Penelope Miller
Estab 1927, dept estab 1970; Maintains non-profit art gallery, part of library, Boone campus; on-campus shop for art supplies; pub; D & E; SC 3, LC 2; D 30, E 15
Activities: Schols offered
Degrees: AA, AS 2 yrs
Courses: Art Appreciation, Art Education, Art History, Art in Elementary School, Drawing, Exploring Art Media, Landscaping, Life Drawing, Painting, Photography, Stage Design, Teacher Training, Theatre Arts

CEDAR FALLS

UNIVERSITY OF NORTHERN IOWA, Dept of Art, 104 Kamerick Art Bldg, Cedar Falls, IA 50614-0362. Tel 319-273-2077; Fax 319-273-7333; Email artdept@uni.edu; Web: www.uni.edu/artdept/Home.html; *Asst Prof* Soo Hostetler, MFA; *Prof* Roy Behrens, MA; *Prof* Charles Adelman PhD; *Prof* JoAnn Schnabel, MFA; *Prof* Thomas Stancliffe, MFA; *Prof, Art Dept Head* Jeff Byrd, MFA; *Prof* Philip Fass, MFA; *Assoc Prof* Aaron Wilson, MFA; *Prof* Richard Colburn, MFA; *Assoc Prof* Tim Dooley, MFA; *Asst Prof* Elizabeth Sutton, PhD; *Secy* Angela Kroemer; *Prof* Mary Frisbee Johnson
Estab 1876, dept estab 1945; Maintain nonprofit art gallery; art library; pub; D & E; Scholarships; SC 65, LC 20, GC 31; 13,500, non-maj 515, maj 400, grad 5
Ent Req: HS dipl, ACT
Degrees: BA & BFA 4 yrs, MA 1 1/2 yr
Tuition: Res—undergrad $2058 per sem, grad $2406 per sem; nonres— $5212 per sem, grad $5618 per sem, campus res—room & board $4148 per yr
Courses: Art Appreciation, Art Education, Art History, Ceramics, Drawing, Graphic Design, Illustration, †Jewelry/Metals, †Painting, Performance Art, Printmaking, Sculpture
Summer School: Dir Mary Frisbee Johnson. Enrl 75

CEDAR RAPIDS

COE COLLEGE, Dept of Art, 1220 1st Ave NE, Cedar Rapids, IA 52402-5008. Tel 319-399-8559; Fax 319-399-8557; Email pthompso@coe.edu; Web: www.coe.edu/academics/art; *Chmn* Peter Thompson, MFA; *Assoc Prof* Andrea Kann; *Asst Prof* Lucy Goodson, MFA; *Lectr* Kathleen Carracio, MFA; *Prof* John Beckelman, MFA; *Adjunct* Priscilla Steele; *Asst Prof* David Webber
Estab 1851; Maintain nonprofit art gallery & library, Marvin Cone Gallery, Eaton-Buchan Gallery, 1220 1st Ave NE, Cedar Rapids IA; on-campus shop where supplies may be purchased; pvt; D & E; Scholarships; SC 15, LC 5; D 1200
Ent Req: HS dipl, SAT, ACT
Degrees: BA 4 yr
Courses: Advertising Design, Aesthetics, Architecture, Art Appreciation, †Art Education, †Art History, †Ceramics, Collage, Costume Design & Construction, Design, Digital Art, Drafting, †Drawing, Film, Graphic Arts, Graphic Design, Mixed Media, †Painting, †Photography, †Printmaking, †Sculpture, †Teacher Training, Video

KIRKWOOD COMMUNITY COLLEGE, Dept of Arts & Humanities, 6301 Kirkwood Blvd SW, 336 Cedar Hall Cedar Rapids, IA 52404-5260. Tel 319-398-4956; Fax 319-398-7135; Email arts@kirkwood.edu; Web: www.kirkwood.edu/artshumanities; *Dean* Jennifer Bradley; *Prof* Helen Gruenwald, MA; *Asst Prof* Tonua Kehoe; *Instr* Arbe Bareis; *Instr* Robert Naujoks; *Prof* Conifer Smith; *Instr* Greta Songe; *Instr* John-Thomas Richard; *Instr* Lisa Lawrence; *Instr* Joe Hall; *Instr* Scott Gay; *Instr* Chris Mortenson; *Instr* Dan McCabe; *Instr* Robert Caputo
Estab 1966; Maintains nonprofit Iowa Hall Gallery, 101 Iowa Hall, 6301 Kirkwood Blvd SW Cedar Rapids, IA 52404; on-campus shop sells art supplies; pub; D & E; Scholarships; SC 18, LC 6; D 180, E 50
Ent Req: HS dipl
Degrees: AA 2 yr
Tuition: $145 per cr hr
Courses: Art Appreciation, Art History, Ceramics, Design, Digital Art, Drawing, Glass, Graphic Arts, Photography, Printmaking, Sculpture
Adult Hobby Classes: Fundamentals of Photography $395

Summer School: Dept Coord, Jennifer Cunningham. Tuition $145 per cr hr. Courses—Art History, Art Appreciation, Ceramics, Design, Drawing, Lettering, Painting, Photography, Printmaking, Sculpture

MOUNT MERCY UNIVERSITY, Art Dept, 1330 Elmhurst Dr NE, Cedar Rapids, IA 52402-4797. Tel 319-363-8213; Fax 319-363-5270; Web: www2.mtmercy.edu; *Prof* Charles Barth, PhD, MFA; *Prof* Jane Gilmor, MFA; *Asst Prof* David VanAllen, MFA
Estab 1928, dept estab 1960; Maintain nonprofit art gallery; Janalyn Hanson White Gallery; art library; Pvt; D & E; Scholarships; SC 12, LC 5; D 1,100, E 300, non-maj 150, maj 45
Ent Req: HS dipl, ACT
Degrees: BA 4 yr
Courses: †Art Education, Art History, Calligraphy, Ceramics, Design, Drawing, Graphic Arts, Graphic Design, Jewelry, Painting, Photography, Sculpture, Textile Design, Travel Study
Summer School: Dir, Susan Pauly, VPres Acad Affairs. Enrl 500; tuition $1,215 per 3 hr course, two 5 wk sessions. Courses—Art Appreciation, Ceramics, Graphic Design, Photography

CENTERVILLE

INDIAN HILLS COMMUNITY COLLEGE, Dept of Art, 721 N 1st St, Centerville, IA 52544-1223. Tel 641-856-2143; Fax 641-856-5527; Web: www.ihcc.cc.iowa.us; WATS 800-670-3641; *Head Dept* Mark McWhorter; *Instr* Enfys McMurrey, MA; *Instr* David Johnson
Estab 1932, dept estab 1967; pub; D & E; Scholarships; SC 10; D 70, E 30, non-maj 50, maj 14
Ent Req: HS dipl or equal, open door
Degrees: AA 2 yr
Courses: Art Appreciation, Art History, Arts & Crafts, Ceramics, †Design, Design, †Drafting, Drawing, †Occupational Therapy, Painting, †Photography, Raku Pottery, †Theatre Arts
Summer School: Chmn, Mark McWhorter. Courses—Art Appreciation, Ceramics, Design, European Art Tours, Painting

CLINTON

ASHFORD UNIVERSITY, (Mount Saint Clare College) Art Dept, 1310 19th Ave NW, Clinton, IA 52732-2752. Tel 563-242-4023; Fax 563-242-2003; Web: www.ashford.edu; *Head Dept* Prof Anna Pagnucci
Estab 1928, dept estab 1940; Maintain non-profit art gallery, Clare Hall (same address); Pvt; D & E; Scholarships; SC 5, LC 1; non-maj 80, maj 8
Ent Req: HS dipl
Degrees: AA, BA, MA
Courses: 2-D & 3-D Design, †Animation, Art Appreciation, †Art Education, †Art History, Calligraphy, Ceramics, Computer Art, Computer Graphics, Design, Desktop Publishing, Drawing, Fiber Art, Fiber Sculpture, †Graphic Arts, †Graphic Design, †Painting, †Photography, †Printmaking, †Sculpture, †Teacher Training, †Video
Summer School: Art Appreciation, Calligraphy, Painting

EASTERN IOWA COMMUNITY COLLEGE, Clinton Community College, 1000 Lincoln Blvd, Clinton, IA 52732-6299. Tel 563-244-7001; Fax 319-244-7026; Web: www.eicc.edu; *Instr* Carolyn Phillips
Estab 1946; Pub; D&E, distance educ; Scholarships
Ent Req: depends on specific scholarship
Degrees: AA
Tuition: Res—$65 fees included per sem; nonres—$97.50 fees included per sem
Courses: Art Appreciation, Art History, Design, Drawing, Painting, Photography, Printmaking

COUNCIL BLUFFS

IOWA WESTERN COMMUNITY COLLEGE, Art Dept, 2700 College Rd, Council Bluffs, IA 51503-1057; PO Box 4C, Council Bluffs, IA 51502-3004. Tel 712-325-3200; Fax 712-325-3424; *Chmn* Frances Parrott
2000
Degrees: BA 4 yr
Tuition: Res—undergrad $79 per cr hr; nonres—undergrad $114
Courses: Art Appreciation, Art History, Ceramics, Design, Drawing, Painting, Photography, Sculpture

CRESTON

SOUTHWESTERN COMMUNITY COLLEGE, Art Dept, 1501 W Townline St, Creston, IA 50801-1098. Tel 641-782-7081; Fax 641-782-3312; Web: www.swcc.cc.ia.us; *Dir Art Dept* Linda Dainty
Estab 1966; pub; D & E; Scholarships; SC 6, LC 3; D 550, E 200, non-maj 40, maj 15, others 15
Ent Req: HS dipl
Degrees: AA 2 yrs
Courses: Art Appreciation, Art Education, Art History, Ceramics, Computer Graphics, Design, Drawing, Graphic Design, Painting, Photography, Teacher Training
Adult Hobby Classes: Enrl 10-30; tuition $30 per sem. Courses—Per regular session
Summer School: Workshops in arts science

DAVENPORT

SAINT AMBROSE UNIVERSITY, Art Dept, 518 W Locust St, Davenport, IA 52803-2898. Tel 563-333-6000; Fax 563-333-6243; Web: www.sau.edu; web.sau.edu/art; *Chair Art Dept & Prof Art History* Dr Terri Switzer, PhD; *Prof Art* Leslie Bell, MFA; *Prof Art* Kristin Quinn, MFA; *Asst Prof Art* Renee Meyer Ernst, MFA; *Asst Prof Art* Joseph Lappie, MFA
Estab 1892; pvt; D & E; Scholarships; SC 33, LC 15; undergrad 2885, maj 140, grad 844
Ent Req: HS dipl
Degrees: BA 4 yrs
Courses: Art Education, Art History, Calligraphy, Drawing, Graphic Arts, Graphic Design, Illustration, Lettering, Painting, Photography, Printmaking, Teacher Training, Web Design
Summer School: Tuition $400 per sem hr. Courses—vary

DECORAH

LUTHER COLLEGE, Art Dept, 700 College Dr, Decorah, IA 52101-1041. Tel 563-387-2000, 387-1114; Fax 563-387-1391; Email martinka@luther.edu; Web: www.luther.edu; *Head Dept* Kate Martinson
Estab 1861; FT 3, PT 2; den; D; Scholarships; SC 13, LC 5; D 160
Ent Req: HS dipl or ent exam
Degrees: BA 4 yr
Courses: †Aesthetics, †Art Education, Art Management, †Ceramics, Computer Art, †Drawing, Fibers, Graphic Arts, Hand Made Paper, †History of Art & Architecture, †Lettering, †Painting, †Printmaking, Spinning, †Stage Design, †Teacher Training, †Theatre Arts
Children's Classes: Enrl 50; Courses offered spring & fall
Summer School: Acad Dean, A Thomas Kraalsel. Enrl 200 June & July. Courses—Drawing, Invitation to Art

DES MOINES

DRAKE UNIVERSITY, Dept Art & Design, 2507 University Ave, Des Moines, IA 50311-4516. Tel 515-271-2863; Fax 515-271-2558; Email admissions@drake.edu; Web: www.drake.edu/art-design/; *Asscc Prof Art & Dept Chmn* Benjamin Gardner
Estab 1881; Maintains nonprofit Anderson Gallery at Harmon Fine Arts Center, 2505 Carpenter Ave, Des Moines, IA 50311; FT 10, PT 8; pvt; D & E; Scholarships; SC 64, LC 15, GC 33; D 140, maj 140
Ent Req: 2 pt average in HS or previous col
Degrees: BA, BFA
Courses: Art Appreciation, †Drawing, †Graphic Design, †History of Art & Architecture, Lettering, Museum Staff Training, †Painting, †Printmaking, †Sculpture

GRAND VIEW COLLEGE, Art Dept, 1200 Grandview Ave, Des Moines, IA 50316-1599. Tel 515-263-2800; Fax 515-263-2974; Web: www.gvc.edu; *Dept Head* Dennis Kaven
Scholarships
Degrees: BA, cert
Tuition: Res—undergrad $6290 per sem
Courses: Art Therapy, Computer Graphics, Drawing, Jewelry, Painting, Photography, Printmaking, Textile Design, Theatre Arts

DUBUQUE

CLARKE COLLEGE, Dept of Art, 1550 Clarke Dr, Dubuque, IA 52001-3198. Tel 563-588-6300; Fax 563-588-6789; Email joan.lingen@clarke.edu; Web: www.clarke.edu; *Chmn & Prof Art* Joan Lingen PhD; *Prof Art* Douglas Schlesier, MFA; *Prof Art* Louise Kamas, MFA; *Assoc Prof* Carmelle Zserdin, MA; *Assoc Prof* Al Grivetti, MFA
Estab 1843; Maintain nonprofit art gallery; Quigley Gallery; pvt, den; D & E; Scholarships; SC 15, LC 4; maj 60, others 1200
Ent Req: HS grad, 16 units and Col Ent Board
Degrees: BFA(studio), BA(studio & art history) & BFA(graphic design)
Courses: Aesthetics, Art Appreciation, †Art Education, Art History, Book Arts, Calligraphy, †Ceramics, Costume Design & Construction, Design, †Drawing, †Graphic Design, History of Art & Architecture, Lettering, Mixed Media, †Painting, Photography, †Printmaking, †Sculpture, Stage Design, †Teacher Training, †Theatre Arts
Adult Hobby Classes: Enrl varies; 3, 4, 7 & 15 wk terms
Children's Classes: Enrl 15 per camp; tuition $60 per wk, summers
Summer School: Dir, Karen Adams. 3-4 wk term. Courses—Varies from yr to yr

LORAS COLLEGE, Dept of Art, 1450 Alta Vista, Dubuque, IA 52001. Tel 563-588-7117; Fax 563-588-7292; Web: www.loras.edu; *Chmn & Prof* Roy Haught; *Assoc Prof* Thomas Jewell Vitale; *Instr* Tom Gibbs
Degrees: MA (Art Educ & Studio Arts), BA
Tuition: Res & nonres—$13,645 per yr
Courses: Art Appreciation, †Art Education, †Art History, Design, Drawing, †Fibers, Painting, Printmaking, Sculpture, †Studio Art
Summer School: Dir, John Hess. Enrl $170 per course

ESTHERVILLE

IOWA LAKES COMMUNITY COLLEGE, Dept of Art, 300 S 18th St, Estherville, IA 51334-2721. Tel 712-362-2604; Fax 712-362-8363
Estab 1967; pub; D & E; Scholarships; SC 26, LC 1
Ent Req: HS dipl
Degrees: AA, AS(Commercial Art) 2 yrs

Tuition: Res—undergrad $917 per sem; nonres—undergrad $941 per sem
Courses: Advertising Design, Art History, Calligraphy, Ceramics, Commercial Art, Commercial Studio Portfolio Preparation, Computer Graphics, Drawing, Graphic Arts, Graphic Design, Illustration, Mixed Media, Painting, Photography
Summer School: Courses—Internships in Commercial Art

FOREST CITY

WALDORF COLLEGE, Art Dept, 106 S Sixth St Forest City, IA 50436. Tel 641-585-2450; Fax 641-582-8194; Web: www.waldorf.edu; *Chair* Kristi Carlson; *Adjunct* Lori Hadacek
Estab 1903; FT 1, PT 2; den; D & E; Scholarships; SC 4; D 80, maj 15
Ent Req: HS dipl, ACT or SAT
Degrees: AA, 2 yr, BA, 3 yr
Courses: Art Appreciation, †Art History, Design, Drawing, Painting, Photography, Printmaking

FORT DODGE

IOWA CENTRAL COMMUNITY COLLEGE, Dept of Art, 330 Ave M, Fort Dodge, IA 50501. Tel 515-576-7201; Web: www.iccc.cc.ia.us; *Chmn* Rusty Farrington
Estab 1966; Pub; D & E; Scholarships; SC 4, LC 2; D 120, E 15, non-maj 153, maj 20
Ent Req: HS dipl
Degrees: AA 2 yr
Courses: Art History, Painting, Studio Art
Summer School: Dir, Rusty Farrington. Enrl 45; tuition $53 per cr hr

GRINNELL

GRINNELL COLLEGE, Dept of Art, 1108 Park St, Grinnell, IA 50112. Tel 641-269-3064, 269-3085; Fax 515-269-4420; Web: www.grinnell.edu; *Prof* Merle W Zirkle; *Interim Dir* Bobbie McKibbin; *Chmn* Tony Crowley
Estab 1846, dept estab 1930; Maintain nonprofit art gallery; Faueconer Art Gallery-Bucksbaum Center for Arts; pvt; D; Scholarships; SC 9, LC 9; D 150, non-maj 125, maj 25
Ent Req: HS dipl, SAT or ACT
Degrees: BA 4 yrs
Courses: Art Education, Art History, Ceramics, Design, Drawing, Jewelry, Painting, Printmaking, Sculpture

IOWA CITY

UNIVERSITY OF IOWA, School of Art & Art History, 150 Art Bldg W, Iowa City, IA 52242-1706. Tel 319-335-1771; Fax 319-335-1774; Web: www.uiowa.edu; *Prof Foil Stamping* Virginia Myers; *Prof Metalsmithing & Jewelry* Chunghi Choo; *Dir* Dorothy Johnson
Estab 1847, school estab 1911; FT 38, PT 3; pub; D & E; Scholarships; SC 60, LC 55, GC 55; D 681, maj 508, grad 173
Ent Req: HS dipl, ACT or SAT, upper rank in HS
Degrees: BA and BFA 4 yr, MA, MFA, PhD
Courses: Aesthetics, †Art Education, †Art History, †Calligraphy, †Ceramics, Conceptual Art, †Design, †Drawing, †Graphic Design, Industrial Design, Interior Design, †Intermedia, †Jewelry, †Multimedia, †Painting, †Photography, †Printmaking, †Sculpture, †Silversmithing, Teacher Training, †Video
Summer School: Dir, Dorothy Johnson. Enrl undergrad 195, grad 115; tuition res—undergrad $1030, grad $1467; nonres—undergrad $3780, grad $4726 for term of 8 wks, beginning June 10. Courses—Full range of Art Education, Art History, Studio Courses

IOWA FALLS

ELLSWORTH COMMUNITY COLLEGE, Dept of Fine Arts, 1100 College Ave, Iowa Falls, IA 50126-1199. Tel 641-648-4611; Fax 641-648-3128; Web: www.iavalley.cc.il.us\eco; *Chmn* Greg Metzen
Estab 1890; pub; D & E; SC 10, LC 1; in dept D 20-25
Ent Req: HS dipl, ACT
Degrees: AA 2 yrs
Courses: †Advertising Design, Art Appreciation, Art History, Ceramics, Commercial Art, Design, Drawing, Graphic Arts, Graphic Design, Illustration, Lettering, Mixed Media, Painting, Photography, Sculpture
Adult Hobby Classes: Enrl 12; tuition $20 per 20 hrs. Courses—Pottery
Summer School: Dir, Dr Del Shepard. Enrl 14; tuition $40 per sem hr for 4 weeks. Courses—Art Interpretation

LAMONI

GRACELAND UNIVERSITY, Fine Arts Div, One University Pl, Lamoni, IA 50140. Tel 641-784-5270; Fax 641-784-5487; Email finearts@graceland.edu; Web: www.graceland.edu; *Dept Coordr & Assoc Prof* Julia Franklin; *Asst Prof* Kitty Miller; *Assoc Prof* Robert Stephens; *Instr* Chuck Manuel; *Instr* Amber McDole
Estab 1895, dept estab 1961; Maintain nonprofit art gallery, Constance Gallery, The Helene Center Art Gallery & The Shaw Center Art Gallery, 1 University Pl, Lamoni, IA; pvt den; D; Scholarships; SC 36, LC 10; D 250, E 15, non-maj 60, maj 85, others 4
Ent Req: HS dipl
Degrees: BA and BS 4 yrs
Courses: Art Appreciation, †Art Education, Art History, Ceramics, Color Theory, †Commercial Design, Computer Graphic Design, Design, Drawing, †Graphic Design, Illustration, †Painting, Photography, †Printmaking, †Sculpture
Children's Classes: 138 summer art camp attendance, one week $75
Summer School: Dir, Dr Velma Ruch

MASON CITY

NORTH IOWA AREA COMMUNITY COLLEGE, Dept of Art, 500 College Dr, Mason City, IA 50401-7213. Tel 641-423-1264, Ext 242, 888-406-4222; Fax 641-423-1711; Email allisway@niacc.edu; Web: www.niacc.cc.edu; *Instr* Melissa Lovingood, MFA; *Instr & Chair* Wayne Allison, MFA; *Adjunct* Ken Anderson; *Adjunct* Ted Bieth; *Adjunct Emer* Peggy Bang; *Adjunct* Dean Swenson; *Adjunct* Paula Hauus, MFA
Estab 1964; Maintains nonprofit NIACC Auditorium Gallery; schols open to art majors; on-campus shop where art supplies may be purchased; pub; D & E; Scholarships; SC 4, LC 2; D 240, E 100, maj 30
Ent Req: HS dipl
Degrees: AA 2 yr
Tuition: Res— $800 per 15 cr hrs; nonres—$1200 per 15 cr hr
Courses: 2-D Design, Art Appreciation, Art Education, Art History, Ceramics, Computer Graphic Design, †Design, Drawing, †Graphic Arts, †Graphic Design, †History of Art & Architecture, †Mixed Media, Painting, Photography

MOUNT PLEASANT

IOWA WESLEYAN COLLEGE, Art Dept, 601 N Main, Mount Pleasant, IA 52641. Tel 319-385-8021; Web: www.iwc.edu; *Chmn* Don R Jones; *Chmn Fine Arts Div* Ann Kligensmith; *Design Ctr Adjunct* Mike Foley; *Art Educ Adjunct* Don Kramer
Estab 1842; den; Scholarships; SC 10, LC 4; maj 32
Degrees: BA 4 yr
Courses: Art Education, Art History, Ceramics, Design, Drawing, Graphic Arts, Introduction to Art, Painting, Photography, Printmaking, Secondary Art, Special Problems, Twentieth Century Art History, †Visual Communication & Design

OTTUMWA

INDIAN HILLS COMMUNITY COLLEGE, OTTUMWA CAMPUS, Dept of Art, 525 Grandview, Ottumwa, IA 52501. Tel 641-683-5111 ext 1825; Fax 641-683-5206; Email mark.mcwhorter@indianhills.edu; Web: www.indianhills.edu; WATS 800-726-2585; *Dean Arts & Sciences* Darlas Shockley; *Dept Head* Mark McWhorter; *Instr* Lisa Fritz
Estab 1965; Maintains nonprofit art gallery, Indian Hills Art Gallery 525 Grandview Ottumwa, IA 52501; schols open to art majors; on-campus shop where art supplies may be purchased; pub; D & E; Scholarships; SC 7, LC 2; D 150, E 70, maj 25
Ent Req: HS dipl, GED, ACT or SAT
Degrees: AA, AAS & AAA 2 yrs
Tuition: Res—$137 per sem cr hr; nonres—$160 per sem cr hr (res acquired after 90 days)
Courses: Advertising Design, Aesthetics, Art Appreciation, Art History, Ceramics, Crafts, Design, Drafting, Drawing, Film, †Graphic Design, Handicrafts, History of Art & Architecture, Lettering, Occupational Therapy, Painting, Photography, Sculpture
Adult Hobby Classes: Enrl 10-20; tuition $35 per sem cr hr. Courses—Ceramics, Painting, Watercolor
Summer School: Dean Arts & Sciences, Darlas Shockley. Enrl 120; 6 wk session. Courses—Liberal Arts, $137 per hr

PELLA

CENTRAL COLLEGE, (Central University of Iowa) Art Dept, 812 University, Pella, IA 50219. Tel 641-628-5261; Web: www.central.edu; *Chmn* J Vruwink, MFA
Estab 1853; pvt; D & E; Scholarships; SC 20, LC 6; D 180, non-maj 140, maj 40
Ent Req: HS dipl, ACT
Degrees: BA 4 yrs
Courses: Art History, Ceramics, Drawing, Glassblowing, Modern Art, Painting, Primitive Art, Studio Art

SIOUX CITY

BRIAR CLIFF UNIVERSITY, Art Dept, 3303 Rebecca St, Sioux City, IA 51104-2324. Tel 712-279-5321 or 800-662-3303; Fax 712-279-1698; Email bill.welu@briarcliff.edu; Web: www.sbc.edu/academic/arts; *Chairperson* William J Welu, MFA; *Assoc Prof* Dr Judith A Welu, MFA, EdD; *Lectr* Jeff Baldus, BA; *Lectr* Noreen Eskildsen, MA
Estab 1930; Maintain nonprofit art gallery; Clausen Art Gallery; pvt, den; D & E; Scholarships; SC 8, LC 5; D 250, non-maj 150, maj 30
Ent Req: HS dipl, ACT
Degrees: BA and BS 4 yr, MA in Educ
Courses: 2, 3 & 4 (major studio areas & independent study), Art 1, Art Appreciation, Art Education, Art History, Ceramics, Collage, Critical Seminar, Design, Drawing, Intermedia, †Mixed Media, †Painting, †Sculpture, †Teacher Training
Summer School: Dr Judith Welu. Enrl 30-40; tuition $210 per cr hr for 5 wk term. Courses—Contemporary Art History, Elementary Art Education, Pottery

MORNINGSIDE COLLEGE, Art Dept, 1501 Morningside Ave, Sioux City, IA 51106-1717. Tel 712-274-5212; Fax 712-274-5101; Email bowitz@morningside.edu; Web: www.morningside.edu; *Chmn* John Bowitz; *Asst*

Prof Terri McGaffin; *Instr* John Kolbo; *Instr* Shannon Sargent; *Instr* Jim Bisenius; *Instr* Amy Foltz; *Instr* Dolie Thompson
Estab 1894; Maintain nonprofit art gallery, Helen Levitt Gallery & Eppley Gallery 3625 Garretson Ave, Sioux City, IA 51106; on-campus shop for art supplies; FT 4; pvt; D & E; Scholarships; SC 17, LC 4; D 161, maj 90
Ent Req: HS dipl
Degrees: BA and BS (Art Educ) 4 yrs
Courses: Advertising Design, Art Education, Art History, Ceramics, Commercial Art, Conceptual Art, Costume Design & Construction, Design, Drawing, Film, Graphic Arts, Graphic Design, Illustration, Mixed Media, Painting, Photography, Printmaking, Sculpture, Stage Design, Studio, Teacher Training, Theatre Arts, Video
Summer School: Dir, John Bowitz. Enrl 50; tuition $270 per cr, May, June, July. Courses—Drawing, Photography

SIOUX CITY ART CENTER, 225 Nebraska St, Sioux City, IA 51101-1712. Tel 712-279-6272; Fax 712-255-2921; Email kwelch@sioux-city.org; Web: www.siouxcityartcenter.org; *Dir* Al Harris-Fernandez; *Chair* Doug Palmer; *Cur* Todd Behrens; *Exhib & Coll Coordr* Shannon Sargent; *Pres* Joe Twidwell; *Sec* Kjersten Welch; *Interim Studio Prog Coordr* Debra Marqusee; *Develop Coordr* Stacie Anderson; *Develop Coordr* Erin Webber-Dreeszen; *Publs Coordr* Lyle Listamann
Estab 1938; Maintains nonprofit art gallery, Atrium Gift Gallery, 225 Nebraska St, Sioux City IA 51101; Margaret Avery Heffernan Reference Library, non-circulating, vis by appt only; pvt & pub partnership; D & E; Scholarships; SC 14-20, LC 1-2, GC 15; D 100, E 400
Courses: Ceramics, Drawing, Mixed Media, Painting, Photography, Printmaking, Stained Glass
Adult Hobby Classes: Enrl 62, tuition $92-$125 (mem) & $100-$156 (non-mem) for 8 wk quarterly terms; Courses—Drawing, Painting (Oil, Watercolor), Stained Glass, Mosaics, Printmaking, Digital Photography, Black & White Film Photography, Adobe Photoshop, Ceramics, Pottery from Wheel, Assemblage Art
Children's Classes: Enrl 252; tuition $5-$80 (mem) & $5 - $96 (non-mem) for 8 wk quarterly term; Courses—Clay, Drawing, Mixed Media, Painting
Summer School: Project SOAR: Dir, Alice Marley; open to HS students; Enrl 10 per workshop; Tuition $10 per student; Courses—Photography, Ceramics, Drawing, Painting. Art Camp: Dir, open to ages 6 - 12; Enrl 24 per AM & PM sessions; $100 half-day, $200 full day (mem) & $123 half-day, $246 full day (non-mem) for 6-day camp offered over 2 wks; 4 - 5 camps offered through summer with AM, PM or full-day options; Courses—Drawing, Painting, Clay, Mixed Media

WAVERLY

WARTBURG COLLEGE, Dept of Art, 100 Wartburg Blvd, Waverly, IA 50677-2200. Tel 319-352-8200; Web: www.wartburg.edu/art; WATS 800-553-1797; *Dept Head* Thomas Payne, MFA; *Asst Prof* Barbara Fedeler, MFA
Estab 1852; Non-profit art gallery; den; D & E; Scholarships; SC 18, LC 4; D 135, non-maj 110, maj 25
Ent Req: HS dipl, PSAT, ACT & SAT, foreign students TOEFL and upper 50 percent of class
Degrees: BA(Art), BA(Art Educ) 4 yrs
Tuition: Res—undergrad $15,510 per yr, $5850 room & board
Courses: Advertising Design, Art Appreciation, Art Education, Art History, Computer Graphic Design, Design, Drawing, Graphic Design, Metal Design, Painting, Photography, Printmaking, Sculpture
Summer School: Courses—Drawing, Independent Study, Painting

KANSAS

ATCHISON

BENEDICTINE COLLEGE, Art Dept, 1020 N Second St, Atchison, KS 66002. Tel 913-367-5340; Fax 913-367-6102; Web: www.benedictine.edu; *Chmn* Dan Carrell
Estab 1971; FT 1; den; D; SC 15, LC 3; D 145, non-maj 123, maj 22
Ent Req: HS dipl, ent exam
Degrees: BA 4 yr
Courses: Art Education, Art History, Calligraphy, Ceramics, Drawing, Graphic Arts, Painting, Photography, Printmaking, Sculpture, Teacher Training

BALDWIN CITY

BAKER UNIVERSITY, Dept of Mass Media & Visual Arts, 618 Eighth St, Baldwin City, KS 66006. Tel 785-594-4509; Fax 785-594-2522; Email bknappe@bakeru.edu; Web: www.bakeru.edu/contact/directories/academic-departments/art; *Chair & Asst Prof Art History* Brett Knappe; *Prof Art* Inge Balch; *Instr Art* Jenn Jarnot
Estab 1858; Maintains nonprofit art gallery: Holt/Russell Gallery, Baker Univ, PO Box 65, Baldwin City, KS 66006; schols open to all incoming students; pvt; D & E; Scholarships; SC 14, LC 9; D 180, maj 25
Ent Req: HS dipl, provision made for entrance without HS dipl by interview & comt action
Degrees: BA (Art) 4 yrs
Tuition: $19,925 per yr
Courses: Art Education, †Art History, Ceramics, Drawing, Graphic Arts, History of Art & Architecture, Painting, †Photography, Printmaking, Sculpture, Teacher Training
Summer School: Available; enrl & courses offered vary

COFFEYVILLE

COFFEYVILLE COMMUNITY COLLEGE, Art Dept, 400 W 11th St, Coffeyville, KS 67337-5064. Tel 620-252-7020; Fax 620-252-7098; Email michaeld@coffeyville.edu; Web: www.ccc.cc.ks.us; *Head Dept* Michael DeRosa
Estab 1923, dept estab 1969; pub; D & E; Scholarships; SC 8, LC 2; D 300, E 60, non-maj 300, maj 25
Ent Req: HS dipl
Degrees: AA
Courses: Art Appreciation, Art Education, Art History, Ceramics, Constructions, Design, Drawing, Film, Handicrafts, Mixed Media, Painting, Photography, Printmaking, Sculpture, Theatre Arts, Video
Adult Hobby Classes: Enrl 15-20; 3 month sem. Courses—Crafts
Children's Classes: Enrl 15; tuition $60 for 2 wks. Courses—Clay, Sculpture
Summer School: Dir, Michael DeRosa. Enrl 25; 2 month session. Courses—Ceramics I, Drawing I

COLBY

COLBY COMMUNITY COLLEGE, Art Dept, 1255 S Range, Colby, KS 67701. Tel 785-462-3984; Fax 785-462-4600; Email rebel.jay@colbycc.edu; Web: www.colby.edu; *Dir* Rebel Jay
Estab 1965, dept estab 1966; Maintains a non-profit gallery; pub; D & E; Scholarships; SC 16, LC 6; D 141, E 210, maj 18
Activities: Bookstore
Ent Req: HS dipl
Degrees: AA 2 yrs
Courses: †Art Appreciation, †Art Education, †Art History, Color Structure & Design, †Drawing, †Graphic Design, Painting, †Printmaking, Visual Arts
Adult Hobby Classes: Enrl 10-20

EL DORADO

BUTLER COMMUNITY COLLEGE, Art Dept, 901 S Haverhill Rd, El Dorado, KS 67042-3225. Tel 316-321-2222; Fax 316-322-3109; Web: www.butlercc.edu; *Dean* Dr Jay Moorman; *Instr* Valerie Haring; *Instr* John Oehm; *Instr* Roger Mathews
Estab 1927, dept estab 1964; Maintain nonprofit art gallery; Erman B White Gallery, 901 S Haverhill, El Dorado KS 67042; on-campus bookstore where art supplies may be purchased; pub; D & E, online courses; Scholarships; SC 13, LC 1; D 168, E 57
Ent Req: HS dipl, ACT, EED
Degrees: AA 2 yr
Tuition: Res—$95 per cr hr; nonres—$153 per cr hr
Courses: Art Appreciation, Ceramics, †Glasswork, Graphic Arts, Painting, Silversmithing, Two-Dimensional Design

EMPORIA

EMPORIA STATE UNIVERSITY, Dept of Art, 1200 Commercial St, Emporia, KS 66801-5057. Tel 620-341-5246; Fax 620-341-6246; Web: www.emporia.edu/art; *Chair* Elaine Henry; *Asst Prof* Matthew Derezinski; *Prof* Dan R Kirchhefer; *Asst Prof* Patrick Martin; *Asst Prof* Andre Piper; *Prof* Larry Schwarm; *Asst* Eric Conrad; *Asst* Roberta Eichenberg; *Lectr* Deborah Maxwell; *Lectr* Susan Nakao; *Lectr* John Hasegawa; *Lectr* Lily Liu; *Asst* Monica Kjellman-Chapin
Estab 1863, dept estab early 1900s; Maintain nonprofit art gallery; Norman R Eppink Art Gallery, Johnkins Hall, Emporia State Univ, Emporia, KS 66801; art supplies available on-campus; pub; D & E; Scholarships; SC 42, LC 15, GC 30; D 920, E 60, maj 182, grad 10
Ent Req: HS dipl, HS seniors may enroll in regular classes, ACT 21
Degrees: BFA, BSE, BS(Art Therapy) 4 yr, MS(Art Therapy)
Courses: Art Appreciation, †Art Education, Art History, †Ceramics, Design, Drawing, Engraving Arts, Fibers, Glass, †Graphic Design, Metals, Mixed Media, †Painting, †Photography, †Printmaking, †Sculpture, Teacher Training
Adult Hobby Classes: Metals, Ceramics & Photography
Summer School: Chair, Elaine Henry. Courses—most of the regular classes

GARDEN CITY

GARDEN CITY COMMUNITY COLLEGE, Art Dept, 801 Campus Dr, Garden City, KS 67846. Tel 316-276-7611; Fax 316-276-9630; *Chmn Human & Fine Arts* Kevin Brungardt
Degrees: AA
Tuition: Res—undergrad $44 per cr hr; nonres—$78 per cr hr
Courses: Art Appreciation, Art History, Ceramics, Design, Drawing, Handicrafts, Interior Design, Jewelry, Painting, Photography, Printmaking, Stage Design, Stained Glass

GREAT BEND

BARTON COUNTY COMMUNITY COLLEGE, Fine Arts Dept, 245 NE 30 Rd, Great Bend, KS 67530-9251. Tel 316-792-9260; Email dudeks@bartonccc.edu; *Dir* Steve Dudek, MFA; *Instr* Bill Forst, MFA
Estab 1965, dept estab 1969; Maintains nonprofit art gallery, Shafer Art Gallery, Fne Arts Bldg; FT 4 PT 3; pub; D & E; Scholarships; SC 15, LC 3; D 150, E 25; Maj 20
Ent Req: HS dipl or GED
Degrees: AA
Tuition: $125 per class
Courses: Art Appreciation, Art Education, Art History, †Ceramics, Design, Digital Photography, Drawing, †Graphic Design, †Painting, †Photography

Adult Hobby Classes: Enrl 25-200; tuition $42 per cr hr. Courses—Ceramics, Computer Graphics, Design, Drawing, Graphic Design, Individual Art Projects, Painting, Photo, Digital Photography
Summer School: Dir, Steve Dudek. Enrl 15-20; tuition $42 per hr for 8 wks. Courses—Ceramics, Individual Art Projects, Painting, Photo, Watercolor

HAYS

FORT HAYS STATE UNIVERSITY, Dept of Art & Design, 600 Park St, Hays, KS 67601-4099. Tel 785-628-4247; Fax 785-628-4087; Email ctaylor@fhsu.edu; Web: www.fhsu.edu/art/; *Chmn* Leland Powers, MFA; *Prof* Joel Dugan, MFA; *Prof* Chaiwat Thumsujarit, MFA; *Prof* Zoran Stevanov, PhD, MFA; *Instr* Erica Bittel, MA; *Asst Prof* Linda Ganstrom, MFA; *Assoc Prof* Allen Craven, MFA; *Prof* Gordon Sherman, MFA; *Asst Prof* Tobias Flores, MFA; *Prof* Karrie Simpson Voth, MFA; *Assoc Prof* Amy Schmierbach, MFA; *Instr* Charmion Arthur, MA; *Instr* Joyce Jilg, MA
Estab 1902, dept estab 1930; maintains nonprofit gallery, Moss-Thorns Gallery of Art, 600 Park St Hays, KS 67601-4009; on-campus art supply shop; pub; D & E; Scholarships; SC 66, LC 19, GC 28; D 742, non-maj 555, maj 286, grad 36, others 7
Ent Req: HS dipl
Degrees: BA & BFA 4 yrs, MFA 2 - 3 yrs
Tuition: Res—undergrad $145.27 per cr hr, grad $200.67 per cr hr; non-res—undergrad $427.37 pr cr hr, grad $510.02 per cr hr; campus res available
Courses: Advertising Design, Art Appreciation, †Art Education, †Art History, †Ceramics, Commercial Art, Design, †Drawing, †Graphic Design, †Handicrafts, Illustration, †Interior Design, Intermedia, Lettering, Mixed Media, †Painting, †Photography, †Printmaking, †Sculpture, †Teacher Training, Textile Design

HESSTON

HESSTON COLLEGE, Art Dept, 325 S College Ave, Hesston, KS 67062-9112; PO Box 3000, Hesston, KS 67062-2093. Tel 316-327-8164; Web: www.hesston.edu; *Head Dept* Lois Misegadis; *Faculty Emeritus* Paul Friesen
Estab 1915; pvt; D; Scholarships; SC 9, SC 1; non-maj 50, maj 5
Ent Req: HS dipl
Degrees: AA 2 yr
Tuition: $8100 annual tuition; campus res available
Courses: Art Appreciation, Art History, Ceramics, Design, Drawing, Graphic Design, Painting, Photography, Printmaking, Sculpture, Theatre Arts

HUTCHINSON

HUTCHINSON COMMUNITY COLLEGE, Visual Arts Dept, 600 E 11th St, Hutchinson, KS 67501-5800. Tel 620-665-3500; Fax 620-665-3310; Email brewerb@hutchcc.edu; Web: www.hutchcc.edu; *Prof* Roy Swanson; *Color & Graphic Instr* Scott Brown; *Ceramics & Sculpture Instr* Jerri Griffin; *Art History Instr* Teresa Preston; *Chmn* William Brewer
Estab 1928; Maintains nonprofit art gallery, Stringer Fyer Gallery; maintains art/architecture library, Parker Library; pub; D & E, on-line; Scholarships; SC 20+; D 215, E 41, non-maj 180, maj 81
Ent Req: HS dipl
Degrees: AA 2 yrs
Courses: Advertising Design, Architecture, Art Appreciation, Art Education, Art History, Ceramics, Commercial Art, Computer Graphics Design, Design, Drafting, Drawing, Graphic Arts, Graphic Design, Jewelry, Jewelry, Painting, Printmaking, Sculpture, Silversmithing, Stage Design, Teacher Training, Theatre Arts, Video
Summer School: Dir, Jeff Adams; Tuition $27 per hr for 6 wk session. Courses—Art Appreciation, Art Education

IOLA

ALLEN COUNTY COMMUNITY COLLEGE, Art Dept, 1801 N Cottonwood, Iola, KS 66749. Tel 316-365-5116; Web: www.allencc.net; *Dept Head* Steven R Greenwall, MFA
Estab 1965; pub; D & E; Scholarships; SC 5, LC 2; D 700, E 1000, non-maj 40, maj 10
Ent Req: HS dipl or GED
Degrees: AA, AS & AAS 2 yr
Courses: 2-D & 3-D Design, Art Appreciation, Art Fundamentals, Ceramics, Commercial Art, Drawing, Painting, Photography, Sculpture
Summer School: Courses—all courses

LAWRENCE

HASKELL INDIAN NATIONS UNIVERSITY, Art Dept, 155 Indian Ave, Lawrence, KS 66046-4817. Tel 785-749-8431, Ext 252; Web: www.haskell.com; *Instr* B J Wahnee, MA
Estab 1884, dept estab 1970; pub; D; SC 14, LC 1; in dept D, non-maj 90, maj 30
Ent Req: HS dipl or GED, at least 1/4 Indian, Eskimo or Aleut and receive agency approval
Degrees: AA & AAS 2 yrs, BA 4 yr
Tuition: Government funded for native Americans only; campus res available
Courses: Art Appreciation, Art History, Ceramics, Design, Drawing, Jewelry, Native American Architecture, Native American Art History, Native American Cultural/Tribal Art Forms, Native American Painting, Painting, Sculpture, Textile Design
Summer School: Enrl 150

UNIVERSITY OF KANSAS, The School of the Arts, Dept of Visual Art, 1467 Jayhawk Blvd, Lawrence, KS 66045-3140. Tel 785-864-4401; Fax 785-864-4404; Email visualart@ku.edu; Web: art.ku.edu; *Assoc Prof* Norman Akers; *Assoc Prof* Jane Asbury; *Asst Prof* Shawn (Daina) Bitters; *Prof Emer* Phillip Blackhurst; *Assoc Prof & Undergrad Coordr* Ruth Bowman; *Asst Prof* David Brackett; *Asst Prof* Matt Burke; *Prof* Carol Ann Carter; *Asst Prof* John Derby; *Lectr* Stacey Fox; *Prof Emer* Norman Gee; *Prof* Dawn Guernsey; *Assoc Prof* John Hachmeister; *Assoc Prof & Grad Dir* Tanya Hartman; *Prof* Jon Havener; *Prof & Chair* Mary Anne Jordan; *Prof* Cima Katz; *Assoc Prof & Assoc Dean* Elizabeth Kowalchuk; *Assoc Prof* Michael Krueger; *Prof* Gerald Lubensky; *Asst Prof* Marshall Maude; *Prof* Judith McCrea; *Assoc Prof* Yoomi Nam; *Assoc Prof* So Yeon Park; *Prof* Lin Stanionis; *Assoc Prof* Denise Stone; *Prof* Jon Swindell; *Asst Prof* Maria Velasco; *Assoc Prof* David Vertacnik; *Assoc Prof* Gina Westergard
Estab 1864; Maintains nonprofit art gallery; art supplies sold at on-campus store; Pub; D & E; Scholarships; Fellowships; SC 70, GC 35; 260
Ent Req: Portfolio review, essays
Degrees: BA, BAE, BFA, MA, MFA 4-5 yr
Tuition: Res—undergrad $262.50, grad $295.50 per cr hr; nonres—undergrad $689.35, grad $691.25 per cr hr
Courses: Art Education, Art History, Ceramics, Drawing, Goldsmithing, Mixed Media, Painting, Printmaking, Sculpture, Silversmithing, Teacher Training, Textile Design, Weaving
Summer School: Dir, Mary Anne Jordon
—**Dept of Art**, 1467 Jayhawk Blvd, Art & Design Bldg Rm 300 Lawrence, KS 66045-7594. Tel 785-864-4401; Fax 785-864-4404; *Chmn* Judith McCrea
Estab 1885; FT 19; Scholarships; SC 50, GC 25; maj 160
Tuition: Res—undergrad $899 per sem, grad $1088 per sem; nonres— $2985 per sem
Courses: †Drawing, New Genres, †Painting, †Printmaking, †Sculpture
Summer School: Dir, Judith McCrea. Enrl 60; tuition $57 for 8 wks. Courses—Life Drawing, Intro to Drawing I & II, Painting I-IV
—**Dept of Design**, 1467 Jayhawk Blvd, Art & Design Bldg Rm 300 Lawrence, KS 66045-7531. Tel 785-864-4401; *Chmn* Lois Greene
Estab 1921; FT 25, PT 5; SC 83, LC 32, GC 26; maj 550, grad 30
Tuition: Res—undergrad $2041.50 per yr, $68.05 per cr hr; nonres—undergrad $8460 per yr, $282 per cr hr
Courses: †Art Education, †Ceramics, Design, †Graphic Design, †Illustration, †Industrial Design, †Interior Design, †Jewelry, Photography, †Textile Design, Textile Printing & Dyeing, Visual Communications, †Weaving
Summer School: Term of 4-8 wks beginning June
—**Kress Foundation Dept of Art History**, Spencer Museum of Art, Rm 209, Lawrence, KS 66045. Tel 785-864-4713; Fax 785-864-5091; Email arthist@lark.cc.ukans.edu; *Dept Chair* Linda Stone-Ferrier; *Prof Emeritus* Chu-tsing Li PhD; *Prof* Charles Eldredge PhD; *Prof* Marilyn Stokstad PhD; *Prof* Stephen Goddard; *Prof & Asian Grad Adv* Marsha Weidner; *Assoc Prof* Edmund Eglinski PhD; *Assoc Prof* Amy McNair; *Assoc Prof* David Cateforts PhD; *Asst Prof* John Teramoto PhD; *Asst Prof* Patrick Frank; *Lectr* Roger Ward; *Dir Mus* Andrea Norris PhD; *Asst Prof* Patricia Darish PhD; *Assoc Prof* John Pultz
Estab 1866, dept estab 1953; pub; D & E; Scholarships; LC 30, GC 10; D 900, E 40, maj 50, grad 70
Ent Req: HS dipl
Degrees: BA, BFA, BGS, MA, PhD
Tuition: Res—undergrad $2041.50 per yr, $68.05 per cr hr; nonres—undergrad $8460 per yr, $282 per cr hr
Courses: African Art, American Art, Art History, Chinese Art, Japanese Art, Photography, Western European Art
Summer School: Enrl 80. Intro courses—Art History, Asian Art History & Modern Art History. Classes in Great Britain & Rome
—**Dept of Art & Music Education & Music Therapy**, 311 Bailey Hall, Lawrence, KS 66045-0001. Tel 785-864-4784; Fax 785-864-5076; *Chmn Dept* Lois Greene; *Asst Prof* Denise Stone PhD; *Asst Prof* Elizabeth Kowalchuk
Estab 1865, dept estab 1969; pub; D & E; Scholarships; GC 12; D 535, maj 123, grad 123, others 289
Ent Req: HS dipl, ent exam
Degrees: BAE 5 yrs, MA 1-6 yrs, PhD 3-6 yrs
Tuition: Res—undergrad $2041.50 per yr, $68.05 per cr hr; nonres—undergrad $8460 per yr, $282 per cr hr
Courses: Visual Arts Education
Summer School: Term of 8 wks beginning June

LEAVENWORTH

UNIVERSITY OF SAINT MARY, Fine Arts Dept, 4100 S 4th St, Leavenworth, KS 66048-5082. Tel 913-682-5151 ext 6608; Fax 913-758-6140; Email prindaville0211@stmary.edu; Web: www.stmary.edu; *Asst Prof & Prog Dir* Shelby Prindaville, MFA; *Assoc Prof* Susan Nelson, MFA
Estab 1923; Maintains a nonprofit art gallery, Goppert Gallery (same address); schols open to new students; Pvt, Catholic; D & E; Scholarships; SC 20, LC 3; non-maj 80, maj 25
Activities: Schols offered
Ent Req: HS dipl
Degrees: BA, BS 4 yr
Tuition: Res—$8,475 per sem
Courses: Advertising Design, Art Appreciation, Art History, Ceramics, Commercial Art, Computer Graphics, Design, Drawing, Graphic Arts, Graphic Design, Illustration, †Mixed Media, Painting, Photography, Printmaking

LIBERAL

SEWARD COUNTY COMMUNITY COLLEGE, Art Dept, 1801 N Kansas, Liberal, KS 67901-2054; PO Box 1137, Liberal, KS 67905-1137. Tel 620-417-1453; Email susan.copas@sccc.edu; Web: www.sccc.edu; *Dept Chair* Susan Copas; *Art Instr* Dustin Farmer
Estab 1969; pub; D & E; online; Scholarships; SC 23, LC 5; D 1,000, E 700
Ent Req: HS dipl
Degrees: AA 2 yrs
Courses: Art Education, Art History, Ceramics, Design, Drawing, Graphic Design, Handicrafts, History of Art & Architecture, Painting, Photography, Sculpture, Silversmithing, Visual Communication

LINDSBORG

BETHANY COLLEGE, Art Dept, 421 N First St, Lindsborg, KS 67456. Tel 785-227-3311, Ext 8145; Fax 785-227-2860; Email kahlerc@bethanylb.edu; Web: www.bethanylb.edu; *Prof* Mary Kay, MFA; *Asst Prof* Frank Shaw, MFA; *Head Art Dept* Caroline Kahler, MFA; *Prof* Ed Pogue, MFA; *Dr* Bruce Kahler; *Instr* James Turner
Estab 1881; Maintain nonprofit art gallery, Mingenback Art Center Gallery, Corner of Olson & Second St, Lindsburg, KS 67456; Den, Private, Denominational, Coed, ELCA - Lutheran Church of America; D & E; Scholarships; SC 26, LC 4, GC 2; D 150, non-maj 120, maj 40
Ent Req: HS dipl
Degrees: BA 4 yr
Courses: †Art Administration, Art Appreciation, †Art Education, Art History, Art Therapy, †Basketry-textiles, †Ceramics, Design, †Drawing, Jewelry, †Painting, Photography, Printmaking, †Sculpture, Studio Concentration, †Teacher Training, †Webpage Design
Summer School: Acad Dean, Dr Gene Bales

MANHATTAN

KANSAS STATE UNIVERSITY, Art Dept, 322 Willard Hall, Manhattan, KS 66506. Tel 785-532-6605; Fax 785-532-0334; Email art@ksu.edu; Web: www.ksu.edu/art; *Head Dept & Prof* Duane Noblett, MFA; *Prof* Yoshiro Ikeda, MFA; *Prof* Elliott Pujol, MFA; *Prof* Glen R Brown, PhD; *Prof* Anna Calluori Holcombe, MFA; *Assoc Prof* Daniel Hunt, MFA; *Assoc Prof* Kathleen King, MFA; *Asst Prof* Barri Lester, MFA; *Asst Prof* Rachel Melis, MFA; *Asst Prof* Nancy Morrow, MFA; *Prof* Lynda Andrus, MFA; *Asst Prof* Thomas Bookwalter, BFA; *Asst Prof* Jason Scuilla, MFA; *Asst Prof* Roger Rouston, MFA; *Prof* Teresa Tempero Schmidt, MFA
Estab 1863, dept estab 1965; Non-Profit art gallery, Chapman Gallery of Art, Kansas State Univ, 116 Willard Hall, Manhattan, KS 66506. Art supplies may be purchased on campus; pub; D & E; Scholarships; Fellowships; SC 45, LC 19, GC 7; D 1940, E 60, non-maj 1800, maj 400, grad 15
Ent Req: HS dipl
Degrees: BS(Art Educ) jointly with Col Educ, BA & BFA 4 yrs, MFA 60 sem cr
Courses: †Art Education, †Art History, †Ceramics, Design, †Drawing, Graphic Arts, †Graphic Design, †Illustration, †Jewelry, †Painting, †Printmaking, †Sculpture
Summer School: Dir, Duane Noblett. Courses—most of above, varies from summer to summer
—**College of Architecture Planning & Design**, 115 Seaton Hall, Manhattan, KS 66506-2900. Tel 785-532-5950; Fax 785-532-6722; Email dela@ksu.edu; Web: aalto.arch.ksu.edu; *Assoc Dean* Ray Weisenburger; *Dean* Dennis Law
Estab 1904; FT 53; 800
Degrees: BA, MA(Archit, Regional Planning & Interior Archit)
Tuition: Res—$75.55 per cr hr; nonres—$301.15 per cr hr
Courses: Architectural Programming, Architecture, Art History, Building Construction, Landscape Architecture, Landscape Design
Adult Hobby Classes: Dean, Lane L Marshall. Courses—Graphic Delineation, Preservation
Children's Classes: Courses—Special Design Program in June
Summer School: Dean, Lane L Marshall. 8 wks of courses beginning June 4th. Courses—Design Discovery Program, Design Studio

MCPHERSON

MCPHERSON COLLEGE, Art Dept, 1600 E Euclid, McPherson, KS 67460-3847; PO Box 1402, McPherson, KS 67460-1402. Tel 316-241-0731; Web: www.mcpherson.edu; *Asst Prof* Kelly Frigard; *Chmn* Wayne Conyers
Estab 1887; den; D & E; Scholarships; SC 14, LC 5; D 150, maj 10, others 140
Ent Req: HS dipl, ACT
Degrees: AB 4 yr
Courses: †Art Education, Art History, Ceramics, Drawing, †Interior Design, Lettering, Museum Staff Training, Painting, Printmaking, Teacher Training, Textile Design

NORTH NEWTON

BETHEL COLLEGE, Dept of Art, 300 E 27th St, North Newton, KS 67117-8061. Tel 316-283-2500; Fax 316-284-5286; Web: www.bethelks.edu; *Chmn* Merrill Kraball; *Assoc Prof* Gail Lutsch, MFA
Estab 1888, dept estab 1959; den; D; Scholarships; SC 11, LC 3; D 240, non-maj 215, maj 25
Ent Req: HS, ACT
Degrees: BA(Art) 4 yrs
Courses: Art Education, Art History, Ceramics, Crafts, Drawing, Graphic Arts, Graphic Design, Painting, Photography, Printmaking, Sculpture
Adult Hobby Classes: Enrl 15; tuition $40 per 6 wk session. Courses—Ceramics, Drawing, Painting
Summer School: Courses—Drawing, Painting

OTTAWA

OTTAWA UNIVERSITY, Dept of Art, 1001 S Cedar St, Ottawa, KS 66067-3399. Tel 785-242-5200; Fax 785-242-7429; Web: www.ottawa.edu; *Chmn* Frank J Lemp
Estab 1865; FT 1; pvt; D; Scholarships; SC 16, LC 5; D 35, maj 5
Ent Req: HS grad, SAT, ACT
Degrees: BA 4 yrs
Courses: Art Education, Art History, Arts Management, Ceramics, Drawing, Graphic Arts, Painting, Photography
Children's Classes: Outreach Progs
Summer School: Dir, Frank Lemp. Tuition $89 per cr hr for 8 wk session. Courses—Art Fundamentals

OVERLAND PARK

JOHNSON COUNTY COMMUNITY COLLEGE, Fine Arts Dept & Art History Dept, 12345 College Blvd, Overland Park, KS 66210-1299. Tel 913-469-8500-ext 3649; Fax 913-469-4409; Email lthomas@jccc.edu; Web: www.jccc.edu; *Adjunct Prof Fine Art* Doug Baker, MFA; *Adjunct Prof Art History* Tracy Boswell, MA; *Adjunct Prof Fine Art* John Carroll, MFA; *Asst Prof Fine Art & Sculpture Dept Coordr* Mark Cowardin, MFA; *Assoc Prof Fine Art & Ceramic Dept Coordr* Laura-Harris Gascogne, MFA; *Adjunct Prof Fine Art* Keiko Kira, MFA; *Adjunct Prof Photog* John Lamberton, MFA; *Adjunct Assoc Prof Art History/Architecture* Ted Meadows, MA; *Adjunct Assoc Prof Art History* Kathleen Mendenhall, MA; *Adjunct Prof Art History* Rajee Mohan, MA; *Adjunct Asst Prof Art History* Jennifer Newlands, MA; *Adjunct Prof Fine Art* Syndey Pener, MFA; *Adjunct Assoc Prof Fine Art* Ruthanne Robertson, MFA; *Adjunct Assoc Prof Fine Art* Angelica Sandoval, MFA; *Assoc Prof Art History & Chair Art History* Allison Smith, PhD; *Adjunct Assoc Prof Fine Art* Bridget Stewart, MFA; *Prof & Chair Fine Art* Larry Thomas, MFA; *Adjunct Prof Art History* Ann Wiklund, MA; *Adjunct Asst Prof Art History* Valerie Zell, MA; *Adjunct Prof Photog* Mary Wessel, MFA; *Adjunct Asst Prof Art History* Marie Dolembo, MA; *Adjunct Assoc Prof Fine Art* Nick Haney, MFA; *Adjunct Asst Prof Photog* Philip Heying, BFA; *Adjunct Asst Prof Art History* Brian Hogarth, MA; *Adjunct Asst Prof Art History* Heather Kauten; *Adjunct Asst Prof Fine Art* Misha Kligman, MFA; *Adjunct Assoc Prof Photog* Adam Long, MFA; *Adjunct Prof Photog* Jeff Nichols, MFA; *Adjunct Prof Photog* Meghan Nichols, MFA; *Adjunct Asst Prof Photog* Craig Sands, BFA; *Adjunct Asst Prof Fine Art* Andrew Shell, MFA; *Prof Emeritus Photog* Tom Tarnowski, MFA
Estab 1969; Maintain non-profit art gallery, JCCC Student Gallery, 3rd Floor Student Center; Nerman Mus of Contemporary Art, (same address as col; on-campus shop sells art supplies; pub; D, E & weekends; Scholarships; SC 30, LC 4; Enrl in Fine Arts & Art History D 1272, E 219
Activities: Schols offered
Ent Req: HS dipl or equivalent
Degrees: AA 2 yr
Tuition: Johnson County Res $88 per hr, out of district $103, out of state $206
Courses: 2-D & 3-D Design, †Architecture, Art History, Ceramics, †Design, †Digital Imaging for Artists, Drawing, Life Drawing, Painting, Photography, Sculpture, Silversmithing, Studio Workshop
Children's Classes: Accelerated fine arts for gifted children
Summer School: Dir, Larry Thomas, Prof & Chair Fine Arts Dept. Enrl 95; tuition $88 per cr hr for term of 8 wks. Courses—Ceramics, Design, Drawing, Painting, Photography, Sculpture, Silversmithing

PITTSBURG

PITTSBURG STATE UNIVERSITY, Art Dept, 1701 S Broadway St, Pittsburg, KS 66762-7500. Tel 620-235-4302; Fax 620-235-4303; Email art@pittstate.edu; Web: www.pittstate.edu/art; *Chairperson & Assoc Prof* Rhona McBain, MFA; *Prof* Marjorie K Schick, MFA; *Assoc Prof* Malcolm E Kucharski, MFA; *Prof* Portico K Bowman, MFA; *Prof* Jr James M Oliver, MFA; *Asst Prof* Josie Mai; *Assoc Prof* Li Li Tseng; *Asst Prof* Emmalyn Gennis; *Instr* Janet Lewis; *Instr* Deann Norris
Estab 1903, dept estab 1921; Maintain nonprofit art gallery, Pittsburg State University Art Gallery, Art Dept - Porter Hall, 1701 S Broadway, Pittsburg, KS 66762-7512; pub; D & E; Scholarships; SC 50, LC 24, GC 22; D 600, E 50, non-maj 300, maj 90, grad 10
Ent Req: HS dipl
Degrees: BFA & BSED 4 yr, MA 36 hr
Courses: Art Appreciation, †Art Education, Art History, Ceramics, †Commercial Art, Crafts, Design, Drawing, Jewelry, Jewelry Design, †Painting, Photography, Printmaking, Sculpture, Teacher Training
Summer School: Enrl 100; tuition res—undergrad $105 per cr hr; grad $141 per cr hr; nonres—undergrad $299 per cr hr, grad $349 per cr hr, for term of 2 4 wk sessions (June & July). Courses—Art Education, Ceramics, Crafts, Drawing, Painting

PRATT

PRATT COMMUNITY COLLEGE, Art Dept, 348 NE SR 61, Pratt, KS 67124. Tel 620-672-5641 Ext 228, 800-794-3091; Fax 620-672-5288; Email marshas@prattcc.edu; Web: www.prattcc.edu, www.pcc.cc.ks.us; *Art Instr* Marsha Shrack, MFA
Maintain Delmar Riney Gallery, PCC 348 NE SR 61, Pratt. Art supplies sold at on campus store; 1; Pub; D & E; Scholarships; SC 6, LC; D 100, E 15, Maj 25
Ent Req: HS dipl
Degrees: AA and AS
Tuition: Res—$39 per cr hr; nonres—$68 per cr hr
Courses: Art Appreciation, Ceramics, Design, Drawing, Elementary School Arts, Graphic Design, Illustration, Introduction to Art, Painting, Photography, Printmaking
Summer School: Dir Marsha Shrack; Graphic Design, Illustration, Introduction to Art

SALINA

KANSAS WESLEYAN UNIVERSITY, Art Dept, 100 E Claflin, Salina, KS 67401. Tel 785-827-5541; Fax 785-827-0927; Email jill.wagner@kwu.edu; Web: www.kwu.edu; *Asst Prof Graphic Design* Jill Wagner; *Asst Prof of Art Dept Chair* Lori Wright
Estab 1886; Maintains nonprofit art gallery - The Gallery at Kansas Wesleyan Univ; pvt; D & E; Scholarships; SC 15, LC 4; maj 15, others 500 for two sem
Degrees: AB 4 yr
Tuition: Res—undergrad $17,000; fees incl room & board

Courses: †Advertising Art, †Art Appreciation, †Art Education, †Art History, †Art Studio, †Ceramics, †Design, †Drawing, †Graphic Arts, †Graphic Design, †Painting, †Photography, †Printmaking, †Sculpture
Summer School: Enrl 125; for term of 8 wks beginning June

STERLING

STERLING COLLEGE, Art & Design Dept, 125 W Cooper St, Sterling, KS 67579-1533. Tel 620-278-2173; Fax 620-278-4375; Email dswartz@sterling.edu; Web: www.sterling.edu; *Chmn* Daniel Swartz
Open Mon - Fri 8 AM - 5 PM; Estab 1876; den; D & E; Scholarships; SC 16, LC 2; D 410
Ent Req: HS dipl
Degrees: BA & BS
Courses: 2-D Color Design, 3-D Design, Ceramics, Costume Design & Construction, Drawing, Fibers, Graphic Arts, Graphic Design, Painting
Adult Hobby Classes: Enrl 25; tuition $20. Courses—all areas
Children's Classes: Art Education

TOPEKA

WASHBURN UNIVERSITY OF TOPEKA, Dept of Art, 1700 SW College, Topeka, KS 66621. Tel 785-670-1125; Fax 785-670-1189; Email art@washburn.edu; Web: www.washburn.edu/cas/art/; *Prof* Azyz Sharafy; *Assoc Prof, Interim Chair* Marguerite Perret; *Asst Prof* Danielle Head; *Assoc Prof* Ye Wang; *Catron Prof of Art* Marin Abell; *Asst Prof* Michael Hager; *Lectr* Lynda Miller; *Asst Prof* Kelly Watt; *Lectr* Monette Mark
Estab 1868; Maintain nonprofit art gallery; Mulvane Art Museum, Washburn University, 1700 SW College, Topeka, KS 66621; on-campus art supplies shop; FT 9; pub; D&E; Scholarships; SC 23, LC 7, GC 1; non-maj 300, maj 100
Ent Req: HS dipl
Degrees: BA and BFA 4 yr
Tuition: Res—$273 per cr hr; nonres—$617 per cr hr
Courses: Art Appreciation, Art History, Art Introduction, Ceramics, Computer Graphic Design, Computer Publication, Computers, Design, Drawing, Etching, Lithography, Painting, Photography, Printmaking, Sculpture, Silkscreen, Watercolor
Children's Classes: Tuition $35 for ten 1 1/2 hr sessions
Summer School: VPres Acad Affairs, Dr Randy Pembrook. $225 per cr hr; courses—Art history, Art studio

WICHITA

FRIENDS UNIVERSITY, Art Dept, 2100 University Ave, Wichita, KS 67213. Tel 316-295-5100, 316-295-5656; Fax 316-263-1092, 316-295-5656; Email maber@friends.edu; Web: www.friends.edu; *Chmn* Ted Krone
Estab 1898; den; D & E; Scholarships; SC 18, LC 4; D 329, E 37
Ent Req: HS dipl
Degrees: MA 6 yrs, BA & BS 4 yrs
Courses: †Aesthetics, †Art Education, †Art History, †Ceramics, †Computer Graphics, †Design, †Drawing, †Fine Arts 2 & 3-D, †Graphic Design, †Painting, Photography, Printmaking, Sculpture, Silversmithing, Teacher Training
Adult Hobby Classes: Courses—Drawing, Jewelry, Painting

WICHITA CENTER FOR THE ARTS, Mary R Koch School of Visual Arts, 9112 E Central, Wichita, KS 67206. Tel 316-634-2787; Fax 316-634-0593; Email arts@wcfta.com; Web: www.wcfta.com; *Exec Dir* Howard W Ellington; *Dir Educ* Pam Bugler; *Dir Gallery* Brian Hinkle; *Dir Arts Based Pre-School* Wayna Buch; *Theatre Develop* John Boldenow; *Pub Rels* Kim Kufahl
Estab 1920; Maintain nonprofit art gallery; Hurst Sales Gallery; art library; 35; pvt; D&E; Scholarships; SC 40; D 450, E 150
Courses: 3-D Design, Art Education, Art History, Ceramics, Drawing, Enameling, Mixed Media, Painting, Photography, Pottery, Printmaking, Sculpture, Teacher Training, Weaving
Adult Hobby Classes: Enrl 300; tuition $130 for 12 wk term. Courses—Performing Arts, 2-D & 3-D Design
Children's Classes: Enrl 300; tuition $70. Courses—Performing Arts, 2-D & 3-D Design
Summer School: Dir Educ, Pam Bugler. Enrl 300; tuition $45-$55 for 6 wk term. Courses—same as regular sessions

WICHITA STATE UNIVERSITY, School of Art & Design, 1845 Fairmount St, Box 67 Wichita, KS 67260-0067. Tel 316-978-3555; Fax 316-978-5418; Web: finearts.wichita.edu/design; *Grad Coordr* Ronald Christ; *Interim Dir* Barry Badgett
Estab 1895, dept estab 1901; pub; D & E; Scholarships; D 1149, E 194, non-maj 78, maj 285, grad 51, others 2
Ent Req: HS dipl
Degrees: BAE, BA & BFA 4 yr, MFA 2 yr, MA 1 yr
Courses: †Art Education, †Art History, †Ceramics, Drawing, †Graphic Design, Illustration, Lettering, †Painting, Photography, †Printmaking, †Sculpture, Teacher Training
Summer School: Tuition as above for term of 8 wks

WINFIELD

SOUTHWESTERN COLLEGE, Art Dept, 100 College St, Winfield, KS 67156-2499. Tel 620-229-6000; Web: www.sckans.edu
Estab 1885; pvt & den; D & E; Scholarships; SC 12, LC 4
Ent Req: HS dipl
Degrees: BA 4 yr
Courses: Art Education
Adult Hobby Classes: Design, History of Art, Life Drawing, Painting
Summer School: Chmn, Michael Wilder. Courses—Art History, Design, Drawing, Painting, Sculpture

KENTUCKY

BARBOURVILLE

UNION COLLEGE, Music and Fine Arts Dept, 310 College St, Barbourville, KY 40906-1499. Tel 606-546-1334; Fax 606-546-1625; Web: www.unionky.edu; *Chmn* Dr Thomas McFarland
Estab 1879; Den; D & E; Scholarships; LC
Ent Req: HS dipl
Degrees: BA, BS and MA (Educ) 4 yr
Courses: Art History

BEREA

BEREA COLLEGE, Art & Art History Program, CPO 2162, Berea, KY 40404-2342. Tel 859-985-9715; Fax 859-985-3541; Email lisa_kriner@berea.edu; Web: www.berea.edu; *Dir & Asst Prof* Meghan C Doherty, PhD; *Asst Prof* Kevin N Gardner, MFA; *Assoc Prof & Prog Chair* Eileen McKiernan Gonzalez, PhD; *Chmn* Lisa L Kriner, MFA; *Asst Prof* Daniel Feinburg, MFA; *Asst Prof* Raymond Gonzalez, MFA; *Asst Prof* Ashley Elston, PhD; *Instr* Anna Youngyeon, MFA
Estab 1855, dept estab 1936; Maintains a nonprofit art gallery - Doris Ulmann Galleries; on-campus shop for purchase of art supplies; pvt; D; Scholarships; SC 31, LC 24; C 1670, E 1 (total); D 350, maj 50
Ent Req: HS dipl (preference given to students from Southern Appalachian region)
Degrees: BA 4 yr
Tuition: None; campus res—room and board $300-$1800 based on income
Courses: Archaeology, †Art History, †Ceramics, Design, †Drawing, †Fashion Arts, Fiber Arts, †Painting, †Printmaking, †Sculpture

BOWLING GREEN

WESTERN KENTUCKY UNIVERSITY, Art Dept, 1906 College Heights Blvd, Bowling Green, KY 42101-1000. Tel 270-745-3944; Fax 270-745-5932; Email art@wku.edu; Web: www.wku.edu/dept/academic/ahss/art/art.html; *Dept Head* Kim Chalmers
Maintains on-campus art supply shop; FT 10, PT 9; Pub; D & E; SC 49, LC 21; maj 187
Ent Req: HS dipl
Degrees: BA & BFA 4 yrs, MA(Art Educ)
Courses: †Art Education, Art History, †Ceramics, Design, Drawing, Graphic Design, †Painting, Photography, †Printmaking, †Sculpture, †Weaving
Summer School: Dept Head Kim Chalmers. Enrl 100; tuition res $97 per cr hr, nonres $265 per cr hr. Courses—Lecture & Studio Art Courses

CAMPBELLSVILLE

CAMPBELLSVILLE UNIVERSITY, Art & Design Department, One University Dr, Campbellsville, KY 42718; UPO 863, 1 University Dr Campbellsville, KY 42718-2190. Tel 270-789-5268; Fax 270-789-5524; Email ljcundiff@campbellsville.edu; Web: www.campbellsville.edu (click on Academics-College of Arts & Sciences); *Prof of Art* Linda Cundiff; *Instr of Art* Susie Trejo Williams; *Instr* Henrietta Scott; *Assoc Prof Art* Davie Reneau; *Instr* Jeffrey Walker; *Instr* Cora Renfro; *Asst Prof of Art* William Morse
Estab 1906, dept estab 1967; Non-profit art gallery - Pence Chowning Art Gallery; 1 University Dr, UPO 863 Campbellsville, KY 42718; Montgomery Library; Pvt; D & E, Online; Scholarships; SC 30, LC 6; D 40, E 10, non-maj 15, maj 40, others 8 minors
Activities: Schols offered
Ent Req: HS dipl, ACT, portfolio
Degrees: BA, BS with/without teacher cert, Bachelor of Fine Arts
Tuition: $9800 per yr
Courses: Aesthetics, †Animation, Art Appreciation, Art Education, Art History, Ceramics, Collage, Commercial Art, Constructions, Design, Drawing, Elementary School Art, †Graphic Arts, Graphic Design, Graphic Design, Mixed Media, Painting, Photography, Printmaking, Sculpture, Secondary School Art, Stage Design, Teacher Training, Theatre Arts
Adult Hobby Classes: Enrl 15; tuition $50 per audit hr. Courses—Understanding Art, courses above as auditors
Summer School: Term of 8 wks. Courses—Art Appreciation,

CRESTVIEW HILLS

THOMAS MORE COLLEGE, Art Dept, 333 Thomas More Pky, Crestview Hills, KY 41017. Tel 859-341-5800, Ext 3420; Fax 859-344-3345; Web: www.thomasmoore.edu; *Chmn* Rebecca Bilbo; *Assoc Prof* Barbara Rauf, MFA
Estab 1921; pvt; D & E; SC 12, LC 4; D 12, E 5, maj 17
Ent Req: HS dipl
Degrees: BA, BES, BS, AA & AES
Courses: Aesthetics, Anatomy, Art Education, Art History, Arts Management, Ceramics, Color, Design, Drawing, Figure Drawing, Painting, Perspective, Photography, Printmaking, Sculpture, Teacher Training, Theatre Arts
Summer School: Dir, Dr Raymond Hebert. Courses—various

GEORGETOWN

GEORGETOWN COLLEGE, Art Dept, Anne Wright Wilson Fine Arts Bldg, Georgetown College Georgetown, KY 40324; 400 E College St, Wilson Art Bldg Rm 106 Georgetown, KY 40324. Tel 502-863-8106; Fax 502-868-8888; Email juilee_decker@georgetowncollege.edu; Web: www.georgetowncollege.edu/art/; *Gallery Dir & Cur Coll* Laura Stewart; *Prof Art History & Dept Chair* Dr Juilee Decker
Estab 1829

HIGHLAND HEIGHTS

NORTHERN KENTUCKY UNIVERSITY, Dept of Visual Arts, Nunn Dr, Highland Heights, KY 41099-0001. Tel 859-572-5421; Fax 859-572-6501; Web: www.nkul~art/; *Chmn* Thomas F McGovern
Estab 1968; Maintains nonprofit University Galleries, Dept of Visual Arts; art supplies sold at on-campus store; FT 20, PT 8; pub; D, E & Summer; Scholarships; SC 13; Enrl 510
Activities: Schols available
Ent Req: HS grad, ACT scores
Degrees: BA(Art Educ), BFA(Studio Art), BFA (Graphic Design), BA(Graphic Design), BA (Studio Art)
Courses: Aesthetics, Art Appreciation, †Art Education, †Art History, †Ceramics, Design, †Drawing, †Graphic Design, History of Art & Architecture, Mixed Media, New Media, †Painting, †Photography, †Printmaking, †Sculpture, Teacher Training, Video
Summer School: Chmn, Thomas McGovern. Enrl 170; tuition $47 per sem hr for sessions. Courses—Art Education, Drawing, Graphic Design, Printmaking, Ceramics

LEXINGTON

TRANSYLVANIA UNIVERSITY, Art Program, 300 N Broadway, Lexington, KY 40508-1776. Tel 859-233-8141, 233-8119; Web: www.transy.edu; *Prof* Dr Nancy Wolsk, PhD; *Prof, Div Chair* Jack Girard, MFA; *Assoc Prof, Prog Dir* Kurt Gohde, MFA; *Prof of Art* Dan S Selter, MA; *Asst Prof* Kimberly Miller; *Gallery Dir* Andrea Fisher, BFA
Estab 1780; Maintain a nonprofit gallery, The Morlan Gallery, Transylvania Univ, 300 N Broadway, Lexington, KY 40508; pvt; D & E; Scholarships; SC 20, LC 3; D 105, E 14, maj 18
Ent Req: HS dipl
Degrees: BA
Courses: †Aesthetics, Art Appreciation, †Art Education, Art History, Ceramics, Collage, Costume Design & Construction, Design, Drawing, Film, †History of Art & Architecture, Mixed Media, Painting, Photography, †Printmaking, Sculpture, Stage Design, Teacher Training, Theatre Arts

UNIVERSITY OF KENTUCKY, Dept of Art, College of Fine Arts, Rm 207 Fine Arts Bldg Lexington, KY 40506-0001. Tel 859-257-8151; Fax 859-257-3042; Web: www.edufinearts; *Dean* Robert Shay; *Chmn* Jack Gron
Estab 1918; FT 22, PT 15; pub; D; Scholarships; Assistantships; SC 23, LC 19, GC 6; maj 200, others 1500
Degrees: BA, BFA, MA & MFA 3 yr
Courses: †Art Education, †Art History, Ceramics, Drawing, Fibers, Graphic Design, Painting, Photography, Printmaking, Sculpture, †Studio Art, Video
Summer School: Dir, Jack Gron. Tuition res—$118 per cr hr, nonres—$341 per cr hr. Courses—varied

LOUISVILLE

JEFFERSON COMMUNITY COLLEGE & TECHNICAL COLLEGE, Fine Arts, 109 E Broadway, Fine Arts Dept Louisville, KY 40202-2000. Tel 502-213-2518; *Fine Art Dept Head* Prof J Barry Motes; *Prof* Dr Amy Stewart; *Asst Prof* Lisa Simon
Estab 1968; Maintain nonprofit art gallery, Krantz Art Gallery, VTI 116, 110 E Chestnut; on-campus shop where art supplies may be purchased; PT 6; pub; D & E; Scholarships; SC 11, LC 6; D 4774, E 4172
Ent Req: HS dipl
Degrees: AA & Assoc in Photography 2 yrs
Tuition: $135/credit hrs
Courses: †Advertising Design, Aesthetics, Art Education, Art History, †Commercial Art, Drawing, Graphic Arts, Graphic Design, Painting, †Photography, Sculpture, †Theatre Arts
Summer School: Dean, Dr Robert Deger. Tuition $45 per cr hr. Courses—Art Appreciation, Drawing, Photography

UNIVERSITY OF LOUISVILLE, Allen R Hite Art Institute, Department of Fine Arts, Belkaap Campus Louisville, KY 40292-0001. Tel 502-852-6794; Fax 502-852-6791; Web: www.art.louisville.edu; *Chmn Dept Fine Arts, Dir Hite Art Institute* James T Grubola, MFA; *Assoc Prof* Moon-he Balk, MFA; *Asst Prof* Todd Burns, MFA; *Assoc Prof* Tom Buser, PhD; *Assoc Prof* Mary Carothers, MFA; *Prof* Ying Kit Chan, MFA; *Assoc Prof* Stow Chapman, MS; *Prof* Robert Douglas, PhD; *Assoc Prof* Mitch Eckert, MFA; *Power Creative Designer-in-Residence* Leslie Friesen, BFA; *Assoc Prof* Christopher Fulton, PhD; *Assoc Prof* Linda Gigante, PhD; *Prof* Lida Gordon, MFA; *Assoc Prof* Barbara Hanger, MFA; *Assoc Prof* Ben Hufbauer, PhD; *Assoc Prof* Jay Kloner, PhD; *Asst Prof* Scott Massey, MFA; *Prof* Stephanie Maloney, PhD; *Assoc Prof* Mark Priest, MFA; *Prof* Steve Skaggs, MS; *Prof* John Whitesell, MFA; *Gallery Dir & Adjunct Assoc Prof* John Begley, MFA; *Adjunct Assoc Prof* Peter Morrin, MFA; *Prof Emeritus* Donald Anderson, MFA; *Prof Emeritus* Henry Chodkowski, MFA; *Prof Emeritus* Dario Cofi, PhD; *Prof Emeritus* Suzanne Mitchell, MFA; *Prof Emeritus* William Morgan, PhD; *Asst Prof* Che Rhodes, MFA; *Asst Prof* Susan Jarosi, PhD
Estab 1846, dept estab 1935; Maintain nonprofit art galleries; Hite Art Institute Galleries, Schneider Hall, Univ of Louisville, Louisville, KY 40292. Library: Margaret Bridwell Art Library; FT 21, PT 18; pub; D & E; Scholarships; SC 60, LC 50, GC 38; D 1,200, E 200, non-maj 50, maj 500, grad 65
Ent Req: HS dipl, CEEB
Degrees: MA 1 to 2 yrs, PhD 3 yrs, BA 4 yrs, BFA 4 yrs
Courses: Aesthetics, †Art Education, †Art History, †Ceramics, †Design, †Drawing, †Fiber, †Glass, †Graphic Design, †History of Art & Architecture, Interior Architecture, †Interior Design, †Jewelry, †Museum Staff Training, †Painting, †Photography, †Printmaking, †Sculpture
Summer School: Dir, James T Grubola. Enrl 100 for May-Aug. Courses—Various Art & Art History Classes

MIDWAY

MIDWAY COLLEGE, Art Dept, 512 E Stephens St, Midway, KY 40347-1120. Tel 859-846-4421, Ext 5809; Fax 859-846-5349; Web: www.midway.edu; *Instr Music & Choir* Wayne Gebb; *Chmn* Steve Davis-Rosenbaum; *Instr* Kate Davis-Rosenbaum
FT 2; Den, W; D; Scholarships; SC 7, LC 3; 55
Ent Req: HS dipl, ACT
Degrees: 2 yr
Courses: Art Education, Art in the Child's World, Basic Design, Ceramics, Drawing, Historical Furniture, Painting, Sculpture, Textile Design

MOREHEAD

MOREHEAD STATE UNIVERSITY, Art & Design Dept, Claypool-Young Art Bldg 211, Morehead, KY 40351; 265 University Blvd Morehead, KY 40351. Tel 606-783-2771, 783-2193; Fax 606-783-5048; Email s.ward@moreheadstate.edu; Web: www.moreheadstate.edu/art; *Chmn* Robert Franzini; *Prof* Elisabeth Mesa-Gaido; *Assoc Prof* Deeno Golding; *Prof* Gary Mesa-Gaido; *Assoc Prof* Joy Gritton; *Asst Prof* Dougfeng Li; *Asst Prof* Jennifer Reis; *Art Instr* Seth Green; *Asst Prof* Christopher Field; *Asst Prof* Jean Petsch; *Asst Prof* Julia Finch; *Vis Asst Prof* Lee Ann Paynter; *Instr* Jennifer Bell; *Instr* Toni Hobbs
Estab 1922; Maintain nonprofit art gallery, Claypool-Young Art Gallery, 265 Univ Blvd, MSU, Morehead, KY 40351, Gallery Dir Jennifer Reis; maintain on-campus art supplies shop; pub; D & E; Scholarships; SC 45, LC 14, GC 26; D 900, E 100, non-maj 815, maj 175, GS 10
Ent Req: HS dipl, ACT
Degrees: BA 4 yr, MA 1 - 2 yr
Tuition: KY residents $3,933 per sem, non-residents $9,833 per sem
Courses: Art Education, Ceramics, Computer Art, Drawing, Graphic Design, Illustration, Mixed Media, Painting, Photography, Printmaking
Children's Classes: Summer Arts Academy
Summer School: SAA Coord Greg Wing.

MURRAY

MURRAY STATE UNIVERSITY, Dept of Art, 218 Wells Hall, Murray, KY 42071-3318. Tel 270-762-3741; Fax 270-762-3920; Web: www.murraystate.edu; *Chmn* Richard Dougherty; *Prof* Dale Leys, MFA; *Prof* Paul Sasso, MFA; *Prof* Jerry Speight, MFA; *Assoc Prof* Michael Johnson, MFA; *Assoc Prof* Camille Sarre, PhD, MFA; *Assoc Prof* Steve Bishop, MFA; *Asst Prof* Peggy Schrock, PhD, MFA; *Gallery Dir* Albert Sperath, MFA; *Asst Prof* Jeanne Beaver; *Asst Prof* Sarah Guthworth; *Asst Prof* Alma Hale; *Asst Prof* Nicole Hard; *Asst Prof* Susan O'Brien; *Lectr* Zbynek Smetana
Estab 1925, dept estab 1931; pub; D & E; Scholarships; SC 117, LC 15, GS 48; non-maj 475, maj 200, grad 13
Ent Req: HS dipl, ACT, portfolio required for grad students
Degrees: BA, BS & BFA 4 yr, MA(Studio) 1 1/2 - 2 yrs
Courses: Art Appreciation, Art Education, Art History, Ceramics, Drawing, Graphic Design, History of Art & Architecture, Jewelry, †Painting, †Photography, †Printmaking, †Sculpture, Silversmithing, Surface Design, Teacher Training, Textile Design, †Weaving, Wood Design
Children's Classes: Summer art workshops for HS students
Summer School: Dir, Dale Leys. Enrl 40-80; tuition res—undergrad $67 per hr, grad $99 per hr; nonres—undergrad $193 per hr, grad $282 per hr for short sessions of 5 wk 7 1/2 wk or 10 wk terms

OWENSBORO

BRESCIA UNIVERSITY, (Brescia College) Art Dept, 717 Frederica St, Owensboro, KY 42301-3019. Tel 502-685-3131; Fax 502-686-4266; Email info@brescia.edu; Web: www.brescia.edu; *Chmn* Sr Mary Diane Taylor; *Prof Fine Arts* David Stratton; *Asst Prof Art* Frank Krevens
Estab 1950; Maintain nonprofit art gallery; Anna Eaton Stout Memorial Art Gallery, 717 Frederica St, Owensboro, KY 42301; on-campus shop where art supplies may be purchased; FT 3; den; D&E, weekend; Scholarships; SC 32, LC 10; 960, maj 30
Ent Req: HS dipl, placement exam, ACT, GED
Degrees: BA 4 yr
Courses: 2-D & 3-D Design, Advertising Design, Art Appreciation, †Art Education, Art History, Calligraphy, †Ceramics, Design, Drawing, Film, †Graphic Design, Mixed Media, Painting, Photography, Printmaking, Stained Glass

KENTUCKY WESLEYAN COLLEGE RALPH CENTER OF FINE ARTS BUILDING, Dept Art, 3000 Frederica St, Owensboro, KY 42302-6055. Tel 270-852-3608; Email hlogsdon@kwc.edu; Web: www.kwc.edu; *Acting Chmn* Monte Hamm; *Art Director & Prof of Art* Heather M Logsdon, MFA; *Art Instructor* Enid Roach, MA; *Art Instructor* Jill Sparks, MA
Dept estab 1950; Maintains a non-profit art gallery: Ralph Gallery of Fine Arts, Kentucky Wesleyan College, 3000 Frederica St, Owensboro, KY 42301 -

270-852-3608 - curator H Logsdon; Private; D, E, Online; Scholarships; SC 15, LC 4; maj 30
Degrees: BA 4 yr
Courses: Aesthetics, Art Appreciation, Art Education, Art Studio, Arts & Crafts, Ceramics, Design, Drawing, Graphic Arts, Graphic Design, Painting, Photography, Printmaking, Sculpture, Teacher Training, Video
Summer School: Enrl 60. Courses—Art for the Elementary Schools, Art Survey

PIKEVILLE

PIKEVILLE COLLEGE, Humanities Division, 147 Sycamore St, Pikeville, KY 41501-9118. Tel 606-218-5250; Fax 606-218-5269; Email webmaster@pc.edu; Web: www.pc.edu; *Gallery Dir* Janice Ford; *Chmn* Dr Brigitte LaTrespo
Estab 1889; Maintain nonprofit art gallery, Weber Art Gallery, 147 Sycamore St, Pikeville, KY 41501; pvt den; D & E; SC 16, LC 5
Ent Req: SAT, ACT
Degrees: BA & BS 4 yrs
Courses: †Art Education, Art History, Ceramics, Drawing, History of Art & Architecture, Painting, Printmaking, Sculpture, †Teacher Training
Summer School: Courses—vary

PIPPA PASSES

ALICE LLOYD COLLEGE, Art Dept, 100 Purpose Rd, Pippa Passes, KY 41844-8884. Tel 606-368-2101, Ext 6083; Fax 606-368-6496; Web: www.alc.edu; *Instr* Mike Ware
Estab 1923; FT 1; pvt; D & E; Scholarships; SC 6, LC 1
Ent Req: HS dipl, ent exam
Degrees: BS & BA 4 yrs
Courses: Art Appreciation, †Art for Elementary Education, Art History Survey No 2, Pottery
Children's Classes: Enrl 10-20; tuition free. Courses—Drawing, Painting, Sculpture

RICHMOND

EASTERN KENTUCKY UNIVERSITY, Art Dept, Campbell 309, Richmond, KY 40475; 521 Lancaster Ave, Richmond, KY 40475-3102. Tel 859-622-1629; Fax 859-622-5904; Email artsmith@acs.eku.edu; Web: www.art.eku.edu; *Chmn* Dr Gil R Smith
Estab 1906; Maintain nonprofit art gallery; Frederick Giles Gallery, Campbell Building 309, Eastern Kentucky University, Richmond, KY 40475-3102; pub; D&E; Scholarships; SC 40, LC 14, GC 12, other 5; non-maj 70, maj 251, grad 6
Ent Req: HS grad
Degrees: BA, BFA & MA(Educ) 4 yrs
Courses: Art Appreciation, †Art Education, Art History, †Ceramics, Drawing, †Graphic Design, †Interior Design, †Metals, †Painting, †Photography, †Sculpture
Adult Hobby Classes: Non-credit courses offered
Summer School: Enrl & courses vary; tuition same as regular sem

WILLIAMSBURG

CUMBERLAND COLLEGE, Dept of Art, 7523 College Station Dr, Williamsburg, KY 40769-1386. Tel 606-549-2200; Fax 606-539-4490; Web: cumberlandcollege.edu; *Chmn* Kenneth R Weedman
Estab 1889; Maintains nonprofit art gallery on campus; den; D & E; Scholarships; SC 20, LC 10; D 1614, E 60, maj 30
Ent Req: HS dipl, ACT test
Degrees: BA and BS 4 yr
Courses: Aesthetics, Art Appreciation, Art Education, Art History, Computer Imaging, Design, Drawing, Film, Painting, Printmaking, Sculpture, Stage Design, Teacher Training, Theatre Arts, Video

WILMORE

ASBURY UNIVERSITY, Art Dept, 1 Macklem Dr, Wilmore, KY 40390-1152. Tel 859-858-3511, Ext 2250; Fax 859-858-3921; Web: www.asbury.edu; *Instr* Prof Linda Stratford; *Art Dept Chair, Instr* Prof Keith Barker; *Instr* Chris Segre-Lewis; *Instr* Prof Margaret Park Smith; *Asst Prof* Josh Smith; *Prof Emeritus* Rudy Medlock
Estab 1890; Maintain nonprofit art gallery, Asbury University Galleries (same address as school); FT 5, PT 6; pvt; D & E; Scholarships; SC 24, LC 6; D 1350, maj 45, others 250
Ent Req: HS dipl
Degrees: AB & BS 4 yr
Courses: Aesthetics, Animation, Art Appreciation, Art Education, Art History, Ceramics, Design, Drawing, Graphic Arts, Graphic Design, History of Art & Architecture, Painting, Photography, Printmaking, Sculpture, Stained Glass, Teacher Training
Summer School: Courses - Photography, Painting, Seminar in France

LOUISIANA

ALEXANDRIA

LOUISIANA STATE UNIVERSITY AT ALEXANDRIA, Dept of Fine Arts & Design, 8100 Hwy 71 S, Coughlin 146 Alexandria, LA 71302-9119. Tel 318-445-3672; Web: www.lsu.edu; *Prof Art* Roy V deVille, MA
Estab 1960; pub; D; Scholarships; D 200, E 50, non-maj 300, maj 15
Ent Req: HS dipl, entrance exam, state exam & ACT
Degrees: Fine Arts Assoc 2-3 yr
Children's Classes: Enrl 50; tuition $189 per course. Courses—Painting, Pottery
Summer School: Enrl 150; tuition $120 per cr. Courses—Art Appreciation, Art History, Painting, Pottery

BATON ROUGE

LOUISIANA STATE UNIVERSITY, School of Art, 123 Art Bldg, Baton Rouge, LA 70803. Tel 225-388-5411; Fax 225-578-5424; Web: www.lsu.edu; *Prof* Richard Cox, PhD, MFA; *Prof* Mark Zucker, PhD, MFA; *Prof* Patricia Lawrence, PhD, MFA; *Prof* Melody Guichet, MFA; *Prof* A J Meek, MFA; *Prof* Christopher Hentz, MFA; *Prof* Kimberly Arp, MFA; *Prof* Robert Hausey, MFA; *Prof* Gerald Bower, MFA; *Assoc Prof* Michael Book, MFA; *Assoc Prof* Gregory Elliot, MFA; *Asst Prof* Paul Dean, MFA; *Asst Prof* Herb Goodman, MFA; *Asst* Larry Livaudais, MFA; *Asst* Lynne Baggett, MFA; *Asst* Susan Ryan, MFA; *Asst* Kirsten Noreen; *Dir* Michael Daugherty, MFA; *Asst* Edward Smith; *Asst Prof* Denyce Celentano; *Asst Prof* Cynthia Handel; *Asst Prof* Robert Silverman; *Asst Prof* Parrott Bacot
Estab 1874, dept estab 1935; pub; D & E; Scholarships
Ent Req: HS dipl, ACT scores
Degrees: BFA 4 yr, MFA 3
Courses: †Art History, †Ceramics, Drawing, †Graphic Design, †Painting, †Printmaking, †Sculpture
Summer School: Tuition res—$273, nonres—$653 for 8 wk course
—**Student Union Art Gallery**, 216 LSU Student Union Art Gallery, Louisiana State University Baton Rouge, LA 70803. Tel 225-578-5162; Fax 225-578-4326; Email unionartgallery@lsu.edu; *Dir* Judy Stahl
Open Mon-Fri 10AM-6PM, Sun 1PM-5PM, cl on major holidays; No admis fee
Collections: paintings; drawings; lithographs; silkscreens; photographs; sculptures

SOUTHERN UNIVERSITY A & M COLLEGE, School of Architecture, PO Box 11947, Southern Branch Baton Rouge, LA 70813-1947. Tel 225-771-3015; Fax 225-771-4709; Web: subr.edu/architecture/awotona; *Dean* Adenrele Awotona; *Instr* Jill Bambury; *Instr* John Delgado; *Instr* Charles Smith; *Instr* Randall Teal; *Instr* Archie Tiner; *Instr* Lonnie Wilkinson; *Instr* Annette Williams; *Instr* Kelley Roberts; *Instr* Henry Thurman
Estab 1956; pub; D & E; Scholarships; SC 14; D 250, non-maj 7, maj 162
Ent Req: HS dipl
Degrees: BA 5 yrs
Courses: Architecture, Art Education, Computer, Graphic Arts, Painting, Printmaking
Summer School: Dir, E D Van Purnell. Term of 8 wks beginning June. Courses—Architectural Design, Construction Materials & Systems, Graphic Presentation, Structures

GRAMBLING

GRAMBLING STATE UNIVERSITY, Art Dept, PO Box 4276, Grambling, LA 71245-1184. Tel 318-274-2274; Web: www.grambling.edu; *Chmn* Karl Norman; *Prof* Donna F McGee; *Assoc Prof* Rodrecas Davis
Estab 1901; Maintains a non-profit gallery
Degrees: BA 4 yr
Tuition: Res—$1044 per sem; nonres—$2019 per sem
Courses: Art Appreciation, †Art Education, Art History, Ceramics, Computer, Design, Drawing, Handicrafts, Illustration, Painting, Printmaking, Sculpture, Teacher Training

HAMMOND

SOUTHEASTERN LOUISIANA UNIVERSITY, Art & Design, SLU 10765, Hammond, LA 70402. Tel 504-549-2193; Fax 985-549-5316; Web: www.selu.edu; *Graphic Design* Gary Keown, MFA; *Art History* C Roy Blackwood, MFA; *Art History* Irene Nero; *New Media & Animation* John Valentine; *Art History* Timothy Silva
Estab 1925; Maintain nonprofit art gallery; Clark Hall Gallery, SLU 10765, Hammond, N 70402; art supplies available on-campus; Pub; D & E; Scholarships; SC 25, LC 4, GC 2; D 121, E 75, maj 122
Ent Req: HS dipl, ACT
Degrees: BA(Educ), BA(Humanities), BA(Cultural Resource Management) 4 yrs
Courses: Art Education, Art History, Ceramics, Digital Design, Drawing, Painting, Photography, Printmaking, Sculpture, Teacher Training
Summer School: Dir, C Roy Blackwood. Enrl 150; 8 wk term. Courses—Art Education, Art Survey for Elementary Teachers

LAFAYETTE

UNIVERSITY OF LOUISIANA AT LAFAYETTE, Dept of Visual Arts, Ullafayette Box 43850, Lafayette, LA 70504. Tel 337-482-6056; Fax 337-482-5907; Web: www.arts.louisiana.edu; *Dept Head, Assoc Prof* Matthew LaRose; *Prof* Brian Kelly; *Prof* Allan Jones; *Prof* John Hathorn; *Prof* John Gargano; *Prof* Steven Breaux
Estab 1900; Maintains a non-profit art gallery: Hillard University Art Museum, campus of Univ Louisiana @ Lafayette; art supplies can be purchased at school store; FT 20, PT 4; pub; D&E; Scholarships; SC, LC; univ 18,000
Degrees: BFA 4-5 yrs
Courses: †Advertising Design, †Art Education, †Ceramics, †Choreographic Design, Drawing, †Fine Arts, Graphic Design, Mixed Media, Painting, †Photography, Printmaking, Sculpture, Silversmithing, Video
Summer School: Dir, Gordon Brooks. Enrl 300; study aboard program in Paris, France & London, England. Courses—Ceramics, Computer Art, Design, Drawing, Film & Video Animation, Painting, Photography

LAKE CHARLES

MCNEESE STATE UNIVERSITY, Dept of Visual Arts, 4205 Ryan St, Lake Charles, LA 70605-4511. Tel 337-475-5060; Fax 337-475-5927; Web: www.mcneeseartonline.org; *Chmn* Lynn Reynolds; *Assoc Prof* Kenneth Baskin; *Prof* Martin Bee; *Assoc Prof* Meghan Fleming; *Prof* Heather Kelley; *Asst Prof* Bridget McDaniel; *Prof* Lisa Reinauer; *Assoc Prof & Dept Head* Lynn Reynolds; *Assoc Prof* Larry Schuh; *Assoc Prof* Lewis Temple; *Admin Asst* Monica Veillon; *Prof* Gerry Wubben
Estab 1950, dept estab 1953; Maintains nonprofit art gallery, Abercrombie Gallery; on-campus shop sells art supplies; FT 9; pub; D & E; Scholarships; SC 24, LC 4, GC 1; D 85, E 15, non-maj 215, maj 150
Ent Req: HS dipl
Degrees: BA (Art Educ) & BA (Studio Arts) 4 yrs
Courses: †Advertising Design, Art Appreciation, †Art Education, Art History, †Ceramics, †Drawing, Graphic Arts, Graphic Design, Mixed Media, †Painting, †Photography, †Printmaking, Survey crafts course

MONROE

UNIVERSITY OF LOUISIANA AT MONROE, (Northeast Louisiana University) Dept of Art, 700 University Ave, Stubbs 141 Monroe, LA 71203-3708. Tel 318-342-1375, 342-5252; Fax 318-342-1369; Web: www.ulm.edu; *Instr* Brian Fassett, MFA; *Instr* Richard Hayes, MFA; *Instr* Gary Ratcliff, MFA; *Instr* Robert Ward, MFA; *Instr* Cynthia Kee, MFA; *Instr* James Norton, MFA; *Instr* Joni Noble, MFA; *Instr* Linda Ward, MFA; *Head Dept* Ronald J Alexander, MFA; *Asst Prof* Cliff Tresner
Estab 1931, dept estab 1956; pub; D & E; Scholarships; SC 28, LC 4, GC 9; non-maj 300, maj 125, GS 3
Ent Req: HS dipl
Degrees: BFA 4 yrs, MEd
Courses: 3-D Design, Advertising Design, Analytical Perspective, Art Appreciation, Block Printing, Ceramics, Drawing, Figure Drawing, Painting, Photography, Printmaking, Sculpture, Silkscreen, Survey Class
Adult Hobby Classes: Enrl 20. May 31 - July 2. Courses—Art 411
Summer School: Dir, Ronald J Alexander. Courses—Art Appreciation, Art Education, Drawing, Painting

NATCHITOCHES

NORTHWESTERN STATE UNIVERSITY OF LOUISIANA, School of Creative & Performing Arts - Dept of Fine & Graphic Arts, 140 Central Ave, Natchitoches, LA 71497-0001. Tel 318-357-5744; Fax 318-357-5906; Email barthelemys@nsula.edu; Web: www.nsula.edu/art; *Prof* Michael Yankowski, MFA; *Assoc Prof* Roger A Chandler, MArch, PhD; *Prof* Clyde Downs, MFA; *Asst Prof* Robert Moreau, MFA; *Asst Prof* F Brooks DeFee, MA; *Asst Prof* W Anthony Watkins; *Asst Prof* Matt DeFord; *Asst Prof* Isaac Powell
Estab 1885; Maintains nonprofit gallery, Hanchey Gallery, AA Fredericks & Alice Dear Fine Art Building, NSU 71497; Watson Libr, NSU 71497; Orville J Hanchey Gallery, 140 Central Ave, Natchitoches, LA 71497. Art supplies may be purchased on campus; Pub; D, E & internet; Scholarships; SC 67, LC 17, GC 36; non-maj 60, maj 101, grad 16
Ent Req: Selective admis
Degrees: BFA 4 yrs, MA 2 yrs, special prog for advanced students MA in Art
Courses: †Advertising Design, Art Appreciation, †Art Education, Art History, Ceramics, Commercial Art, Design, Drawing, Graphic Arts, †Graphic Design, History of Art & Architecture, Painting, Printmaking, Professional Photography, Sculpture, Stained Glass, Stringed Instrument Construction
Adult Hobby Classes: Courses—most of above

NEW ORLEANS

DELGADO COLLEGE, Dept of Fine Arts, 501 City Park Ave, New Orleans, LA 70119-4324. Tel 504-483-4400, 483-4069; Fax 504-483-4954; Email lcoppi@dcc.edu; Web: www.dcc.edu; *Chmn Fine Arts* Lisette Copping
Dept estab 1967. College has 2 campuses; pub; D & E; Scholarships; SC 12-20, LC 12-20; D 150, E 65, maj 60
Ent Req: HS dipl, 18 yr old
Degrees: AA and AS 2 yrs
Courses: Art Appreciation, Art History, Ceramics, Drawing, History of Art & Architecture, Jewelry, Painting, Sculpture

LOYOLA UNIVERSITY OF NEW ORLEANS, Dept of Visual Arts, 6363 Saint Charles Ave, New Orleans, LA 70118. Tel 504-865-2011, 861-5456; Fax 504-861-5457; Web: www.loyno.edu; *Chmn* Carol Leak
Den; D & E; Scholarships; SC 9, LC 3; D 150, E 45, maj 28
Ent Req: HS dipl, ent exam
Degrees: BSA 4 yrs
Courses: Art History, Ceramics, Computer Graphics, Design, Drawing, Painting, Photography, Printmaking, Sculpture, Teacher Training
Summer School: Chmn, John Sears. Enrl 40; term of 6 wks beginning in June. Courses—Drawing, Painting, Printmaking, Sculpture

SOUTHERN UNIVERSITY IN NEW ORLEANS, Fine Arts & Philosophy Dept, 6400 Press Dr, New Orleans, LA 70126-0002. Tel 504-286-5000, 286-5267; Fax 504-286-5296; *Asst Prof* Gary Oaks, MFA; *Music* Roger Dickerson, MFA; *Music* Valeria King, MFA; *Chmn* Sara Hollis, MA; *Instr* Cynthia Ramirez; *Instr* Charlie Johnson; *Instr* Arthur Pindle; *Instr* Tommy Myrick; *Instr* Edward Jordan
Estab 1951, dept estab 1960; pub; D & E; D 21, E 26, non-maj 700, maj 47
Ent Req: HS dipl
Degrees: BA 4 yrs, BS(Art Educ) 4 yrs, BS(Music Educ) 4 yrs
Courses: African & American Art, African Art, Art Education, Art History, Ceramics, Commercial Art, Crafts, Drawing, Painting, Photography, Printmaking, Sculpture, Video
Adult Hobby Classes: Courses offered
Summer School: Courses offered

TULANE UNIVERSITY, School of Architecture, 6823 Saint Charles Ave, 304 Richardson Mem Bldg New Orleans, LA 70118-5665. Tel 504-865-5389; Fax 504-862-8798; Web: www.tsaarch.edu; *Dean* Donald Gatzke
Estab 1907; FT 24, PT 12; pvt; 320
Degrees: BA, MA(Archit)
Tuition: $9380 per sem
Courses: Computer Graphics, Design, Frank Lloyd Wright's Architecture, History, Life Drawing, Structures, Technology, Theory
—**Sophie H Newcomb Memorial College**, 1229 Broadway, Woldenberg Art Ctr New Orleans, LA 70118-5210. Tel 504-865-5327; Fax 504-862-8710; Web: www.2tulane.edu; *Assoc* Theresa Cole; *Prof* Gene H Koss; *Prof* Marilyn R Brown; *Assoc Prof* Ronna Harris; *Assoc Prof* Jeremy Jernegan; *Prof* Barry Bailey; *Prof* Elizabeth Boone; *Chmn* Arthur Okazaki; *Assoc Prof* Sandy Chism; *Asst Prof* Pamela Franco; *Assoc Prof* Michael Plante; *Prof* Bill Tronzo
Estab 1886; pvt; D & E; Scholarships; SC 33, LC 25, GC 29; D 817 per sem, E 37 per sem
Ent Req: HS dipl, CEEB, interview, review of work by chmn & or faculty (optional)
Degrees: BA, BFA, BA(Art Biology), MA, MFA
Tuition: $26,000 incl room & board per yr
Courses: American Art, Ceramics, Drawing, Glass Blowing, Painting, Photography, Pre-Columbian Art, Printmaking, Sculpture
Adult Hobby Classes: Art History, Ceramics, Drawing, Glass, Painting, Photography, Printmaking, Sculpture
Children's Classes: Offered through the Dept of Educ
Summer School: Dean, Richard Marksbury. Courses—Art History, Ceramics, Drawing, Glass, Painting, Photography, Sculpture

UNIVERSITY OF NEW ORLEANS-LAKE FRONT, Dept of Fine Arts, 2000 Lakeshore Dr, New Orleans, LA 70148-0001. Tel 504-280-6410; Fax 504-280-7346; Email cola@uno.edu; Web: www.finearts.uno.edu; *Prof Emeritus* Doyle J Gertjejansen, MFA; *Prof* Richard A Johnson, MFA; *Chair & Assoc Prof* Cheryl A Hayes, MFA; *Vis Artist* Anya Martin, MFA; *Vis Artist* Tony Campbell, MFA; *Vis Artist* Aaron McNamee, MFA; *Asst Prof* Dan Rule, MFA; *Asst Prof* Rebecca Reynolds, PhD; *Vis Lectr* Alexa Arroyo, MA; *Instr* Jeff Rinehart, MFA; *Instr* Kathy Rodriguez, MFA, MA
Estab 1958, dept estab 1968; Maintains 2 non-profit art galleries, Uno-St Claude Gallery, 2429 St. Claude Ave, New Orleans, LA 7017; Uno Fine Arts Gallery, Dept of Fine Arts, 2000 Lakeshore Dr, New Orleans LA 70117; on-campus supply shop; pub; D & E; Scholarships; SC 29, LC 24, GC 34; D 11,000 (university), non-maj 1900, maj 150, grad 20
Ent Req: HS dipl
Degrees: BA 4 yrs, MFA 60 hrs
Tuition: In-state $6,578; Out of state $19,068
Courses: †Art History, †Design, Digital Art, Drawing, Graphic Design, Hyper-Media, †Painting, †Photography, †Printmaking, †Sculpture, Video-Digital
Summer School: Tuition $913 for one credit of 8 wks beginning June. Courses—Art Fundamentals, Art History, Drawing, Painting, Photography, Sculpture, Printmaking

XAVIER UNIVERSITY OF LOUISIANA, Dept of Fine Arts, 1 Drexel Dr New Orleans, LA 70125. Tel 504-483-7556; Web: www.xula.edu; *Chmn* Ron Bechet; *Prof* John T Scott, MFA; *Asst Prof* Mrs Nelson Marsalis, MFA
Estab 1926, dept estab 1935; den; D & E; Scholarships; SC 48, LC 10; D 50, E 12, non-maj 10, maj 52
Ent Req: HS dipl, SAT or ACT, health cert, C average at least
Degrees: BA, BA (Art Ed), BFA, BS & MA
Courses: Art Appreciation, Art History, Black & White Photography, Ceramics, Design, Graphic Ad Design, Painting, Photography, Printmaking
Adult Hobby Classes: Courses—Creative Crafts

PINEVILLE

LOUISIANA COLLEGE, Dept of Art, 1140 College Dr, Pineville, LA 71359; PO Box 561, Pineville, LA 71359-0001. Tel 318-487-7262; Fax 318-487-7337; Email reynoso@lacollege.edu; Web: www.lacollege.edu; *Adjunct Prof* Preston Gilchrist; *Dept Coordr* Rondall Reynoso; *Asst Prof* Wang-Ling Chou; *Adjunct Prof* John Ammons; *Asst Prof* Tim Roper
Estab 1906; Maintains nonprofit gallery, Weathersby Fine Arts Building Gallery, 1140 College Dr, Box 561, Pineville, LA 71359; Den; D & E; Scholarships; SC 42, LC 9, Lab C; D 26
Ent Req: HS grad
Degrees: BA 50 hrs art, 127 total; BFA 78 hrs art, 134 total
Courses: †Art Education, †Ceramics, Commercial Art, Design, Drawing, †Graphic Design, †Painting, Sculpture, †Studio Arts, Teacher Training, †Web Design

RUSTON

LOUISIANA TECH, School of Art, 1 Mayfield St, Ruston, LA 71272; PO Box 3175W, Tech Sta Ruston, LA 71272-0001. Tel 318-257-3909; Fax 318-257-4890; Email ddablow@latech.edu; Web: www.art.latech.edu; *Dir* Dean Dablow
Estab 1894; maintain nonprofit art gallery, School of Art Gallery; art & architecture libr at same address; FT 11, PT 3; pub; D&E; Scholarships; SC 98, LC 8, GC 87; maj 380, Grad 17
Ent Req: HS dipl
Degrees: BID, BFA, MFA 3 yrs
Courses: †Advertising Design, Art Appreciation, Art Education, Art History, †Ceramics, †Commercial Art, Conceptual Art, Design, †Drawing, †Graphic Arts,

†Graphic Design, Illustration, †Interior Design, †Painting, †Photography, †Printmaking, †Sculpture, †Studio Art
Summer School: varies

SHREVEPORT

CENTENARY COLLEGE OF LOUISIANA, Dept of Art, 2911 Centenary Blvd, Shreveport, LA 71104-3396. Tel 318-869-5261, 869-5011; Fax 318-869-5730; Email ballen@bata.centenary.edu; Web: www.centenary.edu/department/art/; *Chmn Dept & Prof* Bruce Allen, MFA; *Lectr* Neil Johnson, BA; *Vis Asst Prof* Lisa Nicoletti, PhD; *Instr* Diane Dufilho, MA
Estab 1825, dept estab 1935; Maintain Turner Art Center Gallery; den; D & E; Scholarships; SC 22, LC 8; D 125 per sem
Ent Req: HS dipl, SAT or ACT
Degrees: BA 4 yrs
Courses: Aesthetics, Art Education, Art History, Ceramics, Drafting, Drawing, Graphic Arts, Painting, Printmaking, Sculpture, Teacher Training

THIBODAUX

NICHOLLS STATE UNIVERSITY, Dept of Art, 906 E 1st St, Thibodaux, LA 70310-6701. Tel 985-448-4597; Fax 985-448-4596; Web: www.nicholls.edu; *Art Dept Head* Dennis Sipiorski
Estab 1948; FT 8; pub; D & E; Scholarships; SC 73, LC 6; D 100, non-maj 20, maj 80, others 20
Ent Req: HS dipl, ACT
Degrees: BA 4 yrs
Courses: Applied Design, Art Appreciation, Art Education, Art History, Ceramics, Design, Drawing, Graphic Design, Illustration, Painting, Papermaking, Photography, Printmaking, Rendering, Sculpture, Water Media

MAINE

AUGUSTA

UNIVERSITY OF MAINE AT AUGUSTA, College of Arts & Humanities, 46 University Dr, University Heights Augusta, ME 04330-9488. Tel 207-621-3000; Fax 207-621-3293; Web: www.uma.maine.edu; *Prof* Philip Paratore, MFA; *Prof* Robert Katz, MFA; *Prof* Karen Gilg, MFA; *Prof* Tom Hoffman, MFA; *Prof* Lizabeth Libbey, MFA; *Prof* Bill Moseley, MFA; *Prof* Mark Polishook, MFA; *Prof* Roger Richman, MFA; *Prof* Donald Stratton, MFA; *Prof* Charles Winfield, MFA; *Assoc Prof* Brooks Stoddard, MFA; *Chmn* Joshua Nadel, MFA
Estab 1965, dept estab 1970; pub; D & E; SC 20, LC 8; D 50, E 40, non-maj 40, maj 60
Ent Req: HS dipl
Degrees: AA(Architectural Studies) 2 yrs
Courses: Advertising Design, Art History, Ceramics, Drawing, Graphic Arts, Mixed Media, Painting, Paper Making, Photography, Sculpture
Summer School: Provost, Richard Randall. Enrl 30-50; tuition $52 per cr hr for term of 7 wks beginning last wk in June. Courses - Drawing, Painting, Sculpture

BRUNSWICK

BOWDOIN COLLEGE, Art Dept, 9300 College Station, Visual Arts Ctr Brunswick, ME 04011-8493. Tel 207-725-3697; Fax 207-725-3996; Web: www.bowdoin.edu; *Prof* Linda Docherty PhD; *Chair* Mark Wethli, MFA; *Dir Art History* Susan Wegner, PhD; *Prof* Thomas B Cornell, AB; *Lectr* John Bisbee, BFA; *Asst Prof* Stephen Perkinson, PhD; *Asst Prof* Pamela Fletcher, PhD; *Asst Prof* Michael Kolster, MFA; *Prof* Jim Mullen, MFA; *Vis Asst Prof* Anna Hepler, MFA; *Asst Prof* De-Nin Lee, MFA; *Prof* Clifton Olds, PhD; *Vis Asst Prof* Meghan Brady, MFA; *Vis Asst Prof* Wiebke Theodore, MArch; *Vis Asst Prof* Meggan Gould, MFA
Estab 1794; maintain a nonprofit art gallery: Bowdoin College Museum of Art, Walker Art Bldg, 9400 College Station Brunswick ME 04011; maintains an art/architecture library: Pierce Art Library, Visual Arts Center, 9300 College Station, Brunswick ME; on-campus shop where art supplies may be purchased; pvt; D & E; Scholarships; SC 12, LC 12; maj 54
Ent Req: HS dipl
Degrees: AB 4 yrs
Courses: Architecture, Art History, Digital Animation, Drawing, History of Art & Architecture, Painting, Photography, Printmaking, Sculpture, Stage Design, Visual Arts

DEER ISLE

HAYSTACK MOUNTAIN SCHOOL OF CRAFTS, PO Box 518, Deer Isle, ME 04627-0518. Tel 207-348-2306; Fax 207-348-2307; Email haystack@haystack-mtn.org; Web: www.haystack-mtn.org; *Dir* Paul Sacaridiz; *Director* D. Samuel Quigley; *Director of External Affairs* Vera Harsh; *Director of Exhibitions & Registrar* Jane LeGrow; *Director of Education* Caitlyn Healy
Estab 1950; Maintains nonprofit art gallery, Haystack's Ctr for Community Progs, 22 Church St, Deer Isle ME 04627; maintains art library; on-campus shop where art supplies may be purchased; FT 36; pvt; D, Summer school; Scholarships; SC; D 82
Collections: Over 15,000 objects from ancient times to the present: artworks from Africa, Asia, the Americas, and Europe, with particularly strong collections of American paintings, decorative arts and Victorian toys and doll houses. Outside a sculpture trail featuring 10 large scale works is surrounded by 12 acres of gardens and lawns.
Exhibitions: The recently renovated Palmer galleries house exhibitions from the permanent collection showcasing prized works from the last 3 centuries. The remaining galleries are used for an additional 12-18 changing exhibitions.
Activities: Art & dance classes for adults & children, homeschool programs,; lectures and concerts, book signings, docent and staff led tours, bus trips and exhibitions related events; books & gifts related to current exhibitions.
Tuition: approx $1,020 Tuition + housing (range $400-2,215) for 2 week sessions; approx $520 tuition + housing (range $225-$1,230) of 1 week sessions
Courses: Basketry, Blacksmithing, Ceramics, Drawing, Fabric, Glassblowing, Graphic Arts, Metalsmithing, Mixed Media, Painting, Papermaking, Printmaking, Quiltmaking, Sculpture, Stained Glass, Weaving, Woodworking, writing
Summer School: Dir, Paul Sacarudiz. Enrl 80; tuition $475 for 1 wk, $890 for 2 wks. Courses—Basketry, Blacksmith, Fabric Arts, Glassblowing, Graphics, Metalsmithing, Papermaking, Quiltmaking, Woodworking

GORHAM

UNIVERSITY OF SOUTHERN MAINE, Dept of Art, 37 College Ave, Gorham, ME 04038-1032. Tel 207-780-5460; Fax 207-780-5759; Web: www.usm.maine.edu/artdepartment; *Internship Coordr* Amy Haqberg; *Dir Exhibs* Carolyn Eyler; *Environmental & Studio Tech* Stephen Walsh; *Prof Art Hist* Donna Cassidy; *Prof Sculpture* Michael Shaughnessy; *Assoc Prof Art Educ* Kelly Hrenko; *Prof Digital & Foundation* Jan Piribeck; *Assoc Prof - Digital* Raphael DiLuzio; *Lectr Painting & Drawing* Jim Flahaven; *Lectr Printmaking and Digital Photo* Damir Porobic; *Instr* J McDermott; *Instr* D Schneider; *Instr* L Lisberger; *Instr* R Goodale; *Instr* V Goodlett; *Instr* J Kagan; *Instr* R Wilson
Estab 1878, dept estab 1956; Maintains nonprofit art gallery, USM Art Gallery; maintains art library, USM Libraries; pub; D & E & weekend; SC 33 LC 14; maj 162
Ent Req: HS dipl
Degrees: BA, BFA
Tuition: Res—undergrad $253 per cr hr; nonres—undergrad $665 per cr hr
Courses: Art Education, Art History, Ceramics, Design, †Digital Art, Drawing, Mixed Media, Painting, Philosophy of Art; Problems in Art, Photography, Printmaking, Sculpture

LEWISTON

BATES COLLEGE, Art & Visual Culture, 2 Andrews Rd, Lewiston, ME 04240-6020; 75 Russell St, Lewiston, ME 04240. Tel 207-786-8212; Fax 207-786-8335; Email aodom@bates.edu; Web: www.bates.edu; *Prof* Rebecca W Corrie; *Pres* Elaine Hansen; *Assoc Prof* Edward S Hardwood; *Prof* Erica Rand; *Asst Prof, Chmn* Trian Nguyen; *Assoc Prof* Pamela Johnson; *Lectr* Susan Denlsnap; *Senior Lectr* Robert Feintuch; *Senior Lectr* Elke Morris
Estab 1864, dept estab 1964; Maintain nonprofit art gallery, Bates College Mus of Art; on-campus shop where art supplies may be purchased; FT 5, PT 4; pvt; D & E; Scholarships; SC 26, LC 37; 1650 total
Degrees: BA 4 yr
Courses: Aesthetics, Art History, Ceramics, Drawing, History of Art & Architecture, Painting, Photography, Printmaking, Sculpture, †Studio Art

ORONO

UNIVERSITY OF MAINE, Dept of Art, 107 Lord, Orono, ME 04469-5712. Tel 207-581-3245; Fax 207-581-3276; Email um.art@umit.maine.edu; Web: www.maine.edu/art; *Prof* Laurie E Hicks PhD; *Prof* Michael H Lewis, MFA; *Assoc Prof* Constant Albertson, PhD; *Assoc Prof & Chair* Michael Grillo, PhD, MA; *Assoc Prof* Andy Mavery, MFA; *Adjunct Assoc Prof* Nina Sutcliffe, MA; *Adjunct Asst Prof* Ed Nadeau, MFA; *Adjunct Asst Prof* Karen Linehan, MA; *Adjunct Asst Prof* Wayne Hall, MFA; *Adjunct Asst Prof* Jorge Gonzalez, MFA; *Adjunct Asst Prof* Kerstin Engman, MFA; *Adjunct Asst Prof* Susan Camp, MFA; *Adjunct Prof* John Eden, MFA; *Prof* James Linehan, MFA; *Prof* Susan Groce, MFA; *Assoc Prof* Justin Wolff, PhD; *Instr* Matthew Smolinsky, MFA; *Adjunct Asst Prof* Greg Ondo, MFA
Estab 1862, dept estab 1946; Maintain nonprofit art gallery, Lord Hall, Dept of Art, Univ of Maine, Orono, ME 04469; on-campus art supply shop; pub; D & E; Scholarships; SC 57, LC 24, GC; maj 175-200; minors 80
Ent Req: HS dipl, 3 CEEB tests
Degrees: BA 4 yrs, BFA
Tuition: Res—undergrad $8480; nonres—undergrad $20,750; campus res—room & board $7484 per yr
Courses: Aesthetics, Art Appreciation, †Art Education, †Art History, Computer Art, Design, Digital Art, Drawing, Graphic Design, History of Art & Architecture, Mixed Media, †New Media, Painting, Photography, Printmaking, Sculpture, †Studio Art, Teacher Training
Children's Classes: Chair, Laurie E Hicks, PhD. Enrl 110-125; tuition $25 for 8 wks during the Fall sem. Courses—Art Education
Summer School: Dir, Robert White. Tuition $105 per cr hr, 3-8 wk courses. Courses—Art Education, Art History, Basic Drawing, Basic Painting, Computer Graphics, Photography, Printmaking

PORTLAND

MAINE COLLEGE OF ART, 522 Congress St # 4, Portland, ME 04101-3378. Tel 207-775-3052; Fax 207-775-5087; Email info@meca.edu; Web: www.meca.edu; *Pres* Christine J Vincent; *Dean* Greg Murphy; *Instr* John Eide, MFA; *Instr* Mark Jamra, BFA; *Instr* John T Ventimiglia, MFA; *Instr* Mark Johnson, MFA; *Instr* George LaRou, MFA; *Instr* Gan Xu, PhD; *Instr* Joan Uraneck, MFA; *Instr* Honour Mack, MFA; *Instr* Paul Diamato, MFA
Estab 1882; pvt; D & E; Scholarships; SC 37, LC 9; D 330, E300, maj 330, others 170 HS, 75 children (4th-9th grades)
Ent Req: HS dipl, portfolio

Degrees: BFA 4 yr (under Maine law, & academically advanced HS Sr may take the freshman yr at Maine College of Art for both HS & Maine College of Art cr), MFA 2 yr
Courses: Art Education, Art History, Art in Service, †Ceramics, Computer Arts, Design, Drawing, †Graphic Design, Illustration, †Jewelry, †Metalsmithing, Mixed Media, New Media Illustration, †Painting, †Photography, †Printmaking, †Sculpture, †Self-Designed Media Arts, †Silversmithing, Video, Woodworking & Furniture Design
Adult Hobby Classes: 300; tuition 325 per 1 cr course plus lab fee $10-$25. Courses—Apparel Design, Cartooning, Ceramics, Design, Drawing, Electronic Imaging, Graphic Design, Illustration, Jewelry, Landscape Design, Metalsmithing, Painting, Photography, Printmaking, Sculpture, Textile Design
Children's Classes: $245; tuition $150 for 10 wk term. Courses—Ceramics, Computer Graphics, Drawing, Graphic Design, Metalsmithing, Photography, Printmaking, Sculpture
Summer School: Dir, Margo Halverson. Courses—Art History, Ceramics, Computer Imaging, Drawing, Graphic Design, Jewelry & Metalsmithing, Painting, Photography, Printmaking, Sculpture, Watercolor, 2 & 3-D Design

PORTLAND POTTERY INC, 118 Washington Ave, Portland, ME 04101-2631. Tel 207-772-3273; Fax 207-780-6451; Web: www.portlandpottery.com
Courses: †Jewelry, †Pottery, †Sculpture

ROCKPORT

MAINE PHOTOGRAPHIC WORKSHOPS, THE INTERNATIONAL T.V. & FILM WORKSHOPS & ROCKPORT COLLEGE, 2 Central St, Rockport, ME 04856-5936; PO Box 200, Rockport, ME 04856-0200. Tel 207-236-8581; Fax 207-236-2558; Email info@theworkshops.com; Web: www.theworkshops.com; *Founder & Dir* David H Lyman; *Registrar* Kerry Curren; *Student Svcs* Christy Smith
Estab 1973; Scholarships; 1200
Degrees: AA 2 yr, MFA
Courses: 3-D Art, Animation, Archaeology, Art History, Collage, Commercial Art, Conceptual Art, Digital Media, Drawing, Film, Graphic Arts, Graphic Design, History of Cinema, History of Photography, Illustration, Interactive Multimedia, Painting, Photography, Printmaking, Psychology of Symbols, Screen Dynamics, Teacher Training, Video
Adult Hobby Classes: Enrl 1000
Summer School: Dir, David H Lyman. Enrl 2000; tuition $250-$600 for 1 wk workshop. Courses—Directing, Editing, Film, Video, Writing

WATERVILLE

COLBY COLLEGE, Art Dept, 4000 Mayflower Hill, Waterville, ME 04901-8840. Tel 207-872-3233; Fax 207-872-3141; *Prof* Harriett Matthews, MFA; *Prof* David Simon, PhD; *Prof* Michael Marlais, PhD; *Assoc Prof* Scott Reed, MFA; *Asst Prof* Ankeney Weitz, PhD; *Assoc Prof* Berin Engman, MFA; *Assoc Prof* Veronique Plesch, PhD; *Asst Prof* Laura Saltz, PhD; *Vis Asst Prof* Dee Peppe, MFA
Estab 1813, dept estab 1944; Maintain nonprofit art gallery; pvt; D & E; Scholarships; SC 25, LC 25; D 500, non-maj 425, maj 75
Ent Req: HS dipl
Degrees: BA 4 yrs
Courses: Art History, †Art History, Ceramics, Drawing, History of Art & Architecture, History of Art & Architecture, †Painting, Painting, Photography, †Printmaking, Printmaking, †Sculpture, Sculpture

MARYLAND

BALTIMORE

BALTIMORE CITY COMMUNITY COLLEGE, Dept of Fine Arts, 2901 Liberty Heights Ave, Main Bldg, Rm 243 Baltimore, MD 21215-7807. Tel 410-462-7605; Web: www.bccc.edu; *Chmn* Rose Monroe; *Assoc Prof* David Bahr, MFA; *Asst Prof* Sally De Marcos, MEd
Estab 1947; Harbor Campus address Lombard St & Market Place, Baltimore, MD 21202; FT 7, PT 20; pub; D & E; Scholarships; D & E 9800, non-maj 505, maj 388
Ent Req: HS dipl or HS equivalency, ent exam
Degrees: AA 2 yrs
Courses: Advertising Design, Art Education, Art History, Ceramics, Commercial Art, Drawing, †Fashion Design, Fashion Illustration, †Fashion Merchandising, Graphic Arts, †Graphic Design, Jewelry, Painting, †Photography, Printmaking, Sculpture, Textile Design
Adult Hobby Classes: Tuition res $56 per cr; nonres $168 per cr. Courses—same as above
Summer School: Dir, Dr Stephen Millman. Enrl 2655. Courses - Ceramics, Crafts, Design, Drawing, Fashion Design, Painting

COLLEGE OF NOTRE DAME OF MARYLAND, Art Dept, 4701 N Charles St, Baltimore, MD 21210-2404. Tel 410-532-5520; Fax 410-532-5795; Email dfirmani@ndm.edu; Web: www.ndm.edu; WATS (Md) 800-435-0200; all other 800-435-0300; *Chmn Prof* Domenico Firmani PhD; *Prof* Kevin Raines, MFA; *Assoc Prof* Geoff Delanoy, MFA
Estab 1899; Maintains nonprofit gallery, Gormley Gallery, 4701 N Charles, Baltimore, MD 21210; den, W; wkend, M; D & E, wkend; Scholarships; SC 32, LC 20, GC 5; D 680, non-maj 480, maj 45
Ent Req: HS dipl, SAT
Degrees: BA 4 yrs
Courses: Advertising Design, Art Education, †Art History, Commercial Art, Design, Drawing, †Graphic Arts, Graphic Design, Illustration, †Museum Staff Training, Painting, †Photography, Printmaking, Sculpture, †Studio, Teacher Training
Adult Hobby Classes: Enrl 55; tuition $150 per cr (1-9 cr). Courses offered in Weekend College & Continuing Education Programs
Summer School: Enrl 35; tuition $95 per cr. Courses—Drawing, History of Art Surveys, Painting, Photography, Printmaking, Sculpture, Teacher Training

COPPIN STATE COLLEGE, Dept Fine & Communication Arts, 2500 W North Ave, Baltimore, MD 21216-3698. Tel 410-383-5400; Fax 410-383-9606; Web: www.coppin.edu; *Chmn* Dr Judith Willner
FT 1, PT 2; Scholarships; SC 6, LC 7; D 350, E 45
Degrees: BS, MA & Doc in Art Education
Courses: Advertising Design, Art Education, Art History, Calligraphy, Ceramics, Drawing, Film, Graphic Design, Lettering, Painting, Photography, Printmaking, Sculpture, Teacher Training, Theatre Arts

GOUCHER COLLEGE, Art & Art History Dept, 1021 Dulaney Valley Rd, Baltimore, MD 21204-2780. Tel 410-337-6000, 337-6570; Web: www.goucher.edu; *Prof, Chair* Allyn Massey; *Prof* Gail Husch; *Prof* Ed Worteck; *Prof* April Osttinger; *Prof* Matthew McConville
Estab 1885; Rosenberg Gallery & Silber Gallery; FT 5, PT 6-7; pvt; D & E; Scholarships; SC 23, LC 19; D 500, non-maj 450, maj (art) 40
Ent Req: HS dipl, SAT, achievement tests (CEEB), American College Testing Program
Degrees: BA 4 yrs (18 depts for undergrads)
Courses: †Aesthetics, †Art Education, †Art History, †Arts Administration, †Ceramics, †Communications, †Conceptual Art, †Constructions, †Mixed Media, †Painting, †Photography, †Printmaking, †Sculpture, †Video

JOHNS HOPKINS UNIVERSITY, Dept of the History of Art, 3400 N Charles St, Baltimore, MD 21218-2680. Tel 410-516-7117; Fax 410-516-5188; Email arthist@jhu.edu; Web: www.jhu.edu; *Chmn* Dr Stephen Campbell
Estab 1947; FT 5, PT 3; pvt; D & E; Scholarships; LC; 10-20 in advanced courses, 80-100 in introductory courses
Tuition: $31,620 per yr
Courses: †Art History, History of Art & Archaeology
Summer School: Enrl 30
—School of Medicine, Dept of Art as Applied to Medicine, 1830 E Monument St, Ste 7000, Baltimore, MD 21205. Tel 410-955-3213; Fax 410-955-1085; Email dbalch1@jhmi.edu; Web: www.hopkinsmedicine.org/medart; *Dir Dept* Gary P Lees, MS; *Assoc Prof* Timothy H Phelps, MS; *Assoc Prof* Howard C Bartner, MA; *Assoc Prof* David Rini, MA; *Asst Prof* Dale R Levitz, MS; *Assoc Prof* Corinne Sandone, MA; *Assoc Prof* Norman Barker, MS; *Asst Prof* Juan R Garcia, MA; *Asst Prof* Anne R Altemus, MA; *Lectr* Joseph Dieter Jr; *Asst Prof* Miguel A Schon, PhD; *Prof Pathology* Grover M Hutchins, MD; *Lectr* Joan A Freedman, MS; *Assoc Prof* Ian Suk; *Instr* Virginia Ferrante
Univ estab 1876, School Medicine estab 1893, dept estab 1911; Maintains an art library; pvt; D; Scholarships; SC 13, LC 5, GC 11
Ent Req: Baccalaureate degree
Degrees: MA
Tuition: $36,100 per yr
Courses: Illustration, Photography, Sculpture, Video

MARYLAND INSTITUTE, College of Art, 1300 W Mt Royal Ave, Baltimore, MD 21217. Tel 410-669-9200; Web: www.mica.edu; *Pres* Samuel Hoi
Estab 1826; FT 45, PT 55; pvt; D & E; Scholarships; D 1107, E 554, Sat 280
Ent Req: HS grad, exam
Degrees: BFA & MFA 4 yrs
Tuition: $46,870 per yr
Courses: Ceramics, Computer Graphics, Drawing, Fibers & Wood, Graphic Design, Illustration, Interior Design, Painting, Photography, Printmaking, Sculpture
Adult Hobby Classes: Evenings & Saturdays, cr-non cr classes
Children's Classes: Saturdays & Summer classes
—Hoffberger School of Painting, 1300 W Mt Royal Ave, Baltimore, MD 21217. Tel 410-669-9200; Fax 410-225-2408; Web: www.mica.edu; *Dir* Joan Waltemath
Fel awarded annually for study at the grad level; limited to 14
—Rinehart School of Sculpture, 1300 W Mt Royal Ave, Baltimore, MD 21217. Tel 410-669-9200; Fax 410-225-2408; Web: www.mica.edu; *Dir* Jann Rosen-Queralt
Courses: Sculpture
—Mount Royal School of Art, 1300 Mount Royal Ave, Baltimore, MD 21217. Tel 410-669-9200; Web: www.mica.edu; *Dir* Luca Buvoli; *Faculty* David B Brody; *Faculty* Patty Chang; *Faculty* Dawn Clements
79
Degrees: MAT 2 yrs
Courses: Aesthetics, Art Education, Art History, Calligraphy, †Ceramics, †Drawing, History of Art & Archeology, Intermedia, †Mixed Media, Painting, Photography, †Sculpture, Studio Art, Teacher Training, Video
—Graduate Photographic & Electronic Media, 1300 W Mount Royal Ave, Baltimore, MD 21217. Tel 410-225-2306; Web: www.mica.edu; *Dir* Timothy Druckrey
Degrees: MFA 2 yrs
Courses: History of Photography, Photography
—Graduate Art Education, 1300 W Mount Royal Ave, Baltimore, MD 21217. Tel 410-669-9200; Web: www.mica.edu; *Dir* Stacey Salazar EdD
Degrees: MFA 2 yrs
Courses: Art Education, Teacher Training

MORGAN STATE UNIVERSITY, Dept of Art, 1700 E Coldspring Lane, Baltimore, MD 21251. Tel 443-885-3021, 885-3333 (Main); Web: www.morgan.edu; *Fine Arts Dept Chmn* Dr Nathan Carter; *Coordr Art Dept* Kenneth Royster
Estab 1867, dept estab 1950; FT 7; pub; D & E; Scholarships; SC 28, LC 11, GC 17; D 340, E 50, non-maj 250, maj 140, GS 11
Ent Req: HS dipl
Degrees: BA(Art & Music Performance) & MA(Music)

Courses: 3-D Design, Architecture, Art Education, Art History, Ceramics, Design, Drawing, †Gallery, Graphic Arts, Graphic Design, Illustration, Painting, Photography, Sculpture, †Theatre Arts

SCHULER SCHOOL OF FINE ARTS, 5 E Lafayette Ave, Baltimore, MD 21202-2880; 7 E Lafayette Ave, Baltimore, MD 21202-2807. Tel 410-685-3568; Email schulerschool@gmail.com; Web: www.schulerschool.com; *Dir* Francesca Schuler Guerin; *Asst Dir* Hans Schuler Guerin
Estab 1959; Maintain library; pvt; D & E, Sat workshops; SC 9, GC 3; D 50, E 30, grad 2
Degrees: 4 yrs; dipl, 5 yr scholarship
Tuition: $5,500 per yr, part-time students pay by schedule for sem
Courses: Art Education, Drawing, Painting, Sculpture
Children's Classes: Tuition $750-$1200 (summer - ages 14 & over). Courses—Drawing, Painting, Sculpture
Summer School: Dir, Francis S. Guerin. Enrl 30; tuition $750 for term of 6 wks beginning June, $1,300 for 6 hrs per day, 6 wks. Courses—Drawing, Oil Painting, Sculpture, Watercolor

UNIVERSITY OF MARYLAND, BALTIMORE COUNTY, Intermedia & Digital Arts (IMDA), Dept of Visual Arts, 1000 Hilltop Cr, FA #111 Baltimore, MD 21250. Tel 410-455-2150; Fax 410-455-1053; Email imda@umbc.edu; Web: imda.umbc.edu; *Assoc Prof* Guenet Abraham; *Prof & Dir Imaging Research Ctr* Dan Bailey; *Affiliate Assoc Prof, Chief Cur AOK Libr & Dir CBSA* Tom Beck; *Asst Prof & Assoc Chair* Kelley Bell; *Undergrad Prog Dir* Melanie Berry; *Affiliate Assoc Prof & Assoc Dir Imaging Research Ctr* Lee Boot; *Assoc Prof* Steve Bradley; *Adjunct Faculty* Susan Campbell; *Assoc Prof* Lynn Cazabon; *Assoc Prof* Irene Chan; *Assoc Prof* Cathy Cook; *Prof* Mark Alice Durant; *Assoc Prof* Eric Dyer; *Adjunct Faculty* Joan Feldman; *Affiliate Assoc Prof & Dir Ctr for Art Design & Visual Culture* Symmes Gardner; *Assoc Prof* Vin Grabill; *Assoc Prof & Assoc Chair* Preminda Jacob; *Affiliate Assoc Prof* James Mahoney; *Prof & Graduate Prog Dir* Carrie Frances Parks; *Prof* Lisa Moren; *Prof & Dir Ctr for Innovative Research in Creative Arts* Sarah Sharp; *Prof* Timothy Nohe; *Assoc Prof* Kathy O'Dell; *Assoc Prof* Peggy Re; *Prof* James Smalls; *Prof* John Sturgeon; *Assoc Prof* Calla Thompson; *Exhib & Tech Dir, Ctr for Art* William-John Tudor; *Assoc Prof* Fred Worden; *Graduate Prog Coordr* Eva Holley; *Asst Prof* Gary Rozanc; *Asst Prof* Viviana Cordova; *Adjunct Faculty* Joe Reinsel
Estab 1966; Maintains coll in Albin O Kuhn Library & Gallery; art supplies sold on campus; pub; D & E; Scholarships; SC 27, LC 12, GC 4; in dept D 485, non-maj 375, maj 110
Library Holdings: Book Volumes, Manuscripts, Maps, Other Holdings Archives; Artifacts; Special Collections, Photographs
Ent Req: HS dipl, SAT
Degrees: BA 4 yrs, BFA, MFA
Courses: Aesthetics, †Art History, Collage, Conceptual Art, †Drawing, †Film, Graphic Arts, †Graphic Design, †History of Art & Architecture, Intermedia, Lettering, †Maker Technologies, Mixed Media, †Painting, †Photography, Physical Computing, Printmaking, Social Practices, †Video

BEL AIR

HARFORD COMMUNITY COLLEGE, Visual, Performing and Applied Arts Division, 401 Thomas Run Rd, Bel Air, MD 21015-1696. Tel 443-412-2000; Fax 443-412-2180; Email vpaa@harford.edu; Web: www.harford.edu; *Dean* Paul Labe Jr; *Prof Art* James McFarland; *Assoc Prof Art* Kenneth Jones; *Assoc Prof Art* Heidi Neff; *Assoc Prof Art* Jeffrey Ball; *Assoc Prof Theatre* Dr Ben Fisler; *Assoc Prof Mass Communs* Wayne Hepler; *Asst Prof Mass Communs* Claudia Brown; *Asst Prof Music* Dr Patricia Burt; *Photog Faculty* Jeffrey Rollinger
Estab 1957; Maintain Chesapeake Gallery, Harford Community College, 401 Thomas Run Rd, Bel Air, MD 21015; FT 10, PT 40; pub; D & E; SC 105, LC 13; FT 6,000, PT 4,500
Ent Req: HS dipl
Degrees: AA 2 yrs
Tuition: Res—undergrad $87 per cr hr; nonres—undergrad $174 (out of county), $261 (out of state) per cr hr
Courses: Architecture, Art History, Audio, Ceramics, Costume Design & Construction, Design, †Design & Technical Theatre, †Digital Imaging, †Digital Media, Drawing, Film, †Fine Art, Graphic Arts, Graphic Design, History of Art & Architecture, Illustration, Mixed Media, †Music, Painting, †Performing Arts, †Photography, Printmaking, Sculpture, Stage Design, Theatre Arts, Video

BOWIE

BOWIE STATE UNIVERSITY, Fine & Performing Arts Dept, 14000 Jericho Park Rd, MLK Bldg, Rm 236 Bowie, MD 20715-3319. Tel 301-860-4000; Fax 301-860-3767; *Coordr Gallery Dir* Robert Ward; *Chmn* Clarence Knight
Estab 1865, dept estab 1968; FT 8; pub; D; SC 7, LC 3; D 1600, E 350, non-maj 180, maj 45
Ent Req: HS dipl
Degrees: BA(Art) 4 yrs
Courses: African & American History, Art History, Ceramics, Cinematography, Computer Graphics, Crafts, Design, Drawing, Graphics, Museum & Gallery Study, Painting, Photography, Sculpture
Summer School: Dir, Dr Ida Brandon. Courses—Ceramics, Media Workshop

CATONSVILLE

COMMUNITY COLLEGE OF BALTIMORE COUNTY, (Catonsville Community College) School of Technology, Art & Design, 800 S Rolling Rd, Catonsville, MD 21228-5317. Tel 443-840-4598; Fax 443-840-5134; Email hrummel@ccbcmd.edu; *Dept Chair* Hal Rummel; *Coordr* Doug McNamara; *Coordr* Debby Ciccarelli; *Interior Design Coordr* Laura Kimball
Estab 1957; pub; D & E; Scholarships; SC 26, LC 6; D 600, E 400, non-maj 200, maj 300, applied arts maj 350
Ent Req: HS dipl
Degrees: cert & AA 2 yrs
Courses: Art Appreciation, Art Education, Art History, Ceramics, Commercial Art, Drawing, Graphic Design, Illustration, Interior Design, Painting, †Photography, Sculpture
Summer School: Same as above

COLLEGE PARK

UNIVERSITY OF MARYLAND, Dept of Art History & Archaeology, 1211-D Art-Sociology Bldg, College Park, MD 20742-1335. Tel 301-405-1479; 405-1494; Fax 301-314-9652; Email jh24@umail.umd.edu; Web: www.inform.umd.edu/EdRes/colleges/ARHU/Depts/ArtHistory; *Chmn* June Hargrove
Estab 1944; FT 17, PT 2; pub; D; Scholarships; SC 39, LC 37, GC 22; 2000 per sem, maj 102, grad 77
Ent Req: 3.0 grade average
Degrees: BA, MA, PhD
Courses: Art History
Adult Hobby Classes: Enrl 500 per yr. Courses—Art History
Summer School: Dir, Dr Melvin Hall. Enrl 350; tuition res—$170; nonres—$280 per cr hr for term of 6 wks. Courses—Art History
—Department of Art, 1211-E Art-Sociology Bldg, College Park, MD 20742-1311. Tel 301-405-1442; Fax 301-314-9740; Email artdept@umail.umd.edu; Web: www.inform.umd.edu/EdRes/colleges/ARHU/Depts/Art; *Chmn* John Ruppert
Estab 1944; FT 19, PT 5; pub; D; Scholarships; SC 39, LC 37, GC 22; 850 per sem, maj 170, grad 20
Ent Req: 3.0 grade average
Degrees: BA, MFA
Courses: 2-D & 3-D Drawing, Art Theory, Artist Survival, Design, Lithography, Mixed Media, Papermaking, Photography, Printmaking
Summer School: Dir, Dr Melvin Berstein. Two six-week sessions. Courses—Design, Drawing, Painting, Printmaking, Sculpture

CUMBERLAND

ALLEGANY COMMUNITY COLLEGE, Art Dept, 12401 Willow Brook Rd SE, Cumberland, MD 21502. Tel 301-724-7700; Fax 301-724-6892; Web: www.ac.cc.md.us; *Chmn* James D Zamagias
Estab 1966; FT 1 PT 3; pub; D & E; Scholarships; SC 6, LC 1; Enrl D 30, E 9
Ent Req: HS dipl
Degrees: AA 2 yrs
Courses: 2-D & 3-D Design, Ceramics, Drawing, Painting, Survey of Art History
Adult Hobby Classes: Courses offered
Summer School: Dir, James D Zamagias. Term of 6 wks beginning July. Courses—Painting, 2-D Design

EMMITSBURG

MOUNT SAINT MARY'S UNIVERSITY, Visual & Performing Arts Dept, 16300 Old Emmitsburg Rd, Emmitsburg, MD 21727-7702. Tel 301-447-6122, Ext 5308; Fax 301-447-5755; Web: www.msmary.edu; *Prof* Margaret Rahaim, MFA; *Art Faculty* Dr Kurt Blaugher; *Prof* Elizabeth Holtry, MFA; *Prof* Dr Andrew Rosenfeld; *Prof* Barry Long, MA
Estab 1808; pvt; D & E; Scholarships; SC 13, LC 3; D 1528, maj 20
Ent Req: HS dipl, SAT
Degrees: BA and BS 4 yrs
Courses: Art Education, †Art History, Ceramics, Design, †Drawing, Graphic Arts, Graphic Design, Mixed Media, †Painting, Photography, Printmaking, †Sculpture, †Theatre Arts

FREDERICK

HOOD COLLEGE, Dept of Art, 401 Rosemont Ave, Frederick, MD 21701-8575. Tel 301-663-3131; Fax 301-694-7653; Web: www.hood.edu; *Assoc Prof* Fred Bohrer; *Chmn* Dr Anne Derbes
Estab 1893; Varies from PT to FT; pvt, W; D; SC 18, LC 16; D 700, maj 60
Ent Req: HS dipl
Degrees: BA 4 yrs
Courses: Art History, Three Areas of Concentration: Studio Arts, Visual Communications
Summer School: Dir, Dr Patricia Bartlett. Tuition by course for term of 6 wks, June-Aug. Courses—Internships and Independent Studies, Photography, Watercolor and Sketching, Woodcut

FROSTBURG

FROSTBURG STATE UNIVERSITY, Dept of Visual Arts, 101 Braddock Rd, Frostburg, MD 21532-2303. Tel 301-687-4797; Fax 301-689-4737; Email ddavis@frostburg.edu; WATS 800-687-8677; *Head Dept* Dustin P Davis
Estab 1898; FT 3; pub; D; Scholarships; SC 25, LC 5; D 230, maj 150, GS 13
Ent Req: HS dipl
Degrees: BFA(Art Educ Cert) 4 yr
Courses: 2-D & 3-D Design, Art Appreciation, Art Criticism, Art Education, Art History, Art Therapy, Ceramics, Crafts, Drawing, Graphic Design, Painting, Photography, Printmaking, Sculpture, Teacher Training, Visual Imagery

HAGERSTOWN

HAGERSTOWN JUNIOR COLLEGE, Art Dept, 11400 Robinwood Dr, Hagerstown, MD 21742-6514. Tel 301-790-2800, Ext 221; Fax 301-739-0737; *Coordr* Ben Culbertson; *Pres* Norman Shea
Estab 1946; pub; D & E; SC 10, LC 4; D 110, E 66
Degrees: AA, 2 yrs
Tuition: Washington County res—$70 per cr hr; out-of-county—$114 per cr hr; nonres—$143 per cr hr
Courses: Art Appreciation, Art History, Art Methods, Basic Design, Ceramics, Drawing, Painting, Photography, Sculpture, Video
Summer School: Courses - Art & Culture, Basic Drawing, Painting, Photography, Special Studies in Ceramics, Parent & Child Art Studio

LARGO

PRINCE GEORGE'S COMMUNITY COLLEGE, Art Dept, 301 Largo Rd, English & Humanities Div Largo, MD 20774-2109. Tel 301-322-0966; Fax 301-808-0960; Web: www.pg.cc.md.us; *Chmn* Gary Kirkeby
Estab 1958, dept estab 1967; 5 FT, 16 PT; pub; D & E; Scholarships; SC 18, LC 2; D 220, E 140, maj 11
Ent Req: HS dipl, CGP test
Degrees: AA
Courses: Art Appreciation, Art Survey, Ceramics, Commercial Advertising, Commercial Design, Computer Graphics, Design, Drawing, Graphic Arts, Graphic Design, Illustration, Lettering, Multimedia, Painting, Photography, Sculpture
Summer School: Dean, Dr Robert Barshay. Courses—Drawing, Intro to Art, Painting, Photography

PRINCESS ANNE

UNIVERSITY OF MARYLAND EASTERN SHORE, Art & Technology Dept, 11868 Academic Oval, Princess Anne, MD 21853-1299. Tel 410-651-6488, 651-2200; Fax 410-351-7959; *Coordr Art Educ* Ernest R Satchell
Degrees: BA 4 yr
Tuition: Res—$124 per cr hr incl room & board per sem; nonres—$265
Courses: Art Appreciation, Art Education, Art History, Calligraphy, Ceramics, Drawing, Handicrafts, Jewelry, Painting, Photography, Printmaking, Sculpture

ROCKVILLE

MONTGOMERY COLLEGE, Dept of Art, 51 Manakee St, Rockville, MD 20850. Tel 240-566-4083; Email artsinstitute@montgomerycollege.edu; Web: artsinstitute.montgomerycollege.edu; *Dean Arts* Deborah Preston; *Art Chair Germantown* Ziki Findikoglu; *Art Chair Rockville* Kay McCrohan; *Art Chair Tacoma Park* Wilfred Brunner; *Acting Dir, School of Art + Design* Maggie Noss; *Chair Commun Art Technology* Ed Riggs
Estab 1946; Maintain nonprofit art galleries, Cafritz Art Center Gallery, Commun Art Technology Gallery, Globe Hall Atrium Gallery, Sarah Silberman Art Gallery; Pub; D & E & W; Scholarships; SC 65, LC 13; 2,800
Ent Req: HS dipl, SA+D portfolio review
Degrees: AA Studio Art, Art Ed, Art History; AFA Studio Art, Graphic Design; AAS Graphic Design
Tuition: County Res—$93; state res— $191; out-of-state—$257
Courses: †Architecture, Art Appreciation, †Art History, Ceramics, Color Crafts, †Commercial Art, Computer Graphics, Design, Drawing, Enameling, Film, Goldsmithing, Graphic Design, History of Art & Architecture, †Illustration, †Interior Design, Jewelry, Metalsmithing, Painting, †Photography, Printmaking, Sculpture, Stage Design, Theatre Arts, Video
Adult Hobby Classes: Tuition & classes vary
Children's Classes: Tuition & classes vary
Summer School: Chmn Prof James L Brown. Tuition $35 per sem hr. Courses—Ceramics, Color, Crafts, Design, Drawing, Painting, Printmaking, Sculpture, Art History

SAINT MARY'S CITY

SAINT MARY'S COLLEGE OF MARYLAND, Art & Art History Dept, 18952 East Fischer Rd Saint Mary's City, MD 20686. Tel 240-895-2000, 895-4250; Fax 240-895-4958; Email srjohnson@smcm.edu; Web: www.smcm.edu; *Dept Chmn* Sue Johnson, MFA; *Prof* Jeffrey Carr, MFA; *Asst Prof* Joe Lucchesi, PhD; *Asst Prof* Rebecca Brown, PhD
Estab 1964; pub; D & E; Scholarships; SC 14, LC 16; D 155, E 43, non-maj 128, maj 70
Ent Req: HS dipl, SAT scores
Degrees: BA
Courses: Art History, Digital Imaging, Drawing, Graphic Arts, Mixed Media, Painting, Photography, Printmaking, Sculpture
Adult Hobby Classes: Art History, Drawing, Mixed Media, Painting, Photography, Printmaking, Sculpture
Summer School: Tuition $110 per cr

SALISBURY

SALISBURY STATE UNIVERSITY, Art Dept, 1101 Camden Ave, Salisbury, MD 21801-6860. Tel 410-543-6270; Fax 410-548-3002; Web: www.ssu.edu; *Chmn* Paul Flexner, PhD; *Assoc Prof* John R Cleary, MFA; *Asst Prof* Ursula M Ehrhardt, MA; *Asst Prof* Dean A Peterson, MA; *Assoc Prof* Marie Cavallaro
Estab 1925, dept estab 1970; Maintain nonprofit art gallery; Atrium Gallery & Fueton Gallery; Pub; D & E; Scholarships; SC 26, LC 7, GC 1; non-maj 500, maj 111, grad 2
Ent Req: HS dipl, SAT verbal & math, ACT
Degrees: BA & BFA 4 yrs,
Courses: †Advertising Design, Art Appreciation, Art Education, Art History, Ceramics, Commercial Art, Design, †European Field Study, Glassblowing, History of Art & Architecture, †Independent Study, Painting, Photography, †Principles of Color, Sculpture, †Visual Communications

SILVER SPRING

MARYLAND COLLEGE OF ART & DESIGN, 7600 Takoma Ave CF 120, Silver Spring, MD 20912. Tel 240-567-4454; Fax 240-567-5820; Web: www.mcadmd.org; *Pres* Wesley E Paulson; *Dean* Don Smith; *Asst Prof* Chris Medley, MFA
Estab 1955; pvt; D & E; Scholarships; Degree Prog 83, Enrichment & Special Students 175
Ent Req: HS dipl, SAT verbal scores, letter of recommendation, portfolio interview
Degrees: AFA 2 yrs
Courses: Advertising Design, Art History, Commercial Art, Computer Graphics, Design, Drawing, Graphic Arts, Graphic Design, Illustration, Intermedia, Lettering, Painting, Photography, Printmaking, Sculpture
Adult Hobby Classes: Enrl 1000; tuition $80-180 for 6-10 wks. Courses—Computer, Design, Drawing, Painting, Photography, Printmaking, Sculpture, Watercolor
Children's Classes: Enrl 1200; tuition $80-100 for 1-8 wks. Courses—Cartooning, Ceramics, Computer, Design, Drawing, Painting, Photography, Printmaking, Sculpture
Summer School: Dir, David Gracyalny. Enrl 1000; tuition $80-250 for 1-9 wks. Courses—Cartooning, Ceramics, Computer, Design, Drawing, Painting, Photography, Printmaking, Sculpture, Watercolor

TOWSON

TOWSON STATE UNIVERSITY, Dept of Art, 8000 York Rd, Towson, MD 21252-0002. Tel 410-704-3682, 704-2808; Fax 410-704-2810; Email jflood@towson.edu; Web: www.towson.edu/art; *Dept Chmn* James Flood
Estab 1866; FT 15, PT 9; pub; D & E
Ent Req: HS grad
Degrees: BA, BS, MEd(Art Educ) 4 yr & MFA; spring sem Florence, Italy, Feb-May
Courses: Art Education, Art History, Ceramics, Drawing, Enameling, Graphic Arts, Jewelry, Painting, Sculpture, Textile Design, Weaving, Wood & Metal
Adult Hobby Classes: Enrl 60
Summer School: Dir, Jim Flood. Enrl 25; 2 five wk sessions. Courses—Art History, Studio

WESTMINSTER

WESTERN MARYLAND COLLEGE, Dept of Art & Art History, 2 College Hill, Westminster, MD 21157-4390. Tel 410-848-8700; Web: www.wmdc.edu; *Prof* Wasyl Palijczuk; *Assoc Prof* Michael Losch; *Dept Head* Sue Bloom
Estab 1867; FT 4, PT 2; independent; D & E; Scholarships; SC 15, LC 12, GC 6; D 1213, maj 40-60, grad 15
Ent Req: HS dipl, ent exam, SAT
Degrees: BA, BS & MEd 4 yrs
Courses: Ceramics, Computer Graphics, Design, Drawing, Graphic Design, †History of Art & Architecture, Jewelry, Lettering, Painting, Photography, Printmaking, Sculpture, †Teacher Training
Summer School: Two 5 wk terms beginning June 21. Courses—Art History, Ceramics, Painting, Printmaking, Sculpture, Weaving

MASSACHUSETTS

AMHERST

AMHERST COLLEGE, Dept of Art & the History of Art, 107 Fayerweather Hall, Amherst, MA 01002-5000; 17 Fayerweather Dr, Rm 107, Amherst, MA 01002-5000. Tel 413-542-2365; Fax 413-542-7917; Email finearts@amherst.edu; Web: www.amherst.edu/~finearts; *Prof* Natasha Staller; *Wm R Mead Prof of Art, Chair* Robert T Sweeney; *John C Newton Prof of Art & History of Art & Black Studies* Rowland O Abiodun; *Prof of Art & History of Art* Nicola M Courtright; *Sr Resident Artist* Betsey Garand; *Sr Resident Artist* David I Gloman; *Prof Art* Carol Keller; *Prof* Justin Kimball; *Howard M & Martha P Mitchell Prof of History of Art & Asian Languages/Civilizations* Samuel C Morse; *Vis Asst Prof Art, Film & Media Studies* Adam Levine; *Vis Asst Prof & RE Keiter '57 Post-Doc Fellow* Yael Rice
Estab 1822; Maintain nonprofit art gallery, The Eli Marsh Gallery, 105 Fayerweather Hall, Amherst College, Amherst, MA 01002-5000 (open during academic yr only); FT 11; pvt; D; Scholarships; SC 15, LC 15
Ent Req: HS dipl
Degrees: BA 4 yrs
Tuition: $32,400 comprehensive fee for yr + room & board
Courses: 3-D Design, Aesthetics, Anatomy, Art History, Drawing, †Film, Painting, Photography, Printmaking, Sculpture

UNIVERSITY OF MASSACHUSETTS, AMHERST, College of Arts & Sciences, Fine Arts Center, Department of Art, Amherst, MA 01003-2510; 151 Presidents Dr, OFC 1 Amherst, MA 01003-9311. Tel 413-545-1902; Fax 413-545-3929; Web: www.umass.edu; *Chmn Dept* Ronald Michaud
Estab 1958; FT 36; Pub; SC 50, LC 19, GC 20; maj undergrad 430, grad 85
Ent Req: HS grad, portfolio & SAT required, 16 units HS
Degrees: BA, BFA, MFA

Courses: Ceramics, Design, Drawing, Painting, Photography, Printmaking, Sculpture
Summer School: Dir, Angel Ramirez. Courses—Architectural Drawing, Design, Drawing, Painting, Photography
—**Art History Program,** 130 Hicks Way, 317 Bartlett Hall Amherst, MA 01003-9269. Tel 413-545-3595; Fax 413-545-3880; Web: www.umass.edu; *Prof* Walter B Denny PhD; *Prof* Craig Harbison PhD; *Assoc Prof* Kristine Haney PhD; *Assoc Prof* Laetitia La Follette PhD; *Prof* Bill Odel; *Dir* Ronald Michaud
Estab 1947, prog estab 1958; pub; D & E; Scholarships; Fellowships; LC 36, GC 16; D 1735, non-maj 1369, maj 105, grad 40
Ent Req: HS dipl & transcript, SAT
Degrees: BA, MA
Courses: Aesthetics, American Art to 1860, Ancient Art, Architecture, †Art History, Greek & Roman Art & Architecture, History of Art & Archeology, Islamic Art, Museum Staff Training, Renaissance to Modern Art, Survey
Adult Hobby Classes: All courses available through Continuing Education
Summer School: Courses—Introduction to Art, Modern Art
—**Dept of Landscape Architecture & Regional Planning,** 111 Thatcher Rd Ofc1, 109 Hills Amherst, MA 01003-9361. Tel 413-545-2255; Fax 413-545-1772; Web: www.umass.edularp; *Asst Dept Head* Merle Willman PhD; *Dept Head* Jack Ahern
Estab 1903; pub; D; SC 6, LC 5; 35
Degrees: MA(Archit, Regional Planning & Landscape Design)
Courses: Aspects of Design Environment, Drafting, Drawing, Drawing & Measuring, Environmental Policy & Planning, Landscape Architecture, Site Planning, Studio Landscape
Summer School: Planning & design short courses

BEVERLY

ENDICOTT COLLEGE, School of Visual & Performing Arts, 376 Hale St, Beverly, MA 01915-2098. Tel 978-232-2250; Fax 978-232-2231; Email htobin@endicott.edu; Web: www.endicott.edu; *Dean* Mark Towner; *Chmn Performing Arts* Rebecca Kenneally; *Visual Arts Coordr* Kathleen Moore; *Chmn, Visual Communs* Sanford Farrier; *Assoc Dean Interior Design* Kevin Renz; *Chair, Fine Arts* Carol Pelletier
Estab 1939; Maintains non-profit art galleries: Heftler Visiting Artist Gallery, Spencer Presentation Gallery, Carol Grillo Gallery; pvt, co-ed; D & E; Scholarships; SC 120, LC 25; 310, non-maj 40, maj 270
Ent Req: HS dipl
Degrees: BS 4 yr, BFA, MA & MFA
Tuition: Res—$30,612 per yr, room & board $14,500
Courses: Advertising Design, Aesthetics, Art History, †Art Therapy, †Ceramics, †Commercial Art, Design, Drafting, Drawing, Film, Graphic Arts, Graphic Design, History of Art & Architecture, Illustration, †Interior Design, †Interior Design, Museum Staff Training, Painting, †Photography, Printmaking, Sculpture, Stage Design, †Studio Art, Theatre Arts, Theatre Arts

MONTSERRAT COLLEGE OF ART, 23 Essex St, Beverly, MA 01915; PO Box 26, Beverly, MA 01915-0026. Tel 978-921-4242; Fax 978-922-4268; Email admiss@montserrat.edu; Web: www.montserrat.edu; *Dean* Laura Tonelli; *Painting* Rob Roy; *Printmaking* Stacy Thomas-Vickory; *Photog* Ron DiRito; *Illustration* Mark Hoffmann; *Graphic Design* John Colan; *Gallery Dir* Leonie Bradbury; *Art Educ* Patricia Palmer; *Pres* Stephen D Immerman, EdD; *Sculpture Chair* Meredith Morten; *Foundation Dept* Judy Brown; *Liberal Arts Chair* Charles Boyer
Estab 1970; Maintain nonprofit art gallery on campus, Montserrat Gallery, Carol Schlosberg Gallery; Paul Scott Library; Pvt; D & E weekend workshops; Scholarships; SC 150, LC 50, Cont Educ; D 270, E 150, Other 300
Activities: Schols offered
Ent Req: Personal interview and portfolio review
Degrees: BFA 4 yr dipl granted
Tuition: $28,250 per yr, $14,125 per sem; $1,350 reg fee per yr, $650 reg fee per sem
Courses: Advertising Design, Animation, Art Education, Art History, †Book Arts, Conceptual Art, Design, Drawing, Fashion Arts, Graphic Arts, †Graphic Design, †Illustration, Lettering, Mixed Media, †Painting, †Photography, †Printmaking, †Sculpture, Video
Adult Hobby Classes: Courses—Drawing, Graphic Design, Painting, Photography, Printmaking
Summer School: Dir of Cont Educ, Marie LeCure. Enrl 60; Pre-College Prog in July & Aug. Courses—Life Drawing, Painting, Illustration, Printmaking

BOSTON

BOSTON CENTER FOR ADULT EDUCATION, 122 Arlington St, Boston, MA 02116-5307. Tel 617-267-4430; Fax 617-247-3606; Web: www.bcae.org; *Exec Dir* Mary McTique
Estab 1933; pvt; D & E; Scholarships; SC 26, LC 2; D 2300, E 20,000
Ent Req: Open to all over 17
Courses: Architecture, Art Appreciation, Art History, Calligraphy, Ceramics, Clay Sculpture, Crafts, Drawing, Interior Design, Painting, Photography, Sculpture, Studio Crafts, Theatre Arts, Video, Weaving
Summer School: Same as winter program

BOSTON UNIVERSITY, Graduate Program - Arts Administration, 808 Commonwealth Ave, 2699, Boston, MA 02215-1206. Tel 617-353-4064; Fax 617-358-1230; Email artsad@bu.edu; Web: www.bu.edu/artsadmin; *Program Director* Lanfranco Aceti; *Senior Lecturer* Douglas DeNatale
Estab 1992; pvt; E; Scholarships; Assistantships; GC 25
Ent Req: BA dipl
Degrees: MS (Arts Administration), 2 yr
Tuition: $830 per credit for part-time students (less than 12 cr); $24,588 per semester for full time students (12 cr or more); The program: 40 cr total; international students must be full-time
Courses: Art History, Museum Staff Training

BOSTON UNIVERSITY, School for the Arts, 855 Commonwealth Ave, Visual Arts Division Boston, MA 02215-1303. Tel 617-353-3371, 3350; Fax 617-353-7217; Email visuarts@bu.edu; Web: www.bu.edu; *Dir School of Visual Arts* Lynne Allen; *Prof* Hugh O'Donnell; *Chmn Graphic Design* Alston Purvis; *Chmn Art Educ* Barry Shauck; *Prof* John Walker
Estab 1869, sch estab 1954; Pvt; D; Scholarships; SC 38, LC 12, GC 15; 395, non-maj 75, maj 260, grad 60
Ent Req: HS dipl, portfolio
Degrees: BFA 4 yrs, MFA 2 yrs
Tuition: $35,000 per yr incl room & board
Courses: †Art Education, Design, Drawing, †Graphic Design, †Painting, Photography, Printmaking, †Sculpture, Studio Teaching (grad level), Teacher Training

EMMANUEL COLLEGE, Art Dept, 400 The Fenway, Boston, MA 02115. Tel 617-735-9807; Fax 617-735-9877; Web: www.emmanuel.edu/; *Chmn Art Dept* Theresa Monaco, MFA; *Prof* Ellen Glavin, ShD; *Prof* C David Thomas, MFA; *Assoc Prof* Kathleen A Soles, MFA
Estab 1919, dept estab 1950; pvt; D & E; Scholarships; SC 30, LC 11; D 300, E 50, non-maj 200, maj 80
Ent Req: HS dipl, SAT
Degrees: BA & BFA 4 yrs
Courses: †Art Education, †Art History, †Art Therapy, Ceramics, Drawing, Graphic Arts, †Graphic Design, Mixed Media, †Painting, †Printmaking, Sculpture, †Teacher Training
Adult Hobby Classes: Enrl 300; tuition $193 per cr. Courses—Art Educ, Art History, Art Theory, In Studio Art
Summer School: Dir, Dr Jacquelyn Armitage. Enrl 230; tuition $143 per cr hr for term of 6 wks in June-Aug

MASSACHUSETTS COLLEGE OF ART, 621 Huntington Ave, Boston, MA 02115-5801. Tel 617-879-7000; Fax 617-879-7250; Web: www.massart.edu; *Dean Grad & Continuing Educ* Richard Aronowitz; *Chmn Fine Arts 2D* Roger Tibbets; *Chmn Fine Arts 3D* Joe Wood; *Chmn Media* Barbara Bosworth; *Chmn Critical Studies* John Russell; *Pres* Katherine Sloan; *Chair Environmental Design* Paul Hajian; *Chair Commun Design* Elizabeth Resnick; *Chair Art Educ* John Crowe
Estab 1873; Maintain a nonprofit art gallery: Arnheim Gallery, Bakalar Gallery, Deren Gallery, 621 Huntington Ave, Boston, MA 02115; maintain an art/architecture library: Martan R Godine Library, 621 Huntington Ave, Boston, MA 02115; on-campus shop where art supplies may be purchased; Pub; D & E; SC 400, LC 250, GC 50; D 1,100, E 1,000, grad 100
Ent Req: HS transcript, college transcript, SAT, statement of purpose, portfolio
Degrees: BFA 4 yrs, MFA 2 yrs, MSAE 2 yrs
Courses: Architectural Design, Art Education, Art History, Ceramics, Fashion Design, Fibers, Film, Film Making, Freshman Artistic Seminars, Glass, Graphic Design, Illustration, Industrial Design, Intermedia, Metals, Painting, Photography, Printmaking, Sculpture, Video
Adult Hobby Classes: Courses—All areas
Children's Classes: Courses—All areas
Summer School: Assoc Dir Continuing Educ, Susan Gately. Courses—all areas

MOUNT IDA COLLEGE, Chamberlayne School of Design & Merchandising, 777 Dedham St, Boston, MA 02459-3310. *School Dir* Phyllis Misite; *Lectr* Rose Botti-Salitsky
Estab 1892, dept estab 1952; pvt; D & E; D 253, E 38, maj 253
Ent Req: HS dipl
Degrees: AA, BA
Courses: Drawing, Fashion Arts, Graphic Arts, Illustration, Interior Design, Jewelry, Merchandising, Painting, Sculpture, Textile Design
Summer School: Dir Susan Holton. Courses—same as regular acad yr

NORTHEASTERN UNIVERSITY, Dept of Art & Architecture, 360 Huntington Ave, Boston, MA 02115-5000. Tel 617-373-2347; Fax 617-373-8535; *Chmn* Elizabeth Cromley, PhD; *Prof* Mardges Bacon PhD; *Assoc Prof* T Neal Rantoul, MFA; *Assoc Prof* Mira Cantor, MFA; *Assoc Prof* George Thrush, MArchit; *Assoc Prof* Julie Curtis, MFA; *Assoc Prof* Edwin Andrews, MFA; *Assoc Prof* Tom Starr, MFA; *Asst Prof* Peter Wiederspahn, MArchit; *Asst Prof* Ann McDonald, MFA
Estab 1898, dept estab 1952; pvt; D & E; Scholarships; D 1200, E 1200, non-maj 1500, maj 380
Ent Req: HS dipl
Degrees: BA & BS 4 yrs
Tuition: Freshmen $4460 per acad qtr; upperclassmen $5775 per acad qtr; campus res available
Courses: Animation, Architectural Design, Architecture, Art History, Computer Aided Design, Design, Drafting, Drawing, Graphic Arts, Graphic Design, History of Art & Architecture, Illustration, Media Design, Mixed Media, Multimedia, Painting, Photography, Video
Adult Hobby Classes: Enrl 180; tuition $116 per 12 wk quarter cr. Courses—same as full-time program
Summer School: Chmn, Peter Serenyi. Enrl 240. Tuition & courses—same as above

SCHOOL OF FASHION DESIGN, 136 Newbury St, Boston, MA 02116-2904. Tel 617-536-9343; Email sfdboston@aol.com; Web: www.schooloffashiondesign.org
Estab 1934; pvt; D, E & Sat; Scholarships; D approx 60, E approx 40
Ent Req: HS dipl
Degrees: No degrees, 2 yr cert or 3 yr dipl
Courses: Costume Design & Construction, Drafting, Drawing, Fashion Arts, Illustration, Textile Design, Theatre Arts
Adult Hobby Classes: 100; tuition $1080 per 3 cr course. Courses—Fashion Design
Summer School: Dir, James Hannon. Enrl 100; tuition $1080 per 3 cr course of 10 wks. Courses—Fashion Design

SCHOOL OF THE MUSEUM OF FINE ARTS, 230 The Fenway, Boston, MA 02115. Tel 617-267-6100, 369-3581; Fax 617-424-6271; Email ddluhy@mfa.org;

Web: www.smfa.edu; *Dean* Deborah H Dluhy PhD; *Provost* Daniel Poteel II; *Dean Faculty* Lorne Falk
Estab 1876; Grossman Gallery; pvt; D & E; Scholarships; SC 190 LC 30 GC 12 CE 78 per sem; D 678 E 646, grad 100
Ent Req: HS dipl, HS and col transcripts, portfolio
Degrees: Dipl, BFA, BFA plus BA or BS, MFA, MAT, BFA-E, Post BA all degrees in affiliation with Tufts University)
Courses: Art Education, Art History, Ceramics, Drawing, Film, Graphic Arts, Graphic Design, Illustration, Jewelry, Mixed Media, Painting, Performance, Photography, Printmaking, Sculpture, Video
Adult Hobby Classes: E & Saturday classes; 1.5 cr or 3 cr per course. Courses—Artists' Books, Ceramics, Drawing, Electronic Arts, Film/Animation, Graphic Design, Jewelry, Mixed Media, Painting, Papermaking, Photography, Printmaking, Sculpture, Stained Glass, Video
Summer School: Dir Continuing Educ, Debra Samdperil

UNIVERSITY OF MASSACHUSETTS - BOSTON, Art Dept, 100 Morrissey Blvd, Harbor Campus Boston, MA 02125-3300. Tel 617-287-5730; Fax 617-287-5757; Web: www.umb.edu; *Prof* Wilfredo Chiesa; *Assoc Prof* Margaret Hart; *Assoc Prof* Victoria Weston, PhD, MFA; *Chair* Ann Torke, PhD; *Assoc Prof* Elizabeth Marran
Sch estab 1965, dept estab 1966; pub; D & E; SC 18, LC 32; D 900, E 100, maj 200
Ent Req: Entrance exam
Degrees: BA
Tuition: Res—$1055 per sem; nonres—$4421 per sem (plus fees)
Courses: Aesthetics, Art History, Drawing, Film, Graphic Arts, History of Art & Architecture, Intermedia, Painting, Photography, Printmaking, Sculpture, Video
Summer School: Enrl 150; tuition $140 per cr, 2 sessions. Courses—American Art in Boston, Ancient to Medieval Art, Drawing, Photography

BRIDGEWATER

BRIDGEWATER STATE COLLEGE, Art Dept, School and Summer Sts, Bridgewater, MA 02325. Tel 508-531-1200; Fax 508-279-6128; Web: www.bridgew.edu; *Prof* Roger Dunn PhD, PhD, MFA; *Prof* Mercedes Nunez, MFA; *Prof* Dorothy Pulsifer, MA; *Assoc Prof* Rob Lorenson, MFA; *Assoc Prof* Collin Asmus, MFA; *Asst Prof* Beatrice St Laurent, PhD; *Asst Prof* Preston Saunders, MFA; *Asst Prof* Ivana George, MFA; *Chmn* Brenda Molife, PhD; *Asst Prof* Shanshan Cui, MFA; *Asst Prof* Magaly Ponce, MFA; *Asst Prof* Mary Dondero, MFA; *Asst Prof* John Hooker, MFA; *Asst Prof* Leigh Craven, MFA; *Asst Prof* Donald Tarallo, MFA
Estab 1840; Maintain nonprofit art gallery; The Wallace Anderson Gallery, 40 School St, Bridgewater, MA 02325; Maintain Maxwell Library, Park Ave, Bridgewater, MA 02325; pub; D & E; SC 35, LC 10, GC 35; D 1000, E 400, non-maj 960, maj 280, grad 10
Ent Req: HS dipl, SAT
Degrees: BA 4 yrs
Courses: †Art Appreciation, Art Education, Art History, Ceramics, †Commercial Art, Drawing, Goldsmithing, Graphic Arts, Graphic Design, Handicrafts, †History of Art & Architecture, Jewelry, †Mixed Media, Painting, †Photography, Printmaking, Sculpture, Silversmithing, †Studio Art, †Teacher Training, †Textile Design, †Video, Watercolor, †Weaving
Adult Hobby Classes: Enrl 100. Courses—Same as day courses; rotational
Summer School: Dir, Brenda Molife, PhD. Enrl 40. Courses—Same as above

CAMBRIDGE

HARVARD UNIVERSITY, Dept of History of Art & Architecture, 485 Broadway, Cambridge, MA 02138-3845. Tel 617-495-2377; Fax 617-495-1769; Web: www.fas.harvard.edu; *Chmn Dept* Ioli Kalavrezou
Estab 1874; FT 24; pvt; Scholarships; LC 26 incl GC 12; undergrad 88, grad 100
Courses: Art History

LESLEY UNIVERSITY, (The Art Institute of Boston at Lesley University) College of Art & Design, 29 Everett St, Cambridge, MA 02138-2702. Tel 617-262-1223; Fax 617-437-1226; Email admissions@lesley.edu; Web: www.lesley.edu/aib; *Dean* Stan Trecker; *Sr Assoc Dean Acad Affairs* Matthew Cherry; *Chair Animation* John Casey; *Chair Art History* Stuart Steck; *Chair Design* Kristina Lamour Sansone; *Chair Fine Arts* Michael David; *Chair Foundation* Arlene Grossman; *Chair Illustration* Susan LeVan; *Chair Photog* Andre Ruesch
Estab 1912; Maintains nonprofit art gallery, art library, Lesley Univ Col of Art & Design - main gallery; Lesley Univ Col of Art & Design Library (both at same address); pvt; D & E; Scholarships; SC 80, LC 20; D 535, E 200
Ent Req: HS dipl, portfolio and interview
Degrees: BFA, MFA
Courses: Animation, Art Education, Art History, Ceramics, Commercial Art, Computer Graphics, Conceptual Art, Design, Drawing, †Film, †Fine Arts, †Graphic Design, †Handicrafts, †History of Art & Architecture, Illustration, †Mixed Media, Painting, †Photography, Printmaking, Sculpture, Typography, Video
Adult Hobby Classes: Courses—Continuing education offers most of the above typically 2-3 cr each
Summer School: Dir, Diana Arcadipone, Assoc Dean Courses—most of above

MASSACHUSETTS INSTITUTE OF TECHNOLOGY, School of Architecture and Planning, 77 Massachusetts Ave, Rm 7-231 Cambridge, MA 02139-4301. *Dean* William J Mitchell; *Head Dept* Stanford Anderson; *Urban Studies & Planning* Bish Sanyal; *Asst to the Dean* Peggy Cain
Estab 1865; FT 62; pvt; Scholarships; SC, LC, GC; 600
Degrees: MA, PhD(Building Technol); Media Arts & Sciences
Tuition: $26,960 per yr
Courses: History of Art & Architecture
—Center for Advanced Visual Studies, 265 Massachusetts Ave, Fl 3 Cambridge, MA 02139-4301; 77 Massachusetts Ave # N52-390, Cambridge, MA 02139-4301. Tel 617-253-4415; Fax 617-253-1660; Web: cavs.mit.edu; *Dir* Steve Benton
Estab dept 1967; pvt; D & E; SC 9, LC 1, GC 5; D & E 250, non-maj 240, grad 10
Ent Req: BA degree
Degrees: MS(Visual Studies)
Tuition: $26,690 per yr
Courses: Art & Technology, Environmental Art, †Video
Summer School: Art Workshop

CHESTNUT HILL

BOSTON COLLEGE, Fine Arts Dept, 140 Commonwealth Ave, Devlin Hall #434 Chestnut Hill, MA 02467-3800. Tel 617-552-4295; Fax 617-552-0134; Web: www.bostoncollege.com; *Chmn* John Michalczyk
FT 11, PT 20
Degrees: BA offered
Courses: Art History, Ceramics, Drawing, Film, Painting, Photography, Sculpture, Studio Art

PINE MANOR COLLEGE, Visual Arts Dept, 400 Heath St, Chestnut Hill, MA 02467-2332. Tel 617-731-7157; Fax 617-731-7199; Web: www.pmc.edu; *Div Chmn* Bob Owcvark; *Prog Coordr Photog Dept* Susan Butler
Estab 1911; pvt; D; SC 25, LC 25; D 80
Ent Req: HS dipl
Degrees: AA & AS 2 yrs, BA 4 yrs
Tuition: Res—undergrad $11,940 per acad yr; campus res—room & board $7450 per acad yr
Courses: Architecture, †Art History, Costume Design & Construction, Drafting, Drawing, Graphic Arts, Interior Design, Museum Staff Training, Painting, Printmaking, Sculpture, Stage Design, Theatre Arts, Visual Arts
Adult Hobby Classes: Studio courses 25, lecture courses 25
Summer School: Dir, Dr Eva I Kampits

CHICOPEE

OUR LADY OF ELMS COLLEGE, Dept of Fine Arts, 291 Springfield St, Chicopee, MA 01013-2839. Tel 413-594-2761; Fax 413-592-4871; *Chmn Dept* Nancy Costanzo
Estab 1928, dept estab 1950; pvt; D & E; Scholarships; SC 14, LC 6; D 210, non-maj 193, maj 17
Ent Req: HS dipl, Col Ent Exam (Verbal and Math)
Degrees: BA 4 yrs
Courses: Art Education, Art History, Calligraphy, Ceramics, Drawing, Painting, Photography, Printmaking, Sculpture

DOVER

CHARLES RIVER SCHOOL, Creative Arts Program, 56 Centre St, Dover, MA 02030-2207; PO Box 339, Dover, MA 02030-0339. Tel 508-785-0068, 785-8250; Fax 508-785-8291; Email crcap@charlesriverschool.edu; Web: www.crcap.org; *Dir* Toby Dewey
Estab 1910, program estab 1970; pvt summer school; D; Scholarships
Ent Req: Open to ages 8-15 years (as of July 1)
Courses: Art, Computer, Dance, Drama, Media, Music, Photography, Textile Design, Writing
Summer School: Dir, Toby Dewy Jr. Enrl 235; tuition $1675 per session. Courses—Computer

FRAMINGHAM

DANFORTH MUSEUM OF ART SCHOOL, 123 Union Ave, Framingham, MA 01702-8291. Tel 508-620-0050; Fax 508-872-5542; Web: www.danforthmuseum.org; *Dir* Patricia Walker
Estab 1975; Maintain nonprofit art museum, Danforth Museum of Art, 123 Union Ave, Framingham, MA 01702; pvt; D&E; Scholarships; SC
Ent Req: None
Tuition: Varies per course; museum members receive a tuition reduction
Courses: Art History, Ceramics, †Collage, Drawing, Graphic Arts, Jewelry, Painting, Photography, Printmaking, Sculpture, Weaving
Adult Hobby Classes: Enrl 200 - 400; tuition varies per 10 wk sessions. Courses—Arts, Crafts, Photography
Children's Classes: Enrl 200 - 400; tuition varies per 8 wk session. Courses—Art Multi-Media, Ceramics
Summer School: Enrl 200-300; tuition varies per 1 wk courses. Courses—Same as above

FRAMINGHAM STATE COLLEGE, Art Dept, 100 State St, Framingham, MA 01701; PO Box 9101, Framingham, MA 01701-9101. Tel 508-620-1220, 626-4831 (Cote); Fax 508-626-4022; Email mcote@fre.mass.edu; Web: www.framingham.edu; *Assoc Prof* Elizabeth Perry; *Prof* Barbara Milot; *Chmn* Marc Cote; *Asst Prof* Erika Schneider; *Asst Prof* Timothy McDonald; *Asst Prof* Keri Straka; *Asst Prof* Brian Bishop; *Prof* John Anderson
Estab 1839, dept estab 1920; Maintain nonprofit art gallery, Mazmarian Gallery 100 State St Framingham MA 01701; Catherine Carter; pub; D & E; Scholarships; SC 20, LC 10, GC 10; D 3,000, E 2500, maj 105, grad 20
Special Subjects: Illustration
Ent Req: HS dipl, portfolio review
Degrees: BA 4 yrs
Courses: Art Appreciation, †Art Education, †Art History, †Ceramics, Collage, Commercial Art, †Fashion Arts, †Graphic Design, Museum Studies, †Printmaking, †Sculpture, †Studio Art
Adult Hobby Classes: Art History, Studio Art

GREAT BARRINGTON

SIMON'S ROCK COLLEGE OF BARD, Visual Arts Dept, 84 Alford Rd, Great Barrington, MA 01230-2499. Tel 413-528-0771; Fax 413-528-7365; Email admit@simons-rock.edu; Web: www.simons-rock.edu; *Prof* William D Jackson; *Prof* Arthur Hillman, MFA; *Prof Ceramics* John Kingston, MFA
Estab 1966; PT 2; pvt; D & E; Scholarships; SC 14, LC 4
Ent Req: Personal interview
Degrees: AA 2-3 yrs, BA 4 yrs
Tuition: $21,740 per yr; campus res—room $3270, board $3430
Courses: 2-D Design, 3-D Design, Aesthetics, Art History, Artist & the Book, Ceramics, Drawing, Graphic Design, Illustration, Intermedia, Introduction to the Arts, Jewelry, Microcomputer Graphics, Painting, Photography, Printmaking, Sculpture

GREENFIELD

GREENFIELD COMMUNITY COLLEGE, Art Dept, One College Dr, Greenfield, MA 01301. Tel 413-775-1241; Web: art.gcc.mass.edu; *Dept Chair* Paul Lindale, MFA; *Prof* John Bross, MFA; *Prof* Penne Krol, MFA; *Prof* Budge Hyde, MFA; *Prof* Tom Young, MFA; *Instr* Jennifer Simms, MFA; *Instr* Joan Qibgirne, MFA; *Instr* Elliott Mitchell, MFA; *Instr* Mikael Petriaccia, MFA; *Art Historian* Breta Yuars Petruccia, MA
Estab 1962; maintains a small gallery & on campus store where art supplies may be purchased; pub; D & E; Scholarships; SC 16; in school D 1400, E 400, maj 110
Ent Req: HS dipl
Degrees: AA, AS 2 yrs
Courses: †Art History, Collage, Conceptual Art, †Drawing, Illustration, †Painting, †Photography, †Printmaking, Video
Summer School: Elizabeth Roop. Tuition $38 per cr for a 7 wk term. Courses—Color, Design, Drawing Workshop, Multi Media Design, Photography

HOLYOKE

HOLYOKE COMMUNITY COLLEGE, Dept of Art, 303 Homestead Ave, Holyoke, MA 01040-1099. Tel 413-538-7000; Fax 413-534-8975; Web: www.hcc.mass.edu; *Dean of Humanities & Fine Arts* John Field
Estab 1946; FT2; pub; D & E; Scholarships; SC 7, LC 4; D 115, E 20, maj 50
Ent Req: HS dipl, portfolio
Degrees: AA 2 yrs
Courses: Art Education, Drawing, Graphic Arts, Graphic Design, History of Art & Architecture, Painting, Photography
Summer School: Dir, William Murphy. Courses—Per regular session, on demand

LEXINGTON

MUNROE CENTER FOR THE ARTS, (Lexington Friends of the Arts, Inc.), 1403 Massachusetts Ave, Lexington, MA 02420-3804. Tel 781-862-6040; Fax 781-674-2787; Web: www.munroecenter.org; *Exec Dir* Christian Herold, MA; *Dir Educ* Hannah Hammond-Hagman
Estab 1994; Maintain nonprofit art gallery; PT 16; pub; D & E; Scholarships; SC 100, LC 20; D 700, E 300
Ent Req: Registration
Courses: Aesthetics, Art Education, Ceramics, †Costume Design & Construction, †Fashion Arts, Illustration, Mixed Media, Painting, Printmaking, Sculpture, Theatre Arts
Adult Hobby Classes: Enrl 300; tuition $150 per class. Courses—Ceramics, Faux Art, Painting, Printmaking, Quilt Making, Sculpture, Yoga
Children's Classes: Enrl 700; tuition $120 per class. Courses—Drama, Drawing, Ceramics, Mixed Media, Painting, Woodworking
Summer School: Enrl 360; tuition $250 per wk, Integrated Creative Arts Camp (ages 6-12)

LINCOLN

DECORDOVA MUSEUM SCHOOL, 51 Sandy Pond Rd, Lincoln, MA 01773-2600. Tel 781-259-0505; Fax 781-259-0507; Email info@decordova.org; Web: www.decordova.org/school/
Open Office: Mon - Fri 9 AM - 4 PM; Studio: Mon - Thurs 9:15 Am - 9:45 PM, Fri - Sun 9:15 AM - 4:45 PM; Gallery: Mon - Thurs 9:30 AM - 9 PM, Fri 9:30 AM - 4 PM, Sat & Sun 10 AM - 4 PM; No admis fee to gallery; tuition for classes varies; Facility has 7 studios dedicated to Calligraphy, Ceramics, Drawing, Jewelry, Painting, Printmaking, Sculpture & Watercolor; also maintains School Gallery
Activities: 100 adult classes/workshops per term; 20 - 30 children's classes/workshops per term; children's progs in July; Professional Development Points available to teachers for all classes; schols available
Courses: Book Arts, Calligraphy, Ceramics, Collage, Color Design, Jewelry, Painting, Photography, Printmaking, Sculpture, Silversmithing, Watercolor

LONGMEADOW

BAY PATH COLLEGE, Dept of Art, 588 Longmeadow St, Longmeadow, MA 01106-2292. Tel 413-567-0621; Fax 413-567-9324; Web: www.baypath.edu; *Dir* Dr John Jarvis
Estab 1947; pvt, W; D & E; SC 18, LC 2; D 660, E 400, maj 10
Ent Req: HS dipl
Degrees: AFA 2 yr
Courses: Ceramics, Drawing, Graphic Arts, Handicrafts, History of Art & Architecture, Painting
Adult Hobby Classes: Enrl 300; tuition $80 per 8 wk course. Courses - Drawing, Painting, Watercolor

LOWELL

UNIVERSITY OF MASSACHUSETTS LOWELL, Dept of Art, 71 Wilder St Ste 8, Lowell, MA 01854-3096. Tel 978-934-3494; Fax 978-934-4050; Web: www.uml.edu; *Chmn Dept* James Coates; *Prof* Brenda Pinardi, MFA; *Prof* Arno Minkkinen, MFA; *Assoc Prof* James Veatch, EdM; *Prof* Fred Faudie; *Assoc Prof* John C Freeman
Estab 1975 (merger of Lowell State College and Lowell Technological Institute); Maintain nonprofit art gallery; Duggan Gallery & University Gallery; Pub; D & E; D 1,200, E 25, non-maj 450, maj 150
Ent Req: HS dipl, SAT
Degrees: BFA 4 yrs
Courses: Graphic Design, Photography, †Studio Art, Visual Communication Design
Adult Hobby Classes: Enrl 15 - 20 per course; tuition $135. Courses—Art Appreciation, Drawing, Painting, Survey of Art
Summer School: Enrl 10-15; tuition $135 per cr for 3 weeks. Courses—Art Appreciation, Drawing, Photography, Survey of Art I & II, Seminars in Italy, Greece, Finland, France

MEDFORD

TUFTS UNIVERSITY, Dept of Art & Art History, 11 Talbot Ave, Medford, MA 02155-5812. Tel 617-627-3567; Email amy.west@tufts.edu; Web: ase.tufts.edu/art; *Prof & Dept Chair* Christina Maranci; *Prof & Dir, Film & Media Studies* Malcom Turvey; *Assoc Prof* Cristelle Baskins, PhD; *Asst Prof* Eva Hoffman, PhD; *Assoc Prof* Ikumi Kaminishi, PhD; *Asst Prof* Diana Martinez; *Assoc Prof* Eric Rosenberg, PhD; *Prof* Peter Probst, PhD; *Asst Prof* Jeremy Melius; *Assoc Prof & Dir Grad Studies* Karen Overbey, PhD; *Assoc Prof* Adriana Zavala; *Prof* Andrew McClellan; *Asst Prof* Jacob Stewart-Halevy
Maintain nonprofit art gallery, Tufts University Art Gallery, 40R Talbot Ave, Medford, MA 02155; maintain art/architecture lib, Tisch Library, Tuft University; FT/PT 18; Pvt; D; Scholarships; maj 100; GS 24
Ent Req: HS dipl
Degrees: BA, BS, BFA, MA, MFA; cert in museum studies
Tuition: $55,172 per yr
Courses: †Architecture, †Art History, Calligraphy, Ceramics, Design, Drawing, Film, Graphic Arts, Graphic Design, History of Architecture, Illustration, Interdisciplinary Studio Art, Jewelry, Lettering, Metal Working, Mixed Media, Museum Staff Training, Museum Studies, Studio
Adult Hobby Classes: Courses offered
Summer School: Courses—Boston Architecture, Modern Art, Survey, Museum History

NORTH DARTMOUTH

UNIVERSITY OF MASSACHUSETTS DARTMOUTH, College of Visual & Performing Arts, 285 Old Westport Rd, North Dartmouth, MA 02747-2300. Tel 508-999-8564; Fax 508-999-9126; Web: www.umassd.edu; *Dean* John Laughton PhD; *Chmn Music Dept* Eleanor Carlson, DMA; *Chmn Art Educ* Arlene Mollo; *Chmn Fine Art* Anthony J Miraglia, MFA; *Chmn Design* Spencer Ladd; *Chmn Art History* Michael Taylor; *Coordr Gallery* Lasse Antonsen, MA
Estab 1895, col estab 1948; Maintain nonprofit art gallery; art supplies available on-campus; FT 46, PT 25; pub; D & E; Scholarships; SC 75, LC 41, GC 7; D 700
Ent Req: HS dipl, SAT, open admis to qualified freshmen
Degrees: BFA and BA 4 yr, MFA and MAE 2-5 yrs
Courses: Art Education, Art History, Ceramics, Design, Electronic Imaging, Illustration, Jewelry, Painting, Photography, Printmaking, Sculpture, Textile Design
Adult Hobby Classes: Enrl 175; tuition $365 for 14 wk session. Courses—13 including Art History, Ceramics, Jewelry
Children's Classes: Enrl 35; tuition $95 for 9 wk session. Courses—Children's Theater
Summer School: Dir, Dean R Waxler. Enrl 240; tuition $365 for 5 wk session. Courses—15 including Art History, Crafts

NORTHAMPTON

SMITH COLLEGE, Art Dept, 22 Elm St, Hillyer Hall Northampton, MA 01063-6304. Tel 413-584-2700, 585-3100; Fax 413-585-3119; Web: www.smith.edu/art; *Prof* John Davis, PhD; *Prof* Brigitte Buettner, PhD; *Prof* Barbara Kellum, PhD; *Prof* Dana Leibsohn, PhD; *Prof* John Moore, PhD; *Prof* Craig Felton Dr, PhD; *Assoc Prof* Frazer Ward, PhD; *Assoc Prof* Laura Kalba, PhD
Estab 1875, dept estab 1877; Maintains Oresman gallery & art library (same address); Hillyer Art Library: BFAC, 22 Elm St. Northhampton, MA 01163; on-campus shop for purchase of art supplies; FT 17; pvt, W; D & E; Scholarships; SC 24, LC 34; maj 170
Ent Req: HS dipl, col board exam
Degrees: BA 4 yrs
Courses: Architecture, Art History, Color, Design with Computer, Drafting, Drawing, Graphic Arts, Graphic Design, History of Art & Architecture, Landscape Architecture, Painting, Photography, Printmaking, Sculpture

NORTON

WHEATON COLLEGE, Art Dept, 26 E Main St, Norton, MA 02766-2322. Tel 508-285-7722; Fax 508-286-3565; *Chmn Dept* Andrew Howard
Estab 1834; Maintain nonprofit arts gallery; Watson Fine Arts Center; FT 6, PT 3; pvt; Scholarships; SC 6, LC 18; 1,500
Degrees: BA (art history) 4 yr, BFA (Studio Art)
Courses: 2-D & 3-D Design, †Art History, Drawing, Painting, Photography, Printmaking, Sculpture

PAXTON

ANNA MARIA COLLEGE, Dept of Art, 50 Sunset Ln, Paxton, MA 01612-1106; PO Box 114, Paxton, MA 01612-0114. Tel 508-849-3441; Web: www.annamaria.edu; *Chmn Dept* Alice Lambert
Estab 1948; FT 2, PT 4; pvt; D & E; Scholarships; SC 15, LC 12; D 397, maj 32
Ent Req: HS dipl, ent exam
Degrees: 4 yr
Courses: †Advertising Design, Aesthetics, †Art Education, Art History, †Art Therapy, Ceramics, Drawing, Enameling, Lettering, Macrame, Modeling, Painting, Photography, Rug Design, Sculpture, Silk Screen, Stitchery, †Studio Art, †Teacher Training, Weaving
Summer School: Dir, Ann McMorrow. Two sessions beginning May.

PITTSFIELD

BERKSHIRE COMMUNITY COLLEGE, Dept of Fine Arts, 1350 West St, Pittsfield, MA 01201-5786. Tel 413-499-4660; Fax 413-447-7840; *Instr* Benigna Chilla, MFA
Estab 1960, dept estab 1961; pub; D & E; Scholarships; SC 16, LC 4; D 72, E 75, non-maj 12, maj 72
Ent Req: HS dipl
Degrees: AA 2 yrs
Courses: 2-D Design, 20th Century Art, 3-D Design, Applied Graphics, Art History, Drawing, Mixed Media, Painting, Photography, Primitive Art, Printmaking
Adult Hobby Classes: Continuing education evening classes, some may be applied to degree program
Summer School: 7 wks beginning June. Courses—Design, Drawing, Painting, Photography

QUINCY

QUINCY COLLEGE, Art Dept, 1250 Hancock St, Ste 101N Quincy, MA 02169-4331. Tel 617-984-1600; Fax 617-984-1779; Web: quincycollege.edu; *Chmn Humanities* Dr Kenneth Bindseil; *Pres* Sue Harris; *Adj Prof* Marylou Clark; *Adj Instruc* Brian Adgate; *Adj Instruc* Tracy Spadafora; *Adjunct Instr* David Tander; *Adj Instr* Robert Littlefield; *Asst Prof* Steve Dooner
In transition from city control to private control; D & E; SC, LC; 3800 (entire college)
Ent Req: Open
Degrees: AA, AS and Cert offered
Tuition: Res & non-res $1700 per sem
Courses: †Art History, †Collage, †Design, Development to American Film, Drawing, Painting, Photography, †Theatre Arts
Summer School: Same format as regular cr courses; Dean Bindseil, Dean of Liberal Arts & Sciences

SALEM

SALEM STATE UNIVERSITY, Art & Design Department, 352 LaFayette St, Salem, MA 01970. Tel 978-542-6222; Fax 978-542-6597; Email mmelilli@salemstate.edu; Web: www.salemstate.edu; *Professor* Benjamin Gross, MFA; *Prof* Richard Lewis, MFA; *Prof* John Volpacchio, MFA; *Prof* Mark Malloy, MFA; *Prof Chairperson* Mary Mellili, MFA; *Asst Prof* Rebecca Plummer Rohloff, PhD; *Prof* Haig Demarjian, MFA; *Prof* Ken Reker, MFA; *Assoc Prof* Brian Alves; *Asst Prof* Gretchen Sinnett
Estab 1854; Maintain nonprofit art gallery, Winfisky Gallery; Pub; D & E; Scholarships; SC 19, LC 8, GC 5; maj 210
Ent Req: HS dipl
Degrees: BA 4 yrs, MAT in Art
Tuition: Res—$910 per yr; nonres—$7,050 per yr; campus res available
Courses: 3-D Studio, †Art Education, †Art History, Ceramics, †Graphic Design, Illustration, †Metals, Mixed Media, Multimedia Design, †Painting, †Photography, †Printmaking, Sculpture
Summer School: Pres, Dr Patricia M. Meservey

SOUTH HADLEY

MOUNT HOLYOKE COLLEGE, Art Dept, 50 College St, South Hadley, MA 01075; Lower Lake Rd, South Hadley, MA 01075-1499. Tel 413-538-2200; Fax 413-538-2167; Web: www.mtholyoke.educ/acad.art/; *Studio Chmn* Rie Hachiyanagi; *Art History* Paul Staiti; *Architecture* Michael T. Davis
Estab 1837; Maintain nonprofit art gallery; Blanchaid Campus Center, and The Mount Holyoke College Art Museum; Pvt, W; D & E; Scholarships; SC 13, LC 32; D 409, maj 52
Ent Req: SAT, college boards
Degrees: BA
Courses: †Architecture, †Art History, Drawing, †Film, †History of Art & Architecture, Painting, Photography, Printmaking, Sculpture
Adult Hobby Classes: Continuing education program leading to BA

SPRINGFIELD

SPRINGFIELD COLLEGE, Dept of Visual & Performing Arts, 263 Alden St, Springfield, MA 01109-3788. Tel 413-748-3540; Fax 413-748-3580; *Chmn* Ronald Maggio; *Asst Prof* Martin Shell, MFA; *Asst Prof* Chris Haynes, MFA; *Asst Prof* Simone Alter-Muri, Ed; *Asst Prof* Cynthia Noble, MA; *Asst Prof* Leslie Abrams, MA; *Instr* Charles Abel, MFA; *Instr* Holly Murray, MFA; *Instr* Ruth West, MFA; *Instr* John Moriarty, MFA; *Instr* Catherine Lydon, MFA; *Instr* Scott Redman; *Instr* Jorge Costa; *Instr* Monika Burzcyk
Estab 1885, dept estab 1971; Maintain nonprofit art gallery; Wieliam Blizard Gallery; Pvt; D & E; Scholarships; SC 30, LC 6; D 400, E 10, non-maj 300, maj 50
Ent Req: HS dipl, SAT, portfolio
Degrees: BA, BS 4 yr, MS(Art Therapy) 2 yr
Courses: Advertising Design, Aesthetics, Art Appreciation, Art Education, Art History, †Art Therapy, Arts Management, Ceramics, Collage, †Computer Graphics, Computer Graphics Animation, Conceptual Art, Constructions, Costume Design & Construction, Design, Drawing, Graphic Arts, Graphic Design, History of Art & Architecture, Illustration, Intermedia, Mixed Media, Museum Staff Training, Painting, Photography, Printmaking, Restoration & Conservation, Sculpture, Stage Design, Teacher Training, Theatre Arts, Video

TRURO

TRURO CENTER FOR THE ARTS AT CASTLE HILL, INC, 10 Meetinghouse Rd, Truro, MA 02666; PO Box 756, Truro, MA 02666-0756. Tel 508-349-7511; Fax 508-349-7513; Email info@castlehill.org; Web: www.castlehill.org; *Pres* Kim Kettler; *Exec Dir* Cherie Mittenthal
Estab 1972; Maintain nonprofit art gallery, Kohl Gallery; over 45 other nationally known instructors; pvt summer school; D & E; Scholarships; SC 50, LC 3; studio courses; lect courses; poetry readings; 730
Ent Req: None
Courses: Book Arts, Ceramics, Drawing, †Illustration, Jewelry, Literature, Painting, Photography, Printmaking, Sculpture, Wood, Writing
Children's Classes: Classes in painting, printmaking, sculpture, jewelry
Summer School: Exec Dir, Cherie Mittenthal. Enrl 700-730; tuition $180-$220 per workshop. Courses—Book, Clay, Drawing, Illustration, Jewelry, Painting, Paper Arts, Photography, Printmaking, Sculpture, Woodwork, Writing

WALTHAM

BRANDEIS UNIVERSITY, Dept of Fine Arts, 415 South St Waltham, MA 02454-9110. Tel 781-736-2655; Web: www.brandeis.edu; *Chmn* Graham Campbell
Estab 1948; FT 12; pvt; D; Scholarships; SC 10, LC 28; 2800
Ent Req: HS dipl, college board ent exam
Degrees: BS 4 yr
Courses: Art History, Design, Drawing, Painting, Sculpture
Summer School: Dir, Sanford Lotlor. Enrl 10-12 per course; tuition $585 per course for 4 week term. Courses—Introduction to History of Art II, Survey of Western Architecture

WELLESLEY

WELLESLEY COLLEGE, Art Dept, 106 Central St, Wellesley, MA 02481-8203. Tel 781-283-2042; Fax 781-283-3647; *Chmn* Patricia Berman; *Prof* Peter J Fergusson, PhD; *Prof* James W Rayen, MFA; *Prof* Richard W Wallace, PhD; *Prof* Miranda Marvin, PhD, MFA; *Prof* Margaret Carroll, PhD; *Prof* Carlos Dorrien, MFA; *Prof* Lilian Armstrong, PhD, MA; *Prof* Bunny Harvey, MFA; *Prof* Alice T Friedman, PhD; *Assoc Prof* Anne Higonnet, PhD; *Assoc Prof* Elaine Spatz-Rabinowitz, MFA; *Assoc Prof* Judy Block, MFA; *Assoc Prof* Phyllis McGibbon, MFA; *Asst Prof* Heping Liu, PhD, MA
Estab 1875, dept estab 1886; pvt; D; SC 19, LC 46; D 1233
Ent Req: HS dipl
Degrees: BA
Courses: †Architecture, †Art History, Drawing, Graphic Arts, Painting, Photography, Printmaking, Sculpture, †Studio Art

WEST BARNSTABLE

CAPE COD COMMUNITY COLLEGE, Art Dept, Humanities Division, Route 132 West Barnstable, MA; 2240 Iyanough Rd, West Barnstable, MA 02668-1532. Tel 508-362-2131; Fax 508-362-8638; Web: www.capecod.mass.edu; *Prof* Sara Ringler, MFA; *Prof* Marie Canaves, MFA; *Coordr Art* Robert McDonald, MFA
Estab 1963, dept estab 1973; pub; D & E; SC 14, LC 7; in school D 2000, E 3000, maj 100
Ent Req: HS dipl
Degrees: AA and AS 2 yrs
Courses: Art History, †Digital Imaging, Drawing, †Film, Graphic Design, Illustration, Life Drawing, Mixed Media, Painting, †Papermaking/Book Arts, †Printmaking, †Quark Express, †Sculpture, Stage Design, Theatre Arts, Video, Visual Fundamentals, †Watercolor Advanced Projects
Adult Hobby Classes: Courses—Art History, Drawing, Graphic Design, Watercolor
Summer School: Assoc Dean, Humanities, Bruce Bell. Courses—Art History, Drawing, Graphic Design, Visual Fundamentals

WESTFIELD

WESTFIELD STATE COLLEGE, Art Dept, 577 Western Ave, Westfield, MA 01086-2501. Tel 413-572-5630; Fax 413-562-3613; *Chmn* Barbara Keim
Estab 1972; Maintain nonprofit art gallery; Arno Maris Art Gallery; Pub; D & E; Scholarships
Ent Req: HS dipl & portfolio review
Degrees: BA (Fine Arts) 4 yrs
Courses: Anatomy, Art Appreciation, Art Education, Art History, Commercial Art, Computer Graphics, Design, Drawing, Illustration, Lettering, Mixed Media, Practicum, Printmaking, Sculpture, Teacher Training
Adult Hobby Classes: Enrl 100. Courses—Design Fundamentals, Studio Courses
Summer School: Dept Chmn, P Conant. Courses—Design Fundamentals, Studio Courses

WESTON

REGIS COLLEGE, Dept of Art, 235 Wellesley St, Weston, MA 02193-1545. Tel 781-768-7000; Fax 781-768-8339; Web: www.regiscollege.edu; *Chmn* Sr Marie de Sales Dinneen
Estab 1927, dept estab 1944; den; D & E; Scholarships; SC 12, LC 12; D 250, non-maj 200, maj 50
Ent Req: HS dipl, SAT, various tests
Degrees: BA 4 yr
Courses: †Art History, Art Therapy, Ceramics, Computer Design, Coordinating Seminars, Drawing, Enameling, Etching, Graphic Techniques, Illustration, †Introduction to Art, Painting, Silk Screen, Stained Glass, Weaving, Woodcut

WILLIAMSTOWN

WILLIAMS COLLEGE, Dept of Art History & Studio Art, WL Spencer Art Bldg, 35 Driscoll Hall Dr Williamstown, MA 01267. Tel 413-597-3578; Fax 413-597-3693; Email arts@williams.edu; Web: art.williams.edu; *Chair & Prof* Elizabeth McGowan; *Dept Adminr Asst* Beverly Sylvester
Estab 1793, dept estab 1903; Maintains nonprofit Williams Museum of Art; FT/PT 26; pvt; D; Scholarships
Ent Req: HS dipl
Degrees: BA 4 yrs, MA(History of Art) 2 yrs
Tuition: $55,140 per yr
Courses: Architecture, Art History, Drawing, Painting, Photography, Printmaking, Sculpture, Video

WORCESTER

ASSUMPTION COLLEGE, Dept of Art, Music & Theatre, 500 Salisbury St, Worcester, MA 01609-1265; PO Box 15005, Worcester, MA 01615-0005. Tel 508-767-7000; Web: www.assumption.edu; *Prof* Rev Donat Lamothe, PhD; *Assoc Prof* Barbara Beall-Fofana, PhD; *Asst Prof* Scott Glushien, MFA; *Vis Asst Prof* Edith Read, MFA; *Vis Asst Prof* Thomas Grady, MFA; *Vis Asst Prof* Jeremy Long, MFA
Estab 1904, dept estab 1976; Maintain a nonprofit art gallery & library at Emmanuel d'Alzen Library; den; D; Scholarships; D 600, E 25
Ent Req: HS dipl
Degrees: BA 4 yr
Tuition: $17,950 per yr; campus res available
Courses: †Advertising Design, Aesthetics, Architecture, Art Education, Art History, †Commercial Art, †Design, Drawing, Graphic Arts, †Graphic Design, History of Art & Architecture, Painting, †Photography, Printmaking, †Sculpture, †Stage Design, Theatre Arts

CLARK UNIVERSITY, Dept of Visual & Performing Arts, 950 Main St, Worcester, MA 01610-1477. Tel 508-793-7113; Fax 508-793-8844; Web: www.clarku.edu; *Dir Studio Art Prog* Elli Crocker, MFA; *Dean Admissions* Harold Wingood; *Chmn* Rhys Townsend; *Prof* Sarah Bule; *Assoc Prof* Sarah Walker; *Instr* Stephen Dirado
Estab 1887; University gallery on campus; FT 4, PT 10; pvt; D & E; Scholarships; SC 50, LC 24; Maj 100, non-maj 450, other 20
Ent Req: HS dipl, CEEB, achievement tests, SAT & ACH
Degrees: BA
Courses: Aesthetics, Costume Design & Construction, Drawing, †Graphic Design, History of Art & Architecture, †Painting, †Photography, Printmaking, Screen Studies, Sculpture, Stage Design, Theatre Arts, Video, Video Production, Visual Design, Visual Studies
Adult Hobby Classes: Offered through Clark University College of Professional and Continuing Education
Summer School: Offered through Clark University College of Professional and Continuing Education

COLLEGE OF THE HOLY CROSS, Dept of Visual Arts, One College St, Worcester, MA 01610; 1 College St, Worcester, MA 01610-2322. Tel 508-793-2011; Web: www.holycross.edu; *Prof* Virginia C Raguin, PhD; *Assoc Prof* Susan S Schmidt, MFA; *Assoc Prof* Robert Parke-Harrison, MFA; *Assoc Prof* Father John Reboli, SJ, PhD; *Assoc Prof* Michael Beatly, MFA; *Prof* Joanna Ziegler, PhD; *Asst Prof* Alison Fleming, PhD; *Asst Prof* Cristi Rinklin, MFA; *Instr* Naomi Ribner, MFA
Estab 1843, dept estab 1954; pvt; D; SC 12, LC 15; D 485, maj 25
Ent Req: HS dipl, SAT, ATS
Degrees: BA 4 yr
Courses: Aesthetics, Architecture, †Art History, †Digital Art, Drawing, Graphic Arts, Graphic Design, History of Art & Architecture, Painting, Photography, Printmaking, Sculpture, †Studio

WORCESTER CENTER FOR CRAFTS, 25 Sagamore Rd, Worcester, MA 01605-3914. Tel 508-753-8183; Fax 508-797-5626; Email wcc@worcestercraftcenter.org; Web: www.worcestercraftcenter.org; *Exec Dir* Honee A Hess; *Gallery Store* Candace Casey; *Registrar* Elaine Cowan; *Ceramics & Photog Dept Head* Tom O'Malley; *Glass & Metals Dept Head* Gale Scott
Estab 1856; Maintain nonprofit art gallery, Krikorian Gallery (same address); James & Carol Donnelly Craft &Art Library (same address); Kristen Kieffer, Pam Faren, Laurie Mader; Pvt, Pub; D & E, weekend; Scholarships; SC 60; D & E 280, continuing ed 1,000
Activities: Schols offered
Ent Req: No req for adult educ
Tuition: Tuition: $50-480
Courses: Art History, Ceramics, Design, Enameling, Glass Blowing, Handicrafts, Jewelry, Lampworking, Photography, Sculpture, Silversmithing, Stained Glass, Surface Design
Adult Hobby Classes: Enrl 1,500; tuition $300 Sept-July. Courses—Ceramics, Enamel, Photography, Stained Glass, Metal Working, Glass Blowing
Children's Classes: Enrl 500; tuition $200 per 6 wks. Courses—Ceramics, glass
Summer School: Enrl 100 adults Courses—Ceramics, Glass, Metal, Photography

WORCESTER STATE COLLEGE, Visual & Performing Arts Dept, 486 Chandler St, Worcester, MA 01602-2861. Tel 508-929-8824, 929-8000; Email cnigro@worcester.edu; Web: www.worcester.edu; *Chmn* Dr Christie Nigro; *Prof* Dr Ellen Kosmere; *Assoc Prof* Michael C Hachey; *Prof* Michel D Merle; *Asst Prof* Bryce Vinokurov
Estab 1874; pub; D & E; SC 18, LC 9; D & E 725
Ent Req: HS dipl, col board exams, completion of systems application form
Degrees: BA and BS 4 yrs
Courses: Art Education, Art History, Collage, Drafting, Drawing, Environmental Design, Graphic Design, Handicrafts, History of Urban Form, Intermedia, Mixed Media, Painting, Printmaking, Sculpture
Summer School: Usually 5-8 courses & workshops

MICHIGAN

ADRIAN

ADRIAN COLLEGE, Art & Design Dept, 110 S Madison St, Adrian, MI 49221-2575. Tel 517-265-5161; Fax 517-264-3153; Email croyer@adrian.edu; Web: www.adrian.edu; *Prof* Pauleve Benio, MFA; *Chmn, Assoc Prof* Catherine M Royer, MFA; *Asst Prof* Garin Horner, MFA; *Asst Prof* Juliana Clendenin, MFA; *Coordr Art Educ* Sue Thompson, MAE; *Instr* Elijah Van Benscheten, MFA; *Instr* Gregory Jones, MFA; *Instr* Brian Pitman, MFA; *Instr* Deborah Campbell, MFA; *Instr* Debra Irvine-Stiver, MAE; *Instr* Robert Stranges, MAE
Estab 1859, dept estab 1962; Maintain nonprofit art gallery; Suptnitz Gallery, Adrian Col, 110 S Madison, Adrian MI 49221; art supplies available on-campus; pvt, den; D & E; Scholarships; SC 32, LC 18; in dept D 300, E 50, non-maj 220, maj 120
Ent Req: HS dipl, ACT, SAT
Degrees: BA, BS in Interior Design & BFA with teaching cert
Courses: Art Education, Art History, Arts Management, Ceramics, Design, Drafting, Drawing, Graphic Design, History of Art & Architecture, Interior Design, Mixed Media, Painting, Photography, Pre-Art Therapy, Printmaking, Sculpture, Textile Design
Children's Classes: youth art prog, 80 per term, $75
Summer School: Dir, Catherine Royer. Enrl 15; May term, summer term June-July. Courses—Advanced Study, Art Education, Design, Drawing

SIENA HEIGHTS UNIVERSITY, Studio Angelico-Art Dept, 1247 Siena Heights Dr, Adrian, MI 49221. Tel 517-264-7860; Fax 517-264-7739; Web: www.sienaheights.edu; *Prof* Joseph Bergman, MFA; *Prof* John Wittershiem, MFA; *Prof & Chmn* Christine Reising, MFA; *Prof* Deborah Danielson, MFA; *Instr* Jamie Goode, MFA; *Instr* Lois DeMots, MA; *Asst Prof* Paul McMullen; *Assoc Prof Art History* Peter Barr, PhD; *Instr* Niki Havekost, MFA; *Instr* Jean Buescher, MFA; *Instr* Todd Marsee, MFA; *Instr* Robert Stranges, MArtEd; *Instr* Jean Lash, MArtEd
Estab 1919; Maintains nonprofit art gallery, Klemm Gallery, Studio Angelico; Pvt; D & E; Scholarships; SC 56; D 200, maj 96
Ent Req: HS dipl
Degrees: BA & BFA 4 yrs
Tuition: Undergrad $6,350 per sem
Courses: Aesthetics, Architecture, Art Appreciation, Art Education, Art History, †Ceramics, †Drawing, †Graphic Design, †Metalsmithing, †Painting, †Photography, †Printmaking, †Sculpture
Summer School: Courses—Bookmaking, Ceramics, Mixed Media, Portrait Painting, Watercolor

ALLENDALE

GRAND VALLEY STATE UNIVERSITY, Art & Design Dept, 1 Campus Dr, Allendale, MI 49401-9401. Tel 616-331-3486; Fax 616-331-3240; Email jenkinsv@gvsu.edu; Web: www.gvsu.edu; *Chmn* Virginia Jenkins MFA; *Prof* Ed Wong-Ligda; *Prof* Beverly Seley; *Prof* Dellas Henke; *Prof* Lorelle Thomas; *Assoc Prof* Richard Weis; *Assoc Prof* Ann Keister; *Assoc Prof* Paul Wittenbraker; *Assoc Prof* Bill Hosterman; *Assoc Prof* Jill Eggers; *Asst Prof* Anna Campbell; *Asst Prof* Hsiao-ping Chen; *Asst Prof* Brett Colley; *Asst Prof* Sigrid Danielson; *Assoc Prof* Tim Fisher; *Asst Prof* Hoon Lee; *Assoc Prof* Kristen Strom; *Asst Prof* Norwood Viviano; *Asst Prof* Katalin Zaszlavik; *Assoc Prof* Renee Zettle-Sterling
Estab 1960; Mem: Maintains non-profit art gallery; on campus shop where supplies can be purchased; pub; D & E; Scholarships; SC 52, LC 12, GC 1; D 380, E 40, maj 1,400, non-maj 420
Ent Req: ACT, Entrance portfolio
Degrees: BA(Studio), BS(Studio), BFA 4 yrs, BA(Art Educ), BA (Art Hist), BA (Art Educ), BS (Art Educ)
Courses: Art Appreciation, †Art Education, Art History, †Ceramics, Drawing, †Goldsmithing, †Graphic Design, †Illustration, †Jewelry, †Painting, †Printmaking, †Sculpture, †Silversmithing, Visual Studies
Summer School: Courses—Introduction to Art, Art for the Classroom Teacher, Workshops, 2-D Design, Color & Design, Intro to Drawing

ALMA

ALMA COLLEGE, Clack Art Center, Dept of Art & Design, 614 W Superior, Alma, MI 48801. Tel 517-463-7220, 463-7111; Fax 517-463-7085; Web: www.alma.edu; *Prof* C Sandy Lopez-Isnardi; *Assoc Prof* Robert Rozier; *Prof* Carrie Anne Parks-Kirby; *Asst Prof* Dr Dan Connolly
Estab 1886; Maintain non-profit art gallery, Flora Kirsch Beck Gallery, same address; coll library; on-campus shop where limited art supplies may be purchased; pvt; D & E; Scholarships; SC 10-20, LC 4-8; D 250, maj 40
Activities: Schols offered

Degrees: BA, BFA
Courses: Advertising Design, Aesthetics, Art Education, Art History, Ceramics, Computer Graphics, †Design, Drawing, Foreign Study, †Graphic Arts, Graphic Design, History of Art & Architecture, Illustration, Jewelry, Mixed Media, Museum Staff Training, Painting, Photography, Printmaking, Scientific Illustration, Sculpture, Weaving

ANN ARBOR

UNIVERSITY OF MICHIGAN, ANN ARBOR, Penny W Stamps School of Art & Design, 2000 Bonisteel Blvd, Ann Arbor, MI 48109-2069. Tel 734-764-0397; Fax 734-615-9753; Web: stamps.umich.edu; *Dean* Gunalan Nadarajan; *Assoc Dean* Jane Prophet; *Assoc Dean* Elona Van Gent; *Asst Dean* Joann McDaniel; *Assoc Prof & Dir MFA Program* Osman Khan; *Assoc Prof & Dir MDes Integrative Design* John Marshall; *Assoc Prof & Undergrad Prog Co-Dir* Stephanie Tharp; *Assoc Prof & Undergrad Prog Co-Dir* Anne Mondro
Estab 1817, sch estab 1974; Maintains nonprofit art galleries: Jean Paul Slusser Gallery & Warren M Robbins Gallery, both on-campus; Work Exhibition Space. Art library, University of Michigan Art, Architecture and Engineering Library.; FT 39, PT 38; pub; D & E; Scholarships
Ent Req: HS dipl, portfolio exam
Degrees: BA, BFA, MFA, MDes
Tuition: Undergrad: Res $7,467, Nonres $24,511; Grad: Res $11,798, Nonres $23,812
Courses: Art History, Ceramics, Collage, Conceptual Art, Constructions, Costume Design & Construction, Design, †Display, Drawing, Graphic Arts, Graphic Design, Lettering, Mixed Media, Painting, Photography, Printmaking, Sculpture, †Textiles, Video, Weaving
—Dept of History of Art, 110 Tappan Hall, 855 South University Ave Ann Arbor, MI 48109-1357. Tel 734-764-5400; Fax 734-647-4121; Email histartadmiss@umich.edu; Web: lsa.umich.edu/histart; *Prof & Chair* Elizabeth Sears; *Prof & Assoc Chair* Celeste Brusati; *Prof & Cur, Kelsey Mus of Archaeology* Elaine K Gazda; *Chief Admin* Jeff Craft
Dept estab 1910; pub; Scholarships; Fellowships
Degrees: BA, MA, PhD
Courses: †Art History, Museum Studies

BATTLE CREEK

KELLOGG COMMUNITY COLLEGE, Arts & Communication Dept, 450 North Ave, Battle Creek, MI 49017-3397. Tel 269-965-3931; Fax 269-965-0280; Web: www.kellogg.edu; *Art Instr* Ryan Flathu; *Art Instr* Peter Williams; *Chmn* Paula Puckett
Estab 1962; Maintains nonprofit art gallery, Davidson Gallery; FT 9, PT 18; pub; D & E; occupational cert; Scholarships; SC, LC; D 2,200, E 2,000, maj 60
Ent Req: None
Degrees: AA 2-4 yr
Courses: †Advertising Design, Animation, †Architecture, Art Appreciation, †Art Education, Art History, †Ceramics, Design, Drafting, †Drawing, †Graphic Design, †Industrial Design, †Mixed Media, †Painting, †Photography, †Sculpture, Stage Design, Teacher Training, Theatre Arts
Adult Hobby Classes: Courses—all areas
Summer School: Courses—Basic Art & Appreciation

BENTON HARBOR

LAKE MICHIGAN COLLEGE, Dept of Art & Science, 2755 E Napier Ave, Benton Harbor, MI 49022-1881. Tel 616-927-3571, Ext 5180; *Instr* Ken Schaber, MFA
Estab 1943; pub; D & E; Scholarships; SC 10, LC 5; 3377 total
Ent Req: Open door policy
Degrees: AA 2 yrs
Courses: 2-D & 3-D Design, Art Appreciation, Art Education, Art History, Ceramics, Design, Drawing, Occupational Therapy, Painting, Photography, Printmaking, Sculpture, Weaving

BERRIEN SPRINGS

ANDREWS UNIVERSITY, Dept of Art, Art History & Design, N US Rt 31, Berrien Springs, MI 49104-0001. Tel 616-471-7771; Fax 616-471-3949; Web: www.andrews.edu; *Chmn* Gregory Constantine; *Prof* Steve Hansen; *Instr* Robert Mason
Estab 1952; FT 4; den; D & E; SC 18, LC 5; enrl 130, maj 20
Ent Req: HS grad
Degrees: BS(Art Educ), BA 4 yrs, BFA 4 yrs
Courses: Art Education, Art History, Ceramics, Drawing, European Study, Graphic Design, Painting, Photography, Printmaking, Sculpture

BIG RAPIDS

FERRIS STATE UNIVERSITY, Visual Communication Dept, 119 South St Bus 302, Big Rapids, MI 49307-2284. Tel 231-591-2442; *Dept Head* Kaaren Denyes
10; Scholarships
Degrees: AAS & BS
Tuition: Res—undergrad $2142 per sem; nonres—undergrad $4838 per sem
Courses: Advertising Design, Air Brush, Art History, Concept Development, Conceptual Art, Creative Writing, Design, Drawing, Figure Drawing, Film, †Graphic Arts, †Graphic Design, Illustration, Intermedia, Lettering, Mixed Media, Painting, Photography, Printmaking, Production Art, Rendering, Typography, Video
Adult Hobby Classes: Enrl 400; tuition $180 per cr hr
Summer School: Dir, Karl Walker. Tuition $180 per qtr

BIRMINGHAM

BIRMINGHAM BLOOMFIELD ART CENTER, 1516 S Cranbrook Rd, Birmingham, MI 48009-1855. Tel 248-644-0866; Fax 248-644-7904; Web: www.bbartcenter.org (ULC); *Pres & Ceo* Annie Van Gelderen; *VPres Programs* Cynthia Mills; *Youth Prog Dir* Susan Owens; *VP Fin* Gwenn Rosseau; *Exec Asst* Diane Taylor
Estab 1957; Maintains Robinson Gallery, Kantgias/Desalle Gallery, LaBan Commons Gallery; maintains art/architecture libr; PT 100; pub; Community School of the Arts; D, E & weekends; Scholarships; SC & LC 500; 3600 total
Activities: Schols offered
Courses: Ceramics, Collage, Conceptual Art, Design, Drawing, Fashion Arts, Figure Drawing, Illustration, Jewelry, Jewelry & Metalsmithing, Mixed Media, Original Watercolor, Painting, Painting-Oil, Perspective Drawing, Photography, Printmaking, Sculpture, Still-Life & Landscape Drawing, Teen & Adult Portfolio Prep, Weaving
Adult Hobby Classes: Enrl 3000-3500; tuition $0-$300 for 3-39 hrs. Courses-Design, Drawing, Fibers, Jewelry, Painting, Pottery, Printmaking, Sculpture
Children's Classes: Enrl 500; tuition $150-$300.
Summer School: Youth Prog Dir, Susan Owens. Enrl 500; 2 wk term. Summer Art Camps, Pre-K - HS

BLOOMFIELD HILLS

CRANBROOK ACADEMY OF ART, 39221 Woodward Ave, PO Box 801 Bloomfield Hills, MI 48303-0801. Tel 877-462-7262; Email info@cranbrook.edu; Web: www.cranbrookart.edu; *Pres* Dominic A DiMarco; *Dir* Susan Ewing; *Mus Dir* Andrew Blauvelt; *Libr Dir* Judy Dyki
Estab 1932; Maintains nonprofit Cranbrook Art Mus, Center for Collections & Research, House & Gardens and Institute of Science; on-campus shop for art supplies; Pvt; D & E; Studio Prog minimum 30 hrs wk; Scholarships; SC, GC 2
Ent Req: Portfolio
Degrees: MFA & MArchit 2 yrs
Tuition: $36,800 per yr
Courses: Architecture, Ceramics, Design, Fiber, †Graphic Design, Metalsmithing, Painting, Photography, Print Media, Sculpture
Summer School: Summer Art Institute offers prog to high school students ages 13 - 18

DEARBORN

HENRY FORD COMMUNITY COLLEGE, McKenzie Fine Art Ctr, 5101 Evergreen Rd, Dearborn, MI 48128-1495. Tel 313-845-9634, 9600; Fax 313-845-6321; Web: www.hfcc.net; *Div Dir* Rick Goward; *Mgr Performing Arts* Dale Van Dorp; *Dept Head* Martin Anderson; *Instr Interior Design* Pamela Banduric; *Mgr Enrichment* Robert Cadez; *Ceramics* Cathy Dambach; *Drawing* Kevin Donahue; *Graphic Design* Kirk McLendon; *Dance* Diane Mancinelli; *Music* Kevin Dewey; *Philosophy* John Azar; *Speech* Stanley Moore; *Radio* Jay Kornek; *Dir Theater* George Popovich
Estab 1938; FT 6, PT 40; pub; D & E; Scholarships; SC 25, LC 9; D 3500, E 7500, maj 600
Ent Req: HS dipl
Degrees: AA 2 yrs
Courses: 2-D Design, 3-D Design, Art Appreciation, Art History, †Ceramics, Drawing, †Graphic Design, †Interior Design, Jewelry, †Painting, Photography, Printmaking, Sculpture, Textile Design
Children's Classes: Ceramics, Jewelry, Painting/Drawing, Sculpture
Summer School: Dir, Martin W Anderson. Tuition res-$30 per cr hr, nonres $42. Courses—Art Appreciation, Art History, Ceramics, Color Photography, Directed Study, Drawing, Black & White Photography, 2-D Design

DETROIT

COLLEGE FOR CREATIVE STUDIES, 201 E Kirby, Detroit, MI 48202. Tel 313-664-7400; Web: www.collegeforcreativestudies.edu; *Pres* Richard L Rogers; *Acad Dean* Imre Molnar; *Chmn Transportation Design* Mark West; *Chmn Crafts* Tom Madden; *Chmn Liberal Arts* Julie Longo; *Chmn Graphic Design* Doug Kisor; *Chmn Entertainment Arts* Scott Bogoniewski; *Chmn Photog* Bruce Feklman; *Chmn Illustration* Gil Ashby; *Chair Advertising Design* Mark Zapico; *Chair Product Design* Vincenzo Iavicoli
Estab 1926; maintain nonprofit art gallery; pvt; D & E; Scholarships; SC, LC; D 950, E 250, others 200; 1307 students
Ent Req: HS dipl & portfolio
Degrees: BFA 4 yrs
Courses: †Advertising Design, †Art History, †Ceramics, †Commercial Art, †Conceptual Art, Crafts, †Design, †Drawing, †Film, Fine Arts, Glass, †Graphic Arts, †Graphic Design, †Illustration, †Industrial Design, †Interior Design, †Jewelry, †Mixed Media, †Painting, †Photography, †Printmaking, †Sculpture, †Silversmithing, †Textile Design, †Video, †Weaving
Adult Hobby Classes: Enrl 281. Courses—Computer Technology, Crafts, Fine Arts, Graphic Commun, Industrial Design, Photography
Children's Classes: Enrl 59. Courses—Art, Music
Summer School: Dean Acad Affairs, Imre Molnar; Dir Continuing Educ, Carla Gonzalez; Enrl 230; tuition $476 per cr hr. Courses—Computer Technology, Crafts, Fine Arts, Industrial Design, Photography

MARYGROVE COLLEGE, Department of Art, 8425 W McNichols Rd, Detroit, MI 48221-2546. Tel 313-927-1370; Fax 313-927-1425; Email mgreene@marygrove.edu; Web: www.marygrove.edu; *Chair* Mary Lou Greene; *Asst Prof* Tim Gralewski; *Asst Prof* Sarah Nesbitt; *Asst Prof* Cindy Read; *Adjunct* Maria Prainito-Wisczaer, MFA

Estab 1910; maintains nonprofit art gallery, The Gallery Marygrove College, 8425 W McNichols, Detroit, MI 48221; pvt; D & E; Scholarships; SC 37, LC 20, GC 5; D 150, E 25, non-maj 60, maj 45, grad 5
Ent Req: Interview with portfolio
Degrees: BA & BFA 4 yrs, AA
Courses: Advertising Design, Art Education, Art History, †Ceramics, Collage, Commercial Art, Conceptual Art, Constructions, †Drawing, Film, †Graphic Arts, Graphic Design, Mixed Media, †Painting, Photography, †Printmaking, Sculpture, †Teacher Training
Adult Hobby Classes: Enrl 65; tuition $35-$90 per course. Courses—Drawing, Painting, Photography
Children's Classes: Enrl 100; tuition $20-$50 per course. Courses—Ceramics, Painting, Photography
Summer School: Dean Continuing Educ, Sr Andrea Lee, PhD. Enrl 40, tuition $86 per cr hr for term of two 6 wk terms. Courses—Basic courses, graduate and undergraduate

UNIVERSITY OF DETROIT MERCY, School of Architecture, 4001 W McNichols Rd, Detroit, MI 48221-3038. Tel 313-993-1532; Fax 313-993-1512; Web: www.architecture.udmercy.edu; *Dean* Stephan P Vogel; *Prof* John C Mueller; *Assoc Dean* Stephan J LaGrassa
Estab 1877, school estab 1964; pvt; D & E; Scholarships; SC 14, LC 36; D 200, maj 200
Ent Req: HS dipl, B average
Degrees: MArch 5 years
Tuition: Undergrad $8235 per 12-18 cr hrs per sem, $420 per 1-11 cr; grad $9075 per 12-18 cr hrs per sem, $605 per 1-11 cr
Courses: Architecture, Design

WAYNE STATE UNIVERSITY, Dept of Art & Art History, 4841 Cass Ave, 150 Arts Bldg Detroit, MI 48202-1203. Tel 313-577-2980; Fax 313-577-3491; *Chmn* Marian Jackson; *Interim Chmn* Robert Marten
FT 25, PT 20
Courses: Art History, Ceramics, Drawing, Fibers, Graphic Design, Industrial Design, Interdisciplinary Electronic Media, Interior Design, Metals, Painting, Photography, Printmaking, Sculpture
Summer School: Tuition same as regular sem for 7 wks. Courses—Art History, Ceramics, Drawing, Fibers, Painting, Photography, Sculpture

DOWAGIAC

SOUTHWESTERN MICHIGAN COLLEGE, Fine & Performing Arts Dept, 58900 Cherry Grove Rd, Dowagiac, MI 49047-9726. Tel 616-782-5113; Web: www.swmich.edu; *Chmn & Instr* Dr John Korzon, DA; *Instr* David R Baker, MFA; *Instr* Patty Bunner, MFA
Estab 1964; pub; D & E; Scholarships; SC 13, LC 3; D 200, E 100, non-maj 200, maj 100
Ent Req: HS dipl
Degrees: AA & AS
Tuition: Res—undergrad $50 per cr hr; nonres—undergrad $85 per cr hr; foreign, in service & out of state $66 per cr hr
Courses: Advertising Design, Architecture, Ceramics, Commercial Art, Drafting, Drawing, Graphic Arts, Lettering, Painting, Photography, Printmaking
Adult Hobby Classes: Art Appreciation, Ceramics, Painting, Photography
Summer School: Dir, Marshall Bishop. Enrl 1000; 7 wk terms

EAST LANSING

MICHIGAN STATE UNIVERSITY, Dept of Art & Art History, 113 Kresge Art Ctr, East Lansing, MI 48824-1119. Tel 517-355-7610; Fax 517-432-3938; Email art@msu.edu; Web: www.art.msu.edu; *Prog Head* Dr Kenneth Haltman; *Dir Grad Prog* Dr Janice Simpson
Estab 1855; FT 30; pub; D & E; Scholarships; SC 77, LC 45, GC 25; D 2500, non-maj 1500, maj 450, grad 60
Ent Req: HS dipl
Degrees: BA & BFA 4 yrs, MA 1 yr, MFA 2 yrs
Courses: Art Education, Art History, Ceramics, Collage, Conceptual Art, Constructions, Design, Drawing, Graphic Design, History of Art & Architecture, Mixed Media, †Museum Studies, Painting, Photography, Printmaking, Sculpture, Teacher Training, Video
Adult Hobby Classes: Tuition $10 per session. Courses—History of Art & Studio Art
Children's Classes: Enrl 150; tuition $50 for 10 wks. Courses—Computer, Drawing, Painting, Photography, Sculpture
Summer School: Dir, Jim Hopfensperger

ESCANABA

BAY DE NOC COMMUNITY COLLEGE, Art Dept, 2001 N Lincoln Rd, Escanaba, MI 49829-2511. Tel 906-786-5802; Fax 906-789-6913; *Instr Drawing & Design* Craig Seckinger; *Instr Art History* Joann Leffel; *Instr Pottery* Al Hansen
Maintain nonprofit art gallery; Scholarships; SC 6, LC 2; D 60, E 20
Degrees: AA, AS
Tuition: County res—$53.50 per cr hr; non-county res—$73.50 per cr hr; non-state res—$117.50 per cr hr
Courses: Art History, Ceramics, Design, Drawing, Painting, Sculpture

FARMINGTON HILLS

OAKLAND COMMUNITY COLLEGE, Art Dept, 27055 Orchard Lake Rd, Orchard Ridge Campus Farmington Hills, MI 48334-4556. Tel 248-522-3400; Fax 248-471-7544; Web: www.oaklandcc.edu; *Chmn* Robert Piepenburg
Degrees: AA and ASA offered
Tuition: District res—$48-70 per cr hr; non-district—$82.40 per cr hr
Courses: Advertising Design, Art Appreciation, Art History, Calligraphy, Ceramics, Design, Drawing, Fashion Arts, Handicrafts, Photography, Sculpture

FLINT

MOTT COMMUNITY COLLEGE, Fine Arts & Social Sciences Division, 1401 E Court St, Flint, MI 48503-2089. Tel 810-762-0332; Fax 810-762-5670; Email marycusack@mcc.edu; Web: www.mcc.edu; *Dean* Mary Cusack; *Prof* Jessie Sirna, MA; *Prof* Thomas Bohnert, MAEd; *Prof* John Dempsey; *Prof* Mara Fulmer; *Asst Prof* James Shurter; *Instr* Dustin Price
Estab 1923; Maintain a non-profit art gallery; pub; D & E; SC 45, LC 7; D & E 250, maj 250
Ent Req: HS dipl or 19 yrs old
Degrees: AFA 2 yrs
Tuition: Fall 2012 $108.05 in district, $161.75 out of district, $215.86 out of state per contact hour
Courses: Art Appreciation, Art Education, Art History, Ceramics, Drawing, Film, Graphic Design, Jewelry, Painting, †Photography, Printmaking, Sculpture, Theatre Arts, Video
Adult Hobby Classes: Classes offered through cont education division
Summer School: Tuition same as above; 7.5 wk sessions

GRAND RAPIDS

AQUINAS COLLEGE, Art Dept, 1607 Robinson Rd SE, Grand Rapids, MI 49506-1799. Tel 616-459-8281, Ext 2413; Fax 616-459-2563; Email zimmekat@aquinas.edu; Web: www.aquinas.edu; *Chmn Dept & Prof* Ron Pederson, MFA; *Prof* Sr Marie Celeste Miller, PhD, MFA; *Prof* Steve Schousen, MFA; *Assoc Prof & Dir Exhibs* Dana Freeman, MFA; *Assoc Prof* Kurt Kaiser, MFA; *Adjunct Assoc Prof Painting* Sharon Sandberg, MFA; *Prof* Joseph Becherer, PhD; *Prof Art History* Lena Meijer; *Adjunct Asst Prof Art Educ* HJ Slider, MA; *Adjunct Prof* Don Kerr, MFA; *Adjunct Assoc Prof* Chris LaPorte, MFA; *Adjunct Instr Ceramics* Madeline Kaczmarczyk
Estab 1940, dept estab 1965; maintains nonprofit art gallery, AMC Gallery, 1607 Robinson Rd SE, Grand Rapids, MI 49506; pvt; den; D & E; Scholarships; SC 30, LC 12; non-maj 80, maj 50
Ent Req: HS dipl
Degrees: BA and BFA 4 yrs
Courses: Art Appreciation, †Art Education, †Art History, †Ceramics, Conceptual Art, Constructions, Design, †History of Art & Architecture, Mixed Media, †Painting, †Photography, †Printmaking, †Sculpture, Stage Design, Theatre Arts

CALVIN COLLEGE, Art Dept, 3201 Burton SE, Grand Rapids, MI 49546. Tel 616-957-6271; Fax 616-957-8551; Web: www.calvin.edu; *Prof* Helen Bonzelaar, PhD, MFA; *Prof* Franklin Spevers, MS; *Assoc Prof* Anna Greidanus Probes, MFA; *Prof* Henry Luhikhuizen, PhD, MFA; *Chmn Dept* Carl Huisman
Estab 1876, dept estab 1965; den; D & E; Scholarships; SC 16, LC 4, GC 5; maj 130, grad 4, others 4
Ent Req: HS dipl, SAT or ACT
Degrees: BA(Art, Art Educ, Art History) & BFA(Art), MAT
Courses: Advertising Design, Aesthetics, Architecture, Art Appreciation, Art Education, Art History, Art Therapy, Ceramics, Commercial Art, Conceptual Art, Constructions, Graphic Design, History of Art & Architecture, Jewelry, Painting, Photography, Printmaking, Sculpture, Silversmithing, Teacher Training
Summer School: Courses vary

GRAND RAPIDS COMMUNITY COLLEGE, Visual Art Dept, 143 Bostwick NE, Grand Rapids, MI 49503. Tel 616-234-3544; Fax 611-234-3368; Email nantonak@grcc.cc.edu; Web: grcc.cc.edu; *Dept Head Visual Arts* Nick Antonakis; *Art Gallery Dir* Robin Van Rooyen
Estab 1914; Maintains nonprofit art gallery, Grand Rapids Community College Art Gallery; FT 7, PT 11; pub; D, E & W; Scholarships; SC 17, LC 2; D 250, E 75, maj 60
Ent Req: HS dipl or ent exam
Degrees: AA 2 yrs & AFA 2 yrs
Courses: 20th Century Art, Art Education, Art History, Ceramics, Color & Design, Drawing, Graphic Design, History of Art & Architecture, Life Drawing, Mixed Media, Painting, Photography, Teacher Training
Summer School: Term of 7 wks beginning May. Courses—Art History, Drawing, Photography, Pottery, Outdoor Painting, Drawing

KENDALL COLLEGE OF ART & DESIGN OF FERRIS STATE UNIVERSITY, 17 Fountain St NW, Grand Rapids, MI 49503-3194. Tel 616-451-2787; Email kcadadmissions@ferris.edu; Web: www.kcad.edu; *Interim Pres* Oliver H Evans PhD; *Dean of Student Serv* Sandy Britton, MBA; *Dir of Talent Acquisition & Recruitment* Kristopher Jones, MFA
Estab 1928; Maintains non-profit art gallery & KCAD Library 17 Fountain St NW, Grand Rapids MI, 49503; pub; D & E; Scholarships; Fellowships; SC 187, LC 37, GC 27; 1438
Ent Req: HS dipl, ACT, SAT, portfolio review, essay
Degrees: BFA, BS, MFA & MAE
Courses: Advertising Design, †Architecture, †Art Education, †Art History, Design, Drafting, †Drawing, †Fashion Arts, †Furniture Design, †Graphic Design, History of Art & Architecture, †Illustration, †Industrial Design, †Interior Design, Mixed Media, †Painting, †Photography, †Printmaking, †Sculpture, †Silversmithing, Video
Adult Hobby Classes: 524; tuition $215 for 7 wk term. Courses—Ceramics, Computer Art, Drawing, Jewelry Design, Painting, Photography
Children's Classes: 826; tuition $125 & up for 6 wk term. Courses—Ceramics, Drawing, Painting, Photography, Sculpture
Summer School: Dir of Continuing Studies, Brenda Sipe. Full semester, May - July; same program as regular session

HANCOCK

FINLANDIA UNIV, International School of Art and Design, 200 Michigan St, Hancock, MI 49930-1427. Tel 906-487-7225; Fax 906-487-7290; Email art&design@finlandia.edu; Web: www.finlandia.edu; *Prof* Phyllis Fredendall, MFA; *Dean* Denise Vandeville, MFA; *Asst Prof* Phillip Faulkner
Estab 1896, dept estab 1997; Maintains two non-profit galleries: Finalandia University Gallery Quincy St, Hancock, MI; Reflections Gallery 200 Michigan St, Hancock, MI 49930; Northwind Books sells art supplies on-campus; pvt; D & E; Scholarships; SC 38, LC 9; E 45
Ent Req: HS dipl, open door policy
Degrees: AA 2 yrs, BFA, BA 4 yrs
Tuition: $9,699 per sem; campus res available
Courses: Advertising Design, Aesthetics, Art Education, Art History, Art Therapy, †Ceramics, Design, Drawing, †Fashion Arts, Fiber, †Graphic Arts, †Graphic Design, History of Art & Architecture, †Integrated Design, †Painting, Photography, Printmaking, Product Design, Sculpture, †Sustainable Design, Teacher Training, †Textile Design, Visual Communications, Weaving

HILLSDALE

HILLSDALE COLLEGE, Art Dept, 33 E College St, Hillsdale, MI 49242-1298. Tel 517-437-7341, Ext 2371; Fax 517-437-3923; Web: www.hillsdale.edu; *Dir* Samuel Knecht, MFA; *Asst Prof* Tony Frudakis, MFA; *Instr* Patrick Forshay; *Instr* Will Bippes
Estab 1844; pvt; Scholarships; SC 12, LC 5; D 1000, non-maj 150, maj 15
Ent Req: HS dipl, SAT
Degrees: BA & BS 4 yrs
Courses: Advertising Design, Art Education, Art History, Ceramics, Drawing, Film, Graphic Arts, History of Art & Architecture, Illustration, Lettering, Painting, Photography, Printmaking, Restoration & Conservation, Sculpture, Stage Design, Teacher Training, Video
Summer School: Dir, Rich Moeggenberg. Courses—Vary

HOLLAND

HOPE COLLEGE, Dept of Art & Art History, 275 Columbia Ave, Art Dept Holland, MI 49423; PO Box 9000, Holland, MI 49422-9000. Tel 616-395-7500; Fax 616-395-7499; Email nelson@hope.edu; Web: www.hope.edu; *Prof* William Mayer, MFA; *Assoc Prof* Katherine Sullivan, MFA; *Prof* Bruce McCombs, MFA; *Assoc Prof & Chmn* Steve Nelson, MFA; *Asst Prof* Stephanie Milanowski, MFA; *Asst Prof* Anne Heath-Wiersma, PhD; *Gallery Dir* Heidi Kraus, PhD
Estab 1866, dept estab 1962; Maintain nonprofit art gallery; DePree Gallery, Hope College, 275 Columbia Ave, Holland, MI 49423; art supplies cam be purchased at college bookstore; den; D & E; Scholarships; SC 18, LC 12; D 185, E 61, non-maj 488, maj 26
Ent Req: HS dipl, CEEB-SAT or ACT
Degrees: BA and BM 4 yrs
Tuition: $13,430 per sem
Courses: 2-D & 3-D Design, †Art Education, †Art History, †Ceramics, Design, †Drawing, †Painting, †Photography, †Printmaking, †Sculpture
Summer School: Registrar, Carol DeJong. Tuition $250 per sem hr. Courses—Vary from yr to yr

INTERLOCHEN

INTERLOCHEN CENTER FOR THE ARTS, Interlochen Arts Academy, Dept of Visual Art, 4000 Hwy M-137, Interlochen, MI 49643-0199; PO Box 199, Interlochen, MI 49643-0199. Tel 231-276-7200; Web: www.interlochen.org; *Dir Visual Arts* Melinda Zacher
Maintain a nonprofit art gallery & art/architecture library; Pvt; D; Scholarships; SC, LC; 440, non-maj 30, maj 50
Ent Req: portfolio, HS dipl, post grad certificate
Tuition: $46,500 per yr, includes room & board
Courses: Art History, Ceramics, Design, Drawing, Fiber Art, Jewelry, Mixed Media, Painting, Photography, Printmaking, Sculpture, Silversmithing, Textile Design, Weaving
Summer School: Dir Visual Arts, Melinda Zacher. Enrl 2,500. Interlochen Arts Camp, formerly National Music Camp Courses & same as above

IRONWOOD

GOGEBIC COMMUNITY COLLEGE, Fine Arts Dept, E 4946 Jackson Rd, Ironwood, MI 49938. Tel 906-932-4231, Ext 283; *Chmn* Jeannie Milakovich
Estab 1932; pub; D & E; Scholarships; SC 14, LC 3; D 37, E 32, non-maj 65, maj 4
Ent Req: HS dipl or equivalent
Degrees: AA 2 yrs
Adult Hobby Classes: Courses—Painting
Summer School: Dean Instruction, Dale Johnson. Courses—Ceramics, Ceramic Sculpture, Drawing, Painting

KALAMAZOO

KALAMAZOO COLLEGE, Art Dept, 1200 Academy St, Kalamazoo, MI 49006-3295. Tel 616-337-7047; Fax 616-337-7067; Email fischer@kzoo.edu; *Prof* Richard Koenig, MFA; *Chmn* Tom Rice, MFA
Estab 1833, dept estab approx 1940; pvt; D; Scholarships; SC 14, LC 10; (school) 1200, non-maj 250 (dept), maj 20, others 5
Ent Req: HS dipl, SAT, ACT, class rank
Degrees: BA 4 yrs
Courses: Aesthetics, Art History, Ceramics, Drawing, Painting, Photography, Printmaking, Sculpture, Teacher Training

KALAMAZOO INSTITUTE OF ARTS, KIA School, 314 S Park St, Kalamazoo, MI 49007-5102. Tel 269-349-7775; Fax 269-349-9313; Email denisel@kiarts.org; Web: www.kiarts.org; *Dir KIA School* Denise Lisiecki, MA; *Head Children's Prog* Corinne Satterlee, BFA; *Head Weaving Dept* Gretchen Huggett, BS; *Head Jewelry Dept* Lauren Tripp; *Chair Ceramics* Brian Hirt, MFA; *Head Jewelry Dept* Kelli Jackson; *Chair Photog & Digital Media* Mary Whalen; *Head Printmaking* Vicki Van Ameyden, MFA
Estab 1924; Maintains nonprofit art gallery, Kalamazoo Institute of Arts; maintains an art library, Mary & Edwin Meader Fine Art Library; PT 50; pvt, nonprofit; D & E; Scholarships; SC 85 LC 1; D 530, E 490
Tuition: $180-$290 depending upon membership; no campus res
Courses: Art Appreciation, Ceramics, Courses for the Handicapped, Design, Digital Media, Drawing, Glass, Home School, Jewelry, Mixed Media, Painting, Photography, Printmaking, Sculpture, Silversmithing, †Video, Weaving
Children's Classes: Enrl 400; tuition $108-$220 for one sem; Courses—Varied
Summer School: Dir, Denise Lisiecki. Enrl 900; tuition $108-$285 June - Aug. Courses—Full schedule

KALAMAZOO VALLEY COMMUNITY COLLEGE, Center for New Media, 100 E Michigan Ave, Kalamazoo, MI 49007; PO Box 4070, Kalamazoo, MI 49003-4070. Tel 269-373-7919; Email thamann@kvcc.edu; Web: www.kvcc.edu; *Dir Ctr for New Media* Thomas Hamann; *Art Chair* David Posther; *ANM Chair* Aubrey Hardaway; *Instr* Linda Rzoska; *Instr* Beth Purdy; *Instr* Mark DeYoung
Estab 1968; Mem: Maintains Arcus Gallery 100 E Michigan Ave Kalamazoo MI 49007; pub; D & E; Scholarships; SC 12, LC, Post Assoc Degree Cert; D 300, E 100
Ent Req: Open Door
Degrees: AA, AS and Cert (1 yr)
Courses: 2-D Design, †Adobe Creative Suite CC, Advertising Design, Aesthetics, Art Appreciation, Art Education, Calligraphy, Ceramics, Commercial Art, Design, Drafting, Drawing, Electronic Publishing, Graphic Design, Illustration, Illustration Media, Illustrator, Lettering, Painting, Photography, Photoshop, Teacher Training
Adult Hobby Classes: Courses—Same as regular session
Children's Classes: Courses—Ceramics
Summer School: Instr, Arleigh Smyrnios; Enrl 1125; tuition $43.25 per cr hr for 8 wk term. Courses—Ceramics, Design, Drawing, Watercolor, Electronic Publishing

WESTERN MICHIGAN UNIVERSITY, Frostic School of Art, R2110 Richmond Center for Visual Arts, 1903 West Michigan Ave Kalamazoo, MI 49008-5213. Tel 269-387-2436; Fax 269-387-2477; Web: www.wmich.edu/art; *Dir* Tricia Hennessy; *Foundation Area Coordr* Karen Bondarchuk; *Art Educ Area Coordr* Bill Charland; *Digital Media Photog Area Coordr* Adriane Little; *Painting Area Coordr* Vince Torano; *Jewelry/Metals Area Coordr* Autumn Brown; *Ceramics Area Coordr* Ed Harkness; *Art History Area Coordr* Mary-Louise Tolton; *Print Media Area Coordr* Nichole Maury; *Art Edu* Christina Chin; *Art Appreciation* Cat Crotchett; *Art History* Andrew Hennlich; *Foundation* Jim Hopfensperger; *Graphic Design* Nicholas Kuder; *Graphic Design* Ryan Lewis; *Photo/Intermedia* Adriane Little; *Photo/Intermedia* Ginger Owen; *Art Appreciation* Paul Solomon; *Graphic Design* Leon Sun; *Painting* Vince Torano; *Art History* Mary-Louise Totton; *Print Media* Patricia Villalobos; *Painting* Dick deDeaux; *Photo/Intermedia* Bill Davis; *Art History* Joyce Kubiski
Estab 1904, dept estab 1939; Maintains a nonprofit art gallery: Albertine Monroe-Brown Gallery, Rose Netzorg & James Wilfrid Kerr Gallery, Robert & Eleanor DeVries Gallery, Richmond Center for Visual Arts; FT 13; pub; D & E; Scholarships; SC 60, LC 9, GC 8; non-maj 400, maj 330, grad 5
Activities: Schls offered
Ent Req: HS dipl, ACT
Degrees: BA, BS & BFA 4 yrs, MA - Art Education
Tuition: Res—undergrad $353-385 per cr hr, grad $510 per cr hr; nonres—undergrad $793-858 per cr hr, grad $1,024 per cr hr; campus res—room & board $8,000
Courses: Art Appreciation, †Art Education, †Art History, †Ceramics, †Drawing, †Graphic Design, †Jewelry/Metals, †Painting, †Photography/Intermedia, Print Media, †Sculpture

LANSING

LANSING COMMUNITY COLLEGE, Visual Arts & Media Dept, PO Box 40010, Lansing, MI 48901-7210; 315 N Grand Ave, Lansing, MI 48933-1213. Tel 517-483-1476; Fax 517-483-1050; Web: www.lcc.edu; *Prof* Constance Peterson, BS; *Prof* Sharon Wood, MFA; *Prof* Ike Lea; *Prof* Fred Clark, MFA; *Prof* Brian Bishop, MFA; *Prof* Susie Stanley, BA; *Prof* Jim Redding, MA
Estab 1957; FT & PT 40; pub; D & E, weekends - online; Scholarships; SC 80, LC 10; D 758, E 506, non-maj 400, maj 560, others 304
Ent Req: HS dipl
Degrees: AA 2 yrs
Courses: Advertising Design, Commercial Art, †Computer Graphics Animation, †Computer Graphics Web Design, †Conceptual Art, Design, †Digital Effects, Drawing, †Film, †Graphic Design, Illustration, †Multimedia, Painting, †Photography, Printmaking, †Sequential Art, Typography
Adult Hobby Classes: Enrl 60; duration 16 wks. Courses— Watercolor, Matting & Framing, Photography, Photoshop
Summer School: Dir, Mary Cusack. Enrl 250. Courses—Same as Fall & Spring sem

LIVONIA

MADONNA UNIVERSITY, College of Arts & Humanities, 36600 Schoolcraft Rd, Livonia, MI 48150-1176. Tel 734-432-5300; Email dsemivan@madonna.edu; Web: www.madonna.edu; *Chmn Art Dept* Douglas Semivan, MFA; *Instr Visual Arts Educ* G Aseneth Andrews, MA; *Instr Art History* Ralph F Glenn, MA; *Instr Visual*

Arts Educ Melissa Liford, MA; *Instr Art History* Jeanne Moore, MA; *Instr Studio Art* Mary Rousseaux, MFA; *Instr Graphic Design* Robin Ward, BFA
Estab 1947; Maintain a nonprofit art gallery; on-campus shop where art supplies may be purchased; pvt; D & E; Scholarships; SC 17, LC 3; D 43, E 22, maj 17
Ent Req: HS dipl, portfolio
Degrees: AA 2 yrs, AB 4 yrs
Courses: †Advertising Design, Architecture, Art Appreciation, Art Education, Art History, Calligraphy, Ceramics, Collage, †Commercial Art, Computer Art, Design, Display, †Drawing, †Film, †Fine Arts, †Graphic Arts, †Graphic Design, History of Art & Architecture, Illustration, Lettering, Mixed Media, Painting, Photography, Printmaking, Sculpture, Teacher Training, Video
Adult Hobby Classes: Enrl 25; tuition $70 per 10 wk course. Courses—Painting
Summer School: Dir, Prof R F Glenn. Enrl 25 for 6-8 wks. Courses—Art History, Printmaking, Teacher Art Education

SCHOOLCRAFT COLLEGE, Dept of Art & Design, 18600 Haggerty Rd, Livonia, MI 48152-2696. Tel 734-462-4400; Fax 734-462-4538; *Prof* Stephen Wroble, MA; *Dean Art Dept* Jean Bonner
Estab 1964; pub; D & E; Scholarships; Fellowships; SC 13, LC 4; D 300, E 150, maj 100
Ent Req: Ent exam
Degrees: AAS & AA 2 yrs
Courses: Ceramics, Computer Aided Art & Design, Design, Drawing, Film, Graphic Arts, History of Art & Design, Jewelry, Painting, Photography, Printmaking, Sculpture
Adult Hobby Classes: Acrylic Painting, Ceramics, Drawing, Jewelry, Macrame, Photography, Stained Glass
Children's Classes: Enrl 40; tuition same as above. Courses—Talented & Gifted Program
Summer School: Design, Drawing, Printmaking, Watercolor

MARQUETTE

NORTHERN MICHIGAN UNIVERSITY, Dept of Art & Design, 1401 Presque Isle, Marquette, MI 49855. Tel 906-227-2194, 227-2279; Fax 906-227-2276; Email art@num.eduðepartmentåd_career.html; Web: www.nmu.edu; *Prof* Thomas Cappuccio; *Prof* John D Hubbard; *Prof* William C Leete; *Prof* Diane D Kordich; *Prof* Dennis Staffne; *Prof* Dale Wedig; *Asst Prof* Jane Milkie; *Asst Prof* Sam Chung; *Head Dept* Michael J Cinelli; *Asst Prof* Derrick Christen; *Asst Prof* Steve Leuthold; *Asst Prof* Stephan Larson
Estab 1899, dept estab 1964; pub; D & E; Scholarships; SC 30, LC 20, GC 18
Ent Req: HS dipl, ACT
Degrees: BS, BFA, BA 4 yrs, MAE
Courses: †Art Education, †Art History, †Ceramics, Computer Graphics, †Drawing, Electronic Imaging, †Film, Graphic Design, Illustration, Industrial Design, Jewelry, Painting, Photography, Printmaking, Sculpture, Silversmithing, Video
Summer School: Dir, Michael J Cinelli. Enrl 15-20; 6 wk terms

MIDLAND

ALDEN B. DOW MUSEUM OF SCIENCE & ART, (Arts Midland Galleries & School) Alden B. Dow Museum School, 1801 W St Andrews, Midland, MI 48640. Tel 517-631-3250; Fax 517-631-7890; Email winslow@mcfta.org; Web: www.mcfta.org; *Dir* B B Winslow; *Mus School Mgr* Armin Mersmann
Estab 1971; Maintains a non-profit art gallery & on-campus art supplies shop.; pvt; D & E; Scholarships; SC 12-20, LC 2; D & E 250
Courses: Aesthetics, Art Appreciation, Art History, Calligraphy, Ceramics, Collage, Conceptual Art, Constructions, Design, Drawing, History of Art & Architecture, Metalsmithing, Mixed Media, Museum Staff Training, Painting, Papermaking, Photography, Printmaking, Sculpture, Stained Glass, Textile Design, Weaving
Adult Hobby Classes: Enrl 200; tuition $85-$120 per sem
Children's Classes: Enrl 50; tuition $50-$65 per sem
Summer School: School Coordr Armin Mersmann

NORTHWOOD UNIVERSITY, Alden B Dow Creativity Center, 4000 Whiting Dr, Midland, MI 48640-2398. Tel 989-837-4478; Fax 989-837-4468; Email creativity@northwood.edu; Web: www.northwood.edu/abd; *Exec Dir* Dr Grover B Proctor Jr; *Asst Dir* Christianna Schartow
Estab 1978; Pvt; Scholarships; Fellowships

MONROE

MONROE COUNTY COMMUNITY COLLEGE, Humanities Division, 1555 S Raisinville Rd, Monroe, MI 48161-9746. Tel 734-384-4153; Fax 734-457-6023; Email reagle@monroeccc.edu; Web: www.monroeccc.edu; *Secy* Rachel Eagle; *Asst Prof Art* Theodore Vassar; *Asst Prof Art* Gary Wilson; *Adjunct Prof Art* Dan Stewart
Maintains a nonprofit art gallery; on-campus shop for purchase of art supplies; FT 2; pub; D & E; Scholarships; SC 16, LC 5
Degrees: AFA offered
Tuition: Res—$102 per cr hr; nonres—$177-197 per cr hr
Courses: Art Appreciation, †Art for Elementary Teachers, Art History, Ceramics, Design, Drawing, †Film, †Graphic Arts, †Graphic Design, Illustration, †Mixed Media, Painting, Printmaking, †Sculpture, †Theatre Arts

MOUNT PLEASANT

CENTRAL MICHIGAN UNIVERSITY, Dept of Art, 163 Wightman Hall, Rm 132 Mount Pleasant, MI 48859. Tel 989-774-3025; Fax 989-774-2278; Web: www.art.cmich.edu; *Chmn Dept* Al Wildey
Estab 1892; Maintain a nonprofit art gallery, CMU Art Gallery, Preston & Franklin, Mt Pleasant, MI 48859; FT 17, PT 2; pub; D & E; Scholarships; Fellowships; SC 81, LC 27; for univ 19,800
Ent Req: HS dipl
Degrees: BA, BFA & BAA 4 yrs
Courses: Aesthetics, Art Appreciation, Art Criticism, Art Education, Art History, Ceramics, Drawing, Fiber Design, Graphic Design, Painting, Photography, Printmaking, Sculpture

MUSKEGON

MUSKEGON COMMUNITY COLLEGE, Dept of Creative & Performing Arts, 221 S Quarterline Rd, Muskegon, MI 49442-1493. Tel 231-773-9131, Ext 324; Fax 231-777-0255; Email tim.norris@muskegoncc.edu; erin.hoffman@muskegoncc.edu; Web: www.muskegoncc.edu; *Dept Chmn* Sheila Wahamaki; *Prog Coordr* Tim Norris; *Prog Coordr* Erin Hoffman
Estab 1926; Maintain nonprofit art gallery, Overbrook Art Gallery; pub; D & E; Scholarships; SC 18, LC 6; D 280, E 60
Ent Req: HS dipl
Degrees: AA 2 yrs
Courses: †Art Appreciation, Art Education, Art History, Beginning Art, Ceramics, Design, Drawing, Painting, Printmaking, Sculpture

OLIVET

OLIVET COLLEGE, Art Dept, 320 S Main St, Olivet, MI 49076-9406. Tel 616-749-7000; *Chmn* Gary Wertheimer, MFA; *Prof* Donald Rowe; *Instr* Susan Rowe, MFA
Estab 1844, dept estab 1870; pvt; D & E; Scholarships; SC 17, LC 8, GC 10; D 610, non-maj 50, maj 20, grad 2
Ent Req: HS dipl
Degrees: BS and BM 4 yrs, MA 1 yr
Courses: Art History, †Commercial Art, †Design, †Drawing, †Painting, †Printmaking, †Sculpture

PETOSKEY

NORTH CENTRAL MICHIGAN COLLEGE, Art Dept, 1515 Howard St, Petoskey, MI 49770-8740. Tel 231-348-6651, 348-6600; Fax 231-348-6628; *Dept Contact* Shanna Robinson, MFA; *Instr* Andrea Gerring; *Instr* Rosemary Gould; *Instr* Richard Cunningham; *Instr* Dawn Swaim; *Instr* Joel Stoppel; *Instr* Bonnie Hill
Art supplies sold at on-campus store; D & E; SC & LC
Degrees: AA offered
Courses: Art Education, Art History, †Ceramics, Design, Drawing, †Graphic Arts, Graphic Design, Painting, Photography, Printmaking, Sculpture, †Silversmithing, Stained Glass, †Textile Design, †Weaving
Adult Hobby Classes: Courses offered
Summer School: Courses offered

PONTIAC

CREATIVE ART CENTER-NORTH OAKLAND COUNTY, Pontiac Creative Arts Center, 47 Williams St, Pontiac, MI 48341-1759. Tel 248-333-7849; Email pcacdirector@gmail.com; Web: www.pontiacarts.org; *Exec Dir* William Dwyer
Open Tues - Sat 10 AM - 5 PM, cl holidays; No admis fee; Estab 1964 to present the best in exhibitions, educational activities & community art outreach; non-profit community arts center serving adults & children with ongoing exhibits; Maintains a non-profit art gallery; Average Annual Attendance: 10,000; Mem: 160; dues organizations $50, family $40, general $35, artists & seniors $20; ann meeting in Apr; pub; D, E & Weekends; Scholarships; SC 9; LC 2; 200
Income: Financed by endowment, mem, city & state appropriation, trust funds, Mich Council for the Arts
Activities: Classes for adults & children; lects open to pub; 6 vis lectrs per year; concerts; exten prog to local schools
Ent Req: Open enrollment
Tuition: Varies; no campus res
Courses: Art Appreciation, Art Education, Ceramics, Dance, Drawing, Mixed Media, Painting, Photography, Sculpture, Theatre Arts, Wood Turning
Adult Hobby Classes: Tuition $45-$150
Children's Classes: Courses—Dance, Drawing, Painting, Sculpture
Summer School: Three wk session. Courses—Dance, Visual Arts, Ceramics, Photography & Woodturner

PORT HURON

SAINT CLAIR COUNTY COMMUNITY COLLEGE, Jack R Hennesey Art Dept, 323 Erie St, Port Huron, MI 48060-3812; PO Box 5015, Port Huron, MI 48061-5015. Tel 810-984-3881; *VPres Acad Svcs* Anita Gliniecki; *Dept Chmn* David Korff; *Advertising Design Faculty* John Henry; *Theater* Nancy Osborn
Estab 1923; pub; D & E; Scholarships; SC 30, LC 5; D 60
Ent Req: HS dipl
Degrees: AA and AAS 2 yrs
Courses: †Advertising Design, Art Appreciation, Art Education, Art History, Calligraphy, †Commercial Art, Costume Design & Construction, †Drafting, Drawing, Mixed Media, Painting, Photography, †Pottery, Printmaking, Sculpture, Stage Design, †Theatre Arts, Weaving
Adult Hobby Classes: Courses—Drawing, Painting, Pottery

ROCHESTER

OAKLAND UNIVERSITY, Dept of Art & Art History, 2200 N Squirrel Rd, Rochester, MI 48309-4402; Oakland Univ College of Arts & Sciences, 310 Wilson Hall Rochester, MI 48309-4401. Tel 248-370-3375; Fax 248-370-3375; Email eis@oakland.edu; Web: www2.oakland.edu/art-history/; *Chmn Dept & Spec Instr* Andrea Eis; *Prof* Susan Wood, PhD; *Prof* Janice Schimmelman, PhD; *Assoc Prof* Claude Baillargeon, PhD; *Assoc Prof* Vagner M Whitehead, MFA; *Asst Prof* John Corso, PhD; *Asst Prof* Susan Evans, MFA; *Asst Prof* Taylor Hokanson, MFA; *Asst Prof* Shuishan Yu, PhD; *Asst Prof* Cody VanderKaay, MFA; *Adjunct Asst Prof* Lynn G Fausone, MFA; *Spec Instr* Sally S Tardella; *Gallery Dir & Spec Instr* Stephen Goody, MFA; *Assoc Prof* Tamara Jhashi, PhD
Estab 1957, dept estab 1960; Maintains Oakland Univ Art Gallery & libr within dept; FT & PT 28; pub; D & E; Scholarships; SC 37, LC 43; Maj 228
Ent Req: HS dipl
Degrees: BA 4 yrs
Courses: †Art History, †Studio Art

SCOTTVILLE

WEST SHORE COMMUNITY COLLEGE, Division of Humanities & Fine Arts, 3000 N Stiles Rd, Scottville, MI 49454-9791. Tel 231-845-6211; Web: www.westshore.cc.mi.us; *Chmn* Sharon Bloom; *Assoc Prof* Rebecca Mott, MA; *Instr* Teresa Soles, MA; *Instr* Judy Peters, BA
Estab 1965; PT 3, FT 7; Pub; D & E; Scholarships; SC 18, LC 10; non-maj 250, maj 10
Ent Req: HS dipl
Degrees: AA 2 yrs
Courses: †Art History, Ceramics, Drafting, Drawing, Graphic Design, Mixed Media, Painting, Photography, Printmaking, Sculpture, Stage Design, †Theatre Arts
Adult Hobby Classes: Art Workshops & Studio, Crafts, Photography
Summer School: Painting, Pottery

SOUTHFIELD

LAWRENCE TECHNOLOGICAL UNIVERSITY, College of Architecture, 21000 W Ten Mile Rd, Southfield, MI 48075-1051. Tel 248-204-2800; Fax 248-204-2900; Web: www.ltu.edu; *Asst Dean* Betty Lee Seydler-Hepworth; *Dean* Neville H Clouten
Estab 1932; Pvt; D&E
Degrees: BArchit, BA(Archit Illustration), BS(Archit), BS(Interior Archit)
Courses: †Architecture, †Interior Architecture
Summer School: Dir, Harold Linton. Enrl 75; tuition $250. Courses—Pre-College Architecture

SPRING ARBOR

SPRING ARBOR COLLEGE, Art Dept, 106 E Main St, Sta 19 Spring Arbor, MI 49283-9701. Tel 517-750-1200, Ext 1364; Web: www.arbor.edu; *Div Dir Music Arts* Bill Bippes, MFA; *Asst Prof* Roger Valand, MFA; *Dir* Paul Wolber, MA
Estab 1873, dept estab 1971; pvt den; D & E; Scholarships; SC 17, LC 6; D 200, E 20, non-maj 20, maj 32
Ent Req: HS dipl
Degrees: AA(Commercial) 2 yrs, BA 4 yrs
Courses: †Advertising Design, Commercial Art, †Drawing, †Graphic Arts, †Illustration, †Painting, †Printmaking, †Sculpture, †Teacher Training

TRAVERSE CITY

NORTHWESTERN MICHIGAN COLLEGE, Art Dept, 1701 E Front St, Traverse City, MI 49686-3016. Tel 231-922-1325; Fax 231-922-1696; Web: www.nmc.edu; *Chmn Dept* Doug Domine, BFA; *Instr* Mike Torre, MA; *Instr* Jill Hinds, BFA; *Art Historian* Jackie Shinners, MFA
Estab 1951, dept estab 1957; FT 4, PT 12; pub; D & E; Scholarships; SC 40, LC 4; non-maj 400, maj 75
Ent Req: HS dipl
Degrees: AA 2 yrs, AAS
Courses: Advertising Design, Art Education, Art History, Commercial Art, Drawing, Goldsmithing, Graphic Arts, Graphic Design, Illustration, Jewelry, Lettering, Life Drawing, Painting, Perspective, Photography, Pottery, Printmaking, Publication Design, Reproduction Techniques, Silversmithing, Typography
Adult Hobby Classes: Enrl 50; tuition $23. Courses - Drawing, Life Drawing, Painting, Pottery, Printmaking
Summer School: Dir, Stephen Ballance. Enrl 100 tuition $53 per billing hr in-district, $87.75 per billing hr other for 8 week terms. Courses—drawing, Photography, Pottery

TWIN LAKE

BLUE LAKE FINE ARTS CAMP, Art Dept, 300 E Crystal Lake Rd, Twin Lake, MI 49457-9499. Tel 231-894-1966; Fax 231-893-5120; Web: www.bluelake.org; *Chmn* Carol Tice; *Exec Asst* Lisa Martin
Estab 1966; Pub; Scholarships
Courses: 2D-3D, Ceramics, Drawing, Fibre Arts, Illustration, Painting, Sculpture, Weaving, Wheel-Work
Adult Hobby Classes: Call for information
Summer School: Summer prog for middle and high school students

UNIVERSITY CENTER

DELTA COLLEGE, Art Dept, 1961 Delta Rd University Center, MI 48710. Tel 517-686-9000, Ext 9101; *Assoc Prof & Dept Chmn* Gina Dominique, MFA; *Prof* Randal Crawford, MFA; *Instr* Michael Glowacki; *Instr* Andrew Rieder
Estab 1960; Maintains a nonprofit gallery, Delta Galleria 1961 Delta Rd University Center MI 48710; art collection in main library; art supplies sold on campus bookstore; pub; D & E, Off Campus Centers; Scholarships; SC 21, LC 5; Non-maj 1000, Maj 150
Ent Req: open door policy
Degrees: AFA 2 yrs
Courses: Art Education, Art History, Ceramics, Design, Digital Imaging, Drawing, Graphic Arts, Graphic Design, Painting, Photography, Printmaking, Sculpture

SAGINAW VALLEY STATE UNIVERSITY, Dept of Art & Design, 7400 Bay Rd, University Center, MI 48710-0001. Tel 517-790-4390; Email mzivich@svsu.edu; *Prof* Matthew Zivich, MFA; *Prof* Barron Hirsch, MFA; *Chmn Dept, Prof* Hideki Kihata, MFA; *Adjunct Instr* Sara B Clark, MFA; *Assoc Prof* Rodney Nowosielski; *Asst Prof* Shaun Bangert; *Asst Prof* Mike Mosher; *Instr* David Littell; *Instr* Craig Prime; *Instr* Terry Basmadjian; *Instr* Marlene Pellcrito
Estab 1960, dept estab 1968; Maintain nonprofit art gallery; University Gallery & Marshall Fredericks Sculpture Gallery; Pub; D & E; Scholarships; SC approx 20, LC approx 15; D 200, E 50, maj 65
Ent Req: HS dipl
Degrees: BA(Art), BFA 4 yrs or less
Courses: Advertising Design, Art Education, Art History, Ceramics, Commercial Art, Design, Drafting, Drawing, Graphic Arts, Graphic Design, Handicrafts, Illustration, Lettering, Occupational Therapy, Painting, Photography, Printmaking, Sculpture, Teacher Training, Theatre Arts
Summer School: Courses vary

YPSILANTI

EASTERN MICHIGAN UNIVERSITY, Dept of Art, 114 Ford Hall, Ypsilanti, MI 48197-2251. Tel 734-487-1268, 487-0192; Fax 734-481-1095; Web: www.art.acad.emich.edu; *Head Dept* Tom Venner
Estab 1849, dept estab 1901; pub; D & E; Scholarships; SC 55, LC 18; undergrad maj 420, non-maj 800, grad 100
Ent Req: HS dipl
Degrees: BA(Art History), BFA(Studio Art), BS & BA(Art Educ) 4 yrs, MA(Art Educ), MA(Studio) & MFA 2 yrs
Courses: Art Education, †Art History, †Ceramics, †Drawing, †Graphic Design, †Jewelry, †Painting, †Photography, †Printmaking, †Sculpture, †Textile Design
Children's Classes: Enrl 40; tuition $35 for 8-10 classes offered on Sat for Art talented & gifted
Summer School: Term of 7 1/2 wks, major & non-major courses

MINNESOTA

BEMIDJI

BEMIDJI STATE UNIVERSITY, Visual Arts Dept, 1500 Birchmont Dr, Bemidji, MN 56601. Tel 218-755-3735; Fax 218-755-4406; Web: www.bemidjistate.edu; *Chmn* MaryAnn Papanek-Miller; *Prof* Kyle Crocker PhD; *Asst Prof* John Holden, MFA; *Asst Prof* Steve Sundahl, MFA; *Asst Prof* Jaineth Skinner, MFA; *Asst Prof* Carol Struve, MFA
Estab 1918; pub; D & E; Scholarships; SC 54, LC 17, GC individual study
Ent Req: HS dipl, ACT, SAT, PSAT, or SCAT
Degrees: BA, BS(Teaching) and BS(Tech Illustration, Commercial Design), BFA
Courses: Advertising Design, Art Appreciation, Art Education, Art History, Ceramics, Crafts, Design, Drawing, Graphic Arts, Graphic Design, Jewelry, Painting, Printmaking, Sculpture, Teacher Training
Adult Hobby Classes: Tuition res—$46.70 per qtr hr. Courses—Graphic Design, Elementary Art Concepts & Methods, Secondary Art Concepts & Methods
Summer School: Dir, M Kaul. Enrl 250; tuition res—undergrad $46.70 per qtr hr, nonres—undergrad $101.40 per qtr hr. Courses—Art, Ceramics, History, Metals, Painting, Printmaking, 3-D Design

BLOOMINGTON

NORMANDALE COMMUNITY COLLEGE, Art Dept, 9700 France Ave S, Bloomington, MN 55431-4399. Tel 952-487-8143; Fax 952-487-8230; Web: www.normandale.mncu.edu; *Instr* D R Peterson, BFA; *Instr* Marilyn Wood, MFA; *Art Coordr* Martha Wittstruck
Estab 1969; Pub; D&E
Degrees: AA
Courses: Art Appreciation, Art History, Ceramics, Design, Drawing, Jewelry, Painting, Photography, Sculpture
Adult Hobby Classes: Courses offered
Summer School: Courses offered

BROOKLYN PARK

NORTH HENNEPIN COMMUNITY COLLEGE, Art Dept, 7411 85th Ave N, Brooklyn Park, MN 55445-2231. Tel 763-424-0775; Fax 763-493-0568; Email will.agar@nhcc.edu; Web: www.nhcc.edu; *Instr* Will Agar; *Instr* Jane Bassuk; *Instr* Jerry Mathiason; *Instr* Steve Pauley; *Instr* Michelle Ranta; *Instr* Jason Schoch; *Instr* Marina Haworth; *Instr* Gina Dabrowski; *Instr* Glenn Grafelman
Estab 1964; Non-profit gallery: Joseph F Gazzuolo Gallery, North Hennepin Community College, 7411 85th Ave N Brooklyn, MN 55445; on-campus shop

where art supplies may be purchased; FT 6; pub; D&E, Wknd, Online; Scholarships; SC 18, LC 4; Total college enrollment: 10,655
Activities: Schols offered
Ent Req: HS dipl. ent exam
Degrees: AA, AS & AAS 2 yr, AFA
Tuition: Tuition: $500 per 3 credits
Courses: 2-D & 3-D Design, Art History, Contemporary Crafts, Digital Photography, Drawing, Graphic Design, Illustration, Introduction to Art, Jewelry, Metalsmithing, Painting, Photography, Printmaking, Studio Arts, Typography, Video, Visual Communications
Adult Hobby Classes: Enrl 28. Courses—Drawing, Jewelry, Painting, Quilt Making
Children's Classes: Enrl 20. Courses—Art Theatre, Computer, Language, Photography, Sports
Summer School: Enrl 28; tuition $234. Courses—Drawing, Introduction of Art, Photography

COLLEGEVILLE

SAINT JOHN'S UNIVERSITY, Art Dept, Box 2000, Collegeville, MN 56321. Tel 320-363-2011, 363-5036; Web: www.csbsju.edu/; *Assoc Prof* James Hendershot, MFA; *Assoc Prof* Bro Alan Reed, MFA; *Assoc Prof* Sr Baulu Kuan, MFA; *Asst Prof* Andrea Shaker, MFA; *Prof* Dennis Frandrup, MFA; *Lectr* Susan Hendershot, MFA; *Instr* Anne Salisbury, PhD; *Lectr* James Rolle, BFA; *Lectr* Robert Wilde, MA
Estab 1856, joint studies with College of Saint Benedict; pvt; Scholarships; SC 20, LC 15
Ent Req: HS dipl
Degrees: BA, BS
Courses: Art History, Ceramics, Drawing, Jewelry, Painting, Photography, Printmaking, Sculpture
Adult Hobby Classes: Occasional adult education classes

COON RAPIDS

ANOKA RAMSEY COMMUNITY COLLEGE, Art Dept, 11200 Mississippi Blvd NW, Coon Rapids, MN 55433-3499. Tel 763-427-2600; Fax 612-422-3341; Web: www.an.cc.mm.us; *Dean* Brenda Robert; *Instr* Robert E Toensing, MFA
Estab 1970; Pub; D&E; Scholarships
Degrees: AA offered
Courses: Advertising Design, Art Appreciation, Art Education, Ceramics, Design, Drawing, Film, Glassblowing, Jewelry, Painting, Photography, Sculpture

DULUTH

UNIVERSITY OF MINNESOTA, DULUTH, Art Dept, 10 University Dr, 317 Humanities Bldg Duluth, MN 55812-2403. Tel 218-726-8225, 800-232-1339; Fax 218-726-6532; Email art@ub.d.umn.edu; Web: www.d.umn.edu/art/; *Prof* Thomas F Hedin, PhD, MFA; *Prof* Dean R Lettenstrom, MFA; *Assoc Prof* Robyn Roslak, PhD, MA; *Prof* James Klueg, MFA; *Asst Prof* Robert Repinski, MFA; *Assoc Prof* Janice Kmetz, MFA; *Prof, Head Dept* Gloria D Brush, MFA; *Assoc Prof* Alyce Coker; *Assoc Prof* Sarah Bauer, MFA; *Asst Prof* Catherine Ishino, MFA; *Asst Prof* Alison Aune, PhD; *Asst Prof* Philip Choo; *Asst Prof* Eun-Kyung Suh
B; Pub; D & E; Scholarships; Fellowships; SC 30, LC 6, GC 10; D 200, E 50, maj 414, grad 3
Ent Req: HS dipl, HS rank & ACT req, col prep req
Degrees: BFA, BA 4 yrs, MFA in Graphic Design
Courses: †2D & 3D Digital Studios, Art Appreciation, Art Education, Art History, †Art in Technologies, Ceramics, Design, Drawing, Fibers, Graphic Design, †History of Art, †Interactive Design, Intermedia, Jewelry, Mixed Media, †Motion Graphics, Museum Staff Training, Painting, Photography, Printmaking, Sculpture, Silversmithing, †Studio Major, Teacher Training, †Typography, Weaving
Adult Hobby Classes: 10 wk courses. Courses—Studio Arts, Graphic Design
Summer School: Dir, Haren Heikel. 5 wk summer sessions. Courses—Art Appreciation, Art Education, Ceramics, Drawing, Graphic Design, Jewelry & Metals, Painting, Photography

ELY

VERMILION COMMUNITY COLLEGE, Art Dept, 1900 E Camp St, Ely, MN 55731-1996. Tel 218-365-7273; Web: www.vcc.edu; WATS 800-657-3608; *Instr* Chris Koivisto
Estab 1922, dept estab 1964; pub; D & E; SC 13, LC 5; D 63, E 15, non-maj 65, maj 13
Ent Req: HS dipl
Degrees: AA 2 yr
Courses: Art Appreciation, Art History, Ceramics, Drawing, Painting, Sculpture
Adult Hobby Classes: $105 per cr. Courses—Drawing, Introduction, Painting, Ceramics

GRAND MARAIS

GRAND MARAIS ART COLONY, PO Box 626, Grand Marais, MN 55604-0626. Tel 218-387-1284; Fax 218-387-1395; Email arts@boreal.org; Web: grandmaraisartcolony.org; *Faculty* Kelly Dupre; *Faculty* Hazel Belvo; *Faculty* Sharon Frykman; *Faculty* Steve Frykman; *Faculty* Naomi Hart; *Faculty* Karen Knutson; *Faculty* Susan Frame; *Instr* Joann Krause; *Instr* Jeanne Larson; *Faculty* Michaelin Otis
Estab 1947; D & E; Scholarships; SC 4; D 200
Ent Req: Open
Courses: Drawing, Painting, Pastels, Personal Creativity
Adult Hobby Classes: Enrl 200; tuition same as above; 15 wks of 1 - 2 wk workshops. Courses—Drawing, Painting,
Children's Classes: Enrl 50; tuition $70 for 1 full wk. Courses—Drawing, Mixed Media, Painting
Summer School: Dir, Jay Andersen. Courses—Drawing, Painting, Watercolor

HIBBING

HIBBING COMMUNITY COLLEGE, Art Dept, 1515 E 25th St, Hibbing, MN 55746-3300. Tel 218-262-6700; Web: www.hcc.mnscu.edu; *Instr* Theresa Chudzik; *Instr* Bill Goodman
Pub; D&E; Scholarships
Degrees: AA & AAS 2 yrs
Courses: Art Appreciation, Ceramics, Design, Drawing, Introduction to Theatre, Painting, Photography, Sculpture, Stage Craft

MANKATO

BETHANY LUTHERAN COLLEGE, Art Dept, 700 Luther Dr, Mankato, MN 56001-6163. Tel 507-344-7000; Fax 507-344-7376; Web: www.blc.edu; *Head of Dept* William Bukowski
Estab 1927, dept estab 1960; FT 2, PT 3; den; D; Scholarships; SC 2, LC 2; D 36, non-maj 40, maj 18
Ent Req: HS dipl, ACT
Degrees: AA 2 yr, dipl
Courses: †3-D Design, Art Appreciation, Art History, Art Structure, Ceramics, †Computer Graphics, Design, Drawing, Painting, †Web Design
Summer School: Dir, William Bukowski. Enrl 20; tuition $130 for 2 wk - 1 1/2 days

MANKATO STATE UNIVERSITY, Art Dept, PO Box 8400, MSU Box 42 Mankato, MN 56002-8400. Tel 507-389-6412; Web: www.mankato.ms.us.edu; WATS 507-389-5887
Estab 1868, dept estab 1938; FT 15; pub; D & E; Scholarships; SC 42, LC 28, GC 54; D 3000 (total), E 500, non-maj 1000, maj 200, grad 25
Ent Req: HS dipl
Degrees: BA, BFA and BS 4 yr, MA and MS 1-1 1/2 yr
Courses: Art Education, Art History, Ceramics, Drawing, Fibers, Graphic Arts, Painting, Photography, Printmaking, Sculpture
Summer School: Tuition same as above

MINNEAPOLIS

ART INSTRUCTION SCHOOLS, Education Dept, 6465 Wayzata Blvd, Ste 240 Minneapolis, MN 55426-1723. Tel 612-362-5060; Email info@artists-ais.com; Web: www.artists-ais.edu; *Dir* Judith Turner
Estab 1914; pvt
Courses: Fundamentals of Art and Specialized Art
Adult Hobby Classes: Enrl 5000; tuition $1495 - $2000. Courses—Fundamentals of Art, Specialized Art

AUGSBURG COLLEGE, Art Dept, 2211 Riverside Ave, Minneapolis, MN 55454-1351. Tel 612-330-1285; Fax 612-330-1649; Email anderso3@augsburg.edu ; *Chmn* Kristin Anderson
Estab 1869, dept estab 1960; FT 3, PT 4; den; D & E; Scholarships; SC 15, LC 6; D 200, maj 60, others 1500
Ent Req: HS dipl
Degrees: BA 4 yrs
Tuition: $7235 per sem; campus res—room & board $4022
Courses: Art Education, Art History, Calligraphy, Ceramics, Communications Design, Drawing, Environmental Design, Handicrafts, History of Art & Architecture, Painting, Photography, Sculpture, Stage Design, Teacher Training, Theatre Arts
Adult Hobby Classes: Enrl 1200; tuition $780 per course. Courses—Art History, Calligraphy, Ceramics, Communications Design, Drawing, Environmental Design, Painting, Publication Design
Summer School: Enrl 350; term of six or four wks beginning end of May

MINNEAPOLIS COLLEGE OF ART & DESIGN, 2501 Stevens Ave S, Minneapolis, MN 55404-4347. Tel 612-874-3700, 874-3754; Fax 612-874-3701; Email admissions@mcad.edu; Web: www.mcad.edu; *Chair Design Dept* Bernard Canniffe; *Prof Design Dept* Tom Garrett; *Prof* Jan Jancourt; *Prof* Elizabeth Erickson; *Prof* Rebecca Alm
Estab 1886; Maintains library; Morrison Bldg Rm 127, 2501 Stevens Ave S, Minneapolis, MN 55404; FT 32, PT 609; pvt; D; Scholarships; SC 82, LC 60, GC 3; D 650, E 325, maj 620, grad 40
Ent Req: HS dipl or GED
Degrees: BS & BFA 4 yr, MFA
Tuition: $21,300 annual tuition off campus, $25,000 annual tuition on campus
Courses: †Advertising Design, †Animation, †Comic Art, Computer Graphics, †Design Theory & Methods, †Drawing, †Film, †Furniture Design, †Graphic Arts, †Graphic Design, †Illustration, †Interactive Media, Liberal Arts, Packaging & Product Design, †Painting, †Photography, †Printmaking, Screen Printing, †Sculpture, Video, Web & Multimedia
Adult Hobby Classes: Continuing Studies
Children's Classes: Courses offered
Summer School: Dir of Continuing Studies, cost & enrollment varies. Professional, youth & enrichment courses.

UNIVERSITY OF MINNESOTA, MINNEAPOLIS, Art History, 271 19th Ave S, 338 Heller Hall Minneapolis, MN 55455-0121. Tel 612-624-4500; Fax 612-626-8679; Email arthist@umn.edu; Web: www.arthist.umn.edu; *Prof* Frederick Asher, PhD; *Prof* Gabriel P Weisberg, PhD; *Prof* Frederick A Cooper; *Prof* Sheila J McNally; *Prof* Karal Ann Marling, PhD; *Prof* Robert Poor, PhD; *Assoc Prof* John

Steyaert, PhD; *Prof* Robert Silberman, PhD; *Prof* Catherine Asher, PhD; *Assoc Prof* Jane Blocker, PhD; *Asst Prof* Michael Gaudio; *Chmn & Prof* Steven Ostrow, PhD
An on-campus shop where art supplies may be purchased; Pub; D & E; Scholarships; Fellowships; LC 28, GC 59; maj 68, grad 52
Ent Req: HS dipl, ent exam, GRE required for grad school
Degrees: BA 4 yrs, MA 2 yrs, PhD
Courses: †Art History, †Film, †History of Art & Archaeology
Adult Hobby Classes: Enrl 200; sem system. Courses—Ancient & Modern Art History, Asian Art History
Summer School: Dir, Steven Ostrow.
—**Dept of Art**, 405 21st Ave S, Minneapolis, MN 55455. Tel 612-625-8096; Fax 612-625-7881; Email artdept@umn.edu; Web: artdept.umn.edu; *Chmn Dept* Clarence Morgan, MFA; *Prof* Karl Bethke, MFA; *Prof* Curtis Hoard, MFA; *Prof* Thomas Rose, MA; *Prof* Mary Diane Katsiaficas, MFA; *Assoc Prof* Thomas Cowette, BFA; *Assoc Prof* David Feinberg, MFA; *Assoc Prof* Gary Hallman, MFA; *Assoc Prof* Lynn Gray, MFA; *Assoc Prof* James Henkel, MFA; *Assoc Prof* Guy Baldwin, MFA; *Assoc Prof* Jerald Krepps, MFA; *Assoc Prof* Thomas Lane, MFA; *Assoc Prof* Susan Lucey, MFA; *Assoc Prof* Marjorie Franklin, MFA; *Assoc Prof* Joyce Lyon, MFA; *Assoc Prof* Alexis Kuhr, MFA; *Assoc Prof* Wayne Potratz, MA; *Asst Prof* Christine Arle Baumler, MFA; *Asst Prof* Margaret Bohls, MFA; *Asst Prof* Lynn Lukkas, MFA; *Asst Prof* Ryuta Wakajima, MFA
Estab 1851, fine arts estab 1939; pub; D & E; Scholarships; SC 39, LC 7; D 1000, E 560, maj 325, grad 55
Ent Req: HS dipl, PSAT, ACT
Degrees: BA, BFA, MFA
Courses: Ceramics, Critical Theory, Drawing, Electronic Art, Neon, Painting, Papermaking, Photography, Printmaking, Sculpture, Silkscreening
Adult Hobby Classes: Courses—same as above
Children's Classes: Summers Honors College for HS students
Summer School: Dir, Carol Ann Dickinson. Courses—same as above
—**Split Rock Arts Program**, 1420 Eckles Ave, 360 Coffey Hall St Paul, MN 55108-1030. Tel 612-624-4000; Fax 612-624-6210; Email splitrockarts@umn.edu; Web: www.cce.umn.edu/splitrockarts; *Dir* Andrea Gilats; *Prog Assoc* Vivien Oja
Estab 1984; Scholarships; Enrl 550; Courses: Creativity Enhancement, Creative Writing, Fine Crafts, Visual Arts
Publications: Split Rock Arts Program catalog, annually
Tuition: $540 plus; campus res—$180-$516 per wk
Courses: Basketry, Beadworking, Bookmaking, †Ceramics, †Collage, Creativity Enhancement Fabric Art, †Design, †Drawing, †Fashion Arts, †Handicrafts, †Jewelry, †Mixed Media, †Painting, †Printmaking, Quiltmaking, †Sculpture, †Textile Design, †Weaving

MOORHEAD

CONCORDIA COLLEGE, Art Dept, 901 S Eighth, Moorhead, MN 56562. Tel 218-299-4623; Fax 218-299-4256, 299-3947; *Assoc Prof* David Boggs, MFA; *Asst Prof* Heidi Allen, MFA; *Asst Prof* Susan Pierson Ellingson, PhD, MFA; *Instr* John Borge, BA; *Prof* Duane Mickelson, MFA; *Asst Prof* Ross Hilgers; *Chair* Robert Meadows Rogers, PhD
Estab 1891; den; D&E; Scholarships; SC 10, LC 5; D 300, maj 80, total 2900
Ent Req: HS dipl, character references
Degrees: BA and BM 4 yrs, independent studio work, work-study prog and special studies
Courses: 2-D Foundations, 3-D Foundations, †Art Education, †Art History, Ceramics, Drawing, Figure Drawing, Graphic Design, Macintosh Computer Design Lab, Painting, Photography, Printmaking, Sculpture, Senior Project, †Studio Art
Summer School: Enrl 40; tuition $1200 for term of 4 wks beginning May 15 & June 12. Courses—Art Education, Art History, Drawing, Graphic Design, Painting, Printmaking, Travel Seminar, 2-D Foundation

MINNESOTA STATE UNIVERSITY-MOORHEAD, Dept of Art & Design, 1104 7th Ave S, Dille Center for the Arts Moorhead, MN 56563-0001. Tel 218-477-2151; 477-2152; Fax 218-477-5039; Email artdept@mnstate.edu; Web: www.mnstate.edu; *Prof* Allen Sheets, MFA; *Asst Prof* Anna Arnar, PhD; *Prof* Carl Oltvedt, MFA; *Asst Prof* Jim Park, MFA; *Assoc Prof* Donald Clark, MFA; *Assoc Prof* Zhimin Guan, MFA; *Asst Prof* Sherry Short, MFA; *Assoc Prof* Wil Shynkaruk, MFA; *Asst Prof* Bjorn Anderson, PhD; *Asst Prof* Brad Bachmeier, MFA; *Asst Prof* John Volk, MFA
Estab 1887; Maintains a nonprofit art gallery, Roland Dille Center for the Arts Gallery, MSUM Campus; Pub; D & E; Scholarships; SC 47, LC 20; D 7,500, maj 400
Ent Req: HS dipl
Degrees: BA, BS, BFA
Courses: †Art Appreciation, Art Education, Art History, Ceramics, †Design, Drawing, Graphic Design, †History of Art & Architecture, Illustration, Painting, Photography, Printmaking, Sculpture, Teacher Training

MORRIS

UNIVERSITY OF MINNESOTA, MORRIS, Humanities Division, 600 E 4th St, Morris, MN 56267. Tel 320-589-2211, 589-6251; Web: www.morris.umn.edu; *Chmn* Frederick Peterson PhD
Estab 1960, dept estab 1963; pub; D; Scholarships; SC 16, LC 8; D 195, non-maj 150, maj 45
Ent Req: top 50% in HS, ACT or PSAT
Degrees: BA 4 yrs
Courses: †Art History, †Studio Art, Teacher Training

NORTH MANKATO

SOUTH CENTRAL TECHNICAL COLLEGE, Commercial & Technical Art Dept, 1920 Lee Blvd, North Mankato, MN 56003-2504. Tel 507-389-7200; Web: www.sctc.mnscu.edu; *Instr* Kevin McLaughlin; *Instr* Robert Williams
Estab 1969; FT 2; pub; D; Scholarships; D 20
Ent Req: Portfolio
Degrees: AA 2 yr
Courses: Advertising Design, Calligraphy, Commercial Art, Conceptual Art, Desktop Publishing, Drafting, Drawing, Fashion Arts, Graphic Arts, Graphic Design, Illustration, Lettering, Mixed Media, Multi-Media, †Web Page Design

NORTHFIELD

CARLETON COLLEGE, Dept of Art & Art History, One N College St, Northfield, MN 55057. Tel 507-646-4341, 646-4000 (main); *Chmn* Alison Kettering
Estab 1921; pvt; Scholarships; SC 30, LC 20; maj 42, others 550
Degrees: 4 yr
Courses: †Art History, †Studio Art

SAINT OLAF COLLEGE, Art Dept, 1520 Saint Olaf Ave, Northfield, MN 55057-1574. Tel 507-786-3248; Web: www.stolaf.edu/art
Estab 1875, dept estab 1932; den; D & E; Scholarships
Ent Req: HS dipl, SAT
Degrees: BA 4 yr
Courses: †Art History

ROCHESTER

ROCHESTER COMMUNITY & TECHNICAL COLLEGE, Art Dept, 851 30th Ave SE, Rochester, MN 55904-4915. Tel 507-285-7215 (Pres), 285-7210 (main); Web: www.roch.edu; *Instr* Terry Richardson, MS; *Instr* Pat Kraemer, MS; *Instr* Terry Dennis, MS
Estab 1920s; pub; D & E; Scholarships; SC 17, LC 4; D & E 4000, maj 50
Ent Req: state req
Degrees: AAS, AA
Courses: Advertising Design, Art Appreciation, Art History, †Ceramics, Craft Design Series, Design, †Drawing, Fibers, †Graphic Design, Interior Design, Jewelry, †Painting, Photography, Printmaking, Sculpture, Stage Design, Theatre Arts, Weaving
Adult Hobby Classes: All areas, cr & non cr for variable tuition. Courses—Cartooning, & others on less regular basis
Summer School: Dir, A Olson. Art workshops are offered for at least one session each summer

SAINT CLOUD

SAINT CLOUD STATE UNIVERSITY, Dept of Art, 720 4th Ave S, KVAC Rm 101 Saint Cloud, MN 56301-4442. Tel 320-308-4283; Fax 320-308-2232; Email art@stcloudstate.edu; Web: www.stcloudstate.edu/~art; *Chair* David Sebberson
Estab 1869; FT 13, PT 6; Pub; D & E; SC 65, LC 15, GC 20; maj 400
Ent Req: HS dipl
Degrees: BA, BFA, BS, 4 yrs
Courses: †2-D Media, †3-D Media, Art History, Ceramics, Drawing, Graphic Design, †Integrated Media, Painting, Photography, Printmaking, Sculpture, Teacher Training
Summer School: Two terms

SAINT JOSEPH

COLLEGE OF SAINT BENEDICT, Art Dept, 37 S College Ave, Saint Joseph, MN 56374. Tel 320-363-5011; Web: www.csbjsu.edu; *Assoc Prof* Sr Baulu Kuan, MA; *Assoc Prof* James Hendershot, MA; *Asst Prof* Andrea Shaker, MFA; *Instr* Robert Wilde, MFA; *Chmn* Sr Dennis Frandrup
Estab 1913; joint studies with St John's University, Collegeville, MN; pvt; D & E; Scholarships; SC 21, LC 15; D 1893, maj 70
Ent Req: HS dipl, SAT, PSAT, ACT
Degrees: BA(Art) & BA(Art History) 4 yr, internships & open studio
Courses: †Art History, †Ceramics, †Drawing, Jewelry, Mixed Media, †Painting, †Photography, †Printmaking, †Sculpture

SAINT PAUL

BETHEL UNIVERSITY, Dept of Art & Design, 3900 Bethel Dr, Saint Paul, MN 55112-6999. Tel 651-638-6263; Fax 651-638-6001; Email cas-art@bethel.edu; Web: www.bethelcollege.edu; *Prof* Wayne L Roosa PhD; *Prof* Ken Steinbach, MFA; *Prof* Kirk Freeman, MFA; *Prof* Jeffrey Wetzig, MFA; *Prof* Lex Thompson, MFA; *Asst Prof* Jessica Henderson, MFA; *Assoc Prof* Michelle Westmark, MFA; *Assoc Prof* Amanda Hamilton, MFA
Estab 1871; Maintains 2 non-profit art galleries, Olson Gallery & Johnson Gallery (same address as school); on campus shop where art supplies may be purchased; FT 7; pvt; D&E; Scholarships; SC 29, LC 7; D, non-maj 100, maj 60
Activities: schols offered
Ent Req: HS dipl, SAT, ACT, PSAT or NMSQT, evidence of a standard of faith & practice that is compatible to Bethel lifestyle
Degrees: BA(Art Educ), BA(Art History) & BA(Studio Arts) 4 yr, BFA
Tuition: $43,000
Courses: 2-D Design, 3-D Design, †Advertising Design, †Art Education, †Art History, †Ceramics, †Drawing, †Graphic Design, †Painting, †Photography, †Printmaking, †Sculpture

CONCORDIA UNIVERSITY, Art and Design Department, 1282 Concordia Avenue, Saint Paul, MN 55104. Tel 651-641-8743; Fax 651-654-0207; Web: www.csp.edu; *Prof* Stephanie Hunder; *Chmn* Keith Williams; *Term Professor* Cate Vermelznd; *Term Professor* John DuFresne; *Instructor* Erin Maurelli; *Instructor* James O'Brien; *Instructor* Brad Daniels; *Instructor* Alonso Sierzha; *Instructor* Kathryn Swan; *Instructor* Megan Johnston; *Instructor* Michelle Daniels

Estab 1897, dept estab 1967; Maintains a non-profit art gallery: Concordia Gallery; Maintains an art/architecture library: H. Williams Teaching Gallery, 1201 Marshall Ave., St. Paul, MN 55104; Maintains an on-campus shop where art supplies may be purchased; den; D & E; Scholarships; SC 14, LC 3; D 84, E 20, others 35
Ent Req: HS dipl
Degrees: BS BA 4 yrs, BFA 4 yrs
Courses: Advertising Design, Aesthetics, Art Education, Art History, Ceramics, Drawing, Graphic Design, Jewelry, Painting, Photography, Printmaking, Sculpture, Teacher Training, Theatre Arts, Typography
Summer School: Courses—Art Educ Methods, Art Fundamentals

HAMLINE UNIVERSITY, Dept of Studio Arts & Art History, 1536 Hewitt Ave, Saint Paul, MN 55104-1205. Tel 651-523-2296; Fax 651-523-3066; Web: www.hamline.edu/depts/art/; *Artist-in-Residence* Leonardo Lasansky, MFA; *Assoc Prof* Andrew Wykes MFA; *Dept Chair, Assoc Prof* Aida Audeh, PhD; *Dir Soeffker Gallery & Permanent Coll, Lectr* John-Mark Schlink, MFA; *Vis Asst Prof* Bruce Thomas; *Vis Asst Prof* Ann Paulk, PhD; *Vis Asst Prof* Elizabeth Avery PhD; *Vis Asst Prof* Kate Fisher, MFA; *Vis Asst Prof* Steve Stenzel, MFA; *Vis Asst Prof* Krista Walsh, MFA; *Vis Asst Prof* Jessica Streit, PhD
Estab 1854; maintain non-profit art gallery, Soeffker Gallery, Drew Fine Arts Bldg, same address; pvt; D & E; Scholarships; SC 18, LC 7; non-maj 70, maj 35
Activities: Schols offered
Ent Req: HS dipl
Degrees: BA 4 yrs
Courses: Art Education, †Art History, Drawing, †Painting, †Photography, †Printmaking, Sculpture
Summer School: Dean, John Matachek

MACALESTER COLLEGE, Art & Art History Dept, 1600 Grand Ave, Saint Paul, MN 55105-1899. Tel 651-696-6279; Fax 651-696-6266; Email godollei@macalester.edu; Web: www.macalester.edu; *Chair & Prof* Ruthann Godollei; *Assoc Prof* Stanton Sears; *Assoc Prof* Christine Willcox; *Assoc Prof* Joanne Inglot; *Asst Prof* Kari Shepherdson-Scott; *Instr* Gary Erickson; *Instr* Megan Vossler; *Instr* Eric Carrol
Estab 1946; Maintains nonprofit Law Warschaw Gallery, Janet Wallace Fine Art Center, 1600 Grand Ave, St Paul, MN 55105 & Macalester College Library; pvt; D & E; Scholarships; SC 31, LC 15, GC 1; Maj 20
Ent Req: 4 yrs secondary school, SAT or ACT test
Degrees: BA(Art) 4 yrs
Tuition: $46,000
Courses: †Architecture, †Art History, Art of China, Art of Japan, †Ceramics, †Design, Dissent, †Drawing, †Graphic Design, †History of Art & Architecture, Intro to Visual Culture, †Painting, †Photography, †Printmaking, Race, Class & Gender in American Art, †Sculpture, The Mural, †Video

ST CATHERINE UNIVERSITY, Art & Art History Dept, 2004 Randolph, Saint Paul, MN 55105. Tel 651-690-6636, 690-6000; Web: www.stkate.edu; *Chmn & Assoc Prof* Todd Deutsch; *Assoc Prof* Pat Olson; *Assoc Prof* Carol Lee Chase; *Asst Prof* Amy Hamlin; *Asst Prof* Tamsie Ringler
Dept estab 1915; Maintains a nonprofit art gallery - Catherine G. Murphy Gallery (same location); maintains an art/architecture library - Visual Resources Library.; FT 3, PT 5; Pvt, (Women only); D & E; Scholarships; SC, LC; Maj 65
Activities: Schols offered
Ent Req: HS dipl
Degrees: BA(Art) 4 yr
Tuition: $510 per cr hr, $21,000 per yr
Courses: Art & Technology, Art Appreciation, Art Education, †Art History, Ceramics, Drawing, Graphic Arts, Graphic Design, Illustration, Jewelry, Mixed Media, Museum Staff Training, Painting, Photography, Pottery, Printmaking, Publication Design, Sculpture, †Studio Art, Typography, Women in Art
Adult Hobby Classes: Special Workshops
Summer School: Enrl 30. Courses—Art Education, Art History, Art Studio

UNIVERSITY OF MINNESOTA, Dept of Design, Housing & Apparel, 1985 Buford Ave, 240 McNeal Hall Saint Paul, MN 55108-6136. Tel 612-624-9700; Web: www.dha.design.umn.edu; *Head Dept* Dr Elizabeth Bye
Dept estab 1851; Maintains non-profit art gallery - Goldstein Museum of Design, 364 McNeal Hall, 1985 Buford Ave, St Pau, MN 55108. Maintains architecture library, 89 Church St, 210 Rapson Hall, Minneapolis, MN 55455. Maintains an on-campus shop where art supplies may be purchased; Pub; D & E; SC 57, LC 54, GC 25; D 750 (fall 2015), grad 70
Ent Req: HS dipl; math requirement
Degrees: BS, BFA, MFA, MS, MA & PhD 4 yr
Tuition: Res—undergrad $1,064 per cr; grad $7,920, 6-14 cr; nonres—undergrad $1,712 per cr
Courses: †Applied Design, †Costume Design & Construction, Costume History, Decorative Arts, Design, Drawing, Graphic Arts, †Housing, †Interior Design, †Retail Merchandising, Textile Design, †Textiles Clothing
Summer School: Courses—vary each yr

UNIVERSITY OF ST THOMAS, Deptartment of Art History, 2115 Summit Ave, Mail 44C Saint Paul, MN 55105-1048. Tel 651-962-5560; Fax 651-962-5861; Email marria.thompson@stthomas.edu; Web: www.stthomas.edu/arthistory; *Prof* Mark Stansbury-O'Donnell; *Chair, Prof* Victoria Young; *Prof* Craig Eliason; *Prof* Shelly Nordtorp-Madson; *Prof* Elizabeth Kindall; *Prof* William Barnes; *Prof* Eric Kjellgren; *Prof* Heather Shirey; *Prof* Jayme Yahr
Estab 1885, dept estab 1978; Maintains a nonprofit art gallery: O'Shaughnessy Educational Center Lobby Gallery, St. Paul American Museum of Asmat Art, St. Paul; FT 8 Adjuncts 6; Pvt; D & E; Scholarships; LC 8, GC 6; D 2847, E 275, maj 10
Ent Req: HS dipl
Degrees: BA 4 yrs, MA 2yrs
Courses: Architecture, †Art History, Design, History of Art & Architecture, Museum Staff Training
Summer School: Dir, Heather Shirey

SAINT PETER

GUSTAVUS ADOLPHUS COLLEGE, Art & Art History Dept, 800 W College Ave, Schaefer Fine Arts Ctr Saint Peter, MN 56082-1485. Tel 507-933-8000, 933-7019; Web: www.gustavus.edu; *Chmn* Linnea Wren
Estab 1876; FT 8, PT 2; den; D; Scholarships; SC 27; 2300 total, 750 art, maj 50
Ent Req: HS grad, ent exam
Degrees: BA 4 yr
Courses: Art Appreciation, †Art Education, †Art History, Basic Design, Bronze Casting, Ceramics, Design, Drawing, Painting, Photography, Printmaking, Sculpture, †Studio Art, Teacher Training
Summer School: Independent Study prog for three 4 wk periods during June, July or Aug

WHITE BEAR LAKE

CENTURY COLLEGE, Humanities Dept, 3300 Century Ave N, White Bear Lake, MN 55110-1842. Tel 651-779-3200; Fax 651-779-3417; Web: www.cedntury.edu; *Instr* Mel Sundby; *Instr* Karin McGinness; *Chmn* Kenneth Maeckelbergh; *Instr* Dawn Saks; *Instr* Larry Vienneau; *Instr* Mary Aspness
Estab 1968; Maintains Century College Art Gallery on campus; pub; D, E & Sat; Scholarships; SC 20, LC 8; D 75, E 30
Degrees: AA
Tuition: Res—$95.76 per sem cr; nonres—$181.41 per sem cr
Courses: American Art, Art Appreciation, Art History, Art Therapy, Calligraphy, Ceramics, Design, Drawing, Film, Graphic Arts, Graphic Design, Interior Design, Lettering, Painting, Photography, Theatre Arts, Video
Adult Hobby Classes: Enrl 6000; tuition varies. 39 courses offered
Children's Classes: Enrl 500; tuition under $100 each course. 30 courses offered
Summer School: Dean Sue Ehlers. Tuition $181.41 per cr

WILLMAR

RIDGEWATER COLLEGE, Art Dept, 2101 15th Ave NW, Willmar, MN 56201-3096. Tel 320-231-5102, 231-5132; Fax 320-231-6602; Web: www.ridgewater.mnscu.edu; *Chmn Art Dept & Coordr Art Gallery* Robert Mattson
Estab 1962-63; pub; D & E; SC 8, LC 3; D 50, maj 15
Ent Req: HS dipl
Degrees: AA & AS 2 yrs
Courses: Art Education, Ceramics, Display, Drawing, Graphic Arts, Graphic Design, History of Art & Architecture, Introduction to Studio Practices, Painting, Structure, Teacher Training
Adult Hobby Classes: Courses—Ceramics, Design, History of Art, Painting

WINONA

SAINT MARY'S UNIVERSITY OF MINNESOTA, Art & Design Dept, 700 Terrace Heights, Winona, MN 55987. Tel 507-457-1593; Fax 507-457-6967; Web: www.smumn.edu; WATS 800-635-5987; *Prof* Margaret Mear, MFA; *Prof* Roderick Robertson, MFA; *Chair* Preston Lawing; *Prof* Robert McCall; *Instr* Michelle Cochran; *Instr* Charles Campbell; *Instr* John Whelan
Estab 1912, dept estab 1970; Nonprofit - Lillian Davis Hogan Galleries, 700 Terrace Heights, Winona, MN 55987; Den; D; Scholarships; SC 20, LC 6; in school D 1,390
Ent Req: HS dipl
Degrees: BA 4 yrs
Courses: Art Appreciation, Art History, Ceramics, Computer Design, Design, Drawing, †Electronic Publishing, †Graphic Design, Illustration, Painting, Photography, Printmaking, Sculpture, †Studio Arts, †Studio Arts, Theatre Arts

WINONA STATE UNIVERSITY, Dept of Art, PO Box 5838, Winona, MN 55987. Tel 507-457-5395; Fax 507-457-5086; Web: www.winona.edu; *Prof* Judy Schlawin, MS; *Assoc Prof* Don Schmidlapp, MFA
Estab 1860; pub; D & E; Scholarships
Degrees: BA and BS
Courses: Art Education, Art History, Ceramics, Drawing, Graphic Design, Interior Design, Lettering, Painting, Printmaking, Sculpture, Weaving
Summer School: Courses offered

MISSISSIPPI

BLUE MOUNTAIN

BLUE MOUNTAIN COLLEGE, Art Dept, Box 296, Blue Mountain, MS 38610. Tel 662-685-4771, Ext 162; Web: www.bmc.edu; *Chmn Dept* William Dowdy, MA
Estab 1873, dept estab 1875; FT 2; den; D & E; Scholarships; SC 16, LC 2; D 28, E 12, non-maj 20, maj 8, others 12
Ent Req: HS dipl
Degrees: BA & BS(Educ) 4 yr
Courses: Art History, Commercial Art, Drawing, Painting
Adult Hobby Classes: Enrl 12; tuition $42 per sem hr. Courses—Drawing, Painting
Summer School: Dir, William Dowdy. Enrl 20

BOONEVILLE

NORTHEAST MISSISSIPPI JUNIOR COLLEGE, Art Dept, 101 Cunningham, Booneville, MS 38829. Tel 662-728-7751, Ext 229; Web: www.necc.cc.ms.us; *Instr*

Terry Anderson; *Instr* Judy Tucci; *Chmn* Jerry Rains; *Chair Visual Arts* Marty McLendon
Estab 1948; Anderson Hall Art Gallery; FT 3, PT 1; pub; D & E; Scholarships; SC 6, LC 3; D 2800, maj 30
Ent Req: HS dipl, ent exam
Degrees: 2 yr Assoc degrees in art educ, fine arts and interior design
Courses: Advertising Design, Aesthetics, Art Education, Art History, Ceramics, Design, Drafting, Drawing, Painting, Teacher Training, Theatre Arts
Adult Hobby Classes: Watercolor

CLARKSDALE

COAHOMA COMMUNITY COLLEGE, Art Education & Fine Arts Dept, 3240 Friars Pt Rd, Clarksdale, MS 38614. Tel 662-627-2571, Ext 208; *Chmn* Henry Dorsey
Degrees: AA
Tuition: In district—$700 per yr; res—$2511.70 per yr; outside district $1100 per yr; outside state $2100 per yr; out of district boarding $2911.70 per yr, out of state boarding $3911.70 per yr
Courses: Art Appreciation, Art Education, Art History, Drawing, Handicrafts, Intro to Art
Adult Hobby Classes: Enrl 15-32; tuition $27.50 per sem hr. Courses—Art & Music Appreciation

CLEVELAND

DELTA STATE UNIVERSITY, Dept of Art, 1003 W Sunflower Rd, Cleveland, MS 38733-0001. Tel 662-846-4720; Web: www.deltastate.edu; *Chmn* Ron Koehler; *Prof* William Carey Lester Jr; *Prof* Kim Rushing; *Prof* Patricia Brown; *Assoc Prof* Joseph Abide; *Asst Prof* M Duncan Baird; *Asst Prof* Benjamin Johnston; *Asst Prof* Allison Melton; *Asst Prof* Cetin Oguz; *Asst Prof* Robyn Moore; *Instr* Mollie Rollins Rushing; *Prof* Dr Cliff McMahon
Estab 1924; Maintain nonprofit art gallery; Wright Art Center Gallery; on-campus shop for art supplies; FT 10 PT 2; pub; D & E; Scholarships; SC 42, LC 10, GC 30; maj 160
Ent Req: HS dipl
Degrees: BA & BFA
Courses: †Advertising Design, †Art Appreciation, †Art Education, Art History, Ceramics, Computer Graphics, †Design, Drawing, Fibers, †Film, †Graphic Design, Illustration, †Painting, †Photography, Printmaking, †Sculpture, †Video, †Weaving
Summer School: Tuition & living expenses $488 per term, June 2 - July 3 or July 7 - Aug 8. Courses—Art for Elementary, Ceramics, Drawing, Internship in Commercial Design, Introduction to Art, Painting, Sculpture

CLINTON

MISSISSIPPI COLLEGE, Art Dept, 200 S Capitol, Box 4020 Clinton, MS 39058-0001. Tel 601-925-3231; Fax 601-925-7732; Email art@mcedu; Web: www.mc.edu/campus/academics/arts; *Head Art Dept* Randy B Miley
Estab 1825, dept estab 1950; Maintains a non-profit art gallery - Samuel Marshal Gore Galleries, 199 Monroe St, Clinton, MS 39056. Also maintains art/architecture library in Aven - 200 S Capitol St, Clinton, MS 39058; FT 5, PT 1; den; D, E & online; Scholarships; Assistantships; SC 71, LC 23, GD 42, OL & HB 14; maj 136, non-maj 350, GS 28
Ent Req: HS dipl, BA, BS, BE(Art), MA(Art) and ME(Art) 4 yr, Freshman Art merit
Degrees: BA, BS, BFA, BSED, MFA, MS, MED
Tuition: $477 per credit hr
Courses: Aesthetics, †Art Education, †Art History, †Ceramics, Design, †Drawing, †Graphic Design, †Interior Design, †Painting, Papermaking, †Sculpture
Adult Hobby Classes: Enrl 50; tuition $35 for 5 weeks. Courses—Calligraphy, Drawing, Flower Arranging, Painting
Summer School: Dir, Dr Randy Miley. Tuition $1,437 for two 6-wk terms. Courses—Ceramics, Drawing, Painting, Printmaking, Papermaking

COLUMBUS

MISSISSIPPI UNIVERSITY FOR WOMEN, Division of Fine & Performing Arts, 1100 College St, W 70, Columbus, MS 39701-5800. Tel 662-329-7341; Web: www.muw.edu/fine_arts/; *Head Dept* Dr Michael Garrett; *Prof* David Frank; *Prof* Thomas Nawrocki, MFA; *Asst Prof* Robert Gibson, MFA; *Asst Prof* John Alford, MFA
Estab 1884; FT 8, PT 3; pub; D & E; Scholarships; SC 49, LC 8; D 263, E 39, non-maj 45, maj 72
Ent Req: HS dipl, ACT, SAT
Degrees: BA, BS and BFA 4 yrs
Courses: Architectural Construction & Materials, †Art Education, Art History, Calligraphy, Ceramics, Commercial Art, Conceptual Art, Graphic Design, Illustration, †Interior Design, Lettering, †Metal Art, Mixed Media, †Painting, Photography, †Printmaking, Sculpture, Stage Design, Teacher Training, †Theatre Arts, Weaving
Adult Hobby Classes: Courses—Drawing, Painting, Weaving
Summer School: Courses—Vary according to demand

DECATUR

EAST CENTRAL COMMUNITY COLLEGE, Art Dept, PO Box 129, Decatur, MS 39327-0129. Tel 601-635-2121; Email bguraedy@eccc.cc.ms.us; Web: www.eccc.edu; *Head Dept* J Bruce Guraedy, MEd; *Art Instr* Todd Eldridge
Estab 1928, dept estab 1965; pub; D, E & Sat; Scholarships; SC 10, LC 8; D 175, E 70, non-maj 100, maj 10
Ent Req: HS dipl, GED
Degrees: AA and AS 2 yrs
Courses: Advertising Design, Art Appreciation, Art Education, Art History, Ceramics, Collage, Design, Drafting, Drawing, Fashion Arts, Handicrafts, Illustration, Industrial Design, Interior Design, Landscape Architecture, Mixed Media, Painting, Printmaking, Sculpture, Stage Design, Theatre Arts
Adult Hobby Classes: Enrl 15; tuition $100 per sem for 10 wks. Courses—Beginning Painting, Drawing, Painting
Children's Classes: Kid's College & pvt lessons available
Summer School: Vice Pres of Continuing Educ, Gene Davis. Enrl 300 - 400; tuition $50 per sem hr for term of 10 wks. Courses—vary according to student demand

ELLISVILLE

JONES COUNTY JUNIOR COLLEGE, Art Dept, 900 S Court St, Ellisville, MS 39437-3999. Tel 601-477-4148, 477-4000; Fax 601-477-4017; *Chmn Fine Arts* Jeff Brown
Estab 1927; pub; D; Scholarships; SC 12, LC 4; D 100, E 12, maj 15, others 12
Ent Req: HS dipl
Degrees: AA 2 yrs
Adult Hobby Classes: Enrl 20. Courses—Painting
Summer School: Term of 4 wks beginning June. Courses—same as regular session

GAUTIER

MISSISSIPPI GULF COAST COMMUNITY COLLEGE-JACKSON COUNTY CAMPUS, Art Dept, PO Box 100, Gautier, MS 39553-0100. Tel 228-497-9602; *Chmn Fine Arts Dept* Johnnie Gray, MA; *Instr (2-D)* Mary Hardy, MA; *Instr (3-D)* Kevin Turner
Maintains nonprofit gallery, MGCCC/Jackson County Campus Fine Arts Gallery P. O. Box 100, Gautier MS 39553; Pub; D & E; Scholarships; SC 9, LC 2; D 90, E 8, non-maj 62, maj 28
Degrees: AA, 2 yrs
Tuition: Res—$65 per cr
Courses: †3-D Design, Art Appreciation, Art Education, †Art for Elementary Teachers, Ceramics, Design, Drawing, Painting, Sculpture

HATTIESBURG

UNIVERSITY OF SOUTHERN MISSISSIPPI, Dept of Art & Design, 118 College Dr (#5033), Hattiesburg, MS 39406-0002. Tel 601-266-4972; Fax 601-266-6379; Email johnhouse@usm.edu; Web: www.vsm.edu/visualarts; *Prof* James Meade, Jr, MFA; *Chair Prof* John House, MFA; *Prof* Janet Gorzegno, MFA; *Prof* Deanna Douglas, MFA; *Mus Dir* Mark Riesby; *Assoc Prof* Jennifer Torres
Estab 1910; Maintain a nonprofit art gallery, USM Museum of Art, also maintain an art/architecture library; on-campus shop where art supplies may be purchased and Barnes & Noble book store; FT 9, PT 6; pub; D & E; Scholarships; SC 64, LC 41, GC 20; non-maj 35, maj 120, grad 5
Ent Req: HS dipl
Degrees: BA, BS, BFA, MAE
Courses: Art History, †Ceramics, †Design, Drawing, †Graphic Design, †Mixed Media, Painting, Photography, Printmaking, Sculpture

ITTA BENA

MISSISSIPPI VALLEY STATE UNIVERSITY, Fine Arts Dept, 14000 Highway 82 W, Itta Bena, MS 38941-1401. Tel 662-254-3482; Fax 662-254-3485; Email lhorn@musu.edu; Web: www.mvsu.edu.com; *Co-Gallery Dir* Dorothy Vaughn; *Co-Dir Gallery* Ronald Minks; *Acting Head* Lawrence Horn; *Assoc Prof Art* Frank Hardmon; *Asst Prof Art* Charles Davis
Estab 1952; SC 8, LC 2; pub; D & E
Ent Req: HS dipl
Degrees: BA & BS
Tuition: Res—undergrad $2094.50 per sem; out-of-state—$3074.50
Courses: 2 & 3-D Design, African American Art History, Art Appreciation, Art History, Arts & Crafts, Ceramics, Color Fundamentals, Commercial Art, Drawing, Graphic Arts, Illustration, Painting, Photography, Printmaking, Public School Art, Typography, Visual Communications
Summer School: Courses—Art Appreciation, Public School Art

JACKSON

BELHAVEN COLLEGE, Art Dept, 1500 Peachtree St, Jackson, MS 39202-1789. Tel 601-968-5950; Fax 601-968-9998; Email mhause@belhaven.edu; Web: belhaven.edu; *Asst Prof Art* William Morse; *Asst Prof Art History* Melissa Hause; *Asst Prof of Art* Nate Theisen; *Instr* Gretchen Haien; *Instr* Sam Beibers
Estab 1883, dept estab 1889; Maintain nonprofit art gallery, Bessie Cary Lemly Gallery, Belhaven College, 1500 Peachtree St, Jackson, MS 39202; den; D & E; Scholarships; SC 6; D 650, E 200, maj 30
Ent Req: HS dipl
Degrees: BA
Courses: Aesthetics, Art Appreciation, Art Education, Art History, Design, Drawing, Graphic Design, Painting, Photography, Printmaking, Sculpture

JACKSON STATE UNIVERSITY, Dept of Art, 1400 John R Lynch St, Jackson, MS 39217-0001. Tel 601-979-2040; Fax 601-968-7010; Email liberalarts@jsums.edu; Web: www.jsums.edu; *Chmn* John M Sullivan; *Assoc Prof* Hyun Chong Kim; *Assoc Prof* Charles W Carraway; *Assoc Prof* Lealan Swanson
Estab 1949; Maintain nonprofit art gallery; pub; D; Scholarships; SC 16, LC 7, GC 1; D 486, maj 57
Ent Req: HS dipl
Degrees: BA & BS(maj in Art) 4 yrs

Courses: Art History, Ceramics, Commercial Art, Drawing, Graphic Arts, Painting, Studio Crafts
Adult Hobby Classes: Athenian Art Club activities
Children's Classes: Enrl 75; tuition $100. Courses—General Art
Summer School: Dir, B Graves. Enrl 3000; tuition $100. Courses—Art Education, Painting

MILLSAPS COLLEGE, Dept of Art, 1701 N State St, Jackson, MS 39210-0001. Tel 601-974-1000, 974-1432; Web: www.millsaps.edu; *Chmn* Elise Smith, MFA; *Asst Prof* Collin Asmus, MA; *Instr* Kay Holloway, MFA; *Instr* Sandra Smithson; *Instr* Steven Jones
Estab 1913, dept estab 1970; priv; D & E; Scholarships; LC 4; non maj 100, maj 20
Ent Req: HS dipl, SAT combined 1100 average
Degrees: BA 4 yr
Courses: Aesthetics, Architecture, Art History, Calligraphy, Ceramics, Design, Drawing, History of Art & Architecture, Lettering, Museum Staff Training, Painting, Photography, Printmaking, Sculpture, Stage Design, Teacher Training, Textile Design, Theatre Arts, Weaving
Adult Hobby Classes: Tuition $35 per class
Children's Classes: Limited courses

LENA

SIMON MICHAEL SCHOOL OF FINE ARTS, 477 Maze Rd, Lena, MS 39094-9681. Tel 361-729-6233; *Head Dept* Simon Michael
Estab 1947; FT 1; pvt; professionals & intermediates
Courses: Drawing, Landscape Architecture, Mixed Media, Painting, Sculpture
Summer School: Enrl varies; tuition varies for each 1 wk workshop. Courses—Travel Art Workshop in USA and Europe

LORMAN

ALCORN STATE UNIVERSITY, Dept of Fine Arts, 1000 ASU Dr, No 29, Lorman, MS 39096-7500. Tel 601-877-6271, 877-6100; Fax 601-877-6262; *Instr* John Buchanan; *Chmn* Joyce Bolden PhD
Estab 1871, dept estab 1973; pub; D & E; SC 9, LC 3
Ent Req: HS dipl, ACT
Courses: Art Appreciation, Art Education, Ceramics, Drawing, Painting
Adult Hobby Classes: Drawing, Graduate Level Art Education, Painting
Summer School: Courses—Art Education, Fine Arts

MOORHEAD

MISSISSIPPI DELTA COMMUNITY COLLEGE, Dept of Fine Arts, Hwy 3 & Cherry St, Moorhead, MS 38761; PO Box 668, Moorhead, MS 38761-0668. Tel 662-246-6322; Fax 662-246-6321; Web: www.mdcc.cc.ms.us; *Coordr* Wallace Mallette; *Coordr* Cindy Ray; *Chmn* Simone Strawbridge; *Instr* Nancy Stone-Street
Estab 1926; pub; D & E; Scholarships; SC 11, LC 2; D 68, E 29, maj 28
Ent Req: HS dipl, ent exam
Degrees: AA 2 yrs
Courses: Advertising Design, Art Appreciation, Art Education, Art History, Ceramics, Design, Drawing, Graphic Arts, Painting, Printmaking, Sculpture, Stage Design, Theatre Arts
Adult Hobby Classes: Enrl 29. Courses—Ceramics, Painting

POPLARVILLE

PEARL RIVER COMMUNITY COLLEGE, Visual Arts, Dept of Fine Arts & Communication, 101 Hwy 11 N, Poplarville, MS 39470-2216. Tel 601-403-1000; Email cnull@prcc.edu; Web: www.prcc.edu; *Chmn* James A Rawls; *Instr* Charleen A Null; *Instr Art* Anna Holsten
Estab 1921; FT 1, PT 2; pub; D & E; Scholarships; SC 4, LC 2; D 85 - 100, non-maj 65 - 75, maj 20 - 25, E 20 - 40, non-maj 20 - 30, maj 10 - 20
Ent Req: HS dipl or ACT Score & GED
Degrees: AA
Courses: Art Appreciation, Art Education, Art History, Calligraphy, Design, Drafting, Drawing, Elementary Art Education, Handicrafts, Interior Design, Introduction to Art, Painting, Photography, Teacher Training

RAYMOND

HINDS COMMUNITY COLLEGE, Dept of Art, 501 E Main St, Raymond, MS 39154-9700; PO Box 1100, Raymond, MS 39154-9799. Tel 601-857-3275; 5261; Fax 601-857-3392; Email info@hindscc.edu; Web: www.hindscc.edu; *Chmn and Gallery Director* Sarah Teasley; *Instr* Melanie Atkinson; *Instr* Randy Minton; *Instr* Lee McCarty
Estab 1917; Maintain nonprofit art gallery; Marie Hull Gallery, Art Department, Hinds Community College, Raymond, MS 39154-1100; FT 4; pub; D & E; Scholarships; SC 12, LC 3; D 500, E 20
Activities: Schls offered
Degrees: AA 2 yr
Tuition: In-state $1,960
Courses: Art Appreciation, Art Education, Art History, Ceramics, Commercial Art, †Computer Art, Design, Drawing, Graphic Arts, Graphic Design, Landscape Architecture, Painting, Photography
Adult Hobby Classes: Courses offered
Summer School: Dir, Sarah Teasley. Enrl 24; tuition $165 for 8 wk term. Courses—Art Appreciation

STARVILLE

MISSISSIPPI STATE UNIVERSITY, Dept of Art, Starville, MS; PO Box 5182, Mississippi State, MS 39762-5182. Tel 662-325-2970, 325-2323 (main), 325-2224 (admis), 325-6900 (art dept); Fax 662-325-3850; Email da@ra.msstate.edu; Web: www.caad.msstate.edu; *Head* Kay DeMarsche, MFA; *Prof* Brent Funderburk, MFA; *Prof* Marita Gootee, MFA; *Prof* Robert Long, MFA; *Prof* Jamie Mixon, MFA; *Prof* Linda Seckinger; *Assoc Prof* Tim McCourt, MFA; *Assoc Prof* Soon Ee Ngoh, MFA; *Assoc Prof* Jeffrey Haupt, MFA; *Assoc Prof* Patrick Miller, MFA; *Assoc Prof* Jamie Runnells, MFA; *Asst Prof* Angi Bourgeois, PhD; *Asst Prof* Ben Harvey, PhD; *Instr* Bill Andrews, MFA; *Asst Prof* Critz Campbell, MFA; *Asst Prof* James Davis, MFA; *Asst Prof* Rebecca Davis, MFA; *Asst Prof* Jason DeMarte, MFA; *Lectr* Chuck Galey, BFA; *Lectr* Jayson Triplett, MFA
Estab 1879, dept estab 1971; maintains nonprofit art gallery, Dept of Art Gallery, PO Box 5182, MS State, MS 39762; maintains art library, Giles Hall, MSU, MS 39759; on-campus shop where art supplies may be purchased; Pub; D&E; Scholarships; SC 80, LC 30; D 750, non-maj 650, maj 300
Ent Req: HS dipl
Degrees: BFA 4-5 yrs
Courses: †Art Appreciation, Art History, Ceramics, †Design, Drawing, †Fine Art, †Graphic Design, †Museum Staff Training, Painting, Photography, Printmaking, Sculpture
Adult Hobby Classes: Enrl 40; tuition $1,700 per yr. Courses—Drawing, Fundamentals, Painting

TOUGALOO

TOUGALOO COLLEGE, Art Dept, 500 W County Line Rd, Tougaloo College Div of Humanities Tougaloo, MS 39174-9700. Tel 601-977-4431; Fax 601-977-4425; Web: www.tougaloo.edu; *Dean Humanities* Andrea Montgomery, PhD
Estab 1869, dept estab 1968

UNIVERSITY

UNIVERSITY OF MISSISSIPPI, Department of Art, Oxford, MS; 116 Meek Hall, University, MS 38677; PO Box 1848, University, MS 38677-1848. Tel 662-915-7193 (art dept); Fax 662-915-5013; Email art@olemiss.edu; Web: www.olemiss.edu/depts/art; *Assoc Prof* Tom Dewey II, PhD, MA; *Prof* Paula Temple, MFA; *Assoc Prof* Betty Crouther, PhD, MFA; *Prof* Aileen Ajootian, PhD, MA; *Prof* Nancy Wicker, PhD; *Prof* Jan Murray, MFA; *Chair & Prof* Sheri Rieth, MFA; *Assoc Prof* Virginia Chavis; *Assoc Prof* Matt Long; *Assoc Prof* Brooke White; *Assoc Prof* Durant Thompson; *Asst Prof* Philip Jackson; *Asst Prof* Lou Haney
Dept estab 1949; Maintains a nonprofit art gallery & on-campus shop where art supplies may be purchased; FT 12, PT 13; pub; D, online; Scholarships; Financial aid; SC 64, LC 45, GC 25, other 9; non-maj 350, maj 265, grad 16
Ent Req: HS dipl
Degrees: BA 4 yr, BFA 4 yr, MFA 3 yr
Tuition: Res—undergrad $2,302 per sem; campus res—room $800-$966
Courses: †Art History, †Ceramics, Drawing, †Graphic Design, †Painting, †Photography, †Printmaking, †Sculpture
Summer School: Two 4 wk sessions beginning June. Courses—Art History, Drawing, Painting, Foundations

MISSOURI

BOLIVAR

SOUTHWEST BAPTIST UNIVERSITY, Art Dept, 1600 University Dr, Bolivar, MO 65613. Tel 417-326-1651, 328-1605; *Chmn* Wesley A Gott, MFA; *Adjunct Prof* Diane Callahan, BFA; *Asst Prof* John Gruber, MFA; *Adjunct Prof* Sandra Maupin, MA
Sch estab 1879, dept estab 1974; Maintains nonprofit gallery, Driskill Art Gallery, 1600 University Ave Bolivar, MO 65613; Den; D & E; Scholarships; SC 30, LC 3; D 150, E 20, maj 35
Ent Req: HS dipl
Degrees: BS, BA, MS, MBA & MPT
Tuition: Res & nonres—undergrad $5,000 per yr; campus res—room & board $3,100 per acad yr
Courses: †Art Education, Art History, †Ceramics, †Commercial Art, Costume Design & Construction, †Drawing, †Graphic Arts, Graphic Design, †Painting, †Photography, †Printmaking, †Sculpture, Stage Design, †Teacher Training, Theatre Arts
Adult Hobby Classes: Enrl 10; per hr for 15 weeks. Courses—Drawing, Painting, Photography
Summer School: Enrl 600; Dir Dr Bill Brown, Dean of Music, Arts & Letters, 4 wk term beginning in June, also a 4 wk term beginning in July. Courses—Internships

CANTON

CULVER-STOCKTON COLLEGE, Art Dept, 1 College Hill Canton, MO 63435-1299. Tel 217-231-6367, 231-6368; Fax 217-231-6611; Email croyer@culver.edu; Email jjorgen@culver.edu; Web: www.culver.edu/; *Assoc Prof* Joseph Jorgensen; *Prof* Gary Thomas
Estab 1853; pvt; D; Scholarships; SC 16, LC 6; 1030, maj 40
Ent Req: HS dipl, ACT or Col Board Ent Exam
Degrees: BFA & BA(Visual Arts), BS(Art Educ) & BS(Arts Management) 4 yrs

Courses: †Art Education, Art History, †Ceramics, Design, Drawing, †Graphic Design, Illustration, †Painting, †Photography, Printmaking, †Sculpture, Teacher Training
Summer School: Reg, Barbara Conover. Tuition $150 per cr hr. Courses—Various studio workshops

CAPE GIRARDEAU

SOUTHEAST MISSOURI STATE UNIVERSITY, Dept of Art, 1 University Plz, Art Bldg 306, Mail Stop 4500 Cape Girardeau, MO 63701-4710. Tel 573-651-2143, 651-2000; Web: www.smsu.edu; *Prof & Interim Chmn* Ron Clayton; *Assoc Prof* Lane Fabrick; *Assoc Prof* Pat Reagan; *Asst Prof* Louise Bodenheimer
Estab 1873, dept estab 1920; FT11; pub; D & E; Scholarships; SC 28, LC 10, GC 18; D 1300
Ent Req: HS dipl
Degrees: BS, BS(Educ) & BA 4 yrs, MAT
Courses: 3-D Design, Advertising Design, Art History, Ceramics, Color Composition, Commercial Art, Design Foundation, Drawing, Fiber, Graphic Design, Illustration, Lettering, Painting, Perceptive Art, Printmaking, Screen Printing, Sculpture, Silversmithing, Typography, Video Art Graphic

COLUMBIA

COLUMBIA COLLEGE, Art Dept, 1001 Rogers, Columbia, MO 65216-0001. Tel 573-875-8700; Fax 573-875-7209; Web: www.ccis.edu; *Instr* Sidney Larson, MA; *Instr* Ben Cameron, MA; *Instr* Richard Baumann, MFA; *Instr* Michael Sledd, MFA; *Chmn* Tom Watson; *Instr Photog & Ceramics* Ed Collings
Estab 1851; FT 5, PT 2; den; D; Scholarships; SC 55, LC 13; D 180, non-maj 80, maj 115
Ent Req: HS dipl or equivalent, ACT or SAT, also accept transfer students
Degrees: AA 2 yrs, BA, BS and BFA 4 yrs
Courses: Art History, Ceramics, Drawing, Fashion Arts, Graphic Arts, Graphic Design, Illustration, Painting, Photography
Adult Hobby Classes: Enrl 15; tuition $75 per cr. Courses—Arts & Crafts, Photography
Summer School: Evening Studies Dir, Dr John Hendricks. Enrl 20; tuition $75 per cr hr

STEPHENS COLLEGE, Art Dept, 1200 E Broadway, Columbia, MO 65215-0001. Tel 573-442-2211, Exten 4363; Email jterry@stephens.edu; Web: www.stephens.edu; *Instr* Robert Friedman; *Chair* Dr James H Terry; *Instr* Lillian Sung
Estab 1833, dept estab 1850; Maintain nonprofit art gallery; Davis Art Gallery; art supplies available on-campus; Pvt; D & E; Scholarships; SC 20, LC 11; D 450, maj 5, others 10
Ent Req: SAT or ACT, recommendations, interview
Degrees: BA 3-4 yrs, BFA 3 1/2-4 yrs
Courses: Advertising Design, Art Education, Art History, Ceramics, Commercial Art, Costume Design & Construction, Drawing, †Fashion Arts, Film, Graphic Arts, †Graphic Design, History of Art & Architecture, Illustration, Occupational Therapy, †Painting, †Photography, †Printmaking, †Sculpture, †Stage Design, Teacher Training, †Theatre Arts, †Video
Children's Classes: Tuition $900 per yr; Stephens Child Study Center, grades K-3, preschool; includes special creative arts emphasis

UNIVERSITY OF MISSOURI - COLUMBIA, Dept of Art, A 126 Fine Arts, Columbia, MO 65211. Tel 573-882-3555; Fax 573-884-6807; Email plattm@missouri.edu; Web: art.missouri.edu; *Dept Chmn & Prof* Melvin Platt; *Assoc Prof (Painting & Drawing)* William Hawk; *Prof, Dir Undergrad Studies (Graphic Design)* Deborah Huelsbergen; *Assoc Prof (Painting & Drawing)* Nathan P Boyer; *Asst Prof (Photog)* Joe Johnson; *Prof (Graphic Design)* Jean Brueggenhohann; *Asst Tchs Prof & Dir Florence Prog* Mark Langeneckert; *Assoc Prof (Sculpture)* James Calvin; *Assoc Prof (Environmental Sculpture, Video & Performance)* Cherie Sampson; *Prof (Ceramics)* Bede Clarke; *Prof (Fibers)* Jo Stealey; *Assoc Prof, Dir Grad Studies (Painting & Drawing)* J Brett Grill; *Assoc Prof (Graphic Design, Interactive Media)* Ric Wilson; *Prof (Painting & Drawing)* Lampo Leong; *Asst Prof* Chris Daniggelis; *Asst Prof* Joe Pintz; *Asst Tchg Prof* Matthew Ballou; *Asst Tchg Prof* Alexis Callender; *Asst Tchg Prof* Travis Shaffer; *Asst Prof* Jessica Thornton
Estab 1839, dept estab 1912; Maintains a nonprofit art gallery, Bingham Gallery of Art, A129 Fine Arts Bldg, University of Missouri, Columbia, MO 65211; FT 19, PT 13; pub; D, E & wknd; Scholarships; SC 100 LC 3, GC 20; non-maj 1000 per sem, maj 270, grad 28
Activities: Schls offered
Ent Req: HS dipl
Degrees: BA, BFA, MFA
Tuition: Res—undergrad $274 per cr hr, grad $347.30 per cr hr; nonres—undergrad $774.90 per cr hr, grad $910.10 per cr hr plus fees
Courses: †Advertising Design, †Art Appreciation, †Art Education, †Art History, †Calligraphy, †Ceramics, Design, †Drawing, †Fibers, †Graphic Design, Introduction to Art, †Mixed Media, †Painting, †Photography, †Printmaking, †Sculpture, †Video
Summer School: Dept Chair, Melvin Platt, Courses—Ceramics, Drawing, Fibers, Painting, Photography, Printmaking, 2D & 3D
—**Art History & Archaeology Dept**, 109 Pickard Hall, Columbia, MO 65211-1420. Tel 573-882-6711; Fax 573-884-5269; Web: www.missouri.edu; *Prof Emeritus* Osmund Overby PhD; *Prof* Norman Land PhD; *Prof Emeritus* William R Biers PhD; *Prof Emeritus* Patricia Crown PhD; *Chmn* Anne Rudloff Stanton PhD; *Prof* Marcus Rautman; *Prof Emeritus* Howard Marshall; *Prof* Kathleen Slane; *Assoc Prof* Keith Eggener; *Assoc Prof* Susan Langdon; *Assoc Prof* Kristin Schwain; *Asst Prof* Michael Yonan; *Instr* Elizabeth Hornbeck, PhD
Estab 1839, dept estab 1892; pub; D & E; Scholarships; LC 42, GC 18; maj 48, grad 39
Ent Req: HS dipl, SAT, GRE for grad students
Degrees: BA 4 yrs, MA 2-3 yrs, PhD 4 yrs
Tuition: Res—undergrad $246 per cr hr; nonres—undergrad $370 per cr hr; campus res available
Courses: Art History, Classical Archaeology, Historic Preservation, History of Art & Archeology
Summer School: Courses offered

FERGUSON

SAINT LOUIS COMMUNITY COLLEGE AT FLORISSANT VALLEY, Liberal Arts Division, 3400 Pershall Rd, Ferguson, MO 63135-1408. Tel 314-513-4375; Fax 314-513-2086; *Acting Chmn Div* Carol Berger; *Prof* Kim Mosley; *Assoc Prof* Jim Gormley; *Assoc Prof* John Ortbals; *Assoc Prof* Larry Byers; *Assoc Prof* Chris Licata; *Assoc Prof* Bob Langnas; *Assoc Prof* Eric Shultis; *Instr II* Janice Nesser-Chu
Estab 1962; Maintains nonprofit gallery, St. Louis Community College at Florissant Valley, 3400 Pershall Rd, St Louis 63135; FT10; pub; D & E; Scholarships; SC 36, LC 4; maj 70
Activities: Art supplies available at on-campus store
Ent Req: HS dipl, ent exam
Degrees: AA, AFA 2 yr, AAS 2 yr
Courses: Advertising Design, Air Brush, Art Appreciation, Art History, Ceramics, Commercial Art, Design, Drawing, Electronic Cert, Graphic Design, Illustration, Lettering, Painting, Photography, Printmaking, Sculpture, Silversmithing, Transfer Art, Typography, Video
Adult Hobby Classes: variable - through continuing educ div
Summer School: Courses—Design, Drawing, Figure Drawing, Lettering, Painting

FULTON

WESTMINSTER COLLEGE, Fine Arts Dept, 501 Westminster Ave, Fulton, MO 65251-1230. Web: www.westminster-mo.edu; *Coord* Dr Natasha Sexton
Estab 1870; Maintain nonprofit art gallery; Champ Art Gallery; Pvt; D & E; Scholarships; SC 54, LC 6; maj 100
Ent Req: HS dipl, SAT or ACT
Degrees: BA, BS & BFA 4 yr
Courses: Advertising Design, Aesthetics, Art Appreciation, Art Education, Art History, Art Therapy, Ceramics, Collage, Commercial Art, Costume Design & Construction, Design, Drawing, Film, Goldsmithing, Graphic Arts, Graphic Design, Handicrafts, History of Art & Architecture, Illustration, Interior Design, Jewelry, Painting, Photography, Printmaking, Sculpture, Silversmithing, Stage Design, Teacher Training, Theatre Arts, Video, Weaving

HANNIBAL

HANNIBAL LA GRANGE COLLEGE, Art Dept, 2800 Palmyra, Hannibal, MO 63401. Tel 573-221-3675; *Instr* Bill Krehmeier; *Instr* Dorothy Hahn; *Chmn* Robin Stone
Scholarships
Degrees: AA, BA(Art)
Tuition: $4425 per sem (12-17 hrs)
Courses: Advertising Design, Art Appreciation, Art Education, Art History, Calligraphy, Cartooning, Ceramics, Commercial Art, Design, Drawing, Handicrafts, Lettering, Mixed Media, Painting, Photography, Printmaking, Sculpture, Textile Design
Summer School: Dean, Dr Woodrow Burt. Term 2-4 wk & one 8 wk. Courses—vary

HILLSBORO

JEFFERSON COLLEGE, Dept of Art, 1000 Viking Dr, Hillsboro, MO 63050-2440. Tel 636-797-3000; Web: www.jeffco.edu

JEFFERSON CITY

LINCOLN UNIVERSITY, Dept Visual and Performing Arts, 820 Chestnut St, Jefferson City, MO 65102-3500. Tel 573-681-5195; Fax 573-681-5004; Email govangd@lincolnu.edu; Web: www.lincolnu.edu/finearts; *Asst Prof* Cheryl Unterschulz; *Prof* James Tatum; *Asst Prof* Rebecca Stonesanders; *Asst Prof* Cynthia Byler; *Asst Prof* James Crow
Estab 1927; Fine arts gallery; Richardson Fine Arts Center; FT 3, PT 4; pub; D&E; Scholarships; SC 19, LC 6; maj 50, others 100
Ent Req: HS dipl
Degrees: BS(Art) & BS(Art Educ) 4 yr
Courses: Applied Art, †Art Appreciation, Art Education, Art History, †Ceramics, †Commercial Art, †Design, †Drawing, †Graphic Arts, †Graphic Design, †Handicrafts, †History of Art & Architecture, †Mixed Media, †Painting, †Photography, †Printmaking, Studio Art, Teacher Training
Summer School: Courses—same as above

JOPLIN

MISSOURI SOUTHERN STATE UNIVERSITY, Dept of Art, 3950 Newman Rd, Joplin, MO 64801-1595. Tel 417-625-9563; Fax 417-625-3046; Email kyle-n@mail.mssc.edu; Web: www.mssu.edu; *Prof* V A Christensen; *Prof* David Noblett; *Adjunct Prof* Alice Knepper; *Dept Head* Nick Kyle; *Prof* Josie Mai; *Prof* Burt Bucher; *Prof* Frank Pishkur; *Adjunct Prof* Peggy Beckham
Estab 1937; Maintains nonprofit art gallery; on-campus art supply shop; FT 7; pub; D & E; Scholarships; SC 24, LC 2, Non-credit 4; D 500, non-maj 15 maj 125, others 10
Ent Req: HS dipl

Degrees: BA & BSE 4 yrs
Courses: Aesthetics, Art Appreciation, Art Education, Art History, Ceramics, Commercial Art, Design, Drawing, †Graphic Communications, Graphic Design, Mixed Media, Painting, Photography, Printmaking, Sculpture, Silversmithing, †Studio, Studio Crafts, Teacher Training, Typography
Adult Hobby Classes: Enrl 60; Tuition varies. Courses—Clay, Jewelry, Photographic (Digital), Watercolor
Summer School: Dir, Nick Kyle. Art Appreciation, Studio Course

KANSAS CITY

AVILA COLLEGE, Art Division, Dept of Humanities, 11901 Wornall Rd, Kansas City, MO 64145-1698. Tel 816-942-8400, Ext 2289; Fax 816-501-2459; Web: www.avila.edu; *Instr* Sharyl Wright; *Instr* Kelly Mills; *Instr* Lisa Sugimoto; *Chmn Humanities* Carol Coburn; *Chmn Art & Design* Susan Lawlor; *Instr* Marci Aylward
Estab 1948; 7 adjunct instrs; den; D & E; Scholarships; SC 35, LC 4; D 140, E 20, non-maj 120, maj 40
Ent Req: HS dipl, SAT and PSAT
Degrees: BA 4 yrs
Courses: Art Appreciation, Art Education, Art History, Ceramics, Commercial Art, Design, Drawing, Graphic Arts, Graphic Design, Illustration, Painting, Photography, Printmaking, Sculpture, Teacher Training
Adult Hobby Classes: Courses offered

KANSAS CITY ART INSTITUTE, 4415 Warwick Blvd, Kansas City, MO 64111-1820. Tel 800-522-5224; Fax 816-802-3309; Email info@kcai.edu; Web: www.kcai.edu; *The Nerman Family President* Tony Jones, CBE; *Prof* Chris Chapin; *The Kathleen Collins Chair & Prof* Cary Esser; *The Ray Beagle Chair & Prof* Michele Fricke, MFA; *Asst Prof* Caleb Taylor
Estab 1885; Maintain nonprofit art gallery; H & R Block Art Space, 16 E 43rd St, Kansas City, MO 64111; library Jannes Library & Learning Ctr, 4538 Warwick Blvd, Kansas City, MO 64111/ on-campus shop for purchase of art supplies; Pvt; D & E; Scholarships; maj areas 7, LC 104 in liberal arts; D 620, E 740
Activities: Book traveling exhibs; originate traveling exhibs
Ent Req: HS dipl, portfolio interview, recommendations, essay
Degrees: BFA 4 yrs
Courses: †Animation, †Art History, †Ceramics, †Creative Writing, †Design, Drawing, Fashion Arts, Film, Graphic Design, †Interactive Arts, Creative Writing, Painting, †Photography, †Printmaking, †Sculpture, †Textile, Weaving
Adult Hobby Classes: tuition varies
Children's Classes: tuition varies
Summer School: tuition varies, contact Director School for Continuing and Professional Studies, Sonja Garrett

MAPLE WOODS COMMUNITY COLLEGE, Dept of Art & Art History, 2601 NE Barry Rd, Kansas City, MO 64156-1299. Tel 816-437-3000, Ext 3226; Web: www.maplewoods.cc.mo.us; *Head Dept* Jennie Frederick
Estab 1969; PT 6; pub; D & E; Scholarships; SC 12, LC 2; D 125, E & Sat 80
Ent Req: HS dipl or GED
Degrees: AA 2 yrs
Courses: Art Education, Art Fundamentals, Art History, Ceramics, Commercial Art, †Computer, †Design, Drawing, †Fiber, Painting, Photography, Printmaking, Sculpture
Adult Hobby Classes: Courses same as above
Children's Classes: Summer classes.
Summer School: Dir, Helen Mary Turner. Courses—Ceramics, Drawing, Painting

METROPOLITAN COMMUNITY COLLEGE - PENN VALLEY, Art Dept, 3201 SW Trafficway, Kansas City, MO 64111. Tel 816-604-4757; Fax 816-759-4606; Email darlene.town@mcckc.edu; Web: www.mcckc.edu/pennvalley/humanities/art; *Div Chmn Humanities* Vicki Raine; *Art Instr/Gallery Dir* Bernadette Torres; *Art Instr* Mary Beth Moley
Maintain nonprofit art gallery, Carter Art Center (same address); schols open to all art majors; on-campus shop where art supplies may be purchased; Pub (Metropolitan Community Col - Kansas City); Scholarships
Degrees: AAS - Graphic Design
Tuition: District res—$87 per sem hr; non-district res—$156 per sem hr; non-state res—$210 per sem hr
Courses: Animation, Art Fundamentals, Art History, Cartooning, Ceramics, †Commercial Art, Computer Graphics, †Digital Prepness, Drawing, Fashion Arts, †Graphic Arts, †Graphic Design, Painting, Photography, Sculpture, †Web Design

ROCKHURST UNIVERSITY, Dept of Communication & Fine Arts, 1100 Rockhurst Rd, Kansas City, MO 64110-2508. Tel 816-501-4000, 816-501-4407 (Gallery); Web: www.rockhurst.edu; *Gallery Dir* Anne Pearce
Maintains Greenlease Art Gallery

UNIVERSITY OF MISSOURI-KANSAS CITY, Dept of Art & Art History, 5100 Rockhill Rd, 204 Fine Art Bldg Kansas City, MO 64110-2446. Tel 816-235-1501; Fax 816-235-5507; Email art@umkc.edu; Web: www.umkc.edu/art; *Chmn* Kati Toivaner
Estab 1933; Average Annual Attendance: 11,000; FT 10, PT 7; pub; D & E; Scholarships; maj 138
Income: $15,000 (financed through city and state)
Ent Req: contact Admis Office
Degrees: BA (Art), (Studio Art) & (Art History)
Courses: Art Appreciation, †Art History, Computer Art, Drawing, Graphic Design, Intermedia, Painting, Photography, Printmaking
Summer School: Dir, B L Dunbar. Enrl 65; 8 wk term. Courses—Art History, Drawing, Painting, Photography, Printmaking

KIRKSVILLE

TRUMAN STATE UNIVERSITY, Art Dept, 100 E Normal St, Kirksville, MO 63501-4200. Tel 660-785-4417; *Head Div Fine Arts* Robert L Jones
Estab 1867; pub; D & E; Scholarships; SC 27, LC 8; D 220, non-maj 45, maj 155
Ent Req: HS dipl
Degrees: BFA(Visual Communications Studio) 4 yrs, BA(Liberal Arts) 4 yrs, BA (Art History) 4 yrs
Courses: †Art History, †Ceramics, Fibers, †Painting, †Photography, †Printmaking, †Sculpture, Visual Communications
Summer School: Enrl 80-100; term of two 5 wk sessions beginning June & July

LIBERTY

WILLIAM JEWELL COLLEGE, Art Dept, 500 College Hill, Liberty, MO 64068. Tel 816-781-7700, Ext 5415; Fax 816-415-5027; *Chmn* Nano Nore, MFA; *Instr* Rebecca Koop, BFA
Estab 1849, dept estab 1966; pvt (cooperates with the Missouri Baptist Convention); D & E; Scholarships; D 120, E 35-40, maj 30
Degrees: BA(Art) & BS 4 yrs
Courses: Art Appreciation, Art Education, Art History, Calligraphy, Ceramics, Computer Graphic, Design, Drawing, Fibers, Painting, Photography, Printmaking, Sculpture, Weaving
Adult Hobby Classes: Enrl 10 - 15; tuition $120 per 14 wk sem. Courses—Drawing, Illustration, Jewelry/Silversmithing, Painting, Photography
Children's Classes: Enrl 10 - 15; tuition $30 - $40 for a 6 wk session. Courses—Ceramics, Drawing, Painting, Photography
Summer School: Dir, Dr Steve Schwegler; Illustration Academy, Dirs John & Mark English

MARYVILLE

NORTHWEST MISSOURI STATE UNIVERSITY, Dept of Fine & Performing Arts, 800 University Dr, Maryville, MO 64468-6001. Tel 660-562-1326; Fax 660-562-1346; Email oehler@nwmissouri.edu; Web: www.nwmissouri.edu/dept/art/index.htm; *Assoc Prof/Chair* Dr David Oehler, PhD; *Prof* Dr Kim Spradling, PhD; *Assoc Prof* Armin Muhsam, MFA; *Assoc Prof* Glen Williams, MFA; *Assoc Prof* Craig Warner, MFA; *Asst Prof* Dr Martha Breckenridge, PhD; *Asst Prof* Chris Graves, MFA; *Instr* Robert Schultz, MFA; *Instr* Veronica Watkins, MFA; *Prof* Phil Laber, MFA; *Instr* Kwok-Pong (Bobby) Tso, MFA
Estab 1905, dept estab 1915; Maintains nonprofit Olive De Luce Fine Art Gallery; art supplies sold at on-campus store; FT 10, PT 2; pub; D & E; Scholarships; SC 74, LC 19; D 475, E 25, non-maj 350, maj 172
Ent Req: HS dipl
Degrees: BA, BFA, BSE & BA 4 yrs
Tuition: In-state 25 cr hr $266; out of state $474.64
Courses: Advertising Design, Art Appreciation, †Art Education, Art History, †Ceramics, Commercial Art, Computer Graphics, Constructions, †Design, †Drawing, †Graphic Design, History of Art & Architecture, Interactive Digital Media, Intl Study in Art History, Intl Study in Studio, Jewelry, Metalsmithing, Mixed Media, †Painting, †Photography, †Printmaking, †Sculpture, Teacher Training, †Weaving
Children's Classes: Courses—Art Educ Club workshops $15
Summer School: Chmn Dept Art, Dave Oehler. Offerings vary yr to yr. Courses—Art Education, Ceramics, Jewelry, Painting, Photography, Watercolor

NEOSHO

CROWDER COLLEGE, Longwell Museum/Art Department, 601 Laclede, Neosho, MO 64850. Tel 417-455-5526, 417-451-3223; Email Caseystueber@crowder.edu; Web: www.longwellmuseum.weebly.com, www.crowder.edu; *Art Instr* Casey Stueber; *Art Instr* Allen Bishop
Estab 1964; Maintain non-profit art gallery, Longwell Museum, same address as school; on-campus shop where art supplies may be purchased; FT 1, PT 1; Pub; D & E; Scholarships; D 1000, E 300, maj 20, others 250
Ent Req: HS grad or equivalent
Degrees: AA & AAS 2 yrs
Courses: †20-30 Design, Art Appreciation, Art History, Ceramic Design, †Ceramics, †Costume Design & Construction, Design, Drawing, Fibers Design, †Graphic Arts, †Graphic Design, Jewelry, Painting, †Photography, Sculpture, †Stage Design, †Theatre Arts, †Weaving

NEVADA

COTTEY COLLEGE, Art Dept, 1000 W Austin, Nevada, MO 64772. Tel 417-667-8181; Email bfulton@cottey.edu; Web: www.cottey.edu; *VPres* Cathryn Pridal, PhD; *Art Faculty* Brianne Fulton, MFA
Estab 1884; maintains nonprofit art gallery, PEO Foundation Gallery; on-campus shop where art supplies may be purchased; FT 3; pvt, W; D; Scholarships; SC 15, LC 4; maj 12-15, total 369
Activities: Schols offered
Ent Req: HS grad, AC Board
Degrees: AA 2 yrs & AS 2 yrs, AFA visual arts, selective BA degrees
Courses: Art Appreciation, Art History, Ceramics, Design, Drawing, Graphic Arts, Handicrafts, Illustration, Jewelry, Metals, Painting, Photography, Printmaking, Weaving

PARKVILLE

PARK UNIVERSITY, Dept of Art & Design, 8700 NW River Park Dr, Box 42 Parkville, MO 64152-4358. Tel 816-741-2000, Ext 6457; Fax 816-741-4911; Email donnabach@mail.park.edu; *Chmn* Donna N Bachman; *Asst Prof* Thomas H Smith; *Asst Prof* Kay M Boehr

Estab 1875; Maintain nonprofit gallery; Campanella Gallery; Pvt; D & E; Scholarships; SC 13, LC 4; D 50, non-maj 40, maj 130
Ent Req: HS dipl, ACT
Degrees: BA, 4 yrs
Tuition: Res—undergrad $165 per cr hr; campus res—$2,425 room & board
Courses: 3-D Design, Advertising Design, Art Education, Art History, Ceramics, Drawing, †Fiber, Graphic Design, History of Art & Architecture, Interior Design, Painting, Photography, Sculpture, Teacher Training
Summer School: Tuition $165 per cr hr for 8 wk term. Courses—Ceramics, Printmaking, varied curriculum

POINT LOOKOUT

COLLEGE OF THE OZARKS, Dept of Art, PO Box 17, Art Dept Point Lookout, MO 65726-0017. Tel 417-334-6411, Ext 3287; Email allman@cofo.edu; Web: www.cofo.edu; *Prof* Anne Allman PhD; *Prof* Jayme Burchett, MFA; *Prof* Jeff Johnston, MFA; *Assoc Prof* Richard Cummings, PhD
Estab 1906, dept estab 1962; Maintain nonprofit art gallery; Boger Art Gallery, Art Dept, PO Box 17, Point Lookout, MO 65726; on-campus shop for art supplies; pvt; D; Scholarships; SC 22, LC 4; D 200, E 25, non-maj 1500, maj 50
Ent Req: HS dipl, ACT
Degrees: BA & BS 4 yr
Tuition: No fees are charged; each student works 960 hrs in on-campus employment
Courses: †Art Education, †Ceramics, †Computer Art, †Design, †Drawing, Fibers, †Graphic Design, †Painting, †Photography, †Printmaking, †Sculpture

SAINT CHARLES

LINDENWOOD COLLEGE, Art Dept, 209 S Kingshighway St, Saint Charles, MO 63301-1693. Tel 636-949-4862, 949-2000; *Chmn Dept, Contact* Elaine Tillinger
Estab 1827; FT 4, PT 4; pvt; D & E; Scholarships; SC 24, LC 16; D 200, E 30, maj 40
Ent Req: HS dipl, ent exam
Degrees: BA, BS, BFA 4 yrs, MA, MFA
Courses: Art Education, Art History, Ceramics, Computer Art, Design, Drawing, Graphic Arts, Painting, Photography, Printmaking, Sculpture, Teacher Training

SAINT JOSEPH

MISSOURI WESTERN STATE UNIVERSITY, School of Fine Arts, 4525 Downs Dr, Saint Joseph, MO 64507-2246. Tel 816-271-4200, Ext 4282; Fax 816-271-4181; Email puriso@missouriwestern.edu; Web: www.missouriwestern.edu/art; *Assoc Prof* David Harris, MFA; *Asst Prof* Neil Lawley, MFA; *Assoc Prof* Teresa Harris, MFA; *Dept Chair, Assoc Prof* Peter Hriso; *Artist in Res* Eric Fuson; *Assoc Prof* Rebecca Foley, MFA; *Asst Prof* Peter Britton, MFA; *Asst Prof* Matt Hepworth, MFA; *Asst Prof* Neil Lawley, MFA; *Asst Prof* Kathy Liao, MFA; *Asst Prof* Dr Madeline Rislow, MFA
Estab 1969; Maintains nonprofit gallery, Gallery 206; MWSU Library; art supplies sold at on-campus store; Pub; D & E & online; Scholarships; SC 25, LC 8; D 355, E 100, non-maj 120, maj 130, grad 10
Ent Req: HS dipl, GED, ACT
Degrees: BSE (Art Educ), BA & BFA (Graphic Design), BFA (Studio, Digital Animation), BFA (Art Therapy)
Courses: Advertising Design, Aesthetics, Animation, Art Appreciation, Art Education, Art History, Ceramics, Commercial Art, Computer Art, Design, Drawing, Graphic Arts, Graphic Design, History of Art & Architecture, Illustration, Painting, Photography, Printmaking, Sculpture, Teacher Training, Tools & Techniques
Adult Hobby Classes: adult classes through western institute prog
Children's Classes: children's classes through western institute prog
Summer School: Tuition res—$130 for 5 or more cr hrs, nonres—$240 for 5 or more cr hrs; term of 8 wks beginning June 1. Courses—Art Education, Ceramics, Introduction to Art, Photomedia, Painting

SAINT LOUIS

FONTBONNE UNIVERSITY, Fine Art Dept, 6800 Wydown Blvd, Saint Louis, MO 63105-3043. Tel 314-889-1431; Fax 314-889-1451; Web: www.fontbonne.edu; *Prof* Hank Knickmeyer, MFA; *Assoc Prof* Victor Wang, MFA; *Assoc Prof* Deanna Jent, MFA; *Assoc Prof* Tim Liddy, MFA; *Asst Prof* Michael Sullivan, MFA; *Assoc Prof* Catherine Connor-Talasek, MFA; *Asst Prof & Chair* Mark Douglas, MFA
Estab 1923; Maintains nonprofit gallery, Gallery of Art 6800 Wydown Blvd, St Louis, MO 63105; Fontbonne University Fine Arts Gallery; pvt; D & E; Scholarships; SC 10, LC 2, GC 6; non-maj 10, maj 46, grad 12, others 5
Ent Req: HS dipl, portfolio
Degrees: BA and BFA 4 yrs, MA 1 yr, MFA 2 yrs
Courses: Art Appreciation, Art Education, Art History, †Ceramics, Design, †Drawing, †Fibers, †Graphic Design, Illustration, †Painting, †Photography, †Sculpture, Teacher Training, Weaving
Adult Hobby Classes: Tuition $150 per cr. Courses—Art History
Summer School: Dir, Mark Douglas. Enrl 75; tuition subject to chg, see website. Courses—Ceramics, Drawing, Modern Art, Painting, Printmaking

MARYVILLE UNIVERSITY OF SAINT LOUIS, Art & Design Program, 650 Maryville University Dr, Saint Louis, MO 63141-7299. Tel 314-529-9300, 529-9381 (art div), 800-627-9855; Fax 314-529-9940; Web: www.maryville.edu; *Assoc Prof Art & Prog Dir Studio Art* John Baltrushunas, MFA; *Assoc Prof & Prog Dir, Interior Design* Darlene Davison, BFA; *Instr Graphic Design* Laurie Eisenbach-Bush, BFA; *Assoc Prof Art History* Todd Brenningmeyer, PhD; *Assoc Prof Interactive Design* Jon Fahnestock, MFA; *Asst Prof Art* Scott Angus, MFA; *Instr Graphic Design* Caren Sehlossberg-Wood, BA; *Asst Prof Interior Design* Jessica Senne, AIA, NCIDQ
Estab 1872, dept estab 1961; Maintains nonprofit gallery, Morton J May Foundation Gallery; on-campus shop for purchase of art supplies; Pvt; D, E & W; Scholarships; SC 74, LC 6; D 200, E 30, non-maj 60, maj 180
Ent Req: HS dipl, ACT or SAT
Degrees: BA, BFA
Tuition: $12,779 per sem; $766 per cr hr; campus res—room & board $10,000 per yr
Courses: 2-D & 3-D Design, 3-D Modeling, Advertising Design, Animation, †Art Education, †Art History, †Art Studio, †Auto CAD, †Ceramics, †Color Theory, Design, †Display, †Drafting, Drawing, Environmental Graphics, †Fibers & Soft Sculpture, †Furniture Design, †Graphic Arts, †Handmade Book, History of Art & Architecture, Identity Design, Illustration, †Interactive Design, †Interior Design, Mixed Media, Motion Graphics, Occupational Therapy, Packaging, †Painting, †Painting the Figure, †Photography, †Printmaking, †Sculpture, †Silversmithing, †Teacher Training, Video, Web Design
Adult Hobby Classes: Enrl & tuition vary. Courses—Art & Architectural History, Art in St Louis, Drawing, Painting, Photography
Summer School: Enrl 60; Director Dr. Todd Brenningmeyer, Assoc Prof Art History; tuition same as regular year. Courses—Photography, Drawing, Painting, Interior Design.

SAINT LOUIS COMMUNITY COLLEGE AT FOREST PARK, Art Dept, 5600 Oakland Ave, Saint Louis, MO 63110-1393. Tel 314-644-9350; Fax 314-644-9752; Web: www.stlcc.cc.mo.us; *Asst Prof* Evann Richards, BA; *Instr* Joe C Angert, MA; *Instr* Allen Arpadi, BA
Estab 1962, dept estab 1963. College maintains three campuses; PT 14; pub; D & E; Scholarships; SC 36, LC 6; D 200, E 100, non-maj 75, maj 75
Ent Req: HS dipl
Degrees: AA & AAS 2 yrs
Courses: Advertising Design, Art Appreciation, Art Education, †Art History, Ceramics, Color, Commercial Art, Commercial Photography, Computer-Assisted Publishing, Design, Drawing, Film, †Graphic Design, Illustration, Lettering, †Painting, †Photography
Adult Hobby Classes: Courses—Drawing, Painting, Photography, Printmaking, Sculpture, Video
Summer School: Chmn, Leon Anderson. Enrl 100. Courses—Same as those above

SAINT LOUIS COMMUNITY COLLEGE AT MERAMEC, Art Dept, 11333 Big Bend Blvd, Saint Louis, MO 63122. Tel 314-984-7500, 984-7632; Web: www.stlcc.edu/mc/dept/art; *Prof* Margaret Keller; *Prof* Chuck Groth; *Prof* Rene Behrend; *Prof* David Hanlon; *Prof* Betsy Morris; *Prof* James Ibur; *Prof* Joe Chesla; *Prof* Erin Leclerc; *Prof* Mary Huelsmann; *Prof* Michael Swoboda; *Prof* Virginia Heisler; *Prof* Ken Wood; *Prof* David Montgomery; *Prof* Bradley Fratello; *Prof* Michael Lorenz; *Prof* Timothy Linder
Estab 1964; Maintain nonprofit art gallery, Meramec Contemporary Art Gallery (on campus); Pub; D & E; Scholarships; SC 130, LC 10
Ent Req: HS dipl
Degrees: AFA 2 yr, AAS 2yr
Courses: Advertising Design, †Architecture, Art History, Ceramics, Commercial Art, Drawing, Illustration, Interior Design, Painting, Photography, Printmaking, Sculpture, †Video
Summer School: Chmn Dept, Tim Linder. Courses—Art Appreciation, Ceramics, Design, Drawing, Photography

SAINT LOUIS UNIVERSITY, Fine & Performing Arts Dept, 221 N Grand Blvd, Saint Louis, MO 63103-2097. Tel 314-977-3030; Fax 314-977-3447; *Chmn* Dr Cindy Stollhans
Maintains McNamee Gallery, St Louis; Scholarships
Degrees: BA
Tuition: Undergrad $6765 full-time per term, $468 part-time per hr
Courses: Approaching the Arts, Art History, Design, Drawing, Painting, Photography, Sculpture, †Studio Art
Summer School: Courses—Drawings, Painting, Studio Art

UNIVERSITY OF MISSOURI, SAINT LOUIS, Dept of Art & Art History, 8001 Natural Bridge Rd, Saint Louis, MO 63121-4499. Tel 314-516-5975; Fax 314-516-5003; Web: www.umsl.edu/~art; *Chmn* Dan Younger, MFA; *Prof* Ken Anderson, MFA; *Prof* Yael Even, PhD, MFA; *Prof* Jeanne Morgan Zarucchi, PhD; *Asst Prof* Terry Suhre, MFA; *Assoc Prof* Gretchen Schisla, MFA; *Sr Lectr* Juliana Yuan, MA; *Des Lee Foundation Prof Art Educ* E Louis Lankford, PhD; *Assoc Prof* Marian Amies, MFA; *Asst Prof* Phillip Robinson, MFA; *Assoc Prof* Jeffrey Sippel, MFA; *Asst Prof* Jennifer McKnight, MFA; *Instr* Luci McMichael, MAT; *Assoc Prof* Ruth Bohan, PhD; *Assoc Prof* Susan Cahan, PhD; *Asst Prof* Susan Waller, PhD
Estab 1963; Maintain nonprofit art gallery; Gallery 210; Pub; D & E; Scholarships; SC 66, LC 52, GC 7; maj 270 (50 Art History, 220 Studio Art)
Ent Req: HS dipl
Degrees: BA(Art Hist), BFA
Courses: Art Education, †Art History, Design, †Drawing, †General Fine Arts, †Graphic Design, Illustration, †Painting, †Photography, †Printmaking

WASHINGTON UNIVERSITY, School of Art, 1 Brookings Dr, Campus Box 1031 Saint Louis, MO 63130-4862. Tel 314-935-6500; Fax 314-935-4862; Email jpike@art.wustl.edu; Web: www.wustl.edu; *Dean School* Jeffrey C Pike; *Assoc Dean School* Georgia Binnington; *Assoc Dean* Michael Byron; *Dir Grad Studies* Eric Troffkin
Estab 1853; Maintain nonprofit art gallery, The Des Lee Gallery, 1627 Washington Ave, St. Louis, MO 63104; pvt; D; Scholarships; Fellowships; SC 62, LC 10, GC 31; maj 320, grad 20
Ent Req: HS dipl, SAT or ACT, portfolio
Degrees: BFA 4 yrs, MFA 2 yrs
Tuition: $26,900 per yr, $13,450 per sem, $1,120 per cr hr; campus res—room & board available
Courses: †Advertising Design, Aesthetics, Architecture, Art Appreciation, Art Education, Art History, †Ceramics, Costume Design & Construction, Design, Drawing, †Fashion Arts, †Fashion Design, †Glass Blowing, Graphic Arts, †Graphic

Design, History of Art & Architecture, †Illustration, Mixed Media, Occupational Therapy, †Painting, †Photography, †Printmaking, †Sculpture, Stage Design, Theatre Arts, Video
Summer School: Enrl 50; tuition $$4565 HS program for term beginning June 12-Jul 16. Courses—Painting, Printmaking, Photography. Drawing, Computer Graphics, Fashion, Sculpture, Ceramics, Florence, Italy, enrl 40; tuition $2850, $750 room, June 1 - June 30. Courses—On-site Drawing, Photography, Book Arts & Painting
—**School of Architecture**, 1 Brookings Dr, Campus Box 1079 Saint Louis, MO 63130-4862. Tel 314-935-6200; Fax 314-935-7656; Web: www.wustl.edu; *Dean School* Cynthia Weese, FAIA
Estab 1910; pvt; D; Scholarships; SC 28, LC 58, GC 42; 300, maj 200, grad 100
Degrees: BA(Arch), March, MA(UD)
Tuition: $18,350 per yr, $765 per cr hr
Courses: †Architecture, Design, Drawing, Interior Design, Landscape Architecture, Photography
Adult Hobby Classes: Enrl 43; tuition $175 per unit. Cert degree program, Bachelor of Technology in Architecture
Summer School: Tuition varies. Courses—Advanced Architectural Design, Fundamentals of Design, Structural Principles

SPRINGFIELD

DRURY COLLEGE, Art & Art History Dept, 900 N Benton Ave, Springfield, MO 65802-3791. Tel 417-873-7263, 873-7879; Fax 417-873-6921; Web: www.drury.edu; *Chmn* Alkis Tsolakis
Estab 1873; FT 6, PT 9; den; D; Scholarships; SC 12, LC 5; 2246
Ent Req: HS dipl
Degrees: 4 yrs
Courses: Architecture, Art History, Ceramics, Commercial Art, Photography, Studio Arts, Teacher Training, Weaving
Adult Hobby Classes: Enrl 25-35; tuition $125 per cr hr. Courses—Studio Art & History of Art
Children's Classes: Summer Scape, gifted children. Courses—Architecture, Design, Photography
Summer School: Dir, Sue Rollins. Enrl 292; tuition $125 per cr hr June-Aug for 9 wk term. Courses—Art History, Ceramics, Drawing, Painting, Photography

EVANGEL UNIVERSITY, Humanities-Art Dept, 1111 N Glenstone Ave, Trask Hall 3rd Floor Springfield, MO 65802-2125. Tel 417-865-2815; Fax 417-865-9599; Web: www.evangel.edu; *Dept Chair* Nathan Nelson
Maintains nonprofit Barnett Fine Art & Design Gallery
Activities: Schols & fels available
Courses: Advertising Design, Art Appreciation, Art Education, Art History, Ceramics, Collage, Commercial Art, Conceptual Art, Costume Design & Construction, Design, Drawing, Film, Graphic Arts, Graphic Design, History of Art & Architecture, Mixed Media, Painting, Photography, Printmaking, Sculpture, Stage Design, Teacher Training, Textile Design, Theatre Arts, Weaving

MISSOURI STATE UNIVERSITY, Dept of Art & Design, 901 S National Springfield, MO 65897-0001. Tel 417-837-2330; Email artanddesign@missouristate.edu; Web: www.art.missouristate.edu; *Head Dept* Prof Carolyn Cardenas
Estab 1901; Maintains nonprofit gallery, Brick City Gallery, 215 W Mill St, Springfield, MO 65806; on-campus art supplies shop; FT 28, PT 15; pub; D & E; Scholarships; SC 70, LC 37, GC 27, Other 8; maj 556, others 22,385
Ent Req: HS dipl, ent exam
Degrees: BFA (Art, Design) BS (Education Comprehensive & Electronic Arts) BA (Art History) 4 yrs; MFA (Visual Arts)
Courses: Art Appreciation, †Art Education, †Art History, †Ceramics, Computer Animation, †Digital Arts, †Drawing, †Electronic Arts, †Graphic Design, Illustration, †Metals/Jewelry, †Painting, †Photography, †Printmaking, †Sculpture
Adult Hobby Classes: Tuition $98 per cr hr for 1 & 2 wk sessions

UNION

EAST CENTRAL COLLEGE, Art Dept, 1964 Prairie Dell Rd, Union, MO 63084-4344. Tel 636-583-5195, Ext 2258; Web: www.eastcentral.edu; *Arts Program Coordr* Adam Watkins
Estab 1968; FT 2, PT 1; pub; D & E; Scholarships; SC 8, LC 8; D 370, E 120, maj 40
Ent Req: HS dipl, ent exam
Degrees: AA & AAS 2 yrs
Courses: Art Appreciation, Art Education, Art History, Business of Art, Design, Drawing, Figure Drawing, Handicrafts, History of Art & Architecture, Lettering, Painting, Photography, Printmaking, Sculpture, Teacher Training
Adult Hobby Classes: Enrl 121; tuition $21-$38 per semester. Courses—Painting
Children's Classes: Tuition $25 for 4 wk summer term. Courses—Art, Drawing, Sculpture, Painting
Summer School: Tuition $21 per cr hr for 8 wk term. Courses—Art Appreciation, Art History

WARRENSBURG

UNIVERSITY OF CENTRAL MISSOURI, (Central Missouri State University) Dept of Art & Design, PO Box 800, Art Ctr 120 Warrensburg, MO 64093-5299. Tel 660-543-4481; Fax 660-543-8786; Web: www.ucmo.edu; *Chair Dept* Mick Luehrman, PhD; *Assoc Prof* David Babcock, MFA; *Prof* Kathleen Desmond, EdD; *Prof* Joyce Jablonski, MFA; *Prof* John Louder, MFA; *Assoc Prof* Melanie Lowrance, MFA; *Assoc Prof* Clint Orr, MFA; *Assoc Prof* Susan Stevenson, PhD; *Assoc Prof* Rahila Weed, PhD; *Prof* Matthew Zupnick, MFA; *Asst Prof* Jasmine Cloud, PhD; *Assoc Prof* Haroom Sattar, MFA; *Asst Prof* Mark Farris, MFA; *Asst Prof* John Malta, MFA; *Asst Prof* Marco Rosichelli, MFA; *Asst Prof* Justin Shaw, MFA; *Asst Prof* Eric Stykel, MFA
Estab 1871; Maintains a nonprofit art gallery, Art Center Gallery, Art Ctr 120, Warrensburg MO 64093; on-campus shop where art supplies may be purchased; pub; D & E; Scholarships; SC 52, LC 10, GC 7; D maj 434, minors 30
Ent Req: HS dipl, Missouri School & Col Ability Test, ACT
Degrees: BSE & BFA 4 yrs
Courses: †Advertising Design, †Art Appreciation, †Art Education, Art History, †Ceramics, †Commercial Art, †Design, Drawing, †Graphic Design, †History of Art & Architecture, Illustration, †Interior Design, Painting, †Printmaking, Sculpture, †Studio Art, Teacher Training, †Textile Design, †Weaving
Children's Classes: Gallery Kids - 2 Saturdays per sem
Summer School: Chair Dept, Mick Luehrman. Term of 12 wks beginning second wk in May. Courses—Ceramics, Drawing, Grad Studio Courses, Painting, Art Educ

WEBSTER GROVES

WEBSTER UNIVERSITY, Department of Art, Design & Art History, 470 E Lockwood Blvd, Webster Groves, MO 63119-3194. Tel 314-968-7171 or 314-961-2660; Fax 314-968-7139; Email art@webster.edu; Web: www.webster.edu; *Chmn* Tom Lang, MFA; *Prof* Carol Hodson, MFA; *Prof* Jeffrey Hughes, PhD, MFA; *Prof* Brad Loudenback, MFA; *Prof* Gary Passanise, MFA; *Assoc Prof* Jeri Au, MFA; *Assoc Prof* Robin Assner, MFA; *Assoc Prof* Noriko Yuasa, MFA; *Asst Prof* Tate Foley, MFA; *Asst Prof* Ryan Gregg, MFA; *Asst Prof* Brian Zimmerman, MFA
Estab 1915, dept estab 1946; Maintains nonprofit Hunt Gallery 8342 Big Bend Blvd, St Louis, MO 63119; pvt; D & E; Scholarships; SC 60, LC 15; 1100, maj 100
Ent Req: HS dipl, SAT or ACT
Degrees: BA & BFA 4 yrs
Courses: †Art Education, †Art History, †Ceramics, Collage, Conceptual Art, †Drawing, Film, †Graphic Design, †Painting, †Papermaking, †Photography, †Printmaking, †Sculpture, †Teacher Training
Adult Hobby Classes: Tuition $175 per cr hr for 16 wk sem. Courses—Art, Photography, Watercolor
Summer School: Assoc Dean Fine Arts, Peter Sargent. Tuition $175 per cr hr for term of 6 or 8 wks beginning June. Courses—Introductory Photography, Sculpture Workshop: Bronze

MONTANA

BILLINGS

MONTANA STATE UNIVERSITY-BILLINGS, Art Dept, 1500 University Dr, Billings, MT 59101-0252. Tel 406-657-2324; Fax 406-657-2187; Email kpitman@msubillings.edu; Web: www.msubilling.edu/art; *Chair* Connie M Landis
Estab 1927; Maintains non profit Northcutt Steele Gallery on campus; Art supplies may be purchased at on-campus shop; FT 6, PT 4; pub; D & E; Scholarships
Ent Req: HS dipl
Degrees: AA, BA(Lib Arts, Studio & Art Educ Option K-12)
Courses: †Art Education, Art History, Ceramics, †Collage, †Computer Graphics, †Design, Drawing, †Lithography, Painting, Photography, †Printmaking, Sculpture
Summer School: Tuition res—$415.55 per cr, nonres—$786.65 per cr for three sessions from May through Aug. Courses—various studio courses and workshops

ROCKY MOUNTAIN COLLEGE, Art Dept, 1511 Poly Dr, Billings, MT 59102-1796. Tel 406-657-1094, 657-1040 (main), 657-1000 (admis); Web: www.rocky.edu; *Chmn* Mark Moak
Estab 1878, dept estab 1957; pvt; D; Scholarships; SC 12, LC 5; 112, non-maj 40, maj 30, others 5
Ent Req: HS dipl, ACT
Degrees: BA & BS 4 yrs
Courses: Art Education, Art History, Ceramics, Drawing, Graphic Design, Painting, Photography, Sculpture, Teacher Training
Adult Hobby Classes: Enrl 100; tuition $20 for 5 wks. Courses—Crafts, Painting, Picture Framing

BOZEMAN

MONTANA STATE UNIVERSITY, School of Art, 213 Haynes Hall, Bozeman, MT 59717. Tel 406-994-4501; Fax 406-994-3680; Email art@montana.edu; Web: www.art.montana.edu; *Dir School of Art* Vaughan Judge; *Adjunct Instr Metalsmithing* Bryan Peterson; *Prof Graphic Design* Jeffrey Conger; *Asst Prof Graphic Design* Meta Newhouse; *Prof Art History* Todd Larkin; *Prof Graphic Design* Stephanie Newman; *Asst Prof Ceramics* Josh DeWeese; *Asst Prof Printmaking* Gesine Janzen; *Asst Prof Painting* Sarah Mast; *Asst Prof - Painting & Drawing* Rollin Beamish; *Asst Prof - Art History* Regina Gee; *Asst Prof - Foundation* Dean Adams; *Assoc Prof Art History* Melissa Ragain; *Assoc Prof Ceramics* Jeremy Hatch; *Assoc Prof Sculpture* Jim Zimpel; *Adjunct Instr Foundations* Denise Reibe; *Adjunct Instr, Art History* Barbara Emberlin
Estab 1893; Maintain nonprofit art gallery; Helene E Copeland Gallery, Montana State Univ, Bozeman, MT 59717; creative arts library; art supplies available in bookstore; 14; pub; D & E; Scholarships; Fellowships; SC 43, LC 21, GC 14; maj 400, grad 15
Activities: Schols offered
Ent Req: HS dipl 2.5 GPA or ACT score of 20
Degrees: BFA, MFA, BA, MA
Tuition: Res—$5,730 per yr, nonres—$15,580 per yr
Courses: †Art Education, †Art History, †Ceramics, Design, †Drawing, Goldsmithing, Graphic Arts, †Graphic Design, History of Art & Architecture, Illustration, Jewelry, Metals, Mixed Media, †Painting, †Printmaking, †Sculpture, †Silversmithing, †Studio Arts, Teacher Training

Summer School: Dir, Richard Helzer. Enrl 65; tuition res—$284.65 per cr, nonres—$695.05 per cr for 12 wk term. Courses—Art History, Ceramics, Drawing, Graphic Design, Metals, Painting, Printmaking, Sculpture, Special Workshops
—**School of Architecture**, Cheever Hall, Rm 160, Bozeman, MT 59717-3760; PO Box 173760, Bozeman, MT 59717-3760. Tel 406-994-4256; Fax 406-994-6696; Email architecture@montana.edu; Web: www.arch.montana.edu/; *Interim Dir* Steven Juroszek; *Interim Assoc Dir* John Brittingham
FT 13, PT 1; Pub; D & E; Scholarships; LabC 31, LC 39; maj 400
Degrees: BA(Environmental Design), MArch
Tuition: Res—$3,079 per yr; nonres—$9,075 per yr
Courses: Architectural Graphics, Architecture, Computer Applications in Architecture, Construction Drawings & Specifications, Design Fundamentals, Environmental Controls, History, Professional Practice, Structures, Theory
Summer School: Res—$171.40 undergrad per cr, $190.35 per cr, nonres—$421.25 undergrad per cr, $440.20 grad per cr

DILLON

THE UNIVERSITY OF MONTANA WESTERN, Art Program, 710 S Atlantic, Dillon, MT 59725. Tel 406-683-7232; Fax 406-683-7493; Email r_horst@umwestern.edu; Web: www.umwestern.edu/; *Chmn Dept* Randy Horst; *Prof* David Regan; *Prof* Eva Mastandrea
Estab 1897; Maintains nonprofit gallery, The University of Montana - Western Art Gallery & Museum, 710 S Atlantic, Dillon, MT 59725. Art supplies may be purchased on campus; FT 3; pub; 3 1/2 block sessions; Scholarships; SC 18, LC 2; maj 30
Ent Req: HS dipl
Degrees: BS & BA 4 yrs
Courses: Art Education, Art History, Ceramics, †Computer Art, Drawing, Glass Blowing, †Illustration, Painting, Photography, Printmaking, Sculpture
Summer School: Dir Anneliese Ripley. Courses—Ceramics, Glassblowing, Travel Study

GREAT FALLS

UNIVERSITY OF GREAT FALLS, Art Dept, 1301 20th St S, Art Bldg Great Falls, MT 59405-4934. Tel 406-761-8210; 791-5375; Fax 406-791-5394; Email jbecker@ufg.edu; Web: www.ugf.edu; *Prof Art* Julia Becker; *Prof Music* Dr John Cubbage; *Adjunct Prof Art* Susan Thomas; *Adjunct Prof Art* David Rothweiler; *Adjunct Prof Art* Sophia Sparklin; *Adjunct Prof Art* Leslie Fontana; *Adjunct Prof Art* Doug Wendt; *Adjunct Prof Art* Rebecca Scott
Estab 1933; Maintain library exhibit space on-campus; UGF Library, same address; on-campus shop where art supplies may be purchased; FT 1, PT 2; pvt; D & E; weekends & special sessions; Scholarships; Fellowships; SC 15, Lab C, LC9; approx 1,000, majs 38
Activities: Schols offered
Ent Req: high school grad, entry tests
Degrees: 4 yrs
Tuition: $10,000 per yr
Courses: †Art Appreciation, Art Education, †Art History, †Book Arts, †Calligraphy, Ceramics, †Collage, †Conceptual Art, Design, Drawing, †Film, †Graphic Design, †Handicrafts, †History of Art & Architecture, †Mixed Media, †Museum Staff Training, †Painting, †Photography, †Printmaking, †Restoration & Conservation, †Sculpture, †Stage Design, †Teacher Training, †Textile Design, †Theatre Arts, †Video
Children's Classes: Enrl 24; summer; pastel painting; drawing in nature; textile design; book arts; life drawing
Summer School: General art classes; Kerri Koteskey, Registrar

HAVRE

MONTANA STATE UNIVERSITY-NORTHERN, Humanities & Social Sciences, PO Box 7751, Havre, MT 59501-7751. Tel 406-265-3751, 265-3700; Fax 406-265-3777; Web: www.montanastateuniv.edu; *Art Dept Chmn* Will Ron
Estab 1929; pub; D & E; Scholarships; SC 15, LC 5, GC 9; D 425, grad 7
Ent Req: HS dipl
Degrees: AA 2 yrs, BS(Educ) and BA 4 yrs, MSc(Educ)
Courses: Art Education, Ceramics, Commercial Art, Drafting, Drawing, Graphic Arts, Painting, Sculpture
Adult Hobby Classes: Enrl 60. Courses—Classroom and Recreational Art, Watercolor Workshop
Summer School: Dir, Dr Gus Korb. Enrl 1390; two 5 wk sessions. Courses—Art Education, Art Methods K-12, Art Therapy

MILES CITY

MILES COMMUNITY COLLEGE, Dept of Fine Arts & Humanities, 2715 Dickinson St, Miles City, MT 59301-4799. Tel 406-234-3031; Web: www.milescc.edu; *Instr* Fred McKee, MFA
Estab 1937, dept estab 1967; pub; D & E; Scholarships; SC 17, LC 1; D 36, E 23, non-maj 55, maj 4
Ent Req: HS dipl, ACT
Degrees: AA 2 yrs, cert
Courses: Art Appreciation, Ceramics, Design, Graphic Arts, Graphic Design, Jewelry, Painting, Photography
Adult Hobby Classes: Enrl 39; tuition $58 per cr hr. Courses—Crafts, Jewelry Making, Painting, Photography, Pottery
Children's Classes: Kids Kamp-2 wks in summer

MISSOULA

UNIVERSITY OF MONTANA, School of Art, 32 Campus Dr (FA205) Missoula, MT 59812. Tel 406-243-4181; Email art.information@mso.umt.edu; Web: www.umt.edu/art; *Prof* Beth Lo, MFA; *Prof* Rafael Chacon, PhD; *Prof* Mary Ann Bonjorni, MFA; *Prof* James Bailey, MFA; *Prof* Elizabeth Dove, MFA; *Prof* Cathryn Mallory; *Assoc Prof* Matt Hamon, MFA; *Asst Prof* Jennifer Combe, MFA; *Prof* Julia Galloway, MFA; *Prof* Valerie Hedquist, PhD; *Assoc Prof* Brad Allen, MFA; *Assoc Prof* Kevin Bell, MFA; *Assoc Prof* Trey Hill, MFA
Pub; D & E; Scholarships
Ent Req: HS dipl
Degrees: BA & BFA 4 yrs, MA & MFA
Courses: Art Appreciation, Art Criticism and Social History of Art, Art Education, †Art History, †Ceramics, †Drawing, History of Art & Architecture, Mixed Media, †Painting, †Photography, †Printmaking, †Sculpture
Summer School: Co-Chairs Bobby Tilton & Cathryn Mallory. Enrl 25 per class; Courses—Various regular & experimental classes

NEBRASKA

BELLEVUE

BELLEVUE COLLEGE, Art Dept, 1000 Galvin Rd S, Bellevue, NE 68005-3058. Tel 402-291-8100; *Chmn* Dr Joyce Wilson PhD
Scholarships
Degrees: BA, BFA, BTS(Commercial Art)
Tuition: Undergrad—$135 per cr hr, grad $265 per cr hr
Courses: Advertising Design, Aesthetics, Art History, Art Management, Ceramics, Commercial Art, Design, Drawing, History of Art & Architecture, Life Drawing, Painting, Papermaking, Photography, Printmaking, Sculpture
Summer School: Tuition $132 per cr hr

CHADRON

CHADRON STATE COLLEGE, Dept of Art, 1000 Main St, Chadron, NE 69337-2690. Tel 308-432-6326; Fax 308-432-6464; Email rbird@asc.edu; Web: www.csc.edu.art; *Chmn* Richard Bird, MFA; *Asst Prof* Mary Donahue, MFA; *Asst Prof* Laura Bentz, MFA; *Instr* Don Ruleaux, MFA; *Instr* Nancy Sharps, MA; *Instr* Daniel Binkard; *Instr* Dewayne Gimeson
Estab 1911, dept estab 1935; Maintain nonprofit art gallery, Gallery 239 & Main Art Gallery, 100 Main, Chadron, NE 69337; Library; on-campus shop where art supplies may be purchased; pub; D & E; Scholarships; SC 24, LC 4, GC 6; D 2000, off-campus 500, non-maj 40, maj 65
Ent Req: HS dipl
Degrees: BS & BA 4 yrs
Tuition: Res—undergrad $180 per hr, grad $220 per hr; nonres—undergrad $315 per hr, grad $388 per hr; campus res—room & board $2,400
Courses: Advertising Design, Art Appreciation, Art Education, Art History, Ceramics, Design, Drawing, Glass, Graphic Design, Jewelry, Painting, Photography, Printmaking, Sculpture
Adult Hobby Classes: Enrl 30. Tuition varies. Courses vary
Summer School: Dir, Dr Taylor. Enrl 30; tuition same as above. Courses—usually 2 - 4 courses on semi-rotation basis

COLUMBUS

CENTRAL COMMUNITY COLLEGE - COLUMBUS CAMPUS, Business & Arts Cluster, 4500 63rd St, Columbus, NE; PO Box 1027, Columbus, NE 68602-1027. Tel 402-564-7132; *Head Dept* Ellen Lake; *Instr* Richard Abraham, MA; *Instr* Kathleen Lohr, MA
Estab 1969, dept estab 1971; pub; D & E; Scholarships; SC 8, LC 1; D 100, E 20, non-maj 77, maj 43
Ent Req: HS dipl, GED
Degrees: AA 2 yrs
Courses: Air Brush, Art History, Ceramics, Color Theory, †Commercial Art, Design, Drafting, Drawing, Graphic Arts, Handicrafts, Interior Design, Life Drawing, Mixed Media, Painting, Photography, Printmaking, Stage Design, Textile Design, Theatre Arts
Summer School: Dir, Richard D Abraham. Enrl 25; tuition $41 per hr for term of 7 wks beginning June. Courses—Drawing, Painting

CRETE

DOANE COLLEGE, Dept of Art, 1014 Boswell Ave, Crete, NE 68333-2426. Tel 402-826-2161, 826-8273; Web: www.doane.edu; *Head Dept* Richard Terrell
Estab 1872, dept estab 1958; FT 3; pvt; D; Scholarships; SC 6, LC 5; 150, non-maj 140, maj 10
Ent Req: HS dipl
Degrees: BA 4 yrs
Courses: Art Education, Art History, Ceramics, Drawing, Film, Graphic Design, Painting, Printmaking, Sculpture, Stage Design

HASTINGS

HASTINGS COLLEGE, Department of Visual Arts, 710 N Turner, Hastings, NE 68901-7621. Tel 402-461-7396; Fax 402-461-7480; Email tmcgehee@hastings.edu; Web: www.hastings.edu; *Dir Pub Rels* Joyce Ore; *Chmn Dept* Turner McGehee; *Prof* Tom Kreager; *Chmn* Tom Kreager; *Prof* Turner McGehee; *Prof* Lynn Cox; *Prof* Aaron Badham

Estab 1925; Maintains a non-profit art gallery; FT 4, PT 4; Private; D & E; Scholarships; SC 16, LC 5; maj 50, others 350
Ent Req: HS grad
Degrees: BA 4 yrs
Courses: †Art Appreciation, Art Education, Art History, Ceramics, Color, †Commercial Art, Commercial Art, Conceptual Art, Design, Drawing, Glass Blowing, Graphic Arts, †Graphic Design, Painting, †Photography, Printmaking, Sculpture, Video

KEARNEY

UNIVERSITY OF NEBRASKA, KEARNEY, Dept of Art & Art History, 905 W 25th St, Kearney, NE 68849-0003. Tel 308-865-8353; Fax 308-865-8806; Web: www.unk.edu; *Chmn & Prof* Doug Waterfield; *Assoc Prof* Jake Jacobson, MFA; *Assoc Prof* Tom Dennis, MFA; *Asst Prof* Richard Schuessler, MFA; *Asst Prof* John Stanko; *Asst Prof* Derrick Burbul; *Asst Prof* Chad Fonfara; *Asst Prof* Donna Alden, PhD; *Asst Prof* Victoria Goro-Rapoport; *Prof* Mark Hartman; *Prof* Lori Santos; *Lectr* John McKirahan; *Lectr* John Franczak
Estab 1905; Maintains nonprofit art gallery, Walker Art Gallery, 2506 12th Ave, Kearney, NE. Campus shop where art supplies may be purchased; FT 13, PT 11; pub; D & E; Scholarships; SC 20, LC 12, GC 18; D 870, E 22, non-maj 1400, maj 250, grad 25
Ent Req: HS dipl, SAT or ACT recommended
Degrees: BFA, BA, BA(Art History), BA(Educ), 4 yrs, MA(Educ-Art)
Courses: Aesthetics, Art Education, Art History, Ceramics, Computer Graphics, †Drawing, Glass Blowing, †Painting, Photography, †Printmaking, †Sculpture, †Teacher Training, Visual Communication & Design
Summer School: Chmn, Doug Waterfield. Enrl 250; Courses—Drawing

LINCOLN

NEBRASKA WESLEYAN UNIVERSITY, Art Dept, 5000 St Paul, Lincoln, NE 68504. Tel 402-465-2273; Fax 402-465-2179; Web: www.nebrwesleyan.edu; *Assoc Prof* Lisa Lockman, MFA; *Adjunct Prof Art* Susan Horn, MFA; *Dept Chair, Prof Art History* Dr Donald Paoletta, PhD; *Asst Prof* David Gracie, MFA
Estab 1888, dept estab 1890; Maintains nonprofit gallery, Elder Gallery 50th & Huntington Sts, Lincoln, NE 68504; FT 3 PT 2; pvt; D & E; Scholarships; SC 22, LC 4; non-maj 300, maj 50
Ent Req: HS dipl, ent exam
Degrees: BA, BFA & BS 4 yrs
Courses: Art Education, Art History, Ceramics, Design, Drawing, Graphic Arts, Graphic Design, Jewelry, Painting, Photography, Printmaking, Sculpture, Silversmithing
Adult Hobby Classes: Enrl 30; tuition $152 per sem hr. Degree Program
Summer School: Enrl 30; tuition $152 per sem hr per 8 wks

UNIVERSITY OF NEBRASKA-LINCOLN, Dept of Art & Art History, Stadium Dr & T St, Richards Hall 120 Lincoln, NE 68588-0114. Tel 402-472-2631; Fax 402-472-9746; Email artdept@unl.edu; Web: www.unl.edu/art; *Chmn Grad Comt* Gail Kendall, MFA; *Chmn Dept* Ed Forde, MFA
Estab 1869, dept 1912; Maintain nonprofit art gallery; Eisentrager/Howard Gallery, 1st Floor Richards Hall, Stadium Dr & T St, Univ Nebr, Lincoln 68588-0114; art supplies available on-campus; FT 20, PT 8; pub; D & E; Scholarships; SC 71, LC 27, GC 45; D 1950, E 175, non-maj 600, maj 400, grad 25
Ent Req: HS dipl
Degrees: BA, BFA, MFA 2-3 Yrs
Courses: †2-D & 3-D Design, Advertising Design, †Art History, Book Art, †Ceramics, †Commercial Art, †Drawing, †Graphic Arts, †Graphic Design, †Illustration, Mixed Media, †Painting, Papermaking, †Photography, †Printmaking, †Sculpture
Summer School: Dir, Nancy Stara. Enrl 250; two 5 wk sessions beginning June & Aug. Courses—Art History, Ceramics, Drawing, Painting, Photography, Printmaking, Special Problems & Topics

NORFOLK

NORTHEAST COMMUNITY COLLEGE, Dept of Liberal Arts, 801 E Benjamin Ave, Norfolk, NE 68701-6831; PO Box 469, Norfolk, NE 68702-0469. Tel 402-371-2020, Ext 480; Fax 402-644-0650; Web: www.northeastcollege.com; *Instr* Julie Noyes, MA; *Instr* Harry Lindner, MA
Estab 1928; FT 3 PT 1; pub; D & E; Scholarships; SC 5, LC 5; D 150, E 50, non-maj 100, maj 50
Ent Req: HS dipl
Degrees: AA & AS 2 yrs
Courses: Art Education, Art History, Drawing, Graphic Design, Painting, Photography
Adult Hobby Classes: Oil Painting
Summer School: Chmn Dept, Patrick Keating. Tuition same as regular yr. Courses—Photography

OMAHA

COLLEGE OF SAINT MARY, Art Dept, 7000 Mercy Rd, Omaha, NE 68106-2632. Tel 402-399-2405; Web: www.csm.edu; *Chmn Dept* Tom Schlosser
Estab 1923; pvt, W; D & E; Scholarships; SC 11, LC 5; D 620, maj 18, special 2
Ent Req: HS dipl
Degrees: BA and BS 4 yrs
Courses: Art History, Ceramics, Computer Graphics, Design, Painting, Photography, Sculpture, Teacher Training, Women in Art
Adult Hobby Classes: Enrl 587; tuition $133 per cr hr. Evening & weekend college offer full range of general education classes
Summer School: Dir, Dr Vernon Lestrud. Enrl 572; tuition $133 per cr hr. Full range of studio & history general education classes

CREIGHTON UNIVERSITY, Fine & Performing Arts Dept, 2500 California Plaza, Omaha, NE 68178. Tel 402-280-2509, 280-2700; Fax 402-280-2320; Web: www.creighton.edu; *Assoc Chair* Fr Michael Flecky SJ, MFA; *Assoc Chair Performing Arts* Alan Klem, MFA; *Dance Coordr* Valerie Roche, ARAD; *Instr* John Thein, MFA; *Instr* Carole Seitz, MFA; *Instr* Bob Bosco, MFA; *Instr* Bill Hutson, MFA; *Instr* Jerry Horning, MFA; *Theater Coordr* Bill Vandest, MFA; *Instr* Don Doll SJ, MFA; *Instr Art History* Roger Aikin; *Instr Sculpture* Littleton Alston; *Gallery Dir* Fr Ted Bohr SJ; *Music Coordr* Dr Fredrick Henna; *Instr Music* Fr Charles Jurgensmeier; *Instr Arts Mgmt* Mike Markey; *Theater Instr* Michael McCandaless; *Instr Set Design* Mark Krejci
Estab 1878, dept estab 1966; den; D & E; Scholarships; SC 87, LC 16; 888, non-maj 850, maj 38, cert prog 24
Ent Req: HS dipl, regular col admis exam
Degrees: BA & BFA 4 yrs
Courses: 3-D Design, Advertising Design, Art Appreciation, Art Education, Art History, Ceramics, Color Theory, Design, Drawing, History of Art & Architecture, Intaglio, Lithography, Painting, Photography, Printmaking, Sculpture, Studio Fundamentals, Teacher Training, †Theatre Arts
Adult Hobby Classes: Advertising, Art History, Ceramics, Design, Life Drawing, Painting, Photography

UNIVERSITY OF NEBRASKA AT OMAHA, School of the Arts, 6001 Dodge St, Omaha, NE 68182-0002. Tel 402-554-2420, 554-2800; Web: www.unomaha.edu; *Prof* Bonnie O'Connell, MFA; *Prof* Barbara Simcoe; *Prof* David Helm; *Asst Prof* Adrian Duran, PhD; *Prof, Unit Coordr* Amy Morris, PhD; *Asst Prof* Bridget Sandhoff, PhD; *Asst Prof* Jeremy L Johnson, PhD; *Asst Prof* Lilly Lu, PhD; *Assoc Prod* Russ Nordman, MFA; *Asst* Jave Yoshimoto, MFA
Estab 1908, dept estab 1910; maintain a non-profit art gallery; on-campus shop where art supplies may be purchased; Maintain non-profit art gallery; FT 12 PT 8; pub; D & E, Online; Scholarships; SC 32, LC 22, GC 10; D 550, E 100
Ent Req: HS dipl
Degrees: BA & BFA 4 yrs
Courses: †Architecture, †Art Education, †Art History, Bookarts, †Ceramics, †Drawing, †Graphic Design, †Painting, Paper Making, †Printmaking, †Sculpture, Visual Technology
Summer School: Chmn Dept, Dr Martin Rosenberg. Tuition same as above for term of 5 wks. Courses—Vary

PERU

PERU STATE COLLEGE, Art Dept, PO Box 10, Peru, NE 68421-0010. Tel 402-872-2271, 872-3815; Email perry@nscs.peru.edu; *Prof* Kenneth Anderson
Scholarships
Degrees: BA, BAEd, BS, MA
Tuition: Res—$65.75 per sem; nonres—$131.50 per sem
Courses: Art Appreciation, Art Education, Art History, Ceramics, Design, Drawing, Figure Drawing, Independent Art Study, Lettering, Painting, Photography, Printmaking, Sculpture, Stage Design
Summer School: $65.75 cr for 5 weeks

SCOTTSBLUFF

WESTERN NEBRASKA COMMUNITY COLLEGE, Division of Language & Arts, 1601 E 27th St, Scottsbluff, NE 69361-1899. Tel 308-635-3606; Web: www.wncc.net; *Chmn Div Language* Paul Jacobson; *Chmn Art* Ziya Sever, MA
Estab 1926; FT 2; pub; D & E; Scholarships; SC 8, LC 3; D 60, E 150, non-maj 50, maj 10
Ent Req: HS dipl
Degrees: AA & AS 2 yrs
Courses: Art Education, Art History, Drawing, History of Film, Music Education, Painting, Photography, Theatre Arts
Adult Hobby Classes: Enrl 150; tuition $15 per course. Courses—Carving, Drawing, Macrame, Pottery, Sculpture, Stained Glass, Watercolor & Oil Painting, Weaving

SEWARD

CONCORDIA UNIVERSITY, Art Dept, 800 N Columbia, Seward, NE 68434. Tel 402-643-3651; Web: www.cune.edu; *Prof* Richard Wiegmann, MFA; *Prof* Lynn Soloway, MFA; *Prof* Jim Bockelman, MFA; *Head Dept* William R Wolfram, MFA; *Prof* Kenneth Schmidt, PhD
Estab 1894; Maintain nonprofit art gallery; Marxhausen Art Gallery, 800 N Columbia Ave, Seward, NE 68434; den; D & E; Scholarships; SC 40, LC 7; non-maj 10, maj 95
Ent Req: HS dipl
Degrees: BS, BA 4 yr, BFA 4 yr
Courses: Advertising Design, †Art Education, Ceramics, Collage, †Commercial Art, Design, Drawing, Graphic Arts, Graphic Design, Illustration, Mixed Media, Painting, Photography, Printmaking, Sculpture, Teacher Training
Summer School: Tuition $210 per cr hr for term of 2 1/2 wks beginning early May

WAYNE

WAYNE STATE COLLEGE, Dept Art & Design, 1111 Main St, Wayne, NE 68787-1172. Tel 402-375-7359; Fax 402-375-7204; Web: www.wsc.edu; *Prof* Steve Elliot; *Prof* Pearl Hansen; *Dept Chair* Wayne Anderson; *Prof* Marlene Mueller; *Prof* Vic Reynolds; *Lectr* Judith Berry
Estab 1910; Maintains nonprofit gallery, Norstrand Visual Arts Gallery, FA, 111 Main, Wayne NE 68787; 8 FT & PT; pub; D&E; Scholarships; SC 21, LC 8; maj 85, others 700, total 4,000
Ent Req: HS grad
Degrees: BA, BS, MA & MS

Courses: †Advertising Design, †Art Appreciation, Art History, †Ceramics, Commercial Art, Design, Drafting, Drawing, Graphic Arts, Handicrafts, Jewelry, Painting, †Printmaking, Sculpture, †Teacher Training
Summer School: Three sessions

YORK

YORK COLLEGE, Art Dept, 1125 E 8TH ST, York, NE 68467-3200. Tel 402-362-4441, Ext 218; *Asst Prof* Paul M Shields
Sch estab 1956, dept estab 1962; Pvt; D; Scholarships; SC 6, LC 1; D 26, non-maj 20, maj 10
Ent Req: HS dipl, ACT
Degrees: AA 2 yrs
Tuition: Res—undergrad $5,150 per sem
Courses: 2-D & 3-D Design, Art Appreciation, Art History, Commercial Design, Drawing, Painting

NEVADA

INCLINE VILLAGE

SIERRA NEVADA COLLEGE, Fine Arts Dept, 999 Tahoe Blvd, Incline Village, NV 89451-9500. Tel 775-831-1314; Email ashipley@sierranevada.edu; Web: www.sierranevada.edu; *Dir Gallery* Russell Dudley; *Chmn* Anne Shipley; *Dir Summer Arts* Sheri Leigh; *Asst Prof* J Damron; *Asst Prof* Mary Kenny; *Asst Prof* Chris Lanier
Estab 1969; Maintains Tahoe Gallery, Abernathy Hall, 800 College Dr, Incline Village, Nev; art supplies available at on-campus shop; pvt; D & E; Scholarships; SC 75, LC 8; D 260, E 40, maj 30
Collections: Contemporary ceramics, Contemporary mixed media
Ent Req: HS dipl, 2.5 grade point avg
Degrees: BA, BFA 4 yr
Courses: Art Appreciation, Art Education, Art History, †Ceramics, Design, Digital Arts, †Drawing, †Film, Graphic Arts, Mixed Media, Music, †Painting, †Photography, †Printmaking, Sculpture, Teacher Training, †Theatre Arts, †Video
Adult Hobby Classes: Enrl 80; tuition per cr. Courses—Ceramics
Summer School: Dir, Sheri Leigh. Enrl 200; tuition $420 per course non cr. Courses—Studio Arts

LAS VEGAS

UNIVERSITY OF NEVADA, LAS VEGAS, Dept of Art, 4505 S Maryland Pkwy, Las Vegas, NV 89154-9900; PO Box 455002, Las Vegas, NV 89154-5002. Tel 702-895-3237; Fax 702-895-4346; Web: http://art.unlv.edu/MFA/; *Assoc Prof* Cathie Kelly; *Prof* Thomas J Holder; *Prof* Jeffrey Burden; *Assoc Prof* Pasha Rafat; *Assoc Prof* Mary Warner; *Prof & Chmn* Mark Burns; *Prof* Catherine Angel; *Asst Prof* Emily Kennerk; *Asst Prof* Louisa McDonald; *Asst Prof* Sang-Duok Seo; *Prof* Bob Tracy; *Asst Prof* Stephen Hendee; *Asst Prof* Helga Watkins; *Asst Prof* Kirsten Swenson
Estab 1955; Maintains Donna Beam Fine Art Gallery, 4505 Maryland Pkwy Box 5002, Las Vegas NV 89154; Pub; D & E; Scholarships; SC 32, LC 18; all courses 551, maj 95
Ent Req: HS dipl, ACT
Degrees: BA and BFA 5 yrs, MFA
Courses: Art Appreciation, Ceramics, Drawing, Graphic Design, Intermedia, Painting, Photography, Printmaking, Sculpture
Summer School: Dir, Thomas Holder. Enrl varies; 5 wk session. Courses—Ceramics, Drawing, Painting, Printmaking

RENO

UNIVERSITY OF NEVADA, RENO, Art Dept, Mail Stop 224, Reno, NV 89557-0001. Tel 775-784-1110, 784-6682; Web: www.unr.edu; *Chmn Dept* Ed W Martinez
Estab 1940; FT 10; pub; D & E; Scholarships; SC 20, LC 6, GC 5; maj 120, others 800
Ent Req: HS grad and 16 units
Degrees: BA 4 yr
Courses: †Art Education, †Art History, †Ceramics, †Drawing, Graphic Design, †Painting, †Photography, †Printmaking, †Sculpture
Adult Hobby Classes: Evening division in all areas
Summer School: Courses in all studio areas

NEW HAMPSHIRE

DURHAM

UNIVERSITY OF NEW HAMPSHIRE, Dept of Art & Art History, 30 Academic Way, Paul Creative Arts Ctr Durham, NH 03824-2617. Tel 603-862-2190; Fax 603-862-2191; Email art-arthistory@unh.edu; Web: cola.unh.edu/art-and-art-history; *Chmn* Prof Craig Hood, MFA; *Prof* Grant Drumheller, MFA; *Prof* Jennifer Moses, MFA; *Prof* Brian Chu; *Prof* Patricia Emison; *Assoc Prof* Benjamin Cariens, MFA; *Assoc Prof* Julee Holcombe, MFA; *Assoc Prof* Leah Woods, MFA; *Asst Prof* Ivo van der Graaff, PhD; *Asst Prof* Susan Wager, PhD; *Asst Prof* Sachiko Akiyama, MFA
Estab 1928, dept estab 1941; Maintains Visual Resource Center, 30 Academic Way, Durham, NH 03824; pub; D & E; Scholarships; Fellowships; SC 55, LC 17, GC 10, Online 4; non-maj 1000, maj 70, grad 5, others 60
Ent Req: HS dipl, portfolio
Degrees: BFA & BA(Studio Arts & Art History) 4 yrs, MAT 5 yrs
Courses: Architecture, Art Education, Art History, Ceramics, Drawing, Painting, Photography, Printmaking, Sculpture

HANOVER

DARTMOUTH COLLEGE, Dept of Art History, 6033 Carpenter Hall, Hanover, NH 03755-3570. Tel 603-646-2306; Fax 603-646-3428; Email art.history@dartmouth.edu; Web: www.dartmouth.edu/~arthist/; *Chair* Ada Cohen; *Admin* Elizabeth Alexander
Estab 1906; Maintain nonprofit art gallery; Hood Museum of Art, Hanover, NH 03755; FT 8; pvt; D; LC 25, other 6; in col 4000, maj 46
Degrees: AB 4 yr
Tuition: $36,915 per yr, room & board $10,930
Courses: †Art History

HENNIKER

NEW ENGLAND COLLEGE, Art & Art History, 98 Bridge St, Henniker, NH 03242-3292. Tel 603-428-2211; Fax 603-428-7230; Web: www.nec.edu; *Prof* Marguerite Walsh, MFA; *Prof* Farid A Haddad, MFA; *Assoc Prof* Inez McDermott, MA; *Asst Prof* Darryl Furtkamp, MFA
Estab 1946; Maintain nonprofit art gallery; New England College Art Gallery, Preston Barn, Henniker, NH 03242; art supplies can be purchased on-campus; Pvt; D; Scholarships; non-maj 250; maj 65
Degrees: BA
Courses: †Art Appreciation, †Art History, Design, Drawing, Graphic Arts, Mixed Media, †Painting, †Photography, Printmaking, Sculpture

MANCHESTER

NEW HAMPSHIRE INSTITUTE OF ART, 148 Concord St, Manchester, NH 03104-4858. Tel 603-623-0313; Web: www.nhia.edu; *Interim Pres* Dr Daniel Lyman
Estab 1898; pvt; cr and adult educ courses; D & E; Scholarships; SC 16; 1000
Ent Req: none
Degrees: BFA
Courses: Aesthetics, Art Appreciation, Art Education, Art History, Calligraphy, †Ceramics, Collage, Design, Fashion Arts, Handicrafts, History of Art & Architecture, Illustration, Jewelry, Mixed Media, †Painting, †Photography, Printmaking, Sculpture, Silversmithing, Theatre Arts, Weaving
Adult Hobby Classes: Enrl 400; tuition $150-$600 for 12-15 wks. Courses—Art History, Ceramics, Drawing, Fiber Arts, Painting, Photography, Printmaking, Sculpture
Children's Classes: Enrl 75; tuition $75-$125 for 6-12 wks. Courses—Artful Hands
Summer School: Courses—Same as in Fall & Spring

SAINT ANSELM COLLEGE, Dept of Fine Arts, 100 Saint Anselm Dr, Manchester, NH 03102-1308. Tel 603-641-7370; Fax 603-641-7116; Email khoffman@anselm.edu; Web: www.anselm.edu; *Chmn* Katherine Hoffman; *Prof* Dr Kate Bentz; *Prof* Dr Francis Kayali; *Prof* Dr Sean Parr; *Prof* Kimberly Ashury
Estab 1889; Maintains a non-profit art gallery: Alva de Mars Megan Chapel Art Center, St Anselm College, 100 St Anselm Dr, Manchester, NH 03102; FT 3; pvt; D & E; Scholarships; SC 2, LC 9; 1500
Ent Req: HS dipl, relative standing, SAT, interview
Degrees: BA 4 yr
Courses: Aesthetics, Architecture, †Art History, Ceramics, Design, Drawing, Film, †Fine Arts, Graphic Arts, Graphic Design, History of Art & Architecture, Mixed Media, Music History, Theory & Performance, Painting, Photography, Printmaking, Sculpture, Teacher Training, Theatre Arts
Summer School: Courses—vary

NASHUA

RIVIER COLLEGE, Art Dept, 420 Main St, Nashua, NH 03060. Tel 603-888-1311, Ext 8276
Estab 1933, dept estab 1940; pvt; D & E; Scholarships; SC 100, LC 25; D 50, E 40, non-maj 20, maj 70
Ent Req: HS dipl, SAT, certain HS equivalencies, preliminary evidence of artistic ability, slide portfolio
Degrees: AA 2 yrs, BA, and BFA 4 yrs
Courses: Aesthetics, Art Appreciation, Art Education, Art History, Calligraphy, Ceramics, Collage, Conceptual Art, Design, †Digital Imaging, Drawing, †Graphic Design, †Illustration, Mixed Media, †Painting, †Photography, Printmaking, Sculpture, Silversmithing, Teacher Training, Weaving
Adult Hobby Classes: Enrl 60; tuition $171 per cr for 15 wk term. Courses—Variety of fine arts & design studio courses
Children's Classes: Enrl 24. Courses—Pre-college summer art program
Summer School: Dir, Rose Arthur, PhD. Tuition $132 per cr for 6 wks. Courses—Master Workshops in Basic Design, Drawing, Etching, Graphic Design, Painting, Sculpture

NEW LONDON

COLBY-SAWYER COLLEGE, Dept of Fine & Performing Arts, 100 Main St, New London, NH 03257. Tel 603-526-3000, 526-3661, Ext 3666 (Chair); Fax 603-526-2135; Email colbyweb@colby-sawyer.edu; Web: www.colby-sawyer.edu;

Prof Loretta Barnett, MFA; *Prof* Jon Keenan, MFA; *Chair & Asst Prof* Brian Clancy, PhD; *Asst Prof* Nicholas Gaffney, MFA; *Asst Prof* Brandy Gibbs-Riley, MFA; *Assoc Prof* Bert Yarborough, MFA
Estab 1837; Maintains nonprofit Marian Graves Mugar Art Gallery & campus shop for purchase of art supplies; FT 6; pvt; D; Scholarships; SC 24, LC 25; 1150 univ; 60 dept
Ent Req: high school dipl
Degrees: BA (Art, Art History & Graphic Design), BFA (Art & Graphic Design)
Courses: Acting, Advertising Design, Aesthetics, American Art, Art Appreciation, †Art History, †Ceramics, Creative Expression, Dance, †Design, †Drawing, †Graphic Design, History of Art & Architecture, Life Drawing, Music, †Painting, †Photography, †Printmaking, †Sculpture, Stage Craft, Theatre Design, Theatre History, Typography

PLYMOUTH

PLYMOUTH STATE COLLEGE, Art Dept, 17 High St, Plymouth, NH 03264-1595. Tel 603-535-2201; Fax 603-535-3892; Email bhaust@mail.plymouth.edu; Web: www.plymouth.edu; *Head Dept* Bill Haust
Estab 1871; FT 11; pub; D & E; Scholarships; SC 17, LC 8; D 3050, maj 90
Ent Req: HS grad, references, health record, transcript, SAT, CEEB, ACT
Degrees: BS, BFA & BA 4 yrs
Courses: Architecture, Art Appreciation, †Art Education, †Art History, †Ceramics, Design, †Drawing, †Graphic Design, Illustration, Museum Staff Training, †Painting, †Photography, †Printmaking, †Sculpture, †Teacher Training
Adult Hobby Classes: Dir, Gail Carr. Enrl 50. Courses—Vary
Children's Classes: Courses available
Summer School: Courses vary

RINDGE

FRANKLIN PIERCE COLLEGE, Dept of Fine Arts & Graphic Communications, 40 University Dr, Rindge, NH 03461-5046. Tel 603-899-4000; Fax 603-899-4308; *Co-Chmn* Robert Diercks
Estab 1962; pvt; D & E; Scholarships; SC 20, LC 2
Ent Req: HS dipl
Degrees: BA(Fine Arts), BA(Graphic Design)
Courses: Art Education, Art History, Ceramics, Color Photography, Commercial Art, Design, Drawing, Graphic Design, Illustration, Painting, Photography, Printmaking, Sculpture, Stage Design, Teacher Training
Summer School: Color Photography, Landscape Painting

SHARON

SHARON ARTS CENTER, School Arts & Crafts, 457 NH Route 123, Sharon, NH 03458-7116. Tel 603-924-7256; Fax 603-924-6074; Email keri@sharonarts.org; Web: www.sharonarts.org
Estab 1947; Maintains a nonprofit art gallery, Sharon Arts Gallery, 30 Grove St, Peterborough, NH 03458, 603-924-7676; PT 30; pvt; D & E; Scholarships; SC 75; classes yr round; D 700, E 100
Ent Req: none
Tuition: $180 members, $215 non-members
Courses: Basketry, Calligraphy, Ceramics, Drawing, †Glassmaking, Jewelry, Painting, Photography, Printmaking, Sculpture, Weaving, Woodcarving
Adult Hobby Classes: Enrl 900. Courses—Visual & Tactile Arts
Children's Classes: Enrl 100. Courses—Visual & Tactile Arts
Summer School: Dir, Deb DeCicco. Courses—Visual & Tactile Arts, Drawing, Painting, Jewelry, Ceramics, Weaving & others; July Art Week for Teens

NEW JERSEY

BLACKWOOD

CAMDEN COUNTY COLLEGE, Visual & Performing Arts Dept, 200 College Dr, Blackwood, NJ 08012-3228; PO Box 200, Blackwood, NJ 08012-0200. Tel 856-227-7200; Fax 856-374-4969; *Prof* L Dell'Olio; *Dean & Prof* J Rowlands
Estab 1966; Scholarships; SC 12, LC 10; 100
Ent Req: HS dipl or equivalent
Degrees: AA 2 yrs
Courses: Art History, Art Therapy, Ceramics, Computer Graphics, Design, Drawing, Painting, Sculpture
Adult Hobby Classes: Special sessions
Children's Classes: Special sessions
Summer School: Courses available

CALDWELL

CALDWELL COLLEGE, Dept of Fine Arts, 120 Bloomfield Ave, Caldwell, NJ 07006-5310. Tel 973-618-3238; Fax 973-618-3915; Email jcroce@caldwell.edu; Web: www.caldwellcollege.edu; *Prof* Lawrence Szycher; *Chmn* Judith Croce; *Prof* Kendall Baker; *Asst Prof* Jennifer Noonan
Estab 1939; Maintain a nonprofit art gallery, Viscegia Art Gallery, same address; library; FT 3, PT 6; pvt; D & E; Scholarships; SC 45+, LC 10+, GC 5; D 1,535, E 1,000, maj 35, dept 90, GS 10
Activities: Schols offered
Ent Req: HS grad, art portfolio
Degrees: BA 3-4 yr, BFA 4-5 yr
Courses: †Advertising Design, †Aesthetics, †Art Appreciation, Art Education, Art History, Art Therapy, Ceramics, †Collage, †Commercial Art, †Conceptual Art, †Design, Drawing, †Graphic Arts, †Graphic Design, †History of Art & Architecture, †Mixed Media, †Museum Staff Training, Painting, Photography, †Printmaking, Sculpture, †Teacher Training, †Video

CAMDEN

RUTGERS UNIVERSITY, CAMDEN, Art Dept, 311 N 5th St, Fine Arts Ctr Camden, NJ 08102-1405. Tel 609-225-6176; Fax 609-225-6330; Web: www.camden.rutgers.edu; *Chmn* John Giannotti
FT 5, PT 9; pub; D; SC 24, LC 13; art D 450, maj 75
Ent Req: HS dipl, must qualify for regular col admis, portfolio
Degrees: BA(Art) 4 yrs
Courses: Art History, Computer Animation, Computer Graphics, Drawing, Graphic Design, Museum Studies, Painting, Photography, Printmaking, Sculpture
Summer School: Chmn, John Giannotti. Courses—Varies

DEMAREST

THE ART SCHOOL AT OLD CHURCH, 561 Piermont Rd, Demarest, NJ 07627-1615. Tel 201-767-7160; Fax 201-767-0497; Email info@tasoc.org; Web: www.tasoc.org; *Admin Dir* Karen Shalom; *Communs* Lorraine Zaloom; *Exec Dir* Maria Danziger; *Opers Dir* Peter Schmidt; *Dir Gallery* Rachael Faillace; *Exec Asst* Melissa Pazcoguin; *Ceramic Studio Mgr* David Shirey
Estab 1974; Maintain nonprofit art gallery; The Mikhail Zakin Gallery at Old Church, 561 Piermont Rd, Demarest, NJ 07627; on-campus shop with limited art supplies; Pub; D & E; Scholarships; Fellowships; SC 75; D 475, E 325
Publications: Centerling, semi-annual
Tuition: Varies per course
Courses: Art Appreciation, †Assemblage, Ceramics, †Collage, †Crocheting, Drawing, Fiber Art, Glass Bead Making, Jewelry, †Knitting, †Metalsmithing, Mixed Media, Painting, Photography, Printmaking, †Quiltmaking, Sculpture, Stained Glass
Adult Hobby Classes: Enrl 450. Courses—Ceramics, Drawing, Metals, Painting, Printmaking, Sculpture, Basketry, Glass
Children's Classes: Enrl 250. Courses—Ceramics, Drawing, Painting, Sculpture, Textiles

DOVER

JOE KUBERT SCHOOL OF CARTOON & GRAPHIC ART, INC, 37 Myrtle Ave, Dover, NJ 07801-4085. Tel 973-361-1327; Fax 973-361-1844; Web: www.kubertsworld.com; *Instr* Hy Eisman; *Instr* Irwin Hasen; *Instr* Douglas Compton; *Instr* Michael Chen; *Instr* Jose Delbo; *Instr* Kim Demulder; *Instr* Jim McWeeney; *Instr* Judy Mates; *Instr* Greg Webb; *Instr* John Troy; *Pres* Joe Kubert
Estab 1976; pvt; D & E; Scholarships; SC all, LC all; D 200, E 100
Ent Req: HS dipl, interview, portfolio
Degrees: 3 yr dipl
Courses: Cartoon Graphics, Cinematic Animation, Commercial Art, Design, Graphic Arts, Illustration, Lettering, Painting, Video
Adult Hobby Classes: Enrl 100; tuition $200 per 12 wks. Courses—Basic & Advanced Paste-Ups & Mechanicals, Cartoon Workshop, Computer Graphic/Animation Workshop
Children's Classes: Enrl 20; tuition $15 per class. Courses—Saturday Cartoon Sketch Class
Summer School: Courses—same as regular session

EDISON

MIDDLESEX COUNTY COLLEGE, Visual Arts Dept, 155 Mill Rd, Edison, NJ 08837-3601; PO Box 3050, Edison, NJ 08818-3050. Tel 732-906-2589; Fax 732-906-2510; *Chmn* Jay Siegfried
Scholarships
Degrees: AA
Tuition: County $57.50 per cr hr; out-of-county $115; out-of-state $115 per cr hr
Courses: Art Appreciation, Art Education, Art Foundation, Art Fundamentals (2-D & 3-D Design), Art History, Art Industry & Communication, Ceramics, Drawing, Painting, Printmaking, Sculpture, Stage Design
Adult Hobby Classes: Courses offered
Summer School: Dir, Warren Kelerme. Courses—Art History, Ceramics, Drawing, Painting

EWING

THE COLLEGE OF NEW JERSEY, School of Arts & Sciences, 2000 Pennington Rd, Ewing, NJ 08628; PO Box 7718, Ewing, NJ 08628-0718. Tel 609-771-2652; Fax 609-637-5134; Web: www.tcnj.edu; *Chmn Dept* Lois Fichner-Rathus; *Prof* Bruce Rigby, MFA; *Assoc Prof* Kenneth Kaplowitz, MFA; *Assoc Prof* Charles Kumnick, MFA; *Assoc Prof* Marcia Taylor, PhD, MAATR; *Assoc Prof* Wendell Brooks, MFA; *Assoc Prof* Elizabeth Mackie, MFA; *Asst Prof* Philip Sanders, MA; *Asst Prof* Charles McVicker, BPA; *Asst Prof* William Nyman, MFA; *Dept Chair* Anita Allyn; *Prof Art History* Lee-Ann Riccardi
Estab 1855; FT 17, PT 18; pub; D & E; Scholarships; SC 40, LC 10, GC 11; non-maj 5200, maj 300
Ent Req: HS dipl
Degrees: BA & BFA 4 yr
Courses: Advertising Design, Art Appreciation, †Art Education, Art History, Ceramics, Computer Animation, Computer Graphics, Design, Display, Drafting, Drawing, †Fine Arts, †Graphic Design, History of Art & Architecture, Illustration, †Interior Design, Intermedia, Jewelry, Lettering, Mixed Media, Painting, Photography, Printmaking, Sculpture, Silversmithing, Teacher Training
Summer School: June & July five wk sessions, Governor's School of the Arts (July)

GLASSBORO

ROWAN UNIVERSITY, Dept of Art, 201 Mullica Hill Rd, Glassboro, NJ 08028-1702. Tel 856-256-4000; Fax 856-256-4814; Web: www.rowan.edu; *Chair* Fred Adelson, PhD; *Asst Chair* Keith Adams
Estab 1925; Maintain nonprofit art gallery, Westby Gallery, Westby Hall, Rowan Univ, Rt #322, Glassboro, NJ 08028; Pub; D & E; Scholarships; SC 80, LC15; D 6,100, E 5,000, maj 300
Ent Req: HS dipl, ent exam, portfolio and SAT
Degrees: BA 4 yrs, BFA 4 yrs, MA
Courses: Advertising Design, Art Appreciation, Art Education, Art History Survey, Batik, Ceramics, Computer Art, Drawing, Enameling, Fiber Arts, Illustration, Jewelry, Puppetry, Sculpture, Theatrical Design
Children's Classes: Enrl 30. Courses—Crafts, Drawing, Mixed Media, Painting
Summer School: Dir, Dean H Sosa. Enrl 100; Courses—Drawing, Painting, Printing

HACKETTSTOWN

CENTENARY COLLEGE, Humanities Dept, 400 Jefferson St, Hackettstown, NJ 07840-2184. Tel 908-852-1400; *Pres* Dr Barbara-Jayne Lewthwaite; *Assoc Prof* Richard Wood, MFA; *Asst Prof Interior Design* Elena Kays, MFA; *Instr* Elizabeth Desabritas, MFA; *Assoc Prof* Carol Yoshimine-Webster, MFA
Estab 1874; pvt; Scholarships; SC 11, LC 2; maj 70, others 367, total 678
Exhibitions: Gallery Exhibitions (BFA students) Architecture Site, Art/Design reviews, Interior Design students
Ent Req: high school dipl
Degrees: BFA(Art & Design), AA(Interior Design), BFA(Interior Design), BS (Communications)
Adult Hobby Classes: Tuition $98 per cr. Courses—Graphic Arts, Interior Design
Summer School: Dir, Larry Friedman. Tuition $98 per cr. Courses—Graphic Art, Interior Design

JERSEY CITY

NEW JERSEY CITY UNIVERSITY, Art Dept, 2039 Kennedy Blvd, Jersey City, NJ 07305. Tel 201-200-3214, Ext 3241; Fax 201-200-3224; Email rosenberg@njcu.edu; Web: www.njcu.edu; *Prof* Ben Jones, MFA; *Prof* Mary Campbell, MFA; *Prof* Jose Rodeiro, PhD, MFA; *Prof* Charles Plosky, MFA; *Prof* Herbert Rosenberg, MFA; *Assoc Prof* Raymond Statlander, MFA; *Asst Prof* Mauro Altamura, MFA; *Asst Prof* Winifred McNeill, MFA; *Asst Prof* Ellen Quinn, MFA; *Art History Prof* Midori Yoshimoto, PhD; *Prof* Dennis Raverty, PhD; *MFA* Dennis Dittrich; *MFA* Hugo Bastidas; *MFA* Brian Gustafson; *MFA* Deborah Jack; *Jewelry & Metals Prof* Ken MacBain, MFA; *Printmaking Prof* Martin Kruck, MFA
Estab 1927, dept estab 1961; Maintains 2 nonprofit art galleries, Lemmerman Gallery at Hepburn Hall, 2039 Kennedy Blvd and Visual Art Gallery, 100 Culver Ave; maintains architecture library, Art Dept 100 Culver Ave Jersey City NJ 07305; FT 13 PT 15; pub; D & E; Scholarships; SC 61, LC 19, GC 31; D 350, E 60, GS 60
Ent Req: HS dipl or equivalent
Degrees: BA & BFA 128 sem hrs, MA, MFA 60 sem hrs, grad assistantship
Courses: Advertising Design, Aesthetics, Art Appreciation, Art Education, Art History, Art Therapy, Ceramics, †Communication Design, Conceptual Art, †Crafts, Design, Digital Imaging, Drawing, †Fine Arts, Graphic Design, History of Art, Industrial Design, Intermedia, Jewelry, Lettering, Metalsmithing, Mixed Media, Painting, †Photography, Printmaking, Sculpture, †Teacher Certification

SAINT PETER'S COLLEGE, Fine Arts Dept, 2641 Kennedy Blvd, Jersey City, NJ 07306. Tel 201-915-9238; Fax 201-915-9240; Web: www.spc.edu; *Chmn* Jon D Boshart PhD
Estab 1872, dept estab 1963; Maintain nonprofit art gallery; St Peter's College Art Gallery; Jesuit; D & E; Scholarships; SC 8, LC 20; D 2,000, E 900, maj 15
Ent Req: HS dipl
Degrees: BA, BA in Cursu Classico, BS 4 yrs
Courses: Advertising Design, Aesthetics, Architecture, Art Appreciation, Art Education, †Art History, Commercial Art, †Drawing, †Graphic Arts, History of Art & Architecture, Mixed Media, †Painting, Photography, Restoration & Conservation, †Sculpture, Teacher Training
Adult Hobby Classes: Tuition $508 per sem. Courses—Art History, Studio
Summer School: Dir, Dr Boshart. Tuition $1,524 per 3 cr, one 3 wk session & two 5 wk sessions. Courses—Art History, Electives, Drawing, Film History, Introduction to Visual Arts, Painting, Photography, Graphic Arts, Museum Courses

LAKEWOOD

GEORGIAN COURT UNIVERSITY, Dept of Art, 900 Lakewood Ave, Lakewood, NJ 08701-2697. Tel 732-987-2437; Web: www.georgian.edu; *Prof* Geraldine Velasquez, EdD; *Assoc Prof* Sr Mary Phyllis Breimayer, PhD; *Assoc Prof* Suzanne Pilgram, MFA; *Asst Prof* Sr Joyce Jacobs, MA; *Lectr* Nicholas Caivano, MA; *Asst Prof* Lisa Festa, PhD
Estab 1908, dept estab 1924; Maintains nonprofit art gallery, Christina Geis Gallery Georgian Court Univ 900 Lakewood Ave Lakewood NJ 08701; pvt; D & E; Scholarships; SC 18, LC 11; 240, non-maj 150, maj 90
Ent Req: HS dipl, col board scores, portfolio
Degrees: BA 4 yr, BFA
Courses: †Art (studio & art history), †Art Education, †Art History, Calligraphy, Ceramics, Color & Design, Commercial Art, Computer Graphics, Drawing, Fashion Arts, Graphic Design, Illustration, Jewelry, Lettering, Painting, Photography, Printmaking, Sculpture, Teacher Training, Textile Design, Weaving
Summer School: Courses in Art History

LAWRENCEVILLE

RIDER UNIVERSITY, Dept of Fine Arts, 2083 Lawrenceville Rd, Lawrenceville, NJ 08648-3099. Tel 609-896-5168; *Chmn* Dr Jerry Rife
Estab 1966; FT 5; pvt; D & E; SC 9, LC 4; D 3500, E 5169, maj 35
Ent Req: HS dipl
Degrees: BA(Fine Arts) 4 yrs
Courses: Drawing, Graphic Arts, Graphic Design, Painting
Summer School: Courses—Drawing, Art & Society

LINCROFT

BROOKDALE COMMUNITY COLLEGE, Center for the Visual Arts, 765 Newman Springs Rd, Lincroft, NJ 07738-1599. Tel 732-224-2000; Fax 732-224-2060; Web: www.brookdale.cc.nj.us; *Chmn* Ed O'Neill
Estab 1968; Pub; D & E
Ent Req: HS dipl
Degrees: AA
Tuition: County res—$90 per cr hr; non-county res—$165 per cr hr; non-state res—$341 per cr hr
Courses: Ceramics, Design, Drawing, Jewelry, Painting, Printmaking

LIVINGSTON

ART CENTRE OF NEW JERSEY, 284 Beaufort Ave Ste 3, Riker Hill Art Pk Bldg 501 Livingston, NJ 07039-1042. Tel 973-227-3488; Fax 973-227-3488; *Pres* Tim Maher; *First VPres* Elaine Denton; *Second VPres* Salomon Kadoche; *Treas* Louis de Smet
Estab 1924 as an art school & presently is a venue for workshops, art events, lects, critiques, exhibitions, etc; Two pub exhibs per yr; Mem: 250; dues $12.50; annual meeting in May; Pub; D (open studies with models, no classes) Mon & Fri 1-3:30, Sat 11-1:30; Scholarships; D 60
Income: Financed by mem & art sales
Publications: Membership newsletter
Courses: Painting
Adult Hobby Classes: Workshops

MADISON

DREW UNIVERSITY, Art Dept, 36 Madison Ave, College of Liberal Arts Madison, NJ 07940-1434. Tel 973-408-3553, 408-3000; Fax 973-408-3768; *Prof* Livio Saganic, MFA; *Dept Chmn* Michael Peglau, PhD; *Asst Prof* Margaret Kuntz, PhD; *Adjunct Asst Prof* William Mutter, MFA; *Adjunct Asst Prof* Raymond Stein; *Prof* Sara Henry-Corrington; *Adjunct Asst Prof* Lisa Solon, MBA; *Adjunct Asst Prof* Anne Gaines, MFA; *Adjunct Asst Prof* Tom Birkner, MFA; *Adjunct Asst Prof* Jim Jeffers, MFA
Estab 1928; Maintain nonprofit art gallery; Korn Gallery, Drew University, Madison, NJ 07940; pvt; D & E; Scholarships; SC 17, LC 10; D 275, E 12, maj 45, minors 15
Ent Req: HS dipl
Degrees: BA 4 yrs
Courses: Aesthetics, †Art History, Ceramics, Computer Graphics, Design, Drawing, History of Art & Architecture, Painting, Photography, Printmaking, Sculpture
Summer School: Dir, Catherine Messer. Enrl 300; tuition $1200 for 4, 5 or 6 wk term. Courses—Art History for the Blind, Ceramics, Computer Graphics, Photography

FAIRLEIGH DICKINSON UNIVERSITY, Fine Arts Dept, 285 Madison Ave, Madison, NJ 07940. Tel 973-443-8500; Web: www.fdu.edu; *Faculty* Judy Moonelis; *Faculty* George Cochrane
Estab 1942, dept estab 1965; pvt; D & E; Scholarships; SC 37, LC 9
Ent Req: HS dipl, SAT
Degrees: degrees BA (Art & Fine Arts)
Tuition: Res—undergrad $367 per cr, room & board; nonres—undergrad $367 per cr hr; campus res available
Courses: Advertising Design, Art Appreciation, Art History, Bio & Wildlife Illustration, Calligraphy, Ceramics, Commercial Art, Computer Animation, Computer Graphics, Design, Desktop Publishing, Drawing, †Graphic Design, History of Art & Architecture, Illustration, Lettering, Mixed Media, Painting, Photography, Printmaking, Sculpture

MAHWAH

RAMAPO COLLEGE OF NEW JERSEY, School of Contemporary Arts, 505 Ramapo Valley Rd, Mahwah, NJ 07430-1680. Tel 201-529-7368; Fax 201-684-7481; Email sperry@ramapo.edu; Web: www.ramapo.edu; *Dean* Steven Perry, MFA; *Prof Painting* W Wada, MFA; *Assoc Prof Photo* Yolanda del Amo, MFA; *Assoc Prof Art History* Meredith Davis, PhD; *Assoc Prof Art History* John Peffer, PhD; *Assoc Prof 3D Design & Animation* Ann LePore, MFA; *Assoc Prof Drawing & Painting* Jackie Skrzynski, MFA; *Prof, Video Art & New Media* Shalom Gorewitz; *Asst Prof, Art Sculpture* Joel Weissman
Estab 1968; Maintain non-profit art galleries, Kresge Foundation Gallery, Andre Z Pascal Gallery & Seldon Rodman Gallery of popular Arts, all on campus; Potter Library, campus; pub; D&E; SC 53, LC 15; maj 110
Ent Req: HS dipl, SAT
Degrees: BA
Courses: †Art & Technology, Art History, †Art Therapy, Ceramics, Costume Design & Construction, Drawing, †Film, Graphic Arts, †Graphic Design, History of Art & Architecture, †Installation Art, Painting, Photography, Printmaking, Sculpture, †Stage Design, †Theatre Arts, †Video Art

Summer School: Dir, Shalom Gorewitz. Tuition $71.50 cr hr, $91.50 out of state. Courses—Computer Graphics, Photography

MONTCLAIR

MONTCLAIR ART MUSEUM, Yard School of Art, 3 S Mountain Ave, Montclair, NJ 07042. Tel 973-746-5555; Fax 973-746-9118; Email mail@montclair-art.com; Web: www.montclair-art.com; *Dir* Jacquelyn Roesch Sanchez
Art school estab 1924; FT 18; pvt; D & E; Scholarships; SC 17; D 300 per term, E 100 per term
Courses: Art Education, Chinese Print, Collage, Drawing, Mixed Media, Painting, Portraiture, Printmaking, Sculpture
Adult Hobby Classes: Enrl 300; tuition $135-$175, duration 8 wks. Courses—Anatomy, Drawing, Painting, Pastels, Portraiture, Still Life, Watercolor
Children's Classes: Enrl 90; tuition $120-$140 per 8 wk sem. Courses—Mixed Media

MONTCLAIR STATE UNIVERSITY, Fine Arts Dept, 1 Normal Ave, College of the Arts Montclair, NJ 07043-1699. Tel 973-655-7295; Web: www.montclair.edu; *Dean* Geoffrey Newman; *Chmn* John Czerkowicz
Estab 1908; FT 18, PT 4; pub; Scholarships; SC 35, LC 18; maj 250, grad maj 200
Ent Req: HS grad and exam, interview, portfolio
Degrees: BA 4 yr, BFA 4 yr, MA
Courses: Art Education, Art History, Ceramics, Drawing, Film, Graphic Design, Illustration, Jewelry, Metalwork, Painting, Photography, Printmaking, Sculpture, Textile Design, TV as Art
Summer School: Life Drawing, Painting, Photography, Sculpture

MORRISTOWN

COLLEGE OF SAINT ELIZABETH, Art Dept, 2 Convent Rd, Morristown, NJ 07960-6989. Tel 973-290-4315; Email vbutera@cse.edu; Web: www.cse.edu; *Chmn Dept* Dr Virginia Fabbri Butera; *Assoc Prof* Sr Anne Haarer; *Adjunct Prof* Elaine Chong; *Adjunct Prof* Raul Villarreal; *Adjunct Prof* Todd Doney; *Adjunct Prof* Rocio Scary; *Adjunct Prof* Will Suarez
Estab 1899, dept 1956; Maintain a nonprofit art gallery, Terese F Maloney Art Gallery, College of St Elizabeth, 2 Convent Rd, Morristown, NJ 07960; www.maloneyartgallery.org; den, W, M & W continuing studies; D & E; Scholarships; SC 17, LC 4; D 250, maj 27
Ent Req: HS dipl, ent exam
Degrees: BA 4 yrs
Courses: Advertising Design, Aesthetics, Art Appreciation, Art History, Calligraphy, Ceramics, †Collage, Color and Design, Conceptual Art, Drawing, Graphic Arts, Graphic Design, Mixed Media, Painting, Photography, Printmaking, Sculpture, Silversmithing, Teacher Training

NEW BRUNSWICK

RUTGERS, THE STATE UNIVERSITY OF NEW JERSEY, Mason Gross School of the Arts, 33 Livingston Ave, New Brunswick, NJ 08901-1959. Tel 848-932-5210; Fax 732-932-2217; Email art.design@mgsa.rutgers.edu; Web: www.masongross.rutgers.edu; *Dean* George B Stauffer; *Chair, Art & Design Dept, Assoc Prof* Gerry Beegan; *Chair & Artistic Dir Dance Dept* Julia M Ritter; *Dir Music Dept* Wiliam Berz; *Interim Chair, Theater Dept, Head of Acting* Barbara Marchant; *Dir Rutgers Filmmaking Ctr* Patrick Stettner
Estab 1766, school estab 1976; maintains nonprofit art gallery, Mason Gross Art Gallery; FT & PT 260; pub; D; Scholarships; SC 50, LC 20, GC 28; Undergrad 815; Grad 329
Ent Req: HS dipl, portfolio
Degrees: BHA, BFA, MFA
Tuition: Res $11,744; Nonres $27,282
Courses: Art History, Dance, Design, Film, Theatre Arts, Visual Arts

NEWARK

RUTGERS UNIVERSITY, NEWARK, Arts, Culture & Media, 110 Warren St, University Heights Bradley Hall Newark, NJ 07102-1809. Tel 973-353-3732; Email idwatson@newark.rutgers.edu; Web: acm.newark.rutgers.edu; WATS 800-648-5600; *Chair* Ian Watson; *Deputy Chair* Paul Sternberger
FT 20; Pub; D; Scholarships
Ent Req: HS dipl, or as specified by col and univ
Degrees: BA 4 yr, BFA(Design)
Tuition: Res $7,215 per yr; Nonres $15,369 per yr
Courses: Art Appreciation, Art Education, Art History, Ceramics, Computer Graphics, Design, Drawing, Graphic Design, History of Art & Architecture, Illustration, Journalism, Painting, Photography, Printmaking, Sculpture, Stage Design, Teacher Training, Theatre Arts
Summer School: Courses—Art History, Ceramics, Drawing, Painting, 2-D Design, 3-D Design

OCEAN CITY

OCEAN CITY ARTS CENTER, 1735 Simpson Ave, Ocean City, NJ 08226-3070. Tel 609-399-7628; Fax 609-399-7089; Email ocarts@pro-usa.net; Web: www.oceancityartscenter.org; *Instr Guitar* Rob Gummel; *Instr Painting* Sue Rau; *Exec Dir* Lorraine Hansen; *Instr* Annie Arena; *Marketing & Pub Rels* Christine Harry; *Bookkeeper* Peg Castagna; *Instr* Lee Kuchler; *Instr* Susan Myers; *Instr* Patty Guckes; *Instr* Marie Natale; *Instr* Kim Weiland; *Instr* Sue Van Duyne
Estab 1966; Maintains nonprofit art gallery, Ocean City Arts Center Gallery; Pvt; D & E; weekends; Scholarships; SC 14, LC 1; D 1, E 8
Ent Req: none
Tuition: Varies
Courses: Ceramics, Collage, Dance, Drawing, Film, Handicrafts, Mixed Media, Painting, Photography, Pottery, Sculpture, Stained Glass, Theatre Arts, Video
Adult Hobby Classes: 50; $65 - $150
Children's Classes: 250; $65 - $350; art camp, performing arts camp, tv/media camp, guitar camp
Summer School: Exec Dir, Lorraine Hansen. Same classes offered during summer plus workshops & demonstrations

PARAMUS

BERGEN COMMUNITY COLLEGE, Visual Art Dept, 400 Paramus Rd, Rm A335, Paramus, NJ 07652. Tel 201-447-7100; Fax 201-612-8225; Web: www.bergen.cc.nj.us; *Dean Art & Humanities* Michael Redmond
pub; D&E; Scholarships
Degrees: AA
Tuition: In county—$57.60 per cr; nonres—$119.70 per cr hr
Courses: Animation, Art Anatomy, Art Appreciation, Art History, Ceramics, Color Theory, Commercial Illustration, Craft Design, Design, Drawing, Fundamentals Art, Graphic Design, Handicrafts, Interior Design, Lettering, Painting, Photography, Printmaking, Sculpture

PATERSON

PASSAIC COUNTY COMMUNITY COLLEGE, Division of Humanities, One College Blvd, Paterson, NJ 07505-1179. Tel 973-684-6555; Fax 973-523-6085; Email mgillan@pccc.cc.nj.us; Web: www.pccc.cc.nj.us/poetry/index.htm; *Prof* Mark G Bialy; *Pres* Steve Rose; *Cur Gallery* Jane Havv; *Exec Dir Cultural Arts* Maria Mazziotti Gillan; *Asst Dir* Aline Papazian
Estab 1969; pub; D & E; SC 4, LC 3; D 100, E 25
Ent Req: HS dipl, New Jersey basic skills exam
Degrees: AA 2 yrs
Courses: Advertising Design, Aesthetics, Art Appreciation, Art History, Commercial Art, Design, Drawing

PEMBERTON

BURLINGTON COUNTY COLLEGE, Humanities & Fine Art Div, 601 Pemberton Browns Mills Rd, Pemberton, NJ 08068-1599. Tel 609-894-9311, Ext 7441; Web: www.bcc.edu; *Art Instr* Jane Yantz; *Art Instr* Jeff Bailey
Estab 1969; pub; D & E; Scholarships
Ent Req: HS dipl, equivalent
Degrees: AA
Tuition: County res—$69.50 per cr hr; non-county res—$84.50 per cr hr; non-state res—$120.50 per cr hr
Courses: Art Appreciation, Art Education, Art History, Art Therapy, Calligraphy, Ceramics, Design, Drawing, Film, Handicrafts, Introduction To Teaching Art, Modernism, Painting, Photography, Sculpture, Theatre Arts, Video
Adult Hobby Classes: 10; tuition $150. Courses—Ceramics
Summer School: Dir, Diane Grimes. Courses—Ceramics, Drawing, Painting, Sculpture

PRINCETON

PRINCETON UNIVERSITY, Dept of Art & Archaeology, 105 McCormick Hall, Princeton, NJ 08544-1018. Tel 609-258-3782; Fax 609-258-0103; Email artarch@princeton.edu; Web: artandarchaeology.princeton.edu; *Dir, Princeton Univ Art Mus* James Steward; *Chair & Prof Art & Archaeology* Michael Koortbojian; *Dept Mgr* Maureen Killeen; *Head Librn* Holly Hatheway
Estab 1783; Maintains nonprofit art museumPrinceton University Art Museum; pvt; Scholarships; LC 16, GC 9
Degrees: PhD
Tuition: $51,870 per yr
Courses: Archaeology, Art History, Film, Video, Visual Arts
—**School of Architecture**, S-110 Architecture Bldg, Princeton, NJ 08544. Tel 609-258-3741; Fax 609-258-4740; Email soa@princeton.edu; Web: soa.princeton.edu; *Dean* Monica Ponce de Leon; *Assoc Dean* Paul Lewis
Estab 1919; FT/PT 42; pvt; D; Scholarships; Fellowships
Ent Req: HS dipl
Degrees: BA, MA, PhD
Tuition: $51,870 per yr
Courses: Acoustics & Lighting, Building & Science Technology, Environmental Engineering, History of Architectural Theory, Modern Architecture, Urban Studies

RANDOLPH

COUNTY COLLEGE OF MORRIS, Art Dept, 214 Center Grove Rd, Randolph, NJ 07869-2086. Tel 973-328-5000; Fax 973-328-5445; *Chmn & Prof* James Gwynne
Estab 1970; pub; D & E; SC 15, LC 3; maj 263
Ent Req: HS dipl
Degrees: AA(Humanities/Art) 2 yrs, AAS(Photography Technology) 2 yrs
Courses: Advertising Design, Art History, Ceramics, Color & Design, Drawing, Major Styles & Historical Periods, Modern Art, Painting, Photography, Printmaking, Sculpture
Summer School: Two 5 week day sessions, one evening session

SEWELL

GLOUCESTER COUNTY COLLEGE, Liberal Arts Dept, 1400 Tanyard Rd, Sewell, NJ 08080-4249. Tel 856-468-5000; Fax 856-488-2018; Web: www.gcc.nj.edu; *Head* John Henzy
Estab 1967; Special program offered for gifted students; art gallery on campus; 130 PT & FT; pub; D & E; Scholarships; SC 6, LC 6
Ent Req: HS dipl
Degrees: AA
Tuition: Res—$79 per cr hr; nonres—$80 per cr hr
Courses: Art History, Arts & Crafts for Handicapped, Ceramics, Drawing, General Design, Graphic Arts, Jewelry, Mixed Media, Painting, Sculpture
Summer School: Dir, Dr Mossman

SHREWSBURY

GUILD OF CREATIVE ART, 620 Broad St, Rte 35 Shrewsbury, NJ 07702-4117. Tel 732-741-1441; Fax 732-741-1441; Email guildofcreativeart@verizon.net; Web: www.guildofcreativeart.org; *Instr & Board of Dirs & Co-Pres* Leslie Backlund; *Board of Dirs & VPres* Marilyn Baldi; *Board of Dirs* Mary Christensen; *Board of Dirs* Donna Colasurdo; *Board of Dirs* Mary Fitzsimmons; *Board of Dirs Secy* Liz Jacobelli; *Board of Dirs & Co-Pres* David Levy Docent; *Board of Dirs & Treas* Sheila Menendez; *Board of Dirs & VPres* Tony Migliaccio; *Instr* Hillary Binder-Klein; *Instr* Karen Dooney; *Instr* James Kent; *Instr* Caroline Klein; *Instr* Mira Welnowska; *Instr* Debbie Redden; *Instr* Randy Mayer; *Instr* Tera Yoshimura; *Instr* Robert J Stetz
Estab 1960; Maintains nonprofit art gallery and art/architecture library: Guild of Creative Art, 620 Broad Street, Shrewsbury, NJ 07702; Non-profit coop; D&E; Scholarships; SC 16; D & E
Ent Req: Membership adult $30 per yr
Tuition: varies per instr
Courses: Art Appreciation, Mixed Media, Painting, Sculpture
Adult Hobby Classes: Courses—Design, Drawing, Painting
Children's Classes: Enrl $250; tuition for 10 wk term. Courses—Design, Life Drawing, Painting
Summer School: Coord Educational Servs, Bill Alcaro. Oil & Acrylic Painting, Watercolor, Figure Drawing, Portfolio Preparation

SOUTH ORANGE

SETON HALL UNIVERSITY, College of Arts & Sciences, 400 S Orange Ave, South Orange, NJ 07079-2697. Tel 973-761-9459; Fax 973-275-2368; Web: www.shu.edu; *Chmn* Charlotte Nichols, PhD; *Prof* Julius Zsako, PhD; *Prof* Barbara Cate; *Prof* Jeanette Hile, MA; *Assoc Prof* Alison Dale, MA; *Asst Prof* Arthur Cook, MM; *Asst Prof* Arline Lowe, MM; *Asst Prof* Joel Friedman, DMA; *Asst Prof* Deborah Gilwood, MA; *Asst Prof* K D Knittel, PhD, MA; *Asst Prof* Susan Leshnoff, EdD; *Asst Prof* Ira Greenberg, MFA
Estab dept 1968; FT 10, PT 9; pvt; D & E; Scholarships; Fellowships; SC 8
Degrees: BA 4 yr, MA
Courses: Advertising, Art Education, Art History, Chinese Brush Painting, Commercial Art, Drawing, Fine Art, Graphic Design, Illustration, Mixed Media, Music Art, Painting, Printmaking, Sculpture
Summer School: Dir, Petra Chu. Enrl 200; May - Aug. Courses—Art, Art History, Fine Arts

TOMS RIVER

OCEAN COUNTY COLLEGE, Humanities Dept, College Dr, Toms River, NJ 08754-2001; PO Box 2001, Toms River, NJ 08754-2001. Tel 732-255-0400; Fax 732-255-0444; Web: www.ocean.edu; *Coordr* Joseph Conrey; *Prof* Patricia Kennedy, MS; *Prof* Lisa Horning, MS; *Prof* Howard Unger, EdD; *Prof* John R Gowen, EdD; *Prof* Arthur Waldman, EdD; *Pres* Stephen McCleary
Estab 1964, dept estab 1964; pub; D & E; Scholarships; SC 19, LC 3; D 1500, E 1500, maj 67
Ent Req: HS dipl
Degrees: AA in Liberal Arts with concentration in Fine Art & AAS(Visual Commun Technology) 2 yrs
Courses: Advertising Design, Aesthetics, Art History, Calligraphy, Ceramics, Commercial Art, Conceptual Art, Costume Design & Construction, Drawing, Film, Graphic Arts, Graphic Design, Handicrafts, Lettering, Painting, Photography, Printmaking, Sculpture, Stage Design, Theatre Arts
Summer School: Enrl 175; tuition $34 for term of 5 wks or 6 wks beginning June. Courses—Arts & Humanities, Basic Drawing, Ceramics, Computer Graphics, Crafts, Photography

TRENTON

JOHNSON ATELIER TECHNICAL INSTITUTE OF SCULPTURE, 60 Sculptors Way, Trenton, NJ 08619-3428. Tel 609-890-7777; Fax 609-890-1816; Email lrn2sculpt@aol.com; Web: www.gotrain.com/schools; *Pres* James Barton, MFA; *Acad Dir* James E Ulry, MFA; *Dir* Dona Warner, BFA; *Acad Asst* E Gyuri Hollosy, MFA
Open by appointment; Estab 1974; pvt; D & E; Scholarships; SC 12; apprentices 20, interns 2
Ent Req: HS dipl, portfolio review
Degrees: The Atelier is a non degree granting institution with a two year apprenticeship program in sculpture
Tuition: $4800 per acad yr, $400 monthly
Courses: Ceramic Shell, Foundry, Metal Chasing, Modeling & Enlarging, Moldmaking, Patina, Restoration & Conservation, Sand Foundry, Sculpture, Structures, Wax Working & Casting

UNION

KEAN UNIVERSITY, Fine Arts Dept, 1000 Morris Ave, Union, NJ 07083-7133. Tel 908-527-2307; Fax 908-527-2804; *Dir Gallery* Alec Nicolescu; *Coordr Interior Design* Linda Fisher; *Coordr Art Educ* Michael DeSiano; *Coordr Art History* Louis Kachur; *Chmn* Jack Cornish
Estab 1855; FT 31; pub; D & E; Scholarships; SC 58, LC 37, GC 24; FT 383, PT 236, maj 656, grad 37
Ent Req: HS dipl, portfolio interview for art maj, SAT
Degrees: BA 4 yrs, BFA 4, MA(Art Educ)
Courses: Advertising Design, Aesthetics, †Art Education, †Art History, Ceramics, †Commercial Art, Display, Drafting, Drawing, Film, Furniture Making, Graphic Arts, Graphic Design, Illustration, †Interior Design, Jewelry, Lettering, Museum Staff Training, Occupational Therapy, Painting, Photography, Printmaking, Sculpture, Textile Design
Summer School: Asst Dir, George Sisko. Courses—Art History, Art in Education, Ceramics, Drawing, Introduction to Art, Introduction to Interior Design, Jewelry, Life Drawing, Painting, Printmaking, Sculpture, Watercolor

VINELAND

CUMBERLAND COUNTY COLLEGE, Arts & Humanities, PO Box 1500, College Drive, Vineland, NJ 08362-1500. Tel 609-691-8600; Fax 609-691-8813, Ext 314; Email art@cccnj.net; *Dean* James Piccone
Maintain nonprofit gallery; pub; D&E; Scholarships; SC 24, LC 8; maj 88
Degrees: AS
Tuition: County res—$737 per sem; out-of-county res—$122.50 per cr hr; out-of-state res—$245 per cr hr
Courses: Art Appreciation, †Art Education, Art History, †Design, Drawing, †Graphic Arts, †Graphic Design, Multi-media, Painting, Photography, Video
Adult Hobby Classes: non-cr
Summer School: Computer Graphics

WAYNE

WILLIAM PATERSON UNIVERSITY, Dept Arts, 300 Pompton Rd, Power Art Wayne, NJ 07470-2103. Tel 973-720-2401; Fax 973-720-3805; Email lazarusa@wpunj.edu; Web: www.wpunj.edu; *Art Dept Chmn* Alejandro Anreus; *Assoc Prof* James Brown; *Assoc Prof* Zhiyuan Cong; *Asst Prof* Angela DeLaura; *Assoc Prof* Leslie Farber; *Prof* Ming Fay; *Assoc Prof* David Horton; *Asst Prof* Elaine Lorenz; *Prof* Charles Magistro; *Asst Prof* Lily Prince; *Asst Prof* Steve Rittler; *Prof* David Shapiro; *Asst Prof* Thomas Uhlein; *Asst Prof* He Zhang; *Asst Prof* Nisha Drinkard; *Asst Prof* Robin Schwartz; *Asst Prof* Deborah Frizzell; *Asst Prof* Lauren Razzore; *Asst Prof* Bruce Gionet; *Asst Prof* Maggie Williams; *Prof* Ofelia Garcia
Dept estab 1958; Maintain a nonprofit art gallery, Ben Shahn Galleries, 300 Pompton Rd, Wayne, NJ 07470; maintain art/architecture library, Askeyy Library, 300 Pompton Rd, Wayne, NJ 07470; FT 24, PT 8; pub; D; Scholarships; SC 135, LC 60, GC 50; maj 450, grad 30, E non-maj 170
Ent Req: SATs, portfolio
Degrees: BA 4 yr, BFA, MFA
Tuition: Res—undergrad $73, grad $131
Courses: Advertising Design, †Art Education, †Art History, Ceramics, †Commercial Art, Computer Animation, Computer Graphics, Computer Illustration, Conceptual Art, †Design, Film, †Furniture Design, †Graphic Arts, Graphic Design, History of Art & Architecture, †Illustration, Lettering, Museum Staff Training, †Painting, †Photography, †Printmaking, Stage Design, †Teacher Training, †Textile Design
Summer School: Dir, Alan Lazarus. Enrl 150; tuition $65 per cr, $90 out of state. Courses—Art History, Drawing, Painting, Photography

WEST LONG BRANCH

MONMOUTH UNIVERSITY, Dept of Art & Design, 400 Cedar Ave, 800 Bldg, Rm 822 West Long Branch, NJ 07764-1804. Tel 732-571-3428; Fax 732-263-5273; Web: www.monmouth.edu; *Chmn* Vincent Dimattio, MFA; *Prof* Pat Cresson; *Assoc Prof* Ellen Garfield, MA; *Assoc Prof* Richard Davis, MFA; *Assoc Prof* Karen Bright, MFA; *Asst Prof* Edward Jankowski, MFA
Estab 1933; pvt; D & E; Scholarships; SC 25, LC 8; in dept D 108, E 6, non-maj 80, maj 108, audits 6
Ent Req: HS dipl, portfolio for transfer students
Degrees: BA(Art), BFA & BA(Art Educ) 4 yr
Courses: Appreciation of Art, †Art Education, Art History, †Ceramics, Drawing, Graphic Arts, Handicrafts, History of Art & Architecture, Metalsmithing, †Painting, Photography, Printmaking, †Sculpture, Teacher Training
Adult Hobby Classes: Courses—Painting
Summer School: Art Appreciation, Ceramics, Independent Study, Painting, Sculpture

WEST WINDSOR

MERCER COUNTY COMMUNITY COLLEGE, Arts, Communication & Engineering Technology, 1200 Old Trenton Rd, West Windsor, NJ 08550-3407. Tel 609-586-4800, Ext 3348; Fax 609-586-2318; Web: www.mccc.edu; *Dean* Robert A Terrano, MFA; *Cur* Tricia Fagan; *Prof* Mel Leipzig, MFA; *Prof* Frank Rivera, MFA; *Instr* Michael Welliver, MFA
Estab 1902, dept estab 1967; FT 10, PT 13; pub; D & E; Scholarships; SC 44, LC 6; E 350, maj 261
Ent Req: HS dipl
Degrees: AA & AAS 2 yrs
Courses: †Advertising Design, †Architecture, Art Education, Art History, †Ceramics, Commercial Art, Design, Drawing, Film, Graphic Arts, Graphic Design,

History of Art & Architecture, Illustration, †Painting, †Photography, Printmaking, †Sculpture, †Theatre Arts, Video
Adult Hobby Classes: Enrl 448. Tuition varies. Courses—Calligraphy, Ceramics, Drawing, Painting, Photography, Stained Glass
Children's Classes: Enrl 1000. Tuition varies. Courses—Drawing, Maskmaking, Painting, Printmaking, Soft Sculpture
Summer School: Dir, R Serofkin. Enrl 712 (camp college); 2 - 4 wk sessions. Dir, M Dietrich. Enrl 22; 4 wks. Courses—Architecture. Dir, M K Gitlick. Enrl 160; Arts Camp 2 - 4 wk sessions. Also regular cr courses

NEW MEXICO

ALBUQUERQUE

UNIVERSITY OF NEW MEXICO, Department of Fine Arts & Art History, 1 University of New Mexico, MSC04 2560 Albuquerque, NM 87131-0001. Tel 505-277-5861; Fax 505-277-5955; Email art@unm.edu; Web: art.unm.edu; *Chair* Mary Tsiongas; *Dir* Kirsten Pai Buick; *Regents Prof* Adrienne Salinger, MFA; *Regents Prof* Joyce M Szabo, PhD; *Prof* Michael D Cook, MFA; *Prof* Constance DeJong, MFA; *Prof* William T Gilbert, MFA; *Prof* Olivia L Lumpkin, PhD; *Prof* Jim Stone, MFA; *Prof* Nancy Pauly, PhD; *Prof* Andrea Polli, MFA; *Prof* Yoshiko Shimano, MFA; *Prof* Linney Wix, PhD; *Assoc Chair & Assoc Prof* Patrick Manning, MFA; *Prof* Laurel Lampela, PhD
Estab 1935; Maintain non-profit art gallery, John Sommers Gallery, Art Bldg, 2nd Fl; Fine Arts & Design Library (same address); on-campus shop sells fine paper only; pub; D&E; Scholarships; SC 56, LC 22, Grad 8; Maj 500+, Grad 111
Activities: Schols offered
Ent Req: (please go to finearts.unm.edu)
Degrees: BA (Art Studio, Art History, Art Educ), BFA (Art Studio), MA (Art Educ, Art History), MFA (Art Studio), PhD (Art History)
Tuition: Res $2,578.50, nonres $10,023.96
Courses: †Architecture, Art Appreciation, Art Ecology, †Art Education, †Art History, †Art Studio, Ceramics, Drawing, Electronic Arts, Film, Music, Painting, Photography, Printmaking, Sculpture, Studio Foundations, Theater, Weaving
Summer School: Arts of the Americas Program, wide variety of courses offered
—Dept of Art & Art History, 1 University of New Mexico, MSC04 2560 Albuquerque, NM 87131-0001. Tel 505-277-5861; Fax 505-277-5955; Web: www.unm.edu/~artdept2/; *Chmn* Joyce Szabo, PhD
Estab 1889; John Sommers Gallery; fine arts library; art supplies available at univ bookstore; pub; D & E; Scholarships; Fellowships; SC 190, LC 43, GC 73; E 511, non-maj 230, maj 227, grad 116
Ent Req: HS dipl
Degrees: BA, BAFA & BFA 4 yrs, MA 2 yrs, MFA 3 yrs, PhD 3+ yrs
Tuition: Per cr hr: res-undergrad $190.45; res-grad $209.30; nonres-undergrad $190.45-$622.60; nonres-grad $209.30-$637.97
Courses: Aesthetics, Architecture, Art Appreciation, Art History, Ceramics, Conceptual Art, Design, †Digital/Electronic Art, Drawing, Film, Graphic Arts, History of Art & Architecture, Metalwork, Mixed Media, Painting, Photography, Printmaking, Sculpture, Video
Children's Classes: Offered through Art Educ Dept
Summer School: Tuition res/nonres-undergrad $190.45; res/nonres-grad $209.30. Two 4 wk terms & one 8 wk term beginning June 9, 2008. Courses—same as above
—Tamarind Institute, 108-110 Cornell Dr SE, Albuquerque, NM 87106. Tel 505-277-3901; Fax 505-277-3920; Email tamarind@unm.edu; Web: finearts.unm.edu/tamarind.htm; *Tamarind Master Printer & Studio Mgr* Bill Lagattuta; *Dir* Marjorie Devon; *Educ Dir* Rodney Hamon
Estab 1960; Maintains nonprofit art gallery; Pub; D; Fellowships; SC, LC; enrl 8
Ent Req: Extensive previous experience in lithography &/or undergrad degree in printmaking
Degrees: Cert as Tamarind Master Printer 2 yrs
Tuition: $160 per cr hr
Courses: †Lithography
Summer School: 4 wk prog; campus res available. Courses—Various lithographic techniques

VSA ARTS OF NEW MEXICO, Enabled Arts Center, 4904 4th St NW, Albuquerque, NM 87107-3906. Tel 505-345-2872; Fax 505-345-2896; Email info@vsartsnm.org; Web: vsartsnm.org; *Exec Dir* Beth Rudolph; *Dir* Deborah Malshibini; *Exhib Coordr* Wendy Zollinger
Estab 1992; Center is a studio program for individuals with disabilities focusing on pre-vocational, vocational & studio skills; maintain nonprofit art gallery, Very Special Arts Gallery, 4904 Fourth St, NW, Albuquerque, NM 87107; pvt; D; D 30-40
Ent Req: 14 years or older
Courses: Art Appreciation, Ceramics, Collage, Drawing, Mixed Media, Painting, Printmaking, Sculpture, †Theatre Arts

FARMINGTON

SAN JUAN COLLEGE, Art Dept, 4601 College Blvd, Farmington, NM 87402-4699. Tel 505-326-3311, Ext 281, 599-0281; Fax 505-599-0385; Web: www.sjc.cc.nm.us; *Dept Chmn* Bill Hatch
Estab 1956; FT 1, PT 5; pub; D & E; Scholarships
Ent Req: HS dipl
Degrees: AA
Tuition: Res—$15 per cr hr; nonres—$25 per cr hr
Courses: Art Appreciation, Art Education, Art History, Calligraphy, Ceramics, Design, Drawing, Film, Graphic Design, Jewelry, Painting, Photography, Printmaking, Sculpture

HOBBS

NEW MEXICO JUNIOR COLLEGE, Arts & Sciences, 5317 Lovington Hwy, Hobbs, NM 88240. Tel 505-392-4510; Fax 505-392-1318; Web: www.nmjc.cc.nm.us; *Dean* Mickey D Best, MFA; *Instr* Lawrence Wilcox, MFA; *Instr* George Biggs, MFA
Estab 1965; pub; D & E; Scholarships; SC 6, LC 1; D 100, E 30, non-maj 200, maj 20
Ent Req: HS dipl, GED or special approval
Degrees: AA 2 yrs
Courses: Advertising Design, †Animation, Ceramics, Collage, Color & Design, Drawing, Interior Design, Painting, Photography, Printmaking
Adult Hobby Classes: Drawing, Painting, Portraiture, Watercolor
Children's Classes: Drawing, Painting
Summer School: Dean, Steve McLeary. Courses—Ceramics, Printmaking

LAS CRUCES

NEW MEXICO STATE UNIVERSITY, Art Dept, PO Box 30001, Dept 3572 Las Cruces, NM 88003-8001. Tel 505-646-1705; Fax 505-646-8036; Email artdept@msu.edu; *Dept Head* Spencer Fidler, MFA; *Assoc Prof* William Green, MFA; *College Asst Prof* Jacklyn St Aubyn, MFA; *Assoc Prof* Julia Barello, MFA; *Assoc Prof* Rachel Stevens, MFA; *Assoc Prof* Elizabeth Zarur, PhD; *College Asst Prof* Julie Fitzsimmons, MFA; *Prof* Joshua Rose, MFA; *Dir Ceramics* Amanda Jaffe; *Photo Dir* David Taylor; *Asst Prof* Stephanie Taylor, PhD; *Asst Prof* Peter Fine
Estab 1975; Maintains nonprofit art gallery, NMSU Art Gallery, DW Williams Art Center, NMSU, Las Cruces, NM 88003; Pub; D & E; Scholarships; Fellowships; SC 52, LC 25, GC 53; maj 280, grad 31
Ent Req: HS dipl
Degrees: BA & BFA 4 yrs, MFA 3 yrs, MA(Studio) & MA(Art Hist) 2 yrs
Courses: Art Appreciation, Art History, Ceramics, Design, Drawing, Graphic Arts, Graphic Design, Illustration, Jewelry, †Metal Arts, Mixed Media, Painting, Photography, Printmaking, Restoration & Conservation, Sculpture, Silversmithing
Summer School: Prof, Spencer Fidler

LAS VEGAS

NEW MEXICO HIGHLANDS UNIVERSITY, Dept of Communications & Fine Arts, 901 University Ave, Las Vegas, NM 87701-4072. Tel 505-454-3238, 454-3573; Fax 505-454-3068; Web: www.nmhu.edu/Department/commarts; *Asst Prof* Arthur Trujillo; *Chmn* Andre Garcia-Nuthmann
Estab 1898; pub; D & E; Scholarships; SC 24, LC 8, GC 12; non-maj 55, maj 51, grad 4
Ent Req: HS dipl, ACT, Early Admis Prog, GED
Degrees: BA 4 yrs, BFA, MA 1 yr
Courses: Art Education, Art History, Calligraphy, Ceramics, Drawing, Graphic Arts, Jewelry, Lettering, Painting, Photography, Printmaking, Sculpture, Silversmithing, Stage Design, Teacher Training, Theatre Arts
Adult Hobby Classes: Courses—Ceramics, Painting, Weaving
Summer School: Mainly studio plus core curriculum, depending upon staffing

PORTALES

EASTERN NEW MEXICO UNIVERSITY, Dept of Art, 1500 S Ave K, Sta 27 Portales, NM 88130-7400. Tel 505-562-2778; Web: www.enmu.edu/; *Chmn* Jim Bryant; *Asst Prof* Mary Finneran, MFA; *Asst Prof* Greg Erf, MFA; *Asst Prof* Phil Geraci, MFA; *Asst Prof* Galina McGuire, MFA; *Asst Prof* Mic Muhlbauer, MFA
Estab 1932; pub; D & E; Scholarships; SC 44, LC 6, GC 25; D 507, E 150, maj 110
Ent Req: HS dipl, GED, ACT
Degrees: AA 2 yrs, BS, BA & BFA 4 yrs
Courses: †Advertising Design, Art Education, Art History, Calligraphy, †Ceramics, †Commercial Art, †Drawing, †Graphic Arts, Graphic Design, Illustration, †Jewelry, Lettering, †Painting, Photography, †Sculpture, †Teacher Training, Theatre Arts, Video
Summer School: Courses—Ceramics, Commercial Art, Crafts, Drawing, Lettering, Photography

SANTA FE

COLLEGE OF SANTA FE, Art Dept, 1600 Saint Michaels Dr, Santa Fe, NM 87505-7615. Tel 505-473-6500; Fax 505-473-6501; Email info@csf.edu; Web: www.csf.edu; *Emeritus* Richard L Cook, MA; *Prof* Ronald Picco, MFA; *Asst Prof* Robert Sorrell, MFA; *Asst Prof* David Schienbaum, MFA; *Asst Prof* James Enyeart, MFA; *Asst Prof* Richard Fisher, MFA; *Asst Prof* Nancy Sutor, MFA; *Asst Prof* Khristaan Villela, PhD; *Asst Prof* Roxanne Malone, MFA; *Asst Prof* Don Messec, MA; *Adjunct Assoc* Steve Fitch, MFA; *Adjunct Assoc* Linda Swanson, MFA; *Dir Gallery* Lake McTighe, MFA; *Chmn* Gerry Snyder, MA
Estab 1947, dept estab 1986; pvt; D & E; Scholarships; SC 35, LC 10; D 350, non-maj 250, maj 95, non-degree 30
Ent Req: HS dipl or GED
Degrees: BA & BFA (Visual Arts)
Courses: Aesthetics, Art, Art Appreciation, Art Education, †Art History, †Art Studio, Art Therapy, Ceramics, Collage, Conceptual Art, Constructions, †Drawing, Film, Intermedia, Mixed Media, Museum Staff Training, †Painting, †Photography, †Printmaking, Psychology, †Sculpture, Theatre Arts, Video
Children's Classes: Enrl 20-25; tuition $500-$750 for 3 wk term. Courses—General Studio Art
Summer School: Dir, Gerry Snyder. Courses—Art History, Drawing, Lifecasting, Painting, Photography, Printmaking, Sculpture

INSTITUTE OF AMERICAN INDIAN ARTS, Museum of Contemporary Native Arts, 108 Cathedral Pl, Santa Fe, NM 87501-2027. Tel 505-428-5900; Fax 505-983-1222; Email pphillips@iaia.edu; Web: www.iaiamuseum.org; *Dir* Patsy Phillips; *Chief Cur* Ryan Rice; *Cur Coll* Tatiana Lomahaftew-Singer; *Registrar* Joy Farley; *Admin & Finance* Ramona Arnold; *Spec Proj & Community Relations* Larry Phillips; *Mus Educ Prog Coordr* Hayes A Locklear; *Mus Shop Mgr* Laura Ellerby; *Chief Security* Thomas Atencio; *Dep Security Office* Maria Favella; *Mus Studies Dept Faculty* Michelle McGeough; *Mus Studies Dept Chair* Jessie Ryker-Crawford; *Primitive Edge Gallery Coordr* Mary Deleary
Estab 1972; Maintain art gallery, Lloyd Kiva, 108 Cathedral Pl, Santa Fe, NM 87501; nonprofit art gallery, Primitive Edge Gallery, 83 Avan Nu Po Rd, Santa Fe, NM 87508, library, 89 Avan Nu Po Rd, Santa Fe, NM 87505; congressionally funded; D, E, Online; Scholarships; SC, LC; D 192
Ent Req: HS dipl
Degrees: AAS, AA, AFA, BFA, BA, Cert
Tuition: $100 per cr hr
Courses: †Ceramics, †Creative Writing, †Film, †Graphic Arts, †Graphic Design, †Indigenous Liberal Arts, †Museum Staff Training, †Museum Studies, †Native Studies, †New Media Arts, †Painting, †Photography, †Sculpture, †Silversmithing, †Studio Art, †Theatre Arts, †Video, †Weaving
Adult Hobby Classes: Beadwork, Dancing, Exhib Techniques, Traditional Clothing, Flute Making, Fiber Arts
Summer School: Dir, Hayes Lewis. Courses—Museum Studies, Summer Film & Television Workshop

SANTA FE ARTS INSTITUTE, 1600 Saint Michaels Dr, Santa Fe, NM 87505-7615; PO Box 24044, Santa Fe, NM 87502-0044. Tel 505-424-5050; Fax 505-424-5051; Web: www.sfai.org; *Dir* Diane R Karp, Dr; *Res Dir* Sheilah Wilson
Estab 1985; pvt; D & E; Scholarships; SC 12; varies
Ent Req: Portfolio review
Courses: Collage, Installation, Mixed Media, Painting, Photography, Sculpture, Video, Video Art
Adult Hobby Classes: Installation & Video Art, Master classes in Printing, Mixed Media, Sculpture
Children's Classes: Summer youth workshops

SILVER CITY

WESTERN NEW MEXICO UNIVERSITY, Expressive Arts Dept, 1000 W College Ave, Silver City, NM 88062; PO Box 680, Dept of Expressive Arts Silver City, NM 88062-0680. Tel 575-538-6618; Fax 575-538-6619; Email admissions@wnmu.edu; Web: www.wnmu.edu; *Asst Prof* Jim Pendergast, MFA; *Asst Prof* John Abbott, MFA; *Prof* Michael Metcalf, MFA; *Co-Chmn Theater* Jack Ellis; *Asst Prof* Jessica Wilson, MFA; *Asst Prof* Danny Reyes
Estab 1893; Mem: Maintains non profit art gallery, McCray Gallery Expressive Arts Dept W NM Univ PO Box 680 Silver City NM 88061; on campus shop where art supplies are purchased; Pub; D & E; Scholarships; SC 10, LC 7; D 211, non-maj 196, maj 15
Ent Req: HS dipl
Degrees: BA, BS, AA, & MA, 4 yrs
Courses: Advertising Design, Art Appreciation, Art Education, Art History, †Ceramics, Costume Design & Construction, Design, Drawing, Fiber Arts, Film, Graphic Arts, Graphic Design, †Painting, †Photography, †Printmaking, †Sculpture, Stage Design, Teacher Training, Textile Design, †Video
Adult Hobby Classes: Ceramics, Fiber, Lapidary
Summer School: Enrl 80-100. Courses—Art Appreciation, Ceramics, Clay Workshop, Elementary Art Methods, Painting & Drawing Workshop, Printmaking, Special Art Tours in New Mexico & Europe

NEW YORK

ALBANY

THE COLLEGE OF SAINT ROSE, The Center For Art and Design, 432 Western Ave, Albany, NY 12203-1490; 324 State Street, Albany, NY 12210. Tel 518-485-3900; Fax 518-485-3920; Email tolmiek@strose.edu; Web: www.strose.edu; *Prof* Paul Mauren, MFA; *Assoc Prof* Ann Breaznell, MFA; *Prof* Scott Brodie, MFA; *Prof* Lucy Bowditch, PhD, MFA; *Prof* Jessica Loy, MFA; *Assoc Prof* Thomas Santelli, MFA; *Asst Prof* Robert O'Neil, MFA; *Assoc Prof* Gina Occhiogrosso, MFA; *Assoc Prof* Theresa Flanigan, PhD; *Chmn, Assoc Prof* Kris Tolmie, MFA; *Assoc Prof* Ben Schwab, MFA; *Asst Prof* Robert Shane, Ph.D; *Asst Prof* Chris St Cyr, MFA; *Asst Prof* Susan Meyer, MFA
Estab 1920, dept estab 1970; Maintain nonprofit art gallery; Esther Massry Art Gallery (same address); art supplies available at on-campus store; pvt; D & E; Scholarships; SC 50, LC12; non-maj 100, maj 200
Activities: Schols offered
Ent Req: HS dipl, SAT or ACT, rank in top 2/5 of class
Degrees: BFA(Graphic Design, Studio Art), BS(Art Educ, Studio Art), MS(Art Educ), MA(Studio Art)
Tuition: $14,410 per sem undergrad (12-18 cr/sem), $958 per sem hr
Courses: Aesthetics, Art History, Design, Drawing, Graphic Design, Painting, Photography, Printmaking, Sculpture, Studio Art, Typography
Adult Hobby Classes: Enrl 20; tuition $250 per cr hr. Courses—Some continuing education courses each sem
Summer School: Chmn Kris Tolmie. Courses— Theories of Art Educ (grad course). Kris Tolmie, Dir Pre-College Summer Experience

THE SAGE COLLEGES, Dept Visual Arts, 140 New Scotland Ave, Albany, NY 12208-3425. Tel 518-292-1778; Fax 518-292-7758; Email bielic@sage.edu; Web: www.sage.edu; *Interim Chair Visual Arts* Kevin Stoner; *Asst to the Chair* Cathleen Bieling
Estab 1957, dept estab 1970; Maintain a nonprofit art gallery - Opaika Gallery, The Sage Colleges, 140 W Scotland Ave, Albany, NY 12208; Pvt; D & E; Scholarships; SC 43, LC 16 (Art); D 700 (total), 200 (art), E 823 (total)
Ent Req: HS dipl, references, records, SAT, portfolio
Degrees: MA (Art Ed), AAS 2 yrs, BA (Theatre), AS-BFA (fine arts, graphic design, interior design)
Courses: Art Education, Art History, Ceramics, Collage, Design, Drafting, Drawing, Fine Arts, Fine Arts Illustration, Graphic Arts, Graphic Design, History of Art & Architecture, Illustration, Interior Design, Intermedia, Lettering, Mixed Media, Painting, Photography, Printmaking, Sculpture, Studio Studies, Teacher Training, Theatre Arts
Children's Classes: Summer courses for High School students
Summer School: Dir, Dierdra Zarrillo. Enrl 60.

STATE UNIVERSITY OF NEW YORK AT ALBANY, Art Dept, 1400 Washington Ave, Albany, NY 12222-1000. Tel 518-442-4020; Fax 518-442-4807; Email bh996@albany.edu; Web: www.albany.edu; *Prof* Roberta Bernstein, PhD; *Prof* Edward Mayer, MFA; *Prof* Phyllis Galembo, MFA; *Assoc Prof* Mark Greenwold, MFA; *Assoc Prof* Marja Vallila, MFA; *Dept Chair & Prof* JoAnne Carson, MFA; *Assoc Prof* David Carbone, MFA; *Assoc Prof* Sarah Cohen, PhD; *Asst Prof* Rachel Dressler, PhD; *Asst Prof* Daniel Goodwin, MFA; *Technician* Roger Bisbing, MFA; *Asst Prof* Leona Christie, MFA; *Asst Prof* Yvette Mattern, MFA; *Assoc Prof* Michael Werner, PhD; *Prof* John Overbeck, PhD
Estab 1848; Art library; art supplies available on-campus; pub; D & E; Scholarships; SC 43, LC 20, GC 33; D 750, E 400, non-maj 600, maj 150, grad 45
Ent Req: HS dipl
Degrees: BA 4 yr, MA 1.5 yr, MFA 2 yr
Tuition: Res—undergrad $1700 per sem, $137 per cr hr, grad $2550 per sem, $213 per cr hr; nonres—undergrad $4150 per sem; $346 per cr hr, grad $4208 per sem, $351 per cr hr; campus res—room & board $3440.50 per sem
Courses: Aesthetics, †Art History, Design, Digital Imaging, †Drawing, Mixed Media, †Painting, †Photography, †Printmaking, †Sculpture, Video
Adult Hobby Classes: Courses in all studio areas
Summer School: Dir, Michael DeRensis. Enrl 350.

ALFRED

NEW YORK STATE COLLEGE OF CERAMICS AT ALFRED UNIVERSITY, School of Art & Design, 2 Pine St, Alfred, NY 14802-1205. Tel 607-871-2441; Fax 607-871-2198; Email fedizel@alfred.edu; Web: art.alfred.edu; *Dean* Gerar Edizel
Estab 1900; Maintains a nonprofit art gallery, Fosdick-Nelson Gallery, 1 Pine St, Alfred NY 14802, Robert Turner Student Gallery & Cohen Gallery; Scholes Library, 2 Pine St, Alfred NY 14802; on campus shop where art supplies may be purchased; FT 15; pvt; D & E; Scholarships; SC, LC, GC
Activities: Schols offered
Ent Req: Portfolio, GPA, SAT, HS dipl, essay, letter(s) of recommendation
Degrees: BS, BFA, MFA
Tuition: Undergrad Res—$32,494, Nonres—$26,308; Grad $22,520
Courses: Art Education, †Art History, †Ceramic Art, Ceramics, †Costume Design & Construction, Digital Imaging, †Dimensional Studies, †Display, Drawing, Electronic Integrated Arts, Glass Arts, Graphic Design, †Interactive Art, †Interactive Media, †Metals, †Mixed Media, Painting, Photography, Pre-Art Therapy, †Print Media, Printmaking, †Sculpture, †Sculpture/Dimensional studies, †Sonic Arts, Sound design, †Stage Design, †Theatre Arts, Video, †Video Arts
Adult Hobby Classes: 3D modeling; Rapid Prototyping
Summer School: Courses—Art History, Ceramics, Glass, Sculpture, Drawing, Painting, Photography

AMHERST

DAEMEN COLLEGE, Art Dept, 4380 Main St, Amherst, NY 14226-3592. Tel 716-839-8241; Fax 716-839-8516; Web: www.daemen.edu; *Assoc Prof* Dennis Barraclough, MFA; *Asst Prof & Chmn* Joseph Kukella, MFA; *Instr* Jane Marinsky, BFA; *Instr* Joan Goldberg, BFA; *Instr* David Cinquino, MFA; *Instr* Dana Hatchett, MFA; *Prof* James Allen, MFA; *Asst Prof* Kevin Kegler, MAH
Estab 1947; pvt; D & E; Scholarships; SC 50; D 1800, non-maj 1740, maj 100
Ent Req: HS dipl, art portfolio
Degrees: BFA(Drawing, Graphic Design, Illustration, Painting, Printmaking, Sculpture), BS(Art), & BS(Art Educ) 4 yrs
Courses: †Advertising Design, Aesthetics, Art Appreciation, †Art Education, Art History, Ceramics, Computer Art, Design, Drawing, †Graphic Design, †Illustration, †Painting, Photography, †Printmaking, †Sculpture, Stage Design, Textile Design, Theatre Arts, Weaving, †Website Design
Summer School: Dean, Charles Reedy

ANNANDALE-ON-HUDSON

BARD COLLEGE, Center for Curatorial Studies Graduate Program, PO Box 5000, Annandale-on-Hudson, NY 12504-5000. Tel 845-758-7598; Fax 845-758-2442; Email ccs@bard.edu; Web: www.bard.edu/ccs/; *Exec Dir* Tom Eccles; *Grad Prog Dir* Paul O'Neill; *Dir Exhibs and Opers* Marcia Acita; *Dir Library & Archives* Ann Butler
Prog estab 1994; Maintains nonprofit art gallery, Hessel Mus of Art & CCS Galleries, Ctr for Curatorial Studies Mus, Bard Col, Annandale-on-Hudson, NY 12504-5000; Art library; on-campus shop where art supplies may be purchased; pvt; D; Scholarships; Fellowships; GC 20; grad 25
Ent Req: BA, BFA or equivalent
Degrees: Master's 2 yr
Courses: Aesthetics, Art History, †Museum Staff Training

BARD COLLEGE, Milton Avery Graduate School of the Arts, PO Box 5000, 30 Campus Rd Annandale-on-Hudson, NY 12504-5000. Tel 845-758-7481; Fax

845-758-7507; Email mfa@bard.edu; Web: www.bard.edu/mfa; *Dir* Arthur Gibbons; *Asst Dir* Mark Wonsidler; *Mng Dir* Lawre Stone
Estab 1981; Maintains a nonprofit art gallery, Bard Hessel Museum of Art; CCS Bard Library; art supplies sold at on-campus store; FT/PT 61; pvt; D, E & Summer; Scholarships; GC
Degrees: MFA
Tuition: $62,039 (two-yr prog)
Courses: Film, Music, Painting, Performance, Photography, Sculpture, Video, Writing

AURORA

WELLS COLLEGE, Dept of Art, 170 Main St, Aurora, NY 13026-1101. Tel 315-364-3440, 364-3266; *Asst Prof* Rosemary Welsh; *Div Chmn* Susan Forbes
Estab 1868; pvt, W; D; Scholarships; SC 19, LC 20; D 500 (total), non-maj 122, maj 18
Ent Req: HS dipl, cr by exam programs
Degrees: BA 4 yrs
Courses: Aesthetics, †Art History, †Ceramics, †Drawing, †Painting, Photography, Printmaking, Teacher Training, †Theatre Arts

BAYSIDE HILLS

QUEENSBOROUGH COMMUNITY COLLEGE, Dept of Art & Photography, 222-05 56th Ave, Bayside Hills, NY 11364. Tel 718-631-6395; Fax 718-631-6612; Web: www.qcc.cuny.edu; *Assoc Prof* Robert Rogers, MFA; *Asst Prof* Jules Allen, MFA; *Asst Prof* Javier Cambre; *Assoc Prof* Kenneth Golden; *Prof* Paul Tschinkel; *Asst Prof* Anissa Mack
Estab 1958, dept estab 1968; Maintains nonprofit art gallery, Queensborough Community College Art Gallery, Oakland Building, 222-05 56th Ave, Bayside, NY 11364; Pub; D & E; Scholarships; SC 21, LC 14; D 9,000, E 4,000
Ent Req: HS dipl, placement exams
Degrees: AA & AS
Courses: Advertising Design, Art History, Artist Apprenticeships, Arts for Teachers of Children, Arts Internships, Ceramics, Color Theory, Design, Digital Art & Design, Drawing, Graphic Design, Illustration, Painting, †Photography, Printmaking, Sculpture, Video
Summer School: Courses—Drawing, Photography, Sculpture, Art History, 2-D Design

BINGHAMTON

BINGHAMTON UNIVERSITY, Art History Department, PO Box 6000, Binghamton, NY 13902-6000. Tel 607-777-2112; Fax 607-777-4466; Email arthist@binghamton.edu; Web: www2.binghampton.edu/art-history; *Dist Prof* John Tagg; *Assoc Prof* Karen Barzman; *Assoc Prof* Tom McDonough; *Assoc Prof* Nancy Um; *Asst Prof* Kevin Hatch; *Asst Prof* Jeffrey Kirkwood; *Asst Prof* Julia Walker; *Assoc Prof* Pamela Smart
Estab 1846; maintains a non-profit art gallery: Art Museum; Maintains an Art library, Battle Lindsay, Location : Lindsay Bldg; Pub; D&E; Scholarships; 679, non-maj 400, maj 40, grad 43
Ent Req: HS dipl, Regents Scholarship, ACT or SAT, Teacher/counselor recommendation
Degrees: BA, MA, PhD
Courses: †Architecture, †Art History, †Cinema, Printmaking, †Studio Art, Video
Summer School: Tuition same as acad yr, 3 separate sessions during summer. Courses—Art History

BROCKPORT

STATE UNIVERSITY OF NEW YORK COLLEGE AT BROCKPORT, Dept of Art, Tower Fine Arts Bldg, Brockport, NY 14420-2985; 350 New Campus Dr, Brockport, NY 14420-2914. Tel 716-395-2209; Fax 716-395-2588; Web: www.brockport.edu; *Chmn* Debra Fisher; *Prof* Jennifer Heuker; *Asst Prof* Alisia Chase; *Asst Prof* Tim Massey; *Assoc Prof* James Morris
Maintain nonprofit art gallery; FT 3, PT 6; Pub; D; Scholarships; SC 33, LC 29; 8188, maj 100, grad 2000, grad 30
Ent Req: HS dipl, ent exam
Degrees: BA, BS & BFA 4 yrs
Courses: Artists Books, †Ceramics, Design, Drawing, †Jewelry, †Painting, †Photography, †Printmaking, †Sculpture, Video
Adult Hobby Classes: Courses—Ceramics, Drawing, Methods, Museum & Gallery Studies, Painting, Photography, Sculpture, 2-D & 3-D Design
Summer School: Dir, Dr Kenneth O'Brien

BRONX

BRONX COMMUNITY COLLEGE, Music & Art Dept, 2155 University Ave, Bliss Hall 303 Bronx, NY 10453-2804. Tel 718-289-55341, 289-5252; Fax 718-289-6433; Web: www.bcc.cuny.edu/artmusic/index.html; *Chmn* Dr Ruth Bass
Pub; AM, PM
Ent Req: HS dipl, equivalent
Degrees: Cert, AS, AAS
Tuition: Res—$1305 per sem; nonres—$1538 per sem
Courses: Art Appreciation, Art History, Ceramics, Commercial Art, Design, Drawing, Modern Art, Painting, Photography, Printmaking, †Sculpture
Adult Hobby Classes: Enrl 25; tuition $45 for 7 wks. Courses—Calligraphy, Drawing

HERBERT H LEHMAN COLLEGE, Art Dept, 250 Bedford Park Blvd W, Bronx, NY 10468-1527. Tel 718-960-8256; Fax 718-960-7203; *Chmn* Herbert R Broderick, MFA; *Assoc Prof* Arvn Bose; *Asst Prof* David Gillison, MFA
Estab 1968; pub; D & E; Scholarships; SC 18, LC 29, GC 31; non-maj 100, major 50, grad 15
Ent Req: HS dipl, ent exam
Degrees: BA & BFA 4 yrs, MA, MFA & MA 2 yrs
Courses: †Art History, †Graphic Arts, †Painting, †Sculpture
Summer School: Dean, Chester Robinson. Enrl 45; Courses—Art History, Drawing, Painting

MANHATTAN COLLEGE, Visual & Performing Arts Dept, 3900 Manhattan College Pkwy, Bronx, NY 10471-3927. Tel 718-862-7373; Fax 718-862-8444; Email mark.pottinger@manhattan.edu; Web: manhattan.edu; *Assoc Prof* Mark A Pottinger; *Assoc Prof* Daniel Savoy; *Asst Prof* Marisa Lerer
Estab 1853; pvt den; D&E; Scholarships; LC 8, Art 4, Music 4; D 3000
Ent Req: HS dipl
Degrees: BA, BS
Courses: Art History, Ceramics, Drawing, Film, Graphic Arts, Graphic Design, History of Art & Architecture, Painting, Photography, Printmaking, Sculpture

BRONXVILLE

CONCORDIA COLLEGE, Art Dept, 171 White Plains Rd, Bronxville, NY 10708-1998. Tel 914-337-9300; Fax 914-395-4500
Estab 1881; pvt; D; Scholarships; SC 4, LC 2
Ent Req: HS dipl, SAT or ACT
Degrees: BA and BS 4 yrs
Courses: Art Education, Art History, Ceramics, Computer Graphics, Drawing, Handicrafts, History of Art & Architecture, Painting, Photography, Sculpture, Teacher Training
Adult Hobby Classes: Courses—Painting

SARAH LAWRENCE COLLEGE, Dept of Art History, 1 Mead Way, Bronxville, NY 10708-5999. Tel 914-337-0700; Web: www.slc.edu; *Dean* Jerrilynn Dodds; *Faculty* David Castriota; *Faculty* Joseph C Forte; *Faculty* Susan Kart; *Faculty* Judith Rodenbeck
Estab 1926; FT 1, PT 9; pvt; D; Scholarships
Ent Req: HS dipl
Degrees: BA 4 yrs
Tuition: $17,280 per yr
Courses: Art History, Drawing, Filmmaking, Painting, Photography, Printmaking, Sculpture, Visual Fundamentals
Summer School: Center for Continuing Education

BROOKHAVEN

INTERNATIONAL COUNCIL FOR CULTURAL EXCHANGE (ICCE), PO Box 361, Brookhaven, NY 11719-0361. Tel 800-690-4223; Fax 212-982-4017; Email info@ICCE-Travel.org; Web: www.icce-travel.org; *Prog Coordr* Stanley I Gochman PhD; *International Planning Dir* Julie Gochman
Estab 1982; pvt, nonprofit; May-Nov International Prog (Europe 2-3 wks); SC, LC
Ent Req: Minimum age - 17
Degrees: college cr
Tuition: Depends on prog
Courses: Art Appreciation, Art History, Drawing, History of Art & Architecture, Mixed Media, Theatre Arts
Summer School: Tuition approx $3698 for 2-3 wk session abroad. Courses—Landscape, Painting

BROOKLYN

BROOKLYN COLLEGE, Art Dept, 2900 Bedford Ave, Brooklyn, NY 11210-2850. Tel 718-951-5181; Fax 718-951-5670; Web: www.brooklyn.cuny.edu; *Chmn* Michael Mallory
Estab 1962; Pub; AM, PM; Scholarships
Degrees: BA, BFA, MA, MFA
Tuition: Res (in state)—undergrad $1,600 per sem, grad $160 per cr hr; non res—undergrad $3,400 per sem, grad $285 per cr hr
Courses: Aesthetics, Art History, Calligraphy, Ceramics, Collage, Computer Graphics, Design, Drawing, Graphic Arts, Graphic Design, History of Art & Architecture, Intermedia, Mixed Media, Museum Staff Training, Painting, Photography, Printmaking, Sculpture
Adult Hobby Classes: Enrl 50. Courses—Studio Art
Summer School: Enrl 100-150; two summer sessions. Courses—Art History, Computer Graphics, Studio Art

KINGSBOROUGH COMMUNITY COLLEGE, Dept of Art, 2001 Oriental Blvd, Brooklyn, NY 11235-2333. Tel 718-368-5000, 368-5718 (art); Fax 718-368-4872; Web: www.kingsborough.edu
Estab 1965, dept estab 1972; Maintains nonprofit Art Gallery, in Arts & Sciences Bldg on campus; pub; D & E; SC 10, LC 8; maj 135
Ent Req: HS dipl
Degrees: AS 2 yrs
Courses: Art History, Ceramics, Design, Drawing, Graphic Design, Illustration, Painting, Photography, Sculpture
Adult Hobby Classes: Overseas travel courses
Summer School: Courses—Art

LONG ISLAND UNIVERSITY, BROOKLYN CAMPUS, Art Dept, 1 University Plz, Bldg 7 Brooklyn, NY 11201-5301. Tel 718-488-1051; *Prof* Liz Rudey; *Chmn* Bob Barry; *Prof* Nancy Grove; *Prof* Cynthia Dantzic; *Prof* Hilary Lorenz
Maintain nonprofit art gallery; The Salena Gallery, The Resnick Gallery & The Kumbie Gallery; FT 5, PT 15; Pvt; D & E; Scholarships; SC 20, LC 6; maj 35
Ent Req: HS dipl, ent exam
Degrees: BA, BFA in Art Educ & Studio Art

Courses: †Art Education, Art History, Arts Management, Calligraphy, Ceramics, †Color, †Computer Graphics, Drawing, Media Arts, Medical-Scientific Illustration, Painting, †Photography, Printmaking, Sculpture, †Teacher Training, Teaching Art to Children, †Video, Visual Experience
Adult Hobby Classes: Courses—Teaching Art to Children
Summer School: Dir, Liz Rudey. Term of two 6 wk sessions. Courses—Ceramics, Drawing, Painting, Art History, Calligraphy

NEW YORK CITY COLLEGE OF TECHNOLOGY OF THE CITY UNIVERSITY OF NEW YORK, Dept of Advertising Design & Graphic Arts, 300 Jay St, Brooklyn, NY 11201-1909. Tel 718-260-5175; Fax 718-254-8555; Email jmason@citytech.cuny.edu; Web: www.citytech.cuny.edu; *Chmn* Joel Mason
Estab 1946; Maintain nonprofit art gallery, Grace Gallery, 300 Jay St, N1124, Brooklyn, NY 11201; pub; D & E; Scholarships; SC 16, LC 3; D 650, E 350
Ent Req: HS dipl
Degrees: AAS 2 yr, BTech 4 yr, BComm 2 yr, AAS Graphic Arts, BTech Graphic Arts 4 yr Cert, Desktop Pub
Courses: 3-D Animation, †Advertising Design, †Computer Graphics, †Digital Graphics, Digital Video, †Digital Video, †Digital Work Flow, Drawing, Graphic Arts, Graphic Design, Illustration, †Multi-Media, Packaging, Painting, Photography, †Photography Binding Finishing, Printmaking, Type Spacing, Video, Web Design
Summer School: Computer Graphics, Design, Illustration, Lettering, Life Drawing, Paste-up, Photography, Video Design

PRATT INSTITUTE, School of Art, 200 Willoughby Ave, Brooklyn, NY 11205-3899. Tel 718-636-3619; Fax 718-636-3410; Email dean-of-art@pratt.edu; Web: www.pratt.edu/academics/school-of-art; *Dean* Gerry Snyder
Pub
Degrees: BA & BFA 4 yr, MA & MFA 2 yr
Tuition: Undergrad $49,810 per yr; grad $1,713 per cr
Courses: †Art & Design Education, Arts & Cultural Management, Creative Arts Therapy, Design Management, Digital Arts & Animation, Film & Video, Fine Arts, Foundation, Photography
Adult Hobby Classes: Various courses offered
Summer School: Enrl for high school students only
—**School of Design**, 200 Willoughby Ave, Brooklyn, NY 11205. Tel 718-687-5744; Email SoD@pratt.edu; Web: www.pratt.edu/academics/school-of-design; *Dean* Anita Cooney
Pub
Degrees: BA & BFA 4 yr, MA & MFA 2 yr
Tuition: Undergrad $49,810 per yr; grad $1,713 per cr
Courses: †Communications Design, †Fashion Arts, Foundation, †Industrial Design, †Interior Design, Package Design
Adult Hobby Classes: Various courses offered
—**School of Architecture**, 61 St James Place, Brooklyn, NY 11238. Tel 718-399-4304; Email hanrahan@pratt.edu; Web: www.pratt.edu/academics/architecture; *Dean* Thomas Hanrahan
Pub
Degrees: BArch, MArch
Tuition: Undergrad $49,810 per yr; grad $1,713 per cr
Courses: Architecture, Art History, City & Regional Planning, Construction Management, Design, Facilities Management, Landscape Architecture, Real Estate, Sustainable Environmental Systems

PROMOTE ART WORKS INC (PAWI), Job Readiness in the Arts-Media-Communication, 123 Smith St, Brooklyn, NY 6218. Tel 718-797-3116; Fax 718-855-1208; Email executive@micromuseum.com; Web: www.micromuseum.com; *Technical Dir* William Laziza
Estab 1993; Internship; ongoing; Scholarships
Ent Req: interview process
Courses: †Conceptual Art, †Interactive Media, †Mixed Media, †Video
Adult Hobby Classes: Tuition $50 per hr. Courses—Video Editing
Children's Classes: Tuition $15 per class. Courses—Dance, Drama, Movement
Summer School: Tuition $15 per class. Courses—Art, Science

BROOKVILLE

C W POST CAMPUS OF LONG ISLAND UNIVERSITY, School of Visual & Performing Arts, 720 Northern Blvd, Brookville, NY 11548-1300. Tel 516-299-2000, 299-2395 (visual & performing arts); Web: www.cwpost.liunet.edu; *Chmn & Prof* Jerome Zimmerman; *Prof* Marilyn Goldstein; *Prof* Howard LaMarcz; *Prof* Robert Yasuda; *Assoc Prof* David Henley; *Assoc Prof* Jacqueline Frank; *Assoc Prof* Frank Olt; *Assoc Prof* Joan Powers; *Asst Prof* John Fekner; *Asst Prof* Richard Mills; *Asst Prof* Carol Huebner-Venezia; *Asst Prof* Donna Tuman; *Asst Prof* Vincent Wright; *Dean Visual & Performing Arts* Lynn Croton
Dept estab 1957; pvt; D & E; Scholarships; SC 70, LC 15, GC 40; D 2000, E 450, non-maj 2000, maj 250, grad 150, others 50
Ent Req: HS dipl, portfolio
Degrees: BA(Art Educ), BA(Art Hist), BA(Studio), BS(Art Therapy) & BFA (Graphic Design) 4 yrs, MA(Photography), MA(Studio), MS(Art Educ) & MFA (Art, Design or Photography) 2 yrs
Courses: †Advertising Design, Aesthetics, †Art Education, †Art History, Ceramics, Collage, Commercial Art, Computer Graphics, Conceptual Art, Constructions, Drawing, Film, Fine Arts, Graphic Arts, Graphic Design, Handicrafts, Illustration, Intermedia, Jewelry, Lettering, Mixed Media, Painting, Photography, Printmaking, Sculpture, Stage Design, Teacher Training, Theatre Arts, Video, Weaving
Adult Hobby Classes: Courses—Varied
Summer School: Prof, Howard LaMarcz. Duration 3-5 wk sessions. Courses—varied

BUFFALO

LOCUST STREET NEIGHBORHOOD ART CLASSES, INC, 138 Locust St, Buffalo, NY 14204-1246. Tel 716-852-4562; Email info.locuststreetart@gmail.com; Web: locuststreetart.org; *Acting Dir* Dorothea Braemer; *Educ Dir* Rachelynn Noworyta; *Prog Dir* Katharine Whitefield; *Instr Photo* Kenn Morgan; *Instr Animation* Roger Scott; *Instr Adult Drawing & Painting* Jess Widmer; *Instr Children's d&p* Darron L Whitsett
Open Tues - Thurs & Sat Noon - 6 PM; Estab 1959; Inc 1971; Maintains an informal on-site art/architecture library; maintains a non-profit art gallery: Locust Street Art, 138 Locust St. Buffalo, NY 14204; Pvt; D & Weekend; SC 4, Other 1; Non-maj 300 per yr
Collections: Permanent collection of paintings by students
Exhibitions: Annual Art Show
Tuition: No tuition fees
Courses: animation, Ceramics, Clay, †Drawing, †Painting, †Photography, Public Art Projects, Spoken Word Poetry
Adult Hobby Classes: Enrl 120. Courses—Clay, Drawing, Painting, Photography
Children's Classes: Enrl 200. Courses—Clay, Drawing, Painting
Summer School: Dir, Molly Bethel, Coordr, Sky Bethel -Enrl adults and children. Course—Drawing, Painting, Photog, children's summer day program

STATE UNIVERSITY OF NEW YORK COLLEGE AT BUFFALO, Fine Arts Dept, 1300 Elmwood Ave, Buffalo, NY 14222-1004. Tel 716-878-6032; Fax 716-878-6697; Web: finearts.buffalostate.edu; *Interim Chair* Lin Xia Jiang
Estab 1875, dept estab 1969; FT 16; pub; D & E; SC 34, LC 17, GC 6; maj 300 (art) 50 (BFA) 12 (art history)
Ent Req: HS dipl
Degrees: BA(Art), BA(Art History) & BFA 4 yrs
Courses: †Art History, †Drawing, †Painting, †Papermaking, †Photography, †Printmaking, †Sculpture
Summer School: Dir, Gerald Accurso. Courses—Art History, Studio

UNIVERSITY AT BUFFALO, STATE UNIVERSITY OF NEW YORK, Dept of Visual Studies, 202 Center for the Arts, Buffalo, NY 14260-6010. Tel 716-645-6878 ext 1350; Fax 716-645-6970; Email art-info@buffalo.edu; Web: www.visualstudies.buffalo.edu; *Painting* David Schirm; *Intermedia* Millie Chen; *Emerging Practices* Paul Vanouse; *Photog & Visual Studies* Gary Nickard; *Sculpture & Undergraduate Director* Reinhard Reitzenstein; *Drawing Chair* Joan Linder; *Print Media* Adele Henderson; *Art History & Visual Studies* Livingston Watrous; *Painting* George Hughes; *Art History & Visual Studies* Elizabeth Otto
Estab 1846; Maintain nonprofit art gallery, Dept of Visual Studies Gallery 202 Center For The Arts, Buffalo, NY 14260-6010; FT 14, PT 14; pub; D & E; Scholarships; Fellowships; SC 80, LC 35, GC 20, Other 30; D & E 350, non-maj 100, maj 325, grad 50
Ent Req: HS dipl
Degrees: BA, BFA & MFA, MA
Courses: Aesthetics, Art History, †Communications Design, †Computer Art, Conceptual Art, Criticism & Theory, Design, Drawing, Foundations, Graphic Design, Installation, Mixed Media, †Painting, †Photography, †Printmaking, Public Art Practice, †Sculpture, Typography, Video
Summer School: Enrl 104; tuition res $180 per cr hr, nonres $389 per cr hr for 3-6 wk term. Courses—Computer Art, Drawing, Painting, Photo, Printmaking

VILLA MARIA COLLEGE OF BUFFALO, Art Dept, 240 Pine Ridge Rd, Buffalo, NY 14225-3999. Tel 716-896-0700; Fax 716-896-0705; Web: www.villa.edu; *Gallery Cur* Brian R Duffy, MFA
Estab 1961; pvt; D & E; Scholarships; SC 27, LC 3; D 450, E 100, maj 170
Ent Req: HS dipl of equivalency
Degrees: AA, AAS & AS 2 yrs
Courses: 3-D Design, Advertising Design, Advertising Graphics, Art History, Color Photo, Commercial Design, Computer-aided Design, Design, Drafting, Drawing, Etching, Graphic Arts, Graphic Design, History of Interior Design, History of Photography, Interior Design, Lettering, Mechanical Systems & Building Materials, Painting, Photography, Printmaking, Rendering & Presentation, Sculpture, Serigraphy, Studio Lighting, Textile Design, View Camera Techniques
Adult Hobby Classes: Courses - Drawing, Painting, Photography
Summer School: Enrl 10-20. Courses—a variety of interest courses, including Drawing, Painting and Photography

CANANDAIGUA

FINGER LAKES COMMUNITY COLLEGE, Visual & Performing Arts Dept, 4355 Lake Shore Dr, Canandaigua, NY 14424. Tel 716-394-3500, Ext 257; Fax 716-394-5005; *Prof* Wayne Williams, MFA; *Asst Prof* John Fox, MFA; *Pres* Daniel T Hayes
Estab 1966; FT 5; pub; D & E; SC 14, LC 2; D 60, non-maj 700, maj 50
Ent Req: HS dipl
Degrees: AA & AAS 2 yrs
Courses: Advertising Design, Art History, Ceramics, Commercial Art, Drawing, Graphic Arts, Graphic Design, Illustration, Painting, Photography, Printmaking, Sculpture, Stage Design, Theatre Arts
Summer School: Courses—Per regular session

CANTON

ST LAWRENCE UNIVERSITY, Dept of Fine Arts, 23 Romoda Dr, Canton, NY 13617. Tel 315-229-5192; Web: www.stlawu.edu; *Assoc Prof* Dorothy Limouze, PhD; *Assoc Prof* Faye Serio, MFA; *Assoc Prof* Chandreyi Basu, PhD; *Assoc Prof* Melissa Schulenberg, PhD; *Asst Prof* Amy Hauber, MFA; *Asst Prof* Mark Denaci, PhD; *Asst Prof* Kasarian Dane, MFA; *Prof* Obiora Udechukwu, MFA; *Instr* Linda Strauss
Estab 1856; Non-Profit art gallery, Richard F Brush Art Gallery. Art supplies may be purchased on campus; pvt; D&E; SC 16, LC 13; maj 80, non-maj 300
Ent Req: HS dipl
Degrees: BA
Courses: Art Education, Art History, Ceramics, Drawing, History of Art & Architecture, Painting, Photography, Printmaking, Sculpture, Video
Summer School: Dir, Donna Fish. Enrl 10-20. Courses—Art History, Studio

CAZENOVIA

CAZENOVIA COLLEGE, Center for Art & Design Studies, 22 Sullivan St, Studio Art Cazenovia, NY 13035-1085. Tel 800-654-3210; Fax 315-655-2190; Web: www.cazevonia.edu; *Pres* Mark Tierno; *Prof* Lillian Ottaviano, MFA; *Prof* Jeanne King, MFA; *Prof* Jo Buffalo, MFA; *Prof & Chmn* Charles Goss, MFA; *Assoc Prof* Kim Waale, MFA; *Assoc Prof* Anita Welych, MFA; *Assoc Prof* Karen Steen, MFA; *Instr* Patricia Beglin, MA; *Asst Prof* Laurie Selleck, MFA; *Asst Prof* Allyn Stewart, MFA; *Asst Prof* Tod Guynn, MFA; *Asst Prof* Elizabeth Moore, MS; *Prof* Josef Ritter, MFA
Estab 1824; pvt; D & E; Scholarships; SC 21, LC 3; D 660
Ent Req: HS dipl
Degrees: AS, AAS, BS, BFA, & BPS 2 yr & 4 yr progs
Courses: †Advanced Studio Art, †Advertising Design, Advertising Layout, Basic Design, Ceramics, Drafting, Drawing, Fashion Design, †Illustration, †Interior Design, Lettering, Office & Mercantile Interiors, Painting, Photography, Printmaking, Rendering, Residential Interiors, Typography
Adult Hobby Classes: Enrl 200; Courses—large variety
Summer School: Dir, Marge Pinet. Enrl 100; Courses—Variety

CHAUTAUQUA

CHAUTAUQUA INSTITUTION, School of Art, 1 Ames Ave, Chautauqua, NY 14722; PO Box 1098, Chautauqua, NY 14722-1098. Tel 716-357-6233; Fax 716-357-9014; Email art@ciweb.org; Web: www.ciweb.org; *Dir Art School* Don Kimes
Estab 1874; maintain nonprofit art gallery, Strohl Art Center & Logan Galleries; pvt; D (summers only) & E; Scholarships; SC 40, LC 20; D 38, maj 38, GS 10, other 28
Ent Req: portfolio review, min 2 yrs previous univ level art studies, coll credit granted
Courses: Ceramics, Drawing, Painting, Printmaking, Sculpture
Summer School: Dir, Don Kimes.

CLAYTON

THOUSAND ISLANDS ARTS CENTER - HOME OF THE HANDWEAVING MUSEUM, 314 John St, Clayton, NY 13624-1017. Tel 315-686-4123; Web: www.tiartscenter.org; *Exec Dir* Leslie W Rowland; *Cur* Jessica Phinney; *Potter* Serena Buchanan; *Cur Emeritus* Sonja Wahl
Estab 1964; Maintain a nonprofit art gallery: Catherine C. Johnson Gallery, 314 John St, Clayton, NY 13624; on-campus shop where art supplies may be purchased; PT 33; brd of trustees, non-profit; D & E (weekdays & weekends); Scholarships; SC 35; D 210, E 10
Degrees: no degrees but transfer cr
Courses: Basketry, Bird Carving, Ceramics, Decoy Carving, Drawing, Fashion Arts, Fiber Arts, Handicrafts, Jewelry, Mixed Media, Painting, Pottery, Quilting, Sculpture, †Sewing, Spinning, Weaving
Children's Classes: Drawing, Painting, Pottery, Weaving
Summer School: Marcia Rogers, Educator - Courses—Country Painting, Decoy Carving, Painting on Silk, Pottery, Quilting, Sculpture, Watercolor Painting, Weaving

CLINTON

HAMILTON COLLEGE, Art Dept, 198 College Hill Rd, Clinton, NY 13323. Tel 315-859-4269; Email art@hamilton.edu; Web: www.hamilton.edu; *Prof* William Salzillo, MFA; *Prof* Robert Muirhead, MFA; *Prof Art* Ella Gant, MFA; *Assoc Prof* Rebecca Murtaugh; *Asst Prof* Robert Knight; *Kevin Kennedy Assoc Prof Art* Katharine Kuharic
Maintains a nonprofit art gallery, Emerson Gallery 198 College Hill Rd, Clinton, NY 13325; Private; D; SC
Degrees: BA

COBLESKILL

STATE UNIVERSITY OF NEW YORK, COBLESKILL, Art Dept, State Rte 7, Cobleskill, NY 12043. Tel 518-255-5700; Web: www.cobleskill.edu
Estab 1950; pub; D & E; SC 2, LC 2; D 95
Ent Req: HS dipl
Degrees: AA & AS 2 yrs, BT 4 yrs
Courses: Art Education, Art History, Drawing, Painting, Sculpture, Teacher Training, Theatre Arts
Adult Hobby Classes: Enrl 4000 per yr; tuition $9 per course. Courses—large variety of mini-courses

CORNING

CORNING COMMUNITY COLLEGE, Division of Humanities, One Academic Dr, Corning, NY 14830. Tel 607-962-9271; Fax 607-962-9456; *Prof* Margaret Brill, MA; *Assoc Prof* Fred Herbst; *Prof* David Higgins, MFA
Estab 1958, dept estab 1963; FT 3; pub; D & E; SC 8, LC 6
Ent Req: HS dipl, SAT
Degrees: AA, AS, AAS 2 yrs
Courses: Architecture, Art Appreciation, Art History, Ceramics, Design, Drawing, History of Art & Architecture, Jewelry, Painting, Photography, Silkscreen, Silversmithing
Adult Hobby Classes: Enrl 18
Summer School: Dir, Betsy Brune

CORTLAND

STATE UNIVERSITY OF NEW YORK, COLLEGE AT CORTLAND, Dept Art & Art History, PO Box 2000, Room 222 Dowd Cortland, NY 13045-0900. Tel 607-753-4316; Fax 607-753-5967; Email anne.mclorn@cortland.edu; Email lori.ellis@cortland.edu; Web: www.cortland.edu/art/; *Chmn & Prof* Lori Ellis; *Prof* Jeremiah Donovan, MFA; *Prof* Barbara Wisch, PhD, MAT; *Prof* Charles Heasley, MFA; *Assoc Prof* Kathryn Kramer, PhD, MFA; *Asst Prof* Martine Barnaby, MFA; *Asst Prof* Jennifer McNamara, MFA; *Asst Prof* Vaughn Randall, MFA
Estab 1868, dept estab 1948; Maintains Dowd Art Gallery; pub; D & E; Scholarships; SC 40, LC 10; D 5600 (total), 1200 (art), maj 80
Ent Req: HS dipl, all college admissions standards based on high school average or scores from SAT, ACTP or Regent's tests
Degrees: BA 4 yrs, BFA 4 yrs
Courses: Art Appreciation, Art Education, †Art History, Ceramics, Computer Generated Prints, Computers in the Visual Arts, Contemporary Art, Design, Drawing, Fabric Design, †Graphic Design (New Media), †History of Art & Architecture, †Lettering Typography, Lithography, Modern Art, Painting, Photography, Printmaking, Sculpture, Silkscreen, Surrealism, Weaving
Summer School: Two terms of 5 wks beginning June 26. Courses—Art History, Studio

DIX HILLS

THE ART LEAGUE OF LONG ISLAND, Stevenson Academy Program, 107 E Deer Park Rd, Dix Hills, NY 11746-4818. Tel 631-462-5400; Email info@thestevensonacademy.com; Web: www.thestevensonacademy.com

ELMIRA

ELMIRA COLLEGE, Art Dept, One Park Pl, Elmira, NY 14901. Tel 607-735-1800, 735-1804 (Acad Affairs), 607-735-1724 (Admis); Fax 607-735-1712; Web: www.elmira.edu; *Chmn* Doug Holtgrewe; *Prof* James Cook; *Asst Prof* Leslie Kramer, MFA; *Asst Prof* Mac Dennis, MFA; *Asst* John Diamond-Nigh, MFA; *Asst* Jan Kather, MFA
Estab 1855; pvt; D & E; Scholarships; SC 26, LC 15, GC 8; D 250, E 125, maj 35, grad 6
Ent Req: HS dipl
Degrees: AA, AS, BA, BS & MEduc
Courses: †Art Education, †Art History, †Ceramics, †Drawing, †Painting, †Photography, †Printmaking, †Sculpture, †Video
Adult Hobby Classes: Tuition $180 - $265 per cr hr. Courses—Art History, Ceramics, Drawing, Landscape Painting & Drawing, Painting, Photography, Video
Summer School: Dir, Lois Webster. Tuition undergrad $180 cr hr, grad $265 per cr hr. Courses—Art History, Ceramics, Drawing, Landscape Painting & Drawing, Painting

FARMINGDALE

STATE UNIVERSITY OF NEW YORK AT FARMINGDALE, Visual Communications, 2350 Broadhollow Rd, Farmingdale, NY 11735-1006. Tel 631-420-2181; Fax 631-420-2034; Web: www.farmingdale.edu/art; *Dept Chmn* Wayne Krush; *Asst Prof* George Fernandez; *Assoc Prof* Thomas Germano; *Assoc Prof* Paul Gustafson; *Assoc Prof* Mark Moscarillo; *Asst Prof* Donna Proper; *Assoc Prof* Allison Puff; *Assoc Prof* Bill Steedle
Estab 1912; 10 FT, 6 PT; pub; D&E
Ent Req: portfolio, drawing test
Degrees: BT
Tuition: Res—$3,700 per yr; nonres—$8,300 per yr
Courses: Calligraphy, Computer Art, Computer Graphics, Design, Drawing, Electronic Publishing, Illustration, Layout, Multi-Media, Painting, Pastels, Photography, Printmaking, Typography, Watercolors, Web Design
Adult Hobby Classes: Tuition $45 per credit hr. Courses same as above
Summer School: Dir, Francis N Pellegrini. Tuition $45 per cr; June-Aug. Courses—Advertising, Art History, Design, Drawing, Lettering, Mechanical Art, Production

FLUSHING

QUEENS COLLEGE, Art Dept, 65-30 Kissena Blvd, Flushing, NY 11367. Tel 718-997-5770, 997-5411; Web: www.qc.edu; *Chmn* James Saslow
Nonprofit art gallery on 4th fl; also a museum; 13 FT instrs
Degrees: BA, BFA, MA, MFA, MSEd
Courses: Advertising Design, Architecture, Art Appreciation, Art Education, Art History, Calligraphy, Ceramics, Design, Drawing, Illustration, Painting, Photography, Printmaking, Sculpture
Summer School: Courses held at Caumsett State Park

FOREST HILLS

FOREST HILLS ADULT AND YOUTH CENTER, 6701 110th St, Forest Hills, NY 11375-2378. Tel 718-263-8066; *Prin HS* Elma Fleming
Degrees: Cert
Tuition: $70 plus materials for 7 wk course
Courses: Art Appreciation, Calligraphy, Drawing, Handicrafts, Painting, Quilting

FREDONIA

STATE UNIVERSITY OF NEW YORK AT FREDONIA, Dept of Art, 280 Central Ave, Rockefeller Art Center Rm 269 Fredonia, NY 14063-1127. Tel

716-673-3537; Email lundem@fredonia.edu; Web: www.fredonia.edu; *Prof* Marvin Bjurlin; *Prof* Robert Booth; *Prof* Paul Bowers; *Prof* John Hughson; *Prof* Daniel Reiff, PhD; *Chmn* Mary Lee Lunde; *Prof* Alberto Rey; *Prof* Liz Lee; *Asst Prof* Jan Conradi
Estab 1867, dept estab 1948; pub; D & E; Scholarships; SC 30, LC 18; D 650, E 70, non-maj 610, major 140
Ent Req: ent req HS dipl, GRE, SAT, portfolio review all students
Degrees: BA 4 yrs, BFA 4 yrs
Courses: Art History, †Ceramics, Drawing, †Graphic Arts, †Illustration, †Painting, †Photography, Printmaking, †Sculpture, Video

GARDEN CITY

ADELPHI UNIVERSITY, Dept of Art & Art History, 1 South Ave, Garden City, NY 11530-4213; PO Box 701, Garden City, NY 11530-0701. Tel 516-877-4460; Fax 516-877-4459; Web: www.adelphi.edu; *Prof* Richard Vaux; *Assoc Prof* Thomas MacNulty; *Asst Prof* Dale Flashner; *Chmn* Harry Davies; *Asst Prof* Geoffrey Grogan; *Asst Prof* Jacob Wisse
Estab 1896; Maintain nonprofit art gallery; FT 7, PT 18; pvt; D & E; Scholarships; SC 50, LC 10, GC 20; D 700, E 100, maj 130, grad 60
Ent Req: HS dipl; portfolio required for undergrad admis, portfolio required for grad admis
Degrees: BA 4 yrs, MA 1 1/2 yrs
Courses: †Advertising Design, Aesthetics, Art Education, Art History, Calligraphy, Ceramics, Design, Drawing, Graphic Arts, Graphic Design, History of Art & Architecture, Jewelry, Lettering, Mixed Media, Painting, Photography, Printmaking, Sculpture, Teacher Training
Summer School: Chmn, Harry Davies. Tuition—same as regular session; two 4 wk summer terms also 2 wk courses. Courses—Crafts, Drawing, Painting, Sculpture, Photography

NASSAU COMMUNITY COLLEGE, Art Dept, One Education Dr, Garden City, NY 11530. Tel 516-572-7162; Fax 516-572-9673; *Prof* Robert Lawn; *Prof* Edward Fox
Estab 1959, dept estab 1960; pub; D & E; Scholarships; SC 22, LC 5; D & E 20,000
Ent Req: HS dipl
Degrees: AA 2 yrs, cert in photography & advertising design 1 yr
Courses: Advertising Art, Art History, Arts & Crafts, Ceramics, Drawing, Fashion Arts, Painting, Photography, Printmaking, Sculpture
Summer School: Two 5 wk terms

GENESEO

STATE UNIVERSITY OF NEW YORK COLLEGE AT GENESEO, Dept of Art, One College Circle, Geneseo, NY 14454. Tel 716-245-5814, 245-5211 (main); Fax 716-245-5815; Web: www.geneseo.edu; *Chmn* Carl Shanahan
Estab 1871; FT 8, PT 3; pub; D & E; Scholarships; SC 35, LC 7; D 1000, E 1150, maj 115
Ent Req: HS dipl, ent exam
Degrees: BA(Art) 3-4 yrs
Courses: 2-D & 3-D Design, Art History, Ceramics, Computer Art, Drawing, Graphic Arts, Jewelry, Painting, Photography, Photolithography, Sculpture, Textile Design, Wood Design
Summer School: Enrl 180; Courses vary

GENEVA

HOBART & WILLIAM SMITH COLLEGES, Art Dept, Houghton House Gallery, 1 Kings Lane Geneva, NY 14456; 300 Pulteney St, Geneva, NY 14456. Tel 315-781-3487; Fax 315-781-3689; Web: www.hws.edu; *Chair* Nicholas Ruth
Estab 1822; FT 6; pvt; D; Scholarships; SC 15, LC 8; D 1,800
Ent Req: HS dipl, ent exam
Degrees: BA & BS 4 yrs
Courses: †Architecture, †Art History, Drawing, Mixed Media, Painting, Photography, Printmaking, Sculpture, †Studio Art

HAMILTON

COLGATE UNIVERSITY, Dept of Art & Art History, 13 Oak Dr, Hamilton, NY 13346-1386. Tel 315-228-7633, 228-1000; Fax 315-824-7787; Web: www.colgate.edu; *Chmn* John Knecht, MFA; *Prof* Eric Van Schaack, PhD, MFA; *Prof* Jim Loveless, MFA; *Assoc Prof* Judith Oliver, PhD, MFA; *Assoc Prof* Robert McVaugh, PhD; *Assoc Prof* Lynn Schwarzer, MFA; *Asst Prof* Padma Kaimal, MA; *Asst Prof* Mary Ann Calo, MA; *Asst Prof* Daniella Dooling, MA; *Asst Prof* Carol Kinne, MA
Estab 1819, dept estab 1905; pvt; D; Scholarships; SC 22, LC 23; D 941, maj 50
Ent Req: HS dipl, CEEB or ACT
Degrees: BA 4 yrs
Courses: Art History, Combined Media, Drawing, Mixed Media, Motion Picture Productions, Painting, Photography, Printmaking, Sculpture

HEMPSTEAD

HOFSTRA UNIVERSITY, Department of Fine Arts, 118A Calkins Hall, Hempstead, NY 11549-1000. Tel 516-463-5475; Fax 516-463-6268; Email fadmh@hofstra.edu; Web: www.hofstra.edu; *Chmn* Douglas Hilson
Estab 1935, dept estab 1945; Maintain nonprofit art gallery, Rosenberg, Calkins Hall, Hofstra Univ, Hempstead, NY 11550; FT 11; pvt; D & E; Scholarships; SC, LC 20, GC 16; D 1610, maj 100, grad 10
Ent Req: HS dipl
Degrees: BA, MA, BS
Tuition: Undergrad $7,140 per sem
Courses: Appraisal of Art and Antiques, Art History, Drawing, Graphic Arts, Jewelry, Painting, †Photography, †Sculpture
Summer School: Dean, Deanna Chitayat. Courses—Art History, Fine Arts

HERKIMER

HERKIMER COUNTY COMMUNITY COLLEGE, Humanities Social Services, 100 Reservoir Rd, Herkimer, NY 13350-1598. Tel 315-866-0300, Ext 200; Fax 315-866-7253; Web: www.hccc.ntcnct.com; *Dean* Jennifer Boulanger, MFA; *Asst Dean* Pat Haag, MFA; *Assoc Prof* James Bruce Schwabach, MFA; *Assoc Prof* Mariann Wrinn, MFA; *Asst Prof* Gale Farley
Estab 1966; pub; D & E; SC 8, LC 4; D 329 (total), maj 16
Ent Req: HS dipl, SAT or ACT; open
Degrees: AA, AS & AAS 2 yrs
Courses: †2-D Design, †3-D Design, Art Appreciation, Art History, †Ceramics, Drawing, Painting, Photography, †Sculpture, Theatre Arts, Video
Adult Hobby Classes: Enrl 40 cr, 100 non-credit; Courses—Art Appreciation, Calligraphy, Pastels, Portraits, Photography
Children's Classes: Enrl 40; tuition varies. Courses—Cartooning Workshop, Introduction to Drawing
Summer School: Dir, John Ribnikac. Enrl 40. Courses—Same as regular session

HOUGHTON

HOUGHTON COLLEGE, Art Dept, One Willard Ave, Houghton, NY 14744. Tel 716-567-2211; *Head Art Dept* Gary Baxter
Estab 1883; den; D & E; Scholarships; SC 8, LC 6
Degrees: AA & AS 2 yrs, BA & BS 4 yrs
Courses: Ceramics, Drawing, Graphic Design, Painting, Photography, Printmaking, Sculpture

ITHACA

CORNELL UNIVERSITY, College of Architecture, Art, and Planning, 129 Sibley Dome, Ithaca, NY 14853. Tel 607-255-9110; Fax 607-255-1900; Email aapdean@cornell.edu; Web: aap.cornell.edu; *Dean* Kieran Donaghy; *Asst Dean for Admin* Thomas E Cole Jr; *Dir Admissions* Maureen Carroll; *Dir Communs* Elise Gold; *Dir IT Solutions* Andre Hafner; *Dir Facilities* Frank Parish; *Dir Business Svc Ctr* Melinda Stelick; *Admin Mgr & Dir of Spec Projects* Lyn Pohl
Estab 1868; Maintain nonprofit art gallery; Olive Tjaden Gallery, Rm 101; Fine Arts Library, Cornell Univ; art supplies available on-campus; FT/PT 51; Pvt; D; Scholarships; Undergrad 507, grad 276
Ent Req: HS dipl, HS transcript, SAT
Degrees: BFA, MFA
Tuition: Undergrad $52,853, grad varies by discipline
Courses: Architecture, Fine Arts, Urban & Regional Studies
—**Dept of Art,** 224 Tjaden Hall, Ithaca, NY 14853. Tel 607-255-3558; Fax 607-255-3462; Email artinfo@cornell.edu; Web: aap.cornell.edu/academics/art; *Dept Chair* Michael Ashkin
Estab 1868, dept estab 1921; pvt; D; Scholarships; SC 25, LC 1, GC 4
Ent Req: HS dipl, HS transcript, SAT
Degrees: BFA, MFA
Tuition: Undergrad $52,853, grad varies by discipline
Courses: Architecture, City & Regional Planning, †Combined Media, Drawing, Painting, Photography, Printmaking, Sculpture
—**Dept of Architecture,** 139 E Sibley Hall, Ithaca, NY 14853. Tel 607-255-5236; Fax 607-255-0291; Email cuarch@cornell.edu; Web: aap.cornell.edu/academics/architecture; *Dept Chair* Andrea Simtich; *Dir Grad Studies* Jenny Sabin
pvt; D; Scholarships; LC 64, GC 12
Ent Req: HS dipl, SAT, grad admis requires GRE
Degrees: BArch 5 yr, MArch, MS, PhD
Tuition: Undergrad $52,853, grad varies by discipline
Courses: Architecture, Architecture History, Building Design & Technology, Computer Graphics

ITHACA COLLEGE, Fine Art Dept, 101 Ceracche Ctr, Ithaca, NY 14850-7277. Tel 607-274-3330; Fax 607-274-1358; Web: www.ithaca.edu; *Prof* Raymond Ghirardo, MFA; *Chmn* Susan Weisend, MFA; *Instr* Pat Hunsinger; *Instr* Bill Hastings; *Instr* Linda Price; *Assoc Prof* Carla Stetson; *Asst Prof* Dora Engler; *Asst Prof* Sarah Sutton; *Asst Prof* Patricia Capaldi; *Instr* Pamela Drix; *Instr* Sara Fersuson; *Instr* Brody Burroughs
Estab 1892, dept estab 1968; Maintain nonprofit art gallery; Handwerker Gallery, 1170 Gannett Center, Ithaca, NY 14850; Pvt; D & E; Scholarships; SC 27; non-maj 300, maj 50
Ent Req: HS dipl, SAT scores
Degrees: BA and BFA 4 yrs & Teacher Education
Courses: 2-D Design, †Art Education, Art History, Computer Art, Drawing, Figure Drawing, †Graphic Design, Painting, Printmaking, Sculpture, Silkscreen
Summer School: Chmn, Susan Weisand. Enrl 10-20. Courses—Intro to Drawing, Computer Art, Painting

JAMAICA

SAINT JOHN'S UNIVERSITY, Dept of Fine Arts, 8000 Utopia Pkwy, Jamaica, NY 11439. Tel 718-990-6161; Fax 718-990-1907; *Gallery Dir* Mohammad Mohsin; *Chmn* Paul Fabozzi
Pvt; D; Scholarships; SC 24, LC 9; D 1300, maj 100
Ent Req: HS dipl, ent exam, portfolio review
Degrees: BFA & BS 4 yrs
Courses: Advertising Design, Aesthetics, Art Appreciation, Art Education, Art History, Ceramics, Collage, Commercial Art, Conceptual Art, Design, Drawing, Film, †Fine Arts, Graphic Arts, †Graphic Design, History of Art & Architecture,

†Illustration, Industrial Design, Intermedia, Jewelry, Lettering, Mixed Media, †Painting, †Photography, †Printmaking, Saturday Scholarship Program, †Sculpture, Video
Adult Hobby Classes: Courses—Drawing, Figure, Painting, Sculpture
Summer School: Courses—Drawing, Painting

YORK COLLEGE OF THE CITY UNIVERSITY OF NEW YORK, Fine & Performing Arts, 94-20 Guy Brewer Blvd, Jamaica, NY 11451. Tel 718-262-2400; Fax 718-262-2998; *Prof* Jane Schuler PhD; *Coordr Fine Arts* Phillips Simkin; *Assoc Prof* Ernest Garthwaite, MA; *Assoc Prof* Arthur Anderson, MFA
Estab 1968; pub; D & E; 4303
Ent Req: HS dipl
Degrees: BA 4 yrs
Courses: Art Education, Art History, Computer Graphics, Drawing, Graphic Arts, Painting, Photography, Printmaking, Sculpture
Summer School: Dean, Wallace Schoenberg. Enrl $20 per course; tuition $47 per cr for term of 6 wks beginning late June. Courses—Art History, Drawing, Painting

JAMESTOWN

JAMESTOWN COMMUNITY COLLEGE, Arts, Humanities & Health Sciences Division, 525 Falconer St, Jamestown, NY 14701-1999. Tel 716-665-5220, Ext 394; Fax 716-665-9110; Email billdisbro@mail.sunyjcc.edu; Web: www.sunyjcc.edu; *Art Coordr* Bill Disbro
Estab 1950, dept estab 1970; Maintain nonprofit art gallery; Week Gallery; FT 1, PT 7; pub; D & E; Scholarships; SC 11, LC 1; D 310, E 254
Ent Req: open
Degrees: AA 60 cr hrs; AS Fine Arts; Studio Art
Courses: Ceramics, Computer Graphics, Design, Drawing, Introduction to Visual Art, Painting, Photography, Survey of Visual Arts, Video
Summer School: Dir, Roslin Newton. Enrl 25-50; Courses—Ceramics, Drawing, Painting, Photography

LOUDONVILLE

SIENA COLLEGE, Dept of Creative Arts, 515 Loudon Rd, Loudonville, NY 12211-1459. Tel 578-783-2325 (Liberal Arts Office); Fax 518-783-4293; Web: www.siena.edu; *Chair & Prof Art History* Patricia Trutty-Coohill; *Asst Prof Photog & Video* Amanda Green, MFA; *Asst Prof Journalism* Rebecca Taylor, JD; *Prof Theatre* Mahmood Karimi-Hakak, DSE; *Asst Prof Theatre Design* Denise Massman, MFA; *Asst Prof Painting & Drawing* Scott Foster, MFA; *Assoc Prof Music* Paul Koyne, PhD; *Asst Prof Music* Timothy Reno, PhD
Estab 1937; Maintain nonprofit art gallery; den; D & E; Scholarships; SC & LC; Enrl 3000, maj 60
Ent Req: HS dipl
Degrees: BA
Tuition: $26,185 per year without room & board
Courses: Aesthetics, †Chorus, †Costume Design & Construction, †Design, Drawing, †Film, Graphic Design, History of Art & Architecture, Mixed Media, †Museum Staff Training, Music, Painting, †Photography, Printmaking, †Stage Design, Theatre Arts, †Video, †Voice
Summer School: Enrl 35; tuition $315 per cr hr for 7 wk term. Courses—Intro to Visual Arts

MIDDLETOWN

ORANGE COUNTY COMMUNITY COLLEGE, Arts & Communication, 115 South St, Middletown, NY 10940-6404. Tel 845-341-4787; Fax 845-341-4775; Web: www.sunyorange.edu; *Chair* Mark Strunsky; *Asst Prof Arts & Communs* Joseph Litow; *Asst Prof Arts & Communs* Susan Slater-Tanner
Estab 1950, dept estab 1950; Maintain a nonprofit art gallery, Harriman Student Gallery, 115 South St, Middletown, NY 10940; Pub; D & E; Scholarships; SC 16, LC 8; D 135, maj 60
Ent Req: HS dipl
Degrees: AA 2 yrs, AAS(Visual Comm Graphics)
Tuition: $1,550 per semester; no campus res
Courses: Art History, Color, Computer Graphic Design, Design, Drawing, Painting, Photography, Sculpture

NEW PALTZ

STATE UNIVERSITY OF NEW YORK AT NEW PALTZ, Art Education Program, 1 Hawk Dr, Smiley Art Bldg 108-A New Paltz, NY 12561-2447. Tel 845-257-3850; Web: www.newpaltz.edu/arted; *Chmn Art Studio & Art Educ* Myra Mimlitsch-Gray; *Prog Dir Art Educ* Margaret Johnson; *Assoc Chair* David Cavallaro
Pub; D & E; SC, LC, GC; maj 600, grad 100
Degrees: BA, MS, MA
Tuition: res—$2,175 per person; nonres—$5,305 per person
Courses: Art Education, Ceramics, Graphic Design, Metal, Painting, Photography, Printmaking, Sculpture

NEW ROCHELLE

THE COLLEGE OF NEW ROCHELLE, School of Arts & Sciences Art Dept, 29 Castle Pl, New Rochelle, NY 10805-2330. Tel 914-654-5274; Email estern@cnr.edu; Web: www.cnr.edu/artdept; *Chair* Emily Stern, MFA; *Prof* William C Maxwell, PhD; *Assoc Prof* Cristina deGennaro, MFA; *Assoc Prof* Margie Neuhaus, MFA; *Prof* Susan Canning, PhD
Estab 1904, dept estab 1929; Maintain nonprofit gallery, Castle Gallery, 29 Castle Pl, New Rochelle, NY 10805; Pvt, women only; D&E; Scholarships; SC 52, LC 14, GC 21; D 150, non-maj 45, maj 105, grad 98
Ent Req: HS dipl, SAT or ACT scores, college preparatory program in high school
Degrees: BA, BFA and BS 4 yrs
Tuition: $9950 per yr; campus res— room and board $4320 per yr
Courses: †Art Education, †Art History, †Art Therapy, Ceramics, Collage, Computer Graphics, Design, Drawing, Fiber Arts, Film, Graphic Design, Jewelry, Metalwork, Mixed Media, Painting, Photography, Printmaking, Sculpture, Teacher Training
Summer School: Painting for non-maj; pre-college prog, other courses available for college students

NEW YORK

AESTHETIC REALISM FOUNDATION, 141 Greene St, New York, NY 10012-3201. Tel 212-777-4490; Fax 212-777-4426; Web: www.aestheticrealism.org; *Chmn Educ* Ellen Reiss; *Exec Dir* Margot Carpenter
Estab 1973, as a not for profit educational foundation to teach Aesthetic Realism, the philosophy founded in 1941 by American poet & critic Eli Siegel (1902-1978), based on his historic principle: "The world, art, and self explain each other: each is the aesthetic oneness of opposites."; Maintains nonprofit art gallery, Terrain Gallery, same location
Publications: The Right of Aesthetic Realism to Be Known, weekly periodical
Courses: Anthropology, Art Criticism, Art History, Drawing, Education, †Film, Marriage, Music, Poetry, Singing, Theatre Arts
Children's Classes: Learning to Like the World

AMERICAN ACADEMY IN ROME, 7 E 60th St, New York, NY 10022-1030. Tel 212-751-7200; Fax 212-751-7220; Web: www.aarome.org; *Pres & CEO* Mark Robbins; *VPres Develop* Christine Begley; *Chmn* Mary Margaret Jones
Estab 1894, chartered by Congress 1905; consolidated with School of Classical Studies 1913; Dept of Musical Composition estab 1921; Fellowships for independent study in Rome at the Acad in the fields of architecture, landscape architecture, design, painting, sculpture, musical composition, classical and post-classical studies, history of art, Italian studies are open to citizens of the United States. Painters and sculptors receive a supplies allowance of $600 per year. Approx 30 fellowships are awarded each year Applicants' material is judged by independent juries of professionals in the field of award. Stipend and travel allowances total $6200, plus room, studio or study, and partial board. Application forms and information sheets are available from the New York office. Applications and supporting material and $25 application fee must be received at the Academy's New York office by November 15 of each year; Mem: Annual meeting Oct; Board in Feb; Scholarships
Summer School: 28 fellowships

AMERICAN UNIVERSITY, Dept of Art, 520 W 43rd St, Apt 21E New York, NY 10036-4352. Tel 202-885-1670; Fax 202-885-1132; Email dkimes@american.edu; *Chmn Dept & Prof* Don Kimes, MFA; *Prof* C Stanley Lewis, MFA; *Prof* Mary Garrard; *Prof* Norma Broude, PhD; *Prof* M Oxman, MFA; *Assoc Prof* Ron Haynie Oxman, MFA; *Assoc Prof* Deborah Kahn, MFA; *Assoc Prof* Michael Graham, MFA; *Asst Prof* Helen Langa, PhD; *Asst Prof* Luis Silva, MFA; *Prof* Barbara Rose, PhD; *Assoc Prof* Chemi Montes, MFA; *Instr* Glenn Goldberg, MFA; *Instr* Steven Cushner, MFA; *Instr* Susan Yanero, MFA; *Instr* Sharo Fischel, MFA; *Instr* Carol Goldberg, MFA; *Instr* Jo Weiss Le, MFA; *Instr* Jeneen Piccuirro, MFA; *Instr* Guy Zoller, MFA; *Instr* Rachel Simons, PhD; *Instr* Laurie Swindull, MFA
Estab 1893, dept estab 1945; Maintain nonprofit art gallery; Watkins Gallery, Dept of Art, 4400 Massachusetts Ave NW, Washington, DC; pvt; D&E; Scholarships; Fellowships; SC 26, LC 15, GC 19 and 6 Art History courses in Italy Program; D & E 1600, maj 191, grad 70
Ent Req: HS dipl
Degrees: BA, BFA(Studio Art), BA(Design), BA(Art History) 4 yrs, MA(Art History) 18 months, MFA(Painting, Sculpture, Printmaking) 2 yrs
Courses: Aesthetics, Art Appreciation, †Art History, Ceramics, Collage, Computer Graphics, Constructions, †Drawing, †Graphic Design, History of Art & Architecture, Lettering, Mixed Media, Multimedia, †Painting, †Printmaking, †Sculpture
Summer School: Dept Adminr, Glenna Haynie. Design, Studio & Art History

ART STUDENTS LEAGUE OF NEW YORK, 215 W 57th St, New York, NY 10019-2193. Tel 212-247-4510; Fax 212-541-7024; Email info@artstudentsleague.org; Web: www.theartstudentsleague.org
Estab 1875; FT 65; pvt; Scholarships; LC; D 1200, E 800, Sat 500 (adults and children)
Ent Req: none
Courses: Drawing, Graphic Arts, Illustration, Painting, †Printmaking, Sculpture
Children's Classes: Classes on Saturday
Summer School: Enrl 800, beginning June

THE ART STUDIO NEW YORK, 145 W 96th St, New York, NY 10025-6403. Tel 212-932-8484; Email info@theartstudiony.com; Web: www.theartstudiony.com; *Founder, Dir & Instr* Rebecca Schweiger
Courses: †Drawing, †Mixed Media, †Painting

BERNARD M BARUCH COLLEGE OF THE CITY UNIVERSITY OF NEW YORK, Art Dept, 1 Bernard Baruch Way, 55 Lexington Ave at 24th St New York, NY 10010-5585. Tel 646-312-4052; Fax 646-312-4051; Web: www.baruch.cuny.edu; *Dept Chair* Anne Swartz; *Deputy Chair Art* Leonard Sussman
Estab 1968; pub; D & E; SC 26, LC 16; D 2000, E 500
Ent Req: HS dipl
Degrees: BA, BBA & BSEd 4 yrs, MBA 5 yrs, PhD
Courses: Advertising Design, Art History, Ceramics, Computer Graphics, Drawing, History of Art & Architecture, Illustration, Painting, Photography, Sculpture
Summer School: Courses - Art History Survey, Ceramics, Crafts, Drawing, Painting, Photography

CITY COLLEGE OF NEW YORK, Art Dept, 160 Convent Ave, New York, NY 10031-9101. Tel 212-650-7420; Fax 212-650-7438; Email art@ccny.cuny.edu;

Web: www.ccny.cuny.edu; *Dir Mus Studies* Prof Harriet Senie, PhD; *Assoc Prof* Ellen Handy, PhD; *Dir* Marit Dewhurst, BFA; *Prof* Colin Chase; *Prof* Sylvia Netzer; *Prof* Ina Saltz; *Chair* Leo Fuentes; *Asst Prof* Molly Aitken; *Assoc Prof* Becca Albee; *Lectr* Patterson Beckwith; *Prog Dir Art Ed Asst Prof* Marit Dewhurst; *Lectr & Co-Dir Art History* Craig Houser; *Assoc Prof & Chair* Anna Indych-Lopez; *Lectr* Lise Kjaer; *DIAP MFA Prog Dir* Hajoe Moderegger; *Assoc Prof* Tom Thayer; *Asst Prof* Mark Addison Smith; *Asst Prof* Abby Kornfeld; *Asst Prof* Joe Moore
Estab 1847; pub; D & E & Sat; Scholarships; SC 125, LC 25, GC 35; D 1600, E 133, maj 400, grad 60
Ent Req: HS dipl, entrance placement exams
Degrees: BA, MA, BFA, MFA
Tuition: Res—undergrad $2415 per sem, $205 per cr hr; nonres—undergrad $435 per cr hr
Courses: Art Education, Art History, Ceramics, Design, Drawing, Graphic Arts, Graphic Design, Intermedia, Mixed Media, Museum Staff Training, Painting, Photography, Printmaking, Sculpture
Adult Hobby Classes: Courses—Advertising & Design, Art History, Ceramics, Drawing, Graphics, Museum Studies, Painting, Photography, Sculpture

CITY UNIVERSITY OF NEW YORK, PhD Program in Art History, 365 5th Ave, The Graduate Center New York, NY 10016-4309. Tel 212-817-8035; Fax 212-817-1502; Email arthistory@gc.cuny.edu; Web: www.gc.cuny.edu; *Prof Emeritus* Jack Flam; *Prof Emerita* Rosemarie Haag Bletter; *Prof* Anna Chave; *Prof Emeritus* George Corbin; *Prof* Mona Hadler; *Prof Emerita* Eloise Quinones-Keber; *Prof Emerita* Diane Kelder; *Prof* Gail Levin; *Prof Emerita* Patricia Mainardi; *Prof Emerita* Sally Webster; *Prof* Romy Golan; *Prof* Barbara Lane; *Prof Emeritus* Stuart Liebman; *Prof* Katherine Manthorne; *Prof* James M Saslow; *Prof* Harriet Senie; *Prof* Judy Sund; *Prof* Emily Braun; *Prof Emerita* Lisa Vergara; *Prof* Claire Bishop; *Prof* David Joselit; *Prof* Jennifer Ball; *Prof* Amanda Wunder; *Prof* M Antonella Pelizzari
Estab 1961, prog estab 1971; Maintain nonprofit art gallery (James Gallery) on campus; art libr within Mina Rees Libr; pub; D & E; Scholarships; Fellowships; LC 10, GC 6; D 200
Ent Req: BA or MA in Art History
Degrees: PhD
Tuition: Res—$2435 per sem, $275 per cr hr; nonres—$3800 per sem, $475 per cr hr
Courses: African, Art History, Modern and Contemporary Art & Architecture, Native American & Pre-Columbian Art & Architecture, Oceanic, Renaissance & Baroque Art & Architecture

COLUMBIA UNIVERSITY, School of the Arts, 2960 Broadway, New York, NY 10027. Tel 212-854-2875; Email arts@columbia.edu; Web: arts.columbia.edu; *Dean of Faculty* Carol Becker; *Dean of Academic Admin* Jana Wright
Estab 1881; Maintains Miriam & Ira D Wallach Art Gallery and Lenfest Center for the Arts.; pvt; Scholarships; Fellowships; 800
Ent Req: Bachelor's degree in appropriate area of study
Degrees: MFA
Tuition: $63,961
Courses: Film, Film & Media Studies, Theatre Arts, Visual Arts, Writing
—**Graduate School of Architecture, Planning & Preservation**, 1172 Amsterdam Ave, New York, NY 10027-7055. Tel 212-854-3414; Fax 212-864-0410; Web: www.arch.columbia.edu; *Dean* Amale Andraos
Estab 1881; FT 31, PT 32; pvt; Scholarships; Fellowships; 400
Ent Req: Bachelor's degree in appropriate area of study
Degrees: MArchit, MS, PhD
Tuition: $28,470
Courses: Architecture, Preservation, Real Estate, Urbanism
—**Dept of Art History & Archaeology**, 826 Schermerhorn Hall, 1190 Amsterdam Ave New York, NY 10027. Tel 212-854-4505; Fax 212-854-7329; Web: www.columbia.edu/cu/arthistory; *Dept Chair* Michael Cole
Pvt
Degrees: BA, MA, MPhil, PhD
Courses: Aesthetics, Architecture, Art Appreciation, Art History, Classical Art & Archeology, Far Eastern Art & Archeology, History & Theory of Art History, History of Architecture, History of Art & Archeology, History of Western Art, Near Eastern Art & Archeology, Primitive & Pre-Columbian Art & Archeology
—**Art & Art Education Program at Teachers College**, 444 Macy Hall, New York, NY 10027. Tel 212-678-3360; Email arted@tc.edu; Web: www.tc.columbia.edu; *Prog Dir* Dr Mary Claire Hafeli
Estab 1888; pvt; Scholarships; Fellowships; Assistantships; GC; 5547
Ent Req: Bachelor's degree & Portfolio review
Degrees: EDD, EDDCT, EDM, MA
Tuition: $1,635 per cr
Courses: Art Appreciation, Art Education, Artistic-Aesthetic Development, Ceramics, Crafts, Curriculum Design, Design, Drawing, Historical Foundations, Museum Studies, Painting, Painting Crafts, Philosophy of Art, Photography, Printmaking, Sculpture, Teacher Education

COOPER UNION, School of Art, 30 Cooper Sq, New York, NY 10003-7120. Tel 212-353-4200; Email artschool@cooper.edu; Web: cooper.edu; *Acting Dean* Mike Essl
Estab 1859; Nonprofit gallery - The Arthur J. Houghton Gallery, 7 E 7th St, New York, NY 10003; FT 10, PT 60; pvt; D & E; Scholarships
Ent Req: HS dipl, ent exam
Degrees: BFA 4 yr
Tuition: Free
Courses: †Calligraphy, †Conceptual Art, †Design, †Drawing, †Film, †Graphic Design, †Painting, †Photography, †Printmaking, †Sculpture, †Video
Adult Hobby Classes: Extended Studies Prog
Children's Classes: Enrl 200. Courses—Pre College Art & Architecture for HS students
Summer School: Dir, Stephanie Hightower. Enrl 100. Courses—Same as above

EDUCATION ALLIANCE, Art School & Gallery, 197 E Broadway, New York, NY 10002-5598. Tel 646-395-4280; Email info@mannycantor.org; Web: www.edalliance.org; *Community Educ* Kristin Eno
Estab 1889; PT 26; priv; D & E; Scholarships
Ent Req: None
Degrees: Cert
Tuition: Varies per course
Courses: Ceramics, Drawing, Metal Sculpture, Mixed Media, Painting, Photography, Sculpture
Adult Hobby Classes: Enrl 150; 15 wk term; Courses—Painting, Drawing, Sculpture, Metal Sculpture, Ceramics, Photography, Photo Silk Screen
Children's Classes: Enrl 20; 30 wk term. Courses—Mixed Media
Summer School: Dir Clare J Kagel. Enrl 60; tuition by the course for 10 wk term. Courses—Painting, Sculpture

FASHION INSTITUTE OF TECHNOLOGY, School of Art & Design, 227 W 27th St, New York, NY 10001-5992. Tel 212-217-7999; Web: www.fitnyc.edu; *Chmn Interior Design* Eric Daniels; *Chmn Fashion Design* Michael Casey; *Chmn Fashion Illustrations* Kam Mak; *Chmn Jewelry Design* Wendy Yothers; *Chmn Fashion Business Mgmt* Naomi Gross; *Chmn Modern Languages & Cultures* Prof Isabella Bertoletti; *Chmn Fine Arts* Joel Werring; *Chmn Commun Design* Suzanne E Anoushian; *Chmn Advertising & Mktg Communs* John F Fraser; *Chmn Technical Design* Deborah Beard; *Chmn Educational Skills* Mark Goldblatt; *Chmn Interior Design* Eric Daniels; *Chmn International Trade* Christine Sala Pomeranz; *Chmn Photog* Brad Paris; *Chmn Production Mgmt* Mario Federici; *Chmn Science & Math* Calvin Williamson; *Chmn Science & Math* Geoffrey Rogers; *Chmn Social Science* Paul Clement; *Chmn Textile Develop & Mktg* Jeffrey Silberman
Estab 1951; pub; D & E; Scholarships; SC 317, LC 26; D 4011, E 7004
Ent Req: HS dipl, ent exam
Degrees: AAS 2 yr, BFA 4 yr
Tuition: Res—undergrad $1200 per sem; nonres—undergrad $2825 per sem; campus res—room & board $4412 per yr
Courses: Accessories Design, †Advertising Design, Art History, †Display, History of Art & Architecture, †Illustration, †Interior Design, †Jewelry, Painting, †Photography, Printmaking, †Restoration & Conservation, Sculpture, Silversmithing, †Textile Design, Toy Design, Weaving
Adult Hobby Classes: Part-time Studies
Summer School: VPres Student Affairs, Stayton Wood. Enrl 4589; tuition $78-$200 per course for term of 3, 5 & 7 wks beginning June. Courses—Same as above

FORDHAM UNIVERSITY, Art Dept, 113 W 60th St, Arts Division, Lincoln Ctr New York, NY 10023-7414. Tel 212-636-6000; Web: www.fordham.edu; *Div Chmn* William Conlon
Estab 1968; FT 7; pvt; D & E; Scholarships; SC 18, LC 25; D 900, E 1750, maj 56
Ent Req: HS dipl
Degrees: BA 4 yrs
Courses: Aesthetics, Costume Design & Construction, Drawing, Graphic Arts, History of Art & Architecture, Painting, Photography, Sculpture, Stage Design, Teacher Training, Theatre Arts
Summer School: Dir, Dr Levak. Four terms per summer for 5 wks each
—**Center Gallery**, 70 Lincoln Center Plz, Lincoln Center Campus New York, NY 10023-6594. Tel 212-636-6000
Call for hours
Collections: Photographs; paintings; sculpture; drawings
—**Push Pin Gallery**, 113 W 60th St, Visual Arts Complex New York, NY 10023. Tel 212-636-6000
Call for hours
Collections: Works by student artists including paintings, drawings, & sculpture

GREENWICH HOUSE INC, Greenwich House Pottery, 16 Jones St, New York, NY 10014-4132. Tel 212-242-4106; Fax 212-645-5486; Email pottery@greenwichhouse.org; Web: www.greenwichhousepottery.org; *Asst Dir* Lynne Lerner; *Dir* Elizabeth Zawada; *Programs Coordr* Gail Heidel; *Studio Mgr* Josephine Burr
Estab 1909, parent organization estab 1902; Maintains nonprofit art gallery, Jane Hartsook Gallery, 16 Jones St, New York, NY 10014; 26; pvt; D & E; Scholarships; SC 32; D 200, E 94
Ent Req: none
Degrees: none
Tuition: No campus res
Courses: Art History, Ceramics, Glazing Chemistry, Sculpture
Adult Hobby Classes: Enrl 200. Courses—Pottery Wheel, Handbuilding, Sculpture
Children's Classes: Enrl 50. Creative technique instruction
Summer School: Dir, Elizabeth Zawada. Enrl 40;

HARRIET FEBLAND ART WORKSHOP, 245 E 63rd St, Ste 1803, New York, NY 10065. Tel 212-759-2215; Email harrietfebland@aol.com; Web: www.harrietfeblandart.com; *Dir & Instr* Harriet FeBland
Estab 1962; Pvt; D; SC 6, LC 1, GC 2; D 90, others 30
Income: Financed by student tuition
Ent Req: Review of previous work, paintings or sculpture
Tuition: $1,800 - $2,000 per 15 wk class, $700 for 5 wk 1 hr critique session
Courses: Collage, †Constructions, Drawing, †Mixed Media, †Moku-Hanga woodcut block printing, †Painting, Sculpture
Adult Hobby Classes: 70; $2,000 per sem (15 wk each sem). Courses—Advanced Painting, Assemblage, Construction, Drawing
Summer School: Dir, Harriet FeBland. Workshops for 2 to 3 wks are given at various universities in US & England

HENRY STREET SETTLEMENT ARTS FOR LIVING CENTER, 466 Grand St, New York, NY 10002-4804. Tel 212-598-0400; Fax 212-505-8329; *Dir* Barbara Tate
Estab 1895; pvt; D; Scholarships; D 60, E 60
Ent Req: None
Courses: Calligraphy, Ceramics, Drawing, Graphic Arts, Mixed Media, Painting, Printmaking, Sculpture
Adult Hobby Classes: Courses—Crafts, Drawing, Painting, Pottery
Children's Classes: Courses—Arts & Crafts, Cartooning, Drawing, Experimental Art, Painting, Pottery, Printmaking

HUNTER COLLEGE, Dept of Art & Art History, 695 Park Ave, North Bldg 11054 New York, NY 10021. Tel 212-772-4995; Email art@hunter.cuny.edu; Web: huntercollegeart.org; *Prof & Galleries Dir* Joachim Pissarro; *Chmn & Galleries Exec Dir* Howard Singerman; *Assoc Chair, Art History* Hendrik Dey; *Assoc Chair, Studio Art* Andrea Blum
Estab 1890, dept estab 1935; Maintain nonprofit art galleries: Bertha & Karl Leubsdorf Art Gallery, 205 Hudson Gallery & East Harlem Gallery; maintains Zabar Art Library; FT 29, PT 53; pub; D & E; Scholarships; Work study; SC 20-25, LC 10, GC 14-20
Ent Req: HS dipl
Degrees: BA & BFA 4 yrs, MA & MFA
Tuition: Undergrad (per cr): res $285, nonres $580; Grad (per cr): res $440, nonres $805
Courses: Art History, Ceramics, Drawing, Painting, Photography, Printmaking, Sculpture, Studio Art

INTERNATIONAL CENTER OF PHOTOGRAPHY, School, 1114 Ave of the Americas at 43rd St, New York, NY 10036. Tel 212-857-0001; Fax 212-857-0091; Email education@icp.org; Web: www.icp.org; *Facilities Supv* H Eugene Foster; *Digital Media Labs* Per Gylfe; *Chair Photog & Photojournalism Prog* Alison Morley
Open Mon - Fri 9:30 AM - 7 PM, Sat 9 AM - 3 PM, cl Sun, July 4, Thanksgiving, Christmas & New Years Days; Maintains classrooms, Bard Studios, color & black-and-white labs, digital labs, professional shooting studio, research ctr w/ library & archives & Rita K Hillman Education Gallery; Average Annual Attendance: 5,000
Exhibitions: Rita K Hillman Gallery: displays work of students, faculty & staff
Activities: Teen Academy; 1-yr cert progs; 2-yr MFA progs; continuing educ progs; travel progs
Courses: Photography

JOHN JAY COLLEGE OF CRIMINAL JUSTICE, Dept of Art, Music & Philosophy, 524 W 59th St, New York, NY 10019-1007. Tel 212-237-8325; Web: www.jjay.cuny.edu; *Chmn* John Pittman; *Prof* Laurie Schneider PhD; *Assoc Prof* Helen Ramsaran, MFA
Estab 1964, dept estab 1971; FT 4, PT 3; pub; D & E; SC 5, LC 6; D 180, E 180
Ent Req: HS dipl
Degrees: BA and BS 4 yr
Courses: Art History, Drawing, Painting, Sculpture

LOWER EAST SIDE PRINTSHOP INC, 306 W 37th St, 6th Fl, New York, NY 10018. Tel 212-673-5390; Fax 212-979-6493; Email info@printshop.org; Web: http://printshop.org; *Exec Dir* Dusica Kirjakovic; *Studio Dir & Master Printer* James Miller; *Progs Dir* Sei Young Kim

MANHATTAN GRAPHICS CENTER, 250 W 40th St, New York, NY 10018. Tel 212-219-8783; Email manhattangraphicscenter@verizon.net; Web: www.manhattangraphicscenter.org; *Pres* Ruth Moscovitch; *VPres* Bob Shore; *VPres* Jaz Graf; *Instr* Frederick Mershimer; *Instr* Vijay Kumar; *Instr* Margaret Nussbaum; *Instr* Arnold Brooks; *Instr* Takuji Hamanaka
Estab 1986; Center is a nonprofit printmaking school & workshops where artists may work in a variety of media, including etching, silkscreen, lithography, woodcut, monotype & other printmaking techniques; schols open to new mems demonstrating financial need; on-campus shop where art supplies may be purchased; Pub; D & E; Weekends; Scholarships; SC 25 LC 3
Tuition: $85-395
Courses: †Graphic Arts, Photography, Printmaking
Adult Hobby Classes: Enrl 10; tuition $30 per wk. Courses—Etching, Lithography, Monotype, Silkscreen, Woodcut

MARYMOUNT MANHATTAN COLLEGE, Fine & Performing Arts Div, 221 E 71st St, New York, NY 10021-4597. Tel 212-774-0760; Fax 212-774-0770; Email mfleischer@mmm.edu; Web: www.marymount.mm.edu; *Prof Theatre* Barbara Adrian; *Asst Prof Theatre* John Basil; *Asst Prof Art History* Adrienne Bell; *Asst Prof Art Dir Hewitt Gallery* Millie Burns; *Assoc Prof Art & Chair Art Dept* Hallie Cohen; *Assoc Prof Theatre* Kevin Connell; *Assoc Prof Theatre* Robert Dutiel; *Assoc Prof Art* Millie Falcaro; *Assoc Prof Dance* Anthony Ferro; *Prof & Chair Theatre* Mary Fleischer; *Assoc Prof Dance* Jens Giersdorf; *Assoc Prof Art* James Holl; *Assoc Prof & Chair Dance* Katie Langan; *Artist in Res, Dance* Nancy Lushington; *Prof Theatre & Chair Fine & Performing Arts* David Mold; *Asst Prof Theatre* Jeff Morrison; *Prof Theatre* Richard Niles; *Assoc Prof Theatre* Ellen Orenstein; *Prof Theatre* Ray Recht; *Artist in Res, Musical Theatre* Christine Riley; *Prof Theatre* Mark Ringer; *Assoc Prof Art History* Jason Rosenfeld; *Asst Prof Art* Nicholas Schneider; *Assoc Prof Theatre* Patricia Simon; *Asst Prof Theatre* Jill Stevenson; *Assoc Prof Dance* Haila Strauss; *Asst Prof Dance* Tami Stronach; *Assoc Prof Dance & Music* Andrew Warshaw; *Asst Prof Theatre* Kirche Zeile
Estab 1936; Maintains nonprofit Hewitt Gallery of Art; FT 25; pvt; D & E; Scholarships; SC & LC; maj 700
Ent Req: HS dipl
Degrees: BA & BFA
Tuition: $22,420 per yr
Courses: Aesthetics, Art Appreciation, Art Education, †Art History, Arts Management, Ceramics, Choreography, †Commercial Art, Conceptual Art, Costume Design & Construction, Dance, Design, Display, Drafting, Drawing, Film, Graphic Arts, Graphic Design, History of Art & Architecture, Illustration, Intermedia, Mixed Media, Musical Theatre, Painting, Photography, Printmaking, Sculpture, Stage Design, †Theatre Arts, Video

NATIONAL ACADEMY SCHOOL, 5 E 89th St, New York, NY 10128-0602. Tel 212-996-1908; Fax 212-426-1711; Email mpellegrin@nationalacademy.org; Web: www.nationalacademy.org; *Dir School* Maurizio Pellegrin
Estab 1826; Maintain nonprofit art gallery 5 E 89th St, New York NY 10028; 45; pvt; D, E & weekends; Scholarships; SC 60, LC 4, GC 1; Enrl 600, Maj, Cont Educ
Activities: Schols offered
Ent Req: Portfolio required for the Studio Intensive
Degrees: cert; dipl
Tuition: varies
Courses: Anatomy, †Art History, Career Development Seminar, Collage, Composition-Portraiture, Drawing, Drawing the Classical Orders, Life Sketch Class, †Mixed Media, Painting, †Photography, Printmaking, Sculpture, †Theory and Criticism, †Video, Workshops
Adult Hobby Classes: Enrl 550; tuition varies per class. Courses—Drawing, Painting, Printmaking, Sculpture & related subjects
Children's Classes: Enrl 25; tuition varies per class. Courses ages 6-16 & older—Drawing & Painting
Summer School: Dir, Maurizio Pellegrin, Enrl 300. Courses—Drawing, Painting, Printmaking, Sculpture, Watercolor, Mixed Media & variety of workshops

THE NEW SCHOOL, Parsons School of Design, 66 Fifth Ave, New York, NY 10011-8802. Tel 212-229-8900; Email communications@newschool.edu; Web: www.newschool.edu/parsons; *Exec Dean* Joel Towers; *Dean School of Art & Design* Sarah Lawrence; *Dean School of Art, Media & Tech* Ann Gaines; *Dean School of Constructed Environments* Robert Kirkbride; *Dean School of Design Strategies* Jane Pirone; *Dean School of Fashion* Burak Cakmak
Estab 1896; FT 150, PT 1,250; pvt; D & E; Scholarships; SC 200, LC 400, GC 25; D & E 5,500
Ent Req: HS dipl, portfolio
Degrees: AAS, BFA, BBA, MA, MFA & MArch
Tuition: Undergrad $1,640 per cr; grad $1,744 per cr
Courses: †Advertising Design, Aesthetics, Architecture, †Art Education, Art History, Calligraphy, †Ceramics, †Commercial Art, Fashion Arts, †Fine Arts, Graphic Design, History of Art & Architecture, †History of Decorative Arts, Illustration, Industrial Design, Interior Design, Jewelry, Lighting Design, Marketing & Fashion Merchandising, Painting, Photography, Product Design, Sculpture, †Textile Design
Adult Hobby Classes: Courses—Advertising, Computer Graphics, Fashion Design, Fine Arts, Floral Design, Illustration, Interior Design, Lighting Design, Marketing & Merchandising, Product Design, Surface Decoration, Theatre Design
Summer School: Courses—Art, Art History, Design

THE NEW SCHOOL PARSONS SCHOOL OF DESIGN, Sheila C Johnson Design Center, 66 Fifth Ave at 13th St, New York, NY 10011; 2 West 13th St, Rm Z101 New York, NY 10011. Tel 212-229-8919; Email sjdc@newschool.edu; Web: www.newschool.edu; *Dir & Chief Cur* Radhika Subramaniam; *Asst Dir* Kristina Kaufman; *Asst Dir* Daisy Wong; *Gallery Tech* Allison Schlegel
Open daily noon - 6 PM & Thurs until 8 PM; No admis fee

NEW YORK ACADEMY OF ART, Graduate School of Figurative Art, 111 Franklin St, New York, NY 10013-2911. Tel 212-966-0300; Fax 212-966-3217; Email michael@nyaa.edu; Web: www.nyaa.edu; *Instr* Randolph Melick; *Chmn* Harvey Citron; *Instr* Edward Schmidt; *Instr* Martha Mayer Erlebacher; *Instr* Vincent Desiderio; *Exec Dir* Stephen Farthing
Estab 1983; Maintain art library; NY Academy of Art Library; pvt; Scholarships
Degrees: MFA 2 yrs, part-time MFA 4 yrs
Courses: Anatomy, Art History, Drawing, †Figurative Art, History of Art & Architecture, Painting, Sculpture
Adult Hobby Classes: Enrl 250; tuition $350-$400 per course for 12 wk term. Courses—Anatomy, Drawing, Painting, Sculpture
Children's Classes: Enrl 60; tuition $0-350 for 8-12 weeks
Summer School: Dir, Jesse Penridge. Enrl 250; tuition $250 per course for 9 wk term. Courses—Anatomy, Drawing, Painting, Sculpture

NEW YORK INSTITUTE OF PHOTOGRAPHY, 192 Lexington Ave, Ste 701 New York, NY 10016. Tel 800-583-1736; Fax 212-867-8122; Email info@nyip.com; Web: www.nyip.com; *Gen Mgr* Robyn Selman
Estab 1910; pvt; Flexible; online learning; Correspondence course in photography approved by New York State and approved for veterans; Enrollment 10,000
Degrees: cert of graduation
Courses: Digital Photography, Photoshop, Still Photography

NEW YORK SCHOOL OF INTERIOR DESIGN, 170 E 70th St, New York, NY 10021-5167. Tel 212-472-1500; Fax 212-472-3800; Email admission@nysid.edu; Web: nysid.edu; *Pres* Inge Heckel; *Dean* Scott Ageloff; *Assoc Dean* Ellen Fisher; *Area Coordr* Peter Brandt; *Area Coordr* Judith Gura; *Area Coordr* Veronica Whitlock
Estab 1916; Maintain nonprofit art gallery & library, 161 E 69 St, New York, NY 10021; art supplies may be purchased on campus; over 80; pvt; D & E & Wknds; Scholarships; Fellowships; SC, LC, GC; 750 maj & grad
Ent Req: HS dipl, application & interview
Degrees: AAS, BFA, MFA
Tuition: No campus res
Courses: Art History, Color, Design Materials, Drafting, Drawing, History of Art & Architecture, †Interior Design, Space Planning
Summer School: Dean, Scott Ageloff. Enrl 275

NEW YORK STUDIO SCHOOL OF DRAWING, PAINTING & SCULPTURE, 8 W Eighth St, New York, NY 10011. Tel 212-673-6466; Fax 212-777-0996; Web: www.nyss.org; *Dean* Graham Nickson; *Dir Prog* Elisa Jensen
Estab 1964; pvt; D; Scholarships; SC 13, LC 2; D100
Ent Req: HS dipl, portfolio of recent work
Degrees: Cert, MFA
Tuition: $4700 per sem; campus res—available
Courses: Drawing, Drawing Marathon, Painting, Sculpture
Adult Hobby Classes: 40; tuition $375 per 13 wks. Courses—Drawing (from the model)
Summer School: Courses—Drawing, Painting, Sculpture

NEW YORK UNIVERSITY, Tisch School of the Arts, 721 Broadway, New York, NY 10003. Tel 212-998-1800; Web: tisch.nyu.edu; *Dean* Allyson Green; *Sr Assoc Dean* Sheril Antonio; *Sr Assoc Dean* Kathleen McDermott; *Sr Assoc Dean* Robert Cameron
Pvt; D & E; Scholarships; Fellowships
Tuition: $56,924 per yr

Courses: Cinema Studies, Collaborative Arts, Dance, Drama, Dramatic Writing, Film & TV, Gaming, Interactive Media Arts, Music, Performance Studies, Photography & Imaging

PACE UNIVERSITY, Theatre & Fine Arts Dept, 156 Williams St, Pace Plaza New York, NY 10038-5300. Tel 212-346-1352; Fax 212-346-1424; Web: www.pace.edu/pace; *Chmn* Dr Lee Evans
Estab 1950; pvt; D & E; Scholarships; SC 4, LC 20; D 200, E 150, 700-800 per yr art only
Ent Req: HS dipl, ent exam
Degrees: 4 yr, Art History Major
Courses: Art History, Drawing, Graphic Design, Modern Art, Oriental Art, Studio Art
Adult Hobby Classes: Courses same as above
Summer School: Two summer sessions. Courses—Studio Art

PRATT INSTITUTE, Pratt Manhattan, 144 W. 14th St, New York, NY 10011. Tel 212-647-7775; Fax 212-461-6026; Web: www.prattinst.edu; *Dir* David Marcincowski
Estab 1892; Maintain nonprofit art gallery, Pratt Manhattan Gallery, 144 W 14th St, 2nd Fl, New York, NY 10011; pvt; D; Scholarships
Ent Req: HS dipl, portfolio, interview
Degrees: AOS, 2 yrs
Tuition: $810 per cr; campus res available
Courses: Advertising Design, Art History, Commercial Art, Computer Graphics, Design, Graphic Design, Illustration

SCHOOL OF VISUAL ARTS, 209 E 23rd St, New York, NY 10010-3994. Tel 212-592-2000; Fax 212-725-3587; Email squidley@sva.edu; Web: www.schoolofvisualarts.edu; *Chmn* Silas H Rhodes; *Pres* David Rhodes
Estab 1947; Maintains a nonprofit art gallery, Visual Arts Gallery, 601 W 26th St, NY, NY; maintains an art/architecture library, Visual Arts Library, 380 2nd Ave, NY, NY; on-campus shop for purchase of art supplies; 800 practicing artists, scholars, critics; pvt; D, E & W; Scholarships; FT 3363, PT 137
Publications: Art & Academe, semi-annual; Portfolio, annual; Words, semi-annual
Ent Req: HS transcript, portfolio review, SAT or ACT test results, interview, 2 letters of recommendation
Degrees: BFA, MFA, MAT (K-12) in Art Educ, MPS Art Therapy
Tuition: $22,080 plus fees per yr
Courses: †Advertising Design, †Animation, †Art Appreciation, †Art Education, Art History, †Cartooning, Ceramics, Commercial Art, †Computer Art, Conceptual Art, Design, Display, Drafting, Drawing, †Film, Graphic Arts, †Graphic Design, History of Art & Architecture, †Illustration, †Interior Design, Intermedia, Mixed Media, †Painting, †Photography, †Printmaking, †Sculpture, Silversmithing, Teacher Training, †Video
Adult Hobby Classes: Enrl 2446; tuition $175 per cr for 12 wks/sem. Courses—Advertising & Graphic Design, Art Education, Art History, Art Therapy, Computer Art, Craft Arts, Film & Video, Fine Arts, Humanities Sciences, Illustration & Cartooning, Interior Design, Photography
Children's Classes: Enrl 200; tuition $200 course 8wks/sem. Courses—Cartooning, Design, Drawing, Film, Interior Design, Painting, Photography, Portfolio Preparation, Sculpture
Summer School: Exec Dir, Joseph Cipri. Enrl 2471; tuition $175 per cr 10 wks. Courses—Same as adult education classes, Archaeology in Greece, Painting in Barcelona

SKOWHEGAN SCHOOL OF PAINTING & SCULPTURE, 136 W 22nd St, Frnt 1 New York, NY 10011-2424. Tel 212-529-0505; Fax 212-473-1342; Email mail@skowheganart.org; Web: www.skowheganart.org; *Exec Dir Develop & Admin* Kate Haw; *Exec Dir Prog* Sarah Workneh
Estab 1946; Maintain art library; Robert Lehman Library; 10; pub, nine wk summer residency prog for independent work; Fellowships; 65
Ent Req: proficient in English, 21 years of age & slide portfolio or video
Degrees: cr recognized for transfer, no degrees
Tuition: $5200 includes room & board
Courses: No acad work; individual critiques only
Summer School: Enrl 65; 9 wk summer res prog in Maine for independent work. Contact admin office at 200 Park Ave S, No 1116, New York, NY 10003

WOOD TOBE-COBURN SCHOOL, 8 E 40th St, New York, NY 10016-0105. Tel 212-686-9040; Fax 212-686-9171; Web: www.woodtobecoburn.com; *Pres* Sandi Gruninger
Estab 1937; FT 7, PT 10; pvt; D; Scholarships; 2 yr course, 16 months, for HS grad; 1 yr course, 9-12 months, for those with 15 or more transferable college sem cr, classroom study alternates with periods of work in stores or projects in fashion field; 250
Degrees: AOS(Occupational Studies)
Courses: Display, Fabrics, Fashion Arts, Fashion Design, Fashion Merchandising, Marketing & Management

NIAGARA FALLS

NIAGARA UNIVERSITY, Fine Arts Dept, PO Box 1913, Niagara Falls, NY 14109. Tel 716-285-1212; Web: www.niagara.edu; *Chmn* Sharon Watkinson
Tuition: $3750 per sem
Courses: Art Appreciation, Art History, Ceramics, Drawing, Painting
Adult Hobby Classes: Enrl 150; tuition $85 per sem. Courses—Ceramics, Painting
Summer School: Dir, L Centofanti. Enrl 25; tuition $185 per sem hr. Courses—Ceramics

OAKDALE

DOWLING COLLEGE, Dept of Visual Arts, 50 Idle Hour Blvd, Oakdale, NY 11769. Tel 631-244-3000; Fax 631-589-6644; Email art@dowling.edu; Web: www.dowling.edu; *Dept Chair, Assoc Prof & Gallery Dir* Stephen Lamia, PhD; *Assoc Prof* Mary Abell, PhD; *Asst Prof* Zach Scher, MA
Estab 1955; maintain a nonprofit art gallery: The Anthony Giordano Gallery, Dir Pam Brown, Dowling College, Idle Hour Blvd, Oakdale, NY 11769; maintain an art/architecture library: Slide Collection-Betty Ann Derbentli, Cur, Dowling College, Fortunoff Hall 323, Idle Hour Blvd, Oakdale, NY 11769; Pvt; D & E; Scholarships; D 1100, E 500
Ent Req: HS dipl
Degrees: BA(Visual Art), BA(Visual Communications), BS and BBA 4 yrs
Courses: 2-D & 3-D Design, Advertising Design, Art Criticism, Art History, Calligraphy, Ceramics, Computer Graphics, Costume Design & Construction, Design, Drawing, Graphic Arts, Graphic Design, History of Art & Architecture, Illustration, Jewelry, Lettering, Life Drawing, Painting, Photography, Printmaking, Sculpture, †Stage Design, Textile Design
Adult Hobby Classes: Software Instruction
Children's Classes: Software Instruction
Summer School: Software Instruction

OLD WESTBURY

NEW YORK INSTITUTE OF TECHNOLOGY, Fine Arts Dept, PO Box 8000, Northern Blvd Old Westbury, NY 11568-8000. Tel 516-686-7516, 686-7542; Fax 516-686-7613; Email pvoci@nyit.edu; Web: www.iris.nyit.edu/finearts; *Chmn & Assoc Prof* Peter Voci; *Prof* Faye Fayerman, MFA; *Adjunct Prof* Albert Prohaska, MA; *Assoc Prof* Nieves Micas, MA; *Asst Prof* Lev Poliakov, MA; *Adjunct Asst Prof* Steven Woodburn, MFA; *Adjunct Instr* Martin Clements, MA; *Adjunct Asst Prof* Richard Shen; *Adjunct Asst Prof* Joanne Hartman; *Asst Prof* Jane Grundy; *Adjunct Asst Prof* Charles DiDiego; *Adjunct Instr* Blase Decelestino; *Adjunct Assoc Prof* Antonio DiSpigna; *Adjunct Asst Prof* Donna Voci
Estab 1910, dept estab 1963; pvt; D; Scholarships; SC 11, LC 85; D 427, non-maj 100, maj 327
Ent Req: HS dipl, portfolio review
Degrees: BFA 4 yr
Tuition: No campus res
Courses: †Advertising Design, Aesthetics, †Architecture, Art Appreciation, †Art Education, Art History, Calligraphy, Computer Graphics, Design, Drafting, Drawing, Film, †Graphic Arts, †Graphic Design, Illustration, †Interior Design, Lettering, Mixed Media, Painting, Photography, Printmaking, Sculpture
Summer School: Courses—Drawing, Interior Design, Painting, Sculpture

STATE UNIVERSITY OF NEW YORK COLLEGE AT OLD WESTBURY, Visual Arts Dept, PO Box 210, Old Westbury, NY 11568-0210. Tel 516-876-3000, 876-3056, 876-3135 (acad affairs); Web: www.oldwestbury.edu; *Prof* William McGowin; *Chmn* Mac Adains
Estab 1968, Dept estab 1969; pub; D & E; SC 10, LC 10; D & E 277
Ent Req: HS dipl, skills proficiency exam, GED, special exception - inquire through admissions
Degrees: BA & BS(Visual Arts) 4 yr
Courses: Collage, Conceptual Art, History of Art & Architecture, Mixed Media, Painting, Photography, Printmaking, Sculpture, TV Production/Editing, Video

ONEONTA

HARTWICK COLLEGE, Art Dept, 1 Hartwick Dr, Oneonta, NY 13820-4000. Tel 607-431-4825; Fax 607-431-4191; *Chmn* Gloria Escobar, MFA; *Prof* Phil Young, MFA; *Prof* Roberta Griffith, MFA; *Asst Prof* Dr Elizabeth Ayer, MFA; *Asst Prof* Terry Slade, MFA; *Assoc Prof* Dr Fiona Dejardin, MFA; *Assoc Prof* Leesa Rittelmann
Estab 1797; FT 7, PT 8; pvt; D; Scholarships; 1500, non-maj 1433, maj 67
Ent Req: HS dipl, SAT or ACT, recommendation from teacher or counselor & personal essay, $35 fee
Degrees: BA 4 yr
Courses: †Art History, Ceramics, Drawing, Graphic Design, Painting, Photography, Printmaking, Sculpture, †Studio, Teacher Training
Summer School: High sch arts workshop, 3 wks in July

STATE UNIVERSITY OF NEW YORK COLLEGE AT ONEONTA, Dept of Art, 222 Fine Arts Ctr, Oneonta, NY 13820. Tel 607-436-3715; Web: www.oneonta.edu; *Assoc Prof* Sven Anderson; *Prof* Nancy Callahan; *Prof* Yolanda Sharpe; *Prof* Ellen Farber; *Prof* Thomas Sakoulas; *Asst Prof* Jian Cui; *Assoc Prof* Rhea Nowak; *Lectr* Katherine Spitzhoff; *Lectr* Kenneth Havenstein
Estab 1889; Maintain non-profit art gallery, Martin-Mullen Art Gallery, Fine Arts Bldg. Maintain Milne Library; pub; D & E; SC 60, LC 7; D 660, E 35, maj 123, 25-30 at Cooperstown Center
Activities: Schols offered
Ent Req: ent req HS dipl, regents scholarship exam, SAT & ACT
Degrees: degrees BA(Studio Art, Art History) other programs include: one leading to MA(Museum History, Folk Art) in conjunction with the New York State Historical Assn at Cooperstown, NY 13326 (Daniel R Porter III, SUNY Dir); a 3-1 program in conjunction with the Fashion Institute of Technology in New York City, with 3 years at Oneonta as a Studio Art major leading to a BS degree and/or 1 year at FIT leading to an AAS, Advertising & Communications, Advertising Design, Apparel Production & Management, Fashion Buying & Merchandising, Fashion Design, Textile Design, and/or Textile Technology
Courses: 2-D Design, 3-D Design, Art History, Ceramics, Computer Art, †Conceptual Art, †Digital Media, Drawing, †Graphic Arts, †Graphic Design, Images of Women in Western Art, †Mixed Media, Painting, †Photography, †Printmaking, †Sculpture, †Video, Visual Arts
Adult Hobby Classes: Offered only on a subscription basis at normal tuition rates through the Office of Continuing Education
Summer School: Enrl 40-50. Tuition same as in regular session for two 4 & 5 wk terms beginning June and July. Courses—Studio

ORANGEBURG

DOMINICAN COLLEGE OF BLAUVELT, Art Dept, 470 Western Hwy, Orangeburg, NY 10962-1295. Tel 845-359-7800; Fax 845-359-2313; Web: www.dc.edu; *Dir Dept Arts & Science* William Hurst
Estab 1952; Independent; D&E
Degrees: BS & BA 4 yr
Courses: Art Education, Art History, Drawing, Painting
Adult Hobby Classes: Enrl 40; tuition $117 per cr. Courses—Art History, Painting
Summer School: Dir, A M DiSiena. Enrl 35: tuition $117 per cr. Courses—History of Art, Watercolor

OSSINING

POLYADAM CONCRETE SYSTEM WORKSHOPS, 11-1 Woods Brooke Circle, Ossining, NY 10562-2070. Tel 914-941-1157; Web: www.polyadam.com; *Dir* George E Adamy, MBA
Estab 1968; Art supplies available on-campus; FT 1, PT 1; pvt; D & E; SC 13, LC 2, GC 13; D 20, E 30
Courses: Collage, Constructions, Museum Staff Training, †Plastics, Polyadam Concrete Casting & Construction, Restoration & Conservation, Sculpture, Teacher Training
Adult Hobby Classes: Courses offered
Children's Classes: Courses offered
Summer School: Courses offered

OSWEGO

STATE UNIVERSITY OF NEW YORK COLLEGE AT OSWEGO, Art Dept, 7060 Rt 104, Tyler Hall Oswego, NY 13126-3599. Tel 315-312-3017; Fax 315-312-5642; Email oertling@oswego.edu; Web: www.oswego.eduårt\; *Chmn* Sewall Oertling
Estab 1861; FT 18; pub; D & E; SC 31, LC 9; maj 150, grad 10
Ent Req: HS dipl, SAT or NYS regents scholarship exam
Degrees: BA 4 yr, BFA 4 yr, MA 2 yr, MAT 2 yr
Courses: Aesthetics, †Art History, †Ceramics, †Drawing, †Graphic Arts, †Graphic Design, Jewelry/Metalsmithing, Museum Staff Training, †Painting, †Photography, †Printmaking
Summer School: Dir, Lewis C Popham III

PLATTSBURGH

CLINTON COMMUNITY COLLEGE, Art Dept, 136 Clinton Point Dr, Plattsburgh, NY 12901-5690. Tel 518-562-4200; Fax 518-561-8261; Web: www.clintoncc.suny.edu; *Chmn* Mark Davison
Estab 1966
Ent Req: HS dipl
Degrees: AS & AA 2 yr
Tuition: Res—$94 per cr hr; nonres—$188 per cr hr
Courses: Art Appreciation, Design, Drawing, Painting, Photography, Sculpture, Theatre Arts

STATE UNIVERSITY OF NEW YORK AT PLATTSBURGH, Art Dept, 101 Broad St, Myers Fine Arts Bldg Plattsburgh, NY 12901-2637. Tel 518-564-2000; Fax 518-564-7827; Web: www.plattsburgh.edu; *Chmn* Rick Mikkelson, MFA
Estab 1789, dept estab 1930; FT 9, PT 4; pub; D & E; Scholarships; SC 30, LC 10; D 700, maj 154
Ent Req: HS dipl, EOP
Degrees: BA & BS 4 yrs
Courses: †Art History, †Ceramics, †Computer Graphics, †Drawing, †Graphic Arts, †Graphic Design, Illustration, Lettering, Mixed Media, †Painting, †Photography, †Printmaking, †Sculpture
Summer School: Dir, J Worthington. Tuition $137 for 5 wks. Courses—Ceramics, Painting, Photography, Sculpture

PLEASANTVILLE

PACE UNIVERSITY, Dyson College of Arts & Sciences, 861 Bedford Rd, Fine Arts Dept Pleasantville, NY 10570-2799. Tel 914-773-3675; Web: www.pace.edu; *Assoc Dean Arts & Science* Joseph Franko; *Chmn* John Mulgrew, MA; *Prof* Barbara Friedman, MFA; *Prof* Janetta Benton, PhD, MFA; *Prof* Linda Gottesfeld, MFA; *Prof* Roger Sayre, MFA; *Prof* Jillian McDonald; *Prof* William Pappenheimer; *Prof* Charlotte Becket
FT 5, PT 12; Pvt; D & E; SC 4, LC 4
Ent Req: HS dipl
Degrees: AA & BS
Tuition: Campus res available
Courses: Advertising Design, Aesthetics, Architecture, Art Appreciation, Art Education, Ceramics, Commercial Art, †Conceptual Art, Design, Drawing, Graphic Arts, Graphic Design, History of Art & Architecture, Illustration, Interior Design, Painting, Photography, Printmaking, Sculpture, Typography
Summer School: Dir, Prof John Mulgrew. Courses—Art History, Ceramics, Drawing, Painting

POTSDAM

STATE UNIVERSITY OF NEW YORK COLLEGE AT POTSDAM, Dept of Fine Arts, 44 Pierrepont Ave, Brainerd Hall 219 Potsdam, NY 13676-2294. Tel 315-267-2251; Fax 315-267-4884; Email downincj@postsdam.edu; Web: www.potsdam.edu; *Prof, Chair* Caroline Downing
Estab 1948; Maintain non-profit art gallery, Roland Gibson Gallery, The Art Mus, Brainerd Hall 125, 44 Pierrepont Ave, Potsdam, NY 13676; on-campus shop where art supplies may be purchased; pub; D & E; SC 120, LC 28
Activities: Schols offered
Ent Req: HS dipl
Degrees: BA & BFA 4 yr, art educ certification, pre-creative arts therapy, Graphic Design & Media
Tuition: In-state $6,470; out-of-state $16.320
Courses: †Art Appreciation, †Art Education, †Art History, †Art Studio, Ceramics, †Costume Design & Construction, †Design, Drawing, †Graphic Arts, †Graphic Design, †Museum Staff Training, Painting, Photography, †Printmaking, †Sculpture, †Stage Design, †Teacher Training, †Theatre Arts, †Video, †Visual Arts (BFA)
Adult Hobby Classes: Enrl 15; tuition $100 for 10 weeks. Courses—watercolor
Children's Classes: Enrl 56; tuition $150 (K-3); $250 (4-8); $299 (8-12). Courses—Creative Arts Camp
Summer School: Chair Theatre & Dance, Jay Pecora.

POUGHKEEPSIE

DUTCHESS COMMUNITY COLLEGE, Dept of Visual Arts, 53 Pendell Rd, Poughkeepsie, NY 12601-1595. Tel 845-431-8000; Fax 845-431-8991; *Dir* Eric Somers
Estab 1957; pub; D & E; Scholarships; SC 24, LC 22; D 660, E 340, maj 100
Ent Req: HS dipl
Degrees: AAS (Commercial Art)
Courses: Glass, Leather, Metal, Painting, Photography, Plastic, Weaving, Wood

VASSAR COLLEGE, Art Dept, 124 Raymond Ave, Box 702 Poughkeepsie, NY 12604-0001. Tel 845-437-5220; Fax 845-437-7707; Email liaguis@vassar.edu; Web: www.art.vassar.edu; *Prof* Nicholas Adams; *Prof* Susan D Kuretsky; *Chair & Assoc Prof* Peter Charlap; *Prof* Brian Lukacher; *Prof* Molly Nesbit; *Prof* Eve D'Ambra; *Prof* Lisa Collins; *Prof* Harry Roseman; *Assoc Prof* Laura Newman; *Asst Prof* Tobias Armborst; *Asst Prof* Andrew Tallon; *Asst Prof* Yvonne Elet; *Vis Instr* Gregory Seiffert; *Adjunct Instr* Patrick McElnea; *Adjunct Asst Prof* Samantha Vernon; *Adjunct Asst Prof* Judith Linn
Estab 1861; Maintain non-profit art gallery, Frances Lehman Loeb Art Ctr; Vassar College Art Library; FT 10, PT 7; pvt; D & E; Scholarships; SC 8, LC; maj 90, others 2400
Activities: Schols offered
Ent Req: HS grad, ent exam
Degrees: BA(Art History) 4 yr
Courses: Architecture, Art History, †Color, Computer Animation, Design, Drafting, Drawing, †History of Art & Architecture, Painting, Photography, Printmaking, Sculpture, Video

PURCHASE

MANHATTANVILLE COLLEGE, Art Dept, 2900 Purchase St, Purchase, NY 10577-2132. Tel 914-323-5331; Fax 914-323-5311; *Head Dept* Ann Bavar
Estab 1841; pvt; D & E; Scholarships; SC 25, LC 10, GC 7; D 180, non-maj 90, maj 90, grad 10
Ent Req: HS dipl, portfolio, interview
Degrees: BA and BFA 4 yrs, MAT 1 yr, special prog MATA (Masters of Art in Teaching Art)
Courses: Advertising Design, Art Education, Art History, Book Design, Ceramics, Commercial Art, Conceptual Art, Constructions, Design, Drawing, Graphic Arts, Graphic Design, Illustration, Lettering, Metal Sculpture, Painting, Photography, Printmaking, Sculpture, Teacher Training
Summer School: Dir, Don Richards. Two sessions June & July. Courses—Art History, Ceramics, Computer Graphics, Drawing, Painting, Sculpture

PURCHASE COLLEGE, STATE UNIVERSITY OF NEW YORK, School of Art+Design, 735 Anderson Hill Rd, Purchase, NY 10577-1499. Tel 914-251-6750; Fax 914-251-6793; Email ade@purchase.edu; Web: www.purchase.edu/academics/art-and-design; *Dir & Assoc Prof* Christopher Robbins; *Prof* Sharon Horvath; *Assoc Prof* Kate Gilmore; *Prof* Warren Lehner; *Assoc Prof* Carol Bankerd; *Assoc Prof* Bill Deere; *Assoc Prof* Robin Lynch; *Assoc Prof* Julian Kreimer; *Asst Prof* Cynthia Lin; *Assoc Prof* Jo Ann Walters; *Assoc Prof* Stella Ebner; *Prof* Cassandra Hooper; *Assoc Prof* Nancy Bowen
Estab 1967; Maintain nonprofit art gallery, Richard & Dolly Maass Gallery & Purchase College library. On-campus shop where art supplies may be purchased; pub; D & E; Scholarships; Fellowships; Grants; SC, LC, GC
Ent Req: HS Dipl/GED, bachelors for MFA, recommendations & test scores required
Degrees: BFA, MA, MFA
Tuition: Res—undergrad $11,760 per yr; nonres—$23,520 per yr; res—grad $16,870 per yr; nonres—grad $33,740 per yr
Courses: Graphic Design, Painting, Photography, Printmaking, Sculpture, Visual Arts
Children's Classes: Summer session art program
—**ART HISTORY BOARD OF STUDY**, 735 Anderson Hill Rd, Purchase, NY 10577-1499. Tel 914-251-6750; Fax 914-251-6793; Web: www.purchase.edu; *Acting Dean* Peggy De Cooke PhD; *Dir* Steven Lam
Estab 1971, dept estab 1977; pub; D & E; Scholarships; 2500, maj 50
Ent Req: HS dipl, essay on application, grades, test scores
Degrees: BA & BALA 4 yrs
Tuition: Res—$3,400 per yr; nonres—$8,300 per yr
Courses: Art History

RIVERDALE

COLLEGE OF MOUNT SAINT VINCENT, Fine Arts Dept, 6301 Riverdale Ave, Riverdale, NY 10471-1093. Tel 718-405-3200; Fax 718-601-6392; *Prof* Richard Barnett, BFA; *Chmn & Prof* Enrico Giordana, BFA

Estab 1911; pvt; D & E; Scholarships; SC 22, LC 10; D 950, E 50
Ent Req: HS dipl and SAT
Degrees: BA, BS and BS(Art Educ) 4 yrs
Courses: Art History, Ceramics, Design, Drawing, Painting, Photography
Summer School: Dir Continuing Education, Dr Marjorie Connelly. Courses—vary each summer

RIVERHEAD

SOUTHAMPTON COLLEGE OF LONG ISLAND UNIVERSITY, Arts & Media Division, 121 Speonk-Riverhead Rd - LIU Bldg, Long Island University at Riverhead Riverhead, NY 11901-3499. Tel 631-287-8010; Fax 631-287-8253; Web: www2.southampton.liu.edu
Estab 1963

ROCHESTER

MONROE COMMUNITY COLLEGE, Art Dept, 1000 E Henrietta Rd, Rochester, NY 14623-5780. Tel 716-292-2000; Fax 716-427-2749; Web: www.monroe.cc.edu; *Assoc Prof* Joe Hendrick, MFA; *Prof* Bruce Brown, MFA
Estab 1961; Monthly art exhibitions in school library; 3 FT, PT varies; pub; D & E; SC 16, LC 4
Ent Req: HS dipl
Degrees: Assoc in Arts 2 yrs, Assoc in Science 2 yrs, Assoc in Applied Science 2 yrs
Tuition: $1525 per nine months
Courses: Art History, Ceramics, †Commercial Art, Drafting, Drawing, Graphic Arts, Graphic Design, Handicrafts, Illustration, Jewelry, Lettering, Painting, Printmaking, Sculpture, Textile Design, Theatre Arts, Video, Weaving
Adult Hobby Classes: Tuition $36 per hr. Courses—Batik, Ceramics, Jewelry, Leatherwork, Macrame, Rugmaking, Soft Sculpture, Weaving
Summer School: Dir, George C McDade

NAZARETH COLLEGE OF ROCHESTER, Art Dept, 4245 East Ave, Rochester, NY 14618-3790. Tel 716-389-2525; Fax 716-586-2452; *Head Dept* Ron Netsky; *Assoc Prof* Kathy Calderwood, BFA; *Prof* Karen Trickey, MSEd; *Assoc Prof* Maureen Brilla, MFA; *Prof* Lynn Duggan, MFA; *Assoc Prof* Mitchell Messina, MFA; *Asst Prof* Catherine Kirby, MFA; *Assoc Prof* Ellen Horovitz, PhD; *Dir* Dorothy Bokelman, PhD
Estab 1926, dept estab 1936; pvt; D & E; Scholarships; SC 40, LC 15, GC 6; D 180, E 74, non-maj 50, maj 200, grad 48
Ent Req: HS dipl
Degrees: BA and BS 4 yrs
Courses: †Art Education, †Art History, Art Therapy, Ceramics, Computer Graphics, Drawing, †Graphic Arts, Jewelry, Painting, Photography, Printmaking, Sculpture, Textile Design
Summer School: 6 wks beginning July 5th. Courses—Grad & undergrad

ROBERTS WESLEYAN COLLEGE, Department of Visual Art, 2301 Westside Dr, Rochester, NY 14624-1997. Tel 585-594-6120; Fax 585-594-6118; Email ciaccia_kathryn@roberts.edu; Web: www.roberts.edu; *Dir Art* Douglas Giebel; *Prof* Scot Bennett; *Asst Prof* Romy Hosford; *Asst Prof* Sue Leo
Estab 1866; Maintains nonprofit Davison Art Gallery; pvt; D & E; Scholarships; SC 34, LC 5; D 1,589, E 246, maj 42
Ent Req: HS dipl
Degrees: BA(Studio Art), BS(Studio Art)
Tuition: $27,036 per yr
Courses: Art Appreciation, Art History, Ceramics, Design, †Digital Media Art, Drawing, Graphic Design, Painting, Photography, Printmaking, Sculpture, †Video

ROCHESTER INSTITUTE OF TECHNOLOGY, College of Imaging Arts & Sciences, 55 Lomb Memorial Dr, Rochester, NY 14623. Tel 585-475-7562; Fax 585-475-5055; Email facpgd@rit.edu; Web: www.rit.edu/cias; *Design Chair* Peter Byrne; *Sr Assoc Dean* Dr Twyla Cummings; *Dean Col* Dr Lorraine Justice; *Art Chair* Glen Hintz; *School for American Crafts Chair* Juan Carlos Cabellero-Perez
Degrees: BFA, MFA
Tuition: Undergrad $17,628 per sem, grad $19,344 per sem
Courses: †Art Education, †Ceramics, Computer Graphics, Design, Drawing, †Film, Fine Art Studio, Graphic Arts, †Graphic Design, History of Art & Architecture, Illustration, Industrial Design, Interior Design, Jewelry, Metals, Painting, †Photography, Printmaking, Sculpture, Silversmithing, Teacher Training, Video, Wood
Adult Hobby Classes: Courses offered
Children's Classes: One wk summer workshop for juniors in HS
Summer School: 5 wk sessions, 2 1/2 wk sessions, & special one wk workshops
—**School of Design**, 73 Lomb Memorial Dr, College of Fine & Applied Arts Rochester, NY 14623-5602. Tel 716-475-2668; Fax 716-475-6447; *Chmn Graphic Design* Mary Anne Begland; *Chmn Industrial, Interior & Packaging Design* Toby Thompson; *Chmn Foundation Studies* Joyce Hertzson; *Chmn Crafts* Michael White; *Prof* Kener E Bond Jr; *Prof* Frederick Lipp, MFA; *Prof* R Roger Remington, MS; *Prof* Joanne Szabla, PhD, MS; *Prof* James E Thomas, MFA; *Prof* Lawrence Williams, MFA; *Prof* Philip W Bornarth, MFA; *Prof* Barbara Hodik, PhD, MFA; *Prof* James Ver Hague, MFA; *Prof* Robert A Cole, MS; *Prof* Robert Heischman, UCFA; *Prof* Craig McArt, MFA; *Prof* William Keyser, MFA; *Prof* Doug Sigler, MFA; *Prof* Robert Schmitz, MFA; *Prof* Richard Hirsch, MFA; *Prof* Richard Tanner, MS; *Prof* Michael Taylor, MFA; *Prof* Mark Stanitz, MA; *Prof* Len Urso, MFA; *Prof* Max Lenderman, MFA; *Prof* Albert Paley, MFA; *Prof* Wendell Castle, MFA; *Prof* Robert C Morgan, PhD, MFA; *Prof* James H Sias, MA; *Prof* Robert Wabnitz, Dipl & Cert; *Assoc Prof* Edward C Miller, MFA; *Assoc Prof* Bruce Sodervick, MFA; *Assoc Prof* Joseph A Watson, MFA; *Assoc Prof* Robert M Kahute, MFA; *Assoc Prof* Steve Loar, MA; *Asst Prof* Heinz Klinkon, BFA; *Asst Prof* Doug Cleminshaw, MFA; *Asst Prof* Elizabeth Fomin, MFA; *Asst Prof* Glen Hintz, MFA; *Asst Prof* Thomas Lightfoot, PhD, MFA
Estab 1829; FT 47, PT 19; pvt; 1000
Ent Req: HS grad, ent exam, portfolio
Degrees: BFA, MFA
Tuition: Undergrad $333 per cr, grad $425 per cr
Courses: Computer Graphics, Drawing, Glass Blowing, History of Art & Archeology, Illustration, †Industrial Design, †Interior Design, Jewelry, Sculpture, †Silversmithing, Stained Glass, †Textile Design, †Weaving
Adult Hobby Classes: Crafts, Design, Painting
Summer School: Enrl 250; tuition undergrad $260 per cr, grad $330 per cr for 8 wk term beginning June. Courses—Ceramics, Computer Graphics, Glass, Graphic Design, Metal, Painting, Printmaking, Textiles, Wood, Industrial, Interior, Packaging Design, Art History, 2-D and 3-D Design
—**School of Photographic Arts & Sciences**, 70 Lomb Memorial Dr, Rochester, NY 14623-5604. Tel 716-475-2716; Fax 716-475-5804; *Assoc Dir* Nancy Stuart, AB; *Chmn Imaging & Photographic Technology* Andrew Davidhazy, MEd; *Chmn Fine Arts Photo* Ken White, MEd; *Chmn Film/Video* Howard Lester, MEd; *Chmn Biomedical Photo Communs* Michael Peres, MEd; *Chmn American Video Institute* John Ciampa, JD; *Chmn Photographic Processing & Finishing Management* James Rice, BS; *Prof* John E Karpen, MFA; *Prof* Weston D Kemp, MFA; *Prof* Lothar K Engelmann, PhD, MFA; *Prof* Russell C Kraus, EdD; *Prof* David J Robertson, BFA; *Assoc Prof* Owen Butler, BFA; *Assoc Prof* Kerry Coppin, BFA; *Assoc Prof* Jeff Weiss, BFA; *Assoc Prof* Patti Ambroge, BFA; *Assoc Prof* Bradley T Hindson, BA; *Assoc Prof* Alan Vogel, BA; *Assoc Prof* Robert Kayser, BS; *Assoc Prof* James Reilly, MA; *Assoc Prof* Guenther Cartwright, BA; *Assoc Prof* Howard LeVant, BS; *Assoc Prof* Elliott Rubenstein, MA; *Assoc Prof* Erik Timmerman, BS; *Assoc Prof* Douglas F Rea, MFA; *Assoc Prof* Steve Diehl, BS; *Assoc Prof* Mark Haven, BA; *Assoc Prof* John Retallack, BA; *Asst Prof* Tom Lopez, MS; *Asst Prof* Stephanie Maxwell, MS; *Asst Prof* Bruce Lane, MS; *Asst Prof* Adrianne Carrageorge, MS; *Asst Prof* Lorett Falkner, MS; *Asst Prof* Deni Defenbaugh, MS; *Asst Prof* Sabrine Susstrink, MS; *Asst Prof* Kaleen Moriority, MS; *Asst Prof* Jack Holm, MS; *Asst Prof* Glen Miller, MS; *Asst Prof* William Osterman, MFA; *Asst Prof* Martha Leinroth, MFA; *Lectr* Dan Larken, MFA; *Dir* William DuBois, MS
900
Degrees: AA, BA, MA
Tuition: Undergrad $333 per cr, grad $425 per cr
Courses: Advertising, Biomedical Photography, Film, Film Studies, Photographic Communications, Photographic Technology, Photography, Processing & Finishing, Video
Summer School: Courses—Photography, Film/Video, Motion Picture Workshops, Narrative/Documentary/Editorial workshop, Nature Photography
—**School of Printing Management & Sciences**, 69 Lomb Memorial Dr, College of Imaging Arts & Sciences Rochester, NY 14623-5602. Tel 716-475-2728; Fax 716-475-7029; *Dir* Harold Gaffin; *Dean* Joan Stone; *Chmn Design Composition Division* Emery E Schneider, BS & MEd; *Coordr Grad Prog* Joseph L Noga, MS; *Paul & Louise Miller Prof* Robert G Hacker, BS; *Prof* Barbara Birkett, BS; *Prof* Miles F Southworth, BS; *Assoc Prof* William H Birkett, BS; *Assoc Prof* Clifton T Frazier, BS; *Assoc Prof* Herbert H Johnson, BS; *Assoc Prof* Archibald D Provan, BS; *Assoc Prof* Werner Rebsamen, dipl; *Asst Prof* Robert Y Chung, BA; *Asst Prof* Hugh R Fox, AB & JD; *Asst Prof* David P Pankow, BA & MA
School has 25 laboratories, occupying 125,000 sq ft. More than 70 courses are offered; 700
Degrees: BS, MS
Tuition: Undergrad $333 per cr, grad $425 per cr
Courses: Color Separation, Flexography, Gravure, Ink & Color, Introduction to Book Production, Newspaper Design, Printmaking, Systems Planning, Typography & Design
Summer School: Graphic Arts, Layout & Printing, Reproduction Photography, Ink & Color, Newspaper & Magazine Design, Hand Papermaking, Web Offset, Gravure, Lithography, Printing Plates, Typography, Bookbinding
—**School for American Craft**, 73 Lomb Memorial Dr, Rochester, NY 14623-5602. Tel 716-475-5778; *Dean* Dr Joan Stone; *Dir* Thomas Morin; *Chmn* Richard Pannen
Degrees: BS, BFA, MS, MST
Tuition: Undergrad $333 per cr, grad $425 per cr
Courses: Ceramics, Furniture & Wood Working, Glass, Metals, Textiles
Adult Hobby Classes: Extensive seminar schedule
Summer School: scholarships

UNIVERSITY OF ROCHESTER, Dept of Art & Art History, PO Box 270038, 424 Morey Hall Rochester, NY 14627-0038. Tel 585-275-9249; Fax 585-442-1692; Email aah_vcs@mail.rochester.edu; Web: www.rochester.edu/college/aah; *Chmn* Allen C Topolski
Estab 1902; Maintain nonprofit art gallery; Hartnett Art Gallery, Rochester NY; FT 11, PT 5; pvt; D; Scholarships; SC 25, LC 25; maj 15, others 600
Degrees: BA, MA, PhD(Visual & Cultural Studies)
Courses: Art History, Drawing, History of Art & Architecture, Painting, Photography, Sculpture, †Video
Summer School: Enrl 40; tuition & duration vary

VISUAL STUDIES WORKSHOP, 31 Prince St, Rochester, NY 14607-1499. Tel 585-442-8676; Fax 585-442-1992; Email info@vsw.org; Web: www.vsw.org; *Dir* Tate Shaw; *Fiscal Officer* Laraine Gallagher; *Ed Afterimage* Karen vanMeenen; *Exhibs Coordr* Rick Hock; *Assoc Ed Afterimage* Lucia Sommer
Open by appt; Gallery open Thurs 3-7 PM, Fri 3-5 PM, Sat - Sun 2-6 PM; Estab 1969 to establish a center for the transmission & study of the visual image; Visual Studies Workshops produce & or present approx 20 exhibitions per yr encompassing contemporary & historical issues; subjects vary from photography, film, video, artists' book works & related media; maintains Siskind Gallery and Bookstore; Mem: Dues artist $35, researcher $75, friend $250, advocate $750; Pub; E, weekend & summer
Library Holdings: Original Documents, Other Holdings, Pamphlets, Periodical Subscriptions, Photographs, Prints, Reels, Slides, Video Tapes
Special Subjects: Mixed Media, Photography
Collections: 19th & 20th century photographs, mechanical prints & artists' books
Exhibitions: Rotating exhibits
Publications: Afterimage, bi-monthly
Activities: Classes for adults; Summer Institute prog with intensive short term workshops for artists & mus professionals; lects open to pub, 15 vis lectrs per yr; gallery talks; tours (by appointment); schols offered; original objects of art lent to institutions with proper exhibs facilities; lending collection contains 27,000

photographs of original artwork; originates traveling exhibs to mus, colleges & universities; mus shop sells books, magazines, original art & prints
Degrees: MFA
Courses: †Artist's Books, †Display, Photography
—**Research Center**, 31 Prince St, Rochester, NY 14607-1499. Tel 716-442-8676; Fax 716-442-1992; Email library@vsw.org; Web: www.vsw.org; *Cur Colls* Jessica McDonald
Open by appt; Estab 1971 to maintain a permanent collection for the study of the function & effect of the visual image; For reference only
Library Holdings: Audio Tapes, Book Volumes 19,000, Cassettes, Clipping Files, Exhibition Catalogs, Kodachrome Transparencies, Lantern Slides, Motion Pictures, Original Art Works, Other Holdings Posters, Pamphlets, Periodical Subscriptions 160, Photographs, Prints, Reproductions, Slides, Video Tapes
Collections: Illustrated book coll, photographic print coll

SANBORN

NIAGARA COUNTY COMMUNITY COLLEGE, Fine Arts Division, 3111 Saunders Settlement Rd, Sanborn, NY 14132-9460. Tel 716-614-6222; Fax 716-614-6700; Web: www.sunyniagara.cc.ny.us; *Dept Coordr MFA* Barbara Buckman; *Prof* Bud Jacobs; *Prof* Nancy Knechtel
Estab 1965; FT 15, PT 14; pub; D & E; Scholarships; SC 12, LC 4; D 400, E 120, maj 140
Ent Req: HS dipl
Degrees: AS(Fine Arts) 2 yrs
Courses: Advertising Design, Aesthetics, Art Appreciation, Art History, Art Therapy, Ceramics, Commercial Art, Conceptual Art, Constructions, Design, Drafting, †Drawing, Film, Graphic Arts, †Graphic Design, Handicrafts, Illustration, Lettering, Mixed Media, Museum Staff Training, †Painting, Photography, Sculpture, Stage Design, Theatre Arts, Visual Art

SARATOGA SPRINGS

SKIDMORE COLLEGE, Dept of Art & Art History, 815 N Broadway, Saratoga Springs, NY 12866-1632. Tel 518-580-5000, 580-5030 (Dept Art & Art History); Fax 518-580-5029; Web: www.skidmore.edu; *Chmn* Peter Stake
Estab 1911; FT 20; pvt; Scholarships; SC 32, LC 18; maj 350, 2000 total
Ent Req: HS grad, 16 cr, ent exam, portfolio
Degrees: BA & BS 4 yrs
Courses: Art History, Ceramics, Computer Imaging, Design, Design, Drawing, Graphic Design, Jewelry/Metalsmithing, Painting, Photography, Printmaking, Sculpture, Weaving
Summer School: Dir, Regis Brodie. Enrl 194 for two 6 wk sessions. Courses—Advanced Studio & Independent Study, Art History, Ceramics, Drawing, Etching, Jewelry, Lettering, Painting, Photography, Sculpture, 2-D Design, Video, Watercolor, Weaving

SCHENECTADY

UNION COLLEGE, Dept of Visual Arts, 807 Union St, Arts Bldg Schenectady, NY 12308-3103. Tel 518-388-6714; Fax 518-388-6567; Web: www.union.edu; *Chmn Visual Arts* Chris Duncan
Estab 1795; FT 7; pvt; D; Scholarships; SC 14, LC 4; maj 35
Ent Req: HS dipl, ent exam
Degrees: BA with emphasis in music, art or theatre arts 4 yr
Courses: 3-D, Art History, Drawing, Painting, Photography, Printmaking, Sculpture, Stage Design, Theatre Arts, †Visual Arts
Adult Hobby Classes: Enrl 30; Courses—Drawing, Photography
Children's Classes: Enrl 15
Summer School: Dean, Jane Zacek. Enrl 30; Courses—Art History, Drawing, 3-D, Painting, Photography, Printmaking

SELDEN

SUFFOLK COUNTY COMMUNITY COLLEGE, Art Dept, 533 College Rd, Selden, NY 11784-2899. Tel 631-451-4110; Web: www.sunysuffolk.edu; *Dept Head* Arthur Kleinfelder
FT 6, PT 6
Ent Req: HS dipl, equivalent
Degrees: AFA
Tuition: Res $98.50 per cr hr; nonres (out of state) $198 per cr hr
Courses: Art Appreciation, Art History, Ceramics, Design, Drawing, Painting, Printmaking
Adult Hobby Classes: Enrl 200; tuition $15 per hr. Courses—Photography, Interior Design
Summer School: Dir, Maurice Flecker. Tuition res $60 per cr for 6-8 wk sessions. Courses—Painting, Sculpture, 2-D Design, Life Drawing, Printmaking & Ceramics

SPARKILL

SAINT THOMAS AQUINAS COLLEGE, Art Dept, 125 Rte 340, Sparkill, NY 10976. Tel 845-398-4000, Ext 4136; Fax 845-398-4071; *Prof* Carl Rattner, MFA, DA; *Assoc Prof* Barbara Yonz, MA, MFA; *Asst Prof* Nina Bellisio, MFA; *Asst Prof* Matthew Finn, MFA; *Asst Prof* Carol Lagsteid, MFD, MSW; *Adj Prof* Annie Sheih, MFA; *Adj Prof* Jane Marcy; *Adj Prof* Rene Smith
Estab 1952, dept estab 1969; Maintain nonprofit art gallery; art supplies furnished for all studio classes; schols vary; Pvt; D & E; Scholarships; SC, LC; D 1,100, maj 50
Ent Req: HS dipl
Degrees: BA and BS 4 yrs
Tuition: $21,140 per yr, incl room & board
Courses: Advertising Design, Art Appreciation, Art History, Art Therapy, Ceramics, Commercial Art, Conceptual Art, Display, Drawing, Graphic Design, Jewelry, Mixed Media, Painting, Photography, Printmaking, Sculpture, Video
Summer School: Dir, Dr Joseph Keane. Tuition $210 for 3 cr course. Courses—Varies 3-6 art courses including Ceramics, Painting, Photography

STATEN ISLAND

COLLEGE OF STATEN ISLAND, Performing & Creative Arts Dept, 2800 Victory Blvd, Bldg IP-203 Staten Island, NY 10314-6609. Tel 718-982-2520; Fax 718-982-2537; Email jonest@mail.csi.cuny.edu; Web: www.csi.cuny.edu; *Coordr Art Prog* Prof Pat Passlof; *Prof* Ralph Martel; *Asst Prof* Tracey Jones; *Adj Assoc Prof* Mor Pipman; *Adj Assoc Prof* Geoffrey Dorfman; *Asst Prof* Beatrix Reinhardt; *Asst Prof* Siona Wilson; *Prof* Nanette Salomon; *Adj Asst Prof* Robert Ludwig; *Adj Asst Prof* Howard Smith; *Adj Asst Prof* Faustino Quintanilla; *Adj Assoc Prof* Janine Coyne; *Adj Asst Prof* Nicole Frocheur; *Adj Asst Prof* Craig Manister; *Adjunct Asst Prof* Robert Morgan Taylor
Maintains nonprofit galleries, The College of Staten Island Art Gallery & The CSI Student Art Gallery; Pub; D, E & W; SC, LC, GC 1
Degrees: BS(Art), BS(Photography), BA(Art), BA(photography)
Tuition: Res—undergrad $170 per cr hr, grad $185 per cr hr
Courses: †Art Appreciation, †Art History, †Design, †Drawing, †History of Art & Architecture, †Museum Staff Training, †Painting, †Photography, †Printmaking, Sculpture
Summer School: Courses offered

INSTITUTE FOR ARTS & HUMANITIES EDUCATION, New Jersey Summer Arts Institute, 270 Lawrence Ave, Staten Island, NY 10310-3026. Tel 732-220-1600; Fax 732-220-1515; Email ihe@ihenj.org; *Exec Dir* Maureen Heckerman
Estab 1980; Students earn HS cr; 4 FT; pvt; D & E; Scholarships; 130
Publications: Quarterly newsletter
Ent Req: audition, master class, portfolio, interview
Courses: Advertising Design, Aesthetics, Architecture, Art Appreciation, Art Education, Art History, Ceramics, Collage, Conceptual Art, Costume Design & Construction, Design, Display, Drawing, Fashion Arts, Film, Graphic Arts, Graphic Design, History of Art & Architecture, Illustration, Intermedia, Jewelry, Mixed Media, Painting, Photography, Printmaking, Sculpture, Stage Design, Teacher Training, Textile Design, Theatre Arts, Video, Weaving

WAGNER COLLEGE, Arts Administration Dept, One Campus Rd, Staten Island, NY 10301. Tel 718-390-3271, 390-3100; Fax 718-390-3223; Email gpsull@wagner.edu; Web: www.wagner.edu; *Chmn* Gary Sullivan; *Instr* Lillian Stausland; *Instr* Robert Williams
Estab 1948; Maintain nonprofit art gallery; pvt; D & E; SC 20, LC 6; maj 35, others 2000
Ent Req: HS grad
Degrees: BA(Art), BS(Art Admin)
Courses: 2-D Design, 3-D Design, Advertising Design, Art History, Arts Administration, Ceramics, Crafts Design, Drawing, Graphic Arts, Mixed Media, Painting, Photography, Printmaking, Sculpture
Summer School: Two sessions of 4 wks, Dir Extensions & Summer Prog, Maureen Connolly

STONE RIDGE

ULSTER COUNTY COMMUNITY COLLEGE/SUNY ULSTER, Dept of Art, Design, Music, Theatre, Communication & Fashion, 491 Cottekill Rd, Stone Ridge, NY 12484. Tel 845-687-5066 (Art Dept); Fax 845-687-5083; Email machelli@sunyulster.edu; Web: www.sunyulster.edu; *Chmn* Iain Machell, MFA; *Prof* Sean Nixon, MFA
Estab 1963; Maintain nonprofit art gallery, Muroff-Kotler Gallery, Vanderlyn Hall, Stone Ridge Campus, Stone Ridge, NY 12484; maintains library, Dewitt Library, Stone Ridge Campus, Stone Ridge, NY 12484; PT 7; pub; D & E; Scholarships; SC 17, LC 6; D 500, E 190, non-maj 590, maj 100
Activities: Schols offered
Ent Req: HS dipl
Degrees: AA 2 yrs, AS 2 yrs
Tuition: Full-time NY res $3,820 per yr; full-time other $7,640 per yr; no campus res
Courses: 2-D Design, 3-D Design, Art Appreciation, Art History, Computer Art, Computer Assisted Graphic Design, Desk-Top Publishing, Drawing, Fashion Arts, †Graphic Design, Life Drawing, Painting, Photography, Web Page Design
Summer School: Visual Arts Coordr, Iain Machell. Enrl 30 - 50; tuition $285 per 3 sem hrs for 6 wks. Courses—Computer Art, Drawing, Painting, Photography

STONY BROOK

STONY BROOK UNIVERSITY, College of Arts & Sciences, Dept of Art, Staller Center for the Arts, State University of NY at Stony Brook Stony Brook, NY 11794-5400. Tel 631-632-7250; Fax 631-632-7261; Email jvotolo@notes.cc.sunysb.edu; Web: www.art.sunysb.edu; *Prof* Melvin H Pekarsky, MA; *Prof* Donald B Kuspit PhD; *Prof* Howardena Pindell, MFA; *Prof* Toby Buonagurio, MA; *Prof* Michele H Bogart, PhD; *Chair & Prof* Anita Moskowitz, PhD; *Prof* Barbara Frank, PhD; *Asst Prof* Grady Gerbracht, MFA; *Asst Prof* Martin Levine, MFA; *Assoc Prof* Stephanie Dinkins, MFA; *Assoc Prof* Christa Erickson, MFA; *Assoc Prof* Nobuho Nagasawa, MFA; *Lectr* Shoki Goodarzi, PhD; *Vis Assoc Prof* Richard Leslie, PhD; *Artist in Res* Gary Schneider, MFA; *Asst Prof* Andrew Uroskie, PhD; *Asst Prof* Zabet Patterson, PhD; *Lectr* Helen Harrison, MA
Estab 1957; Maintains nonprofit gallery, Staller Center for The Arts, Stony Brook University, Stony Brook, NY, 11797-5400; maintains an art library, Frank Melville Jr, Memorial Library; art supplies can be purchased at on-campus shop; FT 7; pub; D, E, winter & summer sessions; SC 41, LC 49, GC 47; D 13,733, E 1,116, non-maj 2,890, maj 12,276, GS 7,675

Ent Req: HS dipl, SAT
Degrees: BA(Art History) & BA(Studio Art), MA(Art History & Criticism), MFA (Studio Art), PhD(Art History & Criticism)
Tuition: Undergrad $4,350 per yr, grad $6,900 per yr
Courses: †Aesthetics, †Art Criticism, †Art History, Ceramics, †Collage, Conceptual Art, †Constructions, †Costume Design & Construction, Drawing, †Electronic Media, History of Art & Architecture, †Mixed Media, Painting, †Performance Art, Photography, Printmaking, Sculpture, †Stage Design, †Studio Art, †Video
Summer School: Tuition res—undergrad $18 per cr hr, grad $288 per cr hr; nonres—undergrad $442 per cr hr, grad $455 per cr hr for term of 6 wks (two sessions). Courses vary in areas of Art Education, Art History & Criticism, Studio Art

SUFFERN

ROCKLAND COMMUNITY COLLEGE, Graphic Arts & Advertising Tech Dept, 145 College Rd, Suffern, NY 10901-3699. Tel 845-574-4251; Fax 845-356-1529; *Discipline Coordr* Emily Harvey
Estab 1965; pub; D & E; SC plus apprenticeships; D 900, E 300, maj 200
Ent Req: open
Degrees: AAS 2 yrs
Courses: Advertising Design, Alternative Processes in Photography, Art Appreciation, Art History, Art Therapy, Color Production, Drawing, Electric Art, Graphic Arts, Graphic Design, Lettering, Lithography, Painting, Photography, Portfolio Workshop, Sculpture, Serigraphy Printing
Adult Hobby Classes: Enrl 528; tuition varies. Courses—Ceramics, Crafts
Summer School: Dir, Emily Harvey. Enrl 180; June - Aug. Courses—Computer Graphics, Drawing, Overseas Program, Painting, Sculpture

SYRACUSE

LE MOYNE COLLEGE, Visual & Performing Arts Dept, 1419 Salt Springs Rd, Syracuse, NY 13214. Tel 315-445-4523; Email pac@lemoyne.edu; Web: www.lemoyne.edu; *Chmn & Asst. Prof* Karel Blakeley; *Dir Music & Arts Admin* Travis Newton; *Area Dir Visual Arts Prog & Adj Asst Prof* David G Moore
Estab 1946; Maintain nonprofit art gallery; Wilson Art Gallery, Lemoyne College, Syracuse, NY 13214; Pvt; D&E; SC 6, LC 5; non-maj 350
Ent Req: HS dipl, SAT or ACT
Degrees: BS & BA 4 yrs
Courses: †Art Appreciation, Art History, Drawing, Graphic Arts, Painting, †Photography, †Printmaking, Sculpture

SYRACUSE UNIVERSITY, College of Visual & Performing Arts, 102 Shaffer Art Bldg, School of Art & Design Syracuse, NY 13244-1010. Tel 315-443-2507; Fax 315-443-1303; *Interim Dir* Barbara Walter, MFA; *Dean* Carole Brzozowski, MS
Estab 1873; Maintain nonprofit art gallery; Lowe Art Gallery, 102 Shaffer Art Bldg, Syracuse Univ, Syracuse, NY 13244; FT 60, PT 52; pvt; D & E; Scholarships; SC 200, LC 25, GC 100; D 1,200
Ent Req: HS dipl, portfolio review
Degrees: BID 5 yrs, BFA 4 yrs, MFA & MA(Museum Studies) 2 yrs
Tuition: Undergrad $13,480 per yr; grad $406 per cr; campus res available
Courses: †Advertising Design, †Art Education, †Art History, †Art Photography, †Ceramics, †Communications Design, †Computer Graphics, Drawing, Environmental Design, †Fashion Arts, Fibers, Film, †Illustration, †Industrial Design, †Interior Design, †Metalsmithing, †Museum Studies Program, †Painting, Papermaking, †Printmaking, †Sculpture, †Surface Pattern Design, †Textile Design, †Video, Weaving
Adult Hobby Classes: Enrl 155; tuition undergrad $276 per cr. Courses—same as above
Children's Classes: Enrl 80; tuition $50 per sem. Courses—general art
Summer School: Tuition undergrad $408 per cr, grad $456 per cr. Courses—same as above
—Dept of Fine Arts (Art History), 308 Bowne Hall, Syracuse, NY 13244-1200. Tel 315-443-4184; Fax 315-443-4186; Email ljstraub@syr.edu; Web: http://finearts.syr.edu/; *Prof* Gary Radke PhD; *Prof* Meredith Lillich PhD; *Prof* Laurinda Dixon PhD; *Prof* Mary Marien PhD; *Prof* Barbara Larson PhD; *Prof* Alan Braddock
Estab 1870, dept estab 1948; Pvt; D & E; Scholarships; LC 25, GC 15; non-maj 900, maj 71, grad 46
Ent Req: HS dipl, SAT
Degrees: BA, MA
Tuition: Undergrad $15,800 per yr
Courses: American Art, Art & Music History, Art Appreciation, Art History, Arts & Ideas, Baroque, History of Art & Archeology, Italian Medieval Art, Photography

TROY

EMMA WILLARD SCHOOL, Dept of Visual & Performing Arts, 285 Pawling Ave, Troy, NY 12180-5294. Tel 518-833-1300; Web: http//www.emmawillard.org; *Dept Chmn* Debra Spiro-Allen
Estab 1814, dept estab 1969; See website for full listing; pvt Women only; D; Scholarships
Ent Req: Grades 9-12 & Post Graduate
Tuition: $19,600 incl room & board
Courses: Advanced Studio Art, Art Appreciation, Art History, Ceramics, Dance, Drawing, Jewelry, Music, Photography, Printmaking, Theatre Arts, Visual Arts Foundation, Weaving

RENSSELAER POLYTECHNIC INSTITUTE, School of Architecture, 110 Eighth St, Troy, NY 12180-3590. Tel 518-276-6466; Fax 518-276-3034; Web: www.arch.rpi.edu; *Dean* Alan Balfour
Estab 1929; FT 18, PT 18; pvt; D; Scholarships; 275
Degrees: BA(Archit), MA(Archit), MS(Lighting)
Tuition: Undergrad $23,525 per yr
Courses: Design, History, Practice, Structure, Studio
Summer School: Architectural Design
—Eye Ear Studio Dept of Art, 110 8th St, School of Humanities, Art & Social Sciences Troy, NY 12180-3522. Tel 518-276-4778; Web: www.arts.rpi.edu; *Chmn* Neil Rolnick PhD; *Asst Dir* Laura Garrison; *Prof* Larry Keegan; *Clerk Specialist* Amy Horowitz
Scholarships; Fellowships
Degrees: MFA (Electronic Arts) 2 1/2 - 3 yrs
Tuition: $15,880 annual tuition
Courses: Animation, Computer Graphics, Computer Music, Drawing, Installation, Painting, Performance, Sculpture, Video

RUSSELL SAGE COLLEGE, Visual & Performing Arts Dept, 65 1st St, Schacht Fine Arts Ctr Troy, NY 12180-4013. Tel 518-244-2000; Fax 518-271-4545; Web: www.sage.edu/rsc; *Chmn & Dir Creative Arts* Leigh Davies
Pvt, W; 20-40 per class
Ent Req: HS grad
Degrees: fine arts and divisional maj in Music, Art and Drama 4 yrs
Courses: 2-D Design, †Arts Management, †Creative Arts Therapy

UTICA

MOHAWK VALLEY COMMUNITY COLLEGE, 1101 Sherman Dr, Utica, NY 13510-5394. Tel 315-792-5446; Fax 315-792-5666; Email lmigliori@mucc.edu; Web: www.mvcc.edu; *Pres* Michael I Schafer PhD; *Prof* Ronald Labuz PhD; *Assoc Prof* Henry Godlewski, BS; *Head Dept* Larry Migliori, MS; *Assoc Prof* E Duane Isenberg, MA; *Assoc Prof* Jerome Lalonde, MA; *Assoc Prof* Robert Clarke, BFA; *Instr* Thomas Maneen, BFA; *Asst Prof* Alex Piejko, BFA; *Instr* James Vitale; *Assoc Prof* Christine Miller; *Instr* Scott Selden; *Assoc Prof* Wayne Freed; *Instr* Christi Harrington; *Instr* Aaron Board; *Instr* Kathleen Partridge; *Instr* David Yahnke; *Instr* Scot Connor; *Instr* Sara Demas
Estab 1947, dept estab 1955; Maintain a nonprofit art gallery: Small Works, an art/architecture library: James O'Looney and on-campus shop where art supplies may be purchased; FT 16, ADJ 14; pub; D & E; Scholarships; SC 42 (over 2 yr period), LC 10 (over 2 yr period); D 450, E varies, maj 450
Ent Req: HS dipl, GED
Degrees: AAS 2 yrs
Tuition: Campus res—available
Courses: †Advertising Design, Aesthetics, Art Appreciation, Art History, Computer Graphics, †Design, Drawing, Graphic Arts, Graphic Design, †Handicrafts, History of Art & Architecture, Illustration, Lettering, Painting, †Photography, Textile Design, Weaving
Adult Hobby Classes: Enrl 440. Courses—Air Brush, Design, Illustration, Painting, Photography, Sketching, Watercolor
Children's Classes: Coll for child
Summer School: Dir, Larry Migliori. Enrl 40. Courses—Drawing, Design, Photography

MUNSON-WILLIAMS-PROCTOR ARTS INSTITUTE, Pratt MWP College of Art, 310 Genesee St, Utica, NY 13502-4799. Tel 315-797-0000; Fax 315-797-9349; Email admissions@mwpai.edu; Web: www.mwpai.org; *Prof* Steve Arnison; *Prof* Daniel Buckingham; *Prof* Chris Irick; *Prof* Nancy Long; *Prof* Ken Marchione; *Prof* Bryan McGrath; *Prof* Keith Sandman; *Asst Prof* Sandra Stephens; *Prof* Lisa Gregg Wightman; *Assoc Prof* Cynthia Koren; *Prof* Greg Lawler
Estab 1941; Maintains nonprofit gallery & library. Art supply store on campus; pvt; d, e; Scholarships; adults 1900, children 533, Pratt at mwp 160
Activities: On-campus shop sells art supplies
Tuition: $12,400/sem
Courses: 2-D & 3-D Design, Advertising Design, Art Education, Ceramics, Color Theory, Dance, Drawing, Goldsmithing, Graphic Arts, Graphic Design, Humanities, Illustration, Metal Arts, Painting, Photography, Pottery, Printmaking, Sculpture, Silversmithing, †Video
Adult Hobby Classes: Enrl 805. Courses—Dance, Design, Drawing, Jewelry, Painting, Photography, Pottery, Printmaking, Sculpture
Children's Classes: Enrl 423. Courses - Dance, Drawing, Painting,
Summer School: Dir, Dean Ken Marchione. Enrl 413, tuition $65 - $110 for 4 wk term. Courses—Dance Drawing, Jewelry Making, Painting, Photography, Pottery

UTICA COLLEGE OF SYRACUSE UNIVERSITY, Division of Art & Science, 1600 Burrstone Rd, Utica, NY 13502-4892. Tel 315-792-3092; Fax 315-792-3831; Web: www.utica.edu; *Dean Arts & Sciences* Lawrence R Aaronson
Estab 1946, school of art estab 1973; pvt; D; Scholarships; SC 20, LC 7; School of Art D 94, Utica College maj 14
Degrees: BS(Fine Arts) 4 yrs
Courses: Art History, †Ceramics, Design, Drafting, Drawing, Film, Graphic Arts, Occupational Therapy, †Painting, Photography, †Sculpture, Stage Design, Theatre Arts, Video

WATERTOWN

JEFFERSON COMMUNITY COLLEGE, Art Dept, 1220 Coffeen St, Watertown, NY 13601-1822. Tel 315-786-2404; Fax 315-788-0716; Email johndeans@ccmgate.sunyjefferson.edu; Web: www.sunyjefferson.edu; *Pres* John Deans
Estab 1963; FT 1; pub; D & E; Scholarships; SC 2, LC 1; 850
Ent Req: HS dipl, GED
Degrees: AA, AS & AAS 2 yr
Courses: 2-D Studio, Art Appreciation, Art History, Ceramics, Computer-Aided Art & Design, Film Appreciation, Photography, Sculpture, Snow Sculpture
Summer School: Pres, John T Henderson

WEST NYACK

ROCKLAND CENTER FOR THE ARTS, 27 S Greenbush Rd, West Nyack, NY 10021-2700. Tel 845-358-0877; Fax 845-358-0971; Email info@rocklandartcenter.org; Web: www.rocklandartcenter.org; *Dir School* Daly Flanagan, MS; *Exec Dir* Julianne Ramos, MFA; *Artistic Dir* Lynn Stein
Estab 1947; Maintain nonprofit galleries: Emerson Gallery (same address), Catherine Konner Sculpture Park, Gallery One; schols open to children, adults, need based; on-campus art shop sells ceramic supplies only; Pvt; D & E, Weekends; Scholarships; SC 100; D 900, E 400
Collections: Contemporary painting & drawing coll
Publications: Artline newsletter; art school catalogues; exhibition catalogues
Degrees: Non-degree
Tuition: Varies per course
Courses: Ceramics, Creative Writing, Drawing, †Fashion Arts, †Glass, Handicrafts, †Jewelry, †Mixed Media, Painting, †Photography, Printmaking, †Silversmithing, †Teacher Training
Adult Hobby Classes: Enrl 300; tuition $170 - $350 for twelve 3 hr sessions. Courses—Ceramics, Fine Arts & Crafts, Writing
Children's Classes: Enrl 300; tuition $155-$200 for ten 1 1/2 hr sessions. Courses—same as above
Summer School: Dir, Daly Flanagan. Enrl 100 children & 200 adults; tuition average $120 per 6 wks. Courses—same as above

WHITE PLAINS

WESTCHESTER COMMUNITY COLLEGE, Westchester Art Workshop, 196 Central Ave, County Ctr White Plains, NY 10606-1102. Tel 914-684-0094; Fax 914-684-0608; *Prog Dir* Abre Chen
Estab 1926; 75; pub; D & E; Scholarships; SC 90 per sem, 5 sem per yr; D 650, E 550, others 700 (cr given for most courses)
Ent Req: no special req
Degrees: AA, AS & AAS
Tuition: No campus res
Courses: Art Appreciation, Art Foundation, Art Therapy, Calligraphy, Ceramics, Commercial Art, Computer Art Animation, Design, Drawing, Faux Finishes, Goldsmithing, Graphic Arts, Graphic Design, Illustration, Jewelry, Lost Wax Casting, Mixed Media, Painting, Photography, Portrait Painting, Printmaking, Quilting, Sculpture, Silversmithing, Stained Glass, Video, Weaving
Adult Hobby Classes: 100
Children's Classes: Enrl 150. Courses—Cartooning, Ceramics, Drawing, Jewelry, Mixed Media, Painting
Summer School: 700. Courses—same as above

WOODSTOCK

WOODSTOCK SCHOOL OF ART, INC, PO Box 338, Woodstock, NY 12498-0338. Tel 845-679-2388; Fax 845-679-3802; Email wsart@earthlink.net; Web: www.woodstockschoolofart.org; *Pres* Kate McGloughlin; *Instr* Karen O'Neil; *Instr* Eric Angeloch; *Instr* Richard Segalman; *Instr* Staats Fasoldt; *Instr* Lois Woolley; *Instr* Pia Oste-Alexander; *Instr* Tricia Cline; *Instr* Ron Netsky; *Instr* Christie Scheele; *Instr* Mary Anna Goetz; *Instr* Donald Elder; *Instr* Tor Gudmundsen; *Instr* Keith Gunderson; *Instr* Robert Carsten; *Instr* Elizabeth Mowry; *Instr* Meredith Rosier; *Instr* Carol Zaloom; *Instr* Julio Valdez; *Instr* Peik Larsen; *Instr* Lisa Mackie; *Instr* Polly M Law; *Instr* Vince Natale; *Instr* Peter Clapper; *Instr* Claire Lambe; *Instr* Jenny Nelson; *Instr* Christopher Seubert; *Instr* Robert Ohnigian
Estab 1968, dept estab 1981; Maintains nonprofit gallery, Woodstock School of Art Gallery; maintains art/architecture libr; on-campus shop for art supplies; pvt nonprofit; D & E, weekend; Scholarships; SC 19, LC 8
Activities: Schols offered as needed
Courses: Collage, †Drawing, †Mixed Media, †Painting, †Pastel, †Printmaking, †Sculpture, †Watercolor
Summer School: Exec Dir, Christopher Seubert. Tuition $400 per wk. Courses—Collage, Drawing, Etching, Landscape, Lithography, Monotype, Painting, Pastel, Portrait, Sculpture, Watercolor, Figure

NORTH CAROLINA

ASHEVILLE

UNIVERSITY OF NORTH CAROLINA AT ASHEVILLE, Dept of Art, One University Heights, Asheville, NC 28804. Tel 828-251-6600, 257-6559 (Art Dept); Email tcooke@enca.edu; Web: www.unca.edu/art/; *Chmn* S Tucker Cooke, MFA
Estab 1927, dept estab 1965; pub; D & E; Scholarships; SC 20, LC 5; 3277, maj 69
Ent Req: HS dipl, ent exam
Degrees: BA, BFA 4-5 yrs
Courses: 2-D & 3-D Design, Art Education, Art History, Ceramics, Drawing, Intermedia, Life Drawing, Mixed Media, Painting, Photography, Printmaking, Sculpture
Adult Hobby Classes: Contact Educ Dept 704-251-6420
Summer School: Dir, S Tucker Cooke. Courses vary

BOONE

APPALACHIAN STATE UNIVERSITY, Dept of Art, Herbert Wey Hall, Rm 232, Boone, NC 28608. Tel 828-262-2000; Fax 828-262-6312; Web: www.appstate.edu; *Prof* Marianne Suggs; *Prof* Glenn Phifer; *Asst Prof* Eli Bentor; *Asst Prof* Joan Durden; *Prof* Judy Humphrey; *Asst Prof* L Kathleen Campbell; *Chmn* Laura Ives; *Prof* Robin Martindale; *Instr* Lilith Eberle-Nielander; *Instr* Tim Ford; *Instr* Henry T Foreman; *Instr* Kyle Van Lusk; *Instr* Margaret Carter Martine; *Instr* Dr Janet Montgomery; *Instr* Mary Perry; *Instr* Mary Prather; *Instr* Nancy Sokolove; *Instr* Sonny Struss; *Instr* Vicki Clift; *Instr* Susie Winters; *Instr* Ann Thompson; *Asst Prof* Christopher Curtin; *Assoc Prof* Ed Midgett; *Assoc Prof* Gary Nemcosky; *Prof* William G Phifer; *Assoc Prof* Eric Purves; *Prof* Marilyn Smith; *Asst Prof* Lisa Stinson; *Assoc Prof* Jim Toub; *Assoc Prof* Gayle Weitz; *Assoc Prof* Barbara Yale-Read; *Asst Prof* Margaret Yaukey
Estab 1960; pub; D; Scholarships; SC 52, LC 14; D 1000, maj 350, grad 45
Ent Req: HS dipl, ent exam
Degrees: BA, BS & BFA (graphic design, art educ, studio art, art marketing & production) 4 yrs
Courses: Art Appreciation, Art History, Fibers, Graphic Arts
Children's Classes: After sch art program enrl 40, $250 per sem
Summer School: Chmn, Laura Ives. Enrl 60; $75 per hr res, $239 per hr non-res. Courses—per regular session

BREVARD

BREVARD COLLEGE, Department of Art, One Brevard College Dr, Brevard, NC 28712. Tel 828-883-8292; Fax 828-884-3790; Web: www.brevard.edu; *Chair Div Fine Arts* Laura L Franklin, DMA; *Coordr Fine Arts* Anne Chapin, PhD; *Prof* Bill Byers, MFA; *Prof* M Jo Pumphrey, MFA; *Assoc Prof* Kyle Lusk, MFA
Estab 1853; Maintains nonprofit art gallery: Spiers Gallery on campus & an on-campus art supplies shop; FT 4, PT 4; pvt, den; D & E; Scholarships; SC 12, LC 2; non-maj 20, maj 60
Ent Req: HS dipl
Degrees: BA
Tuition: $22,100
Courses: †Art Appreciation, Art History, Ceramics, Drawing, Film, Graphic Arts, Graphic Design, †History of Art & Architecture, †Mixed Media, Painting, Photography, Printmaking, Sculpture
Summer School: Courses vary

CHAPEL HILL

UNIVERSITY OF NORTH CAROLINA AT CHAPEL HILL, Art Dept, Hanes Art Ctr, CB#3405 Chapel Hill, NC 27599-3405. Tel 919-962-2015; Fax 919-962-0722; Web: www.unc.edu/depts/art; *Prof* Mary C Sturgeon PhD; *Chm & Prof* Mary Sheriff PhD; *Prof* Jaroslav Folda PhD; *Asst Chm & Prof* Beth Grabowski, MFA; *Prof* Dennis Zaborowski, MFA; *Prof* Jim Hirschfield, MFA; *Prof* Elin O Slavick, MFA; *Assoc Prof* Dorothy Verkerk, MFA; *Prof* Yun-Dong Nam, MFA; *Assoc Prof* Pika Ghosh, PhD; *Asst Prof* Carol Magee, PhD; *Asst Prof* Lyneise Williams, PhD; *Asst Prof* Jeff Whetstone, MFA; *Assoc Prof* Juan Logan, MFA; *Asst Prof* Kimowan McLain, MFA; *Assoc Prof* Mary Pardo, PhD; *Asst Prof* Glaire Anderson, PhD; *Instr* Susan Harbage-Page, MFA; *Asst Prof* Mario Marzan; *Asst Prof* Cary Levine; *Instr* Michael Sonnichsen; *Instr* David Tinapple
Estab 1793, dept estab 1936; Maintain nonprofit art gallery; John & June Allcott Gallery, UNC-CH, Dept of Art, Chapel Hill, NC 27599; on-campus shop where art supplies may be purchased; Pub; D; Scholarships; SC 30, LC 30, GC 10; D 100 undergrad, 55 grad
Ent Req: HS dipl, SAT
Degrees: BA & BFA 4 yr, MFA & MA(Art History) 2 yr, PhD(Art History) to 6 yr
Tuition: Res—undergrad $693 per sem, grad $693 per sem; nonres—undergrad $4,959 per sem, grad $4,959; campus res—available
Courses: Architecture, †Art History, Ceramics, †Drawing, History of Art & Architecture, †Mixed Media, †Painting, Photography, Printmaking, Sculpture
Summer School: Assoc Prof Dorothy Verkerk. Courses—Various Art History & Studio Courses

CHARLOTTE

CENTRAL PIEDMONT COMMUNITY COLLEGE, Visual & Performing Arts, PO Box 35009, Charlotte, NC 28235-5009. Tel 704-330-2722; Web: www.cpcc.cc.nc.us; *Chmn* Mary Lou Paschal
Estab 1963; Scholarships
Ent Req: HS dipl, equivalent
Degrees: AS, AA & AAS 2 yrs
Tuition: Res undergrad $27.50 per cr hr; nonres $169.75 per cr hr
Courses: Advertising Design, Architecture, Art Appreciation, Art History, Artists Books (special topic), Bronze Casting, Ceramics, Computer Aided Design, Design, Drawing, Interior Design, Jewelry, Painting, Photography, Printmaking, Sculpture, Weaving

QUEENS COLLEGE, Fine Arts Dept, 1900 Selwyn Ave, Charlotte, NC 28207-2450. Tel 704-337-2212, 800-849-0202; Email cas@queens.edu; Web: www.queens.edu; *Fine Arts Chmn* Robert F Porter
Estab 1857; Den; Scholarships; SC 19, LC 7
Degrees: BA
Courses: Art History, Ceramics, Commercial Art

UNIVERSITY OF NORTH CAROLINA AT CHARLOTTE, Dept Art, 9201 University City Blvd, Rowe 173 Charlotte, NC 28223-0001. Tel 704-687-2473; Fax 704-687-2591; Web: www.art.uncc.edu; *Prof & Chair* Roy Strassberg; *Gallery Mgr* Dean Butckovitz; *Assoc Prof* Winston Tite; *Asst Prof* Joan Tweedy; *Assoc Prof* Eldred Hudson; *Prof Emeritus* Lili Corbus; *Assoc Prof* Susan Brenner; *Prof Emeritus* Heather Hoover; *Asst Prof* David Brodeur; *Lectr* Keith Bryant; *Assoc Prof* Jamie Franki; *Lectr* Frances Hawthorne; *Lectr* Ann Kluttz; *Assoc Prof* Jeff Murphy; *Asst Prof* Bonnie Noble; *Assoc Prof* Mary Tuma; *Prof* David Edgar; *Asst Prof* Jim Frakes; *Asst Prof* Maja Godlewska; *Lectr* Kristin Rothrock; *Coordr Undergrad Educ* Malena Bergmann; *Asst Prof* John Ford; *Asst Prof* Heather Freeman; *Asst Prof* Pamela Lawton; *Lectr* Michael Simpson; *Lectr* Deborah Wall; *Lectr* Jason Tselentis; *Asst Prof* Angela Herren
Estab 1965, dept estab 1971; Maintain nonprofit art gallery, Rowe Gallery & Cone Center Gallery, Art Dept, UNC Charlotte, NC 28223; pub; D & E; SC 96, LC 32, Other 16; maj 500

Ent Req: HS dipl, SAT, Col Boards, Portfolio Review for studio degrees
Degrees: BA (Art & Art History) & BFA 4 yrs, K - 12 Art Educ Cert 4 yrs
Courses: Art Education, Art History, Ceramics, Design, Drawing, Electronic Media, Fibers, Graphic Design, Illustration, Jewelry, Painting, Photography, Printmaking, Sculpture
Summer School: Prof Roy Strassberg. Enrl 120; tuition res—$413.90, nonres—$1487.90; two 5 wk sessions, one 3 wk session. Courses—Art Appreciation, Ceramics, Design, Drawing, Painting, Photography

CULLOWHEE

WESTERN CAROLINA UNIVERSITY, Dept of Art/College of Arts & Science, 25 University Dr, 340 Stillwell Bldg Cullowhee, NC 28723-9646. Tel 828-227-7210; Fax 828-227-7505; Email wcrawford@wcu.edu; Web: www.wcu.edu/as/arts/; *Head Dept* Robert Godfrey, MFA; *Prof* James Thompson, PhD; *Prof* Jon Jicha, MFA; *Prof* James E Smythe, MFA; *Prof* Joan Byrd, MFA; *Assoc Prof* Louis Petrovich-Mwaniki, PhD; *Assoc Prof* Cathryn Griffin, MFA; *Assoc Prof* Lee P Budahl, PhD; *Asst Prof* Marya Roland, MFA; *Asst Prof* Matt Liddle, MFA
Estab 1889, dept estab 1968; pub; D & E; Scholarships; SC 51, LC 12; non-maj 1200 per sem, maj 150
Ent Req: HS dipl, SAT & C average in HS
Degrees: BFA, BA & BSE 4 yrs, MA, art honors studio
Courses: Art Appreciation, Art Education, Art History, Book Arts, Ceramics, Conceptual Art, Drawing, Graphic Design, Intermedia, Jewelry, Painting, Photography, Printmaking, Sculpture, Silversmithing, Weaving
Summer School: Dir, Dr Oakley Winters. Course—Art History, Studio Courses in Ceramics, Design, Drawing, Experimental Studio, Fibers, Metalsmithing, Painting, Sculpture

DALLAS

GASTON COLLEGE, Art Dept, 201 Hwy 321 S, Dallas, NC 28034. Tel 704-922-6343, 922-6344; *Dept Chmn* Gary Freeman
Estab 1965; pub; D & E; Scholarships; SC 22, LC 3; D 286, E 70, maj 50
Ent Req: HS dipl
Degrees: AA & AFA 2 yrs, cert 1 yr
Courses: 2-D & 3D Design, Ceramics, Commercial Art Fundamentals, Computer Graphics, Drawing, Jewelry, Painting, Photography, Pottery, Printmaking, Sculpture, Wood Design
Summer School: Dir, Gary Freeman. Enrl 20; term of 11 wks beginning June. Courses—Design, Drawing, Painting, Pottery, Sculpture

DAVIDSON

DAVIDSON COLLEGE, Art Dept, 315 N Main St, Belk Visual Arts Center Davidson, NC 28036-9404; PO Box 7117, Davidson, NC 28035-7117. Tel 704-894-2344; Fax 704-894-2691; Email brking@davidson.edu; Web: www.davidson.edu; *Prof* Larry L Ligo, PhD; *Prof* Nina Serebrennikov, PhD; *Chmn* C Shaw Smith, Jr, PhD; *Emeritus Prof* W Herbert Jackson; *Prof* Cort Savage, MFA; *Prof* Tyler Starr, MFA; *Prof* Joelle Dietrick, MFA; *Prof* Katie St. Clair, MFA
Estab 1837, dept estab 1950; Maintains nonprofit art gallery - Van Euery/Smith Galleries, Art Dept, 315 N Main St, Davidson, NC 28035; pvt; D; Scholarships
Ent Req: Col Boards, HS transcripts
Degrees: BA & BS 4 yrs
Tuition: $60,119 total per yr (comprehensive fee); campus res—room & board fee included in tuition
Courses: Aesthetics, Art History, Collage, Conceptual Art, †Digital Art, Drawing, Graphic Design, History of Art & Architecture, Painting, Printmaking, Sculpture, Theatre Arts

DOBSON

SURRY COMMUNITY COLLEGE, Art Dept, 630 South Main St, Dobson, NC 27017. Tel 336-386-8121; Fax 336-386-8951; Web: www.surry.edu; *Instr* William Sanders; *Dean* John Collins
Estab 1966; Varies
Ent Req: HS dipl, equivalent
Degrees: AA
Tuition: Res $27.50 per cr hr; nonres $169.75 per cr hr
Courses: Art Appreciation, Art History, Commercial Art, Design, Drawing, Handicrafts, Painting, Printmaking, Sculpture

DURHAM

DUKE UNIVERSITY, Dept of Art, Art History & Visual Studies, PO Box 90764, Durham, NC 27708-0764. Tel 919-684-2224; Fax 919-684-4398; Email deptaah@duke.edu; Web: www.duke.edu/web/art; *Chair & Prof* Hans J Van Miegroet, PhD; *Assoc Prof & Dir Grad Studies* Gennifer Weisenfeld, PhD; *Assoc Prof & Dir Undergrad Studies* Sheila Dillon, PhD
Pvt; D; Scholarships; SC 36, LC 84, GC 28, Seminars 32; D 1850, maj 134
Ent Req: HS dipl & ent exam for BA
Degrees: BA, PhD in Art History, JD/MA in Law & the History of Art
Tuition: Campus res—available
Courses: Aesthetics, Architecture, Art History, Conceptual Art, Design, Drawing, Film, Graphic Design, History of Art & Architecture, Mixed Media, Museum Staff Training, Painting, Photography, Printmaking, Sculpture, Visual Studies & Culture
Summer School: Dir, Paula E Gilbert. Two 6 wk sessions offered

NORTH CAROLINA CENTRAL UNIVERSITY, Art Dept, 1801 Fayetteville St, Durham, NC 27707-3129; PO Box 19555, Durham, NC 27707-0021. Tel 919-560-6100; Fax 919-560-6391; Web: www.nccu.edu; *Prof* Dr Melvin Carver, MPD, EdD; *Prof* Achameleh Debela, MFA; *Prof* Chad M Hughes, MFA; *Prof* Myongsin Choi, MA; *Prof, Dir Art Museum* Kenneth Rodgers, MFA; *Prof* John Hughley, EdD; *Prof* Michelle Patterson, MA; *Chmn* Connie M Floyd, MFA
Estab 1910, dept estab 1944; pub; D & E; SC 30, LC 11; D 120, E 30, non-maj 1678, maj 120
Ent Req: HS dipl, SAT
Degrees: in Art Studies, Visual Communications & Studio Art 4 yrs
Courses: †Advertising Design, †Art Education, Art History, †Ceramics, Computer Graphics, †Design, †Drawing, †Graphic Design, Illustration, Painting, Printmaking, †Sculpture
Children's Classes: Saturday school

ELIZABETH CITY

ELIZABETH CITY STATE UNIVERSITY, School of Arts & Humanities, Dept of Art, 1704 Weeksville Rd, 125 Fine Arts Bldg, Campus Box 912 Elizabeth City, NC 27909-7977. Tel 252-335-3345; Fax 252-335-3482; Email arjoyner@mail.ecsu.edu; Web: www.ecsu.edu; *Chair* Alexis Joyner, MFA; *Prof* Drusiano Scerbo, MFA; *Assoc Prof* William Drescher, MFA; *Asst Prof* Jeff Whelan, MFA; *Asst Prof Art Educ* Dr Phyllis Hill
Estab 1891, dept 1961; Maintains nonprofit University Gallery; pub; D & E; Scholarships; SC 27, LC 18, advance courses in Studio and History of Art; D 2003, E 455, non-maj 1928, maj 75
Ent Req: HS dipl, portfolio
Degrees: BA & BS, 4 yrs
Courses: Art Appreciation, Art History, Art Studio general, Ceramics, Drawing, Graphic Design, Painting, Photography, Printmaking, Sculpture, Teacher Training
Summer School: Dir, Warren Poole. Enrl 950. Courses—Same as regular session

FAYETTEVILLE

FAYETTEVILLE STATE UNIVERSITY, Performing & Fine Arts, 1200 Murchison Rd, Fayetteville, NC 28301-4298. Tel 910-672-1457, 672-1571; Fax 910-672-1572; *Head Div of Fine Arts & Humanities* Dr Robert G Owens
Estab 1877; pub; D & E; D 60, E 20
Ent Req: HS dipl, ent exam
Degrees: BA & BFA 4 yr
Courses: Advertising Design, Aesthetics, Art Education, Ceramics, Drawing, Graphic Arts, Handicrafts, History of Art & Architecture, Leather Craft, Lettering, Painting, Photography, Sculpture, Weaving
Summer School: Dir, Dr Beeman C Patterson. Courses—Art in Childhood Education, Arts & Crafts, Drawing, Photography, Survey of Art

METHODIST COLLEGE, Art Dept, 5400 Ramsey St, Fayetteville, NC 28311-1498. Tel 910-630-7107; Fax 910-630-2123; Web: www.methodist.edu/; *Chmn* Silvana Foti, MFA; *Prof* Peggy S Hinson
Estab 1960; FT 2, PT 1; den; D & E; Scholarships; SC 6, LC 4; D 650, maj 22
Ent Req: HS dipl, SAT
Degrees: BA & BS 4 yrs
Courses: Art Education, Art History, Design, Drawing, Painting, Papermaking, Photography, Printmaking, Sculpture
Summer School: 3 terms, 3 wk early session, 5 wk main session, 6 wk directed study. Courses—Art Appreciation, Painting, Sculpture, others as needed

GOLDSBORO

THE ARTS COUNCIL OF WAYNE COUNTY, (Goldsboro Art Center), 102 N John St, Goldsboro, NC 27530-3633. Tel 919-736-3300; Fax 919-736-3335; Email artscouncil@artsinwayne.org; Web: www.artsinwayne.org; *Exec Dir* Sarah Merritt; *Gallery Dir* Becca Scott Reynolds; *Admin Asst* Jo Fleischmann
Estab 1963; Maintains nonprofit art gallery; pub; D & E; Scholarships; SC 25; D 150, E 60, others 210
Courses: Drawing, Painting, Pottery, Spinning
Adult Hobby Classes: Enrl 75; tuition $19 for 11 wk term. Courses— Calligraphy, Oil Painting, Pottery, Watercolors

WAYNE COMMUNITY COLLEGE, Liberal Arts Dept, Caller Box 8002, Goldsboro, NC 27533. Tel 919-735-5151; Fax 919-736-3204; Web: www.wayne.cc.nc.us; *Instr* Patricia Turlington; *Chmn* Ann Spicer
Estab 1957; 4 FT, PT varies
Degrees: AA, AS, AAS & AFA 2 yr
Tuition: Res $27.50 per cr hour; nonres $159.75 per cr hr
Courses: Art Appreciation, Art History, Design, Drawing
Adult Hobby Classes: Courses offered

GREENSBORO

GREENSBORO COLLEGE, Dept of Art, Division of Fine Arts, 815 W Market St, Greensboro, NC 27401-1875. Tel 336-272-7102, Ext 301; Fax 336-271-6634; Web: www.gborocollege.edu; *Assoc Prof* Ray Martin, MFA; *Prof* Robert Kowski, MFA; *Instr* James V Langer; *Instr* Ginger Williamson
Estab 1838; Maintain nonprofit art gallery; Irene Cullis Gallery, Greensboro Col; pvt den; D & E, weekends; Scholarships; SC 15, LC 4; D 200, non-maj 50, maj 20
Ent Req: HS dipl
Degrees: BA 4 yrs
Courses: Art Appreciation, †Art Education, Art History, Ceramics, Design, Drawing, †Painting, Photography, Printmaking, †Sculpture, Stage Design, †Theatre Arts
Adult Hobby Classes: Enrl 40; tuition $225 per cr hr. Courses—Art History
Summer School: Dir, Dr John Drayer. Tuition $138 per cr hr for two 5 wk sessions. Courses—Art Appreciation, Art History

GUILFORD COLLEGE, Art Dept, 5800 W Friendly Ave, Greensboro, NC 27410-4173. Tel 336-316-2000; Fax 336-316-2299; Email glorio@guilford.edu; Web: www.guilford.edu; *Prof of Art* David Newton; *Prof of Art* Roy Nydorf; *Prof of Art, Dept Chair* Adele Wayman
Estab 1837, dept estab 1970; Maintain nonprofit art gallery, Hege Library Art Gallery; private; D & E; Scholarships; studio, lectrs; 40 maj
Ent Req: HS dipl, entrance examination
Degrees: BA 4 yr, BFA 4 yr
Courses: Art History, Ceramics, Design, Drawing, History of Art & Architecture, Painting, Photography, Printmaking, Sculpture

NORTH CAROLINA AGRICULTURAL & TECHNICAL STATE UNIVERSITY, Visual Arts Dept, 312 N Dudley St, Greensboro, NC 27411-0001. Tel 336-334-7993; *Chmn* Stephanie Santmyers
Estab 1930; FT 4, PT 1; pub; SC 29, LC 7; maj 50
Courses: 2-D Design, 3-D Design, Advertising Design, Aesthetics, Art Appreciation, †Art Design, †Art Education, Art History, Ceramics, Crafts, Design, Drawing, Graphic Arts, Graphic Design, Handicrafts, Illustration, †Painting, Printmaking, Sculpture, Teacher Training, Textile Design
Summer School: Dir, Dr Ronald Smith. Courses—Crafts, Public School Art, Art History, Art Appreciation

UNIVERSITY OF NORTH CAROLINA AT GREENSBORO, School of Art, 527 Highland Ave, Greensboro, NC 27412-5015; PO Box 26170, Greensboro, NC 27402-6170. Tel 336-334-5248; Fax 336-334-5270; Email e_kane@uncg.edu; Web: www.vpa.uncg.edu/art; *Prof* Michael Ananian; *Prof* George Dimock; *Prof* Patricia Wasserboehr; *Prof* Billy Lee; *Prof* John Maggio; *Lectr* Richard Gantt; *Prof* Amy Lixi Purcell; *Prof* Mariam Stephan; *Prof* Heather Holian; *Prof* Nikki Blair; *Prof* Barbara Campbell; *Director* Christopher Cassidy; *Lectr* Bryan Ellis; *Prof* Leah Sobsey; *Lectr* Christopher Thomas; *Prof* Lee Walton; *Prof* Eun-Hee Lim; *Prof* Elizabeth Perrill; *Prof* Jennifer Meanley; *Prof* Sheryl Oring; *Prof* Sunny Spillane
Dept estab 1935; maintains nonprofit gallery, The Gallery at the Gatewood, UNCG, 527 Highland Ave, Greensboro, NC 27412; art library, UNCG Visual Resources Library, 105 The Weatherspoon Art Museum, PO Box 26170, Greensboro, NC 27402-6170. Campus shop where art supplies may be purchased; FT 20; pub; D&E; Scholarships; Fellowships; SC 78, LC 43, GC 46, other 15; D 450, grad 15
Ent Req: HS grad, ent exam
Degrees: BA, BFA & MFA 2 yrs
Tuition: In-state undergrad $3,932 per yr; out-of-state $18,794 per yr
Courses: †Art Education, †Art History, Ceramics, Conceptual Art, †Design, Digital Design, Drawing, Graphic Design, Mixed Media, Museum Studies, †Painting, Photography, Printmaking, †Sculpture, Teacher Training, Video
Summer School: Head of dept. Lawrence Jenkens. Enrl 180; beginning May - June and July - Aug. Courses—Art Educ, Art History, Design, Drawing, Etching, Painting, Photography, Sculpture

GREENVILLE

EAST CAROLINA UNIVERSITY, School of Art & Design, 2000 Leo Jenkins Fine Arts Ctr, Mail Stop 502 Greenville, NC 27858-2502. Tel 252-328-6665; Fax 252-328-6441; Web: www.ecu.edu; *Dir* Michael H Drought; *Asst Dir* Scott Eagle; *Asst Dir* Dr Kate LaMere
Estab 1907; Maintain nonprofit gallery; Wellington B Gray Art Gallery, Greenville SC; on-campus shop sells art supplies; FT 49, PT 11; pub; D&E; Scholarships; Fellowships; SC 215, LC 25, GC 85; non-maj 1,400, maj 500, grad 50
Activities: Schols offered
Ent Req: HS dipl, 20 units, Col Board Exam
Degrees: BA, BFA, MFA, MAEd
Tuition: Campus res—available
Courses: Animation, Art Appreciation, †Art Education, †Art History, †Ceramics, Color & Design, Drawing, †Fabric Design, Film, Goldsmithing, Graphic Design, History of Art & Architecture, †Illustration, Independent Study, Interactive Design, Interdisciplinary 3-D Design, †Metal Design, †Painting, †Photography, †Printmaking, †Sculpture, Silversmithing, †Teacher Training, †Textile Design, Video, †Weaving, †Wood Design, Work Experience in the Visual Arts & Design
Children's Classes: Children's afterschool art classes
Summer School: Dir, Michael H Drought. Enrl 200; two 5 wk terms. Courses—Foundation & Survey

HICKORY

LENOIR RHYNE COLLEGE, Dept of Art, PO Box 7471, Visual Arts Ctr Hickory, NC 28603-7471. Tel 828-328-1741; Fax 828-328-7338; Web: www.lrc.edu; *Chmn Dept* Robert Winter PhD; *Asst Prof* Douglas Burton, MA; *Instr* Tom Perryman, MA
Estab 1892, dept estab 1976; den; D & E; Scholarships; SC 5; D 1200, E 350
Ent Req: HS dipl
Degrees: AB & BS 4 yrs
Courses: Aesthetics, Art Appreciation, Art Education, Art History, Ceramics, Drawing, Painting, Photography, Printmaking, Sculpture
Adult Hobby Classes: Courses on Tues & Thurs evenings
Children's Classes: Summer courses for gifted & talented
Summer School: Dir, Dr James Lichtenstein. Enrl 900; tuition $175 per sem hr for 2-5 wk terms beginning June. Courses—Art Appreciation, Art Education, Ceramics, Painting

HIGH POINT

HIGH POINT UNIVERSITY, Fine Arts Dept, 932 Montlieu Ave, University Sta High Point, NC 27260; 833 Montlieu Ave, Campus Box 25 High Point, NC 27262-4221. Tel 336-841-9282; Fax 336-841-5123; Email awheless@highpoint.edu ; *Asst Prof* Alexa Schlimmer; *Chmn* Andrea Wheless
Estab 1924, dept estab 1956; pvt den; D & E; Scholarships; SC 16, LC 6; non-maj 950, maj 10
Ent Req: HS dipl, SAT
Degrees: AB & BS 4 yrs
Courses: Advertising Design, Aesthetics, †Art Education, Art History, Ceramics, Crafts, Drawing, History of Art & Architecture, Interior Design, Painting, Printmaking, Sculpture, Stage Design, Teacher Training, †Theatre Arts
Summer School: Enrl 200; two 5 wk sessions. Courses—Art Education, Crafts, Design, Interior Design

JAMESTOWN

GUILFORD TECHNICAL COMMUNITY COLLEGE, Commercial Art Dept, PO Box 309, Jamestown, NC 27282-0309. Tel 336-454-1126, Ext 2230; Fax 336-819-2022; Email reidm@gtcc.cc.nc.us; Web: www.technet.gtcc.cc.nc.us/; *Instr* Awilda Feliciano, BFA; *Instr* Frederick N Jones, MFA; *Instr* Scott Burnette, BA; *Head* Margaret Reid, MFA; *Instr* Michael Swing; *Instr* Alex Forsyth; *Instr* Julie Evans
Estab 1964; pub; D & E; Scholarships; SC 20, LC 4; D 130, E 60
Ent Req: HS dipl, English & math placement
Degrees: AAS 2 yrs
Courses: †Advertising Design, Art History, Commercial Art, Computer Graphics, Drafting, Drawing, Graphic Arts, Illustration, Lettering, Photography
Adult Hobby Classes: Courses—Variety of subjects
Summer School: 9 wk term. Courses—Various

KINSTON

LENOIR COMMUNITY COLLEGE, Dept of Visual Art, PO Box 188, Kinston, NC 28502-0188. Tel 252-527-6223, Ext 923; *Prof* Henry Stindt
Pub; D&E
Degrees: AA, AS & AFA
Tuition: Res—$27.50 per cr hr; nonres—$169.75 per cr hr
Courses: Ceramics, Commercial Art, Design, Drawing, Illustration, Introduction to Art, Painting, Photography, Printmaking
Summer School: Dir, Gerald A Elliott. Enrl 32; tuition $51 for 12 cr hrs. Courses—Lecture & Studio Art

LAURINBURG

SAINT ANDREWS PRESBYTERIAN COLLEGE, Art Program, 1700 Dogwood Mile, Laurinburg, NC 28352. Tel 910-277-5240, Ext 5264, 277-5264; Fax 910-277-5020; Email mcdavids@sapc.edu; Web: www.sapc.edu/art; *Chmn Art Dept & Instr* Stephanie McDavid
Estab 1960; FT 2; den; D; Scholarships; SC 14, LC 2; D 852, maj 20 - 30
Ent Req: HS dipl, SAT, 2.6 grade point average, 12 acad units
Degrees: BA, MS & BM 4 yrs or 32 courses
Courses: Art Appreciation, Art Education, Art History, Computer Graphics, Design, Drawing, Painting, Photography, Printmaking, Sculpture, Video
Summer School: Studio courses offered

ST ANDREWS PRESBYTERIAN COLLEGE, Art Gallery, 1700 Dogwood Mile, Laurinburg, NC 28352. Tel 910-277-5264; Fax 910-277-5020
Open Mon - Fri 9 AM - 4:30 PM; No admis fee
Collections: Paintings; photographs; sculpture

LEXINGTON

DAVIDSON COUNTY COMMUNITY COLLEGE, Humanities Div, PO Box 1287, 2997 DCCC Rd Lexington, NC 27293-1287. Tel 336-249-8186, Ext 253 or 314; Fax 336-249-0379; Web: www.davidson.cc.nc.us/
Estab 1963, dept estab 1966; FT 2, PT 3; pub; D & E; Scholarships; SC 14, LC 4; D 100, E 30, non-maj 195, maj 30
Ent Req: HS dipl
Degrees: AFA, AS & AA 2 yrs
Courses: Art Education, Art History, Design, Drafting, Handicrafts, Independent Studio, Painting, Photography, Printmaking, Sculpture
Adult Hobby Classes: Courses—Variety taught through continuing educ

MARS HILL

MARS HILL COLLEGE, Art Dept, 100 Athletic St, Mars Hill, NC 28754-9134; PO Box 370, Mars Hill, NC 28754-0370. Tel 828-689-1396; Email rcary@mhc.edu; Web: www.mhc.edu; *Chmn* Scott Lowley
Estab 1856, dept estab 1932; pvt and den; D & E; Scholarships; SC 9, LC 6; D 120, non-maj 100, maj 20
Ent Req: HS dipl, ent exam
Degrees: BA 4 yrs
Courses: †Advertising Design, Aesthetics, †Art Education, †Art History, Ceramics, †Graphic Arts, †Painting, Photography, †Printmaking, Sculpture, †Teacher Training, †Theatre Arts
Summer School: Enrl 450; tuition $65 per cr hr for 5 wk term. Courses—Introduction to the Arts & Photography

MISENHEIMER

PFEIFFER UNIVERSITY, Art Program, PO Box 960, Misenheimer, NC 28109-0960. Tel 704-463-1360, Ext 2667; Fax 704-463-1363; Web: www.pfeiffer.edu/; *Dir* James Haymaker
Estab 1965; FT 1; den; D; Scholarships; SC 4, LC 4; D 100
Ent Req: HS dipl
Degrees: BA

Courses: Art Education, Art History, Ceramics, Drawing, Painting, Sculpture

MOUNT OLIVE

MOUNT OLIVE COLLEGE, Dept of Art, 634 Henderson St, Mount Olive, NC 28365-1263. Tel 919-658-2502, 658-7181; Fax 919-658-7180; *Chmn* Larry Lean
Estab 1951; den; D & E; Scholarships; SC 5, LC 3
Degrees: BA & BS
Courses: American Art, Art Appreciation, Art History, Design, Drawing, Painting
Summer School: Courses—Art Appreciation

MURFREESBORO

CHOWAN COLLEGE, Dept. of Communication Arts, Fine and Applied Arts, One University Place, Murfreesboro, NC 27855. Tel 252-398-6358; Email eupscc@chowan.edu; Web: www.chowan.edu; *Dean of School of Fine and Applied Arts, Professor of Art* Christina Rupsch; *Chair, Assoc Prof* Tom Brennan; *Assistant Prof, Art* Rob Buller; *Assistant Prof, Art* Jacob Muldowney; *Assistant Prof, Graphics* Mitch Henke; *Assistant Prof, Graphics* Jennifer Groves; *Prof, Graphics* Michelle Surerus
Estab 1848; maintains non-profit gallery: Green Hall Galleries; Art Library: Small collection within Green Hall, Significant Collection in Main Library on Campus; Art Supplies may be purchased in the student book store; den; D&E; Scholarships; SC, LC; 100+
Ent Req: HS dipl, SAT or ACT
Degrees: AA 2 yrs, BA, BS, Studio Art, Tracks: Pre-Art Therapy, BS Graphic Design, BS Graphic Communications
Courses: Art Appreciation, Art History, Ceramics, Conceptual Art, Design, Drawing, Figure Drawing, Graphic Design, Illustration, Lettering, Painting, Printmaking, Sculpture, Theatre Arts, Typography, Interactive design, Multimedia, Digital Imaging, Color Reproduction, Printing Application, Intro to Packaging Design, Digital Printing, Flexographic and special printing, Video
Summer School: Dir, Doug Eubank. Courses—Art Appreciation, Ceramics, Drawing, Painting

PEMBROKE

UNIVERSITY OF NORTH CAROLINA AT PEMBROKE, Art Dept, PO Box 1510, Pembroke, NC 28372-1510. Tel 910-521-6216; Fax 910-521-6639; Email art@uncp.edu; Web: www.uncp.edu; *Chair* Dr Richard Gay; *Prof* Dr John Antoine Labadie; *Assoc Prof & Dir Grad Art Educ* Dr Ann Horton-Lopez; *Prof & Coordr Undergrad Art Educ* Dr Tulla Lightfoot; *Asst Prof* Brandon Sanderson; *Asst Prof & Gallery Dir* Carla Rokes; *Asst Prof* Adam Walls; *Asst Prof* David Hicks; *Asst Prof* Dr Nancy Palm; *Assoc Prof* Joseph Begnaud
Estab 1887; Maintains nonprofit art galleries: Locklear Hall Art Gallery & A D Gallery; art supplies sold at on campus store; FT 10, PT 3; pub; D & E; Scholarships; SC 46, LC 25, GC 7; non-maj 6,130, maj 115
Ent Req: CEEB scores, HS record, scholastic standing in HS grad class
Degrees: BA 4 yrs, MA(Art Ed) 2 yrs, MAT(Art Ed)
Courses: Art Appreciation, †Art Education, Art History, Ceramics, Computer Graphics, Design, Drawing, History of Art & Architecture, Mixed Media, Painting, Printmaking, Sculpture, Teacher Training
Summer School: Variety of courses

PENLAND

PENLAND SCHOOL OF CRAFTS, Penland Rd, Penland, NC 28765-8000; PO Box 37, Penland, NC 28765-0037. Tel 828-765-2359; Fax 828-765-7389; Web: www.penland.org
Estab 1929; Maintain nonprofit art gallery; Penland Gallery; Nonprofit org; D (summer, spring & fall classes); Scholarships; SC 112; D approx 1,200
Ent Req: age 19 and above, special fall and spring sessions require portfolio and resume
Degrees: none granted but cr may be obtained through agreement with East Tennessee State Univ & Western Carolina Univ
Courses: Basketry, Blacksmithing, Book Arts, Ceramics, †Drawing, Fibers, Glass, Jewelry, Metalsmithing, †Painting, Papermaking, Photography, Printmaking, Sculpture, †Surface Design, †Textiles, Weaving, Woodworking
Summer School: Dir, Jean McLaughlin. Tuition varies for 1, 2 & 2-1/2 wk courses between June & Sept; 8 wk concentrations-spring & fall. Courses—Basketry, Book Arts, Clay, Drawing, Fibers, Glass, Iron, Metal, Paper, Photography, Printmaking, Sculpture, Surface Design, Wood

RALEIGH

MEREDITH COLLEGE, Art Dept, 3800 Hillsborough St, Gaddy-Hamrick Art Ctr Raleigh, NC 27607-5237. Tel 919-760-8332; Fax 919-760-2347; *Chmn* Rebecca Bailey
Estab 1898; den, W; D & E; Scholarships; SC 15, LC 5; D 490, E 130, maj 85, others 30
Ent Req: HS dipl
Degrees: AB 4 yrs
Courses: Advertising Design, Art Appreciation, Art Education, Art History, Calligraphy, Ceramics, Computer Graphics, Costume Design & Construction, Design, Drawing, Graphic Design, Handicrafts
Adult Hobby Classes: Courses—Art History, Ceramics, Drawing, Fibers, Graphic Design, Painting, Photography, Sculpture
Summer School: Dir, John Hiott. Courses—vary

NORTH CAROLINA STATE UNIVERSITY, College of Design, CB 7701, Raleigh, NC 27695-7701. Tel 919-515-8302; Fax 919-515-7330; Email collegeofdesign@ncsu.edu; Web: www.ncsu.edu/design; *Dean* Mark Hoversten, PhD, FASLA, FCELA, AICD
Estab 1948; 63; pub; D&E, Distance Learning; Architecture 217, Art & Design 214, Graphic Design 130, Industrial Design 106, Landscape Architecture 54
Ent Req: col board, ent exam
Degrees: BEnv(Design in Architecture, Design, Graphic & Industrial Design, Landscape Architecture, March), MGraphic Design, MLandscape Arch, 4-6 yrs
Courses: Architecture, Art + Design, Design, Graphic Design, Industrial Design, Landscape Architecture
Summer School: Courses—Undergrad: Architecture, Graphic Design, Industrial Design, Landscape Architecture, Art + Design

PEACE COLLEGE, Art Dept, 15 E Peace St, Raleigh, NC 27604-1194. Tel 919-508-2000; Fax 919-508-2326; Web: www.peace.edu; *Head Dept* Carolyn Parker
Estab 1857; pvt; D & E; SC 8, LC 2; D 600
Ent Req: HS dipl, SAT
Degrees: AA & AFA 2 yrs & 4 yrs
Courses: †Liberal Arts

ROCKY MOUNT

NORTH CAROLINA WESLEYAN COLLEGE, Dept of Visual & Performing Arts, 3400 N Wesleyan Blvd, Rocky Mount, NC 27804-9906. Tel 252-985-5100, 985-5167 (Dept Visual & Art); Fax 252-977-3701; Web: www.ncwc.edu; *Instr* Everett Mayo Adelman; *Instr* Michele A Cruz; *Dir Theater Dept* David Blakely
Founded 1956; opened 1960; Scholarships
Ent Req: HS dipl
Degrees: BA
Tuition: Res—$9,758 per year
Courses: Advertising Design, Architecture, Art Appreciation, Art Education, Visual Communication
Adult Hobby Classes: Enrl 1055; tuition $125 per sem hr. Courses—Art Appreciation, American Architecture

STATESVILLE

MITCHELL COMMUNITY COLLEGE, Visual Art Dept, 500 W Broad St, Statesville, NC 28677-5293. Tel 704-878-3200; Web: www.mitchell.cc.nc.us; *Chmn* Donald Everett Moore, MA; *Instr* James Messer
Estab 1852, dept estab 1974; FT 2, PT 1; pub; D & E; Scholarships; SC 12-15, LC 5; D 85, E 40, non-maj 100, maj 25
Ent Req: HS dipl, HS transcripts, placement test
Degrees: AA & AFA 2 yrs
Courses: Art History, †Ceramics, Color Theory, Drawing, Intermedia, †Painting, Printmaking, †Sculpture
Adult Hobby Classes: Enrl 100; tuition $130 per 10 wks. Courses—Continuing education courses in art & crafts available

SYLVA

SOUTHWESTERN COMMUNITY COLLEGE, Advertising & Graphic Design, 447 College Dr, Sylva, NC 28779-8581. Tel 828-586-4091, Ext 233; Fax 828-586-3129; Web: www.southwest.cc.nc.us/; *Instr* Bob Clark, MS; *Instr* Bob Keeling, BFA; *Photog Instr* Matthew Turlington
Estab 1964, dept estab 1967; Maintains a nonprofit art gallery; FT 2, PT 2; pub; D; Scholarships; SC 19, LC 14; D 36, maj 50
Ent Req: HS dipl
Degrees: AAS
Courses: Advertising Design, †Airbrush, Art Appreciation, Computer Graphics, Conceptual Art, Design, Drafting, Drawing, Graphic Arts, Graphic Design, Illustration, †Painting, †Penstriping, Photography, Screenprinting, Technical Illustration, Typography
Adult Hobby Classes: Enrl 30, tuition $35 per class hr

WHITEVILLE

SOUTHEASTERN COMMUNITY COLLEGE, Dept of Art, PO Box 151, Whiteville, NC 28472-0151. Tel 910-642-7141, Ext 237; Fax 910-642-5658; Web: www.sccnc.edu; *Instr, Chair* September Krueger
Estab 1965; FT 1 PT 1; pub; D & E; SC 18, LC 7
Ent Req: HS dipl or 18 yrs old
Degrees: AFA 2 yrs
Tuition: Res—$27.50 per cr hour; non-res—$169.75
Courses: Art History, Ceramics, Drawing, Painting, Pottery, Printmaking, Sculpture
Adult Hobby Classes: Tuition res—$25 per course
Summer School: Dir, Christa Balogh

WILKESBORO

WILKES COMMUNITY COLLEGE, Arts & Science Division, PO Box 120, Wilkesboro, NC 28697-0120. Tel 336-838-6100; Fax 336-838-6277; Web: www.wilkes.cc.mc.us; *Instr* Dewey Mayes; *Dir* Blair Hancock
Estab 1965, dept estab 1967; pub; D & E; Scholarships; SC 2, LC 2; D 1600, E 800
Ent Req: HS dipl
Degrees: AA, AFA
Courses: Art History, Art Travel Courses, Costume Design & Construction, Drafting, Drawing, Painting, Photography, Sculpture, Theatre Arts
Summer School: Dir, Bud Mayes

WILMINGTON

UNIVERSITY OF NORTH CAROLINA AT WILMINGTON, Dept of Fine Arts - Division of Art, 601 S College Rd, Wilmington, NC 28403-3201. Tel 910-962-3415 (Dept of Art); *Prof* Ann Conner, MFA; *Prof* Donald Furst, MFA; *Prof, Chmn* Kemille Moore, PhD
Estab 1789, dept estab 1952; pub; D & E
Ent Req: HS dipl, ent exam
Degrees: BCA 4 yrs
Courses: Art Appreciation, Art History, Ceramics, Design, Drawing, Painting, Printmaking, Sculpture
Adult Hobby Classes: Courses—Drawing, Painting
Summer School: Dir, David Miller. Two 5 wk sessions. Courses—Varied

WILSON

BARTON COLLEGE, School of Visual, Performing & Communication Arts, PO Box 5000, Wilson, NC 27893-7000. Tel 252-399-6559; Fax 252-399-6572; Email sfecho@barton.edu; Web: www.barton.edu; *Assoc Prof* Gerard Lange, MFA; *Dean* Susan C Fecho, MFA; *Assoc Prof* Mark Gordon, MFA; *Asst Prof Communs* Richard D Stewart, MA; *Assoc Prof Communs* Webster Struthers, MA; *Dir Theatre at Barton & Asst Prof Theatre* Adam J Twiss, MFA; *Asst Prof Communs* Philip J Valera, M.Mus.
Estab 1903, dept estab 1950; Maintains a nonprofit art gallery, Barton College, Rondon Art Galleries, Case Art Bldg (on campus); art library Case Art Bldg, (on campus); Pvt; D, E, weekend, summer; Scholarships; SC 15, LC 8-10; D 100, non-maj 70, maj 50, others 15 (PT)
Activities: Schols offered
Ent Req: HS dipl, ent exam
Degrees: BS, BA & BFA 4 yrs
Tuition: Undergrad—$12,234 per semester, $1,947-$3,043 campus res—room & board $2,506
Courses: †Art Appreciation, †Art Education, †Art History, Audio, †Ceramics, †Collage, †Commercial Art, Costume Design & Construction, †Design, †Drawing, Film, Graphic Arts, †Graphic Design, †Illustration, †Mixed Media, Museum Staff Training, Musical Theatre, †Painting, †Photography, Photojournalism, †Printmaking, †Sculpture, Stage Design, †Teacher Training, Theatre Arts, †Video, †Visual Communication, †Visual Design
Adult Hobby Classes: Enrl 15; $25 per hr 8 work sessions; continuing educ
Summer School: continuing deuce classes offered

WINGATE

WINGATE UNIVERSITY, Art Department, PO Box 3015, Wingate, NC 28174-0159. Tel 704-233-8000; WATS 800-755-5550; *Chmn Div* Louise Napier
Estab 1896, dept estab 1958; den; D & E; Scholarships; D & E 1500
Ent Req: HS grad
Degrees: BA(Art), BA(Art Education) 4 yrs
Courses: 3-D Design, Art Appreciation, Art History, Art Methods, Ceramics, Composition, Drawing, Film, Gallery Tours, Metalsmithing, Painting, Photography, Printmaking, Sculpture, Sketching
Summer School: Pres, Dr Jerry McGee. Term of 4 wks beginning first wk in June. Courses—all regular class work available if demand warrants

WINSTON-SALEM

SALEM ACADEMY & COLLEGE, Art Dept, 601 S Church St, Winston-Salem, NC 27101-5376. Tel 336-721-2600, 721-2683; Fax 336-721-2683; *Asst Prof* Penny Griffin; *Prof* John Hutton; *Assoc Prof* Kimberly Varnadoe
Non-profit art gallery: Salem Fine Arts Center Gallery; Den, W; D & E; Scholarships; D 642, maj 44
Ent Req: HS Dipl
Degrees: BA 4 yrs
Courses: Art History, Design, Drawing, Graphic Design, Painting, Printmaking, Sculpture

SAWTOOTH CENTER FOR VISUAL ART, 251 N Spruce St, Winston-Salem, NC 27101-2735. Tel 336-723-7395; Fax 336-773-0132; Email info@sawtooth.org; Web: sawtooth.org; *Exec Dir* Sherri Nielson; *Youth Coordr* Katie Longinotti; *Registrar* Julie Morgan
Estab 1945 as Community School of Craft & Art; PT 75; D, E & weekends; Scholarships; SC
Degrees: non-degree
Tuition: $25-$250 per 10 wk course
Courses: Basketry, Book Arts, Calligraphy, Ceramics, Computer Graphics, Drawing, Jewelry, Lampwork, Mixed Media, Painting, Papermaking, Photography, Printmaking, Silversmithing, Stained Glass, Teacher Training, Textile Design, Weaving, Wood Carving
Adult Hobby Classes: Enrl 2000; tuition $100-$250 for 5-10 wk term. Courses—All visual arts & craft mediums
Children's Classes: Enrl 1000; tuition $60-$100 for 5 wks. Courses—35 different media oriented courses
Summer School: Enrl 600; tuition $250 for 4 wks

WAKE FOREST UNIVERSITY, Dept of Art, 1834 Wake Forest Rd, Winston-Salem, NC 27106; Box 7232, Art Dept, Reynolda Sta Winston-Salem, NC 27109. Tel 336-758-5310; Fax 336-758-6014; Web: www.wfu.edu/art; *Prof* Page Laughlin; *Prof* Harry B Titus Jr; *Prof* Bernadine Barnes; *Prof* David Finn; *Assoc Prof* David Faber; *Assoc Prof* John Pickel; *Instr* Alix Hitchcock; *Charlotte C Weber Prof Art* David M Lubin; *Asst Prof* John J Curley; *Asst Prof* Morna O'Neill; *Gallery Dir* Paul Bright; *Asst Prof* Joel Tanber
Estab 1834, dept estab 1968; Maintains nonprofit Charlotte & Phillip Hanes Art Gallery & art libr on campus; art supplies sold at on-campus store; Pvt; D; Scholarships; SC 14, LC 28
Ent Req: HS dipl, SAT
Degrees: BA 4 yrs
Courses: Art History, Collage (Summer I), Drawing, Film, Painting, Photography, Printmaking, Restoration & Conservation, Sculpture, †Studio Art
Summer School: Assoc Dean & Dean of Summer Session Toby Hale. Enrl 25; tuition $235 per cr. Courses—Independent Study, Intro to Visual Arts, Practicum, Printmaking Workshop

WINSTON-SALEM STATE UNIVERSITY, Art Dept, Fine Arts Bldg, FA 112, Winston-Salem, NC 27110. Tel 336-750-2520; Fax 336-750-2522; Email legettel@wssul.adp.wssu.edu; Web: www.wssu.edu/academic/arts-sci/finearts.usp; *Prof* Arcenia Davis; *Asst Prof* Marvette Aldrich; *Interim Chmn* Lee David Legette
Estab, 1892, dept estab 1970; pub; D & E; SC 10, LC 7; D 65, nonmaj 275, maj 65
Ent Req: HS Dipl
Degrees: BA 4 yr
Courses: Art Education, Art History, Drawing, Graphic Arts, Painting, Sculpture
Summer School: Courses offered

NORTH DAKOTA

BISMARCK

BISMARCK STATE COLLEGE, Fine Arts Dept, 1500 Edwards Ave, Bismarck, ND 58501-1299. Tel 701-224-5471; Web: www.bsc.edu; *Assoc Prof* Richard Sammons; *Instr* Tom Porter; *Instr* Marietta Turner; *Instr* Michelle Lindblom; *Instr* Dan Rogers; *Instr* Carol Cashman; *Instr* Barbara Cichy; *Chmn* Jonelle Masters
Estab 1961; FT 3 PT 9; pub; D & E
Degrees: AA 2 yrs
Tuition: Res—undergrad $904.32 per sem; nonres—undergrad $2200.08 per sem
Courses: Art Appreciation, Ceramics, Design, Drawing, Elementary Art, Gallery Management, Handicrafts, Introduction to Understanding Art, Jewelry, Lettering, Painting, Photography, Printmaking, Sculpture
—**The Else Forde Gallery**, 1500 Edwards Ave, Schafer Hall Bismarck, ND 58501-1276. Tel 701-224-5601; Email barbara.jirges@bsc.nodak.edu; Web: www.ndga.org/galleries/bscg.html; *Dir* Barbara Jirges
Open Mon - Thurs 7 AM - 9 PM, Fri 7 AM - 4 PM, Sun 6 PM - 9 PM
Collections: Student artwork; works by local, regional & national artists

DICKINSON

DICKINSON STATE UNIVERSITY, Dept of Art, 291 Campus Dr, Div of Fine Arts and Humanities Dickinson, ND 58601-4853. Tel 701-483-2312, 701-483-2060; Email ronald.gingerich@dickinsonstate.edu; *Chmn* Ron Gingerich, MFA; *Gallery Dir & Assoc Prof Art* Carol Eacret-Simmons, MFA; *Assoc Prof* Marilyn Lee, MFA
Estab 1918, dept estab 1959; Maintains nonprofit art gallery, Dickinson State Univ Art Gallery (same address); art supplies may be purchased on-campus; pub; D & E; Scholarships; SC 36, LC 8; D approx 150 per quarter, non-maj 130, maj 20
Ent Req: HS dipl, out-of state, ACT, minimum score 18 or upper-half of class
Degrees: BA, BS and BCS 4 yr
Courses: †Art Education, Art History, †Ceramics, Color, Costume Design & Construction, Display, Drawing, Graphic Arts, †Graphic Arts Minor, Graphic Design, Handicrafts, Intermedia, Jewelry, Lettering, Painting, Photography, Printmaking, Sculpture, Stage Design, Teacher Training, Theatre Arts
Adult Hobby Classes: Enrl varies; courses - Photography; watercolor; ceramics
Children's Classes: Varies

FARGO

NORTH DAKOTA STATE UNIVERSITY, Division of Fine Arts, PO Box 6050, Dept 2330 Fargo, ND 58108-6050. Tel 701-231-8011; Web: www.ndsu.edu; *Asst Prof* Kimble Bromley, MFA; *Lectr* David Swenson, MFA; *Lectr* Jaime Penuel, BFA; *Lectr* Kent Kapplinger, BFA
Estab 1889, dept estab 1964; Maintain Memorial Union Art Gallery at the University; FT 5; pub; D & E; Scholarships; SC 21; D 225, E 60, non-maj 250, maj 30
Ent Req: HS dipl
Degrees: BA & BS 4 yr
Courses: Architecture, Art Appreciation, Art History, Ceramics, Design, Drafting, Drawing, Fashion Arts, History of Art & Architecture, Interior Design, Landscape Architecture, Painting, Photography, Printmaking, Sculpture, Textile Design, Theatre Arts

GRAND FORKS

UNIVERSITY OF NORTH DAKOTA, Art Department, 3350 Campus Rd, Stop 7099 Grand Forks, ND 58202-7099. Tel 701-777-2257; Fax 701-777-2903; Email patrick_luber@und.nodak.edu; Web: www.und.edu/dept/arts2000/; *Chmn* Patrick Luber
Estab 1883; D FT 11; pub; Scholarships; SC 30, LC 4, GC 14; maj 90, others 1000
Degrees: BFA, BA, BSEd, MFA
Tuition: Campus res—available
Courses: Aesthetics, Art Appreciation, †Art Education, Art History, †Ceramics, Design, †Digital Media, Drawing, †Fibers, Goldsmithing, History of Art & Architecture, †Jewelry, Lettering, †Metalsmithing, †Painting, †Photography, †Printmaking, †Sculpture, Silversmithing, †Teacher Training, †Weaving

Adult Hobby Classes: Enrl 800-1000; tuition $2428 per yr. Courses—Various studio art & art history
Summer School: Dir, J McElroy-Edwards. Enrl 100; tuition one half cash of regular sem. Courses—Varies every summer

JAMESTOWN

UNIVERSITY OF JAMESTOWN, (Jamestown College) Art Dept, PO Box 1559, Jamestown, ND 58402-1559. Tel 701-252-3467; Fax 701-253-4318; Email cox@uj.edu; Web: www.uj.edu; *Chmn* Sharon Cox
1883; Maintains Reiland Fine Art Center, 6003 College Ln, c/o Sharon Cox, Dir, University of Jamestown, ND 58405; Raugust Library, 6000 College Ln, c/o Phyllis Bratton, Dir, University of Jamestown 58405; art supplies available on-campus; FT 21; Pvt, den; D & E; Scholarships; SC 13, LC 4; 146, maj 14
Ent Req: HS dipl
Degrees: BA and BS 4 yr, directed study and individual study in advanced studio areas, private studios, M.ED., PhD, Phys Thera
Courses: †2-D Design; Art Business; Fine Arts, Advertising Design, Art Appreciation, Art Education, Art History, Ceramics, Design, Drawing, Eastern Art History, Graphic Design, History of Art & Architecture, Museum Staff Training, Painting, Photography, Printmaking, Sculpture, Stage Design, Teacher Training, Textile Design, Theatre Arts, Weaving
Summer School: Enrl 20-25, 3 sessions of 6 wks beginning in May

MINOT

MINOT STATE UNIVERSITY, Dept of Art, Division of Humanities, 500 University Ave W, Minot, ND 58701-0002. Tel 701-858-3000, 858-3171, 858-3109; Fax 701-839-6933; Email davidsoc@misu.nodak.edu; Web: www.warp6.cs.misu.nodak.edu; *Chmn Div Humanities* Conrad Davidson; *Art Dept Coordr* Walter Piehl
Estab 1913; FT 4; pub; Scholarships; SC 30; per quarter 200, maj 40
Degrees: BA & BS 4 yr
Courses: Advertising Design, Art History, Ceramics, Design, Drawing, Handicrafts, Jewelry, Painting, Photography, Printmaking, Sculpture, Silk Screen, Weaving
Summer School: Courses—same as above

VALLEY CITY

VALLEY CITY STATE COLLEGE, Art Dept, 101 College St SW, Valley City, ND 58072-4098. Tel 701-845-7598, 845-0701; Web: www.vcsu.edu; *Div Chair* Diana P Skroch; *Instr* Richard Nickel; *Dept Chair* Linda Whitney
Estab 1890, dept estab 1921; pub; D & E; Scholarships; SC 20, LC 3; D 1300, E 200, non-maj 120, maj 30
Ent Req: HS dipl, ACT
Degrees: AA 2 yr, BS & BA 4 yr
Courses: †Art Appreciation, †Art Education, Art History, Ceramics, Computer Graphics, Design, Drawing, Mixed Media, Painting, Printmaking, Theatre Arts

OHIO

ADA

OHIO NORTHERN UNIVERSITY, Dept of Art & Design, 525 S Main St, Ada, OH 45810-6000. Tel 419-772-2160; Fax 419-772-2164; Email art@onu.edu; Web: www.onu.edu/a&s/art; *Chmn* William Brit Rowe; *Assoc Prof Art* Melissa Eddings; *Asst Prof Art* William Mancuso; *Instr* Linda Lehman; *Instr* Rhonda Grubbs; *Asst Prof Art* Luke Sheets
Estab 1871; Maintain nonprofit art gallery; Elzay Art Gallery 525 Main St Ada OH 45810; Stambaugh Theatre Gallery; Pvt; D; Scholarships; SC 30, LC 8; non-maj 20, maj 40
Ent Req: HS dipl, ent exam, portfolio
Degrees: BA and BFA 4 yrs
Tuition: Freshman $17,000 per sem
Courses: †Advertising Design, †Art Appreciation, Art Education, Ceramics, Drawing, Graphic Design, History of Art & Architecture, Jewelry, Museum Studies, Painting, Photography, Printmaking, Sculpture, Teacher Training

AKRON

UNIVERSITY OF AKRON, Myers School of Art, 150 E Exchange St, Akron, OH 44325-7801. Tel 330-972-6030; Fax 330-972-5960; Web: http://art.uakron.edu; *Dept Head* Del Rey Loven
Estab 1870; Maintains nonprofit gallery, Emily Davis Gallery, & art / architecture library; Pub; D & E; Scholarships; SC 25, LC 7, GC 8; D 943, E 129, non-maj 493, maj 450
Ent Req: HS dipl
Degrees: BA, BFA 4 yr
Courses: †Advertising Design, Art Appreciation, Art Education, †Art History, †Art Studio, †Ceramics, Computer, †Drawing, †Graphic Design, History of Art & Architecture, Illustration, †Jewelry, †Metalsmithing, Museum Staff Training, †New Media, †Painting, †Photography, †Printmaking, †Sculpture, †Silversmithing, Teacher Training, Video

ALLIANCE

MOUNT UNION COLLEGE, Dept of Art, 1972 Clark Ave, Alliance, OH 44601-3993. Tel 330-823-2590, 823-2083 (Chmn), 823-3860 (Secy of Dept); *Chmn* Joel Collins, MFA
Estab 1846; pvt; D; Scholarships; SC 27, LC 6; D 150, non-maj 125, maj 25
Ent Req: HS dipl, SAT
Degrees: BA
Courses: Aesthetics, Art Education, Art History, Drawing, Painting, Printmaking, Sculpture, Teacher Training

ASHLAND

ASHLAND UNIVERSITY, Art Dept, 401 College Ave, Ashland, OH 44805-3799. Tel 419-289-4142; Web: www.ashland.edu; *Chmn* David Edgar, MFA; *Prof* Carl M Allen, MA; *Assoc Prof* Charles D Caldemeyer, MFA; *Asst Prof* Keith A Dull, MA; *Asst Prof* Robert A Stanley, EdD
Estab 1878; FT 4; den; D & E; Scholarships; D 1460, maj 32, minors 12
Ent Req: HS dipl
Degrees: BA, BS 4 yr
Courses: †Advertising Design, Art Appreciation, Art Education, available through affiliation with the Art Institute of Pittsburgh: Fashion Illustration, †Ceramics, †Commercial Art, Computer Art, Constructions, Costume Design & Construction, Design, Drawing, Fashion Arts, Interior Design, Photography/Multi Media, Visual Communication

ATHENS

OHIO UNIVERSITY, School of Art, 1 Ohio University, School of Art Athens, OH 45701-2942. Tel 740-593-4288, 593-0497; Email boothe@ohio.edu; Web: www.ohiou.edu/art/index; *Dir* Power Boothe
Estab 1936; 39; pub; D & E; Scholarships; Fellowships; SC 88, LC 30, LGC 29, SGC 50; maj 573, others 1718
Ent Req: secondary school dipl, portfolio
Degrees: BFA, MA & MFA 4-5 yrs
Courses: †Art Education, †Art History, †Art Therapy, †Ceramics, Drawing, Fibers, Glass, †Graphic Design, †Illustration, †Painting, †Photography, †Printmaking, †Sculpture, †Studio Arts, †Visual Communication
Summer School: Two 5 wk sessions June-July & July-Aug; 8 qtr hr maximum per session; SC, LC, GC

BEREA

BALDWIN-WALLACE COLLEGE, Dept of Art, 275 Eastland Rd, Berea, OH 44017-2088. Tel 440-826-2900; Web: www.bw.edu; *Prof Art History* Harold D Cole; *Chmn Div* Dr Marc Vincent
Estab 1845; den; D & E; SC 23, LC 12; 1900, maj 65
Degrees: AB 4 yrs
Courses: Art Education, Art History, Ceramics, Design & Color, Drawing, Painting, Photography, Printmaking, Sculpture

BLUFFTON

BLUFFTON UNIVERSITY, Art Dept, 1 University Dr, Bluffton, OH 45817-2104. Tel 419-358-3000; Email luginbuhlg@bluffton.edu; Web: www.bluffton.edu; *Chair* Gregg Luginbuhl
Courses: †Art Education, Graphic Design

BOWLING GREEN

BOWLING GREEN STATE UNIVERSITY, School of Art, 1000 Fine Arts Bldg, Bowling Green, OH 43403. Tel 419-372-2786; Fax 419-372-2544; *Dir Grad Studies* Charlie Kanwischer; *Chmn Design Studies* Mark Zust; *Chmn 3-D Studies* Kathy Hagan; *Chmn 2-D Studies* Lynn Whitney; *Chmn Art Educ* Dr Karen Kakas; *Chmn Art History* John Lavezzi PhD; *Dir Gallery* Jacqueline Nathan
Estab 1910, dept estab 1946; pub; D & E; Scholarships; Fellowships; SC 53, LC 14, GC 33; D 2460, E 150, non-maj 350, maj 750, grad 25, others 15
Ent Req: ACT (undergrad), GRE (grad)
Degrees: BA, BS & BFA 4 yrs, MA 1 yr, MFA 2 yrs
Courses: Advertising Design, †Art Education, †Art History, †Ceramics, †Computer Art, Design, †Drawing, †Fibers, †Glass, †Graphic Design, Jewelry, †Jewelry/Metals, †Painting, †Photography, †Printmaking, †Sculpture, †Silversmithing, Weaving
Children's Classes: Enrl 100; tuition $40 per 10 wk sem of Sat mornings
Summer School: Dir, Lou Krueger. Enrl 300; tuition $1224 for 8 wk & 6 wk session. Undergrad Courses—Drawing, Photography, Printmaking, Sculpture, Special Workshops

CANTON

CANTON MUSEUM OF ART, 1001 Market Ave N, Canton, OH 44702-1075. Tel 330-453-7666; Fax 330-453-1034; Web: www.cantonart.org; *Exec Dir* Manuel J Albacete; *Cur Exhibits & Registrar* Lynnda Arrasmith; *Bus Mgr* Kay McAllister; *Cur Educ* Lauren Kuntzman
Maintain a nonprofit art gallery & an art/architecture library; Pub; D & E; Scholarships; SC 28; D 322, E 984, others 1306
Tuition: Call office for tuition & class schedules
Courses: †Painting, †Pottery, †Sculpture

MALONE UNIVERSITY, Dept of Art, 2600 Cleveland Ave NW, Canton, OH 44709-3308. Tel 330-471-8231; Fax 330-471-8477; Email mhaines@malone.edu; Web: www.malone.edu/art; *Prof* Claire Murray Adams; *Prof* Barbara Drennen; *Chmn Visual Arts* Gary Spangler
Estab 1956; Maintains 2 nonprofit art galleries, Gerald & Mary Ellen McFadden Gallery & Fountain Gallery, Malone Univ, Johnson Ctr, 2600 Cleveland Ave NW, Canton, OH 44709; also maintains 2 art libraries, Art-in-a-Case, Malone Univ, Cattell Library, 2600 Cleveland Ave NW, Canton, OH 44709 & Mary Ellen McFadden Art Library, Malone Univ, 2600 Cleveland Ave NW, Canton, OH 44709.; den; D & E; Scholarships; SC 2, LC 2; D 75, maj 50
Ent Req: HS dipl, ent exam
Degrees: BA & BS(Educ) 4 yrs
Courses: Applied Design, Art Appreciation, †Art Education, Art History, Ceramics, †Drawing, Graphic Design, History and Criticism of Art, †Painting, Photography, Printmaking, Sculpture, Teacher Training, Textile Design
Summer School: Professional Develop Coord, Dr. Nancy Varian; Graduate teacher workshops available during summer session: jewelry, bookmaking, photography, watercolors, fibers & ceramics.

CHILLICOTHE

OHIO UNIVERSITY-CHILLICOTHE CAMPUS, Fine Arts & Humanities Division, 571 W Fifth St, Chillicothe, OH 45601-2209; PO Box 629, Chillicothe, OH 45601-0629. Tel 740-774-7200; Fax 740-774-7214; Email mcadamsm@ohio.edu; Web: www.ohiou.edu; *Assoc Prof* Margaret McAdams, MFA; *Assoc Prof* Dennis Deane, MFA
Estab 1946; FT 2 PT 1; pub; D & E; Scholarships
Ent Req: HS dipl, ACT or SAT
Degrees: campus for freshman & sophomores only
Courses: Art Appreciation, Art Education, Art History, Ceramics, Design, Drawing, Film, Graphic Design, History of Art & Architecture, Painting, Photography, Teacher Training

CINCINNATI

AIC COLLEGE OF DESIGN, 1171 E Kemper Rd, Cincinnati, OH 43246-3322. Tel 513-751-1206; Fax 513-751-1209; Email aic@aic-arts.edu; Web: aic-arts.edu; *Instr Foundation 1st yr* Cyndi Mendell; *CEO* Marion Allman; *Instr Computer Graphics 2nd yr* Randy Zimmerman; *Pres* Sean M Mendell; *Gen Educ* Marlene Shmalo; *Interactive Instr, Computer Graphics 2nd yr* Dave Solko; *Instr Marketing/ Branding* Chris Rowland; *Instr Photography* Ken Knowton; *Instr Foundation/ Illustration* Jim Effler; *Instr Design* Michael Keidel; *Instr Video* Eric Hampton; *Instr Design* Matthew Baugham; *Instr Math* Trevor Presgrave; *Instr Student Sucess* Donna Wakefield; *Instr Leadership* Chris Taylor
Estab 1976; Maintains an non-profit art gallery, and an art/architecture library; On-campus shop sells art supplies; 5 FT, 4 PT; priv; D, E; Scholarships; L 30; S; D 30
Ent Req: HS dipl, portfolio, interview
Degrees: Design & Computer Graphics AD 2 yr; Graphic Design 3 yr Bachelor
Tuition: $17,760 yr (3 semesters)
Courses: Advertising Design, †Art History, Commercial Art, Computer Graphics, Design, †Display, †Drawing, †Graphic Arts, Graphic Design, †History of Art & Architecture, Illustration, Interactive Media, †Lettering, †Mixed Media, Packaging, †Photography, Print, †Textile Design, †Video, Web
Summer School: Sean Mendell, President

ANTONELLI COLLEGE, 124 E Seventh St, Cincinnati, OH 45202. Tel 513-241-4338; Fax 513-241-9396; Email andrea.millette@antonellicollege.edu; Web: www.antonellicollege.edu; *Pres* Traci Fletcher-Garrett; *Dean Students* Corey Bjarnson; *Acad Dean* Andrea Millette
Estab 1947; FT 5, PT 12; Private; D & E; D 200
Activities: Studio Courses; Lecture Courses
Ent Req: HS dipl, review of portfolio
Degrees: AAB, AAS
Courses: †Commercial Art, Drafting, †Interior Design, †Photography
Adult Hobby Classes: Courses offered
Summer School: Courses offered

ART ACADEMY OF CINCINNATI, 1212 Jackson St, Cincinnati, OH 45202-7106. Tel 513-562-6262; Fax 513-562-8778; Web: www.artacademy.edu; *Prof* Anthony Batchelor; *Pres* Gregory A Smith, BFA; *Prof* Mark Thomas, MFA; *Instr* Kenn Knowlton, MFA; *Instr* Calvin Kowal, MS; *Instr* Larry May, MFA; *Chmn Acad Studies Dept* Diane Smith, MA; *Instr* Jay Zumeta, MA; *Instr* April Foster, MFA; *Instr* Rebecca Seeman, MFA; *Instr* Paige Williams; *Chmn Foundation Dept* Claire Darley, MFA; *Instr* Gary Gaffney, MFA; *Instr* Kim Krause, MFA
Estab 1887; pvt; D & E; Scholarships; 220
Ent Req: HS grad, SAT
Degrees: degrees cert offered at the Academy, 4-5 yr
Courses: Advertising Design, Aesthetics, Art Education, Art History, Commercial Art, †Communication Design, Conceptual Art, Constructions, Design, Drawing, Graphic Arts, Graphic Design, Illustration, Museum Staff Training, Painting, Photography, Printmaking, Sculpture
Adult Hobby Classes: Enrl 2000. Courses—Design, Drawing, Illustration, Painting, Photography, Sculpture
Children's Classes: Enrl 500; tuition $100 per class. Courses—Drawing, Painting, 3-D Design

MOUNT SAINT JOSEPH UNIVERSITY, (College of Mount Saint Joseph) Department of Art and Design, 5701 Delhi Pike, Cincinnati, OH 45233-1670. Tel 513-244-4420; Fax 513-244-4222; Email john.griffith@msj.edu; Web: www.msj.edu; *Chmn & Dept Chair* John Griffith, MED; *Co Dir Art Ed* Susan Lawrence; *Co Dir Art Ed* Sylvia Dick; *Prof* Daniel Mader, MA; *Assoc Prof* Craig Lloyd; *Assoc Prof* Walter Loyola, MFA; *Asst Prof* Kurt Grannan, MFA; *Assoc* Beth Belknap, MDES
Estab 1920; Maintains non-profit Studio San Giuseppe Art Gallery; pvt; D & E; Scholarships; SC 35, LC 4; 100 maj
Ent Req: HS dipl, nat testing scores
Degrees: BA & BFA 4 yr
Courses: †Art Education, Art History, †Ceramics, †Drawing, †Fabrics Design, †Graphic Design, †Jewelry, Lettering, †Painting, †Photography, †Printmaking, †Sculpture

UNIVERSITY OF CINCINNATI, School of Art, 6431 Aronoff Bldg, Cincinnati, OH 45221; PO Box 210016, Cincinnati, OH 45221-0016. Tel 513-556-2962; Fax 513-556-2887; Email jonathan.riess@uc.edu; Web: www.daap.uc.edu/art/default; *Dir, School of Art & Prof Fine Arts* Mark Harris MA; *Dir MFA Prog, Chair & Prof Fine Arts* Kimberly Burleigh, MFA; *Dir Art Hist Prog & Asst Prof Art Educ* Theresa Leininger-Miller, PhD; *Dir Art Educ Prog & Asst Prof Art Educ* Flavia Bastos, PhD; *Foundations Coordr, Undergrad Adv & Assoc Prof Fine Arts* Denise Burge, MFA; *Assoc Prof Fine Arts* Benjamin Britton, MFA; *Prof Fine Arts* Roy Cartwright, MFA; *Assoc Prof Fine Arts* Tarrence Corbin, MFA; *Assoc Prof Fine Arts* Linda Einfalt, MFA; *Prof Fine Arts* Wayne Enstice, MA; *Prof Fine Arts* Frank Herrmann, MFA; *Asst Prof Art History* Mikiko Hirayama, PhD; *Prof Fine Arts* Don Kelley, MFA; *Assoc Prof Fine Arts* Diane Mankin, PhD; *Asst Prof Fine Arts* Matthew Lynch, MFA; *Prof Art History* Kristi Nelson, PhD; *Asst Prof Art History* Kimberly Paice, PhD; *Asst Prof Art Educ* Nancy Parks, EdD; *Prof Art History* Jonathan Riess, PhD; *Chmn & Assoc Prof Art Educ* Robert Russell, PhD; *Prof Fine Arts* Jane Alden Stevens, MFA; *Prof Fine Arts* John Stewart, MFA; *Prof Fine Arts* Jim Williams, MFA; *Assoc Prof Fine Arts* Charles Woodman, MFA
Estab 1819, dept estab 1946; Maintain nonprofit gallery; library; art supplies available for purchase on-site; Pub; D & E; Scholarships
Ent Req: HS dipl - top 3rd class rank, transfers to Fine Arts, portfolio optional & MFA, portfolio required
Degrees: BA(Art History) 4 yr, 5 yr with teaching certification, BFA(Fine Arts) 4 yr, 5 yr with teaching certification, MA(Art History) 2 yr, MA(Art Educ) 2 yr, MFA 2 yr
Courses: Art Education, Art History, Ceramics, Conceptual Art, Contemporary Art & Theory, Digital Art, Drawing, Electronic Arts, Museum Staff Training, Painting, Photography, Printmaking, Sculpture, Teacher Training, Video
Adult Hobby Classes: Art Education, Art History
Children's Classes: Enrl 25; tuition $60 for 10 wks. Courses—Intro to Life Drawing
Summer School: Dir, Wayne Enstice. Enrl 200. Courses—Art Education, Art History, Fine Arts

XAVIER UNIVERSITY, Dept of Art, 1658 Herald Ave, Room 190A Cincinnati, OH 45207-7311; 3800 Victory Pkwy, Cincinnati, OH 45207-1035. Tel 513-745-3811; Fax 513-745-1098; Email phelps@xavier.edu; Web: www.xavier.edu/art; *Prof* Marsha Karagheusian-Murphy, MFA; *Prof* Suzanne Chouteau, MFA; *Chair & Assoc Prof* Mr Kelly Phelps, MFA; *Assoc Prof* Bruce Erikson, MFA; *Assoc Prof* Jonathan Gibson, MFA
Estab 1831, dept estab 1935; Maintain nonprofit Xavier University Art Gallery, A. B. Cohen Ctr, 1658 Herald Ave., Cincinnati, OH 45207-7311; Xu McDonald Library, 3800 Victory Pkwy, Cincinnati OH 45207; pvt; D & E & weekend degree; Scholarships; SC 17, LC 20; D 403, E 349, non-maj 349, maj 54
Ent Req: HS dipl, SAT or ACT
Degrees: BA 4 yr, BFA 4 yr
Tuition: Undergrad $16,515 per semester
Courses: Advertising Design, Aesthetics, Art Appreciation, Art Education, Art History, Art Therapy, Ceramics, Collage, Commercial Art, Constructions, Design, Display, Drawing, Graphic Arts, Graphic Design, History of Art, †Illustration, Intermedia, Mixed Media, Painting, Photography, Printmaking, Sculpture, Teacher Training, Textile Design, Weaving
Summer School: Krista Warner, Coordr; School Art, Graphic Design, Web Design, Fiber Arts, Drawing

CLEVELAND

CASE WESTERN RESERVE UNIVERSITY, Dept of Art History & Art, 11201 Euclid Ave, Mather House Cleveland, OH 44106-7110. Tel 216-368-4118; Fax 216-368-4681; Email dxt6@case.edu; Web: http://arthistory.case.edu; *Prof* Henry Adams; *Assoc Prof, Dept Chmn* Catherine Scallen; *Asst Prof* Noelle Giuffrida; *Assoc Prof* Elina Gertsman; *Asst Prof* Erin Benay; *Asst Prof* Maggie Popkin; *Asst Prof* Andrea Rager; *Assoc Vis Prof* Jose Teixeira
Estab 1875; pvt; D & E; Scholarships; SC 24, LC 55, GC 73
Exhibitions: Annual faculty exhibition & MA student shows
Activities: Schols offered
Ent Req: HS transcript, SAT or ACT, TOEFL for foreign students
Degrees: BA, BS, MA and PhD
Tuition: $22,078 per sem—undergrad; campus res available; $30,852 total per sum—grad; $15,426/sem
Courses: Architecture, †Art Education, †Art History, Ceramics, Costume Design & Construction, Enameling, †History of Art & Architecture, Jewelry, Medical Illustration, †Museum Staff Training, Painting, Photography, †Teacher Training, Textile Design, Weaving
Summer School: June & July. Courses—Art Education, Art History, Art Studio, Museum Studies

CLEVELAND INSTITUTE OF ART, 11610 Euchlid Ave, Cleveland, OH 44106-1710. Tel 216-421-7000; Fax 216-421-7438; Email admissions@cia.edu; Web: www.cia.edu; *Dept Head Biomedical Art* Thomas Nowacki; *Dept Head Ceramics* Seth Nagelberg; *Dept Head Jewelry & Metals* Matthew Hollern; *Dept Head Illustration* Jeff Harter; *Dept Head Industrial Design* Daniel Cuffaro; *Dept Head Printmaking* Margaret Denk-Leigh; *Dept Head Interior Architecture* Michael Gollini; *Head Drawing* Sarah Kabot; *Dept Head Photog* Nancy McEntee; *Dept Head Glass* Marc Petrouie; *Pres* Grafton Nunes; *Dept Head Admin & Int Dept Head Game Design* Anthony Scalmato; *Dept Head Graphic Design* Larry O'Neal; *Dept Head Sculpture & Expanded Media* Sarah Paul; *Dept Head Sculpture & Expanded Media* Tina Cassara; *Dept Head Painting* Lane Cooper

Estab 1882; Maintain non-profit art galleries & library: Reinberger Gallery & Ann & Norman Roulet Student & Alumni Gallery & Jessica R Gund Memorial Library (same address); pvt; D & E; Scholarships; SC 90, LC 38; D 550, E 250, non-maj 18, maj 550, others 23
Activities: Schols offered
Ent Req: HS dipl SAT, ACT and transcript, portfolio
Degrees: BFA 4 yrs, BS & MEd (educ with Case Western Reserve Univ) 4 yrs
Tuition: Res $49,941 per yr, incl rm & board; non-res $38,487 per yr
Courses: Aesthetics, Art Education, Art History, †Ceramics, †Drawing, †Film, †Glass, †Graphic Arts, Graphic Design, Handicrafts, †Illustration, †Industrial Design, †Interior Design, †Jewelry, †Medical Illustration, †Painting, †Photography, †Printmaking, †Sculpture, †Silversmithing
Adult Hobby Classes: Enrl 266; tuition varies per course. Course—Calligraphy, Ceramic, Crafts, Design, Drawing, Fiber & Surface Design, Graphic Design, Painting, Printmaking, Sculpture, Silversmithing, Watercolor
Children's Classes: Enrl 210; tuition varies per course. Courses—Art Basics, Ceramic Sculpture, Crafts, Design, Drawing, Painting, Portfolio Preparation, Printmaking, Photography
Summer School: Dir, Tom Berger. Courses—Ceramics, Design, Drawing, Jewelry & Metalsmithing, Photography, Printmaking, Sculpture, Watercolor

CLEVELAND STATE UNIVERSITY, Art Dept, 1901 E 13, AB106 Cleveland, OH 44115-2215. Tel 216-687-2040; Fax 216-687-2275; Web: www.csuohio.edu; *Prof* George Mauersberger, MFA; *Assoc Prof* Kathy Curnow, MFA, PhD; *Assoc Prof* Richard Schneider, MA; *Prof & Chair* Jennifer Nsocky O'Grady, MFA; *Prod* Samantha Baskino, PhD; *Assoc Prod* Marian Bleeke, PhD; *Assoc Prod* Mark Slankard, MFA; *Asst Prod* Ross Revock, MFA; *Asst Prof* Sarah Rutherford, MFA
Estab 1972; Maintain non-profit art galleries, The Galleries at CSU, 1307 Euclid Ave, 44115; pub; D & E; Scholarships; SC 26, LC 32
Activities: Schols offered
Ent Req: HS dipl
Degrees: BA 4 yr
Courses: †Art History, Computer Graphics, †Drawing, †Graphic Design, †Painting, †Photography, †Printmaking, †Sculpture
Summer School: Chmn, John Hunter. Tuition & courses same as regular schedule

CUYAHOGA COMMUNITY COLLEGE, Dept of Art, 2900 Community College Ave, Cleveland, OH 44115-3196. Tel 216-987-4248, 4600; Email Gerald-Kramer@tri-C.cc.oh.us; Web: www.tri-c.cc.oh.us; *Coordr Fine Art Prog* Gerald Kramer, MFA; *Assoc Prof* Richard Karberg; *Assoc Prof* Jacqueline Freedman
Estab 1963. College maintains four campuses; PT 6; pub; D & E; Scholarships; SC 15, LC 4; D 1,000, E 1,000, maj 1,000
Ent Req: HS dipl/GED
Degrees: AA, AS
Courses: Art Appreciation, Art Education, Art History, Calligraphy, Ceramics, Graphic Design, Occupational Therapy, Painting, Photography, Printmaking, Sculpture, Stage Design, Teacher Training, Theatre Arts, Video
Summer School: Courses—various

COLUMBUS

CAPITAL UNIVERSITY, Fine Arts Dept, 2199 E Main St, Huber Hall Columbus, OH 43209-3913. Tel 614-236-6201; Fax 614-236-6169; *Chmn* Gary Ross, MA; *Asst Prof* Donald Duncan, MS; *Instr* Gretchen Crawford, MA, ATR, LPC
FT 3
Degrees: BA, BFA
Tuition: $15,260 per yr, grad $508 per cr hr, room & board $4400 per yr
Courses: Advertising Design, Art Education, Art History, Ceramics, Design, Drawing, Jewelry, Painting, Photography, Sculpture, Stained Glass, Theatre Arts, Weaving

COLUMBUS COLLEGE OF ART & DESIGN, Fine Arts Dept, 60 Cleveland Ave, Columbus, OH 43215. Tel 614-222-3273; Email library@ccad.edu; Web: www.ccad.edu/library; *Dean* Julie Taggart
Open academic yr Mon - Thurs 7:30 AM - 9:30 PM, Fri 7:30 AM - 5 PM, Sun 1 PM - 5 PM, cl Sat; summer & between semesters Mon - Fri 8 AM - 5 PM; No admis fee; Estab 1879; 68; pvt; approved for Veterans; D & E; Scholarships
Ent Req: HS grad, art portfolio
Degrees: BFA 4 yr
Courses: Advertising Design, Fashion Arts, Fine Arts, Graphic Arts, Illustration, Industrial Design, Interior Design, Packaging Design, Painting, Retail Advertising, Sculpture
Children's Classes: Saturday sessions 9 - 11:30 AM

OHIO DOMINICAN COLLEGE, Art Dept, 1216 Sunbury Rd, Columbus, OH 43219-2099. Tel 614-253-2741, 251-4580; Fax 614-252-0776; *Dept Chmn* William Vensel
Estab 1911; den; D & E; Scholarships; SC and LC 709 per sem; D 139, E 105, maj 17
Ent Req: HS dipl
Degrees: BA 4 yrs, also secondary educ cert or special training cert, K-12
Courses: Ceramics, Color & Materials, History of Art, Painting, Sculpture, Studio Humanities

OHIO STATE UNIVERSITY, Austin E Knowlton School of Architecture, 275 W Woodruff Ave, Columbus, OH 43210-1138. Tel 614-292-1012; Fax 614-292-7106; Web: knowlton.osu.edu; *Dir* Michael B Cadwell; *Section Head* Robert S Livesay
Estab 1899; FT 43, PT 23; pub; Scholarships; Archit 450, Landscape Archit 170, City & Regional Planning 65
Degrees: BS(Archit), MA, PhD
Tuition: Res—$5000 per yr
Courses: City Planning, Design, History of Architecture, Landscape Architecture
Adult Hobby Classes: Enrl limited; Tuition $170-$469.
Summer School: Dir, Robert Liveson. Enrl 50-70; tuition $170-$469 for 10 wks.

—**College of the Arts**, 146 Hopkins Hall, 128 N Oval Mall Columbus, OH 43210-1318. Tel 614-292-5171; Fax 614-292-5218; Web: www.arts.osu.edu; *Dean Col* Judith Koroscik
Univ estab 1870, col estab 1968; pub; D & E; Scholarships; SC 106, LC 192, GC 208; D 3678, E varies, non-maj 2300, maj 893, grad 150
Ent Req: HS dipl
Degrees: BA, MA, PhD
Tuition: Res—$1200 per qtr; nonres—$3000 per qtr
Courses: Art, Art History, Dance, Music, †Stage Design, †Teacher Training, †Theatre Arts, †Weaving
Adult Hobby Classes: Courses—art experiences in all media for local adults
Children's Classes: Enrl 300 per quarter; fees $36 per quarter; Saturday School. Courses—art experiences in all media for local children
Summer School: Same as regular session
—**Dept of Art**, 146 Hopkins Hall, 128 N Oval Mall Columbus, OH 43210-1318. Tel 614-292-5072; Fax 614-292-1674; Email art_advisor@osu.edu; Web: www.art.osu.edu; *Chmn* Sergio Soave
Maintain nonprofit art gallery, OSU Urban Arts Space So W Town St, Columbus OH; maintain art/architecture library, maintains OSU Fine Arts Library, Wexner Center; on campus shop where art supplies may be purchased; FT 21, PT 34; Pub; D & E; Scholarships; SC 56, LC 6, GC 30
Degrees: BA, BFA, MFA
Tuition: Res—undergrad $8667 per yr, grad $9592 per year; nonres—undergrad $20,562 per year, grad $22,950 per year
Courses: Art & Technology, †Ceramics, †Drawing, †Glass, †Painting, †Photography, †Printmaking, †Sculpture
Adult Hobby Classes: Offered through CAP (Creative Art Program) & CED (Continuing Education)
—**Dept of Art Education**, 258 Hopkins Hall, 128 N Oval Mall Columbus, OH 43210-1318. Tel 614-292-7183; Fax 614-688-4483; Web: www.art.ohio-state.edu/ArtEducation; *Chmn Dept* James Hutchens PhD; *Prof* Robert Arnold PhD; *Prof* Terry Barrett PhD; *Prof* Judith Koroscik PhD; *Prof* Michael Parsons PhD; *Prof* Margaret Wyszomirski PhD; *Prof Emeritus* Arthur Efland EdD; *Prof Emeritus* Kenneth Marantz EdD; *Assoc Prof* Don Krug PhD; *Assoc Prof* Sydney Walker PhD; *Prof* Patricia Stuhr PhD; *Assoc Prof* Vesta Daniel EdD; *Asst Prof* Christine Ballangee-Morris PhD; *Asst Prof* Georgianna Short PhD
Estab 1907; pub; D & E; Scholarships; Fellowships; SC 2, LC 42, GC 48, other 14; maj 65, grad 110
Ent Req: HS dipl
Degrees: BAE, MA, PhD
Tuition: Res—$1500 per qtr; nonres—$4300 per qtr
Courses: Art Appreciation, †Art Education, †Art History, †Arts Administration, †Arts Policy, Computer Graphics, Ethnic Art, History of Art, †Industrial Design, †Teacher Training
Summer School: Chmn Dept, James Hutchens, PhD. Courses—Art Educ
—**Dept of Industrial Interior & Visual Communication Design**, 280 Hopkins Hall, 128 N Oval Mall Columbus, OH 43210. Tel 614-292-6746; Fax 614-292-0217; Email design@osu.edu; Web: www.arts.ohio-state.edu/design; *Chmn* Wayne E Carlson
FT 11, PT 5; Public; Day & Evening classes; Scholarships; SC 35, LC 10, GC 10
Degrees: BS, MA, MFA
Tuition: Res—$1461 per quarter; nonres—$4244 per quarter
Courses: 3-D Computer Modeling, †Architecture, †Design, †Design Development, †Design Education, †Design Management, †Graphic Design, Manufacturing Materials & Processes, Research Problems & Design, Visual Thinking Design Methodology
Summer School: Advanced Typography
—**Dept of the History of Art**, 215 Pomerene Hall, 1760 Neil Ave Columbus, OH 43210-1221. Tel 614-292-7481; Fax 614-292-4401; Web: www.history-of-art.ohio-state.edu
Estab 1871, dept estab 1968; pub; D & E; Scholarships; Fellowships; LC 56, GC 29; D 854, non-maj 700, maj 71, grad 73
Ent Req: HS dipl
Degrees: BA, MA 2 yrs, PhD 4-6 yrs
Courses: †Art History, History of Art & Archeology
Summer School: Enrl 250; tuition same as regular session for term of ten wks beginning June. Courses—vary each yr

CUYAHOGA FALLS

CUYAHOGA VALLEY ART CENTER, 2131 Front St, Cuyahoga Falls, OH 44221-3219. Tel 330-928-8092; Fax 330-928-8092; Email cvac@cvartcenter.org; Web: www.cvartcenter.org; *Director* Danielle Dieterich; *Instr* Dino Massaroni; *Instr* Jack Liberman; *Instr* Beth Lindenberger; *Instr* Maryann Mosyjowski; *Instr* Tom Baldwin; *Instr* Deanna Clucas; *Instr* Claire Marks; *Pres* Raven Burdette; *Instr* Jack Mulhollen; *Instr* Sally Heston; *Instr* Susan Mencini; *Instr* Linda Hutchinson; *Instr* Elinore Korow
Estab 1934; maintains a nonprofit art gallery and art library, Cuyahoga Valley Art Center, 2131 Front St, Cuyahoga Falls, OH, 44221; Nonprofit; D & E; SC 23; 300 D&E
Exhibitions: Regional Painting; Whiskey Painters of America; Summer Painting Show; Members Show; Cuyahoga Falls High School Showing; Small Painting Show; Student Show; Akron Soc Artists; Abstract Show; Akron Camera Club
Ent Req: none, interest in art
Degrees: none
Courses: Ceramics, Collage, †Design, Drawing, †Mixed Media, Painting, †Pottery, †Printmaking, Special Workshops, †Textile Design, †Weaving
Adult Hobby Classes: 200; tuition $140-169 for members, $165-198 for nonmembers per 10 wks. Courses—Drawing, Painting, Pottery
Children's Classes: 100; tuition $50 for members, $60 for nonmembers per 10 wks

STUDIOS OF JACK RICHARD CREATIVE SCHOOL OF DESIGN, Professional School of Painting & Design, 2250 Front St, Cuyahoga Falls, OH 44221-2510. Tel 330-929-1575; Fax 330-929-2285; Email jackprichard@aol.com; *Dir* Jack Richard
Estab 1960; pvt; D & E; Scholarships; SC 20, LC 10; D 50-60, E 50-60

Degrees: cert of accomplishment
Courses: Aesthetics, †Art Appreciation, Art Education, Color, Design, Drawing, Illustration, Mural, Occupational Therapy, Painting, Photography, †Restoration & Conservation, Sculpture
Adult Hobby Classes: Enrl 200-300 per session; tuition $11 per class. Courses—Design, Drawing, Painting
Children's Classes: Tues morning & evening
Summer School: Dir, Jane Williams. Enrl 90; tuition $10 - $12 per class Courses—Design, Drawing, Painting

DAYTON

SINCLAIR COMMUNITY COLLEGE, Division of Fine & Performing Arts, 444 W Third St, Dayton, OH 45402. Tel 937-512-5313; Fax 937-512-2130; Email kelly.joslin@sinclair.edu; Web: www.sinclair.edu; *Chair Arts & Asst Prof* Kelly Joslin; *Assoc Prof* Kevin Harris; *Prof Reach Coordr* Tess Little; *Prof* George Hageman; *Prof* Mark Echtner; *Prof* Richard Jurus; *Instr* Nancy Mitchell; *Asst Prof* Robert Coates; *Instr* Bridgett Bogle; *Asst Prof* Kay Koeninger
Estab 1973; Maintain nonprofit art gallery on-campus; Pub; D & E, wkend & web; Scholarships; SC 80, LC 8; 1,500 per qtr
Exhibitions: Rotating three week exhibitions of nationally known artists in four different galleries
Ent Req: HS dipl, ent exam
Degrees: AA 2 yrs
Courses: Advertising Design, †Art Appreciation, †Art History, Ceramics, Commercial Art, Digital Photography, Drawing, Graphic Arts, Painting, Photography, Sculpture, Theatre Arts
Adult Hobby Classes: Drawing for seniors - free to those over 60
Summer School: Chair of Art, Kelly Joslin. Enrl 1,200. Courses—Art Appreciation, Ceramics, Computer Photography, Drawing, Printing, Studio Art

UNIVERSITY OF DAYTON, Visual Arts Dept, 300 College Park, Dayton, OH 45469-1690. Tel 937-229-3237; Fax 937-229-3943; Web: www.as.dayton.edu/visualarts; *Prof, Chmn Dept* Fred Niles, MFA; *Assoc Prof* Mary Zahner, PhD, MFA; *Assoc Prof* Tim Wilbers, MFA; *Assoc Prof* Peter Gooch, MFA; *Assoc Prof* Roger Crum, PhD, MFA; *Assoc Prof* Gary Marcinowski, MFA; *Asst Prof* Jayne Whitaker, MFA; *Asst Prof* Lari Gibbons, MFA; *Asst Prof* Joel Whitaker, MFA; *Prof* Sean Wilkinson, MFA; *Asst Prof* Judith Huacuja-Person; *Asst Prof* Matt Rappaport
Estab 1850; pvt; D & E; Scholarships; SC 15, LC 8; D 275, E 75-100, non-maj 100, maj 250
Ent Req: HS dipl
Degrees: BA, BFA
Courses: Animation, †Art Education, †Art History, Ceramics, Computer Modeling, Digital Imaging, Drawing, Illustration, Mixed Media, †Painting, †Photography, †Printmaking, †Sculpture, †Visual Communication Design
Summer School: Tuition $456 per cr hr

WRIGHT STATE UNIVERSITY, Dept of Art & Art History, 3640 Colonel Glenn Hwy, Dayton, OH 45435-0002. Tel 937-775-2896; Fax 937-775-3049; Email glen.cebulash@wright.edu; Web: www.wright.edu/cola/Dept/art; *Prof* Kimberly Vito, MFA; *Chair & Prof* Glen Cebulash, MFA; *Assoc Prof* Penny Park, MFA; *Assoc Prof* Benjamin Montague, MFA; *Assoc Prof* Stefan Chinov, MFA; *Assoc Prof* Tracy Longley-Cook, MFA; *Assoc Prof* Karla Huebner, PhD; *Assoc Prof* Danielle Rante, MFA; *Asst Prof* Caroline Hillard, PhD; *Assoc Prof* Jeremy Long, MFA; *Asst Prof* John Dickinson, MFA
Estab 1964, dept estab 1965; Maintain nonprofit art gallery; University Art Galleries, 3640 Col Glenn Hwy, Dayton, OH 45435; Pub; D & E; Scholarships; SC 67, LC 16, GC 8; D 516, E 43, non-maj 80, maj 150
Ent Req: HS dipl
Degrees: BA(Studio Art), BA(Art History), BFA 4 yr
Tuition: Res—undergrad $4,271 per semester; nonres—undergrad $8,273 per semester
Courses: Art Education, Art History, Drawing, Painting, Photography, Printmaking, Sculpture
Summer School: Chair & Prof, Glen Cebulash. Enrl 65; tuition res $219 per cr hr, nonres $425 per cr hr. Courses—Drawing, Painting, Photography, Printmaking, Sculpture

DELAWARE

OHIO WESLEYAN UNIVERSITY, Fine Arts Dept, 61 S Sandusky St, Delaware, OH 43015. Tel 740-368-3600; Fax 740-368-3299; Web: www.owu.edu; *Prof* Carol Neuman de Vegvar, PhD; *Chmn* James Krehbiel, MFA; *Prof* Cynthia Cetlin, MFA; *Asst Prof* Jonathan Quick, MFA; *Asst Prof* Frank Hobbs, MFA; *Asst Prof* Kristina Bogdanov, MFA; *Asst Prof* Jeffrey Nilan, MFA
Estab 1842, dept estab 1864; Maintains nonprofit Richard M Ross Art Museum, 60 S Sandusky St, Delaware, OH 43015; art supplies sold at on campus store; pvt; D & E; Scholarships; Fellowships; D 1950, non-maj 1850, maj 100
Ent Req: HS dipl, SAT or ACT
Degrees: BA and BFA 4 yrs
Courses: Aesthetics, Art Education, Art History, Ceramics, Computer Imaging, Drawing, Graphic Design, Jewelry, Painting, Photography, Printmaking, Sculpture, Teacher Training
Summer School: Dean, Charles Stinemetz. Tuition $2,160 per unit for 6 wks. Courses—Varies

ELYRIA

LORAIN COUNTY COMMUNITY COLLEGE, Art Dept, 1005 N Abbe Rd, Elyria, OH 44035. Tel 440-366-4032; Fax 440-365-6519; Web: www.lorainccc.edu; *Chmn* Dr Robert Beckstrom
Estab 1966; FT 2 PT varies by sem
Ent Req: HS dipl or equiv
Degrees: AA
Tuition: County res—$72.50 per cr hr; out-of-county res—$87.50 per cr hr; out-of-state res—$178 per cr hr
Courses: Art Appreciation, Ceramics, Design, Drawing, Painting, Photography, Printmaking, Sculpture, Textile Design

FINDLAY

UNIVERSITY OF FINDLAY, Art Program, 1000 N Main St, Findlay, OH 45840-3653. Tel 419-434-4445; Fax 419-434-4531; Web: www.findlay.edu; *Assoc Prof* Valerie Escobedo; *Assoc Prof* Jack (Ed) Corle; *Assoc Prof* Diane Kontar PhD
Estab 1882; Maintain a nonprofit art gallery; Dudley & Mary Marks Lea Gallery, The Univ of Findlay; FT 4, PT 4; pvt; D & E; Scholarships; SC 21, LC 8; maj 60
Ent Req: HS dipl
Degrees: AA 2yr, BA & BS 4 yr
Courses: Advertising Design, Aesthetics, Art Education, Art History, Ceramics, Collage, Drawing, Graphic Design, Painting, Photography, Printmaking, Sculpture, Teacher Training
Adult Hobby Classes: Enrl 10-20. Courses—Ceramics
Children's Classes: Courses—Ceramics, Drawing

GAMBIER

KENYON COLLEGE, Art Dept, 106 College Dr, Horvitz Hall Gambier, OH 43022. Tel 740-427-5459; Fax 740-427-5230; Web: www.kenyon.edu; *Prof* Eugene J Dwyer, PhD, MFA; *Prof* Gregory P Spaid, MFA; *Prof* Claudia Esslinger, MFA; *Prof* Melissa Dabakis, MFA; *Assoc Prof* K Read Baldwin, MFA; *Prof* Sarah Blick; *Prof* Marcella M Hackbardt, MFA; *Prof* Karen F Snouffer, MFA; *Prof* Kristen Van Ausdall; *Asst Prof* Craig Hill, MFA; *Asst Prof* Austin Porter; *Vis Asst Prof* Emily Zeller, MFA; *Adjunct Asst Prof* Yan Zhou; *Instr* Ellen Sheffield; *Vis Instr* Monica Fullerton; *Asst Prof* Sandra Lee, MFA; *Vis Asst Prof* Jill Greenwood
Estab 1824, dept estab 1965; Maintain nonprofit art gallery; Olin Art Gallery, Kenyon College, Gambier, OH 43022; pvt; D; Scholarships; SC 15, LC 10; D 450, non-maj 250, maj 60
Ent Req: HS dipl
Degrees: BA
Courses: †Art History, †Studio Art

GRANVILLE

DENISON UNIVERSITY, Studio Art Program, Bryant Arts Center, 201 W College St (Rm 401) Granville, OH 43023. Tel 740-587-6596; Fax 614-587-6417; Email coudend@denison.edu; Web: www.denison.edu; *Assoc Prof* Michaela Vivero, MFA; *Assoc Prof* Ronald Abram, MFA; *Assoc Prof & Chair* Carrie Olson, MFA; *Asst Prof* Sheila Wilson, MFA; *Asst Prof* Tommy White, MFA
Estab 1831, dept estab 1931; Maintains nonprofit gallery: Denison Mus, Granville, OH 43023; maintains art/ architecture libr; pvt; D; Scholarships; SC 24, LC 16; D 800, maj 65, double maj 35
Ent Req: HS
Degrees: BA, BFA, BS 4 yr
Courses: †Art History, †Ceramics, †Drawing, Mixed Media, †Painting, †Photography, †Printmaking, †Sculpture

HAMILTON

FITTON CENTER FOR CREATIVE ARTS, 101 S Monument Ave, Hamilton, OH 45041-2833. Tel 513-863-8873; Fax 513-863-8865; Email rjatfitton@aol.com; Web: www.fittoncenter.org; *Arts in Common Dir* Henry Cepluch; *Exhib* Cathy Mayhugh; *Exec Dir* Rick H Jones
Estab 1992; pub; D & E; Scholarships; SC 50, LC 2; D & E 400
Ent Req: varies by program
Degrees: MFA
Courses: Aesthetics, Art Appreciation, Art Education, Art History, Drawing, Fashion Arts, Film, Graphic Arts, Graphic Design, Handicrafts, Illustration, Industrial Design, Intermedia, Painting, Photography

MIAMI UNIVERSITY, Dept Fine Arts, 1601 Peck Blvd, Hamilton, OH 45011. Tel 513-529-2900, 785-3000; Fax 513-785-3145; Web: www.ham.muohio.edu; *Prof* Edward Montgomery; *Art Coordr* Phil Joseph
Date estab 1809; Pub; D; Scholarships
Ent Req: HS dipl
Degrees: BA
Tuition: Full-time $1524.45 per sem; part-time $125.85 per cr hr
Courses: Advertising Design, Art Education, Art History, Drawing, Painting, Printmaking
Summer School: Courses—Drawing, Painting

HIRAM

HIRAM COLLEGE, Art Dept, PO Box 67, Hiram, OH 44234-0067. Tel 330-569-5304; Fax 330-569-5309; Email SaffordLB@Hiram.edu; Web: www.hiram.edu; *Assoc Prof, Dept Chair* Chris Ryan; *Prof* George Schroeder Emeriti; *Prof* Linda Bourassa; *Prof* Lisa Stafford
Estab 1850; Maintain nonprofit art gallery; Frohring Art Gallery; FT 3, PT 2; pvt; E & Weekend; Scholarships; SC 21, LC 19; D 400
Ent Req: HS dipl
Degrees: AB 4 yr, MAIS (master arts in interdisciplinary studies)
Tuition: $19,650 per acad yr
Courses: Aesthetics, Art Education, †Art History, Ceramics, Drawing, Painting, Photography, Printmaking, Sculpture, †Studio Art, Teacher Training
Summer School: Enrl 15-20 per course; 6-7 wks. Courses—Art History, Ceramics, Film Studies, Photography

HURON

BOWLING GREEN STATE UNIVERSITY, FIRELANDS COLLEGE, Humanities Dept, One University Dr, Huron, OH 44839. Tel 419-433-5560; Fax 419-433-9696; Web: www.firelands.bgsu.edu/~dsapp; *Prof Art* David Sapp
Estab 1907, col estab 1966; Maintain nonprofit art gallery, Little Gallery; BGSU Firelands, One University Dr, Huron, OH 44839. Art supplies sold at on-campus store; FT 1, PT 3; pub; D & E Sat; Scholarships; SC 12, LC 3; D 2000
Ent Req: HS dipl, SAT
Degrees: AA 2 yr
Courses: Art Appreciation, Art Education, Art History, Drawing, Graphic Design, Mixed Media, Painting, Printmaking, Studio Foundations
Summer School: Term of 5 wks beginning July. Courses—Studio Courses

KENT

KENT STATE UNIVERSITY, School of Art, 400 Janik Dr, Kent, OH 44242; PO Box 5190, Kent, OH 44242-0001. Tel 330-672-2192; Fax 330-672-4729; Email chavice@kent.edu; Web: www.kent.edu/; *Dir* Christine Havice; *Dir Galleries* Anderson Turner
Estab 1910; Maintain nonprofit art gallery: Downtown Gallery, 141 E Main St, Kent; School Gallery, 201 Art Bldg, 400 Janik Dr, Kent. Scholarships to undergrads; Fellowships & Teaching Assistantships to grads for 1 yr given annually & semi-annually; FT 43, PT 6; pub; D & E; Scholarships; Grants; SC 105, LC 35, GC 50; non-maj 600, maj 600, grad 100
Ent Req: HS dipl, ACT
Degrees: BFA, BA 4 yrs, MA 1 - 2 yrs, MFA 2 - 3 yrs
Tuition: Res—undergrad $4673 per sem; grad $4971 per sem; nonres—undergrad $8653 per sem, grad $8729 per sem, campus res—room starts at $2720, board starts at $1555 per sem
Courses: Advertising Design, Art Appreciation, †Art Education, †Art History, Calligraphy, †Ceramics, Collage, Commercial Art, Conceptual Art, Constructions, Design, Display, †Drawing, Goldsmithing, Graphic Arts, †Graphic Design, †History of Art & Architecture, Hot Glass, †Illustration, Intermedia, †Jewelry, Lettering, Mixed Media, Museum Staff Training, †Painting, †Printmaking, †Sculpture, Silversmithing, Teacher Training, †Textile Design, †Weaving
Adult Hobby Classes: Tuition free to adults 50 yr & retired or 60 yr old (non-credit basis)
Children's Classes: Enrl 100; tuition $15 per 10 wk session, two 5 wk sessions, fall & spring
Summer School: Dir, Christine Havice, Enrl 500; tuition $425 per cr hr, 8 wk term. Courses—Art Education, Art History, Blossom Art Crafts

KIRTLAND

LAKELAND COMMUNITY COLLEGE, Fine Arts Department, 7700 Clock Tower Dr, Kirtland, OH 44094. Tel 440-525-7459 (Dept), 525-7000 (main); Web: www.lakelandcc.edu; *Prof* Teresa Hess, MFA; *Assoc Prof* Christopher Berry, MFA; *Instr* Derek O'Brien, MFA
Estab 1967, dept estab 1968; Maintains a nonprofit art gallery, 7700 Clocktower Dr, Kirtland, OH, 44094; FT 3 PT varies; pub; D & E, weekends; Scholarships; D & E 350
Ent Req: HS dipl
Degrees: AA with concentration in Art 2 yrs, AA Technology degree in Graphic Design
Tuition: In-county res—$89.90 per cr hr; out-of-county res—$110.15 per cr hr; out-of-state—$235 per cr hr
Courses: Art Appreciation, Art History, Ceramics, Drawing, Jewelry, Painting, Sculpture
Summer School: Courses—Ceramics, Drawing, Jewelry, Painting, Sculpture

MARIETTA

MARIETTA COLLEGE, Art Dept, 215 Fifth St Marietta, OH 45750. Tel 740-376-4643; Fax 740-376-4529; Email garoza@marietta.edu; Web: www.mcnet.marietta.edu; *Prof* Ron Wright; *Chmn* Valdis Garoza
Estab 1835; 4; pvt; Grants; Loans; SC 20, LC 7; maj 75, total col 1600
Degrees: BA(Studio, Art History, Art Education & Graphic Design), BFA
Courses: Advertising Design, Art Appreciation, Art Education, Art History, Calligraphy, Carving in Wood & Stone, Ceramics, Commercial Art, Computer Graphic, Design, Design, Drawing, Jewelry Making, Life Drawing, Lithography & Silkscreen, Modeling & Casting, Painting, Printmaking, Stained Glass

MOUNT VERNON

MOUNT VERNON NAZARENE UNIVERSITY, Art Dept, 800 Martinsburg Rd, Mount Vernon, OH 43050-9500. Tel 740-397-9000 x 3040; Web: www.mvnc.edu; *Instr* John Donnelly; *Chmn* Jim Hendrickx
Estab 1968, dept estab 1970; Maintain a nonprofit gallery & library; on-campus bookstore sells art supplies; Den; D & E; Scholarships; SC 20, LC 5; D 1,052, non-maj 1,032, maj 20
Ent Req: HS dipl & grad of upper 2/3, ACT
Degrees: BA; Sr project required for graduation
Courses: Aesthetics, Art Education, Art History, Art in the Western World, Ceramics, Design Fundamentals, Drafting, Drawing, Graphic Communication, Graphic Design, Painting, Photography, Printmaking, Sculpture, Selected Topics, Senior Project

NEW CONCORD

MUSKINGUM COLLEGE, Art Department, 163 Stormont St, Johnson Hall New Concord, OH 43762-1118. Tel 740-826-8211, 826-8310; Web: www.muskingum.edu/; *Asst Prof* Ken McCollum; *Chmn* Yan John Sun; *Instr* Rhoda Van Tassel; *Instr* Amy Kennedy
Estab 1837; FT 3; pvt; D; Scholarships; SC 13, LC 6; D 300, maj 15
Ent Req: HS dipl, ent exam, specific school standards
Degrees: BA and BS 4 yr
Courses: †Art Education, Art History, Ceramics, Design, Drawing, Graphic Arts, Painting, Photography, Sculpture, Teacher Training
Adult Hobby Classes: Enrl 60. Courses—Art Educ
Children's Classes: Enrl 10. Courses—Ceramics

OBERLIN

OBERLIN COLLEGE, Dept of Art, 101 N Professor St, Oberlin, OH 44074-1056. Tel 440-775-8411; Fax 440-775-6905; Email college.admissions@oberlin.edu; Web: www.oberlin.edu; *Chmn* Daniel Goulding, PhD; *Prof* John Pearson, MFA; *Assoc Prof* Susan Kane, PhD, MFA; *Assoc Prof* Patricia Mathews, PhD, MFA; *Assoc Prof* Sarah Schuster, MFA; *Assoc Prof* Johnny Coleman, MFA; *Assoc Prof* Nanette Yannuzzi Macias, MFA; *Asst Prof* Paul Yanto; *Asst Prof* Pipo Nguyen-Duy; *Asst Prof* Doug Sanderson; *Asst Prof* Andy Shaken; *Asst Prof* Will Wilson; *Asst Prof* Rian Brown-Urso; *Asst Prof* Julie Davis; *Asst Prof* Erik Inglis; *Dean Admissions* Debra Chermonte
Estab 1833, dept estab 1917; pvt; D & E; Scholarships; SC 28, LC 38, advanced undergrad & grad courses 13; D approx 1200, non-maj 500, maj 100, grad 5
Ent Req: HS dipl, SAT
Degrees: BA 4 yr
Courses: Art History, Drawing, History of Art & Architecture, Interactive Media, Painting, Photography, Sculpture, Silkscreening

OXFORD

MIAMI UNIVERSITY, Art Dept, 501 E High St, New Art Bldg Oxford, OH 45056-1846. Tel 513-529-2900; Fax 513-529-1532; Web: www.miami.muohio.edu; *Dean School Fine Arts* Pamela Fox; *Chmn* Jerry W Morris
Estab 1809, dept estab 1929; pub; D & E; Scholarships; SC 49, LC 35, GC 20; D 2309, non-maj 1890, maj 419, grad 32
Ent Req: HS dipl, class rank, ACT or SAT
Degrees: BFA & BS(Art) 4 yrs, MFA 2 yrs, MA(Art or Art Educ)
Courses: †Advertising Design, Architecture, †Art Education, †Art History, Calligraphy, †Ceramics, Collage, Commercial Art, Display, †Drawing, Graphic Arts, †Graphic Design, †History of Art & Architecture, Illustration, †Jewelry, Lettering, Museum Staff Training, †Painting, †Photography, †Printmaking, †Sculpture, †Silversmithing, Stitchery, †Teacher Training, Weaving
Children's Classes: Enrl 70; tuition $30 per sem. Courses—General Art
Summer School: Dir, Geoff Eacker. Courses—Crafts

PAINESVILLE

LAKE ERIE COLLEGE, Fine Arts Dept, 391 W Washington St, Painesville, OH 44077-3389. Tel 440-375-7455; Fax 440-375-7454; Web: www.lakeerie.edu; *Prof* Paul Gothard; *Assoc Prof Theater* John Huston; *Asst Prof Visual Art* Nancy Prudic; *Asst Prof Dance* Lisa DeCat
Estab 1856; maintains nonprofit gallery, BK Smith Gallery; FT 4, PT 2; pvt; D & E; SC 20, LC 7; 800 total
Ent Req: col board exam
Degrees: BA & BFA 4 yrs
Courses: Art Education, †Art History, †Ceramics, Design, Drawing, Introductory Art, †Painting, †Photography, †Printmaking, Sculpture
Summer School: Courses vary

SAINT CLAIRSVILLE

OHIO UNIVERSITY-EASTERN CAMPUS, Dept Comparative Arts, 45425 National Rd, Saint Clairsville, OH 43950. Tel 740-695-1720; Web: www.eastern.ohiou.edu; *Prof* David Miles
Pub; D & E; Scholarships
Degrees: BA & BS 4 yrs
Tuition: Res—undergrad $92 pr cr hr, grad $100 per cr hr; nonres—undergrad $102 per cr hr, grad $110 per cr hr
Courses: Art Appreciation, Art Education, Design, Drawing, Photography

SPRINGFIELD

SPRINGFIELD MUSEUM OF ART, 107 Cliff Park Rd, Springfield, OH 45501-2501. Tel 937-325-4673; Fax 937-325-4674; Email afortescue@springfieldart.net; Email ktrout@springfield.net; Web: www.springfieldart.museum; *Dir* Ann Fortescue; *Admin Asst* Katherine Trout; *Cur* Charlotte Gordon; *Bookkeeper* Julie Griffin, CPA
Estab 1951; Maintain nonprofit art gallery & library (same address); PT 15; pvt (art school will be a co-op with Clark State Community Col & mus; D & E; Scholarships; D 600
Tuition: $15-$150 for 9 wks sessions
Courses: Ceramics, Drawing, Glass Blowing, Jewelry, Painting, Photography, Sculpture
Adult Hobby Classes: Enrl 287; tuition varies
Children's Classes: Enrl 286; tuition $39 per qtr. Courses—vary

WITTENBERG UNIVERSITY, Art Dept, N Wittenberg Ave Koch Hall, Springfield, OH 45501; PO Box 720, Springfield, OH 45501-0720. Tel 937-327-6231; Fax 937-327-6349; Email jmann@wittenberg.edu; Web: www.wittenberg.edu; *Prof* Jack Mann, MFA; *Asst Prof* Kevin Salzman, MFA; *Assoc Prof* Ed Charney, MFA; *Asst Prof* Scott Douley, MFA; *Instr* Amy Morris, MA
Estab 1842; maintains nonprofit gallery, Ann Miller Gallery in Koch Hall Art Dept; pvt den; D & E; Scholarships; SC 30, LC 17; D 350, non-maj 270, maj 80
Ent Req: HS dipl, class rank, transcript, SAT or ACT test results, recommendations & if possible, a personal interview
Degrees: BA & BFA 4 yr
Courses: †Art Education, †Art History, †Ceramics, †Computer Imaging, Drawing, †Illustration, Jewelry, †Painting, Photography, †Printmaking, †Sculpture, †Teacher Training
Summer School: Provost, William Wiebenga. Courses—Art in the Elementary School, Fundamentals of Art, Painting

SYLVANIA

LOURDES UNIVERSITY, Art Dept, 6832 Convent Blvd, Sylvania, OH 43560-4805. Tel 419-885-3211; Fax 419-882-3987; Email tmatteson@lourdes.edu; Web: www.lourdes.edu; *Chmn Fine Arts & Assoc Prof* Erin Palmer Szavuly; *Instr* Charlene Taylor, MA; *Instr* Tamara Monk-Hilty, MFA; *Instr* Thomas Hilty, MFA; *Instr* Peggy Halbig Martinez, M.Ed; *Instr* Julia Chytil Hayes, MA; *Instr* Lynn Brinkman, MA; *Instr* Patrick Dubrevil, MFA; *Instr* Sr Sharon Havelak, OSF, MA
Estab 1958; pvt, den; D & E; Scholarships; SC 12, LC 9; D 70, E 30, non-maj 60, maj 35
Ent Req: HS dipl, ACT or SAT
Degrees: AA, BA, BIS, MA
Courses: Aesthetics, Art Appreciation, Art Education, Art History, Art Therapy, Calligraphy, Ceramics, Design, Drawing, Fiber Arts, Painting, †Photography, Printmaking, Sculpture, Weaving
Children's Classes: Summer art prog for children
Summer School: Dir, Todd Matteson. Enrl 30; tuition $274 per cr for 10 wk & 5 wk term. Courses—Art History, Studio Courses

TIFFIN

HEIDELBERG COLLEGE, Dept of Art, 310 E Market St, Tiffin, OH 44883-2462. Tel 419-448-2186; *Chmn* Jim Hagemeyer
Estab 1850; FT 2, PT 3; pvt; D; Scholarships; SC 22, LC 9; 200, maj 24
Ent Req: HS dipl, each applicant's qualifications are considered individually
Degrees: AB 4 yrs, independent study, honors work available
Courses: Advertising Design, Aesthetics, Art Education, Ceramics, Chip Carving, Commercial Art, Copper Enameling, Display, Drawing, Graphic Arts, Graphic Design, History of Art & Architecture, Illustration, Jewelry, Lettering, Metal Tooling, Mosaic, Museum Staff Training, Painting, Sculpture, Stage Design, Teacher Training, Textile Design
Summer School: Term of 6 wks beginning June. Courses—Materials & Methods in Teaching, Practical Arts

TOLEDO

UNIVERSITY OF TOLEDO, Dept of Art, 620 Grove Pl, University Art Bldg Toledo, OH 43620-1515. Tel 419-530-8300; Fax 419-530-8337; Web: www.ut.edu; *Chmn* David Guip, PhD; *Prof* Diana Attie, MS; *Prof* Linda Ames-Bell, MFA; *Prof* Peter Elloian, MFA; *Assoc Prof* Carolyn Autry, MFA; *Assoc Prof* Marc Gerstein, PhD, MFA; *Assoc Prof* Rex Fogt, MFA
Estab 1919; FT 13, PT 12; D & E; Scholarships
Ent Req: HS dipl
Degrees: BA, BFA, BEd 4 yr; MEd (Art Educ) 2 yr
Courses: Advertising Design, Art Education, †Art History, †Ceramics, Design, †Drawing, †Metalsmithing, †Painting, †Photography, †Printmaking, †Sculpture
Summer School: Courses offered from those above

UNIVERSITY HEIGHTS

JOHN CARROLL UNIVERSITY, Dept of Art History & Humanities, 20700 N Park Blvd, University Heights, OH 44118-4520. Tel 216-397-4388 (art dept); 397-1886 (main); Web: www.jcu.edu; *Chmn* Dr Gerald Guest
Estab 1886, dept estab 1965; pvt; D & E; SC 3, LC 30; D 400, non-maj 350, maj-humanities 30, art hist 14
Ent Req: HS dipl, SAT
Degrees: BA Art History 4 yrs, BA Humanities 4 yrs
Courses: Art History, Drawing, Film, History of Art & Architecture, Modern History

WESTERVILLE

OTTERBEIN UNIVERSITY, Art Dept, 1 S. Grove St, Westerville, OH 43081. Tel 614-823-1258, 823-1792 (General); Fax 614-823-1782; Web: wwww.otterbein.edu
1847; Maintains nonprofit art galleries, Miller Gallery, 33 Collegeview Rd, Westerville OH 43081; Frank Mus of Art, 39 S Vine St, Westerville; Fisher Gallery, 27 S Grove St, Westerville; Pvt; D & E; Scholarships; SC 29, LC 9, GC 1; maj 100
Activities: Schols offered
Ent Req: HS dipl
Degrees: BA 4 yrs, BFA
Courses: Art Education, Art History, Ceramics, Computer Art, Drawing, Graphic Design, Painting, Photography, Printmaking, Sculpture

WILBERFORCE

CENTRAL STATE UNIVERSITY, Dept of Art, P.O. Box 1004, Wilberforce, OH 45384-1004. Tel 513-376-6011; Email info@csu.sec.edu; Web: www.centralstate.edu/; *Assoc Prof* Abner Cope; *Assoc Prof* Larry Porter; *Assoc Prof* Ronald Claxton; *Asst Prof* Dwayne Daniel
Estab 1856; FT 6; D; SC 20, LC 8; D 175, maj 50, others 130
Ent Req: HS dipl
Degrees: BA and BS 4 yr
Courses: Advertising Design, Art Education, Art History, Ceramics, Drawing, Graphic Arts, Lettering, Painting, Sculpture, Studio, Teacher Training

WILBERFORCE UNIVERSITY, Art Dept, P.O. Box 1001, Wilberforce, OH 45384. Tel 937-376-2911; *Adv* James Padgett, MFA
Estab 1856, dept estab 1973; pvt; D; Scholarships; SC 22, LC 5
Ent Req: HS dipl
Degrees: BA, BS & BA(Educ) 4 yrs
Courses: Commercial Art, Fine Arts, Printmaking, Sculpture, Teacher Training
Summer School: Courses offered

WILLOUGHBY

WILLOUGHBY SCHOOL OF FINE ARTS, Visual Arts Dept, 38660 Mentor Ave, Willoughby, OH 44094-7797. Tel 440-951-7500; Fax 440-975-4592; Email info@fineartsassociation.org; Web: www.fineartsassociation.org/; *Dept Chair* Mary Sarns; *Dir* Charles Lawrence
Estab 1957; pvt; D & E; Scholarships; D 85, E 195
Courses: Ceramics, Drawing, Intermedia, Mixed Media, Painting, Photography

WILMINGTON

WILMINGTON COLLEGE, Art Dept, 1870 Quaker Way, Wilmington, OH 45177-2473. Tel 937-382-6661, Ext 474; Web: www.wchome.wilmington.edu; *Chmn* Hal Shunk; *Prof* Terry Inlow
Scholarships
Degrees: BA
Tuition: $12,790 per yr
Courses: Art Education, Art History, Ceramics, Design, Drawing, Handicrafts, Painting, Photography, Printmaking, Sculpture, Stage Design

WOOSTER

THE COLLEGE OF WOOSTER, Dept of Art and Art History, 1220 Beall Ave, Ebert Art Ctr Wooster, OH 44691. Tel 330-263-2388; Fax 330-263-2633; Email rseling@wooster.edu; Web: www.wooster.edu/en/Academics/Areas-of-Study/Art-and-Art-History.aspx; WATS 800-321-9885; *Asst Prof* Kara Morrow, PhD; *Prof* Walter Zurko, MFA; *Chmn* John Siewert, PhD; *Assoc Prof* Marina Mangubi, MFA; *Assoc Prof* Bridget Murphy Milligan, MFA; *Asst Prof* Diana Presciutti, PhD; *Admin Coordr* Rose Seling
Estab 1866; Maintain non-profit art gallery, The Col of Wooster Art Mus, same address; pvt; D & E; SC 13, LC 19; D 1800, maj 40
Ent Req: HS dipl
Degrees: BA 4 yr
Courses: Architecture, Art Education, †Art History, Ceramics, Drawing, History of Art & Architecture, Mixed Media, Painting, Photography, Printmaking, Sculpture, Studio Art
Adult Hobby Classes: Available through student activities board. Enrl 12-20; tuition varies
Summer School: Dir, Dr Charles Hampton

YELLOW SPRINGS

ANTIOCH COLLEGE, Visual Arts Dept, 1 Morgan Pl, Yellow Springs, OH 45387-1683. Tel 937-581-8201; Web: www.antioch-college.edu; *Prof* Christopher Garcia, MFA; *Prof* Nevin Mercede, MFA; *Prof* David Lapalombara, MFA
Estab 1853; pvt; D & E; SC 48, LC 10; D 665 per sem, non-maj 100, maj 50
Ent Req: HS dipl
Degrees: BA
Courses: Ceramics, Drawing, Painting, Printmaking, Sculpture

YOUNGSTOWN

YOUNGSTOWN STATE UNIVERSITY, Dept of Art, One University Plaza, Youngstown, OH 44555. Tel 330-742-3000 (Main), 742-3627 (Dept); Fax 330-742-7183; Web: www.ysu.edu; *Chmn* Susan Russo
Estab 1908, dept estab 1952; FT 15, PT 13; pub; D & E; SC 44, LC 26, GC 8; D & E 1250, maj 300, grad 15
Ent Req: HS dipl
Degrees: AB, BFA & BS 4 yrs
Courses: Art & Technology, †Art Education, †Art History, †Ceramics, †Commercial Art, Drawing, Graphic Arts, †Graphic Design, Illustration, Jewelry, Museum Staff Training, †Painting, Photography, †Printmaking, †Sculpture, †Teacher Training
Adult Hobby Classes: Courses—Calligraphy, Ceramics, Drawing, Painting, Photography, Weaving
Summer School: Two 5 wk sessions beginning June. Courses—same as above

OKLAHOMA

ADA

EAST CENTRAL UNIVERSITY, School of Fine Arts, 1100 E 14th St, Box L-3 ECU Ada, OK 74820-6915. Tel 580-559-5353; Fax 580-436-4042; Email bjessop@ecok.edu; Web: www.ecok.edu; *Chair* F Bradley Jessop, EdD; *Asst Prof* Gary Batzloff, MFA; *Asst Prof* Katy Seals, MFA; *Asst Prof* Taryn Chubb, PhD; *Asst Prof* John Dougherty, MFA
Estab 1909; Maintains nonprofit art gallery; Pogue Art Gallery, Attn: Dr. Taryn Chubb, Dir, PMB 0-6 ECU, 1100 E 14th St, Ada, OK 74820; on-campus art supply shop; pub; D, E & online; Scholarships; SC 33, LC 10, GC 4; D 400, E 40, non-maj 320, maj 90, grad 4
Activities: Schols offered
Ent Req: HS dipl, ACT
Degrees: BFA (Studio, Graphic Arts, Art Educ) 4 yr, MEd 33 hrs, post grad work, pub service prog
Tuition: Res—undergrad $150.35, grad $192.01; nonres—undergrad $276.94, grad $329.50
Courses: Aesthetics, Art Appreciation, †Art Education, Art History, Ceramics, †Commercial Art, Design, Drawing, †Graphic Arts, Graphic Design, Handicrafts, History of Art & Architecture, Painting, Photography, Printmaking, Sculpture, †Silversmithing
Adult Hobby Classes: Enrl 25 average. Courses - Drawing, Painting
Children's Classes: Drawing, painting
Summer School: Chair, Dr Bradley Jessop. Tuition undergrad $166, grad $211.50. Courses - Art Education, Drawing, Painting, Sculpture

ALTUS

WESTERN OKLAHOMA STATE COLLEGE, Art Dept, 2801 N Main, Altus, OK 73521. Tel 580-477-2000; Fax 580-521-6154; Web: www.western.cc.uk.us; *Chmn* Jerry Bryan
Pub; D&E; Scholarships
Degrees: AA, AS, AT
Tuition: Res—undergrad $45 per hr; nonres—undergrad $67.50 per hr
Courses: Advertising Design, Art Appreciation, Art History, Ceramics, Design, Drawing, Handicrafts, Jewelry, Painting, Photography, Printmaking, Sculpture, Stage Design, Video, Weaving

BETHANY

SOUTHERN NAZARENE UNIVERSITY, Art & Design Department, 6729 NW 39th Expressway, Bethany, OK 73008. Tel 405-789-6400; 491-6631; Fax 405-491-6381; Email mfeisal@snu.edu; Web: www.snu.edu; *Dean Arts & Sciences* Martha Banz; *Dept Chair* Prof Marcia M Feisal; *Assoc Professional Specialist* Prof Whitney Porch; *Adjunct Prof* Prof Brian Mays
Schols open to art & design majors declared for at least one yr with grade point over 3.0. On-campus shop where art supplies may be purchased; pvt; D & E; Scholarships; SC 16, LC 1; D 51, E 6, non-maj 38, maj 13
Ent Req: HS dipl, ACT
Degrees: BA
Courses: Aesthetics, Art Education, Art History, †B&W Digital, Commercial Art, Crafts, †Design, Drawing, †Graphic Design, Painting, Pottery, Printmaking, Sculpture, †Teacher Training
Children's Classes: Enrl 55; tuition $115 one wk summer art camp (grades 3 - 12). Courses—Drawing, Pottery, Watercolor & various crafts
Summer School: Dir, Nila Murrow. Same as children's classes

CHICKASHA

UNIVERSITY OF SCIENCE & ARTS OF OKLAHOMA, Art Dept, 1727 W Alabama, Chickasha, OK 73018. Tel 405-574-1302; Fax 405-574-1220; Email facknappj@usao.edu; Web: www.usao.edu/usao.art; *Chmn, Assoc Prof Art* Jacquelyn Knapp, MFA; *Prof* Steven Brown, MFA; *Asst Prof* Layne Thrift, MFA; *Asst Prof* Blake Morgan; *Asst Prof* Jordan Vinyard; *Adjunct Instr* Kenny Tolman
Estab 1909; pub; D & E; Scholarships; SC 26, LC 3; maj 95, others 180
Activities: Schols offered
Ent Req: ACT: 24
Degrees: BA, BFA
Courses: Art History, Ceramics, Computer Graphics, Design, Drawing, Graphic Arts, Graphic Design, Jewelry, Mixed Media, Painting, Photography, Pottery, Printmaking, Sculpture, †Teacher Certification
Summer School: Enrl 60; Courses—Ceramics, Jewelry, Painting, Photography, Sculpture

CLAREMORE

ROGERS STATE COLLEGE, Art Dept, 1701 W Will Rogers Blvd, Claremore, OK 74017-3252. Tel 918-341-7510, 343-7744; *Dir* Gary E Moeller, MFA
Estab 1971; pub; D & E; Scholarships; SC 22, LC 3; D 126, E 60, non-maj 146, maj 82
Ent Req: HS dipl, ACT
Degrees: AA & AS 2 yr
Courses: Art History, Ceramics, Drawing, †Fine Arts, †Graphic Technology, Lettering, Painting, Photography, Printmaking, Sculpture
Children's Classes: Tuition $42 per hr. Courses—Children's Art
Summer School: Tuition $42 per hr for term of 8 wks beginning June 5th. Courses—Advanced Ceramics, Art Appreciation, Drawing, Graphic Technology, Painting

DURANT

SOUTHEASTERN OKLAHOMA STATE UNIVERSITY, Dept of Art, Communication & Theatre, 1405 N 4th, Durant, OK 74701. Tel 580-745-2352; Fax 580-745-7477; Email gbeach@sosu.edu; Web: www.se.edu; *Chmn* Dell McLain; *Dir Art* Gleny Beach; *Instr* Jack Ousey
Estab 1909; Maintains nonprofit Centre Gallery, Visual & Performing Arts Ctr, 1614 N 1st Ave, Durant, OK 74701; pub; D, E & Online; Scholarships; SC 18, LC 8
Ent Req: HS dipl, col exam
Degrees: BA & BAEduc 4-5 yrs, BS Graphic Design & Visual Commun
Courses: †Aesthetics, Applied Design, Art Appreciation, Art Education, Art History, Ceramics, †Commercial Art, Crafts, Design, Drawing, Graphic Arts, †Graphic Design, Jewelry, †Non-Western Art & Culture, Painting, †Photography, Printmaking, Sculpture
Adult Hobby Classes: Enrl 20; 12 wk term. Courses—Ceramics, Drawing, Jewelry, Painting
Summer School: Dir, Susan H Allen. Enrl 130; tuition same as above. Courses—Art Appreciation, Ceramics

EDMOND

UNIVERSITY OF CENTRAL OKLAHOMA, Dept of Art & Design, 100 N University Dr, Box 84 Edmond, OK 73034. Tel 405-974-5201; Fax 405-341-4964; *Chmn* Dr Bob E Palmer; *Admin Asst* Kay Jones, MEd
Estab 1890; pub; D & E; Scholarships; maj 280, grad 20, dept 1168, school 13,086
Ent Req: HS dipl, health exams, IQ test, scholarship tests
Degrees: BA, BS and MEduc 3-4 yrs
Courses: African Art, Art Appreciation, †Art Education, †Art History, Art in America, Arts & Crafts, Ceramics, Commercial Art, Drawing, Etching, Figure Drawing, †Graphic Arts, †Graphic Design, †History of Art & Architecture, Illustration, Jewelry, Metal Design, Mixed Media, Museum Staff Training, Painting, Photography, Printmaking, Sculpture, †Silversmithing, †Studio Art, Teacher Training
Summer School: Chmn, Dr Bob E Palmer. Enrl 276; tuition $60.20 per cr hr lower div, $61.20 per cr hr upper div. Courses—Art Appreciation, Art History, Ceramics, Computer Graphics, Design, Drawing, European Study Tour, Fibers, Figure Drawing, Jewelry, Painting, Sculpture

LAWTON

CAMERON UNIVERSITY, Art Dept, 2800 W Gore Blvd, Lawton, OK 73505-6320. Tel 580-581-2450; Fax 580-581-2453; Email tammyj@cameron.edu; Web: www.cameron.edu; *Chmn* Edna McMillan; *Prof* Benson Warren; *Assoc Prof* Kathy Liontas-Warren; *Asst Prof* Monika Linehan; *Asst Prof* Elizabeth Tilak
Estab 1970; pub; D & E; Scholarships; SC 22, LC 5; D 417, E 90, maj 60
Ent Req: HS dipl
Degrees: BA & BFA 4 yrs
Courses: Art Appreciation, Art Education, †Art History, Ceramics, Color, Crafts, Design, Drawing, Graphic Arts, Graphic Design, †Mixed Media, Painting, Photography, †Printmaking, †Sculpture
Summer School: Courses—Art Education, Ceramics, Drawing, Graphics, Mixed Media, Painting, Photography, Printmaking

MIAMI

NORTHEASTERN OKLAHOMA A & M COLLEGE, Art Dept, 200 I St NE Miami, OK 74354. Tel 918-542-8441, 540-6354; Fax 918-542-9759; Web: www.neoam.cc.ok.us/; *Instr* Kirsten Couch; *Chmn* David Froman
Estab 1919; pub; D & E; Scholarships; SC 12, LC 3
Ent Req: HS dipl
Degrees: AA 2 yr
Courses: Advertising Design, Art Appreciation, Art Education, Calligraphy, Ceramics, Commercial Art, Costume Design & Construction, Design, Display, Drawing, Fashion Arts, Graphic Arts, Lettering, Painting, Photography, Sculpture, Stage Design, Theatre Arts, Video

NORMAN

UNIVERSITY OF OKLAHOMA, School of Art, 520 Parrington Oval, Rm 202, Norman, OK 73019. Tel 405-325-2691; Fax 405-325-1668; Web: www.ou.edu/finearts/art; *Dir* Dr Andrew Phelan; *Asst Dir Undergrad* Karen Hayes-Thumann; *Asst Dir Grad* Andrew Stout
Estab 1911; pub; D&E; Scholarships; SC 65, LC 25, GC 15; maj 400, others 1200
Degrees: BFA, BA(Art History), MA(Art History) & MFA
Courses: Art Appreciation, Art Education, †Art History, †Ceramics, †Drawing, Figurative Sculpture, †Film, †Graphic Design, Jewelry, Metal Design, Museum Staff Training, †Painting, †Photography, Printmaking, Sculpture, Video

OKLAHOMA CITY

OKLAHOMA CHRISTIAN UNIVERSITY OF SCIENCE & ARTS, Dept of Art & Design, PO Box 11000, Oklahoma City, OK 73136-1100. Tel 405-425-5556; Fax 405-425-5547; Web: www.ocusa.edu; *Assoc Prof* Cherry Tredway, PhD, MFA; *Asst Prof* David Crismon, MFA; *Med Adjunct Prof* Annette Pate, MEd; *Adjunct Prof* Skip McKinstry, MEd; *Adjunct Prof* Donna Watson, PhD, MEd; *Chmn* Michael J O'Keefe, MFA
Estab 1949; FT 2 PT 15; D; Scholarships
Ent Req: Check with admissions
Degrees: BFA
Tuition: $2125 per trimester (12-16 hrs)

Courses: †Advertising Design, Art Appreciation, †Art Education, Art History, Computer Graphics, Design, Drawing, Graphic Design, Illustration, †Interior Design, Painting, Photography, Printmaking, Stage Design

OKLAHOMA CITY UNIVERSITY, Norick Art Center, 2501 N Blackwelder, Oklahoma City, OK 73106. Tel 405-521-5226; Fax 405-557-6029; Web: www.okcu.edu; *Gallery Director* Mike Wimmer
Estab 1904; Maintains a non-profit art gallery: Nona Jean Hulsey Gallery; FT 2, PT 8; Private; D & E; Scholarships; SC 36, LC 6; maj 45
Ent Req: HS dipl or equivalent
Degrees: 4 yr
Courses: Airbrush, Art Education, Art History, Ceramics, Commercial Art, Computer Graphics, Design, Drawing, Film, Graphic Arts, †Graphic Design, History of Art & Architecture, Illustration, Mixed Media, Painting, Photography, Printmaking, Sculpture, †Studio Art, Teacher Training
Adult Hobby Classes: Summer workshops
Summer School: Chmn, Jack Davis. Enrl 15; tuition $335 per cr hr for two 6 wk sessions May to July, July to Aug. Courses—Ceramics, Drawing, Painting, Sculpture

OKMULGEE

OKLAHOMA STATE UNIVERSITY INSTITUTE OF TECHNOLOGY, School of Visual Communications, 1801 E Fourth, Okmulgee, OK 74447. Tel 918-293-5050; 918-293-5068; Fax 918-293-4625; Email james.mccullough@okstate.edu; Web: www.osuit.edu; *Instr* Kurt Stenstrom; *Instr* Mary Miller; *Instr* Brian Caldwell; *Instr* Nathan Harmon; *Dean* James McCullough; *Instr* Tony Johnson; *Instr* Vincent Chung; *Adjunct Instr* Hali Howard; *Instr* Zane Yost
Estab 1946, dept estab 1947; Maintain nonprofit art gallery, Conoco Art Gallery, Student Union, OSU-Okmulgee; on-campus art supply shop; FT 6, PT 2; pub; D & E; Scholarships; LL 22, LC 2; D 140
Ent Req: HS dipl or 18 yrs of age
Degrees: 2-1/2 yr Assoc Applied Science, degree granting technical school
Tuition: Res $170 per cr hr; non-res $357 per cr hr
Courses: †3D Modeling & Animation, †Advertising Design, †Art History, Commercial Art, Drawing, Graphic Arts, †Graphic Design, Illustration, Lettering, Photography, Still, Studio, Video, Video Editing
Summer School: Grd & 30 quick start classes, James McCullough, Dean, director of summer school

SHAWNEE

OKLAHOMA BAPTIST UNIVERSITY, Art & Design Dept, 500 W University, Shawnee, OK 74801. Tel 800-654-3285; 405-585-5000; Fax 405-585-5030; Email admissions@okbu.edu; Web: www.okbu.edu; *Part-Time Instr* Delaynna Trim, MA; *Asst Prof* Julie Blackstone, MA; *Part-Time Instr* Chris Owens, MFA; *Chmn* Prof Steve Hicks, MFA; *Asst Prof* Corey Fuller, MFA; *Part-Time Instr* Brad Price, MA
Estab 1910; On-campus shop where art supplies may be purchased; Lucas Simmons, Lynette Atchley (part time); Den; D & E; Scholarships; SC 23, LC 8, grad 1; D 250, E 15, non-maj 92, maj 70
Activities: Schols offered
Ent Req: HS dipl, SAT-ACT
Degrees: BA & BFA 4 yrs
Tuition: Res—undergrad $29,320 per sem, $661 per hr; nonres—undergrad; campus res—room & board $3,360 per acad yr
Courses: †Advertising Design, Art Appreciation, Art History, Calligraphy, Ceramics, Design, †Drawing, Fibers, Graphic Arts, †Graphic Design, History of Art & Architecture, Museum Staff Training, †Painting, Photography, †Printmaking, Weaving

SAINT GREGORY'S UNIVERSITY, Dept of Art, 1900 W MacArthur Dr, Shawnee, OK 74804. Tel 405-878-5100; Fax 405-878-5198; Email info@stgregorys.edu; *Chmn & Prof Emerita* Shirlie Bowers Wilcoxson, BFA; *Instr* Stephen L Mauldin, MFA
Estab 1898, dept estab 1960; den; D & E; Scholarships; SC 8, LC 4; D 750
Ent Req: HS dipl, ACT or SAT
Degrees: AA 2 yrs, 4 yrs
Courses: †Art Appreciation, Art History, Ceramics, Commercial Art, Drawing, Mixed Media, †Museum Staff Training, †Painting, †Photography, Sculpture

STILLWATER

OKLAHOMA STATE UNIVERSITY, Department of Art, Graphic Design and Art History, 108 Bartlett Ctr for the Visual Arts, Stillwater, OK 74078. Tel 405-744-6016; Fax 405-744-5767; Email artdepartment@okstate.edu; Web: www.art.okstate.edu; *Assoc Prof* Carey Hissey; *Prof* Chris Ramsay; *Assoc Prof* Brandon Reese; *Prof* Mark Sisson; *Prof* Jack Titus; *Assoc Prof* Jennifer Borland; *Assoc Prof* Phil Choo; *Assoc Prof* Cristina Gonzalez; *Lectr* Teresa Holder; *Lectr* Jo Lynch; *Assoc Prof* Angela Piehl; *Lectr* Priscilla Swarz; *Asst Prof* Louise Siddons; *Asst Prof* Shaoqian Zhang; *Asst Prof* Justen Reyner; *Assoc Prof* Liz Roth; *Asst Prof* Irene Backus; *Dept Head Art & Art History* Rebecca Brienen; *Asst Prof* Patrick Finley
Estab 1890, dept estab 1928; Maintain nonprofit art gallery; Gardiner Art Gallery, 108 Bartlett Ctr for the Visual Arts, Okla State U, Stillwater, OK 74078-4085; art library, Visual Resource Library, 106 Bartlett Ctr Art Dept, Stillwater, OK 74078; Pub; D & E; Scholarships; SC 51, LC 17, GC 4; D 850, E 60, non-maj 810, maj 210
Activities: Schols & fels offered
Ent Req: HS dipl
Degrees: BA, BA, MA (Art Hist), BFA, 4 yr
Courses: Advertising Design, Art Appreciation, Art Education, Art History, Ceramics, Commercial Art, Computer Graphics, Constructions, Design, Drawing, Goldsmithing, Graphic Arts, Graphic Design, History of Art & Architecture, Illustration, Jewelry, Museum Staff Training, Painting, Printmaking, Sculpture, Silversmithing, Typography
Adult Hobby Classes: Enrl 169; tuition $950 per sem. Courses—Lecture, Studio

TAHLEQUAH

NORTHEASTERN STATE UNIVERSITY, College of Arts & Letters, 600 N Grand, Tahlequah, OK 74464. Tel 918-456-5511, Ext 2705; Fax 918-458-2348; Web: www.nsuok.edu; *Instr* Jerry Choate, MFA; *Instr* R C Coones, MFA; *Chmn* James Terrell, EdD; *Instr* Bobby Martin; *Instr* Dawn Ward; *Instr Art History* Andrew Vassar; *Asst Dean* Paul Westbrook
Estab 1889; pub; D & E; Scholarships; non-maj 50, maj 30, grad 10
Ent Req: HS dipl
Degrees: BA & BA(Educ) 4 yr
Courses: Art Education, Art History, Ceramics, Commercial Art, Costume Design & Construction, Drafting, Drawing, Graphic Arts, Lettering, Painting, Photography, Printmaking, Sculpture, Stage Design, Teacher Training, Theatre Arts
Adult Hobby Classes: Enrl 20; tuition $20.85 per cr hr for 1 sem. Courses—Indian Art
Summer School: Dir, Tom Cottrill. Courses—Art Education, Fundamentals of Art

TULSA

ORAL ROBERTS UNIVERSITY, Art Dept, 7777 S Lewis Ave, Tulsa, OK 74171-0001. Tel 918-495-6611; Fax 918-495-6033; Email sbranston@oru.edu; Web: www.oru.edu; *Chmn* Stuart Branston, MFA; *Asst Prof* Jason Howell, MFA; *Instr* Nathan Opp, MA; *Adj Prof* Darlene Gaskil
Estab 1965; pvt; D & E; Scholarships; SC 22, LC 3; D 287, maj 100, others 87
Ent Req: HS dipl, SAT
Degrees: BA(Art Educ), BA & BS(Graphic Design Print), BA(Studio Art) & BS (Graphic Design Video) 4 yrs
Courses: Advertising Design, Art Appreciation, †Art Education, Art History, Calligraphy, Ceramics, Constructions, Design, Drawing, Graphic Arts, †Graphic Design, Handicrafts, Illustration, Interior Design, Intermedia, Jewelry, Lettering, Mixed Media, Painting, Photography, Printmaking, Sculpture, †Studio Art, Teacher Training

TULSA COMMUNITY COLLEGE, Center for Creativity, 909 S Boston Ave, Tulsa, OK 74119-2095. Tel 918-595-7000; Fax 918-595-7295; Web: www.tulsa.cc.okay.us; *Instr* Dewayne Pass, MFA; *Instr* William Derrevere, MA; *Instr* Rhonda Davis, MA
Estab 1970; Maintain nonprofit art gallery, TCC Student Art Gallery; PT 8; pub; D & E; Scholarships; SC 16, LC 7; non-maj 40, maj 160
Ent Req: HS dipl
Degrees: AA 2 yrs
Tuition: Campus residency available
Courses: Art Appreciation, Art History, †Ceramics, Commercial Art, Design, Drawing, Glass Blowing, Goldsmithing, Graphic Arts, †Graphic Design, Jewelry, Painting, Photography, Printmaking, Professional Practices, Sculpture, Silversmithing
Adult Hobby Classes: Special prog of art courses & crafts courses
Summer School: Art Appreciation, Fundamentals I, Drawing, Painting

UNIVERSITY OF TULSA, School of Art, 600 S College Ave, Tulsa, OK 74104. Tel 918-631-2202; Fax 918-631-3423; Web: www.utulsa.edu; *Asst Prof, Art Hist & Visual Cult* Michaela Merryday; *Asst Prof, Photog* Glenn Herbert Davis; *Asst Prof, Art Hist* Susan M Dixon
Estab 1898; Maintain nonprofit art gallery, Alexandre Hogue Gallery, financed by University (annual attendance 1,000); pvt; D & E; Scholarships; SC 20, LC 13, GC 22, Continuing Educ; maj 110, others 400
Degrees: BA, BFA, MA, MFA and MTA 4 yrs
Courses: Advertising Design, Architecture, Art Appreciation, †Art Education, Ceramics, Graphic Design, †Painting, Photography, †Printmaking, †Sculpture
Adult Hobby Classes: Courses offered through Continuing Educ
Summer School: H Teresa Valero, Summer School Dir

WEATHERFORD

SOUTHWESTERN OKLAHOMA STATE UNIVERSITY, Art, Communication & Theatre, 100 Campus Dr, Weatherford, OK 73096-3001. Tel 580-772-6611, Ext 3756, 774-3756; Fax 580-774-6770; Email robin.jones@swosu.edu; Web: www.swosu.edu/depts/art/index; *Chair* Robin Jones, PhD; *Assoc Prof* E K Jeong, PhD; *Asst Prof Graphic Design* Siriporn Peters, PhD; *Asst Prof* Todd Parker, MFA; *Instr Art Ed* Marsha Carman
Estab 1901, dept estab 1941; pub; D & E; Scholarships; SC 35, LC 8, GC 43; D 5000
Activities: Schols offered
Ent Req: HS dipl
Degrees: BFA(Art Educ), BFA 2-dimensional, BFA 3-dimen, BFA graphic design
Courses: Advertising Design, Art Education, Art History, Ceramics, Commercial Art, Drawing, Graphic Arts, Graphic Design, Illustration, Jewelry, Lettering, Mixed Media, Painting, Sculpture, Teacher Training
Adult Hobby Classes: Varies
Summer School: Varies

OREGON

ALBANY

LINN BENTON COMMUNITY COLLEGE, Fine & Applied Art Dept, 6500 SW Pacific Blvd, Albany, OR 97321. Tel 541-917-4999; Fax 541-967-6550; *Instr* John Aikman; *Instr* Rich Bergeman; *Instr* Jason Widmer; *Chmn* Doris Litzer
Estab 1968; pub; D & E; SC 14, LC 2; D 2000, E 4000
Ent Req: open entry
Degrees: AA, AS & AAS 2 yrs
Courses: †Advertising Design, Art History, Ceramics, Display, Drafting, Drawing, †Graphic Arts, †Graphic Design, Handicrafts, Illustration, Lettering, Painting, Photography, Sculpture, Textile Design, Theatre Arts
Adult Hobby Classes: Painting, Tole Painting, Watercolor

ASHLAND

SOUTHERN OREGON UNIVERSITY, Art & Art History Dept, 1250 Siskiyou Blvd, Ashland, OR 97520-5001. Tel 541-552-6386; Fax 541-552-6564; Web: www.sou.edu/art; *Dept Chmn* Margaret Sjogren; *Asst Prof Art* David Bithell; *Office Mgr* Zoey Boyles; *Prof* Cody A Bustamante; *Asst Prof* Melissa Geppert; *Prof* Miles Inada; *Prof* Erika Leppmann; *Instr* Jennifer Longshore; *Prod* Margaret Sjogren; *Asst Prof* Robin Strangfeld; *Adjunct Faculty* Brooks Dierdorff; *Adjunct Faculty* Summer Ventis; *Dept Chair* Deborah Rosenberg
Estab 1926; Galleries at the center for visual arts, 1250 Siskiyou Blvd Ashland OR 97520; pub; D & E; Scholarships; SC 53, LC 17; D 120, E 30, non-maj 700, maj 100
Activities: Schols offered
Ent Req: HS dipl, SAT or ACT
Degrees: BFA, BA or BS(Art) 4 yrs
Courses: †Art, Art Appreciation, †Art History, Ceramics, Commercial Art, Computer Art, Conceptual Art, Design, Digital Art, Drawing, Graphic Arts, Illustration, Intermedia, Mixed Media, Museum Staff Training, Painting, Photography, Printmaking, Sculpture
Children's Classes: Summer classes
Summer School: Enrl 210; 1 - 8 wk term. Courses—various

BEND

CENTRAL OREGON COMMUNITY COLLEGE, Dept of Art, 2600 NW College Way, Bend, OR 97701-5933. Tel 541-382-6112, 383-7510; Fax 541-385-5978; Email jhamblin@cocc.edu; Web: www.cocc.edu/finearts/; *Prof* Sara Krempel, MA
Estab 1949; pub; D & E; Scholarships; in col D 2025, E 2000
Ent Req: HS dipl
Degrees: AA, AS, Cert
Courses: Calligraphy, Ceramics, Drawing, Painting, Photography, Printmaking, Stage Design, Theatre Arts
Adult Hobby Classes: Enrl 1500-2000; tuition, duration & courses offered vary
Summer School: Dir, John Weber. Courses—General courses

COOS BAY

COOS ART MUSEUM, 235 Anderson Ave, Coos Bay, OR 97420-1610. Tel 541-267-3901, 267-4877 (art education); Fax 541-267-4877; Email info@coosart.org; Web: www.coosart.org; *Exec Dir* Steven Broocks
Open Tues - Fri 10 AM - 4 PM, Sat 1 - 4 PM; Estab 1966; 5 separate galleries with the Art Mus, one rental/sales gallery; pvt; D & E, Weekends; SC 30, LC 10; D 25, E 15
Tuition: Varies
Courses: Art Appreciation, Art History, Ceramics, Collage, Design, Drawing, Glass Fusing, Painting, Paste Papers, Printmaking
Adult Hobby Classes: Enrl 100; tuition for 10 wks, mem $40/$45, non-mem $48/ $53
Children's Classes: Tuition varies depending on courses & membership status
Summer School: Tuition same as above

SOUTHWESTERN OREGON COMMUNITY COLLEGE, Visual Arts Dept, 1988 Newmark, Coos Bay, OR 97420. Tel 541-888-7322, 888-7321; Fax 541-888-7801; Web: www.socc.edu/; *Div Dir* Bob Bower; *Prof* Melanie Schwartz, MFA; *Prof* James Fritz
Estab 1962, dept estab 1964; pub; D & E; Scholarships; SC 11, LC 1; D 420, E 300, non-maj 250, maj 170
Degrees: AA 2 yrs
Courses: Art History, Calligraphy, Ceramics, Computer Art, Design, Drawing, Handmade Paper, Painting, Printmaking, Sculpture
Adult Hobby Classes: Tuition $396 per qtr. Courses—Art History, Calligraphy, Ceramics, Drawing, Glassworking, Handmade Paper & Prints, Painting
Children's Classes: Only as occasional workshops
Summer School: Dean Instruction, Phill Anderson. Tuition varies. Courses—Ceramics, Painting & Composition, Watercolor

CORVALLIS

OREGON STATE UNIVERSITY, Dept of Art, 106 Fairbanks Hall, Corvallis, OR 97331-8540. Tel 541-737-4745; Fax 541-737-8686; Web: www.oregonstate.edu/dept/arts/, www.oregonstate.edu/dept/arts/gallery/index.htnl; *Chmn* James Folts, MS; *Prof* Harrison Branch, MFA; *Prof* Clinton Brown, MFA; *Prof* Thomas Morandi, MFA; *Prof* Henry Sayre, PhD, MFA; *Assoc Prof* Shelley Jordon, MFA; *Assoc Prof* Barbara Loeb, PhD, MFA; *Asst Prof* Andrea Marks, MFA; *Asst Prof* Yuji Hiratsuka, MFA; *Asst Prof* John Bowers, MFA; *Asst Prof* John Maul, MFA; *Sr Research Assoc* Douglas Russell, BA; *Prof* Elizabeth Pillod, MFA; *Assoc Prof* Kay Campbell; *Asst Prof* Julie Green; *Asst Prof* John Nettleton; *Asst Prof* Muneera U Spence
Estab 1868, dept estab 1908; Maintains nonprofit art gallery, 100 Fairbanks Hall, Corvallis, OR 97331; pub; D & E; Scholarships; SC 63, LC 16, GC 271; non-maj 2000, maj 525
Ent Req: HS dipl
Degrees: BA, BS, BFA & MAIS
Tuition: Res—undergrad $1360 per quarter; res—grad $2542 per quarter; nonres—undergrad $4780 per quarter; nonres—grad $4270 per quarter; campus res available
Courses: 2-D & 3-D Design, Art History, Drawing, Graphic Design, Painting, Photography, Printmaking, Sculpture, Visual Appreciation
Summer School: Dir, John Maul. Enrl 75; 3 wk session beginning 3rd wk in June. Jumpstart-Preschool Visual Arts Workshop for HS students

EUGENE

LANE COMMUNITY COLLEGE, Art & Applied Design Dept, 4000 E 30th Ave, Eugene, OR 97405-0640. Tel 541-463-5409; Fax 541-463-4185; *Art Div* Mary Jo Kreindel
Estab 1964, dept estab 1967; LCC Art Gallery, 4000 E 30th Ave, Eugene OR 97405; Titan Store where art supplies may be purchased; FT 10; pub; D & E; Scholarships; SC 42, LC 4; D 300, E 75, non-maj 240, maj 60
Ent Req: HS dipl
Degrees: AA, AAS 2 yrs
Courses: 2-D & 3-D Design, Advertising Design, Art Appreciation, Art Education, Art History, Ceramics, Commercial Art, Design, Drawing, †Fiber, Film, †Graphic Design, History of Art & Architecture, Illustration, Intermedia, Jewelry, Lettering, Metal Casting, Painting, Photography, Printmaking, Sculpture, Silversmithing, Textile Design, †Video
Adult Hobby Classes: 250; tuition $39 for 30 hrs & fees. Courses—Art Appreciation, Calligraphy, Ceramics, Chinese Brush Painting, Doll Making, Drawing, Jewelry, Oil Painting, Papermaking, Sculpture, Stained Glass, Watercolor
Summer School: Dean, Rick Williams. Enrl 205; tuition $75.50 per cr hr; Courses—Art Appreciation, Drawing, Sculpture, Watercolor, Design

MAUDE KERNS ART CENTER, 1910 E 15th Ave, Eugene, OR 97403-2094. Tel 541-345-1571; Fax 541-345-6248; Email mkac@efn.org; Web: www.mkartcenter.org; *Exec Dir* Karen Marie Pavelec
Estab 1950; pvt; D & E; Scholarships; SC 45; D & E 450
Courses: Calligraphy, Ceramics, Design, Drawing, Glass Blowing, Graphic Design, Handicrafts, Jewelry, Lampworking, Leaded Glass, †Mixed Media, †Painting, Photography, Printmaking, Sculpture, Textile Design, Weaving
Adult Hobby Classes: Enrl 100. Courses—Per regular session
Children's Classes: Enrl 200; tuition $75. Courses—Ceramics, Drawing & other special workshops
Summer School: Courses varied

UNIVERSITY OF OREGON, Dept of Fine & Applied Arts, 5232 University of Oregon, Eugene, OR 97403-5295. Tel 541-346-3610; Fax 541-346-3626; Web: http://art-uo.uoregon.edu; *Assoc Prof* L Alpert
FT 20, PT 10; Pub; D; Scholarships; D 1475, non-maj 350, maj 1050
Degrees: BA, BS 4 yrs, BFA 5 yrs, MFA 2 yrs minimum after BFA or equivalent
Courses: Ceramics, Drawing, Fibers, Jewelry, Metalsmithing, Painting, Photography, Printmaking, Sculpture, Visual Design
Summer School: Dir, Ron Trebon. 8 wks beginning June. Courses—Ceramics, Computer Graphics, Drawing, Fibers, Jewelry, Metalsmithing, Painting, Photography, Printmaking, Sculpture, Visual Design

GRESHAM

MOUNT HOOD COMMUNITY COLLEGE, Visual Arts Center, 26000 SE Stark St, Gresham, OR 97030-3300. Tel 503-491-7309; Fax 503-491-7389; *Assoc Dean* Chris Bruya
Scholarships
Degrees: AA
Courses: Art Education, Art History, Calligraphy, Ceramics, Design, Drawing, Film, Graphic Design, Illustration, Jewelry, Painting, Printmaking, Sculpture
Adult Hobby Classes: Tuition $30 per cr. Courses—All studio courses
Summer School: Dir, Eric Sankey. Enrl 60 - 90; two 5 wk sessions. Courses—Calligraphy, Ceramics, Drawing, Watercolor

LA GRANDE

EASTERN OREGON UNIVERSITY, School of Arts & Science, 1 University Blvd, Division of Arts & Letters La Grande, OR 97850-2807. Tel 541-962-3672; Fax 503-962-3596; Email dimondt@eou.edu; Web: www.eou.edu; *Prof Art* Thomas Dimond, MFA; *Assoc Prof* Terry Gloeckler, MFA; *Dean Arts & Sciences* Denny Swonger; *Prof Art* Kat Galloway, MFA; *Prof Art* Doug Kaigler, MFA; *Assoc Prof* Jason Brown, MFA; *Instr Photog* Mel Buffington; *Instr Art Educ* Lisa Brown
Estab 1929; pub; D & E; SC 35, LC 15; Non-maj 30, maj 65
Ent Req: HS dipl
Degrees: degrees BA & BS in Art, Endorsement in Art
Courses: Aesthetics, †Art Appreciation, Art Education, Art History, †Calligraphy, Ceramics, †Conceptual Art, †Constructions, †Costume Design & Construction, Design, Drawing, †Film, Glass, †Graphic Arts, †Graphic Design, †Handicrafts, †History of Art & Architecture, Jewelry, Life Drawings, †Mixed Media, Painting, Photography, †Printmaking, Sculpture, †Silversmithing, †Stage Design, †Teacher Training, †Textile Design, †Theatre Arts, †Video
Summer School: Dir, Dr Doyle Slater. Enrl 400. Term of 4-8 wks. Courses—Two or three per summer, beginning & advanced level

MARYLHURST

MARYLHURST UNIVERSITY, Art Dept, 17600 Pacific Hwy, Marylhurst, OR 97036; PO Box 261, Marylhurst, OR 97036-0261. Tel 503-636-8141; Fax 503-636-9526; Email studentinfo@marylhurst.edu; Web: www.marylhurst.edu; *Dir* Kelcey Beardsley; *Instr* Kristin Collins; *Instr* Dennis Cunningham; *Instr* Margaret Shirley; *Instr* Rich Rollins; *Instr* Terri Hopkins; *Instr* Martha Pfanschmidt; *Instr* Denise Roy; *Dir* Paul Sutinen; *Instr* Nancy Hiss; *Instr* Trude Parkinson; *Instr* Peggy Suzio; *Instr* Marlene Bauer; *Instr* Libby Farr; *Instr* Louise Farrar-Wegener; *Instr* Carole Hermanson; *Instr* Kathleen Huun; *Instr* Michele Kremers; *Instr* Paul Pavlock; *Instr* Cheryl Schneidermann; *Instr* Elizabeth Spurgeon; *Instr* William Washburn; *Instr* Nancy Wilkins; *Instr* Stephanie Robison Baggs
Estab 1980; Maintain nonprofit art gallery; The Art Gym, Marylhurst University, PO Box 261, Marylhurst, OR 97036; pvt; D&E; Scholarships; SC 35, LC 16, other 4; non-maj 50, maj 140
Ent Req: HS dipl or equivalent
Degrees: BA, BFA, MA (Art Therapy)
Courses: Art History, Art Therapy Program, Design, Drawing, History of Photography, Interior Design, Lighting, Mixed Media, Museum Staff Training, Painting, Photography, Printmaking, Sculpture, Textiles
Summer School: Dir, Paul Sutinen. Enrl 100; tuition $293 per cr for 10 wk term. Courses—Drawing, Interior Design, Painting, Photography, Printmaking, Sculpture

MCMINNVILLE

LINFIELD COLLEGE, Department of Art & Visual Culture, 900 SE Baker, ADD-Ste A466 McMinnville, OR 97128-6808. Tel 503-883-2804; Email wink@linfield.edu; Web: www.linfield.edu/art/; *Chmn Dept* Ph.D. Brian Winkenweder; *Prof* Ron Mills; *Assoc Prof* Liz Obert; *Asst Prof* Scott Ross; *Instr* Totem Shriver; *Instr* Adrianne Santina; *Instr* Laura Johnson; *Curator* Josephine Zarkovich
Estab 1849, dept estab 1964; Mem: Maintains non-profit gallery, Linfield Fine Arts Gallery 900 SE Baker St, McMinnville OR 97128; pvt; D & E; Scholarships; SC 20, LC 6; non-maj 250, maj 35
Activities: Art supplies available at on-campus shop
Ent Req: HS dipl
Degrees: BA 4 yr
Tuition: $30,604 per yr
Courses: †Aesthetics, Art Education, Art History, Ceramics, †Conceptual Art, †Design, Drawing, †Graphic Arts, Mixed Media, Painting, Photography, Printmaking, Sculpture, Teacher Training, Video

MONMOUTH

WESTERN OREGON STATE COLLEGE, Creative Arts Division, Visual Arts, 345 N Monmouth Ave, Monmouth, OR 97361. Tel 503-838-8000; Fax 503-838-8995; Web: www.wou.edu; *Prof* Kim Hoffman; *Chmn Creative Arts* Dr Tom Bergeron
Estab 1856; FT 8, PT 2; pub; D & E; Scholarships; SC 72, LC 21, GC 27; total 3600
Degrees: BA and BS 4 yr
Courses: Art Education, Art History, Art Theory, Ceramics, Design, Drawing, Graphic Design, Individual Studies, Painting, Printmaking, Sculpture

ONTARIO

TREASURE VALLEY COMMUNITY COLLEGE, Art Dept, 650 College Blvd, Ontario, OR 97914-3423. Tel 541-881-8822; Web: www.tvcc.cc.or.us; *Chmn* Robin Jackson
Estab 1961; PT 4; pub; D & E; Scholarships; SC 14, LC 1; D 50, E 35, non-maj 10, maj 15
Ent Req: Placement testing
Degrees: AS & AA 2 yrs
Tuition: Res—$40 per cr; nonres—$54 per cr; out of state—$56; international—$100; campus res available
Courses: Art History, †Ceramics, Drawing, Painting, Sculpture
Summer School: Chmn, Robert M Jackson. Tuition $190 for term of 8 wks beginning June 22. Courses—Ceramics, Drawing, Painting

OREGON CITY

CLACKAMAS COMMUNITY COLLEGE, Art Dept, 19600 S Molalla Ave, Oregon City, OR 97045. Tel 503-657-8400, Ext 2540; Web: www.clackamas.cc.or.us; *Chmn* Rich True
Estab 1969; Pub; D&E
Ent Req: HS dipl
Degrees: AA
Tuition: Res—$37 per cr hr, nonres—$131 per cr hr
Courses: Advertising Design, Art History, Calligraphy, Ceramics, Design, Drawing, Jewelry, Painting, Sculpture

PENDLETON

BLUE MOUNTAIN COMMUNITY COLLEGE, Fine Arts Dept, 2411 NW Carden Ave, Pendleton, OR 97801-1655; PO Box 100, Pendleton, OR 97801-1000. Tel 541-276-1260; Fax 541-276-6119; Web: www.bmcc.or.us; *Chmn* Michael Booth
Estab 1962, dept estab 1964; Maintain nonprofit art gallery; Betty Fevis Memorial Art Gallery; art library; art supplies available at bookstore; pub; D & E; SC 5, LC 2 per qtr; D 150, E 25
Ent Req: HS dipl or equivalent
Degrees: AA, 2 yrs
Tuition: Res—undergrad $50 per cr hr; nonres—undergrad $100
Courses: Art History, Ceramics, Drawing, Painting, Sculpture

PORTLAND

LEWIS & CLARK COLLEGE, Dept of Art, 0615 SW Palatine Hill Rd, Portland, OR 97219-7879. Tel 503-768-7390, 768-7000; Fax 503-768-7401; Email buetther@lclark.edu; Web: www.lclark.edu/~art/; *Prof* Phyllis Yes; *Assoc Prof* Michael Taylor; *Asst Prof* Sherry Fowler; *Asst Prof* Theodore Vogel; *Vis Lect* Robert B Miller; *Vis Lect* Bruce West; *Instr* Debra Beers
Dept estab 1946; pvt; D; Scholarships; SC 10, LC 2
Ent Req: HS dipl
Degrees: BS and BA 4 yr
Courses: Art History, Ceramics, Drawing, Graphic Arts, History of Art & Architecture, Jewelry, Painting, Printmaking, Sculpture, Weaving

PACIFIC NORTHWEST COLLEGE OF ART, 511 NW Broadway, Portland, OR 97209-3404. Tel 800-818-PNCA; Fax 503-226-3587; Email pncainfo@pnca.edu; *Pres* Sally Lawrence; *Instr* William Moore; *Instr* Paul Missal; *Instr* Betsy Lindsay; *Instr* Robert Hanson; *Instr* Frank Irby; *Instr* Anne Johnson; *Instr* Chris Gander; *Instr* Tom Fawkes; *Instr* Judy Cooke; *Dir Enrol* Jennifer Satalino; *Instr* David Ritchie; *Instr* Horatio Law; *Instr* Robert Selby
Estab 1909; FT 19, PT 24; pvt; D & E; Scholarships; SC 54, LC 15; D 258, PT 47, E 249
Ent Req: HS dipl, portfolio, essay
Degrees: BFA 4 yr
Courses: Art History, †Ceramics, †Drawing, †Graphic Design, †Illustration, †Intermedia, †Painting, †Photography, †Printmaking, †Sculpture
Adult Hobby Classes: Enrl 546; tuition $250 per 12 wk term. Courses—Ceramics, Graphic Design, Illustration, Life Drawing, Painting, Photography, Printmaking, Sculpture & other art-related courses
Children's Classes: Enrl 132; tuition $125 per 12 wk term. Courses—Ceramics, Drawing, Painting, Printmaking, Sculpture
Summer School: Dean, Continuing Educ, Lennie Pitkin. Enrl 500; tuition $210 per 12 wk term. Courses—Wide range of Visual Arts

PORTLAND COMMUNITY COLLEGE, Visual & Performing Arts Division, PO Box 19000, Portland, OR 97280-0990. Tel 503-977-4264, Ext 4263; Fax 503-977-4874; *Div Dean* Steve Ward
Estab 1961, dept estab 1963; pub; D & E, Sat; SC 40, LC 5; D 864, E 282, total 1212
Ent Req: none
Degrees: AA 2 yrs
Courses: Art History, Calligraphy, Ceramics, Drawing, Graphic Design, Painting, Photography, Printing Tech, Sculpture, Stage Design, Theatre Arts
Adult Hobby Classes: Tuition varies per quarter. Courses—various
Children's Classes: Courses offered
Summer School: Dept Chmn, Mary Stupp-Greer. Enrl 400; Term of 8 wks beginning June. Courses—same as regular session

PORTLAND STATE UNIVERSITY, Dept of Art, PO Box 751, Portland, OR 97207-0751. Tel 503-725-3515; Fax 503-725-4541; Web: www.art.pdx.edu; *Dept Chmn, Prof* Michihiro Kosuge, MFA; *Prof* William Fosque, MFA; *Asst Prof* William LePore, MA; *Assoc Prof* Elizabeth Mead, MFA; *Assoc Prof* Sue Taylor, PhD; *Assoc Prof* Daniel Pirosky, BA; *Assoc Prof* Jane Kristof, PhD; *Assoc Prof* Susan Agre-Kippenhan, MFA; *Assoc Prof* Eleanor Erskins, MFA; *Assoc Prof* Susan Harlan, MFA; *Assoc Prof* Junghee Lee, MA; *Asst Prof* Lee Charmin, MFA; *Asst Prof* Charles Colbert, PhD; *Asst Prof* Anne McClanan, PhD
Estab 1955; pub; D & E; Scholarships; E 2000, non-maj 1300, maj 600, grad 12, others 70
Ent Req: HS dipl, SAT
Degrees: BS & BA(Art) 4 yr, MFA (Painting, Printmaking, Sculpture) 2 yr
Courses: Art History, †Drawing, †Graphic Design, †Painting, Printmaking, †Sculpture
Summer School: Enrl 4-500; term of 8-12 wks beginning June 28. Courses—vary. Two centers, one in Portland and one at Cannon Beach: The Haystack Program

REED COLLEGE, Dept of Art, 3203 S E Woodstock Blvd, Portland, OR 97202-8199. Tel 503-771-1112; Fax 503-788-6691; Web: www.reed.edu; *Chmn Art History & Humanities* William J Diebold; *Prof Art* Michael Knutson; *Asst Prof Art* Geraldine Ondrizek
Estab 1911; FT 5; pvt; D; Scholarships; SC 7, LC 5; D 1150, E 15
Degrees: BA 3-5 yr
Courses: Aesthetics, Architecture, †Art History, Ceramics, †Conceptual Art, †Drawing, Graphic Arts, History of Art & Architecture, †History of Art & Architecture, Humanities, †Painting, Photography, Printmaking, Restoration & Conservation, †Sculpture, Theory
Adult Hobby Classes: Courses offered & MA degree
Summer School: Courses offered

ROSEBURG

UMPQUA COMMUNITY COLLEGE, Fine & Performing Arts Dept, PO Box 967, Roseburg, OR 97470-0226. Tel 541-440-4600, Ext 691; Email rochess@umpqua.edu; Web: www.umpqua.edu; *Dir Fine Arts* Susan Rochester
Estab 1964; Maintain nonprofit art gallery, Umpqua Community College, 1140 College Rd, Roseburg, OR 97470; pub; D & E; Scholarships; SC 21, LC 3; D 190, E 90, maj 30
Ent Req: HS dipl
Degrees: AA 2 yr
Courses: Art History, Basic Design, Ceramics, Drawing, Painting, Photography, Sculpture, Theatre Arts
Adult Hobby Classes: Enrl 195; tuition $45 & lab fee for 10 weeks. Courses—Ceramics, Drawing, Painting, Photography, Sculpture

SALEM

CHEMEKETA COMMUNITY COLLEGE, Dept of Humanities & Communications, Art Program, 4000 Lancaster Dr NE, Salem, OR 97305-1453; PO Box 14007, Salem, OR 97309-7070. Tel 503-399-5184; Fax 503-399-5214; Email donb@chemeketa.edu; Web: art.chemeketa.edu, artgallery.chemeketa.edu; *Dir* Don Brase; *Instr* Lee Jacobson, MFA; *Instr* Kay Bunnenberg-Boehmer, MFA; *Instr* Carol Bibler, MFA; *Adjunct* Gary Rawlins, BFA; *Adjunct* Deanne Beausoleil, MA; *Instr* Deborah Trousdale, MFA; *Adjunct* Cynthia Herron, MFA; *Instr* Laurce Mack, MFA; *Adjunct* Jane Lieber Mays, BA
Estab 1969, dept estab 1975; Maintain nonprofit art gallery; Chemeketa Community College Art Gallery; art supplies available in bookstore; Pub; D, E & Weekend; Scholarships; SC 40, LC 6; D 175, E 175
Ent Req: none
Degrees: AA 2 yr
Courses: Art Appreciation, Art as a Profession, †Art Glass, Art History, Ceramics, Design, †Drafting, Drawing, Film, Graphic Design, Painting, Photography, Printmaking, Sculpture, †Theatre Arts
Adult Hobby Classes: Enrl 150-200; tuition $56 per cr hr
Summer School: Tuition varies, 8 wk term

PENNSYLVANIA

ALLENTOWN

CEDAR CREST COLLEGE, Art Dept, 100 College Dr, Allentown, PA 18104-6196. Tel 610-606-4666; Web: www.cedarcrest.edu/; *Prof* Nelson Maniscalco, MFA; *Prof* Pat Badt, MFA; *Asst Prof* William Clark, MFA; *Asst Prof* Jill Odegaard; *Asst Prof* Kim Sloane
Estab 1867; Maintain nonprofit art gallery, Tempkins Gallery; FT 3, PT 2; pvt, women only; D & E; Scholarships; SC 10, LC 6; 1000
Ent Req: HS dipl, CEEB
Degrees: BA, BS, Interdisciplinary Fine Arts Maj (art, theatre, music, dance, creative writing), 4 yr
Courses: Aesthetics, Art Education, Art History, Ceramics, Comparative Study of Art, Drawing, Jewelry, Metal Forming, Painting, †Printmaking, Sculpture, Theatre Arts
Summer School: Courses—Ceramics, Jewelry-Metalsmithing, Sculpture, Painting

MUHLENBERG COLLEGE, Dept of Art, 2400 Chew St, Allentown, PA 18104-5586. Tel 484-664-3100; Web: www.muhlenbergcollege/artdept, www.muhlenberg.edu; *Chmn* Jadviga Da Costa Nunes, PhD, MFA; *Assoc Prof* Scott Sherk, MFA; *Asst Prof* Raymond S Barnes, MFA; *Asst Prof* Joseph Elliott, MFA; *Instr* Kevin Tuttle; *Instr* David Haas; *Instr* Carol Heft
Estab 1848; FT 4, PT 6; pvt, pub; D & E; SC 16, LC 17; D 2000, non-maj 284, maj 60
Ent Req: HS dipl, 3 achievement tests & English Composition Achievement required
Degrees: BA 4 yrs
Tuition: Res—$26,700 per yr with room & board
Courses: Art Education, †Art History, Ceramics, †Design, Drawing, Graphic Arts, History of Art & Architecture, Museum Staff Training, Painting, Photography, Printmaking, Sculpture, †Studio Arts, †Teacher Training, †Theatre Arts
Adult Hobby Classes: Courses—Art History, Drawing, Painting, Photography, Photo-Journalism
Summer School: Dean of Evening Coll, S Laposata; Courses—same as adult educ courses

BETHLEHEM

LEHIGH UNIVERSITY, Dept of Art, Architecture & Design, 17 Memorial Dr E, Bethlehem, PA 18015-3029. Tel 610-758-3610; Web: www.lehigh.edu; *Assoc* Bruce Thomas PhD; *Prof* Ricardo Viera, MFA; *Prof* Lucy Gans, MFA; *Prof* Anthony Viscardi, MArch; *Assoc Prof* Berrisford Boothe, MFA; *Prof Practice* Christine Ussler, MArch; *Assoc Prof* Anna Chupa, MFA; *Assoc Prof* Amy Forsyth, MArch; *Prof of Practice* Jason Travers, MFA; *Assoc Prof* Wesley Heiss, M Arch; *Assoc Prof* Marilyn Jones, MFA; *Asst Prof* Hyun Tae Jung, PhD; *Asst Prof* Nikolai Nikolov, M Arch; *Assoc Prof* Nicholas Sawicki, PhD; *Asst Prof* Susan Kart, PhD
Estab 1925; Maintains Art Galleries, Zoellner Art Center, 420 E Packer Ave, Bethlehem, PA 18015; FT 9, PT 1; pvt; D & E; SC 22, LC 16; D & E 100
Ent Req: HS dipl, SAT, CEEB
Degrees: BA 4 yrs
Courses: †Architecture, †Art, †Art History, †Design, Drawing, Graphic Design, Museum Studies, Painting, Photography, Product Design, Sculpture
Summer School: Courses—Architectural Design, Art History, Graphic Design Workshop, Color

MORAVIAN COLLEGE, Dept of Art, Hurd Campus, 99 W Church St Bethlehem, PA 18018-6614; 1200 Main St, Bethlehem, PA 18018-6614. Tel 610-861-1680; Fax 610-861-1682; Email ciganickj@moravian.edu; Web: www.moravian.edu; *Chmn* Angela Fraleigh, MFA; *Dir of Payne Gallery & Prof* Diane Radycki, PhD; *Prof* Kristin Baxter, EdD; *Instr* Jeffrey Hurwitz; *Instr* Renzo Faggioli; *Prof* Camille Murphy; *Instr* Doug Zucco; *Instr* Martha Kearns; *Instr* Elizabeth Krenos; *Instr* Ted Colegrove; *Instr* Kristine Kotsch; *Instr* Jan Ciganick; *Instr* Ashley Kuhn; *Instr* Luke Wynne; *Instr* Michael Lantz; *Vis Artist* Natessa Amin
Estab 1742, dept estab 1963; Maintains Payne Gallery of Moravian College located at same address; pvt; D & E; Scholarships; SC 15, LC 8; D 1200, E 500, non-maj 1200, maj 140
Ent Req: HS dipl
Degrees: BA and BS 4 yrs
Courses: †Advertising Design, †Art Education, †Art History, †Ceramics, Design, Digital Video, †Drawing, Graphic Arts, Graphic Design, Handicrafts, History of Art & Architecture, Museum Staff Training, Painting, Photography, Printmaking, Sculpture, †Teacher Training & Certification
Children's Classes: Summer camp $100 per wk per student

NORTHAMPTON COMMUNITY COLLEGE, Art Dept, 3835 Green Pond Rd, Bethlehem, PA 18020-7599. Tel 610-861-5300, Ext 5485; Fax 610-861-5373; Web: www.northampton.edu; *Asst Prof* Andrew Szoke; *Prog Coordr* Gerald Rowan
Estab 1967; pub; D & E; Scholarships; SC 12, LC 8; D 100, E 350
Ent Req: HS dipl, portfolio
Degrees: AAS(Advertising), cert in photography
Courses: 3-D Materials, Advertising Design, Architecture, Art History, Ceramics, Color & Spatial Concepts, Computer Graphics, Drafting, Drawing, Fashion Arts, Graphic Arts, Graphic Design, Handicrafts, History of Art & Architecture, Illustration, Interior Design, Lettering, Painting, Photography, Pottery, Printmaking, Sculpture
Adult Hobby Classes: Courses—Art, Photography

BLOOMSBURG

BLOOMSBURG UNIVERSITY, Dept of Art & Art History, 400 E 2nd St, Bloomsburg, PA 17815-1399. Tel 570-389-4646; Fax 570-389-4459; Web: www.bloomu.edu; *Chmn* Dr Christine Sperling; *Prof* Vera Viditz-Ward, MFA; *Assoc Prof* Charles Thomas Walter, PhD, MA; *Asst Prof* Meredith Grimsley, MFA; *Assoc Prof* Vincent Hron, MFA; *Assoc Prof* Jason Godeke, MFA; *Asst Prof* Marilee Salvator, MFA; *Asst Prof* Sue O'Donnell, MFA; *Asst Prof* Dr Nogin Chung, PhD
Estab 1839, dept estab 1940; Maintains nonprofit Haas Gallery of Art, 2nd Fl Mitrani Hall, 400 E 2nd St, Bloomsburg PA 17815; art supplies sold at on-campus store; pub; D & E; Scholarships; SC 24, LC 9; D 1000, E 30, maj 100, non-maj 930
Ent Req: HS dipl
Degrees: BA(Art Studio) & BA(Art History)
Courses: Art History, Computer Graphics, Crafts, General Design, Painting, Photography, Printmaking, Sculpture, †Textile Design
Summer School: Dean, Michael Vavrek. Enrl 200. Courses—Art History, General Studio

BLUE BELL

MONTGOMERY COUNTY COMMUNITY COLLEGE, Art Center, 340 De Kalb Pike, Blue Bell, PA 19422. Tel 215-641-6328; Email fshort@mc3.edu; Web: www.mc3.edu; *Coordr* Frank Short; *Assoc Prof* Roger Cairns, MFA; *Asst Prof* Cheryl Gelover, MFA; *Asst Prof* Michael Connelly; *Assoc Prof* Patrick Winston
Estab 1967; Maintains Fine Art Center Gallery & campus shop for limited purchase of art supplies; FT 5, PT 31; Pub; D, E & online; Scholarships; SC 39, LC 6; D 250
Ent Req: HS dipl
Degrees: AA & AFA Fine Arts, AAS Commercial Art & Digital Design
Tuition: Count res—undergrad $96 per cr hr; nonres—$192 per cr hr
Courses: Art History, Ceramics, †Digital Art, †Digital Design*, †Digital Photography, Drawing, †Fine Art, Graphic Design, Illustration, Painting, Photography, Printmaking, Sculpture, Typography, †Woodworking
Summer School: Coord, Frank Short. Enrl 66; tuition $35 per cr. Courses—Ceramics, Drawing, Painting, Photography

BRYN MAWR

BRYN MAWR COLLEGE, Dept of the History of Art, 101 N Merion Ave, Bryn Mawr, PA 19010-2899. Tel 610-526-5210; Email info@brynmawr.edu; Web: www.brynmawr.edu/arts; *Dept Admin* Adrienne Clarke
Estab 1913; maintains library, Rhys Carpenter Library; pvt, W (men in grad school); D; Scholarships; Fellowships; LC 10, GC 8; maj 15, grad 30, others 250
Degrees: BA 4 yr, MA, PhD
Tuition: $21,860 per yr; campus res—room & board $7870
Courses: †Architecture, Art History, †Graphic Arts, †History of Art & Architecture

HARCUM COLLEGE, Fashion Design, 750 Montgomery Ave, Bryn Mawr, PA 19010-3405. Tel 610-526-6050; Web: www.harcum.edu; *Dir* Winifred Curtis; *Assistant Professor* Julian Crooks
Estab 1915; Maintains a non-profit art gallery: Kevin D Marlo Little Theater, 750 Montgomery Avenue, Bryn Mawr, PA 19010; has an on-campus shop where art supplies can be purchased.; FT 1, PT 5; pvt, Co-Ed; D & E; Scholarships; SC 7, LC 1; D 40, E 8, maj 10
Ent Req: HS dipl
Degrees: AA 2 yr
Courses: Art History, Commercial Art, Costume Design & Construction, Design, Display, Drawing, Fashion Arts, Graphic Design, History of Art & Architecture, Lettering, Painting, Photography, Sculpture, Textile Design
Adult Hobby Classes: residential, fashion & digital design

CALIFORNIA

CALIFORNIA UNIVERSITY OF PENNSYLVANIA, Dept of Art, 250 University, California, PA 15419. Tel 724-938-4000, 938-4182; Fax 724-938-4256; Web: www.cup.edu; *Chmn Dept* Richard Mieczinkowski
Estab 1852, dept estab 1968; pub; D & E; SC 20, LC 5; maj 137
Ent Req: SAT
Degrees: Cert(Art Educ), BA 4 yrs
Courses: Advertising Design, Aesthetics, Art Appreciation, Art Education, Art History, Ceramics, Commercial Art, Costume Design & Construction, Design, Drawing, Fashion Arts, Graphic Arts, Handicrafts, Illustration, Interior Design, Jewelry, Mixed Media, Painting, Printmaking, Sculpture, Stage Design, Stained Glass, Textile Design, Weaving
Adult Hobby Classes: Enrl 25 per class. Courses—Pottery, Stained Glass

Summer School: Chmn, Richard Grinstead. Term of 5 or 10 wks beginning June

CARLISLE

DICKINSON COLLEGE, Dept of Art & Art History, PO Box 1773, Weiss Ctr for the Arts Carlisle, PA 17013-2896. Tel 717-245-1053; Fax 717-245-1937; Email millejoa@dickinson.edu; Web: www.dickinson.edu/departments/arts/; *Prof* Barbara Diduk; *Assoc Prof* Ward Davenny; *Prof* Melinda Schlitt, PhD; *Asst Prof* Elizabeth Lee, PhD; *Asst Prof* Anthony Cervino; *Adjunct Faculty* Andrew Bale; *Asst Prof* Todd Arsenault; *Adjunct Faculty* Lisa Dorrill, PhD; *Assoc Prof* Crispin Sartwell
Estab 1773, dept estab 1940; Maintains nonprofit art gallery, The Trout Gallery, Weiss Center for the Arts, PO Box 1773, Carlisle, PA 17013. Campus shop where art supplies may be purchased; pvt; D; SC 10, LC 15; D 2400, non-maj 550, Maj 80
Ent Req: HS dipl, SAT
Degrees: BA and BS 4 yrs
Courses: Art History, Ceramics, †Contemporary Art, Drawing, History of Art & Architecture, Italian Renaissance, Painting, Photography, Printmaking, Sculpture, †Studio Major, †Video
Summer School: Dir, Diane Fleming. Term of 6 wks beginning May. Courses—per regular session

CHELTENHAM

CHELTENHAM CENTER FOR THE ARTS, 439 Ashbourne Rd, Cheltenham, PA 19012-1705. Tel 215-379-4660; Fax 215-663-1946; Email info@cheltenhamarts.org; Web: www.cheltenhamarts.org; *Events & Publicity Coordr* Traci Nelson; *Educ Dir* Joan Phillips
Estab 1940; maintain nonprofit art gallery at same address; community; D & E; 6-wk terms, 6 per yr; Scholarships; SC 50; D 875, E 200, Other 250
Ent Req: children, teens & adults; open to the public
Tuition: Course prices vary
Courses: Ceramics, Drawing, Jewelry, Painting, Pottery, Printmaking, Sculpture, Stained Glass, Theater Classes, Theatre Arts, Video

CHEYNEY

CHEYNEY UNIVERSITY OF PENNSYLVANIA, Dept of Art, 1837 University Cir, Cheyney, PA 19319-0200. Tel 610-399-2000; Web: www.cheyney.edu; *Fine Arts Dept Chmn* J Hank Hamilton Jr
Estab 1937; pub; D & E; Scholarships; SC 16, LC 4
Ent Req: HS dipl, ent exam
Degrees: BA 4 yrs
Courses: Drawing, Handicrafts, Painting, Sculpture

CLARION

CLARION UNIVERSITY OF PENNSYLVANIA, Dept of Art, 840 Wood St, Clarion, PA 16214-1240. Tel 814-393-2000, ext 2291; Fax 814-393-2168; Email mkuntz@clarion.edu; Web: www.clarion.edu; *Asst Prof* Jeremy Boyle; *Asst Prof* James Rose; *Asst Prof* Dr Gary Greenberg; *Assoc Prof* Kaersten Colvin; *Prof* Melissa Kuntz; *Prof* Mark Franchino; *Instr* Benedict Oddi; *Instr* Natalia Jensen
Estab 1867; Maintains nonprofit University Gallery; Pub; D & E; Scholarships; SC 20, LC 10; D & E 925 per sem, day 450, eve 50, non-maj 150, maj 85
Ent Req: HS dipl
Degrees: BFA(Art), BA(Art), BFA (Art, Graphic Design)
Tuition: $6,500 per yr (approx)
Courses: 3-D Design, Art Appreciation, †Art History, †Ceramics, †Conceptual Art, Design, †Drawing, Graphic Design, History of Art & Architecture, Jewelry, Jewelry, †Painting, †Printmaking, †Sculpture
Summer School: Tuition $200 per cr hr (approx) for 3 sessions

EAST STROUDSBURG

EAST STROUDSBURG UNIVERSITY, Fine Arts Center, 200 Prospect St, Fine Arts Bldg East Stroudsburg, PA 18301-2999. Tel 570-422-3759; Fax 570-422-3777; Web: www.esu.edu; *Chmn* Dr Herbert Weigand
Estab 1894; FT 3, PT 2; pub; D & E; Scholarships; SC 17, LC 6, grad 1; D 45
Ent Req: HS dipl, HS equivalency
Degrees: BA in Fine Arts
Tuition: Res—undergrad $1192 per sem, grad $1845 per sem; nonres—undergrad $4301 per sem, grad $3074 per sem; campus res available
Courses: Aesthetics, American Art Communication Graphics, Art Education, Art History, Calligraphy, Ceramics, Design, Drawing, Graphics, Handicrafts, Lettering, Painting, Printmaking, Sculpture
Summer School: Tuition res—grad $89 per cr hr

EASTON

LAFAYETTE COLLEGE, Dept of Art, 317 Hamilton St, Williams Ctr for the Arts Easton, PA 18042. Tel 610-330-5355; Fax 610-330-5355; Email ahldiane@lafayette.edu; *Prof Art* Ed Kerns; *Dept Head* Diane Cole Ahl
Estab 1827; FT 4, PT 4; pvt; D & E; SC 8, LC 12; D 300, E 250, non-maj 1, maj 17
Ent Req: HS dipl, ent exam, selective admis
Degrees: BS and AB 4 yr
Courses: 2-D & 3-D Design, Art History, Drawing, Graphic Design, History of Architecture, Painting, Photography, Printmaking, Sculpture
Summer School: Graphic Design, Painting, Photography

EDINBORO

EDINBORO UNIVERSITY OF PENNSYLVANIA, Art Dept, 219 Meadville St, Doucette Hall Edinboro, PA 16444-0001. Tel 814-732-2406; Web: www.edinboro.edu; *Chmn Crafts* Bernard Maas; *Fine Arts Representative* Ben Gibson; *Dir Gallery* William Mathie; *Chairperson* Dr Connie Mullineaux; *Asst Chmn of Art* Franz Stohn
Estab 1857; FT 34, PT 2; pub; D & E; Scholarships; SC 86, LC 30, GC 20; D 400 art maj, non-maj 6000, grad 30
Ent Req: HS dipl, SAT
Degrees: BSEd, BFA and BA 4 yrs, MA 1 yr, MFA 2 yrs
Courses: Advertising Design, Art Education, Art History, Ceramics, †Communications Graphics, Film, Goldsmithing, Handicrafts, History of Art & Architecture, Jewelry, Mixed Media, †Painting, †Photography, †Printmaking, †Sculpture, †Silversmithing, †Teacher Training, †Textile Design, Video, Weaving
Summer School: Chmn, Ian Short. Tuition $129 per cr for two 5 wk sessions

ERDENHEIM

ANTONELLI INSTITUTE, Professional Photography & Commercial Art, 300 Montgomery Ave, Erdenheim, PA 19038-8242. Tel 215-836-2222; Fax 215-836-2794; Email admissions@antonelli.org; Web: www.antonelli.org; *Pres* John Hayden; *Instr* Joseph Wilk; *Dir Educ* Tricia Fleming; *Placement, Faculty* Andrew Simcox; *Graphic Design* Chris Patchell; *Graphic Design* Ed Zawora; *Photog* Vladmir Hartman; *Photog* Mimi Janosy; *Photog* Todd Murray; *Photog* Robert Wood
Estab 1938; Maintain art library; pvt; D; SC, LC; D 205, Maj 205
Ent Req: HS dipl
Degrees: A (Specialized Technology)
Courses: Advertising Design, Art History, †Commercial Art, Design, Drawing, Film, Graphic Arts, †Graphic Design, History of Art & Architecture, Illustration, †Photography, Typography
Adult Hobby Classes: Workshops as scheduled
Summer School: Workshops

ERIE

MERCYHURST UNIVERSITY, Dept of Art, 501 E 38th St, Erie, PA 16546-0002. Tel 814-824-2000; Fax 814-825-2188; Email jstaniunashopper@mercyhurst.edu; Web: www.mercyhurst.edu; *Prof* Daniel Burke; *Asst Prof* Gary Cardot; *Chair, Assoc Prof* Jodi Staniunas Hopper; *Assoc Prof* Thomas Hubert; *Asst Prof* Dr Deborah John; *Asst Prof* Mary Elizabeth Meier, PhD; *Instr* Peter Stadtmueller
Estab 1926, dept estab1926; Maintain nonprofit art gallery, Sr Angelica Cummings Art Gallery, 501 E 38th St, Erie PA 16546; FT 7, PT 4; pvt; D & E; Scholarships; SC 50, LC 6, Internship/Co-op 6; D 90, E 20, maj 90
Ent Req: HS dipl, col boards
Degrees: BA 4 yr
Courses: 3-D Design, †Advertising Design, Aesthetics, Art Appreciation, †Art Education, Art Foundations, Art History, †Art Therapy, Ceramics, Design, Drawing, Graphic Arts, †Graphic Design, History of Art & Architecture, Independent Study, Individualized Studio, Internship, Painting, Photography, Printmaking, Sculpture, Senior Seminar, †Studio Art, Teaching Internship

FARMINGTON

TOUCHSTONE CENTER FOR CRAFTS, 1049 Wharton Furnace Rd, Farmington, PA 15437-1195. Tel 724-329-1370; Fax 724-329-1371; Web: www.touchstonecrafts.com; *Registrar* Laura Peters
Estab 1983; 90 PT; pvt; D; Scholarships; D 500
Courses: Ceramics, Design, Fashion Arts, Handicrafts, Illustration, Jewelry, Painting, Photography, Printmaking, Sculpture, Silversmithing, Textile Design, Video, Weaving
Adult Hobby Classes: Enrl 400; tuition $100-$250 per wk. Courses—Blacksmithing, Clay, Fibre, Glass, Metal, Painting, Photography, Printmaking, Wood
Children's Classes: Enrl 100. Courses—Art

GETTYSBURG

GETTYSBURG COLLEGE, Dept of Visual Arts, 300 N Washington St, Gettysburg, PA 17325. Tel 717-337-6121; Email atrevely@gettysburg.edu; Web: www.gettysburg.edu; *Prof* Alan Paulson; *Assoc Prof* James Agard; *Asst Prof* Carol Small; *Instr* Lisa Dorrill; *Instr* Jim Ramos; *Instr* Brent Blair; *Instr* John Winship; *Chmn* Mark Warwick
Estab 1832, dept estab 1956; pvt; D; SC 10, LC 15; D 300
Ent Req: HS dipl, ent exam
Degrees: BA 4 yrs
Courses: 2-D & 3-D Design, American Indian Art, Architecture, †Art History, Art of Cinema, Ceramics, Design, Drawing, Film, Gallery Training, History of Art & Architecture, Museum Staff Training, Painting, Printmaking, Sculpture

GLENSIDE

ARCADIA UNIVERSITY, (Beaver College) Dept of Fine Arts, 450 Easton Rd, Glenside, PA 19038. Tel 215-572-2900; Web: www.arcadia.edu; *Asst Prof* Bonnie Hayes, MA, ABD; *Assoc Prof* Betsey Batchelor, MFA; *Asst Prof* Judith Taylor, MFA; *Asst Prof* W Scott Rawlins, MFA; *Chmn* Robert Mauro, MFA
Estab 1853; PT 7; pvt; D & E; Scholarships; SC 43, LC 14; in Col D FT 625, PT 115, non-maj in dept 30, maj in dept 140
Ent Req: HS dipl, SAT, ACT, optional portfolio review

Degrees: BA and BFA 4 yrs, MA(Educ) 1 yr
Courses: Art Education, Art History, †Art Therapy, Ceramics, Design, Drawing, Goldsmithing, Graphic Design, History of Art & Architecture, Interior Design, Jewelry, Painting, Photography, Printmaking, Silversmithing
Summer School: Chmn, Robert Mauro. Enrl approx 30; tuition $1040 per cr hr for term of 7 wks. Courses—Drawing, Painting, Visual Fundamentals

GREENSBURG

SETON HILL UNIVERSITY, Art Program, 1 Seton Hill Dr Greensburg, PA 15601. Tel 724-834-2200, Ext 4255; Fax 724-830-1294; Email admit@setonhill.edu; Web: setonhill.edu; *Asst Prof* Maureen Vissat, MA; *Dir Gallery & Asst Prof* Carol Brode, MA; *Prog Dir & Assoc Prof* Mary Kay Neff, MFA; *Dir Grad Adult Studies* Christine Schaeffer; *Assoc Prof* Patricia Beachley, MFA; *Assoc Prof* Philip Rostek, MFA; *Assoc Prof* Nina Denninger, MA; *Instr* Richard Stoner; *Instr* Jim Andrews; *Instr* Brian Ferrell; *Instr* Nora Thompson; *Instr* Sandy Trimble; *Asst* Dana Elmendorf; *Instr* David Stanger
Estab 1918, dept estab 1950; Maintains nonprofit art gallery, Harlan Gallery & library, Reeves Library (same address); Pvt, den; D & E & Sat; Scholarships; SC 40, LC 8, GC 11; D 1,875, maj 111, minor 15, pt 10, grad 35
Ent Req: HS dipl, review portfolio
Degrees: BA, BFA 4 yr
Courses: 3-D Design, Advanced 2-D Media, Advanced 3-D Media, †Art Education, †Art History, †Art Therapy, †Ceramics, Design, Digital Imaging, †Drawing, Fabrics, †Graphic Design, Jewelry, Metalsmithing, †Painting, Photography, †Printmaking, Professional Practice, †Restoration & Conservation, †Sculpture, †Studio Art, †Theatre Arts, Typography, †Weaving, †Web Design
Adult Hobby Classes: Enrl 25; tuition $425 per cr for 14 wk sem. Courses— Art History, Photography, Design
Summer School: Dir, Christine Schaffer. Enrl 529. 19 art maj, Courses—Art in Elementary Educ, Digital Imaging

GREENVILLE

THIEL COLLEGE, Dept of Art, 75 College Ave, Greenville, PA 16125-2181. Tel 724-589-2094, 589-2000; Web: www.thiel.edu; *Chmn Dept* Ronald A Pivovar, MFA
Estab 1866, dept estab 1965; pvt; D & E; Scholarships; SC 14, LC 11; D 105, non-maj 65, maj 40
Ent Req: HS dipl, interviews
Degrees: BA 4 yrs
Courses: Art History, Ceramics, Drawing, Graphic Arts, Jewelry, Painting, Printmaking, Sculpture, Stage Design, Theatre Arts
Adult Hobby Classes: Classes offered
Summer School: Asst Acad Dean, Richard Houpt. Term of 4 wks beginning June 3. Courses—Art History, Extended Studies, Drawing

HARRISBURG

HARRISBURG AREA COMMUNITY COLLEGE, Division of Communications, Humanities & the Arts, One HACC Dr, Harrisburg, PA 17110. Tel 717-780-2423; 780-2426; Fax 717-780-3281; Web: www.hacc.edu; *Chmn Art Dept* Sara F Meng PhD; *Chmn Theatre* Marnie Brennan, MA; *Instr* Brenda Eppley, MFA; *Instr* Jim Lard, MFA; *Instr* Ronald Talbott, MFA; *Instr* Marjaneh Talebi, MFA; *Instr* Robert Trovell, MFA, PhD; *Instr* Monica Smith-Talbott, MFA
Estab 1964; Maintains Rose Lehrman Art Gallery; pub; D & E; SC 15, LC 5
Ent Req: HS dipl
Degrees: AA 2 yrs
Courses: Art History, Ceramics, Crafts Marketing, Drawing, Graphic Design, Jewelry, Painting, Photography, Printmaking, Sculpture, Theatre Arts
Adult Hobby Classes: Courses—Calligraphy, Drawing, Painting, Photography, Pottery
Children's Classes: Courses—Calligraphy, Creative Dramatics
Summer School: Dir, Michael Dockery. Courses vary

HAVERFORD

HAVERFORD COLLEGE, Fine Arts Dept, 370 Lancaster Ave, Haverford, PA 19041-1392. Tel 610-896-1267 (Art Dept); Fax 610-896-1495; *Prof* R Christopher Cairns, MFA
Estab 1833, dept estab 1969; pvt; D, M; Scholarships; maj 12
Ent Req: HS dipl, programs in cooperation with Bryn Mawr College, Fine Arts Program
Degrees: BA 4 yrs
Courses: Drawing, Graphic Arts, History of Art & Architecture, Painting, Photography, Sculpture
—Cantor Fitzgerald Gallery, Whitehead Campus Ctr, 370 Lancaster Ave Haverford, PA 19041. Tel 610-896-1287; Email hcexhibits@gmail.com; Web: www.haverford.edu/HHC/exhibits; *Campus Exhibit Coordr* Matthew Seamus Callinan
Open Mon-Tues & Thurs-Fri 11AM-5PM, Wed 11AM-8PM, Sat-Sun 12PM-5PM; No admis fee
Collections: paintings; sculpture

MAIN LINE ART CENTER, 746 Panmure Rd, Haverford, PA 19041-1218. Tel 610-525-0272; Fax 610-525-5036; Web: www.mainlineart.org; *Admin Exec Dir* Judy S Herman; *Instr* Carol Cole, BA; *Instr* Liz Goldberg, MFA; *Instr* Robert Finch, BFA; *Instr* Ginny Kendall, BFA; *Instr* Carol Kardon, BFA; *Instr* Bonnie Mettler, BFA; *Instr* Francine Shore, BFA; *Instr* Carson Fox, BFA; *Instr* Sallee Rush, BFA; *Instr* Mimi Oritsky, MFA; *Instr* Val Rossman, MFA; *Instr* Scott Wheelock, MFA; *Instr* Martha Kent Martin, BFA; *Instr* Patrick Arnold, BFA; *Instr* Carol Stirton-Broad, BFA; *Instr* Lydia Lehr, MFA; *Instr* Ann Simon, MFA; *Instr* Kathie Regan-Dalzell, BA; *Instr* Nury Vicens, MFA; *Instr* Susanna T Saunders, BA
Estab 1937; pvt; D & E; Scholarships; SC 45; D 300, E 250
Courses: Art History, Batik, Calligraphy, Ceramics, Collage, Drawing, Faux Painting, Jewelry, Mixed Media, Painting, Photography, Printmaking, Sculpture, Silversmithing, Textile Design, Tie-dyeing
Children's Classes: Enrl 1500, Courses—General Arts, Pottery
Summer School: Admin Dir, Judy S Herman. Tuition varies, classes begin mid-June. Courses—same as above

HUNTINGDON

JUNIATA COLLEGE, Dept of Art & Art History, 1700 Moore St, Huntingdon, PA 16652. Tel 814-641-3657; Web: www.juniata.edu; *Chmn Dept* Jennifer Streb
Estab 1876; FT 3, PT 1; pvt; D; Scholarships; SC, LC; 1400, maj 40
Ent Req: HS dipl
Degrees: BA 4 yrs
Tuition: Campus res
Courses: Aesthetics, Art History, Arts Management, Ceramics, Computer Graphics, Design, Drawing, History of Art & Architecture, Museum Studies, Painting, Photography, studio art, Theatre Arts
Summer School: Courses —Art History, Ceramics, Studio Art

INDIANA

INDIANA UNIVERSITY OF PENNSYLVANIA, College of Fine Arts, 470 S 11th St, Sprowls Hall Rm 110 Indiana, PA 15705-1044. Tel 724-357-2530; Fax 724-357-3296; Email jlstrong@grove.iup.edu; Web: www.arts.iup.edu; *Assoc Prof* Andrew Gillham; *Asst Prof* Lynda LaRoche; *Assoc Prof* Dr Marjorie Mambo; *Assoc Prof* Dr Brenda Mitchell; *Assoc Prof* Dr Irene Kabala; *Asst Prof* Ivan Fortushniak; *Assoc Prof* Fuyuko Matsubara; *Prof* Susan Palmisano; *Assoc Prof* Penny Rode; *Assoc Prof* Kevin Turner; *Dir, Turning & Furniture Design Ctr* Steve Loar
Estab 1875, dept estab 1875; on-campus shop for purchase of art supplies; pub; D & E; Scholarships; Assistantships; SC 26, LC 21, GC 30; D 250, non-maj 1700, maj 270, grad 30
Ent Req: HS dipl, SAT, portfolio review, ACT
Degrees: BS(Art Educ), BA(Art History & Humanities with Art Concentration), BFA(Studio Art Concentration) 4 yr, MA 2 yr & MFA
Courses: Art Education, †Art History, †Art Studio, Ceramics, Computer Graphics, Design, Drawing, Fiber Arts, Goldsmithing, Graphic Design, Jewelry, Painting, Papermaking, Printmaking, Sculpture, Silversmithing, Weaving, Woodworking
Adult Hobby Classes: Enrl 60; Courses—Ceramics, Drawing
Summer School: Dir, Andrew Gillham. Enrl 140; tuition regular acad sem cr cost. Courses—Art Appreciation, Art History, Special Workshops, Studios

JOHNSTOWN

UNIVERSITY OF PITTSBURGH AT JOHNSTOWN, Dept of Fine Arts, 450 Schoolhouse Rd, Johnstown, PA 15904-2990. Tel 814-269-7000 (Main); Fax 814-269-2096; Email vgrash@pitt.edu; Web: www.upj.pitt.edu; *Dept Head* Dr Valerie Grash
Estab 1968; Art supplies sold at on campus store; pub, pvt; D & E; LC 15; D 160, maj 3
Ent Req: HS dipl, SAT
Degrees: BA 4 yrs
Courses: †Art History, Film, History of Art & Architecture, Photography, Stage Design, †Theatre Arts

KUTZTOWN

KUTZTOWN UNIVERSITY, College of Visual & Performing Arts, PO Box 730, Kutztown, PA 19530-0730. Tel 610-683-4500; Fax 610-683-4547; *Dean* William Mowder
Institution estab 1860, art dept estab 1929; pub; D & E; Scholarships; SC 284, LC 40, GC 8; D 943, maj 10
Ent Req: HS dipl
Degrees: BFA 4 yr, BS(Art Educ) 4 yr, MA(Educ)
Courses: Advertising Design, Art Education, Ceramics, Drawing, Fine Metals, Graphic Design, Illustration, Jewelry, Painting, Photography, Printmaking, Sculpture, Weaving, Woodworking
Children's Classes: Young at Art
Summer School: Regular sessions 5 wks. Courses—Art Ed, Studio

LAPLUME

KEYSTONE COLLEGE, Fine Arts Dept, One College Green, LaPlume, PA 18440-1000; PO Box 50, LaPlume, PA 18440-0200. Tel 570-945-5141, Ext 3300, 3301; Fax 570-945-6767; Email cliff.prokop@keystone.edu; Web: www.keystone.edu; *Prof* William Tersteeg, MFA; *Art Dept Coordr* Stacey Donahue-Semenza, BFA; *Prof* Ward V Roe, MFA; *Assoc Prof* Sally Tosti, MFA; *Instr* Nikki Moser, BFA; *Chmn Fine Arts* Clifton Prokop, MFA; *Assoc Prof* Drake Gomez, MFA; *Assoc Prof* Dave Potter, MA; *Instr* Trevor Herceg, MFA; *Instr* Jodi Dunn, PhD; *Instr* Kevin O'Neil, MFA; *Instr* Elizabeth Burkhauser; *Instr* Frank Groyl
Estab 1868, dept estab 1965; Maintains Linder Gallery at the College; pvt; D & E, weekends; Scholarships; SC 15, LC 2; D 100
Ent Req: HS dipl, SAT
Degrees: AFA 2 yrs, BS (Art Educ), BA (Fine Art)
Tuition: Res—$9848 per yr, incl rm & board
Courses: 2-D Design, 3-D Design, Advertising Design, †Art Appreciation, Art History, Ceramics, Color, Commercial Art, †Costume Design & Construction, Design, Drawing, Film, Graphic Design, †History of Art & Architecture, Intro to Commercial Design, Life Drawing, Mixed Media, Painting, Photography,

Printmaking, Sculpture, Silversmithing, †Stage Design, †Teacher Training, †Theatre Arts

LANCASTER

FRANKLIN & MARSHALL COLLEGE, Art & Art History Dept, PO Box 3003, Lancaster, PA 17604-3003. Tel 717-291-4199; Fax 717-358-4599; Web: www.fandm.edu/art; *Dept Chair* Virginia A Maksymowicz; *Prof* Richard K Kent; *Assoc Prof* Linda Aleci; *Assoc Prof* Michael Clapper; *Assoc Prof* Jun-Cheng Liu; *Assoc Prof* James C Paterson; *Assoc Prof* Amelia Rauser; *Asst Prof* John C Holmgren; *Asst Prof* Kostis Kourelis
Estab 1966; pvt; D & E; Scholarships; SC 10, LC 17; in col D 1900, E 580
Ent Req: HS dipl, SAT
Degrees: BA 4 yr
Tuition: Res—$90,810 per yr
Courses: Architecture, Art History, Basic Design, Drawing, History of Art & Architecture, Painting, Printmaking, Sculpture

PENNSYLVANIA SCHOOL OF ART & DESIGN, 204 N Prince St, Lancaster, PA 17603-3528. Tel 717-396-7833; Fax 717-396-1339; Web: www.psad.edu; *Pres* Mary Colleen Heil
Estab 1982; Maintain nonprofit art gallery on-campus; art library; 40 FT & PT; pvt; D & E; Scholarships; SC 160, LC 9; D 200, E 150, non-maj 60, maj 140
Ent Req: HS dipl
Degrees: BFA (Fine Art, Graphic Design, Illustration) 4 yr
Courses: Aesthetics, Art History, †Drawing, †Fine Art, †Graphic Design, †Illustration, Interior Design, †Photography
Adult Hobby Classes: Enrl 800; tuition $380 per cr. Cert Programs in Desktop Publishing, Interior Design. Studio cr & non-credit courses for youths & adults; web site design cert
Children's Classes: Enrl 250; tuition $160 per cr, 20 contact hrs. Courses—Figure Drawing, Studio
Summer School: Dir, Tracy Beyl. Enrl 220; tuition youth $160 for 20 contact hrs, adult $380 per cr for 30 hrs. Courses—Computer, Interior Design, Photography, Studio

LEWISBURG

BUCKNELL UNIVERSITY, Dept of Art, 701 Moore Ave, Lewisburg, PA 17837-2010. Tel 570-524-1307; Web: www.bucknell.edu; *Prof* Janice Mann, PhD, MFA; *Prof* Neil Anderson, MFA; *Prof* James Turnure, PhD, MFA; *Prof* Christiane Andersson, PhD, MFA; *Prof* Jody Blake, PhD, MFA; *Head Dept* Rosalyn Richards, MFA
Estab 1846; pvt; D; Scholarships; SC 19, LC 20, GC 30; D 500, non-maj 450, maj 50, grad 2
Ent Req: HS dipl
Degrees: BA 4 yrs
Courses: Art History, Drawing, Graphic Arts, History of Art & Architecture, Painting, Photography, Printmaking, Sculpture
Summer School: Dir, Lois Huffines. Courses—Lectures, Studio

LOCK HAVEN

LOCK HAVEN UNIVERSITY, Dept of Fine Arts, 401 N Fairview St, Lock Haven, PA 17745-2342. Tel 570-893-2151, 893-2011, 893-2143; Fax 570-893-2432; Web: www.lhup.edu; *Chmn* Bridgett Glenn
FT 4; pvt; D; Scholarships
Degrees: BA
Tuition: Res—$3468 per 2 sem, $144 per cr hr; nonres—$6824 per 2 sem, $284 per cr hr
Courses: 2-D Design, 3-D design, Art Appreciation, Art Education, Art History, Arts & Crafts, Ceramics, Drawing, Jewelry, Painting, Photography, Printmaking, Sculpture, Stage Design, Textile Design, Weaving
Summer School: Courses offered

LORETTO

ST FRANCIS COLLEGE, Fine Arts Dept, 110 Franciscan Way, Loretto, PA 15940-9709. Tel 814-472-3216; Fax 814-472-3044, 472-3000 (main); Email colson@sfcpa.edu; Web: www.sfcpa.edu; *Chmn* Charles Olsen, MFA
Scholarships
Degrees: minor in fine arts
Tuition: $463 per cr hr; campus res—room & board available
Courses: Art Appreciation, Art History, Culture & Values, Design, Drawing, Exploration of Arts, Independent Study, Modern Art, Museum Staff Training, Painting, Photography, Weaving

MANSFIELD

MANSFIELD UNIVERSITY, Art Dept, 135 Stadium Dr, 118 Allen Hall Mansfield, PA 16933-1611. Tel 570-662-4500; Fax 570-662-4114; *Assoc Prof* Tom Loomis, MA; *Asst Prof & Chmn Dept* Dr Bonnie Kutbay, MA
Estab 1857; pub; D; Scholarships; SC 26, LC 18; D 700, maj 90
Ent Req: HS dipl, SAT, portfolio & interview
Degrees: BA & BS(Studio Art), BA(Art History) & BSE(Art Educ) 4 yr, MEd(Art Educ)
Courses: Advertising Design, Aesthetics, Art Education, Art History, Ceramics, Color & Design, Computer Art, Drawing, Fibers, History of Art & Architecture, Jewelry, Lettering, Painting, Printmaking, Sculpture, Studio Crafts, Visual Studies in Aesthetic Experiences, Weaving
Adult Hobby Classes: Enrl 10. Courses—Art History, Studio Art, Graduate Level Art Education
Children's Classes: Enrl 100, tuition $20 for 10 wks, fall sem. Courses—Elementary Art Education
Summer School: Courses—Ceramics, Drawing, Fibers, Graduate Courses, Painting, Printmaking, Sculpture, Studio Courses

MEADVILLE

ALLEGHENY COLLEGE, Art Dept, 520 N Main St, Meadville, PA 16335-3902. Tel 814-332-4365; Email name@allegheny.edu; Web: www.allegheny.edu; *Chair Art Dept* Amara Geffen
Estab 1815, dept estab 1930; pvt; D; Scholarships; SC 10 per sem, LC 6 per sem; 550, maj 30, non-maj 250
Ent Req: HS dipl, ent exam
Degrees: BA and BS 4 yr
Courses: Art History, Ceramics, Costume Design & Construction, †Drawing, Film, Mixed Media, †Painting, †Photography, †Printmaking, †Sculpture, Stage Design, Theatre Arts, †Video

MEDIA

DELAWARE COUNTY COMMUNITY COLLEGE, Communications, Art & Humanities, 901 S Media Line Rd, Media, PA 19063-5382. Tel 610-359-5000, Ext 5398; Fax 610-359-7331; Email craport@dccc.edu; Web: www.dccc.edu; *Prof* Bertha Gutman, MFA; *Prof* Jaime Treadwell, MFA; *Prof* Bob Jones, MFA; *Prof* David Yox, MFA
Estab 1967; Maintains The Art Gallery at DCCC 901 South Media Line Rd Media PA 19063; pub; D, E & online; Studio & lecture courses
Degrees: AFA
Courses: 2-D & 3-D Design, Advertising, Advertising Design, Aesthetics, Art Education, Art History, Commercial Art, Computer Graphics, Design, Desk Top Publishing, Drawing, Graphic Arts, Graphic Design, History of Art & Architecture, Illustration, Lettering, Mixed Media, Painting, Photography, Production Techniques, Sculpture, Teacher Training, Theatre Arts, Typography
Adult Hobby Classes: Enrl varies; tuition varies. Courses—Calligraphy, Crafts, Drawing, Graphic Design, Interior Design, Needlepoint, Photography, Stained Glass, Sketching, Woodcarving
Summer School: Tuition res $27 per cr hr, nonres $81 per cr hr for term of 6 wks. Courses—Drawing, Painting

MIDDLETOWN

PENN STATE HARRISBURG, School of Humanities, 777 W Harrisburg Pike, Middletown, PA 17057-4898. Tel 717-948-6189; Fax 717-948-6724; Web: www.hbg.psu.edu/; *Prof* Irwin Richman PhD; *Assoc Prof* Troy Thomas PhD; *Dir Humanities* Simon J Bronner; *Dir Humanities* Linda Ross
Estab 1965; Maintain nonprofit art gallery; Morrison Gallery, Gallery Lounge; PT 10; pub; D & E; Scholarships; SC 7, LC 15; D & E 60, grad 40
Degrees: BHumanities, MA
Courses: Aesthetics, Architecture, Art Education, Art History, Drawing, Folk Art & Architecture, Graphic Design, †History of Art & Architecture, Mixed Media, Museum Staff Training, Painting, Photography, Theatre Arts, Video, Visual Studies

MILLERSVILLE

MILLERSVILLE UNIVERSITY, Dept of Art & Design, PO Box 1002, Millersville, PA 17551-0302. Tel 717-872-3298; Fax 717-871-2004; Email wanda.doyle@millersville.edu; Web: www.millersville.edu; *Prof Drawing, 2D & Graphic Design* Jeri L Robinson; *Prof Drawing, Painting & Watercolor* Robert Andriulli; *Assoc Prof Art Educ* Dr Barbara J Bensur; *Instr Drawing* Leslie E Brown; *Asst Prof 2D & 3D Design, Drawing & Sculpture* Line Bruntse; *Asst Prof 2D Design & Drawing* Ben J Cunningham; *Asst Prof Art History* Dr Christine Filippone; *Assoc Prof Photog* Shauna L Frischkorn; *Assoc Prof Graphic Design* Nancy R Mata; *Asst Prof Fine Arts Metals* Allyssa Gold; *Asst Prof Graphic & Interactive Design* James Pannafino; *Chair & Assoc Prof Printmaking* Brant D Schuller; *Assoc Prof Ceramics* Deborah S Sigel; *Interim Dept Sec* Wanda Doyle; *Asst Prof Art History* William W Wolfe; *Asst Grad Prof Art Educ* Dr Victoria Weaver
Estab 1855, dept estab 1930; Maintains nonprofit art gallery, library, & campus store for art supply purchase; pub; D & E; SC 65, LC 10, GC 64; maj 330, grad 20
Ent Req: HS dipl
Degrees: BA(Art), BS(Art Educ), BFA 4 yr, MEd(Art Educ) 1 yr
Tuition: Res—$2902 undergrad, $4397.75 - $4663.25 grad per sem; nonres—$7255 undergrad, $6546.75 - $6812.25 grad per sem
Courses: Art Appreciation, Art Education, Art History, Ceramics, Computer Art, Conceptual Art, Design, Drawing, Graphic Arts, Graphic Design, Handicrafts, History of Art & Architecture, Illustration, Jewelry, Mixed Media, Painting, Photography, Printmaking, Sculpture, Silversmithing, Teacher Training, †Visual Communication
Summer School: Chair, Jeri Robinson. Enrl 200; term of 5 wks, two sessions beginning June & July. Courses—Art, Art Education, Art History

MONROEVILLE

COMMUNITY COLLEGE OF ALLEGHENY COUNTY, BOYCE CAMPUS, Art Dept, 595 Beatty Rd, Monroeville, PA 15146-1348. Tel 724-327-1327; *Adjunct Prof* Kathy Gilbert; *Adjunct Prof* Jesse Almasi; *Adjunct Prof* Jamie Boyd
Pub; D & E; SC 13, LC 1; D 200, E 40, non-maj 140, maj 60
Ent Req: HS dipl
Degrees: AS 2 yrs
Tuition: $58 per cr
Courses: Art History, Ceramics, Collage, Color & Design, Constructions, Drawing, Graphic Arts, Mixed Media, Painting, Photography, Printmaking, Sculpture

Adult Hobby Classes: Ceramics, Color & Design, Drawing, History of Art, Mixed Media, Painting, Photography, Printmaking
Children's Classes: Enrl varies. Courses—Drawing, Painting
Summer School: Courses—Vary

NANTICOKE

LUZERNE COUNTY COMMUNITY COLLEGE, Commercial Art Dept, 1333 S Prospect St, Nanticoke, PA 18634-3814. Tel 570-740-0364; Web: www.luzerne.cc.pa.usa; WATS 800-377-5222; *Instr* Mike Molnar, BFA; *Instr & Coordr* Sam Cramer, BFA; *Instr* William Karlotski, BFA; *Coordr* Susan Sponenberg, BFA; *Instr* Chris Veda
Estab 1967; pub; D & E; SC 20, LC 7; D 140, E 60, non-maj 5, maj 60
Ent Req: HS dipl
Degrees: 2 year programs offered
Courses: Advertising Design, Airbrush, Art Education, Art History, Color & Design, Color Photography, †Computer Graphics, Conceptual Art, Design, Drawing, †Graphic Design, Illustration, Life Drawing, Mixed Media, Painting, Photography, Typography
Adult Hobby Classes: Enrl 350 per yr. Courses—Drawing, Graphic Design, Painting, Photography, Printmaking
Children's Classes: Enrl 500 per yr; summer sessions. Courses—Drawing, Painting
Summer School: Dir, Doug Williams, Enrl 20; Pre College Prog in July & Aug. Courses—Illustration, Life Drawing, Painting, Printmaking

NEW WILMINGTON

WESTMINSTER COLLEGE, Art Dept, 319 S Market St, Charles Freeman Hall - Rm 213 New Wilmington, PA 16172-0001; PO Box 162, New Wilmington, PA 16142-0162. Tel 724-946-7239, 946-6260; Fax 724-946-7070; Email barnerdl@westminster.edu; *Chmn* Dr David L Barner
Estab 1852; 3; den; D; Scholarships; maj 30, total 1100
Degrees: BS & BA(Fine Arts, Educ) 4 yrs
Courses: 2-D Design, 3-D Design, Art History, Ceramics, Computer Graphics, Drawing, Oil Painting, Photography, Printmaking, Sculpture
Children's Classes: Enrl 20

NEWTOWN

BUCKS COUNTY COMMUNITY COLLEGE, Fine Arts Dept, 275 Swamp Rd, Newtown, PA 18940-9677. Tel 215-504-8531; Fax 215-504-8530; Email orlando@bucks.edu; Web: www.bucks.edu/gallery; *Instr* Jon Alley; *Instr* Robert Dodge; *Instr* Jack Gevins; *Instr* Alan Goldstein; *Instr* Catherine Jansen; *Instr* Diane Lindenheim; *Instr* Marlene Miller; *Instr* Charlotte Schatz; *Instr* Helen Weisz; *Instr* Mark Sfirri; *Instr* Milt Sigel; *Instr* Gwen Kerber; *Instr* John Mathews; *Chmn Dept* Frank Dominguez
Estab 1965; pub; D & E; D & E 9200 (school)
Ent Req: HS dipl
Degrees: AA
Courses: Art History, Ceramics, Design, Drawing, Glass, Graphic Design, Jewelry, Painting, Photography, Printmaking, Sculpture, Woodworking

PHILADELPHIA

ART INSTITUTE OF PHILADELPHIA, 1622 Chestnut St, Philadelphia, PA 19103-5119. Tel 215-567-7080, 800-275-2474; Email magomez@aii.edu; Web: www.artinstitutes.edu/philadelphia; *Pres* Michael DePrisco
Estab 1966; FT 40, PT 65; pvt; D & E; Scholarships; SC 30, LC 8; D 1125, E 72
Ent Req: HS dipl, portfolio
Degrees: AST 2 yr
Tuition: $4635 per qtr
Courses: Advertising Design, Art History, Computer Graphics, Design, †Fashion Illustration, †Fashion Merchandising, Graphic Design, Illustration, †Interior Design, Lettering, Mixed Media, †Photography, Weaving

FLEISHER ART MEMORIAL, 719 Catharine St, Philadelphia, PA 19147-2811. Tel 215-922-3456; Fax 215-922-5327; Email info@fleisher.org; Web: www.fleisher.org; *Exec Dir* Elizabeth Grimaldi
Estab 1898; administered by the Philadelphia Museum of Art; maintains nonprofit gallery, Dene M Louchheim Galleries, 719 Catharine St; Matilda Rosenbaum Memorial Library (children) 719 Catharine St; pvt; E; Scholarships; SC 80, LC 1; E 2000
Ent Req: none
Degrees: none
Courses: †Calligraphy, Ceramics, Drawing, Painting, Photography, Printmaking, Sculpture
Adult Hobby Classes: Enrl 850; tuition free Sept-May. Courses—Ceramics, Drawing, Painting, Photography, Printmaking, Sculpture
Children's Classes: Enrl 425; tuition free Sept-May. Courses—Drawing, Painting, Papermaking, Sculpture
Summer School: Ceramics, Drawing, Landscape Painting, Painting, Photography, Printmaking, Sculpture

HUSSIAN SCHOOL OF ART, Commercial Art Dept, 111 S Independence Mall E Ste 300, Philadelphia, PA 19106-2521. Tel 215-574-9600; Fax 215-574-9800; Email info@hussianart.edu; Web: www.hussianart.edu; *Pres* Bruce Wartman; *Adminr* Maureen Flanagan; *Dean Acad Affairs* Melissa Morgan
Estab 1946; Maintain library for students & faculty only; on-campus art supplies shop for students only; FT 1, PT 25; pvt; D; Scholarships; SC & LC; D 140
Ent Req: HS dipl, portfolio interview
Degrees: AST
Tuition: No campus res
Courses: †Advertising Design, Airbrush, Art History, Commercial Art, Computer Graphics, †Digital Media, Drawing, Fine Art, Graphic Arts, Graphic Design, †Illustration, Mixed Media, Painting, Photography, Printmaking
Adult Hobby Classes: Courses offered
Summer School: Dir, Wilbur Crawford. Summer workshop in Advertising Design, Drawing, Illustration & Fantasy Illusion

LA SALLE UNIVERSITY, Dept of Art, 1900 W Olney Ave, Philadelphia, PA 19141-1108. Tel 215-951-1126; Web: www.lasalle.edu/; *Chmn Dept Fine Arts* Dr Charles White
Estab 1865, dept estab 1972; den; D & E; SC 2; D 4, maj 2
Ent Req: HS dipl
Degrees: BA 4 yr
Courses: Art History, Painting, Printmaking
Summer School: Selected courses offered

MOORE COLLEGE OF ART & DESIGN, 1920 Race St, 20th St Philadelphia, PA 19103-1108. Tel 215-568-4515; Fax 215-568-8017; Email info@moore.edu; Web: www.moore.edu; *Acad Dean* Dona Lantz; *Chmn Fine Arts* Paul Hubbard; *Chmn Fashion Design* Janice Lewis; *Chmn Liberal Arts* Jonathan Wallis; *Chmn Illustration* Bill Brown; *Chmn Interior Design* Margaret Leahy; *Chmn Textile Design* Deborah Warner; *Chmn Basic Arts* Moe Brooker; *Pres* Happy Craven Fernandez; *Chmn Graphic Design* Gigi McGee; *Chmn Art Educ* Lynne Horoschak; *Chmn Photog & Digital Arts* James Johnson
Estab 1848; Maintains nonprofit art galleries: The Goldie Paley Gallery and the Levy Gallery for the Arts in Philadelphia, 20th St & The Parkway, Philadelphia, PA 19103; also maintains an art/architecture library on site; Pvt, women only; D & E; Scholarships; Fellowships; SC 217, LC 47; D 525, non-maj 1
Ent Req: HS dipl, portfolio, SAT
Degrees: BFA 4 yr
Courses: †2-D & 3-D Design, †Art Education, †Art History, Ceramics, †Curatorial Studies, Design, Display, †Drafting, Drawing, Fashion Arts, Film, Graphic Arts, †Graphic Design, History of Art & Architecture, †Illustration, †Interior Design, Jewelry, Mixed Media, †Painting, †Photography, †Photography & Digital Arts, †Printmaking, Sculpture, Teacher Training, †Textile Design, Weaving
Adult Hobby Classes: Tuition—$970 per design & media classes, 2 cr each; $685 per design & media classes, audit; $565 per art & design fundamentals & fine art classes, 2 cr each; $395 per art & design fundamentals & fine art classes audit; personal enrichment & career development classes: art & design fundamentals, fine arts, digital media for print & web, digital photography, fashion studies, interior designing. Enrl 800 annually
Children's Classes: Enrl 1200 annually; tuition—$310 per class; registration $40 per student; fine art & design classes K-12
Summer School: Dir Continuing Educ, Neil di Sabato

PENNSYLVANIA ACADEMY OF THE FINE ARTS, Office of Admission, 128 N Broad St, Philadelphia, PA 19102-1424. Tel 215-972-7600; Fax 215-972-0839; Email admissions@pafa.edu; Web: www.pafa.edu; *CEO* David R Brigham; *Painting Dept Chair* Al Gury; *Sculpture Dept Chair* Rob Roesch; *Printmaking Dept Chair* Tony Rosati; *Liberal Arts Dept Chair* Dr Kevin Richards
Estab 1805; Maintain a nonprofit art gallery & art/architecture library - Gallery 118 N Broad St, Philadelphia, PA 19102; Library 128 N Broad St. On-campus shop where art supplies may be purchased; Pvt; D & E; Scholarships; SC 15, LC 4, GC
Publications: Newsletter/Calendar, quarterly
Ent Req: HS dipl, portfolio & recommendations
Degrees: Cert, 4 yrs; Academy BFA, BFA Coordinated prog with Univ Pennsylvania, MFA 2 yrs, Post-Baccalaureate prog 1 yr
Tuition: Nonres—undergrad $13,185 per sem, MFA $16,330 per sem, Post-Baccalaureate $14,040 per sem; no campus res
Courses: Anatomy, Drawing, Mixed Media, Painting, Perspective, Printmaking, Sculpture
Adult Hobby Classes: Enrl 310; tuition varies per class; Courses—Drawing, Painting, Printmaking, Sculpture
Children's Classes: Enrl 700; tuition varies; Courses—Theme Camps
Summer School: Dir, Michael Kowbuz. Enrl 500-600; tuition varies; Courses—Drawing, Painting, Printmaking, Sculpture

PHILADELPHIA COMMUNITY COLLEGE, Dept of Art, 1700 Spring Garden St, Philadelphia, PA 19130-3936. Tel 215-751-8771; *Assoc Prof* Karen Aumann, BFA; *Asst Prof & Head Art Dept* Christopher Feiro
Estab 1967; Pub; D & E; SC 10, LC 6; D 80 art maj
Ent Req: HS dipl, portfolio
Degrees: AA 2 yr
Courses: 2-D Design, 3-D Design, Art History, Ceramics, Computer Graphics, Design, Drawing, Graphic Design, Painting, Photography, Transfer Foundation Program
Summer School: Dir, Bob Paige. Tuition $61 per cr Courses—Art History, Ceramics, Design, Drawing, Painting

PHILADELPHIA UNIVERSITY, 4201 Henry Ave, Philadelphia, PA 19144-5497. Tel 215-951-2700; Fax 215-951-2651, 215-951-2651; Web: www.philau.edu; *Exec Dean* Dr Ronald C Kender; *Pres* Dr Stephen Spinell Jr; *Assoc Provost* Lloyd Russolo; *Exec Dean College & Architecture* Dr Louis Padulo
Estab 1884; On-campus shop where art supplies may be purchased; FT 23; pvt; D&E; Scholarships; GC 2700, UG 486
Degrees: BS 4 yrs, MBA, MS Fashion Apparel Studies, MS Interactive Media & Design, MS Industrial Design, MS Textile Design, MS Textile Engineering, Ms Interior Architecture, MS Sustain Design, MS Construction Mgmt
Tuition: $30,356 per yr
Courses: Aesthetics, Architecture, Art History, Chemistry & Dyeing, Constructions, Design, Drawing, Fashion Apparel Management, Fashion Design, Fashion Merchandising, Graphic Design, History of Art & Architecture, Interior Design, Knitted Design, Occupational Therapy, Photography, Print Design, Restoration & Conservation, Textile Design, Textile Engineering, Textile Quality Control & Testing, Weaving Design
Summer School: Dir, Maxine Lentz

SAINT JOSEPH'S UNIVERSITY, Art Dept, 5600 City Ave, Philadelphia, PA 19131-1376. Tel 610-660-1000, 660-1840; Fax 610-660-2278; Email dmcnally@sju.edu; Web: www.sju.edu/int/academics/cas/art/index.htm/; *Chmn & Prof Painting* Dennis McNally, PhD; *Prof Painting* Steve Cope, MFA; *Prof Ceramics* Jury Smith, MFA; *Prof Art History* Emily Hage, PhD; *Photog* Susan Fenton, MFA; *Prof Sculpture/3D* Ron Klein, MFA; *Adj Prof* Peter Bonner, MFA; *Adj Prof* Jeanne Brody, PhD; *Adj Prof* Sabrina DeTurk, PhD; *Adj Prof* Marie Eldin, MED; *Adj Prof* Roberta Fallon, PhD; *Adj Prof* Beverly Fisher, MFA; *Adj Prof* David Freese, BS; *Adj Prof* Marta Sanchez-Dallam, MFA; *Adj Prof* Alison Stigora, MFA; *Adj Prof* Kathleen Vaccaro, MFA
Estab 1851, prog estab 1975; Maintains a non-profit art gallery, Boland Hall, 5600 City Ave, Phila, PA, www.sju.edu/int/resources/gallery; Pvt, den; D & E; Scholarships; SC 58, LC 31; D 4400, maj 55, grad 1500
Ent Req: HS dipl
Degrees: BA
Courses: Architecture, †Art, Art Appreciation, †Art Education, Art History, Ceramics, Digital Photography, Drawing, History of Art & Architecture, †Mixed Media, Mosaics, Painting, Photography, Sculpture

TEMPLE UNIVERSITY, Tyler School of Art, 2001 N 13th St, Philadelphia, PA 19122-6016. Tel 215-777-9000; Email tyler@temple.edu; Web: www.temple.edu/tyler; *Dean* Susan Cahan; *Assoc Dean & Grad Prog Dir* Chad Curtis; *Assoc Dean & Dir, Architecture & Environmental Design* Kate Wingert-Playdon
Dept estab 1935; Maintains nonprofit art gallery: Temple Gallery; Pub; D & E; Scholarships; Fellowships
Ent Req: HS dipl, SAT, portfolio
Degrees: BA, BFA, MFA, MArch, PhD,
Tuition: Res—undergrad $22,632 per yr, Nonres—undergrad $36,504 per yr; Res—grad $1,110 per cr hr; Res—grad $1,521 per cr hr
Courses: Animation, †Architecture, †Art Education, †Art History, †Ceramics, Computers, Drawing, †Fibers Fabric Design, Film, Foundry, †Glass, †Graphic Design, Handmade Cameras, †History of Art & Architecture, Illustration, Metals, †Painting, Papermaking, Performance Art, †Photography, †Printmaking, Sculpture, Video, Weaving
Children's Classes: Courses—Computer & Studio, also programs for HS students

UNIVERSITY OF PENNSYLVANIA, School of Design (PennDesign), 102 Meyerson Hall, 210 S 34th St Philadelphia, PA 19104. Tel 215-898-6520; Fax 215-573-3927; Email admissions@design.upenn.edu; Web: www.design.upenn.edu; *Dean & Prof* Frederick Steiner; *Prof* Eugenie L Birch; *Prof & Chair, Architecture* Winka Dubbeldam; *Prof & Chair, Fine Arts* Ken Lum; *Prof & Chair, Landscape Architecture* Richard Weller; *Chair, Historic Preservation* Frank G Matero; *Prof & Chair, City/Regional Planning* Lisa Servon
Estab 1874; FT/PT 65; pvt; Scholarships; Fellowships; 723
Ent Req: ent exam, portfolio
Degrees: MFA, MArch, MSD, PhD
Tuition: Master's Prog $51,458 per yr, Doctoral Prog $34,882
Courses: Architectural Design, City Planning, Fine Arts, Landscape Architecture
Summer School: Studio courses in Paris, Venice & India

UNIVERSITY OF THE ARTS, Philadelphia Colleges of Art & Design, Performing Arts & Media & Communication, 320 S Broad St, Philadelphia, PA 19102-4901. Tel 215-717-6030 (Univ), 875-1100 (PCAD), 800-616-2787 (Admissions); Fax 215-875-1100 (PCAD); Web: www.uarts.edu; *Pres* Sean T Buffington; *Interim Dean, College of Art & Design* Alida Fish; *Dean, College of Performing Arts* Richard J Lawn; *Dean, Div Liberal Arts* Peter Stambler; *Provost* Kirk E Pillow
Estab 1876; pvt; D & E; Scholarships; undergrad 760, grad 120
Ent Req: ent req HS dipl, portfolio & audition SAT
Degrees: degrees BFA 4 yrs, BS, BM, MA, MFA, MM, Mid, Mat cert
Tuition: $17,250 per yr
Courses: Acting, Aesthetics, Animation Business of the Arts, Art Education, Art History, Calligraphy, †Ceramics, Collage, Conceptual Art, Constructions, Dance Education, Digital Storytelling, Drawing, †Film, Goldsmithing, †Graphic Design, †Illustration, †Industrial Design, Interactive Narrative, Interface Design, Intermedia, Jazz Dance Performance, Jazz Music Theory, Jewelry, Lettering, Media Technology, Mixed Media, Multimedia, Museum Exhibition Design, †Museum Staff Training, Music Education, Music Industry: Modern Ballet, Musical Theater, †Painting, Performance & Composition, †Photography, †Printmaking, †Sculpture, Silversmithing, †Teacher Training, †Textile Design, Weaving
Adult Hobby Classes: Courses—Ceramics, Computer Graphics, Creative Writing, Design, Fine Arts, Illustration, Jewelry & Metalsmithing, Photography, Printmaking, Sculpture, Woodworking
Children's Classes: Courses—Acting, Animation, Bookmaking, Ceramics, Comix, Creative Writing, Dance, Drama, Drawing, Figure Drawing, Graphic Design, Illustration, Jewelry, Musical Theater, Painting, Photography, Sculpture
Summer School: Courses—Acting, Crafts, Design, Fine Arts, Jazz Performing, Media Arts, Musical Theater

PITTSBURGH

ART INSTITUTE OF PITTSBURGH, 420 Blvd of the Allies Pittsburgh, PA 15219. Tel 412-263-6600, 291-6200; Fax 412-263-6667; Email admissions-aip@aii.edu; Web: www.aip.aii.edu; *Pres* George Pry; *Technology* Allan Agamedia, BS; *Digital Media Production/Video Production* Cy Anderson, BS; *Gen Educ* Douglas Anke, BS; *Photog* Karen Antonelli, BA; *Industrial Design Technology* Alan Assad, MEd; *Industrial Design Technology* Cyril Assad, BFA; *Media Arts & Animation* Michele Bamburak, BA; *Multimedia & Web Design* David Barton, BA; *Graphic Design* Mark Bender, BFA; *Media Arts & Animation* Sean Benedict, BA; *Dir Gen Educ* Heather A Bigley, MS; *Gen Educ* Maria Boada, MS; *Gen Educ* Diane Bowser, MA; *Media Arts & Animation/Gen Educ* J Nicholas Brockmann, MFA; *Gen Educ* Chad Brown, BA; *Graphic Design* Stephen M Butler, BS; *Multimedia & Web Design* Michael Cantella, BA; *Media Arts & Animation* Richard Catizone; *Gen Educ* Alberta Patella Certo, MEd; *Industrial Design Technology* Dan-Horia Chinda, MArch; *Gen Educ, Graphic Design* Angelo L Ciotti, MA; *Digital Design* Bob Clements, BS; *Photog* Brian Colkitt, AST; *Computer Animation* Ruth Comley, BA; *Graphic Design* Jeff Davis, MFA; *Graphic Design* Frank J DeGennaro, BS; *Gen Educ* Maura Doern-Danko, MFA; *Photog* Thomas Donley, AST; *Gen Educ* Elizabeth C Dunn, MAT; *Graphic Design* Earl Easter, BS; *Photog* Anderson B English, MFA; *Industrial Design Technology* William Farrell; *Gen Educ* John C Franke, BA; *Video Production* Donald Gabany, BA; *Graphic Design* Deborah Giancola, MPA; *Interior Design* Jordene Gates, BS; *VPres, Dean Educ* Edward A Gill, MEd; *Graphic Design* David S Giuliani, BS; *Graphic Design* Albert Gotlieb, MFA; *Foundations* Maurice Graves; *Gen Educ* Kathy Griffin, MEd; *Industrial Design Technology* Eric Hahn, BFA; *Graphic Design* John L Hassinger; *Gen Educ* Janna L Haubach, MEd; *Prog Chmn Digital Media Production* Douglas N Heaps, BS; *Photog* Bruce Henderson, BA; *Media Arts & Animation* Joseph Herron, BFA; *Interior Design* Margaret Herron, BA; *Video Production* James Hudson, BS; *Multimedia & Web Design* Patricia Adamcik-Huettel, AST; *Gen Educ* Jason Joy, MA; *Video Production* Douglas R Kennedy; *Graphic Design* Amy Kern, MFA; *Graphic Design* Michael W LaMark, MS; *Prof Foundations Studies* Una Charlene Langer-Holt; *Photog* Barry Lavery, MDiv; *Interior Design* Pamela A Lisak; *Graphic Design* Leslie B Lockerman, BFA; *Gen Educ* Frederick Lorini, MFA; *Media Arts & Animation* Angela Love, BS; *Video Production* Andrew Maietta, MLS; *Graphic Design* Michael Malle; *Gen Educ* Edward M Matus, MA; *Gen Educ* Richard Matvey, MEd; *Chair Multimedia & Design* Sharon McGuire, BA; *Photog* G Chris Miller, BS; *Graphic Design* Linda Miller; *Graphic Design* Ronald A Miller, BA; *Graphic Design & Digital Design* Joseph W Milne, BA; *Industrial Design Technology* William R Mitas, BS; *Graphic Design* Connie Moore, MAT; *Gen Educ* Linda Musto, BS; *Industrial Design* Lars Nyquist, BA; *Culinary Arts & Management* Shawn Oddo, AOS; *Digital Design* Shawn O'Mara, BS; *Graphic Design* Michael N Opalko, BFA; *Gen Educ* Robert Peluso, PhD; *Industrial Design Technology* David Pence, BS; *Gen Educ* Stephanie Perry, MBA; *Multimedia & Web Design* Dante Piombino, BA; *Media Arts & Animation* Francis A Pionati, MFA; *Gen Educ* Linda Rathburn, MEd; *Industrial Design Technology* Scott Ritiger, BA; *Industrial Design Technology* Arturo Rivero; *Multimedia & Web Design* Leon L Salvayon, MEd; *Media Arts & Animation* Michael C Schwab, BFA; *Media Arts & Animation* John Simpson, Jr, BA; *Interior Design* James J Smelko, BS; *Interior Design* Kelly JK Spewock, MFA; *Multimedia & Web Design* Jay W Speyerer, BS; *Graphic Design* Mary Jean Stabile, BS; *Media Arts & Animation* Jeffrey Styers, BS; *Gen Educ* Rebecca Suhoza, MA; *Graphic Design, Media Arts & Animation* Andrew Sujdak, BS; *Gen Educ* Michele M Thomas, MS; *Interior Design* John Michael Toth, BA; *Media Arts & Animation* Edward A Urian, BS; *Media Arts & Animation* David M Walters, BA; *Graphic Design, Media Arts & Animation* Helen Webster, BFA; *Media Arts & Animation* Greg Weider, BFA; *Media Arts & Animation* Hans Westman, BA; *Gen Educ* Jialu Wu, PhD; *Industrial Design* James Yedinak, BA; *Graphic Design* Shirley Yee, MFA; *Media Arts & Animation* Jeffrey Zehner, BS; *Graphic Design, Media Arts & Animation* Flavia Zortea, BFA; *Dir Entertainment Technology Center* Douglas Henderson
Estab 1921; Maintain nonprofit art gallery & art library; pvt; D & E; Scholarships; 2300
Ent Req: HS grad
Degrees: AA 2 yrs, dipl
Tuition: $334 per cr hr, AS prog 105 cr, BS prog 180 cr
Courses: Culinary Arts, Digital Design, Digital Media Production, Game Art & Design, Graphic Design, Industrial Design, Interior Design, Media Arts & Animation, Multimedia, Photography, Video, Web Site Administration
Summer School: Dir, Melinda Trempus.

CARLOW COLLEGE, Art Dept, 3333 Fifth Ave, Pittsburgh, PA 15213. Tel 412-578-6000, 578-6003; Web: www.carlow.edu; *Assoc Chmn* Suzanne Steiner; *Chmn Dept of Art* Dale Hussman
Estab 1945; FT 1, PT 3; den; D & E; Scholarships; SC 17, LC 6; 800, maj 35
Ent Req: HS dipl and transcript, col boards
Degrees: BA, Cert Art Education
Tuition: $13,468 per yr; campus res—room & board $5490
Courses: 2-D Design, American Art, Art Education, Art Therapy, Ceramics, Drawing, Fiber Arts, Painting, Printmaking, Sculpture, Survey of Art, Teacher Training, Twentieth Century Art

CARNEGIE MELLON UNIVERSITY, College of Fine Arts, 5000 Forbes Ave, Rm 100, Pittsburgh, PA 15213-3815. Tel 412-268-2349; Email cfa-contact@cmu.edu; Web: www.cmu.edu/cfa; *Dean & Prof* Dan Martin; *Dir Regina Gouger Miller Gallery* Elizabeth Chodos
Estab 1905; Maintain a nonprofit art gallery, Regina Gouger Miller Gallery, Miller Institute of Contemporary Art; maintain an art library, Hunt Library. Art supplies may be purchased on campus; pvt; D & E; Scholarships; Fellowships; SC, LC, GC
Ent Req: col board ent exam plus auditions or portfolio
Degrees: BFA, MFA
Tuition: Undergrad $54,244 per yr; campus res available
Courses: Architecture, Conceptual Art, Constructions, Costume Design & Construction, Design, Graphic Arts, Graphic Design, Mixed Media, Painting, Photography, Printmaking, Restoration & Conservation, Sculpture, Stage Design, Theatre Arts, Video
Summer School: Term of 6 wks. Courses—includes some pre-college courses
—**School of Architecture**, 500 Forbes Ave, College of Fine Arts 201 Pittsburgh, PA 15213-3890. Tel 412-268-2354; Fax 412-268-7819; Web: soa.cmu.edu; *Prof & Head* Stephen R Lee
Undergrad 248; Grad 100
Degrees: BArch, MS, PhD
Courses: Architecture
—**School of Design**, 5000 Forbes Ave, MMCH 110 Pittsburgh, PA 15213-3890. Tel 412-268-2828; Fax 412-268-7838; Email info@design.cmu.edu; Web: design.cmu.edu; *Prof & Head* Terry Irwin
Degrees: BDes, MA, MPS, MDes. DDes, PhD
Courses: Graphic Design, Industrial Design, Product Design
Summer School: Design Studio
—**School of Art**, 5000 Forbes Ave, CFA 300 Pittsburgh, PA 15213-3890. Tel 412-268-2409; Fax 412-268-7817; Email schoolofart@cmu.edu; Web: www.art.cmu.edu; *Prof & Head* Charlie White; *Prof & Dir, Ctr for the Arts in*

Society James Duesing; *Prof & Dir, Frank-Ratchye STUDIO for Creative Inquiry* Golan Levin
FT/PT 25; Scholarships; Undergrad 200; Grad 18
Degrees: BFA & MFA
Courses: †Art, Art History, Ceramic Sculpture, Computer, Conceptual Art, Constructions, Drawing, Mixed Media, Painting, Printmaking, Sculpture, Video
Children's Classes: Courses—same as undergrad prog
Summer School: 6 wk prog. Courses—same as undergrad prog

CHATHAM COLLEGE, Fine & Performing Arts, Woodland Rd, Pittsburgh, PA 15232-2826. Tel 412-365-1100; Web: www.chatham.edu; *Dir* Dr Margaret Ross; *Asst Prof* Michael Pestel; *Chmn* Pat Montley
Estab 1869; FT 2, PT 2; pvt, W; SC 17, LC 7
Ent Req: HS grad
Degrees: BA 4 yrs
Courses: Aesthetics, Art Appreciation, Art Education, †Art History, Conceptual Art, Constructions, Design, Drawing, Film, History of Art & Architecture, Independent Study, Introduction to Art, Mixed Media, †Painting, Photography, Printmaking, †Sculpture

LA ROCHE COLLEGE, Division of Design, 9000 Babcock Blvd, Pittsburgh, PA 15237-5898. Tel 412-367-9300; Fax 412-536-1527; Email maria.ripepi@laroche.edu; Web: www.laroche.edu; *Asst Prof* Neha Agarwal, MFA; *Assoc Prof* Thomas Bates, MA, MPA; *Asst Prof* Patrick Connolly, MA; *Asst Prof* Richard Helfrich, MFA; *Prof* Lauren Lampe, MFA; *Vis Prof* RJ Thompson, BS; *Asst Prof & Dept Chair Interior Design* Nicole Bieak Kreidler, MS; *Prof* Devvrat Nagar, MEd, GD Arch; *Asst Prof* Maria Ripepi, MFA; *Asst Prof* Lisa Kamphaus, BFA
Estab 1963, dept estab 1965; PT 15; pvt; D & E; SC 25, LC 15; D & E 220, non-maj 50, maj 170
Ent Req: HS dipl
Degrees: BA and BS 4 yr
Courses: 3-D Design, Advertising Design, Aesthetics, Airbrush Illustration, Art History, Building Technology, Buyer Behavior, Ceramics, Commercial Art, Communication, Computer Graphics, Contract Documents, Directed & Independent Studies, Display, Drawing, Fashion Design, Foundation Design, †Graphic Arts, †Graphic Design, Illustration, Industrial Design, †Interior Design, Lettering, Marketing Strategy, †Multimedia Design, Package Design, Painting, Photography, Portfolio Preparation, Sculpture, Sr Design Seminar, Textile Design
Summer School: Dir Admis, David McFarland.

POINT PARK COLLEGE, Performing Arts Dept, 201 Wood St, Pittsburgh, PA 15222-1984. Tel 412-392-3450; Fax 412-391-1980; *Chmn* Ronald Allan Lindblom
Degrees: BA & BFA
Tuition: $4300 per sem
Courses: Architecture, Art Appreciation, Art History, †Fashion Illustration, †Film, †Interior Design, †Photography, †Stage Design, Theatre Design, †Visual Arts

UNIVERSITY OF PITTSBURGH, Henry Clay Frick Dept History of Art & Architecture, 104 Frick Fine Arts Bldg, Pittsburgh, PA 15260. Tel 412-648-2400; Fax 412-648-2792; Web: www.haa.pitt.edu; *Chmn* Kirk Savage; *Mellon Prof* Terence Smith, PhD; *Prof Emeritus* David Wilkins; *Asst Prof* Christopher Drew Armstrong, PhD; *Asst Prof* Josh Ellenbogen, PhD; *Assoc Prof* Gao Minglu, PhD; *Assoc Prof* Barbara McCloskey, PhD; *Prof* Franklin Toker, PhD
Estab 1787, dept estab 1927; Maintain nonprofit, University Art Gallery; Fine Arts Library; on-campus shop sells art supplies; Pvt; D & E; Scholarships; Fellowships; LC 35, GC 10; D 750, E 250, grad 30
Ent Req: HS dipl, BA, GRE for grad work
Degrees: BA 4 yrs, MA 2 yrs, PhD
Tuition: Res—grad $6,142 per sem; nonres—grad $11,725 per sem
Courses: †Architectural Studies, †Architecture, Art History, History of Art & Architecture
Summer School: Dir, Kirk Savage. Enrl 150; 6 wks, 2 sessions 3-4 wks, 3 sessions
—Dept of Studio Arts, 118 Frick Fine Arts Bldg, Pittsburgh, PA 15260. Tel 412-648-2430; Fax 412-648-3660; Web: www.pitt.edu/~studio; *Assoc Prof* Michael Morrill; *Assoc Prof* Kenneth Batista; *Prof* Paul Glabicki; *Assoc Prof* Delanie Jenkins; *Asst Prof* Bovey Lee; *Assoc Prof* Edward Powell
Estab 1968; FT 6, PT 4-7; pub; D & E; SC 29; 1,000 non-majors; 75 majors
Degrees: BA
Tuition: Res—$11,000 per yr
Courses: Design, Drawing, Graphic Design, Painting, Print Etching, Sculpture

RADNOR

CABRINI COLLEGE, Dept of Fine Arts, 610 King of Prussia Rd, Radnor, PA 19087-3698. Tel 610-902-8380; Fax 610-902-8539; *Chmn Dept* Adeline Bethany, EdD
Estab 1957; FT 2, PT 3; den; D & E; Scholarships; SC 11, LC 4
Ent Req: HS dipl, satisfactory average & rank in secondary school class, SAT, recommendations
Degrees: BA(Arts Administration, Fine Arts & Graphic Design), BS & BSED
Courses: Art Education, Ceramics, Computer Publication Design, Design & Composition, Drawing, Graphic Design, History of Art & Architecture, Painting, Teacher Training
Adult Hobby Classes: Courses offered
Summer School: Dir, Dr Midge Leahy. Term of 6 wks beginning May & July. Courses—Color Theory, Drawing, Elem Art Methods, Mixed Media, Painting

READING

ALBRIGHT COLLEGE, Dept of Art, 13th & Bern Sts, Reading, PA 19604; PO Box 15234, Reading, PA 19612-5234. Tel 610-921-7715; Fax 610-921-7530; Web: www.alb.edu; *Prof* Tom Watcke; *Chmn* Kristen Woodward; *Asst Prof* Dr Richard Hamwi; *Assoc Prof* Gary Adlestein; *Lectr* Christopher Youngs
Estab 1856, dept estab 1964; maintains nonprofit gallery, Freedman Gallery 13th & Bern St, PO Box 15234, Reading, PA 19612-5234; Pvt; D & E; Scholarships; SC 14, LC 7; D 322, E 41, non-maj 340, maj 14, others 20
Ent Req: HS dipl, SAT
Degrees: BA 4 yrs
Courses: †Art Education, Art History, Ceramics, †Commercial Art, Constructions, †Design, Drawing, Fashion Arts, Film, †Graphic Arts, History of Art & Architecture, Interior Design, Mixed Media, †Painting, Photography, Printmaking, †Sculpture, †Teacher Training, †Textile Design, Theatre Arts
Adult Hobby Classes: Enrl 40; tuition $110 per cr. Courses—Drawing, Photography
Children's Classes: Enrl 25-35; tuition $35-$50 per course. Courses—Crafts, Drawing
Summer School: Enrl 30 - 50; 2 terms of 4 wks beginning in June & July. Courses—Art History, Drawing, Painting

ROSEMONT

ROSEMONT COLLEGE, Art Program, 1400 Montgomery Ave, Rosemont, PA 19010-1699. Tel 610-527-0200; Fax 610-526-2984; Email admissions@rosemont.edu; Web: www.rosemont.edu; *Chmn Div* Tina Walduier Bizzarro, PhD; *Assoc Prof & Dir Gallery* Patricia Nugent, MFA; *Assoc Prof* Michael Willse, MFA; *Asst Prof* Amy Orr, MFA
Estab 1921; FT 6, PT 4; pvt, W (exchange with Villanova Univ, Cabrini College, Eastern College, The Design Schools); D; Scholarships; total col 600, art 200, grad approx 17
Ent Req: HS dipl, SAT
Degrees: BFA (Studio Art), BA (Art History, Studio Art), Teacher cert in Art K-12
Courses: Aesthetics, American Indian Art, Art Criticism, Art Education, Ceramics, Creativity & the Marketplace, Drawing, Fiber History, Graphic Arts, Painting, Photography, Printmaking, Sculpture, Studio Art, Teacher Training
Summer School: Dir, Tina Walduier Bizzarro

SCRANTON

LACKAWANNA COLLEGE, Fine Arts Dept, 501 Vine St, Scranton, PA 18509-3251. Tel 570-961-7827; Web: www.lacka.ljc.edu; *Chmn* John De Nunzio
Estab 1885
Ent Req: HS dipl or equivalent
Degrees: AA
Tuition: $795 per cr, $585 per 3 cr
Courses: Fine Arts, Survey Class

MARYWOOD UNIVERSITY, Art Dept, 2300 Adams Ave, Scranton, PA 18509-1598. Tel 570-348-6211, 348-6278; Fax 570-Fax: 340-6023; Web: www.marywood.edu; *Chmn* Matt Povse
Estab 1915; Maintains 3 nonprofit art galleries, Mahady Gallery, Suraci Gallery, The Maslow Collection Study Gallery for Contemporary Art - all on campus; on-campus shop where art supplies may be purchased; FT 13, PT 36; pvt; D & E; Scholarships; SC 56, LC 14, GC 58; maj 275, grad 100
Ent Req: HS dipl, portfolio & interview
Degrees: BA(Art Educ), BA (Art Therapy, Arts Admin), BFA (Painting, Illustration, Graphic Design, Photography, Ceramics, Sculpture), MA(Studio Art, Art Educ, Art Therapy), MFA (Visual Arts with concentration in Ceramics, Graphic Design, Illustration, Sculpture, Painting, Printmaking, Photography)
Courses: Advertising Design, Aesthetics, †Art Education, Art History, †Art Therapy, †Ceramics, Drawing, Graphic Arts, †Graphic Design, †Illustration, Jewelry, †Painting, †Photography, †Printmaking, †Sculpture, Serigraphy, †Weaving

PENN FOSTER COLLEGE, (Harcourt Learning Direct) School of Interior Design, 925 Oak St, Scranton, PA 18515. Tel 570-342-7701, Ext 341; Fax 570-343-0560; Email russell.day@pennfoster.edu; *Chief Certification Officer* Connie Dempsey; *Dept Chair* Russell Day; *Senior Instr* Sharon Hopkins
Estab 1890, dept estab 1969; FT 1; pvt; distance educ; 4200
Ent Req: completion of high school
Degrees: career diploma, AS Interior Design, AS Graphic Design, Fashion Merchandising
Courses: Art Appreciation, Fashion Arts, Graphic Arts, †Graphic Design, Interior Decorating
Adult Hobby Classes: Interior Decorating
Summer School: Dept Chair, Russell Day
—Art/Graphic Design, 14300 N Northsight Blvd, Scottsdale, AZ 85260. Tel 480-947-6644; Fax 480-951-6030; Web: www.pennfostercollege.edu; *Sr Instr* Sharon Hopkins
Estab 1890; FT 1, PT 2; pvt; open enrollment; Distance Learning
Ent Req: HS dipl
Degrees: Assoc of Science
Courses: Art Appreciation, Drafting, †Graphic Design
Adult Hobby Classes: Drawing, Painting

SHIPPENSBURG

SHIPPENSBURG UNIVERSITY, Art Dept, 1871 Old Main Dr, Huber Art Ctr Shippensburg, PA 17257-2200. Tel 717-477-1530; Fax 717-477-4049; Web: www.shippensburg.edu; *Chmn Art Dept* William Hynes, MFA; *Assoc Prof* Janet Ruby; *Asst Prof* Bill Davis, MFA; *Asst Prof* Dr Stephen Hirshon, MFA; *Asst Prof* Michael Campbell, MFA; *Asst Prof* Steven Dolbin
Estab 1871, dept estab 1920; pub; D & E; Scholarships; SC 17, LC 6; D 400, E 100, non-maj 600, grad 15, continuing educ 20
Ent Req: HS dipl, Portfolio review
Degrees: BA(Art)
Courses: Art History, Arts & Crafts, Ceramics, Drawing, Enameling, Painting, Printmaking, Sculpture

Adult Hobby Classes: Sr citizen tuition waived in regular classes if space is available
Summer School: Dir, William Hynes. Lectr & Studio courses

SLIPPERY ROCK

SLIPPERY ROCK UNIVERSITY OF PENNSYLVANIA, Dept of Art, 1 Morrow Way, Slippery Rock, PA 16057-1313. Tel 724-738-2020; Fax 724-738-4485; *Prof, Chmn* Thomas Como; *Prof* Heather Hertel; *Prof* Sean MacMillan; *Asst Prof* John Shumway, MFA; *Prof* Dr Kurt Pitluga; *Prof* Katherine Mickle, MFA; *Prof* June Edwards, MFA; *Prof* Barbara Westman
Maintain nonprofit art gallery, gaultgallery@maltbycenter; FT 9; Pub; D & E; SC 27, LC 3; maj 70
Ent Req: HS dipl
Degrees: BA(Art), BFA(Art) 4 yr
Courses: Art History, Art Synthesis, Ceramics, Drawing, Graphic Design, Metalsmithing, Mixed Media, Painting, Photography, Printmaking, Sculpture, Teacher Training, Textile Design
Summer School: Tuition $129 per cr hr

SWARTHMORE

SWARTHMORE COLLEGE, Dept of Art & Art History, 500 College Ave, Swarthmore, PA 19081-1390. Tel 610-328-8116, 328-8000; Fax 610-328-7793; Email jcianfr1@swarthmore.edu; Web: www.swarthmore.edu; *Assoc Provost & Assoc Prof* Patricia L Reilly, PhD; *Prof* Constance Cain Hungerford, PhD, MFA; *Chmn & Prof* Michael Cothren, PhD, MFA; *Prof* Brian A Meunier, MFA; *Assoc Prof* Janine Mileaf, PhD; *Prof* Syd Carpenter, MFA; *Prof* Randall L Exxon, MFA
Estab 1864, dept estab 1925; pvt; D; Scholarships; SC 14, LC 33; non-maj 500, maj 25
Ent Req: HS dipl, SAT, CEEB
Degrees: BA 4 yrs
Tuition: $23,020 per yr, campus res—room & board $7500 per yr
Courses: Aesthetics, Architecture, Art, Art History, Ceramics, Drawing, History, History of Architecture, History of Art & Architecture, History of Cinema, Landscape Architecture, Mixed Media, Painting, Philosophy, Photography, Printmaking, Sculpture, Stage Design, Theatre Arts, Theatre Program, Urban History

UNIVERSITY PARK

PENNSYLVANIA STATE UNIVERSITY, UNIVERSITY PARK, Penn State School of Visual Arts, 210 Patterson Bldg, University Park, PA 16802. Tel 814-865-0444; Fax 814-865-1158; Web: www.sova.psu.edu; *Asst Prof Art* Janet Hartranft; *Prof Art & Women's Studies (Drawing/Painting)* Micaela Amato; *Assoc Prof Art Educ* Patricia Amburgy; *Asst Prof Women's Studies & Art (Art Criticism)* Irina Aristarkhova; *Assoc Prof Art (Drawing/Painting)* John Bowman; *Assoc Prof Art (Core Prog & Drawing/Painting)* Paul Chidester; *Assoc Prof Art (Fayette Campus)* David DiPietro; *Prof Art Educ* Yvonne Gaudelius; *Assoc Prof Art (Printmaking)* Robin Gibson; *Asst Prof Art (Photog)* Lonnie Graham; *Prof Art Educ & Women's Studies* Karen Keifer-Boyd; *Asst Prof Art (New Media)* Matthew Kenyon; *Assoc Prof Art Educ* Wanda Knight; *Prof Art (Gen Educ)* Jerrold Maddox; *Asst Prof Art (Sculpture)* Cristin Millet; *Prof Art (Drawing/Painting)* Helen O'Leary; *Assoc Prof Art (Art Criticism)* Simone Osthoff; *Asst Prof Art Educ & Curriculum & Instruction* Kimberly Powell; *Assoc Prof Art (Ceramics)* Elizabeth Quackenbush; *Assoc Prof Art (New Media)* Carlos Rosas; *Assoc Prof Art (Printmaking & New Media)* Jean Sanders; *Asst Prof Integrative Art & Art (Photog)* Keith Shapiro; *Asst Prof Art Educ & Women's Studies* Stephanie Springgay; *Prof Art (Ceramics)* Christopher Staley; *Prof Art Educ* Mary Ann Stankiewicz; *Prof Art Educ* Christine Thompson; *Asst Prof Art (Metal Art & Technology)* James Thurman; *Dir & Prof Art Educ* Charles Garoian; *Distinguished Prof Art (Drawing/ Painting)* Robert Yarber; *Assoc Prof Art & Art Educ* David Ebitz; *Instr Art Educ* Jody Guy; *Asst Prof Art (Photog)* Stephen Rubin; *Asst Prof Art (Sculpture)* Bonnie Collura; *Asst Prof Art (Ceramics)* Del Harrow
Estab 1855, col estab 1963; Maintains nonprofit art gallery, Edwin Zoller Gallery, 210 Patterson Bldg, Penn State Univ, University Park, PA 16802; maintains art library, Pattee Library. Art supplies may be purchased on campus; pub; D & E; SC 282, LC 99, GC 104
Ent Req: HS dipl and GPA, SAT, successful portfolio review
Degrees: PhD, MEd, MFA, MS, BA, BFA, BDES, IDS
Tuition: Res—$6,082 per sem; nonres—$11,097 per sem
Courses: †Art Appreciation, Art Education, †Art History, Ceramics, †Collage, Drawing, †Interdisciplinary Digital Studios, Metals, †Mixed Media, †Museum Staff Training, †New Media, Painting, Photography, Printmaking, Sculpture, †Teacher Training, †Video
Summer School: Courses— limited
—**Dept of Art History,** 229 Arts Bldg, University Park, PA 16802-1920. Tel 814-865-6326; Fax 814-865-1242; Email cxz3@psu.edu; Web: www.arthistory.psu.edu; *Evan Pugh Prof Emeritus* Hellmut Hager, PhD; *Prof Emeritus* Roland E Fleischer, PhD; *Evan Pugh Prof* Anthony Cutler, PhD; *Assoc Prof Emeritus* Jeanne Chenault Porter PhD; *Assoc Prof* Elizabeth B Smith PhD; *Assoc Prof* Elizabeth J Walters PhD; *Assoc Prof* Brian Curran, PhD; *Assoc Prof & Dept Head* Craig Zabel, PhD; *Assoc Prof* Charlotte Houghton, PhD; *Assoc Prof* Nancy Locke, PhD; *Asst Prof* Chika Okeke-Agulu, PhD; *Assoc Prof* Sarah Rich, PhD; *Asst Prof* Madhuri Desai, PhD
Estab 1855, dept estab 1963; pub; D & E; Scholarships; Fellowships; Assistantships; LC 50, GC 36; maj 50, grad 35
Ent Req: HS dipl
Degrees: BA, MA, PhD
Tuition: Res—$3273 per sem; nonres—$7044 per sem
Courses: 19th & 20th century European Art & Architecture, Aesthetics, American Art & Architecture, Ancient Egyptian, †Art History, Contemporary Art, Criticism, Early Christian & Byzantine Art, German Baroque & Rococo Architecture, Greek & Roman Art & Architecture, Historiography, History of Art & Archeology, History of Photography, Iconology, Italian Renaissance & Baroque Art & Architecture, Late Antique, Museum Studies, Northern Renaissance & Baroque Art, Spanish & French Baroque & Rococo Art, Western Medieval Art & Architecture
Adult Hobby Classes: Classes offered through Continuing Education
Summer School: Courses same as regular session, but limited

UPPER BURRELL

PENNSYLVANIA STATE UNIVERSITY AT NEW KENSINGTON, Depts of Art & Architecture, 3550 Seventh St Rd, Upper Burrell, PA 15068. Tel 724-339-5466, 339-5456; Web: www.psu.edu/dept/arts/schools/schools; *Assoc Prof Art* Bud Gibbons
Estab 1968; pub; D; Scholarships; SC 3-4, LC 1 per sem
Ent Req: col boards
Degrees: 2 yr (option for 4 yr at main campus at University Park)
Courses: Art Education, Art History, Ceramics, Design, Drawing, Music, Painting, Theatre Arts
Adult Hobby Classes: Courses—Ceramics, Painting, Theater for Children
Children's Classes: Courses—Art, Drama, Music Workshops
Summer School: Dir, Joseph Ferrino. Enrl 100; 8 wk term. Courses—Art, Drama, Music, Workshops

VILLANOVA

VILLANOVA UNIVERSITY, Dept of Theater, 800 Lancaster Ave, Villanova, PA 19085. Tel 610-519-4610, 519-4660 (History); Web: www.villanova.edu; *Prof* George Radan; *Asst Prof* Dr Mark Sullivan; *Chmn* Bro Richard Cannuli
Estab 1842, dept estab 1971; pvt; D & E; SC 25, LC 6; D 35, maj 35
Ent Req: HS dipl, SAT
Degrees: BFA 4 yrs; courses taught in conjunction with Rosemont College
Courses: †Aesthetics, Archaeology, Art Education, Art History, Conservation, Drawing, Painting, Theatre Arts
Adult Hobby Classes: Enrl 20-30; tuition $585 per course in 14 wk sem. Courses—Calligraphy, Drawing
Summer School: Held in Siena, Italy. Courses—Art History, Language, Studio Art

WASHINGTON

WASHINGTON & JEFFERSON COLLEGE, Art Dept, 50 S Lincoln St, Olin Art Ctr Washington, PA 15301-4812. Tel 724-222-4400, 223-6110; Web: www.wj.edu; *Chmn Art Dept & Assoc Prof* John Lambertson; *Asst Prof* Patrick T Schmidt, MFA; *Adjunct Prof* James McNutt, MA
Estab 1787, dept estab 1959; Maintain nonprofit art gallery; pvt; D & E; Scholarships; SC 14, LC 8; D 162, E 18, non-maj 139, maj 23, others 15
Ent Req: HS dipl, SAT, achievement tests
Degrees: BA 4 yr
Courses: Art Appreciation, Art Education, Art History, Ceramics, Design, Drawing, Framing & Matting, Gallery Management, Lettering, Painting, Photography, Photography, Printmaking, Restoration & Conservation, Sculpture, Teacher Training
Summer School: Dir, Dean Dlugos. Enrl 250, two 4 wk sessions, June-Aug. Courses—Drawing, Framing, Matting, Photography

WAYNE

WAYNE ART CENTER, 413 Maplewood Ave, Wayne, PA 19087-4792. Tel 610-688-3553; Fax 610-995-0478; Email info@wayneart.org; Web: www.wayneart.org; *Instr* Deena Ball, BA; *Instr* Susan Branco; *Instr* Karen Carlin Fogarty; *Instr* Mark Gruener; *Instr* Patricia Jordan; *Instr* Lyn Mueller; *Instr* Wendy Scheirer; *Instr* Georganna Lenssen; *Instr* Chiwishi Joy-Abney; *Instr* Tony Squadroni; *Instr* Abigail Ober; *Instr* Anne Graham; *Instr* Beth Clark; *Instr* Bonnie Mettler; *Instr* Brett Thomas; *Instr* Carol Kardon; *Instr* Cathy Darlington; *Instr* Chris Darway; *Instr* Claire Haik; *Instr* Jennifer Frudakis; *Instr* Martin Campos; *Instr* Jenn Warpole; *Instr* John Wilson; *Instr* Jon Redmond; *Instr* Teresa DeSeve; *Instr* Joseph Sweeny; *Instr* Karen Sacks; *Instr* Kassem Amoudi; *Instr* Kate Hochner; *Instr* Laura Ducceschi; *Instr* Laurie Daddona; *Instr* Mark Kidd; *Instr* Marlene Adler; *Instr* Matthew Courtney; *Instr* Mary Elizabeth Nelson; *Instr* Robert Waddington; *Instr* Michael Doyle; *Instr* Mick McAndrews; *Instr* Nathan Durnin; *Instr* Paris Muchanic; *Instr* Piera Raffaele; *Instr* Robert Deane
Estab 1930; Maintains a non-profit art gallery, and an art/architecture library. Clay may be purchased on-campus.; pvt; D & E; Scholarships; SC 500; D 5000
Ent Req: none; free program for senior citizens
Tuition: $350
Courses: Ceramics, Drawing, Mixed Media, Painting, Photography, Pottery, Sculpture
Children's Classes: Tuition $35 for 10 wk sem, yearly dues $6. Courses—Drawing, Painting, Jewelry, Culinary, Ceramics.
Summer School: Children's program Coordinator: Tessa Downs. Courses—same as above plus Robotics

WAYNESBURG

WAYNESBURG COLLEGE, Dept of Fine Arts, 51 W College St, Waynesburg, PA 15370-1258. Tel 724-627-8191, 852-3296; Fax 724-627-6416; Web: www.waynesburg.edu/~art; *Prof* Susan Phillips, MFA; *Instr* Nathan Sims
Estab 1849, dept estab 1971; pvt; D & E; Scholarships; SC 25, LC 6; D 131, E 3, maj 17
Ent Req: HS dipl
Degrees: BA (Visual Commun) 4 yrs, MBA
Courses: Art Education, Art History, Ceramics, Computer Applications for Visual Communication, Computer Graphics, Design, Desk Top Publishing, Drawing, Graphic Arts, Layout & Photography for Media, Media Presentation, Painting,

Photo-Journalism, Photography, Printmaking, Sculpture, Television, Theatre Arts, Typography, †Visual Art, †Visual Communication, †Visual Communication-Print Media
Adult Hobby Classes: Courses—Art History, Graphic Design, Photography
Summer School: Dept Chmn, Daniel Morris.

WEST MIFFLIN

COMMUNITY COLLEGE OF ALLEGHENY COUNTY, Fine Arts Dept, 1750 Clairton Rd, South Campus West Mifflin, PA 15122-3029. Tel 412-469-1100; Fax 412-469-6370; Web: www.ccac.edu; *Chmn* George Jaber
Estab 1968; FT 2; pub; D&E
Ent Req: HS dipl
Degrees: AA, AS
Tuition: County res—$920 per yr, $68 per cr hr
Courses: Advertising Design, Art Appreciation, Calligraphy, Ceramics, Commercial Art, Computer Graphics, Design, Drawing, Handicrafts, Painting, Photography

WILKES-BARRE

WILKES UNIVERSITY, Dept of Art, Bedford Hall, Wilkes-Barre, PA 18766. Tel 570-826-1135; Web: www.wilkes.edu; *Chmn* Terry Zipay, PhD; *Assoc Prof* Sharon Bowar; *Adjunct Prof* Sedor Sieboda PhD; *Adjunct Prof* Jan Conway, MFA; *Adjunct Prof* Jean Adams, BA
Estab 1947; pvt; D & E; Scholarships; SC 20, LC 7; D 170, E 23, non-maj 120, maj 35
Ent Req: HS dipl, SAT
Degrees: BA 4 yr
Courses: †Art Education, †Art History, †Ceramics, †Communication Design, Drawing, Painting, †Photography, †Printmaking, †Sculpture, Surface Design, Teacher Training, Textile Design
Adult Hobby Classes: Courses variable
Summer School: Dir, Henry Steuben. Tuition $350 per cr for 5 wk day, 8 wk evening or 3 wk pre-session. Courses—Art Studio, Ceramics, Photography, Surface Design

WILLIAMSPORT

LYCOMING COLLEGE, Art Dept, 700 College Pl, Williamsport, PA 17701-5192. Tel 570-321-4000, 321-4002; Email estomin@lycoming.edu; Web: www.lycoming.edu/; *Chmn* B Lynn Estomin, MFA; *Prof* Amy Golahny, PhD, MFA; *Asst Prof* Gustavo Plascencia, MFA; *Prof* Seth Goodman, MFA; *Instr* Katherine Sterngold, MFA; *Asst Prof* Howard Tran, MFA; *Instr* Kim Rhone, MFA
Estab 1812; Maintain nonprofit art gallery; Lycoming Col Art Gallery; art supplies available on-campus; pvt; D & E; Scholarships; SC 18, LC 8; College 1,500, Dept 500, maj 70
Ent Req: HS dipl, ACT or SAT
Degrees: BA 4 yr
Courses: Advertising Design, †Art Education, †Art History, Ceramics, †Commercial Art, Computer Design & Animation, Computer Graphics, †Conceptual Art, Costume Design & Construction, Design, Drawing, †Film History, Graphic Arts, Graphic Design, †History of Art & Architecture, †Painting, †Photography, †Printmaking, †Sculpture, Stage Design, Teacher Training, Theatre Arts

PENNSYLVANIA COLLEGE OF TECHNOLOGY, The Gallery at Penn College, 1 College Ave, Williamsport, PA 17701-5799. Tel 570-320-2445; Email gallery@pct.edu; Web: gallery.pct.edu; *Gallery Director* Penny Lutz
Parent school est 1914; gallery est 2001; On-campus art supplies shop; Maintain a nonprofit art gallery; pub; D & E; Scholarships; SC
Ent Req: HS dipl, placement test
Degrees: AA 2 yr, BGD 4 yr, SD 2 yr
Courses: †Advertising Design, Art History, Ceramics, Drawing, Graphic Arts, †Graphic Design, History of Art & Architecture, Illustration, Painting, Photography, Technical Illustration

YORK

YORK COLLEGE OF PENNSYLVANIA, Dept of Music, Art & Speech Communications, 441 Country Club Rd, York, PA 17405-3651. Tel 717-846-7788; Fax 717-849-1602; Web: www.ycp.edu; *Coordr Div Arts* Pamela Hemzik; *Coordr, Graphic Design* Paul Saikai, BA; *Asst Prof* Otto Tomasch, MFA; *Adjunct* Mary Todenhoff, MFA; *Adjunct* Penelope Grumbine-Hornock, MFA; *Adjunct* Marian Lorence, MPA; *Adjunct* Laure Drogoul, MA
Estab 1941; pvt; D & E; SC 17, LC 7
Ent Req: HS dipl, SAT or ACT
Degrees: BA 4 yrs & AA 2 yrs
Courses: Art Appreciation, Art Education, Art History, Ceramics, Commercial Art, Computer Graphics, Drawing, Graphic Design, Painting, Photography, Sculpture
Adult Hobby Classes: Enrl 40; Courses—per regular session
Summer School: Dir, Thomas Michalski.

RHODE ISLAND

BRISTOL

ROGER WILLIAMS UNIVERSITY, Visual Art Dept, One Old Ferry Rd, Bristol, RI 02809-2921. Tel 401-254-3617; Web: www.rwuonline.cc/; *Prof* Ronald Wilczek; *Assoc Prof* Sharon Delucca; *Asst Prof* Rebecca Leuchak; *Asst Prof* Kathleen Hancock
Estab 1948, dept estab 1967; pvt; D & E; Scholarships; SC 18, LC 8; D 1800, E 1500, maj 42
Ent Req: HS dipl
Degrees: AA 2 yr, BA 4 yr, apprenticeship and senior teaching
Courses: †Graphic Design, †Painting, †Photography, †Printmaking, Sculpture

KINGSTON

UNIVERSITY OF RHODE ISLAND, Dept of Art & Art History, Fine Arts Ctr, 105 Upper College Rd Ste 1 Kingston, RI 02881-0820. Tel 401-874-2131, 874-5821; Fax 401-874-2729; Email artdept@etal.uri.edu; *Chair* Wendy W Roworth, PhD; *Prof* William Klenk PhD; *Prof* Robert Dilworth, MFA; *Prof* Richard Calabro, MFA; *Prof* Gary Richman, MFA; *Prof* Barbara Pagh, MFA; *Assoc Prof* Mary Hollinshead, PhD; *Prof* Ronald Onorato PhD; *Assoc Prof* Sherri Wills, MFA, MA; *Asst Prof* Annu Palakunnathu Matthew, MFA; *Asst Prof* Ron Hutt, MFA
Estab 1892; Maintain nonprofit art gallery, URI Fine Arts Center Galleries, Fine Arts Center URI, Kingston, RI 02881; Ft 12, PT 6; pub; D & E; Scholarships; SC 21, studio seminars 24, LC 23; D 900, E 30, non-maj 725, maj 200, other 10 - 20
Ent Req: same as required for Col of Arts & Sciences
Degrees: BA(Studio), BA(Art History) & BFA(Art Studio) 4 yrs
Courses: Aesthetics, Architecture, †Art Appreciation, Art History, Collage, Conceptual Art, Digital Art, Digital Design, Drawing, Film, Graphic Arts, †Graphic Design, History of Art & Architecture, Painting, Photography, †Printmaking, Sculpture, Studio Art, †Video
Adult Hobby Classes: Art History, Drawing, Painting, Sculpture
Summer School: Courses— Art History, Drawing, Photography

NEWPORT

NEWPORT ART MUSEUM, Coleman Center for Creative Studies, 76 Bellevue Ave, Newport, RI 02840-7411. Tel 401-848-8200; Fax 401-848-8205; Email info@newportartmuseum.com; Web: www.newportartmuseum.com; *Exec Dir* Elizabeth Goddard; *Dir Educ* Maggie Anderson
Estab 1912; D & E; Scholarships; SC 25, LC 3; D 300 (total)
Ent Req: none
Degrees: none
Tuition: Varies by course
Courses: Art History, Ceramics, Collage, Design, Drawing, Etching, Graphic Arts, Graphic Design, Handicrafts, History of Art & Architecture, Jewelry, Multimedia, Painting, Pastels, Photography, Printmaking, Sculpture
Adult Hobby Classes: Enrl 200; tuition varies; 6, 8 or 10 wk courses
Children's Classes: Enrl 100 per term; tuition varies per 6, 8, or 10 wk session
Summer School: Summer school dir - Maggie Anderson, Dir Educ; Enrl 160; tuition varies. Courses—Painting, Drawing, Workshops, Children's Multimedia

SALVE REGINA UNIVERSITY, Art Dept, 100 Ochre Point Ave, Newport, RI 02840-4149. Tel 401-847-6650; *Chmn* Barbara Shamblin, MFA; *Assoc Prof* Daniel Ludwig, MFA; *Asst Prof* Bert Emerson, MAT
Estab 1947; den; D & E; Scholarships; SC 28, LC 8; D 270 per sem (dept), non-maj 95, maj 72
Ent Req: HS dipl, ent exam
Degrees: BA 4 yr
Courses: 2 & 3-D Design, Aesthetics, Anatomy, Art History, Ceramics, Commercial Art, Design, Drawing, Environmental Design, Film, Graphic Arts, Graphic Design, History of Art & Architecture, Illustration, Painting, Photography, Sculpture, Theatre Arts
Summer School: Dir, Jay Lacouture

PROVIDENCE

BROWN UNIVERSITY, Dept of History of Art & Architecture, Box 1855, 64 College St Providence, RI 02912. Tel 401-863-1174; Fax 401-863-7790; Email nancy_safian@brown.edu; Web: www.brown.edu/academics/art-history; *Prof & Chair* Sheila Bonde; *Prof* Jeffrey Muller; *Prof & Dir Grad Studies* Evelyn Lincoln; *Prof* Dietrich Neumann; *Prof* Douglas Nickel
Pvt; D; Scholarships
Degrees: BA, MA, PhD
Tuition: $54,320 per yr
Courses: 19th & 20th Century Architecture & Painting, †Art History, Chinese Art, Greek, History of Art & Archaeology, Introduction to Art, Italian & Roman Art & Architecture
Summer School: Courses—limited
—**Dept of Visual Art,** PO Box 1861, List Art Bldg, 64 College St Providence, RI 02912. Tel 401-863-2423; Fax 401-863-1680; Email olanda_estrada@brown.edu; Web: www.brown.edu/academics/visual-art; *Prof & Chair* Leslie Bostrom; *Prof* Wendy Edwards
FT/PT 17; Pvt; D
Degrees: BA
Tuition: $54,320 per yr
Courses: Art of the Book, Computer Art, Drawing, Painting, Printmaking, Sculpture

PROVIDENCE COLLEGE, Art & Art History Dept, 549 River Ave, Providence, RI 02918-0001. Tel 401-865-2401, 865-2707; Fax 401-865-2410; *Chmn* Dr Ann Wood Norton; *Prof* Joan Branham; *Prof* James Baker; *Assoc Prof* Adrian G Dabash, MFA; *Assoc Prof* Richard A McAlister, MFA; *Assoc Prof* Alice Beckwith, PhD, MFA; *Asst Prof* James Janecek, MFA; *Asst Prof* Richard Elkington, MFA; *Asst Prof* Deborah Johnson, PhD, MFA; *Slide Librn* John DiCicco, MFA
Estab 1917, dept estab 1969; Maintain Hunt - Cavanaogh Gallery in Hunt - Cavanaogh Hall of Providence College; pvt; D & E; SC 49, LC 8; D 254, E 250, non-maj 209, maj 45

Ent Req: HS dipl, portfolio needed for transfer students
Degrees: BA 4 yr
Courses: †Art History, †Ceramics, †Drawing, †Painting, †Photography, †Printmaking, †Sculpture
Adult Hobby Classes: Dean, Dr O'Hara. Courses—History of Architecture, Art History, Calligraphy, Ceramics, Drafting, Drawing, Painting, Photography, Sculpture, Studio Art, Watercolor
Summer School: Dir, James M Murphy. Tuition $180 & $50 lab fee for three cr courses beginning mid-June through July. Courses—Art History, Calligraphy, Ceramics, Drawing, Painting, Photography, Printmaking, Soft and Hard Crafts. A summer program is offered at Pietrasanta, Italy: Dir, Richard A McAlister, MFA. Courses—Art History, Languages, Literature, Religious Studies, Studio Art, Drawing, Painting, Sculpture

RHODE ISLAND COLLEGE, Art Dept, 600 Mt Pleasant, Providence, RI 02908. Tel 401-456-8054; Fax 401-456-4755; Email nbockbrader@ric.edu; Web: www.ric.edu/art; *Prof* Krisjohn O Horvat, MFA; *Prof* Mary Ball Howkins, PhD, MFA; *Assoc Prof* Donna Kelly, PhD, MFA; *Prof* William Martin, MFA; *Prof* Heemong Kim, MFA; *Prof* Stephen Fisher, MFA; *Assoc Prof* Lisa Russell, MFA; *Assoc Prof* Bryan E Steinberg, MFA; *Prof, Chairperson* Nancy Bockbrader, MFA; *Assoc Prof, Found Coordr* Doug Bosch, MFA; *Asst Prof* Richard Whitten, MFA; *Asst Prof* Amy Montali, MFA
Estab 1854, dept estab 1969; Maintain nonprofit gallery, Bannister Gallery, Roberts Hall, 600 Mt Pleasant Ave, Providence, RI 02908; Pub; D & E; Scholarships; SC 48, LC 10, GC 15; D 450, E approx 50, non-maj approx 100, maj 350, grad 25
Ent Req: HS dipl, CEEB and SAT
Degrees: BA(Art History), BA, BS(Art Educ) & BFA(Studio Art) 4 yr, MAT 1 yr
Courses: Aesthetics, Art Appreciation, †Art Education, †Art History, †Ceramics, Design, Drawing, Fibers, †Graphic Design, History of Art & Architecture, †Jewelry, Metals, †Metalsmithing/Jewelry Design, †Painting, †Photography, †Printmaking, †Sculpture, Teacher Training
Adult Hobby Classes: Visual Arts in Society, Drawing, Design, Photography
Summer School: Courses—Ceramics, Drawing, Painting, Photography, Relief Printing

RHODE ISLAND SCHOOL OF DESIGN, 2 College St, Providence, RI 02903-2784. Tel 401-454-6100; Fax 401-454-6309; Email admissions@risd.edu; Web: www.risd.edu; *Pres* Rosanne Somerson; *Provost* Daniel Cavicchi; *Dir Mus of Art* John Smith
Estab 1877; Maintain nonprofit art gallery, Mus of Art, RI School of Design, 224 Benefit St, Providence, RI 02903; Fleet Library, 15 Westminster St; on-campus art supplies shop; Pvt; endowed; D & E; Scholarships; Fellowships; Grants; Loans; SC, LC, GC; under grad 2,030, grad 476
Publications: RISD Views, bimonthly; Catalogue of Degree Programs (annually); Annual Report; Continuing Ed Catalogues, 5 times a year
Ent Req: HS grad, SAT, visual work
Degrees: BFA, BArch, MFA, MID, MLA, MAT, MArch, MA, MDes
Tuition: $49,900
Courses: †Apparel Design, †Architecture, †Art History, †Ceramics, †Digital Media, †Film/Animation/Video, †Furniture Design, †Glass, †Graphic Design, †Illustration, †Industrial Design, †Interior Architecture, †Jewelry & Metalsmithing, †Landscape Architecture, Liberal Arts, †Painting, †Photography, †Printmaking, †Sculpture, †Teaching & Learning in Art/Design, †Textile Design
Adult Hobby Classes: Enrl 4500; tuition varies. Courses—Advertising & Print Design, Apparel Design, Ceramics, Computer Graphics, Culinary Arts, Glass, Illustration, Interior Design, Jewelry, Natural Science Illustration, New Media, Painting, Photography, Printmaking, Sculpture, Textile, Video
Summer School: Art & Design, Graphic Design

WARWICK

COMMUNITY COLLEGE OF RHODE ISLAND, Dept of Art, 400 East Ave, Warwick, RI 02886-1807. Tel 401-825-2220; Fax 401-825-2282; Web: www.ccri.edu/art; *Prof* M Kelman; *Prof* C Smith; *Prof* T Morrissey; *Prof* Natalie Coletta; *Prof* Nancy Wyllie; *Asst Prof* Yvonne Leonard; *Asst Prof* Mazih Adam; *Dept Chmn & Asst Prof* Mark Zellers; *Asst Prof* Mark Hartshorn
Estab 1964; On-campus art supplies shop; FT 10, PT 15; pub; D & E; Scholarships; SC 16, LC 3, seminar 1; D 4600
Ent Req: HS dipl, ent exam, equivalency exam
Degrees: AA, AFA, AS & AAS 2 yr
Tuition: Res—$832 per sem, $77 per cr hr
Courses: Art Appreciation, Art Education, Art History, Ceramics, Commercial Art, Drawing, Graphic Arts, Graphic Design, History of Modern Art, Interior Design, Life Drawing, Mixed Media, Painting, Photography, Sculpture, Survey of Ancient Art
Summer School: Chmn, Rebecca Clark. Enrl 200; 7 wk term. Courses—Ceramics, Crafts History of Modern Art, Drawing

SOUTH CAROLINA

AIKEN

UNIVERSITY OF SOUTH CAROLINA AT AIKEN, Dept of Visual & Performing Arts, 471 University Pkwy, Aiken, SC 29801. Tel 803-641-3305; *Chmn* Jack Benjamin; *Prof* Albin Beyer; *Asst Prof* John Elliot; *Instr* Robert McCreary, BS
Estab 1961, dept estab 1985; pub; D & E; SC 31, LC 6; D 180, E 60
Ent Req: HS dipl, GED, SAT
Degrees: BA & MFA
Courses: Advertising Design, Art History, Ceramics, Commercial Art, Drawing, Graphic Design, Illustration, Painting, Photography, Printmaking, Sculpture, Theatre Arts
Adult Hobby Classes: Tuition $1060 per sem. Courses—Vary
Summer School: Dir, A Beyer. Courses—Vary

CHARLESTON

CHARLESTON SOUTHERN UNIVERSITY, Dept of Language & Visual Art, PO Box 118087, Charleston, SC 29411-8087. Tel 843-863-7000; *Chmn* Dr Pamela Peak
Estab 1960; den; D & E; Scholarships; SC 14, LC 2; D 80, E 71, maj 15
Ent Req: GED or HS dipl
Degrees: BA and BS 4 yrs
Courses: Art Education, Ceramics, Drawing, Graphic Arts, History of Art & Architecture, Painting, Sculpture, Teacher Training
Summer School: Enrl 1500; tui $45 per sem hr; campus res—room and board $240 per sem; two 5 wk sessions beginning June. Courses—same as regular session

COLLEGE OF CHARLESTON, School of the Arts, 44 Saint Philip St, Charleston, SC 29424. Tel 843-953-7766; Fax 843-953-4988; *Chmn Music Dept* Steve Rosenberg; *Chmn Theatre Dept* Mark Landis; *Chmn Studio Art* Michael Tyzack; *Chmn Art History* Diane Johnson; *Dir, Arts Management* Karen Chandler; *Dir, Historic Preservation* Robert Russell; *Dir, Historic Preservation* Ralph Muldrow; *Dean* Valerie B Morris
Estab 1966; Maintain nonprofit art gallery; Halsey Gallery, College of Charleston School of Arts, Charleston, SC 29424; pub; D & E; Scholarships; SC 36, LC 24
Ent Req: HS dipl
Degrees: BA(Fine Arts) 4 yrs
Courses: Art History, Arts Management, Drawing, Historic Preservation, History of Art & Architecture, Painting, Photography, Printmaking, Sculpture, Stage Design, Theatre Arts

GIBBES MUSEUM OF ART, 135 Meeting St, Charleston, SC 29401-2217. Tel 843-722-2706; Fax 843-720-1682; Email wammons@gibbesmuseum.org; Web: www.gibbesmuseum.org; *Exec Dir & Chief Cur* Angela Mack; *Dir Fin & Admin* Courtney Soler; *Dir Coll & Opers* Zinnia Willits; *Opers Mgr & Chief Prep* Greg Jenkins; *Dir Cur Affairs* Sara Arnold; *Exhibs Consultant* Pam Wall; *Assoc Cur Educ* Becca Hiester; *Develop & Visitor Servs Mgr* Wendi Ammons; *Dir Progs & Digital Engagement* Lasley Steever; *Special Events Mgr* Jena Clem
Open Mon - Sat 10 AM - 5 PM, Wed 10 AM - 8 PM, Sun 1 PM - 5 PM; Admis fee adults $15, seniors & military $13, students $10, children 4-17 $6, children 3 & under free; Estab 1905; Mem: dues student $25, individual $55, dual $75, family $125, contributing $250, sustaining $500; D & E; Scholarships; SC, LC; varies
Ent Req: none
Tuition: varies
Courses: †Art Appreciation, †Art Education, †Art History, †Children's Drawing Workshops, †Paints & Drawings, †Photography, †Teacher Training
Children's Classes: Enrl, tuition & courses vary
Summer School: Dir, Rebecca Sailor

CLEMSON

CLEMSON UNIVERSITY, COLLEGE OF ARCHITECTURE, ARTS & HUMANITIES, Art Dept, 2-121 Lee Hall, Clemson, SC 29634-0509. Tel 864-656-3881; Web: http://www.clemson.edu/caah/art; *Pres* James Barker; *Dean, CAAH* Richard E (Rick) Goodstein; *Chair, Art Dept* Greg Shelnutt; *Grad Coordr* David Detrich
Estab 1967; Maintain non-profit art gallery Lee Gallery, Denise Woodward-Detrich, Dir; Gunnin Art & Architecture Library (26,000 vols); on-campus shop where art supplies may be purchased; pub; D; GC 24, SC 40, LC 29 (undergrad courses for service to pre-architecture and other Univ requirements); approx 1500 annually, grad maj 10
Ent Req: available on request
Degrees: BA, BS, BFA-Art 120 hrs, MFA-Art 60 hrs
Tuition: Res—$3592 per sem; nonres—$5890 per sem
Courses: Architecture, Art History, Ceramics, Drawing, Painting, Photography, Printmaking, Sculpture

CLINTON

PRESBYTERIAN COLLEGE, Visual & Theater Arts, PO Box 975, Harper Ctr Clinton, SC 29325-0975. Tel 864-833-2820, 833-8316; Fax 864-833-8600; Web: www.presby.edu; *Asst Prof* Lesley Preston; *Chmn* Mark R Anderson
Estab 1880, Dept estab 1966; den; D & E; Scholarships; SC 8, LC 5; D 200, non-maj 190, maj 10
Ent Req: HS dipl with C average, SAT
Degrees: BA & BS 4 yr
Courses: 2-D & 3-D Design, Art Appreciation, Art Education, Art History, Drawing, Painting
Summer School: Dean, J W Moncrief. Enrl 150; tuition $120 per sem. Courses—Art Appreciation, Painting

COLUMBIA

BENEDICT COLLEGE, School of Humanities, Arts & Social Sciences, 1600 Harden St, Columbia, SC 29204-1058. Tel 803-705-4711; Fax 803-705-6599; Email brooksc@benedict.edu; Web: www.benedict.edu; *Prof Art & Dir Ponder Gallery* Tyrone Geter; *Dir Theatre Ensemble* Charles Brooks; *Prof* Gina Moore; *Asst Prof* Wendell Brown; *Assoc Prof* Jasmin Cyril; *Admin Specialist* Alicia Briggs; *Instr* Brian Rego; *Instr* Sanford Greene; *Instr* Ladymon Stockard
Estab 1870; Maintains a nonprofit Gallery - The Ponder Gallery; maintains an art/architecture library - Fine Arts Dept (art area); on-campus shop where art supplies may be purchased; schols open to art majors vary; pvt; D, E & CE, Sat; Scholarships; SC 11, LC 6; D 20
Ent Req: HS dipl
Degrees: BA(Teaching of Art), BA (Studio Art)
Tuition: $13800 per yr (room & board incl)

Courses: Art Appreciation, Art Education, Art History, Ceramics, Drawing, Graphic Design, Painting, Sculpture, Teacher Training
Summer School: Term of two 5 wk sessions beginning June. Courses—Art Appreciation

COLUMBIA COLLEGE, Dept of Art, 1301 Columbia College Dr, Columbia, SC 29203-5998. Tel 803-786-3012; Fax 803-786-3893; Web: www.columbiacollegesc.edu; *Chmn* Stephen Nevitt
Estab 1854; FT 4, PT 1; pvt; D&E; Scholarships
Degrees: BA (Studio Art), BA (Studio Art with Art Educ Certification)
Tuition: $15,570 per yr; campus res—room & board $5240 per yr; additional fee $300
Courses: 3-D Design, Advertising Design, Art Appreciation, Art History, Ceramics, Design, Drawing, Life Drawing, Painting, Photography, Printmaking, †Sculpture
Adult Hobby Classes: Enrl 20 per class. Courses—Art Appreciation, Art History, Drawing, Photography
Summer School: Dir, Becky Hulion. Enrl 20 per class. Courses—Art Appreciation, Art History, Art Education, Drawing, Photography, Printmaking

UNIVERSITY OF SOUTH CAROLINA, Dept of Art, McMaster College, Columbia, SC 29208-0001. Tel 803-777-4236, 777-0535, 777-7480; Fax 803-777-0535; Web: www.cal.sc.eduÅrtındex.html; *Chmn* Robert F Lyon; *Chmn Studio* Richard Rose; *Chmn Art Educ* Cynthia Colbert, EdD; *Chmn Art History* John Bryan, EdD; *Chmn Media Arts* Sandra Wertz, PhD, EdD; *Asst Chmn* Harry Hansen
Estab 1801, dept estab 1924; pub; D & E; Scholarships; SC 89, LC 57, GC 73; D 1620, E 174, non-maj 1000, maj 520, grad 82
Ent Req: HS dipl
Degrees: BA, BFA & BS 4 yrs, MA & MAT 2 yr, MFA 3 yrs
Courses: †3-D Studies, †Advertising Design, †Art Education, †Art History, †Ceramics, †Commercial Art, †Drawing, †Graphic Arts, †Graphic Design, Illustration, Jewelry, Museum Staff Training, Painting, Photography, Printmaking, Restoration & Conservation
Adult Hobby Classes: Enrl 125; tuition $127 per hr for 16 wk term. Courses—Art for Elementary School, Basic Drawing, Ceramics, Fiber Arts, Fundamentals of Art, Interior Design, Intro to Art
Children's Classes: Enrl 100; tuition $30 for 9 wk term. Courses—Children's Art
Summer School: Enrl 400; tuition undergrad $127 per hr, grad $141 per hr. Courses—Same as acad yr

FLORENCE

FRANCIS MARION UNIVERSITY, Fine Arts Dept, PO Box 100547, Florence, SC 29502-0547. Tel 843-661-1385; Fax 843-661-1529; Web: www.departments.fmarion.edu/finearts; *Prof & Chmn* Lawrence P Anderson
Estab 1969; Maintains nonprofit art gallery: Hyman Fine Arts Center Gallery; Pub; D&E; Scholarships
Degrees: BA
Courses: Art Appreciation, †Art Education, Art History, †Ceramics, Costume Design & Construction, Design, Drafting, Drawing, Film, Graphic Design, †Painting, †Photography, Sculpture, †Stage Design, †Theatre Arts, Video

GAFFNEY

LIMESTONE COLLEGE, Art Dept, 1115 College Dr, Gaffney, SC 29340-3799. Tel 864-489-7151, Ext 513; Web: www.limestone.edu; *Chair & Prof of Art* Carolyn Ford; *Assistant Prof of Art* Chris Neyen; *Instr* Brett Schenning; *Instr* Emily Tuttle
Estab 1845; Maintains a non-profit art gallery: Granberry Gallery, 1115 College Drive, Gaffney, SC 29340; pvt; D & E & Online; Scholarships; SC 19, LC 5; D 1,200, maj 29
Ent Req: HS dipl, ent exam
Degrees: BA (Studio & Graphics)
Courses: 2-D & 3-D Design, Art Appreciation, Art History, Ceramics, Design, Drawing, Graphic Arts, Graphic Design, Handicrafts, History of Art & Architecture, Mixed Media, Painting, Photography, Printmaking, Printmaking, Sculpture

GREENVILLE

BOB JONES UNIVERSITY, School of Fine Arts, Div of Art & Design, 1700 Wade Hampton Blvd, Greenville, SC 29614-1000. Tel 864-242-5100, Ext 2720; Fax 864-233-9829; Email artdesign@bju.edu; Web: www.bju.edu; *Dean* Darren Lawson, PhD; *Chmn* Jay Bopp, MFA; *Design Dept Head* Chris Barnhart, MA; *Instr* Kevin Isgett, MFA; *Studio Dept Head* Kevin Isgett, MFA; *Instr* Michelle Berg Radford, MFA; *Instr* Jared Stanley, MA; *Instr* Diane Mattox, MA; *Instr* Karen Flora, MA; *Instr* Pam Adams, MA; *Instr* Laurilyn Hall, MFA; *Instr* John Nolan, MA; *Instr* Chris Barnhart, MA; *Instr* Amanda West, MFA
Estab 1927, dept estab 1945; Maintain nonprofit art gallery, BJU Museum & Gallery, at univ & JS Mack Library. Campus shop where art supplies may be purchased; pvt; D; Scholarships; SC 29, LC 12; M 59, W 57
Ent Req: HS dipl, letters of recommendation
Degrees: BFA & BS 4 yrs
Tuition: $4980 per yr, $2490 per sem; campus res—room & board $3900 per yr
Courses: Advertising Design, Aesthetics, †Apparel, Art Appreciation, †Art Education, Art History, Bronze Casting, Calligraphy, †Ceramics, Costume Design & Construction, †Design, Drawing, †Fashion Arts, †Film, Goldsmithing, Graphic Arts, †Graphic Design, Handicrafts, History of Art & Architecture, Illustration, †Interior Design, Jewelry, Lettering, Mixed Media, †Occupational Therapy, †Painting, Photography, Printmaking, Sculpture, Silversmithing, †Stage Design, †Teacher Training, †Textile Design, †Theatre Arts, Weaving
Summer School: Dir Jay Bopp, internship; Art Appreciation

FURMAN UNIVERSITY, Art Dept, 3300 Poinsett Hwy, Greenville, SC 29613-1000. Tel 864-294-2074; Web: http://www2.furman.edu/academics/art/pages/default.aspx
Estab 1826; maintains a nonprofit art gallery, Thompson Art Gallery, ROE Art Bldg; pvt; D & E; Scholarships; SC 21, LC 8; D 245, non-maj 205, maj 60
Ent Req: HS dipl, SAT
Degrees: BA 4 yr
Courses: Advertising Design, Art Appreciation, Art Criticism, Art Education, Art History, Ceramics, Crafts, Drawing, Graphic Design, †History of Art, Painting, Photography, Printmaking, Sculpture, Typography, Web Design

GREENVILLE COUNTY MUSEUM OF ART CENTER FOR MUSEUM EDUCATION, 420 College St, Greenville, SC 29601-2099. Tel 864-271-7570, ext 12; Fax 864-271-7579; Email abarr@greenvillemuseum.org; Web: www.greenvillemuseum.org; *Coordr* Anne Q Barr
Estab 1960; Museum collections incl Andrew Wyeth, Jasper Johns, William H Johnson & an extensive collection of American art; PT 35; pub; D & E; Scholarships; SC 12, LC 2, GC 6; D 250, E 170
Tuition: Call for brochure
Courses: Art History, Drawing, Painting, Photography, †Pottery, †Printmaking

GREENVILLE TECHNICAL COLLEGE, Visual Arts Dept, PO Box 5616, Greenville, SC 29606-5616. Tel 864-848-2024, 848-2000; Fax 864-848-2003; Web: www.greenvilletech.com; *Campus Dir* Nancy Welch; *Dept Head* Blake Praytor
Degrees: AA (Fine Art, Graphic Design) Cert Program
Tuition: In-county res—$71 per cr hr, out of county $78 per cr hr, out of state $157 per cr hr
Courses: Art Appreciation, Art History, Film, Graphic Design, Photography
Adult Hobby Classes: Courses offered
Summer School: Dir, Dr David S Trask. Enrl 35. Courses—Art Appreciation

GREENWOOD

LANDER UNIVERSITY, College of Arts & Humanities - Visual Arts, 320 Stanley Ave, Greenwood, SC 29649-2056. Tel 864-388-8323; Fax 864-388-8144; Email jslagle@lander.edu; Web: www.lauder.edu; *Chair & Assoc Prof Art* Jim Slagle; *Assoc Prof Art* Jon Holloway; *Asst Prof Art* Doug McAbee; *Asst Prof Art* Elizabeth Snipes; *Asst Prof Art* Sandy Singletary; *Asst Prof Art* Asma Nazim-Starnes; *Asst Prof Art* Dr Susan Deaton; *Asst Prof Art* Chrystine Kefner
Estab 1872; Maintains nonprofit art gallery, Lander University Gallery, 320 Stanley Ave, Greenwood, SC 29649; on-campus shop sells art supplies; FT 6, PT 4; pub; D & E; Scholarships; SC 28, LC 7, GC 7, Study Tours 2; D 330, E 150, non-maj 250, maj 80, grad 11
Ent Req: HS dipl
Degrees: BS (Art) 4 yrs, BS (K-12 certification), BS (Art/Graphic Design Emphasis), MAT (Art) 14 months
Courses: Advertising Design, Art Appreciation, Art Education, Art History, Ceramics, Commercial Art, Display, Drawing, Graphic Arts, Graphic Design, Handicrafts, Mixed Media, Painting, Photography, Printmaking, Sculpture, Study Tour to Europe, †Teacher Training, Theatre Arts

HARTSVILLE

COKER COLLEGE, Art Dept, 300 E College Ave, Hartsville, SC 29550-3797. Tel 843-383-8150; Email jgrosser@coker.edu; Web: www.coker.edu/art/; *Prof Art, Chair* Jean Grosser; *Assoc Prof Design* Ken Maginnis; *Prof Painting & Drawing* Jim Boden; *Asst Prof & Gallery Dir* Larry Merriman
Estab 1908; Maintain nonprofit art gallery; Cecelia Coker Bell Gallery, 300 E College Ave, Hartsville, SC 29550; FT 3; pvt; D & E; Scholarships; SC 24, LC 12; 1000, maj 50
Ent Req: HS dipl, ent exam
Degrees: BA and BS 4 yrs
Courses: Art Appreciation, †Art Education, Art History, Ceramics, Conceptual Art, Design, Drawing, †Fine Arts, †Graphic Design, Illustration, Painting, †Photography, Sculpture, Teacher Training, Web Design

NEWBERRY

NEWBERRY COLLEGE, Dept of Art, 2100 College St, Newberry, SC 29108-2197. Tel 803-276-5010; Fax 803-321-5627; *Asst Prof* Elizabeth Ruff; *Head Dept* Bruce Nell-Smith
Estab 1856, dept estab 1973; den; D & E; SC 35, LC 2; D 114, non-maj 106, maj 15
Ent Req: HS dipl, SAT
Degrees: BA (Art Studio) 4 yrs, BA (Arts Mgt), two courses in independent study, financial aid available
Courses: Art History, Drawing, Mixed Media, Painting, Printmaking, Stage Design, Theatre Arts

ORANGEBURG

CLAFLIN COLLEGE, Dept of Art, 400 Magnolia St, Orangeburg, SC 29115-6815. Tel 803-535-5335 (Art Dept); Web: www.claflincollege.edu; *Assoc Prof* Dr Kod Igwe; *Instr* Cecil Williams; *Chmn* Herman Keith
School estab 1869, dept estab 1888; pvt; D; Scholarships; SC 10, LC 2; D 20
Ent Req: HS dipl, SAT
Degrees: BA 4 years, BA Teacher Educ 4 years
Courses: Advanced Studio, †Advertising Design, Afro-American Art History, †Art Education, Art History, Ceramics, Drawing, Film, Graphic Arts, Lettering, Painting, Photography, Printmaking, Sculpture, Theatre Arts, Video
Summer School: Dir, Karen Woodfaulk. Enrl 10-12, 6 wk term beginning June. Courses—Art Appreciation, Art-Elem School Crafts, Advertising Art, Textile Design

SOUTH CAROLINA STATE UNIVERSITY, Dept of Visual & Performing Arts, 300 College St NE, Orangeburg, SC 29117-0001. Tel 803-536-7101; Fax 803-536-7192; Email jwalsh@scsu.edu; Web: www.scsu.edu/; *Asst Prof* Johnathon Walsh; *Asst Prof* Kimberly Ledee; *Asst Prof* Leslie Rech; *Asst Prof* Steven Crall; *Instr* Frank Martin II
Dept estab 1972; Maintains nonprofit gallery; music & fine arts libr; pub, state; D & E; SC 15, LC 7; D 73, nonmaj 8, maj 73
Ent Req: HS dipl
Degrees: BA & BS 4 yrs, MS approx 2 yrs
Courses: †Art Education, †Design, †Printmaking, †Sculpture
Adult Hobby Classes: Ceramics, Sculpture, Drawing, Painting
Summer School: Dir, Dr Leroy Davis. Tuition $90 per cr hr. Courses—Art Appreciation, Arts & Crafts for Children

ROCK HILL

WINTHROP UNIVERSITY, Dept of Art & Design, 701 Oakland Ave, Rock Hill, SC 29733. Tel 803-323-2653; Email waldenr@winthrop.edu; Web: www.winthrop.edu; *Prof* Mary Mintich; *Prof* John Olvera; *Prof* David Freeman; *Prof* Alf Ward; *Assoc Prof* Dr Seymour Simmons; *Assoc Prof* Alan Huston; *Assoc Prof* Paul Martyka; *Assoc Prof* Jim Connell; *Assoc Prof* Laura Dufresne; *Assoc Prof* Phil Moody; *Assoc Prof* Margaret Johnson; *Assoc Prof* David Stokes; *Assoc Prof* Dr Peg DeLamater; *Asst Prof* Chad Dresbach; *Asst Prof* Marge Moody; *Asst Prof* Dr Alice Burmeister; *Chmn* Jerry Walden
Estab 1886; pub; D & E; SC 42, LC 10; in college D 5300, non-maj 300, maj 345, grad 10
Ent Req: HS dipl, SAT, CEEB
Degrees: BA and BFA 4 yrs
Courses: Advertising Design, Art Appreciation, †Art Education, †Art History, Calligraphy, †Ceramics, Collage, Commercial Art, Conceptual Art, Design, Display, Drafting, †Drawing, Fashion Arts, Graphic Arts, †Graphic Design, Handicrafts, History of Art & Architecture, Illustration, Industrial Design, †Interior Design, †Jewelry, Lettering, Mixed Media, Museum Staff Training, †Painting, †Photography, †Printmaking, †Sculpture, Silversmithing, Teacher Training, Textile Design, Weaving

SPARTANBURG

CONVERSE COLLEGE, School of the Arts, Dept of Art & Design, 580 E Main St, Spartanburg, SC 29302-1931. Tel 864-596-9000, 596-9181, 596-9178; Fax 864-596-9606; Email artdesign@converse.edu; Web: www.converse.edu; *Asst Prof & Dept Chmn* Susanne Gunter, EdD; *Asst Prof Studio Art* Greg Mueller, MFA; *Instructor & Coordr Educ* Andrea Elliott, MA; *Assoc Prof & Coordr Interior Design* Ruth Beals, MA; *Assoc Prof Studio Art* Andrew Blanchard, MFA; *Asst Prof Interior Design* Jane Hughes, MA; *Assoc Prof & Coordr Art History* Suzanne Schuweiler, PhD; *Asst Prof Studio Art* Jena Thomas, MFA
Estab 1889; Maintains nonprofit Milliken Gallery, 580 E Main St, Spartansburg, SC 29302; art/architecture library not for public use; pvt, women only; D & E; Scholarships; SC 40, LC 17; In dept: non-maj 30, maj 100, grad 30
Ent Req: HS dipl, SAT, CEEB, ACT, Advanced placement in Art & Art History
Degrees: BA & BFA 4 yrs, MEd, MAT
Courses: Art Appreciation, †Art Education, †Art History, †Art Therapy, Ceramics, Design, DraftingAuto CAD, Drawing, Graphic Design, †History of Art & Architecture, †Interior Design, Jewelry, Museum Staff Training, Occupational Therapy, Painting, Photography, Printmaking, Sculpture, †Studio Art, Teacher Training
Summer School: Dir, Joe Dunn

SPARTANBURG COUNTY MUSEUM OF ART, The Art School, 200 E St John St, Spartanburg, SC 29306. Tel 864-582-7616; Fax 864-948-5353; Email artschool@spartanburgartmuseum.org; Web: www.spartanburgartmus.org; *Dir* Bob LoGrippo
Estab 1962; Maintain nonprofit art gallery; schols offered ann; Pvt; D & E; Loans; SC 25; 300-400
Ent Req: none
Tuition: $110-$185 for 8-12 wk classes & weekend workshops
Courses: Calligraphy, Cartooning, Drawing, Figure Drawing, Mixed Media, Painting, Portraiture, Pottery & Ceramic Design, †Printmaking, Sculpture, Stained Glass
Adult Hobby Classes: $110-$185 for Art Appreciation, Fine Arts
Children's Classes: $70-$100 for 4-8 wk classes & weekend workshops
Summer School: Dir, Robert LoGrippo. Enrl 200. Art Camp, 1-6 wk sessions

SOUTH DAKOTA

ABERDEEN

NORTHERN STATE UNIVERSITY, Art Dept, 1200 S Jay St, Aberdeen, SD 57401-7198. Tel 605-626-2514; Fax 605-626-2263; Email kilianp@northern.edu; Web: www.northern.edu/artdept/index.html; *Prof* Mark McGinnis, MFA; *Prof* Bill Hoar, PhD, MFA; *Prof & Coordr* Peter Kilian, MFA; *Asst Prof* Ruth McKinney; *Prof* Mark Shekore, MFA; *Asst Prof & Adjunct* Joel McKinney; *Adjunct Instr* Troy McQuillen; *Adjunct Instr* Roxanne Hinze
Maintain nonprofit art gallery, Northern Galleries, 1200 S Jay St, Aberdeen, SD 57401; Estab 1901, dept estab 1920; pub; D & E; Scholarships; SC 40, LC 14, GC 6; D 385, non-maj 300, maj 85
Ent Req: HS dipl
Degrees: AA 2 yrs, BA, BSEd 4 yrs
Courses: †Advertising Design, Aesthetics, Art Appreciation, Art Education, Art History, Ceramics, Commercial Art, †Computer Graphics, Design, Drawing, Fiber Arts, Graphic Arts, History of Art & Architecture, Mixed Media, Painting, Photography, Printmaking, Sculpture, Teacher Training, Theatre Arts, Video
Adult Hobby Classes: Enrl 30; tuition $74.10 per cr
Summer School: Prof, Peter Kilian, Dir

BROOKINGS

SOUTH DAKOTA STATE UNIVERSITY, Dept of Visual Arts, PO Box 2802, Brookings, SD 57007-0001. Tel 605-688-4103; Fax 605-688-6769; Email SDSU.ArtDept@sdstate.edu; Web: http://sdstate.edu/academic/programs/index.cfm; *Prof Dir School of Design* Michael Steele, MFA; *Assoc Prof* Leda Cempellin, PhD; *Prof* Jeannie French, MFA; *Prof* Scott Wallace, MFA; *Assoc Prof* Cable Hardin, MFA; *Asst Prof* Diana Behl, MFA; *Instr Prog Coordr Studio Art* Mark Stemwedel, MFA; *Instr* Beverly Krumm, MFA; *Instr* Mitch Tobert; *Instr* Peter Reichardt, MFA; *Instr* Molly Wicks, MFA; *Instr* Elijah Van Benschoten, MFA; *Asst Prof* Anthony Carton; *Instr* Shannon Frewaldt
Estab 1881; Maintain nonprofit art gallery; Ritz Gallery, Box 2802, 111 Grove Hall, SDSU Brookings SD 57007; art supplies available on-campus; Pub; D & E, online; Scholarships; SC 42, LC 8, online Art History, Photography, Computer Graphics, Drawing & Digital Art; Enrl non-maj 50, maj 230
Activities: Schols offered
Ent Req: HS dipl, ent ACT
Degrees: BFA (120 credits, certificates)
Tuition: Tuition & fees $8,532 per yr (average)
Courses: †Animation, Art Appreciation, †Art Education, Art History, †Ceramics, Design, Drawing, Film, General Art, †Graphic Design, †History of Art & Architecture, History of Art & Design, Interactive & Web Design, Mixed Media, †Painting, Photography, †Printmaking, †Sculpture, Teacher Training
Summer School: Dir, Michael Steele

MADISON

DAKOTA STATE UNIVERSITY, College of Liberal Arts, 820 N Washington Ave, 114 Beadle Hall Madison, SD 57042-1735. Tel 605-256-5270; Fax 605-256-5021; Web: www.dsu.edu; *Prof* John Laflin; *Prof* Roger Reed; *Assoc Prof* Alan Fisher; *Assoc Prof* James Janke; *Assoc Prof* Nancy Moose; *Assoc Prof* Louise Pope; *Assoc Prof* James Swanson; *Dean* Eric Johnson
Estab 1881; FT 1, PT 1; pub; D; Scholarships; SC 16, LC 5; D 120, maj 20
Ent Req: HS dipl, ACT
Degrees: BS 4 yrs
Tuition: Res—undergrad $1620 per yr; nonres—$5152 per yr
Courses: Art Education, Art History, Ceramics, Drawing, Jewelry, Painting, Sculpture, Teacher Training
Summer School: Term of 8 wks beginning June

MITCHELL

DAKOTA WESLEYAN UNIVERSITY, Art Dept, 1200 W University Ave, Mitchell, SD 57391-4358. Tel 800-333-8506; Web: www.dwu.edu/art/index.htm
Courses: †Art Appreciation, †Art History, †Ceramics, †Design, †Drawing, †Painting

SIOUX FALLS

AUGUSTANA COLLEGE, Art Dept, 2001 S Summit Ave, Sioux Falls, SD 57197-0002. Tel 605-336-5428; WATS 800-727-2844; *Chmn* Carl A Grupp, MFA; *Asst Prof* Tom Shields, MFA; *Instr* John Peters, MFA; *Instr* Gerry Punt, BA
Estab 1860; den; D & E; Scholarships; SC 14, LC 3; total 1861
Ent Req: HS dipl, ent exam
Degrees: BA & MAT
Tuition: $13,960 annual tuition; campus res—room & board $4058
Courses: †Art Education, †Drawing, Etching, †Graphic Design, History of Art & Architecture, Lithography, Painting, Printmaking, Sculpture, Teacher Training
Children's Classes: Enrl 15; tuition $600 fall & spring. Courses—Ceramics, Drawing
Summer School: Dir, Dr Gary D Olson. Term of 7 wks beginning June. Courses—Arts, Crafts, Drawing

UNIVERSITY OF SIOUX FALLS, Dept of Art, 1101 W 22nd St, Division of Fine Arts/Music Sioux Falls, SD 57105-1600. Tel 605-331-5000; Web: www.usiouxfalls.edu; *Chmn* Nancy Olive; *Pres* Mark Benedetto
Estab 1883; pub; Scholarships; SC, LC; 1000
Degrees: BA with maj in Art or Art Educ 4 yrs
Courses: Art Education, Art History, Ceramics, Drawing, Graphic Design, Handicrafts, Painting, Photography, Printmaking, Sculpture
Summer School: Terms one 3 wk session, two 4 wk sessions. Courses—Crafts, Design, Drawing, Education

SPEARFISH

BLACK HILLS STATE UNIVERSITY, Art Dept, University Sta, Box 9003, Spearfish, SD 57799-9003. Tel 605-642-6011, 642-6420; *Prof* Steve Babbitt; *Prof* James Knutson; *Prof* Susan Hore-Pabst; *Prof* Janeen Larson; *Prof* Stephen Parker; *Prof* Randall Royer; *Instr* Abdollah Farrokhi; *Chmn* Jim Cargill
Estab 1883; FT 13; pub; D; Scholarships; SC 15, LC 4; maj 50
Ent Req: HS dipl, transcripts, ACT, physical exam
Degrees: BA 4 yrs
Courses: Art Education, Calligraphy, Ceramics, Commercial Art, Drafting, Drawing, Painting, Photography, Sculpture
Summer School: Art in our Lives, Ceramics, Drawing, Painting, School Arts & Crafts

VERMILLION

UNIVERSITY OF SOUTH DAKOTA, Department of Art, College of Fine Arts, 414 E Clark St, Vermillion, SD 57069-2307. Tel 605-677-5636; 677-5011; Email jday@usd.edu; Web: www.usd.edu/; *Chmn & Dean* John Day, MFA; *Prof* Lloyd Menard, MFA; *Prof* Jeff Freeman, MFA; *Prof* John Banasiak, MFA; *Assoc Prof* Martin Wanserski, MFA; *Assoc Prof* Ann Balakier, PhD, MFA; *Prof* Dennis Wavrat, MFA; *Instr* Michael Hill
Estab 1862, dept estab 1887; pub; D & E; Scholarships; SC 32, LC 9, GC 9; non-maj 300, maj 80, grad 17
Ent Req: HS dipl, ACT
Degrees: BFA, BFA with Teacher Cert, MFA
Courses: Advertising Design, Aesthetics, Art Appreciation, †Art Education, Art History, †Ceramics, Commercial Art, Design, Drawing, †Graphic Design, Graphics, History of Art & Architecture, Lettering, Mixed Media, Museum Staff Training, †Painting, †Photography, †Printmaking, †Sculpture, Teacher Training
Summer School: Chmn, Lawrence Anderson. Tuition per cr hr for terms of 4 wks to 15 wks. Courses—variable offerings in summer-not all disciplines are offered each summer

YANKTON

MOUNT MARTY COLLEGE, Fine Arts Dept, 1105 W 8th St, Yankton, SD 57078. Tel 605-668-1011, 668-1574; Fax 605-668-1607; Email dkahle@mtmc.edu; Web: www.mtmc.edu; *Dept Head* David Kahle, MA
Estab 1936; Maintain non-profit gallery & library; on-campus shop where art supplies may be purchased; S. Carol Baumert (PT); PVT; D&E; SC 17, LC 5; 9
Activities: Schols offered
Ent Req: HS dipl
Degrees: BA 4 yrs, MA(Anesthesia)
Courses: 2-D & 3-D Design, Art Appreciation, Calligraphy, Ceramics, Collage, Design, Drawing, Handicrafts, Mixed Media, Printmaking, Teacher Training
Adult Hobby Classes: Enrl 100-150; tuition $283 per 11 cr hrs, $3390 full time. Courses—Art Appreciation, Calligraphy, Ceramics, Crafts, Design, Painting & Drawing, Photography, Printmaking
Summer School: Dir, Sr Pierre Roberts. Tuition $100 per cr hr for term of wks beginning June & July

TENNESSEE

CHATTANOOGA

CHATTANOOGA STATE TECHNICAL COMMUNITY COLLEGE, Advertising Arts Dept, 4501 Amnicola Hwy, Chattanooga, TN 37406-1018. Tel 423-697-4400, 697-4441; Fax 423-697-2539; Web: www.cstcc.cc.tn.us; *Dir Fine Arts* Denise Frank; *Asst Prof* Alan Wallace
FT 2; pub; D & E; Scholarships; SC 30, LC 5; D 3000, E 2000
Ent Req: HS dipl
Degrees: Cert, AA(Advertising Art)
Tuition: Res—$56 per cr hr; nonres—$168 per cr hr
Courses: Advertising Concepts, Advertising Design, Air Brush, Art Education, Art History, Ceramics, Commercial Art, Drafting, Drawing, Graphic Arts, Graphic Design, Illustration, Internships, Painting, Photography, Production Art, Teacher Training, Typography
Adult Hobby Classes: Tuition $45 per course. Courses—Painting, Photography
Children's Classes: Tuition $20 per course. Courses—Arts & Crafts, Ceramics & Sculpture
Summer School: Tuition $140 per term of 10 wks

UNIVERSITY OF TENNESSEE AT CHATTANOOGA, Dept of Art, 615 McCallie Ave, Chattanooga, TN 37403-2504. Tel 423-755-4178; Fax 423-785-2101; Web: www.utc.edu; *Head & Prof* Matt Greenwell, MFA; *Prof* Anne Lindsey, PhD; *Prof* Maggie McMahon, MFA; *Prof* Gavin Townsend, PhD, MFA; *Prof* E Alan White, MFA; *Prof* Ron Buffington, MFA; *Asst Prof* David Young, MFA; *Clinical Prof* Nandini Makrandi; *Lectr* Robert Cox; *Lectr* Dan Bething; *Lectr* Leslie Jensen-Inman
Estab 1928; Maintains a nonprofit art gallery, Cress Gallery of Art, 615 McCallie Ave, Chattanooga TN 37403; pub; D & E; Scholarships; SC 45, LC 11, other 6; D 501, E 15, non-maj 320, maj 196, grad 1
Ent Req: HS dipl, ACT or SAT, health exam
Degrees: BA, BS, BFA 4 yrs
Courses: †3D, †Art Appreciation, Art Education, Art History, Ceramics, Drawing, Graphic Design, †History of Art & Architecture, †Mixed Media, Painting, †Photography, Printmaking, Sculpture, †Web Media
Summer School: Same as reg semester

CLARKSVILLE

AUSTIN PEAY STATE UNIVERSITY, Dept of Art, 601 College St, Clarksville, TN 37044; PO Box 4677, Clarksville, TN 37044-0001. Tel 931-648-7333; Email marsh@apsu02.apsu.edu; Web: www.apsu.edu/; *Assoc Prof* Kell Black, MFA; *Chair* Cindy Marsh, MFA
Estab 1927, dept estab 1930; pub; D & E; Scholarships; GC 3; D 740, E 75, non-maj 590, maj 150
Ent Req: HS dipl
Degrees: BFA, BA & BS 4 yrs
Courses: †Art Education, Art History, †Ceramics, Drawing, †Graphic Design, Illustration, Lettering, †Painting, †Photography, †Printmaking, †Sculpture
Summer School: tuition $192 per cr

CLEVELAND

CLEVELAND STATE COMMUNITY COLLEGE, Dept of Art, 3535 Adkisson Dr, Cleveland, TN 37312-2813; PO Box 3570, Cleveland, TN 37320-3570. Tel 423-472-7141; Fax 423-478-6255; WATS 800-604-2722; *Head* Jere Chumley, MA
Estab 1967; pub; D & E; Scholarships; SC 6, LC 5; D 95, E 20, non-maj 60, maj 35
Ent Req: HS dipl or GED
Degrees: AA and AS 2 yrs
Tuition: Res—$647 per sem; nonres—$2585 per sem
Courses: Architecture, Art Appreciation, Art Education, Art History, Calligraphy, Ceramics, Design, Drafting, Drawing, History of Art & Architecture, Painting, Photography, Sculpture
Adult Hobby Classes: Drawing, Painting

LEE UNIVERSITY, Dept of Communication & the Arts, 1120 N Ocoee St, Cleveland, TN 37311-4475. Tel 423-614-8240; Fax 423-614-8242; Web: www.leeuniversity.edu; *Chmn* Dr Matthew Melton
Estab 1918; Pvt
Ent Req: HS dipl
Degrees: BA, BS
Tuition: Res—$5500 on campus per sem
Courses: Art Appreciation, Art History, Drawing, Film, Painting, Photography

COLLEGEDALE

SOUTHERN ADVENTIST UNIVERSITY, Art Dept, PO Box 370, Collegedale, TN 37315-0370. Tel 423-238-2732, 237-2111; *Chmn* Wayne Hazen
Estab 1969; den; D & E; Scholarships; LC 4; maj 50
Ent Req: HS dipl, ent exam
Degrees: BA(Art), BA(Art & Educ) & BA(Computer Graphic Design) 4 yr
Courses: Animation, Art, Art Appreciation, Art Education, Art History, Ceramics, Computer Graphic Design, Design, Drawing, Fine Art, Graphic Arts, Graphic Design, Painting, Printmaking, Sculpture

COLUMBIA

COLUMBIA STATE COMMUNITY COLLEGE, Dept of Art, 1665 Hampshire Pike, Columbia, TN 38401-5653. Tel 931-540-2722; Web: www.coscc.cc.tn.us; *Prof* Fred Behrens, MFA; *Div Chm* Marvin Austin PhD
Estab 1966; pub; D & E; Scholarships; SC 17, LC 4; D 230, non-maj 215, maj 12-15
Ent Req: open door institution
Degrees: AA & AS 2 yrs
Courses: Art History, †Art Studio, Design, Drawing, Film, Painting, Photography, Printmaking, Visual Arts
Children's Classes: Enrl 18-20, tuition $30 per session

GATLINBURG

ARROWMONT SCHOOL OF ARTS & CRAFTS, 556 Parkway, Gatlinburg, TN 37738-3202; PO Box 567, Gatlinburg, TN 37738-0567. Tel 865-436-5860; Fax 865-430-4101; Email info@arrowmont.org; Web: www.arrowmont.org; *Dir* Bill May; *Prog Dir* Nick DeFord; *Development Director* Fran Day; *Gallery Manager* Kelly Hider
Estab 1945; Maintains nonprofit gallery, Sandra J Blain Galleries, Geoffrey A Wolpert Gallery, Jerry drown Gallery (same address as school); maintain an art library: Marian G Heard Resource Center, 556 Parkway, Gatlinburg, TN 37738; on-campus shop for purchase of art supplies; Pvt; D & E (operate mostly in spring & summer with special programs for fall & winter); Scholarships; Fellowships; SC 180, GC 30; D 2000, 300
Activities: Schols offered (check website for descriptions)
Ent Req: Must be 18 yrs & older
Degrees: none granted, though cr is offered with approval
Tuition: Tuition varies
Courses: Basketry, Bookbinding, Ceramics, Drawing, Enamel, Fused Glass, Jewelry, Mixed Media, Painting, Papermaking, Photography, Printmaking, Quilting, Sculpture, Silversmithing, Stained Glass, Textile Design, Weaving, Woodturning, Woodworking
Adult Hobby Classes: Winter (evenings) $150-$200
Children's Classes: Winter $100

GREENEVILLE

TUSCULUM COLLEGE, Fine Arts Dept, Division of Arts & Humanities, 2299 Tusculum, Greeneville, TN 37743; PO Box 5084, Greeneville, TN 37743-0001. Tel 423-636-7300; Web: www.tusculum.edu; *Asst Prof Art* Tom Silva
Estab 1794; den; D; Scholarships; SC 25, LC 3; D 445, maj 18
Ent Req: HS dipl
Degrees: BA & BS 4 yrs
Courses: Art Education, Ceramics, Drawing, History of Art & Architecture, Painting, Printmaking, Sculpture
Adult Hobby Classes: Enrl 14. Courses—Painting

HARROGATE

LINCOLN MEMORIAL UNIVERSITY, Division of Humanities, 6965 Cumberland Gap Pkwy, Harrogate, TN 37752-8245. Tel 423-869-3611; Web: www.lmunet.edu; *Assoc Prof Art* Betty DeBord; *Instr* Alex Buckland; *Chmn Humanities* Colun Leckey
Estab 1897, dept estab 1974; pvt; D & E; SC 30, LC 3; D 120, E 75, non-maj 97, maj 98

Ent Req: HS dipl
Degrees: BA 4 yrs
Courses: Aesthetics, Art Education, Art History, Ceramics, Commercial Art, Drawing, Film, Goldsmithing, †Graphic Arts, Jewelry, Lettering, Museum Staff Training, †Painting, †Photography, †Sculpture, Silversmithing, †Teacher Training, †Textile Design, †Theatre Arts, Weaving

JACKSON

LAMBUTH UNIVERSITY, Dept of Human Ecology & Visual Arts, 705 Lambuth Blvd, Jackson, TN 38301-5280. Tel 731-427-4725 (Jackson), 901-678-5087 (Memphis); Email lambuth@memphis.edu; Web: www.lambuth.edu; *Chmn* Lawrence A Ray PhD; *Assoc Prof* June Creasy, MS; *Asst Prof* Lendon H Noe, MS; *Lectr* Susan Haubold, MEd; *Lectr* Belinda A Patterson, BS; *Lectr* Glynn Weatherley, BS; *Lectr* Rosemary Carroway, BA
Estab 1843, dept estab 1950; Methodist; D & E; Scholarships; SC 21, LC 10
Ent Req: HS dipl
Degrees: BA, BS, B(Mus) & B(Bus Ad) 4 yrs
Courses: Advertising Design, Aesthetics, †Art Education, †Art History, †Commercial Art, Crafts, †Drawing, Fiber Crafts, †Graphic Design, Human Ecology, †Interior Design, †Painting, †Photography, †Printmaking, †Sculpture, Stage Design, †Stained Glass, Visual Art
Adult Hobby Classes: Adult Evening Prog. $1800 per term
Children's Classes: Enrl 45-50; tuition $50 for 5 wk term. Courses—Elementary art classes
Summer School: Dir, William Shutowski. Courses—Art Appreciation, Art Education, Basic ID, Painting, Printmaking

UNION UNIVERSITY, Dept of Art, 1050 Union University Dr, Jackson, TN 38305-3697. Tel 901-668-1818; Fax 901-661-5175; Email lbenson@uu.edu; Web: www.uu.edu; *Prof* Chris Nadaskay; *Chmn* Aaron Lee Benson; *Instr* Jonathan Gillette; *Instr* Lori Nolen
Estab 1824, dept estab 1958; Maintain nonprofit art gallery; Union Univ Gallery of Art, Jackson TN; Pvt; D & E; Scholarships; SC 20, LC 5; D 200, E 40, maj 28
Ent Req: HS dipl, portfolio, ACT
Degrees: BA and BS 4 yrs
Courses: Art Appreciation, Art Education, Ceramics, Design, †Drafting, Drawing, Graphic Design, Painting, Photography, Printmaking, Sculpture, Teacher Training
Children's Classes: Enrl 6-8 $185
Summer School: Dir Debra Tayloe

JEFFERSON CITY

CARSON-NEWMAN UNIVERSITY, Art Dept, 1646 S. Russell Ave, Art Dept Jefferson City, TN 37760-2204; 2130 Branner Ave, Art Dept Jefferson City, TN 37760. Tel 865-471-4985; Email sgray@cn.edu; Web: www.cn.edu; *Prof* David Underwood; *Assoc Prof & Dept Chmn* Julie Rabun; *Assoc Prof* Lisa Alanary; *Assoc Prof* Chad Airhart
Col estab 1851; maintain a nonprofit art gallery: The Omega Gallery, Warren Art Bldg, 2130 Branner Ave, Jefferson City, TN 37760; FT 4; pvt; D & E; Scholarships; SC 32, LC 16; maj 85
Ent Req: HS dipl
Degrees: BA(Art & Photography) 4 yrs
Courses: Art Appreciation, Art Education, Art History, Computer Graphics, Design, Drawing, Graphic Arts, Graphic Design, Mixed Media, Painting, Photography, Senior Seminar, Support Systems

JOHNSON CITY

EAST TENNESSEE STATE UNIVERSITY, College of Arts and Sciences, Dept of Art & Design, PO Box 70708, Johnson City, TN 37614-1710. Tel 423-439-4247; Fax 423-439-4393; Web: etsu.edu/cas.art; *Prof* M Wayne Dyer; *Prof* Michael Smith, MFA; *Prof* Vida Hull, PhD; *Prof* Ralph Slatton, MFA; *Assoc Prof* David Dixon, MFA; *Assoc Prof* Don Davis, MFA; *Assoc Prof* Mira Gerard, MFA; *Prof* Anita DeAngelis, MFA; *Assoc Prof* Peter Pawlowicz, PhD; *Prof, Interim Chair* Catherine Murray, MFA; *Assoc Prof* Scott Koterbay, PhD; *Assoc Prof* Pat Mink; *Asst Prof* Travis Graves; *Gallery Dir* Karlota Contreras-Koterbay; *Visual Resource Cur* Lisa Jones
Estab 1911, dept estab 1949; Maintain nonprofit gallery, Slocumb Galleries, Carroll Reece Museum & slide and visual resource library on ETSU campus. On-campus shop sells art supplies; Pub; D & E; Scholarships; SC 102, LC 30, GC 46; maj 400
Ent Req: HS dipl, ACT or SAT
Degrees: BA & BFA 4 yrs, MA, MFA
Courses: †Aesthetics, †Art History, †Ceramics, Commercial Art, Conceptual Art, Design, Drawing, Film, Goldsmithing, †Graphic Design, History of Art & Architecture, Illustration, †Jewelry, †Metalsmithing, Mixed Media, †Painting, †Photography, Printmaking, †Sculpture, Silversmithing, Teacher Training, Video, Weaving, †Weaving/Fibers
Adult Hobby Classes: Cr/no cr classes at night. Courses—Art History, Drawing, Photography, painting
Summer School: Dir, M Wayne Dyer. Term for 2-5 wks. Courses—Book Arts, Ceramics, Computer Art, Stone Carving

KNOXVILLE

UNIVERSITY OF TENNESSEE, KNOXVILLE, School of Art, 1715 Volunteer Blvd, Ste. 213, Knoxville, TN 37996-2410. Tel 865-974-3407; Fax 865-974-3198; Web: www.web.utk.edu/~art; *Dir School of Art* Paul Lee; *Assoc Dir* Tim Hiles
Estab 1794, dept estab 1951; Maintain nonprofit art gallery; Ewing Gallery; art supplies available on campus; FT 27, PT 15; pub; D & E; Scholarships; SC 51, LC 23, GC 50; D 1,600, E 250, non-maj 300, maj 400, grad 40
Ent Req: HS dipl
Degrees: BA & BFA, MFA; both undergraduate & graduate cr may be earned through the affiliated program at Arrowmont School of Arts & Crafts, Gatlinburg, TN
Tuition: Res—undergraduate $1,302 per sem, grad $1,653 per sem; nonres—undergrad $3,034 per sem, campus res—room & board $3,166 per yr
Courses: †Art History, †Ceramics, †Drawing, †Graphic Design, Media Arts, †Painting, †Printmaking, †Sculpture, †Watercolors
Summer School: Dir, Norman Magden. Enrl 400; term of 2 sessions beginning June & Aug. Courses—Art History, Design, Drawing, Media Arts

MARYVILLE

MARYVILLE COLLEGE, Dept of Fine Arts, 502 East Lamar Alexander Pkwy, Maryville, TN 37804. Tel 865-981-8000; Web: www.maryvillecollege.edu; *Asst Prof* Carl Gombert; *Asst Prof* Jeff Turner; *Chmn* Dan Taddie
Estab 1937; FT 2, PT 1; den; D&E; Scholarships; SC 10, LC 6
Degrees: 4 yr
Courses: Art Education, Art History, Ceramics, Computer Graphics, Drawing, Fabric Design, Graphic Design, Painting, Photography, Printmaking, Visual Theory & Design, Weaving
Adult Hobby Classes: Courses offered
Children's Classes: Art Education, Crafts

MEMPHIS

MEMPHIS COLLEGE OF ART, 1930 Poplar Ave, Overton Park Memphis, TN 38104-2756. Tel 901-272-5100; Fax 901-272-5158; Email info@mca.edu; Web: www.mca.edu; *Pres* Dr Ron Jones; *Acad Dean & Div Chair Foundation* Remy Miller, MFA; *Div Chair Fine Arts* Howard Paine, MFA; *Div Chair Design Arts* David Chioffi, MFA; *Div Chair Foundations* Remy Miller, MFA; *Cur Galleries* Cat Blackwell Pence; *Dir Grad Studies* Haley Morris-Cafiero, MFA; *Dir Grad Studies* Dr Cathy Wilson, MA
Estab 1936; maintain art libr & nonprofit art gallery on campus; art supplies available for purchase on campus; FT 22, PT 22; pvt; D & E; Scholarships; SC 132, LC 73, GC 20; D 300, E 300, GS 19
Ent Req: HS dipl
Degrees: BFA 4 yrs, MFA 2 yrs, MA 1 yr
Tuition: $25,600
Courses: †Advertising Design, Aesthetics, Architecture, †Art Education, Art History, †Book Arts, †Ceramics, Collage, †Commercial Art, †Computer Arts, Conceptual Art, †Design, Digital Media Animation, †Drawing, Goldsmithing, †Graphic Arts, †Graphic Design, History of Art & Architecture, †Illustration, Intermedia, †Jewelry, Lettering, Mixed Media, †Painting, †Papermaking, †Photography, †Printmaking, †Sculpture, †Silversmithing, Video
Adult Hobby Classes: Classes vary
Children's Classes: Classes vary
Summer School: Dir, Mary Beth Haas, Cece Palazola, Dir Community Educ

RHODES COLLEGE, Dept of Art, 2000 N Pkwy, Memphis, TN 38112. Tel 901-843-3000, 3442; Fax 901-843-3727; Web: www.rhodes.edu; *Chmn, Asst Prof* Victor Coonin, MFA; *Assoc Prof* David McCarthy; *Assoc Prof* Diane Hoffman, MFA; *Instr* Hallie Charney, MFA; *Asst Prof* Val Vaigardson; *Prof* Jim Lutz; *Asst Prof* Margaret Woodhull
Estab 1848, dept estab 1940; pvt; D & E; SC 17, LC 12; D 250, non-maj 240, maj 10
Ent Req: SAT or ACT, 13 acad cr, 16 overall
Degrees: BA 4 yrs
Tuition: campus res—room & board
Courses: Aesthetics, Architecture, Art History, Drawing, History of Art & Architecture, Museum Staff Training, Painting, Photography, Printmaking, Sculpture

UNIVERSITY OF MEMPHIS, Art Dept, 108 Jones Hall, Memphis, TN 38152-3305. Tel 901-678-2216; Fax 901-678-2735; *Chmn Asst* Wayne Simpkins; *Chmn Asst* Brenda Landman; *Acting Chmn* Sandy Lowrance
Estab 1912; pub; D & E; Scholarships; SC 100, LC 40, GC 30; D 2200, maj 467, grad 80
Ent Req: HS dipl, SAT
Degrees: BA & BFA 4 yrs, MA 1 yr, MFA 2 yrs
Tuition: Campus residence available
Courses: Art Education, Ceramics, Drawing, Graphic Design, History of Art & Architecture, Illustration, Interior Design, Museum Staff Training, Painting, Photography, Printmaking, Sculpture, Teacher Training
Adult Hobby Classes: Courses offered
Summer School: Dir, Robert E Lewis

MURFREESBORO

MIDDLE TENNESSEE STATE UNIVERSITY, Art Dept, 1301 E Main St, Murfreesboro, TN 37132-0001. Tel 615-898-2300; 898-5653 (Gallery); Fax 615-898-2254; Web: www.mtsu.edu; *Instr* Jean Nagy; *Instr* Barry Buxkamper; *Instr* Ollie Fancher; *Instr* Klaus Kallenberger; *Instr* Janet Higgins; *Instr* Christie Nuell; *Instr* Lon Nuell; *Instr* Marissa Recchia; *Instr* Charles Jansen; *Instr* Tanya Tewell; *Instr* Nancy Kelker; *Instr* John O'Connell; *Instr* Doug Schatz; *Instr* David Shaul; *Instr* Shirley Yokley; *Chmn Art Dept* Mark Price; *Instr* Carlyle Johnson
Estab 1911, dept estab 1952; Maintains Todd Gallery; pub; D & E; Scholarships; SC 62, LC 10, GC 35; non-maj 900, maj 200, grad 5
Ent Req: HS dipl
Degrees: BS(Art Educ), & BFA 4 yrs
Courses: †Art Education, †Ceramics, †Commercial Art, Drawing, Goldsmithing, Graphic Design, †Jewelry, †Painting, †Printmaking, †Sculpture, †Silversmithing, Textile Design
Adult Hobby Classes: Courses Offered
Children's Classes: Creative Art Clinic for Children; enrl 45; tuition $25 per term

Summer School: Courses Offered

NASHVILLE

CHEEKWOOD NASHVILLE'S HOME OF ART & GARDENS, Education Dept, 1200 Forrest Park Dr, Nashville, TN 37205-4242. Tel 615-353-9827; Fax 615-353-2162; *Pres* Jane Jerry; *Dir Museum* John Wentenhall; *Cur Coll* Celia Walker; *Dir Botanical Gardens* Bob Brackman; *Dir Educ* Mary Grissim
Estab 1960; pvt; D & E; Scholarships; SC 10-15, LC 5-10
Courses: Art Appreciation, Art History, Ceramics, Drawing, Jewelry, Landscape Design, Painting, Papermaking, Sculpture, Weaving
Adult Hobby Classes: Enrl 750; tuition $110-$137. Courses—Clay on Wheel, Drawing, Horticulture, Landscape Design, Painting, Photography, Sculpture
Children's Classes: Enrl 200; tuition $90-$110. Courses—Clay Jewelry, Drawing, Environmental Science, Film Making, Gardening, Painting, Photography, Sculpture
Summer School: Enrl 900; tuition $90-$110. Courses—Clay Jewelry, Drawing, Environmental Science, Film Making, Gardening, Painting, Photography, Sculpture

FISK UNIVERSITY, Art Dept, 1000 17th Ave N, Nashville, TN 37208-3045. Tel 615-329-8674, 329-8500; Fax 615-329-8551; Web: www.fisk.edu; *Asst Prof* Alicia Henry, MA; *Chmn & Instr* Lifran Fort, MA
Estab 1867, dept estab 1937; pvt; D; Scholarships; SC 10, LC 3; 65, non-maj 40, maj 15
Ent Req: HS dipl, SAT
Degrees: BS & BA 4 yrs
Courses: Aesthetics, African Art, African-American Art, Art History, Drawing, Painting, Sculpture

NOSSI COLLEGE OF ART, 590 Cheron Rd, Nashville, TN 37115. Tel 615-514-2787; Fax 615-514-2788; Email admissions@nossi.edu; Web: www.nossi.edu; *Exec VPres* Cyrus Vatandoost, BA; *Graphic Design Coordr* Bruce Stanley, BFA; *Illustration Coordr* Mark Fleming, BFA; *Founder, CEO & Pres* Nossi Vatandoost, BFA; *VPres Acad Affairs* Dr Byron Edwards, PhD; *Photog Coordr* Reeves Smith, MFA; *Videography Coordr* Hans Chilberg, BFA
Estab 1973; pvt; D, E & online; Scholarships; SC 37, LC 15. Other 25
Activities: Mus shop sells art supplies
Ent Req: HS dipl or GED
Degrees: AOS Interactive Graphic Design, AOS Photography; BA Graphic Art & Design, BA Commercial Illustration, BA Photog, BA Videography
Tuition: $5,900 per sem
Courses: Advertising Design, Architecture, Art Appreciation, Art Education, Art History, †Commercial Art, Conceptual Art, Design, Display, Drawing, †Film, Graphic Arts, †Graphic Design, Illustration, Lettering, Mixed Media, Painting, †Photography, †Video

VANDERBILT UNIVERSITY, Dept of Art, 2301 Vanderbilt Pl, Box 351660-B Nashville, TN 37235-1660. Tel 615-343-7241; Fax 615-322-3467; Web: www.vanderbilt.edu/arts; *Prof Emeritus* Donald H Evans, MFA; *Prof* Michael Aurbach, MFA; *Sr Lectr* Susan DeMay, MFA; *Sr Lectr* Carlton Wilkinson, MFA; *Chair* Marilyn Murphy, MFA; *Sr Lectr* Ron Porter, MFA; *Sr Lectr* Libby Rowe; *Lectr* Robert Durham
Estab 1873, dept estab 1944; Maintain nonprofit gallery; Fine Arts Gallery, Nashville, TN; maintain arts section in gen library; Jean & Alexander Heard Library. Art supplies may be purchased on campus; Pvt; D; Scholarships; Fellowships; SC 19, LC 29, GC 2; D, non-maj 367, maj 9
Ent Req: HS dipl, ent exam
Degrees: BA 4 yrs
Courses: Art Appreciation, Art History, Ceramics, Drawing, Multimedia Design, Painting, Photography, Printmaking, Sculpture, Video
Summer School: Dean, Richard McCarty. Tuition $840 per cr hr for two 4 wk terms beginning early June. Courses—Vary

WATKINS COLLEGE OF ART, DESIGN & FILM, 2298 Rosa L Parks Blvd, Nashville, TN 37228-1573. Tel 615-383-4848; Fax 615-383-4849; Email mklaes@watkins.edu; Web: www.watkins.edu; *Pres* Ellen L Meyer; *VPres Acad Affairs* Joy McKenzie; *Assoc Prof & Chair Film School* Richard Gershman; *Prof Film* Valorie Stover Quarles; *Assoc Prof Film* Robert Gordon; *Prof Fine Art* Terry Thacker; *Assoc Prof & Chair of Fine Art* Kristi Hargrove; *Asst Prof Fine Art & Studio Facilities Mgr* Brady Haston; *Asst Prof Fine Art* Morgan Higby-Flowers; *Asst Prof Fine Art* Ariel Lavery; *Assoc Prof & Chair* Dan Brawner; *Assoc Prof Graphic Design* Judith Sweeney O'Bryan; *Chair & Assoc Prof Interior Design* Cheryl Gulley; *Assoc Prof & Chair Photog* Robin Paris; *Asst Photog* Christine Rogers; *Instr & Dir Gen Educ & BA Prog* Cary Beth Miller; *Prof Film* Steven Womack; *Assoc Prof Graphic Design* Steve Wilkinson; *Asst Prof Art History* Thomas Williams
Estab 1885; Maintain non-profit art galleries, Brownlee O Currey, Jr Gallery (same address); Watkins Arcade Gallery (WAG), 244 5th Ave N #77, Nashville, TN 37246; art library, Watkins Library (same address); FT 18, PT 40; pvt; D&E; Scholarships; SC 81, LC 25; D 305; non-maj 7, maj 290, other 8
Activities: Schols offered
Ent Req: HS graduate ACT 21, college trans 2.6 or better, portfolio req for BFA progs
Degrees: Approved by Tennessee Higher Education Commission, BFA in Fine Art; BFA in Film; BFA in Photography; BFA in Int Design; BFA in Graphic Design; BA in Art; certificate in film; certificate of interior design
Tuition: All programs $20,850 per yr; $695 per cr hr
Courses: †Advertising Design, Aesthetics, Art History, †Ceramics, †Conceptual Art, †Design, Drafting, †Drawing, †Film, †Fine Art, †Graphic Design, †History of Art & Architecture, Illustration, †Interior Design, †Mixed Media, †Painting, †Photography, †Printmaking, †Production Design, †Sculpture, †Video, †Web Design
Adult Hobby Classes: Enrl 910; tuition $105-$275; various courses
Children's Classes: Enrl 127; tuition $325; various courses
Summer School: Dir, Mary Beth Harding.

SEWANEE

UNIVERSITY OF THE SOUTH, Dept of Fine Arts, Carnegie Hall, Sewanee, TN 37383-0001. Tel 913-598-1201; Email pmalde@seraph1.sewaner.edu; Web: www.sewanee.edu; *Chmn Dept* Gregory Clark
FT 6; Pvt, den; D; SC 20, LC 20; D 250, non-maj 225, maj 30
Degrees: BS & BA, MDiv
Courses: Art History, Drawing, Painting, Photography, Printmaking, Sculpture, Video
Summer School: Dir, Dr John Reishman. Enrl 150 for term of 6 wks beginning June; tuition $400 per cr. Courses—History of Western Art II, Painting, Photography

SMITHVILLE

TENNESSEE TECH UNIVERSITY, Appalachian Center for Craft, 1560 Craft Center Dr, Smithville, TN 37166-7352. Tel 931-372-3051; Fax 615-597-6803; Email craftcenter@tntech.edu; Web: www.tntech.edu/craftcenter

TULLAHOMA

MOTLOW STATE COMMUNITY COLLEGE, Art Dept, 6015 Ledford Mill Rd, Dept 245 Tullahoma, TN 37388-7972. Tel 931-455-3804; Fax 931-393-1681; Web: www.mscc.edu; *Art Teacher* Ann Smotherman; *Dean* Dr Mary McLemore; *Art Teacher* Brian Robinson
Estab 1969; Pub; D & E; Scholarships
Ent Req: HS dipl or equivalent
Tuition: In state—$2199 per yr; out of state—$4022.50 per yr
Courses: Art Appreciation, Arts & Crafts, Ceramics, Commercial Art, Design, Drawing, Painting, Photography
Adult Hobby Classes: Enrl 200
Children's Classes: Enrl 40

TEXAS

ABILENE

ABILENE CHRISTIAN UNIVERSITY, Dept of Art & Design, 1 ACU, Abilene, TX 79699-0002. Tel 915-674-2085; Fax 915-674-2051; Email maxwellj@acu.edu; Web: www.acu.edu/academics/cas/art.html; *Head Dept & Chmn* Jack Maxwell; *Prof* Robert Green; *Prof* Ginna Sadler; *Prof* Nil Santana; *Prof* Geoff Broderick; *Prof* Dan McGregor; *Prof* Ronnie Rama; *Prof* Kitty Wasemiller; *Prof* Mike Wiggins
Estab 1906; Maintain nonprofit art gallery, Clover Virginia Shore Art Gallery, 142 Don Morris Center, Box 27987, Abilene, TX 79699-7987; FT 8, PT 2; pvt; D & E; Scholarships; SC 31, LC 8; maj 130
Ent Req: upper 3/4 HS grad class or at 19 standard score ACT composite
Degrees: BA, BA(Educ) & BFA 4 yrs
Courses: Advertising Design, Architecture, Art Appreciation, Art Education, Art History, Ceramics, Design, Drawing, Graphic Design, History of Art & Architecture, †Illustration, Jewelry, Painting, Photography, Pottery, Printmaking, Sculpture
Summer School: Chmn, Jack Maxwell, Enrl 10; tuition $347 per sem hour. Courses— Drawing, Introduction to Art History, Sculpture, Graphic Design

HARDIN-SIMMONS UNIVERSITY, Art Dept, Box 16085, Abilene, TX 79698; 2200 Hickory St, Abilene, TX 79601-2345. Tel 325-671-2223; Email mjones@hsutx.edu; Web: www.hsutx.edu/academics/music_art/art; *Prof* Martha Kiel, MEd; *Prof & Chmn* Mike Jones, MFA; *Assoc Prof* Steve Neves, MFA
Univ estab 1891; Maintains nonprofit Ira Taylor Gallery; den; D & E; Scholarships; SC 27, LC 5; D 110, E 60, non-maj 35, maj 75
Ent Req: HS dipl, SAT, ACT
Degrees: BA, BBS, BFA 4 yrs
Courses: Art Appreciation, Art Education, Art History, †Ceramics, †Drawing, †Graphic Design, †Painting, †Photography, †Printmaking, Sculpture, †Teacher Training
Summer School: Prof & Chair, Mike Jones. Courses—Art Appreciation, Ceramics, Drawing, History of Graphic Design Online, Photography

MCMURRY UNIVERSITY, Art Dept, 1401 Sayles Blvd, McMurray Station Box 278 Abilene, TX 79605-4207. Tel 915-793-4888; Fax 915-793-4662; Web: www.mcm.edu; *Head Dept* Kathy Walker-Millar, BS; *Prof* J Robert Miller, BS; *Asst Prof* Linda Stricklin, BS; *Instr* Judy Deaton
Estab 1923; pvt; D & E; Scholarships; SC 19, LC 1; D 80, E 8, non-maj 18, maj 15
Ent Req: HS dipl
Degrees: BA, BFA & BS 4 yrs
Courses: Art Education, Art History, Assemblage Sculpture, Ceramics, Design, Drawing, Jewelry, Painting, Teacher Training
Adult Hobby Classes: Enrl 24; tuition $360 fall, spring & summer terms. Courses—Art Education I & II
Summer School: Dir, Bob Maniss. Two summer terms. Courses—Art Education I, Exploring the Visual Arts

ALPINE

SUL ROSS STATE UNIVERSITY, Dept of Fine Arts & Communications, C-43, Alpine, TX 79832-0001. Tel 915-837-8130; Fax 915-837-8046; *Prof* Charles R Hext, MFA; *Asst Prof* Carol Fairlie, MFA; *Asst Prof* Jim Bob Salazar, MFA
Estab 1920, dept estab 1922; pub; D & E; Scholarships; SC 21, LC 3, GC 19; D 183, E 32, non-maj 170, maj 25-30, GS 15
Ent Req: HS dipl, ACT or SAT

Degrees: BFA 4 yrs, MEd(Art) 1 1/2 yrs
Courses: Advertising Art, †Advertising Design, †Art Appreciation, †Art Education, †Art History, †Ceramics, Collage, †Commercial Art, Conceptual Art, Constructions, Costume Design & Construction, Design, Drafting, Drawing, †Graphic Arts, †Graphic Design, Handicrafts, †History of Art & Architecture, Illustration, Industrial Design, Interior Design, Jewelry, Landscape Architecture, †Mixed Media, †Painting, Photography, †Printmaking, Restoration & Conservation, †Sculpture, Stage Design, †Teacher Training

ALVIN

ALVIN COMMUNITY COLLEGE, Art Dept, 3110 Mustang Rd, Alvin, TX 77511-4807. Tel 281-756-3752; Fax 281-388-4903; Email dlavalley@alvin.cc.tx.us ; *Chmn* Dennis LaValley
Estab 1949; D & E
Ent Req: HS dipl
Degrees: AA 2 yrs
Courses: Art Appreciation, Art History, †Art Metals, Ceramics, Design Communication, Drawing, Graphic Design, Graphic Media, Painting, †Photography, Sculpture
Summer School: Dir, Bruce Turner. 6-12 wk term. Courses—Vary

AMARILLO

AMARILLO COLLEGE, Visual Art Dept, PO Box 447, Amarillo, TX 79178-0001. Tel 806-371-5000, Ext 5290; Web: www.actx.edu/~visual_arts/; *Asst Prof* Dennis Olson, MFA; *Asst Prof* Steven Cost, MFA; *Instr* Pedro Gonzalez; *Instr* Stephanie Jung, MFA; *Dept Head* Victoria Taylor-Gore, MFA
Estab 1926; Maintains: nonprofit art gallery, Southern Light Gallery, Amarillo College; art library, Art Dept Resource Library, Amarillo College; pub; D & E; Scholarships; SC 18, LC 2; D 142, E 60
Ent Req: HS dipl, CEEB
Degrees: AA 2 yrs
Courses: Art History, Ceramics, Drawing, †Fine Art, †Graphic Design, Illustration, Jewelry, Layout, †Painting, †Sculpture, Typographics

ARLINGTON

UNIVERSITY OF TEXAS AT ARLINGTON, Art & Art History Department, 335 Fine Arts Bldg, Arlington, TX 76019; 502 S Cooper St, Box 19089 Arlington, TX 76019. Tel 817-272-2891; Fax 817-272-2805; Email art@uta.edu; Web: www.uta.edu; *Chmn* Robert Hower; *Asst Prof* Melia Belli; *Sr Lectr* Mark Clive; *Sr Lectr* Bryan Florentin; *Assoc Prof* Lisa Graham; *Assoc Prof* Benito Huerta; *Vis Asst Prof* Kelly Ingelright; *Assoc Prof* Marilyn Jolly; *Prof* David Keens; *Assoc Prof* Leighton McWilliams; *Vis Asst Prof* Fred Miller; *Prof* Kenda North; *Assoc Prof* Andrew Ortiz; *Assoc Prof* Nancy Palmeri; *Prof Emeritus* Jack Plummer; *Adjunct Prof* Erik Tosten; *Assoc Prof* Dr Mary Vaccaro; *Assoc Prof* Barton Weiss; *Assoc Prof* Nicholas Wood; *Prof* Beth Wright; *Adjunct Prof* Paul Benero; *Vis Asst Prof* Stephen Lapthisophon; *Asst Prof* Darryl Lauster; *Adjunct Prof* David Pinkston; *Adjunct Prof* Fred Spaulding; *Adj Asst Prof* Stephanie Clark; *Adj Asst Prof* Debra Dewitte; *Adj Asst Prof* Carlos Donjuan; *Vis Asst Prof* Sedrick Huckaby; *Asst Prof* Seiji Ikeda; *Asst Prof* Benjamin Lima; *Adj Asst Prof* Chaitra Linehan; *Adj Asst Prof* Mark Mueller; *Asst Prof* Ya'Ke Smith; *Asst Prof* Tore Terrasi
Estab 1895, dept estab 1937; Maintain nonprofit art gallery, The Gallery at UTA; maintain art/architecture library, 601 W Nedderman, Architecture Building Rm 104, Arlington, TX 76019; on-campus shop where art supplies may be purchased; pub; D & E; Scholarships; SC 115, LC 51, GC 40; D 764, E 108, non-maj 20, maj 800, grad 27
Ent Req: HS dipl, SAT of ACT
Degrees: BA(Art, Art History), MFA, BFA, Cert Teaching
Tuition: Res—$13,670 per yr; nonres—$21,935 per yr
Courses: Advertising Design, Art Appreciation, Art Education, †Art History, Clay, Conceptual Art, Constructions, Design, Display, †Drawing, Film, Glass, Glass Blowing, †Graphic Design, History of Art & Architecture, Illustration, Intermedia, Mixed Media, Museum Staff Training, †Painting, †Photography, †Printmaking, †Sculpture, Teacher Training, †Video

AUSTIN

AUSTIN COMMUNITY COLLEGE, Dept of Commercial Art, North Ridge Campus, 11928 Stonehollow Dr, Austin, TX 78758-3190. Tel 512-223-7000 (Main), 223-4830 (Dept); Fax 512-223-4444; Web: www.austin.cc.tx.us/; *Head Dept South Campus* Steve Kramer
Estab 1974; FT 3, PT 30; pub; D & E; 386 per sem
Ent Req: HS dipl or GED
Degrees: AAS 2 yr, Multi Media Cert
Courses: Advertising, Animation, Art History, Calligraphy, Ceramics, Commercial Art, Commercial Art History, Computer Layout & Design, Desktop Publishing, Drawing, Environmental Graphics, Figure Drawing, Graphic Arts, Graphic Design, Graphics Practicum, Illustration, Illustrative Techniques, Metalsmithing, Painting, Photography, †Printmaking, Production Art, †Sculpture, Silkscreening, Typography Design, †Video

CONCORDIA UNIVERSITY, Dept of Fine Arts, 11400 Concordia University Dr, Austin, TX 78726-1887. Tel 512-452-7661; Fax 512-459-8517; Web: www.concordia.edu; *Chmn* Dr David Kroft
Estab 1925; FT 1; den; D; Scholarships; SC 1, LC 1; D 350
Ent Req: HS dipl
Degrees: AA 2 yrs
Courses: Art Fundamentals, Ceramics, Design, Drawing, Drawing Media, Relief Printing

UNIVERSITY OF TEXAS, School of Architecture, 1 University Station, B7500 Austin, TX 78712-0803. Tel 512-471-1922; Fax 512-471-0716; Email lwspeck@mail.utexas.edu; Web: www.utexas.edu; *Dean* Lawrence Speck
Estab 1909; FT 38, PT 9; pub; Scholarships; undergrad 450, grad 210
Ent Req: reasonable HS scholastic achievement, SAT, ACT
Degrees: BA, MA, PhD
Tuition: Res—$80 per cr hr, grad $120 per cr hr; nonres—$295 per cr hr, grad $335 per cr hr
Courses: †Architecture, Community & Regional Planning
Adult Hobby Classes: Courses through Division of Continuing Education
Children's Classes: Six week summer program for high school
Summer School: Dir, Harold Box
—**Dept of Art & Art History**, Austin, TX 78712; 1 University Station # D1300, Austin, TX 78712. Tel 512-471-3382; Fax 512-471-7801; Email shanesullivan@mail.utexas.edu; Web: www.finearts.utexas.edu/aah/; *Chair* John Yancey; *Assoc Chair* Lee Chesney; *Asst Dir Develop* Carolyn Porter; *Asst Chair - Art History* Susan Rather; *Asst Chair - Design* Kate Catterall; *Asst Chair - Studio Art* Daniel Sutherland; *Asst Chair - Visual Art Studies* Christopher Adejumo; *Foundations Dir* Robert Anderson; *Undergrad Coordr* Shane Sullivan; *Grad Coordr - Art History* Maureen Howell; *Grad Coordr - Art Educ, Design, Studio Art* Judy Clark
Estab 1938; Maintain nonprofit art gallery; Creative Research Laboratory, 2832 E Martin Luther King Jr Blvd, Austin TX 78705; art library; art supplies may be purchased at university coop; FT & PT 80; pub; D & E; Scholarships; Fellowships; SC 20, LC 15, GC 20; enrl grad 150, 700 undergrad maj
Ent Req: acad & portfolio application
Degrees: BA 4yrs, BFA 4 yrs, MA 2 yrs, MFA 2 yrs, PhD & MFA 3yrs
Tuition: Res—undergrad $4,154 & fees per sem, grad $3,642 & fees per sem; nonres—undergrad $13,293 & fees per sem, grad $7,361 & fees per sem
Courses: Art Appreciation, Art Education, Art History, Ceramics, Design, Digital-Time Arts, Drawing, Metals, Painting, Performance Art, Photography, Printmaking, Sculpture, Teacher Training, †Video Art
Summer School: Two 6 wk terms

BEAUMONT

LAMAR UNIVERSITY, Art Dept, PO Box 10027, LU Sta, Beaumont, TX 77710. Tel 409-880-8141; Fax 409-880-1799; Email donna.meeks@lamar.edu; Web: www.lamar.edu; *Prof* Lynne Lokensgard, PhD; *Prof* Meredith M Jack, MFA; *Prof* Keith Carter, BS; *Assoc Prof* Prince Thomas, MFA; *Chmn & Prof* Donna M Meeks, MFA; *Assoc Prof* Kurt Dyrhaug, MFA; *Assoc Prof* Ann Matlock, MFA; *Asst Prof* Xenia Fedorchenko, MFA; *Instr* Linnis Blanton, BFA; *Instr* Rose Matthis, MFA; *Asst Prof* Fu-Chia-Wen Lien, PhD; *Instr* Jamie Paul Kessler, MFA; *Instr* Ray Daniels, MFA; *Instr* Greg Busceme, MFA
Estab 1923, dept estab 1951; Maintains nonprofit art gallery, Dishman Art Museum, Lamar Univ, PO Box 10027, Beaumont, TX, 77710; pub; D & E; Scholarships; SC 60, LC 76; D 547, E 111, non-maj 300, maj 190
Ent Req: HS dipl, SAT/ACT
Degrees: BFA, BS & MA, 4 yr
Courses: Advertising Design, Aesthetics, Art Appreciation, †Art Education, †Art History, †Ceramics, †Commercial Art, †Computer Graphics, Design, †Drawing, †Graphic Arts, †Graphic Design, †Illustration, Jewelry, Museum Staff Training, †Painting, †Photography, †Printmaking, †Sculpture, †Teacher Training, Textile Design, Weaving
Summer School: Dir, Donna M Meeks. Enrl 125; tuition res $360, nonres $1185 per 3 sem hrs for 5 wk sessions. Courses—Art Appreciation, Computers in Art, Drawing, Watercolor & Illustration

BELTON

UNIVERSITY OF MARY HARDIN-BAYLOR, College of Visual & Performing Arts, 900 College St, UMHB Box 8012 Belton, TX 76513-2578. Tel 254-295-4294; Fax 254-295-4675; Email hseals@umhb.edu; Web: www.umhb.edu; *Chmn* Hershall Seals; *Dean* Ted Barnes; *Prof* John Hancock; *Prof* Helen Kwiatkowski; *Prof* Barbar Fontaine-White; *Asst Prof* Matt Smith; *Asst Pro* David Hill; *Asst Prof* Dr. Sarah Andyshak
Estab 1845; Maintain a nonprofit art gallery Baugh Center for the Visual Arts Art Gallery, 700 College St, UMHB Box 8012, Belton, TX 76513; PT 3; pvt; D & E; Scholarships; SC 29, LC 4, six independent learning course per sem; D 300, E 50, non-maj 250, maj 55
Ent Req: upper half of HS grad class
Degrees: BA, BFA 4 yrs
Tuition: $810 per cr hr
Courses: Art Education, Art History, Ceramics, Design, Drawing, Graphic Design, Jewelry, Mixed Media, Painting, Photography, Printmaking, Sculpture
Children's Classes: Summer Art

BIG SPRING

HOWARD COLLEGE, Art Dept, 1001 Birdwell Ln, Division of Fine Arts Big Spring, TX 79720-5015. Tel 915-264-5000; Fax 915-264-5082; *Prof* Mary Dudley; *Dept Chair* Liz Lowery
Estab 1948, dept estab 1972; pub; D & E; Scholarships; SC 5, LC 1; D 70, E 20, non-maj 60, maj 10
Ent Req: HS dipl, ACT
Degrees: AA
Courses: Art Appreciation, Art Education, Art History, Ceramics, Drawing, Painting, Watercolors

BROWNSVILLE

UNIVERSITY OF TEXAS AT BROWNSVILLE & TEXAS SOUTHMOST COLLEGE, Fine Arts Dept, 1 W University Blvd, Brownsville, TX 78520-4933. Tel 956-544-8200; *Chmn Fine Arts* Terry Tomlin
Estab 1973; pub; D & E; Scholarships; SC 10, LC 10; D 300, E 100
Ent Req: HS dipl
Degrees: AA (Fine Arts) 2-3 yrs, BA 4 yr
Courses: Art Education, Ceramics, Design I and II, Drawing, Graphic Design, History of Art & Architecture, Painting, Photography, Sculpture
Adult Hobby Classes: Courses—Ceramics, Drawing
Summer School: Dir, Terry Tomlin. Courses—Art Appreciation, Art History

BROWNWOOD

HOWARD PAYNE UNIVERSITY, School of Fine Arts, 1000 Fisk St, Brownwood, TX 76801-2715. Tel 325-649-8088; Email dharmon@hputx.edu; Web: www.hputx.edu/art; *Dean* Richard Fiese PhD; *Chmn Dept Art* David Harmon, MFA; *Adjunct* Tim Cooper; *Adjunct* Julie Mize
Estab 1889; Maintains nonprofit art gallery; FT 2, PT 2; pvt; D & E; Scholarships; SC 6, LC 2; D 40, E 10, non-maj 12, maj 15
Ent Req: HS dipl, ent exam
Degrees: BA & BS 4 yrs
Tuition: $275 per credit hours of study
Courses: Aesthetics, Art Appreciation, Art Education, Art History, Ceramics, Commercial Art, Computer Graphics, Design, Drawing, Graphic Arts, Graphic Design, Handicrafts, Painting, Photography, Printmaking, †Sculpture, †Teacher Training, Theatre Arts, Video
Adult Hobby Classes: Enrl 30; tuition $50 per course. Courses—Travel Seminars
Children's Classes: Fall & Spring, 7 - 9. Course—Basic Art
Summer School: Enrl 75; tuition term of 4 wks beginning June. Courses—Art Educ, Crafts, Drawing, Painting

CANYON

WEST TEXAS A&M UNIVERSITY, Art, Theatre & Dance Dept, PO Box 60747, Canyon, TX 79016-0001. Tel 806-651-2799; Fax 806-651-2818; Email dwillard@mail.wtamu.edu; Web: www.wtamu.edu; *Prof* Royal Brantley, MFA; *Assoc Prof* Scott Frish, MFA; *Dept Head* David Willard, MFA; *Assoc Prof* Chad Holliday, MFA; *Assoc Prof* Marcus Melton, MFA; *Asst Prof* Jon Revett, MFA; *Asst Prof* Dr Amy Von Lintel, PhD; *Asst Prof* Stephen Crandell, MFA; *Prof* John Landon, MFA; *Assoc Prof* Anne Medlock, MFA; *Asst Prof* Andrew Lewis, MFA; *Asst Prof* Tana Roberson, MFA; *Assoc Prof* Leslie Williams, MFA; *Assoc Prof* Edward Truitt, MFA; *Instr* Crystal Bertrand, MFA
Estab 1910; Maintain nonprofit art gallery, Northern Hall Art Gallery, same address; maintains an art library at WTAMU; Pub; D & E; Scholarships; SC 70, LC 23, GC 50; maj 120, non-maj 100, grad 8
Ent Req: HS dipl
Degrees: BA, BS, BFA, MA & MFA
Tuition: Res $2,051 per sem, non-res $2,533 per sem
Courses: Aesthetics, Art History, †Ceramics, Computer Art, †Drawing, †Glassblowing, †Graphic Design, †Painting, †Printmaking, †Sculpture, Theatre Arts

COLLEGE STATION

TEXAS A&M UNIVERSITY, College of Architecture, 3137 TAMU, College Station, TX 77843-3137. Tel 979-845-1221; Fax 979-845-4491; Email reganjt@archone.tamu.edu; Web: www.tamu.edu; *Dean* Tom Regan
Estab 1905; FT 92; pub; D; Scholarships; maj Ed 800, total 1750
Ent Req: SAT; Achievement, HS rank
Degrees: BED, BS(Building Construction), BLandscape Arch, March, MLandscape, MUrban Planning, PhD(Urban Science) 4 yr, MS(Construction Mgmt), MS(Land Development), MS(Architecture), PhD(Architecture), MS (Visualization) (Computer Animation)
Courses: Architecture, Art History, Computer Animation, Constructions, Design, Drafting, Drawing, History of Art & Architecture, Illustration, Landscape Architecture, Photography, Restoration & Conservation, Video
Summer School: Dir, Rodney Hill. Enrl 1000; Courses—Arch Design, Arch History, Construction Science, Drawing, Planning

COMMERCE

TEXAS A&M UNIVERSITY COMMERCE, Dept of Art, PO Box 3011, Commerce, TX 75429-3011. Tel 903-886-5208; Fax 903-886-5987; Web: www.tamu-commerce.edu; *Head* William Wadley; *Instr Ceramics* Barbara Frey, MFA; *Instr Printmaking* Lee Baxter Davis, MFA; *Instr Sculpture* Jerry Dodd, MFA; *Coordr Grad Progs & Instr Painting* Michael Miller, MFA; *Instr Art History* Ivana Spalatin, MFA; *Asst Prof* Stan Godwin, MFA; *Prof Photog* Bill McDowell; *Coordr New Media* Lee Whitmarsh; *Gallery Coordr* Brenda Feher-Simonelli
Pub; D & E; Scholarships; SC 64, LC 29, GC 19; maj 300, GS 30
Ent Req: HS dipl, ACT or SAT
Degrees: BA, BS & BFA 4 yr, MFA 2 yr, MA & MS 1 1/2 yr. There is a special prog called the Post Masters-MFA which is worked out on an individual basis
Courses: †Advertising Design, Aesthetics, †Art Education, Art History, †Ceramics, Collage, †Commercial Art, Constructions, Drafting, †Drawing, †Graphic Arts, †Graphic Design, History of Art & Architecture, †Illustration, Industrial Design, †Intermedia, †Jewelry, Lettering, Lithography, †Mixed Media, †Painting, Papermaking & Casting, †Photography, †Printmaking, †Sculpture, Silversmithing, †Teacher Training, Video
Adult Hobby Classes: Enrl 15; tuition $77 per sem. Courses—Bonsai, Ceramics, Drawing, Painting, Watercolor
Summer School: Enrl 15; tuition res—$64.75-$393; nonres—$134.75-$2121, for 2 terms of 2 to 6 wks beginning June. Courses—Art Education, Ceramics, Design, Drawing, Painting, Printmaking

CORPUS CHRISTI

DEL MAR COLLEGE, Art Dept, 101 Baldwin Blvd, Corpus Christi, TX 78404-3894. Tel 361-698-1216; Fax 361-698-1511; Email krosier@delmar.edu; Web: www.delmar.edu; *Chair & Prof* Ken Rosier, MFA; *Prof* Randolph Flowers, MS; *Prof* Cynthia Perkins, MA; *Assoc Prof* Amorette Garza, MFA; *Assoc Prof* Gerardo Cobarruvias, MA; *Asst Prof* Kerstin Dale, MFA
Estab 1941, dept estab 1965; Maintains nonprofit Joseph A Cain Memorial Gallery, Del Mar College, 101 Baldwin Blvd, Corpus Christi, TX 78404; pub; D & E; Scholarships; SC 21, LC 3; D 500, E 100, non-maj 400, maj 139
Ent Req: HS dipl, SAT score or any accepted test including GED
Degrees: AA 2 yr in studio, art educ
Tuition: Res—$353 per 3 sem hrs; nonres—$503+ per 3 sem hrs
Courses: Art Appreciation, †Art Education, Art History, Ceramics, Design, Drawing, Graphic Design, †Life Drawing, Painting, Photography, Printmaking, Sculpture, †Watercolor
Adult Hobby Classes: Tuition varies according to classes. Courses—same as above

CORSICANA

NAVARRO COLLEGE, Art Dept, 3200 W Seventh Ave, Corsicana, TX 75110. Tel 903-874-6501; Fax 903-874-4636; Email tsale@nav.cc.tx.us; WATS 800-NAVARRO; *Dir* Tom Sale
Estab 1946; FT2, PT2; pub; D & E; Scholarships; SC 6, LC 2; D 300, maj 30
Ent Req: HS dipl, ent exam, special permission
Degrees: AA, AS, A Gen Educ & A Appl Sci 60 sem hr
Courses: 2-D & 3-D Design, Advertising Design, Art Appreciation, Ceramics, Commercial Art, †Computer Art, Design, Drafting, Drawing, Graphic Arts, Illustration, Multi-Media, Painting, Photography, Sculpture, Video
Adult Hobby Classes: Enrl 200; tuition $30-$150 for sem of 6-12 wks. Courses—Art Appreciation, Crafts, Design, Drawing, Painting, Photography, Sculpture
Summer School: Enrl 30; Courses—Art Appreciation

DALLAS

THE ART INSTITUTE OF DALLAS, 8080 Park Lane (Ste 100), Dallas, TX 75231-5900. Tel 214-692-8080; Fax 214-692-6541; Web: www.aid.edu; WATS 800-275-4243; *Registrar* Tom Chauvin; *Pres* Thomas W Newsom
Estab 1998; Maintains nonprofit art gallery: Pegasus Art Gallery; Mildred Kellez Library; on-campus shop for purchasing art supplies; pvt; D & E; Scholarships
Ent Req: HS dipl, equivalent
Degrees: AA & BA
Courses: Computer Animation Multimedia, †Culinary & Restaurant Management, Fashion Design, †Film, †Graphic Design, Interior Design, †Management, Photography, Visual Communication
Adult Hobby Classes: Enrl 850; tuition $2050 per quarter. Courses—Commercial Art, Culinary Arts, Fashion Merchandising, Interior Design, Photography, Video

DALLAS BAPTIST UNIVERSITY, Dept of Art, 3000 Mountain Creek Pkwy, Dallas, TX 75211-9299. Tel 214-333-5316, 333-5300; Fax 214-333-6804; Email dawna@dbu.edu; Web: www.dbu.edu; *Head Art Dept* Dawna Hamm Walsh PhD; *Asst Prof* Jim Hutchinson, MFA; *Dean Fine Arts* Dr Ron Bowles; *Instr* Nancy Cole, MFA; *Instr* Dana Hamrick Ferrara, MFA; *Instr* Lee Bowman, MA; *Instr* Tempy Berg-Gilbert, MA; *Instr* Angela Pitts, MFA; *Instr* Mary Morgan, MFA; *Instr* Dawn Gold, MA; *Instr* Tamra Sawyer, MLA; *Instr* Spray Gleaves, MA; *Instr* Shelby Keyes, MLA
Estab 1965; Maintains Learning Center Gallery, Dept of Art, Dallas Baptist Univ, 3000 Creek Pkwy, Dallas, TX 75244-9299; Vance Memorial Library, DBU 3000 Mountain Creek Pkwy, Dallas, TX 75211; FT 3, PT 18; pvt den; D, E, wknds, online; Scholarships; SC 20, LC 6, GC 15, online classes; D 150, E 30, non-maj 50, maj 50, grad 7, online
Activities: Schols offered
Ent Req: HS dipl
Degrees: BA & BS 4 yrs, Grad Art Degree: MLA
Tuition: $846.00 per cr hr
Courses: Advertising Design, Aesthetics, Art Appreciation, Art Education, Art History, Commercial Art, Crafts, Design, Drawing, Fine Arts, Graphic Arts, Graphic Design, History of Art & Architecture, †Mixed Media, †Museum Studies, Painting, Photography, Religious & Christian Art, Sculpture, Theatre Arts
Summer School: Dir, Dr Dawna Walsh, PhD. Tuition $1,000 per cr hr. Courses—Drawing, Painting, Art Travel Program for cr available

SOUTHERN METHODIST UNIVERSITY, Meadows School of the Arts - Division of Art, PO Box 750356, Dallas, TX 75275-0356. Tel 214-768-2489; Fax 214-768-4257; Web: www.smu.edu/meadows; *Prof* Philip VanKeuren; *Prof* Michael Corris; *Prof* Jay Sullivan; *Prof* Mary Vernon; *Prof* Barnaby Fitzgerald; *Asst Prof* Debora Hunter; *Asst Prof* Brittany Ransom; *Asst Prof* Brian Molanphy; *Asst Prof* Mary Walling Blackburn; *Chair* Noah Simblist
Estab 1911, Meadows School of the Arts estab 1964; Maintains nonprofit Pollock Gallery, SMU Division of Art PO Box 750 356, Dallas, TX 75275-0356; maintains Jack & Nancy Hamon Arts Library; pvt; D & E; Scholarships; maj 52, grad 11
Ent Req: selective admis
Degrees: BFA(Art), BA(Art History) 4 yr, MFA(Art) 2 yr, MA(Art History) 2 yr, PhD(Art History) 5 yr
Courses: †Art History, †Ceramics, †Color and Composition, Bronze Casting, †Drawing, †Painting, †Photography, †Printmaking, †Sculpture
Adult Hobby Classes: Ceramics, Color and Composition, Bronze Casting
Summer School: Selected courses in art & art history at Taos, NM

DENISON

GRAYSON COUNTY COLLEGE, Art Dept, 6101 Grayson Dr, Denison, TX 75020-8238. Tel 903-463-8662; Fax 903-463-5284; Web: www.gcc.edu; *Inst* Evette Moorman; *Instr* Terri Blair; *Dept Head* Steve O Black
Estab 1965; PT 2; pub; D & E; Scholarships; LC 3; D 63, E 35
Ent Req: HS dipl
Degrees: AA 2 yrs
Courses: 3-D Design, Art Appreciation, Art Education, Art History, Color & Design, Drawing, Foundations of Art, Painting
Adult Hobby Classes: Ceramics, Drawing, Painting
Summer School: Dir, Steve O Black. Courses—Art Appreciation, Foundations of Art, Drawing, Painting

DENTON

TEXAS WOMAN'S UNIVERSITY, School of the Arts, Dept of Visual Arts, PO Box 425469, Denton, TX 76204-5469. Tel 940-898-2530; Fax 940-898-2496; Email visualarts@twu.edu; Web: www.twu.edu/as/va; *Dir School of the Arts* John Weinkein, MFA; *Prof* Linda Stuckenbruck, MFA; *Prof* Dr John A Calabrese, PhD, MFA; *Prof* Susan Kae Grant, MFA; *Adjunct Assoc Prof* Don Radke, MFA; *Adjunct Assoc Prof* Laurie Weller, MFA; *Asst Prof* Colby Parsons-O'Keefe, MFA; *Instr* David Bieloh, MA
Estab 1901; pub; D & E; Scholarships; SC 21, LC 34, GC 17; non-maj 400, maj 110, undergrad 150, total 750
Ent Req: HS dipl, MA and MFA portfolio review required
Degrees: BA and BFA 4 yrs, MA 1 yr, MFA 2 yrs
Courses: Art Education, Art History, Bookmaking-Topography, Clay, †Graphic Design, Handmade Paper, Painting, Photography, Sculpture
Summer School: tuition same as above for 2 5-wk sessions. Courses—Art Design, Art Education, Art History, Clay, Drawing, Fibers, Painting, Photography

UNIVERSITY OF NORTH TEXAS, College of Visual Arts & Design, 1201 W Mulberry St, Denton, TX 16201; 1155 Union Cir, #305100 Denton, TX 76203-5017. Tel 940-565-2855; Fax 940-565-4717; Email cvad@unt.edu; Web: art.unt.edu; *Assoc Dean* Eric Ligon, MFA; *Chair, Dept Art Educ* Denise Baxter, PhD; *Chair, Dept Studio* Annette Lawrence, MFA; *Assoc Prof Interior Design* Bruce Nacke, MFA; *Assoc Prof Interior Design* Johnnie Stark, MFA; *Assoc Prof Fashion Design* Marian O'Rourke-Kaplan, MA; *Chair, Dept Design* Cynthia Mohr, MA; *Regents Prof Metals* Harlan Butt, MFA; *Prof Drawing & Painting* Vincent Falsetta; *Prof Drawing & Painting* Robert Jessup; *Prof Art Educ* Terry Barrett; *Regents Prof* Elmer Taylor, MFA; *Prof Fashion Design* Myra Walker; *Assoc Prof Art History* Nada Shabout, PhD; *Assoc Prof Art History* Jennifer Way, PhD; *Assoc Prof Communs Design* Michael Gibson; *Assoc Dean & Distinguished Teaching Prof* Eric Ligan, MFA; *Prof Photog* Dornith Doherty, MFA; *Assoc Prof Design* Jane Stidham, PhD; *Assoc Prof Printmaking* Larry Gibbons; *Assoc Prof Art History* Kelly Donahue-Wallace, PhD; *Assoc Prof Drawing & Painting* Matthew Bourbon, MFA; *Prof Sculpture* Richard Davis, MFA; *Assoc Prof Metals* Ana Lopez, MFA, MA; *Assoc Prof Art History* Lisa Owen, PhD; *Assoc Prof Art History* Mickey Abel, PhD; *Assoc Prof Commun Design* Keith Owens, MFA; *Assoc Dean* Jerry Austin, MFA; *Assoc Prof Fashion Design* Li Fen Chang, MFA
Estab 1890, dept estab 1901; Maintain nonprofit art gallery, University Art Gallery, 1201 W Mulberry, Denton, TX 76201; Willis Library; on-campus shop for purchase of art supplies; art library; pub; D & E; Scholarships; Fellowships; SC 212, LC 43, GC 29; maj 2,100, grad 150
Ent Req: HS dipl, SAT, GRE, portfolio for MFA, letters of recommendation for PhD
Degrees: BA 4 yrs, BFA 4 yrs, MFA, MA, PhD
Courses: Art Appreciation, †Art Education, †Art History, †Arts, †Ceramics, †Communication Design, Conceptual Art, Design, Drawing, †Electronic Media Art, †Fashion Arts, †Innovation Studies, †Interior Design, †Jewelry, †Leadership, †Mixed Media, †Photography, †Printmaking, †Sculpture, Teacher Training, Textile Design, †Weaving
Adult Hobby Classes: Tuition determined by class. Courses—Mini-classes in arts and craft related areas. Offered by Mini Course Office.
Children's Classes: Courses—Mini-classes in arts and crafts related areas; special prog for advanced students. Offered by Mini-Course Office
Summer School: Dean, Robert Milues. Enrl 700-900 per session; tuition res—undergrad & grad $99 per sem hr for term of 5 wks; nonres—undergrad $335 per sem hr, grad $531.90 per sem hr for term of 5 wks; 2 summer sessions. Courses—Art Appreciation, Art Education, Art History, Design, Drawing, Fashion, Interior Design, Painting, Photography

EDINBURG

UNIVERSITY OF TEXAS PAN AMERICAN, Art Dept, 1201 W University Dr, Edinburg, TX 78539-2970. Tel 956-381-2011; Fax 210-384-5072; Email nmoyer@panam.edu; Web: www.panam.edu/dept/art/; *Prof Sculpture* Richard P Hyslin; *Prof Painting* Philip S Field; *Prof Printmaking & Drawing* Wilbert R Martin; *Chmn Dept* Nancy Moyer PhD; *Asst Prof Ceramics* Charles Wissinger; *Asst Prof Painting & Printmaking* Lenard Brown; *Asst Prof Art History* Richard Phillips; *Gallery Dir* Dindy Reich; *Art Educ* James Dutremaine
Estab 1927, dept estab 1972; maintain nonprofit art gallery, Charles and Dorothy Clark Gallery, FIAB, Art Dept. UT-PA, Edinburg, TX 78539; University Gallery, CAS, Art Dept. UT-PA, Edinburg, TX 78539; pub; D & E; Scholarships; SC 43, LC 14; D 1200, E 150, non-maj 650, maj 209
Ent Req: immunization, top 50%, GED
Degrees: BA and BFA 4 yrs
Courses: Advertising Design, Aesthetics, Art Appreciation, †Art Education, Art History, †Ceramics, Collage, Computer Graphic, Design, Drawing, †Graphic Design, Illustration, †Jewelry, Lettering, †Painting, Photography, †Printmaking, †Sculpture, Silversmithing
Summer School: Dir, Nancy Moyer. Enrl 20 per class; tuition $31-$78 for term of 5 wks beginning June 2 & July 9. Courses—Art Appreciation, Art Education, Basic Design, Beginning & Advanced Painting, Ceramics, Drawing, Elementary Art Educ, Printing

EL PASO

UNIVERSITY OF TEXAS AT EL PASO, Dept of Art, 500 W University, Fox Fine Arts Bldg El Paso, TX 79902-5816. Tel 915-747-5181, 747-5000; Fax 915-747-6749; Email artdept@utep.edu; Web: www.utep.edu/arts; *Head Dept* Albert Wong
Estab 1939; FT 12, PT 9; pub; D & E; Scholarships; SC 24, GC 8; 200
Degrees: BA & BFA 4 yrs, MA (Studio & Art Ed)
Courses: Art Education, Art History, Ceramics, Design, Drawing, Graphic Design, Metals, Painting, Printmaking, Sculpture
Adult Hobby Classes: Enrl 9; tuition varies from class to class. Courses—offered through Extension Division
Children's Classes: Enrl 25; tuition $25 for 6 week class. Courses—Kidzart

FORT WORTH

SAGER STUDIOS, 320 N Bailey Ave, Fort Worth, TX 76107-1003. Tel 817-626-3105; *Owner* Judy Sager
Estab 1964; pvt; D & E; D 8, E 16
Ent Req: entrance exam, portfolio preparation stressed
Degrees: BFA 4 yr
Tuition: $35 per month
Courses: Ceramics, Collage, Design, Drawing, Lettering, Mixed Media, Painting, Photography, Printmaking, Sculpture, Teacher Training
Children's Classes: Special classes for gifted students ages 10-24

TEXAS WESLEYAN UNIVERSITY, Dept of Art, 1201 Wesleyan St, Fort Worth, TX 76105-1536. Tel 817-531-4444; Fax 817-531-4814; *Dean, Theater Arts* Joe Brown; *Dean Art Dept* Kit Hall; *Dir Art Dept* Bob Pevitts
Den; D & E; Scholarships; SC, LC
Ent Req: HS dipl
Degrees: BA 4 yrs
Courses: Art Education, Ceramics, Drawing, History of Art & Architecture, Painting, Printmaking, Teacher Training

GAINESVILLE

NORTH CENTRAL TEXAS COLLEGE, Division of Communications & Fine Arts, 1525 W California St, Gainesville, TX 76240-4636. Tel 940-668-7731; Fax 940-668-6049; Web: www.nctc.cc.tx.us; *Chmn* Mary Dell Heathington; *Prof* Scott Robinson
Estab 1924; pub; D & E; Scholarships; SC 14, LC 1; D 50
Ent Req: HS dipl, SAT or ACT, individual approval
Degrees: AA and AFA 2 yrs
Courses: Art Appreciation, Art History, Ceramics, Drawing, Figure Drawing, Jewelry, Painting, Sculpture
Adult Hobby Classes: Enrl 120; tuition in county $28 per cr hr, out of county $40 per cr hr, out of state $64 per cr hr; Courses—Basketry, Country Art, Drawing, Flower Arrangement, Painting, Weaving
Children's Classes: Enrl 20; tuition $15. Courses - Art

GEORGETOWN

SOUTHWESTERN UNIVERSITY, Sarofim School of Fine Art, Dept of Art & Art History, PO Box 770, Georgetown, TX 78627-0770. Tel 512-863-1504; Fax 512-863-1422; Email sewelll@southwestern.edu; Web: www.southwestern.edu; *Chair Art History* Thomas Howe PhD; *Chair Art* Victoria Star Varner; *Prof* Kimberly Smith, PhD; *Assoc Prof* Patrick Hojonsky, PhD; *Asst Prof* Allison Miller, PhD; *Prof* Mary Visser, MFA; *Instr* Noel Robbins; *Instr* Kristen Van Patten; *Instr* Kimberly Jones; *Instr* Rowena Dasch Houuhton
Estab 1840, dept estab 1940; Maintains nonprofit art gallery, Sarofim School of Fine Art, Fine Art Gallery & A Frank Smith Library Center, 1001 E University Ave, Georgetown, TX 78626; art supplies may be purchased on- campus; Jonathon Faber, Mat Rebholz, Kimberly Jones, Rowena Dasch Houuhton; pvt; D&E; Scholarships; SC 39, LC 35; D 1515, maj 33
Ent Req: HS dipl, SAT, portfolio
Degrees: BA 4 yrs; BFA 4 yrs
Tuition: Schols offered, tui $37,560
Courses: Architecture, Art Education, Art History, Ceramics, †Computer Imaging, Design, Drawing, Painting, Photography, Printmaking, Sculpture
Summer School: Courses—various

HILLSBORO

HILL COLLEGE, Fine Arts Dept, 112 Lamar Dr, Hillsboro, TX 76645-2799. Tel 254-582-2555, ext 224 (Visual Arts) or ext 270 (Performing Arts); Fax 254-582-5791; Email ccason@hillcollege.edu; Web: www.hillcollege.edu; *Coordr Fine Arts* Phillip Lowe; *Visual Fine Arts Coordr* Christine Cason
Estab 1921; Maintain nonprofit art gallery, Regent's Gallery, Admin Bldg, 112 Lamar Dr, Hillsboro, TX; Pub; D & E; Scholarships; SC & LC
Degrees: AA, cert
Tuition: In district—$73 per sem hr; res—$90.33 per sem hr; nonres—$157 per sem hr
Courses: Art Appreciation, Art History, Costume Design & Construction, Design, Digital Imaging, Drawing, †Graphic Design, Mixed Media, Painting, Photography, Sculpture, Stage Design, Theatre Arts

HOUSTON

ART INSTITUTE OF HOUSTON, 4140 Southwest Fwy Ste 100, Houston, TX 77027-7319. Tel 713-623-2040; Fax 713-966-2700; Web: www.aih.aii.edu; WATS 800-275-4244; *School of Design* John Luukkonen; *Dir Educ* Joe Orlando
Estab 1964; FT 25, PT 15; pvt; D & E; Scholarships; D 800, E 145
Ent Req: ent req HS transcripts & graduation or GED, interview
Degrees: AA
Courses: Fashion Merchandising, Graphic Design, Illustration, Interior Design, Photography
Adult Hobby Classes: Applied Photography, Interior Planning, Layout & Production

HOUSTON BAPTIST UNIVERSITY, Dept of Art, 7502 Fondren Rd, Houston, TX 77074-3298. Tel 281-649-3000; *Chmn* James Busby
Estab 1963; den; D & E; Scholarships; SC 7, LC 9; D 2500, maj 35
Ent Req: HS dipl, ent exam
Degrees: BA & BS
Courses: Art Appreciation, Art Education, Ceramics, Design, Drawing, Elementary Art with Teacher Certification, History of Art & Architecture, Painting, Printmaking, Sculpture

MUSEUM OF FINE ARTS, HOUSTON, Glassell School of Art, 5101 Montrose Blvd, Houston, TX 77005-1803; PO Box 6826, Houston, TX 77256. Tel 713-639-7500; Fax 713-639-7709; Email glassell@mfah.org; Web: www.mfah.org/visit/glassell-school; *Dir* Joseph Havel; *Assoc Dir* Jennifer Cronin; *Faculty Chair & Studio School Dean* Patrick Palmer; *Admin Dean, Junior School* Pamela Perez; *Assoc Dir Core Residency Prog* Mary Leclere
Estab 1979. under the auspices of the Museum of Fine Arts, Houston; Maintains nonprofit art gallery, Laura Lee Blanton Gallery. Affiliate of Museum of Fine Arts, Houston; pvt; D & E; Fellowships; SC 34, LC 5; studio 1087, Jr 3407
Activities: Schols offered
Ent Req: ent req portfolio review, transfer students
Degrees: 4 yr cert
Tuition: Junior school: $150-300; studio school: $600 SC, $400 art history
Courses: Art History, Ceramics, †Design, Digital Media, †Drawing, Enamel, †Jewelry, Painting, Photography, †Printmaking, †Sculpture
Summer School: Jujio school $150 per course, 2984 enrollment

RICE UNIVERSITY, Visual & Dramatic Arts, 6100 Main St, MS 549 Houston, TX 77005-1892; PO Box 1892, MS 549 Houston, TX 77251-1892. Tel 713-348-4882; Fax 713-348-5910; Email arts@rice.edu; Web: arts.rice.edu; *Prof Emeritus* Basilios N Poulos, MA; *Prof* Karin Broker, MFA; *Prof Emeritus* George Smith, MFA; *Prof* Geoffrey Winningham, MFA; *Assoc Prof* Brian Huberman, MFA; *Prof* John Sparagana, MFA; *Assoc Prof* Darra Keeton, MFA; *Assoc Prof* Christopher Sperandio; *Sr Admin* Gaylon Denney
Estab 1912, dept estab 1966-67; Maintains nonprofit art gallery; Rice University Art Gallery, PO Box 1892, MS-55, Houston, TX 77251-1892; Pvt; D & E; Scholarships; Fellowships; D 125, non-maj 75, maj 50, grad 2 (BFA)
Ent Req: HS dipl, CEEB, evaluations of HS counselors and teachers, interview
Degrees: BA 4 yrs, BFA 5 yrs
Tuition: $12,800 per yr, $6,400 per sem, grad $13,300 per yr, $6,650 per sem; PT $740 per yr, $370 per sem; campus res—room & board $6,000 per yr
Courses: †Art History, Design, Drawing, Film, Painting, Photography, Printmaking, Sculpture, Video
Adult Hobby Classes: Classes offered for adults & children at university

SAN JACINTO COLLEGE-NORTH, Art Dept, 5800 Uvalde, Houston, TX 77049. Tel 281-459-7119; Web: www.sjcd.cc.tx.us; *Instr* Ken Luce; *Chmn Fine Arts Dept* Randy Snyder
Estab 1972; pub; D & E; Scholarships; SC 16, LC 3; D 56, E 21, non-maj 50, maj 27
Ent Req: HS dipl
Degrees: AA 2 yrs
Courses: Art Appreciation, Art History, Drawing, Painting, Sculpture
Adult Hobby Classes: Enrl 50; tuition $15 - $40 per 6-18 hrs. Courses—Calligraphy, Ceramics, Origami, Pastel Art, Photography, Stained Glass
Children's Classes: Enrl 15, tuition $30 per 6 wks. Courses—Pastel Art
Summer School: Dir, Kenneth A Luce. Enrl 10 - 25; tuition $78 - $96. Courses—vary beginning May

TEXAS SOUTHERN UNIVERSITY, College of Liberal Arts & Behavioral Sciences, 3100 Cleburne Ave, Houston, TX 77004. Tel 713-313-7337; Fax 713-313-1869; *Assoc Prof* Alvia Wardlaw; *Art Coordr & Assoc Prof* Harvey Johnson; *Chmn* Dianne Jemmson-Pollard; *Assoc Prof* Dr Sarah Trotty; *Assoc Prof* Leamon Green; *Instr* Maya Watson
Estab 1949; Maintains nonprofit art gallery: University Museum & Lobby of Biggers Center; Pub; D & E; Scholarships; SC 31, LC 12, GC 4; maj 50, other 100
Ent Req: HS dipl
Degrees: BA in Art
Courses: Art Education, Ceramics, Design, Drawing, Hot Print Making, Painting, Sculpture, Silk Screen Painting, Weaving

UNIVERSITY OF HOUSTON, Dept of Art, 4800 Calhoun Rd, Houston, TX 77004-2693. Tel 713-743-3001; Fax 713-743-2823; *Chmn* Dr W Jackson Rushing
Estab 1927; FT 29, PT 7; pub; D & E; Scholarships; D 600 maj
Ent Req: HS dipl, SAT
Degrees: BA, BFA, MFA
Courses: Art History, Ceramics, †Graphic Communications, Interior Design, Jewelry/Metals, †Paint/Drawing, Painting, Photography, †Photography/Video, Printmaking, †Sculpture, Silversmithing, Video

UNIVERSITY OF SAINT THOMAS, Fine and Performing Arts Dept, 3800 Montrose Blvd, Houston, TX 77006-4626. Tel 713-522-7911; Fax 713-942-5015; Email stewarca@stthom.edu; Web: www.stthom.edu; *Dept Chmn* Claire McDonald; *Chmn Art History* Bernard Bonario, PhD; *Chmn Studio Arts* Suzanne Manns; *Asst Prof* Charles Anthony Stewart
Estab 1947; Den; D & E; Scholarships; SC 50, LC 22, GC 18; D 220, E 100, non-maj 265, maj 30, GS 25
Ent Req: HS dipl
Degrees: BA (Liberal Arts, Art History emphasis), BA (Studio Arts), BFA (Studio Arts), MLA (Art History)
Courses: Art History, †Ceramics, †Collage, †Costume Design & Construction, †Drawing, †Mixed Media, †Painting, †Photography, †Printmaking, †Sculpture, †Silversmithing, †Stage Design, †Studio Arts, †Teacher Training, †Theatre Arts

HUNTSVILLE

SAM HOUSTON STATE UNIVERSITY, Art Dept, Box 2089, Huntsville, TX 77341. Tel 936-294-1315; Fax 936-294-1251; Web: www.shsu.edu; *Prof* Jimmy Barker, MFA; *Assoc Prof* Kenneth L Zonker, MFA; *Asst Prof* Patrick Lawler, MFA; *Asst Prof* Kate Borcherbing, MFA; *Dept Head* Martin Amorous, MFA; *Prof* Sharon King; *Ceramics* Matt Wilt; *Prof* Tony Shipp; *Asst Prof* Charlotte Drumm
Estab 1879, dept estab 1936; pub; D; SC 26, LC 7, GC 12; D 844, non-maj 100, maj 170, grad 15
Ent Req: HS dipl, ACT or SAT
Degrees: BA, BFA 4 yrs, MFA 2 yrs, MA 1 1/2 yrs
Courses: 2-D & 3-D Design, Advertising Design, Art History, Ceramics, Drawing, Illustration, Jewelry, Life Drawing, Painting, Printmaking, Sculpture, Studio Art
Summer School: Chmn, Jimmy H Barker. Courses—Art History, Crafts, Drawing, Watercolor, 2-D Design

HURST

TARRANT COUNTY COLLEGE NORTHEAST CAMPUS, Art Dept, 828 Harwood Rd, Northeast Campus Hurst, TX 76054-3219. Tel 817-515-6571; Fax 817-515-6256; Email martha.gordon@tccd.edu; Web: www.tccd.net; *Chair & Assoc Prof* Martha Gordon, MFA; *Assoc Prof* Karmien Bowman, MA; *Assoc Prof* Anitra Blayton, MFA; *Assoc Prof & Coordr Graphic Commun* Lynn Dally, MFA; *Assoc Prof* Cynthia Hurt, MFA; *Assoc Prof* Richard (Scott) Parker, MFA; *Instr* Suzanne Perez, MA; *Assoc Prof* Andrew Stalder, MFA; *Assoc Prof Photog* Richard Doherty, MFA; *Assoc Prof Photog* Patricia Richards, MFA; *Instr Graphic Commun* Christopher Flynn, BA; *Instr Graphic Commun* Sean Foushee, BA
Estab 1967, dept estab 1968; Art supplies sold at on-campus store; pub; D, E & weekends; SC 19, LC 3; D 200, E 150, non-maj 150, maj 200
Ent Req: HS dipl, GED, admis by individual approval
Degrees: AA and AAS 2 yrs
Tuition: Res—$50 per hr, minimum; nonres—of county $73, others $165 per sem hr with $200 minimum fee, aliens $120 per sem hr with $200 minimum fee; no campus res
Courses: Advertising Design, Art Appreciation, Art Education, Art History, Ceramics, Collage, Constructions, †Design, Drawing, Jewelry, Mixed Media, Painting, Photography, Printmaking, Sculpture
Adult Hobby Classes: Enrl 50; for 7 wks. Courses—Drawing, Oil-Acrylic, Tole Painting, Ceramics enrl 14, $200
Children's Classes: Enrl 100; 7 wks. Courses—Cartooning, Ceramics, College for Kids, Drawing, Painting
Summer School: Dir, Dr Jane Harper. Enrl 100; tuition as above for term of 6 wks beginning June. Courses—Art Appreciation

KILGORE

KILGORE COLLEGE, Visual Arts Dept, 1100 Broadway, Fine Arts Kilgore, TX 75662-3204. Tel 903-984-8531; Fax 903-983-8600; Web: www.kilgore.edu; *Instr* Larry Kitchen; *Instr* O Rufus Lovett; *Chmn* John Hillier
Estab 1935; D & E; Scholarships; SC 11, LC 3; D 75, E 25, non-maj 25, maj 50
Ent Req: HS dipl
Degrees: AAAS & AA
Tuition: District res—$31 per sem hr; non-district res—$53 per sem hr; non-state res—$239 per sem hr
Courses: †Art Education, †Art History, Commercial Art, †Drawing, Painting, Photography, Printmaking, Sculpture

KINGSVILLE

TEXAS A&M UNIVERSITY-KINGSVILLE, Art Dept, 700 University Blvd, MSC 157 Kingsville, TX 78363-8300. Tel 361-593-2619; Fax 361-593-2662; Web: www.tamuk.edu; *Prof* William Renfro; *Prof* Richard Scherpereel; *Prof* Maurice Schmidt; *Lectr* Peggy Wilkes; *Chmn* Santa Barraza
Estab 1925, dept estab 1930; pub; D & E; SC 21, LC 5, GC 2; D 700, non-maj 300, maj 400, art maj 150, grad 20
Ent Req: HS dipl
Degrees: BFA & BA 4 yr
Courses: Advertising Design, Art Education, Art History, Ceramics, Design, Drawing, Graphic Arts, History of Art & Architecture, Painting, Principles of Art, Printmaking, Sculpture, Teacher Training
Adult Hobby Classes: Courses offered
Summer School: Courses—full schedule

LAKE JACKSON

BRAZOSPORT COLLEGE, Communications & Fine Art, 500 College Dr, Lake Jackson, TX 77566-3199. Tel 979-230-3000; Fax 979-230-3465; Email kfunkhou@brazosport.edu; Web: www.brazosport.edu; *Fine Arts Dept Chmn* Kate Funkhouser; *Asst Prof* Molly I Brauhn; *Instr* Jackson Zorn; *Adjunct Prof* Kamilah Campbell
Estab 1968; Maintains Brazosport Col Art Gallery, 500 Col Dr, Lake Jackson; 0; pub; D & E; Scholarships; SC 10-15, LC 3; D 220 Maj 30
Ent Req: HS dipl or GED

Degrees: AA 2 yrs
Courses: Art Appreciation, Art History, Ceramics, Design, Drawing, Graphic Arts, †Graphic Design, Painting, †Photography, †Printmaking, Sculpture, Theatre Arts
Adult Hobby Classes: Ceramics, China Painting, Painting

LEVELLAND

SOUTH PLAINS COLLEGE, Fine Arts Dept, 1401 S College Ave, FA-133 Levelland, TX 79336-6503. Tel 806-894-9611, Ext 2261; Email vpa@southplainscollege.edu; Web: www.spc.cc.tx.us; *Chmn* Dr Daniel Nazworth; *Asst Prof* Chris Adams; *Asst Prof* Kathy Whiteside; *Assoc Prof* Allison Black; *Assoc Prof* Kara Donatelli; *Assoc Prof* Angela Heath
Estab 1958; Maintains a non-profit art gallery; on-campus shop to purchase art supplies; FT 5, PT 2; pub; D & E; Scholarships; SC 7, LC 3; D 252, E 76, maj 52
Ent Req: HS dipl
Degrees: AA 2 yrs
Courses: 2-D Design, Art Appreciation, Art Education, Art History, Ceramics, Design, Design I, Drawing, Painting, Photography, Silversmithing, Teacher Training
Summer School: Dr Yancy Nunez. Enrl 66; tuition same as regular sem for 6 wk term. Courses—Art History, Life Drawing, Photography

LUBBOCK

LUBBOCK CHRISTIAN UNIVERSITY, Dept of Communication & Fine Art, 5601 19th St, Lubbock, TX 79407-2099. Tel 806-796-8800; Fax 806-796-8917; Web: www.lcu.edu; *Chmn & Instr* Dr Michelle Kraft, MA; *Prof* Karen Randolph, MFA
Estab 1956; Scholarships
Degrees: BA & BSID
Tuition: $3200 annual tuition
Courses: Advertising Design, †Animation, Art Appreciation, Art Education, Art History, Design, †Digital Imaging, Drawing, Fine Arts, Graphic Arts, Graphic Design, Handicrafts, Painting, Sculpture
Summer School: Dir, K Randolph. Tuition $310 per course for 3-4 wk session. Courses—Art, Art & Children, Art History, Desktop Publishing, 2-D Design

TEXAS TECH UNIVERSITY, Dept of Art, P.O. Box 42081 Lubbock, TX 79409-2081. Tel 806-742-3825; Fax 806-742-1971; Web: www.depts.ttu.edu/art; *Dir & Prof* Tina Fuentes, MFA; *Assoc Dir & Assoc Prof* Nancy Slagle, MFA; *Assoc Dir & Assoc Prof* Andrew Martin, MFA
Estab 1925, dept estab 1967; Maintain a nonprofit art gallery Landmark Arts & art library Visual Resource Center; on-campus shop for purchase of art supplies; pub; D & E; Scholarships; SC 60 undergrad, 20 grad, LC 20 undergrad, 15 grad; D 1400, non-maj 950, maj 400, grad 50
Ent Req: HS dipl, SAT or ACT test
Degrees: BFA & BA(Art History), MAE 36 hrs, MFA 60 hrs minimum, PhD 54 hrs beyond MA minimum
Tuition: Variable for res and nonres; campus residence available
Courses: Advertising Design, Aesthetics, Art Appreciation, †Art Education, †Art History, Ceramics, Computer-Aided Design, Design, †Design Communication, Digital Imaging, Drawing, Graphic Design, Illustration, Installation, Intermedia, Jewelry, Lettering, Mixed Media, Painting, Photography, Printmaking, Sculpture, Silversmithing, †Studio Art, Teacher Training, Weaving
Adult Hobby Classes: Computer-Aided Design, Photography, Studio Art
Children's Classes: Art Project for talented high school students, Artery; classes in art for elementary & middle school students
Summer School: Dir, Future Akins-Tillett, Assoc Prof. Courses—Art Education, Ceramics, Drawing, Glassblowing, Jewelry & Metalsmithing, Painting, Papermaking, Photography, Printmaking, Sculpture, Textile Design, Weaving

MESQUITE

EASTFIELD COLLEGE, Humanities Division, Art Dept, 3737 Motley Dr, Mesquite, TX 75150-2099. Tel 972-860-7100; Web: www.efc.dccd.edu; *Dean* Rachel Wolf
Degrees: AA
Tuition: $79 per 3 cr hr
Courses: Art Appreciation, Art History, Ceramics, Design, Drawing, Jewelry, Painting, Sculpture

MIDLAND

MIDLAND COLLEGE, Art Dept, 3600 N Garfield, Midland, TX 79705. Tel 432-685-4624 (fine arts & communs div); Fax 432-685-4769; Email kmoss@midland.edu; Web: www.midland.edu; *Instr* Carol Bailey, MA; *Prof* Kent Moss, MFA; *Dean* William Feeler; *Instr* Susan Randall; *Instr* Michael Hubbard, MFA; *Instr* Dagan Sherman, MFA
Estab 1972; Non-profit art gallery & Library; schols open to financial aid applicants; on-campus art supplies shop; pub; D & E; Scholarships; SC 15, LC 3; D 80, E 75, non-maj 125, maj 25
Ent Req: HS dipl
Degrees: AA and AAA 2 yrs
Tuition: Res—undergrad $327 per 12 hrs plus $40 fee; nonres—undergrad $351 per 12 hrs plus $40 fee; no campus res
Courses: †Art Appreciation, Art History, †Ceramics, Collage, †Design, Drawing, †Graphic Design, Illustration, †Jewelry, Mixed Media, †Painting, †Photography, †Printmaking, †Sculpture, Teacher Training
Adult Hobby Classes: Ceramics, Painting, Photography
Children's Classes: Kid's College
Summer School: Dir, William Feeler, Dean; Enrl 40. Courses—varied

NACOGDOCHES

STEPHEN F AUSTIN STATE UNIVERSITY, School of Art, PO Box 13001, Nacogdoches, TX 75962-0001. Tel 409-468-4804; Fax 409-468-4041; Email talbotck@sfasu.edu; Web: www.sfasu.edu; *Dir* Christopher K Talbot, MFA; *Grad Asst* Linda Post
Estab 1923; Maintains nonprofit art gallery, The Cole Art Center, 329 E Main St, Nacogdoches, TX 75961; maintains library, SFA Steen Library, 1936 North St Nacogdoches, TX 75962; pub; D & E; Scholarships; Fellowships; SC 28, LC 11, GC 11; D 461, non-maj 150, maj 280, grad 20
Ent Req: HS dipl, ACT score 20
Degrees: BA & BFA 4 yrs, MFA 2 yrs, MA 1.5 yrs
Tuition: TX residents $3,600 per 12 credit hours
Courses: Art Appreciation, †Art Education, †Art History, †Ceramics, Cinematography, Design, †Digital Media, †Drawing, †Film, †Graphic Design, Illustration, †Interior Design, †Jewelry, †Museum Staff Training, †Painting, †Photography, †Printmaking, †Sculpture, Silversmithing, Teacher Training, Video
Summer School: Beginning & advanced art classes. Courses—Varies summer to summer

ODESSA

UNIVERSITY OF TEXAS OF PERMIAN BASIN, Dept of Art, 4901 E University Blvd, Odessa, TX 79762-0001. Tel 432-552-2286; Fax 432-552-3285; Email price_p@utpb.edu; Web: utpb.edu; *Chmn* Pam Price, MFA; *Assoc Prof* Chris Stanley, MFA; *Asst Prof* Marianne Berger Woods, PhD; *Asst Prof* David Poindexter, MFA; *Lectr* Dan Askew, MFA
Estab 1972; Maintain nonprofit art gallery, Nancy Fyfe Cardozier Art Gallery, Art Dept, UTPB, 4901 E University, Odessa, TX 79762; art supplies available on-campus; pub; D & E; Scholarships; SC 48, LC 13; non-maj 10, maj 83
Degrees: BA, BFA
Tuition: Campus residency available
Courses: Art Education, Ceramics, Commercial Art, Drawing, Graphic Design, Painting, Photography, Printmaking, Sculpture
Summer School: Courses—varied

PARIS

PARIS JUNIOR COLLEGE, Visual Art Dept, 2400 Clarksville St, Paris, TX 75460-6298. Tel 903-784-0438, 800-441-1398 (TX), 800-232-5804 (US); Fax 903-784-9370; Email smoore@parisjc.edu; Web: www.parisjc.edu; *Instr & Exhib Dir* Susan Moore, MFA
Estab 1924; Maintain nonprofit art gallery, art dept-Foyer Gallery, Attn Susan Moore, Paris Junior College, 2400 Clarksville, Paris, TX 75460; pub; D & E; Scholarships; SC 11, LC 2; D 30-60, E 50-70, non-maj 60-65, maj 15-20
Ent Req: none
Degrees: AA & AS in Art 2 yrs
Courses: Art Appreciation, Art History, †Art Metals (General Art Preparatory Program), Ceramics, Design, Digital Art, Drawing, Life Drawing, Painting, Photography, Sculpture
Adult Hobby Classes: Enrl 20. Courses—Art Appreciation, Art Metals, Ceramics, Design, Drawing, Graphic Art, Painting, Photography, Sculpture
Summer School: Dir, Cathie Tyler. 2-5 wk sessions June-Aug. Courses—Art Appreciation

PASADENA

SAN JACINTO JUNIOR COLLEGE, Division of Fine Arts, 8060 Spencer Hwy, Pasadena, TX 77501-5998. Tel 281-476-1501; Fax 281-478-2711; Web: www.sjcd.cc.tx.us; *Acting Div Chmn & Dean Fine Arts* Dr Jerry Ivins
Estab 1961; pub; D & E; SC 5, LC 1; D 230, E 45, non-maj 120, maj 155
Ent Req: HS dipl, GED or individual approval
Degrees: AA and AS 2 yrs
Courses: Advertising Art, Advertising Design, Art Appreciation, Art History, Ceramics, Commercial Art, Design, Drawing, Free Illustration, Lettering, Painting, Photography, Sculpture
Summer School: Courses—Design, Painting Workshop

PLAINVIEW

WAYLAND BAPTIST UNIVERSITY, Dept of Art, School of Fine Art, School of Fine Arts, Art Dept, Plainview, TX 79072; 1900 West Seventh, WBU #1249 Plainview, TX 79072-6900. Tel 806-291-1083; Fax 806-291-1980; Email kellerc@wbu.edu; Web: www.wbu.edu; *Prof* Candace Keller, PhD; *Assoc Prof* Mark Hilliard, MFA; *Asst Prof* Sam Walker, MA; *Instr* Richard Porter; *Instr* Gordon Zeigler; *Instr* Cindy Carthel; *Adjunct Instr* Dr. Linda Kennedy, PhD; *Instr, Online* Diane Dody, MFA
Estab 1908; Maintains nonprofit art gallery; Malouf Abraham Art Gallery, 1900 W 7th, CMB #1249, Plainview, TX 79072; Maintains art/architecture libr, Mayse Learning Resource Center, 1900 W 7th, Plainview, TX 79072. Art supplies may be purchased on campus; 3; Pvt & Den; D & E; Scholarships; SC 15, LC 5; D 150, E 50, non-maj 160, maj 45, grad 5
Activities: Schols offered
Ent Req: HS dipl, ent exam
Degrees: BA, BS 4 yrs, BFA
Tuition: $480 per sem hr
Courses: Advertising Design, †Art Appreciation, Art Education, Art History, Ceramics, Commercial Art, †Costume Design & Construction, Design, †Drawing, Film, Graphic Arts, †Graphic Design, †History of Art & Architecture, Painting2-D Painting, Photography, Printmaking, Sculpture, †Silversmithing, Stage Design, †Theatre Arts, Watercolor Studio

Adult Hobby Classes: Enrl 90 - 100; 16 wk term. Courses - Art Appreciation, Ceramics, Design, Drawing, Painting, Sculpture, Watercolor
Children's Classes: Enrl 25 - 35; tuition $60 for 2 wk term. Courses offered through Academy of Fine Art on campus
Summer School: Art Cur, Dr Candace Keller. Enrl 30-40; 3 wk term. Courses - Ceramics, Teacher Art Education, Watercolor

SAN ANGELO

ANGELO STATE UNIVERSITY, Visual and Performing Arts, 2601 W Ave N San Angelo, TX 76909. Tel 325-942-2085; Fax 325-942-2152; Email chris.stewart@angelo.edu; Web: www.angelo.edu/; *Chair* Chris Stewart
Estab 1963, dept estab 1976; Scholarships open to art majors for one year annually; for further info contact David Scott, Dept Head; Maintains a non-profit art gallery: Gallery 193 - Carrefa Building; pub; D & E; Scholarships; SC 20, LC 9; D 400 (art), E 50, non-maj 320, maj 80
Ent Req: HS dipl
Degrees: BA(Art) &Teaching Certification, BFA, BA-Music, BA-Theater, BM-Performance, BA-Theater, teaching cert
Courses: Art Education, Art History, Ceramics, Creative Design, Drawing, Etchings, †Graphic Illustration, Greek & Roman Art, History of Contemporary Art, History of Italian Renaissance, Intaglio Processes, Introduction to Art, Jewelry, Painting, Primary Art Theory, †Printmaking, †Sculpture
Summer School: Courses—Art Education, Art History, Ceramics, Introduction to Art, Sculpture, Studio Courses incl Design & Drawing

SAN ANTONIO

OUR LADY OF THE LAKE UNIVERSITY, Dept of Art, 411 SW 24 St, San Antonio, TX 78207-4689. Tel 210-434-6711, Ext 435; Web: www.ollusa.edu/; *Chmn* Alfredo Cruz; *Assoc Prof* Sr Jule Adele Espey PhD; *Assoc Prof* Jody Cariolano; *Dean* Sr Isabel Ball PhD
Estab 1911, dept estab 1920; FT 2, PT 1; den; D & E; Scholarships; SC 12, LC 3; non-maj 62, maj 8
Ent Req: HS dipl, completion of GED tests, 35 on each test or average of 45 on tests
Degrees: BA(Art)
Courses: Art Appreciation, Art Education, Art History, Ceramics, Computer Design, Design, Drawing, Graphic Arts, Painting, Photography, Printmaking, Sculpture
Adult Hobby Classes: Courses offered

SAINT MARY'S UNIVERSITY, Dept of Fine Arts, One Camino Santa Maria, San Antonio, TX 78228. Tel 210-436-3797, 436-3011; *Chmn* Sharon McMahon
Estab 1852; FT 8, PT 12; pvt; D & E; SC 10, LC 20; D 60, maj 58
Ent Req: HS dipl or GED, ent exam
Degrees: BA 4-5 yrs
Tuition: Res $4548, incl rm & board; $365 per cr hr
Courses: 3-D Design, Art Education, Drawing, Graphic Design, History of Art & Architecture, Painting, Photography, Printmaking, Sculpture, Teacher Training, Theatre Arts
Adult Hobby Classes: Enrl 75-100; tuition $25. Courses—vary
Summer School: Courses—vary

SAN ANTONIO COLLEGE, Visual Arts & Technology, 1300 San Pedro Ave, San Antonio, TX 78212-4299. Tel 210-733-2894, 733-2000; Fax 210-733-2338; Web: www.accd.edu/sac; *Chmn* Richard Arredondo; *Fine Arts Program Dir* Mark Pritchett
Estab 1955; FT 17, PT 20; pub; D & E; SC 75, LC 4; D 1000-1300, E 250-450
Ent Req: Ent req HS dipl, GED, TASP, ent exam
Degrees: AA & AS 2 yrs
Courses: Art Appreciation, Art History, Art Metals, Ceramics, Design, Drawing, Electronic Graphics, †Graphic Arts, Graphic Design, Illustration, Painting, Photography, Printmaking, Sculpture
Summer School: Dir, Richard Arredondo. Enrl 500; Courses—Same as for regular school yr

TRINITY UNIVERSITY, Department of Art & Art History, One Trinity Pl, San Antonio, TX 78212-7201. Tel 210-999-7682; Fax 210-999-8035; Email elizabeth.ward@trinity.edu; Web: www.trinity.edu; *Prof* Kate Ritson, MFA; *Chair & Prof* Elizabeth Ward, MFA; *Prof* Patricia Simonite, MFA; *Assoc Prof* Jon Lee, MFA; *Assoc Prof* Jessica Halonen, MFA; *Instr* Holly Goeckler, MFA; *Instr* Randall Wallace, MFA
Estab 1869; Mem: Maintains nonprofit art gallery; collection housed in Elizabeth Huth Coates Library; on-campus shop sells art supplies; pvt; D & E; SC 45; D 144, E 30, non-maj 50, maj 90
Ent Req: HS dipl, CEEB, SAT, 3 achievement tests
Degrees: BA 4 yrs
Courses: Art History, †Book Arts, Ceramics, †Design, Drawing, †History of Art & Architecture, †Outdoor Studio, Painting, †Papermaking, Photography, Printmaking, Sculpture, †Small Metals, †Studio Art
Adult Hobby Classes: Courses offered by Department of Continuing Educ
Summer School: Dir, Dept of Continuing Educ. Courses vary

UNIVERSITY OF TEXAS AT SAN ANTONIO, Dept of Art & Art History, One USTA Cir, San Antonio, TX 78249-0642. Tel 210-458-4352; Fax 210-458-4356; *Prof Emeritus* James Broderick, MA; *Prof* Ronald Binks, MFA; *Prof Emeritus* Charles Field, MFA; *Prof* Judith Sobre PhD; *Prof* Ken Little, MFA; *Dept Chair* Gregory Elliott, MFA; *Prof* Dennis Olsen, MA; *Prof* Constance Lowe, MFA; *Assoc Prof* Richard Armendariz; *Assoc Prof* Ovidio Giberga; *Prof* Kent Rush, MFA; *Assoc Prof* Scott Sherer, PhD; *Assoc Prof* Libby Rowe, MFA; *Asst Prof* Teresa Eckmann, PhD; *Asst Prof* Juliet Wiersema, PhD; *Asst Prof* Julie Johnson, PhD; *Asst Prof* Christine Blizard; *Asst Prof* Mark Mccoin
Estab 1974; Maintain non-profit art gallery, main gallery same location; UTSA Satellite space, 1518 S Alamo St, San Antonio TX 78204; 14; Pub; D & E; Scholarships; SC 31, LC 25, GC 17; non-maj 180, maj 500, grad 46
Ent Req: HS dipl, ACT, grad
Degrees: BFA 4 yrs, MFA 2 yrs, MA 1 yr
Courses: Art Appreciation, Art History, Ceramics, Conceptual Art, Design, Drawing, History of Art & Architecture, New Media/Video, Painting, Photography, Printmaking, Sculpture
Summer School: Chmn Gregory Elliott - Tuition $264 per sem. Courses—Art History, Ceramics, Drawing, Painting, Photography, Printmaking, Sculpture

UNIVERSITY OF THE INCARNATE WORD, Art Dept, 4301 Broadway, San Antonio, TX 78209. Tel 210-829-6000; Web: www.uiw.edu; *Prof* E Stoker, MA; *Lectr* Don Ewers, MA; *Chmn* Kathy Vargas, MFA; *Asst Prof* Miguel Cortinas, MFA; *Asst Prof* John Dawes, MFA
Estab 1881, dept estab 1948; Maintains nonprofit gallery, Semmes Gallery, 4301 Broadway, San Antonio, TX 78209; Den; D & E; Scholarships; SC 14, LC 9; D 195, non-maj 120, maj 30
Ent Req: HS dipl, ent exam
Degrees: BA 4 yrs
Courses: Advertising Design, Art Education, Art History, Ceramics, Costume Design & Construction, Design, Drawing, Fashion Arts, Graphic Arts, Graphic Design, Museum Staff Training, Painting, Photography, Printmaking, Sculpture, Stage Design, Textile Design, Theatre Arts, Weaving

SAN MARCOS

TEXAS STATE UNIVERSITY - SAN MARCOS, Dept of Art and Design, 601 University Dr, San Marcos, TX 78666-4684. Tel 512-245-2611; Fax 512-245-7969; Email en04@tx.state.edu; Web: www.swt.edu; *Chmn* Dr Erik Nielsen; *Prof* Mark Todd; *Prof* Jean Laman, MFA; *Prof* Neal Wilson; *Prof* Roger Bruce Colombik; *Prof* David Shields; *Prof* Beverley Penn; *Prof* Michel Conroy; *Prof* Brian Row; *Prof* Eric Weller; *Prof* Randal Reid; *Prof* William Meek; *Assoc Prof* Jeff Davis; *Assoc Prof* Jeff Dell; *Assoc Prof* James Housefield; *Assoc Prof* Holly Shields; *Assoc Prof* Tom Beono; *Asst Prof* Erica Dugaune; *Asst Prof* Teri Evans Palmer; *Asst Prof* Michelle Hays; *Asst Prof* Alan Pizer
Estab 1903, dept estab 1916; Maintains a nonprofit art gallery; pub; D & E; Scholarships; SC 31, LC 7, GC 6; D 1600, E 150, non-maj 1350, maj 1100
Ent Req: HS dipl, ACT, SAT
Degrees: BFA (Commun Design & Studio), BFA Art Ed all-level & BA(Art History), BA 4 yr, MFA Commun Design
Courses: Advertising Design, Art Appreciation, Art Education, Art History, Communication Design, Computer Graphics, Design, Digital Images, Drawing, Fibers, Graphic Arts, Graphic Design, Illustration, Metals, Multi-Media, Painting, Photography, Printmaking, Sculpture, Teacher Training, Watercolor
Children's Classes: summers only; one week; $15
Summer School: Chmn, Erik Nielson. Two 6 week terms

SEGUIN

TEXAS LUTHERAN UNIVERSITY, Dept of Visual Arts, 1000 W Court St, Seguin, TX 78155-9996. Tel 830-372-8000, Ext 6017; Web: www.tlu.edu; *Chmn* J Nellermoe, MA; *Assoc Prof* T Paul Hernandez; *Asst Prof* Landa King
Estab 1923; FT 2; D; SC 18, LC 3; 1000, maj 10
Ent Req: HS dipl
Degrees: BA(Art) 4 yrs
Courses: Advertising Design, Art Appreciation, Art Concepts, Art Education, Art History, Ceramics, Design, Drawing, Independent Study, Painting, Printmaking, Sculpture
Adult Hobby Classes: Enrl 12; tuition $72 for 6 wk term. Courses—Art Appreciation, Sketching
Summer School: Instr, John Nellermoe. Enrl 12; tuition $75 for 6 wk term. Courses—Ceramics, Painting

SHERMAN

AUSTIN COLLEGE, Art Dept, 900 N Grande, Ste 61587, Sherman, TX 75090-4440. Tel 903-813-2000; Email mmonroe@austinc.edu; Web: www.austinc.edu/; *Prof* Mark Smith; *Chmn* Tim Tracz; *Prof* Mark Monroe, MFA; *Prof* Jeffrey Fontana; *Studio Mgr* Joseph Allison
Estab 1848; Maintains a nonprofit art gallery, Ida Green Gallery, Austin College, 900 N Grand Ave Sherman, TX 75090-4440; pvt; D; Scholarships; SC 9, LC 5, GC 8; D 350, maj 55, grad 2
Ent Req: ent exam plus acceptance by admis comt
Degrees: BA 4 yrs, MA 5 yrs
Courses: Art History, Ceramics, Drawing, History of Art & Architecture, Painting, Photography, Printmaking, Sculpture, Silversmithing, Theatre Arts, Video

TEMPLE

TEMPLE COLLEGE, Art Dept, 2600 S First St, Temple, TX 76504. Tel 254-298-8282; Web: www.templejc.edu; *Chmn* Michael Donahue, MFA
Estab 1926; 43; pub; D & E; Scholarships; SC 4, LC 2; D 100, E 15, non-maj 85, maj 15
Ent Req: HS dipl, ACT or SAT
Degrees: AA 2 yrs
Courses: Art Appreciation, Art History, Ceramics, Communications, Design, Drawing, Figure Drawing, Painting, Printmaking, Sculpture
Adult Hobby Classes: Enrl 15 per class; tuition $19 per 8 sessions. Courses—Arts & Crafts, Calligraphy, Drawing

TEXARKANA

TEXARKANA COLLEGE, Art Dept, 2500 N Robison Rd, Texarkana, TX 75599-0001. Tel 903-838-4541; Fax 903-832-5030; *Prof* Valerie Owens
Estab 1927; D & E; Scholarships
Ent Req: HS dipl
Tuition: District res—$375 for 15 cr hrs; out of district res—$570 for 15 cr hrs
Courses: Art Appreciation, Ceramics, Drawing, Painting, Sculpture, Weaving
Summer School: Enrl 20; tuition $300. Courses—Drawing & Ceramics

TYLER

TYLER JUNIOR COLLEGE, Art Program, PO Box 9020, Tyler, TX 75711-9020. Tel 903-510-2200, 510-2233; Email dwhi@tjc.edu; Web: www.tyler.cc.tx.us, www.tjc.edu; *Prof & Art Dept Chair* Derrick White; *Prof* Paul Jones; *Prof* Philana Pace; *Prof* Chance Dunlap
Estab 1925; Maintains nonprofit Wise Auditorium Art Gallery; art supplies available on-campus; Pub; D & E; Scholarships; SC 13, LC 3; 600+
Degrees: AA
Tuition: Res—undergrad $578 per yr
Courses: Art Appreciation, Art Education, Art History, Ceramics, Design, Drawing, Painting, Sculpture, Weaving
Adult Hobby Classes: Courses—Offered
Children's Classes: Courses—Offered for ages 5-8 & 9-12
Summer School: Courses—Offered

UNIVERSITY OF TEXAS AT TYLER, Department of Art, School of Visual & Performing Arts, 3900 University Blvd, Tyler, TX 75799-0001. Tel 903-566-7250; Fax 903-566-7062; Web: uttgler.edu/arts/studioarts; *Assoc Prof & Chmn* Gary C Hatcher, MFA; *Prof* James R Pace, MFA; *Asst Prof* Jill Blondin, PhD; *Asst Prof* Alexis Serio; *Asst Prof* Dewane Hughes; *Asst Prof* Dr Barbara Airulla; *Asst Prof* Sally Campbell
Estab 1973; Maintain nonprofit art gallery, The Meadowlands Gallery, 3900 University Blvd, Tyler, TX 75799; pub; D & E; Scholarships; SC 32, LC 18, GC 12
Ent Req: AA degree or 60 hrs of college study
Degrees: BA, BFA, MAT, MAIS, MFA
Tuition: Res—$432 per sem; nonres—$2988 per sem
Courses: Aesthetics, †Art Education, †Art History, Ceramics, Drawing, Graphic Arts, Graphic Design, History of Art & Architecture, Interior Design, Mixed Media, Painting, Photography, Printmaking, Sculpture, †Silversmithing, †Studio Art, Teacher Training
Summer School: Dir, Gary C. Hatcher, Courses—vary

VICTORIA

VICTORIA COLLEGE, Fine Arts Dept, 2200 E Red River, Victoria, TX 77901. Tel 361-573-3291; Fax 361-572-3850; Web: www.vc.cc.tx.us/; *Prof* Fred Spaulding; *Head Dept* Dr Marylynn Fletcher
Estab 1925; pub; D & E; SC 9, LC 3; D 100, E 40, non-maj 40, maj 100
Ent Req: HS dipl
Degrees: AA
Courses: Art Appreciation, Art Education, Art Fundamentals, Art History, Ceramics, Design, Drafting, Drawing, Graphic Arts, Graphic Design, †Occupational Therapy, Painting, Sculpture, Stage Design, †Teacher Training, Theatre Arts
Summer School: Courses—as above

WACO

BAYLOR UNIVERSITY - COLLEGE OF ARTS AND SCIENCES, Dept of Art, Waco, TX 76798-7263; 1 Bear Pl, #97344 Waco, TX 76798-7344. Tel 254-710-1867; Fax 254-710-1566; Email Arts_Sciences_Webmaster@baylor.edu; Web: www.baylor.edu; *Chmn* Mark W Anderson, MFA; *Prof & Artist in Res* Karl Umlauf, MFA; *Prof* Berry J Klingman, MFA; *Prof* Terry M Roller, MFA; *Prof & Ceramic in Res* Paul A McCoy, MFA; *Prof* Heidi J Hornik, PhD, MA; *Assoc Prof* Robbie Barber, MFA; *Prof* Mary Ruth Smith, PhD, MFA; *Assoc Prof* Julia Hitchcock, MFA; *Sr Lectr* Karen Pope, PhD; *Asst Prof* Virginia Green, MFA; *Asst Prof* Susan Mullally, MFA; *Lectr* Leah Force, MFA; *Asst Prof* Mack Gingles; *Asst Prof* Nathan Elkins; *Asst Prof* Benny Fountain
Estab 1845, dept estab 1870; Maintains non-profit art gallery: Martin Mus, 1401 S Univ Parks Dr, Waco TX 78706, Karin Gilliam, Dir; maintains Crouch Fine Arts Libr; on-campus art supplies shop; den; D & E; Scholarships; SC 65, LC 24, GC 12; D 1600, E60, non-maj 1300, maj 200
Ent Req: HS dipl, ent exam, SAT/ACT tests
Degrees: BA & BFA(Studio) 4 yrs
Courses: 2-D Design, 3-D Design, †Art History, †Ceramics, Drawing, †Fibers, †Graphic Design, †Painting, †Photography, †Printmaking, †Sculpture
Summer School: Prof, Mark W Anderson

MCLENNAN COMMUNITY COLLEGE, Visual Arts Dept, 1400 College Dr, Waco, TX 76708-1499. Tel 254-299-8000, 299-8791 (art dept); Fax 254-299-8778; Email amurad@mclennan.edu; Web: www.mclennan.edu; *Dir* Donald C Blamos; *Coordr* Andrew Murad
Estab 1965; Maintain nonprofit art gallery; 3 located on campus; Pub; D & E; SC 8, LC 3; D 35, non-maj 20, maj 40
Ent Req: HS dipl
Degrees: AA 2 yrs
Tuition: Res—$34 per sem hr; nonres—$39 per sem hr, out-of-state & international $94; no campus res
Courses: Art Appreciation, Art History, Ceramics, Design, Design Communication, Drafting, Oil Painting, Painting, Photography, Problems in Contemporary Art, Sculpture, Watercolor
Adult Hobby Classes: Tuition depends on the class. Courses—Ceramics, Drawing, Jewelry, Painting, Sculpture, Stained Glass
Summer School: Dir, Andrew Murad. Tuition $55. Courses—Design, Drawing, Watercolor, Art Appreciation

WEATHERFORD

WEATHERFORD COLLEGE, Dept of Speech Fine Arts, 225 College Park Dr, Weatherford, TX 76086-5699. Tel 817-594-5471, Ext 211; Email endy@wc.edu; Web: www.wc.edu/; *Head Visual Arts & Instr* Myrlan Coleman; *Head Speech & Fine Arts* Cal Lewiston; *Instr* Daniel Birdsong; *Instr* Cassie Hannah
Estab 1856, dept estab 1959; Maintains nonprofit art gallery on campus; pub; D & E; Scholarships; SC 12, LC 4; D 58, non-maj 30, maj 16, others 12
Ent Req: HS dipl
Degrees: AA
Courses: Art Appreciation, Art History, Design, Drawing, Intermedia, Mixed Media, Painting, Photography
Summer School: Dir Cal Lewiston.

WHARTON

WHARTON COUNTY JUNIOR COLLEGE, Art Dept, 911 Boling Hwy, Wharton, TX 77488. Tel 979-532-4560; Web: www.wcjc.cc.tx.us
Maintain nonprofit art gallery; pub; D & E; Scholarships; SC 8, LC 2; D 140, E 100
Ent Req: HS dipl, GED
Degrees: 2 yrs
Courses: Art Education, Art Fundamentals, Art History, Calligraphy, Ceramics, Design, Drawing, History of Art & Architecture, Painting, Sculpture, Teacher Training
Summer School: Dir Jess Coleman. Enrl 36; 6 wk term. Courses—Foundation of Art, Drawing

WICHITA FALLS

MIDWESTERN STATE UNIVERSITY, Lamar D. Fain College of Fine Arts, 3410 Taft Blvd, Dept of Art Wichita Falls, TX 76308-2036. Tel 940-397-4264; Fax 940-397-4369; Email art@mwsu.edu; Web: finearts.mwsu.edu/art/; *Chair* Nancy Steele-Hamme; *Dean College of Fine Arts* Dr Ron Fischli
Estab 1926; Maintain a nonprofit art gallery, Midwestern State Univ Art Gallery, 3140 Taft Blvd, Wichita Falls, TX 76308; Pub; D & E; Scholarships
Ent Req: HS dipl, ACT, SAT
Degrees: BA, BFA & BFA with Teacher Cert 4 yrs
Tuition: refer to website
Courses: Art Appreciation, Art Education, Art History, †Ceramics, †Commercial Art, Design, Drawing, †Metals, †Painting, †Photography, †Printmaking, †Sculpture, †Teacher Training
Summer School: Dir, Dr. Nancy Steele-Hamme. Courses—Commercial Art

UTAH

CEDAR CITY

SOUTHERN UTAH STATE UNIVERSITY, Dept of Art, 351 W Center, Cedar City, UT 84720. Tel 435-586-7962, 586-5426; Email felstead@suu.edu; Web: www.suu.edu; *Chmn* Brian P Hoover
Estab 1897; FT 4, PT 2; pub; D & E; Scholarships; SC 29, LC 6; D 300, E 80, maj 60, minors 45
Ent Req: HS dipl ent exam
Degrees: BA and BS 4 yrs
Courses: Ceramics, Commercial Art, Drawing, Graphic Arts, Graphic Design, History of Art & Architecture, Illustration, Painting, Sculpture, Teacher Training
Summer School: Dir, Arlene Braithwaite. Tuition same as regular school. Courses—Drawing, Ceramics, Art Methods for Elementary School, Art Appreciation

EPHRAIM

SNOW COLLEGE, Art Dept, 150 E College Ave, Ephraim, UT 84627. Tel 435-283-7039, 283,7414; Web: www.snow.edu; *Chmn* Carl Purcell
Estab 1888; Pub; D&E; Scholarships
Ent Req: HS dipl
Degrees: AA, AAS
Tuition: Res—$707 per yr; nonres— $2942 per yr
Courses: Art Appreciation, Ceramics, Design, Drawing, Interior Design, Jewelry, Painting, Photography, Printmaking, Sculpture

LOGAN

UTAH STATE UNIVERSITY, Dept of Landscape Architecture Environmental Planning, College of Humanities, Arts & Social Science, Logan, UT 84322-4005. Tel 435-797-0500; Fax 435-797-0503; Email cjohnson@hass.usu.edu; Web: www.usu.edu/~laep/; *Acting Head* Craig Johnson
FT 6, PT 3
Degrees: BA, BLA & MLA 4 yr
Tuition: Res—$309 per cr hr; nonres—$736 per cr hr
Courses: †Landscape Architecture, †Town & Regional Planning
—Dept of Art, UMC 4000, Logan, UT 84322. Tel 435-797-3460 3; Fax 435-797-3412; *Prof* Glen Edwards; *Prof* Craig Law; *Prof* Jon Anderson; *Prof*

Adrian Van Suchtelen; *Assoc Prof* Thomas Toone; *Assoc Prof* John Neely; *Assoc Prof* Marion Hyde; *Assoc Prof* Christopher Terry; *Assoc Prof* Sara Northerner; *Assoc Prof* Greg Schulte; *Assoc Prof* Janet Shapero; *Asst Prof* Jane Catlin; *Asst Prof* Lauren Schiller; *Asst Prof* Alan Hashimoto; *Asst Prof* Julie Johnson; *Asst Prof* Koichi Yamamoto
Estab 1890; D & E; D 500, maj 500, grad 37
Ent Req: HS dipl, HS transcript, ACT
Degrees: BA, BS & BFA 4 yr, MA 2 yr, MFA 3 yr
Tuition: Res—undergrad $1060, grad $935; nonres—undergrad $3182, grad $2751
Courses: †Art Education, †Art History, †Ceramics, †Drawing, †Graphic Arts, †Illustration, †Painting, †Photography, †Printmaking, †Sculpture
Summer School: Head, Prof Craig Shaw. 4 wk session. Courses—Basic Drawing, Ceramics, Exploring Art, Individual Projects, Photography, 3-D Design, 2-D Design, Various Summer Workshops

OGDEN

WEBER STATE UNIVERSITY, Dept of Visual Arts, 2001 University Circle, Ogden, UT 84408-2001. Tel 801-626-6762, 6000; Fax 801-626-6976; Web: www.weber.edu/; *Chair & Assoc Prof* Matthew Choberka, MFA; *Prof* Mark Biddle, MFA; *Prof* Susan Makov, MFA; *Assoc Prof* Angelika Pagel, PhD, MFA; *Asst Prof* Naseem Banerji, PhD, MFA; *Asst Prof* Stephen Wolochowicz, MFA; *Asst Prof* Liese Zahabl, MFA; *Asst Prof* Jason Manley, MFA; *Prof* Kathleen Stevenson, MFA; *Asst Prof* Larry Clarkson, MFA; *Asst Prof* Joshua Winegar, MFA; *Asst Prof* Paul Crow, MFA
Estab 1933, dept estab 1937; Maintains non-profit art gallery, Mary Elizabeth Dee Shaw Gallery, 2001 University Cr, Katie Lee, Dir; on-campus art supplies shop; pub; D & E; Scholarships; SC 66, LC 17; D 2464, E 694, non-maj 700, maj 200
Ent Req: HS dipl, ACT
Degrees: BA, BFA, 4 yr
Courses: †2-D, †3-D, Advertising Design, Art Appreciation, Art Education, Art History, Ceramics, Commercial Art, Conceptual Art, Design, Drawing, Graphic Arts, History of Art & Architecture, Illustration, Painting, Photography, Printmaking, †Sculpture, Silversmithing, Textile Design, Video, Weaving

PROVO

BRIGHAM YOUNG UNIVERSITY, Dept of Visual Arts, 1 BYU, Provo, UT 84602-0002. Tel 801-422-4266; Fax 801-422-0695; Email aliesha_cook@byu.edu; Web: cfac.byu.edu/va/; *Chmn* John Telford; *Assoc Chmn* Gary Barton
Estab 1875, dept estab 1893; Gallery 303, F-303 HFAC, Provo, UT 84602; FT 33, PT 50; den; D & E; Scholarships; SC 50, LC 40, Grad 15; E 1975, maj 908, pre-maj 335, grad 45
Ent Req: HS dipl or ACT
Degrees: BA and BFA 4 yrs, MFA 2 yrs and MA 1 1/2 yrs
Courses: †Art Education, †Art History, Calligraphy, †Ceramics, †Drawing, Graphic Design, Illustration, †Painting, Photography, †Printmaking, †Sculpture, †Teacher Training
Summer School: Courses same as regular session

SAINT GEORGE

DIXIE COLLEGE, Art Dept, 225 S 700 E, Saint George, UT 84770-3875. Tel 435-652-7700, 652-7792; Email hanson@dixie.edu; Web: www.dixie.edu; *Prof* Glen Blakely; *Asst Prof* Del Parson; *Chmn* Brent Hanson; *Asst Prof* Dennis Martinez
Estab 1911; pub; D & E; Scholarships; SC 24, LC 7, GC 1; D 400, maj 30
Ent Req: HS dipl, ACT
Degrees: AA and AS 2 yrs
Courses: 3-D Design, Advertising Design, Art Education, Art History, Ceramics, Commercial Art, Costume Design & Construction, Drafting, Drawing, Film, Illustration, Interior Design, Life Drawing, Painting, Photography, Portrait Drawing, Printmaking, Sculpture, Teacher Training, Textile Design, Theatre Arts, Video, Weaving
Adult Hobby Classes: Weaving
Children's Classes: 10 wk session
Summer School: Varies

SALT LAKE CITY

SALT LAKE COMMUNITY COLLEGE, Graphic Design Dept, 4600 S Redwood Rd, Salt Lake City, UT 84123-3145; PO Box 30808, Salt Lake City, UT 84130-0808. Tel 801-957-4630, 957-4072; Web: www.slcc.edu; *Div & Dept Chair* Steve Mansfield, BA; *Dean* Elwood Zaugg; *Prof* Rob Adamson; *Prof* Rodayne Esmaye; *Prof* Neal Reiland; *Prof* Fred VanDyke, BA; *Prof* Sheila Chambers, BA; *Instr* Richard Graham, BA; *Instr* Terry Martin, BA; *Instr* Lana Gruendell, BA
FT 3, PT 3; Pub; D & E; Scholarships; SC 44, LC 7; D 123, E 10, non-maj 81, maj 42
Ent Req: HS dipl or equivalent, aptitude test
Degrees: Dipl, AAS(Design), AAS(Animation), AAS(Illustration), AAS (Photography), AAS (Multimedia)
Courses: Advertising Design, Art Principles, Computer Graphics, Drawing, †Graphic Design, Illustration, †Lettering, Photography
Summer School: Dean, James Schnirel. Enrl 30; tuition $145 for term of 10 wks beginning June. Courses—Aesthetics, Drawing, Lettering, Media & Techniques

UNIVERSITY OF UTAH, Dept of Art & Art History, 375 South 1530 East, Rm 161, Salt Lake City, UT 84112-0380. Tel 801-581-7200 (Main), 581-8677 (Dept); Fax 801-585-6171; Email info@art.utah.edu; Web: www.art.utah.edu; *Dean* Raymond Tymas-Jones; *Prof* Joseph Marotta, MFA; *Asst Prof Lectr* Laurel Caryn, MFA; *Prof* Sheila Muller, PhD; *Prof* David Pendell, MFA; *Prof* Raymond Morales, BA; *Prof* Roger D (Sam) Wilson, MA; *Chair & Assoc Prof* Elizabeth Peterson, PhD; *Assoc Prof* Kaiti Slater, MFA; *Assoc Prof* Justin Diggle, MFA; *Asst Prof Lectr* Dave Eddy, MFA; *Asst Prof* Paul Stout, MFA; *Asst Prof Lectr* John Erickson, MFA; *Asst Prof* Beth Krensky, PhD; *Asst Prof* Edward Bateman; *Assoc Prof* Kim Martinez, MFA; *Asst Prof* John O'Connell, MFA; *Asst Prof Lectr* Maureen O'Hara Ure, MFA; *Asst Prof* Paul Paret, PhD; *Assoc Prof* Brian Snapp, MFA; *Assoc Prof* Carol Sogard, MFA; *Instr* Sandy Brunvand, MFA; *Instr* Elizabeth DeWitte, MFA; *Instr* Tom Hoffman; *Instr* Kristina Lenzi; *Instr* Maryann Webster; *Asst Prof* Lela Graybill, PhD; *Asst Prof* Alison Denyer, MFA; *Instr* Diana Gardiner; *Asst Prof* Elena Shtromberg; *Instr* Nolan Baumgartner, MFA; *Instr* Michael Dooley, MA; *Instr* Martin Novak, MFA
Estab 1850, dept estab 1888; Maintain nonprofit art gallery, Alvin Gittens Gallery, 375 S, 1530 E, Rm. 161, Salt Lake City, UT 84112-0380; on-campus shop sells art supplies; pub; D & E; Scholarships; SC 148, LC 47, GC 38/semester; D 1736, E 403, non-maj 1043, maj 1428, grad 51
Ent Req: HS dipl
Degrees: degrees BA (Art History) & BFA 4 yrs (Art), MA (Art History) and MFA (Art) 2 yrs
Courses: Art Appreciation, †Art Education, †Art History, †Ceramics, †Drawing, †Graphic Design, Illustration, Lettering, †Mixed Media, †Painting/Drawing, †Photography/Digital Imaging, †Printmaking, †Sculpture/Intermedia, Silversmithing, Teacher Training, †Transmedia, Video

WESTMINSTER COLLEGE OF SALT LAKE CITY, Dept of Arts, 1840 S 1300 E, Salt Lake City, UT 84105-3697. Tel 801-484-7651; Fax 801-484-5579; Web: www.wcslc.edu; *Chmn Fine Arts Prog* Craig Glidden
Estab 1875; FT 2, PT 5; pvt; D; Scholarships; SC 25, LC 2; D 900-1000, maj 25
Ent Req: HS dipl, ent exam acceptable, HS grade point average
Degrees: BA & BS 4 yrs
Courses: Art Education, Art History, Ceramics, Drawing, Painting, Photography, Sculpture, Teacher Training, Weaving

VERMONT

BENNINGTON

BENNINGTON COLLEGE, Visual Arts Division, 1 College Dr, Bennington, VT 05201-6003. Tel 802-442-5401; Fax 802-440-4350; Email feedback@bennington.edu; Web: www.bennington.edu/Home.aspx; *Pres* Elizabeth Coleman; *Dean Admissions & Fin Aid* Ken Himmelman; *Dir Admissions* Lauren Magrath
Estab 1932; FT E 70; pvt; Scholarships
Degrees: AB 4 yrs & MA 2 yrs
Tuition: $28,150 per yr; campus res
Courses: 3-D Modeling, Animation Lithography, Architecture, Art History, CAD, Ceramics, Cultural Studies, Drawing, Etching Studio, Graphics, Painting, Photography, Printmaking, Sculpture, Visual Arts

BURLINGTON

UNIVERSITY OF VERMONT, Dept of Art, 304 Williams Hall, Burlington, VT 05405-0001. Tel 802-656-2014; Fax 802-656-8429; Web: www.uvm.edu; *Chmn* William E Mierse
24; Pub; D & E; D 25
Degrees: BA 4 yrs
Courses: Art Education, Art History, Ceramics, Clay Silkscreen, Computer Art, Design, Design, Drawing, Fine Metals, Lithography, Painting, Photography, Printmaking, Sculpture, Teacher Training, Video, Visual Art
Adult Hobby Classes: College of Continuing Education
Summer School: Dir, Lynne Ballard. Two 9 wk sessions beginning in May

CASTLETON

CASTLETON STATE COLLEGE, Art Dept, 45 Alumni Dr, Fine Arts Ctr Castleton, VT 05735-4454. Tel 802-468-5611; Fax 802-468-5237; Email information@castleton.edu; Web: www.csc.vsc.edu; *Head Dept* Jonathon Scott; *Prof* William Ramage; *Coordr* Mariko Hancock
Estab 1787; Pub; D & E; Scholarships; SC 31, LC 3, GC varies; D 1900, E 1000, non-maj 300, maj 52, grad 5
Ent Req: HS dipl, ACT, SAT, CEEB
Degrees: BA(Art) & BA Art(2nd major Education) 4 yrs
Courses: Advertising Design, Art History, Calligraphy, Computer Graphics, Drawing, Education, Graphic Design, Lettering, Painting, Photography, Printmaking, Professional Studio Arts, Sculpture, Typography, Video
Summer School: Enrl 24. Courses—Introduction to Art History, Introduction to Studio Art

COLCHESTER

ST MICHAEL'S COLLEGE, Fine Arts Dept, One Winooski Park, Box 364 Colchester, VT 05439. Tel 802-654-2000; Web: www.smcvt.edu; *Assoc Prof* Will Mentor, BFA; *Asst Prof* Brian Collier, MFA
Estab 1903, dept estab 1965; den; D & E; SC 8, LC 3
Ent Req: HS dipl
Degrees: BA 4 yrs
Tuition: Res—undergrad $18,615 per yr, campus res—available
Courses: Art Education, Art History, Art Theory, Calligraphy, Costume Design & Construction, Drawing, Graphic Arts, History of Art & Architecture, Painting, Photography, Printmaking, Sculpture, Stage Design, Teacher Training, Theatre Arts
Summer School: Dir, Dr Art Hessler. Session 1, 5 wks beginning mid May, session 2, 6 wks beginning last wk in June. Courses—Calligraphy, Drawing, Painting

JOHNSON

JOHNSON STATE COLLEGE, Dept Fine & Performing Arts, Dibden Center for the Arts, 337 College Hill, Johnson, VT 05656. Tel 802-635-1310; Fax 802-635-1248; Email parizom@badger.jsc.vsc.edu; Web: www.jsc.vsc.edu; *Gallery Dir* Suzanne Ritger; *Photog Dept Head* John M Miller; *Assoc Prof* Lisa Jablow; *Prof Sculpture* Susan Calza; *Dept Painting* Ken Leslie; *Asst Prof Art History* Mary Martin; *Asst Prof Music-Jazz* Steve Blair
Estab 1828; Maintain nonprofit art gallery; Julian Scott Memorial Gallery, Johnson State Col, Johnson VT 05656; art library; art supplies available at Vt Studio Ctr; pub; D & E; Scholarships; SC 30, LC 10, GC 20; D 325, non-maj 200, maj 140
Ent Req: HS dipl
Degrees: BA & BFA 4 yrs, MFA 3 yrs
Tuition: Res—undergrad $177 per cr; nonres—undergrad $400 per cr; campus res—room & board $5,000 per yr
Courses: Art Education, Art History, Ceramics, Design, Drawing, Painting, Photography, Printmaking, Sculpture, Studio Art
Children's Classes: Gifted & talented prog for high school students
Summer School: Dir, Mary Pariyo. Courses—Mixed Media, Painting, Sculpture

MIDDLEBURY

MIDDLEBURY COLLEGE, History of Art & Architecture Dept, 78 Chateau Rd, Johnson Memorial Bldg Middlebury, VT 05753-6133. Tel 802-443-5234; Fax 802-443-2250; Email midd@middlebury.edu; Web: www.middlebury.edu; *Chmn* Peter Broucke; *Coordr* Mary Lousplain; *Prof* John Hunisak; *Prof* Kristen Hovins; *Prof* Glenn Andres; *Vis Asst Prof* Katherine Smith-Abbott; *Prof* Cynthia Atheron; *Vis Asst Prof* Parker Croft; *Robert P Youngman Cur Asian Art* Colin Mackenzie; *Dir College Museum* Richard Saunders
Estab 1800; pvt; D; SC 7, LC 30; maj 77, others 500 per term
Ent Req: exam and cert
Degrees: BA
Courses: Art History, Design, Drawing, Painting, Photography, Printmaking, Sculpture

NORTHFIELD

NORWICH UNIVERSITY, Dept of Architecture and Art, 158 Harmon Dr, Northfield, VT 05663-1000. Tel 802-485-2000; Fax 802-485-2580; Email ddoz@norwich.edu; Web: www.norwich.edu/acad; *Div Head & Assoc Prof* Michael Hoffman, MFA; *Prof* Earl Fechter, MFA; *Asst Prof* Arthur Schaller; *Asst Prof* Kirsten van Aalst; *Prof* Robert Schmidd, MFA; *Assoc Prof* David Woolf, MFA; *Prof* Arnold Aho, MFA; *Architectural History* Dr Lisa Shrenk
Maintains Kreitzberg Library; art supplies can be purchased at on-campus shop; Pvt; D; SC, LC; D 65 (studio art), E 8, non-maj 126
Ent Req: HS dipl
Degrees: BA
Tuition: Campus residency available
Courses: Architecture, Art History, Design, Drawing, Painting, Photography, Printmaking

PLAINFIELD

GODDARD COLLEGE, Dept of Art, 123 Pitkin Rd Plainfield, VT 05667. Tel 802-454-8311; Web: www.goddard.edu; *Instr* Cynthia Ross; *Instr* David Hale; *Head* Jon Batdorff
Estab 1938; pvt; D & E
Degrees: BA 4 yr, MA 1-2 yr
Tuition: Res—undergrad $16,528 (comprehensive) per sem, $8,920 (tuition only) per sem; nonres—undergrad $9,163 per sem, grad $5,105 per sem; campus res available
Courses: Art Education, Art History, Ceramics, Drawing, Holography, Painting, Photography, Printmaking, Sculpture, Video, Weaving

POULTNEY

GREEN MOUNTAIN COLLEGE, Dept of Art, 1 College Circle Poultney, VT 05764. Tel 802-287-8000; Fax 802-287-8099; *Chmn* Susan Smith-Hunter; *Prof* Dick Weis; *Prof* Richard Weinstein
Estab 1834; maj 60
Ent Req: scholarships
Degrees: BFA 4 yrs
Tuition: Res and non-res $17000 per sem
Courses: Art History, Ceramics, Design, Drawing, Fine Art Studio, Graphic Design, Graphic Design Studio, Illustration, Painting, Photography, Printmaking, Sculpture

VIRGINIA

ANNANDALE

NORTHERN VIRGINIA COMMUNITY COLLEGE, Art Dept, 8333 Little River Tpke, Annandale, VA 22003-3796. Tel 703-323-3107; Fax 703-323-4248; Web: www.nv.cc.va.us; *Chmn* Duncan Tebow; *Admin & Prog Specialist* Nancy Minogue; *Prof* Elizabeth Tebon; *Asst Prof* Theresa McFadden; *Asst Prof* Giogio Porta
Estab 1960s; Maintains nonprofit Verizon Gallery, in Campus Community Ctr; Pub; D, E & weekends; Scholarships; SC; D 650, E 200
Ent Req: open admis
Degrees: degrees AA(Art Educ), AA(Art History) AAS(Commercial Art), AA(Fine Arts) & AA(Photography) 2 yrs, AAA(Fine Art)
Courses: Art History, Ceramics, Computer Graphics, Design, Drawing, †Fine Arts, Painting, Sculpture
Summer School: Chmn Humanities Div, Dr Duncan Tebow. Tuition same as regular session; 2 five wk D sessions and 1 ten wk E session during Summer. Courses—varied, incl study abroad

ARLINGTON

MARYMOUNT UNIVERSITY, School of Arts & Sciences Div, 2807 N Glebe Rd, Arlington, VA 22207-4299. Tel 703-522-5600; Fax 703-284-3859; Web: www.marymount.edu; *Prof* Christine Haggerty, MFA; *Prof* Judy Bass, MFA; *Assoc Prof* Bridget Murphy; *Assoc Prof* Mark Trubridge
Estab 1950; Maintain nonprofit art gallery; Barry Gallery; art supplies sold at on-campus shop; pvt; D & E; SC 20, LC 12
Ent Req: HS dipl, SAT results, letter of recommendation
Degrees: BA 4 yrs
Tuition: Res—undergrad $11,580 per sem, grad $750 per cr hr; campus res available
Courses: Advertising Design, †Art Education, Art History, Art of the Book, Clothing Design & Construction, Design, Drawing, Fashion Arts, Figure Drawing, †Graphic Design, Interior Design, Jewelry Design, Painting, Performance Media, Photography, Printmaking, Sculpture, †Studio Arts, Textile Design, Video
Adult Hobby Classes: Courses—any course in fine arts
Summer School: See website

ASHLAND

RANDOLPH-MACON COLLEGE, Dept of the Arts, 204 Henry St, Ashland, VA 23005-1634. Tel 804-798-8375, 798-8372; Fax 804-752-7231; Web: www.rmc.edu; *Prof* R D Ward; *Assoc Prof* Joe Mattys; *Lectr* Evie Terrono; *Chmn* E Raymond Berry; *Instr Music* James Doering; *Dir Coral Act* Dave Greennagle
Estab 1830, dept estab 1953; FT 5, PT 2; pvt; D; SC 4, LC 4; D 200, non-maj 200
Degrees: BA & BS 4 yrs
Tuition: Res—undergrad $9905 per yr; campus res available
Courses: †Art History, †Art Management, †Drama, Drawing, †Music, Painting, †Studio Art

BLACKSBURG

VIRGINIA POLYTECHNIC INSTITUTE & STATE UNIVERSITY, Dept of Art & Art History, 201 Draper Rd, Blacksburg, VA 24061-0001. Tel 540-231-5547; Fax 540-231-5761; Email dmyers@vt.edu; Web: www.art.vt.edu; *Prof Emerita* Jane Aiken PhD; *Prof* Steve Bickley, MFA; *Prof* Derek Myers, MFA; *Prof* Ann-Marie Knoblauch, PhD; *Prof* Robert Fields, MFA; *Prof* Alison Slein, MFA; *Prof* Gregg Bryson, MFA; *Prof* Robert Graham, MFA; *Prof* Ray Kass, MFA; *Prof* Janet Niewald, MFA; *Head Dept* L Bailey Van Hook PhD; *Prof* David Crane, MFA; *Prof* Truman Capone, MFA; *Prof* Sally Cornelius, PhD
Estab 1969; FT 13; pub; D&E; Scholarships; SC 25, LC 12; Maj 300
Degrees: BA 4 yrs, BFA 5 yrs
Tuition: In state N/A; out of state N/A
Courses: Advertising Design, Art Appreciation, Art History, Ceramics, Commercial Art, Computer Art, Design, Drawing, Graphic Arts, Graphic Design, Illustration, Mixed Media, Painting, Sculpture
Summer School: Dir, Derek Myers. Enrl 150; tuition proportional to acad yr for two 5 wk sessions. Courses—Advertising Design, Art History, Ceramics, Computer Art, Design, Drawing, Graphic Design, Illustration, Painting, Sculpture, Watercolor

BRIDGEWATER

BRIDGEWATER COLLEGE, Art Dept, 402 E College St, Bridgewater, VA 22812-1599. Tel 540-828-5396; Fax 540-828-2160; Web: www.bridgewater.edu; *Dept Head* Nan Covert, MFA
FT 2; Scholarships
Ent Req: HS dipl, sophomore review portfolio
Degrees: BA 4 yr
Tuition: $20,000 per yr undergrad
Courses: Art History, †Computer Graphics, Design, Drawing, Painting, Photography, Printmaking, Sculpture

BRISTOL

VIRGINIA INTERMONT COLLEGE, Fine Arts Div, 1013 Moore St, Bristol, VA 24201-4225. Tel 540-669-6101; Fax 540-669-5763; *Chmn* Dr Jon Mehlferber; *Instr* Tedd Blevins, MFA
Estab 1884; den; D & E; Scholarships; SC 15, LC 4; D 35, non-maj 110
Ent Req: HS dipl, review of work
Degrees: BA(Art) & BA(Art Educ) 4 yrs, AA 2 yrs
Tuition: $17510 per yr (incl board)

BUENA VISTA

SOUTHERN VIRGINIA COLLEGE, Division of Arts and Humanities, One College Hill Dr, Buena Vista, VA 24416. Tel 540-261-8471; Fax 540-261-8451; Email bcrawford@southvirginia.edu; Web: www.southernvirginia.edu; *Head Dept* Barbara Crawford
Estab 1867; pvt; D; SC 10, LC 5; D 185, non-maj 175, maj 2
Ent Req: HS dipl, SAT or ACT
Degrees: AA & BA 2 yrs

Courses: Art Education, Art History, Design, Italian Renaissance, Painting, Photography, Study Abroad, Teacher Training

CHARLOTTESVILLE

UNIVERSITY OF VIRGINIA, McIntire Dept of Art, Fayerweather Hall, Charlottesville, VA 22904; PO Box 400130, Charlottesville, VA 22904-4130. Tel 434-924-6123; Fax 434-924-3647; Email mwd2f@virginia.edu; Web: www.virginia.edu/art/; *Art History Instr* Lawrence Goedde; *Art History Instr* Daniel Ehnbom; *Prof* Paul Barolsky; *Prof* Malcolm Bell; *Prof* John Dobbins; *Assoc Prof & Chair* Francesca Fiorani; *Prof* Maurie McInnis; *Prof* David Summers; *Assoc Prof* Dorothy Wong; *Studio Faculty* William Bennett; *Studio Faculty* Richard Crozier; *Studio Faculty* Dean Dass; *Studio Faculty* Kevin Everson; *Studio Faculty* Philip Geiger; *Studio Faculty* Sanda Iliescu; *Studio Faculty* Megan Marlatt; *Studio Faculty* Akemi Ohira-Rollando; *Studio Faculty* Elizabeth Schoyer; *Studio Faculty* William Wylie; *Assoc Prof Art History* Sarah Betzer; *Assoc Prof Art History* Douglas Fordham; *Assoc Prof* Carmenita Higginbotham; *Lectr Arts Admin* George Sampson; *Asst Prof, Art History* Eric Ramirez-Weaver; *Assoc Prof Art History* Tyler Jo-Smith; *Univ Prof* Elizabeth Turner; *Asst Prof Studio Art* Lydia Moyer; *Asst Prof Studio Art* Pamela Pecchio
Estab 1819, dept estab 1951; Maintain nonprofit art gallery, Fralin Mus of Art, 155 Rugby Rd, PO Box 400119, Charlottesville, Va 22904; Fiske Kimball Fine Arts Library; Has on campus shop where art supplies can be purchased; FT 21; pub; D; Scholarships; SC 38, LC 20, GC 10; D 1600, maj 140, grad 45,
Activities: Schols offered
Ent Req: HS dipl
Degrees: BA(Studio and Art History), MA(Art History & Architectural) and PhD (Art History & Architectural)
Courses: Art History, Computer Graphics, Drawing, †Film, †New Media, Painting, Photography, Printmaking, Sculpture
Summer School: Enrl 15; tuition varies. Courses—Art History, Studio Art

DANVILLE

AVERETT COLLEGE, Art Dept, 420 W Main St, Danville, VA 24541-3692. Tel 804-791-5600, 791-5797; Fax 804-791-5647; *Coordr* Diane Kendrick, MFA; *Prof* Robert Marsh, MFA
Estab 1859, dept estab 1930; pvt; D & E; Scholarships; SC 13, LC 5; D 1000, non-maj 250, maj 25
Ent Req: HS dipl
Degrees: AB
Tuition: $10128 per yr
Courses: Advertising Design, Art Education, Art History, Ceramics, Commercial Art, Drawing, Fashion Arts, History of Art & Architecture, Illustration, Jewelry, Lettering, Painting, Printmaking, Sculpture, Teacher Training, Textile Design
Summer School: Two 4 wk sessions

FAIRFAX

GEORGE MASON UNIVERSITY, College of Humanities & Social Sciences, Dept of History & Art History, 4400 University Dr, MS 3G1, Fairfax, VA 22030-4444. Tel 703-993-1250; Fax 703-993-1251; Web: www.gmu.edu/; *Dir Art History Prog* Dr Michele Greet; *Instr* Dr Robert DeCaroli; *Instr* Dr Larry Butler; *Instr* Dr Angela Ho; *Instr* Dr Nicole DeArmendi; *Asst Prof* Jacquelyn Williamson; *Asst Prof* Lisa Bauman; *Asst Prof* Chris Gregg
Estab 1948, dept estab 1981; Maintains library, New Arts & Social Change Research Center; pub; D & E; SC 16, LC 20, GC 5, Seminars; maj 40, grad 20
Ent Req: HS dipl, SAT or CEEB
Degrees: BA, MA
Courses: Architecture, Art Appreciation, Art History, †History of Art & Architecture
Summer School: Courses—Art Appreciation, Art Education, Studio Arts
—College of Visual & Performing Arts, Fine Arts Gallery, Johnson Ctr Rm 123, Fairfax, VA 22030. Tel 703-993-8888; Email ekravitz@gmu.edu; Web: www.gmu.edu/depts/gallery/; *Dir* Walter Kravitz
Open Mon - Fri 9 AM - 9 PM; Gallery 123

FARMVILLE

LONGWOOD UNIVERSITY, Dept of Art, 201 High St Farmville, VA 23909. Tel 434-395-2284; Fax 434-395-2775; Email mcqueenjg@longwood.edu; Web: www.lwc.edu/; *Assoc Prof* Christopher M Register; *Prof* Randall W Edmonson; *Prof* John SJ Burke; *Asst Prof* Claire B McCoy; *Prof* Mark Baldridge; *Asst Prof* Kelly Nelson; *Asst Prof* Martin Brief; *Asst Prof* Johnson Bowles; *Asst Prof* Anna Cox; *Lectr* John Williams
Estab 1839, dept estab 1932; Maintains nonprofit gallery, Longwood Center for the Visual Arts, Main Street, Farmville, VA 23901; pub; D & E; Scholarships; SC 59, LC 15; non-maj 450 per sem maj 225 per sem
Ent Req: HS dipl
Degrees: BFA (Art Educ, Art History, Studio) 4 yr
Courses: 3-D Design, Art Appreciation, Art Education, Art History, Basic Design, Ceramics, Crafts, Design, Drawing, Fibers, Graphic Design, Illustration, Jewelry, Metalsmithing, Painting, Photography, Printmaking, Sculpture, Stained Glass, Teacher Training, Typography, Wood Design
Summer School: Dir, Randall W Edmonson. Tuition varies for one 3-wk & two 4-wk sessions. Courses—Varied

FREDERICKSBURG

UNIVERSITY OF MARY WASHINGTON, Dept of Art & Art History, 1301 College Ave, Fredericksburg, VA 22401-5300. Tel 540-654-2038; Fax 540-654-1952; Web: www.mwc.edu; Others TTY 540-654-1104; *Chair & Assoc Prof* Jean Ann Dabb; *Prof* Joseph Dreiss; *Prof* Lorene Nickel; *Assoc Prof* Steve Griffin; *Asst Prof* Marjorie Och; *Sr Lectr* Carole Garmon
Estab 1904; pub; D & E; Scholarships; SC 18, LC 20; Maj 100
Ent Req: HS dipl, ent exam
Degrees: BA, BS & BLS 4 yrs
Courses: Art History, Ceramics, Drawing, Painting, Photography, Printmaking, Sculpture, †Studio Art

HAMPDEN SYDNEY

HAMPDEN-SYDNEY COLLEGE, Fine Arts Dept, PO Box 34, Winston Studio Hampden Sydney, VA 23943-0034. Tel 434-223-6205; Email dlewis@hsc.edu; Web: www.hsc.edu/academics/finearts; *Chair* David Lewis

HAMPTON

HAMPTON UNIVERSITY, Dept of Fine & Performing Arts, 1 Hampton University, Armstrong Hall Rm 144 Hampton, VA 23668-0100. Tel 757-727-5416, 727-5402; Web: www.hamptonu.edu/academics; *Chmn* Dr Karen Ward
Estab 1869; pvt; D; Scholarships; SC 22, LC 7, GC 9; maj 80, others 300, grad 7
Ent Req: HS grad
Degrees: BA, BS
Courses: Ceramics, Interior Design, Painting, Photography
Summer School: Dir, Sheila May. Courses—Advanced Workshop in Ceramics, Art Educ Methods, Art Methods for the Elementary School, Basic Design, Ceramics, Commercial Art, Design, Drawing & Composition, Graphics, Metalwork & Jewelry, Painting, Understanding the Arts

HARRISONBURG

EASTERN MENNONITE UNIVERSITY, Visual and Communication Arts, 1200 Park Rd, Harrisonburg, VA 22802-2462. Tel 540-432-4360; Fax 540-432-4444; Email steven.johnson@emu.edu; Web: www.emu.edu/vaca; *Associate Professor of Visual and Communication Arts, Department Chair* Steven Johnson; *Assistant Professor of Visual and Communication Arts* Anna Westfall; *Professor of Visual and Communication Arts* Cyndi D. Gusler; *Professor of Visual and Communication Arts* Jerry L. HOlsopple; *Instructor of Visual and Communication Arts* Zeljko Mirkovic
1917; Maintains a non-profit art gallery: Margaret Marting Gelman Gallery, 1307 Park Rd, Harrisonburg, VA 22802; art/architecture collection contained in main library; Denominational; D & E; Scholarships; Financial aid; Total Univ 1,870; undergrad 1,200
Special Subjects: Graphic Design
Degrees: BA, BS, MA
Tuition: Resident - $44,860 (annual tuition only $34,060)
Courses: Art, †Art Education, Ceramics, Communications, Costume Design & Construction, Digital Media, †Digital Media, Drawing, Film, Graphic Arts, Mixed Media, Painting, †Photography, Photography, Printmaking, Stage Design, †Studio Art, Teacher Training, Theatre Arts, Video

JAMES MADISON UNIVERSITY, School of Art & Art History, 800 S Main St, Harrisonburg, VA 22807-0001. Tel 540-568-6216; Fax 540-568-6598; *Dir* Dr Cole H Welter; *Prof* James Crable, MFA; *Prof* Steve Zapton, MFA; *Prof* Barbara Lewis, MFA; *Prof* Kathleen Arthur, PhD, MFA; *Prof* Gary Chatelain, MFA; *Prof* Jack McCaslin, MFA; *Prof* Masako Miyata, MFA; *Prof* Kenneth Szmagaj, MFA; *Assoc Prof* Sang Yoon, MFA; *Assoc Prof* Trudy Cole-Zielanski, MFA; *Asst Prof* William Tate, MArch; *Asst Prof* Peter Ratner, MFA; *Asst Prof* Corinne Diope, MFA; *Instr* Stuart Downs, MA
Estab 1908; pub; D & E; Scholarships; SC 31, LC 21, GC 22; D & E 1254, maj 184, GS 12
Ent Req: HS dipl, grads must submit portfolio, undergrads selected on portfolio & acad merit
Degrees: BA(Art History), BS & BFA(Studio) 4 yrs, MA(Studio, Art History, Art Educ) 1 1/2 to 2 yrs, MFA 60 cr hrs
Tuition: Res—undergrad $56 per cr; undergrad $252 per cr; room & board available
Courses: Advertising Design, Aesthetics, †Art Education, †Art History, Art Therapy, †Ceramics, Computer Graphics, Drafting, †Drawing, Goldsmithing, †Graphic Design, Interior Design, †Jewelry, Museum Staff Training, Painting, Papermaking, Photography, Printmaking, Sculpture, Silversmithing, Stained Glass, Textile Design, Typography, Weaving
Adult Hobby Classes: Tuition res—$250, nonres—$658 for 1-3 cr hr. Courses—Summer workshop, all beginning courses
Children's Classes: Enrl 260; tuition $40 for 8 sessions

LEXINGTON

WASHINGTON AND LEE UNIVERSITY, Div of Art, 204 W Washington St, Lexington, VA 24450-2116. Tel 540-458-8857, 463-8861 (Art Dept); Fax 540-458-8104; Email psimpson@wlu.edu; *Prof* Pamela H Simpson, PhD, MFA; *Prof* Larry M Stene, MFA; *Assoc Prof* Kathleen Olson-Janjic, MFA; *Assoc Prof* Joan O'Mara, PhD, MFA; *Head* George Bent, PhD, MFA
Estab 1749, dept 1949; pvt; D; Scholarships; SC 14, LC 26; D 1700 (in col) non-maj 200, maj 20
Ent Req: HS dipl, SAT, 3 CEEB, one English CEEB plus essay on skills in English, English composition test; entrance requirements most rigorous in English; required of all, including art majors
Degrees: BA 4 yrs
Courses: Art History, Drawing, Graphic Arts, History of Art & Architecture, Museum Staff Training, Painting, Printmaking, Sculpture, Stage Design, †Study Art Abroad (Italy, Greece), Theatre Arts

LYNCHBURG

LYNCHBURG COLLEGE, Art Dept, 1501 Lakeside Dr, Lynchburg, VA 24501-3113. Tel 804-544-8349; Fax 804-544-8277; Web: www.lynchburg.edu/academic/art; *Prof* Richard Pumphrey, MFA; *Prof* Beverly Rhoads, MFA; *Lectr* Barbara Rothermel, MLA
Estab 1903, dept estab 1948; Maintains nonprofit art gallery, The Davra Gallery, Dillard Fine Arts Building, 1501 Lakeside Dr, Lynchburg, VA 24501; pvt; D & E; SC 26, LC 16, GC 2; D 400, E 50, non-maj 410, maj 45
Ent Req: HS dipl
Degrees: BA & BS 4 yrs
Courses: Art Appreciation, Art History, Ceramics, Design, Drawing, Figure Drawing, Graphic Arts, Graphic Design, Painting, Photography, Sculpture
Summer School: Art Education, Art History & Studio

RANDOLPH-MACON WOMAN'S COLLEGE, Dept of Art, 2500 Rivermont Ave, Lynchburg, VA 24503-1526. Tel 804-947-8486; Fax 804-947-8138; Web: www.rmwc.edu; *Acting Chmn* Kathy Muehlemann
Estab 1891; FT 4; pvt, W; D; Scholarships; SC 18, LC 15; maj 35, others 305
Degrees: BA 4 yrs
Courses: American Art, Art History, Art Survey, Ceramics, Drawing, Painting, Printmaking, Sculpture
Summer School: Dir, Dr John Justice. Enrl 30; 4 wk term. Courses—various

NEWPORT NEWS

CHRISTOPHER NEWPORT UNIVERSITY, Dept of Fine Performing Arts, 1 University Pl, Newport News, VA 23606-2949. Tel 757-594-7089, 594-7000; Fax 757-594-7389; Web: cnu.edu; *Chmn* Lawrence Wood, MA; *Asst Prof* B Anglin, BA; *Prof* David Alexick, MA, PhD; *Prof* Belle Pendleton, MA, PhD; *Assoc Prof* Greg Henry, BFA, MFA
Estab 1974; Maintain nonprofit art gallery; pub; D & E; Scholarships; SC 18, LC 9; D 250, E 60, non-maj 200, maj 100
Ent Req: HS dipl, admis comt approval
Degrees: BA & BS 4 yrs
Courses: †Art, †Art Appreciation, Art Education, Art History, Ceramics, Collage, Costume Design & Construction, Drawing, Graphic Arts, †Music (BM), Painting, Photography, †Printmaking, Sculpture, Stage Design, Theatre Arts
Adult Hobby Classes: 100 variable
Summer School: Dir, Dr Barry Woods. Enrl 25; tuition $300. Courses—Ceramics, Drawing, Painting

NORFOLK

NORFOLK STATE UNIVERSITY, Fine Arts Dept, 700 Park Ave Norfolk, VA 23504. Tel 757-823-8844; Email webmaster@nsu.edu; Web: www.nsu.edu/; *Head Dept* Rod A Taylor PhD
Estab 1935; pub; D & E; SC 50, LC 7; D 355, E 18, non-maj 200, maj 155
Ent Req: HS dipl
Degrees: BA(Art Educ), BA(Fine Arts) and BA(Graphic Design) 4 yrs, MA and MFA in Visual Studies
Courses: Advertising Design, Aesthetics, Art Appreciation, †Art Education, Art History, Calligraphy, Ceramics, Commercial Art, †Costume Design & Construction, Design, Drawing, †Fashion Arts, Graphic Arts, †Graphic Design, †Handicrafts, Illustration, Lettering, Mixed Media, Painting, Photography, Printmaking, Sculpture, †Teacher Training
Adult Hobby Classes: Enrl 30. Courses—Ceramics, Crafts
Children's Classes: Enrl 45; tuition none. Courses—all areas

OLD DOMINION UNIVERSITY, Art Dept, 4600 Monarch Way, Barry Arts Building Room 1000 Norfolk, VA 23529. Tel 757-683-4047, 683-3000; Fax 757-683-5923; Email rrlove@odu.edu; Web: www.odu.edu/artdept; *Dir Gallery* Cullen Strawn; *Visiting Assoc Prof* Nikki Webb; *Assoc Prof & Chief Dept Advisor* Elliott Jones; *Assoc Prof* Richard Nickel; *Assoc Prof* John Roth; *Assoc Prof* Dianne deBeixedon; *Lect Sr* Patricia Edwards; *Assoc Prof & Chair* Peter Eudenbach; *Lect Sr* Agnieszka Whelan; *Assoc Prof* Ivanete Blanco; *Assoc Prof* Greta Pratt; *Asst Prof* Anne Muraoka; *Prof* Kenneth Fitzgerald; *Asst Prof* Ming Hong; *Asst Prof* David Shields; *Asst Prof* Alison Stinely; *Asst Prof* Vittorio Colazzi; *Asst Prof* Jared Benton
Estab 1962; Maintain a nonprofit art gallery, Baron & Ellin Gordon Art Galleries, 4509 Monarch Way, Norfolk, VA 23529; maintain an art library, Elise N. Hofheimer Art Libr, Diehn Fine & Performing Arts Ctr, Rm 109, Norfolk, VA 23529; Pub, Commonwealth of Virginia; D, E; Scholarships; Fellowships; Assistantships; SC, LC, GC; 1,244 day; 296 evening; 500 majors; 3 grad stud
Ent Req: HS, dipl, SAT
Degrees: BA(Art History, Art Education or Studio Art), BFA
Tuition: Res—$325 per cr hr; nonres—$891 per cr hr
Courses: 3D Media, Advertising Design, Aesthetics, Art Appreciation, †Art Education, †Art History, Ceramics, Clay, Crafts, Design, †Drawing, Goldsmithing, Graphic Arts, †Graphic Design, History of Art & Architecture, Illustration, Jewelrymaking, Metals, Mixed Media, Museum Staff Training, †Painting, †Photography, †Printmaking, †Sculpture, Silversmithing, †Studio Art, Teacher Training, Textile Design, Weaving
Children's Classes: Saturday morning art classes, enrollment 50, spring semester
Summer School: Chair, Prof Peter Eudenbach. Enrl 125; tuition res $325 per cr hr; nonres $891 per cr hr

VIRGINIA WESLEYAN COLLEGE, Art Dept of the Humanities Div, 1584 Wesleyan Dr, Norfolk, VA 23502-5599. Tel 757-455-3200; Fax 757-461-5025; *Assoc Prof* Barclay Sheaks; *Assoc Prof* Joyce B Howell, MFA, PhD; *Adjunct Instr* Ken Bowen, MA
Pvt, den; D & E; Scholarships; SC 21, LC 8; E 20
Ent Req: HS dipl, SAT
Degrees: BA(Liberal Arts) 4 yrs
Tuition: $16,500 per yr; campus res available
Courses: Aesthetics, Art Appreciation, Art Education, Art History, Ceramics, Computer Art, Drawing, Fabric Enrichment, Graphic Arts, Graphic Design, Handicrafts, History of Art & Architecture, Jewelry, Mixed Media, Painting, Photography, Printmaking, Sculpture, Silversmithing, Stage Design, Teacher Training, Theatre Arts, Weaving
Adult Hobby Classes: Enrl 20

PETERSBURG

RICHARD BLAND COLLEGE, Art Dept, 11301 Johnson Rd, Petersburg, VA 23805-7100. Tel 804-862-6272, 862-6100; *Pres* James B McNeer; *Chmn* David Majewski
Estab 1960, dept estab 1963; pub; D & E; SC 3, LC 3; D 73
Ent Req: HS dipl, SAT, recommendation of HS counselor
Degrees: AA(Fine Arts) 2 yrs
Tuition: Res—undergrad $1140 per sem; nonres—$3125 per sem
Courses: Art Appreciation, Art History, Basic Design, Drawing, Painting, Sculpture
Adult Hobby Classes: Courses—Interior Design, Yoga

VIRGINIA STATE UNIVERSITY, Department of Art & Design, PO Box 9026, Petersburg, VA 23806-0001. Tel 804-524-5944; Fax 804-524-5472; Email sbernard@vsu.edu; Email tlarose@vsu.edu; Web: www.vsu.edu; *Chmn & Dir* Thomas Larose, PhD; *Asst Prof* Ann Ford; *Asst Prof* Meena Khalili; *Instr* Anh Do
Estab 1882, dept estab 1935; Maintains nonprofit art gallery, Meredith Art Gallery, 216 Harris Hall, Petersburg, VA 23806; on-campus art supplies shop; Pub; D & E; SC 16, LC 6; D 400, E 60, non-maj 302, maj 130
Ent Req: HS dipl
Degrees: BFA (Visual Arts) 4 yrs
Tuition: Res—undergrad $1,614 per sem, res grad—$4,600 room & board; nonres undergrad—$1,996 per sem, nonres grad—$4,967
Courses: Animation, Art Appreciation, Art History, Ceramics, Computer Graphics, Drawing, Graphic Design, Illustration, Internship, Lettering, Painting, Photography, Printmaking, Sculpture, Senior Thesis, Silkscreen, †Studio, Typography
Summer School: Dir, Dr V Thota, Art Appreciation. Courses—Drawing, Art Crafts

PORTSMOUTH

TIDEWATER COMMUNITY COLLEGE, Visual Arts Center, 340 High St, Portsmouth, VA 23704-3795. Tel 757-822-6999; Fax 757-822-6800; Web: www.tcc.edu; *Dir* Ed Gibbs; *Prof* Rob Hawkes; *Prof* Craig Nilson; *Asst Prof* Corinne Lilyard-Mitchell; *Asst Prof* Ed Francis; *Asst Prof* Rhonda Todoroff; *Asst Prof* Tom Siefmund; *Assoc Prof* Rosemary Hill; *Instr* Lisa Finley; *Pub Rels Specialist* Janet Sydenstricker
Estab 1968; pub; D & E; SC 12, LC 3; D 120, E 180, non-maj 190, maj 110
Ent Req: HS dipl
Degrees: AA(Fine Arts), AAS(Graphic Arts) 2 yrs
Courses: †Advertising Design, Art Appreciation, Art History, Ceramics, Computer Graphics, Design, Drawing, Illustration, Lettering, Painting, Photography, Sculpture
Adult Hobby Classes: Offered through Continuing Educ Div
Summer School: Dir Anne Iott. Enrl 15 per course; tuition per course beginning May. Courses—Art History, Ceramics, Design, Drawing, Painting

RADFORD

RADFORD UNIVERSITY, Art Dept, 801 E Main St, Radford, VA 24142-0001; PO Box 6965, Radford, VA 24142-6965. Tel 540-831-5754; Email sarbury@radford.edu; Web: www.radford.edu; *Chmn* Dr Steve Arbury, PhD; *Prof* Halide Salam; *Asst Prof* Ed LeShock, MFA; *Assoc Prof* Jennifer Spoon, MFA; *Prof* Charles Brouwer, MFA; *Asst Prof* Dr Eloise Philpot, PhD; *Asst Prof* Matthew Johnston, PhD; *MFA* ZL Feng; *Asst Prof* Richard Bay, EdD; *Asst Prof* Drew Dodson, MFA; *Asst Prof* John O'Connor, MA
Estab 1910, dept estab 1936; Maintains nonprofit art gallery, Radford University Art Museum; Pub; D & E; Scholarships; D 1,250, E 80, non-maj 1,086, maj 202, grad 32
Activities: Limited art supplies sold in campus bookstore
Ent Req: HS dipl, SAT
Degrees: BA, BFA, BS & BS (teaching) 4 yrs, MFA 2 yrs, MS 1 yr
Courses: Animation, Art Appreciation, Art Education, Art Foundations, Art History, Baroque & Rococo Art, Ceramics, Contemporary Art, Drawing, Graphic Design, Jewelry, Lettering, †Museum Staff Training, Painting, Photography, Sculpture, Teacher Training, Visual Arts

RICHMOND

J SARGEANT REYNOLDS COMMUNITY COLLEGE, Humanities & Social Science Division, PO Box 85622, Richmond, VA 23285-5622. Tel 804-371-3263; Web: www.jsr.cc.va.us; *Assoc Div Chmn* Patricia Johnson; *Head Art Prog* Barbara Glenn
Estab 1972
Ent Req: HS dipl or equivalent
Degrees: AA
Tuition: Res—$4.52 per cr hr; nonres—$175.40 per cr hr
Courses: Art Appreciation, Art History, Design, Drawing, Graphic Design, Handicrafts, Interior Design, Painting, Photography, Sculpture

UNIVERSITY OF RICHMOND, Dept of Art and Art History, Modlin Center for the Arts, Richmond, VA 23173. Tel 804-289-8272, 289-8276; Fax 804-287-6006; *Chmn* Charles W Johnson Jr PhD; *Prof* Stephen Addiss, PhD; *Assoc Prof* Margaret Denton, PhD; *Assoc Prof* Mark Rhodes; *Assoc Prof* Tanja Softie; *Asst Prof* Erling Sjovold; *Exec Dir Univ Mus* Richard Waller
Estab 1840; Maintains nonprofit art gallery; Pvt; D & E; Scholarships; SC 29, LC 15

Ent Req: HS dipl, CEEB
Degrees: BA and BS 4 yrs
Tuition: Res—&14,000 per yr
Courses: †Architecture, †Art History, Ceramics, Color & Design, Design, Drawing, History of Art & Architecture, †Mixed Media, Museum Staff Training, Museum Studies, Painting, Photography, Printmaking, Sculpture, †Studio Art

VIRGINIA COMMONWEALTH UNIVERSITY, School of the Arts, 325 N Harrison St, PO Box 842519 Richmond, VA 23284-2519. Tel 804-828-2787; Fax 804-828-6469; Email arts@vcu.edu; Web: arts.vcu.edu; *Dean* Shawn Brixey
Estab 1838; School founded 1928; Maintains nonprofit galleries Anderson Gallery & VCU Institute of Contemporary Art; Cabell Library; on-campus shop sells art supplies; FT 174, PT 60; pub; D & E; Scholarships; Fellowships; Assistantships; LC & GC; 3,021
Ent Req: ent req portfolio or audition
Degrees: BA, BFA, BM, MA, MFA, MAE, PhD
Tuition: Res $12,094; Nonres $32,742
Courses: 2-D Art, Art Education, Art Experience, Art History, Ceramics, Costume Design & Construction, Design, Exceptional Art, Fashion Arts, Film, Fine Arts, Graphic Arts, Graphic Design, Interior Design, Jewelry, Painting, Photography, Printmaking, Theatre Arts
Summer School: Courses 3 - 8 wks, most art disciplines

ROANOKE

HOLLINS UNIVERSITY, Art Dept, PO Box 9583, Roanoke, VA 24020-9583. Tel 540-362-6323; Email huadm@hollins.edu; rsulkin@hollins.edu; Web: www.hollins.edu/academics/art/; *Prof & Chair* Robert Sulkin
Estab 1842; Maintains nonprofit gallery, Eleanor Wilson Museum, 8009 Fishburn Dr, Roanoke VA 24020
Courses: Art History, †Studio

VIRGINIA WESTERN COMMUNITY COLLEGE, Communication Design, Fine Art & Photography, 3097 Colonial Ave SW, Roanoke, VA 24015-4705. Tel 540-857-7385, 857-7255 (Dept Head); Fax 540-857-6096; Email dcurtis@vw.cc.va.us; Web: www.vw.cc.va.us; *Interim Chmn Div Human* Dr John Capps, EdD; *Dept Head* Elizabeth Bailey
PT 10; Pub; D & E; Scholarships; SC 11, LC 2
Ent Req: HS dipl
Degrees: AA(Fine Art), AAS (Commun Design)
Adult Hobby Classes: Oil Painting, Papermaking, Watercolor

SALEM

ROANOKE COLLEGE, Fine Arts Dept-Art, 221 College Ln, Olin Hall Salem, VA 24153-3747. Tel 540-375-2374; Fax 540-375-2559; Email partin@roanoke.edu; Web: www.roanoke.edu; *Chmn* Bruce Partin, PhD; *Prof* Scott Hardwig, MFA; *Assoc Prof* Elizabeth Heil, MFA; *Assoc Prof* Dr Jane Long, MFA; *Asst Prof* Katherine Shortridge; *Asst Prof* James Hargrove
Estab 1842, dept estab 1930; Maintain nonprofit art gallery, Olin Galleries; pvt; D&E; Scholarships; SC 16, LC 8; D 130, non-maj 120, maj 40
Ent Req: HS dipl, SAT or ACT, 13 acad cr - 2 English, 2 Social Sciences, 5 Arts & Humanities, 2 Math, 2 Science
Degrees: BA 4 yrs
Courses: Advertising Design, Art Education, †Art History, Ceramics, Drawing, Graphic Design, Painting, Photography, Printmaking, Sculpture, Stage Design, †Studio Arts
Children's Classes: Ceramics
Summer School: Dir, Ms Leah Russell. Courses—Art History, Studio

STAUNTON

MARY BALDWIN COLLEGE, Dept of Art & Art History, 318 Prospect St, Staunton, VA 24401. Tel 540-887-7196; Fax 540-887-7139; Web: www.mbc.edu; *Assoc Prof* Paul Ryan; *Assoc Prof* Dr Sara N James; *Asst Prof* Jim Sconyers; *Instr* Nancy Ross; *Vis Artist* Anne Hanger; *Adjunct Instr* Beth Young
Estab 1842; Maintain nonprofit gallery, Hunt Gallery at Mary Baldwin College, Staunton, VA 24401; pvt; D & E; Scholarships; SC 40, LC 30; D 173, E 32, non-maj 172, maj 45, others 4 non-credit
Ent Req: HS dipl
Degrees: BA & BS 4 yrs
Courses: Art Appreciation, Art Criticism, Art History, Ceramics, Drawing, Film, Graphic Design, Historical Preservation, Interior Design, Museum Staff Training, Painting, Photography, Printmaking, Teacher Training, Typography, Video

STERLING

MAGNUM OPUS, 20963 Sandstone Sq Sterling, VA 20163-7209. Tel 703-790-0861; *Head Dept* John Fettes
Estab 1955; pvt; D & E; SC 1; D 63, E 12
Courses: Drawing, Painting
Summer School: Dir, John Fettes.

SWEET BRIAR

SWEET BRIAR COLLEGE, Art History Dept, 134 Chapel Rd, Sweet Briar, VA 24595-5001. Tel 804-381-6125 (Art History Dept), 381-6100; Fax 804-381-6152; Email witcombe@sbc.edu; Web: www.sbc.edu/academics/arth/; *Prof* Aileen H Laing PhD; *Chmn* Christopher Witcombe; *Prof* Diane D Moran, PhD
Estab 1901, dept estab 1930; pvt; D; Scholarships; SC 19, LC 19; D 375 per term, maj 32
Ent Req: HS dipl, col boards
Degrees: BA 4 yrs
Courses: †Art History, Drawing, Graphic Arts, History of Art & Architecture
Adult Hobby Classes: Fibre Art History, Graphic Design, Modern Art

WILLIAMSBURG

COLLEGE OF WILLIAM & MARY, Dept of Fine Arts, PO Box 8795, Williamsburg, VA 23187-8795. Tel 757-221-2530 (Dept of Arts); *Ralph H Wark Prof Art & Art History* Dr Alan Wallach, MFA; *Assoc Prof* Marlene Jack, MFA; *Assoc Prof* William Barnes, MFA; *Asst Prof* Lewis Choen, MFA; *Lectr* Joseph Dye, MFA
Estab 1693, dept estab 1936; pub; D; SC 20, LC 22; D 5000, non-maj 825, maj 64
Ent Req: HS dipl
Degrees: BA 4 yrs
Tuition: Res—$1560 per sem; nonres—$4500 per sem; campus res available
Courses: †Architecture, †Art History, †Ceramics, †Drawing, †Painting, †Printmaking, †Sculpture
Summer School: Dir, Nell Jones. Courses—Art History, Design, Painting, Drawing

WISE

CLINCH VALLEY COLLEGE OF THE UNIVERSITY OF VIRGINIA, Visual & Performing Arts Dept, One College Ave, Wise, VA 24293. Tel 540-328-0100; Fax 540-328-0115; *Chmn* Susan Adams-Ramsey
Estab 1954, dept estab 1980; pub; D & E; Scholarships; SC 9, LC 4
Ent Req: HS dipl, SAT or ACT
Degrees: BA & BS 4 yrs
Tuition: Res/non-res—$77 per cr; res/non-res—12-18 cr $1,735
Courses: Applied Music, Art Education, Art History, Ceramics, Costume Design & Construction, Drawing, Film, History of Art & Architecture, Music History & Literature, Music Theory, Painting, Performance, Sculpture, Stage Design, Teacher Training, Theatre Arts
Adult Hobby Classes: Dir, Dr Winston Ely
Summer School: Courses—Same as above

WASHINGTON

AUBURN

GREEN RIVER COMMUNITY COLLEGE, Art Dept, 12401 SE 320th St, Auburn, WA 98092-3699. Tel 253-833-9111; Fax 253-288-3465; Web: www.greenriver.edu; *Faculty* Heather McGeachy; *Faculty* Cindy Small
Estab 1965; pub; D & E; SC 31, LC 4; D 330, E 120
Ent Req: HS dipl or 18 yrs old
Degrees: AA 2 yr
Tuition: Living with parents $7380, other housing $11,052
Courses: Art History, Ceramics, Computer Enhanced Design, Craft, Design, Drawing, Painting, Papermaking, Photography, Weaving
Summer School: Dir, Bruce Haulman. Tuition $193.66. Courses—Ceramics, Drawing, Painting, Photography

BELLEVUE

BELLEVUE COMMUNITY COLLEGE, Art Dept, 3000 Landerholm Circle SE, Bellevue, WA 98007-6484. Tel 206-641-2341; Fax 425-643-2690; *Dept Chmn* Carolyn Luark; *Photo Instr* John Wesley; *Art History Instr* Vicki Artimovich
Estab 1966; pub; D & E; SC 15, LC 5; 600, maj 50
Ent Req: no ent req
Degrees: AA 2 yrs
Tuition: Varies according to courses taken
Courses: Art History, Design, Drawing, Interior Design, Painting, Photography, Sculpture, Textile Design
Adult Hobby Classes: Enrl 600. Courses—Ceramics, Design, Drawing, Jewelry, Painting, Photography, Sculpture

BELLINGHAM

WESTERN WASHINGTON UNIVERSITY, Art Dept, 516 High St, Fine Arts Complex, Rm 116 Bellingham, WA 98225-5946. Tel 360-650-3660; Fax 360-647-6878; Web: www.wwu.edu; *Chmn Dept Art* Thomas Johnston
Estab 1899; FT 15, PT 6; pub; D & E; Scholarships; D 1500, E 200
Ent Req: HS dipl, ent exam
Degrees: BA 4 yr, BA(Educ) 4 yr, BFA 5 yr, MEd 6 yr
Courses: †Art History, †Ceramics, †Drawing, †Fibers, †Graphic Design, †Metals, †Painting, †Sculpture
Adult Hobby Classes: Enrl 200; tuition $43 per cr continuing educ; Courses—Ceramics, Drawing, Fibers, Paintings, Sculpture
Children's Classes: Enrl 100; tuition $125 one wk session; Courses—Adventures in Science/Arts
Summer School: Dir, Shirley Ennons. Tuition $404, six & nine week sessions; Courses—Art Education, Art History, Ceramics, Drawing, Fibers, Painting, Sculpture

BREMERTON

OLYMPIC COLLEGE, Social Sciences & Humanities Div, 1600 Chester Ave, Bremerton, WA 98337-1699. Tel 360-792-6050, 7767; Fax 360-792-7689; Email

rlawrence@oc.ctc.edu; Web: www.oc.ctc.edu/; *Dir* Randy Lawrence; *Instr* Ina Wu, MFA
Estab 1946; Olympic College Art Gallery; pub; D & E; Scholarships; LC 3; D 125, E 75
Ent Req: HS dipl
Degrees: AA, AS & ATA 2 yrs, cert
Courses: Art Appreciation, Art History, Ceramics, Drawing, Jewelry, Life Drawing, Native American Art History, Painting, Papermaking, Photography, Printmaking, Sculpture, Stained Glass
Adult Hobby Classes: Calligraphy, Painting

CHENEY

EASTERN WASHINGTON UNIVERSITY, Dept of Art, 526 Fifth St, Art 1400 Cheney, WA 99004-1619. Tel 509-359-2493; Fax 509-359-7028; Web: www.ewu.edu, www.visual.arts.ewu.edu; *Chmn* Lanny Devono; *Prof Art History* Dr Barbara Miller
Estab 1886; pub; D; Scholarships; SC 58, LC 21, GC 18; D 600, non-maj 200, maj 200, GS 20
Degrees: BA, BEd and BFA 4 yrs, MA and MEd 1 to 2 yrs
Tuition: Res—undergrad $81 per cr hr, grad $130 per cr hr; nonres—undergrad $287 per cr hr, grad $394 per cr hr
Courses: Aesthetics, Art Appreciation, Art Education, Art History, Ceramics, Design, Drawing, Graphic Design, Mixed Media, Painting, Photography, Printmaking, Sculpture, Teacher Training
Summer School: Dir, Richard L Twedt. Enrl 200; tuition $120 per cr undergrad, $190 per cr grad for 8 wk term. Courses—Art History, Art in Humanities, Drawing, Painting, Photography

ELLENSBURG

CENTRAL WASHINGTON UNIVERSITY, Dept of Art, 400 E University Way, Ellensburg, WA 98926-7564. Tel 509-963-2665; Fax 509-963-1918; Email art_dept@cwu.edu; Web: www.cwu.edu/art; *Chmn* Gregg Schlanger
Estab 1891; Maintains nonprofit gallery, Sarah Spurgeon Gallery, Dept Art, 400 E University Way MS 7564 Ellensburg WA 98926-7564; 12; pub; D; Scholarships; maj 200, others 7134
Ent Req: GPA 2
Degrees: BA, BFA, MFA 4-5 yrs
Courses: Art Appreciation, Art History, Ceramics, Computer Art, Design, Drawing, †Graphic Design, Illustration, Jewelry, Painting, Photography, Sculpture, Wood Design
Summer School: Dir, Gregg Schlanger. Tuition $80 per cr for 4, 6, 8 wk sessions. Courses: Art Appreciation, Ceramics, Computer Art, Drawing, Illustration

EVERETT

EVERETT COMMUNITY COLLEGE, Art Dept, 2000 Tower St, Everett, WA 98201-1390. Tel 425-388-9439; Fax 425-388-9129; Email gkammer@everettcc.edu; Web: www.evcc.ctc.edu; *Instr Art* Lowell Hanson; *Instr Art* Thom Lee; *Instr Art* Sandra Lepper; *Dir* Greg Kammer
Maintain nonprofit art gallery, Russell Day Gallery; on-campus shop where art supplies may be purchased; Pub; D&E; Scholarships; SC, LC, Online/Distance Learning
Degrees: AA, AFA & ATA 2 yr
Tuition: $56 per cr hr
Courses: Advertising Design, †Aesthetics, Art Appreciation, Art Education, Art History, Ceramics, Commercial Art, Design, Drawing, Graphic Arts, Graphic Design, Industrial Design, Media Production, Multimedia, Painting, Photography, Printmaking, †Studio Arts, Theatre Arts, †Written Arts

LACEY

ST MARTINS COLLEGE, Humanities Dept, 5300 Pacific Ave SE, Lacey, WA 98503-1297. Tel 360-491-4700; Fax 360-459-4124; Web: www.stmartin.edu; *Pres* David R Spangler, PhD
Dept estab 1895; pvt; D & E
Ent Req: HS dipl
Degrees: BA
Tuition: FT $7780 per sem
Courses: Art Appreciation, Art History, Ceramics, Design, Drawing, Painting, Printmaking

LAKEWOOD

FORT STEILACOOM COMMUNITY COLLEGE, Fine Arts Dept, 9401 Farwest Dr SW, Lakewood, WA 98498-1919. Tel 253-964-6500, 964-6655; Fax 253-964-6318; Email mpederse@pierce.ctc.edu; Web: www.pierce.ctc.edu/; *Chmn* Morrie Pedersen
Estab 1966, dept estab 1972; FT 2, PT 2; pub; D & E; SC 20, LC 5; D 3500
Ent Req: ent exam
Degrees: AA 2yrs
Courses: Drawing, Figure Drawing, Painting, Photography, Printmaking
Adult Hobby Classes: Courses vary
Summer School: Dir, Walt Boyden. Tuition $19 per cr hr. Courses—Ceramics, Drawing, Painting.

LONGVIEW

LOWER COLUMBIA COLLEGE, Art Dept, 1600 Maple St, Longview, WA 98632-3907; PO Box 3010, Longview, WA 98632-0310. Tel 360-577-2300, Ext 3414 (Art Dept); Fax 360-577-3400; Web: lcc.ctc.edu/; *Instr* Yvette O'Neill, MA; *Chmn* Rosemary Powelson, MFA
Estab 1934; pub; D & E; Scholarships; SC 36, LC 8; D 200, E 100
Ent Req: open admis
Degrees: AAS 2 yrs
Courses: Art History, Calligraphy, Ceramics, Design, Drawing, Graphic Arts, Painting, Photography, Printmaking, Sculpture
Adult Hobby Classes: Courses—Matting & Framing, Relief Woodcuts, Recreational Photography

MOSES LAKE

BIG BEND COMMUNITY COLLEGE, Art Dept, 7662 Chanute St, Moses Lake, WA 98837. Tel 509-762-5351 ext 269; Web: www.bbcc.ctc.edu; *Dir* Rie Palkovic; *Art Instr* Francis Palkovic; *Art Instr* Betty Johanssen
Estab 1962; Art supplies can be purchased at on-campus shop; pub; D & E; SC 8, LC 2; D 325, E 60, maj 10-15
Ent Req: HS dipl
Degrees: AA 2 yrs
Courses: Art Appreciation, Basic Design, Ceramics, Drawing, History of Art & Architecture, Lettering, Painting, Photography, Poster Art, Pottery, Sculpture
Adult Hobby Classes: Enrl 15. Courses—Drawing

MOUNT VERNON

SKAGIT VALLEY COLLEGE, Dept of Art, 2405 E College Way, Mount Vernon, WA 98273-5899. Tel 360-416-7724 (Dept Art), 428-1261; Fax 360-416-7690; *Chmn* Ann Chadwick-Reid
Estab 1926; FT 2, PT 6; pub; D & E; Scholarships; SC 32, LC 1; D 2500, E 3500
Ent Req: open
Courses: Art Appreciation, Art History, Ceramics, Design, Drawing, Figure Drawing, Jewelry, Painting, Photography, Printmaking, Sculpture
Adult Hobby Classes: Four nights a week
Summer School: Dir, Bert Williamson

PASCO

COLUMBIA BASIN COLLEGE, Esvelt Gallery, 2600 N 20th Ave, Pasco, WA 99301-4108. Tel 509-547-0511 ext 2374; Fax 509-546-0401; Email mdryburgh@columbiabasin.edu; Web: www.cbc2.org/arts/arts_center; *Art Dept Lead & Instr* James Craig, MFA; *Dean Arts & Humanities* Bill McKay; *Dir Gallery & Instr* Mary Dryburgh; *Instr* Tracy Petre; *Instr* Greg Pierce
Estab 1955; Maintains a non-profit art gallery & on-campus art supplies shop.; FT 3, PT 5; pub; D & E, wkends; Scholarships; SC 12, LC 3
Degrees: AA & AS
Tuition: Res—$178.50; nonres—$684.50
Courses: Art Appreciation, Art History, Ceramics, Design, Drawing, Graphic Design, Metal Casting & Foundry, Photography, Sculpture, Stage Design
Adult Hobby Classes: Enrl 5000; tuition $400 per qtr. Courses—Art Appreciation, Fine Arts, Graphic Design
Summer School: Dir, Bill McKay. Enrl 1500; tuition $400 for 8 wks. Courses—Ceramics, Drawing, Illustration, Introduction to Art

PULLMAN

WASHINGTON STATE UNIVERSITY, Fine Arts Dept, PO Box 647450, Pullman, WA 99164-7450. Tel 509-335-8686; Fax 509-335-7742; *Chmn* Paul Lee
Estab 1890, dept estab 1925; FT 12; pub; D & E; Scholarships; SC 29, LC 13, GC 25; D 1593, E 131, maj 220, GS 25
Ent Req: HS dipl
Degrees: BA(Fine Arts) 4 yrs, BFA 4 yrs, MFA 2 yrs
Tuition: Res—$1829; nonres—$5272
Courses: Ceramics, Drawing, Electronic Imaging, Painting, Photography, Printmaking, Sculpture

SEATTLE

THE ART INSTITUTES, The Art Institute of Seattle, 2323 Elliott Ave, Seattle, WA 98121-1642. Tel 206-448-6600; Fax 206-448-2501; Email aisadm@aii.edu; Web: www.ais.edu; *Pres* Elden Monday; *Dir Interior Design, Industrial Design Tech* William R Edgar; *Dir Graphic Design, Web Design & Interactive Media, Digital Design* Douglas Heinlein
Estab 1946; pvt; D&E; Scholarships; SC 60%, LC 40%; D 2000, E 350
Ent Req: HS dipl, portfolio approval recommended but not required
Degrees: prof dipl, AA 2 yr
Tuition: $13,365 per yr for 3 qtrs
Courses: Advertising Design, †Audio Production, Animation, Culinary Arts, Multimedia, Fashion Marketing, Industrial Design, Commercial Art, Commercial Art Technician, †Costume Design & Construction, †Design, Fashion Arts, Fashion Merchandising, Film, Graphic Arts, Graphic Design, Illustration, Interior Design, Layout & Production, Lettering, Photography, †Textile Design, Video

CITY ART WORKS, Pratt Fine Arts Center, 1902 S Main St, Seattle, WA 98144-2206. Tel 206-328-2200; Fax 206-328-1260; Email info@pratt.org; Web: www.pratt.org; *Exec Dir* Michelle Bufano; *Dir Progs* Brandi Clark
Open daily 9 AM - 9 PM; Estab 1979; pvt; D & E; Scholarships; Fellowships; SC 300; D 1000, E 1000

Ent Req: open enrollment
Degrees: no degree prog
Courses: Collage, Drawing, Glass blowing & casting, Goldsmithing, Illustration, Jewelry, Mixed Media, Painting, Printmaking, Sculpture, Silversmithing
Adult Hobby Classes: Enrl 2000; tuition $100-$500 for 8 wk class. Classes—Drawing, Glass, Jewelry, Painting, Printmaking, Sculpture
Children's Classes: Drawing, Glass, Printmaking, Sculpture
Summer School: Educ Dir, Janet Berkow. Enrl 50; tuition $400-$650 per wk-long class. Classes—Glassblowing, Jewelry, Printmaking, Sculpture

CORNISH COLLEGE OF THE ARTS, Art Dept, 1000 Lenora St, Seattle, WA 98121-2707. Tel 206-726-5151; Fax 206-720-1011; Email admission@cornish.edu; Web: www.cornish.edu; *Pres* Sergei Tschernisch; *Provost* Lois Harris PhD; *Art Dept Chair* David Ulrich; *Design Dept Chair* Grant Donesky
Estab 1914; 18; pvt; D; Scholarships; Fellowships; SC 80, LC 12; D 330, non-maj 10, maj 168 (art), 162 (dos)
Ent Req: HS dipl, application for admission, portfolio review
Degrees: BFA 4 yr, BM 4 yr
Courses: †Animation, Art History, Drawing, Furniture Design, †Gaming Design, Graphic Design, †Illustration, †Interior Design, †Media Art, †Motion Design, †Package Design, Painting, Photography, Printmaking, Sculpture, Video, †Visual Communications, †Web Design

NORTH SEATTLE COLLEGE, North Seattle College Dept of Art, 9600 College Way N, Humanities Division Seattle, WA 98103-3514. Tel 206-934-3709; Fax 206-527-3784; Email kelda.martensen@seattlecolleges.edu; Web: www.northseattle.edu/program/art; *Drawing & Painting* Michelle Kelly, MFA; *Jewelry & Metal Design* Lynne Hull, MFA; *Ceramics* George Rodriguez, MFA; *Digital Photog* Erin Burns, MFA; *Printmaking & Drawing* Amanda Knowles, MFA; *Digital Art* Bo Choi, MFA; *Gallery Cur* Amanda Knowles, MFA; *Sculpture* Paula Rebsom, MFA; *Drawing, Painting, Design & Printmaking* Kelda Martensen, MFA; *Painting & Drawing* Emily Ghevaurd, MFA; *Design & Drawing* Emma Levitt, MFA; *Drawing & Painting* Daphne Monkoff, MFA; *Jewelry* Avan Galligan, MFA; *Art History* Jen Garcia, MA
Estab 1970; Maintains The North Seattle College Art Gallery (same address); pub; D & E; Hybn'd; Scholarships; SC 27, LC 7; D 150, E 65
Income: State funded, foundation endowments, grants
Activities: Schols offered
Ent Req: HS dipl
Degrees: AA 2 yr, AFA, CFA 2 yr, CJD
Tuition: Res—undergrad $657.75 per quarter, $62.752 per cr, nonres—$2,393.75 per quarter; no campus res
Courses: Art Appreciation, Art History, Ceramics, Conceptual Art, Design, Drawing, Goldsmithing, History of Art & Architecture, Jewelry, Painting, Photography, Printmaking, Sculpture, Silversmithing
Adult Hobby Classes: Enrl 6600; tuition $657.75 per quarter for res, $2,393.75 per quarter for nonres. Courses—Art History, Basic Drawing, Ceramics, 2-D & 3-D Design, Intro to Art, Jewelry Design, Painting, Sculptures, Water Solvable Media

SEATTLE CENTRAL COMMUNITY COLLEGE, Humanities - Social Sciences Division, 1701 Broadway, Seattle, WA 98122-2400. Tel 206-587-3800; Fax 206-344-4390; Web: www.seattlecentral.org; *Prof* Ileana Leavens; *Chmn* Audrey Wright; *Prof* Tatiana Garmendia; *Asst Prof* Don Barrie; *Asst Prof* Don Tanze; *Instr* Royal Alley-Bavaes
Estab 1970; pub; D & E; Scholarships; SC 15, LC 5; D 70, E 50
Ent Req: HS dipl, ent exam
Degrees: AA 2 yrs
Tuition: Res—$426 per qtr; nonres—$1692 per qtr; no campus res
Courses: †Aesthetics, †Art Appreciation, Art History, †Design, †Drawing, †History of Art & Architecture, †Mixed Media, Painting, †Printmaking
Summer School: Dir, Ileana Leavens. Courses—Art History, Painting, Sculpture

SEATTLE PACIFIC UNIVERSITY, Art Dept, 3307 Third Ave W, Seattle, WA 98119. Tel 206-281-2079; Fax 206-281-2500; *Prof* Michael Caldwell; *Dean Col Arts & Sciences* Joyce Erickson
Scholarships; Fellowships
Tuition: $4223 per qtr for 12-17 cr; campus res—$1620 room, board & meals
Courses: Art Appreciation, †Art Education, Ceramics, Design, Drawing, Fashion Arts, Handicrafts, Industrial Design, Interior Design, Jewelry, Painting, Printmaking, Sculpture, Textile Design, Weaving
Children's Classes: Tuition $23 for 8 wk session. Courses - General Art for Children
Summer School: Dir, Larry Metcalf. Two 4 wk sessions. Courses - Elementary Art Education Workshops, Fabrics, Monoprinting, Painting, Papermaking, Silkscreening

SEATTLE UNIVERSITY, Dept of Art & Art History, 901 12th Ave, Seattle, WA 98122-4411; PO Box 222000, Seattle, WA 98122-1090. Tel 206-296-5356 (Fine Arts Dept), 296-6000; Fax 206-296-5433; Email venker@seattleu.edu; Web: www.seattleu.edu/artsci/departments/art-arthistory; *Asst Prof* Josef Venker, SJ, MFA; *Assoc Prof* Francisco Guerrero, MFA; *Assoc Prof* Naomi Kasumi, MFA; *Assoc Prof* Claire Garoutte, MFA; *Assoc Prof* Ken Allan, PhD; *Assoc Prof & Chair* Naomi Hume, PhD; *Assoc Prof* Alexander Mouton, MFA; *Asst Prof* Trung Pham, MFA; *Lectr* Wynne Greenwood, MFA
1891; Maintain a nonprofit art gallery - Kinsey Gallery, Hedreen Gallery & Vachon Gallery; on-campus art supplies shop; Jesuit/Catholic; D; Scholarships; SC 25, LC 15; D 160, maj 160
Ent Req: HS dipl and entrance exam
Degrees: BA prog offered
Tuition: $685 per cr hr; FT $30,825 per yr
Courses: †Art History, Calligraphy, Ceramic Sculpture, Ceramics, †Design, Drawing, Film, Graphic Design, History of Art & Architecture, Painting, †Photography, Printmaking, †Studio Art, Video
Summer School: Courses—same as regular session

SHORELINE COMMUNITY COLLEGE, Humanities Division, 16101 Greenwood Ave N, Seattle, WA 98133-5696. Tel 206-546-4741; Fax 206-546-5869; Email mbonar@shoreline.edu; Web: www.shoreline.edu; *Dean* Norma Goldstein, PhD; *Prof* Chris Simons, MFA; *Prof* Bruce Armstutz, MFA; *Prof* K Takechi; *Prof* Christine Shefner; *Prof* Jim Reddin
Estab 1964; On-campus shop sells art supplies; pub; D & E; Scholarships; SC 9, LC Art History Survey; D 5500
Publications: EBBTIDE, biweekly; Spindrift, annual art & literary publication
Ent Req: HS dipl, col ent exam
Degrees: AA & AFA
Courses: †Advertising Design, Aesthetics, Art Appreciation, Art History, Ceramics, †Commercial Art, Conceptual Art, Constructions, †Costume Design & Construction, Design, †Drafting, Drawing, †Fashion Arts, Film, †Graphic Arts, †Graphic Design, History of Art & Architecture, Mixed Media, Multimedia, Painting, †Photography, Sculpture, Stage Design, †Textile Design, †Video
Summer School: Dir, Marie Rosenwasser. Enrl 45 maximum; two 4 wk terms. Courses—Ceramics, Design, Design Appreciation, Drawing, Electronic Design, Graphic Design, Painting, Photography, Sculpture

UNIVERSITY OF WASHINGTON, School of Art, PO Box 353440, Seattle, WA 98195-3440. Tel 206-543-0970 (Admin), 543-0646 (Advising); Fax 206-685-1657; Web: www.art.washington.edu; *Dir* Christopher Ozubko
Estab 1878; Maintain a nonprofit art gallery Jacob Lawrence Gallery, Rm 132, Art Bldg; Art Library, Art Bldg Rm 101; pub; D & E; Scholarships; SC 113, LC 84, GC 30; Maj 1100, grad 125
Ent Req: must meet university admis req, must be matriculated to enroll in art classes in acad yr
Degrees: BFA 4 yrs, BA 4 yrs, MA, PhD and MFA, BDes, MDes
Courses: †Art History, †Ceramics, Drawing, Fibers, †Graphic Design, †Industrial Design, †Interaction Design, Interdisciplinary Visual Arts, †Painting, †Photography, †Printmaking, †Sculpture, Textile Design, Video, Weaving
Summer School: Dir, C Ozubko. Enrl 830; 2-month term. Various courses offered through UW Extension, open to community

SPOKANE

GONZAGA UNIVERSITY, Dept of Art, 502 E Boone, College of Arts & Sciences Spokane, WA 99258-1774. Tel 509-328-4220, Ext 6686; *Prof* R Gilmore; *Prof* Mary Farrell; *Prof Emeritus* Terry Gieber; *Chmn* Shalon Parker; *Asst Prof* Mathew Rude
Estab 1962; Maintain art/architecture library; FT 4, PT 2; pvt; D & E; SC 20, LC 5; D 250 incl maj 40, others 80
Activities: Schols offered
Ent Req: HS dipl
Degrees: BA 4 yrs
Tuition: $17,285 per sem; campus res available
Courses: 2-D Design, Art Education, Ceramics, Drawing, †History of Art, Painting, Printmaking, Teacher Training
Summer School: Dean Arts & Sciences, Elisabeth Mermann-Jozwiak. Term of 8 wks beginning June. Courses— Drawing, Painting, Printmaking

SPOKANE FALLS COMMUNITY COLLEGE, Fine Arts Dept, 3410 W Fort George Wright Dr, Spokane, WA 99204-5288. Tel 509-533-3500; 533-3710 (Art Dept); Fax 509-533-3484; Email finearts@spokanefalls.edu; Email jof@sfcc.spokane.cc.wa.us; Web: www.spokanefalls.edu; *Dean* Bonnie Brunt; *Asst Prof* Tom O'Day; *Dept Chmn* Carolyn Stephens; *Asst Prof* Patty Haag; *Asst Prof* Carl Richardson; *Asst Prof* Mardis Nenno; *Adjunct Asst Prof* Peter Jagoda; *Adjunct Asst Prof* Lee Ayars; *Adjunct Asst Prof* Cindy Wilson; *Adjunct Asst Prof* Kurt Madison; *Adjunct Asst Prof* Margot Casstevens; *Adjunct Asst Prof* Tobe Harvey; *Adjunct asst Prof* Bradd Skubinna; *Adjunct Asst Prof* Leona Lopez Schindler; *Asst Prof* Megan Martens-Haworth; *Asst Prof* Garric Simonsen; *Asst Prof* Bernadette Vielbig
Estab 1963; pub; D & E & Sat; Scholarships; SC 41, LC 5, workshops; D 600, E 200
Ent Req: HS dipl, GED
Degrees: AAA 3 yr, AA, AFA & CFA 2 yr
Tuition: Res—$467 per quarter; nonres—$1837 per quarter; no campus res
Courses: Art Education, Art History, †Bronze Casting, Ceramics, Computer Arts, Design 2D & 3D Advanced, Digital Paint, Drawing, Exhibit, Fiber Arts, Handicrafts, Health/Safety in Art, Illustration, Intro to Art, Jewelry, Lettering, Mat/Frame, Mixed Media, †Mold Making, Non-Western Art, Painting, Photography, Portfolio, Printmaking, Sculpture
Adult Hobby Classes: Enrl 10-20; tuition $25.60 for 6 week term. Courses—Art History, Ceramics, Drawing, Watercolor
Children's Classes: Enrl 20-22; tuition $30 for 4 wks. Art Experiences, Courses—Ceramics, Drawing
Summer School: Enrl 100; tuition $50.30 per cr or $503 per 10-18 cr; 6-8 wk term. Courses—Art Workshops, Ceramics, Color & Design, Drawing, Intro to Art, Watercolor

WHITWORTH UNIVERSITY, (Whitworth College) Art Dept, 300 W Hawthorne Ave, Spokane, WA 99251-0001. Tel 509-777-1000, 777-3258 (Art Dept); Fax 509-466-3781; Web: www.whitworth.edu; *Dept Chair, Prof* Gordon Wilson, MFA; *Assoc Prof* Meredith Shimizu, PhD; *Assoc Prof* Katie Creyts, MFA; *Assoc Prof* Bradley Oiler, MFA
Maintain non-profit art galleries: Bryan Oliver Gallery & Cowles Student Gallery, Lied Art Center; Pvt; D & E; Scholarships; SC 23, LC 18
Ent Req: HS dipl
Degrees: BA 4 yrs, MA, MAT & MEd 2 yrs
Courses: Art Administration, Art Education, Art History, Ceramics, Drawing, Graphic Design, Leaded Glass, Mixed Media, Painting, Printmaking

STANWOOD

PILCHUCK GLASS SCHOOL, 1201-316th St NW, Stanwood, WA 98292. Tel 360-445-3111; Fax 360-445-5515; Email info@pilchuck.com; Web: www.pilchuck.com; *Exec Dir* James Baker

Estab 1971; summer location: 1201 316th St NW, Stanwood, WA 98292-9600, Tel: 206-445-3111, Fax: 206-445-5515; FT & PT 50; pvt; D & E; Scholarships; SC 25; D & E 250
Ent Req: 18 years or older
Courses: Constructions, Glass, Sculpture
Summer School: Exec Dir, Marjorie Levy. Enrl 250; tuition approx $2200 for 2 1/2 wk course. Courses—Casting, Cold Working, Flamework, Fusing, Glassblowing, Mosaic, Stained Glass

TACOMA

PACIFIC LUTHERAN UNIVERSITY, Dept of Art, 12180 Park Ave, Dept Art Tacoma, WA 98447-0001. Tel 253-535-7573; Fax 253-536-5063; Web: www.plu.eduartd; *Chmn* John Hallam PhD; *Prof* David Keyes, Ma; *Assoc Prof* Dennis Cox, MFA; *Assoc Prof* Beatrice Geller, MFA; *Assoc Prof* Lawrence Gold, MFA; *Assoc Prof* Walt Tomsic, MFA
Estab 1890, dept estab 1960; Maintain nonprofit art gallery on-campus; Den; D & E; Scholarships; SC 29, LC 8; D 800, E 75, maj 60
Ent Req: HS dipl, SAT
Degrees: BA, BAEd & BFA 4 yrs
Tuition: $19,000 per yr
Courses: Art Appreciation, Art Education, Art History, †Ceramics, †Drawing, Electronic Imaging, †Graphic Arts, †Graphic Design, Illustration, †Mixed Media, †Painting, †Photography, †Printmaking, †Sculpture

TACOMA COMMUNITY COLLEGE, Art Dept, 6501 S 19th St, Tacoma, WA 98466-6100. Tel 253-566-5000, 566-5260 (Art Dept); Fax 253-566-6070; Web: www.tacoma.ctc.edu; *Art Dept Chmn* Richard Mahaffey
Estab 1965; FT 5; pub; D & E; Scholarships; SC 35, LC 1; D & E 1500
Degrees: AAS & Assoc in Liberal Arts 2 yrs
Courses: 2-D & 3-D Design, Art History, Figure Drawing, Jewelry, Painting, Photography, Pottery, Printmaking, Sculpture

UNIVERSITY OF PUGET SOUND, Dept of Art & Art History, 1500 N Warner St #1072, Tacoma, WA 98416-1072. Tel 253-879-2806; Fax 253-879-3500; Email art@pugetsound.edu; Web: www.pugetsound.edu; *Prof of Art History* Linda Williams; *Prof of Art History* Zaixin Hong; *Prof Art* Janet Marcanage; *Chmn (until 2019), Prof Art* Elise Richman; *Prof Art* Michael Johnson; *Prof of Art History* Kriszta Koatsis; *Prof Art* Chad Gunderson
Estab 1935; maintains nonprofit gallery, Kittredge Gallery, same location; FT 7; pvt; D; Scholarships; SC 17, LC 15; maj 46, undergrad 455
Ent Req: HS grad
Degrees: BA 4 yrs
Courses: †Art History, Asian Art, Ceramics, Drawing, Painting, Printmaking, Sculpture, †Studio Art
Summer School: Courses—Art Education, Art History, Ceramics, Drawing, Painting, Watercolor

VANCOUVER

CLARK COLLEGE, Art Dept, 1800 E McLoughlin Blvd, Vancouver, WA 98663-3598. Tel 360-694-6521; Fax 360-992-2828; Web: www.clark.edu; *Coordr* Chuck Ramsey
Estab 1933, dept estab 1947; pub; D & E; Scholarships; SC 87, LC 3; D 400, E 500
Ent Req: open door
Degrees: Assoc of Arts & Science, Assoc of Applied Science, & Assoc of General Studies 2 yrs
Courses: Art History, Calligraphy, Ceramics, Drawing, Graphic Design, Handicrafts, Jewelry, Lettering, Painting, Photography
Summer School: Dir Chuck Ramsey. Enrl 40 FTE; tuition $27.50 per cr. Courses—Art Appreciation, Art History, Calligraphy, Ceramics, Drawing, Photography, Watercolor

WALLA WALLA

WALLA WALLA COMMUNITY COLLEGE, Fine Arts Dept, 500 Tausick Way, Walla Walla, WA 99362-9267. Tel 509-527-1873; Email lisa.rasmussen@wwcc.edu; Web: www.wwcc.edu; *Coordr & Instr* Lisa Anne Rasmussen; *Instr* Elizabeth Harris; *Instr* Margaret Jamison; *Instr* Warren Rood; *Instr* Sara Wyman
Estab 1967; Maintains a non-profit art gallery; on-campus art supply shop; pub; D, E, online; Scholarships; SC 8, LC 2; D115, E 15, non-maj 100, maj 15
Ent Req: HS dipl, equivalent
Degrees: AA 2 yr
Tuition: $476.16 ea studio class (4) Cr; 5 Cr classes $595.20
Courses: Art Appreciation, Art History, Ceramics, Commercial Art, Design, Drawing, Handicrafts, Photography, Pottery, Printmaking, Sculpture
Adult Hobby Classes: Watercolors, Woodworking 2 Cr
Children's Classes: Kids college $200
Summer School: Tuition same as regular quarter

WHITMAN COLLEGE, Art Dept, 345 Boyer Ave, Olin Hall Walla Walla, WA 99362-2067. Tel 509-527-5204; Fax 509-527-5039; *Chmn* Charles Timm-Ballard; *Instr* Charly Bloomquist; *Vis Asst Prof Art* Mare Bolker; *Asst Prof Art* Michelle Acuff; *Asst Prof Art* Justin Lincoln; *Vis Asst Prof Art* Joe Page; *Instr* Malunda Povlsen-Jones; *Instr* Dawn Forbes
Estab 1883; Maintains nonprofit gallery, Sheehan Gallery & Bleesway Student Gallery; Pvt; D & E; Scholarships; SC 31, LC 3; D 320, E 30, non-maj 200, maj 150
Ent Req: HS dipl, ent exam
Degrees: BA 4 yrs
Tuition: $26,870 per yr
Courses: Aesthetics, Art History, Book Arts, Ceramics, Drawing, History of Art & Architecture, Painting, Photography, Printmaking, Sculpture

WENATCHEE

WENATCHEE VALLEY COLLEGE, Art Dept, 1300 Fifth St, Wenatchee, WA 98801. Tel 509-682-6780; Fax 504-664-2538; Email sbailey@wvc.edu; *Prof* Scott Bailey
Estab 1939; Maintain nonprofit art gallery, Robert Graves Gallery, 1300 Fifth St, Wenatchee, WA 98801; pub; D & E; Scholarships; SC, LC; D 550, E 200, maj 45
Ent Req: HS dipl, open door policy
Degrees: AA 2 yrs
Courses: Aesthetics, Art Appreciation, Art History, Ceramics, Color Theory, Design, Drawing, Graphic Arts, Graphic Design, Illustration, Painting, Printmaking, Sculpture
Summer School: Dir, Dr Joann Schoen

YAKIMA

YAKIMA VALLEY COMMUNITY COLLEGE, Dept of Visual Arts, S 16th Ave & Nob Hill Blvd, Yakima, WA 98907; PO Box 22520, Yakima, WA 98907-2520. Tel 509-574-4844 (chair), 574-4845 (Assoc faculty), 574-4600 (Main); Email jbissonette@yvcc.edu; Email jsaracino@yvcc.edu; Web: www.yvcc.edu; *Faculty* John Bissonette; *Dir* Rachel Dorn; *Faculty* Jennifer Saracino
Estab 1928; Maintain nonprofit art gallery affiliated with Larson Gallery at Yakima Valley Col, PO Box 22520, Yakima, WA 98907; art supplies available on-campus; PT 5; pub; D&E; Scholarships; SC 19, LC 6; D 250, E 100, non-maj 320, maj 30
Ent Req: HS dipl
Degrees: AA & AS offered
Tuition: Res—$118.84 per cr hr; nonres—$131.84 per cr hr with waiver; international $290.84
Courses: Art Appreciation, Art History, Ceramics, Design, Drawing, Graphic Arts, Graphic Design, Painting, Photography, Printmaking, Sculpture
Summer School: Dir, Robert A Fisher. Tuition $530 per quarter, FT

WEST VIRGINIA

ATHENS

CONCORD COLLEGE, Fine Art Division, PO Box 1000, Athens, WV 24712-1000. Tel 304-384-3115; Fax 304-384-9044; *Prof* Gerald C Arrington, MFA; *Asst Prof* Sheila M Chipley, EdD; *Asst Prof* Steve Glazer, EdD
Estab 1872, dept estab 1925; pub; D & E; Scholarships; SC 32, LC 3; non-maj 200, maj 75, D 75
Ent Req: HS dipl
Degrees: BA & BS 4 yrs
Tuition: Res—$1223 per sem; nonres—$2488 per sem; campus res—room & board available
Courses: †Advertising, Advertising Design, Art Education, Art History, Ceramics, Collage, Commercial Art, Drawing, Graphic Arts, Graphic Design, Handicrafts, Illustration, Painting, Printmaking, Sculpture, Teacher Training
Adult Hobby Classes: Enrl varies; tuition based on part-time rates. Courses—Vary
Children's Classes: Enrl varies; tuition none for 4 wk sessions. Courses vary
Summer School: Term of 5 wks beginning June. Courses—varied

BETHANY

BETHANY COLLEGE, Visual & Performing Arts Dept, 31 E Campus Dr, Bethany, WV 26032. Tel 304-829-7824; Email kmorgan@bethanywv.edu; Web: www.bethanywv.edu; *Chair & Prof Fine Arts* Kenneth Morgan
Estab 1840, dept estab 1958; den; D; Scholarships; SC 27, LC 7; D 136, non-maj 106, maj 30
Ent Req: HS dipl
Degrees: BA & BS 4 yrs
Tuition: $14,752 per yr; campus res available
Courses: Art History, Calligraphy, Ceramics, Drawing, Graphic Design, Illustration, Painting, Photography, Sculpture

BLUEFIELD

BLUEFIELD STATE COLLEGE, Division of Arts & Sciences, 219 Rock St, Bluefield, WV 24701-2198. Tel 304-327-4000; Fax 304-325-7747; Web: www.bluefieldstate.edu; *Prof* Joyce Shamro; *Head Dept* Jim Voelker
Estab 1895; pub; D & E; Scholarships; Fellowships; SC 14, LC 4; D 125, E 40, non-maj 150, minor 10, other 5
Ent Req: HS dipl, 18 yrs old
Degrees: BA, BA(Humanities), BS, BS(Educ) & BS(Engineering Technology) 4 yrs
Courses: Art Education, Art History, Ceramics, Computer Art, Drawing, Painting, Photography, Printmaking, Sculpture
Adult Hobby Classes: Enrl 10-15. Courses—Art in Western World, Photography, Television, Woodcarving
Children's Classes: Enrl varies. Courses—Ceramics, Drawing
Summer School: Dir, Dwight Moore. Enrl 15-20; term of 5 wks beginning June/July. Courses—Art Educ & Appreciation (workshops on occasion)

BUCKHANNON

WEST VIRGINIA WESLEYAN COLLEGE, Art Dept, 59 College Ave, Buckhannon, WV 26201-2699. Tel 304-473-8000, 473-8433; Email

mason_k@wvwc.edu; Web: www.wvwc.edu/aca/art/artfront; *Asst Prof* Ellen Mueller; *Asst Prof* Beth Koch; *Asst Prof* Phil McCollam
Estab 1890; Maintains nonprofit art gallery; art supplies available for purchase on campus; Den; D & E; SC 16, LC 6; non-maj 120, maj 20, grad 2
Ent Req: HS dipl, ent exam
Degrees: BA
Courses: Art Education, Art History, Ceramics, Computer Graphics, Computer Illustration, Design, Drawing, Graphic Design, Painting, Printmaking, Sculpture, Theatre Arts

CHARLESTON

UNIVERSITY OF CHARLESTON, Carleton Varney Dept of Art & Design, 2300 MacCorkle Ave SE, Charleston, WV 25304. Tel 304-357-4725; Fax 304-357-4175; Email swatts@ucwv.edu; *Coordr* Steve Watts; *Dir* Joellen Kerr; *Instr* Tracy Wasinger, BS
Estab 1888; FT 3, PT 3; pvt; D & E; Scholarships; maj 55
Ent Req: usual col req
Degrees: 4 yr
Courses: Advanced Studio, Art Administration, Art Appreciation, †Art Education, Art History, Color Theory, Design, Drafting, Drawing, †Interior Design, Painting, Photography, Printmaking, Teacher Training
Children's Classes: Enrl 30; tuition by the wk. Courses—Summer Art Camp Program
Summer School: Dir, Joellen Kerr. Tuition $60 per wk. Courses—Summer Colors

ELKINS

DAVIS & ELKINS COLLEGE, Dept of Art, 100 Campus Dr, Elkins, WV 26241-3996. Tel 304-637-1212; Fax 304-637-1287; Email larosem@DnE.edu; *Head, Assoc Prof* Matthew LaRose; *Adjunct Instr* Holly Adams; *Adjunct Instr* Mary Rayme; *Adjunct Instr* Donna Morgan
Estab 1904; FT 1, PT 3; pvt, den; D & E; Scholarships; SC 18, LC 4; non-maj 30, maj 10
Ent Req: HS dipl
Degrees: BA, BS
Tuition: $5290 per sem; campus res available
Courses: †Art Education, Art History, Ceramics, Costume Design & Construction, Drawing, Graphic Arts, Painting, Pottery, †Printmaking, Sculpture, Stage Design, †Theatre Arts, Weaving
Adult Hobby Classes: Enrl 90
Summer School: Dir Margo Blevin. Augusta Heritage Arts Workshop. Courses—Appalachian Crafts, Basketry, Bushcraft, Calligraphy, Chair Bottoming, Dance, Folkcarving, Folklore Musical Instrument Construction & Repair, Papermaking, Pottery, Stained Glass, Woodworking

FAIRMONT

FAIRMONT STATE COLLEGE, Div of Fine Arts, 1201 Locust Ave, Fairmont, WV 26554-2451. Tel 304-367-4000; Web: www.fscwv.edu; *Prof* John Clovis, MFA; *Prof* Dr Stephen Smigocki, MFA, PhD; *Prof* Barry Snyder, MFA; *Prof* Lynn Boggess, MFA
Pub; D & E; Scholarships; D maj 35, non-maj 15
Ent Req: HS dipl
Degrees: BA(Art Educ) and BS(Graphics, Fine Arts) 4 yrs
Courses: †Art Education, Art History, Ceramics, Commercial Design, Design, Drawing, Graphic Arts, Painting, Photography, Printmaking, Sculpture
Adult Hobby Classes: Two - three times a wk for 16 wks. Courses—same as above
Children's Classes: Enrl 20; tuition $25 per 6 wk term. Courses—Art for children ages 5 - 12, 2 - D & 3 - D Design
Summer School: Dir Dr S Snyder. Enrl 50; 4 wks per sessions. Courses—Art Education, Drawing, Design, Painting, Art Appreciation

GLENVILLE

GLENVILLE STATE COLLEGE, Dept of Fine Arts, 200 High St, Glenville, WV 26351-1200. Tel 304-462-6340; Fax 304-462-4049; Email chris.cosner@glenville.edu; Web: www.glenville.edu; *Chmn* Lloyd E Bone Jr; *Assoc Prof* John Selberg, MFA; *Assoc Prof* Chris Cosner, MFA; *Assoc Prof* Duane Chapman, MFA
Estab 1872, dept estab 1952; Maintains a non-profit art gallery & on-campus supplies shop; pub; D & E; Scholarships; SC 25, LC 3; D 128, E 42, non-maj 14, maj 55
Activities: Schols offered
Ent Req: HS dipl
Degrees: BA 4 yrs
Tuition: $3,516 per semester
Courses: Art Appreciation, †Art Education, Art History, †Ceramics, Drawing, Graphic Arts, Jewelry, Lettering, †Painting, Photography, Printmaking, Sculpture, †Studio Art, Textile Design, Weaving

HUNTINGTON

MARSHALL UNIVERSITY, Dept of Art & Design, 1 John Marshall Dr, Huntington, WV 25755-0003. Tel 304-696-6760; 696-2296 (Gallery); Fax 304-696-6505; Email clercx@marshall.edu; Web: www.marshall.edu; *Chmn* Byron Clercx
Estab 1903; Maintains Birke Art Gallery; FT 10; pub; maj incl grad 108
Ent Req: HS grad
Degrees: BFA & MA in art educ & studio 4 yrs
Courses: Art Education, Ceramics, Graphic Design, Painting, Photography, Printmaking, Sculpture, Weaving
Summer School: Tuition $427.10 for 6 sem hrs, nonres $1247.10 for 5 wk terms

INSTITUTE

WEST VIRGINIA STATE UNIVERSITY, Art Dept, PO Box 1000, Campus Box 4 Institute, WV 25112-1000. Tel 304-766-3196, 766-3198; Fax 304-768-9842; Web: www.wvstateu.edu; *Chair* Reidun Ovrebo PhD; *Asst Prof* Molly Erlandson; *Asst Prof* Paula Clendenin
D & E; Scholarships; SC 26, LC 11
Ent Req: HS dipl
Degrees: AB(Art) and BSEd(Art) 4 yrs
Tuition: Res—$1282 per sem; nonres—$2946 per sem
Courses: Appalachian Art & Crafts, Art Education, Art History, Ceramics, Computer Graphics, Design, Drawing, Figure Drawing, Graphic Design, Painting, Photography, Printmaking, Sculpture, Teacher Training
Summer School: Dir, R Ovrebo. Enrl 75.; 3 or 6 wk session. Courses—Art Appreciation, Basic Studio

KEYSER

POTOMAC STATE COLLEGE, Dept of Art, 101 Fort Ave, Keyser, WV 26726-2600. Tel 304-788-6800; Web: www.wvu.edu; *Pres* Anthony Whitmore, MA; *Chmn* Richard Davis
College estab 1953, dept estab 1974; FT 2; pub; D & E; SC 8, LC 2; D 160, non-maj 150, others 10
Ent Req: HS dipl
Degrees: AA 2 yrs, AAS 2 yrs
Courses: Drawing, Painting, Sculpture, Visual Foundation
Summer School: Dir, Edward Wade. Courses—Art Appreciation, Drawing, Painting

MONTGOMERY

WEST VIRGINIA INSTITUTE OF TECHNOLOGY, Creative Arts Dept, 405 Fayette Pike, Montgomery, WV 25136-2436. Tel 304-442-3302; Web: www.wvutech.edu; *Dept Secy* Dorothy Oliver
Estab 1896; pub; Scholarships; 3500 (total)
Ent Req: HS grad
Degrees: AS, BA and BS 2-4 yrs
Courses: Art Appreciation, Ceramics, Design, Graphic Design, Painting

MORGANTOWN

WEST VIRGINIA UNIVERSITY, College of Creative Arts, School of Art & Design, PO Box 6111, School of Art & Design Morgantown, WV 26506-6111. Tel 304-293-4077/2552; Fax 304-293-5731; Email alison.helm@mail.wvu.edu; Web: www.wvu.edu; *Prof* Janet Snyder, PhD; *Assoc Prof Emeritus* Victoria Fergus, PhD, MFA; *Assoc Prof* Naijun Zhang, MFA; *Assoc Prof* Kristina Olson, MA; *Prof* Eve Faulkes, MFA; *Prof & Dir of Art* Alison Helm, MFA; *Assoc Prof* Joseph Lupo, MFA; *Asst Prof* Dylan Collins, MFA; *Asst Prof* Joseph Galbreath, MFA; *Assoc Prof* Gerald Habarth, MFA; *Assoc Prof* Jason Lee, MFA; *Assoc Prof* Rhonda Reymond, PhD; *Assoc Prof* Shoji Satake, MFA; *Assoc Prof* Michael Sherwin, MFA; *Assoc Prof* Robert Moore, MFA; *Asst Prof* Kofi Opoku, MFA; *Asst Prof* Amy Schissel, MFA; *Asst Prof* Teri Giobbia, PhD; *Teaching Asst Prof* Jeffrey Moser, MFA
Estab 1867, div estab 1897; Maintain nonprofit art gallery; Mesaros Gallery, 1 Fine Arts Dr, WVU, Morgantown, WV 26506-6111; Evansdale Library; 16; Pub; D & E; Scholarships; SC, LC, GC; D 250, non-maj 5, maj 323, grad 20, others 87
Ent Req: HS dipl
Degrees: BFA & certification (Art Educ) and BFA 4 yrs, MA (Art) and MFA (Art) 3 yrs; grad degrees; Visual Therapy certificate
Tuition: $3,840 per sem w/fees in state; undergrad/grad in state $4,653; grad out of state $11,592 w/fees per sem
Courses: Art Appreciation, †Art Education, †Art History, Basic Design, †Ceramics, †Conceptual Art, †Design, Drawing, Electronic Media, †Graphic Arts, †Graphic Design, †History of Art & Architecture, †Interactive Design for Media, †Mixed Media, †Museum Staff Training, †Occupational Therapy, †Painting, Photography, †Printmaking, †Sculpture, Video
Summer School: Dir, Alison Helm. Enrl 80

PARKERSBURG

WEST VIRGINIA UNIVERSITY AT PARKERSBURG, Art Dept, 300 Campus Dr, Parkersburg, WV 26101-8656. Tel 304-424-8000; Fax 304-424-8354; Web: www.wvup.wvnet.edu; *Prof* Beth Sears Cox, MFA
Estab 1961, dept estab 1973; pub; D & E; Scholarships; SC 25, LC 5; D 120, E 80, non-maj 125, maj 8
Ent Req: HS dipl
Degrees: AA 2 yrs, BA
Courses: Art History, Bronze Casting, Ceramics, Drawing, Painting, Photography, Printmaking, Wood Carving

SHEPHERDSTOWN

SHEPHERD UNIVERSITY, Dept of Contemporary Art & Theater, Ctr for Contemporary Art, 92 W Campus Dr Shepherdstown, WV 25443; P.O. Box 5000, Shepherdstown, WV 25443-5000. Tel 304-876-5254; Fax 304-876-5766; Email rsmith@shepherd.edu; Web: www.shepherd.edu/artweb/; WATS 800-826-6807; *Dean* Dow Benedict; *Coordr Photog* Rich Bruner; *Coordr Design* Kristin Kaineg; *Chair & Coordr Non-Toxic Printmaking* Rhonda Smith; *Dir Exhib* Evan Boggess; *Coordr Painting* Sonya Evanisko; *Co-Coordr Photog* Erin Neve; *Coordr Theater*

Ed Herendeen; *Coordr Sculpture* Christian Benefiel; *Coordr Art History* Chris Coltrin; *Coordr Art Educ* David Modler; *Coordr Computer Labs* Kristin Kaineg
Estab 1872; Maintain a nonprofit art gallery - Frank Center Gallery, Frank Center for Creative Arts & Phase II Gallery, Shepherd Univ, Shepherdstown, WV 25443; on-campus shop where art supplies may be purchased; FT 11, PT 15; pub; D & E; Scholarships; SC 58, LC 12, GC 4; maj 250; grad stu 2-5
Ent Req: HS dipl, portfolio
Degrees: BFA, BA(Educ)
Tuition: $2,282/sem full-time
Courses: Advertising Design, Aesthetic Criticism, Aesthetics, Art Appreciation, †Art Education, Art History, Art Therapy, Conceptual Art, Constructions, Design, Design, Drawing, †Graphic Design, History of Art & Architecture, Intermedia, Mixed Media, †Painting, †Photography, †Printmaking, †Sculpture, Teacher Training, Theatre Arts, Video
Summer School: Chair, Rhonda Smith. Enrl 60; courses—Art Appreciation, Studio, Photo

WEST LIBERTY

WEST LIBERTY STATE COLLEGE, Div Art, PO Box 295, 125 Campus Service Center West Liberty, WV 26074-0295. Tel 304-336-8096; Fax 304-336-8056; Email dejaager@wlsc.edu; Web: www.wlsc.edu; *Chmn* Mark Williams, MFA; *Assoc Prof* Robert Villmagna; *Asst Prof* Brian Fencl; *Assoc Prof* Jim Haizlett; *Instr* Brad Johnson; *Instr* Paula Lucas
Estab 1836; pub; D & E; Scholarships; SC 40, LC 6; D 855, E 140, non-maj 900, maj 90, others 12
Ent Req: HS dipl, score of 17 or higher on ACT test or cumulative HS GPA of at least 2.0 or a combined verbal/math score of 680 on the SAT
Degrees: BA and BS 4 yrs
Courses: Advertising Design, Art Appreciation, †Art Education, Art History, Ceramics, Computer Graphics, Costume Design & Construction, Drawing, Film, Graphic Arts, †Graphic Design, History of Art & Architecture, Illustration, Jewelry, Lettering, Painting, Photography, Printmaking, Sculpture, Stage Design, Studio Crafts, Theatre Arts, Weaving
Summer School: Dir, David T Jauersak. Tuition res $100 per sem hr, nonres $190 per sem hr. Courses—Art Education, Special Education

WISCONSIN

APPLETON

LAWRENCE UNIVERSITY, Dept of Art & Art History, Wriston Art Ctr, 613 E College Ave Appleton, WI 54911; 711 E Boldt Way Appleton, WI 54911. Tel 920-832-6621; Fax 920-832-7362; Web: www.lawrence.edu/dept/art; *Prof* Carol Lawton; *Assoc Prof* Robert Neilson; *Asst Prof* Benjamin Tilghman; *Assoc Prof* J Shimon; *Chair & Assoc Prof* Elizabeth Carlson; *Assoc Prof* Benjamin Rhinehart
Estab 1847; Maintain nonprofit art gallery; FT 6; pvt; D; Scholarships; SC 21, LC 21
Ent Req: HS performance, CEEB scores, recommendation
Degrees: BA 4 yrs
Tuition: $40,200 includes room & board per 3 term yr
Courses: 3-D Design, Art Education, †Art History, Ceramics, Drawing, Painting, Photography, Printmaking, Sculpture, †Studio Art, Studio Ceramics

DE PERE

SAINT NORBERT COLLEGE, Div of Humanities & Fine Arts, 100 Grant St, De Pere, WI 54115-2099. Tel 920-403-3119 (Dir of Humanities); Fax 920-403-4086; Web: www.snc.edu/; *Dir* Dr Howard Ebert
Estab 1898; FT 6; pvt den; D; SC 19, LC 5; D 60, maj 60
Ent Req: HS dipl, ent exam
Degrees: BA 4 yrs
Courses: Aesthetics, Art Education, Art History, Ceramics, Drawing, Graphic Arts, Graphic Design, Illustration, Jewelry, Painting, Photography, Sculpture, Teacher Training
Summer School: Terms of 3 or 5 wks beginning June. Courses—Art Education, Ceramics, Drawing, History of Art, Painting, Sculpture

EAU CLAIRE

UNIVERSITY OF WISCONSIN-EAU CLAIRE, Dept of Art & Design, 105 Garfield Ave, Eau Claire, WI 54701-4811; PO Box 4004, Eau Claire, WI 54702-4004. Tel 715-836-3277; Fax 715-836-4882; Web: www.uwec.edu/; *Chmn* Christos Theo; *Prof Art & Design* Li-ying Bao; *Prof* Eugene Hood; *Prof* D Scott Robertson; *Dir Foster Gallery Woodshop Supv* Tom Wagener; *Assoc Prof* Lia Johnson; *Asst Prof* Jyl Kelley; *Asst Prof* Jason Lanka; *Assoc Prof* Jian Luo; *Assoc Prof* Susan O'Brien; *Assoc Prof* Karen O'Day; *Asst Prof* Gill Olon; *Assoc Prof* Sandra Starck; *Asst Prof* Wanrudee Buranakorn; *Asst Prof* Sooyun Im
Estab 1916; Maintains a nonprofit art gallery: Foster Gallery, Univ WI-Eau Claire, 121 Water St. Eau Claire, WI; pub; D & E; Scholarships; SC, LC varies; maj 325
Ent Req: HS dipl
Degrees: BA, BS & BFA 4 yrs
Tuition: Res—$8,148 per yr; nonres—$16,176 per yr
Courses: †Art Education, †Art History, †Ceramics, †Drawing, †Graphic Design, †Illustration, †Painting, †Photography, †Printmaking, †Sculpture

FOND DU LAC

MARIAN UNIVERSITY, Art Dept, 45 S National Ave, Fond Du Lac, WI 54935-4621. Tel 920-923-7612; Fax 920-923-7154; Email mmerline@marianuniversity.edu; Web: www.mariancoll.edu/; *Dean Arts, Humanities & Letters* James van Dyke, PhD; *Chair Art Dept* Mark Merline, MFA; *Assoc Prof* Tom Wallestad; *Instr* Hillary Quella; *Instr* Leah Klapperich; *Instr* Deborah Bartelt; *Instr* Shane McAdams; *Instr* Evelyn McLean-Cowan
Estab 1936; Four yr schols open to all; pvt; D & E; Scholarships; SC 10, LC 10; D 1,200, E 200, maj 50
Ent Req: HS dipl, ACT or SAT
Degrees: BA and BS 4 yrs
Tuition: $19,590 per yr, $300 per cr; campus res available
Courses: †Advertising Design, Aesthetics, Art Appreciation, †Art Education, Art History, †Art Therapy, Ceramics, †Commercial Art, †Conceptual Art, †Constructions, Design, †Display, Drawing, Fiber Arts, †Graphic Arts, Illustration, Jewelry, Mixed Media, Painting, Photography, Printmaking, Puppetry, Sculpture, Teacher Training
Adult Hobby Classes: Workshops, summer sessions, continuing education
Children's Classes: In Relationship with Art Education
Summer School: Workshops, cr art courses

GREEN BAY

UNIVERSITY OF WISCONSIN-GREEN BAY, Arts Dept, 2420 Nicolet, Green Bay, WI 54311-7001. Tel 920-465-2348, 465-2310; Fax 920-465-2890; Web: www.uwgb.edu; *Assoc Prof* Ronald Baba; *Prof* David Damkoehler; *Chmn* Curt Heuer; *Assoc Prof* Jeff Benzow; *Assoc Prof* Christine Style; *Asst Prof* Jennifer Mokren; *Asst Prof* Elizabeth Ament; *Prof* Jery Dell; *Prof* Carol Emmons; *Prof* Karon Winzenz
Estab 1970; FT 3; pub; D & E; SC 29, LC 3; D 5500
Ent Req: HS dipl, ent exam
Degrees: BA and BS 4 yrs
Courses: Acting & Directing, Aesthetics, Art Education, Ceramics, Costume & Makeup Design, Drawing, Environmental Design, Graphic Communications, Graphic Design, Intermedia, Jewelry, Mixed Media, Painting, Photography, Printmaking, Sculpture, Stage Design, Styles, Textile Design, Theatre Arts
Children's Classes: Varies
Summer School: Courses—vary

KENOSHA

CARTHAGE COLLEGE, Art Dept, 2001 Alford Park Dr, Kenosha, WI 53140-1929. Tel 262-551-5859; Fax 262-551-6208; Web: www.carthage.edu; *Chmn* Ed Kalke
Estab 1963; Priv, den; D & E; Scholarships
Degrees: BA
Tuition: Res—$18,205 per term; campus res—room & board $5465
Courses: Advertising Design, Art Education, Art History, Basic Photography, Ceramics, Design, Drawing, Graphic Design

UNIVERSITY OF WISCONSIN-PARKSIDE, Art Dept, 400 Wood Rd, Kenosha, WI 53144; PO Box 2000, Kenosha, WI 53141-2000. Tel 414-595-2581; Fax 414-595-2271; *Prof* Douglas DeVinny, MFA; *Assoc Prof* Dennis Bayuzick, MFA; *Assoc Prof* Alan Goldsmith, MFA; *Prof* David Holmes, MFA; *Asst Prof* Trenton Baylor, MFA; *Asst Prof* Susan Funkenstein, PhD; *Lectr* Rob Miller, MA; *Asst Prof* Lisa Barber; *Asst Prof* Tao Chen
Estab 1965; Maintain nonprofit art gallery; Commun Arts Gallery, Kenosha, WI; art supplies available on-campus; Pub; D & E; Scholarships; SC 25, LC 6
Ent Req: ent req HS dipl, upper 50%
Degrees: BA and BS 4 yrs
Courses: Advertising Design, Aesthetics, †Animation, Art Appreciation, †Art Education, Art History, Art Metals, †Ceramics, †Design, †Drawing, †Graphic Arts, †Graphic Design, History of Art & Architecture, †Illustration, Illustration, Jewelry, Life Drawing, †Painting, †Printmaking, †Sculpture, Silversmithing, Teacher Training, Textile Design, Weaving, †Web Design
Summer School: Tuition $210 res hr for term of 8 wks beginning mid June. Courses—Vary from summer to summer

LA CROSSE

UNIVERSITY OF WISCONSIN-LA CROSSE, Center for the Arts, 1725 State St, La Crosse, WI 54601-3788. Tel 608-785-8230; Fax 608-785-8840; Web: www.uwlax.edu/art; *Chmn* Jennifer Williams Terpstra; *Gallery Dir* John Ready
Estab 1905; University maintains a nonprofit art gallery; on-campus shop for purchase of art supplies; FT 8; pub; D & E; Scholarships; SC 25, LC 5; (univ) 7600
Ent Req: HS dipl
Degrees: BA and BS 4 yrs
Tuition: Res—$155.90 per cr hr; nonres—$468.90 per cr hr
Courses: 2-D & 3-D Design, Aesthetics in Art Criticism in the Visual Arts, Ancient Art of the Western World, Art Appreciation, Art Education, Art Metals, Blacksmithing, Ceramics, Computer Art, Drawing, Figure Drawing, Graphic Arts, History of American Art, Medieval Art of the Western World, Modern Art of the Western World, Multi-Cultural Art Survey, Painting, Printmaking, Renaissance Art of the Western World, Sculpture
Adult Hobby Classes: Courses—Blacksmithing, Ceramics, Outreach Jewelry
Summer School: Courses—vary

VITERBO UNIVERSITY, Art Dept, 815 S Ninth, La Crosse, WI 54601. Tel 608-796-3000, 796-3755; Fax 608-791-0367; Email lschoenfielder@viterbo.edu; Web: www.viterbo.edu/; *Instr* Diane Crane; *Chmn* Lisa Schoenfielder; *Prof* Peter Fletcher; *Asst Prof* Tom Bartel
Estab 1890; pvt; D & E; Scholarships; SC 10-12, LC 6; D 55, maj 55

Degrees: BA, BAEd & BS 4 yrs
Courses: Advertising Design, Art Education, Art History, Ceramics, Commercial Art, Drawing, Fibers, Graphic Arts, Illustration, Painting, Photography, Printmaking, Sculpture, Teacher Training, Weaving

WESTERN WISCONSIN TECHNICAL COLLEGE, Graphics Division, 400 7th St N, La Crosse, WI 54601-3368. Tel 608-785-9200; Fax 608-785-9473; Email west@fahlr.wwtc.edu; Web: wwtc.edu; *Chmn* Richard Westpfahl; *Program Head* Philip Brochhauren; *Instr* Barb Fischer; *Instr* Craig Kunce; *Instr* Lane Butz; *Instr* Eddie Hale; *Instr* Ken Hey; *Instr* Chris Bucheit; *Visual Com Instr* Mark Davini; *Visual Com Instr* Jacob Griggs; *Electronic Imaging & Print Instr* Janet Oglesby; *Electronic Imag & Print Instr* Eugene Van Roy
Estab 1911, dept estab 1964; pub; D & E; Scholarships; SC & LC 16; D 130, E 145, non-maj 132, maj 143
Ent Req: HS dipl or GED
Degrees: AAS 2 yrs
Courses: Advertising Design, †Commercial Art, Computer Graphics, Display, Film, †Graphic Arts, Graphic Design, Illustration, Lettering, Media, Mixed Media, Painting, Photography, Printing & Publishing, Stage Design, Video, Visual Communications
Adult Hobby Classes: Enrl 264. Courses—Color Photo Printing, Painting, Photography, Computer Graphics
Summer School: Dir, Richard Westpfahl. Courses—varied

MADISON

EDGEWOOD COLLEGE, Art Dept, 1000 Edgewood College Dr, Madison, WI 53711-1997. Tel 608-663-2307; Fax 608-663-3291; Email rtarrell@edgewood.edu; Web: www.edgewood.edu/; *Assoc Prof* David Smith; *Assoc Prof* Melanie Herzog; *Instr* Ellen Meyer; *Instr* Mary Lybarger; *Asst Prof* Randy Feig; *Asst Prof* Janice M Havlena; *Prof* Robert Tarrell; *Asst Prof* Alan Luft; *Instr* Tracy Dietzel; *Instr* Jane Fasse
Estab 1941; Maintain nonprofit art gallery; DeRicci Gallery; den; D & E; Grants
Ent Req: HS dipl, ACT
Degrees: BA or BS 4 yrs
Tuition: $7100 per sem; campus res available
Courses: †Art Education, Art History, Art Therapy, Calligraphy, Ceramics, Design, Drawing, Graphic Design, Painting, Photography, †Printmaking, Sculpture, †Teacher Training, Textile Design, Video
Summer School: Dir, Dr Joseph Schmiedicke. Tuition $110 per cr. Courses—vary

MADISON AREA TECHNICAL COLLEGE, Art Dept, 1701 Wright St, Madison, WI 53704-2599. Tel 608-246-6058, 246-6100, 246-6002; Fax 608-246-6880; *Chmn* Jerry E Butler PhD
Estab 1911; Pub; D & E; Scholarships; SC 45, LC 12; D 5,300, E 23,000 (part-time)
Ent Req: HS dipl
Degrees: AA 2 yrs (Commercial Art, Interior Designing, Photography & Visual Communications)
Tuition: $64 per cr
Courses: Advertising Design, Art History, Calligraphy, Ceramics, †Commercial Art, Design, Display, Drawing, Handicrafts, Illustration, Jewelry, Lettering, Painting, †Photography, Printmaking, Visual Communications
Adult Hobby Classes: Enrl 1,000. Courses—same as regular session

UNIVERSITY OF WISCONSIN, MADISON, Dept of Art, 455 N Park St, 6241 Humanities Bldg Madison, WI 53706-1483. Tel 608-262-1660; Fax 608-265-4593; Email artinfo@education.wisc.edu; Web: www.art.wisc.edu; *Prof* Jim Escalante; *Prof* Jack Damer; *Emer Prof* Leslee Nelson; *Emer Prof* Bruce Breckenridge; *Emer Prof* Cavaliere Ketchum; *Emer Prof* Richard Long; *Emer Prof* Truman Lowe; *Emer Prof* George Cramer; *Emer Prof* Doug Marschalek; *Emer Prof* Frances Myers; *Emer Prof* Steve Feren; *Emer Prof* David Becker; *Prof* Elaine Scheer; *Prof* Tom Loeser; *Prof* Derrick Buisch; *Prof* Michael Connors; *Emer Prof* Theresa Marche; *Prof* T L Solien; *Prof* Laurie Beth Clark; *Emer Prof* Patricia Fennell; *Emer Prof* Fred Fenster; *Prof* Aristotle Georgiades; *Prof* Nancy Mladenoff; *Prof* Gail Simpson; *Prof* Lisa Gralnick; *Prof* John Hitchcock; *Prof* Stephen Hilyard; *Assoc Prof* Fred Stonehouse; *Assoc Prof* Tom Jones; *Asst Prof* Faisal Abdu'Allah; *Asst Prof* Emily Arthur; *Asst Prof* Matthew Bakkom; *Asst Prof* Lynda Barry; *Asst Prof* Jeff Clancy; *Asst Prof* Sarah Fitzsimons; *Asst Prof* Gerit Grimm; *Asst Prof* Helen Lee; *Prof* Dennis Miller; *Asst Prof* Meg Mitchell; *Prof* Doug Rosenberg; *Asst Prof* Leslie Smith III; *Faculty Assoc* Michael Villiquette
Estab 1911; Maintains nonprofit Gallery 7 455 N Park St, Madison, WI 53706 & Art Lofts Gallery 111 N Frances St, Madison, WI 53706 and Kohler Art Library 160 Conrad A Elvehjem Bldg, 800 University Ave, Madison, WI 53706; on-campus shop sells art supplies; FT 32; pub; D & E; Scholarships; Fellowships; SC 100, LC 10, GC 50; non maj 200, maj 280, grad 90
Degrees: BS Art, BS Art Educ, BFA, MA, MFA
Tuition: Res—undergrad $5,212 per sem, grad $5,932 per sem; nonres—undergrad $13,327 per sem, grad $12,595 per sem
Courses: Art Education, †Art History, Book Making, Ceramics, †Commercial Art, †Conceptual Art, †Constructions, Design, Drawing, Etching, Glass, †Graphic Arts, Graphic Design, Illustration, Intermedia, Jewelry, Lettering, Lithography, Mixed Media, Painting, Papermaking, Performance, Photography, Printmaking, Sculpture, Serigraphy, †Silversmithing, †Stage Design, Stage Design & Lighting, Typography, Video, Wood, Woodworking
Summer School: Three wk early session, 8 wk session, 4 wk session
—**Dept of Art History**, 800 University Ave, 232 Conrad A Elvehjem Building Madison, WI 53706-1414. Tel 608-263-2340; Fax 608-265-6425; Email arthistory@ls.wisc.edu; Web: arthistory.wisc.edu/; *Prof Art History* Barbara C Buenger; *Prof* Henry J Drewal; *Prof* Narcisco G Menocal; *Prof, Dept Chmn* Gail L Geiger; *Prof* Jane C Hutchison; *Prof* Julia K Murray; *Prof* Quitman E Phillips; *Dept Adminr* Sandra Russell; *Prof* Nicholas D Cahill; *Prof* Thomas E A Dale; *Asst Prof* Anna V Andrzejewski; *Asst Prof* Jill H Casid; *Assoc Prof* Nancy R Marshall; *Assoc Prof* Ann Smart Martin; *Instr* Dan Fuller; *Instr* Gautama Vajracharya
Estab 1848, dept estab 1925; Art supplies available at univ bookstore; Pub; D & E; Scholarships; Fellowships; LC 15, GC 18-20; D 1,200, maj 250, non-maj 1,100, grad 150, continuing educ 100
Ent Req: BA, BS, BFMA
Degrees: MA, PhD
Tuition: Res—$4,160 per sem; nonres—$11,796 per sem
Courses: 20th Century Photography, African Art, American Art, †Art History, Asian Art, Ceramics, Dutch Painting, Greek Art & Society, Material Culture, Modern Art, Printmaking, Sculpture, Venetian Painting, Visual Culture, Western Architecture, Women's Art
—**Graduate School of Business, Bolz Center for Arts Administration,** 975 University Ave, Madison, WI 53706-1324. Tel 608-263-4161; Fax 608-265-2739; Email ataylor@bus.wisc.edu; Web: www.bolzcenter.org/; *Dir* Andrew Taylor
Estab 1969
Degrees: MA
Tuition: Res bus MA $1,777.35 per sem, non-res $4,985.35 per sem
Courses: Arts Administration Seminars, Colloquium in Arts Administration

MANITOWOC

SILVER LAKE COLLEGE, Art Dept, 2406 S Alverno Rd, Manitowoc, WI 54220-9319. Tel 920-684-6691, 686-6181; Fax 920-684-7082; Email merdmann@silver.sl.edu; Web: www.sl.edu/art; *Prof, Chmn* Sr Mariella Erdmann, MFA; *Assoc Prof* Dionne Landgraff, PhD; *Assoc Prof* Tracey Richardson, MFA
Estab 1936, dept estab 1959; pvt; D & E, wkends; SC 21, LC 6; D 50, E 10, non-maj 25, maj 25
Ent Req: HS dipl, ACT or SAT
Degrees: BA(Studio Art) or BA(Art Educ) 4 yrs
Courses: †Art Education, Art History, Calligraphy, Ceramics, †Commercial Art, Computer Graphics, Drawing, Graphic Arts, Graphic Design, Jewelry, Lettering, Mixed Media, Painting, Photography, Printmaking, Sculpture, †Studio Art, Teacher Training, Textile Design
Adult Hobby Classes: Courses—Vary
Children's Classes: Courses—Clay, Drawing, Fibers, Graphics, Painting, Sculpture
Summer School: Dir, Sr Lorita Gaffney. Courses—Vary

MARINETTE

UNIVERSITY OF WISCONSIN COLLEGE - MARINETTE, Art Dept, 750 W Bay Shore St, Marinette, WI 54143-4253. Tel 715-735-4322; Fax 715-735-4307; Email ssinfo@wuc.edu; Web: www.uwc.edu; *Prof* Judith Baker; *Prof* Frank Zetzman; *Prof* Heidi Jensen; *Prof* Diana Budde; *Prof* Tom Fleming; *Prof & Chmn* Kitty Kingston; *Prof* Stephanie Coupolos-Selle; *Prof* James LaMalfa
Estab 1850, dept estab 1946; Maintains nonprofit Fini art Gallery; Theater on the Bay; Library, Lonnie Schofield, Dir; Campus shop where art supplies may be purchased; Pub; D, E & weekend; Scholarships; SC 7, LC 3, live video; D non-maj 100, maj 10
Ent Req: HS dipl or GED
Degrees: AAS 2 yrs
Tuition: Res—undergrad $2,300 per sem; nonres—undergrad $4,203 per sem
Courses: 2-D Design, Art History, †Digital Cinema, †Digital Design, Drawing, Painting, Photography, Sculpture, Survey of Art
Summer School: Dir, Sidney Bremer. Tuition $70 per cr. Courses—Art Appreciation, Art History

MENOMONIE

UNIVERSITY OF WISCONSIN-STOUT, Dept of Art & Design, 324 Applied Art Bldg, Menomonie, WI 54751; PO Box 790, Art & Design Dept Menomonie, WI 54751-0790. Tel 715-232-1141; Fax 715-232-1669; Email jacksonm@uwstout.edu; Web: www.uwstout.edu/cas/; *Head Dept* Ron Verdon, MFA; *Prof* Todd Boppel, MFA; *Prof* Doug Cumming, MFA; *Prof* Eddie Wong, MFA; *Prof* Dr Claudia Smith, PhD, MFA; *Prof* Susan Hunt, MFA; *Prof* Rob Price, MFA; *Prof* Paul De Long, MFA; *Asst Prof* William De Hoff, MFA; *Asst Prof* Mark Kallsen, MFA; *Asst Prof* Kate Maury, MFA; *Asst Prof* Maureen Mitton, MFA; *Asst Prof* Timothy O'Keeffe, MFA; *Asst Prof* Benjamin Pratt, MFA; *Asst Prof* David Gariff, MFA; *Asst Prof* David Morgan, MFA; *Lectr* Nancy Blum-Cumming, MFA
Estab 1893, dept estab 1965; pub; E; SC 60, LC 6; D 24, non-maj 1200, maj 630
Ent Req: HS dipl
Degrees: BS(Art), BFA(Art) 4 yrs
Courses: †Art Education, Art History, Art Metals, Art Period Courses, Blacksmithing, Ceramics, Design, Drawing, Fashion Illustration, †Graphic Design, †Industrial Design, †Interior Design, Painting, Printmaking, Sculpture, Silversmithing
Children's Classes: Sat classes in Art Design, Art History, Fine Arts, Graphic Arts
Summer School: Dir, Gene Bloedorn. Courses—Advanced Graphic Design, Ceramics, Drawing, Design, Life Drawing, Painting, Printmaking

MEQUON

CONCORDIA UNIVERSITY, Division of Performing & Visual Arts, 12800 N Lake Shore Dr, Mequon, WI 53097-2418. Tel 262-243-5700; Fax 262-243-4351; Email gayland.store@con.edu; Web: www.cuw.edu; *Dir* Dr Gene Edward Veith; *Prof* Maaji Bell; *Prof* Jeff Shaarhan; *Prof* Terry Valentine; *Prof* Dean Graf
Estab 1881, dept estab 1971; Maintain nonprofit art gallery, Concordia University Art Gallery; den; D & E; SC 25, LC 4; non-maj 100, maj 60
Ent Req: HS dipl
Degrees: BA
Courses: †Aesthetics, †Art Education, †Art History, †Calligraphy, †Ceramics, Design, †Design, †Drawing, †Graphic Arts, †Graphic Design, †History of Art & Architecture, †Mixed Media, †Painting, †Photography, †Printmaking, †Sculpture, †Teacher Training, †Weaving
Summer School: Dr. William Cario, Asst VPres of Acad, Terms of 6 wks. Courses—Drawing & Painting (outdoors)

MILWAUKEE

ALVERNO COLLEGE, Art Dept, 3400 S 43rd St, Milwaukee, WI 53219-4844; PO Box 343922, Milwaukee, WI 53234-3922. Tel 414-382-6000, 382-6148; Fax 414-382-6354; *Chmn* Nancy Lamers
Estab 1948; pvt, W only in degree program; D & E; Scholarships; SC 20, LC 5; D 2300, E 2300, maj 60
Ent Req: GPA, class rank and ACT or SAT
Degrees: BA 4 yrs (or 128 cr)
Tuition: $6000 per sem; campus res—room & board available, $1900 per sem
Courses: Art Education, Art History, Art Therapy, Ceramics, Computer Graphics, Drawing, Enameling (Cloisonne), Fibers, General Crafts, Introduction to Visual Art, Metal Working, Painting, Printmaking, Sculpture, Teacher Training
Summer School: Term June to Aug. Courses—Art Education, Studio Art

CARDINAL STRITCH UNIVERSITY, Art Dept, 6801 N Yates Rd, Milwaukee, WI 53217-3985. Tel 414-410-4100; Fax 414-351-7516; Email tbernie@stritch.edu; Web: www.stritch.edu/; *Asst Prof* Peter Galante; *Asst Prof* Teri Wagner; *Instr* Michal Ann Carley; *Asst Prof* Steven Sellars; *Asst Prof* Timothy Abler; *Dean Arts & Scis* Dr Dickson K Smith
Estab 1937; den; D & E; Scholarships; SC 29, LC 17; maj 98
Ent Req: HS dipl, ent exam
Degrees: AA, BA, BFA
Courses: †Art Education, †Art History, †Ceramics, Computer Graphics, †Drawing, †Fibers, †Film, †Graphic Design, Illustration, †Jewelry, †Metalsmithing, †Painting, †Photography, †Printmaking, †Sculpture, †Textile Design, †Video
Adult Hobby Classes: Enrl 200; tuition $40-$100 per 8-12 wk sessions. Courses—Basic, Ceramics, Drawing, Mixed Media, Painting, Watercolor
Children's Classes: Enrl 100; tuition $60 per child per 12 classes. Courses—traditional media plus various crafts

MILWAUKEE AREA TECHNICAL COLLEGE, School of Media & Creative Arts, 700 W State St, Milwaukee, WI 53233-1419. Tel 414-297-6433; Fax 414-297-7689; Email carlsobd@matc.edu; Web: www.matc.edu; *Assoc Dean* Brian Carlson, BA & MS; *Instr* Howard Austin, MS; *Instr* Edward Adams, MFA; *Instr* Corrine Kraus, BFA; *Instr* Mark Saxon, AAS; *Instr* Robert Stocki, BFA; *Dean* Mohammad Dakwar, BS
Estab 1912, dept estab 1958; pub; D & E & Online; Scholarships; Financial aid; D 240, E 150
Ent Req: HS dipl
Degrees: AA 2 yrs & 1 yr Technical
Courses: 3-D Modeling & Animation, Advertising Design, Audio Production, Commercial Art, Computer Graphics, Computer Simulation & Gaming, Design, Display, Drawing, eProduction, Graphic Arts, Graphic Design, Illustration, †Mixed Media, Mobile App Design, Multimedia, Music, Photography, Video, Visual Communications
Adult Hobby Classes: Tuition $46.10 per cr

MILWAUKEE INSTITUTE OF ART & DESIGN, 273 E Erie St, Milwaukee, WI 53202-6003. Tel 414-847-3342; Fax 414-291-8077; Web: www.miad.edu; *VPres Academic Affairs* David Martin; *Pres* Jeffrey Morin; *Asst Dir Library Servs* Nancy Siker
Open Mon - Thurs 7:30 AM - 9 PM, Fri 7:30 AM - 5 PM, Sat & Sun 1 PM - 5 PM; Estab 1974; Maintain non-profit art gallery, Frederick Layton Gallery, Books Stevens Gallery, 273 E Erie St, Milwaukee, WI 53202; on-campus shop where art supplies may be purchased; FT 100, PT 60; pvt; D&E; Scholarships; SC, LC; D 400, maj 650, pre-col 320, adult learning 340
Ent Req: HS dipl, portfolio
Degrees: BFA 4 yrs
Tuition: $21,800 per yr
Courses: Advertising Design, Aesthetics, †Architecture, Art History, Conceptual Art, Constructions, Design, Display, Drafting, Drawing, Graphic Design, History of Art & Architecture, Illustration, Industrial Design, Interior Design, Painting, Photography, Printmaking, Sculpture, †Video

MOUNT MARY COLLEGE, Art & Design Division, 2900 N Menomonee River Pkwy, Milwaukee, WI 53222. Tel 414-258-4810; Fax 414-256-1224; Email huebner@mtmary.edu; Web: www.mtmary.edu; *Prof* Angelee Fuchs, MA; *Prof* Joseph Rozman, MFA; *Assoc Prof* Sandra Keiser, MA; *Assoc Prof* Sr Aloyse Hessburg, MA; *Assoc Prof* Pamela Steffen, MBS; *Chmn* Lynn Kapitan, PhD; *Assoc Prof* Sr Carla Huebner, MS, MA; *Assoc Prof* Dennis Klopfer, MS; *Asst Prof* Melody Todd, MS; *Asst Prof* Greg Miller, MS; *Asst Prof* Karen McCormick, MA; *Asst Prof* Troy Gerth, MFA; *Instr* Patty Rass, MA; *Instr* Sue Loesl, MA; *Asst Prof* Nancy Lohmiller, BA; *Prof* Sr Rosemarita Huebner, MFA; *Instr* Janice Stewart, MA; *Instr* Dianne Atkinson, MA; *Instr* Mary Bartling, BA; *Prof* Bruce Moon, PhD; *Asst Prof* Leona Nelson, MA; *Asst Prof* Elizabeth Gaston, PhD; *Instr* Barbara Chappell, MA; *Instr* Sandra Tonz; *Instr* Joan Kadow; *Instr* Marie Perloneo; *Asst Prof* Debra Heermans, MA; *Instr* Jackie Halverson, MA; *Instr* Carol Powers, PhD
Estab 1913, dept estab 1929; Maintains Marian Gallery, 2900 Menomonee River Pkwy, Milwaukee, WI 53222; art supplies available at on-campus shop; pvt, W only; D & E; Scholarships; SC 22, LC 12, GC12; D 200, E 30, non-maj 50, maj 300, grad 50
Ent Req: HS dipl
Degrees: BA 4 yrs, MA(Art Therapy)
Tuition: $11,380 per yr, $5660 per sem; campus res—available; board $750 - $1000 per sem
Courses: †Advertising Design, Aesthetics, Architecture, Art Appreciation, †Art Education, Art History, †Art Therapy, Calligraphy, Ceramics, †Commercial Art, Constructions, †Costume Design & Construction, Design, Display, Drawing, †Fashion Arts, †Graphic Arts, †Graphic Design, Handicrafts, †History of Art & Architecture, †Interior Design, †Lettering, †Mixed Media, †Occupational Therapy, †Painting, †Photography, †Printmaking, †Sculpture, Silversmithing, †Teacher Training, †Textile Design, Video
Adult Hobby Classes: Enrl 1300; tuition variable, on going year round. Courses—Varied, self-interest
Children's Classes: Enrl 125; tuition $65 for 1-6 wk term, summer only. Courses—Arts & Crafts
Summer School: Dir, Toni Wulff

UNIVERSITY OF WISCONSIN-MILWAUKEE, Peck School of the Arts, Dept of Art & Design, 3203 N Downer Ave (MIT371), Milwaukee, WI 53211; PO Box 413, Milwaukee, WI 53201-0413. Tel 414-229-4947; Fax 414-229-2973; Email art-info@uwm.edu; Web: www.arts.uwm.edu; *Chair* Kyoung Ae Cho; *Dir Grad Studies* Jessica Meuninck Ganger; *Dir Foundations* Josie Osborne
Dept of Art & Design estab 1919; Peck School of the Arts estab 1962; Maintain a nonprofit art gallery, INOVA Institute of Visual Art, PO Box 413, Milwaukee, WI 53201; maintains Golda Meier Library; scholarships of $55,000 open to all art students for 1 yr annually; art supplies sold at on-campus store; FT 21, PT 37; pub; D & E; Scholarships; SC 70, LC 9, GC, AE 10; maj 800, grad 22
Ent Req: Portfolio review/application
Degrees: BFA(Art), BFA with teachers cert, BA(Art), MA(Art), MS(Art Educ), MFA(Art)
Tuition: www.bfs.uwm.edu/fees
Courses: Advertising Design, Art Appreciation, Art Education, Ceramics, Collage, Commercial Art, Conceptual Art, Constructions, Costume Design & Construction, Design, Digital Studio Practice, Drawing, Fibers, Graphic Design, Interarts, Metals, Painting, Photography, Printmaking, Sculpture, Teacher Training, Textile Design
Adult Hobby Classes: jewelry & metalsmithing $65-$270 per workshop
Summer School: Kyoung Ae Cho, Chair

OSHKOSH

UNIVERSITY OF WISCONSIN OSHKOSH, Dept of Art, 800 Algoma Blvd, Oshkosh, WI 54901-8651. Tel 920-424-2222; Fax 920-424-1738; Web: www.uwosh.edu/art; *Chmn* Edwin Jager; *Asst Prof* Jaehan Bae; *Asst Prof* Michael Beitz; *Asst Prof* Jessica Calderwood; *Assoc Prof* Karina Cutler-Lake; *Asst Prof* Mary Hoefferie; *Prof* Li Hu; *Prof* Jeff Lipschutz; *Prof* Richard Masters; *Assoc Prof* Susan Maxwell; *Prof* Gail Panske; *Prof* Arthur Pontynen; *Assoc Prof* Andrew Redington; *FT* Barbara Rosenthal; *Asst Prof* Emmet Sandberg; *Assoc Prof* Wendy Strauch-Nelson
Estab 1871; Maintain nonprofit art gallery, Priebe Gallery, Dept. of Art, University of Wisconsin, Oshkosh, WI 54901; schols open to art majors; on-campus art supplies shop; FT 18; pub; D & E; Scholarships; SC 56, LC 14, GC 31; D 10,5000, E 2500, maj 300, minors 70
Ent Req: HS dipl
Degrees: BA, BS(Art) 4 yrs, BFA 82 cr
Tuition: Res—$2606.90; non-res—$8548.90; campus res—room & board $2658
Courses: Advertising Design, †Art Appreciation, Art History, †Art Metals, Ceramics, Commercial Art, †Design, Drawing, †Functional Design, Graphic Arts, Graphic Design, Jewelry, Lettering, Painting, Photography, Printmaking, Sculpture, Teacher Training, Textile Design, Woodcraft

PLATTEVILLE

UNIVERSITY OF WISCONSIN-PLATTEVILLE, Dept of Fine Art, 1 University Plz, Art Bldg 212B Platteville, WI 53818-3099. Tel 608-342-1781; Fax 608-342-1491; Web: www.uwplatt.edu; *Instr* Steve Vance; *Instr* Kaye Winder; *Chmn* David Van Buren
Estab 1866; FT 8; pub; D & E; SC 30, LC 5, GC 3; maj 105
Ent Req: HS dipl, ent exam
Degrees: BA and BS 4 yrs
Tuition: Res—undergrad $3520; nonres—undergrad $12,300; campus res—room & board $1295 per sem
Courses: Art in Elementary Education, Art Survey, Ceramics, Drawing, Ethnic Art, Fiber & Fabrics, Graphic Design, Illustration, Lettering & Typographic, Painting, Photography, Printmaking
Summer School: Enrl 2200; term of 8 wks beginning June. Courses—same as regular session

RICE LAKE

UNIVERSITY OF WISCONSIN, Center-Barron County, Dept of Art, 1800 College Dr, Rice Lake, WI 54868-2414. Tel 715-234-8176, Ext 5408; Fax 715-234-1975; Web: www.uwc.edu; *Prof* Don Ruedy, MFA
Estab 1968; FT 1 PT 1; pub; D & E; Scholarships; SC 8, LC 2; D 63, E 10, non-maj 57, maj 16
Ent Req: HS dipl
Degrees: AA
Tuition: In-state—$1280
Courses: Art History, Calligraphy, Design, Drawing, Jewelry, Lettering, Painting, Printmaking, Theatre Arts
Children's Classes: Enrl 30; tuition $40 for 2 wks in summer. Courses—Art

RIPON

RIPON COLLEGE, Art Dept, 300 Seward St, PO Box 248 Ripon, WI 54971-0248. Tel 920-748-8110; Email kainee@ripon.edu; Web: www.ripon.edu/academics/; *Chmn* Rafael Salas; *Prof* Evelyn Kain; *Asst Prof* Travis Nygard; *Asst Prof* Mollie Oblinger
Estab 1851; Pvt; D; Scholarships; Financial aid; SC 13, LC 8; maj 20
Ent Req: grad from accredited secondary school, SAT or ACT is recommended, but not required
Degrees: BA
Tuition: $18,000 per yr
Courses: †Art History, Design, Drawing, Mixed Media, Painting

RIVER FALLS

UNIVERSITY OF WISCONSIN-RIVER FALLS, Art Dept, 410 S Third St River Falls, WI 54022-5001. Tel 715-425-3266; Fax 715-425-0657; Email michael.a.padgett@uwrf.edu; Web: www.uwrf.edu/art/welcome; *Chmn* Michael Padgett
Estab 1874, major estab 1958; pub; D; Scholarships; SC 26, LC 18; non-maj 400, maj 170
Ent Req: HS dipl
Degrees: BA, BS(Educ), BFA and BS(Liberal Arts) 4 yrs
Courses: Aesthetics, †Art Education, Art History, Ceramics, Costume Design & Construction, Drawing, Fibers, Film, Glass Blowing, Graphic Design, History of Art & Architecture, Jewelry, Painting, Photography, Printmaking, Silversmithing, Stained Glass, Textile Design
Summer School: Dir, Dr Lynn Jermal. Enrl 1600; 4 wk sessions. Courses—Clay, Fibers, Glass, Painting, Printmaking, Sculpture

STEVENS POINT

UNIVERSITY OF WISCONSIN-STEVENS POINT, Dept of Art & Design, 1800 Portage St, College of Fine Arts Stevens Point, WI 54481-1925. Tel 715-346-2669, 346-4066; Fax 715-346-4072; Email rstolzer@uwsp.edu; Web: www.uwsp.edu/acad/cofa/index.htm, www.uwsp.edu/art-design/; *Prof* Rex Dorethy, MFA; *Prof* Robert Stowers, MFA; *Prof* Diane Bywaters, MFA; *Prof* Anne-Bridget Gary, MFA; *Prof* Robert Erickson, MFA; *Prof* Larry Ball, MFA; *Prof* Rob Stolzer, MFA; *Prof* Guillermo Penafiel, MFA; *Prof* John O Smith, MFA; *Lect* Mark Pohlkamp, MFA; *Prof* Susan Morrison, MFA; *Assoc Lectr* Sheila Sullivan; *Acad Dept Assoc* Mimi Johnson; *Dir Gallery* Caren Heft; *Sr Lectr* Mark Brueggeman; *Assoc Lectr* William McKee; *Asst Prof* Diana Black; *Asst Prof* Stuart Morris; *Asst Prof* Kristin Theilking; *Assoc Lect* Mary Rosek; *Assoc Lect* Keven Brunett; *Art Hist Librn* Matthew Sackel; *Prof* Cortney Chaffin, MFA; *Prof* Jillian Noble, MFA
Estab 1894; Maintain a nonprofit art gallery, Edna Carlsten Art Gallery; Pub; D & E; Scholarships; SC 47, LC 8, GC 7; D 866, non-maj 666, maj 325
Ent Req: HS dipl
Degrees: BA(Fine Arts) & BFA(Art-Professional)
Courses: †Advertising Design, †Art Appreciation, †Art Education, †Art History, Ceramics, †Commercial Art, Computer Graphics, †Design, Drawing, †Graphic Arts, Graphic Design, †History of Art & Architecture, †Landscape Architecture, Painting, Photography, Printmaking, Sculpture, †Studio Art
Children's Classes: Art Workshop

SUPERIOR

UNIVERSITY OF WISCONSIN-SUPERIOR, Programs in the Visual Arts, PO Box 2000, Holden Fine Arts Ctr 3101 Belknap & Catlin Superior, WI 54880-4500. Tel 715-394-8391, 394-8101; Email lgrittne@staff.uwsuper.edu; Web: www.uwsuper.edu; *Prof* Mel Olsen, MFA; *Prof* William Morgan, MFA; *Assoc Prof* Laurel Scott, PhD, MFA; *Assoc Prof* Susan Loonsk, MFA; *Lectr* Kim Borst, MFA; *Lectr* Pope Wright, MA; *Chmn* James Grittner, MFA; *Lectr* Tim Cleary
Estab 1896, dept estab 1930; Maintain nonprofit art gallery; Pub; D & E; Scholarships; SC 7, LC 3, GC 8; D 250, E 100-125, non-maj 250, maj 100, grad 30
Ent Req: HS dipl
Degrees: BS, BS(Photography), BS(Art Therapy), BFA & BFA(Photography) 4 yrs, BFA with cert 5 yrs, MA 5 - 6 yrs
Courses: †Art Education, †Art History, †Art Therapy, †Ceramics, Collage, Design, Drawing, †Jewelry, †Painting, †Photography, †Printmaking, †Sculpture, †Silversmithing, †Teacher Training, †Weaving
Adult Hobby Classes: Ceramics, Crafts, Drawing, Fibers, Metalwork, Painting, Photography
Children's Classes: Summer session only
Summer School: Dir, Mel Olsen. Courses—Art History, Ceramics, Drawing, Painting, Photography

WAUKESHA

CARROLL COLLEGE, Art Dept, 100 N East Ave, Waukesha, WI 53186-5593. Tel 262-547-1211, 524-7191; Web: www.cc.edu; *Co-Chmn* Thomas Selle; *Assoc Prof* Philip Krejcarek, MFA
Estab 1846; pvt; D & E; Scholarships; SC 21, LC 4; D 1100, E 350
Ent Req: HS dipl, SAT or ACT
Degrees: BA
Courses: Museum Staff Training, †Pre-Architecture; Commercial Art; Weaving, Sculpture, †Stage Design, †Teacher Training, Textile Design, †Theatre Arts, †Video
Adult Hobby Classes: Enrl 20 per session. Courses—Photographing Your Own Work
Children's Classes: New program
Summer School: Asst Prof, Thomas Selle. Enrl varies; tuition varies for term of 6 wks. Courses—Drawing, Graphics, Photography

WHITEWATER

UNIVERSITY OF WISCONSIN-WHITEWATER, Art Dept, 800 W Main St, Ctr of the Arts 2073 Whitewater, WI 53190-1790. Tel 262-472-1324; Fax 262-472-2808; Email art@uww.edu; Web: www.uww.edu; *Chmn* Chris Henige
Estab 1868; maintain nonprofit art gallery, Crossman Gallery, 800 W Main St, CA1030; FT 16, PT 1; pub; D & E; Scholarships; SC 41, LC 18; D 270, maj 200
Ent Req: HS dipl
Degrees: BA & BS(Art, Art Educ, Art History, Graphic Design), BFA 4 yrs
Courses: Advertising Design, Art Appreciation, Art Education, †Art History, Ceramics, Commercial Art, Drawing, †Graphic Design, Illustration, Jewelry, Painting, Photography, Printmaking, Sculpture, Teacher Training
Adult Hobby Classes: Enrl 240; tuition non res—undergrad $296.40 per cr, res undergrad—$96.90 per cr
Summer School: Dir, Richard Lee. Enrl 80; 3 & 6 wk terms, May-Aug. Courses—Art History, Ceramics, Drawing

WYOMING

CASPER

CASPER COLLEGE, Dept of Visual Arts, 125 College Dr, Casper, WY 82601-4699. Tel 307-268-2060; Fax 307-268-2224; Email lmunns@acad.cc.whecn.edu; *Instr* Justin Hayward; *Prog Dir* Linda Lee Ryan, MFA; *Instr* Nancy Madura, MFA; *Instr* Valerie Innella; *Instr* Michael Keogh, MFA; *Instr* Michael Olson; *Instr* Wendy Riley
Pub; D & E; Scholarships; LC 2; D 3870
Ent Req: HS dipl
Degrees: AA 2 yrs
Courses: Advertising Design, Art History, Ceramics, Collage, Commercial Art, Drafting, Drawing, Handicrafts, Illustration, Jewelry, Painting, Photography, Sculpture, Silversmithing, Textile Design, Theatre Arts
Summer School: Tuition $624 for summer sem or $52 per hr. Courses—Air Brush, Ceramics, Drawing, Jewelry, Painting, Photography

CHEYENNE

LARAMIE COUNTY COMMUNITY COLLEGE, Division of Arts & Humanities, 1400 E College Dr, Cheyenne, WY 82007-3295. Tel 307-778-1158; Fax 307-778-1399; Email kerryhart@lccc.wy.edu; *Dean* Kerry Hart, MA; *Instr* Matt West, MFA; *Instr* Ron Medina, MFA
Estab 1969; maintains nonprofit gallery; pub; D & E; Scholarships; SC 19, LC 3; D 125, E 100, non-maj 150, maj 20
Ent Req: HS dipl
Degrees: AA
Courses: Ceramics, Computer Graphics, Designs & Welded Sculpture, Drawing, Metals, Painting, Photography, Sculpture, Theatre Arts
Summer School: Dean, Chuck Thompson. Enrl 40; tuition $50 per cr hr for 8 wk term. Courses—Ceramics, Computer Graphics, Drawing, Metals, Watercolor

LARAMIE

UNIVERSITY OF WYOMING, Dept of Art, 1000 E University Ave, Dept 3138 Laramie, WY 82071-2000. Tel 307-766-3269; Fax 307-766-5468; Email kwold@uwyo.edu; rlk@uwyo.edu; *Head Dept* Ricki Klages
Estab 1886, dept estab 1946; FT 9; pub; D; Scholarships; SC 23, LC 6, GC 13; D 80, non-maj 600, maj 120, grad 16
Ent Req: HS dipl
Degrees: BA, BS and BFA 4 yrs
Courses: Art Appreciation, †Art Education, Art History, †Ceramics, †Design, †Drawing, †Graphic Design, †Painting, †Printmaking, †Sculpture
Adult Hobby Classes: Courses offered through University of Wyoming Art Museum
Summer School: Dir, Ricki Klages. Enrl 140; tuition res—undergrad $94 per cr hr 1-12, grad $164 per cr hr 1-12; non res—undergrad $322 per cr hr 1-12, grad $470 per cr hr 1-12, 4 & 8 wk sessions. Courses—Art Appreciation, Art History, Ceramics, Drawing, Graphic Design, Painting, Printmaking, Sculpture

POWELL

NORTHWEST COMMUNITY COLLEGE, Dept of Art, 231 W Sixth St, Powell, WY 82435. Tel 307-754-6111, 754-6201; Email mastersm@nwc.cc.wy.us; *Instr & Asst Prof* Lynn Thorpe; *Assoc Prof* John Giarrizzo; *Asst Prof* Morgan Tyree; *Chmn* Mike Masterson; *Asst Prof* Peder Gjovick; *Assoc Prof* Craig Satterlee
Estab 1946, dept estab 1952; pub; D & E; Scholarships; SC 12, LC 4; D 130, E 222, non-maj 317, maj 35
Ent Req: HS dipl, nonres ACT
Degrees: AA 2 yrs
Courses: Advertising Design, Art Education, Ceramics, Commercial Art, Drawing, Graphic Arts, Graphic Design, Handicrafts, History of Graphic Design, Lettering, Painting, Photography, Printmaking
Adult Hobby Classes: Enrl 100. Courses—Vary each sem

RIVERTON

CENTRAL WYOMING COLLEGE, Art Center, 2660 Peck Ave, Riverton, WY 82501-2273. Tel 307-855-2216, 855-2211; Fax 307-855-2090; Email nkehoe@cwc.edu; Web: www.cwc.edu; *Chair Dept* Nita Kehoe; *Prof Photog* Lonnie Slorck; *Ceramics* Markus Urbanik; *Prof 2-D* Matt Flint
Estab 1966; Maintain nonprofit art gallery; Robert A Peck Gallery; pub; D & E; Scholarships; SC 30, LC 2; D 1500, E 500, non-maj 200, maj 100, others 20
Ent Req: HS dipl, GED
Degrees: AA 2 yrs
Courses: Art Appreciation, Art Education, Art History, Bronze Casting, Ceramics, Design, Drawing, Fiber Arts, Graphic Design, Mixed Media, Moldmaking, Painting, Photography, Printmaking, Sculpture, Textile Design, Video
Adult Hobby Classes: Enrl 30 plus; tuition $15-$50. Courses—Varied Art & General Curriculum
Children's Classes: Enrl 200; classes for a day, wk or sem. Courses—varied
Summer School: Dir, Nita Kehoe; Limited Art offerings

ROCK SPRINGS

WESTERN WYOMING COMMUNITY COLLEGE, Art Dept, 2500 College Dr, Rock Springs, WY 82901-5802. Tel 307-382-1600, Ext 723; Email fmcewin@uucc.cc.uy.us; *Head Dept* Dr Florence McEwin
Estab 1969; Maintain nonprofit gallery & library, Hay Library; on-campus shop where art supplies may be purchased; pub; D & E; Scholarships; SC 12, LC 1; D 675, E 600, maj 20
Ent Req: HS dipl
Degrees: AA 2 yrs
Tuition: $1,200 ann
Courses: Advertising Design, Art Appreciation, Art History, Ceramics, Collage, Design, Drafting, Drawing, Film, Graphic Design, History of Art & Architecture, Life Drawing, Mixed Media, Museum Staff Training, Painting, Photography, Printmaking, Sculpture, Stage Design, Theatre Arts, Video
Adult Hobby Classes: Enrl 100. Courses—Crafts, Drawing, Painting, Pottery
Children's Classes: Dance
Summer School: Dir, Florence McEwin. Courses—Ceramics, Photography

SHERIDAN

SHERIDAN COLLEGE, Art Dept, 3059 Coffeen Ave, Sheridan, WY 82801-9133; PO Box 1500, Sheridan, WY 82801-1500. Tel 307-674-6446, ext 3008; Fax 307-674-4293; Email rdugal@sheridan.edu; Web: www.sheridaneollegeart.com; *Prog Chair* Rod Dugal; *Prof* Tawni Shuler; *Prof* Jason Lanka; *Adjunct* Brittney Whisonant; *Adjunct* Arin Wadell
Estab 1951; Maintains on-campus store for art supply sale; PT 3; pub; D & E; Scholarships; SC 35, LC 3; maj 30
Ent Req: HS grad
Degrees: AFA 2 yrs
Courses: Art Appreciation, Ceramics, Design, Drawing, Etching, Graphic Design, Jewelry, Lithography, Painting, Photography, Pottery, Sculpture, Silk Screen
Adult Hobby Classes: Enrl 40-60; tuition varies. Courses—Drawing, Painting, Pottery, Stained Glass
Children's Classes: Enrl 10-15; tuition varies. Courses—Pottery
Summer School: Enrl 10-15; tuition varies. Courses—Painting, Pottery

TORRINGTON

EASTERN WYOMING COLLEGE, Art Dept, 3200 W C St, Torrington, WY 82240-1699. Tel 307-532-8291; Fax 307-532-8225; Email cphillip@ewc.wy.edu; Web: ewc.wy.edu; *Head Dept* Daniel Fielder
Estab 1948; Maintains FA Lobby Art Gallery; art supplies sold at on-campus store; PT 2; pub; D & E; Scholarships; SC 9, LC 1; D 50, maj 4, non-maj 46
Ent Req: varied
Degrees: AA and AAS 2 yrs
Courses: Ceramics, Commercial Art, Design I, Drawing, General Art, Graphic Arts, History of Art & Architecture, Painting, Photography, Sculpture
Adult Hobby Classes: Painting Workshops
Summer School: Head, Daniel Fielder

PUERTO RICO

MAYAGUEZ

UNIVERSITY OF PUERTO RICO, MAYAGUEZ, Dept of Humanities, College of Fine Arts & Theory of Art Programs, PO Box 9000, Mayaguez, PR 00681-9000. Tel 787-832-4040, Ext 3160, 265-3846; Fax 809-265-1225; *Dir* Rafael Jackson PhD; *Prof* Yvette Cabrera, MFA; *Prof* Sandra Aponte, MFA; *Prof* Alfredo Ortiz, MFA; *Prof* Carlos Fajardo, MFA; *Prof* Felix Zapata, MFA; *Prof* Edwin Cordero, MFA; *Prof* Ramon Lopez, MFA
Estab 1970; Maintains nonprofit Art Gallery, Chardon Bldg, UPR - Mayaguez, Mayaguez, PR 00680; FT 40; pub; D; SC 20, LC 15; 402, maj 115
Ent Req: HS dipl
Degrees: BA(Art Theory) and BA(Plastic Arts) 4 yrs
Courses: Aesthetics, Art Appreciation, †Art Criticism, Art Education, Art History, †Art Theory, Calligraphy, Ceramics, Commercial Art, Design, Drawing, Graphic Arts, Illustration, Painting, Photography, Printmaking, Restoration & Conservation, Sculpture, Stage Design, Teacher Training, Theatre Arts
Adult Hobby Classes: Enrl 40

PONCE

PONTIFICAL CATHOLIC UNIVERSITY OF PUERTO RICO, Dept of Fine Arts, 2250 Las Americas Ave, Ste 508 Ponce, PR 00717-9997. Tel 787-841-2000; Email bellas_artes@email.pucpr.edu; Web: www.pucpr.edu; *Head Dept* Edwin J Mattei, MA; *Auxiliary Prof* Beverly Zapata, MA
Estab 1948, dept estab 1964; Maintain nonprofit art gallery, Galeria Diego J Alcala Laboy; den, Pvt; D & E; Scholarships; SC 36, LC 4, GC 10; 66 maj
Ent Req: HS dipl
Degrees: BA 4 yrs, MA 2 yrs
Tuition: Res—undergrad $150 per cr hr, grad $200 per cr hr
Courses: Advertising Design, Aesthetics, Art Appreciation, Art Education, Art History, Ceramics, Conceptual Art, Constructions, Contemporary Form, Design, Drawing, †Graphic Arts, Graphic Design, History in Art in Puerto Rico, †Mixed Media, Painting, Photography, Printmaking, Sculpture

RIO PIEDRAS

UNIVERSITY OF PUERTO RICO, Dept of Fine Arts, Ponce de Leon Ave, Rio Piedras, PR; UPR Sta, PO Box 21849 San Juan, PR 00931-1849. Tel 787-764-0000 Ext 3611; Fax 787-773-1721; Email departmentodebellasartes@yahoo.com
Estab 1902, dept estab 1950; pub; D & E & Sat; Scholarships; SC 25, LC 15; D 200, maj 45
Ent Req: HS dipl
Degrees: BA 4 yrs
Courses: Art Appreciation, Art History, Art in Puerto Rico, †Art Theory, Color Theory, †Conceptual Art, Design, †Digital Images, Drawing, †Graphic Arts, †History of Art & Architecture, †Mixed Media, †Museum Staff Training, Painting, Photography, Pre-Hispanic Art of Antilles, Printmaking, Sculpture, Video

SAN GERMAN

INTER AMERICAN UNIVERSITY OF PUERTO RICO, Fine Arts Dept -Art Program, Call Box 5100, San German, PR 00683. Tel 787-264-1912, Ext 7552; Email interarte@intersg.edu; *Assoc Prof* Fernando Santiago, MA; *Dir Prof* Maria Garcia Vera, MFA; *Assoc Prof* Dr. Paul Vivoni; *Instr* Maria Navedo Rivera, MFA; *Assistant Professor* Janet Leon, MFA; *Instr* Dra. Kalia Toro; *Instr* Prof Roxanne Cepero; *Instr* Prof Eduardo Kugo III
Estab 1912, dept estab 1947; Maintains a non-profit art gallery; pvt; D & E; SC 65, LC 6, GC 24; D 210, maj 135, GS 15
Ent Req: HS dipl, college board, presentation of portfolio
Degrees: BA 4 yrs, MFA 2 yrs
Tuition: Res—undergrad $98 per cr, grad $145 per cr; campus res available
Courses: AA and BA in Graphic Design, Aesthetics, Art Appreciation, †Art Education, Art History, BFA in Fine Arts, †Ceramics, Display, Drawing, Graphic Arts, Graphic Design, History of Art & Architecture, †Painting, †Photography, †Printmaking, †Sculpture, Teacher Training
Summer School: Dir, Jaime Carrero. Enrl 10; tuition $75 per cr hr for 5 wk term. Courses—Art Appreciation, Ceramic, Sculpture

SAN JUAN

ESCUELA DE ARTES PLASTICAS DE PUERTO RICO, El Morro Grounds, School of Fine Arts San Juan, PR 00901; Escuela de Artes Plasticas de Puerto Rico, PO Box 9021112 San Juan, PR 00902-1112. Tel 787-725-8120; Fax 787-725-8111; Email info@eap.edu; Web: eap.edu; *Chancellor* Aro Ivonne Maria Marcial Vega; *Student Aid Coordr* Alfred Diaz; *Acting Dean Acad/Study Affairs* Teresa Lopez; *Institutional Researcher* Shirley A Tavares, EdD
Estab 1966; Maintains nonprofit art gallery on campus (same address); schols open to sophomore, junior & senior students with 3.00 or above GPA; Francisco Oller Learning Resource Center Library; FT 17, PT 48; Pub; D&E; Scholarships; SC 82, LC 40; D 456, E 66
Ent Req: HS dipl, ent exam, portfolio or admis seminar, interview & essay
Degrees: BA 4 yrs
Tuition: In-state $4,404 per yr, $90 per cr; out-of-state $7,644 per yr, $180 per cr
Courses: †Art Education, Design & Visual Computer, †Fashion Design, †Industrial Design, †Painting, †Sculpture
Adult Hobby Classes: Enrl 244; tuition $144 per cr. Courses—Graphic, Painting, Sculpture, Photography

Canadian Art Schools

ALBERTA

BANFF

BANFF CENTRE, 107 Tunnel Mountain Dr, Box 1020 Banff, AB T1L 1H5 Canada. Tel 403-762-6100; Fax 403-762-6345; Email arts_info@banffcentre.ca; Web: www.banffcentre.ca; *Pres* Janice Price; *VPres Arts* Carolyn Warren; *VPres & COO* Luke Sunderland; *VPres & CFO* Bruce Byford; *VPres Develop* Neil Johnson
Open Mon - Fri 8 AM - 7 PM, Sat 9:30 AM - 6 PM, Statutory holidays 9:30 AM - 6 PM; cl Sun, Christmas Day, Boxing Day & New Year's Day; Estab 1933 for summer study, winter cycle prog began 1979; Pub; Day - Mostly Independent Study; Scholarships
Ent Req: Resume, slides of work, post-secondary art training at a university or art school and/or professional experience in field
Tuition: Tuition depends on prog
Courses: Art Studio, Ceramics, Media Arts, Photography, †Theatre Arts, †Video
Adult Hobby Classes: Courses - Art Studio, Ceramics Studio, Photography Studio, Visual Community
Summer School: Courses - Art Studio, Ceramics Studio, Photography Studio, Visual Community

CALGARY

ALBERTA COLLEGE OF ART & DESIGN, 1407 14th Ave NW, Calgary, AB T2N 4R3 Canada. Tel 403-284-7600, 800-251-8290; Fax 403-289-6682; Email admissions@acad.ca; Web: acad.ca; *Sr VPres Fin Corp Srvc* Donald Dart; *Pres & CEO* Daniel Doz; *Assoc VPres Student Affairs* Marianne Elder; *Assoc VPres Research & Academic Affairs* Alison Miyauchi; *Assoc VPres Instruc Affairs* Marc Scholes; *Dir Human Resources* Jill Brown
Open daily 7 AM - 11 PM; Estab 1926; Maintain nonprofit art gallery; The Illingworth Kerr Gallery; pub; D & E; Scholarships; SC 250, LC 14; D 1000, E 500, non-maj 60, maj 850, others 60
Ent Req: HS dipl, portfolio
Degrees: BFA; BDes
Tuition: $9320 per yr plus course costs (Canadian funds)
Courses: Ceramics, Drawing, †Fibre, Glass, †Interdisciplinary, Jewelry, †Media & Digital Technology, Painting, Photographic Arts, Photography, Printmaking, Sculpture, Visual Communications
Adult Hobby Classes: Enrl 1500; tuition varies per course. Courses—Ceramics, Art Fundamentals, Drawing, Jewelry, Painting, Printmaking, Sculpture, Glass, Textiles, Watercolor, Photography
Children's Classes: Enrl 560; tuition $110 per course; Pre-College Studio $135 for 18 hrs. Courses—Ceramics, Jewelry, Mixed Media, Painting, Painting for Teenagers, Puppetry, Sculpture
Summer School: Enrl varies 100 approx

MOUNT ROYAL COLLEGE, Dept of Interior Design, 4825 Mount Royal Gate SW, Calgary, AB T3E 6K6 Canada. Tel 403-440-5143; Fax 403-440-6939; Email pdozois@mtroyal.ca; Web: www.mtroyal.ca; *Chmn* Helen Evans Warren; *Asst to Chair* Sarah Block; *Faculty of Arts Academic Advisor* Rachel Doe; *Interior Design Acad Advisor* Paula Dozois
Estab 1910; FT 5, PT 10; pub; D & E; Scholarships; SC 12, LC 17
Ent Req: HS dipl
Degrees: 2 yr dipl
Tuition: $3857 per sem
Courses: Business Principles & Practices, Design, Graphic Presentation, History of Art & Architecture, History of Furniture, †Interior Design, Sculpture, Stage Design, Technical Design & Drafting
Adult Hobby Classes: Enrl 50. Courses—Interior Design Program

UNIVERSITY OF CALGARY, Dept of Art, 2500 University Dr NW, Art Bldg 612 Calgary, AB T2N 1N4 Canada. Tel 403-220-6817; Fax 403-289-7333; Web: art.ucalgary.ca; *Art Dept Head* Brian Rusted; *Art Dept Mgr* Nicole Ethier
Estab 1965; FT 21, PT 6; pub; D & E; SC 56, LC 19, GC 8; D 263, E 31, all maj
Ent Req: HS dipl
Degrees: BA(Art History), BFA(School Art, Art), MFA(Studio)
Tuition: $2513 per session
Courses: †Architecture, †Art Education, Art Fundamentals, †Art History, Art Theory, Conceptual Art, Costume Design & Construction, Drawing, Film, Graphic Arts, History of Art & Architecture, Intermedia, Mixed Media, Museum Staff Training, †Painting, †Photography, †Printmaking, †Sculpture, Stage Design, †Theatre Arts, Video
Summer School: Two terms of 6 wks, May-July. Courses—Art History, Drawing, Printmaking, Painting, Art Fundamentals, Art Education, Sculpture

EDMONTON

UNIVERSITY OF ALBERTA, Dept of Art & Design, 3-98 Fine Arts Bldg, Univ of Alberta Campus Edmonton, AB T6G 2C9 Canada. Tel 780-492-3261; Fax 780-492-7870; Email artdes@ualberta.ca; Web: www.artdesign.ualberta.ca; *Chair* Cezary Gajewski; *Assoc Chair Grad Studies & Research* Lianne McTavish; *Coordr Visual Communs Design* Bonnie Sadler Takach; *Coordr History of Art, Design & Visual Culture* Natalie Loveless; *Assoc Chair Undergrad Studies & Coordr Printmaking* Prof Sean Caulfield; *Coordr Painting, Drawing & Intermedia* Jesse Thomas; *Coordr History of Art, Design & Visual Culture Honours Advisor* Lisa Claypool; *Coordr Sculpture* Peter Hide; *Coordr Art & Design Fundamentals* Aiden Rowe; *Coordr Industrial Design* Robert Lederer
Estab 1908, dept estab 1946; Maintains a nonprofit art gallery, FAB Gallery & Design Gallery, Fine Arts Bldg; Maintains an art/architecture library. Art supplies may be purchased on campus; Pub; D & E; Scholarships; SC 51, LC 42, grad 23; Maj 748, grad 54
Ent Req: HS dipl, portfolio
Degrees: BFA 4 yrs, BDES 4 yrs, MFA, MA, M Des 2 yrs, PhD
Tuition: Undergrad $6,596 per yr, grad $5,252 per yr; international $8,021
Courses: †Advertising Design, †Art History, †Commercial Art, †Conceptual Art, †Design, Design & Visual Culture, Drawing, †Graphic Arts, †Graphic Design, History of Art, †History of Art & Architecture, †Industrial Design, †Painting, †Printmaking, †Sculpture, †Visual Communication Design
Summer School: Enrl 150; tuition $420 per course. Courses—Art History, Drawing, Painting, Printmaking, Sculpture, Visual Commun Design

LETHBRIDGE

UNIVERSITY OF LETHBRIDGE, Faculty of Fine Arts, 4401 University Dr, Lethbridge, AB T1K 3M4 Canada. Tel 403-329-2126; Fax 403-382-7127; Email finearts@uleth.ca; Web: www.uleth.ca/finearts; *Dean* Edward Jurkowski; *Assoc Dean* Shelly Scott; *Chair Art Dept* Annie Martin; *Chair Music Dept* Deanna Oye; *Chair New Media Dept* Deric Olsen
Estab 1967; pub; D & E; Scholarships; SC 26, LC 9; Undergrad enrl 700
Ent Req: HS dipl
Degrees: BA & BFA 4 yrs
Tuition: Res—undergrad $5184 per sem; nonres—undergrad $10,320 per sem
Courses: Aesthetics, Art Appreciation, Art Education, Art History, Conceptual Art, Costume Design & Construction, Design, Drawing, History of Art & Architecture, Intermedia, Mixed Media, Museum Staff Training, Painting, Photography, Printmaking, Sculpture, Stage Design, Teacher Training, Theatre Arts, Video

RED DEER

RED DEER COLLEGE, School of Creative Arts, 100 College Blvd, PO Box 5005 Red Deer, AB T4N 5H5 Canada. Tel 403-342-3400; Fax 403-340-8940; Email creativearts@rdc.ab.ca; Web: rdc.ab.ca; *Dean* Jason Frizzell; *Assoc Dean* Peter Fielding
Estab 1973; FT 6, PT 2; pub; D & E; Scholarships; max 50 first yr students, 30 second yr
Ent Req: HS dipl, portfolio
Degrees: dipl, BFA 2 yrs
Tuition: undergrad—$2,210-$5,083 per sem
Courses: Art History, Ceramics, Drawing, Fundamentals of Visual Communication, Painting, Printmaking, Sculpture
Adult Hobby Classes: Enrl 300; tuition $74 - $100 per course. Courses—Ceramics, Drawing, Glass Blowing
Children's Classes: Enrl 80; tuition $350 per wk. Courses—Drawing, Painting, Sculpture
Summer School: Enrl 500; tuition $200 per wk. Courses—Applied Arts, Drawing, Glass Blowing, Painting, Printmaking

BRITISH COLUMBIA

KELOWNA

UNIVERSITY OF BRITISH COLUMBIA OKANAGAN, Faculty of Creative & Critical Studies, CCS Bldg, 1148 Research Rd Kelowna, BC V1V 1V7 Canada. Tel 250-807-8000; Fax 250-807-8543; Email fccs.ubco@ubc.ca; Web: ok.ubc.ca; *Dean pro tem* Robert Eggleston; *Assoc Dean Undergrad Studies* Marianne Legault; *Assoc Dean Research & Grad Studies* Stephen Foster; *Dept Head Creative Studies* Ashok Mathur; *Dept Head Critical Studies* Martin Blum

Estab 2005; Maintains a nonprofit art gallery, Fina Gallery, UBC Okanagan, 333 University Way, Kelowna, BC V1V 1V7; 17; pub; D & E; Scholarships; SC 75, LC 18, GC 4; D 200, E 20
Ent Req: HS dipl
Degrees: BFA 4 yr, BA Creative Writing, MFA Interdisciplinary graduate studies
Tuition: Res—undergrad $4,600 per year
Courses: Aesthetics, †Art History, Collage, Conceptual Art, Constructions, †Creative Writing, †Drawing, Film, Graphic Arts, †Intermedia, Mixed Media, †Painting, †Photography, †Printmaking, †Sculpture, Theater Arts, †Video
Summer School: 40 $300 per course, painting, drawing, aramids

VANCOUVER

EMILY CARR UNIVERSITY OF ART + DESIGN, 1399 Johnston St, Granville Island Vancouver, BC V6H 3R9 Canada. Tel 604-844-3800; Fax 604-844-3801; Email reception@ecuad.ca; Web: www.ecuad.ca; *Pres & Vice Chancellor* Dr Ronald Burnett; *VPres Acad & Provost* Bonne Zabalotney; *Dean Faculty of Culture & Community* Susan Stewart
Estab 1925; Maintains nonprofit Charles H Scott Gallery & Media and Concourse Galleries; univ library; pub; D & E; SC 653, LC 188, GC 24; D 1884, E 300, Grad 41
Activities: Schols offered
Ent Req: HS dipl plus presentation of folio of art work
Degrees: 2 yr masters, 4 yr degree
Tuition: res—$2,605; non-res—$9,182
Courses: Animation, Art History, Ceramics, Conceptual Art, Design, Drawing, Film, Graphic Arts, Graphic Design, Illustration, Intermedia Studies, Mixed Media, Painting, Photography, Printmaking, Sculpture, Video
Adult Hobby Classes: Enrl 2000; tuition $250 per course. Courses—Design, Fine Arts
Summer School: Dir, Sadira Rodriques Enrl 700; tuition $250. Courses—Design, Fine Arts

LANGARA COLLEGE, Dept of Fine Arts, 100 W 49th Ave, Vancouver, BC V5Y 2Z6 Canada. Tel 604-323-5511; Fax 604-323-5555; Email swebster@langara.bc.ca; Web: langara.bc.ca; *Dept Chair* Suzi Webster Benwick; *Asst Dept Chair* Jake Hill
Estab 1970; pub; D; Scholarships; SC 7, LC 1; D 160
Ent Req: HS dipl, portfolio
Degrees: Fine Arts dipl
Courses: Art History, Ceramics, Commercial Art, Conceptual Art, Design, Drawing, Graphic Arts, Graphic Design, History of Art & Architecture, Painting, Photography, Printmaking, Sculpture, Typography

UNIVERSITY OF BRITISH COLUMBIA, Dept of Art History, Visual Art & Theory, 400-6333 Memorial Rd, Vancouver, BC V6T 122 Canada. Tel 604-822-2757; Fax 604-822-9003; Email ahva.dept@ubc.ca; Web: www.ahva.ubc.ca; *Admin* Andrea Tuele; *Prof & Dept Head* Scott Watson
Maintain the Morris and Helen Belkin Art Gallery & the AHVA Gallery; there is an on-campus art supply shop; D & E; Scholarships; Fellowships
Degrees: BA, BFA, MA, MFA, PhD
Courses: Art History, †Asian, Graphic Arts, History of Art & Architecture, †Indigenous Arts of the America, Mixed Media, Painting, Photography, Printmaking, Sculpture, †Western

VICTORIA

UNIVERSITY OF VICTORIA, Faculty of Arts, Fine Arts Bldg 116, 3800 Finnerty Rd Victoria, BC V8P 5C2 Canada. Tel 250-721-7755; Fax 250-721-7748; Email fineasst@finearts.uvic.ca; Web: finearts.uvic.ca; *Acting Dean* Susan Lewis; *Assoc Dean* Evanthia Baboula; *Dean's Asst* Ami Cheli
Estab 1963; Maintains Univ of Victoria Legacy Art Galleries; pub; D & E; Scholarships; Fellowships; 50
Ent Req: HS dipl
Degrees: BFA, MFA
Tuition: Undergrad $6,000 per yr
Courses: Digital Multimedia, Drawing, Painting, Photography, Printmaking, Sculpture
Summer School: Drawing, Painting, Printmaking

MANITOBA

WINNIPEG

UNIVERSITY OF MANITOBA, School of Art, 313 ARTlab, 180 Dafoe Rd, Ft Garry Campus Winnipeg, MB R3T 2N2 Canada. Tel 204-474-9367; 800-432-1960; Fax 204-474-7605; Email fineart@umanitoba.ca; Web: umanitoba.ca/schools/art; *Dir* Paul Hess; *Assoc Dir* Dr Mary Ann Steggles, MFA
Estab 1913; Maintains the Univ of Manitoba School of Art Gallery; Pub; D&E; Scholarships; SC 35, LC 16; D 440
Ent Req: HS dipl and portfolio
Degrees: BFA
Tuition: $5,700 per yr
Courses: †Art History, †Ceramics, †Drawing, †Foundations, †Graphic Design, †Painting, †Photography, †Printmaking, †Sculpture
Summer School: Courses—Studio & Art History

NEW BRUNSWICK

FREDERICTON

NEW BRUNSWICK COLLEGE OF CRAFT & DESIGN, 457 Queen St, PO Box 6000 Fredericton, NB E3B 5H1 Canada. Tel 506-453-2305; 877-400-1107; Fax 506-457-7352; Email nbccdrecruiting@gnb.ca; Web: nbccd.ca; *Dir* Keith McAlpine; *Academic Dean* Harriet Taylor; *Dir Admin* Donna Boudreau; *Registrar* Nancy Beaulieu
Estab 1946; pub; D & E; Workshops; 70 plus PT
Ent Req: HS dipl, transcript, questionnaire and interview
Degrees: 3 yr dipl
Courses: Advertising Design, Art History, Ceramics, †Clothing Design & Construction, Colour, †Creative Graphics, Design, Drawing, Fashion Arts, Graphic Arts, Illustration, Jewelry, †Native Arts Studies, Photography, Silversmithing, Textile Design, Weaving
Adult Hobby Classes: Courses—Weekend workshops

UNIVERSITY OF NEW BRUNSWICK, Faculty of Arts, PO Box 4400, Faculty of Arts Fredericton, NB E3B 5A3 Canada. Tel 506-453-4655; Fax 506-453-5102; Email arts@unb.ca; Web: www.unb.ca/arts; *Dean* George A. MacLean; *Assoc Dean* Joanne Wright; *Assoc Dean* Carmen Poulin
Estab 1785
Degrees: BAA (Applied Arts)
Tuition: Res—$7,460 per yr
Courses: Art History, †Craft, †Design
Children's Classes: 70; tuition $15 for 6 weeks, one afternoon per wk

MONCTON

UNIVERSITE DE MONCTON, Dept of Visual Arts, Pavillon Leopold-Taillon, 18 avenue Antonine-Maillet Moncton, NB E1A 3E9 Canada. Tel 506-858-4033; Fax 506-858-4166; Email artsvisuels@umoncton.ca; Web: www.umoncton.ca; *Dir* Jacques Arseneault
Estab 1946, dept estab 1968; pub; D & E; Scholarships; SC 12, LC 1; D 20, E 11, non-maj 25, maj 6
Ent Req: HS dipl
Degrees: BA(Fine Arts) 4 yrs
Tuition: $2430; campus res—room & board $1545 per yr
Courses: Art History, Drawing, Painting, Sculpture

SACKVILLE

MOUNT ALLISON UNIVERSITY, Dept of Fine Arts, 152 Main St, Sackville, NB E4L 1B5 Canada. Tel 506-364-2490; Fax 506-364-2606; Email finearts@mta.ca; Web: www.mta.ca/finearts; *Dept Head* Thaddeus Holownia, BA; *Prof* Erik Edson, MFA; *Assoc Prof* Dr Anne Koval, BA, MA, PhD; *Lectr & Printmaking Tech* Dan Steeves, BFA; *Assoc Prof* Leah Garnett, MFA; *Lectr & Photog Tech* Karen Stentaford, MFA, BFA, BEd; *Assoc Prof* Chris Down, BFA, MFA; *Assoc Prof* Adriana Kuiper, BFA, MFA; *Asst Prof* Jerry Ropson, BFA, MFA; *Lectr & Sculpture Tech* Paul Griffin, BFA, MFA; *Adjunct Prof & Dir Owens Art Gallery* Gemey Kelly
Estab 1854; Maintains Owens Art Gallery; on campus shop where art supplies may be purchased; Pub; D & E 20; Scholarships; SC 34, LC 19; Maj140, non Maj 59
Ent Req: HS dipl
Degrees: BFA 4 yrs
Tuition: Tuition $6,720 (Canadian), $13,440 (non-Canadian) plus meals Various plans from $3,098 to $3,370, residence single $4,204, supersingle $4,501, double $3,636
Courses: †Art History, †Drawing, Open Media, †Painting, †Photography, †Printmaking, †Sculpture

NEWFOUNDLAND

CORNER BROOK

GRENFELL CAMPUS, MEMORIAL UNIVERSITY OF NEWFOUNDLAND, Division of Fine Arts, Visual Arts Program, 20 University Dr, Corner Brook, NF A2H 5G4 Canada. Tel 709-637-6200; Fax 709-637-6203; Email ipercy@grenfell.mun.ca; Web: www.grenfell.mun.ca; *Dean School of Fine Arts* Todd Hennessey; *Prog Chair & Asst Prof* Ingrid Mary Percy; *Art Gallery Dir* Charlotte Jones; *Workshop Supv & Master Carpenter* Bruce Bryne; *Prof* Michael Coyne; *Secy, Fine Arts Div* Linda Humphries
Estab 1975, dept estab 1988; Maintain nonprofit art gallery; Sir Wilfred Grenfell College, Corner Brook, NF A2H6P9; maintain art/architecture library, Ferris Hodgett Library, Grenfell Campus, Memorial Univ of New England Corner Brook, NL A2H6P9; pub; D & E; Scholarships; Studio & lect courses; D 50, Maj 80
Degrees: BFA
Courses: Aesthetics, Art Appreciation, Art History, Design, Digital Imaging, History of Art & Architecture, Mixed Media, Painting, Photography, Printmaking, Sculpture, †Theatre Arts
Adult Hobby Classes: Drawing, Studio Areas
Children's Classes: Art

NOVA SCOTIA

ANTIGONISH

ST FRANCIS XAVIER UNIVERSITY, Art Dept, PO Box 5000, Antigonish, NS B2G 2W5 Canada. Tel 902-867-2300; Fax 902-867-5395; Email artdept@stfx.ca; Web: sites.stfx.ca/art; *Chmn & Assoc Prof Art History* Sharon Gregory
PT 4; Scholarships
Degrees: BA
Tuition: undergrad—$7,536 - $17,010
Courses: Art History, Design, Drawing, Painting, Printmaking, Stained Glass
Adult Hobby Classes: Courses—Drawing, General Studio, Painting
Children's Classes: Courses—Drawing, Painting, Printmaking
Summer School: Enrl 15; 5 wk sem beginning July-Aug. Courses—General Studio

HALIFAX

DALHOUSIE UNIVERSITY, School of Architecture, 5410 Spring Garden Rd, Box 15000 Halifax, NS B3H 4R2 Canada. Tel 902-494-3971; Fax 902-423-6672; Email arch.office@dal.ca; Web: www.dal.ca/architecture; *Prof & Dean, Faculty of Architecture & Planning* Christine Macy; *Assoc Prof & Dir School of Architecture* Diogo Burnay; *Prof & Dir Col of Sustainability* Steven Mannell; *Prof* Brian MacKay-Lyons; *Assoc Prof & Undergrad Coordr* Niall Savage; *Prof & Grad Coordr* Susan Bonnemaison
Estab 1911, faculty estab 1961; pvt; D; Scholarships; approx 200, maj 200, grad 2
Ent Req: previous 2 yrs at univ
Degrees: MArchit 4 yrs, Post-professional MArchit 1 yr minimum
Tuition: $8,662 per yr; differential for foreign students
Courses: Architecture, Art History, Constructions, Drafting, Environmental Studies, Photography, Urban & Rural Planning
Summer School: Three terms per yr

NOVA SCOTIA COLLEGE OF ART & DESIGN, 5163 Duke St, Halifax, NS B3J 3J6 Canada. Tel 902-444-9600; Fax 902-425-2420; Web: nscad.ca; *Pres* Dianne Taylor-Gearing; *VPres Acad & Research* Ann-Barbara Graff; *Assoc Prof & Chair, Design Div* Marlene Ivey; *Chair, Fine Arts Div* Mathew Reichertz; *Asst Prof & Chair, Foundation Studies Div* Craig Leonard; *Chair, Art History & Critical Studies Div* Darrell Varga; *Assoc Prof & Chair, Media Arts Div* Adrian Fish; *Asst Prof & Chair Crafts Div* Gary Markle
Estab 1887; Maintains nonprofit Anna Leonowens Gallery; NSCAD Library; art supplies sold at on campus store; pvt; D & E; Scholarships; Fellowships; SC 67, LC 31, GC 8 each sem; FT 810, PT 183, grad 14
Ent Req: HS dipl, portfolio or project
Degrees: BFA, BD(Graphic Design), BA, MFA & MA(Art Educ), MDES
Tuition: FT Canadian—$3,741 - $4,382 per sem; FT International—$9,420 per sem
Courses: Art Education, Art History, Ceramics, Computer Art, Design, Drawing, Fashion Arts, Film, Graphic Arts, Graphic Design, Jewelry, Mixed Media, Painting, Photography, Printmaking, Sculpture, Textile Design, Video

WOLFVILLE

ACADIA UNIVERSITY, Faculty of Arts, 15 University Ave, Wolfville, NS B4P 2R6 Canada. Tel 902-585-1485; Fax 902-585-1070; Email cheryl.macdonald@acadiau.ca; Web: www.acadiau.ca; *Interim Dean of Arts* Dr Jeffrey Hennessy; *Admin Mgr* Cheryl MacDonald; *Gallery Dir & Cur* Laurie Dalton; *Art Instr* Judith Leidl
Maintains Acadia Univ Art Gallery, 10 Highland Ave, Wolfville, NS, B4P 2R6; Scholarships
Degrees: BA, BAM, BM, MA
Tuition: FT undergrad—$6,661 - $15,903
Courses: Art History, Painting, †Studio Art

ONTARIO

BROCKVILLE

ST LAWRENCE COLLEGE, Visual & Creative Arts Program, 2288 Parkedale Ave, Brockville, ON K6V 5X3 Canada. Tel 613-345-0660; Email cchrysler@sl.on.ca; Web: www.stlawrencecollege.ca; *Prog Contact & Gallery Cur* Christina Chrysler
Maintains the Marianne van Silfhout Gallery, 2288 Parkedale Ave, Brockville, ON K6V 5X3; pub; D & E
Ent Req: Hs dipl & portfolio
Degrees: Dipl (Visual & Creative Arts) 2 yrs
Tuition: res—$2,850; international—$13,420
Courses: Art History, Commercial Art, Communications, Computer Graphics, Drawing, †Graphic Design, Illustration, Marketing, Mixed Media, Painting, Photography, Printmaking

DUNDAS

DUNDAS VALLEY SCHOOL OF ART, 21 Ogilvie St, Dundas, ON L9H 2S1 Canada. Tel 905-628-6357; Fax 905-628-1087; Email info@dvsa.ca; Web: dvsa.ca; *Exec Dir* Claire Loughheed; *Dir Advancement* Heather Vaugeois; *Registrar* Bonnie Wheeler; *Dir Independent Studies* John Wilkinson
Estab 1964; Maintain nonprofit art gallery & art/architecture library, DVSA Gallery & Library. Art supplies may be purchased on campus; pvt; D & E; Scholarships; SC 65, LC 2, GC 1; D 2,000, E 2,000
Ent Req: part time no-req, special programs, interview with portfolio
Tuition: $74 - $329
Courses: Art Appreciation, Art History, Ceramics, Collage, Conceptual Art, Constructions, Design, Drawing, Mixed Media, Painting, Photography, Printmaking, Sculpture
Adult Hobby Classes: Courses—Ceramics, Drawing, Painting, Photography, Printmaking, Sculpture
Children's Classes: Courses—Drawing, Painting, Pottery
Summer School: Enrl 1800

GUELPH

UNIVERSITY OF GUELPH, School of Fine Art & Music, Zavitz Hall, Rm 201, Guelph, ON N1G 2W1 Canada. Tel 519-824-4120, Ext 53988; Fax 519-821-5482; Email rmcginni@uoguelph.ca; Web: www.uoguelph.ca/sofam; *Dir* Sally Hickson; *Admin* Robin McGinnis
Estab 1966; Maintains the Zavitz, Boarding House & G Galleries; FT 23, PT 20; pub; D; Scholarships; SC 30, LC 30 Grad 9; 959, maj 300
Ent Req: HS dipl
Degrees: BA 3 yrs, BA (Hons) 4 yrs
Tuition: Res—undergrad $3,960 per sem; campus res available
Courses: Aesthetics, Alternative Media, †Art History, Collage, †Conceptual Art, †Drawing, History of Art & Architecture, †Intermedia, †Painting, †Photography, †Printmaking, †Sculpture, Video

HAMILTON

MCMASTER UNIVERSITY, School of the Arts, Togo Salmon Hall 414, 1280 Main St W Hamilton, ON L8S 4M2 Canada. Tel 905-525-9140; Fax 905-527-3731; Email sota@mcmaster.ca; Web: sota.humanities.mcmaster.ca; *Dir* Alison McQueen; *Music Counsellor* Andrew Mitchell; *Theatre & Film Studies Counsellor* Joseph Sokalski; *Art Counsellor* Briana Palmer; *Art History Counsellor* Angela Sheng
Estab 1934; FT 21; SC 12, LC 29; 85
Degrees: BA(Art History), Hons BA(Studio & Art History) 3-4 yrs
Tuition: $224 per unit; international $812 per unit; campus res available
Courses: †Art History, †Film, Music, †Studio Art, †Theatre Arts

KINGSTON

QUEEN'S UNIVERSITY, Faculty of Arts & Sciences, Creative Arts Program, Dunning Hall, 1st Fl, 94 University Ave Kingston, ON K7L 3N6 Canada. Tel 613-533-2467; Fax 613-533-6891; Email fineart@queensu.ca; Web: www.queensu.ca/artsci; *Dean* Susan Mumm; *Drama & Music Dir* Craig Walker; *Fine Art Dir* G. Smith; *Film & Media Dir* S. Lord
Open Mon - Fri 8:30 AM - 12 PM & 1 PM - 4:30 PM; Estab 1932; pub; D & E; SC 16, LC 25
Ent Req: Grade XIII
Degrees: BA 3 yrs, BA(hons) & BFA 4 yrs, MA(Conservation), MA(Art History), PhD(Art History)
Tuition: res—$7,502 per year; non-res—$35,505 per year
Courses: Art Conservation, Art History, Drawing, Painting, Printmaking, Restoration & Conservation, Sculpture
Summer School: Drawing, Painting, Sculpture

LONDON

UNIVERSITY OF WESTERN ONTARIO, Dept of Visual Arts, John Labatt Visual Arts Centre, London, ON N6A 5B7 Canada. Tel 519-661-3440; Fax 519-661-2020; Email visarts@uwo.ca; Web: www.uwo.ca/visarts; *Dept Chmn* Joy James; *Grad Chair* Patrick Mahon; *Undergrad Chair* David Merritt; *ArtLab Gallery Dir* Susan Edelstein
Estab 1967; Maintains the ArtLab Gallery, Perth Drive, N6A 5B; pub; D & E; SC 23, LC 31; maj 235
Ent Req: HS dipl, portfolio and/or interview
Degrees: BA, BA(Hons) & BFA
Tuition: res—$4701.01 per year; non-res—$10,483.79 per year
Courses: Drawing, †History of Art & Architecture, Museum Staff Training, †Painting, †Photography, †Printmaking, †Sculpture
Summer School: Enrl limited; term of 6 wks beginning July. Courses—Visual Arts

OAKVILLE

SHERIDAN COLLEGE, Faculty of Animation, Arts & Design, 1430 Trafalgar Rd, Oakville, ON L6H 2L1 Canada. Tel 905-845-9430; Fax 905-815-4041; Web: www.sheridancollege.ca; *Dean* Ronni Rosenberg, MFA, MArch, RGD; *Assoc Dean Design Illustration & Photography* Donna Braggins, MA, RGD; *Assoc Dean Material, Art & Design* Heather Whitton, BFA, MEd; *Assoc Dean Animation & Game Design* Angela Stukator, PhD; *Assoc Dean Film Television & Journalism* Maija Saari, BA; *Assoc Dean Visual & Performing Arts* Michael Rubinoff, BA, LL. B
Estab 1967; Maintains nonprofit art gallery, The Gallery (same address); schols open to qualified students; FT 109; pub; D & E; Scholarships; SC 80%, LC 20%; D 4500
Ent Req: HS dipl
Degrees: BAA 4 yr
Tuition: Canadian res—$4,897 per yr; international—$16,312 per yr
Courses: †Animation & Game Design, †Costume Design & Construction, †Film, TV & Journalism, †Interior Design, †Material Arts & Design, †Visual & Performing Arts

Adult Hobby Classes: Enrl 2800; tuition varies
Summer School: Enrl 600. Programs-various Visual & Performing Arts

OTTAWA

CARLETON UNIVERSITY, School for Studies in Art & Culture, 423 St Patrick's Bldg, 1125 Colonel Bay Dr Ottawa, ON K1S 5B6 Canada. Tel 613-520-5606; Fax 613-520-3575; Web: carleton.ca/ssac; *Dir, School for Studies in Art & Culture* Brian Foss; *Undergrad Admin, Art History & Film Studies* Caroline Karasiuk; *Grad Admin* Barbara Shannon; *Undergrad Admin, Music* Tasneem Ujjainwala; *School Admin* Kristin Guth
Estab 1991; FT 8, PT 2; D & E; Scholarships; SC 2, LC 25, GC 3; D over 700, maj 135
Ent Req: HS dipl
Degrees: BA & MA
Tuition: Res—$7,190-$11,210 per yr
Courses: Art History, †Audio Visual, †Film, †Music

SOUTHAMPTON

SOUTHAMPTON ART CENTRE, ART SCHOOL & GALLERY, 201 High St, Box 115 Southampton, ON N0H 2L0 Canada. Tel 519-797-5068; 800-806-8838; Fax 519-797-2486; Email artschoolsouthampton@gmail.com; Web: www.southamptonartschool.com; *Dir* Darlene McConnachie
Estab 1958 as a summer school; Maintains art gallery; pub; D; Scholarships
Tuition: Varies by course
Courses: Art Appreciation, Art History, Calligraphy, Collage, Design, Drawing, Handicrafts, Jewelry, Mixed Media, Painting, Photography, Printmaking, Sculpture, Textile Design
Adult Hobby Classes: Courses—Culinary, Ferro-Cement Sculpture, Knitting, Photography, Quilting, Rug Hooking
Children's Classes: Courses—Crafts, Drawing, Painting, Sculpture
Summer School: Courses—Acrylic, Collage, Drawing, Figures, Mixed Media, Oil, Printmaking, Portraits, Watercolor

THUNDER BAY

LAKEHEAD UNIVERSITY, Dept of Visual Arts, 955 Oliver Rd, Thunder Bay, ON P7B 5E1 Canada. Tel 807-343-8787; Email kholmes@lakeheadu.ca; Web: www.lakeheadu.ca; *Prof Emeritus* Mark Nissenholt, MFA; *Asst Prof* Roland Martin; *Asst Prof & Chair* Dr Kristy Holmes; *Asst Prof* Sam Shahsahabi
Div estab 1976, dept estab 1988; pub; D & E; Scholarships
Ent Req: HS dipl, portfolio
Degrees: BA, BFA, Dipl in Arts Admin
Courses: Art History, †Ceramics, Drawing, †Painting, †Printmaking, †Sculpture
Adult Hobby Classes: Studio and art history courses

TORONTO

GEORGE BROWN COLLEGE OF APPLIED ARTS & TECHNOLOGY, Centre for Arts, Design & Information Technology, 230 Richmond St E, Toronto, ON M5A 1P4 Canada. Tel 416-415-5000; Web: www.georgebrown.ca/adit; *Dean, School of Design* Luigi Ferrara
Estab 1970; FT 30, PT 60; D & E; D 900, E 2000
Ent Req: HS grade 12 dipl, entr exam
Degrees: Dipl & cert
Tuition: Degree progs—$16,500 per yr; dipl, cert & post-grad progs—$13,520 per yr
Courses: †Advertising Design, Air Brush Techniques, Calligraphy, Cartooning, †Commercial Art, Computer Graphics, †Fashion Arts, Graphic Arts, Graphic Design, Illustration, †Lettering, Marker Rendering Techniques, Painting, Photography, Video

HUMBER COLLEGE, School of Creative & Performing Arts, 205 Humber College Blvd, Toronto, ON M5T 2T9 Canada. Tel 416-675-3111; Email enquiry@humber.ca; Web: creativearts.humber.ca; *Dean* Steve Bellamy; *Prog Dir, Film & TV Acting* John Bourgeois; *Prog Dir, Music* Denny Christianson; *Prog Dir, Comedy* Andrew Clark; *Prog Dir, Theatre Performance* Paul De Jong; *Prog Dir, Arts Admin* Anne Frost; *Prog Dir, Theatre Production* Heather Kent; *Prog Dir, Publishing* Alison Maclean; *Prog Dir, Jazz & Community Music* Catherine Mitro; *Prog Dir, Creative Writing* Antanas Sileika
Estab 1967; pub; D & E; SC 300, LC 75, GC 6; grad 50, PT 25
Ent Req: HS dipl, mature student status, one yr of employment plus 19 yrs of age
Degrees: 2 & 3 yr dipl courses
Tuition: Canadian res—$6,948 per yr; international—$14,200 per yr
Courses: Art History, Drafting, Drawing, Film, Furniture Design, Graphic Arts, †Graphic Design, †Industrial Design, †Interior Design, †Landscape Technology, †Museum Staff Training, †Music, †Packaging Design, Photography, †Theatre Arts, TV Production
Adult Hobby Classes: Enrl 4042; tuition & duration vary. Beginning classes in most regular courses
Children's Classes: Nature studies

KOFFLER CENTER OF THE ARTS, 180 Shaw St, Ste 104-105 Toronto, ON M6J 2W5 Canada. Tel 647-925-0643; Fax 416-636-5813; Email info@kofflerarts.org; Web: kofflerarts.org; *Exec Dir* Cathy Jonasson; *Gallery Dir & Cur* Mona Filip; *Dir Pub Progs & Engagement* Jessica Dargo Caplan; *Dir Literary & Theatre Progs* Natalie Kertes; *Dir Digital Progs* Alex Johnson; *Gallery Asst & Educator* Mary Anderson
Open Tues - Fri Noon - 6 PM, Sat & Sun 11 AM - 5 PM, cl Mon; Estab 1977; Maintains the Koffler Gallery at Artscape Youngplace; pub; D & E; Scholarships; D 400, E 98; SC 35
Courses: Ceramics, Clay, Drawing, Mixed Media, Painting, Sculpture, Stone Sculpture, †Theater Arts
Adult Hobby Classes: Enrl 350-400. Courses—Drawing, Painting, Sculpture
Children's Classes: 50 Drawing, Painting, Ceramics

OCAD UNIVERSITY, 100 McCaul St, Toronto, ON M5T 1W1 Canada. Tel 416-977-6000; Fax 416-977-6006; Email admissions@ocadu.ca; Web: www.ocadu.ca; *Pres* Dr Sara Diamond; *VPres Acad & Provost* Dr Gillian Siddall; *Dean, Faculty of Art* Vladimir Spicanovic; *Dean, Faculty of Design* Gayle Nicoll; *Dean, Faculty of Liberal Arts & Sciences* Caroline Langill
Estab 1876; Maintain art/architecture library: Dorothy H Hoover Library, 113 McCaul St, Toronto; maintain an on-site not for profit art gallery; on-campus shop for purchase of art supplies; pub; D & E; Scholarships; SC 296 LC 53; D 2144, E 2000, grad summer 900
Ent Req: HS dipl, English requirement, interview
Degrees: BA, BFA, BDes, MFA, MDes, MA, EMDes
Tuition: Canadian res—$8,646 per yr; international—$25,842 per yr
Courses: Aboriginal Visual Culture, †Advertising Design, Anthropology, Art History, Arts of Latin American & Asia, †Calligraphy, †Ceramics, Collage, †Commercial Art, Communication Design, Communication studies, Conceptual Art, Contemporary Theory & Criticism, Creative Writing, †Criticism & Curatorial Practice, Cultural Studies, †Design, Digital &n Media Studies, Display, †Drawing, Drawing & Painting, English, English Literature & Composition, Expanded Animation, †Fashion Arts, Film, Film Studies, Furniture Design, †Graphic Arts, †Graphic Design, History of Art & Architecture, History of Design, Humanities, †Illustration, Industrial Ceramics, †Industrial Design, †Integrated Media, †Jewelry, Linguistics, †Material Art & Design, Fiber, Mixed Media, Native Studies, †On-Screen Media, †Painting, Philosophy, †Photography, †Printmaking, Science/Technology/Mathematics, †Sculpture, †Sculpture/Installation, Silversmithing, Social Sciences, Sociology, Stage Design, Sustainability in Design, Video, Visual Culture, Wearable Technology, †Weaving, Women's Studies
Summer School: Summer courses run for three, six or twelve week periods. Classes take place from one to four days per week and may be scheduled mornings, afternoons and/or evenings. Courses—Drawing & Painting, General Art, Photography, Printmaking, General Design, Material Art & Design (Fibre, Jewelry/Metalsmithing, Ceramics) English, History & Theory of Visual Culture, Humanities, Social Sciences, Science, Technology, Mathematics

TORONTO ART THERAPY INSTITUTE, 8 Prince Arthur Ave, 2nd Fl, Toronto, ON M5R 1A9 Canada. Tel 416-924-6221; Fax 416-924-0156; Email torontoarttherapyassistant@gmail.com; Web: www.tati.on.ca; *Exec Dir* Dr Helene Burt
Estab 1968; D & E; Enrl 12 per prog
Degrees: Dipl, BA and MA(Art Therapy) through affiliation with Wilfred Laurier Univ & Nazareth College
Tuition: $7,700 per yr

TORONTO SCHOOL OF ART, 980 Dufferin St, 2nd Floor Toronto, ON M6H 4B4 Canada. Tel 416-504-7910; Fax 416-504-8171; Email info@tsa-art.com; Web: tsa-art.com; *Mng Dir* Elizabeth D'Agostino; *Student & Events Coordr* Renee Castonguay; *Social Media Coordr* Kimberley Lillywhite; *Office Mgr* Stacy Lewis
Estab 1969; pvt; D & E; Scholarships; D 300 E 200 Majs 10 Grads 5
Ent Req: portfolio
Degrees: 3 yr dipl, 1 yr portfolio develop, 1 yr independent studio prog
Tuition: $275 - $590 depending on duration and type of course or workshop
Courses: Drawing, Mixed Media, Painting, Photography, Printmaking, Sculpture

UNIVERSITY OF TORONTO, Dept of Fine Art, 27 King's College Circle, Toronto, ON M5S 1A1 Canada. Tel 416-946-7624; Fax 416-946-7627; Email chairfa@chass.utoronto.ca; Web: www.library.utoronto.ca/fineart; *Chmn* Marc Gotlieb; *Assoc Chmn Grad Studies* Mark Cheetham; *Assoc Chmn Visual Studies* Lisa Steele; *Undergrad Coordr Art History* Alexander Nagel; *Undergrad Coordr Visual Studies* George Hawken
Estab 1934; FT 21, PT 13; pub; Scholarships; Fellowships; LC, GC
Degrees: BA 4 yrs, MA 2 yrs, PhD 5 yrs
Tuition: Nonres—undergrad $12,024; campus res available
Courses: Aesthetics, Architecture, Art History, Art Studio, Conceptual Art, Drawing, Graphic Arts, History of Art & Architecture, Painting, Photography, Printmaking, Sculpture, Video
Adult Hobby Classes: Enrl 250

YORK UNIVERSITY, School of the Arts, Media, Performance & Design, Joan & Martin Goldfarb Centre for Fine Arts, 4700 Keele St Toronto, ON M3J 1P3 Canada. Tel 416-736-2100; Email ampd@yorku.ca; Web: ampd.yorku.ca; *Dean* Shawn Brixey; *Assoc Prof & Chair, Dept of Cinema & Media Arts* Ali Kazimi; *Assoc Prof & Chair, Dept of Dance* Susan Cash; *Assoc Prof & Chair, Dept of Design* Sandra Gabriele; *Assoc Prof & Chair, Dept of Computational Arts* Don Sinclair; *Assoc Prof & Chair, Dept of Music* William Thomas; *Assoc Prof & Chair, Dept of Theatre* Ines Buchli; *Assoc Prof & Chair, Dept Visual Art & Art History* Brandon Vickerd
Estab 1969; FT 26, PT 8; pub; D & E; Scholarships; SC 53, LC 17; D over 400, maj 400, others 120
Ent Req: HS dipl, interview and portfolio evaluation for studio statement for art history
Degrees: BA(Hons), BFA(Hons) 4 yrs, MA in Art History, MFA in Visual Arts
Tuition: Res—$7,102 per year; nonres—$21,419 per year (prices quoted are Canadian dollars)
Courses: Art History, Criticism, †Dance, Design, †Digital Media, Drawing, Graphic Arts, Interdisciplinary Studio, Painting, Photography, Sculpture, †Theatre Arts, Theory

WATERLOO

UNIVERSITY OF WATERLOO, Dept of Fine Arts, 200 University Ave W, ECH Bldg Waterloo, ON N2L 3G1 Canada. Tel 519-888-4567, ext 36923; Fax 519-888-4521; Web: uwaterloo.ca/fine-arts; *Dean of Arts* Douglas Peers; *Assoc Prof & Chair, Dept Fine Arts* Doug Kirton; *Asst Prof & Assoc Chair, Undergrad Studies*

Bojana Videkanic; *Asst Prof & Assoc Chair, Grad Studies* Tara Cooper; *Dir & Cur, Univ of Waterloo Art Gallery* Ivan Jurakic
Estab 1958, dept estab 1968; Maintains nonprofit gallery, University of Waterloo Art Gallery 200 University Ave W, Waterloo Ont N2L3G1, Maintains art/architecture library; Eva McCavley, Paul Dignan; Pub; D & E; Scholarships; SC 25, LC 27, GC; maj 150; Day 150
Ent Req: HS dipl
Degrees: BA 3 yrs, BA(Hons) 4 yrs
Tuition: Res—$3,652 per yr, international—$12,871; campus res available
Courses: †Art History, Ceramic Sculpture, Ceramics, Computer Animation, Computer Imaging, †Drawing, †Film Theory & History, Illustration, †Painting, Photography, †Printmaking, †Sculpture
Summer School: Enrl 30. Courses—Drawing

WINDSOR

UNIVERSITY OF WINDSOR, School of Creative Arts, School of Visual Arts, 401 Sunset Ave Windsor, ON N9B 3P4 Canada. Tel 519-253-3000, Ext 2829; Fax 519-971-3647; Email art@uwindsor.ca; Web: www1.uwindsor.ca/soca; *Dir, School of Creative Arts* Karen Engle; *Undergrad Coordr* Michael Darroch; *Prof, Film & Media Arts* Min Bae; *Prof, Media Art Histories & Visual Culture* Michael Farrell; *Prof, Music & Sound, Sonic Art* Brent Lee; *Prof, Photography* Cyndra MacDowell; *Prof, Film & Media Arts* Kim Nelson; *Prof, Media Art Histories & Visual Culture* Lee Rodney; *Prof, Photography & Studio Art* Brenda Francis Pelkey; *Prof, Integrated Media* Sigi Torinus; *Prof, Print & Bio Art* Jennifer Willet
Estab 1960; Maintains nonprofit art galleries: LeBel Gallery, School of Visual Arts, Univ of Windsor, Windsor, Ontario N9B 3P4; SoVA Projects Art Gallery, School of Visual Arts, Univ Windsor, LeBel Bldg. Art Supplies may be purchased on campus; FT 8, PT 3; pub; D & E; Scholarships; Assistantships; SC 32, LC 10, GC 6; D 250, maj 300, G students 10
Ent Req: Ontario Secondary School Graduation Dipl (OSSD) plus 6 Ontario Acad Courses (OAC) or equivalent
Degrees: BA in Visual Arts or Art History 3 yrs, BA (Hons) in Visual Arts or Art History, Combined honors degree program and BFA 4 yrs, MFA 2 yrs
Tuition: Res—$3,834 per yr; international—$7,577 per yr
Courses: †Art History, Built Environment, †Drawing, †Film, Green Corridor, †Integrated Media, Multi Media, †Painting, Photography, †Printmaking, †Sculpture

PRINCE EDWARD ISLAND

CHARLOTTETOWN

HOLLAND COLLEGE, School of Visual Arts & Journalism, 140 Weymouth St, Charlottetown, PE C1A 4Z1 Canada. Tel 902-629-7032; Fax 902-629-4268; Email info@hollandcollege.com; Web: www.hollandcollege.com; *Fundamental Arts* Gweneth Branch-Rice; *Journalism* Rick MacLean; *Journalism* Wayne Young; *Photography & Digital Imaging* Alex Murchison; *Photography & Digital Imaging* Jean Duchesne; *Video Game Art & Animation* Chris Sharpley; *Video Game Art & Animation* Tiffany Baxter
Estab 1977; Schols open to all; Alex Murchinson, Jean Duchesne; Pub; D; Scholarships; SC, LC; D 25
Ent Req: Grad 12, portfolio, questionnaire
Degrees: Dipl
Tuition: Res—$3,830 per yr; international—$7,695 per yr
Courses: †Animation, †Digital Imaging, †Graphic Design, †Journalism, Photography, †Video Game Art

QUEBEC

MONTREAL

CONCORDIA UNIVERSITY, Faculty of Fine Arts, 1515 Ste Catherine St W, EV 2.705 Montreal, QC H3G 1M8 Canada. Tel 514-848-2424; Fax 514-848-4599; Web: www.concordia.ca/finearts; *Dean, Fine Arts* Rebecca Duclos; *Chair, Art Educ* David Pariser; *Chair, Art History* Elaine Cheasley Paterson; *Chair, Mel Hoppenheim School of Cinema* Catherine Russell; *Chair, Contemporary Dance* Silvy Panet-Raymond; *Coordr, Creative Arts Therapies* Yehudit Silverman; *Chair, Theatre* Ted Little; *Chair, Studio Arts* Eric Simon; *Chair, Music* Mark Corwin; *Chair, Design & Computational Arts* pk langshaw
Maintains Leonard & Bina Ellen Art Gallery, FOFA Galley, Communication Studies Media Gallery, Mobile Media Gallery, VAV Gallery & MFA Gallery; D & E; Scholarships
Ent Req: HS dipl, CEGEP dipl Prov of Quebec
Degrees: BFA, post-BFA Dipl in Art Educ & Art Therapy, full-time leading to teaching cert, MA(Art Educ), MA(Art History), MA(Art Therapy), PhD(Art Educ)
Tuition: Res—$1,850 - $4,219; international—$10,410
Courses: †Art Education, †Art History, †Art Therapy, †Ceramics, †Contemporary Dance, †Design Art, †Drawing, †Fibres, †Film, Interdisciplinary Studies, †Music, †Painting, †Photography, †Printmaking, †Sculpture, †Studio Arts, †Theatre Arts, Women & the Fine Arts
Adult Hobby Classes: Courses offered
Summer School: Courses offered

MCGILL UNIVERSITY, Dept of Art History & Communication Studies, 853 Sherbrooke St W, Arts Bldg, Rm 265 Montreal, QC H3A 2T6 Canada. Tel 514-398-2850; Fax 514-398-8557; Email ahcs@mcgill.ca; Web: www.mcgill.ca/ahcs; *Prof & Dept Chair* Jenny Burman; *Prof & Grad Prog Dir* Matthew Hunter; *Prof & Undergrad Dir, Art History* Charmaine Nelson; *Prof & Undergrad Dir, Commun Studies* Gabriella Coleman
Pvt; D; Assistantships; SC 2, LC 7, GC 12
Ent Req: HS dipl or CEGEP Dipl
Degrees: BA(Art History), MA & PhD(Art History), MA & PhD(Communication Studies)
Tuition: Canadian res—$2,328 - $7,227 per yr, international—$15,942 per yr
Courses: Ancient Greek Art, Baroque Art, †History of Art & Archaeology, Medieval Art, Modern Art, Renaissance Art

UNIVERSITE DE MONTREAL, Dept of Art History & Film Studies, Pavillon Lionel-Groulx, 3150, rue Jean-Brillant Montreal, QC H3T 1N8 Canada. Tel 514-343-6182; Fax 514-343-2393; Email histart@umontreal.ca; Web: histart.umontreal.ca; *Prof & Dept Dir* Silvestra Mariniello
Dept estab 1961; pvt; D & E; SC 20, LC 70, GC 10; D 270, non-maj 113, maj 106, grad 80, others 151
Ent Req: HS dipl
Degrees: BA, MA & PhD
Tuition: Canadian res—$1,146 - $3,515 per session; international—$7,853 per session; campus res available
Courses: Art History, Film, Fine Arts

UNIVERSITE DU QUEBEC A MONTREAL, Faculty of Arts, Pavillon Judith-Jasmin, 405 rue Sainte-Catherine E Montreal, QC H2X 2C4 Canada. Tel 514-987-4545; Fax 514-987-4653; Email arts@uqam.ca; Web: arts.uqam.ca; *Dean* Jean-Christian Pleau
Estab 1969
Ent Req: 2 yrs after HS
Degrees: BA & MA; programs in Dance, Literary Studies, Music, Design, Theatre, Art History, Visual & Media Arts
Courses: †Art History, †Dance, †Design, †Literary Studies, †Music, †Theatre Arts, †Visual & Media Arts
Adult Hobby Classes: Cert in visual arts available

QUEBEC

UNIVERSITE LAVAL, Faculty of Planning, Architecture, Arts & Design, Edifice du Boulevard, 350 boulevard Charest E, 7e etage Quebec, QC G1K 3H5 Canada. Tel 418-656-2546; Email faaad@faaad.ulaval.ca; Web: faaad.ulaval.ca; *Dean Planning, Architecture Art & Design* Alain Rochon; *Assoc Prof & Dir, School of Architecture* GianPiero Moretti; *Prof & Dir, School of Art* Jocelyn Robert; *Prof & Dir, School of Land Management & Regional Planning* Claude Lavoie; *Dir, School of Design* Michel Fleury
Estab 1970; Maintains Visual Arts Gallery, Bldg la Fabrique, boulevard Charest Est, 404, Quebec, G1K 3G8; pub; D
Ent Req: 2 yrs col
Degrees: BA, MA & PhD
Tuition: Res undergrad—$2,900 - $7,637 per yr; international undergrad—$7,637 - $19,676 per yr
Courses: †Animation, †Architecture, Computer Graphic, †Design, Graphic Arts, Graphic Design, †History of Art & Architecture, †Media Arts, †Product Design, †Urban Design, †Visual Arts

TROIS-RIVIERES

UNIVERSITE DU QUEBEC, TROIS-RIVIERES, Department of Philosophy & the Arts, 3351 boulevard des Forges, Trois-Rivieres, QC G9A 5H7 Canada. Tel 819-376-5136; Fax 819-376-5226; Email arts@utqr.ca; Web: www.uqtr.uquebec.ca/arts; *Admin Officer* Elise Lebordais; *Prof & Dept Dir* Aime Zayed, PhD; *Prog Dir* France Joyal
Estab 1969; Maintains R3 Gallery, 3351 boulevard de Forges, Trois-Rivieres, G9A 5H7; pub; D & E; SC 12, LC 8, GC 28; D 150, E 100
Activities: r3 Galerie d'art
Ent Req: ent exam or DEC
Degrees: BA(Fine Arts) & BA(Art Education)
Courses: †Art Education, †Art History, †Fine Arts, †Theatre Arts
Adult Hobby Classes: Courses—Art History, Painting, Printmaking

SASKATCHEWAN

REGINA

UNIVERSITY OF REGINA, Faculty of Media, Art & Performance, Riddell Centre, Regina, SK S4S 0A2 Canada. Tel 306-585-5510; Fax 306-585-5544; Email media.art.performance@uregina.ca; Web: www.uregina.ca/mediaartperformance; *Prof & Dean* Rae Staseson; *Assoc Prof & Head, Theatre Dept* Kathryn Bracht; *Asst Prof & Head, Music Dept* Lynn Cavanagh; *Prof & Head, Visual Arts Dept* Leesa Streifler
Maintain nonprofit art gallery; FT 9; pub; D&E; Scholarships; Fellowships; SC, LC, GC; 650
Ent Req: HS grad
Degrees: 2 yr cert, BA 3 yrs, BA 4 yrs, BFA 4 yrs, MFA 2 yrs
Tuition: Res undergrad—$3,373 per sem; international undergrad—$9,703
Courses: †Art Appreciation, †Art History, †Ceramics, †Drawing, †Film, Intermedia, †Music, Painting, †Photography, †Printmaking, †Sculpture, †Theatre Arts
Summer School: Introductory courses offered

SASKATOON

UNIVERSITY OF SASKATCHEWAN, Art & Art History Dept, Murray Bldg, 3 Campus Dr Saskatoon, SK S7N 5A5 Canada. Tel 306-966-6185; Fax

306-966-5782; Email art.arthistory@usask.ca; Web: www.arts.usask.ca/art; *Asst Prof* Jon Bath; *Prof* Keith Bell; *Prof* Lynne Bell; *Assoc Prof* Jennifer Crane; *Asst Prof* Allyson Glenn; *Asst Prof* John David Graham; *Assoc Prof* Mary Longman; *Prof* Alison Norlen; *Dept Head, Art & Art History* Tim Nowlin; *Prof* Susan Shantz
Estab 1936; Maintains Gordon Snelgrove Gallery; FT 13, PT 4; pub; D; Scholarships; SC, LC, GC; approx 880, BFA prog 130, grad 9
Ent Req: HS grad
Degrees: BA 3 yrs, BAHons(Art History), BA(Advanced) 4 yrs, BFA 4 yrs, MFA (Studio Art), BEd(Art)
Tuition: Canadian res—$193 per cr unit; international—$501 per cr unit
Courses: †Art Education, †Art History, †Drawing, †History of Art & Architecture, †Painting, †Photography, †Printmaking, †Sculpture
Summer School: Enrl 200. Courses—Art Educ, Art History, Drawing, Painting, Photography, Printmaking, Sculpture

III ART INFORMATION

Major Museums Abroad

Major Art Schools Abroad

State Arts Councils

State Directors and Supervisors of Art Education

Art Magazines

Museums Abroad

ALBANIA

TIRANA

M **MEZURAJ MUSEUM,** Sun Business Center, Kavaja Ave 1st Fl Tirana, Albania. Tel 355 4 226 7196; Fax 355 4 226 7199; Email info@mezuraj.museum; Web: mezuraj.museum; *Pres* Eduart Mezuraj
Open Mon - Sat 9 AM - 6 PM; cl Sun; Admis 300 ALL or 3 EUR, children under 12 w/ parent & students free; Estab for the protection & admin of mus objects, memory preservation, archaeological searching & enterprise; Private mus with 2 exhib rooms, 1 hall of exhibs, 2 offices; Average Annual Attendance: 200,000
Purchases: Purchases are made for enriching archaeological collections & that of contemporary & traditional art
Library Holdings: CD-ROMs, Cassettes, Compact Disks, DVDs, Exhibition Catalogs, Original Art Works, Original Documents, Photographs, Prints, Reproductions, Sculpture, Video Tapes
Special Subjects: Archaeology, Art History, Bronzes, Ceramics, Coins & Medals, Historical Material, History of Art & Archaeology, Jewelry, African Art
Collections: Archeological objects, pre-historic, antique & middle-aged, iconographic art, many other works of Albanian artists, Traditional painters' & contemporary Albanian painters' collections
Publications: Mezuraj Album; Mezuraj Collection of Helidon Haliti; Mezuraj Collection of Artur Muharremi
Activities: Lectrs open to the public; gallery talks; schols; book traveling exhibs; mus shop sells books, original art, reproductions, prints

ALGERIA

ALGIERS

M **MUSEE NATIONAL DES ANTIQUITES ET DES ARTS ISLAMIQUES,** National Museum of Antiquities & Islamic Arts, 177, Boulevard krim Belkacem, Parc de la libertï 1/2 Algiers, 16100 Algeria. Tel 213 (0) 21 68 11 29; Fax 213 (0) 21 68 12 56; Email museemna@musee-antiquites.art.dz; Web: www.musee-antiquites.art.dz; *Dir* Drias Lakhdar; *Cur* Mohammed Temmam
Open Sat - Thurs 9 AM - 12 PM & 1 PM - 4:30 PM; Admis 200 DZD
Collections: Algerian antiquities & Islamic art

M **MUSEE NATIONAL DES BEAUX ARTS D'ALGER,** National Museum of Fine Arts of Algiers, 178, Place Dar Essalem, El Hamma, Belouizdad Algiers, Algeria. Tel 213 0 21 66 49 16; Email directrice@musee-beauxarts.dz; Web: www.musee-beauxarts.dz; *Dir* Dalila Mohamed-Orfali
Open Sat - Thurs 9 AM - 12 PM & 1 PM - 5 PM; Admis 200 DZD, children under 16 & seniors over 65 free; 1930; art gallery; Ground floor & two floors & two major entrances
Purchases: Annual commission of acquisitions
Collections: Contemporary Algerian art, paintings, drawings, bronze reliefs, ancient paintings 14th - 19th century (European)
Publications: Guides; exhibition catalogues; collections catalogues
Activities: Exhibitions; commemorations; conferences; concerts; tours

ARGENTINA

BUENOS AIRES

M **FUNDACION FEDERICO JORGE KLEMM,** Federico Jorge Klemm Foundation, Marcelo T de Alvear 626, Buenos Aires, Argentina. Tel 4312-3334/ 4443; Email admin@fundacionfjklemm.org; Web: www.fundacionfjklemm.org; *Pres* Matilde Marín; *Cultural Mgmnt* Valeria Fiterman; *Cultural Mgmnt* Fernando Ezpeleta; *Admin* Maria Fernanda Quiroga
Open Mon - Fri 11 AM - 8 PM; No admis fee

M **FUNDACION PROA,** PROA Foundation, Avenida Pedro de Mendoza 1929, La Boca, Caminito Buenos Aires, C1169AAD Argentina. Tel (54-11) 4104-1000; Email info@proa.org; Web: www.proa.org; *Dir* Adriana Rosenberg
Open Tues - Sun 11 AM - 7 PM, cl Mon; Admis 40 ARS, students 30 ARS, pensioners 20 ARS

M **MUSEO DE ARTE ESPANOL ENRIQUE LARRETA,** Larreta Museum of Spanish Art, Avenida Juramento 2291, Buenos Aires, 1428 Argentina. Tel 54 (11) 4784-4040; Fax 54 (11) 4783-2640; Email museolarreta@buenosaires.gob.ar; Web: www.buenosaires.gob.ar/museolarreta; *Dir* Nicolas Helft
Open Tue - Fri 12 - 7 PM, Sat, Sun & holidays 10 AM - 8 PM; Admis general 30 ARS, children free
Collections: 13th - 16th century wood carvings, gilt objects and painted panels, paintings of Spanish School of 16th and 17th centuries, tapestries, furniture

M **MUSEO DE ARTE HISPANOAMERICANO ISAAC FERNANDEZ BLANCO,** Isaac Fernandez Blanco Museum of Hispano-American Art, Suipacha 1422, Buenos Aires, CP 1011 Argentina. Tel 5411-4327-0228; Email mifb_prensa@buenosaires.gob.ar; Web: www.buenosaires.gob.ar/museofernandezblanco; *Dir* Jorge Cometti
Palacio Noel: open Tues - Fri 1 - 7 PM, Sat & Sun 11 AM - 7 PM, cl Mon; Casa Fernandez Blanco: open Tues - Fri 12 PM - 6 PM, Sat & Sun 11 AM - 5 PM, cl Mon; Admis 90 ARS, Wed free; Estab 1922
Collections: Personal collection of Don Isaac White Fernandez, Dona Celina Gonzalez Garano & others; paintings, furniture, silverware, and other decorative arts

M **MUSEO DE ARTE LATINOAMERICANO DE BUENOS AIRES,** Latin American Art Museum of Buenos Aires, Avenida Figueroa Alcorat 3415, Buenos Aires, C1425CLA Argentina. Tel 54 11 4808 6500; Email informes@malba.org.ar; Web: www.malba.org.ar; *Pres* Eduardo Costantini; *Gen Mgr* Emilio Xarrier; *Artistic Dir* Agustin Perez Rubio
Open Sun, Mon, Thurs-Sat & holidays noon - 8 PM, Wed noon - 9 PM, cl Tues; Admis adults 140 ARS, students, teachers & seniors 45 ARS, children under 5 & persons with disabilities free
Collections: History of Spanish American art; Avant-garde movement from beginning to present, Costantini Collection

M **MUSEO DE ARTE MODERNO,** Museum of Modern Art, Avenida San Juan 350, Buenos Aires, C1143AAO Argentina. Tel 54 11 4361-6919; Email informesmoderno@gmail.com; Web: www.buenosaires.gob.ar/museoartemoderno.; *Dir* Victoria Noorthoorn
Open Tues - Fri 11 AM - 7 PM, Sat, Sun & holidays 11 AM - 8 PM, cl Mon; Admis 20 ARS, Tues free; Estab 1956
Collections: Latin American paintings, especially Argentine, and contemporary schools

M **MUSEO DE BELLAS ARTES DE LA BOCA DE ARTISTAS ARGENTINOS - BENITO QUINQUELA MARTIN,** Benito Quinquela Martin Museum of Fine Argentine Arts, La Boca, Avenida Don Pedro de Mendoza 1843/35, La Boca Buenos Aires, 1169 Argentina. Tel 54 11 4301-1080; Email museoquinquelamartin@buenosaires.gov.ar; Web: www.buenosaires.gob.ar/museoquinquelamartin; *Dir* Victor Fernandez
Open Tues - Fri 10 AM - 6 PM (winter) & Tues - Fri 11:15 AM - 6 PM (summer), Sat, Sun & holidays 11 AM - 6 PM, cl Mon; No admis fee, donations accepted; Estab 1938
Collections: Paintings, sculptures, engravings & maritime museum

M **MUSEO NACIONAL DE ARTE DECORATIVO,** National Museum of Decorative Art, Avda del Libertador 1902, Buenos Aires, C1425AAS Argentina. Tel 54 (11) 4801-8248; Fax 54 (11) 4802-6606; Email museo@mnad.org; Web: www.mnad.org; *Dir* Alberto Guillermo Bellucci
Open Special guided tour in English: Tues - Fri 2:30 PM; Admis 20 ARS, seniors & children 12 & under free; Open Jan Tues - Sat 2 - 7 PM, Feb - Dec Tues - Sun 2 - 7 PM
Collections: European works, furniture, sculptures and tapestries, glasses, porcelains, hardstones, Oriental lacquers

M **MUSEO NACIONAL DE BELLAS ARTES,** National Museum of Fine Arts, Avda del Libertador 1473, Buenos Aires, 1425 Argentina. Tel 54 (11) 5288-9900; Email info@mnba.gob.ar; Web: www.bellasartes.gob.ar; *Exec Dir* Marcela Cardillo
Open Tues - Fri 11 AM - 8 PM, Sat & Sun 10 AM - 8 PM; cl Mon; No admis fee; Opened in 1896, the Nat Mus of Fine Arts has on display more than 12,000 pieces of art across 24 exhibit halls with state of the art technology for both traditional & multimedia shows.
Collections: Latin American and European art, both modern and classical

CORDOBA

M **MUSEO MUNICIPAL DE BELLAS ARTES GENARO PEREZ,** Genaro Perez Museum of Fine Arts, Avda Gral Paz 33, Cordoba, 5000 Argentina. Tel 351 434-1646; Fax 351 433-2720; Email museogenaroperez@gmail.com; Web: museogenaroperez.wordpress.com; *Dir* Raul Lafuret Pereyra

Open Tues - Sun 10 AM - 8 PM; No admis fee; Estab 1943
Collections: Permanent collection of Argentine and Cordovan painting from 1868 to the present; 19th century pieces; generation of the 1930s; nonfigurative avant-garde of the 1950s; movements from 1960 to the present
Exhibitions: Changing contemporary art exhibits

M **MUSEO PROVINCIAL DE BELLAS ARTES EMILIO CARAFFA,** Emilio Caraffa Museum of Fine Arts, Av Poeta Lugones 411, Cordoba, X5000HZE Argentina. Tel 54 (351) 434-3348/49; Email comunicacion@museocaraffa.org.ar; Web: www.museocaraffa.org.ar; *Dir* Jorge Torres
Open Tues - Fri 10 AM - 8 PM, Sat, Sun & holidays 10:30 AM - 7 PM, cl Mon; Admis 15 ARS, children, students & seniors free; Estab 1916; Neoclassical building housing contemporary art
Collections: Provincial art center, including art library and archives, Argentine and foreign paintings, sculptures, drawings and engravings

LA PLATA

M **MUSEO DE ARTE CONTEMPORANEO LATINOAMERICANO,** Museum of Contemporary Latin American Art, Centro Cultural Pasaje Dardo Rocha, Calle 50 entre 6 y 7, 2 Piso La Plata, CP 1900 Argentina. Tel 0221 427-1843; Fax 0221 427-1843; Email prensa@macla.com.ar; Web: www.macla.com.ar; *Dir Gen* Maria de las Mercedes Reitano
Open Tues - Sun & holidays 10 AM - 10 PM, cl Mon; No admis fee; Estab 2001 to provide a space where artists, researchers, students and the public in general can get to know and value contemporary Latin American art.
Collections: Exhibitions of contemporary Latin American art
Activities: mus shop sells carefully selected works by local, national and international contemporary artists

ROSARIO

M **MUSEO MUNICIPAL DE ARTE DECORATIVO FIRMA Y ODILO ESTEVEZ,** Firma y Odilo Estevez Museum of Decorative Art, Santa Fe 748, Rosario, S2000ATH Argentina. Tel 54 341 4802547; Email museo@museoestevez.gob.ar; Web: www.museoestevez.gob.ar; *Dir* Analia Garcia
Open Wed - Sun 9 AM - 5 PM, public holidays 9 AM - 1 PM, cl Mon & Tues; No admis fee; Estab 1968
Collections: Antique glass, paintings by Van Utrecht, Antolinez, De Hondecoeter, Gerard, Lucas, 16th - 18th centuries furniture & silver, ceramics, antique glass, ivories, silver

M **MUSEO MUNICIPAL DE BELLAS ARTES JUAN B CASTAGNINO,** Juan B Castagnino Museum Museum of Fine Arts, Av Pellegrini 2202, Rosario, Santa Fe CP 2000 Argentina. Tel 54 341 4802542/43; Email direccion@castagninomacro.org; Web: www.castagninomacro.org.ar; *Dir* Marcela Romer
Open Jan & Feb Thurs - Sun 5 PM - 9 PM, cl Mon - Wed; No admis fee; Estab 1937; Library with 3000 vols, two floors, totaling 35 rooms with 700 linear meters available for exhibitions
Collections: Works by Jose de Ribera, Goya, Valdes Leal & a complete collection of Argentine art from 19th century to present

SANTA FE

M **MUSEO PROVINCIAL DE BELLAS ARTES ROSA GALISTEO DE RODRIGUEZ,** Rosa Galisteo de Rodriguez Museum of Fine Arts, 4 de Enero 1510, Santa Fe, 3000 Argentina. Tel 54 342 457 3577; Email museorosagalisteo@santafe.gov.ar; Web: www.museorosagalisteo.gobn.ar; *Dir* Analia Solomonoff
Open Tues - Fri 8 AM - noon & 4 - 9 PM, Sat, Sun & holidays 4 - 9 PM, cl Mon; No admis fee; Library with 4000 vols
Collections: Contemporary Argentine & modern art

TANDIL

M **MUSEO MUNICIPAL DE BELLAS ARTES DE TANDIL,** Tandil Museum of Fine Arts, Chacabuco 357, Tandil, 7000 Argentina. Tel 54 (0249) 443-2067; Email mumbattandil@gmail.com; Web: mumbat.com; *Dir* Indiana Gnocchini
Open Tues - Fri 9 AM - noon & 5 - 8 PM, Sat & Sun 5 - 8 PM, cl Mon; No admis fee
Collections: Paintings of classical, impressionist, cubist and modern schools

ARMENIA

YEREVAN

M **NATIONAL GALLERY OF ARMENIA,** 1 Arami St, Republic Sq Yerevan, 0010 Armenia. Tel (374-10) 567472, 582161; Fax (374-10) 580812; Email galleryarmenia@gmail.com; Web: www.gallery.am; *Dir* Arman Tsaturyan; *Chief Cur* Vehanush Pounarjyan
Open Tues - Sat 11 AM - 5:30 PM, Sun 11 AM - 5 PM, cl Mon; Admis adults 800 AMD, school children, students & pensioners 300 AMD, children (7 & under), art students, artists union members, veterans, disabled, mus workers, delegations & servicemen free
Collections: Collection of more than 19,000 Russian, Armenian and western European paintings, sculptures, & graphic and applied arts

AUSTRALIA

ADELAIDE

M **ART GALLERY OF SOUTH AUSTRALIA,** North Terrace, Adelaide, SA 5000 Australia. Tel 61 8 8207-7000; Fax 61 8 8207-7070; Email agsainformation@artgallery.sa.gov.au; Web: www.artgallery.sa.gov.au; *Co-Dir* Mark Horton; *Co-Dir* Lisa Slade; *Cur of Australian Paintings & Sculpture* Tracey Lock; *Sr Cur of Prints, Drawings & Photographs* Julie Robinson; *Cur of Asian Art* James Bennett; *Cur of European & Australian Decorative Arts* Rebecca Evans; *Cur of European & North American Art* Tony Magnusson; *Cur Contemporary Art* Leigh Robb; *Cur Aboriginal & Torres Strait Islander Art* Nici Cumpston
Open daily 10 AM - 5 PM daily, cl Dec 25; No admis fee; charges for some exhibs; Estab 1881; Main art gallery of the state of South Australia; Average Annual Attendance: 600,000
Income: Financed by South Australian state government
Purchases: Continually adding to the permanent collection
Library Holdings: Auction Catalogs, Book Volumes, CD-ROMs, Cards, Clipping Files, Exhibition Catalogs, Fiche, Original Documents, Pamphlets, Periodical Subscriptions, Records
Special Subjects: Asian Art, Ceramics, Decorative Arts, Drawings, Etchings & Engravings, Furniture, Glass, Islamic Art, Jewelry, Laces, Painting-Australian, Painting-British, Photography, Porcelain, Pottery, Prints, Sculpture, Silver, Textiles, Watercolors, Woodcuts, Painting-European
Collections: Representative selection of Australian, British and European paintings, prints, drawings and sculpture, large coll of ceramics, glass and silver, extensive Australian Colonial Coll, Asian Arts; SE Asian ceramics, furniture, photography
Exhibitions: Several temporary exhibitions per year
Publications: Exhibition catalogues, collection catalogues, newsletter, ann report
Activities: Classes for children; docent training; lects open to pub, lectrs for mems only; concerts; gallery talks; tours; traveling exhibs to Australian & New Zealand galleries; mus shop sells books, magazines, reproductions; prints, gifts, postcards & posters

BALLARAT

M **ART GALLERY OF BALLARAT,** 40 Lydiard St N, Ballarat, Victoria 3350 Australia. Tel 03 5320 5858; Fax 03 5320 5791; Email artgal@ballarat.vic.gov.au; Web: www.artgalleryofballarat.com.au; *Dir* Gordon Morrison; *Registrar* Anne Rowland
Open daily 10 AM - 5 PM; cl Christmas Day & Boxing Day; No admis fee, charges may apply for some exhibs; Estab 1884
Collections: Australian art including paintings, drawings, sculptures & decorative arts

BENALLA

M **BENALLA ART GALLERY,** Botanical Gardens, Bridge St Benalla, Victoria 3672 Australia; PO Box 227, Benalla, Victoria 3671 Australia. Tel 61 3 5760 2619; Email gallery@benalla.vic.gov.au; Web: www.benallaartgallery.com; *Mgr Arts Communs & Events* Julian Mulally; *Dir* Bryony Nainby
Open Wed - Mon 10 AM - 5 PM; cl Good Friday, Christmas Day & Boxing Day
Collections: Collection includes paintings, printmaking, works on paper, photography, textiles, ceramics, sculpture & decorative arts
Activities: Gallery shop sells handmade crafts, books, cards & children's toys

BRISBANE

M **INSTITUTE OF MODERN ART,** 420 Brunswick St, Fortitude Valley Brisbane, QLD 4006 Australia. Tel 61 7 3252 5750; Fax 61 7 3252 5072; Email ima@ima.org.au; Web: www.ima.org.au; *Exec Dir* Aileen Burns; *Exec Dir* Johan Lundh; *Sr Mgr* Madeleine King; *Assoc Ed* Evie Franzidis; *Bookkeeper* Jewel Mackenzie
Open Tues, Wed, Fri & Sat noon - 6 PM, Thurs noon - 8 PM, cl public holidays, Easter wkend, Christmas/New Year break; No admis fee; Estab 1975; Second oldest contemporary art space; progs of exhibs & events featuring emerging & established local, nat, & international artists; Mem: Dues family $85 AUD, individual $55 AUD, artist, student & seniors $30 AUD
Collections: Modern and contemporary art in various media, Rotating exhibitions; See website for details
Activities: Lects open to pub; 72 vis lectrs per yr; concerts; gallery talks; tours; organize traveling exhibs; mus shop sells books, magazines

M **QUEENSLAND ART GALLERY,** Gallery of Modern Art, Stanley Pl, Cultural Precinct, South Bank Brisbane, Queensland 4101 Australia. Tel 61 (07) 3840 7303; Fax 61 (07) 3844 8865; Email gallery@qagoma.qld.gov.au; Web: www.qagoma.qld.gov.au; *Dir* Chris Saines; *Deputy Dir Coll & Exhibs* Maud Page; *Asst Dir Learning & Pub Engagement* Simon Wright; *Asst Dir Devel & Commercial Servs* Tarragh Cunningham; *Asst Dir Opers & Governance* Adam Lindsay
Open daily 10 AM - 5 PM, Anzac Day 12 noon - 5 PM, cl Good Friday & Christmas & Boxing Day; Admis free, except for special exhibs; Estab 1895; pub art mus for the state of Queensland
Collections: Predominantly Australian art, ceramics, decorative arts, paintings and drawings, British and European paintings and sculpture, historical & contemporary Asian & Pacific art
Activities: Classes for children; lects open to the pub; lects for mems only; gallery talks; tours; extension prog serves regional Queensland; lending of original objects of art; organize traveling exhibs; mus shop sells books, magazines, & collectibles

BULLEEN

M **HEIDE MUSEUM OF MODERN ART,** 7 Templestowe Rd, Bulleen, Victoria VIC 3105 Australia. Tel 61 3-9850-1500; Fax 61 3-9852-0154; Email info@heide.com.au; Web: www.heide.com.au; *Dir & CEO* Kirsty Grant; *Deputy Dir & Sr Cur* Linda Michael
Open Tues - Sun & pub holidays 10 AM - 5 PM; Admis $18 AUD, concession $14 AUD, children under 12 & mems free; Estab 1981, to continue the legacy of founders, John & Sunday Reed; Three separate gallery spaces showing modern & contemporary Australian art; Average Annual Attendance: 40,000; Mem: 1,500
Collections: Over 2,000 works of art & a unique body of cultural material that documents the social & artistic history of Heide
Activities: Classes for adults & children; lects open to pub; lects for mems only; gallery talks; tours; mus shop sells books, magazines, Australian designed gifts, accessories & exhib catalogues

BUNBURY

M **BUNBURY REGIONAL ART GALLERIES,** 64 Wittenoom St, Bunbury, WA 6230 Australia. Tel 08 9792 7323; Email artgallery@bunbury.wa.gov.au; Web: www.brag.org.au; *Gallery Officer* Donna Fortescue; *Dir* Julian Bowron
Open daily 10 AM - 4 PM; cl New Year's Day, Good Friday, ANZAC Day (morning), Christmas Day & Boxing Day; No admis fee, donations accepted; Five exhibiting spaces totaling 540 sq meters and 121 running meters

CANBERRA

M **NATIONAL GALLERY OF AUSTRALIA,** Parkes Pl, Parkes Canberra, ACT 2600 Australia; GPO Box 1150, Canberra, ACT 2601 Australia. Tel 61 2 6240 6411; Email information@nga.gov.au; Web: www.nga.gov.au; *Dir* Nick Mitzevich; *Deputy Dir* Kirsten Paisley; *Asst Dir Exhibs & Coll Servs* Adam Worrall; *Asst Dir Engagement & Devel* Alison Wright; *CFO* Tony Lawless
Open daily 10 AM - 5 PM, cl Christmas Day; No admis fee (special exhibs costs may apply); 1982
Library Holdings: Auction Catalogs, Audio Tapes, Book Volumes, Clipping Files, Exhibition Catalogs, Manuscripts, Memorabilia, Original Documents, Pamphlets, Periodical Subscriptions
Collections: Australian coll includes fine and decorative arts, folk art, commercial art, architecture and design, International coll contains arts from Asia, Southeast Asia, Oceania, Africa, Pre-Columbian America and Europe
Activities: Classes for adults & children; lectrs open to the pub; lectrs for mems only; concerts; gallery talks; tours; galley shop sells books, magazines, reproductions, prints; children's gallery

L **Research Library**, GPO Box 1150, Canberra, ACT 2601 Australia. Tel 61 2 6240 6533; Fax 61 2 6240 6753; Email rlr@nga.gov.au; Web: www.nga.gov.au/research/library; *Research Library & Archives* Katie Russell
Open Mon - Tues & Thurs - Fri 10 AM - 5PM, cl Wed; Estab 1975; Natl Gallery of Australia
Library Holdings: Auction Catalogs 54,000, Book Volumes 140,000, Clipping Files 75,000, DVDs 500, Exhibition Catalogs 15,000, Fiche 35,000, Manuscripts 70, Other Holdings Serials 2,000, Periodical Subscriptions 800, Video Tapes 300
Special Subjects: Painting-Japanese, Asian Art, Bookplates & Bindings, Ceramics, Collages, Conceptual Art, Costume Design & Constr, Crafts, Decorative Arts, Display, Drawings, Etchings & Engravings, Fashion Arts, Folk Art, Furniture, Glass, Graphic Arts, Graphic Design, Handicrafts, Illustration, Islamic Art, Jewelry, Landscapes, Manuscripts, Mixed Media, Oriental Art, Painting-American, Painting-Australian, Painting-British, Painting-European, Painting-French, Painting-Italian, Painting-New Zealand, Painting-Scandinavian, Photography, Portraits, Posters, Printmaking, Prints, Restoration & Conservation, Sculpture, Tapestries, Textiles, Video, Watercolors, Woodcarvings, Woodcuts, Painting-German
Activities: Docent training; concerts; gallery talks; tours; sponsoring of competitions; lectrs for mem only; mus shop sells books, magazines, original art, reproductions & prints

CASTLEMAINE

M **CASTLEMAINE ART GALLERY AND HISTORICAL MUSEUM,** 14 Lyttleton St, PO Box 248 Castlemaine, VIC 3450 Australia. Tel 03 5472 2292; Fax 03 5470 6184; Email info@castlemainegallery.com; Web: www.castlemainegallery.com; *Dir* Jennifer Kalionis; *Cur* Emma Busowsky Cox
Open Mon, Wed - Fri 10 AM - 5 PM, Sat & Sun noon - 5 PM; cl Tues, Good Fri & Christmas Day; Admis adults $10 AUD, concession/pension $8 AUD, mems & children under 18 free; Estab 1913
Collections: Collection of historical artworks, photographs, costumes, decorative arts & objects specifically relating to the Mount Alexander district

HAMILTON

M **HAMILTON ART GALLERY,** 107 Brown St, Hamilton, VIC 3300 Australia. Tel 03 5573-0460; Fax 03 5571-1017; Email info@hamiltongallery.org; Web: www.hamiltongallery.org; *Dir* Sarah Schmidt
Open Mon - Fri 10 AM - 5 PM, Sat 10 AM - noon & 2 - 5 PM, Sun 2 - 5 PM; No admis fee
Collections: Ceramics, Asian art, paintings, prints, furniture, metalwork, contemporary art

HOBART

M **TASMANIAN MUSEUM AND ART GALLERY,** Dunn Pl, Hobart, TAS 7000 Australia; GPO Box 1164, Hobart, TAS 7001 Australia. Tel (03) 6211 4112; Fax (03) 6165 7000; Email tmagmail@tmag.tas.gov.au; Web: www.tmag.tas.gov.au; *Dir* Janet Carding; *Deputy Dir Coll & Res* Steven de Haan; *Deputy Dir Audience Engagement* Andy Baird; *Deputy Dir Bus & Opers* Laurence Paine
Open Tues - Sun 10 AM - 4 PM; cl Good Friday, Anzac Day & Christmas Day; No admis fee; Estab 1840 by Royal Society of Tasmania; Gallery contains art, science, humanities
Library Holdings: Auction Catalogs, Book Volumes, Clipping Files, Exhibition Catalogs, Kodachrome Transparencies, Pamphlets, Periodical Subscriptions
Collections: Australian and Tasmanian art
Activities: Classes & holiday programs for children; lects open to pub; concerts; gallery talks; tours; lending of original art to galleries & museums; mus shop sells books, magazines, reproductions, prints

HORSHAM

M **HORSHAM REGIONAL ART GALLERY,** 78 Wilson St, Horsham, Victoria 3400 Australia. Tel 61 3 5362-2888; Fax 61 3 5382-5407; Email boxoffice@hrcc.vic.gov.au; Web: www.horshamartgallery.com.au; *Dir* Adam Harding; *Cur* Alison Eggleton
Open Tues - Fri 10 AM - 5 PM, Sat 11 AM - 4:30 PM, Sun 1 - 4:30 PM; cl Mon & public holidays; No admis fee, suggested donation; Estab 1973
Collections: Australian photography, painting & drawing

LAUNCESTON

M **QUEEN VICTORIA MUSEUM AND ART GALLERY,** Art Gallery at Royal Park, 2 Wellington St Launceston, TAS 7250 Australia; Museum at Inveresk, 2 Invermay Rd Launceston, TAS 7248 Australia. Tel (03) 6323-3777; Email enquiries@qvmag.tas.gov.au; Web: www.qvmag.tas.gov.au; *Dir* Mr Richard Mulvaney; *Colls Mgr* Martin George; *Exhibs Mgr* Andrew Johnson; *Visitor Opers Mgr* Janet Keeling
Open daily 10 AM - 4 PM, cl Good Friday & Christmas day; No admis fee; Estab 1891; Museum, art gallery & planetarium on two separate sites; Average Annual Attendance: 135,000
Library Holdings: Auction Catalogs, Audio Tapes, Book Volumes, CD-ROMs, Clipping Files, Compact Disks, DVDs, Exhibition Catalogs, Manuscripts, Maps, Memorabilia, Pamphlets, Periodical Subscriptions, Photographs, Records
Special Subjects: Ceramics, Costumes, Crafts, Decorative Arts, Drawings, Etchings & Engravings, Ethnology, Furniture, Glass, Laces, Metalwork, Painting-Australian, Photography, Porcelain, Portraits, Pottery, Prints, Scrimshaw, Sculpture, Silver, Textiles, Watercolors, Woodcuts
Collections: Pure & applied art, Tasmanian history: Tasmanian & general anthropology, Tasmanian botany, geology, paleontology & zoology
Activities: Classes for children & children; lects open to pub; lects for mems only; concerts; gallery talks; tours; schols; mus shops & art gallery sells books, reproductions, prints & giftware

LISMORE

M **LISMORE REGIONAL GALLERY,** 131 Molesworth St, Lismore, New South Wales 2480 Australia. Tel 61 2-6622-2209; Fax 61 2-6622-2228; Email artgallery@lismore.nsw.gov.au; Web: www.lismoregallery.org; *Dir* Brett Adington; *Cur* Kezia Geddes
Open Tues - Fri 10 AM - 4 PM, Sat 10 AM - 2 PM; cl Sun, Mon & pub holidays; No admis fee; Facilitate the exchange of ideas locally & nationally through a distinctive & innovative program of exhibitions & events

MELBOURNE

M **MONASH UNIVERSITY MUSEUM OF ART,** 900 Dandenong Rd, Ground Fl, Bldg F, Caulfield Campus Melbourne, VIC 3145 Australia. Tel 61 3-9905-4217; Email muma@monash.edu; Web: monash.edu.au/muma; *Dir* Charlotte Day; *Sr Cur* Hannah Mathews; *Cur Coll* Kirrily Hammond; *Cur Exhib* Francis Parker; *Cur Research* Helen Hughes
Open Tues - Fri 10 AM - 5 PM, Sat noon - 5 PM; No admis fee; Estab 1961; University art museum, found on contemporary art; Average Annual Attendance: 30,000
Collections: Monash Univ Coll
Publications: Please refer to www.monash.edu.au/muma/publications
Activities: Lects open to the pub; gallery talks; tours; lending of original objects of art to college mus & galleries; mus shop sells books & magazines

M **NATIONAL GALLERY OF VICTORIA,** 180 St Kilda Rd, PO Box 7259 Melbourne, Victoria VIC 3004 Australia. Tel 61 (0)3 8620 2222; Email enquiries@ngv.vic.gov.au; Web: www.ngv.vic.gov.au; *Dir* Tony Ellwood; *Deputy Dir* Andrew Clark; *Asst Dir Curatorial & Coll Management* Dr Isobel Crombie; *Asst Dir Exhibs Mgmt & Des* Don Heron
Open 10 AM - 5 PM, cl Christmas Day; No admis fee (fees may apply for some temporary exhibs); Estab 1861; Library with 20,000 vols
Collections: Asian art, Australian art, pre-Columbian art, modern European art, antiquities, costumes, textiles, old master and modern drawings, paintings, photography, prints and sculpture

MILDURA

M **MILDURA ARTS CENTRE,** 199 Cureton Ave, Mildura, VIC 3500 Australia; PO Box 105, Mildura, Victoria 3502 Australia. Tel (03) 5018 8330; Fax (03) 5021 1462; Email arts_centre@mildura.vic.gov.au; Web: www.milduraarts.net.au; *Arts & Culture Devel Mgr* Antonette Zema
Open daily 10 AM - 5 PM, Anzac Day 1 - 5 PM, cl Good Friday & Christmas Day; No admis fee; Estab 1956; 444 seat performing arts theatre, art gallery, Rio Vista Historic House, sculpture garden & licensed cafe

Collections: Estimated 1700 items of art, includes Australia's best Degas & Australia's most important collection of sculpture of the period 1960-1980

PERTH

M **ART GALLERY OF WESTERN AUSTRALIA,** Perth Cultural Centre, Perth, WA 6000 Australia; PO Box 8363, Perth Business Centre Perth, WA 6849 Australia. Tel 61 8 9492 6622; Email admin@artgallery.wa.gov.au; Web: www.artgallery.wa.gov.au; *Dir* Stefano Carboni, PhD
Open Wed - Mon 10 AM - 5 PM, cl Tues, Good Friday & Christmas Day, Anzac Day; No admis fee, donations accepted; Estab 1895
Collections: Australian Aboriginal Artifacts, British, European & Australian paintings, prints, drawings, sculptures & crafts
Activities: Docent training; lects open to pub; 500 vis lectrs per yr; gallery talks; tours; Western Australian Indigenous Art Award; mus shop sells books, magazines, reproductions, prints & giftware

SYDNEY

M **ART GALLERY OF NEW SOUTH WALES,** Art Gallery Rd, The Domain Sydney, NSW 2000 Australia. Tel 02-9225 1700; Fax 02-9225 1701; Email artmail@ag.nsw.gov.au; Web: www.artgallery.nsw.gov.au; *Dir* Dr Michael Brand; *Deputy Dir & Dir Colls* Maud Page
Open daily 10 AM - 5 PM, Wed 5 AM - 10 PM; No admis fee (fees may apply for special exhibits); Estab 1871, place of experience & inspiration through collections, exhibitions, programs & research; Average Annual Attendance: 1,200,000
Collections: Australian Aboriginal and Melanesian art, Australian art, collections of British and European painting and sculpture, Asian art, including Japanese ceramics and painting and Chinese ceramics, contemporary art; photography; prints & drawings
Activities: Classes for children; lects open to public; lects for members only; concerts; gallery talks; tours; films; scholarships offered; mus shop sells books, magazines, original art & reproductions

M **MUSEUM OF APPLIED ARTS & SCIENCES,** Powerhouse Museum, 500 Harris St, Ultimo, Sydney, NSW 2007 Australia. Tel 61 (02) 9217 0111; Email info@phm.gov.au; Web: maas.museum/powerhouse-museum; *Dir* Dolla Merrilles; *Dir Pub Engagement* Michael Parry; *Dir Devel & External Affairs* Leann Meiers
Open daily 10 AM - 5 PM, cl Christmas Day; Admis adults $15 AUD, NSW srs card holders pension & concessions & student card holders $8 AUD, children 16 & under free; additional fees apply for temporary exhibitions; Estab 1879; Library with 20,000 vols; Average Annual Attendance: 600,000; Mem: 30,000
Collections: Scientific Instruments, Numismatics, Philately, Astronomy, Technology, Design, Decorative Arts, History
Activities: Classes for adults & children; lects open to public & mems only; 5-10; books, magazines, reproductions, prints, gifts

M **MUSEUM OF CONTEMPORARY ART,** 140 George St, The Rocks Sydney, NSW 2000 Australia. Tel 612 9245-2400; Fax 612 9252-4361; Email reception@mca.com.au; Web: www.mca.com.au; *Dir* Liz Ann Macgregor; *Dir Finance & Corp Servs* Richard Drysdale; *Dir Develop & Enterprises* Heidi Forbes; *Dir Curatorial & Digital* Blair French; *Dir Audience Engagement* Gill Nicol; *Chief Financial Officer* Anh Thi Do; *Chief Cur* Rachel Kent; *Sr Cur* Natasha Bullock
Open daily 10 AM - 5 PM, Wed 10 AM - 9 PM, cl Christmas Day; No admis fee
Collections: Contemporary art archives, J W Power Collection, Loti & Victor Smorgon Collection of Contemporary Australian Art, Maningrida Collection of Aboriginal Art, Ramingining Collection of Aboriginal Art, Arnotts Biscuits Collection of Aboriginal bark painting
Activities: Educ progs for adults & children; tours

M **UNIVERSITY OF SYDNEY MUSEUMS,** University of Sydney, Sydney, NSW 2006 Australia. Tel 61 2 9351 7305; Fax 61 2 9351 8746; Email university.museums@sydney.edu.au; Web: sydney.edu.au/museums/; *Dir* David Ellis; *Assoc Dir, Mus Content* Paul Donnelly; *Sr Cur, Macleay Museum* Jude Philip; *Sr Cur, Nicholson Museum* Michael Turner; *Sr Cur, University Art Gallery* Ann Stephen
Open Mon - Fri 10 AM - 4:30 PM, first Sat of month noon - 4 PM, cl other Sats, Sun & pub holidays; No admis fee; Estab 1860; Two campus art museums, Nicholson Museum & Macleay Museum and University Art Gallery; Average Annual Attendance: 45,000; Mem: 500; ann dues $50 AUD
Income: Financed through university grant
Collections: Antiquities of Egypt, Near East, Europe, Greece, Italy, Australian & Aboriginal art, historic photographs, natural history collections and scientific instruments
Activities: Classes for adults & children; school educ prog; lects for members only, 6 vis lectrs per yr, gallery talks, tours; sales shop sells books, reproductions, greeting cards, mugs, cards, bookmats, mousemats, key rings

AUSTRIA

BREGENZ

M **KUNSTHAUS BREGENZ,** Bregenz Art House, Karl Tizian Platz, Postbox 45 Bregenz, 6900 Austria. Tel 43-5574-485 94-0; Fax 43-5574-485 94-408; Email kub@kunsthaus-bregenz.at; Web: www.kunsthaus-bregenz.at; *Dir* Thomas D Trummer; *Chief Exec* Werner Doring; *Cur* Dr Rudolf Sagmeister
Open Tues, Wed, Fri - Sun 10 AM - 6 PM, Thurs 10 AM - 9 PM, cl Mon; Admis adults 9 EUR, reductions 7 EUR, children & youths free
Collections: Collection of contemporary Austrian art, Paintings, sculpture, object and conceptual art, video art, mixed-media and photography, International works in art and architecture
Activities: Classes for adults & children; lects open to the pub; mus shop sells books

M **VORARLBERG MUSEUM,** Kornmarktplatz 1, Bregenz, 6900 Austria. Tel 43 0 5574 460 50; Email info@vorarlbergmuseum.at; Web: www.vorarlbergmuseum.at; *Dir* Dr Andreas Rudigier
Open Tues, Wed, Fri - Sun 10 AM - 6 PM, Thurs 10 AM - 8 PM, cl Mon; Admis 9 EUR, reduced 7 EUR
Library Holdings: Auction Catalogs, Book Volumes, DVDs, Exhibition Catalogs, Maps, Original Documents
Special Subjects: Antiquities-Roman, Archaeology, Crafts, Decorative Arts, Drawings, Graphics, Painting-European, Portraits, Religious Art, Textiles
Collections: Visual art, history & archaeological artifacts
Activities: Classes for adults & children; lects open to pub; lects for mems only; tours; lending of original objects of art to other mus

EISENSTADT

M **LANDESMUSEUM BURGENLAND,** Burgenland Provincial Museum, Museumgasse 1-5, Eisenstadt, Burgenland 7000 Austria. Tel 43 2682 719 4000; Fax 43 2682 719 4051; Email office@landesmuseum-burgenland.at; Web: landesmuseum-burgenland.at; *Dir* Gert Polster
Open Jan 7 - May 31 Tues - Sat 9 AM - 5 PM; June 1 - Nov 11 Mon - Sat 9 AM - 5 PM; Nov 12 - Dec 23 Mon - Fri 9 AM - 5 PM; holidays, 10 AM - 5 PM; Admis 5.50 EUR, reduced 4.50 EUR, students 2 EUR, family 12 EUR
Collections: art, folklore & historic artifacts

GRAZ

M **KUNSTHAUS GRAZ,** Graz Art House, Lendkai 1, Graz, 8020 Austria. Tel 43-316/8017-9200; Fax 43-316/8017-9212; Email kunsthausgraz@museum-joanneum.at; Web: www.museum-joanneum.at/kunsthaus-graz; *Chief Cur* Katrin Rosalind Bucher Trantow; *Cur* Katia Huemer; *Artistic Dir* Gabriele Hofbauer
Open Tues - Sun 10 AM - 5 PM, cl Christmas Eve & Day; Admis adults 9 EUR, groups of 7 or more, seniors, people with disabilities 7 EUR, students up to 27 yrs 3 EUR, students in school groups 2 EUR, families 18 EUR, children 6 and under free; Estab 2003; international contemporary art; Average Annual Attendance: 80,000
Collections: Multi-disciplinary contemporary art

M **UNIVERSALMUSEUM JOANNEUM,** Joanneum Universal Museum, Mariahilferstrasse 2-4, Graz, 8020 Austria. Tel 43-316/8017-0; Fax 43-316/8017-9699; Email welcome@museum-joanneum.at; Web: www.museum-joanneum.at; *Dir* Dr Wolfgang Muchitsch
See website for hours & admission fees; Estab 1811; Operating company of nine museum departments in Austria; Average Annual Attendance: 500,000
Library Holdings: Audio Tapes, Book Volumes, CD-ROMs, Cards, Compact Disks, DVDs, Exhibition Catalogs, Framed Reproductions
Special Subjects: Archaeology, Baroque Art, Coins & Medals, Drawings, Ethnology, Folk Art, Glass, Graphics, Historical Material, Metalwork, Military Art, Painting-European, Painting-German, Period Rooms, Photography, Portraits, Religious Art, Renaissance Art, Sculpture, Textiles
Activities: Educ prog; classes for adults & children; lects open to pub; gallery talks; tours; sponsoring of competitions; The Council of Europe Museum Prize, 1983; fels available; sales shop sells books, magazines & souvenirs

INNSBRUCK

M **TIROLER LANDESMUSEUM FERDINANDEUM,** Tyrolean State Museum Ferdinandeum, Museumstrasse 15, Innsbruck, 6020 Austria. Tel 43 512 594 89 111; Fax 43 512 594 89 109; Email info@tiroler-landesmuseum.at; Web: www.tiroler-landesmuseum.at; *Dir* Dr Wolfgang Meighorner
Open Tues - Sun 9 AM - 5 PM; Admis combi-ticket for admis to five mus buildings: 11 EUR, reduced 8 EUR, children & teenagers up to 19 free
Collections: Pre-historic, Roman, Early Middle-Ages and modern era art, Romanesque & Gothic masterpieces, Dutch art collection, musical instruments, modern art gallery

KLAGENFURT

M **MUSEUM MODERNER KUNST KARNTEN,** Carinthian Museum of Modern Art, Burggasse 8, Klagenfurt, 9020 Austria. Tel 43 (0)50 536 16252; Email office.museum@ktn.gv.at; Web: www.mmkk.at; *Dir* Christine Wetzlinger-Grundnig
Open Tues, Wed, Fri - Sun 10 AM - 6 PM, Thurs 10 AM - 8 PM; Admis adults 5 EUR, concessions 2.50 EUR, children & teenagers free
Collections: Art and cultural artifacts of the Province of Carinthia

KLOSTERNEUBURG

M **ESSL MUSEUM,** An der Donau-Au 1, Klosterneuburg, 3400 Austria. Tel 43 (0) 2243-370 50 150; Email info@essl.museum; Web: www.essl.museum; *Exec Dir* Prof Karlheinz Essl
Coll available for loan only, exhibition activities have ceased.

LINZ

M **LENTOS KUNSTMUSEUM LINZ,** Lentos Art Museum, Ernst-Koref-Promenade 1, Linz, 4020 Austria. Tel 43-732-7070-3600, 43-732-7070-3614; Fax 43-732-7070-3604; Email info@lentos.at; Web: www.lentos.at; *Dir* Stella Rollig

Open Tues, Wed, Fri - Sun 10 AM - 6 PM, Thurs 10 AM - 9 PM, cl Mon; Admis adults 8 EUR, concessions 4.50 - 6 EUR, school groups & children under 7 free; Estab 2003 as successor to the New Gallery of the City of Linz
Collections: Wolfgang Gurlitt Collection

M **NORDICO STADTMUSEUM LINZ,** Nordico City Museum, Damentzstrasse 23, Linz, 4020 Austria. Tel 43 732-7070-1912, 1901; Email nordico@nordico.at; Web: www.nordico.at; *Mus Mgr* Andrea Bina
Open Tues, Wed, Fri - Sun 10 AM - 6 PM, Thurs 10 AM - 9 PM, cl Mon; Admis adults 6.50 EUR, reduced 2.50 - 4.50 EUR, student groups & children 7 & under free
Collections: Historical and archaeological collection of the City of Linz

MIESENBACH

M **GAUERMANN MUSEUM,** Scheuchenstein 127, Miesenbach, 2761 Austria. Tel 43 676 59621 48; Email museum.gauermann@gmail.com; Web: www.miesenbach.at/gauermannmuseum; *Cur* Bernhard Kratzig
Admis adults 5 EUR, seniors 3.50 EUR, children 2 EUR; Open Sat, Sun & holidays 10 AM - 5 PM or by appointment, cl Dec; Estab 1976

SALZBURG

M **MUSEUM DER MODERNE SALZBURG,** Salzburg Museum of Modern Art Monchsberg, Monchsberg 32, Salzburg, 5020 Austria. Tel 43 662 842220-403; Fax 43 662 842220-700; Email info@mdmsalzburg.at; Web: www.museumdermoderne.at; *Dir* Dr Sabine Breitwieser; *Cur & Head of Coll* Beatrice von Bormann; *Head of Educ* Martina Pohn
Open Tues, Thurs - Sun 10 AM - 6 PM, Wed 10 AM - 8 PM cl Mon; Admis regular 8 EUR, reduced 6 EUR
Collections: 20th century paintings, sculpture, graphics and photography, art in between the war periods, contemporary Austrian and international art

M **Salzburg Museum of Modern Art Rupertinum**, Wiener-Philharmoniker-Gasse 9, Salzburg, 5020 Austria. Tel 43 662 842220-451
Closed for renovations.

M **RESIDENZGALERIE SALZBURG,** Salzburg Residence Gallery, Franziskanergasse 5a, Salzburg, 5010 Austria. Tel 0043 662 8042-2109; Email office@domquartier.at; Web: residenzgalerie.at; *Dir* Dr Gabriele Groschner; *Cur* Dr Erika Mayr-Oehring; *Cur* Dr Thomas Habersatter
Open Mon, Wed - Sun 10 AM - 5 PM, cl Tues; Admis full access 12 EUR, reduced 10 EUR; partial access 10 EUR, reduced 8 EUR; European paintings of the 16th - 19th centuries; Average Annual Attendance: 60,000
Income: Income from public collection of the govt of Salzburg
Collections: European paintings, 16th - 19th centuries
Publications: Exhibition catalogues
Activities: Classes for adults & children; lects open to pub; 200 vis lectrs per yr; concerts; gallery talks; tours; literature, cinema, modern art lent to mus, official collections; mus shops sells books, magazines, reproductions, postcards, souvenirs

M **SALZBURG MUSEUM,** Mozartplatz 1, Salzburg, 5010 Austria. Tel 43 662 620808-0; Fax 43 662 620808-720; Email office@salzburgmuseum.at; Web: www.salzburgmuseum.at; *Cur* Peter Husty
Open Tues - Sun 9 AM - 5 PM, Jan 1 1 - 5 PM, Dec 24 & 31 9 AM - 2 PM, cl Nov 1; Admis adults 7 EUR, reduced 6 EUR, young people 16-26 4 EUR, children 6-15 3 EUR; Estab 1834; Library with 100,000 vols including 7 mus; Mem: 5,000
Collections: Art, coins, musical instruments, costumes, peasant art, Prehistoric & Roman archaeology, Toy, fortress, folk and excavation museums
Exhibitions: 18 different exhibs per yr
Activities: Classes for adults & children; lects open to pub; 2,500 vis lectrs per yr; concerts; gallery talks; tours; sponsoring of competitions; Mus of the Year Award 2009; lending of original art to mus around the world; originate traveling exhibs; mus shop sells books; reproductions; prints; jr mus Kinderwell (children's world)

TULLN

M **EGON SCHIELE MUSEUM,** Donaulande 28, Tulln, 3430 Austria. Tel 43 2272 64 570; Email info@egon-schiele.eu; Web: www.egon-schiele.eu; *Gen Mgr* Brigitte Schlogl; *Gen Mgr* Peter Weiss; *Cur* Christian Bauer; *Art Dir* Carl Aigner
Open Tues - Sun & holidays 10 AM - 5 PM, cl Mon; Admis adult 5.50 EUR, reduced 4.50 EUR, children 3.50 EUR
Collections: Oil paintings

VIENNA

M **ALBERTINA MUSEUM,** Albertinaplatz 1, Vienna, 1010 Austria. Tel 43 1 534 83-0; Fax 43 1 534 83-430; Email info@albertina.at; Web: www.albertina.at; *Dir* Prof Dr Klaus Albrecht Schroder; *Deputy Dir* Dr Christian Benedik
Open daily 10 AM - 6 PM, Wed 10 AM - 9 PM; Admis adults 12.90 EUR, seniors 65 & over 9.90 EUR, students with ID up to 26 yrs 8.50 EUR, children under 19 free; Estab 1796; Average Annual Attendance: 600,000
Library Holdings: Auction Catalogs, Book Volumes, Exhibition Catalogs, Periodical Subscriptions
Special Subjects: Drawings, Miniatures, Posters, Prints, Watercolors
Collections: Drawings 44,000, sketchbooks, miniatures & posters, The Batlinger Collection, Masterwork of Modern Art from the Albertina
Exhibitions: 5-6 exhibs per year
Activities: Classes for adults & children; lects open to pub; mus shop sells books, magazines, reproductions, prints

M **GEMALDEGALERIE DER AKADEMIE DER BILDENDEN KUNSTE WIEN,** Picture Gallery of the Academy of Fine Arts Vienna, Schillerplatz 3, Vienna, 1010 Austria. Tel 43 01 58816 2222; Fax 43 01 58633 46; Email gemgal@akbild.ac.at; Web: www.akademiegalerie.at; *Dir* Dr Julia Nauhaus; *Cur* Claudia Koch
Open Tues - Sun & holidays 10 AM - 6 PM, cl Mon; Admis regular 8 EUR, reduced 5 EUR, children and adolescents under 19 free; Estab 1692; old masters 15 - 19th century
Income: Financed by government
Special Subjects: Painting-Dutch, Painting-European, Painting-Flemish, Painting-French, Painting-German, Painting-Italian, Painting-Spanish
Collections: European Paintings of the 14th - 20th centuries - Hieronymus Bosch, Hans Baldung Grien, 17th century Dutch (Rembrandt, Ruisdael, van Goyen, Jan Both & others), Flemish, (Rubens, Jordaens, van Dyck), Guardi, Magnasco, Tiepolo, bequests by Count Lamberg, Prince Liechtenstein, Wolfgang von Wurzbach, Glyptotheque (Coll 19th-century sculpture)
Activities: Lects open to public; gallery talks; books, slides, postcards

M **KUNST HAUS WIEN MUSEUM HUNDERTWASSER,** Vienna Art House, Hundertwasser Museum, Untere Weissgerberstrasse 13, Vienna, 1030 Austria. Tel +43-1-712-04-95; Fax +43-1-712-04-96; Email info@kunsthauswien.com; Web: www.kunsthauswien.com; *Dir* Bettina Leidl; *Exhib Mgr* Sophie Haslinger; *Cur* Verena Kaspar-Eisert
Open daily 10 AM - 6 PM; Admis 12 EUR; Estab 1991; Average Annual Attendance: 160,000
Collections: Paintings, graphic works, applied art & architectural designs by Austrian artist Friedensreich Hundertwasser
Activities: Mus shop sells books, reproductions & prints

M **KUNSTHISTORISCHES MUSEUM WIEN,** Museum of Fine Arts, Maria-Theresien-Platz, Vienna, 1010 Austria. Tel 43 1 525 24 0; Email info@khm.at; Web: www.khm.at; *Gen Dir* Dr Sabine Haag; *Comm Dir* Dr Paul Frey
Open (Sept-May) Tue-Wed & Fri-Sun 10-6, Thu 10-9; (June-Aug) Mon-Wed & Fri-Sun 10-6, Thu 10-9; Admis ann ticket 44 EUR, ann ticket U25 25 EUR, adults 15 EUR, concessions 11 EUR, children & teens under 19 no admis fee; Average Annual Attendance: 1,300,000
Special Subjects: Antiquities-Assyrian, Antiquities-Byzantine, Antiquities-Egyptian, Antiquities-Etruscan, Antiquities-Greek, Antiquities-Oriental, Antiquities-Persian, Antiquities-Roman, Baroque Art, Bronzes, Coins & Medals, Costumes, Decorative Arts, Embroidery, Enamels, Glass, Gold, Ivory, Jewelry, Manuscripts, Medieval Art, Painting-Dutch, Painting-European, Painting-Flemish, Painting-French, Painting-German, Painting-Italian, Painting-Spanish, Portraits, Pottery, Religious Art, Renaissance Art, Sculpture, Silver, Tapestries, Textiles, Woodcuts
Collections: Egyptian coll, antiquities, ceramics, historical carriages & costumes, jewelry, old musical instruments, paintings, tapestries, weapons, coll of secular & ecclesiastical treasures of Holy Roman Empire & Hapsburg Dynasty
Activities: Classes for adults & children; lects open to pub; concerts; gallery talks; mus shop sells books, reproductions, prints & jewelry

M **MUMOK - MUSEUM MODERNER KUNST STIFTUNG LUDWIG WIEN,** Ludwig Foundation Museum of Modern Art, Museumsplatz 1, Vienna, 1070 Austria. Tel 43-1-525 00-0; Fax 43-1-525 00-1300; Email info@mumok.at; Web: www.mumok.at; *Dir* Karola Kraus; *Mng Dir* Cornelia Lamprechter; *Head of Coll* Susanne Neuburger
Open Mon 2 PM - 7 PM, Tues, Wed, Fri - Sun 10 AM -7 PM, Thurs 10 AM - 9 PM; Admis 11 EUR, reduced 7.50 - 8 EUR; Estab 1962; Museum modern & contemporary art
Library Holdings: Book Volumes, Exhibition Catalogs, Filmstrips, Pamphlets
Collections: Works of the 20th century; artists represented include: Archipenko, Arp, Bartach, Beckman, Boeckl, Bonnard, Delaunay, Ernst, Gleizes, Hofer, Hoflehner, Jawlensky, Kandinsky, Kirchner, Klee, Kokoschka, Laurens, Leger, Marc, Matisse, Miro, Moore, Munch, Nolde, Picasso, Rodin, Rosso, Wotruba & others, Classical Modernism, Nouveau Realisme, Fluxus Pop Art; concept art; sand art; Vienna Actionism
Publications: Catalogues
Activities: Classes for adults & children; lects open to pub; lects for mems only; gallery talks; tours; school progs; schls & fels offered; organize traveling exhibs; mus shop sells books, magazines, catalogues, design, editions, posters

M **OSTERREICHISCHE GALERIE BELVEDERE VIENNA,** Belvedere Museum Vienna, Prinz Eugen-Strasse 27, Vienna, 1030 Austria. Tel 43 1 795 57 134; Fax 43 1 795 57 136; Email public@belvedere.at; Email info@belvedere.at; Web: www.belvedere.at; *Artistic Dir & CEO* Stella Rolligdirektion@belvedere.at; *CFO* Wolfgang Bergmanndirektion@belvedere.at
Open Upper & Lower Belvedere Mon - Thurs & Sat - Sun 9 AM - 6 PM, Fri 9 AM - 9 PM; Belvedere 21: Wed & Fri 11 AM - 9 PM, Thurs - Sun 11 AM - 6 PM; Admis (Klimt-Ticket, valid 30 days after purchase for all collections) adults 22 EUR, seniors 65 & over & students 26 & under 19 EUR, children & teenagers no admis fee; Mus incls Upper & Lower Belvedere, Belvedere 21 - Museum of Contemporary Art; Average Annual Attendance: 1,100,000
Library Holdings: Auction Catalogs, Audio Tapes, Book Volumes, CD-ROMs, Cards, Compact Disks, DVDs, Exhibition Catalogs, Kodachrome Transparencies, Lantern Slides, Manuscripts, Memorabilia, Original Art Works, Original Documents, Other Holdings, Pamphlets, Periodical Subscriptions, Photographs, Prints, Records, Reproductions, Slides, Video Tapes
Special Subjects: Baroque Art, Bronzes, Landscapes, Medieval Art, Painting-French, Period Rooms, Portraits, Religious Art, Restorations, Sculpture, Watercolors
Collections: Upper Belvedere includes permanent collections of Austrian art from the Middle Ages to the present, an International art collection by artists such as Claude Monet, Vincent Van Gogh & Max Beckman, French Impressionism & a collection of Viennese Biedermeier
Exhibitions: Lower Belvedere stages temporary exhibits with artwork from around the world; The 21er Haus stages contemporary, Austrian art exhibits
Publications: Exhibition Catalogues, Catalogues Raisonnes, Collection Guides
Activities: Classes for adults & children; docent training; lects open to pub; 2-3 vis lectrs per yr; concerts; gallery talks, tours; fellowships; BC21 Art Award; extension

progs directed to schools & sr citizens; artmobile; mus shop sells books, reproductions & prints

AZERBAIJAN

BAKU

M **BAKU MUSEUM OF MODERN ART,** 5 Yusuph Safarov St, Baku, 1025 Azerbaijan. Tel 99-412 490 84 04; Fax 99-412 490 84 03; Email office@mim.az; Web: www.mim.az; *Exec Dir* Khayyam Abdinov
Open Tues - Sun 11 AM - 9 PM, cl Mon; Admis regular 5 AZN, students 2 AZN, children & preschoolers free; Estab 2009
Collections: Contemporary paintings and sculpture from the second half of the 20th century to the present

BAHAMAS

NASSAU

M **NATIONAL ART GALLERY OF THE BAHAMAS,** Villa Doyle, West and West Hill Sts Nassau, Bahamas. Tel 242-328-5800; Fax 242-322-1180; Email info@nagb.org.bs; Web: nagb.org.bs; *Dir* Amanda Coulson
Open Tues - Sat 10 AM - 5 PM, Sun noon - 5 PM, cl Mon & public holidays; Admis non-res $10, res $7, seniors & students $5, children under 12 free
Collections: Contemporary Bahamian and international art in various media

BANGLADESH

DHAKA

M **BANGLADESH NATIONAL MUSEUM,** Shahbag Rd, Dhaka, 1000 Bangladesh. Tel 88 02 586 14842; Fax 88 02 966 7381; Email dgmuseum@yahoo.com; Web: bangladeshmuseum.gov.bd; *Dir Gen* Faizul Latif Chowdhury
Open Apr - Sept, Sat - Wed 10:30 AM - 5:30 PM, Fri 3 - 8 PM; Oct - Mar, Sat - Wed 9:30 AM - 4:30 PM, Fri 2:30 - 7:30 PM; Admis res 20 BDT, non-res 100 BDT, children under 3 free; Estab 1913 to collect, preserve & display antiquities
Library Holdings: Book Volumes, Cards, DVDs, Exhibition Catalogs, Memorabilia, Photographs, Sculpture
Special Subjects: African Art, American Indian Art, American Western Art, Anthropology, Antiquities-Egyptian, Antiquities-Greek, Antiquities-Oriental, Antiquities-Persian, Antiquities-Roman, Archaeology, Archaeology, Architecture, Art Education, Art History, Asian Art, Bronzes, Calligraphy, Carpets & Rugs, Cartoons, Ceramics, Coins & Medals, Collages, Costumes, Crafts, Decorative Arts, Dioramas, Dolls, Drawings, Embroidery, Enamels, Ethnology, Folk Art, Furniture, Glass, Gold, Graphics, Historical Material, Interior Design, Islamic Art, Ivory, Jade, Jewelry, Leather, Manuscripts, Maps, Metalwork, Miniatures, Mosaics, Oriental Art, Painting-American, Painting-British, Painting-Canadian, Painting-Dutch, Painting-European, Painting-Flemish, Painting-French, Painting-German, Painting-Italian, Painting-Japanese, Painting-Russian, Painting-Scandinavian, Painting-Spanish, Photography, Portraits, Posters, Pottery, Pre-Columbian Art, Primitive art, Prints, Religious Art, Renaissance Art, Reproductions, Restorations, Scrimshaw, Sculpture, Silver, Southwestern Art, Tapestries, Textiles, Watercolors, Woodcarvings, Woodcuts
Collections: 44 galleries, Buddhist & Brahminical stone sculptures, architectural pieces, Arabic and Persian inscriptions, calligraphy, coin cabinet, Sanskrit & Bengali manuscripts, plaques, figures, stamped and inscribed slabs, votive seals, moulded and decorated brick, Paintings, arms & armament, porcelain, metal work, embroidered quilts, ivory works, Furniture, tribal and folk arts and crafts, Objects related to Liberation War
Exhibitions: Nakshi Kantha, Ornament, Rare Book Coin Exhib Etc
Publications: Research Oriented Books, magazines, catalogues, booklets, view-card and many more
Activities: Classes for adults & children; publish & sale of publ; guide to school students & general pub (visitor); concerts; gallery talks; sponsoring of competitions; awards, occasional prog to minimum of 128 students; mus shop sells books, magazines, reproductions, prints, slides, pens, t-shirts, paper weights, research oriented publs & other items; junior mus include: Ahsasn Manzil Mus, Dhake; Osmany Mus, Sylhet; Zia Memorial Mus, Chittagong; Shilpacharya Zaninul, Abedin; Sangrahashala, Mymensingh; Palli Kavi JasImuddin, Sangrahashala

M **BENGAL GALLERY OF FINE ARTS,** House 42, Road 16 (New), Sheikh Kamal Saranl Dhanmondi Dhaka, 1209 Bangladesh. Tel 880 1746 297554; Email gallery@bengalfoundation.org; Web: www.bengalfoundation.org/gallery; *Dir-Gen* Luva Nahid Choudhury
Open 12 PM - 8 PM; Estab 2000; first modern art gallery in Bangladesh; Display area 76M, spread over 188 Sq M; Average Annual Attendance: 20,000; Mem: Private limited company
Income: Sponsored by Bengal Foundation Trust
Publications: Over 250 catalogues, brochures & flyers
Activities: Host art exhibs; lects open to pub; book launches; 10 vis lectrs per yr; gallery talks; mus shop sells books, magazines, original art, reproductions, prints, CDs & DVDs

BELARUS

MINSK

M **NATIONAL ART MUSEUM OF THE REPUBLIC OF BELARUS,** 20 Lenin St, Minsk, 220030 Belarus. Tel 375-17-227-71-63; Fax 375-17-328-68-44; Email nmmrb@bk.ru; Web: www.artmuseum.by; *Dir Gen* Vladimir Prokoptsov; *Dep Dir Gen, Scientific Work* Natalya Selitskaya; *Dep Dir Gen, Gen Affairs* Igor Shostak
Open Mon & Wed - Sun 11 AM - 7 PM, cl Tues; Admis adults 50,000 BYR, pupils & students 25,000 BYR, children under 7 free; Estab 1939
Collections: More than 25,600 exhibits, modern Belarusian art, painting, sculpture, drawing, applied art, national Belarusian art, 17th-20th century, ancient Belarusian art, paintings, icons, ceramics, porcelain, arts and crafts, manuscripts and books, 16th-19th century, West European art, 16th-20th century; Russian art, 18-20th century, Eastern Art, 15th - 20th century

BELGIUM

ANTWERP

M **KONINKLIJK MUSEUM VOOR SCHONE KUNSTEN ANTWERPEN,** Royal Museum of Fine Arts Antwerp, Lange Kievitstraat 111-113, Box 100 Antwerp, 2018 Belgium. Tel 32 (03) 224 95 50; Email info@kmska.be; Web: www.kmska.be; *Gen Dir & Head Cur* Manfred Sellink; *Head Coll Dept* Elsje Janssen
Closed for renovations until 2018; Estab 1890; Library with 35,000 vols
Library Holdings: Auction Catalogs, Book Volumes, CD-ROMs, Exhibition Catalogs, Fiche, Periodical Subscriptions
Special Subjects: Drawings, Painting-European, Sculpture
Collections: Five Centuries of Flemish Painting: Flemish Primitives, early foreign schools, 16th-17th century Antwerp School, 17th century Dutch School, 19th and 20th century Belgian artists, works of De Braekeleer, Ensor, Leys, Permeke, Smits and Wouters
Publications: Yearbook
Activities: Classes for adults & children; dramatic progs; docent training; lects open to pub; concerts; gallery talks; tours; lending of original objects of art; mus shop sells books, magazines & reproductions

M **MUSEUM AAN DE STROOM,** Hanzestedenplaats 1, Antwerp, 2000 Belgium. Tel 323 338 4400; Email mas@stad.antwerpen.be; Web: www.mas.be; *Dir* Marieke van Bommel; *Coordr, Coll Acquisition* Cathy Pelgrims
Open April - Oct Tues - Fri 10 AM - 5 PM, Sat & Sun 10 AM - 6 PM; Nov - March Tues - Sun 10 AM - 5 PM, cl Mon; Admis adults 10 EUR, students 12 - 25 & seniors 65 & up 8 EUR, children under 12 free; Estab 2011; Average Annual Attendance: 650,000
Collections: Cultural art of the port city of Antwerp

M **MUSEUM MAYER VAN DEN BERGH,** Lange Gasthuisstraat 19, Antwerp, 2000 Belgium. Tel 32 3 338 81 88; Fax 32 3 338 81 99; Email museum.mayervandenbergh@stad.antwerpen.be; Web: www.museummayervandenbergh.be; *Cur* Claire Baisier; *Coll Mgr* Rita Van Dooren; *Exhib Coordr* Tonia Dhaese
Admis adults 8 EUR, students 12 - 25 & seniors 65 & up 6 EUR, children under 12 free; Open Tues - Sun 10 AM - 5 PM, cl Mon
Collections: Masterpieces from the Middle Ages and the Renaissance as well as 19th century works, Paintings by artists including Breughel, Metsys, Aertsen, Mostaert, Bronzino, Heda & de Vos, medieval sculptures, tapestries, drawings and stained glass windows

M **MUSEUM PLANTIN-MORETUS,** Vrijdagmarkt 22, Antwerp, 2000 Belgium. Tel 32 3 221 14 50; Fax 32 3 221 14 71; Email museum.plantin.moretus@stad.antwerpen.be; Web: www.museumplantinmoretus.be; *Mgr* Iris Kockelbergh; *Cur Print Cabinet* Marijke Hellemans; *Cur Books & Archives* Dirk Imhof; *Cur Historical House* Werner Van Hoof
Open Tues - Sun 10 AM - 5 PM, cl Mon; Admis adults 8 EUR, students 12 - 25 yrs & seniors 65 & over 6 EUR, under 12 yrs free; House built 16th c, Mus estab 1877; Library of 30,000 books of 15th - 18th centuries; print cabinet 80,000 drawing & print from 1500 to 21st century; Average Annual Attendance: 80,000
Library Holdings: Auction Catalogs, Book Volumes, Exhibition Catalogs, Manuscripts, Original Documents, Periodical Subscriptions
Special Subjects: Baroque Art, Bookplates & Bindings, Calligraphy, Carpets & Rugs, Ceramics, Drawings, Etchings & Engravings, Furniture, Historical Material, Leather, Manuscripts, Maps, Painting-Flemish, Period Rooms, Porcelain, Portraits, Prints, Religious Art, Renaissance Art, Reproductions, Restorations, Sculpture, Tapestries, Watercolors, Woodcarvings, Woodcuts, Decorative Arts
Collections: Designs, copper and wood engravings, printing presses, typography, Coll of Antwerp Iconographics; modern drawings: Jensor, F Jespers, H leys, W Vaes, Rik Wovters; modern engravings: Cantre, Ensor, Masereel, J Minne, W Vaes; old drawings: Jordaens, E and A Quellin, Rubens, Schut, Van Dyck; old engravings: Galle, Goltzius, Hogenbergh, W Hollar, Yegher, Wiericx, etc, typographical coll
Activities: Classes for children; lects open to pub; gallery talks; tours; lending coll incl printing & books, & serves museums & exhibitions; mus shop sells books, original art, prints, reproductions, gifts, objects about colls

M **MUSEUM ROCKOXHUIS,** Rockox House Museum, Keizerstraat 10-12, Antwerp, 2000 Belgium. Tel 32 03 201 92 50; Fax 32 03 201 92 51; Email inforockoxhuis@kbc.be; Web: www.rockoxhuis.be
Open Tues - Sun 10 AM - 5 PM, cl Mon; Admis adult 8 EUR, seniors 6 EUR, students 19 - 25 1 EUR, visitors under 18 & under free; Estab 1949

M **MUSEUM VAN HEDENDAAGSE KUNST ANTWERPEN,** Museum of Contemporary Art Antwerp, Leuvenstraat 32, Antwerp, 2000 Belgium. Tel 32 03

260 9999; Fax 32 03 216 2486; Email info@muhka.be; Web: www.muhka.be; *Dir* Bart De Baere
Open Tues, Wed, Fri - Sun 11 AM - 6 PM, Thurs 11 AM - 9 PM, cl Mon; Admis adults 10 EUR, seniors 65 & up 5 EUR, students 1 EUR, children under 13 free; Estab 1987
Collections: International contemporary art

M **RUBENSHUIS,** Rubens House, Wapper 9-11, Antwerp, 2000 Belgium. Tel 32 3-201-15-55; Fax 32 3-227-36-92; Email rubenshuis@stad.antwerpen.be; Web: www.rubenshuis.be; *Dir* Ben van Beneden; *Conservator* Martine Maris; *Coll, Preservation & Bldg Mgr* Georges Delcart
Open Tues - Sun 10 AM - 5 PM, cl Mon; Admis adults 8 EUR, students 12 - 25 & seniors 65 & up 6 EUR, children under 12 free
Collections: Works by Baroque painter Peter Paul Rubens, sculptures and masterpieces by various artists

BRUGES

M **MUSEA BRUGGE,** Bruges Museum, Dijver 12, Bruges, 8000 Belgium. Tel 32 50 44 87 11; Fax 32 50 44 87 78; Email musea@brugge.be; Web: www.museabrugge.be
Museum consists of 14 institutions throughout the Flemish city of Bruges.

M **Gruuthusemuseum - Gruuthuse Museum**, Dijver 17, Brugge, 8000 Belgium. Tel 32-50-44-87-11; Fax 32-50-44-87-78; Email musea@brugge.be; Web: www.museabrugge.be
Closed for renovations until 2018; Admis adults 8 EUR, reduced 6 EUR, children under 12 free; City palace
Special Subjects: Pottery, Silver, Tapestries
Collections: Room of Honor: tapestries, fireplace, decorated timber
Exhibitions: History of Bruges & its inhabitants; Room of Honor
Activities: Mus shop sells books, prints

M **Volkskundemuseum - Museum of Folk Life**, Balstraat 43, Bruges, 8000 Belgium. Tel 32-50-44-87-43; Fax 32-50-44-87-78; Email musea@brugge.be; Web: www.museabrugge.be
Open Tues - Sun 9:30 AM - 5 PM, cl Mon; Admis adults 4 EUR, reduced 3 EUR, children under 12 free; 8 almshouses from 17th c with modern architectural extension, incl classroom, cobbler's workshop, hatter's workshop, Flemish living room, confectioner's bakery, pharmacy, inn, tailor's workshop, bedroom
Special Subjects: Folk Art, Period Rooms, Laces
Collections: Old objects in different decors

M **Sint-Janshospitaal - St. John's Hospital**, Mariastraat 38, Bruges, 8000 Belgium. Tel 32-50-44-87-43; Fax 32-50-44-87-78; Email musea@brugge.be; Web: www.museabrugge.be
Open Tues - Sun 9:30 AM - 5 PM, cl Mon; Admis adults 8 EUR, reduced 6 EUR, children under 12 free; Preserved hospital building, chapel, attic displaying monumental roof-truss system, apothecary chamber & herb garden, masterpieces by Hans Memling
Special Subjects: Furniture, Painting-European, Pewter, Sculpture, Silver
Collections: Works by Hans Memling
Activities: Mus shop sells books, prints & other items

M **Onze-Lieve-Vrouw-Ter-Potterie - Our Lady of the Potterie**, Potterierei 79 B, Bruges, 8000 Belgium. Tel 32-50-44-87-43; Fax 32-50-44-87-78; Email musea@brugge.be; Web: www.museabrugge.be
Open Tues - Sun 9:30 AM - 12:30 PM & 1:30 - 5 PM, cl Mon; Admis adults 4 EUR, reduced 3 EUR, children under 12 free; Baroque church & historic hospital served by monks & nuns in the 13th century
Collections: Works of art, incl objects related to healthcare, worship & the monastery

M **Arentshuis - Arents House**, Dijver 16, Bruges, 8000 Belgium. Tel 32-50-44-87-43; Fax 32-50-44-87-78; Email musea@brugge.be; Web: www.museabrugge.be
Open Tues - Sun 9:30 AM - 5 PM, cl Mon; Admis adults 4 EUR, reduced 3 EUR, children under 12 free; 18th century mansion with drawing colls of the Steinmet-Kabinet & permanent presentation around the British-Bruges artist Frank Brangwyn
Collections: Works of British-Bruges artist Frank Brangwyn (1867-1956), paintings, watercolors, engravings, furniture & carpet designs
Exhibitions: Located on ground floor ever changing exhibits of expressive art, usually in association with the Groeninge Museum

M **Groeningemuseum - Groeninge Museum**, Dijver 12, Bruges, 8000 Belgium. Tel 32-50-44-87-43; Fax 32-50-44-87-78; Email musea@brugge.be; Web: www.museabrugge.be
Open Tues - Sun 9:30 AM - 5 PM, cl Mon; Admis individual 8 EUR, reduced 6 EUR, children under 12 free; A rich & fascinating array of artworks from the southern Netherlands (Belgium) over a period of six centuries (15th-21st)
Collections: The Flemish Primitives & Expressionists and various Renaissance & Baroque masters, pieces from the Neo-classical & Realistic periods & milestones from the Symbolist & Modernist movement, a selection of post 1345 modern art

M **Stadhuis - City Hall**, Burg 12, Bruges, 8000 Belgium. Tel 32-50-44-87-43; Fax 32-50-44-87-78; Email musea@brugge.be; Web: www.museabrugge.be
Open daily 9:30 AM - 5 PM; Admis adults 4 EUR, reduced 3 EUR, children under 12 free; Bruges Town Hall, dating from 1376, with Gothic Chamber
Special Subjects: Period Rooms
Collections: Gothic Chamber: 19th c wall paintings, polychrome ceiling, painted figures
Exhibitions: Governors & Governed

M **Gentpoort - Gate of Ghent**, Gentpoortvest, Bruges, 8000 Belgium. Tel 32-50-44-87-43; Fax 32-50-44-87-78; Email musea@brugge.be; Web: www.museabrugge.be
Open Sat & Sun 9:30 AM - 12:30 PM & 1:30 PM - 5 PM, cl Mon - Thurs; Admis adults 4 EUR, reduced 3 EUR, children under 12 free; Ghent Gate, 1 of 4 medieval Bruges city gates which have survived to contemporary times

M **Sint-Janshuismolen - Sint-Janshuis Mill**, Kruisvest, Bruges, 8000 Belgium. Tel 32-50-44-87-43; Fax 32-50-44-87-78; Email musea@brugge.be; Web: www.museabrugge.be
Open Tues - Sun 9:30 AM - 12:30 PM & 1:30 PM - 5 PM, cl Mon; Admis adults 3 EUR, reduced 2 EUR, children under 12 free; Sint-Janshuis Mill circa 1770, historic active grain mill located at its original site; Koelewei Mill circa 1765, historic active grain mill transplanted near Dampoort (Dam Gate) in 1996

M **Belfort - Belfry & Carillon**, Markt 7, Bruges, 8000 Belgium. Tel 32-50-44-87-43; Fax 32-50-44-87-78; Email musea@brugge.be; Web: www.museabrugge.be
Open daily 9:30 AM - 6 PM; Admis adults 10 EUR, reduced 8 EUR, children under 6 free; Historic Belfry tower, 83 meters high with 366 steps, contains treasury room, clock mechanism & carillon with 47 bells
Activities: Mus shop sells books, magazines, reproductions, prints

M **Brugse Vrije - Liberty of Bruges**, Burg 11 a, Bruges, 8000 Belgium. Tel 32-50-44-87-43; Fax 32-50-44-87-78; Email musea@brugge.be; Web: www.museabrugge.be
Open daily 9:30 AM - 12:30 PM & 1:30 PM - 5PM; Admis adults 4 EUR, reduced 3 EUR, children under 12 free; Former location of city courts, now houses Municipal Archives; contains Court of Justice & Renaissance Chamber
Collections: Renaissance Chamber: contains monumental 16th c fireplace with wood, marble & alabaster mantle designed by Lanceloot Blondeel

M **Archeologiemuseum - Archaeology Museum**, Mariastraat 36 a, Bruges, 8000 Belgium. Tel 32-50-44-87-43; Fax 32-50-44-87-78; Email musea@brugge.be; Web: www.museabrugge.be
Open Tues - Sun 9:30 AM - 12:30 PM & 1:30 PM - 5 PM, cl Mon; Admis individual 4 EUR, reduced 3 EUR, children under 12 free; Mus confronts aspects of life from prehistory, the roman period & the middle ages (early & late) through a series of do & search tasks
Collections: Archaeological finds

M **Onze-Lieve-Vrouwekerk - Museum of the Church of Our Lady**, Mariastraat, Bruges, 8000 Belgium. Tel 32-50-44-87-11; Fax 32-50-44-87-78; Email musea@brugge.be; Web: www.museabrugge.be
Open Mon - Sat 9:30 AM - 5 PM, Sun 1:30 PM - 5 PM; Admis adults 6 EUR, reduced 5 EUR, children under 12 free; Church with 122 meter high brick steeple
Special Subjects: Renaissance Art, Woodcarvings
Collections: Madonna & Child, by Michaelangelo, 16th century ceremonial tombs of Mary of Burgundy & Charles the Bold, painted tombs from 13th & 14th centuries, choir aisle: paintings & woodcarvings

M **Gezellemuseum - Gezelle Museum**, Rolweg 64, Bruges, 8000 Belgium. Tel 32-50-44-87-43; Fax 32-50-44-87-78; Email musea@brugge.be; Web: www.museabrugge.be
Open Tues - Sun 9:30 AM - 12:30 PM & 1:30 PM - 5 PM, cl Mon; Admis adults 4 EUR, reduced 3 EUR, children under 12 free; Birthplace of Flemish writer Guido Gezelle, with garden & biological kitchen garden
Collections: The Man Who Gives Fire by Jan Fabre
Exhibitions: Displays on the art of the written word

BRUSSELS

L **BIBLIOTHEQUE ROYALE DE BELIQUE,** Royal Library of Belgium, 4 blvd de l'Empereur, Brussels, 1000 Belgium. Tel 32 2 519 53 11; Fax 32 2 519 53 33; Email info@kbr.be; Web: www.kbr.be; *Dir* Patrick Lefevre
Open Mon - Fri 9 AM - 6:45 PM, Sat 9 AM - noon & 1 PM - 4:45 PM, cl Sun; Reading Room Access Annual Pass 25 EUR, Annual Student Pass 15 EUR, Individual Day Pass 5 EUR; Estab 1559
Collections: Coins, medals, maps, manuscripts, prints, rare printed books housed in Belgian National Library

M **BOZAR CENTRE FOR FINE ARTS, BRUSSELS,** Ravensteinstraat 23, Brussels, 1000 Belgium. Tel 02-507-82-00; Fax 02-507-85-15; Email info@bozar.be; Web: www.bozar.be; *CEO & Artistic Dir* Paul Dujarain
Exhibs open Tues, Wed, Fri - Sun 10 AM - 9 PM, Thurs 10 AM - 9 PM, cl Mon

M **ERASMUS HOUSE & BEGUINAGE MUSEUM,** Erasmus House, Rue du Chapitre 31 Brussels, 1070 Belgium; Beguinage, Rue du Chapelain 8 Brussels, 1070 Belgium. Tel 32-2-527-12-69; Fax 32-2-521-13-83; Email info@erasmushouse.museum; Web: www.erasmushouse.museum; *Cur* Ann Arend; *Dep Cur* Helen Haug
Open Erasmus House: Tues - Sun 10 AM - 6 PM; Beguinage: Tues - Sun 10 AM - noon & 2 PM - 5 PM; Admis 1.25 EUR; Mus dedicated to Erasmus of Rotterdam, 16th century house, printings & furniture; library with 4000 vols.; Two locations form the oldest communal mus in Belgium
Collections: Documents, paintings, manuscripts relating to Erasmus & other humanists of the 16th century

M **MUSEE HORTA,** Horta Museum, 25 rue Americaine, Brussels, 1060 Belgium. Tel 02 543 04 90; Email info@hortamuseum.be; Web: www.hortamuseum.be; *Dir* Francoise Aubry
Open Tues - Sun 2 PM - 5:30 PM, cl Mon; open to tour groups in the morning; Admis adults 10 EUR, seniors 6 EUR, student 5 EUR, pupils 6 - 18 yrs 3 EUR; Estab 1969; Art Nouveau building & World Heritage Site
Library Holdings: Exhibition Catalogs, Manuscripts, Original Documents, Photographs, Slides
Collections: Works of art by V Horta, architecture & furniture
Activities: Classes for children; mus shop sells books, prints, jewelry, postcards, calendars

M **MUSEES ROYAUX D'ART ET D'HISTOIRE,** Royal Museums of Art and History, Parc du Cinquantenaire 10, Brussels, 1000 Belgium. Tel 02-741-72-11; Fax 02-733-77-68; Email info@kmkg.be; Web: www.kmkg-mrah.be, www.mim.be; *Gen Dir* Alexandra De Poorter
Open Cinquantenaire Mus, Halle Gate & Musical Instruments Mus Tues - Fri 9:30 AM - 5 PM, Sat - Sun 10 AM - 5 PM, cl Mon; Mus of the Far East closed until further notice; Admis Cinquantenaire Mus & Musical Instruments Mus adults 8 EUR, sr citizens & students 19 - 25 6 EUR, pupils 6 - 18 2 EUR, children 3 & under free; Halle Gate adults 5 EUR, sr citizens 65 & up 4 EUR, students 6 - 25 1.50 EUR; Cultural and art history museum consisting of four sites: Cinquantenaire Museum, Musical Instruments Museum, Halle Gate & Museums of the Far East; Average Annual Attendance: 165,000
Income: Financed by federal state
Library Holdings: Auction Catalogs, Book Volumes, Exhibition Catalogs

Special Subjects: American Indian Art, Anthropology, Antiquities-Assyrian, Antiquities-Byzantine, Antiquities-Egyptian, Antiquities-Etruscan, Antiquities-Greek, Antiquities-Oriental, Antiquities-Persian, Antiquities-Roman, Archaeology, Asian Art, Baroque Art, Carpets & Rugs, Ceramics, Coins & Medals, Costumes, Crafts, Decorative Arts, Embroidery, Enamels, Eskimo Art, Ethnology, Flasks & Bottles, Folk Art, Furniture, Glass, Gold, Graphics, Historical Material, Islamic Art, Ivory, Jade, Jewelry, Laces, Medieval Art, Metalwork, Miniatures, Mosaics, Oriental Art, Photography, Porcelain, Pottery, Pre-Columbian Art, Primitive art, Prints, Renaissance Art, Silver, Stained Glass, Tapestries, Textiles
Collections: Pre-Columbian art, Belgian, Egyptian, Greek, Roman and classical art, Medieval, Renaissance and modern art - ceramics, furniture, glass, lace, silver, tapestries, textiles, ethnography, folklore, Oceanic, South-East Asia, American Indian, India, Merovingians, stone, modern & historical instruments, Islamic Art
Activities: Classes for adults & children; lects open to pub; tours; mus shop sells books, magazines, original art, reproductions

M **MUSEES ROYAUX DES BEAUX-ARTS DE BELGIQUE,** Royal Museums of Fine Arts of Belgium, Rue de la régence 3, Brussels, 1000 Belgium. Tel 32 02 508 32 11; Fax 32 0 2 508 32 32; Email info@fine-arts-museum.be; Web: www.fine-arts-museum.be; *Dir Gen* Michel Draguet
Open Tues - Fri 10 AM - 5 PM, Sat - Sun 11 AM - 6 PM, cl Mon; Admis adults 14,50 EUR, seniors 65 & up 12,50 EUR, students 20-26 & school teachers 8 EUR, children & young people under 19 no charge; Federal institution consisting of various museum entities distinct by the nature of their exhibits and located throughout the city of Brussels
Activities: Classes for adults & children; lects open to public, gallery talks, tours; scholarships, fellowships; mus shop sells books, magazines, reproductions, prints, slides

M **Musee Fin-de-Siecle Museum**, Rue de la Regence 3, Brussels, 1000 Belgium. Tel 32 02 508 32 11; Email info@fine.arts.museum.be; Web: www.fin-de-siecle-museum.be
Open Tues - Fri 10 AM - 5 PM, Sat & Sun 11 Am - 6 PM, cl Mon; Admis adults 8 EUR, seniors 65 & up 6 EUR, children & young people 6 - 25 2 EUR, children 5 & under no admis fee
Collections: Paintings, drawings, sculptures and decorative arts from the 1900s

M **Musee Modern Museum**, Rue de la Regence 3, Brussels, 1000 Belgium. Tel 32 02 508 32 11; Email info@fine.arts.museum.be; Web: www.fine-arts-museum.be
Open Tues - Fri 10 AM - 5 PM, Sat & Sun 11 AM - 6 PM, cl Mon; Admis adults 8 EUR, seniors 65 & up 6 EUR, children & young people 6 - 25 2 EUR, children 5 & under no admis fee
Collections: Paintings, drawings & sculptures from the late 18th century to the present day
Activities: Classes for adults & children; lects open to public, gallery talks, tours; scholarships, fellowships; books, magazines, reproductions, prints & slides

M **Musee Meunier Museum**, Rue de l'Abbaye 59, Brussels, 1050 Belgium. Tel 32 02 648 44 49; Email info@fine-arts-museum.be; Web: www.fine-arts-museum.be
Open Tues - Fri 10 AM - noon & 12:45 PM - 5 PM; No admis fee
Collections: Paintings, drawings & sculptures by Constantin Meunier

M **Musee Wiertz Museum**, Rue Vautier 62, Brussels, 1050 Belgium. Tel 32 02 648 17 18; Email info@fine-arts-museum.be; Web: www.fine-arts-museum.be
Open Tues - Fri 10 AM - noon & 12:45 PM - 5 PM; No admis fee
Collections: Works by Belgian Romantic artist Antoine Wiertz

M **Musee Old Masters Museum**, Rue De La Regence 3, Brussels, 1000 Belgium. Tel 32 02 508 32 11; Email info@fine-arts-museum.be; Web: www.fine-arts-museum.be
Tues - Fri 10 AM - 5 PM; admis adults 8 EUR, seniors 65 & up 6 EUR, children & young people 6 - 25 2 EUR, children 5 & under free
Special Subjects: Painting-British, Painting-European, Painting-Dutch, Painting-Flemish, Painting-French, Renaissance Art, Period Rooms
Collections: Paintings from the 15th - 18th centuries
Activities: Classes for adults & children; lects open to public, gallery talks, tours; scholarships, fellowships; mus shop sells books, magazines, reproductions, prints, slides

M **Musee Magritte Museum**, Place royale, Brussels, 1000 Belgium. Tel 32 02 508 32 11; Email info@fine-arts-museum.be; Web: www.musee-magritte-museum.be
Open Tues - Fri 10 AM - 5 PM, Sat & Sun 11 AM - 6 PM, cl Mon; Admis adults 8 EUR, seniors 65 & up 6 EUR, children & young people 6 - 25 2 EUR, children 5 & under free
Collections: Works by Belgian Surrealist artist Rene Magritte

GHENT

M **MUSEUM VOOR SCHONE KUNSTEN GENT,** Museum of Fine Arts Ghent, Fernand Scribedreef 1, Citadelpark Ghent, 9000 Belgium. Tel 32-09-240-07-00; Fax 32-09-240-07-90; Email museum.msk@gent.be; Web: www.mskgent.be; *Dir* Catherine de Zegher
Open Tues - Sun 10 AM - 6 PM, cl Mon; Admis adults 8 EUR, seniors 65 & up 6 EUR, young people 19 - 26 2 EUR, citizens & children under 12 free
Special Subjects: Baroque Art, Drawings, Etchings & Engravings, Landscapes, Marine Painting, Medieval Art, Painting-Dutch, Painting-European, Painting-Flemish, Painting-French, Painting-Italian, Portraits, Religious Art, Renaissance Art, Sculpture, Watercolors, Woodcuts
Collections: Developments in visual arts from the middle ages to the first half of the 20th century, Painting of the Southern Netherlands, Sculpture and other European paintings

LIEGE

M **LE GRAND CURTIUS,** The Grand Curtius, Feronstree 136, Liege, 4000 Belgium. Tel 32 42 21 6817; Fax 32 42 21 6809; Email infograndcurtius@liege.be; Web: www.grandcurtiusliege.be; *Dir* Jean-Marc Gay; *Asst Cur* Pauline Bovy
Open Mon, Wed - Sun 10 AM - 6 PM; cl Tues; Admis 5 EUR, children under 12 free; Estab 2009; 16th - 18th century bldg connected by contemporary spaces; Average Annual Attendance: 85,000
Income: Municipal Mus
Special Subjects: Antiquities-Roman, Baroque Art, Coins & Medals, Crafts, Decorative Arts, Enamels, Furniture, Glass, Medieval Art, Metalwork, Painting-European, Religious Art, Renaissance Art, Sculpture, Silver, Stained Glass
Collections: 18th century decorative arts of Liege, housed in a mansion of the same period, Archaeology, decorative arts, religious art, glass, arms & weapons, ancient clocks
Publications: Catalogue of coll & temporary exhib
Activities: Classes for children; lects open to pub; 5 vis lectrs per yr; mus shop sells books, postcards, small gifts; Le Petit Curtius

M **MUSEE LA BOVERIE,** Boverie Museum, Parc de la Boverie, Liege, 4020 Belgium. Tel 32 4 221 93 19; Email info@laboverie.com; Web: www.laboverie.com; *Dir* Jean-Marc Gay
Open Tues - Sun 10 AM - 6 PM, cl Mon; Admis adults 12 EUR, children 14 - 25 & senior citizens 8 EUR, children under 14 free; Estab 2016; Fine arts museum and expo center
Collections: Paintings & sculptures from the 16th - 21st century
Activities: Classes for adults & children; visits; mus shop sells books, magazines & reproductions

MORLANWELZ

M **MUSEE ROYAL DE MARIEMONT,** Royal Mariemont Museum, Chaussee de Mariemont 100, Morlanwelz, 7140 Belgium. Tel 32 (0) 64 21 21 93; Fax 32 (0) 64 26 29 24; Email info@musee-mariemont.be; Web: www.musee-mariemont.be; *Scientific Dir* Marie-Cecile Bruwier; *Opers Dir* Roland Van der Hoeven
Open Apr - Sept Tues - Sun 10 AM - 6 PM, Oct - Mar Tues - Sun 10 AM - 5 PM, cl Mon; Admis adults 5 EUR, sr citizens 2.50 EUR, students 2 EUR; Maintains library with 150,000 volumes
Library Holdings: Auction Catalogs, Book Volumes, Cards, Exhibition Catalogs, Manuscripts, Maps, Original Art Works, Original Documents, Pamphlets, Periodical Subscriptions, Photographs, Prints, Reproductions, Sculpture
Special Subjects: Antiquities-Egyptian, Antiquities-Etruscan, Antiquities-Greek, Antiquities-Roman, Archaeology, Asian Art, Bookplates & Bindings, Bronzes, Calligraphy, Cartoons, Ceramics, Coins & Medals, Decorative Arts, Drawings, Embroidery, Enamels, Etchings & Engravings, Furniture, Glass, Gold, Graphics, Historical Material, Islamic Art, Ivory, Jade, Jewelry, Manuscripts, Maps, Metalwork, Miniatures, Mosaics, Oriental Art, Pewter, Porcelain, Pottery, Sculpture, Textiles
Collections: Belgian archaeology, porcelain from Tournai, Egyptian, Grecian, Roman, Chinese & Japanese antiquities, rare books & manuscripts
Publications: catalogues of exhibitions; monographic, scientific review: Les Cahiers de Mariemont
Activities: Classes for children & children; lects open to public; lects for mems only; concerts; tours; competitions; award: Prix des musees-wallonie, 2007, Prix de bonne pratique-reflexions sur le musee et L'integration sociale, 2009, Prix des enfants-wallonne, 2012, Tripadvisor-Certificat d'excellence, 2013; mus shop sells books, reproductions & prints

NAMUR

M **MUSEE FELICIEN ROPS,** Felicien Rops Museum, Rue Fumal 12 B, Namur, 5000 Belgium. Tel 32 81 77 67 55; Fax 32 81 77 69 25; Email info@museerops.be; Web: www.museerops.be; *Dir* Veronique Carpiaux
Open Tues - Sun 10:00 AM - 6 PM; cl Jan 1st, Dec 24, 25, & 31; Admis 3 EUR, students & seniors 1.50 EUR, school groups 1 EUR, children under 12 & visitors first Sun of month free; Mus is situated in Old Namur in a 19th century residence
Income: provincial institution of Namur
Purchases: bookshop with postcards, posters
Library Holdings: Auction Catalogs, Book Volumes, Exhibition Catalogs, Original Documents, Periodical Subscriptions
Special Subjects: Art History, Drawings, Painting-European, Prints, Embroidery
Collections: Coll of Rop's prints, drawings & paintings
Exhibitions: Three exhibs per yr
Publications: 3 publ per yr
Activities: Classes for children; lects open to the pub; 2 vis lectrs per yr; concerts; gallery talks; schols; traveling exhibs to other mus worldwide; mus shop sells books, reproductions

M **MUSEE PROVINCIAL DES ARTS ANCIENS DU NAMUROIS,** Provincial Museum of Ancient Arts, Namur, Hotel de Gaiffier d'Hestroy, rue de Fer 24 Namur, 5000 Belgium. Tel 32 0 81 77 67 54; Fax 32 0 81 77 69 24; Email musee.arts.anciens@province.namur.be; Web: www.province.namur.be/trema; *Dir* Marie-Francoise Degembe
Open Tues - Sun 10 AM - 6 PM, cl Mon; Admis adult 3 EUR, students, senior citizens & groups 1.5 EUR, children under 12 free
Library Holdings: Book Volumes, Exhibition Catalogs, Manuscripts, Maps, Periodical Subscriptions
Special Subjects: Archaeology, Art History, Coins & Medals, Drawings, Embroidery, Enamels, Glass, Gold, History of Art & Archaeology, Ivory, Manuscripts, Maps, Medieval Art, Metalwork, Miniatures, Painting-European, Painting-European, Religious Art, Renaissance Art, Sculpture, Silver, Textiles
Collections: Medieval & Renaissance collection of sculptures, paintings, silver and other artifacts, Treasure of Hugo d'Oignies
Publications: Catalog of Exhib
Activities: Educ prog; classes for children; lects open to pub; mus shop sells books, reproductions, prints, DVDs

VERVIERS

M **MUSEE DES BEAUX-ARTS ET DE LA CERAMIQUE,** Museum of Fine Arts and Ceramics, Rue Renier 17, Verviers, 4800 Belgium. Tel 087 33 16 95; Fax 087 44 62 98; Email musees.verviers@verviers.be; Web: musee.verviers.be; *Cur* Marie-Paule Deblanc-Magnee

Open Mon, Wed & Sat 2 PM - 5 PM, Sun 3 PM - 6 PM
Collections: European & Asian painting and sculpture, ceramics, & folk arts

BERMUDA

HAMILTON

M **BERMUDA NATIONAL GALLERY,** City Hall & Arts Centre, Church St Hamilton, Bermuda. Tel 441-295-9428; Fax 441-295-2055; Email director@bng.bm; Web: bermudanationalgallery.com; *Dir* Lisa Howie
Open Mon - Fri 10 AM - 4 PM, Sat 10 AM - 2 PM, cl pub holidays; Admis non-mems $5; Estab 1992; Home of the national art collection
Collections: Diverse masks, paintings, photographs, prints, sculptures, decorative arts and more, African coll, Bermuda Coll, Contemporary coll, European Watlington coll, Photography & Print coll

BHUTAN

PARO

M **NATIONAL MUSEUM OF BHUTAN,** PO Box 1227, Paro, Bhutan. Tel 975 27 1511; Fax 975 27 1510; Email nmb@druknet.bt; Web: www.nationalmuseum.gov.bt; *Dir* Khenpo Phuntsok Tashi
Open Winter: Nov - Mar daily 9 AM - 4 PM; Summer April - Oct daily 9 AM - 5 PM; Admis res 10 BTN, SAARC country citizens 25 BTN, non-SAARC country citizens 150 BTN, monks, nuns and children under 10 free; Estab 1968; Located in the ancient 'Ta Dzong' watchtower
Collections: Works from 4000 BCE to the present representing the multicultural heritage of the Kingdom of Bhutan

BOLIVIA

LA PAZ

M **MUSEO NACIONAL DE ARQUEOLOGIA,** National Museum of Archaeology, Calle Tiwanaku 93, Casilla Oficial 64 La Paz, Bolivia. Tel 591-2 231 1621; Web: www.bolivian.com/arqueologia; *Dir* Michel Marcos
Open Mon - Fri 9 AM - 12:30 PM & 3 - 7 PM, Sat 9 AM - noon; Admis 10 BOB
Collections: Anthropology, archaeology, ethnology, folklore, Lake Titicaca district exhibitions, traditional native arts and crafts

M **MUSEO NACIONAL DE ARTE,** National Museum of Art, Calle Comercio esq Socabaya, La Paz, 11390 Bolivia. Tel 591-2 240 8600; Fax 591-2 2408542; Email mna@mna.org.bo; Web: www.mna.org.bo; *Dir* Galo Coca Soto; *Cur* Jose Bedoya; *Cur* Fatima Olivarez
Open Tues - Fri 9:30 AM - 12:30 PM & 1 PM - 7 PM, Sat 10 AM - 5:30 PM, Sun 10 AM - 1:30 PM, cl Mon; Admis res 5 BOB, non-res 15 BOB; Estab 1965; Colonial-era and contemporary art galleries
Library Holdings: Audio Tapes, Book Volumes, CD-ROMs, Cards, Cassettes, Clipping Files, Compact Disks, Exhibition Catalogs, Fiche, Framed Reproductions, Memorabilia, Original Art Works, Original Documents, Other Holdings, Pamphlets, Periodical Subscriptions, Photographs, Prints, Records, Reels, Sculpture, Slides, Video Tapes
Collections: Colonial & local modern art, Latin American art
Publications: Hemoria 1990-2002. Postales, Catalogs
Activities: Lect open to public, concerts, gallery talks, tours; lending original objects of art; books, magazines

BOTSWANA

GABORONE

M **BOTSWANA NATIONAL MUSEUM,** 331 Independence Ave, Private Bag 00114 Gaborone, Botswana. Tel 267 374 616; Fax 267 302 797; Email national.museum@gov.bw; Web: www.botswana-museum.gov.bw; *Sr Cur* Marumo Kedumetse; *Prin Cur* Gertrude Matswiri
Open Tues - Fri 9 AM - 6 PM, Sat & Sun 9 AM - 5 PM, cl Mon; No admis fee; Estab 1968; Cultural heritage museum and art gallery
Income: Financed by govt
Library Holdings: Auction Catalogs, Book Volumes, Cards, Periodical Subscriptions, Slides, Video Tapes
Special Subjects: African Art, Anthropology, Archaeology, Bronzes, Ceramics, Coins & Medals, Costumes, Crafts, Decorative Arts, Dioramas, Drawings, Ethnology, Folk Art, Graphics, Photography, Porcelain, Portraits, Posters, Pottery, Primitive art, Reproductions, Sculpture, Tapestries, Textiles, Watercolors
Collections: Art of all races of Africa south of the Sahara, scientific colls relating to Botswana
Exhibitions: Artists in Botswana (annual); HIV/AIDS (annual); Basket & Craft Exhibition (annual); Photographic (annual)
Publications: Zebra's Voice (quarterly); annual report; exhib catalogue
Activities: Classes for children; tours; sponsoring of competition; annual visual arts awards; lending of objects of art to other ministries; originate traveling exhibs to other countries; mus shop sells books, magazines, original art

BRAZIL

OURO PRETO

M **MUSEU DA INCONFIDENCIA,** Museum of Conspiracy, Praca Tiradentes, 139, Ouro Preto, Minas Gerais 35400 Brazil. Tel 55 (31) 3551-1121; 3551-5233; Web: www.museudainconfidencia.gov.br; *Dir* Rui Mourao
Open Tues - Sun noon - 6 PM; Admis adult 8 BRL, children 4 BRL; Average Annual Attendance: 150,000-200,000
Collections: Objects & documents related to the 1789 Revolutionaries of Minas Gerais (the Inconfidentes), Antonio Francisco Lisboa's coll of works, Religious art, Furniture from the 18th & 19th century, Religious music from the 18th century in Minas Gerais, Objects related to the Empire period (19th century), Objects related to the Vila Rica (the old Ouro Preto)
Publications: Oficina do Inconfidencis, Revista de Trabalho (annual issue) and Isto e Inconfidencia (bulletin published four times a year), Museu da Inconfidencia (institutional book of the museum)
Activities: Educ prog; activities for adults & children; guided tours; student training; ext prog offers film exhibs; mus shop sells books, magazines, reproductions, slides, postal cards, CD-ROMs, compact disks, DVDs, exhibs catalogs

RIO DE JANEIRO

M **MUSEU DE ARTE MODERNA DE RIO DE JANEIRO,** Museum of Modern Art, Av Infante Dom Henrique 85, Parque do Flamengo Rio de Janeiro, 20021-140 Brazil. Tel 55 (21) 3883-5600; Fax 55 (21) 3883-5612; Email mam@mamrio.org.br; Web: mamrio.org.br; *Pres* Carlos Alberto Gouvea Chateaubriand; *VPres* Joao Mauricio de Araujo Pinho Filho; *Dir* Luiz Schymura
Open Tues - Fri noon - 6 PM, Sat & Sun noon - 7 PM; Admis 14 BRL; students & seniors 60 & up 7 BRL; Estab 1948
Collections: Collections representing different countries

M **MUSEU NACIONAL DE BELAS ARTES,** National Museum of Fine Arts, Ave Rio Branco 199, Rio de Janeiro, 20040 Brazil. Tel 55 (21) 3299-0600; Web: mnba.gov.br; *Dir* Monica Xexeo
Open Tues - Fri 10 AM - 5 PM, Sat - Sun & holidays 1 PM - 5 PM; Admis 8 BRL, Sun free; Estab 1937; Library with 12,000 vols
Collections: 19th & 20th century Brazilian art, works by outstanding painters, European paintings & sculptures - works by Dutch, English, French, German, Italian, Portuguese & Spanish masters, masterpieces of foreign coll: Dutch school - eight Brazilian landscapes by Frans Post, French school - 20 Paintings by Eugene Boudin, Ventania (Storm) by Alfred Sisley, Italian School Portrait of the Cardinal Amadei by Giovanni Battista Gaulli, Baciccia, Sao Caetano (c 1730) by Giambattista Tiepolo. Graphic art department: Prints & drawings by Annibale Carracci, Chagall, Daumier, Durer, Toulouse Lautrec, Picasso, Guido Reni, Renoir, Tiepolo, etc

SALVADOR

M **MUSEU HENRIQUETA CATHARINO,** Henriqueta Catharino Museum, Rua Monsenhor Flaviano 02, Salvador, 40-080-136 Brazil. Tel (071) 3329 5520; Fax (071) 3329 5681; Email contato@institutofeminino.com.br; Web: www.institutofeminino.org.br; *Exec Dir* Sonia Bastos
Open Tues - Fri 10 AM - Noon, 1 PM - 6 PM, Sat 2 PM - 6 PM; Admis fee adults 5 BRL, students & seniors 3 BRL; Estab 1923; Circ 20,000; House-museum and decorative art collection of the Fundacao Instituto Feminino Da Bahia; Average Annual Attendance: 4000
Income: Property investments & rent
Collections: Religious art, Brazilian art, women's apparel, jewelry, gold, silver, Costumes & Textiles
Publications: Catalogue, Costume and Textile Museum
Activities: Classes for children; concerts; gallery talks; mus shop sells books

SAO PAULO

A **CENTRO CULTURAL BANCO DO BRASIL,** Bank of Brazil Cultural Center, Rua Alvares Penteado, 112, Centro Sao Paulo, 01012-000 Brazil. Web: culturabancodobrasil.com.br
Estab 1986; Cultural institutions dedicated to the arts with centers in Sao Paulo, Rio de Janiero, Brasilia and Belo Horizonte, Brazil.
Special Subjects: Drawings, Video, Photography, Prints, Sculpture, Theatre Arts, Film
Exhibitions: Temporary exhibs programmed permanently
Activities: Classes for adults, children & families; docent training; gallery talks; guided tours; lending of original objects of art to several mus & institutions on contemporary art; mus shop sells books, magazines

M **Bank of Brazil Cultural Center - Rio de Janeiro**, Rua Primeiro de Marco 66, Centro CEP Rio de Janeiro, 200100-000 Brazil. Tel 21 3808-2020; Email ccbbrio@bb.com.br; Web: culturabancodobrasil.com.br; *Contact* Bianca Mello
Open Wed. - Mon 9 AM - 9 PM; Centrally located neoclassical building housing a theater, cinema, museum, archives and library
Collections: Paintings, drawings, photographs, video installations, mixed media
Activities: Educ progs, cultural attractions; tours

M **Bank of Brazil Cultural Center - Brasilia**, SCES, Tranche 02, lot 22, Brasilia, 70200-002 Brazil. Tel 61 3108-7600; Email ccbbdf@bb.com.br; Web: culturabancodobrasil.com.br; *Contact* Michele Lira Rodrigues
Open Tues - Sun 9 AM - 9 PM; Renovated, two-story structure housing theaters, galleries and multipurpose spaces
Collections: Paintings, drawings, photographs, video installations, mixed media
Activities: Educ progs for adults & children, cultural events; tours

M **Bank of Brazil Cultural Center - Belo Horizonte**, Praca da Liberdade, 450, Belo Horizonte, 30140-010 Brazil. Tel 31 3431-9400; Email ccbbbh@bb.com.br; Web: culturabancodobrasil.com.br; *Contact* Barbara Campos Guimaraes
Open Wed - Mon 9 AM - 9 PM; Renovated, former public administration building housing a theater, gallery and multipurpose room
Collections: Paintings, drawings, photographs, video installations, mixed media
Activities: Educ progs; tours

M **Bank of Brazil Cultural Center - Sao Paulo**, Rua Alvares Penteado, 112, Sao Paulo, 01012-000 Brazil. Tel 11 3113-3651; Email ccbbsp@bb.com.br; Web: culturabancodobrasil.com.br; *Contact* Leonardo Guarniero
Open Wed - Mon 9 AM - 9 PM; Centrally located, former bank building housing theaters, galleries and an auditorium
Collections: Paintings, drawings, photographs, video installations, mixed media
Activities: Art and educ progs, visual art shows; tours

M **MUSEU DE ARTE CONTEMPORANEA DA UNIVERSIDADE DE SAO PAULO,** Contemporary Art Museum of Sao Paulo University, Avenida Pedro Alvares Cabral 1301, Sao Paulo, 04094-050 Brazil. Tel 55 11 2648 0254; Email mac@usp.br; Web: www.mac.usp.br; *Vice-Dir* Katia Canton
Open Tues - Sun 10 AM - 6 PM, cl Mon; No admis fee; Estab 1963
Collections: Painting, sculptures, prints & drawings by masters of the international school & Brazilian Art

M **MUSEU DE ARTE DE SAO PAULO ASSIS CHATEAUBRIAND,** Sao Paulo Museum of Art, Ave Paulista 1578, Sao Paulo, 01310-200 Brazil. Tel 11 3149 5959; Fax 11 3284 0574; Email atendimento@masp.art.br; Web: masp.art.br; *Pres* Heitor Martins; *VPres* Miguel Chaia
Open Tues, Wed, Fri - Sun 10 AM - 6 PM, 10 AM - 8 PM, cl Mon; Admis adults 35 BRL, seniors 65 & up & students 17 BRL, children under 10 & mems free; Estab 1947
Collections: Representative works by Portinari & Lasar Segall, ancient & modern paintings & sculptures: American, 19th - 20th Centuries, Brazilian, 17th - 20th Centuries, British, 18th - 20th Centuries, Dutch, Flemish & German, 15th - 20th Centuries, French, 16th - 20th Centuries, Italian, 13th - 20th Centuries, Spanish & Portuguese, 16th - 19th Centuries

M **MUSEU DE ARTE MODERNA DE SAO PAULO,** Sao Paulo Museum of Modern Art, Parque Ibirapuera, portao 3, Sao Paulo, 04094-000 Brazil. Tel 55 11 5085-1300; Fax 55 11 5049-2342; Email atendimento@mam.org.br; Web: mam.org.br; *Pres* Milu Villela; *Cur* Felipe Chaimovich; *Mng Dir* Bertrando Molinari; *Mgr* Nelma Raphael dos Santos
Open Tues - Sun 10 AM - 5:30 PM, cl Mon; Admis 6 BRL, vistors under 10 & over 60 free, Sun free; Estab 1948
Collections: Multidisciplinary modern art from the 1950's to the present
Exhibitions: Panorama of Brazilian Art

BRUNEI DARUSSALAM

BANDAR SERI BAGAWAN

M **MUZIUM BRUNEI,** Brunei Museum, Jalan Korta Batu, Bandar Seri Bagawan, 1510 Brunei Darussalam. Tel 673 238 1672; Karim Pg Hj Osman
Open Sat - Thur 9 AM - 5 PM, Fri 9 - 11:30 AM & 2:30 - 5 PM; No admis fee; Estab 1965; Average Annual Attendance: 98,000

BULGARIA

PLOVDIV

M **REGIONAL ARCHAEOLOGICAL MUSEUM - PLOVDIV,** Pl Saedinenie 1, Plovdiv, 4000 Bulgaria. Tel 032 633106; Fax 032 633106; Email ram.plovdiv@gmail.com; Web: www.archaeologicalmuseumplovdiv.org; *Dir* Dr Kostadin Kisyov
Open winter: Tues - Sat 9:30 AM - 5 PM, cl Sun & Mon; summer: Tues - Sun 10 AM - 6 PM, cl Mon; Admis 5 BGN, disabled & children under 7 free; Estab 1882; Library with 15,000 vols
Income: Municipal budget
Library Holdings: Book Volumes, CD-ROMs, Compact Disks, DVDs, Exhibition Catalogs, Maps, Other Holdings, Photographs, Reels, Slides
Collections: Prehistory, classical & medieval archaeology, epigraphic monuments, jewelry, numismatics, toreutics & vessels
Activities: Excavations; mus shop sells books, original art, reproductions, prints & other items

SOFIA

M **NATSIONALNA HUDOJESTVENA GALERIA,** National Art Gallery, St Alexander Nevski Sq, 1 19th of February St Sofia, 1000 Bulgaria. Tel 359-2-980-0071; Fax 359-2-980-3320; Email nag.bg@abv.bg; Web: www.nationalartgallerybg.org; *Dir* Slava Ivanova; *Deputy Dir, Bulgarian Art* Bistra Rangelova; *Deputy Dir, Bulgarian Art* Ivan Milev; *Deputy Dir, Foreign Art* Iaroslava Bubnova
Open Tues, Wed, Fri & Sun 10 AM - 6 PM, Thurs & Sat noon - 8 PM, cl Mon; Admis adults 10 BGN, students & seniors 5 BGN; Estab 1948; National museum for Bulgarian art
Income: Ministry of Culture
Library Holdings: Auction Catalogs, CD-ROMs, Compact Disks, DVDs, Exhibition Catalogs, Framed Reproductions, Kodachrome Transparencies, Original Art Works, Original Documents, Photographs, Prints, Reproductions, Sculpture, Slides
Collections: National & foreign art, permanent expositions of paintings & sculpture, Old Bulgarian Art, Art of the Middle Ages (10th - 14th century), Bulgarian Christian Art (18th - 19th century)
Exhibitions: Temporary exhibitions of Bulgarian & foreign art
Activities: Classes for children; concerts, gallery talks, tours; lending of original art objects to galleries within the country; originates traveling exhibs to municipality & private galleries; mus shop sells books, magazines, original art, reproductions & prints

CAMBODIA

PHNOM PENH

M **NATIONAL MUSEUM OF CAMBODIA,** Street 13, Sangkat Chey Chumneas, Kahn Daun Penh Phnom Penh, Cambodia. Tel 855 023 211 753; Email museum_cam@camnet.com.kh; Web: www.cambodiamuseum.info; *Dir* Kong Vireak
Open daily 8 AM - 5 PM; Admis 5 KHR; Estab 1917
Collections: Over 5000 objects on display; Khmer artifacts, statues, pre-Angkorian pottery & Brahmanist lingas; coins

CHILE

SANTIAGO

M **MUSEO CHILENO DE ARTE PRECOLOMBINO,** Chilean Museum of Pre-Columbian Art, Bandera 361, Santiago, Chile. Tel (56 2) 2 928 1500; Email informaciones@museoprecolombino.cl; Web: www.precolombino.cl; *Dir* Carlos Aldunate del Solar; *Gen Mgr* Alicia Leiva Brosius; *Chief Cur* Jose Berenguer Rodriguez
Open Tues - Sun 10 AM - 6 PM, cl Mon; Gen admis 4 CLP, univ students 2 CLP, student groups free
Collections: Permanent exhibition of items predating Spanish conquest, 3000 specimens of ceramics, textiles, sculptures and others

M **MUSEO DE ARTE COLONIAL DE SAN FRANCISCO,** San Francisco Museum of Colonial Art, PO Box 1220, Alameda Bernardo O'Higgins 834 Santiago, Chile. Tel (56 2) 2 639 8737; Email administracion@museosanfrancisco.com; Web: museosanfrancisco.com; *Mng Dir* Santiago Andrade; *Exec Dir* Manuel Alvarado
Open Mon - Fri 9:30 AM to 1:30 PM and 3 PM - 6 PM, Sat & Sun 10 AM - 2 PM; Admis adults 1,000 CLP, students & seniors 500 CLP
Income: Income from pvt support
Collections: 16th - 19th century art, collection of 17th century paintings in Chile, the life of St Francis depicted in 53 pictures, other religious works of art, furniture
Exhibitions: Arte religioso de la Escuela quiteña
Publications: Pinturas de la Serie de San Francisco Edic Morgan Antártica; Catÿlogo del Museo de San Francisco
Activities: Mus shop sells books, original art, reproductions, prints, handicrafts, ceramics, oil paintings & religious articles

M **MUSEO DE ARTE CONTEMPORANEO,** Museum of Contemporary Art, Parque Forestal, Ismael Valdes Vergara 506 Santiago, Chile. Tel 56 2 2977 1755; Email dirmac@uchile.cl; Web: www.mac.uchile.cl; *Dir* Francisco Brugnoli
Open Tues - Sat 11 AM - 7 PM, Sun 11 AM - 6 PM, cl Mon; No admis fee; Estab 1946; Part of the University of Chile Faculty of Arts
Collections: Over 2000 pieces of art produced in Chile since the late 19th century to the present, 600 paintings, 130 drawings, 80 sculptures, contemporary and modern work by local and international artists

M **MUSEO DE ARTE POPULAR AMERICANO TOMAS LAGO,** Tomas Lago American Popular Art Museum, Centro Gabriela Mistral, Av Libertador Bernardo O'Higgins 227 Santiago, Chile. Tel 562 2639 6139; Email mapa@uchile.cl; Web: www.mapa.uchile.cl; *Dir* Nury Gonzalez
Open Tues - Fri 10 AM - 8 PM, Sat, Sun & holidays 11 AM - 8 PM; No admis fee; Estab 1944; Part of the University of Chile Faculty of Arts
Collections: Araucanian silver, American folk arts of pottery, basketware, metal & wood

M **MUSEO NACIONAL DE BELLAS ARTES,** National Museum of Fine Arts, Parque Forestal, s/n Casilla 3209 Santiago, Chile. Tel (56 2) 224 991 600; Email contacto@mnba.cl; Web: www.mnba.cl; *Dir* Roberto Farriol; *Cur & Asst Dir* Gloria Cortes; *Cur & Asst Dir* Paula Honorato
Open Tues - Sun 10 AM - 6:45 PM; No admis fee; Estab 1880; maintain Chilean artistic heritage; Chilean & foreign painting, sculpture, engraving etc; Average Annual Attendance: 253,000
Library Holdings: Book Volumes, CD-ROMs, Clipping Files, Compact Disks, DVDs, Exhibition Catalogs, Manuscripts, Original Documents, Photographs, Prints, Records, Reproductions, Slides, Video Tapes
Special Subjects: Etchings & Engravings, Landscapes, Latin American Art, Marine Painting, Painting-Dutch, Painting-Flemish, Painting-French, Painting-Italian, Painting-Spanish, Photography, Portraits, Religious Art, Sculpture
Collections: Baroque, Chilean & Spanish paintings, sculpture, engravings, contemporary art
Activities: Classes for children; docent training; lects open to the public; opening events; gallery talks; guided tours; Museo Sin Muros, Salas MNBA Mall Plaza; lending of original objects of art to mus & cultural ctrs; organize traveling exhibs to

Chilean regions; mus shop sells books, magazines, original art, reproductions, prints & memorabilia

CHINA

BEIJING

M **NATIONAL ART MUSEUM OF CHINA,** 1 Wusi St, Dongcheng Dist Beijing, 100010 China. Tel 86 10 64017076; Fax 86 10 64034953; Email bgs@namoc.org; Web: www.namoc.org; *Dir* Wu Weishan; *Sec* Zhang Shijun; *Deputy Dir* Xie Xiaofan; *Deputy Dir* An Yuanyuan; *Deputy Dir* Zhang Qing
Open Tues - Sun 9 AM - 5 PM, cl Mon; No admis fee
Collections: More than 60,000 fine art works, Chinese paintings, prints, sculptures, sketches, iconography, folk and traditional arts and crafts, puppets, toys, kites, textiles, embroidery, decorative arts

M **NATIONAL MUSEUM OF CHINA,** 16 E Chang'an Ave, Dongcheng Dist Beijing, 100006 China. Tel 86 10 6511 6400; Email info@chnmuseum.cn; Web: chnmuseum.cn; *Dir* Lu Zhangshen
Open Tues - Sun 9 AM - 5 PM, cl Mon; No admis fee; Estab 1912; To protect and impart China's culture, continue China's civilizational lineage and carry forward China's national spirit
Collections: 1.3 million exhibition pieces including masterpieces, historical itmes and contemporary items, traditional Chinese arts & crafts, jade & ivory carvings, lacquer, handicrafts of gold inlaid ware, antique porcelain, ancient bronze, embroidery, furniture, paintings and calligraphy

M **THE PALACE MUSEUM,** The Forbidden City, 4 Jingshan Qianjie, Beijing, 100009 China. Tel 8610 8500-7421; Fax 8610 8500-7079; Email gugong@dpm.org.cn; Web: www.dpm.org.cn; *Dir* Shan Jixiang; *Deputy Dir & Sec Party Comt* Ji Tianbin; *Exec Deputy Dir* Wang Yamin
Open April - Oct daily 8:30 AM - 5 PM; Nov - March 8:30 AM - 4:30 PM; Admis April - Oct 60 CNY, Nov - March 40 CNY students 20 CNY, children under 120 cm in height free; Located in the former palace of the Ming & Qing dynasties, the museum covers an area of 720,000 sq meters and comprises a collection of nearly one million artifacts spanning 5,000 years of Chinese history.
Special Subjects: Asian Art, Calligraphy, Antiquities-Oriental, Decorative Arts, Costumes, Jade, Oriental Art
Collections: Chinese paintings and calligraphy of Ming and Qing dynasties, textiles, coins, pottery, porcelains, enamels, carved lacquer ware, ivory & wood carving, bronze & jade
Publications: Forbidden City Publishing House

GUANGZHOU

M **GUANGDONG MUSEUM OF ART,** 38 Yanyu Rd, Ersha Island Guangzhou, 510105 China. Tel 020 873 51 468; Web: www.gdmoa.org; *Dir* Luo Yiping
Open Tues - Sun 9 AM - 5 PM, cl Mon; No admis fee; Twelve indoor exhib halls covering 8,000 sq meters and an outdoor sculpture park covering 5,000 sq meters
Collections: Sculpture, painting and ceramic work, Contemporary art of the coastal areas of China and Guangdong Province
Exhibitions: Triennial Exhibition of Contemporary Art

SHANGHAI

M **MUSEUM OF CONTEMPORARY ART SHANGHAI,** Gate 7 People's Park, 231 Nanjing West Rd Shanghai, 200003 China. Tel 86 216 327 9900; Fax 86 216 327 1257; Email info@mocashanghai.org; Web: www.mocashanghai.org; *Chm & Dir* Samuel Kung
Open daily 10 AM - 6 PM; Admis adults 50 CNY, students, senior citizens, military & handicapped 25 CNY, children under 1.3 m in height & members free; Estab 2005
Collections: Chinese and international contemporary art

M **SHANGHAI MUSEUM,** No 201 Renmin Ave, Shanghai, 200003 China. Tel (021) 637 23 500 132; Email webmaster@shanghai-museum.org; Web: www.shanghaimuseum.net; *Dir* Chen Xiejun
Open daily 9 AM - 5 PM; No admis fee; Estab 1952; Collection of more than one million ancient Chinese artifacts
Special Subjects: Bronzes, Ceramics, Sculpture, Calligraphy, Jade, Furniture
Collections: Ancient Chinese bronze, ceramics, painting & calligraphy

CHINA, REPUBLIC OF

KAOHSIUNG CITY

M **KAOHSIUNG MUSEUM OF FINE ARTS,** 80 Meishuguan Rd, Gushan Dist Kaohsiung City, Taiwan China, Republic of. Tel 07-555-0331; Fax 07-555-0307; Email servicemail@kmfa.gov.tw; Web: www.kmfa.gov.tw; *Dir* Dr Pei-ni Beatrice Hsieh
Open Tues - Sun 9 AM - 5 PM, cl Mon; No admis fee
Collections: Collection of more than 2,500 works in 18 categories including calligraphy, sculptures, oil paintings, watercolors and sketches

TAICHUNG

M **NATIONAL TAIWAN MUSEUM OF FINE ARTS,** No 2 Sec 1 Wuquan W Rd, West Dist Taichung, 403 Taiwan China, Republic of. Tel 886 04 2372-3552; Fax 886-04-2372-1195; Web: www.ntmofa.gov.tw; *Dir* Tsung-Huang Hsiao
Open Tues - Fri 9 AM - 5 PM, Sat - Sun 9 AM - 6 PM, cl Mon; No admis fee; Estab 1980
Collections: Over 10,000 items created over various centuries from the Ming & Qing dynasties to the present

TAIPEI

M **MUSEUM OF CONTEMPORARY ART, TAIPEI,** No 39 Chang'An W Rd, Datong Dist Taipei, 103 Taiwan China, Republic of. Tel 886-2-2552-3721; Fax 886-2-2559-3874; Email services@mocataipei.org.tw; Web: www.mocataipei.org.tw; *Dir* Jui-Jen Shih; *Cur* Yu-Chieh Lin
Open Tues - Sun 10 AM - 6 PM, cl Mon; Gen admis 50 TWD, under 6 & over 65 free; Estab 2001
Library Holdings: Exhibition Catalogs, Kodachrome Transparencies
Special Subjects: Archaeology
Collections: International and local contemporary art in various media
Activities: Classes for adults & children; gallery talks; serving Zhong Shan Book Street; mus shop sells books

M **NATIONAL PALACE MUSEUM,** No 221 Sec 2 Zhishan Rd, Shillin Dist Taipei, 11143 Taiwan China, Republic of. Tel 886-2-6610-3600; Email service@npm.gov.tw; Web: www.npm.gov.tw; *Dir* Chi-Nan Chen
Open daily 8:30 AM - 6:30 PM; Admis adults 350 TWD, students (with ID) 150 TWD; Estab 1925 in Peking, 1965 in Wai-Shuang-hsi, Taipei
Income: Income: 125,001,000 TWD
Purchases: 91 pieces of Vietnamese under glaze blue doyce lain, 16 pieces of Southeast Asian textile, 1 Gandharan standing bodhisattva sculpture, and 1 Kashmiri seated Buddha sculpture
Library Holdings: Auction Catalogs, Audio Tapes, Book Volumes, CD-ROMs, Cassettes, Clipping Files, Compact Disks, DVDs, Exhibition Catalogs, Fiche, Maps, Original Documents, Periodical Subscriptions, Photographs, Slides, Video Tapes
Special Subjects: Bronzes, Calligraphy, Ceramics, Crafts, Embroidery, Enamels, Ivory, Jade, Jewelry, Manuscripts, Miniatures, Oriental Art, Porcelain, Portraits, Pottery, Religious Art, Tapestries, Woodcarvings
Collections: Bronzes, calligraphy, carved lacquer, embroidery, enamelware, jades, miniature crafts, oracle bones, paintings, porcelain, pottery, rare and old books & documents from Shang Dynasty to Ch'ing Dynasty, tapestry, writing implements
Exhibitions: Compassion and Wisdom: Religious Sculptural Arts; Orientation Gallery; Gems in the Rare Books Collection; Heaven-Sent Conveyances: Highlights of Ch'ing Historical Documents; Arts from Ch'Ing Imperial Collection; Splendors of Ch'ing Furniture (1800-1911); Transitions and Convergences (221-960); Oversized Hanging and Hand Scrolls Selections; Prototypes of Modern Styles (960-1350); The Ancient Art of Writing: Selections from the History of Chinese Calligraphy; The New Era of Ornamentation (1350-1521); The Contest of Craft: Ming Dynasty's Chia-Ching to Ch'ung-chen (1522-1644); Painting and Calligraphy Donated and Entrusted to the National Palace Museum; Treasures from an Age of Prosperity: The Reigns of Emperors K'ang-hsi, Yung-cheng and Ch'ien-Jung (1662-1795); Toward Modernity: Late Ch'ing Dynasty (1796-1911); NPM Outdoor Public Art: Intertia/Exertion; The Mystery of Bronzes; The Neolithic Age: The Beginning of Civilization (6200-1600 B.C.E); Classical Civilization: The Bronze Age (1600-221 B.C.E.); From Classic to Tradition (221 B.C.E.-220 C.E.); Dazzling Gems of the Collection: Famous Pieces from the Ch'ing Dynasty Palaces
Publications: The National Palace Museum Monthly of Chinese Art; The National Palace Museum Research Quarterly; Exploring Asia: Episode One of the NPM Southern Branch; The Tradition of Re-Presenting Art; Diagrams Showing the Reconstruction of Various Structures in the Prefecture of Taiwan; Illustrated Catalog of Painting and Calligraphy in the National Palace Mus; The Heavenly Collection: Treasures from the Emperor Ch'ien-lung Library; Kanjur Manuscript: Tibetan-language edition, hand-copied in gold ink K'ang-hsi reign, Ch'ing Dynasty-Illuminations I & III; Exquisite Beauty-Islamic Jades; New Visions at the Ch'ing Court: Giuseppe Castiglione and Western-Style Trends; Lasting Impressions: Seals from the Museum Collection (in Chinese); Treasures of the Forbidden City: Palace Imprints of the Ch'ing Dynasty (in Chinese); The Old is New NPM Guidebook: Splendors of the New National Palace Museum; Treasures of the National Palace Museum (Painting and Calligraphy & Books and Documents); Treasures from the Working of Nature: Eight Thousand Years of Antiquities; Marvelous Sparks of the Brush: Painting & Calligraphy, Books & Documents
Activities: Docent training, classes for children, teenagers & adults; teacher training workshops; dramatic progs; lects open to pub; 150 per yr; concerts, tours, sponsoring of competitions; teacher's workshops & reproduction exhibs throughout Taiwan; originate traveling exhibs on education upon invitation; shop sells books, reproductions, prints; children's gallery within mus's main building

L **Library,** Wai-shuang-hsi, Shih-Lin, Taipei, Taiwan China, Republic of. Tel 886-2-2881-2021; Fax 886-2-2882-1440; Email service@npm.gov.tw; Web: www.npm.gov.tw
Open Mon - Sat 9 AM - 5 PM
Library Holdings: Book Volumes 48,000, Other Holdings Documents 395,000; Rare books 191,000, Periodical Subscriptions 683

COLOMBIA

BOGOTA

M **EL MUSEO DEL ORO DEL BANCO DE LA REPUBLICA,** The Gold Museum, Santander Park, Carrera 5 & 16th St Bogota, Colombia. Tel 571 343

2222; Fax 571 284 7450; Web: www.banrepcultural.org/museo-del-oro; *Dir* Ms Maria Alicia Uribe
Open Tues - Sat 9 AM - 6 PM, Sun & pub holidays 10 AM - 4 PM, cl Mon; Admis adults 3,000 COP, under 12 and over 60 free, Sun free; Estab 1939; Part of the Cultural Division of Banco de la Republica
Special Subjects: Anthropology, Archaeology, Gold, Metalwork, Pottery, Pre-Columbian Art, Restorations, Textiles
Collections: Pre-Hispanic Goldwork Collection, Pottery, stone, shell, wood & textile archaeological objects
Publications: Boletin Museo del Oro
Activities: International exhibs displayed in recognized mus & cultural institutions around the world; mus shop sells books, reproductions & other items

M **MUSEO COLONIAL,** Colonial Museum, Carrera 6, No 9-77, Bogota, Colombia. Tel (57-1) 341 6017; Email ctoquica@mincultura.gov.co; Web: www.museocolonial.gov.co; *Dir* María Constanza Toquica Clavijo
Open Tues - Fri 9 AM - 5 PM, Sat - Sun 10 AM - 4 PM, cl Mon; Admis adults 3,000 COP, students with ID 2,000 COP, children 5 - 12 500 COP, children under 5 & seniors over 60 free; Estab 1942
Collections: Spanish colonial period art work: paintings, sculpture, furniture, gold and silver work, drawing

M **MUSEO NACIONAL DE COLOMBIA,** National Museum of Colombia, Carrera 7, No 28 - 66 Bogota, Colombia. Tel 571 381 6470; Fax 571 381 6490; Email info@museonacional.gov.co; Web: museonacional.gov.co; *Dir* Daniel Castro Benitez
Open Tues - Sat 10 AM - 6 PM, Sun 10 AM - 5 PM, cl Mon; No admis fee; Estab 1824
Collections: Colombian art and artifacts from the earliest inhabitants to present

COSTA RICA

SAN JOSE

M **MUSEO DE ARTE COSTARRICENSE,** Costa Rican Museum of Art, Parque Metropolitano La Sabana, 42 & Paseo Colon Paseo San Jose, 10108 Costa Rica. Tel 506 2256-1281; Email macprensa@musarco.go.cr; Web: www.musarco.go.cr; *Dir* Sofia Soto-Maffioli
Open Tues - Sun 9 AM - 4 PM; No admis fee; Estab 1978; Average Annual Attendance: 60,000
Collections: Representative Costa Rican art
Activities: Classes for adults & children; docent training

M **MUSEO NACIONAL DE COSTA RICA,** National Museum of Costa Rica, Calle 17, Avenidas Central y Segunda, Antiguo Cuartel Bella Vista San Jose, 1000 Costa Rica. Tel 506 257 1433; Fax 506 257 7427; Email informacion@museocostarica.go.cr; Web: www.museocostarica.go.cr; *Dir* Francisco Corrales Ulloa
Open Tues - Sat 8:30 AM - 4:30 PM, Sun 9 AM - 4:30 PM, cl Mon; Admis adult nationals 1,500 CRC, children under 12, students & seniors with ID & Sun free; foreign visitors $9 USD, students with ID $4 USD, children under 12 free; Estab 1887
Collections: Pre-Columbian & colonial religious art, natural history
Publications: Vinculos; Brenesia

COTE D'IVOIRE

ABIDJAN

M **MUSEE DES CIVILISATIONS DE COTE D'IVOIRE,** Ivory Coast Museum of Civilizations, 32 Boulevard Carde, Abidjan, Cote d'Ivoire. Tel 225-20-22-20-56; Email museeciv@aviso.ci; *Dir* Silvie Memel Kassi
Open Tues - Fri 9 AM - 6:30 PM, Sat 9 AM - 5 PM, cl Mon; Estab 1942; National museum of Cote d'Ivoire
Collections: Art, ethnographic, scientific & sociological exhibits

CROATIA

RIJEKA

M **MUZEJ MODERNE I SUVREMENE UMJETNOSTI,** Museum of Modern and Contemporary Art, Dolac 1/II, Rijeka, 51000 Croatia. Tel 385-51-492-611; Fax 385-51-330-982; Email mmsu-rijeka@ri.t-com.hr; Web: www.mmsu.hr; *Dir* Slaven Tolj
Open May - Sept Tues - Fri 11 AM - 8 PM, Sat & Sun 11 AM - 2 PM & 6 PM - 9 PM; Oct - April Tues - Fri 11 AM - 6 PM, Sat & Sun 11 AM - 1 PM & 5 PM - 8 PM; cl Mon; No admis fee; Estab 1948; Modern & contemporary art
Library Holdings: Audio Tapes, Book Volumes, CD-ROMs, DVDs, Exhibition Catalogs, Filmstrips, Video Tapes
Special Subjects: Drawings, Graphics, Photography, Posters, Prints, Sculpture
Collections: Paintings, sculptures & graphics, drawings, photographs, mixed media, video
Publications: Catalogues of temporary exhibitions
Activities: Classes for adults & children; Lects open to pub; gallery talks; tours

SPLIT

M **ARHEOLOSKI MUZEJ U SPLITU,** Archaeological Museum in Split, Zrinjsko-Frankopanska 25, Split, 21000 Croatia. Tel (021) 329-340; Fax (021) 329-360; Email info@armus.hr; Web: www.armus.hr; *Dir & Sr Cur* Damir Kliskic
Open June - Sept Mon - Sat 9 AM - 2 PM & 4 PM - 8 PM, cl Sun; Oct - May: Mon - Fri 9 AM - 2 PM & 4 PM - 8 PM, Sat 9 AM - 2 PM, cl Sun; Admis adults 20 HRK, children, students & senior citizens 10 HRK; Estab 1820; Library with 30,000 vols
Collections: Relics from the Greek colonies, prehistoric & numismatic coll, medieval monuments from the 9th to the 13th century

M **GALERIJA UMJETNINA,** Gallery of Fine Arts, Ulica kralja Tomislava 15, Split, 21000 Croatia. Tel 385-21-350-110; Fax 385-21-350-111; Email galerija-umjetnina@galum.hr; Web: www.galum.hr; *Dir* Branko Franceschi
Open Tues - Sun 10 AM - 9 PM, cl Mon & holidays; Admis adults 40 HRK, students & seniors 20 HRK, children under 7 free; Estab 1931; Library with 10,000 vols
Collections: Paintings & sculptures, ancient & modern art

VELIKA GORICA

M **MUZEJ TUROPOLJA,** Turopolja Museum, Trg kralja Tomislava 1, Velika Gorica, 10410 Croatia. Tel 385 1 6221 325; Fax 385 1 6225 077; Email muzej-turopolja@muzej-turopolja.hr; Web: www.muzej-turopolja.hr; *Dir* Margareta Biskupic
Open Tues - Fri 9 AM - 5:30 PM, Sat & Sun 10 AM - 1 PM, cl Mon; Admis 10 HRK, students 8 HRK; Estab 1960

ZAGREB

M **ARHEOLOSKI MUZEJ U ZAGREBU,** Archaeological Museum in Zagreb, 19 Nikola Subic Zrinski Sq, PO Box 13 Zagreb, 10000 Croatia. Tel 385-1-4873-100; Fax 385-1-4873-102; Email amz@amz.hr; Web: www.amz.hr; *Dir* Sanjin Mihelic; *Asst Dir* Vesna Herak; *Sr Cur* Sanja Mijak Bozek
Open Tues, Wed, Fri & Sat 10 AM - 6 PM, Thurs 10 AM - 8 PM, Sun 10 AM - 1 PM, cl Mon & holidays; Admis family 30 HRK, adults 20 HRK, children, students & seniors 10 HRK; Estab 1846
Income: City of Zagreb
Library Holdings: Book Volumes
Collections: Neolithic 13th century
Publications: Vjesnik AM2; catalogues & monographs of the archaeological mus in Zagreb
Activities: Mus shop sells books, reproductions, & other items

M **MODERNA GALERIJA,** Modern Gallery - National Museum of Modern Art, Andrije Hebranga 1, Zagreb, 10000 Croatia. Tel 385 1 60 410 40; Fax 385 1 60 410 44; Email moderna-galerija@zg.t-com.hr; Web: www.moderna-galerija.hr; *Dir* Biserka Rauter Plancic
Open Tues - Fri 11 AM - 7 PM, Sat & Sun 11 AM - 1 PM, cl Mon & holidays; Admis family 70 HRK, adults 40 HRK, students & seniors 30 HRK, groups 20 HRK, toddlers free; Estab 1905; Library with 4000 vols
Library Holdings: Cards 2,000, Exhibition Catalogs 1,500, Video Tapes 200
Special Subjects: Coins & Medals, Drawings, Graphics, Landscapes, Marine Painting, Painting-European, Painting-French, Painting-German, Photography, Portraits, Primitive art, Sculpture, Tapestries, Watercolors, Woodcarvings, Woodcuts, Prints
Collections: Collection of sculptures, graphic arts & paintings, medals, video & new media
Exhibitions: Studio Josip Racic young artist exhibs (10 per yr); 13 temporary exhibs per yr in Moderna Galerija
Publications: Dossier
Activities: Classes for children; lects open to pub; 4 vis lectrs per yr; original objects of art lent to other museums & galleries in & around Croatia; mus shop sells reproductions, books, magazines

M **MUZEJ SUVREMENE UMJETNOSTI ZAGREB,** Museum of Contemporary Art Zagreb, Av. Dubrovnik 17, Zagreb, 10000 Croatia. Tel 385-1-60-52-700; Fax 385-1-60-52-798; Email msu@msu.hr; Web: www.msu.hr; *Dir* Snjezanda Pintaric; *Deputy Dir* Natasa Ivancevic; *Chief Cur* Nada Beros
Open Tues - Fri & Sun 11 AM - 6 PM, Sat 11 AM - 8 PM, cl Mon & holidays; Admis family 50 HRK, adults 30 HRK, concessions 15 HRK; Estab 1954; Galleries exhibiting contemporary Croatian art
Collections: Drawings, graphics, prints, art on paper, sculpture & paintings, film & video, photography & media art, Toso Dabac Archive, Kozaric Studio, Seissel Donation, Benko Horvat Collection

M **Galerija Primitivne Umjetnosti, Gallery of Naive Art**, Cirilometodska 3, Zagreb, 41000 Croatia. Tel 041 423 669; *Cur* Mrzljak Franjo

M **MUZEJ ZA UMJETNOST I OBRT,** Museum of Arts & Crafts, Trg Marsala Tita 10, Zagreb, 10000 Croatia. Tel 385-1-4882-111; Fax 385-1-4828-088; Email muo@muo.hr; Web: www.muo.hr; *Dir* Miroslav Gasparovic
Open Tues - Sat 11 AM - 8 PM, Sun 10 AM - 2 PM, cl Mon & pub holidays; Admis families 70 HRK, adults 40 HRK, students & retired 20 HRK; Estab 1880, collecting art and decorative arts from 13th - 20th century; Library with 70,000 vols; Mem: 100,000
Library Holdings: Auction Catalogs, Book Volumes, CD-ROMs, Exhibition Catalogs, Fiche, Framed Reproductions, Manuscripts, Maps, Original Art Works, Original Documents, Pamphlets, Periodical Subscriptions, Photographs, Prints, Reproductions
Special Subjects: Architecture, Baroque Art, Bookplates & Bindings, Bronzes, Carpets & Rugs, Ceramics, Coins & Medals, Costumes, Crafts, Decorative Arts, Dolls, Drawings, Embroidery, Etchings & Engravings, Flasks & Bottles, Furniture, Glass, Gold, Graphics, Ivory, Jewelry, Judaica, Laces, Landscapes, Leather, Manuscripts, Metalwork, Miniatures, Painting-British, Painting-European,

Painting-Flemish, Painting-French, Painting-German, Painting-Italian, Painting-Spanish, Pewter, Photography, Porcelain, Portraits, Posters, Pottery, Religious Art, Renaissance Art, Restorations, Sculpture, Silver, Stained Glass, Tapestries, Textiles, Watercolors
Collections: Applied arts from the 14th to the 20th century, ceramics, glass, tapestries, textiles, paintings & sculptures, furniture, clocks & watches, metal, photography, design architecture, Anka Gvozdanovic Coll
Activities: Classes for adults & children; children's workshops; lects open to pub; 10 vis lectrs per yr; concerts; gallery talks; tours; lending of original objects of art to other mus & galleries in Croatia; organize traveling exhibs throughout Europe; mus shop sells books, original art, reproductions, prints & other items

M **STROSSMAYEROVA GALERIJA STARIH MAJSTORA,** Strossmayer Gallery of Old Masters, Zrinski trg 11, Zagreb, 10000 Croatia. Tel 385-1-489-5117; Fax 385-1-481-9979; Email sgallery@hazu.hr; Web: info.hazu.hr; *Dir* Prof Borivoj Popovcak
Open Tues 10 AM - 7 PM, Wed - Fri 10 AM - 4 PM, Sat-Sun 10 AM - 1 PM; Gen admis 30 HRK, students 10 HRK; Estab 1884; A unit of the Croatian Academy of Sciences and Arts; Average Annual Attendance: 9,000
Income: Ministry of Science; Ministry of Culture
Library Holdings: Book Volumes 10,000, Exhibition Catalogs 2,000
Collections: Gallery of old masters from 13th - 19th century, French coll, mostly 18th-19th century, Italian coll, Fra Angelico - Piazzetta, nine rooms, paintings & sculpture, 13th-19th century, Dutch coll, 15th-18th century
Activities: Classes for children; gallery talks, 50 vis lectrs per yr; mus shop sells books & reproductions

CUBA

HAVANA

M **MUSEO DE ARTES DECORATIVAS,** Museum of Decorative Arts, Calle 17, No 502, Vedado Havana, 10400 Cuba. Tel 53-7-7832-0924; Email artdeco@cubarte.cult.cu; Web: www.cubarte.cult.cu; *Dir* Katia Varela Ortaz
Open Tues - Sat 10:30 AM - 5:30 PM, Sun 10 AM - 12:30 PM, cl Mon; Admis 3 CUC, children under 12 free; Estab 1964; Library with 2500 vols
Collections: Porcelain, bronzes, gold & silver work, furniture & tapestries

M **MUSEO NACIONAL DE BELLAS ARTES,** National Museum of Fine Arts, Trocadero St, entre Zulueta y Monserate Havana, 10200 Cuba. Tel (53-7) 7863-9042; Email direccion@bellasartes.cult.cu; Web: www.bellasartes.cult.cu; *Dir* Ana Cristina Perera Escalona; *Deputy Dir* Heriberto Rodriguez Perez
Open Tues - Sun 10 AM - 6 PM, cl Mon; Gen admis 8 CUC, children under 14 free; Estab 1913; Fine arts collection housed in a Spanish Renaissance style edifice
Collections: Renaissance and other European art, Cuban art from colonial times to the present

CYPRUS

NICOSIA

M **CENTRE OF VISUAL ARTS AND RESEARCH,** 285 Ermou St, Nicosia, 1017 Cyprus. Tel 357 2230 0999; Fax 357 2230 0989; Email cvar@severis.org; Web: cvar.severis.org; *Exec Dir* Rita C Severis; *Cur* Aliki Yiannakou
Open Winter: Tues - Thurs & Sat - Sun 9:30 AM - 5 PM, Fri 9:30 AM - 8 PM, cl Mon; Summer: Mon - Thurs & Sat 10 AM - 6 PM, Fri 10 AM - 8 PM, cl Sun; Gen admis 5 EUR, children & students free; Estab 2014; Mem: Library with 5,000 vols
Collections: Costas & Rita Severis collections containing paintings, antique costumes and memorabilia of Cyprus and its neighbors, 18th - 20th century works of arts by foreign artists

M **CYPRUS MUSEUM,** 1 Mouseiou St, PO Box 22024 Nicosia, 1516 Cyprus. Tel 357 2286 5801; Fax 357 2286 5888; Email antiquitiesdept@da.mcw.gov.cy; Web: www.mcw.gov.cy/da; *Dir, Dept of Antiquities* Marina Solomidou-Ieronymidou
Open Tues - Fri 8 AM - 6 PM, Sat 9 AM - 5 PM, Sun 10 AM - 1 PM, cl Mon; Admis 4.50 EUR; Estab 1910; 14 exhibition galleries from the Neolithic to the Roman period, early Christian period; Average Annual Attendance: 150,000; Mem: ICOM
Income: Government budget through the Department of Antiquities
Library Holdings: Auction Catalogs, Book Volumes, CD-ROMs, Compact Disks, DVDs, Exhibition Catalogs, Fiche, Filmstrips, Framed Reproductions, Manuscripts, Maps, Memorabilia, Motion Pictures, Original Art Works, Original Documents, Pamphlets, Periodical Subscriptions, Photographs, Prints, Reproductions, Sculpture, Slides, Video Tapes
Special Subjects: Afro-American Art, Antiquities-Byzantine, Antiquities-Greek, Antiquities-Roman, Archaeology, Bronzes, Ceramics, Coins & Medals, Enamels, Etchings & Engravings, Furniture, Glass, Gold, Ivory, Jewelry, Metalwork, Military Art, Mosaics, Antiquities-Assyrian, Antiquities-Oriental
Collections: Bronze cauldron from Salamis, middle and late Bronze-age Geometric, Archaic, Classical, Hellenistic and Graeco-Roman pottery, Mycenaean vases, Neolithic stone tools and vessels, sculpture from Archaic to Greco-Roman Age, including the Fine Arsos Head, the Aphrodite of Soli, and the bronze statue of Septimus Severus, silver trays from Lambousa
Publications: ARDAC, Monographs; RDAC (Report of the Department of Antiquities)
Activities: Classes for children; lects open to pub; concerts; lending of original objects of art to mus & academies in Europe & USA; organize traveling exhibs to mus & academies; originate traveling exhibs to Europe and America; sales shop sells books, reproductions, slides, postcards

CZECH REPUBLIC

BRNO

M **MORAVSKA GALERIE V BRNE,** Moravian Gallery in Brno, Prazak Palace, Husova 18 Brno, 662 26 Czech Republic. Tel 420 532 169 131; Email info@moravska-galerie.cz; Web: www.moravska-galerie.cz; *Dir* Jan Press
Open Wed & Fri - Sun 10 AM - 6 PM, Thurs 10 AM - 7 PM, cl Mon & Tues; No admis fee; Estab 1873; Library with 120,000 vols; Average Annual Attendance: 100,000
Income: National institution, main source of financing is the state budget
Library Holdings: Auction Catalogs, Book Volumes, CD-ROMs, Compact Disks, DVDs, Exhibition Catalogs, Manuscripts
Special Subjects: Antiquities-Oriental, Baroque Art, Bookplates & Bindings, Ceramics, Costumes, Decorative Arts, Drawings, Etchings & Engravings, Furniture, Glass, Gold, Graphics, Jewelry, Landscapes, Manuscripts, Medieval Art, Metalwork, Oriental Art, Painting-Dutch, Painting-European, Painting-Flemish, Painting-German, Painting-Italian, Painting-Russian, Photography, Porcelain, Portraits, Posters, Pottery, Prints, Religious Art, Renaissance Art, Restorations, Sculpture, Tapestries, Textiles, Watercolors, Woodcarvings, Woodcuts
Collections: European Art Collection - ceramics, furniture, glass, graphic design, jewelry, photography, textiles, Fine Art Collection - graphic art, painting, sculpture, 14th century to present, Oriental Art Collection, Design, architecture
Activities: Classes for adults & children; art workshops; lects open to pub; 20 vis lectrs per yr; concerts; gallery talks; tours; awards, Michal Ranny Prize; lending of original objects of art to other mus; mus shop sells books, magazines, reproductions, prints, gifts, jewelry & accessories

JABLONEC NAD NISOU

M **MUZEUM SKLA A BIZUTERIE V JABLONCI NAD NISOU,** Museum of Glass & Jewelry in Jablonec Nad Nisou, U Muzea 398/4, Jablonec nad Nisou, 466 01 Czech Republic. Tel 420-483-369-011; Fax 420-483-369-012; Email info@msb-jablonec.cz; Web: www.msb-jablonec.cz; *Dir* Milada Valeckova
Open Tues - Sun 9 AM - 5 PM; July - Aug daily 9 AM - 5 PM; Admis adults 80 CZK, children 6 - 15, students, seniors & disabled persons 50 CZK; Estab 1904; Library with 11,500 vols
Collections: Bohemian glass making & jewelry, exhibitions

LIBEREC

M **OBLASTNI GALERIE V LIBERCI,** Regional Art Gallery in Liberec, U Tiskarny 81/1, Liberec, 460 01 Czech Republic. Tel 420-485-106-325; Fax 420-485-106-321; Email oblgal@ogl.cz; Web: www.ogl.cz; *Dir* Jan Randacek; *Deputy Dir* Marcela Vostrakova
Open Tues, Wed, Fri - Sun 10 AM - 6 PM, Thurs 10 AM - 9 PM, cl Mon; Admis adults 50 CZK, students, children over 10 & pensioners 20 CZK, children under 10 free; Estab 1945; Regional, collecting Museum of European Art
Collections: Paintings, drawings, graphic arts & sculptures, 16th - 19th century Dutch paintings, 19th century French, German & Austrian paintings, 20th century Czech art

LITOMERICE

M **SEVEROCESKA GALERIE VYTVARNEHO UMENI V LITOMERICICH,** North Bohemian Gallery of Fine Arts in Litomerice, Michalska 7, Litomerice, 412-01 Czech Republic. Tel 416-732-382; Fax 416-732-383; Email info@galerie-ltm.cz; Web: www.galerie-ltm.cz; *Dir* Jan Stibr, PhD
Open April - Sep Tues - Sun 9 AM - noon & 1 - 6 PM, cl Mon; Oct - Mar Tues - Sun 9 AM - noon & 1 PM - 5 PM, cl Mon; Admis adults 50 CZK, students & seniors 25 CZK, children 6 - 12 10 CZK, children under 6 free; Estab 1956; Early art colls from the 13th-16th centuries, Baroque art colls & art of the 19th-21st centuries, Naiv art, works from the Litomerice area & Northwest Bohemia, works of leading artists in Czech fine art; Average Annual Attendance: 17,000
Special Subjects: Baroque Art, Drawings, Etchings & Engravings, Graphics, Landscapes, Medieval Art, Painting-European, Prints, Religious Art, Renaissance Art, Sculpture
Collections: Gothic Art Coll, Renaissance Art coll, Baroque Art coll, art of the 19th, 20th & 21st centuries, Naiv Art coll
Publications: Exhib catalogs
Activities: Classes for adults & children; lects open to the pub; 218 vis lectrs per yr; concerts; tours; lending of original objects of art to mus & art galleries in Czech Republic & abroad; mus shop sells exhib catalogs

PRAGUE

M **CESKE MUZEUM VYTVARNYCH UMENI V PRAZE,** Czech Museum of Fine Arts in Prague, 19-21 Husova St, Old Town Prague, 110 00 Czech Republic. Tel 420-222-220-218; Fax 420-222-221-190; Email muzeum@cmvu.cz; Web: www.cmvu.cz; *Dir* Ivan Neumann; *Deputy Dir & Chief Cur* Richard Drury
Open Tues - Sun 10 AM - 6 PM, cl Mon; Admis adults 50 CZK, concessions 20 CZK, children under 6 free; Estab 1963; dedicated to collecting, documenting and promoting 20th & 21st century Czech artworks
Collections: Series of work acquired at the beginning of the 1960s, 19th century art and the turn of the 20th century; realist trends

M **GALERIE HLAVNIHO MESTA PRAHY,** City Gallery Prague, Old Town Sq 605/13, Prague, 110 00 Czech Republic. Tel 420 224 828 245; Email office@ghmp.cz; Web: ghmp.cz; *Dir* Magdalena Jurikova
Open Tues - Sun 10 AM - 6 PM, cl Mon; Admis adult 120 CZK, children & students 60 CZK, seniors over 65 30 CZK, children under 10 free; Estab 1963;

Modern & contemporary art institution exhibiting in eight buildings across the City of Prague
Collections: Pragensia work, 19th & 20th centuries Czech artists
Activities: Classes for children; lects open to pub; concerts; tours; Museum shop sells books & magazines

M **GALERIE RUDOLFINUM,** Rudolfinum Gallery, Alsovo Nabrezi 12, Prague, 110 01 Czech Republic. Tel 420-227-059-205; Fax 420-222-319-293; Email galerie@rudolfinum.org; Web: www.galerierudolfinum.cz; *Dir* Petr Nedoma; *Registrar & Cur* David Korecky
Open Tues - Wed & Fri - Sun 10 AM - 6 PM, Thurs 10 AM - 8 PM, cl Mon; Admis 130 CZK, reduced 80 CZK, children under 15 free; Estab 1994; Contemporary art gallery housed in a historic Neo-Renaissance building

M **MUCHOVO MUZEUM PRAHA,** Mucha Museum Prague, Kaunicky palac, Panska 7 Prague, 110 00 Czech Republic. Tel 420 224 216 415; Email museum@mucha.cz; Web: www.mucha.cz; *Pres* John Mucha; *Dir* Sarah Mucha; *Cur* Tomoko Sato
Open daily 10 AM - 6 PM; Admis adults 240 CZK, seniors, students & children 160 CZK; Estab 1998
Collections: Extensive overview of the artistic work of Alphonse Mucha

M **MUSEUM KAMPA,** U Sovovych mlynu 503/2, Prague, 118 00 Czech Republic. Tel 420 257 286 144; Email jana.pelouchova@museumkampa.cz; Web: www.museumkampa.cz; *Chm* Jiri Pospisil; *Dir* Jan Smetana; *Chief Cur* Helena Musilova; *Head Colls & Exhibs Dept* Sandra Prusa; *Head Lect Dept* Eliska Pychova; *Pub Rels* Jana Pelouchova
Open Mon - Sun 10 AM - 6 PM; Gen admis adults 350 CZK, students 7 seniors 250 CZK, under 6 no charge; Estab 1999; Contemporary art museum housed in a restored 10th century mill.
Income: Financed by the Jan and Meda Mladek Foundation
Special Subjects: Painting-European, Photography
Collections: 19th - 21st century contemporary art, Central European art
Activities: Educ progs; lects open to pub

M **NARODNI GALERIE V PRAZE,** National Gallery in Prague, Kinsky Palace, Staromestske nam 12 Prague, 110 15 Czech Republic. Tel 420 224 301 122; Fax 420 222 324 641; Email info@ngprague.cz; Web: www.ngprague.cz; *Dir* Jiri Fajt; *Chief Cur* Adam Budak
Open Tues - Sun 10 AM - 6 PM, cl Mon; Gen admis 300 CZK, reduced 150 CZK, children under 6 free; Estab 1796; Library with 75,000 vols
Collections: Architecture, Czech sculpture of the 19th and 20th century, French and European art of the 19th and 20th century, Old Czech art, Old European Art, graphic art, modern art, Oriental art, European Old Masters, Bohemian Art from the Era of Emperor Rudolf II to the Close of the Baroque, Medieval Art in Bohemia and Central Europe (1200 - 1550), 19th and 20th Century Art, Asian Art
Activities: Classes for adults & children; lectrs open to pub; lects for mems only; 85 vis lectrs per yr; concerts; gallery talks; fellowships offered; mus shop sells books, prints, reproductions, slides

M **UMELECKOPRUMYSLOVE MUZEUM V PRAZE,** Museum of Decorative Arts in Prague, Ulice 17 listopadu 2, Prague, 110 00 Czech Republic. Tel 420 778 543 901; Email info@upm.cz; Web: www.upm.cz; *Dir* Dr Helena Koenigsmarkova; *Chief Cur* Radim Vondracek
Museum closed for renovation; Estab 1885; Art Library with 150,000 vols; permanent coll; stories of material; Mem: The Society of Friends of the Museum of Decorative Arts in Prague
Income: Financed by the Ministry of Culture of the Czech Republic
Library Holdings: Auction Catalogs, Book Volumes, CD-ROMs, DVDs, Exhibition Catalogs, Original Documents, Pamphlets, Periodical Subscriptions, Slides
Special Subjects: Ceramics, Costumes, Decorative Arts, Flasks & Bottles, Furniture, Glass, Graphics, Historical Material, Jewelry, Metalwork, Mosaics, Oriental Art, Painting-American, Painting-Australian, Painting-British, Painting-Canadian, Painting-Dutch, Painting-European, Painting-Flemish, Painting-French, Painting-German, Painting-Israeli, Painting-Italian, Painting-Japanese, Painting-New Zealand, Painting-Polish, Painting-Russian, Painting-Scandinavian, Painting-Spanish, Photography, Porcelain, Posters, Prints, Religious Art, Renaissance Art, Silver, Tapestries, Textiles, Woodcuts
Collections: European applied art from 12th to 21st century, collections of glass, ceramics, china, furniture, textiles, tapestries, gold & silver work, iron, ivory, clocks, prints, posters, photography, contemporary design, fashion, toys, porcelain, jewelry, watches, UPM holdings Mus of Textile in Ceska Skalice, 20th century furniture, Kamenice nad Lipou
Activities: Classes for adults & children; lects open to pub; tours; gallery talks; awards; schols offered; lends original objects of art to museums worldwide; originates traveling exhibs to museums worldwide; mus shop sells books, magazines, original art, reproductions, prints & other items; Josef Sudek Gallery, The Chateau at Kamenice nad Lipou

M **ZIDOVSKE MUZEUM V PRAZE,** Jewish Museum in Prague, U Stare skoly 1, Prague, 110 01 Czech Republic. Tel 420 221 749 211; Fax 420 222 749 300; Email office@jewishmuseum.cz; Web: www.jewishmuseum.cz; *Dir* Dr Leo Pavlat; *Deputy Dir* Michal Frankl
Open Sun - Fri 9 AM - 4:30 PM, summer 9 AM - 6 PM, cl Sat & Jewish holidays; Admis fee adults 300 CZK, children 6 - 15 yrs & students under 26 yrs 200 CZK, under 6 yrs free; Library with 100,000 vols
Special Subjects: Judaica
Collections: Historical archival materials of Bohemian & Moravian Jewish religious communities, library of ancient books with a coll of Hebrew manuscripts, children's drawings & works of painters from the Terezin concentration camp, silver from Czech synagogues, textiles from synagogues of historic interest, Holocaust memorial
Activities: Classes for children; 50 vis lectrs per yr; concerts; gallery talks

DENMARK

AALBORG

M **KUNSTEN MUSEUM OF MODERN ART,** Kong Christians Alle 50, Aalborg, 9000 Denmark. Tel 45 99 82 41 00; Email kunsten@aalborg.dk; Web: www.kunsten.dk; *Dir* Gitte Orskou
Open Tues - Sun 10 AM - 5 PM, cl Mon; Admis adults 95 DKK, students 50 DKK, children up to 18 free; Estab 1879, building inaugurated 1972; Museum contains 3,700 art works; Average Annual Attendance: 70,000
Income: Self-governing institution with state, county & municipal funding
Purchases: Modern & contemporary art
Collections: Collection of graphics, painting & sculpture from 1900 to the present, Danish and international
Exhibitions: 8-10 spec exhibitions annually
Publications: Approx 4 exhibition catalogs annually
Activities: Concerts; gallery talks; tours; exten prog to school district of Nordjylland County; traveling exhibition within school district of Nordjylland County; sales shop sells books, reproductions, scarves, T-shirts, magazines, prints; occasional exhibitions for children; occasional workshops for children

AARHUS

M **AROS AARHUS KUNSTMUSEUM,** ARoS Aarhus Art Museum, Aros Alle 2, Aarhus, 8000 Denmark. Tel 45 87 30 66 00; Email info@aros.dk; Web: www.aros.dk; *Dir* Erlend Hoyersten; *Chief Cur* Lise Pennington
Open Tues, Thurs - Sun 10 AM - 5 PM, Wed 10 AM - 10 PM, cl Mon; Admis adults 120 DKK, students & visitors under 28 yrs 90 DKK; children under 18 free; Library with 1000 vols
Collections: Danish & European art, Danish Golden ages, Danish modernism-Asger Jorn, Richard Mortensen, contemp Danish & international, Jeff Koons, Gilbert & George

CHARLOTTENLUND

M **ORDRUPGAARDSAMLINGEN,** Ordrupgaard Museum, Vilvordevej 110, Charlottenlund, 2920 Denmark. Tel 45 39 64 11 83; Email ordrupgaard@ordrupgaard.dk; Web: ordrupgaard.dk; *Dir* Anne-Birgitte Fonsmark
Open Tues, Thurs & Fri 1 PM - 5 PM, Wed 1 PM - 9 PM, Sat, Sun & holidays 11 AM - 5 PM, cl Mon; Finn Juhl's House: Sat, Sun & holidays 11 AM - 4:45 PM; Admis adults 110 DKK, students 100 DKK, visitors under18 free; Masterpieces by French impressionists; Danish art from the 19th and 20th centuries; art museum set in a large, lovely park; the famous Danish architect Finn Fuhl's house
Library Holdings: Auction Catalogs, Book Volumes, Exhibition Catalogs, Kodachrome Transparencies, Manuscripts, Memorabilia, Photographs, Video Tapes
Special Subjects: Architecture, Painting-French, Painting-Scandinavian, Period Rooms
Collections: Wilhelm Hansen Collection, paintings by Cezanne, Corot, Courbet, Degas, Delacroix, Gauguin, Manet, Pissarro, Renoir, Sisley & other French & Danish artists from the 19th century & the beginning of the century
Activities: Classes for children; Lects open to pub; lects for mems only; gallery talks; mus shop sells books, magazines, reproductions, prints & Souvenirs

COPENHAGEN

L **DANMARKS KUNSTBIBLIOTEK,** Danish National Art Library, Nyhavn 2, Postbnoks 1053 Copenhagen, 1007 Denmark. Tel 45 33 74 48 02; Email dkb@kunstbib.dk; Web: www.kunstbib.dk; *Dir* Steen Sondergaard Thomsen
Open Mon - Thurs 11 AM - 5:30 PM, Fri 11 AM - 4 PM, July & August Mon - Fri 11 AM - 4 PM, cl weekends & pub holidays; No admis fee; Estab 1754; Circ 80,000
Income: Government financed
Library Holdings: Book Volumes 175,000, Other Holdings Architectural Drawings 350,000, Photographs 350,000, Slides 170,000
Activities: Classes adults; docent training; lects open to pub, 3 vis lectrs per yr; lending of original objects of art of exhib on architecture

M **DESIGNMUSEUM DANMARK,** Danish Design Museum, Bredgade 68, Copenhagen, 1260 Denmark. Tel 33 18-56 56; Fax 33 18 56 66; Email info@designmuseum.dk; Web: www.designmuseum.dk; *Dir* Anne-Louise Sommer; *Head, Library & Research* Lars Dybdahl; *Head, Exhibs & Colls* Christian Holmsted Olesen; *Cur* Ulla Houkjaer
Open Tues, Thurs, Fri - Sun 10 AM - 6 PM, Wed 10 AM - 9 PM; cl Mon; Gen admis 100 DKK, students & visitors under 26 free; Estab 1890; Library with 100,000 vols
Library Holdings: Auction Catalogs, Book Volumes, Exhibition Catalogs, Periodical Subscriptions
Special Subjects: Architecture, Art Education, Art History, Carpets & Rugs, Ceramics, Costumes, Decorative Arts, Embroidery, Furniture, Glass, Graphics, Interior Design, Laces, Porcelain, Posters, Pottery, Silver, Tapestries, Textiles, Asian Art, Baroque Art, Oriental Art, Renaissance Art
Collections: Chinese and Japanese art and handicrafts, European decorative and applied art from the Middle Ages to present - bookbindings, carpets and tapestries, furniture, jewelry, porcelain and pottery, silverware, glass and textiles

M **GLYPTOTEKET,** Ny Carlsberg Glyptotek, Dantes Plads 7, Copenhagen, 1556 Denmark. Tel 45 33 41 81 41; Fax 45 33 91 20 58; Email info@glyptoteket.dk; Web: www.glyptoteket.dk; *Dir* Flemming Friborg; *Deputy Dir* Louise Rue Moos; *Head of Colls* Rune Frederiksen
Open Tues, Wed, Fri - Sun 11 AM - 6 PM, Thurs 11 AM - 10 PM, cl Mon; Admis adults 95 DKK, visitors under 27 50 DKK, children under 18 & Tues free; Art museum built around the personal coll of Carl Jacobsen; Average Annual Attendance: 350,000

Collections: Danish & French paintings & sculptures from 19th & 20th centuries, Egyptian, Etruscan, Greek & Roman sculpture
Activities: Mus shop sells books, magazines, reproductions

M **KOEBENHAVNS MUSEUM,** Museum of Copenhagen, Vesterbrogade 59, Copenhagen, 1620 Denmark. Tel 45 24 94 96 12; Email museum@kff.kk.dk; Web: www.cphmuseum.kk.dk; *Dir* Louise Jacobsen
Museum closed for relocation; Estab 1891; Copenhagen's more than 800 yrs long history
Collections: Objects, paintings and models from the history of Copenhagen

M **KONGERNES SAMLING,** The Royal Danish Collection, Rosenborg Castle, Oster Voldgade 4A Copenhagen, 1350K Denmark. Tel 45 33 15 32 86; Email kosa@kosa.dk; Web: www.kongernessamling.dk; *Mus Dir* Jorgen Selmer; *Dir Chamberlain* Henning Fode; *Senior Cur* Jorgen Hein; *Asst Cur* Peter Kristiansen; *Cur* Alex Harms
Open Rosenborg: Jan - Apr & Nov - mid-Dec Tues - Sun 11 AM - 2 PM, May - mid-June & Sept - Oct daily 10 AM - 4 PM, mid-June - Aug daily 9 AM - 5 PM; Amalienborg: Jan - Apr & Nov - Dec Tues - Sun 11 AM - 4 PM, May - Oct daily 10 AM - 4 PM; Admis Rosenborg: adults 105 DKK, students 70 DKK, children 17 & under free; Amalienborg: adults 75 DKK, students 55 DKK, children 17 & under free; Estab 1833; Museum of Danish royal history from 1600-1850 located on the grounds of two castles; Average Annual Attendance: 250,000
Library Holdings: Auction Catalogs, Book Volumes, CD-ROMs, Exhibition Catalogs, Kodachrome Transparencies, Original Documents, Pamphlets, Periodical Subscriptions, Photographs, Prints
Special Subjects: Historical Material
Collections: Danish royal crown jewels & regalia, arms, apparel, jewelry & furniture from period 1470-1863
Publications: Guidebooks
Activities: Concerts; lending of original art to other mus; Mus shop sells books, prints & souvenirs

M **NATIONALMUSEET,** National Museum of Denmark, Prinsens Palae, Ny Vestergade 10 Copenhagen, 1471 Denmark. Tel 45 33 13 44 11; Fax 45 33 47 33 33; Web: natmus.dk; *Dir* Per Kristian Madsen
Open Tues - Sun 10 AM - 5 PM, cl Mon; Admis adult 75 DKK, adult & child 60 DKK, children under 18 free; Museum of Danish cultural history
Collections: Museum has 5 divisions, including Danish historical collection, folk museum, ethnographic collection, classical antiquities collection, royal coin & medal collection, Danish Prehistory (13000 BC - 1050 AD), Middle Ages & Renaissance Denmark (1050-1660), 18th Century Denmark, Stories of Denmark: 1660-2000, The Royal Collection of Coins & Medals, The Collection of Egyptian and Classical Antiquities, Ethnographic Collection, The Children's Museum, The National Museum's Victorian Home
Activities: Classes for children; mus shop sells books, reproductions, prints

M **STATENS MUSEUM FOR KUNST,** National Gallery of Denmark, Solvgade 48-50, Copenhagen, 1307 Denmark. Tel 45 33 74 84 94; Fax 45 33 74 84 04; Email smk@smk.dk; Web: www.smk.dk; *Dir* Mikkel Bogh
Open Tues & Thurs - Sun 10 AM - 5 PM, Wed 10 AM - 8 PM, cl Mon; Admis adults 110 DKK, one adult & one child 90 DKK, visitors under 30 85 DKK, visitors under 18 free; Estab 1896; Average Annual Attendance: 350,000
Collections: Danish paintings and sculpture, various other works by 19th and 20th century Scandinavian artists, old masters of Italian, Flemish, Dutch and German Schools, modern French art, 700 years of art history, from 1300-today
Exhibitions: LA Ring on the Edge of the World; Andre Derain
Publications: Publications for each exhib
Activities: Classes for adults & children; lects open to pub; concerts; gallery talks; tours; lending of original objects of art to domestic & foreign museums; book traveling exhibs; originates traveling exhibs; mus shop sells books, magazines & prints; junior mus

M **THORVALDSENSMUSEUM,** Thorvaldsens Museum, Bertel Thorvaldsens Plads 2, Copenhagen, 1213 Denmark. Tel 45-33-32-15-32; Email thm@thorvaldsensmuseum.dk; Web: www.thorvaldsensmuseum.dk; *Dir* Stig Miss; *Cur* William Gelius; *Cur* Margrethe Floryan; *Cur* Kristine Bulow Clausen; *Head of Communs* Bettina Weiland; *Head of Educ* Line Esbjorn
Open Tues - Sun 10 AM - 5 PM, cl Mon; Admis adults 50 DKK, youth & children under 18 & Wed free; Estab 1848; Sculptures, paintings, antiquities
Special Subjects: Drawings, Sculpture
Collections: Sculpture & drawings by Bertel Thorvaldsen (1770 - 1844) & his collections of contemporary paintings, drawings & prints, Painting coll containing works by leading European & Scandinavian painters from Thorvaldsen's own time, Thorvaldsen's Collections of ancient artifacts, gems & coins
Activities: Classes for adults & children; lects open to pub; concerts; gallery talks; tours; mus shop sells books, prints, slides, plaster casts

EBELTOFT

M **GLASMUSEET EBELTOFT,** Ebeltoft Glass Museum, Strandvejen 8, Ebeltoft, 8400 Denmark. Tel 45 86 34 17 99; Fax 45 86 34 60 60; Email glasmuseet@glasmuseet.dk; Web: www.glasmuseet.dk; *Exec Dir* Dan Molgaard; *Exhib Coordr* Sandra F Blach; *Head Pub Rels & Communs* Pia S Bittner
Open Jan - Mar Thurs - Sun 10 AM - 4 PM; April - June daily 10 AM - 5 PM; July - mid-Aug daily 10 AM - 6 PM; mid-Aug - Oct daily 10 AM - 5 PM; Nov - Dec Thurs - Sun 10 AM - 4 PM; Admis adults 175 DKK, children 50 DKK; Estab 1985; Contemporary art in glass; Average Annual Attendance: 40,000
Library Holdings: Auction Catalogs, Book Volumes, Exhibition Catalogs, Periodical Subscriptions
Special Subjects: Crafts, Decorative Arts, Glass, Historical Material
Collections: More than 1500 glass objects from over 700 Danish & international artists
Exhibitions: Solo & group exhibs throughout the yr
Publications: Exhib catalogs
Activities: Classes for children; lects open to pub, 4-6 vis lectrs per yr; concerts; gallery talks; tours; originate traveling exhibs worldwide; mus shop sells books, magazines & original art, works of glass

FAABORG

M **FAABORG MUSEUM,** Gronnegade 75, Faaborg, 5600 Denmark. Tel 45 62 61 06 45; Fax 45 62 61 06 65; Email info@faaborgmuseum.dk; Web: www.faaborgmuseum.dk; *Dir* Gertrude Hvidberg-Hansen; *Cur* Gry Hedin
Open Nov - March 10 AM - 3 PM; April, May, Sept & Oct 10 AM - 4 PM; June - Aug 10 - 4 & Wed 10 - 6; Admis adults 70 DKK, concessions 60 DKK, students 35 DKK, children & under 26 free; Museum housed in a Carl Petersen design building
Special Subjects: Painting-European, Furniture, Sculpture, Architecture
Collections: Funen-based painting, sculpture, architecture & furniture design made from 1885-1925

HORSENS

M **HORSENS KUNSTMUSEUM,** Horsens Art Museum, Carolinelundsvej 2, Horsens, 8700 Denmark. Tel 76 29 23 50; Fax 75 61 86 21; Email horsensmuseum@horsens.dk; Web: www.horsenskunstmuseum.dk; *Dir* Claus Hagedorn-Olsen
Open July - Aug daily 10 AM - 4PM, Sep - June Tues - Sun 11 PM - 4 PM, cl Mon; Admis adults 40 DKK, under 18 free; Estab 1984; Contemporary Danish art museum
Special Subjects: Painting-European, Sculpture, Architecture
Collections: Paintings, drawings and graphic works by Danish artist Michael Kvium, works by Christian Lemmerz, Erik Frandsen, Nina Sten-Knudsen and Lars Norgard, paintings from the Danish Golden Age of the 19th century, Danish Modernist works from the 1940's to the 1960's, international contemporary art

HUMLEBAEK

M **LOUISIANA MUSEUM OF MODERN ART,** Gammel Strandvej 13, Humlebaek, 3050 Denmark. Tel 45 4919 0719; Fax 45 4919 3505; Email curatorial@louisiana.dk; Web: www.louisiana.dk; *Dir* Poul Erik Tojner; *Cur* Kirsten Degel; *Cur* Kjeld Kjeldsen; *Cur* Anders Kold; *Cur* Marie Laurberg; *Cur* Tine Colstrup; *Cur* Mathias Ussing Seeberg
Open Tues - Fri 11 AM - 10 PM, Sat - Sun & pub holidays 11 AM - 6 PM, cl Mon; Admis adults 115 DKK, students 100 DKK, children under 18 & members free; Estab 1958; International modern art museum; Average Annual Attendance: 500,000
Special Subjects: Painting-American, Painting-European, Sculpture
Collections: Danish, international & modern art from 1950, including sculpture & paintings
Activities: Classes for children; concerts; cinema; theatre; lect for members only

ISHOJ

M **ARKEN MUSEUM FOR MODERNE KUNST,** ARKEN Museum of Modern Art, Skovvej 100, Ishoj, 2635 Denmark. Tel 45-43-54-02-22; Email info@arken.dk; Web: www.arken.dk; *Dir* Christian Gether
Open Tues, Thurs - Sun 10 AM - 5 PM, Wed 10 AM - 9 PM, cl Mon; Admis adults 110 DKK, students 90 DKK, children 17 & under free; Estab 1996
Collections: Danish, Nordic & international contemporary art

KOLDING

M **TRAPHOLT,** Trapholt, Museum of Modern Art and Design, Aeblehaven 23, Kolding, 6000 Denmark. Tel 45-76-30-05-30; Fax 45-76-30-05-33; Email kunstmuseum@trapholt.dk; Web: www.trapholt.dk; *Dir* Karen Gron; *Exhibs* Vera Westergaard; *Head of Colls* Sara Staunsager
Open Tues - Sun 10 AM - 5 PM, Wed 10 AM - 8 PM, cl Mon; Admis adults 100 DKK, seniors 80 DKK, students 50 DKK, under 18 free; Estab 1988; Modern art & design; Average Annual Attendance: 65,000
Collections: Danish furniture design, modern Danish visual art & sculpture from the 19th century to the present, ceramics, textiles & product designs

RODOVRE

M **HEERUP MUSEUM,** Kirkesvinget 1, Rodovre, 2610 Denmark. Tel 45 3637 8700; Email heerupmuseum@rk.dk; Web: www.heerup.dk; *Dir* Anni Lave Nielsen
Open Tues - Sun 11 AM - 4 PM, cl Mon; Admis adults 45 DKK, students, groups & senior citizens 30 DKK, children under 16 & members no charge
Collections: Works of Henry Heerup

SILKEBORG

M **MUSEUM JORN, SILKEBORG,** Gudenavej 7-9, Silkeborg, 8600 Denmark. Tel 45 8682 5388; Fax 45 8681 5131; Email info@museumjorn.dk; Web: www.museumjorn.dk; *Dir* Jacob Thage; *Cur* Karen Friis Herbsleb; *Cur* Lucas Haberkorn
Open late June - early Sept daily 10 AM - 5 PM; early Sept - early Dec Tues, Wed, Fri - Sun 10 AM - 5 PM, Thurs 10 AM - 9 PM, cl Mon; Admis adults 90 DKK, seniors 80 DKK, students 70 DKK, children under 18 free; Estab 1951
Collections: Danish and European works
Activities: Mus shop sells books, magazines, reproductions, souvenirs, toys, & prints

DOMINICAN REPUBLIC

SANTO DOMINGO

M **GALERIA NACIONAL DE BELLAS ARTES,** National Gallery of Fine Arts, Av Maximo Gomez esq Independencia, Santo Domingo, Dominican Republic. Tel 809-687-0504; Web: ganabasd.com; *Dir* Marianne de Tolentino
Open Tues, Wed & Fri 10 AM - 5 PM, Thurs 10 AM - 9 PM, Sat & Sun noon - 6 PM, cl Mon; No admis fee; Estab 1955; Fine arts housed in the renovated Palace of Fine Arts
Collections: Fine arts, including paintings and sculptures, from the Dominican Republic and abroad

M **MUSEO DE ARTE MODERNO,** Museum of Modern Art, Av Pedro Henriquez Urena, Plaza de la Cultura Juan Pablo Duarte Santo Domingo, Dominican Republic. Tel 809-685-2154; Web: cultura.gob.do; *Dir* Maria Elena Ditren
Open Tues - Sun 10 AM - 6 PM; Admis adults 50 DOP, students 20 DOP; Estab 1976; Average Annual Attendance: 125,000
Collections: More than 1000 pieces; paintings, drawings, sculptures, videos, architecture, models, engravings, photographs, Dominican, Caribbean and Latin American art

ECUADOR

QUITO

M **CENTRO DE ARTE CONTEMPORANEO,** Center for Contemporary Art, Montevideo y Luis Davila, Barrio de San Juan Quito, Ecuador. Tel 593 2 394 6990; Email mediacioncentrodeartec@gmail.com; Web: www.centrodeartecontemporaneo.gob.ec; *Dir* Maria Elena Machuca
Open Tues - Sun 9 AM - 5:30 PM; No admis fee; Contemporary art exhibition space
Collections: Contemporary art from Ecuador and Latin America

M **MUSEO DE ARTE COLONIAL,** Museum of Colonial Art, Calles Cuenca y Mejia, Quito, Ecuador. Tel 593 2 228 2297; Email museo.artecolonial@casadelacultura.gob.ec; Web: www.casadelacultura.gob.ec; Guido Diaz Navarrete
Open Tues - Sat 9:30 AM - 5 PM; Admis foreigners $2 USD, nationals $1 USD, seniors $.50, children under 12 free; Estab 1914
Collections: Art from the Escuela Quitena of the Colonial epoch - 17th, 18th and 19th century art and some contemporary art

EGYPT

ALEXANDRIA

M **GRAECO-ROMAN MUSEUM,** 5 Sharia al-Mathaf ar-Romani, Alexandria, Egypt. Tel (03) 487 6434; Web: www.sca-egypt.org; *Head, Mus Section* Ahmed Sharaf
Currently closed for renovations; Estab 1892; Library with 15,000 vols
Collections: 40,000 piece collection with sculptures, mosaics, woodwork, and coins from the Byzantine, Greek and Roman eras

ASWAN

M **NUBIA MUSEUM,** El Fanadek St, Aswan, 81111 Egypt. Tel 20 97 319 333; Fax 20 97 317 998; Web: www.sca-egypt.org; *Dir* Ossama Abdel-Meguid
Open winter 9 AM - 1 PM & 5 PM - 9 PM; summer 9 AM - 1 PM & 6 PM - 10 PM; Admis adults 60 EGP, children 30 EGP; Estab 1997; Cultural history museum founded in cooperation with UNESCO
Collections: Prehistoric Nubian and Egyptian artifacts, Coptic & Islamic art, pottery, furniture, jewelry, clothing & armor

CAIRO

M **COPTIC MUSEUM,** 3 Sharia Mar Girgis, Old Cairo Cairo, Egypt. Tel 20 2 2362 8766; Email info@coptic-cairo.com; Web: www.coptic-cairo.com; *Dir* Mervet Megalli
Open daily 9 AM - 5 PM; Admis foreign adults 40 EGP, foreign students 20 EGP, Egyptian adults 2 EGP, Egyptian students 1 EGP; Estab 1910; Library with 6500 vols
Special Subjects: Antiquities-Byzantine, Antiquities-Egyptian, Archaeology, Religious Art
Collections: Coptic art dating back to Egypt's Christian era, architecture, bone, ebony, frescos, glass, icons, ivory, manuscripts, metalwork, pottery, sculpture, textiles, woodcarvings

M **MUSEUM OF EGYPTIAN ANTIQUITIES,** Midan El Tahrir, Cairo, 11511 Egypt. Tel 20 112 152 0515; Email egyptianmuseum@hotmail.com; Web: www.egyptianmuseum.gov.eg; *Dir* Sabah Abdel-Razek
Open daily 9 AM - 7 PM, 9 AM - 5 PM during Ramadan; Admis foreign adults 60 EGP, foreign students 30 EGP, Egyptian adults 4 EGP, Egyptian students 2 EGP; additional charges for the Royal Mummies Room & Centennial Gallery; Estab 1902; Library with 39,000 vols; 160,000 object in 107 halls covering 5,000 years of Egyptian history
Special Subjects: Antiquities-Egyptian
Collections: Ancient Egyptian art from prehistoric times through 6th century AD (excluding Coptic & Islamic periods), tombs & pharaonic antiquities, papyrus & coins, sculptures, busts & statues

M **MUSEUM OF ISLAMIC ART,** Midan Bab al-Khalq, Cairo, 11638 Egypt. Tel 02 2390 1520; Web: www.sca-egypt.org; *Dir* Ahmed El-Shoky
Open Mon - Thurs, Sat & Sun 9 AM - 5 PM, Fri 9 AM - noon & 2 PM - 5 PM; Admis adults 50 EGP, children 30 EGP; Estab 1881; Museum maintains library with 14,000 volumes
Collections: Works of art showing evolution of Islamic art from the 7th - 19th centuries, ceramics, textiles, carpets, metalwork, carved wood, stone artifacts, funerary art, epigraphy, calligraphy, geometry, astronomy & medicine
Publications: Islamic Archaeological studies, 5 vols

GIZA

M **GRAND EGYPTIAN MUSEUM,** El Remaya Sq, Giza, Egypt. Tel 202 33 776 893; Fax 202 33 777 263; Email administration@gem.gov.eg; Web: www.gem.gov.eg; *Dir* Tarek Taufik
Under construction; expected opening in 2018; 480,000 sq ft site with library, research center, restoration laboratories & children's museum neighboring the Giza Pyramids
Collections: Egyptian antiquities, pharaonic history

EL SALVADOR

SAN SALVADOR

M **MUSEO DE ARTE DE EL SALVADOR,** El Salvador Museum of Art, Final Avenida la Revolucion, Colonia San Benito San Salvador, El Salvador. Tel 503 2243-6099; Fax 503 2243-1726; Email informacion.marte@gmail.com; Web: marte.org.sv; *Exec Dir* Roberto Galicia; *Prog Dir* Rafael Alas; *Educ Prog Dir* Violeta Renderos
Open Tues - Sun 10 AM - 6 PM, cl Mon; Admis adults 1.50 SVC, students 0.50 SVC, under 12 and seniors free; Estab 2003
Collections: Three exhibit halls dedicated to temporal national and international work, Great Hall filled with Salvadoran paintings, MARTE's collection mainly formed of Salvadoran works (265)
Exhibitions: Artist of the month from collection
Publications: One pub per yr
Activities: Classes for adults & children; docent training; lects open to pub; 6 vis lectrs per yr; concerts; tours; mus shop sells prints, jewelry, textiles & accessories of local & international

ENGLAND

BATH

M **AMERICAN MUSEUM IN BRITAIN,** Claverton Manor, Bath, BA2 7BD England. Tel 44 0 1225 460 503; Fax 44 0 1225 469 160; Email enquiries@americanmuseum.org; Web: americanmuseum.org; *Dir* Richard Wendorf
Open mid-March - Oct Tues - Sun noon - 5 PM, cl Mon accept Aug & bank holidays; Christmas season late Nov - mid Dec noon - 4:30 PM; Admis adults 11 GBP, seniors over 60 & students 9.50 GBP, children 5 - 18 6.50 GBP, family 28.50 GBP; Estab 1961; Regency Manor House built in 1820; Average Annual Attendance: 40,000
Library Holdings: Auction Catalogs 400, Audio Tapes 60, Book Volumes approx 10,000, CD-ROMs, Compact Disks, DVDs, Exhibition Catalogs, Manuscripts, Photographs 500, Records 80, Slides 400, Video Tapes 20
Collections: American decorative arts from 17th to 19th centuries, Early printed maps
Publications: America in Britain jour yearly; newsletter biannually
Activities: Classes for adults & children; docent training; lects open to pub, 4 vis lectrs per yr; concerts; gallery talks; tours; original objects of art lent to other mus; mus shop sells books, original art

M **HOLBURNE MUSEUM OF ART,** Great Pulteney St, Bath, Avon BA2 4DB England. Tel 44-1225 388569; Fax (1225) 333121; Email enquiries@holburne.org; Web: www.bath.ac.uk/Holburne; *Dir* Jennifer Scott; *Cur* Amina Wright
Open Mon - Sun 10 AM - 5 PM, Sun 11 AM - 5 PM; No admis fee; Estab 1916
Collections: Paintings by 17th & 18th century masters, including Gainsborough, Turner, British & Continental, fine art, porcelain & silver
Activities: Educ prog; classes for adults & children; docent training; lects open to pub; 30 vis lectrs per yr; gallery talks; tours; concerts; originates traveling exhibs; mus shop sells books, reproductions, prints

M **VICTORIA ART GALLERY,** Bridge St, Bath, BA2 4AT England. Tel 44 (0) 1225 477233; Fax 44 (0) 1225 477231; Email victoria_enquiries@bathnes.gov.uk; Web: www.victoriagal.org.uk; *Mgr* Joe Benington; *Colls Mgr* Katherine Wall
Open Mon - Sun 10 AM - 5 PM; No admis fee; Estab 1900; a purpose-built facility with permanent collection & temporary exhibs; Average Annual Attendance: 105,000
Purchases: Howard Hodgkin: Silence 1997-2004, Oil on Wood; William Brooker: Pink Chair 1953, Oil on Canvas
Collections: British & European paintings from 17th to 20th century, English pottery, porcelain, antique glass

BIRMINGHAM

M **BIRMINGHAM MUSEUMS TRUST,** Birmingham Museums and Art Gallery, Chamberlain Sq, Birmingham, B3 3DH England. Tel (121) 348 8038; Fax (121) 303 1394; Email bmag.enquiries@birminghammuseums.org.uk; Web: www.birminghammuseums.org.uk; *Dir* Ellen MacAdam; *Dir of Collections* Toby Watley
Open Mon - Thurs & Sat & Sun 10 AM - 5 PM, Fri 10:30 AM - 5 PM; No admis fee, except for some temp exhibs; Estab 1867 Museum & Art Gallery; Average Annual Attendance: 682,000
Income: Birmingham City Council 6M pa, Arts Council England, plus Trusts & charities
Purchases: Purchases made according to published collecting policy
Collections: Fine and applied art, including English works since 17th century, foreign schools from Renaissance, Pre-Raphaelite works, silver, ceramics, coin, textile colls, Old and New World archeology, ethnography and local history colls, branch museums house furniture, machinery and applied arts, Pinto Collection of Treen, Staffordshire Hoard
Exhibitions: ongoing prog of temporary exhibs
Publications: world Art from Birmingham Museums & Art Gallery
Activities: Classes for children in school parties; family activities; lects open to pub; gallery talks; tours; mus shop sells books, reproductions, prints, jewelry & gifts

BRIGHTON

M **ROYAL PAVILION & MUSEUMS,** Brighton Museum & Art Gallery, Royal Pavilion Gardens, Brighton, East Sussex BN1 1EE England. Tel (03000) 290900; Fax 01273 292871; Email visitor.services@brighton-hove.gov.uk; Web: www.brightonmuseums.org.uk; *Cur Fine Art* Jenny Lund
Open Tues - Sun 10 AM - 5 PM, cl Mon; No admis fee for Brighton or Hove residents. Adults 5.20 GBP, children 3 GBP; Estab 1873 - mus, art gallery, library
Income: Brighton & City Council; owned by local authority, grants & funding
Special Subjects: Ceramics, Costumes, Crafts, Decorative Arts, Drawings, Ethnology, Furniture, Glass
Collections: Fashion & Style, World Art, 20th Century Art & Design, Mr Willett's Popular Pottery & Local History, Fine Art
Exhibitions: Ongoing temporary exhib programming
Activities: Classes for adults & children; lects open to public; Gallery talks; mus shop sells books, reproductions, prints, gen gifts & souvenirs

BRISTOL

M **BRISTOL MUSEUMS AND ART GALLERY,** Queen's Rd, Bristol, BS8 1RL England. Tel (0117) 922 3571; Fax (0117) 922 2047; Email general.museum@bristol.gov.uk; Web: www.bristol-city.gov.uk/museums; *Divisional Dir, Museums & Heritage* Hilary McGowan
Open Mon - Fri 10 AM - 5 PM, Sat & Sun 10 AM - 6 PM; No admis fee
Collections: Fine and applied arts of Great Britain, archaeological and ethnological collection, Oriental Art

CAMBRIDGE

M **UNIVERSITY OF CAMBRIDGE,** The Fitzwilliam Museum, Trumpington St, Cambridge, CB2 1RB England. Tel (01223) 332900; Fax (01223) 332923; Email fitzmuseum-enquiries@lists.cam.ac.uk; Web: www.fitzmuseum.cam.ac.uk; *Dir* Dr Timothy Potts; *Keeper of Applied Art* Dr Victoria Avery; *Sr Asst Keeper, Applied Art* Dr James Lin; *Keeper of Antiquities* Dr Lucilla Burn; *Sr Asst Keeper Antiquities* Julie Dawson; *Keeper of Coins and Medals* Dr Mark Blackburn; *Asst Keeper Coins and Medals* Dr Adrian Popescu; *Asst Dir & Keeper of Paintings, Drawings & Prints* David Scrase; *Sr Asst Keeper Paintings, Drawings & Prints* Jane Munro; *Sr Asst Keeper Prints* Craig Hartley; *Keeper of Manuscripts & Printed Books* Dr Stella Panayotova; *Asst Dir Central Serv* Kate Carreno; *Sr Asst Keeper Admin* Thyrza Smith; *Head of Educ* Julia Tozer; *Sr Asst Keeper Antiquities* Dr Sally Ann Ashton; *Asst Keeper Coins & Medals* Dr Martin Allen; *Asst Dir Conservation* Rupert Featherstone
Open Tues - Sat 10 AM - 5 PM, Sun & Bank Holidays Noon - 5 PM, cl Jan 1, Dec 24 - Dec 26 & Dec 31; No admis fee; Estab 1848; Mus & gallery; library with 300,000 vols; Average Annual Attendance: 300,000
Collections: European ceramics, Greek, Roman, western Asiatic & Egyptian antiquities, arms & armor, coins, drawings, furniture, illuminated manuscripts, manuscripts, paintings, prints, sculpture, textiles
Activities: Classes for adults & children; dramatic prog; lects open to pub; concerts; gallery talks; tours; lending of original objects of art; mus shop sells books, reproductions, stationery goods & jewelry

DONCASTER

M **DONCASTER MUSEUM AND ART GALLERY,** Chequer Rd, Doncaster, Yorks DN1 2AE England. Tel 1302-734293; Fax 1302 73 5409; Email museum@doncaster.gov.uk; Web: www.doncaster.gov.uk/museums; *Mus Mgr* C Dalton; *Mus Officer Art & Exhibs* Neil McGregor
Open Mon - Fri 10 AM - 4:30 PM, Sat & Sun 10:30 AM - 4 PM; cl Sun, New Year's Day, Good Friday, Christmas Day, Boxing Day; No admis fee; Estab 1909; 7 gallery areas with permanent and temporary exhibs; Average Annual Attendance: 78,000
Income: By local authority
Special Subjects: African Art, Antiquities-Roman, Archaeology, Ceramics, Coins & Medals, Costumes, Decorative Arts, Drawings, Etchings & Engravings, Glass, Jewelry, Laces, Landscapes, Maps, Marine Painting, Painting-British, Painting-Flemish, Painting-French, Painting-Italian, Painting-Russian, Pewter, Photography, Porcelain, Portraits, Posters, Pottery, Prints, Prints, Religious Art, Reproductions, Sculpture, Silver, Tapestries, Textiles, Watercolors, Woodcarvings, Woodcuts
Collections: European painting, ceramics and glass, silver and jewelry, The King's Own Yorkshire Light Infantry Regimental Collection, Archaeology & Natural History
Publications: The Don Pottery, 1801-1893 (March 2001)
Activities: Classes for adults & children; lects open to pub; 20 vis lectrs per yr; concerts; gallery talks; books traveling exhibs 5 per yr; mus shop sells books, prints

EAST MOLESEY

M **HISTORIC ROYAL PALACES,** Hampton Court Palace, East Molesey, Surrey KT8 9AU England. Tel 0844 482 7777 (from UK), 44 (0)20 3166 6000 (from outside UK); Email hamptoncourt@hrp.org.uk; *Palace Dir* Hugh Player; *Supt Royal Coll* Chris Stevens
Open Mar - Oct 25 Mon - Sun 10 AM - 6 PM; Oct 26 - Mar 28 Mon - Sun 10 AM - 4:30 PM; Admis adult 18.20 GBP, children 9:10 GBP, children under 5 free; Represents art, architecture & gardens from the Tudor Period to Georgian Period
Special Subjects: Woodcarvings
Collections: Paintings & tapestries, including Andrea Mantegna's 9 paintings of The Triumphs of Caesar
Activities: Classes for adults & children; dramatic progs; lects open to pub; tours; sales of books

KENDAL

M **ABBOT HALL ART GALLERY & MUSEUM OF LAKELAND LIFE & INDUSTRY,** Kendal, Cumbria LA9 5AL England. Tel (01539) 722464; Fax (01539) 722494; Email info@abbothall.org.uk; Web: www.abbothall.org.uk; *Dir* Edward King; *Deputy Dir* Cherrie Trelogan; *Head of Publicity & Mktg* Sandy Kitching; *Head of Finance & Admin* Beryl Tulley
Open Jan 17 - Dec 20 Mon - Sat 10:30 AM - 5 PM; July & Aug Sun noon - 4 PM; Nov - Feb 10:30 AM - 4 PM; Admis adults 9 GBP; Estab 1962; 18th house beside the river bank, 18 rooms plus active modern and contemporary exhib prog; Average Annual Attendance: 35,000
Library Holdings: Cards, Exhibition Catalogs, Pamphlets, Photographs, Sculpture
Collections: Gallery provides changing exhibitions of local and international interest, houses permanent colls of 18th century furniture, paintings and objects d'art, modern paintings, sculpture, drawings, museum features working and social life of the area, 18th century portraits, Esp Romney, watercolors & drawings, including Ruskin, Constable, Turner, lake district landscapes, modern British art, Post-Lucian Freud, Bridget Riley, Paula Rego, Bridget Riley
Publications: Exhibition Catalogues
Activities: Classes for children; lects open to public; books

LEEDS

M **LEEDS MUSEUMS & GALLERIES,** Leeds City Museum, Millennium Sq, Leeds, LS2 8BH England. Tel 0113 224 3732; Email city.museum@leeds.gov.uk; Web: www.leeds.gov.uk/museumsandgalleries; *Head Museums & Galleries* John Roles; *Cur Exhibs* Ruth Leach; *Asst Cur* Marek Romaniszyn; *Prin Keeper* Sam Flavin; *Learning & Access Officer* Natalie Burns
Open Tues - Fri 10 AM - 5 PM, Sat & Sun 11 AM - 5 PM, cl Mon; No admis fee; Estab 1819
Income: Local Government
Library Holdings: Auction Catalogs, Photographs, Prints, Sculpture
Special Subjects: Antiquities-Greek, Antiquities-Oriental, Architecture, Art Education, Art History, Asian Art, Baroque Art, Carpets & Rugs, Cartoons, Ceramics, Costumes, Crafts, Decorative Arts, Dolls, Drawings, Embroidery, Furniture, Glass, Gold, Historical Material, Ivory, Jade, Jewelry, Landscapes, Manuscripts, Oriental Art, Painting-American, Painting-British, Painting-Dutch, Painting-European, Painting-French, Painting-Italian, Painting-Spanish, Period Rooms, Pewter, Porcelain, Pottery, Prints, Religious Art, Renaissance Art, Restorations, Sculpture, Silver, Tapestries, Textiles, Watercolors
Collections: Natural, industrial, contemporary, fine & decorative arts
Activities: Classes for adults & children; concerts; gallery talks; tours; mus shop sells books, reproductions, prints

M **Leeds Art Gallery,** The Headrow, Leeds, LS1 3AA England. Tel 0113 247 8248; Fax 0113 244 9689; Email city.art.gallery@leeds.gov.uk; *Learning & Access Officer* Amanda Phillips; *Cur Exhibs* Sarah Brown
Open Mon & Tues, Thurs - Sat 10 AM - 5 PM, Wed Noon - 5 PM, Sun 1 - 5 PM; No admis fee; Estab 1888; Gallery with outstanding collections of British 19th & 20th centuries & changing exhib progs; Average Annual Attendance: 500,000
Income: Local Government
Collections: English watercolors, English & European paintings of 19th century, modern British paintings & sculpture
Exhibitions: Temporary exhibition programme
Activities: Educ prog; classes for adults & children; Artspace interactive family zone; lects open to pub; gallery talks; tours; Exten prog Picture Lending Scheme; original objects of art lent to individual & corporate subscribers; originate traveling exhibs; mus shop sells book, reproductions, prints, postcards, souvenirs & other items

M **Lotherton Hall,** Off Collier Ln, Aberford Leeds, LS25 3EB England. Tel 0113 378 2959; Fax 0113 281 2100; Email lotherton.hall@leeds.gov.uk; *Keeper* Michael Thaw; *Learning & Access Officer* Dionne Matthews; *Asst Community Cur* Stephanie Davies
Open Mar - Oct daily 10 AM - 5 PM, Nov - Feb daily 10 AM - 4 PM; last admission 45 minutes before cl; Admis 5.50 GBP, concessions 4.40 GBP; Historic house open as mus with gardens; Gascoigne family coll; special costume; Average Annual Attendance: 30,000
Income: Local Government
Collections: Gascoigne Collection of 17th to 20th century paintings, ceramics, silver, furniture, jewelry costumes, British historic furniture; silver; ceramics

Activities: Classes for adults & children; dramatic progs; six lectrs per yr; concerts; gallery talks; tours; mus shop sells books, reproductions, prints

LEICESTER

M **NEW WALK MUSEUM AND ART GALLERY,** 53 New Walk, Leicester, LE1 7EA England. Tel 0116 225 4900; Email museums@leicester.gov.uk; Web: www.leicester.gov.uk/museums; *Head Museums & Heritage* Sarah Leavitt; *Asst Dir Museums, Libraries & Arts* Linden Rowley
Open Mon - Sat 10 AM - 5 PM, Sun 11 AM - 5 PM; No admis fee; Estab 1849
Collections: Major special collections include 18th, 19th and 20th century British Art, European art from Renaissance to present including Victorian & German Expressionists, Picasso ceramics, contemporary art, arts & crafts collection

LINCOLN

M **LINCOLNSHIRE COUNTY COUNCIL,** Library & Heritage Services, County Offices, Newland Lincoln, LN1 1YL England. Tel 01522-550586; Fax 01522-516720; Email customer_services@lincolnshire.gov.uk; Web: www.lincolnshire.gov.uk; *Head of Libraries & Heritage* Jonathan Platt
Oversees 3 museums & Lincolnshire Archives, 49 libraries, 10 mobile libraries, 3 hospital libraries, 2 prison libraries, 1 Immigration & Repatriation Centre Library; Average Annual Attendance: 350,000
Library Holdings: Book Volumes, CD-ROMs, Cards, Clipping Files, Compact Disks, DVDs, Manuscripts, Maps, Memorabilia, Original Art Works, Original Documents, Other Holdings, Pamphlets, Periodical Subscriptions, Photographs, Prints, Records, Reels, Reproductions, Sculpture, Slides, Video Tapes
Special Subjects: Archaeology, Ceramics, Coins & Medals, Costumes, Crafts, Decorative Arts, Dolls, Ethnology, Furniture, Glass, Leather, Manuscripts, Maps, Medieval Art, Metalwork, Military Art, Painting-British, Period Rooms, Photography, Porcelain, Portraits, Pottery, Sculpture, Watercolors
Collections: Over 3 million items of historical interest relating to Lincolnshire
Activities: Classes for adults & children; lects open to pub; concerts; gallery talks; tours; lending of original objects of art to pub & pvt bodies & individuals; mus shop sells books, magazines, original art, reproductions, & prints

M **Museum of Lincolnshire Life**, Burton Rd, Lincoln, LN1 3LY England. Tel (1522) 528448; *Prin Keeper* J Finch; *Keeper Collections Mgmt* A Martin; *Keeper Visitor & Community Serv* K Howard
Open Mon - Sun 10 AM - 4:30 PM; cl Jan 1, Dec 24 - 26 & 31
Collections: Displays illustrating the social, agricultural & industrial history of Lincolnshire over the last three centuries

M **The Collection: Art & Archaeology in Lincolnshire**, Danes Terr, Lincoln, LN2 1LP England. Tel (01522) 782040; Email thecollection@lincolnshire.gov.uk; Web: www.thecollectionmuseum.com; *District Mgr* William Mason; *Keeper of Art* Dawn Heywood; *Keeper of Archaeology* Antony Lee
Open daily 10 AM - 4 PM; No admis fee; Art gallery estab 1927, Museum estab 1906 (new bldg opened 2005); Collection brings together award winning Archaeology Mus & region's premier art gallery, The Usher; Average Annual Attendance: 120,000
Special Subjects: Antiquities-Egyptian, Antiquities-Greek, Antiquities-Roman, Archaeology, Ceramics, Coins & Medals, Costumes, Decorative Arts, Drawings, Enamels, Etchings & Engravings, Ethnology, Furniture, Glass, Gold, Landscapes, Metalwork, Miniatures, Mosaics, Porcelain, Portraits, Pottery, Prints, Sculpture, Silver, Watercolors
Collections: Exhibits the Usher coll of watches, miniatures, porcelain, special coll of works by Peter De Wint, a general coll of paintings, sculpture & decorative art, coll of coins & tokens from Lincolnshire, archaeological coll spanning 300,000 yrs from stone age to later medieval period, geology, ethnography, arms & armour
Activities: Classes for adults & children; lectrs open to pub; tours; mus shop sells books, magazines & prints

LIVERPOOL

M **WALKER ART GALLERY,** William Brown St, Liverpool, L3 8EL England. Tel 44 151 478 4199; Fax (151) 478-4190; Email thewalker@liverpoolmuseums.org.uk; Web: www.liverpoolmuseums.org.uk; *Cur Brit Art* Charlotte Keenan; *Head Fine Art* Ann Bukantas; *Cur Fine Art* Xanthe Brooke
Open daily 10 AM - 5 PM; No admis fee; 1878; Historic, modern, & contemporary fine & applied arts from 12th - 21st century; Average Annual Attendance: 250,000
Income: (funded direct from UK government)
Special Subjects: Afro-American Art, Baroque Art, Bronzes, Ceramics, Costumes, Decorative Arts, Drawings, Etchings & Engravings, Furniture, Glass, Graphics, Hispanic Art, Ivory, Landscapes, Manuscripts, Medieval Art, Metalwork, Miniatures, Painting-British, Painting-Dutch, Painting-European, Painting-Flemish, Painting-German, Painting-Italian, Painting-Polish, Painting-Scandinavian, Painting-Spanish, Porcelain, Portraits, Pottery, Prints, Religious Art, Renaissance Art, Sculpture, Silver, Stained Glass, Tapestries, Watercolors, Woodcuts
Collections: English & European drawings, paintings, prints, sculpture, watercolors, incl colls of Italian & Netherlandish primitives, pop art, 17th - 19th century European
Exhibitions: 3 major shows per yr
Activities: Classes for adults & children; concerts; gallery talks; tours; lending of original art to Northwest England region; originates traveling exhibs; mus shop sells books, reproductions, prints, postcards, jewelry & ceramics; big art for little children

LONDON

M **BRITISH MUSEUM,** Great Russell St, London, WC1B 3DG England. Tel 44 (0) 20 7323 8000; Email info@thebritishmuseum.org; Web: www.britishmuseum.org; *Dir* Hartwig Fischer
Open daily 10 AM - 5:30 PM, Fri until 8:30 PM cl Good Friday, Dec 24 - 26 & Jan 1; No admis fee; Estab 1753
Collections: Ancient Egypt & The Sudan, Ancient Near East, Greek & Roman, Prehistory & Europe, Asia, Africa, Oceania & the Americas, coins & medals, prints & drawings
Activities: Educ prog; lects open to pub; mus shop

M **THE COURTAULD INSTITUTE OF ART,** The Courtauld Gallery, Somerset House, Strand London, WC2R 0RN England. Tel 44 (0) 20 7848 2526; Fax (020) 7848 2589; Email galleryinfo@courtauld.ac.uk; Web: www.courtauld.ac.uk; *Dir* Deborah Swallow; *Head of Gallery* Ernst Vegelin; *Cur Drawings* Stephanie Buck; *Asst Cur Works on Paper* Rachel Sloan; *Cur Decorative Arts* Alexandra Gerstein; *Cur 20th Century Art* Barnaby Wright; *Registrar* Julia Blanks; *Paper Conservator* Kate Edmondson; *Paintings Conservator* Graeme Barraclough
Open Mon - Sun 10 AM - 6 PM; Admis adults 6 euro; Estab 1932; Collection of paintings, prints, drawings & decorative arts 14th - 20th century; Average Annual Attendance: 250,000
Special Subjects: Baroque Art, Bronzes, Ceramics, Decorative Arts, Drawings, Islamic Art, Landscapes, Medieval Art, Painting-British, Painting-European, Painting-Flemish, Painting-French, Painting-German, Painting-Italian, Portraits, Prints, Renaissance Art, Silver, Sculpture
Collections: Samuel Courtauld Collection of Impressionist & Post-Impressionist Art, other colls include old masters, early 20th century French and English paintings, modern British art, English landscape paintings and drawings, 550 paintings, ranging from 1300-1950, 500 items of sculpture, furniture & decorative art, 7000 drawings, 20,000 prints
Exhibitions: 3 exhibs per yr
Activities: Classes for adults & children; lect open to public; gallery talks; tours; junction outreach to schools & hospitals; originates traveling exhibs; mus shop sells books

M **DALI UNIVERSE,** County Hall Gallery, Riverside Bldg, County Hall London, SE1 7PB England. Tel 0870 744 7485; Fax 020 7620 3120; Email operations@countyhallgallery.com; Web: www.daliuniverse.com
Open daily 10 AM - 5:30 PM, Thurs 10 AM - 8 PM; Admis adults $21 ages 18-64, seniors 65+, military police & firefighters $19, children 13-17 & students 18 with ID $15, children 6-12 $7, children 5 & under free
Collections: Works by Dali

M **THE DESIGN MUSEUM,** 224-238 Kensington High St, London, W8 6AG England. Tel 020-3862-5900; Email info@designmuseum.org; Web: www.designmuseum.org; *Dir* Deyan Sudjic
Open daily 10 AM - 5:45 PM, cl Dec 25 & 26; Admis adults 12.40 GBP, child 6.20 GBP, under 12 free; Estab 1989; International design mus; Average Annual Attendance: 250,000; Mem: 2,000
Collections: Devoted to contemporary design in every format; furniture, graphics, architecture and industrial design
Activities: Classes for adults & children; lects open to pub; gallery talks; tours; Design of the Year award; organize traveling exhibs; mus shop sells books, magazines, original art, reproductions, prints & slides

M **DULWICH PICTURE GALLERY,** A/B, Gallery Rd, London, SE21 7AD England. Tel (0208) 693-5254; Fax (0208) 299-8700; Email enquiries@dulwichpicturegallery.org.uk; *Dir* Ian DeJardin; *Dir Learning & Pub Affairs* Gillian Wolfe; *Head of Communications* Ellie Manwell; *Dir Develop & Communs* Lily Harriss; *Dir Finance* Paula Dimond; *Chief Cur* Xavier Bray
Open Tues - Sun 10 AM - 5 PM, cl Mon; Admis Exhib: adult 11 GBP, senior 10 GBP; Permanent Coll: adult 7 GBP, senior 6 GBP, Srs, concessions fee; Estab 1811; 17th & 18th century European Old Master paintings in oldest public gallery in England; Average Annual Attendance: 150,000; Mem: Friends of Dulwich Picture Gallery
Library Holdings: Book Volumes, Clipping Files, Exhibition Catalogs, Original Documents, Pamphlets, Photographs, Prints, Slides
Collections: Collections of Old Masters from 1626 onwards, including Claude, Cuyp, Gainsborough, Murillo, Poussin, Raphael, Rembrandt, Rubens, Teniers, Tiepolo, Van Dyck, Watteau & others
Publications: catalogues
Activities: Classes for adults & children; lects open to pub; concerts; gallery talks; tours; small vis attraction of the yr 2005; Sandford Award for Heritage Educ 2006; extension prog in London; book traveling exhibs vary; organize traveling exhibs; mus shop sells books, magazines, reproductions, prints, gift items, exhib posters, merchandise, jewelry, cards & Christmas gifts

M **ENGLISH HERITAGE,** (Victoria and Albert Museum) Victoria & Albert Museum, Cromwell Rd, South Kensington London, SW7 2RL England. Tel 44 020 7942 2000; Email hello@vam.ac.uk; Email comments@vam.ac.uk; Web: www.vam.ac.uk; *Dir* Dr Tristram Hunt
Open daily 10 AM - 5:45 PM, Fri until 10 PM; No admis fee to the mus, some exhib & events carry a separate charge; Estab 1857, to enable everyone to enjoy its coll & explore the cultures that created them, and to inspire those who shape contemporary design; Average Annual Attendance: 2,700,000
Income: Grant-in-aid from government plus fundraising
Special Subjects: Prints, Drawings, Furniture, Woodcarvings, Textiles, Ceramics, Glass, Metalwork, Sculpture
Collections: Fine and applied arts of all countries, periods and styles, including Oriental art. European colls are mostly post-classical, architectural details, art of the book, bronzes, calligraphy, carpets, ceramics, clocks, costumes, cutlery, drawings, embroidery, enamels, engravings, fabrics, furniture, glass, gold and silversmiths' work, ironwork, ivories, jewelry, lace, lithographs, manuscripts, metalwork, miniatures, musical instruments, oil paintings, posters, pottery and porcelain, prints, sculpture, stained glass, tapestries, theatre art, vestments, watches, watercolors, woodwork
Activities: Classes for adults & children; lects open to pub; concerts; gallery talks; tours; fellowships; originates traveling exhibs to mus & galleries in UK & internationally; mus shop sells books, magazines, original art; reproductions & prints

M **Apsley House (Wellington Collection)**, 149 Piccadilly, Hyde Park Corner London, W1J 7NT England. Tel 44-20-7499-5676; Fax 011-44-207-4936576; Web: www.english-heritage.eng.uk; *Keeper of the Wellington Coll* Dr Josephine Oxley

Open Wed - Sun 11 AM - 5 PM, cl Mon & Tues; Admis adults 8.80 GBP, children 5-15 5.20 GBP; Opened to the public 1952; Old Masters, silver, sculpture & porcelain; Average Annual Attendance: 50,000
Income: Income from govt grants
Special Subjects: Architecture, Ceramics, Coins & Medals, Decorative Arts, Furniture, Gold, Metalwork, Painting-British, Painting-Dutch, Painting-French, Painting-European, Painting-Flemish, Painting-Spanish, Period Rooms, Porcelain, Portraits, Silver, Sculpture
Collections: Paintings, silver, porcelain, sculpture, orders and decorations, and personal relics of the first Duke of Wellington
Activities: Classes for children; lects open to pub; lects for mems only; concerts; gallery talks; shop sells books, reproductions, slides

M **V&A Museum of Childhood**, Cambridge Heath Rd, London, E2 9PA England. Tel 0208 983 5200; Fax 020-8983-5225; Email moc@vam.ac.uk; Web: www.museumofchildhood.org.uk; *Cur, Dir* Rhian Harris
Open 10 AM - 5:45 PM; No admis fee; Estab 1972; National Museum of Childhood; Average Annual Attendance: 390,000
Income: Government funded
Library Holdings: Auction Catalogs, Memorabilia, Original Documents, Periodical Subscriptions
Special Subjects: Costumes, Crafts, Dolls, Drawings, Embroidery, Furniture, Jewelry, Photography
Collections: Dolls, ceramics, costumes, textiles, furniture & toys, articles related to childhood, British Toy Making Archive
Activities: Classes for adults & children, art activities, inset envelopes for address and spec events on school holidays & weekends; drop in activities & workshops for families & children; lects open to pub; gallery talks; tours; lending of original objects of art; organize traveling exhibs; mus shop sells books, magazines

M **IMPERIAL WAR MUSEUM LONDON,** Lambeth Rd, London, SE1 6HZ England. Tel 02074165000; Web: www.iwm.org.uk; *Dir-Gen* Diane Lees
Open daily 10 AM - 6 PM, cl Dec 24 - 26; No admis fee; Estab in 1919 to tell the story of modern war and conflict involving Britain, the Commonwealth and former empire countries
Special Subjects: Historical Material, Photography, Posters, Prints, Film, Manuscripts
Collections: 800,000 technical, social, economic, political, personal & cultural artifacts, wartime personal items such as letters, diaries & trickets
Exhibitions: Permanent & temporary exhibits
Activities: Family educ progs; outreach & resources; interactive progs; lects open to pub; gallery talks; tours; Mus shop sells posters, prints, books, media & gifts

M **INSTITUTE OF CONTEMPORARY ARTS,** The Mall, London, London, SW1Y 5AH England. Tel 44-0-20-7930-3647; Web: www.ica.org.uk; *Exec Dir* Gregor Muir
Open Tues - Sun 11 AM - 11 PM, exhibs open 11 AM - 6 PM; Daily membership costs 1 GBP
Collections: Changing exhibits of contemporary art in various media; painting, graphic art, video, photography, film

M **THE NATIONAL GALLERY,** Trafalgar Sq, London, WC2N 5DN England. Tel 44 (0) 20 7747 2885; Email information@ng.london.org.uk; Web: www.nationalgallery.org.uk; *Dir* Gabriele Finaldi; *Chair* Hannah Rothschild
Open daily 10 AM - 6 PM, Fri 10 - 9 PM cl Dec 24 - 26 & Jan 1; No admis fee; Estab 1824; Houses one of the great collections of Western European painting in the world; Average Annual Attendance: 4,300,000
Collections: Western European paintings from the 13th to the 19th centuries
Activities: Classes for adults & children; concerts; gallery talks; tours; sales shop sells books, magazines, prints

M **NATIONAL PORTRAIT GALLERY,** St Martin's Place, London, WC2H 0HE England. Tel 44 (0) 20 7306 0055; Email archiveenquiry@npg.org.uk; Web: www.npg.org.uk; *Dir* Dr Nicholas Cullinan; *Cur Dir* Tarnya Cooper
Open daily 10 AM - 6 PM, Fri until 9 PM; No admis fee; Estab 1856; home to the largest Collection of portraiture in the world, featuring men & women who have made a significant contribution to British history & culture from the Middle Ages until the present day; Average Annual Attendance: 1.27 million; Mem: Membership & patrons scheme
Library Holdings: Clipping Files, Exhibition Catalogs, Manuscripts, Original Documents, Photographs, Prints, Reproductions
Special Subjects: Drawings, Painting-British, Photography, Portraits, Prints, Sculpture
Collections: National collection of portraits spanning the last 500 years, including sculpture, photographs & digital media
Publications: Vanity Fair Portraits; Beatles to Bowie: The 60s Exposed; Twiggy: A Life in Photographs; Lucian Freud Portraits; Man Ray Portraits
Activities: Educ prog; classes for adults & children; school groups/workshops; lects open to pub; concerts; gallery talks; tours; competitions; annual BP Portrait Award; annual Taylor Wessing Photographic Portrait Prize; lending of original objects of art to touring exhibs; originate traveling exhibs to UK mus & galleries & international orgs; mus shop sells book, magazines, reproductions, prints, slides & other gift items

M **QUEEN'S GALLERY,** Buckingham Palace Rd, London, SW1A 1AA England. Tel (20) 7839-1377; Web: www.royal.gov.uk
March - July open daily 10 AM - 5:30 PM; July - Oct 9:15 AM - 5:30 PM; Oct - Apr 10 AM - 5:30 PM; Admis adult 10.30 GBP, over 60 & student with ID 9.40 GBP, under 17 5.30 GBP, under 5 free

M **ROYAL ACADEMY OF ARTS,** Burlington House, Piccadilly London, W1J 0BD England. Tel 020 7300 8000; Fax 020 7300 8001; Email comment@royalacademy.org.uk; Web: www.royalacademy.org.uk; *Pres* Christopher Le Brun, RA; *Keeper* Rebecca Salter, RA
Open Sat - Thurs 10 AM - 6 PM, Fri 10 AM - 10 PM; No admis fee, exhib pricing may vary; Estab 1768; Average Annual Attendance: 750,000
Income: Exhib ticket sales & pvt corporate sponsors
Library Holdings: Book Volumes, Exhibition Catalogs, Original Documents
Collections: Paintings, prints, architectural collection
Exhibitions: Six exhibs per yr
Publications: Exhib Catalogues for exhib listed
Activities: Educ prog; classes for adults & children; 3 yr post-grad arts course (full time); lects open to the pub; gallery talks; lend original objects of art to other galleries for exhibs; sales shop sells books, magazines, cards, jewelry & clothing

L **Library**, Burlington House, Piccadilly London, W1J 0BD England. Tel 020 7300 5737; Email library@royalacademy.org.uk; Web: www.royalacademy.org.uk; *Head Library Servs* Adam Waterton
Open Tues - Fri 10 AM - 1 PM & 2 PM - 5 PM by appointment; No admis fee; Estab 1768
Library Holdings: Book Volumes 40,000, Clipping Files 500, Exhibition Catalogs 8,000, Manuscripts, Other Holdings Engravings; Fine arts books 20,000; Manuscripts; Original drawings

M **SOUTH LONDON GALLERY,** 65 Peckham Rd, London, SE5 8UH England. Tel +44(0) 20 7703 6120; Fax +44(0) 20 7252 4730; Email mail@southlondongallery.org; Web: www.southlondongallery.org; *Gallery Dir* Margot Heller; *Prog Mgr* Simon Parris
Open Tues - Sun 11 AM - 6 PM, Wed 11 AM - 9 PM, cl Mon; No admis fee; Estab 1891; Since 1993 the gallery has staged ground-breaking solo & group exhibitions of works by artists such as Gilbert & George, Tracey Emin, Gavin Turk, Mona Hatoum, Bill Viola, Barbara Kruger, Tom Friedman; Average Annual Attendance: 30,000
Collections: Contemporary British art, 20th century original prints, paintings of the Victorian period, topographical paintings & drawings of local subjects permanent coll exhibited periodically
Exhibitions: Exhibitions from permanent collection
Activities: Educ prog; classes for adults & children; lects open to pub; concerts; gallery talks; tours; shop sells books & postcards

M **TATE GALLERY,** Bankside, London, SE1 9TG England. Tel 44 (0) 20 7887 8888; Email ticketing@tate.org.uk; Web: www.tate.org.uk; *Dir* Maria Balshaw; *Mng Dir* Kerstin Mogull; *Dir Tate Britain* Dr Alex Farquharson; *Dir Tate Modern* Frances Morris
Open Sun - Thurs 10 AM - 6 PM Fri - Sat 10 AM - 10 PM; No admis fee; Institution consists of four galleries: Tate Britain & Tate Modern in London, Tate Liverpool in Liverpool and Tate St Ives in Corwall
Collections: Works of Blake, Constable, Hogarth, Turner and the Pre-Raphaelites, British painting from the 16th century to present, modern foreign painting from Impressionism onward, modern sculpture, collection totals 12,000, including 5500 prints

M **THE WALLACE COLLECTION,** Hertford House, Manchester Sq London, W1U 3BN England. Tel 44 (0) 207 563-9500; Fax 44 (0) 207 224 2155; Email collections@wallacecollection.org; Web: www.wallacecollection.org; *Dir* Dr Christopher Martin Vogtherr
Open daily 10 AM - 5 PM; No admis fee; Estab 1900; Circ Reference library; Average Annual Attendance: 380,000
Income: Government of UK plus 30% generated income
Purchases: Cl coll, purchases not permitted
Library Holdings: Auction Catalogs, Book Volumes, Exhibition Catalogs, Fiche, Periodical Subscriptions, Reels
Special Subjects: Art History, Bronzes, Ceramics, Decorative Arts, Enamels, Glass, Ivory, Manuscripts, Miniatures, Painting-British, Painting-Dutch, Painting-European, Painting-Flemish, Painting-French, Painting-German, Painting-Italian, Porcelain, Portraits, Sculpture, Silver, Watercolors
Collections: Arms & Armour, French Furniture, Sevres Porcelain, paintings & works of art of all European schools, miniatures, sculpture, maiolica, renaissance glass & enamels
Publications: The Noble Art of the Sword: Fashion & Fencing in Renaissance Europe; Catalogue of European Arms & Armour; Catalogue of Glass & Limoges Painted Enamels
Activities: Classes for adults & children; docent training; lects open to pub; concerts; gallery talks; mus shop sells books, reproductions & other items

M **WHITECHAPEL ART GALLERY,** 80-82 Whitechapel High St, London, E1 7QX England. Tel (020) 7522 7888; Fax (020) 7377 1685; Email info@whitechapel.org; Web: www.whitechapel.org; *Dir* Iwona Blazwick; *Press Officer* David Gleeson; *Head Admin* Alison Digance; *Finance Officer* Raksha Patel
Open Tues - Wed & Fri - Sun 11 AM - 6 PM, Thurs 11 AM - 9 PM, cl Mon; No admis fee except one spec exhib per year; Estab 1901; Established & emerging contemporary artists; Mem: Membership fees start at 40 GBP
Collections: Changing exhibitions, primarily of modern & contemporary art
Activities: Classes for adults, classes for children; lects for members only, gallery talks, tours; mus shop sells books, magazines, prints

M **WILLIAM MORRIS GALLERY,** Lloyd Park, Forest Rd London, E17 4PP England. Tel 0208 496 4390; Email wmg.enquires@walthamforest.gov.uk; Web: www.wmgallery.org.uk; *Mus, Gallery & Archives Mgr* Anna Mason; *Exhib & Coll Officer* Carien Kremer; *Activities & Events Officer* Rebecca Jacobs; *Learning & Outreach Officer* Sharon Trotter; *Operations Support Officer* Linda Weston
Open Wed - Sun 10 AM - 5 PM, Tues pre-booked groups & school visits 10 AM - 5 PM; No admis fee; Estab 1950; Promotes the life, work & continuing influence of William Morris through its internationally renowned coll; Average Annual Attendance: 130,000; Mem: Friends of the William Morris Gallery
Income: Local government
Library Holdings: Auction Catalogs, Book Volumes, CD-ROMs, Exhibition Catalogs, Manuscripts, Memorabilia, Original Art Works, Original Documents, Pamphlets, Periodical Subscriptions, Photographs, Prints, Records
Special Subjects: Architecture, Carpets & Rugs, Ceramics, Crafts, Decorative Arts, Drawings, Embroidery, Furniture, Stained Glass, Tapestries, Textiles, Woodcuts
Collections: Morris's original designs, textiles, wallpapers, furniture, stained glass, ceramics, metalwork, books, archival materials, personal items (coffee cup & satchel), Works by Edward Burne-Jones, Dante Gabriel Rossetti & Philip Webb also represented, Wide range coll of arts & crafts material (includes works by

Arthur Heygate Mackmurdo & the Century Guild, William De Morgan, Walter Crane, May Morris, George Jack, Frank Brangwyn & Christopher Whall & others)
Publications: William Morris in 50 Objects, by Anna Mason & Carien Kremer
Activities: Classes for adults & children; dramatic progs; docent training; lects opent to pub; 9 vis lectrs per yr; concerts; gallery talks; tours; awards, ArtFund: Mus of the Year 2013, Mus & Heritage Awards: Best Permanent Exhib; mus shop sells books, magazines, original art by local artists, prints, postcards, stationery, accessories & clothing, branded items, household, tiles & ceramics, jewelry, exhib merchandise

MANCHESTER

M **MANCHESTER CITY GALLERIES,** (Wythenshawe Hall, City Art Galleries) Manchester Art Gallery, Mosley St, Manchester, M2 3JL England. Tel 0161 235 8888; Fax 0161 274 7146; Web: www.manchesterartgallery.org; *Head of Galleries* Moira Stevenson
Open Mon - Sun - 10 AM - 5 PM, Thurs until 9 PM; No admis fee; Estab1882; reopened following major refurbishment in 2002
Income: owned & managed by Manchester city council
Special Subjects: Crafts, Decorative Arts, Painting-British, Painting-European, Silver
Collections: British art, English costume, enamels, silver and decorative arts, Old Master and Dutch 17th century painting, pre-Raphaelite painting
Activities: Classes for adults & children; lectrs open to the public; lectrs for mems only; gallery talks; tours; mus shop sells books, reproductions, prints

M **UNIVERSITY OF MANCHESTER,** Whitworth Art Gallery, Oxford Rd, Manchester, M15 6ER England. Tel 0161-275-7450; Fax 0161-275-7451; Email whitworth@manchester.ac.uk; Web: www.whitworth.manchester.ac.uk; *Dir* Dr Maria Balshaw
Open Mon - Wed 10 AM - 5 PM; Thurs 10 AM - 9 PM, Fri - Sun 10 AM - 5 PM; No admis fee; Estab 1889; Collections of fine art & design; Average Annual Attendance: 87,000
Income: 130,000
Library Holdings: Exhibition Catalogs
Special Subjects: Drawings, Embroidery, Etchings & Engravings, Painting-British, Portraits, Prints, Textiles, Watercolors
Collections: British drawings and watercolors, contemporary British paintings and sculpture, Old Master and modern prints, textiles, wallpapers
Exhibitions: Programs change regularly, see website for latest info
Activities: Classes for adults & children; family workshops; lects open to pub; 10-20 vis lectrs per yr; concerts; gallery talks; tours; mus shop sells books, magazines, reproductions, prints, gifts, postcards

NEWCASTLE-UPON-TYNE

M **TYNE AND WEAR ARCHIVES & MUSEUMS,** Laing Art Gallery, Newcastle Discovery, New Bridge St Newcastle-upon-Tyne, NE1 8AG England. Tel (0191) 232 7734; Fax (0191) 222 0952; Email info@laingartgallery.org.uk; Web: www.twmuseums.org.uk; *Dir Tyne & Wear Museums* Alec Coles; *Cur Laing Art Gallery* Julie Milne
Open Tues - Sat 10 AM - 5 PM, Sun 2 - 5 PM; No admis fee; Estab 1904; The Laing Art Gallery is the premier art gallery in Newcastle. Show exhibitions of contemporary and historical art; Average Annual Attendance: 295,000
Collections: British oil paintings since 1700 (with works by Burne-Jones, Gainsborough, Landsear, Reynolds, Turner), British prints & watercolors, British (especially local) ceramics, costume, glass, pewter, silver of all periods, modern works by Ben Nicholson, Henry Moore & Stanley Spencer
Activities: Educ prog; classes for adults & children; 40 vis lectrs per yr; tours; lending of original objects of art to various galleries; mus shop sells books, magazines, original art, reproductions, prints, original craft & design

M **Sunderland Museum & Winter Gardens**, Burdon Rd, Sunderland, SR1 1PP England. Tel 191-561 2323, 180010191553 (text phone); Email info@sunderlandmuseum.org.uk; Web: www.sunderlandmuseum.org.uk; *Mgr* Jo Cunningham; *Learning Officer* Jennie Lambert; *Keeper of Art* Shaura Gregg; *Keeper of Art History* Martin Rovtledge
Open Mon - Sat 10 AM - 5 PM, Sun 2 PM - 5 PM; No admis fee; Estab 1846; mus, art gallery, winter gardens; Average Annual Attendance: 300,000; Mem: Friends of Sunderland Museums (FOSUMS)
Income: local authority
Special Subjects: Archaeology, Ceramics, Decorative Arts, Drawings, Embroidery, Etchings & Engravings, Ethnology, Glass, Historical Material, Landscapes, Marine Painting, Painting-British, Photography, Porcelain, Portraits, Pottery, Prints, Silver, Textiles, Watercolors, Woodcuts
Collections: Local history, pottery, fine art, natural history & archaeology
Activities: Classes for adults & children; lects open to pub; awards; mus shop sells books, magazines, reproductions, prints, unique gifts

M **Shipley Art Gallery**, Prince Consort Rd, Newcastle, England. Tel 191-477-1495; Email info@shipleyartgallery.org.uk
Open Tues - Fri 10 AM - 4 PM, Sat 10 AM - 5 PM, cl Sun & Mon; No admis fee
Collections: Contemporary craft & paintings from the old masters

M **South Shields Museum & Art Gallery**, Ocean Rd, South Shields Tyne and Wear, NE33 2JA England. Tel (0191) 211-5599; Email info@southshieldsmuseum.org.uk
Open Mon - Fri 10 AM - PM, 5 Sat 11 AM - 4 PM, cl Sun; No admis fee
Collections: Local art history

NEWPORT

M **BOROUGH OF NEWPORT MUSEUM AND ART GALLERY,** John Frost Sq, Newport, Gwent NP20 1PA England. Tel 1633 656656; Fax (1633) 222615; Email museum@newport.gov.uk; Web: www.newport.gov.uk/museum; *Cur* Robert Trett
Open Tues - Fri 9:30 AM - 5 PM, Sat 9:30 - 4 PM. cl Sun & bank holidays; No admis fee
Collections: Early English watercolors, oil paintings by British artists, local archeology (especially Roman), natural & social history

OXFORD

M **MODERN ART OXFORD,** 30 Pembroke St, Oxford, 0X1 1BP England. Tel (01865) 722733; Fax (01865) 722573; Email info@modernartoxford.org.uk; Web: www.modernartoxford.org.uk; *Exec Dir* Paul Hobson
Open Tues - Sat 11 AM - 6 PM, Sun 12 - 5 PM, cl Mon; No admis fee; Purpose to pioneer progs of contemp art; Library with 15,000 vols; Average Annual Attendance: 200,000; Mem: 300 mems; 30 GBP
Income: UK charity reg; public funding
Library Holdings: Exhibition Catalogs, Periodical Subscriptions
Exhibitions: Features changing international exhibitions of 20th century painting, photography, prints, sculpture, drawing, film & video
Activities: Classes for adults & children; lects open to pub; 10 vis lectrs per yr; concerts; gallery talks; tours; mus shop sells books, magazines, prints

M **OXFORD UNIVERSITY,** Ashmolean Museum, Beaumont St, Oxford, OX1 2PH England. Tel (01865) 278000; Fax (01865) 278018; Web: www.ashmolean.org; *Dir* Dr Xa Sturgis
Open Tues - Sun 10 AM - 5 PM, bank holidays Mon 10 AM - 5 PM; cl Dec 24 - 26; No admis fee; Estab 1683
Collections: British, European, Egyptian, Mediterranean & Near Eastern archaeology, Chinese Bronzes, Chinese & Japanese porcelain, painting & lacquer, Dutch, English, Flemish, French & Italian oil paintings, Indian sculpture & painting, Hope Collection of engraved portraits, Tibetan, Indian and Islamic art objects, collection of coins from various countries and times, Old Master and modern drawings, prints and watercolors

PLYMOUTH

M **PLYMOUTH CITY MUSEUM AND ART GALLERY,** Drake Circus, Plymouth, Devon PL4 8AJ England. Tel (01752) 304774; Fax (01752) 304775; Email plymouth.museum@plymouth.gov.uk; Web: www.plymouthmuseum.gov.uk; *Cur* Nicola Moyle
Open Tues - Fri 10 AM - 5:30 PM, Sat 10 AM - 5 PM; cl Sun & Mon; No admis fee; Estab 1838 to illustrate arts of the West Country; Average Annual Attendance: 70,000
Collections: The Clarendon Collection of Portraits of 16th & 17th Century English worthies, Collection of Cookworthy's Plymouth & Bristol Porcelain, The Cottonian Collection of early printed & illuminated books
Activities: Classes for adults & children, dramatic progs, concerts & gallery talks; lects open to pub; books, magazines, reproductions, prints, gifts & souvenirs

SHEFFIELD

M **FRIENDS OF BISHOPS HOUSE,** (Weston Park Museum), Weston Park, Western Bank Sheffield, Yorks S10 2TP England. Tel (114) 2768588; Fax 114-275-0957; Email info@sheffieldgalleries.co.uk; *Dir* Kim Streets; *Sr Prin* Janet Barnes
Open year round Sat & Sun 10 AM - 4 PM; cl New Year's Day, Easter, Christmas Day; No admis fee; Estab 1875
Collections: Sheffield silver, Old Sheffield Plate, British and European cutlery, coins and medals, ceramics

M **Abbeydale Hamlet**, Abbeydale Rd S, Sheffield, S7 2QW England. Tel (114) 272 2106; Email ask@simt.co.uk; Web: www.simt.co.uk/abbeydale-industrial-hamlet; *Mus Srvcs Mgr* Alison Duce
Open Mon - Thurs 10 AM - 4 PM, Sun 11 AM - 4:45 PM, cl Fri & Sat; Adult 4 GBP, concessions 3 GBP
Collections: An 18th century scytheworks with Huntsman type crucible steel furnace, tilt-hammers, grinding-shop and hand forges

M **Bishop's House**, Norton Lees Lane, Sheffield, S8 9BE England. Tel 0114 255 7701; Email enquiries@bishophouse.org.uk; Web: www.friendsofbishopshouse.org.uk; *Dir (Museums Sheffield)* K Streets
Open Sat & Sun 10 AM - 4 PM; Admis free, donations welcome; Estab 1974; Former Yedman Farmer's house; Average Annual Attendance: 1500
Income: (financed by donations & shop sales)
Collections: A late 15th century timber-framed domestic building with 16th - 17th century additions, Artifacts from Sheffield Castle
Activities: Classes for children; dramatic progs; tours; mus shop sells books, reproductions, prints crafts & souvenirs

SOUTHAMPTON

M **SOUTHAMPTON CITY ART GALLERY,** Civic Centre, Southampton, Hants S014 7LP England. Tel 023-8083-3007; Fax 023-8083-2153; Email art.gallery@southampton.gov.uk; *Cur* Adrian B Rance; *Prin Officer Arts* Elizabeth Goodall; *Head* Margaret Heller
Open Mon - Fri 10 AM - 3 PM, Sat 10 AM - 5 PM; cl Sun; No admis fee
Collections: Continental Old Masters, French 19th & 20th centuries schools, British painting from the 18th century to present, contemporary sculpture & painting

SOUTHPORT

M **ATKINSON ART GALLERY,** Lord St, Southport, Merseyside PR8 1DB England. Tel 1704 533333; Fax (151) 934-2109; *Dir* Emma Anderson
Open Mon - Fri 10 AM - 5 PM, Sat 11 AM - 4 PM, Sun 11 AM - 4 PM; No admis fee; Estab 1878; Average Annual Attendance: 25,000
Collections: British art - local, contemporary & historic, British 18th, 19th & 20th centuries oils, drawings, prints, sculptures & watercolors

Activities: Gallery talks; sales shop sells books, postcards & cards

STOKE-ON-TRENT

M **THE POTTERIES MUSEUM & ART GALLERY,** Bethesda St, Stoke-On-Trent, Staffs ST1 3DW England. Tel 01782-232323; Fax 01782-232500; Email museums@stoke.gov.uk; Web: www.stokemuseums.org.uk/visit/pmag; *Mgr* Pamela Mallalieu; *Head of Mus* Ian Lawley
Open Mon - Sat 10 AM - 5 PM, Sun 11 AM - 4 PM; No admis fee; Average Annual Attendance: 170,000
Collections: English ceramics coll incl Staffordshire ware, fine & decorative arts, 20th Century British Art
Activities: Educ prog; classes for adults; drop-in art craft for children; lects open to pub; gallery talks; tours; concerts; sponsoring of competitions; 2 book traveling exhibs; originate traveling exhibs; mus shop sells books, magazines

WOLVERHAMPTON

M **WOLVERHAMPTON ARTS & HERITAGE,** Wolverton Art Gallery, Lichfield St, West Midlands Wolverhampton, West Midlands WV1 1DU England. Tel 44 (0) 1902 552055; Fax 44 (0) 1902 552053; Email artgallery@wolverhampton.gov.uk; Web: www.wolverhamptonart.org.uk; *Art Galleries & Museums Officer* Corinne Miller; *Head Mktg & Opers* Zoe Papiernik
Open Mon - Sat 10:30 AM - 4:30 PM, Sun 11 AM - 4 PM, Bank HolidaysCafe open Mon - Sat 10:30 AM - 4:30 PM; No admis fee; Estab 1884, giving Wulfrunians their permanent art display; Average Annual Attendance: 150,000
Special Subjects: Asian Art, Enamels, Painting-British
Collections: Contemporary British art, 18th century British paintings, 19th & 20th centuries British painting & watercolors, branch museums have English enamels, japanning & porcelain, Victorian & Georgian, over 12,000 items in coll
Activities: Classes for adults & children; lects open to pub; gallery talks; tours; mus shop sells books, reproductions, prints, general arts & crafts products

YORK

M **YORK CITY ART GALLERY,** Exhibition Sq, York, Y01 7EW England. Tel 01 904 687687; Fax (01904) 551866; Web: www.yorkartgallery.org.uk; *Asst Cur Decorative Art* Helen Walsh; *Asst Cur Fine Arts* Jennifer Alexander; *Cur Fine Arts* Laura Turner
Open daily 10 AM - 5 PM, Sat 10 AM - 6 PM, Sun 11 AM - 4 PM; Dec 24th & 31st 10 AM - 2:30 PM with last admis at 2:15 PM, cl Dec 25, 26 & Jan 1; Adult admis 7.50 GBP child admis free with adult.; Estab 2000; Displays of fine paintings & ceramics
Collections: British and European paintings, including the Lycett Green Collection of Old Masters, modern stoneware pottery, paintings and drawings by York artists, notably William Etty, watercolors, drawings and prints, mostly local topography
Activities: Classes for adults & children; lects open to pub; gallery talks; mus shop sells books, original art, prints, slides, cards

ESTONIA

TALLINN

M **EESTI KUNSTIMUUSEUM,** Art Museum of Estonia, Weizenbergi 34, Valge 1 Tallinn, 10127 Estonia. Tel 372-602-6001; Fax 372-602-6002; Email press@ekm.ee; Web: kunstimuuseum.ekm.ee; *Dir-Gen* Sirje Helme
Joint ticket admis for all five branches adults 14 EUR, families 28 EUR; Estab 1919; National art museum of Estonia consisting of five museums across the city of Tallinn

M **Kumu Art Museum**, Weizenbergi 34, Valge 1 Tallinn, 10127 Estonia. Tel 372-602-6001; Fax 372-602-6002; Email kumu.info@ekm.ee; Web: kunstimuuseum.ekm.ee/en; *Dir Gen* Sirje Helme
Open April - Sept Tue & Thurs - Sun 10 AM - 6 PM, Wed 10 AM - 8 PM, cl Mon, Oct - March Wed 10 AM - 8 PM, Thurs - Sun 10 Am - 6 PM; Admis adults 6 EUR, concessions 4 EUR, families 12 EUR; Estab 2006; Contemporary art museum & headquarters for the Art Museum of Estonia
Library Holdings: Auction Catalogs, Book Volumes, CD-ROMs, Cards, Cassettes, DVDs, Exhibition Catalogs, Manuscripts, Periodical Subscriptions, Reproductions
Collections: Classics of Estonian art from the 18th century to World War II, Estonian art from 1945-1991 and contemporary art
Activities: Classes for adults & children; dramatic progs; docent training; lectrs for mems only; concerts; gallery talks; tours; schols; fels; awarded European Mus Award; mus shop sells books, magazines

M **Adamson-Eric Museum**, Luhike Jalg 3, Tallinn, 10130 Estonia. Tel 372-644-5838; Fax 372-602-6002; Email adamson-eric@ekm.ee; Web: adamson-eric.ekm.ee; *Dir* Ulle Kruus
Open May - Sept Tues - Sun 11 AM - 6 PM, cl Mon; Oct - April Wed - Sun 11 AM - 6 PM, cl Mon & Tues; Admis adults 5.50 EUR, concessions 3.50 EUR, families 11 EUR
Collections: Art of Estonian painter Adamson-Eric

M **Kadriorg Art Museum**, Weizenbergi 37, Tallinn, 10127 Estonia. Tel 372-606-6400; Fax 372-606-6401; Email kadriorg@ekm.ee; Web: kadriorumuuseum.ekm.ee; *Dir* Aleksandra Murre
Open May - Sept Tues, Thurs - Sun 10 AM - 6 PM, Wed 10 AM - 8 PM; Oct - April Wed 10 AM - 8 PM, Thurs - Sun 10 AM - 5 PM; Admis adults 5.50 EUR, concessions 3.50 EUR, families 11 EUR
Collections: European and Russian art between 16th and 20th century, 16th to 20th century Western European, Russian and Chinese art

M **Niguliste Museum**, Niguliste 3, Tallinn, 10130 Estonia. Tel 372-631-4330; Fax 372-602-6002; Email niguliste@ekm.ee; Web: nigulistemuuseum.ekm.ee; *Dir Gen* Sirje Helme
Open May - Sept Tues - Sun 10 AM - 5 PM, cl Mon; Oct - April Wed - Sun 10 AM - 5 PM, cl Mon & Tues; Admis adults 5 EUR, concessions 3 EUR, families 10 EUR; Estab 1984 to collect & exhibit ecclesiastical art; Late Gothic architecture
Collections: Ecclesiastical Medieval and Baroque art between the 13th and 18th centuries, Silverware of guilds, crafts, Brotherhood of the Black Heads and church
Publications: Mand, Ann. Bernt Notke: Between Innovation & Tradition; Tallinn: Art Museum of Estonia (exhib catalog)
Activities: Educ prog; classes for adults & children; lects open to pub; concerts; gallery talks; mus shop sells books, magazines, reproductions

M **Mikkel Museum**, Weizenbergi 28, Tallinn, 10127 Estonia. Tel 372-670-6400; Fax 372-602-6002; Email kadriorg@ekm.ee; Web: mikkelmuuseum.ekm.ee; *Admin* Maila Kuriks
Open May - Sept Tues, Thurs - Sun 10 AM - 6 PM, Wed 10 AM - 8 PM, cl Mon; Oct - April Wed 10 AM - 8 PM, Thurs - Sun 10 AM - 5 PM, cl Mon & Tues; Admis adults 3.50 EUR, students 2 EUR, families 7 EUR; Estab 1997; Housed in the kitchen building of the Kadriorg Palace
Collections: Private collection of Johannes Mikkel, Western European, Russian, Chinese & Estonian art from the 16th to 20th centuries

TARTU

M **EESTI RAHVA MUUSEUM,** Estonian National Museum, Veski 32, Tartu, 51014 Estonia. Tel 372-735-0400; Email erm@erm.ee; Web: www.erm.ee; *Dir* Tonis Lukas
Open daily 7 AM - 10 PM; Admis adult 1.80 EUR, discounted 1.20 EUR, family 5 EUR; Estab 1909
Collections: Estonian artifacts, drawings, photographs & films

ETHIOPIA

ADDIS ABABA

M **NATIONAL MUSEUM OF ETHIOPIA,** King George VI St, Addis Ababa, Ethiopia. Tel 251-940-637-476; *Dir* Mamitu Yilma
Open 8:30 AM - 5 PM; Admis 10 ETB
Special Subjects: African Art, Archaeology, Ethnology, Religious Art
Collections: Ethiopian ethnographic artifacts & cultural history documents, early Christian religious art, archaeological & palaeontological displays, traditional weapons, jewelry, utensils, clothing and musical instruments

FIJI

SUVA

M **FIJI MUSEUM,** Ratu Cakobau Rd, Suva, Fiji. Tel 679-331-5944; Fax 679-330-5143; Email fijimuseum@kidanet.net.fj; Web: www.fijimuseum.org.fj; *Dir* Adi Mere Ratunabuabua
Open Mon - Thurs & Sat 9 AM - 4:30 PM, Fri 9 AM - 4 PM; Admis adults 7 FJD, children & students 5 FJD
Collections: Five main galleries of pre-history, Indo-Fijian work, Fiji history, Masi & art, historical, ethnographical, sculptures, textiles, fine arts

FINLAND

ESPOO

M **ESPOON MODERNIN TAITEEN MUSEO,** Espoo Museum of Modern Art, Ahertajantie 5, Tapiola Espoo, 02100 Finland; PO Box 6661, Espoon Kaupunki, 02070 Finland. Tel 358 09 8165 0493; Email info@emma.museum; Web: www.emma.museum; *Chief Cur* Pilvi Kalhama; *Chief Cur* Paivi Talasmaa
Open Tues & Thurs 11 AM - 6 PM, Wed & Fri 11 AM - 7 PM, Sat & Sun 11 AM - 5 PM, cl Mon; Admis adults 12 EUR, visitors under 18 & over 70 (Fri free from 5 - 7 PM); Estab 2006; 5,000 sq meter exhib space
Collections: Primarily post-war Finnish art (Saastamoinen Foundation Art Collection
Activities: Lects open to pub; mus shop

M **GALLEN-KALLELAN MUSEO,** Gallen-Kallelan Museum, Gallen-Kallelan tie 27, Espoo, 02600 Finland. Tel 358-9-849-2340; Fax 358-9-541-6426; Email info@gallen-kallela.fi; Web: www.gallen-kallela.fi; *Dir* Tuija Wahlroos
Open summer daily 11 AM - 6PM; autumn, winter & spring Tues - Sat 11 AM - 4 PM, Sun 11 AM - 5 PM, cl Mon; Admis adults 8 EUR, seniors 6 EUR, students 4 EUR, under 18 free; Located in the castle-like Tarvaspaa studio & residence
Collections: Works by Finnish artist Akseli Gallen-Kallela, contemporary art

HELSINKI

M **ARKKITEHTUURIMUSEO,** Museum of Finnish Architecture, Kasarmikatu 24, Helsinki, 00130 Finland. Tel 358-9-8567-5100; Email mfa@mfa.fi; Web: www.mfa.fi; *Dir* Juulia Kauste

Open Tues - Sun 11 AM - 6 PM, Wed 11 AM - 8 PM; Admis adults 8 EUR, students 4 EUR, children under 18 free; Estab 1956; Library with 30,000 vols
Special Subjects: Architecture, Art Education, Art History, Decorative Arts, Furniture, History of Art & Archaeology, Interior Design, Landscape Architecture, Landscapes
Collections: Finnish architecture coll (mainly on post 1900 architecture) includes 85,000 photographs, 32,000 slides, 500,000 original drawings
Exhibitions: Changing exhibs on Finnish & international architecture; Permanent Exhibition: Decades of Finnish Architecture 1900-1970
Activities: Classes for children; lects open to pub; gallery talks; tours; originates traveling exhibs; mus shop sells books & magazines

M **DESIGNMUSEO,** Design Museum, Korkeavuorenkatu 23, Helsinki, 00130 Finland. Tel 3589-6220-540; Email info@designmuseum.fi; Web: www.designmuseum.fi; *Dir* Jukka Savolainen; *Chief Cur & Deputy Dir* Merja Vilhunen
Open winter Tues 11 AM - 8 PM, Wed - Sun 11 AM - 6 PM, cl Mon; summer daily 11 AM - 6 PM; Admis adults 10 EUR, seniors 8 EUR, students 5 EUR, children free
Collections: History and development of Finnish design with over 35,000 objects, 40,000 drawings and 100,000 images

M **DIDRICHSENIN TAIDEMUSEO,** Didrichsen Art Museum, Kuusilahdenkuja 1, Helsinki, 00340 Finland. Tel 358-010-2193-974; Email office@didrichsenmuseum.fi; Web: www.didrichsenmuseum.fi; *Dir* Peter Didrichsen; *Chief Cur* Maria Didrichsen
Open Tues - Sun 11 AM - 5 PM, cl Mon; Admis adults 12 EUR, reduced 10 EUR, children under 7 & seniors over 75 free; Art museum located in a private, seaside residence on Kuusisaari Island
Collections: Finnish art, modern international art & architecture, Pre-Columbian art, Oriental art

M **HELSINGIN TAIDEMUSEO,** Helsinki Art Museum, Etalainen Rautatiekatu 8, Helsinki, 00100 Finland. Tel 358-09-310-1051; Email ham@hel.fi; Web: www.hamhelsinki.fi; *Dir & Cur* Maija Tanninen-Mattila
Open Tues - Sun 11 AM - 7 PM, cl Mon; Adults 10 EUR, reduced admis 8 EUR, under 18 free; Average Annual Attendance: 93,000
Collections: 9,000 works of art acquired by the city of Helsinki since the 19th century, Various other donated small collections; contemporary art

M **Tennis Palace Art Museum,** Etelainen Rautatiekatu 8, Helsinki, 00100 Finland. Tel 358-09-310-87001; Fax 358-09-310-87000; Email ham@hel.fi; Web: www.hamhelsinki.fi; *Dir* Mr Maija Tanninen-Mattila; *Chief Cur Exhibs* Ms Pirkko Siitari; *Chief Cur Colls* Ms Elina Leskela; *Cur Educ* Nanne Raivio
Open Tues - Sun 11 AM - 7 PM, cl Mon; Admis 10 EUR, discount 8 EUR, under 18 free
Collections: Emphasis of the colls is on 20th and 21st century Finnish art, donated and accessioned colls, public art & sculptures

M **KANSALLISGALLERIA,** Finnish National Gallery, Kaivokatu 2, Helsinki, 00100 Finland. Tel 358-0294-500-200; Web: www.kansallisgalleria.fi; *Dir Gen* Ruohonen Risto; *Fundraising Dir* Tawast Jyri
National cultural institution comprised of three museum units located throughout Helsinki; Average Annual Attendance: 500,000
Collections: State-owned coll of more than 35,000 works of Finnish and international art

M **Ateneum Art Museum,** Kaivokatu 2, Helsinki, 00100 Finland. Tel 358-0294-500-401; Email ainfo@ateneum.fi; Web: www.ateneum.fi; *Dir* Susanna Pettersson
Open Tue & Fri 10 AM - 6 PM, Wed & Thurs 10 AM - 8 PM, Sat & Sun 10 AM - 5 PM, cl Mon; Admis adults 13 EUR, reduced under 18 free
Collections: 4300 paintings and 750 sculptures from 18th century to the early 60s, 650 works from international artists, prints from the late 19th century to the present; Nordic and European prints; Japanese woodcuts

M **Museum of Contemporary Art Kiasma,** Mannerheiminaukio 2, Helsinki, 00100 Finland. Tel 358-0294-500-501; Email info@kiasma.fi; Web: www.kiasma.fi; *Dir* Leevi Haapala
Open Tue 10 AM - 5 PM, Wed - Fri 10 AM - 8:30 PM, Sat 10 AM - 6 PM, Sun 10 AM - 5 PM, cl Mon; Admis adults 12 EUR, reduced 8 EUR, under 18 free
Collections: More than 9,000 works of art, international and national contemporary art, painting, photography, graphics, prints
Activities: Classes for adults & children; lects open to pub; concerts; gallery talks; tours; mus shop sells books, prints & other items

M **Sinebrychoff Art Museum,** Bulevardi 40, Helsinki, 00120 Finland. Tel 358-0294-500-460; Fax 358-0294-500-476; Email siff.info@siff.fi; Web: www.sinebrychoffintaidemuseo.fi; *Dir* Kirsi Eskelinen
Open Tue & Fri 10 AM - 6 PM, Wed - Thurs 10 AM - 8 PM, Sat - Sun 10 AM - 5 PM; Admis adults 12 EUR, reduced 10 EUR, under 18 free; Estab 2003
Library Holdings: Auction Catalogs, Exhibition Catalogs, Prints
Collections: Paul & Fanny Sinebrychoff Collection, European art from the 14th to the 19th century, Swedish portraits, icons, graphics and miniatures, glassware, porcelain, silverware, statues, clocks, and furniture
Activities: Lects open to pub; concerts; tours; mus shop sells reproductions, prints, postcards

M **SUOMEN KANSALLISMUSEO,** National Museum of Finland, Mannerheimintie 34, Helsinki, 00100 Finland; PO Box 913, Helsinki, 00101 Finland. Tel 358-295-33-6000; Fax 358-295-33-6999; Email kansallismuseo@kansallismuseo.fi; Web: www.kansallismuseo.fi; *Dir Gen* Elina Anttila, PhD; *Dir Mus Svcs* Tiina Mertanen; *Chief Exhibs* Minerva Keltanen
Open Tues - Sun 11 AM - 6 PM, cl Mon; Admis adults 10 EUR, reduced 7 EUR, under 18 yrs old free; Estab 1893; Numerous branch galleries throughout Finland; Average Annual Attendance: 100,000
Special Subjects: American Indian Art, Anthropology, Archaeology, Asian Art, Baroque Art, Carpets & Rugs, Ceramics, Coins & Medals, Costumes, Crafts, Decorative Arts, Dolls, Drawings, Embroidery, Eskimo Art, Ethnology, Flasks & Bottles, Folk Art, Furniture, Glass, Gold, Graphics, Historical Material, Islamic Art, Ivory, Jade, Jewelry, Judaica, Laces, Leather, Medieval Art, Metalwork, Miniatures, Oriental Art, Painting-Scandinavian, Period Rooms, Pewter, Photography, Porcelain, Portraits, Pottery, Primitive art, Prints, Religious Art, Renaissance Art, Scrimshaw, Silver, Stained Glass, Textiles
Collections: Ethnographical colls with Finnish, Finno-Ugrian & comparative ethnographical colls, Finnish historical colls with a coll of coins & medals, archaeological colls with finnish & comparative colls
Activities: Classes for children; dramatic progs; lects open to pub; ten vis lectrs per yr; concerts; tours; gallery talks; mus shop sells books, reproductions & prints; Workshop Vintti

KUOPIO

M **KUOPIAN TAIDEMUSEO,** Kuopio Art Museum, Kauppakatu 35, Kuopio, 70100 Finland. Tel 358-017-182-633; Email taidemuseo@kuopio.fi; Web: taidemuseo.kuopio.fi; *Dir* Aija Jaatinen
Open Tues - Sat 10 AM - 5 PM, cl Sun & Mon; Admis adults 6 EUR, reduced 4 EUR, under 18 free; Estab 1980
Collections: 6,700 pieces of mainly Finnish art with emphasis on contemporary art from the North Savo area from the 19th century to the present

PORI

M **PORIN TAIDEMUSEO,** Pori Art Museum, Etelaranta, Pori, 28100 Finland. Tel 358-44-701-1080; Fax 358-2-634-9410; Email taidemuseo@pori.fi; Web: www.poriartmuseum.fi; *Dir* Esko Nummelin
Open Tues - Sun 11 AM - 6 PM, Wed 11 AM - 8 PM; cl Mon; Admis adults 5 EUR, reduced 2.50 EUR, families 10 EUR; Estab 1981
Collections: Two permanent colls of nearly 2,800 works of contemporary Finnish art with emphasis on art from Western Finland and the Satakunta region

TAMPERE

M **SARA HILDENIN TAIDEMUSEO,** Sara Hilden Art Museum, Laiturikatu 13, Tampere, 33230 Finland. Tel 358-3-5654-3500; Email sara.hilden@tampere.fi; Web: www.tampere.fi/sarahilden; *Dir* Paivi Loimaala; *Chief Cur* Sarianne Soikkonen
Open Jan - Aug Mon - Sun 10 AM - 6 PM; Sept - Dec: Tues - Sun 10 AM - 6 PM, cl Mon; Admis adults 10 EUR, groups 6 EUR, pensioners, students & children 7-16 4 EUR, under 7 free; Estab 1979
Library Holdings: Auction Catalogs, Audio Tapes, Cassettes, Compact Disks, DVDs, Exhibition Catalogs, Original Documents, Periodical Subscriptions, Slides, Video Tapes
Collections: Comprehensive coll of nearly 5,000 works of modern Finnish & contemporary art
Activities: Classes for children; senior art educ; lectrs open to the pub; gallery talks; tours; mus shop sells books, cards & posters

TURKU

M **TURUN TAIDEMUSEO,** Turku Art Museum, Aurakatu 26, Turku, 20100 Finland. Tel 358-2-2627-100; Fax 358-2-2627-090; Web: www.turuntaidemuseo.fi; *Dir* Kari Immonen; *Cur* Christian Hoffmann; *Cur* Mia Haltia; *Cur* Annina Siren
Open Tues - Fri 11 AM - 7 PM, Sat - Sun 11 AM - 5 PM, cl Mon; Admis adults 9 EUR, students, seniors, unemployed & groups of 10 or more 5 EUR, visitors under 16 yrs free; Estab 1904; Average Annual Attendance: 35,000
Library Holdings: Auction Catalogs, Exhibition Catalogs, Periodical Subscriptions, Slides, Video Tapes
Collections: 19th & 20th centuries Finnish & Scandinavian art, drawings, paintings, prints & sculpture, 19th & 20th centuries international print coll
Activities: Lects open to pub; concerts; gallery talks; tours; mus shop sells books, magazines, original art, reproductions, prints, slides

FRANCE

AIX-EN-PROVENCE

M **MUSEE GRANET,** Granet Museum, Place Saint Jean de Malte, Aix-en-Provence, 13100 France. Tel 33 04 4252 8832; Fax 33 04 4252 8802; Web: www.museegranet-aixenprovence.fr; *Dir & Chief Cur* Bruno Ely
Open Tues - Sun 10 AM - 7 PM; Admis full 8 EUR, reduced 6 EUR, children under 18 & students under 26 free; Average Annual Attendance: 166,500
Collections: More than 12,000 European works & masterpieces, paintings, sculpture & artifacts

ALENCON

M **MUSEE DES BEAUX-ARTS ET DE LA DENTELLE D'ALENCON,** Museum of Fine Arts and Lace, Cour Carree de la Dentelle, Alencon, 61000 France. Tel 02-33-32-40-07; Fax 02-33-26-51-66; Email musee@ville-alencon.fr; Web: www.museedentelle-alencon.fr; *Cur* Johanna Mauboussin
Open Sept - June: Tues - Sun 10 AM - Noon & 2 - 6 PM, cl Mon; July & Aug daily 10 AM - Noon & 2 - 6 PM; Admis adult 4.10 EUR, reduced 3.05 EUR, under 26 free
Collections: 17th - 19th century French, Dutch & Flemish paintings, 16th - 19th century French, Italian & Dutch drawings, 16th - 20th century Alencon, Flemish, Italian & Eastern European lace

ANGERS

M **MUSEE DES BEAUX-ARTS D'ANGERS,** Museum of Fine Arts, 10 rue du Musee, Angers, 49100 France. Tel 33-2-41-05-38-00; Fax 33-2-41-05-38-09; Email musees@ville.angers.fr; Web: musees.angers.fr; *Dir & Cur* Anne Esnault
Open Oct - May Tues - Sun 10 AM - noon & 2 - 6 PM, cl Mon; June - Sept daily 10 AM - 6:30 PM; Admis general 4 EUR, reduced 3 EUR, under 26 free; Average Annual Attendance: 109,367 visitors
Income: Municipal budget
Library Holdings: Auction Catalogs, Book Volumes, CD-ROMs, Cards, Exhibition Catalogs, Framed Reproductions, Kodachrome Transparencies, Manuscripts, Original Documents, Periodical Subscriptions, Photographs, Slides
Collections: Paintings of the 17th & 18th centuries, Dutch, Flemish & French schools, sculpture, including busts by Houdon
Activities: Classes for adults & children; 3-4 book traveling exhibs per yr; mus shop sells books, magazines, reproductions, prints, slides, jewelry

ANGOULEME

M **MUSEE D'ANGOULEME,** Angouleme Museum, Sq Girard II, rue Corneille, Angouleme, 16000 France. Tel 05-45-95-79-88; Web: musee-angouleme.fr; *Dir & Chief Cur* Beatrice Rolin
Open May - Sept Tues - Sun 10 AM - 6 PM, cl Mon; Oct - April Tues, Wed & Fri 10 AM - 12:30 PM & 1:45 PM - 6 PM, Thurs 10 AM - 6 PM, Sat & Sun 2 PM - 6 PM, cl Mon; Admis general 5 EUR, reduced 3 EUR, under 18 free
Collections: European art, fine art and archeology colls

ANTIBES

M **MUSEE PICASSO,** Picasso Museum, Place Mariejol, Antibes, 06600 France. Tel 33-04-92-90-54-28; Email musee.picasso@ville-antibes.fr; Web: www.antibes-juanlespins.com/culture/musee-picasso; *Dir & Chief Cur* Jean-Louis Andral
Open mid-Sept - mid-June: Tues - Sun 10 AM - noon & 2 PM - 6 PM, cl Mon; mid-June - mid-Sept: Tues - Sun 10 AM - 6 PM; Admis full price 6 EUR, reduced 3 EUR, 17 & under & disabled visitors free
Income: Income from Assn des Amis du musee Picasso
Collections: Modern and contemporary art, works by Picasso, Nicholas de Stael, Germaine Richier, Hans Hartung, Anna-Eva Bergman
Activities: Classes for adults & children; lects open to pub; 6 lectrs per yr; mus shop sells books, magazines, reproductions, prints cards, cosmetics, DVDs

AVIGNON

M **COLLECTION LAMBERT EN AVIGNON,** Lambert Collection in Avignon, 5 rue Violette, Avignon, 84000 France. Tel 0490 165 620; Fax 0490 165 621; Email information@collectionlambert.com; Web: www.collectionlambert.fr; *Dir* Eric Mezil; *CEO* Igor Boiko
Open Sept - June: Tues - Sun 11 AM - 6 PM, cl Mon; July & Aug: daily 11 AM - 7 PM; Admis general 10 EUR, reduced 8 EUR, children 6 & under free; Estab 2000
Collections: Personal art collection of noted French art dealer Yvon Lambert, contemporary art

M **MUSEE DU PETIT PALAIS,** Petit Palace Museum, Place du Palais des Papes, Avignon, 84000 France. Tel 04-90-86-44-58; Fax 04-90-82-18-72; Email musee.petitpalais@mairie-avignon.com; Web: www.petit-palais.org; *Dir* Dominique Vingtain
Open Wed - Mon 10 AM - 1 PM and 2 - 6 PM, cl Tues; Admis full 6 EUR, reduced 3 EUR, children 12 & under free; Estab 1976
Library Holdings: Cards, Exhibition Catalogs, Reproductions
Collections: Italian paintings covering the period from 14th - 16th century, Medieval sculpture from Avignon from 12th - 15th century, paintings of the Avignon School of 14th - 15th centuries
Publications: Peinture Italienne, musee de Petit Palais Avignon RMN, 2005
Activities: Classes for adults & children; concerts, gallery tours; mus shop sells books, reproductions, & prints

BORDEAUX

M **MUSEE DES ARTS DECORATIFS ET DU DESIGN,** Museum of Decorative Arts and Design, 39 rue Bouffard, Bordeaux, 33000 France. Tel 33 05 56 10 14 00; Email madd@mairie-bordeaux.fr; Web: www.madd-bordeaux.fr; *Dir* Constance Rubini
Open Wed - Mon 11 AM - 6PM, cl Tues; Admis 4 EUR, reduced 2 EUR; Estab in 1955; Installed in a former private residence and municipal building
Collections: 18th & 19th century French decorative arts including furnishings, ceramics, glassware, gold & silver work, musical & measuring instruments, miniatures, tableware & personal items, French design items

M **MUSEE DES BEAUX-ARTS,** Museum of Fine Arts, 20 Cors d'Albert, Bordeaux, 33000 France. Tel 33 05 56 10 20 56; Fax 33 05 56 10 25 13; Email musbaxa@mairie-bordeaux.fr; Web: www.musba-bordeaux.fr; *Dir* Sophie Barthelemy
Open Wed - Mon 11 AM - 6 PM, cl Tues; Admis general 4 EUR, reduced 2 EUR,
Collections: 15th - 16th century European Renaissance paintings & sculptures, 17th century Caravaggesque, Flemish & Dutch paintings, 17th - 18th century Italian & French paintings, 18th century English, German & Flemish paintings

BOURGES

M **MUSEE ESTEVE,** Esteve Museum, 13 rue Edouard Branly, Bourges, France. Tel 02-48-24-75-38; Fax 02-48-24-29-48; Email musee-esteve@ville-bourges.fr; Web: www.ville-bourges.fr; *Conservation & Educ* Helene Mathiau
Open Wed - Mon 10 - noon & 2 - 6 PM, cl Tues; No admis fee; Estab 1987
Collections: Works by French painter Maurice Esteve, paintings, drawings, watercolors, collages, tapestries & lithographs

BREST

M **MUSEE DES BEAUX-ARTS DE BREST,** Museum of Fine Arts, 24 rue Traverse, Brest, 29200 France. Tel 02-98-00-87-96; Fax 02-98-00-87-78; Email musee-beaux-arts@brest-metropole-oceane.fr; Web: www.musee-brest.fr; *Dir & Chief Cur* Pascal Aumasson
Open Tues - Sat 10 AM - noon, 2 - 6 PM, Sun 2 - 6 PM, cl Mon; Admis general 5 EUR, reduced 3 EUR, under 25 free; Estab 1968
Library Holdings: Cards, Exhibition Catalogs
Special Subjects: Asian Art, Baroque Art, Ceramics, Landscapes, Painting-French, Painting-Italian, Painting-European
Collections: Paintings, sculptures & graphic arts, Pont-Aven School
Exhibitions: Autour de Charles Estienne
Publications: Catalogues d'exposition
Activities: Classes for children; concerts; lects open to pub; mus shop sells books

CERET

M **MUSEE D'ART MODERNE DE CERET,** Museum of Modern Art, 8, Bd Marechal Joffre, Ceret, 66400 France; BP 60413, Ceret, Cedex 66403 France. Tel 33-04-68-87-27-76; Fax 33-04-68-87-31-92; Email contact@musee-ceret.com; Web: www.musee-ceret.com; *Dir & Cur* Nathalie Gallissot
Open Jul - Sept: daily 10 AM - 7 PM; Oct - June: Tues - Sun 10 AM - 5:30 PM, cl Mon; Admis general 8 EUR, reduced 6 EUR, children under 12 free; Estab 1950; Modern & contemporary art school of Paris - catalamish art
Special Subjects: Ceramics, Drawings, Landscapes, Painting-French, Painting-Spanish, Prints, Sculpture
Collections: Modern Art, European Art, Works by: Picasso, Gris, Chagall, Soutine, Herbin, Nasson, Nanolo, Tapies, Grano, Brossa
Activities: Classes for children; concerts; mus shop sells books, reproductions, prints & other items

CHANTILLY

M **MUSEE CONDE,** Conde Museum, 7 rue du Connetable, Chantilly, 60500 France. Tel 33 03 44 27 31 80; Fax 33 03 44 24 56 83; Email nicole.garnier@domainedechantilly.com; Web: www.musee-conde.fr, www.domainedechantilly.com; *Dir & Chief Cur* Nicole Garnier; *Heritage Cur* Mathieu Deldicque
Open (Domaine de Chantilly) late Mar - Oct 10 AM - 6 PM; Nov - late March 10:30 AM - 5 PM, cl Tues; Admis (Domaine de Chantilly) full 17 EUR, reduced 10 EUR; Collection of Henri d'Orleans, Duke of Aumale, located on the grounds of the Domaine de Chantilly; Average Annual Attendance: 265,000
Library Holdings: Book Volumes, Exhibition Catalogs, Manuscripts, Maps, Original Documents, Periodical Subscriptions, Photographs, Prints
Special Subjects: Antiquities-Egyptian, Antiquities-Greek, Antiquities-Roman, Archaeology, Art History, Asian Art, Baroque Art, Decorative Arts, Drawings, Graphics, Manuscripts, Painting-European, Painting-Flemish, Painting-French, Painting-Italian, Religious Art, Renaissance Art, Sculpture, Woodcarvings, Tapestries
Collections: Paintings from the 15th - 19th centuries, drawings from the 16th - 18th centuries, Italian Renaissance, photographs from the 1850s, prints & portraits from the 16th - 19th centuries, furniture, miniatures & bone china
Publications: Exhibition Catalogue, Fra Angelico
Activities: Classes for children; lects open to the public; 5 vis lectrs per yr; concerts; gallery talks; tours; mus shop sells books, magazines, original art, reproductions, prints, slides, porcelain, tapestries, etc

DIJON

M **MUSEE DES BEAUX-ARTS DE DIJON,** Museum of Fine Arts, Palais des Ducs et des Etats de Bourgogne, Dijon, 21000 France. Tel 03 80 74 52 09; Fax 03 80 74 53 44; Email museedesbeauxarts@ville-dijon.fr; Web: mba.dijon.fr; *Dir* David Liot
Open May - Oct: Wed - Mon 9:30 AM - 6 PM, cl Tues; Nov - April: Wed - Mon 10 AM - 5 PM, cl Tues; No admis fee; Estab 1799
Collections: Furniture, objects of art, paintings of French & foreign schools, sculpture, Granville Collection

FONTAINEBLEAU

M **CHATEAU DE FONTAINEBLEAU,** Chateau de Fontainebleau, Fontainebleau, 77300 France. Tel 33 (01) 60-71-50-70; Fax 33 (01) 60-71-50-71; Email reservation@chateaudefontainebleau.fr; Web: www.musee-chateau-fontainebleau.fr; *Pres* Jean-Frangois Hebert; *Dir Heritage & Colls* Vincent Droguet
Open Chateau: April - Sept Wed - Mon 9:30 AM - 5 PM, cl Tues; Oct - Mar Wed - Mon 9:30 AM - 5 PM, cl Tues; Courtyard & Gardens: Mar, April & Oct daily 9 AM - 6 PM; May - Sep daily 9 AM - 7 PM; Nov - Feb daily 9 AM - 5 PM; Admis 11 EUR, reduced 9 EUR; Estab to show 8 centuries of history; Former sovereign residence & palace comprised of state apartments, small apartments, galleries, a theatre, museums, chapels, courtyards & gardens
Collections: Paintings, furniture and interiors of 1st Empire and 17th, 18th and 19th centuries

Publications: Visitor's guide (French, English, German, Russian, Italian, Spanish, Japanese, Chinese edits); many other publs of the cur of the castle
Activities: Educ prog; classes for children; lect open to public; 20-30 vis lectrs per yr; concerts; theater

GRENOBLE

M **MUSEE DE GRENOBLE,** Grenoble Museum, 5, place de Lavalette, Grenoble, 38010 France. Tel 04-76-63-44-44; Fax 04-76-63-44-10; Email musee-de-grenoble@grenoble.fr; Web: www.museedegrenoble.fr; *Dir* Guy Tosatto
Open Wed - Sun 10 AM - 6:30 PM, cl Tues; Admis 8 EUR, reduced 5 EUR, under 18 & first Sun of month free; Estab 1798
Collections: Western paintings from the 13th - 20th centuries, masterpieces of classical Dutch, Flemish, Italian & Spanish painting, 20th century European coll, post-1945 contemporary art

LENS

M **MUSEE DU LOUVRE - LENS,** The Louvre - Lens, 99 rue Paul Bert, Lens, 62300 France. Tel 33 (0)3 21 18 62 62; Fax 33 (0)3 21 18 62 65; Email info@louvrelens.fr; Web: www.louvrelens.fr; *Dir* Xavier Dectot
Open Mon, Wed - Sun 10 AM - 6 PM, cl Tues & May 1; No admis fee; Regional branch of The Louvre in Paris located in the Nord-Pas de Calais region of France.; Average Annual Attendance: 470000
Library Holdings: Book Volumes, Cards, DVDs, Exhibition Catalogs
Activities: Classes for adults & children; lects open to public; concerts, gallery talks, tours; mus shop sells books, magazines

LILLE

M **PALAIS DES BEAUX-ARTS DE LILLE,** Palace of Fine Arts, Place de la Republique, Lille, 59000 France. Tel 33-03-20-06-78-00; Fax 33-03-20-06-78-15; Web: www.pba-lille.fr; *Dir* Bruno Girveau
Open Mon 2 - 6 PM, Wed - Sun 10 AM - 6 PM, cl Tues; Admis general 7 EUR, reduced 4 EUR, under 18 free
Library Holdings: Auction Catalogs, Book Volumes, Exhibition Catalogs, Original Documents, Periodical Subscriptions, Photographs, Prints, Slides
Collections: Western European paintings from 15th - 20th centuries, collection of ceramics, objects of art and sculptures
Publications: Catalogue de Ceramiques; Catalogue de Sculpture
Activities: Classes for adults & children; mus shop sells books, reproductions, prints

LYON

M **MUSEE DES BEAUX-ARTS DE LYON,** Museum of Fine Arts, 20 Place des Terreaux, Lyon, 69001 France. Tel 33 04 72 10 17 40; Fax 33 04 78 28 12 45; Email contact@mba-lyon.fr; Web: www.mba-lyon.fr; *Dir* Sylvie Ramond
Open Sun, Mon, Wed, Thurs & Sat 10 AM - 6 PM, Fri 10:30 AM - 6 PM, cl Tues & holidays; Admis general 7 EUR, reduced 4 EUR; Estab 1792
Library Holdings: Cards, Exhibition Catalogs
Collections: Ancient, Medieval & Modern sculpture, Egyptian, Greek & Roman antiquities, French art since the Middle Ages, French, Hispano-Moorish, Italian & Oriental ceramics, Gothic & Renaissance art, Islamic art, modern art & murals by Puvis de Chavannes, painting of the French, Flemish, Dutch, Italian & Spanish schools
Activities: Classes for adults & children; lect open to public; concerts; gallery talks; mus shop sells books

M **MUSEE DES TISSUS, MUSEE DES ARTS DECORATIFS DE LYON,** Museum of Textiles, Museum of Decorative Arts, 34 rue de la Charite, Lyon, 69002 France. Tel 33-04-78-38-42-00; Fax 33-04-72-40-25-12; Email info@museedestissus.com; Web: www.mtmad.fr; *Dir* Maximilien Durand
Open Tues - Sun 10 AM - 5:30 PM, cl Mon; Admis adults 10 EUR, reduced 7.50 EUR; Estab 1856 by the Chamber of Commerce of Lyon; Displays textile history from the Coptic antiquity to the 20th century & decorative arts from the 16th - 20th century; Average Annual Attendance: 90,000
Library Holdings: Auction Catalogs, Book Volumes, Cards, Exhibition Catalogs, Manuscripts, Original Art Works, Original Documents, Periodical Subscriptions, Photographs, Prints
Special Subjects: Textiles, Costumes, Decorative Arts
Collections: Re-created French 18th century salons with furniture, objects d'art & decorative pieces, 15th & 16th centuries Italian majolicas, tapestries of Middle Ages & Renaissance, European drawings from 16th to 19th century, History of textiles, embroidery & lace from the Coptic antiquity to modern
Publications: Museum of Decorative Arts, handbook of the colls; exhibs catalogs
Activities: Classed for adults & children; lects open to pub; concerts; scholarships offered; mus shop sells books, magazines, reproductions, prints

MARSEILLE

M **MUSEE DES BEAUX-ARTS DE MARSEILLE,** Museum of Fine Arts, Palais Longchamp, 7 rue Edouard Stephan Marseille, 13004 France. Tel 33 04 91 14 59 30; Email dgac-musee-beauxarts@marie-marseille.fr; Web: culture.marseiile.fr; *Dir* Marie-Paule Vial; *Chief Cur* Luc Georget
Open Tues - Sun 10 AM - 6 PM, cl Mon; Admis general 5 EUR, reduced 3 EUR, under 18 free; Estab 1801
Collections: More than 8,000 drawings, paintings & sculptures from the 16th - 19th centuries, works by Baroque artist Pierre Puget

ORLEANS

M **MUSEE DES BEAUX-ARTS D'ORLEANS,** Museum of Fine Arts, 1, rue Fernand Rabier, Orleans, 45000 France. Tel 02 38 79 21 83; Fax 02 38 79 20 08; Email musee-ba@orleans-agglo.fr; Web: www.orleans-agglo.fr; *Deputy Dir & Cur* Benedicte De Donker
Open Tues - Thurs & Sat 10 AM - 6 PM, Fri 10 AM - 8 PM, Sun 1 - 6 PM, cl Mon; Admis 4 EUR, reduced 2 EUR, under 18 free; Estab 1797; European artwork from the 16th to the 20th century
Library Holdings: Auction Catalogs, Book Volumes, CD-ROMs, Cards, DVDs, Exhibition Catalogs, Fiche, Framed Reproductions, Manuscripts, Memorabilia, Original Documents, Other Holdings, Periodical Subscriptions, Photographs, Reproductions, Slides
Special Subjects: Decorative Arts, Drawings, Enamels, Etchings & Engravings, Furniture, Ivory, Landscapes, Medieval Art, Painting-Dutch, Painting-European, Painting-Flemish, Painting-French, Painting-German, Painting-Italian, Painting-Spanish, Portraits, Prints, Religious Art, Renaissance Art, Sculpture, Silver, Watercolors, Woodcuts, Miniatures
Collections: Dutch, French, Flemish, German, Italian & Spanish paintings, prints, & drawings, primarily from 17th & 18th centuries, 19th & 20th century art works, sculptures
Publications: Quick book, exhibition catalogue
Activities: Classes for children; visits for adults in groups; lects open to the pub; lects for mems only; 190 vis lectrs per yr; concerts; gallery talks; lending original object of art to French & international mus & institutions; mus shop sells books, magazines, reproductions; prints, slides & other items

PARIS

M **CENTRE NATIONAL D'ART ET DE CULTURE GEORGES POMPIDOU,** Georges Pompidou National Center of Arts and Culture, Place Georges Pompidou, Paris, 75004 France. Tel 33 (0) 1 44 78 12 33; Email info@centrepompidou.fr; Web: www.centrepompidou.fr; *Pres* Serge Lasvignes; *Exec Dir* Julie Narbey
Open museum & exhibs: 11 AM - 9 PM, Thurs 11 AM - 11 PM cl Tues & May 1; Admis adult 14 EUR, concessions 11 EUR, under 18, mems, teachers, journalists & unemployed (proof of status required) no admis fee; Circ 1,500,000; Center composed of museum, Musee National d'Art Moderne; library, Bibliotheque Publique d'Information; research centre, Institut de Recherche et Coordination Acoustique/Musique; The Atelier Brancusi; 2 cinemas; 2 theatres; Average Annual Attendance: 3,600,000; Mem: 46,700; meet 2-3 times a week
Income: Mem & mus friends
Library Holdings: Auction Catalogs, Audio Tapes, Book Volumes, CD-ROMs, Cards, Cassettes, Clipping Files, Compact Disks, DVDs, Exhibition Catalogs, Framed Reproductions, Manuscripts, Original Documents 380,000, Periodical Subscriptions, Photographs, Reproductions, Slides, Video Tapes
Collections: 20th century paintings, prints, drawings & sculpture, art films & photographs, designs & architecture
Publications: Catalogues & numerous other publs
Activities: Classes for adults & children; docent training; lects open to the pub; 33,600 vis lectrs per yr; concerts; gallery talks; tours; award, Price Marcel Duchamp; schols; fels; lending original objects of art to Centre Pompidou mobile; 20 book traveling exhibs per yr; originates traveling exhibs to co-productions with main mus & art centers around the world; mus shop sells books, magazines, reproductions, prints, slides; jr gallery

L **ECOLE NATIONALE SUPERIEURE DES BEAUX-ARTS - LE SERVICE DE COLLECTIONS,** National School of Fine Arts Collections Service, 14 rue Bonaparte, Paris, 75272 France. Tel 01-47-03-54-35; Email consultation-collections@beauxartsparis.fr; Web: www.beauxartsparis.com; *Head Cur Colls* Anne-Marie Garcia
Open Mon, Wed & Fri 1:30 - 5:30 PM; No admis fee; Estab 1819; 120,000 vol library & 500,000 works of art
Income: Ministere de la Culture
Library Holdings: Auction Catalogs, Audio Tapes, Book Volumes, CD-ROMs, Cassettes, DVDs, Exhibition Catalogs, Manuscripts, Original Art Works, Original Documents, Periodical Subscriptions, Photographs, Prints, Sculpture, Video Tapes
Special Subjects: Antiquities-Greek, Antiquities-Roman, Archaeology, Architecture, Art Education, Art History, Bookplates & Bindings, Calligraphy, Coins & Medals, Constructions, Decorative Arts, Drawings, Etchings & Engravings, Graphic Arts, Illustration, Landscape Architecture, Manuscripts, Miniatures, Painting-European, Painting-French, Photography, Prints, Reproductions, Sculpture
Collections: paintings, sculptures, plaster casts, prints, photographs, manuscripts
Activities: Classes for adults; lects open to pub; 50 vis lectrs per yr; traveling exhibs varies, Princeton Art Mus, Dahesh Mus (NY); mus shop sells books

M **LES ARTS DECORATIFS - MUSEE DES ARTS DECORATIFS,** Museum of Decorative Arts, 107, rue de Rivoli, Paris, 75001 France. Tel 33-01-44-55-57-50; Email presse@lesartsdecoratifs.fr; Web: www.lesartsdecoratifs.fr; *Pres* Pierre-Alexis Dumas; *Dir* Olivier Gabet
Open Tues, Wed, Fri - Sun 11 AM - 6 PM, Thurs 11 AM - 9 PM, cl Mon; Admis 11 EUR, reduced 8. 50 EUR; Estab 1901
Library Holdings: Auction Catalogs, Book Volumes, Exhibition Catalogs, Original Art Works
Collections: Decorative arts coll from Middle Ages to present, exhibs of decorative arts, design, textiles & costumes, graphism, exhibs of publicity, toys & jewels, library with 100,000 vols
Activities: Classes for adults and children; lects open to public; organize traveling exhibs; mus shop sells original art, reproductions, design and decorative arts

M **MAISON EUROPEENNE DE LA PHOTOGRAPHIE,** European House of Photography, 5/7 rue de Fourcy, Paris, 75004 France. Tel 33 144 78 75 00; Fax 33 144 78 75 15; Web: www.mep-fr.org; *Pres* Henry Chapier; *Dir* Jean-Luc Monterosso
Open Wed - Sun 11 AM - 8 PM, cl Mon & Tues; Admis adults 8 EUR, reduced 4.50 EUR, children under 8 free

Collections: International coll of photographs from the 1950s to the present, video coll

M **MUSEE CARNAVALET,** Carnavalet Museum, 16 rue des Francs-Bourgeois, Paris, 75003 France. Tel 01 44 59 58 58; Fax 01 44 59 58 11; Email carnavalet.actionculturelle@paris.fr; Web: www.carnavalet.paris.fr; *Chief Cur* Valerie Guillaume; *Secy Gen* Daniele Desideri
Open Tues - Sun 10 AM - 6 PM, cl Mon; Admis 5 EUR; Estab 1880; Average Annual Attendance: 250,000
Special Subjects: Archaeology, Architecture, Ceramics, Decorative Arts, Drawings, Graphics, Painting-French, Period Rooms, Photography, Portraits, Prints, Sculpture
Collections: History and archaeology of Paris, prints, drawings, photography & sculpture
Activities: Classes for adults & children; lects open to pub; concerts; mus shop sells books, magazines, reproductions, slides

M **MUSEE COGNACQ-JAY,** Cognacq-Jay Museum, 8, rue Elzevir, Paris, 75003 France. Tel 33 01 40 27 07 21; Email reservation.cognacq-jay@paris.fr; Web: www.cognacq-jay.paris.fr; *Dir & Cur* Rose-Marie Herda-Mousseaux; *Asst to the Dir & Cur* Benjamin Couilleaux
Open Tues - Sun 10 AM - 6 PM, cl Mon; No admis fee, except for temp exhibs; Estab 1929; Gallery contains European art of the 18th Century
Special Subjects: Decorative Arts, Drawings, Furniture, Jewelry, Miniatures, Painting-British, Painting-French, Painting-Italian, Porcelain, Portraits, Sculpture, Tapestries, Watercolors
Collections: 18th century works of art, English and French furniture, pastels, paintings, porcelain, sculpture, miniatures, drawings
Publications: Catalogue of furniture; Catalogue of miniatures; Catalogue of paintings; Catalogue of drawings & pastels; Catalogue of gold boxes & objects of virtue
Activities: Classes for children; lects open to pub; gallery talks; tours; mus shop sells books, reproductions; catalogues & mus collections

M **MUSEE D'ART MODERNE DE LA VILLE DE PARIS,** City of Paris Museum of Modern Art, 12 Avenue de New York, Paris, 75116 France. Tel 33 1 53 67 40 00; Web: www.mam.paris.fr; *Dir* Fabrice Hergott; *Sec Gen* Anne-Sophie De Gasquet
Open Tues - Sun 10 AM - 6 PM, Thurs until 10 PM, cl Mon & public holidays; Perm colls: no admis fee; spec exhibs: adults 5 - 12 EUR, disabled, children 18 & under free
Collections: Modern painting and sculpture

M **MUSEE D'ORSAY,** 62 rue de Lille, Paris, 75343 France. Tel 33 (0)1 40 49 48 14; Web: www.musee-orsay.fr; *Dir* Laurence des Cars; *Chief Cur* Sylvie Patry
Open Tues - Sun 9:30 AM - 6 PM, Thurs 9:30 AM - 9:45 PM, cl Mon, May 1 & Dec 25; Admis 14 EUR, concessions 11 EUR, under 18 & mems free; Estab 1986; 17,000 sq ft; Average Annual Attendance: 3,000,000; Mem: 20,000
Library Holdings: Book Volumes, CD-ROMs, Cards, Compact Disks, DVDs, Exhibition Catalogs, Framed Reproductions, Reproductions, Sculpture
Collections: French art from 1848 - 1914, Paintings, sculptures, furniture, photography, decorative arts, graphic arts, architecture, collection of impressionist masterpieces, Louvre Museum Collection, Musee du Jeu de Paume Collection
Activities: Educ progs; concerts; mus shop sells books, magazines, reproductions, cards, exhib catalogs, CD Roms, DVD's, sculptures & stationary

M **Musee de l'Orangerie**, Jardin des Tuileries, Paris, 75001 France. Tel 33 (0)1 44 50 43 00; Email information@musee-orangerie.fr; Web: www.musee-orangerie.fr; *Pres* Guy Cogeval
Open Mon - Sun 9 AM - 6 PM, cl Tues, May 1, morning of July 14 & Dec 25; Admis 9 EUR, discount 6.50 EUR, first Sun of month free
Collections: coll of Jean Walter & Paul Guillaume; Les Nympheas, Hebert: paintings by Ernest Hebert

M **MUSEE DE CLUNY - MUSEE NATIONAL DU MOYEN AGE,** Cluny Museum - National Museum of the Middle Ages, 6 place Paul Painleve, Paris, 75005 France. Tel 33 01 53 73 78 00; Fax 33 01 53 73 78 35; Email contact.musee-moyenage@culture.gouv.fr; Web: www.musee-moyenage.fr; *Dir & Cur* Elisabeth Taburet-Delahaye
Open Wed - Mon 9:15 AM - 5:45 PM, cl Tues; Admis general 8 EUR, reduced 6 EUR, under 18 free; Estab 1843 (first pub opening 1844); Two joined bldgs: 1st century Roman Bath & Cluny Abbots 15 century residence; Average Annual Attendance: 300,000; Mem: 600
Collections: Enamels, furniture, goldsmithery, ivories, paintings, sculptures & tapestries of the Middle Ages-from the 10th to the beginning of the 16th centuries, Gallo-Roman antiquities
Publications: Catalogues; guidebooks
Activities: Classes for adults & children; concerts; gallery talks; tours; mus shop sells books, reproductions

M **MUSEE DES MONUMENTS FRANCAIS,** Museum of French Monuments, Palais de Chaillot, 1 place du Trocadero Paris, 75116 France. Tel 33 01 58 51 52 00; Fax 33 01 47 55 40 13; Web: www.citechaillot.fr; *Dir & Chief Cur* Laurence de Finance
Open Wed, Fri - Sun 11 AM - 7 PM, Thurs 11 AM - 9 PM, cl Mon & Tues; Admis general 8 EUR, reduced 6 EUR, under 18 free; Estab 1882; Museum of the Cite de l'Architecture et du Patrimoine; library with 10,000 works on art history
Collections: Full scale casts of the principal French monuments and sculpture from the beginning of Christianity to the 19th century, full scale reproductions of Medieval murals

M **MUSEE DU LOUVRE,** The Louvre, Paris Cedex 01, Paris, 75058 France. Tel 33 (0)1 40 20 53 17; Email info@louvre.fr; Web: www.louvre.fr; *Pres & Dir* Jean-Luc Martinez; *Mng Dir* Maxence Langlois-Berthelot
Open Mon, Thurs, Sat & Sun 9 AM - 6 PM, Wed & Fri 9 AM - 9:45 PM, cl Tues, May 1 & Dec 25; Admis gen 15 EUR; Estab 1793; Fine art museum housed in a former French palace; Average Annual Attendance: 8,300,000
Collections: Art of Islam, The Edmond de Rothschild Collection, Oriental, Greek, Roman Etruscan and Egyptian antiquities, objets d'art, drawings, paintings, Medieval & Renaissance sculpture, History of the Louvre
Activities: Classes for adults & children; lects open to public; concerts, gallery talks, tours; mus shop sells books, magazines, reproductions, prints, slides, jewels, post cards

M **The Carrousel & Tuileries Gardens**, 99 rue de Rivoli, Paris, 75039 France.
Open daily Oct - March 7:30 AM - 7:30 PM, April, May, Sept 7 Am - 9 PM, June - Aug 7 AM - 11 PM; No admis fee; 24-hectare public, open-air sculpture museum and gardens
Collections: 17th - 21st century statues and vases, Aristide Maillol sculptures
Activities: Guided tours

M **MUSEE MARMOTTAN MONET,** Marmottan Monet Museum, 2 rue Louis Boilly, Paris, 75016 France. Tel 33-01-44-96-50-33; Fax 33-01-40-50-65-84; Email marmottan@marmottan.fr; Web: www.marmottan.fr; *Dir* Patrick de Carolis
Open Tues, Wed, Fri - Sun 10 AM - 6 PM, Thurs 10 AM - 8 PM, cl Mon; Admis 11 EUR, reduced 6.50 EUR, children under 8 free
Collections: Coll of Primitives, Renaissance, Empire and Impressionist works, medieval miniatures in Wildenstein coll
Activities: Educ prog; classes for children; mus shop sells books, magazines, original art, reproductions, prints

M **MUSEE NATIONAL EUGENE-DELACROIX,** National Museum of Eugene Delacroix, 6 rue de Furstenberg, Paris, 75006 France. Tel 33 01 44 41 86 50; Email contact.musee-delacroix@louvre.fr; Web: www.musee-delacroix.fr; *Dir* Dominique de Font-Reaulx
Open Wed - Mon 9:30 AM - 5:30 PM; Admis 7 EUR; Estab 1932; Art museum housed in the former apartment of French artist Eugene Delacroix
Special Subjects: Drawings, Landscapes, Painting-French, Portraits, Prints, Watercolors
Collections: Artwork, writings & personal belongings of Eugene Delacroix
Activities: Educ and outreach progs for adults & children; family workshops, conferences, concerts, tours

M **MUSEE NATIONAL FRANCAIS DES ARTS ASIATIQUES - GUIMET,** Guimet National Museum of Asian Art, 6 place d'Iena, Paris, 75116 France. Tel 33 1 56 52 53 00; Fax 33 1 56 52 53 54; Email contact@guimet.fr; Web: www.guimet.fr; *Pres* Sophie Makariou; *Dir* Thierry Jopeck
Open Mon & Wed - Sun 10 AM - 6 PM; cl Tues; Admis 7.50 EUR, reduced 5.50 EUR; temp exhibs: 8 EUR, reduced 6 EUR; Estab 1889; Maintains library with 100,000 vols. Main exhib contains 4,000+ works on 5,500 Sq m; Average Annual Attendance: 300,000
Income: Admis fees & state funds
Library Holdings: Auction Catalogs, Book Volumes, CD-ROMs, Compact Disks, Exhibition Catalogs, Filmstrips, Manuscripts, Maps, Micro Print, Original Art Works, Original Documents, Photographs, Prints, Records, Reproductions
Special Subjects: Antiquities-Oriental, Archaeology, Asian Art, Bronzes, Calligraphy, Carpets & Rugs, Ceramics, Costumes, Drawings, Furniture, Glass, Gold, Ivory, Jade, Jewelry, Manuscripts, Photography, Porcelain, Pottery, Sculpture, Textiles
Collections: Art, archaeology, religions, history of India, Afghanistan, Central Asia, China, Korea, Japan, Khmer, Tibet, Thailand and Indonesia
Activities: Classes for adults & children; lects open to pub; concerts; mus shop sells books, reproductions, prints

M **MUSEE NATIONAL GUSTAVE-MOREAU,** Gustave Moreau National Museum, 14 rue de La Rochefoucauld, Paris, F-75009 France. Tel 33-1-48-74-38-50; Fax 33-1-48-74-18-71; Email info@musee-moreau.fr; Web: musee-moreau.fr; *Dir* Marie-Cecile Forest; *Secy Gen* David Ben Si Mohand
Open Mon, Wed & Thurs 10 AM - 12:45 PM & 2 - 5:15 PM, Fri - Sun 10 AM - 5:15 PM, cl Tues; Admis general 6 EUR, reduced 4 EUR; Housed in the family home of French painter Gustave Moreau
Collections: Several of Gustave Moreau's masterpieces with preparatory work, more than 4,800 drawings and 450 watercolors, collection of personal artifacts and souvenirs in former apartment

M **MUSEE NATIONAL PICASSO - PARIS,** National Picasso Museum, 5 rue de Thorigny, Paris, 75003 France. Tel 33-01-85-56-00-36; Email contact@museepicassoparis.fr; Web: www.museepicassoparis.fr; *Chief Cur & Pres* Laurent Le Bon
Open Tues - Sun 9:30 AM - 6 PM, cl Mon; Admis regular 12.50 EUR, reduced 11 EUR, under 18 free; Located in the Hotel Sale
Collections: Works of Pablo Picasso from 1848 to 1972 following chronological stylistic changes, 200 paintings, 3000 drawings, sculptures, collages, illustrated books and manuscripts, Picasso personal collection and collection of friends

M **MUSEE RODIN,** Rodin Museum, 77 rue de Varenne, Paris, 75007 France. Tel 33-01-44-18-61-10; Fax 33-01-44-18-61-30; Email goldberger@musee-rodin.fr; Web: www.musee-rodin.fr; *Dir & Chief Cur* Catherine Chevillot
Open Tues - Sun 10 AM - 5:45 PM, cl Mon; Admis full 10 EUR, reduced 7 EUR, under 18 free; Estab 1919; Located in the Hotel Biron and features a chapel & sculpture garden; Average Annual Attendance: 700,000
Library Holdings: Auction Catalogs, Audio Tapes, CD-ROMs, Exhibition Catalogs, Manuscripts, Maps, Original Documents, Periodical Subscriptions, Video Tapes
Special Subjects: Sculpture
Collections: 6,600 sculptures by Rodin, Drawings, paintings, engravings, photographs, archives and personal coll
Exhibitions: Prog on website
Activities: Mus shop sells books, magazines, reproductions

M **PETIT PALAIS, MUSEE DES BEAUX-ARTS DE LA VILLE DE PARIS,** City of Paris Fine Arts Museum, Ave Winston Churchill, Paris, 75008 France. Tel 33 01 53 43 40 00; Fax 33 01 53 43 40 52; Web: www.petitpalais.paris.fr; *Dir* Christophe Leribault; *Secy Gen* Bruno Leuvrey

Open Tues - Thurs & Sat - Sun 10 AM - 6 PM, Fri 10 AM - 9 PM temporary exhibs, cl Mon & pub holidays; No admis fee to permanent coll & interior garden; Estab 1900
Collections: Egyptian, Etruscan and Greek antiquities, paintings, sculpture and other works of art to 19th century
Activities: Classes for children; lects open to pub; concerts; originate traveling exhibs; mus shop sells books & magazines

RENNES

M **MUSEE DES BEAUX-ARTS DE RENNES,** Museum of Fine Arts, 20 quai Emile Zola, Rennes, 35000 France. Tel 02-23-62-17-45; Fax 02-23-62-17-49; Email museebeauxarts@ville-rennes.fr; Web: www.mbar.org; *Dir* Anne Dary
Open Tues - Fri 10 AM - 5 PM, Sat & Sun 10 AM - 6 PM, cl Mon; Admis regular 5 EUR, reduced 3 EUR, under 18 free; Estab 1794
Library Holdings: Cards, Exhibition Catalogs
Collections: Drawings, paintings and sculptures from 15th - 21st centuries, Egyptian, Greek & Celtic artifacts, contemporary art
Exhibitions: Objects of the 18th century
Activities: Classes for children & children; lects for mems only; 6 vis lectrs per yr; concerts; gallery talks; fels; lending of original art to other mus; mus shop sells books

STRASBOURG

M **MUSEE DES BEAUX-ARTS DE STRASBOURG,** Museum of Fine Arts, 2 place du Chateau, Strasbourg, Cedex 67076 France. Tel 33-03-68-98-51-60; Fax 33-03-68-98-57-67; Email dominique.jacquot@strasbourg.eu; Web: www.musees.strasbourg.eu; *Dir* Joelle Pijaudier-Cabot; *Cur* Dominique Jacquot; *Cur* Michele Lavallee
Open Mon, Wed - Fri 10 AM - 6 PM; Admis regular 6.50 EUR, reduced 3.50 EUR, under 18 free; Located on the first floor of Rohan Palace
Collections: European paintings from the 17th - 19th centuries, Italian & Flemish primitives, Renaissance & Mannerism, 17th & 18th century Baroque, Naturalism & Classicism

TOULOUSE

M **MUSEE DES AUGUSTINS - MUSEE DES BEAUX-ARTS DE TOULOUSE,** Augustins Museum - Museum of Fine Arts, 21 rue de Metz, Toulouse, 31000 France. Tel 33 05 61 22 21 82; Fax 33 05 61 22 34 69; Email augustins@mairie-toulouse.fr; Web: www.augustins.org; *Dir* Pierre Cohen
Open Wed 10 AM - 9 PM, Thurs - Mon, 10 AM - 6 PM, cl Tues; Admis regular 5 EUR, reduced 3 EUR, under 18 free; Estab 1793; Average Annual Attendance: 120,000
Library Holdings: Book Volumes, Cards, Exhibition Catalogs, Kodachrome Transparencies, Periodical Subscriptions, Photographs, Slides
Special Subjects: Medieval Art, Painting-European, Painting-Flemish, Painting-French, Painting-Italian, Religious Art, Sculpture
Collections: More tha 4,000 paintings and sculptures dating from the early Middle Ages to the beginning of the 20th century
Publications: Guides to collection
Activities: Classes for children; lects open to pub, 6 vis lectrs per year, concerts, gallery talks, tours; mus shop sells books

TOURS

M **MUSEE DES BEAUX-ARTS DE TOURS,** Museum of Fine Arts, 18 place Francois Sicard, Tours, 37000 France. Tel 33-02-47-05-68-73; Fax 33-02-47-05-38-91; Email musee-beauxarts@ville-tours.fr; Web: www.mba.tours.fr; *Dir* Sophie Join-Lambert; *Chief Cur* Annie Gilet
Open Wed - Mon 9 - 11:45 AM & 2:15 - 6 PM, cl Tues; Admis regular 6 EUR, reduced 3 EUR, children under 12 free; Estab 1801; Located in the Palais des Archeveques
Library Holdings: Auction Catalogs, CD-ROMs, Cards, DVDs, Exhibition Catalogs, Framed Reproductions, Kodachrome Transparencies, Lantern Slides
Special Subjects: Antiquities-Etruscan, Antiquities-Greek, Antiquities-Roman, Asian Art, Baroque Art, Bronzes, Calligraphy, Carpets & Rugs, Cartoons, Ceramics, Coins & Medals, Collages, Costumes, Crafts, Decorative Arts, Drawings, Embroidery, Enamels, Furniture, Glass, Gold, Graphics, Hispanic Art, Historical Material, Islamic Art, Ivory, Jewelry, Landscapes, Leather, Manuscripts, Maps, Marine Painting, Medieval Art, Metalwork, Military Art, Miniatures, Painting-American, Painting-Dutch, Painting-European, Painting-Flemish, Painting-French, Painting-German, Painting-Italian, Painting-Japanese, Painting-Scandinavian, Painting-Spanish, Photography, Porcelain, Portraits, Pottery, Prints, Religious Art, Renaissance Art, Sculpture, Tapestries, Textiles, Watercolors, Silver, Woodcarvings
Collections: Ancient and Modern Tapestries, Furniture, French School of 18th Century, including Boucher and Lancret, Italian Paintings of 13th to 16th Century, including Mantegna and primitives, 17th Century Paintings, including Rembrandt and Rubens, 19th Century Paintings, including Degas, Delacroix and Monet, Sculptures: Bourdelle, Houdon, Lemoyne, Rodin, Davidson, Calder
Activities: Classes for adults & children; lects open to pub; 4 vis lectrs per yr; concerts; mus shop sells books, reproductions & prints

VERSAILLES

M **CHATEAU DE VERSAILLES,** Palace of Versailles, Chateau de Versailles, RP 834 Versailles, 78008 France. Tel 33-01-30-83-78-00; Email documentation@chateauversailles.fr; Web: www.chateauversailles.fr; *Pres* Catherine Pegard
Open Apr - Oct: Tues - Sun 9 AM - 6:30 PM; Nov - March: Tues - Sun 9 - 5:30; Admis 18 EUR, reduced 13 EUR; under 18 free; Visiting areas include the Palace, Garden, Grand Trianon, Marie-Antoinette's Estate, Marly Estate & Royal Stables; Average Annual Attendance: 4,500,000
Income: Property of the Etablissement public du château, du musée et du domaine national de Versailles, a national public institution
Library Holdings: Auction Catalogs, Book Volumes, Clipping Files, Exhibition Catalogs, Periodical Subscriptions
Special Subjects: Architecture, Decorative Arts, Drawings, Furniture, Landscape Architecture, Landscapes, Painting-European, Painting-French, Porcelain, Portraits, Restorations, Sculpture, Tapestries, Tapestries, Woodcarvings
Collections: Paintings, sculptures & carriages from 17th to 19th centuries, decorative arts from 17th - 19th century, drawings & prints
Activities: Classes for children; lects open to pub; lects for mems only; concerts; tours; mus shop sells books, reproductions, prints, souvenirs & spin-offs

GABON

LIBREVILLE

M **MUSEE NATIONAL DES ARTS ET TRADITIONS DU GABON,** National Museum of Art & Culture, Au Bord de Mer, Libreville, Gabon. Tel 241-01-76-14-56; *Dir* Ayme Sylvain Ibouili
Open Mon - Fri 8:30 AM - 3:30 PM; Admis general 1,000 CFA, guided tour 2,000 CFA
Collections: 2,500 objects of Gabon ethnography, history and art

GAMBIA

BANJUL

M **NATIONAL CENTRE FOR ARTS & CULTURE,** The Gambia National Museum, Independence Dr, Banjul, Gambia. Tel 220-422-6244; Fax 220-422-7461; Email info@ncac.gm; Web: www.ncac.gm; *Dir Gen* Baba A Ceesay
Open Mon - Thurs 9 AM - 6 PM, Fri - Sun, 9 AM - 5 PM; Admis 50 GMD; Estab 1985; History & ethnography of The Gambia housed in an old colonial building
Library Holdings: CD-ROMs, Cassettes
Collections: Permanent collection of cultural objects, Artifacts, works of art, books, historical documents and photographs relating to the ethnographic and historical culture of the region
Activities: Classes for children; sales shop sells books, reproductions, prints, slides & attire; Wassu Museum, Wassu

GEORGIA

TBILISI

M **GEORGIAN NATIONAL MUSEUM,** 1 Lado Gudiashvili str, Tbilisi, 0105 Georgia. Tel 995-32-2-99-80-22; Email info@museum.ge; Web: www.museum.ge; *Gen Dir* Dr David Lordkipanidze
Open Tues - Sun 10 AM - 6 PM, cl Mon; Admis adult 3.50 GEL, visitors under 18 .50 GEL, children under 6 free; Estab 2004; Unification of 10 museums, the National Gallery, four house museums & two research centers
Collections: Best-known samples of Georgian & Eurasian artwork, Medieval Christian art, Islamic art, Colchis gold & silver jewelry, masterpieces of the Russian, Western European and Asian decorative arts, modern & contemporary Georgian paintings

GERMANY

AACHEN

M **SUERMONDT-LUDWIG-MUSEUM,** Wilhelmstrasse 18, Aachen, 52070 Germany. Tel 49 0241 47980 40; Fax 49 0241 37075; Email info@suermondt-ludwig-museum.de; Web: www.suermondt-ludwig-museum.de; *Dir* Peter van den Brink
Open Tues, Thurs & Fri noon - 6 PM, Wed noon - 8 PM, Sat & Sun 11 AM - 6 PM, cl Mon; Admis full 5 EUR, reduced 3 EUR; Estab 1877; Library with 55,000 books & periodicals
Collections: Paintings from the Middle Ages to the Baroque, portraits from Middle Ages to present, sculpture from the Middle Ages, graphic art (ceramics, textiles)

BERLIN

M **BRUCKE-MUSEUM,** Bussardsteig 9, Berlin, 14195 Germany. Tel 030-831-2029; Fax 030-831-5961; Email bruecke-museum@t-online.de; Web: www.bruecke-museum.de; *Dir & Prof* Dr Magdalena M Moeller
Open Wed - Mon 11 AM - 5 PM, cl Tues; Admis full 6 EUR, reduced 4 EUR; Estab 1967 upon the donation of Karl Schmidt-Rottluff; Dedicated to the works by mems of the 20th century expressionist artist's group Die Brucke.
Library Holdings: Other Holdings publs on the Brucke group, Expressionism &

Collections: German expressionism, paintings, sculptures & graphic art of the Brucke group
Publications: Brucke Archiv-Meft, appears at irregular intervals
Activities: Tours; originate traveling exhibs; mus shop sells catalogues accompanying exhibs

M **DEUTSCHES HISTORISCHES MUSEUM,** German Historical Museum, Unter den Linden 2, Berlin, 10117 Germany. Tel 49 30 20304-751; Fax 49 30 20304-759; Email info@dhm.de; Web: www.dhm.de; *Pres & Dir Exhibs* Dr Ralph Gross; *Deputy Dir* Ulrike Kretzschmar; *Dir Svcs* Bernd Burmeister; *Dir Communs* Barbara Wolf; *Coll Dir* Fritz Backhaus
Open daily 10 AM - 6 PM, cls Dec 24; Admis adults 8 EUR, reduced 4 EUR, children under 18 free; Estab 1987
Library Holdings: Auction Catalogs, CD-ROMs, Exhibition Catalogs
Special Subjects: Coins & Medals, Drawings, Historical Material, Manuscripts, Medieval Art, Military Art, Painting-German, Photography, Posters, Textiles
Collections: Objects documenting everyday life, historical documents, maps, house archive, contemporary documents after 1914, arts & posters, paintings before 1900, paintings, 20th century sculpture, photographs, numismatics, applied arts & plastic, everyday life culture: medical equipment, household supplies, textiles, badges, toys, postcards, militaria: weapons, harnesses, military devices, medals, uniforms, flags
Exhibitions: Permanent Exhib: German History in Images & Artifacts from Two Millennia; German history in pictures & documents
Activities: Educ progs for adults & children; lectrs open to the pub; lending of original objects of art to mus; mus shop sells books, magazines

M **JUDISCHES MUSEUM BERLIN,** Jewish Museum Berlin, Lindenstrasse 9-14, Berlin, 10969 Germany. Tel 49 (0)30 259 93 300; Fax 49 (0)30 259 93 409; Email info@jmberlin.de; Web: www.jmberlin.de; *Dir* Peter Schafer; *Prog Dir* Cilly Kugelmann; *Mng Dir* Martin Michaelis; *Organizational Dir* Bulent Durmus
Open Mon 10 AM - 10 PM, Tues - Sun 10 AM - 8 PM; Admis regular 8 EUR, reduced 3 EUR, children 6 & under free; Estab 2001
Collections: Jewish ceremonial objects, applied arts, fine arts, photography, archival documents on the lives of German Jewish individuals & families

M **SAMMLUNG BOROS,** Bunker, Reinhardtstr 20, Berlin, 10117 Germany. Tel 49 30 2759 4065; Email info@sammlung-boros.de; Web: www.sammlung-boros.de; *Dir* Juliet Kothe; *Asst to the Dir* Thyra Fermann
Open Thurs - Sat w/ advance reservations, to groups of up to 12 people; Admis 15 EUR, reduced 9 EUR; Pvt coll of international artists from 1990-present; 3,000 sq meter converted air-raid bunker
Special Subjects: Sculpture
Collections: Modern & contemporary art
Exhibitions: Temporary & rotating exhibits
Activities: Educ progs; coll educ; gallery interpreting; gallery talks; tours

M **STAATLICHE MUSEEN ZU BERLIN STIFTUNG PREUSSISCHER KULTURBESITZ,** National Museums in Berlin, Prussian Cultural Heritage Foundation, Stauffenbergstrasse 41, Berlin, 10785 Germany. Tel 49 (0)30 266 424242; Fax 49 (0)30 266 422290; Email service@smb.museum; Web: www.smb.museum; *Gen Dir* Prof Dr Michael Eissenhauer
Special Subjects: African Art, Antiquities-Assyrian, Antiquities-Byzantine, Antiquities-Etruscan, Antiquities-Greek, Antiquities-Oriental, Antiquities-Persian, Antiquities-Roman, Archaeology, Asian Art, Baroque Art, Bronzes, Calligraphy, Carpets & Rugs, Cartoons, Ceramics, Coins & Medals, Collages, Costumes, Crafts, Drawings, Embroidery, Enamels, Etchings & Engravings, Ethnology, Flasks & Bottles, Folk Art, Furniture, Glass, Graphics, Islamic Art, Jewelry, Laces, Landscapes, Leather, Manuscripts, Medieval Art, Miniatures, Oriental Art, Painting-American, Painting-British, Painting-Dutch, Painting-European, Painting-French, Painting-German, Painting-Italian, Painting-Japanese, Painting-Spanish, Period Rooms, Photography, Porcelain, Portraits, Posters, Pottery, Pre-Columbian Art, Prints, Religious Art, Renaissance Art, Reproductions, Restorations, Sculpture, Silver, Tapestries, Textiles, Watercolors, Woodcuts
Collections: Supervises 19 museums and departments, in addition to an art library and a museum library & research laboratory
Activities: lects open to pub; tours; mus shop sells books, magazines, reproductions, prints & merchandising products; Junior mus: Kindergaline in Bode-Museum, Am Kupfergraben1, 10778 Berlin

M **Ethnologisches Museum - Ethnological Museum**, Lanstrasse 8, Arnimallee 27, Berlin, 14195 Germany. Tel 49 (0)30 8301273; Fax 49 (0)30 8301261; Email em@smb.spk-berlin.de; Web: www.smb.museum/em; *Dir* Prof Dr Viola Konig; *Deputy Dir* Dr Richard Haas
Open Tues - Fri 10 AM - 5 PM, Sat - Sun 11 AM - 6 PM; Admis 8 EUR, concessions 4 EUR
Collections: Material and immaterial goods and archaeological artifacts from outside of Europe

M **Museum fur Europaischer Kulturen - Museum of European Cultures**, Lansstrasse 8, Arnimallee 25, Berlin, 14195 Germany. Tel 49 (0)03 266 426801; Fax 49 (0)30 266 426804; Email mek@.smb.spk-berlin.de; Web: www.smb.museum; *Dir* Prof Dr Elisabeth Tietmeyer; *Deputy Dir* Dr Leontine Meijer-van Mensch
Open Tues - Fri 10 AM - 5 PM, Sat & Sun 11 AM - 6 PM; Admis 8 EUR, concessions 4 EUR
Collections: Ethnographic items & objects of cultural history and popular art from throughout Europe

M **Hamburger Bahnhof, Museum fur Gegenwart - Hamburger Bahnhof, Museum for Contemporary Art**, Invalidenstrasse 50-51, Berlin, 10557 Germany. Tel 49 (0) 30 39783411; Fax 49 (0)30 39783413; Email hbf@smb.spk-berlin.de; Web: www.smb.museum/hbf; *Mus Head* Prof Dr Eugen Blume
Open Tues, Wed, Fri 10 AM - 6 PM, Thurs 10 AM - 8 PM, Sat-Sun 11 AM - 6 PM, cl Mon; Admis 14 EUR, concessions 7 EUR
Collections: Contemporary art including paintings, sculpture & object art, photography and multimedia concepts in film & video

M **Alte Nationalgalerie - Old National Gallery**, Bodestrasse, Berlin, 10178 Germany. Tel 49 (0)30 266 424401; Fax 49 (0)30 266 424402; Email ang@smb.spk-berlin.de; Web: www.smb.museum/ang; *Dir* Udo Kittelmann; *Gallery Head* Dr Philipp Demandt
Open Tues, Wed, Fri - Sun 10 AM - 6 PM, Thurs 10 AM - 8 PM, cl Mon; Admis 12 EUR, concessions 6 EUR
Collections: Romantic & Impressionist masterpieces, 19th century paintings & sculptures

M **Bode Museum**, Am Kupfergraben, Berlin, 10117 Germany. Tel 49 (0)30 266 425401; Fax 49 (0)30 266 425402; Web: www.smb.museum/bm; *Coll Dir* Prof Dr Bernhard Weissner; *Coll Dir* Prof Dr Bernd Lindemann
Open Tues, Wed, Fri-Sun 10 AM - 6 PM, Thurs 10 AM - 8 PM, cl Mon; Admis 12 EUR, concessions 6 EUR
Collections: Byzantine art collection, sculpture collection, numismatic collection

M **Neues Museum**, Bodestrasse, Berlin, 10178 Germany. Tel 49 (0)30 266 425001; Fax 49 (0)30 266 425002; Email aemp@smb.spk-berlin.de; Web: www.smb.museum/en/; *Dir* Prof Dr Friederike Seyfried
Open daily 10 AM - 6 PM, Thurs 10 AM - 8 PM; Admis 12 EUR, concessions 6 EUR
Collections: Art & cultural history of ancient Egypt, prehistory & early history, classical antiquities

M **Pergamonmuseum - Pergamon Museum**, Bodestrasse, Berlin, 10178 Germany. Tel 49 (0)30 266 425101; Fax 49 (0)30 266 425102; Web: www.smb.museum/pm; *Dir* Dr Michael Eissenhauer
Open daily 10 AM - 6 PM, Thurs 10 AM - 8 PM; Admis 12 EUR, concessions 6 EUR
Collections: Greek & Roman antiquities, 6,000 years of art & culture from Mesopotamia, Syria and Anatolia, deocorative & archaeological Islamic art from the 7th to the 19th century

M **Gemaldegalerie - Picture Gallery**, Matthaikirchplatz, Berlin, 10785 Germany. Tel 49 (0)30 266 424001; Fax 49 (3)30 266 424003; Email gg@smb.spk-berlin.de; Web: www.smb.museum/gg; *Dir* Prof Dr Bernd Lindemann; *Deputy Dir* Dr Rainer Michaelis
Open Tues, Wed & Fri 10 AM - 6 PM, Thurs 10 AM - 8 PM, Sat & Sun 11 AM - 6 PM, cl Mon; Admis 10 EUR, concessions 5 EUR
Collections: European masterpiece paintings from the 13th - 18th centuries

M **Kunstgewerbemuseum - Museum of Decorative Arts**, Matthaikirchplatz, Berlin, 10785 Germany. Tel 030 266 424242; Email kgm@smb.spk-berlin.de; Web: www.smb.museum; *Dir* Dr Sabine Thummler; *Deputy Dir* Lothar Lambacher
Open Tues - Fri 10 AM - 6 PM, Sat - Sun 11 AM - 6 PM, cl Mon; Admis 8 EUR, concessions 4 EUR
Collections: European arts & crafts and masterpieces of interior design from the 16th to 18th centuries

M **Kupferstichkabinett - Museum of Prints and Drawings**, Matthaikirchplatz, Berlin, 10785 Germany. Tel 49 (0)30 266 424242; Web: www.smb.museum; *Dir* Prof Dr Heinrich Schulze Altcappenberg; *Deputy Dir* Dr Holm Bevers
Open Tues - Fri 10 AM - 6 PM, Sat - Sun 11 AM - 6 PM, cl Mon; Admis 6 EUR, concessions 3 EUR; Library with 40,000 vols
Collections: European drawings, prints & illustrated books

M **Museum fur Asiatische Kunst - Asian Art Museum**, Lansstrasse 8, Arnimallee 25, Berlin, 14195 Germany. Tel 49 (0)30 8301361; Fax 49 (0)30 8301502; Email aku@smb.spk-berlin.de; Web: www.smb.museum/aku; *Dir* Prof Dr Klaas Ruitenbeek; *Deputy Dir* Raffael Dedo Gadebusch
Open Tues - Fri 10 AM - 5 PM, Sat & Sun 11 AM - 6 PM, cl Mon; Admis 8 EUR, concessions 4 EUR
Collections: Buddhist paintings & sculptures from 3rd - 13th century China, Japanese & Korean Buddhist bronze, ceramic, porcelain and lacquer art, Japanese & East Asian lacquer art, Indian stone, bronze & terracotta religious art

M **Altes Museum**, Am Lustgarten, Berlin, 10178 Germany. Tel 49 (0)30 266 425101; Fax 49 (0)30 266 425102; Web: www.smb.museum/am; *Dir* Udo Kittelmann; *Head* Dr Phillip Demandt
Open Tues, Wed, Fri - Sun 10 AM - 6 PM, Thurs 10 AM - 8 PM, cl Mon; Admis 10 EUR, concessions 5 EUR
Collections: Greek, Roman and Etruscan art & archaeology, gold & silver jewellery & ancient coins

M **Museum fur Fotografie - Museum of Photography**, Jebensstrasse 2, Berlin, 10623 Germany. Tel 49 (0)30 266 424183; Fax 49 (0)30 266 424197; Email mf@smb.spk-berlin.de; Web: www.smb.museum/mf; *Head Photography Coll* Moritz Wullen, Prof Dr
Open Tues, Wed, Fri - Sun 11 AM - 7 PM, Thurs 11 AM - 8 PM cl Mon; Admis 10 EUR, concessions 5 EUR
Collections: All forms of photography from the 19th century to the present day

BIELEFELD

M **KUNSTHALLE BIELEFELD,** Bielefeld Art Gallery, Artur-Ladebeck-Strasse 5, Bielefeld, 33602 Germany. Tel 0521 32999500; Fax 0521 329995050; Email info@kunsthalle-bielefeld.de; Web: www.kunsthalle-bielefeld.de; *Dir* Dr Friedrich Meschede; *Deputy Dir* Dr Jutta Hulsewig-Johnen; *Mgr* Gabriela Spengemann
Open Tues, Thurs, Fri & Sun 11 AM - 6 PM, Wed 11 AM - 9 PM, Sat 10 AM - 6 PM, cl Mon; Admis adults 8 EUR, concessions 4 EUR, students 12 & under 2 EUR, children under 6 free; Estab 1968; Art museum & exhib space
Library Holdings: Auction Catalogs, Book Volumes, CD-ROMs, Compact Disks, DVDs, Exhibition Catalogs, Maps, Prints, Video Tapes
Collections: Expressionist painting, Bauhaus art, American painting after 1945, Cubistic sculpture, graphics-library, children's atelier
Publications: Catalogues
Activities: Classes for adults & children; docent training; classes for the blind; lects open to pub; 5 vis lectrs per yr; concerts; gallery talks; tours; mus shop sells books

BONN

M **KUNST- UND AUSSTELLUNGSHALLE DER BUNDESREPUBLIK DEUTSCHLAND,** Art & Exhibition Hall of the Federal Republic of Germany, Museumsmeile Bonn, Friedrich-Ebert-Allee 4 Bonn, 53113 Germany. Tel 49 228 9171-200; Fax 49 228 234154; Email info@bundeskunsthalle.de; Web: www.bundeskunsthalle.de; *Dir* Rein Wolfs; *Comm Dir* Patrick Schmeing; *Educ Progs* Christian Gansicke; *Exib* Ulrike Klein; *Registrar* Karin Weber

Tues & Wed 10 AM - 9 PM, Thurs - Sun 10 AM - 7 PM; Admis 15 EUR, reduced 10 EUR, family 24 EUR, children 18 and under free; Estab 1992 to provide a forum for a varied program of exhibitions of devoted to art, cultural history, science, technology, and the environment; Small, medium & large rooms with 5,600 sq meters of indoor exhib space, 8,000 sq meter landscaped roof garden, library
Special Subjects: Drawings, Conceptual Art, Watercolors, Video, Sculpture, Photography, Graphic Arts, Metalwork, Painting-European
Exhibitions: Rotating exhibits
Publications: newsletter
Activities: Educ progs; classes for adults & children; artist workshops; lects open to pub; concerts; gallery talks; tours; art programming; symposiums; seminars; workshops; integrated art events; film screenings; arts festivals; competitions with awards; original objects of art lent; organize traveling exhibs; mus shop sells books, reproductions, prints, gifts

M **KUNSTMUSEUM BONN,** Bonn Art Museum, Friedrich-Ebert-Allee 2, Bonn, 53113 Germany. Tel 49 0228 77 6260; Fax 49 0228 77 6220; Email kunstmuseum@bonn.de; Web: www.kunstmuseum-bonn.de; *Dir* Prof Dr Stephan Berg; *Deputy Dir* Dr Christoph Schreier; *Head Exhibs & Cur* Dr Volker Adolphs; *Head Admin* Gabriele Kuhn
Open Tues - Sun 11 AM - 6 PM, Wed 11 AM - 9 PM, cl Mon; Admis regular 7 EUR, reduced 3.50 EUR, under 12 free; Estab 1948; Average Annual Attendance: 100,000
Library Holdings: Auction Catalogs, Book Volumes, Exhibition Catalogs
Collections: Art of the 20th century, especially August Macke & the Rhenish expressionists, German Art since 1945, contemporary international graphic arts
Activities: Classes for adults & children; lects open to pub; concerts; gallery talks; tours; originates traveling exhib to art mus in Europe & USA; Kunstladen sells books, original art, reproductions, prints & t-shirts, wine-bottles, etc

M **LANDSCHAFTSVERBANDES RHEINLAND LANDESMUSEUM BONN,** Rhineland State Museum, Colmantstr 14-16, Bonn, 53115 Germany. Tel 49 0228 2070 0, 49 0228 2070 299; Email info.landesmuseum-bonn@lvr.de; Web: www.landesmuseum-bonn.lvr.de; *Dir* Dr Gabriele Uelsberg; *Deputy Dir* Lothar Altringer
Open Tues - Fri & Sun 11 AM - 6 PM, Sat 1 - 6 PM, cl Mon; Admis adults 8 EUR, reduced 6 EUR, children under 18 free; Estab 1820; Average Annual Attendance: 120,000
Library Holdings: Auction Catalogs, Book Volumes, Exhibition Catalogs, Fiche, Maps, Pamphlets, Periodical Subscriptions, Photographs, Prints, Slides
Collections: Rhenish sculpture, painting & applied arts from the Middle Ages up to the present, finds from the Stone Age, Roman times up to the Middle Ages, Renaissance, modern art, photographic coll
Publications: Das Rhein Landemuseum Bonn, Bonner Jahrbucher; Jule im Museum; several series of research reports & catalogs
Activities: Educ prog; classes for children; docent training; holiday activities for children; concerts, tours; lects open to pub; gallery talks; Ceram-Preis fur das archaol. Sachbuch (every 5 yrs), Leo Breur-Förderpreis (every 2 yrs); organize traveling exhibs; mus shop sells books

BRAUNSCHWEIG

M **HERZOG ANTON ULRICH-MUSEUM,** Art Museum of Lower Saxony, Museumstrasse 1, Braunschweig, 38100 Germany. Tel 0531-1225-0; Fax 0531-1225-2408; Email info.haum@3landesmuseen.de; Web: www.3landesmuseen.de; *Dir & Sr Cur* Dr Jochen Luckhardt; *Dir Bus & Communs* Sigrid Eissfeller
Open Tues, Thurs - Sun 10 AM - 5 PM, Wed 10 AM - 8 PM, cl Mon; Admis 5 EUR, reduced 3 EUR; Estab 1754; Library with 60,000 vols, 170,000 objects of art in the collection; Average Annual Attendance: 60,000
Library Holdings: Auction Catalogs, Book Volumes, Exhibition Catalogs
Collections: European Paintings - Renaissance & Baroque, European Renaissance & Baroque decorative art, including bronzes, clocks, French 16th century enamels, Italian majolica, furniture, glass, ivory & wood carvings, laces, Medieval art, prints & drawings from the 15th century to present, East Asian decorative art, graphic works; print room
Exhibitions: Epochal Masterpieces of the Herzog Anton Ulrich-Museum from Antiquity to Present
Publications: Exhibition catalogue; inventory catalogue
Activities: Educ prog; classes for adults & children; docent training; lects open to pub; lects for members only; 20 vis lectrs per year; concerts; gallery talks; tours; lending of original objects of art to other museums; mus shop sells books, prints, postcards, reproductions

BREMEN

M **KUNSTHALLE BREMEN,** Bremen Art Gallery, Am Wall 207, Bremen, 28195 Germany. Tel 49 (0)421 329 08-0; Fax 49 (0)421 329 08-470; Email info@kunsthalle-bremen.de; Web: www.kunsthalle-bremen.de; *Dir* Dr Christoph Grunenberg; *Exec Dir* Stefan Schnier
Open Wed - Sun 10 AM - 5 PM, Tues 10 AM - 9 PM, cl Mon; Admis adults 9 EUR, reduced 5 EUR, ages 6-21 3.50 EUR, children under 6 free; Estab 1823; Art museum; Mem: 8,000
Library Holdings: Auction Catalogs, Book Volumes, Exhibition Catalogs
Special Subjects: Drawings, Graphics, Painting-European, Painting-French, Painting-German, Sculpture
Collections: Japanese drawings and prints, European paintings, Middle Ages to modern, especially French and German Art of the 19th century, 17th - 21st century sculpture, illustrated books
Activities: Educ prog; classes for adults & children; lectrs open to the public; lectrs for mems only; 20 vis lectrs per year; concerts; Kunstpreis der Boettcherstrasse in Bremen; tours; mus shop sells books, magazines, gifts, reproductions

COLOGNE

M **MUSEEN DER STADT KOLN,** Museums of the City of Cologne, Stadthaus Deutz - Ostgebaude, Willy-Brandt-Platz 3 Cologne, 50679 Germany. Tel 0221 221 26764; Fax 0221 221 29240; Web: www.museenkoeln.de; *Coord Cultural Educ* Jorg Kaminke
Estab 1888; Municipal museums located throughout the German city of Cologne

M **Romisch-Germanisches Museum - Romano-Germanic Museum**, Roncalliplatz 4, Cologne, 50667 Germany. Tel 0221 221 22305; Fax 0221 221 24030; Email romisch-germanisches-museum@stadt-koeln.de; Web: www.museenkoeln.de/romisch-germanisches-museum; *Dir* Dr Marcus Trier
Open Tues - Sun 10 AM - 5 PM, 1st Thurs of the month 10 AM - 10 PM, cl Mon; Admis adults 9 EUR, reduced 5 EUR, under 18 free; Estab 1946; archaeological collections; Roman art, migration period collection; Average Annual Attendance: 300,000
Special Subjects: Antiquities-Roman, Archaeology, Crafts, Gold, Jewelry, Medieval Art, Metalwork, Mosaics
Collections: Early and pre-historic discoveries, Roman art, inscriptions, sculptures, gold ornaments, glass and industrial arts
Activities: Classes for adults & children; dramatic progs, docent training; lects open to pub & mem; 5 vis lectrs per yr; gallery talks; tours; shop sells books, magazines, reproductions, prints, slides

L **NS Dokumentationszentrum der Stadt Koln - National Socialist Documentation Center of the City of Cologne**, Appellhofplatz 23-25, Cologne, 50667 Germany. Tel 0221 221 26332; Fax 0221 221 25512; Email nsdok@stadt.koeln.de; Web: www.museenkoeln.de/ns-dokumentationszentrum; *Dir* Dr Werner Jung
Open Tues - Sun 10 AM - 5 PM, 1st Thurs of the month 10 AM - 10 PM, cl Mon; Admis adults 4.50 EUR, reduced 2 EUR, children 6 & under free; Estab 1979; Memorial to victims of National Socialism in Germany housed in former Gestapo prison
Collections: Media installations, preserved graffiti

M **Museum Schnutgen - Schnutgen Museum**, Kulturquartier am Neumarkt, Cacilienstrasse 29-33 Cologne, 50667 Germany. Tel 221 221 23620; Fax 221 221 28489; Email museum.schnuetgen@stadt-koeln.de; Web: www.museum.schnuetgen.de; *Dir* Dr Moritz Woelk
Open Tues, Wed, Fri - Sun 10 AM - 6 PM, Thurs 10 AM - 8 PM, 1st Thurs of the 10 AM - 10 PM, cl Mon; Admis adults 6 EUR, reduced 3.50 EUR, children 6 & under free; Estab 1910 & 1956; Medieval art housed in a Romanesque church
Library Holdings: Auction Catalogs, Exhibition Catalogs, Fiche, Periodical Subscriptions, Slides
Special Subjects: Baroque Art, Enamels, Furniture, Glass, Ivory, Manuscripts, Medieval Art, Religious Art, Renaissance Art, Sculpture, Silver, Stained Glass, Textiles, Woodcarvings
Collections: Art of the early Middle Ages to the Baroque period, sculpture, textiles, stained glass
Activities: Classes for adults & children; concerts

M **Wallraf-Richartz-Museum & Fondation Corboud - Wallraf-Richartz Museum & Corboud Foundation**, Obenmarspforten at Cologne City Hall, Cologne, 50677 Germany. Tel 0221 221 21119; Fax 0221 221 22629; Email info@wallraf.museum; Web: www.wallraf.museum; *Dir* Dr Andreas Bluhm
Open Tues - Sun 10 AM - 6 PM, 1st & 3rd Thurs of the month 10 AM - 10 PM, cl Mon; Admis adults 9 EUR, reduced 6 EUR, children 6 & under free; Picture gallery
Special Subjects: Baroque Art, Drawings, Etchings & Engravings, Graphics, Medieval Art, Painting-Dutch, Painting-European, Painting-Flemish, Painting-French, Painting-German, Painting-Italian, Painting-Spanish, Portraits, Religious Art, Renaissance Art, Sculpture, Watercolors
Collections: 13th to 19th century paintings and sculptures, Baroque, German Romantic and French paintings, Impressionist & Neo-Impressionist German art
Activities: Shop sells books, reproductions, slides

M **Museum fur Angewandte Kunst Koln - Museum of Applied Art**, An der Rechtschule, Cologne, 50667 Germany. Tel 0221 221 23860; Fax 0221 221 23885; Email maak@stadt-koeln.de; Web: www.museenkoeln.de/museum-fuer-angewandte-kunst; *Dir* Dr Petra Hesse
Open Tues - Sun 11 AM - 5 PM, cl Mon; Admis adults 6 EUR, reduced 3.50 EUR, under 18 free; Estab 1989
Collections: European craft arts, jewelry coll

M **Kolnisches Stadtmuseum - Cologne Municipal Museum**, Zeughausstrasse 1-3, Cologne, 50667 Germany. Tel 0221 221 25789; Fax 0221 221 24154; Email ksm@museenkoeln.de; Web: www.museenkoeln.de/ksm; *Dir* Dr Mario Kramp
Open Tues 10 AM - 8 PM, Wed-Sun 10 AM - 5 PM, 1st Thurs of the month 10 AM - 10 PM, cl Mon; Admis general 5 EUR, reduced 3 EUR, children under 6 free; Estab 1888
Library Holdings: Auction Catalogs, Book Volumes, CD-ROMs, Cassettes, Compact Disks, DVDs, Exhibition Catalogs, Manuscripts, Maps, Memorabilia, Original Documents, Pamphlets, Periodical Subscriptions, Records, Video Tapes
Collections: Graphic Arts of Cologne and the Rhineland, photograph coll of the Rhineland, industrial arts of Cologne, religious and rural art and culture, Paintings - local art, Local history, Ceramics, Musical instruments
Activities: Classes for adults & children; docent training; lects open to pub, 5-10 vis lectrs per yr; mus shop sells books, magazines, reproductions, prints, ceramics, replicas of original art

M **Museum fuer Ostasiatische Kunst - Museum for East Asian Art**, Universitatsstrasse 100, Cologne, 50674 Germany. Tel 0221 221 28608; Fax 0221 221 28610; Email mok@museenkoeln.de; Web: www.museum-fuer-ostasiatische-kunst.de; *Dir* Dr Adele Schlombs
Open Tues - Sun 11 AM - 5 PM, 1st Thurs of the month 11 AM - 10 PM, cl Mon; Admis adults 3.50 EUR, reduced 2 EUR, under 18 free; Estab 1909; Library with 18,000 vols
Library Holdings: Auction Catalogs, Book Volumes 11,000, Exhibition Catalogs
Collections: Art of China, Korea and Japan
Publications: Exhib catalogue, bilingual (German & English); Exhibition guide (German)
Activities: Classes for adults & children; docent training; mus shop sells books, magazines, original art

M **Museum Ludwig - Ludwig Museum**, Bischofsgartenstrasse 1, Cologne, 50667 Germany. Tel 0221 221 26165; Fax 0221 221 24114; Email info@museum-ludwig.de; Web: www.museum-ludwig.de; *Dir* Dr Yilmaz Dziewior
Open Tues - Sun 10 AM - 6 PM, 1st Thurs of the month 10 AM-10 PM, cl Mon; Admis 11 EUR, reduced 7.50 EUR; Contemporary art museum; Average Annual Attendance: 350,000
Library Holdings: Auction Catalogs, Exhibition Catalogs, Fiche, Periodical Subscriptions
Special Subjects: Drawings, Graphics, Photography, Prints, Sculpture
Collections: Painting & sculpture from 1900 to present, 20th century art, contemporary art, expressionism, Picasso, pop art, media art, photography from the beginnings to present, Russian avant-garde
Publications: Regular exhibition catalogues
Activities: Classes for adults & children, docent training; lects open to public, gallery talks; concerts; tours, Wolfgang Hahn Prize of Gesellschaft for Modern Artist at Museum Ludwig; lending of original art to patron's clubs; mus shop sells books, magazines & prints

M **Rautenstrauch-Joest-Museum, Kulturen de Welt - Rautenstrauch-Joest Museum, Cultures of the World**, Kulturquartier am Neumarkt, Cäcilienstrasse Str 29-33 Cologne, 50667 Germany. Tel 0221 221 31301; Fax 0221 221 31333; Email rjm@stadt-koeln.d; Web: www.museenkoeln.de/rjm; *Dir* Dr Klaus Schneider
Open Tues - Sun 10 AM - 6 PM, 1st Thurs of the month 10 AM - 8 PM, cl Mon; Admis adults 7 EUR, reduced 4.50 EUR; Estab 1901
Library Holdings: Book Volumes, Exhibition Catalogs, Periodical Subscriptions
Collections: Ethnological museum, folk culture (non European)
Activities: Classes for adults & children; mus shop sells books, magazines, catalogs, ethnographic art

DRESDEN

M **STAATLICHE KUNSTSAMMLUNGEN DRESDEN,** Dresden State Art Collections, Residenzschloss, Taschenberg 2 Dresden, 01067 Germany. Tel 49 0351 49 14 2000; Fax 49 0351 49 14 2001; Email besucherservice@skd.museum; Web: www.skd.museum; *Dir Gen* Dr Marion Ackerman
Visitor Centre open daily 10 AM - 6 PM; Consists of 14 galleries & museums
Library Holdings: Auction Catalogs, Book Volumes, CD-ROMs, Cards, Cassettes, DVDs, Exhibition Catalogs, Maps, Periodical Subscriptions, Video Tapes
Special Subjects: Antiquities-Assyrian, Antiquities-Egyptian, Antiquities-Etruscan, Antiquities-Greek, Antiquities-Roman, Asian Art, Baroque Art, Bronzes, Calligraphy, Carpets & Rugs, Ceramics, Coins & Medals, Collages, Costumes, Crafts, Decorative Arts, Dolls, Drawings, Embroidery, Enamels, Flasks & Bottles, Folk Art, Furniture, Glass, Gold, Graphics, Islamic Art, Ivory, Jade, Jewelry, Juvenile Art, Laces, Landscape Architecture, Leather, Maps, Medieval Art, Metalwork, Miniatures, Mosaics, Oriental Art, Painting-American, Painting-Australian, Painting-British, Painting-Dutch, Painting-European, Painting-Flemish, Painting-French, Painting-German, Painting-Italian, Painting-Japanese, Painting-Polish, Painting-Russian, Painting-Scandinavian, Painting-Spanish, Period Rooms, Pewter, Photography, Porcelain, Portraits, Posters, Pottery, Primitive art, Prints, Religious Art, Renaissance Art, Reproductions, Restorations, Sculpture, Silver, Southwestern Art, Stained Glass, Tapestries, Textiles, Watercolors, Woodcarvings, Woodcuts
Activities: Classes for adults & children; lects open to pub; concerts; gallery talks; tours; mus shop sells books, magazines, prints, slides, CDs & DVDs

M **Old Masters Picture Gallery**, Zwinger Theaterplatz 1, Dresden, 01067 Germany. Tel 49 0351 49 14 6679; Fax 49 0351 49 14 6694; Email gam@skd.museum; Web: www.skd.museum; *Dir* Dr Stephan Koja
Open Tues - Sun 10 AM - 6 PM, cl Mon; Admis normal 10 EUR, reduced 7.50 EUR
Collections: 16th - 18th century European masterpieces, Raphael's Sistine Madonna
Exhibitions: Semiannual special exhibs on several subjects
Activities: Classes for adults & children; docent training; lects open to the pub; lectrs for mems only; concerts; extension prog; lending of original objects of art; mus shop sells books, original art, magazines, reproductions, slides & other items

M **New Masters Gallery**, Albertinum Tzschirnerplatz 2, Dresden, 01067 Germany. Tel 49 0351 49 14 9731; Fax 49 0351 49 14 9732; Email albertinum@skd.museum; Web: www.skd.museum; *Dir* Dr Hilke Wagner
Open Tues - Sun 10 AM - 6 PM, cl Mon; Admis normal 10 EUR, reduced 7.50 EUR; Estab 1959
Collections: Romantic masterpieces to present-day contemporary art, new media installations, sculptures

DUSSELDORF

L **KUNSTAKADEMIE DUSSELDORF, HOCHSCHULE FUR BILDENDE KUNST - BIBLIOTHEK,** State Academy of Art - Library, Eiskellerstrasse 1, Dusseldorf, 40213 Germany. Tel (0211) 1396-0; Fax (0211) 1396-225; Email postmaster@kunstakademie-duesseldorf.de; Web: www.kunstakademie-duesseldorf.de; *Librn* Brigitte Blockhaus, MA
Open Mon - Wed 9 AM - 5 PM, Thurs 9 AM - 7 PM, Fri 10 AM - 2 PM, holidays 10 AM - 1 PM & 2 PM - 5 PM; Estab 1774; Library with 130,000 vols
Purchases: E 40 000 p a
Library Holdings: Auction Catalogs, Book Volumes, CD-ROMs, DVDs, Exhibition Catalogs, Fiche, Manuscripts 13, Periodical Subscriptions 110, Slides 50,000

M **KUNSTHALLE DUSSELDORF,** Dusseldorf Art Gallery, Grabbeplatz 4, Dusseldorf, 40213 Germany. Tel 49 0211 899-6243; Fax 49 0211 892-9168; Email mail@kunsthalle-duesseldorf.de; Web: www.kunsthalle-duesseldorf.de; *Dir* Dr Gregor Jansen; *Cur* Anna Brohm; *Cur* Jasmina Merz; *Mng Dir* Ariane Berger
Open Tues - Sun 11 AM - 6 PM; Admis adults 6 EUR, reduced 3 EUR, under 18 free; Estab 1967; Modern & contemporary art
Exhibitions: Contemporary art exhibitions
Activities: Classes for adults & children; docent training; dramatic progs; lects open to pub; concerts; gallery talks; originate traveling exhibs to museums in Europe; sales shops sell books, magazines, reproductions, prints; Kit Kurstin Tunnel

M **MUSEUM KUNSTPALAST,** Art Palace Museum, Ehrenhof 4-5, Dusseldorf, 40479 Germany. Tel 49 0211 566-4200; Fax 49 0211 892-9307; Email info@smkp.de; Web: www.smkp.de; *Gen Dir* Beat Wismer; *Deputy Head Colls* Barbara Til
Open Tues - Sun 11 AM - 6 PM, Thurs 11 AM - 9 PM, cl Mon; Admis adults 12 EUR, reduced 9.50 EUR, visitors 7 - 17 1 EUR, children 6 & under free; Estab 2001
Collections: Collections of European & applied art from middle ages to 1800, prints, drawings & contemporary art
Activities: Classes for adults & children

FRANKFURT

M **FOTOGRAFIE FORUM FRANKFURT,** Photography Forum, Braubachstrasse 30-32, Frankfurt, 60311 Germany. Tel 49 069 29 1726; Fax 49 069 28 639; Email contact@fffrankfurt.de; Web: www.fffrankfurt.org; *Artistic Dir* Celina Lunsford; *Mng Dir* Sabine Seitz
Open Tues & Thurs - Sun 11 AM - 6 PM, Wed 11 AM - 8 PM, cl Mon; Admis regular 6 EUR, reduced 3 EUR, children 12 & under free; Estab 1984
Library Holdings: Book Volumes, Exhibition Catalogs
Special Subjects: Photography
Collections: Photographs
Activities: Classes for Adults; lects open to pub; gallery talks

M **LIEBIEGHAUS SKULPTURENSAMMLUNG,** Liebieghaus Sculpture Collection, Schaumainkai 71, Frankfurt, 60596 Germany. Tel 49 069 605098-0; Fax 49 069 605098-112; Email info@liebieghaus.de; Web: www.liebieghaus.de; *Dir* Phillip Demandt
Open Tues, Wed, Fri - Sun 10 AM - 6 PM, Thurs 10 AM - 9 PM, cl Mon; Admis adults 10 EUR, reduced 8 EUR, families 18 EUR, children 12 & under free; Sculpture from antiquities to neo-classicism housed in the Grunderzeit villa
Library Holdings: Book Volumes, Cards, Exhibition Catalogs, Lantern Slides
Collections: Sculpture of Egypt, Greece, Rome Medieval period, East Asia, Rococo style, Baroque period & neo-classicism
Activities: Classes for adults & children; dramatic prog; docent training; lects open to pub; lects for members only; concerts; tours; mus shop sells books, slides & other items

M **MUSEUM FUR ANGEWANDTE KUNST FRANKFURT,** Museum of Applied Arts, Schaumainkai 17, Frankfurt, 60594 Germany. Tel 49 69 212 31286; Fax 49 69 212 30703; Email info@museumangewandtekunst.de; Web: www.museumangewandtekunst.de; *Dir* Matthias K Wagner; *Vice Dir* Grit Weber
Open Tues & Thurs - Sun 10 AM - 5 PM, Wed 10 AM - 9 PM; cl Mon; Admis regular 9 EUR, reduced 4.50 EUR; Estab 1877; Historical villa with nine epoche halls; Average Annual Attendance: 120,000
Library Holdings: Auction Catalogs, Audio Tapes, Book Volumes, Compact Disks, DVDs, Exhibition Catalogs, Kodachrome Transparencies, Lantern Slides, Manuscripts, Photographs, Slides
Special Subjects: Asian Art, Calligraphy, Carpets & Rugs, Ceramics, Costumes, Crafts, Furniture, Glass, Gold, Islamic Art, Jewelry, Baroque Art
Collections: 12th - 21st century European applied art from Gothic to art nouveau, Far Eastern & Islamic works of art, book art & industrial product design
Activities: Classes for adults & children; lects open to pub; lects for members only, 10 vis lectrs per yr; concerts; gallery talks; tours; originate traveling exhibs; mus shop sells contemporary jewelry; jr mus Museum with the Suitcase

M **STADELSCHES KUNSTINSTITUT UND STADTISCHE GALERIE,** Stadel Museum, Schaumainkai 63, Frankfurt, 60596 Germany. Tel 49 069 605098 200; Fax 49 069 605098 111; Email info@staedelmuseum.de; Web: www.staedelmuseum.de; *Acting Dir* Jochen Sander; *Acting Dir* Heinz-Jurgen Bokler
Open Tues, Wed, Sat & Sun 10 AM - 6 PM, Thurs & Fri 10 AM - 9 PM, cl Mon; Admis adults 14 EUR, reduced 12 EUR, children under 12 free; Library with 100,000 vols
Library Holdings: Auction Catalogs, Audio Tapes, Book Volumes, Cards, Exhibition Catalogs, Reproductions, Slides
Collections: Paintings, sculptures, prints, drawings
Publications: Exhibition catalog
Activities: Classes for adults & children; dramatic progs; lects for mems only; concerts; gallery talks; tours; mus shop sells books; magazines; reproductions, prints; slide posters, toys

HAMBURG

M **HAMBURGER KUNSTHALLE,** Hamburg Art Gallery, Glockengiesserwall 5, Hamburg, 20095 Germany. Tel 49 040 428131 200; Fax 49 040 4283 409; Email info@hamburger-kunsthalle.de; Web: www.hamburger-kunsthalle.de; *Dir* Prof Dr Hubertus Gassner; *Mng Dir* Dr Stefan Brandt
Open Tues, Wed, Fri - Sun 10 AM - 6 PM, Thurs 10 AM - 9 PM, cl Mon; Admis adults 12 - 14 EUR, reduced 6 - 7 EUR, children free; Estab 1869; Library with 70,000 vols; Average Annual Attendance: 300,000; Mem: 13,000
Library Holdings: Auction Catalogs, Book Volumes, Exhibition Catalogs, Maps, Original Documents, Pamphlets, Periodical Subscriptions, Sculpture
Collections: Drawings, engravings & masterworks of painting from 14th century to present, sculpture from 19th and 20th centuries
Publications: Catalogues
Activities: Classes for adults & children; docent training; lects open to pub; 15 vis lectrs per year; concerts; gallery talks; tours; sponsoring of competitions; mus shop sells books, magazines & prints

M **MUSEUM FUR KUNST UND GEWERBE HAMBURG,** Museum of Arts & Crafts, Steintorplatz, Hamburg, 20099 Germany. Tel 49 040 428134 880; Fax 49 040 428134 999; Email service@mkg-hamburg.de; Web: www.mkg-hamburg.de; *Dir* Prof Sabine Schulze; *Dir Fin* Udo Goerke

Open Tues, Wed & Fri - Sun 10 AM - 6 PM, Thurs 10 AM - 9 PM, cl Mon; Admis regular 12 EUR, reduced 8 EUR, under 18 free; Estab 1877; Average Annual Attendance: 250,000
Library Holdings: Auction Catalogs, Book Volumes, Exhibition Catalogs, Maps, Original Art Works, Original Documents, Periodical Subscriptions, Photographs, Sculpture
Special Subjects: Antiquities-Byzantine, Antiquities-Egyptian, Antiquities-Etruscan, Antiquities-Greek, Antiquities-Oriental, Antiquities-Persian, Antiquities-Roman, Archaeology, Architecture, Art Education, Art History, Asian Art, Baroque Art, Bookplates & Bindings, Bronzes, Calligraphy, Carpets & Rugs, Cartoons, Ceramics, Coins & Medals, Costumes, Crafts, Decorative Arts, Drawings, Enamels, Etchings & Engravings, Furniture, Glass, Gold, Graphics, Historical Material, History of Art & Archaeology, Illustration, Interior Design, Islamic Art, Ivory, Jade, Jewelry, Judaica, Landscape Architecture, Leather, Manuscripts, Maps, Medieval Art, Metalwork, Miniatures, Mosaics, Oriental Art, Painting-German, Period Rooms, Photography, Porcelain, Portraits, Posters, Pottery, Primitive art, Prints, Religious Art, Reproductions, Restorations, Sculpture, Silver, Silversmithing, Tapestries, Textiles, Woodcuts, Renaissance Art
Collections: Near & Far East art, European applied art, art nouveau; modern applied art & industrial design; East Asia & Islamic art, Graphic Design; Photography; Musical Instruments; Fashion & Textiles; Posters, rare books
Activities: Classes for adults & children; Lects open to pub; concerts; gallery talks; tours; awards; mus shop sells books, magazines, prints, original art; Hubertus Wald Kinderreich

HANOVER

M **MUSEUM AUGUST KESTNER,** August Kestner Museum, Trammplatz 3, Hanover, 30159 Germany. Tel 49 511 168 42730; Fax 49 511 168 46530; Email museen-kulturegeschichte@hannover-stadt.de; Web: www.museum-august-kestner.de; *Dir* Dr Wolfgang Schepers
Open Tues, Thurs - Sun 11 AM - 6 PM, Wed 11 AM - 8 PM, cl Mon; Admis adults 7 EUR, reduced 5 EUR, free on Fri; Estab 1889; Neo-Renaissance building
Library Holdings: Auction Catalogs, Book Volumes, Exhibition Catalogs, Kodachrome Transparencies, Periodical Subscriptions, Photographs, Prints
Collections: Ancient, medieval & modern coins & medals, Egyptian, Greek, Etruscan & Roman art objects & medieval art, illustrated manuscripts & incunabula of the 15th - 20th centuries, product design 1900-2000
Activities: Classes for adults & children; lects open to pub; 2-3 traveling exhibs per yr; originate traveling exhibs; mus shop sells books, reproductions, prints, slides

KARLSRUHE

M **BADISCHES LANDESMUSEUM,** Baden State Museum, Schlossplatz 1, Karlsruhe, 76131 Germany. Tel 49 (0)721 / 926 6514; Fax 49 (0)721 / 926 6537; Email info@landesmuseum.de; Web: www.landesmuseum.de; *Dir* Prof Dr Eckart Kohne; *Bus Dir* Susanne SchulenbUrg
Open Tues - Thurs 10 AM - 5 PM, Fri - Sun & public holidays 10 AM - 6 PM, cl Mon; Admis adults 4 EUR, reduced 3 EUR, students .50 EUR; Estab 1921; Maintains library with 70,000 vols; Average Annual Attendance: 300,000
Library Holdings: Auction Catalogs, Book Volumes, Exhibition Catalogs, Periodical Subscriptions
Special Subjects: Antiquities-Byzantine, Antiquities-Egyptian, Antiquities-Greek, Antiquities-Oriental, Antiquities-Roman, Archaeology, Baroque Art, Bronzes, Carpets & Rugs, Ceramics, Coins & Medals, Costumes, Crafts, Decorative Arts, Furniture, Glass, Islamic Art, Ivory, Jewelry, Medieval Art, Oriental Art, Porcelain, Pottery, Religious Art, Renaissance Art, Sculpture
Collections: Antiquities of Egypt, Greece & Rome, art from middle ages to present, medieval, Renaissance & baroque sculpture, coins, weapons & folklore
Activities: Classes for adults & children; lects open to pub; concerts; tours; originate diverse traveling exhibs; mus shop sells books, magazines, original art, reproductions & prints

M **STAATLICHE KUNSTHALLE KARLSRUHE,** State Art Gallery, Hans-Thoma-Strasse 2-6, Karlsruhe, 76133 Germany. Tel 49 0721 926 3359; Fax 49 0721 926 6788; Email info@kunsthalle-karlsruhe.de; Web: www.kunsthalle-karlsruhe.de; *Head* Prof Dr Pia Muller-Tamm; *Deputy Dir* Otmar Bohmes
Open Tues - Sun & pub holidays 10 AM - 6 PM; Admis 8 EUR, reduced 6 EUR, children 5 & under & students free; Estab 1846; Coll spanning eight hundred years of art - 800 works permanently on display; Average Annual Attendance: 125,000
Library Holdings: Auction Catalogs, Book Volumes, CD-ROMs, Exhibition Catalogs, Fiche, Periodical Subscriptions
Collections: 15th - 20th century German painting & graphics, 16th - 20th century Dutch, Flemish & French paintings & graphics, more than 90,000 prints & drawings, sculptures, 19th - 20th century, contemporary art
Publications: Staatliche Kunsthalle (mus guide in German, English & French)
Activities: Classes for adults & children; docent training; training for adults; lects open to pub; gallery talks; concerts; tours; mus shop sells books, reproductions, prints, Junge Kunsthalle

KASSEL

M **MUSEUMSLANDSCHAFT HESSEN KASSEL,** State Museums of Kassel, Schloss Wilhelmshohe, Kassel, 34131 Germany. Tel 49 0561 31680 0; Fax 49 0561 31680 111; Email info@museum-kassel.de; Web: www.museum-kassel.de; *Dir* Dr Bernd Kuster
Open Tues, Thurs - Sun 10 AM - 5 PM, Wed 10 AM - 8 PM, cl Mon; Admis normal 6 EUR, reduced 4 EUR, children under 18 free; Library with 60,000 vols; collection of paintings, antiquities, graphics
Library Holdings: Auction Catalogs, Exhibition Catalogs
Collections: Department of classical antiquities gallery of 15th - 18th century old master paintings, coll of drawings & engravings
Activities: Educ prog; classes for adults & children; concerts; mus shop sells books

MUNICH

M **BAYERISCHE STAATSGEMALDESAMMLUNGEN,** Bavarian State Painting Collections, Barerstrasse 40, Munich, 80333 Germany. Tel 49 089 23805 360; Email info@pinakothek.de; Web: www.pinakothek.de; *Gen Dir* Dr Bernhard Maaz
Consists of five independent museums in Munich: the Neue Pinakothek, the Alte Pinakothek, the Sammlung Schack, the Museum Brandhorst and the Sammlung Moderne Kunst (located in the Pinakothek der Moderne); and 13 public art galleries across Bavaria.
Library Holdings: Book Volumes, CD-ROMs, Cards, Cassettes, Compact Disks, DVDs, Exhibition Catalogs, Maps, Memorabilia, Photographs, Reproductions, Video Tapes
Special Subjects: American Western Art, Architecture, Asian Art, Collages, Crafts, Drawings, Flasks & Bottles, Furniture, Glass, Graphic Arts, Jewelry, Painting-American, Painting-British, Painting-Dutch, Painting-European, Painting-German, Painting-Israeli, Painting-Italian, Painting-Japanese, Painting-Russian, Painting-Scandinavian, Period Rooms, Photography, Portraits, Sculpture, Porcelain, Watercolors
Collections: works of classical modernists, works by Bacon, Baselitz, Beuys, Judd, de Kooning, Polke, Twombley & Warhol, contemporary art, 20th & 21st century applied art, National collection of works on paper
Activities: Classes for adults & children, docent training, progs for disadvantaged persons; concerts, seminars, tours; mus shop sells books, magazines, slides, gifts, postcards, reproductions, prints & design objects

M **Neue Pinakothek - New Picture Gallery**, Barestrasse 29, Eingang Theresienstrasse Munich, 80799 Germany. Tel 49 089 23805 195; Email info@pinakothek.de; Web: www.pinakothek.de
Open Mon, Thurs - Sun 10 AM - 6 PM, Wed 10 AM - 8 PM, cl Tues; Admis regular 7 EUR, reduced 5 EUR
Library Holdings: Book Volumes, CD-ROMs, Cards, Cassettes, Compact Disks, DVDs, Exhibition Catalogs, Maps, Memorabilia, Photographs, Reproductions, Video Tapes
Special Subjects: Landscapes, Painting-British, Painting-Dutch, Painting-European, Painting-Flemish, Painting-French, Painting-German, Painting-Italian, Painting-Polish, Painting-Russian, Painting-Scandinavian, Painting-Spanish, Portraits, Sculpture
Collections: 18th century sculpture, international art
Activities: Classes for adults & children; lects open to pub, seminars, concerts, gallery talks, tours; mus shop sells books, reproductions, prints, slides, gifts, postcards

M **Alte Pinakothek - Old Picture Gallery**, Barerstrasse 27, Eingang Theresienstrasse Munich, 80333 Germany. Tel 49 089 23805 216; Email info@pinakothek.de; Web: www.pinakothek.de
Open Tues 10 AM - 8 PM, Wed - Sun 10 AM - 6 PM, cl Mon; Admis regular 7 EUR, reduced 5 EUR
Library Holdings: Book Volumes, CD-ROMs, Cards, Cassettes, Compact Disks, DVDs, Exhibition Catalogs, Maps, Memorabilia, Photographs, Reproductions, Video Tapes
Special Subjects: Baroque Art, Landscapes, Marine Painting, Medieval Art, Painting-European, Painting-Flemish, Painting-German, Painting-Italian, Painting-Spanish, Portraits, Religious Art, Renaissance Art
Collections: 14th - 18th century Flemish, Spanish, Italian, German & other European paintings
Activities: Classes for adults & children; lects open to pub; seminars; tours; concerts; gallery talks; mus shop sells books, reproductions, prints, slides, gifts, postcards

M **Sammlung Schack - Schack Collection**, Prinzregentenstrasse 9, Munich, 80538 Germany. Tel 49 089 23805 224; Email info@pinakothek.de; Web: www.schack-galerie.de
Open Wed - Sun 10 AM - 6 PM, every 1st & 3rd Wed of month 10 AM - 8 PM, cl Mon & Tues; Admis regular 4 EUR, reduced 3 EUR; Estab 1939
Library Holdings: Book Volumes, CD-ROMs, Cards, Cassettes, Compact Disks, DVDs, Exhibition Catalogs, Maps, Memorabilia, Photographs, Reproductions, Video Tapes
Special Subjects: Painting-German
Collections: 19th century German paintings
Activities: Classes for adults & children; lects open to pub; concerts; gallery talks; tours; mus shop sells books, reproductions, prints, slides, postcards, gifts

M **Museum Brandhorst**, Turkenstrasse 19, Munich, 80333 Germany. Tel 49 (0)89 23805-2286; Email info@pinakothek.de; Web: www.museum-brandhorst.de
Open Tues - Sun 10 AM - 6 PM, Thurs 10 AM - 8 PM, cl Mon; Admis regular 7 EUR, reduced 5 EUR
Special Subjects: Sculpture, Drawings, Photography
Collections: Modern art from the 1960s to the present, works by Pop Art artists including Andy Warhol, Cy Twombley, Damien Hirst, Mike Kelley and Robert Gober
Activities: Classes for adults & children; lects open to pub, seminars, concerts, gallery talks, tours; mus shop sells books, reproductions, prints, slides, gifts, postcards

Pinakothek der Moderne - Modern Picture Gallery, Barerstrasse 40, Munich, 80333 Germany. Tel 49 (0)89 23805-360; Email info@pinakothek.de; Web: www.pinakothek.de
Open Tues, Wed, Fri - Sun 10 AM - 6 PM, Thurs 10 AM - 8 PM, cl Mon; Average Annual Attendance: Admis regular 10 EUR, reduced 7 EUR
Special Subjects: Graphic Arts, Architecture
Collections: 20th - 21st century modern contmeporary art, graphics, architecture & design
Activities: Classes for adults; lects open to pub; seminars; tours; gallery talks; mus shop sells books, reproductions, prints, slides, gifts, postcards

M **BAYERISCHES NATIONALMUSEUM,** Bavarian National Museum, Prinzregentenstrasse 3, Munich, 80538 Germany. Tel 49 089 211 24 01; Email bay.nationalmuseum@bnm.mwn.de; Web: www.bayerisches-nationalmuseum.de; *Dir Gen* Dr Renate Eikelmann
Open Tues, Wed & Fri - Sun 10 AM - 5 PM, Thurs 10 AM - 8 PM, cl Mon; Admis adults 7 EUR, reduced 6 EUR, Sun 1 euro; 1855 (founded), 1862 (opened), 1900

(opening of the present building); One of Europe's major art and cultural history museums
Special Subjects: Baroque Art, Bronzes, Ceramics, Costumes, Decorative Arts, Dolls, Enamels, Flasks & Bottles, Folk Art, Furniture, Glass, Gold, Ivory, Jewelry, Medieval Art, Metalwork, Miniatures, Silver, Tapestries
Collections: European fine arts: decorative arts, paintings, folk art, sculpture, most valuable and extensive crib coll in the world, ceramic art; furniture; textiles
Activities: Educ prog; classes for children, classes for adults; docent training; workshops; lects open to public; concerts; gallery talks; tours; Mus shop sells books, magazines, reproductions, prints, ceramics, glass, paper

M **DEUTSCHES MUSEUM,** Museumsinsel 1, Munich, 80538 Germany. Tel 49 0 89 2179-333; Fax 49 0 89 2179-324; Email visitorservice@deutsches-museum.de; *Dir Gen* Dr Wolfgang M Heckl; *Exhibs & Colls* Ulrich Kernbach; *Exhibs & Colls* Dr Andreas Gundelwein; *Research, Archive & Library* Prof Dr Helmuth Trischler
Open daily 9 AM - 5 PM, cls major holidays; Admis family 25 EUR, adults 12 EUR, seniors & disabled persons 7 EUR, children, teenagers & students 4 EUR; Estab 1903 as a science & technology museum; Exhib space of 66,000 sq meters; storage facilities of 30,000 sq meters
Special Subjects: Historical Material
Collections: More than 113,000 archived science & technology items from 53 different fields, machines, vehicles, musical instruments, models, scientific equipment
Exhibitions: Permanent, rotating & temporary exhibits
Publications: Brochures & catalogs
Activities: Educ progs; classes for adults & children; visiting research progs; lects open to pub; gallery talks; tours; ; symposiums; workshops; outreach progs; individual objects lent

M **HAUS DER KUNST,** House of Art, Prinzregentenstrabe 1, Munich, 80538 Germany. Tel 49 089 21127-113; Fax 49 089 21127-157; Email mail@hausderkunst.de; Web: www.hausderkunst.de; *Dir* Okwui Enwezor; *Chief Cur* Ulrich Wilmes
Open Mon - Wed & Fri - Sun 10 AM - 8 PM, Thurs 10 AM - 10 PM; Admis 12 EUR, reduced 10 EUR, teenagers under 18 & students 5 EUR, children under 12 free; Estab 1937; Non-collecting art museum
Collections: Contemporary art
Activities: Classes for adults & children; lects open to pub; gallery talks; tours; mus shop sells books & magazines

M **STAATLICHE GRAPHISCHE SAMMLUNG MUNCHEN,** State Prints & Drawings Collection, Katharina von Bora Str 10, Munich, D-80333 Germany. Tel 49 089 28 92 76 50; Fax 49 089 28 92 76 53; Email info@sgsm.eu; Web: www.sgsm.eu; *Exec Dir* Dr Michael Hering; *Cur* Dr Achim Riether; *Cur* Dr Andreas Strobl; *Cur* Dr Kurt Zeitler; *Cur* Dr Susanne Wagini
Open Tues 10 AM - 12:30 PM, Thurs 10 AM - 1 PM & 4 PM - 6 PM; No admis fee; Estab 1758; Library with 50,000 vols
Special Subjects: Graphics
Collections: French, 15th to 20th century German, Italian & Dutch prints & drawings, international prints & drawings, portraits & landscapes
Exhibitions: Three to four exhibs per yr
Activities: Lects for members & different unions only; 350 vis lectrs per year; originates traveling exhibs to other graphic departments

M **STAATLICHE MUNZSAMMLUNG,** State Coin Collection, Residenzstrasse 1, Munich, 80333 Germany. Tel 49 089 22 72 21; Fax 49 089 29 98 59; Email info@staatliche-muenzsammlung.de; Web: www.staatliche-muenzsammlung.de; *Dir* Dr Dietrich Klose
Open Tues - Sun 10 AM - 5 PM, cl Mon; Admis adults 2.50 EUR, seniors & students 2 EUR & Sun 1 EUR, children free; Estab 1565; Library with 14,000 vols
Library Holdings: Auction Catalogs, Book Volumes, Exhibition Catalogs
Special Subjects: Metalwork, Coins & Medals
Collections: Coins and medals from different countries & centuries, precious stones from antiquity, Middle Ages & Renaissance, Banknotes, shares, 17th century Japanese lacquer cabinets
Exhibitions: Special exhibs every year
Publications: Sylloge Nummorum Graecorum, exhibition catalogues
Activities: Lects open to pub; 15 vis lectrs per yr; originates traveling exhibs to museums, banks, universities, schools; mus shop sells books & reproductions

M **STAATLICHES MUSEUM AGYPTISCHER KUNST MUNCHEN,** State Museum of Egyptian Art, Gabelsbergerstr 35, Munich, 80333 Germany. Tel 49 089 289 27 630; Email sylvia.schoske@smaek.de; Web: www.smaek.de; *Dir* Dr Sylvia Schoske
Open Tues 10 AM - 8 PM, Wed - Sun 10 AM - 6 PM, cl Mon; Admis adults 7 EUR, reduced 5 EUR, Sun 1 EUR, under 18 free; Estab 1970
Collections: Permanent Exhibitions
Activities: Classes for children; lects open to pub; gallery talks; mus & exhibs halls; books & various items

M **STADTISCHE GALERIE IM LENBACHHAUS,** Lenbach House Municipal Gallery, Luisenstr 33, Munich, 80333 Germany. Tel 49 089 233 320 00; Fax 49 089 233 320-03; Email lenbachhaus@muenchen.de; Web: www.lenbachhaus.de; *Dir* Matthias Muhling; *Admin Dir* Sonja Schamberger
Open Wed - Sun 10 AM - 6 PM, Tues 10 AM - 9 PM, cl Mon; Admis regular 10 EUR, reduced 5 EUR; Estab 1929 as an art museum
Collections: Collection of 19th- & 20th-century contemporary, art by Franz Van Lenbach, the Blue Riders & Joseph Beuys, New Objectivity art of the 1920s & 1930s, post World War II art

NUREMBERG

M **GERMANISCHES NATIONALMUSEUM,** German National Museum, Kartausergasse 1, Nuremberg, 90402 Germany. Tel 49 0911 1331-0; Fax 49 0911-1331-200; Email info@gnm.de; Web: www.gnm.de; *Head* Prof Dr. G Ulrich Grossmann; *Dir Prints & Drawings* Dr Daniel Hess; *Dir Folk toys* Dr Claudia Selheim; *Dir Archives* Dr Birgit Jooss; *Dir Mgmt* Stefan Rosenberger; *Dir Mktg & Commun* Dr Andrea Langer; *Dir Library* Dr Johannes Pommeranz
Open Tue, Thurs - Sun 10 AM - 6 PM, Wed 10 AM - 9 PM, cl Mon; Admis regular 8 EUR, reduced 5 EUR; Estab 1852; mus archive, library for art and culture of the German speaking world; Library with 500,000 vols. Mus of German art & culture from the stone age to present
Library Holdings: Auction Catalogs, Book Volumes, CD-ROMs, Exhibition Catalogs, Fiche, Manuscripts, Maps, Original Art Works, Original Documents, Pamphlets, Periodical Subscriptions, Photographs, Prints
Special Subjects: Archaeology, Baroque Art, Carpets & Rugs, Coins & Medals, Decorative Arts, Dolls, Drawings, Etchings & Engravings, Folk Art, Furniture, Glass, Gold, Graphics, Historical Material, Ivory, Landscapes, Manuscripts, Maps, Medieval Art, Metalwork, Military Art, Painting-European, Painting-German, Porcelain, Pottery, Renaissance Art, Sculpture, Silver, Stained Glass, Tapestries, Textiles, Watercolors, Woodcarvings, Woodcuts
Collections: Ancient historical objects, archives, books, folk art, furniture, manuscripts, musical instruments, paintings, sculpture, textiles, toys, weapons
Exhibitions: Traveling Companions; Witnesses to Mobility; The Fruit of Promise; Citrus Fruits in Art & Culture
Publications: Museum yearbook, catalogues of exhibitions and permanent collections, museum guides, popular books on the museum's collections
Activities: Classes for adults & children at Art Educ Center; docent training; lects open to pub & mem; concerts; gallery talks; tours; lending of original object of art to scientifically relevant exhibs & museums for special exhibs; book traveling exhibs, 1 per year; originates traveling exhibs, 1-2 per yr; mus shop sells books, magazines, reproductions, prints, postcards, souvenirs

RECKLINGHAUSEN

M **KUNSTHALLE RECKLINGHAUSEN,** Recklinghausen Art Gallery, Grosse Perdekamp Str 25-27, Recklinghausen, 45657 Germany. Tel 49 02361 50 1935; Fax 49 02361 50 1932; Email info@kunst-re.de; Web: kunsthall-recklinghausen.com; *Dir* Dr Ferdinand Ullrich; *Deputy Dir* Dr Hans-Jurgen Schwalm
Open Tues - Sun 11 AM - 6 PM; Admis regular 5 EUR, reduced 2.50 EUR; Estab 1950; Contemporary city art gallery
Library Holdings: Auction Catalogs, Book Volumes, Exhibition Catalogs
Collections: Paintings, sculpture, drawings & prints by contemporary artists, outsider art
Activities: Award, Kunstpreis: Junger westen; since 1948 for artists younger than 35; lending of original objects of art to Artothek; mus shop sells books, original art, reproductions & slides

STUTTGART

M **STAATSGALERIE STUTTGART,** Stuttgart National Gallery, Konrad-Adenauer-Strasse 30-32, Stuttgart, 70173 Germany. Tel 49 711 470 40 0; Fax 49 711 236 99 83; Email info@staatsgalerie.de; Web: www.staatsgalerie.de; *Dir* Dr Christiane Lange; *Mng Dir* Dirk Rieker; *Deputy Scientific Dir* Dr Ina Conzen
Open Tues, Wed, Fri - Sun 10 AM - 6 PM, Thurs 10 AM - 8 PM, cl Mon; Admis regular 7 EUR, reduced 5 EUR, Wed free; additional fees for special exhibs; Estab 1843; Comprised of the Alte Staatsgalerie, Neue Staatsgalerie & Alte Staatsgalerie Exten; Average Annual Attendance: 200,000
Library Holdings: Auction Catalogs, Book Volumes, Clipping Files, Exhibition Catalogs
Special Subjects: Drawings, Etchings & Engravings, Graphics, Medieval Art, Painting-Dutch, Painting-European, Painting-German, Painting-Italian, Period Rooms, Photography, Posters, Prints, Sculpture
Collections: 14th - 21st century European art, 14th - 16th century Old German Masters, 16th - 18th century Dutch paintings, 14th - 18th century Italian paintings, Baroque paintings, 19th century paintings, 20th century international art, 21st century paintings & sculptures, contemporary art, photography & graphic art
Exhibitions: (For future exhibs please use website)
Publications: exhib catalogs
Activities: Classes for adults & children; docent training; lects open to pub; tours for children & handicapped persons; concerts; gallery talks; mus shop sells books, reproductions, prints

WITTEN

M **MARKISCHES MUSEUM DER STADT WITTEN,** Markisches Museum of the City of Witten, Husemannstrasse 12, Witten, 58452 Germany. Tel 49 02302 581 25 50; Fax 49 02302 581 25 69; Email maerkisches.museum@stadt-witten.de; Web: www.kulturforum-witten.de/maerkischesmuseumwitten; *Dir* Dr Dirk Steimann; *Cur* Christoph Kohl
Open Wed, Fri - Sun noon - 6 PM, Thurs noon - 8 PM; Admis regular 4 EUR, reduced 2 EUR, under 18 free; Estab 1886
Collections: 20th century German paintings, drawings & graphics

GHANA

ACCRA

M **NATIONAL MUSEUM OF GHANA, ACCRA,** 2 Barnes Rd, Adabraka, PO Box GP 3343 Accra, Ghana. Tel 233 302 221633; Fax 233 302 222401; Email gmmb-acc@gmail.com; Web: nationalmuseum.ghana-net.com; *Exec Dir, Mus & Monuments Bd* Dr Zagba Narh Oyortey; *Mus Dir* Dr Prosper Yao Dzemefe
Open daily 9 AM - 4:30 PM; Admis Ghanaian adults 5 GHS, Ghanaian children 1-3 GHS, foreign adults 40 GHS, foreign children 5 GHS; Estab 1957
Collections: Art, archeological and ethnological colls for Ghana and West Africa

GREECE

ANDROS

M **MUSEUM OF CONTEMPORARY ART, BASIL AND ELISE GOULANDRIS FOUNDATION,** Hora, Andros, 84500 Greece. Tel 30 22820-22444; Fax 30 22820-22490; Email info@moca-andros.gr; Web: www.moca-andros.gr; *Dir* Dr Kyriakos Koutsomallis; *Art Historian - Mgr* Marie Koutsomallis; *Admin Secy* Alexandra Papakostopoulou
Open Nov - Mar Sat, Sun & Mon 10 AM - 2 PM, cl Tues - Fri, April - July Wed - Mon 10 AM - 2 PM, July - Sep Mon 11 AM - 3 PM, Wed - Sun 11 AM - 3 PM & 6 - 9 PM, cl Tues; Admis July - Sept: general 5 EUR, reduced 3 EUR; Oct - June: general 3 EUR, reduced 1.50 EUR; children under 12 free; Estab 1979; 3 levels, 8 rooms
Income: Self-financed
Library Holdings: Auction Catalogs, Book Volumes, Cards, Exhibition Catalogs, Pamphlets
Collections: The Basil & Elise Goulandris Collection, Greek 20th century art, contemporary Greek sculptures
Publications: Isamu Noguchi: Between East & West (exhib catalogs)
Activities: Classes for children; lects open to pub; gallery talks; tours; schols available; lending original object of art to other mus; mus shop sells books, original art, reproductions, prints, decorative artistic items, jewelry

ATHENS

M **ACROPOLIS MUSEUM,** 15 Dionysiou Areopagitou st, Athens, 11742 Greece. Tel 30 210 9000900; Email info@theacropolismuseum.gr; Web: www.theacropolismuseum.gr; *Pres Bd Dirs* Dimitrios Pandermalis
Open Nov - March: Mon - Thurs 9 AM - 5 PM, Fri 9 AM - 10 PM, Sat & Sun 9 AM - 8 PM; April - Oct Mon 8 AM - 4 PM, Tues - Thurs, Sat & Sun 8 AM - 8 PM, Fri 8 AM - 10 PM; Admis 5 EUR; Estab 1863 on the site of the Parthenon; Total area of 25,000 sq meters with a 14,000 sq meter exhib space, 250 sq meter theater, 700 sq meter restaurant & two 125 sq meter shops; Average Annual Attendance: 1,475,000
Special Subjects: Antiquities-Greek, Antiquities-Roman, Architecture, Art History, Ceramics, Bronzes, Sculpture, Archaeology, Furniture, Pottery
Exhibitions: More than 300 exhibits
Publications: Educational booklets
Activities: Educ progs; classes for adults & children; teacher training, outreach & resources; progs for overseas schools; lects open to pub; gallery talks; tours; conferences; seminars; film screenings; mus shop sells books, magazines, reproductions, prints, gifts; jewelry

M **BENAKI MUSEUM,** 1 Koumbari St & Vas Sofias Ave, Athens, 10674 Greece. Tel 210 367 1000; Fax 210 367 1063; Email benaki@benaki.gr; Web: www.benaki.gr; *Dir* Dr Oliver Descotes; *Deputy Dir* Irine Geroulanou; *CFO & COO* Haris Siampanis
Open Wed & Fri 9 AM - 5 PM, Thurs & Sat 9 AM - midnight, Sun 9 AM - 3 PM; Admis full 9 EUR, reduced 7 EUR; Library, historical archives and photographic archives are maintained
Collections: Ancient Greek art, chiefly jewelry, Byzantine and post-Byzantine art, icons and crafts, collections of Islamic art and Chinese porcelain, Greek popular art and historical relics, textiles from Far East and Western Europe

M **BYZANTINE & CHRISTIAN MUSEUM, ATHENS,** 22 Vasilissis Sophias Ave, Athens, 10675 Greece. Tel 30 213 213 9500; Fax 30 72 31 883; Email info.bma@culture.gr; Web: www.byzantinemuseum.gr; *Dir* Dr Katerina P Dellaporta
Open winter: Tues - Sun 9 AM - 4 PM, cl Mon; summer: daily 8 AM - 8 PM; Admis full 8 EUR, reduced 4 EUR, under 18 free; Founded 1914; Library & photo archives are maintained
Library Holdings: Fiche, Periodical Subscriptions, Reproductions
Special Subjects: Antiquities-Byzantine, Antiquities-Greek, Archaeology, Architecture, Ceramics, Coins & Medals, Costumes, Decorative Arts, Embroidery, Islamic Art, Jewelry, Manuscripts, Medieval Art, Metalwork, Mosaics, Painting-European, Painting-Russian, Religious Art, Tapestries, Textiles
Collections: Byzantine & Post-Byzantine icons, ceramics, marbles, metalwork, Christian & Byzantine sculpture & pottery, liturgical items, Greek manuscripts, historic photographs
Exhibitions: Permanent exhib (Byzantine coll)
Publications: European & Hellenic Ceramic of 18th century
Activities: Classes for adults & children; disabled group; lects open to pub; concerts; gallery talks; 5 vis lectrs per year; artmobile; lending of original objects of art to museums & institutions in Europe & America; book 1 traveling exhib per yer; mus shop sells books, cards, posters, video cassettes, CDs, CD-ROMs, reproductions, prints, slides, replicas, engravings, wall-paintings & accessories

M **FRISSIRAS MUSEUM,** 3 & 7 Monis Asteriou, Plaka Athens, Greece. Tel 30 210 32 34678; Fax 30 210 33 16027; Email info@frissirasmuseum.com; Web: www.frissirasmuseum.com; *Founder* Vlassis Frissiras
Open Wed - Fri 10 AM - 5 PM, Sat & Sun 11 AM - 5 PM, cl Mon & Tues; Admis full 6 EUR, reduced 3 EUR; Estab 2000
Collections: Contemporary Greek & European paintings

M **MUSEUM OF CYCLADIC ART,** 4 Neophytou Douka St, Athens, 106 74 Greece. Tel 30 210 7228321-3; Fax 30 210 7239382; Email museum@cycladic.gr; Web: www.cycladic.gr; *Pres* Sandra Marinopoulos; *Dir* Prof Nicholas C Stampolidis
Open Mon, Wed, Fri & Sat 10 AM - 5 PM, Thurs 10 AM - 8 PM, Sun 11 AM - 5 PM, cl Tues; Admis full 7 EUR, reduced 3.50 EUR, under 18 free; Estab 1986, study & promotion of art culture of the Aegean & Cyprus
Special Subjects: Antiquities-Greek, Antiquities-Roman, Archaeology
Collections: Greek art & artifacts of the Cycladic era, Thanos Zintilis Cypriot art coll
Publications: Catalogue of the colls; catalogue of the temporary exhibs; Timelines; educational booklets
Activities: Classes for adults & children; lects open to the pub; gallery talks; tours; mus shop sells books, original art, reproductions

M **NATIONAL ARCHAEOLOGICAL MUSEUM,** 44 Patission St, Athens, 10682 Greece. Tel 30 213 214 4800; Fax 30 210 821 3573; Email eam@culture.gr; Web: www.namuseum.gr; *Dir* Dr Maria Lagogianni
Open daily 8 AM - 8 PM; Admis full 10 EUR, reduced 5 EUR, students free; Estab 1889; 9.000 sq meters of exhib galleries housed in 19th century neoclassical building; Mem: Soc of Friends of the Nat Arch Mus
Income: Financed by the state
Library Holdings: Auction Catalogs, Book Volumes, CD-ROMs, DVDs, Exhibition Catalogs, Periodical Subscriptions, Photographs, Prints, Reproductions, Slides, Video Tapes
Special Subjects: Antiquities-Egyptian, Antiquities-Etruscan, Antiquities-Greek, Antiquities-Roman, Archaeology, Art History, Bronzes, Ceramics, Glass, Gold, History of Art & Archaeology, Ivory, Jewelry, Miniatures, Sculpture, Silver
Collections: Original Greek sculptures, Roman period sculptures, Bronze Age relics, Mycenaean treasures, Greek vases, terracottas, jewels, Egyptian antiquities, neolithic coll, cyclodic collection, Stathetes jewelry collection, coll of Cypriot Antiquities, vases & minor arts collection (terracotta figurines), Vlastos-Serpieris, glass vessels, gold jewelry & silver vessels, Hellenistic pottery Coll
Publications: Worshiping Women (catalogue); Eretria (catalogue); Myth & Colnage (catalogue)
Activities: Classes for deaf children & elderly people; fire educ progs every yr for school-classes; musical & theatrical performances; lectrs for mems only; 12 vis lectrs per year; concerts; lending of original objects of art to scientific archaeological exhibitions; European & US mus; sales shop sells books, reproductions, prints, slides, jewelry, painting art, toys (puzzles), accessories, bags, cravates, mantilla

M **NATIONAL GALLERY - ALEXANDROS SOUTZOS MUSEUM,** Alsos, Goudi, Athens, 11525 Greece. Tel 30 210 7235857; Fax 30 210 7224889; Email secretary@nationalgallery.gr; Web: www.nationalgallery.ge; *Dir* Marina Lambraki-Plaka; *Cur* Efi Agathonikou; *Mgmt Art Main & Res* Michalis Dougelidis
Open Mon & Wed - Fri: 9 - 8, Sat - Sun: 9 - 4, cl Tues; Admis 5 EUR, reduced 3 EUR; Estab 1900; Mus of modern Greek art from the 1500s to the present; Average Annual Attendance: 100,000
Income: State & sponsoring
Library Holdings: Book Volumes, CD-ROMs, Cards, Cassettes, Exhibition Catalogs, Framed Reproductions, Memorabilia, Reproductions
Collections: 14th - 21st century European painting, 17th - 20th century Greek engravings, paintings & sculpture, Impressionist, Post-Impressionist & contemporary drawings
Activities: Classes for children; concerts; gallery talks; tours; extension prog serves other Mus; organize traveling exhibs to other mus in Greece & abroad; sales shop sells books, original art, reproductions, prints

M **Coumantaros Art Gallery of Sparta**, 123 Konstantinou Paloiologou & Thermopylon St, Sparta, 23100 Greece. Tel 30 273 1081822; Web: www.nationalgallery.gr; *Cur* Dr Georgia Chroni
Open Mon - Sat & Sun 9 AM - 3 PM, cl Tues
Collections: Modern Greek art

M **Corfu Annex**, Castellino, Kato Korakiana, Corfu, 49100 Greece. Tel 30 26610 93333; Fax 30 26610 80233; Email marinapapasotiriou@nationalgallery.gr; Web: corfu.nationalgallery.gr; *Cur* Marina Papassotiriou
Open Mon & Wed - Sun 8:30 AM - 3:30 PM, Fri 10 AM - 2 PM & 6 PM - 9 PM; Admis full 2 EUR, reduced 1 EUR; Estab 1993; Housed in the Castellino & Castelleto historic buildings
Collections: Modern Greek art from the beginning of Greek independence to today

M **Nafplion Annex**, 23 Sidiras Merarchias St, Nafplion, 21100 Greece. Tel 30 27520 21915; Fax 30 27520 21935; Email labrinikarakourti@nationalgallery.gr; Web: www.nationalgallery.gr; *Cur* Lambrini Karakourti
Open Mon, Thurs & Sat 10 AM -3 PM, Wed & Fri 10 AM - 3 PM & 5 PM - 8 PM, Sun 10 AM - 2 PM, cl Tues; Admis full 3 EUR, reduced 1.50 EUR, Mon free; Estab 2004; Housed in neo-classical building
Collections: Paintings related to the Greek War of Independence (1821-1829)

M **Kapralos Museum**, Nikou Kazantzaki, 180 10, Aegina, Greece. Tel 30 22970 22001; Web: www.nationalgallery.gr
Open Wed - Fri 8 AM - 4 PM, Sat & Sun 9:30 AM - 5 PM, cl Mon & Tues; Estab 1995; Housed in six rooms of Christos Kapralos's studio on Aegina
Collections: Works by Greek artist Christos Kapralos

M **National Glyptotheque**, Hellenic Army Park, Athens, 15700 Greece. Tel 30 210 7709855; Web: www.nationalgallery.gr
Open Mon & Wed - Sun 9 AM - 4 PM, cl Tues; Estab 2004; Housed on the grounds of the former royal stables at Army Park in Goudi
Collections: 19th & 20th century modern Greek sculpture, Neoclassical, Realist, Modernist, Traditional, Anthropocentric, Post-Modernist, folk, funeral & abstract sculptures, Yannoulis Chalepas, foreign artists

M **NATIONAL MUSEUM OF CONTEMPORARY ART,** Kallirrois Ave & Amvr Frantzi St, Athens, 11743 Greece. Tel 30 210 9242111; Fax 30 210 9245200; Email protocol@emst.culture.gr; Web: www.emst.gr; *Dir* Katrina Koskina
Museum temporarily closed for relocation; Admis full 3 EUR, reduced 1.50 EUR, children under 12 & seniors over 65 free; Estab 2000
Library Holdings: Auction Catalogs, Audio Tapes, CD-ROMs, Compact Disks, DVDs, Exhibition Catalogs, Original Documents, Pamphlets, Periodical Subscriptions, Photographs, Records, Slides, Video Tapes
Collections: Painting and three-dimensional work, historical and contemporary, photography, new media, architecture & design
Publications: Catalogues (included with all art exhibs)
Activities: Classes for adults & children; gallery talks; tours; organize traveling exhibs to other cities in Greece; sales shop sells books, magazines

CORINTH

M **ARCHAEOLOGICAL MUSEUM OF ANCIENT CORINTH,** Ancient Corinth, Corinth, 20007 Greece. Tel 30 27410 31207; Fax 30 27410 31480; Email efakor@culture.gr; Web: odysseus.culture.gr; *Cur* Socrates Koursoumi
Open April - Oct daily 8 AM - 8 PM, cl Nov - March; Admis full 8 EUR, reduced 4 EUR; Estab 1932; Museum & archaeological site; Average Annual Attendance: 160,000
Collections: Prehistoric, Classical, Roman & Asklepieion galleries, statues, sculptures, Greek & Roman inscriptions & antiquities

DELPHI

M **DELPHI ARCHAEOLOGICAL MUSEUM,** Delphi, 33054 Greece. Tel 30 22650 82313; Fax 30 22650 82966; Email efafok@culture.gr; Web: odysseus.culture.gr; *Dir* Nancy Psalti
Open Mon & Tues 10 AM - 5 PM, Wed - Sun 8 AM - 8 PM; Admis full 12 EUR, reduced 6 EUR, under 18 free; Estab 1903; Two-story building, 14 exhib rooms, 2,270 sq meters of exhib space; library with 4,800 vols; Average Annual Attendance: 350,000
Library Holdings: Book Volumes, CD-ROMs, Cards, Exhibition Catalogs, Maps, Periodical Subscriptions, Photographs, Slides
Special Subjects: Antiquities-Egyptian, Antiquities-Greek, Antiquities-Roman, Archaeology, Architecture, Asian Art, Bronzes, Ceramics, Coins & Medals, Crafts, Glass, Gold, Historical Material, History of Art & Archaeology, Ivory, Landscapes, Metalwork, Mosaics, Jewelry, Sculpture, Silver
Collections: Permanent exhibition of ancient sculpture, vases, inscriptions, statuettes, bronze weapons, tools of different periods
Activities: Mus shop sells books, reproductions, prints, slides, corporate gifts, office & paper products, accessories, games

HERAKLION

M **HERAKLION ARCHAEOLOGICAL MUSEUM,** Xanthoudidou 2 Str, Heraklion, TK 71202 Greece. Tel 30 2810 279000; Fax 30 2810 279001; Email amh@culture.gr; Web: odysseus.culture.gr; *Dir* Mandalaki Stiliani
Open summer: daily 8 AM - 8 PM; winter: Mon 11 AM - 5 PM, Tues - Sun & bank holidays 8 AM - 3 PM; Admis full 10 EUR, reduced 5 EUR; Estab 1883; Temporary exhibs including highlights from the permanent colls across 27 galleries
Income: Pub sector
Library Holdings: Book Volumes, CD-ROMs, Exhibition Catalogs, Other Holdings, Pamphlets, Periodical Subscriptions
Collections: Development of Cretan & Minoan art from the Prehistoric to the late Roman periods, Classical & late antiquity exhibits
Publications: N Dimopoulou - Rethemiotaki; The Meraklion Archaeological Museum; Latsis Foundation; Athens, 2005
Activities: Classes for children; lending of original objects of art to Greece & other countries; mus shop sells books, prints & slides

OLYMPIA

M **ARCHAEOLOGICAL MUSEUM OF OLYMPIA,** Ancient Olympia, Olympia, 27065 Greece. Tel 30 26240 22742; Fax 30 26240 22529; Email zepka@culture.gr; Web: odysseus.culture.gr; *Dir* Georgia Chatzi-Spiliopoulou
Open winter Mon 10 AM - 5 PM, Tues - Fri 8 AM - 3 PM; summer 8 AM - 8 PM; Admis full 12 EUR, reduced 6 EUR, under 18 free; Old Museum estab 1885; New Museum estab 1982; Prehistoric, classical & Roman antiquities; Average Annual Attendance: 440,000
Library Holdings: Book Volumes, CD-ROMs, Cards, DVDs, Exhibition Catalogs, Maps, Pamphlets, Periodical Subscriptions
Special Subjects: Antiquities-Greek, Antiquities-Roman, Archaeology, Bronzes, Ceramics
Collections: Ancient Greek sculpture, bronzes, ceramics & glass
Publications: Arapoyanni Xeni, Olympia; Vikatou Olympia, Olympia archaeological site and museums; Chatzi Spiliopoulou Georgia, Archaeological Museum of Olympia
Activities: Classes for children; docent training; educational material for school classes; family trail for the Bronzes Gallery of the mus; mus shop sells books, reproductions, slides, cards

PAIANIA

M **VORRES MUSEUM OF CONTEMPORARY GREEK ART AND FOLK ART,** 1 Parodos Diadochou Constantinou St, Paiania, 190 02 Greece. Tel 30 210 6642520 / 6644771; Fax 30 210 6645775; Email info@vorresmuseum.gr; Web: www.vorresmuseum.gr; *Dir* George Vorres
Open Mon - Fri by appointment only, Sat - Sun 10 AM - 2 PM; Admis full 5 EUR, reduced 3 EUR; Estab 1983; New 2000 sq meter wing to the Museum of Contemporary Greek Art; Average Annual Attendance: 70,000 - 80,000
Income: Sale of tickets & catalogues, rental of space for receptions
Library Holdings: Book Volumes, Exhibition Catalogs, Reproductions
Special Subjects: Antiquities-Greek, Ceramics, Coins & Medals, Folk Art, Furniture, Glass
Collections: Contemporary Greek art, Greek Folk art
Publications: Catalogues & volumes for each part of the museum in Greek & English
Activities: Classes for children; special guided tours

RETHYMNON

M **MUSEUM OF CONTEMPORARY ART OF CRETE,** 32 Mesologhiou Str, Rethymnon, Crete 74131 Greece. Tel 30 28310 52530; Fax 30 28310 52689; Email info@cca.gr; Web: www.rca.gr; *Artistic Dir & Cur* Maria Marangou
Open May - Oct: Tues - Fri 9 AM - 2 PM & 7 - 9 PM, Sat & Sun 10 AM - 3 PM, cl Mon; Nov - April: Tues & Thurs 9 AM - 2 PM, Wed & Fri 9 AM - 2 PM & 6 - 9 PM, Sat & Sun 10 AM - 3 PM, cl Mon; Admis general 3 EUR, groups 2 EUR, undergraduates 1.50 EUR, Thurs free; Estab 1992; Housed in Venetian building
Collections: Paintings of Leuteris Kanakakis including oil, drawings and watercolors, contemporary artists depicting modern Greek art since the 1950s with emphasis on the 1970s, 1980 & 1990s

THESSALONIKI

M **ARCHAEOLOGICAL MUSEUM OF THESSALONIKI,** 6 Manolis Andronikou St, PO Box 540 19 Thessaloniki, 54013 Greece. Tel 30 2313 310201; Fax 30 2310 861306; Email amth@culture.gr; Web: www.amth.gr; *Dir* Dr Polyxeni Adam-Veleni
Open daily 8 AM - 8 PM; Admis full 8 EUR, reduced 4 EUR, under 18 free; Estab 1962; Archaeological collections displayed in one building gallery; Average Annual Attendance: 100,000
Income: Financed by state
Library Holdings: Auction Catalogs, Book Volumes, Exhibition Catalogs, Filmstrips, Photographs, Slides
Special Subjects: Antiquities-Greek, Antiquities-Roman, Archaeology, Architecture, Bronzes, Ceramics, Coins & Medals, Glass, Gold, Ivory, Jewelry, Metalwork, Mosaics
Collections: Macedonian archaeology, mainly from Thessaloniki, Chalkidiki, Kilkis & Pieria (from the prehistoric times to late antiquity)
Activities: Nat progs for children, hands-on activities; periodic exhibs inspired by themes both from ancient & modern culture; lects open to public, 12 vis lectrs per yr; concerts; tours; gallery talks; workshops; lending original objects of art to museums in Europe and elsewhere; Originates traveling exhibitions on Alexander the Great that circulate to other regions in Macedonia supports archaeology research; mus shop sells books, reproductions, prints, slides, puzzles, scarves, ties, t-shirts, bags

M **STATE MUSEUM OF CONTEMPORARY ART,** 21 Kolokotroni St, Moni Lazariston, Stavroupoli Thessaloniki, 56430 Greece. Tel 30 2310 589140 1; Fax 30 2310 600123; Email info@greekstatemuseum.com; Web: www.greekstatemuseum.com; *Mus Dir* Dr Maria Tsantsanoglou; *Ctr Dir* Syrago Tsiara
Open Tues - Sat 10 AM - 6 PM; Admis adults 3 EUR, students 1.5 EUR; Estab 1997; Contemporary art museum & art center
Income: State funded
Library Holdings: Book Volumes, Exhibition Catalogs, Fiche
Collections: George Costakis Collection; Russian avant-garde art, 1,275 oil paintings, constructions, and drawings, 100 works of art, 200 paintings and sculptures, contemporary art by Greek artists
Exhibitions: Variety of exhibs throughout yr
Publications: List of publs accompanying the exhibs
Activities: Classes for adults & children, access prog for visual impaired people; concerts, gallery talks & tours; originates traveling exhibs to all visitors; sales shop sells books & promotional objects

GREENLAND

NUUK

M **GRONLANDS NATIONALMUSEUM,** Greenland National Museum, Hans Egedevej 8, PO Box 145 Nuuk, 3900 Greenland. Tel 299 322 611; Fax 299 322 622; Email nka@natmus.gl; Web: www.natmus.gl; *Dir* Daniel Thorleifsen; *Deputy Dir* Bo Albrecthsen
Open June - mid-Sept Mon - Sun 10 AM - 4 PM; mid-Sept - May Tues - Sun 1 - 4 PM, cl Mon; Admis 30 DKK, children & students free
Special Subjects: Archaeology, Crafts, Eskimo Art, Ethnology, Scrimshaw, Watercolors
Collections: Inuit Archaeological colls, Gustav Holm Collection of Ammassalik in the 1880s, Inughuit-Polareskimos around 1900, kayaks, art and handicrafts, early Inuit art of the 19th century, Modern and contemporary Inuit art, Photography coll, Norse Coll

GUATEMALA

GUATEMALA CITY

MUSEO NACIONAL DE ARQUEOLOGIA Y ETNOLOGIA, National Museum of Archaeology & Ethnology, 7ta Avenida 6a Calle Zona 13, Salon 5 Finca la Aurora Guatemala City, Guatemala. Tel 502 2475 4399; 2475 4406; 2475 4010; Email info@munae.gob.gt; Web: www.munae.gob.gt; *Dir* Patricia del Aguila Flores
Open Tues - Fri 9 AM - 4 PM, Sat - Sun 9 AM - noon & 1:30 PM - 4 PM; Admis domestic 5 GTQ, foreigners 60 GTQ, children under 9 free; Estab 1931; Average Annual Attendance: 85,000
Collections: 20,000 archaeological & 5,000 ethnological artifacts, Mayan & pre-Hispanic art, handcrafted ceramic, stone, shell, bone & jade, fabrics, clothing, ceremonial objects
Publications: Simposio de Investigaciones Arqueologicas en Guatemala

Activities: Sales shop sells books, magazines, slides

M **MUSEO NACIONAL DE ARTE MODERNO CARLOS MERIDA,** Carlos Merida National Museum of Modern Art, Salon No 6, Finca La Aurora Zona 13 Guatemala City, Guatemala. Tel 502 2471 1422; 2472 0467; Web: mcd.gob.gt/meseo-de-arte-moderno-carlos-merida; *Dir* Jose Mario Ponce O Maza
Open Tues - Fri 9 AM - 4 PM, Sat & Sun 9 AM - noon & 1:30 - 4 PM, cl Mon; Admis domestic 5 GTQ, foreigners 50 GTQ; Estab 1935
Collections: Contemporary art by Guatemalan artists, paintings, sculpture, engravings, drawings

M **UNIVERSIDAD FRANCISCO MARROQUIN ORGANIZACION PARA LAS ARTES,** Francisco Marroquin University Organization for the Arts, Centro Cultural Auditorio Juan Bautista, 6 Calle Final Zona 10 Guatemala City, 01010 Guatemala. Tel 502 2338 7810 y 09; Email arteopa@ufm.edu; Email orpafm@ufm.edu; Web: organizacionparalasartes.org; *Pres & Artistic Dir* Geraldina Baca-Spross
Estab 1983; Univ cultural organization dedicated to the presentation of the arts

M **Museo Popol Vuh - Popol Vuh Museum,** 6 Calle Final Zona 10, Guatemala City, 01010 Guatemala. Tel 502 2338 7896; Fax 502 2338 7924; Email popolvuh@ufm.edu; Web: www.popolvuh.ufm.edu; *Cur* Dr Oswaldo Chinchilla
Open Mon - Fri 9 AM - 5 PM, Sat 9 AM - 1 PM, cl Sun; Admis adults 35 GTQ, students 15 GTQ, children 2-12 10 GTQ
Collections: Collection of pre-Hispanic art, stone sculptures and ceramics, pre-classic, classic and post-classic Maya eras, colonial art, folk art, textiles, clothing, masks and decorative arts

M **Museo Ixchel de Traje Indigena - Ixchel Museum of Indigenous Dress,** 6 Calle Final Zona 10, Guatemala City, 01010 Guatemala. Tel 502 2331 3739; 2331-3622; Email info@museoixchel.org; Web: www.museoixchel.org; *Gen Dir* Claudia Monzon; *Dir Admin* Rosa Amparo Lopez de Enriquez
Open Mon - Fri 9 AM - 5 PM, Sat 9 AM - 1 PM; Admis English tour 15 GTQ, Spanish tour 10 GTQ; Estab 1977; Two large spaces to collect, conserve, document, recover and exhibit the Maya textiles of Guatemala, with emphasis on the cultural, technical and artistic significance of the Maya weavings
Income: Financed by admissions, donations, activities, conferences, workshops
Library Holdings: Kodachrome Transparencies, Photographs
Collections: Indigenous clothing and handwoven fabrics from 120 highland communities, Sculptures, photographs, paintings, ceramics, jewelry and more, Pre-Hispanic Maya clothing, Maya-Hispanic clothing, Historic Maya clothing, Contemporary Maya clothing, Embroidery: Stitches that Unite Cultures
Publications: Exhibit & collection catalogs; Books, calendars
Activities: Classes for adults & children; docent training; workshops; tours; mus shop sells books, reproductions, handicrafts, Mayan weavings & dress

GUINEA

CONAKRY

M **MUSEE NATIONAL DE GUINEE,** National Museum of Guinea, 2nd Ave, Conakry, Guinea. Tel 224 30 45 10 66; *Dir Gen* Hadja Kade Seck
Open Tues - Sun 9 AM - 5:30 PM, cl Mon; Admis nationals 500 GNF, students 100 GNF, foreigners 1000 GNF
Collections: Ethnographic coll of masks, statues, musical instruments & archaeological artifacts

HAITI

PORT-AU-PRINCE

M **MUSEE DU PANTHEON NATIONAL HAITIEN,** Haitian National Pantheon Museum, Rue de la Republique, Place des Heros de l'Independence Port-au-Prince, 6110 Haiti. Tel 509 34 17 4435; Web: www.facebook.com/Mupanah; *Dir Gen* Michele Gardere Frisch; *Admin Dir* Andre Thomas; *Head Coll & Conservation* Dukernst Biamby
Open daily 8 AM - 4 PM; Admis 175 HTG; Estab 1983
Collections: Haitian history from the time of the Arawak & Taino people to the 1940s including works dedicated to Spanish and French colonization, the trans-Atlantic slave trade & the Haitian revolution & independence

HONDURAS

TEGUCIGALPA

M **GALERIA NACIONAL DE ARTE,** National Art Gallery, Col Trejo 24 Ave SO, 11 Calle San Pedro Sula Tegucigalpa, Honduras. Tel 504 9970-1661; Email info@galerianacionaldeartehonduras.org; Web: . www.galerianacionaldeartehonduras.org; *Exec Dir* Jose Jorge Salgado
Open Mon - Sat 9 AM - 3 PM; Estab 1996
Collections: Paleolithic cave paintings & sculptures, pre-Columbian stonework & pottery, colonial religious paintings, silverwork, contemporary Honduran art

HONG KONG

KOWLOON

M **HONG KONG MUSEUM OF ART,** 10 Salisbury Rd, Tsimshatsui Kowloon, Hong Kong. Tel 852 2721 0116; Fax 852 2723 7666; Email enquiries@lcsd.gov.hk; Web: hk.art.museum; *Mus Dir* Eve Tam
Closed for renovations; scheduled to reopen in 2019; No admis fee; Estab 1962
Collections: Chinese antiquities, Chinese paintings & calligraphy with a specialization of Cantonese artists, historical collection of paintings, prints & drawings of Hong Kong, Macau & China, local & contemporary art

POKFULAM

M **UNIVERSITY MUSEUM AND ART GALLERY,** University of Hong Kong, 90 Bonham Rd, Pokfulam, Hong Kong. Tel 852 2241-5500; Fax 852 2546-9659; Email museum@hku.hk; Web: www.hkumag.hku.hk; *Dir* Dr Florian Knothe; *Cur* Anita Wong
Open Mon - Sat 9:30 AM - 6 PM, Sun 1 PM - 6 PM; No admis fee; Estab 1953; Housed in the Fung Ping Shan Bldg & TT Tsui Bldg
Special Subjects: Antiquities-Oriental, Asian Art, Calligraphy, Crafts, Decorative Arts, Folk Art, Religious Art, Woodcarvings
Collections: Houses over 2,000 items of Chinese antiquities, Ceramics, bronze, paintings; examples dating from Neolithic period to Qing dynasty, Bronze from Shang to Tang dynasties and coll of Yuan dynasty Nestorian crosses, Jade, wood, and stone carvings; Chinese oil paintings, Old Hong Kong photographs
Activities: Workshops; Lects open to the pub; gallery talks; mus shop sells books, reproductions, souvenirs

HUNGARY

BUDAPEST

M **LUDWIG MUZEUM - KORTARS MUVESZETI MUZEUM,** Ludwig Museum - Museum of Contemporary Art, Mupa Budapest, Komor Marcell u 1 Budapest, 1095 Hungary. Tel 361 555-3444; Fax 361 555-3458; Email info@ludwigmuseum.hu; Web: www.ludwigmuseum.hu; *Dir* Julia Fabyeni; *Head Conservation & Coll Care* Bela Tamas Konya; *Head of Colls* Krisztina Szipocs
Open Tues - Sun 10 AM - 6 PM; cl Mon; Admis adult 8,000 HUF, concession 4,000 HUF, children under 6 & EU seniors over 70 free; Estab 1989; Contemporary art gallery; Average Annual Attendance: 90,000
Library Holdings: Book Volumes, Exhibition Catalogs, Periodical Subscriptions
Special Subjects: Painting-American, Painting-French, Painting-German, Painting-Polish, Painting-Russian, Photography, Prints, Sculpture
Collections: Museum of contemporary art in Hungary to collecting international art, Collection from end of 1960s to present, Pieces of American Pop art and hyperrealism, Eastern-European avant-garde from the 1960's and 70's; geometric, minimalist work; international New painting from 1980s, Conceptual and Action art, International Contemporary Art
Publications: Collection of Ludwig Museum - Museum of Contemporary Art Budapest
Activities: Classes for children; film clubs; screenings; concerts; gallery talks; auxiliary family progs; museum educ; conferences; sales shop sells books; magazines

M **MAGYAR NEMZETI GALERIA,** Hungarian National Gallery, Buda Palace, Buildings A-B-C-D, Szent Gyorgy ter 2 Budapest, 1014 Hungary; PO Box 31, Budapest, 1250 Hungary. Tel 361 201 9082; Fax 361 2126 631; Email info@mng.hu; Web: mng.hu; *Dir* Laszlo Bean
Open Tues - Sun 10 AM - 6 PM; cl Mon; Admis full 1800 HUF, concessions 900 HUF; Estab 1957; Hungarian art from the 11th century to date located in Buda Castle; Average Annual Attendance: 600,000
Income: Financed by the state
Library Holdings: Auction Catalogs, Book Volumes, Exhibition Catalogs
Collections: Ancient & modern Hungarian paintings & sculpture, medal cabinet, panel paintings
Activities: Classes for children; docent training; lects open to pub; 2,000 vis lectrs per yr; concerts; gallery talks; tours; mus shop sells books, reproductions, slides, magazines, prints

M **MAGYAR NEMZETI MUZEUM,** Hungarian National Museum, Muzeum krt 14-16, Budapest, 1088 Hungary. Tel 361 338-2122; 317-7806; 327-7773; Fax 362 317 7806; Email info@hnm.hu; Web: hnm.edu; *Dir Gen* Benedek Varga; *Deputy Dir* Dr Tunde Csasztvay; *Coll Deputy Dir Gen* Gabor Tomka
Open Tues - Sun 10 AM - 6 PM, cl Mon; Admis full 1400 HUF, concession 800 HUF
Special Subjects: Anthropology, Antiquities-Byzantine, Antiquities-Egyptian, Antiquities-Etruscan, Antiquities-Greek, Antiquities-Oriental, Antiquities-Roman, Archaeology, Architecture, Bronzes, Carpets & Rugs, Ceramics, Coins & Medals, Costumes, Decorative Arts, Drawings, Embroidery, Enamels, Ethnology, Folk Art, Furniture, Glass, Gold, Graphics, Jewelry, Landscapes, Leather, Manuscripts, Maps, Medieval Art, Metalwork, Military Art, Miniatures, Painting-European, Photography, Portraits, Prints, Religious Art, Renaissance Art, Restorations, Sculpture, Silver, Textiles, Woodcarvings, Woodcuts
Collections: Archaeological coll from Paleolithic to present, posters, decorative arts, silverware, arts and crafts, textiles, household items, ceramics, glassware, seals, stamps, weapons, musical instruments, toys, pewter, metalwork, photography & coin coll
Activities: Concerts; tours; lending of art objects to var museums; mus shop sells books & reproductions

M **MUCSARNOK,** Palace of Art, Dozsa Gyorgy, UT 37 Budapest, 1146 Hungary. Tel 36 1 460 7000; Fax 36 1 363 7205; Email mucsarnok@mucsarnok.hu; Web: www.mucsarnok.hu; *Artistic Dir* Gyorgy Szego; *Financial Dir* Piroska Medgyes; *Chief Cur* Andras Ban
Open Tue, Wed, Fri - Sun 10 AM - 6 PM, Thurs noon - 8 PM, cl Mon; Admis normal 1800 HUF, students, educators & seniors 900 HUF, reduced 300 HUF; Estab 1877; Library with 15,000 vols
Collections: Hungarian & foreign contemporary art, paintings & sculptures

M **SZEPMUVESZETI MUZEUM,** Museum of Fine Arts, Dozsa Gyorgy ut 41, Budapest, 1146 Hungary. Tel 361 469 7100; Fax 361 469 7171; Email info@szepmuveszeti.hu; Web: www.szepmuveszeti.hu; *Gen Dir* Dr Laszlo Baan; *Deputy Dir* Maria Mihaly; *Head of Research* Dr Orsolya Radvanyi; *Financial Dir* Agnes Pinter Banoszi
Closed for renovations; scheduled to reopen in 2018; Estab 1896; Museum's coll is made up of international art, including all periods of European art & comprises more than 100,000 pieces; Average Annual Attendance: 550,000; Mem: Ministry for human resources
Income: State supported
Library Holdings: Auction Catalogs, Book Volumes, CD-ROMs, Compact Disks, Exhibition Catalogs, Fiche, Kodachrome Transparencies, Manuscripts, Original Documents, Other Holdings, Periodical Subscriptions, Photographs, Prints, Reproductions, Sculpture
Special Subjects: Antiquities-Egyptian, Antiquities-Greek, Antiquities-Roman, Baroque Art, Drawings, Etchings & Engravings, Graphics, Landscapes, Marine Painting, Medieval Art, Painting-British, Painting-Dutch, Painting-European, Painting-Flemish, Painting-French, Painting-Spanish, Sculpture
Collections: Old Master, paintings Egyptian, 19th & 20th century art, old sculpture collection, Vasarely Collections, classical antiquities, prints & drawings after 1800
Exhibitions: Permanent Exhibs of the collections; 6-8 temporary exhibs per yr
Publications: Bulletin, exhib catalogues, monographics, educ materials; catalogues of certain parts of colls
Activities: Classes for adults, children & mentally disabled; dramatic progs; docent training; exhibs; lects open to pub & lects for mems only; 5,000 vis lectrs per yr; concerts; gallery talks; tours; sponsoring of competitions; awards, 2011 mus magazine (Museum Cafe) Bronze Medal; artmobile; lending of original objects of art to national & international art institutions; mus shop sells books, magazines, original art, reproductions, prints slides & other items

ESZTERGOM

M **KERESZTENY MUZEUM,** Christian Museum, Mindszenty ter 2, Esztergom, H-2500 Hungary. Tel 36 33 413 880; Fax 36 33 413 880; Email keresztenymuzeum@gmail.com; Web: www.keresztenymuzeum.hu; *Pres* Pal Csefalvay
Open Mar - Nov Tues, Wed, Fri - Sun 10 AM - 5 PM, cl Mon & Thurs & Dec - Feb; Admis individual 900 Huf, reduced 450 huf; Estab 1875; Old Hungarian and European ecclesiastical art
Library Holdings: Book Volumes, Exhibition Catalogs, Periodical Subscriptions
Special Subjects: Baroque Art, Carpets & Rugs, Ceramics, Coins & Medals, Crafts, Decorative Arts, Drawings, Embroidery, Enamels, Etchings & Engravings, Ethnology, Flasks & Bottles, Folk Art, Furniture, Glass, Ivory, Jewelry, Medieval Art, Metalwork, Painting-Dutch, Painting-European, Painting-Flemish, Painting-German, Painting-Italian, Painting-Spanish, Porcelain, Religious Art, Renaissance Art, Sculpture, Silver, Stained Glass, Tapestries, Textiles, Woodcarvings, Painting-Russian, Portraits, Pottery, Prints, Watercolors, Woodcuts
Collections: Hungarian, Austrian, Dutch, French, German & Italian medieval paintings and silver artwork, miniatures, porcelain, statues & tapestries
Publications: Catalogues of temporary exhib
Activities: Lects open to public; 4 vis lectrs per year; concerts; gallery talks; mus shop sells books, reproductions, prints & CD-ROMs

KECSKEMET

M **MAGYAR FOTOGRAFIAI MUZEUM,** Hungarian Museum of Photography, Katona Jozsef ter 12, Kecskemet, 6000 Hungary. Tel 36-76-483-221; Fax 36-76-508-259; Email fotomuzeum@fotomuzeum.hu; Web: www.fotomuzeum.hu; *Dir* Dr Peter Baki
Open Tues - Sat 12 AM - 5 PM; Admis adults HUF 500, students & pensioners HUF 300
Collections: Collection of more than 1 million photographs from the 1840s to the present, original negatives, cameras, photographic history, artifacts, relics, medals, awards, posters, stamps, postcards, videos, Andre Kertesz coll, Pal Rosti album, Rudolf Baloghs WWII negative collection, Laszlo Moholy-Nagy Collection

M **MAGYAR NAIV MUVESZEK MUZEUMA,** Museum of Hungarian Native Art, Gaspar A U 11, Kecskemet, 6000 Hungary. Tel 76 324 767; Fax 76 481 122; Email kecskem1@t-online.hu; *Dir* Dr Barth Janos
Open Tues - Sun 10 AM - 5 PM, cl Mon; Admis adults 150 HUF, students & seniors 100 HUF; Estab 1976
Collections: Classic & contemporary art by native Hungarian painters and sculptors

PECS

M **JANUS PANNONIUS MUZEUM,** Janus Pannonius Museum, Kaptalan u 5, Pecs, 7621 Hungary. Tel 36 072 514-040; Fax 36 072 514-042; Email jpm@jpm.hu; Web: www.jpm.hu; *Dir* Dr Csorney Boldizsar Laszlo
Open Tues - Sun 10 AM - 6 PM, cl Mon; Admis adults 1200 HUF, seniors & students 600 HUF; Estab 1904; Collective of 12 museums throughout Pecs, Baranja County
Library Holdings: Auction Catalogs, Book Volumes, Cassettes, Exhibition Catalogs, Manuscripts, Memorabilia, Periodical Subscriptions
Special Subjects: Antiquities-Byzantine, Antiquities-Roman, Watercolors
Collections: Modern Hungarian art from the 1800s onwards, fine & applied arts, natural history, local history, archaeology, ethnography
Exhibitions: Zsolnay Ceramics (1955); Vasarely (1973); Csontvary (1983)
Publications: Catalogs of exhibs
Activities: Classes for adults & children; lects open to pub; 10 vis lectrs per year; concerts; gallery talks; tours; lending of original art objects; originate traveling exhibs; mus shop sells books, prints & reproductions

SOPRON

M **SOPRONI MUZEUM,** Sopron Museum, Fo ter 8, Sopron, 9400 Hungary. Tel 36 99 311-327; Fax 36 99 311 347; Email muzeum.titkarsag@muzeum.sopron.hu; Web: www.muzeum.sopron.hu; *Dir* Dr Imre Toth; *Head of Colls* Dr Istvan Keleman; *Opers Dir* Katalin Toth
Open Tues - Sun 10 AM - 6 PM, summer hours 10 AM - 8 PM, cl Mon; Admis full 500 - 1150 HUF reduced 250 - 580 HUF; Estab 1847; Collective of 11 exhibitions throughout the city of Sopron; library with 20,000 vols
Collections: Folk & local Baroque art

SZENTENDRE

M **FERENCZY MUZEUM CENTRUM,** Ferenczy Museum Center, Fo ter 2-5, Szentendre, 2000 Hungary. Tel 36 20 779 6657; Email info@muzeumicentrum.hu; Web: www.humuzeumicentrum.hu; *Dir* Gulyas Gabor
Open Tues - Sun 10 AM - 6 PM, cl Mon; No admis fee; Estab 1951
Income: Supported by county govt
Library Holdings: Book Volumes, Exhibition Catalogs
Special Subjects: Archaeology, Carpets & Rugs, Ceramics, Dolls, Drawings, Folk Art, Graphics, Pottery, Sculpture, Tapestries
Collections: Paintings, sculptures, drawings, archaeological, ethnographic & local history collections, Gobelin tapestries, Kmetty-Kerenyi Collection, Kovoes Margil Ceramic Collection, Barcsay Collection, Vajda Collection, Anna-Ames Collection, Kovacs Margit Ceramic Coll
Exhibitions: Roman lapidarium, dolls & toy soldiers exhibition
Activities: Classes for adults & children; excavations in Pest County, scientific researches, temporary exhibs; concerts; lending of original art objects to fellow institutions & other museums; mus shop sells books, reproductions, stamps & DVDs & other gift items

ZALAEGERSZEG

M **GOCSEJI MUZEUM,** Gocseji Museum, Batthyany u 2, Zalaegerszeg, 8900 Hungary. Tel 36 92 314 537; Fax 36 92 511 972; Email muzeum@zmmi.hu; Web: gocsejimuzeum.hu; *Dir* Dr Imre Kajan; *Deputy Dir, Chief Cur & Head History Dept* Laszlo Kostyal
Open Summer: Tues - Sun 10 AM - 6 PM, cl Mon; Winter: Tues - Sat 9 AM - 5 PM, cl Sun & Mon; Admis full 700 HUF, reduced 350 HUF, children under 6 & seniors over 70 free; Library with 12,000 vols
Special Subjects: Archaeology, Folk Art, Furniture, Hispanic Art, Historical Material, Photography, Sculpture
Collections: Fine & applied arts, ethnography, history & archaeology colls, regional paintings & sculptures, Zsigmond Kisfaludi Strobl sculptures, Janos Neineth ceramics

ICELAND

REYKJAVIK

M **BORGARSOGUSAFN REYKJAVIKUR,** Reykjavik City Museum, Grandagardur 8, Reykjavik, 101 Iceland. Tel 354 411 6300; Email citymuseum@reykjavik.is; Web: borgarsogusafn.is; *Mus Dir* Gudbrandur Benediktsson; *Head Cultural Heritage & Research* Maria Karen Sigurdardottir
Open Arbaer Open Air Museum: June - Aug daily 10 AM - 7 PM, Sept - May daily guided tours only; The Settlement Exhibition: daily 9 AM - 8 PM; Maritime Museum: daily 10 AM - 5 PM; Museum of Photography: Mon - Fri 10 AM - 4 PM; Videy Island: summer daily 10:15 AM - 6:30 PM, winter weekends 1:15 - 4:30 PM; Admis Arbaer Open Air Museum: adults 1,500 ISK, groups 820 ISK, under 18 & over 70 free; The Settlement Exhibition: adults 1,500 ISK, groups 820 ISK, under 18 & over 70 free; Maritime Museum adults 1,500 ISK, groups 820 ISK, under 18 & over 70 free; Museum of Photography no admis fee; Videy Island adults 1,200 ISK, visitors 70 & up 1,000 ISK, visitors 7 - 15 550 ISK, visitors 0 - 6 free; Museum collective includes: Arbaer Open Air Museum; The Settlement Exhibition; Maritime Museum; Photography Museum; Videy Island
Collections: Collections & artifacts relevant to the cultural heritage of the city of Reykjavik
Activities: Mus shop sells books, magazines & reproductions

M **LISTASAFAN REYKJAVIKUR,** Reykjavik Art Museum, PO Box 110, Reykjavik, 121 Iceland. Tel 354 411 6400; Email listasafn@reykjavic.is; Web: artmuseum.is; *Mus Dir* Olaf Sigurdardottir; *Head Exhib Dept* Yean Fee Quay; *Head Coll Dept* Helga Lara Porsteinsdottir; *Office Mgr* Anna Fridbertsdottir
Office open Mon - Fri 8:20 AM - 4:15 PM; Estab 1973; City visual arts institution occupying three locations throughout the capital city of Reykjavik: Hafnarhus, Kjarvalsstadir & Asmundarsafn
Collections: In charge of general art coll and outdoor sculpture coll for city of Reykjavik, diverse exhibitions of Icelandic and international contemporary and experimental art, regularly exhibits works by three of Iceland's most renowed artists: Erro, Kjarval & Asmundur Sveinsson
M **Halfnarhus - Harbor House,** Tryggvagata 17, Reykjavik, Iceland. Tel 354 411 6400; Web: artmuseum.is/harnarhus; *Reception Mgr* Adalheidur Gylfadottir

Open Fri - Wed 10 AM - 5 PM, Thurs 10 AM - 10 PM; Admis adults 1,500 ISK, students 820 ISK, under 18 free
Collections: Coll by Icelandic contemporary artist Erro

M **Kjarvalsstadir,** Flokagata 24, Reykjavik, Iceland. Tel 354 411 6420; Web: artmuseum.is/kjarvalsstadir; *Reception Mgr* Jona Palina Brynjolfsdottir
Open daily 10 AM - 5 PM; Admis adults 1,500 ISK, students 820 ISK, under 18 free
Collections: Paintings & sculptures by Icelandic artist Johannes S Kjarval, Icelandic and international modern art

M **Asmundarsafn,** Sigtun 105, Reykjavik, Iceland. Tel 354 411 6430; Web: artmuseum.is/asmundarsafn; *Reception Project Mgr* Elisabet Bjarklind Porisdottir
Open daily May - Sept 10 AM - 5 PM, Oct - Apr 1 PM - 5 PM; Admis adults 1,500 ISK, students 820 ISK, under 18 free; Estab 1983
Collections: Sculptures by Icelandic artist Asmundur Sveinsson

M **LISTASAFN EINARS JONSSONAR,** Einar Jonsson Museum, Eiriksgata 3, Reykjavik, 101 Iceland. Tel 354 551 3797; Email lej@lej.is; Web: www.lej.is; *Dir* Sigridur Melros Olafsdottir
Open Tues - Sun 1 - 5 PM; Admis adults 1,000 ISK, concessions 500 ISK, under 18 free; Estab 1923
Collections: Sculpture and paintings by Einar Jonsson
Activities: Classes for adults & children; mus shop sells books, reproductions

M **LISTASAFN ISLANDS,** National Gallery of Iceland, Frikirkjuvegi 7, Reykjavik, 101 Iceland. Tel 354 515 9600; Fax 354 515 9601; Email list@listasafn.is; Web: www.listasafn.is; *Mng Dir* Anna Maria Urbancic; *Mus Dir* Halldor Bjorn Runolfsson; *Head Coll* Dagny Heiddal; *Head Exhibs* Birta Gugjonsdottir
Open summer: daily 10 AM - 5 PM, cl Mon; winter Tues - Sun 11 AM - 5 PM, cl Mon; Admis adults 1,500 ISK, 67 & up, disabled & groups of 10+ 750 ISK, children under 18 free; National Gallery also includes the Asgrimur Jonsson Collection & the Sigurjon Olafsson Museum
Collections: Principal collection of Icelandic visual art, international and national Icelandic art from the 19th and 20th centuries, 5,000 drawings, 3,800 paintings, 850 graphic works, 600 sculptures, 200 new media works, 100 photographs, 50 montages, 30 textile works

M **THJODMINJASAFN ISLANDS,** National Museum of Iceland, Sudurgotu 41, Reykjavik, 101 Iceland. Tel 354 530 2200; Fax 354 530 2201; Email thjodminjasafn@thjodminjasafn.is; Web: www.thjodminjasafn.is; *Dir Gen* Margret Hallgrimsdottir
Open summer: May - mid-Sep daily 10 AM - 5 PM; winter: mid-Sep - April Tues - Sun 10 AM - 5 PM, cl Mon; Admis adults 1,500 ISK, senior citizens 67 & up & students 750 ISK, children under 18 free; Estab 1863; Library with 20,000 vols
Library Holdings: Book Volumes 20,000
Collections: Archaeological & ethnological artifacts, Icelandic antiquities, portraits, folk art

INDIA

CALCUTTA

M **INDIAN MUSEUM,** 27 Jawaharlal Nehru Rd, Calcutta, 700016 India. Tel 91 33 2286 1699; Fax 91 33 2286 1696; Email educationofficerim@gmail.com; Web: indianmuseumkolkata.org; *Dir* Dr Jayanta Sengupta; *Educ Officer* Sayan Bhattacharya
Open Mar - Nov Tues - Sun 10 AM - 5 PM, Dec - Feb Tues - Sun 10 AM - 4:30 PM, cl Mon & National Holidays; Admis Indians 20 INR, foreigners 500 INR; Estab 1814
Collections: Bronzes and bronze figures, ceramics, coins, copper and stone implements of prehistoric and proto-historic origin, geology, botany and zoology collections

CHENNAI

M **GOVERNMENT MUSEUM CHENNAI,** 406 Pantheon Rd, Egmore Chennai, 600 008 India. Tel 91 44 2819 3238; Fax 91 44 2819 3035; Email govtmuse@tngov.in; Web: www.chennaimuseum.org; *Cur Art Sect* Tmt A Prema Deepa Rani
Open Sat - Thurs 9:30 AM - 5 PM, cl Fri; Admis Indians: adults 15 INR, children 10 INR, students 5 INR; foreigners: adults 250 INR, children 125 INR, students 75 INR; Estab 1851; 47 galleries across six buildings; Average Annual Attendance: 10,000,000
Library Holdings: Book Volumes, Pamphlets
Collections: Ancient & modern Indian art, Buddhist sculptures, bronzes, archaeology, natural sciences coll
Publications: 164 books & publications issued;
Activities: Classes for children; dramatic progs; docent training as well as training in handcrafts; plant preservation; & chemical conservation; extension progs to schools & other countries; mus shop sells books, prints, slides & postcards

JUNAGADH

M **JUNAGADH MUSEUM,** Sakkarbaug, Junagadh, 362001 India. Tel 0285 2661382; *Cur* Shri KV Vyas
Open Thurs - Tues 10 AM - 1:30 PM & 2:30 - 6 PM; Admis Indian visitors 5 INR, foreign visitiors 50 INR, students 2 INR; Estab 1901
Collections: More than 34,000 collection pieces including miniature paintings, manuscripts, stone inscriptions, sculptures, bronzes, silver & copper art, glass, porcelain, wood acrvings, textiles, folk art, decorative & applied arts

MUMBAI

M **CHHATRAPATI SHIVAJI MAHARAJ VASTU SANGRAHALAYA,** Formerly Prince of Wales Museum of Western India, 159-61 Mahatma Gandhi Rd, Fort Mumbai, 400023 India. Tel 91 022 2284484; 22844519; Fax 91 022 22045430; Email csmvsmumbai@gmail.com; Web: www.csmvs.in; *Dir* Sabyasachi Mukherjee; *Asst Dir* Manisha Nene; *Sr Cur* Vandana Prapanna
Open daily 10:15 AM - 6 PM; Admis foreigners above 12 yrs 500 INR, Indians above 12 yrs 70 INR, seniors above 60 yrs & groups 50 INR, college students with ID 35 INR, children 5 - 12 yrs & students 20 INR; Estab 1922; Library with 20,000 books & 9,000 journals; Average Annual Attendance: 5 million
Income: Financed by charitable giving
Library Holdings: Auction Catalogs, Book Volumes, Exhibition Catalogs, Periodical Subscriptions
Special Subjects: Anthropology, Antiquities-Oriental, Archaeology, Architecture, Bronzes, Calligraphy, Ceramics, Crafts, Decorative Arts, Ethnology, History of Art & Archaeology, Islamic Art, Ivory, Jade, Jewelry, Manuscripts, Miniatures, Oriental Art, Religious Art, Reproductions, Textiles, Sculpture, Painting-British, Painting-European, Painting-Flemish, Painting-French, Painting-German, Photography, Porcelain, Portraits, Pottery, Primitive art, Renaissance Art, Watercolors, Woodcuts
Collections: Sculptures, miniature paintings, numismatics, textiles, decorative art, prints, pre & proto history and natural history, European paintings, Chinese & Japanese antiquities, Jehangir Nicholson Collection
Publications: Indian Life & Landscape by Western Artists; The Tata Collection of Chinese Antiquities in the CSMVS; The Dream of an Inhabitant of Mogul; A Centennial Bouquet; Jewels on the Crescent; Indian Coinage; The Museum Mumbai Guidebook; Tibet through the Eyes of Li Gotami; Gita Govinda Love Poems of Krishna - The Blue God
Activities: Classes for adults & children; lects for mems only; concerts; gallery talks; tours; schols; fels; Sant Ghadge Maharaj Brihanmumbai Municipal Corp Cleanliness Award, 2008; renovation of children's creativity centre; Arms Gallery, pre & proto history complex; mus shop sells books, magazines, reproductions, prints, CDs, DVDs, bags, greeting cards, artificial jewelry, & other gift items

M **HERAS MUSEUM FOR RESEARCH IN INDIAN HISTORY AND CULTURE,** St Xavier's College Campus, 5, Mahapalika Marg Mumbai, 400001 India. Tel 91 022 22620661; Fax 91 022 22659484; Email webadmin@xaviers.edu; Web: xaviers.edu; *Dir* Joan Dias, MA, PhD
Open 9 AM - 4:40 PM by appt only; No admis fee; Estab 1926; Library with 30,000 vols; attached to the Heras Institute of Indian History & Culture; Average Annual Attendance: 500
Library Holdings: Book Volumes, CD-ROMs, Maps, Sculpture
Special Subjects: Archaeology, Bronzes, Coins & Medals, Portraits, Religious Art
Collections: Indian stone sculptures, terracottas, woodwork, paintings, old rare maps, books, metal artifacts, coins, ivories, Indian Christian art
Exhibitions: Heras week, last week in July
Publications: INDICA, research journal
Activities: Research methodology; workshops; seminars; lects open to pub; scholarships offered

NEW DELHI

M **LALIT KALA AKADEMI RABINDRA BHAVAN ART GALLERIES,** National Academy of Art, New Delhi, 35 Ferozeshah Rd, New Delhi, 110001 India. Tel 011 23009200; Fax 011 23009292; Email lka@lalitkala.gov.in; Web: lalitkala.gov.in; *Chmn* Dr Kalyan Kumar Chakravarty; *Secy* Mr Ramaprishnar Vedala
Open Mon - Fri 10 AM - 5:30 PM, cl Sat & Sun; No admis fee; Estab 1954 to provide reference to art patrons; 9 galleries under one roof; bldg 144 running ft ea gallery
Income: Govt of India funding
Purchases: Books, periodicals, DVDs, newspaper, etc
Library Holdings: Book Volumes, CD-ROMs, Clipping Files, Compact Disks, DVDs, Exhibition Catalogs, Manuscripts, Original Art Works, Pamphlets, Periodical Subscriptions, Photographs, Reels, Reproductions, Sculpture, Slides, Video Tapes
Special Subjects: Afro-American Art, American Indian Art, American Western Art, Archaeology, Architecture, Art Education, Art History, Asian Art, Bronzes, Calligraphy, Ceramics, Coins & Medals, Conceptual Art, Crafts, Decorative Arts, Drawings, Folk Art, Glass, Hispanic Art, History of Art & Archaeology, Ivory, Jade, Landscape Architecture, Latin American Art, Manuscripts, Metalwork, Mexican Art, Miniatures, Mixed Media, Mosaics, Oriental Art, Photography, Porcelain, Pottery, Religious Art, Restorations, Sculpture, Southwestern Art, Textiles, Woodcarvings, Woodcuts
Collections: Permanent collection of graphics, paintings, sculpture, graphics & mix media work
Exhibitions: Triennale India; National Exhibition of Art; Internal & external exhibs
Activities: Camps & workshops for artists; gallery talks; National Academy award; Triennial award; fels; schols; NEA Award; scholarships and fels offered; sales shop sells books, magazines, reproductions, slides, prints

M **NATIONAL GALLERY OF MODERN ART, NEW DELHI,** Jaipur House India Gate, New Delhi, 110003 India. Tel 91 011 2338 6111; Fax 91 011 2338 4560; Email ngma.delhi@gmail.com; Web: www.ngmaindia.gov.in; *Dir* Prof Rajeev Lochan
Open Tues - Sun 10 AM - 5 PM, cl Mon & national holidays; Admis foreign visitors 500 INR, Indians 20 INR; Estab 1954
Collections: Indian contemporary paintings, sculptures, graphics, drawings, architecture, industrial design, prints and minor arts from the 1850s to the present

M **NATIONAL MUSEUM, NEW DELHI,** Janpath, New Delhi, 110011 India. Tel 91 011 23019272; Email dgnationalmuseum11@gmail.com; Web: www.nationalmuseumindia.gov.in; *Dir Gen* Shri Padma Lochan; *Dir Colls & Admin* Prem Kumar Nagta

Open Tues - Sun 10 AM - 5 PM, cl Mon; Admis foreign visitors 650 INR, Indians 20 INR; Estab 1949; Library with 30,000 vols
Collections: Arabic, Indian, Persian, Sanskrit language manuscripts, Central Asian antiquities and murals, paintings, decorative arts, numismatic & epigraphy, archaeology & anthropology, arms & armour, Pre-Columbian & Western Art, Pre-Historic archaeology

VADODARA

M **BARODA MUSEUM AND PICTURE GALLERY,** Sayajigunj, Vadodara, 390 018 India. Tel 91 265 793589; Fax 91 265 791959; *Dir* R D Parmar; *Cur* Vijay Patel
Open 10:30 AM - 5 PM, cl public holidays; Admis Indian visitors 10 INR, foreign visitors 200 INR; Estab 1894; Library with 23,000 books
Income: financed by government of Gujarat
Special Subjects: Antiquities-Assyrian, Antiquities-Byzantine, Antiquities-Egyptian, Antiquities-Etruscan, Antiquities-Greek, Antiquities-Oriental, Antiquities-Persian, Antiquities-Roman, Archaeology, Architecture, Art Education, Art History, Asian Art, Baroque Art, Bronzes, Calligraphy, Carpets & Rugs, Ceramics, Coins & Medals, Costumes, Crafts, Decorative Arts, Dolls, Embroidery, Enamels, Etchings & Engravings, Ethnology, Flasks & Bottles, Folk Art, Furniture, Glass, Graphics, Historical Material, History of Art & Archaeology, Interior Design, Islamic Art, Ivory, Jade, Jewelry, Landscapes, Leather, Manuscripts, Maps, Medieval Art, Metalwork, Miniatures, Mosaics, Oriental Art, Painting-British, Painting-Dutch, Painting-European, Painting-Flemish, Painting-French, Painting-Italian, Painting-Japanese, Painting-Russian, Painting-Spanish, Photography, Porcelain, Portraits, Pottery, Prints, Renaissance Art, Restorations, Sculpture, Silver, Tapestries, Textiles, Watercolors, Woodcarvings, Scrimshaw, Stained Glass
Collections: Indian archeology & art, numismatic colls, Asiatic & Egyptian Colls, Greek, Roman, European civilizations & art, European paintings

INDONESIA

JAKARTA

M **GALERI NASIONAL INDONESIA,** Indonesia National Gallery, Jl Medan Merdeka Timur No 14, Jakarta, 10110 Indonesia. Tel 62-21-34833954/5; Fax 62-21-3813021; Email galnas@indosat.net.id; Web: www.galeri-nasional.or.id; *Dir* Tubagus Sukmana; *Drs* Eddy Susilo
Open Tues - Sun 9 AM - 4 PM, cl Mon & National Holidays; No admis fee; 1998
Library Holdings: Audio Tapes, Cassettes, Clipping Files, Exhibition Catalogs, Pamphlets, Photographs, Slides
Collections: Modern and contemporary art in paintings, drawings, prints, statues, photography and installation, 1700 works by Indonesian and international artists, Painting, Drawing, Installations
Publications: Newspaper, E-Mail, Pamphlets
Activities: Socialization; Books traveling exhibits twice a year; Originates exhibs that circulate based on purpose; Mus shop sells books, magazines

M **MUSEUM NASIONAL INDONESIA,** Jl Medan Merdeka Barat 12, Jakarta, Pusat Indonesia. Tel 021-3811551; Fax 62-21-3447778; Email museumnasional_ina@yahoo.co.id; Web: www.museumnasional.org; *Dir* Dr Retno Sulristianingsih, MM
Open Tues - Thurs & Sun 8:30 AM - 2:30 PM, Fri 8 :30 - 11:30 AM, Sat 8:30 AM - 1:30 PM, cl Mon & public holidays; Admis adults IDR 750, under 17 & students IDR 250; Apr 24, 1778, the purpose is to promote research in the field of arts & science, especially in history, archaeology, ethnography & physics
Collections: Over 141,000 cultural objects relating to Indonesian culture and history, Bronze, ceramics, textiles, numismatics, relics, sculpture, Chinese ceramics of the Han, Tang and Ming dynasties, Bronze and gold coll from Indonesian classical period
Exhibitions: Museum Volkenkunde
Publications: Catalogues, magazines, newspapers, brochures, leaflets, posters
Activities: Classes for adults & children; lectrs open to the public; 400 vis lectrs per yr; tours; sponsoring of competitions; fels; lending of original objects of art to Museum Volkenkunde, Leiden; 2 book traveling exhibs per yr; originates traveling exhibs to Province mus; mus shop sells books, magazines, original art, prints

SURABAYA

M **MUSEUM MPU TANTULAR,** State Museum of East Java Province, Jl Lebak Rejo 7, Surabaya, East Java 60134 Indonesia. Tel 62 031 8056688; Fax 62 031 8056688; Email mputantular68@yahoo.com; Web: www.museum-mputantular.com
Open Tues - Thurs 8 AM - 3 PM, Fri 7 AM - 2 PM, Sat & Sun 8 AM - 12:30 PM, cl Mon & national holidays; Admis adults 4,000 IDR, children 3,000 IDR; Estab 1937
Collections: Pre-history, archaeology, weapons, carvings, traditional ceremonial instruments, transportation & communication, ceramics, numismatics

UBUD

M **AGUNG RAI MUSEUM OF ART,** ARMA Museum & Resort, Jalan Raya Pengosekan, Ubud, Bali 80571 Indonesia. Tel 62 361 976 659; Fax 62 361 975 332; Email info@armabali.com; Web: www.armabali.com/museum; *Owner & Cur* Agung Rai
Open Mon - Fri 9 AM - 6 PM; Admis adults 60,000 IDR, children free; Estab 1996; Museum housed in a family owned & operated resort in Bali
Collections: Balinese, modern Indonesian & international paintings, traditional art

IRAN

TEHRAN

M **NATIONAL MUSEUM OF IRAN,** Imam Khoemeini Ave, Si-e-Tir Corner Tehran, 11369 Iran. Tel 6 6670 2061; Web: nmi.ichto.ir; *Dir* Dr Jebrael Nokandeh
Admis 300,000 IRR; Estab 1937
Collections: Ancient history & art, Islamic art, calligraphy, ceramics, glass, textiles

M **TEHRAN MUSEUM OF CONTEMPORARY ART,** N Karegar St, Tehran, Iran. Tel 98 2188989374; Fax 98 2188951323; Email info@tmoca.com; Web: www.tmoca.com; *Dir* Majid Mola-Nourozi
Open Sun - Thurs 10 AM - 6 PM, Fri 3 - 6 PM, cl Sat; Admis 47,000 IRR; Estab 1977; Museum maintains library
Collections: Modern & contemporary Iranian art, 19th - 20th century Western paintings, drawings & sculptures

IRAQ

BAGHDAD

A **DIRECTORATE - GENERAL OF ANTIQUITIES AND HERITAGE,** Sahat Al-Risafi, Baghdad, Iraq. Tel 4165317; *Dir* Nawala al Mutawali
M **Babylon Museum**, Sahat Al-Risafi, Babylon, Iraq. Tel 4165317; *Dir* Nawala al Mutawali
Collections: Models, pictures & paintings of the remains at Babylon

M **IRAQI MUSEUM,** Salhiya Quarter, Baghdad, Iraq. Tel 36121-5; Web: www.iraqmuseum.org; *Dir* Dr Hana' Abdul Khaleq
Collections: Antiquities from the Stone Age to the 17th century, including Islamic objects

IRELAND

CORK

M **CRAWFORD ART GALLERY,** Emmet Pl, Cork, Ireland. Tel 353-0-21 480 5042; Fax 353-0-21-4805043; Email info@crawfordartgallery.ie; Web: www.crawfordartgallery.ie; *Dir* Peter Murray
Open Mon - Wed & Fri - Sat 10 AM - 5 PM, Thurs 10 AM - 8 PM, cl Sun; No admis fee

DUBLIN

M **DUBLIN CITY GALLERY THE HUGH LANE,** Charlemont House, Parnell Sq N Dublin, 1 Ireland. Tel 353 1 222 5564; Fax 353 1 872 2182; Email info.hughlane@dublincity.ie; Web: www.hughlane.ie; *Dir* Barbara Dawson
Open Tues - Thurs 9:45 AM - 6 PM, Fri 9:45 AM - 5 PM, Sat 10 AM - 5 PM, Sun 11 AM - 5 PM, cl Mon; No admis fee; Estab 1908
Special Subjects: Sculpture
Collections: Works of Irish, English & European artists, Sir Hugh Lane Collection, Francis Bacon studio
Activities: Educ prog; classes for adults & children; lects open to pub; concerts; gallery talks; tours; mus shop sells books, magazines & prints

M **GALLERY OF PHOTOGRAPHY,** Meeting House Sq, Temple Bar Dublin, 2 Ireland. Tel 353-1-671-4654; Fax 353-1-670-9293; Email info@galleryofphotography.ie; Web: www.galleryofphotography.ie; *Dir* Tanya Kiang; *Projects Mgr* Trish Lambe
Open Tue - Sat 11 AM - 6 PM; No admis fee
Collections: contemporary photography

M **IRISH MUSEUM OF MODERN ART,** Royal Hospital, Military Rd, Kilmainham Dublin, 8 Ireland. Tel 353-1-6129900; Fax 353-1-6129999; Email info@imma.ie; Web: www.imma.ie; *Dir* Sarah Glennie; *Sr Cur* Rachael Thomas; *Sr Cur* Helen O'Donoghue; *Sr Cur* Christina Kennedy; *Cur* Sean Kissane; *Cur* Lisa Moran
Open Tues - Fri 11:30 AM - 5:30 PM, Sat 10 AM - 5:30 PM, Sun & bank holidays noon - 5:30, cl Mon; No admis fee except for occasional special exhibs; 1991; coll & presentation of modern & contemporary art; Average Annual Attendance: 450,000; Mem: Dues patron 4,000 euro, benefactor 350 euro, supporter 150 euro, family 70 euro, concession 30 euro, individual 50 euro
Income: Financed by the government of Ireland
Collections: Comprises 4,500 works; permanent coll of 1,650 works by Irish & international artists, Madden Arnholz Collection of 2,000 old master prints
Exhibitions: Temporary exhibs which run throughout the yr
Publications: IMMA publishes catalogues for all exhibs
Activities: Artists' residency prog; workshops etc; lectrs open to the public; concerts; gallery talks; guided tours; Mus shop sells books, magazines

M **NATIONAL GALLERY OF IRELAND,** Merrion Sq W, Dublin, 2 Ireland. Tel 353 1 661 5133; Email info@ngi.ie; Web: nationalgallery.ie; *Chmn* Michael Cush; *Dir* Sean Rainbird; *Cur* Dr Adriaan Waiboer
Open Mon - Wed & Fri - Sat 9:15 AM - 5:30 PM, Thurs 9:15 AM - 8:30 PM, Sun 11 AM - 5:30 PM, cl Good Fri & Dec 24 - 26; No admis fee; Estab 1854; Fine art mus housing Irish & European paintings; library with 30,000 vols, painting, sculpture, and the fine arts in Dublin; Average Annual Attendance: 800,000; Mem: The Friends of the NGI

Income: State funded
Library Holdings: Auction Catalogs, Book Volumes, Exhibition Catalogs, Original Art Works, Original Documents, Other Holdings, Pamphlets
Special Subjects: Art History, Bookplates & Bindings, Etchings & Engravings, Historical Material, Miniatures, Painting-American, Painting-British, Painting-Dutch, Painting-European, Painting-Flemish, Painting-French, Painting-German, Painting-Italian, Painting-Spanish, Portraits, Prints
Collections: British, Dutch, Flemish, French, German, Italian, Irish, Russian & Spanish masters since 1250, drawings, prints, oil paintings, sculptures, watercolors, The Yeats Museum (works by Jack B. Yeats, 1871 - 1957), National Portrait Collection (16th-21st century), Fine arts library archival material relates to study of Irish Art & NGI
Activities: Classes for adults & children; family progs; workshops; outreach progs; lects open to pub; 10 vis lectrs per year; gallery talks; tours; concerts; NGI awarded full accreditation (2007) under the mus standards prog for Ireland; fels available; lend original objects of art to sister institutions & accredited international museums; mus shop sells books, magazines, reproductions, prints, slides & other items

M **NATIONAL MUSEUM OF IRELAND,** Kildare St, Dublin, 2 Ireland. Tel 353 1 6777444; Fax 353 1 6777450; Web: www.museum.ie; *Dir* Raghnall O'Floinn
Open Tues - Sat 10 AM - 5 PM, Sun 2 - 5 PM, cl Mon, bank holidays, Good Friday & Christmas Day; No admis fee
Special Subjects: Archaeology
Collections: Art and Industrial Division, Irish Antiquities Division, Irish Folklife Division, Natural History Division

M **NATIONAL PRINT MUSEUM,** Old Garrison Chapel Beggars Bush, Haddington Rd Dublin, 4 Ireland. Tel 353 1 660 3770; Fax 353 1 667 3545; Email info@nationalprintmuseum.ie; Web: www.nationalprintmuseum.ie; *Mgr* Carla Marrinan
Open Mon - Fri 9 AM - 5 PM, Sat - Sun 2 - 5 PM; Admis 3.50 EUR, reduced 2 EUR
Collections: Artifacts related to print history

KILKENNY

M **BUTLER GALLERY,** The Castle Kilkenny, Ireland. Tel 353-0-56-776-1106; Fax 353-0-56-777-0031; Email info@butlergallery.com; Web: www.butlergallery.com; *Head Col & Exhib* Naomi O'Nolan
Open daily Jan & Feb: 10 AM - 1 PM, 2 - 4:30 PM; Mar: 10 AM - 1 PM, 2 - 5 PM; April: 10 AM - 1 PM, 2 - 5:30 PM; May - Sep: 10 AM - 5 PM; Oct - Dec 10 AM - 1 PM, 2 - 4:30 PM; Adult admis 6 EUR, discounted 4 EUR, children 2.50 EUR

LIMERICK

M **THE HUNT MUSEUM,** Rutland St, Limerick, Ireland. Tel 353-61-312833; Fax 353-61-312834; Email info@huntmuseum.com; Web: www.huntmuseum.com; *Dir* Dr Hugh Maguire
Open Mon - Sat 10 AM - 5 PM, Sun & bank holidays 2 - 5 PM; Admis adult 5 EUR, senior & 3rd level student 3.50 EUR, child 2.50 EUR, family 12 EUR

M **LIMERICK CITY GALLERY OF ART,** Pery Sq, Carnegie Bldg Limerick, Ireland. Tel 061-310633; Fax 061-310228; Email artgallery@limerickcity.ie; Web: gallery.limerick.ie; *Dir & Cur* Una McCarthy
Open Mon - Wed & Fri - Sat - 10 AM - 5:30 PM, Thurs 10 AM - 8 PM, Sun noon - 5:30 PM; No admis fee

SLIGO

M **THE MODEL,** The Niland Collection, The Mall, Sligo, Ireland. Tel 353-071-914-1405; Fax 353-071-914-3694; Email info@themodel.ie; Web: www.themodel.ie; *Acting Dir.* Emer McGarry
Open Tues - Sat 10 AM - 5 PM, Sun 10:30 AM - 3:30 PM, cl Mon; No admis fee; Estab 2001; multi-disciplinary art center; Suite of contemporary galleries & galleries specifically designed for coll purposes; Average Annual Attendance: 90,000
Income: public funding
Collections: The Niland Collection
Exhibitions: Changing schedule of exhibs
Publications: Books, 3 published per yr
Activities: Classes for adults & children; ten vis lectrs per yr; concerts; gallery talks; tours; lending of original objects of art; mus shop sells books & magazines

ISRAEL

HAIFA

M **HAIFA MUSEUM OF ART,** 26 Shabbetai Levi St, Haifa, 3304331 Israel. Tel (04) 911 5991; Fax (04) 855 2714; Email info@hms.org.il; *Cur* Tal Nissim
Open Sun - Wed 10 AM - 4 PM, Thurs 10 AM - 7 PM, Fri 10 AM - 1 PM, Sat 10 AM - 3 PM; Admis adults 45 ILS, children 5-18, policemen, soldiers, students, senior citizens 30 ILS; Library with 10,000 vols
Collections: Israeli paintings, sculpture, drawings & prints, modern American, French, German & English paintings, art posters

M **HAIFA MUSEUMS NATIONAL MARITIME MUSEUM,** 198 Allenby St, Haifa, Israel. Tel (04) 8536622; Fax (04) 8539286; Email nautic@netvision.net.il; *Dir Gen* Nissim Tal
Open Sun - Thurs 10 AM - 4 PM, Fri 10 AM - 1 PM, Sat 10 AM - 3 PM; Admis adults 35 ILS, children 5-18, policemen, students, soldiers 20 ILS, senior citizens 23 ILS; Estab 1953; Includes Archaeological collection; Circ Reference only
Library Holdings: Book Volumes approx 5,000, Exhibition Catalogs, Maps, Original Art Works, Periodical Subscriptions 35
Collections: Ancient Haifa, ancient coins from Israel, antiquities from the excavations of Shikmona from the Bronze Age to Byzantine period, Biblical, Cypriot and Greek pottery and sculpture, Near Eastern figurines, Ship models, Maps, Maritime artifacts and gear
Exhibitions: Pirates - the Skull & Crossbones; Maritime paintings by Moshe Rosenthalis
Publications: Exhib catalogues; postcards
Activities: Classes for adults, classes for children; prog school classes; lects open to public, gallery talks, tours

M **HAIFA MUSEUMS TIKOTIN MUSEUM OF JAPANESE ART,** 89 Hanassi Ave, Haifa, 3464217 Israel. Tel (04) 8383554; Fax (04) 8379824; Email info@hms.org.il; Web: www.haifamuseums.org.il; *Dir Gen* Nissim Tal
Open Sun - Wed 10 AM - 7 PM, Fri 10 AM - 1 PM, Sat 10 AM - 7 PM; Admis adults 35 ILS, children 5-18, policemen, students, soldiers 23 ILS, senior citizens 17.50 ILS; Estab May 1960
Library Holdings: Auction Catalogs, Book Volumes, Exhibition Catalogs, Periodical Subscriptions
Collections: Ceramics, folk art, drawings, metalwork, netsuke, prints, paintings
Publications: Catalogs
Activities: Classes for adults & children; lects open to public, concerts, gallery talks, tours; mus shop sells books, reproductions, slides, posters & Japanese handicrafts

M **HECHT MUSEUM,** Univ of Haifa, Mt Carmel Haifa, 31905 Israel. Tel 04-8257773, 04-8240308; Fax 04-8240724; Email mshunit@univ.haifa.ac.il; Web: mushecht.haifa.ac.il; *Dir & Cur* Shunit Marmelstein
Open Sun - Mon & Wed - Thurs 10 AM - 4 PM, Tue 10 AM - 7 PM, Fri 10 AM - 1 PM, Sat 10 AM - 2 PM; No admis fee; Archaeology of Israel; Art; Barlizon School; Impressionists; School of Paris & more
Special Subjects: Antiquities-Assyrian, Antiquities-Byzantine, Antiquities-Egyptian, Antiquities-Etruscan, Antiquities-Greek, Antiquities-Oriental, Antiquities-Persian, Antiquities-Roman, Archaeology, Art Education, Art History, Bronzes, Ceramics, Crafts, Drawings, Etchings & Engravings, Glass, Gold, Historical Material, History of Art & Archaeology, Ivory, Jewelry, Judaica, Landscapes, Manuscripts, Metalwork, Mosaics, Painting-Dutch, Painting-European, Painting-French, Painting-German, Painting-Israeli, Painting-Italian, Painting-Polish, Pottery, Restorations, Sculpture, Silver, Watercolors, Woodcarvings, Coins & Medals
Collections: Archaeological period beginning with the Chalcolithic period and ending in the Byzantine period, Art gallery with works from Hecht Family Collection, French painting of the Barbizon School, Impressionism, Post-Impressionism, School of Paris and Jewish art of the 19th and 20th century, Coins, seals, weights, jewelry, toys, oil lamps, metalwork, woodwork, glass, mosaics and stone
Exhibitions: The Ma'agan Mikhael Ancient Ship; The Great Revolt in the Galilee; Ancient Crafts and Industries; Phoenicians at the Northern Coast of Israel in the Biblical Period; Hoards & Genizot as Chapters in History; The Great Revolt in the Galilee
Publications: Exhib catalog
Activities: Classes for adults and children; concerts, gallery talks, tours; schols available; mus shop sells books, reproductions & other items

HERZLIYA

M **HERZLIYA MUSEUM OF CONTEMPORARY ART,** 4 Ha'banim St, Herzliya, 46379 Israel. Tel 972 9 9500762; Fax 972 9 9500043; Email info@herzliyamuseum.co.il; Web: www.herzliyamuseum.co.il; *Dir* Dr Aya Lurie
Open Sun - Thurs 9 AM - 1 PM; Flat admis fee of NIS 20
Collections: Contemporary art

JAFFA

M **OLD JAFFA MUSEUM OF ANTIQUITIES,** Mifrats Shlomo 10, Jaffa, 68038 Israel. Tel 972 3 682 5375; Email naama@oldjaffa.co.il; Web: www.oldjaffa.co.il; *Mus Mgr* Na'ama Meirovitz
Open Mon - Thurs & Sat 10 AM - 6 PM, Fri 10 AM - 2 PM, cl Sun; Admis adult 40 ILS, children 35 ILS; Estab 1960; Housed in former Ottoman government complex
Special Subjects: Archaeology, Ceramics, Coins & Medals, Glass
Collections: Archaeological findings from the Tel Aviv-Jaffa area from the Neolithic to Roman-Byzantine periods, contemporary art

JERUSALEM

M **BEIT HA'OMANIM,** The Jerusalem Artists' House, 12 Shmuel Hanagid St, Jerusalem, 94592 Israel. Tel (972-2) 6253653; Fax (972-2) 6258594; Email artists@zahav.net.il; Web: www.art.org.il; *Dir* Ruth Zadka; *Asst Dir* Idit Helman; *Asst* T Keller; *Gallery Mgr* Shulamith Efrat
Open Sun - Thurs 10 AM - 1 PM, 4 PM - 7 PM; Fri 10 - 1 PM; Sat 11 AM - 2 PM; No admis fee; Estab 1965
Library Holdings: Exhibition Catalogs
Collections: Artwork of Israeli & Jerusalemite artists
Exhibitions: International Exhibitions
Publications: Research catalogues following exhibitions
Activities: Lects open to pub, gallery talks, tours; mus shop sells original art, reproductions, prints

M **THE ISRAEL MUSEUM, JERUSALEM,** Derech Ruppin 11, Jerusalem, 9171002 Israel; PO Box 71117, Jerusalem, 9171002 Israel. Tel 972 2 670 8811; Fax 972 2 677 1332; Email info@imj.org.il; Web: www.imj.org.il; *Dir.* Prof Ido Bruno
Open Sun, Mon, Wed, Thurs, Sat 10 AM - 5 PM, Tues 10 PM - 4 PM, Fri 10 AM - 2 PM; Admis adults 54 ILS, students 39 ILS, children 5-17 yrs, senior citizens & disabled 27 ILS; Estab 1965
Library Holdings: Auction Catalogs, Book Volumes, Exhibition Catalogs, Periodical Subscriptions
Special Subjects: African Art, American Indian Art, Anthropology, Antiquities-Assyrian, Antiquities-Byzantine, Antiquities-Egyptian, Antiquities-Etruscan, Antiquities-Greek, Antiquities-Oriental, Antiquities-Persian, Antiquities-Roman, Archaeology, Architecture, Asian Art, Baroque Art, Calligraphy, Carpets & Rugs, Ceramics, Coins & Medals, Collages, Costumes, Crafts, Decorative Arts, Drawings, Embroidery, Enamels, Etchings & Engravings, Ethnology, Flasks & Bottles, Furniture, Glass, Gold, Graphics, Islamic Art, Jewelry, Judaica, Landscapes, Latin American Art, Manuscripts, Maps, Medieval Art, Miniatures, Mosaics, Painting-American, Painting-Dutch, Painting-European, Painting-Flemish, Painting-French, Painting-Israeli, Painting-Italian, Painting-Japanese, Period Rooms, Photography, Porcelain, Portraits, Posters, Pottery, Pre-Columbian Art, Prints, Renaissance Art, Sculpture, Watercolors, Woodcarvings, Woodcuts
Collections: Judaica & Jewish ethnography, Fine arts comprising separate department for Israeli art, European art, modern art, contemporary art, prints, drawings, photography design & architecture, Asian art, arts of Africa, Oceania & the Americas
Exhibitions: Approx 20 per yr & permanent collections
Publications: Catalogues, IM Journal in archaeology; IM Magazine; IM Studies
Activities: Classes for adults & children; summer camps; family activities; concerts; gallery talks; tours; sponsoring of competitions; lending of original objects of art to museums worldwide; originates traveling exhibs to museums worldwide; mus shop sells books, reproductions, prints & gift items

M **Rockefeller Archaeological Museum,** 27 Sultan Suleiman St, Jerusalem, Israel. Tel 02 670 8074; Fax 02 670 8063; Email fawziib@imj.org.il; Web: www.imj.org.il; *Cur* Fawzi Ibrahim
Open Sun, Mon, Wed, Thurs 10 AM - 3 PM, Sat 10 AM - 2 PM, cl Tues & Fri; No admis fee
Collections: Archaeological finds of the Land of Israel from prehistory to Ottoman Empire

M **Billy Rose Art Garden**, 11 Ruppin Blvd, Jerusalem, 91710 Israel. Tel 972 2 670 8811; Fax 972 2 677 1332; Email info@imj.org.il; Web: www.imj.org.il
Open Sun - Thurs, Sat 10 AM - 5 PM, Fri 10 AM - 2 PM
Special Subjects: African Art, American Indian Art, Anthropology, Antiquities-Assyrian, Antiquities-Byzantine, Antiquities-Egyptian, Antiquities-Etruscan, Antiquities-Oriental, Antiquities-Persian, Antiquities-Roman, Archaeology, Asian Art, Baroque Art, Bronzes, Calligraphy, Costumes, Drawings, Enamels, Eskimo Art, Etchings & Engravings, Ethnology, Flasks & Bottles, Furniture, Gold, Graphics, Hispanic Art, Historical Material, Islamic Art, Ivory, Jewelry, Judaica, Landscapes, Latin American Art, Manuscripts, Maps, Medieval Art, Mexican Art, Miniatures, Mosaics, Oriental Art, Painting-American, Painting-British, Painting-Canadian, Painting-Dutch, Painting-Flemish, Painting-French, Painting-German, Painting-Israeli, Painting-Italian, Painting-Japanese, Painting-Polish, Painting-Russian, Painting-Scandinavian, Painting-Spanish, Period Rooms, Photography, Porcelain, Portraits, Posters, Pottery, Pre-Columbian Art, Primitive art, Religious Art, Restorations, Scrimshaw, Sculpture, Silver, Southwestern Art, Tapestries, Textiles, Watercolors, Woodcarvings, Woodcuts
Collections: Modern European, American & Israeli sculpture & Reuven Lipchitz collection of Jacques Lipchitz's bronze sketches

M **Samuel & Saidye Bronfman Archaeology Wing**, 11 Ruppin Blvd, Hakyria, Jerusalem, 91710 Israel. Tel 972 2 670 8811; Fax 972 2 670 8906; Web: www.imj.org.il; *Tamar & Teddy Kollek Chief Cur Archaeology* Dr Chaim Gitler
Open Sun - Thurs, Sat 10 AM - 5 PM, Fri 10 AM - 2 PM
Special Subjects: African Art, Anthropology, Antiquities-Assyrian, Antiquities-Byzantine, Antiquities-Egyptian, Antiquities-Etruscan, Antiquities-Greek, Antiquities-Oriental, Antiquities-Persian, Antiquities-Roman, Archaeology, Asian Art, Baroque Art, Calligraphy, Carpets & Rugs, Ceramics, Coins & Medals, Decorative Arts, Drawings, Etchings & Engravings, Ethnology, Folk Art, Furniture, Glass, Gold, Graphics, Historical Material, Islamic Art, Ivory, Jade, Jewelry, Judaica, Latin American Art, Manuscripts, Maps, Medieval Art, Metalwork, Miniatures, Mosaics, Oriental Art, Painting-American, Painting-Dutch, Painting-European, Painting-Flemish, Painting-French, Painting-German, Painting-Israeli, Painting-Italian, Painting-Russian, Painting-Spanish, Photography, Pre-Columbian Art, Prints, Renaissance Art, Sculpture, Silver, Tapestries, Watercolors, Woodcarvings
Collections: Collection of archaeology of Israel from Prehistoric times to Islamic & Crusader periods, material found in excavations since 1948, Collections of Picasso
Activities: Classes for children

L **Shrine of the Book**, 11 Ruppin Blvd, Hakyria, Jerusalem, 91710 Israel. *Lizbeth & George Krupp Cur & Head* Dr Adolfo Roitman
Open Sun - Thurs, Sat 10 AM - 5 PM, Fri 10 AM - 2 PM
Collections: Houses the Dead Sea Scrolls (discovered in Qumran) & manuscripts from adjacent sites on western shore of the Dead Sea, Masada & Nahal Hever

M **MUSEUM ON THE SEAM,** 4 Chel Handassa St, Jerusalem, 9101601 Israel; PO Box 1649, Jerusalem, 9101601 Israel. Tel 972-2-6281278; Fax 972-72-2765452; Email info@mots.org.il; Web: www.mots.org.il; *Exec Dir* Merav Maor Komlosh
Open Mon, Wed, Thurs 10 AM - 5 PM, Tues 2 - 8 PM, Fri 10 AM - 2 PM, cl Sat & Sun; Admis adult 30 nis, student, senior citizen & soldier 25 nis

KEFAR-MENAHEM

M **SHEPHELA MUSEUM,** Kibbutz Kefar-Menahem Post, Kefar-Menahem, 79875 Israel. Tel (08) 850 1827; Fax 08 8508486; Email museum_hash@kfar-menachem.org.11; Web: www.touryoav.org.11/museums; *Dir* Ora Dvir; *Cur* Lea Fait; *Cur* Moshe Saidi
Open Mon - Fri & Sun 8:30 AM - 12:30 PM; Sat 11 AM - 4 PM; Admis $2.50; Estab 1975; archaeology; Average Annual Attendance: 10,000
Income: $100,000
Special Subjects: Painting-Israeli, Historical Material
Collections: Collection of fine arts, children's art & antiquities, New Hebrew Settlement (1930s)
Exhibitions: 4 art exhibitions per year of Israeli contemporary art
Activities: Educ progs for classes and kindergartens in the various exhibs

TEL AVIV

M **ERETZ ISRAEL MUSEUM,** 2 Haim Levanon St, Tel Aviv, 61 170 Israel; PO Box 17068, Ramat Aviv Tel Aviv, 61 170 Israel. Tel (972) 3 6415244; Fax (972) 36412408; Web: www.eretzmuseum.org.il; *Dir Gen* Ilan Cohen; *Deputy Dir Gen* Zachi Becker
Open Sun - Wed 10 AM - 4 PM, Thurs 10 AM - 8 PM, Fri 10 AM - 2 PM, Sat 10 AM - 4 PM; Admis adult 52 ILS, adult Tel Aviv resident 42 ILS, student w/ID 35 ILS, children under 18 free; Estab 1958; Consists of 15 museum spaces & collections
Collections: Historical documents of Tel Aviv-Yafo, Jewish ritual & secular art objects, ancient glass, ceramics, coins, prehistoric finds, scientific & technical apparatus, traditional work tools & methods

M **TEL AVIV MUSEUM OF ART,** 27 Shaul Hamelech Blvd, POB 33288 Tel Aviv, 61332012 Israel. Tel 972 (03) 607 7020; Fax 972 (03) 695 8099; Email info@tamuseum.com; Web: www.tamuseum.com; *Dir* Suzanne Landau; *CFO* Baruch Meidan, CPA (Isr.); *Chief Cur* Doron Rabina
Open Mon, Wed & Sat 10 AM - 6 PM, Tues & Thurs 10 AM - 9 PM; Fri 10 AM - 2 PM; cl Sun; Admis adult 50 ILS, Tel Aviv resident & student with international ID 40 ILS, senior citizens & enlisted soldiers 25 ILS, enlisted solider in uniform & children 18 & under free; Estab 1932; Library with 50,000 vols
Collections: Works from 17th century to present, Israeli art
Activities: Classes for adults & children; lects open to pub, concerts, gallery talks, tours; mus shop sells books, magazines & reproductions

ITALY

ARDEA

M **RACCOLTA MANZU,** Giacomo Manzu Museum, Via Laurentina km. 32, Ardea, 00040 Italy. Tel +39-06-9135022; Email pm-laz.museomanzu@beniculturali.it; Web: www.museomanzu.beniculturali.it
Open Mon 2 - 7 PM, Tues - Sun 9 aM - 7 PM; No admis fee
Special Subjects: Sculpture, Graphic Arts, Bronzes
Collections: Collection includes bronzes, sculptures, engravings & drawings

BARI

M **PINACOTECA DI BARI CORRADO GIAQUINTO,** Corrado Giaquinto Painting Gallery of Bari, Via Spalato 19, Bari, 70121 Italy. Tel 080 54 12 420; Fax 080 55 83 401; Email pincoteca@cittametropolitana.ba.it; Web: www.pinacotecabari.it; *Dir* Dr Clara Gelao; *Press Officer* Anna Martucci
Open Tues - Sat 9:30 AM - 7 PM, Sun 9 AM - 1 PM, cl Mon; Adult admis 3 EUR; Estab 1928; The gallery is located in the Palazzo della Province, a building constructed in the 1930s
Special Subjects: Baroque Art, Bronzes, Ceramics, Watercolors, Drawings, Etchings & Engravings, Folk Art, Furniture, Landscapes, Medieval Art, Painting-European, Painting-Italian, Photography, Portraits, Pottery, Religious Art, Renaissance Art, Sculpture
Collections: Apulian, Venetian & Neapolitan paintings & sculptures from 11th - 19th century, Grieco coll: 50 paintings from Fattom to Morandi, 23 paintings from the Banco di Napoli coll
Publications: Catalogues of all the collections
Activities: Classes for adults & children; concerts; gallery talks; mus shop sells books, reproductions

BERGAMO

M **GALLERIA D'ARTE MODERNA CONTEMPORAENEA DI BERGAMO,** Bergamo Gallery of Modern and Contemporary Art, Via San Tomaso, 53, Bergamo, 24121 Italy. Tel 035 270272; Web: gamec.it; *Pres* Lorenzo Giusti; *Cur* Sara Fumagalli; *Head, Colls* Angela Fabrizia Previtali
Open Mon - Sun 10 AM - 7 PM, Thurs until 10 PM; Admis fee 12 EUR, reduced admis 10 EUR
Collections: Spajani Collection of modern masterpieces, Manzu Collection of sculptures, paintings, drawings and engravings, Stucchi Collection of 1950s - 1960s paintings

M **MUSEO ADRIANO BERNAREGGI,** Adriano Bernareggi Museum, Bergamo via Pignolo 76, Bergamo, Italy. Tel 39-035.248772; Fax 39-035.215517; Email info@fondazionebernareggi.it; Web: www.fondazionebernareggi.it; *Cur* Simone Facchinetti, Dr
Open Tues - Sun 3 PM - 6:30 PM, cl Mon; Admis 5 EUR, reduced 3 EUR; Estab 2000
Special Subjects: Religious Art
Collections: Religious paintings, sculptures, carvings, etchings

BOLOGNA

M **MUSEO D'ARTE MODERNA DI BOLOGNA,** Bologna Museum of Modern Art, via Don Minzoni 14, Bologna, 40121 Italy. Tel 39 051 6496611; Fax 39 051 6496637; Email info@mambo-bologna.org; Web: www.mambo-bologna.org; *Dir* Lara Carlini Fanfogna
Open Tues - Wed & Fri noon - 6 PM, Thurs, Sat, Sun & holidays noon - 8 PM, cl Mon; Admis 6 EUR, reduced 4 EUR, 18 & under free; Ground floor permanent collection, first floor temporary exhibs of contemporary art; Average Annual Attendance: 100,000
Income: Comune di Bologna Istituzione Bologna Musei
Collections: Collection of modern art from the late 18th century to the present
Activities: Classes for adults & children; lects open to pub; concerts; gallery talks; tours

M **Museo Morandi - Morandi Museum**, via Don Minzoni 14, Bologna, 40121 Italy. Tel 39 051 6496611; Fax 39 051 6496637; Email casamorandi@comune.bologna.it; *Mus Mgr* Alessia Masi
Open Tues - Sun 10 AM - 7 PM, cl Mon; Full admis 6 EUR, reduced admis 4 EUR
Collections: Giorgio Morandi Collection, 62 oil paintings, 18 watercolors, 92 drawings, 78 etchings, sculptures and engravings
Exhibitions: Casa Morandi in Ula Fondazia Has
Activities: Classes for adults & children; mus shop sells books, reproductions, prints

M **Villa delle Rose**, via Saragozza 228/230, Bologna, 40135 Italy. Tel 39 051 6496611; Fax 39 051 6496637; Email info@mambo-bologna.org; *Educ Svcs Coordr* Veronica Ceruti
Open only during exhibs
Collections: Temporary exhibitions of Italian and international artists

M **PINACOTECA NAZIONALE DI BOLOGNA,** National Art Gallery of Bologna, Via Belle Arti 56, Bologna, 40126 Italy. Tel 39 051 4209411; Fax 39 051 251368; Email sbas-bo@iperbolt.bologna.it; *Supr* Dr Luigi Ficacci
Open Mon Tues & Wed 9 A - 1:30 PM, Thurs - Sun & holidays 2 - 7 PM, cl Mon; Admis 4 EUR, reduced 2 EUR, free admis first Sun of each month; Estab 1882; Gallery contains dept of prints and drawings; Average Annual Attendance: 150,000
Library Holdings: Book Volumes, CD-ROMs, Cards, Exhibition Catalogs, Photographs, Slides
Collections: 14th - 18th century Bolognese paintings, German & Italian engravings
Activities: Classes for adults & children; concerts; gallery talks; tours; lending of original objects of art to museums in different countries; mus shop sells books, reproductions

BOLZANO

M **MUSEION - MUSEO DI ARTE MODERNA E CONTEMPORANEA,** Museum of Modern & Contemporary Art, Piazza piero Siena, Bolzano, 39100 Italy. Tel +39-0471 223413; Fax +39-0471 223412; Email info@museion.it; *Dir* Leitizia Ragaglia
Open Tues - Sun 10 AM - 6 PM, Thurs 10 AM - 10 PM, cl Mon & holidays; Admis 6 EUR, reduced 3.50 EUR

FLORENCE

M **FONDAZIONE CASA BUONARROTI,** (Museo della Casa Buonarroti) Casa Buonarroti Foundation, Via Ghibellina 70, Florence, 50122 Italy. Tel (055) 241-752; Fax (055) 241-698; Email fond@casabuonarroti.it; Web: www.casabuonarroti.it; *Dir* Pina Ragionieri; *Pres* Antonio Paolucci
Open Nov 1 - Feb 28 10 AM - 4 PM, Mar 1 - Oct 31 10 AM - 5 PM, cl Tues; Admis adults 6.50 EUR, groups & upper secondary school parties 4.50 EUR, primary schools & lower secondary school parties 3.50 EUR
Collections: Works by Michelangelo & others, items from the Buonarroti Family colls
Activities: Mus shop sells books, magazines, reproductions, prints, slides

M **GALLERIA DEGLI UFFIZI,** Uffizi Gallery, Piazzale degli Uffizi, 6, Florence, 50122 Italy. Tel 39 055 294883; Email infouffizi@beniculturali.it; Web: www.uffizi.it; *Dir* Eike Schmidt
Open Tues - Sun 8:15 AM - 6:50 PM, cl Mon, Jan 1, May 1 & Dec 25; Mar 1 - Oct 31 reg 20 EUR, reduced 10 Eur; Nov 1 - Feb 28 reg 12 EUR, reduced 6 EUR
Library Holdings: Auction Catalogs, Audio Tapes, Book Volumes, CD-ROMs, Cards, Compact Disks, DVDs, Exhibition Catalogs, Maps, Photographs, Prints, Records, Reproductions, Slides, Video Tapes
Collections: 14th century and Renaissance paintings, Italian, German, Dutch & Flemish masterpieces, statues & busts
Activities: Classes for children; mus shop sells books, magazines, reproductions, prints & slides

M **Pitti Palace**, Piazza Pitti 1, Florence, 50125 Italy. Tel 39 055 294883; Email infouffizi@beniculturali.it; Web: www.uffizi.it; *Dir* Eike Schmidt
Open Tues - Sun 8:15 AM - 6:50 PM, cl Mon, Jan 1 & Dec 25; Mar 1 - Oct 31 reg 16 EUR, reduced 8 Eur; Nov 1 - Feb 28 reg 10 EUR, reduced 5 EUR; Former royal palace currently houses four galleries: Palatine Gallery & Royal Apartments; Modern Art Gallery; Treasury of the Grand Dukes; and Costume & Fashion Gallery
Collections: Paintings and sculptures of the 19th and 20th century, furniture, tapestries & regalia

M **GALLERIA DELL'ACCADEMIA DI FIRENZE,** Gallery of the Academy of Florence, Via Ricasoli 58/60, Florence, 50122 Italy. Tel 39 055 2388609; Email ga-afi@beniculturali.it; Web: www.galleriaaccademiafirenze.beniculturali.it; *Dir* Dr Cecilie Hollberg
Open Tues - Sun 8:15 AM - 6:50 PM, cl Mon, Jan 1 & Dec 25; Admis 8 EUR, reduced 4 EUR; Estab 1784; Gallery includes 2 floors & 2 bookshops.; Average Annual Attendance: 1,000,000
Collections: Michelangelo's statues in Florence & works of art of 13th - 19th century masters, mostly Tuscan, 19th century plaster models, 18th-19th century Russian icons, ancient musical instruments
Activities: Classes for children; concerts; Mus shop sells books, reproductions, prints, slides

M **MUSEO NAZIONALE DEL BARGELLO,** Bargello National Museum, Via del Proconsolo 4, Florence, 50122 Italy. *Dir* Paola D'Agostino
Open daily 8:15 AM - 1:50 PM; Admis full 4 EUR, reduced 2 EUR; Estab 1865; Collective of galleries housed in a former barracks & prison
Collections: Sculptures and decorative arts from the Renaissance, masterpieces by Donatello, Luca della Robbia, Verrocchio, Michaelangelo & Cellini, bronzes, majolica, waxes, enamels, medals & coins, ivories, furniture, seals, jewelry & regalia, weapons, textiles, tapestries

M **MUSEO NAZIONALE DI SAN MARCO,** National Museum of San Marco, Piazza San Marco 3, Florence, 50121 Italy; Via La Pira 1, Florence, 50121 Italy. Tel 39 055 2388608/704; Email pm-tos.mussanmarco-fi@beniculturali.it; Web: www.polomusealetoscana.beniculturali.it; *Dir* Marilena Tamassia
Open Mon - Fri 8:15 AM - 1:50 PM, Sat & Sun 8:15 AM - 4:50 PM, cl 1st, 3rd & 5th Sun & 2nd & 4th Mon of the month; Admis 4 EUR, reduced 2 EUR; Estab 1869; Art museum housed in a medieval Dominican friary.
Income: Polo Museale della Toscana
Special Subjects: Renaissance Art
Collections: Fra Angelico frescoes, paintings & panels, qui lasciarono traccia di se pittori come Domenico Chirlandaio e Giovanni Antonio Sogliani, che affrescaronoi due Refettori, e Fra' Bartolomeo, l'altro grande artista che visse nel convento all'inizio del Cinquecento, mentre nel'area un tempo destinata a Foresteria sono collocati i reperti architettonici e decorativi provenienti dagli edifici dell'antico Centro di Firenze demolito alla fine del' Ottocento, Al primo piano del Museo, insieme alle celle del Dormitorio, si trova la Biblioteca Monumentale, opera di Michelozzo, che ospita un' esposizione di corali miniati che fanno parte della ricca collezione appartenente al Museo

GENOA

M **GENOVA DI MUSEI,** Genoa Museum, Palazzo Tursi, Via Garibaldi 9 Genoa, 16124 Italy. Tel 010 5574708 4712; Email museibiblioteche@comune.genova.it; Web: www.museidigenova.it; *Exec Mgr Specialty Museums & Libraries* Cristiana Benetti Alessandrini
Collective of museums, galleries and places of cultural significance located throughout the Italian city of Genoa

M **Musei di Strada Nuova - Strada Nuova Museums**, Via Garibaldi 11, Genova, 16124 Italy. Tel 010 5572193; Fax 010 5572269; Email museidistradanuova@comune.genova.it; *Dir* Piero Boccardo
Open Tues - Fri 9 AM - 7 PM, Sat & Sun 10 AM - 7:30 PM, cl Mon; Admis full 9 EUR, reduced 7 EUR; Museum collective consisting of three historic mansions: Palazzo Rosso, Palazzo Bianco & Palazzo Tursi; Average Annual Attendance: 110,000
Special Subjects: Baroque Art, Drawings, Period Rooms, Portraits, Sculpture, Renaissance Art
Collections: Paintings by Van Dyck, Durer, Guercino, Veronese, Reni, Preti, Strozzi, drawings & prints by Guercino, Carracci, Cambiaso, Reni & Genoese Artists of XVII & XVIII centuries
Publications: Exhib catalogs
Activities: Classes for adults & children; docent training; Lectrs open to pub, concerts, guided tours; Mus shop, books, reproductions, prints

M **Musei di Nervi - Nervi Museums**, Villa Saluzzo Serra, Via Capolungo 3 Genova, 16167 Italy. Tel 010 3726025; Fax 010 3200333; Email gam@comune.genova.it; *Dir* Maria Flora Giubile
Admis Modern Art Gallery: full 6 EUR, reduced 3 - 5 EUR; Giannettino Luxoro Museum full 5 EUR, reduced 3 EUR; Frugone Collection full 5 EUR, reduced 3 EUR; Wolfsoniana full 5 EUR, reduced 3- 4 EUR; Open Modern Art Gallery: summer Tues - Fri 11 AM - 6 PM, Sat & Sun 12 - 7 PM & winter Tues - Sun 11 AM - 5 PM, cl Mon; Giannettino Luxoro Museum summer Tues - Fri 9 AM - 2 PM, Sat 2:30 - 7:30 PM & winter Tues - Thurs 9 AM - 2 PM, Fri 9 AM - 1 PM, Sat 2 - 6:30 PM; Frugone Collection summer Tues - Fri 9 AM - 7 PM, Sat & Sun 10 AM - 7:30 PM & Winter Tues - Fri 9 AM - 6:30 PM, Sat & Sun 9:30 - 6:30 PM, cl Mon; Wolfsoniana summer Tues - Fri 11 AM - 6 PM, Sat & Sun 12 - 7 PM & winter Tues - Sun 11 AM - 5 PM, cl Mon; Museum collective consisting of the Modern Art Gallery, Giannettino Luxoro Museum, Frugone Collection, and Wolfsoniana
Collections: 17th & 18th centuries paintings & sculptures, 19th & 20th century modern art, decorative arts & propaganda from 1880-1945
Exhibitions: Kodomono Hi; Tanabata Matsuri; Hina Matsuri
Activities: Concerts, gallery talks, tours; mus shop sells books

LIVORNO

M **MUSEO CIVICO GIOVANNI FATTORI,** Giovanni Fattori City Museum, Via S. Jacopo in, Acquaviva, 65 Livorno, 57127 Italy. Tel +39-0586-808001-804847; Fax +39-0586-806118; Email museofattori@comune.livorno.it; Web: pegaso.comune.livorno.it/index; *Mgr* Dr Francesca Giampaolo; *Asst Mgr* Francesco Luschi
Open 10 AM - 1 PM & 4 PM - 7 PM, cl Mon; Admis 6 EUR, reduced 4 EUR; Fine art mus; Average Annual Attendance: 12,000
Library Holdings: Book Volumes, Exhibition Catalogs, Original Documents
Special Subjects: Antiquities-Byzantine, Antiquities-Etruscan, Antiquities-Roman, Archaeology, Art History, Coins & Medals, Graphics, Painting-Italian, Prints, Sculpture
Collections: Giovanni Fattori & Macchiaioli paintings, 19th & 20th Tuscan & Italian paintings; Byzantine icons; numismatics; archeology
Publications: Exhib catalogs
Activities: Educ activities for children & students; temporary exhibs; lects open to pub; gallery talks; tours; schols; fels; extension prog serves town & province of Livorno; lending of original art to mus & institutions; mus shop sells books, reproductions, prints, postcards & posters

LUCCA

M **MUSEO E PINACOTECA NAZIONALE DI PALAZZO MANSI,** National Museum and Picture Gallery of the Palazzo Mansi, Via Galli Tassi 43, Lucca, 55100 Italy. Tel (0583) 55570; Fax (0583) 312221; Email sbappsae-lu.museilucchesi@beniculturali.it; Web: www.luccamuseinazionali.it; *Dir* Dr Antonia d'Aniello; *Sezione Architettonica* Glauco Borella; *Opers* Dr Ilaria Pergola
Open Tue - Sat 8:30 AM - 7:30 PM, cl Sun & holidays; Admis general 4 EUR, reduced 2 EUR; Est 1977; Paintings, sculptures, frescos, furniture, tapestries; Average Annual Attendance: 15,000
Income: Ministero Beni Culturali
Collections: Works of Tuscan, Venetian, French & Flemish Schools, paintings by such masters as Titian & Tintoretto, Paintings and sculptures XVIII-XX
Activities: Classes for adults & children; concerts, gallery talks; tours, scholarships

M **MUSEO NAZIONALE DI VILLA GUINIGI,** National Museum of Villa Guinigi, Via della Quarquonia, Lucca, 55100 Italy. Tel (0583) 496033; Fax (0583) 496033; Email pm-tos.museilucchesi@beniculturali.it; Web: www.luccamuseinazionali.it; *Dir* Dr Antonia d'Aniello; *Dir Sezione Architectomica* Glauco Borella
Open Tues - Sat 9:30 AM - 5:30 PM, cl Sun, Mon & holidays; Admis 4 EUR, reduced 2 EUR; Estab 1924; 15th century historical bldg; Average Annual Attendance: 10,000
Income: Ministero Culturali
Collections: Roman and late Roman sculptures and mosaics, Romanesque, Gothic and Renaissance Sculpture, paintings from 12th to 18th century, Ancient coins, medals, Italian ceramics, & silverware
Publications: Matteo Civitali
Activities: Classes for adults & children; docent training; lects open to pub; 350 vis lectrs per year; concerts, gallery talks, tours

MANTUA

M **MUSEO DI PALAZZO DUCALE,** Ducale Palace Museum, Piazza Sordello 40, Mantua, 46100 Italy. Tel (0376) 352100 (Museum), 352111 (Soprintendenza), 352104 (Segreteria Soprintendenza); Fax (0376) 366274; Email sbsae-mn@beniculturali.it; Web: www.mantovaducale.beniculturali.it; *Dir* Peter Assmann; *Conservatore* Dr Stefano L'occaso; *Vice Dir* Dr Renata Casarin; *Cur* Dr Stefano L'Occaso
Open Tues - Sun 8:15 AM - 7:15 PM, Fri 8 - 10 PM, cl Mon, Jan 1, May 1, & Dec 25; Admis 12 EUR, reduced 7.50 EUR; Estab 1882; Huge monumental architecture (XIII-XIX centuries) with paintings by Andrea Mantegna, Pisanello, Peter Paul Rubens, tapestries by Raphael; Average Annual Attendance: 200,000
Income: State museum
Library Holdings: Book Volumes, CD-ROMs, DVDs, Exhibition Catalogs, Framed Reproductions, Maps, Micro Print, Motion Pictures, Video Tapes
Special Subjects: Antiquities-Egyptian, Antiquities-Greek, Antiquities-Roman, Archaeology, Architecture, Baroque Art, Carpets & Rugs, Cartoons, Ceramics, Coins & Medals, Collages, Crafts, Decorative Arts, Dolls, Drawings, Etchings & Engravings, Ethnology, Glass, Ivory, Landscapes, Maps, Marine Painting, Medieval Art, Mosaics, Painting-Dutch, Painting-European, Painting-Flemish, Painting-French, Painting-German, Painting-Italian, Photography, Porcelain, Portraits, Prints, Religious Art, Renaissance Art, Sculpture, Silver, Tapestries, Woodcarvings, Watercolors
Collections: Classical Antiquities & Sculpture, picture gallery, modern sculptures, tapestries, prints, drawings
Publications: S L'occaso, The Ducal Palace - Mantua, Milano 2009; G Algeri; Palazzo Ducale di Mantova, Montova 2003
Activities: Classes for adults & children; lects open to pub; 4-5 vis lectrs per yr; concerts; gallery talks; tours; lending of original objects of art to exhibs worldwide; artmobil; mus shop sells books, magazines, reproductions, prints & other items

MILAN

M **MUSEO POLDI PEZZOLI,** Poldi Pezzoli Museum, Via Alessandro Manzoni 12, Milan, 20121 Italy. Tel 39 02 794889; Email ferraris@museopoldipezzoli.it; Web: www.museopoldipezzoli.it; *Dir* Dr Annalisa Zanni; *Cur* Lavinia Galli; *Cur* Andrea Di Lorenzo; *Registrar* Federica Manoli
Admis 10 EUR full price, 7 EUR reduced; Estab 1881
Library Holdings: Exhibition Catalogs, Manuscripts, Photographs, Prints, Sculpture
Collections: Paintings from 14th - 18th century, armor, tapestries, rugs, jewelry, porcelain, glass, textiles, furniture, clocks and watches, Netsuke and Okimono
Publications: The Poldi Pezzoli Visitors' Guide; Masterpieces of Painting
Activities: Classes for adults & children; docent training; concerts; gallery talks; tours; schols; mus shop sells books, original art, reproductions, prints, slides & cards

M **PINACOTECA AMBROSIANA,** Ambrosiana Art Gallery, Piazza Pio XI, 2, Milan, 20123 Italy. Tel (02) 806-921; Fax (02) 806-92210; Email info@ambrosiana.eu; Web: www.ambrosiana.eu; *Dir* DrBuzzi
Open Tues - Sun 10 AM - 6 PM, cl Mon, Jan 1, Easter, May 1, Dec 25; Admis adults 15 EUR, reduced 10 EUR
Collections: Leonardo da Vinci, Botticelli, Caravaggio, Luini, Raphael, Titian, drawings, miniatures, ceramics and enamels

M **PINACOTECA DI BRERA,** Brera Art Gallery, Via Brera 28, Milan, 20121 Italy. Tel 39 02 72263 264; Fax 39 02 720 011 40; Email pin-br@beniculturali.it; Web: www.brera.beniculturali.it; *Dir* James Bradburn
Open Tues - Sun 8:30 AM - 7:15 PM, Thurs until 10:15 PM, cl Mon, Jam 1, May 1, Dec 25; Admis 10 EUR, reduced 7 EUR; The gallery is located in the 17th century Palazza di Brera
Collections: Pictures of all schools, especially Lombard and Venetian, paintings by Mantegna, Bellini, Crivelli, Lotto, Titian, Veronese, Tintoretto, Tiepolo, Foppa, Bergognone, Luini, Piero della Francesca, Bramante, Raphael, Caravaggio, Rembrandt, Van Dyck, Rubens, also Italian 20th century works
Activities: Mus shop sells books, original art, slides

M **RACCOLTE ARTISTICHE DEL CASTELLO SFORZESCO,** Sforzesco Castle Art Collections, Castello Sforzesco, Milan, 20121 Italy. Tel 02-884 63700; Fax 02-884 63650; Email c.unitacastello@comune.milano.it; Web: www.milanocastello.it; *Culture Gen Dir* Dr Francesca Tasso
Open Tues - Sun 9 AM - 5 :30 PM; Admis 5 EUR, reduced 3 EUR; Castle grounds and art collection consisting of museums, libraries and archives.
Activities: Classes for adults & children; guided tours; lects open to pub; vis lectrs; concerts; mus shop sells books, reproductions

M **Museo delle Arti Decorativo - Museum of Decorative Art**, Castello Sforzesco, Milan, 20121 Italy. Tel 02 88463700; Email francesca.tasso@comune.milano.it; Web: artidecorative.milanocastello.it; *Cur* Francesca Tasso
Open Tues - Sun 9 AM - 5 PM, cl Mon; Admis 5 EUR; reduced 3 EUR
Collections: Decorative and applied arts from antiquity to the 1950s, tapestries, weapons, ivories, bronzes, ceramics, leather, wrought iron, majolica, jewellery, clocks, porcelain, enamels, fabrics, scientific instruments and glass

M **Raccolta delle Stampe Achille Bertarelli - Achille Bertarelli Print Collection**, Castello Sforzesco, Milan, 20121 Italy. Tel 02 88463837; Email c.craaibertarelli@comune.milano.it; Web: bertarelli.milanocastello.it; *Cur* Giovanna Mori
Open Mon - Fri 9 AM - 3 PM by appointment only, cl Sat & Sun; No admis fee; Print collection
Collections: Artistic prints, ranging from the first 15th century xylographs to modern graphic design, maps and views, historic, art & popular prints, graphic design, editorial design, conceptual design, bookplates, fashion plates, fans, games & playing cards, business & greeting cards, colored papers, postcards, almanacs & calendars, letterheads, paper money & paper values, heraldry & flags
Activities: Reading room; temporary exhibs; conferences; Mus shop sells books

M **Museo Archeologico - Archaeology Museum**, Castello Sforzesco, Milan, 20121 Italy. Tel 02 88445201; Email c.museoarcheologico@comune.milano.it; Web: museiarcheologici.milanocastello.it; *Cur* Anna Provenzali
Open Tues - Sun 9 AM - 5:30 PM, cl Mon; Admis 5 EUR, reduced 3 EUR
Collections: Ancient Egyptian artifacts including writing instruments & writing surfaces, sculptures & bronze statues, funerary items, amulets, canopic jars, wooden utensils, toiletry items and toys, Neolithic artifacts including stone tools, vessels & vases and tools for spinning & weaving, Bronze Age artifacts including metal & ore pieces, bellows & bronze items, pins & needles and bone, horn & wood artifacts, Golasecca burial pieces including bracelets, swords & ceramics, Roman artifacts
Activities: Guided tours

M **Pinacoteca - Art Gallery**, Castello Sforzesco, Milan, 20121 Italy. Tel 02 88463700; Email c.craaiapplicata@comune.milano.it; Web: pinacoteca.milanocastello.it; *Chief Cur* Francesca Tasso
Open Tues - Sun 9 AM - 5:30 PM; Admis fee 3 euro, reduced 1,50 euro
Collections: Lombard painting from the mid-15th century to early neoclassicism, sculpted wooden reliefs, terracotta busts, medals, large altar pieces, devotional paintings, painted & frescoed murals, Lombard polyptych and miniatures
Activities: Classes for adults & children; conferences; tours; gallery talks; mus shop sells books, prints & reproductions

M **Museo d'Arte Antica - Museum of Ancient Art**, Castello Sforzesco, Milan, 20121 Italy. Tel 02 88463700; Email c.museiartistici@comune.milano.it; Web: arteantica.milanocastello.it; *Chief Cur* Francesca Tasso
Open Tues - Sun 9 AM - 5:30 PM, cl Mon; Admis 5 EUR, reduced 3 EUR
Collections: Stone artifacts including, architectural fragments, funerary & celebratory monuments, statues, coats of arms, reliefs, plaster casts and terracottas originating from buildings and structures from medieval Milan
Activities: Guided tours

M **Archivio Fotographico - Photographic Archives**, Castello Sforzesco, Milan, 20121 Italy. Tel 02 88463664; Email c.craaifotografico@comune.milano.it; Web: archiviofotografico.milanocastello.it
Open Tues - Thurs 10 AM - 1 PM, by appointment only; No admis fee; Archives
Collections: 850,000 photographs from 1840 to the present, historic & artistic heritage of Milan & Lombardy, portraits, photojournalism, Italian landscapes, views of European and world cities
Activities: Conferences; online catalog; vis lects; lects open to pub; mus shop sells books

M **Museo degli Strumenti Musicali - Museum of Musical Instruments**, Castello Sforzesco, Milan, 20121 Italy. Tel 02 88463700; Email c.museiartistici@comune.milano.it; Web: strumentimusicali.milanocastello.it; *Cur* Francesca Tasso; *Cur* Valentina Ricetti
Open Tues - Sun 9 AM - 5:30 PM, cl Mon; Admis 5 EUR, reduced 3 EUR
Collections: Musical instruments from XVI-XX century including plucked instruments, wind instruments, harps, violins, violas, hurdy gurdies & keyboard instruments, musical recording studio
Activities: Guided tours; progs for adults & children; lects; concerts; exhibs

MODENA

M **GALLERIA ESTENSE,** Estense Gallery, Largo Porta Sant'Agostino, 337, Modena, 41121 Italy. Tel 39 059 4395711; Fax 39 059 230196; Email ga-esten@beniculturali.it; Web: www.gallerie-estensi.beniculturali.it; *Dir* Martina Bagnoli; *Libr Dir* Annalisa Battini
Open: (Galleria Estense) Tues - Sat 8:30 AM - 7:30 PM, Sun 2 - 7:30 PM, cl Mon; (Museo Lapidario Estense) Sun 10 AM - 7:30 PM, Mon 8 AM - 7:30 PM, Sat 8:30 AM - 7:30 PM, cl Tues - Fri; Admis 4 EUR, reduced 2 EUR; Two galleries, Galleria Estense & Museo Lapidario Estense and a library Biblioteca Estense Universitaria.
Collections: 14th to the 18th century Italian paintings, bronzes, coins, drawings, medals, minor arts, prints & sculptures from the collection of the House of Este.
Publications: See web site

NAPLES

M **MUSEO CIVICO GAETANO FILANGIERI,** Gaetano Filangieri Civic Museum, Via Duomo 288, Naples, 80138 Italy. Tel 081 203175; Web: www.museofilangieri.org; *Dir* Antonio Buccino Grimaldi
Open Mon - Sat 10 AM - 4 PM, Sun 10 AM - 2 PM; Admis 5 EUR, reduced 3 EUR
Collections: paintings, furniture, archives, photographs, coins, books, Collected works of Gaetano Filangieri, Prince of Satriano

M **MUSEO DI CAPODIMONTE,** Capodimonte Museum, Palazzo di Capodimonte, Via Miano 2, Naples, 80131 Italy. Tel 39 081 7499111; Fax 39 081 7445032; Email mu-cap@beniculturali.it; Web: www.museocapodimonte.beniculturali.it; *Dir* Sylvain Bellenger; *Chief Cur* Linda Martino
Open 8:30 AM - 7:30 PM, cl Wed; Admis 8 EUR, reduced 4 EUR, children under 18 & seniors over 65 yrs no charge; Art museum located in a Bourbon palace
Special Subjects: Ceramics, Coins & Medals, Decorative Arts, Glass, Islamic Art, Ivory, Medieval Art, Metalwork, Oriental Art, Painting-Dutch, Painting-Flemish, Painting-French, Painting-Italian, Painting-Spanish, Porcelain, Portraits, Sculpture, Tapestries
Collections: Paintings from 13th to 18th century, paintings and sculptures of 19th century, arms and armor, medals and bronzes of the Renaissance, porcelain, contemporary art, 20th century
Activities: Classes for adults & children; concerts; mus shop sells books, reproductions

M **MUSEO NAZIONALE DI SAN MARTINO,** National Museum of San Martino, Largo San Martino 5, Naples, 80129 Italy. Tel 39-0817944021; Web: http://www.musis.it/sanmartino.asp?museo=3; *Dir* Antonella Cucciniello
Open Thurs - Tues 8:30 AM - 7:30 PM; Admis 6 euro
Collections: 16th - 18th century pictures & paintings, 13th - 19th century sculpture, majolicas & porcelains, section of modern prints, paintings & engravings, Neapolitan historical collection

PADUA

M **MUSEI CIVICI DI PADOVA,** Padova City Museums, Piazza Eremitani 8, Padua, 35121 Italy. Tel 39 049 8204551; Fax 39 049 8204585; Email musei@comune.padova.it; Web: padovacultura.padovanet.it; *Dir* Davide Banzato; *Funzionario Archeological M* Francesca Verdvese; *Funzionario Art Mus* Elisabetta Gastaldi; *Funzionario Numismatic Mus* Valeria Vettorato; *Librn* Dr Gilda Mantovani; *Mus Mgmnt* Marilena Varotto
Open year round 9 AM - 7 PM; Admis 13 EUR, reduced 8 EUR; Estab 1825; Museum complex housed in an Eremitani monk monastery. Includes the Archaeology Museum, the Museum of Medieval & Modern Art, the Scrovegni Chapel and the City Library.
Library Holdings: Book Volumes, Exhibition Catalogs
Special Subjects: Antiquities-Byzantine, Antiquities-Egyptian, Antiquities-Etruscan, Antiquities-Greek, Antiquities-Roman, Archaeology, Art History, Bronzes, Ceramics, Coins & Medals, Decorative Arts, Drawings, Furniture, Glass, Gold, Graphics, History of Art & Archaeology, Ivory, Jewelry, Landscapes, Medieval Art, Mosaics, Painting-Dutch, Painting-European, Painting-Flemish, Painting-German, Painting-Italian, Pewter, Porcelain, Restorations, Sculpture, Portraits, Renaissance Art
Collections: Archaeological Museum, bronzes, ceramics, industrial arts, painting, sculpture, Greco-Roman, Italian, Paduan, Venetian, Napoleonic coins and medals, Renaissance gallery, Medieval and Modern Art, Archeological Collection, Numismatic Collection, Stone Tablets, multimedia room for the Scrovegni, Chapel & multimedia point in Egyptian room
Publications: Bollettino del Museo Civico
Activities: Classes for children; concerts; Mus shop sells books, reproductions, prints, slides

PARMA

M **COMPLESSO MONUMENTALE DELLA PILOTTA,** Pilotta Monument Complex, Piazzale della Pilotta, 15, Parma, 43121 Italy. Tel 0521 233309-233617; Fax 0521 206336; Email cm-pil@beniculturali.it; Web: pilotta.beniculturali.it; *Dir* Simone Green
Open Tues - Sat 8:30 AM - 7 PM, Sun 1 PM - 7 PM; Admis 10 EUR, reduced 5 EUR; Pilotta Palace complex and National Gallery, Archaeological Museum, Bodonian Museum, Farnese Theater and Palatina Library.
Income: Ministero Beni Culturali
Library Holdings: Book Volumes, Exhibition Catalogs, Manuscripts
Collections: Paintings from 13th to 19th century, including works by Correggio, Parmigianino, Cima, El Greco, Piazzetta, Tiepolo, Holbein, Van Dyck, Mor, Nattier & several painters of the school of Parma, modern art
Activities: Classes for adults & children; guided tours

PERGOLA

M **MUSEO DEI BRONZI DORATI E DELLA CITTà DI PERGOLA,** Perogla Gilded Bronzes Museum, Largo San Giacomo 2, Pergola, 61045 Italy. Tel 0721-734090 / 7373278; Email museo.bronzidorati@libero.it; Web: www.bronzidorati.com
Open daily 10 AM - 12:30 PM, 3:30 PM - 6:30 PM, cl Mon; July & Aug: daily 10 AM - 12:30 PM & 3:30 - 7 PM; Admis 6 EUR, reduced 5 EUR, schools 4 EUR, children 6-11 3 EUR
Collections: Collection of gilded bronzes
Activities: Traveling exhibs; guided tours

PERUGIA

M **GALLERIA NAZIONALE DELL'UMBRIA,** Umbrian National Gallery, Corso Vannucci 19, Palazzo dei Priori Perugia, 06123 Italy. Tel 39 075 5866 8410; Fax 39 075 5866 8400; Email gnu@sistemamuseo.it; Web: www.artiumbria.beniculturali.it; *Dir* Marco Pierini
Open Tues - Sun 8:30 AM - 7:30 PM, cl Mon; Admis fee 8 EUR, children 18-25 yrs 4 EUR; 1863, civic museum; Average Annual Attendance: 80,000
Special Subjects: Baroque Art, Bronzes, Ceramics, Drawings, Furniture, Gold, Ivory, Jewelry, Medieval Art, Painting-Italian, Renaissance Art, Sculpture, Stained Glass, Textiles
Collections: Jewels, paintings from the Umbrian School from the 13th - 18th century, 13th-15th century sculptures, Umbrian clothes from 13th century
Activities: Classes for adults & children; docent training; concerts; gallery talks; tours; museum sells books, magazines, original art, reproductions, prints, slides

PISA

M **MUSEO NAZIONALE DI SAN MATTEO,** National Museum of San Matteo, Piazza San Matteo in Soarta, Pisa, Italy. Tel 39 050 541865; Fax 39 050 542640; Email pm-tos.museosanmatteo@beniculturali.it; Web: www.polomusealetoscana.beniculturali.it; *Interim Dir* Stefano Casciu
Open Tues - Sat 8:30 AM - 7 PM, Sun 8:30 AM - 1:30 PM, cl Mon; Admis adult 5 EUR, reduced 2.50 EUR
Collections: Sculptures by the Pisanos and their school, collection of the Pisan school of the 13th and 14th centuries, and paintings of the 15th, 16th, and 17th centuries, ceramics, collection of coins and medals

POSSAGNO

M **GYPSOTHECA E MUSEO ANTONIO CANOVA,** Antonio Canova Gypsotheca & Museum, Via Canova 74, Possagno, 31054 Italy. Tel 39 0423 544323; Fax 39 0423 922007; Email posta@museocanova.it; Web: www.museocanova.it; *Pres* Franca Coin; *Sec* Alberto Signor; *Dir* Mario Guderzo
Open Tues - Sun 9:30 AM - 6 PM, cl Mon, New Year's Day, Easter & Christmas; Admis 10 EUR, reduced 6 EUR, school children 4 EUR; Average Annual Attendance: 30,000
Library Holdings: Book Volumes, CD-ROMs, Exhibition Catalogs, Prints, Sculpture
Collections: Plaster cast models, paintings, drawings
Activities: Guided tours; concerts; schols; mus shop sells books, original art, reproductions, prints, postcards, gadgets, slides

ROME

M **GALLERIA BORGHESE,** Borghese Gallery, Piazzale Scipione Borghese, 5, Rome, 00197 Italy. Tel 39 068413979; Fax 06 8840756; Email ga-bor@beniculturali.it; Web: galleriaborghese.beniculturali.it/it; *Dir* Anna Coliva
Open Tues - Sun 9 AM - 7 PM, cl Mon, Christmas & New Year's Day, ticket reservation suggested; Admis 13 EUR (plus 2 EUR service charge), reduced 6.50 EUR (plus 2 EUR service charge); Greek, Roman & ancient art, sculptures & paintings from the 15th & 20th centuries
Income: Pub & private
Collections: Baroque & Classical, 580 paintings about XV-XVII-XVIII, 450 sculptures
Exhibitions: One or two exhibs ann
Publications: Catalogues
Activities: Classes for adults & children; concerts; Mus shop, books, reproductions, prints

M **GALLERIA DORIA PAMPHILJ,** Doria Pamphilj Gallery, Piazza del Collegio Romano 2, Rome, 00186 Italy; Piazza Grazioli 5, Rome, 00186 Italy. Tel 39 06 6797323; Fax 39 06 6780939; Email info@dopart.it; Web: www.doriapomphilj.it; *Dir* Jonathan Doria Pamphilj; *Scientific Cur* Andrea G de Marchi
Open daily 9 AM - 7 PM, cl Jan 1, Easter, Dec 25; Admis 12 EUR, reduced 8 EUR
Special Subjects: Antiquities-Roman, Bookplates & Bindings, Bronzes, Painting-European, Painting-Flemish, Painting-Italian, Porcelain, Pottery
Collections: Paintings by Caravaggio, Carracci, Correggio, Filippo Lippi, Lorrain, del Piombo, Titian, Velazquez
Activities: Mus shop sells books, prints, slides, jewelry & other items

M **GALLERIA NAZIONALE PALAZZO BARBERNI,** National Gallery of Rome, Via Quattro Fontane 13, Rome, 00186 Italy. Tel 39 06 481 4591; Fax (06) 4880560; Email sspsae-rni.gnaa@beniculturali.it; *Dir* Flaminia Gennari Santori; *Registrar* Giuliano Forti; *Dir Art History* Dr Michele Di Monte; *Supt* Rossella Vodret; *Registrar* Michela Ulivi; *Pub Relations* Simona Baldi
Open Tues - Sun 8:30 AM - 7 PM; Admis full 7 EUR, reduced 3.50 EUR; Paintings from XIII to XVIII Century, Raphael Caravage, etc, 34 rooms 3 floors; Average Annual Attendance: 240,000
Library Holdings: Audio Tapes, Book Volumes, Cards, Exhibition Catalogs, Maps, Photographs, Reproductions
Collections: Italian & European paintings from 12th - 18th century, Baroque architecture, Sculptures by Bernini, Algardi & others
Activities: Classes for adults & children; lectrs open to pub; 10-12 vis lectrs per yr; concerts; sponsored competitions; museum shop sells books, magazines, reproductions, slides & gadgets

M **ISTITUTO NAZIONALE PER LA GRAFICA,** National Institute for Graphic Arts, Calcografia, Via della Stamperia 6 Rome, 00187 Italy. Tel 39 (6) 230 69 980; Fax 39 (6) 69 921 454; Web: www.grafica.arti.beniculturali.it; *Dir* Doff Serenita Papaldo
Open 10 AM - 7 PM, cl Jan 1, Dec 25; No admis fee
Collections: Italian & foreign prints; drawings from the 14th century to the present

M **MUSEI CAPITOLINI,** Capitolini Museums, Piazza del Campidoglio 1, Rome, 00186 Italy. Tel 39 06 0608; Email info.museicapitolini@comune.roma.it; Web: www.museicapitolini.org; *Dir* Claudio Parisi Presicce
Open daily 9:30 AM - 7:30 PM; Admis 15 EUR, reduced 13 EUR; Collective of art & archaeological museums in Rome, Italy.
Library Holdings: Auction Catalogs, Book Volumes, CD-ROMs, Cards, Exhibition Catalogs, Reproductions
Special Subjects: Antiquities-Egyptian, Antiquities-Etruscan, Antiquities-Greek, Archaeology, Baroque Art, Bronzes, Carpets & Rugs, Ceramics, Coins & Medals, Decorative Arts, Furniture, Medieval Art, Mosaics, Painting-European, Painting-Italian, Porcelain, Sculpture, Tapestries
Collections: Ancient sculptures, Art History
Publications: Musei Capitolini, Guida, Electa 2005 (rist. 2011)
Activities: Guided tours; 5 vis lectrs per yr; concerts; lending of original objects of art to international exhibs; mus shop sells books, postcards, reproductions

M **MUSEO D'ARTE CONTEMPORANEA ROMA,** Museum of Contemporary Art, Rome, Via Nizza 138, Rome, Italy. Tel 39 06 696271; Email macro@comune.roma.it; Web: www.museomacro.it; *Dir* Frederica Pirani
Open Tues - Fri & Sun 10:30 AM - 7 PM, cl Mon; Admis 11 EUR, reduced 9 EUR
Collections: Permanent collection of significant contemporary Italian art since the 1960s

M **MUSEO NAZIONALE ROMANO,** National Museum of Rome, Piazza Sant'Apollinare 44, Rome, Italy. Tel 39 06 480201; Fax 39 06 6787689; Email ssba-rm@beniculturali.it; *Dir* Alessandra Capodiferro
Open Tues - Sun 9 AM - 7:45 PM; Admis 7 EUR, reduced 3.50 EUR
Collections: Archaeological coll, Roman bronzes and sculpture, numismatics

ROVIGO

M **PINACOTECA DELL'ACADEMIA DEI CONCORDI PALAZZO ROVERELLA,** Art Gallery of the Academy of Concordi and of the Rovigo Episcopal Seminary, Piazza V. Emanuele II, 14, Rovigo, 45100 Italy. Tel 0425 460093; Email info@palazzoroverella.com; Web: www.palazzoroverella.com
Open Mon - Fri daily 9 AM - 6:30 PM, Sat 9:30 AM - 1:30 PM; Admis 9 EUR
Collections: Venetian paintings from the 14th to 18th century, Flemish paintings, contemporary art
Activities: Classes for children, schools' progs; concerts; gallery talks; guided tours; museum shop sells books, reproductions, prints

SASSARI

M **MUSEO NAZIONALE ARCHEOLOGICO ED ETNOGRAFICO GIOVANNI ANTONIO SANNA,** Giovanni Antonio Sanna National Archaeological and Ethnographic Museum, Via Roma 64, Sassari, 07100 Italy. Tel 39 079 272203; Email pm-sar.museoarcheo.sassari@beniculturali.it; Web: www.beniculturali.it; *Dir* Giovanna Damiani
Open Tues - Sun 9 AM - 8 PM; Admis 3 EUR, reduced admis 1.50 EUR; Estab 1931
Collections: Archeological Collections, Collection of Sardinian Ethnography

TURIN

M **GALLERIA CIVICA D'ARTE MODERNA E CONTEMPORANEA, TORINO,** Gallery of Modern and Contemporary Art, Turin, Via Magenta 31, Turin, 10128 Italy. Tel 39 011 4429518; Fax 39 011 4429929; Email gam@fondazionetorinomusei.it; Web: www.gamtorino.it; *Dir* Riccardo Passoni
Open Tues - Sun 11 AM - 7 PM, cl Mon; Admis 10 EUR, reduced admis 8 EUR, free 1st Tues each month; Estab 1863; Coll with more than 45,000 art works
Income: Turin Museum Foundation
Library Holdings: Auction Catalogs, Book Volumes, CD-ROMs, Exhibition Catalogs, Kodachrome Transparencies, Original Documents, Pamphlets, Periodical Subscriptions, Prints, Reproductions, Sculpture, Slides, Video Tapes
Collections: modern art, paintings, sculpture, installations from 1800 - 1900 & contemporary art, video coll, graphic art; photography
Publications: Catalogs for each exhibition
Activities: Classes for adults & children; lects open to pub; concerts; gallery talks; mus shop sells books, magazines, reproductions; photographic archive

M **MUSEI REALI TORINO,** Royal Museum of Turin, Piazzetta Reale 1, Turin, 10122 Italy. Tel (011) 5211106; Email mr-to@beniculturali.it; Web: www.meseireali.beniculturali.it; *Dir* Enrica Pagella
Open Tues - Sun 8:30 AM - 7:30 PM; cl Mon; Admis 12 EUR, reduced 6 EUR
Collections: Paintings, decorative arts, prints, textiles & sculpture, House of Savoy Royal Art Collection, arms & armour, antiques, gardens & fountains, portolan charts, incunabula. ballet albums, coins & medals, furniture & carpets
Activities: Classes for adults & children; docent training; lects open to pub; tours; schols; fels

VENICE

A **BIENNALE DI VENEZIA,** The Venice Biennale, S Marco, Ca' Giustinian Venice, 30124 Italy. Tel 39 041 5218711; Fax 39 041 2728329; Email info@labiennale.org; Web: www.labiennale.org; *Pres* Paolo Baratta; *Dir Gen* Andrea Del Mercato
Open 10 AM - 6 PM, cl Mon; Admis 25 EUR, reduced 22 EUR; Estab 1895; Cultural institution that organizes and hosts exhibitions and festivals in art, architecture, cinema, dance, music and theater.
Collections: Visual arts, architecture, cinema, dance, music, theater, historical archives of contemporary art

M **FONDAZIONE MUSEI CIVICI DI VENEZIA,** Venice Civic Museums Foundation, Piazza San Marco, 52, Venice, 30124 Italy. Tel 39 041 2405211; Fax 39 041 5200935; Email info@fmcvenezia.it; Web: www.visitmuve.it; *Pres* Mariacristina Gribaudi; *Vice Pres* Luigi Brugnaro; *Dir* Gabriella Belli
Manages and promotes 10 centuries of architecture, decorations and literature in 11 museums and 5 libraries. The collection contains more than 200,000 works of art, 2,000,000 naturalist exhibits and 200,000 volumes across 40,000 sq meters of exhibition space.; Average Annual Attendance: 2000000

M **Museo Correr - Correr Museum**, San Marco, 52, Venice, 30124 Italy. Tel 39 041 2405211; Fax 39 041 5200935; Email info@fmcvenezia.it; Web: correr.visitmuve.it; *Dir* Gabriella Belli
Open April 1 - Oct 31 10 AM - 7 PM; Nov 1 - Mar 31 10 AM - 5 PM; Admis 20 EUR, reduced 13 EUR; Estab 1922; Former royal residence that houses the Correr Art Collection, Neoclassical & Imperial period rooms and art gallery.
Library Holdings: Auction Catalogs, Book Volumes, CD-ROMs, Cards, Cassettes, DVDs, Exhibition Catalogs, Micro Print, Photographs, Prints, Reproductions
Special Subjects: Architecture, Bronzes, Ceramics, Coins & Medals, Decorative Arts, Etchings & Engravings, Furniture, Glass, Graphics, Landscapes, Manuscripts, Maps, Medieval Art, Military Art, Miniatures, Painting-British, Painting-European, Painting-Flemish, Painting-German, Period Rooms, Porcelain, Portraits, Prints, Religious Art, Renaissance Art, Sculpture, Silver, Tapestries, Textiles
Collections: Coll comprises various area of interest: neoclassical rooms, historical colls throwing light on city's institutions, urban affairs & everyday life, Picture gallery colls of Venetian painting from early 16th century
Publications: Museum Guide
Activities: Classes for adults & children; docent training; lects open to pub; conferences; concerts; gallery talks; tours; schols & fels; lending original object of art for international exhibs; originates traveling exhibs; mus shop sells books, magazines, original art, reproductions, prints, slides & merchandising

M **Casa di Carlo Goldoni - Carlo Goldoni's House**, San Polo, 2794, Venice, 30125 Italy. Tel 39 041 2759325; Fax 39 041 2440081; Email segreteria.casagoldoni@fmcvenezia.it; Web: carlogoldoni.visitmuve.it; *Dir* Chiara Squarcina
Open April - Oct 31: 10 AM - 5 PM; Nov - Mar 31: 10 AM - 4 PM, cl Wed, Jan 1, May 1 & Dec 25; Admis 5 EUR, reduced 3.50 EUR; The archive & library contains more than 30,000 works with theatrical texts, studies & original manuscripts.
Library Holdings: Auction Catalogs, Book Volumes, CD-ROMs, Cards, Cassettes, DVDs, Exhibition Catalogs, Micro Print, Photographs, Prints, Reproductions
Collections: Puppet theatre from Cá Grimani ai Servi, formerly part of the Cá Rezzonico collection
Activities: Educ prog for schools & families; docent training; conferences; conventions

M **Palazzo Fortuny - Fortuny Palace**, San Marco, 3780, Venice, 30124 Italy. Tel 39 041 5200995; Fax 39 041 5223088; Email fortuny@fmcvenezia.it; Web: fortuny.visitmuve.it; *Dir* Daniela Ferretti
Open Mon, Wed - Sun 10 AM - 6 PM, cl Tues, Jan 1 & Dec 25; Admis 12 EUR, reduced 10 EUR; Once owned by the Pesaro family, this large Gothic palazzo in Campo San Beneto was transformed by Mariano Fortuny into his own atelier of photography, stage-design, textile-design & painting. The piano nobile & ground floor spaces are used for special exhibs.
Collections: Fortuny tapestries & colls
Publications: Museum Guide
Activities: Educ prog for schools & families; docent training; conferences; conventions

M **Ca' Rezzonico**, Dorsoduro, 3136, Venice, 30123 Italy. Tel 39 041 2410100; Fax 390 41 2410100; Email carezzonico@fmcvenezia.it; Web: carezzonico.visitmuve.it; *Dir* Gabriella Belli
Open April 1 - Oct 31: 10 AM - 6 PM, Nov 1 - Mar 31: 10 AM - 4 PM, cl Tues, Dec 25 & Jan 1; Admis general 10 EUR, reduced: 7.50 EUR; Former palace contains important 18th century Venetian paintings amid furnishings of the age.; Average Annual Attendance: 100,000
Library Holdings: Auction Catalogs, Book Volumes, CD-ROMs, Cards, Cassettes, DVDs, Exhibition Catalogs, Micro Print, Photographs, Prints, Reproductions
Special Subjects: Architecture, Baroque Art, Bronzes, Ceramics, Drawings, Etchings & Engravings, Furniture, Glass, Painting-Italian, Porcelain, Portraits, Tapestries, Textiles
Collections: 18th century Venetian art, sculpture, etc, Egidio Martini Picture Gallery, Mestrovich Collection
Publications: Museum Guide; Martini's Collection Guide; Mestrovich's Collection Guide
Activities: Classes for adults & children; docent training; lects open to pub; concerts; gallery talks; tours; conferences; theatre lects; schols & fels; lend original art objects for international exhibs; mus sells books, magazines, original art, reproductions, prints, slides & merchandising

M **Museo del Vetro - Glass Museum**, Fondamenta Giustinian, 8, Murano, 30141 Italy. Tel 39 041 739586; Fax 39 041 5275120; Email museo.vetro@fmcvenezia.it; Web: museovetro.visitmuve.it; *Dir* Chiara Squarcina
Open April - Oct 31: 10 AM - 6 PM; Nov - Mar 31 10 AM - 5 PM, cl Jan 1, May 1 & Dec 25; Admis 10 EUR, reduced 7.50 EUR; Estab 1861; Former palace dedicated to the art of glassmaking.
Collections: Venetian glass from middle ages to the present
Publications: Museum Guide
Activities: Educ prog for adults & children; docent training; lects open to pub; concerts; gallery talks, tours; conferences; theatre lect; schols & fels; lend original art object for international exhibs; mus sells books, magazines, original art, reproductions, prints, slides & merchandising

M **Museo di Palazzo Mocenigo - Mocenigo Palace Museum**, Santa Croce, 1992, Venice, 30135 Italy. Tel 39 041 721798; Email info@fmcvenezia.it; Web: mocenigo.visitmuve.it; *Dir* Chiara Squarcina
Open April - Oct 31 Tues - Sun 10 AM - 5 PM; Nov - Mar 31 Tues - Sun 10 AM - 4 PM, cl Mon, Jan 1, May 1 & Dec 25; Admis 8 EUR, reduced 5.50 EUR; Former palace exhibiting 17th - 19th century paintings, clothing & furnishings and Venetian perfumes.
Library Holdings: Auction Catalogs, Book Volumes, CD-ROMs, Cards, Cassettes, DVDs, Exhibition Catalogs, Micro Print, Photographs, Prints, Reproductions
Special Subjects: Flasks & Bottles
Collections: Palace of the Doges, coll of fabrics & costumes, library on history of fashion
Publications: Museum Guide

Activities: Classes for schools & families; docent training; conferences; concerts; theatrical lects

M **Ca' Pesaro Galleria Nazionale d'Arte Moderna - Ca' Pesaro Gallery of Modern Art**, Santa Croce, 2076, Venice, 30135 Italy. Tel 39 041 721127; Fax 39 041 5241075; Email capesaro@fmcvenezia.it; Web: capesaro.visitmuve.it; *Dir* Daniela Ferretti
Open April - Oct 31 10 AM - 6 PM, Nov - March 31 10 AM - 5 PM, cl Mon, Jan 1, May 1, Dec 25; Admis general 10 EUR, reduced 7.50 EUR; Modern art gallery housed in a former Venetian palace.
Library Holdings: Auction Catalogs, Book Volumes, CD-ROMs, Cards, Cassettes, DVDs, Exhibition Catalogs, Micro Print, Photographs, Prints, Reproductions
Special Subjects: Art History, Conceptual Art, Decorative Arts, Drawings, Etchings & Engravings, Glass, Painting-American, Painting-European, Painting-Italian, Photography, Restorations, Sculpture
Collections: 19th & 20th centuries works of art
Publications: Museum Guide
Activities: Educ prog for schools & families; docent training; conferences; mus shop

M **Museo del Merletto - Lace Museum**, Piazza Galuppi, 187, Burano, 30142 Italy. Tel 39 041 730034; Fax 39 041 735471; Email museo.merletto@fmcvenezia.it; Web: museomerletto.visitmuve.it; *Dir* Chiara Squarcina
Open April - Oct 31: Tues - Sun 10 AM - 6 PM; Nov - March 31: Tues - Sun 10 AM - 5 PM; cl Mon, Jan 1, May 1, Dec 25; Admis 5 EUR, reduced 3.50 EUR; Mus houses archives of Andriana Marcello Lace School founded in 1872. It played an important role in the city's cultural & economic life for over a century.
Library Holdings: Book Volumes
Special Subjects: Laces
Collections: Two hundred rare & precious examples of Venetian lace from the 16th to 20th century
Activities: Educ prog for adults & children; docent training; lects open to pub; tours; lend original art objects for international exhibs; mus sells books, original art, reproductions, prints, slides & merchandising

M **Museo di Storia Naturale di Venezia - Venice Museum of Natural History**, Santa Croce, 1730, Venice, 30135 Italy. Tel 39 041 2750206; Fax 39 041 721000; Email nat.mus.ve@fmcvenezia.it; Web: msn.visitmuve.it; *Cur* Luca Mizzan
Open June - Oct 31: daily 10 AM - 6 PM, Nov - May 31: Tues - Fri 9 AM - 5 PM, Sat & Sun 10 AM - 6 PM, cl Mon, Jan 1, Dec 25, May 1; Admis 8 EUR, reduced 5.50 EUR; An important scientific institution, this contains various collections & an important library. It is also a centre for research & surveys regarding the Venetian lagoon & its fauna.
Library Holdings: Auction Catalogs, Book Volumes, CD-ROMs, Cards, Cassettes, DVDs, Exhibition Catalogs, Micro Print, Photographs, Prints, Reproductions
Collections: Atmospheric account of the Ligabue Expedition in the discovery of the Ouranosaurus nigeriensis dinosaur, aquarium reproduction of the tegnue, a formation of seabed rocks of the Venetian coast
Publications: Scientific reviews
Activities: Educ prog for schools & families; docent training

M **Palazzo Ducale - Doge's Palace**, San Marco, 1, Venice, 30135 Italy. Tel 39 041 2715911; Fax 39 041 5285028; Email info@fmcvenezia.it; Web: palazzoducale.visitmuve.it; *Dir* Belli; *Dir* Gabriella Belli
Open Nov 1 - Mar 25: 8:30 AM - 5:30 PM; Mar 26 - Oct 31: 8:30 AM - 7 PM; Fri - Sun 8:30 AM - 11 PM; Admis 19 EUR, reduced 12 EUR; Formerly the Doge's residence & seat of Venetian government, the palace is Gothic architecture. The bldg & its sculptural decoration date from various periods. Along the facades of the Palace run loggias that overlook St. Mar's Square & the lagoon.
Collections: Works by Titian, Veronese, Tintoretto, Vittoria & Tiepolo comprises vast council chambers, delicately-decorated residential apartments & austere prison-cells
Publications: Museum Guide
Activities: Educ progs for schools & families; docent training; conferences; conventions

M **Torre dell'Orologio - Clock Tower**, Piazza San Marco, Venice, 30124 Italy. Email info@fmcvenezia.it; Web: torreorologio.visitmuve.it; *Dir* Gabriella Belli
Open to visits with specialized guide, only upon prior booking; Admis 12 EUR, reduced 7 EUR; Mus dedicated to the history of one of Venice's most famous architectural landmarks.

M **FONDAZIONE QUERINI STAMPALIA,** Querini Stampalia Foundation, Palazzo Querini-Stampalia, Castello 5252 Venice, 30122 Italy. Tel 041 2711411; Fax 041 2711445; Email fondazione@querinistampalia; Web: www.querinistampalia.it; *Dir* Marigusta Lazzari; *Pres* Marino Cortese
Open Tues - Sun 10 AM - 6 PM, cl Mon; Library: Tues - Sat 10 AM - 10 PM, Sun 10 AM - 6 PM, cl Mon; Admis 10 EUR, reduced admis 8 EUR; Estab 1869; 18th century Patrician house-museum and library.; Average Annual Attendance: 150,000
Income: 3,500,000 EUR
Library Holdings: Book Volumes, CD-ROMs, DVDs, Manuscripts, Maps, Original Art Works, Original Documents, Pamphlets, Periodical Subscriptions, Photographs, Prints
Special Subjects: Architecture, Ceramics, Decorative Arts, Furniture, Painting-European, Painting-Italian, Porcelain, Portraits
Collections: 14th - 19th century Italian paintings, contemporary art colls, manuscripts, drawings
Exhibitions: Contemporary art exhibs during the year
Publications: Various publications
Activities: Classes for adults & children; lectrs open to the public; concerts, gallery talks; tours; lending of original objects of art to mus & art exhibs; organize traveling exhibs to other mus; mus shop sells books, design objects, jewelry & other items

M **GALLERIA GIORGIO FRANCHETTI ALLA CA' D'ORO,** Giorgio Franchetti Gallery at the Ca' d'Oro, Calle Ca d'Oro, Canal Grande Venice, 30100 Italy. Tel 041 522349; Fax 041 5238790; Email info@cadoro.org; Web: www.cadoro.org; *Dir* Dr Adriana Augusti; *Cur* Claudia Cremonini
Open Mon 8:15 AM - 2 PM, Tues - Sun 8:15 AM - 7:15 PM; Admis 8.50 EUR, students & seniors 4.25 EUR; House-museum and art gallery housed in a late-Gothic era residence.
Collections: Paintings, furniture, medals, tapestries, bronzes, sculptures, ceramics
Activities: Guided tours; mus shop sells books, postcards, posters & videos

M **GALLERIE DELL'ACCADEMIA DI VENEZIA,** Gallery of the Academy of Venice, Campo della Carita, Dorsoduro 1050 Venice, 30100 Italy. Tel 39 041 5222247; Fax 39 041 5212709; Email ga-ave@beniculturali.it; Web: www.gallerieaccademia.it; *Dir* Paola Marini
Open Mon 8:15 AM - 1 PM, Tues - Sun 8:15 AM - 6:15 PM, cl Jan 1, May 1, Dec 25; Admis 12 EUR, reduced admis 6 EUR; 24 room art gallery housed in the former Santa Maria della Carita church & convent complex.
Collections: Venetian paintings from the 1300s to the 1700s, works by Bellini, Carpaccio, Canaletto, Veronese, Tintoretto, Tiziano, Tiepolo, Titian, Veronese

M **MUSEO ARCHEOLOGICO NAZIONALE DI VENEZIA,** National Archaeological Museum of Venice, Piazza San Marco 17/52, Venice, 30124 Italy. Tel 041 296 7663; Fax 041 296 7606; Email pm-ven.archeologico@beniculturali.it; Web: www.polomusealeveneto.beniculturali.it; *Dir* Annamaria Larese
Open Mon - Fri 9 AM - 5 PM; Admis fee 19 EUR, reduced fee 12 EUR
Collections: Greek & Roman sculpture, jewels, coins

M **MUSEO CAPELLA SANSEVERO,** Sansevero Chapel Museum, Via Francesco de Sanctis 19/21, Naples, 80134 Italy. Tel 39 081 5518470; Email info@museosansevero.it; Web: www.museosansevero.it
Open daily 9 AM - 7 PM, cl Tues; Admis 7 EUR, reduced 5 EUR
Special Subjects: Religious Art, Sculpture, Painting-Italian
Collections: Paintings and marble statues including the Veiled Christ
Activities: Guided tours

M **PEGGY GUGGENHEIM COLLECTION MUSEUM,** Palazzo Venier dei Leoni, Dorsoduro 701 Venice, I-30123 Italy. Tel 39-041-2405-411; Fax 39-041-520-6885; Email info@guggenheim-venice.it; Web: www.guggenheim-venice.it; *Dir* Philip Rylands
Open Wed - Mon 10 AM - 6 PM, cl Tues & Christmas Day; Admis adults 15 EUR, over 65 13 EUR, students under 26 9 EUR, under 10 free
Library Holdings: Exhibition Catalogs, Photographs
Collections: European and American art of the first half of the 20th century, Personal art collection of Peggy Guggenheim in former home, Gianni Mattioli Collection, Nasher Sculpture Garden Collection, Temporary exhibitions
Activities: Classes for children; docent training; lects mems only; concerts; tours; mus shop sells books magazines & reproductions

VERONA

M **MUSEI CIVICI D' ARTE DI VERONA,** Civic Art Museums of Verona, Corso Castelvecchio, 2, Verona, 37121 Italy. Tel 39 045 8062611; Fax 39 045 8062652; Email castelvecchio@comune.verona.it; Web: museicivici.comune.verona.it; *Museums Dir* Francesca Rossi; *Dir Archaeology Unit* Margherita Bolla; *Mgmnt Sec* Alberta Faccini
Collective of eight art galleries and museums throughout Verona, Italy.

M **Galleria d' Arte Moderna Achille Forti - Achille Forti Gallery of Modern Art**, Cortile Mercato Vecchio, Verona, 37121 Italy. Tel 39 045 8001903; Fax 39 045 8031394; Email castelvecchio@comune.verona.it; Web: gam.comune.verona.it; *Dir* Francesca Rossi; *Artistic Dir* Patrizia Nuzzo
Open Tues - Fri 10 AM - 6 PM, Sat, Sun & holidays 11 AM - 7 PM; Admis 8 EUR, reduced 4 EUR

M **Museo Archaeologico al Teatro Romano - Archaeology Museum at the Roman Theater**, Regaste Redentore, 2, Verona, 37129 Italy. Tel 39 045 8000360; Fax 39 045 8010587; Email museoarcheologico@comune.verona.it; Web: museoarcheologico.comune.verona.it; *Dir Archaeology* Margherita Bolla; *Dir* Francesca Rossi
Open Mon 1:30 PM - 7:30 PM, Tues - Sun 8:30 AM - 7:30 PM; Admis 4.50 EUR, reduced 3 EUR

M **Museo di Castelvecchio - Castelvecchio Museum**, Corso Castelvecchio, 2, Verona, 37121 Italy. Tel 39 045 8062611; Fax 39 045 8062652; Email castelveccio@commune.verona.it; Web: museodicastelvecchio.comune.verona.it; *Dir.* Francesca Rossi
Open Mon 1:30 - 7 PM, Tues - Sun 9 AM - 7 PM; Admis general 6 EUR, groups of 15+, seniors & students 4.50 EUR, children 8-14 w/adult 1 EUR; Paintings and sculptures mainly from Northern Italy.; Average Annual Attendance: 150,000

M **Museo Lapidario Maffeiano - Lapidario Maffeiano Museum**, Piazza Bra, 28, Verona, 37121 Italy. Tel 39 045 590087; Fax 39 045 8062652; Email castelvecchio@comune.verona.it; Web: museomaffeiano.comune.verona.it; *Dir* Francesca Rossi
Open Tues - Sun 8:30 AM - 2 PM, cl Mon; Admin 4.50 EUR, reduced 3 EUR

M **Museo degli Affreschi Giovanni Battista Cavalcaselle e Tomba di Giulietta - Giovanni Battista Cavalcaselle Fresco Museum and Juliet's Tomb**, Via Luigi da Porto, 5, Verona, 37122 Italy. Tel 39 045 8000361; Fax 39 045 8062652; Email castelvecchio@comune.verona.it; Web: museodegliaffreschi.comune.verona.it; *Dir* Francesca Rossi
Open Mon 1:30 PM - 7:30 PM, Tues - Sun 8:30 AM - 7:30 PM; Admis 4.50 EUR, reduced 3 EUR

JAMAICA

KINGSTON

M **INSTITUTE OF JAMAICA,** National Gallery of Jamaica, 12 Ocean Blvd, Block C Kingston, Jamaica. Tel 876-922-1561/3; Fax 876-922-8544; Email info@natgalja.org.jm; Web: natgalja.org.jm; *Exec Dir* Dr Veerle Poupeye; *Chief Cur* Charles Campbell
Open Tue - Thurs 10 AM - 4:30 PM, Fri 10 AM - 4 PM, Sat 10 AM - 3 PM, cl Sun & Mon; Admis adults $400 JMD, seniors $200 JMD, students w/ID and children free; Estab 1974; Pub art gallery; Average Annual Attendance: 16,000

Collections: Permanent coll includes overview of 20th century Jamaican art since 1922 in ten galleries, Pre-twentieth century collection of Taino artifacts, Jamaican & West Indian art of the Spanish and English colonial periods, International coll of pre and post 1950 trends, Larry Wirth Collection of paintings and sculptures by Mallica Reynolds, Cecil Baugh gallery of ceramics, Edna Manley Memorial Collection, A D Scott Collection, Matalon Collection
Activities: Classes for children; lectrs open to the pub; 5 vis lectrs per yr; gallery talks; tours; Aaron Matalon Award (Nat Biennial); lending of original art to Jamaican government offices & foreign missions; mus shop sells books, magazines, reproductions & other gift items

JAPAN

AOMORI

M **AOMORI CONTEMPORARY ART CENTRE,** 152-6 Yamazaki Goshizawa, Aomori, 030-0134 Japan. Tel +81-17-764-5200; Fax +81-17-764-5201; Email acac-1@acac-aomori.jp; Web: www.acac-aomori.jp; *Cur* Hukushi Koji
Open 9 AM - 7 PM; No admis fee; Estab 2001; to provide opportunities to appreciate various art productions & to create a new art culture unique to Aomori City; Made up of three main halls: the linear Creative Hall & Residential Hall both designed with the image of bridges & the horseshoe-shaped Exhib Hall equipped with a gallery & circular rooftop stage
Library Holdings: Book Volumes
Activities: Classes for adults & children; lects open to pub; concerts; gallery talks; tours; fels

ASHIYA

M **ASHIYA CITY MUSEUM OF ART & HISTORY,** 12-25 Ise-cho, Ashiya, 659-0052 Japan. Tel +81-797-38-5432; Fax +81-797-38-5434; Web: ashiya-museum.jp
Open Tues - Sun 10 AM - 5 PM, cl Mon; Admis fee changes with exhibs; Estab 1991; art & history mus
Activities: Lects open to pub; gallery talks; mus shop sells books

ATAMI

M **MOA MUSEUM OF ART,** 26-2 Momoyama-cho, Atami, Shizuoka 413-8511 Japan. Tel 81 557 84 2511; Fax 81 557 84 2570; Web: www.moaart.or.jp; *Dir* Dr Tokugu Uchida
Open 9:30 AM - 4:30 PM, cl Thurs; Admis adults 1600 JPY, seniors 1200 JPY, high school & col students w/ID 800 JPY, children under junior high school free; Estab 1982; Mus overlooks the ocean
Collections: Paintings, calligraphies & crafts from the East

FUKUOKA

M **FUKUOKA ART MUSEUM,** 1-6 Ohori-Koen Park, Chuo-ku Fukuoka, 810-0051 Japan. Tel 092-714-6051; Email faam_e@faam.ajibi.jp; Web: www.fukuoka-art-museum.jp
Open Tues - Sat 9:30 AM - 5:30 PM, July - Aug 9:30 AM - 7:30 PM, cl Mon; Admis adults 200 JPY, high school & coll students 150 JPY, elementary & jr high school students free; Estab 1979
Collections: Modern art gallery of 20th century Japanese and international art, Small works of print and drawings, Japanese paintings, Crafts galleries, Matsunaga Collection of tea ceremony utensils and Buddhist art from Tokoin Temple, Buddhist sculptures, Pre-modern gallery, Honda Collection of Southeast Asian Ceramics, Kusuma Collection of textiles

M **FUKUOKA ASIAN ART MUSEUM,** Riverain Center Bldg 7th-8th Fl, 3-1 Shimokawabata-machi, Hakata-ku Fukuoka, Japan. Tel 092 263 1100; Fax 092 263 1105; Email faam_e@faam.ajibi.jp; Web: faam.city.fukuoka.lg.jp/eng/home.html; *Dir* Raiji Kuroda
Open 10 AM - 8 PM, cl Wed; Admis adults 200 JPY, high school & college students 150 JPY, jr high & under no charge; Estab 1999; Average Annual Attendance: 250,000
Library Holdings: Auction Catalogs, Book Volumes, DVDs, Exhibition Catalogs, Pamphlets, Periodical Subscriptions, Photographs, Prints
Collections: Modern & contemporary Asian art, Asia Collection 70: From the Collection of the Fukuoka Asian Art Mus
Activities: Classes for children; residency progs; workshops for adults & children; lects open to pub; 6 vis lectrs per yr; concerts; gallery talks; tours; artist researcher in residence; mus shop sells books, reproductions

HATSUKAICHI

M **ITSUKUSHIMA JINJA HOMOTSUKAN,** Treasure Hall of the Isukushima Shinto Shrine, Miyajima-cho, Itsukushima Hatsukaichi, Hiroshima Japan; Naruto-koen Park Service Center, Tosadomari-Ura Fukuchi 65-20 Naruto, Tokushima Japan. Tel 0829-44-2020; Fax 0829-44-0517; *Cur & Chief Priest* Motoyoshi Nozaka
Open 8 AM - 5 PM; Admis 300 JPY, high school students 200 JPY, elementary students 100 JPY
Collections: Paintings, calligraphy, sutras, swords, and other ancient weapons

HIROSHIMA

M **HIROSHIMA MUSEUM OF ART,** 3-2 Motomachi, Naka-ku Hiroshima, 730-0011 Japan. Tel 082 223 2530; Fax 082 223 2519; Email info@hiroshima-museum.jp; Web: www.hiroshima-museum.jp
Open 9 AM - 5 PM, cl Mon; Admis adults 1000 JPY, high school students 500 JPY, jr high & elementary school students 200 JPY; Estab 1978; art mus; Modern art
Collections: Modern European & Japanese Western-Style paintings
Activities: 3-4 book traveling exhibs per yr; Mus shop sells books, original art, reproductions, prints & other items

IKARUGA

M **HORYUJI,** Horyuji Temple, 1-1 Horyuji Sannai, Ikoma Ikaruga, Nara 636-0115 Japan. Tel 81 745-75-2555
Open 8 AM - 5 PM; Admis 1500 JPY; Ancient Buddhist temple
Collections: Buddhist images and paintings, the buildings date from the Asuka, Nara, Heian, Kamakura, Ashikaga, Tokugawa periods

KAGAWA

M **BENESSE ART SITE NAOSHIMA,** Chichu Art Museum, 3449-1 Naoshima, Kagawa, 761-3110 Japan. Tel +81-(0) 87-892-3755; Fax +81-(0) 87-840-8285; Email chichu-info@fukutake-artmuseum.jp; Web: www.benesse-artsite.jp; *Pres* Soichiro Fukutake
Open Mar - Sep: 10 AM - 6 PM; Oct - Feb: 10 AM - 5 PM, cl Mon; Admis adult 2060 JPY, children 15 yrs & under free; Estab 2004, as a site to rethink the relationship between nature & people; Average Annual Attendance: 120,000
Income: Managed by the Naoshima Fukutake Art Museum Foundation
Collections: Artworks of Claude Monet, Walter De Maria & James Turrell
Activities: Classes for adults & children; lects open to the pub; tours; mus shop sells books, original art, prints

KOMAKI

M **MENARD ART MUSEUM,** 5-250 Komaki, Komaki, Aichi Aichi 485-0041 Japan. Tel +81-568-75-5787; Fax +81-568-77-0626; Email museum@menard.co.jp; Web: museum.menard.co.jp; *Dir* Norimichi Aiba
Open Tues - Sun 10 AM - 5 PM (last entry 4:30 PM); Admis gen 900 JPY, high school & univ students 600 JPY, elementary & jr high school students 300 JPY; (prices for special exhibs may vary); Estab 1987

KOYASAN

M **KOYASAN SHINGON BUDDHISM SOHONZAN KONGOBUJI,** Koyasan Reihokan Museum, Yubinbango648-0211 Wakayama Koya-cho, Ito-gun Koyasan, 648-0211 Japan. Tel 0736 56 2029; Fax 0736 56 2806; Web: www.reihokan.or.jp; *Chief Cur* Shoryu Omori
Open May - Oct: 8:30 AM - 5:30 PM; Nov - April 9:30 AM - 5 PM; Admis adults 600 JPY, high school & college students 350 JPY, elementary & jr high school students 250 JPY; Estab 1921 to protect the cultural assets of Koyasan Shingon Buddhism
Collections: Buddhist paintings and images, sutras and old documents, some of them registered National Treasures and Important Cultural Properties

KURASHIKI

M **OHARA MUSEUM OF ART,** 1-1-15 Chuo, Kurashiki, Okayama 710-8575 Japan. Tel 86-422-0005; Fax 86-427-3677; Email info@ohara.or.jp; Web: www.ohara.or.jp; *Dir* Shuji Takashina
Open Tues - Sun 9 AM - 5 PM, cl Mon; Admis gen 1300 JPY, coll students 800 JPY, elementary, jr & high school students 500 JPY; Estab 11-6-1930; 4 bldgs; Main Gallery with Western Art, Annex with Japanese Art, & Craft Art & Asian Art Gallery; Kojima Torajiro Memorial Hall with Kojima's works - Ancient Egypt & Orient artifacts
Special Subjects: Antiquities-Egyptian, Antiquities-Oriental, Antiquities-Persian, Asian Art, Painting-American, Painting-European, Painting-French, Pottery, Prints, Textiles
Collections: Ancient Egyptian, Persian & Turkish ceramics & sculpture, 19th & 20th century European paintings & sculpture, modern Japanese oil paintings, pottery, sculpture & textiles, Asiatic Art, Contemporary Japanese Art
Activities: Classes for adults; classes for children; lects open to public; gallery talks; mus shop sells books, reproductions, prints, accessories, stationery

KYOTO

M **KYOTO KOKURITSU HAKUBUTSUKAN,** Kyoto National Museum, 527 Chaya-cho, Higashiyama-ku Kyoto, 605-0931 Japan. Tel (075) 541-1151; Web: www.kyohaku.go.jp; *Dir* Johei Sasaki
Open Tues - Sun 9:30 AM - 5 PM, cl Mon; Admis adult 520 JPY, university students w/ID 260 JPY, high school students or younger free; Estab 1897; Permanent coll gallery now under construction, renewal open expected 2013
Collections: Fine art, handicrafts & historical collections of Asia, chiefly Japan, over 65,000 research photographs

M **KYOTO KOKURITSU KINDAI BIJUTSUKAN,** The National Museum of Modern Art, Kyoto, Okazaki Enshoji-cho, Sakyo-ku Kyoto, 606 - 8344 Japan. Tel (81) 75-761-4111; Fax (81) 75-771-5792; Email info@ma7.momak.go.jp; Web: www.momak.go.jp; *Dir* Masaaki Ozaki; *Chief Cur* Ryuichi Matsubara; *Cur* Yuko

Ikeda; *Cur* Jitsuko Ogura; *Asst Cur* Chinatsu Makiguchi; *Assoc Cur* Yui Nakao; *Cur Advisor* Shinji Kohmoto
Open Tues - Sun 9:30 AM - 5 PM, cl Mon & cl Tues if Mon is a national holiday; Gen admis adults 430 JPY, univ students 130 JPY, high school students & jr high students & younger free; discounts to groups of 20 or more; Estab 1963; modern and contemporary art of Japan & the world
Collections: Painting (Japanese style, oil, watercolor), drawing, print, photography, sculpture, craft, and new Modern Contemporary media, Drawings, prints, photography, sculpture, crafts (ceramics, textiles, metalworks, wood and bamboo works, lacquers, jewelry), New Modern/Contemporary Media
Publications: Book on the complete collection of Japanese paintings, collection of oil on canvas, collection of prints, & collection of photography; collection catalog of photography, Nojima Yasuzo, Hasegawa Kiyoshi, Japanese-style painting, western-style painting, Kawai Kanjiro, Ikeda Masuo, W. Eugene Smith; exhibition catalogues; annual reports; Cross Sections (bulletins), Miru newsletter
Activities: Classes for adults & children; docent training; lects open to public, approx 20 per yr; concerts; gallery talks; lending of original objects of art to pub museums in Japan; Japanese painting, oil painting; approx 3 book traveling exhibs per yr; originates traveling exhibs to the National Museum of Modern Art, Tokyo & to museums in Japan; mus shop sells books, magazines, reproductions, postcards, calendars, designer goods, accessories & tableware

M **KYOTO-SHI BIJUTSUKAN,** Kyoto Municipal Museum of Art, Okazaki Park, Sakyo-ku Kyoto, 606-8344 Japan. Tel (075) 771-4107; Fax (075) 761-0444; Web: www.city.kyoto.jp/bunshi/kmma; *Dir* Kozo Shioe
Open Tues - Sun 9 AM - 5 PM, cl Mon; Admis fee depends on exhib; Estab 1933; Colls & exhibs feature modern & contemporary Kyoto
Collections: Contemporary fine art objects, including Japanese pictures, sculptures, decorative art exhibits and prints

MARUGAME

M **MARUGAME GENICHIRO-INOKUMA MUSEUM OF CONTEMPORARY ART,** 80-1 Hama-machi, Marugame, Kagawa 763-0022 Japan. Tel 0877-24-7755; Fax 0877-24-7766; Email mimoca_info@mimoca.org; Web: www.mimoca.org
Open 10 AM - 6 PM, cl Dec 25 - 30; Admis adults 300 JPY, college & univ students 200 JPY, youth under 18 yrs free; Estab 1991
Collections: 20,000 works by Japanese artist Genichiro Inokuma, contemporary art

MATSUMOTO

M **THE JAPAN UKIYO-E MUSEUM,** 2206-1 Koshiba, Shimadachi, Matsumoto, 390-0852 Japan. Tel 0263-47-4440; Fax 0263-48-0208; Web: www.japan-ukiyoe-museum.com; *Dir* Kunio Sakai
Open 10 AM - 5 PM, cl Mon; Admis adults 1200 JPY, children 600 JPY; Estab 1982
Collections: Japanese Ukiyo-e art

M **MATSUMOTO CITY MUSEUM OF ART,** 4-2-22 Chuo, Matsumoto, Nagano 390-0811 Japan. Tel 81-263-39-7400; Fax 81-263-39-3400; Email museum@city.matsumoto.nagano.jp; Web: www.city.matsumoto.nagano.jp
Open Tues - Sun 9 AM - 5 PM; Admis adults 410 JPY, 200 JPY college students, children free; Estab 2002
Collections: Art by local Japanese artists, landscapes & calligraphy

MITO

M **ART TOWER MITO, CONTEMPORARY ART CENTER,** 1-6-8 Goken-cho, Mito, Ibaraki 310-0063 Japan. Tel +81-0-29-227-8111; Fax +81-0-29-227-8110; Email webstaff@arttowermito.or.jp; Web: arttowermito.or.jp; *Dir Gen* Seiji Ozawa
Open Art Gallery: Tues - Sun 9:30 AM - 6 PM; Tower: Tues - Fri 9:30 AM - 6 PM, Sat - Sun & holidays 9:30 AM - 7 PM; Admis Art Gallery: adults 800 JPY, children under 15 yrs & seniors free; Tower: 200 JPY, children 100 JPY; Estab 1990

M **MUSEUM OF MODERN ART, IBARAKI,** 666-1, Higashi Kubo, Senba-cho Mito, Ibaraki Ibaraki 310-0851 Japan. Tel 029-243-5111; Fax 029-243-9992; Email info@modernart.museum.ibk.ed.jp; Web: www.modernart.museum.ibk.ed.jp; *Dir* Masanori Ichikawa
Open Tues - Sun 9:30 AM - 5 PM, cl Mon; Admis varies depending on exhib; Estab 1988 as a center of Ibaraki's art & culture; 2 galleries of special exhibs & 2 galleries of mus coll; Average Annual Attendance: 150,000
Special Subjects: Bronzes, Painting-French, Prints, Sculpture, Watercolors, Woodcuts
Collections: 3,400 works of modern & contemporary art

NAGAOKA

M **NIIGATA PREFECTURAL MUSEUM OF MODERN ART,** 3-278-14 Senshu, Nagaoka, Niigata 940-2083 Japan. Tel 0258-28-4111; Fax 0258-28-4115; Email kinbi@coral.ocn.ne.jp; Web: www.kinbi.pref.niigata.lg.jp; *Dir* Kenichi Tokunaga
Open Tues - Sun 9 AM - 5 PM, cl Mon; Admis 430 JPY, high school & college students 200 JPY, elementary & jr high school students free; discounts for groups; Estab 1993
Special Subjects: Calligraphy, Crafts, Drawings, Painting-French, Painting-German, Painting-Japanese, Photography, Porcelain, Posters, Pottery, Prints, Sculpture, Woodcuts
Collections: 6,000 works
Exhibitions: 4-5 exhibs of various art genres per yr
Publications: Exhib catalogs; coll catalogs
Activities: Classes for adults & children; lects open to pub; concerts; gallery talks; exten prog serves schools & community ctrs in Niigata; originates traveling exhibs; mus shop sells books, reproductions, art goods

NAGOYA

M **AICHI PREFECTURAL MUSEUM OF ART,** 1-13-2 Higashisakura, Higashi-ku Nagoya, 461-8525 Japan. Tel 052 971 5511; Fax 052 971 5604; Email apma-webmaster@aac.pref.aichi.jp; Web: www-art.aac.pref.aichi.jp
Open Tues - Thurs & Sat - Sun 10 AM - 6 PM, Fri 10 AM - 8 PM, cl Mon; Admis adults 500 JPY, high school & college students 300 JPY, children under 13 & handicapped no charge; Estab 1992; 3 exhib galleries & 5 coll galleries; Average Annual Attendance: 200,000
Collections: 20th-century fine arts, Kimura Teizo Collection

M **THE TOKUGAWA ART MUSEUM,** 1017 Tokugawa-cho, Higashi-ku Nagoya, 461-0023 Japan. Tel 81 52 935-6262; Fax 81 52 935-6261; Email info@tokugawa.or.jp; Web: www.tokugawa-art-museum.jp; *Dir* Yoshitaka Tokugawa
Open Tues - Sun 10 AM - 5 PM, cl Mon; Admis adults 1400 JPY, students 700 JPY, children 7 - 14 yrs 500 JPY; Estab 1935; Mus of the Owari Tokugawa family art collection; includes library and garden.; Mem: approx 1,000 people, 3,150-26,250 yen
Income: Financed by Owari Tokugawa Reimeikai Foundation
Special Subjects: Antiquities-Oriental, Calligraphy, Ceramics, Costumes, Maps, Painting-Japanese, Textiles
Collections: Tokugawa Family Collection of 12,000 treasures, including scrolls, swords, calligraphy & pottery
Publications: Kinko Sosho Bulletin of The Tokugawa Reimeikai Foundation; The Tokugawa Institute for the History of Forestry

NARA

M **NARA KOKURITSU HAKUBUTSU-KAN,** Nara National Museum, 50 Noborioji-Cho, Nara, 630-8213 Japan. Tel 81 (50) 5542-8600; Fax 81 (742) 26-7218; Web: www.narahaku.go.jp; *Dir* Nobuyuki Matsumoto
Open Tues - Sun 9:30 AM - 5 PM, cl Mon; Admis adults 520 JPY, univ students 260 JPY, high school students and below free; Incls a conservation ctr consisting of 3 laboratories working on restoration of National Treasures & Important Cultural Properties; also incls a tea house for tea ceremony built in 18th century
Library Holdings: Auction Catalogs, Audio Tapes, Book Volumes, CD-ROMs, Cards, Clipping Files, Compact Disks, DVDs, Exhibition Catalogs, Filmstrips, Framed Reproductions, Kodachrome Transparencies, Maps, Original Art Works, Pamphlets, Periodical Subscriptions, Photographs
Special Subjects: Asian Art, Calligraphy, Crafts, Decorative Arts, Hispanic Art, Historical Material, Manuscripts, Painting-Japanese, Religious Art, Restorations, Sculpture
Collections: Art objects of Buddhist art, mainly of Japan, including decorative arts and archaeological relics, calligraphy, paintings, sculptures, Ancient Chinese Bronzes (Sakamoto coll)
Exhibitions: The 65th Annual Exhibition of Shoso-in Treasures; See website for additional exhibs
Publications: See website
Activities: Classes for adults & children; lects open to pub; 3,000 vis lectrs per yr; guided tours available to general public, schools & company groups; concerts; gallery talks; mus store sells books, magazines, reproductions, prints, post cards& souvenirs

L **Buddhist Art Library**
Open Wed & Fri 9:30 AM - 4:30 PM; Estab 1980
Library Holdings: Auction Catalogs, Exhibition Catalogs, Periodical Subscriptions, Photographs
Special Subjects: Art History, Asian Art, Historical Material, History of Art & Archaeology, Religious Art

OSAKA

M **FUJITA BIJUTSUKAN,** Fujita Museum of Art, No 10 & 32 Youbinbango 534-0026, Miyakojima-ku Amijima-cho Osaka, 534-0026 Japan. Tel (06) 6351-0582; Fax (06) 6351-0583; Web: fujita-museum.or.jp
Open Tues - Sun 10 AM - 4:30 PM; Admis adults 800 JPY, high school & college students 500 JPY, elementary & jr high school students 300 JPY; Estab 1951
Collections: Scroll paintings, Ceramics, Japanese Paintings, Calligraphy, Buddhist Art
Activities: Mus shop sells books & prints

M **NATIONAL MUSEUM OF ART, OSAKA,** 4-2-55 Nakanoshima, Kita-ku Osaka, 530-0005 Japan. Tel 81-06-6447-4680; Fax 81-06-6447-4699; Web: www.nmao.go.jp; *Dir* Akira Tatehata
Open Tues - Sun 10 AM - 5 PM, Fri until 7 PM, cl Mon & Tues when Mon falls on national holiday; Admis adults 430 JPY, univ students 130 JPY, youth under 18 yrs & seniors free; Estab 1977
Library Holdings: Book Volumes, CD-ROMs, Compact Disks, DVDs, Exhibition Catalogs, Periodical Subscriptions, Photographs, Slides, Video Tapes
Collections: Japanese and international modern art in various media
Activities: Classes for children; Lects open to the public, concerts, gallery talks

M **OSAKA-SHIRITSU HAKUBUTSUKAN,** Osaka Municipal Museum of Art, 1-82 Chausuyama-Cho, Tennoji-ku Osaka, 543-0063 Japan. Tel (06) 6771-4874; Fax (06) 6771-4856; Web: www.osaka-art-museum.jp; *Dir* Yutaka Mino
Open Tues - Sun 9:30 AM - 5 PM, cl Mon; Admis fee adults 300 JPY, high school students 200 JPY, jr high students & under free; Estab 1936
Collections: Art of China, Korea & Japan

OTSU

M **THE MUSEUM OF MODERN ART, SHIGA,** 1740-1 Seta-Minamiogaya-Cho, Otsu, Shiga 520 2122 Japan. Tel 077-543-2111; Fax 077-543-4220; Email info@shiga-kinbi.jp; Web: www.shiga-kinbi.jp
Open Tues - Sun 9:30 AM - 5 PM, cl Mon; Admis adults 500 JPY, high school & univ students 300 JPY, jr high school students & younger free
Collections: Contemporary art, modern Japanese style painting & crafts

TOKYO

M **BRIDGESTONE BIJUTSUKAN,** Bridgestone Museum of Art, 1-10-1 Kyobashi, Chuo-ku Tokyo, 104-0031 Japan. Tel (03) 3563-0241; *Chief Cur* Tsuyoshi Kaizuka
Open Tues - Thurs, Sat & Sun 10 AM - 6 PM, Fri 10 AM - 8 PM, cl Mon; Admis fee adults 800 JPY, seniors 600 JPY, students 500 JPY, children 15 yrs & under free; Estab 1952
Collections: Foreign paintings, mainly Impressionism and after, western style paintings late 19th century to present

M **THE NATIONAL ART CENTER, TOKYO,** 7-22-2 Roppongi Minato-ku, Tokyo, 106-8558 Japan. Tel 03-5777-8600; Fax 03-3405-2531; Web: www.nact.jp; *Dir Gen* Tamosu Aoki
Open Mon, Wed, Thurs & Sun 10 AM - 6 PM, Fri & Sat 10 AM - 8 PM, cl Tues; Admis varies per exhib; 14,000 sq meters of exhib space; art library
Income: Independent Administrative Institution National Museum of Art
Special Subjects: Asian Art, Painting-Japanese, Crafts, Mixed Media, Photography, Sculpture, Decorative Arts, Landscapes, Portraits
Collections: Modern & contemporary art, post-WWII Japanese art
Exhibitions: Rotating exhibits; spec exhibs of works on loan from around the world
Publications: Exhib catalouges
Activities: Educ progs; artist workshops; lects open to pub; gallery talks; tours; art programming; conferences; symposiums; outreach progs; educ exten projects; mus shop sells books, original art, reproductions, gifts

TOKYO

M **IDEMITSU MUSEUM OF ARTS,** 3-1-1 Marunouchi, Teigeki Bldg, Fl 9, Chiyoda-ku Tokyo, 100-0005 Japan. Tel 03-3213-9402; Fax 03-3213-8473; Web: www.idemitsu.co.jp/museum; *Mng Dir* Hiroyasu Yamato
Open Tues - Thurs & Sat - Sun 10 AM - 5 PM, Fri 10 AM - 7 PM, cl Mon; Admis adults 1000 JPY, high school & college students 700 JPY, jr high school students & younger free; Estab 1966; Average Annual Attendance: 150,000; Mem: 700 mems; ann dues 8,000 yen
Income: Financed by donations
Special Subjects: Asian Art, Painting-American, Painting-French, Painting-Japanese
Collections: Oriental art & ceramics, Japanese paintings, calligraphy, Chinese bronzes, lacquer wares & paintings by Georges Rouault, Sam Francis
Activities: Lects open to pub; lects for members only; mus shop sells books & reproductions

M **THE NATIONAL MUSEUM OF MODERN ART, TOKYO,** 3-1 Kitanomaru-koen, Chiyoda-ku Tokyo, 102-8322 Japan. Tel (03) 5777-8600; Web: www.momat.go.jp; *Dir* Hisashi Okajima; *Chief Cur* Kuraya Mika
Open Tues - Thurs & Sun 10 AM - 5 PM, Fri & Sat 10 AM - 8 PM, cl Mon (except when Mon is a holiday, the mus is open & cl on Tues) yr-end & New Year holidays and during change of exhib; Admis adults 500 JPY, college students 250 JPY, high school students, seniors over 65 & children under 18 free; Estab 1952
Income: Independent Administrative Institution National Museum of Art
Library Holdings: Auction Catalogs, Book Volumes, CD-ROMs, Clipping Files, Compact Disks, DVDs, Exhibition Catalogs, Fiche, Micro Print, Other Holdings, Pamphlets, Periodical Subscriptions, Photographs, Reels, Video Tapes
Special Subjects: Bronzes, Calligraphy, Ceramics, Collages, Crafts, Dolls, Drawings, Drawings, Etchings & Engravings, Glass, Gold, Graphics, Painting-Japanese, Photography, Prints, Sculpture, Watercolors, Landscapes, Manuscripts, Porcelain, Portraits, Posters, Prints
Collections: Drawings, paintings, photographs, prints, sculptures, watercolors, videos
Publications: Mus Newsletter, Gendai no Me (Japanese); Catalogue (Bilingual); Annual Report (Bilingual); Bulletin (Bilingual)
Activities: Classes for adults & children offered in Japanese only; docent training; lects open to pub; concerts; gallery talks; tours; lending of original objects of art to museums (world); originates traveling exhib to museums mainly in Japan; mus shop sells books, magazines, original art, reproductions & prints; jr mus located at Crafts Gallery, 1-1 Kitanomaru-Koen, Chiyoda-Ku, Tokyo 102-0091; Nat Film Ctr, 3-7-6 Kyobashi, Chao-Ku, Tokyo 104-0031

M **Crafts Gallery**, 1-1 Kitanomaru-koen, Chiyoda-ku Tokyo, 102-0091 Japan. *Chief Cur* Mitsuhiki Hasebe
Collections: Ceramics, lacquer ware, metalworks, Works by Living National Treasures

M **National Film Center**, 3-7-6 Kyobashi, Chuo-ku Tokyo, 104-0031 Japan.
Open Tues - Sun 11 AM - 6:30 PM; Admis adults 520 JPY, high school & university students & seniors 310 JPY, elementary & jr high students 100 JPY

M **THE NATIONAL MUSEUM OF WESTERN ART,** 7-7 Ueno-koen, Taito-ku, Tokyo, 110-0007 Japan. Tel 81-3-5777-8600; Fax 81-3-3828-5135; Email info@nmwa.go.jp; Web: www.nmwa.go.jp; *Dir Gen* Akiko Mabuchi; *Deputy Dir & Chief Cur* Hiroya Murakami
Open Tues - Thurs & Sun 9:30 AM - 5:30 PM, Fri & Sat 9:30 AM - 8 PM, cl Mon and Dec 28 - Jan 1; Admis adults 500 JPY, college students 250 JPY, high school students or younger, persons under 18 yrs & over 65 yrs free; Estab 1959; Average Annual Attendance: 989,344
Income: Independent Administrative Institution National Museum of Art
Library Holdings: Auction Catalogs, Book Volumes, Clipping Files, Exhibition Catalogs, Fiche, Pamphlets, Periodical Subscriptions, Reproductions
Special Subjects: Baroque Art, Bronzes, Decorative Arts, Drawings, Etchings & Engravings, Jewelry, Landscapes, Medieval Art, Painting-British, Painting-Dutch, Painting-European, Painting-Flemish, Painting-French, Painting-German, Painting-Italian, Painting-Scandinavian, Painting-Spanish, Portraits, Prints, Religious Art, Renaissance Art, Sculpture, Tapestries, Watercolors
Collections: Western paintings from late medieval period through the early 20th century, French modern sculpture
Activities: Classes for adults & children; lects open to pub, concerts, gallery talks; mus shop sells books, magazines, reproductions, prints, others

M **NEZU BIJUTSUKAN,** Nezu Museum, 6-5-1 Minami-Aoyama, Minato-ku Tokyo, 107-0062 Japan. Tel (3) 3400 2536; Fax (3) 3400 2436; Web: www.nezu-muse.or.jp; *Dir* Nezu Koichi; *Deputy Dir* Hiroko Nishida
Open Tues - Sun 10 AM - 5 PM, cl Mon; Admis special exhib 1200 JPY, mus coll exhib 1000 JPY; Estab 1940, opened 1941, to preserve & exhib East Asian arts; 6 galleries for exhib different types of Japanese & East Asian arts; Mem: Nezu Club: 3,000 JPY per yr
Collections: Nezu Kaichiro, Sr's private collection & donations, incl about 7,000 items of calligraphy, sculpture, paintings, sword fittings, ceramics, lacquer-ware, archeological exhibits, 7 items designated as national treasures, 87 items designated as Important Cultural Properties
Exhibitions: 8 exhibs per yr
Publications: Coll catalog; exhib catalog; annual bulletin
Activities: Classes for adults; lects open to pub; gallery talks; tea ceremonies (limited for guests & mems); exten dept serves other mus; mus shop sells books, magazines, original art

M **NIHON MINGEIKAN,** Japan Folk Crafts Museum, 4-3-33 Komaba, Meguro-ku, Tokyo, 153-0041 Japan. Tel 81 3 3467 4527; Fax 81 3 3467 4537; Email intl@mingeikan.or.jp; Web: www.mingeikan.or.jp; *Dir* Naota Fukasawa
Open 10 AM - 5 PM, cl Mon; Admis 1100 JPY, high school & univ students 600 JPY, elementary & jr high students 200 JPY; Estab 1936; to introduce Mingei (the arts of the people); 4 large exhibits per yr; two-story building of stone and stucco with black tile roof, designed after traditional Japanese architecture by Soetsu Yanagi (1889-1961) founder of the museum; Average Annual Attendance: 50,000; monthly magazine Mingei; Mem: Dues 5,000 yen
Income: Nonprofit organization
Library Holdings: Book Volumes, CD-ROMs, Cassettes, Clipping Files, Compact Disks, DVDs, Kodachrome Transparencies, Manuscripts, Maps, Micro Print, Original Art Works, Original Documents, Pamphlets, Periodical Subscriptions, Photographs, Prints, Records, Slides, Video Tapes
Special Subjects: African Art, Watercolors
Collections: Folk-craft art objects from all parts of the world, works by Shoji Hamada, Kanjiro Kawai, Shiko Munakota, Keisuke, Serizawa, Bernard Leach, other Mingei Movement advocators
Activities: Educ prog; weaving; dyeing; letter painting; lacquerware; Lects open to pub; 5-6 vis lectrs per year; lects open to the pub; 4 lectrs per yr; annual New Works competition awards every fall; Japan Folk Crafts Mus Encouragement prizes; gallery talks; tours; lending of original objects of art to other high quality mus worldwide; book traveling exhibs, 1-2 per yr worldwide; mus shop sells books, prints, pottery, textiles, lacquered woodwork; original art; magazines, porcelain, ceramics, weaving, paper

M **TOKYO NATIONAL MUSEUM,** 13-9 Ueno Park, Taito-ku, Tokyo, 110-8712 Japan. Tel 81-(3)-5777-8600; Web: www.tnm.jp; *Exec Dir* Zeniya Masami; *Pres* Keiji Matsumura
Open Tues - Sun 9:30 AM - 5 PM, cl Mon & year-end holidays; Admis adults 620 JPY, univ students 410 JPY, seniors, elementary, jr & high school students & persons under 18 free; Estab 1872; Average Annual Attendance: 2,416,281; Mem: dues 10,300 JPY
Income: Independent Administrative Institution National Institutes for Cultural Heritage
Special Subjects: Antiquities-Oriental, Archaeology, Asian Art, Bronzes, Calligraphy, Carpets & Rugs, Ceramics, Coins & Medals, Costumes, Crafts, Decorative Arts, Dolls, Drawings, Embroidery, Etchings & Engravings, Ethnology, Folk Art, Furniture, Glass, Gold, Graphics, Historical Material, Ivory, Jade, Jewelry, Laces, Leather, Manuscripts, Maps, Metalwork, Miniatures, Oriental Art, Painting-Japanese, Pewter, Photography, Porcelain, Sculpture, Silver, Tapestries, Textiles, Woodcarvings, Prints, Primitive art, Pottery
Collections: Eastern fine arts, including paintings, calligraphy, sculpture, metal work, ceramic art, textiles, lacquer ware, archaeological exhibits
Exhibitions: Exhibs throughout the yr; 6-5 special exhibs annually
Activities: Classes for adults & children; lects open to pub; concerts; gallery talks; tours; mus shop sells books, magazines, original art, reproductions

M **TOKYO UNIVERSITY OF THE ARTS,** The University Art Museum, 12-8 Ueno Park, Taito-ku, Yubinbangol110-0007 Tokyo, 110-8714 Japan. Tel +81-50-5525-2200; Web: www.geidai.ac.jp; *Mgr* Katsuyuki Matsui
Open during exhibs only; Admis varies with exhibs; Estab 1970
Special Subjects: Archaeology, Architecture, Asian Art, Bronzes, Calligraphy, Ceramics, Crafts, Drawings, Metalwork, Painting-Japanese, Porcelain, Pottery, Sculpture, Textiles, Woodcuts
Collections: Paintings, sculptures & crafts of Japan, China & Korea
Publications: Tokyo Geijutsu Daigaku Daigaku Bijutsukan Nenpo
Activities: Mus shop sells books

M **TOKYOTO BIJUTSUKAN,** Tokyo Metropolitan Art Museum, 8-36 Ueno-koen, Taito-ku Tokyo, 110-007 Japan. Fax (03) 3823-6920, (03) 3823-6921; Web: www.tobikan.jp; *Dir* Shinshitsu KeiTakeshi
Open Mon - Thurs & Sat - Sun 9:30 AM - 5:30 PM, Fri 9:30 AM - 8 PM, cl every 1st & 3rd Mon of month; Free admis; Estab 1926
Collections: Sculptures

YOKOHAMA

M **YOKOHAMA MUSEUM OF ART,** 3-4-1 Minatomirai, Nishi-ku Yokohama, 220-0012 Japan. Tel +81-(0) 45-221-0300; Fax +81-(0) 45-221-0317; Email yma-mado@yaf.or.jp; Web: www.yokohama.art.museum; *Dir* Eriko Osaka
Open 10 AM - 6 PM; Admis adults 500 JPY, high school & college students 300 JPY, jr high school students 100 JPY, children of & below elementary school age free; Estab 1989; Average Annual Attendance: 700,000
Income: 100 million JPY
Library Holdings: Auction Catalogs, Book Volumes, DVDs, Periodical Subscriptions, Video Tapes
Special Subjects: Architecture, Art Education, Asian Art, Bronzes, Ceramics, Collages, Crafts, Drawings, Etchings & Engravings, Glass, Graphics, Landscapes, Latin American Art, Painting-American, Painting-British, Painting-French, Painting-German, Painting-Japanese, Painting-Russian, Painting-Spanish, Photography, Photography, Porcelain, Portraits, Pottery, Prints, Reproductions, Sculpture, Tapestries, Watercolors, Woodcarvings, Woodcuts
Collections: Works of European & Japanese modern art, contemporary decorative arts, graphic design, architecture & film
Activities: Classes for adults & children; lects open to pub; 1,500 vis lectrs per year; concerts; gallery talks; tours; mus shop sells books, magazines, original art, reproductions, prints

JORDAN

AMMAN

M **DARAT AL FUNUN - THE KHALID SHOMAN FOUNDATION,** 13 Nadeem al Mallah St., PO Box 5223 Amman, 11183 Jordan. Tel 962 6 4643251; Fax 962 6 4643253; Email darat@daratalfununorg; Web: daratalfunun.org; *Founder* Suha Shoman; *Dir* Luma Hamdan; *Art Dir* Eline van der Vlist
Open Sat - Thurs 10 AM - 7 PM; Ramadan 10 AM - 3 PM; Estab 1988 to spread awareness in the fields of the arts, architecture & archaeology; Cultural institution housed across eight buildings and archaeological site
Collections: Paintings, prints, sculptures, drawings, photographs & illustrations by 69 Arab artists, Khalid Shoman Collection
Activities: Educ progs; artist-in-res progs

M **JORDAN NATIONAL GALLERY OF FINE ARTS,** PO Box 9068, Amman, 11191 Jordan. Tel 00-962-6-463-0128; Fax 00-962-6-465-1119; Email info@nationalgallery.org; Web: www.nationalgallery.org; *Dir Gen* Dr Khalid Khreis
Open summer Mon, Wed - Thurs & Sat - Sun 9 AM - 7 PM, winter Mon, Wed - Thurs & Sat - Sun 9 AM - 5 PM, cl Tues & Fri; Admis 7 JOD; Estab 1980; Contemporary art from the developing world
Library Holdings: CD-ROMs, Cards, DVDs, Exhibition Catalogs
Special Subjects: African Art, Architecture, Art Education, Art History, Asian Art, Calligraphy, Ceramics, Collages, Drawings, Etchings & Engravings, Furniture, Graphics, History of Art & Archaeology, Illustration, Islamic Art, Landscape Architecture, Landscapes, Manuscripts, Miniatures, Mixed Media, Painting-American, Painting-British, Painting-French, Painting-Italian, Painting-Japanese, Painting-Russian, Painting-Spanish, Photography, Portraits, Prints, Sculpture, Tapestries, Textiles, Watercolors, Woodcarvings, Woodcuts
Collections: Over 2000 permanent works including paintings, prints, sculptures, photographs, installations, weavings, and ceramics by more than 900 artists from 60 countries, Neo Orientalist Coll
Activities: Classes for adults & children in graphic art; lects open to the pub; concerts, gallery talks; tours; sponsoring of competitions; touring mus to the pub living in distant areas; organize traveling exhibs worldwide; mus shop sells books, magazines, reproductions, prints & other mus items; jr mus

KAZAKHSTAN

ALMATY

M **A KASTEYEV STATE MUSEUM OF FINE ARTS,** 22/1 Koktem-3 md, Almaty, 480070 Kazakhstan. Tel 7-727-394-55-19; Web: www.gmirk.kz; *Dir* Gulmira Shalabeyeva
Open Tues - Sun 11 AM - 7 PM; Admis adults 500 KZT, seniors & students 300 KZT, children 200 KZT; Estab 1976
Collections: Over 20,000 pieces of painting, graphics, sculpture, and decorative art from local and international artists

KOREA, REPUBLIC OF

GWACHEON

M **NATIONAL MUSEUM OF MODERN AND CONTEMPORARY ART, KOREA,** 313 Gwangmyeong-ro, Gwacheon, Gyeonggi-do 13829 Korea, Republic of. Tel 82-2-2188-6000; Fax 82-2-2188-6124; Web: www.moca.go.kr; *Dir* Bartomeu Mari
Open Mar - Oct Tues - Fri & Sun 10 AM - 6 PM, Sat 10 AM - 9 PM; Nov - Feb Tues - Fri & Sun 10 AM - 5 PM, Sat 10 AM - 9 PM; Admis fee varies according to exhib, under 24 or over 65, college students, members, veterans, and persons with disabilities free; Estab 1969; Modern and contemporary art mus with branches in Gwacheon, Seoul, Deoksugung and Cheongju
Income: Government
Library Holdings: Auction Catalogs, Audio Tapes, Book Volumes, CD-ROMs, Clipping Files, Compact Disks, Exhibition Catalogs, Fiche, Memorabilia, Pamphlets, Periodical Subscriptions, Photographs, Prints, Slides, Video Tapes
Collections: Collection of contemporary Korean painting from 1910 to the present, Sculptures, craft, and decorative art, media art, installation art
Activities: Classes for adults & children; docent training; 10-15 vis lectrs per yr; concerts; gallery talks; tours; extension prog in Seoul & Gwacheon; mus shop sells books, magazines; National Museum of Art, Deoksugung, 99 Sejongdae-ro, Jung-gu Seoul

SEOUL

M **NATIONAL MUSEUM OF KOREA,** 137 Seoubinggo-ro (168-6 Yongsan-dong 6-ga), Yongsan-gu Seoul, 04383 Korea, Republic of. Tel 82-2-2077-9000; Email sywoo@korea.kr; Web: www.museum.go.kr; *Dir Gen* Bae Kidong
Open Mon, Tues, Thurs & Fri 10 AM - 6 PM, Wed & Sat 10 AM - 9 PM, Sun & holidays 10 AM - 7 PM, cl Jan 1; Admis is free for permanent exhibs; Twelve branch mus & library
Collections: Korean archaeology, culture & folklore

M **SEOUL MUSEUM OF ART,** 61 Deoksugung-gil (37 Seosomun-dong), Jung-gu, Seoul, 04515 Korea, Republic of. Tel 82-02-2124-8800; Email sema@seoul.go.kr; Web: sema.seoul.go.kr; *Dir Gen* Kim Hong-hee
Admis adults 700 KRW, youth & military/police 300 KRW, over 65 and under 12 free; Open March - Oct Tues - Fri 10 AM - 8 PM, Sat - Sun 10 AM - 7 PM, Nov - Feb Tues - Fri 10 AM - 8 PM, Sat - Sun 10 AM - 6 PM; Representative art mus of Seoul, the capital of Korea
Collections: Currently holds 3,500 pieces of art incl painting, sculpture, installation & media art as well as works from the masters in Korean art history

KUWAIT

JABRIYA

M **TAREQ RAJAB MUSEUM OF ISLAMIC ART,** Block 12 St 5, Bldg 22 Jabriya, 32036 Kuwait. Tel 965 2531-7358; Fax 965 2533-9063; Email ziad@trmkt.com; Web: www.trmkt.com; *Dir* Dr Ziad TS Rajab
Open daily 9 AM - noon & 4 PM - 7 PM, Fri 9 AM - noon; Admis 2 KWD; Estab 1980
Collections: Calligraphy, manuscripts, miniatures, ceramics, metalwork, glass, carvings, Artifacts from the Islamic world of the past 250 years; costumes, textiles, jewelry, and musical instruments, 30,000 items collected over last 50 years

KYRGYZSTAN

BISHKEK

M **GAPAR AITIEV KYRGYZ NATIONAL MUSEUM OF FINE ARTS,** ul. Abdrakhmanov 196, Bishkek, 720000 Kyrgyzstan. Tel 996-312-661623, 664959; Fax 996-312-620548; Email knmii@mail.ru; Web: www.knmii.kg; *Dir* Shygaev Yuristanbek Abdievich
Open Tues - Fri 10 AM - 4:30 PM, cl Mon & last Fri of the month; Admis adults 40 KGS, students 20 KGS; Estab 1935 and dedicated to Kyrgyz folk & applied art
Income: Government institution
Collections: 18,000 works of art; paintings, drawings, sculptures and traditional decorative and applied art, Several galleries of paintings from Soviet period, Replica Egyptian, Greek and classical Western sculptures, Collection of linocuts based on Manas epic
Activities: Classes for adults & children; mus shop sells books, magazines, prints, souvenirs

LATVIA

RIGA

M **LATVIJAS NACIONALAIS MAKSLAS MUZEJS,** Latvian National Museum of Art, 10 K Valdemara St, Riga, 1010 Latvia. Tel 371-67-324 461; Fax 371-67-357408; Email lnmm@lnmm.lv; Web: www.inmm.lv; *Dir* Mara Lace; *Deputy Dir Admin* Iveta Derkusova; *Deputy Dir Coll Servs* Ruta Lapina
Open Tues - Thur 10 AM - 6 PM, Fri 10 AM - 8 PM, Sat 10 AM - 5 PM, Sun 10 AM - 5 PM; Admis adults 3 LVL, students, children & seniors 1.50 LVL; Estab 1905; National art mus of Latvia; Average Annual Attendance: 100,000
Income: financed by government of Latvia
Special Subjects: Sculpture
Collections: More than 52,000 works of art reflecting the development of art in the Baltic area and Latvia from 18th century to present, Russian art from the 19th century to early 20th century, Latvian art of 2nd half of 20th century
Exhibitions: Permanent & special exhibs
Publications: Catalogues; research publs; mus writings, ann
Activities: Classes for adults & children; creative workshops; exhib hall arsenals showing contemporary exhibs; lects open to pub; 1,000 vis lectrs per yr; gallery talks; tours; organize traveling exhibs to other mus; mus shop sells books, reproductions, prints, & souvenirs

M **Arsenals Exhibition Hall,** 1 Torna St, Riga, 1050 Latvia. Tel 371-67-357527; Fax 371-67-357520; Email pr.service@lnmm.lv; Web: www.lnmm.lv; *Adminr* Velga

Pule; *Head of Colls & Scientific Research Dept* Elita Ansone; *Cur Press, Information & Publicity* Natalie Suyunshalieva
Open Tues, Wed, Fri 12 - 6 PM, Thurs 12 - 8 PM, Sat, Sun 12 - 5 PM; cl Mon & pub holidays; Admis adults 2.50 LVL, students, children & seniors 1.50 LVL; Estab 1989; Exhib hall; Average Annual Attendance: 50,000
Library Holdings: Book Volumes, Compact Disks, Exhibition Catalogs, Original Documents, Periodical Subscriptions, Photographs
Special Subjects: Coins & Medals, Collages, Drawings, Etchings & Engravings, Glass, Graphics, Landscapes, Miniatures, Painting-Russian, Photography, Porcelain, Portraits, Posters, Prints, Restorations, Sculpture, Watercolors, Woodcarvings, Woodcuts
Collections: Latvian art of the late 20th century to the present
Activities: Classes for adults & children; lects open to the pub; concerts; gallery talks; tours; extension prog; lending of original art on request; organize traveling exhibs on request; mus shop sells books & magazines

LEBANON

BEIRUT

M **AMERICAN UNIVERSITY OF BEIRUT ARCHAEOLOGICAL MUSEUM,** Bliss St, Beirut, Lebanon; PO Box 11-0236, Beirut, Lebanon. Tel 961-1-759665; Fax 961-1-363235; Email museum@aub.edu.lb; Web: www.aub.edu.lb; *Dir* Dr Leila Badre; *Admin Asst* Amale Feghali; *Research Asst* Nesrine Aad; *Mus Asst* Reine Mady
Open winter Mon - Fri 9 AM - 5 PM, summer 10 AM - 4 PM, cl holidays; No admis fee; Estab 1868; Average Annual Attendance: 3700; Mem: 330; dues Fellows $500; Contributors $200; Family $150; Members $100; Students $10
Library Holdings: Auction Catalogs, Audio Tapes, Cards, Cassettes, Compact Disks, Kodachrome Transparencies, Lantern Slides, Maps, Memorabilia, Motion Pictures, Pamphlets, Photographs
Special Subjects: Archaeology, Bronzes, Ceramics, Coins & Medals, Glass, Gold, Islamic Art, Ivory, Jewelry, Mosaics
Collections: Bronze and Iron Age Near Eastern pottery colls, bronze figurines, weapons and implements of the Bronze Age Near East, Greco-Roman imports of pottery from Near East sites, Paleolithic-Neolithic flint coll, Phoenician glass coll, pottery coll of Islamic periods, substantial coin coll
Activities: Classes for children; dramatic programs; docent training; lects for members & pub; 10 vis lectrs per yr; gallery talks & tours; lending of original objects of art to museums abroad; mus shop sells books, magazines, original art & reproductions, prints, pottery & jewelry

M **DAHESHITE MUSEUM AND LIBRARY,** PO Box 202, Beirut, 04309 Lebanon. *Dir* Dr A S M Dahesh
Library with 30,000 vols
Collections: Aquarelles, gouaches, original paintings, engravings, sculptures in marble, bronze, ivory and wood carvings

M **NATIONAL MUSEUM OF BEIRUT,** Rue de Damas & Ave Abdallah Yafi, Beirut, Lebanon. Tel 961-1 426704; Email info@beirutnationalmuseum.com; Web: www.beirutnationalmuseum.com; *Cur* Anne Marie Maila-Afeiche
Open Tues - Sun 9 AM - 5 PM; Admis 5000 LBP, students & under 18 1000 LBP; Estab 1923 to house all antiquities uncovered on Lebanese territory
Collections: Anthropological sarcophagi of the Greco-Persian period, Byzantine mosaics, royal arms, jewels and statues of the Phoenician epoch, Dr C Ford Collection of 25 sarcophagi of the Greek and Hellenistic epoch, goblets, mosaics, relief and sarcophagi of the Greco-Roman period, Arabic woods and ceramics

M **NICOLAS IBRAHIM SURSOCK MUSEUM,** Rue Sursock, Ashrafieh Beirut, 2071 5509 Lebanon. Tel 961-1-202-001; Email info@sursock.museum; *Dir* Zeina Arida
Open during exhibs
Collections: Exhibitions of contemporary Lebanese and international artists

LIBERIA

MONROVIA

M **NATIONAL MUSEUM OF LIBERIA,** Broad & Buchanan Sts, PO Box 3223 Monrovia, Liberia. Tel 218-21-3330292; *Dir* Albert S. Markeh
Open Mon - Sat 9 AM - 4 PM, Sun 2 PM - 4 PM; Admis 5 LRD
Collections: Liberian history & art

LIBYA

TRIPOLI

M **ASSARAYA ALHAMRA MUSEUM,** Red Castle Museum, Old City, Tripoli, Libya. Tel 38116/7; *Dir Dept of Antiquities* Dr Salah Agab
Estab 1919; Administered by Dept of Antiquities
Collections: Archaeology from Libyan sites

LIECHTENSTEIN

VADUZ

M **KUNSTMUSEUM LIECHTENSTEIN,** Liechtenstein Art Museum, Stadtle 32, Postfach 370 Vaduz, 9490 Liechtenstein. Tel 423-235 03 00; Fax 423-235 03 29; Email mail@kunstmuseum.li; Web: www.kunstmuseum.li; *Dir* Dr Friedemann Malsch; *Cur* Christiane Meyer-Stoll; *Mktg & Commun* Melanie Buchel
Open Tues - Sun 10 AM - 5 PM, Thurs 10 AM - 8 PM; Admis 15 CHF, reduced 10 CHF; Estab 2000; Mus of modern & contemporary art.
Activities: Educ prog; lects open to pub; mus shop sells books

LITHUANIA

KAUNAS

M **M K CIURLIONIS NATIONAL MUSEUM OF ART,** Vlado Putvinskio 55, Kaunas, LT-44248 Lithuania. Tel 370-37 229475; Fax 370-37 222606; Email mkc.info@takas.lt; Web: www.ciurlionis.lt; *Dir* Osvaldas Daugelis
Open Sept - May Tues - Sun 11 AM - 5 PM, June - Aug Tues - Sun 11 AM - 7 PM; Admis 2 EUR; Estab 1921
Collections: Lithuanian, European & Oriental art, 5 related galleries & museums in Kaunas & Druskininkai

VILNIUS

M **CONTEMPORARY ART CENTRE,** Vokieciu 2, Vilnius, 01130 Lithuania. Tel 370-5-2121945; Fax 370-5-2623954; Email info@cac.lt; Email renata@cac.lt; Web: www.cac.lt; *Cur & Editor* Asta Vaiciulyte; *Dir* Kestutis Kuizinas
Open Tues - Sun 12 PM - 8 PM; Admis 8 LTL; Estab 1969

M **LITHUANIAN ART MUSEUM,** Didzioji St 4, Vilnius, LT 01128 Lithuania. Tel 370-5 2628030; Fax 370-5 2126006; Email muziejus@ldm.lt; Web: www.ldm.lt; *Dir* Romualdas Budrys
Open Tues - Sat 11 AM - 5:30 PM, Sun & before national holiday noon - 5 PM, cl Mon & national holidays; Admis 6 LTL, students 3 LTL, children under 7 yrs, disabled & ICOM mem free; Estab 1907; Average Annual Attendance: 170500; Mem: ICOM, ICOM-Lietuva, Assn of Lithuanian Museums
Income: State budget funding provided
Purchases: Avg 17% of annual budget amount
Library Holdings: Book Volumes, CD-ROMs, Cards, Cassettes, Compact Disks, DVDs, Exhibition Catalogs, Lantern Slides, Manuscripts, Maps, Memorabilia, Original Art Works, Original Documents, Pamphlets, Periodical Subscriptions, Photographs, Prints, Reproductions, Video Tapes
Collections: Folk Art, Lithuanian & foreign fine and decorative arts from 14th century to present
Activities: Classes for adults & children; dramatic progs; docent training; family & specialized progs; Lects for members only; concerts, tours; originate traveling exhibs countrywide, worldwide, & to Europe; mus shop sells books, magazines, reproductions

LUXEMBOURG

LUXEMBOURG CITY

M **MUSEE NATIONAL D'HISTOIRE ET D'ART LUXEMBOURG,** Luxembourg National Museum of History and Art, Marche-aux-Poissons, Luxembourg City, 2345 Luxembourg. Tel 352-47-93-30-1; Fax 352-47-93-30-271; Email musee@mnha.etat.lu; Web: www.mnha.lu; *Prof Dir* Michel Polfer; *Chief Cur Fine Arts* Dr Malgorzata Nowara; *Chief Cur Numismatics* Francois Reinert; *Chief Cur Applied Arts* Jean-Luc Mousset
Open Tues - Wed & Fri - Sun 10 AM - 6 PM, Thurs 10 AM - 8 PM, cl Mon; Admis 7 EUR; Estab 1939, new bldg 2002; National collection of archaeology, history, fine & applied arts.; Average Annual Attendance: 60,000
Library Holdings: Auction Catalogs, Book Volumes, CD-ROMs, DVDs, Exhibition Catalogs, Kodachrome Transparencies, Manuscripts, Maps, Original Documents, Other Holdings, Periodical Subscriptions, Photographs, Prints, Slides
Special Subjects: Antiquities-Roman, Archaeology, Baroque Art, Ceramics, Coins & Medals, Collages, Crafts, Decorative Arts, Drawings, Etchings & Engravings, Folk Art, Furniture, Glass, Gold, Graphics, Historical Material, Maps, Medieval Art, Metalwork, Mosaics, Painting-Dutch, Painting-European, Painting-Flemish, Painting-French, Painting-German, Painting-Italian, Photography, Porcelain, Portraits, Pottery, Prints, Religious Art, Renaissance Art, Restorations, Sculpture, Silver, Stained Glass, Textiles, Watercolors
Collections: Archaeological and ethnographic items from Luxembourg from pre-history through the 9th century, Decorative arts, medals, and weapons, Old Master paintings (4th century - 9th century), Modern & contemporary art
Activities: Classes for children; lectrs open to the public; 6 vis lectrs per year; gallery talks; tours; original objects of art lent to national & foreign institutions; mus shop sells books, magazines, reproductions, prints, slides, & games etc

MACAU

NAPE

M **MACAU MUSEUM OF ART,** Macau Cultural Centre, Avenida Xian Xing Hai s/n NAPE, Macau. Tel 853-8791-9814; Fax 853-2875 3174; Email mam@icm.gov.mo; Web: www.mam.gov.mo; *Chmn Admin Comt* Tam Vai Man; *Dir* Chan Hou Seng
Open Mus 10 AM - 7 PM, no admis after 6:30 PM, cl Mon; Libr Tues - Fri 2 PM - 7 PM, Sat & Sun 11 AM - 7 PM, cl Mon & pub holidays; Admis adults 5 MOP, student 2 MOP, under 12 & over 65 free, free on Sun; Estab 1999; Average Annual Attendance: 90,000; Mem: Annual 30 - 50 MOP
Income: Financed by Macau Civic and Municipal Affairs Bureau
Library Holdings: Book Volumes, DVDs, Exhibition Catalogs, Maps, Photographs, Prints
Special Subjects: Asian Art, Calligraphy, Ceramics, Photography, Primitive art, Watercolors
Collections: Chinese calligraphy and paintings, seals, ceramics, copperwares, Western paintings, contemporary art, photography and more, Performance Art, Furniture
Exhibitions: A Glimpse of the Past: Old Macau Photos; Historical Paintings of Macau in the 19th Century
Publications: Exhibition Catalogs
Activities: Courses for children, adults, teenagers, & the handicapped, art seminars and courses; lects open to pub; Mus shop sells books, reproductions

MACEDONIA

SKOPJE

M **MUSEUM OF CONTEMPORARY ART - SKOPJE,** Samoilova bb, PO Box 482 Skopje, 1000 Macedonia. Tel 389-02-311-77-34; Fax 389-02-311-01-23; Email msu-info@msuskopje.org.mk; Web: www.msuskopje.org.mk; *Dir* Eliza Sulevska
Open Tues - Sat 10 AM - 5 PM, Sun 9 AM - 1 PM, cl Mon; Admis 50 MKD
Collections: 4630 exhibits of international and national contemporary art, Art movements through 50s, 60s and 70s

MALAYSIA

KUALA LUMPUR

M **MUZIM NEGARA,** National Museum, Jalan Damansara, Kuala Lumpur, 50566 Malaysia. Tel (03) 2267 1111; Fax (02) 2267 1011; Email prmuziumnegara@jmm.gov.my; Web: www.muziumnegara.gov.my; *Dir Gen* Dato Ibrahim bin Ismail; *Deputy Dir Gen* Wan Jamaluddin bin Yusoff; *Dir Nat Mus* Kamarul Baharin bin A Kasim
Open daily 9 AM - 6 PM; Admis citizens 2 RM, senior citizens & children 1 RM, non-citizens 5 RM, children 2 RM; Estab 1963; Average Annual Attendance: 330,000
Income: Financed by Malaysian Dept of Museums
Special Subjects: Antiquities-Oriental, Archaeology, Asian Art, Bronzes, Ceramics, Costumes, Ethnology, Historical Material, Metalwork
Collections: Oriental & Islamic arts, ethnographical, archaeological & historical collections
Activities: Docent training; young volunteer classes; lects open to pub; gallery talks; tours; originates traveling exhibs to state mus; mus shop sells books, original art, reproductions, crafts

M **NATIONAL VISUAL ARTS GALLERY MALAYSIA,** Balai Seni Lukis Negara 2, Jalan Temerloh Kuala Lumpur, 53200 Malaysia. Tel 603-4025-4990; Fax 603-4025-4987; Email info@artgallery.gov.my; Web: www.artgallery.gov.my; *Dir Gen* Dr Dato Mohamed Najib bin Ahmad Dawa
Open Tues - Sun 10 AM - 6 PM; No admis fee
Collections: Permanent collection of more than 2500 pieces, Ceramics, Chinese ink painting, drawing, watercolors, installation, photography, prints, sculpture, textiles

MALDIVES

MALÉ

M **NATIONAL ART GALLERY OF MALDIVES,** Museum Bldg Block A, Medhuziyaarai Magu Malé, 20131 Maldives. Tel 960-334 3832; Email nationalartgallery@tourism.gov.mv; Web: artgallery.gov.mv; *Dir* Ali Waheed
Open Sun - Thurs 9 AM - 6 PM; No admis fee
Collections: Exhibitions of Maldivian and international contemporary art

MALTA

VALLETTA

M **HERITAGE MALTA,** National Museum of Fine Arts, South St, Valletta, 1101 Malta. Tel 356-21 225 769; Web: www.heritagemalta.org; *CEO Heritage Malta* Kenneth Gambin; *Sr Cur* Sandro Debono
Open daily 9 AM - 5 PM, cl Dec 24, 25, 31, Jan 1 & Good Fri; Admis adults 5 EUR, youth, students & seniors 3.50 EUR, seniors over 60 & students 2.50 EUR, infants free; Estab 1975; Contains fine arts from the 14th century to present day
Library Holdings: Cards, Exhibition Catalogs, Original Documents, Pamphlets, Photographs
Special Subjects: Baroque Art, Bronzes, Ceramics, Drawings, Etchings & Engravings, Furniture, Medieval Art, Painting-Dutch, Painting-European, Painting-Flemish, Painting-French, Painting-Italian, Painting-Spanish, Prints, Religious Art, Sculpture, Silver, Watercolors
Collections: Fine arts, majolica & pharmacy jars of 16th-19th century
Exhibitions: Changing exhibitions of contemporary art & historical themes
Publications: Exhibitions catalogues & postcards

MEXICO

COYOACAN

M **MUSEO FRIDA KAHLO (CASA AZUL),** Frida Kahlo Museum (The Blue House), Londres 247, Col Del Carmen Coyoacan, 04000 Mexico. Tel 55-54-59-99; Fax 56-58-32-56; Email relacionespublicas@museofridakahlo.org.mx; Web: www.museofridakahlo.org.mx; *Dir* Diego Rivera Anahuacalli
Open Tues, Thurs - Sun 10 AM - 5:30 PM, Wed 11 AM - 5:45 PM; Gen admis 200 MXN, Mexican citizens 80 MXN, teachers & students 40 MXN, children & seniors 15 MXN; Estab in 1958 to preserve, maintain & exhibit the house, works of art, collection & personal items of Frida Kahlo & Diego Rivera.; The residence of artist Frida Kahlo.; Average Annual Attendance: 250,000
Library Holdings: Book Volumes, Cards
Special Subjects: Archaeology, Architecture, Folk Art, Mexican Art, Photography, Portraits, Sculpture
Collections: Former residence of Frida Kahlo, Household and personal items and artifacts, decorative arts, paintings, textiles, Private collection of work by other Mexican artists
Activities: Children's progs, darmatizations; guided tours; mus shop sells books, magazines, prints, jewelry, textiles, decorative art & catalogues

GUADALAJARA

M **MUSEO REGIONAL DE GUADALAJARA,** Guadalajara Regional Museum, Liceo No 60, Guadalajara, Jalisco 441000 Mexico. Tel 01 333 613 2703, 01 333 614 2227; Email museoregionalguadalajara@hotmail.com; Web: www.inah.gob.mx; *Dir* Ricardo Ortega Gonzalez
Open daily 9 AM - 5 PM; Gen admis 60 MXN
Collections: Archaeological discoveries, early Mexican objects, folk art & costumes

M **MUSEO TALLER JOSE CLEMENTE OROZCO,** Jose Clemente Orozco Taller Museum, Aurelio Aceves 27, Col Arcos Vallarta Guadalajara, Jalisco 44120 Mexico. Tel 33 3616 8329; Email cabanas@jalisco.gob.mx; Web: sc.jalisco.gob.mx; *Dir Gen* Cecilia Wolf
Open Tues - Sat 12 PM - 6 PM; No admis fee; The last studio J Corozco that shows contemporary art.; Average Annual Attendance: 20,000
Collections: Paintings and sketches by the artist

MEXICO CITY

M **LABORATORIO ARTE ALAMEDA,** Alameda Art Laboratory, Dr Mora 7, Centro Historico Mexico City, 06050 Mexico. Tel 5510 2793; Fax 5512 2079; Email info.artealameda@gmail.com; Web: www.artealameda.bellasartes.gob.mx; *Dir* Tania Aedo Arankowsky; *Deputy Dir* Miranda Ibanez; *Adminr* Jose Antonio Hernandez
Open Tues - Sun 9 AM - 5 PM; Gen admis 21 MXN; students, teachers & seniors free; Estab 2000, dedicated to the exhib, documentation, production & research on artistic practices that explore & setup a dialogue on the art technology relationship
Special Subjects: Intermedia
Collections: Under auspices of Instituto Nacional de Bellas Artes, paintings of the colonial era in Mexico
Activities: Classes for adults & children; concerts & gallery talks

M **MUSEO DE ARTE CARRILLO GIL,** Carrillo Gil Museum of Art, Av Revolucion 1608, Col San Angel Mexico City, DF 01000 Mexico. Tel 86 47 5450; Web: www.museodeartecarrillogil.com; *Dir* Vania Rojas; *Chief Cur* Guillermo Santamarina
Open Tues - Sun 10 AM - 6 PM; Admis 50 MXN, Sun free
Collections: Jose Clemente Orozco Collection, Work by Siqueiros, Rivera and many other 20th century Mexican artists

M **MUSEO DE ARTE MODERNO,** Museum of Modern Art, Paseo de la Reforma y Gandhi s/n, Bosque de Chapultepec Mexico City, 11560 Mexico. Tel (55) 864 75530; Fax (5) 553-62-11; Email infoamigos@mam.org.mx; Web: www.museoartemoderno.com
Open Tues - Sun 10:15 AM - 5:30 PM; Gen admis fee 60 MXN, discounts for teachers & students, Sun free; Estab 1964

Collections: International and Mexican coll of modern art
Activities: Classes for adults & children; lects open to pub; organize traveling exhibs Nat & International; mus shop sells books, magazines, prints, slides

M **MUSEO DE ARTE POPULAR,** Museum of Popular Art, Revillagigedo 11, Cuauhtemoc Mexico City, 06010 Mexico. Tel 5510-2201; Email infomap@cdmx.gob.mx; Web: www.map.cdmx.gob.mx; *Dir Gen* Walther Boelsterly Urrutia
Open Tues - Sun 10 AM - 6 PM, Wed 10 AM - 9 PM, cl Mon; Gen Admis 40 MXN; Estab 2006
Collections: Major permanent collections of Mexican popular arts and crafts

M **MUSEO FRANZ MAYER,** Franz Mayer Museum, Hidalgo 45, Centro Historico Mexico City, DF 06300 Mexico. Tel 5518-2266; Email museo@franzmayer.org.mx; Web: www.franzmayer.org.mx; *Dir Gen* Hector Rivero Borrell Miranda
Open Tues - Fri 10 AM - 5 PM, Sat - Sun 10 AM - 7 PM; Admis 50 MXN, teachers & students 25 MXN, senior citizens & children free
Collections: Collection of decorative arts in Mexico from 16th - 19th centuries, Temporary exhibits of photography & design, International & national origins, Silverwork, ceramics, furniture, textiles, sculpture, paintings, feather art, lacquer, ivory, tortoise shell, glass and enamel

M **MUSEO NACIONAL DE ANTROPOLOGIA,** National Museum of Anthropology, Av Paseo de la Reforma y Calzada Gandhi s/n, Col Chapultepec Mexico City, 11560 Mexico. Tel 52-55 5553-6266 ext. 412322; Email attention.mna@inah.gob.mx; Web: www.mna.inah.gob.mx; *Dir* Antonio Saborit
Open Tues - Sun 9 AM - 7 PM, cl Mon; Gen admis 70 MXN, seniors, persons with disabilities, profs & students with ID & children under 13 free
Collections: Anthropological, archaeological & ethnographical colls

M **MUSEO NACIONAL DE HISTORIA,** National Historical Museum, Castillo de Chapultepec, Primera seccion del Bosque de Chapultepec Mexico City, 11580 Mexico. Tel 52-4040 5214, 5206; Email difusion.mnh@inah.gob.mx; Web: www.mnh.inah.gob.mx; *Dir* Salvador Rueda Smithers
Open Tues - Sun 9AM - 5 PM; Gen admis 65 MXN
Collections: The history of Mexico from the Spanish Conquest to the 1917 Constitution, through collections of ceramics, costumes, documents, flags and banners, furniture, jewelry & personal objects

M **MUSEO NACIONAL DE SAN CARLOS,** San Carlos National Museum, Puente de Alvarado No 50 Col Tabacalera, Del Cuauhtemoc Mexico City, 06030 Mexico. Tel 86 47 58 00; Email cgaitan@inba.gob.mx; Web: www.bellasartes.gob.mx; *Dir* Carmen Gaitan Rojo
Open Tues - Sun 10 AM - 6 PM; Admis 45 MXN, Sun free; Estab 1986; European Art and works by the Old Masters.
Library Holdings: Book Volumes, Cassettes, Exhibition Catalogs, Prints, Records
Collections: English, Flemish, French, German, Hungarian, Italian, Polish, Netherlandish and Spanish paintings from 14th - 19th centuries, Mexican Art
Activities: Lects open to the pub; 1,000 vis lectrs per yr; concerts; gallery talks; mus shop sells books

L **Biblioteca Eric Larsen - Eric Larsen Library**, Puente de Alvarado No 50, Col Tabacalera Mexico City, 06030 Mexico. Tel 86-47-5800 ext. 5486; Email bibliomnsc@gmail.com; Web: www.mnsancarlos.com; *Bibliotecaria* Mariana Mendez Vergara; *Bibliotecaria* Gemma Cruz Salvador
Open Mon - Fri 10 AM - 4 PM; Circ 5,000
Library Holdings: Book Volumes 2000, Cassettes, Exhibition Catalogs, Prints, Records
Activities: Lects open to the pub; 1,000 vis lectrs per yr; concerts; gallery talks

M **MUSEO SOUMAYA,** Soumaya Museum, Plaza Carso, Blvd Cervantes Saavedra esq Presa Falcon, Ampliacion Granada Mexico City, CP 11529 Mexico. Tel 55 1103 9800; Email museo@soumaya.org.mx; Web: www.soumaya.com.mx; *Dir Gen* Alfonso Miranda Marquez; *Asst Dir* Ana Paula Robleda Betancourt; *Cur* Monica Lopez Velarde Estrada
Open daily 10:30 AM - 6:30 PM; No admis fee; Estab 1994 to collect, research, conserve and exhibit the artistic heritage of Mexico & Europe.; Asymmetric, 46 meter high, avant-garde designed building covered in 16,000 hexagonal aluminum plates.
Income: Financed by Fundacion Carlos Slim
Special Subjects: Painting-Italian, Painting-French, Painting-German, Painting-Spanish, Hispanic Art, Sculpture, Ivory, Woodcarvings, Furniture, Portraits, Landscapes, Coins & Medals, Fashion Arts, Commercial Art, Photography
Collections: 15th - 18th century European Old Masters, New Spain & South American works, Mexican & European avant-garde, works by Rodin, Picasso, Dali, Tamayo, Siqueiros & Rivera
Exhibitions: Permanent & temporary exhibits
Publications: Catalogues & monthly publs
Activities: Educ progs; interactive progs; lects open to pub; gallery talks; tours; film screenings; cultural events; sculptures & original objects of art lent; organize traveling exhibs

PUEBLA

M **MUSEO JOSE LUIS BELLO Y ZETINA,** Jose Luis Bello and Zetina Museum, 5 de Mayo, 409, Centro Historico Puebla, 72000 Mexico. Tel 52 222 232 4720; Email contacto@museobello.org; Web: museobello.org
Open Tues - Sun 10 AM - 4 PM, cl Mon; No admis fee; House-museum and art collection.
Collections: Ivories, porcelain, wrought iron, furniture, clocks, watches, musical instruments, Mexican, Chinese and European paintings, sculptures, pottery, vestments, tapestries, ceramics, miniatures

TOLUCA

M **MUSEO DE BELLAS ARTES,** Museum of Fine Arts, Calle de Santos Degollado 102, Toluca, Mexico. Tel 722 2 15 53 29; Email bellasartestoluca@gmail.com; *Dir* Itzel Vargas
Open Tues - Sun 10 AM - 6 PM; Admis adults 10 MXN, children 5 MXN; Estab 1945 as a mus
Collections: Paintings, sculptures, Mexican colonial art

MOLDOVA

CHISINAU

M **NATIONAL ART MUSEUM OF MOLDOVA,** str 31 August 1989 nr 115, Chisinau, 2012 Moldova. Tel 022-24-17-30; Fax 022-24-53-32; Web: www.mnam.md; *Dir Gen* Tudor Zbarnea; *Deputy Dir* Veronica Galcenco
Open Tues - Sun, April - Oct 10 AM - 6 PM, Nov - March 10 AM - 4:30 PM, cl Mon; Admis adult 10 MDL, student & seniors 5 MDL; Estab 1939 to exhibit, conserve & restore art works; Display permanent and temporary exhibitions; Average Annual Attendance: 14,000
Special Subjects: Antiquities-Greek, Antiquities-Persian, Antiquities-Roman, Bronzes, Cartoons, Ceramics, Coins & Medals, Collages, Crafts, Decorative Arts, Drawings, Embroidery, Flasks & Bottles, Glass, Gold, Graphics, Ivory, Juvenile Art, Laces, Landscapes, Marine Painting, Medieval Art, Miniatures, Oriental Art, Painting-European, Painting-French, Painting-German, Painting-Italian, Painting-Japanese, Painting-Polish, Painting-Russian, Painting-Spanish, Photography, Porcelain, Portraits, Pottery, Religious Art, Renaissance Art, Restorations, Sculpture, Silver, Tapestries, Textiles, Watercolors, Woodcarvings
Collections: More than 39 thousand pieces of Moldavian fine and decorative arts from the middle ages to the present, Painting, drawing, sculpture, crafts, Iconography, books, manuscripts, Permanent exhibitions of Russian, European and Asian art
Activities: Classes for adults & children; lects open to public; concerts; tours

MONGOLIA

ULAANBAATAR

M **NATIONAL MUSEUM OF MONGOLIA,** Juulchin St - 1, POB 332 Ulaanbaatar, 210646 Mongolia. Tel 326 802; Email nmm@nationalmuseum.mn; Web: www.nationalmuseum.mn; *Dir* J Saruulbuyan
Open Tues - Sat 9:30 AM - 5:30 PM, cl Sun, Mon & pub holidays; Admis adult 5000 MNT, student 2500 MNT; Estab 1924
Collections: Early bronzes, statues, thangkas, applique, embroidered work and textiles, iconography, ritual artifacts, furniture, household items and decorative arts

M **ZANABAZAR NATIONAL FINE ARTS MUSEUM,** Juulchid St, Chingeltei Dist Ulaanbaatar, 38 Mongolia. Tel 976-11-326060, 326061; Fax 976-11-326060; Email info@zanabazarfam.mn; Web: www.zanabazarfam.mn; *Dir* Batdorj Damndinsuren
Open Summer - Autumn daily 8 AM - 5 PM, Winter - Spring daily 10 AM - 5 PM; Admis adults 5000 MNT, students 2000 MNT, children 600 MNT; Estab 1966
Collections: Collection incl 10,000+ objects, Prehistoric art, work by Zanabazar, painted thangkas, silk appliques, Buddhist artifacts, traditional arts and crafts of Mongolia, Paintings by B Sharav

MONTENEGRO

CETINJE

M **NARODNI MUZEJ CRNE GORE,** National Museum of Montenegro, Novice Cerovica bb, Cetinje, 81250 Montenegro. Tel 382-41-230-310; Fax 382-41-230-310; Email nmcg@t-com.me; Web: www.mnmuseum.org; *Dir* Pavle Pejovic
Open 9 AM - 5 PM
Special Subjects: Archaeology, Ceramics, Coins & Medals, Costumes, Drawings, Ethnology, Graphics, Historical Material, Manuscripts, Photography, Portraits, Religious Art, Sculpture, Southwestern Art

M **Historical Museum**
Open 9 AM - 5 PM; Admis adults 3 EUR, children 2.50 EUR
Collections: General development of Montenegrin people and history through various periods, 1500 museum pieces, 300 archived items, 1500 photographs, maps, graphs, architecture & art

M **Ethnographic Museum**
Open 9 AM - 5 PM; Admis adults 2 EUR, children 1 EUR
Collections: Ethnographic history of Montenegro through various traditional arts and crafts, Textiles, embroidery, musical instruments, material culture

M **Modern Art Gallery**
Open 9 AM - 5 PM; Admis adults 4 EUR, children 2 EUR
Collections: Five colls; Arts of Yugoslav nations and ethnic groups, icons, Montenegrin fine art, Milica Saric-Vukmanovic Memorial Coll and a coll of frescoes

M **Biljarda - Peter II Petrovic Njegos Museum**
Open 9 AM - 5 PM; Admis adults 3 EUR, children 1.50 EUR
Collections: Former residence of bishop and poet Peter II Petrovic Njegos, Personal artifacts, decorative arts, furniture, architecture, armaments

M **King Nikola's Museum**

Open 9 AM - 5 PM; Admis adults 5 EUR, children 2.50 EUR
Collections: Montenegrin history and artifacts in former residence of royal family, Decorations, photographs, weapons, jewelry

MOROCCO

MARRAKECH

M **DAR SI SAID MUSEUM,** Museum of Moroccan Arts, Riad Ez-Zaitoun El Jadid, Marrakech, Morocco. Tel 212-4-44-24-64; *Pres, Foundation of Museums* Mehdi Qotbi
Open Mon, Wed - Thur, Sat - Sun 9 AM - 11:45 AM & 2:30 PM - 5: 45 PM, Fri 9 AM - 11:45 AM & 2:30 PM - 5:45 PM, cl Tues; Admis adults 20 dirham; children 5 dirham
Collections: Berber silver jewelry, oil lamps, embroidered leather, rustic pottery and marble, furniture, carpets and other decorative and architectural arts

MYANMAR

YANGON

M **NATIONAL MUSEUM OF MYANMAR,** 66/74 Pyay Rd, Dagon Yangon, Myanmar. Tel 951-378652, 371540; Fax 951-378652; Email dcicoci@mptmail.net.mm; *Dir Gen* U Kyaw Oo Lwin
Open Tues - Thurs, Sat - Sun 9 AM - 4 PM, cl Mon & Fri; Gen admis 5000 MMK
Collections: Regalia of King Thibaw of Mandalay

NAMIBIA

WINDHOEK

M **NATIONAL ART GALLERY OF NAMIBIA,** c/o John Meinert St & Robert Mugabe Ave, PO Box 994 Windhoek, Namibia. Tel 264-61-231160; Fax 264-61-240930; Email secretary@nagn.org.na; Web: www.nagn.org.na; *Dir* Hercules Viljoen
Open Mon - Fri 9 AM - 5 PM, Sat 9 AM - 2 PM
Collections: Namibian art past and present, African and South African contemporary art; traditional crafts and decorative arts, textiles

NEPAL

BHAKTAPUR

M **NATIONAL ART GALLERY OF NEPAL,** Singhadhoka Bldg Bhaktapur Palace, Durbar Sq Bhaktapur, Nepal. Tel 97716610004
Open Tues - Sun 10:45 AM - 3:45 PM, cl Mon; Admis nationals RPR 40, visitors NPR 100; Estab 1960
Collections: Rare Nepalese paintings, Paubha scroll paintings, bronze, brass, stone and wooden artifacts

KATHMANDU

M **NATIONAL MUSEUM OF NEPAL,** Museum Rd, Chhauni Kathmandu, Nepal. Tel 977-1 427 1504; Email info@nationalmuseum.gov.np; Web: www.nationalmuseum.gov.np; *Dir* Bhesh Narayan Dahal
Open Mon 10:30 AM - 2:30 PM, Wed - Sun 10:30 AM - 4:30 PM, cl Tues & govt holidays; Admis nationals 25 NPR, visitors 150 NPR; Estab 1928
Collections: Art, history, culture, ethnology & natural history colls

M **NEPAL ASSOCIATION OF FINE ARTS,** National Birendra Art Museum, Sitabhawan, Naxal Kathmandu, Nepal. Tel 4411729, 4421206; Fax 4221175, 4414665; Email nafa@wlink.com.np; Web: www.nafa.org.np
Open Sun - Fri 9 AM - 5 PM, cl Sat; Admis nationals NPR 25, international visitors NPR 75; Estab 1986
Collections: 189 pieces of contemporary and historical art by over 60 prominent Nepalese artists

NETHERLANDS

ALKMAAR

M **STEDELIJK MUSEUM ALKMAAR,** Alkmaar Municipal Museum, Canadaplein 1, Alkmaar, 1811 Netherlands. Tel 0031 72-5489798; Email info@museumalkmaar.nl; Web: www.stedelijkmuseumalkmaar.nl; *Dir* Lidewij de Koekkoek; *Cur* Christi Klinkert; *Mktg Mgr* Hans Duncker; *Educator* Aafje Moonen
Open Tues - Sun 10 AM - 5 PM, cl Mon, New Year's Day, King's Day & Christmas Day; Admis adults 10 EUR, seniors 6 EUR, children up to 18 no fee; Average Annual Attendance: 40,000
Income: Financed by city
Special Subjects: Decorative Arts, Dolls, Furniture, Historical Material, Landscapes, Painting-Dutch, Painting-European, Porcelain, Portraits, Sculpture, Silver
Collections: Collection from Alkmaar region, including archaeological items, dolls and other toys, modern sculpture, paintings, silver, tiles, works by Gerard van Honthorst, Caesar van Everdingen, William van de Velde the Elder, Pieter Saenredam Maerten van Heemskerck
Activities: mus shop sells books, reproductions, prints & gifts

AMSTELVEEN

M **MUSEUM JAN VAN DER TOGT,** Dorpstraat 50, Amstelveen, 1182 JE Netherlands. Tel 31-0 20 641 57 54; Email info@jvdtogt.nl; Web: www.jvdtogt.nl; *Dir* Jan Verschoor
Open Wed - Fri 11 AM - 5 PM, Sat - Sun 1 PM - 5 PM; Admis adults 8 EUR, children no fee

AMSTERDAM

M **AMSTERDAM MUSEUM,** Kalverstraat 92, Nieuwezijds Voorburgwal 359 Amsterdam, 1012 Netherlands. Tel 31 020 5231 822; Email info@amsterdammuseum.nl; Web: www.amsterdammuseum.nl; *Dir* Judikje Kiers
Open daily 10 AM - 5 PM; Admis adult 13.50 EUR, student card 11 EUR, children 0-17 free; Estab 1926 to display the history of Amsterdam; Housed in former city orphanage
Special Subjects: Painting-European, Painting-Dutch, Painting-Flemish, Renaissance Art, Glass, Textiles, Furniture, Metalwork, Sculpture, Silver, Bronzes, Portraits, Archaeology
Collections: More than 70,000 items, Dutch Golden Age art
Exhibitions: Permanent, rotating & temporary exhibits
Publications: Travel guides & exhib catalogs
Activities: Educ progs; classes for adults & children; gallery interpreting; interactive progs; lects open to pub; gallery talks; tours; art programming; cultural events; individual objects of art lent; mus shop sells books & souvenirs

M **HERMITAGE AMSTERDAM,** Amstel 51, Amsterdam, Netherlands. Tel 31 (0) 20-530 87 55 & 58; Email mail@hermitage.nl; Web: www.hermitage.nl; *Dir* Cathelijne Broers
Open daily 10 AM - 5 PM, cl King's Day & Christmas Day; Admis adults 25 EUR; children under 17 & Amsterdam City Card holders no admis fee

M **MUSEUM HET REMBRANDTHUIS,** The Rembrandt House Museum, Jodenbreestraat 4, Amsterdam, 1011 NK Netherlands. Tel 020-520-0400; Fax 020-520-0401; Email museum@rembrandthuis.nl; Web: www.rembrandthuis.nl; *Exec Dir* Michael Huijser
Open daily 10 AM - 6 PM, cl King's Day & Christmas Day; Admis adults 13 EUR, children 6 - 17 4 EUR, children under 6 no fee; The house where Rembrandt lived for nearly 20 years; Average Annual Attendance: 250,000
Collections: Rembrandt's etchings and drawings, drawings and paintings by Rembrandt's pupils, contemporary artists influenced by Rembrandt
Activities: Educ prog; classes for children; tours; originate traveling exhibs; mus shop sells books, prints, & reproductions

M **RIJKSMUSEUM,** National Museum, Museumstraat 1, PO Box 74888 Amsterdam, 1070 DN Netherlands. Tel 31 (0) 20 6747 000; Email info@rijksmuseum.nl; Web: www.rijksmuseum.nl; *Gen Dir* Taco Dibbits; *Dir Finance & Opers* Erik van Ginkel; *Dir Devel & Media* Hendrikje Crebolder
Open daily 9 AM - 5 PM; Admis adults 17.50 EUR, 18 yrs & under free; 1800; Library with 200,000 vols
Library Holdings: Exhibition Catalogs, Framed Reproductions, Memorabilia, Photographs, Reproductions
Collections: Asiatic art, Dutch history & paintings, prints & drawings from all parts of the world, sculpture & applied art
Activities: Classes for adults & children; lects open to pub; tours; mus shop sells books, reproductions, prints & slides

M **STEDELIJK MUSEUM AMSTERDAM,** Amsterdam Municipal Museum, Museumplein 10, Amsterdam, 1071 DJ Netherlands; PO Box 75082, Amsterdam, 1070 AB Netherlands. Tel 31 (0) 20 5732 911; Fax 31 (0) 20 6752 716; Email info@stedelijk.nl; Web: www.stedelijk.nl; *Dir* Jan Willem Sieburgh; *Chief Cur* Bart van der Heide
Open Sat - Thurs 10 AM - 6 PM, Fri 10 AM - 10 PM; Admis adult 17.50 EUR, students 29 & under 7.50 EUR, children 18 & under no fee; Estab 1895; municipal mus, now modern & contemporary art; Library with 180,000 vols; Average Annual Attendance: 500,000; Mem: Urban friends
Library Holdings: Book Volumes, CD-ROMs, Clipping Files, Compact Disks, DVDs, Periodical Subscriptions
Collections: Applied art & design, European & American trends after 1960 in paintings & sculptures
Activities: Classes for adults & children; lects open to pub; concerts; gallery talks; tours; lending of original objects of art to mus; mus shop sells books, magazines, reproductions & designer gifts

M **VAN GOGH MUSEUM,** Museumplein 6, PO Box 75366 Amsterdam, 1070 AJ Netherlands. Tel 31 (0)20 570 5200; Fax 31 (0)20 570 5222; Email info@vangoghmuseum.nl; Web: www.vangoghmuseum.nl; *Dir* Axel Ruger; *Mng Dir* Adriaan Donszelmann
Open daily 9 AM - 6 PM, Fri 9 AM - 9 PM, cl public holidays; Admis adults 18 EUR, children 17 & under free; Estab 1973; fine arts; Average Annual Attendance: 1,300,000
Library Holdings: Auction Catalogs, Audio Tapes, Book Volumes, CD-ROMs, Cassettes, Clipping Files, Exhibition Catalogs, Fiche, Filmstrips, Memorabilia, Motion Pictures, Original Art Works, Original Documents, Periodical Subscriptions, Photographs, Prints, Reproductions, Slides, Video Tapes

Special Subjects: Painting-Dutch, Prints, Sculpture, Watercolors, Woodcuts, Manuscripts
Collections: Some 550 drawings, 200 paintings & 700 letters by Vincent Van Gogh, Van Gogh's personal collection of English & French prints & Japanese woodcuts, Varied collection of 19th century art by contemporaries
Activities: Classes for children; lects open to pub; vis lectrs 8-10 per yr; guided tours; audio tours; group visits; originate traveling exhibs to Art Institute of Chicago; mus shop sells books, magazines, reproductions, prints & slides

APELDOORN

M **NATIONAAL MUSEUM PALEIS HET LOO,** Het Loo Palace National Museum, Koninklijk Park 1, Apeldoorn, 7315 JA Netherlands. Tel 31 55 577 2400; Fax 31 55 577 2408; Email info@paleishetloo.nl; Web: www.paleishetloo.nl; *Dir* Michel van Maarseveen
Open Tues - Sun 10 AM - 5 PM; Admis adults 14.50 EUR; Estab 1984 as a state museum open to the pub.; Palace museum, gardens, park, stables and royal art collection.
Collections: Paintings, sculptures, furniture, arts & crafts, textile & costumes, drawing, prints & photos, orders and decorations, books and carriages & vehicles, Dutch deltfware ceramics, knightly heraldry, insignia & decorations

ARNHEM

M **MUSEUM ARNHEM,** Utrechtseweg 87, Arnhem, Gelderland 6812 AA Netherlands. Tel 31 (0) 26 3031 400; Email info@museumarnhem.nl; Web: www.museumarnhem.nl; *Dir* Hedwig Saam; *Head Mus Affairs* Miriam Windhausen; *Head Pub Affairs* Peter de Kok; *Head Bus Affairs* Bart Weggemans
Open Tues - Sun 11 AM - 5 PM, cl Mon, New Year's Day, King's Day & Christmas Day; Admis adults 9 EUR, youth 13 - 17, students & seniors 5 EUR, children 12 & under free; Average Annual Attendance: 50,000
Income: 3 million euro (financed by the city of Arnhem), 200.000 euro (additional funding)
Library Holdings: Auction Catalogs, Book Volumes, Exhibition Catalogs, Kodachrome Transparencies, Manuscripts, Original Documents, Periodical Subscriptions, Slides, Video Tapes
Collections: Design, Dutch and international paintings, drawings and prints, Dutch contemporary applied art, sculpture gardens, video, on design; realism; contemporary art
Activities: Classes for adults & children; docent training; four visiting lectrs per year; concerts; tours; lending of original objects of art to other art institutions; sales shop sells books, reproductions & bric-a-brac

DELFT

M **MUSEUM PRINSENHOF DELFT,** Sint Agathaplein 1, Delft, 2611 HR Netherlands; Postbus 78, Delft, 2600 ME Netherlands. Tel 31 (015) 260 2358; Fax 31 (015) 213 8744; Email info-prinsenhof@delft.nl; Web: prinsenhof-delft.nl; *Dir* Patrick Van Mil
Open Tues - Sun 11 AM - 5 PM, cl New Year's Day, Easter Sun, King's Day, Whit Sun & Christmas Day; Admis adults 12 EUR, youth 13 -18 6 EUR, children 12 & under free; Library with 6000 vols
Special Subjects: Archaeology, Ceramics, Historical Material, Maps, Painting-Dutch, Painting-European, Portraits, Pottery, Religious Art, Restorations, Silver, Tapestries, Textiles
Collections: Delft silver, tapestries and ware, paintings of the Delft School, modern art, Delftware, ceramics
Activities: Classes for adults & children; mus shop sells books & prints

DORDRECHT

M **DORDRECHTS MUSEUM,** Museumstraat 40, Dordrecht, 3311 XP Netherlands. Tel 31 (0) 78 7708708; Web: www.dordrechtsmuseum.nl; *Mng Dir* Peter Schoon
Open Mon - Sun 10 AM - 5 PM; Admis adults 11 EUR, students 18 & up 6 EUR, youth 13 - 18 5 EUR, children 13 & under free; Estab 1842
Collections: Dutch paintings, prints, drawings & sculpture, 17th to 20th century drawings, paintings & prints

EINDHOVEN

M **VAN ABBEMUSEUM,** Bilderdijklaan 10, Eindhoven, 5611 NH Netherlands; PO Box 235, Eindhoven, 5600 AE Netherlands. Tel 31 40 238 1000; Fax 31 40 246 0680; Email info@vanabbemuseum.nl; Web: www.vanabbemuseum.nl; *Dir* Charles Esche
Open Tues - Sun 11 AM - 5 PM, first Thurs of month 11 AM - 9 PM; Admis adults 12 EUR, groups 9 EUR, youth 13 - 18 yrs & students 6 EUR, children 12 yrs & under free; Estab 1936; Contemporary art museum.; Average Annual Attendance: 110,000
Library Holdings: Audio Tapes, Book Volumes, CD-ROMs, Clipping Files, Compact Disks, DVDs, Exhibition Catalogs, Kodachrome Transparencies, Original Documents, Pamphlets, Photographs, Slides, Video Tapes
Collections: Modern and contemporary art, Lissitzky Collection
Activities: Classes for adults & children; lects open to pub; concerts; tours; mus shop sells books, magazines, & other design items

ENSCHEDE

M **RIJKSMUSEUM TWENTHE,** Twenthe National Museum, Lasondersingel 129, Enschede, 7514 BP Netherlands. Tel 31 53 435 8675; Email info@rijksmuseumtwenthe.nl; Web: www.rijksmuseumtwenthe.nl; *Dir* Drs Arnoud Odding
Open Tues - Sun & pub holidays 11 AM - 5 PM, cl Mon, New Year's Day & Christmas Day; Admis adults 9 EUR, students 7 EUR, children up to 18 free; Estab 1930; wide & varied collection of art & applied art from the Middle Ages to present day. The museum wants to provide a space in which the visitor can walk through the history of art.; Library with 24,000 vols; mus with ca. 8600 objects; Average Annual Attendance: 45,000
Library Holdings: Auction Catalogs, Compact Disks, DVDs, Exhibition Catalogs, Manuscripts, Original Art Works
Special Subjects: American Western Art, Art Education, Art History, Bookplates & Bindings, Bronzes, Ceramics, Collages, Conceptual Art, Crafts, Decorative Arts, Drawings, Etchings & Engravings, Flasks & Bottles, Furniture, Glass, Ivory, Landscape Architecture, Manuscripts, Metalwork, Miniatures, Mixed Media, Painting-American, Painting-Dutch, Painting-European, Pewter, Porcelain, Portraits, Pottery, Prints, Religious Art, Sculpture, Silver, Tapestries, Watercolors, Woodcarvings, Woodcuts
Collections: Coll of paintings & sculptures from middle ages to present
Activities: Classes for adults & children; film programme; lects open to pub; lects for mems only; gallery talks; tours; mus shop sells books, magazines, original art, reproductions

GRONINGEN

M **GRONINGER MUSEUM,** Museumeiland 1, Groningen, 9711ME Netherlands; PO Box 90, Groningen, 9700ME Netherlands. Tel (050) 366 6555; Fax (050) 312 0815; Email info@groningermuseum.nl; Web: www.groningermuseum.nl; *Mng Dir* Dr Andreas Bluhm
Open Tues - Sun 10 AM - 5PM, cl Mon; Admis adults 13 EUR, students 10 EUR, youth 6 - 16 yrs & school groups 3 EUR, children 5 yrs & under free; Estab 1894; Library with 35,000 vols; Average Annual Attendance: 200,000
Library Holdings: Auction Catalogs, Audio Tapes, Book Volumes, CD-ROMs, DVDs, Exhibition Catalogs, Periodical Subscriptions
Collections: Paintings & drawings from the 16th - 20th century, mainly Dutch, including Averkamp, Cuyp, Fabritius, Jordaens, Rembrandt, Rubens, Teniers, Oriental ceramics, local archaeology & history, contemporary photography, design, fashion
Activities: Classes for adults & children; lects open to pub; tours; mus shop sells books, original art

HAARLEM

M **FRANS HALS MUSEUM,** Groot Heiligland 62, Haarlem, 2011 ES Netherlands; PO Box 3365, Haarlem, 2001 DJ Netherlands. Tel 023-5115775; Fax 023-5115776; Email office@franshalsmuseum.nl; Web: www.franshalsmuseum.nl; *Dir* Ann Demeester
Open Tues - Sat 11 AM - 5 PM, Sun & pub holidays noon - 5 PM, cl Dec 25 & Jan 1; Admis adults 12.50 EUR, groups 9 EUR per person, students 6 EUR, children & youth 0 - 18 yrs free; 16th & 17th century art, that focused on Haarlem painters from that period; Average Annual Attendance: 100,000
Collections: Works by Frans Hals & Haarlem school, antique furniture, modern & contemporary art coll
Activities: Mus shop

M **TEYLERS MUSEUM,** Spaarne 16, Haarlem, 2011 CH Netherlands. Tel (023) 516 0960; Fax (023) 531 2004; Email info@teylersmuseum.nl; Web: www.teylersmuseum.nl; *Dir* Dr Marian Scharloo
Open Tues - Fri 10 AM - 5 PM, Sat - Sun & pub holidays 11 AM - 5 PM, cl Mon; Admis adults 12.50 EUR, groups 10 or more 8.50 EUR, youth 6 - 17 yrs 2 EUR, children 5 & under free; Library with 150,000 vols
Collections: Coins, drawings, fossils, historical physical instruments, medals, minerals & paintings
Exhibitions: For current exhibs check website
Activities: Classes for adults & children; lects open to pub; tours; mus shop sells books, magazines, reproductions & fossils

HOORN

M **WESTFRIES MUSEUM,** Roode Steen 1, Hoorn, 1621 CV Netherlands; Achterom 2-4, Hoorn, 1621 KV Netherlands. Tel (229) 280028; Fax (229) 280029; Email info@wfm.nl; Web: www.wfm.nl; *Dir* Ad Geerdink
Open Tues - Fri 11 AM - 5 PM, Sat & Sun 1 PM - 5 PM; Admis adults 6.50 EUR, seniors 5 EUR, youth free; Estab 1880; Historical museum
Special Subjects: Archaeology, Glass, Historical Material, Painting-Dutch, Period Rooms, Pewter, Porcelain, Portraits, Silver
Collections: 17th & 18th century paintings, prints, oak paneling, glass, pottery, furniture, costumes, interiors, folk art, historical objects from Hoorn & West Friesland, West Friesland native painting, prehistoric finds
Activities: Classes for children; lects open to pub; mus shop sells books, magazines, reproductions

LEERDAM

M **NATIONAAL GLASMUSEUM,** National Glass Museum, Lingedijk 28-30, Leerdam, 4142 LD Netherlands. Tel 0345 614 960; Email info@stichtingglas.nl; Web: www.nationaalglasmuseum.nl; *Dir* Arend-Jan Weijsters
Open Tues - Sat 10 AM - 5 PM, Sun noon - 5 PM, cl Mon; Admis adults 8 EUR, youth 6 - 12 yrs 6.50 EUR, children under 6 yrs free
Collections: Antique, machine-made & packaging glass, art glass, unique pieces, contemporary Dutch collection & works from America & Europe

LEEUWARDEN

M **FRIES MUSEUM,** Wilhelminaplein 92, Leeuwarden, 8911 BS Netherlands. Tel 058 255 5500; Email info@friesmuseum.nl; Web: www.friesmuseum.nl; *Gen Dir* Kris Callens
Open Tues - Sun 11 AM - 5 PM, cl Mon; Admis adults 10 EUR, children 4 - 17 yrs, students & teachers 5 EUR, toddlers 3 & under free; Estab 1881
Collections: Archaeology, ceramics, costumes, folk art, historical items, painting, prints and drawings, sculpture

LEIDEN

M **MUSEUM DE LAKENHAL,** Oude Singel 28-32, Leiden, 2312 RA Netherlands; PO Box 2044, Leiden, 2301 CA Netherlands. Tel 31-0-71-5165360; Fax 31-0-71-5134489; Email info@lakenhal.nl; Web: www.lakenhal.nl; *Dir* Meta Knol; *Head Pub Affairs* Minke Schat; *Cur Old Master Paintings* Dr Christiaan Vogelaar; *Head Programs & Coll* Dr Rob Wolthoorn; *Cur Modern Art* Dr Doris Wintgens Hotte; *Cur Leiden History* Dr Jori Zijlmans
Open Tues - Fri 10 AM - 5 PM, Sat - Sun & holidays noon - 5 PM, cl Mon, New Year's Day, King's Day & Christmas Day; Admis 19 - 65 yrs 7.50 EUR, CJP & over 65 yrs 4.50 EUR, 18 yrs & under free; Estab 1874; History & Art of Leiden from the Middle Ages to the present; Average Annual Attendance: 40,000
Special Subjects: Carpets & Rugs, Ceramics, Coins & Medals, Crafts, Decorative Arts, Drawings, Furniture, Glass, Gold, Graphics, Landscapes, Maps, Medieval Art, Painting-Dutch, Painting-European, Period Rooms, Pewter, Photography, Porcelain, Portraits, Portraits, Pottery, Religious Art, Renaissance Art, Sculpture, Silver, Stained Glass, Tapestries, Textiles
Collections: Altar pieces by Lucas van Leyden, paintings by Rembrandt, Steen, van Goyen, pictures of Leiden School & modern Leiden School, arms, ceramics, furniture, glass, period rooms, pewter, silver
Activities: Classes for children; lect open to pub; 4 vis lectrs per yr; concerts; tours; mus shop sells books, magazines, original art, reproductions & slides

M **RIJKSMUSEUM VAN OUDHEDEN,** National Museum of Antiques, Rapenburg 28, Leiden, 2311 EW Netherlands; PO Box 11114, Leiden, 2301 EC Netherlands. Tel 31-0-71-5163-163; Fax 31-0-71-5149-941; Email info@rmo.nl; Web: www.rmo.nl; *Dir* Wim Weijland
Open Tues - Sun 10 AM - 5 PM; Admis adults 9.50 EUR, seniors 7.50 EUR, children 5 - 17 yrs 3 EUR, children 4 yrs & under free
Collections: Consists of more than 80,000 objects; statues of Roman emperors, prehistoric gold jewelry, Egyptian mummy cases and Etruscan masterpieces in bronze

MUIDEN

M **RIJKSMUSEUM MUIDERSLOT,** Muiden National Museum, Herengracht 1, Muiden, 1398 AA Netherlands. Tel (0294) 256262; Fax (0294) 261056; Email info@muiderslot.nl; Web: www.muiderslot.nl; *Dir* Bert Boer; *Cur* Rik van Wegen
Open Apr - Nov: Mon - Fri 10 AM - 5 PM, Sat - Sun & pub holidays noon - 5 PM; Nov - Apr: Sat - Sun noon - 5 PM; Admis adults 13.50 EUR, children 4 - 11 yrs 9 EUR, children up to 3 yrs free; Estab 1878; Castle museum and grounds.
Collections: 13th century castle furnished in early Dutch Renaissance 17th century style, paintings, tapestries, furniture & armory, sculptures, modern; reconstructed Dutch herb & vegetable gardens
Activities: Classes for adults & children; historical flower arrangements; educ prog; concerts; mus shop sells books

NIJMEGEN

M **MUSEUM HET VALKHOF,** Kelfkensbos 59, Nijmegen, 6511 TB Netherlands; PO Box 1474, Nijmegen, 6501 BL Netherlands. Tel 31 024 360 88 05; Email info@museumhetvalkhof.nl; Web: www.museumhetvalkhof.nl; *Dir* Drs Marijke Brouwer
Open Tues - Sun 11 AM - 5 PM; Admis adults 11 EUR, youth 6 - 18 yrs & students 5.50 EUR; Estab 1999
Collections: Roman antiquities, old masters and modern art

OTTERLO

M **KROLLER-MULLER MUSEUM,** Nationale Park de Hoge Veluwe, Houtkampweg 6 Otterlo, 6731 AW Netherlands; PO Box 1, Otterlo, 6730 AA Netherlands. Tel 31 318 591241; Email info@krollermuller.nl; Web: www.krollermuller.nl; *Dir* Drs Lisette Pelsers; *Bus Dir* Rinus Vonhof; *Cur Research* Drs Toos van Kooten; *Mktg & Sponsoring* Lies Boelryk; *Exec Sec Press & Publicity* Drs Wanda Vermeulen; *Educ* Drs Herman Tibosch
Open Tues - Sun 10 AM - 5 PM, cl Mon & Jan 1; Admis park & mus adults 18.30 EUR, children 6-12 yrs 9.15 EUR, children 6 & under free; Estab 1938; Library with 35,000 vols/no pub library; Average Annual Attendance: 275,000
Special Subjects: Drawings, Painting-Dutch, Painting-European, Painting-Flemish, Sculpture
Collections: Van Gogh Collection, 19th and 20th century art - drawings, paintings, sculpture garden, ceramics, graphic arts, sculpture and sculpture drawings, Contemporary Art
Publications: Sculpture Garden - Van Gogh Drawings & Paintings
Activities: Educ prog; printed tax children 4+; lects open to pub; concerts; mus shop sells books, magazines, original art, reproductions, prints & gifts

ROTTERDAM

M **MUSEUM BOIJMANS VAN BEUNINGEN,** Museumpark 18-20, Rotterdam, 3015 CX Netherlands; POB 2277, Rotterdam, 3000 CG Netherlands. Tel 31 (0)10 44-19-400; Email info@boijmans.nl; Web: www.boijmans.nl; *Bus Mgr & Deputy Dir* Mrs Ina Klaassen; *Head of Presentations* Mrs Cathy Jacob; *Dir* Sjarel Ex
Open Tues - Sun 11 AM - 5 PM, cl Mon, New Year's Day, King's Day & Christmas Day; Admis adults 15.00 EUR, students 7.50 EUR, youth under 18 yrs, ICOM card holders free; Average Annual Attendance: 200,000
Collections: Dutch school paintings including Bosch, Hals, Rembrandt, Van Eyck, 15th-20th century Dutch, Flemish, French, German, Italian & Spanish works, Baroque School, Impressionists, old, modern & contemporary sculpture, Dutch, Italian, Persian & Spanish pottery & tiles, Dutch design
Activities: Classes for children and adults; lects open to pub; concerts, gallery talks, tours, scholarships; mus shop sells books, reproductions, prints; Museumpark 18-20 POB 2277 3000 CG Rotterdam

THE HAGUE

M **GEMEENTEMUSEUM DEN HAAG,** Municipal Museum of The Hague, Stadhouderslaan 41, The Hague, 2517 HV Netherlands; PO Box 72, The Hague, 2501 CB Netherlands. Tel 31 (070) 338 1111; Email info@gemeentemuseum.nl; Web: www.gemeentemuseum.nl; *Gen Mgr* Benno Tempel; *Dep Dir* Hans Buurman
Open Tues - Sun 10 AM - 5 PM, cl Mon; Admis adults 15 EUR, students & CJP 11.50 EUR, children up to 18 yrs & museumcard free
Collections: Decorative Arts Collection includes ceramics, furniture, glass, silver, modern art of 19th & 20th century, musical instruments, history of The Hague

M **HET MAURITSHUIS,** Royal Picture Gallery Mauritshuis, Plein 29, The Hague, 2511 CS Netherlands; PO Box 536, The Hague, 2501 CM Netherlands. Tel (070) 3023456; Email mail@Mauritshuis.nl; Web: www.mauritshuis.nl; *Dir* Dr Emilie E. S. Gordenker
Open Mon 1 - 6 PM; Tues, Wed, Fri - Sun 10 AM - 6 PM; Thurs 10 AM - 8 PM; Admis Mauritshuis: adults 14 EUR, children free; Prince William V Gallery: adults 5 EUR, children 2.50 EUR; Estab 1822; Picture gallery; Average Annual Attendance: 200,000
Library Holdings: Auction Catalogs, Book Volumes, Exhibition Catalogs, Kodachrome Transparencies, Periodical Subscriptions, Photographs, Reproductions
Collections: Paintings of the Dutch and Flemish Masters of the 15th, 16th, mainly 17th and 18th centuries, including G David, Holbein, Hals, Rembrandt, Van Dyck, Vermeer, Steen, Rubens
Publications: Made in Holland; Jan Steen In the Mauritshuis
Activities: Classes & progs for children; docent training; lects for mems; 12 vis lectrs per yr; guided tours; Frits Duparc Prize; mus shop sells books, magazines, reproductions, prints, slides & other gift items

S-HERTOGENBOSCH

M **HET NOORDBRABANTS MUSEUM,** Verwersstraat 41, PO Box 1004 s-Hertogenbosch, 5200 BA Netherlands. Tel 073-6877877; Email info@hnbm.nl; Web: www.hetnoordbrabantsmuseum.nl; *Dir* Charles de Mooij
Open Tues - Sun 11 AM - 7 PM, cl Mon; Admis adults 12 EUR, group of 15 or more 9 EUR, youth free; Average Annual Attendance: 85,000
Library Holdings: Auction Catalogs, Book Volumes, Compact Disks, DVDs, Exhibition Catalogs, Fiche, Pamphlets, Periodical Subscriptions, Photographs, Slides, Video Tapes
Special Subjects: Archaeology, Architecture, Art Education, Art History, Baroque Art, Coins & Medals, Crafts, Drawings, Glass, Painting-Dutch, Painting-Flemish, Photography, Religious Art, Sculpture, Silver, Tapestries, Woodcarvings, Renaissance Art
Collections: All colls have an emphasis on local history: archaeology, arts & crafts, coins & medals, painting & sculpture
Activities: Classes for adults & children; lects for members only; 4 vis lectrs per yr; gallery talks; tours; originate to other museums; sales of books, magazines, reproductions, prints & slides

NEW ZEALAND

AUCKLAND

M **AUCKLAND ART GALLERY TOI O TAMAKI,** Corner of Kitchener & Wellesley Sts, Auckland, 1010 New Zealand; PO Box 5449, Wellesley St Auckland, 1141 New Zealand. Tel 64 9 379 1349; Web: www.aucklandartgallery.com; *Dir* Rhana Devenport
Open daily 10 AM - 5 PM, cl Christmas Day; Admis is free; Estab 1888; Library with 33,000 vols
Collections: American & Australian paintings, general collection of European paintings & sculpture from 12th century on, historical & contemporary New Zealand painting, sculpture & prints

L **UNIVERSITY OF AUCKLAND,** Elam School of Fine Arts Library, Fine Arts Library Exten, 20 Whitaker Pl Level 2 Rm 432-235 Auckland, 1010 New Zealand. Tel 64 (0) 9 923 7902; Email j.carroll@auckland.ac.nz; Web: www.library.auckland.ac.nz; *Librn for Art History & Fine Arts* Jayne Carroll
Library with 30,000 vols

M **WAITAKERE CONTEMPORARY GALLERY,** Corner of Titirangi & S Titirangi Rds, Auckland, 0604 New Zealand; PO Box 60109, Titirangi Auckland, 0642 New Zealand. Tel +64-9-817-8087; Fax +64-9 817 3340; Email info@lopdell.org.nz; Web: www.lopdell.org.nz; *Dir* Andrew Clifford
Open daily 10 AM - 4:30 PM; No admis fee; Estab 1990 as art gallery; Waitakere City Regional Art Gallery; Average Annual Attendance: 30,000
Publications: Len Castle: Making the Molecules Dance; Blast! Pat Hanley - the Painter & his Protests by Trish Cribben; To the Harbour by Stanley Palmer

Activities: Classes for adults & children; lects open to pub; concerts; gallery talks; tours; Secondary School Art Awards; Portage Ceramic Awards; exten dept lends original objects of art to schools; originates traveling exhibs to New Zealand Art Galleries; sales shop sells books, magazines, original art, reproductions, prints

CHRISTCHURCH

M **CHRISTCHURCH ART GALLERY TE PUNA O WAIWHETU,** 58 Gloucester St, PO Box 2626 Christchurch, 8140 New Zealand. Tel 64-3-941-7300; Fax 64-3-941-7301; Email art.gallery@ccc.govt.nz; Web: www.christchurchartgallery.org.nz; *Dir* Jenny Harper
No admis fee; Currently closed for repairs
Collections: Permanent collection of historical, 20th century and contemporary art, Collections of works on paper, glass, and traditional craft

DUNEDIN

M **DUNEDIN PUBLIC ART GALLERY,** 30 The Octagon, Dunedin, 9016 New Zealand. Tel (+643) 474 3240; Fax (+643) 474 3250; Email dpagmail@dcc.govt.nz; Web: dunedin.art.museum; *Dir* Cam McCracken
Open daily 10 AM - 5 PM, cl Christmas Day; No admis fee, except for special exhibs; Estab 1884; Average Annual Attendance: 180,000
Income: Local authority supplemented with grants, sponsorship, retail, hire of commercial spaces
Collections: 15th - 19th century European paintings, New Zealand paintings since 1876, Australian paintings 1900-60, British watercolors, portraits and landscapes, ancillary colls of furniture, ceramics, glass, silver, oriental rugs, De Beer coll of Old Masters, including Monet, Contemporary New Zealand Art
Activities: Classes for children; lects open to pub; concerts; gallery talks; tours; film screenings; 3 - 4 book traveling exhibs; originate traveling exhibs throughout New Zealand; mus shop sells books, magazines & reproductions

HAMILTON

M **WAIKATO MUSEUM,** 1 Grantham St, South end of Victoria St Hamilton, New Zealand; Private Bag 3010, Hamilton, 3240 New Zealand. Tel 07-838-6606; Email museum@hcc.govt.nz; Web: www.waikatomuseum.co.nz; *Dir* Cherie Meecham
Open daily 10 AM - 4:30 PM, cl Christmas Day; No admis fee; Maintains 8 galleries with various collections
Collections: Art coll is made up of 2500 pieces, Early years of European settlement; Images and artists of the Waikato region, Wood and stone carvings, flax weaving, adzes, waka, korowai, taiaha, ritual and archaeological materials, photographs

NAPIER

M **MTG HAWKES BAY,** Tai Ahuriri, 1 Tennyson St Napier, 4110 New Zealand; PO Box 248, Napier, 4140 New Zealand. Tel (6) 835-7781; Fax (6) 835-3984; Email info@mtghawkesbay.com; Web: www.mtghawkesbay.com; *Dir* Laura Vodanovich
Open Mon - Sun 10 AM - 5 PM, cl Christmas Day; Admis adults $10, seniors & students 15 & up $7.50, youth under 15 free; Average Annual Attendance: 220,000; Mem: 1200; Friends of the Heart
Library Holdings: Audio Tapes, Book Volumes, Cassettes, Clipping Files, Exhibition Catalogs, Kodachrome Transparencies, Lantern Slides, Manuscripts, Maps, Memorabilia, Original Art Works, Original Documents, Pamphlets, Periodical Subscriptions, Photographs, Prints, Records, Sculpture, Slides, Video Tapes
Special Subjects: Architecture, Art History, Ceramics, Costumes, Crafts, Decorative Arts, Drawings, Embroidery, Etchings & Engravings, Furniture, Glass, Historical Material, Jewelry, Landscapes, Manuscripts, Maps, Photography, Portraits, Pottery, Primitive art, Prints, Sculpture, Tapestries, Textiles
Collections: Antiques, Maori & Pacific artifacts, New Zealand painting & sculpture
Activities: Classes for children; Lects open to pub & members only; vis lectrs every year; Mus shop sells books, magazines, reproductions, prints, cards, and other items

PORIRUA CITY

M **PATAKA MUSEUM AND GALLERY,** Cnr Norrie and Parumoana St, PO Box 50240 Porirua City, 5240 New Zealand. Tel 64-4-237-1511; Fax 64-4-237-4527; Email pataka@pcc.govt.nz; Web: www.pataka.org.nz; *Dir* Reuben Friend
Open Mon - Sat 10 AM - 5 PM, Sun 11 AM - 4:30 PM; No admis fee
Collections: Contemporary Maori, Pacific Island and New Zealand art; historical & ethnographic artifacts

WELLINGTON

M **MUSEUM OF NEW ZEALAND TE PAPA TONGAREWA,** 55 Cable St, PO Box 467 Wellington, New Zealand. Tel 64 (4) 381 7000; Fax 64 (4) 381 7070; Email mail@tepapa.govt.nz; Web: www.tepapa.govt.nz; *Acting CEO & Kaihautu (Maori Leader)* Arapata Hakiwai; *Head Arts & Visual Culture* Jonathan Mane-Wheoki
Open daily 10 AM - 6 PM; No admis fee; Estab Feb 1998; Library with 20,000 vols; Average Annual Attendance: 1,300,000
Collections: Australian, British, European & New Zealand art, Sir Harold Beauchamp Collection of early English drawings, illustrations & watercolors, Sir John Ilott Collection of prints, Nan Kivell Collection of British original prints, Monrad Collection of early European graphics, collection of Old Master drawings
Activities: Classes for children; lects open to pub, concerts; gallery talks; tours; mus shop sells books, magazines, original art, reproductions & prints

WHANGANUI

M **SARJEANT GALLERY TE WHARE O REHUA O WHANGANUI,** Sarjeant on the Quay, 38 Taupo Quay, Whanganui, 4500 New Zealand; PO Box 998, Queen's Park Whanganui, 4540 New Zealand. Tel (06) 349 0506; Fax (06) 349 0507; Email info@sarjeant.org.nz; Web: www.sarjeant.org.nz; *Sr Cur* Greg Anderson; *Cur/Pub Prog Mgr* Greg Donson; *Events & Communs Officer* Raewyne Johnson; *Educ Officer* Sietske Jansma; *Educ Officer* Andrea Gardner; *Technician* Garry George; *Opers Mgr* Paula Allen; *Asst Cur* Sarah McClintock; *Admin Officer* Teresa Wakefield
Open daily 10:30 AM - 4:30 PM, Anzac Day 1 PM - 4:30 PM, cl Good Fri & Christmas Day; No admis fee, donations welcome; Estab 1919; built as Art Gallery
Income: Financed by Wanganie Dist Council
Library Holdings: Auction Catalogs, Book Volumes, Clipping Files, Exhibition Catalogs, Periodical Subscriptions
Collections: New Zealand art with a strong photographic focus & regional art, First World War cartoons & posters, 19th & early 20th Century British & European art
Exhibitions: Approx 22 per year
Activities: Classes for children; artist in residence prog; shop specializes in glass & jewelry; gallery talks; events; venue for private functions

NICARAGUA

MANAGUA

M **EL MUSEO NACIONAL DE NICARAGUA DIOCLESIANO CHAVEZ,** National Museum of Nicaragua, National Palace, Plaza de la Republica Managua, Nicaragua. Web: www.inc.gob.ni; *Dir Gen* Vilma de la Rocha Areas
Open Mon - Sun 9 AM - 4 PM; Admis Nicaraguans: adult & college students 20 NIO, primary & high school students 10 NIO; non-citizens: adults 80 NIO, children under 18 yrs 40 NIO
Collections: National archaeological and ethnographic history artifacts, Pre-Columbian ceramics & traditional art, Latin American paintings, metate stone artifacts, Gueguense room, Rodrigo Penalba Collection

NIGERIA

LAGOS

M **OMENKA GALLERY,** 24 Ikoyi Crescent, Ikoyi Lagos, Nigeria. Tel 234 900 846 9991; Email info@omenkagallery.com; Web: www.omenkagallery.com; *Dir* Oliver Enwonwu; *Opers Mgr* Ladun Ogidan
Open Mon - Fri 10 AM - 7 PM, Sat 12 PM - 7 PM, Sun 2 PM - 7 PM; Estab 2003; Modern art gallery
Special Subjects: African Art, Photography, Sculpture
Collections: Modern & contemporary African paintings, installations, photographs & sculptures
Publications: Exhib catalogues
Activities: Educ progs; tours; art fairs

M **RELE GALLERY,** 5 Military St, Onikan Lagos, 4400 Nigeria. Tel 234 0809 321 5460; Email art@rele.co; Web: www.rele.co; *Dir* Adenrele Sonariwo; *Gallery Mgr* Kehinde Afolabi
Open Tues - Fri 10 AM - 6 PM, Sat 12 PM - 6 PM, Sun 2 PM - 6 PM; Estab 2015; Modern art galley
Special Subjects: African Art, Photography
Collections: Modern and contemporary African art
Activities: Art projects; gallery talks; tours; original works of art for sale

NORWAY

BERGEN

M **KODE ART MUSEUMS OF BERGEN,** Rasmus Meyers alle 9, Bergen, 5015 Norway. Tel +47-55-56-80-00; Fax +47-55-56-80-11; Email post@kodebergen.no; Web: kodebergen.no; *Dir* Karin Hindsbo
Open summer: daily 11 AM - 5 PM; winter: Tues - Sun 11 AM - 6 PM, cl Mon; Admis adults NOK 100, students NOK 50, children under 16 yrs free; Estab in 2006 and consists of the Edvard Grieg Museum Troldhaugen, Harald Saeverud Museum Siljustol, Ole Bull Museum Lysoen, Bergen Art Museum & West Norway Museum of Decorative Art

HAUGESUND

M **HAUGESUND BILLEDGALLERI,** Haugesund Picture Gallery, Erling Skjalgssonsgt 4, Haugesund, 5501 Norway; Postboks 147, Haugesund, 5501 Norway. Tel 52-74 41 80; Fax 52-74 41 81; Email postmottak.billedgalleriet@haugesund.kommune.no; Web: www.haugesund-billedgalleri.net; *Gallery Dir* Grethe Lunde Ovrebo
Open Tues - Wed & Fri - Sat noon - 3 PM, Thurs noon - 7 PM, Sun noon - 5 PM, cl Mon.; Admis adults NOK 50, seniors & students NOK 30, children free

HORTEN

M **PREUS MUSEUM,** Kommandorkaptein Klicks vei 7, Horten, 3183 Norway; Karljohansvern, PO Box 254 Horten, 3192 Norway. Tel 47-33 03 1630; Email post@preusmuseum.no; Web: www.preusmuseum.no; *Dir* Ingrid Nilsson; *Asst Dir & Chief Cur* Malfrid Grimstvedt
Open Tues - Sun 11 AM - 4 PM; Admis adults NOK 60, seniors NOK 50, students NOK 40, children under 16 yrs free; National museum of photography

LILLEHAMMER

M **LILLEHAMMER KUNSTMUSEUM,** Lillehammer Municipal Art Gallery, Stortorget 2, Postboks 264 Lillehammer, 2602 Norway. Tel 61 05 44 60; Fax 61 25 19 44; Email post@lillehammerartmuseum.com; Web: www.lillehammerartmuseum.com; *Exec Dir* Svein Olav Hoff
Open daily 11 AM - 4 PM; Admis adults NOK 100, children free
Collections: Norwegian paintings, sculpture and graphic art from 19th and 20th centuries

OSLO

M **INTERKULTURELT MUSEUM,** Intercultural Museum, Toyenbekken 5, Oslo, 0188 Norway; Postboks 3078, Elisenberg Oslo, 0207 Norway. Tel 47-22 05 2830; Email post.ikm@oslomuseum.no; Web: www.oslomuseum.no; *Dir* Lars Emil Hansen
Open Tues - Sun 11 AM - 4 PM; Admis free; Part of the Oslo Museum
Collections: Documentation on immigration history & cultural changes in Norwegian society., visual arts

L **KUNSTHOGSKOLEN OSLO BIBLIOTEKET,** National Academy of the Arts - The Library, Fossveien 24, Oslo, 0551 Norway; PO Box 6853, St Olavs pl Oslo, 0130 Norway. Tel 47-22 99 5510; Email bibliotek@khio.no; Web: www.khio.no; *Sr Librn* Bjornulf Aasen
Open Mon - Thurs 9 AM - 7 PM, Fri 9 AM - 3:30 PM; Library with 6000 volumes to support training by 14 teachers of 130 students

M **KUNSTINDUSTRIMUSEET I OSLO,** Museum of Decorative Arts & Design, Oslo, St Olavs Gate 1, Oslo, 0165 Norway; PO Box 7014, St Olavs plass Oslo, 0130 Norway. Tel 47-21 98 2093; Fax 47-21 98 2000; Email info@nasjonalmuseet.no; Web: www.nasjonalmuseet.no; *Dir, National Museum* Audun Eckhoff; *Dir of Design & Decorative Arts* Widar Halen; *Sr Cur* Knut Astrup Bull
Open Tues, Wed & Fri 10 AM - 5 PM, Thurs 10 AM - 7 PM, Sat & Sun 11 AM - 4 PM, cl Mon; Admis adults NOK 100, students & seniors NOK 50, children under 18 yrs & Sun free; Estab 1876, part of the National Museum of Art, Architecture & Design; Library with 52,000 vols
Collections: Collection from the 600s to the present of applied arts, fashion & design with ceramics, furniture, glass, silver, textiles from Norway, Europe & Far East

M **NASJONALGALLERIET,** The National Gallery, Universitetsgaten 13, Oslo, Norway; Post Box 7014, St Olavs plass Oslo, 0130 Norway. Tel 47-21 98 2093; Fax 47-21 98 2000; Email info@nasjonalmuseet.no; Web: www.nasjonalmuseet.no; *Dir, National Museum* Audun Eckhoff; *Dir of Old Masters & Modern Art* Nils Ohlsen
Open Tues, Wed & Fri 10 AM - 6 PM, Thurs 10 AM - 7 PM, Sat & Sun 11 AM - 5 PM, cl Mon; Admis adults NOK 100, seniors & students NOK 50, children under 18 & Sun free; Estab 1837, part of the National Museum of Art, Architecture & Design; Library with 80,000 vols; Average Annual Attendance: 350,000
Income: Government grants
Library Holdings: Auction Catalogs, Book Volumes, Exhibition Catalogs, Pamphlets, Periodical Subscriptions, Slides
Collections: Norwegian paintings & sculpture, Old European paintings, icon coll, especially of modern French, Danish & Swedish art, a coll of prints & drawings, a small coll of Greek & Roman sculptures, the colls of paintings & sculpture up to 1945
Activities: Educ prog; lects open to pub; concerts; gallery talks

M **NORSK FOLKEMUSEUM,** Norwegian Museum of Cultural History, Museumsv.10, Oslo, 0287 Norway; PO Box 720, Skoyen Oslo, 0214 Norway. Tel 47-22 12 3700; Fax 47-22 12 3777; Email post@norskfolkemuseum.no; Web: www.norskfolkemuseum.no; *Dir* Inger Jensen
Open daily 10 AM - 6 PM; Admis adults NOK 110, seniors & students NOK 85, children 6 - 15 yrs NOK 30, children under 6 yrs free; Estab 1894; Average Annual Attendance: 250,000
Collections: The Sami section provides an insight into the ancient culture of the Sami people. The Open Air Museum totals about 160 old buildings, all original. Among them are the 13th century Gol stave church, farmsteads from different districts of the country, single buildings of particular interest, The Old Town: 17th, 18th, 19th & 20th centuries town houses; Urban Colls, other colls include folk art & church history
Activities: Classes for adults & children; dramatic progs; lects open to pub; concerts; tours; mus shop sells books, replicas, gift items & souvenirs

M **NORSK MARITIMT MUSEUM,** Norwegian Maritime Museum, Bygdoynesveien 37, Oslo, 0286 Norway. Tel 47-24 11 4151; Fax 47-24 11 4150; Email fellespost@marmuseum.no; Web: www.marmuseum.no; *Asst Dir* Eyvind Bagle
Open May 15 - Aug 31: daily 10 AM - 5 PM, Sept 1 - May 14: Tues - Fri 10 AM - 3 PM, Sat & Sun 10 AM - 4 PM; Admis adults NOK 80, students & seniors NOK 40, children 6 - 16 yrs NOK 30, children under 6 yrs free; Estab 1914; Library with 30,000 vols; Mem: Friends of Norsk Sjofartsmuseum
Library Holdings: Clipping Files, Manuscripts, Maps, Original Documents, Pamphlets, Periodical Subscriptions, Photographs, Prints
Special Subjects: Archaeology, Dioramas, Drawings, Historical Material, Marine Painting, Miniatures, Painting-Scandinavian, Photography, Prints, Sculpture
Collections: Amundsen's Gjoa, archives pertaining to maritime history, instruments, paintings, photographs of ships, ship models, tools & other items pertaining to maritime colls, shop and boat plans
Publications: Yearbook
Activities: Classes for adults; panoramic movies of the Coast of Norway and Oslo; lects open to pub; mus shop sells books, reproductions, prints, maritime objects

M **UIO KULTURHISTORIK MUSEUM,** University of Oslo Museum of Cultural History, Frederiksgate 2, Oslo, 0164 Norway; PO Box 6762, St Olavs plass Oslo, 0130 Norway. Tel 47-22 85 1900; Fax 47-22 85 1938; Email postmottak@khm.uio.no; Web: www.khm.uio.no; *Mus Dir* Hakon Glorstad
Open Historical Mus: Tues - Sun mid-May - mid-Sept 10 AM - 5 PM & mid-Sept - mid-May 11 AM - 4 PM; Viking Ship Mus: daily May - Oct 9 AM - 6 PM & Oct - May 10 AM - 4 PM; Admis Historical Mus: adults NOK 50, seniors & students NOK 25, children under 16 yrs free; Viking Ship Mus: adults NOK 60, seniors & students NOK 35, children 6 - 16 years NOK 30, children under 6 yrs free; Contains the Historical Museum and the Viking Ship Museum
Collections: Archaeological finds from Norwegian Stone, Bronze & Iron Ages, also Medieval age, including religious art, 70,000 exhibits from prehistoric & Viking times, including Middle Ages

M **VIGELAND MUSEUM,** Nobels gate 32, Oslo, 0268 Norway; Kulturetaten Vigeland-museet, Postboks 1453 VIka Oslo, 0166 Norway. Tel 47-23 49 3700; Email postmottak.vigeland@vigeland.museum.no; Web: www.vigeland.museum.no; *Mus Dir* Jarle Stromodden
Open Sept - May Tue - Sun noon - 4 PM; May - Sept Tue - Sun 10 AM - 5 PM, cl Mon; Admis adults NOK 60, children 7 - 16 yrs, students & seniors NOK 30, children under 7 yrs free; Estab 1947
Collections: Entire production of work by Gustav Vigeland, Sculptures in plaster, granite, bronze, marble, wrought iron, Thousands of drawings, woodcuts, woodcarvings, Original casts of sculpture work

OMAN

MUSCAT

M **BAIT AL ZUBAIR MUSEUM,** House of Al Zubair, Al Saidiyah St, PO Box 257 Muscat, 100 Oman. Tel 968-24 736 688; Fax 968-24 740 913; Email museum@baitalzubairmuseum.com; Web: www.baitalzubairmuseum.com; *Gen Mgr & Cur* Paul Doubleday
Open Sat - Thurs 9:30 AM - 6 PM; Nominal admis fee of 1-2 OMR, children under 10 yrs free; Estab 1998 to exhibit the Al Zubair family private collection
Collections: Detailed archaeological and ethnographic items of Omani history and culture, Omani weaponry, jewelry, costumes, furniture, maps, photographs, coins, stamps, musical instruments, documents, manuscripts and books

M **NATIONAL MUSEUM OF OMAN,** National Museum of Oman, Muscat, Oman. Tel 246 41 300; Fax 246 41 331; Email info@mhc.gov.om; Web: www.mhc.gov.om; *Chmn* HH Sayyid Haitham bin Tariq Al Said
Estab 2013; Modern, 4,000 sq meter museum with more than 7,000 objects on display in 12 galleries & 250 showcases
Collections: Omani traditional handcrafts, costumes, jewelry, photographs, manuscripts, fine arts & paintings, household items, tools, stamps & coins and Omani archaeology

PAKISTAN

KARACHI

M **NATIONAL MUSEUM OF PAKISTAN,** Burns Garden, Karachi, 74200 Pakistan. Tel 021-26 33 881, 26 28 280, 26 39 930; Web: nationalheritage.gov.pk; *Supt* Mohammad Arif
Open daily 10 AM - 5 PM, cl Wed; Admis 4 PKR, students free; Estab 1971 as archaeological & history mus for preservation of cultural heritage & educ; Average Annual Attendance: 150,000
Collections: Antiquities dating from 7000 BC to modern times, large coll of coins and miniature paintings spreading from 6th century BC to present, ethnological material from the various regions of Pakistan, Buddhist and Hindu sculptures, paleolithic implements, handicrafts and manuscripts of the Muslim period, collection of defunct Victoria Museum
Activities: Originates traveling exhibs to USA, Germany, Japan, Korea & various other countries

LAHORE

M **LAHORE MUSEUM,** Shahrah-e-Quaid-e-Azam, The Mall Rd Lahore, 54000 Pakistan. Tel 92 42 99210809; Fax 92 42 9210810; Email lhrmuseum@wol.net.pk; Web: www.lahoremuseum.org; *Dir* Sumaira Samad; *Pub Rels Officer* Nomia Khadim
Open daily 9 AM - 5 PM; Admis foreigner 100 PKR, adults 10 PKR, children PKR 2; Estab 1864 to showcase cultural heritage; Average Annual Attendance: 282,213
Income: Punjab Provincial Government, Pakistan
Purchases: Through acquisition comt - purchase comt
Library Holdings: Audio Tapes, Book Volumes 30,000, CD-ROMs, Cards, Cassettes, Clipping Files, Compact Disks, DVDs, Exhibition Catalogs, Fiche, Filmstrips, Framed Reproductions, Kodachrome Transparencies, Lantern Slides, Manuscripts, Maps, Memorabilia, Micro Print, Motion Pictures, Original Art Works, Original Documents, Pamphlets, Periodical Subscriptions, Photographs, Prints, Records, Reels, Reproductions, Sculpture, Slides, Video Tapes

Special Subjects: Antiquities-Persian, Archaeology, Architecture, Asian Art, Baroque Art, Bronzes, Carpets & Rugs, Ceramics, Coins & Medals, Costumes, Crafts, Decorative Arts, Embroidery, Furniture, Historical Material, Islamic Art, Leather, Manuscripts, Miniatures, Renaissance Art, Reproductions, Restorations, Textiles, Watercolors
Collections: Greco-Buddhist sculpture, Indo-Pakistan coins, miniature paintings, local arts, armor, stamps, Oriental porcelain & manuscripts, Islamic calligraphy, Stone Age material, pre and pro historic antiquities
Publications: Guides, catalogues on collection, research journal (Lahore Museum Bulletin)
Activities: Classes for adults & children; dramatic prog; internships; lects open to pub; 6 vis lectrs per yr; concerts; tours; lending original objects of art to world mus on governmental basis and to museums within the country; mus shop sells books, magazines, reproductions, prints, slides & other replicas of mus objects; Lahore City Heritage Museum as part of Lahore Museum

PALAU

KOROR

M **BELAU NATIONAL MUSEUM,** Ngerbeched Hamlet, PO Box 666 Koror, 96940 Palau. Tel 680-488-2265; Fax 680-488-3183; Email bnm@palaunet.com; Web: www.belaunationalmuseum.net; *Dir & Cur* Olympia Esel Morei
Open Mon - Fri 8 AM - 5 PM, Sat 10 AM - 4 PM, Sun 1 PM - 4 PM; Admis resident/foreign adult residents $3 - $10 USD, children 6 - 17 yrs $3 - $5 USD, local student $1 USD; Estab 1955
Collections: Five major colls including cultural objects, media, traditional and contemporary art, natural history and a research library, 4000 items relating to anthropology, art, and history, Over 20,000 photographic slides, 6000 prints, negatives, films, videos and recordings, Photos of Palau and Micronesia from the 18th century to the present, Ethnographic history of Palau people and culture

PANAMA

PANAMA CITY

M **MUSEO DE ARTE CONTEMPORANEO,** Museum of Contemporary Art, Av de los Martires, Calle San Blas, Ancon Panama City, Panama. Tel 262-8012, 3380; Fax 262-3376; Web: www.macpanama.org; *Exec Dir* Silvia Estaras Manzano
Open Tues - Sat 10 AM - 5 PM, Sun 10 AM - 4 PM, cl Mon & nat holidays; Admis adults $5, children & seniors $2.50, students $2
Collections: Permanent coll of watercolor and oil paintings by contemporary Panamanian artists

PAPUA NEW GUINEA

BOROKO

M **PAPUA NEW GUINEA NATIONAL MUSEUM & ART GALLERY,** PO Box 5560, Boroko, Papua New Guinea. Tel 675-325 2458, 325 5364; Fax 675-325 1779; Email nationalmuseum@museumpng.gov.pg; Web: www.museumpng.gov.pg; *Dir* Dr Andrew Moutu
Open Mon - Fri 9 AM - 3 PM, Sun 1 PM - 3 PM, cl Sat; Collection of the natural, cultural & contemporary heritage of Papua New Guinea
Collections: Anthropological, archaeological, natural science, war relic and contemporary art collections

PARAGUAY

ASUNCION

M **CENTRO DE ARTES VISUALES/MUSEO DEL BARRO,** Visual Arts Center/ Barro Museum, Grabadores del Cabichui 2716, e/ Emeterio Miranda y Canada Asuncion, 1827 Paraguay. Tel 595 21 607 996; Email info@museodelbarro.org; Web: www.museodelbarro.org; *Dir, Centro de Artes Visuales* Ticio Escobar; *Dir, Museo del Barro* Osvaldo Salerno
Open Wed - Sat 9 AM - noon & 1:30 PM - 8 PM; No admis fee; Estab 1979
Collections: Popular art by professional and amateur artists in Paraguay, more than 4,000 pieces including carvings, furniture, pottery, textiles & religious sculptures
Activities: Guided tours

M **Museo de Arte Indigena - Museum of Indigenous Art**, Centro de Artes Visuales, Asuncion, Paraguay. *Dir* Lia Colombino
Open Wed - Sat 9 AM - noon & 1:30 PM - 8 PM; No admis fee
Collections: Indigenous and traditional arts & crafts of Paraguay, vessels, carvings, feather & fabric ornaments, masks, baskets
Activities: Guided tours

M **Museo Paraguayo de Arte Contemporaneo - Paraguayan Museum of Contemporary Art**, Centro de Artes Visuales, Asuncion, Paraguay. *Dir* Felix Toranzos
Open Wed - Sat 9 AM - noon & 1:30 PM - 8 PM; No admis fee
Collections: Contemporary and modern art from international and local artists, 300 engravings of Jose Guadalupe Posada, Guerra Grande photographic coll, Ignacio Nunez Soler Photography Coll, Miguel Acevedo drawing coll, Dora Guimaraes coll of 1175 drawings and engravings, Oscar Manesi Spanish and Latin American coll
Activities: Guided tours

M **MUSEO NACIONAL DE BELLAS ARTES,** National Museum of Fine Arts, Eligio Ayala 1345, e/ Pai Perez Curupayty Asuncion, Paraguay. Tel 595-21 211578; Email museobellasartes@cultura.gov.py; Web: www.cultura.gov.py; *Dir* Regina Duarte
Open Mon - Fri 7 AM - 6 PM, Sat 8 AM - 2 PM; Estab 1909
Collections: Paintings and sculptures

PERU

LIMA

M **MUSEO DE ARTE DE LIMA,** Lima Museum of Art, Paseo Colon 125, Exposition Park Lima, 1 Peru. Tel (51-1) 20 40000; Fax (51-1) 331 0126; Email informes@mali.pe; Web: www.mali.pe; *Dir* Natalia Majluf; *Gen Mgr* Flavio Calda; *Cur Contemporary Art* Sharon Lerner
Open Tues - Fri & Sun 10 AM - 8 PM, Sat 10 AM - 5 PM; Admis is 30 PEN, 15 PEN for residents
Collections: Peruvian art throughout history, Colonial painting, carvings, ceramics, furniture, metals, modern paintings, religious art, sculpture, textiles

M **MUSEO NACIONAL DE LA CULTURA PERUANA,** National Museum of Peruvian Culture, Avenida Alfonso Ugarte 650, Lima, 100 Peru. Tel 511-423-5892; Email mncp@cultura.gob.pe; Web: www.cultura.gob.pe; *Dir* Sara Acevedo Basurto
Open Tues - Sat 10 Am - 5 PM; Admis adults 5 PEN, students 2 PEN, children 1 PEN; Estab 1946
Collections: Ethnology, folklore, popular art

PHILIPPINES

MAKATI CITY

M **AYALA MUSEUM,** Makati Ave cnr De La Rosa St, Greenbelt Park Ayala Center Makati City, 1224 Philippines. Tel 632-759-8288; Email hello@ayalamuseum.org; Web: www.ayalamuseum.org; *Dir* Mariles L. Gustilo
Open Tues - Sun 9 AM - 6 PM, cl Mon; Admis non-resident: adults 350-425 PHP, children, students & seniors PHP 250; resident: adults PHP 150, children, students & seniors PHP 75
Collections: Dioramas of Philippine history, boat gallery, 19th century paintings, work by Fernando Amorsolo, Fernando Zoebel de Ayala y Montojo, Ethnographic coll of artifacts from Philippine history

MANILA

M **METROPOLITAN MUSEUM OF MANILA,** Bangko Sentral ng Pilipinas Complex, Roxas Blvd Manila, 1554 Philippines. Tel (632) 708-7829; Fax (632) 708-7828; Email info@metmuseum.ph; Web: www.metmuseum.ph; *DIr* Sandra Palomar-Quan
Open Mon - Sat 10 AM to 5:30 PM; Gen admis PHP 100, seniors & persons with disabilities PHP 80; Estab 1976; maintains exhibitions of pre-colonial, modern & contemporary Philippine art; Average Annual Attendance: 240,000
Income: Financed from foundation
Library Holdings: Audio Tapes, Book Volumes, Cassettes, Exhibition Catalogs, Kodachrome Transparencies, Manuscripts, Pamphlets, Periodical Subscriptions, Photographs, Prints, Slides
Special Subjects: Pottery, Asian Art
Collections: Fine arts museum, paintings, graphic arts, sculptures & decorative arts
Publications: Catalogues, books on Filipino art & artists
Activities: Classes for adults & children; docent training; lects open to pub; 4 vis lectrs per year; gallery talks; provincial capitals; originate non-traditional rural traveling exhibs; sales of books

M **NATIONAL MUSEUM OF THE PHILIPPINES,** Padre Burgos Dr, Manila, 1000 Philippines. Tel (632) 527-1215; Fax (632) 527-0306; Email director4@nationalmuseum.gov.ph; Web: www.nationalmuseum.gov.ph; *Dir IV* Jeremy Barns
Open Tues - Sun 10 AM - 5 PM; No admis fee; Estab October 29, 1901 - to protect, preserve & disseminate the heritage of the Filipino people; Arts/Anthropological/ Archaeological/Zoological/Botanical & Geological; Average Annual Attendance: 201,383
Income: Varies yearly/financed by Philippine gov
Purchases: Paintings, specimens
Library Holdings: Audio Tapes, Book Volumes, CD-ROMs, Cassettes, Clipping Files, Compact Disks, DVDs, Exhibition Catalogs, Kodachrome Transparencies, Manuscripts, Original Art Works, Original Documents, Pamphlets, Periodical Subscriptions, Photographs, Prints, Reproductions, Sculpture, Slides, Video Tapes
Special Subjects: Anthropology, Archaeology, Asian Art, Ceramics, Costumes, Crafts, Decorative Arts, Dioramas, Drawings, Embroidery, Ethnology, Folk Art, Islamic Art, Ivory, Landscapes, Sculpture, Textiles
Collections: Fine arts, cultural, archaeological, sciences colls, Textile, arts & crafts, paintings, photographs, drawings
Exhibitions: Best of Philippine Art; San Diego Exhibits; Cloth Traditions; Juan Luna Exhibs; 5 Centuries of Maritime Trade before the Coming of the West; National Art Gallery permanent exhib
Publications: Nat Museum Papers; Ann Reports; A Voyage of 100 Years; Art-i-facts (newsletter)

Activities: Docent training; gallery talks; tours; sponsoring of competitions; lects for staff only; lectrs minimum one per month, concerts; metro Manila & suburbs; schools, universities & other institutions; nationwide; 19 Branches countrywide; Branches, schools, universities, local government units & other institutions; mus shop sells books, slides, magazines, crafts, prints & contemporary productions

PASIG CITY

M **LOPEZ MEMORIAL MUSEUM,** Lopez Museum & Library, G/F Benpres Bldg, Exchange Rd & Meralco Ave, Ortigas Ctr Pasig City, Philippines. Tel 632-631-2417; Email lmmpasig@gmail.com; Web: lopez-museum.com; *Dir* Mercedes Lopez-Vargas
Open Mon - Sat 8 AM - 5 PM; Admis adults PHP 100, students PHP 80; 1960
Library Holdings: Book Volumes, CD-ROMs, Cards, Cassettes, Clipping Files, Compact Disks, DVDs, Manuscripts, Memorabilia, Original Art Works, Original Documents, Other Holdings, Pamphlets, Periodical Subscriptions, Photographs, Prints, Records, Reels, Reproductions, Sculpture
Collections: 600 years of Filipino art and artistic history, 14th-15th century artifacts, Maps, rare books, manuscripts, Ming Dynasty porcelain
Activities: Classes for adults & children; lects open to pub; concerts; gallery talks; tours; museum shop sells books, reproductions, prints

POLAND

BARANOW SANDOMIERSKI

M **CASTLE IN BARANOW SANDOMIERSKI,** Zamkowa St 20, 39-450, Baranow Sandomierski, Poland. Tel 48 15 811 80 39; Fax 48 15 811 80 40; Email muzeum@arp.com.pl; Web: www.baranow.com.pl
Open Apr 1 - Oct 30 Tues - Sun 9 AM - 7 PM; Admis adults 15 PLN; seniors, students & children 7 & over 8 PLN, children 6 & under no charge; 16th-century castle
Collections: Period furnishings

GNIEZNO

M **MUZEUM POCZATKOW PANSTWA POLSKIEGO W GNIEZNIE,** Museum of the Origins of the Polish State in Gnieznie, ul. Kostrzewskiego 1, Gniezno, 62-200 Poland. Tel 61-426-46-41; Fax 61-426-48-41; Email sekretariat@muzeumgniezno.pl; Web: www.muzeumgniezno.pl; *Dir* Dr. Michal Bogacki
Open Tues - Sun 9 AM - 6 PM; Gen admis costs 10 PLN, reduced admis 7 PLN; Estab 1973; Regional & early Polish history museum.
Collections: Archaeological artifacts, costumes & regalia, jewelry, pottery, photographs
Activities: Guided tours

KIELCE

M **MUZEUM NARODOWE W KIELCACH,** National Museum in Kielce, pl Zamkowy 1, Kielce, 25-010 Poland. Tel (41) 344 4015; Fax (41) 344 8261; Email b.sabat@mnki.pl; Web: mnki.pl; *Dir* Dr Robert Kotowski; *Deputy Dir* Ilona Daria Dyktyriska
Open Tues - Sun 10 AM - 6 PM, cl Mon; Admis adults 10 PLN, children 8 PLN, free admis on Sun; Estab 1908; Library with 31,500 vols; Average Annual Attendance: 93,000
Library Holdings: Book Volumes 33,300, Exhibition Catalogs 2760, Periodical Subscriptions 3315
Special Subjects: Baroque Art, Decorative Arts, Folk Art, Furniture, Glass, Graphics, Landscapes, Military Art, Oriental Art, Painting-European, Painting-Polish, Photography, Porcelain, Portraits, Sculpture, Silver, Tapestries, Textiles, Gold
Collections: Polish paintings from 17th to 20th century, Polish baroque interiors, European-paintings, graphics, glass, pottery, gold, silver, furniture, arms & armour, coins, medals, historical and biographical materials, archaeology, natural history, folk art, car models, Polish archaeology, Polish folk art
Exhibitions: Historic interiors of 17th and 18th century; Gallery of Polish Painting and Decorative Arts; Old European and Oriental Arms and Armour; Sanctuary of Marshal Jozef Pilsudski; Paintings by Piotr Michatowski, Henryk Czarnecki, Jozef Deskur, Jozef Czapski; Polish archaeology; Polish folk art; natural history
Publications: The Ann of Nat Mus in Kielce; Corpus Inscriptionum Poloniae, vol 1-5; exhibit catalogs
Activities: Classes for adults & children; lects open to pub; 2000 vis lectrs per year; concerts; gallery talks; sponsoring of competitions; mus shop sells books & reproductions

KRAKOW

L **BIBLIOTEKA GLOWNA AKADEMII SZTUK PIEKNYCH,** Central Library of the Academy of Fine Arts, ul Smolensk 9, Krakow, 31-108 Poland. Tel 48 12 292 62 77; Email biblioteka@asp.krakow.pl; Web: bg.asp.krakow.pl/bg/; *Dir* Jadwiga Wielgut-Walczak
Open Mon - Thurs 9 AM - 7 PM, Fri 9 AM - 2:30 PM, Sat 9 AM - 1 PM; Admis for our professors & students is free; Estab 1869, mus of Technology and Industry; Average Annual Attendance: 39,500
Library Holdings: Auction Catalogs, Book Volumes, CD-ROMs, Cards, Cassettes, Compact Disks, Exhibition Catalogs, Manuscripts, Maps, Original Art Works, Periodical Subscriptions, Photographs, Prints, Reproductions, Sculpture, Slides
Collections: Over 75,000 vols, 30,000 other items in collection, poster room, print room

M **MUZEUM NARODOWE W KRAKOWIE,** National Museum in Kracow, al. 3 Maja 1, Krakow, 30-062 Poland. Tel (012) 433 55 00; Fax (012) 433 55 55; Email dyrekcja@muzeum.krakow.pl; Web: www.muzeum.krakow.pl; *Dir* Zofia Golubiew
Open Tues - Sat 10 AM - 6 PM, Sun 10 AM - 4 PM; Admis adults 11 PLN, children, students & seniors 6 PLN, free admis on Sun; Estab 1879
Collections: National Museum in Krakow consists of several departments with various colls: 3 galleries exhibit Polish painting and sculpture from 14th to 20th century, Emeryk Hutten-Czapski Dept has graphic, numismatic and old book coll, Jan Matejko's House exhibits relics and paintings of the eminent Polish painter, Czartoryski Coll contains national relics, armory, Polish and foreign crafts and paintings, archaeology, Czartoryski Library and Archives holds colls of documents, codices, books and incunabula, Stanislaw Wyspianski Museum exhibits works by the Polish Modernist artist, handicrafts, architecture and town planning, Karol Szymanowski Museum contains exhibits relating to the life of the eminent composer

M **ZAMEK KROLEWSKI NA WAWELU-PANSTWOWE ZBIORY SZTU,** Wawel Royal Castle - State Art Collections, Wawel 5, Krakow, 31 001 Poland. Tel +48-12-422-5155; Fax +48-12-421-5177; Email zamek@wawel.org.pl; Web: www.wawel.krakow.pl; *Dir* Jan K Ostrowski; *Deputy Dir* Jerzy T Petrus; *Deputy Dir* Prof Marcin Fabianski; *Deputy Dir* Danuta Ziernicka
Open: Nov - Feb 9 AM - 5 PM, March & Oct 9 AM - 6 PM, April & Sept 9 AM - 7 PM, May - Aug 9 AM - 8 PM; Admis fees vary with exhibs, reductions for children, students & seniors; Estab 1930; Library with 20,912 vols; Average Annual Attendance: 1,000,000
Income: Financed by Ministry of Culture & Nat Heritage
Purchases: Polish regalia & items linked with the castle & royal ct
Library Holdings: Auction Catalogs, Book Volumes, CD-ROMs, Exhibition Catalogs, Original Documents, Periodical Subscriptions, Photographs
Collections: Colls of art in the royal castle, 16th century coll of Flemish tapestries, Italian & Dutch paintings, Oriental objects of art
Publications: Studia Waweliana; Acta Archaeological Waweliana; catalogues of collections & temporary exhibitions
Activities: Classes for children; docent training; lects open to pub; 3,000 vis lectrs per yr; works lent to Polish & foreign mus; mus shop sells books, magazines, reproductions, prints & slides

LODZ

M **MUZEUM SZTUKI W LODZI,** Museum of Art in Lodz, ul Wieckowskiego 36, Lodz, 90-734 Poland. Tel (00 48 42) 633 9790; Fax (00 48 42) 632 9941; Email muzeum@msl.org.pl; Web: www.msl.org.pl; *Dir* Jaroslaw Suchan
Open Tues 10 AM - 6 PM, Wed - Sun 11 AM - 7 PM, cl Mon; Admis adult 6 PLN, children & youth under 16 yrs 1 PLN, no admis fee on Thurs; Estab 1931; International contemporary art.
Library Holdings: Auction Catalogs, Book Volumes, Exhibition Catalogs, Original Documents, Pamphlets, Periodical Subscriptions, Prints
Collections: Contemporary, modern and Avant-garde art, Polish photography and multimedia collections
Publications: 111 Works from the Collection of Museum Sztuki in Lodzi
Activities: Classes for adults and children; music progs; lects open to pub; concerts; gallery talks; tours; schols and fellowships offered; mus shop sells books, reproductions, prints, slides

POZNAN

M **MUZEUM NARODOWE W POZNANIU,** National Museum in Poznan, Aleje Marcinkowskiego 9, Poznan, 61-745 Poland. Tel 0048 61 85 68 000; Fax 0048 61 85 15 898; Email mnp@mnp.art.pl; Web: www.mnp.art.pl; *Dir* Jaroslaw Suchan; *Dep Dir* Ursula Tracz
Open Tues - Thurs 9 AM - 3 PM, Fri noon - 9 PM, Sat - Sun 11 AM - 6 PM, cl Mon; Admis adult 12 PLN, reduces 8 PLN, no admis fee on Sat; Estab 1857; Library has 85,000 vols; 8 branch museums; Average Annual Attendance: 191,329
Library Holdings: Auction Catalogs, Book Volumes, Cards, Exhibition Catalogs, Periodical Subscriptions, Photographs, Slides
Special Subjects: Antiquities-Greek, Baroque Art, Bronzes, Ceramics, Coins & Medals, Collages, Costumes, Crafts, Decorative Arts, Drawings, Ethnology, Folk Art, Furniture, Glass, Gold, Graphics, Jewelry, Landscapes, Medieval Art, Military Art, Miniatures, Painting-British, Painting-Dutch, Painting-European, Painting-Flemish, Painting-French, Painting-German, Painting-Italian, Painting-Polish, Painting-Spanish, Photography, Portraits, Posters, Pottery, Prints, Religious Art, Renaissance Art, Reproductions, Restorations, Sculpture, Silver
Collections: Polish paintings from 15th to 20th century, prints, drawings, sculpture, medieval art, European paintings from 14th to 19th century, modern art
Activities: Classes for adults & children; lects open to pub; concerts; gallery talks; original art lent to other mus; mus shop sells books, magazines, reproductions, prints, slides, posters & other gadgets

WARSAW

L **BIBLIOTEKA UNIWERSYTECKA W WARSZAWIE,** University of Warsaw Library, Dobra 56/66, Warsaw, 00-312 Poland. Tel 48 22 55 25 178, 55 25 179; Email oin.buw@uw.edu.pl; Web: www.buw.uw.edu.pl; *Gen Dir* Jolanta Talbierska PhD
Open Mon - Fri 9 AM - 9 PM, Sat noon - 7 PM, Sun 3 PM - 8 PM; Estab 1817
Collections: Prints & drawings from 15th - 20th century, various memorial colls

M **CENTRUM SZTUKI WSPOLCZESNEJ ZAMEK UJAZDOWSKI,** Centre for Contemporary Art Ujazdowski Castle, ul. Jazdow 2, Warsaw, 00-467 Poland. Tel 48-22-628-76-83; Fax 48-22-628-95-50; Email csw@csw.art.pl; Web: www.csw.art.pl; *Dir* Malgorzata Ludwisiak

Open Tues - Thurs, Sat & Sun 11 AM - 7 PM, Fri 12 AM - 9 PM, cl Mon; Admis 12 PLN, discounted 6 PLN
Library Holdings: CD-ROMs, DVDs, Exhibition Catalogs, Kodachrome Transparencies, Video Tapes
Collections: Exhibitions of contemporary art in various media
Activities: Classes for adults & children; lects open to public, concerts, gallery tours

M **MUZEUM NARODOWE W WARSZAWIE,** National Museum in Warsaw, Aleje Jerozolimskie 3, Warsaw, 00-495 Poland. Tel 48 22 621 10 31; Fax 48 22 622 85 59; Email muzeum@mnw.art.pl; Web: www.mnw.art.pl; *Dir* Agnieszka Morawinska; *Deputy Dir, Communs & Pub Affairs* Mateusz Labuda; *Deputy Dir, Research* Piotr Rypson; *Deputy Dir, Management* Elzbieta Sobiecka
Open Tues, Wed, Fri, Sat & Sun 10 AM - 6 PM, Thurs 10 AM - 9 PM, cl Mon; Admis 15 PLN, reduced 10 PLN, no admis fee on Tues; Estab 1862
Library Holdings: Auction Catalogs, Audio Tapes, Book Volumes, CD-ROMs, Exhibition Catalogs, Fiche, Manuscripts, Maps, Memorabilia, Original Documents, Periodical Subscriptions, Prints
Collections: Paintings, sculptures & drawings, Medieval & modern Polish 12th century art, Ancient Art Coll, Eastern Christian Art Coll, Oriental Art Coll, Decorative Art Coll, Miniature Room, European painting coll, Gallery of European Old Masters, Gallery of 18th century art; gallery of 20th & 21st century art, Dept of coins & medals; gallery of old Polish & European Portrait
Publications: Bulletin du Musee National de Varsouie, quarterly
Activities: Educ prog; classes for children; lects open to pub; concerts; gallery talks; tours; lending of original objects of art to mus and galleries all over the world; originate traveling exhibs to mus in Europe and US; mus shop sells books, magazines, reproductions, prints

M **ZACHETA - NATIONAL GALLERY OF ART,** (Narodowe Centrum Kultury), pl. Malachowskiego 3, Warsaw, 00-916 Poland. Tel 48-22-556-96-00; Fax 48-22-827-78-86; Email office@zacheta.art.pl; Web: www.zacheta.art.pl; *Dir* Hanna Wroblewska; *Deputy Dir* Justyna Markiewicz
Open Tues - Sun noon - 8 PM, cl Mon; Admis 15 PLN, concession 10 PLN, no admis fee on Thurs; Built in 1860-1900 for the presentation and promotion of contemporary art; Popularize & promote contemporary art; Average Annual Attendance: 35,000
Library Holdings: Audio Tapes, Book Volumes, CD-ROMs, Cassettes, Clipping Files, DVDs, Exhibition Catalogs, Original Documents, Photographs, Slides, Video Tapes
Collections: Oldest exhibition site in Warsaw, Contemporary and modern art in various media from Polish and international artists, Contemporary Polish Art in various media, Extensive permanent coll
Exhibitions: Organize only temporary exhibs
Activities: Classes for adults, children & artists; lects open to public; concerts; gallery talks and tours; lending of original art to other cultural institutions; Culture to go project; mus shop sells books, magazines, prints, reproductions, DVDs & gadgets

M **Kordegarda Gallery**, ul. Krakowskie Przedmiescie 15/17, Warsaw, 00-071 Poland. Tel 22-42-10-125; Email kordegarda@nck.pl; Web: www.kordegarda.org; *Gallery Coord* Aleksandra Chrzanowska-Purchla
Open Tues - Sun 11 AM - 7 PM; No admis fee; Estab 2011; Kordegarda works as a place of presentation of contemporary Polish culture
Income: Financed from the budget of Ministry & Culture
Special Subjects: Graphics, Jewelry, Painting-Polish, Portraits, Posters, Prints, Sculpture, Woodcuts
Activities: Lects open to pub; concerts; gallery talks; tours; mus shop sells books, DVD's

WROCLAW

M **MUZEUM ARCHITEKTURY,** Museum of Architecture, ul. Bernardynska 5, Wroclaw, 50-156 Poland. Tel (48) (71) 344-82-79, 343-36-75; Fax (48) (71) 344-65-77; Email muzeum@ma.wroc.pl; Web: www.ma.wroc.pl; *Dir* Jerzy Ilkosz, MA; *Deputy Dir* Ewa Jasienko
Open Tues, Fri - Sun 11 AM - 5 PM, Wed 10 AM - 4 PM, Thurs 12 PM - 7 PM; Gen admis 10 PLN, reduced ticket 7 PLN; Estab 1965; Museum housed in beautiful former Bernardine 14th Century Cloister Complex
Income: State budget, City of Wroclaw, Sponsors
Purchases: Architectural books and catalogues from other museums and institutions
Library Holdings: Audio Tapes, Book Volumes, CD-ROMs, Cassettes, Compact Disks, Exhibition Catalogs, Maps, Original Documents, Photographs, Reproductions, Sculpture, Slides, Video Tapes
Collections: Polish & other architecture, modern art, individual architecture, documents, photographs, projects
Publications: Books about architecture, art - Polish and foreign
Activities: Classes for adults & children; seminars for students; research conferences; lects open to public, concerts, gallery talks; awards: SYBILLA 2005, 2006, 2007; lending original objects of art to other museums; co-operation with traveling exhibs; mus shop sells books

M **MUZEUM NARODOWE WE WROCLAWIU,** National Museum in Wroclaw, Pl. Powstancow Warszawy 5, Wroclaw, 50-153 Poland. Tel (71) 372-51-50; Fax (71) 343-56-43; Email muzeumnarodowe@wr.onet.pl; Web: www.mnwr.art.pl; *Dir* Piotr Oszczanowski
Open Winter: Tues - Fri 10 AM - 4 PM, Sat - Sun 10 AM - 5 PM; Summer: Tuers - Fri & Sun 10 AM - 5 PM, Sat 10 AM - 6 PM; cl Mon & Tues (except last Tues of month, open 10 AM - 5 PM); Admis adult 15 PLN, reduced 10 PLN, youth 7 - 16 yrs 1 PLN, children under 7 yrs free; Estab 1947; Library with 91,000 vols; 102,000 mus objects
Collections: Medieval art, Polish paintings from 17th - 20th century, European paintings, decorative arts, prints, ethnography & history relating to Silesia, numismatics
Publications: Exhibition catalogs
Activities: Classes for adults & children; books & magazines

ZAGAN

M **PALACE IN ZAGAN,** Ul. Szprotawska 4, Zagan, 68-100 Poland. Tel 48 684772831; Email sekretariat@palac.zagan.pl; Web: www.palac.zagan.pl
Open Mon - Fri 7 AM - 4 PM; Admis 3 - 5 PLN
Collections: Period furnishings

PORTUGAL

EVORA

M **MUSEU DE EVORA,** Evora Museum, Largo Conde de Vila Flor, Evora, 7000-804 Portugal. Tel 266 730 480; Fax 266 702 604; Email mevora@cultura-alentejo.pt; Web: museudevora.imc-ip.pt; *Dir* Antonio Miguel Alegria
Open Tues - Sun 9:30 AM - 5:30 PM, cl Mon; Admis 3 EUR; Estab 1840; Average Annual Attendance: 30,000; Mem: Amigos do Museu de Evora: 140; dues junior 12 EUR, standard 24 EUR, family 48 EUR, enterprise 120 EUR, benefactor 240 EUR, contrib enterprise 1200 EUR; mem req 120 hrs vol work
Special Subjects: Antiquities-Roman, Archaeology, Architecture, Baroque Art, Bronzes, Carpets & Rugs, Ceramics, Coins & Medals, Costumes, Decorative Arts, Drawings, Embroidery, Ethnology, Furniture, Glass, Islamic Art, Jewelry, Landscape Architecture, Medieval Art, Metalwork, Painting-Dutch, Painting-European, Painting-Flemish, Painting-French, Painting-Italian, Painting-Spanish, Portraits, Pottery, Religious Art, Renaissance Art, Sculpture, Textiles, Silver, Tapestries, Watercolors
Collections: Paintings: 16th century Flemish & Portuguese works, local prehistoric tools & Roman art & archaeology, sculpture from middle ages to the 19th century, 18th century Portuguese furniture & silver, textiles & paramounts from the 16th - 19th centuries
Publications: Exhib catalogs
Activities: Lects open to pub; gallery talks; mus shop sells books, magazines, reproductions, prints

LAMEGO

M **MUSEU DE LAMEGO,** Lamego Musuem, Largo de Camoes, Lamego, 5100-147 Portugal. Tel 351 254 600 230; Email mlamego@culturanorte.gov.pt; Web: www.museudelamego.gov.pt; *Dir* Luis Sebastian
Open daily 10 AM - 6 PM; Gen admis 3 EUR, reduced 1.50 EUR; Estab 1915, opened 1918; Regional mus housed in a former episcopal palace.
Income: Financed by Direcao Regional de Cultura do Norte
Collections: Portuguese 16th - 18th century paintings, 16th century Belgian tapestries, sculpture, ceramics, drawings & engravings, furniture, goldsmith, religious ornaments
Activities: Educ svcs; guided tours

LISBON

M **CASA MUSEU - DR ANASTACIO GONCALVES,** Dr Anastacio Goncalves House Museum, Ave 5 de Outubro, 6-8, Lisbon, 1050-055 Portugal. Fax 351-213 548 754; Email cmag@imc-ip.pt; Web: www.cmag-imc-ip.pt; TWX 351-213 540 823; *Dir* Ana Mantua
Open Tues 2 PM - 6 PM, Wed - Sun 10 AM - 6 PM, cl Mon; Gen admis 3 EUR, seniors 65 & up & youth under 25 1.50 EUR; Museum housed in the former residence of Portuguese painter José Malhoa.
Collections: Portuguese 19th century paintings, decorative art, Chinese porcelain
Activities: Guided tours; concerts; colloquiums; conferences

M **CASA-MUSEU MEDEIROS E ALMEIDA,** Rua Rosa Araujo, n 41, Lisbon, 1250-194 Portugal. Tel 213 547 892; Fax 213 561 951; Email inf@casa-museumedeirosealmeida.pt; Web: www.casa-museumedeirosealmeida.pt; *Admin Dir* Luis Macara; *Asst Dir* Fernando Silva; *Mus Dir* Teresa Cancela
Open Mon - Sat 10 AM - 5 PM; Admis 5 EUR, seniors 3 EUR; Estab 1972; House museum and foundation collection across 27 galleries.
Special Subjects: Painting-Dutch, Painting-Flemish, Furniture, Portraits, Silver, Jewelry, Tapestries, Porcelain, Jade, Religious Art, Sculpture
Collections: 2,000 displayed objects including Flemish masterpieces, clocks & pocket watches, Chinese Ming porcelain, Imperial Chinese jade, gilded silver utensils, European fans

M **MUSEU CALOUSTE GULBENKIAN,** Calouste Gulbenkian Museum, Av de Berne 45 A, Lisbon, 1067-001 Portugal. Tel 351-217 823 030; Fax 351-217 823 032; Email museu@gulbenkian.pt; Web: www.gulbenkian.pt; *Dir* Joao Castel-Branco Pereira
Open Tues - Sun 10 AM - 6 PM, cl Mon; Admis 12 EUR, reduced 6 EUR, youth under 12 & Sun no admis fee; Estab 1969; Ancient & contemporary art mus; includes an art library and a garden.
Income: Financed by Calouste Gulbenkian Foundation
Library Holdings: Book Volumes, Exhibition Catalogs
Special Subjects: Landscapes, Graphics, Watercolors, Tapestries, Etchings & Engravings, Photography, Prints, Drawings, Collages
Collections: Gulbenkian art collection covering the period 2800 BC to present, Egyptian, Greco-Roman, Islamic & Oriental art, manuscripts, furniture, gold & silver, medals, European paintings, tapestries & decorative arts, Portuguese & foreign art from the 20th & 21st century, Portuguese Contemporary Art
Publications: Catalogues of the exhibs & guide to the coll
Activities: Classes for adults, children & families; docent training; gallery talks; lending of original objects of art to several mus & institutions on contemporary art; mus shop sells books, magazines

M **MUSEU COLECAO BERARDO,** Berardo Collection Museum, Praca do Imperio, Lisbon, 1449-003 Portugal. Tel 351 213 612 878; Fax 351 213 612 570; Email museuberardo@museuberardo.pt; Web: www.museuberardo.pt; *Dir Gen* Pedro Bernardes; *Artistic Dir* Rita Lougares
Open daily 10 AM - 7 PM, cl Dec 52; Admis 5 EUR, Sat & children 6 & under free admission; Estab as a museum of modern and contemporary art
Special Subjects: Painting-European, Watercolors, Drawings, Prints, Photography, Sculpture, Furniture, Textiles
Collections: 900 modern & contemporary works of art across 70 disciplines
Exhibitions: Permanent & temporary exhibits
Publications: Books, brochures, exhib catalogs
Activities: Educ progs; classes for adults & children; gallery interpreting; interactive progs; gallery talks; tours; art programming; public art projects; arts festivals; cultural events; mus shop sells books, magazines, original art, reproductions, prints; gifts

M **MUSEU NACIONAL DE ARTE ANTIGA,** National Museum of Ancient Art, Rua das Janelas Verdes, Lisbon, 1249-017 Portugal. Tel 351-21 391 2800; Fax 351-21 397 3703; Email geral@mnaa.dgpc.pt; Web: www.museudearteantiga.pt; *Dir* Antonio Filipe Pimentel
Open Tues - Sun 10 AM - 6 PM; Admis general 6 EUR; Estab 1884; Library with 36,000 vols; Average Annual Attendance: 150,000; Mem: 650; 25 EUR
Library Holdings: Auction Catalogs, Book Volumes, Exhibition Catalogs, Periodical Subscriptions
Collections: Portuguese and foreign plastic and ornamental art from 12th-19th century
Activities: Educ prog; docent training; lects open to pub; vis lectrs; gallery talks; mus shop has books, reproductions, original art, slides & prints

M **MUSEU NACIONAL DE ARTE CONTEMPORANEA DO CHIADO,** National Museum of Contemporary Art, Museu Do Chiado, Rua de Serpa Pinto 4, Lisbon, 1200-444 Portugal. Tel 351-213 432 148; Fax 351-213 432 151; Email museuchiado@mnac.dgpc.pt; Web: www.museuartecontemporanea.pt; *Dir* David Santos
Open Tues - Sun 10 AM - 6 PM, cl Mon; Gen admis 4.50 EUR; Estab 1911, Nat Museum of Contemporary Art; Gallery includes 5 rooms with total area of 1200M
Special Subjects: Drawings, Period Rooms, Portraits, Sculpture
Collections: Contemporary painting and sculpture
Activities: Classes & workshops for children; originate traveling exhibs to Spain

PORTO

M **MUSEU NACIONAL DE SOARES DOS REIS,** National Museum of Soares Dos Reis, Palacio dos Carrancas, Rua de D Manuel II 44 Porto, 4050-342 Portugal. Tel 351-223 393 770; Fax 351-222 082 851; Email mnsr@ipmuseus.pt; Web: www.museusoaresdoreis.pt; *Dir* Maria Joao Vasconcelos
Open Tues - Sun 10 AM - 6 PM, cl Mon; Gen admis 5 EUR; reduced 2.50 EUR
Collections: Furniture, glass, jewelry, old and modern paintings, porcelain, pottery, sculpture

M **MUSEU SERRALVES DE ARTE CONTEMPORANEA,** Serralves Foundation Museum of Contemporary Art, Rua Dom Joao de Castro, 210, Porto, 4150-417 Portugal. Tel 351 226 156 500; Fax 351 22 615 6533; Email serralves@serralves.pt; Web: www.serralves.pt; *Mus Dir* João Ribas; *Museum Dept Dir* Marta Almeida
Open Oct - Mar: Mon - Fri 10 AM - 6 PM, Sat - Sun 10 AM - 7 PM; Apr - Sept: Mon - Fri 10 AM - 7 PM, Sat - Sun 10 Am - 8 PM, cl Dec 25 & Jan 1; Admis Museum & Park 10 EUR, under 12 & Sun 10 AM - 1 PM free; 1999
Collections: National and international contemporary art from the 1960s to the present

VISEU

M **MUSEU GRAO VASCO,** Grão Vasco Museum, Adro da Se, Viseu, 3500-195 Portugal. Tel 351-232 422 049; Fax 351-232 421 241; Email mngv@mngv.dgpc.pt; Web: www.patrimoniocultural.pt; *Dir* Agostinho Paiva Ribeiro
Open Tues 2 PM - 6 PM, Wed - Sun 10 AM - 6 PM, cl Mon; Gen admis 4 EUR; Estab 1916; Circ 446; Average Annual Attendance: 45,597
Library Holdings: Book Volumes, Exhibition Catalogs, Manuscripts, Pamphlets, Periodical Subscriptions
Special Subjects: Carpets & Rugs, Ceramics, Coins & Medals, Decorative Arts, Furniture, Medieval Art, Painting-Flemish, Porcelain, Portraits, Pottery, Religious Art, Renaissance Art, Sculpture, Silver, Textiles
Collections: Flemish & Portuguese paintings, furniture, tapestries, ceramics & glassware, drawings, paintings
Activities: Thematic visits; lending of original objects of art to other museums; mus shop sells books & reproductions

QATAR

DOHA

M **MATHAF: ARAB MUSEUM OF MODERN ART,** PO Box 2777, Education City Doha, Qatar. Tel 974 4402 8855; Web: www.mathaf.org.qa; *Dir* Abdellah Karroum
Open Sat - Thurs 9 AM - 7 PM, Fri 1:30 PM - 7 PM; Estab 2010; Modern art museum housed in a renovated school building
Income: Financed by Qatar Museums & Qatar Foundation
Special Subjects: Asian Art, Sculpture, Video
Collections: Contemporary art coll of more than 9,000 pieces from the Arab world including paintings, sculptures, works on paper and installation & video works
Activities: Educ progs for schools, adults & families; creative workshops, mus talks

M **MUSEUM OF ISLAMIC ART,** Corniche, Doha, Qatar. Tel 974 4422 4444; Web: www.mia.org.qa; *Dir* Julia Gonnella
Open Sat - Thurs 9 AM - 7 PM, Fri 1:30 - 7 PM; No admis fee; Estab in 2008 to display Islamic art masterpieces from three continents over 1,400 years; Located on the artificial peninsula of Corniche covering more than 45,000 sq meters
Special Subjects: Islamic Art, Antiquities-Persian, Textiles, Manuscripts, Metalwork, Ceramics, Glass, Calligraphy, Bronzes, Costumes
Collections: Kitchen wares, elaborate tile panels, mosque lamps, goblets & vases,, 800 manuscripts including 7th century Qurans & Ottoman works, bronze, brass & vessels, armor, scientific instruments precious metal pieces, carpets, costumes & fabrics
Exhibitions: Permanent exhibits
Publications: Exhib catalogs
Activities: Art educ & calligraphy workshops; classes for children; gallery talks, tours; cultural events; art programming; Mus shop sells home decor, gifts & accessories

ROMANIA

ARAD

M **COMPLEXUL MUZEAL ARAD,** Arad Museum Complex, Piata George Enescu 1, Arad, 310131 Romania. Tel 0257 281847; Fax 0257 280114; Email office@museumarad.ro; Web: www.museumarad.ro; *Dir* Peter Hugel
Open Tues - Sun 9 AM - 5 PM, cl Mon; Admis adults 2 RON, children, military, students & seniors 1 RON; Estab 1893
Collections: Archeological artifacts, Romanian & European art

BUCHAREST

L **BIBLIOTECA ACADEMIEI ROMANE,** Library of the Romanian Academy, Calea Victoriei 125, Sector 1 Bucharest, 71102 Romania. Tel 021 212 8284, 8285; Fax 021 212 5856; Email biblacad@biblacad.ro; Web: www.biblacad.ro; *Dir Gen* Florin Gheorghe Filip
Estab 1867
Library Holdings: Other Holdings Items over 9 million
Collections: National depository for Romanian & United Nations publications, Romania, Latin, Greek, Oriental & Slavonic manuscripts, engravings, documents, maps, medals & coins

M **MUZEUL NATIONAL DE ARTA AL ROMANIEI,** National Museum of Art of Romania, Calea Victoriei 49-53, Bucharest, 70101 Romania. Tel 40 21 313 30 30; Fax 40 21 312 43 27; Email national.art@art.museum.ro; Web: www.mnar.arts.ro; *Gen Dir* Calin Stegerean
Open May - Sept: Wed - Sun 11 AM - 7 PM; Oct - Apr: Wed - Sun 10 AM - 6 PM; Admis fee National Gallery 10 RON, European Art Gallery 8 RON, combined tickets National Gallery & European Art Gallery 15 RON; Estab 1948; Average Annual Attendance: 120,000
Income: The National Museum of Art of Romania is a public nonprofit cultural institution. Finance sources include visiting fees, subsidy of Ministry of Culture and from the Friends of The National Museum of Art Assn
Library Holdings: Exhibition Catalogs, Kodachrome Transparencies, Lantern Slides
Special Subjects: Antiquities-Byzantine, Antiquities-Egyptian, Antiquities-Oriental, Antiquities-Persian, Antiquities-Roman, Archaeology, Architecture, Asian Art, Baroque Art, Bookplates & Bindings, Bronzes, Calligraphy, Carpets & Rugs, Ceramics, Costumes, Crafts, Decorative Arts, Drawings, Embroidery, Enamels, Etchings & Engravings, Ethnology, Flasks & Bottles, Folk Art, Furniture, Glass, Gold, Graphics, Hispanic Art, Historical Material, Islamic Art, Ivory, Jade, Jewelry, Judaica, Laces, Landscapes, Leather, Manuscripts, Marine Painting, Medieval Art, Metalwork, Military Art, Miniatures, Oriental Art, Painting-British, Painting-Dutch, Painting-European, Painting-Flemish, Painting-French, Painting-German, Painting-Italian, Painting-Japanese, Painting-Polish, Painting-Russian, Painting-Spanish, Period Rooms, Pewter, Photography, Porcelain, Portraits, Posters, Pottery, Religious Art, Renaissance Art, Reproductions, Restorations, Sculpture, Silver, Tapestries, Textiles, Watercolors, Woodcarvings, Woodcuts
Collections: Romanian Medieval Art - 14th to early 19th century, Romanian Modern Art - 19th to first half of the 20th century, European Art - 14th to early 20th century
Publications: Exhibition catalogs
Activities: Classes for adults, children & teachers; workshops; concerts; gallery talks; tours; lending of original objects of art; books, magazines, reproductions, prints, puzzles, promotional objects

M **The Art Collections Museum**, Calea Victoriei 111, Bucharest, 010071 Romania. Tel 40 21 212 17 49, 40 21 212 96 41
Open May - Sep: Sat - Wed 11 AM - 7 PM; Oct - Apr: Sat - Wed 10 AM - 6 PM; Admis 15 RON
Collections: Romanian folk art, decorative arts, paintings, sculpture, graphic arts

M **K. H. Zambaccian Museum**, 21A Muzeul Zambaccian St, Bucharest, 011871 Romania. Tel 40 21 230 19 20
Open May - Sep: Wed - Sun 11 AM - 7 PM; Oct - Apr: Wed - Sun 10 AM - 6 PM; Admis 7 RON
Collections: Romanian & European 19th & 20th century art
Publications: Museum's brochure

M **Theodor Pallady Museum**, 22 Spatarului St, Bucharest, 020772 Romania. Tel 40 21 211 49 79
Open May - Sep: Wed - Sun 11 AM - 7 PM; Oct - Apr: Wed - Sun 10 AM - 6 PM

M **MUZEUL NATIONAL DE ARTA CONTEMPORANA,** National Museum of Contemporary Art, str Izvor 2-4, Palatul Parlamentului Wing E-4 Bucharest, 050563 Romania. Tel 0040-21-3189137, 3139115; Fax 0040-21-3189138, 3121502;

Email info@mnac.ro; Web: www.mnac.ro; *Gen Dir* Calin Dan; *Artistic Dir* Ruxandra Balaci; *Head Curatorial Dept* Raluca Velisar
Open Wed - Sun 10 AM - 6 PM; Gen admis 10 RON, reduced 5 RON; Estab 2004
Collections: Contemporary national and international art in various media

CLUJ-NAPOCA

M **MUZEUL DE ARTA CLUJ-NAPOCA,** Museum of Art Cluj-Napoca, Piata Unirii 30, Cluj-Napoca, 400098 Romania. Tel 0264 596952; 596953; Fax 0753 066791; Email info.muzeu@macluj.ro; Web: www.macluj.ro; *Mgr* Lucian Kovacs
Open Wed - Sun 9 AM - 5 PM; cl Mon & Tues; Admis permanent exhibs 8 RON
Collections: Romanian & universal art, including graphics, paintings, sculpture and decorative arts from 16th - 20th century
Activities: mus shop sells books, magazines, reproductions & prints

M **MUZEUL ETNOGRAFIC AL TRANSILVANIEI,** Transylvanian Museum of Ethnography, Str Memorandumului, Cluj-Napoca, 3400 Romania. Tel 4 0264 592344; Fax 4 0264 592148; Email contact@muzeul-etnografic.ro; Web: www.muzeul-etnografic.ro; *Dir* Tiberiu Graur
Open winter: 9 AM - 4 PM; summer: 10 AM - 6 PM
Collections: Exhibits of Transylvanian traditional occupations, primitive people, Ethnographical Park, the first open-air museum in Romania

CONSTANTA

M **MUZEUL DE ISTORIE NATIONALA SI ARHEOLOGIE CONSTANTA,** National History & Archaeology Museum, Piata Ovidiu nr. 12, Constanta, 900745 Romania. Tel 0241 618 763; Email secretariat@minac.ro; Web: www.minac.ro; *Dir* Dr Gabriel Custurea
Open May - Nov: daily 8 AM - 8 PM; Nov - May Wed - Sun 9 AM - 5 PM; Gen admis 10 RON, reduced 5 RON; Estab 1878; Library with 40,000 vols; Average Annual Attendance: 80,000
Library Holdings: Book Volumes, CD-ROMs, Compact Disks, DVDs, Maps, Photographs
Special Subjects: Anthropology, Antiquities-Egyptian, Antiquities-Etruscan, Antiquities-Greek, Antiquities-Oriental, Antiquities-Roman, Archaeology, Archaeology, Architecture, Art Education, Art History, Ceramics, Coins & Medals, Costumes, Crafts, Dioramas, Ethnology, Furniture, Glass, Glass, Gold, Gold, Graphics, Historical Material, History of Art & Archaeology, Jewelry, Manuscripts, Maps, Medieval Art, Mosaics, Photography, Posters, Pottery, Primitive art, Religious Art, Restorations, Scrimshaw, Sculpture, Silver, Silver, Islamic Art
Collections: Prehistory, history & archaeology of the region, statues, coins, Neolithic vessels, Smoking pipes collection
Exhibitions: Temporary exhibitions in summer
Publications: Pontica
Activities: Classes for children; mus shop sells books, magazines, reproductions, CDs & prints; Edificiu Roman cu Mozaic

PLOIESTI

M **MUZEUL JUDETEAN DE ARTA PRAHOVA - ION IONESCU-QUINTUS,** Art Museum of Prahova County, Blvd Independentei nr 1, Ploiesti, Romania. Tel 40 244 522264; Fax 40 244 511375; Email office@artmuseum.ro; Web: www.artmuseum.ro; *Dir* Florin Sicoie
Open Tues - Sun 9 AM - 5 PM, cl Mon
Collections: Modern & contemporary Romanian painting, graphics, sculpture & decorative arts

SIBIU

M **MUZEUL NATIONAL BRUKENTHAL,** Brukenthal Palace & European Art Gallery, Piata Mare 4-5, Sibiu, 550163 Romania. Tel 40 269 217 691; Fax 40 269 211 545; Email info@brukenthalmuseum.ro; Web: www.brukenthalmuseum.ro; *Gen Dir* Dr Sabin Adrian Luca; *Deputy Dir* Dana Roxana
Open Summer: Tues - Sun 10 AM - 6 PM, cl Mon & first Tues of month; Winter: Wed - Sun 10 AM - 6 PM, cl Mon & Tues; Gen admis 20 RON, students 5 RON; Estab 1817; pub mus; European, Romanian & Contemporary Art from the 15th-21st century; Average Annual Attendance: 366,410; Mem: CODART, ICOM
Income: Governmental funding
Purchases: through donations
Library Holdings: Book Volumes, DVDs, Exhibition Catalogs, Fiche, Framed Reproductions, Manuscripts, Maps, Memorabilia, Original Documents, Pamphlets, Periodical Subscriptions, Reproductions
Special Subjects: Antiquities-Egyptian, Antiquities-Greek, Antiquities-Roman, Archaeology, Art History, Asian Art, Baroque Art, Bronzes, Carpets & Rugs, Ceramics, Coins & Medals, Costumes, Crafts, Decorative Arts, Drawings, Embroidery, Etchings & Engravings, Flasks & Bottles, Furniture, Glass, Graphics, Hispanic Art, Historical Material, History of Art & Archaeology, Islamic Art, Jewelry, Landscapes, Manuscripts, Maps, Marine Painting, Medieval Art, Metalwork, Mexican Art, Miniatures, Oriental Art, Painting-Dutch, Painting-European, Painting-Flemish, Painting-French, Painting-German, Painting-Italian, Painting-Russian, Painting-Spanish, Period Rooms, Pewter, Photography, Porcelain, Portraits, Pottery, Primitive art, Prints, Religious Art, Renaissance Art, Restorations, Sculpture, Silver, Textiles, Watercolors, Woodcarvings
Collections: Personal collections of Samuel von Brukenthal, German & Austrian painting, Flemish, Dutch, Italian painting, Transylvanian Sculpture in Stone, Plaster-Cast copies of famous sculptures, cartography cabinet, print works & drawings cabinet, reception rooms (the Baroque Salons with original wallpaper), Anatolian Rug Coll, Romanian Art paintings (from 18th-20th century, Liturgical vestments (from 14th-16th c), Transylvanian Altars (15th & 16th c)
Exhibitions: Permanent & temporary exhibs
Publications: Brukenthal Acta Musei; Bibliotheca Brukenthal Book Series; guides; albums; exhib catalogues; booklets
Activities: Classes for adults & children; docent training; workshops; lects for mems only; concerts, gallery talks; tours; sponsoring of competitions; schols; awards to Prof Sabin Adrian Luca, Dr Elena Popescu & Dr Maria Ordeanu; European Union Prize for Cultural Heritage; lending original objects of art to mus from abroad for special exhibs; mus shop sells books, magazines, reproductions, prints, slides, DVD's, chocolate, personalized products & souvenirs

M **Altemberger House: The Museum of History**, Str Mitropoliei 2, Sibiu, 550179 Romania. Tel 40 269 218143; *Dept Head* Raluca Teodorescu
Collections: Material & ethnographic history of Sibiu and Southern Transylvania

M **Romanian Art Gallery**, Piata Mare 5, Sibiu, 550163 Romania. Tel 40 269 217691; *Dept Head* Alexandru Sonoc; *Deputy Dept Head* Daniela Damboiu
European, Romanian & Contemporary Art from the 17th-20th century; Average Annual Attendance: 366,410
Income: Government financial support & donations
Library Holdings: Book Volumes, CD-ROMs, Compact Disks, DVDs, Exhibition Catalogs
Special Subjects: Baroque Art, Bronzes, Carpets & Rugs, Ceramics, Decorative Arts, Drawings, Etchings & Engravings, Furniture, Glass, Graphics, Islamic Art, Medieval Art, Religious Art, Renaissance Art, Sculpture, Stained Glass, Textiles, Watercolors, Woodcarvings, Woodcuts, Painting-American
Collections: Romanian painting, sculpture, decorative arts, graphics
Exhibitions: Permanent: Romanian painting 17th - 20th century
Publications: Bruckenthal Acta Musei Guide; exhib catalogues; Eurographics
Activities: Classes for children; docent training; tours; loaning for temporary exhibs; organize traveling exhibs to country & abroad; mus shop sells books, magazines, reproductions, prints, post cards & personalized objects

L **The Brukenthal Library**, Piata Mare 4, Sibiu, 550163 Romania. Tel 40 269 217691; *Head of Brukenthal Library* Dr Constantin Ittu
Open Mon - Fri 10 AM - 3 PM
Library Holdings: Book Volumes, Exhibition Catalogs, Manuscripts, Maps, Original Documents, Periodical Subscriptions, Photographs, Prints

M **Contemporary Art Gallery**, Str Tribunei 6, Sibiu, 550176 Romania. Tel 40 0269 250431; *Dept Head* Alexandru Sonoc; *Deputy Dept Head* Daniela Damboiu
European, Romanian & Contemporary Art from the 15th-21st century

RUSSIA

KAZAN

M **THE STATE MUSEUM OF FINE ARTS OF TATARSTAN REPUBLIC,** Ul K Marska 64, Kazan, 420015 Russia. Tel 7 843 236 6931; Email muzei.izo@yandex.ru; Web: www.izo-museum.ru; *Dir* Rozaliya Naurgaleyeva
Open Tues - Sun 10 AM - 6 PM, Thurs 10 AM - 8 PM; Admis 200 RUB, reduced 130 RUB; Estab 1967; Library with 10,000 exhibits; Average Annual Attendance: 160,000
Special Subjects: Antiquities-Oriental, Asian Art, Baroque Art, Calligraphy, Carpets & Rugs, Ceramics, Costumes, Decorative Arts, Drawings, Embroidery, Enamels, Etchings & Engravings, Flasks & Bottles, Folk Art, Furniture, Glass, Gold, Graphics, Islamic Art, Laces, Landscapes, Leather, Maps, Medieval Art, Military Art, Painting-Dutch, Painting-European, Painting-French, Painting-German, Painting-Italian, Painting-Russian, Porcelain, Portraits, Primitive art, Religious Art, Restorations, Sculpture, Silver, Stained Glass, Textiles, Watercolors, Woodcarvings
Collections: West European & Soviet paintings, Russian & National Art
Exhibitions: Permanent exhibs: Russian 16th-20th century; West-European 16th-19th century; Shishkin Feshin
Publications: Catalogues, monographies
Activities: Classes for children; lects for mems only; concerts; gallery talks; tours; schols; organize traveling exhibs to Europe & Russia; mus shop sells books, magazines, prints, monographies & booklets

MOSCOW

M **MOSCOW KREMLIN STATE HISTORICAL AND CULTURAL MUSEUM AND HERITAGE SITE,** Moscow Kremlin Museums, Lebyazhiy per 4, Moscow, 125009 Russia. Tel 7 495 624 55 03; Fax 7 495 621 63 23; Email head@kremlin.museum.ru; Web: www.kreml.ru; *Gen Dir* Elena Gagarina
May 15- Sept 30: 9:30 AM - 6 PM; Oct 1 - May 14: 10 AM - 5 PM; cl Thurs; Admis 250 - 700 RUB; children under 16 free
Collections: Collections housed in Armoury & various Kremlin cathedrals

M **Kremlin Cathedrals**, Lebyazhir per 4, Moscow, 125009 Russia.
Open Mon - Wed & Fri - Sun 10 AM - 6 PM, cl Thurs; Admis 500 RUB
Collections: Icons, tombs & applied arts found in Cathedral of the Assumption, Cathedral of the Annunciation, Archangel Cathedral, Rizpolozhensky Cathedral & Cathedral of the Twelve Apostles

M **MOSCOW MUSEUM OF MODERN ART,** Petrovka 25, Moscow, 125009 Russia. Tel 7 495 694 28 90; Email info@mmoma.ru; Web: www.mmoma.ru; *Gen Dir* Zurab Tsereteli; *Exec Dir* Vasili Tsereteli; *First Deputy Dir* Manana Popova; *Deputy Dir* Georgy Patashuri; *Deputy Dir Exhib Activities* Ljudmila Andreeva; *Chief Cur* Elena Nasonova
Tues - Sun 12 PM - 9 PM, cl Mon; Admis standard 500 RUB, discounted 300 RUB, children under 7 free; Estab 1999 as the first state museum in Russia solely dedicated to art of the 20th & 21st centuries; Five venues across Moscow, the main building is a former 18th century mansion
Special Subjects: Painting-Russian, Painting-European, Conceptual Art, Sculpture, Photography, Drawings, Illustration, Mixed Media
Collections: 20th - 21st century contemporary art
Exhibitions: Rotating exhibits
Publications: Dialogue of Arts magazine

Activities: Educ progs for young & emerging artists, educ art workshops; lects open to pub; gallery talks; tours; art programming; conferences; arts festivals; outreach progs; individual sculptures & original objects of art lent; organize traveling exhibs; mus shop sells books, magazines, original art, reproductions, gifts; jewelry

M **MOSCOW MUSEUM OF OUTSIDER ART,** Izmailovski blvd 30, Moscow, 105043 Russia. Tel 095-465-6304; Fax 095-164-3738; Email outsider@t-com.me; Web: www.museum.ru/outsider; *Dir* Vladimir Abakumov
Estab 1989
Collections: Collection of national outsider art, neuve invention, and naive art

M **THE STATE MUSEUM OF ORIENTAL ART,** Nikitskij Blvd 12a, Moscow, 119019 Russia. Tel 7 (495) 691-0212; Fax 7 (495) 695-4846; Email info@orientmuseum.ru; Web: www.orientmuseum.ru; *Dir* Alekeaudr V Sedov
Open Tuess, Fri - Sun 11 AM - 8 PM, Wed & Thurs 12 - 9 PM cl Mon; Admis adults 150 RUB, students & pensioners 50 RUB, foreigners 300 RUB; Estab 1918; storage, study & popularization of art & material culture of the East; Average Annual Attendance: 72,400
Income: Federal budget from the revenues in the main & auxiliary scientific funds
Library Holdings: Auction Catalogs, Book Volumes, Exhibition Catalogs, Manuscripts, Periodical Subscriptions, Photographs
Special Subjects: Antiquities-Assyrian, Antiquities-Egyptian, Antiquities-Oriental, Antiquities-Persian, Archaeology, Asian Art, Bronzes, Calligraphy, Carpets & Rugs, Ceramics, Enamels, Etchings & Engravings, Islamic Art, Miniatures, Oriental Art, Painting-Dutch, Painting-French, Painting-Israeli, Painting-Japanese, Painting-Russian, Textiles
Collections: Art of the Republics of Soviet Central Asia, Chinese art, monuments of art of Japan, India, Vietnam, Korea, Mongolia, Iran and other countries of the Middle and Far East
Activities: Classes for children; lects open to pub; concerts; gallery talks; tours; 4 book traveling exhibs per yr; organize traveling exhibs for the museums of Russia; mus shop sells books, magazines, original art, reproductions, prints, slides, souvenirs

M **STATE TRETYAKOV GALLERY,** Str Lavrushinsky per 10, Moscow, 119017 Russia. Tel 499 230 7788; Fax 495 953 1051; Email tretyakov@tretyakov.ru; Web: www.tretyakovgallery.ru; *Dir Gen* Zelphira Tregulova
Open Tues, Wed, & Sun 10 AM - 6 PM, Thurs, Fri, & Sat 10 AM - 9 PM, cl Mon; Admis adults 450 RUB, students 300 RUB
Collections: 40,000 Russian icons, Russian & Soviet paintings, sculpture & graphic arts from 11th century to present

SAINT PETERSBURG

M **THE STATE HERMITAGE MUSEUM,** The Hermitage, 2, Palace Sq, Saint Petersburg, 1900000 Russia. Tel 7 812 571 34 65; Fax 7 812 570 47 58; Email chancery@hermitage.ru; Web: www.hermitagemuseum.org; *Dir* Dr Mikhail Piotrovski
Open Tues, Thurs, Sat - Sun 10:30 AM - 6 PM, Wed & Fri 10:30 AM - 9 PM, cl Mon, Jan 1 & May 9; Admis adults 700 RUB, Russian Federation & Belarusian citizens 400 RUB, all children & students free
Collections: Collection of the arts of prehistoric, ancient Eastern, Greco - Roman and medieval times, preserves over 2,600,000 objects d'art, including 40,000 drawings, 500,000 engravings, works by Leonardo da Vinci, Raphael, Titian, Rubens and Rembrandt, coins, weapons, applied art, porcelain & glass

M **STATE RUSSIAN MUSEUM,** Inzhenernaya Str 4, Saint Petersburg, 191011 Russia. Tel (812) 595-42-48; Email info@rusmuseum.ru; Web: www.rusmuseum.ru; *Dir* V A Gusev
Open Mon, Wed, Fri - Sun 10 AM - 6 PM, Thurs 1 PM - 9 PM, cl Tues; Admis adults 450 RUB, students & children 200 RUB; Estab 1895
Collections: Collection of Russian icons, paintings, sculptures & drawings from the 11th to the 19th centuries

SARATOV

M **MUZEY RADISHCHEVA,** Saratov Radishchev State Museum of Art, Ul Radishcheva 39, Saratov, 410600 Russia. Tel (8 845 2) 26 16 06; Email radmuseumart@radmuseumart.ru; Web: radmuseumart.ru; *Dir Gen* T V Grodskova
Open Tues - Wed 10 AM - 6 PM, Thurs noon - 8 PM, Fri - Sun 10 AM - 6 PM, cl Mon; Admis foreign nationals 200 RUB, Russian adults 120 RUB, Russian seniors 50 RUB, Russian students 20 - 25 RUB; Estab 1885; Circ Library circulation: 8,400; Library with 34,000 vols & 20,000 exhibitions; Average Annual Attendance: Library attendance: 2,500
Library Holdings: Book Volumes 34,000, Manuscripts 7, Periodical Subscriptions 26
Collections: The Books from Bogolyubov AP; Russian Books XVIII - XX Centuries; Foreign Books XVIII - XX Centuries; Miniature Books; The History of Library
Publications: Russian Books XVIII century

TVER

M **TVER REGIONAL ART GALLERY,** str Sovetskaya 3, Tver, 170100 Russia. Tel 4822 34 25 61; Fax 4822 34 25 61; Email tvergallery@mail.ru; Web: gallery.tver.ru; *Dir* Tatyana S Kuyukina
Open Tues - Sun 11 AM - 5 PM; Admis 100 RUB; Estab 1866; Library with 28,000 vols; 36,000 exhibits; Average Annual Attendance: 72,000
Library Holdings: Auction Catalogs, Book Volumes, Compact Disks, Periodical Subscriptions
Special Subjects: Archaeology, Architecture, Asian Art, Baroque Art, Bookplates & Bindings, Bronzes, Carpets & Rugs, Ceramics, Coins & Medals, Collages, Costumes, Decorative Arts, Drawings, Embroidery, Enamels, Etchings & Engravings, Flasks & Bottles, Folk Art, Furniture, Glass, Gold, Graphics, Historical Material, Islamic Art, Ivory, Jewelry, Judaica, Laces, Landscapes, Leather, Manuscripts, Maps, Marine Painting, Medieval Art, Metalwork, Miniatures, Mosaics, Oriental Art, Painting-American, Painting-British, Painting-Dutch, Painting-European, Painting-Flemish, Painting-French, Painting-German, Painting-Italian, Painting-Japanese, Painting-Polish, Painting-Russian, Painting-Scandinavian, Painting-Spanish, Pewter, Photography, Porcelain, Portraits, Posters, Pottery, Primitive art, Prints, Religious Art, Renaissance Art, Reproductions, Restorations, Sculpture, Silver, Stained Glass, Tapestries, Textiles, Watercolors, Woodcarvings, Woodcuts
Collections: Paintings, graphics, sculptures, decorative arts
Exhibitions: 58 exhibs & 6 additional
Publications: 96 publs
Activities: Classes for children; dramatic progs; lects open to pub; 4,746 vis lectrs per yr; concerts; gallery talks; tours; schols; awards; lending of original art to Russian Mus, Tretjakov Gallery; mus shop sells books, original art, reproductions, prints; junior mus Vladimir Serov's mus, Tver region Emmaus; Valentine Serov's Mus, Tver region Do-motkanovo

YAKUTSK

M **NATIONAL FINE ARTS MUSEUM OF THE REPUBLIC OF SAKHA - YAKUTIA,** Yakutia National Fine Arts Museum, Kiroiv str 9, Yakutsk, 677000 Russia. Tel 7 4112 33 52 74; Email sakhamuseum@mail.ru; *Dir* Asya Gabysheva
Open Tues - Sat 10 AM - 5 PM, cl Sun & Mon; Estab 1946
Collections: Russian art of the 18th to 19th centuries, 20th century art, art of the Yakutia, Western European art

RWANDA

BUTARE

M **NATIONAL MUSEUMS OF RWANDA,** PO Box 630, Butare, Rwanda. Tel 250-730-07410193; Email info@museum.gov.rw; Web: www.museum.gov.rw; *Dir Gen* Alphonse B Umuliisa
Open daily 8 AM - 6 PM; Admis EAC & CEPGL nationals & citizens: adults 1,000 RWF, students 500 RWF; international: adults 6,000 RWF, students 3,000 RWF; Estab 1989 to preserve the history & cultivate cultural knowledge of Rwanda through six locations
Collections: Ethnographic and artistic artifacts of Rwandan history and region

M **National Art Gallery - Rwesero**, Rwesero Hill, Nyanza, Rwanda. *Gallery Mgr* Ndabaga Karekezi Andre
Collections: Contemporary Rwandan visual arts, sculpture, decorative art, and traditional crafts

SAN MARINO

SAN MARINO CITY

M **MUSEI DI STATO REPUBBLICA DI SAN MARINO,** State Museums of the Republic of San Marino, Palazzo Pergami Belluzzi, Piazzetta del Titano 1 San Marino City, San Marino. Tel 0549-882670, 0549-883835; Fax 0549-882679; Email info@museidistato.sm; Email museodistato@omniway.sm; Web: www.museidistato.sm
Open Mar 20 - Sept 20 8 AM - 8 PM, Sept 21 - Mar 19 8:50 AM - 5 PM; Admis 3 EUR, reduced 1.50 EUR; Estab 1899
Collections: Over 5,000 artifacts of San Marino ethnographic and artistic history, Archaeological finds from Neolithic to the early Middle Ages, Architectural remains of the ancient Basilica, Paintings from 17th century convent, Fine art and sculpture by San Marino artists, Coins and medals

M **St Francis Museum**, Via Basilicius, San Marino, 47890 San Marino. Tel 0549-885132
Collections: Sacred arts and gallery housed in 14th century loggias Franciscian Monastery, Panel paintings, frescoes, canvases, furnishings, paraments, Emilio Ambron Collection

M **Museum of Ancient Arms**, Via Salita alla Cesta, San Marino, San Marino. Tel 0549-991295
Collections: History and development of ancient arms and armors of the San Marino region

M **Contemporary & Modern Art Gallery**, Galleria di via Eugippo, Via Eugippo San Marino, San Marino. Tel 0549-883002, 885414; Fax 0549-883003; Email galleria@museidistato.sm
Collections: 750 works from the early 20th century to the present in various media

SAUDI ARABIA

RIYADH

M **NAILA ART GALLERY,** Al Takhassosi St Bldg 247, #2, Riyadh, Saudi Arabia. Tel 966 11 880 5352; Email info@gallerynaila.com; Web: www.gallerynaila.com; *Founder* Naifa al-Fayez
Open Sun - Thurs 10 AM - 10 PM, Sat 2 pm - 10 PM; Estab 2012
Collections: Contemporary art including paintings, sculptures and design pieces
Activities: Educ programs; tours

M **NATIONAL MUSEUM OF SAUDI ARABIA,** King Saud Rd, PO Box 3734 Riyadh, 11481 Saudi Arabia. Tel 966-1-402-9500; Email info@saudimuseum.com; Web: www.nationalmuseum.org.sa; *Dir Gen* Dr Abdullah bin Saud Al-Saud
Open Mon - Thurs 8 AM - 12 PM & 2 PM - 8 PM, Fri 4 PM - 8 PM, Sat 8 AM - 8 PM, Sun 8 AM - 2 PM; Admis 10 SAR, children & students free; Estab 1999
Collections: History of Islam and the Saudi region in 10 galleries, Manuscripts, documents, antiques, decorative arts, traditional crafts

SCOTLAND

ABERDEEN

M **ABERDEEN ART GALLERY & MUSEUMS,** Schoolhill, Aberdeen, AB10 1FQ Scotland. Tel 03000 200 293; Fax 44 (0) 1224 623666; Email info@aagm.co.uk; Web: www.aagm.co.uk; *Art Gallery & Mus Mgr* Christine Rew
Open Tues - Sat 10 AM - 5 PM, Sun 2 PM - 5 PM; No admis fee
Collections: 20th century British art, fine & decorative arts, James McBey print room
Activities: Classes for children; lects open to public; concerts; gallery talks; sales shop sells books, magazines

DUNDEE

M **LEISURE & CULTURE DUNDEE,** (Dundee Arts & Heritage) The McManus: Dundee's Art Gallery & Museum, Albert Sq, Dundee, DD1 1DA Scotland. Tel 44 01382 307200; Fax 44 01382 432369; Email themcmanus@leisureandculturedundee.com; Web: www.mcmanus.co.uk; *Head Mus Services* Fiona Sinclair; *Cur* Christine Miller; *Cur* Anna Robertson
Open Mon - Sat 10 AM - 5 PM, Sun 12:30 - 4:30 PM; No admis fee; Estab 1872; Large regl mus with colls of art, history & natural history; Average Annual Attendance: 250,000
Income: Funded by Dundee City Council
Special Subjects: Antiquities-Greek, Antiquities-Roman, Archaeology, Ceramics, Coins & Medals, Costumes, Decorative Arts, Drawings, Etchings & Engravings, Ethnology, Glass, Historical Material, Landscapes, Marine Painting, Painting-British, Painting-European, Photography, Portraits, Prints, Renaissance Art, Scrimshaw, Sculpture, Silver, Stained Glass, Textiles, Watercolors, Woodcarvings
Collections: 18th, 19th and 20th Century Scottish and English paintings, 17th Century Venetian and Flemish works, varied selection of watercolors and prints from the 18th - 20th Century, regional archaeology, Whaling history
Activities: Classes for adults & children; outreach program; lectrs open to the public; gallery talks; tours; Dundee Visual Arts Awards; lending of original objects of art to various institutions; mus shop sells prints & other merchandise

EDINBURGH

M **NATIONAL GALLERIES OF SCOTLAND,** Scottish National Gallery, The Mound, Edinburgh, EH2 2EL Scotland. Tel 44 (0)131 624 6200; Fax 44 (0)131 220 0917; Email enquiries@nationalgalleries.org; Web: www.nationalgalleries.org; *Dir Gen* Sir John Leighton; *COO* Nicola Catterall; *Dir Collection & Research* Prof Christopher Breward; *Dir Conservation & Collection Mgmt* Jacqueline Ridge; *Dir Public Engagement* Jo Coomber
Open daily 10 AM - 5 PM, Thurs until 7 PM; No admis fee; Estab 1850; Average Annual Attendance: 897,014
Library Holdings: Auction Catalogs, Book Volumes, Exhibition Catalogs, Fiche, Pamphlets, Periodical Subscriptions, Reproductions, Slides
Special Subjects: Coins & Medals, Drawings, Etchings & Engravings, Furniture, Landscapes, Painting-American, Painting-British, Painting-Dutch, Painting-European, Painting-French, Painting-German, Painting-Italian, Painting-Spanish, Religious Art, Renaissance Art, Tapestries, Watercolors
Collections: European & Scottish drawings, paintings, prints & sculpture, 14th - 19th centuries
Activities: Classes for adults & children; lects open to pub; concerts; gallery talks; mus shop sells books, magazines, reproductions & other gift items

M **Scottish National Gallery of Modern Art,** 75 Belford Rd, Edinburgh, EH4 3DR Scotland. Tel 44 (0)131 624 6200; Fax 44 (0)131 343 2802; Email enquiries@nationalgalleries.org; Web: www.nationalgalleries.org; *Dir-Gen* Sir John Leighton; *Dir* Simon Groom
Open daily 10 AM - 6 PM; No admis fee; Estab 1959; Two separate gallery bldgs set in extensive grounds and holding a coll of 20th & 21st century art; Average Annual Attendance: 300,000
Library Holdings: Auction Catalogs, Audio Tapes, Book Volumes, CD-ROMs, Cards, Cassettes, Clipping Files, Compact Disks, DVDs, Exhibition Catalogs, Manuscripts, Original Documents, Pamphlets, Periodical Subscriptions, Photographs, Prints, Records, Reels, Slides, Video Tapes
Collections: Western art from 20th & 21st centuries including painting, sculpture and graphic art; incl Matisse, Picasso, Dali & Scottish Art from Peploe to Douglas Gordon, Surrealism
Activities: Classes for adults & children; art clubs; lects open to public; gallery talks; tours; traveling exhibs circulated within the UK & internationally; mus shop sells books, magazines, reproductions, prints, slides & gifts

M **NATIONAL MUSEUMS SCOTLAND,** National Museum of Scotland, Chambers St, Edinburgh, EH1 1JF Scotland. Tel 44 (0) 300 123 6789; Email info@nms.ac.uk; Web: www.nms.ac.uk; *Dir* Dr Gordon Rintoul CBE
Open daily 10 AM - 5 PM, cl Dec 25; No admis fee; Four museums including: National Museum of Scotland, National War Museum, National Museum of Rural Life, National Museum of Flight; Average Annual Attendance: 2,500,000
Library Holdings: Auction Catalogs, Book Volumes, Exhibition Catalogs, Maps, Pamphlets, Periodical Subscriptions
Special Subjects: Scrimshaw, American Indian Art, Antiquities-Assyrian, Antiquities-Egyptian, Antiquities-Roman, Archaeology, Carpets & Rugs, Ceramics, Coins & Medals, Costumes, Decorative Arts, Eskimo Art, Furniture, Glass, Islamic Art, Ivory, Jade, Jewelry, Metalwork, Military Art, Miniatures, Photography, Porcelain, Pottery, Sculpture, Silver, Textiles
Collections: Collections of international applied arts, archaeology, natural sciences, science & tech, Scotland & Europe, world cultures
Activities: Classes for adults & children; dramatic progs; lect open to public; lect for mems only; gallery talks; tours; sponsoring of competitions; original works of art are lent to museums and cultural institutions; book traveling exhibs; originates traveling exhibs; mus shop sells books, magazines, reproductions, prints, toys, cards & jewelry

GLASGOW

M **GLASGOW MUSEUMS,** Glasgow Life, 220 High St Glasgow, G4 0QW Scotland. Tel (0141) 276-9500; Fax (0141) 276-9540; Email museums@glasgowlife.org.uk; Web: www.glasgowlife.org.uk; *CEO* Bridget McConnell
Open Mon - Thurs & Sat 10 AM - 5 PM, Fri & Sun 11 AM - 5 PM; Admis to all museums is free; Nine museums located throughout the city of Glasgow
Collections: Archaeology, British and Scottish art, Decorative Art Collection of ceramics, glass, jewelry, silver (especially Scottish), ethnography, Fine Art Collection representing the Dutch, Flemish, French and Italian schools, history, natural history

M **GLASGOW UNIVERSITY,** The Hunterian, University Ave, Glasgow, Gl2 8QQ Scotland. Tel (0141) 330 4221; Fax (0141) 330 3617; Email hunterian-enquiries@glasgow.ac.uk; Web: www.glasgow.ac.uk/hunterian; *Cur Palaeontology* Dr N Clark; *Cur Mineralogy* Dr J Faithfull; *Cur Archaeology* Dr S Coupar; *Cur Numismatics* Dr D Bateson; *Dir* Dr David Gaimster; *Cur Zoology* Maggie Reilly; *Senior Cur Art* Prof Pamela Robertson; *Cur Art* Peter Black; *Cur Art* Anne Dulau; *Deputy Dir* Mungo Campbell; *Head Mktg & Communications* Susan Ferguson; *Head Colls Management* Malcolm Chapman
Open Tues - Sat 10 AM - 5 PM, Sun 11 AM - 4 PM; All permanent galleries are free; Estab 1807 to serve the university and public; Three main sites on Univ Campus; Average Annual Attendance: 120,000
Income: Income from the university
Purchases: Purchases in areas of expertise of current colls
Special Subjects: Anthropology, Antiquities-Byzantine, Antiquities-Egyptian, Antiquities-Greek, Antiquities-Roman, Archaeology, Ceramics, Coins & Medals, Costumes, Ethnology, Furniture, Gold, Historical Material, Ivory, Jade, Painting-Dutch, Painting-Flemish, Porcelain, Pottery, Prints, Silver, Drawings
Collections: Prehistoric, Roman, ethnographical & coin colls, Paleontology, rocks & minerals, art, archaeology, medicine & anatomy, scientific instruments, zoology
Activities: Classes for adults & children; lect open to pub; gallery talks; exten prog serves scientific community, public, students, mus; shop sells books, reproductions, slides, toys

M **KELVINGROVE ART GALLERY & MUSEUM,** Argyle St, Glasgow, UK G3 8AG Scotland. Tel 0141 287 4350; Email info@glasgowlife.org.uk; Web: www.glasgowlife.org.uk/museums/kelvingrove; *CEO* Dr Bridget McConnell CBE; *Dir City Mktg & External Relations* Susan Deighan; *Dir Fin & Corporate Svcs* Martin Booth; *Dir Cultural Svcs* Jill Miller OBE; *Dir Sport* Billy Garrett
Open Mon - Thurs & Sat 10 AM - 5 PM, Fri & Sun 11 AM - 5 PM; No admis fee; Estab 1901; Scottish Recognised Collection of National Significance across 22 themed galleries; Average Annual Attendance: 1,000,000
Special Subjects: Painting-British, Painting-Dutch, Painting-Flemish, Antiquities-Egyptian, Antiquities-Roman, Antiquities-Greek, Metalwork, Sculpture, Archaeology, Historical Material
Collections: Dutch Old Masters, French Impressionists, Scottish Art, Salvador Dali, Charles Rennie Mackintosh & Glasgow Style, Scottish history & archaeology, arms & armor, ancient Egypt, natural history, world cultures
Exhibitions: Permanent, rotating & temporary exhibits
Activities: Educ progs; classes for families, adults, young people & children; artist workshops; interactive progs; lects open to pub; gallery talks; tours; workshops; competitions with awards; public art projects; arts festivals

SENEGAL

DAKAR

M **MUSEE THEODORE MONOD D'ART AFRICAIN,** Theodore Monod Museum of African Art, Place Soweto, BP 6167 Dakar, Senegal. Tel 221 33 823 9268; Web: ifan.ucad.sn; *Dir, IFAN* Papa Ndiaye
Open Tues - Sun 9 AM - 6 PM; Admis 2300 CFA, children 200 CFA; Part of l'Institut Fondamental d'Afrique Noire - IFAN
Collections: African art, ethnography, folk art, contemporary art

SERBIA

BELGRADE

M **MUZEJ GRADA BEOGRADA,** Belgrade City Museum, Zmaj Jovina Str 1, Belgrade, 11000 Serbia. Tel 011 263 0825; Fax 011-3283 504; Email office@mgb.org.rs; Web: www.mgb.org.rs; *Dir* Tatiana Koricanac
Open Tues, Wed & Fri 10 AM - 5 PM, Thurs, noon - 8 PM, Sat 11 AM - 5 PM, Sun 10 AM - 2 PM, cl Mon; Admis 200 CSD; Estab 1903

M **MUZEJ SAVREMENE UMETNOSTI BEOGRAD,** Museum of Contemporary Art Belgrade, Usce 10 blok 15, Belgrade, 11070 Serbia. Tel 381 011 3115 713; Email msub@msub.org.rs; Web: msub.org.rs; *Dir* Slobodan Nakarada; *Head Colls & Exhibs Dept and Cur New Art Media* Dr Zoran Eric; *Cur 1900-1950 Paintings* Misela Blanusa; *Cur Post-WWII Paintings* Svetlana Mitic; *Cur Prints & Drawings* Zaklina Ratkovic; *Cur Center for Visual Culture* Dr Dejan Sretenovic; *Cur Museum Contemporary Art Salon* Una Popovic
Open Mon, Wed, Fri - Sun 10 AM - 6 PM, Thurs 10 AM - 10 PM; Admis 300 RSD, reduced 150 RSD, groups 200 RSD; Estab 1958 to develop, collect & display art produced from Serbia and former Yugoslavia since 1900
Special Subjects: Painting-European, Sculpture, Prints, Drawings, Mixed Media, Photography, Film, Video
Collections: More than 8,000 pieces of art from Serbia, the Balkans, Europe & worldwide
Exhibitions: Permanent, rotating & temporary exhibits
Activities: Educ progs; classes for adults; gallery interpreting; artist residencies; artist workshops; interactive progs; lects open to pub; public art projects; gallery talks; tours; workshops; film screenings; individual objects of art lent

M **NATIONAL MUSEUM OF SERBIA,** National Museum in Belgrade, Trg Republike 1a, Belgrade, Serbia. Tel 381-11-33-060-48; Fax 381-11-26 277-21; Email kontakt@narodnimuzej.rs; Web: www.narodnimuzej.rs; *Dir* Dr Bojana Boric-Breskovic
Open Tues, Wed & Fri 10 AM - 5 PM, Thurs & Sat noon - 8 PM, Sun 10 AM - 2 PM, cl Mon; Adult admis 200 RSD, children & students 100 RSD
Library Holdings: Book Volumes 36,000, CD-ROMs 120, Manuscripts 10, Other Holdings 132, Periodical Subscriptions 22 titles
Special Subjects: Archaeology
Collections: Ethnographic and material history of Serbian culture and region, Over 400,000 archaeological artifacts, pieces of medieval art, post-medieval art, modern and contemporary art and more, European Art coll
Publications: Exhibition & collections catalogues; monographies; periodicals
Activities: Classes for adults & children; concerts; gallery talks; tours

M **Gallery of Frescoes**, Cara Urosa 20, Belgrade, 11000 Serbia. Email galerijafresaka@narodnimuzej.rs; *Cur & Gallery Mgr* Bojan Popovic
Estab 1953; Average Annual Attendance: 6000
Special Subjects: Medieval Art
Collections: Copies of Frescoes; icons; miniatures; sculptures
Exhibitions: Five temporary exhibits per yr
Activities: Concerts; tours

M **Museum of Vuk and Dositej**, Gospodar Jevremova 21, Belgrade, 11000 Serbia. Email mvd@narodnimuzej.rs; *Cur & Mus Mgr* Ljiljana Cubric

M **Memorial Museum of Nadezda and Rastko Petrovic**, Ljube Stojanovica 25, Belgrade, 11000 Serbia. Email dokumentacija@narodnimuzej.rs

M **Lepenski Vir Museum**, Boljetin Village, Donji Milanovac, 19220 Serbia. Tel 381 030 501 389
Mesolithic archaeological site

NOVI SAD

M **RAJKO MAMUZIC GALLERY OF FINE ARTS,** Vase Stajica 1, Novi Sad, 21000 Serbia. Tel 381-21-520-223, 381-21-520-467; Fax 381-21-520-223; Email glurm@mts.rs; Web: www.galerijamamuzic.org.rs; *Sr Cur* Joan Stolic
Open Wed - Sun 9 AM - 5 PM; No admis fee; Estab 1972; Anthology of Serbian fine arts from second half of the 20th century; Average Annual Attendance: 15,000
Income: Financed by the state
Library Holdings: Audio Tapes, Book Volumes, Cards, Clipping Files, Compact Disks, DVDs, Exhibition Catalogs, Manuscripts, Motion Pictures, Original Documents, Pamphlets, Photographs
Special Subjects: Art Education, Art History
Collections: Anthology of Serbian fine arts from second half of the 20th century, 800 works by 35 artists; paintings, sculptures, drawings, Serbian painting from second half 20th cen collected by Rajko Mamuzic
Activities: Classes for adults; concerts; gallery talks; tours; lend original object of art to various mus researching the same period & making exhibs; mus shop sells postcards

SINGAPORE, REPUBLIC OF

SINGAPORE

M **NATIONAL UNIVERSITY OF SINGAPORE CENTER FOR THE ARTS,** NUS Museum, University Cultural Centre, 50 Kent Ridge Crescent Singapore, 119279 Singapore, Republic of. Tel 65-6516-8817; Fax 65-6778-3738; Email museum@nus.edu.sg; Web: www.nus.edu.sg/cfa; *Dir* Christine Khor; *Mus Head, Sr Assoc Dir* Ahmad Bin Mashadi
Open Center for the Arts: Mon - Thurs 8:30 AM - 6 PM, Fri 8:30 AM - 5:30 PM, cl weekends & pub holidays; NUS Museum: Tues - Sat 10 AM - 6 PM, cl Mon & pub holidays; No admis fee; Estab 1955
Collections: Lee Kong Chian Collection of Chinese art spanning 7000 years, Ng Eng Teng Collection of sculpture, South and Southeast Asian collection of ceramics, textiles, sculptures, paintings and more, Straights Chinese collection
Activities: Classes for adults & children; docent training; mus shop sells exhibit catalogs

M **SINGAPORE ART MUSEUM,** 71 Bras Basah Rd, Singapore, 189555 Singapore, Republic of; 61 Stamford Rd #02-02, Singapore, 178892 Singapore, Republic of. Tel 65-65899-580; Email enquiries@singaporeartmuseum.sg; Web: www.singaporeartmuseum.sg
Open Mon - Sun 10 AM - 7 PM, Fri 10 AM - 9 PM; Admis adults $10 SGD, students & seniors $5 SGD, citizens/permanent residents & Fri 6 PM - 9 PM free; Estab 1996
Special Subjects: Asian Art, Photography
Collections: Permanent collection of over 7,500 pieces of modern and contemporary Southeast Asian art
Publications: Exhib catalogs; contemporary artists from Singapore
Activities: Classes for adults & children; dramatic progs; docent training; lectrs open to the public; gallery talks; tours; exten prog lends original objects of art to corp & pvt institutions; organize traveling exhibs internationally; mus shop sells books, magazines, reproductions, prints, merchandise, jewelry

SLOVAKIA

BANSKA BYSTRICA

M **STREDOSLOVENSKA GALERIA,** Central Slovakian Gallery, Dolna 8, Banska Bystrica, 975-50 Slovakia. Tel 421-48-470 16 15; Email ssgbb@ssgbb.sk; Web: www.ssgbb.sk; *Dir* Maros Rovnak, ArtD
Open Mon - Fri 10 AM - 5 PM, Sat - Sun 10 AM - 4 PM, cl Mon; Admis adults 2 EUR, students & seniors 0.50 EUR
Collections: 8,250 works of modern and contemporary Slovakian art

BRATISLAVA

M **DANUBIANA MEULENSTEEN ART MUSEUM,** 851 10 Bratislava-Cunovo, Bratislava, 810 00 Slovakia; P.O. Box 9, Bratislava, 81107 Slovakia. Tel 421-2 62 52 8501; Fax 421-2 62 52 8502; Email danubiana@danubiana.sk; Web: www.danubiana.sk; *Dir* Vincent Polakovic; *Gen Mgr* Katarina Polakovicova
Open summer: Tues - Sun 11 AM - 7 PM; winter: Tues - Sun 10 AM - 6 PM; Admis adults 10 EUR, children & students 5 EUR, family 20 EUR; Estab 2000

M **GALERIA MESTA BRATISLAVY,** Bratislava City Gallery, Mirbach Palace, Frantiskanske nam 11 Bratislava, 815 35 Slovakia. Tel 421-2-5443-1556; Fax 421-2-5443-2611; Email gmb@gmb.sk; Web: www.gmb.bratislava.sk; *Dir* Dr Ivan Jancar; *Mgr* Zuzana Jakabova
Open Tues - Sun 11 AM - 6 PM, cl Mon; Admis adults 4 EUR, children, students, seniors, disabled, natl mus assoc mems 2 EUR; family 6 EUR; Estab 1961; Public, owned by City of Bratislava; Average Annual Attendance: 35,000
Income: Financed partially by town
Library Holdings: Auction Catalogs, Book Volumes, Exhibition Catalogs, Video Tapes
Special Subjects: Restorations, Art History
Collections: 18th-20th century art, Gothic painting & sculpture, permanent Baroque art exhibition (central Europe's)
Activities: Classes for children; lects open to pub; concerts; gallery talks; 2007, 2010, 2012 gallery of the year award (for Slovak Republic only); lending original objects of art to sister institutions; mus shop sells books, reproductions & prints

M **SLOVENSKA NARODNA GALERIA,** Slovak National Gallery, Riecna 1, Bratislava, 815 13 Slovakia. Tel 421-2 204 761 00; Email info@sng.sk; Web: www.sng.sk; *Dir Gen* Alexandra Kusa, PhD; *Deputy Dir Gen* Alexandra Homolova, PhD
Open Tues - Wed & Fri - Sun 10 AM - 6 PM, Thurs noon - 8 PM; cl Mon; Gen admis 3.50 EUR; Estab 1948; Circ Circulation 5,500; Gallery contains art history, art collections, scientific research, culture & educ; Average Annual Attendance: 110,000; Mem: friends of SNG, 150
Library Holdings: Auction Catalogs, Book Volumes, CD-ROMs, Clipping Files, Compact Disks, Exhibition Catalogs, Fiche, Filmstrips, Manuscripts, Maps, Memorabilia, Micro Print, Original Documents, Periodical Subscriptions, Photographs, Reproductions, Slides, Video Tapes
Special Subjects: Antiquities-Roman, Archaeology, Architecture, Art Education, Baroque Art, Bronzes, Calligraphy, Ceramics, Collages, Conceptual Art, Costumes, Crafts, Drawings, Folk Art, Renaissance Art, Graphics, Hispanic Art, History of Art & Archaeology, Illustration, Interior Design, Jewelry, Landscape Architecture, Medieval Art, Miniatures, Mixed Media, Mosaics, Oriental Art, Painting-British, Painting-Dutch, Painting-European, Painting-Flemish, Painting-French, Painting-Italian, Painting-Spanish, Photography, Porcelain, Portraits, Posters, Prints, Religious Art, Restorations, Sculpture, Silver, Textiles, Watercolors
Collections: Applied arts, European & Slovak paintings, Dutch, Flemish and Italian works of art, graphics and drawings, sculpture
Publications: Renaissance (exhib & publ)
Activities: Classes for adults; classes for children; dramatic progs & other art of Slovakia; lects open to pub; 6-8 vis lectrs per yr; concerts; gallery talks; tours; schols; mus shop sells books, magazines, original art, reproductions, prints

DOLNY KUBIN

M **ORAVSKA GALERIA,** Orava Gallery, Hviezdoslavovo Sq 11, 026 01 Dolny Kubin, Slovakia. Tel 632-12 421-43-58; Fax 421-43-586-43-95; Email orgaldk@vuczilina.sk; ogaleria@nextra.sk; Web: www.oravskagaleria.sk; *Dir & Cur* Eva Luptakova
Open Tues - Sun 10 AM - 5 PM; Admis adults to permanent exhibs 2 EUR, temp exhibs 1 euro, seniors 1 EUR, children & students 0.50 EUR, res students 0.25 EUR, disabled & children under 6 free; Estab 1971
Collections: 7,472 works in 8 disciplines; craft of the 15th - 19th centuries, icons, Slovak artworks of the 20th century, traditional folk art

M **Mary Medveckej Gallery**, Medvedzie 1/1, Tvrdosin, 02744 Slovakia. Tel 421-043-532-2793; Web: www.oravskagaleria.sk
Open Apr 1 - Sept 30 Tues - Sun 10 AM - 4 PM; Admis to permanent exhibs: adults 1 EUR, children, disabled & seniors 0.50 EUR; admis to exhib hall: adults 0.50 EUR, children, disabled & seniors 0.25 euro, children under 6 free; family cardholder pass rates apply
Collections: Permanent collection of Slovakian artist Maria Medvecka

MEZILABORCE

M **ANDY WARHOL MUSEUM OF MODERN ART,** A Warhol St, Mezilaborce, 06801 Slovakia. Tel 421-57 74 800 72; Email awmuseum@centrum.sk; Web: andywarhol.sk; *Dir* Valika Madarova; *Deputy Dir & Chief Cur* Michal Bycko
Open May - Sept Mon - Fri 10 AM - 5 PM, Sat & Sun noon - 5 PM; October - April Mon - Fri 10 AM - 4 PM, Sat & Sun noon - 4 PM; Admis adults 3.50 EUR, students & seniors 1.70 EUR; Estab 1991

SLOVENIA

KOBARID

M **KOBARISKI MUZEJ,** Kobarid Museum, Gregorciceva ulica 10, Kobarid, 5222 Slovenia. Tel 386 05 389 00 00; Fax 386 05 389 00 02; Email info@kobariski-muzej.si; Web: www.kobariski-muzej.si; *Dir* Joze Serbec
Open Apr - Sept daily 9 AM - 6 PM; Oct - Mar daily 10 AM - 5 PM; Admis adults 6 EUR, seniors, high school & university students 4 EUR, children 2.5 EUR; Estab 1990
Collections: WWI history on the Isonzo front

LJUBLJANA

M **MESTNI MUZEJ LJUBLJANA,** City Museum of Ljubljana, Gosposka 15, Ljubljana, 1000 Slovenia. Tel 386 1 2412 500; Fax 386 1 2412 540; Email info@mgml.si; Web: www.mgml.si; *Dir* Dr Blaz Persin
Open Tues, Wed Fri - Sun 10 AM - 6 PM, Thurs 10 AM - 9 PM, cl Mon; Admis adults 4 EUR, students children & seniors 2.5 EUR; Housed in Auersperg Palace
Collections: 200,000 piece collection tracing the cultural history of the City of Ljubljana from prehistoric to modern times

M **City Art Gallery**, Mestni trg 5, Ljubljana, 1000 Slovenia. Tel 386 1 2411 770; Email mestna.galerija@mgml.si; Web: www.mgml.si; *Dir* Alenka Premov
Open Tues, Wed, Fri - Sat 11 AM - 7 PM, Thurs 11 AM - 9 PM, Sun 11 AM - 3 PM, cl mon; No admis fee
Collections: Works by all prominent exponents of Slovenian art of the 20th century
Activities: Classes for adults & children; lects open to the public; 15 vis lectrs per yr; gallery talks; tours; mus shop sells books, magazines, reproductions & prints

M **Jakopic Gallery**, Slovenska cesta 9, Ljubljana, 1000 Slovenia. Tel 386-0-1-2412-500; Email galerija.jakopic@mgml.si; Web: www.mgml.si; *Dir* Marija Skocir
Open Tues, Wed, Sun 10 AM - 6 PM; Thurs, Fri, Sat 10 AM - 9 PM; cl Mon; Adults 8 EUR, students, children, the disabled and the unemployed 5.50 EUR
Collections: Temporary exhibitions of international and national Slovakian artwork in various media

M **MODERNA GALERIJA & MUZEJ SODOBNE UMETNOSTI METELKOVA,** Museum of Modern Art & Museum of Contemporary Art Metelkova, Tomsiceva 14, Ljubljana, 1000 Slovenia. Tel 00386 12416 834; Email info@mg-lj.si; Web: www.mg-lj-si; *Dir* Zdenka Badovinac
Open 10 AM - 6 PM, open Thurs until 8 PM, cl Mon; Admis adults 5 EUR, students & pensioners 2.5 EUR, adult groups 3.5 EUR, student groups 2 EUR, family 8 EUR; Estab 1948; Library with 45,000 vols; Average Annual Attendance: 50,000
Income: Public funds
Library Holdings: Book Volumes, Exhibition Catalogs
Collections: Slovene art from Impressionists to present, international coll containing works of major artists of contemporary world art, Arteast 2000 (in Museum of Contemporary Art Metelkova)
Exhibitions: 20th Century Continuities & Ruptures (in Museum of Modern Art); The Present and Presence (in Museum of Contemporary Art Metelkova)
Activities: Classes for children; gallery talks; mus sells books & reproductions

M **NARODNA GALERIJA,** National Gallery of Slovenia, Puharjeva 9, Ljubljana, 1000 Slovenia. Tel 00386-(0) 1 24 15 400; Fax 00386-(0) 1-24 15 403; Email info@ng-slo.si; Web: www.ng-slo.si; *Dir* Barbara Jaki, PhD; *Head Cur* Mateja Brescak, MA; *Head Conservation-Restoration* Andrej Hirci, MA; *Head Educ* Kristina Preininger
Open Tues - Sun 10 AM - 6 PM, Thurs until 8 PM, cl Mon; Admis general 7 EUR, reduced 5 EUR; Estab 1918 for the purpose of collection of art in Slovenia; Library with 37,000 vols; 15,000 works of art (paintings, sculptures, works on paper); Average Annual Attendance: 250,000
Income: Government
Library Holdings: Auction Catalogs, CD-ROMs, Clipping Files, DVDs, Exhibition Catalogs, Framed Reproductions, Manuscripts, Maps, Original Documents, Pamphlets, Periodical Subscriptions, Records, Reproductions, Video Tapes
Special Subjects: Baroque Art, Coins & Medals, Drawings, Etchings & Engravings, Graphics, Landscapes, Manuscripts, Medieval Art, Painting-Dutch, Painting-European, Painting-Flemish, Painting-French, Painting-German, Painting-Italian, Painting-Polish, Painting-Spanish, Photography, Portraits, Prints, Religious Art, Renaissance Art, Sculpture, Watercolors, Woodcarvings, Woodcuts, Restorations, Sculpture
Collections: Copies of medieval frescoes, European Masters from the 14th century to the beginning of the 20th century, Slovenian sculptures and paintings from the 13th to the 20th century, Slovenian graphic arts, Coll of posters, Archival-documentary coll, Photo-Library
Publications: Exhib Catalogues
Activities: Classes for adults & children, dramatic progs, docent training, workshops; lects open to the pub; 6 vis lectrs per yr, concerts, gallery talks, tours; lending of original objects of art to European galleries & mus; originate traveling exhibs to Slovenian mus; mus shop sells books, magazines, reproductions, prints & slides

SOUTH AFRICA

CAPE TOWN

M **IZIKO MUSEUMS OF SOUTH AFRICA,** (Iziko Michaelis Collection) Michaelis Collection, Iziko Old Town House, Greenmarket Sq Cape Town, South Africa; PO Box 61, Cape Town, 8000 South Africa. Tel 27 (0) 21 481-3933; Email info@iziko.org.za; Web: www.iziko.org.za; *Cur* Hayden Proud
Open Mon - Sat 10 AM - 5 PM, cl Sun; Admis adults 20 ZAR, youth 6 - 18 yrs, SA students & seniors 10 ZAR, children 5 and under free; Estab 1914; Old Master Collection; Mem: 150 mems; friends of the Michaelis Coll R75.00; ann meeting Sep
Income: state funded
Library Holdings: Book Volumes
Collections: Dutch and Flemish graphic art and paintings of the 16th - 18th centuries, historical colls of the Iziko SA National Gallery
Exhibitions: Vis Artist's Residency Program
Activities: Classes for adults & children; lects open to pub; 2-3 vis lectrs per yr; concerts; gallery talks; lending of original objects of art to Haus der Kunst, Munich, schools from disadvantaged areas; progs for blind & disabled pupils; occasional travel exhibs to Sanlam Art Gallery, Bellville; mus shop sells books, postcards, brochures, current exhibs catalogues

M **SOUTH AFRICAN NATIONAL GALLERY,** Government Ave, Company's Garden Cape Town, 8000 South Africa. Tel 27 (0) 21 481 3970; Fax 27 (0) 21 467 4680; Web: www.iziko.org.za; *Cur* Hayden Proud
Open daily 10 AM - 5 PM; Admis adults 30 ZAR, youth 6 - 18 yrs, SA students & seniors 15 ZAR, children 5 & under no fee
Collections: 19th and 20th century South African art, 15th - 20th century, European art, including drawings, paintings, prints, sculptures and watercolors, traditional African art, 20th century American Art

DURBAN

M **DURBAN ART GALLERY,** City Hall, 2nd Fl, Anton Lembede St Durban, 4000 South Africa. Tel (031) 311 2264; Fax (031) 311 2273; Email mduduzi.xakaza@durban.gov.za; Web: www.durban.gov.za; *Educ Officer* Mduduzi Xakaza
Open Mon - Sat 8:30 AM - 4:00 PM, Sun 11 AM - 4 PM; No admis fee
Library Holdings: Auction Catalogs, Audio Tapes, CD-ROMs, Cassettes, Clipping Files, Compact Disks, Exhibition Catalogs, Slides, Video Tapes
Collections: Archaeology, paintings, graphic art, porcelain, sculptures, local history
Activities: Classes for adults & children; lects open to public

JOHANNESBURG

M **GOODMAN GALLEY,** 163 Jan Smuts Ave, Parkwood Johannesburg, 2193 South Africa. Tel 27-11-788-1113; Fax 27-11-788-9887; Email jhb@goodman-gallery.com; Web: www.goodman-gallery.com; *Dir* Liza Essers
Open Tues - Fri 9:30 AM - 5:30 PM, Sat 9:30 AM - 4 PM, cl Mon; Estab 1966; International contemporary art gallery
Collections: International modern and contemporary art & installations, African art, paintings, photographs, video installations. sculptures
Publications: Exhib catalogues
Activities: Educ progs; art projs; gallery talks; panel discussions; confs; tours

M **JOHANNESBURG ART GALLERY,** Cnr Klein & King George Sts, Joubert Park Johannesburg, 2044 South Africa. Tel (011) 725 3130; Fax (011) 720 6000; Email jag@joburg.org.za; Web: www.joburg.org.za; *Cur Contemp Art* Musha Neluheni
Open Tues - Sun 10 AM - 5 PM; No admis fee; Estab 1910; Art Gallery
Library Holdings: Auction Catalogs, Book Volumes, CD-ROMs, Clipping Files, Compact Disks, Exhibition Catalogs, Original Documents, Other Holdings Archives, Pamphlets, Periodical Subscriptions, Slides, Video Tapes
Collections: South African & international painting & sculpture, print coll, small coll of ceramics, textiles & fans
Activities: Classes for adults & children; lects open to pub; mus shop sells books

KIMBERLEY

M **WILLIAM HUMPHREYS ART GALLERY,** Cullinan Crescent, Civic Centre, PO Box 885 Kimberley, Cape Province 8300 South Africa. Tel (053) 8311724; Fax (053) 8322221; Email info@whag.co.za; Web: www.whag.co.za; *Dir* Mrs Ann Pretorius; *Comm Proj Ldr* Mrs Hesta Maree
Open Mon - Fri 8 AM - 4:45 PM, Sat 10 AM - 4:45, Sun & holidays 9 AM - 11:45 AM; Admis adults 5 ZAR adults, children 2 ZAR; Estab 1952; Circ 100; Art Mus; Average Annual Attendance: 22,000
Income: Central State: Dept Arts & Culture
Library Holdings: Auction Catalogs, Audio Tapes, Book Volumes, Cassettes, DVDs, Pamphlets, Periodical Subscriptions, Video Tapes
Collections: collection of Old Masters, collection of South African works of art, traditional and contemp SA ceramics, traditional SA artifacts, European & Cape furniture
Exhibitions: Traveling temporary exhibs
Publications: Newsletter; Carter, ACR The Work of War Artists in S.A. (reprints of the London Art Jour 1900)
Activities: Classes for adults & children; lects open to public; 10 vis lectrs per year; concerts; gallery talks; tours; sponsoring of competitions; Heritage; lending of original objects of art; mus shop sells books, original art, reproductions, prints

PIETERMARITZBURG

M **TATHAM ART GALLERY,** Chief Albert Luthuli (Commercial Rd) opposite City Hall, PO Box 321 Pietermaritzburg, 3200 South Africa. Tel 27 033 392 2801; Fax 27 033 394 9831; Web: www.tatham.org.za; *Dir* Brendan Bell; *Asst Dir* Bryony Clark; *Educ Officer* Pinky Madlabane-Nkabinde; *Technical Officer* Phumlani Ntshangase; *Admin Officer* Vimla Moodley
Open Mon - Fri 8 AM - 5 PM; No admis fee; Estab 1903
Collections: 18th century English & French paintings & sculpture, 19th & 20th century English graphics, modern European graphics, South African painting & sculpture

PORT ELIZABETH

M **NELSON MANDELA METROPOLITAN ART MUSEUM,** (King George VI Art Gallery), One Park Dr, Port Elizabeth, 6001 South Africa. Tel 27 (041) 506 2000; Fax 27 (041) 586 3234; Email artmuseum@mandelametro.gov.za; Web: www.artmuseum.co.za; *Dir* Dr Melanie Hillebrand
Open Mon & Wed - Fri 9 AM - 5 PM, Tues Noon - 5 PM, Sat, Sun 1 - 5 PM, pub holidays 2 - 5 PM, last Sun of month 9 AM - 2 PM; No admis fee
Library Holdings: Auction Catalogs, Audio Tapes, Book Volumes, CD-ROMs, Cassettes, DVDs, Exhibition Catalogs, Original Documents, Pamphlets, Periodical Subscriptions
Special Subjects: Anthropology, Art Education, Art History, Asian Art, Bronzes, Carpets & Rugs, Cartoons, Ceramics, Collages, Conceptual Art, Costumes, Crafts, Decorative Arts, Drawings, Embroidery, Eskimo Art, Etchings & Engravings, Ethnology, Graphics, History of Art & Archaeology, Jewelry, Landscapes, Miniatures, Mosaics, Oriental Art, Painting-British, Painting-European, Photography, Porcelain, Portraits, Posters, Pottery, Prints, Restorations, Sculpture, Stained Glass, Textiles, Watercolors, Woodcarvings, Woodcuts, Marine Painting
Collections: South African art (Eastern Cape), British art, international printmaking & Oriental art (including Indian miniatures & Chinese textiles)
Exhibitions: Active prog of temporary exhibs
Activities: Classes for adults & children; teacher training; lects open to pub; 5 vis lectrs per yr; concerts; gallery talks; tours; sponsoring of competitions; biennial exhib & award; extension prog serves Eastern Cape Province; artmobile; lending of original objects of art to other mus; organize traveling exhibs to other mus; mus shop sells books, reproductions, prints, gifts & other items

PRETORIA

M **PRETORIA ART MUSEUM,** Municipal Art Gallery, Arcadia Park, Pretoria, 0083 South Africa; PO Box 40925, Arcadia, 0007 South Africa. Tel 27 (012) 358-6750; Fax 27 (012) 344-1809; Email art.museum@tshwane.gov.za; Web: www.tshwane.gov.za; *Dir* Dirk Oegema
Open Tues - Sun 10 AM - 5 PM; Admis adults 22 ZAR, seniors 11 ZAR, students 5 ZAR; Estab 1964
Library Holdings: Auction Catalogs, Book Volumes, Clipping Files, Exhibition Catalogs, Pamphlets, Periodical Subscriptions
Special Subjects: African Art, Ceramics, Crafts, Drawings, Etchings & Engravings, Graphics, Painting-Dutch, Painting-Flemish, Photography, Pottery, Prints, Sculpture, Tapestries, Textiles, Woodcarvings
Collections: European graphics, 17th century Dutch art, 19th & 20th centuries South African art

SPAIN

ALZUZA

M **MUSEO JORGE OTEIZA,** Jorge Oteiza Museum, C/de la Cuesta 7, Alzuza, Navarra 31486 Spain. Tel 948 332 074; Fax 948 332 066; Email info@museooteiza.org; Web: www.museooteiza.org; *Dir* Gregorio Diaz Ereno; *Deputy Dir* Juan Pablo Huercanos; *Cur* Elena Martin; *Head Didactic Dept* Aitziber Urtasun; *Head Research Ctr* Borja Gonzalez Riera
Open summer: July 1 - Aug 31 Tues - Sat 11 AM - 7 PM, Sun & pub holidays 11 AM - 3 PM; winter: Sept 1 - June 30 Thurs -Fri 10 AM - 3 PM, Sat 11 AM - 7 PM, Sun & pub holidays 11 AM-3 PM; Admis adults 4 EUR, students 2 EUR; seniors, children under 18 & people with disabilities free
Collections: 1,690 sculptures; 800 drawings; 2,000 chalk laboratory studies

BARCELONA

M **FUNDACIO ANTONI TAPIES,** Antoni Tapies Foundation, Calle Arago 255, Barcelona, 08007 Spain. Tel 34 934 870 315; Fax 34 934 870 009; Web: www.fundaciotapies.org; *Dir* Carles Guerra; *Cur* Nuria Homs Serra
Open Tues - Sun 10 AM - 7 PM, cl Mon; Admis adults 7 EUR, students & seniors 5.60 EUR; Foundation museum.
Collections: Anoni Tapies paintings

M **MUSEU D'ART CONTEMPORANI DE BARCELONA,** Museum of Contemporary Art, Placa dels Angels 1, Barcelona, 08001 Spain. Tel 34 93 481 33 68; Fax 34 93 412 46 02; Email comunicacio@macba.cat; Web: www.macba.cat; *Dir* Ferran Barenblit; *CEO* Josep M Carrete
Open Mon - Fri 11 AM - 8 PM, Sat 10 AM - 8 PM, Sun & holidays 10 AM - 3 PM, Tues cl; Gen admis 10 EUR; students, journalists & teachers 8 EUR; reduced 5 EUR
Collections: Many works from Catalonian, Spanish & international artists ranging from the 1950s to the present

M **MUSEU DEL DISSENY DE BARCELONA,** Design Museum of Barcelona, Placa de les Glories Catalanes 37-38, Disseny Hub Barcelona Bldg Barcelona, 08018 Spain. Tel 00 34 93 256 3465; Fax (93) 2054518; Email museudeldisseny@bcn.cat; Web: www.museudeldisseny.cat; *Dir* Pilar Velez
Open Mon 10 PM - 8 PM; Adults 6 EUR, reduced admis 4 EUR; Rooms dedicated historical and contemporary decorative arts, ceramics, industrial design, textiles, clothing & graphic arts; Average Annual Attendance: 65,000
Income: financed by the municipality
Library Holdings: Auction Catalogs, Kodachrome Transparencies, Manuscripts, Periodical Subscriptions, Photographs, Slides
Collections: Collections dedicated to European decorative art, Spanish industrial design, Spanish ceramics, Occidental textiles, Spanish fashion, graphic art & topography
Exhibitions: Mexican Colonial Pottery, Margit Denz; Between East and West, Pere Noguera, Lusterware, Picasso, Miro, Barcelo
Publications: Exhib catalogues
Activities: Classes for adults & children; conservation courses; lects open to pub; 3 vis lectrs per yr; concerts; gallery talks; tours; awards: Critic Assn 1982 & 2003; lending of original objects of art to temporary exhibs in mus all over the world; originate traveling exhibs to Spanish mus; sales shop sells books, original art, reproductions, postcards, catalogues

M **MUSEU EUROPEU D'ART MODERN,** European Museum of Modern Art, Barra de Ferro 5, Barcelona, 08003 Spain. Tel 34 933 195 693; Fax 34 934 179 360; Email info@meam.es; Web: www.meam.es; *Dir* Jose Manuel Infiesta
Open 10 AM - 8 PM; Admis standard 9 EUR, reduced 7 EUR, children under 12 yrs free
Income: Owned by Fundacion Privada de las Artes y los Artistas
Collections: Figurative art of the 20th & 21st centuries

M **MUSEU NACIONAL D'ART DE CATALUNYA,** Catalona National Museum of Art, Parc de Montjuic, Palau Nacional Barcelona, 08038 Spain. Tel (00 34) 93 622 03 60; Fax (00 34) 93 622 03 74; Email mnac@mnac.cat; Web: www.museunacional.cat; *Dir* Pepe Serra Villalba; *Admin* Víctor Magrans Julià
Open May - Sep: Tues -Sat 10 AM - 8 PM, Sun & holidays 10 AM - 3 PM; Oct - Apr: Tues - Sat 10 AM - 6 PM, Sun & pub holidays 10 AM - 3 PM, cl Mon, Jan 1, May 1 & Dec 25; Admis 12 EUR, temporary exhibs 6 EUR, children under 16 & seniors over 65 free; Circ 105,000 documents; Medieval, Romanesque, Gothic, Renaissance & Baroque modern art collections.; Average Annual Attendance: 8,000,000; Mem: Friends of the museum
Library Holdings: Book Volumes, Cards, Compact Disks, DVDs, Exhibition Catalogs, Lantern Slides, Manuscripts, Original Documents, Pamphlets, Periodical Subscriptions, Photographs, Prints, Reproductions, Slides, Video Tapes
Special Subjects: Coins & Medals, Decorative Arts, Drawings, Enamels, Etchings & Engravings, Furniture, Jewelry, Landscapes, Medieval Art, Metalwork, Painting-European, Painting-European, Painting-Spanish, Photography, Portraits, Posters, Prints, Religious Art, Renaissance Art, Restorations, Sculpture, Silver, Stained Glass, Tapestries, Watercolors, Woodcarvings
Collections: Baroque & Renaissance paintings & sculpture, Catalan Gothic & Romanesque paintings & sculpture; modern paintings, sculpture & arts and crafts; photography; drawings & prints; numismatics
Publications: Publications on temporary and permanent collections
Activities: Classes for adults & children; docent training; dramatic progs; lects open to pub; concerts; gallery talks; tours; schols & fels offered; lending of original objects of art to other museums; mus shop sells books, magazines, original art; prints; reproductions, slides, gifts

M **MUSEU PICASSO,** Picasso Museum, Calle Montcada 15-23, Barcelona, 08003 Spain. Tel 34 93 256 30 00; Fax 34 93 315 01 02; Email museupicasso@bcn.cat; Web: www.museupicasso.bcn.cat; *Dir* Emmanuel Guigon
Open Tues - Wed, Fri - Sun (including pub holidays) 9 AM - 8:30 PM, Thurs 9 AM - 9:30 PM, Mon 10 AM - 5 PM; Admis includes collection & temporary exhib 14 EUR, collection only 12 EUR; Estab 1963; Average Annual Attendance: 950,000
Collections: Pablo Picasso, 1890-1972: 4,000 paintings, sculpture, drawings, ceramics and prints, including the series Las Meninas, photography on Picasso
Publications: Cartoons on the Front Line; Picasso in Paris: 1900-1907; Picasso 1936: Traces of an exhib (2011); Xavier Vilato: 1921-2000 The Road to Freedom; Economy: Picasso; Ceramica (2012)
Activities: Classes for adults & children; docent training; lects open to pub; concerts; gallery talks; tours; lending of original objects of art; organize traveling exhibs; mus shop sells books, magazines, prints, slides, reproductions

M **REIAL ACADEMIA CATALANA DE BELLAS ARTES DE SANT JORDI,** Catalonian Royal Academy of Fine Arts of Saint George, Casa Lonja, Paseo de Isabel II, n 1, 2 Barcelona, 08003 Spain. Tel 93 319 2432; Fax 93 319 0216; Email museu@racba.org; Web: www.racba.org; *Pres & Exec Sr Dir* Joan Antoni Solans Huguet; *Conservador Mus & Ilmo Sr* Josep Bracons Clapes
Open Mon - Fri 10 AM - 2 PM, cl Aug; No admis fee; Estab 1849; Private collection of the Royal Academy of Fine Arts in Barcelona, Spain.
Library Holdings: Book Volumes, Exhibition Catalogs, Memorabilia, Periodical Subscriptions
Activities: Lects open to pub; concerts; Mus shop sells books

BILBAO

M **GUGGENHEIM MUSEUM BILBAO,** Avenida Abandoibarra, Bilbao, 2 48009 Spain. Tel 34 944 35 90 00; Email informacion@guggenheim-bilbao.es; Web: www.guggenheim-bilbao.es; *Dir Gen* Juan Ignacio Vidarte
Open Tues - Sun 10 AM - 8 PM, cl Mon, Jan 1 & Dec 25; Admis adult 10 EUR, seniors & students 6 EUR, children free; Estab 1997
Collections: Modern and contemporary art from the mid-20th century to the present

M **MUSEO DE BELLAS ARTES DE BILBAO,** Bilbao Fine Arts Museum, Museo Plaza, 2, Bilbao, 48009 Spain. Tel 34 944 396 060; Fax 34 944 396 145; Email info@museobilbao.com; Web: www.museobilbao.com; *Dir* Javier Viar Olloqui

Open Wed - Mon 10 AM - 8 PM; Admis general 7 EUR, reduced 5 EUR, children under 12 yrs & Wed no admis fee
Library Holdings: Auction Catalogs, Audio Tapes, Book Volumes, CD-ROMs, Cards, Cassettes, Clipping Files, Compact Disks, DVDs, Exhibition Catalogs, Fiche, Filmstrips, Original Documents, Pamphlets, Periodical Subscriptions, Photographs, Prints
Collections: Paintings, sculpture, famous works by El Greco, Goya, Gauguin, Velazquez, general contemporary art, early Spanish paintings
Activities: Classes for adults & children; dramatic progs; docent training; lectrs open to the pub; lectrs for mems only; vis lectrs; schols; gallery talks; tours; mus shop sells books, original art, reproductions, prints & other items

CADIZ

M **FUNDACION MONTENMEDIO ARTE CONTEMPORANEO,** Montenmedio Contemporary Art Foundation, Dehesa de Montenmedio, Carretera A-48 (N-340) Cadiz, 11150 Spain. Tel 34 956 455 134; Fax 34 956 445 135; Email correo@fundacionnmac.org; Web: fundacionnmac.org; *Pres* Antonio Blazquez; *Dir* Jimena Blazquez Abascal
Open Tues - Sun 10 AM - 2PM & 5 - 9 PM, cl Mon; Gen admis 3 EUR, reduced admis 2 EUR, children under 8 free; Foundation collection and library.
Collections: Works by more than 40 contemporary artists with more than 20 on permanent display
Activities: Educ & cultural progs for adults and children

FIGUERES

M **GALA-SALVADOR DALI FOUNDATION MUSEUMS,** Salvador Dali Foundation, Torre Galatea, Pujada del Castell 28 Figueres, Catalonia E-17600 Spain. Tel 34-972-677-505; Fax 34-972-501-666; Email secgeneral@fundaciodali.org; Web: www.salvador-dali.org; *Chmn* Jordi Mercader; *Dir* Montse Aguer
Special Subjects: Drawings, Etchings & Engravings, Jewelry, Photography, Sculpture
Collections: Permanent Collection: thousands of objects dating from all the various periods of Dali's life, 4000+ works of art in various media

M **Teatre Museu-Dali**, Gala Dali Sq 5, Figueres, Catalonia E-17600 Spain. Tel 34-972-677-500; Fax 34-972-501-666; Email tmgrups@fundaciodali.org
Open Nov 1 - Feb 28 10:30 AM - 6 PM; Mar 1 - June 30 9:30 AM - 6 PM; July 1 - Sept 30 9 AM - 8 PM; Oct 1 - Oct 30 9:30 AM - 6 PM, cl Mon from Oct 1 to May 31, Jan 1, Dec 25; Admis 14 EUR, reduced 10 EUR, children under 8 free
Collections: Dali designed architectural piece

M **Dali - Joyas**, Ma Angels Vayreda St, Pujada del Castell St Figueres, E-17600 Spain. Tel 34-972-677-500; Fax 34 972-501-666; Email tmgrups@fundaciodali.org
Open Nov 1 - Feb 28 10:30 AM - 6 PM, Mar 1 - June 30 9:30 AM - 6 PM, July 1 - Sept 30 9 AM - 8 PM, Oct 1 - Oct 30 9:30 AM - 6 PM, cl Mon Oct 1 to May 31, Jan 1, Dec 25; Admis 7 EUR, reduced 5 EUR, children under 8 free
Collections: Collection of 37 jewels in gold and precious stones, Drawings and paintings made during design of jewels from 1940-1970

M **Casa Salvador Dali Portiligat**, Torre Galatea, Portlligat Cadaques, E-17488 Spain. Tel 34-972-251-015; Fax 34-972-251-083; Email pll@fundaciodali.org
Open Jan 1 - 6 & Feb 11 - Jun 14 10:30 AM - 6 PM, Jun 15 - Sept 15 9:30 AM - 9 PM, Sept 16 - Dec 31 10:30 AM - 6 PM, cl Mon, Jan 1, Jan 7 - Feb 11 & Dec 25 Reservations must be made in advance.; Admis 11 EUR, reduced 8 EUR, children under 8 free.; Average Annual Attendance: 99,717
Special Subjects: Decorative Arts, Furniture
Collections: Dali's only fixed residence from 1930-1982
Activities: Mus shop sells books & reproductions

M **Castillo Gala Dali Pubol**, Gala Dali Square, Pubol-la Pera, E-17120 Spain. Tel 34-972-488-655; Email pubol@fundaciodali.org
Open Jan 1 - Jan 10: 10 AM - 5 PM Jan 11 - Mar 14: cl Mar 15 - Jun 14: 10 AM - 6 PM Jun 15 - Sept 15: 10 AM - 8 PM Sept 16 - Nov 1: 10 AM - 6 PM Nov 2 - Dec 31: 10 AM - 5 PM; Admis 8 EUR, reduced 6 EUR, children under 8 free; 1996; Average Annual Attendance: 104,081
Special Subjects: Architecture, Costumes, Crafts, Decorative Arts, Drawings, Furniture, Glass, Painting-Spanish, Sculpture, Tapestries, Watercolors
Collections: Castle with interior designed and decorated with Dali artifacts and pieces, 2nd floor - clothes created by Dalí and dresses belonging to Gala by the world's leading fashion designers
Publications: Guide book of castle & catalog of temporary exhib
Activities: Prog of guided visits for school groups; concerts; tours; mus shop sells books, reproductions, & souvenirs

LEON

M **MUSEO DE ARTE CONTEMPORANEO DE CASTILLA Y LEON,** Avenida de los Reyes Leoneses 24, Leon, 24008 Spain. Tel 34-987-09-00-00; Fax 34-987-09-11-11; Email musac@musac.es; Web: musac.es; *Dir* Manuel Olveira
Open Tues - Fri 11 AM - 2 PM, 5 PM - 8 PM, Sat, Sun & holidays 11 AM - 3 PM, 5 PM - 9 PM; Admis 3 EUR, students 17 - 25 yrs & families 2 EUR, children 8 - 18 yrs 1 EUR, Sun 5 PM - 9 PM, children under 8 yrs & seniors free; Estab 2005, mus for the present; 6 main galleries, 1 project room, 1 showcase; Average Annual Attendance: 100,000
Income: Financed through regional government
Library Holdings: Audio Tapes, Book Volumes, CD-ROMs, Cards, Clipping Files, Compact Disks, DVDs, Exhibition Catalogs, Filmstrips, Kodachrome Transparencies, Lantern Slides, Manuscripts, Memorabilia, Micro Print, Motion Pictures, Original Art Works, Original Documents, Other Holdings, Pamphlets, Periodical Subscriptions, Photographs, Prints, Records, Reels, Reproductions, Slides, Video Tapes
Special Subjects: Architecture, Conceptual Art, Graphics, Illustration, Latin American Art, Mixed Media, Painting-Spanish
Activities: Workshops; performances, films; lects; guided tours

LLEIDA

M **MUSEU D'ART JAUME MORERA,** Jaume Morera Museum of Art, Calle Mayor 31 o Avinguda de Blondel 38-40, Edifici Casino Principal Lleida, 25007 Spain. Tel 0034-973-700-419; Fax 0034-973-700-487; Email mmorera@paeria.cat; Web: mmorera.paeria.es; *Dir* Jesus Navarro Guitart
Sept - May: Open Tues - Sat noon - 2 PM & 5 PM - 8 PM, Sun & holidays 11 AM - 2 PM, cl Mon June - Sept: Tues - Sat 10 AM - 1 PM & 6 - 8 PM, Sun 10 AM - 1 PM, cl Mon; No admis fee; Estab 1914 as the Art Museum of Lleida
Collections: paintings by Jaume Morera

MADRID

M **MUSEO CERRALBO,** Cerralbo Museum, Ventura Rodriguez 17, Madrid, 28008 Spain. Tel 34 915 473 646; Fax 34 915 591 171; Email museo.cerralbo@cultura.gob.es; Web: www.mecd.gob.es; *Dir* Lurdes Vaquero Arguelles; *Cur* M Angeles Granados Ortega; *Cur* Rebeca C Recio Martin
Open Tues - Sat 9:30 AM - 3:00 PM, Thurs 5 PM - 8 PM, Sun & pub holidays 10 AM - 3:00 PM; Admis 3 EUR, reduced 1.50 EUR; Estab 1924; pub institution; Foundation and house museum.; Average Annual Attendance: 80,000
Library Holdings: Auction Catalogs, Book Volumes, CD-ROMs, DVDs, Exhibition Catalogs, Memorabilia, Original Documents, Periodical Subscriptions
Special Subjects: Antiquities-Egyptian, Antiquities-Etruscan, Antiquities-Greek, Antiquities-Roman, Archaeology, Archaeology, Architecture, Asian Art, Baroque Art, Bronzes, Carpets & Rugs, Ceramics, Coins & Medals, Costumes, Decorative Arts, Drawings, Embroidery, Enamels, Etchings & Engravings, Ethnology, Glass, Gold, Graphics, Hispanic Art, Islamic Art, Ivory, Jewelry, Judaica, Laces, Manuscripts, Maps, Medieval Art, Metalwork, Military Art, Miniatures, Oriental Art, Painting-British, Painting-Dutch, Painting-European, Painting-Flemish, Painting-French, Painting-German, Painting-Italian, Painting-Spanish, Pewter, Photography, Porcelain, Portraits, Pottery, Religious Art, Renaissance Art, Restorations, Sculpture, Silver, Stained Glass, Tapestries, Textiles, Watercolors, Woodcarvings, Woodcuts, Furniture
Collections: Paintings, drawings, engravings, porcelain arms, carpets, coins, furniture; photographs; clocks; tapestries; books; sculptures; wood carvings, includes paintings by: El Greco, Ribera, Titian, Van Dyck & Tintoretto, library with 15,000 vols (historical library); archive (historical)
Publications: check website
Activities: Classes for children; educ progs include conferences; courses; families & children workshops; school activities; concerts; schols; awards, Europa Nostra; lending of original art to other mus; mus shop sells reproductions, books, slides, office objects & other items

M **MUSEO DEL ROMANTICISMO,** (Museo Romantico) Museum of the Romantic Period, Calle de San Mateo 13, Madrid, 28004 Spain. Tel (34) 914 481 045; Fax (34) 914 456 940; Email informacion.romanticismo@mcu.es; Web: museoromanticismo.mcu.es; *Dir* Asuncion Cardona Suanzes
Open winter: Tues - Sat 9:30 AM - 8 PM, Sun 10 AM - 3 PM, cl Mon; summer: Tues - Sat 9:30 AM - 8:30 PM, Sun 10 AM - 3 PM, cl Mon; Gen admis 3 EUR, reduced 1.50 EUR
Special Subjects: Ceramics, Decorative Arts, Dolls, Drawings, Furniture, Glass, Gold, Graphics, Jewelry, Miniatures, Painting-Spanish, Period Rooms, Photography, Porcelain, Portraits
Collections: Books, decorations, furniture and paintings of the Spanish Romantic period

M **MUSEO LAZARO GALDIANO,** Lazaro Galdiano Museum, Serrano 122, Madrid, 28006 Spain. Tel 34 915 616 084; Fax 34 915 617 793; Email info@museolazarogaldiano.es; Web: www.flg.es; *Dir* Elena Hernando; *Sec* Rosa Gonzalez; *Conservation* Carmen Espinosa; *Conservation* Amparo Lopez
Open Mon, Wed - Sat 10 AM - 4:30 PM, Sun 10 AM - 3 PM, cl Tues; Admis visitors 6 EUR, seniors, families 3 EUR, children under 12 yrs, teachers, unemployed, Sun 2 PM - 3 PM free; Estab 1951; Foundation museum and library.
Collections: Ivories, enamels, furniture, manuscripts, tapestries, prints, coins, textiles, drawings, bindings, rare books, European paintings & sculpture XV-XIX, paintings by Francisco de Goya, medals, pottery, antiquities
Activities: Docent training; concerts; mus shop sells books, magazines & reproductions

M **MUSEO NACIONAL CENTRO DE ARTE REINA SOFIA,** Queen Sofia National Art Center Museum, Calle Santa Isabel 52, Madrid, 28012 Spain. Tel 34 91 744 1000; Fax 34 91 774 1056; Email info@museoreinasofia.es; Email quejasysugerencias@museoreinasofia.es; Web: www.museoreinasofia.es; *Dir* Manuel Borja-Viuel; *Dep Dir* Joao Fernandes; *Head Exhibs* Teresa Velazquez
Open Mon & Wed - Sat 10 AM - 9 PM, Sun 10 AM - 7 PM, cl Tues, Jan 1 & 6, May 1, Nov 9, Dec 24, 25 & 31; Gen admis 10 EUR, temporary exhibs are 4 EUR, children under 18 & sr citizens over 65 free; The primary aim of the Museo Nacional Centro de Arte Reina Sofia is to encourage public access to various manifestations in modern & contemporary art in order to broaden knowledge, promote education & foster social communication of the arts.; Average Annual Attendance: 2,705,529
Collections: Works produced between the end of the 19th century up to the present, 16,200 works of art in various media; 4000 paintings, 1400 sculptures, 3000 drawings, more than 5000 prints, more than 2600 photographs, 80 videos & 30 installations, 100 decorative art pieces and 30 pieces of architecture
Activities: Classes for adults & children; dramatic progs; decent training; lects open to pub; concerts; gallery talks; tours; schols & fels; 2 book traveling exhibs per yr; organize 5-7 traveling exhibs to Serpentine Gallery, London; Tate Modern, London; Museum of Modern Art (MoMA), New York, Whitney Museum, New York; Centre Georges Pompidou, Paris; Pinacoteca de Sao Paul, Brasil; Museu de Arte Contemporanea de Serralves, Oporto, Portugal; Stedelijk Van Abbemuseum Eidenhaven, Netherlands; Museum fur Neve Kunst ZKM, Karlsruhe, Germany; Sammlung Falckenberg, Hamburg, Germany; mus shop sells books, mags, reproductions, prints & slides

M **MUSEO NACIONAL DEL PRADO,** The Prado Museum, Calle Ruiz de Alarcon 23, Madrid, 28014 Spain. Tel 34 91 330 2800; Email museo.nacional@museodelprado.es; Web: www.museodelprado.es; *Dir* Miguel Falomir Faus
Open Mon - Sat 10 AM - 8 PM, Sun & holidays 10 AM - 7 PM, cl Jan 1, May 1 & Dec 25; Gen admis 15 EUR, reduced 7.50 EUR, students & children under 18 free; Estab 1819; National museum.
Income: Financed by Govt of Spain
Collections: Paintings by: Botticelli, Rembrandt, Velazquez, El Greco, Goya, Murillo, Raphael, Bosch, Van der Weyden, Zurbaran, Van Dyck, Tiepolo, Ribalta, Rubens, Titian, Veronese, Tintoretto, Moro, Juanes, Menendez, Poussin, Ribera, classical and Renaissance sculpture, jewels and medals, drawings & prints
Activities: Educ and research progs for adults & children; pub progs & projects; guided tours

M **MUSEO SOROLLA,** Sorolla Museum, General Martinez Campos 37, Madrid, 28010 Spain. Tel 0034-91-3101584; Fax 0034-91-3085925; Email museo.sorolla@mecd.es; Web: museosorolla.mcu.es; *Dir* Consuelo Luca de Tena
Open Tues - Sat 9:30 AM - 8 PM, Sun & holidays 10 AM - 3 PM; Gen admis 3 EUR, reduced 1.50 EUR, retirees, seniors over 65 yrs, children under 18 yrs, Sat 2 PM - 8 PM & Sun free

M **MUSEO THYSSEN-BORNEMISZA,** Thyssen-Bornemisza Museum, Paseo del Prado 8, Madrid, 28014 Spain. Tel (34) 917 911 370; Email cav@museothyssen.org; Email mtb@museothyssen.org; Web: www.museothyssen.org; *Mng Dir* Evelio Acevedo; *Artistic Dir* Guillermo Solana
Open Mon 12 PM - 4 PM, Tues - Sun 10 AM - 7 PM, cl Jan 1, May 1 & Dec 25; Gen admis 12 EUR, reduced 8 EUR, children under 12 free; Estab 1992
Collections: 14th- to 20th-century fine art

M **PATRIMONIO NACIONAL,** National Heritage, Calle de Bailen s/n, Madrid, 28071 Spain. Tel 91-542-87-00; Fax 91-542-69-47; Email info@patrimonionacional.es; Web: www.patrimonionacional.es; *Pres* Jose Rodriguez-Spiteri Palazuelo; *Mng Dir* Alicia Pastor Mor
Estab 1940 to administer former Crown property; responsible for all the museums situated in Royal Palaces & properties; governed by a board of directors.; Manages and maintains 20 royal sites, four natural areas and the royal collections.; Average Annual Attendance: 829,604
Library Holdings: Book Volumes, Cards, Exhibition Catalogs, Maps, Reels, Reproductions
Special Subjects: Costumes, Architecture, Bronzes, Carpets & Rugs, Tapestries, Ceramics, Decorative Arts, Dioramas, Drawings, Furniture, Porcelain, Sculpture, Etchings & Engravings, Painting-European
Collections: armor, textiles & tapestries, paintings, sculptures, clocks, musical instruments, carriages, furniture
Publications: Guides to all the Museums
Activities: Educ progs; concerts; competitions; awards; mus shop sells books, reproductions

M **Palacio Real de Madrid - Royal Palace of Madrid**, Calle de Bailen s/n, Madrid, 28071 Spain. Tel 91 542 0059
Open Oct - March: daily 10 AM - 6 PM; April - Sept: daily 10 AM - 8 PM; Gen admis 10 EUR, reduced 5 EUR; Built 1738-1751; Former royal palace with library.
Collections: Special room devoted to 16th-18th century tapestries, clocks, paintings & porcelain from the Royal Palaces & Pharmacy
Activities: Tours

M **Palacio Real de La Granja de San Ildefonso - Royal Palace of La Granja de San Ildefonso**, Plaza de Espana 17, La Granja de San Ildefonso Segovia, 40100 Spain. Tel 92 147 0019
Open Oct - Mar: Tues - Sun 10 AM - 6 PM; Apr - Sept: Tues - Sun 10 AM - 8 PM, cl Mon; Gen admis 9 EUR, reduced 4EUR; Built 1720-1724; Former royal palace and summer residence.
Library Holdings: Book Volumes, Cards, Exhibition Catalogs, Reproductions
Collections: Gardens & fountains in imitation of Versailles, botanical garden, chapel, garden maze, tapestry museum
Activities: Tours

M **Palacio Real de Riofrio - Royal Palace of Riofrio**, 40420, Real Sitio de San Ildefonso Segovia, Spain. Tel 91 542 0059
Open Oct - March: Tues - Sun 10 AM - 6PM; April - Sept Tues - Sun 10 AM - 8 PM; Admin 7 EUR, reduced 4 EUR; Built 1751-1762; Former royal palace & hunting lodge with surrounding forest area.
Collections: Furnishings, paintings, carpets, tapestries, ceramics
Activities: Tours

M **Palacio Real de la Almudaina - Royal Palace of La Almudaina**, Calle Palau Reial S/N, Palma de Mallorca Balearic Is, 07001 Spain. Tel 97 172 7145
Open Oct - March: daily 10 AM - 6 PM, April - Sept: daily 10 AM - 8 PM; Gen admis 7 EUR, reduced 4 EUR; Built 1305-1314; Official royal residence built on the remains of a Roman settlement and Arabic fortress.
Collections: Furnishings, tapestries
Activities: Tours

M **Palacio Real de Aranjuez - Royal Palace of Aranjuez**, Ave de Palacio, Aranjuez, 28300 Spain. Tel 91 891 1344
Open Oct - March: Tues - Sun 10 AM - 6PM; April - Sept Tues - Sun 10 AM - 8 PM; Gen admis 9 EUR, reduced 4 EUR; Built 1564-1752; Former royal palace and country retreat
Collections: 18th century art, sculptures, furnishings, gardens & country house, barge museum
Activities: Tours

M **Real Sitio de San Lorenzo de El Escorial - Royal Site of San Lorenzo de El Escorial**, R Monasterio de San Lorenzo de El Escorial, Patrimonio Nacional Av D Juan de Borbon y Battenberg s/n Madrid, 28200 Spain. Tel 91 890 5903
Open Oct - Mar: Tues - Sun 10 AM - 6 PM; Apr - Sept: Tues - Sun 10 AM - 8 PM; Gen admis 10 EUR, reduced 5 EUR; Built 1562-1584; Former monastery, royal residence & gardens; Average Annual Attendance: 635,062
Library Holdings: Book Volumes, Cards, Exhibition Catalogs, Reproductions
Collections: Royal Collection of famous international work by artists of 16th & 18th centuries, paintings, sculptures, tapestries, mobiliary, clocks, lamps, porcelains, maps & prints
Activities: Concerts; mus shop sells books, reproductions

M **Monasterio de Sta Maria la Real de Las Huelgas - Monastery of Santa Maria la Real de Las Huelgas**, Calle Campas de Adentro s/n, Burgos, 09001 Spain. Tel 94 720 1630
Open Tues - Sat 10 AM - 2 PM & 4 PM - 6:30 PM, Sun & holidays 10: 30 AM - 3 PM; Gen admis 6 EUR; Founded 1187; Former Cistercian convent.
Collections: Works of sacred art, furnishings, paintings, medieval textiles, chapel, chapter house, cloisters & gardens
Activities: Tours

M **Real Monasterio de Santa Clara de Tordesillas - Royal Monastery of Santa Clara de Tordesillas**, Calle Alonso del Castillo Solorzano 21, Tordesillas, 47100 Spain. Tel 98 377 0071
Open Tues - Sat 10 AM - 2 PM & 4 PM - 6:30 PM, Sun & holidays 10:30 AM - 3 PM; Gen admis 6 EUR; Founded 1363; Former Mudejar palace, convent and Gothic church.
Collections: 14th century art, sacred works of art, tilework, plasterwork, courtyard galleries, cloisters
Activities: Tours

M **Real Monasterio de la Encarnacion - Royal Monastery of La Encarnacion**, Plaza de la Encarnacion 1, Madrid, 28013 Spain. Tel 91 542 0059
Open Tues - Sat 10 AM - 2 PM & 4 PM - 6:30 PM, Sun & holidays 10 AM - 3 PM; Gen admis 6 EUR; Estab 1611; Former convent and royal residence.
Collections: Decorative art, furnishings, royal portraits, relics & works of sacred art

M **Monasterio de las Descalzas Reales - Monastery of Las Descalzas Reales**, Plaza de las Descalzas s/n, Madrid, 28013 Spain. Tel 91 542 0059
Open Tues - Sat 10 AM - 2 PM & 4 PM - 6:30 PM, Sun & holidays 10 AM - 3 PM; Gen admis 6 EUR; Estab 1559; Former convent and royal residence.
Collections: Showing monastic life in the 16th & 17th centuries, furnishings, mosaics, works of sacred art
Activities: Tours

MALAGA

M **MUSEO PICASSO MALAGA,** Picasso Museum, Malaga, Palacio de Buenavista San Augustin 8, Malaga, 29015 Spain. Tel 34 952 12 76 00; Fax 34 952 60 45 70; Email info@museopicassomalaga.org; Web: www.museopicassomalaga.org; *Artistic Dir* Jose Lebrero Stals
Open July - Aug: daily 10 AM - 8 PM; Sept - Oct: daily 10 AM - 7 PM; Nov - Feb: daily 10 AM - 6 PM; Mar - June: daily 10 AM - 7 PM; Admis for perm collection plus temp exhbis 10 EUR, reduced 5 EUR; Estab 2003
Collections: Selected, donated Works by Pablo Picasso, Roberto Otero photographic archive
Activities: Educ & cultural progs; tours

MALPARTIDA DE CACERES

M **MUSEO VOSTELL MALPARTIDA,** Vostell Malpartida Museum, Apartado de correos 20, Malpartida de Caceres, Spain. Tel 927-01-08-12; Fax 927-01-08-14; Email museo@museovostell.org; Web: museovostell.org; *Dir* Josefa Cortes Morillo
Open Tues - Sat 9:30 AM - 1:30 PM, 4 - 6:30 PM; Sun 9:30 AM - 2:30 PM, cl Mon; Estab 1976
Collections: Conceptual art, sculptures, paintings, video installations

MARBELLA

M **MUSEO DEL GRABADO ESPANOL CONTEMPORANEO,** Museum of Contemporary Spanish Prints, c/ Hospital Bazan s/n, Marbella, 29601 Spain. Tel 952-765-741; Fax 952-764-591; Email info@mgec.es; Web: www.mgec.es; *Dir* German Borrachero
Open Summer: Mon 9 AM - 2 PM, Tues - Fri 9 AM - 7 PM; Sat 9 AM - 2 PM, cl Sun; Fall - Spring Mon & Sat 10 AM - 2 PM, Tues-Fri 10 AM - 2 PM & 6 PM - 10 PM; Admis adults 3 EUR, students 1.50 EUR, retired & children free; Estab 1992; preservation, promotion & exhib of 20th & 21st century engravings & Spanish artwork; Gallery located in the restored rooms of the former 16th century Hospital de la Encarnacion; Average Annual Attendance: 5725; Mem: 65; annual dues 60 EUR
Income: 100,000 EUR (own resources); 300,000 EUR (public admin)
Purchases: 400,000 EUR
Library Holdings: Book Volumes, CD-ROMs, Compact Disks, DVDs, Exhibition Catalogs, Pamphlets, Periodical Subscriptions
Collections: prints & graphic works from the 19th century to the present, 15th - 18th century
Exhibitions: Collection of works by Goya, Fortuny, Baroja, Picasso, Miro, Dali, Chillida, Saura, Tapies, Barcelo & Plensa
Publications: Exhib catalogs (10 per yr)
Activities: Classes for adults & children; Techniques engraving courses; lects open to pub; concerts; 2 fellowships; Premios Nacionales De Grabado award; lending original objects of art to different institutions & organizations; organize traveling exhibs to different institutions & organizations; mus shop sells books, prints, slides, T-shirts & mugs

PAMPLONA

M **MUSEO DE NAVARRA,** Museum of Navarra, Santo Domingo 47, Pamplona, E-31001 Spain. Tel 848-428-880; Email museo@navarra.es; Web: www.museodenavarra.navarra.es; *Dir* Mercedes Jover Hernando
Open Tues - Sat 9:30 AM - 2 PM & 5 PM - 7 PM; Sun & holidays 11 AM - 2 PM; Admis adults 2 EUR; Sat afternoon, Sun, children under 18 & seniors over 65 free
Special Subjects: Coins & Medals, Drawings, Embroidery, Hispanic Art, Islamic Art, Ivory, Medieval Art, Mosaics, Painting-European, Photography, Portraits, Religious Art, Renaissance Art, Sculpture, Silver
Collections: documentation on Navarre artists

Activities: Classes for children; dramatic progs; docent training; lects open to pub; concerts; mus shop sells books, reproductions, slides

SEGOVIA

M **MUSEO DE ARTE CONTEMPORANEO ESTEBAN VICENTE,** Esteban Vicente Museum of Contemporary Art, Plazuela de las Bellas Artes, Segovia, 40001 Spain. Tel 34 921 46 2010; Fax 34 921 46 2277; Email museo@museoestebanvicente.es; Web: www.museoestebanvicente.es; *Mgr* Luis Miguel del Pozo Gomez; *Cur* Ana Doldan de Caceres
Open Tues - Fri 11 Am - 2 PM & 4 PM - 7 PM, Sat 11 AM - 8 PM, Sun & holidays 11 AM - 3 PM, cl Mon; Gen admis 3 EUR, reduced 1.50 EUR, youth under 18 yrs & seniors over 65 yrs free; Contemporary art museum housed in a 15th century medieval palace.
Collections: Oil paintings, watercolors, drawings, collages, sculptures, tapestries, lithographs & silkscreens

SEVILLA

M **CENTRO ANDALUZ DE ARTE CONTEMPORANEO,** Andalusian Center for Contemporary Art, Avda Americo Vespucio 2, Camino de los Descubrimientos s/n Sevilla, 41092 Spain. Tel 34-955-03-70-70; Fax 34-955-03-70-52; Email prensa.caac@juntadeandalucia.es; Web: www.caac.es; *Dir* Juan Antonio Alvarel Reyes
Open Tues - Sat 11 AM - 9 PM, Sun 11 AM - 3:30 PM, cl Mon; Gen admis 3.01 EUR, Tues - Fri 7 PM - 9 PM & Sat free; Estab 1997; Contemporary art center and housed in a former monastery.
Income: Financed by Govt of Andalucia
Special Subjects: Photography
Activities: Educ progs; lects open to pub; concerts; organize traveling exhibs

M **MUSEO DE BELLAS ARTES DE SEVILLA,** Museum of Fine Arts of Seville, Plaza del Museo 9, Sevilla, 41001 Spain. Tel 0034-954-78-65-00; Fax 0034-954-78-64-90-; Email museobellasartessevilla.ccd@juntadeandalucia.es; Web: www.museodebellasartesdesevilla.es; *Dir* Maria del Valme Munoz Rubio
Open mid-Sept - mid-June: Tues - Sat 10 AM - 8:30 PM, Sun & pub holidays 10 AM - 5 PM, cl Mon; mid-June - mid-Sept: Tues - Sun & pub holidays 10 AM - 5 PM, cl Mon; Admis 1.50 EUR, European Union citizens & ICOM mems free; Estab 1835
Library Holdings: Exhibition Catalogs
Collections: Painting & sculpture XV - XX century; Sevillian mainly
Publications: Exhib catalogues
Activities: Exhibs; painters prog; lects open to pub; mus shop sells books, & other merchandise

TOLEDO

M **MUSEO DEL GRECO,** Paseo del Transito s/n, Toledo, 45002 Spain. Tel 925 22 36 65; Fax 925 22 58 31; Email museodelgreco@mecd.es; Web: museodelgreco.mcu.es; *Dir* Consolacion Pastor Cremades
Open April - Sept: Tues - Sat 9:30 AM - 8 PM, Sun & holidays 10 AM - 3 PM; Oct - Mar: Tues - Sat 9:30 AM - 6:30 PM, Sun & holidays 10 AM - 3 PM; Gen admis 3 EUR, reduced 1.50 EUR, youth under 18 yrs, seniors over 65 and families free
Income: Spanish Ministry of Education, Culture & Sport
Collections: El Greco's paintings, including portraits of Christ and the Apostles and other 16th and 17th century paintings & furniture

VALENCIA

M **MUSEO DE BELLAS ARTES DE VALENCIA,** Valencia Museum of Fine Arts, c/ San Pio V, No 9, Valencia, 46010 Spain. Tel 96 387 0300; Email museobellasartesvalencia@gva.es; Web: museobellasartesvalencia.gva.es; *Dir* Jose Ignacio Cazar Pinazo
Open Tues - Sun 10 AM - 8 PM; No admis fee
Income: Financed by Govt of Valencia
Collections: 14th -17th century paintings, landscapes & portraits, sculptures, religious works
Activities: Educ progs; presentations; guided tours

VALLADOLID

M **MUSEO NACIONAL DE ESCULTURA,** National Museum of Sculpture, c/ Cadenas de San Gregorio 1, 2 y 3, Valladolid, 47011 Spain. Tel 00-34-983-250-375; Fax 00-34-983-259-300; Email museoescultura@mecd.es; Web: museoescultura.mcu.es; *Dir* Maria Bolanos Atienza; *Deputy Dir* Manuel Arias Martinez
Open Tues - Sat 10 AM - 2 PM & 4 - 7:30 PM, Sun & holidays 10 AM - 2 PM; Admis 3 EUR, groups 1.50 EUR, children & students free
Special Subjects: Religious Art, Sculpture
Collections: Sculptures from the Middle Ages to the 19th century in various media, Collection de Repadaucciones Artisticas
Activities: Classes for adults & children; docent training; concerts; gallery talks; tours; mus shop sells books

M **MUSEO PATIO HERRERIANO DE ARTE CONTEMPORANEO ESPANOL,** Patio Herreriano Museum of Contemporary Spanish Art, Calle Jorge Guillen 6, Valladolid, 47003 Spain. Tel 34 983 362 908; Fax 34 983 375 295; Email patioherreriano@museoph.org; Web: www.museopatioherreriano.org; *Dir* Cristina Fontaneda Berthet
Open Tues - Fri 11 AM - 2 PM & 5 PM - 8 PM, Sat 11 AM - 8 PM, Sun 11 AM - 3 PM, cl Mon; No admis fee; Estab 2002; Contemporary art museum housed in a former monastery.
Collections: Contemporary Spanish art from 1918 to the present
Activities: Educ progs for adults and children; tours

SRI LANKA

ANURADHAPURA

M **ANURADHAPURA FOLK MUSEUM,** Old Town, Anuradhapura, Sri Lanka. Tel 00 94 25 223 4624; Web: www.museum.gov.lk; *Ed Officer* G. P. G. Pushpakumara
Open Tues - Sat 9 AM - 5 PM, cl Sun, Mon & pub holidays; Admis Sri Lankan nationals: adults 20 LKR, children 10 LKR; foreign nationals: adults 300 LKR, children 150 LKR; Estab 1971
Income: Sri Lanka Dept of National Museums
Collections: Local cultural & religious objects

COLOMBO

M **NATIONAL MUSEUMS OF SRI LANKA,** Colombo National Museum, Sir Marcus Fernando Mw, PO Box 854 Colombo, 7 Sri Lanka. Tel 94-0094 112 694 366; Email ranjith.shewage@gmail.com; Web: www.museum.gov.lk; *Dir, Dept of Nat Museums* Sanuja Kasthuriarachchi; *Mus Keeper* SH Ranjith
Open daily 9 AM - 6 PM, cl public holidays; Admis Sri Lankan nationals: adults 25 LKR, children 15 LKR; foreign nationals: adults 500 LKR, children 300 LKR; Est 1877; Cultural objects; Average Annual Attendance: 1.5 million
Income: government financed & donations
Library Holdings: Book Volumes, CD-ROMs, Cards, Cassettes, Clipping Files, Compact Disks, Exhibition Catalogs, Manuscripts, Maps, Micro Print, Original Art Works, Original Documents, Other Holdings, Pamphlets, Periodical Subscriptions, Photographs, Prints, Records
Collections: Art, folk culture and antiquities of Sri Lanka
Publications: Spolia Zeylanica
Activities: Classes for children; lects open to the pub, gallery talks; books traveling exhibs; originates traveling exhibs; mus shop sells books, magazines, original art

SWEDEN

GOTEBORG

M **GOTEBORGS KONSTMUSEUM,** Gothenburg Museum of Art, Gotaplatsen, Goteborg, 41256 Sweden. Tel 46 31 368 3500; Fax 46 31 368 3526; Email info.konstmuseum@kultur.goteborg.se; Web: konstmuseum.goteborg.se; *Dir* Isabella Nilsson
Open Tues 11 AM - 6 PM, Wed 11 AM - 8 PM, Thurs 11 AM - 6 PM, Fri - Sun & holidays 11 AM - 5 PM, cl Mon; Admis adults 40 SEK, groups 10 SEK, youth under 25 free
Collections: 15th - 17th century European art, 18th century Swedish art, 19th century Nordic art, French art

HELSINGBORG

M **DUNKERS KULTURHUS,** Dunkers Cultural Center, Kungsgatan 11, Helsingborg, 251 89 Sweden. Tel 46-042-10-74-00; Fax 46-042-10-74-10; Web: www.dunkerskulturhus.se; *Opers Mgr* Katti Hoflin
Open Tues - Fri 10 AM - 6 PM, Sat & Sun 10 AM - 5 PM; cl Mon; Admis to exhib adults 70 SEK, children under 18 free
Collections: artwork

LANDSKRONA

M **LANDSKRONA MUSEUM,** Slottsgatan, Linnankatu Landskrona, 261 80 Sweden. Tel 0418 47 31 20; Fax 0418 47 48 33; Web: www.landskrona.se/museum; *Dir* Christin Nielsen
Open Tues - Fri 10 AM - 5 PM, cl Mon; No admis fee
Collections: Swedish paintings since 1900, modern Swiss art, Nell Walden collection of paintings & ethnology, local history
Exhibitions: Temporary exhibs
Activities: Classes for children; lects open to public; concerts; mus shop sells books, reproductions, crafts

MORA

M **ZORNMUSEET,** Zorn Museum, Vasagatan 36, Mora, 792 21 Sweden; Box 32, Mora, 792 21 Sweden. Tel 46-0-250-592310; Fax 46-0-250-18460; Email info@zorn.se; Web: www.zorn.se; *Mus Dir* Johan Cederlund
Open June - Aug Mon - Sun 9 AM - 5 PM; Sept - Dec daily 11:45 AM - 4 PM; Jan - May 11:45 AM - 4 PM; Admis adults 70 SEK, pensioners & students 60 SEK, children 15 & under free; Estab 1939; Art by Anders Zorn & his art coll
Collections: Anders Zorn Collection
Activities: Mus shop sells books, reproductions, postcards, gifts

NORRKOPING

M **NORRKOPINGS KONSTMUSEUM,** Norrkoping Art Museum, Kristinaplatsen, Norrkoping, 602-34 Sweden. Tel 46-0-11-15-26-00; Fax 46-0-11-13-58-97; Email

konstmuseet@norrkoping.se; Web: www.norrkoping.se/konstmuseet; *Dir* Kristina Arnerud Mejhammer
Open Sept - May Tues - Sun 11 AM - 5 PM, Wed 11 AM - 8 PM; June - Aug Tues - Sun noon - 4 PM, Wed Noon - 8 PM, cl Mon; No admis fee
Collections: Collection of Swedish art from the 1600s to the present, incl Modernism & graphic art
Activities: Classes for adults & children; dramatic programs; lects open to pub, 4 -6 vis lectrs per yr; concerts; gallery talks; tours; serves Ostergutland, Sweden, Abroad; originates traveling exhibs to mus in Sweden & abroad; mus shop sells books, magazines, reproductions, prints

SKARHAMN

M **NORDISKA AKVARELLMUSEET,** Nordic Watercolour Museum, Sodra hamnen 6, Skarhamn, 471 32 Sweden. Tel 46-304-60-00-80; Email info@akvarellmuseet.org; Web: akvarellmuseet.org; *Dir* Bera Nordal; *Chrmn* Bjorn Springfeldt
Open daily 11 AM - 6 PM; Gen admis May - Sept 100 SEK, Oct - April 50 SEK, children under 25 free; Estab 2000
Collections: artwork by contemporary international watercolorists

STOCKHOLM

M **ARKITEKTUR - OCH DESIGNCENTRUM,** (Arkitektur Museet) Architecture and Design Center, Skeppsholmen, Stockholm, 11149 Sweden. Tel 08-520235 00; Email info@arkdes.se; Web: www.arkdes.se; *Supt* Kerstin Brunnberg; *Project Mgr* Ulrika Behm
Open Tues 10 AM - 8 PM, Wed - Sun 10 AM - 6 PM; No admis fee; Estab 1978
Collections: Some 2 million drawings and sketches, 600,000 photographs and more than 2000 models assoc with the history of Swedish buildings and national and international architects, books & periodicals
Publications: Yearly book, exhib catalogues occasionally; Swedish modernism

M **MODERNA MUSEET,** The Modern Museum, Skeppsholmen, Box 16382 Stockholm, 103 27 Sweden. Tel 46 8 5202 3500; Email info@modernamuseet.se; Web: www.modernamuseet.se; *Dir* Daniel Birnbaum; *Co-Dir* Ann-Sofi Noring
Open Tues & Fri 10 AM - 8 PM, Wed & Thurs 10 AM - 6 PM, Sat & Sun 11 AM - 6 PM, cl Mon; Admis varies by exhibs; Estab to collect, preserve, exhibit and promote knowledge about 20th and 21st century art
Income: Financed by the Swedish Ministry of Culture
Collections: Coll includes 5,000 paintings, sculptures & installations; 25,000 watercolors, drawings & prints; 400 art videos & films; 100,000 photographs, modern & contemporary art from 1900 to the present including key works by artists such as Duchamp, Picasso, Dali, Matisse and Rauschenberg, photographic collection of work from the 1840s to the present
Activities: Educ & research progs; tours; long-term loans

M **NATIONALMUSEUM,** National Museum of Sweden, Sodra Blasieholmshamnen, Stockholm, Sweden; PO Box 16176, Stockholm, 103 24 Sweden. Tel 46 (08) 5195 4300; Fax 46 (08) 5195 4450; Email info@nationalmuseum.se; Web: www.nationalmuseum.se; *Dir Gen* Berndt Arell; *Deputy Dir Gen* Birgitta Castenfors
Open May 15 - Aug 31 & Oct 2 - Jan 11 Mon, Wed, Fri - Sun 10 AM - 6 PM, Tues & Thurs 10 AM - 8 PM; Regular admis 100 SEK, reduced 80 SEK; Estab 1792 to preserve cultural heritage and promote art, interest in art and knowledge of art.; Renovated, c. 1866 Florentine & Venetian Renaissance building.; Average Annual Attendance: 500,000
Library Holdings: Book Volumes, Exhibition Catalogs, Original Documents
Special Subjects: Crafts, Decorative Arts, Drawings, Etchings & Engravings, Furniture, Glass, Miniatures, Painting-Dutch, Painting-European, Painting-Flemish, Painting-French, Painting-German, Painting-Italian, Painting-Scandinavian, Painting-Spanish, Porcelain, Portraits, Prints, Sculpture, Textiles
Collections: 16,000 works of paintings, icons & miniatures, sculptures, including antiquities, 500,000 drawings & prints, 30,000 items of applied art, collections of several royal castles with 7500 works of art from the middle ages to early 20th century applied arts also contemporary
Activities: Educ prog; classes for adults & children; lects open to pub; lectrs for mems only; gallery talks; tours; traveling exhibs to regl Swedish museums; mus shop sells books, reproductions, prints, jewelry, applied arts, glass & furniture

M **NORDISKA MUSEET,** Nordic Museum, Djurgardsvagen 6-16, PO Box 27820 Stockholm, 115 93 Sweden. Tel (8) 519 546 00; Fax (8) 519 545 80; Email nordiska@nordiskamuseet.se; Web: www.nordiskamuseet.se; *Dir* Sanne Houby-Nielson
Open Mon, Tues, Thurs - Sun 10 AM - 5 PM, Wed 10 AM - 8 PM; Admis adults 100 SEK, children under 18 yrs free
Collections: Costumes, industrial art, handcrafts, period furnishings, over one million exhibits

M **STOCKHOLMS STADSMUSEUM,** Stockholm City Museum, Ryssgarden Sodermalmstorg, PO Box 150 25 Stockholm, 104 65 Sweden. Tel 46 8 508 316 00; Fax 46 8 508 316 99; Email info.stadsmuseum@stockholm.se; Web: www.stadsmuseet.stockholm.se; *Mus & City Conservation Dir* Ann-Charlotte Backlund
Open Tues, Wed, Fri - Sun 11 AM - 5 PM, Thurs 11 AM - 8 PM; Admis adults 100 SEK, youth 19 yrs & under free
Collections: The Lohe Treasure, naive 19th century paintings of Josabeth Sjoberg & armed 15th century vessel, photographs, paintings, drawings, sketches & engravings
Activities: Classes for children; lects open to public, tours; mus shop sells books

M **VARLDSKULTUR MUSEERNA - OSTASIATISKA MUSEET,** Museums of World Culture Museum of Far Eastern Antiquities, Tyghusplan, Skeppsholmen, PO Box 16381 Stockholm, 103 27 Sweden. Tel 46 010 456 1200; Email info@ostasiatiskamuseet.se; Web: www.varldskulturmuseerna.se; *Dir Gen* Sanne Houby-Nielsen
Open Tues 11 AM - 8 PM, Wed - Sun 11 AM - 5 PM, cl Mon; No admis fee; Estab 1926
Collections: Chinese archaeology, Buddhist sculpture, bronzes, painting & porcelain, Stone-age pottery, Indian, Japanese & Korean art, Southeast Asian art and archaeology
Publications: Bulletin of Museum of Far Eastern Antiquities; Exhib catalogues; Monographs
Activities: Lects open to pub; concerts; gallery talks; tours; originate traveling exhibs; mus shop sells books, magazines, reproductions, prints, slides, ikebana tools, and souvenirs

SWITZERLAND

AARAU

M **AARGAUER KUNSTHAUS,** Aargauer Art House, Aargauerplatz, Aarau, 5001 Switzerland. Tel 0041 (062) 8352330; Fax 0041 (062) 8352329; Email kunsthaus@ag.ch; Web: www.aargauerkunsthaus.ch; *Dir* Madeleine Schuppli; *Cur & Deputy Dir* Thomas Schmutz
Open Tues - Sun 10 AM - 5 PM; Thurs 10 AM - 8 PM, cl Mon; Admis adults 15 CHF, students 10 CHF, 16 and under free; Contemporary art art museum.
Collections: Swiss painting and sculpture from 1750 to the present day, Caspar Wolf paintings (1735-1783) - art of the first painter of the Alps, landscape painter Adolf Staebli and Auberjonois, Bruhlmann, Amiet, G Giacometti, Hodler, Meyer-Amden, Louis Soutter, Vallotton
Activities: Classes for children; concerts; gallery talks; tours; mus shop sells books

BASEL

M **ANTIKENMUSEUM BASEL UND SAMMLUNG LUDWIG,** Basel Museum of Ancient Art & Ludwig Collection, St Albangraben 5, Basel, 4010 Switzerland. Tel 41-0-61-201-12-12; Fax 41-0-61-201-12-10; Email info@antikenmuseumbasel.ch; Web: www.antikenmuseumbasel.ch; *Dir* Dr Andrea Bignasca
Open Tues - Sun 10 AM - 5 PM, cl Mon; Admis adults 10 CHF, groups 13 CHF, youth under 20 yrs & students under 30 yrs 5 CHF, children under 13 yrs free; Estab 1961
Collections: Only Swiss museum devoted to the art and culture of the Mediterranean area, Collection dates mainly from Greek, Italian, Etruscan, Roman and Egyptian periods, Sculptures, pottery, gold jewelry, bronze statues, clay figures
Activities: Classes for adults & children; lects open to pub; concerts; lending of original objects of art to other mus; mus shop sells books, magazines & reproductions

M **KUNSTMUSEUM BASEL,** Basel Art Museum, Gegenwert, St Alban-Rheinweg 60, Basel, 4052 Switzerland; Hauptbau & Neubau, St Alban-Graben 16, Basel, 4051 Switzerland; St Alban-Graben 20, Basel, 4010 Switzerland. Tel 41 61 206 6262; Email pressoffice@kunstmuseumbasel.ch; Web: www.kunstmuseumbasel.ch; *Dir* Dr Josef Helfenstein
Open: Hauptbau & Neubau Tues - Sun 10 AM - 6 PM, Wed 10 AM - 8 PM, cl Mon; Gegenwert: Tues - Sun 11 AM - 6 PM, cl Mon; Admis for all exhibs adults 32 CHF, groups 23 CHF, students 20 - 30 yrs 16 CHF, youth 13 - 19 yrs, 8 CHF; Coll estab 1661; Municipal art collection housed in three locations: Hauptbau, Neubau and Gegenwart.
Library Holdings: Auction Catalogs, Book Volumes, CD-ROMs, Exhibition Catalogs, Manuscripts, Original Documents, Periodical Subscriptions
Collections: Old Masters from the 15th–18th centuries, 19th century & modern art, 19th century art and classic modernism, contemporary art after 1960, prints & drawings
Activities: Educ prog; classes for adults & children; lects open to pub; 20 vis lectrs per yr; concerts; gallery talks; tours; originates traveling exhibs to partner mus; mus shop sells books, magazines, reproductions, prints & slides

M **NATURHISTORISCHES MUSEUM BASEL,** Natural History Museum of Basel, Augustinergasse 2, Postfach Basel, 4001 Switzerland. Tel 41 61 266 55 00; Email nmb@bs.ch; Web: www.nmb.bs.ch; *Dir* Dr Christian A Meyer
Open Tues - Sun 10 AM - 5 PM, cl Mon; Admis adults 7 CHF, youth & students 5 CHF, children under 13 yrs free; Estab 1821; Library with 58,000 vols
Collections: Anthropology, Entomology, mineralogy, fossils, animals, zoology, Western European Center for Ocean Drulling Prog, micropaleontological reference coll
Activities: Classes for adults; classes for children; docent training; mus shop sells books, magazines, other objects

M **S AM SCHWEIZERISCHES ARCHITEKTURMUSEUM,** S AM Swiss Architecture Museum, Steinenberg 7, PO Box 911 Basel, 4001 Switzerland. Tel 41-(0) 61-261-14-13; Fax 41-(0) 61-261-14-28; Email info@sam-basel.org; Web: www.sam-basel.org; *Dir* Andreas Ruby
Open Tues, Wed, Fri 11 AM - 6 PM, Thurs 11 AM - 8:30 PM, Sat & Sun 11 AM - 5 PM; cl Mon; Admis adults 12 CHF, youth under 18 yrs, students, seniors, pensioners & unemployed 8 CHF, children under 15 yrs free; Estab 1984; Architecture mus; Mem: 350
Income: Mems, fundraising, sponsoring & other
Special Subjects: Architecture
Activities: Classes for adults & children; lects open to pub; tours; book traveling exhibs, 0-1; organize traveling exhibs to mus; mus shop sells books, magazines, original art & reproductions

BERN

M **KUNSTMUSEUM BERN,** Museum of Fine Arts Bern, Hodlerstrasse 8-12, Bern, 3000 Bern 7 Switzerland. Tel 031 328 09 44; Fax 031 328 09 55; Email

info@kunstmuseumbern.ch; Web: www.kunstmuseumbern.ch; *Dir* Dr Marcel Brulhart
Open Tues 10 AM - 9 PM, Wed - Sun 10 AM - 5 PM, cl Mon; Gen admis 7 CHF, reduced 5 CHF
Special Subjects: Drawings, Graphics, Landscapes, Painting-European, Painting-French, Painting-German, Painting-Italian, Painting-Russian, Painting-Spanish, Photography, Sculpture
Collections: Dutch & contemporary artists, French & other European Masters of the 19th & 20th centuries, Italian Masters, collection of Paul Klee works of 46 items, Niklaus Manuel, Hermann & Margrit Rupf Foundation, Adolf Wolfli Foundation, Swiss Baroque Masters, Swiss 19th & 20th Century Masters, 38,000 drawings & engravings, illustrations, works by Sophie Taeuber-Arp
Exhibitions: See website
Activities: Classes for adults and children; pvt & pub guided tours; mus shop or sales shop sells books, magazines, reproductions, prints & cards

M **ZENTRUM PAUL KLEE,** Paul Klee Center, Monument im Fruchtland 3, Postfach Bern, 30006 Switzerland. Tel +41-031-359-01-01; Fax +41-031-359-01-02; Email info@zpk.org; Web: www.zpk.org; *Dir* Marcel Bruhart; *Head Coll, Exhib & Research* Dr Michael Baumgatner
Open Tues - Sun 10 AM - 5 PM, cl Mon; Admis adults 20 CHF, senior citizens / concessions & groups 18 CHF, students & apprentices 10 CHF, children 6 -16 yrs 7 CHF
Special Subjects: Painting-German, Watercolors
Collections: More than 10,000 pieces of artwork by Paul Klee
Activities: Music, literature, theater & dance progs; concerts; tours

CHUR

M **BUNDNER KUNSTMUSEUM,** Bundner Art Museum, Bahnhofstrasse 35, Chur, 7000 Switzerland. Tel 41 81 257 2870; Fax 41 81 257 2172; Email info@bkm.gr.ch; Web: www.buendner-kunstmuseum.ch; *Co-Dir* Stephan Kunz; *Co-Dir* Nicole Seeberger; *Cur* Lynn Kost
Open Tues, Wed, Fri - Sun 10 AM - 5 PM, Thurs 10 AM - 8 PM, cl Mon; Gen admis 15 CHF, seniors, apprentices, students & groups 12 CHF, youth 16 yrs & under free; Modern & contemporary art museum housed in a 19th century villa.
Library Holdings: Auction Catalogs, Book Volumes, CD-ROMs, Exhibition Catalogs, Photographs, Video Tapes
Collections: Alberto, Augusto & Giovanni Giacometti, Angelika Kauffmann, E L Kirchner, Swiss painting, Contemporary Swiss Art
Activities: Classes for adults & children; concerts; gallery talks; tours; awards given, Manor-Kunstpreis, Suedostschweiz Medien; lending of original art to employees of canto Graubunden; mus shop sells books, prints, postcards, reproductions

DAVOS

M **KIRCHNER MUSEUM DAVOS,** Ernst Ludwig Kirchner Platz, Promenade 82 Davos, CH-7270 Switzerland. Tel +41-81-410-63-00; Fax +41-81-410-63-01; Email info@kirchnermuseum.ch; Web: www.kirchnermuseum.ch; *Dir* Thorsten Sadowsky
Open Tues - Sun 11 AM - 6 PM; Admis adults 12 CHF, seniors & groups 10 CHF, children & students 5 CHF; 1982; Average Annual Attendance: 25,000
Special Subjects: Drawings, Etchings & Engravings, Furniture, Painting-European, Photography, Portraits, Prints, Sculpture, Tapestries, Textiles, Watercolors, Woodcuts
Collections: Works by Ernst Ludwig Kirchner & his contemporaries
Exhibitions: 2 exhibs per yr
Publications: Exhibs catalogues
Activities: Classes for adults & children; concerts; gallery talks; tours; extension prog includes research; mus shop sells books, reproductions, prints

GENEVA

M **MUSEE D'ART MODERNE ET CONTEMPORAIN,** Museum of Modern & Contemporary Art, 10 rue das Vieux-Grenadiers, Geneva, 1205 Switzerland. Tel 41-22-320-61-22; Fax 41-22-781-56-81; Web: www.mamco.ch; *Dir* Lionel Bovier
Open Tues - Fri noon - 6 PM, Sat - Sun 11 AM - 6 PM, cl Mon; Admis 8 CHF, reduced 6 CHF, groups 4 CHF, under 18 yrs free, first Sun & Wed evening free
Collections: More than 3,000 works of art and 300 photographs; largest museum in Switzerland for contemporary & modern art

M **MUSEES D'ART ET D'HISTOIRE,** Museum of Art & History, rue Charles-Galland 2, 1206 Geneva, Switzerland. Tel 41 (0) 22 418 26 00; Fax 41 (0) 22 418 26 01; Email mah@ville-ge.ch; Web: www.institutions.ville-geneve.ch/fr/mah; *Dir* Jean-Yves Marin; *Cur Archaeology* Jean-Luc Chappaz; *Cur Applied Art & Textile* Marielle Martiniani-Reber; *Cur Numismatic Coll* Matteo Campagnolo; *Cur Fine Art* Laurence Madeline
Open Tues - Sun 11 AM - 6 PM, cl Mon; Free admission to the perm collections. Temp exhibs cost between 5 CHF & 20 CHF; Estab 1970; an encyclopedic museum, it houses colls in such diverse fields as archaeology, the fine arts and applied arts; largest Swiss coll of Egyptian antiques; also Near-East, Greek, Etruscan and Roman colls; Average Annual Attendance: 350,000 for the 5 museums
Library Holdings: Book Volumes, Cards, Exhibition Catalogs
Collections: Swiss art works, primitive Italian, French, German & Flemish art, modern art, archaeology, European sculpture & decorative arts, six attached museums
Exhibitions: See website
Activities: Classes for children; concerts; tours; Mus shop sells books, magazines & reproductions

GRUYERES

M **MUSEUM HR GIGER,** Chateau St Germain, Gruyeres, 1663 Switzerland. Tel 41-26-921-22-00; Fax 41-26-921-22-11; Email info@hrgigermuseum.com; Web: www.hrgigermuseum.com; *Adminr* Sandra Mivelaz
Open Apr - Oct daily 10 AM - 6 PM, Nov - Mar Tues - Fri 1 PM - 5 PM, Sat - Sun 10 AM - 6 PM, cl Mon; Admis adults 12.50 CHF, students, seniors & military 8.50 CHF, children 4 CHF; Estab 1998; Art museum housed in a medieval chateau.
Collections: Paintings, sculptures, furniture & film designs by HR Giger
Activities: Tours; mus shop sells books, CDs, furniture, prints & posters, sculptures, and jewelry

LAUSANNE

M **COLLECTION DE L'ART BRUT,** Art Brut Collection, 11 Av des Bergieres, Lausanne, 1004 Switzerland. Tel 41 21 315 25 70; Fax 41 21 315 25 71; Email art.brut@lausanne.ch; Web: www.artbrut.ch; *Dir* Sarah Lombardi
Open July & Aug daily 11 AM - 6 PM; Sept - June Tues - Sun 11 AM - 6 PM; cl Dec 25 & Jan 1; Admis adults 10 CHF, reduced 5 CHF, children under 16 free; Estab in 1945 to collect and display international works of Art Brut; Four-floor, 18th-century Swiss chateau; Mem: dues 50 CHF - 2,000 CHF
Special Subjects: Prints, Drawings, Watercolors, Film, Video, Sculpture
Collections: More than 70,000 works by 1,000 artists
Exhibitions: Rotating exhibits
Publications: Catalogs & monographs
Activities: Educ progs; classes for adults & children; gallery talks; tours; film screenings; original objects of art lent; organize traveling exhibs

LIGORNETTO

M **MUSEO VINCENZO VELA,** Vincenzo Vela Museum, PO Box 8, Ligornetto, 6853 Switzerland. Tel 41 58 481 30 40; Fax 41 91 647 32 41; Email museo.vela@bak.admin.ch; Web: www.museo-vela.ch; *Dir* Dr Gianna A Mina
Open Jan - May 10 AM - 5 PM; June - Sept 10 AM - 6 PM; Oct - Dec 10 AM - 5 PM; Sun 10 AM - 6 PM; Gen admis 12 CHF, reduced 8 CHF; 19th century villa and house-museum.
Library Holdings: Auction Catalogs, Book Volumes, Exhibition Catalogs, Periodical Subscriptions
Collections: Works of art by Vela family, paintings from eighteenth & nineteenth centuries Italian schools, original monument plasters by Vinceno Vela (1820-1891), plasters by Lorenzo Vela (1812-1897), Pictures by Spartaco, Lombard & Piemontese paintings from the eighteenth & nineteenth centuries
Activities: Classes for children; concerts; gallery talks; Mus shop sells books

LUCERNE

M **KUNSTMUSEUM LUCERNE,** Museum of Art Lucerne, Europaplatz 1, Lucerne, 6002 Switzerland. Tel (041) 226 78 00; Fax (041) 226 78 01; Email info@kunstmuseumluzern.ch; Web: www.kunstmuseumluzern.ch; *Dir* Fanni Fetzer
Open Tues, Thurs - Sun 10 AM - 5 PM, Wed 10 AM - 8 PM, cl Mon; Admis adults 15 CHF, groups of 10 or more 10 CHF, youth & students up to 16 yrs 6 CHF, children up to 6 yrs free; Average Annual Attendance: 50,000
Library Holdings: Book Volumes, Cards, Exhibition Catalogs
Collections: Swiss art from ancient times to 20th century, European expressionism and contemporary works
Activities: Classes for adults & children; lects open to pub; 2-4 vis lectrs per yr; gallery talks; tours; mus shop sells books, magazines, original art, reproductions, prints & various shop articles

SCHAFFHAUSEN

M **MUSEUM ZU ALLERHEILIGEN,** Klosterstrasse 16, Schaffhausen, 8200 Switzerland. Tel +41 (0) 52 633 07 77; Fax +41 (0) 52 633 07 88; Email admin.allerheiligen@stsh.ch; Web: www.allerheiligen.ch; *Dir* Dr Katarina Epprecht; *Deputy Dir & Cur Natural History* Dr Urs Weibel; *Cur History* Daniel Gruetter; *Cur Archaeology* Markus Honeisen; *Cur Art* Dr Matthias Fischer
Open Tues - Sun 11 AM - 5 PM, cl Mon; Admis adults 12 CHF, reduced 9 CHF, groups & youth 25 yrs & under & free; Estab 1921; Art & historical museum housed in am 11th century monastery.
Library Holdings: Auction Catalogs, Book Volumes, Exhibition Catalogs
Special Subjects: Antiquities-Assyrian, Antiquities-Etruscan, Antiquities-Greek, Antiquities-Persian, Antiquities-Roman, Archaeology, Asian Art, Baroque Art, Bronzes, Carpets & Rugs, Ceramics, Coins & Medals, Collages, Costumes, Crafts, Dioramas, Dolls, Drawings, Embroidery, Enamels, Etchings & Engravings, Ethnology, Furniture, Glass, Gold, Graphics, Historical Material, Ivory, Jade, Jewelry, Latin American Art, Leather, Manuscripts, Maps, Medieval Art, Metalwork, Military Art, Miniatures, Mosaics, Oriental Art, Painting-European, Period Rooms, Pewter, Photography, Porcelain, Portraits, Posters, Pottery, Pre-Columbian Art, Prints, Religious Art, Renaissance Art, Restorations, Sculpture, Silver, Stained Glass, Tapestries, Textiles, Watercolors, Woodcarvings, Woodcuts
Collections: Prehistory, natural history and art, graphics, numismatics, playing cards, Sturzenegger Collection, Stemmler Collection, Ebnother Collection
Exhibitions: Permanent exhibs of the colls & changing exhibs
Publications: Interdisciplinary editions of the mus
Activities: Classes for children & families; workshops; lectrs; gallery talks; guided tours; lending of original objects of art to mems of Kunstverein Schaffhausen; mus shop sells books, original art, reproductions, prints & other items

SOLOTHURN

M **KUNSTMUSEUM SOLOTHURN,** Solothurn Art Museum, Werkhofstrasse 30, Solothurn, 4500 Switzerland. Tel (032) 624 40 00; Fax (032) 622 50 01; Email kunstmuseum@solothurn.ch; Web: www.kunstmuseum-so.ch; *Cur* Dr Christoph Vogele; *Asst* Patricia Bieder; *Registrar* Anna Burkli
Open Tues - Fri 11 AM - 5 PM, Sat - Sun 10 AM - 5 PM, cl Mon; No admis fee; donatins accepted; Estab 1902; Art mus, mainly Swiss art; Average Annual Attendance: 20,000
Income: Financed mainly by city of Solothurn
Special Subjects: Baroque Art, Drawings, Landscapes, Painting-European, Painting-French, Painting-German, Portraits, Religious Art, Renaissance Art, Sculpture, Watercolors
Collections: Swiss art from 1850 to present, including Amiet, Hodler, Giacometti, Oppenheim, Raetz, Signer, small old master coll, small international coll includes Van Gogh, Matisse, Klimt, Leger
Exhibitions: 8 exhibs per yr
Publications: Broad selection of own exhib catalogues
Activities: Classes for adults & children; concerts; gallery talks; tours; mus shop sells books, prints, reproductions, postcards

ST GALLEN

M **HISTORISCHES UND VOLKERKUNDEMUSEUM,** Museum of History and Ethnology, Museumstrasse 50, St Gallen, CH-9000 Switzerland. Tel 41 071 242 0642; Fax 41 071 242 0644; Email info@hvmsg.ch; Web: www.hmsg.ch; *Dir* Dr Daniel Studer
Open Tues - Sun 10 AM - 5 PM; Admis adults 12 CHF, groups 10 CHF, youth up to 16 yrs without an adult, students & teachers 6 CHF, youth up to 16 yrs with an adult free; Historical & cultural museum located in a city park.
Special Subjects: African Art, American Indian Art, Archaeology, Asian Art, Ceramics, Costumes, Embroidery, Eskimo Art, Glass, Graphics, Period Rooms, Porcelain, Pre-Columbian Art, Prints, Religious Art, Sculpture, Textiles
Collections: Furniture, glass & glass painting, graphics, period rooms, pewter, porcelain, stoves, weapons, archeology, artifacts of different people from Egypt, Africa, N & S America & Asia
Activities: Educ progs for adults & children; tours; cus shop sells books, magazines & original art; children's museum

M **KUNSTMUSEUM ST GALLEN,** St Gallen Art Museum, Museumstrasse 32, St Gallen, CH-9000 Switzerland. Tel 41-71-242-06-71; Fax 41-71-242-06-72; Email info@kunstmuseumsg.ch; Web: www.kunstmuseumsg.ch; *Dir* Roland Waspe; *Cur* Nadia Veronese
Open Tues, Thurs - Sun 10 AM - 5 PM, Wed 10 AM - 8 PM, cl Mon; Admis adults 12 CHF, reduced 6 CHF
Collections: Paintings and sculptures from the late Middle Ages, Significant prints by Durer, Rembrandt and Callot, 17th century Dutch and Flemish painting, 19th century Swiss, German and French painting from Romanticism to Impressionism, Turn of the century modern and contemporary art
Activities: Art educ program; tours

THUN

M **KUNSTMUSEUM THUN,** Thun Art Museum, Hofstettenstrasse 14, Thun, CH-3602 Switzerland. Tel 41-0-33-225-84-20; Fax 41-0-33-225-89-06; Email kunstmuseum@thun.ch; Web: www.kunstmuseumthun.ch; *Dir* Helen Hirsch
Open Tues, Thurs - Sun 10 AM - 5 PM, Wed 10 AM - 7 PM, cl Mon; Admis adults 14 CHF, students & apprentices 12 CHF, youth 16 yrs and under free; Estab 1948; Mus with mainly contemporary art exhibs & coll of Swiss art.
Income: Financed by City of Thun & Canton of Bern
Purchases: Swiss Art
Library Holdings: Auction Catalogs, Book Volumes, CD-ROMs, DVDs, Exhibition Catalogs
Special Subjects: Collages, Drawings, Historical Material, Photography, Portraits, Posters, Prints, Reproductions, Restorations, Sculpture, Watercolors, Woodcuts
Collections: More than 7000 works; paintings, videos, sculpture, graphic arts, drawings, Minor and major Swiss artists both past and present, (see website)
Exhibitions: (see website)
Activities: Classes for adults & children; docent training; lects open to pub; concerts; gallery talks; tours; organize traveling exhibs; mus shop sells books, original art

WINTERTHUR

M **FOTOMUSEUM WINTERTHUR,** Winterthur Photo Museum, Gruzenstrasse 44 & 45, Winterthur, 8400 Switzerland. Tel 41-52-234-10-60; Fax 41-52-233-60-97; Email fotomuseum@fotomuseum.ch; Web: www.fotomuseum.ch; *Co-Dir & Cur* Duncan Forbes
Open Tues, Thurs - Sun 11 AM - 6 PM, Wed 11 AM - 8 PM, cl Mon; Admis 10 CHF, reduced 8 CHF; Estab 1993; contemporary as well as traditional for masters of 19th & 20th century; cultural-historical, sociological mus of applied photography; Average Annual Attendance: 54,550; Mem: 2,050 mems; dues 50 - 5,000
Income: 75% privately financed
Special Subjects: Photography, Porcelain
Collections: Contemporary photography in some 4000 photographs; rotating exhibitions
Activities: Classes for adults & children; lects open to pub; mus shop sells books, magazines & postcards

M **KUNST MUSEUM WINTERTHUR,** Winterthur Art Museum, Museumstrasse 52, PO Box 235 Winterthur, 8402 Switzerland. Tel 41 052 267 5162; Fax 41 052 267 5317; Email info@kmw.ch; Web: www.kmw.ch; *Dir* Dr Konrad Bitterli
Open Tues 10 AM - 8 PM, Wed - Sun 10 AM - 5 PM, cl Mon; Admis 15 CHF, reduced 12 CHF, children under 16 yrs free; Estab 1848; Mem: Open to everyone
Collections: French, Italian, German and Swiss painting and sculpture of 19th and 20th centuries, including Monet, Degas, Picasso, Gris, Leger, Klee, Schlemmer, Schwitters, Arp, Kandinsky, Renoir, Bonnard, Maillol, Van Gogh, Rodin, Brancusi, Morandi, Giacometti, de Stael, drawings and prints, European and American painting and sculpture after 1960: Agnes M Martin, Kelly, Marden, Mangold, Guston
Activities: Classes for children; lects open to pub; concerts; gallery talks, tours

M **Reinhart am Stadtgarten - Reinhart at the City Garden,** Stadthausstrasse 6, Winterthur, CH-8400 Switzerland. Tel 41 052 267 5172; Email info@kmw.ch; Web: www.kmw.ch; *Cur* Andrea Lutz
Open Tues - Sun 10 AM - 5 PM, Thurs 10 AM - 8 PM, cl Mon; Admis 19 CHF, reduced 15 CHF; Estab 1951
Collections: Pictures & drawings by German, Swiss & Austrian Masters of the 18th to 20th centuries, drawings & prints
Publications: Catalogues of paintings on permanent display
Activities: Classes for children; concerts

ZURICH

M **KUNSTHAUS ZURICH,** Zurich Art Gallery, Heimplatz 1, Zurich, 8001 Switzerland; Winkelwiese 4, Zurich, CH-8001 Switzerland. Tel 41 044 253 84 84; Fax 41 044 253 84 33; Email info@kunsthaus.ch; Web: www.kunsthaus.ch; *Dir* Dr Christoph Becker; *Secretariat* Christa Meienberg
Open Tues, Fri - Sun 10 AM - 6 PM, Wed & Thurs 10 AM - 8 PM, cl Mon; Admis 16 CHF, reduced 11 CHF; Estab 1910 for exhibs; Average Annual Attendance: 300,000; Mem: 18,000
Income: CHF 15 million budget
Library Holdings: Auction Catalogs, Book Volumes, CD-ROMs, DVDs, Exhibition Catalogs, Original Documents, Pamphlets, Periodical Subscriptions, Photographs, Prints, Sculpture, Video Tapes
Collections: Alberto Giacometti works, medieval and modern sculptures, paintings, graphic arts, 16th - 20th centuries, mainly 19th and 20th, photo and video coll
Activities: Educ prog; classes for adults & children; docent training; 4500 vis lectrs per yr; concerts; gallery talks; mus shop sells books, magazines, reproductions, prints & gifts

M **LANDESMUSEUM ZURICH,** Swiss National Museum, Museumstrasse 2, Zurich, 8021 Switzerland. Tel 41 (044) 218 65 11; Fax 41 (044) 211 29 49; Email info@snm.admin.ch; Web: www.nationalmuseum.ch; *Dir* Dr Andreas Spillmann
Open Tues - Wed, Fri - Sun 10 AM - 5 PM, Thurs 10 AM - 7 PM, cl Mon; Admis adults 10 CHF, reduced 8 CHF, children up to 16 yrs free; Library with 85,000 vols
Collections: History & cultural development of Switzerland since prehistoric times
Activities: Sales of books, prints, souvenirs

M **MUSEUM RIETBERG,** Gablerstrasse 15, Zurich, 8002 Switzerland. Tel (01) 206-31-31; Fax (01) 206-31-32; Email museum.rietberg@zuerich.ch; Web: www.rietberg.ch; *Dir* Dr Albert Lutz; *Deputy Dir* Dr Johannes Beltz
Open Tues, Thurs - Sun 10 AM - 5 PM, Wed 10 AM - 8 PM, cl Mon; Admis 18 CHF, reduced 14 CHF, youth 16 yrs & under free; Estab 1952, mus for non-European art; Gallery contains art from Asia, Africa, Oceania and the Americas; Average Annual Attendance: 80,000; Mem: 4,000
Library Holdings: Auction Catalogs, Book Volumes, Exhibition Catalogs
Collections: Asian, Oceanic and African art, Chinese bronzes, Baron von der Heydt Collection, The Berti Aschmann Foundation of Tibetan bronzes
Activities: Classes for adults & children; lects open to pub, 75 vis lectrs per yr; concerts; gallery talks; tours; 3 book traveling exhibs per yr; mus shop sells books, magazines, original art, reproductions, prints, posters, jewelry, stationery

M **STIFTUNG SAMMLUNG E G BUHRLE,** E.G. Buhrle Foundation Collection, Pfingstweidstrasse 96, Zurich, CH-8008 Switzerland. Tel 41-42-422-00-86; Email info@buehrle.ch; Web: www.buehrle.ch; *Dir & Cur* Dr Lukas Gloor
Open First Sun of month; group visits by appointment only; Pub tour admis 25 CHF; Estab 1960
Collections: private coll of Emil Georg Buhrle, French Impressionism and Post-Impressionism; 19th century French art; French avant-garde after 1900, Dutch painting of the 17th century and Italian painting of the 16th - 18th centuries, Gothic wood sculptures

M **ZURICH UNIVERSITY OF THE ARTS (ZHDK),** Zurich Museum of Design, Ausstellungsstrasse 60, Zurich, CH-8005 Switzerland; PO Box, Zurich, CH-8031 Switzerland. Tel 41-(0)-43-446-46-46; Fax 41-(0)-43-446-45-87; Email hs.admin@zhdk.ch; Web: www.zhdk.ch, www.museum-bellerive.ch; *Dir* Christian Brändle; *Cur* Sabine Flaschberger
Open Tues, Thurs - Sun 10 AM - 5 PM, Wed 10 AM - 8 PM, cl Mon; Admis Hall & Gallery 12 CHF, reduced 8 CHF, children under 12 yrs free; Estab 1875; Mem: See www.museum-gestaltung.ch
Library Holdings: Audio Tapes, Book Volumes, CD-ROMs, Clipping Files, Compact Disks, DVDs, Exhibition Catalogs, Maps, Motion Pictures, Original Documents, Periodical Subscriptions, Photographs, Prints, Records, Video Tapes
Special Subjects: Architecture, Cartoons, Ceramics, Decorative Arts, Drawings, Furniture, Glass, Graphics, Photography, Posters, Prints, Textiles, Crafts
Collections: Posters, graphic arts, design objects, illustrations of 20th century cultural production & applied art, Book covers, textiles, ceramics, glass, works in metal and wood, puppets, industrial design
Exhibitions: Please see website
Publications: Please see website
Activities: Workshops for children/students; lects open to pub; galley talks & tours; traveling exhibs organized; mus shop sells books, magazines & design objects

SYRIA

DAMASCUS

M **AZEM PALACE - MUSEUM OF POPULAR ARTS AND TRADITIONS,** Old Town, Suq al-Buzuriyya Damascus, Syria. Tel 963-11-221-0122, 222-1737; Email min-tourism@mail.sy
Open Wed - Mon 8 AM - 1 PM & 4 PM - 7 PM, cl Tues; Admis 150 SYP
Collections: Former palace divided into quarters; examines Syria's past through domestic artifacts and decorative arts, Textiles, household items, traditional craft; brass, Damascene procar material, wood mosaics

M **NATIONAL MUSEUM OF DAMASCUS,** Qasr el Heir St, Damascus, Syria. Tel 963 11 223 4331; Fax 963 11 224 7983; *Dir Gen* Heba Al Sakhel
Estab 1919
Collections: Ancient, Byzantine, Greek, Islamic, Modern, Oriental, Prehistoric and Roman art

TANZANIA

DAR ES SALAAM

M **NATIONAL MUSEUM OF TANZANIA,** National Museum & House of Culture, Shaaban Roberts St, PO Box 511 Dar es Salaam, Tanzania. Tel (51) 22030; Email director@houseofculture.or.tz; Web: www.houseofculture.or.tz; *Dir* Jumanne Mghembe
Open daily 9:30 AM - 6 PM; Admis foreign nationals: adults 6,500 TZS, students 2,600 TZS; Tanzanian citizens: adults & college students 1,500 TZS, elementary students 500 TZS; Estab 1934
Collections: Archaeology from Stone Age sites, ethnography & history collections

THAILAND

BANGKOK

M **NATIONAL GALLERY BANGKOK,** 4 Chao Fa Rd, Ko Rattanakosin Dist Bangkok, 10200 Thailand. Tel 662 281-2224; Web: ngbangkok.wordpress.com; *Dir* Ajara Kangsarikijja
Open Wed - Sun 9 AM - 4 PM; Admis 200 THB
Collections: Traditional and contemporary Thai art by Thai artists from the 17th century onward

M **NATIONAL MUSEUM BANGKOK,** Na Phrothat Rd, Amphoe Phda Nakhon Bangkok, 10200 Thailand. Tel 66 (0)2 215 8173; Web: www.bangkok.com/attraction-museum/national-museum.htm; *Dir* Khun Riam Pumpongpaet
Open Wed - Sun 9 AM - 4 PM, cl Mon & Tues; Admis 200 THB; Estab 1928
Collections: Bronze & stone sculptures, prehistoric artifacts, textiles, weapons, wood-carvings, royal regalia, theatrical masks, marionettes, shadow-play figures

M **SUAN PAKKAD PALACE MUSEUM,** 352-354 Sri Ayudhya Rd, Rajathevi Bangkok, 10400 Thailand. Tel (662) 245-4934, 246-1775-6 #229; Fax (662) 247-2079; Email info@suanpakkad.com; Web: www.suanpakkad.com; *Chmn* Sukhumbhand Paribatra
Open daily 9 AM - 4 PM; Admis local 50 baht, visitor 100 baht; Estab 1944-1945; Art & archaeology; Average Annual Attendance: 20,000
Library Holdings: Cards, Photographs
Special Subjects: Bronzes, Ceramics, Coins & Medals, Crafts, Dolls, Drawings, Furniture, Glass, Gold, Ivory, Jade, Jewelry, Manuscripts, Metalwork, Photography, Porcelain, Pottery, Sculpture, Silver, Stained Glass, Woodcarvings, Painting-French
Collections: Combination of fine arts and ancient artifacts from private coll, Reconstructed traditional houses; pottery, jewelry, bronze objects, architecture, The Lacquer Pavilion, Buddha images
Publications: The Suan Pakkad Palace Coll; The Lacquer Pavilion
Activities: Tours; sales shop sells books & CDs

TONGA

NUKU'ALOFA

M **TONGA NATIONAL CULTURAL CENTRE,** Taufa'ahau Rd, PO Box 2598 Nuku'alofa, Tonga. Tel 676-23-022; Fax 676-23-520; Email tongaculturecentre@gmail.com; *Dir* 'Etuate Lavulavu
Open Mon - Fri 9 AM - 4 PM; No admis fee
Collections: Local historical and ethnographic artifacts, contemporary art and cultural handicrafts, Wood carvings, canoe making, jewelry, textiles, basket weaving

TRINIDAD AND TOBAGO

PORT OF SPAIN

M **NATIONAL MUSEUM & ART GALLERY OF TRINIDAD AND TOBAGO,** 117 Frederick St, Port of Spain, Trinidad and Tobago. Tel 868-623-5941; Fax 868-623-7116; Email nationalmuseum117@gmail.com; Web: www.culture.gov.tt; *Cur* Lorraine Johnson
Open Tues - Sat 10 AM - 6 PM, Sun 2 PM - 6 PM; Admis is free; Estab 1892 to preserve the heritage of Trinidad and Tobago; 12,000 sq ft exhibit space; Average Annual Attendance: 60,000
Income: Financed by Ministry of Community Development, Culture and the Arts
Library Holdings: Book Volumes, Exhibition Catalogs, Original Documents, Pamphlets, Periodical Subscriptions, Photographs, Slides
Special Subjects: Archaeology, Cartoons, Ceramics, Coins & Medals, Collages, Costumes, Dioramas, Drawings, Flasks & Bottles, Historical Material, Landscapes, Maps, Military Art, Photography, Portraits, Pottery, Pre-Columbian Art, Prints, Reproductions, Restorations, Sculpture, Watercolors, Woodcarvings, Woodcuts
Collections: Fine art, archaeology, history & natural history colls
Exhibitions: August-Annual Independence Art Exhibition
Publications: Art catalogues
Activities: Museum theatre; children art & heritage workshop; lects open to pub; 6 vis lectrs per yr; concerts; gallery talks; guided tours; competitions; The Master Artist Award; lending of original objects of art to diplomatic missions abroad; originate traveling exhibs to governmental organizations; sales shop sells books, reproductions & prints

TUNISIA

KAIROUAN

M **RAQQADA NATIONAL MUSEUM OF ISLAMIC ART,** Sfax Rd, Kairouan, Tunisia. Tel 216-71-782-264; Fax 216-71-781-993; Web: www.patrimoinedetunisie.com.tn; *Dir* Mourad Rammah; *Cur* Lotfi Abd El Jaoued
Open Sept 1 - June 16 9 AM - 4 PM; June 17 - July 17 8 AM - 5 PM; July 18 - Sept 15 8:15 AM - 2:15 PM; cl Mon; Admis 5 TND
Collections: Archaeological finds from Kairouan, Art & crafts from the Aghlabid residences at Reqqada and Al Abbasiya, Houses coll of Islamic art in Tunisia; ceramics, medals, bronze & glass, calligraphy & manuscripts

SOUSSE

M **SOUSSE ARCHAEOLOGICAL MUSEUM,** Rue Abou Kacem Echabi, Sousse, Tunisia. Tel 216-71-782-264; Fax 216-71-781-993; Web: www.patrimoinedetunisie.com.tn
Open Tues - Sun April 1 - Sept 15: 9 AM - noon & 2 PM - 6 PM; Sept 16 - March 31: 8 AM - noon & 3 PM - 7 PM; Admis 5 TND; Estab 1951
Collections: Vast collection of mosaics; vases, masks, statues, burial tombs, Punic, Roman and early Christian period items and artifacts

TUNIS

M **MUSEE NATIONAL DU BARDO,** National Bardo Museum, Rue Mongi Slim, Tunis, 2000 Tunisia. Tel 216 71 513 650; Fax 216 71 514 050; Web: www.bardomuseum.tn; *Chief Cur* Taher Ghalia
Open May - Oct 9 AM - 5 PM, Oct - May 9:30 AM - 4: 30 PM; Admis 11 TND
Collections: Ancient & modern Islamic art, Greek & Roman antiquities, Roman mosaics

TURKEY

ANKARA

M **ANADOLU MEDENIYETLERI MUZESI,** Museum of Anatolian Civilizations, Gozcu Sokak No 2, Ulus Ankara, 06240 Turkey. Tel 90-312-324-31-60, 61, 65; Fax 90-312-311-28-39; Email anmedmuz@gmail.com; Web: www.anadolumedeniyetlerimuzesi.gov.tr
Open daily 8:30 AM - 7 PM; Admis 15 TRY; Estab 1921
Collections: Vast archaeological and ethnographic coll detailing Turkish history throughout every civilization in the region, Gold, silver, marble, bronze, coin colls, jewelry and more
Activities: Classes for children; lects open to pub; 10-15 vis lectrs per yr; concerts; schols; awards, European Mus of the Year Award (1997); sales shop sells books, reproductions, & prints; junior mus, Gordion Museum, Yassihoyuk Village, Polatli-Ankara

ISTANBUL

M **ELGIZ MUSEUM,** Elgiz Museum, Meydan Sokak Beybi Giz Plaza B Blok, Maslak Istanbul, 34398 Turkey. Tel 90-212-290-25-25; Fax 90-212-290-25-26; Email info@www.elgizmuseumistanbul.org; Web: www.elgizmuseum.org
Open Tues by appointment, Wed - Fri 10 AM - 5 PM, Sat 10 AM - 4 PM, cl Sun, Mon & nat holidays; No admis fee; Estab 2001
Collections: artworks by Turkish & international artists

M **ISTANBUL ARKEOLOJI MUZELERI,** Istanbul Archaeological Museums, Alemdar Cad Osman Hamdi, Bey Yokusu Sk Istanbul, 34122 Turkey. Tel 90 212 520 77 40, 41; Fax 90 212 527 43 00; Email info@istanbularkeoloji.gov.tr; Web: www.istanbularkeoloji.gov.tr; *Dir* Zeynep S Kiziltan; *Librn* Havva Koc
Open Tues - Sun 9 AM - 7 PM, cl Mon; Gen admis 20 TRY; Estab 1902; Library with 80,000 plus vols; Average Annual Attendance: 400-500
Purchases: Donation library
Library Holdings: Auction Catalogs, Book Volumes, Exhibition Catalogs, Manuscripts, Maps, Original Documents, Pamphlets, Periodical Subscriptions, Photographs
Special Subjects: Archaeology, American Western Art
Collections: Architectural pieces, Turkish tiles, Akkadian, Assyrian, Byzantine, Egyptian, Greek, Hittite, Roman, Sumerian and Urartu works of art
Publications: The Annual of the Istanbul Archaeological Museum
Activities: Concerts, shows & painting exhibitions; lectrs in all topics (archaeology, philology & numismatics)

M **ISTANBUL MUSEUM OF MODERN ART,** Meclis-i Mebusan Cad, Liman Isletmeleri, Sahasi Antrepo No: 4 Karakoy Istanbul, 99 344330 Turkey. Tel 90-212-334-73-00; Fax 90-212-243-43-19; Email info@istanbulmodern.org; Web: www.istanbulmodern.org; *Dir* Levent Calikoglu; *COO* Yasemin Sumer
Open Tues, Wed & Fri-Sun 10 AM - 6 PM, Thurs 10 AM - 8 PM, cl Mon, Jan 1 & on the 1st day of religious holidays; Regular admis 55 TL,groups 42 TL; students & seniors 65 & over 35 TL; discounts for residents of Turkey
Collections: Modern & contemporary art

M **TOPKAPI PALACE MUSEUM,** Sultanahmet, Fatih Istanbul, Turkey. Tel 0212 512 04 80; Fax 0212 526 98 40; Email topkapisarayimuzesi@kultur.gov.tr; Web: topkapisarayi.gov.tr; *Pres* Haluk Dursun
Open Oct 30 - April 15: Wed - Mon 9 AM - 4:45 PM; April 15 - Oct 30: Wed - Mon 9 AM - 6:45 PM, cl Tues & first day of religious holidays; Admis Museum: 40 TL, Harem: 25 TL, Hagia Irene 20 TL; children 6 yrs and under free; Library with 18,000 manuscripts and 23,000 archival documents
Collections: Chinese & Japanese porcelains, miniatures & portraits of Sultans, private colls of Kenan Ozbel, Sami Ozgiritli's collection of furniture, Islamic relics, Sultan's costumes, Turkish embroideries, armor, tiles, applied arts, paintings

M **TURK VE ISLAM ESERLERI MUZESI,** Museum of Turkish and Islamic Art, Ibrahim Pasa Sarayi No 44, 34122 Sultanahmet, Fatih Istanbul, Turkey. Tel 212 518 18 06; Fax 212 518 18 07; Email tiem@tiem.gov.tr; Web: www.tiem.gov.tr
Open Tues - Sun 9 AM - 5 PM; Gen admis 25 TRY
Special Subjects: Antiquities-Oriental, Woodcuts
Collections: Illuminated manuscripts, monuments of Islamic art, metalwork and ceramics, Turkish and Islamic carpets, sculpture in stone and stucco, wood carvings, traditional crafts gathered from Turkish mosques and tombs
Activities: Mus shop sells books, magazines, original art, reproductions, prints, slides

TURKMENISTAN

ASHGABAT

M **THE STATE MUSEUM OF THE STATE CULTURAL CENTRE OF TURKMENISTAN,** Ave Archabil 30, Ashgabat, Turkmenistan. Tel 48-25-92; Fax 48-25-93; Web: www.museum.gov.tm; *Dir* Dr Ovez Mammetnurov
Open Wed - Mon 10 AM - 5 PM, cl Tue; Admis for citizens 3 TMT, foreign visitors 10 USD; Estab 1998
Collections: Middle Ages, Household objects, national costumes, Turkmen crafts, books, ethnography, jewels, carpets, Ancient world, antiquity (3rd century B.C. to 3 century A.D.)
Activities: Educ progs; confs; tours

UGANDA

KAMPALA

M **UGANDA MUSEUM,** Kira Rd, Plot No 5 Kampala, Uganda. Tel 256-41-423-2707; Web: www.ugandamuseums.ug; *Dir* Rose Nkaale Mwanga
Open daily 8 AM - 7 PM; Admis foreign nationals: adults 5,000 UGX, children 1,500 UGX; Ugandan citizens: adults 2,000 UGX, children 1,000 UGX; Estab 1908
Collections: Ethnographic collections from various regions of Uganda

UKRAINE

KYIV

M **BOHDAN AND VERVARA KHANENKO MUSEUM OF ART,** Museum of Western & Oriental Art, 15 Tereshenkovskaya St, Kyiv, UkrainianUkraine. Tel 38 (0) 44 235 32 90; Fax 38 (0) 44 235 02 06; Email khanenkomuseum@ukr.net; Web: www.khanenkomuseum.kiev.ua; *Deputy Gen Dir* Elena Viktorovna
Open Wed - Sun 10:30 AM - 5:30 PM, cl Mon & Tues; Admis adults 15 UAH, students 10 UAH, children & seniors 5 UAH; Estab 1919; European art (14-19 cent) Byzantine icons, Asian art; Average Annual Attendance: 45,000
Income: State-run
Collections: 20,000 items
Exhibitions: 5 - 8 temporary exhib per yr
Publications: Oriental Collection
Activities: Mus shop sells books, reproductions, prints, souvenirs, cards & bookmarks

M **KYIV MUSEUM OF RUSSIAN ART,** 9 Tereschenkivska St, Kyiv, Ukrainian 01004 Ukraine. Tel 38 (044) 287-73-24; Email museumru@ukr.net; Web: www.kmrm.com.ua; *Dir* Yuri Vakulenko
Open Tues, Wed, Fri, Sat & Sun 10 AM - 6 PM, cl Mon & Thurs; Gen admis 25 UAH, students 10 UAH, children & seniors 5 UAH; Estab 1922; Average Annual Attendance: 70,000; Mem: 15 comt mems
Special Subjects: Baroque Art, Bronzes, Ceramics, Coins & Medals, Decorative Arts, Drawings, Etchings & Engravings, Folk Art, Furniture, Glass, Graphics, Landscapes, Marine Painting, Medieval Art, Metalwork, Miniatures, Painting-Russian, Porcelain, Portraits, Religious Art, Sculpture, Watercolors
Collections: 12,000 art objects
Activities: Classes for adults & children; workshops; lects open to pub, 720 vis lectrs per yr; concerts; tours; mus shop sells reproductions, magazines, prints; Children Picture Gallery

M **NATIONAL ART MUSEUM OF UKRAINE,** Hrushevskogo St 6, Kyiv, 01001 Ukraine. Tel 38 (044) 278-13-57; Fax 38 (044) 278-74-54; Email info@namu.kiev.ua; Web: www.namu.kiev.ua; *Dir* Yuliya Lytvynets
Open Wed - Thurs & Sun 10 AM - 6 PM, Fri noon - 8 PM, Sat 11 AM - 7 PM, cl Mon & Tues; Admis adults 20 UAH, students 10 UAH, children & seniors 5 UAH; Average Annual Attendance: 120,000
Income: Financed by state budget
Collections: Portraits, icons, wood carvings & paintings from the Middle Ages, exhibits covering 8 centuries, modern art, Soviet art, Avant-Garde, Japanese calligraphy
Publications: Ukrainian Painting; Ukrainian Portrait XVI-XVIII; Monographies
Activities: Classes for adults & children; concerts; gallery talks; original objects of art lent to state museums in other countries; originates traveling exhibs to Tretiakov Gallery, Guggenheim Mus, Winnipeg Art Gallery, Chicago Cultural Ctr, New Church of Amsterdam, New York Ukrainian Mus; mus shop sells books, magazines, reproductions, almanacs

M **NATIONAL MUSEUM OF UKRAINIAN DECORATIVE FOLK ART,** 9 Lavra St., Bldg 29, Kyiv, Ukrainian 01015 Ukraine. Tel 38 (044) 280 13 43; Email musukrndm@kv.ukrtel.net; Web: www.mundm.kiev.ua; *Dir* Lyudmila String
Open Mon, Wed - Sun 10 AM - 6 PM; Admis adults 20 UAH, seniors 7 UAH, students 5 UAH, children 3 UAH
Collections: Wood carvings, ceramics, weaving & applied arts from 16th century to present

ODESSA

M **MUSEUM OF ODESSA MODERN ART,** Belinskogo str 5, Odessa, 65014 Ukraine. Tel 38 (048) 777-1250; Email info@msio.com.ua; Web: msio.com.ua; *Dir* Semen Kantor; *Cur* Mikhail Raskovetsky
Open Wed - Sat noon - 7 PM, Sun noon - 6 PM, cl Mon & Tues; Estab 2008
Collections: Modern & contemporary Odessa art

UNITED ARAB EMIRATES

ABU DHABI

M **THE LOUVRE ABU DHABI,** Saadiyat Cultural Dist, Abu Dhabi, United Arab Emirates. Tel 971 600 56 55 56; Email contact@louvreabudhabi.ae; Web: www.louvreabudhabi.ae; *Dir* Manuel Rabate; *Scientific, Curatorial & Colls Mgmnt Dir* Dr Souraya Noujaim
Open Sat, Sun, Tues & Wed 10 AM - 8 PM, Thurs & Fri 10 AM - 10 PM; Admis 63 AED; reduced 31.5 AED; Estab 2006, opened 2017; Collaborative art & civilization museum between France and the United Arab Emirates made up of 23 galleries across 55 buildings spread out from under a 7,500 ton geometric dome.
Income: Financed buy Abu Dhabi Dept of Culture & Tourism and Agence France-Museums
Collections: Prehistoric art, contemporary art, Egyptian, Asian, Mediterranean, Middle Eastern artifacts, paintings & portraits, sculpture, armor, furniture, ceramics, religious & cosmographic pieces
Activities: Educ progs for adults & children; guided tours; children's mus

AL AIN

M **AL AIN NATIONAL MUSEUM,** Zayed bin Sultan St, Al Hosn Dist Al Ain, United Arab Emirates; Historic Environment Dept, PO Box 15715 Al Ain, United Arab Emirates. Tel 971 3 711 8200; Fax 971 3 765 8311; Email historic-environment@tcaabudhabi.ae; Web: tcaabudhabi.ae; *Dir* Mohammad Amer Mur Al Nayadi
Open Tues - Thurs & Sat - Sun 8 AM - 7:30 PM, Fri 3 PM - 7:30 PM; Admis adults 3 AED, children under 10 yrs 1 AED; Estab 1969
Special Subjects: Archaeology, Bronzes, Ceramics, Coins & Medals, Ethnology, Glass, Gold, Jewelry
Collections: Archaeology and ethnography of UAE region; artifacts, ceramics, coins, weapons, jewelry, textiles, costumes, and decorative arts
Activities: Classes for children

DUBAI

M **CUADRO FINE ART GALLERY,** Gate Village Bldg 10, Dubai International Financial Center Dubai, 506586 United Arab Emirates; PO Box 506586, Dubai,

United Arab Emirates. Tel 9714 425 0400; Email info@cuadroart.com; Web: www.cuadroart.com; *Mgr* Bashar Al Shroogi
Open Tues - Sun 10 AM - 8 PM; Estab 2008 to provide exhibitions, education, residency & consultation of the fine arts; Two-floor, seven gallery, 13,000 sq ft exhib space located in the Dubai International Financial Center
Special Subjects: Mixed Media, Sculpture, Photography
Collections: Modern & contemporary art
Exhibitions: Temporary exhibits
Activities: Educ progs; artist residencies; lects open to pub; gallery talks; tours; workshops; panel discussions

M **MEEM GALLERY,** Umm Suqeim Rd, PO Box 290, Al Qouz Dubai, United Arab Emirates. Tel 971 04 347 7883; Fax 971 04 340 1640; Email info@meemartgallery.com; Web: www.meemartgallery.com; *Mng Dir* Charles Pocock
Open Sat - Thurs 10 AM - 6 PM; Estab in 2007 to collect and exhibit modern and contemporary Arab & Iranian art
Special Subjects: NOSculpture, Drawings, Watercolors, Photography, Mixed Media
Collections: Modern & contemporary art
Exhibitions: Temporary exhibits
Publications: Exhib catalogs
Activities: Gallery talks; tours; integrated art events; arts festivals; Mus sells original works of art

SHARJAH

M **SHARJAH ART MUSEUM,** PO Box 19989, Al Shuwaihean Arts Area Sharjah, United Arab Emirates. Tel 971-6-568 8222; Fax 971-6-568 6229; Email info@sarjahmuseums.ae; Web: www.sharjahmuseums.ae; *Dir* Sheikh Dr Mohammed Al Qasimi
Open Sat - Thurs 8 AM - 8 PM, Fri 4 PM - 8 PM; No admis fee; Estab 1997
Collections: Various works by European painters depicting the Far and Near East, 8 sets of colls donated by H H Saikah Dr Sultan bin Mohammad Al Qasimi

URUGUAY

MALDONADO

M **MUSEO DE ARTE AMERICANO DE MALDONADO,** Maldonado Museum of American Art, Calle Treinta y Tres 823, Maldonado, Uruguay. Tel 598 42 222276; Email jpaez@adinet.com.uy; Web: maam-uruguay.blogspot.com; Jorge Paez Algorta
Open summer 6 PM - 10 PM; all other times by appointment; No admis fee; Estab 1973; Foundation, museum and cultural center founded by artist Jorge Paez Vilaro housed in a historic house
Collections: Pre-Columbian art, art of the colonial period, contemporary art, traditional & folk art, and art from Africa and Oceania

MONTEVIDEO

M **MUSEO DE ARTES DECORATIVAS,** Museum of Decorative Arts, 25 de Mayo 376, Montevideo, CP-11100 Uruguay. Tel 598-2-915-6060; Email artesdecorativas@mec.gub.uy; Web: www.mec.gub.uy; *Dir* Fernando Loustaunau
Open Mon - Fri 12:30 PM - 5:30 PM; Estab 1972; Art museum housed in a historic house
Collections: European painting and decorative arts; ancient Greek and Roman art, Islamic ceramics of the 10th - 18th century

M **MUSEO DE BELLAS ARTES JUAN MANUEL BLANES,** Juan Manuel Blanes Museum of Fine Arts, Avda Millan 4015, Montevideo, Uruguay. Tel 598-23362248; Fax 598-23367134; Email museojuanmanuelblanes@gmail.com; Web: blanes.montevideo.gub.uy; *Dir* Gabriel Peluffo Linari
Open Tues - Sun 12:15 PM - 5:45 PM
Collections: Paintings, sculptures, drawings, wood-carvings

M **MUSEO NACIONAL DE ARTES VISUALES,** National Museum of Visual Arts, Tomas Giribaldi 2283 esq Julio Herrera y Reissig, Parque Rodo Montevideo, 11300 Uruguay. Tel 598-27116054; Email director@mnav.gub.uy; Web: mnav.gub.uy; *Dir* Enrique Aguerre
Open Tues - Sun 2 PM - 7 PM
Collections: 4217 ceramics, drawings, engravings, paintings & sculptures

UZBEKISTAN

NUKUS

M **KARAKALPAK STATE ART MUSEUM,** K Rzaev St, Nukus, Republic of Karakalpakstan 230100 Uzbekistan; Dosliq Prospekt 115, Nukus, 230100 Uzbekistan. Tel 998-61-222-25-56; Email museum_savitsky@mail.ru; Web: www.savitskycollection.org; www.museum.kr.uz; *Dir* Marinika Maratovna Babanazarova; *Cur* Valentina Egorovna Sycheva
Open Mon - Fri 9 AM - 1 PM & 2 PM - 5 PM, Sat - Sun 10 AM - 4 PM; Admis Uzbekistan citizens: adults 6000 UZS, students 4000 UZS, children 2000 UZS; foreign visitors: adults 25000 UZS, students 15000 UZS, children 10000 UZS; 1966; Russian Uzbek avant-garde artists, Karakalpak artists, folk applied art, art of ancient Khorezm; Average Annual Attendance: 70,000
Library Holdings: Auction Catalogs, Audio Tapes, Book Volumes, CD-ROMs, Cassettes, DVDs, Exhibition Catalogs, Lantern Slides, Manuscripts, Memorabilia, Motion Pictures, Pamphlets, Periodical Subscriptions, Photographs, Slides, Video Tapes
Special Subjects: Archaeology, Architecture, Art History, Carpets & Rugs, Coins & Medals, Costumes, Decorative Arts, Drawings, Graphics, History of Art & Archaeology, Oriental Art, Painting-American, Painting-British, Painting-French, Restorations, Sculpture, Textiles, Watercolors
Collections: Uzbek avant-garde of the 1920's and 1930s; Russian avant-garde of the 20th century and contemporary art of Karakalpakstan, Unique medieval ceramics, silver, jewelry and traditional textiles and ethnographic material
Activities: Classes for adults & children; dramatic progs; lects open to pub; gallery talks; tours; sponsoring of competitions; awards; ext prog serving rural areas; lending of original objects of art; mus shop sells books; magazines, reproductions, souvenirs

TASHKENT

M **MUSEUM OF APPLIED ART,** 15 Rakatboshi St, Tashkent, 100031 Uzbekistan. Tel (998) 71-256-40-42, (998) 71-256-39-43; Fax (998) 71-25213-67; Email muzeyart@mail.ru
Open daily 9 AM - 6 PM
Collections: More than 7000 pieces of traditional folk art from the 19th century to the present, Ceramics, glass and porcelain plates, hand-made and machine embroidery, national fabrics and textiles, carpets, works of wood engraving, miniatures, jewelry

M **STATE MUSEUM OF ARTS OF UZBEKISTAN,** 16 Movarounnahr St, Tashkent, Uzbekistan. Tel 99871-136-7436, 136-7740
Open Mon 10 AM - 1:30 PM, Wed - Sun 10 AM - 5 PM, cl Tues
Collections: Consists of more than 50,000 exhibits presenting decorative folk art and fine arts of Uzbekistan, Russia, Western European & Asian artists, Engraving, ceramics, wood engravings, painting, textiles, embroidery, carpets and decorative metal works

VANUATU

PORT VILA

M **VANUATU CULTURAL CENTRE & NATIONAL MUSEUM,** Rue d'Artois St, Port Vila, Vanuatu; PO Box 184, Port Vila, Vanuatu. Tel 678 22 129; Fax 678 26 590; Email vks@vanuatu.com.vu; Web: vanuatuculturalcenter.vu; *Dir* Marcellin Abong
Open Cultural Centre: Mon - Fri 7:30 AM - 11:30 AM & 1:30 PM - 4:30 PM; National Museum: Mon - Fri 9 AM - 4 PM, Sat 9 AM - 11:30 AM; Estab 1970
Collections: Over 3500 artifacts relating to Vanuatu ethnographic history, Masks, gongs, mats, scale models, canoes; traditional and contemporary art, headdresses and examples of Lapita and Wusi pottery

VATICAN CITY

VATICAN CITY

M **MONUMENTI, MUSEI E GALLERIE PONTIFICIE,** Vatican Museums and Galleries, Viale Vaticano, Vatican City, 00165 Vatican City. Tel 00 39 06 6988 4676; Fax 00 39 06 6988 3145; Email info.mv@scv.va; Web: www.museivaticani.va; *Dir* Barbara Jatta; *Mng Dir* Monsingnor Paolo Nicolini
Open Mon-Sat 9 AM - 6 PM, last Sun of each month except holidays 9 AM - 2 PM; cl Sun, holidays; Admis 16 EUR, reduced 8 EUR, scholastic 4 EUR; Estab 1506 by Pope Julius II
Collections: Twelve museum sections with Byzantine, medieval & modern art, classical sculpture, liturgical art, minor arts

M **Museo Pio Clementino**, Viale Vaticano, Vatican City, 00165 Vatican City.
Founded by Pope Clement XIV (1770-74) & enlarged by his successor, Pius VI; exhibits include the Apollo of Belvedere, the Apoxyomenos by Lysippus, the Laocoon Group, the Meleager of Skopas, the Apollo Sauroktonous by Praxiteles

M **Pinacoteca Vaticana**, Viale Vaticano, Vatican City, 00165 Vatican City.
Inaugurated by Pope Pius XI in 1932
Collections: Paintings by Fra Angelico, Raphael, Leonardo da Vinci, Titian & Caravaggio, & the Raphael Tapestries

M **Collezione d'Arte Religiosa Moderna**, Vilae Vaticano, Vatican City, 00165 Vatican City.
Founded in 1973 by Pope Paul VI; paintings, sculptures & drawings offered to the Pope by artists & donors

M **Vatican Palaces**, Viale Vaticano, Vatican City, 00165 Vatican City.
Chapel of Beato Angelico (or Niccolo V, 1448-1450); Sistine Chapel constructed for Sixtus IV (1471-1484); Borgia Apartment decorated by Pinturicchio; Chapel of Urbano VIII (1631-1635); rooms & loggias decorated by Raphael; Gallery of the Maps (1580-83)

M **Museo Sacro**, Viale Vaticano, Vatican City, 00165 Vatican City.
Founded in 1756 by Pope Benedict XIV; administered by the Apostolic Vatican Library
Collections: Objects of liturgical art, historical relics & curios from the Lateran, objects of Paleolithic, medieval & Renaissance minor arts, paintings of the Roman era

M **Museo Profano**, Citta del Vaticano, Vatican City, 00120 Vatican City.
Founded in 1767 by Pope Clement XIII; administered by the Vatican Apostolic Library
Collections: Bronze sculpture & minor art of the classical era

M **Museo Chiaramonti e Braccio Nuovo**, Viale Vaticano, Vatican City, 00165 Vatican City.

Founded by Pope Pius VII at the beginning of the 19th century, to house the many new findings excavated in that period
Collections: Statues of the Nile, of Demosthenes & of the Augustus of Prima Porta

M **Museo Gregoriano Etrusco**, Viale Vaticano, Vatican City, 001695 Vatican City. Founded by Pope Gregory XVI in 1837
Collections: Objects from the Tomba Regolini Galassi of Cerveteri, the bronzes, terracottas & jewelry, & Greek vases from Etruscan tombs

M **Museo Gregoriano Egizio**, Viale Vaticano, Vatican City, 00165 Vatican City. Inaugurated by Pope Gregory XVI in 1839
Collections: Egyptian papyri, mummies, sarcophagi & statues, including statue of Queen Tuia (1300 BC)

M **Museo Gregoriano Profano**, Viale Vaticano, Vatican City, 00165 Vatican City. Founded by Gregory XVI in 1844 & housed in the Lateran Palace, it was transferred to a new building in the Vatican & opened to the public in 1970
Collections: Roman sculptures from the Pontifical States, Portrait-statue of Sophocles, the Marsyas of the Myronian group of Athena & Marsyas, the Flavian reliefs from the Palace of the Apostolic Chancery

M **Museo Pio Cristiano**, Viale Vaticano, Vatican City, 00165 Vatican City. Founded by Pius IX in 1854 & housed in the Lateran Palace; transferred to a new building in the Vatican & opened to the public in 1970
Collections: Sarcophagi, Latin & Greek inscriptions from Christian cemeteries & basilicas, the Good Shepherd

M **Museo Missionario Etnologico**, Viale Vaticano, Vatican City, 00165 Vatican City. Founded by Pius XI in 1926 & housed in the Lateran Palace; transferred to a new building in the Vatican & opened to the public in 1973
Collections: Ethnographical colls from all over the world
Publications: Annali

VENEZUELA

CARACAS

M **GALERIA DE ARTE NACIONAL,** National Art Gallery, Avenida Mexico, La Candelaria Caracas, Venezuela. Tel 58 0212 339 75 07; Email gan@fmn.gob.ve; Web: vereda.ula.ve; *Dir* Giovanni Covino
Open Tues - Fri 9 AM - 5 PM, Sat - Mon & holidays 10 AM - 5 PM; No admis fee; Estab 1974
Collections: Visual arts of Venezuela throughout history

M **MUSEO ALEJANDRO OTERO,** Alejandro Otero Museum, Complejo Cultural la Rinconada, Caracas, Venezuela. Tel 58 212 682-0102, 58 212 682-0941; Web: www.fmn.gob.ve; *Dir* Clemente Martinez
Open Tues - Fri 9 AM - 4 PM, Sat - Sun & holidays 10 AM - 4 PM; No admis fee; Estab 1990
Collections: Contemporary art including major works by Alejandro Otero and other Venezuelan artists

M **MUSEO DE ARTE COLONIAL DE CARACAS QUINTA DE ANAUCO,** Quinta de Anauco Colonial Art Museum of Caracas, Ave Panteon, San Bernardino Caracas, 1011 Venezuela. Tel 58 212 551-8190; Fax 58 212 551-8517; Email infoanauco@quintadeanauco.org.ve; Web: www.quintadeanauco.org.ve; *Dir* Carlos F Duarte
Open Tues - Fri 9 AM - noon & 2 PM - 4:00 PM, Sat - Sun 10 AM - 4 PM; Admis adults 250 VEF, students and children 200 VEF; Estab 1942; Colonial art museum housed in a former country mansion; Mem: 500 mems
Income: financed by private funds
Collections: works of Venezuelan colonial period art; furniture, sculpture, ceramics, glass, silver, paintings, metalwork, textiles, glass, decorative arts and more
Activities: Classes for children; lects open to pub; 6 vis lectrs per yr; concerts; tours; conferences

M **MUSEO DE ARTE CONTEMPORANEO,** Museum of Contemporary Art, Zona Cultural de Parque Central, Nivel Lecuna Caracas, Venezuela. Tel 58 212 573-8289; Web: www.fmn.gob.ve; *Dir* Daniel Briceno
Open Tues - Fri 9 AM - 5 PM, Sat - Sun & holidays 10 AM - 5 PM; No admis fee; Estab 1973
Collections: Temporary exhibitions of national and international contemporary arts; painting, sculpture, drawing, cinema, video and photography

M **MUSEO DE BELLAS ARTES,** Museum of Fine Arts, Plaza de los Museos, Parque Los Caobos Bellas Artes Caracas, Venezuela. Tel 58 212 578 02 75; Web: www.fmn.gob.ve; *Dir* Ruben Witzoski
Open Tues - Fri 9 AM - 5 PM, weekends and holidays 10 AM - 5 PM; No admis fee; Estab 1917; museum of fine arts and study of the arts; Average Annual Attendance: 40,000
Income: Private and public funds
Purchases: Installation by Bernardi Roig
Library Holdings: Auction Catalogs, Audio Tapes, Book Volumes, CD-ROMs, Clipping Files, Exhibition Catalogs, Pamphlets
Special Subjects: Antiquities-Egyptian, Watercolors
Collections: Latin American & foreign paintings & sculpture, Cubism (old masters), Egyptian coll, Chinese ceramics, prints, drawings and photographs cabinet
Exhibitions: Gego: 1955-1990; Perú Milenario: 3,000 years of ancestral art; IV Bienal del Barro de América Roberto Guevara; Chema Madoz: Objetos 1990-1999; Sobre la Marcha: Dibujos de Pablo Benavides; Del Cuerpo a la Imagen; 150 Años de Fotografía en España; Chinese ceramics, Egyptian art, Cubism, drawings, prints and photographs cabinet, sculpture garden
Publications: Exhibition catalogs
Activities: Classes for children; dramatic progs; docent training; lects open to pub; concerts; gallery talks; tours; Daniela Chappard juried exhib; Josune Dorronsoro contest; originate traveling exhibs to mus internationally; mus shop sells books, magazines, original art, reproductions, prints, slides, artisan crafts from Venezuela

VIETNAM

HANOI

M **BAO TANG MY THUAT VIET NAM,** Vietnam Fine Arts Museum, 66 Nguyen Thai Hoc St, Ba Dinh Dist Hanoi, Vietnam. Tel (84-4) 373 32 131; Fax (84-4) 373 41 427; Email btmtvn@vnfam.vn; Web: vnfam.vn; *Dir* Phan Van Tien
Open daily 8:30 AM - 5 PM; Admis adults 30,000 VND, college students 15,000 VND, children 6 - 16 yrs 10,000 VND, children under 6 yrs free; Estab 26 June 1966; preserving and highlighting the nation's characteristic aesthetic values, the essence of Vietnamese plastic art from ancient times up to now
Purchases: Artwork and art books
Library Holdings: Book Volumes, Clipping Files, Fiche, Filmstrips, Manuscripts, Original Documents, Photographs, Records
Special Subjects: Bronzes, Ceramics, Collages, Costumes, Crafts, Decorative Arts, Drawings, Embroidery, Enamels, Etchings & Engravings, Folk Art, Graphics, Primitive art, Prints, Restorations, Sculpture, Textiles, Watercolors, Woodcarvings, Woodcuts
Collections: Ancient & modern ceramics, fine arts & handicrafts, Vietnamese cultural heritage, specialized library of over 1100 vols, Folk fine arts, Traditional Applied fine arts
Exhibitions: Ceramics & porcelain, excavations from wrecks in Vietnamese waters; Vietnamese fine arts from the doi moi (renewal) period up to present
Publications: Nguyen Phan Chanh's silk paintings, Vietnam Fine Arts Museum Guidebook of Vietnam Fine Arts Museum, VCD on Vietnamese Fine Arts Museum
Activities: Classes for children; exten program includes lending of original objects of art to art museums of Finland, Japan, Belgium; 5-7 book traveling exhibs per yr; organize traveling exhibs to local cities in Vietnam & abroad; mus shop sells books, magazines, original art, prints, reproductions, CD's, handcrafts & ceramics

HO CHI MINH

M **HO CHI MINH CITY FINE ARTS MUSEUM,** 97A Pho Duc Chinh St, Dist 1 Ho Chi Minh, Vietnam. Tel 08-38-294-441; *Dir* Ma Thanh Cao
Open Tues - Sun 9 AM - 5 PM; Admis 10,000 VND
Collections: Changing exhibits of contemporary art by local and international artists, Permanent collection of sketches, paintings, statues; works from the 1st century to the early 20th century

WALES

CARDIFF

M **AMGUEDDFA CYMRU - NATIONAL MUSEUM WALES,** National Museum Cardiff, Cathays Park, Cardiff, CF10 3NP Wales. Tel 029 2039 7951; Fax 029 2057 3321; Email post@museumwales.ac.uk; Web: www.museumwales.ac.uk; *Pres* Elizabeth Elias; *Dir Gen* David Anderson; *Dir Operations & Deputy Dir Gen* Mark Richards; *Dir Colls & Research* Peter Wakelin; *Dir Learning, Exhibs & Digital Media* Janice Lane; *Dir Finance & Corporate Resources* Neil Wicks
Open Tues - Sun 10 AM - 5 PM; No admis fee; Estab 1907; Natural sciences & art galleries; Average Annual Attendance: 350,000
Income: Sponsored by the Nat Assembly for Wales
Purchases: Include Thomas Girtin, Near Beddgelet, Leon Kossott From Wilksden Gieln, Autumn
Collections: Art, natural sciences, archaeology & industry of Wales, British and European fine and applied art, coll of Impressionist Art
Publications: Things of Beauty; National Museum of Wales - celebrating the first 100 years
Activities: Classes for adults & children, dramatic progs; lects open to pub, 30 vis lectrs per yr; concerts; gallery talks; tours; originate traveling exhibs; UK mus & galleries world-wide; mus shop sells books, reproductions, prints, slides

ZAMBIA

LUSAKA

M **LUSAKA NATIONAL MUSEUM,** Independence Ave & Nasser Rd, PO Box 50491 Lusaka, 10101 Zambia. Tel 260-1-228805/6/7; Email lusamus@zamnet.zm; Web: www.museumszambia.org; *Dir* Friday Mufuzi
Open daily 9 AM - 4:30 PM; Admis: adults $5 USD, children $3 USD; Estab 1996; Museum of national history, archaeology & ethnography
Income: Financed by govt grants
Library Holdings: Book Volumes, Original Documents, Pamphlets, Periodical Subscriptions, Photographs
Special Subjects: African Art, Anthropology, Archaeology, Art History, Bookplates & Bindings, Crafts, Decorative Arts, Dioramas, Etchings & Engravings, Ethnology, Historical Material, History of Art & Archaeology, Maps, Woodcarvings
Collections: Ethnography, pre-history, history and natural history of Zambian region, Collection of artifacts, tools, traditional craft and ritual objects, masks, costumes, textiles, statues, Modern and Makonde art, traditional Chitenge body wraps
Activities: Classes for adults & children; outreach progs; concerts; gallery tours; sponsoring of competitions; traveling exhibs to other mus; organize traveling exhibs to surrounding villages & towns; mus shop sells books, magazines, original art, prints, crafts & souvenirs

ZIMBABWE

HARARE

M **NATIONAL GALLERY OF ZIMBABWE,** 20 Julius Nyerere Way, Parklane Harare, Zimbabwe; PO Box CY 848, Causeway Harare, Zimbabwe. Tel 263 86 7700 2043; Email info@nationalgallery.co.zw; Web: www.nationalgallery.co.zw; *Exec Dir* Doreen Sibanda; *Deputy Dir* Raphael Chikukwa

Open Tues - Sun 9 AM - 5 PM; Admis $1 USD; Estab 1957; Mem: 400
Income: Commission on sales & government grant
Collections: African traditional & local contemporary sculpture & paintings, ancient & modern European paintings & sculpture, including works by Bellini, Caracciolo, Gainsborough, Murillo, Reynolds, Rodin, Showa sculpture
Activities: Classes for adults & children, dramatic progs; lects open to pub; mus shop sells books, magazines & original art

Art Schools Abroad

ARGENTINA

BUENOS AIRES

UNIVERSIDAD DEL MUSEO SOCIAL ARGENTINO, Dept of Visual Arts, Av Corrientes 1723, Buenos Aires, C1042AAD Argentina. Tel 54 11 5330-7600; Fax 54 11 5530-7614; Email informes@umsa.edu.ar; Web: www.umsa.edu.ar; *Dean Faculty of Arts* Roxana Amodeo
Estab 1956
Activities: Schols offered
Courses: †Art History, †Drawing, †Painting, †Sculpture

AUSTRALIA

BARTON

ROYAL AUSTRALIAN INSTITUTE OF ARCHITECTS, 7 National Circuit, Barton, ACT 2600 Australia; Level 2, National Circuit, PO Box 3373 Barton, ACT 2608 Australia. Tel 61 2 6121 2000; Fax 61 2 6121 2001; Email national@architecture.com.au; Web: www.architecture.com.au; *CEO* Jennifer Cunich
Estab 1930; Maintains architecture library, RAIA Chap, 2A Mugga Way, Red Hill, ACT, Australia 2603

DARLINGHURST

NATIONAL ART SCHOOL, Forbes St, Darlinghurst, NSW 2010 Australia. Tel 61 02 9339 8744; Fax 61 02 9339 8740; Email enquiries@nas.edu.au; Web: www.nas.edu.au; *Mng Dir* David Grayce
Approx 1850; Maintains a nonprofit art gallery, National Art School Gallery, Forbes St, Darlinghurst, NSW 2010 Australia; maintains art/architecture library, National Art School Library. Art supplies may be purchased on campus; Pub, NSN Dept of Education & Training; D & E; Scholarships; Fellowships; SC 6, LC 1, GC 2; enrl D 900, GS 50, other 1200
Ent Req: Portfolio of usual artwork & interview
Degrees: Bachelor of Fine Art, BFA (Honours); Master of Fine Art
Courses: Aesthetics, Art History, Ceramics, Drawing, History of Art & Architecture, Painting, Photography, Printmaking, Sculpture
Adult Hobby Classes: Pub Programs
Summer School: Dir Jayne Dyer

FITZROY

AUSTRALIAN CATHOLIC UNIVERSITY, 115 Victoria Parade, Fitzroy, VIC 3065 Australia; Locked Bag 4115 DC, Fitzroy, VIC 3065 Australia. Tel 03 9953 3000; Email studentcentre@patrick.acu.edu.au; *Exec Dean* Tania Aspland; *Provost & Deputy Vice-Chancellor, Acad* Prof Pauline Nugent
Activities: Schols offered
Courses: †Advertising Design, †Design, †Graphic Design, †Illustration, †Museum Staff Training, †Painting, †Photography, †Printmaking, †Sculpture

HOBART

UNIVERSITY OF TASMANIA, Tasmanian School of Art, Private Bag 132, Hobart, Tasmania TAS 7001 Australia. Tel 61 3 6226 7814; Fax 61 3 6226 6291; Email arts.faculty@utas.edu.au; Web: www.utas.edu.au/arts; *Deputy Dean, Faculty of Art* Prof Noel Frankham; *Head Tasmanian College of the Arts* Kit Wise

LILYFIELD

UNIVERSITY OF SYDNEY, College of the Arts, Kirkbride Way, Lilyfield, NSW NSW 2040 Australia; Locked Bag 15, Rozelle, NSW 2039 Australia. Tel 61-(2) 9351-1002; Email sca.dean@sydney.edu.au; Web: sydney.edu.au/sca; *Dean* Prof Colin Rhodes; *Head Dept Contemp Art* Oliver Smith; *Assoc Dean Learning & Teaching* Andrew Lavery; *Assoc Dean Research* Jacqueline Millner; *Dir SCA Graduate School* Debra Dawes
Estab 1976; Maintains non profit art gallery, SCA Galleries, Locked Bag 15, Rozelle NSW, 2039 Australia; maintains art library, SCA LIbrary; Pub; D
Degrees: BVA, MVA, PhD
Courses: †Ceramics, Conceptual Art, Design, Drawing, †Film, †Glass, Handicrafts, †Jewelry, Mixed Media, †Painting, †Photography, †Printmaking, †Sculpture, Theories of Art Practice, Video

MELBOURNE

VICTORIAN COLLEGE OF THE ARTS, School of Art, 234 St Kilda Rd, Southbank Melbourne, Victoria 3006 Australia. Tel 61 3 9035 9200 (HR); Email vcam-er@unimelb.edu.au; Web: vca.unimelb.edu.au; *Head School of Art, Honours Coordr* Jan Murray

PADDINGTON

UNIVERSITY OF NEW SOUTH WALES, College of Fine Arts, Greens Rd, Paddington, NSW 2021 Australia; PO Box 259, Paddington, NSW 2021 Australia. Tel 61 2 8936 0684; Fax 612 8936 0706; Email artdesign@unsw.edu.au; Web: www.artdesign.unsw.edu.au/home; *Dean* Prof Ross Harley
Courses: †Art Education, †Ceramics, †Design, †Drawing, †Film, †Graphic Design, †Jewelry, †Painting, †Printmaking, †Sculpture, †Textile Design, †Video

SYDNEY

JULIAN ASHTON ART SCHOOL, PO Box N676, Grosvenor Pl Sydney, NSW 1220 Australia. Tel 61 2 9241 1641; Web: www.julianashtonartschool.com.au; *Prin* Paul Ashton Delprat
Estab 1890
Courses: †Drawing, †Sculpture

UNIVERSITY OF SYDNEY, School of Philosophical and Historical Inquiry, Quadrangle A14, Sydney, NSW 2006 Australia. Tel 61-2-9351-2862; Fax 61-2-9351-3918; Email sophi.enquiries@sydney.edu.au; Web: www.usyd.edu.au; *Prof* Margaret C Miller; *Prof* Alison Betts
Estab 1850; Maintains a nonprofit art gallery, Nicholson Museum, Main Quadrance A-14, Univ Sydney; 4; pub; D; LC, GC, LAB

AUSTRIA

SALZBURG

INTERNATIONALE SOMMERAKADEMIE FUR BILDENDE KUNST SALZBURG, Salzburg International Summer Academy of Fine Arts, Franziskanergasse 5a/1 Stock, Salzburg, 5010 Austria; PO Box 18, Salzburg, 5010 Austria. Tel 43 662 842113; Fax 43 662 849638; Email office@summeracademy.at; Web: www.summeracademy.at; *Dir* Hildegund Amanshauser
Estab 1953; pub; D; Scholarships; SC 20
Activities: Schols available
Ent Req: Over 17 yrs of age
Degrees: BA, MA, PhD
Tuition: 440 - 1,160 EUR depending on duration of course
Courses: †Architecture, †Conceptual Art, Curatorial Practice, †Display, †Drawing, †Fashion Arts, †Film, †Goldsmithing, †Graphic Arts, †Mixed Media, †Painting, †Photography, Printmaking, †Sculpture, †Silversmithing, †Textile Design, †Video
Summer School: Dir Hildegund Amanshauser

VIENNA

UNIVERSITAT FUR ANGEWANDTE KUNST WIEN, Studienabteilung, Oskar Kokoschka Platz 2 Vienna, A-1010 Austria. Tel 43 1 71133 2060; Email studien@uni-ak.ac.at; Web: www.dieangewandte.at; *Rector* Gerald Bast; *Dean Studies* Prof Mag art Josef Kaiser
Estab 1868; Maintains art library, Universitatsibibliothek, Oskar Kokoschka-Platz 2, A-1010 Wien Austria; Pub; D; GC 12
Activities: Schols offered
Ent Req: Austrian Maturazeugnis or equivalent; entrance exam; for foreigners proof of admis to a univ in home country
Degrees: BA, MA
Courses: †Advertising Design, †Aesthetics, †Architecture, †Art Appreciation, †Art Education, †Art History, †Calligraphy, †Ceramics, †Collage, †Commercial Art, †Conceptual Art, †Constructions, †Costume Design & Construction, †Crafts,

†Design, †Drawing, †Fashion Arts, †Film, †Fine Arts, †Graphic Arts, †Graphic Design, †History of Art & Architecture, †Industrial Design, †Landscape Design, †Lettering, †Mixed Media, †Painting, †Photography, Printmaking, †Restoration & Conservation, †Sculpture, †Stage Design, Teacher Training, †Textile Design, †Theatre Arts, †Video, †Weaving

BARBADOS

CAVE HILL

UNIVERSITY OF THE WEST INDIES CAVE HILL CAMPUS, Errol Barrow Centre for Creative Imagination, Cave Hill Campus, Cave Hill, Barbados. Tel 246-417 4776; Fax 246-417-8903; Email ebcci@cavehill.uwi.edu; Web: www.cavehill.uwi.edu/ebcci; *Mngr* Prof Carla Springer

BELARUS

MINSK

BELARUSIAN STATE ACADEMY OF ARTS, Prospect Nezavisimosti 81, Minsk, 220012 Belarus. Tel 375 17 292 15 42; Fax 375 17 292 20 41; Email info@bdam.by; Web: bdam.by/en/; *Assoc Prof, Rector* Mikhail Barazna, PhD
Estab 1945
Courses: †Applied Arts, †Design, Painting, Sculpture, †Theatre Arts

BELGIUM

ANTWERP

KONINKLIJKE ACADEMIE VOOR SCHONE KUNSTEN, Royal Academy of Fine Arts Antwerp, Mustsaardstraat 31, Antwerp, B-2000 Belgium. Tel 03 213 71 60; Fax 03 213 71 69; Email kaska.dko@antigon.be; Web: www.academieantwerpendko.org; *Dir* Prof Eric Ubben; *Prof* Nedda El-Asmar; *Prof* Walter Van Beirendonck; *Prof* Johan Pas
Estab 1663; Nadia Naveau, Vaast Colson, Tina Gillen; pub; D; SC 20, LC 10,; D 650, grad 100
Ent Req: artistic entrance exam plus high school diploma
Degrees: BA (hons), MA (visual arts, conservation studies), PhD
Courses: †Art History, †Costume Design & Construction, †Design, †Drawing, †Fashion Arts, †Graphic Arts, †Graphic Design, †History of Art & Architecture, †Museum Staff Training, †Painting, †Photography, †Printmaking, †Restoration & Conservation, †Sculpture, †Silversmithing, †Stage Design, †Teacher Training, †Theatre Arts

BRUSSELS

ECOLE NATIONALE SUPERIEURE DES ARTS VISUELS DE LA CAMBRE, 21 Abbaye de la Cambre, Brussels, B-1000 Belgium. Tel 00 32 2 626 17 80; Fax 00 32 2 640 96 93; Email lacambre@lacambre.be; Web: www.lacambre.be; *Dir* Caroline Mierop; *Deputy Dir* Barbara Cuglietta
Estab 1926

BOLIVIA

CASILLA

UNIVERSIDAD NUR, Dept Arts, Av Cristo Redentor 100 Casilla, Santa Cruz de la Sie, Santa Cruz Casilla, 3273 Bolivia. Tel 591 3 333 7432; Web: www.nur.edu; *Coordr Career Teaching* Jorge Braulio

BOSNIA AND HERZEGOVINA

SARAJEVO

UNIVERSITY OF SARAJEVO, Academy of Fine Arts, Obala Kulina Bana br 7/11, Sarajevo, 71000 Bosnia and Herzegovina. Tel 387 (0) 33 210 369; Fax 387 (0) 33 210 530; Email alu@alu.unsa.ba; Web: www.unsa.ba; *Prof, Dean* Marina Finci

BRAZIL

BELO HORIZONTE

UNIVERSIDADE FEDERAL DE MINAS GERAIS (UFMG), Escola de Belas Artes, Av Antonio Carlos, 6627 Pampulha Belo Horizonte, MG 31270-901 Brazil. Tel (31) 3409-53 77; Fax (31) 3409-52 70; Email cecor@eba.ufmg.br; Web: www.eba.ufmg.br; *Dir* Prof Maria Beatriz Braga Mendonca
Courses: †Animation & Digital Film, †Conservation & Restoration, †Dance, †Fashion Arts, †Theatre Arts, †Visual Arts

RIO DE JANEIRO

ESCOLA DE ARTES VISUAIS, School of Visual Arts of Parque Lage, Rua Jardim Botanico, 414, Parque Lage Rio de Janeiro, 22461-000 Brazil. Tel 55 21 2334 4088; Email cursos.eavparquelage@gmail.com; Web: www.eavparquelage.rj.gov.br; *Dir* Lisette Lagnado
Estab 1975; maintains art/architecture library; on-campus shop where art supplies may be purchased; pub; D & E, Mon - Sat; SC 39, LC 19; 1,475
Activities: Schols offered
Ent Req: Free courses
Tuition: $120-$125 per month
Courses: Aesthetics, Art Appreciation, Art Education, Art History, †Conceptual Art, Drawing, †Engraving, Film, Graphic Arts, Mixed Media, Painting, Photography, Sculpture, Video

BULGARIA

SOFIA

NIKOLAJ PAVLOVIC HIGHER INSTITUTE OF FINE ARTS, National Academy of Arts, Shipka 1, Sofia, 1000 Bulgaria. Tel 3592 987 33 28; Email art_academy@nha.bg; Web: www.nha.bg; *Institutional Coord* Mitko Dinev
Estab 1896; Maintains nonprofit Acadmia Gallery & art/architecture library; Pub; D; Enrollment 1,000
Ent Req: Entrance exams
Degrees: BA, MA, DA
Courses: †Art Education, †Art History, †Book & Graphic Design, †Ceramics, †Digital Arts, †Graphic Arts, †Industrial Design, †Metalworking, †Painting, †Photography, †Poster & Visual Communication, †Sculpture, †Stage Design, †Textile Design, †Woodcarving

CAMBODIA

PHNOM PENH

ROYAL UNIVERSITY OF FINE ARTS (RUFA), 72 St 19 (Preah Ang Yukunthor), Sangkat Chey Chumneas Khan Daun Penh Phnom Penh, Cambodia. Tel 855 0 23 986 417; Email rufa@camnet.com.kh; Web: www.rufa.edu.kh; *Rector* His Excellency Tuy Koeun; *Vice Rector* Mao Ngyhong; *Vice Rector* Proeung Chheang

CHILE

SANTIAGO

UNIVERSIDAD DE CHILE, Faculty of Arts, Sede Alfonso Letelier Llona Company 1264, Santiago, Chile. Tel 886-2-22722181; Fax 886-2-29687563; Web: www.artes.uchile.cl; *Dean* Prof Clara Cardenas Squella
Courses: †Painting, †Photography, †Pottery, †Sculpture, †Silversmithing, †Textile Design

CHINA

JINAN

SHANDONG UNIVERSITY OF ART & DESIGN, 23 Qianfoshan E Rd, Jinan, Shandong Province 250014 China. Tel 0086-531-2619385; Fax 0086-531-2619550; Web: www.at0086.com/SUAD; *Pres* Pan Lusheng
Courses: †Architecture, †Digital Arts, †Drafting, †Fashion Arts, †Handicrafts, †Landscape Architecture

CHINA, REPUBLIC OF

TAIPEI

NATIONAL TAIWAN ACADEMY OF ARTS, Pan-chiao Park, Taipei, 22055 Taiwan China, Republic of. Tel 967-6414; Web: m.ntua.edu.tw/ntuaen/index.htm; *Pres* S L Ling

COLOMBIA

BOGOTA

PONTIFICIA UNIVERSIDAD JAVERIANA, Carrera 7, No 40-62, Apdo Aereo 56710 Bogota, 11001000 Colombia. Tel 571-320-83-20; Fax 571-288-23-35; Email contacto@javeriana.edu.co; Web: www.javeriana.edu.co; *Rector* Rev. Jorge Humberto Pelaez Piedrahita S.J.
Estab 1622; Pvt

UNIVERSIDAD NACIONAL DE COLOMBIA, School of Visual Arts, Ciudad Universitaria - Bogota, Ave Carrera 30' 45-03, Bldg 303 Bogota, 111321 Colombia. Tel 57 1 3165000; Email ogutierrezr@unal.edu.co; Web: www.unal.edu.co; *Dir* Oscar Gutierrez Rodriguez; *Dir* Jose David Lozano Moreno

CROATIA

ZAGREB

AKADEMIJA IIKOVNIH UMJETNOSTI, Academy of Fine Arts of the University of Zagreb, Ilica 85, Zagreb, HR-10000 Croatia. Tel 385 1 3777 300; Fax 385 1 3711 440; Email alu@alu.hr; Web: www.alu.hr; *Prof* Damir Sokic; *Head Graphics Dept* Mirjana Vodopija; *Head Sculpture Dept* Neven Bilic; *Head Animation & New Media Dept* Ivana Keser Battista; *Head Restoration Dept* Andrej Aranicki
Estab 1907; Maintain nonprofit gallery; maintain art/architecture library; Pub; D; SC 100, LC 60, GC 40; Enrl D 400, maj 400, grad students 50
Ent Req: High school dipl
Degrees: BA, MA, PhD
Courses: Advertising Design, Aesthetics, Animation, †Art Education, Art History, Calligraphy, Collage, Costume Design & Construction, Drawing, Film, Graphic Arts, Graphic Design, History of Art & Architecture, Mixed Media, †Painting, Photography, †Printmaking, Restoration & Conservation, Sculpture, Stage Design, Teacher Training, Video

CZECH REPUBLIC

PRAGUE

AKADEMIE VYTVARNYCH UMENI, Academy of Fine Arts in Prague, U Akademie 4, Praha 7 Prague, 17022 Czech Republic. Tel 420 220 408 200; Fax 420 233 381 662; Email martina.krizkova@avu.cz; Web: www.avu.cz; *Contact Person, Coordr* Martina Krizkova
Estab 1799; Maintains nonprofit art gallery, art/architecture library; art supplies sold at campus store; pub; D
Ent Req: Passing entrance exam
Degrees: HS educ
Courses: Architecture, Art History, Conceptual Art, Drawing, Graphic Arts, History of Art & Architecture, Mixed Media, Painting, Printmaking, Restoration & Conservation, Sculpture, Video
Adult Hobby Classes: Courses—Drawing (E)
Summer School: Dir Dr Roman Franta. Courses: Drawing, Painting

VYSOKA SKOLA UMELECKO-PRUMYSLOVA V PRAZE, Academy of Arts, Architecture & Design, Jan Palach 80, Prague, 116 93 Czech Republic. Tel 420-251-098-241; Fax 420-251-098-240; Email studijni@vsup.cz; Web: www.vsup.cz; *Rector* Jindrich Smetana, Prof. Ak. Arch.
Estab 1885; Maintains nonprofit art gallery & library; Pub; D; Scholarships; 450 D
Degrees: MgA
Courses: Aesthetics, Animation, Architecture, Art History, Calligraphy, Ceramics, Conceptual Art, Design, Drawing, Fashion Arts, Goldsmithing, Graphic Arts, Graphic Design, History of Art & Architecture, Lettering, Mixed Media, Museum Staff Training, Painting, Photography, Printmaking, Sculpture, Silversmithing, Textile Design

DENMARK

AARHUS

ARKITEKTSKOLEN AARHUS, Aarhus School of Architecture, Norreport 20, Aarhus, C 8000 Denmark. Tel 45 89-36-00-00; Email a@aarch.dk; Web: www.aarch.dk; *Rector* Torben Nielsen
1965; Maintain an art/architecture library, Norreport 20, DK-8000 Aarhus C; on-campus shop where art supplies can be purchased; pub; D
Degrees: BA (Architecture), MA (Architecture)
Courses: †Architecture, †Design

COPENHAGEN

KONGELIGE DANSKE KUNSTAKADEMI, The Royal Danish Academy of Fine Arts, Kongens Nytorv 1, Copenhagen, DK-1050 Denmark. Tel 0045-33-74-46-01; Email bks@kunstakademiet.dk; Web: www.kunstakademiet.dk; *Rector* Sanne Kofod Olsen
Estab 1754; Maintains nonprofit art gallery Q gallery, Peder Skrams Gade 2, Copenhagen DK-1054; maintains art library; Pub; D; SC, LC, other; 200
Ent Req: Competitive
Degrees: BFA, MFA, MA
Courses: †Art Theory, Film, Graphic Arts, Mixed Media, Painting, Sculpture, Video, †Visual Art

ENGLAND

BIRMINGHAM

BIRMINGHAM CITY UNIVERSITY, Faculty of Art & Design, University House, 15 Bartholomew Row Birmingham, B5 5JU England. Tel 44 (0)121 331 5000; Email international.enquiries@bcu.ac.uk; Web: www.bcu.ac.uk; *Pro-Chancellor & Chmn* Mark Hopton

BRIGHTON

UNIVERSITY OF BRIGHTON, Faculty of Arts, Lewes Rd, Mithras House Brighton, BN2 4AT England. Tel (1273) 600900; Email a.boddington@brighton.ac.uk; Web: arts.brighton.ac.uk/faculty-of-arts-brighton; *Dean, Faculty of Arts* Anne Boddington
Estab 1859; Maintains a nonprofit art gallery as main bldg; maintains art/ architecture library, St Peters House, University of Brighton. Scholarships offered to international students, see university website for details; Art supplies may be purchased on campus; Pub; D & E & summer schools classes; Scholarships; SC, LC, GC; Maj 3250, GS 450, PhD 80
Ent Req: Various as applicable
Degrees: PhD, MPhil, MA, MDes, MFA, BA, FDA
Tuition: See website
Courses: Aesthetics, Architecture, Art Education, Art History, Ceramics, Commercial Art, Conceptual Art, Costume Design & Construction, Design, Fashion Arts, Film, Graphic Arts, Graphic Design, Handicrafts, History of Art & Architecture, Mixed Media, Museum Staff Training, Painting, Photography, Printmaking, Sculpture, †Silversmithing, Teacher Training, Textile Design, Theatre Arts, Weaving
Adult Hobby Classes: See website
Summer School: Anne Asha, Dir; courses: Humanities, Arts & Design

GLOUCESTER

GLOUCESTERSHIRE COLLEGE, Llanthony Rd, Gloucester, GL2 5JQ England. Tel 0345 155 2020; Email info@gloscol.ac.uk; Web: www.gloscal.ac.uk; *Prin* Matthew Burgess; *Chair* Trish Burton
Enrollment 21,000

LEICESTER

DE MONTFORT UNIVERSITY, Faculty of Art and Design, The Gateway, Leicester, LE1 9BH England. Tel 44 116 255 1551; Email enquiry@dmu.ac.uk; Web: www.dmu.ac.uk; *Vice Chancellor* Prof Dominic Shellard

LIVERPOOL

LIVERPOOL JOHN MOORES UNIVERSITY, Aldham Robarts Learning Resource Centre, 70 Mount Pleasant, Rodney House Liverpool, L3 5UX England. Tel (151) 231 2121; Email enquiry@ljmu.ac.uk; Web: www.ljmu.ac.uk; *Chancellor* Sir Brian Leveson

LONDON

CAMBERWELL COLLEGE OF ARTS, 45-65 Peckham Rd, London, SE5 8UF England. Tel (020) 7514-6302; Email info@camberwell.arts.ac.uk; Web: www.arts.ac.uk/camberwell; *Pro Vice Chancelor CCW* David Crow
Degrees: BA, MA
Courses: †Ceramics, †Drawing, †Graphic Design, †Illustration, †Metalwork, †Painting, †Photography, †Restoration & Conservation, †Sculpture, †Silversmithing

CHELSEA COLLEGE OF ART & DESIGN, 16 John Islip St, London, SW1P4JU England. Tel 207 514 7751; Fax (0171) 514 7777; Email info@chelsea.arts.ac.uk; *Vice Chancellor* Nigel Carrington; *Prog Dir* Martin Newth

CITY AND GUILDS OF LONDON ART SCHOOL, 124 Kennington Park Rd, London, SE11 4DJ England. Tel 020 7735 2306; Fax 020 7582 5361; Email info@cityandguildsartschool.ac.uk; Web: www.cityandguildsartschool.ac.uk; *Prin* Tamiko O'Brien; *Vice Prin* Magnus von Wistinghausen
Estab 1879; Maintains art library same location; art supplies available on campus; Independent; D & E; Scholarships; Degree & Grad Courses, Other
Activities: Schols available
Degrees: BA Hons & MA
Courses: †Art Appreciation, Art Education, Art History, †Drawing, Historical Stone carving, †History of Art & Architecture, †Lettering, Ornamental Wood carving, Painting, Printmaking, †Restoration & Conservation, †Sculpture

ROYAL ACADEMY SCHOOLS, Fine Art, Burlington House, Piccadilly, London, W1J OBD England. Tel 020 7300 5650; Email

schools@royalacademy.org.uk; Web: www.royalacademy.org.uk; *Pres* Christopher Le Brun; *Keeper* Eileen Cooper
Estab 1768; Maintains a nonprofit art gallery. Schols open annually to American residents with an MA degree in Fine Arts. Art supplies may be purchased on campus; Independent Royal Instn, pvt; D; Scholarships; Grad Course in Fine Arts, 3 yr Post Grad Course in Fine Art
Activities: Schols available
Ent Req: University Honours Degree, Bachelor's Degree in Fine Art
Degrees: Postgrad Dipl
Courses: Fine Arts, Painting, Printmaking, Sculpture

ROYAL COLLEGE OF ART, Kensington Gore, London, SW7 2EU England. Tel 0207 590 4444; Fax 0207 590 4500; Email info@rca.ac.uk; Web: www.rca.ac.uk; *Rector* Dr Paul Thompson
Estab 1837; Maintain library, same address; on-campus shop where art supplies may be purchased; Pub; D; SC 19
Ent Req: Undergrad degree
Degrees: MA, MPM, PhD
Courses: †Architecture, †Ceramics, Critical Writing in Art & Design, †Design, †Drawing, †Fashion Arts, †Goldsmithing, †Graphic Arts, †Graphic Design, †History of Art & Architecture, †Painting, †Photography, †Printmaking, †Sculpture, †Silversmithing, †Textile Design

SAINT MARTIN'S SCHOOL OF ART, 107 Charing Cross Rd, London, WC2H 0DU England. Tel 44-020-7514-7022; Fax 44-020-7514-7254; *Pro Vice-Chancellor* Jeremy Till

SLADE SCHOOL OF FINE ART, University College, Gower St London, WC1E 6BT England. Tel 44 (020) 7679 2313; Fax 44 (020) 7679 7801; Email slade.enquiries@ucl.ac.uk; Web: www.ucl.ac.uk; *Dir* Prof Susan Collins
Estab 1871

UNIVERSITY OF LONDON, Goldsmiths' University of London, Lewisham Way, New Cross London, SE14 6NW England. Tel +44 (0) 207 919 7171; Email international@gold.ac.uk; Web: www.gold.ac.uk; *Warden* Patrick Loughrey
On-campus shop where art supplies may be purchased; British Univ; D
Activities: Schols offered
Degrees: Yes
Courses: †Advertising Design, †Art Education, †Art History, †Ceramics, †Collage, †Conceptual Art, †Constructions, †Costume Design & Construction, †Design, †Drawing, †Fashion Arts, †Film, †Graphic Arts, †Graphic Design, †Mixed Media, †Museum Staff Training, †Occupational Therapy, †Painting, †Photography, †Printmaking, †Sculpture, †Stage Design, †Textile Design, †Theatre Arts, †Video

UNIVERSITY OF THE ARTS LONDON, Central Saint Martins, Granary Building 1 Granary Sq, Kings Cross London, N1C 4AA England. Tel 44-20 7514 7444; Email info@arts.ac.uk; Web: www.arts.ac.uk/csm/; *Head of College* Jeremy Till
Maintains nonprofit Lethaby Gallery

WIMBLEDON COLLEGE OF ARTS, Merton Hall Rd, London, SW19 3QA England. Tel 44 020 7514 9641; Email info@wimbledon.arts.ac.uk; Web: www.arts.ac.uk/wimbledon; *Pro Vice Chancellor CCW* David Crow
—**Dept of Foundation Studies**, 1 Wilson Rd, Foundation Bldg London, SE5 8LU England. Tel 020 7514 6311; Email ccwshortcourses@arts.ac.uk; Web: www.arts.ac.uk/camberwell; *Prog Leader* Claire McCormack
—**Dept of Theatre**, Merton Hall Rd, London, SW19 3QA England. Tel 020 7514 7514; *Course Leader* Abigail Hammond; *Course Leader* Elizabeth Dawson; *Course Leader* Eli Bo; *Course Leader* Grant Hicks
—**Dept of Fine Arts**, Merton Hall Rd, London, SW19 3QA England. Tel 020 7514 9641; Web: www.arts.ac.uk/wimbledon; *Course Leader* Dereck Harris
—**Department of History of Art & Contextual Studies**, Merton Hall Rd, London, SW19 3QA England. Tel 181-540-0231; *Course Leader* Dr Betti Marenko

MANCHESTER

MANCHESTER METROPOLITAN UNIVERSITY, School of Art, Cavendish St, Manchester, M15 6BR England. Tel 44 (0)161 247 1751; Email artschool@mmu.ac.uk; Web: www.art.mmu.ac.uk; *Acting Head Faculty* Nikhil Gomes

NOTTINGHAM

NOTTINGHAM TRENT UNIVERSITY, School of Art and Design, Burton St, Nottingham, NG1 4BU England. Tel 44 0 115 941 8418; Email events.team@ntu.ac.uk; Web: www.ntu.ac.uk/art/; *Dean* Marjolijn Brussaard
Estab 1843; Maintains nonprofit Bonington Gallery; art supplies sold at Boningtons Art Shop; 2,500
Courses: †Costume Design & Construction, †Decorative Arts, †Fashion Arts, †Fine Art, †Graphic Design, †Photography, †Stage Design, †Textile Design

OXFORD

UNIVERSITY OF OXFORD, Ruskin School of Art, 74 High St, Oxford, OX1 4BG England. Tel +44 (0) 1865 276 940; Email info@rsa.ox.ac.uk; Web: www.rsa.ox.ac.uk; *Head of School* Anthony Gardner, PhD
Maintains art library
Degrees: BFA, MFA, DPhil in Fine Art

SUFFOLK

SUFFOLK NEW COLLEGE, Department of Art & Design, Ipswich, Suffolk, IP4 1LT England. Tel 01473-382200; Fax 01473 382441; Email info@suffolk.ac.uk; Web: www.suffolk.ac.uk; *Prin* Viv Gillespie

SURREY

UNIVERSITY FOR THE CREATIVE ARTS AT FARNAM, Falkner Rd, Farnham Surrey, GU9 7DS England. Tel 44 (0) 1252-722441; Fax 44 (0) 1252-892616; Web: www.ucreative.ac.uk; *Chancellor* Dame Zandra Rhodes
Estab 2008, (founder col 1866); UCA campuses also at Canterbury, Epsom, Maidstone & Rochester; Art supplies available on-campus; pub; D; SC, LC, GC; Enrl 6,500
Degrees: BA (Hons); MA
Courses: Advertising Design, †Architecture, †Ceramics, Costume Design & Construction, Design, †Fashion Arts, †Film, Goldsmithing, Graphic Arts, Graphic Design, Mixed Media, Painting, Photography, Printmaking, Sculpture, Silversmithing, Textile Design, Video

ESTONIA

TALLINN

EESTI KUNSTIAKADEEMIA, Estonian Academy of Arts, Estonia pst 7, Teatri valjak 1 Tallinn, 10143 Estonia. Tel (372) 626 7301; Email artun@artun.ee; Web: www.artun.ee; *Rector* Prof Mart Kalm
Estab 1914; Pub; D & E
Ent Req: Secondary educ, passing of entry exam
Degrees: Bachelor, Master, Doctor, dipl
Courses: †Architecture, †Art History, †Ceramics, †Design, †Fashion Arts, †Glass Art, †Goldsmithing, †Graphic Arts, †Graphic Design, †Interior Architecture, †Mixed Media, †Photography, †Restoration & Conservation, †Sculpture, †Stage Design, †Textile Design
Adult Hobby Classes: Open Academy, diploma level educ

FINLAND

HELSINKI

KUVATAIDEAKATEMIA, Academy of Fine Arts, Elimaenkatu 25 A, Helsinki, 00510 Finland; PO Box 10, Helsinki, 00097 Finland. Tel 0294 47 2000; Email kuva.info@uniarts.fi; Web: www.uniarts.fi; *Rector* Jari Perkiomaki
Academy estab 1848; Maintains nonprofit art galleries, FAFA Gallery, Lonnrotinkatu 35, 00180 Helsinki, Finland, Kuva/Tila Merimiehenkatu 36, 00150 Helsinki, Finland; maintains FAFA Library, Elimaenkatu 25 A, 00510, Helsinki, Finland; Pub; D
Degrees: BFA, MFA, DFA
Tuition: No tuition fee for degree students
Courses: Painting, Printmaking, Sculpture, Time and Space Arts

FRANCE

PARIS

ECOLE DU LOUVRE, School of the Louvre, Palais du Louvre Porte Jaujard, Place du Carrousel Paris, 75038 Paris cedex 01 France. Tel 01 55 35 1800; Fax 01 55 35 1850; Web: www.ecoledulouvre.fr; *Dir* Philippe Durey
Estab 1882
Courses: †Anthropology, †Archaeology, †Art History, †Epigraphy, †Museology

ECOLE NATIONALE SUPERIEURE DES ARTS DECORATIFS, National College of Decorative Arts, 31 rue d'Ulm, Paris, 75240 cedex 05 France. Tel 33 01 42 34 9700; Fax 33 01 42 34 9785; Web: www.ensad.fr
Estab 1766; Maintains art library; 180; 700
Degrees: Master's (5 yrs)
Tuition: 646 EUR per yr
Courses: †Animation, †Art, †Fashion Arts, †Graphic Design, †Instruction, †Interior Architecture, †Photography, †Printmaking, †Product Design, †Stage Design, †Textile Design, †Video

ECOLE NATIONALE SUPERIEURE DES BEAUX-ARTS, National College of Fine Arts, 14 rue Bonaparte, Paris, 75006 France. Tel 01 47 03 5000; Fax 01 47 03 5080; Email info@beauxartsparis.fr; Web: www.beauxartsparis.fr; *Dir* Jean-Marc Bustamante
Estab 1648; Maintains temp exhibs of contemporary art or heritage coll; cabinet of drawings with 3 exhibs per yr; Mediatheque open access libr for students & Servile de Collections, research libr for art historians, both on site; pub; D, E & Summer; SC, LC & GC
Ent Req: BA
Degrees: Dipl
Courses: Aesthetics, Art History, Conceptual Art, Drawing, Graphic Arts, Mixed Media, Painting, Photography, Printmaking, Sculpture, Video
Adult Hobby Classes: Summer courses only

ECOLE SPECIALE D'ARCHITECTURE, 254 blvd Raspail, Paris, 75014 France. Tel 33 01 40 47 40 47; Email info@esa-paris.fr; Web: www.esa-paris.fr; *Pres* Raed Skhiri; *Dir* Francois Bouvard
Estab 1865; Maintains a nonprofit Gallerie Speciale & art/architecture library; Pvt; D; Scholarships; SC 10, LC, GC
Activities: Schols available
Ent Req: HS dipl
Degrees: DESA
Courses: Aesthetics, Architecture, Art Education, Art History, Constructions, Design, Drawing, History of Art & Architecture, Mixed Media, Photography, Restoration & Conservation

UNIVERSITE DE PARIS I, PANTHEON-SORBONNE, UFR d'Art et d'Archeologie, Sorbonne Center, 17 rue de la Sorbonne Paris, 75005 France. Tel 01 44 07 80 00; Email art1@univ-paris1.fr; Web: www.univ-paris1.fr; *Dir* Alain Duplouy
Estab 1971

VILLENEUVE D'ASCQ

ECOLE NATIONALE SUPERIEURE D'ARCHITECTURE ET DE PAYSAGE DE LILLE, ENSAP Lille, 2 rue Verte Villeneuve d'Ascq, 59650 France. Tel 03-20 61 95 50; Fax 03-20 61 95 51; Email ensap@lille.archi.fr; Web: www.lille.archi.fr; *Dir* Jean Marc Zuretti

GERMANY

BERLIN

UNIVERSITAT DER KUNSTE BERLIN, Postfach 12 05 44, Berlin, 10595 Germany; Einsteinufer 43-53, Berlin, 10587 Germany. Tel 49 030-3185-0; Fax 49 030 3185 2635; Web: www.udk-berlin.de; *Pres* Prof Martin Rennert; *First VPres* Prof Ulrike Hentschel; *Chancellor* Wolfgang Abramowski
Estab 1975
Activities: Classes held days; studio course, lect courses, grad courses; schols available

BRAUNSCHWEIG

HOCHSCHULE FUR BILDENDE KUNSTE BRAUNSCHWEIG, Braunschweig University of Art, Johannes-Selenka-Platz 1, Braunschweig, 38118 Germany. Tel 49 (531) 391 91 22; Fax 49 (531) 391 93 07; Email hvp@hbk-bs.de; Web: www.hbk-bs.de; *Pres* Vanessa Ohlraun
Estab 1963; Maintains nonprofit art gallery; maintains art library; Schols offered semi-annually; Pub; bd of trustees; D; Scholarships; SC, LC, GC; enrl 1,200
Ent Req: High school dipl, display of art & design work
Degrees: BA, MA, MEd
Tuition: 500 EUR per semester
Courses: Advertising Design, Aesthetics, Art Appreciation, Art History, Art Mediation, Communication Arts, Communication Design, Conceptual Art, Constructions, Design, Display, Drawing, Fashion Arts, Film, Fine Arts, Goldsmithing, Graphic Arts, Graphic Design, Industrial Design, Lettering, Mixed Media, Painting, Photography, Sculpture, Theatre Arts, Transportation Design, Video
Adult Hobby Classes: Classes for senior citizens

DRESDEN

HOCHSCHULE FUR BILDENDE KUNSTE DRESDEN, Dresden Academy of Art, Bruhlsche Terrasse 1, Dresden, 01067 Germany; Postfach 160153, Dresden, 01287 Germany. Tel (351) 4402-260; Fax (351) 4402-2655; Web: www.hfbk-dresden.de; *Rector* Matthias Flugge; *Chancellor* Jochen Beibert
Estab 1764; Maintains nonprofit gallery & art/architecture library; Pub; D & E; Scholarships; SC, LC, GC; enrl 650
Ent Req: Abitur or equivalent, portfolio and entry exam
Degrees: Dipl after 5 years
Courses: Art History, †Conceptual Art, †Costume Design & Construction, †Drawing, †Graphic Arts, †Mixed Media, †Painting, †Restoration & Conservation, †Sculpture, †Stage Design, Theatre Arts, Video

DUSSELDORF

KUNSTAKADEMIE DUSSELDORF, Dusseldorf Academy of Art, Eiskellerstrasse 1, Dusseldorf, 40213 Germany. Tel 0211 1396 0; Fax 0211 1396 225; Email postmaster@kunstakademie-duesseldorf.de; Web: www.kunstakademie-duesseldorf.de; *Rector* Rita McBride; *Dean, Art* Thomas Grunfeld; *Gallery Dir* Prof Dr Robert Fleck
No admis fee; Estab 1773; Maintains nonprofit Akademie-Galerie, Burgplatz 1, 40213 Dusseldorf, Germany
Courses: †Architecture, †Art Education, †Art History, †Film, †Painting, †Photography, †Sculpture, †Video

FRANKFURT

STAATLICHE HOCHSCHULE FUR BILDENDE KUENSTE - STAEDELSCHULE, Academy of Fine Arts, Durerstrasse 10, Frankfurt, D 60596 Germany. Tel 0049 069 6050 08-0; Fax 0049 069 6050 08-66; Web: www.staedelschule.de; *Rector & Prof Art History & Cultural Educ* Philippe Pirotte; *Vice Rector* Judith Hopf
Estab 1817; Maintains art gallery, Portikus, Alte Brucke 2, 60594 Frankfurt, Germany; pub; D & E; SC, LC
Ent Req: application with portfolio
Courses: Art History, Painting, Photography, Printmaking, Sculpture, Video

HAMBURG

HOCHSCHULE FUR BILDENDE KUNSTE, University of Fine Arts of Hamburg, Lerchenfeld 2, Hamburg, 22081 Germany. Tel 49-40 428989-0; Fax 49-40 428989-271; Email kanzlerin@hbfk.hamburg.de; Web: www.hfbk-hamburg.de; *Chanc* Dr. Anna Neubauer
Estab 1767; Maintains HFBK Gallery & Library; art supplies sold at campus store; pub; D & E; Scholarships; SC, LC & GC
Activities: Schols available
Ent Req: Higher educ entrance qualification, outstanding artistic ability, portfolio
Degrees: BA & MA (Fine Arts), PhD
Tuition: 375 EUR per sem
Courses: Art Appreciation, Art Education, Art History, Ceramics, Commercial Art, Conceptual Art, Design, Drawing, Film, Goldsmithing, Graphic Arts, Graphic Design, Handicrafts, History of Art & Architecture, Mixed Media, Painting, Photography, Printmaking, Sculpture, Silversmithing, Stage Design, Teacher Training, Textile Design, Video

KARLSRUHE

STAATLICHE AKADEMIE DER BILDENDEN KUNSTE KARLSRUHE, State Academy of Fine Arts Karlsruhe, Reinhold-Frank-Strasse 67, Karlsruhe, 76133 Germany. Tel 0721-926-5210; Fax 0721-926-5213; Web: www.kunstakademie-karlsruhe.de; *Rector* Prof Ernst Caramelle
Estab 1854; Maintains art library; pub; D; SC, LC
Courses: Drawing, Painting, Sculpture

LEIPZIG

HOCHSCHULE FUR GRAFIK UND BUCHKUNST, Academy of Visual Arts Leipzig, Wachterstrasse 11, Leipzig, 04107 Germany. Tel 49 0 341 2135 168; Email hgb@hgb-leipzig.de; Web: www.hgb-leipzig.de; *Rector* Ralf Hartmann
Maintains nonprofit art gallery; Pub; other

MUNICH

AKADEMIE DER BILDENDEN KUNSTE MUNCHEN, Academy of Fine Arts in Munich, Akademiestrasse 2-4, Munich, 80799 Germany. Tel 49 89-3852-0; Fax 49 89-3852-206; Web: www.adbk.de; *Pres* Prof Dieter Rehm
Estab 1770

NUREMBERG

AKADEMIE DER BILDENDEN KUNSTE IN NURNBERG, Academy of Fine Arts in Nuremberg, Bingstrasse 60, Nuremberg, 90480 Germany. Tel 49 911 9404 0; Email info@adbk-nuernberg.de; Web: www.adbk-nuernberg.de; *Pres* Ottmar Horl
Estab 1662; Pub; D
Ent Req: Qualifying examination, aptitude test
Degrees: State exam, dipl, cert, master schiler, dipl postgrad, master of architecture
Courses: Advertising Design, Architecture, Art Education, Art History, Conceptual Art, Design, Goldsmithing, Graphic Arts, Graphic Design, History of Art & Architecture, Mixed Media, Painting, Photography, Printmaking, Sculpture, Silversmithing, Teacher Training, Video

STUTTGART

STAATLICHE AKADEMIE DER BILDENDEN KUNSTE STUTTGART, Stuttgart State Academy of Art and Design, Am Weissenhof 1, Stuttgart, 70191 Germany. Tel 49 (0) 711-28440-0; Fax 49 (0) 711-28440-225; Email info@abk-stuttgart.de; Web: www.abk-stuttgart.de; *Rector* Prof Dr Barbara Bader

GREECE

ATHENS

ECOLE FRANCAISE D'ATHENES, French School of Athens, 6 rue Didotou, Athens, 10680 Greece. Tel (30) 210 36 79 900; Fax (30) 210 36 32 101; Email efa@efa.gr; Web: www.efa.gr; *Dir* Marie-Dominique Nenna
Estab 1846; Pub

HUNGARY

BUDAPEST

MAGYAR KEPZOMUVESZETI EGYETEM, Hungarian University of Fine Arts, 1062 Andrassy ut 69-71, Budapest, 1062 Hungary. Tel 361 342 1738; Fax 361 342 7563; Email info@mke.hu; Web: www.mke.hu; *Rector* Prof Judit Csanadi
Estab 1871; Pub; D; SC, LC, GC, Postgrad
Ent Req: Final exam at secondary sch, entrance exam
Degrees: MA
Courses: †Art Education, †Art History, †Costume Design & Construction, †Drawing, †Graphic Arts, †Graphic Design, †Mixed Media, †Painting, †Photography, †Printmaking, †Restoration & Conservation, †Sculpture, †Stage Design, †Teacher Training, †Video

INDIA

BARODA

MAHARAJA SAYAJIRAO UNIVERSITY OF BARODA, Faculty of Fine Arts, M. S. University of Baroda, Pratapgunj, Baroda, GujaratIndia. Tel 0265 279 5555; Email info@msubaroda.ac.in; Web: www.msubaroda.ac.in; *Chanc* Dr Rajmata Shubhangini Raje Gaekwad
Estab 1949; Maintain non-profit art gallery & art library; Pub; D; SC 4, LC 6, GC 6
Activities: Schols offered
Ent Req: 10+2 (higher secondary or equivalent)
Degrees: BVA, MVA, B.Des, M.Des, M.Muse, PhD
Courses: †Art History, †Commercial Art, †Design, †Drawing, †Graphic Design, †History of Art & Architecture, †Museum Staff Training, †Painting, †Printmaking, †Sculpture

LUCKNOW

UNIVERSITY OF LUCKNOW, College of Arts and Crafts, Faculty of Fine Arts, Badshah Bagh, Lucknow, UP 226 007 India. Tel 91 522 2740086; Email update@lkouniv.ac.in; Web: www.lkouniv.ac.in; *Chanc* Shri Ram Naik

MUMBAI

RACHANA SANSAD, Academy of Architecture, 278, Shankar Ghaneker Marg, Prabhadevi Mumbai, 400025 India. Tel (022) 2430 1024; Fax (022) 2430 1724; Email contact@rachanasansad.edu.in; Web: rachanasansad.edu.in; *Prin* Suresh M Singh; *Prof* Rohit Shinkre; *Asst Prof* Arun Narwekar; *Asst Prof* Uttara Mone
Estab 1955; Maintains a nonprofit art gallery, Rachana Sansad's Art Gallery, 278, Shankar Ghaneker Marg, Prabhadevi, Mumbai, 400 025, India. Art supplies may be purchased on campus; Pvt; D; Scholarships; SC, LC, GC; 300 students
Ent Req: 10+2 course
Degrees: B Architecture of Univ of Mumbai
Tuition: As per government norms
Courses: Architecture

IRELAND

BALLYVAUGHAN

BURREN COLLEGE OF ART, Newtown Castle, County Clare Ballyvaughan, County ClareIreland. Tel 353-65-7077200; Email anna@burrencollege.ie; Web: www.burrencollege.ie; *Pres* Mary Hawkes-Greene; *Dean & Head Painting & Drawing* Conor McGrady; *Head Sculpture* Aine Phillips; *Head of Irish Studies* Gordon D'Arcy; *Head Creative Writing* Frank Golden
Estab 1993; Maintains nonprofit art gallery, BCA Gallery, Newtown Castle, Ballyvaughan, Co Clare; maintains art & architecture libr, maintains on-campus shop where art supplies can be purchased; Pvt; D Acad yr and summer; SC, LC, GC 8
Activities: Schols offered
Ent Req: GPA 3 on Scale 4 per sem or yr (undergrad) BFA degree for MFA
Degrees: MFA, Post-Bac, PhD, JYA transfer cr for undergraduate, MA, postgraduate diploma
Courses: †Art & Ecology, Art History, Drawing, Painting, Photography, Sculpture
Adult Hobby Classes: Enrl 10-20 Summer Costs Vary
Summer School: Director Martina Cleary Head of Photography; max enrollment 12, tuition 3500 EUR

DUBLIN

COLAISTE NAISIUNTA EALAINE IS DEARTHA, National College of Art & Design, 100 Thomas St, Dublin, 8 Ireland. Tel 353 1 636 4200; Fax 353 1 636 4207; Email fios@ncad.ie; Web: www.ncad.ie; *Chmn* Prof Niamh Brennan; *Head Design* Prof Alex Milton; *Head Educ* Prof Dervil Jordan; *Head Fine Art* Prof Philip Napier; *Head Visual Culture* Prof David Crowley; *Head Acad Affairs and Research* Prof Siun Hanrahan; *Head First Yr Art & Design* Mary Avril Gillan
Estab 1746; Art supplies may be purchased on campus; Pub; D, E & Easter & Summer periods; SC 12, LC 2 GC 5, Art, Design & Teacher Educ
Degrees: BA, BDes, MA, MFA, MLitt, PhD
Courses: Aesthetics, †Art Education, Art History, †Ceramics, Conceptual Art, †Design, Drawing, †Fashion Arts, †Goldsmithing, Graphic Design, Handicrafts, †Mixed Media, †Painting, Photography, †Printmaking, †Sculpture, Silversmithing, †Textile Design, Video, Weaving

ISRAEL

JERUSALEM

BEZALEL ACADEMY OF ARTS & DESIGN, Mount Scopus, PO Box 24046 Jerusalem, 9124001 Israel. Tel (2) 5893333; Fax (2) 5823094; Email mail@bezalel.ac.il; Web: www.bezalel.ac.il; *Pres* Adi Stern
Estab 1906; Maintains art & architecture lib, Bezalel Lib, Bezalel Acad, 7 Bezalel St, Mt Scopes Jerusalem 91260; maintains gift shop; 2,000
Degrees: BArch, B.DES, BFA, MFA, M.DES, M. Urban Des.
Courses: Advertising Design, †Architecture, Art History, Calligraphy, †Ceramics, †Design, Drawing, †Film, †Glass Design, †Goldsmithing, †Graphic Arts, †Graphic Design, †Industrial Design, †Painting, †Photography, †Printmaking, †Sculpture, †Video

ITALY

BOLOGNA

ACCADEMIA DI BELLE ARTI DI BOLOGNA, Academy of Fine Arts, Via delle Belle Arti 54, Bologna, 40126 Italy. Tel 39-051-4226411; Fax 39-051-253032; Email direzione@ababo.net; Web: www.ababo.it; *Dir* Prof Mauro Mazzali

FLORENCE

ACCADEMIA DI BELLE ARTI DI FIRENZE, Academy of Fine Arts, via Ricasoli 66, Florence, 50122 Italy. Tel 39 055 215 449; Fax 39 055 239 6921; Email abafi@accademia.firenze.it; Web: www.accademia.firenze.it; *Dir* Prof Eugenio Cecioni

MILAN

ACCADEMIA DI BELLE ARTI DI BRERA, Academy of Fine Arts, via Brera 28, Milan, 20121 Italy; Via Fiori Oscuri 7, Milan, 20121 Italy. Tel 39 02 8695 51; Fax 39 02 8640 3643; Email accademia@pec.accademiadibrera.milano.it; Web: www.accademiadibrera.milano.it; *Dir* Franco Marrocco
Estab 1776; Maintains art/architecture library; Ministero Univ & Research, pub; D; Scholarships; GC 28
Activities: Schols available
Ent Req: Secondary level school
Degrees: 1o Level, 3 yrs; 2o Level, 2 yrs
Tuition: See website for tuition

PERUGIA

ACCADEMIA DI BELLE ARTI DI PERUGIA PIETRO VANNUCCI, Academy of Fine Arts, Piazza San Francesco al Prato 5, Perugia, 06123 Italy. Tel 39 075 5730631; Fax 39 075 5730632; Email info@abaperugia.org; Web: www.abaperugia.com; *Dir* Paolo Belardi

ROME

ACCADEMIA DI BELLE ARTI DI ROMA, Academy of Fine Arts, via Ripetta 222, Rome, 00186 Italy. Tel 39 06-322-70-25; Fax 39 06-321 80 07; Email direzione@accademiabelleartiroma.it; Web: www.accademiabelleartiroma.it; *Pres* Mario Ali; *Dir* Prof Tiziana D'Acchille
Estab 1873; pub; D; D 365
Activities: Schols
Tuition: 500 to 1500 EUR
Courses: Decoration, Fashion Arts, Graphic Arts, Graphic Design, Painting, Scenography, Sculpture

AMERICAN ACADEMY IN ROME, School of Fine Arts, Via Angelo Masina 5, Rome, 00153 Italy. Tel 39 06-58461; Fax 39 06-5810788; Email info@aarome.org; Web: www.aarome.org; *Pres & CEO* Mark Robbins; *Dir* John Ochsendorf
Estab 1894; Fellowships
Courses: †Architecture, †Design, †Historic Preservation & Conservation, †Landscape Architecture, †Literature, †Musical Composition, †Visual Arts

BRITISH SCHOOL AT ROME, via Gramsci 61, Rome, 00197 Italy. Tel +39 06 326 4939; Fax +39 06 322 1201; Email info@bsrome.it; Web: www.bsr.ac.uk; *Dir* Stephen J Milner, MA, DPhil; *Asst Dir* Thomas Leo-True, MA, PhD
Estab 1901

ISTITUTO SUPERIORE PER LA CONSERVAZIONE ED IL RESTAURO, Institute for Conservation and Restoration, Via di San Michele 23, Rome, 00153 Italy. Tel 06 67236300; Fax 06 67236409; Email is-cr.segreteria@beniculturali.it; Web: www.iscr.beniculturali.it; *Dir* Gisella Capponi
Estab 1939

TURIN

ACCADEMIA ALBERTINA DI BELLE ARTI DI TORINO, Albertina Academy of Fine Arts, via Accademia Albertina 6, Turin, 10123 Italy. Tel 011-889020; Fax 011 812 5688; Email accademia.torino@pec.it; Web: www.accademialbertina.torino.it; *Pres* Fiorenzo Alfieri; *Dir* Prof Salvatore Bitonti
Estab 1652

VENICE

ACCADEMIA DI BELLE ARTI DI VENEZIA, Academy of Fine Arts, Dorsoduro 423, Venice, 30123 Italy. Tel 39 041 2413752; Fax 39 041 5230129; Email info@accademiavenezia.it; Web: www.accademiavenezia.it; *Pres* Luana Zanella; *Dir* Giuseppe La Bruna
Estab 1750

JAMAICA

KINGSTON

EDNA MANLEY COLLEGE OF THE VISUAL AND PERFORMING ARTS, School of Visual Arts, 1 Arthur Wint Dr, Kingston, 5 St Andrew Jamaica. Tel 876-619-3362; Email info@emc.edu.jm; Web: emc.edu.jm; *Principal* Nicholeen Degrasse-Johnson; *Vice Principal Academic & Tech Studies* Mrs Carol Hamilton; *Vice Principal Admin & Resource Devel* Denise Salmon
Estab 1950; SC, LC
Ent Req: 5 CXC, portfolio review, drawing exam
Degrees: UWI/EMCUDA, BA, Dipl Studio Art, JBTE
Courses: †Advertising Design, †Aesthetics, †Art Education, †Art History, †Ceramics, †Design, †Display, †Drawing, †Goldsmithing, †Graphic Arts, †Graphic Design, †History of Art & Architecture, †Painting, †Photography, †Printmaking, †Sculpture, †Silversmithing, †Stage Design, †Teacher Training, †Textile Design, †Theatre Arts, †Weaving

JAPAN

KANAZAWA

KANAZAWA COLLEGE OF ART, 5-11-1 Kodatsuno, Kanazawa, Ishikawa 920 8656 Japan. Tel (81) 76-262-3531; Fax (81) 76-262-6594; Email admin@kanazawa-bidai.ac.jp; Web: www.kanazawa-bidai.ac.jp; *Pres* Masahiko Maeda
Estab 1946; Maintains arts library; Pub; D
Degrees: BA 4 yrs, MFA, PhD
Tuition: Entrance fee: Kanazawa residents or Kanazawa College of Art graduates 28,200 JPY, others 56,400 JPY; lecture fee 14,880 JPY per credit
Courses: Craft, Design, Fine Art, Liberal Arts

KYOTO

KYOTO CITY UNIVERSITY OF ARTS, Faculty of Fine Arts, 13-6 Kutsukake-cho, Oe, Nishikyo-ku Kyoto, 610-1197 Japan. Tel 81 75 334-2200; Email admin@kcua.ac.jp; Web: www.kcua.ac.jp; *Pres* Kiyokazu Washida
Courses: †Ceramics, †Concept & Media Planning, †Dyeing & Weaving, †Environmental Design, †General Science of Art, †Nihonga, †Painting, †Printmaking, †Product Design, †Sculpture, †Urushi Lacquering, †Visual Design

TOKYO

TAMA ART UNIVERSITY, 3-15-34 Kaminoge, Setagaya-Ku Tokyo, 158 8558 Japan. Tel 81 42 679 5602; Email nyushi@tamabi.ac.jp; Web: www.tamabi.ac.jp; *Pres* Igarashi Takenobu
Estab 1953; Maintains Tama Art University Museum and Library; Pvt; D & E; Scholarships; D 3000, E 800, GS 200
Tuition: 1,899,000 - 1,930,000 JPY
Courses: †Art Science, †Ceramics, †Design, †Environmental Design, †Glass, †Graphic Arts, †Graphic Design, †Information Design, †Japanese Painting, †Metal Design, †Oil Painting, †Painting, †Printmaking, †Product Design, †Sculpture, †Teacher Training, †Textile Design, †Theatre Arts

TOKYO GEIJUTSU DAIGAKU, Tokyo University of the Arts, 12-8 Ueno Park, Taito-Ku, Tokyo, 110 8714 Japan. Tel 8150 5525 2013; Email toiawase@ml.geidai.ac.jp; Web: www.geidai.ac.jp; *Dean, Faculty of Fine Arts* Katsuhiko Hibino; *Pres* Kazuki Sawa; *Dir, Grad School of Film & New Media* Takashi Kiriyama; *Dir, Univ Library* Kei Matsushita
Estab 1949; Maintains University Art Museum and Library; Undergrad 2,045 & grad 1,172

KOREA, REPUBLIC OF

SEOUL

SEOUL NATIONAL UNIVERSITY, College of Fine Arts, 1 Gwanak-ro, Gwanak-gu Seoul, 151-742 Korea, Republic of. Tel 82 2-880-6883; Web: art.snu.ac.kr/en/; *Dean* Soon-jong Lee
Estab 1946
Degrees: Undergrad 4 yrs, master's 2 yrs, doctorate 3 yrs
Courses: †Crafts, †Design, †Oriental Painting, †Painting, †Sculpture

LATVIA

RIGA

LATVIJAS MAKSLAS AKADEMIJA, Art Academy of Latvia, Kalpaka blvd 13, Riga, 1867 Latvia. Tel 371 67332202; Fax 371 67228963; Email info@lma.lv; Web: www.lma.lv; *Rector* Prof Kristaps Zarins
Estab 1919
Degrees: Undergrad 4 yrs, master's 2 yrs, doctorate 3 yrs
Courses: †2-D & 3-D Visual Arts, †Art History, †Audio-Video Media Art, †Design

LEBANON

SIN EL-FIL

UNIVERSITE DE BALAMAND - ACADEMIE LIBANAISE DES BEAUX-ARTS, Lebanese Academy of Fine Arts, Avenue Emile Edde, BP 55251 Sin El-Fil, Lebanon. Tel 961 1-480056; Fax 961 1-500779; Email alba@alba.edu.lb; Web: www.alba.edu.lb; *Dean* Andre Bekhazi

MEXICO

CHOLULA

UNIVERSIDAD DE LAS AMERICAS, School of Arts and Humanities, Santa Catarina Martir, Cholula, Puebla CP 72810 Mexico. Tel 52 222 229 20 00; Web: www.udlap.mx; *Rector* Luis Ernesto Derbez Bautista; *Dean* Martha Laura Ramirez Dorantes
Courses: †Architecture, †Art History, †Fine Arts, †Interior Design, †Visual Information Design

MEXICO CITY

INSTITUTO NACIONAL DE BELLAS ARTES, National Institute of Fine Arts, Paseo Reforma y Campo Marte, Mexico City, Mexico; Paseo de la Reforma y Campo, Marte s/n, Modula A, Piso 1, Col Chapultepec Polanco Mexico City, 11560 Mexico. Tel 01 800 904 4000; Email infoinba@inba.gob.mx; Web: www.inba.gob.mx; *Gen Dir* Lidia Camacho
Estab 1946

UNIVERSIDAD NACIONAL AUTONOMA DE MEXICO, Faculty of Arts and Design, Ave Constitution 600, Col Bo La Concha, Del. Xochimilco Mexico City, DF CP 16210 Mexico. Tel 54-89-49-14, 20, 21 & 22; Web: www.fad.unam.mx; *Dir* Dr Elizabeth Fuentes Rojas
Estab 1781; Maintains nonprofit art galleries; maintains an art/architecture library; on campus shop sells art supplies; schols offered annually to internal students; Pub; D & E; Scholarships; E, NM, M, Grad C; 3,500 students
Ent Req: High school dipl
Courses: †Advertising Design, †Aesthetics, †Art Appreciation, †Art Education, †Art History, †Calligraphy, †Ceramics, †Collage, †Commercial Art, †Conceptual Art, †Design, †Drawing, Engraving, †Film, †Graphic Arts, †Graphic Design, †Mixed Media, †Painting, †Photography, †Printmaking, †Restoration & Conservation, †Sculpture, †Silversmithing, †Stage Design, †Teacher Training, †Video
Adult Hobby Classes: Several courses
Children's Classes: Courses for children 6-12 yrs
Summer School: Courses of continuing educ

NETHERLANDS

AMSTERDAM

ACADEMIE VAN BOUWKUNST, Academy of Architecture, Waterlooplein 211, Amsterdam, 1011 PG Netherlands. Tel 020-531-8218; Fax 020-623-2519; Email avb-info@ahk.nl; Web: www.academievanbouwkunst.nl; *Dir* Aart Oxenaar
Courses: †Architecture, †Landscape Architecture, †Urban Design

RIJKSAKADEMIE VAN BEELDENDE KUNSTEN, State Academy of Fine Arts, Sarphatistraat 470, Amsterdam, 1018 GW Netherlands. Tel 31 (20) 52 70 300;

Fax 31 (20) 52 70 301; Email info@rijksakademie.nl; Web: www.rijksakademie.nl; *Dir* Dr Els van Odijk
Estab 1870
Activities: Open to young artists from all over the world

BREDA

AVANS HOGESCHOOL, School of Fine Art and Design/St Joost, Beukenlaan 1, Breda, 4834 CR Netherlands. Tel 31 (0) 88-5257302; Email info.akvstjoost@avans.nl; Web: www.akvstjoost.nl
Estab 1812; Maintains art/architecture library
Courses: †Animation, †Audiovisual Design, †Graphic Design, †Illustration, †Photography

THE HAGUE

KONINKLIJKE ACADEMIE VAN BEELDENDE KUNSTEN, Royal Academy of Art, Prinsessegracht 4, The Hague, 2514 AN Netherlands. Tel 070-315-47-77; Fax 070-315-47-78; Email post@kabk.nl; Web: www.kabk.nl; *Dir* Marieke Schoenmakers
Open to visitors Mon - Thurs 8 AM - 9:30 PM, Fri 8 Am - 6:30 PM, Sat 10 AM - 4:30 PM; Estab 1682

NORWAY

OSLO

KUNSTHOGSKOLEN I OSLO, (Statens Kunstakademi) Oslo National Academy of the Arts, Fossveien 24, Oslo, 0551 Norway; PO Box 6853, St. Olavs plass Oslo, 0130 Norway. Tel 47 22 99 55 00; Fax 47 22 99 55 02; Email postmottak@khio.no; Web: www.khio.no; *Rector* Jorn Mortensen
Estab 1996; Maintains a nonprofit art gallery; Pub; D & E; D 550
Ent Req: General univ admis cert & entrance examination
Degrees: BA, MA
Courses: Advertising Design, Ceramics, Costume Design & Construction, Fashion Arts, Goldsmithing, Graphic Arts, Graphic Design, Opera, Painting, Printmaking, Sculpture, Silversmithing

PERU

LIMA

ESCUELA NACIONAL SUPERIOR AUTONOMA DE BELLAS ARTES DEL PERU, National School of Fine Arts, Jiron Ancash 681, Lima, Peru. Tel 427-2200; Fax 427-0799; Email ensabap@ensabap.edu.pe; Web: www.ensabap.edu.pe; *Dir Acad* Ana Moreno Salvatierra
Estab 1918; D, E & N
Ent Req: Seundaria completa, examen de admision, documentas personales (test)
Degrees: Titulo de artista plastico y docente anombre de la nacion
Adult Hobby Classes: Enrl 600; courses—painting & drawing
Children's Classes: Enrl 600; courses—painting & drawing
Summer School: Enrl 1200; courses— painting, drawing & graphic design; Dir Ana Moreno Salvatierra

POLAND

KRACOW

AKADEMIA SZTUK PIEKNYCH IM JANA MATEJKI W KRAKOWIE, Jan Matejko Academy of Fine Arts, pl Jana Matekji 13, Kracow, 31-157 Poland. Tel 0048 12 299 20 00; Fax 0048 12 422 65 66; Email rektor@asp.krakow.pl; Web: www.asp.krakow.pl; *Rector* Prof Stanislaw Rodzinski; *Chancellor* Jolanta Ewartowska, MEng
Estab 1818; Pub; D & E
Degrees: BA, MA
Courses: †Industrial Design, †Interior Design, †Intermedia, †Painting, †Restoration & Conservation, †Sculpture

LODZ

AKADEMIA SZTUK PIEKNYCH IM WLADYSLAWA STRZEMINSKIEGO W LODZ, Strzeminski Academy of Art Lodz, ul Wojska Polskiego 121, Lodz, 91-726 Poland. Tel 48 42 2547 408; Fax 48 42 2547 418; Email kancelaria@asp.lodz.pl; Web: www.asp.lodz.pl; *Rector* Jolanta Rudzka-Habisiak; *Pro-rector Science* Mariusz Wlodarczyk; *Pro-rector Teaching* Mariusz Lukawski; *Chancellor* Piotr Statucki
Estab 1945; Maintains art galleries: Galeria Kobro, Galeria OdNowa, Galeria Parter, Galeria Wolna Przestrzen, Galeria Biala Sciana, Galeria Nasza Sciana, Galeria Pomiedzy, Galeria 144 Grafiki, Galeria Pod Napieciem, Galeria Strefa Erasmusa
Courses: †Fashion Arts, †Graphics, †Industrial Design, †Interior Design, †Painting, †Textile Design, †Visual Arts

WARSAW

AKADEMIA SZTUK PIEKNYCH, Academy of Fine Arts, ul Krakowskie Przedmiescie 5, Warsaw, 00-068 Poland. Tel 22 826 19 72; Fax 22 320 02 14; Email rektorat@asp.waw.pl; Web: www.asp.waw.pl; *Rector* Maria Widlinska; *Vice Rector Student Affairs* Wojciech Zubala; *Vice Rector Arts & Sciences* Pawel Nowak; *Deputy Rector* Jerzy Boguslawski
Estab 1904; Maintains Academy of Fine Arts Museum & Central Library

WROCLAW

AKADEMIA SZTUK PIEKNYCH, (Panstwowa Wyzsza Szkola Sztuk Plastyczynch) Academy of Fine Arts, Pl Polski 3/4, Wroclaw, 50-156 Poland. Tel 48 71 343 80 31; Email rector@asp.wroc.pl; Web: www.asp.wroc.pl; *Rector* Piotr Kielan

PORTUGAL

LISBON

UNIVERSIDADE DE LISBOA, Faculty of Fine Arts, Largo da Academia Nacional de Belas-Artes 2, Lisbon, 1249-058 Portugal. Tel 351 217 967 624; Fax 351 210 113 402; Email reitoria@ulisboa.pt; Web: www.ulisboa.pt; *Rector* Antonio Manuel da Cruz Serra
Art supplies may be purchased on campus; Pub; D; Scholarships; SC, LC, GC
Degrees: Licenciatura, Mestrado, Douturamento
Courses: Advertising Design, Art Education, Art History, Ceramics, Design, Drawing, Graphic Arts, Graphic Design, Museum Staff Training, Painting, Photography, Sculpture

PORTO

UNIVERSIDADE DO PORTO, Faculty of Fine Arts, Av Rodrigues de Freitas 265, Porto, 4049-021 Portugal. Tel 351 225 192 400; Fax 351 225 367 036; Email expediente@fba.up.pt; Web: www.fba.up.pt; *Dir* Jose Carlos de Paiva e Silva
Maintains museum and library
Courses: †Art Education, †Communication Design, †Drawing, †Fine Arts, †Graphic Design, †Industrial Design, †Mixed Media, †Painting, †Printmaking, †Product Design, †Sculpture

RUSSIA

MOSCOW

MOSCOW STATE ACADEMIC ART INSTITUTE NAMED AFTER V I SURIKOV, The Surikov Art Institute in Moscow, 30 Tovarishcheskii Pereulok, Moscow, 109004 Russia. Tel 495 912 1875; Fax 495 912 5672; Email artinst@mail.ru; *Rector* Anatoly Lubanov
Courses: †Art History, †Graphic Arts, †Painting, †Sculpture

SAINT PETERSBURG

ST PETERSBURG REPIN INSTITUTE OF PAINTING, SCULPTURE & ARCHITECTURE, Universitetskaya Nab 17, Saint Petersburg, 199034 Russia. Tel 812-323 6496; *Rector* Semyon Mikahilovsky

SCOTLAND

DUNDEE

UNIVERSITY OF DUNDEE, Duncan of Jordanstone College of Art & Design, 13 Perth Rd, Dundee, DD1 4HT Scotland. Tel 440-1382-385 828; Fax 440-1382-388 363; Email djcad@dundee.ac.uk; Web: www.dundee.ac.uk; *Deputy Principal, Knowledge Exchange in the Creative Arts* Georgina Follett; *Programme Dir Design & Craft* Prof Mike Press
Maintains nonprofit art gallery; art supplies may be purchased on campus; Pub; D & E; Scholarships; S 14, GC 5; D 1426, Maj 1426, GS 52
Ent Req: 3 Scottish Highers (including Art & English) or 2 A Levels plus portfolio or equivalent
Degrees: BDesign, BA Fine Art, BSc Architecture, BA in Art, Philosophy, Contemporary Studies, BSci Interactive Media Design, Innovative Product Design MArch, MSc Electronic Imaging, MFA, M Design, MPhil, PhD
Courses: †Animation & Electronic Imaging, †Architecture, †Art History, †Design, †Drawing, †Goldsmithing, †Graphic Design, †History of Art & Architecture, †Illustration, Innovative Product Design, †Interactive Media Design, †Interior Design, †Jewelry & Metalwork, †Painting, †Printmaking, †Sculpture, †Textile Design, †Video, †Weaving
Adult Hobby Classes: Embroidery, Pressmaking, Making Soft Furnishings, Printing for Pleasure & Life Drawing
Children's Classes: Creative Textile Design
Summer School: Various subjects available

EDINBURGH

UNIVERSITY OF EDINBURGH, Edinburgh College of Art, Lauriston Pl, Edinburgh, EH3 9DF Scotland. Tel 44 0131-651 5800; Email eca@ed.ac.uk; Web: www.eca.ed.ac.uk; *Prin* Chris Breward; *Head Reid School of Music* Dr Elaine Kelly; *Head School of Design* Juliette MacDonald; *Head School of History of Art* Richard Williams; *Head School of Art* Dean Hughes
Maintains Talbot Rice Gallery
Courses: †Architecture, †Design, †History of Art & Architecture, †Landscape Architecture

GLASGOW

THE GLASGOW SCHOOL OF ART, 167 Renfrew St, Glasgow, UK G3 6RQ Scotland. Tel 0141-353-4500; Fax 0141-353-4408; Email info@gsa.ac.uk; Web: www.gsa.ac.uk; *Dir* Prof Tom Inns, BEng (Hons), DIC, MDes (RCA), PhD, FRSA
Estab 1845; Pub; D & E; Scholarships; SC 10, GC 5
Ent Req: portfolio
Degrees: BA, BDes, MEDes, BEng, MEng, MFA, MA, MLitt, MPhil, PhD
Courses: †Architecture, †Art Education, †Conceptual Art, †Design, †Graphic Arts, †Graphic Design, †Painting, †Photography, †Printmaking, †Textile Design

SLOVAKIA

BRATISLAVA

VYSOKA SKOLA VYTVARNYCH UMENI, Academy of Fine Arts & Design Bratislava, Hviezdoslavovo 18, Bratislava, 814 37 Slovakia. Tel 02 5942 8500; Email rector@vsvu.sk; Web: www.vsvu.sk; *Rector* Stanislav Stankoci
Estab 1949; Maintain non-profit gallery & non-profit library at same address; on-campus shop where art supplies may be purchased; Pub; D; SC, LC, GC
Ent Req: admis exam
Degrees: Bachelor's, Master's & Doctoral
Courses: Architecture, Design, Graphic Arts, Graphic Design, Handicrafts, Painting, Photography, Printmaking, Restoration & Conservation, Sculpture, Textile Design, Video

SOUTH AFRICA

CAPE TOWN

UNIVERSITY OF CAPE TOWN, Michaelis School of Fine Art, 31-37 Orange St, Gardens Cape Town, 8001 South Africa. Tel 021 650 7111; Fax 021 424 2889; Web: www.michaelis.uct.ac.za; *Dir* Berni Searle
Estab 1925; Maintains art gallery
Courses: †Art History, †Curatorship, †Fine Arts

DOORNFONTEIN

UNIVERSITY OF JOHANNESBURG, Faculty of Art, Design & Architecture, Bunting Rd Campus, Auckland Park, PO Box 17011 Doornfontein, 2028 South Africa. Tel 27 011 559-4555; Email myfuture@uj.ac.za; Web: www.uj.ac.za; *Prin & Vice Chanc* Ihron Rensburg
Estab 1930; Maintains nonprofit FADA Gallery; pub; D; 950
Degrees: B Tech, M Tech, D Tech
Courses: Architecture, Art Appreciation, Art History, Ceramics, Design, Drawing, Fashion Arts, Goldsmithing, History of Art & Architecture, †Industrial Design, Interior Design, †Multimedia, Painting, Printmaking, Sculpture, Silversmithing, Teacher Training

SPAIN

SEVILLA

REAL ACADEMIA DE BELLAS ARTES DE SANTA ISABEL DE HUNGRIA DE SEVILLE, The Royal Academy of Fine Arts of Saint Isabel of Hungary of Sevilla, Abades 14, Casa de los Pinos Sevilla, 41004 Spain. Tel 0034 954 221198; Email rabasih@insacan.org; Web: www.insacan.org; *Pres* Roman de la Calle
Estab 1850
Courses: †Archeology, †Architecture, †Audiovisual, †Music, †Painting, †Scenic Art, †Sculpture, †Sumptuary Art

SWEDEN

STOCKHOLM

KUNGLIGA KONSTHOGSKOLAN, Royal Institute of Art, Flaggmansvagen 1, PO Box 163 15 Stockholm, 103 26 Sweden. Tel 46 (08) 614 40 00; Fax 46 (08) 679 86 26; Email info@kkh.se; Web: www.kkh.se; *Vice-Chancellor* Sara Arrhenius; *Pro Rector* Peter Geschwind
Maintains Royal Academy of Fine Arts Library & Architecture Library; Profs 13, lectrs & teachers 25; 230
Courses: †Advertising Design, †Architectural Conservation, Theory & History, †Architecture, †Art History, †Digital Media, †Drawing, †Painting, †Photography, †Sculpture

SWITZERLAND

GENEVA

ECOLES D'ART DE GENEVE, Geneva University of Art & Design, Boulevard James-Fazy 15, Geneva, 1201 Switzerland. Tel 41 22 388 51 00; Fax 41 22 388 51 59; Email info.head@hesge.ch; Web: www.hesge.ch/head; *Dir* Jean-Pierre Greff
Estab 2006; Maintains art library; 115; 659
Degrees: Bachelor's & Master's in Visual Arts or Design

LAUSANNE

ECOLE CANTONALE D'ART DE LAUSANNE, Lausanne College of Art, 5 avenue du Temple, PO Box 555 Lausanne, 1001 Switzerland. Tel 41 021 316-99-33; Fax 41 021 316-92-66; Email ecal@ecal.ch; Web: www.ecal.ch; *Dir* Alexis Georgacopoulos
Degrees: Bachelor's & Master's
Courses: †Film, †Fine Arts, †Graphic Arts, †Industrial Design, †Media & Interaction Design, †Photography

State Arts Councils

NATIONAL ENDOWMENT FOR THE ARTS

Mary Anne Carter, Acting Chairman
400 7th St, SW Washington, DC 20506
Tel 202-682-5414
E-mail: carterm@arts.gov
Website: arts.gov

REGIONAL ORGANIZATIONS

Arts Midwest
David Fraher, Pres & CEO
2908 Hennepin Ave, Ste 200
Minneapolis, MN 55408-1954
Tel 612-341-0755 ext 8024; Fax 612-341-0902
(IA, IL, IN, MI, MN, ND, OH, SD, WI)
E-mail: david@artsmidwest.org
Website: www.artsmidwest.org

Mid-America Arts Alliance
Ed Clifford, Pres & CEO
2018 Baltimore Ave
Kansas City, MO 64108
Tel 816-421-1388; Fax 816-421-3918 TDD: 800-735-2966
(AR, KS, MO, NE, OK, TX) E-mail: artistinc@maaa.org
Website: www.maaa.org; eusa.org

Mid-Atlantic Arts Foundation
Theresa Colvin, Exec Dir
201 North Charles St, Ste 401
Baltimore, MD 21201
Tel 410-539-6656; Fax 410-837-5517 TDD: 410-779-1593
(DC, DE, MD, NJ, NY, PA, VA, VI, WV)
E-mail: info@midatlanticarts.org, theresa@midatlanticarts.org
Website: www.midatlanticarts.org

New England Foundation for the Arts
Cathy Edwards, Exec Dir
145 Tremont St, 7th floor
Boston, MA 02111
Tel 617-951-0010; Fax 617-951-0016
(CT, MA, ME, NH, RI, VT)
E-mail: info@nefa.org
Website: www.nefa.org

South Arts
Suzette M Surkamer, Exec Dir
1800 Peachtree St NW, Ste 808
Atlanta, GA 30309
Tel 404-874-7244; Fax 404-873-2148 TTD: 800-255-0056
(AL, FL, GA, KY, LA, MS, NC, SC, TN)
E-mail: ssurkamer@southarts.org
Website: www.southarts.org

Western States Arts Federation
Anthony Radich, Exec Dir
1743 Wazee St, Ste 300
Denver, CO 80202
Tel 303-629-1166; 888-562-7232; Fax 303-629-9717
(AK, AZ, CA, CO, HI, ID, MT, NV, NM, OR, UT, WA, WY)
E-mail: staff@westaf.org, anthony.radich@westaf.org
Website: www.westaf.org

STATE ART AGENCIES

Alabama State Council on the Arts
Albert B Head, Exec Dir
201 Monroe St
Montgomery, AL 36130-1800
Tel 334-242-4076; Fax 334-240-3269
E-mail: al.head@arts.alabama.gov
Website: arts.alabama.gov

Alaska State Council on the Arts
Benjamin Brown, Chair
Andrea Noble-Pelant, Exec Dir
161 Klevin St, Ste 102
Anchorage, AK 99508-1506
Tel 907-269-6610, 888-278-7424; Fax 907-269-6601 TTD: 800-770-8973
E-mail: aksca.info@alaska.gov, andrea.noble-pelant@alaska.gov
Website: education.alaska.gov/aksca

Arizona Commission on the Arts
Mark Feldman, Chair
Jaime Dempsey, Exec Dir
417 W Roosevelt St
Phoenix, AZ 85003-1326
Tel 602-771-6501; Fax 602-256-0282
E-mail: info@azarts.gov, jdempsey@azarts.gov
Website: azarts.gov

Arkansas Arts Council
Gay Bechtelheimer, Chair
Patrick Ralston, Dir
1100 N St
Little Rock, AR 72201-2606
Tel 501-324-9150, 501-324-9207; Fax 501-324-9207 TDD 501-324-9811
E-mail: info@arkansasarts.com, patrick.ralston@arkansas.gov
Website: www.arkansasarts.org

California Arts Council
Donn K Harris, Chair
Anne Bown-Crawford, Exec Dir
1300 I St, Ste 930
Sacramento, CA 95814
Tel 916-322-6555; 800-201-6201; Fax 916-322-6575
E-mail: anne.bown.crawford@arts.ca.gov
Website: www.cac.ca.gov

Colorado Creative Industries
Tim Schultz, Chair
Margaret Hunt, Exec Dir
1625 Broadway, Ste 2700
Denver, CO 80202
Tel 303-892-3840; Fax 303-892-3848
E-mail: margaret.hunt@state.co.us
Website: www.coloradocreativeindustries.org

Connecticut Office of the Arts
Fitz Jellinghaus, Chair
Culture One Constitution Plaza, 2nd Fl
Hartford, CT 06103
Tel 860-256-2800; Fax 860-256-2811
E-mail: kristina.newmanscott@ct.gov
Website: www.cultureandtourism.org

Delaware Division of the Arts
Joseph Mack Wathen, Chair
Paul Weagraff, Dir
Carvel State Office Bldg 820 N French St, 4th Fl
Wilmington, DE 19801
Tel 302-577-8278; Fax 302-577-6561
E-mail: delarts@state.de.us; paul.weagraff@state.de.us
Website: arts.delaware.gov

DC Commission on the Arts and Humanities
Kay Kendall, Chair
Angie Gates, Interim Exec Dir
200 I St SE, Ste 1400
Washington, DC 20003
Tel 202-724-5613; Fax 202-727-4135 TTY: 202-724-4493
E-mail: cah@dc.gov; angie.gates@dc.gov
Website: dcarts.dc.gov

Florida Division of Cultural Affairs
Glenn Lochrie, Chair
Sandy Shaughnessy, Dir
329 N Meridian St
Tallahassee, FL 32308
Mailing Address: R A Gray Bldg, 500 S Bronough St
Tallahassee, FL 32399-0250
Tel 850-245-6470; Fax 850-245-6454
E-mail: info@florida-arts.org; sandy.shaughnessy@dos.myflorida.com
Website: dos.myflorida.com/cultural

Georgia Council for the Arts
J Barry Schrenk, Chair
Karen L Paty, Exec Dir
75 5th St NW, Ste 1200
Atlanta, GA 30308
Tel 404-962-4015
E-mail: gaarts@gaarts.org; kpaty@gaarts.org
Website: gaarts.org

Hawai'i State Foundation on Culture and the Arts
Patricia Hamamoto, Chair
Jonathan Johnson, Exec Dir
250 S Hotel St, 2nd Fl
Honolulu, HI 96813
Tel 808-586-0300; Fax 808-586-0308
E-mail: jonathan.johnson@hawaii.gov
Website: sfca.hawaii.gov

Idaho Commission on the Arts
Kay Hardy, Chair
Michael Faison, Exec Dir
2410 N Old Penitentiary Rd
Boise, ID 83712
Mailing Address: PO Box 83720
Boise, ID 83720-0008
Tel 208-334-2119; 800-278-3863; Fax 208-334-2488
E-mail: info@arts.idaho.gov; michael.faison@arts.idaho.gov
Website: www.arts.idaho.gov

Illinois Arts Council Agency
Shirley R Madigan, Chair
Joshua Davis, Exec Dir
James R Thompson Center 100 W Randolph, Ste 10-500
Chicago, IL 60601
Tel 312-814-6750; 800-237-6994; Fax 312-814-1471
E-mail: iac.info@illinois.gov; joshua.davis@illinois.gov
Website: www.arts.illinois.gov

Indiana Arts Commission
Kathy Ziliak Anderson, Chair
Lewis Ricci, Exec Dir
100 N Senate Ave, Rm N505
Indianapolis, IN 46204
Tel 317-232-1268; Fax 317-232-5595
E-mail: indianaartscommission@iac.in.gov; lricci@iac.in.gov
Website: www.in.gov/arts

Iowa Arts Council
Paul Dennison, Chair
Matthew Harris, Div Admin
Chris Kramer, Acting Dir
600 E Locust
Des Moines, IA 50319-0290
Tel 515-281-5111; Fax 515-242-6498
E-mail: matthew.harris@iowa.gov; chris.kramer@iowa.gov
Website: iowaculture.gov

Kansas Creative Arts Industries Commission
Larry Meeker, Chair
Peter Jasso, Dir
1000 SW Jackson St, Ste 100
Topeka, KS 66612-1354
Tel 785-296-2178
E-mail: pjasso@kansascommerce.com
Website: www.kansascommerce.com/index.aspx?nid=541

Kentucky Arts Council
Mary Michael Corbett, Chair
Chris Cathers, Interim Exec Dir
1025 Capital Center Dr, 3rd Fl
Frankfort, KY 40601
Tel 502-564-3757; 888-833-2787; Fax 502-564-2839
E-mail: kyarts@ky.gov; christopher.cathers@ky.gov
Website: artscouncil.ky.gov

Louisiana Division of the Arts
Mary D Lee, Chair
Cheryl Castille, Exec Dir
Louisiana Division of the Arts 1051 N 3rd St, Rm 405
Baton Rouge, LA 70802
Mailing Address: PO Box 44247
Baton Rouge, LA 70804-4247
Tel 225-342-8180; Fax 225-342-8173
E-mail: arts@crt.la.gov; ccastille@crt.la.gov
Website: www.crt.state.la.us/cultural-development/arts/index

Maine Arts Commission
Charles V Stanhope, Chair
Julie A Richard, Exec Dir
193 State St, 25 State House Station
Augusta, ME 04333-0025
Tel 207-287-2724; Fax 207-287-2725 TTY 877-887-3878
E-mail: mainearts.info@maine.gov; julie.richard@maine.gov
Website: mainearts.maine.gov

Maryland State Arts Council
Catherine Leggett, Chair
Ken Skrzesz, Exec Dir
175 W Ostend St, Ste E
Baltimore, MD 21230
Tel 410-767-6555; Fax 410-333-1062
E-mail: msac.commerce@maryland.gov
Website: www.msac.org

Massachusetts Cultural Council
Nina Fialkow, Chair
Anita Walker, Exec Dir
10 St James Ave, 3rd Fl
Boston, MA 02116-3803
Tel 617-858-2700; 800-232-0960 (MA Only); Fax: 617-574-7305
E-mail: mcc@art.state.ma.us; anita.walker@art.state.ma.us
Website: www.massculturalcouncil.org

Michigan Council for Arts and Cultural Affairs
Omari Rush, Chair
John Bracey, Exec Dir
Michigan Economic Development Corporation 300 N Washington Sq
Lansing, MI 48913
Tel 517-241-4011; 888-522-0103; Fax 517-241-3979
E-mail: braceyj@michigan.org
Website: www.michiganbusiness.org/arts

Minnesota State Arts Board
Sean Dowse, Chair
Sue Gens, Exec Dir
Park Square Ct 400 Sibley St, Ste 200
Saint Paul, MN 55101-1928
Tel 651-215-1600; 800-866-2787; Fax 651-215-1602
E-mail: msab@arts.state.mn.us; sue.gens@arts.state.mn.us
Website: www.arts.state.mn.us

Mississippi Arts Commission
Steve Edds, Chair
Malcolm White, Exec Dir
501 N West St, Ste 1101A, Woolfork Bldg
Jackson, MS 39201
Tel 601-359-6030; Fax 601-359-6008
E-mail: mwhite@arts.ms.gov
Website: www.arts.state.ms.us

Missouri Arts Council
Sharon Beshore, Chair
Michael Donovan, Exec Dir
815 Olive St, Ste 16
Saint Louis, MO 63101-1503
Tel 314-340-6845; 866-407-4752; Fax 314-340-7215 TTD: 800-735-2966
E-mail: moarts@ded.mo.gov; michael.donovan@ded.mo.gov
Website: www.missouriartscouncil.org

Montana Arts Council
Cynthia Andrus, Chair
Tatiana Gant, Exec Dir 830 N Warren St, 1st Fl
Helena, MT 59620
Mailing Address: PO Box 202201
Helena, MT 59620
Tel 406-444-6430; Fax 406-444-6548
E-mail: mac@mt.gov; tatiana.gant@mt.gov
Website: art.mt.gov

Nebraska Arts Council
Candy Henning, Chair
Suzanne Wise, Exec Dir
1004 Farnam St, Plaza Level
Omaha, NE 68102
E-mail: nac.info@nebraska.gov; suzanne.wise@nebraska.gov
Tel 402-595-2122; 800-341-4067
Website: www.artscouncil.nebraska.gov

Nevada Arts Council
Julia Arger, Chair
Tony Manfredi, Exec Dir
716 N Carson St, Ste A
Carson City, NV 89701
Tel 775-687-6680; Fax 775-687-6688
E-mail: infonvartscouncil@nevadaculture.org; tmanfredi@nevadaculture.org
Website: nevadaculture.org/nac

New Hampshire State Council on the Arts
Dr Roger C Brooks, Chair
Ginnie Lupi, Dir
19 Pillsbury St, 1st Fl
Concord, NH 03301-3570
Tel 603-271-2789; Fax 603-271-3584 TTY/TTD: 800-735-2964
E-mail: virginia.lupi@dncr.nh.gov
Website: www.nh.gov/nharts/

New Jersey State Council on the Arts
Elizabeth A Mattson, Chair
Nicholas Paleologos, Exec Dir
225 W State St
Trenton, NJ 08608
Mailing Address: PO Box 306
Trenton, NJ 08625-0306
Tel 609-292-6130; Fax 609-989-1440
E-mail: nicholas.paleologos@sos.state.nj.us
Website: nj.gov/state/njsca/index.html

New Mexico Arts
Sherry Davis, Chair
Loie Fecteau, Exec Dir
Bataan Memorial Bldg 407 Galisteo St, Ste 270
Santa Fe, NM 87501
Tel 505-827-6490; 800-879-4278; Fax 505-827-6043
E-mail: loie.fecteau@state.nm.us
Website: www.nmarts.org

New York State Council on the Arts
Dr Barbaralee Diamondstein-Spielvogel, Chair
Megan White, Dep Dir, Programs
Mara Manus, Exec Dir, Agency Opers
300 Park Ave S, 10th Fl
New York, NY 10010
Tel 212-459-8800; 800-510-0021
E-mail: info@arts.ny.gov; mara.manus@arts.ny.gov
Website: www.nysca.org

North Carolina Arts Council
Stephen Hill, Chair
Wayne Martin, Exec Dir
109 E Jones St
Raleigh, NC 27601
Mailing Address: MSC #4632, Dept of Cultural Resources
Raleigh, NC 27699-4632
Tel 919-807-6500; Fax 919-807-6532
E-mail: ncarts@ncdcr.gov; wayne.martin@ncdcr.gov
Website: www.ncarts.org

North Dakota Council on the Arts
David "White Thunder" Trottier, Chair
Kim Konikow, xec Dir
1600 E Century Ave, Ste 6
Bismarck, ND 58503
Tel 701-328-7590; Fax 701-328-7595
E-mail: comserv@nd.gov; kkonikow@nd.gov
Website: www.nd.gov/arts/

Ohio Arts Council
Geraldine Warner, Chair
Donna S Collins, Exec Dir
Rhodes State Office Tower 30 E Broad St, 33rd Fl
Columbus, OH 43215-3414
Tel 614-466-2613; 888-243-8622; Fax 614-466-4494 TTY/TDD: 800-750-0750
E-mail: webmaster@oac.state.oh.us; donna.collins@oac.state.oh.us
Website: www.oac.ohio.gov

Oklahoma Arts Council
Ann Neal, Chair
Amber Sharples, Exec Dir
Jim Thorpe Bldg 2101 N Lincoln Blvd, Ste 640

Oklahoma City, OK 73105
Mailing Address: PO Box 52001-2001
Oklahoma City, OK 73152-2001
Tel 405-521-2931; Fax 405-521-6418
E-mail: okarts@art.ok.gov; amber.sharples@arts.ok.gov
Website: www.arts.ok.gov

Oregon Arts Commission
Christopher Acebo, Chair
Brian Rogers, Exec Dir
775 Summer St NE, Ste 200
Salem, OR 97301-1280
Tel 503-986-0082; Fax 503-986-0260
E-mail: oregon.artscomm@state.or.us; brian.rogers@oregon.gov
Website: www.oregonartscommission.org

Pennsylvania Council on the Arts
Jeff Parks, Chair
Karl Blischke, Exec Dir
216 Finance Bldg Commonwealth & North Sts
Harrisburg, PA 17120
Tel 717-787-6883; Fax 717-783-2538
E-mail: ra-arts@pa.gov; kablischke@pa.gov
Website: www.arts.pa.gov

Rhode Island State Council on the Arts
Libby Slader, Chair
Randall Rosenbaum, Exec Dir
One Capitol Hill, 3rd Fl
Providence, RI 02908
Tel 401-222-3880; Fax 401-222-3018
E-mail: donna.fiske@arts.ri.gov; randall.rosenbaum@arts.ri.gov
Website: www.arts.ri.gov

South Carolina Arts Commission
Henry Horowitz, Chair
Ken May, Exec Dir
1026 Sumter St, Ste 200
Columbia, SC 29201-3746
Tel 803-734-8696; Fax 803-734-8526
E-mail: info@arts.sc.gov; kmay@arts.sc.gov
Website: www.southcarolinaarts.com

South Dakota Arts Council
Lynne Byrne, Chair
Patrick Baker, Dir
711 E Wells Ave
Pierre, SD 57501-3369
Tel 605-773-3301; 800-952-3625; Fax 605-773-5977
E-mail: sdac@state.sd.us; patrick.baker@state.sd.us
Website: www.artscouncil.sd.gov

Tennessee Arts Commission
Ritche Bowden, Chair
Anne B Pope, Exec Dir
401 Charlotte Ave
Nashville, TN 37243
Tel 615-741-1701; Fax 615-741-8559
E-mail: anne.b.pope@tn.gov
Website: tnartscommission.org

Texas Commission on the Arts
Dale W Brock, Chair
Gary Gibbs, PhD, Exec Dir
E O Thompson Office Bldg 920 Colorado, Ste 501
Austin, TX 78701
Mailing Address: PO Box 13406
Austin, TX 78711-3406
Tel 512-463-5535; 800-252-9415; Fax 512-475-2699 TTY: 512-475-3327
E-mail: front.desk@arts.texas.gov; ggibbs@arts.texas.gov
Website: www.arts.state.gov

Utah Division of Arts and Museums
Ken Verdoia, Chair
Victoria Panella Bourns, Dir
617 E South Temple
Salt Lake City, UT 84102
Tel 801-236-7555; Fax 801-236-7556
E-mail: vbourns@utah.gov
Website: heritage.utah.gov/utah-division-of-arts-museums

Vermont Arts Council
Bob Stannard, Chair
Karen Mittelman, Exec Dir
136 State St,
Montpelier, VT 05633-6001
Tel 802-828-3291; Fax 802-828-3363
E-mail: info@vermontartscouncil.org; kmittelman@vermontartscouncil.org
Website: www.vermontartscouncil.org

Virginia Commission for the Arts
Shelley Kruger Weisberg, Chair
Janet Starke, Exec Dir
1001 E Broad St, Ste 330
Richmond, VA 23219
Tel 804-225-3132; Fax 804-225-4327
E-mail: arts@arts.virginia.gov; janet.starke@vca.virginia.gov
Website: www.arts.virginia.gov

Washington State Arts Commission (ArtsWA)
Sue Coliton, Chair
Karen Hanan, Exec Dir
711 Capitol Way S, Ste 600
Olympia, WA 98501
Mailing Address: PO Box 42675
Olympia, WA 98504-2675
Tel 360-753-3860; Fax 360-586-5351
E-mail: info@arts.wa.gov; karen.hanan@arts.wa.gov
Website: www.arts.wa.gov

West Virginia Commission on the Arts
Harold M Forbes, Chair
Lance Schrader, Dir
The Culture Center Capitol Complex 1900 Kanawha Blvd E
Charleston, WV 25305-0300
Tel 304-558-0240; Fax 304-558-3560
E-mail: lance.e.schrader@wv.gov
Website: www.wvculture.org/arts

Wisconsin Arts Board
Kevin Miller, Chair
George Tzougros, Exec Dir
Tommy G. Thompson Commerce Bldg
201 W Washington Ave
Madison, WI 53703
Mailing Address: PO Box 8690
Madison, WI 53708-8690
Tel 608-266-0190; Fax 608-267-0380
E-mail: artsboard@wisconsin.gov; gtzougros@travelwisconsin.com
Website: artsboard.wisconsin.gov

Wyoming Arts Council
Holly Turner, Chair
Michael Lange, Exec Dir
Barrett Bldg 2301 Central Ave, 2nd Fl
Cheyenne, WY 82002
Tel 307-777-7742; Fax 307-777-5499
E-mail: michael.lange@wyo.gov
Website: wyoarts.state.wy.us

TERRITORIAL ART AGENCIES

American Samoa Council on Culture, Arts and Humanities
Paogofie Fiaigoa, Exec Chair
PO Box 1540
Pago Pago, AS 96799
Tel 684-633-4347; Fax 684-633-2059
E-mail: info@as.gov
Website: www.americansamoa.gov/arts-council

Guam Council on the Arts and Humanities Agency
Francis Guerrero, Interim Chair
Joyce Bamba, Deputy Dir
Terlaje Professional Bldg 194 Hernan Cortez Ave, 1st Fl
Hagatna, GU 96910
Mailing Address: PO Box 2950
Hagatna, GU 96932
Tel 671-300-1204; Fax 671-300-1209
E-mail: info@caha.guam.gov; joyce.bamba@caha.guam.gov
Website: www.guamcaha.org

Commonwealth Council for Arts and Culture (Northern Mariana Islands)
Joseph M Diaz, Chair
Angel Hocog, Exec Dir
Dept of Community & Cultural Affairs
PO Box 5553, CHRB
Saipan, MP 96950
Tel 670-322-9982; Fax 670-322-9028
E-mail: angelshocog@gmail.com

Institute of Puerto Rican Culture
Jose Luis Ramos Escobar, Chair
Jorge Irizarry Vizcarrondo, Exec Dir
Antiguo Asilo de Beneficencia, Barrio Ballaja Viejo
San Juan, PR
Mailing Address: PO Box 902-4184
San Juan, PR 00902-4184
Tel 787-724-0700; Fax 787-724-8393
E-mail: merodriguez@icp.gobierno.pr

Virgin Islands Council on the Arts
Jose Raul Carrillo, Chair
Tasida H Kelch, Exec Dir
5070 Norre Gade, Ste 1
Saint Thomas, VI 00802-6762
Tel 340-774-5984; Fax 340-774-6206
E-mail: tasidakelch@yahoo.com
Website: www.vicouncilonarts.org

State Directors and Representatives of Art Education

ALABAMA

Andy Meadows, Arts Education Specialist
Alabama State Department of Education Instructional Services Section
50 N Ripley St, PO Box 302101
Montgomery, AL 36104
Tel 334-353-1191
E-mail: ameadows@alsde.edu

ALASKA

Laura Forbes, Arts in Education
Alaska State Council on the Arts
161 Klevin St, Ste 102
Anchorage, AK 99508-1506
Tel 907-269-6682
E-mail: laura.forbes@alaska.gov

ARIZONA

Dustin Loehr, Dir Arts in Education & Title IV-A
Arizona Department of Education
1535 W Jefferson
Phoenix, AZ 85007
Tel 602-364-3015
E-mail: dustin.loehr@azed.gov

ARKANSAS

Lana Hallmark, Fine Arts Specialist
Arkansas Department of Education Division of Learning Services
4 Capitol Mall, Rm 301-B
Little Rock, AR 72201
Tel 501-682-7590
E-mail: lana.hallmark@arkansas.gov

CALIFORNIA

Jack Mitchell, CTE Consultant for Art, Media & Entertainment
California Department of Education 1430 N St, Ste 4202
Sacramento, CA 95814
Tel 916-319-0504
E-mail: jmitchell@cde.ca.gov

COLORADO

Karol Gates, Director
Colorado Department of Education Standards and Instructional Support Office
1580 Logan St, Ste 300
Denver, CO 80203
Tel 303-866-6576
E-mail: gates_k@cde.state.co.us

CONNECTICUT

Arts & Standards, Connecticut State Department of Education Office of Academics
165 Capitol Ave
Hartford, CT 06145
Tel 860-713-6592

DELAWARE

Debora Hansen, Education Associate for Visual & Performing Arts, Gifted & Talented Program
Delaware Department of Education 401 Federal St
Dover, DE 19901
Tel 302-735-4190
E-mail: deb.hansen@doe.k12.de.us

DISTRICT OF COLUMBIA

Heather Holaday, Deputy Chief Arts, Global Education, Health, Physical Education
District of Columbia Public Schools Office of Teaching & Learning
1200 First St NE
Washington, DC 20002
Tel 202-442-9439
E-mail: heather.holaday@dc.gov

FLORIDA

Jennifer Infinger, Fine Arts Education Specialist
Florida Department of Education Bureau of Standards and Instructional Support
325 W Gaines St
Tallahassee, FL 32399-0400
Tel 850-245-0762
E-mail: jennifer.infinger@fldoe.org

GEORGIA

Jessica Booth, Fine Arts Program
Georgia Department of Education 1754 Twin Towers E 205 Jesse Hill Jr Dr SE
Atlanta, GA 30334
Tel 404-656-2800
E-mail: jbooth@doe.k12.ga.us

HAWAII

Una Chan, Fine Arts & World Languages Education Specialist
Hawaii State Department of Education 1390 Miller St
Honolulu, HI 96816
Tel 808-305-9709
E-mail: una_chan@hawaiidoe.org

IDAHO

Dr Peggy Wenner, Arts & Humanities Coordinator
Idaho State Department of Education 650 W State St, PO Box 83720
Boise, ID 83720-0027
Tel 208-332-6949
E-mail: pjwenner@sde.idaho.gov

ILLINOIS

Susan Dickson, Program Director
Illinois Arts Council Agency 100 W Randolph, Ste 10-500
Chicago, IL 60601
Tel 312-814-6750
Email: susan.dickson@illinois.gov

INDIANA

Stephanie Haines, Arts Education and Accessibility Manager
Indiana Arts Commission 100 N Senate Ave, Rm N505
Indianapolis, IN 46204
Tel 317-232-1274; Fax 317-232-5595
E-mail: shaines@iac.in.gov

IOWA

Angela Matsuoka, Arts Consultant
Iowa Department of Education Grimes State Office Bldg 400 E 14th St
Des Moines, IA 50319
Tel 515-281-3933
E-mail: angela.matsuoka@iowa.gov

KANSAS

Joyce Huser, Fine Arts Education Program Consultant
State Department of Education 120 SE 10th Ave
Topeka, KS 66612
Tel 785-296-4932
E-mail: jhuser@ksde.org

KENTUCKY

Robert Duncan, Arts & Humanities Consultant
Kentucky Department of Education Capital Plaza Tower 500 Mero St, 18th Fl
Frankfort, KY 40601
Tel 502-564-2106; Fax 502-564-9848
E-mail: robert.duncan@education.ky.gov

LOUISIANA

Danny Belanger, Director of Arts Education & Accessibility
Louisiana Division of the Arts 1051 N 3rd St, Rm 4005
Baton Rouge, LA 70802
Tel 225-342-8209
E-mail: dbelanger@crt.la.gov

MAINE

Nathaniel Menifield, Visual & Performing Arts Specialist
Maine Department of Education 23 State House Station
Augusta, ME 04333
Tel 207-624-6824
E-mail: nathaniel.j.menifield@maine.gov

MARYLAND

Alysia Lee, Coordinator of Fine Arts
Maryland State Department of Education 200 W Baltimore St
Baltimore, MD 21201
Tel 410-767-0352
E-mail: alysia.lee@maryland.gov

MASSACHUSETTS

Dr. Lurline Munoz-Bennett, Arts Education & Equity Coordinator
Massachusetts Department of Elementary & Secondary Education 75 Pleasant St
Malden, MA 02148-4906
Tel 781-338-6285
E-mail: lmunoz-bennett@doe.mass.edu

MICHIGAN

Dr. Kathy Dewsbury-White, Project Director
Michigan Arts Education Instruction & Assessment (MAEIA)
1001 Centennial Way, Suite 300 Lansing, MI 48917
Tel 517-816-4520
E-mail: Kdwhite@michiganassessmentconsortium.org

MINNESOTA

Dr Pam Paulson, Director of Professional Development & Resources
Perpich Center for Arts Education 6125 Olson Memorial Hwy
Golden Valley, MN 55422
Tel 763-591-4708
E-mail: pam.paulson@pcae.k12.mn.us

MISSISSIPPI

Limeul Eubanks, Division Director II
Mississippi Department of Education 359 N West St, Ste 313, PO Box 771
Jackson, MS 39205-0771
Tel 601-359-2586; Fax 601-359-2040 E-mail: leubanks@mde.k12.ms.us

MISSOURI

Tom Tobias, Arts Education Director
Missouri Department of Education Office of College and Career Readiness
205 Jefferson St
Jefferson City, MO 65101
Tel 573-751-9610; Fax 573-526-0812
E-mail: tom.tobias@dese.mo.gov

MONTANA

Monica Grable, Director of Arts Education
Montana Arts Council 830 N Warren St, 1st Fl
Helena, MT 59601
Tel 406-444-6522; Fax 406-444-6548

NEBRASKA

Debbie DeFrain, State Director of Fine Arts Education
Nebraska Department of Education 301 Centennial Mall S, PO Box 94987
Lincoln, NE 68509-4987
Tel 402-471-3142; Fax 402-471-0117
E-mail: debbie.defrain@nebraska.gov

NEVADA

Brenda Bledsoe, Education Programs Professional
Nevada Department of Education Office of Standards and Instructional Support
9890 S Maryland Parkway, 2nd Fl
Las Vegas, NV 89183
Tel 775-687-9183
E-mail: brendabledsoe@doe.nv.gov

NEW HAMPSHIRE

Marcia McCaffrey, Arts Consultant
New Hampshire Department of Education
101 Pleasant St
Concord, NH 03301-3860
Tel 603-271-3193
E-mail: marcia.mccaffrey@doe.nh.gov

NEW JERSEY

Dale Schmid, Visual & Performing Arts Coordinator
New Jersey Department of Education 100 River View Plaza, PO Box 500
Trenton, NJ 08625-0500
Tel 609-984-6308
E-mail: dale.schmid@doe.state.nj.us

NEW MEXICO

Vicki Breen, Arts Education Administrator
New Mexico Public Education Department
Jerry Apodaca Education Bldg 300 Don Gaspar Ave
Santa Fe, NM 87501
Tel 505-827-4278
E-mail: vicki.breen@state.nm.us

NEW YORK

Leslie Yolen, Associate in Arts Education
New York State Education Department 89 Washington Ave
Albany, NY 12234
Tel 518-474-5922; 518-473-4884
E-mail: lyolen@nysed.gov

NORTH CAROLINA

Slater Mapp, Theater Arts & Visual Arts Education Consultant
North Carolina Department of Public Instruction 301 N Wilmington St
Raleigh, NC 27601
Tel 919-807-3758; Fax 919-807-3823
E-mail: slater.mapp@dpi.nc.gov

NORTH DAKOTA

Anne Ellefeson, Director, Office of Academic Support
North Dakota Department of Public Instruction 600 E Boulevard Ave, #201
Bismarck, ND 58505
Tel 701-328-2488
E-mail: aellefson@nd.gov

OHIO

Nancy Pistone, Fine Arts Consultant
Ohio Department of Education 25 S Front St
Columbus, OH 43215-4183
Tel 614-466-7908
E-mail: nancy.pistone@education.ohio.gov

OKLAHOMA

Elizabeth Maughan, Ph.D. Director of Fine Arts
Oklahoma State Department of Education 2500 N Lincoln Blvd, Ste 315
Oklahoma City, OK 73105-4599
Tel 405-522-3219
E-mail: elizabeth.maughan@sde.ok.gov

OREGON

Christie Dudley, Director of Standards and Instructional Supports Oregon Department of Education
Office of Teaching Learning & Assessment 255 Capitol St NE
Salem, OR 97310-0203 Tel 503-947-5713

PENNSYLVANIA

O David Deitz, Arts Consultant
Pennsylvania Department of Education
333 Market St
Harrisburg, PA 17126
Tel 717-512-1472
Email: c-odeitz@pa.gov

RHODE ISLAND

Maggie Anderson, Director, Arts in Education
Rhode Island State Council on the Arts 1 Capitol Hill, 3rd Fl
Providence, RI 02908
Tel 401-222-6994; Fax 401-222-3018
E-mail: maggie.anderson@arts.ri.gov

SOUTH CAROLINA

Carrie Ann Power, Visual & Performing Arts Education Associate
South Carolina Department of Education 1429 Senate St, Rm 607-B
Columbia, SC 29201
Tel 803-734-0323
E-mail: cpower@ed.sc.gov

SOUTH DAKOTA

Becky Nelson, Director Division of Learning & Instruction
South Dakota Department of Education 800 Governors Dr
Pierre, SD 57501-2291
Tel 605-773-5529; Fax 605-773-4236
E-mail: becky.nelson@state.sd.us

TENNESSEE

Ann Brown, Director of Arts Education
Tennessee Arts Commission 401 Charlotte Ave
Nashville, TN 37243-0780
Tel 615-532-5939; Fax 615-741-8559
E-mail: ann.brown@tn.gov

TEXAS

Mackie V Spradley, Director of Enrichment Education & Programs
Texas Education Agency 1701 N Congress Ave
Austin, TX 78701-1494
Tel 512-463-9581
E-mail: mackie.spradley@tea.texas.gov

UTAH

Cathy Jensen, Fine Arts Curriculum Specialist
Utah State Office of Education 250 East 500 South, PO Box 144200
Salt Lake City, UT 84114-4200
Tel 801-538-7793
E-mail: cathy.jensen@schools.utah.gov

VERMONT

Emily Titterton, Arts Content Specialist
Vermont Agency of Education 219 N Main St, Ste 402
Barre, VT 05641
Tel 802-479-1378
E-mail: emily.titterton@vermont.gov

VIRGINIA

Cheryle Cuddy Gardner, Principal Specialist of Fine Arts
Virginia Department of Education James Monroe Bldg 101 N 14th St
Richmond, VA 23219
Tel 804-225-2881
E-mail: cherry.gardner@doe.virginia.gov

WASHINGTON

Anne Banks, Arts Program Supervisor
Office of Superintendent of Public Instruction Old Capitol Bldg
600 Washington St, SE, PO Box 47200
Olympia, WA 98504-7200
Tel 360-725-4966
Email: anne.banks@k12.wa.us

WEST VIRGINIA

Dr. Raymond WS Lowther, Arts Coordinator
West Virginia Department of Education Office of Middle/Secondary
Learning Capitol Complex, Bldg 6, Rm 722
1900 Kanawha Blvd E
Charleston, WV 25305
Tel 304-558-5325; Fax 304-558-1834
E-mail: ray.lowther@k12.wv.us

WISCONSIN

Dr Julie A Palkowski, Fine Arts & Creativity Education Consultant
Wisconsin Department of Public Instruction 125 S Webster St, PO Box 7841
Madison, WI 53707-7841
Tel 608-261-7494
E-mail: julie.palkowski@dpi.wi.gov

WYOMING

Tera Hernandez, Language Arts, Fine & Performing Arts Consultant
Wyoming Department of Education 2300 Capitol Ave, Hathaway Bldg, 2nd Fl
Cheyenne, WY 82002-0050
Tel 307-777-8595
E-mail: terra.hernandez@wyo.gov

Art Magazines

A for Annuals; Bi-M for Bimonthlies; Bi-W for Biweeklies;

M for Monthlies; Q for Quarterlies; Semi-A for Semiannually; W for Weeklies

African Arts (Q)—Leslie Ellen Jones, Exec Ed & Art Dir.
African Studies Center, University of California, 10244 Bunche Hall, 405 Hilgard Ave, Los Angeles, CA 90095. Tel 310-825-3686; Fax 310-206-2250; E-mail afriartsedit@international.ucla.edu; Website www.mitpressjournals.org/aa. Yearly $100.00

Afterimage (Bi-M)—Karen vanMeenen, Ed.
Visual Studies Workshop Inc, 31 Prince St, Rochester, NY 14607. Tel 585-442-8676 ext 26; E-mail afterimageeditor@yahoo.com; Website vsw.org/afterimage. Yearly $33.00

American Art—Robin Veder, Exec Ed.
Smithsonian American Art Museum, 750 9th St NW, Ste 3100, Washington, DC 20001- 4505. Tel 202-633-7970; E-mail AmericanArtJournal@si.edu; Website http://www.journals.uchicago.edu/toc/amart/current. Yearly $40.00 individuals; $35.00 students

American Craft (Bi-M)—Monica Moses, Ed in Chf.
American Craft Council, 1224 Marshall St, NE, Ste 200, Minneapolis, MN 55413. Tel 612-206-3100; E-mail council@craftcouncil.org; Website craftcouncil.org/magazine. Yearly $40.00 US; $55.00 Canada & international

American Journal of Archaeology (Q)—Jane B. Carter, Ed in Chf.
44 Beacon St, 2nd Fl, Boston, MA 02215-2006; Tel 617-353-9361; Fax 617-353-6550; E-mail: aja@aia.bu.edu; Website ww.ajaonline.org. Yearly $80.00 individuals; $50.00 students; $295.00 institutions

American Watercolor Society Newsletter (2 Issues)—Susannah Hart Thomer, Ed.
American Watercolor Society, 47 Fifth Ave, New York, NY 10003. Tel 212-206-8986; Fax 212-206-1960; E-mail info@americanwatercolorsociety.org; Website www.americanwatercolorsociety.org. Assoc. Membership yearly $50.00

Aperture (Q)—Michael Famighetti, Ed.
Aperture Foundation, 547 W 27th St, 4th Fl, New York, NY 10001. Tel 212-505-5555; Fax 212-979-7759; E-mail customerservice@aperture.org; Website www.aperture.org. Yearly $75.00 US; $95.00 Canada; $105.00 international

Archaeology (Bi-M)—Jarrett A. Lobell, Ed in Chf.
Archaeological Institute of America, 36-36 33rd St, Long Island City, NY 11106. Tel 1-718-472-3050; Fax 718-472-3051; E-mail editorial@archaeology.org; Website www.archaeology.org. Yearly $14.97

Architectural Digest (M)—Amy Astley, Ed in Chf.
Architectural Digest, 4 Times Sq, 18th Fl, New York, NY 10036. Tel 800-365-8032; E-mail contact@archdigest.com; Website www.architecturaldigest.com. Yearly $24.99 US; $70.00 Canada; $70.00 international

Archives of American Art Journal (Semi-A)—Emily Shapiro, Ed.
Victor Bldg Ste 2200, PO Box 37012, MRC 937, Washington DC 20013-7012. Tel 202-633-7940; Fax 212-633-7994; Website www.aaa.si.edu/publications/journal. Yearly $40 individual

Art & Antiques (10 Issues)—John Dorfman, NY Sr Ed.
1319-cc Military Cutoff Rd #192, Wilmington, NC 28405. Tel 910-679-4402; Fax 919-869-1864; E-mail info@artandantiquesmag.com; Website www.artandantiquesmag.com. Yearly $29.50

A&U—David Waggoner, Ed in Chf & Publr.
25 Monroe St, Ste 205, Albany, NY 12210. Tel 518-426-9010; Fax 518-436-5354; E-mail mailbox@aumag.org; Website www.aumag.org. Yearly $24.95 individual; Free digital.

Art Bulletin (Q)—Nina Athanassoglou-Kallmyer, Ed in Chf.
College Art Association, 50 Broadway, 21st Fl, New York, NY 10004. Tel 212-691-1051; Fax 212-627-2381; E-mail nyoffice@collegeart.org; Website www.collegeart.org.

Art Business News—(Q) Linda Mariano, Mng Ed.
PO Box 91447, Long Beach, CA 90809. Tel 888-881-5861; E-mail letters@artbusinessnews.com.; Website artbusinessnews.com. Yearly $20.00

Art Documentation (Semi-A)—Judy Dyki, Ed.
ARLIS/ NA Publications, 7044 S 13th St, Oak Creek, WI 53154. Tel 800- 817-0621 ext 450; E-mail customercare@arlisna.org; Website www.arlisna.org. Free to members

Artforum International Magazine (10 Issues)—David Velasco, Ed in Chf.
Artforum International Magazine, 350 7th Ave, New York, NY 10001. Tel 212-475-4000; Fax 212-529-1257; E-mail generalinfo@artforum.com; Website www.artforum.com. Yearly $50.00 US; $70.00 Canada; $120.00 international

Art in America (M)—William S. Smith, Ed
110 Greene St, 5th 2nd Fl, New York, NY 10012. Tel 212-398-1690; E-mail aiaeditor@artinamericamag.com; Website www.artinamericamagazine.com. Yearly $45.00 US; $85.00 Canada; $100.00 international

Artist's Magazine (10 Issues)—Maureen Bloomfield, Ed in Chf.
F + W Media, 10151 Carver Rd, Ste 200, Blue Ash, OH 45242. Tel 513- 531-2222; Fax 513-891-7153; E-mail tamedit@fwmedia.com; Website www.artistsnetwork.com/the-artists-magazine. Yearly $23.99 US; $33.99 Canada; $39.99 international

Art Journal (Q)—Rebecca M Brown, Ed in Chf.
College Art Association, 50 Broadway, 21st Fl, New York, NY 10004. Tel 212- 691-1051; Fax 212-627-2381; E-mail nyoffice@collegeart.org Website www.collegeart.org. Free for members

Art New England (6 Issues)—Sarah Baker, Ed in Chf.
560 Harrison Ave, Ste 412, Boston, MA 02118. Tel 617-259-1040; Fax 617-259-1039; E-mail: editorial@artnewengland.com; Website artnewengland.com. Yearly $28.00

Artnews (11 Issues)—Sarah Douglas, Ed in Chf.
110 Greene St, New York, NY 10012. Tel 212-398-1690; Fax 212-819-0394; E-mail info@artmediaholdings.com; Website www.artnews.com. Yearly $19.95

Art of the West (7 Issues)—Vicki Stavig, Ed.
15612 Hwy 7, Ste 235, Minnetonka, MN 55345. Tel 952-935-5850; Fax 952-935-6546; E-mail: aotw@aotw.com; Website www.aotw.com. Yearly $25.00; $43.00 international

Art Papers (Bi-M)—Sarah Higgins, Ed & Art Dir.
1083 Austin Ave, NE, Ste 206, Atlanta, GA 30307. Tel 404-588-1837; Fax 404-588-1836; E-mail info@artpapers.org; Website ww.artpapers.org. Yearly $35.00 US; $45.00 Canada & Mexico; $70.00 international

Arts—Kaywin Feldman, Pres & Dir.
Minneapolis Institute of Arts, 2400 Third Ave S, Minneapolis, MN 55404. Tel 612-870- 6314; Fax 612-870-3004; Website www.artsmia.org. Free for members

Arts Link Newsletter (Q)—Steve Custer, Mgr Publs & Communs.
Americans for the Arts 1000 Vermont Ave, NW 6th Fl, Washington, DC 20005. Tel 202-371-2830; Fax 203-271-0424; Website www.americansforthearts.org. Free for members

Arts Quarterly (Q)—David Johnson, Ed.
New Orleans Museum of Art, 1 Collins C Diboll Cir, City Park, New Orleans, LA 70124. Tel 504-658-4100; Fax 504-658-4199; Website www.noma.org. Free for members

Art Therapy (Q)—
American Art Therapy Association, 4875 Eisenhower Ave, Ste 240, Alexandria, VA 22304. Tel 888-290-0878; Fax 703-783-8468; E-mail info@arttherapy.org; Website www.arttherapy.org. Yearly $199.00 (individuals, print); $273.00 (institutions, online); $312.00 (institutions, print & online)

Art Times (Q)—Raymond J Steiner, Ed.
PO Box 730, Mount Marion, NY 12456. Tel 845-246-6944; Fax 845-246-6944; E-mail info@arttimesjournal.com; Website www.arttimesjournal.com. Yearly $18.00 US; $35.00 international

Aviso (M)—
American Alliance of Museums, 1575 Eye St, NW, Ste 400, Washington, DC 20005. Tel 202-289- 1818; Fax 202-289-6578; E-mail infocenter@aam-us.org; Website www.aam-us.org. Free for members

Blouin Art + Auction (11 Issues)—Louise Blouin, Publr
Louise Blouin Media (US), 88 Laight St, New York, NY 10013. Tel 212- 447-9555; E-mail generalinfo@artinfo.com; Website www.blouinartinfo.com. Yearly $129.99 US; $149.99 Canada; $169.99 international

Bomb (Q)—Betsy Sussler, Publr & Ed in Chf.
80 Hanson Pl, Ste 703, Brooklyn, NY 11217-1506. Tel 718-636-9100; Fax 718-636- 9200; Email generalinquiries@bombsite.com; Website www.bombmagazine.org. Yearly $32.00

Bulletin of the Detroit Institute of Arts—Kirk Ambrose, Ed in Chf.
Publishing & Colls Info, 5200 Woodward Ave, Detroit, MI 48202. Tel 313-833-7960; E-Mail operator@dia.org; Website www.dia.org. Yearly $15.00

Canadian Art (Q)—David Balzer, Ed in Chf & Publr.
Canadian Art Foundation, 215 Spadina Ave, Ste 320, Toronto, ON M5T 2C7, Canada. Tel 416-368-8854; Fax 416-368-6135; E-Mail info@canadianart.ca; Website www.canadianart.ca. Yearly $29.95 US.

Ceramics Monthly (M)—Jennifer Poellot Harnetty, Ed.
Ceramics Monthly, 600 N Cleveland Ave, Ste 210 Westerville, OH 43082. Tel 614-794- 5843; Fax 614-794-5842; E-mail: editorial@ceramicsmonthly.org; Website www.ceramicartsnetwork.org. Monthly $4.97

C Magazine (Q)—Jaclyn Bruneau, Ed.
PO Box 5 Sta B, Toronto, ON M5T 2T2, Canada. Tel 416-539-9495; Fax 416-539-9903; E-mail info@cmagazine.com; Website www.cmagazine.com. Yearly $31.00 US; $26.00 Canada

City Arts Magazine (M)—Leah Baltus, Ed in Chf.
Encore Media Group, 425 N 85th St, Seattle, WA 98103. Tel 206-443-0445; Fax 206-443-1246; E-mail info@cityartsmagazine.com; Website www.cityartsonline.com. Yearly $36.00

Cleveland Museum of Art Members Magazine (Bi-M)—Gregory Donley & Kathleen Mills, Eds.
Publications Dept, 11150 East Blvd, Cleveland, OH 44106. Tel 216-421-7350; E-mail magazine@clevelandart.org; Website www.clevelandart.org. Free for members

Columbia Journal of Law & the Arts (Q)—David Manella, Ed in Chf.
Columbia University School of Law, 435 W 116th St, New York, NY 10027. Tel 212-854-1607; E-mail columbiajla@gmail.com; Website www.lawandarts.org. Yearly $60.00 domestic; $75.00 international

Communication Arts (6 Issues) Patrick Coyne, Publr.
110 Constitution Dr, Menlo Park, CA 94025. Tel 650-326-6040; Fax 650- 326-1648; E-mail editorial@commarts.com; Website Yearly $53.00 US; $70.00 Canada; $110.00 international

Conscious Community Magazine (M)—Kasia Szumal, Publr.
47 W Polk St, Ste 153 Chicago, IL 60605. Tel 847-966-1110; E-mail themonthlyaspectarian@gmail.com; Website consciouscommunitymagazine.com. Yearly $36.00

Gesta (2 Issues)—Linda Safran & Adam S Cohen, Eds.
International Center of Medieval Art, The Cloisters, Fort Tryon Park, New York, NY 10040. Tel 212-928-1146; E-mail gesta@medievalart.org; Website www.medievalart.org. Free for ICMA members

IFAR Journal (Q)—Sharon Flescher, Ed in Chf.
International Foundation for Art Research, 500 Fifth Ave, Ste 935, New York, NY 10110. Tel 212-391-6234; Fax 212-391-8794; E-mail kferg@ifar.org; Website www.ifar.org. Yearly $75.00; free with membership minimum of $250.00

Journal of Aesthetics & Art Criticism (Q)—Robert Stecker & Theodore Gracyk, Eds.
American Society for Aesthetics, 1550 Larimer St #644 Denver CO 80202-1602; Website www.aesthetics-online.site-ym.com. Free for members

Journal of Canadian Art History (Semi-A)—Martha Langford, Ed in Chf.
Concordia University, 1455 De Maissonneuve Blvd West, Montreal, QC H3G 1M8, Canada. Tel 514-848-2424, ext 4699; Fax 514-848-4584; E-mail jcah@concordia.ca; Website jcah-ahac.concordia.ca/en. Yearly $75.00 US, $60.00 Canada

Leonardo (5 Issues)—Roger Malina, Exec Ed.
Leonardo/SAST, 211 Sutter St, Ste 501, San Francisco, CA 94108. Tel 415-391-1110; Fax 415-391-2385; E-mail isast@leonardo.info; Website www.leonardo.info. Yearly (print and electronic access) $94.00 individuals; $741.00 institutions

Letter Arts Review (Q)—Christopher Calderhead, Ed.
1833 Spring Garden St, 1st Fl, Greensboro, NC 27403. Tel 800-369-9598; Fax 336-272-9015; E-mail info@johnnealbooks.com; Website www.johnnealbooks.com. Yearly $48.00 US; $56.00 Canada; $70.00 international

Linea—Stephanie Cassidy, Ed.
The Art Students League of New York 215 W 57th St, New York, NY 10019. Tel 212-247-4510; Fax 212-541-7024; E-mail linea@artstudentsleague.org; Website www.asllinea.org. Online only

Master Drawings (Q)—Jane Turner, Ed.
Master Drawings Association Inc, 225 Madison Ave, New York, NY 10016-3405. Tel 212-590-0369; Fax 212-685-4740; E-mail administrator@masterdrawings.org; Website www.masterdrawings.org. Yearly $125.00 domestic; $160.00 international

Metropolitan Museum of Art Bulletin (Q)—Daniel H Weiss, Exec Dir.
1000 Fifth Ave, New York, NY 10028-0198. Tel 212-535- 7710; Website www.metmuseum.org. Free for members

Museum (Bi-M)—Cecelia Walls, Content & Editorial Strategist
American Alliance of Museums, 1575 Eye St, NW, Ste 400, Washington, DC 20005. Tel 202-289-1818; Fax 202-289-6578; Website www.aam-us.org. Yearly $38.00 US; $56.00 Canada & Mexico; $80.00 international

October (Q)—Adam Lehner, Mng Ed.
MIT Press Journals, 350 Fifth Ave, #7401, New York, NY 10118. Tel 212-253-7012; E-mail octobermagazine@gmail.com; Website www.mitpressjournals.org Yearly (print and electronic access) $70.00

Ornament (5 issues)—Robert Liu & Carolyn Benesh, Eds.
Ornament Inc, PO Box 2349, San Marcos, CA 92079-2349. Tel 760- 599-0222; E-mail editorial@ornamentmagazine.com; Website www.ornamentmagazine.com. Yearly $29.99

Professional Artist (Bi-M)—Gigi Rosenberg, Ed.
938 Lake Baldwin Ln, Orlando, FL 32814. Tel 407-258-3109; Fax 407-258-3109; E-mail info@professionalartistmag.com; Website www.professionalartistmag.com. Yearly $43.00

SchoolArts (9 Issues)—Nancy Walkup, Ed.
Davis Publications Inc, 50 Portland St, Worcester, MA 01608. Tel 508-754-7201; Fax 508-753-3834; Website www.davisart.com. Yearly $24.95

Sculpture (M)—Glenn Harper, Ed.
International Sculpture Center, 1633 Connecticut Ave, NW, 4th Fl, Washington, DC 20009. Tel 202-234-0555; Fax 202-234-2663; E-mail editor@sculpture.org; Website www.sculpture.org. Yearly $60.00

Sculpture Review (Q)—Giancarlo Biagi, Ed in Chf & Art Dir.
National Sculpture Society, 75 Varick St, 11th Fl, New York, NY 10013. Tel 212-764-5645; 10; Fax 212-764-5651; Website www.sculpturereview.com. Yearly $30.00 US

Society of Architectural Historians Newsletter (M)—Karen Kingsley, Ed in Chief
Society of Architectural Historians, 1365 N Astor St, Chicago IL, 60610. Tel 312-573-1365; E-Mail info@sah.org; Website www.sah.org.

Southwest Art (M)—Kristin Hoerth, Ed in Chf.
10901 W 120th Ave, Ste 350, Broomfield, CO 80021. Tel 303-442-0427; Fax 303-449- 0279; E-mail southwestart@fwmedia.com; Website www.southwestart.com. Yearly $36.95 US

Stained Glass Quarterly (Q)—Richard Gross, Ed.
Stained Glass Association of America, 9313 E 63rd St, Raytown, MO 64133. Tel 800-438-9581; Fax 816-737-2801; Email stainedglassquarterly@gmail.com; Website stainedglassquarterly.com. Yearly $29.00 US; $47.00 Canada & Mexico; $59.00 international

Studies in Art Education (Q)—Elizabeth Snow, Ed.
National Art Education Association, 901 Prince St, Alexandria, VA 22314. Tel 703-860-8000; Fax 703-860-2960; E-mail info@arteducators.org; Website www.arteducators.org. Yearly $30.00 US; $45.00 Canada & international

Studio Potter (Semi-A)—Elenor Wilson, Ed.
PO Box 257, Shelburne Falls, MA 03107. Tel 413-625-6000; E-mail editor@studiopotter.org; Website www.studiopotter.org. Membership Yearly $70.00 US; $95.00 Canada; $105.00 international

Sunshine Artist (M)—Stephanie Hintz, Mng Ed
N7528 Aanstad Rd PO Box 5000 Iola, WI 54945. E-mail business@sunshineartist.com; Website www.sunshineartist.com. Yearly $34.95; $54.95 Canada; $64.95 international

Vie des Arts (Q)—Bernard Levy, Ed in Chf.
5605 Ave de Gaspe, Local 603, Montreal, QC H2T 2A4, Canada. Tel 514-282-0205; Fax 514-282-0235; E-mail: admin@viedesarts.com Website www.viedesarts.com. Yearly $52.00 US; $32.00 Canada; $72.00 international

Woman's Art Journal (2 Issues)—Joan Marter & Margaret Barlow, Eds.
Rutgers University, Dept of Art History, Voorhees Hall, 71 Hamilton St, New Brunswick, NJ 08901. Tel 732-932-7041, ext 20; Fax 732-932-1261; E-mail waj@womansartjournal.org; Website www.womansartjournal.org. Yearly $47.00

IV INDEXES

Subject

Personnel

Organizational

Subject Index

Major Subjects are listed first, followed by named collections.

AFRICAN ART

Academy of the New Church, Glencairn Museum, Bryn Athyn PA
The Africa Center, New York NY
African American Atelier, Greensboro NC
African American Museum of Iowa, Cedar Rapids IA
African Art Museum of Maryland, Columbia MD
Albany Museum of Art, Albany GA
Albion College, Bobbitt Visual Arts Center, Albion MI
Amherst College, Mead Art Museum, Amherst MA
Art Gallery of Ontario, Toronto ON
The Art Museum of Eastern Idaho, Idaho Falls ID
Arts Council of Fayetteville-Cumberland County, The Arts Center, Fayetteville NC
The Baltimore Museum of Art, Baltimore MD
Bangladesh National Museum, Dhaka
Barnes Foundation, Merion PA
Beck Cultural Exchange Center, Inc, Knoxville TN
Berea College, Doris Ulmann Galleries, Berea KY
Birmingham Museum of Art, Birmingham AL
Blanden Memorial Art Museum, Fort Dodge IA
Blauvelt Demarest Foundation, Hiram Blauvelt Art Museum, Oradell NJ
Botswana National Museum, Gaborone
Bowers Museum, Santa Ana CA
Brown University, Haffenreffer Museum of Anthropology, Providence RI
Bucknell University, Edward & Marthann Samek Art Gallery, Lewisburg PA
The Buffalo Fine Arts Academy, Albright-Knox Art Gallery, Buffalo NY
C W Post Campus of Long Island University, Hillwood Art Museum, Brookville NY
California African-American Museum, Los Angeles CA
California State University, East Bay, C E Smith Museum of Anthropology, Hayward CA
Capital University, Schumacher Gallery, Columbus OH
Center for Puppetry Arts, Atlanta GA
The Children's Museum of Indianapolis, Indianapolis IN
Cincinnati Art Museum, Cincinnati Art Museum, Cincinnati OH
City of Fayette, Alabama, Fayette Art Museum, Fayette AL
The Columbus Museum, Columbus GA
Concordia Historical Institute, Saint Louis MO
Cornell Museum of Art and American Culture, Delray Beach FL
Cornell University, Herbert F Johnson Museum of Art, Ithaca NY
Craft and Folk Art Museum (CAFAM), Los Angeles CA
Crocker Art Museum, Sacramento CA
The Currier Museum of Art, Manchester NH
Dallas Museum of Art, Dallas TX
Dartmouth College, Hood Museum of Art, Hanover NH
Denver Art Museum, Denver CO
Detroit Institute of Arts, Detroit MI
Detroit Zoological Institute, Wildlife Interpretive Gallery, Royal Oak MI
Dickinson College, The Trout Gallery, Carlisle PA
Doncaster Museum and Art Gallery, Doncaster Yorks
East Carolina University, Wellington B Gray Gallery, Greenville NC
East Los Angeles College, Vincent Price Art Museum, Monterey Park CA
Edmundson Art Foundation, Inc, Des Moines Art Center, Des Moines IA
Emory University, Michael C Carlos Museum, Atlanta GA
En Foco, Inc, Bronx NY
Evansville Museum of Arts, History & Science, Evansville IN
Everhart Museum, Scranton PA
Fairbanks Museum & Planetarium, Saint Johnsbury VT
Fine Arts Museums of San Francisco, Legion of Honor, San Francisco CA
Fisk University, Aaron Douglas Gallery, Nashville TN
Fitchburg Art Museum, Fitchburg MA
Fitton Center for Creative Arts, Hamilton OH
Flint Institute of Arts, Flint MI
Florida State University and Central Florida Community College, The Appleton Museum of Art, Ocala FL
Fuller Craft Museum, Brockton MA
General Board of Discipleship, The United Methodist Church, The Upper Room Chapel & Museum, Nashville TN
Grand Rapids Art Museum, Grand Rapids MI
Hammonds House Museum, Atlanta GA
Heard Museum, Phoenix AZ
Historisches und Volkerkundemuseum, Museum of History and Ethnology, St Gallen
Honolulu Museum of Art, Honolulu HI
Illinois State Museum, ISM Lockport Gallery, Chicago Gallery & Southern Illinois Art Gallery, Springfield IL
Institute of Contemporary Art, Los Angeles, Los Angeles CA
The Interchurch Center, Galleries at the Interchurch Center, New York NY
Intermedia Arts, Minneapolis MN
International Museum of Art, El Paso TX
The Israel Museum, Jerusalem, Jerusalem
Jacksonville University, Alexander Brest Museum & Gallery, Jacksonville FL
Johns Hopkins University, Homewood Museum, Baltimore MD
Jordan National Gallery of Fine Arts, Amman
Joslyn Art Museum, Omaha NE
Kalamazoo Institute of Arts, Kalamazoo MI
Keene State College, Thorne-Sagendorph Art Gallery, Keene NH
Kenosha Public Museums, Kenosha WI
Kimbell Art Foundation, Kimbell Art Museum, Fort Worth TX
The Kreeger Museum, Washington DC
La Salle University Art Museum, Philadelphia PA
Langston University, Melvin B Tolson Black Heritage Center, Langston OK
Las Vegas Natural History Museum, Las Vegas NV
Lighthouse ArtCenter Museum & School of Art, Tequesta FL
Lightner Museum, Saint Augustine FL
Lillian & Coleman Taube Museum of Art, Minot ND
Louisiana Arts & Science Museum, Baton Rouge LA
Lusaka National Museum, Lusaka
Mabee-Gerrer Museum of Art, Shawnee OK
Madison Museum of Fine Art, Madison GA
Maine College of Art, The Institute of Contemporary Art, Portland ME
Marietta College, Grover M Hermann Fine Arts Center, Marietta OH
Marquette University, Haggerty Museum of Art, Milwaukee WI
Martin and Osa Johnson, Chanute KS
McPherson Museum and Arts Foundation, McPherson KS
Meredith College, Frankie G Weems Gallery & Rotunda Gallery, Raleigh NC
Mezuraj Museum, Tirana
Michelson Museum of Art, Marshall TX
Michigan State University, Eli & Edythe Broad Art Museum, East Lansing MI
Minneapolis Institute of Art, Minneapolis MN
The Mint Museum, Charlotte NC
The Mint Museum, Mint Museum of Craft & Design, Charlotte NC
Missoula Art Museum, Missoula MT
Mobile Museum of Art, Mobile AL
Modern Art Museum, Fort Worth TX
Montreal Museum of Fine Arts, Montreal QC
Morris Museum, Morristown NJ
Musee des Augustines de l'Hotel Dieu de Quebec, Quebec QC
The Museum, Greenwood SC
Museum of African American Art, Los Angeles CA
The Museum of Arts & Sciences Inc, Daytona Beach FL
Museum of Contemporary Art, North Miami FL
Museum of Fine Arts, Houston, Houston TX
Museum of Fine Arts, Saint Petersburg, Florida, Inc, Saint Petersburg FL
Museum of Vancouver, Vancouver BC
Museum of York County, Rock Hill SC
National Museum of African Art, Smithsonian Institution, Washington DC
National Museum of Ethiopia, Addis Ababa
The Nelson-Atkins Museum of Art, Kansas City MO
Nemeth Art Center, Park Rapids MN
New Brunswick Museum, Saint John NB
New Orleans Museum of Art, New Orleans LA
New Visions Gallery, Inc, Marshfield WI
Nihon Mingeikan, Japan Folk Crafts Museum, Tokyo
North Carolina Central University, NCCU Art Museum, Durham NC
North Carolina Museum of Art, Raleigh NC
Norwich Free Academy, Slater Memorial Museum, Norwich CT
Oakland University, Oakland University Art Gallery, Rochester MI
Ohio University, Kennedy Museum of Art, Athens OH
Okanagan Heritage Museum, Kelowna BC
Okefenokee Heritage Center, Inc, Waycross GA
Omenka Gallery, Lagos
Omniplex Science Museum, Oklahoma City OK
Owensboro Museum of Fine Art, Owensboro KY
Page-Walker Arts & History Center, Cary NC
Peabody Essex Museum, Salem MA
Pensacola Museum of Art, Pensacola FL
Peoria Riverfront Museum, Peoria IL
Philbrook Museum of Art, Tulsa OK
Piedmont Arts Association, Martinsville VA
Plains Art Museum, Fargo ND
Polk Museum of Art, Lakeland FL
The Pomona College, Claremont CA
Portland Art Museum, Portland OR
Purchase College, Neuberger Museum of Art, Purchase NY
Queens College, City University of New York, Godwin-Ternbach Museum, Flushing NY
Reading Public Museum, Reading PA
Rele Gallery, Lagos
Royal Ontario Museum, Toronto ON
Saint Mary's College of California, Museum of Art, Moraga CA
Saint Olaf College, Flaten Art Museum, Northfield MN
Santa Barbara Museum of Art, Santa Barbara CA
Santa Clara University, de Saisset Museum, Santa Clara CA
Scripps College, Ruth Chandler Williamson Gallery, Claremont CA

Sheldon Art Galleries, Saint Louis MO
Southern Oregon University, Schneider Museum of Art, Ashland OR
The Speed Art Museum, Louisville KY
St Mary's College of Maryland, The Dwight Frederick Boyden Gallery, St Mary's City MD
Staatliche Museen zu Berlin Stiftung Preussischer Kulturbesitz, National Museums in Berlin, Prussian Cultural Heritage Foundation, Berlin
Stanford University, Cantor Arts Center at Stanford University, Stanford CA
State University of New York at New Paltz, Samuel Dorsky Museum of Art, New Paltz NY
State University of New York at Oswego, Tyler Art Gallery, Oswego NY
State University of New York at Plattsburgh, Art Museum, Plattsburgh NY
Staten Island Museum, Staten Island NY
Topeka & Shawnee County Public Library, Alice C Sabatini Gallery, Topeka KS
Tubman African American Museum, Macon GA
University of Georgia, Georgia Museum of Art, Athens GA
University of Illinois at Urbana-Champaign, Krannert Art Museum and Kinkead Pavilion, Champaign IL
University of Illinois at Urbana-Champaign, Spurlock Museum, Urbana IL
University of Kansas, Spencer Museum of Art, Lawrence KS
The University of Kentucky Art Museum, Lexington KY
University of Miami, Lowe Art Museum, Coral Gables FL
University of Notre Dame, Snite Museum of Art, Notre Dame IN
University of Pennsylvania, Arthur Ross Gallery, Philadelphia PA
University of Richmond, University Museums, Richmond VA
University of Utah, Utah Museum of Fine Arts, Salt Lake City UT
University of Wisconsin-Madison, Chazen Museum of Art, Madison WI
University of Wisconsin-Stout, J Furlong Gallery, Menomonie WI
Wadsworth Atheneum Museum of Art, Hartford CT
The Walker African American Museum & Research Center, Las Vegas NV
Wayne Center for the Arts, Wooster OH
Wheaton College, Beard and Weil Galleries, Norton MA
William Paterson University, University Galleries, Wayne NJ
Winston-Salem State University, Diggs Gallery, Winston-Salem NC

AFRO-AMERICAN ART

African American Atelier, Greensboro NC
African American Museum in Philadelphia, Philadelphia PA
African American Museum of Iowa, Cedar Rapids IA
Albany Museum of Art, Albany GA
Alton Museum of History & Art, Inc, Alton IL
American Folk Art Museum, New York NY
American Sport Art Museum and Archives, Daphne AL
Amherst College, Mead Art Museum, Amherst MA
Amon Carter Museum of American Art, Fort Worth TX
Art Museum of Greater Lafayette, Lafayette IN
Art Without Walls Inc, Sayville NY
Arts Council of Fayetteville-Cumberland County, The Arts Center, Fayetteville NC
ArtSpace/Lima, Lima OH
Asheville Art Museum, Asheville NC
The Baltimore Museum of Art, Baltimore MD
Baruch College of the City University of New York, Sidney Mishkin Gallery, New York NY
Baton Rouge Gallery, Center For Contemporary Art, Baton Rouge LA
Beck Cultural Exchange Center, Inc, Knoxville TN
Birmingham Museum of Art, Birmingham AL
Booth Western Art Museum, Cartersville GA
California African-American Museum, Los Angeles CA
California State University, Chico, Janet Turner Print Museum, CSU, Chicago, Chico CA
Cartoon Art Museum, San Francisco CA
Cedar Rapids Museum of Art, Cedar Rapids IA
Center for Puppetry Arts, Atlanta GA
Central United Methodist Church, Swords Into Plowshares Peace Center & Gallery, Detroit MI
City of El Paso, El Paso TX
City of Fayette, Alabama, Fayette Art Museum, Fayette AL
Colgate University, Picker Art Gallery, Hamilton NY
College of William & Mary, Muscarelle Museum of Art, Williamsburg VA
The Columbus Museum, Columbus GA
The Contemporary Austin, Austin TX
County of Henrico, Meadow Farm Museum, Glen Allen VA
Craft and Folk Art Museum (CAFAM), Los Angeles CA
Crocker Art Museum, Sacramento CA
Cyprus Museum, Nicosia
Dallas Museum of Art, Dallas TX
Danville Museum of Fine Arts & History, Danville VA
Dartmouth College, Hood Museum of Art, Hanover NH
Davidson College, William H Van Every Jr & Edward M Smith Galleries, Davidson NC
Delta Blues Museum, Clarksdale MS
Detroit Institute of Arts, Detroit MI
Detroit Repertory Theatre Gallery, Detroit MI
DuSable Museum of African American History, Chicago IL
East Carolina University, Wellington B Gray Gallery, Greenville NC
Elmhurst Art Museum, Elmhurst IL
En Foco, Inc, Bronx NY
Eubie Blake National Jazz Institute and Cultural Center, Baltimore MD
Fairfield University, Art Museum, Fairfield CT
Fine Arts Museums of San Francisco, Legion of Honor, San Francisco CA
Fisk University, Aaron Douglas Gallery, Nashville TN
Fitchburg Art Museum, Fitchburg MA
Fitton Center for Creative Arts, Hamilton OH
Florence County Museum, Florence SC
Folk Art Society of America, Richmond VA
General Board of Discipleship, The United Methodist Church, The Upper Room Chapel & Museum, Nashville TN
Grand Rapids Art Museum, Grand Rapids MI
Greenville County Museum of Art, Greenville SC
Hammonds House Museum, Atlanta GA
High Museum of Art, Atlanta GA
Huntington Museum of Art, Huntington WV
Illinois State Museum, ISM Lockport Gallery, Chicago Gallery & Southern Illinois Art Gallery, Springfield IL
Institute of Contemporary Art, Los Angeles, Los Angeles CA
INTAR Gallery, New York NY
The Interchurch Center, Galleries at the Interchurch Center, New York NY
Intermedia Arts, Minneapolis MN
Intuit: The Center for Intuitive & Outsider Art, Chicago IL
Iredell Museums, Statesville NC
Jerald Melberg Gallery, Charlotte NC
Kentucky Museum of Art and Craft, Louisville KY
Knoxville Museum of Art, Knoxville TN
Lafayette Science Museum & Planetarium, Lafayette LA
LaGrange Art Museum, LaGrange GA
Lalit Kala Akademi Rabindra Bhavan Art Galleries, National Academy of Art, New Delhi, New Delhi
Langston University, Melvin B Tolson Black Heritage Center, Langston OK
Lehman College Art Gallery, Bronx NY
Lillian & Coleman Taube Museum of Art, Minot ND
Longview Museum of Fine Art, Longview TX
Louise Hopkins Underwood Center for the Arts, Lubbock TX
Louisiana Department of Culture, Recreation & Tourism, Louisiana State Museum, New Orleans LA
Maryland Hall for the Creative Arts, Chaney Gallery, Annapolis MD
Mennello Museum of American Art, Orlando FL
Meredith College, Frankie G Weems Gallery & Rotunda Gallery, Raleigh NC
Michigan State University, Eli & Edythe Broad Art Museum, East Lansing MI
The Mint Museum, Charlotte NC
Mississippi River Museum at Mud-Island River Park, Memphis TN
Missoula Art Museum, Missoula MT
Mobile Museum of Art, Mobile AL
Modern Art Museum, Fort Worth TX
Montclair Art Museum, Montclair NJ
Morehead State University, Kentucky Folk Art Center, Morehead KY
Morris Museum of Art, Augusta GA
Mount Vernon Hotel Museum & Garden, New York NY
Museum of African American Art, Los Angeles CA
The Museum of Arts & Sciences Inc, Daytona Beach FL
Museum of Contemporary Art, North Miami FL
Museum of Contemporary Art Chicago, Chicago IL
Museum of the National Center of Afro-American Artists, Boston MA
National Museum of Women in the Arts, Washington DC
Nebraska Game and Parks Commission, Arbor Lodge State Historical Park & Morton Mansion, Nebraska City NE
The Nelson-Atkins Museum of Art, Kansas City MO
New Britain Museum of American Art, New Britain CT
New Orleans Museum of Art, New Orleans LA
Niagara University, Castellani Art Museum, Niagara NY
North Carolina Museum of Art, Raleigh NC
Norwich Free Academy, Slater Memorial Museum, Norwich CT
Ogden Museum of Southern Art, University of New Orleans, New Orleans LA
Ohio History Connection, National Afro-American Museum & Cultural Center, Wilberforce OH
Okefenokee Heritage Center, Inc, Waycross GA
Opelousas Museum of Art, Inc (OMA), Opelousas LA
Owensboro Museum of Fine Art, Owensboro KY
Page-Walker Arts & History Center, Cary NC
Panhandle-Plains Historical Museum, Canyon TX
Pennsylvania Academy of the Fine Arts, Philadelphia PA
Piedmont Arts Association, Martinsville VA
Polk Museum of Art, Lakeland FL
Portsmouth Historical Society, John Paul Jones House & Discover Portsmouth, Portsmouth NH
Pump House Center for the Arts, Chillicothe OH
Rollins College, George D & Harriet W Cornell Fine Arts Museum, Winter Park FL
Roswell Museum & Art Center, Roswell NM
Saint Joseph Museum, Inc., Saint Joseph MO
San Antonio Museum of Art, San Antonio TX
Scripps College, Ruth Chandler Williamson Gallery, Claremont CA
Scripps College, Clark Humanities Museum, Claremont CA
Sheldon Art Galleries, Saint Louis MO
South Carolina Artisans Center, Walterboro SC
South Carolina State Museum, Columbia SC
South Dakota State University, South Dakota Art Museum, Brookings SD
Southeastern Center for Contemporary Art, Winston-Salem NC
The Speed Art Museum, Louisville KY
Springfield Art Museum, Springfield MO
St Mary's College of Maryland, The Dwight Frederick Boyden Gallery, St Mary's City MD
Stanford University, Cantor Arts Center at Stanford University, Stanford CA
State University of New York at Geneseo, Bertha V B Lederer Gallery, Geneseo NY
Stone Quarry Hill Art Park, Winner Gallery, Cazenovia NY
The Studio Museum in Harlem, New York NY
Taft Museum of Art, Cincinnati OH
Thomas Jefferson Foundation, Inc, Monticello, Charlottesville VA
Tubman African American Museum, Macon GA
University of California, Berkeley, Phoebe Apperson Hearst Museum of Anthropology, Berkeley CA
University of Georgia, Georgia Museum of Art, Athens GA
University of Houston, Blaffer Art Museum, Houston TX
University of Illinois at Urbana-Champaign, Krannert Art Museum and Kinkead Pavilion, Champaign IL
The University of Kentucky Art Museum, Lexington KY
University of Miami, Lowe Art Museum, Coral Gables FL

University of North Carolina at Greensboro, Weatherspoon Art Museum, Greensboro NC
University of Notre Dame, Snite Museum of Art, Notre Dame IN
University of Pennsylvania, Arthur Ross Gallery, Philadelphia PA
University of Richmond, University Museums, Richmond VA
University of Texas at Austin, Blanton Museum of Art, Austin TX
The University of Texas at San Antonio, Institute of Texan Cultures, San Antonio TX
University of Wisconsin-Madison, Chazen Museum of Art, Madison WI
Viridian Artists Inc, New York NY
Wadsworth Atheneum Museum of Art, Hartford CT
The Walker African American Museum & Research Center, Las Vegas NV
Walker Art Gallery, Liverpool
Waterloo Center of the Arts, Waterloo IA
Waterworks Visual Arts Center, Salisbury NC
Wichita State University, Ulrich Museum of Art, Wichita KS
Winston-Salem State University, Diggs Gallery, Winston-Salem NC
Wiregrass Museum of Art, Dothan AL
Woodmere Art Museum Inc, Philadelphia PA
World Erotic Art Museum, Miami Beach FL
Yerba Buena Center for the Arts, San Francisco CA
Zigler Art Museum, Jennings LA

AMERICAN INDIAN ART

Academy of the New Church, Glencairn Museum, Bryn Athyn PA
Adams County Historical Society, Gettysburg PA
Alaska Department of Education, Division of Libraries, Archives & Museums, Sheldon Jackson Museum, Sitka AK
Alaska Heritage Museum at Wells Fargo, Anchorage AK
Alaska State Museum, Juneau AK
Albany Institute of History & Art, Albany NY
Albany Museum of Art, Albany GA
The Albrecht-Kemper Museum of Art, Saint Joseph MO
American Folk Art Museum, New York NY
American Sport Art Museum and Archives, Daphne AL
Amon Carter Museum of American Art, Fort Worth TX
Anchorage Museum at Rasmuson Center, Anchorage AK
Appaloosa Museum and Heritage Center, Moscow ID
Archaeological Society of Ohio, Indian Museum of Lake County, Ohio, Willoughby OH
Arnot Art Museum, Elmira NY
Art Museum of Greater Lafayette, Lafayette IN
Art Without Walls Inc, Sayville NY
Arts Council of Fayetteville-Cumberland County, The Arts Center, Fayetteville NC
ArtSpace/Lima, Lima OH
Asheville Art Museum, Asheville NC
Ataloa Lodge Museum, Muskogee OK
Aurora University, Schingoethe Center for Native American Cultures & The Schingoethe Art Gallery, Aurora IL
The Baltimore Museum of Art, Baltimore MD
Bangladesh National Museum, Dhaka
Bay County Historical Society, Historical Museum of Bay County, Bay City MI
Bent Museum & Gallery, Taos NM
Berkshire Museum, Pittsfield MA
Berman Museum, Anniston AL
Besser Museum for Northeast Michigan, Alpena MI
Birmingham Museum of Art, Birmingham AL
Bone Creek Museum of Agrarian Art, David City NE
Bowdoin College, Peary-MacMillan Arctic Museum, Brunswick ME
Bowers Museum, Santa Ana CA
Brandeis University, Rose Art Museum, Waltham MA
Brown University, Haffenreffer Museum of Anthropology, Providence RI
Bruce Museum, Inc, Greenwich CT
Bullion Plaza Cultural Center & Museum, Miami AZ
C M Russell Museum, Great Falls MT
C W Post Campus of Long Island University, Hillwood Art Museum, Brookville NY
California State Parks, State Indian Museum, Sacramento CA
California State University, Chico, Janet Turner Print Museum, CSU, Chicago, Chico CA
Cambridge Museum, Cambridge NE
Capital University, Schumacher Gallery, Columbus OH
Carlsbad Museum & Art Center, Carlsbad NM
Carson County Square House Museum, Panhandle TX
Cayuga Museum of History & Art, Auburn NY
Cedar Rapids Museum of Art, Cedar Rapids IA
Central United Methodist Church, Swords Into Plowshares Peace Center & Gallery, Detroit MI
Chelan County Public Utility District, Rocky Reach Dam, Wenatchee WA
Chief Plenty Coups Museum State Park, Pryor MT
Cincinnati Art Museum, Cincinnati Art Museum, Cincinnati OH
City of El Paso, El Paso Museum of Archaeology, El Paso TX
City of Springdale, Shiloh Museum of Ozark History, Springdale AR
City of Ukiah, Grace Hudson Museum & The Sun House, Ukiah CA
Clark County Historical Society, Pioneer - Krier Museum, Ashland KS
Colgate University, Picker Art Gallery, Hamilton NY
College of William & Mary, Muscarelle Museum of Art, Williamsburg VA
The Columbus Museum, Columbus GA
Cornell College, Peter Paul Luce Gallery, Mount Vernon IA
Cornell Museum of Art and American Culture, Delray Beach FL
Coutts Museum of Art, Inc, El Dorado KS
Craft and Folk Art Museum (CAFAM), Los Angeles CA
Cripple Creek District Museum, Cripple Creek CO
Crocker Art Museum, Sacramento CA
The Currier Museum of Art, Manchester NH
Dacotah Prairie Museum, Lamont Art Gallery, Aberdeen SD
Dallas Museum of Art, Dallas TX
Dartmouth College, Hood Museum of Art, Hanover NH
Deming-Luna Mimbres Museum, Deming NM
Denver Art Museum, Denver CO
Dickinson College, The Trout Gallery, Carlisle PA
Dickinson State University, Art Gallery, Dickinson ND
Dixie State University, Sears Art Museum Gallery, Saint George UT
East Carolina University, Wellington B Gray Gallery, Greenville NC
East Los Angeles College, Vincent Price Art Museum, Monterey Park CA
Eastern Washington State Historical Society, Northwest Museum of Arts & Culture, Spokane WA
Eiteljorg Museum of American Indians & Western Art, Indianapolis IN
En Foco, Inc, Bronx NY
Erie County Historical Society, Erie PA
Eula Mae Edwards Museum & Gallery, Clovis NM
Evanston Historical Society, Charles Gates Dawes House, Evanston IL
Fairbanks Museum & Planetarium, Saint Johnsbury VT
Favell Museum of Western Art & Indian Artifacts, Klamath Falls OR
Fetherston Foundation, Packwood House Museum, Lewisburg PA
Fine Arts Museums of San Francisco, Legion of Honor, San Francisco CA
Five Civilized Tribes Museum, Muskogee OK
Flint Institute of Arts, Flint MI
Florence County Museum, Florence SC
Folk Art Society of America, Richmond VA
The Frank Phillips Foundation Inc, Woolaroc Museum, Bartlesville OK
Fruitlands Museum, Inc, Harvard MA
Fulton County Historical Society Inc, Fulton County Museum (Tetzlaff Reference Room), Rochester IN
General Board of Discipleship, The United Methodist Church, The Upper Room Chapel & Museum, Nashville TN
George Phippen, Phippen Museum - Art of the American West, Prescott AZ
Gloridale Partnership, National Museum of Woodcarving, Custer SD
Goshen Historical Society, Goshen CT
Grand Rapids Art Museum, Grand Rapids MI
Grand Rapids Public Museum, Grand Rapids MI
Grand River Museum, Lemmon SD
Hamilton College, Emerson Gallery, Clinton NY
Hastings Museum of Natural & Cultural History, Hastings NE
Heard Museum, Phoenix AZ
Henry County Museum & Cultural Arts Center, Clinton MO
Heritage Center, Inc, Pine Ridge SD
Heritage Museums & Gardens, Sandwich MA
Herrett Center for Arts & Sciences, Jean B King Art Gallery, Twin Falls ID
Hershey Museum, Hershey PA
Hidalgo County Historical Museum, Edinburg TX
High Desert Museum, Bend OR
Historic Arkansas Museum, Little Rock AR
Historisches und Volkerkundemuseum, Museum of History and Ethnology, St Gallen
The History Center in Tompkins County, Ithaca NY
History Colorado Center Museum, Denver CO
Holter Museum of Art, Helena MT
Honolulu Museum of Art, Honolulu HI
Illinois State Museum, ISM Lockport Gallery, Chicago Gallery & Southern Illinois Art Gallery, Springfield IL
Imperial Calcasieu Museum, Gibson-Barham Gallery, Lake Charles LA
Independence Historical Museum & Art Center, Independence KS
Indian Arts & Crafts Board, US Dept of the Interior, Sioux Indian Museum, Rapid City SD
Indian Pueblo Cultural Center, Albuquerque NM
INTAR Gallery, New York NY
The Interchurch Center, Galleries at the Interchurch Center, New York NY
Intermedia Arts, Minneapolis MN
Iowa State University, Brunnier Art Museum, Ames IA
Iroquois Indian Museum, Howes Cave NY
The Israel Museum, Jerusalem, Jerusalem
Jefferson County Open Space, Hiwan Homestead Museum, Evergreen CO
The John L. Clarke Western Art Gallery & Memorial Museum, East Glacier Park MT
Johnson-Humrickhouse Museum, Coshocton OH
Joslyn Art Museum, Omaha NE
Juniata College Museum of Art, Huntingdon PA
Kateri Tekakwitha Shrine/St. Francis Xavier Mission, Kahnawake QC
Kelly-Griggs House Museum, Red Bluff CA
Kenosha Public Museums, Kenosha WI
Klein Museum, Mobridge SD
Knoxville Museum of Art, Knoxville TN
Koshare Indian Museum, Inc, La Junta CO
L D Brinkman, Kerrville TX
Lac du Flambeau Band of Lake Superior Chippewa Indians, George W Brown Jr Ojibwe Museum & Cultural Center, Lac Du Flambeau WI
LaGrange Art Museum, LaGrange GA
Lalit Kala Akademi Rabindra Bhavan Art Galleries, National Academy of Art, New Delhi, New Delhi
Leelanau Historical Museum, Leland MI
Lightner Museum, Saint Augustine FL
Lillian & Coleman Taube Museum of Art, Minot ND
Lincoln County Historical Association, Inc, 1811 Old Lincoln County Jail & Lincoln County Museum, Wiscasset ME
Louise Hopkins Underwood Center for the Arts, Lubbock TX
Loveland Museum/Gallery, Loveland CO
Mabee-Gerrer Museum of Art, Shawnee OK
Maricopa County Historical Society, Desert Caballeros Western Museum, Wickenburg AZ
Marquette University, Haggerty Museum of Art, Milwaukee WI
Maryhill Museum of Art, Goldendale WA
Massillon Museum, Massillon OH
McNay Art Museum, San Antonio TX
McPherson Museum and Arts Foundation, McPherson KS
Mennello Museum of American Art, Orlando FL
Meredith College, Frankie G Weems Gallery & Rotunda Gallery, Raleigh NC
Michelson Museum of Art, Marshall TX
Mid-America All-Indian Center, Indian Center Museum, Wichita KS
Middle Border Museum & Oscar Howe Art Center, Mitchell SD
Millicent Rogers Museum, Taos NM
Minneapolis Institute of Art, Minneapolis MN
The Mint Museum, Charlotte NC
Mission San Luis Rey de Francia, Mission San Luis Rey Museum, Oceanside CA

Mission San Miguel Museum, San Miguel CA
Mississippi River Museum at Mud-Island River Park, Memphis TN
Missoula Art Museum, Missoula MT
Mobile Museum of Art, Mobile AL
Mohave Museum of History & Arts, Kingman AZ
Montana State University, Helen E Copeland Gallery, Bozeman MT
Montclair Art Museum, Montclair NJ
Morris Museum, Morristown NJ
Musee des Augustines de l'Hotel Dieu de Quebec, Quebec QC
Musee des Maitres et Artisans du Quebec, Montreal QC
Musees Royaux d'Art et d'Histoire, Royal Museums of Art and History, Brussels
The Museum of Arts & Sciences Inc, Daytona Beach FL
Museum of Fine Arts, Saint Petersburg, Florida, Inc, Saint Petersburg FL
Museum of Northern Arizona, Flagstaff AZ
Museum of the Plains Indian & Crafts Center, Browning MT
Museum of the Southwest, Midland TX
Museum of Vancouver, Vancouver BC
National Hall of Fame for Famous American Indians, Anadarko OK
National Museum of the American Indian, George Gustav Heye Center, New York NY
National Museum of Wildlife Art of the Unites States, Jackson WY
National Museum of Women in the Arts, Washington DC
National Museums Scotland, National Museum of Scotland, Edinburgh
National Park Service, Hubbell Trading Post National Historic Site, Ganado AZ
The National Shrine of the North American Martyrs, Fultonville NY
Nelda C & H J Lutcher Stark Foundation, Stark Museum of Art, Orange TX
The Nelson-Atkins Museum of Art, Kansas City MO
Nevada Museum of Art, Reno NV
New Britain Museum of American Art, New Britain CT
New Brunswick Museum, Saint John NB
New Orleans Museum of Art, New Orleans LA
New Visions Gallery, Inc, Marshfield WI
North Carolina Museum of Art, Raleigh NC
Norwich Free Academy, Slater Memorial Museum, Norwich CT
The Ohio Historical Society, Inc, Campus Martius Museum & Ohio River Museum, Marietta OH
Ohio History Connection, National Road-Zane Grey Museum, Norwich OH
Ohio University, Kennedy Museum of Art, Athens OH
Okanagan Heritage Museum, Kelowna BC
Okefenokee Heritage Center, Inc, Waycross GA
Oklahoma Historical Society, State Museum of History, Oklahoma City OK
Opelousas Museum of Art, Inc (OMA), Opelousas LA
Oshkosh Public Museum & Library, Oshkosh WI
Owensboro Museum of Fine Art, Owensboro KY
Page-Walker Arts & History Center, Cary NC
Palm Springs Art Museum, Palm Springs CA
Panhandle-Plains Historical Museum, Canyon TX
Peabody Essex Museum, Salem MA
Philbrook Museum of Art, Tulsa OK
Piatt Castles, West Liberty OH
Piedmont Arts Association, Martinsville VA
Pine Bluff/Jefferson County Historical Museum, Pine Bluff AR
Plains Art Museum, Fargo ND
Plumas County Museum, Quincy CA
The Pomona College, Claremont CA
Ponca City Cultural Center & Museum, Ponca City OK
Port Huron Museum, Port Huron MI
Portland Art Museum, Portland OR
Principia College, School of Nations Museum, Elsah IL
Pueblo Museum, Desert Hot Springs CA
Pump House Center for the Arts, Chillicothe OH
Purdue University Galleries, West Lafayette IN
Queens College, City University of New York, Godwin-Ternbach Museum, Flushing NY
Reading Public Museum, Reading PA
Red River Valley Museum, Vernon TX
Red Rock Park, Red Rock Park, Church Rock NM
Regina Public Library, Dunlop Art Gallery, Regina SK
Riverside Metropolitan Museum, Riverside CA
Roberts County Museum, Miami TX
The Rockwell Museum, Corning NY
Rollins College, George D & Harriet W Cornell Fine Arts Museum, Winter Park FL
Roswell Museum & Art Center, Roswell NM
Ryerss Victorian Museum & Library, Philadelphia PA
Safety Harbor Museum and Cultural Arts Center, Safety Harbor FL
Saginaw Art Museum, Saginaw MI
Saint Joseph Museum, Inc., Saint Joseph MO
San Bernardino County Museum, Redlands CA
The San Joaquin Pioneer & Historical Society, The Haggin Museum, Stockton CA
Seneca-Iroquois National Museum, Salamanca NY
Sheldon Art Galleries, Saint Louis MO
Sheldon Museum & Cultural Center, Inc, Sheldon Museum & Cultural Center, Haines AK
Sooke Region Museum & Art Gallery, Sooke BC
South Carolina Artisans Center, Walterboro SC
South Dakota State University, South Dakota Art Museum, Brookings SD
Southern Plains Indian Museum, Anadarko OK
The Speed Art Museum, Louisville KY
Springfield Art Museum, Springfield MO
Stamford Museum & Nature Center, Stamford CT
Stanford University, Cantor Arts Center at Stanford University, Stanford CA
State Capital Museum, Olympia WA
State University of New York at Geneseo, Bertha V B Lederer Gallery, Geneseo NY
Ste Genevieve Museum, Sainte Genevieve MO
Strasburg Museum, Strasburg VA
Stratford Historical Society, Catharine B Mitchell Museum, Stratford CT
Suomen Kansallismuseo, National Museum of Finland, Helsinki
Tacoma Art Museum, Tacoma WA
Texas Ranger Hall of Fame & Museum, Waco TX
Thomas Jefferson Foundation, Inc, Monticello, Charlottesville VA
Tohono Chul Park, Tucson AZ
Topeka & Shawnee County Public Library, Alice C Sabatini Gallery, Topeka KS
Trust Authority, Museum of the Great Plains, Lawton OK
Tubac Center of the Arts, Santa Cruz Valley Art Association, Tubac AZ
Turtle Bay Exploration Park, Redding CA
United States Coast Guard Museum, New London CT
United States Military Academy, West Point Museum, West Point NY
University of California, Berkeley, Phoebe Apperson Hearst Museum of Anthropology, Berkeley CA
University of Illinois at Urbana-Champaign, Krannert Art Museum and Kinkead Pavilion, Champaign IL
The University of Kentucky Art Museum, Lexington KY
University of Miami, Lowe Art Museum, Coral Gables FL
University of Minnesota Duluth, Tweed Museum of Art, Duluth MN
University of Nebraska-Lincoln, Great Plains Art Museum, Lincoln NE
University of Notre Dame, Snite Museum of Art, Notre Dame IN
University of Utah, Utah Museum of Fine Arts, Salt Lake City UT
University of Victoria, The Legacy Art Gallery, Victoria BC
University of Washington, Burke Museum of Natural History and Culture, Seattle WA
University of Wisconsin-Madison, Chazen Museum of Art, Madison WI
Vermilion County Museum Society, Danville IL
Wadsworth Atheneum Museum of Art, Hartford CT
Wheaton College, Beard and Weil Galleries, Norton MA
Wheelwright Museum of the American Indian, Santa Fe NM
Wichita State University, Ulrich Museum of Art, Wichita KS
Wildling Art Museum, Solvang CA
Wisconsin Historical Society, Wisconsin Historical Museum, Madison WI
Witte Museum, San Antonio TX
World Erotic Art Museum, Miami Beach FL
Wounded Knee Museum, Wall SD
Wyoming State Museum, Cheyenne WY
Yellowstone County Museum, Billings MT
Yosemite Museum, Yosemite National Park CA
Zigler Art Museum, Jennings LA

AMERICAN WESTERN ART

The Albrecht-Kemper Museum of Art, Saint Joseph MO
Albuquerque Museum of Art & History, Albuquerque NM
Amon Carter Museum of American Art, Fort Worth TX
Appaloosa Museum and Heritage Center, Moscow ID
Arnot Art Museum, Elmira NY
Art Gallery of Hamilton, Hamilton ON
The Art Museum of Eastern Idaho, Idaho Falls ID
Art Without Walls Inc, Sayville NY
Artesia Historical Museum and Art Center, Artesia NM
ArtSpace/Lima, Lima OH
The Baltimore Museum of Art, Baltimore MD
Bangladesh National Museum, Dhaka
Bayerische Staatsgemaldesammlungen, Bavarian State Painting Collections, Munich
Berkshire Museum, Pittsfield MA
Berman Museum, Anniston AL
Birmingham Museum of Art, Birmingham AL
Blauvelt Demarest Foundation, Hiram Blauvelt Art Museum, Oradell NJ
Bone Creek Museum of Agrarian Art, David City NE
Booth Western Art Museum, Cartersville GA
Brookgreen Gardens, Murrells Inlet SC
C M Russell Museum, Great Falls MT
California State University, Chico, Janet Turner Print Museum, CSU, Chicago, Chico CA
Cambridge Museum, Cambridge NE
Cape Ann Museum, Gloucester MA
Carlsbad Museum & Art Center, Carlsbad NM
Cartoon Art Museum, San Francisco CA
Cayuga Museum of History & Art, Auburn NY
Cedar Rapids Museum of Art, Cedar Rapids IA
Chatillon-DeMenil House Foundation, Chatillon-DeMenil Mansion, Saint Louis MO
Cheekwood-Tennessee Botanical Garden & Museum of Art, Nashville TN
City of El Paso, El Paso TX
City of Ukiah, Grace Hudson Museum & The Sun House, Ukiah CA
Columbus Museum of Art, Columbus OH
Coutts Museum of Art, Inc, El Dorado KS
Cripple Creek District Museum, Cripple Creek CO
Crocker Art Museum, Sacramento CA
Crook County Museum & Art Gallery, Sundance WY
The Currier Museum of Art, Manchester NH
Dallas Museum of Art, Dallas TX
Dartmouth College, Hood Museum of Art, Hanover NH
Denver Art Museum, Denver CO
Dixie State University, Sears Art Museum Gallery, Saint George UT
East Carolina University, Wellington B Gray Gallery, Greenville NC
Eiteljorg Museum of American Indians & Western Art, Indianapolis IN
Elisabet Ney, Austin TX
Ellen Noel Art Museum of the Permian Basin, Odessa TX
Elmhurst Art Museum, Elmhurst IL
Favell Museum of Western Art & Indian Artifacts, Klamath Falls OR
Forest Lawn Museum, Glendale CA
The Frank Phillips Foundation Inc, Woolaroc Museum, Bartlesville OK
Frederic Remington, Ogdensburg NY
Freer Gallery of Art & Arthur M Sackler Gallery, Freer Gallery of Art, Washington DC
Frontier Times Museum, Bandera TX
George Phippen, Phippen Museum - Art of the American West, Prescott AZ
Gloridale Partnership, National Museum of Woodcarving, Custer SD
Grand Rapids Art Museum, Grand Rapids MI
Hastings Museum of Natural & Cultural History, Hastings NE
Heard Museum, Phoenix AZ
Hidalgo County Historical Museum, Edinburg TX
High Desert Museum, Bend OR
High Museum of Art, Atlanta GA
Historical Museum at Fort Missoula, Missoula MT
History Colorado Center Museum, Denver CO
Honolulu Museum of Art, Honolulu HI
Huntington Museum of Art, Huntington WV

Illinois State Museum, ISM Lockport Gallery, Chicago Gallery & Southern Illinois Art Gallery, Springfield IL
Independence Historical Museum & Art Center, Independence KS
Intermedia Arts, Minneapolis MN
Istanbul Arkeoloji Muzeleri, Istanbul Archaeological Museums, Istanbul
James Dick Foundation, Festival - Institute, Round Top TX
Jefferson County Open Space, Hiwan Homestead Museum, Evergreen CO
JMW Turner Museum, Sarasota FL
Joe Gish's Old West Museum, Fredericksburg TX
The John L. Clarke Western Art Gallery & Memorial Museum, East Glacier Park MT
Johns Hopkins University, Evergreen Museum & Library, Baltimore MD
Joslyn Art Museum, Omaha NE
Keystone Gallery, Scott City KS
Kirkland Museum of Fine & Decorative Art, Denver CO
Klein Museum, Mobridge SD
Knoxville Museum of Art, Knoxville TN
Koshare Indian Museum, Inc, La Junta CO
L D Brinkman, Kerrville TX
Laguna Art Museum, Laguna Beach CA
Lalit Kala Akademi Rabindra Bhavan Art Galleries, National Academy of Art, New Delhi, New Delhi
Leanin' Tree Museum & Sculpture Garden of Western Art, Boulder CO
Lillian & Coleman Taube Museum of Art, Minot ND
Lincoln County Historical Association, Inc, 1811 Old Lincoln County Jail & Lincoln County Museum, Wiscasset ME
Louise Hopkins Underwood Center for the Arts, Lubbock TX
Loveland Museum/Gallery, Loveland CO
Maricopa County Historical Society, Desert Caballeros Western Museum, Wickenburg AZ
Marietta College, Grover M Hermann Fine Arts Center, Marietta OH
Mennello Museum of American Art, Orlando FL
The Mexican Museum, San Francisco CA
Michelson Museum of Art, Marshall TX
Middle Border Museum & Oscar Howe Art Center, Mitchell SD
Millicent Rogers Museum, Taos NM
Minot State University, Northwest Art Center, Minot ND
Missoula Art Museum, Missoula MT
Mobile Museum of Art, Mobile AL
Montana State University, Helen E Copeland Gallery, Bozeman MT
Montreal Museum of Fine Arts, Montreal QC
Muhlenberg College, Martin Art Gallery, Allentown PA
Museo De Las Americas, Denver CO
The Museum of Arts & Sciences Inc, Daytona Beach FL
Museum of Fine Arts, Saint Petersburg, Florida, Inc, Saint Petersburg FL
Museum of Northern Arizona, Flagstaff AZ
Museum of the Southwest, Midland TX
The Museum of Western Art, Kerrville TX
National Museum of Wildlife Art of the Unites States, Jackson WY
National Museum of Women in the Arts, Washington DC
National Park Service, Hubbell Trading Post National Historic Site, Ganado AZ
Natural History Museum of Los Angeles County, Los Angeles CA
Nebraska Game and Parks Commission, Arbor Lodge State Historical Park & Morton Mansion, Nebraska City NE
Nelda C & H J Lutcher Stark Foundation, Stark Museum of Art, Orange TX
The Nelson-Atkins Museum of Art, Kansas City MO
Nevada Museum of Art, Reno NV
New Britain Museum of American Art, New Britain CT
Northeastern Nevada Museum, Elko NV
Ogden Union Station, Union Station Museums, Ogden UT
Ohio History Connection, National Road-Zane Grey Museum, Norwich OH
Oklahoma Historical Society, State Museum of History, Oklahoma City OK
Opelousas Museum of Art, Inc (OMA), Opelousas LA
Owensboro Museum of Fine Art, Owensboro KY
Page-Walker Arts & History Center, Cary NC
Palm Springs Art Museum, Palm Springs CA
Panhandle-Plains Historical Museum, Canyon TX
Pasadena Museum of California Art, Pasadena CA
Philbrook Museum of Art, Tulsa OK
Phillips Academy, Addison Gallery of American Art, Andover MA
Piedmont Arts Association, Martinsville VA
Pioneer Town, Pioneer Museum of Western Art, Wimberley TX
Plains Art Museum, Fargo ND
Pueblo Museum, Desert Hot Springs CA
Red Rock Park, Red Rock Park, Church Rock NM
The Rockwell Museum, Corning NY
Ross Memorial Museum, Saint Andrews NB
Roswell Museum & Art Center, Roswell NM
Saginaw Art Museum, Saginaw MI
Saint Joseph Museum, Inc., Saint Joseph MO
San Antonio Museum of Art, San Antonio TX
San Bernardino County Museum, Redlands CA
The San Joaquin Pioneer & Historical Society, The Haggin Museum, Stockton CA
Santa Paula Art Museum, Santa Paula CA
Sheldon Art Galleries, Saint Louis MO
South Dakota State University, South Dakota Art Museum, Brookings SD
The Speed Art Museum, Louisville KY
Springfield Art Museum, Springfield MO
Springville Museum of Art, Springville UT
Stone Quarry Hill Art Park, Winner Gallery, Cazenovia NY
Swope Art Museum, Terre Haute IN
Taos Historic Museums, Ernest Blumenschein Home & Studio, Taos NM
Texas Ranger Hall of Fame & Museum, Waco TX
Topeka & Shawnee County Public Library, Alice C Sabatini Gallery, Topeka KS
Trust Authority, Museum of the Great Plains, Lawton OK
Tubac Center of the Arts, Santa Cruz Valley Art Association, Tubac AZ
Turtle Bay Exploration Park, Redding CA
United States Military Academy, West Point Museum, West Point NY
University of California, Berkeley, Phoebe Apperson Hearst Museum of Anthropology, Berkeley CA
University of Georgia, Georgia Museum of Art, Athens GA
University of Illinois at Urbana-Champaign, Krannert Art Museum and Kinkead Pavilion, Champaign IL
University of Miami, Lowe Art Museum, Coral Gables FL
University of Nebraska-Lincoln, Great Plains Art Museum, Lincoln NE
University of New Mexico, The Harwood Museum of Art, Taos NM
University of Notre Dame, Snite Museum of Art, Notre Dame IN
University of Southern California, USC Fisher Museum of Art, Los Angeles CA
University of Texas at Austin, Blanton Museum of Art, Austin TX
University of Victoria, The Legacy Art Gallery, Victoria BC
VU Centre De Diffusion Et De Production De La Photographie, Quebec QC
Wildling Art Museum, Solvang CA
Wisconsin Historical Society, Wisconsin Historical Museum, Madison WI
Wyoming State Museum, Cheyenne WY
Wyoming Trails Gallery, Wheatland WY
Yellowstone County Museum, Billings MT

ANTHROPOLOGY

Alaska Department of Education, Division of Libraries, Archives & Museums, Sheldon Jackson Museum, Sitka AK
Alaska Heritage Museum at Wells Fargo, Anchorage AK
Alaska State Museum, Juneau AK
Anchorage Museum at Rasmuson Center, Anchorage AK
Art Without Walls Inc, Sayville NY
ArtSpace/Lima, Lima OH
Bangladesh National Museum, Dhaka
Bay County Historical Society, Historical Museum of Bay County, Bay City MI
Beloit College, Wright Museum of Art, Beloit WI
Berkshire Museum, Pittsfield MA
Besser Museum for Northeast Michigan, Alpena MI
Botswana National Museum, Gaborone
Bowdoin College, Peary-MacMillan Arctic Museum, Brunswick ME
Brown University, Haffenreffer Museum of Anthropology, Providence RI
Buena Vista Museum of Natural History, Bakersfield CA
Buffalo Niagara Heritage Village, Amherst NY
C M Russell Museum, Great Falls MT
California State Parks, State Indian Museum, Sacramento CA
California State University, East Bay, C E Smith Museum of Anthropology, Hayward CA
Canadian Museum of History, Gatineau QC
Carlsbad Museum & Art Center, Carlsbad NM
Carson County Square House Museum, Panhandle TX
Cayuga Museum of History & Art, Auburn NY
Chelan County Public Utility District, Rocky Reach Dam, Wenatchee WA
The Children's Museum of Indianapolis, Indianapolis IN
Children's Museum of Manhattan, New York NY
City of Ukiah, Grace Hudson Museum & The Sun House, Ukiah CA
College of William & Mary, Muscarelle Museum of Art, Williamsburg VA
Craft and Folk Art Museum (CAFAM), Los Angeles CA
Crocker Art Museum, Sacramento CA
Crook County Museum & Art Gallery, Sundance WY
Dartmouth College, Hood Museum of Art, Hanover NH
Deming-Luna Mimbres Museum, Deming NM
East Carolina University, Wellington B Gray Gallery, Greenville NC
Evansville Museum of Arts, History & Science, Evansville IN
Everhart Museum, Scranton PA
Fairbanks Museum & Planetarium, Saint Johnsbury VT
Fort Morgan Heritage Foundation, Fort Morgan CO
The Frank Phillips Foundation Inc, Woolaroc Museum, Bartlesville OK
Freer Gallery of Art & Arthur M Sackler Gallery, Arthur M Sackler Gallery, Washington DC
Frontier Times Museum, Bandera TX
Glasgow University, The Hunterian, Glasgow
Grand Rapids Public Museum, Grand Rapids MI
Hancock Shaker Village, Inc, Pittsfield MA
Heart of West Texas Museum, Colorado City TX
Heritage Center, Inc, Pine Ridge SD
Herrett Center for Arts & Sciences, Jean B King Art Gallery, Twin Falls ID
Hidalgo County Historical Museum, Edinburg TX
High Desert Museum, Bend OR
The History Center in Tompkins County, Ithaca NY
History Colorado Center Museum, Denver CO
Illinois State Museum, ISM Lockport Gallery, Chicago Gallery & Southern Illinois Art Gallery, Springfield IL
Independence Historical Museum & Art Center, Independence KS
Indian Pueblo Cultural Center, Albuquerque NM
Indiana State Museum, Indianapolis IN
Indiana University, The Mathers Museum of World Cultures, Bloomington IN
Institute of Puerto Rican Culture, Museo Fuerte Conde de Mirasol, Vieques PR
Iredell Museums, Statesville NC
Iroquois Indian Museum, Howes Cave NY
The Israel Museum, Jerusalem, Jerusalem
Jacques Marchais Museum of Tibetan Art, Staten Island NY
Kenosha Public Museums, Kenosha WI
Lafayette Science Museum & Planetarium, Lafayette LA
Lehigh Valley Heritage Center, Allentown PA
Lightner Museum, Saint Augustine FL
Loveland Museum/Gallery, Loveland CO
Loyola University Chicago, Loyola University Museum of Art, Chicago IL
Lusaka National Museum, Lusaka
The Mariners' Museum, Newport News VA
McLean County Historical Society, McLean County Museum of History, Bloomington IL
McPherson Museum and Arts Foundation, McPherson KS
Milwaukee Public Museum, Milwaukee WI

ANTIQUITIES-ASSYRIAN

ANTIQUITIES-BYZANTINE

ANTIQUITIES-EGYPTIAN

Detroit Zoological Institute, Wildlife Interpretive Gallery, Royal Oak MI
Dickinson College, The Trout Gallery, Carlisle PA
Emory University, Michael C Carlos Museum, Atlanta GA
Evansville Museum of Arts, History & Science, Evansville IN
Everhart Museum, Scranton PA
Fairbanks Museum & Planetarium, Saint Johnsbury VT
Fetherston Foundation, Packwood House Museum, Lewisburg PA
Fine Arts Museums of San Francisco, Legion of Honor, San Francisco CA
Fitchburg Art Museum, Fitchburg MA
Florence County Museum, Florence SC
Florida State University and Central Florida Community College, The Appleton Museum of Art, Ocala FL
Freer Gallery of Art & Arthur M Sackler Gallery, Arthur M Sackler Gallery, Washington DC
Glasgow University, The Hunterian, Glasgow
Grand Rapids Art Museum, Grand Rapids MI
Grand Rapids Public Museum, Grand Rapids MI
Hamilton College, Emerson Gallery, Clinton NY
Harvard University, Semitic Museum, Cambridge MA
Hebrew Union College - Jewish Institute of Religion, Skirball Museum Cincinnati, Cincinnati OH
Hecht Museum, Haifa
Hermitage Museum & Gardens, Norfolk VA
Iredell Museums, Statesville NC
The Israel Museum, Jerusalem, Jerusalem
Johns Hopkins University, Evergreen Museum & Library, Baltimore MD
Joslyn Art Museum, Omaha NE
Kelvingrove Art Gallery & Museum, Glasgow UK
Kimbell Art Foundation, Kimbell Art Museum, Fort Worth TX
Kunsthistorisches Museum Wien, Museum of Fine Arts, Vienna
Lightner Museum, Saint Augustine FL
Lincolnshire County Council, The Collection: Art & Archaeology in Lincolnshire, Lincoln
Louisiana Arts & Science Museum, Baton Rouge LA
Mabee-Gerrer Museum of Art, Shawnee OK
The Metropolitan Museum of Art, New York NY
Michigan State University, Eli & Edythe Broad Art Museum, East Lansing MI
Milwaukee Art Museum, Milwaukee WI
Montreal Museum of Fine Arts, Montreal QC
Musees Royaux d'Art et d'Histoire, Royal Museums of Art and History, Brussels
Museo De Bellas Artes, Museum of Fine Arts, Caracas
Museo di Palazzo Ducale, Ducale Palace Museum, Mantua
The Museum, Greenwood SC
Museum of Egyptian Antiquities, Cairo
Museum of Fine Arts, Boston MA
Museum of Fine Arts, Saint Petersburg, Florida, Inc, Saint Petersburg FL
Museum of Vancouver, Vancouver BC
Muzeul de Istorie Nationala Si Arheologie Constanta, National History & Archaeology Museum, Constanta
Muzeul National de Arta al Romaniei, National Museum of Art of Romania, Bucharest
National Archaeological Museum, Athens
National Museums Scotland, National Museum of Scotland, Edinburgh
The Nelson-Atkins Museum of Art, Kansas City MO
North Carolina Museum of Art, Raleigh NC
Norwich Free Academy, Slater Memorial Museum, Norwich CT
Ohara Museum of Art, Kurashiki
Okanagan Heritage Museum, Kelowna BC
Panhandle-Plains Historical Museum, Canyon TX
Putnam Museum of History and Natural Science, Davenport IA
Pyramid Hill Sculpture Park & Museum, Hamilton OH
Queens College, City University of New York, Godwin-Ternbach Museum, Flushing NY
Reading Public Museum, Reading PA
Rollins College, George D & Harriet W Cornell Fine Arts Museum, Winter Park FL
Rosemount Museum, Inc, Pueblo CO
The Rosenbach Museum & Library, Philadelphia PA
Royal Arts Foundation, Belcourt Castle, Newport RI
Saint Anselm College, Alva de Mars Megan Chapel Art Center, Manchester NH
San Antonio Museum of Art, San Antonio TX
The San Joaquin Pioneer & Historical Society, The Haggin Museum, Stockton CA
Scripps College, Ruth Chandler Williamson Gallery, Claremont CA
Southern Baptist Theological Seminary, Joseph A Callaway Archaeological Museum, Louisville KY
The Speed Art Museum, Louisville KY
Stanford University, Cantor Arts Center at Stanford University, Stanford CA
The State Museum of Oriental Art, Moscow
State University of New York at New Paltz, Samuel Dorsky Museum of Art, New Paltz NY
Szepmuveszeti Muzeum, Museum of Fine Arts, Budapest
Toledo Museum of Art, Toledo OH
University of California, Berkeley, Phoebe Apperson Hearst Museum of Anthropology, Berkeley CA
University of Illinois at Urbana-Champaign, Krannert Art Museum and Kinkead Pavilion, Champaign IL
University of Illinois at Urbana-Champaign, Spurlock Museum, Urbana IL
University of Miami, Lowe Art Museum, Coral Gables FL
University of Michigan, Kelsey Museum of Archaeology, Ann Arbor MI
University of Notre Dame, Snite Museum of Art, Notre Dame IN
University of Richmond, University Museums, Richmond VA
University of Utah, Utah Museum of Fine Arts, Salt Lake City UT
Vassar College, The Frances Lehman Loeb Art Center, Poughkeepsie NY
Virginia Museum of Fine Arts, Richmond VA
Walters Art Museum, Baltimore MD
Worcester Art Museum, Worcester MA
World Erotic Art Museum, Miami Beach FL

ANTIQUITIES-ETRUSCAN

Academy of the New Church, Glencairn Museum, Bryn Athyn PA
Amherst College, Mead Art Museum, Amherst MA
Arnot Art Museum, Elmira NY
Baroda Museum and Picture Gallery, Vadodara
Berkshire Museum, Pittsfield MA
Brown University, Haffenreffer Museum of Anthropology, Providence RI
Bucknell University, Edward & Marthann Samek Art Gallery, Lewisburg PA
The Buffalo Fine Arts Academy, Albright-Knox Art Gallery, Buffalo NY
Cincinnati Art Museum, Cincinnati Art Museum, Cincinnati OH
Cornell Museum of Art and American Culture, Delray Beach FL
Crocker Art Museum, Sacramento CA
Dallas Museum of Art, Dallas TX
Dartmouth College, Hood Museum of Art, Hanover NH
Detroit Institute of Arts, Detroit MI
Emory University, Michael C Carlos Museum, Atlanta GA
Fetherston Foundation, Packwood House Museum, Lewisburg PA
Fine Arts Museums of San Francisco, Legion of Honor, San Francisco CA
Florence County Museum, Florence SC
Florida State University and Central Florida Community College, The Appleton Museum of Art, Ocala FL
Hecht Museum, Haifa
The Israel Museum, Jerusalem, Jerusalem
Kimbell Art Foundation, Kimbell Art Museum, Fort Worth TX
Kunsthistorisches Museum Wien, Museum of Fine Arts, Vienna
The Metropolitan Museum of Art, New York NY
Michigan State University, Eli & Edythe Broad Art Museum, East Lansing MI
Montreal Museum of Fine Arts, Montreal QC
Musee des Beaux-Arts de Tours, Museum of Fine Arts, Tours
Musees Royaux d'Art et d'Histoire, Royal Museums of Art and History, Brussels
Museum of Fine Arts, Saint Petersburg, Florida, Inc, Saint Petersburg FL
Museum zu Allerheiligen, Schaffhausen
Muzeul de Istorie Nationala Si Arheologie Constanta, National History & Archaeology Museum, Constanta
National Archaeological Museum, Athens
Norwich Free Academy, Slater Memorial Museum, Norwich CT
Putnam Museum of History and Natural Science, Davenport IA
Pyramid Hill Sculpture Park & Museum, Hamilton OH
Queens College, City University of New York, Godwin-Ternbach Museum, Flushing NY
Reading Public Museum, Reading PA
Rollins College, George D & Harriet W Cornell Fine Arts Museum, Winter Park FL
Saginaw Art Museum, Saginaw MI
The Speed Art Museum, Louisville KY
Staatliche Museen zu Berlin Stiftung Preussischer Kulturbesitz, National Museums in Berlin, Prussian Cultural Heritage Foundation, Berlin
Stanford University, Cantor Arts Center at Stanford University, Stanford CA
Tampa Museum of Art, Tampa FL
University of California, Berkeley, Phoebe Apperson Hearst Museum of Anthropology, Berkeley CA
University of Wisconsin-Madison, Chazen Museum of Art, Madison WI
Vassar College, The Frances Lehman Loeb Art Center, Poughkeepsie NY
Walters Art Museum, Baltimore MD
Wheaton College, Beard and Weil Galleries, Norton MA
World Erotic Art Museum, Miami Beach FL

ANTIQUITIES-GREEK

Academy of the New Church, Glencairn Museum, Bryn Athyn PA
Acropolis Museum, Athens
Albany Museum of Art, Albany GA
Amherst College, Mead Art Museum, Amherst MA
Archaeological Museum of Olympia, Olympia
Archaeological Museum of Thessaloniki, Thessaloniki
Arnot Art Museum, Elmira NY
Art Without Walls Inc, Sayville NY
Bangladesh National Museum, Dhaka
Baroda Museum and Picture Gallery, Vadodara
Beloit College, Wright Museum of Art, Beloit WI
Berkshire Museum, Pittsfield MA
Blanden Memorial Art Museum, Fort Dodge IA
Bob Jones University Museum & Gallery Inc, Greenville SC
Brown University, Haffenreffer Museum of Anthropology, Providence RI
Bucknell University, Edward & Marthann Samek Art Gallery, Lewisburg PA
The Buffalo Fine Arts Academy, Albright-Knox Art Gallery, Buffalo NY
Byzantine & Christian Museum, Athens, Athens
C W Post Campus of Long Island University, Hillwood Art Museum, Brookville NY
Carleton College, Art Gallery, Northfield MN
The Children's Museum of Indianapolis, Indianapolis IN
Chrysler Museum of Art, Norfolk VA
Cincinnati Art Museum, Cincinnati Art Museum, Cincinnati OH
The Cleveland Museum of Art, Cleveland OH
Corcoran Gallery of Art, Washington DC
Crocker Art Museum, Sacramento CA
Cyprus Museum, Nicosia
Dallas Museum of Art, Dallas TX
Dartmouth College, Hood Museum of Art, Hanover NH
Delphi Archaeological Museum, Delphi
Detroit Institute of Arts, Detroit MI
Dumbarton Oaks, Dumbarton Oaks Museum, Washington DC
Emory University, Michael C Carlos Museum, Atlanta GA
Everhart Museum, Scranton PA
Fetherston Foundation, Packwood House Museum, Lewisburg PA
Fine Arts Museums of San Francisco, Legion of Honor, San Francisco CA
Fitchburg Art Museum, Fitchburg MA
Florence County Museum, Florence SC
Florida State University and Central Florida Community College, The Appleton Museum of Art, Ocala FL
Forest Lawn Museum, Glendale CA

ANTIQUITIES-ORIENTAL

ANTIQUITIES-PERSIAN

Florida State University and Central Florida Community College, The Appleton Museum of Art, Ocala FL
Freer Gallery of Art & Arthur M Sackler Gallery, Arthur M Sackler Gallery, Washington DC
Harvard University, Semitic Museum, Cambridge MA
Hecht Museum, Haifa
Henry County Museum & Cultural Arts Center, Clinton MO
Hermitage Museum & Gardens, Norfolk VA
Huntington Museum of Art, Huntington WV
The Israel Museum, Jerusalem, Jerusalem
Jacksonville University, Alexander Brest Museum & Gallery, Jacksonville FL
Johns Hopkins University, Evergreen Museum & Library, Baltimore MD
Kimbell Art Foundation, Kimbell Art Museum, Fort Worth TX
Kunsthistorisches Museum Wien, Museum of Fine Arts, Vienna
Lahore Museum, Lahore
Mabee-Gerrer Museum of Art, Shawnee OK
The Metropolitan Museum of Art, New York NY
Michigan State University, Eli & Edythe Broad Art Museum, East Lansing MI
The Mint Museum, Charlotte NC
Montreal Museum of Fine Arts, Montreal QC
Musees Royaux d'Art et d'Histoire, Royal Museums of Art and History, Brussels
The Museum of Arts & Sciences Inc, Daytona Beach FL
Museum of Fine Arts, Saint Petersburg, Florida, Inc, Saint Petersburg FL
Museum of Islamic Art, Doha
Museum zu Allerheiligen, Schaffhausen
Muzeul National de Arta al Romaniei, National Museum of Art of Romania, Bucharest
National Art Museum of Moldova, Chisinau
Norwich Free Academy, Slater Memorial Museum, Norwich CT
Ohara Museum of Art, Kurashiki
Putnam Museum of History and Natural Science, Davenport IA
Reading Public Museum, Reading PA
Royal Arts Foundation, Belcourt Castle, Newport RI
The Speed Art Museum, Louisville KY
Staatliche Museen zu Berlin Stiftung Preussischer Kulturbesitz, National Museums in Berlin, Prussian Cultural Heritage Foundation, Berlin
Stanford University, Cantor Arts Center at Stanford University, Stanford CA
The State Museum of Oriental Art, Moscow
The University of Kentucky Art Museum, Lexington KY
University of Notre Dame, Snite Museum of Art, Notre Dame IN
Walters Art Museum, Baltimore MD
Woodmere Art Museum Inc, Philadelphia PA
World Erotic Art Museum, Miami Beach FL

ANTIQUITIES-ROMAN

Academy of the New Church, Glencairn Museum, Bryn Athyn PA
Acropolis Museum, Athens
Albany Museum of Art, Albany GA
Amherst College, Mead Art Museum, Amherst MA
Archaeological Museum of Olympia, Olympia
Archaeological Museum of Thessaloniki, Thessaloniki
Art Without Walls Inc, Sayville NY
Bangladesh National Museum, Dhaka
Baroda Museum and Picture Gallery, Vadodara
Beloit College, Wright Museum of Art, Beloit WI
Blanden Memorial Art Museum, Fort Dodge IA
Bob Jones University Museum & Gallery Inc, Greenville SC
Bucknell University, Edward & Marthann Samek Art Gallery, Lewisburg PA
The Buffalo Fine Arts Academy, Albright-Knox Art Gallery, Buffalo NY
C W Post Campus of Long Island University, Hillwood Art Museum, Brookville NY
Carleton College, Art Gallery, Northfield MN
Cedar Rapids Museum of Art, Cedar Rapids IA
The Children's Museum of Indianapolis, Indianapolis IN
Chrysler Museum of Art, Norfolk VA
Cincinnati Art Museum, Cincinnati Art Museum, Cincinnati OH
The Cleveland Museum of Art, Cleveland OH
Crocker Art Museum, Sacramento CA
Cyprus Museum, Nicosia
Dallas Museum of Art, Dallas TX
Delphi Archaeological Museum, Delphi
Detroit Institute of Arts, Detroit MI
Dickinson College, The Trout Gallery, Carlisle PA
Doncaster Museum and Art Gallery, Doncaster Yorks
Dumbarton Oaks, Dumbarton Oaks Museum, Washington DC
Emory University, Michael C Carlos Museum, Atlanta GA
Everhart Museum, Scranton PA
Fetherston Foundation, Packwood House Museum, Lewisburg PA
Fine Arts Museums of San Francisco, Legion of Honor, San Francisco CA
Fitchburg Art Museum, Fitchburg MA
Florence County Museum, Florence SC
Florida State University and Central Florida Community College, The Appleton Museum of Art, Ocala FL
Forest Lawn Museum, Glendale CA
Freer Gallery of Art & Arthur M Sackler Gallery, Arthur M Sackler Gallery, Washington DC
Glasgow University, The Hunterian, Glasgow
Harvard University, Semitic Museum, Cambridge MA
Hebrew Union College - Jewish Institute of Religion, Skirball Museum Cincinnati, Cincinnati OH
Hecht Museum, Haifa
Hermitage Museum & Gardens, Norfolk VA
Iredell Museums, Statesville NC
Isabella Stewart Gardner Museum, Boston MA
The Israel Museum, Jerusalem, Jerusalem
James Madison University, Duke Hall Gallery of Fine Art, Harrisonburg VA
Johns Hopkins University, Evergreen Museum & Library, Baltimore MD
Joslyn Art Museum, Omaha NE
Kelvingrove Art Gallery & Museum, Glasgow UK
Kenosha Public Museums, Kenosha WI
Kimbell Art Foundation, Kimbell Art Museum, Fort Worth TX
Kunsthistorisches Museum Wien, Museum of Fine Arts, Vienna
Le Grand Curtius, The Grand Curtius, Liege
Lightner Museum, Saint Augustine FL
Lincolnshire County Council, The Collection: Art & Archaeology in Lincolnshire, Lincoln
Louisiana Arts & Science Museum, Baton Rouge LA
Mabee-Gerrer Museum of Art, Shawnee OK
Massillon Museum, Massillon OH
The Metropolitan Museum of Art, New York NY
Michigan State University, Eli & Edythe Broad Art Museum, East Lansing MI
Milwaukee Art Museum, Milwaukee WI
Minneapolis Institute of Art, Minneapolis MN
The Mint Museum, Charlotte NC
Mobile Museum of Art, Mobile AL
Montreal Museum of Fine Arts, Montreal QC
Musee des Beaux-Arts de Tours, Museum of Fine Arts, Tours
Musees Royaux d'Art et d'Histoire, Royal Museums of Art and History, Brussels
Museo di Palazzo Ducale, Ducale Palace Museum, Mantua
The Museum, Greenwood SC
Museum of Cycladic Art, Athens
Museum of Fine Arts, Boston MA
Museum of Fine Arts, Saint Petersburg, Florida, Inc, Saint Petersburg FL
Museum of Vancouver, Vancouver BC
Museum zu Allerheiligen, Schaffhausen
Muzeul de Istorie Nationala Si Arheologie Constanta, National History & Archaeology Museum, Constanta
Muzeul National de Arta al Romaniei, National Museum of Art of Romania, Bucharest
National Archaeological Museum, Athens
National Art Museum of Moldova, Chisinau
National Museums Scotland, National Museum of Scotland, Edinburgh
The Nelson-Atkins Museum of Art, Kansas City MO
New Brunswick Museum, Saint John NB
North Carolina Museum of Art, Raleigh NC
Norwich Free Academy, Slater Memorial Museum, Norwich CT
Okanagan Heritage Museum, Kelowna BC
Panhandle-Plains Historical Museum, Canyon TX
Putnam Museum of History and Natural Science, Davenport IA
Pyramid Hill Sculpture Park & Museum, Hamilton OH
Queen's University, Agnes Etherington Art Centre, Kingston ON
Queens College, City University of New York, Godwin-Ternbach Museum, Flushing NY
Reading Public Museum, Reading PA
Rollins College, George D & Harriet W Cornell Fine Arts Museum, Winter Park FL
San Antonio Museum of Art, San Antonio TX
The San Joaquin Pioneer & Historical Society, The Haggin Museum, Stockton CA
Santa Barbara Museum of Art, Santa Barbara CA
Scripps College, Ruth Chandler Williamson Gallery, Claremont CA
Seattle Art Museum, Seattle WA
Slovenska Narodna Galeria, Slovak National Gallery, Bratislava
The Society of the Cincinnati at Anderson House, Washington DC
The Speed Art Museum, Louisville KY
Spertus Institute of Jewish Studies, Chicago IL
St Mary's College of Maryland, The Dwight Frederick Boyden Gallery, St Mary's City MD
Staatliche Museen zu Berlin Stiftung Preussischer Kulturbesitz, National Museums in Berlin, Prussian Cultural Heritage Foundation, Berlin
Stanford University, Cantor Arts Center at Stanford University, Stanford CA
Staten Island Museum, Staten Island NY
Szepmuveszeti Muzeum, Museum of Fine Arts, Budapest
Tampa Museum of Art, Tampa FL
Toledo Museum of Art, Toledo OH
University of California, Berkeley, Phoebe Apperson Hearst Museum of Anthropology, Berkeley CA
University of Chicago, Smart Museum of Art, Chicago IL
University of Illinois at Urbana-Champaign, Krannert Art Museum and Kinkead Pavilion, Champaign IL
University of Illinois at Urbana-Champaign, Spurlock Museum, Urbana IL
The University of Kentucky Art Museum, Lexington KY
University of Miami, Lowe Art Museum, Coral Gables FL
University of Michigan, Kelsey Museum of Archaeology, Ann Arbor MI
University of Notre Dame, Snite Museum of Art, Notre Dame IN
University of Vermont, Robert Hull Fleming Museum, Burlington VT
University of Wisconsin-Madison, Chazen Museum of Art, Madison WI
Vassar College, The Frances Lehman Loeb Art Center, Poughkeepsie NY
Vizcaya Museum & Gardens, Miami FL
Vorarlberg Museum, Bregenz
Walters Art Museum, Baltimore MD
Wheaton College, Beard and Weil Galleries, Norton MA
Worcester Art Museum, Worcester MA
World Erotic Art Museum, Miami Beach FL

ARCHAEOLOGY

Academy of the New Church, Glencairn Museum, Bryn Athyn PA
Acropolis Museum, Athens
African American Museum in Philadelphia, Philadelphia PA
African Art Museum of Maryland, Columbia MD
Al Ain National Museum, Al Ain
Alaska Heritage Museum at Wells Fargo, Anchorage AK
Alaska Museum of Science & Nature, Anchorage AK
Alaska State Museum, Juneau AK
American Architectural Foundation, Museum, Washington DC
American University of Beirut Archaeological Museum, Beirut
Amherst College, Mead Art Museum, Amherst MA
Amsterdam Museum, Amsterdam
Anchorage Museum at Rasmuson Center, Anchorage AK
Archaeological Museum of Olympia, Olympia
Archaeological Museum of Thessaloniki, Thessaloniki
Archaeological Society of Ohio, Indian Museum of Lake County, Ohio, Willoughby OH
Art Without Walls Inc, Sayville NY
ArtSpace/Lima, Lima OH

Augustana University, Eide-Dalrymple Gallery, Sioux Falls SD
Aurora University, Schingoethe Center for Native American Cultures & The Schingoethe Art Gallery, Aurora IL
Balzekas Museum of Lithuanian Culture, Chicago IL
Bangladesh National Museum, Dhaka
Baroda Museum and Picture Gallery, Vadodara
Bay County Historical Society, Historical Museum of Bay County, Bay City MI
Beloit College, Wright Museum of Art, Beloit WI
Berea College, Doris Ulmann Galleries, Berea KY
Berman Museum, Anniston AL
Besser Museum for Northeast Michigan, Alpena MI
Beverly Historical Society, Cabot, Hale & Balch House Museums, Beverly MA
Bob Jones University Museum & Gallery Inc, Greenville SC
Botswana National Museum, Gaborone
Bronx Community College (CUNY), Hall of Fame for Great Americans, Bronx NY
Brown University, Haffenreffer Museum of Anthropology, Providence RI
Bruce Museum, Inc, Greenwich CT
Byzantine & Christian Museum, Athens, Athens
C M Russell Museum, Great Falls MT
California State University, East Bay, C E Smith Museum of Anthropology, Hayward CA
Calvert Marine Museum, Solomons MD
Cambridge Museum, Cambridge NE
Canadian Museum of History, Gatineau QC
Carlsbad Museum & Art Center, Carlsbad NM
Carson County Square House Museum, Panhandle TX
Cayuga Museum of History & Art, Auburn NY
Chelan County Public Utility District, Rocky Reach Dam, Wenatchee WA
The Children's Museum of Indianapolis, Indianapolis IN
City of El Paso, El Paso Museum of Archaeology, El Paso TX
The City of Petersburg Museums, Petersburg VA
Clark County Historical Society, Pioneer - Krier Museum, Ashland KS
The Columbus Museum, Columbus GA
Concord Museum, Concord MA
Coptic Museum, Cairo
County of Henrico, Meadow Farm Museum, Glen Allen VA
Crook County Museum & Art Gallery, Sundance WY
Crow Wing County Historical Society, Brainerd MN
Cyprus Museum, Nicosia
Dallas Museum of Art, Dallas TX
Delaware Division of Historical & Cultural Affairs, Dover DE
Delphi Archaeological Museum, Delphi
Department of Economic & Community Development, State of Connecticut DECD Eric Sloane Museum, Kent CT
Detroit Institute of Arts, Detroit MI
Doncaster Museum and Art Gallery, Doncaster Yorks
Edgecombe County Cultural Arts Council, Inc, Blount-Bridgers House, Hobson Pittman Memorial Gallery, Tarboro NC
Emory University, Michael C Carlos Museum, Atlanta GA
Essex Historical Society and Shipbuilding Museum, Essex MA
Everhart Museum, Scranton PA
Fairbanks Museum & Planetarium, Saint Johnsbury VT
Fairfield University, Art Museum, Fairfield CT
Farmington Village Green & Library Association, Stanley-Whitman House, Farmington CT
Fetherston Foundation, Packwood House Museum, Lewisburg PA
Fishkill Historical Society, Van Wyck Homestead Museum, Fishkill NY
Florence County Museum, Florence SC
Forges du Saint-Maurice National Historic Site, Trois Rivieres QC
Fort Morgan Heritage Foundation, Fort Morgan CO
Fort Ticonderoga Association, Ticonderoga NY
The Frank Phillips Foundation Inc, Woolaroc Museum, Bartlesville OK
Freer Gallery of Art & Arthur M Sackler Gallery, Arthur M Sackler Gallery, Washington DC
Glasgow University, The Hunterian, Glasgow
Grand Rapids Public Museum, Grand Rapids MI
Hancock Shaker Village, Inc, Pittsfield MA
Harvard University, Semitic Museum, Cambridge MA
Heard Museum, Phoenix AZ
Heart of West Texas Museum, Colorado City TX
Hebrew Union College, Skirball Cultural Center, Los Angeles CA
Hebrew Union College - Jewish Institute of Religion, Skirball Museum Cincinnati, Cincinnati OH
Hebrew Union College - Jewish Institute of Religion Museum, Jewish Institute of Religion, New York NY
Hecht Museum, Haifa
Henry County Museum & Cultural Arts Center, Clinton MO
Heras Museum for Research in Indian History and Culture, Mumbai
Herrett Center for Arts & Sciences, Jean B King Art Gallery, Twin Falls ID
Het Noordbrabants Museum, s-Hertogenbosch
High Desert Museum, Bend OR
Historic Arkansas Museum, Little Rock AR
Historic Huguenot Street, New Paltz NY
Historic Newton, Newton MA
Historical Museum at Fort Missoula, Missoula MT
Historical Society of Cheshire County, Keene NH
Historical Society of Martin County, Elliott Museum, Stuart FL
Historical Society of Rockland County, New City NY
Historisches und Volkerkundemuseum, Museum of History and Ethnology, St Gallen
The History Center in Tompkins County, Ithaca NY
History Colorado Center Museum, Denver CO
History Museum of Mobile, Mobile AL
i.d.e.a. Museum, Mesa AZ
Idaho Historical Museum, Boise ID
Illinois Historic Preservation Agency, Bishop Hill State Historic Site, Bishop Hill IL
Illinois State Museum, ISM Lockport Gallery, Chicago Gallery & Southern Illinois Art Gallery, Springfield IL
Independence Historical Museum & Art Center, Independence KS
Independence National Historical Park, Philadelphia PA
Independence Seaport Museum, Philadelphia PA
Indian Pueblo Cultural Center, Albuquerque NM
Indiana State Museum, Indianapolis IN
Institute of Puerto Rican Culture, Museo Fuerte Conde de Mirasol, Vieques PR
Institute of Puerto Rican Culture, Museo y Parque Historico Ruinas de Caparra, Guaynabo PR
Iroquois Indian Museum, Howes Cave NY
The Israel Museum, Jerusalem, Jerusalem
Istanbul Arkeoloji Muzeleri, Istanbul Archaeological Museums, Istanbul
The Jewish Museum, New York NY
Johns Hopkins University, Homewood Museum, Baltimore MD
Karakalpak State Art Museum, Nukus Republic of Karakalpakstan
Kelly-Griggs House Museum, Red Bluff CA
Kelvingrove Art Gallery & Museum, Glasgow UK
Kenosha Public Museums, Kenosha WI
Kern County Museum, Bakersfield CA
Klein Museum, Mobridge SD
Koshare Indian Museum, Inc, La Junta CO
Lac du Flambeau Band of Lake Superior Chippewa Indians, George W Brown Jr Ojibwe Museum & Cultural Center, Lac Du Flambeau WI
Lafayette Science Museum & Planetarium, Lafayette LA
Lahore Museum, Lahore
Lalit Kala Akademi Rabindra Bhavan Art Galleries, National Academy of Art, New Delhi, New Delhi
Lehigh Valley Heritage Center, Allentown PA
Lincoln County Historical Association, Inc, 1811 Old Lincoln County Jail & Lincoln County Museum, Wiscasset ME
Lincolnshire County Council, Library & Heritage Services, Lincoln
Lincolnshire County Council, The Collection: Art & Archaeology in Lincolnshire, Lincoln
Livingston County Historical Society, Museum, Geneseo NY
Loveland Museum/Gallery, Loveland CO
Lusaka National Museum, Lusaka
Maine Historical Society, MHS Museum, Portland ME
Massillon Museum, Massillon OH
Maui Historical Society, Hale Hoike ike at the Bailey House, Wailuku HI
McLean County Historical Society, McLean County Museum of History, Bloomington IL
McPherson Museum and Arts Foundation, McPherson KS
Mezuraj Museum, Tirana
Mission San Luis Rey de Francia, Mission San Luis Rey Museum, Oceanside CA
Mission San Miguel Museum, San Miguel CA
Mississippi River Museum at Mud-Island River Park, Memphis TN
Mohave Museum of History & Arts, Kingman AZ
Moncur Gallery, Boissevain MB
Montclair Art Museum, Montclair NJ
Montreal Museum of Fine Arts, Montreal QC
Morris Museum, Morristown NJ
Morris Museum of Art, Augusta GA
Mount Vernon Hotel Museum & Garden, New York NY
Musee Regional de lu Cote-Nord, Sept-Iles QC
Musees Royaux d'Art et d'Histoire, Royal Museums of Art and History, Brussels
Museo de Arte de Ponce, The Luis A Ferre Foundation Inc, Ponce PR
Museo De Las Americas, Denver CO
Museo di Palazzo Ducale, Ducale Palace Museum, Mantua
The Museum, Greenwood SC
The Museum of Arts & Sciences Inc, Daytona Beach FL
Museum of Arts & Sciences, Inc, Macon GA
Museum of Contemporary Art, Taipei, Taipei
Museum of Cycladic Art, Athens
Museum of Northern Arizona, Flagstaff AZ
Museum of Northern British Columbia, Ruth Harvey Art Gallery, Prince Rupert BC
Museum of the Southwest, Midland TX
Museum of Vancouver, Vancouver BC
Museum of West Louisiana, Leesville LA
Museum of York County, Rock Hill SC
Museum Prinsenhof Delft, Delft
Museum zu Allerheiligen, Schaffhausen
Muzeul de Istorie Nationala Si Arheologie Constanta, National History & Archaeology Museum, Constanta
Muzeul National de Arta al Romaniei, National Museum of Art of Romania, Bucharest
Muzim Negara, National Museum, Kuala Lumpur
National Archaeological Museum, Athens
National Museum & Art Gallery of Trinidad and Tobago, Port of Spain
National Museum of Ethiopia, Addis Ababa
National Museum of Ireland, Dublin
National Museum of the American Indian, George Gustav Heye Center, New York NY
National Museum of the Philippines, Manila
National Museums Scotland, National Museum of Scotland, Edinburgh
National Park Service, Hubbell Trading Post National Historic Site, Ganado AZ
Natural History Museum of Los Angeles County, Los Angeles CA
Naval Historical Center, National Museum of the US Navy, Washington DC
New Gallery of Modern Art, Charlotte NC
New Jersey Historical Society, Newark NJ
Norsk Maritimt Museum, Norwegian Maritime Museum, Oslo
Northern Maine Museum of Science, Presque Isle ME
The Ohio Historical Society, Inc, Campus Martius Museum & Ohio River Museum, Marietta OH
Okanagan Heritage Museum, Kelowna BC
Oklahoma Historical Society, State Museum of History, Oklahoma City OK
Old Jaffa Museum of Antiquities, Jaffa
Oshkosh Public Museum & Library, Oshkosh WI
Panhandle-Plains Historical Museum, Canyon TX
Pennsylvania Historical & Museum Commission, The State Museum of Pennsylvania, Harrisburg PA
Peoria Riverfront Museum, Peoria IL
Ponca City Cultural Center & Museum, Ponca City OK
Port Huron Museum, Port Huron MI
Preservation Virginia, John Marshall House, Richmond VA
Putnam Museum of History and Natural Science, Davenport IA
Red Rock Park, Red Rock Park, Church Rock NM
Riverside Metropolitan Museum, Riverside CA
Roberson Museum & Science Center, Binghamton NY
Roberts County Museum, Miami TX
Rollins College, George D & Harriet W Cornell Fine Arts Museum, Winter Park FL
Roswell Museum & Art Center, Roswell NM

Royal Alberta Museum, Royal Alberta Museum, Edmonton AB
Royal Ontario Museum, Toronto ON
Saco Museum, Saco ME
Safety Harbor Museum and Cultural Arts Center, Safety Harbor FL
Saint Joseph Museum, Inc., Saint Joseph MO
San Antonio Museum of Art, San Antonio TX
San Bernardino County Museum, Redlands CA
The San Joaquin Pioneer & Historical Society, The Haggin Museum, Stockton CA
Scripps College, Ruth Chandler Williamson Gallery, Claremont CA
Seneca-Iroquois National Museum, Salamanca NY
Shaker Village of Pleasant Hill, Harrodsburg KY
Shirley Plantation Foundation, Charles City VA
Slater Mill, Old Slater Mill Association, Pawtucket RI
Slovenska Narodna Galeria, Slovak National Gallery, Bratislava
Sooke Region Museum & Art Gallery, Sooke BC
South Street Seaport Museum, New York NY
Southern Baptist Theological Seminary, Joseph A Callaway Archaeological Museum, Louisville KY
Spertus Institute of Jewish Studies, Chicago IL
Staatliche Museen zu Berlin Stiftung Preussischer Kulturbesitz, National Museums in Berlin, Prussian Cultural Heritage Foundation, Berlin
The State Museum of Oriental Art, Moscow
Ste Genevieve Museum, Sainte Genevieve MO
Stone Quarry Hill Art Park, Winner Gallery, Cazenovia NY
Suomen Kansallismuseo, National Museum of Finland, Helsinki
Tallahassee Museum of History & Natural Science, Tallahassee FL
Thomas Jefferson Foundation, Inc, Monticello, Charlottesville VA
Tokyo National Museum, Tokyo
Trust Authority, Museum of the Great Plains, Lawton OK
Tryon Palace, New Bern NC
Turtle Bay Exploration Park, Redding CA
Turtle Mountain Chippewa Historical Society, Turtle Mountain Heritage Center, Belcourt ND
Tver Regional Art Gallery, Tver
Tyne and Wear Archives & Museums, Sunderland Museum & Winter Gardens, Sunderland
United Methodist Historical Society, Lovely Lane Museum, Baltimore MD
University of California, Berkeley, Phoebe Apperson Hearst Museum of Anthropology, Berkeley CA
University of Illinois at Urbana-Champaign, Spurlock Museum, Urbana IL
University of Victoria, The Legacy Art Gallery, Victoria BC
University of Washington, Burke Museum of Natural History and Culture, Seattle WA
University of Wisconsin-Madison, Chazen Museum of Art, Madison WI
Vassar College, The Frances Lehman Loeb Art Center, Poughkeepsie NY
Vorarlberg Museum, Bregenz
Wadsworth Atheneum Museum of Art, Hartford CT
Westfries Museum, Hoorn
Whalers Village Museum, Lahaina HI
Wisconsin Historical Society, Wisconsin Historical Museum, Madison WI
Woodlawn/The Pope-Leighey, Alexandria VA
Yellowstone County Museum, Billings MT

ARCHITECTURE

1890 House-Museum & Center for the Arts, Cortland NY
Academy of the New Church, Glencairn Museum, Bryn Athyn PA
Acropolis Museum, Athens
African Art Museum of Maryland, Columbia MD
Allentown Art Museum, Allentown PA
Alton Museum of History & Art, Inc, Alton IL
American Swedish Institute, Minneapolis MN
Archaeological Museum of Thessaloniki, Thessaloniki
Arkkitehtuurimuseo, Museum of Finnish Architecture, Helsinki
Arnot Art Museum, Elmira NY
Art Without Walls Inc, Sayville NY
Artesia Historical Museum and Art Center, Artesia NM
Arts Council of Fayetteville-Cumberland County, The Arts Center, Fayetteville NC
ArtSpace/Lima, Lima OH
Asheville Art Museum, Asheville NC
Asian Art Museum of San Francisco, Chong-Moon Lee Ctr for Asian Art and Culture, San Francisco CA
Athenaeum of Philadelphia, Philadelphia PA
Atlanta Historical Society Inc, Atlanta History Center, Atlanta GA
The Baltimore Museum of Art, Baltimore MD
Bangladesh National Museum, Dhaka
Baroda Museum and Picture Gallery, Vadodara
The Bartlett Museum, Amesbury MA
Bayerische Staatsgemaldesammlungen, Bavarian State Painting Collections, Munich
Beloit College, Wright Museum of Art, Beloit WI
Blanden Memorial Art Museum, Fort Dodge IA
Board of Parks & Recreation, The Parthenon, Nashville TN
Boston Public Library, Albert H Wiggin Gallery & Print Department, Boston MA
The Bostonian Society, Old State House Museum, Boston MA
Brick Store Museum, Kennebunk ME
Bronx Community College (CUNY), Hall of Fame for Great Americans, Bronx NY
Buffalo Niagara Heritage Village, Amherst NY
Burchfield Penney Art Center, Buffalo NY
Bush-Holley Historic Site & Storehouse Gallery, Greenwich Historical Society, Cos Cob CT
Byzantine & Christian Museum, Athens, Athens
Canadian Clay and Glass Gallery, Waterloo ON
Central United Methodist Church, Swords Into Plowshares Peace Center & Gallery, Detroit MI
Charleston Museum, Heyward-Washington House, Charleston SC
Charleston Museum, Joseph Manigault House, Charleston SC
Chateau de Versailles, Palace of Versailles, Versailles
Chatham Historical Society, The Atwood House Museum, Chatham MA
Chatillon-DeMenil House Foundation, Chatillon-DeMenil Mansion, Saint Louis MO
Chicago Architecture Foundation, Chicago IL
Chicago Athenaeum, Museum of Architecture & Design, Galena IL
Chinati Foundation, Marfa TX
The City of Petersburg Museums, Petersburg VA
Columbia County Historical Society, Luykas Van Alen House, Kinderhook NY
The Columbus Museum, Columbus GA
Contemporary Calgary, Calgary AB
County of Henrico, Meadow Farm Museum, Glen Allen VA
Craigdarroch Castle Historical Museum Society, Victoria BC
Cranbrook Art Museum, Bloomfield Hills MI
Crocker Art Museum, Sacramento CA
Crow Wing County Historical Society, Brainerd MN
The Currier Museum of Art, Manchester NH
Dallas Museum of Art, Dallas TX
Dalnavert Museum, Winnipeg MB
Danville Museum of Fine Arts & History, Danville VA
Davidson College, William H Van Every Jr & Edward M Smith Galleries, Davidson NC
Delaware Division of Historical & Cultural Affairs, Dover DE
Delaware Historical Society, Read House and Gardens, New Castle DE
DeLeon White Gallery, Toronto ON
Delphi Archaeological Museum, Delphi
Delta Blues Museum, Clarksdale MS
Denver Art Museum, Denver CO
Designmuseum Danmark, Danish Design Museum, Copenhagen
Detroit Institute of Arts, Detroit MI
Eastern Washington State Historical Society, Northwest Museum of Arts & Culture, Spokane WA
Edgecombe County Cultural Arts Council, Inc, Blount-Bridgers House, Hobson Pittman Memorial Gallery, Tarboro NC
Edsel & Eleanor Ford House, Grosse Pointe Shores MI
Elisabet Ney, Austin TX
Elmhurst Art Museum, Elmhurst IL
Elverhoj Museum of History and Art, Solvang CA
Evanston Historical Society, Charles Gates Dawes House, Evanston IL
Faaborg Museum, Faaborg
Fairbanks Museum & Planetarium, Saint Johnsbury VT
Farmington Village Green & Library Association, Stanley-Whitman House, Farmington CT
Fishkill Historical Society, Van Wyck Homestead Museum, Fishkill NY
Florence County Museum, Florence SC
Folk Art Society of America, Richmond VA
Fondazione Musei Civici Di Venezia, Museo Correr - Correr Museum, Venice
Fondazione Musei Civici Di Venezia, Ca' Rezzonico, Venice
Forest Lawn Museum, Glendale CA
Frank Lloyd Wright's, Alexandria VA
Freer Gallery of Art & Arthur M Sackler Gallery, Arthur M Sackler Gallery, Washington DC
Genesee Country Village & Museum, John L Wehle Art Gallery, Mumford NY
Georgian Court University, M Christina Geis Gallery, Lakewood NJ
Germantown Historical Society, Philadelphia PA
Girard College, Stephen Girard Collection, Philadelphia PA
Glanmore National Historic Site of Canada, Belleville ON
Glessner House Museum, Chicago IL
Hancock Shaker Village, Inc, Pittsfield MA
Headquarters Fort Monroe, Dept of Army, Casemate Museum, Hampton VA
Hebrew Union College, Skirball Cultural Center, Los Angeles CA
Hebrew Union College - Jewish Institute of Religion Museum, Jewish Institute of Religion, New York NY
Henry County Museum & Cultural Arts Center, Clinton MO
Henry Morrison Flagler Museum, Palm Beach FL
Henry Sheldon Museum of Vermont History and Research Center, Middlebury VT
Het Noordbrabants Museum, s-Hertogenbosch
High Museum of Art, Atlanta GA
Hill-Stead Museum, Farmington CT
Hillel Foundation, Hillel Jewish Student Center Gallery, Cincinnati OH
Historic Arkansas Museum, Little Rock AR
Historic Holyoke at Wistariahurst & City of Holyoke, Holyoke MA
Historic Hudson Valley, Pocantico Hills NY
Historic Huguenot Street, New Paltz NY
Historical Museum at Fort Missoula, Missoula MT
Historical Society of Cheshire County, Keene NH
Historical Society of Old Newbury, Cushing House Museum, Newburyport MA
Historical Society of Washington DC, The City Museum of Washington DC, Washington DC
The History Center in Tompkins County, Ithaca NY
The Hudson River Museum, Yonkers NY
The Huntington Library, Art Collections & Botanical Gardens, San Marino CA
The Hyde Collection, Glens Falls NY
Illinois Historic Preservation Agency, Bishop Hill State Historic Site, Bishop Hill IL
Indiana Landmarks, Morris-Butler House, Indianapolis IN
Indiana State Museum, Indianapolis IN
Institute of Contemporary Art, Los Angeles, Los Angeles CA
Institute of Puerto Rican Culture, Museo Fuerte Conde de Mirasol, Vieques PR
Intermedia Arts, Minneapolis MN
International Museum of Art, El Paso TX
The Israel Museum, Jerusalem, Jerusalem
James Dick Foundation, Festival - Institute, Round Top TX
Jefferson County Open Space, Hiwan Homestead Museum, Evergreen CO
The Jewish Museum, New York NY
Joe Gish's Old West Museum, Fredericksburg TX
Johns Hopkins University, Evergreen Museum & Library, Baltimore MD
Johns Hopkins University, Homewood Museum, Baltimore MD
Jordan National Gallery of Fine Arts, Amman
Joslyn Art Museum, Omaha NE
Karakalpak State Art Museum, Nukus Republic of Karakalpakstan
Kern County Museum, Bakersfield CA
Kimbell Art Foundation, Kimbell Art Museum, Fort Worth TX
King Kamehameha V Judiciary History Center, Honolulu HI
Kirkland Museum of Fine & Decorative Art, Denver CO
The Kreeger Museum, Washington DC

LACE (Los Angeles Contemporary Exhibitions), Los Angeles CA
Lahore Museum, Lahore
Lalit Kala Akademi Rabindra Bhavan Art Galleries, National Academy of Art, New Delhi, New Delhi
Landis Valley Village and Farm Museum, PA Historical & Museum Commission, Lancaster PA
Lehigh Valley Heritage Center, Allentown PA
Liberty Hall Historic Site, Liberty Hall Museum, Frankfort KY
Lincoln County Historical Association, Inc, 1811 Old Lincoln County Jail & Lincoln County Museum, Wiscasset ME
Livingston County Historical Society, Museum, Geneseo NY
Lockwood-Mathews Mansion Museum, Norwalk CT
Longfellow-Evangeline State Commemorative Area, Saint Martinville LA
Longue Vue House & Gardens, New Orleans LA
Louisiana Department of Culture, Recreation & Tourism, Louisiana State Museum, New Orleans LA
Loveland Museum/Gallery, Loveland CO
Loyola University Chicago, Loyola University Museum of Art, Chicago IL
Maine Historical Society, Wadsworth-Longfellow House, Portland ME
Marblehead Museum & Historical Society, Marblehead MA
Marblehead Museum & Historical Society, Jeremiah Lee Mansion, Marblehead MA
Maryland Historical Society, Museum of Maryland History, Baltimore MD
Massachusetts Institute of Technology, MIT Museum, Cambridge MA
McDowell House & Apothecary Shop, Danville KY
McLean County Historical Society, McLean County Museum of History, Bloomington IL
Meredith College, Frankie G Weems Gallery & Rotunda Gallery, Raleigh NC
Middle Border Museum & Oscar Howe Art Center, Mitchell SD
Millicent Rogers Museum, Taos NM
Milwaukee Art Museum, Milwaukee WI
The Mint Museum, Charlotte NC
Mission San Luis Rey de Francia, Mission San Luis Rey Museum, Oceanside CA
Mission San Miguel Museum, San Miguel CA
Mississippi River Museum at Mud-Island River Park, Memphis TN
Missoula Art Museum, Missoula MT
Modern Art Museum, Fort Worth TX
Moore College of Art & Design, The Galleries at Moore, Philadelphia PA
Morris Museum of Art, Augusta GA
Morris-Jumel Mansion, Inc, New York NY
Mount Vernon Hotel Museum & Garden, New York NY
MTG Hawkes Bay, Napier
Museo de Arte Contemporaneo de Castilla y Leon, Leon
Museo De Las Americas, Denver CO
Museo di Palazzo Ducale, Ducale Palace Museum, Mantua
Museum of Art & History, Santa Cruz, Santa Cruz CA
The Museum of Arts & Sciences Inc, Daytona Beach FL
Museum of Chinese in America, New York NY
Museum of Contemporary Art, North Miami FL
Museum of Modern Art, New York NY
The Museum of Western Art, Kerrville TX
Muzej za Umjetnost i Obrt, Museum of Arts & Crafts, Zagreb
Muzeul de Istorie Nationala Si Arheologie Constanta, National History & Archaeology Museum, Constanta
Muzeul National de Arta al Romaniei, National Museum of Art of Romania, Bucharest
The National Museum of Puerto Rican Arts & Culture, Chicago IL
National Park Service, Weir Farm National Historic Site, Wilton CT
National Society of Colonial Dames of America in the State of Maryland, Mount Clare Museum House, Baltimore MD
National Society of the Colonial Dames of America in The Commonwealth of Virginia, Wilton House Museum, Richmond VA
National Trust for Historic Preservation, Shadows-on-the-Teche, New Iberia LA
National Trust for Historic Preservation, Chesterwood, Stockbridge MA
Naval Historical Center, National Museum of the US Navy, Washington DC
Nebraska Game and Parks Commission, Arbor Lodge State Historical Park & Morton Mansion, Nebraska City NE
Nebraska State Capitol, Lincoln NE
Nevada Museum of Art, Reno NV
New Canaan Historical Society, New Canaan CT
New York State Office of Parks, Recreation & Historic Preservation, Staatsburgh State Historic Site, Staatsburg NY
Norwich Free Academy, Slater Memorial Museum, Norwich CT
Ogden Museum of Southern Art, University of New Orleans, New Orleans LA
Olana State Historic Site, Hudson NY
The Old Jail Art Center, Albany TX
Opelousas Museum of Art, Inc (OMA), Opelousas LA
Oshkosh Public Museum & Library, Oshkosh WI
Owensboro Museum of Fine Art, Owensboro KY
Page-Walker Arts & History Center, Cary NC
Panhandle-Plains Historical Museum, Canyon TX
Pasadena Museum of History, Pasadena CA
Patrick Henry, Red Hill National Memorial, Brookneal VA
Peabody Essex Museum, Salem MA
Pennsylvania Academy of the Fine Arts, Philadelphia PA
Philip Johnson Glass House, National Trust for Historic Preservation, New Canaan CT
Piatt Castles, West Liberty OH
Pioneer Town, Pioneer Museum of Western Art, Wimberley TX
Plumas County Museum, Quincy CA
Preservation Virginia, John Marshall House, Richmond VA
PS1 Contemporary Art Center, Long Island City NY
Pueblo Museum, Desert Hot Springs CA
Pyramid Hill Sculpture Park & Museum, Hamilton OH
Reynolda House Museum of American Art, Winston-Salem NC
Riverside Metropolitan Museum, Riverside CA
Ross Memorial Museum, Saint Andrews NB
Royal Arts Foundation, Belcourt Castle, Newport RI
Royal Ontario Museum, Toronto ON
Ryerss Victorian Museum & Library, Philadelphia PA
Saco Museum, Saco ME
Saginaw Art Museum, Saginaw MI
Saint Anselm College, Alva de Mars Megan Chapel Art Center, Manchester NH
Saint Johnsbury Athenaeum, Saint Johnsbury VT
Saint Joseph Museum, Inc., Saint Joseph MO
San Francisco Museum of Modern Art, San Francisco CA
Santarella Museum & Gardens, Tyringham MA
Seneca Falls Historical Society Museum, Seneca Falls NY
Shaker Village of Pleasant Hill, Harrodsburg KY
Sheldon Art Galleries, Saint Louis MO
Shirley Plantation Foundation, Charles City VA
Slovenska Narodna Galeria, Slovak National Gallery, Bratislava
Sonoma Valley Museum of Art, Sonoma CA
South Street Seaport Museum, New York NY
The Speed Art Museum, Louisville KY
Spertus Institute of Jewish Studies, Chicago IL
State University of New York College at Fredonia, Cathy and Jesse Marion Art Gallery, Fredonia NY
Stone Quarry Hill Art Park, Winner Gallery, Cazenovia NY
Stratford Historical Society, Catharine B Mitchell Museum, Stratford CT
Suffolk University, Gallery, Boston MA
The Summit County Historical Society of Akron, OH, Akron OH
Tacoma Art Museum, Tacoma WA
Taft Museum of Art, Cincinnati OH
Tallahassee Museum of History & Natural Science, Tallahassee FL
Taos Historic Museums, Ernest Blumenschein Home & Studio, Taos NM
Thomas Jefferson Foundation, Inc, Monticello, Charlottesville VA
Topeka & Shawnee County Public Library, Alice C Sabatini Gallery, Topeka KS
Trust Authority, Museum of the Great Plains, Lawton OK
Tryon Palace, New Bern NC
Turtle Mountain Chippewa Historical Society, Turtle Mountain Heritage Center, Belcourt ND
Tver Regional Art Gallery, Tver
United Society of Shakers, Shaker Museum, New Gloucester ME
United States Capitol, Architect of the Capitol, Washington DC
University of California, San Diego, Stuart Collection, La Jolla CA
University of Minnesota, Goldstein Museum of Design, Saint Paul MN
University of New Mexico, The Harwood Museum of Art, Taos NM
University of Victoria, The Legacy Art Gallery, Victoria BC
University of Wisconsin-Madison, Chazen Museum of Art, Madison WI
Vancouver Art Gallery, Vancouver BC
Vassar College, The Frances Lehman Loeb Art Center, Poughkeepsie NY
Vesterheim Norwegian-American Museum, Decorah IA
Victoria Mansion - Morse Libby House, Portland ME
Villa Terrace Decorative Arts Museum, Milwaukee WI
Wadsworth Atheneum Museum of Art, Hartford CT
Warner House Association, MacPheadris-Warner House, Portsmouth NH
Western Pennsylvania Conservancy, Fallingwater, Mill Run PA
Westover Plantation, Charles City VA
White House, Washington DC
Willard House & Clock Museum, Inc, North Grafton MA
William Morris Gallery, London
Wisconsin Historical Society, Wisconsin Historical Museum, Madison WI
Woodlawn/The Pope-Leighey, Alexandria VA
Woodmere Art Museum Inc, Philadelphia PA
Woodrow Wilson, Washington DC
Workman & Temple Family Homestead Museum, City of Industry CA
Wornall Majors House Museums, John Wornall House Museum, Kansas City MO
Yale University, Yale Center for British Art, New Haven CT
Yokohama Museum of Art, Yokohama

ART EDUCATION

African Art Museum of Maryland, Columbia MD
Arkkitehtuurimuseo, Museum of Finnish Architecture, Helsinki
Bangladesh National Museum, Dhaka
Baroda Museum and Picture Gallery, Vadodara
Brickton Art Center, Park Ridge IL
Burke Arts Council, Jailhouse Galleries, Morganton NC
Bush-Holley Historic Site & Storehouse Gallery, Greenwich Historical Society, Cos Cob CT
Cape Ann Museum, Gloucester MA
Craft and Folk Art Museum (CAFAM), Los Angeles CA
Designmuseum Danmark, Danish Design Museum, Copenhagen
Dublin Arts Council, Dublin OH
Elverhoj Museum of History and Art, Solvang CA
Fisher Art Gallery, Marshalltown IA
Genesee Country Village & Museum, John L Wehle Art Gallery, Mumford NY
George Phippen, Phippen Museum - Art of the American West, Prescott AZ
Hecht Museum, Haifa
Het Noordbrabants Museum, s-Hertogenbosch
High Museum of Art, Atlanta GA
International Museum of Art & Science, McAllen TX
JMW Turner Museum, Sarasota FL
Jordan National Gallery of Fine Arts, Amman
LACE (Los Angeles Contemporary Exhibitions), Los Angeles CA
Lalit Kala Akademi Rabindra Bhavan Art Galleries, National Academy of Art, New Delhi, New Delhi
Latino Art Museum, Pomona CA
Morris Museum of Art, Augusta GA
The Museum, Greenwood SC
Muzeul de Istorie Nationala Si Arheologie Constanta, National History & Archaeology Museum, Constanta
National Museum of Ceramic Art, Baltimore MD
National Silk Art Museum, Weston MO

Nelson Mandela Metropolitan Art Museum, Port Elizabeth
Nevada Museum of Art, Reno NV
New York State Office of Parks, Recreation & Historic Preservation, Staatsburgh State Historic Site, Staatsburg NY
Palm Springs Art Museum, Palm Springs CA
Rajko Mamuzic Gallery of Fine Arts, Novi Sad
San Antonio Museum of Art, San Antonio TX
Slovenska Narodna Galeria, Slovak National Gallery, Bratislava
South Dakota State University, South Dakota Art Museum, Brookings SD
Stone Quarry Hill Art Park, Winner Gallery, Cazenovia NY
Texas A&M University, J Wayne Stark University Center Galleries, College Station TX
Volcano Art Center Gallery, Hawaii Volcanoes National Park HI
Walter Anderson Museum of Art, Ocean Springs MS
Wilkes Art Gallery, North Wilkesboro NC
Yokohama Museum of Art, Yokohama

ART HISTORY

Acropolis Museum, Athens
Akron Art Museum, Akron OH
Amon Carter Museum of American Art, Fort Worth TX
Arkkitehtuurimuseo, Museum of Finnish Architecture, Helsinki
Bangladesh National Museum, Dhaka
Baroda Museum and Picture Gallery, Vadodara
Belskie Museum, Closter NJ
Berea College, Doris Ulmann Galleries, Berea KY
Birger Sandzen Memorial Gallery, Lindsborg KS
Brickton Art Center, Park Ridge IL
Bush-Holley Historic Site & Storehouse Gallery, Greenwich Historical Society, Cos Cob CT
Cape Ann Museum, Gloucester MA
Crocker Art Museum, Sacramento CA
Dalnavert Museum, Winnipeg MB
Danville Museum of Fine Arts & History, Danville VA
Designmuseum Danmark, Danish Design Museum, Copenhagen
Elverhoj Museum of History and Art, Solvang CA
Fetherston Foundation, Packwood House Museum, Lewisburg PA
Fisher Art Gallery, Marshalltown IA
Folk Art Society of America, Richmond VA
Fondazione Musei Civici Di Venezia, Ca' Pesaro Galleria Nazionale d'Arte Moderna - Ca' Pesaro Gallery of Modern Art, Venice
Galeria Mesta Bratislavy, Bratislava City Gallery, Bratislava
General Board of Discipleship, The United Methodist Church, The Upper Room Chapel & Museum, Nashville TN
Genesee Country Village & Museum, John L Wehle Art Gallery, Mumford NY
George Phippen, Phippen Museum - Art of the American West, Prescott AZ
Hecht Museum, Haifa
Het Noordbrabants Museum, s-Hertogenbosch
High Museum of Art, Atlanta GA
Historical Society of Cheshire County, Keene NH
Illinois State Museum, ISM Lockport Gallery, Chicago Gallery & Southern Illinois Art Gallery, Springfield IL
Indian Pueblo Cultural Center, Albuquerque NM
International Museum of Art & Science, McAllen TX
James Dick Foundation, Festival - Institute, Round Top TX
JMW Turner Museum, Sarasota FL
Johns Hopkins University, Evergreen Museum & Library, Baltimore MD
Jordan National Gallery of Fine Arts, Amman
Karakalpak State Art Museum, Nukus Republic of Karakalpakstan
LACE (Los Angeles Contemporary Exhibitions), Los Angeles CA
Lalit Kala Akademi Rabindra Bhavan Art Galleries, National Academy of Art, New Delhi, New Delhi
Laumeier Sculpture Park, Saint Louis MO
Lighthouse ArtCenter Museum & School of Art, Tequesta FL
Lusaka National Museum, Lusaka
Mezuraj Museum, Tirana
Mission San Luis Rey de Francia, Mission San Luis Rey Museum, Oceanside CA
Morris Museum of Art, Augusta GA
MTG Hawkes Bay, Napier
Museum of Fine Arts, Saint Petersburg, Florida, Inc, Saint Petersburg FL
Muzeul de Istorie Nationala Si Arheologie Constanta, National History & Archaeology Museum, Constanta
National Archaeological Museum, Athens
National Gallery of Ireland, Dublin
National Silk Art Museum, Weston MO
Nelson Mandela Metropolitan Art Museum, Port Elizabeth
Nevada Museum of Art, Reno NV
New York State Office of Parks, Recreation & Historic Preservation, Staatsburgh State Historic Site, Staatsburg NY
Photographic Resource Center, Inc, Cambridge MA
Rajko Mamuzic Gallery of Fine Arts, Novi Sad
Salisbury University, Ward Museum of Wildfowl Art, Salisbury MD
San Antonio Museum of Art, San Antonio TX
Springfield Art Museum, Springfield MO
Stone Quarry Hill Art Park, Winner Gallery, Cazenovia NY
Suffolk University, Gallery, Boston MA
Texas A&M University, J Wayne Stark University Center Galleries, College Station TX
United States Figure Skating Association, World Figure Skating Museum & Hall of Fame, Colorado Springs CO
University Art Gallery at California State University, Dominguez Hills, Carson CA
VU Centre De Diffusion Et De Production De La Photographie, Quebec QC
The Wallace Collection, London
Walter Anderson Museum of Art, Ocean Springs MS

ASIAN ART

Academy of the New Church, Glencairn Museum, Bryn Athyn PA
Albion College, Bobbitt Visual Arts Center, Albion MI
Amherst College, Mead Art Museum, Amherst MA
Arnot Art Museum, Elmira NY
Art Gallery of Greater Victoria, Victoria BC
Art Gallery of South Australia, Adelaide
Art Without Walls Inc, Sayville NY
ArtSpace/Lima, Lima OH
Asia Society Museum, New York NY
Asian Art Museum of San Francisco, Chong-Moon Lee Ctr for Asian Art and Culture, San Francisco CA
The Baltimore Museum of Art, Baltimore MD
Bangladesh National Museum, Dhaka
Barnes Foundation, Merion PA
Baroda Museum and Picture Gallery, Vadodara
Bayerische Staatsgemaldesammlungen, Bavarian State Painting Collections, Munich
Beloit College, Wright Museum of Art, Beloit WI
Berea College, Doris Ulmann Galleries, Berea KY
Billie Trimble Chandler, Texas State Museum of Asian Cultures, Corpus Christi TX
Birger Sandzen Memorial Gallery, Lindsborg KS
Birmingham Museum of Art, Birmingham AL
Boise Art Museum, Boise ID
Bowers Museum, Santa Ana CA
Brandeis University, Rose Art Museum, Waltham MA
Brown University, Haffenreffer Museum of Anthropology, Providence RI
Bucknell University, Edward & Marthann Samek Art Gallery, Lewisburg PA
The Buffalo Fine Arts Academy, Albright-Knox Art Gallery, Buffalo NY
C W Post Campus of Long Island University, Hillwood Art Museum, Brookville NY
California State University, Chico, Janet Turner Print Museum, CSU, Chicago, Chico CA
Cameron Art Museum, Wilmington NC
Canadian Clay and Glass Gallery, Waterloo ON
Capital University, Schumacher Gallery, Columbus OH
Carleton College, Art Gallery, Northfield MN
Center for Puppetry Arts, Atlanta GA
The Children's Museum of Indianapolis, Indianapolis IN
Children's Museum of Manhattan, New York NY
Cincinnati Art Museum, Cincinnati Art Museum, Cincinnati OH
Colgate University, Picker Art Gallery, Hamilton NY
College of William & Mary, Muscarelle Museum of Art, Williamsburg VA
The Columbus Museum, Columbus GA
Concordia Historical Institute, Saint Louis MO
Cornell University, Herbert F Johnson Museum of Art, Ithaca NY
Coutts Museum of Art, Inc, El Dorado KS
Craft and Folk Art Museum (CAFAM), Los Angeles CA
Crocker Art Museum, Sacramento CA
The Currier Museum of Art, Manchester NH
Dallas Museum of Art, Dallas TX
Dartmouth College, Hood Museum of Art, Hanover NH
Davidson College, William H Van Every Jr & Edward M Smith Galleries, Davidson NC
Delphi Archaeological Museum, Delphi
Denver Art Museum, Denver CO
Designmuseum Danmark, Danish Design Museum, Copenhagen
Detroit Institute of Arts, Detroit MI
Detroit Zoological Institute, Wildlife Interpretive Gallery, Royal Oak MI
Dickinson College, The Trout Gallery, Carlisle PA
Dublin Arts Council, Dublin OH
Edsel & Eleanor Ford House, Grosse Pointe Shores MI
Elmhurst Art Museum, Elmhurst IL
Emory University, Michael C Carlos Museum, Atlanta GA
En Foco, Inc, Bronx NY
Erie Art Museum, Erie PA
Erie County Historical Society, Erie PA
Everhart Museum, Scranton PA
Fairbanks Museum & Planetarium, Saint Johnsbury VT
Fetherston Foundation, Packwood House Museum, Lewisburg PA
Fine Arts Center for the New River Valley, Pulaski VA
Fitton Center for Creative Arts, Hamilton OH
Flint Institute of Arts, Flint MI
Florence County Museum, Florence SC
Florida State University and Central Florida Community College, The Appleton Museum of Art, Ocala FL
Folk Art Society of America, Richmond VA
Freer Gallery of Art & Arthur M Sackler Gallery, Arthur M Sackler Gallery, Washington DC
General Board of Discipleship, The United Methodist Church, The Upper Room Chapel & Museum, Nashville TN
Glanmore National Historic Site of Canada, Belleville ON
Grand Rapids Public Museum, Grand Rapids MI
Headley-Whitney Museum, Lexington KY
Heard Museum, Phoenix AZ
Henry County Museum & Cultural Arts Center, Clinton MO
Hill-Stead Museum, Farmington CT
Hillwood Museum & Gardens Foundation, Hillwood Estate Museum & Gardens, Washington DC
Historisches und Volkerkundemuseum, Museum of History and Ethnology, St Gallen
Honolulu Museum of Art, Honolulu HI
The Hyde Collection, Glens Falls NY
Idemitsu Museum of Arts, Tokyo
Institute of Contemporary Art, Los Angeles, Los Angeles CA
The Interchurch Center, Galleries at the Interchurch Center, New York NY
International Museum of Art, El Paso TX
The Israel Museum, Jerusalem, Jerusalem
Jacksonville University, Alexander Brest Museum & Gallery, Jacksonville FL
Jacques Marchais Museum of Tibetan Art, Staten Island NY
James Madison University, Duke Hall Gallery of Fine Art, Harrisonburg VA
Johns Hopkins University, Evergreen Museum & Library, Baltimore MD
Jordan National Gallery of Fine Arts, Amman
Joslyn Art Museum, Omaha NE
Kenosha Public Museums, Kenosha WI
Kimbell Art Foundation, Kimbell Art Museum, Fort Worth TX
LA County Museum of Art, Los Angeles CA
La Salle University Art Museum, Philadelphia PA
Lahore Museum, Lahore
Lalit Kala Akademi Rabindra Bhavan Art Galleries, National Academy of Art, New Delhi, New Delhi
Lawrence University, Wriston Art Center Galleries, Appleton WI
Lightner Museum, Saint Augustine FL
Lillian & Coleman Taube Museum of Art, Minot ND

Lizzadro Museum of Lapidary Art, Elmhurst IL
Los Angeles County Museum of Art, Los Angeles CA
Louise Hopkins Underwood Center for the Arts, Lubbock TX
Mabee-Gerrer Museum of Art, Shawnee OK
Macau Museum of Art, NAPE
Mathaf: Arab Museum of Modern Art, Doha
McPherson Museum and Arts Foundation, McPherson KS
Memphis Brooks Museum of Art, Memphis TN
The Metropolitan Museum of Art, New York NY
Metropolitan Museum of Manila, Manila
Michigan State University, Eli & Edythe Broad Art Museum, East Lansing MI
The Mint Museum, Charlotte NC
Mississippi Museum of Art, Jackson MS
Mobile Museum of Art, Mobile AL
Montreal Museum of Fine Arts, Montreal QC
Morris Museum, Morristown NJ
Musee des Beaux-Arts de Tours, Museum of Fine Arts, Tours
Musees Royaux d'Art et d'Histoire, Royal Museums of Art and History, Brussels
The Museum, Greenwood SC
Museum fur Angewandte Kunst Frankfurt, Museum of Applied Arts, Frankfurt
The Museum of Arts & Sciences Inc, Daytona Beach FL
Museum of Chinese in America, New York NY
Museum of Contemporary Art Chicago, Chicago IL
Museum of Fine Arts, Houston, Houston TX
Museum of Fine Arts, Saint Petersburg, Florida, Inc, Saint Petersburg FL
Museum of Vancouver, Vancouver BC
Museum zu Allerheiligen, Schaffhausen
Muzeul National de Arta al Romaniei, National Museum of Art of Romania, Bucharest
Muzim Negara, National Museum, Kuala Lumpur
Nara Kokuritsu Hakubutsu-Kan, Nara National Museum, Nara
The National Art Center, Tokyo, Tokyo
National Gallery of Canada, Ottawa ON
National Museum of the Philippines, Manila
National Museum of Women in the Arts, Washington DC
Naval Historical Center, National Museum of the US Navy, Washington DC
Nelson Mandela Metropolitan Art Museum, Port Elizabeth
The Nelson-Atkins Museum of Art, Kansas City MO
New Orleans Museum of Art, New Orleans LA
New Visions Gallery, Inc, Marshfield WI
Norton Simon Museum, Pasadena CA
Norwich Free Academy, Slater Memorial Museum, Norwich CT
Noyes Art Gallery, Lincoln NE
Oakland University, Oakland University Art Gallery, Rochester MI
Oberlin College, Allen Memorial Art Museum, Oberlin OH
Ohara Museum of Art, Kurashiki
Okanagan Heritage Museum, Kelowna BC
The Old Jail Art Center, Albany TX
Owensboro Museum of Fine Art, Owensboro KY
Palm Beach County Parks & Recreation Department, Morikami Museum & Japanese Gardens, Delray Beach FL
Panhandle-Plains Historical Museum, Canyon TX
Peabody Essex Museum, Salem MA
Philbrook Museum of Art, Tulsa OK
Phoenix Art Museum, Phoenix AZ
Plumas County Museum, Quincy CA
Polk Museum of Art, Lakeland FL
The Pomona College, Claremont CA
Portland Art Museum, Portland OR
Principia College, School of Nations Museum, Elsah IL
Putnam Museum of History and Natural Science, Davenport IA
Queens College, City University of New York, Godwin-Ternbach Museum, Flushing NY
Reading Public Museum, Reading PA
Rollins College, George D & Harriet W Cornell Fine Arts Museum, Winter Park FL
Royal Arts Foundation, Belcourt Castle, Newport RI
Royal Ontario Museum, Toronto ON
Rubin Museum of Art, New York NY
Ryerss Victorian Museum & Library, Philadelphia PA
Saginaw Art Museum, Saginaw MI
Saint Olaf College, Flaten Art Museum, Northfield MN
San Antonio Museum of Art, San Antonio TX
The San Joaquin Pioneer & Historical Society, The Haggin Museum, Stockton CA
Santa Barbara Museum of Art, Santa Barbara CA
Scripps College, Ruth Chandler Williamson Gallery, Claremont CA
Seattle Art Museum, Seattle WA
Sheldon Art Galleries, Saint Louis MO
Singapore Art Museum, Singapore
The Society of the Cincinnati at Anderson House, Washington DC
The Speed Art Museum, Louisville KY
Springfield Art Museum, Springfield MO
St Mary's College of Maryland, The Dwight Frederick Boyden Gallery, St Mary's City MD
Staatliche Museen zu Berlin Stiftung Preussischer Kulturbesitz, National Museums in Berlin, Prussian Cultural Heritage Foundation, Berlin
Stanford University, Cantor Arts Center at Stanford University, Stanford CA
The State Museum of Fine Arts of Tatarstan Republic, Kazan
The State Museum of Oriental Art, Moscow
State University of New York at New Paltz, Samuel Dorsky Museum of Art, New Paltz NY
State University of New York at Plattsburgh, Art Museum, Plattsburgh NY
Stone Quarry Hill Art Park, Winner Gallery, Cazenovia NY
Suomen Kansallismuseo, National Museum of Finland, Helsinki
Tacoma Art Museum, Tacoma WA
Taft Museum of Art, Cincinnati OH
Tokyo National Museum, Tokyo
Topeka & Shawnee County Public Library, Alice C Sabatini Gallery, Topeka KS
Tver Regional Art Gallery, Tver
Tyler Museum of Art, Tyler TX
University of California, Berkeley, Phoebe Apperson Hearst Museum of Anthropology, Berkeley CA
University of California, Davis, Jan Shrem and Maria Manetti Shrem Museum of Art, Davis CA
University of Chicago, Smart Museum of Art, Chicago IL
University of Florida, Samuel P Harn Museum of Art, Gainesville FL
University of Georgia, Georgia Museum of Art, Athens GA
University of Houston, Blaffer Art Museum, Houston TX
University of Illinois at Urbana-Champaign, Krannert Art Museum and Kinkead Pavilion, Champaign IL
University of Illinois at Urbana-Champaign, Spurlock Museum, Urbana IL
University of Kansas, Spencer Museum of Art, Lawrence KS
The University of Kentucky Art Museum, Lexington KY
University of Mary Washington, University of Mary Washington Galleries, Fredericksburg VA
University of Miami, Lowe Art Museum, Coral Gables FL
University of Nevada, Reno, Sheppard Contemporary & University Galleries, Reno NV
University of North Carolina at Greensboro, Weatherspoon Art Museum, Greensboro NC
University of Richmond, University Museums, Richmond VA
University of Utah, Utah Museum of Fine Arts, Salt Lake City UT
University of Victoria, The Legacy Art Gallery, Victoria BC
University of Washington, Burke Museum of Natural History and Culture, Seattle WA
University of Wisconsin-Madison, Chazen Museum of Art, Madison WI
Vancouver Art Gallery, Vancouver BC
Vassar College, The Frances Lehman Loeb Art Center, Poughkeepsie NY
Villa Terrace Decorative Arts Museum, Milwaukee WI
Virginia Museum of Fine Arts, Richmond VA
Walters Art Museum, Baltimore MD
Washburn University, Mulvane Art Museum, Topeka KS
Wheaton College, Beard and Weil Galleries, Norton MA
Wing Luke Asian Museum, Seattle WA
Woodmere Art Museum Inc, Philadelphia PA
Worcester Art Museum, Worcester MA
World Erotic Art Museum, Miami Beach FL
Yokohama Museum of Art, Yokohama
Zigler Art Museum, Jennings LA

BAROQUE ART

Allentown Art Museum, Allentown PA
Amherst College, Mead Art Museum, Amherst MA
Arnot Art Museum, Elmira NY
Art Gallery of Hamilton, Hamilton ON
Art Without Walls Inc, Sayville NY
Baroda Museum and Picture Gallery, Vadodara
Bass Museum of Art, Miami Beach FL
Bayerisches Nationalmuseum, Bavarian National Museum, Munich
Beloit College, Wright Museum of Art, Beloit WI
Birmingham Museum of Art, Birmingham AL
Blanden Memorial Art Museum, Fort Dodge IA
Bob Jones University Museum & Gallery Inc, Greenville SC
Bruce Museum, Inc, Greenwich CT
Bucknell University, Edward & Marthann Samek Art Gallery, Lewisburg PA
The Buffalo Fine Arts Academy, Albright-Knox Art Gallery, Buffalo NY
Canadian Clay and Glass Gallery, Waterloo ON
Cincinnati Art Museum, Cincinnati Art Museum, Cincinnati OH
City of El Paso, El Paso TX
College of William & Mary, Muscarelle Museum of Art, Williamsburg VA
Cornell College, Peter Paul Luce Gallery, Mount Vernon IA
The Courtauld Institute of Art, The Courtauld Gallery, London
Crocker Art Museum, Sacramento CA
The Currier Museum of Art, Manchester NH
Dallas Museum of Art, Dallas TX
Dartmouth College, Hood Museum of Art, Hanover NH
Denver Art Museum, Denver CO
Designmuseum Danmark, Danish Design Museum, Copenhagen
Detroit Institute of Arts, Detroit MI
Dickinson College, The Trout Gallery, Carlisle PA
Fairfield University, Art Museum, Fairfield CT
Fine Arts Center for the New River Valley, Pulaski VA
Flint Institute of Arts, Flint MI
Fondazione Musei Civici Di Venezia, Ca' Rezzonico, Venice
Galleria Nazionale dell'Umbria, Umbrian National Gallery, Perugia
Hartwick College, Foreman Gallery, Oneonta NY
Het Noordbrabants Museum, s-Hertogenbosch
The Huntington Library, Art Collections & Botanical Gardens, San Marino CA
The Hyde Collection, Glens Falls NY
The Israel Museum, Jerusalem, Jerusalem
Kereszteny Muzeum, Christian Museum, Esztergom
Kimbell Art Foundation, Kimbell Art Museum, Fort Worth TX
Kunsthistorisches Museum Wien, Museum of Fine Arts, Vienna
Kunstmuseum Solothurn, Solothurn Art Museum, Solothurn
Kyiv Museum of Russian Art, Kyiv Ukrainian
La Salle University Art Museum, Philadelphia PA
Lahore Museum, Lahore
Le Grand Curtius, The Grand Curtius, Liege
Loyola University Chicago, Loyola University Museum of Art, Chicago IL
Michigan State University, Eli & Edythe Broad Art Museum, East Lansing MI
The Mint Museum, Charlotte NC
Montreal Museum of Fine Arts, Montreal QC
Moravska Galerie v Brne, Moravian Gallery in Brno, Brno
Musee des Beaux-Arts de Tours, Museum of Fine Arts, Tours
Museen der Stadt Koln, Wallraf-Richartz-Museum & Fondation Corboud - Wallraf-Richartz Museum & Corboud Foundation, Cologne
Musees Royaux d'Art et d'Histoire, Royal Museums of Art and History, Brussels
Museo De Las Americas, Denver CO
Museo di Palazzo Ducale, Ducale Palace Museum, Mantua
Museum fur Angewandte Kunst Frankfurt, Museum of Applied Arts, Frankfurt
The Museum of Arts & Sciences Inc, Daytona Beach FL

Museum of Fine Arts, Houston, Houston TX
Museum Plantin-Moretus, Antwerp
Museum zu Allerheiligen, Schaffhausen
Muzej za Umjetnost i Obrt, Museum of Arts & Crafts, Zagreb
Muzeul National de Arta al Romaniei, National Museum of Art of Romania, Bucharest
Muzeum Narodowe W Kielcach, National Museum in Kielce, Kielce
Muzeum Narodowe w Poznaniu, National Museum in Poznan, Poznan
Narodna Galerija, National Gallery of Slovenia, Ljubljana
National Gallery of Canada, Ottawa ON
The National Museum of Western Art, Tokyo
The Nelson-Atkins Museum of Art, Kansas City MO
North Carolina Museum of Art, Raleigh NC
Noyes Art Gallery, Lincoln NE
Osterreichische Galerie Belvedere Vienna, Belvedere Museum Vienna, Vienna
Panhandle-Plains Historical Museum, Canyon TX
Phoenix Art Museum, Phoenix AZ
Queens College, City University of New York, Godwin-Ternbach Museum, Flushing NY
Reading Public Museum, Reading PA
Rollins College, George D & Harriet W Cornell Fine Arts Museum, Winter Park FL
San Angelo Museum of Fine Arts, San Angelo TX
San Antonio Museum of Art, San Antonio TX
San Diego Museum of Art, San Diego CA
Slovenska Narodna Galeria, Slovak National Gallery, Bratislava
The Society of the Cincinnati at Anderson House, Washington DC
Southern Methodist University, Meadows Museum, Dallas TX
The Speed Art Museum, Louisville KY
Staatliche Museen zu Berlin Stiftung Preussischer Kulturbesitz, National Museums in Berlin, Prussian Cultural Heritage Foundation, Berlin
Stanford University, Cantor Arts Center at Stanford University, Stanford CA
The State Museum of Fine Arts of Tatarstan Republic, Kazan
Staten Island Museum, Staten Island NY
Suomen Kansallismuseo, National Museum of Finland, Helsinki
Szepmuveszeti Muzeum, Museum of Fine Arts, Budapest
Timken Museum of Art, San Diego CA
Tver Regional Art Gallery, Tver
University of Chicago, Smart Museum of Art, Chicago IL
University of Georgia, Georgia Museum of Art, Athens GA
University of Illinois at Urbana-Champaign, Krannert Art Museum and Kinkead Pavilion, Champaign IL
University of Kansas, Spencer Museum of Art, Lawrence KS
The University of Kentucky Art Museum, Lexington KY
University of Miami, Lowe Art Museum, Coral Gables FL
University of Nevada, Reno, Sheppard Contemporary & University Galleries, Reno NV
University of Notre Dame, Snite Museum of Art, Notre Dame IN
University of Richmond, University Museums, Richmond VA
University of Texas at Austin, Blanton Museum of Art, Austin TX
University of Utah, Utah Museum of Fine Arts, Salt Lake City UT
University of Wisconsin-Madison, Chazen Museum of Art, Madison WI
Wadsworth Atheneum Museum of Art, Hartford CT
Walker Art Gallery, Liverpool
Walters Art Museum, Baltimore MD
Wheaton College, Beard and Weil Galleries, Norton MA
Worcester Art Museum, Worcester MA

BOOKPLATES & BINDINGS

Adams National Historic Park, Quincy MA
Artspace, Richmond VA
Athenaeum of Philadelphia, Philadelphia PA
Beloit College, Wright Museum of Art, Beloit WI
Brick Store Museum, Kennebunk ME
C W Post Campus of Long Island University, Hillwood Art Museum, Brookville NY
Cameron Art Museum, Wilmington NC
Canadian Museum of History, Gatineau QC
College of William & Mary, Muscarelle Museum of Art, Williamsburg VA
Cripple Creek District Museum, Cripple Creek CO
Crocker Art Museum, Sacramento CA
The Currier Museum of Art, Manchester NH
Farmington Village Green & Library Association, Stanley-Whitman House, Farmington CT
Fort Ticonderoga Association, Ticonderoga NY
Freer Gallery of Art & Arthur M Sackler Gallery, Arthur M Sackler Gallery, Washington DC
Fuller Craft Museum, Brockton MA
Germantown Historical Society, Philadelphia PA
Glessner House Museum, Chicago IL
Hebrew Union College - Jewish Institute of Religion Museum, Jewish Institute of Religion, New York NY
Hillwood Museum & Gardens Foundation, Hillwood Estate Museum & Gardens, Washington DC
Independence Seaport Museum, Philadelphia PA
The Interchurch Center, Galleries at the Interchurch Center, New York NY
JMW Turner Museum, Sarasota FL
Johns Hopkins University, Evergreen Museum & Library, Baltimore MD
La Casa del Libro Museum, San Juan PR
Lafayette Science Museum & Planetarium, Lafayette LA
Lauren Rogers, Laurel MS
Lusaka National Museum, Lusaka
The Mariners' Museum, Newport News VA
Minnesota State University, Mankato, Mankato MN
Moravska Galerie v Brne, Moravian Gallery in Brno, Brno
Museum Plantin-Moretus, Antwerp
Muzej za Umjetnost i Obrt, Museum of Arts & Crafts, Zagreb
Muzeul National de Arta al Romaniei, National Museum of Art of Romania, Bucharest
National Gallery of Canada, Ottawa ON
National Gallery of Ireland, Dublin
Natural History Museum of Los Angeles County, Los Angeles CA
Panhandle-Plains Historical Museum, Canyon TX
Shirley Plantation Foundation, Charles City VA
The Society of the Cincinnati at Anderson House, Washington DC
South Carolina Artisans Center, Walterboro SC
Spertus Institute of Jewish Studies, Chicago IL
Stanford University, Cantor Arts Center at Stanford University, Stanford CA
Tver Regional Art Gallery, Tver
United Methodist Historical Society, Lovely Lane Museum, Baltimore MD
University of Georgia, Georgia Museum of Art, Athens GA
Valley Art Gallery, Forest Grove OR
Woodmere Art Museum Inc, Philadelphia PA
Yale University, Yale Center for British Art, New Haven CT

BRONZES

Acropolis Museum, Athens
African Art Museum of Maryland, Columbia MD
Al Ain National Museum, Al Ain
Albin Polasek Museum & Sculpture Gardens, Winter Park FL
Albuquerque Museum of Art & History, Albuquerque NM
Allentown Art Museum, Allentown PA
Alton Museum of History & Art, Inc, Alton IL
American Sport Art Museum and Archives, Daphne AL
American University of Beirut Archaeological Museum, Beirut
Amherst College, Mead Art Museum, Amherst MA
Amon Carter Museum of American Art, Fort Worth TX
Amsterdam Museum, Amsterdam
Appaloosa Museum and Heritage Center, Moscow ID
Archaeological Museum of Olympia, Olympia
Archaeological Museum of Thessaloniki, Thessaloniki
Arnot Art Museum, Elmira NY
ArtSpace/Lima, Lima OH
Asian Art Museum of San Francisco, Chong-Moon Lee Ctr for Asian Art and Culture, San Francisco CA
Bangladesh National Museum, Dhaka
Baroda Museum and Picture Gallery, Vadodara
Bayerisches Nationalmuseum, Bavarian National Museum, Munich
Berman Museum, Anniston AL
Billie Trimble Chandler, Texas State Museum of Asian Cultures, Corpus Christi TX
Blanden Memorial Art Museum, Fort Dodge IA
Blauvelt Demarest Foundation, Hiram Blauvelt Art Museum, Oradell NJ
Bob Jones University Museum & Gallery Inc, Greenville SC
Boise Art Museum, Boise ID
Booth Western Art Museum, Cartersville GA
Botswana National Museum, Gaborone
Bronx Community College (CUNY), Hall of Fame for Great Americans, Bronx NY
Brookgreen Gardens, Murrells Inlet SC
Bucknell University, Edward & Marthann Samek Art Gallery, Lewisburg PA
Burchfield Penney Art Center, Buffalo NY
C M Russell Museum, Great Falls MT
Canadian Clay and Glass Gallery, Waterloo ON
Canadian Museum of History, Gatineau QC
Cape Ann Museum, Gloucester MA
Cape Cod Museum of Art Inc, Dennis MA
Carlsbad Museum & Art Center, Carlsbad NM
Carson County Square House Museum, Panhandle TX
Cincinnati Art Museum, Cincinnati Art Museum, Cincinnati OH
Colgate University, Picker Art Gallery, Hamilton NY
College of William & Mary, Muscarelle Museum of Art, Williamsburg VA
Corcoran Gallery of Art, Washington DC
Cornell Museum of Art and American Culture, Delray Beach FL
The Courtauld Institute of Art, The Courtauld Gallery, London
Crocker Art Museum, Sacramento CA
Crook County Museum & Art Gallery, Sundance WY
Cyprus Museum, Nicosia
Dahesh Museum of Art, Greenwich CT
Dallas Museum of Art, Dallas TX
Dartmouth College, Hood Museum of Art, Hanover NH
DeLeon White Gallery, Toronto ON
Delphi Archaeological Museum, Delphi
Denver Art Museum, Denver CO
Detroit Institute of Arts, Detroit MI
Dixie State University, Sears Art Museum Gallery, Saint George UT
Dublin Arts Council, Dublin OH
Eiteljorg Museum of American Indians & Western Art, Indianapolis IN
Ellen Noel Art Museum of the Permian Basin, Odessa TX
Erie Art Museum, Erie PA
Erie County Historical Society, Erie PA
Favell Museum of Western Art & Indian Artifacts, Klamath Falls OR
Fetherston Foundation, Packwood House Museum, Lewisburg PA
Fine Arts Museums of San Francisco, Legion of Honor, San Francisco CA
Five Civilized Tribes Museum, Muskogee OK
Flint Institute of Arts, Flint MI
Florida State University and Central Florida Community College, The Appleton Museum of Art, Ocala FL
Fondazione Musei Civici Di Venezia, Museo Correr - Correr Museum, Venice
Fondazione Musei Civici Di Venezia, Ca' Rezzonico, Venice
Forest Lawn Museum, Glendale CA
The Frank Phillips Foundation Inc, Woolaroc Museum, Bartlesville OK
Frankfort Community Public Library, Anna & Harlan Hubbard Gallery, Frankfort IN
Frederic Remington, Ogdensburg NY
Freer Gallery of Art & Arthur M Sackler Gallery, Arthur M Sackler Gallery, Washington DC
The Frick Art & Historical Center, Inc, Frick Art Museum, Pittsburgh PA
Frick Collection, New York NY
Galerie Montcalm, Gatineau QC
Galleria Nazionale dell'Umbria, Umbrian National Gallery, Perugia
Gallery One Visual Arts Center, Ellensburg WA

General Board of Discipleship, The United Methodist Church, The Upper Room Chapel & Museum, Nashville TN
George Phippen, Phippen Museum - Art of the American West, Prescott AZ
Glanmore National Historic Site of Canada, Belleville ON
Glessner House Museum, Chicago IL
Headley-Whitney Museum, Lexington KY
Heard Museum, Phoenix AZ
Hebrew Union College - Jewish Institute of Religion, Skirball Museum Cincinnati, Cincinnati OH
Hebrew Union College - Jewish Institute of Religion Museum, Jewish Institute of Religion, New York NY
Hecht Museum, Haifa
Henry County Museum & Cultural Arts Center, Clinton MO
Heras Museum for Research in Indian History and Culture, Mumbai
Hermitage Museum & Gardens, Norfolk VA
High Desert Museum, Bend OR
Hill-Stead Museum, Farmington CT
Hillwood Museum & Gardens Foundation, Hillwood Estate Museum & Gardens, Washington DC
Honolulu Museum of Art, Honolulu HI
The Huntington Library, Art Collections & Botanical Gardens, San Marino CA
The Hyde Collection, Glens Falls NY
International Museum of Art, El Paso TX
Jacksonville University, Alexander Brest Museum & Gallery, Jacksonville FL
Jacques Marchais Museum of Tibetan Art, Staten Island NY
The John L. Clarke Western Art Gallery & Memorial Museum, East Glacier Park MT
Johns Hopkins University, Evergreen Museum & Library, Baltimore MD
Joslyn Art Museum, Omaha NE
Kalamazoo Institute of Arts, Kalamazoo MI
Kenosha Public Museums, Kenosha WI
Kentucky Derby Museum, Louisville KY
Kimbell Art Foundation, Kimbell Art Museum, Fort Worth TX
Kirkland Museum of Fine & Decorative Art, Denver CO
Knoxville Museum of Art, Knoxville TN
Koshare Indian Museum, Inc, La Junta CO
Kunsthistorisches Museum Wien, Museum of Fine Arts, Vienna
Kyiv Museum of Russian Art, Kyiv Ukrainian
L D Brinkman, Kerrville TX
Lahore Museum, Lahore
Lalit Kala Akademi Rabindra Bhavan Art Galleries, National Academy of Art, New Delhi, New Delhi
Latino Art Museum, Pomona CA
League of New Hampshire Craftsmen, Grodin Permanent Collection Museum, Concord NH
Leanin' Tree Museum & Sculpture Garden of Western Art, Boulder CO
Leigh Yawkey Woodson Art Museum, Wausau WI
Lightner Museum, Saint Augustine FL
Los Angeles County Museum of Natural History, William S Hart Museum, Newhall CA
Louise Hopkins Underwood Center for the Arts, Lubbock TX
Louisiana Arts & Science Museum, Baton Rouge LA
Louisiana Department of Culture, Recreation & Tourism, Louisiana State Museum, New Orleans LA
Loveland Museum/Gallery, Loveland CO
Loyola University Chicago, Loyola University Museum of Art, Chicago IL
Maricopa County Historical Society, Desert Caballeros Western Museum, Wickenburg AZ
Mennello Museum of American Art, Orlando FL
Mezuraj Museum, Tirana
Michigan State University, Eli & Edythe Broad Art Museum, East Lansing MI
Middle Border Museum & Oscar Howe Art Center, Mitchell SD
Midwest Museum of American Art, Elkhart IN
Minnesota Museum of American Art, Saint Paul MN
Missoula Art Museum, Missoula MT
Mobile Museum of Art, Mobile AL
Mohawk Valley Heritage Association, Inc, Walter Elwood Museum, Amsterdam NY
Montreal Museum of Fine Arts, Montreal QC
Morris Museum, Morristown NJ
Musee des Beaux-Arts de Tours, Museum of Fine Arts, Tours
Musee National des Beaux Arts du Quebec, Quebec QC
Museo De Las Americas, Denver CO
The Museum of Arts & Sciences Inc, Daytona Beach FL
Museum of Fine Arts, Saint Petersburg, Florida, Inc, Saint Petersburg FL
Museum of Islamic Art, Doha
Museum of Latin American Art, Long Beach CA
Museum of Modern Art, Ibaraki, Mito Ibaraki
Museum of the Plains Indian & Crafts Center, Browning MT
Museum of the Southwest, Midland TX
The Museum of Western Art, Kerrville TX
Museum zu Allerheiligen, Schaffhausen
Muzej za Umjetnost i Obrt, Museum of Arts & Crafts, Zagreb
Muzeul National de Arta al Romaniei, National Museum of Art of Romania, Bucharest
Muzeum Narodowe w Poznaniu, National Museum in Poznan, Poznan
Muzim Negara, National Museum, Kuala Lumpur
National Archaeological Museum, Athens
National Art Museum of Moldova, Chisinau
National Baseball Hall of Fame & Museum, Cooperstown NY
National Gallery of Canada, Ottawa ON
National Hall of Fame for Famous American Indians, Anadarko OK
The National Museum of Modern Art, Tokyo, Tokyo
National Museum of Racing, National Museum of Racing & Hall of Fame, Saratoga Springs NY
The National Museum of Western Art, Tokyo
National Museum of Wildlife Art of the Unites States, Jackson WY
National Palace Museum, Taipei
National Trust for Historic Preservation, Chesterwood, Stockbridge MA
Naval Historical Center, National Museum of the US Navy, Washington DC
Nebraska Game and Parks Commission, Arbor Lodge State Historical Park & Morton Mansion, Nebraska City NE
Nelda C & H J Lutcher Stark Foundation, Stark Museum of Art, Orange TX
Nelson Mandela Metropolitan Art Museum, Port Elizabeth
The Nelson-Atkins Museum of Art, Kansas City MO
Nevada Museum of Art, Reno NV
New Britain Museum of American Art, New Britain CT
New Orleans Museum of Art, New Orleans LA
Newfields, Indianapolis IN
Norton Simon Museum, Pasadena CA
Norwich Free Academy, Slater Memorial Museum, Norwich CT
Noyes Art Gallery, Lincoln NE
Ohio University, Kennedy Museum of Art, Athens OH
Ohrmann Museum and Gallery, Drummond MT
Okanagan Heritage Museum, Kelowna BC
The Old Jail Art Center, Albany TX
Order Sons of Italy in America, Garibaldi & Meucci Museum, Staten Island NY
Osterreichische Galerie Belvedere Vienna, Belvedere Museum Vienna, Vienna
Owensboro Museum of Fine Art, Owensboro KY
Palm Springs Art Museum, Palm Springs CA
Panhandle-Plains Historical Museum, Canyon TX
Pennsylvania Academy of the Fine Arts, Philadelphia PA
Pioneer Town, Pioneer Museum of Western Art, Wimberley TX
Plumas County Museum, Quincy CA
Portland Art Museum, Portland OR
Queens College, City University of New York, Godwin-Ternbach Museum, Flushing NY
Reading Public Museum, Reading PA
The Rockwell Museum, Corning NY
Rollins College, George D & Harriet W Cornell Fine Arts Museum, Winter Park FL
Ross Memorial Museum, Saint Andrews NB
Roswell Museum & Art Center, Roswell NM
Saginaw Art Museum, Saginaw MI
Saint Olaf College, Flaten Art Museum, Northfield MN
San Antonio Museum of Art, San Antonio TX
Santarella Museum & Gardens, Tyringham MA
Scripps College, Ruth Chandler Williamson Gallery, Claremont CA
Shanghai Museum, Shanghai
Slovenska Narodna Galeria, Slovak National Gallery, Bratislava
The Society of the Cincinnati at Anderson House, Washington DC
The Speed Art Museum, Louisville KY
Springfield Art Museum, Springfield MO
Springville Museum of Art, Springville UT
Staatliche Museen zu Berlin Stiftung Preussischer Kulturbesitz, National Museums in Berlin, Prussian Cultural Heritage Foundation, Berlin
The State Museum of Oriental Art, Moscow
State University of New York at Plattsburgh, Art Museum, Plattsburgh NY
Staten Island Museum, Staten Island NY
Stone Quarry Hill Art Park, Winner Gallery, Cazenovia NY
Suan Pakkad Palace Museum, Bangkok
Tampa Museum of Art, Tampa FL
Timken Museum of Art, San Diego CA
Tokyo National Museum, Tokyo
Topeka & Shawnee County Public Library, Alice C Sabatini Gallery, Topeka KS
Tver Regional Art Gallery, Tver
Ukrainian Institute of Modern Art, Chicago IL
UMLAUF Sculpture Garden & Museum, Austin TX
United States Capitol, Architect of the Capitol, Washington DC
United States Figure Skating Association, World Figure Skating Museum & Hall of Fame, Colorado Springs CO
United States Military Academy, West Point Museum, West Point NY
University of Florida, Samuel P Harn Museum of Art, Gainesville FL
University of Georgia, Georgia Museum of Art, Athens GA
University of Illinois at Urbana-Champaign, Krannert Art Museum and Kinkead Pavilion, Champaign IL
University of Kansas, Spencer Museum of Art, Lawrence KS
The University of Kentucky Art Museum, Lexington KY
University of Michigan, Kelsey Museum of Archaeology, Ann Arbor MI
University of Nebraska-Lincoln, Great Plains Art Museum, Lincoln NE
University of Richmond, University Museums, Richmond VA
University of Utah, Utah Museum of Fine Arts, Salt Lake City UT
University of Wisconsin-Madison, Chazen Museum of Art, Madison WI
Vero Beach Museum of Art, Vero Beach FL
Villa Terrace Decorative Arts Museum, Milwaukee WI
Virginia Museum of Fine Arts, Richmond VA
Vizcaya Museum & Gardens, Miami FL
Walker Art Gallery, Liverpool
The Wallace Collection, London
Waterworks Visual Arts Center, Salisbury NC
Wayne Center for the Arts, Wooster OH
Wheaton College, Beard and Weil Galleries, Norton MA
Wichita State University, Ulrich Museum of Art, Wichita KS
Wildling Art Museum, Solvang CA
World Erotic Art Museum, Miami Beach FL
Wyoming Trails Gallery, Wheatland WY
Yokohama Museum of Art, Yokohama
Zigler Art Museum, Jennings LA

CALLIGRAPHY

Academy of the New Church, Glencairn Museum, Bryn Athyn PA
American Sport Art Museum and Archives, Daphne AL
Arlington Arts Center (AAC), Arlington VA
Arnot Art Museum, Elmira NY
Art Center of Battle Creek, Battle Creek MI
ArtSpace/Lima, Lima OH
Asian Art Museum of San Francisco, Chong-Moon Lee Ctr for Asian Art and Culture, San Francisco CA
Bangladesh National Museum, Dhaka
Baroda Museum and Picture Gallery, Vadodara
Beloit College, Wright Museum of Art, Beloit WI
Billie Trimble Chandler, Texas State Museum of Asian Cultures, Corpus Christi TX
Blanden Memorial Art Museum, Fort Dodge IA

Bucknell University, Edward & Marthann Samek Art Gallery, Lewisburg PA
Canadian Museum of History, Gatineau QC
Central United Methodist Church, Swords Into Plowshares Peace Center & Gallery, Detroit MI
Cincinnati Art Museum, Cincinnati Art Museum, Cincinnati OH
College of William & Mary, Muscarelle Museum of Art, Williamsburg VA
Crocker Art Museum, Sacramento CA
Dallas Museum of Art, Dallas TX
Detroit Institute of Arts, Detroit MI
Dickinson College, The Trout Gallery, Carlisle PA
Fine Arts Center for the New River Valley, Pulaski VA
Freer Gallery of Art & Arthur M Sackler Gallery, Arthur M Sackler Gallery, Washington DC
General Board of Discipleship, The United Methodist Church, The Upper Room Chapel & Museum, Nashville TN
Georgian Court University, M Christina Geis Gallery, Lakewood NJ
Glessner House Museum, Chicago IL
Hebrew Union College - Jewish Institute of Religion, Skirball Museum Cincinnati, Cincinnati OH
Hebrew Union College - Jewish Institute of Religion Museum, Jewish Institute of Religion, New York NY
The Interchurch Center, Galleries at the Interchurch Center, New York NY
The Israel Museum, Jerusalem, Jerusalem
Jacques Marchais Museum of Tibetan Art, Staten Island NY
Jordan National Gallery of Fine Arts, Amman
Kenosha Public Museums, Kenosha WI
Kimbell Art Foundation, Kimbell Art Museum, Fort Worth TX
LACE (Los Angeles Contemporary Exhibitions), Los Angeles CA
Lalit Kala Akademi Rabindra Bhavan Art Galleries, National Academy of Art, New Delhi, New Delhi
Landis Valley Village and Farm Museum, PA Historical & Museum Commission, Lancaster PA
League of New Hampshire Craftsmen, Grodin Permanent Collection Museum, Concord NH
Lighthouse ArtCenter Museum & School of Art, Tequesta FL
Macau Museum of Art, NAPE
Michigan State University, Eli & Edythe Broad Art Museum, East Lansing MI
The Mint Museum, Charlotte NC
Missoula Art Museum, Missoula MT
Musee des Augustines de l'Hotel Dieu de Quebec, Quebec QC
Musee des Beaux-Arts de Tours, Museum of Fine Arts, Tours
Museum fur Angewandte Kunst Frankfurt, Museum of Applied Arts, Frankfurt
The Museum of Arts & Sciences Inc, Daytona Beach FL
Museum of Islamic Art, Doha
Museum Plantin-Moretus, Antwerp
Muzeul National de Arta al Romaniei, National Museum of Art of Romania, Bucharest
Nara Kokuritsu Hakubutsu-Kan, Nara National Museum, Nara
The National Museum of Modern Art, Tokyo, Tokyo
National Museum of Women in the Arts, Washington DC
National Palace Museum, Taipei
Naval Historical Center, National Museum of the US Navy, Washington DC
The Nelson-Atkins Museum of Art, Kansas City MO
Niigata Prefectural Museum of Modern Art, Nagaoka
Panhandle-Plains Historical Museum, Canyon TX
Phoenix Art Museum, Phoenix AZ
Portland Art Museum, Portland OR
Saint John's University, Dr. M.T. Geoffrey Yeh Art Gallery, Queens NY
San Antonio Museum of Art, San Antonio TX
Scripps College, Ruth Chandler Williamson Gallery, Claremont CA
Shanghai Museum, Shanghai
Slovenska Narodna Galeria, Slovak National Gallery, Bratislava
Staatliche Museen zu Berlin Stiftung Preussischer Kulturbesitz, National Museums in Berlin, Prussian Cultural Heritage Foundation, Berlin
Stanford University, Cantor Arts Center at Stanford University, Stanford CA
The State Museum of Fine Arts of Tatarstan Republic, Kazan
The State Museum of Oriental Art, Moscow
State University of New York at Geneseo, Bertha V B Lederer Gallery, Geneseo NY
State University of New York at New Paltz, Samuel Dorsky Museum of Art, New Paltz NY
The Tokugawa Art Museum, Nagoya
Tokyo National Museum, Tokyo
United Methodist Historical Society, Lovely Lane Museum, Baltimore MD
University of Illinois at Urbana-Champaign, Krannert Art Museum and Kinkead Pavilion, Champaign IL
University of Indianapolis, Christel DeHaan Fine Arts Gallery, Indianapolis IN
University of Kansas, Spencer Museum of Art, Lawrence KS
University of North Dakota, Hughes Fine Arts Center-Col Eugene Myers Art Gallery, Grand Forks ND
University of Richmond, University Museums, Richmond VA
University of Wisconsin-Madison, Chazen Museum of Art, Madison WI
Willard House & Clock Museum, Inc, North Grafton MA

CARPETS & RUGS

Academy of the New Church, Glencairn Museum, Bryn Athyn PA
Albion College, Bobbitt Visual Arts Center, Albion MI
American Folk Art Museum, New York NY
Anchorage Museum at Rasmuson Center, Anchorage AK
Asian Art Museum of San Francisco, Chong-Moon Lee Ctr for Asian Art and Culture, San Francisco CA
Bangladesh National Museum, Dhaka
Barnes Foundation, Merion PA
Baroda Museum and Picture Gallery, Vadodara
Brick Store Museum, Kennebunk ME
Bruce Museum, Inc, Greenwich CT
Bucknell University, Edward & Marthann Samek Art Gallery, Lewisburg PA
Buffalo Niagara Heritage Village, Amherst NY
Canadian Museum of History, Gatineau QC
Carlsbad Museum & Art Center, Carlsbad NM
Carson County Square House Museum, Panhandle TX
Chatham Historical Society, The Atwood House Museum, Chatham MA
Cincinnati Art Museum, Cincinnati Art Museum, Cincinnati OH
Clark County Historical Society, Pioneer - Krier Museum, Ashland KS
Columbus Museum of Art, Columbus OH
Contemporary Calgary, Calgary AB
Cornell College, Peter Paul Luce Gallery, Mount Vernon IA
County of Henrico, Meadow Farm Museum, Glen Allen VA
Coutts Museum of Art, Inc, El Dorado KS
Craft and Folk Art Museum (CAFAM), Los Angeles CA
Craigdarroch Castle Historical Museum Society, Victoria BC
Crocker Art Museum, Sacramento CA
Crow Wing County Historical Society, Brainerd MN
Dallas Museum of Art, Dallas TX
Dalnavert Museum, Winnipeg MB
Danville Museum of Fine Arts & History, Danville VA
DAR Museum, National Society Daughters of the American Revolution, Washington DC
Designmuseum Danmark, Danish Design Museum, Copenhagen
Detroit Institute of Arts, Detroit MI
Dixie State University, Sears Art Museum Gallery, Saint George UT
Edsel & Eleanor Ford House, Grosse Pointe Shores MI
Erie County Historical Society, Erie PA
Evanston Historical Society, Charles Gates Dawes House, Evanston IL
Fetherston Foundation, Packwood House Museum, Lewisburg PA
Fine Arts Museums of San Francisco, Legion of Honor, San Francisco CA
Florence County Museum, Florence SC
Florida State University and Central Florida Community College, The Appleton Museum of Art, Ocala FL
Fuller Craft Museum, Brockton MA
General Board of Discipleship, The United Methodist Church, The Upper Room Chapel & Museum, Nashville TN
Glanmore National Historic Site of Canada, Belleville ON
Glessner House Museum, Chicago IL
Grand Rapids Public Museum, Grand Rapids MI
Greene County Historical Society, Bronck Museum, Coxsackie NY
Hebrew Union College - Jewish Institute of Religion, Skirball Museum Cincinnati, Cincinnati OH
Henry County Museum & Cultural Arts Center, Clinton MO
Henry Morrison Flagler Museum, Palm Beach FL
Hermitage Museum & Gardens, Norfolk VA
Hill-Stead Museum, Farmington CT
Hillwood Museum & Gardens Foundation, Hillwood Estate Museum & Gardens, Washington DC
Historic Arkansas Museum, Little Rock AR
Historic Huguenot Street, New Paltz NY
The History Center in Tompkins County, Ithaca NY
History Colorado Center Museum, Denver CO
The Huntington Library, Art Collections & Botanical Gardens, San Marino CA
Huntington Museum of Art, Huntington WV
The Hyde Collection, Glens Falls NY
Illinois Historic Preservation Agency, Bishop Hill State Historic Site, Bishop Hill IL
Imperial Calcasieu Museum, Gibson-Barham Gallery, Lake Charles LA
Indiana Landmarks, Morris-Butler House, Indianapolis IN
International Museum of Art, El Paso TX
Iredell Museums, Statesville NC
The Israel Museum, Jerusalem, Jerusalem
Jacksonville University, Alexander Brest Museum & Gallery, Jacksonville FL
Jacques Marchais Museum of Tibetan Art, Staten Island NY
James Dick Foundation, Festival - Institute, Round Top TX
The Jewish Museum, New York NY
JMW Turner Museum, Sarasota FL
Johns Hopkins University, Evergreen Museum & Library, Baltimore MD
Karakalpak State Art Museum, Nukus Republic of Karakalpakstan
Kenosha Public Museums, Kenosha WI
Kereszteny Muzeum, Christian Museum, Esztergom
Kings County Historical Society & Museum, Hampton NB
Kirkland Museum of Fine & Decorative Art, Denver CO
Koshare Indian Museum, Inc, La Junta CO
Lac du Flambeau Band of Lake Superior Chippewa Indians, George W Brown Jr Ojibwe Museum & Cultural Center, Lac Du Flambeau WI
LaGrange Art Museum, LaGrange GA
Lahore Museum, Lahore
League of New Hampshire Craftsmen, Grodin Permanent Collection Museum, Concord NH
Lightner Museum, Saint Augustine FL
The Long Island Museum of American Art, History & Carriages, Stony Brook NY
Longue Vue House & Gardens, New Orleans LA
Los Angeles County Museum of Natural History, William S Hart Museum, Newhall CA
Louise Hopkins Underwood Center for the Arts, Lubbock TX
Marblehead Museum & Historical Society, Marblehead MA
Marblehead Museum & Historical Society, Jeremiah Lee Mansion, Marblehead MA
Maricopa County Historical Society, Desert Caballeros Western Museum, Wickenburg AZ
Marquette University, Haggerty Museum of Art, Milwaukee WI
Massillon Museum, Massillon OH
McDowell House & Apothecary Shop, Danville KY
McLean County Historical Society, McLean County Museum of History, Bloomington IL
Meredith College, Frankie G Weems Gallery & Rotunda Gallery, Raleigh NC
Mississippi River Museum at Mud-Island River Park, Memphis TN
Mississippi Valley Conservation Authority, R Tait McKenzie Memorial Museum, Almonte ON
Mohawk Valley Heritage Association, Inc, Walter Elwood Museum, Amsterdam NY
Montreal Museum of Fine Arts, Montreal QC

Morris Museum, Morristown NJ
Mount Vernon Hotel Museum & Garden, New York NY
Muscatine Art Center, Muscatine IA
Musee des Beaux-Arts de Tours, Museum of Fine Arts, Tours
Musees Royaux d'Art et d'Histoire, Royal Museums of Art and History, Brussels
Museo di Palazzo Ducale, Ducale Palace Museum, Mantua
The Museum, Greenwood SC
Museum De Lakenhal, Leiden
Museum fur Angewandte Kunst Frankfurt, Museum of Applied Arts, Frankfurt
The Museum of Arts & Sciences Inc, Daytona Beach FL
Museum of Northern Arizona, Flagstaff AZ
Museum Plantin-Moretus, Antwerp
Museum zu Allerheiligen, Schaffhausen
Muzej za Umjetnost i Obrt, Museum of Arts & Crafts, Zagreb
Muzeul National de Arta al Romaniei, National Museum of Art of Romania, Bucharest
National Museums Scotland, National Museum of Scotland, Edinburgh
Nebraska Game and Parks Commission, Arbor Lodge State Historical Park & Morton Mansion, Nebraska City NE
Nelda C & H J Lutcher Stark Foundation, Stark Museum of Art, Orange TX
Nelson Mandela Metropolitan Art Museum, Port Elizabeth
The Nelson-Atkins Museum of Art, Kansas City MO
New Brunswick Museum, Saint John NB
New Visions Gallery, Inc, Marshfield WI
New York State Office of Parks, Recreation & Historic Preservation, Staatsburgh State Historic Site, Staatsburg NY
Nichols House Museum, Inc, Boston MA
Norwich Free Academy, Slater Memorial Museum, Norwich CT
Ohio University, Kennedy Museum of Art, Athens OH
The Old Jail Art Center, Albany TX
Owensboro Museum of Fine Art, Owensboro KY
Panhandle-Plains Historical Museum, Canyon TX
Pasadena Museum of History, Pasadena CA
Plumas County Museum, Quincy CA
Polk Museum of Art, Lakeland FL
Port Huron Museum, Port Huron MI
Portland Art Museum, Portland OR
Putnam Museum of History and Natural Science, Davenport IA
Queens College, City University of New York, Godwin-Ternbach Museum, Flushing NY
Rensselaer County Historical Society, Hart-Cluett Mansion, 1827, Troy NY
Rhode Island Historical Society, John Brown House, Providence RI
Riverside Metropolitan Museum, Riverside CA
The Rockwell Museum, Corning NY
The Rosenbach Museum & Library, Philadelphia PA
Ross Memorial Museum, Saint Andrews NB
Rubin Museum of Art, New York NY
Saginaw Art Museum, Saginaw MI
Saint Anselm College, Alva de Mars Megan Chapel Art Center, Manchester NH
Saint Olaf College, Flaten Art Museum, Northfield MN
Schweinfurth Art Center, Auburn NY
The Society of the Cincinnati at Anderson House, Washington DC
South Carolina Artisans Center, Walterboro SC
South Dakota State University, South Dakota Art Museum, Brookings SD
The Speed Art Museum, Louisville KY
Spertus Institute of Jewish Studies, Chicago IL
Springville Museum of Art, Springville UT
Staatliche Museen zu Berlin Stiftung Preussischer Kulturbesitz, National Museums in Berlin, Prussian Cultural Heritage Foundation, Berlin
The State Museum of Fine Arts of Tatarstan Republic, Kazan
The State Museum of Oriental Art, Moscow
State University of New York at Geneseo, Bertha V B Lederer Gallery, Geneseo NY
The Summit County Historical Society of Akron, OH, Akron OH
Suomen Kansallismuseo, National Museum of Finland, Helsinki
Swedish American Museum, Chicago IL
Taos Historic Museums, Ernest Blumenschein Home & Studio, Taos NM
Textile Museum of Canada, Toronto ON
Tohono Chul Park, Tucson AZ
Tokyo National Museum, Tokyo
Topeka & Shawnee County Public Library, Alice C Sabatini Gallery, Topeka KS
Tryon Palace, New Bern NC
Tver Regional Art Gallery, Tver
Ukrainian Canadian Archives & Museum of Alberta, Edmonton AB
University of Calgary, Nickle Galleries, Calgary AB
University of Georgia, Georgia Museum of Art, Athens GA
University of Kansas, Spencer Museum of Art, Lawrence KS
The University of Kentucky Art Museum, Lexington KY
University of Minnesota, Goldstein Museum of Design, Saint Paul MN
University of Pennsylvania, Arthur Ross Gallery, Philadelphia PA
University of Utah, Utah Museum of Fine Arts, Salt Lake City UT
Vesterheim Norwegian-American Museum, Decorah IA
Victoria Mansion - Morse Libby House, Portland ME
Vizcaya Museum & Gardens, Miami FL
Willard House & Clock Museum, Inc, North Grafton MA
William Morris Gallery, London
Wisconsin Historical Society, Wisconsin Historical Museum, Madison WI
Woodlawn/The Pope-Leighey, Alexandria VA
Woodmere Art Museum Inc, Philadelphia PA

CARTOONS

Alaska State Museum, Juneau AK
American Museum of Cartoon Art, Inc, Sunland CA
American Museum of the Moving Image, Astoria NY
The Art Gallery of Grand Prairie, Grande Prairie AB
Art Without Walls Inc, Sayville NY
ArtSpace/Lima, Lima OH
Bangladesh National Museum, Dhaka
Barker Character, Comic and Cartoon Museum, Cheshire CT
Beck Cultural Exchange Center, Inc, Knoxville TN
Bruce Museum, Inc, Greenwich CT
Burchfield Penney Art Center, Buffalo NY
C M Russell Museum, Great Falls MT
Cartoon Art Museum, San Francisco CA
Central United Methodist Church, Swords Into Plowshares Peace Center & Gallery, Detroit MI
The Children's Museum of Indianapolis, Indianapolis IN
Children's Museum of Manhattan, New York NY
City of Fremont, Olive Hyde Art Gallery, Fremont CA
Colgate University, Picker Art Gallery, Hamilton NY
Coutts Museum of Art, Inc, El Dorado KS
Cripple Creek District Museum, Cripple Creek CO
Crocker Art Museum, Sacramento CA
Erie Art Museum, Erie PA
Fort George G Meade Museum, Fort Meade MD
Galerie Montcalm, Gatineau QC
Hartwick College, Foreman Gallery, Oneonta NY
Headquarters Fort Monroe, Dept of Army, Casemate Museum, Hampton VA
Intermedia Arts, Minneapolis MN
Intuit: The Center for Intuitive & Outsider Art, Chicago IL
The Jewish Museum, New York NY
Kansas State Historical Society, Kansas Museum of History, Topeka KS
Kelly-Griggs House Museum, Red Bluff CA
Lafayette College, Lafayette College Art Galleries, Easton PA
Longue Vue House & Gardens, New Orleans LA
Marylhurst University, The Art Gym, Marylhurst OR
McCord Museum of Canadian History, Montreal QC
Musee des Beaux-Arts de Tours, Museum of Fine Arts, Tours
Museo di Palazzo Ducale, Ducale Palace Museum, Mantua
Museum of Chinese in America, New York NY
The Museum of Western Art, Kerrville TX
National Art Museum of Moldova, Chisinau
National Baseball Hall of Fame & Museum, Cooperstown NY
National Museum & Art Gallery of Trinidad and Tobago, Port of Spain
Naval Historical Center, National Museum of the US Navy, Washington DC
Nelson Mandela Metropolitan Art Museum, Port Elizabeth
New Britain Museum of American Art, New Britain CT
Norwich Free Academy, Slater Memorial Museum, Norwich CT
Noyes Art Gallery, Lincoln NE
Panhandle-Plains Historical Museum, Canyon TX
Port Huron Museum, Port Huron MI
Queens College, City University of New York, Godwin-Ternbach Museum, Flushing NY
Rollins College, George D & Harriet W Cornell Fine Arts Museum, Winter Park FL
The San Joaquin Pioneer & Historical Society, The Haggin Museum, Stockton CA
The Speed Art Museum, Louisville KY
Spertus Institute of Jewish Studies, Chicago IL
Staatliche Museen zu Berlin Stiftung Preussischer Kulturbesitz, National Museums in Berlin, Prussian Cultural Heritage Foundation, Berlin
United States Military Academy, West Point Museum, West Point NY
The University of Kentucky Art Museum, Lexington KY
Wisconsin Historical Society, Wisconsin Historical Museum, Madison WI
World Erotic Art Museum, Miami Beach FL

CERAMICS

A.E. Backus Museum & Gallery, Fort Pierce FL
Academy of the New Church, Glencairn Museum, Bryn Athyn PA
Acropolis Museum, Athens
Adams National Historic Park, Quincy MA
African American Atelier, Greensboro NC
African Art Museum of Maryland, Columbia MD
Al Ain National Museum, Al Ain
Alaska State Museum, Juneau AK
Albany Institute of History & Art, Albany NY
Alberta College of Art & Design, Illingworth Kerr Gallery, Calgary AB
Albion College, Bobbitt Visual Arts Center, Albion MI
Albuquerque Museum of Art & History, Albuquerque NM
Allentown Art Museum, Allentown PA
American Folk Art Museum, New York NY
American Museum of Ceramic Art, Pomona CA
American Swedish Institute, Minneapolis MN
American University of Beirut Archaeological Museum, Beirut
Amherst College, Mead Art Museum, Amherst MA
Archaeological Museum of Olympia, Olympia
Archaeological Museum of Thessaloniki, Thessaloniki
Arkansas Arts Center, Little Rock AR
Arnot Art Museum, Elmira NY
Art Community Center, Art Center of Corpus Christi, Corpus Christi TX
The Art Gallery of Cornwall, Cornwall ON
Art Gallery of Nova Scotia, Halifax NS
Art Gallery of South Australia, Adelaide
Art Museum of Greater Lafayette, Lafayette IN
ArtSpace/Lima, Lima OH
Asheville Art Museum, Asheville NC
Asian Art Museum of San Francisco, Chong-Moon Lee Ctr for Asian Art and Culture, San Francisco CA
Audrain County Historical Society, Graceland Museum & American Saddlehorse Museum & Fire Brick Industry Museum, Mexico MO
Bainbridge Arts & Crafts Gallery, Bainbridge Island WA
Baldwin Historical Society Museum, Baldwin NY
The Baltimore Museum of Art, Baltimore MD
Balzekas Museum of Lithuanian Culture, Chicago IL
Bangladesh National Museum, Dhaka
Barnes Foundation, Merion PA
Baroda Museum and Picture Gallery, Vadodara
Bass Museum of Art, Miami Beach FL
Baton Rouge Gallery, Center For Contemporary Art, Baton Rouge LA
Bayerisches Nationalmuseum, Bavarian National Museum, Munich
Belger Arts Center, Kansas City MO
Bellevue Arts Museum, Bellevue WA
Bemis Center for Contemporary Arts, Omaha NE
Bennington Museum, Bennington VT

Berea College, Doris Ulmann Galleries, Berea KY
Berkshire Museum, Pittsfield MA
Berman Museum, Anniston AL
Besser Museum for Northeast Michigan, Alpena MI
Bethany College, Mingenback Art Center, Lindsborg KS
Beverly Historical Society, Cabot, Hale & Balch House Museums, Beverly MA
Biggs Museum of American Art, Dover DE
Billie Trimble Chandler, Texas State Museum of Asian Cultures, Corpus Christi TX
Birger Sandzen Memorial Gallery, Lindsborg KS
Birmingham Museum of Art, Birmingham AL
Blanden Memorial Art Museum, Fort Dodge IA
Blowing Rock Art and History Museum, Blowing Rock NC
Bob Jones University Museum & Gallery Inc, Greenville SC
Bone Creek Museum of Agrarian Art, David City NE
The Bostonian Society, Old State House Museum, Boston MA
Botswana National Museum, Gaborone
Brown University, Haffenreffer Museum of Anthropology, Providence RI
Bruce Museum, Inc, Greenwich CT
Bucknell University, Edward & Marthann Samek Art Gallery, Lewisburg PA
Bullion Plaza Cultural Center & Museum, Miami AZ
Burchfield Penney Art Center, Buffalo NY
Burke Arts Council, Jailhouse Galleries, Morganton NC
Byzantine & Christian Museum, Athens, Athens
Cameron Art Museum, Wilmington NC
Canadian Clay and Glass Gallery, Waterloo ON
Canadian Museum of History, Gatineau QC
Canadian Museum of Nature, Musee Canadien de la Nature, Ottawa ON
Canton Museum of Art, Canton OH
Cape Cod Museum of Art Inc, Dennis MA
Carlsbad Museum & Art Center, Carlsbad NM
Cedar Rapids Museum of Art, Cedar Rapids IA
Central United Methodist Church, Swords Into Plowshares Peace Center & Gallery, Detroit MI
Charles Allis Art Museum, Milwaukee WI
Charleston Museum, Charleston SC
Chatham Historical Society, The Atwood House Museum, Chatham MA
The Children's Museum of Indianapolis, Indianapolis IN
Cincinnati Art Museum, Cincinnati Art Museum, Cincinnati OH
City of Cedar Falls, Iowa, James & Meryl Hearst Center for the Arts & Sculpture Garden, Cedar Falls IA
City of Fremont, Olive Hyde Art Gallery, Fremont CA
The City of Petersburg Museums, Petersburg VA
City of Springdale, Shiloh Museum of Ozark History, Springdale AR
Clark Art Institute, Williamstown MA
The Clay Studio, Philadelphia PA
Clayworks Gallery, Charlotte NC
Clear Lake Arts Center, Clear Lake IA
The Cleveland Museum of Art, Cleveland OH
Coastal Arts League Museum, Half Moon Bay CA
Cohasset Historical Society, Pratt Building (Society Headquarters), Cohasset MA
Colgate University, Picker Art Gallery, Hamilton NY
College of William & Mary, Muscarelle Museum of Art, Williamsburg VA
Colonial Williamsburg Foundation, Abby Aldrich Rockefeller Folk Art Museum, Williamsburg VA
The Columbus Museum, Columbus GA
Concord Museum, Concord MA
Concordia University, Marxhausen Art Gallery, Seward NE
Contemporary Calgary, Calgary AB
County of Henrico, Meadow Farm Museum, Glen Allen VA
The Courtauld Institute of Art, The Courtauld Gallery, London
Coutts Museum of Art, Inc, El Dorado KS
Craft and Folk Art Museum (CAFAM), Los Angeles CA
Craigdarroch Castle Historical Museum Society, Victoria BC
Cranbrook Art Museum, Bloomfield Hills MI
Cripple Creek District Museum, Cripple Creek CO
Crocker Art Museum, Sacramento CA
The Currier Museum of Art, Manchester NH
Cyprus Museum, Nicosia
Dallas Museum of Art, Dallas TX
Dalnavert Museum, Winnipeg MB
DAR Museum, National Society Daughters of the American Revolution, Washington DC
Dartmouth College, Hood Museum of Art, Hanover NH
Dartmouth Heritage Museum, Dartmouth NS
Daum Museum of Contemporary Art, Sedalia MO
Davidson College, William H Van Every Jr & Edward M Smith Galleries, Davidson NC
Deines Cultural Center, Russell KS
Delaware Division of Historical & Cultural Affairs, Dover DE
Delphi Archaeological Museum, Delphi
Denver Art Museum, Denver CO
Designmuseum Danmark, Danish Design Museum, Copenhagen
Detroit Institute of Arts, Detroit MI
Detroit Zoological Institute, Wildlife Interpretive Gallery, Royal Oak MI
Dickinson College, The Trout Gallery, Carlisle PA
Dickinson State University, Art Gallery, Dickinson ND
Dixie State University, Sears Art Museum Gallery, Saint George UT
The Dixon Gallery & Gardens, Memphis TN
Doncaster Museum and Art Gallery, Doncaster Yorks
Dublin Arts Council, Dublin OH
Edgecombe County Cultural Arts Council, Inc, Blount-Bridgers House, Hobson Pittman Memorial Gallery, Tarboro NC
Edsel & Eleanor Ford House, Grosse Pointe Shores MI
Ella Sharp Museum, Jackson MI
Ellen Noel Art Museum of the Permian Basin, Odessa TX
Elmhurst Art Museum, Elmhurst IL
Emory University, Michael C Carlos Museum, Atlanta GA
Erie Art Museum, Erie PA
Erie County Historical Society, Erie PA
Evanston Historical Society, Charles Gates Dawes House, Evanston IL
Everhart Museum, Scranton PA
Everson Museum of Art, Syracuse NY
Fairbanks Museum & Planetarium, Saint Johnsbury VT
Farmington Village Green & Library Association, Stanley-Whitman House, Farmington CT
Fetherston Foundation, Packwood House Museum, Lewisburg PA
Fine Arts Center for the New River Valley, Pulaski VA
Fine Arts Museums of San Francisco, Legion of Honor, San Francisco CA
Fireweed Gallery, Homer AK
Fisher Art Gallery, Marshalltown IA
Flint Institute of Arts, Flint MI
Florence County Museum, Florence SC
Florida CraftArt, Saint Petersburg FL
Folk Art Society of America, Richmond VA
Fondazione Musei Civici Di Venezia, Museo Correr - Correr Museum, Venice
Fondazione Musei Civici Di Venezia, Ca' Rezzonico, Venice
Forest Lawn Museum, Glendale CA
Freer Gallery of Art & Arthur M Sackler Gallery, Freer Gallery of Art, Washington DC
Freer Gallery of Art & Arthur M Sackler Gallery, Arthur M Sackler Gallery, Washington DC
The Frick Art & Historical Center, Inc, Frick Art Museum, Pittsburgh PA
Fuller Craft Museum, Brockton MA
Galleria Nazionale dell'Umbria, Umbrian National Gallery, Perugia
Gallery One Visual Arts Center, Ellensburg WA
General Board of Discipleship, The United Methodist Church, The Upper Room Chapel & Museum, Nashville TN
Genesee Country Village & Museum, John L Wehle Art Gallery, Mumford NY
George R Gardiner Museum of Ceramic Art, Toronto ON
Georgian Court University, M Christina Geis Gallery, Lakewood NJ
Girard College, Stephen Girard Collection, Philadelphia PA
Glanmore National Historic Site of Canada, Belleville ON
Glasgow University, The Hunterian, Glasgow
Glessner House Museum, Chicago IL
Grand Rapids Art Museum, Grand Rapids MI
Grand Rapids Public Museum, Grand Rapids MI
Harrison County Historical Museum, Marshall TX
Haystack Mountain School of Crafts, Deer Isle ME
Headley-Whitney Museum, Lexington KY
Headquarters Fort Monroe, Dept of Army, Casemate Museum, Hampton VA
Heard Museum, Phoenix AZ
Hebrew Union College - Jewish Institute of Religion Museum, Jewish Institute of Religion, New York NY
Hecht Museum, Haifa
Henry Sheldon Museum of Vermont History and Research Center, Middlebury VT
Heritage Center, Inc, Pine Ridge SD
Hermitage Museum & Gardens, Norfolk VA
Hershey Museum, Hershey PA
High Museum of Art, Atlanta GA
Hill-Stead Museum, Farmington CT
Hillwood Museum & Gardens Foundation, Hillwood Estate Museum & Gardens, Washington DC
Historic Arkansas Museum, Little Rock AR
Historic Cherry Hill, Albany NY
Historic Deerfield, Inc, Deerfield MA
Historic Hudson Valley, Pocantico Hills NY
Historic Huguenot Street, New Paltz NY
Historic Newton, Newton MA
Historical Society of Bloomfield, Bloomfield NJ
Historical Society of Cheshire County, Keene NH
Historisches und Volkerkundemuseum, Museum of History and Ethnology, St Gallen
History Colorado Center Museum, Denver CO
History Museum of Mobile, Mobile AL
Holter Museum of Art, Helena MT
Honolulu Museum of Art, Honolulu HI
Hot Shops Art Center, Omaha NE
Hui No'eau Visual Arts Center, Gallery and Gift Shop, Makawao Maui HI
The Huntington Library, Art Collections & Botanical Gardens, San Marino CA
Huntington Museum of Art, Huntington WV
Hyde Park Art Center, Chicago IL
i.d.e.a. Museum, Mesa AZ
Illinois State Museum, ISM Lockport Gallery, Chicago Gallery & Southern Illinois Art Gallery, Springfield IL
Imperial Calcasieu Museum, Gibson-Barham Gallery, Lake Charles LA
Independence Seaport Museum, Philadelphia PA
Indiana Landmarks, Morris-Butler House, Indianapolis IN
Indiana State Museum, Indianapolis IN
Institute of Contemporary Art, Los Angeles, Los Angeles CA
Institute of Puerto Rican Culture, Museo Fuerte Conde de Mirasol, Vieques PR
The Interchurch Center, Galleries at the Interchurch Center, New York NY
Intermedia Arts, Minneapolis MN
Iowa State University, Brunnier Art Museum, Ames IA
Iredell Museums, Statesville NC
Iroquois Indian Museum, Howes Cave NY
The Israel Museum, Jerusalem, Jerusalem
Jacksonville University, Alexander Brest Museum & Gallery, Jacksonville FL
James Dick Foundation, Festival - Institute, Round Top TX
James Monroe Museum, Fredericksburg VA
The Jewish Museum, New York NY
Johns Hopkins University, Evergreen Museum & Library, Baltimore MD
Johns Hopkins University, Homewood Museum, Baltimore MD
Jordan National Gallery of Fine Arts, Amman
Kalamazoo Institute of Arts, Kalamazoo MI
Kelly-Griggs House Museum, Red Bluff CA
Kenosha Public Museums, Kenosha WI
Kentucky Museum of Art and Craft, Louisville KY
Kereszteny Muzeum, Christian Museum, Esztergom
Kimbell Art Foundation, Kimbell Art Museum, Fort Worth TX
Kings County Historical Society & Museum, Hampton NB
Kirkland Museum of Fine & Decorative Art, Denver CO
Kyiv Museum of Russian Art, Kyiv Ukrainian
La Salle University Art Museum, Philadelphia PA
Lafayette College, Lafayette College Art Galleries, Easton PA
LaGrange Art Museum, LaGrange GA
Laguna Art Museum, Laguna Beach CA
Lahore Museum, Lahore

Lalit Kala Akademi Rabindra Bhavan Art Galleries, National Academy of Art, New Delhi, New Delhi
Latino Art Museum, Pomona CA
League of New Hampshire Craftsmen, Grodin Permanent Collection Museum, Concord NH
Lighthouse ArtCenter Museum & School of Art, Tequesta FL
Lightner Museum, Saint Augustine FL
Lillian & Coleman Taube Museum of Art, Minot ND
Lincoln County Historical Association, Inc, 1811 Old Lincoln County Jail & Lincoln County Museum, Wiscasset ME
Lincolnshire County Council, Library & Heritage Services, Lincoln
Lincolnshire County Council, The Collection: Art & Archaeology in Lincolnshire, Lincoln
Livingston County Historical Society, Museum, Geneseo NY
The Long Island Museum of American Art, History & Carriages, Stony Brook NY
Longfellow-Evangeline State Commemorative Area, Saint Martinville LA
Longue Vue House & Gardens, New Orleans LA
Longview Museum of Fine Art, Longview TX
Louise Hopkins Underwood Center for the Arts, Lubbock TX
Louisiana Arts & Science Museum, Baton Rouge LA
Louisiana Department of Culture, Recreation & Tourism, Louisiana State Museum, New Orleans LA
Loyola Marymount University, Laband Art Gallery, Los Angeles CA
Loyola University Chicago, Loyola University Museum of Art, Chicago IL
Mabee-Gerrer Museum of Art, Shawnee OK
Macau Museum of Art, NAPE
Madison & Main Gallery, Greeley CO
Madison Museum of Fine Art, Madison GA
Maine Historical Society, Wadsworth-Longfellow House, Portland ME
Marblehead Museum & Historical Society, Marblehead MA
Marblehead Museum & Historical Society, Jeremiah Lee Mansion, Marblehead MA
The Mariners' Museum, Newport News VA
Mark Twain, Hartford CT
Maryland Art Place, Baltimore MD
Marylhurst University, The Art Gym, Marylhurst OR
Massillon Museum, Massillon OH
Maude Kerns Art Center, Eugene OR
McCord Museum of Canadian History, Montreal QC
McLean County Historical Society, McLean County Museum of History, Bloomington IL
Mennello Museum of American Art, Orlando FL
Meredith College, Frankie G Weems Gallery & Rotunda Gallery, Raleigh NC
Mesa Arts Center, Mesa Contemporary Arts Museum, Mesa AZ
The Mexican Museum, San Francisco CA
Mezuraj Museum, Tirana
Michigan State University, Eli & Edythe Broad Art Museum, East Lansing MI
Midwest Museum of American Art, Elkhart IN
Millicent Rogers Museum, Taos NM
Minnesota Museum of American Art, Saint Paul MN
Minot State University, Northwest Art Center, Minot ND
The Mint Museum, Charlotte NC
The Mint Museum, Mint Museum of Craft & Design, Charlotte NC
Missoula Art Museum, Missoula MT
Mobile Museum of Art, Mobile AL
Modern Art Museum, Fort Worth TX
Montana State University, Helen E Copeland Gallery, Bozeman MT
Montclair Art Museum, Montclair NJ
Montreal Museum of Fine Arts, Montreal QC
Moore College of Art & Design, The Galleries at Moore, Philadelphia PA
Moravska Galerie v Brne, Moravian Gallery in Brno, Brno
Morris Museum, Morristown NJ
Morris-Jumel Mansion, Inc, New York NY
Mount Vernon Hotel Museum & Garden, New York NY
MTG Hawkes Bay, Napier
Musee des Augustines de l'Hotel Dieu de Quebec, Quebec QC
Musee des Beaux-Arts de Tours, Museum of Fine Arts, Tours
Musee des Maitres et Artisans du Quebec, Montreal QC
Musee Regional de lu Cote-Nord, Sept-Iles QC
Musees Royaux d'Art et d'Histoire, Royal Museums of Art and History, Brussels
Museo De Las Americas, Denver CO
Museo Del Romanticismo, Museum of the Romantic Period, Madrid
Museo di Palazzo Ducale, Ducale Palace Museum, Mantua
The Museum, Greenwood SC
Museum De Lakenhal, Leiden
Museum fur Angewandte Kunst Frankfurt, Museum of Applied Arts, Frankfurt
Museum of Art & History, Santa Cruz, Santa Cruz CA
Museum of Art - Deland FL, Inc, Deland FL
Museum of Art, Fort Lauderdale, Fort Lauderdale FL
Museum of Arts & Design, New York NY
The Museum of Arts & Sciences Inc, Daytona Beach FL
Museum of Arts & Sciences, Inc, Macon GA
Museum of Contemporary Art, North Miami FL
Museum of Fine Arts, Saint Petersburg, Florida, Inc, Saint Petersburg FL
Museum of Islamic Art, Doha
Museum of Latin American Art, Long Beach CA
Museum of Northern Arizona, Flagstaff AZ
Museum of Northern British Columbia, Ruth Harvey Art Gallery, Prince Rupert BC
Museum of Northwest Art, La Conner WA
Museum of the Plains Indian & Crafts Center, Browning MT
Museum of the Southwest, Midland TX
Museum of Vancouver, Vancouver BC
Museum of York County, Rock Hill SC
Museum Plantin-Moretus, Antwerp
Museum Prinsenhof Delft, Delft
Museum zu Allerheiligen, Schaffhausen
Muzej za Umjetnost i Obrt, Museum of Arts & Crafts, Zagreb
Muzeul de Istorie Nationala Si Arheologie Constanta, National History & Archaeology Museum, Constanta
Muzeul National de Arta al Romaniei, National Museum of Art of Romania, Bucharest
Muzeum Narodowe w Poznaniu, National Museum in Poznan, Poznan
Muzim Negara, National Museum, Kuala Lumpur
National Archaeological Museum, Athens
National Art Museum of Moldova, Chisinau
National Baseball Hall of Fame & Museum, Cooperstown NY
National Museum & Art Gallery of Trinidad and Tobago, Port of Spain
National Museum of Ceramic Art, Baltimore MD
The National Museum of Modern Art, Tokyo, Tokyo
National Museum of the American Indian, George Gustav Heye Center, New York NY
National Museum of the Philippines, Manila
National Museum of Women in the Arts, Washington DC
National Museums Scotland, National Museum of Scotland, Edinburgh
National Palace Museum, Taipei
National Society of Colonial Dames of America in the State of Maryland, Mount Clare Museum House, Baltimore MD
National Society of the Colonial Dames of America in The Commonwealth of Virginia, Wilton House Museum, Richmond VA
National Veterans Art Museum, Chicago IL
Naval Historical Center, National Museum of the US Navy, Washington DC
Nelson Mandela Metropolitan Art Museum, Port Elizabeth
The Nelson-Atkins Museum of Art, Kansas City MO
Neue Galerie New York, New York NY
Nevada Museum of Art, Reno NV
New Britain Museum of American Art, New Britain CT
New Brunswick Museum, Saint John NB
New England Maple Museum, Pittsford VT
New Visions Gallery, Inc, Marshfield WI
New York State Office of Parks Recreation & Historic Preservation, John Jay Homestead State Historic Site, Katonah NY
New York State Office of Parks, Recreation & Historic Preservation, Staatsburgh State Historic Site, Staatsburg NY
Newfields, Indianapolis IN
Norwich Free Academy, Slater Memorial Museum, Norwich CT
Nova Scotia College of Art and Design, Anna Leonowens Gallery, Halifax NS
Noyes Art Gallery, Lincoln NE
Ogden Museum of Southern Art, University of New Orleans, New Orleans LA
Ohio History Connection, National Road-Zane Grey Museum, Norwich OH
Ohio University, Kennedy Museum of Art, Athens OH
Okanagan Heritage Museum, Kelowna BC
Olana State Historic Site, Hudson NY
Old Island Restoration Foundation Inc, Oldest House in Key West, Key West FL
Old Jaffa Museum of Antiquities, Jaffa
The Old Jail Art Center, Albany TX
Old Salem Museums & Gardens, Museum of Early Southern Decorative Arts, Winston-Salem NC
Orange County Museum of Art, Newport Beach CA
Oshkosh Public Museum & Library, Oshkosh WI
Owensboro Museum of Fine Art, Owensboro KY
Panhandle-Plains Historical Museum, Canyon TX
Pasadena Museum of History, Pasadena CA
Peabody Essex Museum, Salem MA
Pewabic Society Inc, Pewabic, Detroit MI
Philadelphia History Museum, Philadelphia PA
Philbrook Museum of Art, Tulsa OK
Phillips County Museum, Holyoke CO
Plains Art Museum, Fargo ND
Plumas County Museum, Quincy CA
Polk Museum of Art, Lakeland FL
Portland Art Museum, Portland OR
Portsmouth Historical Society, John Paul Jones House & Discover Portsmouth, Portsmouth NH
Preservation Virginia, John Marshall House, Richmond VA
Principia College, School of Nations Museum, Elsah IL
Purdue University Galleries, West Lafayette IN
Putnam Museum of History and Natural Science, Davenport IA
Queen Victoria Museum and Art Gallery, Launceston TAS
Queens College, City University of New York, Godwin-Ternbach Museum, Flushing NY
Randall Junior Museum, San Francisco CA
Randolph College, Maier Museum of Art, Lynchburg VA
Reading Public Museum, Reading PA
Rensselaer County Historical Society, Hart-Cluett Mansion, 1827, Troy NY
Rhode Island Historical Society, John Brown House, Providence RI
Rollins College, George D & Harriet W Cornell Fine Arts Museum, Winter Park FL
Rose Lehrman Art Gallery, Harrisburg PA
Ross Memorial Museum, Saint Andrews NB
Roswell Museum & Art Center, Roswell NM
Royal Arts Foundation, Belcourt Castle, Newport RI
Ryerss Victorian Museum & Library, Philadelphia PA
Saco Museum, Saco ME
Saginaw Art Museum, Saginaw MI
Saint Anselm College, Alva de Mars Megan Chapel Art Center, Manchester NH
Saint Bonaventure University, Regina A Quick Center for the Arts, Saint Bonaventure NY
Saint Joseph Museum, Inc., Saint Joseph MO
Saint Olaf College, Flaten Art Museum, Northfield MN
San Angelo Museum of Fine Arts, San Angelo TX
San Antonio Museum of Art, San Antonio TX
The San Joaquin Pioneer & Historical Society, The Haggin Museum, Stockton CA
Santa Clara University, de Saisset Museum, Santa Clara CA
Scripps College, Ruth Chandler Williamson Gallery, Claremont CA
Seneca-Iroquois National Museum, Salamanca NY
Shanghai Museum, Shanghai
Shirley Plantation Foundation, Charles City VA
Slovenska Narodna Galeria, Slovak National Gallery, Bratislava
Society for Contemporary Craft, Pittsburgh PA
The Society of the Cincinnati at Anderson House, Washington DC
South Carolina Artisans Center, Walterboro SC
South Dakota State University, South Dakota Art Museum, Brookings SD
Southeastern Center for Contemporary Art, Winston-Salem NC
Spartanburg Art Museum, Spartanburg SC

The Speed Art Museum, Louisville KY
Spertus Institute of Jewish Studies, Chicago IL
Springfield Art Museum, Springfield MO
St Mary's College of Maryland, The Dwight Frederick Boyden Gallery, St Mary's City MD
Staatliche Museen zu Berlin Stiftung Preussischer Kulturbesitz, National Museums in Berlin, Prussian Cultural Heritage Foundation, Berlin
Stanford University, Cantor Arts Center at Stanford University, Stanford CA
The State Museum of Fine Arts of Tatarstan Republic, Kazan
The State Museum of Oriental Art, Moscow
State University of New York at Geneseo, Bertha V B Lederer Gallery, Geneseo NY
State University of New York at New Paltz, Samuel Dorsky Museum of Art, New Paltz NY
The State University of New York at Potsdam, The Art Museum, Potsdam NY
State University of New York College at Cortland, Dowd Fine Arts Gallery, Cortland NY
Staten Island Museum, Staten Island NY
Stone Quarry Hill Art Park, Winner Gallery, Cazenovia NY
Strasburg Museum, Strasburg VA
Stratford Historical Society, Catharine B Mitchell Museum, Stratford CT
Suan Pakkad Palace Museum, Bangkok
The Summit County Historical Society of Akron, OH, Akron OH
Suomen Kansallismuseo, National Museum of Finland, Helsinki
Swedish American Museum, Chicago IL
T C Steele State Historic Site, Nashville IN
Tacoma Art Museum, Tacoma WA
Taft Museum of Art, Cincinnati OH
Tallahassee Museum of History & Natural Science, Tallahassee FL
Tampa Museum of Art, Tampa FL
Taos Historic Museums, Ernest Blumenschein Home & Studio, Taos NM
Temiskaming Art Gallery, Haileybury ON
Thomas Jefferson Foundation, Inc, Monticello, Charlottesville VA
Thomas More College, Eva G Farris Art Gallery, Crestview KY
Tohono Chul Park, Tucson AZ
The Tokugawa Art Museum, Nagoya
Tokyo National Museum, Tokyo
Toledo Museum of Art, Toledo OH
Topeka & Shawnee County Public Library, Alice C Sabatini Gallery, Topeka KS
Traffic Zone Center for Visual Art, Minneapolis MN
Trenton City Museum, Trenton NJ
Triton Museum of Art, Santa Clara CA
Tryon Palace, New Bern NC
Tubac Center of the Arts, Santa Cruz Valley Art Association, Tubac AZ
Tubman African American Museum, Macon GA
Tver Regional Art Gallery, Tver
Tyne and Wear Archives & Museums, Sunderland Museum & Winter Gardens, Sunderland
Ukrainian Canadian Archives & Museum of Alberta, Edmonton AB
Ukrainian Institute of Modern Art, Chicago IL
The Ukrainian Museum, New York NY
UMLAUF Sculpture Garden & Museum, Austin TX
United Society of Shakers, Shaker Museum, New Gloucester ME
United States Coast Guard Museum, New London CT
United States Figure Skating Association, World Figure Skating Museum & Hall of Fame, Colorado Springs CO
University of Calgary, Nickle Galleries, Calgary AB
University of California, Berkeley, Phoebe Apperson Hearst Museum of Anthropology, Berkeley CA
University of California, Davis, Jan Shrem and Maria Manetti Shrem Museum of Art, Davis CA
University of Florida, Samuel P Harn Museum of Art, Gainesville FL
University of Georgia, Georgia Museum of Art, Athens GA
University of Illinois at Urbana-Champaign, Krannert Art Museum and Kinkead Pavilion, Champaign IL
University of Illinois at Urbana-Champaign, Spurlock Museum, Urbana IL
University of Indianapolis, Christel DeHaan Fine Arts Gallery, Indianapolis IN
The University of Kentucky Art Museum, Lexington KY
University of Miami, Lowe Art Museum, Coral Gables FL
University of Minnesota, Katherine E Nash Gallery, Minneapolis MN
University of Minnesota, Goldstein Museum of Design, Saint Paul MN
University of Montana, Montana Museum of Art & Culture, Missoula MT
University of Nevada, Reno, Sheppard Contemporary & University Galleries, Reno NV
University of New Mexico, The Harwood Museum of Art, Taos NM
University of North Dakota, Hughes Fine Arts Center-Col Eugene Myers Art Gallery, Grand Forks ND
University of Richmond, University Museums, Richmond VA
University of Utah, Utah Museum of Fine Arts, Salt Lake City UT
University of Victoria, The Legacy Art Gallery, Victoria BC
University of Wisconsin-Eau Claire, Foster Gallery, Eau Claire WI
University of Wisconsin-Madison, Chazen Museum of Art, Madison WI
USS Constitution Museum, Boston MA
The Valentine, Richmond VA
Vassar College, The Frances Lehman Loeb Art Center, Poughkeepsie NY
Venice Art Center, Venice FL
Vesterheim Norwegian-American Museum, Decorah IA
Victoria Mansion - Morse Libby House, Portland ME
Villa Terrace Decorative Arts Museum, Milwaukee WI
Vizcaya Museum & Gardens, Miami FL
Volcano Art Center Gallery, Hawaii Volcanoes National Park HI
Vorres Museum of Contemporary Greek Art and Folk Art, Paiania
Wadsworth Atheneum Museum of Art, Hartford CT
The Walker African American Museum & Research Center, Las Vegas NV
Walker Art Gallery, Liverpool
Walker Fine Art, Denver CO
The Wallace Collection, London
Walter Anderson Museum of Art, Ocean Springs MS
Warner House Association, MacPheadris-Warner House, Portsmouth NH
Washburn University, Mulvane Art Museum, Topeka KS
Waterloo Center of the Arts, Waterloo IA
Waterworks Visual Arts Center, Salisbury NC
Wayne Center for the Arts, Wooster OH
Wharton Esherick Museum, Paoli PA
Wheaton College, Beard and Weil Galleries, Norton MA
Wheelwright Museum of the American Indian, Santa Fe NM
Willard House & Clock Museum, Inc, North Grafton MA
William Morris Gallery, London
Wiregrass Museum of Art, Dothan AL
Wisconsin Historical Society, Wisconsin Historical Museum, Madison WI
Woodlawn/The Pope-Leighey, Alexandria VA
Woodmere Art Museum Inc, Philadelphia PA
Worcester Art Museum, Worcester MA
World Erotic Art Museum, Miami Beach FL
Wyoming State Museum, Cheyenne WY
Yellowstone County Museum, Billings MT
Yokohama Museum of Art, Yokohama
Zigler Art Museum, Jennings LA

COINS & MEDALS

Academy of the New Church, Glencairn Museum, Bryn Athyn PA
Adams County Historical Society, Gettysburg PA
African American Museum in Philadelphia, Philadelphia PA
Al Ain National Museum, Al Ain
Alaska Heritage Museum at Wells Fargo, Anchorage AK
Alaska State Museum, Juneau AK
Albany Institute of History & Art, Albany NY
Albuquerque Museum of Art & History, Albuquerque NM
Alton Museum of History & Art, Inc, Alton IL
American University of Beirut Archaeological Museum, Beirut
Archaeological Museum of Thessaloniki, Thessaloniki
ArtSpace/Lima, Lima OH
Balzekas Museum of Lithuanian Culture, Chicago IL
Bangladesh National Museum, Dhaka
Baroda Museum and Picture Gallery, Vadodara
Bennington Museum, Bennington VT
Berkshire Museum, Pittsfield MA
Bob Jones University Museum & Gallery Inc, Greenville SC
The Bostonian Society, Old State House Museum, Boston MA
Botswana National Museum, Gaborone
Brick Store Museum, Kennebunk ME
Bronx Community College (CUNY), Hall of Fame for Great Americans, Bronx NY
Brookgreen Gardens, Murrells Inlet SC
Buffalo Niagara Heritage Village, Amherst NY
Byzantine & Christian Museum, Athens, Athens
Cambridge Museum, Cambridge NE
Canadian Museum of History, Gatineau QC
Canadian War Museum, Ottawa ON
Cape Ann Museum, Gloucester MA
Cedar Rapids Museum of Art, Cedar Rapids IA
Chatillon-DeMenil House Foundation, Chatillon-DeMenil Mansion, Saint Louis MO
The Children's Museum of Indianapolis, Indianapolis IN
Cincinnati Art Museum, Cincinnati Art Museum, Cincinnati OH
Clark County Historical Society, Pioneer - Krier Museum, Ashland KS
College of William & Mary, Muscarelle Museum of Art, Williamsburg VA
Concordia Historical Institute, Saint Louis MO
Cornell University, Herbert F Johnson Museum of Art, Ithaca NY
Craft and Folk Art Museum (CAFAM), Los Angeles CA
Cripple Creek District Museum, Cripple Creek CO
Crocker Art Museum, Sacramento CA
Crook County Museum & Art Gallery, Sundance WY
Cyprus Museum, Nicosia
Dallas Museum of Art, Dallas TX
Dalnavert Museum, Winnipeg MB
Danville Museum of Fine Arts & History, Danville VA
DAR Museum, National Society Daughters of the American Revolution, Washington DC
Dartmouth College, Hood Museum of Art, Hanover NH
Dawson City Museum, Dawson City YT
Delphi Archaeological Museum, Delphi
Detroit Institute of Arts, Detroit MI
Doncaster Museum and Art Gallery, Doncaster Yorks
Everhart Museum, Scranton PA
Fairbanks Museum & Planetarium, Saint Johnsbury VT
Farmington Village Green & Library Association, Stanley-Whitman House, Farmington CT
Favell Museum of Western Art & Indian Artifacts, Klamath Falls OR
Fetherston Foundation, Packwood House Museum, Lewisburg PA
Florence County Museum, Florence SC
Florida State University, John & Mable Ringling Museum of Art, Sarasota FL
Fondazione Musei Civici Di Venezia, Museo Correr - Correr Museum, Venice
Forest Lawn Museum, Glendale CA
Freer Gallery of Art & Arthur M Sackler Gallery, Arthur M Sackler Gallery, Washington DC
Frontier Times Museum, Bandera TX
Fulton County Historical Society Inc, Fulton County Museum (Tetzlaff Reference Room), Rochester IN
General Board of Discipleship, The United Methodist Church, The Upper Room Chapel & Museum, Nashville TN
Glanmore National Historic Site of Canada, Belleville ON
Glasgow University, The Hunterian, Glasgow
Grand Rapids Art Museum, Grand Rapids MI
Grand Rapids Public Museum, Grand Rapids MI
Harvard University, Semitic Museum, Cambridge MA
Hastings Museum of Natural & Cultural History, Hastings NE
Headquarters Fort Monroe, Dept of Army, Casemate Museum, Hampton VA
Hebrew Union College, Skirball Cultural Center, Los Angeles CA
Hecht Museum, Haifa
Henry Sheldon Museum of Vermont History and Research Center, Middlebury VT

Heras Museum for Research in Indian History and Culture, Mumbai
Heritage Glass Museum, Glassboro NJ
Heritage Museum & Cultural Center, Baker LA
Hermitage Museum & Gardens, Norfolk VA
Het Noordbrabants Museum, s-Hertogenbosch
Hillwood Museum & Gardens Foundation, Hillwood Estate Museum & Gardens, Washington DC
Historic Hudson Valley, Pocantico Hills NY
Historic Huguenot Street, New Paltz NY
Historical Society of Cheshire County, Keene NH
History Colorado Center Museum, Denver CO
History Museum of Mobile, Mobile AL
Huntington Museum of Art, Huntington WV
Imperial Calcasieu Museum, Gibson-Barham Gallery, Lake Charles LA
Independence Historical Museum & Art Center, Independence KS
Independence Seaport Museum, Philadelphia PA
Institute of Puerto Rican Culture, Museo Fuerte Conde de Mirasol, Vieques PR
International Museum of Art, El Paso TX
The Israel Museum, Jerusalem, Jerusalem
Jacksonville University, Alexander Brest Museum & Gallery, Jacksonville FL
James Dick Foundation, Festival - Institute, Round Top TX
The Jewish Museum, New York NY
Johns Hopkins University, Evergreen Museum & Library, Baltimore MD
Joslyn Art Museum, Omaha NE
Karakalpak State Art Museum, Nukus Republic of Karakalpakstan
Kenosha Public Museums, Kenosha WI
Kereszteny Muzeum, Christian Museum, Esztergom
Kings County Historical Society & Museum, Hampton NB
Koochiching Museums, International Falls MN
Kunsthistorisches Museum Wien, Museum of Fine Arts, Vienna
Kyiv Museum of Russian Art, Kyiv Ukrainian
Lahore Museum, Lahore
Lalit Kala Akademi Rabindra Bhavan Art Galleries, National Academy of Art, New Delhi, New Delhi
Le Grand Curtius, The Grand Curtius, Liege
Lightner Museum, Saint Augustine FL
Lincolnshire County Council, Library & Heritage Services, Lincoln
Lincolnshire County Council, The Collection: Art & Archaeology in Lincolnshire, Lincoln
The Long Island Museum of American Art, History & Carriages, Stony Brook NY
Longfellow-Evangeline State Commemorative Area, Saint Martinville LA
Marblehead Museum & Historical Society, Marblehead MA
Marblehead Museum & Historical Society, Jeremiah Lee Mansion, Marblehead MA
The Mariners' Museum, Newport News VA
McDowell House & Apothecary Shop, Danville KY
McLean County Historical Society, McLean County Museum of History, Bloomington IL
Medina Railroad Museum, Medina NY
Mezuraj Museum, Tirana
Michigan State University, Eli & Edythe Broad Art Museum, East Lansing MI
Mississippi River Museum at Mud-Island River Park, Memphis TN
Moderna Galerija, Modern Gallery - National Museum of Modern Art, Zagreb
Musee des Augustines de l'Hotel Dieu de Quebec, Quebec QC
Musee des Beaux-Arts de Tours, Museum of Fine Arts, Tours
Musees Royaux d'Art et d'Histoire, Royal Museums of Art and History, Brussels
Museo De Las Americas, Denver CO
Museo di Palazzo Ducale, Ducale Palace Museum, Mantua
Museu Nacional D'Art De Catalunya, Catalona National Museum of Art, Barcelona
The Museum, Greenwood SC
Museum De Lakenhal, Leiden
The Museum of Arts & Sciences Inc, Daytona Beach FL
Museum of Northern British Columbia, Ruth Harvey Art Gallery, Prince Rupert BC
Museum of Vancouver, Vancouver BC
Museum zu Allerheiligen, Schaffhausen
Muzej za Umjetnost i Obrt, Museum of Arts & Crafts, Zagreb
Muzeul de Istorie Nationala Si Arheologie Constanta, National History & Archaeology Museum, Constanta
Muzeum Narodowe w Poznaniu, National Museum in Poznan, Poznan
Narodna Galerija, National Gallery of Slovenia, Ljubljana
National Art Museum of Moldova, Chisinau
National Baseball Hall of Fame & Museum, Cooperstown NY
National Museum & Art Gallery of Trinidad and Tobago, Port of Spain
National Museum of the American Indian, George Gustav Heye Center, New York NY
National Museums Scotland, National Museum of Scotland, Edinburgh
Naval Historical Center, National Museum of the US Navy, Washington DC
New Brunswick Museum, Saint John NB
New Jersey Historical Society, Newark NJ
Norwich Free Academy, Slater Memorial Museum, Norwich CT
Ohio History Connection, National Afro-American Museum & Cultural Center, Wilberforce OH
Old Jaffa Museum of Antiquities, Jaffa
Order Sons of Italy in America, Garibaldi & Meucci Museum, Staten Island NY
Oshkosh Public Museum & Library, Oshkosh WI
Panhandle-Plains Historical Museum, Canyon TX
Pennsylvania Academy of the Fine Arts, Philadelphia PA
Philadelphia History Museum, Philadelphia PA
Plainsman Museum, Aurora NE
Plumas County Museum, Quincy CA
Polish Museum of America (PMA), Chicago IL
Portland Art Museum, Portland OR
Putnam Museum of History and Natural Science, Davenport IA
Queens College, City University of New York, Godwin-Ternbach Museum, Flushing NY
Reading Public Museum, Reading PA
Rhode Island Historical Society, John Brown House, Providence RI
Rollins College, George D & Harriet W Cornell Fine Arts Museum, Winter Park FL
Royal Alberta Museum, Royal Alberta Museum, Edmonton AB
Saco Museum, Saco ME
Saint Mary's College of California, Museum of Art, Moraga CA
San Antonio Museum of Art, San Antonio TX
Schweinfurth Art Center, Auburn NY
Shirley Plantation Foundation, Charles City VA
The Society of the Cincinnati at Anderson House, Washington DC
The Speed Art Museum, Louisville KY
Spertus Institute of Jewish Studies, Chicago IL
Staatliche Munzsammlung, State Coin Collection, Munich
Staatliche Museen zu Berlin Stiftung Preussischer Kulturbesitz, National Museums in Berlin, Prussian Cultural Heritage Foundation, Berlin
Stanford University, Cantor Arts Center at Stanford University, Stanford CA
Staten Island Museum, Staten Island NY
Ste Genevieve Museum, Sainte Genevieve MO
Suan Pakkad Palace Museum, Bangkok
Suomen Kansallismuseo, National Museum of Finland, Helsinki
Swedish American Museum, Chicago IL
Tampa Museum of Art, Tampa FL
Tokyo National Museum, Tokyo
Tubman African American Museum, Macon GA
Tver Regional Art Gallery, Tver
The Ukrainian Museum, New York NY
United Society of Shakers, Shaker Museum, New Gloucester ME
United States Coast Guard Museum, New London CT
United States Military Academy, West Point Museum, West Point NY
University of Calgary, Nickle Galleries, Calgary AB
University of California, Berkeley, Phoebe Apperson Hearst Museum of Anthropology, Berkeley CA
University of Georgia, Georgia Museum of Art, Athens GA
University of Illinois at Urbana-Champaign, Spurlock Museum, Urbana IL
University of Indianapolis, Christel DeHaan Fine Arts Gallery, Indianapolis IN
The University of Kentucky Art Museum, Lexington KY
University of Richmond, University Museums, Richmond VA
University of Saskatchewan, Diefenbaker Canada Centre, Saskatoon SK
University of Wisconsin-Madison, Chazen Museum of Art, Madison WI
USS Constitution Museum, Boston MA
Vesterheim Norwegian-American Museum, Decorah IA
Vorres Museum of Contemporary Greek Art and Folk Art, Paiania
The Walker African American Museum & Research Center, Las Vegas NV
Wheaton College, Beard and Weil Galleries, Norton MA
Willard House & Clock Museum, Inc, North Grafton MA
Wisconsin Historical Society, Wisconsin Historical Museum, Madison WI
Woodlawn/The Pope-Leighey, Alexandria VA
Worcester Art Museum, Worcester MA
World Erotic Art Museum, Miami Beach FL
Yellowstone County Museum, Billings MT

COLLAGES

African American Atelier, Greensboro NC
African American Museum in Philadelphia, Philadelphia PA
Alaska State Museum, Juneau AK
Albuquerque Museum of Art & History, Albuquerque NM
American Sport Art Museum and Archives, Daphne AL
Amherst College, Mead Art Museum, Amherst MA
Arnot Art Museum, Elmira NY
Art and History Museums - Maitland, Maitland FL
Art Without Walls Inc, Sayville NY
Arts Council of Fayetteville-Cumberland County, The Arts Center, Fayetteville NC
ArtSpace/Lima, Lima OH
Bangladesh National Museum, Dhaka
Bayerische Staatsgemaldesammlungen, Bavarian State Painting Collections, Munich
Beaumont Art League, Beaumont TX
Bucknell University, Edward & Marthann Samek Art Gallery, Lewisburg PA
Burchfield Penney Art Center, Buffalo NY
Cameron Art Museum, Wilmington NC
Canadian Clay and Glass Gallery, Waterloo ON
Canadian Museum of History, Gatineau QC
Children's Museum of Manhattan, New York NY
City of Fremont, Olive Hyde Art Gallery, Fremont CA
College of William & Mary, Muscarelle Museum of Art, Williamsburg VA
The Columbus Museum, Columbus GA
Contemporary Calgary, Calgary AB
Coutts Museum of Art, Inc, El Dorado KS
Craft and Folk Art Museum (CAFAM), Los Angeles CA
Dallas Museum of Art, Dallas TX
Daum Museum of Contemporary Art, Sedalia MO
Davidson College, William H Van Every Jr & Edward M Smith Galleries, Davidson NC
Deines Cultural Center, Russell KS
DeLeon White Gallery, Toronto ON
Detroit Institute of Arts, Detroit MI
Detroit Repertory Theatre Gallery, Detroit MI
Dublin Arts Council, Dublin OH
Ellen Noel Art Museum of the Permian Basin, Odessa TX
Erie Art Museum, Erie PA
Fairbanks Museum & Planetarium, Saint Johnsbury VT
Fine Arts Center for the New River Valley, Pulaski VA
Flint Institute of Arts, Flint MI
Florence County Museum, Florence SC
Folk Art Society of America, Richmond VA
Freer Gallery of Art & Arthur M Sackler Gallery, Arthur M Sackler Gallery, Washington DC
Fuller Craft Museum, Brockton MA
Galerie Montcalm, Gatineau QC
Gallery One Visual Arts Center, Ellensburg WA
Grand Rapids Art Museum, Grand Rapids MI
Hammonds House Museum, Atlanta GA
Hebrew Union College, Skirball Cultural Center, Los Angeles CA

Hebrew Union College - Jewish Institute of Religion Museum, Jewish Institute of Religion, New York NY
Heritage Center, Inc, Pine Ridge SD
Hickory Museum of Art, Inc, Hickory NC
Huntington Museum of Art, Huntington WV
i.d.e.a. Museum, Mesa AZ
Illinois State Museum, ISM Lockport Gallery, Chicago Gallery & Southern Illinois Art Gallery, Springfield IL
The Interchurch Center, Galleries at the Interchurch Center, New York NY
Intermedia Arts, Minneapolis MN
The Israel Museum, Jerusalem, Jerusalem
Jordan National Gallery of Fine Arts, Amman
Kentucky Museum of Art and Craft, Louisville KY
La Salle University Art Museum, Philadelphia PA
Latino Art Museum, Pomona CA
League of New Hampshire Craftsmen, Grodin Permanent Collection Museum, Concord NH
Lighthouse ArtCenter Museum & School of Art, Tequesta FL
The Long Island Museum of American Art, History & Carriages, Stony Brook NY
Longview Museum of Fine Art, Longview TX
Louise Hopkins Underwood Center for the Arts, Lubbock TX
Maryland Art Place, Baltimore MD
Marylhurst University, The Art Gym, Marylhurst OR
Mennello Museum of American Art, Orlando FL
Meredith College, Frankie G Weems Gallery & Rotunda Gallery, Raleigh NC
Mesa Arts Center, Mesa Contemporary Arts Museum, Mesa AZ
Michigan State University, Eli & Edythe Broad Art Museum, East Lansing MI
Midwest Museum of American Art, Elkhart IN
Miller Art Center Foundation Inc, Miller Art Museum, Sturgeon Bay WI
Minnesota Museum of American Art, Saint Paul MN
The Mint Museum, Charlotte NC
Missoula Art Museum, Missoula MT
Mobile Museum of Art, Mobile AL
Modern Art Museum, Fort Worth TX
Monroe County Historical Association, Elizabeth D Walters Library, Stroudsburg PA
Morris Museum, Morristown NJ
Morris Museum of Art, Augusta GA
Musee des Beaux-Arts de Tours, Museum of Fine Arts, Tours
Museo di Palazzo Ducale, Ducale Palace Museum, Mantua
Museum of Contemporary Art, North Miami FL
Museum of Contemporary Art Chicago, Chicago IL
Museum of Latin American Art, Long Beach CA
Museum of Northwest Art, La Conner WA
Museum zu Allerheiligen, Schaffhausen
Muzeum Narodowe w Poznaniu, National Museum in Poznan, Poznan
Nassau County Museum of Art, Roslyn Harbor NY
National Art Museum of Moldova, Chisinau
National Baseball Hall of Fame & Museum, Cooperstown NY
National Gallery of Canada, Ottawa ON
National Museum & Art Gallery of Trinidad and Tobago, Port of Spain
The National Museum of Modern Art, Tokyo, Tokyo
National Veterans Art Museum, Chicago IL
Nelson Mandela Metropolitan Art Museum, Port Elizabeth
New Britain Museum of American Art, New Britain CT
New Brunswick Museum, Saint John NB
Niagara University, Castellani Art Museum, Niagara NY
Norwich Free Academy, Slater Memorial Museum, Norwich CT
Nova Scotia College of Art and Design, Anna Leonowens Gallery, Halifax NS
Noyes Art Gallery, Lincoln NE
Oakland University, Oakland University Art Gallery, Rochester MI
Opelousas Museum of Art, Inc (OMA), Opelousas LA
Owensboro Museum of Fine Art, Owensboro KY
Pennsylvania Academy of the Fine Arts, Philadelphia PA
Polk Museum of Art, Lakeland FL
PS1 Contemporary Art Center, Long Island City NY
Randolph College, Maier Museum of Art, Lynchburg VA
Rollins College, George D & Harriet W Cornell Fine Arts Museum, Winter Park FL
Roswell Museum & Art Center, Roswell NM
Saginaw Art Museum, Saginaw MI
Saint Anselm College, Alva de Mars Megan Chapel Art Center, Manchester NH
San Bernardino County Museum, Redlands CA
Schweinfurth Art Center, Auburn NY
Slovenska Narodna Galeria, Slovak National Gallery, Bratislava
South Carolina Artisans Center, Walterboro SC
Southeastern Center for Contemporary Art, Winston-Salem NC
The Speed Art Museum, Louisville KY
Springfield Art Museum, Springfield MO
Staatliche Museen zu Berlin Stiftung Preussischer Kulturbesitz, National Museums in Berlin, Prussian Cultural Heritage Foundation, Berlin
Stanford University, Cantor Arts Center at Stanford University, Stanford CA
State University of New York at Geneseo, Bertha V B Lederer Gallery, Geneseo NY
State University of New York College at Cortland, Dowd Fine Arts Gallery, Cortland NY
Temiskaming Art Gallery, Haileybury ON
Tohono Chul Park, Tucson AZ
Tubman African American Museum, Macon GA
Tver Regional Art Gallery, Tver
University of Chicago, Smart Museum of Art, Chicago IL
University of Florida, Samuel P Harn Museum of Art, Gainesville FL
University of Georgia, Georgia Museum of Art, Athens GA
University of Illinois at Urbana-Champaign, Krannert Art Museum and Kinkead Pavilion, Champaign IL
The University of Kentucky Art Museum, Lexington KY
University of Richmond, University Museums, Richmond VA
University of Wisconsin-Eau Claire, Foster Gallery, Eau Claire WI
Vero Beach Museum of Art, Vero Beach FL
Viridian Artists Inc, New York NY
The Walker African American Museum & Research Center, Las Vegas NV
Wiregrass Museum of Art, Dothan AL
Wyoming State Museum, Cheyenne WY
Yokohama Museum of Art, Yokohama

CONCEPTUAL ART

Alaska Heritage Museum at Wells Fargo, Anchorage AK
Art Metropole, Toronto ON
Brickton Art Center, Park Ridge IL
Burke Arts Council, Jailhouse Galleries, Morganton NC
Canadian Clay and Glass Gallery, Waterloo ON
Crocker Art Museum, Sacramento CA
eMediaLoft.org, New York NY
Fondazione Musei Civici Di Venezia, Ca' Pesaro Galleria Nazionale d'Arte Moderna - Ca' Pesaro Gallery of Modern Art, Venice
High Museum of Art, Atlanta GA
LACE (Los Angeles Contemporary Exhibitions), Los Angeles CA
Lalit Kala Akademi Rabindra Bhavan Art Galleries, National Academy of Art, New Delhi, New Delhi
Latino Art Museum, Pomona CA
Loyola University Chicago, Loyola University Museum of Art, Chicago IL
Maine College of Art, The Institute of Contemporary Art, Portland ME
Morris Museum of Art, Augusta GA
Moscow Museum of Modern Art, Moscow
Museo de Arte Contemporaneo de Castilla y Leon, Leon
Nelson Mandela Metropolitan Art Museum, Port Elizabeth
San Antonio Museum of Art, San Antonio TX
Slovenska Narodna Galeria, Slovak National Gallery, Bratislava
Stone Quarry Hill Art Park, Winner Gallery, Cazenovia NY
VU Centre De Diffusion Et De Production De La Photographie, Quebec QC

COSTUMES

Abington Art Center, Jenkintown PA
Academy of the New Church, Glencairn Museum, Bryn Athyn PA
Adams County Historical Society, Gettysburg PA
African American Museum in Philadelphia, Philadelphia PA
African Art Museum of Maryland, Columbia MD
Alaska Department of Education, Division of Libraries, Archives & Museums, Sheldon Jackson Museum, Sitka AK
Alaska State Museum, Juneau AK
Albuquerque Museum of Art & History, Albuquerque NM
American Museum of the Moving Image, Astoria NY
American Textile History Museum, Lowell MA
Anchorage Museum at Rasmuson Center, Anchorage AK
The Andy Warhol Museum, Pittsburgh PA
Appaloosa Museum and Heritage Center, Moscow ID
Arapahoe Community College, Colorado Gallery of the Arts, Littleton CO
Arizona Historical Society-Yuma, Sanguinetti House Museum & Garden, Yuma AZ
Art Center of Battle Creek, Battle Creek MI
Art Metropole, Toronto ON
Art Without Walls Inc, Sayville NY
ArtSpace/Lima, Lima OH
Atlanta Historical Society Inc, Atlanta History Center, Atlanta GA
Baldwin Historical Society Museum, Baldwin NY
Balzekas Museum of Lithuanian Culture, Chicago IL
Bangladesh National Museum, Dhaka
Barker Character, Comic and Cartoon Museum, Cheshire CT
Baroda Museum and Picture Gallery, Vadodara
The Bartlett Museum, Amesbury MA
Bayerisches Nationalmuseum, Bavarian National Museum, Munich
Bennington Museum, Bennington VT
Berkshire Museum, Pittsfield MA
Besser Museum for Northeast Michigan, Alpena MI
Billie Trimble Chandler, Texas State Museum of Asian Cultures, Corpus Christi TX
Birmingham Museum of Art, Birmingham AL
The Bostonian Society, Old State House Museum, Boston MA
Botswana National Museum, Gaborone
Brick Store Museum, Kennebunk ME
Brown University, Haffenreffer Museum of Anthropology, Providence RI
Bruce Museum, Inc, Greenwich CT
Buffalo Niagara Heritage Village, Amherst NY
Byzantine & Christian Museum, Athens, Athens
Cambridge Museum, Cambridge NE
Canadian Museum of History, Gatineau QC
Canadian Museum of Nature, Musee Canadien de la Nature, Ottawa ON
Canton Museum of Art, Canton OH
Carson County Square House Museum, Panhandle TX
Centenary College of Louisiana, Meadows Museum of Art, Shreveport LA
Center for Puppetry Arts, Atlanta GA
Chatham Historical Society, The Atwood House Museum, Chatham MA
The Children's Museum of Indianapolis, Indianapolis IN
Children's Museum of Manhattan, New York NY
Cincinnati Art Museum, Cincinnati Art Museum, Cincinnati OH
City of Atlanta, Atlanta Cyclorama & Civil War Museum, Atlanta GA
The City of Petersburg Museums, Petersburg VA
Cohasset Historical Society, Pratt Building (Society Headquarters), Cohasset MA
The Columbus Museum, Columbus GA
Concord Museum, Concord MA
Concordia Historical Institute, Saint Louis MO
Craft and Folk Art Museum (CAFAM), Los Angeles CA
Cranford Historical Society, Cranford NJ
Cripple Creek District Museum, Cripple Creek CO
Crocker Art Museum, Sacramento CA
Crow Wing County Historical Society, Brainerd MN
Dalnavert Museum, Winnipeg MB
Danville Museum of Fine Arts & History, Danville VA
DAR Museum, National Society Daughters of the American Revolution, Washington DC
Dartmouth College, Hood Museum of Art, Hanover NH

Dartmouth Heritage Museum, Dartmouth NS
Delta Blues Museum, Clarksdale MS
Designmuseum Danmark, Danish Design Museum, Copenhagen
Detroit Institute of Arts, Detroit MI
Doncaster Museum and Art Gallery, Doncaster Yorks
Edsel & Eleanor Ford House, Grosse Pointe Shores MI
Ella Sharp Museum, Jackson MI
Erie County Historical Society, Erie PA
Evanston Historical Society, Charles Gates Dawes House, Evanston IL
Fairbanks Museum & Planetarium, Saint Johnsbury VT
Fall River Historical Society, Fall River MA
Farmington Village Green & Library Association, Stanley-Whitman House, Farmington CT
Fetherston Foundation, Packwood House Museum, Lewisburg PA
Fine Arts Museums of San Francisco, Legion of Honor, San Francisco CA
Fishkill Historical Society, Van Wyck Homestead Museum, Fishkill NY
Fitchburg Art Museum, Fitchburg MA
Folk Art Society of America, Richmond VA
Fort George G Meade Museum, Fort Meade MD
Fort Morgan Heritage Foundation, Fort Morgan CO
Fort Ticonderoga Association, Ticonderoga NY
Freer Gallery of Art & Arthur M Sackler Gallery, Arthur M Sackler Gallery, Washington DC
Fulton County Historical Society Inc, Fulton County Museum (Tetzlaff Reference Room), Rochester IN
Genesee Country Village & Museum, John L Wehle Art Gallery, Mumford NY
Germantown Historical Society, Philadelphia PA
Girard College, Stephen Girard Collection, Philadelphia PA
Glasgow University, The Hunterian, Glasgow
Glessner House Museum, Chicago IL
Grand Rapids Art Museum, Grand Rapids MI
Grand Rapids Public Museum, Grand Rapids MI
Greene County Historical Society, Bronck Museum, Coxsackie NY
Harvard University, Semitic Museum, Cambridge MA
Hebrew Union College, Skirball Cultural Center, Los Angeles CA
Henry County Museum & Cultural Arts Center, Clinton MO
Henry Sheldon Museum of Vermont History and Research Center, Middlebury VT
Heritage Glass Museum, Glassboro NJ
Heritage Museum & Cultural Center, Baker LA
Hermitage Museum & Gardens, Norfolk VA
High Desert Museum, Bend OR
Hillwood Museum & Gardens Foundation, Hillwood Estate Museum & Gardens, Washington DC
Historic Arkansas Museum, Little Rock AR
Historic Cherry Hill, Albany NY
Historic Deerfield, Inc, Deerfield MA
Historic Holyoke at Wistariahurst & City of Holyoke, Holyoke MA
Historic Hudson Valley, Pocantico Hills NY
Historic Huguenot Street, New Paltz NY
Historic Newton, Newton MA
Historic Northampton Museum & Education Center, Northampton MA
Historic Paris - Bourbon County, Inc, Hopewell Museum, Paris KY
Historical Society of Bloomfield, Bloomfield NJ
Historisches und Volkerkundemuseum, Museum of History and Ethnology, St Gallen
The History Center in Tompkins County, Ithaca NY
History Colorado Center Museum, Denver CO
Honolulu Museum of Art, Honolulu HI
i.d.e.a. Museum, Mesa AZ
Idaho Historical Museum, Boise ID
Imperial Calcasieu Museum, Gibson-Barham Gallery, Lake Charles LA
Independence Seaport Museum, Philadelphia PA
Indiana State Museum, Indianapolis IN
International Clown Hall of Fame & Research Center, Inc, West Allis WI
International Museum of Art, El Paso TX
Iredell Museums, Statesville NC
The Israel Museum, Jerusalem, Jerusalem
James Dick Foundation, Festival - Institute, Round Top TX
Jefferson County Historical Society, Watertown NY
Jefferson County Open Space, Hiwan Homestead Museum, Evergreen CO
Joe Gish's Old West Museum, Fredericksburg TX
Karakalpak State Art Museum, Nukus Republic of Karakalpakstan
Kelly-Griggs House Museum, Red Bluff CA
Kenosha Public Museums, Kenosha WI
Kentucky Derby Museum, Louisville KY
Kentucky Museum of Art and Craft, Louisville KY
Kern County Museum, Bakersfield CA
Kings County Historical Society & Museum, Hampton NB
Kunsthistorisches Museum Wien, Museum of Fine Arts, Vienna
LA County Museum of Art, Los Angeles CA
Lac du Flambeau Band of Lake Superior Chippewa Indians, George W Brown Jr Ojibwe Museum & Cultural Center, Lac Du Flambeau WI
Lafayette Science Museum & Planetarium, Lafayette LA
Lahore Museum, Lahore
Lehigh Valley Heritage Center, Allentown PA
Liberty Hall Historic Site, Liberty Hall Museum, Frankfort KY
Lightner Museum, Saint Augustine FL
Lincoln County Historical Association, Inc, 1811 Old Lincoln County Jail & Lincoln County Museum, Wiscasset ME
Lincolnshire County Council, Library & Heritage Services, Lincoln
Lincolnshire County Council, The Collection: Art & Archaeology in Lincolnshire, Lincoln
Lockwood-Mathews Mansion Museum, Norwalk CT
The Long Island Museum of American Art, History & Carriages, Stony Brook NY
Longue Vue House & Gardens, New Orleans LA
Los Angeles County Museum of Art, Los Angeles CA
Louise Hopkins Underwood Center for the Arts, Lubbock TX
Louisiana Arts & Science Museum, Baton Rouge LA
Louisiana Department of Culture, Recreation & Tourism, Louisiana State Museum, New Orleans LA
Loveland Museum/Gallery, Loveland CO
Maine Historical Society, MHS Museum, Portland ME
Maine Historical Society, Wadsworth-Longfellow House, Portland ME
Marblehead Museum & Historical Society, Marblehead MA
Marblehead Museum & Historical Society, Jeremiah Lee Mansion, Marblehead MA
Maricopa County Historical Society, Desert Caballeros Western Museum, Wickenburg AZ
Massillon Museum, Massillon OH
McCord Museum of Canadian History, Montreal QC
McLean County Historical Society, McLean County Museum of History, Bloomington IL
McPherson Museum and Arts Foundation, McPherson KS
Meredith College, Frankie G Weems Gallery & Rotunda Gallery, Raleigh NC
The Metropolitan Museum of Art, New York NY
Millicent Rogers Museum, Taos NM
The Mint Museum, Charlotte NC
The Mint Museum, Mint Museum of Craft & Design, Charlotte NC
Mississippi River Museum at Mud-Island River Park, Memphis TN
Missouri Department of Natural Resources, Missouri State Museum, Jefferson City MO
Montana State University, Helen E Copeland Gallery, Bozeman MT
Montclair Art Museum, Montclair NJ
Moravska Galerie v Brne, Moravian Gallery in Brno, Brno
Morris Museum, Morristown NJ
Morris-Jumel Mansion, Inc, New York NY
Mount Mary College, Marian Gallery, Milwaukee WI
MTG Hawkes Bay, Napier
Muscatine Art Center, Muscatine IA
Musee des Beaux-Arts de Tours, Museum of Fine Arts, Tours
Musees Royaux d'Art et d'Histoire, Royal Museums of Art and History, Brussels
The Museum, Greenwood SC
Museum fur Angewandte Kunst Frankfurt, Museum of Applied Arts, Frankfurt
Museum of Art & History, Santa Cruz, Santa Cruz CA
Museum of Chinese in America, New York NY
Museum of Islamic Art, Doha
Museum of Ossining Historical Society, Ossining NY
Museum of Vancouver, Vancouver BC
Museum of York County, Rock Hill SC
Museum zu Allerheiligen, Schaffhausen
Muzej za Umjetnost i Obrt, Museum of Arts & Crafts, Zagreb
Muzeul de Istorie Nationala Si Arheologie Constanta, National History & Archaeology Museum, Constanta
Muzeul National de Arta al Romaniei, National Museum of Art of Romania, Bucharest
Muzeum Narodowe w Poznaniu, National Museum in Poznan, Poznan
Muzim Negara, National Museum, Kuala Lumpur
Nanticoke Indian Museum, Millsboro DE
National Baseball Hall of Fame & Museum, Cooperstown NY
National Museum & Art Gallery of Trinidad and Tobago, Port of Spain
National Museum of the American Indian, George Gustav Heye Center, New York NY
National Museum of the Philippines, Manila
National Museum of Women in the Arts, Washington DC
National Museums Scotland, National Museum of Scotland, Edinburgh
National Society of Colonial Dames of America in the State of Maryland, Mount Clare Museum House, Baltimore MD
Naval Historical Center, National Museum of the US Navy, Washington DC
Naval War College Museum, Newport RI
Nebraska Game and Parks Commission, Arbor Lodge State Historical Park & Morton Mansion, Nebraska City NE
Nelson Mandela Metropolitan Art Museum, Port Elizabeth
The Nelson-Atkins Museum of Art, Kansas City MO
Neville Public Museum of Brown County, Green Bay WI
New Brunswick Museum, Saint John NB
New Canaan Historical Society, New Canaan CT
New Jersey Historical Society, Newark NJ
New York State Military Museum and Veterans Research Center, Saratoga Springs NY
Norwich Free Academy, Slater Memorial Museum, Norwich CT
Ogden Museum of Southern Art, University of New Orleans, New Orleans LA
The Ohio Historical Society, Inc, Campus Martius Museum & Ohio River Museum, Marietta OH
Okanagan Heritage Museum, Kelowna BC
Old Dartmouth Historical Society, New Bedford Whaling Museum, New Bedford MA
Old Island Restoration Foundation Inc, Oldest House in Key West, Key West FL
Palm Beach County Parks & Recreation Department, Morikami Museum & Japanese Gardens, Delray Beach FL
Panhandle-Plains Historical Museum, Canyon TX
Pasadena Museum of History, Pasadena CA
Philadelphia History Museum, Philadelphia PA
Philadelphia University, Paley Design Center, Philadelphia PA
Phoenix Art Museum, Phoenix AZ
Pine Bluff/Jefferson County Historical Museum, Pine Bluff AR
Please Touch Museum, Philadelphia PA
Plumas County Museum, Quincy CA
Polish Museum of America (PMA), Chicago IL
Port Huron Museum, Port Huron MI
Portsmouth Historical Society, John Paul Jones House & Discover Portsmouth, Portsmouth NH
Preservation Virginia, John Marshall House, Richmond VA
Pueblo Museum, Desert Hot Springs CA
Putnam County Historical Society, Foundry School Museum, Cold Spring NY
Putnam Museum of History and Natural Science, Davenport IA
Queen Victoria Museum and Art Gallery, Launceston TAS
Red Rock Park, Red Rock Park, Church Rock NM
Rensselaer County Historical Society, Hart-Cluett Mansion, 1827, Troy NY
Reynolda House Museum of American Art, Winston-Salem NC
Rhode Island Historical Society, John Brown House, Providence RI
Rollins College, George D & Harriet W Cornell Fine Arts Museum, Winter Park FL
Roswell Museum & Art Center, Roswell NM
Royal Arts Foundation, Belcourt Castle, Newport RI

Saco Museum, Saco ME
Saginaw Art Museum, Saginaw MI
San Francisco Maritime National Historical Park, Maritime Museum, San Francisco CA
The San Joaquin Pioneer & Historical Society, The Haggin Museum, Stockton CA
Scripps College, Ruth Chandler Williamson Gallery, Claremont CA
Sea Cliff Village Museum, Sea Cliff NY
Seneca Falls Historical Society Museum, Seneca Falls NY
Seneca-Iroquois National Museum, Salamanca NY
Shaker Museum & Library, Old Chatham NY
Shaker Village of Pleasant Hill, Harrodsburg KY
Sheldon Art Galleries, Saint Louis MO
Shores Memorial Museum, Lyndon Center VT
Slater Mill, Old Slater Mill Association, Pawtucket RI
Slovenska Narodna Galeria, Slovak National Gallery, Bratislava
The Society of the Cincinnati at Anderson House, Washington DC
Sooke Region Museum & Art Gallery, Sooke BC
Southern Lorain County Historical Society, Spirit of '76 Museum, Elyria OH
The Speed Art Museum, Louisville KY
St Mary's College of Maryland, The Dwight Frederick Boyden Gallery, St Mary's City MD
Staatliche Museen zu Berlin Stiftung Preussischer Kulturbesitz, National Museums in Berlin, Prussian Cultural Heritage Foundation, Berlin
The State Museum of Fine Arts of Tatarstan Republic, Kazan
Staten Island Museum, Staten Island NY
Strasburg Museum, Strasburg VA
The Summit County Historical Society of Akron, OH, Akron OH
Suomen Kansallismuseo, National Museum of Finland, Helsinki
Swedish American Museum, Chicago IL
Tallahassee Museum of History & Natural Science, Tallahassee FL
The Tokugawa Art Museum, Nagoya
Tokyo National Museum, Tokyo
Trust Authority, Museum of the Great Plains, Lawton OK
Tryon Palace, New Bern NC
Tubman African American Museum, Macon GA
Turtle Bay Exploration Park, Redding CA
Tver Regional Art Gallery, Tver
Ukrainian Canadian Archives & Museum of Alberta, Edmonton AB
The Ukrainian Museum, New York NY
United Society of Shakers, Shaker Museum, New Gloucester ME
United States Coast Guard Museum, New London CT
United States Figure Skating Association, World Figure Skating Museum & Hall of Fame, Colorado Springs CO
University of Georgia, Georgia Museum of Art, Athens GA
The University of Kentucky Art Museum, Lexington KY
University of Minnesota, Goldstein Museum of Design, Saint Paul MN
University of Nevada, Reno, Sheppard Contemporary & University Galleries, Reno NV
University of Saskatchewan, Diefenbaker Canada Centre, Saskatoon SK
University of Utah, Utah Museum of Fine Arts, Salt Lake City UT
University of Vermont, Robert Hull Fleming Museum, Burlington VT
University of Victoria, The Legacy Art Gallery, Victoria BC
USS Constitution Museum, Boston MA
The Valentine, Richmond VA
Vesterheim Norwegian-American Museum, Decorah IA
Wadsworth Atheneum Museum of Art, Hartford CT
The Walker African American Museum & Research Center, Las Vegas NV
Walker Art Gallery, Liverpool
Waterville Historical Society, Redington Museum, Waterville ME
Waterworks Visual Arts Center, Salisbury NC
Western Kentucky University, Kentucky Library & Museum, Bowling Green KY
Western Reserve Historical Society, Cleveland OH
Wheelwright Museum of the American Indian, Santa Fe NM
Willard House & Clock Museum, Inc, North Grafton MA
Wiregrass Museum of Art, Dothan AL
Wisconsin Historical Society, Wisconsin Historical Museum, Madison WI
Witte Museum, San Antonio TX
Woodlawn/The Pope-Leighey, Alexandria VA
Wyoming State Museum, Cheyenne WY

CRAFTS

African American Museum in Philadelphia, Philadelphia PA
African Art Museum of Maryland, Columbia MD
Alaska State Museum, Juneau AK
Albany Institute of History & Art, Albany NY
Albuquerque Museum of Art & History, Albuquerque NM
American Art Museum, Renwick Gallery, Washington DC
American Folk Art Museum, New York NY
American Swedish Institute, Minneapolis MN
Anchorage Museum at Rasmuson Center, Anchorage AK
Appaloosa Museum and Heritage Center, Moscow ID
Arkansas Arts Center, Little Rock AR
Art and History Museums - Maitland, Maitland FL
The Art Gallery of Cornwall, Cornwall ON
Art Gallery of Nova Scotia, Halifax NS
Art Museum of Greater Lafayette, Lafayette IN
Arts Council of Fayetteville-Cumberland County, The Arts Center, Fayetteville NC
ArtSpace/Lima, Lima OH
Asheville Art Museum, Asheville NC
Associates for Community Development, The Arts Center, Inc, Martinsburg WV
Balzekas Museum of Lithuanian Culture, Chicago IL
Bangladesh National Museum, Dhaka
Baroda Museum and Picture Gallery, Vadodara
Bay County Historical Society, Historical Museum of Bay County, Bay City MI
Bayerische Staatsgemaldesammlungen, Bavarian State Painting Collections, Munich
Bellevue Arts Museum, Bellevue WA
Besser Museum for Northeast Michigan, Alpena MI
Botswana National Museum, Gaborone
Bucks County Historical Society, Mercer Museum, Doylestown PA
Buffalo Niagara Heritage Village, Amherst NY
Burchfield Penney Art Center, Buffalo NY
Bush-Holley Historic Site & Storehouse Gallery, Greenwich Historical Society, Cos Cob CT
Cameron Art Museum, Wilmington NC
Canadian Clay and Glass Gallery, Waterloo ON
Canadian Museum of Nature, Musee Canadien de la Nature, Ottawa ON
Carson County Square House Museum, Panhandle TX
Children's Museum of Manhattan, New York NY
City of Fremont, Olive Hyde Art Gallery, Fremont CA
City of Pittsfield Office of Cultural Development, Lichtenstein Center for the Arts, Pittsfield MA
City of Springdale, Shiloh Museum of Ozark History, Springdale AR
The Columbus Museum, Columbus GA
Concordia Historical Institute, Saint Louis MO
Confederation Centre Art Gallery and Museum, Charlottetown PE
County of Henrico, Meadow Farm Museum, Glen Allen VA
Craft and Folk Art Museum (CAFAM), Los Angeles CA
Cranbrook Art Museum, Bloomfield Hills MI
Cripple Creek District Museum, Cripple Creek CO
Crocker Art Museum, Sacramento CA
Crook County Museum & Art Gallery, Sundance WY
Dallas Museum of Art, Dallas TX
Dalnavert Museum, Winnipeg MB
Delphi Archaeological Museum, Delphi
Delta Blues Museum, Clarksdale MS
Detroit Institute of Arts, Detroit MI
Durham Art Guild, Durham NC
Erie Art Museum, Erie PA
Erie County Historical Society, Erie PA
Essex Historical Society and Shipbuilding Museum, Essex MA
Evanston Historical Society, Charles Gates Dawes House, Evanston IL
Farmington Village Green & Library Association, Stanley-Whitman House, Farmington CT
Fetherston Foundation, Packwood House Museum, Lewisburg PA
Fine Arts Center for the New River Valley, Pulaski VA
Fine Arts Museums of San Francisco, Legion of Honor, San Francisco CA
Folk Art Society of America, Richmond VA
Freer Gallery of Art & Arthur M Sackler Gallery, Arthur M Sackler Gallery, Washington DC
Fuller Craft Museum, Brockton MA
Galerie Montcalm, Gatineau QC
Gallery One Visual Arts Center, Ellensburg WA
Genesee Country Village & Museum, John L Wehle Art Gallery, Mumford NY
Grand Rapids Art Museum, Grand Rapids MI
Hambidge Center for Creative Arts & Sciences, Rabun Gap GA
Hancock Shaker Village, Inc, Pittsfield MA
Haystack Mountain School of Crafts, Deer Isle ME
Hebrew Union College, Skirball Cultural Center, Los Angeles CA
Hebrew Union College - Jewish Institute of Religion Museum, Jewish Institute of Religion, New York NY
Hecht Museum, Haifa
Henry Sheldon Museum of Vermont History and Research Center, Middlebury VT
Heritage Museum & Cultural Center, Baker LA
Hermitage Museum & Gardens, Norfolk VA
Hershey Museum, Hershey PA
Het Noordbrabants Museum, s-Hertogenbosch
High Museum of Art, Atlanta GA
Hillwood Museum & Gardens Foundation, Hillwood Estate Museum & Gardens, Washington DC
Historic Arkansas Museum, Little Rock AR
Historic Paris - Bourbon County, Inc, Hopewell Museum, Paris KY
The History Center in Tompkins County, Ithaca NY
Huntington Museum of Art, Huntington WV
Hyde Park Art Center, Chicago IL
i.d.e.a. Museum, Mesa AZ
Illinois Historic Preservation Agency, Bishop Hill State Historic Site, Bishop Hill IL
Illinois State Museum, ISM Lockport Gallery, Chicago Gallery & Southern Illinois Art Gallery, Springfield IL
Imperial Calcasieu Museum, Gibson-Barham Gallery, Lake Charles LA
Independence Seaport Museum, Philadelphia PA
Indian Arts & Crafts Board, US Dept of the Interior, Sioux Indian Museum, Rapid City SD
Institute of Puerto Rican Culture, Museo Fuerte Conde de Mirasol, Vieques PR
The Interchurch Center, Galleries at the Interchurch Center, New York NY
International Clown Hall of Fame & Research Center, Inc, West Allis WI
Iroquois Indian Museum, Howes Cave NY
The Israel Museum, Jerusalem, Jerusalem
James Dick Foundation, Festival - Institute, Round Top TX
Kenosha Public Museums, Kenosha WI
Kentucky Museum of Art and Craft, Louisville KY
Kereszteny Muzeum, Christian Museum, Esztergom
Koochiching Museums, International Falls MN
Koshare Indian Museum, Inc, La Junta CO
LA County Museum of Art, Los Angeles CA
Lac du Flambeau Band of Lake Superior Chippewa Indians, George W Brown Jr Ojibwe Museum & Cultural Center, Lac Du Flambeau WI
Lafayette Science Museum & Planetarium, Lafayette LA
Lahore Museum, Lahore
Lalit Kala Akademi Rabindra Bhavan Art Galleries, National Academy of Art, New Delhi, New Delhi
Landis Valley Village and Farm Museum, PA Historical & Museum Commission, Lancaster PA
Le Grand Curtius, The Grand Curtius, Liege
League of New Hampshire Craftsmen, Grodin Permanent Collection Museum, Concord NH
Leelanau Historical Museum, Leland MI
Lehigh Valley Heritage Center, Allentown PA
Lincoln County Historical Association, Inc, 1811 Old Lincoln County Jail & Lincoln County Museum, Wiscasset ME
Lincolnshire County Council, Library & Heritage Services, Lincoln
Livingston County Historical Society, Museum, Geneseo NY
The Long Island Museum of American Art, History & Carriages, Stony Brook NY

Longfellow-Evangeline State Commemorative Area, Saint Martinville LA
Loyola University Chicago, Loyola University Museum of Art, Chicago IL
Lusaka National Museum, Lusaka
Maison Saint-Gabriel Museum, Montreal QC
Marietta College, Grover M Hermann Fine Arts Center, Marietta OH
The Mariners' Museum, Newport News VA
Maude Kerns Art Center, Eugene OR
McLean County Historical Society, McLean County Museum of History, Bloomington IL
Meredith College, Frankie G Weems Gallery & Rotunda Gallery, Raleigh NC
Mesa Arts Center, Mesa Contemporary Arts Museum, Mesa AZ
The Mexican Museum, San Francisco CA
Millicent Rogers Museum, Taos NM
Minnesota Museum of American Art, Saint Paul MN
Minnesota State University, Mankato, Mankato MN
The Mint Museum, Charlotte NC
The Mint Museum, Mint Museum of Craft & Design, Charlotte NC
Missoula Art Museum, Missoula MT
Mobile Museum of Art, Mobile AL
Montana State University, Helen E Copeland Gallery, Bozeman MT
Moore College of Art & Design, The Galleries at Moore, Philadelphia PA
Morris Museum, Morristown NJ
Morris Museum of Art, Augusta GA
MTG Hawkes Bay, Napier
Musee des Beaux-Arts de Tours, Museum of Fine Arts, Tours
Musee des Maitres et Artisans du Quebec, Montreal QC
Musees Royaux d'Art et d'Histoire, Royal Museums of Art and History, Brussels
Museo De Las Americas, Denver CO
Museo di Palazzo Ducale, Ducale Palace Museum, Mantua
The Museum, Greenwood SC
Museum De Lakenhal, Leiden
Museum fur Angewandte Kunst Frankfurt, Museum of Applied Arts, Frankfurt
Museum of Arts & Design, New York NY
Museum of Chinese in America, New York NY
Museum of Northern Arizona, Flagstaff AZ
Museum of Northern British Columbia, Ruth Harvey Art Gallery, Prince Rupert BC
Museum of the Plains Indian & Crafts Center, Browning MT
Museum zu Allerheiligen, Schaffhausen
Muzej za Umjetnost i Obrt, Museum of Arts & Crafts, Zagreb
Muzeul de Istorie Nationala Si Arheologie Constanta, National History & Archaeology Museum, Constanta
Muzeul National de Arta al Romaniei, National Museum of Art of Romania, Bucharest
Muzeum Narodowe w Poznaniu, National Museum in Poznan, Poznan
Nara Kokuritsu Hakubutsu-Kan, Nara National Museum, Nara
The National Art Center, Tokyo, Tokyo
National Art Museum of Moldova, Chisinau
National Museum of Ceramic Art, Baltimore MD
The National Museum of Modern Art, Tokyo, Tokyo
National Museum of the Philippines, Manila
National Museum of Women in the Arts, Washington DC
National Palace Museum, Taipei
The National Quilt Museum, Paducah KY
Nelson Mandela Metropolitan Art Museum, Port Elizabeth
New Brunswick Museum, Saint John NB
New England Maple Museum, Pittsford VT
New Visions Gallery, Inc, Marshfield WI
Niigata Prefectural Museum of Modern Art, Nagaoka
The Nippon Gallery at the Nippon Club, New York NY
North Light Gallery, Millinocket ME
Norwich Free Academy, Slater Memorial Museum, Norwich CT
Nova Scotia College of Art and Design, Anna Leonowens Gallery, Halifax NS
Nova Scotia Museum, Maritime Museum of the Atlantic, Halifax NS
Noyes Art Gallery, Lincoln NE
Ogden Museum of Southern Art, University of New Orleans, New Orleans LA
The Ohio Historical Society, Inc, Campus Martius Museum & Ohio River Museum, Marietta OH
Ohio History Connection, National Afro-American Museum & Cultural Center, Wilberforce OH
Okanagan Heritage Museum, Kelowna BC
Okefenokee Heritage Center, Inc, Waycross GA
Old Dartmouth Historical Society, New Bedford Whaling Museum, New Bedford MA
Owensboro Museum of Fine Art, Owensboro KY
Palm Beach County Parks & Recreation Department, Morikami Museum & Japanese Gardens, Delray Beach FL
Panhandle-Plains Historical Museum, Canyon TX
Pasadena Museum of History, Pasadena CA
Pioneer Town, Pioneer Museum of Western Art, Wimberley TX
Please Touch Museum, Philadelphia PA
Plumas County Museum, Quincy CA
Principia College, School of Nations Museum, Elsah IL
Queen Victoria Museum and Art Gallery, Launceston TAS
Randall Junior Museum, San Francisco CA
Rawls Museum Arts, Courtland VA
Red Rock Park, Red Rock Park, Church Rock NM
Regina Public Library, Dunlop Art Gallery, Regina SK
Rensselaer County Historical Society, Hart-Cluett Mansion, 1827, Troy NY
Rhode Island Historical Society, John Brown House, Providence RI
Roberson Museum & Science Center, Binghamton NY
Rollins College, George D & Harriet W Cornell Fine Arts Museum, Winter Park FL
Rose Lehrman Art Gallery, Harrisburg PA
Roswell Museum & Art Center, Roswell NM
Saginaw Art Museum, Saginaw MI
Saint Anselm College, Alva de Mars Megan Chapel Art Center, Manchester NH
Salisbury University, Ward Museum of Wildfowl Art, Salisbury MD
San Francisco Maritime National Historical Park, Maritime Museum, San Francisco CA
Schweinfurth Art Center, Auburn NY
Seneca-Iroquois National Museum, Salamanca NY
Shaker Village of Pleasant Hill, Harrodsburg KY
Slovenska Narodna Galeria, Slovak National Gallery, Bratislava
Society for Contemporary Craft, Pittsburgh PA
Sooke Region Museum & Art Gallery, Sooke BC
South Carolina Artisans Center, Walterboro SC
South Carolina State Museum, Columbia SC
Southeastern Center for Contemporary Art, Winston-Salem NC
Southern Plains Indian Museum, Anadarko OK
The Speed Art Museum, Louisville KY
Spertus Institute of Jewish Studies, Chicago IL
St Mary's College of Maryland, The Dwight Frederick Boyden Gallery, St Mary's City MD
Staatliche Museen zu Berlin Stiftung Preussischer Kulturbesitz, National Museums in Berlin, Prussian Cultural Heritage Foundation, Berlin
Stamford Museum & Nature Center, Stamford CT
Staten Island Museum, Staten Island NY
Strasburg Museum, Strasburg VA
Suan Pakkad Palace Museum, Bangkok
Suomen Kansallismuseo, National Museum of Finland, Helsinki
Swedish American Museum, Chicago IL
Tallahassee Museum of History & Natural Science, Tallahassee FL
Tampa Museum of Art, Tampa FL
Tohono Chul Park, Tucson AZ
Tokyo National Museum, Tokyo
Trust Authority, Museum of the Great Plains, Lawton OK
Tubac Center of the Arts, Santa Cruz Valley Art Association, Tubac AZ
Tubman African American Museum, Macon GA
Ukrainian Canadian Archives & Museum of Alberta, Edmonton AB
The Ukrainian Museum, New York NY
United Society of Shakers, Shaker Museum, New Gloucester ME
University of California, Berkeley, Phoebe Apperson Hearst Museum of Anthropology, Berkeley CA
University of Georgia, Georgia Museum of Art, Athens GA
The University of Kentucky Art Museum, Lexington KY
University of Minnesota, Goldstein Museum of Design, Saint Paul MN
University of Saskatchewan, Diefenbaker Canada Centre, Saskatoon SK
University of Victoria, The Legacy Art Gallery, Victoria BC
Utah Arts Council, Chase Home Museum of Utah Folk Arts, Salt Lake City UT
Vermont State Craft Center at Frog Hollow, Burlington VT
Vesterheim Norwegian-American Museum, Decorah IA
Volcano Art Center Gallery, Hawaii Volcanoes National Park HI
Vorarlberg Museum, Bregenz
Wadsworth Atheneum Museum of Art, Hartford CT
The Walker African American Museum & Research Center, Las Vegas NV
Waterworks Visual Arts Center, Salisbury NC
Wharton Esherick Museum, Paoli PA
Whatcom Museum, Bellingham WA
Wheelwright Museum of the American Indian, Santa Fe NM
Wilkes Art Gallery, North Wilkesboro NC
William Morris Gallery, London
Wisconsin Historical Society, Wisconsin Historical Museum, Madison WI
Yokohama Museum of Art, Yokohama

DECORATIVE ARTS

1890 House-Museum & Center for the Arts, Cortland NY
Abington Art Center, Jenkintown PA
Academy of the New Church, Glencairn Museum, Bryn Athyn PA
Adams National Historic Park, Quincy MA
African Art Museum of Maryland, Columbia MD
Akron Art Museum, Akron OH
Alaska State Museum, Juneau AK
Albany Institute of History & Art, Albany NY
Albany Museum of Art, Albany GA
Albion College, Bobbitt Visual Arts Center, Albion MI
Albuquerque Museum of Art & History, Albuquerque NM
Allentown Art Museum, Allentown PA
American Architectural Foundation, Museum, Washington DC
American Art Museum, Renwick Gallery, Washington DC
American Folk Art Museum, New York NY
American Museum of Ceramic Art, Pomona CA
Americas Society Art Gallery, New York NY
Amherst College, Mead Art Museum, Amherst MA
Arkansas Arts Center, Little Rock AR
Arkkitehtuurimuseo, Museum of Finnish Architecture, Helsinki
Arnot Art Museum, Elmira NY
Art Center of Battle Creek, Battle Creek MI
The Art Gallery of Cornwall, Cornwall ON
The Art Gallery of Grand Prairie, Grande Prairie AB
Art Gallery of Greater Victoria, Victoria BC
Art Gallery of Guelph, Guelph ON
Art Gallery of Nova Scotia, Halifax NS
Art Gallery of South Australia, Adelaide
Art Museum of Greater Lafayette, Lafayette IN
Art Museum of Southeast Texas, Beaumont TX
Arts Council of Fayetteville-Cumberland County, The Arts Center, Fayetteville NC
ArtSpace/Lima, Lima OH
Asian Art Museum of San Francisco, Chong-Moon Lee Ctr for Asian Art and Culture, San Francisco CA
Athenaeum of Philadelphia, Philadelphia PA
Atlanta Historical Society Inc, Atlanta History Center, Atlanta GA
Audrain County Historical Society, Graceland Museum & American Saddlehorse Museum & Fire Brick Industry Museum, Mexico MO
The Baltimore Museum of Art, Baltimore MD
Balzekas Museum of Lithuanian Culture, Chicago IL
Bangladesh National Museum, Dhaka
Barnes Foundation, Merion PA
Baroda Museum and Picture Gallery, Vadodara
Bass Museum of Art, Miami Beach FL
Bay County Historical Society, Historical Museum of Bay County, Bay City MI
Bayerisches Nationalmuseum, Bavarian National Museum, Munich

Beaverbrook Art Gallery, Fredericton NB
Belger Arts Center, Kansas City MO
Bellevue Arts Museum, Bellevue WA
Beloit College, Wright Museum of Art, Beloit WI
Bemis Center for Contemporary Arts, Omaha NE
Bennington Museum, Bennington VT
Berkshire Museum, Pittsfield MA
Besser Museum for Northeast Michigan, Alpena MI
Beverly Historical Society, Cabot, Hale & Balch House Museums, Beverly MA
Biggs Museum of American Art, Dover DE
Birmingham Museum of Art, Birmingham AL
Bob Jones University Museum & Gallery Inc, Greenville SC
The Bostonian Society, Old State House Museum, Boston MA
Botswana National Museum, Gaborone
Brick Store Museum, Kennebunk ME
Bruce Museum, Inc, Greenwich CT
Bucknell University, Edward & Marthann Samek Art Gallery, Lewisburg PA
Buffalo Niagara Heritage Village, Amherst NY
Burchfield Penney Art Center, Buffalo NY
Bush-Holley Historic Site & Storehouse Gallery, Greenwich Historical Society, Cos Cob CT
Byzantine & Christian Museum, Athens, Athens
C M Russell Museum, Great Falls MT
Cameron Art Museum, Wilmington NC
Canadian Clay and Glass Gallery, Waterloo ON
Canadian Museum of History, Gatineau QC
Canton Museum of Art, Canton OH
Cape Ann Museum, Gloucester MA
Captain Forbes House Museum, Milton MA
Carnegie Museums of Pittsburgh, Carnegie Museum of Art, Pittsburgh PA
Carson County Square House Museum, Panhandle TX
Cayuga Museum of History & Art, Auburn NY
Cedar Rapids Museum of Art, Cedar Rapids IA
Charleston Museum, Charleston SC
Charleston Museum, Heyward-Washington House, Charleston SC
Charleston Museum, Joseph Manigault House, Charleston SC
Chateau de Versailles, Palace of Versailles, Versailles
Chatham Historical Society, The Atwood House Museum, Chatham MA
Chatillon-DeMenil House Foundation, Chatillon-DeMenil Mansion, Saint Louis MO
Cheekwood-Tennessee Botanical Garden & Museum of Art, Nashville TN
Chicago Athenaeum, Museum of Architecture & Design, Galena IL
The Children's Museum of Indianapolis, Indianapolis IN
Chrysler Museum of Art, Norfolk VA
Cincinnati Art Museum, Cincinnati Art Museum, Cincinnati OH
City of Austin Parks & Recreation, O Henry Museum, Austin TX
City of Fremont, Olive Hyde Art Gallery, Fremont CA
The City of Petersburg Museums, Petersburg VA
Clark Art Institute, Williamstown MA
Clemson University, Fort Hill Plantation, Clemson SC
The Cleveland Museum of Art, Cleveland OH
Cohasset Historical Society, Pratt Building (Society Headquarters), Cohasset MA
Columbia County Historical Society, Luykas Van Alen House, Kinderhook NY
Columbia Museum of Art, Columbia SC
The Columbus Museum, Columbus GA
Columbus Museum of Art, Columbus OH
Concord Museum, Concord MA
Confederation Centre Art Gallery and Museum, Charlottetown PE
Corcoran Gallery of Art, Washington DC
County of Henrico, Meadow Farm Museum, Glen Allen VA
The Courtauld Institute of Art, The Courtauld Gallery, London
Coutts Museum of Art, Inc, El Dorado KS
Craft and Folk Art Museum (CAFAM), Los Angeles CA
Cranbrook Art Museum, Bloomfield Hills MI
Cripple Creek District Museum, Cripple Creek CO
Crocker Art Museum, Sacramento CA
Cuneo Mansion & Gardens, Vernon Hills IL
Dallas Museum of Art, Dallas TX
Dalnavert Museum, Winnipeg MB
DAR Museum, National Society Daughters of the American Revolution, Washington DC
Dartmouth College, Hood Museum of Art, Hanover NH
Delaware Art Museum, Wilmington DE
Delaware Historical Society, Read House and Gardens, New Castle DE
Deming-Luna Mimbres Museum, Deming NM
Denver Art Museum, Denver CO
Designmuseum Danmark, Danish Design Museum, Copenhagen
Detroit Institute of Arts, Detroit MI
Detroit Repertory Theatre Gallery, Detroit MI
Dickinson College, The Trout Gallery, Carlisle PA
The Dixon Gallery & Gardens, Memphis TN
Doncaster Museum and Art Gallery, Doncaster Yorks
Dumbarton Oaks, Dumbarton Oaks Museum, Washington DC
Edgecombe County Cultural Arts Council, Inc, Blount-Bridgers House, Hobson Pittman Memorial Gallery, Tarboro NC
Edsel & Eleanor Ford House, Grosse Pointe Shores MI
Eiteljorg Museum of American Indians & Western Art, Indianapolis IN
Ella Sharp Museum, Jackson MI
Ellis County Museum Inc, Waxahachie TX
Elverhoj Museum of History and Art, Solvang CA
Environment Canada - Parks Canada, Laurier House, National Historic Site, Ottawa ON
Erie Art Museum, Erie PA
Erie County Historical Society, Erie PA
Essex Historical Society and Shipbuilding Museum, Essex MA
The Ethel Wright Mohamed Stitchery Museum, Belzoni MS
Evanston Historical Society, Charles Gates Dawes House, Evanston IL
Evansville Museum of Arts, History & Science, Evansville IN
Everhart Museum, Scranton PA
Everson Museum of Art, Syracuse NY
Fall River Historical Society, Fall River MA
Farmington Village Green & Library Association, Stanley-Whitman House, Farmington CT
Fetherston Foundation, Packwood House Museum, Lewisburg PA
Fine Arts Museums of San Francisco, Legion of Honor, San Francisco CA
Fishkill Historical Society, Van Wyck Homestead Museum, Fishkill NY
Fitchburg Art Museum, Fitchburg MA
Fitton Center for Creative Arts, Hamilton OH
Flint Institute of Arts, Flint MI
Florence County Museum, Florence SC
Florida State University, John & Mable Ringling Museum of Art, Sarasota FL
Florida State University and Central Florida Community College, The Appleton Museum of Art, Ocala FL
Fondazione Musei Civici Di Venezia, Museo Correr - Correr Museum, Venice
Fondazione Musei Civici Di Venezia, Ca' Pesaro Galleria Nazionale d'Arte Moderna - Ca' Pesaro Gallery of Modern Art, Venice
Forest Lawn Museum, Glendale CA
Fort Ticonderoga Association, Ticonderoga NY
Freer Gallery of Art & Arthur M Sackler Gallery, Arthur M Sackler Gallery, Washington DC
The Frick Art & Historical Center, Inc, Frick Art Museum, Pittsburgh PA
Frontier Times Museum, Bandera TX
Fuller Craft Museum, Brockton MA
Galerie Montcalm, Gatineau QC
Gallery One Visual Arts Center, Ellensburg WA
General Board of Discipleship, The United Methodist Church, The Upper Room Chapel & Museum, Nashville TN
Genesee Country Village & Museum, John L Wehle Art Gallery, Mumford NY
Germantown Historical Society, Philadelphia PA
Girard College, Stephen Girard Collection, Philadelphia PA
Glanmore National Historic Site of Canada, Belleville ON
Glessner House Museum, Chicago IL
Grand Rapids Public Museum, Grand Rapids MI
Gunston Hall Plantation, Mason Neck VA
Hammonds House Museum, Atlanta GA
Hancock Shaker Village, Inc, Pittsfield MA
Hastings Museum of Natural & Cultural History, Hastings NE
Haystack Mountain School of Crafts, Deer Isle ME
Headley-Whitney Museum, Lexington KY
Headquarters Fort Monroe, Dept of Army, Casemate Museum, Hampton VA
Heard Museum, Phoenix AZ
Hebrew Union College, Skirball Cultural Center, Los Angeles CA
Henry County Museum & Cultural Arts Center, Clinton MO
Henry Morrison Flagler Museum, Palm Beach FL
Henry Sheldon Museum of Vermont History and Research Center, Middlebury VT
Heritage Center, Inc, Pine Ridge SD
Hermitage Museum & Gardens, Norfolk VA
Herrett Center for Arts & Sciences, Jean B King Art Gallery, Twin Falls ID
Hershey Museum, Hershey PA
High Museum of Art, Atlanta GA
Hill-Stead Museum, Farmington CT
Hillwood Museum & Gardens Foundation, Hillwood Estate Museum & Gardens, Washington DC
Historic Arkansas Museum, Little Rock AR
Historic Cherry Hill, Albany NY
Historic Deerfield, Inc, Deerfield MA
Historic Holyoke at Wistariahurst & City of Holyoke, Holyoke MA
Historic Hudson Valley, Pocantico Hills NY
Historic Huguenot Street, New Paltz NY
Historic Northampton Museum & Education Center, Northampton MA
Historic Paris - Bourbon County, Inc, Hopewell Museum, Paris KY
Historical Society of Martin County, Elliott Museum, Stuart FL
Historical Society of Old Newbury, Cushing House Museum, Newburyport MA
Historical Society of Washington DC, The City Museum of Washington DC, Washington DC
The History Center in Tompkins County, Ithaca NY
History Colorado Center Museum, Denver CO
History Museum of Mobile, Mobile AL
Honolulu Museum of Art, Honolulu HI
Houston Museum of Decorative Arts, Chattanooga TN
The Hudson River Museum, Yonkers NY
The Huntington Library, Art Collections & Botanical Gardens, San Marino CA
Huntington Museum of Art, Huntington WV
The Hyde Collection, Glens Falls NY
i.d.e.a. Museum, Mesa AZ
Idaho Historical Museum, Boise ID
Illinois Historic Preservation Agency, Bishop Hill State Historic Site, Bishop Hill IL
Illinois State Museum, ISM Lockport Gallery, Chicago Gallery & Southern Illinois Art Gallery, Springfield IL
Imperial Calcasieu Museum, Gibson-Barham Gallery, Lake Charles LA
Independence National Historical Park, Philadelphia PA
Independence Seaport Museum, Philadelphia PA
Indiana Landmarks, Morris-Butler House, Indianapolis IN
Indiana State Museum, Indianapolis IN
Institute of Puerto Rican Culture, Museo Fuerte Conde de Mirasol, Vieques PR
The Interchurch Center, Galleries at the Interchurch Center, New York NY
Intermedia Arts, Minneapolis MN
International Museum of Art, El Paso TX
Iowa State University, Brunnier Art Museum, Ames IA
Iredell Museums, Statesville NC
The Israel Museum, Jerusalem, Jerusalem
Jacksonville University, Alexander Brest Museum & Gallery, Jacksonville FL
Jacques Marchais Museum of Tibetan Art, Staten Island NY
James Dick Foundation, Festival - Institute, Round Top TX
Jefferson County Open Space, Hiwan Homestead Museum, Evergreen CO
The Jewish Museum, New York NY
Johns Hopkins University, Evergreen Museum & Library, Baltimore MD
Johns Hopkins University, Homewood Museum, Baltimore MD
Johnson-Humrickhouse Museum, Coshocton OH
Joslyn Art Museum, Omaha NE
Juniata College Museum of Art, Huntingdon PA
Karakalpak State Art Museum, Nukus Republic of Karakalpakstan
Kenosha Public Museums, Kenosha WI

Kentucky Museum of Art and Craft, Louisville KY
Kereszteny Muzeum, Christian Museum, Esztergom
Kern County Museum, Bakersfield CA
Kings County Historical Society & Museum, Hampton NB
Kirkland Museum of Fine & Decorative Art, Denver CO
Knoxville Museum of Art, Knoxville TN
Koshare Indian Museum, Inc, La Junta CO
Kunsthistorisches Museum Wien, Museum of Fine Arts, Vienna
Kyiv Museum of Russian Art, Kyiv Ukrainian
Lac du Flambeau Band of Lake Superior Chippewa Indians, George W Brown Jr Ojibwe Museum & Cultural Center, Lac Du Flambeau WI
Lafayette College, Lafayette College Art Galleries, Easton PA
Lahore Museum, Lahore
Lalit Kala Akademi Rabindra Bhavan Art Galleries, National Academy of Art, New Delhi, New Delhi
Landis Valley Village and Farm Museum, PA Historical & Museum Commission, Lancaster PA
Le Grand Curtius, The Grand Curtius, Liege
League of New Hampshire Craftsmen, Grodin Permanent Collection Museum, Concord NH
Lehigh Valley Heritage Center, Allentown PA
Leigh Yawkey Woodson Art Museum, Wausau WI
Liberty Hall Historic Site, Liberty Hall Museum, Frankfort KY
Lightner Museum, Saint Augustine FL
Lincoln County Historical Association, Inc, 1811 Old Lincoln County Jail & Lincoln County Museum, Wiscasset ME
Lincolnshire County Council, Library & Heritage Services, Lincoln
Lincolnshire County Council, The Collection: Art & Archaeology in Lincolnshire, Lincoln
Lockwood-Mathews Mansion Museum, Norwalk CT
The Long Island Museum of American Art, History & Carriages, Stony Brook NY
Longfellow's Wayside Inn Museum, Sudbury MA
Longfellow-Evangeline State Commemorative Area, Saint Martinville LA
Longue Vue House & Gardens, New Orleans LA
Los Angeles County Museum of Art, Los Angeles CA
Los Angeles County Museum of Natural History, William S Hart Museum, Newhall CA
Louisiana Department of Culture, Recreation & Tourism, Louisiana State Museum, New Orleans LA
Loveland Museum/Gallery, Loveland CO
Loyola University Chicago, Loyola University Museum of Art, Chicago IL
Lusaka National Museum, Lusaka
Lyman Allyn Art Museum, New London CT
Mabee-Gerrer Museum of Art, Shawnee OK
Madison County Historical Society, Cottage Lawn, Oneida NY
Maine Historical Society, MHS Museum, Portland ME
Maine Historical Society, Wadsworth-Longfellow House, Portland ME
Mamie McFaddin Ward, Beaumont TX
Marblehead Museum & Historical Society, Marblehead MA
Marblehead Museum & Historical Society, Jeremiah Lee Mansion, Marblehead MA
Maricopa County Historical Society, Desert Caballeros Western Museum, Wickenburg AZ
The Mariners' Museum, Newport News VA
Mark Twain, Hartford CT
Marquette University, Haggerty Museum of Art, Milwaukee WI
Maryhill Museum of Art, Goldendale WA
Massillon Museum, Massillon OH
McCord Museum of Canadian History, Montreal QC
McDowell House & Apothecary Shop, Danville KY
McLean County Historical Society, McLean County Museum of History, Bloomington IL
McNay Art Museum, San Antonio TX
McPherson Museum and Arts Foundation, McPherson KS
Mennello Museum of American Art, Orlando FL
Meridian Museum of Art, Meridian MS
The Metropolitan Museum of Art, New York NY
Michigan State University, Eli & Edythe Broad Art Museum, East Lansing MI
Midwest Museum of American Art, Elkhart IN
Millicent Rogers Museum, Taos NM
Milwaukee Public Museum, Milwaukee WI
Minneapolis Institute of Art, Minneapolis MN
The Mint Museum, Charlotte NC
The Mint Museum, Mint Museum of Craft & Design, Charlotte NC
Missoula Art Museum, Missoula MT
Mobile Museum of Art, Mobile AL
Monroe County Historical Association, Elizabeth D Walters Library, Stroudsburg PA
Montana State University, Helen E Copeland Gallery, Bozeman MT
Montgomery Museum of Fine Arts, Montgomery AL
Montreal Museum of Fine Arts, Montreal QC
Moravian Historical Society, Nazareth PA
Moravska Galerie v Brne, Moravian Gallery in Brno, Brno
Morris Museum, Morristown NJ
Morris Museum of Art, Augusta GA
Morris-Jumel Mansion, Inc, New York NY
Morven Museum & Garden, Princeton NJ
Mount Vernon Hotel Museum & Garden, New York NY
MTG Hawkes Bay, Napier
Muscatine Art Center, Muscatine IA
Musee Cognacq-Jay, Cognacq-Jay Museum, Paris
Musee des Beaux-Arts d'Orleans, Museum of Fine Arts, Orleans
Musee des Beaux-Arts de Tours, Museum of Fine Arts, Tours
Musee National des Beaux Arts du Quebec, Quebec QC
Musees Royaux d'Art et d'Histoire, Royal Museums of Art and History, Brussels
Museo de Arte de Ponce, The Luis A Ferre Foundation Inc, Ponce PR
Museo Del Romanticismo, Museum of the Romantic Period, Madrid
Museo di Palazzo Ducale, Ducale Palace Museum, Mantua
Museu Nacional D'Art De Catalunya, Catalona National Museum of Art, Barcelona
Museum De Lakenhal, Leiden
Museum of Art & History, Santa Cruz, Santa Cruz CA
Museum of Arts & Design, New York NY
The Museum of Arts & Sciences Inc, Daytona Beach FL
Museum of Chinese in America, New York NY
Museum of Fine Arts, Boston MA
Museum of Fine Arts, Houston, Houston TX
Museum of Fine Arts, Saint Petersburg, Florida, Inc, Saint Petersburg FL
Museum of Vancouver, Vancouver BC
Museum of West Louisiana, Leesville LA
The Museum of Western Art, Kerrville TX
Museum of Wisconsin Art, West Bend WI
Museum of York County, Rock Hill SC
Museum Plantin-Moretus, Antwerp
Muzej za Umjetnost i Obrt, Museum of Arts & Crafts, Zagreb
Muzeul National de Arta al Romaniei, National Museum of Art of Romania, Bucharest
Muzeum Narodowe W Kielcach, National Museum in Kielce, Kielce
Muzeum Narodowe w Poznaniu, National Museum in Poznan, Poznan
Nara Kokuritsu Hakubutsu-Kan, Nara National Museum, Nara
The National Art Center, Tokyo, Tokyo
National Art Museum of Moldova, Chisinau
National Baseball Hall of Fame & Museum, Cooperstown NY
National Gallery of Canada, Ottawa ON
National Heritage Museum, Lexington MA
National Museum of Ceramic Art, Baltimore MD
National Museum of the American Indian, George Gustav Heye Center, New York NY
National Museum of the Philippines, Manila
The National Museum of Western Art, Tokyo
National Museum of Women in the Arts, Washington DC
National Museums Scotland, National Museum of Scotland, Edinburgh
National Park Service, Weir Farm National Historic Site, Wilton CT
The National Quilt Museum, Paducah KY
The National Shrine of the North American Martyrs, Fultonville NY
National Silk Art Museum, Weston MO
National Society of Colonial Dames of America in the State of Maryland, Mount Clare Museum House, Baltimore MD
National Society of the Colonial Dames of America in The Commonwealth of Virginia, Wilton House Museum, Richmond VA
National Trust for Historic Preservation, Washington DC
National Trust for Historic Preservation, Shadows-on-the-Teche, New Iberia LA
National Trust for Historic Preservation, Chesterwood, Stockbridge MA
Naval Historical Center, National Museum of the US Navy, Washington DC
Nebraska State Capitol, Lincoln NE
Nelda C & H J Lutcher Stark Foundation, Stark Museum of Art, Orange TX
Nelson Mandela Metropolitan Art Museum, Port Elizabeth
The Nelson-Atkins Museum of Art, Kansas City MO
Neue Galerie New York, New York NY
Neustadt Collection of Tiffany Glass, Long Island City NY
Nevada Museum of Art, Reno NV
New Brunswick Museum, Saint John NB
New Canaan Historical Society, New Canaan CT
New Orleans Artworks at New Orleans Glassworks & Printmaking Studio, New Orleans LA
New Orleans Museum of Art, New Orleans LA
New Visions Gallery, Inc, Marshfield WI
New York State Museum, Albany NY
New York State Office of Parks Recreation & Historic Preservation, John Jay Homestead State Historic Site, Katonah NY
New York State Office of Parks, Recreation & Historic Preservation, Staatsburgh State Historic Site, Staatsburg NY
New York State Office of Parks: Recreation and Historic Preservation, Senate House State Historic Site, Kingston NY
Newburyport Maritime Society, Inc, Custom House Maritime Museum, Newburyport MA
Newfields, Indianapolis IN
Nichols House Museum, Inc, Boston MA
The Noble Maritime Collection, Staten Island NY
North Carolina Museum of Art, Raleigh NC
North End Gallery, Leonardtown MD
Norwich Free Academy, Slater Memorial Museum, Norwich CT
Noyes Art Gallery, Lincoln NE
Ogden Museum of Southern Art, University of New Orleans, New Orleans LA
The Ohio Historical Society, Inc, Campus Martius Museum & Ohio River Museum, Marietta OH
Okanagan Heritage Museum, Kelowna BC
Oklahoma Historical Society, State Museum of History, Oklahoma City OK
Olana State Historic Site, Hudson NY
Old Barracks Museum, Trenton NJ
Old Dartmouth Historical Society, New Bedford Whaling Museum, New Bedford MA
Old Salem Museums & Gardens, Museum of Early Southern Decorative Arts, Winston-Salem NC
Opelousas Museum of Art, Inc (OMA), Opelousas LA
Order Sons of Italy in America, Garibaldi & Meucci Museum, Staten Island NY
Oshkosh Public Museum & Library, Oshkosh WI
Owensboro Museum of Fine Art, Owensboro KY
Palm Beach County Parks & Recreation Department, Morikami Museum & Japanese Gardens, Delray Beach FL
Panhandle-Plains Historical Museum, Canyon TX
Pasadena Museum of History, Pasadena CA
Peabody Essex Museum, Salem MA
Pennsylvania Historical & Museum Commission, The State Museum of Pennsylvania, Harrisburg PA
Pensacola Museum of Art, Pensacola FL
Philadelphia History Museum, Philadelphia PA
Phillips Academy, Addison Gallery of American Art, Andover MA
Phoenix Art Museum, Phoenix AZ
Piatt Castles, West Liberty OH
Pioneer Town, Pioneer Museum of Western Art, Wimberley TX
Plumas County Museum, Quincy CA
Polish Museum of America (PMA), Chicago IL
Polk Museum of Art, Lakeland FL
The Pomona College, Claremont CA
Port Huron Museum, Port Huron MI
Portland Art Museum, Portland OR
Portland Museum of Art, Portland ME
Portsmouth Historical Society, John Paul Jones House & Discover Portsmouth, Portsmouth NH

Preservation Virginia, John Marshall House, Richmond VA
Principia College, School of Nations Museum, Elsah IL
Putnam County Historical Society, Foundry School Museum, Cold Spring NY
Putnam Museum of History and Natural Science, Davenport IA
Quapaw Quarter Association, Inc, Villa Marre, Little Rock AR
Queen Victoria Museum and Art Gallery, Launceston TAS
Queens College, City University of New York, Godwin-Ternbach Museum, Flushing NY
Reading Public Museum, Reading PA
Rensselaer County Historical Society, Hart-Cluett Mansion, 1827, Troy NY
Reynolda House Museum of American Art, Winston-Salem NC
Rhode Island Historical Society, John Brown House, Providence RI
Ringwood Manor House Museum, Ringwood NJ
Riverside County Museum, Edward-Dean Museum & Gardens, Cherry Valley CA
Roberson Museum & Science Center, Binghamton NY
Rock Ford Foundation, Inc, Rock Ford Plantation, Lancaster PA
Rollins College, George D & Harriet W Cornell Fine Arts Museum, Winter Park FL
Roosevelt-Vanderbilt National Historic Sites, Hyde Park NY
Ross Memorial Museum, Saint Andrews NB
Roswell Museum & Art Center, Roswell NM
Royal Alberta Museum, Royal Alberta Museum, Edmonton AB
Ryerss Victorian Museum & Library, Philadelphia PA
Saco Museum, Saco ME
Saginaw Art Museum, Saginaw MI
Saint Anselm College, Alva de Mars Megan Chapel Art Center, Manchester NH
Saint Bonaventure University, Regina A Quick Center for the Arts, Saint Bonaventure NY
Salisbury University, Ward Museum of Wildfowl Art, Salisbury MD
San Angelo Museum of Fine Arts, San Angelo TX
San Antonio Museum of Art, San Antonio TX
San Diego Museum of Art, San Diego CA
The San Joaquin Pioneer & Historical Society, The Haggin Museum, Stockton CA
Santa Paula Art Museum, Santa Paula CA
Santarella Museum & Gardens, Tyringham MA
Schuyler-Hamilton House, Morristown NJ
Schweinfurth Art Center, Auburn NY
Seneca-Iroquois National Museum, Salamanca NY
Shaker Museum & Library, Old Chatham NY
Shaker Village of Pleasant Hill, Harrodsburg KY
Sheldon Art Galleries, Saint Louis MO
Shirley Plantation Foundation, Charles City VA
Slater Mill, Old Slater Mill Association, Pawtucket RI
The Society of the Cincinnati at Anderson House, Washington DC
South Carolina Artisans Center, Walterboro SC
South Carolina State Museum, Columbia SC
South Dakota State University, South Dakota Art Museum, Brookings SD
The Speed Art Museum, Louisville KY
Spertus Institute of Jewish Studies, Chicago IL
Springfield Art Museum, Springfield MO
St Mary's College of Maryland, The Dwight Frederick Boyden Gallery, St Mary's City MD
Stanford University, Cantor Arts Center at Stanford University, Stanford CA
The State Museum of Fine Arts of Tatarstan Republic, Kazan
Staten Island Museum, Staten Island NY
Stedelijk Museum Alkmaar, Alkmaar Municipal Museum, Alkmaar
The Stewart Museum, Montreal QC
Stone Quarry Hill Art Park, Winner Gallery, Cazenovia NY
Suffolk University, Gallery, Boston MA
The Summit County Historical Society of Akron, OH, Akron OH
Suomen Kansallismuseo, National Museum of Finland, Helsinki
Susquehanna University, Lore Degenstein Gallery, Selinsgrove PA
Swedish American Museum, Chicago IL
Swetcharnik Art Studio, Mount Airy MD
T C Steele State Historic Site, Nashville IN
Taft Museum of Art, Cincinnati OH
Tallahassee Museum of History & Natural Science, Tallahassee FL
Telfair Museums, Savannah GA
Thomas Jefferson Foundation, Inc, Monticello, Charlottesville VA
Timken Museum of Art, San Diego CA
Tohono Chul Park, Tucson AZ
Tokyo National Museum, Tokyo
Toledo Museum of Art, Toledo OH
Tubac Center of the Arts, Santa Cruz Valley Art Association, Tubac AZ
Tver Regional Art Gallery, Tver
Tyne and Wear Archives & Museums, Sunderland Museum & Winter Gardens, Sunderland
Ukrainian Canadian Archives & Museum of Alberta, Edmonton AB
The Ukrainian Museum, New York NY
United Methodist Historical Society, Lovely Lane Museum, Baltimore MD
United Society of Shakers, Shaker Museum, New Gloucester ME
United States Capitol, Architect of the Capitol, Washington DC
United States Coast Guard Museum, New London CT
United States Figure Skating Association, World Figure Skating Museum & Hall of Fame, Colorado Springs CO
University of California, Berkeley, Phoebe Apperson Hearst Museum of Anthropology, Berkeley CA
University of Chicago, Smart Museum of Art, Chicago IL
University of Georgia, Georgia Museum of Art, Athens GA
University of Houston, Blaffer Art Museum, Houston TX
University of Illinois at Urbana-Champaign, Krannert Art Museum and Kinkead Pavilion, Champaign IL
The University of Kentucky Art Museum, Lexington KY
University of Minnesota, Goldstein Museum of Design, Saint Paul MN
University of New Mexico, The Harwood Museum of Art, Taos NM
University of Notre Dame, Snite Museum of Art, Notre Dame IN
University of Richmond, University Museums, Richmond VA
University of Saskatchewan, Diefenbaker Canada Centre, Saskatoon SK
University of Victoria, The Legacy Art Gallery, Victoria BC
University of Wisconsin-Madison, Chazen Museum of Art, Madison WI
The Valentine, Richmond VA
Vermilion County Museum Society, Danville IL
Vesterheim Norwegian-American Museum, Decorah IA
Victoria Mansion - Morse Libby House, Portland ME
Villa Terrace Decorative Arts Museum, Milwaukee WI
Virginia Museum of Fine Arts, Richmond VA
Vizcaya Museum & Gardens, Miami FL
Volcano Art Center Gallery, Hawaii Volcanoes National Park HI
Vorarlberg Museum, Bregenz
Wadsworth Atheneum Museum of Art, Hartford CT
The Walker African American Museum & Research Center, Las Vegas NV
Walker Art Gallery, Liverpool
The Wallace Collection, London
Walters Art Museum, Baltimore MD
Warner House Association, MacPheadris-Warner House, Portsmouth NH
Waterloo Center of the Arts, Waterloo IA
Waterville Historical Society, Redington Museum, Waterville ME
Waterworks Visual Arts Center, Salisbury NC
Western Kentucky University, Kentucky Library & Museum, Bowling Green KY
Western Reserve Historical Society, Cleveland OH
Westmoreland Museum of American Art, Greensburg PA
Whalers Village Museum, Lahaina HI
Wharton Esherick Museum, Paoli PA
Wheaton College, Beard and Weil Galleries, Norton MA
White House, Washington DC
Wilkes Art Gallery, North Wilkesboro NC
Willard House & Clock Museum, Inc, North Grafton MA
William Morris Gallery, London
The Winnipeg Art Gallery, Winnipeg MB
Wiregrass Museum of Art, Dothan AL
Witte Museum, San Antonio TX
Woodlawn/The Pope-Leighey, Alexandria VA
Woodmere Art Museum Inc, Philadelphia PA
Woodrow Wilson, Staunton VA
Woodrow Wilson, Washington DC
Worcester Art Museum, Worcester MA
Workman & Temple Family Homestead Museum, City of Industry CA
World Erotic Art Museum, Miami Beach FL
Wornall Majors House Museums, John Wornall House Museum, Kansas City MO
Wyoming State Museum, Cheyenne WY
Yellowstone County Museum, Billings MT
Yeshiva University Museum, New York NY

DIORAMAS

Academy of the New Church, Glencairn Museum, Bryn Athyn PA
African American Museum of Iowa, Cedar Rapids IA
Alton Museum of History & Art, Inc, Alton IL
Atlanta Historical Society Inc, Atlanta History Center, Atlanta GA
Bangladesh National Museum, Dhaka
The Bartlett Museum, Amesbury MA
Berkshire Museum, Pittsfield MA
Besser Museum for Northeast Michigan, Alpena MI
Billie Trimble Chandler, Texas State Museum of Asian Cultures, Corpus Christi TX
Blauvelt Demarest Foundation, Hiram Blauvelt Art Museum, Oradell NJ
Botswana National Museum, Gaborone
Brick Store Museum, Kennebunk ME
Bruce Museum, Inc, Greenwich CT
Buffalo Niagara Heritage Village, Amherst NY
Canadian Clay and Glass Gallery, Waterloo ON
Canadian Museum of History, Gatineau QC
Canadian Museum of Nature, Musee Canadien de la Nature, Ottawa ON
Cape Ann Museum, Gloucester MA
Carlsbad Museum & Art Center, Carlsbad NM
Carnegie Center for Art & History, New Albany IN
Carson County Square House Museum, Panhandle TX
The Children's Museum of Indianapolis, Indianapolis IN
Clark County Historical Society, Pioneer - Krier Museum, Ashland KS
Cohasset Historical Society, Pratt Building (Society Headquarters), Cohasset MA
Craft and Folk Art Museum (CAFAM), Los Angeles CA
Cripple Creek District Museum, Cripple Creek CO
Crook County Museum & Art Gallery, Sundance WY
Department of Economic & Community Development, State of Connecticut DECD Eric Sloane Museum, Kent CT
Dublin Arts Council, Dublin OH
Evanston Historical Society, Charles Gates Dawes House, Evanston IL
Everhart Museum, Scranton PA
Fairbanks Museum & Planetarium, Saint Johnsbury VT
Favell Museum of Western Art & Indian Artifacts, Klamath Falls OR
Fetherston Foundation, Packwood House Museum, Lewisburg PA
Florida Department of Environmental Protection, Stephen Foster Folk Culture Center State Park, White Springs FL
Fruitlands Museum, Inc, Harvard MA
Fulton County Historical Society Inc, Fulton County Museum (Tetzlaff Reference Room), Rochester IN
Grand Rapids Public Museum, Grand Rapids MI
Great Lakes Historical Society, Inland Seas Maritime Museum, Vermilion OH
Hastings Museum of Natural & Cultural History, Hastings NE
Historical Society of Bloomfield, Bloomfield NJ
History Colorado Center Museum, Denver CO
Illinois State Museum, ISM Lockport Gallery, Chicago Gallery & Southern Illinois Art Gallery, Springfield IL
Independence Seaport Museum, Philadelphia PA
Kenosha Public Museums, Kenosha WI
Lac du Flambeau Band of Lake Superior Chippewa Indians, George W Brown Jr Ojibwe Museum & Cultural Center, Lac Du Flambeau WI

Lafayette Science Museum & Planetarium, Lafayette LA
Lehigh Valley Heritage Center, Allentown PA
Lizzadro Museum of Lapidary Art, Elmhurst IL
Loveland Museum/Gallery, Loveland CO
Lusaka National Museum, Lusaka
Maricopa County Historical Society, Desert Caballeros Western Museum, Wickenburg AZ
The Mariners' Museum, Newport News VA
Medina Railroad Museum, Medina NY
Mission San Miguel Museum, San Miguel CA
Mississippi River Museum at Mud-Island River Park, Memphis TN
The Museum, Greenwood SC
Museum of the Plains Indian & Crafts Center, Browning MT
Museum of York County, Rock Hill SC
Museum zu Allerheiligen, Schaffhausen
Muzeul de Istorie Nationala Si Arheologie Constanta, National History & Archaeology Museum, Constanta
National Museum & Art Gallery of Trinidad and Tobago, Port of Spain
National Museum of the Philippines, Manila
Naval Historical Center, National Museum of the US Navy, Washington DC
New England Maple Museum, Pittsford VT
Norsk Maritimt Museum, Norwegian Maritime Museum, Oslo
Ogden Union Station, Union Station Museums, Ogden UT
Ohio History Connection, National Road-Zane Grey Museum, Norwich OH
Okefenokee Heritage Center, Inc, Waycross GA
Old Island Restoration Foundation Inc, Oldest House in Key West, Key West FL
Oshkosh Public Museum & Library, Oshkosh WI
Panhandle-Plains Historical Museum, Canyon TX
Pennsylvania Historical & Museum Commission, Railroad Museum of Pennsylvania, Strasburg PA
Plumas County Museum, Quincy CA
Reading Public Museum, Reading PA
Royal Alberta Museum, Royal Alberta Museum, Edmonton AB
Safety Harbor Museum and Cultural Arts Center, Safety Harbor FL
Scripps College, Ruth Chandler Williamson Gallery, Claremont CA
Seneca-Iroquois National Museum, Salamanca NY
The Society of the Cincinnati at Anderson House, Washington DC
Southern Plains Indian Museum, Anadarko OK
Tinkertown Museum, Sandia Park NM
Tohono Chul Park, Tucson AZ
United States Military Academy, West Point Museum, West Point NY
University of Minnesota, The Bell Museum of Natural History, Minneapolis MN
University of Saskatchewan, Diefenbaker Canada Centre, Saskatoon SK
The Walker African American Museum & Research Center, Las Vegas NV
Whatcom Museum, Bellingham WA
Wyoming State Museum, Cheyenne WY
Yellowstone County Museum, Billings MT
Zigler Art Museum, Jennings LA

DOLLS

Adams County Historical Society, Gettysburg PA
African American Atelier, Greensboro NC
African American Museum in Philadelphia, Philadelphia PA
Alaska Heritage Museum at Wells Fargo, Anchorage AK
Alaska State Museum, Juneau AK
Alton Museum of History & Art, Inc, Alton IL
Anchorage Museum at Rasmuson Center, Anchorage AK
Arizona Historical Society-Yuma, Sanguinetti House Museum & Garden, Yuma AZ
Art Without Walls Inc, Sayville NY
Arts Council of Fayetteville-Cumberland County, The Arts Center, Fayetteville NC
ArtSpace/Lima, Lima OH
Atlanta Historical Society Inc, Atlanta History Center, Atlanta GA
Bangladesh National Museum, Dhaka
Barker Character, Comic and Cartoon Museum, Cheshire CT
Baroda Museum and Picture Gallery, Vadodara
Bayerisches Nationalmuseum, Bavarian National Museum, Munich
Bennington Museum, Bennington VT
Berkshire Museum, Pittsfield MA
Besser Museum for Northeast Michigan, Alpena MI
Billie Trimble Chandler, Texas State Museum of Asian Cultures, Corpus Christi TX
Brick Store Museum, Kennebunk ME
Brooklyn Historical Society, Brooklyn OH
Buffalo Niagara Heritage Village, Amherst NY
Cambridge Museum, Cambridge NE
Canadian Museum of History, Gatineau QC
Cape Ann Museum, Gloucester MA
Carnegie Museums of Pittsburgh, Carnegie Museum of Art, Pittsburgh PA
Carson County Square House Museum, Panhandle TX
Chatham Historical Society, The Atwood House Museum, Chatham MA
The Children's Museum of Indianapolis, Indianapolis IN
City of Fremont, Olive Hyde Art Gallery, Fremont CA
Clark County Historical Society, Pioneer - Krier Museum, Ashland KS
Cohasset Historical Society, Pratt Building (Society Headquarters), Cohasset MA
The Columbus Museum, Columbus GA
Craigdarroch Castle Historical Museum Society, Victoria BC
Cripple Creek District Museum, Cripple Creek CO
Crook County Museum & Art Gallery, Sundance WY
Crow Wing County Historical Society, Brainerd MN
Dalnavert Museum, Winnipeg MB
DAR Museum, National Society Daughters of the American Revolution, Washington DC
Dartmouth Heritage Museum, Dartmouth NS
Deines Cultural Center, Russell KS
Deming-Luna Mimbres Museum, Deming NM
Erie Art Museum, Erie PA
Erie County Historical Society, Erie PA
Evanston Historical Society, Charles Gates Dawes House, Evanston IL
Evansville Museum of Arts, History & Science, Evansville IN
Everhart Museum, Scranton PA
Fairbanks Museum & Planetarium, Saint Johnsbury VT
Farmington Village Green & Library Association, Stanley-Whitman House, Farmington CT
Fetherston Foundation, Packwood House Museum, Lewisburg PA
Fishkill Historical Society, Van Wyck Homestead Museum, Fishkill NY
The Frank Phillips Foundation Inc, Woolaroc Museum, Bartlesville OK
Frontier Times Museum, Bandera TX
Fruitlands Museum, Inc, Harvard MA
Fulton County Historical Society Inc, Fulton County Museum (Tetzlaff Reference Room), Rochester IN
Gadsden Museum, Mesilla NM
Gallery One Visual Arts Center, Ellensburg WA
Germantown Historical Society, Philadelphia PA
Glanmore National Historic Site of Canada, Belleville ON
Grand Rapids Public Museum, Grand Rapids MI
Hancock Shaker Village, Inc, Pittsfield MA
Heard Museum, Phoenix AZ
Heart of West Texas Museum, Colorado City TX
Hebrew Union College, Skirball Cultural Center, Los Angeles CA
Henry County Museum & Cultural Arts Center, Clinton MO
Henry Sheldon Museum of Vermont History and Research Center, Middlebury VT
Heritage Center, Inc, Pine Ridge SD
Historic Cherry Hill, Albany NY
Historic Huguenot Street, New Paltz NY
Historic Newton, Newton MA
Historical Society of Martin County, Elliott Museum, Stuart FL
History Colorado Center Museum, Denver CO
Houston Museum of Decorative Arts, Chattanooga TN
Illinois State Museum, ISM Lockport Gallery, Chicago Gallery & Southern Illinois Art Gallery, Springfield IL
Imperial Calcasieu Museum, Gibson-Barham Gallery, Lake Charles LA
Independence Historical Museum & Art Center, Independence KS
Indiana State Museum, Indianapolis IN
The Interchurch Center, Galleries at the Interchurch Center, New York NY
International Clown Hall of Fame & Research Center, Inc, West Allis WI
International Museum of Art, El Paso TX
Iowa State University, Brunnier Art Museum, Ames IA
Iredell Museums, Statesville NC
Iroquois Indian Museum, Howes Cave NY
Jefferson County Open Space, Hiwan Homestead Museum, Evergreen CO
Kelly-Griggs House Museum, Red Bluff CA
Kenosha Public Museums, Kenosha WI
Kings County Historical Society & Museum, Hampton NB
Klein Museum, Mobridge SD
Koochiching Museums, International Falls MN
LA County Museum of Art, Los Angeles CA
Lac du Flambeau Band of Lake Superior Chippewa Indians, George W Brown Jr Ojibwe Museum & Cultural Center, Lac Du Flambeau WI
League of New Hampshire Craftsmen, Grodin Permanent Collection Museum, Concord NH
Lightner Museum, Saint Augustine FL
Lincolnshire County Council, Library & Heritage Services, Lincoln
Livingston County Historical Society, Museum, Geneseo NY
The Long Island Museum of American Art, History & Carriages, Stony Brook NY
Longfellow-Evangeline State Commemorative Area, Saint Martinville LA
Longue Vue House & Gardens, New Orleans LA
Louise Hopkins Underwood Center for the Arts, Lubbock TX
Louisiana Arts & Science Museum, Baton Rouge LA
Louisiana Department of Culture, Recreation & Tourism, Louisiana State Museum, New Orleans LA
Loveland Museum/Gallery, Loveland CO
Lyman Allyn Art Museum, New London CT
Marblehead Museum & Historical Society, Marblehead MA
Marblehead Museum & Historical Society, Jeremiah Lee Mansion, Marblehead MA
Maricopa County Historical Society, Desert Caballeros Western Museum, Wickenburg AZ
Marquette University, Haggerty Museum of Art, Milwaukee WI
Massillon Museum, Massillon OH
McCord Museum of Canadian History, Montreal QC
McDowell House & Apothecary Shop, Danville KY
McLean County Historical Society, McLean County Museum of History, Bloomington IL
McPherson Museum and Arts Foundation, McPherson KS
Meredith College, Frankie G Weems Gallery & Rotunda Gallery, Raleigh NC
The Mexican Museum, San Francisco CA
Middle Border Museum & Oscar Howe Art Center, Mitchell SD
Montana State University, Helen E Copeland Gallery, Bozeman MT
Musee des Augustines de l'Hotel Dieu de Quebec, Quebec QC
Museo Del Romanticismo, Museum of the Romantic Period, Madrid
Museo di Palazzo Ducale, Ducale Palace Museum, Mantua
The Museum, Greenwood SC
Museum of Art & History, Santa Cruz, Santa Cruz CA
Museum of the Plains Indian & Crafts Center, Browning MT
Museum of Vancouver, Vancouver BC
Museum of West Louisiana, Leesville LA
Museum zu Allerheiligen, Schaffhausen
Muzej za Umjetnost i Obrt, Museum of Arts & Crafts, Zagreb
The National Museum of Modern Art, Tokyo, Tokyo
National Society of Colonial Dames of America in the State of Maryland, Mount Clare Museum House, Baltimore MD
Nebraska Game and Parks Commission, Arbor Lodge State Historical Park & Morton Mansion, Nebraska City NE
Neville Public Museum of Brown County, Green Bay WI
New Brunswick Museum, Saint John NB
New Canaan Historical Society, New Canaan CT
New Jersey Historical Society, Newark NJ

Norwich Free Academy, Slater Memorial Museum, Norwich CT
The Ohio Historical Society, Inc, Campus Martius Museum & Ohio River Museum, Marietta OH
Ohio History Connection, National Afro-American Museum & Cultural Center, Wilberforce OH
Okefenokee Heritage Center, Inc, Waycross GA
Old Dartmouth Historical Society, New Bedford Whaling Museum, New Bedford MA
Old Island Restoration Foundation Inc, Oldest House in Key West, Key West FL
Oshkosh Public Museum & Library, Oshkosh WI
Palm Beach County Parks & Recreation Department, Morikami Museum & Japanese Gardens, Delray Beach FL
Panhandle-Plains Historical Museum, Canyon TX
Pasadena Museum of History, Pasadena CA
Philadelphia History Museum, Philadelphia PA
Pine Bluff/Jefferson County Historical Museum, Pine Bluff AR
Pioneer Historical Museum of South Dakota, Hot Springs SD
Plainsman Museum, Aurora NE
Please Touch Museum, Philadelphia PA
Plumas County Museum, Quincy CA
Port Huron Museum, Port Huron MI
Presidential Museum & Leadership Library, Odessa TX
Principia College, School of Nations Museum, Elsah IL
Putnam Museum of History and Natural Science, Davenport IA
Reading Public Museum, Reading PA
Red River Valley Museum, Vernon TX
Rensselaer County Historical Society, Hart-Cluett Mansion, 1827, Troy NY
Rhode Island Historical Society, John Brown House, Providence RI
Riverside Metropolitan Museum, Riverside CA
Roswell Museum & Art Center, Roswell NM
Royal Alberta Museum, Royal Alberta Museum, Edmonton AB
Saco Museum, Saco ME
Saint Joseph Museum, Inc., Saint Joseph MO
San Antonio Museum of Art, San Antonio TX
The San Joaquin Pioneer & Historical Society, The Haggin Museum, Stockton CA
Sea Cliff Village Museum, Sea Cliff NY
Seneca-Iroquois National Museum, Salamanca NY
Shaker Museum & Library, Old Chatham NY
Shores Memorial Museum, Lyndon Center VT
Sooke Region Museum & Art Gallery, Sooke BC
South Carolina Artisans Center, Walterboro SC
The Speed Art Museum, Louisville KY
Ste Genevieve Museum, Sainte Genevieve MO
Stedelijk Museum Alkmaar, Alkmaar Municipal Museum, Alkmaar
Stratford Historical Society, Catharine B Mitchell Museum, Stratford CT
Suan Pakkad Palace Museum, Bangkok
The Summit County Historical Society of Akron, OH, Akron OH
Suomen Kansallismuseo, National Museum of Finland, Helsinki
Tallahassee Museum of History & Natural Science, Tallahassee FL
Tinkertown Museum, Sandia Park NM
Tohono Chul Park, Tucson AZ
Tokyo National Museum, Tokyo
Ukrainian Canadian Archives & Museum of Alberta, Edmonton AB
United Society of Shakers, Shaker Museum, New Gloucester ME
University of Saskatchewan, Diefenbaker Canada Centre, Saskatoon SK
Vesterheim Norwegian-American Museum, Decorah IA
The Walker African American Museum & Research Center, Las Vegas NV
Waterville Historical Society, Redington Museum, Waterville ME
Wellfleet Historical Society & Museum, Inc, Wellfleet MA
Westmoreland Museum of American Art, Greensburg PA
Whatcom Museum, Bellingham WA
Wheelwright Museum of the American Indian, Santa Fe NM
Willard House & Clock Museum, Inc, North Grafton MA
Witte Museum, San Antonio TX
World Erotic Art Museum, Miami Beach FL
Wyoming State Museum, Cheyenne WY
Yankton County Historical Society, Dakota Territorial Museum, Yankton SD

DRAWINGS

1708 Gallery, Richmond VA
A.E. Backus Museum & Gallery, Fort Pierce FL
Abington Art Center, Jenkintown PA
Academy Art Museum, Easton MD
Academy of the New Church, Glencairn Museum, Bryn Athyn PA
African American Atelier, Greensboro NC
African American Museum in Philadelphia, Philadelphia PA
Alaska Heritage Museum at Wells Fargo, Anchorage AK
Alaska State Museum, Juneau AK
Albany Institute of History & Art, Albany NY
Albany Museum of Art, Albany GA
Albertina Museum, Vienna
Albin Polasek Museum & Sculpture Gardens, Winter Park FL
The Albrecht-Kemper Museum of Art, Saint Joseph MO
Albuquerque Museum of Art & History, Albuquerque NM
Alexandria Museum of Art, Alexandria LA
Allentown Art Museum, Allentown PA
Alton Museum of History & Art, Inc, Alton IL
American Folk Art Museum, New York NY
American University, Museum at the Katzen, Washington DC
Amherst College, Mead Art Museum, Amherst MA
Amon Carter Museum of American Art, Fort Worth TX
Anchorage Museum at Rasmuson Center, Anchorage AK
Appaloosa Museum and Heritage Center, Moscow ID
Arizona Historical Society-Yuma, Sanguinetti House Museum & Garden, Yuma AZ
Arkansas Arts Center, Little Rock AR
Arnot Art Museum, Elmira NY
Art and History Museums - Maitland, Maitland FL
Art Center of Battle Creek, Battle Creek MI
The Art Center of Waco, Waco TX
Art Community Center, Art Center of Corpus Christi, Corpus Christi TX
The Art Gallery of Cornwall, Cornwall ON
Art Gallery of Nova Scotia, Halifax NS
Art Gallery of South Australia, Adelaide
The Art Museum of Eastern Idaho, Idaho Falls ID
Art Museum of Greater Lafayette, Lafayette IN
Art Museum of Southeast Texas, Beaumont TX
Art Museum of the Americas, Washington DC
Art Without Walls Inc, Sayville NY
Artesia Historical Museum and Art Center, Artesia NM
Arts Council of Fayetteville-Cumberland County, The Arts Center, Fayetteville NC
Artspace, Richmond VA
ArtSpace/Lima, Lima OH
Augustana University, Eide-Dalrymple Gallery, Sioux Falls SD
Baldwin Gallery, Aspen CO
Baldwin-Wallace College, Fawick Art Gallery, Berea OH
The Baltimore Museum of Art, Baltimore MD
Balzekas Museum of Lithuanian Culture, Chicago IL
Bangladesh National Museum, Dhaka
Barnes Foundation, Merion PA
Baruch College of the City University of New York, Sidney Mishkin Gallery, New York NY
Bayerische Staatsgemaldesammlungen, Bavarian State Painting Collections, Munich
Bellevue Arts Museum, Bellevue WA
Bennington Museum, Bennington VT
Berkshire Museum, Pittsfield MA
Besser Museum for Northeast Michigan, Alpena MI
Biggs Museum of American Art, Dover DE
Birmingham Museum of Art, Birmingham AL
Blauvelt Demarest Foundation, Hiram Blauvelt Art Museum, Oradell NJ
Blowing Rock Art and History Museum, Blowing Rock NC
Bone Creek Museum of Agrarian Art, David City NE
Booth Western Art Museum, Cartersville GA
Boston Public Library, Albert H Wiggin Gallery & Print Department, Boston MA
The Bostonian Society, Old State House Museum, Boston MA
Botswana National Museum, Gaborone
Brickton Art Center, Park Ridge IL
Bruce Museum, Inc, Greenwich CT
Bucknell University, Edward & Marthann Samek Art Gallery, Lewisburg PA
Burchfield Penney Art Center, Buffalo NY
Burke Arts Council, Jailhouse Galleries, Morganton NC
Bush-Holley Historic Site & Storehouse Gallery, Greenwich Historical Society, Cos Cob CT
C M Russell Museum, Great Falls MT
C W Post Campus of Long Island University, Hillwood Art Museum, Brookville NY
The California Historical Society, San Francisco CA
Cameron Art Museum, Wilmington NC
Canadian Clay and Glass Gallery, Waterloo ON
Canadian Museum of History, Gatineau QC
Canadian Museum of Nature, Musee Canadien de la Nature, Ottawa ON
Cape Ann Museum, Gloucester MA
Carnegie Mellon University, Hunt Institute for Botanical Documentation, Pittsburgh PA
Carnegie Museums of Pittsburgh, Carnegie Museum of Art, Pittsburgh PA
Carson County Square House Museum, Panhandle TX
Cartoon Art Museum, San Francisco CA
Cedar Rapids Museum of Art, Cedar Rapids IA
Centenary College of Louisiana, Meadows Museum of Art, Shreveport LA
Chateau de Versailles, Palace of Versailles, Versailles
Chatham Historical Society, The Atwood House Museum, Chatham MA
The Children's Museum of Indianapolis, Indianapolis IN
Children's Museum of Manhattan, New York NY
City of Atlanta, Chastain Arts Center & Gallery, Atlanta GA
City of Cedar Falls, Iowa, James & Meryl Hearst Center for the Arts & Sculpture Garden, Cedar Falls IA
City of Fayette, Alabama, Fayette Art Museum, Fayette AL
City of Fremont, Olive Hyde Art Gallery, Fremont CA
City of Pittsfield Office of Cultural Development, Lichtenstein Center for the Arts, Pittsfield MA
City of Springdale, Shiloh Museum of Ozark History, Springdale AR
Clark Art Institute, Williamstown MA
Clear Lake Arts Center, Clear Lake IA
Colgate University, Picker Art Gallery, Hamilton NY
College of William & Mary, Muscarelle Museum of Art, Williamsburg VA
The Columbus Museum, Columbus GA
Columbus Museum of Art, Columbus OH
Concordia University, Leonard & Bina Ellen Art Gallery, Montreal QC
Confederation Centre Art Gallery and Museum, Charlottetown PE
Contemporary Art Center, Peoria IL
Contemporary Calgary, Calgary AB
Corcoran Gallery of Art, Washington DC
Cornell College, Peter Paul Luce Gallery, Mount Vernon IA
Cornell Museum of Art and American Culture, Delray Beach FL
Cornell University, Herbert F Johnson Museum of Art, Ithaca NY
The Courtauld Institute of Art, The Courtauld Gallery, London
Coutts Museum of Art, Inc, El Dorado KS
Craft and Folk Art Museum (CAFAM), Los Angeles CA
Cranbrook Art Museum, Bloomfield Hills MI
Cripple Creek District Museum, Cripple Creek CO
Crocker Art Museum, Sacramento CA
Crook County Museum & Art Gallery, Sundance WY
Crow Wing County Historical Society, Brainerd MN
The Currier Museum of Art, Manchester NH
Dahesh Museum of Art, Greenwich CT
Dallas Museum of Art, Dallas TX
Dalnavert Museum, Winnipeg MB
Danville Museum of Fine Arts & History, Danville VA
Dartmouth College, Hood Museum of Art, Hanover NH
Daum Museum of Contemporary Art, Sedalia MO
Davidson College, William H Van Every Jr & Edward M Smith Galleries, Davidson NC

Del Mar College, Joseph A Cain Memorial Art Gallery, Corpus Christi TX
DeLeon White Gallery, Toronto ON
Denver Art Museum, Denver CO
Detroit Institute of Arts, Detroit MI
Detroit Repertory Theatre Gallery, Detroit MI
Dickinson College, The Trout Gallery, Carlisle PA
Dixie State University, Sears Art Museum Gallery, Saint George UT
Doncaster Museum and Art Gallery, Doncaster Yorks
Eastern Illinois University, Tarble Arts Center, Charleston IL
Edsel & Eleanor Ford House, Grosse Pointe Shores MI
Eiteljorg Museum of American Indians & Western Art, Indianapolis IN
Ellen Noel Art Museum of the Permian Basin, Odessa TX
Elmhurst Art Museum, Elmhurst IL
eMediaLoft.org, New York NY
Environment Canada - Parks Canada, Laurier House, National Historic Site, Ottawa ON
Erie Art Museum, Erie PA
Erie County Historical Society, Erie PA
Essex Historical Society and Shipbuilding Museum, Essex MA
Everhart Museum, Scranton PA
Farmington Village Green & Library Association, Stanley-Whitman House, Farmington CT
Fine Arts Museums of San Francisco, Legion of Honor, San Francisco CA
Fishkill Historical Society, Van Wyck Homestead Museum, Fishkill NY
Fisk University, Aaron Douglas Gallery, Nashville TN
Fitchburg Art Museum, Fitchburg MA
Flint Institute of Arts, Flint MI
Florence County Museum, Florence SC
Florida Southern College, Melvin Art Gallery, Lakeland FL
Florida State University, John & Mable Ringling Museum of Art, Sarasota FL
Folk Art Society of America, Richmond VA
Fondazione Musei Civici Di Venezia, Ca' Rezzonico, Venice
Fondazione Musei Civici Di Venezia, Ca' Pesaro Galleria Nazionale d'Arte Moderna - Ca' Pesaro Gallery of Modern Art, Venice
Forest Lawn Museum, Glendale CA
Fort Hays State University, Moss-Thorns Gallery of Arts, Hays KS
Fort Smith Regional Art Museum, Fort Smith AR
The Frank Phillips Foundation Inc, Woolaroc Museum, Bartlesville OK
Freer Gallery of Art & Arthur M Sackler Gallery, Arthur M Sackler Gallery, Washington DC
The Frick Art & Historical Center, Inc, Frick Art Museum, Pittsburgh PA
Frick Collection, New York NY
Frontier Times Museum, Bandera TX
Fruitlands Museum, Inc, Harvard MA
Fuller Craft Museum, Brockton MA
Galerie Montcalm, Gatineau QC
Galleria Nazionale dell'Umbria, Umbrian National Gallery, Perugia
Gallery One Visual Arts Center, Ellensburg WA
George Phippen, Phippen Museum - Art of the American West, Prescott AZ
Georgia O'Keeffe Museum, Santa Fe NM
Georgian Court University, M Christina Geis Gallery, Lakewood NJ
Germantown Historical Society, Philadelphia PA
Gertrude Herbert Institute of Art, Augusta GA
Glanmore National Historic Site of Canada, Belleville ON
Glasgow University, The Hunterian, Glasgow
Grand Rapids Public Museum, Grand Rapids MI
Great Lakes Historical Society, Inland Seas Maritime Museum, Vermilion OH
Greene County Historical Society, Bronck Museum, Coxsackie NY
Greenville College, Richard W Bock Sculpture Collection, Almira College House, Greenville IL
Hamilton College, Emerson Gallery, Clinton NY
Hancock Shaker Village, Inc, Pittsfield MA
Hartwick College, Foreman Gallery, Oneonta NY
Headquarters Fort Monroe, Dept of Army, Casemate Museum, Hampton VA
Heard Museum, Phoenix AZ
Hebrew Union College, Skirball Cultural Center, Los Angeles CA
Hebrew Union College - Jewish Institute of Religion, Skirball Museum Cincinnati, Cincinnati OH
Hecht Museum, Haifa
The Heckscher Museum of Art, Huntington NY
Henry County Museum & Cultural Arts Center, Clinton MO
Henry Sheldon Museum of Vermont History and Research Center, Middlebury VT
Heritage Center, Inc, Pine Ridge SD
Hermitage Museum & Gardens, Norfolk VA
Het Noordbrabants Museum, s-Hertogenbosch
Hickory Museum of Art, Inc, Hickory NC
High Desert Museum, Bend OR
High Museum of Art, Atlanta GA
Hill-Stead Museum, Farmington CT
Hillwood Museum & Gardens Foundation, Hillwood Estate Museum & Gardens, Washington DC
Historic Arkansas Museum, Little Rock AR
Historic Huguenot Street, New Paltz NY
Historic Newton, Newton MA
The History Center in Tompkins County, Ithaca NY
Hui No'eau Visual Arts Center, Gallery and Gift Shop, Makawao Maui HI
The Huntington Library, Art Collections & Botanical Gardens, San Marino CA
The Hyde Collection, Glens Falls NY
Hyde Park Art Center, Chicago IL
i.d.e.a. Museum, Mesa AZ
Illinois State Museum, ISM Lockport Gallery, Chicago Gallery & Southern Illinois Art Gallery, Springfield IL
Illinois Wesleyan University, Merwin & Wakeley Galleries, Bloomington IL
Imperial Calcasieu Museum, Gibson-Barham Gallery, Lake Charles LA
Independence Historical Museum & Art Center, Independence KS
Independence Seaport Museum, Philadelphia PA
Institute of Contemporary Art, Los Angeles, Los Angeles CA
The Interchurch Center, Galleries at the Interchurch Center, New York NY
Intermedia Arts, Minneapolis MN
International Museum of Art, El Paso TX
Intuit: The Center for Intuitive & Outsider Art, Chicago IL
Iredell Museums, Statesville NC
Iroquois Indian Museum, Howes Cave NY
The Israel Museum, Jerusalem, Jerusalem
Jacksonville University, Alexander Brest Museum & Gallery, Jacksonville FL
James A Michener Art Museum, Doylestown PA
Jerald Melberg Gallery, Charlotte NC
The Jewish Museum, New York NY
JMW Turner Museum, Sarasota FL
Johns Hopkins University, Evergreen Museum & Library, Baltimore MD
Jordan National Gallery of Fine Arts, Amman
Joslyn Art Museum, Omaha NE
Juniata College Museum of Art, Huntingdon PA
Kalamazoo Institute of Arts, Kalamazoo MI
Kamloops Art Gallery, Kamloops BC
Karakalpak State Art Museum, Nukus Republic of Karakalpakstan
Kenosha Public Museums, Kenosha WI
Kentucky Museum of Art and Craft, Louisville KY
Kereszteny Muzeum, Christian Museum, Esztergom
Kimbell Art Foundation, Kimbell Art Museum, Fort Worth TX
Kirchner Museum Davos, Davos
Kirkland Museum of Fine & Decorative Art, Denver CO
Kitchener-Waterloo Art Gallery, Kitchener ON
Klein Museum, Mobridge SD
Knoxville Museum of Art, Knoxville TN
Koninklijk Museum voor Schone Kunsten Antwerpen, Royal Museum of Fine Arts Antwerp, Antwerp
The Kreeger Museum, Washington DC
Kroller-Muller Museum, Otterlo
Kunsthalle Bremen, Bremen Art Gallery, Bremen
Kunstmuseum Solothurn, Solothurn Art Museum, Solothurn
Kyiv Museum of Russian Art, Kyiv Ukrainian
La Salle University Art Museum, Philadelphia PA
Lac du Flambeau Band of Lake Superior Chippewa Indians, George W Brown Jr Ojibwe Museum & Cultural Center, Lac Du Flambeau WI
LACE (Los Angeles Contemporary Exhibitions), Los Angeles CA
Lafayette College, Lafayette College Art Galleries, Easton PA
Lafayette Science Museum & Planetarium, Lafayette LA
LaGrange Art Museum, LaGrange GA
Laguna Art Museum, Laguna Beach CA
Lalit Kala Akademi Rabindra Bhavan Art Galleries, National Academy of Art, New Delhi, New Delhi
Latino Art Museum, Pomona CA
Lawrence University, Wriston Art Center Galleries, Appleton WI
Lehigh Valley Heritage Center, Allentown PA
Lighthouse ArtCenter Museum & School of Art, Tequesta FL
Lightner Museum, Saint Augustine FL
Lincolnshire County Council, The Collection: Art & Archaeology in Lincolnshire, Lincoln
The Long Island Museum of American Art, History & Carriages, Stony Brook NY
Longue Vue House & Gardens, New Orleans LA
Los Angeles County Museum of Art, Los Angeles CA
Louise Hopkins Underwood Center for the Arts, Lubbock TX
Louisiana Arts & Science Museum, Baton Rouge LA
Louisiana Department of Culture, Recreation & Tourism, Louisiana State Museum, New Orleans LA
Loveland Museum/Gallery, Loveland CO
Mabee-Gerrer Museum of Art, Shawnee OK
Madison Museum of Contemporary Art, Madison WI
Madison Museum of Fine Art, Madison GA
Maricopa County Historical Society, Desert Caballeros Western Museum, Wickenburg AZ
The Mariners' Museum, Newport News VA
Marquette University, Haggerty Museum of Art, Milwaukee WI
Maryhill Museum of Art, Goldendale WA
Maryland Art Place, Baltimore MD
Maryland Hall for the Creative Arts, Chaney Gallery, Annapolis MD
Marylhurst University, The Art Gym, Marylhurst OR
Massachusetts Institute of Technology, MIT Museum, Cambridge MA
Massillon Museum, Massillon OH
Maude Kerns Art Center, Eugene OR
McCord Museum of Canadian History, Montreal QC
McDowell House & Apothecary Shop, Danville KY
McLean County Historical Society, McLean County Museum of History, Bloomington IL
Meem Gallery, Dubai
Mennello Museum of American Art, Orlando FL
Meredith College, Frankie G Weems Gallery & Rotunda Gallery, Raleigh NC
Meridian Museum of Art, Meridian MS
Mesa Arts Center, Mesa Contemporary Arts Museum, Mesa AZ
The Metropolitan Museum of Art, New York NY
The Mexican Museum, San Francisco CA
Michelson Museum of Art, Marshall TX
Michigan State University, Eli & Edythe Broad Art Museum, East Lansing MI
Midwest Museum of American Art, Elkhart IN
Miller Art Center Foundation Inc, Miller Art Museum, Sturgeon Bay WI
Millicent Rogers Museum, Taos NM
Millikin University, Perkinson Gallery, Decatur IL
Mills College Art Museum, Oakland CA
Minneapolis Institute of Art, Minneapolis MN
Minnesota Museum of American Art, Saint Paul MN
Minnesota State University, Mankato, Mankato MN
Minot State University, Northwest Art Center, Minot ND
The Mint Museum, Charlotte NC
Mississippi Museum of Art, Jackson MS
Mobile Museum of Art, Mobile AL
Moderna Galerija, Modern Gallery - National Museum of Modern Art, Zagreb
Montana State University, Helen E Copeland Gallery, Bozeman MT
Montclair Art Museum, Montclair NJ
Montgomery Museum of Fine Arts, Montgomery AL
Montreal Museum of Fine Arts, Montreal QC
Moore College of Art & Design, The Galleries at Moore, Philadelphia PA
Moravian College, Payne Gallery, Bethlehem PA
Moravska Galerie v Brne, Moravian Gallery in Brno, Brno
Morris Museum of Art, Augusta GA
Moscow Museum of Modern Art, Moscow
MTG Hawkes Bay, Napier

Muhlenberg College, Martin Art Gallery, Allentown PA
Muscatine Art Center, Muscatine IA
Musee Cognacq-Jay, Cognacq-Jay Museum, Paris
Musee des Augustines de l'Hotel Dieu de Quebec, Quebec QC
Musee des Beaux-Arts d'Orleans, Museum of Fine Arts, Orleans
Musee des Beaux-Arts de Tours, Museum of Fine Arts, Tours
Musee National des Beaux Arts du Quebec, Quebec QC
Musee Regional de lu Cote-Nord, Sept-Iles QC
Museen der Stadt Koln, Museum Ludwig - Ludwig Museum, Cologne
Museen der Stadt Koln, Wallraf-Richartz-Museum & Fondation Corboud - Wallraf-Richartz Museum & Corboud Foundation, Cologne
Museo de Arte de Ponce, The Luis A Ferre Foundation Inc, Ponce PR
Museo De Las Americas, Denver CO
Museo Del Romanticismo, Museum of the Romantic Period, Madrid
Museo di Palazzo Ducale, Ducale Palace Museum, Mantua
Museu Nacional D'Art De Catalunya, Catalona National Museum of Art, Barcelona
Museu Nacional de Arte Contemporanea do Chiado, National Museum of Contemporary Art, Museu Do Chiado, Lisbon
The Museum, Greenwood SC
Museum De Lakenhal, Leiden
Museum of Art & History, Santa Cruz, Santa Cruz CA
Museum of Art - Deland FL, Inc, Deland FL
The Museum of Arts & Sciences Inc, Daytona Beach FL
Museum of Arts & Sciences, Inc, Macon GA
Museum of Chinese in America, New York NY
Museum of Contemporary Art, North Miami FL
Museum of Contemporary Art Chicago, Chicago IL
Museum of Contemporary Art San Diego, San Diego CA
Museum of Fine Arts, Houston, Houston TX
Museum of Fine Arts, Saint Petersburg, Florida, Inc, Saint Petersburg FL
Museum of Latin American Art, Long Beach CA
Museum of Modern Art, New York NY
Museum of Northwest Art, La Conner WA
Museum of the Hudson Highlands, Cornwall On Hudson NY
Museum of the Plains Indian & Crafts Center, Browning MT
Museum of the Southwest, Midland TX
Museum of Vancouver, Vancouver BC
The Museum of Western Art, Kerrville TX
Museum of Wisconsin Art, West Bend WI
Museum Plantin-Moretus, Antwerp
Museum zu Allerheiligen, Schaffhausen
Muzej Moderne I Suvremene Umjetnosti, Museum of Modern and Contemporary Art, Rijeka
Muzej za Umjetnost i Obrt, Museum of Arts & Crafts, Zagreb
Muzeul National de Arta al Romaniei, National Museum of Art of Romania, Bucharest
Muzeum Narodowe w Poznaniu, National Museum in Poznan, Poznan
Narodna Galerija, National Gallery of Slovenia, Ljubljana
Nassau County Museum of Art, Roslyn Harbor NY
National Art Museum of Moldova, Chisinau
National Baseball Hall of Fame & Museum, Cooperstown NY
National Gallery of Canada, Ottawa ON
National Museum & Art Gallery of Trinidad and Tobago, Port of Spain
The National Museum of Modern Art, Tokyo, Tokyo
National Museum of the Philippines, Manila
The National Museum of Western Art, Tokyo
National Museum of Wildlife Art of the Unites States, Jackson WY
National Portrait Gallery, London
National Veterans Art Museum, Chicago IL
Naval Historical Center, National Museum of the US Navy, Washington DC
Nelda C & H J Lutcher Stark Foundation, Stark Museum of Art, Orange TX
Nelson Mandela Metropolitan Art Museum, Port Elizabeth
The Nelson-Atkins Museum of Art, Kansas City MO
Neue Galerie New York, New York NY
Nevada Museum of Art, Reno NV
Neville Public Museum of Brown County, Green Bay WI
New Britain Museum of American Art, New Britain CT
New Brunswick Museum, Saint John NB
New England Maple Museum, Pittsford VT
New Jersey Historical Society, Newark NJ
New Visions Gallery, Inc, Marshfield WI
New York State Military Museum and Veterans Research Center, Saratoga Springs NY
Newfields, Indianapolis IN
Newport Art Museum and Association, Newport RI
Niigata Prefectural Museum of Modern Art, Nagaoka
The Noble Maritime Collection, Staten Island NY
Norman Rockwell Museum, Stockbridge MA
Norsk Maritimt Museum, Norwegian Maritime Museum, Oslo
Norwich Free Academy, Slater Memorial Museum, Norwich CT
Nova Scotia College of Art and Design, Anna Leonowens Gallery, Halifax NS
Noyes Art Gallery, Lincoln NE
Ogden Museum of Southern Art, University of New Orleans, New Orleans LA
Ogunquit Museum of American Art, Ogunquit ME
The Ohio Historical Society, Inc, Campus Martius Museum & Ohio River Museum, Marietta OH
Ohio University, Kennedy Museum of Art, Athens OH
Okanagan Heritage Museum, Kelowna BC
Oklahoma City Museum of Art, Oklahoma City OK
Olana State Historic Site, Hudson NY
Old Dartmouth Historical Society, New Bedford Whaling Museum, New Bedford MA
The Old Jail Art Center, Albany TX
Opelousas Museum of Art, Inc (OMA), Opelousas LA
Orange County Museum of Art, Newport Beach CA
Owensboro Museum of Fine Art, Owensboro KY
Panhandle-Plains Historical Museum, Canyon TX
Parrish Art Museum, Water Mill NY
Pasadena Museum of California Art, Pasadena CA
Peabody Essex Museum, Salem MA
Philadelphia History Museum, Philadelphia PA
Phillips Academy, Addison Gallery of American Art, Andover MA
Plains Art Museum, Fargo ND
Polk Museum of Art, Lakeland FL
The Pomona College, Claremont CA
Portland Art Museum, Portland OR
PS1 Contemporary Art Center, Long Island City NY
Pueblo Museum, Desert Hot Springs CA
Purchase College, Neuberger Museum of Art, Purchase NY
Purdue University Galleries, West Lafayette IN
Putnam Museum of History and Natural Science, Davenport IA
Queen Victoria Museum and Art Gallery, Launceston TAS
Queens College, City University of New York, Godwin-Ternbach Museum, Flushing NY
Quincy University, The Gray Gallery, Quincy IL
Rahr-West Art Museum, Manitowoc WI
Randall Junior Museum, San Francisco CA
Randolph College, Maier Museum of Art, Lynchburg VA
Rawls Museum Arts, Courtland VA
Reading Public Museum, Reading PA
Rensselaer County Historical Society, Hart-Cluett Mansion, 1827, Troy NY
Roberson Museum & Science Center, Binghamton NY
Robert Louis Stevenson Museum, Saint Helena CA
Rose Lehrman Art Gallery, Harrisburg PA
The Rosenbach Museum & Library, Philadelphia PA
Roswell Museum & Art Center, Roswell NM
Saginaw Art Museum, Saginaw MI
Saint Anselm College, Alva de Mars Megan Chapel Art Center, Manchester NH
Saint Bonaventure University, Regina A Quick Center for the Arts, Saint Bonaventure NY
Saint Joseph College, Art Gallery, University of Saint Joseph, West Hartford CT
Saint Mary's College of California, Museum of Art, Moraga CA
Saint Olaf College, Flaten Art Museum, Northfield MN
San Antonio Museum of Art, San Antonio TX
San Francisco Maritime National Historical Park, Maritime Museum, San Francisco CA
The San Joaquin Pioneer & Historical Society, The Haggin Museum, Stockton CA
San Jose Museum of Art, San Jose CA
Santa Barbara Museum of Art, Santa Barbara CA
Scripps College, Ruth Chandler Williamson Gallery, Claremont CA
Seneca-Iroquois National Museum, Salamanca NY
Shaker Museum & Library, Old Chatham NY
Shirley Plantation Foundation, Charles City VA
Slovenska Narodna Galeria, Slovak National Gallery, Bratislava
The Society of the Cincinnati at Anderson House, Washington DC
Solomon R Guggenheim Museum, New York NY
South Carolina Artisans Center, Walterboro SC
South Dakota State University, South Dakota Art Museum, Brookings SD
South Street Seaport Museum, New York NY
Southeastern Center for Contemporary Art, Winston-Salem NC
Southern Oregon University, Schneider Museum of Art, Ashland OR
The Speed Art Museum, Louisville KY
Spertus Institute of Jewish Studies, Chicago IL
Springfield Art Museum, Springfield MO
St Mary's College of Maryland, The Dwight Frederick Boyden Gallery, St Mary's City MD
Staatliche Museen zu Berlin Stiftung Preussischer Kulturbesitz, National Museums in Berlin, Prussian Cultural Heritage Foundation, Berlin
Stamford Museum & Nature Center, Stamford CT
Stanford University, Cantor Arts Center at Stanford University, Stanford CA
Stanley Museum, Inc, Kingfield ME
The State Museum of Fine Arts of Tatarstan Republic, Kazan
State University of New York at Geneseo, Bertha V B Lederer Gallery, Geneseo NY
The State University of New York at Potsdam, The Art Museum, Potsdam NY
State University of New York at Ulster, Muroff-Kotler Visual Arts Gallery, Stone Ridge NY
State University of New York College at Cortland, Dowd Fine Arts Gallery, Cortland NY
The Stewart Museum, Montreal QC
Stone Quarry Hill Art Park, Winner Gallery, Cazenovia NY
Stratford Historical Society, Catharine B Mitchell Museum, Stratford CT
Suan Pakkad Palace Museum, Bangkok
Suffolk University, Gallery, Boston MA
Suomen Kansallismuseo, National Museum of Finland, Helsinki
Susquehanna University, Lore Degenstein Gallery, Selinsgrove PA
Swetcharnik Art Studio, Mount Airy MD
Szepmuveszeti Muzeum, Museum of Fine Arts, Budapest
Taft Museum of Art, Cincinnati OH
Tampa Museum of Art, Tampa FL
Taos Historic Museums, Ernest Blumenschein Home & Studio, Taos NM
Temiskaming Art Gallery, Haileybury ON
Texas Christian University, Fort Worth Contemporary Art, Fort Worth TX
Thomas Jefferson Foundation, Inc, Monticello, Charlottesville VA
Thomas More College, Eva G Farris Art Gallery, Crestview KY
Tinkertown Museum, Sandia Park NM
Tohono Chul Park, Tucson AZ
Tokyo National Museum, Tokyo
Topeka & Shawnee County Public Library, Alice C Sabatini Gallery, Topeka KS
Tubman African American Museum, Macon GA
Tver Regional Art Gallery, Tver
Tyne and Wear Archives & Museums, Sunderland Museum & Winter Gardens, Sunderland
Ukrainian Institute of Modern Art, Chicago IL
The Ukrainian Museum, New York NY
UMLAUF Sculpture Garden & Museum, Austin TX
United Society of Shakers, Shaker Museum, New Gloucester ME
United States Coast Guard Museum, New London CT
United States Figure Skating Association, World Figure Skating Museum & Hall of Fame, Colorado Springs CO
United States Military Academy, West Point Museum, West Point NY
University of Calgary, Nickle Galleries, Calgary AB
University of California, Davis, Jan Shrem and Maria Manetti Shrem Museum of Art, Davis CA

University of California, San Diego, Stuart Collection, La Jolla CA
University of Chicago, Smart Museum of Art, Chicago IL
University of Florida, Samuel P Harn Museum of Art, Gainesville FL
University of Georgia, Georgia Museum of Art, Athens GA
University of Illinois at Urbana-Champaign, Krannert Art Museum and Kinkead Pavilion, Champaign IL
University of Indianapolis, Christel DeHaan Fine Arts Gallery, Indianapolis IN
University of Kansas, Spencer Museum of Art, Lawrence KS
The University of Kentucky Art Museum, Lexington KY
University of Louisville, Hite Art Institute, Louisville KY
University of Manchester, Whitworth Art Gallery, Manchester
University of Mary Washington, University of Mary Washington Galleries, Fredericksburg VA
University of Miami, Lowe Art Museum, Coral Gables FL
University of Minnesota, The Bell Museum of Natural History, Minneapolis MN
University of Minnesota Duluth, Tweed Museum of Art, Duluth MN
University of Nebraska-Lincoln, Great Plains Art Museum, Lincoln NE
University of Nevada, Reno, Sheppard Contemporary & University Galleries, Reno NV
University of New Mexico, The Harwood Museum of Art, Taos NM
University of North Carolina at Greensboro, Weatherspoon Art Museum, Greensboro NC
University of North Dakota, Hughes Fine Arts Center-Col Eugene Myers Art Gallery, Grand Forks ND
University of Notre Dame, Snite Museum of Art, Notre Dame IN
University of Pennsylvania, Arthur Ross Gallery, Philadelphia PA
University of Richmond, University Museums, Richmond VA
University of Saskatchewan, Diefenbaker Canada Centre, Saskatoon SK
University of Texas at Austin, Blanton Museum of Art, Austin TX
University of Utah, Utah Museum of Fine Arts, Salt Lake City UT
University of Vermont, Robert Hull Fleming Museum, Burlington VT
University of Victoria, The Legacy Art Gallery, Victoria BC
University of Wisconsin Oshkosh, Allen Priebe Gallery, Oshkosh WI
University of Wisconsin-Eau Claire, Foster Gallery, Eau Claire WI
University of Wisconsin-Madison, Chazen Museum of Art, Madison WI
University of Wisconsin-Stout, J Furlong Gallery, Menomonie WI
Ursinus College, Philip & Muriel Berman Museum of Art, Collegeville PA
USS Constitution Museum, Boston MA
Valparaiso University, Brauer Museum of Art, Valparaiso IN
Vancouver Art Gallery, Vancouver BC
Vassar College, The Frances Lehman Loeb Art Center, Poughkeepsie NY
Venice Art Center, Venice FL
Vero Beach Museum of Art, Vero Beach FL
Vesterheim Norwegian-American Museum, Decorah IA
Virginia Museum of Fine Arts, Richmond VA
Viridian Artists Inc, New York NY
Volcano Art Center Gallery, Hawaii Volcanoes National Park HI
Vorarlberg Museum, Bregenz
Wadsworth Atheneum Museum of Art, Hartford CT
The Walker African American Museum & Research Center, Las Vegas NV
Walker Art Center, Minneapolis MN
Walker Art Gallery, Liverpool
Walker Fine Art, Denver CO
Walter Anderson Museum of Art, Ocean Springs MS
Washington County Museum of Fine Arts, Hagerstown MD
Waterworks Visual Arts Center, Salisbury NC
Wesleyan University, Davison Art Center, Middletown CT
Westmoreland Museum of American Art, Greensburg PA
Whatcom Museum, Bellingham WA
Wheaton College, Beard and Weil Galleries, Norton MA
Wheelwright Museum of the American Indian, Santa Fe NM
Whitney Museum of American Art, New York NY
Wichita Art Museum, Wichita KS
Wichita State University, Ulrich Museum of Art, Wichita KS
Wildling Art Museum, Solvang CA
Wilfrid Laurier University, Robert Langen Art Gallery, Waterloo ON
Wilkes Art Gallery, North Wilkesboro NC
William Morris Gallery, London
The Winnipeg Art Gallery, Winnipeg MB
Wiregrass Museum of Art, Dothan AL
Wisconsin Historical Society, Wisconsin Historical Museum, Madison WI
Woodlawn/The Pope-Leighey, Alexandria VA
Woodmere Art Museum Inc, Philadelphia PA
Worcester Art Museum, Worcester MA
Wyoming State Museum, Cheyenne WY
Wyoming Trails Gallery, Wheatland WY
Yale University, Yale Center for British Art, New Haven CT
Yellowstone County Museum, Billings MT
Yerba Buena Center for the Arts, San Francisco CA
Yokohama Museum of Art, Yokohama
Zigler Art Museum, Jennings LA

EMBROIDERY

Academy of the New Church, Glencairn Museum, Bryn Athyn PA
Alaska State Museum, Juneau AK
Albany Institute of History & Art, Albany NY
Albuquerque Museum of Art & History, Albuquerque NM
Allentown Art Museum, Allentown PA
American Folk Art Museum, New York NY
Arizona Historical Society-Yuma, Sanguinetti House Museum & Garden, Yuma AZ
The Art Gallery of Cornwall, Cornwall ON
Art Gallery of Nova Scotia, Halifax NS
Artesia Historical Museum and Art Center, Artesia NM
Asian Art Museum of San Francisco, Chong-Moon Lee Ctr for Asian Art and Culture, San Francisco CA
Balzekas Museum of Lithuanian Culture, Chicago IL
Bangladesh National Museum, Dhaka
Baroda Museum and Picture Gallery, Vadodara
Bellevue Arts Museum, Bellevue WA
Bennington Museum, Bennington VT
Beverly Historical Society, Cabot, Hale & Balch House Museums, Beverly MA
Billie Trimble Chandler, Texas State Museum of Asian Cultures, Corpus Christi TX
Bob Jones University Museum & Gallery Inc, Greenville SC
Buffalo Niagara Heritage Village, Amherst NY
Byzantine & Christian Museum, Athens, Athens
Cambridge Museum, Cambridge NE
Canadian Museum of History, Gatineau QC
Cape Ann Museum, Gloucester MA
Central United Methodist Church, Swords Into Plowshares Peace Center & Gallery, Detroit MI
Chatham Historical Society, The Atwood House Museum, Chatham MA
The Children's Museum of Indianapolis, Indianapolis IN
City of Fremont, Olive Hyde Art Gallery, Fremont CA
The City of Petersburg Museums, Petersburg VA
City of Springdale, Shiloh Museum of Ozark History, Springdale AR
Cohasset Historical Society, Pratt Building (Society Headquarters), Cohasset MA
County of Henrico, Meadow Farm Museum, Glen Allen VA
Craft and Folk Art Museum (CAFAM), Los Angeles CA
Craigdarroch Castle Historical Museum Society, Victoria BC
Cripple Creek District Museum, Cripple Creek CO
Crocker Art Museum, Sacramento CA
Crook County Museum & Art Gallery, Sundance WY
Crow Wing County Historical Society, Brainerd MN
The Currier Museum of Art, Manchester NH
Dalnavert Museum, Winnipeg MB
Danville Museum of Fine Arts & History, Danville VA
DAR Museum, National Society Daughters of the American Revolution, Washington DC
Dartmouth Heritage Museum, Dartmouth NS
Davidson College, William H Van Every Jr & Edward M Smith Galleries, Davidson NC
Designmuseum Danmark, Danish Design Museum, Copenhagen
Detroit Institute of Arts, Detroit MI
Detroit Zoological Institute, Wildlife Interpretive Gallery, Royal Oak MI
Ellen Noel Art Museum of the Permian Basin, Odessa TX
Erie Art Museum, Erie PA
Erie County Historical Society, Erie PA
Farmington Village Green & Library Association, Stanley-Whitman House, Farmington CT
Fetherston Foundation, Packwood House Museum, Lewisburg PA
Fine Arts Museums of San Francisco, Legion of Honor, San Francisco CA
Fishkill Historical Society, Van Wyck Homestead Museum, Fishkill NY
Flint Institute of Arts, Flint MI
Florence County Museum, Florence SC
Freer Gallery of Art & Arthur M Sackler Gallery, Arthur M Sackler Gallery, Washington DC
Fruitlands Museum, Inc, Harvard MA
Fuller Craft Museum, Brockton MA
General Board of Discipleship, The United Methodist Church, The Upper Room Chapel & Museum, Nashville TN
Glanmore National Historic Site of Canada, Belleville ON
Glessner House Museum, Chicago IL
Haystack Mountain School of Crafts, Deer Isle ME
Hebrew Union College, Skirball Cultural Center, Los Angeles CA
Henry County Museum & Cultural Arts Center, Clinton MO
Henry Sheldon Museum of Vermont History and Research Center, Middlebury VT
Hermitage Museum & Gardens, Norfolk VA
Hillwood Museum & Gardens Foundation, Hillwood Estate Museum & Gardens, Washington DC
Historic Arkansas Museum, Little Rock AR
Historic Deerfield, Inc, Deerfield MA
Historic Holyoke at Wistariahurst & City of Holyoke, Holyoke MA
Historic Huguenot Street, New Paltz NY
Historic Newton, Newton MA
Historical Society of Old Newbury, Cushing House Museum, Newburyport MA
Historisches und Volkerkundemuseum, Museum of History and Ethnology, St Gallen
The Hyde Collection, Glens Falls NY
Illinois State Museum, ISM Lockport Gallery, Chicago Gallery & Southern Illinois Art Gallery, Springfield IL
Imperial Calcasieu Museum, Gibson-Barham Gallery, Lake Charles LA
Independence Seaport Museum, Philadelphia PA
The Interchurch Center, Galleries at the Interchurch Center, New York NY
Intermedia Arts, Minneapolis MN
Iredell Museums, Statesville NC
The Israel Museum, Jerusalem, Jerusalem
The Jewish Museum, New York NY
Kelly-Griggs House Museum, Red Bluff CA
Kereszteny Muzeum, Christian Museum, Esztergom
Kings County Historical Society & Museum, Hampton NB
Klein Museum, Mobridge SD
Koochiching Museums, International Falls MN
Kunsthistorisches Museum Wien, Museum of Fine Arts, Vienna
LA County Museum of Art, Los Angeles CA
Lac du Flambeau Band of Lake Superior Chippewa Indians, George W Brown Jr Ojibwe Museum & Cultural Center, Lac Du Flambeau WI
Lafayette Science Museum & Planetarium, Lafayette LA
Lahore Museum, Lahore
League of New Hampshire Craftsmen, Grodin Permanent Collection Museum, Concord NH
Lehigh Valley Heritage Center, Allentown PA
Lightner Museum, Saint Augustine FL

Lincoln County Historical Association, Inc, 1811 Old Lincoln County Jail & Lincoln County Museum, Wiscasset ME
Livingston County Historical Society, Museum, Geneseo NY
The Long Island Museum of American Art, History & Carriages, Stony Brook NY
Longfellow-Evangeline State Commemorative Area, Saint Martinville LA
Longue Vue House & Gardens, New Orleans LA
Louise Hopkins Underwood Center for the Arts, Lubbock TX
Loveland Museum/Gallery, Loveland CO
Maine Historical Society, Wadsworth-Longfellow House, Portland ME
Maison Saint-Gabriel Museum, Montreal QC
Marblehead Museum & Historical Society, Marblehead MA
Marblehead Museum & Historical Society, Jeremiah Lee Mansion, Marblehead MA
McCord Museum of Canadian History, Montreal QC
McDowell House & Apothecary Shop, Danville KY
McLean County Historical Society, McLean County Museum of History, Bloomington IL
The Mexican Museum, San Francisco CA
Middle Border Museum & Oscar Howe Art Center, Mitchell SD
Millicent Rogers Museum, Taos NM
Missoula Art Museum, Missoula MT
Monroe County Historical Association, Elizabeth D Walters Library, Stroudsburg PA
Montreal Museum of Fine Arts, Montreal QC
MTG Hawkes Bay, Napier
Musee des Augustines de l'Hotel Dieu de Quebec, Quebec QC
Musee des Beaux-Arts de Tours, Museum of Fine Arts, Tours
Musees Royaux d'Art et d'Histoire, Royal Museums of Art and History, Brussels
Museo De Las Americas, Denver CO
The Museum, Greenwood SC
Museum of Art & History, Santa Cruz, Santa Cruz CA
Museum of Arts & Design, New York NY
Museum of Fine Arts, Houston, Houston TX
Museum zu Allerheiligen, Schaffhausen
Muzej za Umjetnost i Obrt, Museum of Arts & Crafts, Zagreb
Muzeul National de Arta al Romaniei, National Museum of Art of Romania, Bucharest
National Art Museum of Moldova, Chisinau
National Museum of the Philippines, Manila
National Palace Museum, Taipei
The National Quilt Museum, Paducah KY
National Silk Art Museum, Weston MO
National Society of Colonial Dames of America in the State of Maryland, Mount Clare Museum House, Baltimore MD
Naval Historical Center, National Museum of the US Navy, Washington DC
Nelson Mandela Metropolitan Art Museum, Port Elizabeth
Neville Public Museum of Brown County, Green Bay WI
New Brunswick Museum, Saint John NB
New Jersey Historical Society, Newark NJ
Norwich Free Academy, Slater Memorial Museum, Norwich CT
Ogden Museum of Southern Art, University of New Orleans, New Orleans LA
Old Dartmouth Historical Society, New Bedford Whaling Museum, New Bedford MA
Panhandle-Plains Historical Museum, Canyon TX
Pasadena Museum of History, Pasadena CA
Philadelphia History Museum, Philadelphia PA
Plainsman Museum, Aurora NE
Plumas County Museum, Quincy CA
Port Huron Museum, Port Huron MI
Portsmouth Historical Society, John Paul Jones House & Discover Portsmouth, Portsmouth NH
Preservation Virginia, John Marshall House, Richmond VA
Putnam Museum of History and Natural Science, Davenport IA
Queens College, City University of New York, Godwin-Ternbach Museum, Flushing NY
Rensselaer County Historical Society, Hart-Cluett Mansion, 1827, Troy NY
Rhode Island Historical Society, John Brown House, Providence RI
Royal Alberta Museum, Royal Alberta Museum, Edmonton AB
Royal Arts Foundation, Belcourt Castle, Newport RI
Rubin Museum of Art, New York NY
Saginaw Art Museum, Saginaw MI
San Antonio Museum of Art, San Antonio TX
Schweinfurth Art Center, Auburn NY
Shaker Museum & Library, Old Chatham NY
South Dakota State University, South Dakota Art Museum, Brookings SD
The Speed Art Museum, Louisville KY
Staatliche Museen zu Berlin Stiftung Preussischer Kulturbesitz, National Museums in Berlin, Prussian Cultural Heritage Foundation, Berlin
The State Museum of Fine Arts of Tatarstan Republic, Kazan
Staten Island Museum, Staten Island NY
Ste Genevieve Museum, Sainte Genevieve MO
Stratford Historical Society, Catharine B Mitchell Museum, Stratford CT
The Summit County Historical Society of Akron, OH, Akron OH
Suomen Kansallismuseo, National Museum of Finland, Helsinki
Swedish American Museum, Chicago IL
Tallahassee Museum of History & Natural Science, Tallahassee FL
Taos Historic Museums, La Hacienda de Los Martinez, Taos NM
Tohono Chul Park, Tucson AZ
Tokyo National Museum, Tokyo
Tver Regional Art Gallery, Tver
Tyne and Wear Archives & Museums, Sunderland Museum & Winter Gardens, Sunderland
Ukrainian Canadian Archives & Museum of Alberta, Edmonton AB
Ukrainian Institute of Modern Art, Chicago IL
The Ukrainian Museum, New York NY
United Society of Shakers, Shaker Museum, New Gloucester ME
University of Georgia, Georgia Museum of Art, Athens GA
University of Illinois at Urbana-Champaign, Krannert Art Museum and Kinkead Pavilion, Champaign IL
University of Kansas, Spencer Museum of Art, Lawrence KS
The University of Kentucky Art Museum, Lexington KY
University of Manchester, Whitworth Art Gallery, Manchester
University of Minnesota, Goldstein Museum of Design, Saint Paul MN
University of Richmond, University Museums, Richmond VA
University of Utah, Utah Museum of Fine Arts, Salt Lake City UT
Vesterheim Norwegian-American Museum, Decorah IA
Wadsworth Atheneum Museum of Art, Hartford CT
Wheaton College, Beard and Weil Galleries, Norton MA
Wheelwright Museum of the American Indian, Santa Fe NM
Willard House & Clock Museum, Inc, North Grafton MA
William Morris Gallery, London
Witte Museum, San Antonio TX
Woodlawn/The Pope-Leighey, Alexandria VA
Woodmere Art Museum Inc, Philadelphia PA

ENAMELS

Academy of the New Church, Glencairn Museum, Bryn Athyn PA
Arnot Art Museum, Elmira NY
ArtSpace/Lima, Lima OH
Bangladesh National Museum, Dhaka
Baroda Museum and Picture Gallery, Vadodara
Bayerisches Nationalmuseum, Bavarian National Museum, Munich
Bellevue Arts Museum, Bellevue WA
Birmingham Museum of Art, Birmingham AL
Bob Jones University Museum & Gallery Inc, Greenville SC
Canadian Clay and Glass Gallery, Waterloo ON
Canadian Museum of History, Gatineau QC
The Children's Museum of Indianapolis, Indianapolis IN
City of Fremont, Olive Hyde Art Gallery, Fremont CA
College of William & Mary, Muscarelle Museum of Art, Williamsburg VA
The Currier Museum of Art, Manchester NH
Cyprus Museum, Nicosia
Detroit Institute of Arts, Detroit MI
Fine Arts Museums of San Francisco, Legion of Honor, San Francisco CA
Forest Lawn Museum, Glendale CA
Freer Gallery of Art & Arthur M Sackler Gallery, Arthur M Sackler Gallery, Washington DC
Fuller Craft Museum, Brockton MA
Gallery One Visual Arts Center, Ellensburg WA
Glanmore National Historic Site of Canada, Belleville ON
Hermitage Museum & Gardens, Norfolk VA
Hillwood Museum & Gardens Foundation, Hillwood Estate Museum & Gardens, Washington DC
Illinois State Museum, ISM Lockport Gallery, Chicago Gallery & Southern Illinois Art Gallery, Springfield IL
The Interchurch Center, Galleries at the Interchurch Center, New York NY
Iowa State University, Brunnier Art Museum, Ames IA
The Israel Museum, Jerusalem, Jerusalem
Jacksonville University, Alexander Brest Museum & Gallery, Jacksonville FL
Johns Hopkins University, Evergreen Museum & Library, Baltimore MD
Kenosha Public Museums, Kenosha WI
Kereszteny Muzeum, Christian Museum, Esztergom
Kimbell Art Foundation, Kimbell Art Museum, Fort Worth TX
Kirkland Museum of Fine & Decorative Art, Denver CO
Kunsthistorisches Museum Wien, Museum of Fine Arts, Vienna
Le Grand Curtius, The Grand Curtius, Liege
League of New Hampshire Craftsmen, Grodin Permanent Collection Museum, Concord NH
Lightner Museum, Saint Augustine FL
Lincolnshire County Council, The Collection: Art & Archaeology in Lincolnshire, Lincoln
Louise Hopkins Underwood Center for the Arts, Lubbock TX
Loyola University Chicago, Loyola University Museum of Art, Chicago IL
Meredith College, Frankie G Weems Gallery & Rotunda Gallery, Raleigh NC
Mesa Arts Center, Mesa Contemporary Arts Museum, Mesa AZ
Michigan State University, Eli & Edythe Broad Art Museum, East Lansing MI
The Mint Museum, Charlotte NC
Mobile Museum of Art, Mobile AL
Montreal Museum of Fine Arts, Montreal QC
Musee des Beaux-Arts d'Orleans, Museum of Fine Arts, Orleans
Musee des Beaux-Arts de Tours, Museum of Fine Arts, Tours
Musees Royaux d'Art et d'Histoire, Royal Museums of Art and History, Brussels
Museu Nacional D'Art De Catalunya, Catalona National Museum of Art, Barcelona
The Museum of Arts & Sciences Inc, Daytona Beach FL
Museum zu Allerheiligen, Schaffhausen
Muzeul National de Arta al Romaniei, National Museum of Art of Romania, Bucharest
National Palace Museum, Taipei
New Brunswick Museum, Saint John NB
New Orleans Artworks at New Orleans Glassworks & Printmaking Studio, New Orleans LA
Norwich Free Academy, Slater Memorial Museum, Norwich CT
Noyes Art Gallery, Lincoln NE
Panhandle-Plains Historical Museum, Canyon TX
Reading Public Museum, Reading PA
San Antonio Museum of Art, San Antonio TX
Schweinfurth Art Center, Auburn NY
Scripps College, Ruth Chandler Williamson Gallery, Claremont CA
Society for Contemporary Craft, Pittsburgh PA
The Speed Art Museum, Louisville KY
Spertus Institute of Jewish Studies, Chicago IL
Staatliche Museen zu Berlin Stiftung Preussischer Kulturbesitz, National Museums in Berlin, Prussian Cultural Heritage Foundation, Berlin
The State Museum of Fine Arts of Tatarstan Republic, Kazan
The State Museum of Oriental Art, Moscow

Taft Museum of Art, Cincinnati OH
Topeka & Shawnee County Public Library, Alice C Sabatini Gallery, Topeka KS
Tver Regional Art Gallery, Tver
University of Illinois at Urbana-Champaign, Krannert Art Museum and Kinkead Pavilion, Champaign IL
The University of Kentucky Art Museum, Lexington KY
University of Wisconsin-Madison, Chazen Museum of Art, Madison WI
Villa Terrace Decorative Arts Museum, Milwaukee WI
Virginia Museum of Fine Arts, Richmond VA
The Wallace Collection, London
Wilkes Art Gallery, North Wilkesboro NC

ESKIMO ART

Alaska Department of Education, Division of Libraries, Archives & Museums, Sheldon Jackson Museum, Sitka AK
Alaska Heritage Museum at Wells Fargo, Anchorage AK
Alaska State Museum, Juneau AK
Anchorage Museum at Rasmuson Center, Anchorage AK
Archaeological Society of Ohio, Indian Museum of Lake County, Ohio, Willoughby OH
Arnot Art Museum, Elmira NY
Art and History Museums - Maitland, Maitland FL
Art Gallery of Guelph, Guelph ON
Art Gallery of Hamilton, Hamilton ON
Art Gallery of Nova Scotia, Halifax NS
Art Without Walls Inc, Sayville NY
Aurora University, Schingoethe Center for Native American Cultures & The Schingoethe Art Gallery, Aurora IL
Blauvelt Demarest Foundation, Hiram Blauvelt Art Museum, Oradell NJ
Bowdoin College, Peary-MacMillan Arctic Museum, Brunswick ME
Brown University, Haffenreffer Museum of Anthropology, Providence RI
California State University, Chico, Janet Turner Print Museum, CSU, Chicago, Chico CA
Canadian Clay and Glass Gallery, Waterloo ON
Canadian Museum of History, Gatineau QC
Capital University, Schumacher Gallery, Columbus OH
Cedar Rapids Museum of Art, Cedar Rapids IA
Centenary College of Louisiana, Meadows Museum of Art, Shreveport LA
The Children's Museum of Indianapolis, Indianapolis IN
College of William & Mary, Muscarelle Museum of Art, Williamsburg VA
The Columbus Museum, Columbus GA
Columbus Museum of Art, Columbus OH
Dartmouth College, Hood Museum of Art, Hanover NH
Deming-Luna Mimbres Museum, Deming NM
Denver Art Museum, Denver CO
Detroit Institute of Arts, Detroit MI
Detroit Zoological Institute, Wildlife Interpretive Gallery, Royal Oak MI
Eiteljorg Museum of American Indians & Western Art, Indianapolis IN
Eskimo Museum, Churchill MB
Fairbanks Museum & Planetarium, Saint Johnsbury VT
Fine Arts Museums of San Francisco, Legion of Honor, San Francisco CA
Fireweed Gallery, Homer AK
Flint Institute of Arts, Flint MI
Folk Art Society of America, Richmond VA
Fruitlands Museum, Inc, Harvard MA
Henry County Museum & Cultural Arts Center, Clinton MO
Heritage Center, Inc, Pine Ridge SD
Herrett Center for Arts & Sciences, Jean B King Art Gallery, Twin Falls ID
Historisches und Volkerkundemuseum, Museum of History and Ethnology, St Gallen
Illinois State Museum, ISM Lockport Gallery, Chicago Gallery & Southern Illinois Art Gallery, Springfield IL
The Interchurch Center, Galleries at the Interchurch Center, New York NY
Kenosha Public Museums, Kenosha WI
Koshare Indian Museum, Inc, La Junta CO
Louisiana Arts & Science Museum, Baton Rouge LA
McCord Museum of Canadian History, Montreal QC
Michelson Museum of Art, Marshall TX
Michigan State University, Eli & Edythe Broad Art Museum, East Lansing MI
Missoula Art Museum, Missoula MT
Mobile Museum of Art, Mobile AL
Montreal Museum of Fine Arts, Montreal QC
Moravian Historical Society, Nazareth PA
Musee Regional de lu Cote-Nord, Sept-Iles QC
Musees Royaux d'Art et d'Histoire, Royal Museums of Art and History, Brussels
Museum of the Plains Indian & Crafts Center, Browning MT
Museum of Vancouver, Vancouver BC
National Museum of the American Indian, George Gustav Heye Center, New York NY
National Museums Scotland, National Museum of Scotland, Edinburgh
Nelson Mandela Metropolitan Art Museum, Port Elizabeth
New Brunswick Museum, Saint John NB
Norwich Free Academy, Slater Memorial Museum, Norwich CT
Okanagan Heritage Museum, Kelowna BC
Panhandle-Plains Historical Museum, Canyon TX
Portland Art Museum, Portland OR
Pueblo Museum, Desert Hot Springs CA
Queens College, City University of New York, Godwin-Ternbach Museum, Flushing NY
Reading Public Museum, Reading PA
Riverside Metropolitan Museum, Riverside CA
Royal Alberta Museum, Royal Alberta Museum, Edmonton AB
San Francisco Maritime National Historical Park, Maritime Museum, San Francisco CA
The San Joaquin Pioneer & Historical Society, The Haggin Museum, Stockton CA
Sheldon Museum & Cultural Center, Inc, Sheldon Museum & Cultural Center, Haines AK
South Dakota State University, South Dakota Art Museum, Brookings SD
State University of New York at Plattsburgh, Art Museum, Plattsburgh NY
The State University of New York at Potsdam, The Art Museum, Potsdam NY
Suomen Kansallismuseo, National Museum of Finland, Helsinki
United States Coast Guard Museum, New London CT
University of California, Berkeley, Phoebe Apperson Hearst Museum of Anthropology, Berkeley CA
University of Miami, Lowe Art Museum, Coral Gables FL
University of Richmond, University Museums, Richmond VA
University of Saskatchewan, Diefenbaker Canada Centre, Saskatoon SK
University of Washington, Burke Museum of Natural History and Culture, Seattle WA
University of Wisconsin-Madison, Chazen Museum of Art, Madison WI
Wilfrid Laurier University, Robert Langen Art Gallery, Waterloo ON
The Winnipeg Art Gallery, Winnipeg MB
World Erotic Art Museum, Miami Beach FL

ETCHINGS & ENGRAVINGS

1708 Gallery, Richmond VA
Academy Art Museum, Easton MD
African American Museum in Philadelphia, Philadelphia PA
Alaska State Museum, Juneau AK
Albion College, Bobbitt Visual Arts Center, Albion MI
The Albrecht-Kemper Museum of Art, Saint Joseph MO
Albuquerque Museum of Art & History, Albuquerque NM
Allentown Art Museum, Allentown PA
American University, Museum at the Katzen, Washington DC
Amherst College, Mead Art Museum, Amherst MA
Amon Carter Museum of American Art, Fort Worth TX
Anchorage Museum at Rasmuson Center, Anchorage AK
Arnot Art Museum, Elmira NY
Art and History Museums - Maitland, Maitland FL
Art Community Center, Art Center of Corpus Christi, Corpus Christi TX
Art Gallery of Hamilton, Hamilton ON
Art Gallery of Nova Scotia, Halifax NS
Art Gallery of South Australia, Adelaide
The Art Museum of Eastern Idaho, Idaho Falls ID
Art Museum of Greater Lafayette, Lafayette IN
Art Museum of Southeast Texas, Beaumont TX
Artspace, Richmond VA
ArtSpace/Lima, Lima OH
Asheville Art Museum, Asheville NC
Audrain County Historical Society, Graceland Museum & American Saddlehorse Museum & Fire Brick Industry Museum, Mexico MO
Augustana University, Eide-Dalrymple Gallery, Sioux Falls SD
Baldwin Historical Society Museum, Baldwin NY
Baroda Museum and Picture Gallery, Vadodara
Baruch College of the City University of New York, Sidney Mishkin Gallery, New York NY
Baton Rouge Gallery, Center For Contemporary Art, Baton Rouge LA
Belger Arts Center, Kansas City MO
Bennington Museum, Bennington VT
Berkshire Museum, Pittsfield MA
Besser Museum for Northeast Michigan, Alpena MI
Birmingham Museum of Art, Birmingham AL
Blanden Memorial Art Museum, Fort Dodge IA
Bob Jones University Museum & Gallery Inc, Greenville SC
Bone Creek Museum of Agrarian Art, David City NE
Boston Public Library, Albert H Wiggin Gallery & Print Department, Boston MA
Bruce Museum, Inc, Greenwich CT
Bucknell University, Edward & Marthann Samek Art Gallery, Lewisburg PA
The Buffalo Fine Arts Academy, Albright-Knox Art Gallery, Buffalo NY
Bush-Holley Historic Site & Storehouse Gallery, Greenwich Historical Society, Cos Cob CT
C M Russell Museum, Great Falls MT
California State University, Chico, Janet Turner Print Museum, CSU, Chicago, Chico CA
Cameron Art Museum, Wilmington NC
Canadian Clay and Glass Gallery, Waterloo ON
Canadian Museum of History, Gatineau QC
Cape Ann Museum, Gloucester MA
Cape Cod Museum of Art Inc, Dennis MA
Carnegie Mellon University, Hunt Institute for Botanical Documentation, Pittsburgh PA
Carson County Square House Museum, Panhandle TX
Cartoon Art Museum, San Francisco CA
Centenary College of Louisiana, Meadows Museum of Art, Shreveport LA
Center for Book Arts, New York NY
Central United Methodist Church, Swords Into Plowshares Peace Center & Gallery, Detroit MI
Channel Islands Maritime Museum, Oxnard CA
Charleston Museum, Heyward-Washington House, Charleston SC
The Children's Museum of Indianapolis, Indianapolis IN
City of Cedar Falls, Iowa, James & Meryl Hearst Center for the Arts & Sculpture Garden, Cedar Falls IA
City of Fremont, Olive Hyde Art Gallery, Fremont CA
Clark Art Institute, Williamstown MA
Clark County Historical Society, Pioneer - Krier Museum, Ashland KS
Clinton Art Association, River Arts Center, Clinton IA
Colgate University, Picker Art Gallery, Hamilton NY
College of William & Mary, Muscarelle Museum of Art, Williamsburg VA
The Columbus Museum, Columbus GA
Columbus Museum of Art, Columbus OH
Concordia Historical Institute, Saint Louis MO
Concordia University, Leonard & Bina Ellen Art Gallery, Montreal QC
Contemporary Calgary, Calgary AB
Cornell Museum of Art and American Culture, Delray Beach FL
Coutts Museum of Art, Inc, El Dorado KS
Craft and Folk Art Museum (CAFAM), Los Angeles CA
Cranbrook Art Museum, Bloomfield Hills MI
Cripple Creek District Museum, Cripple Creek CO
Crocker Art Museum, Sacramento CA
Crow Wing County Historical Society, Brainerd MN
The Currier Museum of Art, Manchester NH
Cyprus Museum, Nicosia
Dahesh Museum of Art, Greenwich CT
Dalnavert Museum, Winnipeg MB
Danville Museum of Fine Arts & History, Danville VA

Dartmouth College, Hood Museum of Art, Hanover NH
Daum Museum of Contemporary Art, Sedalia MO
Davidson College, William H Van Every Jr & Edward M Smith Galleries, Davidson NC
deCordova Sculpture Park & Museum, Lincoln MA
Deines Cultural Center, Russell KS
Delaware Art Museum, Wilmington DE
Detroit Institute of Arts, Detroit MI
Detroit Repertory Theatre Gallery, Detroit MI
Dickinson College, The Trout Gallery, Carlisle PA
Dixie State University, Sears Art Museum Gallery, Saint George UT
Doncaster Museum and Art Gallery, Doncaster Yorks
Durham Art Guild, Durham NC
Eastern Illinois University, Tarble Arts Center, Charleston IL
Eiteljorg Museum of American Indians & Western Art, Indianapolis IN
Ellen Noel Art Museum of the Permian Basin, Odessa TX
Elmhurst Art Museum, Elmhurst IL
Emory University, Michael C Carlos Museum, Atlanta GA
Erie Art Museum, Erie PA
Evansville Museum of Arts, History & Science, Evansville IN
Farmington Village Green & Library Association, Stanley-Whitman House, Farmington CT
Fetherston Foundation, Packwood House Museum, Lewisburg PA
Fine Arts Center for the New River Valley, Pulaski VA
Fine Arts Museums of San Francisco, Legion of Honor, San Francisco CA
Flint Institute of Arts, Flint MI
Florence County Museum, Florence SC
Florida Southern College, Melvin Art Gallery, Lakeland FL
Fondazione Musei Civici Di Venezia, Museo Correr - Correr Museum, Venice
Fondazione Musei Civici Di Venezia, Ca' Rezzonico, Venice
Fondazione Musei Civici Di Venezia, Ca' Pesaro Galleria Nazionale d'Arte Moderna - Ca' Pesaro Gallery of Modern Art, Venice
Fort Ticonderoga Association, Ticonderoga NY
The Frank Phillips Foundation Inc, Woolaroc Museum, Bartlesville OK
Freer Gallery of Art & Arthur M Sackler Gallery, Arthur M Sackler Gallery, Washington DC
Frontier Times Museum, Bandera TX
Fruitlands Museum, Inc, Harvard MA
Frye Art Museum, Seattle WA
Fuller Craft Museum, Brockton MA
Gallery One Visual Arts Center, Ellensburg WA
Glanmore National Historic Site of Canada, Belleville ON
Glessner House Museum, Chicago IL
Grand Rapids Art Museum, Grand Rapids MI
Grand Rapids Public Museum, Grand Rapids MI
Hamilton College, Emerson Gallery, Clinton NY
Headquarters Fort Monroe, Dept of Army, Casemate Museum, Hampton VA
Hebrew Union College, Skirball Cultural Center, Los Angeles CA
Hebrew Union College - Jewish Institute of Religion Museum, Jewish Institute of Religion, New York NY
Hecht Museum, Haifa
Henry Sheldon Museum of Vermont History and Research Center, Middlebury VT
Heritage Center, Inc, Pine Ridge SD
Hickory Museum of Art, Inc, Hickory NC
High Museum of Art, Atlanta GA
Hill-Stead Museum, Farmington CT
Hillwood Museum & Gardens Foundation, Hillwood Estate Museum & Gardens, Washington DC
Historic Arkansas Museum, Little Rock AR
Honolulu Museum of Art, Honolulu HI
Hui No'eau Visual Arts Center, Gallery and Gift Shop, Makawao Maui HI
The Huntington Library, Art Collections & Botanical Gardens, San Marino CA
The Hyde Collection, Glens Falls NY
Hyde Park Art Center, Chicago IL
i.d.e.a. Museum, Mesa AZ
Illinois State Museum, ISM Lockport Gallery, Chicago Gallery & Southern Illinois Art Gallery, Springfield IL
Imperial Calcasieu Museum, Gibson-Barham Gallery, Lake Charles LA
Independence Seaport Museum, Philadelphia PA
The Interchurch Center, Galleries at the Interchurch Center, New York NY
Intermedia Arts, Minneapolis MN
International Museum of Art, El Paso TX
Iredell Museums, Statesville NC
The Israel Museum, Jerusalem, Jerusalem
Jacksonville University, Alexander Brest Museum & Gallery, Jacksonville FL
The Jewish Museum, New York NY
JMW Turner Museum, Sarasota FL
Johns Hopkins University, Evergreen Museum & Library, Baltimore MD
Jordan National Gallery of Fine Arts, Amman
Joslyn Art Museum, Omaha NE
Juniata College Museum of Art, Huntingdon PA
Kalamazoo Institute of Arts, Kalamazoo MI
Kamloops Art Gallery, Kamloops BC
Kenosha Public Museums, Kenosha WI
Kereszteny Muzeum, Christian Museum, Esztergom
Kimbell Art Foundation, Kimbell Art Museum, Fort Worth TX
Kirchner Museum Davos, Davos
Kirkland Museum of Fine & Decorative Art, Denver CO
Knoxville Museum of Art, Knoxville TN
Kyiv Museum of Russian Art, Kyiv Ukrainian
La Salle University Art Museum, Philadelphia PA
Lac du Flambeau Band of Lake Superior Chippewa Indians, George W Brown Jr Ojibwe Museum & Cultural Center, Lac Du Flambeau WI
Lafayette College, Lafayette College Art Galleries, Easton PA
Lafayette Science Museum & Planetarium, Lafayette LA
LaGrange Art Museum, LaGrange GA
Latino Art Museum, Pomona CA
League of New Hampshire Craftsmen, Grodin Permanent Collection Museum, Concord NH
Lightner Museum, Saint Augustine FL
Lincolnshire County Council, The Collection: Art & Archaeology in Lincolnshire, Lincoln
Lockwood-Mathews Mansion Museum, Norwalk CT
The Long Island Museum of American Art, History & Carriages, Stony Brook NY
Longview Museum of Fine Art, Longview TX
Louise Hopkins Underwood Center for the Arts, Lubbock TX
Louisiana Department of Culture, Recreation & Tourism, Louisiana State Museum, New Orleans LA
Loyola University Chicago, Loyola University Museum of Art, Chicago IL
Lusaka National Museum, Lusaka
Lyme Historical Society, Florence Griswold Museum, Old Lyme CT
Mabee-Gerrer Museum of Art, Shawnee OK
Madison Museum of Fine Art, Madison GA
The Mariners' Museum, Newport News VA
Marquette University, Haggerty Museum of Art, Milwaukee WI
Maryhill Museum of Art, Goldendale WA
Marylhurst University, The Art Gym, Marylhurst OR
Maude Kerns Art Center, Eugene OR
McCord Museum of Canadian History, Montreal QC
Mennello Museum of American Art, Orlando FL
Meredith College, Frankie G Weems Gallery & Rotunda Gallery, Raleigh NC
Mesa Arts Center, Mesa Contemporary Arts Museum, Mesa AZ
The Mexican Museum, San Francisco CA
Miami-Dade College, MDC Museum of Art & Design, Miami FL
Michigan State University, Eli & Edythe Broad Art Museum, East Lansing MI
Middle Border Museum & Oscar Howe Art Center, Mitchell SD
Midwest Museum of American Art, Elkhart IN
Miller Art Center Foundation Inc, Miller Art Museum, Sturgeon Bay WI
Minnesota Museum of American Art, Saint Paul MN
Minot State University, Northwest Art Center, Minot ND
The Mint Museum, Charlotte NC
Mississippi Museum of Art, Jackson MS
Missoula Art Museum, Missoula MT
Mobile Museum of Art, Mobile AL
Mohawk Valley Heritage Association, Inc, Walter Elwood Museum, Amsterdam NY
Montana State University, Helen E Copeland Gallery, Bozeman MT
Montgomery Museum of Fine Arts, Montgomery AL
Montreal Museum of Fine Arts, Montreal QC
Moravian Historical Society, Nazareth PA
Moravska Galerie v Brne, Moravian Gallery in Brno, Brno
Morris Museum, Morristown NJ
Morris Museum of Art, Augusta GA
Morris-Jumel Mansion, Inc, New York NY
Mount Mary College, Marian Gallery, Milwaukee WI
MTG Hawkes Bay, Napier
Muhlenberg College, Martin Art Gallery, Allentown PA
Musee des Beaux-Arts d'Orleans, Museum of Fine Arts, Orleans
Museen der Stadt Koln, Wallraf-Richartz-Museum & Fondation Corboud - Wallraf-Richartz Museum & Corboud Foundation, Cologne
Museo De Las Americas, Denver CO
Museo di Palazzo Ducale, Ducale Palace Museum, Mantua
Museo Nacional de Bellas Artes, National Museum of Fine Arts, Santiago
Museu Nacional D'Art De Catalunya, Catalona National Museum of Art, Barcelona
Museum of Art & History, Santa Cruz, Santa Cruz CA
Museum of Art - Deland FL, Inc, Deland FL
The Museum of Arts & Sciences Inc, Daytona Beach FL
Museum of Contemporary Art, North Miami FL
Museum of Fine Arts, Saint Petersburg, Florida, Inc, Saint Petersburg FL
Museum of Latin American Art, Long Beach CA
Museum of Northwest Art, La Conner WA
Museum of the Plains Indian & Crafts Center, Browning MT
Museum of the Southwest, Midland TX
Museum of Vancouver, Vancouver BC
Museum of Wisconsin Art, West Bend WI
Museum Plantin-Moretus, Antwerp
Museum zu Allerheiligen, Schaffhausen
Muzej za Umjetnost i Obrt, Museum of Arts & Crafts, Zagreb
Muzeul National de Arta al Romaniei, National Museum of Art of Romania, Bucharest
Narodna Galerija, National Gallery of Slovenia, Ljubljana
National Gallery of Canada, Ottawa ON
National Gallery of Ireland, Dublin
The National Museum of Modern Art, Tokyo, Tokyo
The National Museum of Western Art, Tokyo
National Museum of Wildlife Art of the Unites States, Jackson WY
National Museum of Women in the Arts, Washington DC
National Park Service, Weir Farm National Historic Site, Wilton CT
National Society of Colonial Dames of America in the State of Maryland, Mount Clare Museum House, Baltimore MD
Naval Historical Center, National Museum of the US Navy, Washington DC
Nelda C & H J Lutcher Stark Foundation, Stark Museum of Art, Orange TX
Nelson Mandela Metropolitan Art Museum, Port Elizabeth
The Nelson-Atkins Museum of Art, Kansas City MO
Nevada Museum of Art, Reno NV
Neville Public Museum of Brown County, Green Bay WI
New Britain Museum of American Art, New Britain CT
New Brunswick Museum, Saint John NB
New Gallery of Modern Art, Charlotte NC
New Orleans Artworks at New Orleans Glassworks & Printmaking Studio, New Orleans LA
New Visions Gallery, Inc, Marshfield WI
New York State Office of Parks Recreation & Historic Preservation, John Jay Homestead State Historic Site, Katonah NY
New York State Office of Parks, Recreation & Historic Preservation, Staatsburgh State Historic Site, Staatsburg NY
Newport Art Museum and Association, Newport RI
The Noble Maritime Collection, Staten Island NY
Northwestern College, Te Paske Gallery, Orange City IA

Norwich Free Academy, Slater Memorial Museum, Norwich CT
Nova Scotia College of Art and Design, Anna Leonowens Gallery, Halifax NS
Ogden Museum of Southern Art, University of New Orleans, New Orleans LA
Ohio University, Kennedy Museum of Art, Athens OH
Oklahoma City Museum of Art, Oklahoma City OK
Old Dartmouth Historical Society, New Bedford Whaling Museum, New Bedford MA
Opelousas Museum of Art, Inc (OMA), Opelousas LA
Owensboro Museum of Fine Art, Owensboro KY
Page-Walker Arts & History Center, Cary NC
Panhandle-Plains Historical Museum, Canyon TX
Parrish Art Museum, Water Mill NY
Pennsylvania Academy of the Fine Arts, Philadelphia PA
Pensacola Museum of Art, Pensacola FL
Philadelphia History Museum, Philadelphia PA
The Phillips Collection, Washington DC
Polish Museum of America (PMA), Chicago IL
The Pomona College, Claremont CA
Portland Art Museum, Portland OR
Pueblo Museum, Desert Hot Springs CA
Purdue University Galleries, West Lafayette IN
Queen Victoria Museum and Art Gallery, Launceston TAS
Queens College, City University of New York, Godwin-Ternbach Museum, Flushing NY
Randolph College, Maier Museum of Art, Lynchburg VA
Reading Public Museum, Reading PA
Rensselaer County Historical Society, Hart-Cluett Mansion, 1827, Troy NY
Rhode Island Historical Society, John Brown House, Providence RI
Robert Louis Stevenson Museum, Saint Helena CA
The Rockwell Museum, Corning NY
Rose Lehrman Art Gallery, Harrisburg PA
Roswell Museum & Art Center, Roswell NM
Rutgers University, Stedman Art Gallery, Camden NJ
Saginaw Art Museum, Saginaw MI
Saint Anselm College, Alva de Mars Megan Chapel Art Center, Manchester NH
Saint Bonaventure University, Regina A Quick Center for the Arts, Saint Bonaventure NY
Saint Joseph College, Art Gallery, University of Saint Joseph, West Hartford CT
Saint Mary's College of California, Museum of Art, Moraga CA
Saint Olaf College, Flaten Art Museum, Northfield MN
San Antonio Museum of Art, San Antonio TX
San Francisco Maritime National Historical Park, Maritime Museum, San Francisco CA
The San Joaquin Pioneer & Historical Society, The Haggin Museum, Stockton CA
Santa Barbara Museum of Art, Santa Barbara CA
Shirley Plantation Foundation, Charles City VA
The Society of the Cincinnati at Anderson House, Washington DC
Southern Methodist University, Meadows Museum, Dallas TX
The Speed Art Museum, Louisville KY
Spertus Institute of Jewish Studies, Chicago IL
Springfield Art Museum, Springfield MO
St Mary's College of Maryland, The Dwight Frederick Boyden Gallery, St Mary's City MD
Staatliche Museen zu Berlin Stiftung Preussischer Kulturbesitz, National Museums in Berlin, Prussian Cultural Heritage Foundation, Berlin
Stanford University, Cantor Arts Center at Stanford University, Stanford CA
State Capital Museum, Olympia WA
The State Museum of Fine Arts of Tatarstan Republic, Kazan
The State Museum of Oriental Art, Moscow
State University of New York at Geneseo, Bertha V B Lederer Gallery, Geneseo NY
State University of New York at New Paltz, Samuel Dorsky Museum of Art, New Paltz NY
State University of New York at Plattsburgh, Art Museum, Plattsburgh NY
State University of New York College at Cortland, Dowd Fine Arts Gallery, Cortland NY
Staten Island Museum, Staten Island NY
The Stewart Museum, Montreal QC
Stone Quarry Hill Art Park, Winner Gallery, Cazenovia NY
The Summit County Historical Society of Akron, OH, Akron OH
Susquehanna University, Lore Degenstein Gallery, Selinsgrove PA
Swedish American Museum, Chicago IL
Szepmuveszeti Muzeum, Museum of Fine Arts, Budapest
Tacoma Art Museum, Tacoma WA
Tampa Museum of Art, Tampa FL
Temiskaming Art Gallery, Haileybury ON
Thomas Jefferson Foundation, Inc, Monticello, Charlottesville VA
Tohono Chul Park, Tucson AZ
Tokyo National Museum, Tokyo
Topeka & Shawnee County Public Library, Alice C Sabatini Gallery, Topeka KS
Tubman African American Museum, Macon GA
Turtle Bay Exploration Park, Redding CA
Tver Regional Art Gallery, Tver
Tyne and Wear Archives & Museums, Sunderland Museum & Winter Gardens, Sunderland
Ukrainian Institute of Modern Art, Chicago IL
The Ukrainian Museum, New York NY
United States Capitol, Architect of the Capitol, Washington DC
United States Coast Guard Museum, New London CT
United States Figure Skating Association, World Figure Skating Museum & Hall of Fame, Colorado Springs CO
United States Military Academy, West Point Museum, West Point NY
University of Arkansas at Little Rock, Art Galleries, Little Rock AR
University of California, Davis, Jan Shrem and Maria Manetti Shrem Museum of Art, Davis CA
University of Chicago, Smart Museum of Art, Chicago IL
University of Georgia, Georgia Museum of Art, Athens GA
University of Illinois at Urbana-Champaign, Krannert Art Museum and Kinkead Pavilion, Champaign IL
University of Indianapolis, Christel DeHaan Fine Arts Gallery, Indianapolis IN
University of Kansas, Spencer Museum of Art, Lawrence KS
The University of Kentucky Art Museum, Lexington KY
University of Manchester, Whitworth Art Gallery, Manchester
University of Mary Washington, University of Mary Washington Galleries, Fredericksburg VA
University of Miami, Lowe Art Museum, Coral Gables FL
University of Minnesota, The Bell Museum of Natural History, Minneapolis MN
University of Minnesota Duluth, Tweed Museum of Art, Duluth MN
University of Nevada, Reno, Sheppard Contemporary & University Galleries, Reno NV
University of New Mexico, The Harwood Museum of Art, Taos NM
University of Notre Dame, Snite Museum of Art, Notre Dame IN
University of Pennsylvania, Arthur Ross Gallery, Philadelphia PA
University of Richmond, University Museums, Richmond VA
University of Saskatchewan, Diefenbaker Canada Centre, Saskatoon SK
University of Texas at Austin, Blanton Museum of Art, Austin TX
University of Victoria, The Legacy Art Gallery, Victoria BC
University of Wisconsin-Eau Claire, Foster Gallery, Eau Claire WI
University of Wisconsin-Madison, Chazen Museum of Art, Madison WI
Ursinus College, Philip & Muriel Berman Museum of Art, Collegeville PA
USS Constitution Museum, Boston MA
Vassar College, The Frances Lehman Loeb Art Center, Poughkeepsie NY
Vero Beach Museum of Art, Vero Beach FL
Vesterheim Norwegian-American Museum, Decorah IA
Virginia Museum of Fine Arts, Richmond VA
Volcano Art Center Gallery, Hawaii Volcanoes National Park HI
Walker Art Gallery, Liverpool
Washburn University, Mulvane Art Museum, Topeka KS
Waterworks Visual Arts Center, Salisbury NC
Wesleyan University, Davison Art Center, Middletown CT
Westmoreland Museum of American Art, Greensburg PA
Wheaton College, Beard and Weil Galleries, Norton MA
Wichita State University, Ulrich Museum of Art, Wichita KS
Wildling Art Museum, Solvang CA
Wilfrid Laurier University, Robert Langen Art Gallery, Waterloo ON
Wiregrass Museum of Art, Dothan AL
Wisconsin Historical Society, Wisconsin Historical Museum, Madison WI
Woodlawn/The Pope-Leighey, Alexandria VA
Woodmere Art Museum Inc, Philadelphia PA
Worcester Art Museum, Worcester MA
World Erotic Art Museum, Miami Beach FL
Yale University, Yale Center for British Art, New Haven CT
Yokohama Museum of Art, Yokohama
Zigler Art Museum, Jennings LA

ETHNOLOGY

African Art Museum of Maryland, Columbia MD
Al Ain National Museum, Al Ain
Alaska Department of Education, Division of Libraries, Archives & Museums, Sheldon Jackson Museum, Sitka AK
Alaska Heritage Museum at Wells Fargo, Anchorage AK
Alaska State Museum, Juneau AK
Anchorage Museum at Rasmuson Center, Anchorage AK
Arizona Historical Society-Yuma, Sanguinetti House Museum & Garden, Yuma AZ
Art Without Walls Inc, Sayville NY
ArtSpace/Lima, Lima OH
Aurora University, Schingoethe Center for Native American Cultures & The Schingoethe Art Gallery, Aurora IL
Bangladesh National Museum, Dhaka
Baroda Museum and Picture Gallery, Vadodara
Berkshire Museum, Pittsfield MA
Botswana National Museum, Gaborone
Bowdoin College, Peary-MacMillan Arctic Museum, Brunswick ME
Brown University, Haffenreffer Museum of Anthropology, Providence RI
Bruce Museum, Inc, Greenwich CT
C M Russell Museum, Great Falls MT
California State University, East Bay, C E Smith Museum of Anthropology, Hayward CA
Canadian Museum of History, Gatineau QC
Carson County Square House Museum, Panhandle TX
Centenary College of Louisiana, Meadows Museum of Art, Shreveport LA
Chief Plenty Coups Museum State Park, Pryor MT
The Children's Museum of Indianapolis, Indianapolis IN
City of Ukiah, Grace Hudson Museum & The Sun House, Ukiah CA
The Columbus Museum, Columbus GA
Cornell University, Herbert F Johnson Museum of Art, Ithaca NY
Craft and Folk Art Museum (CAFAM), Los Angeles CA
Davidson College, William H Van Every Jr & Edward M Smith Galleries, Davidson NC
Dawson City Museum, Dawson City YT
Eskimo Museum, Churchill MB
Evansville Museum of Arts, History & Science, Evansville IN
Everhart Museum, Scranton PA
Fairbanks Museum & Planetarium, Saint Johnsbury VT
Fetherston Foundation, Packwood House Museum, Lewisburg PA
Folk Art Society of America, Richmond VA
The Frank Phillips Foundation Inc, Woolaroc Museum, Bartlesville OK
Glasgow University, The Hunterian, Glasgow
Grand Rapids Public Museum, Grand Rapids MI
Grand River Museum, Lemmon SD
Hebrew Union College, Skirball Cultural Center, Los Angeles CA
Henry County Museum & Cultural Arts Center, Clinton MO
Heritage Center, Inc, Pine Ridge SD
High Desert Museum, Bend OR

Historic Arkansas Museum, Little Rock AR
Historic Holyoke at Wistariahurst & City of Holyoke, Holyoke MA
The History Center in Tompkins County, Ithaca NY
History Colorado Center Museum, Denver CO
Huntington Museum of Art, Huntington WV
Illinois State Museum, ISM Lockport Gallery, Chicago Gallery & Southern Illinois Art Gallery, Springfield IL
Iroquois Indian Museum, Howes Cave NY
The Israel Museum, Jerusalem, Jerusalem
Jacques Marchais Museum of Tibetan Art, Staten Island NY
Johns Hopkins University, Evergreen Museum & Library, Baltimore MD
Kenosha Public Museums, Kenosha WI
Kereszteny Muzeum, Christian Museum, Esztergom
Kern County Museum, Bakersfield CA
Kings County Historical Society & Museum, Hampton NB
LA County Museum of Art, Los Angeles CA
Lac du Flambeau Band of Lake Superior Chippewa Indians, George W Brown Jr Ojibwe Museum & Cultural Center, Lac Du Flambeau WI
Lafayette Science Museum & Planetarium, Lafayette LA
Leelanau Historical Museum, Leland MI
Lehigh Valley Heritage Center, Allentown PA
Lincolnshire County Council, Library & Heritage Services, Lincoln
Lincolnshire County Council, The Collection: Art & Archaeology in Lincolnshire, Lincoln
Louisiana Department of Culture, Recreation & Tourism, Louisiana State Museum, New Orleans LA
Loyola Marymount University, Laband Art Gallery, Los Angeles CA
Lusaka National Museum, Lusaka
Mabee-Gerrer Museum of Art, Shawnee OK
The Mariners' Museum, Newport News VA
Maryhill Museum of Art, Goldendale WA
Massillon Museum, Massillon OH
McCord Museum of Canadian History, Montreal QC
McLean County Historical Society, McLean County Museum of History, Bloomington IL
Michigan State University, Eli & Edythe Broad Art Museum, East Lansing MI
Missoula Art Museum, Missoula MT
Mohave Museum of History & Arts, Kingman AZ
Montclair Art Museum, Montclair NJ
Musee Regional de lu Cote-Nord, Sept-Iles QC
Musees Royaux d'Art et d'Histoire, Royal Museums of Art and History, Brussels
Museo De Las Americas, Denver CO
Museo di Palazzo Ducale, Ducale Palace Museum, Mantua
The Museum, Greenwood SC
The Museum of Arts & Sciences Inc, Daytona Beach FL
Museum of Chinese in America, New York NY
Museum of Northern Arizona, Flagstaff AZ
Museum of Northern British Columbia, Ruth Harvey Art Gallery, Prince Rupert BC
Museum of Vancouver, Vancouver BC
Museum of York County, Rock Hill SC
Museum zu Allerheiligen, Schaffhausen
Muzeul de Istorie Nationala Si Arheologie Constanta, National History & Archaeology Museum, Constanta
Muzeul National de Arta al Romaniei, National Museum of Art of Romania, Bucharest
Muzeum Narodowe w Poznaniu, National Museum in Poznan, Poznan
Muzim Negara, National Museum, Kuala Lumpur
National Museum of Ethiopia, Addis Ababa
National Museum of the American Indian, George Gustav Heye Center, New York NY
National Museum of the Philippines, Manila
Nelson Mandela Metropolitan Art Museum, Port Elizabeth
New Brunswick Museum, Saint John NB
New York State Museum, Albany NY
Newburyport Maritime Society, Inc, Custom House Maritime Museum, Newburyport MA
Norwich Free Academy, Slater Memorial Museum, Norwich CT
Ohio History Connection, National Afro-American Museum & Cultural Center, Wilberforce OH
Okanagan Heritage Museum, Kelowna BC
Oklahoma Historical Society, State Museum of History, Oklahoma City OK
Old Dartmouth Historical Society, New Bedford Whaling Museum, New Bedford MA
Palm Beach County Parks & Recreation Department, Morikami Museum & Japanese Gardens, Delray Beach FL
Panhandle-Plains Historical Museum, Canyon TX
Queen Victoria Museum and Art Gallery, Launceston TAS
Queen's University, Agnes Etherington Art Centre, Kingston ON
Red Rock Park, Red Rock Park, Church Rock NM
Riverside Metropolitan Museum, Riverside CA
Roberson Museum & Science Center, Binghamton NY
Roswell Museum & Art Center, Roswell NM
Royal Alberta Museum, Royal Alberta Museum, Edmonton AB
Saint Joseph Museum, Inc., Saint Joseph MO
Saint Mary's College of California, Museum of Art, Moraga CA
San Antonio Museum of Art, San Antonio TX
Seneca-Iroquois National Museum, Salamanca NY
Sheldon Art Galleries, Saint Louis MO
Sheldon Museum & Cultural Center, Inc, Sheldon Museum & Cultural Center, Haines AK
Sooke Region Museum & Art Gallery, Sooke BC
Staatliche Museen zu Berlin Stiftung Preussischer Kulturbesitz, National Museums in Berlin, Prussian Cultural Heritage Foundation, Berlin
Staten Island Museum, Staten Island NY
The Stewart Museum, Montreal QC
Stone Quarry Hill Art Park, Winner Gallery, Cazenovia NY
Suomen Kansallismuseo, National Museum of Finland, Helsinki
Tohono Chul Park, Tucson AZ
Tokyo National Museum, Tokyo
Trust Authority, Museum of the Great Plains, Lawton OK
Turtle Bay Exploration Park, Redding CA
Tyne and Wear Archives & Museums, Sunderland Museum & Winter Gardens, Sunderland
The Ukrainian Museum, New York NY
University of California, Berkeley, Phoebe Apperson Hearst Museum of Anthropology, Berkeley CA
University of Illinois at Urbana-Champaign, Spurlock Museum, Urbana IL
The University of Kentucky Art Museum, Lexington KY
The University of Texas at San Antonio, Institute of Texan Cultures, San Antonio TX
University of Vermont, Robert Hull Fleming Museum, Burlington VT
University of Victoria, The Legacy Art Gallery, Victoria BC
University of Washington, Burke Museum of Natural History and Culture, Seattle WA
Whatcom Museum, Bellingham WA
Wheelwright Museum of the American Indian, Santa Fe NM
World Erotic Art Museum, Miami Beach FL
Wyoming State Museum, Cheyenne WY

FLASKS & BOTTLES

Adams County Historical Society, Gettysburg PA
Alaska State Museum, Juneau AK
Albany Institute of History & Art, Albany NY
Albuquerque Museum of Art & History, Albuquerque NM
Amherst College, Mead Art Museum, Amherst MA
Arizona Historical Society-Yuma, Sanguinetti House Museum & Garden, Yuma AZ
Baroda Museum and Picture Gallery, Vadodara
Bayerische Staatsgemaldesammlungen, Bavarian State Painting Collections, Munich
Bayerisches Nationalmuseum, Bavarian National Museum, Munich
Berman Museum, Anniston AL
Brick Store Museum, Kennebunk ME
Buffalo Niagara Heritage Village, Amherst NY
Canadian Clay and Glass Gallery, Waterloo ON
Canadian Museum of History, Gatineau QC
The Children's Museum of Indianapolis, Indianapolis IN
City of Springdale, Shiloh Museum of Ozark History, Springdale AR
Clark Art Institute, Williamstown MA
Cripple Creek District Museum, Cripple Creek CO
Crook County Museum & Art Gallery, Sundance WY
Detroit Institute of Arts, Detroit MI
Fetherston Foundation, Packwood House Museum, Lewisburg PA
Flint Institute of Arts, Flint MI
Fondazione Musei Civici Di Venezia, Museo di Palazzo Mocenigo - Mocenigo Palace Museum, Venice
Frontier Times Museum, Bandera TX
Germantown Historical Society, Philadelphia PA
Grand Rapids Public Museum, Grand Rapids MI
Henry Sheldon Museum of Vermont History and Research Center, Middlebury VT
Heritage Glass Museum, Glassboro NJ
Hillwood Museum & Gardens Foundation, Hillwood Estate Museum & Gardens, Washington DC
Historical Society of Cheshire County, Keene NH
The History Center in Tompkins County, Ithaca NY
Illinois State Museum, ISM Lockport Gallery, Chicago Gallery & Southern Illinois Art Gallery, Springfield IL
Iredell Museums, Statesville NC
The Israel Museum, Jerusalem, Jerusalem
Kenosha Public Museums, Kenosha WI
Kentucky Derby Museum, Louisville KY
Kereszteny Muzeum, Christian Museum, Esztergom
Kimbell Art Foundation, Kimbell Art Museum, Fort Worth TX
Kings County Historical Society & Museum, Hampton NB
The Long Island Museum of American Art, History & Carriages, Stony Brook NY
McDowell House & Apothecary Shop, Danville KY
McLean County Historical Society, McLean County Museum of History, Bloomington IL
Medina Railroad Museum, Medina NY
Musees Royaux d'Art et d'Histoire, Royal Museums of Art and History, Brussels
The Museum, Greenwood SC
Museum of Fine Arts, Houston, Houston TX
Muzej za Umjetnost i Obrt, Museum of Arts & Crafts, Zagreb
Muzeul National de Arta al Romaniei, National Museum of Art of Romania, Bucharest
National Art Museum of Moldova, Chisinau
National Museum & Art Gallery of Trinidad and Tobago, Port of Spain
National Society of Colonial Dames of America in the State of Maryland, Mount Clare Museum House, Baltimore MD
New Brunswick Museum, Saint John NB
New Canaan Historical Society, New Canaan CT
New Jersey Historical Society, Newark NJ
Norwich Free Academy, Slater Memorial Museum, Norwich CT
Panhandle-Plains Historical Museum, Canyon TX
Philadelphia History Museum, Philadelphia PA
Pine Bluff/Jefferson County Historical Museum, Pine Bluff AR
Pioneer Historical Museum of South Dakota, Hot Springs SD
Reading Public Museum, Reading PA
San Antonio Museum of Art, San Antonio TX
The Speed Art Museum, Louisville KY
Staatliche Museen zu Berlin Stiftung Preussischer Kulturbesitz, National Museums in Berlin, Prussian Cultural Heritage Foundation, Berlin
The State Museum of Fine Arts of Tatarstan Republic, Kazan
Staten Island Museum, Staten Island NY
Strasburg Museum, Strasburg VA
Suomen Kansallismuseo, National Museum of Finland, Helsinki
Tohono Chul Park, Tucson AZ
Tubman African American Museum, Macon GA
Tver Regional Art Gallery, Tver
United Society of Shakers, Shaker Museum, New Gloucester ME
University of California, Berkeley, Phoebe Apperson Hearst Museum of Anthropology, Berkeley CA
The University of Kentucky Art Museum, Lexington KY
University of Utah, Utah Museum of Fine Arts, Salt Lake City UT
USS Constitution Museum, Boston MA
Vesterheim Norwegian-American Museum, Decorah IA
Waterville Historical Society, Redington Museum, Waterville ME

Wheaton College, Beard and Weil Galleries, Norton MA
World Erotic Art Museum, Miami Beach FL
Yellowstone County Museum, Billings MT

FOLK ART

Adams County Historical Society, Gettysburg PA
Akron Art Museum, Akron OH
Alaska State Museum, Juneau AK
Albany Institute of History & Art, Albany NY
Albany Museum of Art, Albany GA
Albion College, Bobbitt Visual Arts Center, Albion MI
Albuquerque Museum of Art & History, Albuquerque NM
Alexandria Museum of Art, Alexandria LA
Allentown Art Museum, Allentown PA
Alton Museum of History & Art, Inc, Alton IL
American Folk Art Museum, New York NY
American Museum of Ceramic Art, Pomona CA
American Swedish Institute, Minneapolis MN
Amon Carter Museum of American Art, Fort Worth TX
Arizona Historical Society-Yuma, Sanguinetti House Museum & Garden, Yuma AZ
Arnold Mikelson Mind & Matter Art Gallery, Surrey BC
The Art Gallery of Cornwall, Cornwall ON
The Art Gallery of Grand Prairie, Grande Prairie AB
Art Gallery of Nova Scotia, Halifax NS
Art Museum of Greater Lafayette, Lafayette IN
Art Museum of Southeast Texas, Beaumont TX
Art Without Walls Inc, Sayville NY
ArtSpace/Lima, Lima OH
Asheville Art Museum, Asheville NC
Aurora University, Schingoethe Center for Native American Cultures & The Schingoethe Art Gallery, Aurora IL
Balzekas Museum of Lithuanian Culture, Chicago IL
Bangladesh National Museum, Dhaka
Baroda Museum and Picture Gallery, Vadodara
Bayerisches Nationalmuseum, Bavarian National Museum, Munich
Bellevue Arts Museum, Bellevue WA
Bennington Museum, Bennington VT
Berkshire Museum, Pittsfield MA
Besser Museum for Northeast Michigan, Alpena MI
Beverly Historical Society, Cabot, Hale & Balch House Museums, Beverly MA
Birmingham Museum of Art, Birmingham AL
Bone Creek Museum of Agrarian Art, David City NE
The Bostonian Society, Old State House Museum, Boston MA
Botswana National Museum, Gaborone
Bucks County Historical Society, Mercer Museum, Doylestown PA
Buffalo Niagara Heritage Village, Amherst NY
Bush-Holley Historic Site & Storehouse Gallery, Greenwich Historical Society, Cos Cob CT
C M Russell Museum, Great Falls MT
Cahoon Museum of American Art, Cotuit MA
Cameron Art Museum, Wilmington NC
Canadian Clay and Glass Gallery, Waterloo ON
Canadian Museum of History, Gatineau QC
Carnegie Center for Art & History, New Albany IN
Carson County Square House Museum, Panhandle TX
Cartoon Art Museum, San Francisco CA
Cayuga Museum of History & Art, Auburn NY
Center for Puppetry Arts, Atlanta GA
Central United Methodist Church, Swords Into Plowshares Peace Center & Gallery, Detroit MI
Chatham Historical Society, The Atwood House Museum, Chatham MA
Chesapeake Bay Maritime Museum, Saint Michaels MD
The Children's Museum of Indianapolis, Indianapolis IN
City of Fayette, Alabama, Fayette Art Museum, Fayette AL
City of Gainesville, Thomas Center Galleries - Cultural Affairs, Gainesville FL
City of Springdale, Shiloh Museum of Ozark History, Springdale AR
Colonial Williamsburg Foundation, Abby Aldrich Rockefeller Folk Art Museum, Williamsburg VA
The Columbus Museum, Columbus GA
Columbus Museum of Art, Columbus OH
Contemporary Calgary, Calgary AB
Cornell Museum of Art and American Culture, Delray Beach FL
Cortland County Historical Society, Suggett House Museum, Cortland NY
County of Henrico, Meadow Farm Museum, Glen Allen VA
Coutts Museum of Art, Inc, El Dorado KS
Craft and Folk Art Museum (CAFAM), Los Angeles CA
Cripple Creek District Museum, Cripple Creek CO
Crocker Art Museum, Sacramento CA
Crook County Museum & Art Gallery, Sundance WY
The Currier Museum of Art, Manchester NH
Danville Museum of Fine Arts & History, Danville VA
Davidson College, William H Van Every Jr & Edward M Smith Galleries, Davidson NC
Deines Cultural Center, Russell KS
Delta Blues Museum, Clarksdale MS
Deming-Luna Mimbres Museum, Deming NM
Denver Art Museum, Denver CO
Detroit Repertory Theatre Gallery, Detroit MI
East Carolina University, Wellington B Gray Gallery, Greenville NC
Eastern Illinois University, Tarble Arts Center, Charleston IL
Ellen Noel Art Museum of the Permian Basin, Odessa TX
Elmhurst Art Museum, Elmhurst IL
Erie Art Museum, Erie PA
Erie County Historical Society, Erie PA
The Ethel Wright Mohamed Stitchery Museum, Belzoni MS
Evansville Museum of Arts, History & Science, Evansville IN
Everhart Museum, Scranton PA
Fairbanks Museum & Planetarium, Saint Johnsbury VT
Farmington Village Green & Library Association, Stanley-Whitman House, Farmington CT
Fetherston Foundation, Packwood House Museum, Lewisburg PA
Fine Arts Center for the New River Valley, Pulaski VA
Fishkill Historical Society, Van Wyck Homestead Museum, Fishkill NY
Fisk University, Aaron Douglas Gallery, Nashville TN
Flint Institute of Arts, Flint MI
Florida Department of Environmental Protection, Stephen Foster Folk Culture Center State Park, White Springs FL
Florida Southern College, Melvin Art Gallery, Lakeland FL
Folk Art Society of America, Richmond VA
Frankfort Community Public Library, Anna & Harlan Hubbard Gallery, Frankfort IN
Frontier Times Museum, Bandera TX
Frostburg State University, The Stephanie Ann Roper Gallery, Frostburg MD
Fruitlands Museum, Inc, Harvard MA
Fulton County Historical Society Inc, Fulton County Museum (Tetzlaff Reference Room), Rochester IN
Gadsden Museum of Art, Gadsden AL
Galeria de la Raza, Studio 24, San Francisco CA
General Board of Discipleship, The United Methodist Church, The Upper Room Chapel & Museum, Nashville TN
Genesee Country Village & Museum, John L Wehle Art Gallery, Mumford NY
Grand Rapids Art Museum, Grand Rapids MI
Grassroots Art Center, Lucas KS
Greene County Historical Society, Bronck Museum, Coxsackie NY
Hambidge Center for Creative Arts & Sciences, Rabun Gap GA
Hammonds House Museum, Atlanta GA
Hancock Shaker Village, Inc, Pittsfield MA
Hebrew Union College, Skirball Cultural Center, Los Angeles CA
Hebrew Union College - Jewish Institute of Religion, Skirball Museum Cincinnati, Cincinnati OH
Hebrew Union College - Jewish Institute of Religion Museum, Jewish Institute of Religion, New York NY
Henry Sheldon Museum of Vermont History and Research Center, Middlebury VT
Heritage Center, Inc, Pine Ridge SD
Heritage Museums & Gardens, Sandwich MA
Hershey Museum, Hershey PA
Hickory Museum of Art, Inc, Hickory NC
High Desert Museum, Bend OR
High Museum of Art, Atlanta GA
Hillwood Museum & Gardens Foundation, Hillwood Estate Museum & Gardens, Washington DC
Historic Arkansas Museum, Little Rock AR
Historic Hudson Valley, Pocantico Hills NY
Historic Huguenot Street, New Paltz NY
The History Center in Tompkins County, Ithaca NY
Holter Museum of Art, Helena MT
Honolulu Museum of Art, Honolulu HI
Huntington Museum of Art, Huntington WV
Hyde Park Art Center, Chicago IL
Illinois Historic Preservation Agency, Bishop Hill State Historic Site, Bishop Hill IL
Illinois State Museum, ISM Lockport Gallery, Chicago Gallery & Southern Illinois Art Gallery, Springfield IL
Imperial Calcasieu Museum, Gibson-Barham Gallery, Lake Charles LA
Independence Seaport Museum, Philadelphia PA
Indiana University, The Mathers Museum of World Cultures, Bloomington IN
Institute of Puerto Rican Culture, Museo Fuerte Conde de Mirasol, Vieques PR
Intermedia Arts, Minneapolis MN
International Museum of Art & Science, McAllen TX
Intuit: The Center for Intuitive & Outsider Art, Chicago IL
Iredell Museums, Statesville NC
Iroquois Indian Museum, Howes Cave NY
James Dick Foundation, Festival - Institute, Round Top TX
Jefferson County Open Space, Hiwan Homestead Museum, Evergreen CO
Kenosha Public Museums, Kenosha WI
Kentucky Museum of Art and Craft, Louisville KY
Kereszteny Muzeum, Christian Museum, Esztergom
Key West Art & Historical Society, East Martello Museum & Gallery, Key West FL
Kings County Historical Society & Museum, Hampton NB
Knoxville Museum of Art, Knoxville TN
Koshare Indian Museum, Inc, La Junta CO
Kyiv Museum of Russian Art, Kyiv Ukrainian
LA County Museum of Art, Los Angeles CA
Lac du Flambeau Band of Lake Superior Chippewa Indians, George W Brown Jr Ojibwe Museum & Cultural Center, Lac Du Flambeau WI
Lafayette Science Museum & Planetarium, Lafayette LA
LaGrange Art Museum, LaGrange GA
Lalit Kala Akademi Rabindra Bhavan Art Galleries, National Academy of Art, New Delhi, New Delhi
Landis Valley Village and Farm Museum, PA Historical & Museum Commission, Lancaster PA
League of New Hampshire Craftsmen, Grodin Permanent Collection Museum, Concord NH
Leelanau Historical Museum, Leland MI
Lehigh Valley Heritage Center, Allentown PA
Lightner Museum, Saint Augustine FL
Lincoln County Historical Association, Inc, 1811 Old Lincoln County Jail & Lincoln County Museum, Wiscasset ME
Livingston County Historical Society, Museum, Geneseo NY
The Long Island Museum of American Art, History & Carriages, Stony Brook NY
Longfellow-Evangeline State Commemorative Area, Saint Martinville LA
Louise Hopkins Underwood Center for the Arts, Lubbock TX
Louisiana Arts & Science Museum, Baton Rouge LA
Louisiana Department of Culture, Recreation & Tourism, Louisiana State Museum, New Orleans LA
Loveland Museum/Gallery, Loveland CO
Loyola Marymount University, Laband Art Gallery, Los Angeles CA
Madison Museum of Fine Art, Madison GA
Maine Historical Society, MHS Museum, Portland ME
Marblehead Museum & Historical Society, Marblehead MA
Marblehead Museum & Historical Society, Jeremiah Lee Mansion, Marblehead MA
Maricopa County Historical Society, Desert Caballeros Western Museum, Wickenburg AZ
The Mariners' Museum, Newport News VA
Maryland Art Place, Baltimore MD
Marylhurst University, The Art Gym, Marylhurst OR
McCord Museum of Canadian History, Montreal QC
McDowell House & Apothecary Shop, Danville KY
McLean County Historical Society, McLean County Museum of History, Bloomington IL
McPherson Museum and Arts Foundation, McPherson KS

Mennello Museum of American Art, Orlando FL
The Mexican Museum, San Francisco CA
Midwest Museum of American Art, Elkhart IN
Miles B Carpenter Folk Art Museum, Waverly VA
Millicent Rogers Museum, Taos NM
Milwaukee Public Museum, Milwaukee WI
Mississippi Museum of Art, Jackson MS
Mississippi River Museum at Mud-Island River Park, Memphis TN
Mobile Museum of Art, Mobile AL
Montana State University, Helen E Copeland Gallery, Bozeman MT
Montgomery Museum of Fine Arts, Montgomery AL
Moore College of Art & Design, The Galleries at Moore, Philadelphia PA
Moravian Historical Society, Nazareth PA
Morehead State University, Kentucky Folk Art Center, Morehead KY
Morris Museum of Art, Augusta GA
Musee des Maitres et Artisans du Quebec, Montreal QC
Musees Royaux d'Art et d'Histoire, Royal Museums of Art and History, Brussels
Museo De Las Americas, Denver CO
The Museum, Greenwood SC
Museum of Art & History, Santa Cruz, Santa Cruz CA
Museum of Art - Deland FL, Inc, Deland FL
The Museum of Arts & Sciences Inc, Daytona Beach FL
Museum of Chinese in America, New York NY
Museum of Fine Arts, Saint Petersburg, Florida, Inc, Saint Petersburg FL
Museum of Northern Arizona, Flagstaff AZ
Museum of Vancouver, Vancouver BC
Museum of West Louisiana, Leesville LA
Muzeul National de Arta al Romaniei, National Museum of Art of Romania, Bucharest
Muzeum Narodowe W Kielcach, National Museum in Kielce, Kielce
Muzeum Narodowe w Poznaniu, National Museum in Poznan, Poznan
National Baseball Hall of Fame & Museum, Cooperstown NY
National Museum of Mexican Art, Chicago IL
The National Museum of Puerto Rican Arts & Culture, Chicago IL
National Museum of the Philippines, Manila
National Museum of Wildlife Art of the Unites States, Jackson WY
The National Quilt Museum, Paducah KY
The National Shrine of the North American Martyrs, Fultonville NY
National Society of Colonial Dames of America in the State of Maryland, Mount Clare Museum House, Baltimore MD
Naval Historical Center, National Museum of the US Navy, Washington DC
Neville Public Museum of Brown County, Green Bay WI
New Brunswick Museum, Saint John NB
New England Maple Museum, Pittsford VT
New Orleans Museum of Art, New Orleans LA
The Noble Maritime Collection, Staten Island NY
Norman Rockwell Museum of Vermont, Rutland VT
Norwich Free Academy, Slater Memorial Museum, Norwich CT
Noyes Art Gallery, Lincoln NE
Ogden Museum of Southern Art, University of New Orleans, New Orleans LA
The Ohio Historical Society, Inc, Campus Martius Museum & Ohio River Museum, Marietta OH
Ohio History Connection, National Afro-American Museum & Cultural Center, Wilberforce OH
Okanagan Heritage Museum, Kelowna BC
Old Dartmouth Historical Society, New Bedford Whaling Museum, New Bedford MA
Old Island Restoration Foundation Inc, Oldest House in Key West, Key West FL
Old Salem Museums & Gardens, Museum of Early Southern Decorative Arts, Winston-Salem NC
Opelousas Museum of Art, Inc (OMA), Opelousas LA
Owensboro Museum of Fine Art, Owensboro KY
Page-Walker Arts & History Center, Cary NC
Palm Beach County Parks & Recreation Department, Morikami Museum & Japanese Gardens, Delray Beach FL
Panhandle-Plains Historical Museum, Canyon TX
Pasadena Museum of History, Pasadena CA
Pensacola Museum of Art, Pensacola FL
Peoria Riverfront Museum, Peoria IL
Philadelphia History Museum, Philadelphia PA
The Phillips Collection, Washington DC
Pioneer Historical Museum of South Dakota, Hot Springs SD
Plains Art Museum, Fargo ND
Plainsman Museum, Aurora NE
Polish Museum of America (PMA), Chicago IL
Polk Museum of Art, Lakeland FL
Port Huron Museum, Port Huron MI
Queens College, City University of New York, Godwin-Ternbach Museum, Flushing NY
Randolph College, Maier Museum of Art, Lynchburg VA
Rangeley Lakes Region Logging Museum, Rangeley ME
Reading Public Museum, Reading PA
Regina Public Library, Dunlop Art Gallery, Regina SK
Rensselaer County Historical Society, Hart-Cluett Mansion, 1827, Troy NY
Riverside Metropolitan Museum, Riverside CA
Rollins College, George D & Harriet W Cornell Fine Arts Museum, Winter Park FL
Roswell Museum & Art Center, Roswell NM
Royal Alberta Museum, Royal Alberta Museum, Edmonton AB
Saco Museum, Saco ME
Saginaw Art Museum, Saginaw MI
Salisbury University, Ward Museum of Wildfowl Art, Salisbury MD
San Antonio Museum of Art, San Antonio TX
San Francisco Maritime National Historical Park, Maritime Museum, San Francisco CA
Shaker Village of Pleasant Hill, Harrodsburg KY
Sheldon Art Galleries, Saint Louis MO
Slovenska Narodna Galeria, Slovak National Gallery, Bratislava
South Carolina Artisans Center, Walterboro SC
South Carolina State Museum, Columbia SC
South Dakota State University, South Dakota Art Museum, Brookings SD
South Street Seaport Museum, New York NY
Southeastern Center for Contemporary Art, Winston-Salem NC
Spartanburg Art Museum, Spartanburg SC
The Speed Art Museum, Louisville KY
Spertus Institute of Jewish Studies, Chicago IL
Springfield Art Museum, Springfield MO
Staatliche Museen zu Berlin Stiftung Preussischer Kulturbesitz, National Museums in Berlin, Prussian Cultural Heritage Foundation, Berlin
The State Museum of Fine Arts of Tatarstan Republic, Kazan
Stone Quarry Hill Art Park, Winner Gallery, Cazenovia NY
Stratford Historical Society, Catharine B Mitchell Museum, Stratford CT
The Summit County Historical Society of Akron, OH, Akron OH
Suomen Kansallismuseo, National Museum of Finland, Helsinki
Swedish American Museum, Chicago IL
Tallahassee Museum of History & Natural Science, Tallahassee FL
Tampa Museum of Art, Tampa FL
Tinkertown Museum, Sandia Park NM
Tohono Chul Park, Tucson AZ
Tokyo National Museum, Tokyo
Tubman African American Museum, Macon GA
Tver Regional Art Gallery, Tver
Ukrainian Canadian Archives & Museum of Alberta, Edmonton AB
The Ukrainian Museum, New York NY
United Society of Shakers, Shaker Museum, New Gloucester ME
United States Military Academy, West Point Museum, West Point NY
University of California, Berkeley, Phoebe Apperson Hearst Museum of Anthropology, Berkeley CA
University of Georgia, Georgia Museum of Art, Athens GA
University of Illinois at Urbana-Champaign, Krannert Art Museum and Kinkead Pavilion, Champaign IL
University of Indianapolis, Christel DeHaan Fine Arts Gallery, Indianapolis IN
The University of Kentucky Art Museum, Lexington KY
University of Minnesota, Goldstein Museum of Design, Saint Paul MN
University of Nevada, Reno, Sheppard Contemporary & University Galleries, Reno NV
University of Richmond, University Museums, Richmond VA
The University of Texas at San Antonio, Institute of Texan Cultures, San Antonio TX
University of Victoria, The Legacy Art Gallery, Victoria BC
University of Washington, Burke Museum of Natural History and Culture, Seattle WA
Ursinus College, Philip & Muriel Berman Museum of Art, Collegeville PA
Utah Arts Council, Chase Home Museum of Utah Folk Arts, Salt Lake City UT
Vesterheim Norwegian-American Museum, Decorah IA
Vorres Museum of Contemporary Greek Art and Folk Art, Paiania
The Walker African American Museum & Research Center, Las Vegas NV
Waterworks Visual Arts Center, Salisbury NC
Wendell Gilley, Southwest Harbor ME
Western Kentucky University, Kentucky Library & Museum, Bowling Green KY
Westmoreland Museum of American Art, Greensburg PA
Whalers Village Museum, Lahaina HI
Whatcom Museum, Bellingham WA
Wheelwright Museum of the American Indian, Santa Fe NM
Wilkes Art Gallery, North Wilkesboro NC
Willard House & Clock Museum, Inc, North Grafton MA
Wiregrass Museum of Art, Dothan AL
Wisconsin Historical Society, Wisconsin Historical Museum, Madison WI
Witte Museum, San Antonio TX
Woodmere Art Museum Inc, Philadelphia PA
World Erotic Art Museum, Miami Beach FL
Yellowstone County Museum, Billings MT

FURNITURE

Academy of the New Church, Glencairn Museum, Bryn Athyn PA
Acropolis Museum, Athens
Adams County Historical Society, Gettysburg PA
Adams National Historic Park, Quincy MA
African American Museum in Philadelphia, Philadelphia PA
African Art Museum of Maryland, Columbia MD
Alaska State Museum, Juneau AK
Albany Institute of History & Art, Albany NY
Albany Museum of Art, Albany GA
Albin Polasek Museum & Sculpture Gardens, Winter Park FL
Albion College, Bobbitt Visual Arts Center, Albion MI
Albuquerque Museum of Art & History, Albuquerque NM
Allentown Art Museum, Allentown PA
Alton Museum of History & Art, Inc, Alton IL
American Folk Art Museum, New York NY
Americas Society Art Gallery, New York NY
Amherst College, Mead Art Museum, Amherst MA
Amsterdam Museum, Amsterdam
Anna Maria College, Saint Luke's Gallery, Paxton MA
Anson County Historical Society, Inc, Wadesboro NC
Arizona Historical Society-Yuma, Sanguinetti House Museum & Garden, Yuma AZ
Arkkitehtuurimuseo, Museum of Finnish Architecture, Helsinki
Arnot Art Museum, Elmira NY
Art Gallery of South Australia, Adelaide
Artesia Historical Museum and Art Center, Artesia NM
ArtSpace/Lima, Lima OH
Asheville Art Museum, Asheville NC
Athenaeum of Philadelphia, Philadelphia PA
Audrain County Historical Society, Graceland Museum & American Saddlehorse Museum & Fire Brick Industry Museum, Mexico MO
Baldwin Historical Society Museum, Baldwin NY
The Baltimore Museum of Art, Baltimore MD
Bangladesh National Museum, Dhaka
Barnes Foundation, Merion PA
Barnes Museum, Southington CT
Baroda Museum and Picture Gallery, Vadodara
The Bartlett Museum, Amesbury MA
Bass Museum of Art, Miami Beach FL
Bayerische Staatsgemaldesammlungen, Bavarian State Painting Collections, Munich
Bayerisches Nationalmuseum, Bavarian National Museum, Munich

Kenosha Public Museums, Kenosha WI
Kentucky Museum of Art and Craft, Louisville KY
Kereszteny Muzeum, Christian Museum, Esztergom
King Kamehameha V Judiciary History Center, Honolulu HI
Kings County Historical Society & Museum, Hampton NB
Kirchner Museum Davos, Davos
Kirkland Museum of Fine & Decorative Art, Denver CO
Klein Museum, Mobridge SD
Koochiching Museums, International Falls MN
Kyiv Museum of Russian Art, Kyiv Ukrainian
LA County Museum of Art, Los Angeles CA
Lafayette Science Museum & Planetarium, Lafayette LA
Lahore Museum, Lahore
Landis Valley Village and Farm Museum, PA Historical & Museum Commission, Lancaster PA
Le Grand Curtius, The Grand Curtius, Liege
League of New Hampshire Craftsmen, Grodin Permanent Collection Museum, Concord NH
Lehigh Valley Heritage Center, Allentown PA
Liberty Hall Historic Site, Liberty Hall Museum, Frankfort KY
Lightner Museum, Saint Augustine FL
Lincoln County Historical Association, Inc, 1811 Old Lincoln County Jail & Lincoln County Museum, Wiscasset ME
Lincolnshire County Council, Library & Heritage Services, Lincoln
Lincolnshire County Council, The Collection: Art & Archaeology in Lincolnshire, Lincoln
Livingston County Historical Society, Museum, Geneseo NY
Lockwood-Mathews Mansion Museum, Norwalk CT
The Long Island Museum of American Art, History & Carriages, Stony Brook NY
Longfellow's Wayside Inn Museum, Sudbury MA
Longfellow-Evangeline State Commemorative Area, Saint Martinville LA
Longue Vue House & Gardens, New Orleans LA
Los Angeles County Museum of Natural History, William S Hart Museum, Newhall CA
Louise Hopkins Underwood Center for the Arts, Lubbock TX
Louisiana Department of Culture, Recreation & Tourism, Louisiana State Museum, New Orleans LA
Loveland Museum/Gallery, Loveland CO
Lyman Allyn Art Museum, New London CT
Maine Historical Society, Wadsworth-Longfellow House, Portland ME
Maison Saint-Gabriel Museum, Montreal QC
Marblehead Museum & Historical Society, Marblehead MA
Marblehead Museum & Historical Society, Jeremiah Lee Mansion, Marblehead MA
Maricopa County Historical Society, Desert Caballeros Western Museum, Wickenburg AZ
Mark Twain, Hartford CT
Marquette University, Haggerty Museum of Art, Milwaukee WI
Maryhill Museum of Art, Goldendale WA
Marylhurst University, The Art Gym, Marylhurst OR
Massillon Museum, Massillon OH
Maude Kerns Art Center, Eugene OR
Maui Historical Society, Hale Hoike ike at the Bailey House, Wailuku HI
McCord Museum of Canadian History, Montreal QC
McDowell House & Apothecary Shop, Danville KY
McLean County Historical Society, McLean County Museum of History, Bloomington IL
McPherson Museum and Arts Foundation, McPherson KS
Medina Railroad Museum, Medina NY
Meredith College, Frankie G Weems Gallery & Rotunda Gallery, Raleigh NC
Mesa Arts Center, Mesa Contemporary Arts Museum, Mesa AZ
Middle Border Museum & Oscar Howe Art Center, Mitchell SD
Millicent Rogers Museum, Taos NM
The Mint Museum, Mint Museum of Craft & Design, Charlotte NC
Mission San Luis Rey de Francia, Mission San Luis Rey Museum, Oceanside CA
Mississippi River Museum at Mud-Island River Park, Memphis TN
Mississippi Valley Conservation Authority, R Tait McKenzie Memorial Museum, Almonte ON
Mobile Museum of Art, Mobile AL
Modern Art Museum, Fort Worth TX
Monroe County Historical Association, Elizabeth D Walters Library, Stroudsburg PA
Montreal Museum of Fine Arts, Montreal QC
Moravian Historical Society, Nazareth PA
Moravska Galerie v Brne, Moravian Gallery in Brno, Brno
Morris Museum of Art, Augusta GA
Morris-Jumel Mansion, Inc, New York NY
Mount Mary College, Marian Gallery, Milwaukee WI
Mount Vernon Hotel Museum & Garden, New York NY
MTG Hawkes Bay, Napier
Musee Cognacq-Jay, Cognacq-Jay Museum, Paris
Musee des Augustines de l'Hotel Dieu de Quebec, Quebec QC
Musee des Beaux-Arts d'Orleans, Museum of Fine Arts, Orleans
Musee des Beaux-Arts de Tours, Museum of Fine Arts, Tours
Musee des Maitres et Artisans du Quebec, Montreal QC
Musee Regional de lu Cote-Nord, Sept-Iles QC
Musee Regional de Vaudreuil-Soulanges, Vaudreuil-Dorion QC
Musees Royaux d'Art et d'Histoire, Royal Museums of Art and History, Brussels
Museo De Las Americas, Denver CO
Museo Del Romanticismo, Museum of the Romantic Period, Madrid
Museu Nacional D'Art De Catalunya, Catalona National Museum of Art, Barcelona
The Museum, Greenwood SC
Museum De Lakenhal, Leiden
Museum fur Angewandte Kunst Frankfurt, Museum of Applied Arts, Frankfurt
Museum of Art & History, Santa Cruz, Santa Cruz CA
Museum of Arts & Design, New York NY
The Museum of Arts & Sciences Inc, Daytona Beach FL
Museum of Contemporary Art, North Miami FL
Museum of Fine Arts, Saint Petersburg, Florida, Inc, Saint Petersburg FL
Museum of Vancouver, Vancouver BC
Museum of West Louisiana, Leesville LA
Museum of Wisconsin Art, West Bend WI
Museum Plantin-Moretus, Antwerp
Museum zu Allerheiligen, Schaffhausen
Muzej za Umjetnost i Obrt, Museum of Arts & Crafts, Zagreb
Muzeul de Istorie Nationala Si Arheologie Constanta, National History & Archaeology Museum, Constanta
Muzeul National de Arta al Romaniei, National Museum of Art of Romania, Bucharest
Muzeum Narodowe W Kielcach, National Museum in Kielce, Kielce
Muzeum Narodowe w Poznaniu, National Museum in Poznan, Poznan
National Baseball Hall of Fame & Museum, Cooperstown NY
National Gallery of Canada, Ottawa ON
National Museums Scotland, National Museum of Scotland, Edinburgh
National Park Service, Weir Farm National Historic Site, Wilton CT
National Society of Colonial Dames of America in the State of Maryland, Mount Clare Museum House, Baltimore MD
National Society of the Colonial Dames of America in The Commonwealth of Virginia, Wilton House Museum, Richmond VA
National Trust for Historic Preservation, Washington DC
National Trust for Historic Preservation, Shadows-on-the-Teche, New Iberia LA
The National Trust for Historic Preservation, Lyndhurst, Tarrytown NY
National Trust for Historic Preservation, Chesterwood, Stockbridge MA
National Trust for Historic Preservation, Decatur House, Washington DC
Naval Historical Center, National Museum of the US Navy, Washington DC
Nebraska Game and Parks Commission, Arbor Lodge State Historical Park & Morton Mansion, Nebraska City NE
Nebraska State Capitol, Lincoln NE
Nelda C & H J Lutcher Stark Foundation, Stark Museum of Art, Orange TX
The Nelson-Atkins Museum of Art, Kansas City MO
Neue Galerie New York, New York NY
Neville Public Museum of Brown County, Green Bay WI
New Brunswick Museum, Saint John NB
New Jersey Historical Society, Newark NJ
New Orleans Artworks at New Orleans Glassworks & Printmaking Studio, New Orleans LA
New Orleans Museum of Art, New Orleans LA
New York State Military Museum and Veterans Research Center, Saratoga Springs NY
New York State Office of Parks Recreation & Historic Preservation, John Jay Homestead State Historic Site, Katonah NY
New York State Office of Parks, Recreation & Historic Preservation, Staatsburgh State Historic Site, Staatsburg NY
Newfields, Indianapolis IN
Nichols House Museum, Inc, Boston MA
The Noble Maritime Collection, Staten Island NY
Norwich Free Academy, Slater Memorial Museum, Norwich CT
Noyes Art Gallery, Lincoln NE
Oatlands Plantation, Leesburg VA
Ogden Museum of Southern Art, University of New Orleans, New Orleans LA
Ogden Union Station, Union Station Museums, Ogden UT
The Ohio Historical Society, Inc, Campus Martius Museum & Ohio River Museum, Marietta OH
Okanagan Heritage Museum, Kelowna BC
Okefenokee Heritage Center, Inc, Waycross GA
Olana State Historic Site, Hudson NY
Old Dartmouth Historical Society, New Bedford Whaling Museum, New Bedford MA
Old Island Restoration Foundation Inc, Oldest House in Key West, Key West FL
The Old Jail Art Center, Albany TX
Old Salem Museums & Gardens, Museum of Early Southern Decorative Arts, Winston-Salem NC
Osborne Homestead Museum, Derby CT
Owensboro Museum of Fine Art, Owensboro KY
Page-Walker Arts & History Center, Cary NC
Panhandle-Plains Historical Museum, Canyon TX
Pasadena Museum of California Art, Pasadena CA
Pasadena Museum of History, Pasadena CA
Patrick Henry, Red Hill National Memorial, Brookneal VA
Peabody Essex Museum, Salem MA
Philadelphia History Museum, Philadelphia PA
Philbrook Museum of Art, Tulsa OK
Phillips Academy, Addison Gallery of American Art, Andover MA
Piatt Castles, West Liberty OH
Pioneer Historical Museum of South Dakota, Hot Springs SD
Plainsman Museum, Aurora NE
Plumas County Museum, Quincy CA
Port Huron Museum, Port Huron MI
Portsmouth Historical Society, John Paul Jones House & Discover Portsmouth, Portsmouth NH
Preservation Virginia, John Marshall House, Richmond VA
Pueblo Museum, Desert Hot Springs CA
Putnam County Historical Society, Foundry School Museum, Cold Spring NY
Putnam Museum of History and Natural Science, Davenport IA
Quapaw Quarter Association, Inc, Villa Marre, Little Rock AR
Queen Victoria Museum and Art Gallery, Launceston TAS
Queens College, City University of New York, Godwin-Ternbach Museum, Flushing NY
Rahr-West Art Museum, Manitowoc WI
Reading Public Museum, Reading PA
Rensselaer County Historical Society, Hart-Cluett Mansion, 1827, Troy NY
Reynolda House Museum of American Art, Winston-Salem NC
Rhode Island Historical Society, John Brown House, Providence RI
Riverside Metropolitan Museum, Riverside CA
Roberson Museum & Science Center, Binghamton NY
Robert Louis Stevenson Museum, Saint Helena CA
Roberts County Museum, Miami TX

Rock Ford Foundation, Inc, Rock Ford Plantation, Lancaster PA
Rosemount Museum, Inc, Pueblo CO
Ross Memorial Museum, Saint Andrews NB
Royal Alberta Museum, Royal Alberta Museum, Edmonton AB
Royal Arts Foundation, Belcourt Castle, Newport RI
Ryerss Victorian Museum & Library, Philadelphia PA
Saco Museum, Saco ME
Saint Anselm College, Alva de Mars Megan Chapel Art Center, Manchester NH
Saint-Gaudens National Historic Site, Cornish NH
San Antonio Museum of Art, San Antonio TX
San Diego Museum of Art, San Diego CA
The San Joaquin Pioneer & Historical Society, The Haggin Museum, Stockton CA
Santa Clara University, de Saisset Museum, Santa Clara CA
Seneca Falls Historical Society Museum, Seneca Falls NY
Seneca-Iroquois National Museum, Salamanca NY
Shaker Museum & Library, Old Chatham NY
Shaker Village of Pleasant Hill, Harrodsburg KY
Shanghai Museum, Shanghai
Shirley Plantation Foundation, Charles City VA
Shores Memorial Museum, Lyndon Center VT
Slater Mill, Old Slater Mill Association, Pawtucket RI
Society for Contemporary Craft, Pittsburgh PA
The Society of the Cincinnati at Anderson House, Washington DC
South Carolina Artisans Center, Walterboro SC
South Dakota State University, South Dakota Art Museum, Brookings SD
Southern Lorain County Historical Society, Spirit of '76 Museum, Elyria OH
The Speed Art Museum, Louisville KY
Springfield Art Museum, Springfield MO
Staatliche Museen zu Berlin Stiftung Preussischer Kulturbesitz, National Museums in Berlin, Prussian Cultural Heritage Foundation, Berlin
Stanford University, Cantor Arts Center at Stanford University, Stanford CA
Stanley Museum, Inc, Kingfield ME
The State Museum of Fine Arts of Tatarstan Republic, Kazan
Staten Island Museum, Staten Island NY
Stedelijk Museum Alkmaar, Alkmaar Municipal Museum, Alkmaar
Stone Quarry Hill Art Park, Winner Gallery, Cazenovia NY
Stratford Historical Society, Catharine B Mitchell Museum, Stratford CT
Suan Pakkad Palace Museum, Bangkok
Suffolk University, Gallery, Boston MA
The Summit County Historical Society of Akron, OH, Akron OH
Suomen Kansallismuseo, National Museum of Finland, Helsinki
Susquehanna University, Lore Degenstein Gallery, Selinsgrove PA
Swedish American Museum, Chicago IL
T C Steele State Historic Site, Nashville IN
Taft Museum of Art, Cincinnati OH
Taos Historic Museums, Taos NM
Taos Historic Museums, Ernest Blumenschein Home & Studio, Taos NM
Taos Historic Museums, La Hacienda de Los Martinez, Taos NM
Thomas Jefferson Foundation, Inc, Monticello, Charlottesville VA
Tohono Chul Park, Tucson AZ
Tokyo National Museum, Tokyo
Tryon Palace, New Bern NC
Tubman African American Museum, Macon GA
Tver Regional Art Gallery, Tver
U Gallery, San Francisco CA
Ukrainian Canadian Archives & Museum of Alberta, Edmonton AB
University of California, Berkeley, Phoebe Apperson Hearst Museum of Anthropology, Berkeley CA
University of Chicago, Smart Museum of Art, Chicago IL
University of Georgia, Georgia Museum of Art, Athens GA
University of Illinois at Urbana-Champaign, Krannert Art Museum and Kinkead Pavilion, Champaign IL
The University of Kentucky Art Museum, Lexington KY
University of Minnesota, Goldstein Museum of Design, Saint Paul MN
University of Montana, Montana Museum of Art & Culture, Missoula MT
University of Nevada, Reno, Sheppard Contemporary & University Galleries, Reno NV
University of New Mexico, The Harwood Museum of Art, Taos NM
University of Notre Dame, Snite Museum of Art, Notre Dame IN
University of Saskatchewan, Diefenbaker Canada Centre, Saskatoon SK
University of Tampa, Henry B Plant Museum, Tampa FL
University of Utah, Utah Museum of Fine Arts, Salt Lake City UT
University of Wisconsin-Madison, Chazen Museum of Art, Madison WI
Ursinus College, Philip & Muriel Berman Museum of Art, Collegeville PA
USS Constitution Museum, Boston MA
Van Cortlandt House Museum, Bronx NY
Vermilion County Museum Society, Danville IL
Vesterheim Norwegian-American Museum, Decorah IA
Victoria Mansion - Morse Libby House, Portland ME
Villa Terrace Decorative Arts Museum, Milwaukee WI
Virginia Museum of Fine Arts, Richmond VA
Vizcaya Museum & Gardens, Miami FL
Volcano Art Center Gallery, Hawaii Volcanoes National Park HI
Vorres Museum of Contemporary Greek Art and Folk Art, Paiania
Wadsworth Atheneum Museum of Art, Hartford CT
Walker Art Gallery, Liverpool
Walter Anderson Museum of Art, Ocean Springs MS
Warner House Association, MacPheadris-Warner House, Portsmouth NH
Waterville Historical Society, Redington Museum, Waterville ME
Westmoreland Museum of American Art, Greensburg PA
Wharton Esherick Museum, Paoli PA
White House, Washington DC
Wichita State University, Ulrich Museum of Art, Wichita KS
Willard House & Clock Museum, Inc, North Grafton MA
William Morris Gallery, London
Wisconsin Historical Society, Wisconsin Historical Museum, Madison WI
Witte Museum, San Antonio TX
Woodlawn/The Pope-Leighey, Alexandria VA
Woodmere Art Museum Inc, Philadelphia PA
Woodrow Wilson, Washington DC
Workman & Temple Family Homestead Museum, City of Industry CA
World Erotic Art Museum, Miami Beach FL
Wornall Majors House Museums, John Wornall House Museum, Kansas City MO
Wyoming State Museum, Cheyenne WY
Yankton County Historical Society, Dakota Territorial Museum, Yankton SD
Yellowstone County Museum, Billings MT

GLASS

A.E. Backus Museum & Gallery, Fort Pierce FL
Academy of the New Church, Glencairn Museum, Bryn Athyn PA
Adams County Historical Society, Gettysburg PA
Al Ain National Museum, Al Ain
Alaska State Museum, Juneau AK
Albany Institute of History & Art, Albany NY
Albion College, Bobbitt Visual Arts Center, Albion MI
Albuquerque Museum of Art & History, Albuquerque NM
Alice Moseley Folk Art and Antique Museum, Bay Saint Louis MS
Alton Museum of History & Art, Inc, Alton IL
American Swedish Institute, Minneapolis MN
American University of Beirut Archaeological Museum, Beirut
Amherst College, Mead Art Museum, Amherst MA
Amsterdam Museum, Amsterdam
Archaeological Museum of Thessaloniki, Thessaloniki
Arizona Historical Society-Yuma, Sanguinetti House Museum & Garden, Yuma AZ
Arkansas Arts Center, Little Rock AR
Arnot Art Museum, Elmira NY
Art and History Museums - Maitland, Maitland FL
Art Community Center, Art Center of Corpus Christi, Corpus Christi TX
Art Gallery of South Australia, Adelaide
Arts Council of Fayetteville-Cumberland County, The Arts Center, Fayetteville NC
ArtSpace/Lima, Lima OH
ArtsQuest, Bethlehem PA
Asheville Art Museum, Asheville NC
Audrain County Historical Society, Graceland Museum & American Saddlehorse Museum & Fire Brick Industry Museum, Mexico MO
Bainbridge Arts & Crafts Gallery, Bainbridge Island WA
Baldwin Historical Society Museum, Baldwin NY
Bangladesh National Museum, Dhaka
Barker Character, Comic and Cartoon Museum, Cheshire CT
Baroda Museum and Picture Gallery, Vadodara
Bayerische Staatsgemaldesammlungen, Bavarian State Painting Collections, Munich
Bayerisches Nationalmuseum, Bavarian National Museum, Munich
Bellevue Arts Museum, Bellevue WA
Bennington Museum, Bennington VT
Bergstrom-Mahler Museum of Glass, Neenah WI
Berkshire Museum, Pittsfield MA
Besser Museum for Northeast Michigan, Alpena MI
Beverly Historical Society, Cabot, Hale & Balch House Museums, Beverly MA
Birmingham Museum of Art, Birmingham AL
Brick Store Museum, Kennebunk ME
Brooklyn Historical Society, Brooklyn OH
The Buffalo Fine Arts Academy, Albright-Knox Art Gallery, Buffalo NY
Buffalo Niagara Heritage Village, Amherst NY
Burchfield Penney Art Center, Buffalo NY
Cameron Art Museum, Wilmington NC
Canadian Clay and Glass Gallery, Waterloo ON
Canadian Museum of History, Gatineau QC
Cape Cod Museum of Art Inc, Dennis MA
Center for Art & Education, Van Buren AR
Charleston Museum, Charleston SC
Charleston Museum, Heyward-Washington House, Charleston SC
Charleston Museum, Joseph Manigault House, Charleston SC
Chatham Historical Society, The Atwood House Museum, Chatham MA
Chatillon-DeMenil House Foundation, Chatillon-DeMenil Mansion, Saint Louis MO
Chicago Athenaeum, Museum of Architecture & Design, Galena IL
The Children's Museum of Indianapolis, Indianapolis IN
Chrysler Museum of Art, Norfolk VA
City of Fremont, Olive Hyde Art Gallery, Fremont CA
City of Gainesville, Thomas Center Galleries - Cultural Affairs, Gainesville FL
The City of Petersburg Museums, Petersburg VA
City of Pittsfield Office of Cultural Development, Lichtenstein Center for the Arts, Pittsfield MA
City of Springdale, Shiloh Museum of Ozark History, Springdale AR
Clark Art Institute, Williamstown MA
Clark County Historical Society, Pioneer - Krier Museum, Ashland KS
Clinton Art Association, River Arts Center, Clinton IA
College of William & Mary, Muscarelle Museum of Art, Williamsburg VA
Columbus Chapel & Boal Mansion Museum, Boalsburg PA
The Columbus Museum, Columbus GA
Columbus Museum of Art, Columbus OH
Contemporary Calgary, Calgary AB
Coutts Museum of Art, Inc, El Dorado KS
Craft and Folk Art Museum (CAFAM), Los Angeles CA
Cripple Creek District Museum, Cripple Creek CO
Crocker Art Museum, Sacramento CA
Crook County Museum & Art Gallery, Sundance WY
Crow Wing County Historical Society, Brainerd MN
The Currier Museum of Art, Manchester NH
Cyprus Museum, Nicosia
Dalnavert Museum, Winnipeg MB
DAR Museum, National Society Daughters of the American Revolution, Washington DC
Dartmouth College, Hood Museum of Art, Hanover NH
Dartmouth Heritage Museum, Dartmouth NS
Dawson City Museum, Dawson City YT

deCordova Sculpture Park & Museum, Lincoln MA
Delaware Division of Historical & Cultural Affairs, Dover DE
Delphi Archaeological Museum, Delphi
Deming-Luna Mimbres Museum, Deming NM
Denver Art Museum, Denver CO
Designmuseum Danmark, Danish Design Museum, Copenhagen
Detroit Institute of Arts, Detroit MI
Doncaster Museum and Art Gallery, Doncaster Yorks
Dublin Arts Council, Dublin OH
Edsel & Eleanor Ford House, Grosse Pointe Shores MI
Emory University, Michael C Carlos Museum, Atlanta GA
Environment Canada - Parks Canada, Laurier House, National Historic Site, Ottawa ON
Evanston Historical Society, Charles Gates Dawes House, Evanston IL
Evansville Museum of Arts, History & Science, Evansville IN
Everhart Museum, Scranton PA
Farmington Village Green & Library Association, Stanley-Whitman House, Farmington CT
Fetherston Foundation, Packwood House Museum, Lewisburg PA
Fine Arts Center for the New River Valley, Pulaski VA
Fine Arts Museums of San Francisco, Legion of Honor, San Francisco CA
Fireweed Gallery, Homer AK
Flint Institute of Arts, Flint MI
Florence County Museum, Florence SC
Florida CraftArt, Saint Petersburg FL
Florida Southern College, Melvin Art Gallery, Lakeland FL
Florida State University, John & Mable Ringling Museum of Art, Sarasota FL
Florida State University and Central Florida Community College, The Appleton Museum of Art, Ocala FL
Fondazione Musei Civici Di Venezia, Museo Correr - Correr Museum, Venice
Fondazione Musei Civici Di Venezia, Ca' Rezzonico, Venice
Fondazione Musei Civici Di Venezia, Ca' Pesaro Galleria Nazionale d'Arte Moderna - Ca' Pesaro Gallery of Modern Art, Venice
Forest Lawn Museum, Glendale CA
Frederic Remington, Ogdensburg NY
Freer Gallery of Art & Arthur M Sackler Gallery, Arthur M Sackler Gallery, Washington DC
The Frick Art & Historical Center, Inc, Frick Art Museum, Pittsburgh PA
Fuller Craft Museum, Brockton MA
Gadsden Museum, Mesilla NM
Gadsden Museum of Art, Gadsden AL
Gallery One Visual Arts Center, Ellensburg WA
Girard College, Stephen Girard Collection, Philadelphia PA
Glanmore National Historic Site of Canada, Belleville ON
Glessner House Museum, Chicago IL
Grand Rapids Art Museum, Grand Rapids MI
Grand Rapids Public Museum, Grand Rapids MI
Greene County Historical Society, Bronck Museum, Coxsackie NY
Hastings Museum of Natural & Cultural History, Hastings NE
Haystack Mountain School of Crafts, Deer Isle ME
Headley-Whitney Museum, Lexington KY
Headquarters Fort Monroe, Dept of Army, Casemate Museum, Hampton VA
Heard Museum, Phoenix AZ
Heart of West Texas Museum, Colorado City TX
Hebrew Union College, Skirball Cultural Center, Los Angeles CA
Hecht Museum, Haifa
Henry County Museum & Cultural Arts Center, Clinton MO
Henry Morrison Flagler Museum, Palm Beach FL
Henry Sheldon Museum of Vermont History and Research Center, Middlebury VT
Heritage Glass Museum, Glassboro NJ
Hermitage Museum & Gardens, Norfolk VA
Hershey Museum, Hershey PA
Het Noordbrabants Museum, s-Hertogenbosch
Hickory Museum of Art, Inc, Hickory NC
Hill-Stead Museum, Farmington CT
Hillwood Museum & Gardens Foundation, Hillwood Estate Museum & Gardens, Washington DC
Historic Arkansas Museum, Little Rock AR
Historic Deerfield, Inc, Deerfield MA
Historic Holyoke at Wistariahurst & City of Holyoke, Holyoke MA
Historic Huguenot Street, New Paltz NY
Historic Paris - Bourbon County, Inc, Hopewell Museum, Paris KY
Historical Society of Bloomfield, Bloomfield NJ
Historical Society of Cheshire County, Keene NH
Historical Society of Martin County, Elliott Museum, Stuart FL
Historisches und Volkerkundemuseum, Museum of History and Ethnology, St Gallen
The History Center in Tompkins County, Ithaca NY
Holter Museum of Art, Helena MT
Houston Museum of Decorative Arts, Chattanooga TN
Hunter Museum of American Art, Chattanooga TN
Huntington Museum of Art, Huntington WV
Illinois State Museum, ISM Lockport Gallery, Chicago Gallery & Southern Illinois Art Gallery, Springfield IL
Independence Historical Museum & Art Center, Independence KS
Independence Seaport Museum, Philadelphia PA
Indiana Landmarks, Morris-Butler House, Indianapolis IN
International Museum of Art, El Paso TX
Iowa State University, Brunnier Art Museum, Ames IA
Iredell Museums, Statesville NC
The Israel Museum, Jerusalem, Jerusalem
Jacksonville University, Alexander Brest Museum & Gallery, Jacksonville FL
James Dick Foundation, Festival - Institute, Round Top TX
Jefferson County Historical Society, Watertown NY
Johns Hopkins University, Evergreen Museum & Library, Baltimore MD
Johns Hopkins University, Homewood Museum, Baltimore MD
Joslyn Art Museum, Omaha NE
Kelly-Griggs House Museum, Red Bluff CA
Kenosha Public Museums, Kenosha WI
Kentucky Derby Museum, Louisville KY
Kentucky Museum of Art and Craft, Louisville KY
Kereszteny Muzeum, Christian Museum, Esztergom
Kimbell Art Foundation, Kimbell Art Museum, Fort Worth TX
Kings County Historical Society & Museum, Hampton NB
Kirkland Museum of Fine & Decorative Art, Denver CO
Klein Museum, Mobridge SD
Koochiching Museums, International Falls MN
Kunsthistorisches Museum Wien, Museum of Fine Arts, Vienna
Kyiv Museum of Russian Art, Kyiv Ukrainian
LA County Museum of Art, Los Angeles CA
Lalit Kala Akademi Rabindra Bhavan Art Galleries, National Academy of Art, New Delhi, New Delhi
Landis Valley Village and Farm Museum, PA Historical & Museum Commission, Lancaster PA
Latino Art Museum, Pomona CA
Le Grand Curtius, The Grand Curtius, Liege
League of New Hampshire Craftsmen, Grodin Permanent Collection Museum, Concord NH
Lehigh Valley Heritage Center, Allentown PA
Lightner Museum, Saint Augustine FL
Lillian & Coleman Taube Museum of Art, Minot ND
Lincoln County Historical Association, Inc, 1811 Old Lincoln County Jail & Lincoln County Museum, Wiscasset ME
Lincolnshire County Council, Library & Heritage Services, Lincoln
Lincolnshire County Council, The Collection: Art & Archaeology in Lincolnshire, Lincoln
Livingston County Historical Society, Museum, Geneseo NY
Lockwood-Mathews Mansion Museum, Norwalk CT
The Long Island Museum of American Art, History & Carriages, Stony Brook NY
Longfellow-Evangeline State Commemorative Area, Saint Martinville LA
Longue Vue House & Gardens, New Orleans LA
Los Angeles County Museum of Natural History, William S Hart Museum, Newhall CA
Louise Hopkins Underwood Center for the Arts, Lubbock TX
Louisiana Department of Culture, Recreation & Tourism, Louisiana State Museum, New Orleans LA
Loveland Museum/Gallery, Loveland CO
Maine Historical Society, MHS Museum, Portland ME
Maricopa County Historical Society, Desert Caballeros Western Museum, Wickenburg AZ
Mark Twain, Hartford CT
Marquette University, Haggerty Museum of Art, Milwaukee WI
Maryhill Museum of Art, Goldendale WA
Maryland Historical Society, Museum of Maryland History, Baltimore MD
Massillon Museum, Massillon OH
Maude Kerns Art Center, Eugene OR
McCord Museum of Canadian History, Montreal QC
McDowell House & Apothecary Shop, Danville KY
McLean County Historical Society, McLean County Museum of History, Bloomington IL
McPherson Museum and Arts Foundation, McPherson KS
Memphis Brooks Museum of Art, Memphis TN
Mennello Museum of American Art, Orlando FL
Mesa Arts Center, Mesa Contemporary Arts Museum, Mesa AZ
Michigan State University, Eli & Edythe Broad Art Museum, East Lansing MI
Middle Border Museum & Oscar Howe Art Center, Mitchell SD
Midwest Museum of American Art, Elkhart IN
Minnesota Museum of American Art, Saint Paul MN
The Mint Museum, Mint Museum of Craft & Design, Charlotte NC
Mississippi Museum of Art, Jackson MS
Mississippi River Museum at Mud-Island River Park, Memphis TN
Mobile Museum of Art, Mobile AL
Modern Art Museum, Fort Worth TX
Montgomery Museum of Fine Arts, Montgomery AL
Montreal Museum of Fine Arts, Montreal QC
Moravian Historical Society, Nazareth PA
Moravska Galerie v Brne, Moravian Gallery in Brno, Brno
Morris Museum, Morristown NJ
Morris Museum of Art, Augusta GA
Morris-Jumel Mansion, Inc, New York NY
Mount Vernon Hotel Museum & Garden, New York NY
MTG Hawkes Bay, Napier
Muscatine Art Center, Muscatine IA
Musee des Augustines de l'Hotel Dieu de Quebec, Quebec QC
Musee des Beaux-Arts de Tours, Museum of Fine Arts, Tours
Musees Royaux d'Art et d'Histoire, Royal Museums of Art and History, Brussels
Museo De Las Americas, Denver CO
Museo Del Romanticismo, Museum of the Romantic Period, Madrid
Museo di Palazzo Ducale, Ducale Palace Museum, Mantua
The Museum, Greenwood SC
Museum De Lakenhal, Leiden
Museum fur Angewandte Kunst Frankfurt, Museum of Applied Arts, Frankfurt
Museum of American Glass in WV, Weston WV
Museum of Art - Deland FL, Inc, Deland FL
Museum of Arts & Design, New York NY
The Museum of Arts & Sciences Inc, Daytona Beach FL
Museum of Contemporary Art, North Miami FL
Museum of Fine Arts, Saint Petersburg, Florida, Inc, Saint Petersburg FL
Museum of Islamic Art, Doha
Museum of Latin American Art, Long Beach CA
Museum of Northwest Art, La Conner WA
Museum of Vancouver, Vancouver BC
Museum zu Allerheiligen, Schaffhausen
Muzej za Umjetnost i Obrt, Museum of Arts & Crafts, Zagreb
Muzeul de Istorie Nationala Si Arheologie Constanta, National History & Archaeology Museum, Constanta
Muzeul National de Arta al Romaniei, National Museum of Art of Romania, Bucharest
Muzeum Narodowe W Kielcach, National Museum in Kielce, Kielce
Muzeum Narodowe w Poznaniu, National Museum in Poznan, Poznan
National Archaeological Museum, Athens
National Art Museum of Moldova, Chisinau
National Baseball Hall of Fame & Museum, Cooperstown NY
National Museum of Ceramic Art, Baltimore MD

The National Museum of Modern Art, Tokyo, Tokyo
National Museums Scotland, National Museum of Scotland, Edinburgh
National Society of Colonial Dames of America in the State of Maryland, Mount Clare Museum House, Baltimore MD
National Society of the Colonial Dames of America in The Commonwealth of Virginia, Wilton House Museum, Richmond VA
The National Trust for Historic Preservation, Lyndhurst, Tarrytown NY
Naval Historical Center, National Museum of the US Navy, Washington DC
Nelda C & H J Lutcher Stark Foundation, Stark Museum of Art, Orange TX
The Nelson-Atkins Museum of Art, Kansas City MO
Neustadt Collection of Tiffany Glass, Long Island City NY
Nevada Museum of Art, Reno NV
Neville Public Museum of Brown County, Green Bay WI
New Brunswick Museum, Saint John NB
New Jersey Historical Society, Newark NJ
New Orleans Museum of Art, New Orleans LA
New Visions Gallery, Inc, Marshfield WI
The Noble Maritime Collection, Staten Island NY
Norwich Free Academy, Slater Memorial Museum, Norwich CT
Noyes Art Gallery, Lincoln NE
Ogden Museum of Southern Art, University of New Orleans, New Orleans LA
The Ohio Historical Society, Inc, Campus Martius Museum & Ohio River Museum, Marietta OH
Okanagan Heritage Museum, Kelowna BC
Oklahoma City Museum of Art, Oklahoma City OK
Old Dartmouth Historical Society, New Bedford Whaling Museum, New Bedford MA
Old Jaffa Museum of Antiquities, Jaffa
Old Salem Museums & Gardens, Museum of Early Southern Decorative Arts, Winston-Salem NC
Orange County Museum of Art, Newport Beach CA
Oshkosh Public Museum & Library, Oshkosh WI
Ouachita River Art Gallery, Monroe LA
Owensboro Museum of Fine Art, Owensboro KY
Page-Walker Arts & History Center, Cary NC
Panhandle-Plains Historical Museum, Canyon TX
Pasadena Museum of History, Pasadena CA
Pensacola Museum of Art, Pensacola FL
Philadelphia History Museum, Philadelphia PA
Philbrook Museum of Art, Tulsa OK
Phillips Academy, Addison Gallery of American Art, Andover MA
Phillips County Museum, Holyoke CO
Pioneer Historical Museum of South Dakota, Hot Springs SD
Plains Art Museum, Fargo ND
Plainsman Museum, Aurora NE
Plumas County Museum, Quincy CA
Polk Museum of Art, Lakeland FL
Port Huron Museum, Port Huron MI
Portland Museum of Art, Portland ME
Portsmouth Historical Society, John Paul Jones House & Discover Portsmouth, Portsmouth NH
Preservation Virginia, John Marshall House, Richmond VA
Principia College, School of Nations Museum, Elsah IL
Putnam Museum of History and Natural Science, Davenport IA
Queen Victoria Museum and Art Gallery, Launceston TAS
Queens College, City University of New York, Godwin-Ternbach Museum, Flushing NY
Rahr-West Art Museum, Manitowoc WI
Rawls Museum Arts, Courtland VA
Reading Public Museum, Reading PA
Rensselaer County Historical Society, Hart-Cluett Mansion, 1827, Troy NY
Rhode Island Historical Society, John Brown House, Providence RI
The Rockwell Museum, Corning NY
Rose Lehrman Art Gallery, Harrisburg PA
Ryerss Victorian Museum & Library, Philadelphia PA
Saco Museum, Saco ME
Saginaw Art Museum, Saginaw MI
San Angelo Museum of Fine Arts, San Angelo TX
San Antonio Museum of Art, San Antonio TX
The San Joaquin Pioneer & Historical Society, The Haggin Museum, Stockton CA
Scripps College, Ruth Chandler Williamson Gallery, Claremont CA
Shaker Museum & Library, Old Chatham NY
Shirley Plantation Foundation, Charles City VA
Society for Contemporary Craft, Pittsburgh PA
The Society of the Cincinnati at Anderson House, Washington DC
South Carolina Artisans Center, Walterboro SC
South Dakota State University, South Dakota Art Museum, Brookings SD
Southeastern Center for Contemporary Art, Winston-Salem NC
The Speed Art Museum, Louisville KY
Spertus Institute of Jewish Studies, Chicago IL
Springfield Art Museum, Springfield MO
Staatliche Museen zu Berlin Stiftung Preussischer Kulturbesitz, National Museums in Berlin, Prussian Cultural Heritage Foundation, Berlin
Stanford University, Cantor Arts Center at Stanford University, Stanford CA
The State Museum of Fine Arts of Tatarstan Republic, Kazan
State University of New York at Geneseo, Bertha V B Lederer Gallery, Geneseo NY
Staten Island Museum, Staten Island NY
The Stewart Museum, Montreal QC
Stone Quarry Hill Art Park, Winner Gallery, Cazenovia NY
Stratford Historical Society, Catharine B Mitchell Museum, Stratford CT
Suan Pakkad Palace Museum, Bangkok
The Summit County Historical Society of Akron, OH, Akron OH
Suomen Kansallismuseo, National Museum of Finland, Helsinki
Susquehanna University, Lore Degenstein Gallery, Selinsgrove PA
Swedish American Museum, Chicago IL
Tacoma Art Museum, Tacoma WA
Tampa Museum of Art, Tampa FL
Tokyo National Museum, Tokyo
Toledo Museum of Art, Toledo OH
Topeka & Shawnee County Public Library, Alice C Sabatini Gallery, Topeka KS
Triton Museum of Art, Santa Clara CA
Tryon Palace, New Bern NC
Tver Regional Art Gallery, Tver
Tyne and Wear Archives & Museums, Sunderland Museum & Winter Gardens, Sunderland
United Society of Shakers, Shaker Museum, New Gloucester ME
University of California, Berkeley, Phoebe Apperson Hearst Museum of Anthropology, Berkeley CA
University of Chicago, Smart Museum of Art, Chicago IL
University of Georgia, Georgia Museum of Art, Athens GA
University of Illinois at Urbana-Champaign, Krannert Art Museum and Kinkead Pavilion, Champaign IL
University of Illinois at Urbana-Champaign, Spurlock Museum, Urbana IL
University of Kansas, Spencer Museum of Art, Lawrence KS
The University of Kentucky Art Museum, Lexington KY
University of Miami, Lowe Art Museum, Coral Gables FL
University of Minnesota, Goldstein Museum of Design, Saint Paul MN
University of Nevada, Reno, Sheppard Contemporary & University Galleries, Reno NV
University of Notre Dame, Snite Museum of Art, Notre Dame IN
University of Richmond, University Museums, Richmond VA
University of Saskatchewan, Diefenbaker Canada Centre, Saskatoon SK
University of Utah, Utah Museum of Fine Arts, Salt Lake City UT
University of Wisconsin-Madison, Chazen Museum of Art, Madison WI
USS Constitution Museum, Boston MA
The Valentine, Richmond VA
Valley Art Gallery, Forest Grove OR
Vassar College, The Frances Lehman Loeb Art Center, Poughkeepsie NY
Vero Beach Museum of Art, Vero Beach FL
Vesterheim Norwegian-American Museum, Decorah IA
Victoria Mansion - Morse Libby House, Portland ME
Villa Terrace Decorative Arts Museum, Milwaukee WI
Virginia Museum of Fine Arts, Richmond VA
Volcano Art Center Gallery, Hawaii Volcanoes National Park HI
Vorres Museum of Contemporary Greek Art and Folk Art, Paiania
Walker Art Gallery, Liverpool
The Wallace Collection, London
Washburn University, Mulvane Art Museum, Topeka KS
Washington County Museum of Fine Arts, Hagerstown MD
Waterville Historical Society, Redington Museum, Waterville ME
Waterworks Visual Arts Center, Salisbury NC
Westfries Museum, Hoorn
Westmoreland Museum of American Art, Greensburg PA
Wheaton Arts & Cultural Center, Museum of American Glass, Millville NJ
Wheaton College, Beard and Weil Galleries, Norton MA
White House, Washington DC
Wilkes Art Gallery, North Wilkesboro NC
Willard House & Clock Museum, Inc, North Grafton MA
Winkler Gallery of Fine Art, DuBois PA
Wiregrass Museum of Art, Dothan AL
Woodlawn/The Pope-Leighey, Alexandria VA
World Erotic Art Museum, Miami Beach FL
Yokohama Museum of Art, Yokohama
Zigler Art Museum, Jennings LA

GOLD

Al Ain National Museum, Al Ain
Alaska Heritage Museum at Wells Fargo, Anchorage AK
American University of Beirut Archaeological Museum, Beirut
Archaeological Museum of Thessaloniki, Thessaloniki
The Baltimore Museum of Art, Baltimore MD
Bangladesh National Museum, Dhaka
Bayerisches Nationalmuseum, Bavarian National Museum, Munich
Bellevue Arts Museum, Bellevue WA
Beloit College, Wright Museum of Art, Beloit WI
Berman Museum, Anniston AL
Canadian Museum of History, Gatineau QC
City of Springdale, Shiloh Museum of Ozark History, Springdale AR
College of William & Mary, Muscarelle Museum of Art, Williamsburg VA
Contemporary Calgary, Calgary AB
Cripple Creek District Museum, Cripple Creek CO
Crocker Art Museum, Sacramento CA
Cyprus Museum, Nicosia
Delphi Archaeological Museum, Delphi
Denver Art Museum, Denver CO
Detroit Institute of Arts, Detroit MI
Forest Lawn Museum, Glendale CA
Galleria Nazionale dell'Umbria, Umbrian National Gallery, Perugia
Glanmore National Historic Site of Canada, Belleville ON
Glasgow University, The Hunterian, Glasgow
Haystack Mountain School of Crafts, Deer Isle ME
Headley-Whitney Museum, Lexington KY
Hecht Museum, Haifa
Hillwood Museum & Gardens Foundation, Hillwood Estate Museum & Gardens, Washington DC
Illinois State Museum, ISM Lockport Gallery, Chicago Gallery & Southern Illinois Art Gallery, Springfield IL
The Israel Museum, Jerusalem, Jerusalem
Jacksonville University, Alexander Brest Museum & Gallery, Jacksonville FL
Kimbell Art Foundation, Kimbell Art Museum, Fort Worth TX
Kunsthistorisches Museum Wien, Museum of Fine Arts, Vienna
League of New Hampshire Craftsmen, Grodin Permanent Collection Museum, Concord NH
Lincolnshire County Council, The Collection: Art & Archaeology in Lincolnshire, Lincoln
The Long Island Museum of American Art, History & Carriages, Stony Brook NY
Loyola University Chicago, Loyola University Museum of Art, Chicago IL
Montreal Museum of Fine Arts, Montreal QC

Moravska Galerie v Brne, Moravian Gallery in Brno, Brno
Musee des Beaux-Arts de Tours, Museum of Fine Arts, Tours
Musees Royaux d'Art et d'Histoire, Royal Museums of Art and History, Brussels
Museo De Las Americas, Denver CO
Museo Del Romanticismo, Museum of the Romantic Period, Madrid
Museum De Lakenhal, Leiden
Museum fur Angewandte Kunst Frankfurt, Museum of Applied Arts, Frankfurt
Museum of Art & History, Santa Cruz, Santa Cruz CA
The Museum of Arts & Sciences Inc, Daytona Beach FL
Museum of Fine Arts, Saint Petersburg, Florida, Inc, Saint Petersburg FL
Museum of Northern British Columbia, Ruth Harvey Art Gallery, Prince Rupert BC
Museum zu Allerheiligen, Schaffhausen
Muzej za Umjetnost i Obrt, Museum of Arts & Crafts, Zagreb
Muzeul de Istorie Nationala Si Arheologie Constanta, National History & Archaeology Museum, Constanta
Muzeul National de Arta al Romaniei, National Museum of Art of Romania, Bucharest
Muzeum Narodowe W Kielcach, National Museum in Kielce, Kielce
Muzeum Narodowe w Poznaniu, National Museum in Poznan, Poznan
National Archaeological Museum, Athens
National Art Museum of Moldova, Chisinau
The National Museum of Modern Art, Tokyo, Tokyo
National Society of Colonial Dames of America in the State of Maryland, Mount Clare Museum House, Baltimore MD
New Brunswick Museum, Saint John NB
Norwich Free Academy, Slater Memorial Museum, Norwich CT
Old Salem Museums & Gardens, Museum of Early Southern Decorative Arts, Winston-Salem NC
Panhandle-Plains Historical Museum, Canyon TX
Plumas County Museum, Quincy CA
Polk Museum of Art, Lakeland FL
Royal Arts Foundation, Belcourt Castle, Newport RI
San Angelo Museum of Fine Arts, San Angelo TX
San Antonio Museum of Art, San Antonio TX
The Speed Art Museum, Louisville KY
Stanford University, Cantor Arts Center at Stanford University, Stanford CA
The State Museum of Fine Arts of Tatarstan Republic, Kazan
Suan Pakkad Palace Museum, Bangkok
Suomen Kansallismuseo, National Museum of Finland, Helsinki
Taft Museum of Art, Cincinnati OH
Tokyo National Museum, Tokyo
Tver Regional Art Gallery, Tver
United States Figure Skating Association, World Figure Skating Museum & Hall of Fame, Colorado Springs CO
University of California, Berkeley, Phoebe Apperson Hearst Museum of Anthropology, Berkeley CA
University of Georgia, Georgia Museum of Art, Athens GA
University of Illinois at Urbana-Champaign, Krannert Art Museum and Kinkead Pavilion, Champaign IL
University of Notre Dame, Snite Museum of Art, Notre Dame IN
Virginia Museum of Fine Arts, Richmond VA
Willard House & Clock Museum, Inc, North Grafton MA
World Erotic Art Museum, Miami Beach FL

GRAPHICS

Abington Art Center, Jenkintown PA
African American Museum in Philadelphia, Philadelphia PA
Alaska State Museum, Juneau AK
Alberta College of Art & Design, Illingworth Kerr Gallery, Calgary AB
Albuquerque Museum of Art & History, Albuquerque NM
Alton Museum of History & Art, Inc, Alton IL
The Andy Warhol Museum, Pittsburgh PA
Arnot Art Museum, Elmira NY
Art and History Museums - Maitland, Maitland FL
Art Center of Battle Creek, Battle Creek MI
The Art Center of Waco, Waco TX
Art Community Center, Art Center of Corpus Christi, Corpus Christi TX
Art Gallery of Hamilton, Hamilton ON
Art Gallery of Nova Scotia, Halifax NS
Art Museum of Greater Lafayette, Lafayette IN
Art Museum of Southeast Texas, Beaumont TX
Art Without Walls Inc, Sayville NY
Balzekas Museum of Lithuanian Culture, Chicago IL
Bangladesh National Museum, Dhaka
Baroda Museum and Picture Gallery, Vadodara
Beloit College, Wright Museum of Art, Beloit WI
Besser Museum for Northeast Michigan, Alpena MI
Biggs Museum of American Art, Dover DE
Bone Creek Museum of Agrarian Art, David City NE
Booth Western Art Museum, Cartersville GA
Botswana National Museum, Gaborone
Bucknell University, Edward & Marthann Samek Art Gallery, Lewisburg PA
The Buffalo Fine Arts Academy, Albright-Knox Art Gallery, Buffalo NY
The California Historical Society, San Francisco CA
California State University, Chico, Janet Turner Print Museum, CSU, Chicago, Chico CA
Canadian Museum of History, Gatineau QC
Canton Museum of Art, Canton OH
Cape Cod Museum of Art Inc, Dennis MA
Capital University, Schumacher Gallery, Columbus OH
Central United Methodist Church, Swords Into Plowshares Peace Center & Gallery, Detroit MI
Channel Islands Maritime Museum, Oxnard CA
Cheekwood-Tennessee Botanical Garden & Museum of Art, Nashville TN
Chelan County Public Utility District, Rocky Reach Dam, Wenatchee WA
Chicago Athenaeum, Museum of Architecture & Design, Galena IL
Children's Museum of Manhattan, New York NY
City of Cedar Falls, Iowa, James & Meryl Hearst Center for the Arts & Sculpture Garden, Cedar Falls IA
City of El Paso, El Paso TX
City of Fayette, Alabama, Fayette Art Museum, Fayette AL
City of Fremont, Olive Hyde Art Gallery, Fremont CA
City of Gainesville, Thomas Center Galleries - Cultural Affairs, Gainesville FL
College of William & Mary, Muscarelle Museum of Art, Williamsburg VA
Columbia Museum of Art, Columbia SC
The Columbus Museum, Columbus GA
Contemporary Calgary, Calgary AB
Craft and Folk Art Museum (CAFAM), Los Angeles CA
Cranbrook Art Museum, Bloomfield Hills MI
Crocker Art Museum, Sacramento CA
Dahesh Museum of Art, Greenwich CT
Danville Museum of Fine Arts & History, Danville VA
Dartmouth Heritage Museum, Dartmouth NS
deCordova Sculpture Park & Museum, Lincoln MA
Delaware Art Museum, Wilmington DE
Designmuseum Danmark, Danish Design Museum, Copenhagen
Detroit Institute of Arts, Detroit MI
Dickinson College, The Trout Gallery, Carlisle PA
Dickinson State University, Art Gallery, Dickinson ND
Edmundson Art Foundation, Inc, Des Moines Art Center, Des Moines IA
Erie Art Museum, Erie PA
Fine Arts Museums of San Francisco, Legion of Honor, San Francisco CA
Fitton Center for Creative Arts, Hamilton OH
Flint Institute of Arts, Flint MI
Florence County Museum, Florence SC
Fondazione Musei Civici Di Venezia, Museo Correr - Correr Museum, Venice
Fort George G Meade Museum, Fort Meade MD
The Frank Phillips Foundation Inc, Woolaroc Museum, Bartlesville OK
Fuller Craft Museum, Brockton MA
Gadsden Museum of Art, Gadsden AL
Galerie Montcalm, Gatineau QC
Gallery One Visual Arts Center, Ellensburg WA
The George Washington University, Luther W Brady Art Gallery, Washington DC
Gertrude Herbert Institute of Art, Augusta GA
Girard College, Stephen Girard Collection, Philadelphia PA
Grand Rapids Art Museum, Grand Rapids MI
Grand Rapids Public Museum, Grand Rapids MI
Haystack Mountain School of Crafts, Deer Isle ME
Headquarters Fort Monroe, Dept of Army, Casemate Museum, Hampton VA
Hebrew Union College, Skirball Cultural Center, Los Angeles CA
Hebrew Union College - Jewish Institute of Religion Museum, Jewish Institute of Religion, New York NY
The Heckscher Museum of Art, Huntington NY
Henry Sheldon Museum of Vermont History and Research Center, Middlebury VT
Heritage Center, Inc, Pine Ridge SD
Hickory Museum of Art, Inc, Hickory NC
Hidalgo County Historical Museum, Edinburg TX
Hillwood Museum & Gardens Foundation, Hillwood Estate Museum & Gardens, Washington DC
Historisches und Volkerkundemuseum, Museum of History and Ethnology, St Gallen
Huntington Museum of Art, Huntington WV
i.d.e.a. Museum, Mesa AZ
Illinois State Museum, ISM Lockport Gallery, Chicago Gallery & Southern Illinois Art Gallery, Springfield IL
Imperial Calcasieu Museum, Gibson-Barham Gallery, Lake Charles LA
Independence Seaport Museum, Philadelphia PA
Institute of Puerto Rican Culture, Museo Fuerte Conde de Mirasol, Vieques PR
The Interchurch Center, Galleries at the Interchurch Center, New York NY
Intermedia Arts, Minneapolis MN
The Israel Museum, Jerusalem, Jerusalem
James Dick Foundation, Festival - Institute, Round Top TX
The Jewish Museum, New York NY
JMW Turner Museum, Sarasota FL
Jordan National Gallery of Fine Arts, Amman
Joslyn Art Museum, Omaha NE
Juniata College Museum of Art, Huntingdon PA
Karakalpak State Art Museum, Nukus Republic of Karakalpakstan
Kenosha Public Museums, Kenosha WI
Kentucky Museum of Art and Craft, Louisville KY
Keystone Gallery, Scott City KS
Kunsthalle Bremen, Bremen Art Gallery, Bremen
Kyiv Museum of Russian Art, Kyiv Ukrainian
L'Universite Laval, Ecole des Arts Visuels, Quebec QC
La Salle University Art Museum, Philadelphia PA
Lafayette College, Lafayette College Art Galleries, Easton PA
Lafayette Science Museum & Planetarium, Lafayette LA
LaGrange Art Museum, LaGrange GA
Latino Art Museum, Pomona CA
Lawrence University, Wriston Art Center Galleries, Appleton WI
Lightner Museum, Saint Augustine FL
The Long Island Museum of American Art, History & Carriages, Stony Brook NY
Louisiana Arts & Science Museum, Baton Rouge LA
Louisiana Department of Culture, Recreation & Tourism, Louisiana State Museum, New Orleans LA
The Mariners' Museum, Newport News VA
Maryland Art Place, Baltimore MD
Marylhurst University, The Art Gym, Marylhurst OR
Maude Kerns Art Center, Eugene OR
McCord Museum of Canadian History, Montreal QC
McNay Art Museum, San Antonio TX
Mennello Museum of American Art, Orlando FL
Michigan State University, Eli & Edythe Broad Art Museum, East Lansing MI
Midwest Museum of American Art, Elkhart IN
Minot State University, Northwest Art Center, Minot ND
Mississippi River Museum at Mud-Island River Park, Memphis TN
Mobile Museum of Art, Mobile AL
Moderna Galerija, Modern Gallery - National Museum of Modern Art, Zagreb
Montgomery Museum of Fine Arts, Montgomery AL
Moravska Galerie v Brne, Moravian Gallery in Brno, Brno
Morris Museum of Art, Augusta GA
Mount Allison University, Owens Art Gallery, Sackville NB
Muscatine Art Center, Muscatine IA
Musee des Beaux-Arts de Tours, Museum of Fine Arts, Tours

Museen der Stadt Koln, Museum Ludwig - Ludwig Museum, Cologne
Museen der Stadt Koln, Wallraf-Richartz-Museum & Fondation Corboud - Wallraf-Richartz Museum & Corboud Foundation, Cologne
Musees Royaux d'Art et d'Histoire, Royal Museums of Art and History, Brussels
Museo de Arte Contemporaneo de Castilla y Leon, Leon
Museo de Arte de Ponce, The Luis A Ferre Foundation Inc, Ponce PR
Museo De Las Americas, Denver CO
Museo Del Romanticismo, Museum of the Romantic Period, Madrid
Museum De Lakenhal, Leiden
Museum of Art - Deland FL, Inc, Deland FL
Museum of Art, Fort Lauderdale, Fort Lauderdale FL
The Museum of Arts & Sciences Inc, Daytona Beach FL
Museum of Contemporary Art, North Miami FL
Museum of Discovery & Science, Fort Lauderdale FL
Museum of Latin American Art, Long Beach CA
Museum of Modern Art, New York NY
Museum of Northern British Columbia, Ruth Harvey Art Gallery, Prince Rupert BC
Museum of Northwest Art, La Conner WA
Museum zu Allerheiligen, Schaffhausen
Muzej Moderne I Suvremene Umjetnosti, Museum of Modern and Contemporary Art, Rijeka
Muzej za Umjetnost i Obrt, Museum of Arts & Crafts, Zagreb
Muzeul de Istorie Nationala Si Arheologie Constanta, National History & Archaeology Museum, Constanta
Muzeul National de Arta al Romaniei, National Museum of Art of Romania, Bucharest
Muzeum Narodowe W Kielcach, National Museum in Kielce, Kielce
Muzeum Narodowe w Poznaniu, National Museum in Poznan, Poznan
Narodna Galerija, National Gallery of Slovenia, Ljubljana
National Art Museum of Moldova, Chisinau
National Baseball Hall of Fame & Museum, Cooperstown NY
National Gallery of Canada, Ottawa ON
The National Museum of Modern Art, Tokyo, Tokyo
The National Museum of Puerto Rican Arts & Culture, Chicago IL
National Society of Colonial Dames of America in the State of Maryland, Mount Clare Museum House, Baltimore MD
Naval Historical Center, National Museum of the US Navy, Washington DC
Nelson Mandela Metropolitan Art Museum, Port Elizabeth
New Orleans Museum of Art, New Orleans LA
New Visions Gallery, Inc, Marshfield WI
New York State Military Museum and Veterans Research Center, Saratoga Springs NY
Niagara University, Castellani Art Museum, Niagara NY
The Noble Maritime Collection, Staten Island NY
Norton Simon Museum, Pasadena CA
Norwich Free Academy, Slater Memorial Museum, Norwich CT
Nova Scotia College of Art and Design, Anna Leonowens Gallery, Halifax NS
Noyes Art Gallery, Lincoln NE
Ogden Museum of Southern Art, University of New Orleans, New Orleans LA
Ohio University, Kennedy Museum of Art, Athens OH
Owensboro Museum of Fine Art, Owensboro KY
Palm Beach County Parks & Recreation Department, Morikami Museum & Japanese Gardens, Delray Beach FL
Panhandle-Plains Historical Museum, Canyon TX
Pasadena Museum of California Art, Pasadena CA
Pennsylvania Academy of the Fine Arts, Philadelphia PA
Philadelphia History Museum, Philadelphia PA
Phillips Academy, Addison Gallery of American Art, Andover MA
The Phillips Collection, Washington DC
Plains Art Museum, Fargo ND
Plumas County Museum, Quincy CA
The Pomona College, Claremont CA
Portland Art Museum, Portland OR
Putnam County Historical Society, Foundry School Museum, Cold Spring NY
Queen's University, Agnes Etherington Art Centre, Kingston ON
Queens College, City University of New York, Godwin-Ternbach Museum, Flushing NY
Rahr-West Art Museum, Manitowoc WI
Rensselaer County Historical Society, Hart-Cluett Mansion, 1827, Troy NY
Rose Lehrman Art Gallery, Harrisburg PA
Roswell Museum & Art Center, Roswell NM
Saginaw Art Museum, Saginaw MI
Saint Mary's College of California, Museum of Art, Moraga CA
San Francisco Maritime National Historical Park, Maritime Museum, San Francisco CA
The San Joaquin Pioneer & Historical Society, The Haggin Museum, Stockton CA
Santa Clara University, de Saisset Museum, Santa Clara CA
Scripps College, Ruth Chandler Williamson Gallery, Claremont CA
Simon Fraser University, Simon Fraser University Gallery, Burnaby BC
Slovenska Narodna Galeria, Slovak National Gallery, Bratislava
The Society of the Cincinnati at Anderson House, Washington DC
South Dakota State University, South Dakota Art Museum, Brookings SD
Spertus Institute of Jewish Studies, Chicago IL
Staatliche Graphische Sammlung Munchen, State Prints & Drawings Collection, Munich
Staatliche Museen zu Berlin Stiftung Preussischer Kulturbesitz, National Museums in Berlin, Prussian Cultural Heritage Foundation, Berlin
Stanford University, Cantor Arts Center at Stanford University, Stanford CA
The State Museum of Fine Arts of Tatarstan Republic, Kazan
State University of New York at Geneseo, Bertha V B Lederer Gallery, Geneseo NY
State University of New York at New Paltz, Samuel Dorsky Museum of Art, New Paltz NY
State University of New York College at Cortland, Dowd Fine Arts Gallery, Cortland NY
Staten Island Museum, Staten Island NY
Stephens College, Lewis James & Nellie Stratton Davis Art Gallery, Columbia MO
Suomen Kansallismuseo, National Museum of Finland, Helsinki
Szepmuveszeti Muzeum, Museum of Fine Arts, Budapest
Thomas More College, Eva G Farris Art Gallery, Crestview KY
Tokyo National Museum, Tokyo
Tver Regional Art Gallery, Tver
The Ukrainian Museum, New York NY
United States Military Academy, West Point Museum, West Point NY
University of California, Davis, Jan Shrem and Maria Manetti Shrem Museum of Art, Davis CA
University of California, Los Angeles, Grunwald Center for the Graphic Arts at Hammer Museum, Los Angeles CA
University of Chicago, Smart Museum of Art, Chicago IL
University of Georgia, Georgia Museum of Art, Athens GA
University of Houston, Blaffer Art Museum, Houston TX
University of Illinois at Urbana-Champaign, Krannert Art Museum and Kinkead Pavilion, Champaign IL
University of Indianapolis, Christel DeHaan Fine Arts Gallery, Indianapolis IN
University of Kansas, Spencer Museum of Art, Lawrence KS
The University of Kentucky Art Museum, Lexington KY
University of Minnesota, Goldstein Museum of Design, Saint Paul MN
University of Richmond, University Museums, Richmond VA
University of Utah, Utah Museum of Fine Arts, Salt Lake City UT
University of Victoria, The Legacy Art Gallery, Victoria BC
University of Wisconsin-Eau Claire, Foster Gallery, Eau Claire WI
University of Wisconsin-Madison, Chazen Museum of Art, Madison WI
USS Constitution Museum, Boston MA
Vassar College, The Frances Lehman Loeb Art Center, Poughkeepsie NY
Virginia Museum of Fine Arts, Richmond VA
Volcano Art Center Gallery, Hawaii Volcanoes National Park HI
Vorarlberg Museum, Bregenz
The Walker African American Museum & Research Center, Las Vegas NV
Walker Art Gallery, Liverpool
Washburn University, Mulvane Art Museum, Topeka KS
Waterworks Visual Arts Center, Salisbury NC
Wheaton College, Beard and Weil Galleries, Norton MA
Wilkes Art Gallery, North Wilkesboro NC
Wiregrass Museum of Art, Dothan AL
Wisconsin Historical Society, Wisconsin Historical Museum, Madison WI
Woodmere Art Museum Inc, Philadelphia PA
Yokohama Museum of Art, Yokohama

HISPANIC ART

Albuquerque Museum of Art & History, Albuquerque NM
Amherst College, Mead Art Museum, Amherst MA
Art Community Center, Art Center of Corpus Christi, Corpus Christi TX
The Art Museum of Eastern Idaho, Idaho Falls ID
Art Museum of Greater Lafayette, Lafayette IN
Art Without Walls Inc, Sayville NY
Arts Council of Fayetteville-Cumberland County, The Arts Center, Fayetteville NC
Baruch College of the City University of New York, Sidney Mishkin Gallery, New York NY
Baton Rouge Gallery, Center For Contemporary Art, Baton Rouge LA
Bowers Museum, Santa Ana CA
Bucknell University, Edward & Marthann Samek Art Gallery, Lewisburg PA
California State University, Chico, Janet Turner Print Museum, CSU, Chicago, Chico CA
Cartoon Art Museum, San Francisco CA
The Children's Museum of Indianapolis, Indianapolis IN
City of El Paso, El Paso TX
City of Pittsfield Office of Cultural Development, Lichtenstein Center for the Arts, Pittsfield MA
Concordia Historical Institute, Saint Louis MO
Craft and Folk Art Museum (CAFAM), Los Angeles CA
Davidson College, William H Van Every Jr & Edward M Smith Galleries, Davidson NC
Detroit Institute of Arts, Detroit MI
East Carolina University, Wellington B Gray Gallery, Greenville NC
Ellen Noel Art Museum of the Permian Basin, Odessa TX
En Foco, Inc, Bronx NY
Fitchburg Art Museum, Fitchburg MA
Fitton Center for Creative Arts, Hamilton OH
General Board of Discipleship, The United Methodist Church, The Upper Room Chapel & Museum, Nashville TN
Heard Museum, Phoenix AZ
Henry Sheldon Museum of Vermont History and Research Center, Middlebury VT
Hidalgo County Historical Museum, Edinburg TX
History Colorado Center Museum, Denver CO
Illinois State Museum, ISM Lockport Gallery, Chicago Gallery & Southern Illinois Art Gallery, Springfield IL
Institute of Puerto Rican Culture, Museo Fuerte Conde de Mirasol, Vieques PR
The Interchurch Center, Galleries at the Interchurch Center, New York NY
Intermedia Arts, Minneapolis MN
International Museum of Art, El Paso TX
Johns Hopkins University, Evergreen Museum & Library, Baltimore MD
Kalamazoo Institute of Arts, Kalamazoo MI
Kelly-Griggs House Museum, Red Bluff CA
Kenosha Public Museums, Kenosha WI
Knoxville Museum of Art, Knoxville TN
Koshare Indian Museum, Inc, La Junta CO
LA County Museum of Art, Los Angeles CA
Lalit Kala Akademi Rabindra Bhavan Art Galleries, National Academy of Art, New Delhi, New Delhi
Latino Art Museum, Pomona CA
Latino Center of Art and Culture, Sacramento CA

Lightner Museum, Saint Augustine FL
Lillian & Coleman Taube Museum of Art, Minot ND
Louise Hopkins Underwood Center for the Arts, Lubbock TX
Loyola Marymount University, Laband Art Gallery, Los Angeles CA
Mabee-Gerrer Museum of Art, Shawnee OK
Maryland Art Place, Baltimore MD
Mennello Museum of American Art, Orlando FL
Mesa Arts Center, Mesa Contemporary Arts Museum, Mesa AZ
The Mexican Museum, San Francisco CA
Miami-Dade College, MDC Museum of Art & Design, Miami FL
Millicent Rogers Museum, Taos NM
Modern Art Museum, Fort Worth TX
Musee des Beaux-Arts de Tours, Museum of Fine Arts, Tours
Museo De Las Americas, Denver CO
Museum of Art - Deland FL, Inc, Deland FL
The Museum of Arts & Sciences Inc, Daytona Beach FL
Museum of Contemporary Art, North Miami FL
Museum of Fine Arts, Saint Petersburg, Florida, Inc, Saint Petersburg FL
Museum of Latin American Art, Long Beach CA
Museum of Northern Arizona, Flagstaff AZ
Muzeul National de Arta al Romaniei, National Museum of Art of Romania, Bucharest
Nara Kokuritsu Hakubutsu-Kan, Nara National Museum, Nara
Nassau County Museum of Art, Roslyn Harbor NY
The Nelson-Atkins Museum of Art, Kansas City MO
New Mexico Department of Cultural Affairs, Palace of Governors, Santa Fe NM
Norwich Free Academy, Slater Memorial Museum, Norwich CT
Opelousas Museum of Art, Inc (OMA), Opelousas LA
Owensboro Museum of Fine Art, Owensboro KY
Panhandle-Plains Historical Museum, Canyon TX
Phoenix Art Museum, Phoenix AZ
Queens College, City University of New York, Godwin-Ternbach Museum, Flushing NY
Roswell Museum & Art Center, Roswell NM
Royal Ontario Museum, Toronto ON
Saginaw Art Museum, Saginaw MI
Saint Mary's College of California, Museum of Art, Moraga CA
San Antonio Museum of Art, San Antonio TX
Santa Paula Art Museum, Santa Paula CA
Sheldon Art Galleries, Saint Louis MO
Slovenska Narodna Galeria, Slovak National Gallery, Bratislava
South Carolina State Museum, Columbia SC
Southeastern Center for Contemporary Art, Winston-Salem NC
Southern Methodist University, Meadows Museum, Dallas TX
Stanford University, Cantor Arts Center at Stanford University, Stanford CA
Taos Historic Museums, La Hacienda de Los Martinez, Taos NM
Tohono Chul Park, Tucson AZ
University of Florida, Samuel P Harn Museum of Art, Gainesville FL
University of Georgia, Georgia Museum of Art, Athens GA
University of Illinois at Urbana-Champaign, Krannert Art Museum and Kinkead Pavilion, Champaign IL
University of Miami, Lowe Art Museum, Coral Gables FL
University of New Mexico, The Harwood Museum of Art, Taos NM
University of Notre Dame, Snite Museum of Art, Notre Dame IN
University of Texas at Austin, Blanton Museum of Art, Austin TX
University of Utah, Utah Museum of Fine Arts, Salt Lake City UT
University of Wisconsin-Madison, Chazen Museum of Art, Madison WI
Walker Art Gallery, Liverpool
Wichita State University, Ulrich Museum of Art, Wichita KS
World Erotic Art Museum, Miami Beach FL
Yerba Buena Center for the Arts, San Francisco CA

HISTORICAL MATERIAL

Abraham Lincoln Presidential Library & Museum, Springfield IL
Academy of the New Church, Glencairn Museum, Bryn Athyn PA
Adams County Historical Society, Gettysburg PA
Adams National Historic Park, Quincy MA
African American Museum in Philadelphia, Philadelphia PA
African American Museum of Iowa, Cedar Rapids IA
African Art Museum of Maryland, Columbia MD
Aiken County Historical Museum, Aiken SC
Alaska Heritage Museum at Wells Fargo, Anchorage AK
Alaska Museum of Science & Nature, Anchorage AK
Alaska State Museum, Juneau AK
Albany Institute of History & Art, Albany NY
Albany Museum of Art, Albany GA
Albin Polasek Museum & Sculpture Gardens, Winter Park FL
Albuquerque Museum of Art & History, Albuquerque NM
Allentown Art Museum, Allentown PA
Alton Museum of History & Art, Inc, Alton IL
American Textile History Museum, Lowell MA
Americas Society Art Gallery, New York NY
Amherst College, Mead Art Museum, Amherst MA
Amon Carter Museum of American Art, Fort Worth TX
Anchorage Museum at Rasmuson Center, Anchorage AK
Ancient Spanish Monastery, North Miami Beach FL
Arizona Historical Society-Yuma, Sanguinetti House Museum & Garden, Yuma AZ
Arnot Art Museum, Elmira NY
The Art Gallery of Grand Prairie, Grande Prairie AB
Art Gallery of Nova Scotia, Halifax NS
Art Without Walls Inc, Sayville NY
Artesia Historical Museum and Art Center, Artesia NM
Athenaeum of Philadelphia, Philadelphia PA
Atlanta Historical Society Inc, Atlanta History Center, Atlanta GA
Audrain County Historical Society, Graceland Museum & American Saddlehorse Museum & Fire Brick Industry Museum, Mexico MO
Aurora Regional Fire Museum, Aurora IL
Baker University, Old Castle Museum, Baldwin City KS
Bangladesh National Museum, Dhaka
Barnes Museum, Southington CT
Baroda Museum and Picture Gallery, Vadodara
The Bartlett Museum, Amesbury MA
Bay County Historical Society, Historical Museum of Bay County, Bay City MI
Baycrest Centre for Geriatric Care, The Morris & Sally Justein of Baycrest Heritage Museum, Toronto ON
Bennington Museum, Bennington VT
Beverly Historical Society, Cabot, Hale & Balch House Museums, Beverly MA
Big Horn County Historical Museum, Hardin MT
Blanden Memorial Art Museum, Fort Dodge IA
Bodley-Bullock House Museum, Lexington KY
Booth Western Art Museum, Cartersville GA
Boston Public Library, Albert H Wiggin Gallery & Print Department, Boston MA
The Bostonian Society, Old State House Museum, Boston MA
Bowdoin College, Peary-MacMillan Arctic Museum, Brunswick ME
Brick Store Museum, Kennebunk ME
Bronx Community College (CUNY), Hall of Fame for Great Americans, Bronx NY
Brookgreen Gardens, Murrells Inlet SC
Brooklyn Historical Society, Brooklyn OH
Bucknell University, Edward & Marthann Samek Art Gallery, Lewisburg PA
Buena Vista Museum of Natural History, Bakersfield CA
Buffalo Niagara Heritage Village, Amherst NY
Burchfield Penney Art Center, Buffalo NY
Bush-Holley Historic Site & Storehouse Gallery, Greenwich Historical Society, Cos Cob CT
C M Russell Museum, Great Falls MT
Calvert Marine Museum, Solomons MD
Cambridge Museum, Cambridge NE
Canadian Clay and Glass Gallery, Waterloo ON
Canadian Museum of History, Gatineau QC
Canadian War Museum, Ottawa ON
Cape Ann Museum, Gloucester MA
Carlsbad Museum & Art Center, Carlsbad NM
Carson County Square House Museum, Panhandle TX
Cartoon Art Museum, San Francisco CA
Casa Amesti, Monterey CA
Cayuga Museum of History & Art, Auburn NY
Center for Puppetry Arts, Atlanta GA
Channel Islands Maritime Museum, Oxnard CA
Chatham Historical Society, The Atwood House Museum, Chatham MA
Chatillon-DeMenil House Foundation, Chatillon-DeMenil Mansion, Saint Louis MO
Chelan County Public Utility District, Rocky Reach Dam, Wenatchee WA
Chesapeake Bay Maritime Museum, Saint Michaels MD
Chief Plenty Coups Museum State Park, Pryor MT
The Children's Museum of Indianapolis, Indianapolis IN
Children's Museum of Manhattan, New York NY
City of Atlanta, Atlanta Cyclorama & Civil War Museum, Atlanta GA
City of Austin Parks & Recreation, O Henry Museum, Austin TX
City of Gainesville, Thomas Center Galleries - Cultural Affairs, Gainesville FL
City of Springdale, Shiloh Museum of Ozark History, Springdale AR
Clark County Historical Society, Pioneer - Krier Museum, Ashland KS
Cliveden, Philadelphia PA
Cohasset Historical Society, Pratt Building (Society Headquarters), Cohasset MA
Cohasset Historical Society, Cohasset Maritime Museum, Cohasset MA
Cohasset Historical Society, Captain John Wilson Historical House, Cohasset MA
College of William & Mary, Muscarelle Museum of Art, Williamsburg VA
Columbus Historic Foundation, Blewett-Harrison-Lee Museum, Columbus MS
The Columbus Museum, Columbus GA
Communications and History Museum of Sutton, Sutton QC
Concord Museum, Concord MA
Conrad-Caldwell House Museum, Louisville KY
Craigdarroch Castle Historical Museum Society, Victoria BC
Cranford Historical Society, Cranford NJ
Cripple Creek District Museum, Cripple Creek CO
Crook County Museum & Art Gallery, Sundance WY
The Currier Museum of Art, Manchester NH
Dacotah Prairie Museum, Lamont Art Gallery, Aberdeen SD
Dalnavert Museum, Winnipeg MB
Danville Museum of Fine Arts & History, Danville VA
Davidson College, William H Van Every Jr & Edward M Smith Galleries, Davidson NC
Deines Cultural Center, Russell KS
Delaware Division of Historical & Cultural Affairs, Dover DE
Delphi Archaeological Museum, Delphi
Deming-Luna Mimbres Museum, Deming NM
Department of Economic & Community Development, State of Connecticut DECD Eric Sloane Museum, Kent CT
Deutsches Museum, Munich
Dickinson College, The Trout Gallery, Carlisle PA
The Dinosaur Museum, Blanding UT
East Bay Asian Local Development Corp (EBALDC), Asian Resource Gallery, Oakland CA
Eastern Washington State Historical Society, Northwest Museum of Arts & Culture, Spokane WA
Edgecombe County Cultural Arts Council, Inc, Blount-Bridgers House, Hobson Pittman Memorial Gallery, Tarboro NC
Elisabet Ney, Austin TX
Elmhurst Art Museum, Elmhurst IL
Erie County Historical Society, Erie PA
Essex Historical Society and Shipbuilding Museum, Essex MA
Evanston Historical Society, Charles Gates Dawes House, Evanston IL
Fairbanks Museum & Planetarium, Saint Johnsbury VT
Favell Museum of Western Art & Indian Artifacts, Klamath Falls OR
Fetherston Foundation, Packwood House Museum, Lewisburg PA
Fishkill Historical Society, Van Wyck Homestead Museum, Fishkill NY
Fitton Center for Creative Arts, Hamilton OH

Florence County Museum, Florence SC
Florida Department of Environmental Protection, Stephen Foster Folk Culture Center State Park, White Springs FL
Folk Art Society of America, Richmond VA
Fort George G Meade Museum, Fort Meade MD
Fort Morgan Heritage Foundation, Fort Morgan CO
Fort Ticonderoga Association, Ticonderoga NY
The Frank Phillips Foundation Inc, Woolaroc Museum, Bartlesville OK
Frontier Gateway Museum, Glendive MT
Frontier Times Museum, Bandera TX
Fulton County Historical Society Inc, Fulton County Museum (Tetzlaff Reference Room), Rochester IN
Gadsden Museum of Art, Gadsden AL
General Board of Discipleship, The United Methodist Church, The Upper Room Chapel & Museum, Nashville TN
Genesee Country Village & Museum, John L Wehle Art Gallery, Mumford NY
George Phippen, Phippen Museum - Art of the American West, Prescott AZ
The George Washington University, Luther W Brady Art Gallery, Washington DC
Germantown Historical Society, Philadelphia PA
Girard College, Stephen Girard Collection, Philadelphia PA
Glanmore National Historic Site of Canada, Belleville ON
Glasgow University, The Hunterian, Glasgow
Glenbow Museum, Calgary AB
Glessner House Museum, Chicago IL
Gloridale Partnership, National Museum of Woodcarving, Custer SD
Goshen Historical Society, Goshen CT
Grand Rapids Public Museum, Grand Rapids MI
Grand River Museum, Lemmon SD
Great Lakes Historical Society, Inland Seas Maritime Museum, Vermilion OH
Greene County Historical Society, Bronck Museum, Coxsackie NY
Gunston Hall Plantation, Mason Neck VA
Hammonds House Museum, Atlanta GA
Hancock Shaker Village, Inc, Pittsfield MA
Harold Warp, Minden NE
Harrison County Historical Museum, Marshall TX
Hastings Museum of Natural & Cultural History, Hastings NE
Headquarters Fort Monroe, Dept of Army, Casemate Museum, Hampton VA
Heard Museum, Phoenix AZ
Heart of West Texas Museum, Colorado City TX
Hebrew Union College, Skirball Cultural Center, Los Angeles CA
Hebrew Union College - Jewish Institute of Religion, Skirball Museum Cincinnati, Cincinnati OH
Hebrew Union College - Jewish Institute of Religion Museum, Jewish Institute of Religion, New York NY
Hecht Museum, Haifa
Hendricks Hill Museum, Southport ME
Henry County Museum & Cultural Arts Center, Clinton MO
Henry Morrison Flagler Museum, Palm Beach FL
Henry Sheldon Museum of Vermont History and Research Center, Middlebury VT
Heritage Center, Inc, Pine Ridge SD
Heritage Glass Museum, Glassboro NJ
Heritage Museum & Cultural Center, Baker LA
Hershey Museum, Hershey PA
High Desert Museum, Bend OR
Hill-Stead Museum, Farmington CT
Hillwood Museum & Gardens Foundation, Hillwood Estate Museum & Gardens, Washington DC
Historic Arkansas Museum, Little Rock AR
Historic Holyoke at Wistariahurst & City of Holyoke, Holyoke MA
Historic Huguenot Street, New Paltz NY
Historic Newton, Newton MA
Historical Society of Cheshire County, Keene NH
Historical Society of Old Newbury, Cushing House Museum, Newburyport MA
Historical Society of Rockland County, New City NY
Historical Society of Washington DC, The City Museum of Washington DC, Washington DC
History Colorado Center Museum, Denver CO
History Museum of Mobile, Mobile AL
Hui No'eau Visual Arts Center, Gallery and Gift Shop, Makawao Maui HI
Illinois Historic Preservation Agency, Bishop Hill State Historic Site, Bishop Hill IL
Imperial Calcasieu Museum, Gibson-Barham Gallery, Lake Charles LA
Imperial War Museum London, London
Independence Historical Museum & Art Center, Independence KS
Independence Seaport Museum, Philadelphia PA
Indiana State Museum, Indianapolis IN
Indiana University, The Mathers Museum of World Cultures, Bloomington IN
Institute of Puerto Rican Culture, Museo Fuerte Conde de Mirasol, Vieques PR
Institute of Puerto Rican Culture, Dr Jose C Barbosa Museum, Bayamon PR
Institute of Puerto Rican Culture, Museo y Parque Historico Ruinas de Caparra, Guaynabo PR
International Clown Hall of Fame & Research Center, Inc, West Allis WI
Iredell Museums, Statesville NC
Iroquois Indian Museum, Howes Cave NY
Jacques Marchais Museum of Tibetan Art, Staten Island NY
James Dick Foundation, Festival - Institute, Round Top TX
Jefferson County Historical Society, Watertown NY
Jefferson County Open Space, Hiwan Homestead Museum, Evergreen CO
Johns Hopkins University, Evergreen Museum & Library, Baltimore MD
Jordan Historical Museum of The Twenty, Jordan ON
Joslyn Art Museum, Omaha NE
Kansas State Historical Society, Kansas Museum of History, Topeka KS
Kelly-Griggs House Museum, Red Bluff CA
Kelvingrove Art Gallery & Museum, Glasgow UK
Kenosha Public Museums, Kenosha WI
Kern County Museum, Bakersfield CA
Keystone Gallery, Scott City KS
Kings County Historical Society & Museum, Hampton NB
Klamath County Museum, Klamath Falls OR
Kongernes Samling, The Royal Danish Collection, Copenhagen
Lac du Flambeau Band of Lake Superior Chippewa Indians, George W Brown Jr Ojibwe Museum & Cultural Center, Lac Du Flambeau WI
LACE (Los Angeles Contemporary Exhibitions), Los Angeles CA
Lafayette Science Museum & Planetarium, Lafayette LA
Lahore Museum, Lahore
League of New Hampshire Craftsmen, Grodin Permanent Collection Museum, Concord NH
Leelanau Historical Museum, Leland MI
Lehigh Valley Heritage Center, Allentown PA
LeSueur Museum, Le Sueur MN
Lincoln County Historical Association, Inc, 1811 Old Lincoln County Jail & Lincoln County Museum, Wiscasset ME
Livingston County Historical Society, Museum, Geneseo NY
Lockwood-Mathews Mansion Museum, Norwalk CT
Long Branch Historical Association Church of the Presidents Museum, Long Branch NJ
The Long Island Museum of American Art, History & Carriages, Stony Brook NY
Longfellow-Evangeline State Commemorative Area, Saint Martinville LA
Longue Vue House & Gardens, New Orleans LA
Los Angeles County Museum of Natural History, William S Hart Museum, Newhall CA
Louise Hopkins Underwood Center for the Arts, Lubbock TX
Louisiana Department of Culture, Recreation & Tourism, Louisiana State Museum, New Orleans LA
Loveland Museum/Gallery, Loveland CO
Lusaka National Museum, Lusaka
Lyme Historical Society, Florence Griswold Museum, Old Lyme CT
Maine Historical Society, MHS Museum, Portland ME
Marblehead Museum & Historical Society, Marblehead MA
Marblehead Museum & Historical Society, Jeremiah Lee Mansion, Marblehead MA
Maricopa County Historical Society, Desert Caballeros Western Museum, Wickenburg AZ
The Mariners' Museum, Newport News VA
Maryhill Museum of Art, Goldendale WA
Massachusetts Institute of Technology, MIT Museum, Cambridge MA
McCord Museum of Canadian History, Montreal QC
McDowell House & Apothecary Shop, Danville KY
McLean County Historical Society, McLean County Museum of History, Bloomington IL
McPherson Museum and Arts Foundation, McPherson KS
Medina Railroad Museum, Medina NY
Meredith College, Frankie G Weems Gallery & Rotunda Gallery, Raleigh NC
Mezuraj Museum, Tirana
Middle Border Museum & Oscar Howe Art Center, Mitchell SD
Millicent Rogers Museum, Taos NM
The Mint Museum, Mint Museum of Craft & Design, Charlotte NC
Mission San Luis Rey de Francia, Mission San Luis Rey Museum, Oceanside CA
Mission San Miguel Museum, San Miguel CA
Mississippi River Museum at Mud-Island River Park, Memphis TN
Missouri Department of Natural Resources, Missouri State Museum, Jefferson City MO
Missouri Department of Natural Resources, Elizabeth Rozier Gallery, Jefferson City MO
Mohave Museum of History & Arts, Kingman AZ
Mohawk Valley Heritage Association, Inc, Walter Elwood Museum, Amsterdam NY
Monroe County Historical Association, Elizabeth D Walters Library, Stroudsburg PA
Montana State University, Helen E Copeland Gallery, Bozeman MT
Moravian Historical Society, Nazareth PA
Morris Museum of Art, Augusta GA
Morris-Jumel Mansion, Inc, New York NY
Morven Museum & Garden, Princeton NJ
Mount Vernon Hotel Museum & Garden, New York NY
MTG Hawkes Bay, Napier
Muscatine Art Center, Muscatine IA
Musee des Beaux-Arts de Tours, Museum of Fine Arts, Tours
Musee Regional de lu Cote-Nord, Sept-Iles QC
Musees Royaux d'Art et d'Histoire, Royal Museums of Art and History, Brussels
Museo De Las Americas, Denver CO
Museo Italo Americano, San Francisco CA
The Museum, Greenwood SC
Museum of American Glass in WV, Weston WV
Museum of Art & History, Santa Cruz, Santa Cruz CA
Museum of Chinese in America, New York NY
Museum of Northern Arizona, Flagstaff AZ
Museum of Northern British Columbia, Ruth Harvey Art Gallery, Prince Rupert BC
Museum of Northwest Art, La Conner WA
Museum of Science & History, Jacksonville FL
Museum of the Southwest, Midland TX
Museum of Vancouver, Vancouver BC
Museum of Ventura County, Ventura CA
Museum of York County, Rock Hill SC
Museum Plantin-Moretus, Antwerp
Museum Prinsenhof Delft, Delft
Museum zu Allerheiligen, Schaffhausen
Muzeul de Istorie Nationala Si Arheologie Constanta, National History & Archaeology Museum, Constanta
Muzeul National de Arta al Romaniei, National Museum of Art of Romania, Bucharest
Muzim Negara, National Museum, Kuala Lumpur
Nanticoke Indian Museum, Millsboro DE
Nara Kokuritsu Hakubutsu-Kan, Nara National Museum, Nara
Nathan Hale Homestead Museum, Coventry CT
National Archives & Records Administration, John F Kennedy Presidential Library & Museum, Boston MA
National Archives & Records Administration, Franklin D Roosevelt Museum, Hyde Park NY
National Baseball Hall of Fame & Museum, Cooperstown NY
National Churchill Museum, Fulton MO
National Gallery of Ireland, Dublin
National Heritage Museum, Lexington MA
National Museum & Art Gallery of Trinidad and Tobago, Port of Spain
National Museum of the American Indian, George Gustav Heye Center, New York NY
National Museum of Wildlife Art of the Unites States, Jackson WY

National Park Service, Weir Farm National Historic Site, Wilton CT
The National Shrine of the North American Martyrs, Fultonville NY
National Silk Art Museum, Weston MO
National Society of Colonial Dames of America in the State of Maryland, Mount Clare Museum House, Baltimore MD
Naval War College Museum, Newport RI
Nebraska Game and Parks Commission, Arbor Lodge State Historical Park & Morton Mansion, Nebraska City NE
Nebraska State Capitol, Lincoln NE
Neustadt Collection of Tiffany Glass, Long Island City NY
Nevada Northern Railway Museum, Ely NV
New Brunswick Museum, Saint John NB
New Canaan Historical Society, New Canaan CT
New England Maple Museum, Pittsford VT
New Jersey Historical Society, Newark NJ
New Mexico Department of Cultural Affairs, Palace of Governors, Santa Fe NM
New York State Office of Parks Recreation & Historic Preservation, John Jay Homestead State Historic Site, Katonah NY
New York State Office of Parks, Recreation & Historic Preservation, Staatsburgh State Historic Site, Staatsburg NY
Newburyport Maritime Society, Inc, Custom House Maritime Museum, Newburyport MA
The Noble Maritime Collection, Staten Island NY
Norsk Maritimt Museum, Norwegian Maritime Museum, Oslo
Northeastern Nevada Museum, Elko NV
Norwich Free Academy, Slater Memorial Museum, Norwich CT
Ogden Union Station, Union Station Museums, Ogden UT
The Ohio Historical Society, Inc, Campus Martius Museum & Ohio River Museum, Marietta OH
Ohio History Connection, National Afro-American Museum & Cultural Center, Wilberforce OH
Ohio University, Kennedy Museum of Art, Athens OH
Okefenokee Heritage Center, Inc, Waycross GA
Oklahoma Historical Society, State Museum of History, Oklahoma City OK
Old Barracks Museum, Trenton NJ
Old Dartmouth Historical Society, New Bedford Whaling Museum, New Bedford MA
Old Island Restoration Foundation Inc, Oldest House in Key West, Key West FL
The Old Jail Art Center, Albany TX
Old Salem Museums & Gardens, Museum of Early Southern Decorative Arts, Winston-Salem NC
Opelousas Museum of Art, Inc (OMA), Opelousas LA
Osborne Homestead Museum, Derby CT
Owen Sound Historical Society, Marine & Rail Heritage Museum, Owen Sound ON
Page-Walker Arts & History Center, Cary NC
Palm Beach County Parks & Recreation Department, Morikami Museum & Japanese Gardens, Delray Beach FL
Panhandle-Plains Historical Museum, Canyon TX
Pasadena Museum of History, Pasadena CA
Pennsylvania Academy of the Fine Arts, Philadelphia PA
Pennsylvania Historical & Museum Commission, The State Museum of Pennsylvania, Harrisburg PA
Pennsylvania Historical & Museum Commission, Railroad Museum of Pennsylvania, Strasburg PA
Penobscot Marine Museum, Searsport ME
Philadelphia History Museum, Philadelphia PA
Philbrook Museum of Art, Tulsa OK
Philipse Manor Hall State Historic Site, Yonkers NY
Photographic Resource Center, Inc, Cambridge MA
Pine Bluff/Jefferson County Historical Museum, Pine Bluff AR
Pioneer Historical Museum of South Dakota, Hot Springs SD
Plainsman Museum, Aurora NE
Plumas County Museum, Quincy CA
Polish Museum of America (PMA), Chicago IL
Portsmouth Historical Society, John Paul Jones House & Discover Portsmouth, Portsmouth NH
Preservation Virginia, John Marshall House, Richmond VA
Pueblo Museum, Desert Hot Springs CA
Putnam County Historical Society, Foundry School Museum, Cold Spring NY
Putnam Museum of History and Natural Science, Davenport IA
Queens College, City University of New York, Godwin-Ternbach Museum, Flushing NY
Rangeley Lakes Region Logging Museum, Rangeley ME
Red River Valley Museum, Vernon TX
Red Rock Park, Red Rock Park, Church Rock NM
RedMill Museum Village, Clinton NJ
Rensselaer County Historical Society, Hart-Cluett Mansion, 1827, Troy NY
Rhode Island Historical Society, John Brown House, Providence RI
Ringwood Manor House Museum, Ringwood NJ
Roberson Museum & Science Center, Binghamton NY
Robert Louis Stevenson Museum, Saint Helena CA
Roswell Museum & Art Center, Roswell NM
Royal Alberta Museum, Royal Alberta Museum, Edmonton AB
Royal Arts Foundation, Belcourt Castle, Newport RI
Royal Ontario Museum, Toronto ON
Safety Harbor Museum and Cultural Arts Center, Safety Harbor FL
Saginaw Art Museum, Saginaw MI
Saint Anselm College, Alva de Mars Megan Chapel Art Center, Manchester NH
Saint Mary's College of California, Museum of Art, Moraga CA
San Bernardino County Museum, Redlands CA
San Francisco Maritime National Historical Park, Maritime Museum, San Francisco CA
The San Joaquin Pioneer & Historical Society, The Haggin Museum, Stockton CA
Santa Paula Art Museum, Santa Paula CA
Schuyler Mansion State Historic Site, Albany NY
Sea Cliff Village Museum, Sea Cliff NY
Seneca Falls Historical Society Museum, Seneca Falls NY
Seneca-Iroquois National Museum, Salamanca NY
Shaker Museum & Library, Old Chatham NY
Shaker Village of Pleasant Hill, Harrodsburg KY
Shephela Museum, Kefar-Menahem
Ships of the Sea Maritime Museum, Savannah GA
Shirley Plantation Foundation, Charles City VA
Shoreline Historical Museum, Shoreline WA
Shores Memorial Museum, Lyndon Center VT
Sitka Historical Society, Sitka History Museum, Sitka AK
Slater Mill, Old Slater Mill Association, Pawtucket RI
Sloss Furnaces National Historic Landmark, Birmingham AL
The Society of the Cincinnati at Anderson House, Washington DC
South Dakota State University, South Dakota Art Museum, Brookings SD
South Street Seaport Museum, New York NY
Southern Lorain County Historical Society, Spirit of '76 Museum, Elyria OH
Spertus Institute of Jewish Studies, Chicago IL
St George Art Museum, Saint George UT
Stanford University, Cantor Arts Center at Stanford University, Stanford CA
State University of New York College at Cortland, Dowd Fine Arts Gallery, Cortland NY
Staten Island Museum, Staten Island NY
Ste Genevieve Museum, Sainte Genevieve MO
Stedelijk Museum Alkmaar, Alkmaar Municipal Museum, Alkmaar
The Stewart Museum, Montreal QC
Stone Quarry Hill Art Park, Winner Gallery, Cazenovia NY
The Summit County Historical Society of Akron, OH, Akron OH
Suomen Kansallismuseo, National Museum of Finland, Helsinki
Susquehanna University, Lore Degenstein Gallery, Selinsgrove PA
Swedish American Museum, Chicago IL
T C Steele State Historic Site, Nashville IN
Tallahassee Museum of History & Natural Science, Tallahassee FL
Taos Historic Museums, Ernest Blumenschein Home & Studio, Taos NM
Taos Historic Museums, La Hacienda de Los Martinez, Taos NM
Tennessee State Museum, Nashville TN
Thomas Jefferson Foundation, Inc, Monticello, Charlottesville VA
Tokyo National Museum, Tokyo
Transylvania University, Morlan Gallery, Lexington KY
Trust Authority, Museum of the Great Plains, Lawton OK
Tryon Palace, New Bern NC
Tubac Center of the Arts, Santa Cruz Valley Art Association, Tubac AZ
Tubman African American Museum, Macon GA
Turtle Bay Exploration Park, Redding CA
Turtle Mountain Chippewa Historical Society, Turtle Mountain Heritage Center, Belcourt ND
Tver Regional Art Gallery, Tver
Tyne and Wear Archives & Museums, Sunderland Museum & Winter Gardens, Sunderland
Ukrainian Canadian Archives & Museum of Alberta, Edmonton AB
The Ukrainian Museum, New York NY
United Methodist Church General Commission on Archives & History, Madison NJ
United Methodist Historical Society, Lovely Lane Museum, Baltimore MD
United Society of Shakers, Shaker Museum, New Gloucester ME
United States Figure Skating Association, World Figure Skating Museum & Hall of Fame, Colorado Springs CO
United States Navy Supply Corps School, US Navy Supply Corps Museum, Newport RI
University of California, Davis, Jan Shrem and Maria Manetti Shrem Museum of Art, Davis CA
University of Georgia, Georgia Museum of Art, Athens GA
University of Illinois at Urbana-Champaign, Spurlock Museum, Urbana IL
University of Indianapolis, Christel DeHaan Fine Arts Gallery, Indianapolis IN
University of New Mexico, The Harwood Museum of Art, Taos NM
University of Saskatchewan, Diefenbaker Canada Centre, Saskatoon SK
USS Constitution Museum, Boston MA
Van Cortlandt House Museum, Bronx NY
Vermilion County Museum Society, Danville IL
Vesterheim Norwegian-American Museum, Decorah IA
Victoria Mansion - Morse Libby House, Portland ME
The Walker African American Museum & Research Center, Las Vegas NV
Warner House Association, MacPheadris-Warner House, Portsmouth NH
Washington & Lee University, Lee Chapel & Museum, Lexington VA
Waterville Historical Society, Redington Museum, Waterville ME
Waterworks Visual Arts Center, Salisbury NC
Wedell-Williams Memorial Aviation Museum, Patterson LA
Western Reserve Historical Society, Cleveland OH
Westfries Museum, Hoorn
Whalers Village Museum, Lahaina HI
Whatcom Museum, Bellingham WA
Wheelwright Museum of the American Indian, Santa Fe NM
White House, Washington DC
Wilfrid Laurier University, Robert Langen Art Gallery, Waterloo ON
Willard House & Clock Museum, Inc, North Grafton MA
Witte Museum, San Antonio TX
Woodlawn/The Pope-Leighey, Alexandria VA
Woodrow Wilson, Staunton VA
Woodrow Wilson, Washington DC
Workman & Temple Family Homestead Museum, City of Industry CA
Wornall Majors House Museums, The 1859 Jail, Marshal's Home & Museum, Independence MO
Wounded Knee Museum, Wall SD
Wyoming Trails Gallery, Wheatland WY
Yankton County Historical Society, Dakota Territorial Museum, Yankton SD

HISTORY OF ART & ARCHAEOLOGY

Arkkitehtuurimuseo, Museum of Finnish Architecture, Helsinki
Athenaeum of Philadelphia, Philadelphia PA
Baroda Museum and Picture Gallery, Vadodara
Carlsbad Museum & Art Center, Carlsbad NM

Delphi Archaeological Museum, Delphi
Fetherston Foundation, Packwood House Museum, Lewisburg PA
Hecht Museum, Haifa
Illinois State Museum, ISM Lockport Gallery, Chicago Gallery & Southern Illinois Art Gallery, Springfield IL
James Dick Foundation, Festival - Institute, Round Top TX
JMW Turner Museum, Sarasota FL
Johns Hopkins University, Evergreen Museum & Library, Baltimore MD
Jordan National Gallery of Fine Arts, Amman
Karakalpak State Art Museum, Nukus Republic of Karakalpakstan
Lalit Kala Akademi Rabindra Bhavan Art Galleries, National Academy of Art, New Delhi, New Delhi
Lusaka National Museum, Lusaka
Mezuraj Museum, Tirana
Mission San Luis Rey de Francia, Mission San Luis Rey Museum, Oceanside CA
Muzeul de Istorie Nationala Si Arheologie Constanta, National History & Archaeology Museum, Constanta
National Archaeological Museum, Athens
National Silk Art Museum, Weston MO
Nelson Mandela Metropolitan Art Museum, Port Elizabeth
San Antonio Museum of Art, San Antonio TX
Slovenska Narodna Galeria, Slovak National Gallery, Bratislava
Stone Quarry Hill Art Park, Winner Gallery, Cazenovia NY

ILLUSTRATION

Art Gallery of Nova Scotia, Halifax NS
Crocker Art Museum, Sacramento CA
Houston Museum of Decorative Arts, Chattanooga TN
JMW Turner Museum, Sarasota FL
Jordan National Gallery of Fine Arts, Amman
LACE (Los Angeles Contemporary Exhibitions), Los Angeles CA
Morris Museum of Art, Augusta GA
Moscow Museum of Modern Art, Moscow
Museo de Arte Contemporaneo de Castilla y Leon, Leon
National Baseball Hall of Fame & Museum, Cooperstown NY
National Museum of Ceramic Art, Baltimore MD
Slovenska Narodna Galeria, Slovak National Gallery, Bratislava
Suffolk University, Gallery, Boston MA
University of Nevada, Reno, Sheppard Contemporary & University Galleries, Reno NV

INTERIOR DESIGN

Arkkitehtuurimuseo, Museum of Finnish Architecture, Helsinki
Avant Gallery, Miami FL
Bangladesh National Museum, Dhaka
Baroda Museum and Picture Gallery, Vadodara
Crocker Art Museum, Sacramento CA
Designmuseum Danmark, Danish Design Museum, Copenhagen
James Dick Foundation, Festival - Institute, Round Top TX
Johns Hopkins University, Evergreen Museum & Library, Baltimore MD
The New York Public Library, The New York Public Library for the Performing Arts, New York NY
New York State Office of Parks, Recreation & Historic Preservation, Staatsburgh State Historic Site, Staatsburg NY
Slovenska Narodna Galeria, Slovak National Gallery, Bratislava
Stone Quarry Hill Art Park, Winner Gallery, Cazenovia NY
Suffolk University, Gallery, Boston MA
University of Minnesota, Goldstein Museum of Design, Saint Paul MN

INTERMEDIA

Stone Quarry Hill Art Park, Winner Gallery, Cazenovia NY

ISLAMIC ART

Academy of the New Church, Glencairn Museum, Bryn Athyn PA
African Art Museum of Maryland, Columbia MD
American University of Beirut Archaeological Museum, Beirut
Art Gallery of South Australia, Adelaide
Art Without Walls Inc, Sayville NY
Asian Art Museum of San Francisco, Chong-Moon Lee Ctr for Asian Art and Culture, San Francisco CA
Bangladesh National Museum, Dhaka
Baroda Museum and Picture Gallery, Vadodara
Byzantine & Christian Museum, Athens, Athens
The Children's Museum of Indianapolis, Indianapolis IN
Children's Museum of Manhattan, New York NY
Cincinnati Art Museum, Cincinnati Art Museum, Cincinnati OH
College of William & Mary, Muscarelle Museum of Art, Williamsburg VA
The Courtauld Institute of Art, The Courtauld Gallery, London
Craft and Folk Art Museum (CAFAM), Los Angeles CA
Crocker Art Museum, Sacramento CA
Denver Art Museum, Denver CO
Detroit Institute of Arts, Detroit MI
Dickinson College, The Trout Gallery, Carlisle PA
Fairbanks Museum & Planetarium, Saint Johnsbury VT
Fetherston Foundation, Packwood House Museum, Lewisburg PA
Florence County Museum, Florence SC
Florida State University and Central Florida Community College, The Appleton Museum of Art, Ocala FL
Forest Lawn Museum, Glendale CA
Harvard University, Semitic Museum, Cambridge MA
Honolulu Museum of Art, Honolulu HI
Intermedia Arts, Minneapolis MN
The Israel Museum, Jerusalem, Jerusalem
Johns Hopkins University, Evergreen Museum & Library, Baltimore MD
Jordan National Gallery of Fine Arts, Amman
Kenosha Public Museums, Kenosha WI
Lahore Museum, Lahore
Los Angeles County Museum of Art, Los Angeles CA
Louise Hopkins Underwood Center for the Arts, Lubbock TX
Loyola University Chicago, Loyola University Museum of Art, Chicago IL
Mobile Museum of Art, Mobile AL
Musee des Beaux-Arts de Tours, Museum of Fine Arts, Tours
Musees Royaux d'Art et d'Histoire, Royal Museums of Art and History, Brussels
Museum fur Angewandte Kunst Frankfurt, Museum of Applied Arts, Frankfurt
Museum of Fine Arts, Houston, Houston TX
Museum of Islamic Art, Doha
Muzeul de Istorie Nationala Si Arheologie Constanta, National History & Archaeology Museum, Constanta
Muzeul National de Arta al Romaniei, National Museum of Art of Romania, Bucharest
National Museum of the Philippines, Manila
National Museums Scotland, National Museum of Scotland, Edinburgh
Norwich Free Academy, Slater Memorial Museum, Norwich CT
Panhandle-Plains Historical Museum, Canyon TX
Queens College, City University of New York, Godwin-Ternbach Museum, Flushing NY
Reading Public Museum, Reading PA
San Antonio Museum of Art, San Antonio TX
Sheldon Art Galleries, Saint Louis MO
Staatliche Museen zu Berlin Stiftung Preussischer Kulturbesitz, National Museums in Berlin, Prussian Cultural Heritage Foundation, Berlin
Stanford University, Cantor Arts Center at Stanford University, Stanford CA
The State Museum of Fine Arts of Tatarstan Republic, Kazan
The State Museum of Oriental Art, Moscow
State University of New York at New Paltz, Samuel Dorsky Museum of Art, New Paltz NY
Stone Quarry Hill Art Park, Winner Gallery, Cazenovia NY
Suomen Kansallismuseo, National Museum of Finland, Helsinki
Tver Regional Art Gallery, Tver
University of California, Berkeley, Phoebe Apperson Hearst Museum of Anthropology, Berkeley CA
University of Illinois at Urbana-Champaign, Krannert Art Museum and Kinkead Pavilion, Champaign IL
The University of Kentucky Art Museum, Lexington KY
University of Victoria, The Legacy Art Gallery, Victoria BC
University of Wisconsin-Madison, Chazen Museum of Art, Madison WI
Virginia Museum of Fine Arts, Richmond VA
Walters Art Museum, Baltimore MD

IVORY

Academy of the New Church, Glencairn Museum, Bryn Athyn PA
African Art Museum of Maryland, Columbia MD
Alaska Department of Education, Division of Libraries, Archives & Museums, Sheldon Jackson Museum, Sitka AK
Alaska Heritage Museum at Wells Fargo, Anchorage AK
Albany Institute of History & Art, Albany NY
American University of Beirut Archaeological Museum, Beirut
Amherst College, Mead Art Museum, Amherst MA
Anchorage Museum at Rasmuson Center, Anchorage AK
Archaeological Museum of Thessaloniki, Thessaloniki
Art Without Walls Inc, Sayville NY
Asian Art Museum of San Francisco, Chong-Moon Lee Ctr for Asian Art and Culture, San Francisco CA
Bangladesh National Museum, Dhaka
Baroda Museum and Picture Gallery, Vadodara
Bayerisches Nationalmuseum, Bavarian National Museum, Munich
Beloit College, Wright Museum of Art, Beloit WI
Billie Trimble Chandler, Texas State Museum of Asian Cultures, Corpus Christi TX
Blauvelt Demarest Foundation, Hiram Blauvelt Art Museum, Oradell NJ
Bob Jones University Museum & Gallery Inc, Greenville SC
Bowdoin College, Peary-MacMillan Arctic Museum, Brunswick ME
Brown University, Haffenreffer Museum of Anthropology, Providence RI
Canadian Museum of History, Gatineau QC
Chatham Historical Society, The Atwood House Museum, Chatham MA
The Children's Museum of Indianapolis, Indianapolis IN
The Columbus Museum, Columbus GA
Cyprus Museum, Nicosia
Dalnavert Museum, Winnipeg MB
Delphi Archaeological Museum, Delphi
Detroit Institute of Arts, Detroit MI
Elmhurst Art Museum, Elmhurst IL
Fairbanks Museum & Planetarium, Saint Johnsbury VT
Fetherston Foundation, Packwood House Museum, Lewisburg PA
Fine Arts Museums of San Francisco, Legion of Honor, San Francisco CA
Flint Institute of Arts, Flint MI
Florence County Museum, Florence SC
Florida State University and Central Florida Community College, The Appleton Museum of Art, Ocala FL
Forest Lawn Museum, Glendale CA
Galleria Nazionale dell'Umbria, Umbrian National Gallery, Perugia
Glanmore National Historic Site of Canada, Belleville ON
Glasgow University, The Hunterian, Glasgow
Grand Rapids Public Museum, Grand Rapids MI
Headley-Whitney Museum, Lexington KY
Hecht Museum, Haifa
Henry Sheldon Museum of Vermont History and Research Center, Middlebury VT
Hillwood Museum & Gardens Foundation, Hillwood Estate Museum & Gardens, Washington DC
Illinois State Museum, ISM Lockport Gallery, Chicago Gallery & Southern Illinois Art Gallery, Springfield IL
Jacksonville University, Alexander Brest Museum & Gallery, Jacksonville FL
Joslyn Art Museum, Omaha NE
Kenosha Public Museums, Kenosha WI
Keresztény Muzeum, Christian Museum, Esztergom

Kimbell Art Foundation, Kimbell Art Museum, Fort Worth TX
Kings County Historical Society & Museum, Hampton NB
Koshare Indian Museum, Inc, La Junta CO
Kunsthistorisches Museum Wien, Museum of Fine Arts, Vienna
Lalit Kala Akademi Rabindra Bhavan Art Galleries, National Academy of Art, New Delhi, New Delhi
Lightner Museum, Saint Augustine FL
Lizzadro Museum of Lapidary Art, Elmhurst IL
Loyola University Chicago, Loyola University Museum of Art, Chicago IL
Mabee-Gerrer Museum of Art, Shawnee OK
The Mariners' Museum, Newport News VA
Musee des Beaux-Arts d'Orleans, Museum of Fine Arts, Orleans
Musee des Beaux-Arts de Tours, Museum of Fine Arts, Tours
Musees Royaux d'Art et d'Histoire, Royal Museums of Art and History, Brussels
Museo di Palazzo Ducale, Ducale Palace Museum, Mantua
The Museum, Greenwood SC
The Museum of Arts & Sciences Inc, Daytona Beach FL
Museum of Vancouver, Vancouver BC
Museum zu Allerheiligen, Schaffhausen
Muzej za Umjetnost i Obrt, Museum of Arts & Crafts, Zagreb
Muzeul National de Arta al Romaniei, National Museum of Art of Romania, Bucharest
National Archaeological Museum, Athens
National Art Museum of Moldova, Chisinau
National Museum of the Philippines, Manila
National Museums Scotland, National Museum of Scotland, Edinburgh
National Palace Museum, Taipei
National Society of Colonial Dames of America in the State of Maryland, Mount Clare Museum House, Baltimore MD
Naval Historical Center, National Museum of the US Navy, Washington DC
The Nelson-Atkins Museum of Art, Kansas City MO
Norwich Free Academy, Slater Memorial Museum, Norwich CT
Old Dartmouth Historical Society, New Bedford Whaling Museum, New Bedford MA
Omniplex Science Museum, Oklahoma City OK
Panhandle-Plains Historical Museum, Canyon TX
Peabody Essex Museum, Salem MA
Queens College, City University of New York, Godwin-Ternbach Museum, Flushing NY
Rahr-West Art Museum, Manitowoc WI
Reading Public Museum, Reading PA
Rensselaer County Historical Society, Hart-Cluett Mansion, 1827, Troy NY
Ryerss Victorian Museum & Library, Philadelphia PA
Saint Bonaventure University, Regina A Quick Center for the Arts, Saint Bonaventure NY
Saint John's University, Dr. M.T. Geoffrey Yeh Art Gallery, Queens NY
San Antonio Museum of Art, San Antonio TX
San Francisco Maritime National Historical Park, Maritime Museum, San Francisco CA
Santa Clara University, de Saisset Museum, Santa Clara CA
Sheldon Museum & Cultural Center, Inc, Sheldon Museum & Cultural Center, Haines AK
The Society of the Cincinnati at Anderson House, Washington DC
The Speed Art Museum, Louisville KY
Staten Island Museum, Staten Island NY
Suan Pakkad Palace Museum, Bangkok
Suomen Kansallismuseo, National Museum of Finland, Helsinki
Taft Museum of Art, Cincinnati OH
Tokyo National Museum, Tokyo
Tver Regional Art Gallery, Tver
University of Illinois at Urbana-Champaign, Krannert Art Museum and Kinkead Pavilion, Champaign IL
The University of Kentucky Art Museum, Lexington KY
University of Michigan, Kelsey Museum of Archaeology, Ann Arbor MI
University of Richmond, University Museums, Richmond VA
University of Utah, Utah Museum of Fine Arts, Salt Lake City UT
University of Victoria, The Legacy Art Gallery, Victoria BC
University of Wisconsin-Madison, Chazen Museum of Art, Madison WI
Villa Terrace Decorative Arts Museum, Milwaukee WI
The Walker African American Museum & Research Center, Las Vegas NV
Walker Art Gallery, Liverpool
The Wallace Collection, London
Walters Art Museum, Baltimore MD
Warther Museum Inc, Dover OH
Wheaton College, Beard and Weil Galleries, Norton MA
World Erotic Art Museum, Miami Beach FL

JADE

Alaska Heritage Museum at Wells Fargo, Anchorage AK
Allentown Art Museum, Allentown PA
Amherst College, Mead Art Museum, Amherst MA
Art Without Walls Inc, Sayville NY
Asian Art Museum of San Francisco, Chong-Moon Lee Ctr for Asian Art and Culture, San Francisco CA
Bangladesh National Museum, Dhaka
Baroda Museum and Picture Gallery, Vadodara
Beloit College, Wright Museum of Art, Beloit WI
Billie Trimble Chandler, Texas State Museum of Asian Cultures, Corpus Christi TX
Birger Sandzen Memorial Gallery, Lindsborg KS
Birmingham Museum of Art, Birmingham AL
Cape Ann Museum, Gloucester MA
Casa-Museu Medeiros e Almeida, Lisbon
The Children's Museum of Indianapolis, Indianapolis IN
College of William & Mary, Muscarelle Museum of Art, Williamsburg VA
The Columbus Museum, Columbus GA
Denver Art Museum, Denver CO
Detroit Institute of Arts, Detroit MI
Emory University, Michael C Carlos Museum, Atlanta GA
Erie Art Museum, Erie PA
Fetherston Foundation, Packwood House Museum, Lewisburg PA
Flint Institute of Arts, Flint MI
Florence County Museum, Florence SC
Florida State University and Central Florida Community College, The Appleton Museum of Art, Ocala FL
Forest Lawn Museum, Glendale CA
Glasgow University, The Hunterian, Glasgow
Headley-Whitney Museum, Lexington KY
Hermitage Museum & Gardens, Norfolk VA
Hillwood Museum & Gardens Foundation, Hillwood Estate Museum & Gardens, Washington DC
Honolulu Museum of Art, Honolulu HI
Iowa State University, Brunnier Art Museum, Ames IA
Jacksonville University, Alexander Brest Museum & Gallery, Jacksonville FL
Johns Hopkins University, Evergreen Museum & Library, Baltimore MD
Joslyn Art Museum, Omaha NE
Kenosha Public Museums, Kenosha WI
Kimbell Art Foundation, Kimbell Art Museum, Fort Worth TX
Lalit Kala Akademi Rabindra Bhavan Art Galleries, National Academy of Art, New Delhi, New Delhi
Lightner Museum, Saint Augustine FL
Lizzadro Museum of Lapidary Art, Elmhurst IL
Musees Royaux d'Art et d'Histoire, Royal Museums of Art and History, Brussels
Museo De Las Americas, Denver CO
The Museum of Arts & Sciences Inc, Daytona Beach FL
Museum of Vancouver, Vancouver BC
Museum zu Allerheiligen, Schaffhausen
Muzeul National de Arta al Romaniei, National Museum of Art of Romania, Bucharest
National Museums Scotland, National Museum of Scotland, Edinburgh
National Palace Museum, Taipei
Newfields, Indianapolis IN
Norwich Free Academy, Slater Memorial Museum, Norwich CT
Panhandle-Plains Historical Museum, Canyon TX
Plumas County Museum, Quincy CA
Queens College, City University of New York, Godwin-Ternbach Museum, Flushing NY
Reading Public Museum, Reading PA
Saint Bonaventure University, Regina A Quick Center for the Arts, Saint Bonaventure NY
Saint John's University, Dr. M.T. Geoffrey Yeh Art Gallery, Queens NY
San Antonio Museum of Art, San Antonio TX
The San Joaquin Pioneer & Historical Society, The Haggin Museum, Stockton CA
Santa Barbara Museum of Art, Santa Barbara CA
Seattle Art Museum, Seattle WA
Shanghai Museum, Shanghai
The Society of the Cincinnati at Anderson House, Washington DC
The Speed Art Museum, Louisville KY
Staten Island Museum, Staten Island NY
Suan Pakkad Palace Museum, Bangkok
Suomen Kansallismuseo, National Museum of Finland, Helsinki
Taft Museum of Art, Cincinnati OH
Tokyo National Museum, Tokyo
University of California, Berkeley, Phoebe Apperson Hearst Museum of Anthropology, Berkeley CA
University of Illinois at Urbana-Champaign, Krannert Art Museum and Kinkead Pavilion, Champaign IL
The University of Kentucky Art Museum, Lexington KY
University of Miami, Lowe Art Museum, Coral Gables FL
University of Utah, Utah Museum of Fine Arts, Salt Lake City UT
University of Wisconsin-Madison, Chazen Museum of Art, Madison WI
Vassar College, The Frances Lehman Loeb Art Center, Poughkeepsie NY
Villa Terrace Decorative Arts Museum, Milwaukee WI
Virginia Museum of Fine Arts, Richmond VA
Walker Fine Art, Denver CO
Washington County Museum of Fine Arts, Hagerstown MD
Worcester Art Museum, Worcester MA
World Erotic Art Museum, Miami Beach FL
Wyoming Trails Gallery, Wheatland WY

JEWELRY

A.E. Backus Museum & Gallery, Fort Pierce FL
Academy of the New Church, Glencairn Museum, Bryn Athyn PA
African Art Museum of Maryland, Columbia MD
Al Ain National Museum, Al Ain
Albany Institute of History & Art, Albany NY
Albany Museum of Art, Albany GA
Alberta College of Art & Design, Illingworth Kerr Gallery, Calgary AB
Albuquerque Museum of Art & History, Albuquerque NM
Allentown Art Museum, Allentown PA
American University of Beirut Archaeological Museum, Beirut
Amherst College, Mead Art Museum, Amherst MA
Archaeological Museum of Thessaloniki, Thessaloniki
Arkansas Arts Center, Little Rock AR
Arnold Mikelson Mind & Matter Art Gallery, Surrey BC
The Art Center of Waco, Waco TX
Art Gallery of Bancroft Inc, Bancroft ON
Art Gallery of South Australia, Adelaide
Art Without Walls Inc, Sayville NY
ArtsQuest, Bethlehem PA
Asian Art Museum of San Francisco, Chong-Moon Lee Ctr for Asian Art and Culture, San Francisco CA
Bainbridge Arts & Crafts Gallery, Bainbridge Island WA
Baldwin Historical Society Museum, Baldwin NY
The Baltimore Museum of Art, Baltimore MD
Balzekas Museum of Lithuanian Culture, Chicago IL
Bangladesh National Museum, Dhaka
Barker Character, Comic and Cartoon Museum, Cheshire CT
Baroda Museum and Picture Gallery, Vadodara
Bayerische Staatsgemaldesammlungen, Bavarian State Painting Collections, Munich
Bayerisches Nationalmuseum, Bavarian National Museum, Munich
Bellevue Arts Museum, Bellevue WA
Beloit College, Wright Museum of Art, Beloit WI
Berkshire Museum, Pittsfield MA
Billie Trimble Chandler, Texas State Museum of Asian Cultures, Corpus Christi TX
Buffalo Niagara Heritage Village, Amherst NY
Burchfield Penney Art Center, Buffalo NY

Byzantine & Christian Museum, Athens, Athens
Canadian Museum of History, Gatineau QC
Casa-Museu Medeiros e Almeida, Lisbon
The Children's Museum of Indianapolis, Indianapolis IN
City of Atlanta, Chastain Arts Center & Gallery, Atlanta GA
City of Fremont, Olive Hyde Art Gallery, Fremont CA
College of William & Mary, Muscarelle Museum of Art, Williamsburg VA
The Columbus Museum, Columbus GA
Contemporary Calgary, Calgary AB
Craft and Folk Art Museum (CAFAM), Los Angeles CA
Cripple Creek District Museum, Cripple Creek CO
Crocker Art Museum, Sacramento CA
Crook County Museum & Art Gallery, Sundance WY
Crow Wing County Historical Society, Brainerd MN
Cyprus Museum, Nicosia
Dalnavert Museum, Winnipeg MB
DAR Museum, National Society Daughters of the American Revolution, Washington DC
Deines Cultural Center, Russell KS
Delphi Archaeological Museum, Delphi
Denver Art Museum, Denver CO
Detroit Institute of Arts, Detroit MI
Doncaster Museum and Art Gallery, Doncaster Yorks
Dublin Arts Council, Dublin OH
Eiteljorg Museum of American Indians & Western Art, Indianapolis IN
Ellen Noel Art Museum of the Permian Basin, Odessa TX
Emory University, Michael C Carlos Museum, Atlanta GA
Environment Canada - Parks Canada, Laurier House, National Historic Site, Ottawa ON
Erie County Historical Society, Erie PA
Evanston Historical Society, Charles Gates Dawes House, Evanston IL
Favell Museum of Western Art & Indian Artifacts, Klamath Falls OR
Fetherston Foundation, Packwood House Museum, Lewisburg PA
Fine Arts Center for the New River Valley, Pulaski VA
Fireweed Gallery, Homer AK
Fishkill Historical Society, Van Wyck Homestead Museum, Fishkill NY
Fitton Center for Creative Arts, Hamilton OH
Florence County Museum, Florence SC
Florida CraftArt, Saint Petersburg FL
Florida Department of Environmental Protection, Stephen Foster Folk Culture Center State Park, White Springs FL
Forest Lawn Museum, Glendale CA
Fuller Craft Museum, Brockton MA
Fulton County Historical Society Inc, Fulton County Museum (Tetzlaff Reference Room), Rochester IN
Galleria Nazionale dell'Umbria, Umbrian National Gallery, Perugia
Gallery One Visual Arts Center, Ellensburg WA
Glanmore National Historic Site of Canada, Belleville ON
Haystack Mountain School of Crafts, Deer Isle ME
Headley-Whitney Museum, Lexington KY
Heard Museum, Phoenix AZ
Hebrew Union College, Skirball Cultural Center, Los Angeles CA
Hecht Museum, Haifa
Henry County Museum & Cultural Arts Center, Clinton MO
Henry Sheldon Museum of Vermont History and Research Center, Middlebury VT
Heritage Center, Inc, Pine Ridge SD
Hillwood Museum & Gardens Foundation, Hillwood Estate Museum & Gardens, Washington DC
Holter Museum of Art, Helena MT
Hot Shops Art Center, Omaha NE
Hui No'eau Visual Arts Center, Gallery and Gift Shop, Makawao Maui HI
Imperial Calcasieu Museum, Gibson-Barham Gallery, Lake Charles LA
The Interchurch Center, Galleries at the Interchurch Center, New York NY
Iroquois Indian Museum, Howes Cave NY
The Israel Museum, Jerusalem, Jerusalem
James Dick Foundation, Festival - Institute, Round Top TX
James Monroe Museum, Fredericksburg VA
Kelly-Griggs House Museum, Red Bluff CA
Kenosha Public Museums, Kenosha WI
Kentucky Museum of Art and Craft, Louisville KY
Kereszteny Muzeum, Christian Museum, Esztergom
Keystone Gallery, Scott City KS
Kimbell Art Foundation, Kimbell Art Museum, Fort Worth TX
Kings County Historical Society & Museum, Hampton NB
Klein Museum, Mobridge SD
Koochiching Museums, International Falls MN
Koshare Indian Museum, Inc, La Junta CO
Kunsthistorisches Museum Wien, Museum of Fine Arts, Vienna
Lac du Flambeau Band of Lake Superior Chippewa Indians, George W Brown Jr Ojibwe Museum & Cultural Center, Lac Du Flambeau WI
Latino Art Museum, Pomona CA
Latino Center of Art and Culture, Sacramento CA
League of New Hampshire Craftsmen, Grodin Permanent Collection Museum, Concord NH
Lillian & Coleman Taube Museum of Art, Minot ND
The Loading Dock Gallery, Lowell MA
The Long Island Museum of American Art, History & Carriages, Stony Brook NY
Louise Hopkins Underwood Center for the Arts, Lubbock TX
Louisiana Department of Culture, Recreation & Tourism, Louisiana State Museum, New Orleans LA
Loveland Museum/Gallery, Loveland CO
Madison & Main Gallery, Greeley CO
Marblehead Museum & Historical Society, Marblehead MA
Marblehead Museum & Historical Society, Jeremiah Lee Mansion, Marblehead MA
Maricopa County Historical Society, Desert Caballeros Western Museum, Wickenburg AZ
Maude Kerns Art Center, Eugene OR
McCord Museum of Canadian History, Montreal QC
McDowell House & Apothecary Shop, Danville KY
McLean County Historical Society, McLean County Museum of History, Bloomington IL
Meredith College, Frankie G Weems Gallery & Rotunda Gallery, Raleigh NC
Mesa Arts Center, Mesa Contemporary Arts Museum, Mesa AZ
The Mexican Museum, San Francisco CA
Mezuraj Museum, Tirana
Millicent Rogers Museum, Taos NM
The Mint Museum, Mint Museum of Craft & Design, Charlotte NC
Mississippi River Museum at Mud-Island River Park, Memphis TN
Missoula Art Museum, Missoula MT
Mobile Museum of Art, Mobile AL
Montana State University, Helen E Copeland Gallery, Bozeman MT
Moravska Galerie v Brne, Moravian Gallery in Brno, Brno
MTG Hawkes Bay, Napier
Musee Cognacq-Jay, Cognacq-Jay Museum, Paris
Musee des Beaux-Arts de Tours, Museum of Fine Arts, Tours
Musees Royaux d'Art et d'Histoire, Royal Museums of Art and History, Brussels
Museo De Las Americas, Denver CO
Museo Del Romanticismo, Museum of the Romantic Period, Madrid
Museu Nacional D'Art De Catalunya, Catalona National Museum of Art, Barcelona
Museum fur Angewandte Kunst Frankfurt, Museum of Applied Arts, Frankfurt
Museum of Art - Deland FL, Inc, Deland FL
Museum of Arts & Design, New York NY
The Museum of Arts & Sciences Inc, Daytona Beach FL
Museum of Contemporary Art, North Miami FL
Museum of Northern Arizona, Flagstaff AZ
Museum of Northern British Columbia, Ruth Harvey Art Gallery, Prince Rupert BC
Museum of Northwest Art, La Conner WA
Museum of Vancouver, Vancouver BC
Museum zu Allerheiligen, Schaffhausen
Muzej za Umjetnost i Obrt, Museum of Arts & Crafts, Zagreb
Muzeul de Istorie Nationala Si Arheologie Constanta, National History & Archaeology Museum, Constanta
Muzeul National de Arta al Romaniei, National Museum of Art of Romania, Bucharest
Muzeum Narodowe w Poznaniu, National Museum in Poznan, Poznan
National Archaeological Museum, Athens
National Baseball Hall of Fame & Museum, Cooperstown NY
The National Museum of Western Art, Tokyo
National Museum of Women in the Arts, Washington DC
National Museums Scotland, National Museum of Scotland, Edinburgh
National Palace Museum, Taipei
National Society of Colonial Dames of America in the State of Maryland, Mount Clare Museum House, Baltimore MD
Nebraska Game and Parks Commission, Arbor Lodge State Historical Park & Morton Mansion, Nebraska City NE
Nelson Mandela Metropolitan Art Museum, Port Elizabeth
The Nelson-Atkins Museum of Art, Kansas City MO
Neue Galerie New York, New York NY
New Britain Museum of American Art, New Britain CT
New Brunswick Museum, Saint John NB
North End Gallery, Leonardtown MD
Norwich Free Academy, Slater Memorial Museum, Norwich CT
Nova Scotia College of Art and Design, Anna Leonowens Gallery, Halifax NS
The Ohio Historical Society, Inc, Campus Martius Museum & Ohio River Museum, Marietta OH
Ohio University, Kennedy Museum of Art, Athens OH
Okanagan Heritage Museum, Kelowna BC
Ouachita River Art Gallery, Monroe LA
Pacific Island Ethnic Art Museum, Long Beach CA
Page-Walker Arts & History Center, Cary NC
Panhandle-Plains Historical Museum, Canyon TX
Plainsman Museum, Aurora NE
Pocatello Art Center, Pocatello ID
Port Huron Museum, Port Huron MI
Queens College, City University of New York, Godwin-Ternbach Museum, Flushing NY
Randall Junior Museum, San Francisco CA
Reading Public Museum, Reading PA
Rensselaer County Historical Society, Hart-Cluett Mansion, 1827, Troy NY
Rhode Island Historical Society, John Brown House, Providence RI
Royal Alberta Museum, Royal Alberta Museum, Edmonton AB
Royal Arts Foundation, Belcourt Castle, Newport RI
Ryerss Victorian Museum & Library, Philadelphia PA
Saint Anselm College, Alva de Mars Megan Chapel Art Center, Manchester NH
San Antonio Museum of Art, San Antonio TX
Seneca-Iroquois National Museum, Salamanca NY
Slovenska Narodna Galeria, Slovak National Gallery, Bratislava
Society for Contemporary Craft, Pittsburgh PA
The Society of the Cincinnati at Anderson House, Washington DC
South Carolina Artisans Center, Walterboro SC
South Dakota State University, South Dakota Art Museum, Brookings SD
The Speed Art Museum, Louisville KY
Spertus Institute of Jewish Studies, Chicago IL
Staatliche Museen zu Berlin Stiftung Preussischer Kulturbesitz, National Museums in Berlin, Prussian Cultural Heritage Foundation, Berlin
Stanford University, Cantor Arts Center at Stanford University, Stanford CA
Staten Island Museum, Staten Island NY
Ste Genevieve Museum, Sainte Genevieve MO
Suan Pakkad Palace Museum, Bangkok
Suomen Kansallismuseo, National Museum of Finland, Helsinki
Swedish American Museum, Chicago IL
Tacoma Art Museum, Tacoma WA
Taft Museum of Art, Cincinnati OH
Tohono Chul Park, Tucson AZ
Tokyo National Museum, Tokyo
Topeka & Shawnee County Public Library, Alice C Sabatini Gallery, Topeka KS
Tubman African American Museum, Macon GA
Tver Regional Art Gallery, Tver
The Ukrainian Museum, New York NY
University of Georgia, Georgia Museum of Art, Athens GA
University of Illinois at Urbana-Champaign, Krannert Art Museum and Kinkead Pavilion, Champaign IL

The University of Kentucky Art Museum, Lexington KY
University of North Dakota, Hughes Fine Arts Center-Col Eugene Myers Art Gallery, Grand Forks ND
University of Saskatchewan, Diefenbaker Canada Centre, Saskatoon SK
University of Utah, Utah Museum of Fine Arts, Salt Lake City UT
University of Victoria, The Legacy Art Gallery, Victoria BC
University of Wisconsin-Madison, Chazen Museum of Art, Madison WI
USS Constitution Museum, Boston MA
The Valentine, Richmond VA
Valley Art Gallery, Forest Grove OR
Vassar College, The Frances Lehman Loeb Art Center, Poughkeepsie NY
Venice Art Center, Venice FL
Vesterheim Norwegian-American Museum, Decorah IA
Virginia Museum of Fine Arts, Richmond VA
Volcano Art Center Gallery, Hawaii Volcanoes National Park HI
Wadsworth Atheneum Museum of Art, Hartford CT
The Walker African American Museum & Research Center, Las Vegas NV
Walters Art Museum, Baltimore MD
Waterworks Visual Arts Center, Salisbury NC
Wheelwright Museum of the American Indian, Santa Fe NM
Wilkes Art Gallery, North Wilkesboro NC
Willard House & Clock Museum, Inc, North Grafton MA
Wiregrass Museum of Art, Dothan AL
Wisconsin Historical Society, Wisconsin Historical Museum, Madison WI
Woodlawn/The Pope-Leighey, Alexandria VA
World Erotic Art Museum, Miami Beach FL
Wyoming Trails Gallery, Wheatland WY

JUDAICA

Arnot Art Museum, Elmira NY
Art Without Walls Inc, Sayville NY
Arts Council of Fayetteville-Cumberland County, The Arts Center, Fayetteville NC
B'nai B'rith International, B'nai B'rith Klutznick National Jewish Museum, Washington DC
Barbara & Ray Alpert Jewish Community Center, Pauline & Zena Gatov Gallery, Long Beach CA
Baycrest Centre for Geriatric Care, The Morris & Sally Justein of Baycrest Heritage Museum, Toronto ON
The Children's Museum of Indianapolis, Indianapolis IN
Congregation Beth Israel's Plotkin Judaica Museum, Scottsdale AZ
Craft and Folk Art Museum (CAFAM), Los Angeles CA
Denver Art Museum, Denver CO
Detroit Institute of Arts, Detroit MI
Florence County Museum, Florence SC
General Board of Discipleship, The United Methodist Church, The Upper Room Chapel & Museum, Nashville TN
Hebrew Union College, Skirball Cultural Center, Los Angeles CA
Hebrew Union College - Jewish Institute of Religion, Skirball Museum Cincinnati, Cincinnati OH
Hebrew Union College - Jewish Institute of Religion Museum, Jewish Institute of Religion, New York NY
Hecht Museum, Haifa
Hillel Foundation, Hillel Jewish Student Center Gallery, Cincinnati OH
Hillwood Museum & Gardens Foundation, Hillwood Estate Museum & Gardens, Washington DC
The Israel Museum, Jerusalem, Jerusalem
The Jewish Museum, New York NY
Lightner Museum, Saint Augustine FL
Longue Vue House & Gardens, New Orleans LA
Muzej za Umjetnost i Obrt, Museum of Arts & Crafts, Zagreb
Muzeul National de Arta al Romaniei, National Museum of Art of Romania, Bucharest
National Baseball Hall of Fame & Museum, Cooperstown NY
New Brunswick Museum, Saint John NB
Norwich Free Academy, Slater Memorial Museum, Norwich CT
Reading Public Museum, Reading PA
The Rosenbach Museum & Library, Philadelphia PA
San Antonio Museum of Art, San Antonio TX
The Sherwin Miller Museum of Jewish Art, Tulsa OK
Spertus Institute of Jewish Studies, Chicago IL
Stanford University, Cantor Arts Center at Stanford University, Stanford CA
Suomen Kansallismuseo, National Museum of Finland, Helsinki
Tver Regional Art Gallery, Tver
University of Illinois at Urbana-Champaign, Spurlock Museum, Urbana IL
Waterworks Visual Arts Center, Salisbury NC
World Erotic Art Museum, Miami Beach FL
Yeshiva University Museum, New York NY
Zidovske Muzeum v Praze, Jewish Museum in Prague, Prague

JUVENILE ART

The Art Center of Waco, Waco TX
Art Community Center, Art Center of Corpus Christi, Corpus Christi TX
Art Without Walls Inc, Sayville NY
Arts Council of Fayetteville-Cumberland County, The Arts Center, Fayetteville NC
Canadian Museum of History, Gatineau QC
Cartoon Art Museum, San Francisco CA
The Children's Museum of Indianapolis, Indianapolis IN
Children's Museum of Manhattan, New York NY
Contemporary Calgary, Calgary AB
Deines Cultural Center, Russell KS
Ellen Noel Art Museum of the Permian Basin, Odessa TX
Elmhurst Art Museum, Elmhurst IL
Erie Art Museum, Erie PA
Hebrew Union College, Skirball Cultural Center, Los Angeles CA
Hebrew Union College - Jewish Institute of Religion Museum, Jewish Institute of Religion, New York NY
Henry Sheldon Museum of Vermont History and Research Center, Middlebury VT
Kenosha Public Museums, Kenosha WI
Kentucky Museum of Art and Craft, Louisville KY
LaGrange Art Museum, LaGrange GA
Lillian & Coleman Taube Museum of Art, Minot ND
The Long Island Museum of American Art, History & Carriages, Stony Brook NY
Louise Hopkins Underwood Center for the Arts, Lubbock TX
Meredith College, Frankie G Weems Gallery & Rotunda Gallery, Raleigh NC
Montgomery Museum of Fine Arts, Montgomery AL
Musee Regional de lu Cote-Nord, Sept-Iles QC
Museum of Art - Deland FL, Inc, Deland FL
Museum of Northern Arizona, Flagstaff AZ
National Art Museum of Moldova, Chisinau
New Visions Gallery, Inc, Marshfield WI
Norwich Free Academy, Slater Memorial Museum, Norwich CT
Opelousas Museum of Art, Inc (OMA), Opelousas LA
Owensboro Museum of Fine Art, Owensboro KY
Polk Museum of Art, Lakeland FL
San Antonio Museum of Art, San Antonio TX
Sheldon Art Galleries, Saint Louis MO
South Carolina State Museum, Columbia SC
Southeastern Center for Contemporary Art, Winston-Salem NC
Spartanburg Art Museum, Spartanburg SC
Tohono Chul Park, Tucson AZ
University of Utah, Utah Museum of Fine Arts, Salt Lake City UT
The Walker African American Museum & Research Center, Las Vegas NV
Waterworks Visual Arts Center, Salisbury NC
Wiregrass Museum of Art, Dothan AL
Woodmere Art Museum Inc, Philadelphia PA
Yerba Buena Center for the Arts, San Francisco CA

LACES

Allentown Art Museum, Allentown PA
Alton Museum of History & Art, Inc, Alton IL
The Art Gallery of Cornwall, Cornwall ON
Art Gallery of South Australia, Adelaide
Art Without Walls Inc, Sayville NY
Artesia Historical Museum and Art Center, Artesia NM
Besser Museum for Northeast Michigan, Alpena MI
Brick Store Museum, Kennebunk ME
Brooklyn Historical Society, Brooklyn OH
Buffalo Niagara Heritage Village, Amherst NY
Canadian Museum of History, Gatineau QC
Carson County Square House Museum, Panhandle TX
Clark County Historical Society, Pioneer - Krier Museum, Ashland KS
Cripple Creek District Museum, Cripple Creek CO
Crook County Museum & Art Gallery, Sundance WY
Dalnavert Museum, Winnipeg MB
Danville Museum of Fine Arts & History, Danville VA
Designmuseum Danmark, Danish Design Museum, Copenhagen
Detroit Institute of Arts, Detroit MI
Doncaster Museum and Art Gallery, Doncaster Yorks
Evanston Historical Society, Charles Gates Dawes House, Evanston IL
Fine Arts Museums of San Francisco, Legion of Honor, San Francisco CA
Fishkill Historical Society, Van Wyck Homestead Museum, Fishkill NY
Flint Institute of Arts, Flint MI
Fuller Craft Museum, Brockton MA
Grand Rapids Public Museum, Grand Rapids MI
Hebrew Union College, Skirball Cultural Center, Los Angeles CA
Henry Morrison Flagler Museum, Palm Beach FL
Hillwood Museum & Gardens Foundation, Hillwood Estate Museum & Gardens, Washington DC
Historic Arkansas Museum, Little Rock AR
Illinois State Museum, ISM Lockport Gallery, Chicago Gallery & Southern Illinois Art Gallery, Springfield IL
Imperial Calcasieu Museum, Gibson-Barham Gallery, Lake Charles LA
Indiana Landmarks, Morris-Butler House, Indianapolis IN
James Dick Foundation, Festival - Institute, Round Top TX
Kelly-Griggs House Museum, Red Bluff CA
Kern County Museum, Bakersfield CA
Koochiching Museums, International Falls MN
Leelanau Historical Museum, Leland MI
Lightner Museum, Saint Augustine FL
The Long Island Museum of American Art, History & Carriages, Stony Brook NY
Longfellow-Evangeline State Commemorative Area, Saint Martinville LA
Loveland Museum/Gallery, Loveland CO
McCord Museum of Canadian History, Montreal QC
McLean County Historical Society, McLean County Museum of History, Bloomington IL
Mississippi River Museum at Mud-Island River Park, Memphis TN
Morris-Jumel Mansion, Inc, New York NY
Musees Royaux d'Art et d'Histoire, Royal Museums of Art and History, Brussels
The Museum, Greenwood SC
Museum of Arts & Design, New York NY
Muzej za Umjetnost i Obrt, Museum of Arts & Crafts, Zagreb
Muzeul National de Arta al Romaniei, National Museum of Art of Romania, Bucharest
National Art Museum of Moldova, Chisinau
National Society of Colonial Dames of America in the State of Maryland, Mount Clare Museum House, Baltimore MD
New Brunswick Museum, Saint John NB
Norwich Free Academy, Slater Memorial Museum, Norwich CT
Old Dartmouth Historical Society, New Bedford Whaling Museum, New Bedford MA
Plainsman Museum, Aurora NE
Portland Art Museum, Portland OR
Preservation Virginia, John Marshall House, Richmond VA
Queen Victoria Museum and Art Gallery, Launceston TAS
Rensselaer County Historical Society, Hart-Cluett Mansion, 1827, Troy NY
Saginaw Art Museum, Saginaw MI
San Antonio Museum of Art, San Antonio TX
Slater Mill, Old Slater Mill Association, Pawtucket RI
The Speed Art Museum, Louisville KY
Staatliche Museen zu Berlin Stiftung Preussischer Kulturbesitz, National Museums in Berlin, Prussian Cultural Heritage Foundation, Berlin
The State Museum of Fine Arts of Tatarstan Republic, Kazan

Staten Island Museum, Staten Island NY
Ste Genevieve Museum, Sainte Genevieve MO
Suomen Kansallismuseo, National Museum of Finland, Helsinki
Textile Museum of Canada, Toronto ON
Tohono Chul Park, Tucson AZ
Tokyo National Museum, Tokyo
Tver Regional Art Gallery, Tver
University of Georgia, Georgia Museum of Art, Athens GA
University of Minnesota, Goldstein Museum of Design, Saint Paul MN
The Valentine, Richmond VA
Vesterheim Norwegian-American Museum, Decorah IA
Wadsworth Atheneum Museum of Art, Hartford CT
Washington County Museum of Fine Arts, Hagerstown MD
Wheaton College, Beard and Weil Galleries, Norton MA
Witte Museum, San Antonio TX
Woodmere Art Museum Inc, Philadelphia PA

LANDSCAPE ARCHITECTURE

Arkkitehtuurimuseo, Museum of Finnish Architecture, Helsinki
Athenaeum of Philadelphia, Philadelphia PA
Chateau de Versailles, Palace of Versailles, Versailles
Crocker Art Museum, Sacramento CA
Germantown Historical Society, Philadelphia PA
James Dick Foundation, Festival - Institute, Round Top TX
JMW Turner Museum, Sarasota FL
Johns Hopkins University, Evergreen Museum & Library, Baltimore MD
Jordan National Gallery of Fine Arts, Amman
Lalit Kala Akademi Rabindra Bhavan Art Galleries, National Academy of Art, New Delhi, New Delhi
Laumeier Sculpture Park, Saint Louis MO
Morris Museum of Art, Augusta GA
Nevada Museum of Art, Reno NV
New Canaan Historical Society, New Canaan CT
New York State Office of Parks, Recreation & Historic Preservation, Staatsburgh State Historic Site, Staatsburg NY
Patrick Henry, Red Hill National Memorial, Brookneal VA
Slovenska Narodna Galeria, Slovak National Gallery, Bratislava
St Mary's College of Maryland, The Dwight Frederick Boyden Gallery, St Mary's City MD
Stone Quarry Hill Art Park, Winner Gallery, Cazenovia NY
Suffolk University, Gallery, Boston MA
Villa Terrace Decorative Arts Museum, Milwaukee WI
Wilkes Art Gallery, North Wilkesboro NC

LANDSCAPES

A.E. Backus Museum & Gallery, Fort Pierce FL
Academy Art Museum, Easton MD
Academy of the New Church, Glencairn Museum, Bryn Athyn PA
Alaska State Museum, Juneau AK
Albany Institute of History & Art, Albany NY
The Albrecht-Kemper Museum of Art, Saint Joseph MO
Albuquerque Museum of Art & History, Albuquerque NM
Allentown Art Museum, Allentown PA
Alton Museum of History & Art, Inc, Alton IL
American Folk Art Museum, New York NY
Amherst College, Mead Art Museum, Amherst MA
Amon Carter Museum of American Art, Fort Worth TX
Anchorage Museum at Rasmuson Center, Anchorage AK
Appaloosa Museum and Heritage Center, Moscow ID
Arkkitehtuurimuseo, Museum of Finnish Architecture, Helsinki
Arnold Mikelson Mind & Matter Art Gallery, Surrey BC
Arnot Art Museum, Elmira NY
Art and History Museums - Maitland, Maitland FL
The Art Center of Waco, Waco TX
Art Community Center, Art Center of Corpus Christi, Corpus Christi TX
Art Gallery of Nova Scotia, Halifax NS
Art Museum of Southeast Texas, Beaumont TX
Art Without Walls Inc, Sayville NY
Artesia Historical Museum and Art Center, Artesia NM
Arts Council of Fayetteville-Cumberland County, The Arts Center, Fayetteville NC
Baroda Museum and Picture Gallery, Vadodara
Baton Rouge Gallery, Center For Contemporary Art, Baton Rouge LA
Bay County Historical Society, Historical Museum of Bay County, Bay City MI
Belger Arts Center, Kansas City MO
Bennington Museum, Bennington VT
Berkshire Museum, Pittsfield MA
Besser Museum for Northeast Michigan, Alpena MI
Birmingham Museum of Art, Birmingham AL
Blowing Rock Art and History Museum, Blowing Rock NC
Bone Creek Museum of Agrarian Art, David City NE
Booth Western Art Museum, Cartersville GA
Brick Store Museum, Kennebunk ME
Brickton Art Center, Park Ridge IL
Brooklyn Botanic Garden, Steinhardt Conservatory Gallery, Brooklyn NY
Bruce Museum, Inc, Greenwich CT
Bryan Memorial Gallery, Cambridge VT
Bucknell University, Edward & Marthann Samek Art Gallery, Lewisburg PA
Cahoon Museum of American Art, Cotuit MA
Cambridge Museum, Cambridge NE
Cameron Art Museum, Wilmington NC
Canadian Museum of History, Gatineau QC
Cape Ann Museum, Gloucester MA
Cayuga Museum of History & Art, Auburn NY
Cedar Rapids Museum of Art, Cedar Rapids IA
Centenary College of Louisiana, Meadows Museum of Art, Shreveport LA
Center for Art & Education, Van Buren AR
Central United Methodist Church, Swords Into Plowshares Peace Center & Gallery, Detroit MI
Chateau de Versailles, Palace of Versailles, Versailles
Chatham Historical Society, The Atwood House Museum, Chatham MA
Cincinnati Art Museum, Cincinnati Art Museum, Cincinnati OH
City of Cedar Falls, Iowa, James & Meryl Hearst Center for the Arts & Sculpture Garden, Cedar Falls IA
City of Fayette, Alabama, Fayette Art Museum, Fayette AL
City of Fremont, Olive Hyde Art Gallery, Fremont CA
City of Gainesville, Thomas Center Galleries - Cultural Affairs, Gainesville FL
City of Pittsfield Office of Cultural Development, Lichtenstein Center for the Arts, Pittsfield MA
Clark Art Institute, Williamstown MA
Colgate University, Picker Art Gallery, Hamilton NY
College of William & Mary, Muscarelle Museum of Art, Williamsburg VA
The Columbus Museum, Columbus GA
Columbus Museum of Art, Columbus OH
Concordia University, Leonard & Bina Ellen Art Gallery, Montreal QC
Contemporary Calgary, Calgary AB
The Courtauld Institute of Art, The Courtauld Gallery, London
Coutts Museum of Art, Inc, El Dorado KS
Crocker Art Museum, Sacramento CA
The Currier Museum of Art, Manchester NH
Dahesh Museum of Art, Greenwich CT
Danville Museum of Fine Arts & History, Danville VA
Dartmouth College, Hood Museum of Art, Hanover NH
Daum Museum of Contemporary Art, Sedalia MO
deCordova Sculpture Park & Museum, Lincoln MA
Deines Cultural Center, Russell KS
Delaware Art Museum, Wilmington DE
Delaware Historical Society, Read House and Gardens, New Castle DE
DeLeon White Gallery, Toronto ON
Delphi Archaeological Museum, Delphi
Denver Art Museum, Denver CO
Department of Economic & Community Development, State of Connecticut DECD Eric Sloane Museum, Kent CT
Detroit Institute of Arts, Detroit MI
Dickinson College, The Trout Gallery, Carlisle PA
Dixie State University, Sears Art Museum Gallery, Saint George UT
Doncaster Museum and Art Gallery, Doncaster Yorks
Dublin Arts Council, Dublin OH
Durham Art Guild, Durham NC
Eastern Illinois University, Tarble Arts Center, Charleston IL
Eiteljorg Museum of American Indians & Western Art, Indianapolis IN
Ellen Noel Art Museum of the Permian Basin, Odessa TX
Environment Canada - Parks Canada, Laurier House, National Historic Site, Ottawa ON
Erie Art Museum, Erie PA
Essex Historical Society and Shipbuilding Museum, Essex MA
Evanston Historical Society, Charles Gates Dawes House, Evanston IL
Fetherston Foundation, Packwood House Museum, Lewisburg PA
Fine Arts Center for the New River Valley, Pulaski VA
Fisher Art Gallery, Marshalltown IA
Fitchburg Art Museum, Fitchburg MA
Fitton Center for Creative Arts, Hamilton OH
Flint Institute of Arts, Flint MI
Florence County Museum, Florence SC
Florida Southern College, Melvin Art Gallery, Lakeland FL
Florida State University and Central Florida Community College, The Appleton Museum of Art, Ocala FL
Fondazione Musei Civici Di Venezia, Museo Correr - Correr Museum, Venice
Forest Lawn Museum, Glendale CA
Fort Smith Regional Art Museum, Fort Smith AR
Fort Ticonderoga Association, Ticonderoga NY
Fruitlands Museum, Inc, Harvard MA
Gadsden Museum of Art, Gadsden AL
Galerie Montcalm, Gatineau QC
Gallery One Visual Arts Center, Ellensburg WA
George Eastman Museum, Rochester NY
George Phippen, Phippen Museum - Art of the American West, Prescott AZ
Germantown Historical Society, Philadelphia PA
Glanmore National Historic Site of Canada, Belleville ON
Greene County Historical Society, Bronck Museum, Coxsackie NY
Hebrew Union College, Skirball Cultural Center, Los Angeles CA
Hecht Museum, Haifa
The Heckscher Museum of Art, Huntington NY
Henry Sheldon Museum of Vermont History and Research Center, Middlebury VT
Heritage Center, Inc, Pine Ridge SD
Hermitage Museum & Gardens, Norfolk VA
Hickory Museum of Art, Inc, Hickory NC
Hill-Stead Museum, Farmington CT
Hillwood Museum & Gardens Foundation, Hillwood Estate Museum & Gardens, Washington DC
Historic Cherry Hill, Albany NY
Historic Holyoke at Wistariahurst & City of Holyoke, Holyoke MA
Historic Newton, Newton MA
Historical Society of Cheshire County, Keene NH
The History Center in Tompkins County, Ithaca NY
Holter Museum of Art, Helena MT
Honolulu Museum of Art, Honolulu HI
Hui No'eau Visual Arts Center, Gallery and Gift Shop, Makawao Maui HI
The Hyde Collection, Glens Falls NY
Illinois State Museum, ISM Lockport Gallery, Chicago Gallery & Southern Illinois Art Gallery, Springfield IL
Independence Historical Museum & Art Center, Independence KS
Independence Seaport Museum, Philadelphia PA
Indiana Landmarks, Morris-Butler House, Indianapolis IN
The Interchurch Center, Galleries at the Interchurch Center, New York NY
Intermedia Arts, Minneapolis MN
International Museum of Art, El Paso TX
Iredell Museums, Statesville NC
The Israel Museum, Jerusalem, Jerusalem
James Dick Foundation, Festival - Institute, Round Top TX
JMW Turner Museum, Sarasota FL
Johns Hopkins University, Evergreen Museum & Library, Baltimore MD
Jordan National Gallery of Fine Arts, Amman
Joslyn Art Museum, Omaha NE
Juniata College Museum of Art, Huntingdon PA
Kalamazoo Institute of Arts, Kalamazoo MI

Kenosha Public Museums, Kenosha WI
Kimbell Art Foundation, Kimbell Art Museum, Fort Worth TX
Kirkland Museum of Fine & Decorative Art, Denver CO
Knoxville Museum of Art, Knoxville TN
Koochiching Museums, International Falls MN
The Kreeger Museum, Washington DC
Kunstmuseum Solothurn, Solothurn Art Museum, Solothurn
Kyiv Museum of Russian Art, Kyiv Ukrainian
La Salle University Art Museum, Philadelphia PA
Lafayette College, Lafayette College Art Galleries, Easton PA
Lafayette Science Museum & Planetarium, Lafayette LA
Laguna Art Museum, Laguna Beach CA
Latino Art Museum, Pomona CA
Leigh Yawkey Woodson Art Museum, Wausau WI
Lighthouse ArtCenter Museum & School of Art, Tequesta FL
Lightner Museum, Saint Augustine FL
Lillian & Coleman Taube Museum of Art, Minot ND
Lincolnshire County Council, The Collection: Art & Archaeology in Lincolnshire, Lincoln
Livingston County Historical Society, Museum, Geneseo NY
The Long Island Museum of American Art, History & Carriages, Stony Brook NY
Longfellow-Evangeline State Commemorative Area, Saint Martinville LA
Longue Vue House & Gardens, New Orleans LA
Longview Museum of Fine Art, Longview TX
Louise Hopkins Underwood Center for the Arts, Lubbock TX
Louisiana Arts & Science Museum, Baton Rouge LA
Lyman Allyn Art Museum, New London CT
Lyme Historical Society, Florence Griswold Museum, Old Lyme CT
Mabee-Gerrer Museum of Art, Shawnee OK
Madison Museum of Fine Art, Madison GA
Maine Historical Society, Wadsworth-Longfellow House, Portland ME
Maricopa County Historical Society, Desert Caballeros Western Museum, Wickenburg AZ
Marquette University, Haggerty Museum of Art, Milwaukee WI
Maryland Art Place, Baltimore MD
Marylhurst University, The Art Gym, Marylhurst OR
Massillon Museum, Massillon OH
Maui Historical Society, Hale Hoike ike at the Bailey House, Wailuku HI
McCord Museum of Canadian History, Montreal QC
McPherson Museum and Arts Foundation, McPherson KS
Mennello Museum of American Art, Orlando FL
Meridian Museum of Art, Meridian MS
Mesa Arts Center, Mesa Contemporary Arts Museum, Mesa AZ
Miami-Dade College, MDC Museum of Art & Design, Miami FL
Midwest Museum of American Art, Elkhart IN
Miller Art Center Foundation Inc, Miller Art Museum, Sturgeon Bay WI
Minot State University, Northwest Art Center, Minot ND
Missoula Art Museum, Missoula MT
Mobile Museum of Art, Mobile AL
Modern Art Museum, Fort Worth TX
Moderna Galerija, Modern Gallery - National Museum of Modern Art, Zagreb
Montana State University, Helen E Copeland Gallery, Bozeman MT
Montclair Art Museum, Montclair NJ
Montgomery Museum of Fine Arts, Montgomery AL
Moravska Galerie v Brne, Moravian Gallery in Brno, Brno
Morris Museum of Art, Augusta GA
Mount Vernon Hotel Museum & Garden, New York NY
MTG Hawkes Bay, Napier
Muscatine Art Center, Muscatine IA
Musee des Beaux-Arts d'Orleans, Museum of Fine Arts, Orleans
Musee des Beaux-Arts de Tours, Museum of Fine Arts, Tours
Musee Regional de lu Cote-Nord, Sept-Iles QC
Museo di Palazzo Ducale, Ducale Palace Museum, Mantua
Museo Italo Americano, San Francisco CA
Museo Nacional de Bellas Artes, National Museum of Fine Arts, Santiago
Museu Nacional D'Art De Catalunya, Catalona National Museum of Art, Barcelona
Museum De Lakenhal, Leiden
Museum of Art & History, Santa Cruz, Santa Cruz CA
Museum of Art - Deland FL, Inc, Deland FL
The Museum of Arts & Sciences Inc, Daytona Beach FL
Museum of Contemporary Art, North Miami FL
Museum of Latin American Art, Long Beach CA
Museum of Northern Arizona, Flagstaff AZ
Museum of Northwest Art, La Conner WA
Museum of the Southwest, Midland TX
The Museum of Western Art, Kerrville TX
Muzej za Umjetnost i Obrt, Museum of Arts & Crafts, Zagreb
Muzeul National de Arta al Romaniei, National Museum of Art of Romania, Bucharest
Muzeum Narodowe W Kielcach, National Museum in Kielce, Kielce
Muzeum Narodowe w Poznaniu, National Museum in Poznan, Poznan
Narodna Galerija, National Gallery of Slovenia, Ljubljana
The National Art Center, Tokyo, Tokyo
National Art Museum of Moldova, Chisinau
National Gallery of Canada, Ottawa ON
National Museum & Art Gallery of Trinidad and Tobago, Port of Spain
The National Museum of Modern Art, Tokyo, Tokyo
National Museum of the Philippines, Manila
The National Museum of Western Art, Tokyo
National Museum of Wildlife Art of the Unites States, Jackson WY
National Museum of Women in the Arts, Washington DC
National Park Service, Weir Farm National Historic Site, Wilton CT
National Society of Colonial Dames of America in the State of Maryland, Mount Clare Museum House, Baltimore MD
National Trust for Historic Preservation, Shadows-on-the-Teche, New Iberia LA
National Trust for Historic Preservation, Chesterwood, Stockbridge MA
Nebraska Game and Parks Commission, Arbor Lodge State Historical Park & Morton Mansion, Nebraska City NE
Nelson Mandela Metropolitan Art Museum, Port Elizabeth
The Nelson-Atkins Museum of Art, Kansas City MO
Nevada Museum of Art, Reno NV
New Britain Museum of American Art, New Britain CT
New Brunswick Museum, Saint John NB
New Jersey Historical Society, Newark NJ
New York State Office of Parks, Recreation & Historic Preservation, Staatsburgh State Historic Site, Staatsburg NY
The Noble Maritime Collection, Staten Island NY
Norton Simon Museum, Pasadena CA
Norwich Free Academy, Slater Memorial Museum, Norwich CT
Noyes Art Gallery, Lincoln NE
Ogden Museum of Southern Art, University of New Orleans, New Orleans LA
The Ohio Historical Society, Inc, Campus Martius Museum & Ohio River Museum, Marietta OH
Ohio University, Kennedy Museum of Art, Athens OH
Oklahoma City Museum of Art, Oklahoma City OK
The Old Jail Art Center, Albany TX
Old Salem Museums & Gardens, Museum of Early Southern Decorative Arts, Winston-Salem NC
Opelousas Museum of Art, Inc (OMA), Opelousas LA
Osterreichische Galerie Belvedere Vienna, Belvedere Museum Vienna, Vienna
Owensboro Museum of Fine Art, Owensboro KY
Panhandle-Plains Historical Museum, Canyon TX
Pasadena Museum of California Art, Pasadena CA
Pasadena Museum of History, Pasadena CA
Pennsylvania Academy of the Fine Arts, Philadelphia PA
Philip Johnson Glass House, National Trust for Historic Preservation, New Canaan CT
Plains Art Museum, Fargo ND
Port Huron Museum, Port Huron MI
Putnam County Historical Society, Foundry School Museum, Cold Spring NY
Queens College, City University of New York, Godwin-Ternbach Museum, Flushing NY
Randolph College, Maier Museum of Art, Lynchburg VA
Reading Public Museum, Reading PA
Regina Public Library, Dunlop Art Gallery, Regina SK
Rensselaer County Historical Society, Hart-Cluett Mansion, 1827, Troy NY
Rhode Island Historical Society, John Brown House, Providence RI
Rose Lehrman Art Gallery, Harrisburg PA
Ross Memorial Museum, Saint Andrews NB
Roswell Museum & Art Center, Roswell NM
Ryerss Victorian Museum & Library, Philadelphia PA
Saco Museum, Saco ME
Saginaw Art Museum, Saginaw MI
Saint Anselm College, Alva de Mars Megan Chapel Art Center, Manchester NH
Saint Bonaventure University, Regina A Quick Center for the Arts, Saint Bonaventure NY
Saint Johnsbury Athenaeum, Saint Johnsbury VT
Saint Joseph College, Art Gallery, University of Saint Joseph, West Hartford CT
Saint Mary's College of California, Museum of Art, Moraga CA
Saint Olaf College, Flaten Art Museum, Northfield MN
San Antonio Museum of Art, San Antonio TX
The San Joaquin Pioneer & Historical Society, The Haggin Museum, Stockton CA
Santa Paula Art Museum, Santa Paula CA
Schweinfurth Art Center, Auburn NY
Scripps College, Ruth Chandler Williamson Gallery, Claremont CA
Shirley Plantation Foundation, Charles City VA
South Dakota State University, South Dakota Art Museum, Brookings SD
Southeastern Center for Contemporary Art, Winston-Salem NC
Southern Methodist University, Meadows Museum, Dallas TX
Southern Oregon University, Schneider Museum of Art, Ashland OR
Spartanburg Art Museum, Spartanburg SC
The Speed Art Museum, Louisville KY
Springfield Art Museum, Springfield MO
Staatliche Museen zu Berlin Stiftung Preussischer Kulturbesitz, National Museums in Berlin, Prussian Cultural Heritage Foundation, Berlin
Stanford University, Cantor Arts Center at Stanford University, Stanford CA
The State Museum of Fine Arts of Tatarstan Republic, Kazan
State University of New York at Geneseo, Bertha V B Lederer Gallery, Geneseo NY
State University of New York at New Paltz, Samuel Dorsky Museum of Art, New Paltz NY
State University of New York College at Cortland, Dowd Fine Arts Gallery, Cortland NY
Staten Island Museum, Staten Island NY
Stedelijk Museum Alkmaar, Alkmaar Municipal Museum, Alkmaar
Stone Quarry Hill Art Park, Winner Gallery, Cazenovia NY
Susquehanna University, Lore Degenstein Gallery, Selinsgrove PA
Szepmuveszeti Muzeum, Museum of Fine Arts, Budapest
T C Steele State Historic Site, Nashville IN
Tacoma Art Museum, Tacoma WA
Temiskaming Art Gallery, Haileybury ON
Thomas Jefferson Foundation, Inc, Monticello, Charlottesville VA
Timken Museum of Art, San Diego CA
Tohono Chul Park, Tucson AZ
Topeka & Shawnee County Public Library, Alice C Sabatini Gallery, Topeka KS
Tubac Center of the Arts, Santa Cruz Valley Art Association, Tubac AZ
Tucson Museum of Art and Historic Block, Tucson AZ
Turtle Bay Exploration Park, Redding CA
Tver Regional Art Gallery, Tver
Tyne and Wear Archives & Museums, Sunderland Museum & Winter Gardens, Sunderland
Ukrainian Canadian Archives & Museum of Alberta, Edmonton AB
The Ukrainian Museum, New York NY
United Society of Shakers, Shaker Museum, New Gloucester ME
United States Capitol, Architect of the Capitol, Washington DC

University of Florida, Samuel P Harn Museum of Art, Gainesville FL
University of Georgia, Georgia Museum of Art, Athens GA
University of Illinois at Urbana-Champaign, Krannert Art Museum and Kinkead Pavilion, Champaign IL
University of Indianapolis, Christel DeHaan Fine Arts Gallery, Indianapolis IN
The University of Kentucky Art Museum, Lexington KY
University of Mary Washington, University of Mary Washington Galleries, Fredericksburg VA
University of Miami, Lowe Art Museum, Coral Gables FL
University of Nebraska-Lincoln, Great Plains Art Museum, Lincoln NE
University of Nevada, Reno, Sheppard Contemporary & University Galleries, Reno NV
University of New Mexico, The Harwood Museum of Art, Taos NM
University of Notre Dame, Snite Museum of Art, Notre Dame IN
University of Richmond, University Museums, Richmond VA
University of Saskatchewan, Diefenbaker Canada Centre, Saskatoon SK
University of Utah, Utah Museum of Fine Arts, Salt Lake City UT
University of Wisconsin-Madison, Chazen Museum of Art, Madison WI
Ursinus College, Philip & Muriel Berman Museum of Art, Collegeville PA
Vancouver Art Gallery, Vancouver BC
Vesterheim Norwegian-American Museum, Decorah IA
Viridian Artists Inc, New York NY
Walker Art Gallery, Liverpool
Walker Fine Art, Denver CO
Waterworks Visual Arts Center, Salisbury NC
Whatcom Museum, Bellingham WA
Wheaton College, Beard and Weil Galleries, Norton MA
Wichita State University, Ulrich Museum of Art, Wichita KS
Wildling Art Museum, Solvang CA
Wilfrid Laurier University, Robert Langen Art Gallery, Waterloo ON
Wilkes Art Gallery, North Wilkesboro NC
William Paterson University, University Galleries, Wayne NJ
Wiregrass Museum of Art, Dothan AL
Woodmere Art Museum Inc, Philadelphia PA
Worcester Art Museum, Worcester MA
Wyoming State Museum, Cheyenne WY
Wyoming Trails Gallery, Wheatland WY
Yale University, Yale Center for British Art, New Haven CT
Yokohama Museum of Art, Yokohama
Zigler Art Museum, Jennings LA

LATIN AMERICAN ART

Akron Art Museum, Akron OH
Albuquerque Museum of Art & History, Albuquerque NM
Americas Society Art Gallery, New York NY
Amherst College, Mead Art Museum, Amherst MA
Arnot Art Museum, Elmira NY
Art Community Center, Art Center of Corpus Christi, Corpus Christi TX
Art Without Walls Inc, Sayville NY
Aurora University, Schingoethe Center for Native American Cultures & The Schingoethe Art Gallery, Aurora IL
The Baltimore Museum of Art, Baltimore MD
Beloit College, Wright Museum of Art, Beloit WI
Bone Creek Museum of Agrarian Art, David City NE
Bucknell University, Edward & Marthann Samek Art Gallery, Lewisburg PA
C M Russell Museum, Great Falls MT
California State University, Chico, Janet Turner Print Museum, CSU, Chicago, Chico CA
Cartoon Art Museum, San Francisco CA
Center for Puppetry Arts, Atlanta GA
City of El Paso, El Paso TX
City of Gainesville, Thomas Center Galleries - Cultural Affairs, Gainesville FL
The Contemporary Austin, Austin TX
Coutts Museum of Art, Inc, El Dorado KS
Craft and Folk Art Museum (CAFAM), Los Angeles CA
Dartmouth College, Hood Museum of Art, Hanover NH
Davidson College, William H Van Every Jr & Edward M Smith Galleries, Davidson NC
Denver Art Museum, Denver CO
Detroit Institute of Arts, Detroit MI
East Carolina University, Wellington B Gray Gallery, Greenville NC
Emory University, Michael C Carlos Museum, Atlanta GA
En Foco, Inc, Bronx NY
Fitchburg Art Museum, Fitchburg MA
Fitton Center for Creative Arts, Hamilton OH
Folk Art Society of America, Richmond VA
Forest Lawn Museum, Glendale CA
Galerie Montcalm, Gatineau QC
Hidalgo County Historical Museum, Edinburg TX
Institute of Puerto Rican Culture, Museo Fuerte Conde de Mirasol, Vieques PR
INTAR Gallery, New York NY
The Interchurch Center, Galleries at the Interchurch Center, New York NY
Intermedia Arts, Minneapolis MN
International Museum of Art, El Paso TX
The Israel Museum, Jerusalem, Jerusalem
Kalamazoo Institute of Arts, Kalamazoo MI
Kenosha Public Museums, Kenosha WI
Knoxville Museum of Art, Knoxville TN
LA County Museum of Art, Los Angeles CA
Lalit Kala Akademi Rabindra Bhavan Art Galleries, National Academy of Art, New Delhi, New Delhi
Latino Art Museum, Pomona CA
Lehman College Art Gallery, Bronx NY
Lillian & Coleman Taube Museum of Art, Minot ND
Louise Hopkins Underwood Center for the Arts, Lubbock TX
Loyola Marymount University, Laband Art Gallery, Los Angeles CA
Loyola University Chicago, Loyola University Museum of Art, Chicago IL
Marquette University, Haggerty Museum of Art, Milwaukee WI
Mesa Arts Center, Mesa Contemporary Arts Museum, Mesa AZ
The Mexican Museum, San Francisco CA
Miami-Dade College, MDC Museum of Art & Design, Miami FL
Midwest Museum of American Art, Elkhart IN
Mission San Luis Rey de Francia, Mission San Luis Rey Museum, Oceanside CA
Modern Art Museum, Fort Worth TX
Museo de Arte Contemporaneo de Castilla y Leon, Leon
Museo de Arte de Puerto Rico, San Juan PR
Museo De Las Americas, Denver CO
Museo Nacional de Bellas Artes, National Museum of Fine Arts, Santiago
Museum of Art - Deland FL, Inc, Deland FL
Museum of Art, Fort Lauderdale, Fort Lauderdale FL
The Museum of Arts & Sciences Inc, Daytona Beach FL
Museum of Contemporary Art, North Miami FL
Museum of Fine Arts, Houston, Houston TX
Museum of Fine Arts, Saint Petersburg, Florida, Inc, Saint Petersburg FL
Museum of Latin American Art, Long Beach CA
Museum of Northwest Art, La Conner WA
Museum zu Allerheiligen, Schaffhausen
Nassau County Museum of Art, Roslyn Harbor NY
National Museum of Mexican Art, Chicago IL
National Museum of the American Indian, George Gustav Heye Center, New York NY
National Museum of Women in the Arts, Washington DC
New Orleans Museum of Art, New Orleans LA
Okanagan Heritage Museum, Kelowna BC
Oklahoma City Museum of Art, Oklahoma City OK
Opelousas Museum of Art, Inc (OMA), Opelousas LA
Page-Walker Arts & History Center, Cary NC
Panhandle-Plains Historical Museum, Canyon TX
Phoenix Art Museum, Phoenix AZ
Polk Museum of Art, Lakeland FL
Queens College, City University of New York, Godwin-Ternbach Museum, Flushing NY
Reading Public Museum, Reading PA
Roswell Museum & Art Center, Roswell NM
Saint Joseph College, Art Gallery, University of Saint Joseph, West Hartford CT
Saint Mary's College of California, Museum of Art, Moraga CA
San Angelo Museum of Fine Arts, San Angelo TX
San Antonio Museum of Art, San Antonio TX
The San Joaquin Pioneer & Historical Society, The Haggin Museum, Stockton CA
Santa Barbara Museum of Art, Santa Barbara CA
Sheldon Art Galleries, Saint Louis MO
Southeastern Center for Contemporary Art, Winston-Salem NC
Southern Oregon University, Schneider Museum of Art, Ashland OR
Stanford University, Cantor Arts Center at Stanford University, Stanford CA
State University of New York at Geneseo, Bertha V B Lederer Gallery, Geneseo NY
State University of New York College at Cortland, Dowd Fine Arts Gallery, Cortland NY
Stone Quarry Hill Art Park, Winner Gallery, Cazenovia NY
Tampa Museum of Art, Tampa FL
Topeka & Shawnee County Public Library, Alice C Sabatini Gallery, Topeka KS
Tucson Museum of Art and Historic Block, Tucson AZ
University of California, Berkeley, Phoebe Apperson Hearst Museum of Anthropology, Berkeley CA
University of Florida, Samuel P Harn Museum of Art, Gainesville FL
University of Georgia, Georgia Museum of Art, Athens GA
University of Houston, Blaffer Art Museum, Houston TX
The University of Kentucky Art Museum, Lexington KY
University of Miami, Lowe Art Museum, Coral Gables FL
University of Nevada, Reno, Sheppard Contemporary & University Galleries, Reno NV
University of North Carolina at Greensboro, Weatherspoon Art Museum, Greensboro NC
University of Notre Dame, Snite Museum of Art, Notre Dame IN
University of Southern California, USC Fisher Museum of Art, Los Angeles CA
University of Texas at Austin, Blanton Museum of Art, Austin TX
University of Utah, Utah Museum of Fine Arts, Salt Lake City UT
University of Washington, Burke Museum of Natural History and Culture, Seattle WA
University of Wisconsin-Madison, Chazen Museum of Art, Madison WI
Ursinus College, Philip & Muriel Berman Museum of Art, Collegeville PA
Wadsworth Atheneum Museum of Art, Hartford CT
Wiregrass Museum of Art, Dothan AL
Yerba Buena Center for the Arts, San Francisco CA
Yokohama Museum of Art, Yokohama

LEATHER

Albuquerque Museum of Art & History, Albuquerque NM
Appaloosa Museum and Heritage Center, Moscow ID
Art Without Walls Inc, Sayville NY
Artesia Historical Museum and Art Center, Artesia NM
Arts Council of Fayetteville-Cumberland County, The Arts Center, Fayetteville NC
Bangladesh National Museum, Dhaka
Baroda Museum and Picture Gallery, Vadodara
Bowdoin College, Peary-MacMillan Arctic Museum, Brunswick ME
Buffalo Niagara Heritage Village, Amherst NY
Canadian Museum of History, Gatineau QC
Carlsbad Museum & Art Center, Carlsbad NM
Carson County Square House Museum, Panhandle TX
The Children's Museum of Indianapolis, Indianapolis IN
City of Springdale, Shiloh Museum of Ozark History, Springdale AR
Craft and Folk Art Museum (CAFAM), Los Angeles CA
Cripple Creek District Museum, Cripple Creek CO
Crook County Museum & Art Gallery, Sundance WY
Dalnavert Museum, Winnipeg MB
Deming-Luna Mimbres Museum, Deming NM
Detroit Institute of Arts, Detroit MI
Fitton Center for Creative Arts, Hamilton OH
Flint Institute of Arts, Flint MI
Fuller Craft Museum, Brockton MA

George Phippen, Phippen Museum - Art of the American West, Prescott AZ
Glanmore National Historic Site of Canada, Belleville ON
Headquarters Fort Monroe, Dept of Army, Casemate Museum, Hampton VA
Henry County Museum & Cultural Arts Center, Clinton MO
Henry Sheldon Museum of Vermont History and Research Center, Middlebury VT
Heritage Center, Inc, Pine Ridge SD
Hillwood Museum & Gardens Foundation, Hillwood Estate Museum & Gardens, Washington DC
Illinois State Museum, ISM Lockport Gallery, Chicago Gallery & Southern Illinois Art Gallery, Springfield IL
Independence Historical Museum & Art Center, Independence KS
Iroquois Indian Museum, Howes Cave NY
Kelly-Griggs House Museum, Red Bluff CA
Kenosha Public Museums, Kenosha WI
Koshare Indian Museum, Inc, La Junta CO
Lac du Flambeau Band of Lake Superior Chippewa Indians, George W Brown Jr Ojibwe Museum & Cultural Center, Lac Du Flambeau WI
Lahore Museum, Lahore
League of New Hampshire Craftsmen, Grodin Permanent Collection Museum, Concord NH
Lehigh Valley Heritage Center, Allentown PA
Lincolnshire County Council, Library & Heritage Services, Lincoln
The Long Island Museum of American Art, History & Carriages, Stony Brook NY
The Mexican Museum, San Francisco CA
Musee des Augustines de l'Hotel Dieu de Quebec, Quebec QC
Musee des Beaux-Arts de Tours, Museum of Fine Arts, Tours
Museo De Las Americas, Denver CO
Museum Plantin-Moretus, Antwerp
Museum zu Allerheiligen, Schaffhausen
Muzej za Umjetnost i Obrt, Museum of Arts & Crafts, Zagreb
Muzeul National de Arta al Romaniei, National Museum of Art of Romania, Bucharest
National Baseball Hall of Fame & Museum, Cooperstown NY
Naval Historical Center, National Museum of the US Navy, Washington DC
Nebraska Game and Parks Commission, Arbor Lodge State Historical Park & Morton Mansion, Nebraska City NE
Nebraska State Capitol, Lincoln NE
Nevada Museum of Art, Reno NV
New Brunswick Museum, Saint John NB
New York State Military Museum and Veterans Research Center, Saratoga Springs NY
Norwich Free Academy, Slater Memorial Museum, Norwich CT
Panhandle-Plains Historical Museum, Canyon TX
Plainsman Museum, Aurora NE
Queens College, City University of New York, Godwin-Ternbach Museum, Flushing NY
Roswell Museum & Art Center, Roswell NM
San Antonio Museum of Art, San Antonio TX
Seneca-Iroquois National Museum, Salamanca NY
South Carolina Artisans Center, Walterboro SC
The Speed Art Museum, Louisville KY
Staatliche Museen zu Berlin Stiftung Preussischer Kulturbesitz, National Museums in Berlin, Prussian Cultural Heritage Foundation, Berlin
The State Museum of Fine Arts of Tatarstan Republic, Kazan
Suomen Kansallismuseo, National Museum of Finland, Helsinki
Tokyo National Museum, Tokyo
Tver Regional Art Gallery, Tver
United Society of Shakers, Shaker Museum, New Gloucester ME
University of Minnesota, Goldstein Museum of Design, Saint Paul MN
University of Saskatchewan, Diefenbaker Canada Centre, Saskatoon SK
Vesterheim Norwegian-American Museum, Decorah IA
Wheelwright Museum of the American Indian, Santa Fe NM
Wisconsin Historical Society, Wisconsin Historical Museum, Madison WI
Woodlawn/The Pope-Leighey, Alexandria VA
World Erotic Art Museum, Miami Beach FL

MANUSCRIPTS

Academy of the New Church, Glencairn Museum, Bryn Athyn PA
Adams County Historical Society, Gettysburg PA
African American Museum of Iowa, Cedar Rapids IA
Alaska Heritage Museum at Wells Fargo, Anchorage AK
Albany Institute of History & Art, Albany NY
Albin O Kuhn Library & Gallery, Baltimore MD
Albuquerque Museum of Art & History, Albuquerque NM
Alton Museum of History & Art, Inc, Alton IL
American Textile History Museum, Lowell MA
The Andy Warhol Museum, Pittsburgh PA
Appaloosa Museum and Heritage Center, Moscow ID
Arizona Historical Society-Yuma, Sanguinetti House Museum & Garden, Yuma AZ
Art Without Walls Inc, Sayville NY
Artesia Historical Museum and Art Center, Artesia NM
Arts Council of Fayetteville-Cumberland County, The Arts Center, Fayetteville NC
Aspen Art Museum, Aspen CO
Atlanta Historical Society Inc, Atlanta History Center, Atlanta GA
Baldwin Historical Society Museum, Baldwin NY
Bangladesh National Museum, Dhaka
Baroda Museum and Picture Gallery, Vadodara
The Bartlett Museum, Amesbury MA
Bennington Museum, Bennington VT
Besser Museum for Northeast Michigan, Alpena MI
Bone Creek Museum of Agrarian Art, David City NE
The Bostonian Society, Old State House Museum, Boston MA
Bucknell University, Edward & Marthann Samek Art Gallery, Lewisburg PA
Byzantine & Christian Museum, Athens, Athens
C M Russell Museum, Great Falls MT
Calvert Marine Museum, Solomons MD
Canadian Museum of History, Gatineau QC
Cape Ann Museum, Gloucester MA
Carson County Square House Museum, Panhandle TX
Cartoon Art Museum, San Francisco CA
Channel Islands Maritime Museum, Oxnard CA
Chatham Historical Society, The Atwood House Museum, Chatham MA
Chesapeake Bay Maritime Museum, Saint Michaels MD
The Children's Museum of Indianapolis, Indianapolis IN
City of Austin Parks & Recreation, O Henry Museum, Austin TX
City of Cedar Falls, Iowa, James & Meryl Hearst Center for the Arts & Sculpture Garden, Cedar Falls IA
The City of Petersburg Museums, Petersburg VA
City of Springdale, Shiloh Museum of Ozark History, Springdale AR
City of Ukiah, Grace Hudson Museum & The Sun House, Ukiah CA
Clark County Historical Society, Pioneer - Krier Museum, Ashland KS
Cohasset Historical Society, Pratt Building (Society Headquarters), Cohasset MA
Colgate University, Picker Art Gallery, Hamilton NY
College of William & Mary, Muscarelle Museum of Art, Williamsburg VA
Concordia Historical Institute, Saint Louis MO
Craft and Folk Art Museum (CAFAM), Los Angeles CA
Cripple Creek District Museum, Cripple Creek CO
Crocker Art Museum, Sacramento CA
Crook County Museum & Art Gallery, Sundance WY
Crow Wing County Historical Society, Brainerd MN
The Currier Museum of Art, Manchester NH
Detroit Institute of Arts, Detroit MI
Eastern Washington State Historical Society, Northwest Museum of Arts & Culture, Spokane WA
Edgecombe County Cultural Arts Council, Inc, Blount-Bridgers House, Hobson Pittman Memorial Gallery, Tarboro NC
Emory University, Michael C Carlos Museum, Atlanta GA
Erie County Historical Society, Erie PA
Evanston Historical Society, Charles Gates Dawes House, Evanston IL
Evansville Museum of Arts, History & Science, Evansville IN
Fairbanks Museum & Planetarium, Saint Johnsbury VT
Fetherston Foundation, Packwood House Museum, Lewisburg PA
Fitton Center for Creative Arts, Hamilton OH
Florence County Museum, Florence SC
Fondazione Musei Civici Di Venezia, Museo Correr - Correr Museum, Venice
Forest Lawn Museum, Glendale CA
Fort George G Meade Museum, Fort Meade MD
Fort Morgan Heritage Foundation, Fort Morgan CO
Fort Ticonderoga Association, Ticonderoga NY
Freer Gallery of Art & Arthur M Sackler Gallery, Freer Gallery of Art, Washington DC
Fruitlands Museum, Inc, Harvard MA
Fulton County Historical Society Inc, Fulton County Museum (Tetzlaff Reference Room), Rochester IN
General Board of Discipleship, The United Methodist Church, The Upper Room Chapel & Museum, Nashville TN
Germantown Historical Society, Philadelphia PA
Girard College, Stephen Girard Collection, Philadelphia PA
Glanmore National Historic Site of Canada, Belleville ON
Glessner House Museum, Chicago IL
Grand Rapids Public Museum, Grand Rapids MI
Hancock Shaker Village, Inc, Pittsfield MA
Headquarters Fort Monroe, Dept of Army, Casemate Museum, Hampton VA
Hebrew Union College, Skirball Cultural Center, Los Angeles CA
Hebrew Union College - Jewish Institute of Religion, Skirball Museum Cincinnati, Cincinnati OH
Hebrew Union College - Jewish Institute of Religion Museum, Jewish Institute of Religion, New York NY
Hecht Museum, Haifa
Henry Sheldon Museum of Vermont History and Research Center, Middlebury VT
Heritage Glass Museum, Glassboro NJ
Hidalgo County Historical Museum, Edinburg TX
Hillwood Museum & Gardens Foundation, Hillwood Estate Museum & Gardens, Washington DC
Historic Arkansas Museum, Little Rock AR
Historic Cherry Hill, Albany NY
Historic Holyoke at Wistariahurst & City of Holyoke, Holyoke MA
Historic Huguenot Street, New Paltz NY
Historic Newton, Newton MA
Historical Society of Cheshire County, Keene NH
Historical Society of Old Newbury, Cushing House Museum, Newburyport MA
History Colorado Center Museum, Denver CO
History Museum of Mobile, Mobile AL
The Huntington Library, Art Collections & Botanical Gardens, San Marino CA
Imperial Calcasieu Museum, Gibson-Barham Gallery, Lake Charles LA
Imperial War Museum London, London
Independence Historical Museum & Art Center, Independence KS
Independence Seaport Museum, Philadelphia PA
Indiana State Museum, Indianapolis IN
Institute of Puerto Rican Culture, Museo Fuerte Conde de Mirasol, Vieques PR
Iredell Museums, Statesville NC
The Israel Museum, Jerusalem, Jerusalem
James Dick Foundation, Festival - Institute, Round Top TX
JMW Turner Museum, Sarasota FL
Johns Hopkins University, Evergreen Museum & Library, Baltimore MD
Jordan National Gallery of Fine Arts, Amman
Kenosha Public Museums, Kenosha WI
Kentucky Derby Museum, Louisville KY
King Kamehameha V Judiciary History Center, Honolulu HI
Kings County Historical Society & Museum, Hampton NB
Koffler Centre of the Arts, Koffler Gallery, Toronto ON
Koochiching Museums, International Falls MN
Kunsthistorisches Museum Wien, Museum of Fine Arts, Vienna
La Casa del Libro Museum, San Juan PR
Lac du Flambeau Band of Lake Superior Chippewa Indians, George W Brown Jr Ojibwe Museum & Cultural Center, Lac Du Flambeau WI

Lafayette Science Museum & Planetarium, Lafayette LA
Lahore Museum, Lahore
Lalit Kala Akademi Rabindra Bhavan Art Galleries, National Academy of Art, New Delhi, New Delhi
Leelanau Historical Museum, Leland MI
Lehigh Valley Heritage Center, Allentown PA
Lincolnshire County Council, Library & Heritage Services, Lincoln
The Long Island Museum of American Art, History & Carriages, Stony Brook NY
Louisiana Department of Culture, Recreation & Tourism, Louisiana State Museum, New Orleans LA
Loveland Museum/Gallery, Loveland CO
Maine Historical Society, Wadsworth-Longfellow House, Portland ME
Maricopa County Historical Society, Desert Caballeros Western Museum, Wickenburg AZ
The Mariners' Museum, Newport News VA
McCord Museum of Canadian History, Montreal QC
McLean County Historical Society, McLean County Museum of History, Bloomington IL
The Mexican Museum, San Francisco CA
Mission San Miguel Museum, San Miguel CA
Mississippi River Museum at Mud-Island River Park, Memphis TN
Mohave Museum of History & Arts, Kingman AZ
Moravian Historical Society, Nazareth PA
Moravska Galerie v Brne, Moravian Gallery in Brno, Brno
Mount Vernon Hotel Museum & Garden, New York NY
MTG Hawkes Bay, Napier
Musee des Augustines de l'Hotel Dieu de Quebec, Quebec QC
Musee des Beaux-Arts de Tours, Museum of Fine Arts, Tours
Museum of Art & History, Santa Cruz, Santa Cruz CA
The Museum of Arts & Sciences Inc, Daytona Beach FL
Museum of Chinese in America, New York NY
Museum of Islamic Art, Doha
Museum Plantin-Moretus, Antwerp
Museum zu Allerheiligen, Schaffhausen
Muzej za Umjetnost i Obrt, Museum of Arts & Crafts, Zagreb
Muzeul de Istorie Nationala Si Arheologie Constanta, National History & Archaeology Museum, Constanta
Muzeul National de Arta al Romaniei, National Museum of Art of Romania, Bucharest
Nara Kokuritsu Hakubutsu-Kan, Nara National Museum, Nara
Narodna Galerija, National Gallery of Slovenia, Ljubljana
National Baseball Hall of Fame & Museum, Cooperstown NY
The National Museum of Modern Art, Tokyo, Tokyo
National Museum of the American Indian, George Gustav Heye Center, New York NY
National Museum of Wildlife Art of the Unites States, Jackson WY
National Palace Museum, Taipei
The National Shrine of the North American Martyrs, Fultonville NY
National Society of Colonial Dames of America in the State of Maryland, Mount Clare Museum House, Baltimore MD
Naval Historical Center, National Museum of the US Navy, Washington DC
Naval War College Museum, Newport RI
Nelda C & H J Lutcher Stark Foundation, Stark Museum of Art, Orange TX
Nevada Museum of Art, Reno NV
New Brunswick Museum, Saint John NB
New Canaan Historical Society, New Canaan CT
New York State Office of Parks Recreation & Historic Preservation, John Jay Homestead State Historic Site, Katonah NY
Newburyport Maritime Society, Inc, Custom House Maritime Museum, Newburyport MA
The Noble Maritime Collection, Staten Island NY
Norwich Free Academy, Slater Memorial Museum, Norwich CT
Ohio History Connection, National Afro-American Museum & Cultural Center, Wilberforce OH
Old Dartmouth Historical Society, New Bedford Whaling Museum, New Bedford MA
The Old Jail Art Center, Albany TX
Oshkosh Public Museum & Library, Oshkosh WI
Page-Walker Arts & History Center, Cary NC
Panhandle-Plains Historical Museum, Canyon TX
Pennsylvania Historical & Museum Commission, Railroad Museum of Pennsylvania, Strasburg PA
Preservation Virginia, John Marshall House, Richmond VA
Putnam Museum of History and Natural Science, Davenport IA
Queens College, City University of New York, Godwin-Ternbach Museum, Flushing NY
Reading Public Museum, Reading PA
Rensselaer County Historical Society, Hart-Cluett Mansion, 1827, Troy NY
Robert Louis Stevenson Museum, Saint Helena CA
The Rosenbach Museum & Library, Philadelphia PA
Saco Museum, Saco ME
Saint Johnsbury Athenaeum, Saint Johnsbury VT
San Francisco Maritime National Historical Park, Maritime Museum, San Francisco CA
Seneca Falls Historical Society Museum, Seneca Falls NY
Shaker Village of Pleasant Hill, Harrodsburg KY
Shirley Plantation Foundation, Charles City VA
Slater Mill, Old Slater Mill Association, Pawtucket RI
The Society of the Cincinnati at Anderson House, Washington DC
South Street Seaport Museum, New York NY
The Speed Art Museum, Louisville KY
Spertus Institute of Jewish Studies, Chicago IL
Staatliche Museen zu Berlin Stiftung Preussischer Kulturbesitz, National Museums in Berlin, Prussian Cultural Heritage Foundation, Berlin
Stanford University, Cantor Arts Center at Stanford University, Stanford CA
State University of New York College at Cortland, Dowd Fine Arts Gallery, Cortland NY
Staten Island Museum, Staten Island NY
Stone Quarry Hill Art Park, Winner Gallery, Cazenovia NY
Stratford Historical Society, Catharine B Mitchell Museum, Stratford CT
Suan Pakkad Palace Museum, Bangkok
The Summit County Historical Society of Akron, OH, Akron OH
Susquehanna University, Lore Degenstein Gallery, Selinsgrove PA
Swedish American Museum, Chicago IL
Thomas Jefferson Foundation, Inc, Monticello, Charlottesville VA
Tokyo National Museum, Tokyo
Trust Authority, Museum of the Great Plains, Lawton OK
Tryon Palace, New Bern NC
Turtle Bay Exploration Park, Redding CA
Turtle Mountain Chippewa Historical Society, Turtle Mountain Heritage Center, Belcourt ND
Tver Regional Art Gallery, Tver
United Methodist Historical Society, Lovely Lane Museum, Baltimore MD
United Society of Shakers, Shaker Museum, New Gloucester ME
United States Capitol, Architect of the Capitol, Washington DC
United States Figure Skating Association, World Figure Skating Museum & Hall of Fame, Colorado Springs CO
University of Georgia, Georgia Museum of Art, Athens GA
University of Illinois at Urbana-Champaign, Krannert Art Museum and Kinkead Pavilion, Champaign IL
University of Notre Dame, Snite Museum of Art, Notre Dame IN
University of Saskatchewan, Diefenbaker Canada Centre, Saskatoon SK
University of Wisconsin-Madison, Chazen Museum of Art, Madison WI
USS Constitution Museum, Boston MA
Van Gogh Museum, Amsterdam
Vermilion County Museum Society, Danville IL
Vesterheim Norwegian-American Museum, Decorah IA
Victoria Mansion - Morse Libby House, Portland ME
The Walker African American Museum & Research Center, Las Vegas NV
Walker Art Gallery, Liverpool
The Wallace Collection, London
Waterville Historical Society, Redington Museum, Waterville ME
Wheaton College, Beard and Weil Galleries, Norton MA
Wheelwright Museum of the American Indian, Santa Fe NM
White House, Washington DC
Yale University, Yale Center for British Art, New Haven CT
Yeshiva University Museum, New York NY

MAPS

Academy of the New Church, Glencairn Museum, Bryn Athyn PA
Adams County Historical Society, Gettysburg PA
African American Museum of Iowa, Cedar Rapids IA
African Art Museum of Maryland, Columbia MD
Alaska Heritage Museum at Wells Fargo, Anchorage AK
Alaska State Museum, Juneau AK
Albuquerque Museum of Art & History, Albuquerque NM
Alton Museum of History & Art, Inc, Alton IL
Amherst College, Mead Art Museum, Amherst MA
Amon Carter Museum of American Art, Fort Worth TX
Anchorage Museum at Rasmuson Center, Anchorage AK
Appaloosa Museum and Heritage Center, Moscow ID
Arizona Historical Society-Yuma, Sanguinetti House Museum & Garden, Yuma AZ
Arnot Art Museum, Elmira NY
Art Gallery of Nova Scotia, Halifax NS
Art Without Walls Inc, Sayville NY
Artesia Historical Museum and Art Center, Artesia NM
Athenaeum of Philadelphia, Philadelphia PA
Atlanta Historical Society Inc, Atlanta History Center, Atlanta GA
Audrain County Historical Society, Graceland Museum & American Saddlehorse Museum & Fire Brick Industry Museum, Mexico MO
Baldwin Historical Society Museum, Baldwin NY
Balzekas Museum of Lithuanian Culture, Chicago IL
Bangladesh National Museum, Dhaka
Baroda Museum and Picture Gallery, Vadodara
The Bartlett Museum, Amesbury MA
Bennington Museum, Bennington VT
Besser Museum for Northeast Michigan, Alpena MI
Beverly Historical Society, Cabot, Hale & Balch House Museums, Beverly MA
The Bostonian Society, Old State House Museum, Boston MA
Bowdoin College, Peary-MacMillan Arctic Museum, Brunswick ME
Brick Store Museum, Kennebunk ME
Brooklyn Historical Society, Brooklyn OH
Bruce Museum, Inc, Greenwich CT
Buffalo Niagara Heritage Village, Amherst NY
Bush-Holley Historic Site & Storehouse Gallery, Greenwich Historical Society, Cos Cob CT
Calvert Marine Museum, Solomons MD
Cambridge Museum, Cambridge NE
Canadian Museum of History, Gatineau QC
Cape Ann Museum, Gloucester MA
Carson County Square House Museum, Panhandle TX
Cayuga Museum of History & Art, Auburn NY
Central United Methodist Church, Swords Into Plowshares Peace Center & Gallery, Detroit MI
Channel Islands Maritime Museum, Oxnard CA
Chatham Historical Society, The Atwood House Museum, Chatham MA
The Children's Museum of Indianapolis, Indianapolis IN
The City of Petersburg Museums, Petersburg VA
City of Springdale, Shiloh Museum of Ozark History, Springdale AR
Clark County Historical Society, Pioneer - Krier Museum, Ashland KS
Cohasset Historical Society, Pratt Building (Society Headquarters), Cohasset MA
College of William & Mary, Muscarelle Museum of Art, Williamsburg VA
The Columbus Museum, Columbus GA
Cripple Creek District Museum, Cripple Creek CO
Crocker Art Museum, Sacramento CA
Crook County Museum & Art Gallery, Sundance WY
Crow Wing County Historical Society, Brainerd MN
Danville Museum of Fine Arts & History, Danville VA
Delta Blues Museum, Clarksdale MS
Detroit Institute of Arts, Detroit MI
Doncaster Museum and Art Gallery, Doncaster Yorks

Eastern Washington State Historical Society, Northwest Museum of Arts & Culture, Spokane WA
Edgecombe County Cultural Arts Council, Inc, Blount-Bridgers House, Hobson Pittman Memorial Gallery, Tarboro NC
Ella Sharp Museum, Jackson MI
Erie County Historical Society, Erie PA
Essex Historical Society and Shipbuilding Museum, Essex MA
Evanston Historical Society, Charles Gates Dawes House, Evanston IL
Evansville Museum of Arts, History & Science, Evansville IN
Fairbanks Museum & Planetarium, Saint Johnsbury VT
Fetherston Foundation, Packwood House Museum, Lewisburg PA
Five Civilized Tribes Museum, Muskogee OK
Florida State University and Central Florida Community College, The Appleton Museum of Art, Ocala FL
Fondazione Musei Civici Di Venezia, Museo Correr - Correr Museum, Venice
Fort George G Meade Museum, Fort Meade MD
Fort Ticonderoga Association, Ticonderoga NY
Fruitlands Museum, Inc, Harvard MA
Fulton County Historical Society Inc, Fulton County Museum (Tetzlaff Reference Room), Rochester IN
Gadsden Museum of Art, Gadsden AL
Germantown Historical Society, Philadelphia PA
Glanmore National Historic Site of Canada, Belleville ON
Grand Rapids Public Museum, Grand Rapids MI
Great Lakes Historical Society, Inland Seas Maritime Museum, Vermilion OH
Hancock Shaker Village, Inc, Pittsfield MA
Headquarters Fort Monroe, Dept of Army, Casemate Museum, Hampton VA
Hebrew Union College - Jewish Institute of Religion Museum, Jewish Institute of Religion, New York NY
Henry County Museum & Cultural Arts Center, Clinton MO
Henry Sheldon Museum of Vermont History and Research Center, Middlebury VT
Heritage Glass Museum, Glassboro NJ
Hermitage Museum & Gardens, Norfolk VA
Hidalgo County Historical Museum, Edinburg TX
Hillwood Museum & Gardens Foundation, Hillwood Estate Museum & Gardens, Washington DC
Historic Arkansas Museum, Little Rock AR
Historic Deerfield, Inc, Deerfield MA
Historic Holyoke at Wistariahurst & City of Holyoke, Holyoke MA
Historic Hudson Valley, Pocantico Hills NY
Historic Huguenot Street, New Paltz NY
Historic Newton, Newton MA
Historical Society of Cheshire County, Keene NH
The History Center in Tompkins County, Ithaca NY
History Colorado Center Museum, Denver CO
History Museum of Mobile, Mobile AL
Illinois State Museum, ISM Lockport Gallery, Chicago Gallery & Southern Illinois Art Gallery, Springfield IL
Imperial Calcasieu Museum, Gibson-Barham Gallery, Lake Charles LA
Independence Historical Museum & Art Center, Independence KS
Independence Seaport Museum, Philadelphia PA
Institute of Puerto Rican Culture, Museo Fuerte Conde de Mirasol, Vieques PR
Iredell Museums, Statesville NC
The Israel Museum, Jerusalem, Jerusalem
Jacques Marchais Museum of Tibetan Art, Staten Island NY
James Dick Foundation, Festival - Institute, Round Top TX
JMW Turner Museum, Sarasota FL
Johns Hopkins University, Evergreen Museum & Library, Baltimore MD
Kenosha Public Museums, Kenosha WI
Kern County Museum, Bakersfield CA
King Kamehameha V Judiciary History Center, Honolulu HI
Kings County Historical Society & Museum, Hampton NB
Koochiching Museums, International Falls MN
La Casa del Libro Museum, San Juan PR
Lac du Flambeau Band of Lake Superior Chippewa Indians, George W Brown Jr Ojibwe Museum & Cultural Center, Lac Du Flambeau WI
Lafayette Science Museum & Planetarium, Lafayette LA
Lehigh Valley Heritage Center, Allentown PA
Lincoln County Historical Association, Inc, 1811 Old Lincoln County Jail & Lincoln County Museum, Wiscasset ME
Lincolnshire County Council, Library & Heritage Services, Lincoln
The Long Island Museum of American Art, History & Carriages, Stony Brook NY
Louisiana Department of Culture, Recreation & Tourism, Louisiana State Museum, New Orleans LA
Lusaka National Museum, Lusaka
Marblehead Museum & Historical Society, Marblehead MA
Marblehead Museum & Historical Society, Jeremiah Lee Mansion, Marblehead MA
The Mariners' Museum, Newport News VA
Massachusetts Institute of Technology, MIT Museum, Cambridge MA
McCord Museum of Canadian History, Montreal QC
McDowell House & Apothecary Shop, Danville KY
McLean County Historical Society, McLean County Museum of History, Bloomington IL
Medina Railroad Museum, Medina NY
Middle Border Museum & Oscar Howe Art Center, Mitchell SD
Mississippi River Museum at Mud-Island River Park, Memphis TN
Moravian Historical Society, Nazareth PA
Mount Vernon Hotel Museum & Garden, New York NY
MTG Hawkes Bay, Napier
Muscatine Art Center, Muscatine IA
Musee des Beaux-Arts de Tours, Museum of Fine Arts, Tours
Museo De Las Americas, Denver CO
Museo di Palazzo Ducale, Ducale Palace Museum, Mantua
Museum De Lakenhal, Leiden
Museum of Art & History, Santa Cruz, Santa Cruz CA
The Museum of Arts & Sciences Inc, Daytona Beach FL
Museum of Chinese in America, New York NY
Museum of Northern British Columbia, Ruth Harvey Art Gallery, Prince Rupert BC
Museum Plantin-Moretus, Antwerp
Museum Prinsenhof Delft, Delft
Museum zu Allerheiligen, Schaffhausen
Muzeul de Istorie Nationala Si Arheologie Constanta, National History & Archaeology Museum, Constanta
National Churchill Museum, Fulton MO
National Museum & Art Gallery of Trinidad and Tobago, Port of Spain
National Museum of Wildlife Art of the Unites States, Jackson WY
The National Shrine of the North American Martyrs, Fultonville NY
National Society of the Colonial Dames of America in The Commonwealth of Virginia, Wilton House Museum, Richmond VA
Naval Historical Center, National Museum of the US Navy, Washington DC
Naval War College Museum, Newport RI
New Brunswick Museum, Saint John NB
New Canaan Historical Society, New Canaan CT
New York State Office of Parks Recreation & Historic Preservation, John Jay Homestead State Historic Site, Katonah NY
Newburyport Maritime Society, Inc, Custom House Maritime Museum, Newburyport MA
The Noble Maritime Collection, Staten Island NY
Norwich Free Academy, Slater Memorial Museum, Norwich CT
Ogden Union Station, Union Station Museums, Ogden UT
Oklahoma City Museum of Art, Oklahoma City OK
Old Dartmouth Historical Society, New Bedford Whaling Museum, New Bedford MA
The Old Jail Art Center, Albany TX
Old Salem Museums & Gardens, Museum of Early Southern Decorative Arts, Winston-Salem NC
Opelousas Museum of Art, Inc (OMA), Opelousas LA
Oshkosh Public Museum & Library, Oshkosh WI
Page-Walker Arts & History Center, Cary NC
Panhandle-Plains Historical Museum, Canyon TX
Pennsylvania Historical & Museum Commission, Railroad Museum of Pennsylvania, Strasburg PA
Philadelphia History Museum, Philadelphia PA
Pioneer Historical Museum of South Dakota, Hot Springs SD
Plainsman Museum, Aurora NE
Please Touch Museum, Philadelphia PA
Polish Museum of America (PMA), Chicago IL
Port Huron Museum, Port Huron MI
Portsmouth Historical Society, John Paul Jones House & Discover Portsmouth, Portsmouth NH
Putnam County Historical Society, Foundry School Museum, Cold Spring NY
Putnam Museum of History and Natural Science, Davenport IA
Rensselaer County Historical Society, Hart-Cluett Mansion, 1827, Troy NY
Rhode Island Historical Society, John Brown House, Providence RI
Saco Museum, Saco ME
Safety Harbor Museum and Cultural Arts Center, Safety Harbor FL
Saint Johnsbury Athenaeum, Saint Johnsbury VT
San Francisco Maritime National Historical Park, Maritime Museum, San Francisco CA
Sea Cliff Village Museum, Sea Cliff NY
Seneca Falls Historical Society Museum, Seneca Falls NY
Seneca-Iroquois National Museum, Salamanca NY
Shirley Plantation Foundation, Charles City VA
The Society of the Cincinnati at Anderson House, Washington DC
South Street Seaport Museum, New York NY
The Speed Art Museum, Louisville KY
Spertus Institute of Jewish Studies, Chicago IL
Stanford University, Cantor Arts Center at Stanford University, Stanford CA
The State Museum of Fine Arts of Tatarstan Republic, Kazan
Staten Island Museum, Staten Island NY
Ste Genevieve Museum, Sainte Genevieve MO
Stone Quarry Hill Art Park, Winner Gallery, Cazenovia NY
Stratford Historical Society, Catharine B Mitchell Museum, Stratford CT
The Summit County Historical Society of Akron, OH, Akron OH
Thomas Jefferson Foundation, Inc, Monticello, Charlottesville VA
The Tokugawa Art Museum, Nagoya
Tokyo National Museum, Tokyo
Trust Authority, Museum of the Great Plains, Lawton OK
Tryon Palace, New Bern NC
Turtle Bay Exploration Park, Redding CA
Turtle Mountain Chippewa Historical Society, Turtle Mountain Heritage Center, Belcourt ND
Tver Regional Art Gallery, Tver
United Methodist Historical Society, Lovely Lane Museum, Baltimore MD
United Society of Shakers, Shaker Museum, New Gloucester ME
University of California, Berkeley, Phoebe Apperson Hearst Museum of Anthropology, Berkeley CA
University of Richmond, University Museums, Richmond VA
University of Saskatchewan, Diefenbaker Canada Centre, Saskatoon SK
USS Constitution Museum, Boston MA
Vermilion County Museum Society, Danville IL
Vesterheim Norwegian-American Museum, Decorah IA
Villa Terrace Decorative Arts Museum, Milwaukee WI
Wadsworth Atheneum Museum of Art, Hartford CT
The Walker African American Museum & Research Center, Las Vegas NV
Waterville Historical Society, Redington Museum, Waterville ME
Woodlawn/The Pope-Leighey, Alexandria VA
Wornall Majors House Museums, John Wornall House Museum, Kansas City MO
Yale University, Yale Center for British Art, New Haven CT

MARINE PAINTING

The Albrecht-Kemper Museum of Art, Saint Joseph MO

American Sport Art Museum and Archives, Daphne AL
Arnold Mikelson Mind & Matter Art Gallery, Surrey BC
Arnot Art Museum, Elmira NY
Art Community Center, Art Center of Corpus Christi, Corpus Christi TX
Art Gallery of Nova Scotia, Halifax NS
Art Without Walls Inc, Sayville NY
Besser Museum for Northeast Michigan, Alpena MI
Beverly Historical Society, Cabot, Hale & Balch House Museums, Beverly MA
The Bostonian Society, Old State House Museum, Boston MA
Brick Store Museum, Kennebunk ME
Bruce Museum, Inc, Greenwich CT
Cahoon Museum of American Art, Cotuit MA
Calvert Marine Museum, Solomons MD
Canadian Museum of History, Gatineau QC
Cape Ann Museum, Gloucester MA
Channel Islands Maritime Museum, Oxnard CA
Chatham Historical Society, The Atwood House Museum, Chatham MA
Chesapeake Bay Maritime Museum, Saint Michaels MD
Cohasset Historical Society, Pratt Building (Society Headquarters), Cohasset MA
Cohasset Historical Society, Cohasset Maritime Museum, Cohasset MA
College of William & Mary, Muscarelle Museum of Art, Williamsburg VA
Columbia River Maritime Museum, Astoria OR
The Columbus Museum, Columbus GA
Crocker Art Museum, Sacramento CA
Detroit Institute of Arts, Detroit MI
Doncaster Museum and Art Gallery, Doncaster Yorks
Erie County Historical Society, Erie PA
Essex Historical Society and Shipbuilding Museum, Essex MA
Florida State University and Central Florida Community College, The Appleton Museum of Art, Ocala FL
Gallery One Visual Arts Center, Ellensburg WA
Great Lakes Historical Society, Inland Seas Maritime Museum, Vermilion OH
The Heckscher Museum of Art, Huntington NY
Hickory Museum of Art, Inc, Hickory NC
Hillwood Museum & Gardens Foundation, Hillwood Estate Museum & Gardens, Washington DC
Historic Hudson Valley, Pocantico Hills NY
Hui No'eau Visual Arts Center, Gallery and Gift Shop, Makawao Maui HI
Independence Seaport Museum, Philadelphia PA
The Interchurch Center, Galleries at the Interchurch Center, New York NY
JMW Turner Museum, Sarasota FL
Kyiv Museum of Russian Art, Kyiv Ukrainian
LaGrange Art Museum, LaGrange GA
The Long Island Museum of American Art, History & Carriages, Stony Brook NY
Louisiana Department of Culture, Recreation & Tourism, Louisiana State Museum, New Orleans LA
Maine Maritime Museum, Bath ME
Marblehead Museum & Historical Society, Marblehead MA
Marblehead Museum & Historical Society, Jeremiah Lee Mansion, Marblehead MA
The Mariners' Museum, Newport News VA
Maritime Museum of San Diego, San Diego CA
Massachusetts Institute of Technology, MIT Museum, Cambridge MA
Mobile Museum of Art, Mobile AL
Moderna Galerija, Modern Gallery - National Museum of Modern Art, Zagreb
Monterey History & Art Association, Maritime Museum of Monterey, Monterey CA
Morris Museum of Art, Augusta GA
Musee des Beaux-Arts de Tours, Museum of Fine Arts, Tours
Museo di Palazzo Ducale, Ducale Palace Museum, Mantua
Museo Nacional de Bellas Artes, National Museum of Fine Arts, Santiago
The Museum of Arts & Sciences Inc, Daytona Beach FL
Museum of Northwest Art, La Conner WA
Muzeul National de Arta al Romaniei, National Museum of Art of Romania, Bucharest
National Art Museum of Moldova, Chisinau
Naval Historical Center, National Museum of the US Navy, Washington DC
Naval War College Museum, Newport RI
Nelson Mandela Metropolitan Art Museum, Port Elizabeth
Nevada Museum of Art, Reno NV
New Britain Museum of American Art, New Britain CT
New Brunswick Museum, Saint John NB
Newburyport Maritime Society, Inc, Custom House Maritime Museum, Newburyport MA
The Noble Maritime Collection, Staten Island NY
Norsk Maritimt Museum, Norwegian Maritime Museum, Oslo
Norwich Free Academy, Slater Memorial Museum, Norwich CT
Nova Scotia Museum, Maritime Museum of the Atlantic, Halifax NS
The Ohio Historical Society, Inc, Campus Martius Museum & Ohio River Museum, Marietta OH
Old Dartmouth Historical Society, New Bedford Whaling Museum, New Bedford MA
Old Island Restoration Foundation Inc, Oldest House in Key West, Key West FL
Opelousas Museum of Art, Inc (OMA), Opelousas LA
Panhandle-Plains Historical Museum, Canyon TX
Peabody Essex Museum, Salem MA
Pennsylvania Academy of the Fine Arts, Philadelphia PA
Penobscot Marine Museum, Searsport ME
Port Huron Museum, Port Huron MI
Portsmouth Historical Society, John Paul Jones House & Discover Portsmouth, Portsmouth NH
Queens College, City University of New York, Godwin-Ternbach Museum, Flushing NY
Randolph College, Maier Museum of Art, Lynchburg VA
Reading Public Museum, Reading PA
Rhode Island Historical Society, John Brown House, Providence RI
Saginaw Art Museum, Saginaw MI
Saint Joseph College, Art Gallery, University of Saint Joseph, West Hartford CT
San Antonio Museum of Art, San Antonio TX
San Francisco Maritime National Historical Park, Maritime Museum, San Francisco CA
Scripps College, Ruth Chandler Williamson Gallery, Claremont CA
Ships of the Sea Maritime Museum, Savannah GA
South Street Seaport Museum, New York NY
The Speed Art Museum, Louisville KY
St Mary's College of Maryland, The Dwight Frederick Boyden Gallery, St Mary's City MD
Stanford University, Cantor Arts Center at Stanford University, Stanford CA
Staten Island Museum, Staten Island NY
The Stewart Museum, Montreal QC
Stratford Historical Society, Catharine B Mitchell Museum, Stratford CT
Szepmuveszeti Muzeum, Museum of Fine Arts, Budapest
Timken Museum of Art, San Diego CA
Tver Regional Art Gallery, Tver
Tyne and Wear Archives & Museums, Sunderland Museum & Winter Gardens, Sunderland
University of Georgia, Georgia Museum of Art, Athens GA
University of Illinois at Urbana-Champaign, Krannert Art Museum and Kinkead Pavilion, Champaign IL
The University of Kentucky Art Museum, Lexington KY
University of Richmond, University Museums, Richmond VA
University of Wisconsin-Madison, Chazen Museum of Art, Madison WI
Ursinus College, Philip & Muriel Berman Museum of Art, Collegeville PA
USS Constitution Museum, Boston MA
Vesterheim Norwegian-American Museum, Decorah IA
Wheaton College, Beard and Weil Galleries, Norton MA
Wichita State University, Ulrich Museum of Art, Wichita KS
Wilfrid Laurier University, Robert Langen Art Gallery, Waterloo ON
Yale University, Yale Center for British Art, New Haven CT
Zigler Art Museum, Jennings LA

MEDIEVAL ART

Academy of the New Church, Glencairn Museum, Bryn Athyn PA
Amherst College, Mead Art Museum, Amherst MA
Ancient Spanish Monastery, North Miami Beach FL
Arnot Art Museum, Elmira NY
Art Gallery of Nova Scotia, Halifax NS
Art Without Walls Inc, Sayville NY
Baroda Museum and Picture Gallery, Vadodara
Bayerisches Nationalmuseum, Bavarian National Museum, Munich
Beaverbrook Art Gallery, Fredericton NB
Beloit College, Wright Museum of Art, Beloit WI
Blanden Memorial Art Museum, Fort Dodge IA
Bob Jones University Museum & Gallery Inc, Greenville SC
Byzantine & Christian Museum, Athens, Athens
California State University, Chico, Janet Turner Print Museum, CSU, Chicago, Chico CA
The Children's Museum of Indianapolis, Indianapolis IN
Cincinnati Art Museum, Cincinnati Art Museum, Cincinnati OH
Colgate University, Picker Art Gallery, Hamilton NY
College of William & Mary, Muscarelle Museum of Art, Williamsburg VA
The Courtauld Institute of Art, The Courtauld Gallery, London
The Currier Museum of Art, Manchester NH
Danville Museum of Fine Arts & History, Danville VA
Denver Art Museum, Denver CO
Detroit Institute of Arts, Detroit MI
Florida State University and Central Florida Community College, The Appleton Museum of Art, Ocala FL
Fondazione Musei Civici Di Venezia, Museo Correr - Correr Museum, Venice
Forest Lawn Museum, Glendale CA
The Frick Art & Historical Center, Inc, Frick Art Museum, Pittsburgh PA
Galleria Nazionale dell'Umbria, Umbrian National Gallery, Perugia
Hebrew Union College, Skirball Cultural Center, Los Angeles CA
Hebrew Union College - Jewish Institute of Religion Museum, Jewish Institute of Religion, New York NY
Honolulu Museum of Art, Honolulu HI
The Hyde Collection, Glens Falls NY
The Israel Museum, Jerusalem, Jerusalem
Joslyn Art Museum, Omaha NE
Kereszteny Muzeum, Christian Museum, Esztergom
Kimbell Art Foundation, Kimbell Art Museum, Fort Worth TX
Knoxville Museum of Art, Knoxville TN
Kunsthistorisches Museum Wien, Museum of Fine Arts, Vienna
Kyiv Museum of Russian Art, Kyiv Ukrainian
Le Grand Curtius, The Grand Curtius, Liege
Lincolnshire County Council, Library & Heritage Services, Lincoln
Mabee-Gerrer Museum of Art, Shawnee OK
McNay Art Museum, San Antonio TX
The Metropolitan Museum of Art, New York NY
Moravska Galerie v Brne, Moravian Gallery in Brno, Brno
Musee des Beaux-Arts d'Orleans, Museum of Fine Arts, Orleans
Musee des Beaux-Arts de Tours, Museum of Fine Arts, Tours
Museen der Stadt Koln, Wallraf-Richartz-Museum & Fondation Corboud - Wallraf-Richartz Museum & Corboud Foundation, Cologne
Musees Royaux d'Art et d'Histoire, Royal Museums of Art and History, Brussels
Museo di Palazzo Ducale, Ducale Palace Museum, Mantua
Museu Nacional D'Art De Catalunya, Catalona National Museum of Art, Barcelona
Museum De Lakenhal, Leiden
The Museum of Arts & Sciences Inc, Daytona Beach FL
Museum zu Allerheiligen, Schaffhausen
Muzeul de Istorie Nationala Si Arheologie Constanta, National History & Archaeology Museum, Constanta
Muzeul National de Arta al Romaniei, National Museum of Art of Romania, Bucharest
Muzeum Narodowe w Poznaniu, National Museum in Poznan, Poznan

Narodna Galerija, National Gallery of Slovenia, Ljubljana
National Art Museum of Moldova, Chisinau
National Gallery of Canada, Ottawa ON
The National Museum of Western Art, Tokyo
National Museum of Wildlife Art of the Unites States, Jackson WY
The Nelson-Atkins Museum of Art, Kansas City MO
Opelousas Museum of Art, Inc (OMA), Opelousas LA
Osterreichische Galerie Belvedere Vienna, Belvedere Museum Vienna, Vienna
Panhandle-Plains Historical Museum, Canyon TX
Queens College, City University of New York, Godwin-Ternbach Museum, Flushing NY
Reading Public Museum, Reading PA
Royal Ontario Museum, Toronto ON
Saginaw Art Museum, Saginaw MI
Saint Mary's College of California, Museum of Art, Moraga CA
San Antonio Museum of Art, San Antonio TX
Slovenska Narodna Galeria, Slovak National Gallery, Bratislava
Southern Methodist University, Meadows Museum, Dallas TX
The Speed Art Museum, Louisville KY
Staatliche Museen zu Berlin Stiftung Preussischer Kulturbesitz, National Museums in Berlin, Prussian Cultural Heritage Foundation, Berlin
Stanford University, Cantor Arts Center at Stanford University, Stanford CA
The State Museum of Fine Arts of Tatarstan Republic, Kazan
Staten Island Museum, Staten Island NY
Suomen Kansallismuseo, National Museum of Finland, Helsinki
Szepmuveszeti Muzeum, Museum of Fine Arts, Budapest
Taft Museum of Art, Cincinnati OH
Toledo Museum of Art, Toledo OH
Tver Regional Art Gallery, Tver
University of Illinois at Urbana-Champaign, Krannert Art Museum and Kinkead Pavilion, Champaign IL
University of Kansas, Spencer Museum of Art, Lawrence KS
The University of Kentucky Art Museum, Lexington KY
University of Miami, Lowe Art Museum, Coral Gables FL
University of Notre Dame, Snite Museum of Art, Notre Dame IN
University of Utah, Utah Museum of Fine Arts, Salt Lake City UT
University of Vermont, Robert Hull Fleming Museum, Burlington VT
University of Victoria, The Legacy Art Gallery, Victoria BC
University of Wisconsin-Madison, Chazen Museum of Art, Madison WI
Vassar College, The Frances Lehman Loeb Art Center, Poughkeepsie NY
Walker Art Gallery, Liverpool
Walters Art Museum, Baltimore MD
Worcester Art Museum, Worcester MA

METALWORK

Academy of the New Church, Glencairn Museum, Bryn Athyn PA
Albany Institute of History & Art, Albany NY
Albuquerque Museum of Art & History, Albuquerque NM
American Folk Art Museum, New York NY
Amherst College, Mead Art Museum, Amherst MA
Amsterdam Museum, Amsterdam
Archaeological Museum of Thessaloniki, Thessaloniki
Arkansas Arts Center, Little Rock AR
Arnot Art Museum, Elmira NY
Art Community Center, Art Center of Corpus Christi, Corpus Christi TX
Art Without Walls Inc, Sayville NY
Asheville Art Museum, Asheville NC
Asian Art Museum of San Francisco, Chong-Moon Lee Ctr for Asian Art and Culture, San Francisco CA
Bangladesh National Museum, Dhaka
Baroda Museum and Picture Gallery, Vadodara
Bayerisches Nationalmuseum, Bavarian National Museum, Munich
Bellevue Arts Museum, Bellevue WA
Beloit College, Wright Museum of Art, Beloit WI
Belskie Museum, Closter NJ
Buffalo Niagara Heritage Village, Amherst NY
Burchfield Penney Art Center, Buffalo NY
Byzantine & Christian Museum, Athens, Athens
Canadian Museum of History, Gatineau QC
Center for Art & Education, Van Buren AR
The Children's Museum of Indianapolis, Indianapolis IN
City of Fayette, Alabama, Fayette Art Museum, Fayette AL
Clark County Historical Society, Pioneer - Krier Museum, Ashland KS
College of William & Mary, Muscarelle Museum of Art, Williamsburg VA
The Columbus Museum, Columbus GA
Concord Museum, Concord MA
Contemporary Calgary, Calgary AB
Craft and Folk Art Museum (CAFAM), Los Angeles CA
Cranbrook Art Museum, Bloomfield Hills MI
Crocker Art Museum, Sacramento CA
Cyprus Museum, Nicosia
Dalnavert Museum, Winnipeg MB
Delphi Archaeological Museum, Delphi
Denver Art Museum, Denver CO
Detroit Institute of Arts, Detroit MI
Detroit Zoological Institute, Wildlife Interpretive Gallery, Royal Oak MI
Dublin Arts Council, Dublin OH
Durham Art Guild, Durham NC
Edsel & Eleanor Ford House, Grosse Pointe Shores MI
Evanston Historical Society, Charles Gates Dawes House, Evanston IL
Fetherston Foundation, Packwood House Museum, Lewisburg PA
Fireweed Gallery, Homer AK
Flint Institute of Arts, Flint MI
Florida CraftArt, Saint Petersburg FL
Florida State University and Central Florida Community College, The Appleton Museum of Art, Ocala FL
Forges du Saint-Maurice National Historic Site, Trois Rivieres QC
Fuller Craft Museum, Brockton MA
Galerie Montcalm, Gatineau QC
Gallery One Visual Arts Center, Ellensburg WA
Germantown Historical Society, Philadelphia PA
Girard College, Stephen Girard Collection, Philadelphia PA
Glessner House Museum, Chicago IL
Grand Rapids Art Museum, Grand Rapids MI
Grassroots Art Center, Lucas KS
Haystack Mountain School of Crafts, Deer Isle ME
Hebrew Union College, Skirball Cultural Center, Los Angeles CA
Hecht Museum, Haifa
Henry County Museum & Cultural Arts Center, Clinton MO
Henry Sheldon Museum of Vermont History and Research Center, Middlebury VT
Hillwood Museum & Gardens Foundation, Hillwood Estate Museum & Gardens, Washington DC
Historic Arkansas Museum, Little Rock AR
Historic Hudson Valley, Pocantico Hills NY
Holter Museum of Art, Helena MT
Hot Shops Art Center, Omaha NE
Hui No'eau Visual Arts Center, Gallery and Gift Shop, Makawao Maui HI
Independence Historical Museum & Art Center, Independence KS
Intermedia Arts, Minneapolis MN
Iredell Museums, Statesville NC
Jacques Marchais Museum of Tibetan Art, Staten Island NY
Johns Hopkins University, Evergreen Museum & Library, Baltimore MD
Kelvingrove Art Gallery & Museum, Glasgow UK
Kenosha Public Museums, Kenosha WI
Kereszteny Muzeum, Christian Museum, Esztergom
Kings County Historical Society & Museum, Hampton NB
Kirkland Museum of Fine & Decorative Art, Denver CO
Kyiv Museum of Russian Art, Kyiv Ukrainian
Lalit Kala Akademi Rabindra Bhavan Art Galleries, National Academy of Art, New Delhi, New Delhi
Le Grand Curtius, The Grand Curtius, Liege
League of New Hampshire Craftsmen, Grodin Permanent Collection Museum, Concord NH
Lightner Museum, Saint Augustine FL
Lillian & Coleman Taube Museum of Art, Minot ND
Lincolnshire County Council, Library & Heritage Services, Lincoln
Lincolnshire County Council, The Collection: Art & Archaeology in Lincolnshire, Lincoln
The Long Island Museum of American Art, History & Carriages, Stony Brook NY
Louise Hopkins Underwood Center for the Arts, Lubbock TX
Maryland Historical Society, Museum of Maryland History, Baltimore MD
McCord Museum of Canadian History, Montreal QC
Mesa Arts Center, Mesa Contemporary Arts Museum, Mesa AZ
Millicent Rogers Museum, Taos NM
The Mint Museum, Mint Museum of Craft & Design, Charlotte NC
Missoula Art Museum, Missoula MT
Mobile Museum of Art, Mobile AL
Modern Art Museum, Fort Worth TX
Moravska Galerie v Brne, Moravian Gallery in Brno, Brno
Musee des Beaux-Arts de Tours, Museum of Fine Arts, Tours
Musee des Maitres et Artisans du Quebec, Montreal QC
Musee Regional de lu Cote-Nord, Sept-Iles QC
Musees Royaux d'Art et d'Histoire, Royal Museums of Art and History, Brussels
Museo De Las Americas, Denver CO
Museu Nacional D'Art De Catalunya, Catalona National Museum of Art, Barcelona
Museum of Art - Deland FL, Inc, Deland FL
Museum of Arts & Design, New York NY
Museum of Islamic Art, Doha
Museum of Northwest Art, La Conner WA
Museum zu Allerheiligen, Schaffhausen
Muzej za Umjetnost i Obrt, Museum of Arts & Crafts, Zagreb
Muzeul National de Arta al Romaniei, National Museum of Art of Romania, Bucharest
Muzim Negara, National Museum, Kuala Lumpur
National Museums Scotland, National Museum of Scotland, Edinburgh
National Society of Colonial Dames of America in the State of Maryland, Mount Clare Museum House, Baltimore MD
Naval Historical Center, National Museum of the US Navy, Washington DC
Neue Galerie New York, New York NY
Neustadt Collection of Tiffany Glass, Long Island City NY
New Brunswick Museum, Saint John NB
New Orleans Artworks at New Orleans Glassworks & Printmaking Studio, New Orleans LA
New York State Office of Parks Recreation & Historic Preservation, John Jay Homestead State Historic Site, Katonah NY
Norwich Free Academy, Slater Memorial Museum, Norwich CT
Nova Scotia College of Art and Design, Anna Leonowens Gallery, Halifax NS
Noyes Art Gallery, Lincoln NE
Ohio University, Kennedy Museum of Art, Athens OH
Okanagan Heritage Museum, Kelowna BC
Olana State Historic Site, Hudson NY
Old Salem Museums & Gardens, Museum of Early Southern Decorative Arts, Winston-Salem NC
Panhandle-Plains Historical Museum, Canyon TX
Philadelphia History Museum, Philadelphia PA
Pioneer Town, Pioneer Museum of Western Art, Wimberley TX
Plumas County Museum, Quincy CA
Principia College, School of Nations Museum, Elsah IL
Queen Victoria Museum and Art Gallery, Launceston TAS
Queens College, City University of New York, Godwin-Ternbach Museum, Flushing NY
Reading Public Museum, Reading PA
Rubin Museum of Art, New York NY
Saco Museum, Saco ME
Saint Clair County Community College, Jack R Hennesey Art Galleries, Port Huron MI
San Antonio Museum of Art, San Antonio TX
San Francisco Maritime National Historical Park, Maritime Museum, San Francisco CA
Schweinfurth Art Center, Auburn NY
Seneca-Iroquois National Museum, Salamanca NY
Sheldon Museum & Cultural Center, Inc, Sheldon Museum & Cultural Center, Haines AK

Shirley Plantation Foundation, Charles City VA
Sloss Furnaces National Historic Landmark, Birmingham AL
Society for Contemporary Craft, Pittsburgh PA
The Society of the Cincinnati at Anderson House, Washington DC
South Carolina Artisans Center, Walterboro SC
Southeastern Center for Contemporary Art, Winston-Salem NC
The Speed Art Museum, Louisville KY
Spertus Institute of Jewish Studies, Chicago IL
Staatliche Munzsammlung, State Coin Collection, Munich
Stanford University, Cantor Arts Center at Stanford University, Stanford CA
State University of New York at New Paltz, Samuel Dorsky Museum of Art, New Paltz NY
The Stewart Museum, Montreal QC
Suan Pakkad Palace Museum, Bangkok
Suomen Kansallismuseo, National Museum of Finland, Helsinki
Taos Historic Museums, La Hacienda de Los Martinez, Taos NM
Tokyo National Museum, Tokyo
Topeka & Shawnee County Public Library, Alice C Sabatini Gallery, Topeka KS
Tubman African American Museum, Macon GA
Tver Regional Art Gallery, Tver
The Ukrainian Museum, New York NY
University of Georgia, Georgia Museum of Art, Athens GA
University of Illinois at Urbana-Champaign, Krannert Art Museum and Kinkead Pavilion, Champaign IL
University of Indianapolis, Christel DeHaan Fine Arts Gallery, Indianapolis IN
The University of Kentucky Art Museum, Lexington KY
University of Minnesota, Katherine E Nash Gallery, Minneapolis MN
University of Minnesota, Goldstein Museum of Design, Saint Paul MN
University of Wisconsin-Madison, Chazen Museum of Art, Madison WI
Vesterheim Norwegian-American Museum, Decorah IA
Villa Terrace Decorative Arts Museum, Milwaukee WI
Walker Art Gallery, Liverpool
Walker Fine Art, Denver CO
Wheelwright Museum of the American Indian, Santa Fe NM
White House, Washington DC
Wilfrid Laurier University, Robert Langen Art Gallery, Waterloo ON
Wilkes Art Gallery, North Wilkesboro NC
Workman & Temple Family Homestead Museum, City of Industry CA
World Erotic Art Museum, Miami Beach FL

MEXICAN ART

Americas Society Art Gallery, New York NY
Amherst College, Mead Art Museum, Amherst MA
Art Community Center, Art Center of Corpus Christi, Corpus Christi TX
The Art Museum of Eastern Idaho, Idaho Falls ID
Art Without Walls Inc, Sayville NY
Arts Council of Fayetteville-Cumberland County, The Arts Center, Fayetteville NC
Aurora University, Schingoethe Center for Native American Cultures & The Schingoethe Art Gallery, Aurora IL
The Baltimore Museum of Art, Baltimore MD
Brown University, Haffenreffer Museum of Anthropology, Providence RI
Bucknell University, Edward & Marthann Samek Art Gallery, Lewisburg PA
The Buffalo Fine Arts Academy, Albright-Knox Art Gallery, Buffalo NY
C M Russell Museum, Great Falls MT
California State University, Chico, Janet Turner Print Museum, CSU, Chicago, Chico CA
Centenary College of Louisiana, Meadows Museum of Art, Shreveport LA
The Children's Museum of Indianapolis, Indianapolis IN
City of El Paso, El Paso TX
City of Fremont, Olive Hyde Art Gallery, Fremont CA
The Contemporary Austin, Austin TX
Coutts Museum of Art, Inc, El Dorado KS
Craft and Folk Art Museum (CAFAM), Los Angeles CA
Crocker Art Museum, Sacramento CA
Dartmouth College, Hood Museum of Art, Hanover NH
Davidson College, William H Van Every Jr & Edward M Smith Galleries, Davidson NC
DeLeon White Gallery, Toronto ON
Denver Art Museum, Denver CO
Detroit Institute of Arts, Detroit MI
East Carolina University, Wellington B Gray Gallery, Greenville NC
Edsel & Eleanor Ford House, Grosse Pointe Shores MI
Ellen Noel Art Museum of the Permian Basin, Odessa TX
Emory University, Michael C Carlos Museum, Atlanta GA
En Foco, Inc, Bronx NY
Figge Art Museum, Davenport IA
Flint Institute of Arts, Flint MI
Folk Art Society of America, Richmond VA
Fresno Arts Center & Museum, Fresno CA
General Board of Discipleship, The United Methodist Church, The Upper Room Chapel & Museum, Nashville TN
Heard Museum, Phoenix AZ
Hermitage Museum & Gardens, Norfolk VA
Hidalgo County Historical Museum, Edinburg TX
Independence Historical Museum & Art Center, Independence KS
INTAR Gallery, New York NY
The Interchurch Center, Galleries at the Interchurch Center, New York NY
Intermedia Arts, Minneapolis MN
International Museum of Art, El Paso TX
Jefferson County Open Space, Hiwan Homestead Museum, Evergreen CO
Johns Hopkins University, Evergreen Museum & Library, Baltimore MD
Kenosha Public Museums, Kenosha WI
Knoxville Museum of Art, Knoxville TN
Koshare Indian Museum, Inc, La Junta CO
LA County Museum of Art, Los Angeles CA
Lalit Kala Akademi Rabindra Bhavan Art Galleries, National Academy of Art, New Delhi, New Delhi
Latino Art Museum, Pomona CA
Latino Center of Art and Culture, Sacramento CA
Lillian & Coleman Taube Museum of Art, Minot ND
Louise Hopkins Underwood Center for the Arts, Lubbock TX
Mabee-Gerrer Museum of Art, Shawnee OK
Madison Museum of Contemporary Art, Madison WI
The Mexican Museum, San Francisco CA
Mission San Luis Rey de Francia, Mission San Luis Rey Museum, Oceanside CA
Mission San Miguel Museum, San Miguel CA
Modern Art Museum, Fort Worth TX
Montana State University, Helen E Copeland Gallery, Bozeman MT
Museo De Las Americas, Denver CO
The Museum, Greenwood SC
Museum of Latin American Art, Long Beach CA
National Museum of Mexican Art, Chicago IL
Opelousas Museum of Art, Inc (OMA), Opelousas LA
Palm Springs Art Museum, Palm Springs CA
Panhandle-Plains Historical Museum, Canyon TX
Phoenix Art Museum, Phoenix AZ
Purdue University Galleries, West Lafayette IN
Queens College, City University of New York, Godwin-Ternbach Museum, Flushing NY
Reading Public Museum, Reading PA
Roswell Museum & Art Center, Roswell NM
Saint Joseph College, Art Gallery, University of Saint Joseph, West Hartford CT
Saint Mary's College of California, Museum of Art, Moraga CA
San Angelo Museum of Fine Arts, San Angelo TX
San Antonio Museum of Art, San Antonio TX
Santa Paula Art Museum, Santa Paula CA
Scripps College, Ruth Chandler Williamson Gallery, Claremont CA
The Speed Art Museum, Louisville KY
Stanford University, Cantor Arts Center at Stanford University, Stanford CA
Stone Quarry Hill Art Park, Winner Gallery, Cazenovia NY
Taos Historic Museums, La Hacienda de Los Martinez, Taos NM
Tohono Chul Park, Tucson AZ
Topeka & Shawnee County Public Library, Alice C Sabatini Gallery, Topeka KS
Tucson Museum of Art and Historic Block, Tucson AZ
Tyler Museum of Art, Tyler TX
University of California, Berkeley, Phoebe Apperson Hearst Museum of Anthropology, Berkeley CA
University of Georgia, Georgia Museum of Art, Athens GA
University of Houston, Blaffer Art Museum, Houston TX
University of Illinois at Urbana-Champaign, Krannert Art Museum and Kinkead Pavilion, Champaign IL
The University of Kentucky Art Museum, Lexington KY
University of Miami, Lowe Art Museum, Coral Gables FL
University of Southern California, USC Fisher Museum of Art, Los Angeles CA
University of Texas at Austin, Blanton Museum of Art, Austin TX
University of Utah, Utah Museum of Fine Arts, Salt Lake City UT
University of Washington, Burke Museum of Natural History and Culture, Seattle WA
University of Wisconsin-Madison, Chazen Museum of Art, Madison WI
Wichita Art Museum, Wichita KS
World Erotic Art Museum, Miami Beach FL

MILITARY ART

Adams County Historical Society, Gettysburg PA
African American Museum in Philadelphia, Philadelphia PA
Arizona Historical Society-Yuma, Sanguinetti House Museum & Garden, Yuma AZ
Arnot Art Museum, Elmira NY
Aroostook County Historical & Art Museum, Houlton ME
Arts Council of Fayetteville-Cumberland County, The Arts Center, Fayetteville NC
Bennington Museum, Bennington VT
Bone Creek Museum of Agrarian Art, David City NE
Booth Western Art Museum, Cartersville GA
The Bostonian Society, Old State House Museum, Boston MA
Bullion Plaza Cultural Center & Museum, Miami AZ
Canadian Museum of History, Gatineau QC
Cyprus Museum, Nicosia
Danville Museum of Fine Arts & History, Danville VA
Detroit Institute of Arts, Detroit MI
Evanston Historical Society, Charles Gates Dawes House, Evanston IL
Fairbanks Museum & Planetarium, Saint Johnsbury VT
Florence County Museum, Florence SC
Fondazione Musei Civici Di Venezia, Museo Correr - Correr Museum, Venice
Fort George G Meade Museum, Fort Meade MD
Fort Ticonderoga Association, Ticonderoga NY
Gadsden Museum, Mesilla NM
George Phippen, Phippen Museum - Art of the American West, Prescott AZ
Headquarters Fort Monroe, Dept of Army, Casemate Museum, Hampton VA
Henry County Museum & Cultural Arts Center, Clinton MO
Hillwood Museum & Gardens Foundation, Hillwood Estate Museum & Gardens, Washington DC
Huntington Museum of Art, Huntington WV
Kenosha Public Museums, Kenosha WI
Lightner Museum, Saint Augustine FL
Lincolnshire County Council, Library & Heritage Services, Lincoln
Louise Hopkins Underwood Center for the Arts, Lubbock TX
Louisiana Department of Culture, Recreation & Tourism, Louisiana State Museum, New Orleans LA
Mabee-Gerrer Museum of Art, Shawnee OK
The Mariners' Museum, Newport News VA
Massillon Museum, Massillon OH
Mohawk Valley Heritage Association, Inc, Walter Elwood Museum, Amsterdam NY
Musee des Beaux-Arts de Tours, Museum of Fine Arts, Tours
Museum of West Louisiana, Leesville LA
Museum zu Allerheiligen, Schaffhausen
Muzeul National de Arta al Romaniei, National Museum of Art of Romania, Bucharest

Muzeum Narodowe W Kielcach, National Museum in Kielce, Kielce
Muzeum Narodowe w Poznaniu, National Museum in Poznan, Poznan
National Museum & Art Gallery of Trinidad and Tobago, Port of Spain
National Museums Scotland, National Museum of Scotland, Edinburgh
National Society of Colonial Dames of America in the State of Maryland, Mount Clare Museum House, Baltimore MD
National Veterans Art Museum, Chicago IL
Naval Historical Center, National Museum of the US Navy, Washington DC
Naval War College Museum, Newport RI
New Brunswick Museum, Saint John NB
New York State Military Museum and Veterans Research Center, Saratoga Springs NY
Oklahoma Historical Society, State Museum of History, Oklahoma City OK
Opelousas Museum of Art, Inc (OMA), Opelousas LA
Panhandle-Plains Historical Museum, Canyon TX
Polish Museum of America (PMA), Chicago IL
Portsmouth Historical Society, John Paul Jones House & Discover Portsmouth, Portsmouth NH
Saginaw Art Museum, Saginaw MI
The Society of the Cincinnati at Anderson House, Washington DC
The State Museum of Fine Arts of Tatarstan Republic, Kazan
The Stewart Museum, Montreal QC
The Summit County Historical Society of Akron, OH, Akron OH
United States Military Academy, West Point Museum, West Point NY
United States Navy Supply Corps School, US Navy Supply Corps Museum, Newport RI
USS Constitution Museum, Boston MA
Wisconsin Historical Society, Wisconsin Historical Museum, Madison WI

MINIATURES

Albany Institute of History & Art, Albany NY
Albertina Museum, Vienna
Amherst College, Mead Art Museum, Amherst MA
Bangladesh National Museum, Dhaka
Barker Character, Comic and Cartoon Museum, Cheshire CT
Baroda Museum and Picture Gallery, Vadodara
Bayerisches Nationalmuseum, Bavarian National Museum, Munich
Bronx Community College (CUNY), Hall of Fame for Great Americans, Bronx NY
Bruce Museum, Inc, Greenwich CT
Carolina Art Association, Gibbes Museum of Art, Charleston SC
Center for Art & Education, Van Buren AR
The Children's Museum of Indianapolis, Indianapolis IN
Cincinnati Art Museum, Cincinnati Art Museum, Cincinnati OH
City of Fayette, Alabama, Fayette Art Museum, Fayette AL
City of Fremont, Olive Hyde Art Gallery, Fremont CA
Coutts Museum of Art, Inc, El Dorado KS
Cripple Creek District Museum, Cripple Creek CO
Crocker Art Museum, Sacramento CA
DAR Museum, National Society Daughters of the American Revolution, Washington DC
Detroit Institute of Arts, Detroit MI
Everhart Museum, Scranton PA
Favell Museum of Western Art & Indian Artifacts, Klamath Falls OR
Fine Arts Center for the New River Valley, Pulaski VA
Fishkill Historical Society, Van Wyck Homestead Museum, Fishkill NY
Florence County Museum, Florence SC
Fondazione Musei Civici Di Venezia, Museo Correr - Correr Museum, Venice
Fuller Craft Museum, Brockton MA
Galerie Montcalm, Gatineau QC
George Phippen, Phippen Museum - Art of the American West, Prescott AZ
Glanmore National Historic Site of Canada, Belleville ON
Grand Rapids Art Museum, Grand Rapids MI
Grassroots Art Center, Lucas KS
Headley-Whitney Museum, Lexington KY
Hebrew Union College - Jewish Institute of Religion Museum, Jewish Institute of Religion, New York NY
Henry County Museum & Cultural Arts Center, Clinton MO
Henry Sheldon Museum of Vermont History and Research Center, Middlebury VT
Hillwood Museum & Gardens Foundation, Hillwood Estate Museum & Gardens, Washington DC
Historic Holyoke at Wistariahurst & City of Holyoke, Holyoke MA
Illinois State Museum, ISM Lockport Gallery, Chicago Gallery & Southern Illinois Art Gallery, Springfield IL
Independence Historical Museum & Art Center, Independence KS
International Clown Hall of Fame & Research Center, Inc, West Allis WI
Iredell Museums, Statesville NC
The Israel Museum, Jerusalem, Jerusalem
Jacques Marchais Museum of Tibetan Art, Staten Island NY
Johns Hopkins University, Evergreen Museum & Library, Baltimore MD
Jordan National Gallery of Fine Arts, Amman
Kenosha Public Museums, Kenosha WI
Knoxville Museum of Art, Knoxville TN
Kyiv Museum of Russian Art, Kyiv Ukrainian
Lahore Museum, Lahore
Lalit Kala Akademi Rabindra Bhavan Art Galleries, National Academy of Art, New Delhi, New Delhi
Latino Art Museum, Pomona CA
League of New Hampshire Craftsmen, Grodin Permanent Collection Museum, Concord NH
Lincolnshire County Council, The Collection: Art & Archaeology in Lincolnshire, Lincoln
The Long Island Museum of American Art, History & Carriages, Stony Brook NY
Louise Hopkins Underwood Center for the Arts, Lubbock TX
Louisiana Department of Culture, Recreation & Tourism, Louisiana State Museum, New Orleans LA
Maine Historical Society, Wadsworth-Longfellow House, Portland ME
McCord Museum of Canadian History, Montreal QC
McDowell House & Apothecary Shop, Danville KY
Medina Railroad Museum, Medina NY
Musee Cognacq-Jay, Cognacq-Jay Museum, Paris
Musee des Beaux-Arts d'Orleans, Museum of Fine Arts, Orleans
Musee des Beaux-Arts de Tours, Museum of Fine Arts, Tours
Musees Royaux d'Art et d'Histoire, Royal Museums of Art and History, Brussels
Museo Del Romanticismo, Museum of the Romantic Period, Madrid
Museum zu Allerheiligen, Schaffhausen
Muzej za Umjetnost i Obrt, Museum of Arts & Crafts, Zagreb
Muzeul National de Arta al Romaniei, National Museum of Art of Romania, Bucharest
Muzeum Narodowe w Poznaniu, National Museum in Poznan, Poznan
National Archaeological Museum, Athens
National Art Museum of Moldova, Chisinau
National Baseball Hall of Fame & Museum, Cooperstown NY
National Gallery of Ireland, Dublin
National Museum of Wildlife Art of the Unites States, Jackson WY
National Museums Scotland, National Museum of Scotland, Edinburgh
National Palace Museum, Taipei
National Society of Colonial Dames of America in the State of Maryland, Mount Clare Museum House, Baltimore MD
Naval Historical Center, National Museum of the US Navy, Washington DC
Naval War College Museum, Newport RI
Nelson Mandela Metropolitan Art Museum, Port Elizabeth
New Brunswick Museum, Saint John NB
New Jersey Historical Society, Newark NJ
Norsk Maritimt Museum, Norwegian Maritime Museum, Oslo
Norwich Free Academy, Slater Memorial Museum, Norwich CT
Noyes Art Gallery, Lincoln NE
Okanagan Heritage Museum, Kelowna BC
Old Dartmouth Historical Society, New Bedford Whaling Museum, New Bedford MA
Panhandle-Plains Historical Museum, Canyon TX
Phoenix Art Museum, Phoenix AZ
Pine Bluff/Jefferson County Historical Museum, Pine Bluff AR
Pioneer Historical Museum of South Dakota, Hot Springs SD
Polish Museum of America (PMA), Chicago IL
Portland Art Museum, Portland OR
Rhode Island Historical Society, John Brown House, Providence RI
The Rosenbach Museum & Library, Philadelphia PA
Saco Museum, Saco ME
Saint Olaf College, Flaten Art Museum, Northfield MN
San Antonio Museum of Art, San Antonio TX
Slovenska Narodna Galeria, Slovak National Gallery, Bratislava
The Society of the Cincinnati at Anderson House, Washington DC
South Carolina State Museum, Columbia SC
The Speed Art Museum, Louisville KY
Staatliche Museen zu Berlin Stiftung Preussischer Kulturbesitz, National Museums in Berlin, Prussian Cultural Heritage Foundation, Berlin
The State Museum of Oriental Art, Moscow
Staten Island Museum, Staten Island NY
The Stewart Museum, Montreal QC
Suomen Kansallismuseo, National Museum of Finland, Helsinki
Taft Museum of Art, Cincinnati OH
Tinkertown Museum, Sandia Park NM
Tohono Chul Park, Tucson AZ
Tokyo National Museum, Tokyo
Tver Regional Art Gallery, Tver
United Society of Shakers, Shaker Museum, New Gloucester ME
University of Georgia, Georgia Museum of Art, Athens GA
University of Illinois at Urbana-Champaign, Krannert Art Museum and Kinkead Pavilion, Champaign IL
The University of Kentucky Art Museum, Lexington KY
University of Wisconsin-Madison, Chazen Museum of Art, Madison WI
Vesterheim Norwegian-American Museum, Decorah IA
The Walker African American Museum & Research Center, Las Vegas NV
Walker Art Gallery, Liverpool
The Wallace Collection, London
Wheelwright Museum of the American Indian, Santa Fe NM
Woodlawn/The Pope-Leighey, Alexandria VA
World Erotic Art Museum, Miami Beach FL
Wyoming Trails Gallery, Wheatland WY
Yale University, Yale Center for British Art, New Haven CT
Zigler Art Museum, Jennings LA

MIXED MEDIA

Artspace, Richmond VA
Brickton Art Center, Park Ridge IL
Clear Lake Arts Center, Clear Lake IA
Contemporary Art Center, Peoria IL
Crocker Art Museum, Sacramento CA
Cuadro Fine Art Gallery, Dubai
Dublin Arts Council, Dublin OH
Eula Mae Edwards Museum & Gallery, Clovis NM
Florida CraftArt, Saint Petersburg FL
Glenwood Center for the Arts, Glenwood Springs CO
Haystack Mountain School of Crafts, Deer Isle ME
Hot Shops Art Center, Omaha NE
JMW Turner Museum, Sarasota FL
Jordan National Gallery of Fine Arts, Amman
LACE (Los Angeles Contemporary Exhibitions), Los Angeles CA
Lalit Kala Akademi Rabindra Bhavan Art Galleries, National Academy of Art, New Delhi, New Delhi
Latino Art Museum, Pomona CA
Meem Gallery, Dubai
Moscow Museum of Modern Art, Moscow
Museo de Arte Contemporaneo de Castilla y Leon, Leon
The National Art Center, Tokyo, Tokyo
Palm Springs Art Museum, Palm Springs CA
San Antonio Museum of Art, San Antonio TX
Slovenska Narodna Galeria, Slovak National Gallery, Bratislava

Society for Contemporary Craft, Pittsburgh PA
South Dakota State University, South Dakota Art Museum, Brookings SD
Spertus Institute of Jewish Studies, Chicago IL
Springfield Art Museum, Springfield MO
Stone Quarry Hill Art Park, Winner Gallery, Cazenovia NY

MOSAICS

Academy of the New Church, Glencairn Museum, Bryn Athyn PA
American University of Beirut Archaeological Museum, Beirut
Amherst College, Mead Art Museum, Amherst MA
Archaeological Museum of Thessaloniki, Thessaloniki
Art Community Center, Art Center of Corpus Christi, Corpus Christi TX
Art Without Walls Inc, Sayville NY
The Baltimore Museum of Art, Baltimore MD
Bangladesh National Museum, Dhaka
Baroda Museum and Picture Gallery, Vadodara
Bob Jones University Museum & Gallery Inc, Greenville SC
Byzantine & Christian Museum, Athens, Athens
Cameron Art Museum, Wilmington NC
Canadian Museum of History, Gatineau QC
Children's Museum of Manhattan, New York NY
Craft and Folk Art Museum (CAFAM), Los Angeles CA
Cyprus Museum, Nicosia
Dartmouth College, Hood Museum of Art, Hanover NH
Delphi Archaeological Museum, Delphi
Detroit Institute of Arts, Detroit MI
Dumbarton Oaks, Dumbarton Oaks Museum, Washington DC
Fairbanks Museum & Planetarium, Saint Johnsbury VT
Flint Institute of Arts, Flint MI
Forest Lawn Museum, Glendale CA
The Frank Phillips Foundation Inc, Woolaroc Museum, Bartlesville OK
Fuller Craft Museum, Brockton MA
Grassroots Art Center, Lucas KS
Hecht Museum, Haifa
Henry County Museum & Cultural Arts Center, Clinton MO
Illinois State Museum, ISM Lockport Gallery, Chicago Gallery & Southern Illinois Art Gallery, Springfield IL
The Interchurch Center, Galleries at the Interchurch Center, New York NY
Intermedia Arts, Minneapolis MN
The Israel Museum, Jerusalem, Jerusalem
Johns Hopkins University, Evergreen Museum & Library, Baltimore MD
Kenosha Public Museums, Kenosha WI
Kentucky Museum of Art and Craft, Louisville KY
Kimbell Art Foundation, Kimbell Art Museum, Fort Worth TX
Lalit Kala Akademi Rabindra Bhavan Art Galleries, National Academy of Art, New Delhi, New Delhi
Latino Art Museum, Pomona CA
League of New Hampshire Craftsmen, Grodin Permanent Collection Museum, Concord NH
Lincolnshire County Council, The Collection: Art & Archaeology in Lincolnshire, Lincoln
Lizzadro Museum of Lapidary Art, Elmhurst IL
Louise Hopkins Underwood Center for the Arts, Lubbock TX
Mesa Arts Center, Mesa Contemporary Arts Museum, Mesa AZ
Musees Royaux d'Art et d'Histoire, Royal Museums of Art and History, Brussels
Museo di Palazzo Ducale, Ducale Palace Museum, Mantua
Museum zu Allerheiligen, Schaffhausen
Muzeul de Istorie Nationala Si Arheologie Constanta, National History & Archaeology Museum, Constanta
Nelson Mandela Metropolitan Art Museum, Port Elizabeth
Neustadt Collection of Tiffany Glass, Long Island City NY
Norwich Free Academy, Slater Memorial Museum, Norwich CT
Noyes Art Gallery, Lincoln NE
Panhandle-Plains Historical Museum, Canyon TX
Plainsman Museum, Aurora NE
Queens College, City University of New York, Godwin-Ternbach Museum, Flushing NY
San Antonio Museum of Art, San Antonio TX
Slovenska Narodna Galeria, Slovak National Gallery, Bratislava
Society for Contemporary Craft, Pittsburgh PA
South Dakota State University, South Dakota Art Museum, Brookings SD
The Speed Art Museum, Louisville KY
Stanford University, Cantor Arts Center at Stanford University, Stanford CA
Tohono Chul Park, Tucson AZ
Tver Regional Art Gallery, Tver
University of Utah, Utah Museum of Fine Arts, Salt Lake City UT
University of Wisconsin-Madison, Chazen Museum of Art, Madison WI
Wadsworth Atheneum Museum of Art, Hartford CT
Waterworks Visual Arts Center, Salisbury NC
Wheaton College, Beard and Weil Galleries, Norton MA
Winkler Gallery of Fine Art, DuBois PA
Wiregrass Museum of Art, Dothan AL
Worcester Art Museum, Worcester MA

ORIENTAL ART

Academy of the New Church, Glencairn Museum, Bryn Athyn PA
Alexandria Museum of Art, Alexandria LA
Allentown Art Museum, Allentown PA
Amherst College, Mead Art Museum, Amherst MA
Arnot Art Museum, Elmira NY
Art Gallery of Greater Victoria, Victoria BC
Art Gallery of Nova Scotia, Halifax NS
Art Without Walls Inc, Sayville NY
Arts Council of Fayetteville-Cumberland County, The Arts Center, Fayetteville NC
Asian Art Museum of San Francisco, Chong-Moon Lee Ctr for Asian Art and Culture, San Francisco CA
Bangladesh National Museum, Dhaka
Baroda Museum and Picture Gallery, Vadodara
Beloit College, Wright Museum of Art, Beloit WI
Billie Trimble Chandler, Texas State Museum of Asian Cultures, Corpus Christi TX
Birger Sandzen Memorial Gallery, Lindsborg KS
Birmingham Museum of Art, Birmingham AL
Blanden Memorial Art Museum, Fort Dodge IA
Bob Jones University Museum & Gallery Inc, Greenville SC
Bruce Museum, Inc, Greenwich CT
Bucknell University, Edward & Marthann Samek Art Gallery, Lewisburg PA
The Buffalo Fine Arts Academy, Albright-Knox Art Gallery, Buffalo NY
California State University, Chico, Janet Turner Print Museum, CSU, Chicago, Chico CA
Carnegie Museums of Pittsburgh, Carnegie Museum of Art, Pittsburgh PA
Carolina Art Association, Gibbes Museum of Art, Charleston SC
Chrysler Museum of Art, Norfolk VA
Cincinnati Art Museum, Cincinnati Art Museum, Cincinnati OH
City of Gainesville, Thomas Center Galleries - Cultural Affairs, Gainesville FL
The Cleveland Museum of Art, Cleveland OH
College of William & Mary, Muscarelle Museum of Art, Williamsburg VA
The Columbus Museum, Columbus GA
Columbus Museum of Art, Columbus OH
Coutts Museum of Art, Inc, El Dorado KS
Craft and Folk Art Museum (CAFAM), Los Angeles CA
Crocker Art Museum, Sacramento CA
The Currier Museum of Art, Manchester NH
Dayton Art Institute, Dayton OH
Denver Art Museum, Denver CO
Designmuseum Danmark, Danish Design Museum, Copenhagen
Detroit Institute of Arts, Detroit MI
Dickinson College, The Trout Gallery, Carlisle PA
Emory University, Michael C Carlos Museum, Atlanta GA
Erie Art Museum, Erie PA
Evansville Museum of Arts, History & Science, Evansville IN
Everhart Museum, Scranton PA
Fairbanks Museum & Planetarium, Saint Johnsbury VT
Fetherston Foundation, Packwood House Museum, Lewisburg PA
Figge Art Museum, Davenport IA
Flint Institute of Arts, Flint MI
Florence County Museum, Florence SC
Florida State University and Central Florida Community College, The Appleton Museum of Art, Ocala FL
Fresno Arts Center & Museum, Fresno CA
Glanmore National Historic Site of Canada, Belleville ON
Grand Rapids Art Museum, Grand Rapids MI
Grand Rapids Public Museum, Grand Rapids MI
Greenville College, Richard W Bock Sculpture Collection, Almira College House, Greenville IL
Headley-Whitney Museum, Lexington KY
Hebrew Union College, Skirball Cultural Center, Los Angeles CA
Henry County Museum & Cultural Arts Center, Clinton MO
Hermitage Museum & Gardens, Norfolk VA
Hillwood Museum & Gardens Foundation, Hillwood Estate Museum & Gardens, Washington DC
Historic Cherry Hill, Albany NY
Historic Holyoke at Wistariahurst & City of Holyoke, Holyoke MA
Honolulu Museum of Art, Honolulu HI
Illinois State Museum, ISM Lockport Gallery, Chicago Gallery & Southern Illinois Art Gallery, Springfield IL
The Interchurch Center, Galleries at the Interchurch Center, New York NY
International Museum of Art, El Paso TX
Iowa State University, Brunnier Art Museum, Ames IA
Iredell Museums, Statesville NC
Isabella Stewart Gardner Museum, Boston MA
Jacksonville University, Alexander Brest Museum & Gallery, Jacksonville FL
Jacques Marchais Museum of Tibetan Art, Staten Island NY
JMW Turner Museum, Sarasota FL
Johns Hopkins University, Evergreen Museum & Library, Baltimore MD
Johnson-Humrickhouse Museum, Coshocton OH
Karakalpak State Art Museum, Nukus Republic of Karakalpakstan
Kenosha Public Museums, Kenosha WI
Kentucky Museum of Art and Craft, Louisville KY
Kimbell Art Foundation, Kimbell Art Museum, Fort Worth TX
Lalit Kala Akademi Rabindra Bhavan Art Galleries, National Academy of Art, New Delhi, New Delhi
Lawrence University, Wriston Art Center Galleries, Appleton WI
Lightner Museum, Saint Augustine FL
Lillian & Coleman Taube Museum of Art, Minot ND
Lizzadro Museum of Lapidary Art, Elmhurst IL
Lyman Allyn Art Museum, New London CT
Memphis Brooks Museum of Art, Memphis TN
The Metropolitan Museum of Art, New York NY
Minneapolis Institute of Art, Minneapolis MN
Mobile Museum of Art, Mobile AL
Montana State University, Helen E Copeland Gallery, Bozeman MT
Moravska Galerie v Brne, Moravian Gallery in Brno, Brno
Muscatine Art Center, Muscatine IA
Musees Royaux d'Art et d'Histoire, Royal Museums of Art and History, Brussels
The Museum of Arts & Sciences Inc, Daytona Beach FL
Museum of Contemporary Art Chicago, Chicago IL
Museum of Fine Arts, Boston MA
Museum of Northwest Art, La Conner WA
Museum zu Allerheiligen, Schaffhausen
Muzeul National de Arta al Romaniei, National Museum of Art of Romania, Bucharest
Muzeum Narodowe W Kielcach, National Museum in Kielce, Kielce
National Art Museum of Moldova, Chisinau
National Palace Museum, Taipei
National Silk Art Museum, Weston MO
Nelson Mandela Metropolitan Art Museum, Port Elizabeth
New Orleans Museum of Art, New Orleans LA
New Visions Gallery, Inc, Marshfield WI
Newfields, Indianapolis IN
Norwich Free Academy, Slater Memorial Museum, Norwich CT
Oklahoma City Museum of Art, Oklahoma City OK

Olana State Historic Site, Hudson NY
Omniplex Science Museum, Oklahoma City OK
Owensboro Museum of Fine Art, Owensboro KY
Panhandle-Plains Historical Museum, Canyon TX
Parrish Art Museum, Water Mill NY
Peabody Essex Museum, Salem MA
Philbrook Museum of Art, Tulsa OK
Polk Museum of Art, Lakeland FL
The Pomona College, Claremont CA
Portland Art Museum, Portland OR
Purdue University Galleries, West Lafayette IN
Queens College, City University of New York, Godwin-Ternbach Museum, Flushing NY
Reading Public Museum, Reading PA
Riverside County Museum, Edward-Dean Museum & Gardens, Cherry Valley CA
Royal Arts Foundation, Belcourt Castle, Newport RI
Saginaw Art Museum, Saginaw MI
Saint John's University, Dr. M.T. Geoffrey Yeh Art Gallery, Queens NY
Saint Olaf College, Flaten Art Museum, Northfield MN
San Antonio Museum of Art, San Antonio TX
San Diego Museum of Art, San Diego CA
The San Joaquin Pioneer & Historical Society, The Haggin Museum, Stockton CA
Santa Barbara Museum of Art, Santa Barbara CA
Scripps College, Ruth Chandler Williamson Gallery, Claremont CA
Scripps College, Clark Humanities Museum, Claremont CA
Seattle Art Museum, Seattle WA
Slovenska Narodna Galeria, Slovak National Gallery, Bratislava
The Society of the Cincinnati at Anderson House, Washington DC
Southern Oregon University, Schneider Museum of Art, Ashland OR
Spertus Institute of Jewish Studies, Chicago IL
Staatliche Museen zu Berlin Stiftung Preussischer Kulturbesitz, National Museums in Berlin, Prussian Cultural Heritage Foundation, Berlin
Stanford University, Cantor Arts Center at Stanford University, Stanford CA
The State Museum of Oriental Art, Moscow
Staten Island Museum, Staten Island NY
Stone Quarry Hill Art Park, Winner Gallery, Cazenovia NY
Stratford Historical Society, Catharine B Mitchell Museum, Stratford CT
Suomen Kansallismuseo, National Museum of Finland, Helsinki
Taft Museum of Art, Cincinnati OH
Tokyo National Museum, Tokyo
Topeka & Shawnee County Public Library, Alice C Sabatini Gallery, Topeka KS
Tucson Museum of Art and Historic Block, Tucson AZ
Tver Regional Art Gallery, Tver
University of Chicago, Smart Museum of Art, Chicago IL
University of Illinois at Urbana-Champaign, Krannert Art Museum and Kinkead Pavilion, Champaign IL
The University of Kentucky Art Museum, Lexington KY
University of Miami, Lowe Art Museum, Coral Gables FL
University of Notre Dame, Snite Museum of Art, Notre Dame IN
University of Richmond, University Museums, Richmond VA
University of Utah, Utah Museum of Fine Arts, Salt Lake City UT
University of Vermont, Robert Hull Fleming Museum, Burlington VT
University of Victoria, The Legacy Art Gallery, Victoria BC
University of Washington, Burke Museum of Natural History and Culture, Seattle WA
University of Wisconsin-Madison, Chazen Museum of Art, Madison WI
Vassar College, The Frances Lehman Loeb Art Center, Poughkeepsie NY
Villa Terrace Decorative Arts Museum, Milwaukee WI
Walters Art Museum, Baltimore MD
Washington County Museum of Fine Arts, Hagerstown MD
Wayne Center for the Arts, Wooster OH
Wilfrid Laurier University, Robert Langen Art Gallery, Waterloo ON
Woodmere Art Museum Inc, Philadelphia PA
World Erotic Art Museum, Miami Beach FL
Yerba Buena Center for the Arts, San Francisco CA

PAINTING-AMERICAN

1708 Gallery, Richmond VA
1890 House-Museum & Center for the Arts, Cortland NY
A.E. Backus Museum & Gallery, Fort Pierce FL
A.I.R. Gallery, Brooklyn NY
Abington Art Center, Jenkintown PA
Academy Art Museum, Easton MD
Academy of the New Church, Glencairn Museum, Bryn Athyn PA
African American Museum in Philadelphia, Philadelphia PA
Akron Art Museum, Akron OH
Alaska Heritage Museum at Wells Fargo, Anchorage AK
Albany Institute of History & Art, Albany NY
Albany Museum of Art, Albany GA
Albin Polasek Museum & Sculpture Gardens, Winter Park FL
Albion College, Bobbitt Visual Arts Center, Albion MI
The Albrecht-Kemper Museum of Art, Saint Joseph MO
Albright College, Freedman Gallery, Reading PA
Albuquerque Museum of Art & History, Albuquerque NM
Alice Moseley Folk Art and Antique Museum, Bay Saint Louis MS
Allentown Art Museum, Allentown PA
Alton Museum of History & Art, Inc, Alton IL
American Folk Art Museum, New York NY
American Sport Art Museum and Archives, Daphne AL
American University, Museum at the Katzen, Washington DC
Amon Carter Museum of American Art, Fort Worth TX
Anchorage Museum at Rasmuson Center, Anchorage AK
The Andy Warhol Museum, Pittsburgh PA
Anna Maria College, Saint Luke's Gallery, Paxton MA
Appaloosa Museum and Heritage Center, Moscow ID
ARC Gallery and Educational Foundation, Chicago IL
Arkansas Arts Center, Little Rock AR
Arnot Art Museum, Elmira NY
Art and History Museums - Maitland, Maitland FL
Art Community Center, Art Center of Corpus Christi, Corpus Christi TX
Art Gallery of Alberta, Edmonton AB
The Art Gallery of Grand Prairie, Grande Prairie AB
Art Gallery of Hamilton, Hamilton ON
Art Gallery of Nova Scotia, Halifax NS
Art Gallery of Ontario, Toronto ON
The Art Museum of Eastern Idaho, Idaho Falls ID
Art Museum of Greater Lafayette, Lafayette IN
Art Museum of Southeast Texas, Beaumont TX
Art Without Walls Inc, Sayville NY
Artesia Historical Museum and Art Center, Artesia NM
Artists' Cooperative Gallery, Omaha NE
Arts Council of Fayetteville-Cumberland County, The Arts Center, Fayetteville NC
Artspace, Richmond VA
Asheville Art Museum, Asheville NC
Athenaeum of Philadelphia, Philadelphia PA
Attleboro Arts Museum, Attleboro MA
Audrain County Historical Society, Graceland Museum & American Saddlehorse Museum & Fire Brick Industry Museum, Mexico MO
Augustana University, Eide-Dalrymple Gallery, Sioux Falls SD
Bakersfield Art Foundation, Bakersfield Museum of Art, Bakersfield CA
Baldwin Gallery, Aspen CO
Baldwin Historical Society Museum, Baldwin NY
Baldwin-Wallace College, Fawick Art Gallery, Berea OH
The Baltimore Museum of Art, Baltimore MD
Bangladesh National Museum, Dhaka
Barnes Foundation, Merion PA
The Bartlett Museum, Amesbury MA
Baruch College of the City University of New York, Sidney Mishkin Gallery, New York NY
Bass Museum of Art, Miami Beach FL
Baton Rouge Gallery, Center For Contemporary Art, Baton Rouge LA
Bayerische Staatsgemaldesammlungen, Bavarian State Painting Collections, Munich
Beaumont Art League, Beaumont TX
Belger Arts Center, Kansas City MO
Beloit College, Wright Museum of Art, Beloit WI
Belskie Museum, Closter NJ
Bennington Museum, Bennington VT
Bergstrom-Mahler Museum of Glass, Neenah WI
Berkshire Museum, Pittsfield MA
Berman Museum, Anniston AL
Besser Museum for Northeast Michigan, Alpena MI
Beverly Historical Society, Cabot, Hale & Balch House Museums, Beverly MA
Biggs Museum of American Art, Dover DE
Birger Sandzen Memorial Gallery, Lindsborg KS
Birmingham Museum of Art, Birmingham AL
Biscoe Western Art Museum, San Antonio TX
Blanden Memorial Art Museum, Fort Dodge IA
Blauvelt Demarest Foundation, Hiram Blauvelt Art Museum, Oradell NJ
Blowing Rock Art and History Museum, Blowing Rock NC
Board of Parks & Recreation, The Parthenon, Nashville TN
Bob Jones University Museum & Gallery Inc, Greenville SC
Boise Art Museum, Boise ID
Bone Creek Museum of Agrarian Art, David City NE
Booth Western Art Museum, Cartersville GA
The Bostonian Society, Old State House Museum, Boston MA
Bowdoin College, Peary-MacMillan Arctic Museum, Brunswick ME
Brick Store Museum, Kennebunk ME
Bruce Museum, Inc, Greenwich CT
Bryan Memorial Gallery, Cambridge VT
Bucknell University, Edward & Marthann Samek Art Gallery, Lewisburg PA
The Buffalo Fine Arts Academy, Albright-Knox Art Gallery, Buffalo NY
Burchfield Penney Art Center, Buffalo NY
Burke Arts Council, Jailhouse Galleries, Morganton NC
Bush-Holley Historic Site & Storehouse Gallery, Greenwich Historical Society, Cos Cob CT
C M Russell Museum, Great Falls MT
C W Post Campus of Long Island University, Hillwood Art Museum, Brookville NY
Cambridge Museum, Cambridge NE
Cameron Art Museum, Wilmington NC
Canadian Wildlife & Wilderness Art Museum, Ottawa ON
Canton Museum of Art, Canton OH
Cape Ann Museum, Gloucester MA
Cape Cod Museum of Art Inc, Dennis MA
Capital University, Schumacher Gallery, Columbus OH
Carleton College, Art Gallery, Northfield MN
Carlsbad Museum & Art Center, Carlsbad NM
Carnegie Center for Art & History, New Albany IN
Carnegie Museums of Pittsburgh, Carnegie Museum of Art, Pittsburgh PA
Carolina Art Association, Gibbes Museum of Art, Charleston SC
Carson County Square House Museum, Panhandle TX
Cartoon Art Museum, San Francisco CA
Cayuga Museum of History & Art, Auburn NY
Cedar Rapids Museum of Art, Cedar Rapids IA
Center for Art & Education, Van Buren AR
Center for the Arts Piper Gallery, Crested Butte CO
Central Methodist University, Ashby-Hodge Gallery of American Art, Fayette MO
Central United Methodist Church, Swords Into Plowshares Peace Center & Gallery, Detroit MI
Channel Islands Maritime Museum, Oxnard CA
Charles Allis Art Museum, Milwaukee WI
Charleston Museum, Heyward-Washington House, Charleston SC
Charleston Museum, Joseph Manigault House, Charleston SC
Chatham Historical Society, The Atwood House Museum, Chatham MA
Chatillon-DeMenil House Foundation, Chatillon-DeMenil Mansion, Saint Louis MO
Cheekwood-Tennessee Botanical Garden & Museum of Art, Nashville TN
The Children's Museum of Indianapolis, Indianapolis IN
Chrysler Museum of Art, Norfolk VA
City of Atlanta, Atlanta Cyclorama & Civil War Museum, Atlanta GA

City of Cedar Falls, Iowa, James & Meryl Hearst Center for the Arts & Sculpture Garden, Cedar Falls IA
City of El Paso, El Paso TX
City of Fayette, Alabama, Fayette Art Museum, Fayette AL
City of Fremont, Olive Hyde Art Gallery, Fremont CA
City of Gainesville, Thomas Center Galleries - Cultural Affairs, Gainesville FL
The City of Petersburg Museums, Petersburg VA
City of Pittsfield Office of Cultural Development, Lichtenstein Center for the Arts, Pittsfield MA
City of Springdale, Shiloh Museum of Ozark History, Springdale AR
City of Ukiah, Grace Hudson Museum & The Sun House, Ukiah CA
Clark Art Institute, Williamstown MA
Clark County Historical Society, Pioneer - Krier Museum, Ashland KS
The Cleveland Museum of Art, Cleveland OH
Clinton Art Association, River Arts Center, Clinton IA
Coastal Arts League Museum, Half Moon Bay CA
Cohasset Historical Society, Pratt Building (Society Headquarters), Cohasset MA
Colgate University, Picker Art Gallery, Hamilton NY
The College of Idaho, Rosenthal Art Gallery, Caldwell ID
College of William & Mary, Muscarelle Museum of Art, Williamsburg VA
Columbia Museum of Art, Columbia SC
Columbus Chapel & Boal Mansion Museum, Boalsburg PA
The Columbus Museum, Columbus GA
Columbus Museum of Art, Columbus OH
Concord Museum, Concord MA
Concordia Historical Institute, Saint Louis MO
Coos Art Museum, Coos Bay OR
Corcoran Gallery of Art, Washington DC
Cornell College, Peter Paul Luce Gallery, Mount Vernon IA
Cornell Museum of Art and American Culture, Delray Beach FL
Cornell University, Herbert F Johnson Museum of Art, Ithaca NY
Coutts Museum of Art, Inc, El Dorado KS
Craigdarroch Castle Historical Museum Society, Victoria BC
Cranbrook Art Museum, Bloomfield Hills MI
Crane Collection, Gallery of American Painting and Sculpture, Magnolia MA
Crary Art Gallery, Warren PA
Crazy Horse Memorial, Indian Museum of North America, Native American Educational & Cultural Center & Crazy Horse Memorial Library (Reference), Crazy Horse SD
Cripple Creek District Museum, Cripple Creek CO
Crocker Art Museum, Sacramento CA
Crook County Museum & Art Gallery, Sundance WY
Crow Wing County Historical Society, Brainerd MN
The Currier Museum of Art, Manchester NH
Danville Museum of Fine Arts & History, Danville VA
DAR Museum, National Society Daughters of the American Revolution, Washington DC
Dartmouth College, Hood Museum of Art, Hanover NH
Daum Museum of Contemporary Art, Sedalia MO
Davidson College, William H Van Every Jr & Edward M Smith Galleries, Davidson NC
Dayton Art Institute, Dayton OH
deCordova Sculpture Park & Museum, Lincoln MA
Deines Cultural Center, Russell KS
Delaware Art Museum, Wilmington DE
Delaware Division of Historical & Cultural Affairs, Dover DE
DeLeon White Gallery, Toronto ON
Delta Blues Museum, Clarksdale MS
Denver Art Museum, Denver CO
Department of Economic & Community Development, State of Connecticut DECD Eric Sloane Museum, Kent CT
Detroit Institute of Arts, Detroit MI
Detroit Zoological Institute, Wildlife Interpretive Gallery, Royal Oak MI
Dickinson College, The Trout Gallery, Carlisle PA
Dickinson State University, Art Gallery, Dickinson ND
Discovery Museum, Bridgeport CT
Dixie State University, Sears Art Museum Gallery, Saint George UT
The Dixon Gallery & Gardens, Memphis TN
Dublin Arts Council, Dublin OH
Dumbarton Oaks, Dumbarton Oaks Museum, Washington DC
East Carolina University, Wellington B Gray Gallery, Greenville NC
Eastern Illinois University, Tarble Arts Center, Charleston IL
Eastern Washington State Historical Society, Northwest Museum of Arts & Culture, Spokane WA
Edmundson Art Foundation, Inc, Des Moines Art Center, Des Moines IA
Edsel & Eleanor Ford House, Grosse Pointe Shores MI
Edward Hopper, Nyack NY
Eiteljorg Museum of American Indians & Western Art, Indianapolis IN
Elmhurst Art Museum, Elmhurst IL
Erie Art Museum, Erie PA
Evanston Historical Society, Charles Gates Dawes House, Evanston IL
Evansville Museum of Arts, History & Science, Evansville IN
Everhart Museum, Scranton PA
Everson Museum of Art, Syracuse NY
Fairfield University, Art Museum, Fairfield CT
Fall River Historical Society, Fall River MA
Fetherston Foundation, Packwood House Museum, Lewisburg PA
Figge Art Museum, Davenport IA
Fine Arts Center for the New River Valley, Pulaski VA
Fisher Art Gallery, Marshalltown IA
Fishkill Historical Society, Van Wyck Homestead Museum, Fishkill NY
Fisk University, Aaron Douglas Gallery, Nashville TN
Fitchburg Art Museum, Fitchburg MA
Fitton Center for Creative Arts, Hamilton OH
Flint Institute of Arts, Flint MI
Florence County Museum, Florence SC
Florida Southern College, Melvin Art Gallery, Lakeland FL
Florida State University, John & Mable Ringling Museum of Art, Sarasota FL
Florida State University and Central Florida Community College, The Appleton Museum of Art, Ocala FL
Folk Art Society of America, Richmond VA
Fondazione Musei Civici Di Venezia, Ca' Pesaro Galleria Nazionale d'Arte Moderna - Ca' Pesaro Gallery of Modern Art, Venice
Fort Hays State University, Moss-Thorns Gallery of Arts, Hays KS
Fort Morgan Heritage Foundation, Fort Morgan CO
Fort Smith Regional Art Museum, Fort Smith AR
Fort Ticonderoga Association, Ticonderoga NY
Fort Wayne Museum of Art, Inc, Fort Wayne IN
The Frank Phillips Foundation Inc, Woolaroc Museum, Bartlesville OK
Frankfort Community Public Library, Anna & Harlan Hubbard Gallery, Frankfort IN
Frederic Remington, Ogdensburg NY
The Frick Art & Historical Center, Inc, Frick Art Museum, Pittsburgh PA
Fruitlands Museum, Inc, Harvard MA
Frye Art Museum, Seattle WA
Fuller Craft Museum, Brockton MA
Fulton County Historical Society Inc, Fulton County Museum (Tetzlaff Reference Room), Rochester IN
Gadsden Museum, Mesilla NM
Galerie Montcalm, Gatineau QC
Gallery Moos Ltd, Toronto ON
Gallery One Visual Arts Center, Ellensburg WA
Gaston County Museum of Art & History, Dallas NC
General Board of Discipleship, The United Methodist Church, The Upper Room Chapel & Museum, Nashville TN
Genesee Country Village & Museum, John L Wehle Art Gallery, Mumford NY
George Phippen, Phippen Museum - Art of the American West, Prescott AZ
The George Washington University, Luther W Brady Art Gallery, Washington DC
Georgia O'Keeffe Museum, Santa Fe NM
Germantown Historical Society, Philadelphia PA
Gertrude Herbert Institute of Art, Augusta GA
Girard College, Stephen Girard Collection, Philadelphia PA
Glenwood Center for the Arts, Glenwood Springs CO
Gloridale Partnership, National Museum of Woodcarving, Custer SD
Grand Rapids Art Museum, Grand Rapids MI
Grand Rapids Public Museum, Grand Rapids MI
Greene County Historical Society, Bronck Museum, Coxsackie NY
Greenville College, Richard W Bock Sculpture Collection, Almira College House, Greenville IL
Greenville County Museum of Art, Greenville SC
Gunston Hall Plantation, Mason Neck VA
Hamilton College, Emerson Gallery, Clinton NY
Harness Racing Museum & Hall of Fame, Goshen NY
Hartwick College, Foreman Gallery, Oneonta NY
Hays Arts Center, Hays KS
Headquarters Fort Monroe, Dept of Army, Casemate Museum, Hampton VA
Heard Museum, Phoenix AZ
Hebrew Union College - Jewish Institute of Religion, Skirball Museum Cincinnati, Cincinnati OH
Hebrew Union College - Jewish Institute of Religion Museum, Jewish Institute of Religion, New York NY
The Heckscher Museum of Art, Huntington NY
Henry County Museum & Cultural Arts Center, Clinton MO
Henry Morrison Flagler Museum, Palm Beach FL
Henry Sheldon Museum of Vermont History and Research Center, Middlebury VT
Heritage Center, Inc, Pine Ridge SD
Hermitage Museum & Gardens, Norfolk VA
Hershey Museum, Hershey PA
Hickory Museum of Art, Inc, Hickory NC
High Desert Museum, Bend OR
Hill-Stead Museum, Farmington CT
Hillwood Museum & Gardens Foundation, Hillwood Estate Museum & Gardens, Washington DC
Historic Arkansas Museum, Little Rock AR
Historic Cherry Hill, Albany NY
Historic Deerfield, Inc, Deerfield MA
Historic Hudson Valley, Pocantico Hills NY
Historic Huguenot Street, New Paltz NY
Historic Newton, Newton MA
Historical Society of Cheshire County, Keene NH
Historical Society of Martin County, Elliott Museum, Stuart FL
Historical Society of Old Newbury, Cushing House Museum, Newburyport MA
The History Center in Tompkins County, Ithaca NY
History Colorado Center Museum, Denver CO
Holter Museum of Art, Helena MT
Honolulu Museum of Art, Honolulu HI
The Hudson River Museum, Yonkers NY
Hui No'eau Visual Arts Center, Gallery and Gift Shop, Makawao Maui HI
Hunter Museum of American Art, Chattanooga TN
Huntington Museum of Art, Huntington WV
Huntsville Museum of Art, Huntsville AL
The Hyde Collection, Glens Falls NY
Hyde Park Art Center, Chicago IL
i.d.e.a. Museum, Mesa AZ
Idemitsu Museum of Arts, Tokyo
Illinois Historic Preservation Agency, Bishop Hill State Historic Site, Bishop Hill IL
Illinois State Museum, ISM Lockport Gallery, Chicago Gallery & Southern Illinois Art Gallery, Springfield IL
Illinois Wesleyan University, Merwin & Wakeley Galleries, Bloomington IL
Imperial Calcasieu Museum, Gibson-Barham Gallery, Lake Charles LA
Independence National Historical Park, Philadelphia PA
Independence Seaport Museum, Philadelphia PA
Indiana Landmarks, Morris-Butler House, Indianapolis IN
Indiana State Museum, Indianapolis IN
Institute of Contemporary Art, Los Angeles, Los Angeles CA
International Museum of Art, El Paso TX
International Museum of Art & Science, McAllen TX
Iredell Museums, Statesville NC
Irvine Museum, Irvine CA
Isabella Stewart Gardner Museum, Boston MA
The Israel Museum, Jerusalem, Jerusalem
Jacksonville University, Alexander Brest Museum & Gallery, Jacksonville FL
James A Michener Art Museum, Doylestown PA
James D Veatch Camp Breckinridge Museum & Arts Center, Morganfield KY
James Dick Foundation, Festival - Institute, Round Top TX
Jefferson County Open Space, Hiwan Homestead Museum, Evergreen CO
Jerald Melberg Gallery, Charlotte NC

JMW Turner Museum, Sarasota FL
Joe Gish's Old West Museum, Fredericksburg TX
John D Barrow, Skaneateles NY
The John L. Clarke Western Art Gallery & Memorial Museum, East Glacier Park MT
Johns Hopkins University, Evergreen Museum & Library, Baltimore MD
Jordan National Gallery of Fine Arts, Amman
Joslyn Art Museum, Omaha NE
Juniata College Museum of Art, Huntingdon PA
Kalamazoo Institute of Arts, Kalamazoo MI
Karakalpak State Art Museum, Nukus Republic of Karakalpakstan
Kean University, James Howe Gallery, Union NJ
Keene State College, Thorne-Sagendorph Art Gallery, Keene NH
Kelly-Griggs House Museum, Red Bluff CA
Kenosha Public Museums, Kenosha WI
Kentucky Derby Museum, Louisville KY
Kentucky Museum of Art and Craft, Louisville KY
Knoxville Museum of Art, Knoxville TN
Koochiching Museums, International Falls MN
Koshare Indian Museum, Inc, La Junta CO
The Kreeger Museum, Washington DC
L D Brinkman, Kerrville TX
La Salle University Art Museum, Philadelphia PA
Lafayette College, Lafayette College Art Galleries, Easton PA
Lafayette Science Museum & Planetarium, Lafayette LA
LaGrange Art Museum, LaGrange GA
Laguna Art Museum, Laguna Beach CA
Langston University, Melvin B Tolson Black Heritage Center, Langston OK
Lauren Rogers, Laurel MS
Leanin' Tree Museum & Sculpture Garden of Western Art, Boulder CO
Lehigh Valley Heritage Center, Allentown PA
Liberty Hall Historic Site, Liberty Hall Museum, Frankfort KY
Lighthouse ArtCenter Museum & School of Art, Tequesta FL
Lightner Museum, Saint Augustine FL
Lillian & Coleman Taube Museum of Art, Minot ND
Lincoln County Historical Association, Inc, 1811 Old Lincoln County Jail & Lincoln County Museum, Wiscasset ME
Livingston County Historical Society, Museum, Geneseo NY
Lockwood-Mathews Mansion Museum, Norwalk CT
The Long Island Museum of American Art, History & Carriages, Stony Brook NY
Longfellow's Wayside Inn Museum, Sudbury MA
Longfellow-Evangeline State Commemorative Area, Saint Martinville LA
Longue Vue House & Gardens, New Orleans LA
Longview Museum of Fine Art, Longview TX
Los Angeles County Museum of Art, Los Angeles CA
Los Angeles County Museum of Natural History, William S Hart Museum, Newhall CA
Louise Hopkins Underwood Center for the Arts, Lubbock TX
Louisiana Arts & Science Museum, Baton Rouge LA
Louisiana Department of Culture, Recreation & Tourism, Louisiana State Museum, New Orleans LA
Louisiana Museum of Modern Art, Humlebaek
Loveland Museum/Gallery, Loveland CO
Lycoming College Gallery, Williamsport PA
Lyman Allyn Art Museum, New London CT
Lyme Historical Society, Florence Griswold Museum, Old Lyme CT
Mabee-Gerrer Museum of Art, Shawnee OK
Madison Museum of Contemporary Art, Madison WI
Madison Museum of Fine Art, Madison GA
Maine College of Art, The Institute of Contemporary Art, Portland ME
Maine Historical Society, MHS Museum, Portland ME
Marblehead Museum & Historical Society, Jeremiah Lee Mansion, Marblehead MA
Maricopa County Historical Society, Desert Caballeros Western Museum, Wickenburg AZ
Marietta College, Grover M Hermann Fine Arts Center, Marietta OH
Marietta-Cobb Museum of Art, Marietta GA
The Mariners' Museum, Newport News VA
Mark Twain, Hartford CT
Marquette University, Haggerty Museum of Art, Milwaukee WI
Maryhill Museum of Art, Goldendale WA
Maryland Art Place, Baltimore MD
Maryland Historical Society, Museum of Maryland History, Baltimore MD
Marylhurst University, The Art Gym, Marylhurst OR
Maryville University Saint Louis, Morton J May Foundation Gallery, Saint Louis MO
Massillon Museum, Massillon OH
McDowell House & Apothecary Shop, Danville KY
McLean County Historical Society, McLean County Museum of History, Bloomington IL
McNay Art Museum, San Antonio TX
McPherson College Gallery, McPherson KS
McPherson Museum and Arts Foundation, McPherson KS
Memphis Brooks Museum of Art, Memphis TN
Mennello Museum of American Art, Orlando FL
Meredith College, Frankie G Weems Gallery & Rotunda Gallery, Raleigh NC
Meridian Museum of Art, Meridian MS
Merrick Art Gallery, New Brighton PA
Mesa Arts Center, Mesa Contemporary Arts Museum, Mesa AZ
The Metropolitan Museum of Art, New York NY
Miami-Dade College, MDC Museum of Art & Design, Miami FL
Michelson Museum of Art, Marshall TX
Middle Border Museum & Oscar Howe Art Center, Mitchell SD
Midwest Museum of American Art, Elkhart IN
Miller Art Center Foundation Inc, Miller Art Museum, Sturgeon Bay WI
Millikin University, Perkinson Gallery, Decatur IL
Mills College Art Museum, Oakland CA
Milwaukee Art Museum, Milwaukee WI
Minneapolis Institute of Art, Minneapolis MN
Minnesota Museum of American Art, Saint Paul MN
Minnesota State University, Mankato, Mankato MN
Minot State University, Northwest Art Center, Minot ND
The Mint Museum, Mint Museum of Craft & Design, Charlotte NC
Mission San Luis Rey de Francia, Mission San Luis Rey Museum, Oceanside CA
Mississippi Museum of Art, Jackson MS
Missoula Art Museum, Missoula MT
Missouri Department of Natural Resources, Missouri State Museum, Jefferson City MO
Mobile Museum of Art, Mobile AL
Modern Art Museum, Fort Worth TX
Modernism, San Francisco CA
Mohawk Valley Heritage Association, Inc, Walter Elwood Museum, Amsterdam NY
Monroe County Historical Association, Elizabeth D Walters Library, Stroudsburg PA
Montana State University, Helen E Copeland Gallery, Bozeman MT
Montclair Art Museum, Montclair NJ
Montgomery Museum of Fine Arts, Montgomery AL
Moravian College, Payne Gallery, Bethlehem PA
Moravian Historical Society, Nazareth PA
Morehead State University, Kentucky Folk Art Center, Morehead KY
Morris Museum, Morristown NJ
Morris Museum of Art, Augusta GA
Morris-Jumel Mansion, Inc, New York NY
Morven Museum & Garden, Princeton NJ
Mount Allison University, Owens Art Gallery, Sackville NB
Mount Vernon Hotel Museum & Garden, New York NY
Muhlenberg College, Martin Art Gallery, Allentown PA
Muscatine Art Center, Muscatine IA
Musee des Beaux-Arts de Tours, Museum of Fine Arts, Tours
Musee National des Beaux Arts du Quebec, Quebec QC
Musee Regional de Vaudreuil-Soulanges, Vaudreuil-Dorion QC
Museo de Arte de Ponce, The Luis A Ferre Foundation Inc, Ponce PR
Museo De Las Americas, Denver CO
The Museum, Greenwood SC
Museum of Art & History, Santa Cruz, Santa Cruz CA
Museum of Art - Deland FL, Inc, Deland FL
Museum of Art, Fort Lauderdale, Fort Lauderdale FL
The Museum of Arts & Sciences Inc, Daytona Beach FL
Museum of Arts & Sciences, Inc, Macon GA
Museum of Contemporary Art, North Miami FL
Museum of Contemporary Art Chicago, Chicago IL
Museum of Contemporary Art Jacksonville, Jacksonville FL
Museum of Contemporary Art San Diego, San Diego CA
Museum of Fine Arts, Saint Petersburg, Florida, Inc, Saint Petersburg FL
Museum of Modern Art, New York NY
Museum of Northern Arizona, Flagstaff AZ
Museum of Northwest Art, La Conner WA
Museum of the Southwest, Midland TX
Museum of Ventura County, Ventura CA
The Museum of Western Art, Kerrville TX
Museum of Wisconsin Art, West Bend WI
Museum of York County, Rock Hill SC
Napa Valley Museum, Yountville CA
Nassau County Museum of Art, Roslyn Harbor NY
Nathan Hale Homestead Museum, Coventry CT
National Baseball Hall of Fame & Museum, Cooperstown NY
National Gallery of Canada, Ottawa ON
National Gallery of Ireland, Dublin
National Heritage Museum, Lexington MA
National Museum of the American Indian, George Gustav Heye Center, New York NY
National Museum of Wildlife Art of the Unites States, Jackson WY
National Museum of Women in the Arts, Washington DC
National Park Service, Weir Farm National Historic Site, Wilton CT
National Park Service, Hubbell Trading Post National Historic Site, Ganado AZ
The National Shrine of the North American Martyrs, Fultonville NY
National Society of Colonial Dames of America in the State of Maryland, Mount Clare Museum House, Baltimore MD
National Society of the Colonial Dames of America in The Commonwealth of Virginia, Wilton House Museum, Richmond VA
National Trust for Historic Preservation, Chesterwood, Stockbridge MA
National Veterans Art Museum, Chicago IL
Naval Historical Center, National Museum of the US Navy, Washington DC
Nebraska Game and Parks Commission, Arbor Lodge State Historical Park & Morton Mansion, Nebraska City NE
Nebraska State Capitol, Lincoln NE
Nebraska Wesleyan University, Elder Gallery, Lincoln NE
Nelda C & H J Lutcher Stark Foundation, Stark Museum of Art, Orange TX
The Nelson-Atkins Museum of Art, Kansas City MO
Nevada Museum of Art, Reno NV
Neville Public Museum of Brown County, Green Bay WI
New Britain Museum of American Art, New Britain CT
New Brunswick Museum, Saint John NB
New Canaan Historical Society, New Canaan CT
New England Maple Museum, Pittsford VT
New Gallery of Modern Art, Charlotte NC
New Jersey Historical Society, Newark NJ
New Orleans Museum of Art, New Orleans LA
New Visions Gallery, Inc, Marshfield WI
New York State Military Museum and Veterans Research Center, Saratoga Springs NY
New York State Office of Parks Recreation & Historic Preservation, John Jay Homestead State Historic Site, Katonah NY
New York State Office of Parks, Recreation & Historic Preservation, Staatsburgh State Historic Site, Staatsburg NY
Newburyport Maritime Society, Inc, Custom House Maritime Museum, Newburyport MA
Newfields, Indianapolis IN
Newport Art Museum and Association, Newport RI
Niagara University, Castellani Art Museum, Niagara NY
The Noble Maritime Collection, Staten Island NY
Norman Rockwell Museum, Stockbridge MA
Norman Rockwell Museum of Vermont, Rutland VT
North Carolina Central University, NCCU Art Museum, Durham NC
North Carolina Museum of Art, Raleigh NC
Northeastern Nevada Museum, Elko NV
Norton Simon Museum, Pasadena CA

Norwich Free Academy, Slater Memorial Museum, Norwich CT
Noyes Art Gallery, Lincoln NE
Oberlin College, Allen Memorial Art Museum, Oberlin OH
Ogden Museum of Southern Art, University of New Orleans, New Orleans LA
Ogunquit Museum of American Art, Ogunquit ME
Ohara Museum of Art, Kurashiki
The Ohio Historical Society, Inc, Campus Martius Museum & Ohio River Museum, Marietta OH
Ohio History Connection, National Afro-American Museum & Cultural Center, Wilberforce OH
Ohio University, Kennedy Museum of Art, Athens OH
Ohrmann Museum and Gallery, Drummond MT
Okanagan Heritage Museum, Kelowna BC
Okefenokee Heritage Center, Inc, Waycross GA
Oklahoma City Museum of Art, Oklahoma City OK
Oklahoma Historical Society, State Museum of History, Oklahoma City OK
Olana State Historic Site, Hudson NY
Old Dartmouth Historical Society, New Bedford Whaling Museum, New Bedford MA
Old Island Restoration Foundation Inc, Oldest House in Key West, Key West FL
The Old Jail Art Center, Albany TX
Omniplex Science Museum, Oklahoma City OK
Opelousas Museum of Art, Inc (OMA), Opelousas LA
Orange County Museum of Art, Newport Beach CA
Ouachita River Art Gallery, Monroe LA
Owensboro Museum of Fine Art, Owensboro KY
Page-Walker Arts & History Center, Cary NC
Panhandle-Plains Historical Museum, Canyon TX
Parrish Art Museum, Water Mill NY
Pasadena Museum of California Art, Pasadena CA
Pasadena Museum of History, Pasadena CA
Passaic County Community College, Broadway, LRC, and Hamilton Club Galleries, Paterson NJ
Peabody Essex Museum, Salem MA
Pearson Lakes Art Center, Okoboji IA
Pennsylvania Academy of the Fine Arts, Philadelphia PA
Pennsylvania Historical & Museum Commission, Railroad Museum of Pennsylvania, Strasburg PA
Pensacola Museum of Art, Pensacola FL
Philadelphia History Museum, Philadelphia PA
Philbrook Museum of Art, Tulsa OK
Phillips Academy, Addison Gallery of American Art, Andover MA
The Phillips Collection, Washington DC
Phillips County Museum, Holyoke CO
Phoenix Art Museum, Phoenix AZ
Piedmont Arts Association, Martinsville VA
Plains Art Museum, Fargo ND
Plainsman Museum, Aurora NE
Plumas County Museum, Quincy CA
Polk Museum of Art, Lakeland FL
The Pomona College, Claremont CA
Port Huron Museum, Port Huron MI
Portland Art Museum, Portland OR
Portland Museum of Art, Portland ME
Portsmouth Historical Society, John Paul Jones House & Discover Portsmouth, Portsmouth NH
Preservation Virginia, John Marshall House, Richmond VA
PS1 Contemporary Art Center, Long Island City NY
Pueblo Museum, Desert Hot Springs CA
Pump House Center for the Arts, Chillicothe OH
Purchase College, Neuberger Museum of Art, Purchase NY
Putnam County Historical Society, Foundry School Museum, Cold Spring NY
Queens College, City University of New York, Godwin-Ternbach Museum, Flushing NY
Radio-Canada SRC CBC, Georges Goguen CBC Art Gallery, Moncton NB
Rahr-West Art Museum, Manitowoc WI
Randolph College, Maier Museum of Art, Lynchburg VA
Rapid City Arts Council, Dahl Arts Center, Rapid City SD
Rawls Museum Arts, Courtland VA
Reading Public Museum, Reading PA
Red Rock Park, Red Rock Park, Church Rock NM
Remai Modern, Saskatoon SK
Reynolda House Museum of American Art, Winston-Salem NC
Rhode Island Historical Society, John Brown House, Providence RI
Roberson Museum & Science Center, Binghamton NY
The Rockwell Museum, Corning NY
Rogue Community College, Wiseman Gallery - FireHouse Gallery, Grants Pass OR
Rollins College, George D & Harriet W Cornell Fine Arts Museum, Winter Park FL
Ross Memorial Museum, Saint Andrews NB
Roswell Museum & Art Center, Roswell NM
Royal Arts Foundation, Belcourt Castle, Newport RI
Rutgers University, Stedman Art Gallery, Camden NJ
Ryerss Victorian Museum & Library, Philadelphia PA
Saco Museum, Saco ME
Saginaw Art Museum, Saginaw MI
Saint Anselm College, Alva de Mars Megan Chapel Art Center, Manchester NH
Saint Bonaventure University, Regina A Quick Center for the Arts, Saint Bonaventure NY
Saint Clair County Community College, Jack R Hennesey Art Galleries, Port Huron MI
Saint Johnsbury Athenaeum, Saint Johnsbury VT
Saint Joseph College, Art Gallery, University of Saint Joseph, West Hartford CT
Saint Joseph Museum, Inc., Saint Joseph MO
Saint Mary's College of California, Museum of Art, Moraga CA
Saint Olaf College, Flaten Art Museum, Northfield MN
Salisbury University, Ward Museum of Wildfowl Art, Salisbury MD
San Angelo Museum of Fine Arts, San Angelo TX
San Antonio Museum of Art, San Antonio TX
San Bernardino County Museum, Redlands CA
San Diego Museum of Art, San Diego CA
San Francisco Maritime National Historical Park, Maritime Museum, San Francisco CA
San Francisco Museum of Modern Art, San Francisco CA
The San Joaquin Pioneer & Historical Society, The Haggin Museum, Stockton CA
Santa Barbara Museum of Art, Santa Barbara CA
Santa Clara University, de Saisset Museum, Santa Clara CA
Santa Paula Art Museum, Santa Paula CA
The Schoolhouse Gallery, Provincetown MA
Schweinfurth Art Center, Auburn NY
Scripps College, Ruth Chandler Williamson Gallery, Claremont CA
Seattle Art Museum, Seattle WA
Seneca-Iroquois National Museum, Salamanca NY
Sheldon Art Galleries, Saint Louis MO
Ships of the Sea Maritime Museum, Savannah GA
Shirley Plantation Foundation, Charles City VA
Slater Mill, Old Slater Mill Association, Pawtucket RI
The Society of the Cincinnati at Anderson House, Washington DC
Solomon R Guggenheim Museum, New York NY
South Carolina Artisans Center, Walterboro SC
South Carolina State Museum, Columbia SC
South Dakota State University, South Dakota Art Museum, Brookings SD
Southeastern Center for Contemporary Art, Winston-Salem NC
Southern Lorain County Historical Society, Spirit of '76 Museum, Elyria OH
Southern Oregon University, Schneider Museum of Art, Ashland OR
Southern Utah University, Braithwaite Fine Arts Gallery, Cedar City UT
Spartanburg Art Museum, Spartanburg SC
The Speed Art Museum, Louisville KY
Spertus Institute of Jewish Studies, Chicago IL
Springfield Art Museum, Springfield MO
Springville Museum of Art, Springville UT
Spruce Forest Artisan Village, Grantsville MD
St George Art Museum, Saint George UT
St Mary's College of Maryland, The Dwight Frederick Boyden Gallery, St Mary's City MD
Staatliche Museen zu Berlin Stiftung Preussischer Kulturbesitz, National Museums in Berlin, Prussian Cultural Heritage Foundation, Berlin
Stamford Museum & Nature Center, Stamford CT
Stanford University, Cantor Arts Center at Stanford University, Stanford CA
Stanley Museum, Inc, Kingfield ME
State University of New York at Geneseo, Bertha V B Lederer Gallery, Geneseo NY
State University of New York at New Paltz, Samuel Dorsky Museum of Art, New Paltz NY
State University of New York at Oswego, Tyler Art Gallery, Oswego NY
State University of New York at Plattsburgh, Art Museum, Plattsburgh NY
The State University of New York at Potsdam, The Art Museum, Potsdam NY
State University of New York at Ulster, Muroff-Kotler Visual Arts Gallery, Stone Ridge NY
State University of New York College at Cortland, Dowd Fine Arts Gallery, Cortland NY
Staten Island Museum, Staten Island NY
Stephens College, Lewis James & Nellie Stratton Davis Art Gallery, Columbia MO
Stratford Historical Society, Catharine B Mitchell Museum, Stratford CT
The Summit County Historical Society of Akron, OH, Akron OH
Susquehanna University, Lore Degenstein Gallery, Selinsgrove PA
SVACA - Sheyenne Valley Arts & Crafts Association, Bjarne Ness Gallery at Bear Creek Hall, Fort Ransom ND
Swope Art Museum, Terre Haute IN
T C Steele State Historic Site, Nashville IN
T W Wood Gallery, Montpelier VT
Tacoma Art Museum, Tacoma WA
Taft Museum of Art, Cincinnati OH
Tampa Museum of Art, Tampa FL
Taos Historic Museums, Ernest Blumenschein Home & Studio, Taos NM
Texas A&M University, J Wayne Stark University Center Galleries, College Station TX
Texas Ranger Hall of Fame & Museum, Waco TX
Thomas Jefferson Foundation, Inc, Monticello, Charlottesville VA
Timken Museum of Art, San Diego CA
Tinkertown Museum, Sandia Park NM
Toledo Museum of Art, Toledo OH
Topeka & Shawnee County Public Library, Alice C Sabatini Gallery, Topeka KS
Traffic Zone Center for Visual Art, Minneapolis MN
Triton Museum of Art, Santa Clara CA
Tubac Center of the Arts, Santa Cruz Valley Art Association, Tubac AZ
Tubman African American Museum, Macon GA
Tucson Museum of Art and Historic Block, Tucson AZ
Turtle Bay Exploration Park, Redding CA
Tver Regional Art Gallery, Tver
Twin City Art Foundation, Masur Museum of Art, Monroe LA
Tyler Museum of Art, Tyler TX
U Gallery, San Francisco CA
Ucross Foundation, Big Red Barn Gallery, Clearmont WY
Ukrainian Institute of Modern Art, Chicago IL
UMLAUF Sculpture Garden & Museum, Austin TX
United States Capitol, Architect of the Capitol, Washington DC
United States Military Academy, West Point Museum, West Point NY
University of Arkansas at Little Rock, Art Galleries, Little Rock AR
University of California, Davis, Jan Shrem and Maria Manetti Shrem Museum of Art, Davis CA
University of California, Los Angeles, Hammer Museum, Los Angeles CA
University of Chicago, Smart Museum of Art, Chicago IL
University of Florida, Samuel P Harn Museum of Art, Gainesville FL
University of Georgia, Georgia Museum of Art, Athens GA
University of Houston, Blaffer Art Museum, Houston TX
University of Illinois at Urbana-Champaign, Krannert Art Museum and Kinkead Pavilion, Champaign IL
University of Indianapolis, Christel DeHaan Fine Arts Gallery, Indianapolis IN
University of Kansas, Spencer Museum of Art, Lawrence KS
The University of Kentucky Art Museum, Lexington KY
University of Mary Washington, University of Mary Washington Galleries, Fredericksburg VA
University of Miami, Lowe Art Museum, Coral Gables FL
University of Minnesota, Katherine E Nash Gallery, Minneapolis MN
University of Minnesota, The Bell Museum of Natural History, Minneapolis MN
University of Minnesota Duluth, Tweed Museum of Art, Duluth MN
University of Montana, Montana Museum of Art & Culture, Missoula MT

University of Nebraska-Lincoln, Great Plains Art Museum, Lincoln NE
University of Nevada, Las Vegas, Donna Beam Fine Art Gallery, Las Vegas NV
University of Nevada, Reno, Sheppard Contemporary & University Galleries, Reno NV
University of New Mexico, The Harwood Museum of Art, Taos NM
University of North Carolina at Greensboro, Weatherspoon Art Museum, Greensboro NC
University of Notre Dame, Snite Museum of Art, Notre Dame IN
University of Pennsylvania, Arthur Ross Gallery, Philadelphia PA
University of Richmond, University Museums, Richmond VA
University of Southern California, USC Fisher Museum of Art, Los Angeles CA
University of Texas at Austin, Blanton Museum of Art, Austin TX
University of Utah, Utah Museum of Fine Arts, Salt Lake City UT
University of Wisconsin-Eau Claire, Foster Gallery, Eau Claire WI
University of Wisconsin-Madison, Chazen Museum of Art, Madison WI
University of Wisconsin-Stout, J Furlong Gallery, Menomonie WI
Ursinus College, Philip & Muriel Berman Museum of Art, Collegeville PA
The Valentine, Richmond VA
Valparaiso University, Brauer Museum of Art, Valparaiso IN
Vancouver Art Gallery, Vancouver BC
Vassar College, The Frances Lehman Loeb Art Center, Poughkeepsie NY
Vero Beach Museum of Art, Vero Beach FL
Vesterheim Norwegian-American Museum, Decorah IA
Victoria Mansion - Morse Libby House, Portland ME
Viridian Artists Inc, New York NY
Wadsworth Atheneum Museum of Art, Hartford CT
Walker Art Center, Minneapolis MN
Walker Fine Art, Denver CO
Walter Anderson Museum of Art, Ocean Springs MS
Walters Art Museum, Baltimore MD
Warner House Association, MacPheadris-Warner House, Portsmouth NH
Washburn University, Mulvane Art Museum, Topeka KS
Washington & Lee University, Lee Chapel & Museum, Lexington VA
Washington County Museum of Fine Arts, Hagerstown MD
Waterloo Center of the Arts, Waterloo IA
Waterworks Visual Arts Center, Salisbury NC
Wayne Center for the Arts, Wooster OH
Westmoreland Museum of American Art, Greensburg PA
Wharton Esherick Museum, Paoli PA
Whatcom Museum, Bellingham WA
Wheaton College, Beard and Weil Galleries, Norton MA
White House, Washington DC
Whitney Museum of American Art, New York NY
Wichita Art Museum, Wichita KS
Wichita State University, Ulrich Museum of Art, Wichita KS
Wildling Art Museum, Solvang CA
Wilfrid Laurier University, Robert Langen Art Gallery, Waterloo ON
Wilkes Art Gallery, North Wilkesboro NC
Wilkes University, Sordoni Art Gallery, Wilkes-Barre PA
Willard House & Clock Museum, Inc, North Grafton MA
William Paterson University, University Galleries, Wayne NJ
The Winnipeg Art Gallery, Winnipeg MB
Winston-Salem State University, Diggs Gallery, Winston-Salem NC
Wiregrass Museum of Art, Dothan AL
Wisconsin Historical Society, Wisconsin Historical Museum, Madison WI
Witte Museum, San Antonio TX
Woodlawn/The Pope-Leighey, Alexandria VA
Woodmere Art Museum Inc, Philadelphia PA
Woodrow Wilson, Staunton VA
Woodrow Wilson, Washington DC
Worcester Art Museum, Worcester MA
World Erotic Art Museum, Miami Beach FL
Wustum Museum Art Association, Charles A Wustum Museum of Fine Arts, Racine WI
Wyoming State Museum, Cheyenne WY
Wyoming Trails Gallery, Wheatland WY
Yellowstone County Museum, Billings MT
Yerba Buena Center for the Arts, San Francisco CA
Yokohama Museum of Art, Yokohama
Zigler Art Museum, Jennings LA

PAINTING-AUSTRALIAN

American Sport Art Museum and Archives, Daphne AL
Art Gallery of South Australia, Adelaide
Art Without Walls Inc, Sayville NY
Bakehouse Art Complex, Inc, Miami FL
Central United Methodist Church, Swords Into Plowshares Peace Center & Gallery, Detroit MI
The Children's Museum of Indianapolis, Indianapolis IN
City of Fayette, Alabama, Fayette Art Museum, Fayette AL
College of William & Mary, Muscarelle Museum of Art, Williamsburg VA
Dartmouth College, Hood Museum of Art, Hanover NH
Detroit Institute of Arts, Detroit MI
Fine Arts Center for the New River Valley, Pulaski VA
Institute of Contemporary Art, Los Angeles, Los Angeles CA
Iredell Museums, Statesville NC
Longview Museum of Fine Art, Longview TX
Mobile Museum of Art, Mobile AL
Modern Art Museum, Fort Worth TX
The Museum of Arts & Sciences Inc, Daytona Beach FL
New Visions Gallery, Inc, Marshfield WI
Owensboro Museum of Fine Art, Owensboro KY
PS1 Contemporary Art Center, Long Island City NY
Queen Victoria Museum and Art Gallery, Launceston TAS
San Antonio Museum of Art, San Antonio TX
The Speed Art Museum, Louisville KY
Stanford University, Cantor Arts Center at Stanford University, Stanford CA
University of Houston, Blaffer Art Museum, Houston TX
University of Wisconsin-Madison, Chazen Museum of Art, Madison WI
Wadsworth Atheneum Museum of Art, Hartford CT

PAINTING-BRITISH

Arnot Art Museum, Elmira NY
Art Gallery of Greater Victoria, Victoria BC
Art Gallery of Hamilton, Hamilton ON
Art Gallery of Nova Scotia, Halifax NS
Art Gallery of South Australia, Adelaide
Art Without Walls Inc, Sayville NY
Bangladesh National Museum, Dhaka
Baroda Museum and Picture Gallery, Vadodara
Bass Museum of Art, Miami Beach FL
Bayerische Staatsgemaldesammlungen, Bavarian State Painting Collections, Munich
Beaverbrook Art Gallery, Fredericton NB
Beloit College, Wright Museum of Art, Beloit WI
Berkshire Museum, Pittsfield MA
Birmingham Museum of Art, Birmingham AL
Blauvelt Demarest Foundation, Hiram Blauvelt Art Museum, Oradell NJ
Bob Jones University Museum & Gallery Inc, Greenville SC
Bruce Museum, Inc, Greenwich CT
Bucknell University, Edward & Marthann Samek Art Gallery, Lewisburg PA
The Buffalo Fine Arts Academy, Albright-Knox Art Gallery, Buffalo NY
Capital University, Schumacher Gallery, Columbus OH
Channel Islands Maritime Museum, Oxnard CA
Clark Art Institute, Williamstown MA
Colgate University, Picker Art Gallery, Hamilton NY
College of William & Mary, Muscarelle Museum of Art, Williamsburg VA
The Columbus Museum, Columbus GA
Columbus Museum of Art, Columbus OH
Corcoran Gallery of Art, Washington DC
Cornell Museum of Art and American Culture, Delray Beach FL
The Courtauld Institute of Art, The Courtauld Gallery, London
Coutts Museum of Art, Inc, El Dorado KS
Crocker Art Museum, Sacramento CA
The Currier Museum of Art, Manchester NH
Dahesh Museum of Art, Greenwich CT
Dartmouth College, Hood Museum of Art, Hanover NH
Delaware Art Museum, Wilmington DE
Denver Art Museum, Denver CO
Detroit Institute of Arts, Detroit MI
The Dixon Gallery & Gardens, Memphis TN
Doncaster Museum and Art Gallery, Doncaster Yorks
Evansville Museum of Arts, History & Science, Evansville IN
Figge Art Museum, Davenport IA
Fine Arts Center for the New River Valley, Pulaski VA
Flint Institute of Arts, Flint MI
Florence County Museum, Florence SC
Florida State University, John & Mable Ringling Museum of Art, Sarasota FL
Fondazione Musei Civici Di Venezia, Museo Correr - Correr Museum, Venice
The Frick Art & Historical Center, Inc, Frick Art Museum, Pittsburgh PA
General Board of Discipleship, The United Methodist Church, The Upper Room Chapel & Museum, Nashville TN
Glanmore National Historic Site of Canada, Belleville ON
Gunston Hall Plantation, Mason Neck VA
Hillwood Museum & Gardens Foundation, Hillwood Estate Museum & Gardens, Washington DC
Huntington Museum of Art, Huntington WV
The Hyde Collection, Glens Falls NY
Iredell Museums, Statesville NC
JMW Turner Museum, Sarasota FL
Jordan National Gallery of Fine Arts, Amman
Joslyn Art Museum, Omaha NE
Juniata College Museum of Art, Huntingdon PA
Karakalpak State Art Museum, Nukus Republic of Karakalpakstan
Kelvingrove Art Gallery & Museum, Glasgow UK
Kimbell Art Foundation, Kimbell Art Museum, Fort Worth TX
La Salle University Art Museum, Philadelphia PA
Lafayette College, Lafayette College Art Galleries, Easton PA
Lincolnshire County Council, Library & Heritage Services, Lincoln
Marquette University, Haggerty Museum of Art, Milwaukee WI
Maryhill Museum of Art, Goldendale WA
McCord Museum of Canadian History, Montreal QC
Memphis Brooks Museum of Art, Memphis TN
Mobile Museum of Art, Mobile AL
Modern Art Museum, Fort Worth TX
Mount Vernon Hotel Museum & Garden, New York NY
Musee Cognacq-Jay, Cognacq-Jay Museum, Paris
Museo de Arte de Ponce, The Luis A Ferre Foundation Inc, Ponce PR
The Museum of Arts & Sciences Inc, Daytona Beach FL
Museum of Fine Arts, Saint Petersburg, Florida, Inc, Saint Petersburg FL
Muzej za Umjetnost i Obrt, Museum of Arts & Crafts, Zagreb
Muzeul National de Arta al Romaniei, National Museum of Art of Romania, Bucharest
Muzeum Narodowe w Poznaniu, National Museum in Poznan, Poznan
National Gallery of Canada, Ottawa ON
National Gallery of Ireland, Dublin
The National Museum of Western Art, Tokyo
National Museum of Wildlife Art of the Unites States, Jackson WY
National Portrait Gallery, London
Nelson Mandela Metropolitan Art Museum, Port Elizabeth
New Brunswick Museum, Saint John NB
Niagara University, Castellani Art Museum, Niagara NY
North Carolina Museum of Art, Raleigh NC
Oklahoma City Museum of Art, Oklahoma City OK
Owensboro Museum of Fine Art, Owensboro KY
Panhandle-Plains Historical Museum, Canyon TX

Passaic County Community College, Broadway, LRC, and Hamilton Club Galleries, Paterson NJ
Philadelphia Museum of Art, John G Johnson Collection, Philadelphia PA
Phoenix Art Museum, Phoenix AZ
Piedmont Arts Association, Martinsville VA
Queens College, City University of New York, Godwin-Ternbach Museum, Flushing NY
Reading Public Museum, Reading PA
The Rosenbach Museum & Library, Philadelphia PA
Royal Arts Foundation, Belcourt Castle, Newport RI
Saginaw Art Museum, Saginaw MI
Saint Olaf College, Flaten Art Museum, Northfield MN
San Antonio Museum of Art, San Antonio TX
San Diego Museum of Art, San Diego CA
Shirley Plantation Foundation, Charles City VA
Slovenska Narodna Galeria, Slovak National Gallery, Bratislava
The Society of the Cincinnati at Anderson House, Washington DC
The Speed Art Museum, Louisville KY
Spertus Institute of Jewish Studies, Chicago IL
Springfield Art Museum, Springfield MO
Springville Museum of Art, Springville UT
Staatliche Museen zu Berlin Stiftung Preussischer Kulturbesitz, National Museums in Berlin, Prussian Cultural Heritage Foundation, Berlin
Stanford University, Cantor Arts Center at Stanford University, Stanford CA
State University of New York at Oswego, Tyler Art Gallery, Oswego NY
Szepmuveszeti Muzeum, Museum of Fine Arts, Budapest
Tacoma Art Museum, Tacoma WA
Taft Museum of Art, Cincinnati OH
Tver Regional Art Gallery, Tver
Tyne and Wear Archives & Museums, Sunderland Museum & Winter Gardens, Sunderland
University of California, Los Angeles, Hammer Museum, Los Angeles CA
University of Chicago, Smart Museum of Art, Chicago IL
University of Georgia, Georgia Museum of Art, Athens GA
University of Houston, Blaffer Art Museum, Houston TX
University of Illinois at Urbana-Champaign, Krannert Art Museum and Kinkead Pavilion, Champaign IL
University of Kansas, Spencer Museum of Art, Lawrence KS
The University of Kentucky Art Museum, Lexington KY
University of Manchester, Whitworth Art Gallery, Manchester
University of Miami, Lowe Art Museum, Coral Gables FL
University of Notre Dame, Snite Museum of Art, Notre Dame IN
University of Southern California, USC Fisher Museum of Art, Los Angeles CA
University of Utah, Utah Museum of Fine Arts, Salt Lake City UT
University of Wisconsin-Madison, Chazen Museum of Art, Madison WI
Ursinus College, Philip & Muriel Berman Museum of Art, Collegeville PA
Vancouver Art Gallery, Vancouver BC
Wadsworth Atheneum Museum of Art, Hartford CT
Walker Art Gallery, Liverpool
The Wallace Collection, London
Walters Art Museum, Baltimore MD
Waterworks Visual Arts Center, Salisbury NC
Wheaton College, Beard and Weil Galleries, Norton MA
Wilfrid Laurier University, Robert Langen Art Gallery, Waterloo ON
Woodlawn/The Pope-Leighey, Alexandria VA
Worcester Art Museum, Worcester MA
Yale University, Yale Center for British Art, New Haven CT
Yokohama Museum of Art, Yokohama
Zigler Art Museum, Jennings LA

PAINTING-CANADIAN

Americas Society Art Gallery, New York NY
Arnot Art Museum, Elmira NY
Art Gallery of Alberta, Edmonton AB
Art Gallery of Bancroft Inc, Bancroft ON
The Art Gallery of Cornwall, Cornwall ON
The Art Gallery of Grand Prairie, Grande Prairie AB
Art Gallery of Greater Victoria, Victoria BC
Art Gallery of Nova Scotia, Halifax NS
Art Gallery of Swift Current, Swift Current SK
Art Without Walls Inc, Sayville NY
Bangladesh National Museum, Dhaka
Beaverbrook Art Gallery, Fredericton NB
Blauvelt Demarest Foundation, Hiram Blauvelt Art Museum, Oradell NJ
Bowdoin College, Peary-MacMillan Arctic Museum, Brunswick ME
Bucknell University, Edward & Marthann Samek Art Gallery, Lewisburg PA
Canadian Museum of History, Gatineau QC
Canadian Museum of Nature, Musee Canadien de la Nature, Ottawa ON
Canadian War Museum, Ottawa ON
Cartoon Art Museum, San Francisco CA
Central United Methodist Church, Swords Into Plowshares Peace Center & Gallery, Detroit MI
City of Fayette, Alabama, Fayette Art Museum, Fayette AL
Concordia University, Leonard & Bina Ellen Art Gallery, Montreal QC
Confederation Centre Art Gallery and Museum, Charlottetown PE
Craigdarroch Castle Historical Museum Society, Victoria BC
Dalnavert Museum, Winnipeg MB
Dartmouth Heritage Museum, Dartmouth NS
DeLeon White Gallery, Toronto ON
Environment Canada - Parks Canada, Laurier House, National Historic Site, Ottawa ON
Frye Art Museum, Seattle WA
Galerie Montcalm, Gatineau QC
Gallery Moos Ltd, Toronto ON
Glanmore National Historic Site of Canada, Belleville ON
Glenhyrst Art Gallery of Brant, Brantford ON
Heritage Center, Inc, Pine Ridge SD
Huntington Museum of Art, Huntington WV
Institute of Contemporary Art, Los Angeles, Los Angeles CA
Kamloops Art Gallery, Kamloops BC
Kings County Historical Society & Museum, Hampton NB
Kitchener-Waterloo Art Gallery, Kitchener ON
The Lindsay Gallery Inc, Lindsay ON
McCord Museum of Canadian History, Montreal QC
Mobile Museum of Art, Mobile AL
Modern Art Museum, Fort Worth TX
Musee National des Beaux Arts du Quebec, Quebec QC
Musee Regional de lu Cote-Nord, Sept-Iles QC
Museum of Contemporary Canadian Art, Toronto ON
Museum of Fine Arts, Saint Petersburg, Florida, Inc, Saint Petersburg FL
Museum of Northern British Columbia, Ruth Harvey Art Gallery, Prince Rupert BC
National Gallery of Canada, Ottawa ON
National Museum of Wildlife Art of the Unites States, Jackson WY
New Brunswick Museum, Saint John NB
Niagara University, Castellani Art Museum, Niagara NY
Opelousas Museum of Art, Inc (OMA), Opelousas LA
Plains Art Museum, Fargo ND
Port Huron Museum, Port Huron MI
PS1 Contemporary Art Center, Long Island City NY
Radio-Canada SRC CBC, Georges Goguen CBC Art Gallery, Moncton NB
Red Deer & District Museum & Archives, Red Deer AB
Regina Public Library, Dunlop Art Gallery, Regina SK
Remai Modern, Saskatoon SK
The Robert McLaughlin Gallery, Oshawa ON
Ross Memorial Museum, Saint Andrews NB
The Speed Art Museum, Louisville KY
Spertus Institute of Jewish Studies, Chicago IL
Stanford University, Cantor Arts Center at Stanford University, Stanford CA
State University of New York at Plattsburgh, Art Museum, Plattsburgh NY
Surrey Art Gallery, Surrey BC
Temiskaming Art Gallery, Haileybury ON
Two Rivers Art Gallery, Prince George BC
Ukrainian Institute of Modern Art, Chicago IL
University of Calgary, Nickle Galleries, Calgary AB
University of Minnesota Duluth, Tweed Museum of Art, Duluth MN
University of Saskatchewan, Diefenbaker Canada Centre, Saskatoon SK
Vancouver Art Gallery, Vancouver BC
Wadsworth Atheneum Museum of Art, Hartford CT
Wilfrid Laurier University, Robert Langen Art Gallery, Waterloo ON
The Winnipeg Art Gallery, Winnipeg MB

PAINTING-DUTCH

Allentown Art Museum, Allentown PA
Amsterdam Museum, Amsterdam
Arnot Art Museum, Elmira NY
The Art Gallery of Grand Prairie, Grande Prairie AB
Art Without Walls Inc, Sayville NY
Bangladesh National Museum, Dhaka
Barnes Foundation, Merion PA
Baroda Museum and Picture Gallery, Vadodara
Bass Museum of Art, Miami Beach FL
Bayerische Staatsgemaldesammlungen, Bavarian State Painting Collections, Munich
Berkshire Museum, Pittsfield MA
Birmingham Museum of Art, Birmingham AL
Bob Jones University Museum & Gallery Inc, Greenville SC
Brick Store Museum, Kennebunk ME
Bucknell University, Edward & Marthann Samek Art Gallery, Lewisburg PA
Casa-Museu Medeiros e Almeida, Lisbon
Channel Islands Maritime Museum, Oxnard CA
Chrysler Museum of Art, Norfolk VA
Clark Art Institute, Williamstown MA
College of William & Mary, Muscarelle Museum of Art, Williamsburg VA
Corcoran Gallery of Art, Washington DC
Crocker Art Museum, Sacramento CA
The Currier Museum of Art, Manchester NH
Dartmouth College, Hood Museum of Art, Hanover NH
Detroit Institute of Arts, Detroit MI
Elmhurst Art Museum, Elmhurst IL
Environment Canada - Parks Canada, Laurier House, National Historic Site, Ottawa ON
Evansville Museum of Arts, History & Science, Evansville IN
Fine Arts Center for the New River Valley, Pulaski VA
Flint Institute of Arts, Flint MI
Florida State University, John & Mable Ringling Museum of Art, Sarasota FL
The Frick Art & Historical Center, Inc, Frick Art Museum, Pittsburgh PA
Frye Art Museum, Seattle WA
Gemaldegalerie der Akademie der Bildenden Kunste Wien, Picture Gallery of the Academy of Fine Arts Vienna, Vienna
General Board of Discipleship, The United Methodist Church, The Upper Room Chapel & Museum, Nashville TN
Glasgow University, The Hunterian, Glasgow
Grand Rapids Art Museum, Grand Rapids MI
Hecht Museum, Haifa
Het Noordbrabants Museum, s-Hertogenbosch
Hillwood Museum & Gardens Foundation, Hillwood Estate Museum & Gardens, Washington DC
Historic Huguenot Street, New Paltz NY
Huntington Museum of Art, Huntington WV
The Hyde Collection, Glens Falls NY
Institute of Contemporary Art, Los Angeles, Los Angeles CA
Isabella Stewart Gardner Museum, Boston MA
The Israel Museum, Jerusalem, Jerusalem
Jacksonville University, Alexander Brest Museum & Gallery, Jacksonville FL
Joslyn Art Museum, Omaha NE
Juniata College Museum of Art, Huntingdon PA
Kelvingrove Art Gallery & Museum, Glasgow UK
Kereszteny Muzeum, Christian Museum, Esztergom
Kimbell Art Foundation, Kimbell Art Museum, Fort Worth TX
Kroller-Muller Museum, Otterlo
Kunsthistorisches Museum Wien, Museum of Fine Arts, Vienna
La Salle University Art Museum, Philadelphia PA
The Mariners' Museum, Newport News VA
Marquette University, Haggerty Museum of Art, Milwaukee WI
Memphis Brooks Museum of Art, Memphis TN
Mobile Museum of Art, Mobile AL
Modern Art Museum, Fort Worth TX

Moravska Galerie v Brne, Moravian Gallery in Brno, Brno
Musee des Beaux-Arts d'Orleans, Museum of Fine Arts, Orleans
Musee des Beaux-Arts de Tours, Museum of Fine Arts, Tours
Museen der Stadt Koln, Wallraf-Richartz-Museum & Fondation Corboud - Wallraf-Richartz Museum & Corboud Foundation, Cologne
Museo de Arte de Ponce, The Luis A Ferre Foundation Inc, Ponce PR
Museo di Palazzo Ducale, Ducale Palace Museum, Mantua
Museo Nacional de Bellas Artes, National Museum of Fine Arts, Santiago
Museum De Lakenhal, Leiden
Museum of Art, Fort Lauderdale, Fort Lauderdale FL
The Museum of Arts & Sciences Inc, Daytona Beach FL
Museum of Fine Arts, Saint Petersburg, Florida, Inc, Saint Petersburg FL
Museum Prinsenhof Delft, Delft
Muzeul National de Arta al Romaniei, National Museum of Art of Romania, Bucharest
Muzeum Narodowe w Poznaniu, National Museum in Poznan, Poznan
Narodna Galerija, National Gallery of Slovenia, Ljubljana
National Gallery of Canada, Ottawa ON
National Gallery of Ireland, Dublin
The National Museum of Western Art, Tokyo
National Museum of Wildlife Art of the Unites States, Jackson WY
New Orleans Museum of Art, New Orleans LA
North Carolina Museum of Art, Raleigh NC
Oberlin College, Allen Memorial Art Museum, Oberlin OH
Panhandle-Plains Historical Museum, Canyon TX
Philadelphia Museum of Art, John G Johnson Collection, Philadelphia PA
Phoenix Art Museum, Phoenix AZ
PS1 Contemporary Art Center, Long Island City NY
Pump House Center for the Arts, Chillicothe OH
Queens College, City University of New York, Godwin-Ternbach Museum, Flushing NY
Saginaw Art Museum, Saginaw MI
Saint Bonaventure University, Regina A Quick Center for the Arts, Saint Bonaventure NY
San Antonio Museum of Art, San Antonio TX
San Diego Museum of Art, San Diego CA
The San Joaquin Pioneer & Historical Society, The Haggin Museum, Stockton CA
Slovenska Narodna Galeria, Slovak National Gallery, Bratislava
The Speed Art Museum, Louisville KY
Springfield Art Museum, Springfield MO
St Mary's College of Maryland, The Dwight Frederick Boyden Gallery, St Mary's City MD
Staatliche Museen zu Berlin Stiftung Preussischer Kulturbesitz, National Museums in Berlin, Prussian Cultural Heritage Foundation, Berlin
Stanford University, Cantor Arts Center at Stanford University, Stanford CA
The State Museum of Fine Arts of Tatarstan Republic, Kazan
The State Museum of Oriental Art, Moscow
Staten Island Museum, Staten Island NY
Stedelijk Museum Alkmaar, Alkmaar Municipal Museum, Alkmaar
Szepmuveszeti Muzeum, Museum of Fine Arts, Budapest
Taft Museum of Art, Cincinnati OH
Timken Museum of Art, San Diego CA
Tver Regional Art Gallery, Tver
United States Figure Skating Association, World Figure Skating Museum & Hall of Fame, Colorado Springs CO
University of Chicago, Smart Museum of Art, Chicago IL
University of Illinois at Urbana-Champaign, Krannert Art Museum and Kinkead Pavilion, Champaign IL
University of Kansas, Spencer Museum of Art, Lawrence KS
The University of Kentucky Art Museum, Lexington KY
University of Miami, Lowe Art Museum, Coral Gables FL
University of Southern California, USC Fisher Museum of Art, Los Angeles CA
University of Utah, Utah Museum of Fine Arts, Salt Lake City UT
University of Wisconsin-Madison, Chazen Museum of Art, Madison WI
Ursinus College, Philip & Muriel Berman Museum of Art, Collegeville PA
Van Gogh Museum, Amsterdam
Vancouver Art Gallery, Vancouver BC
Wadsworth Atheneum Museum of Art, Hartford CT
Walker Art Gallery, Liverpool
The Wallace Collection, London
Westfries Museum, Hoorn
Wheaton College, Beard and Weil Galleries, Norton MA
Worcester Art Museum, Worcester MA
Zigler Art Museum, Jennings LA

PAINTING-EUROPEAN

Akron Art Museum, Akron OH
Albin Polasek Museum & Sculpture Gardens, Winter Park FL
Allentown Art Museum, Allentown PA
American Sport Art Museum and Archives, Daphne AL
American University, Museum at the Katzen, Washington DC
Amsterdam Museum, Amsterdam
Arkansas Arts Center, Little Rock AR
Arnot Art Museum, Elmira NY
Art Gallery of Alberta, Edmonton AB
The Art Gallery of Grand Prairie, Grande Prairie AB
Art Gallery of Greater Victoria, Victoria BC
Art Gallery of Hamilton, Hamilton ON
Art Gallery of Nova Scotia, Halifax NS
Art Gallery of Ontario, Toronto ON
Art Gallery of South Australia, Adelaide
Art Without Walls Inc, Sayville NY
The Baltimore Museum of Art, Baltimore MD
Bangladesh National Museum, Dhaka
Barnes Foundation, Merion PA
Baroda Museum and Picture Gallery, Vadodara
Bass Museum of Art, Miami Beach FL
Bayerische Staatsgemaldesammlungen, Bavarian State Painting Collections, Munich
Beaverbrook Art Gallery, Fredericton NB
Beloit College, Wright Museum of Art, Beloit WI
Belskie Museum, Closter NJ
Berman Museum, Anniston AL
Birmingham Museum of Art, Birmingham AL
Blanden Memorial Art Museum, Fort Dodge IA
Blauvelt Demarest Foundation, Hiram Blauvelt Art Museum, Oradell NJ
Bob Jones University Museum & Gallery Inc, Greenville SC
Bruce Museum, Inc, Greenwich CT
Bucknell University, Edward & Marthann Samek Art Gallery, Lewisburg PA
The Buffalo Fine Arts Academy, Albright-Knox Art Gallery, Buffalo NY
Byzantine & Christian Museum, Athens, Athens
Cameron Art Museum, Wilmington NC
Capital University, Schumacher Gallery, Columbus OH
Carnegie Museums of Pittsburgh, Carnegie Museum of Art, Pittsburgh PA
Cartoon Art Museum, San Francisco CA
Channel Islands Maritime Museum, Oxnard CA
Chateau de Versailles, Palace of Versailles, Versailles
City of El Paso, El Paso TX
Clark Art Institute, Williamstown MA
The Cleveland Museum of Art, Cleveland OH
Colgate University, Picker Art Gallery, Hamilton NY
College of William & Mary, Muscarelle Museum of Art, Williamsburg VA
Columbia Museum of Art, Columbia SC
Columbus Museum of Art, Columbus OH
Corcoran Gallery of Art, Washington DC
Cornell Museum of Art and American Culture, Delray Beach FL
Cornell University, Herbert F Johnson Museum of Art, Ithaca NY
The Courtauld Institute of Art, The Courtauld Gallery, London
Coutts Museum of Art, Inc, El Dorado KS
Crocker Art Museum, Sacramento CA
Dahesh Museum of Art, Greenwich CT
Danville Museum of Fine Arts & History, Danville VA
Dartmouth College, Hood Museum of Art, Hanover NH
Dartmouth Heritage Museum, Dartmouth NS
Dayton Art Institute, Dayton OH
Denver Art Museum, Denver CO
Detroit Institute of Arts, Detroit MI
Dumbarton Oaks, Dumbarton Oaks Museum, Washington DC
Elverhoj Museum of History and Art, Solvang CA
Evansville Museum of Arts, History & Science, Evansville IN
Faaborg Museum, Faaborg
Figge Art Museum, Davenport IA
Fine Arts Center for the New River Valley, Pulaski VA
Fisk University, Aaron Douglas Gallery, Nashville TN
Flint Institute of Arts, Flint MI
Florence County Museum, Florence SC
Florida State University, John & Mable Ringling Museum of Art, Sarasota FL
Florida State University and Central Florida Community College, The Appleton Museum of Art, Ocala FL
Fondazione Musei Civici Di Venezia, Museo Correr - Correr Museum, Venice
Fondazione Musei Civici Di Venezia, Ca' Pesaro Galleria Nazionale d'Arte Moderna - Ca' Pesaro Gallery of Modern Art, Venice
Frederic Remington, Ogdensburg NY
Frick Collection, New York NY
Gemaldegalerie der Akademie der Bildenden Kunste Wien, Picture Gallery of the Academy of Fine Arts Vienna, Vienna
General Board of Discipleship, The United Methodist Church, The Upper Room Chapel & Museum, Nashville TN
Hecht Museum, Haifa
Henry Morrison Flagler Museum, Palm Beach FL
Hermitage Museum & Gardens, Norfolk VA
Hillwood Museum & Gardens Foundation, Hillwood Estate Museum & Gardens, Washington DC
Honolulu Museum of Art, Honolulu HI
The Hyde Collection, Glens Falls NY
International Museum of Art & Science, McAllen TX
The Israel Museum, Jerusalem, Jerusalem
JMW Turner Museum, Sarasota FL
Joslyn Art Museum, Omaha NE
Kenosha Public Museums, Kenosha WI
Kereszteny Muzeum, Christian Museum, Esztergom
Kimbell Art Foundation, Kimbell Art Museum, Fort Worth TX
Kirchner Museum Davos, Davos
Kitchener-Waterloo Art Gallery, Kitchener ON
Knoxville Museum of Art, Knoxville TN
Koninklijk Museum voor Schone Kunsten Antwerpen, Royal Museum of Fine Arts Antwerp, Antwerp
Kroller-Muller Museum, Otterlo
Kunsthalle Bremen, Bremen Art Gallery, Bremen
Kunsthistorisches Museum Wien, Museum of Fine Arts, Vienna
Kunstmuseum Solothurn, Solothurn Art Museum, Solothurn
La Salle University Art Museum, Philadelphia PA
Lafayette College, Lafayette College Art Galleries, Easton PA
Latino Art Museum, Pomona CA
Lauren Rogers, Laurel MS
Le Grand Curtius, The Grand Curtius, Liege
Los Angeles County Museum of Art, Los Angeles CA
Louisiana Arts & Science Museum, Baton Rouge LA
Louisiana Museum of Modern Art, Humlebaek
Loyola University Chicago, Loyola University Museum of Art, Chicago IL
Lyman Allyn Art Museum, New London CT
Mabee-Gerrer Museum of Art, Shawnee OK
Madison Museum of Fine Art, Madison GA
Marquette University, Haggerty Museum of Art, Milwaukee WI
McNay Art Museum, San Antonio TX
Meredith College, Frankie G Weems Gallery & Rotunda Gallery, Raleigh NC
Merrick Art Gallery, New Brighton PA
The Metropolitan Museum of Art, New York NY
Milwaukee Art Museum, Milwaukee WI
Minneapolis Institute of Art, Minneapolis MN
Mission San Luis Rey de Francia, Mission San Luis Rey Museum, Oceanside CA
Mississippi Museum of Art, Jackson MS
Mobile Museum of Art, Mobile AL
Modern Art Museum, Fort Worth TX
Moderna Galerija, Modern Gallery - National Museum of Modern Art, Zagreb

Moravska Galerie v Brne, Moravian Gallery in Brno, Brno
Moscow Museum of Modern Art, Moscow
Musee d'art de Joliette, Joliette QC
Musee des Augustines de l'Hotel Dieu de Quebec, Quebec QC
Musee des Beaux-Arts d'Orleans, Museum of Fine Arts, Orleans
Musee des Beaux-Arts de Tours, Museum of Fine Arts, Tours
Museen der Stadt Koln, Wallraf-Richartz-Museum & Fondation Corboud - Wallraf-Richartz Museum & Corboud Foundation, Cologne
Museo di Palazzo Ducale, Ducale Palace Museum, Mantua
Museu Nacional D'Art De Catalunya, Catalona National Museum of Art, Barcelona
Museum De Lakenhal, Leiden
Museum Kampa, Prague
The Museum of Arts & Sciences Inc, Daytona Beach FL
Museum of Arts & Sciences, Inc, Macon GA
Museum of Fine Arts, Saint Petersburg, Florida, Inc, Saint Petersburg FL
Museum Prinsenhof Delft, Delft
Museum zu Allerheiligen, Schaffhausen
Muzej za Umjetnost i Obrt, Museum of Arts & Crafts, Zagreb
Muzeul National de Arta al Romaniei, National Museum of Art of Romania, Bucharest
Muzeum Narodowe W Kielcach, National Museum in Kielce, Kielce
Muzeum Narodowe w Poznaniu, National Museum in Poznan, Poznan
Narodna Galerija, National Gallery of Slovenia, Ljubljana
Nassau County Museum of Art, Roslyn Harbor NY
National Art Museum of Moldova, Chisinau
National Gallery of Canada, Ottawa ON
National Gallery of Ireland, Dublin
The National Museum of Western Art, Tokyo
National Museum of Wildlife Art of the Unites States, Jackson WY
National Trust for Historic Preservation, Chesterwood, Stockbridge MA
Nelson Mandela Metropolitan Art Museum, Port Elizabeth
Nemeth Art Center, Park Rapids MN
Nevada Museum of Art, Reno NV
New Orleans Museum of Art, New Orleans LA
New York State Office of Parks, Recreation & Historic Preservation, Staatsburgh State Historic Site, Staatsburg NY
Newfields, Indianapolis IN
North Carolina Museum of Art, Raleigh NC
Norton Simon Museum, Pasadena CA
Norwich Free Academy, Slater Memorial Museum, Norwich CT
Ohara Museum of Art, Kurashiki
Oklahoma City Museum of Art, Oklahoma City OK
Olana State Historic Site, Hudson NY
Panhandle-Plains Historical Museum, Canyon TX
Passaic County Community College, Broadway, LRC, and Hamilton Club Galleries, Paterson NJ
Philadelphia Museum of Art, John G Johnson Collection, Philadelphia PA
Philbrook Museum of Art, Tulsa OK
The Phillips Collection, Washington DC
Phoenix Art Museum, Phoenix AZ
Piedmont Arts Association, Martinsville VA
Port Huron Museum, Port Huron MI
Portland Art Museum, Portland OR
Portland Museum of Art, Portland ME
Purchase College, Neuberger Museum of Art, Purchase NY
Queens College, City University of New York, Godwin-Ternbach Museum, Flushing NY
Radio-Canada SRC CBC, Georges Goguen CBC Art Gallery, Moncton NB
Reading Public Museum, Reading PA
Rollins College, George D & Harriet W Cornell Fine Arts Museum, Winter Park FL
Royal Arts Foundation, Belcourt Castle, Newport RI
Saginaw Art Museum, Saginaw MI
Saint Bonaventure University, Regina A Quick Center for the Arts, Saint Bonaventure NY
Saint Johnsbury Athenaeum, Saint Johnsbury VT
Saint Olaf College, Flaten Art Museum, Northfield MN
San Antonio Museum of Art, San Antonio TX
San Diego Museum of Art, San Diego CA
The San Joaquin Pioneer & Historical Society, The Haggin Museum, Stockton CA
Santa Barbara Museum of Art, Santa Barbara CA
Seattle Art Museum, Seattle WA
Shirley Plantation Foundation, Charles City VA
Slovenska Narodna Galeria, Slovak National Gallery, Bratislava
The Society of the Cincinnati at Anderson House, Washington DC
The Speed Art Museum, Louisville KY
Spertus Institute of Jewish Studies, Chicago IL
Staatliche Museen zu Berlin Stiftung Preussischer Kulturbesitz, National Museums in Berlin, Prussian Cultural Heritage Foundation, Berlin
Stanford University, Cantor Arts Center at Stanford University, Stanford CA
The State Museum of Fine Arts of Tatarstan Republic, Kazan
Staten Island Museum, Staten Island NY
Stedelijk Museum Alkmaar, Alkmaar Municipal Museum, Alkmaar
Swiss Institute, New York NY
Szepmuveszeti Muzeum, Museum of Fine Arts, Budapest
Tacoma Art Museum, Tacoma WA
Taft Museum of Art, Cincinnati OH
Timken Museum of Art, San Diego CA
Toledo Museum of Art, Toledo OH
Tucson Museum of Art and Historic Block, Tucson AZ
Tver Regional Art Gallery, Tver
United States Figure Skating Association, World Figure Skating Museum & Hall of Fame, Colorado Springs CO
United States Military Academy, West Point Museum, West Point NY
University of California, Los Angeles, Hammer Museum, Los Angeles CA
University of Chicago, Smart Museum of Art, Chicago IL
University of Florida, Samuel P Harn Museum of Art, Gainesville FL
University of Georgia, Georgia Museum of Art, Athens GA
University of Illinois at Urbana-Champaign, Krannert Art Museum and Kinkead Pavilion, Champaign IL
University of Kansas, Spencer Museum of Art, Lawrence KS
The University of Kentucky Art Museum, Lexington KY
University of Miami, Lowe Art Museum, Coral Gables FL
University of Minnesota Duluth, Tweed Museum of Art, Duluth MN
University of Notre Dame, Snite Museum of Art, Notre Dame IN
University of Southern California, USC Fisher Museum of Art, Los Angeles CA
University of Texas at Austin, Blanton Museum of Art, Austin TX
University of Utah, Utah Museum of Fine Arts, Salt Lake City UT
University of Wisconsin-Madison, Chazen Museum of Art, Madison WI
Ursinus College, Philip & Muriel Berman Museum of Art, Collegeville PA
Vassar College, The Frances Lehman Loeb Art Center, Poughkeepsie NY
Virginia Museum of Fine Arts, Richmond VA
Vorarlberg Museum, Bregenz
Wadsworth Atheneum Museum of Art, Hartford CT
Walker Art Gallery, Liverpool
The Wallace Collection, London
Walters Art Museum, Baltimore MD
Waterworks Visual Arts Center, Salisbury NC
Wilfrid Laurier University, Robert Langen Art Gallery, Waterloo ON
Wilkes University, Sordoni Art Gallery, Wilkes-Barre PA
Woodmere Art Museum Inc, Philadelphia PA
World Erotic Art Museum, Miami Beach FL
Zigler Art Museum, Jennings LA

PAINTING-FLEMISH

Allentown Art Museum, Allentown PA
Amsterdam Museum, Amsterdam
Arnot Art Museum, Elmira NY
The Art Gallery of Grand Prairie, Grande Prairie AB
Art Without Walls Inc, Sayville NY
Bangladesh National Museum, Dhaka
Barnes Foundation, Merion PA
Baroda Museum and Picture Gallery, Vadodara
Bass Museum of Art, Miami Beach FL
Beaverbrook Art Gallery, Fredericton NB
Berkshire Museum, Pittsfield MA
Bob Jones University Museum & Gallery Inc, Greenville SC
Bruce Museum, Inc, Greenwich CT
Bucknell University, Edward & Marthann Samek Art Gallery, Lewisburg PA
Casa-Museu Medeiros e Almeida, Lisbon
Channel Islands Maritime Museum, Oxnard CA
Chrysler Museum of Art, Norfolk VA
Cincinnati Art Museum, Cincinnati Art Museum, Cincinnati OH
City of El Paso, El Paso TX
Clark Art Institute, Williamstown MA
Clemson University, Fort Hill Plantation, Clemson SC
College of William & Mary, Muscarelle Museum of Art, Williamsburg VA
Columbus Chapel & Boal Mansion Museum, Boalsburg PA
Columbus Museum of Art, Columbus OH
Corcoran Gallery of Art, Washington DC
The Courtauld Institute of Art, The Courtauld Gallery, London
Crocker Art Museum, Sacramento CA
The Currier Museum of Art, Manchester NH
Dartmouth College, Hood Museum of Art, Hanover NH
Detroit Institute of Arts, Detroit MI
Doncaster Museum and Art Gallery, Doncaster Yorks
Evansville Museum of Arts, History & Science, Evansville IN
Fine Arts Center for the New River Valley, Pulaski VA
Flint Institute of Arts, Flint MI
Florence County Museum, Florence SC
Florida State University, John & Mable Ringling Museum of Art, Sarasota FL
Fondazione Musei Civici Di Venezia, Museo Correr - Correr Museum, Venice
The Frick Art & Historical Center, Inc, Frick Art Museum, Pittsburgh PA
Gemaldegalerie der Akademie der Bildenden Kunste Wien, Picture Gallery of the Academy of Fine Arts Vienna, Vienna
General Board of Discipleship, The United Methodist Church, The Upper Room Chapel & Museum, Nashville TN
Glasgow University, The Hunterian, Glasgow
Het Noordbrabants Museum, s-Hertogenbosch
Honolulu Museum of Art, Honolulu HI
The Hyde Collection, Glens Falls NY
Institute of Contemporary Art, Los Angeles, Los Angeles CA
Isabella Stewart Gardner Museum, Boston MA
The Israel Museum, Jerusalem, Jerusalem
Jacksonville University, Alexander Brest Museum & Gallery, Jacksonville FL
Joslyn Art Museum, Omaha NE
Kelvingrove Art Gallery & Museum, Glasgow UK
Kereszteny Muzeum, Christian Museum, Esztergom
Kimbell Art Foundation, Kimbell Art Museum, Fort Worth TX
Kroller-Muller Museum, Otterlo
Kunsthistorisches Museum Wien, Museum of Fine Arts, Vienna
La Salle University Art Museum, Philadelphia PA
Loyola University Chicago, Loyola University Museum of Art, Chicago IL
Madison Museum of Fine Art, Madison GA
Marquette University, Haggerty Museum of Art, Milwaukee WI
Memphis Brooks Museum of Art, Memphis TN
Modern Art Museum, Fort Worth TX
Moravska Galerie v Brne, Moravian Gallery in Brno, Brno
Musee des Augustines de l'Hotel Dieu de Quebec, Quebec QC
Musee des Beaux-Arts d'Orleans, Museum of Fine Arts, Orleans
Musee des Beaux-Arts de Tours, Museum of Fine Arts, Tours
Museen der Stadt Koln, Wallraf-Richartz-Museum & Fondation Corboud - Wallraf-Richartz Museum & Corboud Foundation, Cologne
Museo de Arte de Ponce, The Luis A Ferre Foundation Inc, Ponce PR
Museo di Palazzo Ducale, Ducale Palace Museum, Mantua

Museo Nacional de Bellas Artes, National Museum of Fine Arts, Santiago
Museum of Fine Arts, Saint Petersburg, Florida, Inc, Saint Petersburg FL
Museum Plantin-Moretus, Antwerp
Muzej za Umjetnost i Obrt, Museum of Arts & Crafts, Zagreb
Muzeul National de Arta al Romaniei, National Museum of Art of Romania, Bucharest
Muzeum Narodowe w Poznaniu, National Museum in Poznan, Poznan
Narodna Galerija, National Gallery of Slovenia, Ljubljana
National Gallery of Canada, Ottawa ON
National Gallery of Ireland, Dublin
The National Museum of Western Art, Tokyo
New Orleans Museum of Art, New Orleans LA
North Carolina Museum of Art, Raleigh NC
Norton Simon Museum, Pasadena CA
Norwich Free Academy, Slater Memorial Museum, Norwich CT
Oberlin College, Allen Memorial Art Museum, Oberlin OH
Panhandle-Plains Historical Museum, Canyon TX
Passaic County Community College, Broadway, LRC, and Hamilton Club Galleries, Paterson NJ
Philadelphia Museum of Art, John G Johnson Collection, Philadelphia PA
Phoenix Art Museum, Phoenix AZ
Piedmont Arts Association, Martinsville VA
Queens College, City University of New York, Godwin-Ternbach Museum, Flushing NY
Reading Public Museum, Reading PA
Saint Bonaventure University, Regina A Quick Center for the Arts, Saint Bonaventure NY
San Antonio Museum of Art, San Antonio TX
San Diego Museum of Art, San Diego CA
Shirley Plantation Foundation, Charles City VA
Slovenska Narodna Galeria, Slovak National Gallery, Bratislava
The Speed Art Museum, Louisville KY
St Mary's College of Maryland, The Dwight Frederick Boyden Gallery, St Mary's City MD
Stanford University, Cantor Arts Center at Stanford University, Stanford CA
Szepmuveszeti Muzeum, Museum of Fine Arts, Budapest
Taft Museum of Art, Cincinnati OH
Timken Museum of Art, San Diego CA
Tver Regional Art Gallery, Tver
University of Chicago, Smart Museum of Art, Chicago IL
University of Illinois at Urbana-Champaign, Krannert Art Museum and Kinkead Pavilion, Champaign IL
The University of Kentucky Art Museum, Lexington KY
University of Miami, Lowe Art Museum, Coral Gables FL
University of Southern California, USC Fisher Museum of Art, Los Angeles CA
University of Utah, Utah Museum of Fine Arts, Salt Lake City UT
University of Wisconsin-Madison, Chazen Museum of Art, Madison WI
Ursinus College, Philip & Muriel Berman Museum of Art, Collegeville PA
Virginia Museum of Fine Arts, Richmond VA
Wadsworth Atheneum Museum of Art, Hartford CT
Walker Art Gallery, Liverpool
The Wallace Collection, London
Worcester Art Museum, Worcester MA
Zigler Art Museum, Jennings LA

PAINTING-FRENCH

Arnot Art Museum, Elmira NY
The Art Gallery of Grand Prairie, Grande Prairie AB
Art Without Walls Inc, Sayville NY
Bangladesh National Museum, Dhaka
Barnes Foundation, Merion PA
Baroda Museum and Picture Gallery, Vadodara
Birmingham Museum of Art, Birmingham AL
Bob Jones University Museum & Gallery Inc, Greenville SC
Bucknell University, Edward & Marthann Samek Art Gallery, Lewisburg PA
The Buffalo Fine Arts Academy, Albright-Knox Art Gallery, Buffalo NY
Cartoon Art Museum, San Francisco CA
Centenary College of Louisiana, Meadows Museum of Art, Shreveport LA
Central United Methodist Church, Swords Into Plowshares Peace Center & Gallery, Detroit MI
Charles Allis Art Museum, Milwaukee WI
Chateau de Versailles, Palace of Versailles, Versailles
Chrysler Museum of Art, Norfolk VA
Cincinnati Art Museum, Cincinnati Art Museum, Cincinnati OH
City of El Paso, El Paso TX
Clark Art Institute, Williamstown MA
Colgate University, Picker Art Gallery, Hamilton NY
College of William & Mary, Muscarelle Museum of Art, Williamsburg VA
Columbus Museum of Art, Columbus OH
Corcoran Gallery of Art, Washington DC
The Courtauld Institute of Art, The Courtauld Gallery, London
Coutts Museum of Art, Inc, El Dorado KS
Crocker Art Museum, Sacramento CA
The Currier Museum of Art, Manchester NH
Dahesh Museum of Art, Greenwich CT
Dartmouth College, Hood Museum of Art, Hanover NH
DeLeon White Gallery, Toronto ON
Denver Art Museum, Denver CO
Dickinson College, The Trout Gallery, Carlisle PA
The Dixon Gallery & Gardens, Memphis TN
Doncaster Museum and Art Gallery, Doncaster Yorks
Edsel & Eleanor Ford House, Grosse Pointe Shores MI
Elmhurst Art Museum, Elmhurst IL
Figge Art Museum, Davenport IA
Fine Arts Center for the New River Valley, Pulaski VA
Fisher Art Gallery, Marshalltown IA
Flint Institute of Arts, Flint MI
Florence County Museum, Florence SC
Florida State University, John & Mable Ringling Museum of Art, Sarasota FL
Florida State University and Central Florida Community College, The Appleton Museum of Art, Ocala FL
Folk Art Society of America, Richmond VA
The Frick Art & Historical Center, Inc, Frick Art Museum, Pittsburgh PA
Frye Art Museum, Seattle WA
Galerie Montcalm, Gatineau QC
Gemaldegalerie der Akademie der Bildenden Kunste Wien, Picture Gallery of the Academy of Fine Arts Vienna, Vienna
General Board of Discipleship, The United Methodist Church, The Upper Room Chapel & Museum, Nashville TN
Glanmore National Historic Site of Canada, Belleville ON
Hecht Museum, Haifa
Henry County Museum & Cultural Arts Center, Clinton MO
Hermitage Museum & Gardens, Norfolk VA
Hill-Stead Museum, Farmington CT
Hillwood Museum & Gardens Foundation, Hillwood Estate Museum & Gardens, Washington DC
Honolulu Museum of Art, Honolulu HI
The Hyde Collection, Glens Falls NY
Idemitsu Museum of Arts, Tokyo
Institute of Contemporary Art, Los Angeles, Los Angeles CA
Isabella Stewart Gardner Museum, Boston MA
The Israel Museum, Jerusalem, Jerusalem
Johns Hopkins University, Evergreen Museum & Library, Baltimore MD
Jordan National Gallery of Fine Arts, Amman
Joslyn Art Museum, Omaha NE
Juniata College Museum of Art, Huntingdon PA
Karakalpak State Art Museum, Nukus Republic of Karakalpakstan
Kateri Tekakwitha Shrine/St. Francis Xavier Mission, Kahnawake QC
Kimbell Art Foundation, Kimbell Art Museum, Fort Worth TX
The Kreeger Museum, Washington DC
Kunsthalle Bremen, Bremen Art Gallery, Bremen
Kunsthistorisches Museum Wien, Museum of Fine Arts, Vienna
Kunstmuseum Solothurn, Solothurn Art Museum, Solothurn
La Salle University Art Museum, Philadelphia PA
Lafayette College, Lafayette College Art Galleries, Easton PA
Latino Art Museum, Pomona CA
Lightner Museum, Saint Augustine FL
Lockwood-Mathews Mansion Museum, Norwalk CT
Longfellow-Evangeline State Commemorative Area, Saint Martinville LA
Loyola University Chicago, Loyola University Museum of Art, Chicago IL
Lyman Allyn Art Museum, New London CT
Madison Museum of Fine Art, Madison GA
The Mariners' Museum, Newport News VA
Marquette University, Haggerty Museum of Art, Milwaukee WI
McCord Museum of Canadian History, Montreal QC
Memphis Brooks Museum of Art, Memphis TN
Michelson Museum of Art, Marshall TX
The Mint Museum, Charlotte NC
Mobile Museum of Art, Mobile AL
Modern Art Museum, Fort Worth TX
Moderna Galerija, Modern Gallery - National Museum of Modern Art, Zagreb
Muscatine Art Center, Muscatine IA
Musee Cognacq-Jay, Cognacq-Jay Museum, Paris
Musee des Augustines de l'Hotel Dieu de Quebec, Quebec QC
Musee des Beaux-Arts d'Orleans, Museum of Fine Arts, Orleans
Musee des Beaux-Arts de Tours, Museum of Fine Arts, Tours
Museen der Stadt Koln, Wallraf-Richartz-Museum & Fondation Corboud - Wallraf-Richartz Museum & Corboud Foundation, Cologne
Museo de Arte de Ponce, The Luis A Ferre Foundation Inc, Ponce PR
Museo di Palazzo Ducale, Ducale Palace Museum, Mantua
Museo Nacional de Bellas Artes, National Museum of Fine Arts, Santiago
The Museum of Arts & Sciences Inc, Daytona Beach FL
Museum of Fine Arts, Saint Petersburg, Florida, Inc, Saint Petersburg FL
Museum of Modern Art, Ibaraki, Mito Ibaraki
Muzej za Umjetnost i Obrt, Museum of Arts & Crafts, Zagreb
Muzeul National de Arta al Romaniei, National Museum of Art of Romania, Bucharest
Muzeum Narodowe w Poznaniu, National Museum in Poznan, Poznan
Narodna Galerija, National Gallery of Slovenia, Ljubljana
Nassau County Museum of Art, Roslyn Harbor NY
National Art Museum of Moldova, Chisinau
National Gallery of Canada, Ottawa ON
National Gallery of Ireland, Dublin
The National Museum of Western Art, Tokyo
National Museum of Wildlife Art of the Unites States, Jackson WY
New Orleans Museum of Art, New Orleans LA
Niagara University, Castellani Art Museum, Niagara NY
Niigata Prefectural Museum of Modern Art, Nagaoka
North Carolina Museum of Art, Raleigh NC
Norton Simon Museum, Pasadena CA
Norwich Free Academy, Slater Memorial Museum, Norwich CT
Ohara Museum of Art, Kurashiki
Oklahoma City Museum of Art, Oklahoma City OK
The Old Jail Art Center, Albany TX
Opelousas Museum of Art, Inc (OMA), Opelousas LA
Osterreichische Galerie Belvedere Vienna, Belvedere Museum Vienna, Vienna
Owensboro Museum of Fine Art, Owensboro KY
Panhandle-Plains Historical Museum, Canyon TX
Passaic County Community College, Broadway, LRC, and Hamilton Club Galleries, Paterson NJ
Philadelphia Museum of Art, John G Johnson Collection, Philadelphia PA
The Phillips Collection, Washington DC
Piedmont Arts Association, Martinsville VA
PS1 Contemporary Art Center, Long Island City NY
Radio-Canada SRC CBC, Georges Goguen CBC Art Gallery, Moncton NB
Reading Public Museum, Reading PA
Ryerss Victorian Museum & Library, Philadelphia PA
Saginaw Art Museum, Saginaw MI
Saint Bonaventure University, Regina A Quick Center for the Arts, Saint Bonaventure NY
San Antonio Museum of Art, San Antonio TX
The San Joaquin Pioneer & Historical Society, The Haggin Museum, Stockton CA
Santa Barbara Museum of Art, Santa Barbara CA

Scripps College, Ruth Chandler Williamson Gallery, Claremont CA
Shirley Plantation Foundation, Charles City VA
Slovenska Narodna Galeria, Slovak National Gallery, Bratislava
The Society of the Cincinnati at Anderson House, Washington DC
Solomon R Guggenheim Museum, New York NY
The Speed Art Museum, Louisville KY
St Mary's College of Maryland, The Dwight Frederick Boyden Gallery, St Mary's City MD
Staatliche Museen zu Berlin Stiftung Preussischer Kulturbesitz, National Museums in Berlin, Prussian Cultural Heritage Foundation, Berlin
Stanford University, Cantor Arts Center at Stanford University, Stanford CA
The State Museum of Fine Arts of Tatarstan Republic, Kazan
The State Museum of Oriental Art, Moscow
Suan Pakkad Palace Museum, Bangkok
Szepmuveszeti Muzeum, Museum of Fine Arts, Budapest
Tacoma Art Museum, Tacoma WA
Taft Museum of Art, Cincinnati OH
Telfair Museums, Savannah GA
Timken Museum of Art, San Diego CA
Tver Regional Art Gallery, Tver
Ukrainian Institute of Modern Art, Chicago IL
University of California, Los Angeles, Hammer Museum, Los Angeles CA
University of Chicago, Smart Museum of Art, Chicago IL
University of Georgia, Georgia Museum of Art, Athens GA
University of Houston, Blaffer Art Museum, Houston TX
University of Illinois at Urbana-Champaign, Krannert Art Museum and Kinkead Pavilion, Champaign IL
University of Miami, Lowe Art Museum, Coral Gables FL
University of Minnesota Duluth, Tweed Museum of Art, Duluth MN
University of Notre Dame, Snite Museum of Art, Notre Dame IN
University of Pennsylvania, Arthur Ross Gallery, Philadelphia PA
University of Southern California, USC Fisher Museum of Art, Los Angeles CA
University of Utah, Utah Museum of Fine Arts, Salt Lake City UT
University of Wisconsin-Madison, Chazen Museum of Art, Madison WI
Ursinus College, Philip & Muriel Berman Museum of Art, Collegeville PA
Wadsworth Atheneum Museum of Art, Hartford CT
The Wallace Collection, London
Walters Art Museum, Baltimore MD
Wheaton College, Beard and Weil Galleries, Norton MA
Worcester Art Museum, Worcester MA
World Erotic Art Museum, Miami Beach FL
Yokohama Museum of Art, Yokohama

PAINTING-GERMAN

Allentown Art Museum, Allentown PA
Arnot Art Museum, Elmira NY
The Art Gallery of Grand Prairie, Grande Prairie AB
Art Without Walls Inc, Sayville NY
Bangladesh National Museum, Dhaka
Barnes Foundation, Merion PA
Bayerische Staatsgemaldesammlungen, Bavarian State Painting Collections, Munich
Beloit College, Wright Museum of Art, Beloit WI
Blanden Memorial Art Museum, Fort Dodge IA
Bob Jones University Museum & Gallery Inc, Greenville SC
Bucknell University, Edward & Marthann Samek Art Gallery, Lewisburg PA
The Buffalo Fine Arts Academy, Albright-Knox Art Gallery, Buffalo NY
Central United Methodist Church, Swords Into Plowshares Peace Center & Gallery, Detroit MI
Cincinnati Art Museum, Cincinnati Art Museum, Cincinnati OH
College of William & Mary, Muscarelle Museum of Art, Williamsburg VA
Columbus Chapel & Boal Mansion Museum, Boalsburg PA
Columbus Museum of Art, Columbus OH
Cornell University, Herbert F Johnson Museum of Art, Ithaca NY
The Courtauld Institute of Art, The Courtauld Gallery, London
Crocker Art Museum, Sacramento CA
The Currier Museum of Art, Manchester NH
DeLeon White Gallery, Toronto ON
Detroit Institute of Arts, Detroit MI
Figge Art Museum, Davenport IA
Fine Arts Center for the New River Valley, Pulaski VA
Flint Institute of Arts, Flint MI
Florida State University, John & Mable Ringling Museum of Art, Sarasota FL
Florida State University and Central Florida Community College, The Appleton Museum of Art, Ocala FL
Fondazione Musei Civici Di Venezia, Museo Correr - Correr Museum, Venice
Frye Art Museum, Seattle WA
Gemaldegalerie der Akademie der Bildenden Kunste Wien, Picture Gallery of the Academy of Fine Arts Vienna, Vienna
Hecht Museum, Haifa
The Hyde Collection, Glens Falls NY
Institute of Contemporary Art, Los Angeles, Los Angeles CA
Johns Hopkins University, Evergreen Museum & Library, Baltimore MD
Juniata College Museum of Art, Huntingdon PA
Kereszteny Muzeum, Christian Museum, Esztergom
Kimbell Art Foundation, Kimbell Art Museum, Fort Worth TX
Kitchener-Waterloo Art Gallery, Kitchener ON
The Kreeger Museum, Washington DC
Kunsthalle Bremen, Bremen Art Gallery, Bremen
Kunsthistorisches Museum Wien, Museum of Fine Arts, Vienna
Kunstmuseum Solothurn, Solothurn Art Museum, Solothurn
La Salle University Art Museum, Philadelphia PA
Lightner Museum, Saint Augustine FL
Longue Vue House & Gardens, New Orleans LA
Loyola University Chicago, Loyola University Museum of Art, Chicago IL
Marquette University, Haggerty Museum of Art, Milwaukee WI
The Metropolitan Museum of Art, New York NY
Michelson Museum of Art, Marshall TX
Milwaukee Art Museum, Milwaukee WI
The Mint Museum, Charlotte NC
Modern Art Museum, Fort Worth TX
Moderna Galerija, Modern Gallery - National Museum of Modern Art, Zagreb
Moravska Galerie v Brne, Moravian Gallery in Brno, Brno
Musee des Beaux-Arts d'Orleans, Museum of Fine Arts, Orleans
Musee des Beaux-Arts de Tours, Museum of Fine Arts, Tours
Museen der Stadt Koln, Wallraf-Richartz-Museum & Fondation Corboud - Wallraf-Richartz Museum & Corboud Foundation, Cologne
Museo di Palazzo Ducale, Ducale Palace Museum, Mantua
The Museum of Arts & Sciences Inc, Daytona Beach FL
Museum of Contemporary Art Chicago, Chicago IL
Museum of Fine Arts, Saint Petersburg, Florida, Inc, Saint Petersburg FL
Muzej za Umjetnost i Obrt, Museum of Arts & Crafts, Zagreb
Muzeul National de Arta al Romaniei, National Museum of Art of Romania, Bucharest
Muzeum Narodowe w Poznaniu, National Museum in Poznan, Poznan
Narodna Galerija, National Gallery of Slovenia, Ljubljana
Nassau County Museum of Art, Roslyn Harbor NY
National Art Museum of Moldova, Chisinau
National Gallery of Canada, Ottawa ON
National Gallery of Ireland, Dublin
The National Museum of Western Art, Tokyo
Neue Galerie New York, New York NY
Niagara University, Castellani Art Museum, Niagara NY
Niigata Prefectural Museum of Modern Art, Nagaoka
North Carolina Museum of Art, Raleigh NC
Norwich Free Academy, Slater Memorial Museum, Norwich CT
Oklahoma City Museum of Art, Oklahoma City OK
The Old Jail Art Center, Albany TX
Opelousas Museum of Art, Inc (OMA), Opelousas LA
Panhandle-Plains Historical Museum, Canyon TX
Passaic County Community College, Broadway, LRC, and Hamilton Club Galleries, Paterson NJ
Philadelphia Museum of Art, John G Johnson Collection, Philadelphia PA
Piedmont Arts Association, Martinsville VA
PS1 Contemporary Art Center, Long Island City NY
Queens College, City University of New York, Godwin-Ternbach Museum, Flushing NY
Reading Public Museum, Reading PA
Saginaw Art Museum, Saginaw MI
Saint Anselm College, Alva de Mars Megan Chapel Art Center, Manchester NH
The San Joaquin Pioneer & Historical Society, The Haggin Museum, Stockton CA
Sheldon Art Galleries, Saint Louis MO
Solomon R Guggenheim Museum, New York NY
The Speed Art Museum, Louisville KY
Spertus Institute of Jewish Studies, Chicago IL
Staatliche Museen zu Berlin Stiftung Preussischer Kulturbesitz, National Museums in Berlin, Prussian Cultural Heritage Foundation, Berlin
Stanford University, Cantor Arts Center at Stanford University, Stanford CA
The State Museum of Fine Arts of Tatarstan Republic, Kazan
State University of New York at New Paltz, Samuel Dorsky Museum of Art, New Paltz NY
Telfair Museums, Savannah GA
Tver Regional Art Gallery, Tver
United States Figure Skating Association, World Figure Skating Museum & Hall of Fame, Colorado Springs CO
University of Chicago, Smart Museum of Art, Chicago IL
University of Houston, Blaffer Art Museum, Houston TX
University of Illinois at Urbana-Champaign, Krannert Art Museum and Kinkead Pavilion, Champaign IL
The University of Kentucky Art Museum, Lexington KY
University of Miami, Lowe Art Museum, Coral Gables FL
University of Utah, Utah Museum of Fine Arts, Salt Lake City UT
University of Wisconsin-Madison, Chazen Museum of Art, Madison WI
Ursinus College, Philip & Muriel Berman Museum of Art, Collegeville PA
Wadsworth Atheneum Museum of Art, Hartford CT
Walker Art Gallery, Liverpool
The Wallace Collection, London
Wheaton College, Beard and Weil Galleries, Norton MA
World Erotic Art Museum, Miami Beach FL
Yokohama Museum of Art, Yokohama
Zigler Art Museum, Jennings LA

PAINTING-ISRAELI

Art Without Walls Inc, Sayville NY
The Baltimore Museum of Art, Baltimore MD
Bayerische Staatsgemaldesammlungen, Bavarian State Painting Collections, Munich
The Buffalo Fine Arts Academy, Albright-Knox Art Gallery, Buffalo NY
Central United Methodist Church, Swords Into Plowshares Peace Center & Gallery, Detroit MI
Detroit Institute of Arts, Detroit MI
Hebrew Union College - Jewish Institute of Religion, Skirball Museum Cincinnati, Cincinnati OH
Hebrew Union College - Jewish Institute of Religion Museum, Jewish Institute of Religion, New York NY
Hecht Museum, Haifa
Institute of Contemporary Art, Los Angeles, Los Angeles CA
The Israel Museum, Jerusalem, Jerusalem
Longue Vue House & Gardens, New Orleans LA
Modern Art Museum, Fort Worth TX
North Carolina Museum of Art, Raleigh NC
Opelousas Museum of Art, Inc (OMA), Opelousas LA
Piedmont Arts Association, Martinsville VA
PS1 Contemporary Art Center, Long Island City NY
Sheldon Art Galleries, Saint Louis MO
Shephela Museum, Kefar-Menahem
The Speed Art Museum, Louisville KY
Spertus Institute of Jewish Studies, Chicago IL

Stanford University, Cantor Arts Center at Stanford University, Stanford CA
The State Museum of Oriental Art, Moscow
Ursinus College, Philip & Muriel Berman Museum of Art, Collegeville PA
Wadsworth Atheneum Museum of Art, Hartford CT
World Erotic Art Museum, Miami Beach FL

PAINTING-ITALIAN

Allentown Art Museum, Allentown PA
Arnot Art Museum, Elmira NY
Art Without Walls Inc, Sayville NY
Bangladesh National Museum, Dhaka
Baroda Museum and Picture Gallery, Vadodara
Bayerische Staatsgemaldesammlungen, Bavarian State Painting Collections, Munich
Berkshire Museum, Pittsfield MA
Birmingham Museum of Art, Birmingham AL
Bob Jones University Museum & Gallery Inc, Greenville SC
Bucknell University, Edward & Marthann Samek Art Gallery, Lewisburg PA
The Buffalo Fine Arts Academy, Albright-Knox Art Gallery, Buffalo NY
Canton Museum of Art, Canton OH
Chrysler Museum of Art, Norfolk VA
Cincinnati Art Museum, Cincinnati Art Museum, Cincinnati OH
City of El Paso, El Paso TX
Clark Art Institute, Williamstown MA
Colgate University, Picker Art Gallery, Hamilton NY
College of William & Mary, Muscarelle Museum of Art, Williamsburg VA
Columbia Museum of Art, Columbia SC
Columbus Chapel & Boal Mansion Museum, Boalsburg PA
Columbus Museum of Art, Columbus OH
The Courtauld Institute of Art, The Courtauld Gallery, London
Crocker Art Museum, Sacramento CA
Cuneo Mansion & Gardens, Vernon Hills IL
The Currier Museum of Art, Manchester NH
Dartmouth College, Hood Museum of Art, Hanover NH
Denver Art Museum, Denver CO
Detroit Institute of Arts, Detroit MI
Doncaster Museum and Art Gallery, Doncaster Yorks
Edsel & Eleanor Ford House, Grosse Pointe Shores MI
Environment Canada - Parks Canada, Laurier House, National Historic Site, Ottawa ON
Fine Arts Center for the New River Valley, Pulaski VA
Flint Institute of Arts, Flint MI
Florida State University, John & Mable Ringling Museum of Art, Sarasota FL
Fondazione Musei Civici Di Venezia, Ca' Rezzonico, Venice
Fondazione Musei Civici Di Venezia, Ca' Pesaro Galleria Nazionale d'Arte Moderna - Ca' Pesaro Gallery of Modern Art, Venice
The Frick Art & Historical Center, Inc, Frick Art Museum, Pittsburgh PA
Frick Collection, New York NY
Frye Art Museum, Seattle WA
Galleria Nazionale dell'Umbria, Umbrian National Gallery, Perugia
Gemaldegalerie der Akademie der Bildenden Kunste Wien, Picture Gallery of the Academy of Fine Arts Vienna, Vienna
General Board of Discipleship, The United Methodist Church, The Upper Room Chapel & Museum, Nashville TN
Hecht Museum, Haifa
Hillwood Museum & Gardens Foundation, Hillwood Estate Museum & Gardens, Washington DC
Honolulu Museum of Art, Honolulu HI
The Hyde Collection, Glens Falls NY
Indiana Landmarks, Morris-Butler House, Indianapolis IN
Institute of Contemporary Art, Los Angeles, Los Angeles CA
Isabella Stewart Gardner Museum, Boston MA
The Israel Museum, Jerusalem, Jerusalem
Jordan National Gallery of Fine Arts, Amman
Joslyn Art Museum, Omaha NE
Juniata College Museum of Art, Huntingdon PA
Kereszteny Muzeum, Christian Museum, Esztergom
Kimbell Art Foundation, Kimbell Art Museum, Fort Worth TX
Kunsthistorisches Museum Wien, Museum of Fine Arts, Vienna
La Salle University Art Museum, Philadelphia PA
Latino Art Museum, Pomona CA
Lightner Museum, Saint Augustine FL
Loyola University Chicago, Loyola University Museum of Art, Chicago IL
Lyman Allyn Art Museum, New London CT
Mabee-Gerrer Museum of Art, Shawnee OK
Madison Museum of Fine Art, Madison GA
Marquette University, Haggerty Museum of Art, Milwaukee WI
Memphis Brooks Museum of Art, Memphis TN
Meredith College, Frankie G Weems Gallery & Rotunda Gallery, Raleigh NC
The Mint Museum, Charlotte NC
Mississippi Museum of Art, Jackson MS
Mobile Museum of Art, Mobile AL
Modern Art Museum, Fort Worth TX
Moravska Galerie v Brne, Moravian Gallery in Brno, Brno
Morris-Jumel Mansion, Inc, New York NY
Musee Cognacq-Jay, Cognacq-Jay Museum, Paris
Musee des Augustines de l'Hotel Dieu de Quebec, Quebec QC
Musee des Beaux-Arts d'Orleans, Museum of Fine Arts, Orleans
Musee des Beaux-Arts de Tours, Museum of Fine Arts, Tours
Museen der Stadt Koln, Wallraf-Richartz-Museum & Fondation Corboud - Wallraf-Richartz Museum & Corboud Foundation, Cologne
Museo de Arte de Ponce, The Luis A Ferre Foundation Inc, Ponce PR
Museo di Palazzo Ducale, Ducale Palace Museum, Mantua
Museo Italo Americano, San Francisco CA
Museo Nacional de Bellas Artes, National Museum of Fine Arts, Santiago
The Museum of Arts & Sciences Inc, Daytona Beach FL
Museum of Contemporary Art Chicago, Chicago IL
Museum of Fine Arts, Saint Petersburg, Florida, Inc, Saint Petersburg FL
Muzej za Umjetnost i Obrt, Museum of Arts & Crafts, Zagreb
Muzeul National de Arta al Romaniei, National Museum of Art of Romania, Bucharest
Muzeum Narodowe w Poznaniu, National Museum in Poznan, Poznan
Narodna Galerija, National Gallery of Slovenia, Ljubljana
National Art Museum of Moldova, Chisinau
National Gallery of Canada, Ottawa ON
National Gallery of Ireland, Dublin
The National Museum of Western Art, Tokyo
National Trust for Historic Preservation, Chesterwood, Stockbridge MA
North Carolina Museum of Art, Raleigh NC
Norwich Free Academy, Slater Memorial Museum, Norwich CT
Oklahoma City Museum of Art, Oklahoma City OK
The Old Jail Art Center, Albany TX
Opelousas Museum of Art, Inc (OMA), Opelousas LA
Order Sons of Italy in America, Garibaldi & Meucci Museum, Staten Island NY
Panhandle-Plains Historical Museum, Canyon TX
Philadelphia Museum of Art, John G Johnson Collection, Philadelphia PA
Philbrook Museum of Art, Tulsa OK
The Phillips Collection, Washington DC
The Pomona College, Claremont CA
PS1 Contemporary Art Center, Long Island City NY
Queens College, City University of New York, Godwin-Ternbach Museum, Flushing NY
Reading Public Museum, Reading PA
Saint Olaf College, Flaten Art Museum, Northfield MN
San Antonio Museum of Art, San Antonio TX
San Diego Museum of Art, San Diego CA
Sheldon Art Galleries, Saint Louis MO
Slovenska Narodna Galeria, Slovak National Gallery, Bratislava
Solomon R Guggenheim Museum, New York NY
The Speed Art Museum, Louisville KY
Staatliche Museen zu Berlin Stiftung Preussischer Kulturbesitz, National Museums in Berlin, Prussian Cultural Heritage Foundation, Berlin
Stanford University, Cantor Arts Center at Stanford University, Stanford CA
The State Museum of Fine Arts of Tatarstan Republic, Kazan
The State University of New York at Potsdam, The Art Museum, Potsdam NY
Timken Museum of Art, San Diego CA
Tver Regional Art Gallery, Tver
University of Chicago, Smart Museum of Art, Chicago IL
University of Georgia, Georgia Museum of Art, Athens GA
University of Houston, Blaffer Art Museum, Houston TX
University of Illinois at Urbana-Champaign, Krannert Art Museum and Kinkead Pavilion, Champaign IL
University of Kansas, Spencer Museum of Art, Lawrence KS
The University of Kentucky Art Museum, Lexington KY
University of Miami, Lowe Art Museum, Coral Gables FL
University of Notre Dame, Snite Museum of Art, Notre Dame IN
University of Southern California, USC Fisher Museum of Art, Los Angeles CA
University of Utah, Utah Museum of Fine Arts, Salt Lake City UT
University of Wisconsin-Madison, Chazen Museum of Art, Madison WI
Ursinus College, Philip & Muriel Berman Museum of Art, Collegeville PA
Vassar College, The Frances Lehman Loeb Art Center, Poughkeepsie NY
Virginia Museum of Fine Arts, Richmond VA
Wadsworth Atheneum Museum of Art, Hartford CT
Walker Art Gallery, Liverpool
The Wallace Collection, London
World Erotic Art Museum, Miami Beach FL
Zigler Art Museum, Jennings LA

PAINTING-JAPANESE

Arnot Art Museum, Elmira NY
Art Without Walls Inc, Sayville NY
Asian Art Museum of San Francisco, Chong-Moon Lee Ctr for Asian Art and Culture, San Francisco CA
Bangladesh National Museum, Dhaka
Baroda Museum and Picture Gallery, Vadodara
Bayerische Staatsgemaldesammlungen, Bavarian State Painting Collections, Munich
Billie Trimble Chandler, Texas State Museum of Asian Cultures, Corpus Christi TX
Birmingham Museum of Art, Birmingham AL
Bucknell University, Edward & Marthann Samek Art Gallery, Lewisburg PA
Central United Methodist Church, Swords Into Plowshares Peace Center & Gallery, Detroit MI
The Cleveland Museum of Art, Cleveland OH
Columbus Museum of Art, Columbus OH
Crocker Art Museum, Sacramento CA
DeLeon White Gallery, Toronto ON
Denver Art Museum, Denver CO
Detroit Institute of Arts, Detroit MI
Environment Canada - Parks Canada, Laurier House, National Historic Site, Ottawa ON
Fine Arts Center for the New River Valley, Pulaski VA
Fitton Center for Creative Arts, Hamilton OH
Florence County Museum, Florence SC
Folk Art Society of America, Richmond VA
Frye Art Museum, Seattle WA
Galerie Montcalm, Gatineau QC
General Board of Discipleship, The United Methodist Church, The Upper Room Chapel & Museum, Nashville TN
Grand Rapids Art Museum, Grand Rapids MI
Henry County Museum & Cultural Arts Center, Clinton MO
Honolulu Museum of Art, Honolulu HI
Idemitsu Museum of Arts, Tokyo
Institute of Contemporary Art, Los Angeles, Los Angeles CA
International Museum of Art, El Paso TX
The Israel Museum, Jerusalem, Jerusalem
Jordan National Gallery of Fine Arts, Amman
Kenosha Public Museums, Kenosha WI
Kimbell Art Foundation, Kimbell Art Museum, Fort Worth TX
Lightner Museum, Saint Augustine FL
The Mariners' Museum, Newport News VA
The Mint Museum, Charlotte NC
Modern Art Museum, Fort Worth TX

Musee des Beaux-Arts de Tours, Museum of Fine Arts, Tours
Museum of Fine Arts, Saint Petersburg, Florida, Inc, Saint Petersburg FL
Muzeul National de Arta al Romaniei, National Museum of Art of Romania, Bucharest
Nara Kokuritsu Hakubutsu-Kan, Nara National Museum, Nara
The National Art Center, Tokyo, Tokyo
National Art Museum of Moldova, Chisinau
National Baseball Hall of Fame & Museum, Cooperstown NY
The National Museum of Modern Art, Tokyo, Tokyo
New Orleans Museum of Art, New Orleans LA
New Visions Gallery, Inc, Marshfield WI
Niigata Prefectural Museum of Modern Art, Nagaoka
Norwich Free Academy, Slater Memorial Museum, Norwich CT
Noyes Art Gallery, Lincoln NE
Palm Beach County Parks & Recreation Department, Morikami Museum & Japanese Gardens, Delray Beach FL
Panhandle-Plains Historical Museum, Canyon TX
PS1 Contemporary Art Center, Long Island City NY
Reading Public Museum, Reading PA
Saginaw Art Museum, Saginaw MI
Saint John's University, Dr. M.T. Geoffrey Yeh Art Gallery, Queens NY
Saint Olaf College, Flaten Art Museum, Northfield MN
San Antonio Museum of Art, San Antonio TX
Santa Barbara Museum of Art, Santa Barbara CA
Scripps College, Ruth Chandler Williamson Gallery, Claremont CA
Seattle Art Museum, Seattle WA
Sheldon Art Galleries, Saint Louis MO
The Society of the Cincinnati at Anderson House, Washington DC
The Speed Art Museum, Louisville KY
Springfield Art Museum, Springfield MO
St Mary's College of Maryland, The Dwight Frederick Boyden Gallery, St Mary's City MD
Staatliche Museen zu Berlin Stiftung Preussischer Kulturbesitz, National Museums in Berlin, Prussian Cultural Heritage Foundation, Berlin
Stanford University, Cantor Arts Center at Stanford University, Stanford CA
The State Museum of Oriental Art, Moscow
State University of New York at New Paltz, Samuel Dorsky Museum of Art, New Paltz NY
The State University of New York at Potsdam, The Art Museum, Potsdam NY
Tacoma Art Museum, Tacoma WA
Temiskaming Art Gallery, Haileybury ON
The Tokugawa Art Museum, Nagoya
Tokyo National Museum, Tokyo
Tver Regional Art Gallery, Tver
Ukrainian Institute of Modern Art, Chicago IL
University of Chicago, Smart Museum of Art, Chicago IL
University of Houston, Blaffer Art Museum, Houston TX
University of Illinois at Urbana-Champaign, Krannert Art Museum and Kinkead Pavilion, Champaign IL
University of Kansas, Spencer Museum of Art, Lawrence KS
The University of Kentucky Art Museum, Lexington KY
University of Utah, Utah Museum of Fine Arts, Salt Lake City UT
University of Wisconsin-Madison, Chazen Museum of Art, Madison WI
Ursinus College, Philip & Muriel Berman Museum of Art, Collegeville PA
Viridian Artists Inc, New York NY
Yokohama Museum of Art, Yokohama
Zigler Art Museum, Jennings LA

PAINTING-NEW ZEALAND

The Art Gallery of Grand Prairie, Grande Prairie AB
Art Without Walls Inc, Sayville NY
Detroit Institute of Arts, Detroit MI
Institute of Contemporary Art, Los Angeles, Los Angeles CA
Modern Art Museum, Fort Worth TX
PS1 Contemporary Art Center, Long Island City NY
Stanford University, Cantor Arts Center at Stanford University, Stanford CA
University of Illinois at Urbana-Champaign, Krannert Art Museum and Kinkead Pavilion, Champaign IL

PAINTING-POLISH

Art Without Walls Inc, Sayville NY
Bucknell University, Edward & Marthann Samek Art Gallery, Lewisburg PA
College of William & Mary, Muscarelle Museum of Art, Williamsburg VA
Detroit Institute of Arts, Detroit MI
Fine Arts Center for the New River Valley, Pulaski VA
Forest Lawn Museum, Glendale CA
Frye Art Museum, Seattle WA
Galerie Montcalm, Gatineau QC
Grand Rapids Art Museum, Grand Rapids MI
Hecht Museum, Haifa
Institute of Contemporary Art, Los Angeles, Los Angeles CA
International Museum of Art, El Paso TX
Muzeul National de Arta al Romaniei, National Museum of Art of Romania, Bucharest
Muzeum Narodowe W Kielcach, National Museum in Kielce, Kielce
Muzeum Narodowe w Poznaniu, National Museum in Poznan, Poznan
Narodna Galerija, National Gallery of Slovenia, Ljubljana
National Art Museum of Moldova, Chisinau
Panhandle-Plains Historical Museum, Canyon TX
Phoenix Art Museum, Phoenix AZ
Polish Museum of America (PMA), Chicago IL
PS1 Contemporary Art Center, Long Island City NY
Reading Public Museum, Reading PA
Saginaw Art Museum, Saginaw MI
The Speed Art Museum, Louisville KY
Spertus Institute of Jewish Studies, Chicago IL
St Mary's Galeria, Orchard Lake MI
Stanford University, Cantor Arts Center at Stanford University, Stanford CA
Tver Regional Art Gallery, Tver
U Gallery, San Francisco CA
University of Georgia, Georgia Museum of Art, Athens GA
University of Wisconsin-Madison, Chazen Museum of Art, Madison WI
Walker Art Gallery, Liverpool
Zigler Art Museum, Jennings LA

PAINTING-RUSSIAN

Art Without Walls Inc, Sayville NY
Bangladesh National Museum, Dhaka
Baroda Museum and Picture Gallery, Vadodara
Bayerische Staatsgemaldesammlungen, Bavarian State Painting Collections, Munich
Bob Jones University Museum & Gallery Inc, Greenville SC
Bucknell University, Edward & Marthann Samek Art Gallery, Lewisburg PA
Byzantine & Christian Museum, Athens, Athens
College of William & Mary, Muscarelle Museum of Art, Williamsburg VA
Coutts Museum of Art, Inc, El Dorado KS
Crocker Art Museum, Sacramento CA
The Currier Museum of Art, Manchester NH
Detroit Institute of Arts, Detroit MI
Doncaster Museum and Art Gallery, Doncaster Yorks
Fine Arts Center for the New River Valley, Pulaski VA
Frye Art Museum, Seattle WA
General Board of Discipleship, The United Methodist Church, The Upper Room Chapel & Museum, Nashville TN
Grand Rapids Art Museum, Grand Rapids MI
Hebrew Union College - Jewish Institute of Religion Museum, Jewish Institute of Religion, New York NY
Hillwood Museum & Gardens Foundation, Hillwood Estate Museum & Gardens, Washington DC
Huntington Museum of Art, Huntington WV
Institute of Contemporary Art, Los Angeles, Los Angeles CA
International Museum of Art, El Paso TX
James Dick Foundation, Festival - Institute, Round Top TX
Johns Hopkins University, Evergreen Museum & Library, Baltimore MD
Jordan National Gallery of Fine Arts, Amman
Joslyn Art Museum, Omaha NE
Kereszteny Muzeum, Christian Museum, Esztergom
Kyiv Museum of Russian Art, Kyiv Ukrainian
Longue Vue House & Gardens, New Orleans LA
Loyola University Chicago, Loyola University Museum of Art, Chicago IL
Meredith College, Frankie G Weems Gallery & Rotunda Gallery, Raleigh NC
Michelson Museum of Art, Marshall TX
The Mint Museum, Charlotte NC
Moravska Galerie v Brne, Moravian Gallery in Brno, Brno
Moscow Museum of Modern Art, Moscow
The Museum of Arts & Sciences Inc, Daytona Beach FL
Muzeul National de Arta al Romaniei, National Museum of Art of Romania, Bucharest
Nassau County Museum of Art, Roslyn Harbor NY
National Art Museum of Moldova, Chisinau
National Gallery of Canada, Ottawa ON
Noyes Art Gallery, Lincoln NE
Panhandle-Plains Historical Museum, Canyon TX
Pearson Lakes Art Center, Okoboji IA
The Phillips Collection, Washington DC
PS1 Contemporary Art Center, Long Island City NY
Queens College, City University of New York, Godwin-Ternbach Museum, Flushing NY
Reading Public Museum, Reading PA
Rollins College, George D & Harriet W Cornell Fine Arts Museum, Winter Park FL
Saginaw Art Museum, Saginaw MI
Saint Olaf College, Flaten Art Museum, Northfield MN
San Antonio Museum of Art, San Antonio TX
Solomon R Guggenheim Museum, New York NY
The Speed Art Museum, Louisville KY
Spertus Institute of Jewish Studies, Chicago IL
Springville Museum of Art, Springville UT
Stanford University, Cantor Arts Center at Stanford University, Stanford CA
The State Museum of Fine Arts of Tatarstan Republic, Kazan
The State Museum of Oriental Art, Moscow
Timken Museum of Art, San Diego CA
Tver Regional Art Gallery, Tver
University of Wisconsin-Madison, Chazen Museum of Art, Madison WI
Ursinus College, Philip & Muriel Berman Museum of Art, Collegeville PA
World Erotic Art Museum, Miami Beach FL
Yokohama Museum of Art, Yokohama

PAINTING-SCANDINAVIAN

American Swedish Institute, Minneapolis MN
Arnot Art Museum, Elmira NY
Art Without Walls Inc, Sayville NY
Bangladesh National Museum, Dhaka
Bayerische Staatsgemaldesammlungen, Bavarian State Painting Collections, Munich
Blauvelt Demarest Foundation, Hiram Blauvelt Art Museum, Oradell NJ
Bucknell University, Edward & Marthann Samek Art Gallery, Lewisburg PA
Colgate University, Picker Art Gallery, Hamilton NY
Crocker Art Museum, Sacramento CA
Detroit Institute of Arts, Detroit MI
Fine Arts Center for the New River Valley, Pulaski VA
Frye Art Museum, Seattle WA
Galerie Montcalm, Gatineau QC
Grand Rapids Art Museum, Grand Rapids MI
Huntington Museum of Art, Huntington WV
Institute of Contemporary Art, Los Angeles, Los Angeles CA
James Dick Foundation, Festival - Institute, Round Top TX
Musee des Beaux-Arts de Tours, Museum of Fine Arts, Tours
The National Museum of Western Art, Tokyo
National Museum of Wildlife Art of the Unites States, Jackson WY
Norsk Maritimt Museum, Norwegian Maritime Museum, Oslo
Panhandle-Plains Historical Museum, Canyon TX
Passaic County Community College, Broadway, LRC, and Hamilton Club Galleries, Paterson NJ
The Phillips Collection, Washington DC
PS1 Contemporary Art Center, Long Island City NY
Reading Public Museum, Reading PA
Saint Olaf College, Flaten Art Museum, Northfield MN
The Speed Art Museum, Louisville KY
Stanford University, Cantor Arts Center at Stanford University, Stanford CA
Suomen Kansallismuseo, National Museum of Finland, Helsinki

Swedish American Museum, Chicago IL
Tver Regional Art Gallery, Tver
University of Wisconsin-Madison, Chazen Museum of Art, Madison WI
Vesterheim Norwegian-American Museum, Decorah IA
Walker Art Gallery, Liverpool

PAINTING-SPANISH

Albuquerque Museum of Art & History, Albuquerque NM
American Sport Art Museum and Archives, Daphne AL
Arnot Art Museum, Elmira NY
The Art Gallery of Grand Prairie, Grande Prairie AB
Art Without Walls Inc, Sayville NY
Bakehouse Art Complex, Inc, Miami FL
The Baltimore Museum of Art, Baltimore MD
Bangladesh National Museum, Dhaka
Baroda Museum and Picture Gallery, Vadodara
Beaverbrook Art Gallery, Fredericton NB
Blanden Memorial Art Museum, Fort Dodge IA
Bucknell University, Edward & Marthann Samek Art Gallery, Lewisburg PA
Canton Museum of Art, Canton OH
Cincinnati Art Museum, Cincinnati Art Museum, Cincinnati OH
City of El Paso, El Paso TX
College of William & Mary, Muscarelle Museum of Art, Williamsburg VA
Columbus Chapel & Boal Mansion Museum, Boalsburg PA
Cornell Museum of Art and American Culture, Delray Beach FL
Coutts Museum of Art, Inc, El Dorado KS
Crocker Art Museum, Sacramento CA
The Currier Museum of Art, Manchester NH
Detroit Institute of Arts, Detroit MI
Dickinson College, The Trout Gallery, Carlisle PA
Flint Institute of Arts, Flint MI
Frye Art Museum, Seattle WA
Gemaldegalerie der Akademie der Bildenden Kunste Wien, Picture Gallery of the Academy of Fine Arts Vienna, Vienna
General Board of Discipleship, The United Methodist Church, The Upper Room Chapel & Museum, Nashville TN
Grand Rapids Art Museum, Grand Rapids MI
Huntington Museum of Art, Huntington WV
Institute of Contemporary Art, Los Angeles, Los Angeles CA
International Museum of Art, El Paso TX
Jerald Melberg Gallery, Charlotte NC
Johns Hopkins University, Evergreen Museum & Library, Baltimore MD
Jordan National Gallery of Fine Arts, Amman
Joslyn Art Museum, Omaha NE
Kereszteny Muzeum, Christian Museum, Esztergom
The Kreeger Museum, Washington DC
Kunsthistorisches Museum Wien, Museum of Fine Arts, Vienna
Latino Art Museum, Pomona CA
Marquette University, Haggerty Museum of Art, Milwaukee WI
The Mint Museum, Charlotte NC
Mission San Luis Rey de Francia, Mission San Luis Rey Museum, Oceanside CA
Mission San Miguel Museum, San Miguel CA
Musee des Augustines de l'Hotel Dieu de Quebec, Quebec QC
Musee des Beaux-Arts d'Orleans, Museum of Fine Arts, Orleans
Musee des Beaux-Arts de Tours, Museum of Fine Arts, Tours
Museen der Stadt Koln, Wallraf-Richartz-Museum & Fondation Corboud - Wallraf-Richartz Museum & Corboud Foundation, Cologne
Museo de Arte Contemporaneo de Castilla y Leon, Leon
Museo de Arte de Ponce, The Luis A Ferre Foundation Inc, Ponce PR
Museo De Las Americas, Denver CO
Museo Del Romanticismo, Museum of the Romantic Period, Madrid
Museo Nacional de Bellas Artes, National Museum of Fine Arts, Santiago
Museu Nacional D'Art De Catalunya, Catalona National Museum of Art, Barcelona
The Museum of Arts & Sciences Inc, Daytona Beach FL
Museum of Fine Arts, Saint Petersburg, Florida, Inc, Saint Petersburg FL
Muzej za Umjetnost i Obrt, Museum of Arts & Crafts, Zagreb
Muzeul National de Arta al Romaniei, National Museum of Art of Romania, Bucharest
Muzeum Narodowe w Poznaniu, National Museum in Poznan, Poznan
Narodna Galerija, National Gallery of Slovenia, Ljubljana
National Art Museum of Moldova, Chisinau
National Gallery of Canada, Ottawa ON
National Gallery of Ireland, Dublin
The National Museum of Western Art, Tokyo
New Mexico Department of Cultural Affairs, Palace of Governors, Santa Fe NM
North Carolina Museum of Art, Raleigh NC
Norwich Free Academy, Slater Memorial Museum, Norwich CT
The Old Jail Art Center, Albany TX
Opelousas Museum of Art, Inc (OMA), Opelousas LA
Panhandle-Plains Historical Museum, Canyon TX
The Phillips Collection, Washington DC
PS1 Contemporary Art Center, Long Island City NY
Queens College, City University of New York, Godwin-Ternbach Museum, Flushing NY
Reading Public Museum, Reading PA
Saint Olaf College, Flaten Art Museum, Northfield MN
San Antonio Museum of Art, San Antonio TX
San Diego Museum of Art, San Diego CA
The San Joaquin Pioneer & Historical Society, The Haggin Museum, Stockton CA
Santa Barbara Museum of Art, Santa Barbara CA
Sheldon Art Galleries, Saint Louis MO
Slovenska Narodna Galeria, Slovak National Gallery, Bratislava
Solomon R Guggenheim Museum, New York NY
Southern Methodist University, Meadows Museum, Dallas TX
The Speed Art Museum, Louisville KY
Springfield Art Museum, Springfield MO
Staatliche Museen zu Berlin Stiftung Preussischer Kulturbesitz, National Museums in Berlin, Prussian Cultural Heritage Foundation, Berlin
Stanford University, Cantor Arts Center at Stanford University, Stanford CA
Szepmuveszeti Muzeum, Museum of Fine Arts, Budapest
Taft Museum of Art, Cincinnati OH
Timken Museum of Art, San Diego CA
Tver Regional Art Gallery, Tver
University of Georgia, Georgia Museum of Art, Athens GA
University of Houston, Blaffer Art Museum, Houston TX
University of Illinois at Urbana-Champaign, Krannert Art Museum and Kinkead Pavilion, Champaign IL
The University of Kentucky Art Museum, Lexington KY
University of Miami, Lowe Art Museum, Coral Gables FL
University of Utah, Utah Museum of Fine Arts, Salt Lake City UT
University of Wisconsin-Madison, Chazen Museum of Art, Madison WI
Ursinus College, Philip & Muriel Berman Museum of Art, Collegeville PA
Walker Art Gallery, Liverpool
Yokohama Museum of Art, Yokohama

PERIOD ROOMS

1890 House-Museum & Center for the Arts, Cortland NY
Academy of the New Church, Glencairn Museum, Bryn Athyn PA
Adams County Historical Society, Gettysburg PA
Adams National Historic Park, Quincy MA
Allentown Art Museum, Allentown PA
American Art Museum, Renwick Gallery, Washington DC
American Swedish Institute, Minneapolis MN
Amherst College, Mead Art Museum, Amherst MA
Arizona Historical Society-Yuma, Sanguinetti House Museum & Garden, Yuma AZ
Arnot Art Museum, Elmira NY
Art Without Walls Inc, Sayville NY
Artesia Historical Museum and Art Center, Artesia NM
Atlanta Historical Society Inc, Atlanta History Center, Atlanta GA
Audrain County Historical Society, Graceland Museum & American Saddlehorse Museum & Fire Brick Industry Museum, Mexico MO
Barnes Museum, Southington CT
The Bartlett Museum, Amesbury MA
Bartow-Pell Mansion Museum & Gardens, Bronx NY
Bay County Historical Society, Historical Museum of Bay County, Bay City MI
Bayerische Staatsgemaldesammlungen, Bavarian State Painting Collections, Munich
Blanden Memorial Art Museum, Fort Dodge IA
Bob Jones University Museum & Gallery Inc, Greenville SC
Brooklyn Historical Society, Brooklyn OH
Buffalo Niagara Heritage Village, Amherst NY
Bush-Holley Historic Site & Storehouse Gallery, Greenwich Historical Society, Cos Cob CT
C M Russell Museum, Great Falls MT
Cambridge Museum, Cambridge NE
Canadian Museum of History, Gatineau QC
Cape Ann Museum, Gloucester MA
Captain Forbes House Museum, Milton MA
Carson County Square House Museum, Panhandle TX
Charleston Museum, Heyward-Washington House, Charleston SC
Charleston Museum, Joseph Manigault House, Charleston SC
Chateau Ramezay Museum, Montreal QC
Chatham Historical Society, The Atwood House Museum, Chatham MA
Chatillon-DeMenil House Foundation, Chatillon-DeMenil Mansion, Saint Louis MO
City of Austin Parks & Recreation, O Henry Museum, Austin TX
City of Gainesville, Thomas Center Galleries - Cultural Affairs, Gainesville FL
The City of Petersburg Museums, Petersburg VA
City of Springdale, Shiloh Museum of Ozark History, Springdale AR
Clark County Historical Society, Pioneer - Krier Museum, Ashland KS
Clemson University, Fort Hill Plantation, Clemson SC
Cliveden, Philadelphia PA
Colonial Williamsburg Foundation, Abby Aldrich Rockefeller Folk Art Museum, Williamsburg VA
Colonial Williamsburg Foundation, DeWitt Wallace Decorative Arts Museum, Williamsburg VA
The Columbus Museum, Columbus GA
Concord Museum, Concord MA
Congregation Beth Israel's Plotkin Judaica Museum, Scottsdale AZ
Conrad-Caldwell House Museum, Louisville KY
Craigdarroch Castle Historical Museum Society, Victoria BC
Crane Collection, Gallery of American Painting and Sculpture, Magnolia MA
Creek Council House Museum, Okmulgee OK
Cripple Creek District Museum, Cripple Creek CO
Crook County Museum & Art Gallery, Sundance WY
Cuneo Mansion & Gardens, Vernon Hills IL
Danville Museum of Fine Arts & History, Danville VA
DAR Museum, National Society Daughters of the American Revolution, Washington DC
Delaware Division of Historical & Cultural Affairs, Dover DE
Detroit Institute of Arts, Detroit MI
Edgecombe County Cultural Arts Council, Inc, Blount-Bridgers House, Hobson Pittman Memorial Gallery, Tarboro NC
Edsel & Eleanor Ford House, Grosse Pointe Shores MI
Environment Canada - Parks Canada, Laurier House, National Historic Site, Ottawa ON
Erie County Historical Society, Erie PA
Evanston Historical Society, Charles Gates Dawes House, Evanston IL
Evansville Museum of Arts, History & Science, Evansville IN
Florida Department of Environmental Protection, Stephen Foster Folk Culture Center State Park, White Springs FL
Florida State University, John & Mable Ringling Museum of Art, Sarasota FL
Fondazione Musei Civici Di Venezia, Museo Correr - Correr Museum, Venice
The Frick Art & Historical Center, Inc, Frick Art Museum, Pittsburgh PA
Frontier Gateway Museum, Glendive MT
Fruitlands Museum, Inc, Harvard MA

Fulton County Historical Society Inc, Fulton County Museum (Tetzlaff Reference Room), Rochester IN
Genesee Country Village & Museum, John L Wehle Art Gallery, Mumford NY
George Washington's Mount Vernon, Mount Vernon VA
Gibson Society, Inc, Gibson House Museum, Boston MA
Girard College, Stephen Girard Collection, Philadelphia PA
Glanmore National Historic Site of Canada, Belleville ON
Glessner House Museum, Chicago IL
Grand Rapids Public Museum, Grand Rapids MI
Greene County Historical Society, Bronck Museum, Coxsackie NY
Hancock Shaker Village, Inc, Pittsfield MA
Headquarters Fort Monroe, Dept of Army, Casemate Museum, Hampton VA
Heart of West Texas Museum, Colorado City TX
Henry County Museum & Cultural Arts Center, Clinton MO
Henry Morrison Flagler Museum, Palm Beach FL
Henry Sheldon Museum of Vermont History and Research Center, Middlebury VT
High Desert Museum, Bend OR
Hill-Stead Museum, Farmington CT
Historic Arkansas Museum, Little Rock AR
Historic Cherry Hill, Albany NY
Historic Deerfield, Inc, Deerfield MA
Historic Holyoke at Wistariahurst & City of Holyoke, Holyoke MA
Historic Huguenot Street, New Paltz NY
Historical Society of Cheshire County, Keene NH
Historical Society of Martin County, Elliott Museum, Stuart FL
Historical Society of Old Newbury, Cushing House Museum, Newburyport MA
Historisches und Volkerkundemuseum, Museum of History and Ethnology, St Gallen
Hopewell Museum, Hopewell NJ
Huntington Museum of Art, Huntington WV
The Hyde Collection, Glens Falls NY
Idaho Historical Museum, Boise ID
Illinois State Museum, ISM Lockport Gallery, Chicago Gallery & Southern Illinois Art Gallery, Springfield IL
Imperial Calcasieu Museum, Lake Charles LA
Imperial Calcasieu Museum, Gibson-Barham Gallery, Lake Charles LA
Independence Historical Museum & Art Center, Independence KS
Independence National Historical Park, Philadelphia PA
Indiana Landmarks, Morris-Butler House, Indianapolis IN
The Israel Museum, Jerusalem, Jerusalem
Jacques Marchais Museum of Tibetan Art, Staten Island NY
James Dick Foundation, Festival - Institute, Round Top TX
Johns Hopkins University, Homewood Museum, Baltimore MD
Jordan Historical Museum of The Twenty, Jordan ON
Kateri Tekakwitha Shrine/St. Francis Xavier Mission, Kahnawake QC
Kelly-Griggs House Museum, Red Bluff CA
Kern County Museum, Bakersfield CA
Kings County Historical Society & Museum, Hampton NB
Klein Museum, Mobridge SD
Knoxville Museum of Art, Knoxville TN
Koochiching Museums, International Falls MN
La Salle University Art Museum, Philadelphia PA
Lauren Rogers, Laurel MS
Lehigh Valley Heritage Center, Allentown PA
Liberty Hall Historic Site, Liberty Hall Museum, Frankfort KY
Lincoln County Historical Association, Inc, 1811 Old Lincoln County Jail & Lincoln County Museum, Wiscasset ME
Lincolnshire County Council, Library & Heritage Services, Lincoln
Lockwood-Mathews Mansion Museum, Norwalk CT
Longfellow's Wayside Inn Museum, Sudbury MA
Longfellow-Evangeline State Commemorative Area, Saint Martinville LA
Longue Vue House & Gardens, New Orleans LA
Los Angeles County Museum of Natural History, William S Hart Museum, Newhall CA
Louisiana Department of Culture, Recreation & Tourism, Louisiana State Museum, New Orleans LA
Loveland Museum/Gallery, Loveland CO
Lyme Historical Society, Florence Griswold Museum, Old Lyme CT
Maine Historical Society, Wadsworth-Longfellow House, Portland ME
Mamie McFaddin Ward, Beaumont TX
Marblehead Museum & Historical Society, Marblehead MA
Marblehead Museum & Historical Society, Jeremiah Lee Mansion, Marblehead MA
Maricopa County Historical Society, Desert Caballeros Western Museum, Wickenburg AZ
Mark Twain, Hartford CT
McDowell House & Apothecary Shop, Danville KY
Middle Border Museum & Oscar Howe Art Center, Mitchell SD
Minneapolis Institute of Art, Minneapolis MN
The Mint Museum, Charlotte NC
Mission San Miguel Museum, San Miguel CA
Mississippi River Museum at Mud-Island River Park, Memphis TN
Monroe County Historical Association, Elizabeth D Walters Library, Stroudsburg PA
Morris Museum, Morristown NJ
Morris-Jumel Mansion, Inc, New York NY
Morven Museum & Garden, Princeton NJ
Mount Vernon Hotel Museum & Garden, New York NY
Muscatine Art Center, Muscatine IA
Musee des Augustines de l'Hotel Dieu de Quebec, Quebec QC
Museo Del Romanticismo, Museum of the Romantic Period, Madrid
Museu Nacional de Arte Contemporanea do Chiado, National Museum of Contemporary Art, Museu Do Chiado, Lisbon
The Museum, Greenwood SC
Museum De Lakenhal, Leiden
Museum of Art, Fort Lauderdale, Fort Lauderdale FL
Museum of Chinese in America, New York NY
Museum of Fine Arts, Boston MA
Museum of Fine Arts, Saint Petersburg, Florida, Inc, Saint Petersburg FL
Museum Plantin-Moretus, Antwerp
Museum zu Allerheiligen, Schaffhausen
Muzeul National de Arta al Romaniei, National Museum of Art of Romania, Bucharest
Nassau County Museum of Art, Roslyn Harbor NY
Nathan Hale Homestead Museum, Coventry CT
National Park Service, Hubbell Trading Post National Historic Site, Ganado AZ
National Society of Colonial Dames of America in the State of Maryland, Mount Clare Museum House, Baltimore MD
National Society of the Colonial Dames of America in The Commonwealth of Virginia, Wilton House Museum, Richmond VA
National Trust for Historic Preservation, Shadows-on-the-Teche, New Iberia LA
National Trust for Historic Preservation, Decatur House, Washington DC
Nebraska Game and Parks Commission, Arbor Lodge State Historical Park & Morton Mansion, Nebraska City NE
The Nelson-Atkins Museum of Art, Kansas City MO
Nemeth Art Center, Park Rapids MN
Nevada Northern Railway Museum, Ely NV
New Brunswick Museum, Saint John NB
New Canaan Historical Society, New Canaan CT
New Mexico Department of Cultural Affairs, Palace of Governors, Santa Fe NM
New Orleans Museum of Art, New Orleans LA
New York State Office of Parks Recreation & Historic Preservation, John Jay Homestead State Historic Site, Katonah NY
New York State Office of Parks, Recreation & Historic Preservation, Staatsburgh State Historic Site, Staatsburg NY
Newfields, Indianapolis IN
Newport Art Museum and Association, Newport RI
Nichols House Museum, Inc, Boston MA
Norwich Free Academy, Slater Memorial Museum, Norwich CT
Oatlands Plantation, Leesburg VA
The Ohio Historical Society, Inc, Campus Martius Museum & Ohio River Museum, Marietta OH
Okefenokee Heritage Center, Inc, Waycross GA
Oklahoma Historical Society, State Museum of History, Oklahoma City OK
Old Barracks Museum, Trenton NJ
Old Fort Harrod State Park Mansion Museum, Harrodsburg KY
Old Island Restoration Foundation Inc, Oldest House in Key West, Key West FL
Oshkosh Public Museum & Library, Oshkosh WI
Osterreichische Galerie Belvedere Vienna, Belvedere Museum Vienna, Vienna
Owensboro Museum of Fine Art, Owensboro KY
Panhandle-Plains Historical Museum, Canyon TX
Pasadena Museum of History, Pasadena CA
Passaic County Community College, Broadway, LRC, and Hamilton Club Galleries, Paterson NJ
Penobscot Marine Museum, Searsport ME
Peoria Historical Society, Peoria IL
Piatt Castles, West Liberty OH
Pioneer Historical Museum of South Dakota, Hot Springs SD
Plainsman Museum, Aurora NE
Portsmouth Historical Society, John Paul Jones House & Discover Portsmouth, Portsmouth NH
Preservation Virginia, John Marshall House, Richmond VA
Pueblo Museum, Desert Hot Springs CA
Putnam County Historical Society, Foundry School Museum, Cold Spring NY
Rahr-West Art Museum, Manitowoc WI
Red Deer & District Museum & Archives, Red Deer AB
Rhode Island Historical Society, John Brown House, Providence RI
Rock Ford Foundation, Inc, Rock Ford Plantation, Lancaster PA
Royal Arts Foundation, Belcourt Castle, Newport RI
Ryerss Victorian Museum & Library, Philadelphia PA
Saco Museum, Saco ME
Saint Johnsbury Athenaeum, Saint Johnsbury VT
Saint Joseph Museum, Inc., Saint Joseph MO
Saint-Gaudens National Historic Site, Cornish NH
The San Joaquin Pioneer & Historical Society, The Haggin Museum, Stockton CA
Schuyler-Hamilton House, Morristown NJ
Seneca Falls Historical Society Museum, Seneca Falls NY
Shirley Plantation Foundation, Charles City VA
Shoreline Historical Museum, Shoreline WA
Shores Memorial Museum, Lyndon Center VT
The Society of the Cincinnati at Anderson House, Washington DC
Sooke Region Museum & Art Gallery, Sooke BC
The Speed Art Museum, Louisville KY
Springville Museum of Art, Springville UT
Staatliche Museen zu Berlin Stiftung Preussischer Kulturbesitz, National Museums in Berlin, Prussian Cultural Heritage Foundation, Berlin
Stan Hywet, Akron OH
Strasburg Museum, Strasburg VA
Stratford Historical Society, Catharine B Mitchell Museum, Stratford CT
The Summit County Historical Society of Akron, OH, Akron OH
Suomen Kansallismuseo, National Museum of Finland, Helsinki
T C Steele State Historic Site, Nashville IN
Tallahassee Museum of History & Natural Science, Tallahassee FL
Taos Historic Museums, Taos NM
Taos Historic Museums, Ernest Blumenschein Home & Studio, Taos NM
Taos Historic Museums, La Hacienda de Los Martinez, Taos NM
Telfair Museums, Savannah GA
Trust Authority, Museum of the Great Plains, Lawton OK
The Trustees of Reservations, The Mission House, Ipswich MA
Tryon Palace, New Bern NC
Tucson Museum of Art and Historic Block, Tucson AZ
United Society of Shakers, Shaker Museum, New Gloucester ME
United States Capitol, Architect of the Capitol, Washington DC
University of Miami, Lowe Art Museum, Coral Gables FL
University of Saskatchewan, Diefenbaker Canada Centre, Saskatoon SK
Vermilion County Museum Society, Danville IL

Vesterheim Norwegian-American Museum, Decorah IA
Victoria Mansion - Morse Libby House, Portland ME
Villa Terrace Decorative Arts Museum, Milwaukee WI
Vizcaya Museum & Gardens, Miami FL
Warner House Association, MacPheadris-Warner House, Portsmouth NH
Washington & Lee University, Lee Chapel & Museum, Lexington VA
Western Reserve Historical Society, Cleveland OH
Westfries Museum, Hoorn
Whatcom Museum, Bellingham WA
White House, Washington DC
Willard House & Clock Museum, Inc, North Grafton MA
Woodlawn/The Pope-Leighey, Alexandria VA
Woodmere Art Museum Inc, Philadelphia PA
Woodrow Wilson, Staunton VA
Woodrow Wilson, Washington DC
World Erotic Art Museum, Miami Beach FL
Wornall Majors House Museums, The 1859 Jail, Marshal's Home & Museum, Independence MO

PEWTER

Albany Institute of History & Art, Albany NY
Allentown Art Museum, Allentown PA
American Folk Art Museum, New York NY
Amherst College, Mead Art Museum, Amherst MA
Baker University, Old Castle Museum, Baldwin City KS
Beverly Historical Society, Cabot, Hale & Balch House Museums, Beverly MA
Cameron Art Museum, Wilmington NC
Canadian Museum of History, Gatineau QC
Cape Ann Museum, Gloucester MA
The Children's Museum of Indianapolis, Indianapolis IN
College of William & Mary, Muscarelle Museum of Art, Williamsburg VA
Concord Museum, Concord MA
The Currier Museum of Art, Manchester NH
DAR Museum, National Society Daughters of the American Revolution, Washington DC
Dartmouth College, Hood Museum of Art, Hanover NH
Detroit Institute of Arts, Detroit MI
The Dixon Gallery & Gardens, Memphis TN
Doncaster Museum and Art Gallery, Doncaster Yorks
Dublin Arts Council, Dublin OH
Fairbanks Museum & Planetarium, Saint Johnsbury VT
Gallery One Visual Arts Center, Ellensburg WA
George Phippen, Phippen Museum - Art of the American West, Prescott AZ
Glanmore National Historic Site of Canada, Belleville ON
Grand Rapids Public Museum, Grand Rapids MI
Henry County Museum & Cultural Arts Center, Clinton MO
Henry Sheldon Museum of Vermont History and Research Center, Middlebury VT
Hillwood Museum & Gardens Foundation, Hillwood Estate Museum & Gardens, Washington DC
Historic Deerfield, Inc, Deerfield MA
Historic Hudson Valley, Pocantico Hills NY
Historic Huguenot Street, New Paltz NY
Historic Newton, Newton MA
Historical Society of Cheshire County, Keene NH
Illinois State Museum, ISM Lockport Gallery, Chicago Gallery & Southern Illinois Art Gallery, Springfield IL
Imperial Calcasieu Museum, Gibson-Barham Gallery, Lake Charles LA
James Dick Foundation, Festival - Institute, Round Top TX
Johns Hopkins University, Homewood Museum, Baltimore MD
Kings County Historical Society & Museum, Hampton NB
Latino Art Museum, Pomona CA
Lehigh Valley Heritage Center, Allentown PA
Lincoln County Historical Association, Inc, 1811 Old Lincoln County Jail & Lincoln County Museum, Wiscasset ME
Livingston County Historical Society, Museum, Geneseo NY
Longfellow-Evangeline State Commemorative Area, Saint Martinville LA
Longue Vue House & Gardens, New Orleans LA
Loyola University Chicago, Loyola University Museum of Art, Chicago IL
McDowell House & Apothecary Shop, Danville KY
The Mexican Museum, San Francisco CA
Mount Vernon Hotel Museum & Garden, New York NY
The Museum, Greenwood SC
Museum De Lakenhal, Leiden
The Museum of Arts & Sciences Inc, Daytona Beach FL
Museum of Fine Arts, Saint Petersburg, Florida, Inc, Saint Petersburg FL
Museum zu Allerheiligen, Schaffhausen
Muzej za Umjetnost i Obrt, Museum of Arts & Crafts, Zagreb
Muzeul National de Arta al Romaniei, National Museum of Art of Romania, Bucharest
National Society of Colonial Dames of America in the State of Maryland, Mount Clare Museum House, Baltimore MD
New Brunswick Museum, Saint John NB
New Canaan Historical Society, New Canaan CT
Norwich Free Academy, Slater Memorial Museum, Norwich CT
The Ohio Historical Society, Inc, Campus Martius Museum & Ohio River Museum, Marietta OH
Oshkosh Public Museum & Library, Oshkosh WI
Panhandle-Plains Historical Museum, Canyon TX
Pump House Center for the Arts, Chillicothe OH
Rhode Island Historical Society, John Brown House, Providence RI
Rollins College, George D & Harriet W Cornell Fine Arts Museum, Winter Park FL
Saco Museum, Saco ME
Shirley Plantation Foundation, Charles City VA
Society for Contemporary Craft, Pittsburgh PA
South Carolina Artisans Center, Walterboro SC
The Speed Art Museum, Louisville KY
Spertus Institute of Jewish Studies, Chicago IL
The Stewart Museum, Montreal QC
Stratford Historical Society, Catharine B Mitchell Museum, Stratford CT
Suomen Kansallismuseo, National Museum of Finland, Helsinki
Tokyo National Museum, Tokyo
Tryon Palace, New Bern NC
Tver Regional Art Gallery, Tver
United Society of Shakers, Shaker Museum, New Gloucester ME
United States Figure Skating Association, World Figure Skating Museum & Hall of Fame, Colorado Springs CO
University of Chicago, Smart Museum of Art, Chicago IL
University of Illinois at Urbana-Champaign, Krannert Art Museum and Kinkead Pavilion, Champaign IL
University of Minnesota, Goldstein Museum of Design, Saint Paul MN
University of Saskatchewan, Diefenbaker Canada Centre, Saskatoon SK
Vesterheim Norwegian-American Museum, Decorah IA
Westfries Museum, Hoorn
Willard House & Clock Museum, Inc, North Grafton MA
Wisconsin Historical Society, Wisconsin Historical Museum, Madison WI
Woodlawn/The Pope-Leighey, Alexandria VA
World Erotic Art Museum, Miami Beach FL

PHOTOGRAPHY

1708 Gallery, Richmond VA
A.E. Backus Museum & Gallery, Fort Pierce FL
A.I.R. Gallery, Brooklyn NY
Abington Art Center, Jenkintown PA
Academy of the New Church, Glencairn Museum, Bryn Athyn PA
African American Atelier, Greensboro NC
African American Museum in Philadelphia, Philadelphia PA
African Art Museum of Maryland, Columbia MD
AKA Artist Run Centre, Saskatoon SK
Akron Art Museum, Akron OH
Alaska Heritage Museum at Wells Fargo, Anchorage AK
Alaska State Museum, Juneau AK
Albany Museum of Art, Albany GA
Alberta College of Art & Design, Illingworth Kerr Gallery, Calgary AB
Albin O Kuhn Library & Gallery, Baltimore MD
Albright College, Freedman Gallery, Reading PA
Albuquerque Museum of Art & History, Albuquerque NM
Alexandria Museum of Art, Alexandria LA
Allentown Art Museum, Allentown PA
American Sport Art Museum and Archives, Daphne AL
American Textile History Museum, Lowell MA
Americas Society Art Gallery, New York NY
Amherst College, Mead Art Museum, Amherst MA
Amon Carter Museum of American Art, Fort Worth TX
Anchorage Museum at Rasmuson Center, Anchorage AK
The Andy Warhol Museum, Pittsburgh PA
Anthology Film Archives, New York NY
Appaloosa Museum and Heritage Center, Moscow ID
Arizona Historical Society-Yuma, Sanguinetti House Museum & Garden, Yuma AZ
Arnot Art Museum, Elmira NY
Aroostook County Historical & Art Museum, Houlton ME
Art and History Museums - Maitland, Maitland FL
Art Center of Battle Creek, Battle Creek MI
The Art Center of Waco, Waco TX
Art Community Center, Art Center of Corpus Christi, Corpus Christi TX
Art Gallery of Alberta, Edmonton AB
Art Gallery of Bancroft Inc, Bancroft ON
The Art Gallery of Cornwall, Cornwall ON
Art Gallery of Hamilton, Hamilton ON
Art Gallery of Nova Scotia, Halifax NS
Art Gallery of South Australia, Adelaide
Art Museum of Greater Lafayette, Lafayette IN
Art Museum of Southeast Texas, Beaumont TX
Art Without Walls Inc, Sayville NY
Artesia Historical Museum and Art Center, Artesia NM
Arts Council of Fayetteville-Cumberland County, The Arts Center, Fayetteville NC
Artspace, Richmond VA
ArtsQuest, Bethlehem PA
Asheville Art Museum, Asheville NC
Associates for Community Development, The Arts Center, Inc, Martinsburg WV
Atlanta Historical Society Inc, Atlanta History Center, Atlanta GA
Avant Gallery, Miami FL
Bainbridge Arts & Crafts Gallery, Bainbridge Island WA
Baker Arts Center, Liberal KS
Baldwin Gallery, Aspen CO
Baldwin Historical Society Museum, Baldwin NY
The Baltimore Museum of Art, Baltimore MD
Balzekas Museum of Lithuanian Culture, Chicago IL
Bangladesh National Museum, Dhaka
Barnes Museum, Southington CT
Baroda Museum and Picture Gallery, Vadodara
Baruch College of the City University of New York, Sidney Mishkin Gallery, New York NY
Baton Rouge Gallery, Center For Contemporary Art, Baton Rouge LA
Bay County Historical Society, Historical Museum of Bay County, Bay City MI
Bayerische Staatsgemaldesammlungen, Bavarian State Painting Collections, Munich
Beloit College, Wright Museum of Art, Beloit WI
Belskie Museum, Closter NJ
Bemis Center for Contemporary Arts, Omaha NE
Bennington Museum, Bennington VT
Berea College, Doris Ulmann Galleries, Berea KY
Besser Museum for Northeast Michigan, Alpena MI
Beverly Historical Society, Cabot, Hale & Balch House Museums, Beverly MA
Birger Sandzen Memorial Gallery, Lindsborg KS
Birmingham Museum of Art, Birmingham AL
Blanden Memorial Art Museum, Fort Dodge IA
Blauvelt Demarest Foundation, Hiram Blauvelt Art Museum, Oradell NJ
Blue Sky Gallery, Oregon Center for the Photographic Arts, Portland OR
Boise Art Museum, Boise ID
Bone Creek Museum of Agrarian Art, David City NE
Booth Western Art Museum, Cartersville GA
Boston Public Library, Albert H Wiggin Gallery & Print Department, Boston MA
Botswana National Museum, Gaborone
Bowdoin College, Peary-MacMillan Arctic Museum, Brunswick ME
Brickton Art Center, Park Ridge IL

Bruce Museum, Inc, Greenwich CT
Bucknell University, Edward & Marthann Samek Art Gallery, Lewisburg PA
The Buffalo Fine Arts Academy, Albright-Knox Art Gallery, Buffalo NY
Buffalo Niagara Heritage Village, Amherst NY
Bullion Plaza Cultural Center & Museum, Miami AZ
Burchfield Penney Art Center, Buffalo NY
Bush-Holley Historic Site & Storehouse Gallery, Greenwich Historical Society, Cos Cob CT
C M Russell Museum, Great Falls MT
C W Post Campus of Long Island University, Hillwood Art Museum, Brookville NY
Cameron Art Museum, Wilmington NC
Canadian Museum for Human Rights, Winnipeg MB
Canadian Museum of History, Gatineau QC
Canadian Museum of Nature, Musee Canadien de la Nature, Ottawa ON
Cape Ann Museum, Gloucester MA
Carleton College, Art Gallery, Northfield MN
Carlsbad Museum & Art Center, Carlsbad NM
Carnegie Museums of Pittsburgh, Carnegie Museum of Art, Pittsburgh PA
Carson County Square House Museum, Panhandle TX
Cartoon Art Museum, San Francisco CA
Cayuga Museum of History & Art, Auburn NY
Cedar Rapids Museum of Art, Cedar Rapids IA
Centenary College of Louisiana, Meadows Museum of Art, Shreveport LA
Center for Fine Art Photography, Fort Collins CO
Center for Puppetry Arts, Atlanta GA
Center for the Arts Piper Gallery, Crested Butte CO
Central Methodist University, Ashby-Hodge Gallery of American Art, Fayette MO
Channel Islands Maritime Museum, Oxnard CA
Chatham Historical Society, The Atwood House Museum, Chatham MA
Chatillon-DeMenil House Foundation, Chatillon-DeMenil Mansion, Saint Louis MO
Chesapeake Bay Maritime Museum, Saint Michaels MD
Chicago Athenaeum, Museum of Architecture & Design, Galena IL
The Children's Museum of Indianapolis, Indianapolis IN
Chrysler Museum of Art, Norfolk VA
City of Cedar Falls, Iowa, James & Meryl Hearst Center for the Arts & Sculpture Garden, Cedar Falls IA
City of El Paso, El Paso TX
City of Fremont, Olive Hyde Art Gallery, Fremont CA
City of Gainesville, Thomas Center Galleries - Cultural Affairs, Gainesville FL
The City of Petersburg Museums, Petersburg VA
City of Pittsfield Office of Cultural Development, Lichtenstein Center for the Arts, Pittsfield MA
City of Springdale, Shiloh Museum of Ozark History, Springdale AR
Clark Art Institute, Williamstown MA
Clark County Historical Society, Pioneer - Krier Museum, Ashland KS
Clear Lake Arts Center, Clear Lake IA
Clinton Art Association, River Arts Center, Clinton IA
Coastal Arts League Museum, Half Moon Bay CA
Colgate University, Picker Art Gallery, Hamilton NY
College of William & Mary, Muscarelle Museum of Art, Williamsburg VA
Colorado Photographic Arts Center, Denver CO
The Columbus Museum, Columbus GA
Columbus Museum of Art, Columbus OH
Congregation Beth Israel's Plotkin Judaica Museum, Scottsdale AZ
Contemporary Art Center, Peoria IL
The Contemporary Austin, Austin TX
Corcoran Gallery of Art, Washington DC
Cornell Museum of Art and American Culture, Delray Beach FL
Cornell University, Herbert F Johnson Museum of Art, Ithaca NY
Coutts Museum of Art, Inc, El Dorado KS
Cranbrook Art Museum, Bloomfield Hills MI
Cranford Historical Society, Cranford NJ
Crary Art Gallery, Warren PA
Cripple Creek District Museum, Cripple Creek CO
Crocker Art Museum, Sacramento CA
Crow Wing County Historical Society, Brainerd MN
Cuadro Fine Art Gallery, Dubai
The Currier Museum of Art, Manchester NH
Dartmouth College, Hood Museum of Art, Hanover NH
Dartmouth Heritage Museum, Dartmouth NS
Daum Museum of Contemporary Art, Sedalia MO
Daytona State College, Southeast Museum of Photography, Daytona Beach FL
deCordova Sculpture Park & Museum, Lincoln MA
Deines Cultural Center, Russell KS
Delaware Art Museum, Wilmington DE
DeLeon White Gallery, Toronto ON
Delta Blues Museum, Clarksdale MS
Denver Art Museum, Denver CO
Detroit Institute of Arts, Detroit MI
Detroit Repertory Theatre Gallery, Detroit MI
Detroit Zoological Institute, Wildlife Interpretive Gallery, Royal Oak MI
Dickinson College, The Trout Gallery, Carlisle PA
Dixie State University, Sears Art Museum Gallery, Saint George UT
Doncaster Museum and Art Gallery, Doncaster Yorks
Dublin Arts Council, Dublin OH
Durham Art Guild, Durham NC
DuSable Museum of African American History, Chicago IL
East Bay Asian Local Development Corp (EBALDC), Asian Resource Gallery, Oakland CA
Eastern Washington State Historical Society, Northwest Museum of Arts & Culture, Spokane WA
Edward Hopper, Nyack NY
Eiteljorg Museum of American Indians & Western Art, Indianapolis IN
Ella Sharp Museum, Jackson MI
Ellen Noel Art Museum of the Permian Basin, Odessa TX
eMediaLoft.org, New York NY
Emory University, Michael C Carlos Museum, Atlanta GA
En Foco, Inc, Bronx NY
Erie Art Museum, Erie PA
Erie County Historical Society, Erie PA
Essex Historical Society and Shipbuilding Museum, Essex MA
Eula Mae Edwards Museum & Gallery, Clovis NM
Eureka Fine Art Gallery, Eureka Springs AR
Evan Lurie Fine Art Gallery, Carmel IN
Evanston Historical Society, Charles Gates Dawes House, Evanston IL
Everhart Museum, Scranton PA
Everson Museum of Art, Syracuse NY
Fairbanks Museum & Planetarium, Saint Johnsbury VT
Fetherston Foundation, Packwood House Museum, Lewisburg PA
Fireweed Gallery, Homer AK
Fishkill Historical Society, Van Wyck Homestead Museum, Fishkill NY
Fisk University, Aaron Douglas Gallery, Nashville TN
Fitchburg Art Museum, Fitchburg MA
Fitton Center for Creative Arts, Hamilton OH
Five Civilized Tribes Museum, Muskogee OK
Flint Institute of Arts, Flint MI
Florida Southern College, Melvin Art Gallery, Lakeland FL
Florida State University, John & Mable Ringling Museum of Art, Sarasota FL
Folk Art Society of America, Richmond VA
Fondazione Musei Civici Di Venezia, Ca' Pesaro Galleria Nazionale d'Arte Moderna - Ca' Pesaro Gallery of Modern Art, Venice
Forest Lawn Museum, Glendale CA
Fort George G Meade Museum, Fort Meade MD
Fort Smith Regional Art Museum, Fort Smith AR
Fort Ticonderoga Association, Ticonderoga NY
Frontier Gateway Museum, Glendive MT
Frontier Times Museum, Bandera TX
Fuller Craft Museum, Brockton MA
Fulton County Historical Society Inc, Fulton County Museum (Tetzlaff Reference Room), Rochester IN
Gadsden Museum of Art, Gadsden AL
Gallery One Visual Arts Center, Ellensburg WA
George Eastman Museum, Rochester NY
George Phippen, Phippen Museum - Art of the American West, Prescott AZ
The George Washington University, Luther W Brady Art Gallery, Washington DC
Georgia O'Keeffe Museum, Santa Fe NM
Georgian Court University, M Christina Geis Gallery, Lakewood NJ
Germantown Historical Society, Philadelphia PA
Gertrude Herbert Institute of Art, Augusta GA
Girard College, Stephen Girard Collection, Philadelphia PA
Glanmore National Historic Site of Canada, Belleville ON
Glessner House Museum, Chicago IL
Goshen Historical Society, Goshen CT
Grand Rapids Public Museum, Grand Rapids MI
Grand River Museum, Lemmon SD
Great Lakes Historical Society, Inland Seas Maritime Museum, Vermilion OH
Grossmont Community College, Hyde Art Gallery, El Cajon CA
Hamilton College, Emerson Gallery, Clinton NY
Hammonds House Museum, Atlanta GA
Hays Arts Center, Hays KS
Headquarters Fort Monroe, Dept of Army, Casemate Museum, Hampton VA
Heard Museum, Phoenix AZ
Hebrew Union College - Jewish Institute of Religion, Skirball Museum Cincinnati, Cincinnati OH
Hebrew Union College - Jewish Institute of Religion Museum, Jewish Institute of Religion, New York NY
The Heckscher Museum of Art, Huntington NY
Henry County Museum & Cultural Arts Center, Clinton MO
Henry Sheldon Museum of Vermont History and Research Center, Middlebury VT
Hermitage Museum & Gardens, Norfolk VA
Het Noordbrabants Museum, s-Hertogenbosch
Hickory Museum of Art, Inc, Hickory NC
Hidalgo County Historical Museum, Edinburg TX
High Desert Museum, Bend OR
High Museum of Art, Atlanta GA
Hill-Stead Museum, Farmington CT
Hillwood Museum & Gardens Foundation, Hillwood Estate Museum & Gardens, Washington DC
Historic Huguenot Street, New Paltz NY
Historic Newton, Newton MA
Historic Northampton Museum & Education Center, Northampton MA
Historical Society of Cheshire County, Keene NH
The History Center in Tompkins County, Ithaca NY
Holter Museum of Art, Helena MT
Honolulu Museum of Art, Honolulu HI
Hot Shops Art Center, Omaha NE
The Hudson River Museum, Yonkers NY
Hui No'eau Visual Arts Center, Gallery and Gift Shop, Makawao Maui HI
Hunter Museum of American Art, Chattanooga TN
Huntington Museum of Art, Huntington WV
Huntsville Museum of Art, Huntsville AL
The Hyde Collection, Glens Falls NY
Hyde Park Art Center, Chicago IL
i.d.e.a. Museum, Mesa AZ
Illinois State Museum, ISM Lockport Gallery, Chicago Gallery & Southern Illinois Art Gallery, Springfield IL
Imperial Calcasieu Museum, Gibson-Barham Gallery, Lake Charles LA
Imperial War Museum London, London
Independence Historical Museum & Art Center, Independence KS
Independence Seaport Museum, Philadelphia PA
Indiana State Museum, Indianapolis IN
Institute of Contemporary Art, Los Angeles, Los Angeles CA
Institute of Puerto Rican Culture, Museo Fuerte Conde de Mirasol, Vieques PR
INTAR Gallery, New York NY
International Center of Photography, Rita K Hillman Education Gallery, New York NY
International Museum of Art & Science, McAllen TX
Iredell Museums, Statesville NC
Iroquois Indian Museum, Howes Cave NY
The Israel Museum, Jerusalem, Jerusalem
Jacques Marchais Museum of Tibetan Art, Staten Island NY
James A Michener Art Museum, Doylestown PA
James D Veatch Camp Breckinridge Museum & Arts Center, Morganfield KY
James Dick Foundation, Festival - Institute, Round Top TX
JMW Turner Museum, Sarasota FL
Joe Gish's Old West Museum, Fredericksburg TX
John B Aird Gallery, Toronto ON
The John L. Clarke Western Art Gallery & Memorial Museum, East Glacier Park MT
Jordan National Gallery of Fine Arts, Amman
Joseph Bellows Gallery, La Jolla CA
Joslyn Art Museum, Omaha NE
Juniata College Museum of Art, Huntingdon PA

Kalamazoo Institute of Arts, Kalamazoo MI
Kamloops Art Gallery, Kamloops BC
Kenosha Public Museums, Kenosha WI
Kentucky Derby Museum, Louisville KY
Kentucky Museum of Art and Craft, Louisville KY
Kern County Museum, Bakersfield CA
Keystone Gallery, Scott City KS
Kings County Historical Society & Museum, Hampton NB
Kirchner Museum Davos, Davos
Kitchener-Waterloo Art Gallery, Kitchener ON
Klein Museum, Mobridge SD
Knoxville Museum of Art, Knoxville TN
Koochiching Museums, International Falls MN
La Salle University Art Museum, Philadelphia PA
Lac du Flambeau Band of Lake Superior Chippewa Indians, George W Brown Jr Ojibwe Museum & Cultural Center, Lac Du Flambeau WI
Lafayette College, Lafayette College Art Galleries, Easton PA
Lafayette Science Museum & Planetarium, Lafayette LA
LaGrange Art Museum, LaGrange GA
Laguna Art Museum, Laguna Beach CA
Lalit Kala Akademi Rabindra Bhavan Art Galleries, National Academy of Art, New Delhi, New Delhi
Latino Art Museum, Pomona CA
Lehigh Valley Heritage Center, Allentown PA
Liberty Hall Historic Site, Liberty Hall Museum, Frankfort KY
Lighthouse ArtCenter Museum & School of Art, Tequesta FL
Lillian & Coleman Taube Museum of Art, Minot ND
Lincoln County Historical Association, Inc, 1811 Old Lincoln County Jail & Lincoln County Museum, Wiscasset ME
Lincolnshire County Council, Library & Heritage Services, Lincoln
The Long Island Museum of American Art, History & Carriages, Stony Brook NY
Longfellow-Evangeline State Commemorative Area, Saint Martinville LA
Longview Museum of Fine Art, Longview TX
Louise Hopkins Underwood Center for the Arts, Lubbock TX
Louisiana Department of Culture, Recreation & Tourism, Louisiana State Museum, New Orleans LA
Loveland Museum/Gallery, Loveland CO
Loyola Marymount University, Laband Art Gallery, Los Angeles CA
Lyme Historical Society, Florence Griswold Museum, Old Lyme CT
Lyon College Kresge Gallery, Batesville AR
Mabee-Gerrer Museum of Art, Shawnee OK
MacArthur Memorial, Norfolk VA
Macau Museum of Art, NAPE
Madison & Main Gallery, Greeley CO
Madison Museum of Contemporary Art, Madison WI
Maine College of Art, The Institute of Contemporary Art, Portland ME
Marblehead Museum & Historical Society, Marblehead MA
Maricopa County Historical Society, Desert Caballeros Western Museum, Wickenburg AZ
The Mariners' Museum, Newport News VA
Mark Twain, Hartford CT
Maryland Hall for the Creative Arts, Chaney Gallery, Annapolis MD
Marylhurst University, The Art Gym, Marylhurst OR
Massachusetts Institute of Technology, MIT Museum, Cambridge MA
Massillon Museum, Massillon OH
McLean County Historical Society, McLean County Museum of History, Bloomington IL
Medina Railroad Museum, Medina NY
Meem Gallery, Dubai
Mennello Museum of American Art, Orlando FL
Meredith College, Frankie G Weems Gallery & Rotunda Gallery, Raleigh NC
Meridian Museum of Art, Meridian MS
Mesa Arts Center, Mesa Contemporary Arts Museum, Mesa AZ
The Metropolitan Museum of Art, New York NY
The Mexican Museum, San Francisco CA
Miami-Dade College, MDC Museum of Art & Design, Miami FL
Middle Border Museum & Oscar Howe Art Center, Mitchell SD
Middle Tennessee State University, Baldwin Photographic Gallery, Murfreesboro TN
Midwest Museum of American Art, Elkhart IN
Miller Art Center Foundation Inc, Miller Art Museum, Sturgeon Bay WI
Millicent Rogers Museum, Taos NM
Mills College Art Museum, Oakland CA
Milwaukee Public Museum, Milwaukee WI
Minneapolis Institute of Art, Minneapolis MN
Minnesota Museum of American Art, Saint Paul MN
Minot State University, Northwest Art Center, Minot ND
The Mint Museum, Charlotte NC
Mississippi Museum of Art, Jackson MS
Mississippi Valley Conservation Authority, R Tait McKenzie Memorial Museum, Almonte ON
Missoula Art Museum, Missoula MT
Mobile Museum of Art, Mobile AL
Moderna Galerija, Modern Gallery - National Museum of Modern Art, Zagreb
Modernism, San Francisco CA
Montclair Art Museum, Montclair NJ
Montgomery Museum of Fine Arts, Montgomery AL
Moore College of Art & Design, The Galleries at Moore, Philadelphia PA
Moravian College, Payne Gallery, Bethlehem PA
Moravska Galerie v Brne, Moravian Gallery in Brno, Brno
Morris Museum of Art, Augusta GA
Moscow Museum of Modern Art, Moscow
MTG Hawkes Bay, Napier
Muhlenberg College, Martin Art Gallery, Allentown PA
Musee des Augustines de l'Hotel Dieu de Quebec, Quebec QC
Musee des Beaux-Arts de Tours, Museum of Fine Arts, Tours
Musee National des Beaux Arts du Quebec, Quebec QC
Musee Regional de lu Cote-Nord, Sept-Iles QC
Museen der Stadt Koln, Museum Ludwig - Ludwig Museum, Cologne
Musees Royaux d'Art et d'Histoire, Royal Museums of Art and History, Brussels
Museo de Arte de Ponce, The Luis A Ferre Foundation Inc, Ponce PR
Museo De Las Americas, Denver CO
Museo Del Romanticismo, Museum of the Romantic Period, Madrid
Museo di Palazzo Ducale, Ducale Palace Museum, Mantua
Museo Italo Americano, San Francisco CA
Museo Nacional de Bellas Artes, National Museum of Fine Arts, Santiago
Museu Nacional D'Art De Catalunya, Catalona National Museum of Art, Barcelona
The Museum, Greenwood SC
Museum De Lakenhal, Leiden
Museum Kampa, Prague
Museum of Art & History, Santa Cruz, Santa Cruz CA
Museum of Art - Deland FL, Inc, Deland FL
The Museum of Arts & Sciences Inc, Daytona Beach FL
Museum of Chinese in America, New York NY
Museum of Contemporary Art Chicago, Chicago IL
Museum of Contemporary Art Jacksonville, Jacksonville FL
Museum of Contemporary Art San Diego, San Diego CA
Museum of Fine Arts, Houston, Houston TX
Museum of Fine Arts, Saint Petersburg, Florida, Inc, Saint Petersburg FL
Museum of Latin American Art, Long Beach CA
Museum of Modern Art, New York NY
Museum of Northern Arizona, Flagstaff AZ
Museum of Northern British Columbia, Ruth Harvey Art Gallery, Prince Rupert BC
Museum of Northwest Art, La Conner WA
Museum of the Plains Indian & Crafts Center, Browning MT
Museum of the Southwest, Midland TX
Museum zu Allerheiligen, Schaffhausen
Muzej Moderne I Suvremene Umjetnosti, Museum of Modern and Contemporary Art, Rijeka
Muzej za Umjetnost i Obrt, Museum of Arts & Crafts, Zagreb
Muzeul de Istorie Nationala Si Arheologie Constanta, National History & Archaeology Museum, Constanta
Muzeul National de Arta al Romaniei, National Museum of Art of Romania, Bucharest
Muzeum Narodowe W Kielcach, National Museum in Kielce, Kielce
Muzeum Narodowe w Poznaniu, National Museum in Poznan, Poznan
Nanticoke Indian Museum, Millsboro DE
Napa Valley Museum, Yountville CA
Narodna Galerija, National Gallery of Slovenia, Ljubljana
The National Art Center, Tokyo, Tokyo
National Art Museum of Moldova, Chisinau
National Baseball Hall of Fame & Museum, Cooperstown NY
National Gallery of Canada, Ottawa ON
National Museum & Art Gallery of Trinidad and Tobago, Port of Spain
National Museum of Mexican Art, Chicago IL
The National Museum of Modern Art, Tokyo, Tokyo
National Museum of the American Indian, George Gustav Heye Center, New York NY
National Museum of Wildlife Art of the Unites States, Jackson WY
National Museum of Women in the Arts, Washington DC
National Museums Scotland, National Museum of Scotland, Edinburgh
National Park Service, Hubbell Trading Post National Historic Site, Ganado AZ
National Portrait Gallery, London
National Trust for Historic Preservation, Shadows-on-the-Teche, New Iberia LA
National Veterans Art Museum, Chicago IL
Naval Historical Center, National Museum of the US Navy, Washington DC
Nebraska Game and Parks Commission, Arbor Lodge State Historical Park & Morton Mansion, Nebraska City NE
Nelson Mandela Metropolitan Art Museum, Port Elizabeth
The Nelson-Atkins Museum of Art, Kansas City MO
Neue Galerie New York, New York NY
Nevada Museum of Art, Reno NV
Neville Public Museum of Brown County, Green Bay WI
New Britain Museum of American Art, New Britain CT
New England Maple Museum, Pittsford VT
New Jersey Historical Society, Newark NJ
New Mexico Department of Cultural Affairs, Palace of Governors, Santa Fe NM
New Orleans Museum of Art, New Orleans LA
New Visions Gallery, Inc, Marshfield WI
New York State Military Museum and Veterans Research Center, Saratoga Springs NY
New York State Office of Parks Recreation & Historic Preservation, John Jay Homestead State Historic Site, Katonah NY
Newburyport Maritime Society, Inc, Custom House Maritime Museum, Newburyport MA
Newport Art Museum and Association, Newport RI
Niagara University, Castellani Art Museum, Niagara NY
Niigata Prefectural Museum of Modern Art, Nagaoka
Norman Rockwell Museum, Stockbridge MA
Norsk Maritimt Museum, Norwegian Maritime Museum, Oslo
North End Gallery, Leonardtown MD
Northeastern Nevada Museum, Elko NV
Northwestern University, Mary & Leigh Block Museum of Art, Evanston IL
Norton Simon Museum, Pasadena CA
Norwich Free Academy, Slater Memorial Museum, Norwich CT
Noyes Art Gallery, Lincoln NE
Oakland University, Oakland University Art Gallery, Rochester MI
Ogden Museum of Southern Art, University of New Orleans, New Orleans LA
The Ohio Historical Society, Inc, Campus Martius Museum & Ohio River Museum, Marietta OH
Ohio History Connection, National Afro-American Museum & Cultural Center, Wilberforce OH
Ohio University, Kennedy Museum of Art, Athens OH
Oklahoma City Museum of Art, Oklahoma City OK
Olana State Historic Site, Hudson NY
Old Dartmouth Historical Society, New Bedford Whaling Museum, New Bedford MA
The Old Jail Art Center, Albany TX
Omenka Gallery, Lagos

Opelousas Museum of Art, Inc (OMA), Opelousas LA
Orange County Museum of Art, Newport Beach CA
Oshkosh Public Museum & Library, Oshkosh WI
Ouachita River Art Gallery, Monroe LA
Owensboro Museum of Fine Art, Owensboro KY
Page-Walker Arts & History Center, Cary NC
Palm Beach County Parks & Recreation Department, Morikami Museum & Japanese Gardens, Delray Beach FL
Palm Springs Art Museum, Palm Springs CA
Panhandle-Plains Historical Museum, Canyon TX
Parrish Art Museum, Water Mill NY
Pasadena Museum of California Art, Pasadena CA
Patrick Henry, Red Hill National Memorial, Brookneal VA
Peabody Essex Museum, Salem MA
Pennsylvania Historical & Museum Commission, Railroad Museum of Pennsylvania, Strasburg PA
Penobscot Marine Museum, Searsport ME
Pensacola Museum of Art, Pensacola FL
Philadelphia History Museum, Philadelphia PA
Phillips Academy, Addison Gallery of American Art, Andover MA
The Phillips Collection, Washington DC
Phoenix Art Museum, Phoenix AZ
Photo Center NW, Seattle WA
Photographic Resource Center, Inc, Cambridge MA
Piedmont Arts Association, Martinsville VA
Pier 24 Photography, San Francisco CA
Pioneer Historical Museum of South Dakota, Hot Springs SD
Plains Art Museum, Fargo ND
Plainsman Museum, Aurora NE
Plumas County Museum, Quincy CA
Pocatello Art Center, Pocatello ID
Polk Museum of Art, Lakeland FL
The Pomona College, Claremont CA
Port Huron Museum, Port Huron MI
Portland Art Museum, Portland OR
Preservation Virginia, John Marshall House, Richmond VA
PS1 Contemporary Art Center, Long Island City NY
Pueblo Museum, Desert Hot Springs CA
Pump House Center for the Arts, Chillicothe OH
Purchase College, Neuberger Museum of Art, Purchase NY
Purdue University Galleries, West Lafayette IN
Putnam County Historical Society, Foundry School Museum, Cold Spring NY
Queen Victoria Museum and Art Gallery, Launceston TAS
Queens College, City University of New York, Godwin-Ternbach Museum, Flushing NY
Radio-Canada SRC CBC, Georges Goguen CBC Art Gallery, Moncton NB
Randall Junior Museum, San Francisco CA
Randolph College, Maier Museum of Art, Lynchburg VA
Rawls Museum Arts, Courtland VA
Reading Public Museum, Reading PA
Real Art Ways (RAW), Hartford CT
Red Deer & District Museum & Archives, Red Deer AB
Regina Public Library, Dunlop Art Gallery, Regina SK
Rele Gallery, Lagos
Remai Modern, Saskatoon SK
Riverside Metropolitan Museum, Riverside CA
Roberson Museum & Science Center, Binghamton NY
Robert Louis Stevenson Museum, Saint Helena CA
The Robert McLaughlin Gallery, Oshawa ON
Robischon Gallery, Denver CO
Rollins College, George D & Harriet W Cornell Fine Arts Museum, Winter Park FL
The Rosenbach Museum & Library, Philadelphia PA
Rutgers University, Stedman Art Gallery, Camden NJ
Saco Museum, Saco ME
Saginaw Art Museum, Saginaw MI
Saint Anselm College, Alva de Mars Megan Chapel Art Center, Manchester NH
Saint Bonaventure University, Regina A Quick Center for the Arts, Saint Bonaventure NY
Saint Joseph College, Art Gallery, University of Saint Joseph, West Hartford CT
Saint Joseph Museum, Inc., Saint Joseph MO
Saint Mary's College of California, Museum of Art, Moraga CA
Saint Olaf College, Flaten Art Museum, Northfield MN
Salisbury University, Ward Museum of Wildfowl Art, Salisbury MD
San Antonio Museum of Art, San Antonio TX
San Francisco Maritime National Historical Park, Maritime Museum, San Francisco CA
San Francisco Museum of Modern Art, San Francisco CA
The San Joaquin Pioneer & Historical Society, The Haggin Museum, Stockton CA
San Jose Museum of Art, San Jose CA
Santa Barbara Museum of Art, Santa Barbara CA
Santa Clara University, de Saisset Museum, Santa Clara CA
The Schoolhouse Gallery, Provincetown MA
Schweinfurth Art Center, Auburn NY
Scripps College, Ruth Chandler Williamson Gallery, Claremont CA
Seneca Falls Historical Society Museum, Seneca Falls NY
Seneca-Iroquois National Museum, Salamanca NY
Sheldon Art Galleries, Saint Louis MO
Sheldon Museum & Cultural Center, Inc, Sheldon Museum & Cultural Center, Haines AK
Shores Memorial Museum, Lyndon Center VT
Singapore Art Museum, Singapore
Slovenska Narodna Galeria, Slovak National Gallery, Bratislava
Solomon R Guggenheim Museum, New York NY
South Carolina Artisans Center, Walterboro SC
South Carolina State Museum, Columbia SC
South Dakota State University, South Dakota Art Museum, Brookings SD
South Shore Arts, Munster IN
South Street Seaport Museum, New York NY
Southeastern Center for Contemporary Art, Winston-Salem NC
Spark Gallery, Denver CO
Spartanburg Art Museum, Spartanburg SC
The Speed Art Museum, Louisville KY
Spertus Institute of Jewish Studies, Chicago IL
Springfield Art Museum, Springfield MO
Springville Museum of Art, Springville UT
St Mary's College of Maryland, The Dwight Frederick Boyden Gallery, St Mary's City MD
Staatliche Museen zu Berlin Stiftung Preussischer Kulturbesitz, National Museums in Berlin, Prussian Cultural Heritage Foundation, Berlin
Stamford Museum & Nature Center, Stamford CT
Stanford University, Cantor Arts Center at Stanford University, Stanford CA
Stanley Museum, Inc, Kingfield ME
State University of New York at New Paltz, Samuel Dorsky Museum of Art, New Paltz NY
The State University of New York at Potsdam, The Art Museum, Potsdam NY
State University of New York at Ulster, Muroff-Kotler Visual Arts Gallery, Stone Ridge NY
State University of New York College at Cortland, Dowd Fine Arts Gallery, Cortland NY
Staten Island Museum, Staten Island NY
Stephen Bulger Gallery, Toronto ON
Stratford Historical Society, Catharine B Mitchell Museum, Stratford CT
The Studio Museum in Harlem, New York NY
Suan Pakkad Palace Museum, Bangkok
The Summit County Historical Society of Akron, OH, Akron OH
Suomen Kansallismuseo, National Museum of Finland, Helsinki
Surrey Art Gallery, Surrey BC
Swedish American Museum, Chicago IL
Swetcharnik Art Studio, Mount Airy MD
Tacoma Art Museum, Tacoma WA
Tampa Museum of Art, Tampa FL
Temiskaming Art Gallery, Haileybury ON
Texas Christian University, Fort Worth Contemporary Art, Fort Worth TX
Texas Ranger Hall of Fame & Museum, Waco TX
Thomas More College, Eva G Farris Art Gallery, Crestview KY
Tohono Chul Park, Tucson AZ
Tokyo National Museum, Tokyo
Traffic Zone Center for Visual Art, Minneapolis MN
Triton Museum of Art, Santa Clara CA
Troy-Pike Cultural Arts Center, Troy AL
Trust Authority, Museum of the Great Plains, Lawton OK
Tubman African American Museum, Macon GA
Tucson Museum of Art and Historic Block, Tucson AZ
Turtle Bay Exploration Park, Redding CA
Tver Regional Art Gallery, Tver
Twin City Art Foundation, Masur Museum of Art, Monroe LA
Tyler Museum of Art, Tyler TX
Tyne and Wear Archives & Museums, Sunderland Museum & Winter Gardens, Sunderland
Ukrainian Canadian Archives & Museum of Alberta, Edmonton AB
Ukrainian Institute of Modern Art, Chicago IL
The Ukrainian Museum, New York NY
United Methodist Historical Society, Lovely Lane Museum, Baltimore MD
United Society of Shakers, Shaker Museum, New Gloucester ME
United States Figure Skating Association, World Figure Skating Museum & Hall of Fame, Colorado Springs CO
University of Arizona, Center for Creative Photography, Tucson AZ
University of Arkansas at Little Rock, Art Galleries, Little Rock AR
University of Calgary, Nickle Galleries, Calgary AB
University of California, Berkeley, Phoebe Apperson Hearst Museum of Anthropology, Berkeley CA
University of California, Davis, Jan Shrem and Maria Manetti Shrem Museum of Art, Davis CA
University of Chicago, Smart Museum of Art, Chicago IL
University of Florida, Samuel P Harn Museum of Art, Gainesville FL
University of Georgia, Georgia Museum of Art, Athens GA
University of Houston, Blaffer Art Museum, Houston TX
University of Illinois at Urbana-Champaign, Krannert Art Museum and Kinkead Pavilion, Champaign IL
University of Indianapolis, Christel DeHaan Fine Arts Gallery, Indianapolis IN
University of Kansas, Spencer Museum of Art, Lawrence KS
The University of Kentucky Art Museum, Lexington KY
University of Mary Washington, University of Mary Washington Galleries, Fredericksburg VA
University of Miami, Lowe Art Museum, Coral Gables FL
University of Minnesota, Katherine E Nash Gallery, Minneapolis MN
University of Minnesota Duluth, Tweed Museum of Art, Duluth MN
University of Nebraska-Lincoln, Great Plains Art Museum, Lincoln NE
University of Nevada, Las Vegas, Donna Beam Fine Art Gallery, Las Vegas NV
University of Nevada, Reno, Sheppard Contemporary & University Galleries, Reno NV
University of New Mexico, The Harwood Museum of Art, Taos NM
University of North Carolina at Greensboro, Weatherspoon Art Museum, Greensboro NC
University of Notre Dame, Snite Museum of Art, Notre Dame IN
University of Pennsylvania, Arthur Ross Gallery, Philadelphia PA
University of Richmond, University Museums, Richmond VA
University of Saskatchewan, Diefenbaker Canada Centre, Saskatoon SK
University of Utah, Utah Museum of Fine Arts, Salt Lake City UT
University of Victoria, The Legacy Art Gallery, Victoria BC
University of Wisconsin-Eau Claire, Foster Gallery, Eau Claire WI
University of Wisconsin-Madison, Chazen Museum of Art, Madison WI
USS Constitution Museum, Boston MA
Utah Arts Council, Chase Home Museum of Utah Folk Arts, Salt Lake City UT
The Valentine, Richmond VA
Vancouver Art Gallery, Vancouver BC
Vassar College, The Frances Lehman Loeb Art Center, Poughkeepsie NY
Venice Art Center, Venice FL
Vero Beach Museum of Art, Vero Beach FL
Vesterheim Norwegian-American Museum, Decorah IA
Victoria Mansion - Morse Libby House, Portland ME
Viridian Artists Inc, New York NY
Volcano Art Center Gallery, Hawaii Volcanoes National Park HI
VU Centre De Diffusion Et De Production De La Photographie, Quebec QC

The Walker African American Museum & Research Center, Las Vegas NV
Walker Art Center, Minneapolis MN
Walker Fine Art, Denver CO
Walter Anderson Museum of Art, Ocean Springs MS
Waterworks Visual Arts Center, Salisbury NC
Wesleyan University, Davison Art Center, Middletown CT
Westmoreland Museum of American Art, Greensburg PA
Whalers Village Museum, Lahaina HI
Whatcom Museum, Bellingham WA
Wheelwright Museum of the American Indian, Santa Fe NM
Wichita State University, Ulrich Museum of Art, Wichita KS
Wilfrid Laurier University, Robert Langen Art Gallery, Waterloo ON
Wilkes Art Gallery, North Wilkesboro NC
William Paterson University, University Galleries, Wayne NJ
Winkler Gallery of Fine Art, DuBois PA
The Winnipeg Art Gallery, Winnipeg MB
Winston-Salem State University, Diggs Gallery, Winston-Salem NC
Wiregrass Museum of Art, Dothan AL
Woodmere Art Museum Inc, Philadelphia PA
World Erotic Art Museum, Miami Beach FL
Wounded Knee Museum, Wall SD
Wyoming State Museum, Cheyenne WY
Yellowstone County Museum, Billings MT
Yeshiva University Museum, New York NY
Yokohama Museum of Art, Yokohama
Yosemite Museum, Yosemite National Park CA
Zigler Art Museum, Jennings LA

PORCELAIN

Albany Institute of History & Art, Albany NY
Allentown Art Museum, Allentown PA
American Swedish Institute, Minneapolis MN
Amherst College, Mead Art Museum, Amherst MA
Arizona Historical Society-Yuma, Sanguinetti House Museum & Garden, Yuma AZ
Arnot Art Museum, Elmira NY
Art and History Museums - Maitland, Maitland FL
The Art Center of Waco, Waco TX
Art Community Center, Art Center of Corpus Christi, Corpus Christi TX
The Art Gallery of Cornwall, Cornwall ON
Art Gallery of Nova Scotia, Halifax NS
Art Gallery of South Australia, Adelaide
Art Museum of Greater Lafayette, Lafayette IN
Art Without Walls Inc, Sayville NY
Asian Art Museum of San Francisco, Chong-Moon Lee Ctr for Asian Art and Culture, San Francisco CA
Baroda Museum and Picture Gallery, Vadodara
Bayerische Staatsgemaldesammlungen, Bavarian State Painting Collections, Munich
Beaverbrook Art Gallery, Fredericton NB
Bellevue Arts Museum, Bellevue WA
Bellingrath Gardens & Home, Theodore AL
Beloit College, Wright Museum of Art, Beloit WI
Besser Museum for Northeast Michigan, Alpena MI
Beverly Historical Society, Cabot, Hale & Balch House Museums, Beverly MA
Birmingham Museum of Art, Birmingham AL
Blanden Memorial Art Museum, Fort Dodge IA
Bob Jones University Museum & Gallery Inc, Greenville SC
Boise Art Museum, Boise ID
Botswana National Museum, Gaborone
The Bradford Group, Niles IL
Brick Store Museum, Kennebunk ME
Bush-Holley Historic Site & Storehouse Gallery, Greenwich Historical Society, Cos Cob CT
Canadian Clay and Glass Gallery, Waterloo ON
Canadian Museum of History, Gatineau QC
Cape Ann Museum, Gloucester MA
Captain Forbes House Museum, Milton MA
Casa-Museu Medeiros e Almeida, Lisbon
Charleston Museum, Heyward-Washington House, Charleston SC
Charleston Museum, Joseph Manigault House, Charleston SC
Chateau de Versailles, Palace of Versailles, Versailles
Chatham Historical Society, The Atwood House Museum, Chatham MA
Chatillon-DeMenil House Foundation, Chatillon-DeMenil Mansion, Saint Louis MO
Cheekwood-Tennessee Botanical Garden & Museum of Art, Nashville TN
The Children's Museum of Indianapolis, Indianapolis IN
City of Austin Parks & Recreation, O Henry Museum, Austin TX
City of Fremont, Olive Hyde Art Gallery, Fremont CA
Clark Art Institute, Williamstown MA
Clark County Historical Society, Pioneer - Krier Museum, Ashland KS
College of William & Mary, Muscarelle Museum of Art, Williamsburg VA
The Columbus Museum, Columbus GA
Columbus Museum of Art, Columbus OH
Craft and Folk Art Museum (CAFAM), Los Angeles CA
Cranbrook Art Museum, Bloomfield Hills MI
Cripple Creek District Museum, Cripple Creek CO
Crocker Art Museum, Sacramento CA
The Currier Museum of Art, Manchester NH
DAR Museum, National Society Daughters of the American Revolution, Washington DC
Dartmouth Heritage Museum, Dartmouth NS
Daum Museum of Contemporary Art, Sedalia MO
Designmuseum Danmark, Danish Design Museum, Copenhagen
Detroit Institute of Arts, Detroit MI
The Dixon Gallery & Gardens, Memphis TN
Doncaster Museum and Art Gallery, Doncaster Yorks
Edsel & Eleanor Ford House, Grosse Pointe Shores MI
Ellen Noel Art Museum of the Permian Basin, Odessa TX
Elverhoj Museum of History and Art, Solvang CA
Erie Art Museum, Erie PA
Evanston Historical Society, Charles Gates Dawes House, Evanston IL
Everhart Museum, Scranton PA
Everson Museum of Art, Syracuse NY
Fetherston Foundation, Packwood House Museum, Lewisburg PA
Fishkill Historical Society, Van Wyck Homestead Museum, Fishkill NY
Flint Institute of Arts, Flint MI
Florida State University and Central Florida Community College, The Appleton Museum of Art, Ocala FL
Fondazione Musei Civici Di Venezia, Museo Correr - Correr Museum, Venice
Fondazione Musei Civici Di Venezia, Ca' Rezzonico, Venice
Fort Smith Regional Art Museum, Fort Smith AR
Frederic Remington, Ogdensburg NY
The Frick Art & Historical Center, Inc, Frick Art Museum, Pittsburgh PA
Frick Collection, New York NY
Fulton County Historical Society Inc, Fulton County Museum (Tetzlaff Reference Room), Rochester IN
Gadsden Museum of Art, Gadsden AL
Galerie Montcalm, Gatineau QC
Gallery One Visual Arts Center, Ellensburg WA
General Board of Discipleship, The United Methodist Church, The Upper Room Chapel & Museum, Nashville TN
Girard College, Stephen Girard Collection, Philadelphia PA
Glanmore National Historic Site of Canada, Belleville ON
Glasgow University, The Hunterian, Glasgow
Glessner House Museum, Chicago IL
Grand Rapids Public Museum, Grand Rapids MI
Haystack Mountain School of Crafts, Deer Isle ME
Headley-Whitney Museum, Lexington KY
Headquarters Fort Monroe, Dept of Army, Casemate Museum, Hampton VA
Henry County Museum & Cultural Arts Center, Clinton MO
Henry Sheldon Museum of Vermont History and Research Center, Middlebury VT
Hershey Museum, Hershey PA
Hill-Stead Museum, Farmington CT
Hillwood Museum & Gardens Foundation, Hillwood Estate Museum & Gardens, Washington DC
Historic Arkansas Museum, Little Rock AR
Historic Cherry Hill, Albany NY
Historic Hudson Valley, Pocantico Hills NY
Historic Huguenot Street, New Paltz NY
Historisches und Volkerkundemuseum, Museum of History and Ethnology, St Gallen
Holter Museum of Art, Helena MT
Honolulu Museum of Art, Honolulu HI
Hui No'eau Visual Arts Center, Gallery and Gift Shop, Makawao Maui HI
Illinois State Museum, ISM Lockport Gallery, Chicago Gallery & Southern Illinois Art Gallery, Springfield IL
Independence Historical Museum & Art Center, Independence KS
Independence Seaport Museum, Philadelphia PA
Indiana Landmarks, Morris-Butler House, Indianapolis IN
International Museum of Art, El Paso TX
Iowa State University, Brunnier Art Museum, Ames IA
The Israel Museum, Jerusalem, Jerusalem
Jacksonville University, Alexander Brest Museum & Gallery, Jacksonville FL
James Dick Foundation, Festival - Institute, Round Top TX
Johns Hopkins University, Evergreen Museum & Library, Baltimore MD
Johns Hopkins University, Homewood Museum, Baltimore MD
Kelly-Griggs House Museum, Red Bluff CA
Kenosha Public Museums, Kenosha WI
Kereszteny Muzeum, Christian Museum, Esztergom
Kimbell Art Foundation, Kimbell Art Museum, Fort Worth TX
Kings County Historical Society & Museum, Hampton NB
Knoxville Museum of Art, Knoxville TN
Koochiching Museums, International Falls MN
Kyiv Museum of Russian Art, Kyiv Ukrainian
Lalit Kala Akademi Rabindra Bhavan Art Galleries, National Academy of Art, New Delhi, New Delhi
Latino Art Museum, Pomona CA
Lehigh Valley Heritage Center, Allentown PA
Lightner Museum, Saint Augustine FL
Lillian & Coleman Taube Museum of Art, Minot ND
Lincoln County Historical Association, Inc, 1811 Old Lincoln County Jail & Lincoln County Museum, Wiscasset ME
Lincolnshire County Council, Library & Heritage Services, Lincoln
Lincolnshire County Council, The Collection: Art & Archaeology in Lincolnshire, Lincoln
The Long Island Museum of American Art, History & Carriages, Stony Brook NY
Longfellow-Evangeline State Commemorative Area, Saint Martinville LA
Longue Vue House & Gardens, New Orleans LA
Louise Hopkins Underwood Center for the Arts, Lubbock TX
Madison Museum of Fine Art, Madison GA
Marblehead Museum & Historical Society, Marblehead MA
Marblehead Museum & Historical Society, Jeremiah Lee Mansion, Marblehead MA
Marquette University, Haggerty Museum of Art, Milwaukee WI
Maryland Historical Society, Museum of Maryland History, Baltimore MD
McDowell House & Apothecary Shop, Danville KY
McLean County Historical Society, McLean County Museum of History, Bloomington IL
Memphis Brooks Museum of Art, Memphis TN
Middle Border Museum & Oscar Howe Art Center, Mitchell SD
The Mint Museum, Charlotte NC
The Mint Museum, Mint Museum of Craft & Design, Charlotte NC
Missoula Art Museum, Missoula MT
Mobile Museum of Art, Mobile AL
Montana State University, Helen E Copeland Gallery, Bozeman MT
Montgomery Museum of Fine Arts, Montgomery AL
Moravska Galerie v Brne, Moravian Gallery in Brno, Brno
Morris Museum of Art, Augusta GA
Mount Vernon Hotel Museum & Garden, New York NY
Musee Cognacq-Jay, Cognacq-Jay Museum, Paris
Musee des Augustines de l'Hotel Dieu de Quebec, Quebec QC
Musee des Beaux-Arts de Tours, Museum of Fine Arts, Tours
Musee Regional de lu Cote-Nord, Sept-Iles QC
Musees Royaux d'Art et d'Histoire, Royal Museums of Art and History, Brussels
Museo De Las Americas, Denver CO
Museo Del Romanticismo, Museum of the Romantic Period, Madrid

Museo di Palazzo Ducale, Ducale Palace Museum, Mantua
The Museum, Greenwood SC
Museum De Lakenhal, Leiden
Museum of Art - Deland FL, Inc, Deland FL
Museum of Arts & Design, New York NY
The Museum of Arts & Sciences Inc, Daytona Beach FL
Museum of Fine Arts, Boston MA
Museum of Northern British Columbia, Ruth Harvey Art Gallery, Prince Rupert BC
Museum of Northwest Art, La Conner WA
Museum Plantin-Moretus, Antwerp
Museum zu Allerheiligen, Schaffhausen
Muzej za Umjetnost i Obrt, Museum of Arts & Crafts, Zagreb
Muzeul National de Arta al Romaniei, National Museum of Art of Romania, Bucharest
Muzeum Narodowe W Kielcach, National Museum in Kielce, Kielce
National Art Museum of Moldova, Chisinau
National Baseball Hall of Fame & Museum, Cooperstown NY
The National Museum of Modern Art, Tokyo, Tokyo
National Museums Scotland, National Museum of Scotland, Edinburgh
National Palace Museum, Taipei
Naval Historical Center, National Museum of the US Navy, Washington DC
Nelda C & H J Lutcher Stark Foundation, Stark Museum of Art, Orange TX
Nelson Mandela Metropolitan Art Museum, Port Elizabeth
Neue Galerie New York, New York NY
Neville Public Museum of Brown County, Green Bay WI
New Britain Museum of American Art, New Britain CT
New Orleans Museum of Art, New Orleans LA
New Visions Gallery, Inc, Marshfield WI
New York State Office of Parks Recreation & Historic Preservation, John Jay Homestead State Historic Site, Katonah NY
Newfields, Indianapolis IN
Niigata Prefectural Museum of Modern Art, Nagaoka
Norwich Free Academy, Slater Memorial Museum, Norwich CT
The Ohio Historical Society, Inc, Campus Martius Museum & Ohio River Museum, Marietta OH
Oshkosh Public Museum & Library, Oshkosh WI
Owensboro Museum of Fine Art, Owensboro KY
Palm Beach County Parks & Recreation Department, Morikami Museum & Japanese Gardens, Delray Beach FL
Panhandle-Plains Historical Museum, Canyon TX
Peabody Essex Museum, Salem MA
Penobscot Marine Museum, Searsport ME
Philadelphia History Museum, Philadelphia PA
Piedmont Arts Association, Martinsville VA
Plumas County Museum, Quincy CA
Pocatello Art Center, Pocatello ID
Preservation Virginia, John Marshall House, Richmond VA
Pump House Center for the Arts, Chillicothe OH
Queen Victoria Museum and Art Gallery, Launceston TAS
Queens College, City University of New York, Godwin-Ternbach Museum, Flushing NY
Rahr-West Art Museum, Manitowoc WI
Red Deer & District Museum & Archives, Red Deer AB
Rhode Island Historical Society, John Brown House, Providence RI
The Rosenbach Museum & Library, Philadelphia PA
Royal Arts Foundation, Belcourt Castle, Newport RI
Ryerss Victorian Museum & Library, Philadelphia PA
Saco Museum, Saco ME
Saginaw Art Museum, Saginaw MI
Saint Bonaventure University, Regina A Quick Center for the Arts, Saint Bonaventure NY
Saint John's University, Dr. M.T. Geoffrey Yeh Art Gallery, Queens NY
San Antonio Museum of Art, San Antonio TX
Seattle Art Museum, Seattle WA
Shirley Plantation Foundation, Charles City VA
Slovenska Narodna Galeria, Slovak National Gallery, Bratislava
The Society of the Cincinnati at Anderson House, Washington DC
South Carolina Artisans Center, Walterboro SC
South Dakota State University, South Dakota Art Museum, Brookings SD
The Speed Art Museum, Louisville KY
Spertus Institute of Jewish Studies, Chicago IL
Staatliche Museen zu Berlin Stiftung Preussischer Kulturbesitz, National Museums in Berlin, Prussian Cultural Heritage Foundation, Berlin
The State Museum of Fine Arts of Tatarstan Republic, Kazan
State University of New York at Plattsburgh, Art Museum, Plattsburgh NY
Staten Island Museum, Staten Island NY
Stedelijk Museum Alkmaar, Alkmaar Municipal Museum, Alkmaar
Stone Quarry Hill Art Park, Winner Gallery, Cazenovia NY
Stratford Historical Society, Catharine B Mitchell Museum, Stratford CT
Suan Pakkad Palace Museum, Bangkok
Suomen Kansallismuseo, National Museum of Finland, Helsinki
Swedish American Museum, Chicago IL
Taft Museum of Art, Cincinnati OH
Tohono Chul Park, Tucson AZ
Tokyo National Museum, Tokyo
Trenton City Museum, Trenton NJ
Tryon Palace, New Bern NC
Tubman African American Museum, Macon GA
Tver Regional Art Gallery, Tver
Tyne and Wear Archives & Museums, Sunderland Museum & Winter Gardens, Sunderland
United Society of Shakers, Shaker Museum, New Gloucester ME
United States Figure Skating Association, World Figure Skating Museum & Hall of Fame, Colorado Springs CO
University of California, Berkeley, Phoebe Apperson Hearst Museum of Anthropology, Berkeley CA
University of Georgia, Georgia Museum of Art, Athens GA
University of Illinois at Urbana-Champaign, Krannert Art Museum and Kinkead Pavilion, Champaign IL
The University of Kentucky Art Museum, Lexington KY
University of Miami, Lowe Art Museum, Coral Gables FL
University of Minnesota, Goldstein Museum of Design, Saint Paul MN
University of Notre Dame, Snite Museum of Art, Notre Dame IN
University of Richmond, University Museums, Richmond VA
University of Tampa, Henry B Plant Museum, Tampa FL
University of Utah, Utah Museum of Fine Arts, Salt Lake City UT
University of Victoria, The Legacy Art Gallery, Victoria BC
University of Wisconsin-Madison, Chazen Museum of Art, Madison WI
Vesterheim Norwegian-American Museum, Decorah IA
Victoria Mansion - Morse Libby House, Portland ME
Villa Terrace Decorative Arts Museum, Milwaukee WI
Virginia Museum of Fine Arts, Richmond VA
Wadsworth Atheneum Museum of Art, Hartford CT
The Walker African American Museum & Research Center, Las Vegas NV
Walker Art Gallery, Liverpool
Walker Fine Art, Denver CO
The Wallace Collection, London
Walters Art Museum, Baltimore MD
Wayne Center for the Arts, Wooster OH
Westfries Museum, Hoorn
White House, Washington DC
Wichita Art Museum, Wichita KS
Wiregrass Museum of Art, Dothan AL
Woodlawn/The Pope-Leighey, Alexandria VA
Woodmere Art Museum Inc, Philadelphia PA
World Erotic Art Museum, Miami Beach FL
Yokohama Museum of Art, Yokohama
Zigler Art Museum, Jennings LA

PORTRAITS

Academy of the New Church, Glencairn Museum, Bryn Athyn PA
Adams County Historical Society, Gettysburg PA
Adams National Historic Park, Quincy MA
African American Atelier, Greensboro NC
African American Museum in Philadelphia, Philadelphia PA
Alaska State Museum, Juneau AK
Albany Institute of History & Art, Albany NY
Albany Museum of Art, Albany GA
Albin Polasek Museum & Sculpture Gardens, Winter Park FL
Albuquerque Museum of Art & History, Albuquerque NM
American Folk Art Museum, New York NY
Amherst College, Mead Art Museum, Amherst MA
Amon Carter Museum of American Art, Fort Worth TX
Amsterdam Museum, Amsterdam
The Andy Warhol Museum, Pittsburgh PA
Arizona Historical Society-Yuma, Sanguinetti House Museum & Garden, Yuma AZ
Arnot Art Museum, Elmira NY
Art Community Center, Art Center of Corpus Christi, Corpus Christi TX
Art Gallery of Alberta, Edmonton AB
The Art Gallery of Cornwall, Cornwall ON
Art Gallery of Nova Scotia, Halifax NS
The Art Museum of Eastern Idaho, Idaho Falls ID
Art Museum of Greater Lafayette, Lafayette IN
Art Without Walls Inc, Sayville NY
Arts Council of Fayetteville-Cumberland County, The Arts Center, Fayetteville NC
Asheville Art Museum, Asheville NC
Asian Art Museum of San Francisco, Chong-Moon Lee Ctr for Asian Art and Culture, San Francisco CA
Bakehouse Art Complex, Inc, Miami FL
The Baltimore Museum of Art, Baltimore MD
Bangladesh National Museum, Dhaka
Baroda Museum and Picture Gallery, Vadodara
The Bartlett Museum, Amesbury MA
Bayerische Staatsgemaldesammlungen, Bavarian State Painting Collections, Munich
Beaverbrook Art Gallery, Fredericton NB
Beloit College, Wright Museum of Art, Beloit WI
Bennington Museum, Bennington VT
Beverly Historical Society, Cabot, Hale & Balch House Museums, Beverly MA
Biggs Museum of American Art, Dover DE
Birmingham Museum of Art, Birmingham AL
Blanden Memorial Art Museum, Fort Dodge IA
Blauvelt Demarest Foundation, Hiram Blauvelt Art Museum, Oradell NJ
Bob Jones University Museum & Gallery Inc, Greenville SC
Boise Art Museum, Boise ID
Booth Western Art Museum, Cartersville GA
Boston Public Library, Albert H Wiggin Gallery & Print Department, Boston MA
The Bostonian Society, Old State House Museum, Boston MA
Botswana National Museum, Gaborone
Brick Store Museum, Kennebunk ME
Bruce Museum, Inc, Greenwich CT
Bucknell University, Edward & Marthann Samek Art Gallery, Lewisburg PA
Buffalo Niagara Heritage Village, Amherst NY
C M Russell Museum, Great Falls MT
Cahoon Museum of American Art, Cotuit MA
Cameron Art Museum, Wilmington NC
Canadian Museum for Human Rights, Winnipeg MB
Canadian Museum of History, Gatineau QC
Canton Museum of Art, Canton OH
Cape Ann Museum, Gloucester MA
Carnegie Center for Art & History, New Albany IN
Carolina Art Association, Gibbes Museum of Art, Charleston SC
Cartoon Art Museum, San Francisco CA
Casa-Museu Medeiros e Almeida, Lisbon
Cayuga Museum of History & Art, Auburn NY
Cedar Rapids Museum of Art, Cedar Rapids IA
Chateau de Versailles, Palace of Versailles, Versailles
Chatham Historical Society, The Atwood House Museum, Chatham MA
Chatillon-DeMenil House Foundation, Chatillon-DeMenil Mansion, Saint Louis MO
Chelan County Public Utility District, Rocky Reach Dam, Wenatchee WA
City of Cedar Falls, Iowa, James & Meryl Hearst Center for the Arts & Sculpture Garden, Cedar Falls IA
City of Fayette, Alabama, Fayette Art Museum, Fayette AL
City of Fremont, Olive Hyde Art Gallery, Fremont CA

City of Gainesville, Thomas Center Galleries - Cultural Affairs, Gainesville FL
The City of Petersburg Museums, Petersburg VA
Clark Art Institute, Williamstown MA
Clark County Historical Society, Pioneer - Krier Museum, Ashland KS
Clemson University, Fort Hill Plantation, Clemson SC
Cohasset Historical Society, Cohasset Maritime Museum, Cohasset MA
Colgate University, Picker Art Gallery, Hamilton NY
College of William & Mary, Muscarelle Museum of Art, Williamsburg VA
The Columbus Museum, Columbus GA
Columbus Museum of Art, Columbus OH
Concord Museum, Concord MA
The Courtauld Institute of Art, The Courtauld Gallery, London
Coutts Museum of Art, Inc, El Dorado KS
Cripple Creek District Museum, Cripple Creek CO
Crocker Art Museum, Sacramento CA
Crow Wing County Historical Society, Brainerd MN
The Currier Museum of Art, Manchester NH
Danville Museum of Fine Arts & History, Danville VA
DAR Museum, National Society Daughters of the American Revolution, Washington DC
Dartmouth College, Hood Museum of Art, Hanover NH
Dartmouth Heritage Museum, Dartmouth NS
deCordova Sculpture Park & Museum, Lincoln MA
Delaware Art Museum, Wilmington DE
Delaware Division of Historical & Cultural Affairs, Dover DE
Delaware Historical Society, Read House and Gardens, New Castle DE
Delta Blues Museum, Clarksdale MS
Denver Art Museum, Denver CO
Department of Economic & Community Development, State of Connecticut DECD Eric Sloane Museum, Kent CT
Detroit Institute of Arts, Detroit MI
Detroit Repertory Theatre Gallery, Detroit MI
Dickinson College, The Trout Gallery, Carlisle PA
Dixie State University, Sears Art Museum Gallery, Saint George UT
Doncaster Museum and Art Gallery, Doncaster Yorks
Dublin Arts Council, Dublin OH
Durham Art Guild, Durham NC
Eiteljorg Museum of American Indians & Western Art, Indianapolis IN
Elisabet Ney, Austin TX
Ellen Noel Art Museum of the Permian Basin, Odessa TX
Elmhurst Art Museum, Elmhurst IL
Environment Canada - Parks Canada, Laurier House, National Historic Site, Ottawa ON
Erie County Historical Society, Erie PA
Evanston Historical Society, Charles Gates Dawes House, Evanston IL
Everhart Museum, Scranton PA
Everson Museum of Art, Syracuse NY
Fetherston Foundation, Packwood House Museum, Lewisburg PA
Fishkill Historical Society, Van Wyck Homestead Museum, Fishkill NY
Fitton Center for Creative Arts, Hamilton OH
Flint Institute of Arts, Flint MI
Florence County Museum, Florence SC
Florida Southern College, Melvin Art Gallery, Lakeland FL
Florida State University and Central Florida Community College, The Appleton Museum of Art, Ocala FL
Folk Art Society of America, Richmond VA
Fondazione Musei Civici Di Venezia, Museo Correr - Correr Museum, Venice
Fondazione Musei Civici Di Venezia, Ca' Rezzonico, Venice
Fort Ticonderoga Association, Ticonderoga NY
The Frick Art & Historical Center, Inc, Frick Art Museum, Pittsburgh PA
Frontier Times Museum, Bandera TX
Fuller Craft Museum, Brockton MA
Fulton County Historical Society Inc, Fulton County Museum (Tetzlaff Reference Room), Rochester IN
Gadsden Museum, Mesilla NM
Gadsden Museum of Art, Gadsden AL
Galerie Montcalm, Gatineau QC
George Phippen, Phippen Museum - Art of the American West, Prescott AZ
Germantown Historical Society, Philadelphia PA
Girard College, Stephen Girard Collection, Philadelphia PA
Glanmore National Historic Site of Canada, Belleville ON
Grand Rapids Public Museum, Grand Rapids MI
Greene County Historical Society, Bronck Museum, Coxsackie NY
Greenville County Museum of Art, Greenville SC
Hancock Shaker Village, Inc, Pittsfield MA
Harness Racing Museum & Hall of Fame, Goshen NY
Headley-Whitney Museum, Lexington KY
The Heckscher Museum of Art, Huntington NY
Henry County Museum & Cultural Arts Center, Clinton MO
Henry Sheldon Museum of Vermont History and Research Center, Middlebury VT
Heras Museum for Research in Indian History and Culture, Mumbai
Heritage Center, Inc, Pine Ridge SD
Hickory Museum of Art, Inc, Hickory NC
Hidalgo County Historical Museum, Edinburg TX
Hill-Stead Museum, Farmington CT
Hillwood Museum & Gardens Foundation, Hillwood Estate Museum & Gardens, Washington DC
Historic Arkansas Museum, Little Rock AR
Historic Cherry Hill, Albany NY
Historic Holyoke at Wistariahurst & City of Holyoke, Holyoke MA
Historic Hudson Valley, Pocantico Hills NY
Historic Huguenot Street, New Paltz NY
Historic Newton, Newton MA
Historical Society of Cheshire County, Keene NH
The History Center in Tompkins County, Ithaca NY
Hunter Museum of American Art, Chattanooga TN
Illinois Historic Preservation Agency, Bishop Hill State Historic Site, Bishop Hill IL
Illinois State Museum, ISM Lockport Gallery, Chicago Gallery & Southern Illinois Art Gallery, Springfield IL
Independence Historical Museum & Art Center, Independence KS
Independence National Historical Park, Philadelphia PA
Indiana Landmarks, Morris-Butler House, Indianapolis IN
Institute of Contemporary Art, Los Angeles, Los Angeles CA
International Museum of Art, El Paso TX
Iredell Museums, Statesville NC
The Israel Museum, Jerusalem, Jerusalem
Jacques Marchais Museum of Tibetan Art, Staten Island NY
James Monroe Museum, Fredericksburg VA
Jekyll Island Museum, Jekyll Island GA
JMW Turner Museum, Sarasota FL
Johns Hopkins University, Evergreen Museum & Library, Baltimore MD
Jordan National Gallery of Fine Arts, Amman
Joslyn Art Museum, Omaha NE
Kalamazoo Institute of Arts, Kalamazoo MI
Kenosha Public Museums, Kenosha WI
Kentucky Museum of Art and Craft, Louisville KY
Kereszteny Muzeum, Christian Museum, Esztergom
Kimbell Art Foundation, Kimbell Art Museum, Fort Worth TX
Kings County Historical Society & Museum, Hampton NB
Kirchner Museum Davos, Davos
Kirkland Museum of Fine & Decorative Art, Denver CO
Knoxville Museum of Art, Knoxville TN
Koochiching Museums, International Falls MN
Koshare Indian Museum, Inc, La Junta CO
Kunsthistorisches Museum Wien, Museum of Fine Arts, Vienna
Kunstmuseum Solothurn, Solothurn Art Museum, Solothurn
Kyiv Museum of Russian Art, Kyiv Ukrainian
La Salle University Art Museum, Philadelphia PA
Lafayette College, Lafayette College Art Galleries, Easton PA
Laguna Art Museum, Laguna Beach CA
Latino Art Museum, Pomona CA
Lehigh Valley Heritage Center, Allentown PA
Liberty Hall Historic Site, Liberty Hall Museum, Frankfort KY
Lillian & Coleman Taube Museum of Art, Minot ND
Lincoln County Historical Association, Inc, 1811 Old Lincoln County Jail & Lincoln County Museum, Wiscasset ME
Lincolnshire County Council, Library & Heritage Services, Lincoln
Lincolnshire County Council, The Collection: Art & Archaeology in Lincolnshire, Lincoln
Livingston County Historical Society, Museum, Geneseo NY
The Long Island Museum of American Art, History & Carriages, Stony Brook NY
Longfellow-Evangeline State Commemorative Area, Saint Martinville LA
Longview Museum of Fine Art, Longview TX
Louisiana Department of Culture, Recreation & Tourism, Louisiana State Museum, New Orleans LA
MacArthur Memorial, Norfolk VA
Marblehead Museum & Historical Society, Marblehead MA
Marblehead Museum & Historical Society, Jeremiah Lee Mansion, Marblehead MA
The Mariners' Museum, Newport News VA
Marylhurst University, The Art Gym, Marylhurst OR
Massachusetts Institute of Technology, MIT Museum, Cambridge MA
Massillon Museum, Massillon OH
McDowell House & Apothecary Shop, Danville KY
McLean County Historical Society, McLean County Museum of History, Bloomington IL
Meridian Museum of Art, Meridian MS
The Mexican Museum, San Francisco CA
Michelson Museum of Art, Marshall TX
Midwest Museum of American Art, Elkhart IN
Miller Art Center Foundation Inc, Miller Art Museum, Sturgeon Bay WI
Minnesota Museum of American Art, Saint Paul MN
Minot State University, Northwest Art Center, Minot ND
The Mint Museum, Charlotte NC
Missoula Art Museum, Missoula MT
Mobile Museum of Art, Mobile AL
Moderna Galerija, Modern Gallery - National Museum of Modern Art, Zagreb
Montclair Art Museum, Montclair NJ
Montgomery Museum of Fine Arts, Montgomery AL
Moore College of Art & Design, The Galleries at Moore, Philadelphia PA
Moravian Historical Society, Nazareth PA
Moravska Galerie v Brne, Moravian Gallery in Brno, Brno
Morris Museum of Art, Augusta GA
Morris-Jumel Mansion, Inc, New York NY
Mount Vernon Hotel Museum & Garden, New York NY
MTG Hawkes Bay, Napier
Muscatine Art Center, Muscatine IA
Musee Cognacq-Jay, Cognacq-Jay Museum, Paris
Musee des Augustines de l'Hotel Dieu de Quebec, Quebec QC
Musee des Beaux-Arts d'Orleans, Museum of Fine Arts, Orleans
Musee des Beaux-Arts de Tours, Museum of Fine Arts, Tours
Musee National des Beaux Arts du Quebec, Quebec QC
Musee Regional de lu Cote-Nord, Sept-Iles QC
Musee Regional de Vaudreuil-Soulanges, Vaudreuil-Dorion QC
Museen der Stadt Koln, Wallraf-Richartz-Museum & Fondation Corboud - Wallraf-Richartz Museum & Corboud Foundation, Cologne
Museo De Las Americas, Denver CO
Museo Del Romanticismo, Museum of the Romantic Period, Madrid
Museo di Palazzo Ducale, Ducale Palace Museum, Mantua
Museo Nacional de Bellas Artes, National Museum of Fine Arts, Santiago
Museu Nacional D'Art De Catalunya, Catalona National Museum of Art, Barcelona
Museu Nacional de Arte Contemporanea do Chiado, National Museum of Contemporary Art, Museu Do Chiado, Lisbon
Museum De Lakenhal, Leiden
Museum of Art - Deland FL, Inc, Deland FL
The Museum of Arts & Sciences Inc, Daytona Beach FL
Museum of Fine Arts, Saint Petersburg, Florida, Inc, Saint Petersburg FL
Museum of Latin American Art, Long Beach CA
Museum of Northern British Columbia, Ruth Harvey Art Gallery, Prince Rupert BC

Museum of Northwest Art, La Conner WA
Museum Plantin-Moretus, Antwerp
Museum Prinsenhof Delft, Delft
Museum zu Allerheiligen, Schaffhausen
Muzej za Umjetnost i Obrt, Museum of Arts & Crafts, Zagreb
Muzeul National de Arta al Romaniei, National Museum of Art of Romania, Bucharest
Muzeum Narodowe W Kielcach, National Museum in Kielce, Kielce
Muzeum Narodowe w Poznaniu, National Museum in Poznan, Poznan
Narodna Galerija, National Gallery of Slovenia, Ljubljana
Nathan Hale Homestead Museum, Coventry CT
The National Art Center, Tokyo, Tokyo
National Art Museum of Moldova, Chisinau
National Baseball Hall of Fame & Museum, Cooperstown NY
National Gallery of Canada, Ottawa ON
National Gallery of Ireland, Dublin
National Museum & Art Gallery of Trinidad and Tobago, Port of Spain
The National Museum of Modern Art, Tokyo, Tokyo
The National Museum of Western Art, Tokyo
National Palace Museum, Taipei
National Portrait Gallery, London
National Silk Art Museum, Weston MO
National Society of Colonial Dames of America in the State of Maryland, Mount Clare Museum House, Baltimore MD
National Society of the Colonial Dames of America in The Commonwealth of Virginia, Wilton House Museum, Richmond VA
National Trust for Historic Preservation, Shadows-on-the-Teche, New Iberia LA
National Trust for Historic Preservation, Chesterwood, Stockbridge MA
Naval Historical Center, National Museum of the US Navy, Washington DC
Nebraska Game and Parks Commission, Arbor Lodge State Historical Park & Morton Mansion, Nebraska City NE
Nelson Mandela Metropolitan Art Museum, Port Elizabeth
Neue Galerie New York, New York NY
Nevada Museum of Art, Reno NV
New Britain Museum of American Art, New Britain CT
New Canaan Historical Society, New Canaan CT
New Jersey Historical Society, Newark NJ
New Orleans Museum of Art, New Orleans LA
New York State Military Museum and Veterans Research Center, Saratoga Springs NY
New York State Office of Parks Recreation & Historic Preservation, John Jay Homestead State Historic Site, Katonah NY
New York State Office of Parks, Recreation & Historic Preservation, Staatsburgh State Historic Site, Staatsburg NY
Newburyport Maritime Society, Inc, Custom House Maritime Museum, Newburyport MA
Newfields, Indianapolis IN
Norman Rockwell Museum, Stockbridge MA
Norton Simon Museum, Pasadena CA
Norwich Free Academy, Slater Memorial Museum, Norwich CT
Noyes Art Gallery, Lincoln NE
Ogden Museum of Southern Art, University of New Orleans, New Orleans LA
The Ohio Historical Society, Inc, Campus Martius Museum & Ohio River Museum, Marietta OH
Oklahoma City Museum of Art, Oklahoma City OK
Old Dartmouth Historical Society, New Bedford Whaling Museum, New Bedford MA
Oshkosh Public Museum & Library, Oshkosh WI
Osterreichische Galerie Belvedere Vienna, Belvedere Museum Vienna, Vienna
Owensboro Museum of Fine Art, Owensboro KY
Panhandle-Plains Historical Museum, Canyon TX
Pasadena Museum of California Art, Pasadena CA
Pasadena Museum of History, Pasadena CA
Patrick Henry, Red Hill National Memorial, Brookneal VA
Pearson Lakes Art Center, Okoboji IA
Pennsylvania Academy of the Fine Arts, Philadelphia PA
Pennsylvania Historical & Museum Commission, Railroad Museum of Pennsylvania, Strasburg PA
Pensacola Museum of Art, Pensacola FL
Philadelphia History Museum, Philadelphia PA
Philadelphia Museum of Art, John G Johnson Collection, Philadelphia PA
Philipse Manor Hall State Historic Site, Yonkers NY
The Phillips Collection, Washington DC
Phoenix Art Museum, Phoenix AZ
Piedmont Arts Association, Martinsville VA
Pioneer Historical Museum of South Dakota, Hot Springs SD
Plains Art Museum, Fargo ND
Plainsman Museum, Aurora NE
Port Huron Museum, Port Huron MI
Preservation Virginia, John Marshall House, Richmond VA
Presidential Museum & Leadership Library, Odessa TX
Pueblo Museum, Desert Hot Springs CA
Pump House Center for the Arts, Chillicothe OH
Putnam County Historical Society, Foundry School Museum, Cold Spring NY
Queen Victoria Museum and Art Gallery, Launceston TAS
Queens College, City University of New York, Godwin-Ternbach Museum, Flushing NY
Randolph College, Maier Museum of Art, Lynchburg VA
Rawls Museum Arts, Courtland VA
Reading Public Museum, Reading PA
Remai Modern, Saskatoon SK
Rensselaer County Historical Society, Hart-Cluett Mansion, 1827, Troy NY
Rhode Island Historical Society, John Brown House, Providence RI
Robert Louis Stevenson Museum, Saint Helena CA
The Robert McLaughlin Gallery, Oshawa ON
Rollins College, George D & Harriet W Cornell Fine Arts Museum, Winter Park FL
Ross Memorial Museum, Saint Andrews NB
Roswell Museum & Art Center, Roswell NM
Ryerss Victorian Museum & Library, Philadelphia PA
Saco Museum, Saco ME
Saginaw Art Museum, Saginaw MI
Saint Anselm College, Alva de Mars Megan Chapel Art Center, Manchester NH
Saint Johnsbury Athenaeum, Saint Johnsbury VT
Saint Joseph College, Art Gallery, University of Saint Joseph, West Hartford CT
Saint Olaf College, Flaten Art Museum, Northfield MN
San Antonio Museum of Art, San Antonio TX
Shirley Plantation Foundation, Charles City VA
Slovenska Narodna Galeria, Slovak National Gallery, Bratislava
The Society of the Cincinnati at Anderson House, Washington DC
South Dakota State University, South Dakota Art Museum, Brookings SD
Southern Lorain County Historical Society, Spirit of '76 Museum, Elyria OH
Southern Methodist University, Meadows Museum, Dallas TX
Spartanburg Art Museum, Spartanburg SC
The Speed Art Museum, Louisville KY
Spertus Institute of Jewish Studies, Chicago IL
Springfield Art Museum, Springfield MO
Springville Museum of Art, Springville UT
St Mary's College of Maryland, The Dwight Frederick Boyden Gallery, St Mary's City MD
Staatliche Museen zu Berlin Stiftung Preussischer Kulturbesitz, National Museums in Berlin, Prussian Cultural Heritage Foundation, Berlin
Stanford University, Cantor Arts Center at Stanford University, Stanford CA
The State Museum of Fine Arts of Tatarstan Republic, Kazan
The State University of New York at Potsdam, The Art Museum, Potsdam NY
State University of New York College at Cortland, Dowd Fine Arts Gallery, Cortland NY
Staten Island Museum, Staten Island NY
Stedelijk Museum Alkmaar, Alkmaar Municipal Museum, Alkmaar
The Stewart Museum, Montreal QC
Stone Quarry Hill Art Park, Winner Gallery, Cazenovia NY
Stratford Historical Society, Catharine B Mitchell Museum, Stratford CT
The Summit County Historical Society of Akron, OH, Akron OH
Suomen Kansallismuseo, National Museum of Finland, Helsinki
Swedish American Museum, Chicago IL
T C Steele State Historic Site, Nashville IN
Tacoma Art Museum, Tacoma WA
Taft Museum of Art, Cincinnati OH
Taos Historic Museums, Ernest Blumenschein Home & Studio, Taos NM
Telfair Museums, Savannah GA
Temiskaming Art Gallery, Haileybury ON
Thomas Jefferson Foundation, Inc, Monticello, Charlottesville VA
Timken Museum of Art, San Diego CA
Transylvania University, Morlan Gallery, Lexington KY
Triton Museum of Art, Santa Clara CA
Tryon Palace, New Bern NC
Tubac Center of the Arts, Santa Cruz Valley Art Association, Tubac AZ
Tubman African American Museum, Macon GA
Tucson Museum of Art and Historic Block, Tucson AZ
Tver Regional Art Gallery, Tver
Tyne and Wear Archives & Museums, Sunderland Museum & Winter Gardens, Sunderland
Ukrainian Canadian Archives & Museum of Alberta, Edmonton AB
United Methodist Historical Society, Lovely Lane Museum, Baltimore MD
United Society of Shakers, Shaker Museum, New Gloucester ME
United States Capitol, Architect of the Capitol, Washington DC
United States Figure Skating Association, World Figure Skating Museum & Hall of Fame, Colorado Springs CO
United States Military Academy, West Point Museum, West Point NY
University of California, Berkeley, Phoebe Apperson Hearst Museum of Anthropology, Berkeley CA
University of Chicago, Smart Museum of Art, Chicago IL
University of Georgia, Georgia Museum of Art, Athens GA
University of Illinois at Urbana-Champaign, Krannert Art Museum and Kinkead Pavilion, Champaign IL
University of Indianapolis, Christel DeHaan Fine Arts Gallery, Indianapolis IN
The University of Kentucky Art Museum, Lexington KY
University of Manchester, Whitworth Art Gallery, Manchester
University of Mary Washington, University of Mary Washington Galleries, Fredericksburg VA
University of Miami, Lowe Art Museum, Coral Gables FL
University of Nebraska-Lincoln, Great Plains Art Museum, Lincoln NE
University of Nevada, Reno, Sheppard Contemporary & University Galleries, Reno NV
University of New Mexico, The Harwood Museum of Art, Taos NM
University of Richmond, University Museums, Richmond VA
University of Saskatchewan, Diefenbaker Canada Centre, Saskatoon SK
University of Southern California, USC Fisher Museum of Art, Los Angeles CA
University of Texas at Austin, Blanton Museum of Art, Austin TX
University of Utah, Utah Museum of Fine Arts, Salt Lake City UT
University of Victoria, The Legacy Art Gallery, Victoria BC
University of Wisconsin-Madison, Chazen Museum of Art, Madison WI
Ursinus College, Philip & Muriel Berman Museum of Art, Collegeville PA
USS Constitution Museum, Boston MA
Vancouver Art Gallery, Vancouver BC
Vassar College, The Frances Lehman Loeb Art Center, Poughkeepsie NY
Vero Beach Museum of Art, Vero Beach FL
Vesterheim Norwegian-American Museum, Decorah IA
Victoria Mansion - Morse Libby House, Portland ME
Viridian Artists Inc, New York NY
Vorarlberg Museum, Bregenz
The Walker African American Museum & Research Center, Las Vegas NV
Walker Art Gallery, Liverpool
Walker Fine Art, Denver CO
The Wallace Collection, London

Warner House Association, MacPheadris-Warner House, Portsmouth NH
Washington & Lee University, Lee Chapel & Museum, Lexington VA
Waterworks Visual Arts Center, Salisbury NC
Westfries Museum, Hoorn
Westmoreland Museum of American Art, Greensburg PA
Whatcom Museum, Bellingham WA
White House, Washington DC
Wichita State University, Ulrich Museum of Art, Wichita KS
Wilfrid Laurier University, Robert Langen Art Gallery, Waterloo ON
Willard House & Clock Museum, Inc, North Grafton MA
Wiregrass Museum of Art, Dothan AL
Wisconsin Historical Society, Wisconsin Historical Museum, Madison WI
Woodlawn/The Pope-Leighey, Alexandria VA
Woodmere Art Museum Inc, Philadelphia PA
Wyoming State Museum, Cheyenne WY
Wyoming Trails Gallery, Wheatland WY
Yale University, Yale Center for British Art, New Haven CT
Yellowstone County Museum, Billings MT
Yokohama Museum of Art, Yokohama
Zigler Art Museum, Jennings LA

POSTERS

African American Atelier, Greensboro NC
African American Museum in Philadelphia, Philadelphia PA
Alaska State Museum, Juneau AK
Albertina Museum, Vienna
American Sport Art Museum and Archives, Daphne AL
American University, Museum at the Katzen, Washington DC
Amherst College, Mead Art Museum, Amherst MA
The Andy Warhol Museum, Pittsburgh PA
Art and History Museums - Maitland, Maitland FL
Art Without Walls Inc, Sayville NY
Arts Council of Fayetteville-Cumberland County, The Arts Center, Fayetteville NC
Asheville Art Museum, Asheville NC
Bangladesh National Museum, Dhaka
Besser Museum for Northeast Michigan, Alpena MI
Beverly Historical Society, Cabot, Hale & Balch House Museums, Beverly MA
Blanden Memorial Art Museum, Fort Dodge IA
Bone Creek Museum of Agrarian Art, David City NE
Booth Western Art Museum, Cartersville GA
Boston Public Library, Albert H Wiggin Gallery & Print Department, Boston MA
Botswana National Museum, Gaborone
Bucknell University, Edward & Marthann Samek Art Gallery, Lewisburg PA
The Buffalo Fine Arts Academy, Albright-Knox Art Gallery, Buffalo NY
Buffalo Niagara Heritage Village, Amherst NY
C W Post Campus of Long Island University, Hillwood Art Museum, Brookville NY
Canadian Museum of History, Gatineau QC
Canadian Museum of Nature, Musee Canadien de la Nature, Ottawa ON
Cartoon Art Museum, San Francisco CA
Cayuga Museum of History & Art, Auburn NY
Center for Puppetry Arts, Atlanta GA
Central United Methodist Church, Swords Into Plowshares Peace Center & Gallery, Detroit MI
Chicago Athenaeum, Museum of Architecture & Design, Galena IL
The Children's Museum of Indianapolis, Indianapolis IN
City of Cedar Falls, Iowa, James & Meryl Hearst Center for the Arts & Sculpture Garden, Cedar Falls IA
Clark Art Institute, Williamstown MA
Colgate University, Picker Art Gallery, Hamilton NY
College of William & Mary, Muscarelle Museum of Art, Williamsburg VA
The Columbus Museum, Columbus GA
Craft and Folk Art Museum (CAFAM), Los Angeles CA
Cripple Creek District Museum, Cripple Creek CO
Crocker Art Museum, Sacramento CA
Crook County Museum & Art Gallery, Sundance WY
Dartmouth College, Hood Museum of Art, Hanover NH
Dartmouth Heritage Museum, Dartmouth NS
Delaware Art Museum, Wilmington DE
Delaware Division of Historical & Cultural Affairs, Dover DE
Delta Blues Museum, Clarksdale MS
Department of Economic & Community Development, State of Connecticut DECD Eric Sloane Museum, Kent CT
Designmuseum Danmark, Danish Design Museum, Copenhagen
Detroit Institute of Arts, Detroit MI
Dickinson College, The Trout Gallery, Carlisle PA
Doncaster Museum and Art Gallery, Doncaster Yorks
Edward Hopper, Nyack NY
Ellen Noel Art Museum of the Permian Basin, Odessa TX
Erie County Historical Society, Erie PA
Evanston Historical Society, Charles Gates Dawes House, Evanston IL
Fairfield University, Art Museum, Fairfield CT
Fitton Center for Creative Arts, Hamilton OH
Folk Art Society of America, Richmond VA
Fort George G Meade Museum, Fort Meade MD
Fulton County Historical Society Inc, Fulton County Museum (Tetzlaff Reference Room), Rochester IN
Galerie Montcalm, Gatineau QC
Germantown Historical Society, Philadelphia PA
Greenville College, Richard W Bock Sculpture Collection, Almira College House, Greenville IL
Hammonds House Museum, Atlanta GA
Hancock Shaker Village, Inc, Pittsfield MA
Headquarters Fort Monroe, Dept of Army, Casemate Museum, Hampton VA
Henry County Museum & Cultural Arts Center, Clinton MO
Henry Sheldon Museum of Vermont History and Research Center, Middlebury VT
Hidalgo County Historical Museum, Edinburg TX
Hillwood Museum & Gardens Foundation, Hillwood Estate Museum & Gardens, Washington DC
The History Center in Tompkins County, Ithaca NY
Hunter Museum of American Art, Chattanooga TN
Illinois State Museum, ISM Lockport Gallery, Chicago Gallery & Southern Illinois Art Gallery, Springfield IL
Imperial War Museum London, London
Independence Historical Museum & Art Center, Independence KS
Independence Seaport Museum, Philadelphia PA
Institute of Puerto Rican Culture, Museo Fuerte Conde de Mirasol, Vieques PR
International Clown Hall of Fame & Research Center, Inc, West Allis WI
Iowa State University, Brunnier Art Museum, Ames IA
Iroquois Indian Museum, Howes Cave NY
The Israel Museum, Jerusalem, Jerusalem
JMW Turner Museum, Sarasota FL
Joe Gish's Old West Museum, Fredericksburg TX
Juniata College Museum of Art, Huntingdon PA
Kenosha Public Museums, Kenosha WI
Kirkland Museum of Fine & Decorative Art, Denver CO
La Casa del Libro Museum, San Juan PR
Lac du Flambeau Band of Lake Superior Chippewa Indians, George W Brown Jr Ojibwe Museum & Cultural Center, Lac Du Flambeau WI
Lafayette Science Museum & Planetarium, Lafayette LA
Latino Art Museum, Pomona CA
Livingston County Historical Society, Museum, Geneseo NY
The Long Island Museum of American Art, History & Carriages, Stony Brook NY
Longview Museum of Fine Art, Longview TX
Louise Hopkins Underwood Center for the Arts, Lubbock TX
Louisiana Department of Culture, Recreation & Tourism, Louisiana State Museum, New Orleans LA
The Mariners' Museum, Newport News VA
Marquette University, Haggerty Museum of Art, Milwaukee WI
McLean County Historical Society, McLean County Museum of History, Bloomington IL
Medina Railroad Museum, Medina NY
Meredith College, Frankie G Weems Gallery & Rotunda Gallery, Raleigh NC
Miami-Dade College, MDC Museum of Art & Design, Miami FL
Minnesota Museum of American Art, Saint Paul MN
Minot State University, Northwest Art Center, Minot ND
Mobile Museum of Art, Mobile AL
Montana State University, Helen E Copeland Gallery, Bozeman MT
Moravska Galerie v Brne, Moravian Gallery in Brno, Brno
Musee Regional de lu Cote-Nord, Sept-Iles QC
Museo De Las Americas, Denver CO
Museu Nacional D'Art De Catalunya, Catalona National Museum of Art, Barcelona
Museum of Art - Deland FL, Inc, Deland FL
The Museum of Arts & Sciences Inc, Daytona Beach FL
Museum of Modern Art, New York NY
Museum of York County, Rock Hill SC
Museum zu Allerheiligen, Schaffhausen
Muzej Moderne I Suvremene Umjetnosti, Museum of Modern and Contemporary Art, Rijeka
Muzej za Umjetnost i Obrt, Museum of Arts & Crafts, Zagreb
Muzeul de Istorie Nationala Si Arheologie Constanta, National History & Archaeology Museum, Constanta
Muzeul National de Arta al Romaniei, National Museum of Art of Romania, Bucharest
Muzeum Narodowe w Poznaniu, National Museum in Poznan, Poznan
National Baseball Hall of Fame & Museum, Cooperstown NY
The National Museum of Modern Art, Tokyo, Tokyo
The National Shrine of the North American Martyrs, Fultonville NY
Naval Historical Center, National Museum of the US Navy, Washington DC
Nebraska State Capitol, Lincoln NE
Nelson Mandela Metropolitan Art Museum, Port Elizabeth
Neue Galerie New York, New York NY
New Britain Museum of American Art, New Britain CT
New Jersey Historical Society, Newark NJ
New Visions Gallery, Inc, Marshfield WI
Niigata Prefectural Museum of Modern Art, Nagaoka
Norman Rockwell Museum of Vermont, Rutland VT
Ogden Museum of Southern Art, University of New Orleans, New Orleans LA
Panhandle-Plains Historical Museum, Canyon TX
Pennsylvania Academy of the Fine Arts, Philadelphia PA
Pennsylvania Historical & Museum Commission, Railroad Museum of Pennsylvania, Strasburg PA
Peoria Riverfront Museum, Peoria IL
Piedmont Arts Association, Martinsville VA
Plains Art Museum, Fargo ND
Pump House Center for the Arts, Chillicothe OH
Queens College, City University of New York, Godwin-Ternbach Museum, Flushing NY
Radio-Canada SRC CBC, Georges Goguen CBC Art Gallery, Moncton NB
Rawls Museum Arts, Courtland VA
Saginaw Art Museum, Saginaw MI
Slovenska Narodna Galeria, Slovak National Gallery, Bratislava
The Society of the Cincinnati at Anderson House, Washington DC
South Dakota State University, South Dakota Art Museum, Brookings SD
South Street Seaport Museum, New York NY
The Speed Art Museum, Louisville KY
Spertus Institute of Jewish Studies, Chicago IL
St Mary's College of Maryland, The Dwight Frederick Boyden Gallery, St Mary's City MD
Staatliche Museen zu Berlin Stiftung Preussischer Kulturbesitz, National Museums in Berlin, Prussian Cultural Heritage Foundation, Berlin
State University of New York at New Paltz, Samuel Dorsky Museum of Art, New Paltz NY
State University of New York at Oswego, Tyler Art Gallery, Oswego NY
Staten Island Museum, Staten Island NY
Stone Quarry Hill Art Park, Winner Gallery, Cazenovia NY
Stratford Historical Society, Catharine B Mitchell Museum, Stratford CT
Tver Regional Art Gallery, Tver

Ukrainian Canadian Archives & Museum of Alberta, Edmonton AB
United Society of Shakers, Shaker Museum, New Gloucester ME
United States Figure Skating Association, World Figure Skating Museum & Hall of Fame, Colorado Springs CO
United States Military Academy, West Point Museum, West Point NY
University of California, Davis, Jan Shrem and Maria Manetti Shrem Museum of Art, Davis CA
University of Georgia, Georgia Museum of Art, Athens GA
University of Illinois at Urbana-Champaign, Krannert Art Museum and Kinkead Pavilion, Champaign IL
The University of Kentucky Art Museum, Lexington KY
University of Nebraska-Lincoln, Great Plains Art Museum, Lincoln NE
University of Saskatchewan, Diefenbaker Canada Centre, Saskatoon SK
University of Wisconsin-Madison, Chazen Museum of Art, Madison WI
Ursinus College, Philip & Muriel Berman Museum of Art, Collegeville PA
USS Constitution Museum, Boston MA
Volcano Art Center Gallery, Hawaii Volcanoes National Park HI
The Walker African American Museum & Research Center, Las Vegas NV
Waterworks Visual Arts Center, Salisbury NC
World Erotic Art Museum, Miami Beach FL

POTTERY

Academy of the New Church, Glencairn Museum, Bryn Athyn PA
Acropolis Museum, Athens
Alaska State Museum, Juneau AK
Albany Institute of History & Art, Albany NY
Albuquerque Museum of Art & History, Albuquerque NM
Alexandria Museum of Art, Alexandria LA
American Folk Art Museum, New York NY
American Sport Art Museum and Archives, Daphne AL
Amherst College, Mead Art Museum, Amherst MA
Arizona Historical Society-Yuma, Sanguinetti House Museum & Garden, Yuma AZ
Arnold Mikelson Mind & Matter Art Gallery, Surrey BC
Arnot Art Museum, Elmira NY
Art and History Museums - Maitland, Maitland FL
The Art Association of Jacksonville, The David Strawn Art Gallery, Jacksonville IL
The Art Center of Waco, Waco TX
Art Community Center, Art Center of Corpus Christi, Corpus Christi TX
Art Gallery of Bancroft Inc, Bancroft ON
The Art Gallery of Cornwall, Cornwall ON
Art Gallery of Nova Scotia, Halifax NS
Art Gallery of South Australia, Adelaide
Art Museum of Greater Lafayette, Lafayette IN
Art Without Walls Inc, Sayville NY
Artesia Historical Museum and Art Center, Artesia NM
Arts Council of Fayetteville-Cumberland County, The Arts Center, Fayetteville NC
Asheville Art Museum, Asheville NC
Asian Art Museum of San Francisco, Chong-Moon Lee Ctr for Asian Art and Culture, San Francisco CA
Baker University, Old Castle Museum, Baldwin City KS
Bangladesh National Museum, Dhaka
Barnes Foundation, Merion PA
Baroda Museum and Picture Gallery, Vadodara
Bellevue Arts Museum, Bellevue WA
Belskie Museum, Closter NJ
Bennington Museum, Bennington VT
Besser Museum for Northeast Michigan, Alpena MI
Beverly Historical Society, Cabot, Hale & Balch House Museums, Beverly MA
Billie Trimble Chandler, Texas State Museum of Asian Cultures, Corpus Christi TX
Birmingham Museum of Art, Birmingham AL
Blowing Rock Art and History Museum, Blowing Rock NC
Bone Creek Museum of Agrarian Art, David City NE
Booth Western Art Museum, Cartersville GA
Botswana National Museum, Gaborone
Brevard College, Spiers Gallery, Brevard NC
Brown University, Haffenreffer Museum of Anthropology, Providence RI
Burke Arts Council, Jailhouse Galleries, Morganton NC
Bush-Holley Historic Site & Storehouse Gallery, Greenwich Historical Society, Cos Cob CT
C M Russell Museum, Great Falls MT
Cambridge Museum, Cambridge NE
Cameron Art Museum, Wilmington NC
Canadian Clay and Glass Gallery, Waterloo ON
Canadian Museum of History, Gatineau QC
Cape Ann Museum, Gloucester MA
Carlsbad Museum & Art Center, Carlsbad NM
Cedar Rapids Museum of Art, Cedar Rapids IA
Center for the Arts Piper Gallery, Crested Butte CO
Central United Methodist Church, Swords Into Plowshares Peace Center & Gallery, Detroit MI
Chatham Historical Society, The Atwood House Museum, Chatham MA
The Children's Museum of Indianapolis, Indianapolis IN
City of Atlanta, Chastain Arts Center & Gallery, Atlanta GA
City of Austin Parks & Recreation, O Henry Museum, Austin TX
City of Cedar Falls, Iowa, James & Meryl Hearst Center for the Arts & Sculpture Garden, Cedar Falls IA
City of Fremont, Olive Hyde Art Gallery, Fremont CA
City of Gainesville, Thomas Center Galleries - Cultural Affairs, Gainesville FL
City of Pittsfield Office of Cultural Development, Lichtenstein Center for the Arts, Pittsfield MA
City of Springdale, Shiloh Museum of Ozark History, Springdale AR
Clinton Art Association, River Arts Center, Clinton IA
Coastal Arts League Museum, Half Moon Bay CA
College of William & Mary, Muscarelle Museum of Art, Williamsburg VA
Colonial Williamsburg Foundation, Abby Aldrich Rockefeller Folk Art Museum, Williamsburg VA
Colonial Williamsburg Foundation, DeWitt Wallace Decorative Arts Museum, Williamsburg VA
The Columbus Museum, Columbus GA
Columbus Museum of Art, Columbus OH
Craft and Folk Art Museum (CAFAM), Los Angeles CA
Cranbrook Art Museum, Bloomfield Hills MI
Cripple Creek District Museum, Cripple Creek CO
Crocker Art Museum, Sacramento CA
DAR Museum, National Society Daughters of the American Revolution, Washington DC
Dartmouth Heritage Museum, Dartmouth NS
Deines Cultural Center, Russell KS
Delta Blues Museum, Clarksdale MS
Deming-Luna Mimbres Museum, Deming NM
Denver Art Museum, Denver CO
Designmuseum Danmark, Danish Design Museum, Copenhagen
Detroit Institute of Arts, Detroit MI
Dickinson College, The Trout Gallery, Carlisle PA
Dixie State University, Sears Art Museum Gallery, Saint George UT
Doncaster Museum and Art Gallery, Doncaster Yorks
Dublin Arts Council, Dublin OH
Eiteljorg Museum of American Indians & Western Art, Indianapolis IN
Emory University, Michael C Carlos Museum, Atlanta GA
Erie Art Museum, Erie PA
Erie County Historical Society, Erie PA
Favell Museum of Western Art & Indian Artifacts, Klamath Falls OR
Fetherston Foundation, Packwood House Museum, Lewisburg PA
Fitton Center for Creative Arts, Hamilton OH
Five Civilized Tribes Museum, Muskogee OK
Flint Institute of Arts, Flint MI
Florence County Museum, Florence SC
Folk Art Society of America, Richmond VA
The Frank Phillips Foundation Inc, Woolaroc Museum, Bartlesville OK
Frontier Times Museum, Bandera TX
Fuller Craft Museum, Brockton MA
Fulton County Historical Society Inc, Fulton County Museum (Tetzlaff Reference Room), Rochester IN
Gadsden Museum, Mesilla NM
Gadsden Museum of Art, Gadsden AL
Galerie Montcalm, Gatineau QC
Gallery One Visual Arts Center, Ellensburg WA
Genesee Country Village & Museum, John L Wehle Art Gallery, Mumford NY
George Phippen, Phippen Museum - Art of the American West, Prescott AZ
Glasgow University, The Hunterian, Glasgow
Glenwood Center for the Arts, Glenwood Springs CO
Grand Rapids Public Museum, Grand Rapids MI
Greene County Historical Society, Bronck Museum, Coxsackie NY
Grossmont Community College, Hyde Art Gallery, El Cajon CA
Headquarters Fort Monroe, Dept of Army, Casemate Museum, Hampton VA
Heard Museum, Phoenix AZ
Hecht Museum, Haifa
Henry County Museum & Cultural Arts Center, Clinton MO
Henry Sheldon Museum of Vermont History and Research Center, Middlebury VT
Heritage Center, Inc, Pine Ridge SD
Hermitage Museum & Gardens, Norfolk VA
Hershey Museum, Hershey PA
Hickory Museum of Art, Inc, Hickory NC
Hill-Stead Museum, Farmington CT
Hillwood Museum & Gardens Foundation, Hillwood Estate Museum & Gardens, Washington DC
Historic Cherry Hill, Albany NY
Historic Deerfield, Inc, Deerfield MA
Historic Hudson Valley, Pocantico Hills NY
Historic Huguenot Street, New Paltz NY
Historical Society of Cheshire County, Keene NH
Holter Museum of Art, Helena MT
Hui No'eau Visual Arts Center, Gallery and Gift Shop, Makawao Maui HI
Hunter Museum of American Art, Chattanooga TN
Illinois State Museum, ISM Lockport Gallery, Chicago Gallery & Southern Illinois Art Gallery, Springfield IL
Imperial Calcasieu Museum, Gibson-Barham Gallery, Lake Charles LA
Independence Historical Museum & Art Center, Independence KS
Institute of Contemporary Art, Los Angeles, Los Angeles CA
Iowa State University, Brunnier Art Museum, Ames IA
Iredell Museums, Statesville NC
Iroquois Indian Museum, Howes Cave NY
The Israel Museum, Jerusalem, Jerusalem
John B Aird Gallery, Toronto ON
Johns Hopkins University, Evergreen Museum & Library, Baltimore MD
Johnson-Humrickhouse Museum, Coshocton OH
Joslyn Art Museum, Omaha NE
Kenosha Public Museums, Kenosha WI
Kentucky Museum of Art and Craft, Louisville KY
Kereszteny Muzeum, Christian Museum, Esztergom
Kings County Historical Society & Museum, Hampton NB
Kirkland Museum of Fine & Decorative Art, Denver CO
Klein Museum, Mobridge SD
Koochiching Museums, International Falls MN
Koshare Indian Museum, Inc, La Junta CO
Kunsthistorisches Museum Wien, Museum of Fine Arts, Vienna
LA County Museum of Art, Los Angeles CA
La Salle University Art Museum, Philadelphia PA
Lafayette College, Lafayette College Art Galleries, Easton PA
LaGrange Art Museum, LaGrange GA
Lalit Kala Akademi Rabindra Bhavan Art Galleries, National Academy of Art, New Delhi, New Delhi
Latino Art Museum, Pomona CA
Lighthouse ArtCenter Museum & School of Art, Tequesta FL
Lightner Museum, Saint Augustine FL
Lillian & Coleman Taube Museum of Art, Minot ND
Lincolnshire County Council, Library & Heritage Services, Lincoln
Lincolnshire County Council, The Collection: Art & Archaeology in Lincolnshire, Lincoln
Livingston County Historical Society, Museum, Geneseo NY
The Loading Dock Gallery, Lowell MA
The Long Island Museum of American Art, History & Carriages, Stony Brook NY
Longfellow-Evangeline State Commemorative Area, Saint Martinville LA
Longue Vue House & Gardens, New Orleans LA

Louise Hopkins Underwood Center for the Arts, Lubbock TX
Louisiana Arts & Science Museum, Baton Rouge LA
Louisiana Department of Culture, Recreation & Tourism, Louisiana State Museum, New Orleans LA
Loyola University Chicago, Loyola University Museum of Art, Chicago IL
Madison Museum of Fine Art, Madison GA
The Mariners' Museum, Newport News VA
Maryland Historical Society, Museum of Maryland History, Baltimore MD
Massillon Museum, Massillon OH
McDowell House & Apothecary Shop, Danville KY
McLean County Historical Society, McLean County Museum of History, Bloomington IL
McPherson Museum and Arts Foundation, McPherson KS
Mennello Museum of American Art, Orlando FL
Meridian Museum of Art, Meridian MS
Mesa Arts Center, Mesa Contemporary Arts Museum, Mesa AZ
Metropolitan Museum of Manila, Manila
The Mexican Museum, San Francisco CA
Miami-Dade College, MDC Museum of Art & Design, Miami FL
Middle Border Museum & Oscar Howe Art Center, Mitchell SD
Midwest Museum of American Art, Elkhart IN
Millicent Rogers Museum, Taos NM
Mills College Art Museum, Oakland CA
Minnesota Museum of American Art, Saint Paul MN
Minot State University, Northwest Art Center, Minot ND
The Mint Museum, Mint Museum of Craft & Design, Charlotte NC
Mississippi River Museum at Mud-Island River Park, Memphis TN
Mobile Museum of Art, Mobile AL
Montclair Art Museum, Montclair NJ
Moravian Historical Society, Nazareth PA
Moravska Galerie v Brne, Moravian Gallery in Brno, Brno
Morehead State University, Kentucky Folk Art Center, Morehead KY
Morris Museum, Morristown NJ
Morris Museum of Art, Augusta GA
Mount Vernon Hotel Museum & Garden, New York NY
MTG Hawkes Bay, Napier
Muscatine Art Center, Muscatine IA
Musee des Augustines de l'Hotel Dieu de Quebec, Quebec QC
Musee des Beaux-Arts de Tours, Museum of Fine Arts, Tours
Musee Regional de lu Cote-Nord, Sept-Iles QC
Musee Regional de Vaudreuil-Soulanges, Vaudreuil-Dorion QC
Musees Royaux d'Art et d'Histoire, Royal Museums of Art and History, Brussels
Museo De Las Americas, Denver CO
The Museum, Greenwood SC
Museum De Lakenhal, Leiden
Museum of Art & History, Santa Cruz, Santa Cruz CA
Museum of Arts & Design, New York NY
The Museum of Arts & Sciences Inc, Daytona Beach FL
Museum of NC Traditional Pottery, Seagrove NC
Museum of Northern Arizona, Flagstaff AZ
Museum of Northwest Art, La Conner WA
Museum of the Southwest, Midland TX
Museum Prinsenhof Delft, Delft
Museum zu Allerheiligen, Schaffhausen
Muzej za Umjetnost i Obrt, Museum of Arts & Crafts, Zagreb
Muzeul de Istorie Nationala Si Arheologie Constanta, National History & Archaeology Museum, Constanta
Muzeul National de Arta al Romaniei, National Museum of Art of Romania, Bucharest
Muzeum Narodowe w Poznaniu, National Museum in Poznan, Poznan
Nanticoke Indian Museum, Millsboro DE
National Art Museum of Moldova, Chisinau
National Baseball Hall of Fame & Museum, Cooperstown NY
National Museum & Art Gallery of Trinidad and Tobago, Port of Spain
National Museum of Ceramic Art, Baltimore MD
National Museum of the American Indian, George Gustav Heye Center, New York NY
National Museums Scotland, National Museum of Scotland, Edinburgh
National Palace Museum, Taipei
National Society of Colonial Dames of America in the State of Maryland, Mount Clare Museum House, Baltimore MD
Nelson Mandela Metropolitan Art Museum, Port Elizabeth
The Nelson-Atkins Museum of Art, Kansas City MO
New Visions Gallery, Inc, Marshfield WI
Niigata Prefectural Museum of Modern Art, Nagaoka
North End Gallery, Leonardtown MD
Norwich Free Academy, Slater Memorial Museum, Norwich CT
Noyes Art Gallery, Lincoln NE
Ogden Museum of Southern Art, University of New Orleans, New Orleans LA
Ohara Museum of Art, Kurashiki
The Ohio Historical Society, Inc, Campus Martius Museum & Ohio River Museum, Marietta OH
Ohio History Connection, National Road-Zane Grey Museum, Norwich OH
Okefenokee Heritage Center, Inc, Waycross GA
Olana State Historic Site, Hudson NY
The Old Jail Art Center, Albany TX
Oshkosh Public Museum & Library, Oshkosh WI
Ouachita River Art Gallery, Monroe LA
Owensboro Museum of Fine Art, Owensboro KY
Palm Beach County Parks & Recreation Department, Morikami Museum & Japanese Gardens, Delray Beach FL
Panhandle-Plains Historical Museum, Canyon TX
Peoria Historical Society, Peoria IL
Piedmont Arts Association, Martinsville VA
Pioneer Historical Museum of South Dakota, Hot Springs SD
Plains Art Museum, Fargo ND
Pueblo Museum, Desert Hot Springs CA
Pump House Center for the Arts, Chillicothe OH
Queen Victoria Museum and Art Gallery, Launceston TAS
Queens College, City University of New York, Godwin-Ternbach Museum, Flushing NY
Rawls Museum Arts, Courtland VA
Reading Public Museum, Reading PA
Rensselaer County Historical Society, Hart-Cluett Mansion, 1827, Troy NY
The Rockwell Museum, Corning NY
Roswell Museum & Art Center, Roswell NM
Saginaw Art Museum, Saginaw MI
Saint Bonaventure University, Regina A Quick Center for the Arts, Saint Bonaventure NY
Saint Olaf College, Flaten Art Museum, Northfield MN
San Antonio Museum of Art, San Antonio TX
The San Joaquin Pioneer & Historical Society, The Haggin Museum, Stockton CA
Schweinfurth Art Center, Auburn NY
Seneca-Iroquois National Museum, Salamanca NY
Shirley Plantation Foundation, Charles City VA
Society for Contemporary Craft, Pittsburgh PA
South Carolina Artisans Center, Walterboro SC
South Dakota State University, South Dakota Art Museum, Brookings SD
Southern Baptist Theological Seminary, Joseph A Callaway Archaeological Museum, Louisville KY
Spartanburg Art Museum, Spartanburg SC
The Speed Art Museum, Louisville KY
Springfield Art Museum, Springfield MO
Springville Museum of Art, Springville UT
Spruce Forest Artisan Village, Grantsville MD
Staatliche Museen zu Berlin Stiftung Preussischer Kulturbesitz, National Museums in Berlin, Prussian Cultural Heritage Foundation, Berlin
Stanford University, Cantor Arts Center at Stanford University, Stanford CA
State University of New York at Geneseo, Bertha V B Lederer Gallery, Geneseo NY
State University of New York at New Paltz, Samuel Dorsky Museum of Art, New Paltz NY
State University of New York at Oswego, Tyler Art Gallery, Oswego NY
Staten Island Museum, Staten Island NY
Stone Quarry Hill Art Park, Winner Gallery, Cazenovia NY
Strasburg Museum, Strasburg VA
Suan Pakkad Palace Museum, Bangkok
The Summit County Historical Society of Akron, OH, Akron OH
Suomen Kansallismuseo, National Museum of Finland, Helsinki
Swedish American Museum, Chicago IL
Tallahassee Museum of History & Natural Science, Tallahassee FL
Taos Historic Museums, Ernest Blumenschein Home & Studio, Taos NM
Temiskaming Art Gallery, Haileybury ON
Tokyo National Museum, Tokyo
Topeka & Shawnee County Public Library, Alice C Sabatini Gallery, Topeka KS
Tubman African American Museum, Macon GA
Tucson Museum of Art and Historic Block, Tucson AZ
Tver Regional Art Gallery, Tver
Tyne and Wear Archives & Museums, Sunderland Museum & Winter Gardens, Sunderland
Ukrainian Canadian Archives & Museum of Alberta, Edmonton AB
The Ukrainian Museum, New York NY
United Society of Shakers, Shaker Museum, New Gloucester ME
University of California, Berkeley, Phoebe Apperson Hearst Museum of Anthropology, Berkeley CA
University of Florida, Samuel P Harn Museum of Art, Gainesville FL
University of Georgia, Georgia Museum of Art, Athens GA
University of Illinois at Urbana-Champaign, Krannert Art Museum and Kinkead Pavilion, Champaign IL
The University of Kentucky Art Museum, Lexington KY
University of Miami, Lowe Art Museum, Coral Gables FL
University of Michigan, Kelsey Museum of Archaeology, Ann Arbor MI
University of Minnesota, Goldstein Museum of Design, Saint Paul MN
University of Minnesota Duluth, Tweed Museum of Art, Duluth MN
University of Nevada, Reno, Sheppard Contemporary & University Galleries, Reno NV
University of New Mexico, The Harwood Museum of Art, Taos NM
University of Notre Dame, Snite Museum of Art, Notre Dame IN
University of Richmond, University Museums, Richmond VA
University of Wisconsin-Madison, Chazen Museum of Art, Madison WI
Ursinus College, Philip & Muriel Berman Museum of Art, Collegeville PA
Valley Art Gallery, Forest Grove OR
Venice Art Center, Venice FL
Vesterheim Norwegian-American Museum, Decorah IA
Villa Terrace Decorative Arts Museum, Milwaukee WI
Virginia Museum of Fine Arts, Richmond VA
Volcano Art Center Gallery, Hawaii Volcanoes National Park HI
The Walker African American Museum & Research Center, Las Vegas NV
Walker Art Gallery, Liverpool
Walker Fine Art, Denver CO
Walter Anderson Museum of Art, Ocean Springs MS
Warner House Association, MacPheadris-Warner House, Portsmouth NH
Waterworks Visual Arts Center, Salisbury NC
Westmoreland Museum of American Art, Greensburg PA
Wheelwright Museum of the American Indian, Santa Fe NM
Wilkes Art Gallery, North Wilkesboro NC
Winston-Salem State University, Diggs Gallery, Winston-Salem NC
Wiregrass Museum of Art, Dothan AL
Wyoming Trails Gallery, Wheatland WY
Yellowstone County Museum, Billings MT
Yokohama Museum of Art, Yokohama
Zigler Art Museum, Jennings LA

PRE-COLUMBIAN ART

Americas Society Art Gallery, New York NY
Amherst College, Mead Art Museum, Amherst MA
Anchorage Museum at Rasmuson Center, Anchorage AK
Arnot Art Museum, Elmira NY
The Art Association of Jacksonville, The David Strawn Art Gallery, Jacksonville IL
Art Without Walls Inc, Sayville NY

Aurora University, Schingoethe Center for Native American Cultures & The Schingoethe Art Gallery, Aurora IL
The Baltimore Museum of Art, Baltimore MD
Bangladesh National Museum, Dhaka
Birmingham Museum of Art, Birmingham AL
Blanden Memorial Art Museum, Fort Dodge IA
Bowers Museum, Santa Ana CA
Brandeis University, Rose Art Museum, Waltham MA
Bruce Museum, Inc, Greenwich CT
C M Russell Museum, Great Falls MT
C W Post Campus of Long Island University, Hillwood Art Museum, Brookville NY
California State University, East Bay, C E Smith Museum of Anthropology, Hayward CA
Capital University, Schumacher Gallery, Columbus OH
Carlsbad Museum & Art Center, Carlsbad NM
Center for Puppetry Arts, Atlanta GA
The Children's Museum of Indianapolis, Indianapolis IN
Cincinnati Art Museum, Cincinnati Art Museum, Cincinnati OH
City of El Paso, El Paso TX
Colgate University, Picker Art Gallery, Hamilton NY
The Columbus Museum, Columbus GA
Columbus Museum of Art, Columbus OH
Concordia University, Leonard & Bina Ellen Art Gallery, Montreal QC
Cornell Museum of Art and American Culture, Delray Beach FL
Cornell University, Herbert F Johnson Museum of Art, Ithaca NY
Dartmouth College, Hood Museum of Art, Hanover NH
Denver Art Museum, Denver CO
Detroit Institute of Arts, Detroit MI
Detroit Zoological Institute, Wildlife Interpretive Gallery, Royal Oak MI
Dickinson College, The Trout Gallery, Carlisle PA
Dumbarton Oaks, Dumbarton Oaks Museum, Washington DC
Emory University, Michael C Carlos Museum, Atlanta GA
Erie Art Museum, Erie PA
Everhart Museum, Scranton PA
Fairbanks Museum & Planetarium, Saint Johnsbury VT
Fetherston Foundation, Packwood House Museum, Lewisburg PA
Fitchburg Art Museum, Fitchburg MA
Fitton Center for Creative Arts, Hamilton OH
Flint Institute of Arts, Flint MI
Florence County Museum, Florence SC
Florida State University and Central Florida Community College, The Appleton Museum of Art, Ocala FL
Fuller Craft Museum, Brockton MA
Grand Rapids Public Museum, Grand Rapids MI
Henry County Museum & Cultural Arts Center, Clinton MO
Herrett Center for Arts & Sciences, Jean B King Art Gallery, Twin Falls ID
Hill-Stead Museum, Farmington CT
Historisches und Volkerkundemuseum, Museum of History and Ethnology, St Gallen
Honolulu Museum of Art, Honolulu HI
Illinois State Museum, ISM Lockport Gallery, Chicago Gallery & Southern Illinois Art Gallery, Springfield IL
Institute of Puerto Rican Culture, Museo Fuerte Conde de Mirasol, Vieques PR
Iredell Museums, Statesville NC
The Israel Museum, Jerusalem, Jerusalem
Jacksonville University, Alexander Brest Museum & Gallery, Jacksonville FL
Kalamazoo Institute of Arts, Kalamazoo MI
Kenosha Public Museums, Kenosha WI
Kimbell Art Foundation, Kimbell Art Museum, Fort Worth TX
La Salle University Art Museum, Philadelphia PA
Latino Art Museum, Pomona CA
Mabee-Gerrer Museum of Art, Shawnee OK
The Mariners' Museum, Newport News VA
The Mexican Museum, San Francisco CA
Miami-Dade College, MDC Museum of Art & Design, Miami FL
Millicent Rogers Museum, Taos NM
Minneapolis Institute of Art, Minneapolis MN
Mississippi Museum of Art, Jackson MS
Montana State University, Helen E Copeland Gallery, Bozeman MT
Musee d'art de Joliette, Joliette QC
Musees Royaux d'Art et d'Histoire, Royal Museums of Art and History, Brussels
Museum of Art, Fort Lauderdale, Fort Lauderdale FL
The Museum of Arts & Sciences Inc, Daytona Beach FL
Museum of Contemporary Art Jacksonville, Jacksonville FL
Museum of Fine Arts, Saint Petersburg, Florida, Inc, Saint Petersburg FL
Museum of the Southwest, Midland TX
Museum zu Allerheiligen, Schaffhausen
National Museum & Art Gallery of Trinidad and Tobago, Port of Spain
National Museum of the American Indian, George Gustav Heye Center, New York NY
National Museum of Wildlife Art of the Unites States, Jackson WY
New Orleans Museum of Art, New Orleans LA
Niagara University, Castellani Art Museum, Niagara NY
North Carolina Museum of Art, Raleigh NC
The Old Jail Art Center, Albany TX
Omniplex Science Museum, Oklahoma City OK
Palm Springs Art Museum, Palm Springs CA
Panhandle-Plains Historical Museum, Canyon TX
Polk Museum of Art, Lakeland FL
Portland Art Museum, Portland OR
Purdue University Galleries, West Lafayette IN
Queens College, City University of New York, Godwin-Ternbach Museum, Flushing NY
Riverside Metropolitan Museum, Riverside CA
Roswell Museum & Art Center, Roswell NM
Royal Ontario Museum, Toronto ON
Saint Bonaventure University, Regina A Quick Center for the Arts, Saint Bonaventure NY
Saint Mary's College of California, Museum of Art, Moraga CA
Saint Olaf College, Flaten Art Museum, Northfield MN
San Antonio Museum of Art, San Antonio TX
The San Joaquin Pioneer & Historical Society, The Haggin Museum, Stockton CA
Scripps College, Ruth Chandler Williamson Gallery, Claremont CA
Sheldon Art Galleries, Saint Louis MO
Staatliche Museen zu Berlin Stiftung Preussischer Kulturbesitz, National Museums in Berlin, Prussian Cultural Heritage Foundation, Berlin
Stanford University, Cantor Arts Center at Stanford University, Stanford CA
State University of New York at New Paltz, Samuel Dorsky Museum of Art, New Paltz NY
Staten Island Museum, Staten Island NY
Stone Quarry Hill Art Park, Winner Gallery, Cazenovia NY
Tucson Museum of Art and Historic Block, Tucson AZ
University of California, Berkeley, Phoebe Apperson Hearst Museum of Anthropology, Berkeley CA
University of Florida, Samuel P Harn Museum of Art, Gainesville FL
University of Illinois at Urbana-Champaign, Krannert Art Museum and Kinkead Pavilion, Champaign IL
The University of Kentucky Art Museum, Lexington KY
University of Notre Dame, Snite Museum of Art, Notre Dame IN
University of Richmond, University Museums, Richmond VA
University of Utah, Utah Museum of Fine Arts, Salt Lake City UT
University of Wisconsin-Madison, Chazen Museum of Art, Madison WI
The Walker African American Museum & Research Center, Las Vegas NV
Wheaton College, Beard and Weil Galleries, Norton MA
Wichita Art Museum, Wichita KS
Wilkes Art Gallery, North Wilkesboro NC
Worcester Art Museum, Worcester MA
World Erotic Art Museum, Miami Beach FL

PRIMITIVE ART

Academy of the New Church, Glencairn Museum, Bryn Athyn PA
Alaska Heritage Museum at Wells Fargo, Anchorage AK
Alton Museum of History & Art, Inc, Alton IL
Anchorage Museum at Rasmuson Center, Anchorage AK
Art Gallery of Greater Victoria, Victoria BC
The Art Museum of Eastern Idaho, Idaho Falls ID
Artesia Historical Museum and Art Center, Artesia NM
Augustana University, Eide-Dalrymple Gallery, Sioux Falls SD
Bangladesh National Museum, Dhaka
Birmingham Museum of Art, Birmingham AL
Bone Creek Museum of Agrarian Art, David City NE
Botswana National Museum, Gaborone
Bowdoin College, Peary-MacMillan Arctic Museum, Brunswick ME
Brown University, Haffenreffer Museum of Anthropology, Providence RI
Canadian Museum of History, Gatineau QC
Capital University, Schumacher Gallery, Columbus OH
Carson County Square House Museum, Panhandle TX
City of Fayette, Alabama, Fayette Art Museum, Fayette AL
City of Springdale, Shiloh Museum of Ozark History, Springdale AR
Colgate University, Picker Art Gallery, Hamilton NY
Colonial Williamsburg Foundation, Abby Aldrich Rockefeller Folk Art Museum, Williamsburg VA
The Columbus Museum, Columbus GA
Cornell University, Herbert F Johnson Museum of Art, Ithaca NY
Craft and Folk Art Museum (CAFAM), Los Angeles CA
Cripple Creek District Museum, Cripple Creek CO
Crocker Art Museum, Sacramento CA
Davidson College, William H Van Every Jr & Edward M Smith Galleries, Davidson NC
Delta Blues Museum, Clarksdale MS
Dickinson College, The Trout Gallery, Carlisle PA
Field Museum, Chicago IL
Fitton Center for Creative Arts, Hamilton OH
Florence County Museum, Florence SC
Folk Art Society of America, Richmond VA
Galerie Montcalm, Gatineau QC
Heard Museum, Phoenix AZ
Heritage Museums & Gardens, Sandwich MA
Hermitage Museum & Gardens, Norfolk VA
Hickory Museum of Art, Inc, Hickory NC
Illinois Historic Preservation Agency, Bishop Hill State Historic Site, Bishop Hill IL
Illinois State Museum, ISM Lockport Gallery, Chicago Gallery & Southern Illinois Art Gallery, Springfield IL
Independence Historical Museum & Art Center, Independence KS
Indiana Landmarks, Morris-Butler House, Indianapolis IN
Intuit: The Center for Intuitive & Outsider Art, Chicago IL
Iredell Museums, Statesville NC
Kenosha Public Museums, Kenosha WI
Kentucky Museum of Art and Craft, Louisville KY
Lafayette Science Museum & Planetarium, Lafayette LA
Louisiana Department of Culture, Recreation & Tourism, Louisiana State Museum, New Orleans LA
Mabee-Gerrer Museum of Art, Shawnee OK
Macau Museum of Art, NAPE
The Mariners' Museum, Newport News VA
The Metropolitan Museum of Art, New York NY
Midwest Museum of American Art, Elkhart IN
Mississippi Museum of Art, Jackson MS
Missoula Art Museum, Missoula MT
Moderna Galerija, Modern Gallery - National Museum of Modern Art, Zagreb
Morehead State University, Kentucky Folk Art Center, Morehead KY
Morris Museum, Morristown NJ
Morris Museum of Art, Augusta GA
MTG Hawkes Bay, Napier
Musees Royaux d'Art et d'Histoire, Royal Museums of Art and History, Brussels
The Museum, Greenwood SC
Museum of Art, Fort Lauderdale, Fort Lauderdale FL
The Museum of Arts & Sciences Inc, Daytona Beach FL
Museum of Northern British Columbia, Ruth Harvey Art Gallery, Prince Rupert BC
Muzeul de Istorie Nationala Si Arheologie Constanta, National History & Archaeology Museum, Constanta

National Society of Colonial Dames of America in the State of Maryland, Mount Clare Museum House, Baltimore MD
Ogden Museum of Southern Art, University of New Orleans, New Orleans LA
Olivet College, Armstrong Collection, Olivet MI
Panhandle-Plains Historical Museum, Canyon TX
Peoria Riverfront Museum, Peoria IL
Pueblo Museum, Desert Hot Springs CA
Queens College, City University of New York, Godwin-Ternbach Museum, Flushing NY
Red Deer & District Museum & Archives, Red Deer AB
Riverside Metropolitan Museum, Riverside CA
Rollins College, George D & Harriet W Cornell Fine Arts Museum, Winter Park FL
Royal Ontario Museum, Toronto ON
Scripps College, Ruth Chandler Williamson Gallery, Claremont CA
Seattle Art Museum, Seattle WA
Stanford University, Cantor Arts Center at Stanford University, Stanford CA
The State Museum of Fine Arts of Tatarstan Republic, Kazan
Staten Island Museum, Staten Island NY
Stephens College, Lewis James & Nellie Stratton Davis Art Gallery, Columbia MO
Stone Quarry Hill Art Park, Winner Gallery, Cazenovia NY
Stratford Historical Society, Catharine B Mitchell Museum, Stratford CT
Suomen Kansallismuseo, National Museum of Finland, Helsinki
Tattoo Art Museum, San Francisco CA
Tohono Chul Park, Tucson AZ
Tokyo National Museum, Tokyo
Topeka & Shawnee County Public Library, Alice C Sabatini Gallery, Topeka KS
Tubman African American Museum, Macon GA
Tver Regional Art Gallery, Tver
The Ukrainian Museum, New York NY
University of California, Berkeley, Phoebe Apperson Hearst Museum of Anthropology, Berkeley CA
University of California, Davis, Jan Shrem and Maria Manetti Shrem Museum of Art, Davis CA
University of Florida, Samuel P Harn Museum of Art, Gainesville FL
University of Illinois at Urbana-Champaign, Krannert Art Museum and Kinkead Pavilion, Champaign IL
The University of Kentucky Art Museum, Lexington KY
University of Miami, Lowe Art Museum, Coral Gables FL
University of Richmond, University Museums, Richmond VA
University of Utah, Utah Museum of Fine Arts, Salt Lake City UT
University of Victoria, The Legacy Art Gallery, Victoria BC
University of Wisconsin-Madison, Chazen Museum of Art, Madison WI
Volcano Art Center Gallery, Hawaii Volcanoes National Park HI
Wheelwright Museum of the American Indian, Santa Fe NM
Winston-Salem State University, Diggs Gallery, Winston-Salem NC
Wyoming State Museum, Cheyenne WY

PRINTS

1708 Gallery, Richmond VA
A.E. Backus Museum & Gallery, Fort Pierce FL
Abington Art Center, Jenkintown PA
Academy Art Museum, Easton MD
African American Atelier, Greensboro NC
African American Museum in Philadelphia, Philadelphia PA
Alaska Heritage Museum at Wells Fargo, Anchorage AK
Alaska State Museum, Juneau AK
Albany Institute of History & Art, Albany NY
Albertina Museum, Vienna
Albion College, Bobbitt Visual Arts Center, Albion MI
The Albrecht-Kemper Museum of Art, Saint Joseph MO
Albright College, Freedman Gallery, Reading PA
Albuquerque Museum of Art & History, Albuquerque NM
Aldrich Museum of Contemporary Art, Ridgefield CT
Alexandria Museum of Art, Alexandria LA
Allentown Art Museum, Allentown PA
Alton Museum of History & Art, Inc, Alton IL
American Sport Art Museum and Archives, Daphne AL
American Textile History Museum, Lowell MA
American University, Museum at the Katzen, Washington DC
Americas Society Art Gallery, New York NY
Amherst College, Mead Art Museum, Amherst MA
Amon Carter Museum of American Art, Fort Worth TX
Anchorage Museum at Rasmuson Center, Anchorage AK
Appaloosa Museum and Heritage Center, Moscow ID
Arkansas Arts Center, Little Rock AR
Arnot Art Museum, Elmira NY
Art and History Museums - Maitland, Maitland FL
Art Center of Battle Creek, Battle Creek MI
The Art Galleries of Ramapo College, Mahwah NJ
The Art Gallery of Cornwall, Cornwall ON
Art Gallery of Guelph, Guelph ON
Art Gallery of Nova Scotia, Halifax NS
Art Gallery of South Australia, Adelaide
Art Museum of Greater Lafayette, Lafayette IN
Art Museum of Southeast Texas, Beaumont TX
Art Museum of the Americas, Washington DC
Art Without Walls Inc, Sayville NY
Artspace, Richmond VA
Asheville Art Museum, Asheville NC
Attleboro Arts Museum, Attleboro MA
Audrain County Historical Society, Graceland Museum & American Saddlehorse Museum & Fire Brick Industry Museum, Mexico MO
Augustana University, Eide-Dalrymple Gallery, Sioux Falls SD
Austin College, Ida Green Gallery, Sherman TX
Baldwin-Wallace College, Fawick Art Gallery, Berea OH
The Baltimore Museum of Art, Baltimore MD
Balzekas Museum of Lithuanian Culture, Chicago IL
Bangladesh National Museum, Dhaka
Baroda Museum and Picture Gallery, Vadodara
Baruch College of the City University of New York, Sidney Mishkin Gallery, New York NY
Belger Arts Center, Kansas City MO
Bellevue Arts Museum, Bellevue WA
Bennington Museum, Bennington VT
Berea College, Doris Ulmann Galleries, Berea KY
Besser Museum for Northeast Michigan, Alpena MI
Beverly Historical Society, Cabot, Hale & Balch House Museums, Beverly MA
Biggs Museum of American Art, Dover DE
Birger Sandzen Memorial Gallery, Lindsborg KS
Birmingham Museum of Art, Birmingham AL
Blanden Memorial Art Museum, Fort Dodge IA
Blauvelt Demarest Foundation, Hiram Blauvelt Art Museum, Oradell NJ
Boise Art Museum, Boise ID
Bone Creek Museum of Agrarian Art, David City NE
Booth Western Art Museum, Cartersville GA
Boston Public Library, Albert H Wiggin Gallery & Print Department, Boston MA
The Bostonian Society, Old State House Museum, Boston MA
Brandeis University, Rose Art Museum, Waltham MA
Brevard College, Spiers Gallery, Brevard NC
Bruce Museum, Inc, Greenwich CT
Bucknell University, Edward & Marthann Samek Art Gallery, Lewisburg PA
Buffalo Niagara Heritage Village, Amherst NY
Burchfield Penney Art Center, Buffalo NY
Burke Arts Council, Jailhouse Galleries, Morganton NC
Burnaby Art Gallery, Burnaby BC
Bush-Holley Historic Site & Storehouse Gallery, Greenwich Historical Society, Cos Cob CT
C M Russell Museum, Great Falls MT
C W Post Campus of Long Island University, Hillwood Art Museum, Brookville NY
California State University, Chico, Janet Turner Print Museum, CSU, Chicago, Chico CA
Cameron Art Museum, Wilmington NC
Canadian Museum for Human Rights, Winnipeg MB
Canadian Museum of History, Gatineau QC
Canadian Museum of Nature, Musee Canadien de la Nature, Ottawa ON
Cape Ann Museum, Gloucester MA
Cape Cod Museum of Art Inc, Dennis MA
Carleton College, Art Gallery, Northfield MN
Carnegie Mellon University, Hunt Institute for Botanical Documentation, Pittsburgh PA
Carnegie Museums of Pittsburgh, Carnegie Museum of Art, Pittsburgh PA
Carolina Art Association, Gibbes Museum of Art, Charleston SC
Carson County Square House Museum, Panhandle TX
Cartoon Art Museum, San Francisco CA
Cedar Rapids Museum of Art, Cedar Rapids IA
Centenary College of Louisiana, Meadows Museum of Art, Shreveport LA
Center for Book Arts, New York NY
Central United Methodist Church, Swords Into Plowshares Peace Center & Gallery, Detroit MI
Channel Islands Maritime Museum, Oxnard CA
Chesapeake Bay Maritime Museum, Saint Michaels MD
Cincinnati Art Museum, Cincinnati Art Museum, Cincinnati OH
City of Atlanta, Chastain Arts Center & Gallery, Atlanta GA
City of Cedar Falls, Iowa, James & Meryl Hearst Center for the Arts & Sculpture Garden, Cedar Falls IA
City of Fremont, Olive Hyde Art Gallery, Fremont CA
The City of Petersburg Museums, Petersburg VA
City of Pittsfield Office of Cultural Development, Lichtenstein Center for the Arts, Pittsfield MA
Clark Art Institute, Williamstown MA
Clinton Art Association, River Arts Center, Clinton IA
Colgate University, Picker Art Gallery, Hamilton NY
The College of Idaho, Rosenthal Art Gallery, Caldwell ID
College of William & Mary, Muscarelle Museum of Art, Williamsburg VA
The Columbus Museum, Columbus GA
Columbus Museum of Art, Columbus OH
Concordia University, Leonard & Bina Ellen Art Gallery, Montreal QC
Concordia University, Marxhausen Art Gallery, Seward NE
Confederation Centre Art Gallery and Museum, Charlottetown PE
Contemporary Art Center, Peoria IL
Coos Art Museum, Coos Bay OR
Cornell College, Peter Paul Luce Gallery, Mount Vernon IA
Cornell University, Herbert F Johnson Museum of Art, Ithaca NY
The Courtauld Institute of Art, The Courtauld Gallery, London
Coutts Museum of Art, Inc, El Dorado KS
Craft and Folk Art Museum (CAFAM), Los Angeles CA
Cranbrook Art Museum, Bloomfield Hills MI
Crary Art Gallery, Warren PA
Cripple Creek District Museum, Cripple Creek CO
Crocker Art Museum, Sacramento CA
The Currier Museum of Art, Manchester NH
Danville Museum of Fine Arts & History, Danville VA
Dartmouth College, Hood Museum of Art, Hanover NH
Dartmouth Heritage Museum, Dartmouth NS
Daum Museum of Contemporary Art, Sedalia MO
Davidson College, William H Van Every Jr & Edward M Smith Galleries, Davidson NC
deCordova Sculpture Park & Museum, Lincoln MA
Deines Cultural Center, Russell KS
Delaware Art Museum, Wilmington DE
DeLeon White Gallery, Toronto ON
Detroit Institute of Arts, Detroit MI
Detroit Repertory Theatre Gallery, Detroit MI
Detroit Zoological Institute, Wildlife Interpretive Gallery, Royal Oak MI
Dickinson College, The Trout Gallery, Carlisle PA
Dixie State University, Sears Art Museum Gallery, Saint George UT
The Dixon Gallery & Gardens, Memphis TN
Doncaster Museum and Art Gallery, Doncaster Yorks
Dublin Arts Council, Dublin OH
Durham Art Guild, Durham NC
DuSable Museum of African American History, Chicago IL
Eastern Illinois University, Tarble Arts Center, Charleston IL
Eastern Washington State Historical Society, Northwest Museum of Arts & Culture, Spokane WA
Eiteljorg Museum of American Indians & Western Art, Indianapolis IN

El Camino College Art Gallery, Torrance CA
Ellen Noel Art Museum of the Permian Basin, Odessa TX
Elmhurst Art Museum, Elmhurst IL
Erie Art Museum, Erie PA
Erie County Historical Society, Erie PA
Essex Historical Society and Shipbuilding Museum, Essex MA
Everhart Museum, Scranton PA
Fairfield University, Art Museum, Fairfield CT
Fisk University, Aaron Douglas Gallery, Nashville TN
Fitchburg Art Museum, Fitchburg MA
Fitton Center for Creative Arts, Hamilton OH
Flint Institute of Arts, Flint MI
Florence County Museum, Florence SC
Florida Southern College, Melvin Art Gallery, Lakeland FL
Florida State University, John & Mable Ringling Museum of Art, Sarasota FL
Fondazione Musei Civici Di Venezia, Museo Correr - Correr Museum, Venice
Fort Hays State University, Moss-Thorns Gallery of Arts, Hays KS
Fort Smith Regional Art Museum, Fort Smith AR
Fort Ticonderoga Association, Ticonderoga NY
Fort Wayne Museum of Art, Inc, Fort Wayne IN
The Frank Phillips Foundation Inc, Woolaroc Museum, Bartlesville OK
Frankfort Community Public Library, Anna & Harlan Hubbard Gallery, Frankfort IN
Frederic Remington, Ogdensburg NY
Frick Collection, New York NY
Frontier Times Museum, Bandera TX
Frostburg State University, The Stephanie Ann Roper Gallery, Frostburg MD
Frye Art Museum, Seattle WA
Fuller Craft Museum, Brockton MA
Fulton County Historical Society Inc, Fulton County Museum (Tetzlaff Reference Room), Rochester IN
Gadsden Museum of Art, Gadsden AL
Galerie Montcalm, Gatineau QC
Gallery Moos Ltd, Toronto ON
Gallery One Visual Arts Center, Ellensburg WA
George Phippen, Phippen Museum - Art of the American West, Prescott AZ
The George Washington University, Luther W Brady Art Gallery, Washington DC
Germantown Historical Society, Philadelphia PA
Gertrude Herbert Institute of Art, Augusta GA
Girard College, Stephen Girard Collection, Philadelphia PA
Glasgow University, The Hunterian, Glasgow
Glenhyrst Art Gallery of Brant, Brantford ON
Glessner House Museum, Chicago IL
Grand Rapids Public Museum, Grand Rapids MI
The Graphic Eye Gallery, Port Washington NY
Great Lakes Historical Society, Inland Seas Maritime Museum, Vermilion OH
Grossmont Community College, Hyde Art Gallery, El Cajon CA
Hamilton College, Emerson Gallery, Clinton NY
Hammonds House Museum, Atlanta GA
Hancock Shaker Village, Inc, Pittsfield MA
Harness Racing Museum & Hall of Fame, Goshen NY
Hartwick College, Foreman Gallery, Oneonta NY
Headquarters Fort Monroe, Dept of Army, Casemate Museum, Hampton VA
Heard Museum, Phoenix AZ
Hebrew Union College, Skirball Cultural Center, Los Angeles CA
Hebrew Union College - Jewish Institute of Religion, Skirball Museum Cincinnati, Cincinnati OH
Hebrew Union College - Jewish Institute of Religion Museum, Jewish Institute of Religion, New York NY
The Heckscher Museum of Art, Huntington NY
Henry County Museum & Cultural Arts Center, Clinton MO
Henry Sheldon Museum of Vermont History and Research Center, Middlebury VT
Heritage Center, Inc, Pine Ridge SD
Hermitage Museum & Gardens, Norfolk VA
Hickory Museum of Art, Inc, Hickory NC
Hill-Stead Museum, Farmington CT
Hillwood Museum & Gardens Foundation, Hillwood Estate Museum & Gardens, Washington DC
Historisches und Volkerkundemuseum, Museum of History and Ethnology, St Gallen
History Colorado Center Museum, Denver CO
Honolulu Museum of Art, Honolulu HI
Hui No'eau Visual Arts Center, Gallery and Gift Shop, Makawao Maui HI
Hunter Museum of American Art, Chattanooga TN
Huntsville Museum of Art, Huntsville AL
The Hyde Collection, Glens Falls NY
i.d.e.a. Museum, Mesa AZ
Illinois State Museum, ISM Lockport Gallery, Chicago Gallery & Southern Illinois Art Gallery, Springfield IL
Illinois Wesleyan University, Merwin & Wakeley Galleries, Bloomington IL
Imperial Calcasieu Museum, Gibson-Barham Gallery, Lake Charles LA
Imperial War Museum London, London
Independence Historical Museum & Art Center, Independence KS
Independence Seaport Museum, Philadelphia PA
Indiana Landmarks, Morris-Butler House, Indianapolis IN
Institute of Contemporary Art, Los Angeles, Los Angeles CA
Institute of Puerto Rican Culture, Museo Fuerte Conde de Mirasol, Vieques PR
International Clown Hall of Fame & Research Center, Inc, West Allis WI
International Museum of Art & Science, McAllen TX
Iowa State University, Brunnier Art Museum, Ames IA
Iredell Museums, Statesville NC
The Israel Museum, Jerusalem, Jerusalem
James A Michener Art Museum, Doylestown PA
Jerald Melberg Gallery, Charlotte NC
JMW Turner Museum, Sarasota FL
Joe Gish's Old West Museum, Fredericksburg TX
The John L. Clarke Western Art Gallery & Memorial Museum, East Glacier Park MT
Johnson-Humrickhouse Museum, Coshocton OH
Jordan National Gallery of Fine Arts, Amman
Joslyn Art Museum, Omaha NE
Juniata College Museum of Art, Huntingdon PA
Kalamazoo Institute of Arts, Kalamazoo MI
Kamloops Art Gallery, Kamloops BC
Keene State College, Thorne-Sagendorph Art Gallery, Keene NH
Kenosha Public Museums, Kenosha WI
Kentucky Museum of Art and Craft, Louisville KY
Kereszteny Muzeum, Christian Museum, Esztergom
Kings County Historical Society & Museum, Hampton NB
Kirchner Museum Davos, Davos
Kirkland Museum of Fine & Decorative Art, Denver CO
Kitchener-Waterloo Art Gallery, Kitchener ON
Knoxville Museum of Art, Knoxville TN
Koshare Indian Museum, Inc, La Junta CO
La Salle University Art Museum, Philadelphia PA
Lafayette College, Lafayette College Art Galleries, Easton PA
Lafayette Science Museum & Planetarium, Lafayette LA
LaGrange Art Museum, LaGrange GA
Latino Art Museum, Pomona CA
Lauren Rogers, Laurel MS
Lawrence University, Wriston Art Center Galleries, Appleton WI
Leigh Yawkey Woodson Art Museum, Wausau WI
Lillian & Coleman Taube Museum of Art, Minot ND
Lincoln County Historical Association, Inc, 1811 Old Lincoln County Jail & Lincoln County Museum, Wiscasset ME
Lincolnshire County Council, The Collection: Art & Archaeology in Lincolnshire, Lincoln
Lindenwood University, Harry D Hendren Gallery, Saint Charles MO
The Loading Dock Gallery, Lowell MA
The Long Island Museum of American Art, History & Carriages, Stony Brook NY
Longfellow's Wayside Inn Museum, Sudbury MA
Longfellow-Evangeline State Commemorative Area, Saint Martinville LA
Longue Vue House & Gardens, New Orleans LA
Longview Museum of Fine Art, Longview TX
Los Angeles County Museum of Art, Los Angeles CA
Louise Hopkins Underwood Center for the Arts, Lubbock TX
Louisiana Arts & Science Museum, Baton Rouge LA
Louisiana Department of Culture, Recreation & Tourism, Louisiana State Museum, New Orleans LA
Loyola University Chicago, Loyola University Museum of Art, Chicago IL
Lycoming College Gallery, Williamsport PA
Lyman Allyn Art Museum, New London CT
Mabee-Gerrer Museum of Art, Shawnee OK
Madison Museum of Contemporary Art, Madison WI
Madison Museum of Fine Art, Madison GA
Maine College of Art, The Institute of Contemporary Art, Portland ME
Marietta-Cobb Museum of Art, Marietta GA
The Mariners' Museum, Newport News VA
Marquette University, Haggerty Museum of Art, Milwaukee WI
Maryhill Museum of Art, Goldendale WA
Marylhurst University, The Art Gym, Marylhurst OR
Massachusetts Institute of Technology, MIT Museum, Cambridge MA
McLean County Historical Society, McLean County Museum of History, Bloomington IL
McPherson College Gallery, McPherson KS
McPherson Museum and Arts Foundation, McPherson KS
Mennello Museum of American Art, Orlando FL
Meridian Museum of Art, Meridian MS
Mesa Arts Center, Mesa Contemporary Arts Museum, Mesa AZ
The Mexican Museum, San Francisco CA
Michelson Museum of Art, Marshall TX
Middle Border Museum & Oscar Howe Art Center, Mitchell SD
Midwest Museum of American Art, Elkhart IN
Miller Art Center Foundation Inc, Miller Art Museum, Sturgeon Bay WI
Millikin University, Perkinson Gallery, Decatur IL
Mills College Art Museum, Oakland CA
Minneapolis Institute of Art, Minneapolis MN
Minnesota Museum of American Art, Saint Paul MN
Minnesota State University, Mankato, Mankato MN
Minot State University, Northwest Art Center, Minot ND
Mississippi Museum of Art, Jackson MS
Missoula Art Museum, Missoula MT
Mobile Museum of Art, Mobile AL
Moderna Galerija, Modern Gallery - National Museum of Modern Art, Zagreb
Montana State University, Helen E Copeland Gallery, Bozeman MT
Montclair Art Museum, Montclair NJ
Montgomery Museum of Fine Arts, Montgomery AL
Moravian College, Payne Gallery, Bethlehem PA
Moravska Galerie v Brne, Moravian Gallery in Brno, Brno
Morehead State University, Claypool-Young Art Gallery, Morehead KY
Morris Museum of Art, Augusta GA
Mount Mary College, Marian Gallery, Milwaukee WI
Mount Vernon Hotel Museum & Garden, New York NY
MTG Hawkes Bay, Napier
Muhlenberg College, Martin Art Gallery, Allentown PA
Muscatine Art Center, Muscatine IA
Musee des Beaux-Arts d'Orleans, Museum of Fine Arts, Orleans
Musee des Beaux-Arts de Tours, Museum of Fine Arts, Tours
Museen der Stadt Koln, Museum Ludwig - Ludwig Museum, Cologne
Musees Royaux d'Art et d'Histoire, Royal Museums of Art and History, Brussels
Museo de Arte de Ponce, The Luis A Ferre Foundation Inc, Ponce PR
Museo De Las Americas, Denver CO
Museo di Palazzo Ducale, Ducale Palace Museum, Mantua
Museu Nacional D'Art De Catalunya, Catalona National Museum of Art, Barcelona
Museum of American Glass in WV, Weston WV
Museum of Art & History, Santa Cruz, Santa Cruz CA
Museum of Art - Deland FL, Inc, Deland FL
The Museum of Arts & Sciences Inc, Daytona Beach FL
Museum of Arts & Sciences, Inc, Macon GA
Museum of Contemporary Art Chicago, Chicago IL
Museum of Contemporary Art Jacksonville, Jacksonville FL
Museum of Contemporary Art San Diego, San Diego CA
Museum of Discovery & Science, Fort Lauderdale FL
Museum of Fine Arts, Boston MA
Museum of Fine Arts, Houston, Houston TX

Museum of Fine Arts, Saint Petersburg, Florida, Inc, Saint Petersburg FL
Museum of Latin American Art, Long Beach CA
Museum of Modern Art, New York NY
Museum of Modern Art, Ibaraki, Mito Ibaraki
Museum of Northern British Columbia, Ruth Harvey Art Gallery, Prince Rupert BC
Museum of Northwest Art, La Conner WA
Museum of the Plains Indian & Crafts Center, Browning MT
Museum of the Southwest, Midland TX
The Museum of Western Art, Kerrville TX
Museum Plantin-Moretus, Antwerp
Museum zu Allerheiligen, Schaffhausen
Muzej Moderne I Suvremene Umjetnosti, Museum of Modern and Contemporary Art, Rijeka
Muzeum Narodowe w Poznaniu, National Museum in Poznan, Poznan
Narodna Galerija, National Gallery of Slovenia, Ljubljana
Nassau Community College, Firehouse Art Gallery, Garden City NY
Nassau County Museum of Art, Roslyn Harbor NY
National Baseball Hall of Fame & Museum, Cooperstown NY
National Gallery of Ireland, Dublin
National Museum & Art Gallery of Trinidad and Tobago, Port of Spain
National Museum of Mexican Art, Chicago IL
The National Museum of Modern Art, Tokyo, Tokyo
National Museum of Racing, National Museum of Racing & Hall of Fame, Saratoga Springs NY
The National Museum of Western Art, Tokyo
National Museum of Wildlife Art of the Unites States, Jackson WY
National Portrait Gallery, London
National Society of Colonial Dames of America in the State of Maryland, Mount Clare Museum House, Baltimore MD
Naval Historical Center, National Museum of the US Navy, Washington DC
Nebraska Wesleyan University, Elder Gallery, Lincoln NE
Nelda C & H J Lutcher Stark Foundation, Stark Museum of Art, Orange TX
Nelson Mandela Metropolitan Art Museum, Port Elizabeth
The Nelson-Atkins Museum of Art, Kansas City MO
Neue Galerie New York, New York NY
Nevada Museum of Art, Reno NV
Neville Public Museum of Brown County, Green Bay WI
New Britain Museum of American Art, New Britain CT
New Brunswick Museum, Saint John NB
New Gallery of Modern Art, Charlotte NC
New Orleans Artworks at New Orleans Glassworks & Printmaking Studio, New Orleans LA
New Visions Gallery, Inc, Marshfield WI
New York State Military Museum and Veterans Research Center, Saratoga Springs NY
Newfields, Indianapolis IN
Newport Art Museum and Association, Newport RI
Niagara University, Castellani Art Museum, Niagara NY
Nichols House Museum, Inc, Boston MA
Niigata Prefectural Museum of Modern Art, Nagaoka
The Noble Maritime Collection, Staten Island NY
Norman Rockwell Museum of Vermont, Rutland VT
Norsk Maritimt Museum, Norwegian Maritime Museum, Oslo
North Light Gallery, Millinocket ME
Northwestern University, Mary & Leigh Block Museum of Art, Evanston IL
Norton Simon Museum, Pasadena CA
Norwich Free Academy, Slater Memorial Museum, Norwich CT
Nova Scotia College of Art and Design, Anna Leonowens Gallery, Halifax NS
Ogden Museum of Southern Art, University of New Orleans, New Orleans LA
Ohara Museum of Art, Kurashiki
Ohio University, Kennedy Museum of Art, Athens OH
Okefenokee Heritage Center, Inc, Waycross GA
Oklahoma City Museum of Art, Oklahoma City OK
Olana State Historic Site, Hudson NY
Old Dartmouth Historical Society, New Bedford Whaling Museum, New Bedford MA
The Old Jail Art Center, Albany TX
Olivet College, Armstrong Collection, Olivet MI
Omniplex Science Museum, Oklahoma City OK
Order Sons of Italy in America, Garibaldi & Meucci Museum, Staten Island NY
Owensboro Museum of Fine Art, Owensboro KY
Panhandle-Plains Historical Museum, Canyon TX
Passaic County Community College, Broadway, LRC, and Hamilton Club Galleries, Paterson NJ
Pennsylvania Academy of the Fine Arts, Philadelphia PA
Pennsylvania Historical & Museum Commission, Railroad Museum of Pennsylvania, Strasburg PA
Pensacola Museum of Art, Pensacola FL
Philbrook Museum of Art, Tulsa OK
Phillips Academy, Addison Gallery of American Art, Andover MA
The Phillips Collection, Washington DC
Phoenix Art Museum, Phoenix AZ
Piedmont Arts Association, Martinsville VA
Plains Art Museum, Fargo ND
Plumas County Museum, Quincy CA
Polish Museum of America (PMA), Chicago IL
Polk Museum of Art, Lakeland FL
The Pomona College, Claremont CA
Port Huron Museum, Port Huron MI
Portland Art Museum, Portland OR
Portland Museum of Art, Portland ME
Pump House Center for the Arts, Chillicothe OH
Purchase College, Neuberger Museum of Art, Purchase NY
Purdue University Galleries, West Lafayette IN
Putnam County Historical Society, Foundry School Museum, Cold Spring NY
Putnam Museum of History and Natural Science, Davenport IA
Queen Victoria Museum and Art Gallery, Launceston TAS
Queen's University, Agnes Etherington Art Centre, Kingston ON
Queens College, City University of New York, Godwin-Ternbach Museum, Flushing NY
Quincy University, The Gray Gallery, Quincy IL
Radio-Canada SRC CBC, Georges Goguen CBC Art Gallery, Moncton NB
Rahr-West Art Museum, Manitowoc WI
Randolph College, Maier Museum of Art, Lynchburg VA
Rapid City Arts Council, Dahl Arts Center, Rapid City SD
Real Art Ways (RAW), Hartford CT
Reed College, Douglas F Cooley Memorial Art Gallery, Portland OR
Remai Modern, Saskatoon SK
Rensselaer County Historical Society, Hart-Cluett Mansion, 1827, Troy NY
Reynolda House Museum of American Art, Winston-Salem NC
Roberson Museum & Science Center, Binghamton NY
The Robert McLaughlin Gallery, Oshawa ON
The Rockwell Museum, Corning NY
Rogue Community College, Wiseman Gallery - FireHouse Gallery, Grants Pass OR
Rollins College, George D & Harriet W Cornell Fine Arts Museum, Winter Park FL
The Rosenbach Museum & Library, Philadelphia PA
Roswell Museum & Art Center, Roswell NM
Rutgers University, Stedman Art Gallery, Camden NJ
Ryerss Victorian Museum & Library, Philadelphia PA
Saginaw Art Museum, Saginaw MI
Saint Anselm College, Alva de Mars Megan Chapel Art Center, Manchester NH
Saint Bonaventure University, Regina A Quick Center for the Arts, Saint Bonaventure NY
Saint Clair County Community College, Jack R Hennesey Art Galleries, Port Huron MI
Saint Joseph College, Art Gallery, University of Saint Joseph, West Hartford CT
Saint Mary's College, Moreau Galleries, Notre Dame IN
Saint Mary's College of California, Museum of Art, Moraga CA
Saint Olaf College, Flaten Art Museum, Northfield MN
Salisbury University, Ward Museum of Wildfowl Art, Salisbury MD
San Angelo Museum of Fine Arts, San Angelo TX
San Antonio Museum of Art, San Antonio TX
San Diego Museum of Art, San Diego CA
San Jose Museum of Art, San Jose CA
Santa Barbara Museum of Art, Santa Barbara CA
The Schoolhouse Gallery, Provincetown MA
Schweinfurth Art Center, Auburn NY
Scripps College, Ruth Chandler Williamson Gallery, Claremont CA
Seattle Art Museum, Seattle WA
Shirley Plantation Foundation, Charles City VA
Slovenska Narodna Galeria, Slovak National Gallery, Bratislava
The Society of the Cincinnati at Anderson House, Washington DC
South Carolina Artisans Center, Walterboro SC
South Dakota State University, South Dakota Art Museum, Brookings SD
South Shore Arts, Munster IN
South Street Seaport Museum, New York NY
Southeastern Center for Contemporary Art, Winston-Salem NC
Southern Methodist University, Meadows Museum, Dallas TX
Southern Oregon University, Schneider Museum of Art, Ashland OR
Spartanburg Art Museum, Spartanburg SC
The Speed Art Museum, Louisville KY
Spertus Institute of Jewish Studies, Chicago IL
Springfield Art Museum, Springfield MO
St Mary's College of Maryland, The Dwight Frederick Boyden Gallery, St Mary's City MD
Staatliche Museen zu Berlin Stiftung Preussischer Kulturbesitz, National Museums in Berlin, Prussian Cultural Heritage Foundation, Berlin
Stamford Museum & Nature Center, Stamford CT
Stanford University, Cantor Arts Center at Stanford University, Stanford CA
State University of New York at New Paltz, Samuel Dorsky Museum of Art, New Paltz NY
The State University of New York at Potsdam, The Art Museum, Potsdam NY
State University of New York at Ulster, Muroff-Kotler Visual Arts Gallery, Stone Ridge NY
State University of New York College at Cortland, Dowd Fine Arts Gallery, Cortland NY
State University of New York College at Fredonia, Cathy and Jesse Marion Art Gallery, Fredonia NY
Staten Island Museum, Staten Island NY
Stratford Historical Society, Catharine B Mitchell Museum, Stratford CT
The Summit County Historical Society of Akron, OH, Akron OH
Suomen Kansallismuseo, National Museum of Finland, Helsinki
Surrey Art Gallery, Surrey BC
Swedish American Museum, Chicago IL
Swope Art Museum, Terre Haute IN
T W Wood Gallery, Montpelier VT
Tacoma Art Museum, Tacoma WA
Tampa Museum of Art, Tampa FL
Texas Christian University, Fort Worth Contemporary Art, Fort Worth TX
Tohono Chul Park, Tucson AZ
Tokyo National Museum, Tokyo
Toledo Museum of Art, Toledo OH
Topeka & Shawnee County Public Library, Alice C Sabatini Gallery, Topeka KS
Traffic Zone Center for Visual Art, Minneapolis MN
Triton Museum of Art, Santa Clara CA
Tryon Palace, New Bern NC
Tubman African American Museum, Macon GA
Tucson Museum of Art and Historic Block, Tucson AZ
Turtle Bay Exploration Park, Redding CA
Tver Regional Art Gallery, Tver
Twin City Art Foundation, Masur Museum of Art, Monroe LA
Tyne and Wear Archives & Museums, Sunderland Museum & Winter Gardens, Sunderland
Ukrainian Canadian Archives & Museum of Alberta, Edmonton AB
United Society of Shakers, Shaker Museum, New Gloucester ME
United States Capitol, Architect of the Capitol, Washington DC
United States Figure Skating Association, World Figure Skating Museum & Hall of Fame, Colorado Springs CO
United States Military Academy, West Point Museum, West Point NY
University of Arkansas at Little Rock, Art Galleries, Little Rock AR
University of Calgary, Nickle Galleries, Calgary AB
University of California, Davis, Jan Shrem and Maria Manetti Shrem Museum of Art, Davis CA
University of Chicago, Smart Museum of Art, Chicago IL

University of Findlay, Dudley & Mary Marks Lea Gallery, Findlay OH
University of Florida, Samuel P Harn Museum of Art, Gainesville FL
University of Georgia, Georgia Museum of Art, Athens GA
University of Illinois at Urbana-Champaign, Krannert Art Museum and Kinkead Pavilion, Champaign IL
University of Indianapolis, Christel DeHaan Fine Arts Gallery, Indianapolis IN
University of Kansas, Spencer Museum of Art, Lawrence KS
The University of Kentucky Art Museum, Lexington KY
University of Louisville, Hite Art Institute, Louisville KY
University of Manchester, Whitworth Art Gallery, Manchester
University of Mary Washington, University of Mary Washington Galleries, Fredericksburg VA
University of Miami, Lowe Art Museum, Coral Gables FL
University of Minnesota, Katherine E Nash Gallery, Minneapolis MN
University of Minnesota, The Bell Museum of Natural History, Minneapolis MN
University of Minnesota Duluth, Tweed Museum of Art, Duluth MN
University of Nebraska-Lincoln, Great Plains Art Museum, Lincoln NE
University of Nevada, Las Vegas, Donna Beam Fine Art Gallery, Las Vegas NV
University of Nevada, Reno, Sheppard Contemporary & University Galleries, Reno NV
University of New Mexico, The Harwood Museum of Art, Taos NM
University of North Carolina at Greensboro, Weatherspoon Art Museum, Greensboro NC
University of Notre Dame, Snite Museum of Art, Notre Dame IN
University of Pennsylvania, Arthur Ross Gallery, Philadelphia PA
University of Richmond, University Museums, Richmond VA
University of Saskatchewan, Diefenbaker Canada Centre, Saskatoon SK
University of Texas at Austin, Blanton Museum of Art, Austin TX
University of Vermont, Robert Hull Fleming Museum, Burlington VT
University of Wisconsin Oshkosh, Allen Priebe Gallery, Oshkosh WI
University of Wisconsin-Eau Claire, Foster Gallery, Eau Claire WI
University of Wisconsin-Madison, Chazen Museum of Art, Madison WI
University of Wisconsin-Stout, J Furlong Gallery, Menomonie WI
Ursinus College, Philip & Muriel Berman Museum of Art, Collegeville PA
USS Constitution Museum, Boston MA
The Valentine, Richmond VA
Valparaiso University, Brauer Museum of Art, Valparaiso IN
Van Gogh Museum, Amsterdam
Vancouver Art Gallery, Vancouver BC
Vero Beach Museum of Art, Vero Beach FL
Vesterheim Norwegian-American Museum, Decorah IA
Viridian Artists Inc, New York NY
Volcano Art Center Gallery, Hawaii Volcanoes National Park HI
Wadsworth Atheneum Museum of Art, Hartford CT
The Walker African American Museum & Research Center, Las Vegas NV
Walker Art Center, Minneapolis MN
Walker Art Gallery, Liverpool
Walker Fine Art, Denver CO
Washburn University, Mulvane Art Museum, Topeka KS
Washington County Museum of Fine Arts, Hagerstown MD
Waterloo Center of the Arts, Waterloo IA
Waterworks Visual Arts Center, Salisbury NC
Wayne Center for the Arts, Wooster OH
Wayne State College, Nordstrand Visual Arts Gallery, Wayne NE
Wendell Gilley, Southwest Harbor ME
Wesleyan University, Davison Art Center, Middletown CT
Wheaton College, Beard and Weil Galleries, Norton MA
Wheelwright Museum of the American Indian, Santa Fe NM
White House, Washington DC
Whitney Museum of American Art, New York NY
Wichita Falls Museum & Art Center, Wichita Falls TX
Wichita State University, Ulrich Museum of Art, Wichita KS
Wildling Art Museum, Solvang CA
Wilfrid Laurier University, Robert Langen Art Gallery, Waterloo ON
Wilkes Art Gallery, North Wilkesboro NC
William Paterson University, University Galleries, Wayne NJ
The Winnipeg Art Gallery, Winnipeg MB
Winston-Salem State University, Diggs Gallery, Winston-Salem NC
Wiregrass Museum of Art, Dothan AL
Wisconsin Historical Society, Wisconsin Historical Museum, Madison WI
Witter Gallery, Storm Lake IA
Woodmere Art Museum Inc, Philadelphia PA
Worcester Art Museum, Worcester MA
Wustum Museum Art Association, Charles A Wustum Museum of Fine Arts, Racine WI
Yale University, Yale Center for British Art, New Haven CT
Yokohama Museum of Art, Yokohama
Zigler Art Museum, Jennings LA

RELIGIOUS ART

Academy of the New Church, Glencairn Museum, Bryn Athyn PA
Adams County Historical Society, Gettysburg PA
African American Museum in Philadelphia, Philadelphia PA
Albin Polasek Museum & Sculpture Gardens, Winter Park FL
Amherst College, Mead Art Museum, Amherst MA
Anchorage Museum at Rasmuson Center, Anchorage AK
Ancient Spanish Monastery, North Miami Beach FL
Archives of the Archdiocese of St Paul & Minneapolis, Saint Paul MN
Arnot Art Museum, Elmira NY
Art Gallery of Alberta, Edmonton AB
The Art Gallery of Cornwall, Cornwall ON
Art Gallery of Hamilton, Hamilton ON
Art Gallery of Nova Scotia, Halifax NS
Art Museum of Greater Lafayette, Lafayette IN
Asian Art Museum of San Francisco, Chong-Moon Lee Ctr for Asian Art and Culture, San Francisco CA
Balzekas Museum of Lithuanian Culture, Chicago IL
Bangladesh National Museum, Dhaka
Beaverbrook Art Gallery, Fredericton NB
Berman Museum, Anniston AL
Birmingham Museum of Art, Birmingham AL
Bob Jones University Museum & Gallery Inc, Greenville SC
Bucknell University, Edward & Marthann Samek Art Gallery, Lewisburg PA
The Buffalo Fine Arts Academy, Albright-Knox Art Gallery, Buffalo NY
Burke Arts Council, Jailhouse Galleries, Morganton NC
Byzantine & Christian Museum, Athens, Athens
Canadian Museum of History, Gatineau QC
Casa-Museu Medeiros e Almeida, Lisbon
Cathedral of Saint John the Divine, New York NY
Center for Art & Education, Van Buren AR
Center for Puppetry Arts, Atlanta GA
Central United Methodist Church, Swords Into Plowshares Peace Center & Gallery, Detroit MI
Chatham Historical Society, The Atwood House Museum, Chatham MA
The Children's Museum of Indianapolis, Indianapolis IN
Cincinnati Art Museum, Cincinnati Art Museum, Cincinnati OH
Clark Art Institute, Williamstown MA
Colgate University, Picker Art Gallery, Hamilton NY
College of William & Mary, Muscarelle Museum of Art, Williamsburg VA
Columbus Museum of Art, Columbus OH
Congregation Beth Israel's Plotkin Judaica Museum, Scottsdale AZ
Coptic Museum, Cairo
Cripple Creek District Museum, Cripple Creek CO
Crocker Art Museum, Sacramento CA
Dartmouth College, Hood Museum of Art, Hanover NH
Denver Art Museum, Denver CO
Detroit Institute of Arts, Detroit MI
Dickinson College, The Trout Gallery, Carlisle PA
Doncaster Museum and Art Gallery, Doncaster Yorks
Dumbarton Oaks, Dumbarton Oaks Museum, Washington DC
Ellen Noel Art Museum of the Permian Basin, Odessa TX
Environment Canada - Parks Canada, Laurier House, National Historic Site, Ottawa ON
Flint Institute of Arts, Flint MI
Florence County Museum, Florence SC
Florida State University and Central Florida Community College, The Appleton Museum of Art, Ocala FL
Folk Art Society of America, Richmond VA
Fondazione Musei Civici Di Venezia, Museo Correr - Correr Museum, Venice
Forest Lawn Museum, Glendale CA
The Frick Art & Historical Center, Inc, Frick Art Museum, Pittsburgh PA
Gadsden Museum, Mesilla NM
General Board of Discipleship, The United Methodist Church, The Upper Room Chapel & Museum, Nashville TN
Gloridale Partnership, National Museum of Woodcarving, Custer SD
Heard Museum, Phoenix AZ
Hebrew Union College - Jewish Institute of Religion, Skirball Museum Cincinnati, Cincinnati OH
Hebrew Union College - Jewish Institute of Religion Museum, Jewish Institute of Religion, New York NY
Henry County Museum & Cultural Arts Center, Clinton MO
Heras Museum for Research in Indian History and Culture, Mumbai
Hermitage Museum & Gardens, Norfolk VA
Het Noordbrabants Museum, s-Hertogenbosch
Hickory Museum of Art, Inc, Hickory NC
Hillwood Museum & Gardens Foundation, Hillwood Estate Museum & Gardens, Washington DC
Historisches und Volkerkundemuseum, Museum of History and Ethnology, St Gallen
Honolulu Museum of Art, Honolulu HI
The Hyde Collection, Glens Falls NY
Illinois State Museum, ISM Lockport Gallery, Chicago Gallery & Southern Illinois Art Gallery, Springfield IL
Institute of Puerto Rican Culture, Museo de Arte Religioso Porta Coeli, San German PR
International Museum of Art, El Paso TX
Jacksonville University, Alexander Brest Museum & Gallery, Jacksonville FL
Jacques Marchais Museum of Tibetan Art, Staten Island NY
Jefferson County Open Space, Hiwan Homestead Museum, Evergreen CO
JMW Turner Museum, Sarasota FL
Kateri Tekakwitha Shrine/St. Francis Xavier Mission, Kahnawake QC
Kenosha Public Museums, Kenosha WI
Kereszteny Muzeum, Christian Museum, Esztergom
Kimbell Art Foundation, Kimbell Art Museum, Fort Worth TX
Kunsthistorisches Museum Wien, Museum of Fine Arts, Vienna
Kunstmuseum Solothurn, Solothurn Art Museum, Solothurn
Kyiv Museum of Russian Art, Kyiv Ukrainian
La Salle University Art Museum, Philadelphia PA
Lalit Kala Akademi Rabindra Bhavan Art Galleries, National Academy of Art, New Delhi, New Delhi
Le Grand Curtius, The Grand Curtius, Liege
Longfellow-Evangeline State Commemorative Area, Saint Martinville LA
Los Angeles County Museum of Art, Los Angeles CA
Loyola Marymount University, Laband Art Gallery, Los Angeles CA
Loyola University Chicago, Loyola University Museum of Art, Chicago IL
Mabee-Gerrer Museum of Art, Shawnee OK
Madison Museum of Fine Art, Madison GA
Marquette University, Haggerty Museum of Art, Milwaukee WI
Maryhill Museum of Art, Goldendale WA
The Mexican Museum, San Francisco CA

Millicent Rogers Museum, Taos NM
Mission San Luis Rey de Francia, Mission San Luis Rey Museum, Oceanside CA
Mission San Miguel Museum, San Miguel CA
Mobile Museum of Art, Mobile AL
Moravian Historical Society, Nazareth PA
Moravska Galerie v Brne, Moravian Gallery in Brno, Brno
Muhlenberg College, Martin Art Gallery, Allentown PA
Musee d'art de Joliette, Joliette QC
Musee des Augustines de l'Hotel Dieu de Quebec, Quebec QC
Musee des Beaux-Arts d'Orleans, Museum of Fine Arts, Orleans
Musee des Beaux-Arts de Tours, Museum of Fine Arts, Tours
Museen der Stadt Koln, Wallraf-Richartz-Museum & Fondation Corboud - Wallraf-Richartz Museum & Corboud Foundation, Cologne
Museo De Las Americas, Denver CO
Museo di Palazzo Ducale, Ducale Palace Museum, Mantua
Museo Nacional de Bellas Artes, National Museum of Fine Arts, Santiago
Museu Nacional D'Art De Catalunya, Catalona National Museum of Art, Barcelona
Museum De Lakenhal, Leiden
The Museum of Arts & Sciences Inc, Daytona Beach FL
Museum of Fine Arts, Saint Petersburg, Florida, Inc, Saint Petersburg FL
Museum Plantin-Moretus, Antwerp
Museum Prinsenhof Delft, Delft
Museum zu Allerheiligen, Schaffhausen
Muzej za Umjetnost i Obrt, Museum of Arts & Crafts, Zagreb
Muzeul de Istorie Nationala Si Arheologie Constanta, National History & Archaeology Museum, Constanta
Muzeul National de Arta al Romaniei, National Museum of Art of Romania, Bucharest
Muzeum Narodowe w Poznaniu, National Museum in Poznan, Poznan
Nara Kokuritsu Hakubutsu-Kan, Nara National Museum, Nara
Narodna Galerija, National Gallery of Slovenia, Ljubljana
National Art Museum of Moldova, Chisinau
National Museum of Ethiopia, Addis Ababa
The National Museum of Western Art, Tokyo
National Palace Museum, Taipei
The National Shrine of the North American Martyrs, Fultonville NY
National Silk Art Museum, Weston MO
North Park University, Carlson Tower Art Gallery, Chicago IL
Norton Simon Museum, Pasadena CA
Norwich Free Academy, Slater Memorial Museum, Norwich CT
Noyes Art Gallery, Lincoln NE
Ogden Museum of Southern Art, University of New Orleans, New Orleans LA
Osterreichische Galerie Belvedere Vienna, Belvedere Museum Vienna, Vienna
Owensboro Museum of Fine Art, Owensboro KY
Page-Walker Arts & History Center, Cary NC
Panhandle-Plains Historical Museum, Canyon TX
Philadelphia Museum of Art, John G Johnson Collection, Philadelphia PA
Piedmont Arts Association, Martinsville VA
Polish Museum of America (PMA), Chicago IL
Queens College, City University of New York, Godwin-Ternbach Museum, Flushing NY
Radio-Canada SRC CBC, Georges Goguen CBC Art Gallery, Moncton NB
Randolph College, Maier Museum of Art, Lynchburg VA
Reading Public Museum, Reading PA
Remai Modern, Saskatoon SK
Rubin Museum of Art, New York NY
Ryerss Victorian Museum & Library, Philadelphia PA
Saginaw Art Museum, Saginaw MI
Saint Anselm College, Alva de Mars Megan Chapel Art Center, Manchester NH
Saint Bonaventure University, Regina A Quick Center for the Arts, Saint Bonaventure NY
Saint Johnsbury Athenaeum, Saint Johnsbury VT
Saint Mary's College of California, Museum of Art, Moraga CA
Saint Olaf College, Flaten Art Museum, Northfield MN
San Antonio Museum of Art, San Antonio TX
San Carlos Cathedral, Monterey CA
Seneca-Iroquois National Museum, Salamanca NY
Shaker Village of Pleasant Hill, Harrodsburg KY
Slovenska Narodna Galeria, Slovak National Gallery, Bratislava
The Society of the Cincinnati at Anderson House, Washington DC
Southern Baptist Theological Seminary, Joseph A Callaway Archaeological Museum, Louisville KY
Southern Methodist University, Meadows Museum, Dallas TX
The Speed Art Museum, Louisville KY
Spertus Institute of Jewish Studies, Chicago IL
Springville Museum of Art, Springville UT
Staatliche Museen zu Berlin Stiftung Preussischer Kulturbesitz, National Museums in Berlin, Prussian Cultural Heritage Foundation, Berlin
Stanford University, Cantor Arts Center at Stanford University, Stanford CA
The State Museum of Fine Arts of Tatarstan Republic, Kazan
Staten Island Museum, Staten Island NY
Stone Quarry Hill Art Park, Winner Gallery, Cazenovia NY
Suomen Kansallismuseo, National Museum of Finland, Helsinki
Swedish American Museum, Chicago IL
Taft Museum of Art, Cincinnati OH
Taos Historic Museums, La Hacienda de Los Martinez, Taos NM
Thomas Jefferson Foundation, Inc, Monticello, Charlottesville VA
Timken Museum of Art, San Diego CA
Tohono Chul Park, Tucson AZ
Topeka & Shawnee County Public Library, Alice C Sabatini Gallery, Topeka KS
Tver Regional Art Gallery, Tver
Ukrainian Canadian Archives & Museum of Alberta, Edmonton AB
UMLAUF Sculpture Garden & Museum, Austin TX
United Methodist Church General Commission on Archives & History, Madison NJ
United Methodist Historical Society, Lovely Lane Museum, Baltimore MD
United Society of Shakers, Shaker Museum, New Gloucester ME
University of Chicago, Smart Museum of Art, Chicago IL
University of Georgia, Georgia Museum of Art, Athens GA
University of Illinois at Urbana-Champaign, Krannert Art Museum and Kinkead Pavilion, Champaign IL
The University of Kentucky Art Museum, Lexington KY
University of Miami, Lowe Art Museum, Coral Gables FL
University of New Mexico, The Harwood Museum of Art, Taos NM
University of Notre Dame, Snite Museum of Art, Notre Dame IN
University of Texas at Austin, Blanton Museum of Art, Austin TX
University of Utah, Utah Museum of Fine Arts, Salt Lake City UT
University of Wisconsin-Madison, Chazen Museum of Art, Madison WI
Ursinus College, Philip & Muriel Berman Museum of Art, Collegeville PA
Valparaiso University, Brauer Museum of Art, Valparaiso IN
Vesterheim Norwegian-American Museum, Decorah IA
Vorarlberg Museum, Bregenz
Walker Art Gallery, Liverpool
Walters Art Museum, Baltimore MD
Waterworks Visual Arts Center, Salisbury NC
Wheelwright Museum of the American Indian, Santa Fe NM
Winston-Salem State University, Diggs Gallery, Winston-Salem NC
Worcester Art Museum, Worcester MA
World Erotic Art Museum, Miami Beach FL
Yeshiva University Museum, New York NY
Zigler Art Museum, Jennings LA

RENAISSANCE ART

Amherst College, Mead Art Museum, Amherst MA
Amsterdam Museum, Amsterdam
Arkansas Arts Center, Little Rock AR
Arnot Art Museum, Elmira NY
Art Gallery of Nova Scotia, Halifax NS
Art Without Walls Inc, Sayville NY
The Baltimore Museum of Art, Baltimore MD
Bangladesh National Museum, Dhaka
Baroda Museum and Picture Gallery, Vadodara
Beaverbrook Art Gallery, Fredericton NB
Birmingham Museum of Art, Birmingham AL
Blanden Memorial Art Museum, Fort Dodge IA
Bob Jones University Museum & Gallery Inc, Greenville SC
Bucknell University, Edward & Marthann Samek Art Gallery, Lewisburg PA
Charles Allis Art Museum, Milwaukee WI
Cincinnati Art Museum, Cincinnati Art Museum, Cincinnati OH
City of El Paso, El Paso TX
Colgate University, Picker Art Gallery, Hamilton NY
College of William & Mary, Muscarelle Museum of Art, Williamsburg VA
Columbia Museum of Art, Columbia SC
Columbus Museum of Art, Columbus OH
The Courtauld Institute of Art, The Courtauld Gallery, London
The Currier Museum of Art, Manchester NH
Dartmouth College, Hood Museum of Art, Hanover NH
Denver Art Museum, Denver CO
Designmuseum Danmark, Danish Design Museum, Copenhagen
Detroit Institute of Arts, Detroit MI
Dickinson College, The Trout Gallery, Carlisle PA
East Los Angeles College, Vincent Price Art Museum, Monterey Park CA
Ellen Noel Art Museum of the Permian Basin, Odessa TX
Fairfield University, Art Museum, Fairfield CT
Flint Institute of Arts, Flint MI
Florence County Museum, Florence SC
Florida State University, John & Mable Ringling Museum of Art, Sarasota FL
Fondazione Musei Civici Di Venezia, Museo Correr - Correr Museum, Venice
Forest Lawn Museum, Glendale CA
The Frick Art & Historical Center, Inc, Frick Art Museum, Pittsburgh PA
Frick Collection, New York NY
Galleria Nazionale dell'Umbria, Umbrian National Gallery, Perugia
General Board of Discipleship, The United Methodist Church, The Upper Room Chapel & Museum, Nashville TN
Hartwick College, Foreman Gallery, Oneonta NY
Het Noordbrabants Museum, s-Hertogenbosch
Hillwood Museum & Gardens Foundation, Hillwood Estate Museum & Gardens, Washington DC
Honolulu Museum of Art, Honolulu HI
The Hyde Collection, Glens Falls NY
The Israel Museum, Jerusalem, Jerusalem
Joslyn Art Museum, Omaha NE
Kereszteny Muzeum, Christian Museum, Esztergom
Kimbell Art Foundation, Kimbell Art Museum, Fort Worth TX
Kunsthistorisches Museum Wien, Museum of Fine Arts, Vienna
Kunstmuseum Solothurn, Solothurn Art Museum, Solothurn
La Salle University Art Museum, Philadelphia PA
Lahore Museum, Lahore
Le Grand Curtius, The Grand Curtius, Liege
Mabee-Gerrer Museum of Art, Shawnee OK
Marquette University, Haggerty Museum of Art, Milwaukee WI
Massillon Museum, Massillon OH
Memphis Brooks Museum of Art, Memphis TN
Moravska Galerie v Brne, Moravian Gallery in Brno, Brno
Musee des Beaux-Arts d'Orleans, Museum of Fine Arts, Orleans
Musee des Beaux-Arts de Tours, Museum of Fine Arts, Tours
Museen der Stadt Koln, Wallraf-Richartz-Museum & Fondation Corboud - Wallraf-Richartz Museum & Corboud Foundation, Cologne
Musees Royaux d'Art et d'Histoire, Royal Museums of Art and History, Brussels
Museo di Palazzo Ducale, Ducale Palace Museum, Mantua

Museu Nacional D'Art De Catalunya, Catalona National Museum of Art, Barcelona
Museum De Lakenhal, Leiden
The Museum of Arts & Sciences Inc, Daytona Beach FL
Museum of Fine Arts, Houston, Houston TX
Museum Plantin-Moretus, Antwerp
Museum zu Allerheiligen, Schaffhausen
Muzej za Umjetnost i Obrt, Museum of Arts & Crafts, Zagreb
Muzeul National de Arta al Romaniei, National Museum of Art of Romania, Bucharest
Muzeum Narodowe w Poznaniu, National Museum in Poznan, Poznan
Narodna Galerija, National Gallery of Slovenia, Ljubljana
Nassau County Museum of Art, Roslyn Harbor NY
National Art Museum of Moldova, Chisinau
The National Museum of Western Art, Tokyo
North Carolina Museum of Art, Raleigh NC
Norton Simon Museum, Pasadena CA
Norwich Free Academy, Slater Memorial Museum, Norwich CT
Panhandle-Plains Historical Museum, Canyon TX
Philadelphia Museum of Art, John G Johnson Collection, Philadelphia PA
Phoenix Art Museum, Phoenix AZ
The Pomona College, Claremont CA
Portland Art Museum, Portland OR
Queens College, City University of New York, Godwin-Ternbach Museum, Flushing NY
Reading Public Museum, Reading PA
Royal Arts Foundation, Belcourt Castle, Newport RI
Saint Bonaventure University, Regina A Quick Center for the Arts, Saint Bonaventure NY
Saint Mary's College of California, Museum of Art, Moraga CA
San Antonio Museum of Art, San Antonio TX
San Diego Museum of Art, San Diego CA
Slovenska Narodna Galeria, Slovak National Gallery, Bratislava
The Society of the Cincinnati at Anderson House, Washington DC
Southern Methodist University, Meadows Museum, Dallas TX
The Speed Art Museum, Louisville KY
Staatliche Museen zu Berlin Stiftung Preussischer Kulturbesitz, National Museums in Berlin, Prussian Cultural Heritage Foundation, Berlin
Stanford University, Cantor Arts Center at Stanford University, Stanford CA
Staten Island Museum, Staten Island NY
Suomen Kansallismuseo, National Museum of Finland, Helsinki
Taft Museum of Art, Cincinnati OH
Tver Regional Art Gallery, Tver
University of Chicago, Smart Museum of Art, Chicago IL
University of Georgia, Georgia Museum of Art, Athens GA
University of Illinois at Urbana-Champaign, Krannert Art Museum and Kinkead Pavilion, Champaign IL
University of Kansas, Spencer Museum of Art, Lawrence KS
The University of Kentucky Art Museum, Lexington KY
University of Miami, Lowe Art Museum, Coral Gables FL
University of Minnesota Duluth, Tweed Museum of Art, Duluth MN
University of Texas at Austin, Blanton Museum of Art, Austin TX
University of Utah, Utah Museum of Fine Arts, Salt Lake City UT
University of Victoria, The Legacy Art Gallery, Victoria BC
University of Wisconsin-Madison, Chazen Museum of Art, Madison WI
Vassar College, The Frances Lehman Loeb Art Center, Poughkeepsie NY
Villa Terrace Decorative Arts Museum, Milwaukee WI
Virginia Museum of Fine Arts, Richmond VA
Vizcaya Museum & Gardens, Miami FL
Walker Art Gallery, Liverpool
Walters Art Museum, Baltimore MD
Woodmere Art Museum Inc, Philadelphia PA
Worcester Art Museum, Worcester MA

REPRODUCTIONS

A.E. Backus Museum & Gallery, Fort Pierce FL
Albin Polasek Museum & Sculpture Gardens, Winter Park FL
Amherst College, Mead Art Museum, Amherst MA
Amon Carter Museum of American Art, Fort Worth TX
Appaloosa Museum and Heritage Center, Moscow ID
Art Gallery of Nova Scotia, Halifax NS
Art Without Walls Inc, Sayville NY
Bangladesh National Museum, Dhaka
Botswana National Museum, Gaborone
C M Russell Museum, Great Falls MT
Canadian Museum of History, Gatineau QC
Cartoon Art Museum, San Francisco CA
Central United Methodist Church, Swords Into Plowshares Peace Center & Gallery, Detroit MI
City of Cedar Falls, Iowa, James & Meryl Hearst Center for the Arts & Sculpture Garden, Cedar Falls IA
Clark County Historical Society, Pioneer - Krier Museum, Ashland KS
Coutts Museum of Art, Inc, El Dorado KS
Cripple Creek District Museum, Cripple Creek CO
Crocker Art Museum, Sacramento CA
Detroit Repertory Theatre Gallery, Detroit MI
Doncaster Museum and Art Gallery, Doncaster Yorks
Edgecombe County Cultural Arts Council, Inc, Blount-Bridgers House, Hobson Pittman Memorial Gallery, Tarboro NC
Edward Hopper, Nyack NY
Environment Canada - Parks Canada, Laurier House, National Historic Site, Ottawa ON
Fitton Center for Creative Arts, Hamilton OH
Forest Lawn Museum, Glendale CA
General Board of Discipleship, The United Methodist Church, The Upper Room Chapel & Museum, Nashville TN
George Phippen, Phippen Museum - Art of the American West, Prescott AZ
Glessner House Museum, Chicago IL
Gloridale Partnership, National Museum of Woodcarving, Custer SD
Great Lakes Historical Society, Inland Seas Maritime Museum, Vermilion OH
Headquarters Fort Monroe, Dept of Army, Casemate Museum, Hampton VA
Hermitage Museum & Gardens, Norfolk VA
The History Center in Tompkins County, Ithaca NY
Independence Historical Museum & Art Center, Independence KS
International Museum of Art, El Paso TX
Jacques Marchais Museum of Tibetan Art, Staten Island NY
JMW Turner Museum, Sarasota FL
Kenosha Public Museums, Kenosha WI
Lahore Museum, Lahore
Lincoln County Historical Association, Inc, 1811 Old Lincoln County Jail & Lincoln County Museum, Wiscasset ME
Longfellow-Evangeline State Commemorative Area, Saint Martinville LA
Medina Railroad Museum, Medina NY
The Mexican Museum, San Francisco CA
Miami-Dade College, MDC Museum of Art & Design, Miami FL
Mission San Miguel Museum, San Miguel CA
Mount Vernon Hotel Museum & Garden, New York NY
Museo De Las Americas, Denver CO
Museum of Chinese in America, New York NY
Museum Plantin-Moretus, Antwerp
Muzeul National de Arta al Romaniei, National Museum of Art of Romania, Bucharest
Muzeum Narodowe w Poznaniu, National Museum in Poznan, Poznan
Nathan Hale Homestead Museum, Coventry CT
National Museum & Art Gallery of Trinidad and Tobago, Port of Spain
National Society of Colonial Dames of America in the State of Maryland, Mount Clare Museum House, Baltimore MD
New York State Office of Parks Recreation & Historic Preservation, John Jay Homestead State Historic Site, Katonah NY
Norwich Free Academy, Slater Memorial Museum, Norwich CT
Panhandle-Plains Historical Museum, Canyon TX
Parrish Art Museum, Water Mill NY
Piedmont Arts Association, Martinsville VA
Polish Museum of America (PMA), Chicago IL
Pump House Center for the Arts, Chillicothe OH
Queens College, City University of New York, Godwin-Ternbach Museum, Flushing NY
Red River Valley Museum, Vernon TX
San Antonio Museum of Art, San Antonio TX
Seneca-Iroquois National Museum, Salamanca NY
Shirley Plantation Foundation, Charles City VA
South Carolina Artisans Center, Walterboro SC
South Dakota State University, South Dakota Art Museum, Brookings SD
Springville Museum of Art, Springville UT
Staatliche Museen zu Berlin Stiftung Preussischer Kulturbesitz, National Museums in Berlin, Prussian Cultural Heritage Foundation, Berlin
State University of New York at Geneseo, Bertha V B Lederer Gallery, Geneseo NY
Staten Island Museum, Staten Island NY
Tacoma Art Museum, Tacoma WA
Tallahassee Museum of History & Natural Science, Tallahassee FL
Thomas Jefferson Foundation, Inc, Monticello, Charlottesville VA
Turtle Bay Exploration Park, Redding CA
Tver Regional Art Gallery, Tver
University of California, Berkeley, Phoebe Apperson Hearst Museum of Anthropology, Berkeley CA
University of Saskatchewan, Diefenbaker Canada Centre, Saskatoon SK
University of Texas at Austin, Blanton Museum of Art, Austin TX
USS Constitution Museum, Boston MA
Vesterheim Norwegian-American Museum, Decorah IA
The Walker African American Museum & Research Center, Las Vegas NV
Walker Fine Art, Denver CO
Walter Anderson Museum of Art, Ocean Springs MS
Wiregrass Museum of Art, Dothan AL
World Erotic Art Museum, Miami Beach FL
Wyoming Trails Gallery, Wheatland WY
Yokohama Museum of Art, Yokohama

RESTORATIONS

Alton Museum of History & Art, Inc, Alton IL
Amon Carter Museum of American Art, Fort Worth TX
Arnot Art Museum, Elmira NY
Art Without Walls Inc, Sayville NY
Bakehouse Art Complex, Inc, Miami FL
Bangladesh National Museum, Dhaka
Baroda Museum and Picture Gallery, Vadodara
Canadian Museum of History, Gatineau QC
Center for Puppetry Arts, Atlanta GA
Chateau de Versailles, Palace of Versailles, Versailles
City of Austin Parks & Recreation, O Henry Museum, Austin TX
City of San Rafael, Falkirk Cultural Center, San Rafael CA
Coastal Arts League Museum, Half Moon Bay CA
Craigdarroch Castle Historical Museum Society, Victoria BC
Cranford Historical Society, Cranford NJ
Cripple Creek District Museum, Cripple Creek CO
Crocker Art Museum, Sacramento CA
Denver Art Museum, Denver CO
Detroit Institute of Arts, Detroit MI
Edgecombe County Cultural Arts Council, Inc, Blount-Bridgers House, Hobson Pittman Memorial Gallery, Tarboro NC
Elisabet Ney, Austin TX
Florence County Museum, Florence SC
Fondazione Musei Civici Di Venezia, Ca' Pesaro Galleria Nazionale d'Arte Moderna - Ca' Pesaro Gallery of Modern Art, Venice
Galeria Mesta Bratislavy, Bratislava City Gallery, Bratislava
Genesee Country Village & Museum, John L Wehle Art Gallery, Mumford NY
Glanmore National Historic Site of Canada, Belleville ON
Glessner House Museum, Chicago IL
Gunston Hall Plantation, Mason Neck VA
Heard Museum, Phoenix AZ
Hecht Museum, Haifa
Heritage Museum & Cultural Center, Baker LA
Historic Holyoke at Wistariahurst & City of Holyoke, Holyoke MA
Historic Hudson Valley, Pocantico Hills NY

Historic Huguenot Street, New Paltz NY
Illinois Historic Preservation Agency, Bishop Hill State Historic Site, Bishop Hill IL
Indiana Landmarks, Morris-Butler House, Indianapolis IN
JMW Turner Museum, Sarasota FL
Joe Gish's Old West Museum, Fredericksburg TX
Johns Hopkins University, Homewood Museum, Baltimore MD
Karakalpak State Art Museum, Nukus Republic of Karakalpakstan
Lafayette Science Museum & Planetarium, Lafayette LA
Lahore Museum, Lahore
Lalit Kala Akademi Rabindra Bhavan Art Galleries, National Academy of Art, New Delhi, New Delhi
Laumeier Sculpture Park, Saint Louis MO
Lincoln County Historical Association, Inc, 1811 Old Lincoln County Jail & Lincoln County Museum, Wiscasset ME
Lockwood-Mathews Mansion Museum, Norwalk CT
McDowell House & Apothecary Shop, Danville KY
Mission San Luis Rey de Francia, Mission San Luis Rey Museum, Oceanside CA
Mission San Miguel Museum, San Miguel CA
Mohave Museum of History & Arts, Kingman AZ
Moravska Galerie v Brne, Moravian Gallery in Brno, Brno
Mount Vernon Hotel Museum & Garden, New York NY
Museu Nacional D'Art De Catalunya, Catalona National Museum of Art, Barcelona
Museum of Chinese in America, New York NY
Museum Plantin-Moretus, Antwerp
Museum Prinsenhof Delft, Delft
Museum zu Allerheiligen, Schaffhausen
Muzej za Umjetnost i Obrt, Museum of Arts & Crafts, Zagreb
Muzeul de Istorie Nationala Si Arheologie Constanta, National History & Archaeology Museum, Constanta
Muzeul National de Arta al Romaniei, National Museum of Art of Romania, Bucharest
Muzeum Narodowe w Poznaniu, National Museum in Poznan, Poznan
Nara Kokuritsu Hakubutsu-Kan, Nara National Museum, Nara
Narodna Galerija, National Gallery of Slovenia, Ljubljana
National Art Museum of Moldova, Chisinau
National Museum & Art Gallery of Trinidad and Tobago, Port of Spain
National Society of Colonial Dames of America in the State of Maryland, Mount Clare Museum House, Baltimore MD
National Trust for Historic Preservation, Shadows-on-the-Teche, New Iberia LA
Nebraska State Capitol, Lincoln NE
Nelda C & H J Lutcher Stark Foundation, Stark Museum of Art, Orange TX
Nelson Mandela Metropolitan Art Museum, Port Elizabeth
The Nelson-Atkins Museum of Art, Kansas City MO
Nevada Northern Railway Museum, Ely NV
New York State Office of Parks Recreation & Historic Preservation, John Jay Homestead State Historic Site, Katonah NY
New York State Office of Parks, Recreation & Historic Preservation, Staatsburgh State Historic Site, Staatsburg NY
The Noble Maritime Collection, Staten Island NY
Norwich Free Academy, Slater Memorial Museum, Norwich CT
The Ohio Historical Society, Inc, Campus Martius Museum & Ohio River Museum, Marietta OH
Old Dartmouth Historical Society, New Bedford Whaling Museum, New Bedford MA
Oshkosh Public Museum & Library, Oshkosh WI
Osterreichische Galerie Belvedere Vienna, Belvedere Museum Vienna, Vienna
Page-Walker Arts & History Center, Cary NC
Panhandle-Plains Historical Museum, Canyon TX
Pennsylvania Historical & Museum Commission, Railroad Museum of Pennsylvania, Strasburg PA
Piatt Castles, West Liberty OH
Please Touch Museum, Philadelphia PA
Preservation Virginia, John Marshall House, Richmond VA
Queens College, City University of New York, Godwin-Ternbach Museum, Flushing NY
Red Deer & District Museum & Archives, Red Deer AB
Ringwood Manor House Museum, Ringwood NJ
Shirley Plantation Foundation, Charles City VA
Slovenska Narodna Galeria, Slovak National Gallery, Bratislava
Staatliche Museen zu Berlin Stiftung Preussischer Kulturbesitz, National Museums in Berlin, Prussian Cultural Heritage Foundation, Berlin
The State Museum of Fine Arts of Tatarstan Republic, Kazan
Thomas Jefferson Foundation, Inc, Monticello, Charlottesville VA
Trust Authority, Museum of the Great Plains, Lawton OK
Tver Regional Art Gallery, Tver
U Gallery, San Francisco CA
United States Capitol, Architect of the Capitol, Washington DC
United States Figure Skating Association, World Figure Skating Museum & Hall of Fame, Colorado Springs CO
Vermilion County Museum Society, Danville IL
Victoria Mansion - Morse Libby House, Portland ME
Villa Terrace Decorative Arts Museum, Milwaukee WI
Wilfrid Laurier University, Robert Langen Art Gallery, Waterloo ON
Willard House & Clock Museum, Inc, North Grafton MA
Woodlawn/The Pope-Leighey, Alexandria VA

SCRIMSHAW

Academy of the New Church, Glencairn Museum, Bryn Athyn PA
Alaska Department of Education, Division of Libraries, Archives & Museums, Sheldon Jackson Museum, Sitka AK
Alaska Heritage Museum at Wells Fargo, Anchorage AK
American Folk Art Museum, New York NY
Bangladesh National Museum, Dhaka
Baroda Museum and Picture Gallery, Vadodara
Blauvelt Demarest Foundation, Hiram Blauvelt Art Museum, Oradell NJ
The Bostonian Society, Old State House Museum, Boston MA
Cayuga Museum of History & Art, Auburn NY
Channel Islands Maritime Museum, Oxnard CA
Chatham Historical Society, The Atwood House Museum, Chatham MA
The Children's Museum of Indianapolis, Indianapolis IN
Dartmouth Heritage Museum, Dartmouth NS
Dawson City Museum, Dawson City YT
Denver Art Museum, Denver CO
Detroit Institute of Arts, Detroit MI
Eiteljorg Museum of American Indians & Western Art, Indianapolis IN
Gallery One Visual Arts Center, Ellensburg WA
Henry Sheldon Museum of Vermont History and Research Center, Middlebury VT
Heritage Museums & Gardens, Sandwich MA
Illinois State Museum, ISM Lockport Gallery, Chicago Gallery & Southern Illinois Art Gallery, Springfield IL
Independence Seaport Museum, Philadelphia PA
Kings County Historical Society & Museum, Hampton NB
Koshare Indian Museum, Inc, La Junta CO
Lincoln County Historical Association, Inc, 1811 Old Lincoln County Jail & Lincoln County Museum, Wiscasset ME
The Mariners' Museum, Newport News VA
Mennello Museum of American Art, Orlando FL
The Museum, Greenwood SC
Muzeul de Istorie Nationala Si Arheologie Constanta, National History & Archaeology Museum, Constanta
National Museums Scotland, National Museum of Scotland, Edinburgh
Naval Historical Center, National Museum of the US Navy, Washington DC
New Canaan Historical Society, New Canaan CT
Norwich Free Academy, Slater Memorial Museum, Norwich CT
Old Dartmouth Historical Society, New Bedford Whaling Museum, New Bedford MA
Peabody Essex Museum, Salem MA
Penobscot Marine Museum, Searsport ME
Pump House Center for the Arts, Chillicothe OH
Queen Victoria Museum and Art Gallery, Launceston TAS
Reading Public Museum, Reading PA
San Francisco Maritime National Historical Park, Maritime Museum, San Francisco CA
Sheldon Museum & Cultural Center, Inc, Sheldon Museum & Cultural Center, Haines AK
Ships of the Sea Maritime Museum, Savannah GA
South Street Seaport Museum, New York NY
Staten Island Museum, Staten Island NY
Suomen Kansallismuseo, National Museum of Finland, Helsinki
University of Miami, Lowe Art Museum, Coral Gables FL
Volcano Art Center Gallery, Hawaii Volcanoes National Park HI
Whalers Village Museum, Lahaina HI
World Erotic Art Museum, Miami Beach FL

SCULPTURE

1708 Gallery, Richmond VA
A.I.R. Gallery, Brooklyn NY
Abington Art Center, Jenkintown PA
Academy Art Museum, Easton MD
Academy of the New Church, Glencairn Museum, Bryn Athyn PA
Acropolis Museum, Athens
African American Atelier, Greensboro NC
African American Museum in Philadelphia, Philadelphia PA
Akron Art Museum, Akron OH
Alaska Heritage Museum at Wells Fargo, Anchorage AK
Alaska State Museum, Juneau AK
Albany Institute of History & Art, Albany NY
Alberta College of Art & Design, Illingworth Kerr Gallery, Calgary AB
Albin Polasek Museum & Sculpture Gardens, Winter Park FL
Albright College, Freedman Gallery, Reading PA
Albuquerque Museum of Art & History, Albuquerque NM
Alexandria Museum of Art, Alexandria LA
Allentown Art Museum, Allentown PA
Alton Museum of History & Art, Inc, Alton IL
American Folk Art Museum, New York NY
American Sport Art Museum and Archives, Daphne AL
American Swedish Institute, Minneapolis MN
American University, Museum at the Katzen, Washington DC
Americas Society Art Gallery, New York NY
Amherst College, Mead Art Museum, Amherst MA
Amon Carter Museum of American Art, Fort Worth TX
Amsterdam Museum, Amsterdam
Anchorage Museum at Rasmuson Center, Anchorage AK
Ancient Spanish Monastery, North Miami Beach FL
Anna Maria College, Saint Luke's Gallery, Paxton MA
ARC Gallery and Educational Foundation, Chicago IL
Arkansas Arts Center, Little Rock AR
Arnold Mikelson Mind & Matter Art Gallery, Surrey BC
Arnot Art Museum, Elmira NY
Art and History Museums - Maitland, Maitland FL
Art Center of Battle Creek, Battle Creek MI
The Art Center of Waco, Waco TX
Art Community Center, Art Center of Corpus Christi, Corpus Christi TX
Art Gallery of Alberta, Edmonton AB
Art Gallery of Bancroft Inc, Bancroft ON
The Art Gallery of Cornwall, Cornwall ON
Art Gallery of Nova Scotia, Halifax NS
Art Gallery of Ontario, Toronto ON
Art Gallery of South Australia, Adelaide
Art Museum of Greater Lafayette, Lafayette IN
Art Museum of Southeast Texas, Beaumont TX
Art Museum of the Americas, Washington DC
Art Without Walls Inc, Sayville NY
Arts Council of Fayetteville-Cumberland County, The Arts Center, Fayetteville NC
Asian Art Museum of San Francisco, Chong-Moon Lee Ctr for Asian Art and Culture, San Francisco CA
Aspen Art Museum, Aspen CO
Associates for Community Development, The Arts Center, Inc, Martinsburg WV
Avant Gallery, Miami FL

Bainbridge Arts & Crafts Gallery, Bainbridge Island WA
Baker Arts Center, Liberal KS
Baldwin Gallery, Aspen CO
Baldwin-Wallace College, Fawick Art Gallery, Berea OH
The Baltimore Museum of Art, Baltimore MD
Bangladesh National Museum, Dhaka
Baroda Museum and Picture Gallery, Vadodara
The Bartlett Museum, Amesbury MA
Baruch College of the City University of New York, Sidney Mishkin Gallery, New York NY
Baton Rouge Gallery, Center For Contemporary Art, Baton Rouge LA
Bayerische Staatsgemaldesammlungen, Bavarian State Painting Collections, Munich
Beaumont Art League, Beaumont TX
Belger Arts Center, Kansas City MO
Bellevue Arts Museum, Bellevue WA
Beloit College, Wright Museum of Art, Beloit WI
Belskie Museum, Closter NJ
Bemis Center for Contemporary Arts, Omaha NE
The Benini Foundation & Sculpture Ranch, Johnson City TX
Bennington Museum, Bennington VT
Bergstrom-Mahler Museum of Glass, Neenah WI
Berman Museum, Anniston AL
Bethany College, Mingenback Art Center, Lindsborg KS
Biggs Museum of American Art, Dover DE
Birger Sandzen Memorial Gallery, Lindsborg KS
Birmingham Museum of Art, Birmingham AL
Biscoe Western Art Museum, San Antonio TX
Blanden Memorial Art Museum, Fort Dodge IA
Blauvelt Demarest Foundation, Hiram Blauvelt Art Museum, Oradell NJ
Board of Parks & Recreation, The Parthenon, Nashville TN
Bob Jones University Museum & Gallery Inc, Greenville SC
Boise Art Museum, Boise ID
Bone Creek Museum of Agrarian Art, David City NE
Booth Western Art Museum, Cartersville GA
The Bostonian Society, Old State House Museum, Boston MA
Botswana National Museum, Gaborone
Bowdoin College, Peary-MacMillan Arctic Museum, Brunswick ME
Brick Store Museum, Kennebunk ME
Bronx Community College (CUNY), Hall of Fame for Great Americans, Bronx NY
Brookgreen Gardens, Murrells Inlet SC
Brown University, Haffenreffer Museum of Anthropology, Providence RI
Bruce Museum, Inc, Greenwich CT
Bucknell University, Edward & Marthann Samek Art Gallery, Lewisburg PA
Burchfield Penney Art Center, Buffalo NY
Burke Arts Council, Jailhouse Galleries, Morganton NC
C M Russell Museum, Great Falls MT
Cameron Art Museum, Wilmington NC
Canadian Clay and Glass Gallery, Waterloo ON
Canadian Museum of History, Gatineau QC
Canadian Wildlife & Wilderness Art Museum, Ottawa ON
Canton Museum of Art, Canton OH
Cape Ann Museum, Gloucester MA
Cape Cod Museum of Art Inc, Dennis MA
Capital University, Schumacher Gallery, Columbus OH
Carlsbad Museum & Art Center, Carlsbad NM
Carnegie Center for Art & History, New Albany IN
Carnegie Museums of Pittsburgh, Carnegie Museum of Art, Pittsburgh PA
Casa-Museu Medeiros e Almeida, Lisbon
Cedar Rapids Museum of Art, Cedar Rapids IA
Centenary College of Louisiana, Meadows Museum of Art, Shreveport LA
Central Methodist University, Ashby-Hodge Gallery of American Art, Fayette MO
Chateau de Versailles, Palace of Versailles, Versailles
The Children's Museum of Indianapolis, Indianapolis IN
Chinati Foundation, Marfa TX
Chrysler Museum of Art, Norfolk VA
Cincinnati Art Museum, Cincinnati Art Museum, Cincinnati OH
City of Cedar Falls, Iowa, James & Meryl Hearst Center for the Arts & Sculpture Garden, Cedar Falls IA
City of Fayette, Alabama, Fayette Art Museum, Fayette AL
City of Fremont, Olive Hyde Art Gallery, Fremont CA
The City of Petersburg Museums, Petersburg VA
City of Pittsfield Office of Cultural Development, Lichtenstein Center for the Arts, Pittsfield MA
Clark Art Institute, Williamstown MA
Clayworks Gallery, Charlotte NC
The Cleveland Museum of Art, Cleveland OH
Clinton Art Association, River Arts Center, Clinton IA
Coastal Arts League Museum, Half Moon Bay CA
Colgate University, Picker Art Gallery, Hamilton NY
College of William & Mary, Muscarelle Museum of Art, Williamsburg VA
Colonial Williamsburg Foundation, Abby Aldrich Rockefeller Folk Art Museum, Williamsburg VA
Colonial Williamsburg Foundation, DeWitt Wallace Decorative Arts Museum, Williamsburg VA
The Columbus Museum, Columbus GA
Columbus Museum of Art, Columbus OH
Concord Museum, Concord MA
Concordia University, Leonard & Bina Ellen Art Gallery, Montreal QC
Congregation Beth Israel's Plotkin Judaica Museum, Scottsdale AZ
Contemporary Art Center, Peoria IL
Coos Art Museum, Coos Bay OR
Cornell Museum of Art and American Culture, Delray Beach FL
Cornell University, Herbert F Johnson Museum of Art, Ithaca NY
The Courtauld Institute of Art, The Courtauld Gallery, London
Coutts Museum of Art, Inc, El Dorado KS
Craft and Folk Art Museum (CAFAM), Los Angeles CA
Cranbrook Art Museum, Bloomfield Hills MI
Crazy Horse Memorial, Indian Museum of North America, Native American Educational & Cultural Center & Crazy Horse Memorial Library (Reference), Crazy Horse SD
Cripple Creek District Museum, Cripple Creek CO
Crocker Art Museum, Sacramento CA
Cuadro Fine Art Gallery, Dubai
The Currier Museum of Art, Manchester NH
Dahesh Museum of Art, Greenwich CT
Danville Museum of Fine Arts & History, Danville VA
Dartmouth College, Hood Museum of Art, Hanover NH
Daum Museum of Contemporary Art, Sedalia MO
Davidson College, William H Van Every Jr & Edward M Smith Galleries, Davidson NC
deCordova Sculpture Park & Museum, Lincoln MA
Deines Cultural Center, Russell KS
Del Mar College, Joseph A Cain Memorial Art Gallery, Corpus Christi TX
Delaware Art Museum, Wilmington DE
DeLeon White Gallery, Toronto ON
Delphi Archaeological Museum, Delphi
Delta Blues Museum, Clarksdale MS
Denver Art Museum, Denver CO
Detroit Institute of Arts, Detroit MI
Detroit Zoological Institute, Wildlife Interpretive Gallery, Royal Oak MI
The Dinosaur Museum, Blanding UT
Dixie State University, Sears Art Museum Gallery, Saint George UT
Doncaster Museum and Art Gallery, Doncaster Yorks
Dublin Arts Council, Dublin OH
Dublin City Gallery The Hugh Lane, Dublin
Dumbarton Oaks, Dumbarton Oaks Museum, Washington DC
Durham Art Guild, Durham NC
DuSable Museum of African American History, Chicago IL
Eastern Illinois University, Tarble Arts Center, Charleston IL
Edmundson Art Foundation, Inc, Des Moines Art Center, Des Moines IA
Edsel & Eleanor Ford House, Grosse Pointe Shores MI
Eiteljorg Museum of American Indians & Western Art, Indianapolis IN
El Camino College Art Gallery, Torrance CA
Elisabet Ney, Austin TX
Ella Sharp Museum, Jackson MI
Ellen Noel Art Museum of the Permian Basin, Odessa TX
Elmhurst Art Museum, Elmhurst IL
Emory University, Michael C Carlos Museum, Atlanta GA
Environment Canada - Parks Canada, Laurier House, National Historic Site, Ottawa ON
Erie Art Museum, Erie PA
Eskimo Museum, Churchill MB
Eula Mae Edwards Museum & Gallery, Clovis NM
Eureka Fine Art Gallery, Eureka Springs AR
Evan Lurie Fine Art Gallery, Carmel IN
Evanston Historical Society, Charles Gates Dawes House, Evanston IL
Evansville Museum of Arts, History & Science, Evansville IN
Everhart Museum, Scranton PA
Everson Museum of Art, Syracuse NY
Faaborg Museum, Faaborg
Fairbanks Museum & Planetarium, Saint Johnsbury VT
Fetherston Foundation, Packwood House Museum, Lewisburg PA
Fireweed Gallery, Homer AK
Fisk University, Aaron Douglas Gallery, Nashville TN
Fitton Center for Creative Arts, Hamilton OH
Five Civilized Tribes Museum, Muskogee OK
Flint Institute of Arts, Flint MI
Florida State University, John & Mable Ringling Museum of Art, Sarasota FL
Florida State University and Central Florida Community College, The Appleton Museum of Art, Ocala FL
Folk Art Society of America, Richmond VA
Fondazione Musei Civici Di Venezia, Museo Correr - Correr Museum, Venice
Fondazione Musei Civici Di Venezia, Ca' Pesaro Galleria Nazionale d'Arte Moderna - Ca' Pesaro Gallery of Modern Art, Venice
Forest Lawn Museum, Glendale CA
Fort Smith Regional Art Museum, Fort Smith AR
Fort Wayne Museum of Art, Inc, Fort Wayne IN
Franconia Sculpture Park, Franconia MN
Frederic Remington, Ogdensburg NY
The Frick Art & Historical Center, Inc, Frick Art Museum, Pittsburgh PA
Frick Collection, New York NY
Fruitlands Museum, Inc, Harvard MA
Fuller Craft Museum, Brockton MA
Gadsden Museum of Art, Gadsden AL
Galerie Montcalm, Gatineau QC
Galleria Nazionale dell'Umbria, Umbrian National Gallery, Perugia
Gallery Moos Ltd, Toronto ON
Gallery One Visual Arts Center, Ellensburg WA
Gaston County Museum of Art & History, Dallas NC
General Board of Discipleship, The United Methodist Church, The Upper Room Chapel & Museum, Nashville TN
Genesee Country Village & Museum, John L Wehle Art Gallery, Mumford NY
George Phippen, Phippen Museum - Art of the American West, Prescott AZ
The George Washington University, Luther W Brady Art Gallery, Washington DC
Georgia O'Keeffe Museum, Santa Fe NM
Georgian Court University, M Christina Geis Gallery, Lakewood NJ
Gertrude Herbert Institute of Art, Augusta GA
Girard College, Stephen Girard Collection, Philadelphia PA
Glanmore National Historic Site of Canada, Belleville ON
Gloridale Partnership, National Museum of Woodcarving, Custer SD
Greenville College, Richard W Bock Sculpture Collection, Almira College House, Greenville IL
Grounds for Sculpture, Hamilton NJ
Harness Racing Museum & Hall of Fame, Goshen NY
Hartwick College, Foreman Gallery, Oneonta NY
Hays Arts Center, Hays KS
Headley-Whitney Museum, Lexington KY
Heard Museum, Phoenix AZ
Hebrew Union College, Skirball Cultural Center, Los Angeles CA
Hebrew Union College - Jewish Institute of Religion Museum, Jewish Institute of Religion, New York NY
Hecht Museum, Haifa
The Heckscher Museum of Art, Huntington NY
Henry County Museum & Cultural Arts Center, Clinton MO
Henry Morrison Flagler Museum, Palm Beach FL

Henry Sheldon Museum of Vermont History and Research Center, Middlebury VT
Heritage Center, Inc, Pine Ridge SD
Hermitage Museum & Gardens, Norfolk VA
Het Noordbrabants Museum, s-Hertogenbosch
Hickory Museum of Art, Inc, Hickory NC
High Desert Museum, Bend OR
Hill-Stead Museum, Farmington CT
Hillwood Museum & Gardens Foundation, Hillwood Estate Museum & Gardens, Washington DC
Historical Society of Cheshire County, Keene NH
Historisches und Volkerkundemuseum, Museum of History and Ethnology, St Gallen
History Colorado Center Museum, Denver CO
Holter Museum of Art, Helena MT
Hot Shops Art Center, Omaha NE
The Hudson River Museum, Yonkers NY
Hunter Museum of American Art, Chattanooga TN
Huntsville Museum of Art, Huntsville AL
The Hyde Collection, Glens Falls NY
Hyde Park Art Center, Chicago IL
i.d.e.a. Museum, Mesa AZ
Illinois State Museum, ISM Lockport Gallery, Chicago Gallery & Southern Illinois Art Gallery, Springfield IL
Imago Galleries, Palm Desert CA
Independence Historical Museum & Art Center, Independence KS
Indiana Landmarks, Morris-Butler House, Indianapolis IN
Indiana State Museum, Indianapolis IN
Institute of Contemporary Art, Los Angeles, Los Angeles CA
Institute of Puerto Rican Culture, Museo Fuerte Conde de Mirasol, Vieques PR
INTAR Gallery, New York NY
International Museum of Art, El Paso TX
Iredell Museums, Statesville NC
Iroquois Indian Museum, Howes Cave NY
Isamu Noguchi, Isamu Noguchi Garden Museum, Long Island City NY
The Israel Museum, Jerusalem, Jerusalem
Jacksonville University, Alexander Brest Museum & Gallery, Jacksonville FL
Jacques Marchais Museum of Tibetan Art, Staten Island NY
James A Michener Art Museum, Doylestown PA
James Monroe Museum, Fredericksburg VA
JMW Turner Museum, Sarasota FL
Joe Gish's Old West Museum, Fredericksburg TX
John B Aird Gallery, Toronto ON
The John L. Clarke Western Art Gallery & Memorial Museum, East Glacier Park MT
Jordan National Gallery of Fine Arts, Amman
Joslyn Art Museum, Omaha NE
Kamloops Art Gallery, Kamloops BC
Karakalpak State Art Museum, Nukus Republic of Karakalpakstan
Kelvingrove Art Gallery & Museum, Glasgow UK
Kenosha Public Museums, Kenosha WI
Kentucky Derby Museum, Louisville KY
Kentucky Museum of Art and Craft, Louisville KY
Kereszteny Muzeum, Christian Museum, Esztergom
Keystone Gallery, Scott City KS
Kimbell Art Foundation, Kimbell Art Museum, Fort Worth TX
Kings County Historical Society & Museum, Hampton NB
Kirchner Museum Davos, Davos
Kirkland Museum of Fine & Decorative Art, Denver CO
Kitchener-Waterloo Art Gallery, Kitchener ON
Knoxville Museum of Art, Knoxville TN
Koninklijk Museum voor Schone Kunsten Antwerpen, Royal Museum of Fine Arts Antwerp, Antwerp
Krasl Art Center, Saint Joseph MI
The Kreeger Museum, Washington DC
Kroller-Muller Museum, Otterlo
Kunsthalle Bremen, Bremen Art Gallery, Bremen
Kunsthistorisches Museum Wien, Museum of Fine Arts, Vienna
Kunstmuseum Solothurn, Solothurn Art Museum, Solothurn
Kyiv Museum of Russian Art, Kyiv Ukrainian
L'Universite Laval, Ecole des Arts Visuels, Quebec QC
La Salle University Art Museum, Philadelphia PA
Lafayette College, Lafayette College Art Galleries, Easton PA
Lafayette Science Museum & Planetarium, Lafayette LA
Laguna Art Museum, Laguna Beach CA
Lalit Kala Akademi Rabindra Bhavan Art Galleries, National Academy of Art, New Delhi, New Delhi
Langston University, Melvin B Tolson Black Heritage Center, Langston OK
Latino Art Museum, Pomona CA
Laumeier Sculpture Park, Saint Louis MO
Le Grand Curtius, The Grand Curtius, Liege
Leanin' Tree Museum & Sculpture Garden of Western Art, Boulder CO
Leigh Yawkey Woodson Art Museum, Wausau WI
Lighthouse ArtCenter Museum & School of Art, Tequesta FL
Lightner Museum, Saint Augustine FL
Lillian & Coleman Taube Museum of Art, Minot ND
Lincolnshire County Council, Library & Heritage Services, Lincoln
Lincolnshire County Council, The Collection: Art & Archaeology in Lincolnshire, Lincoln
The Lindsay Gallery Inc, Lindsay ON
Lockwood-Mathews Mansion Museum, Norwalk CT
The Long Island Museum of American Art, History & Carriages, Stony Brook NY
Longue Vue House & Gardens, New Orleans LA
Longview Museum of Fine Art, Longview TX
Los Angeles County Museum of Art, Los Angeles CA
Louise Hopkins Underwood Center for the Arts, Lubbock TX
Louisiana Arts & Science Museum, Baton Rouge LA
Louisiana Department of Culture, Recreation & Tourism, Louisiana State Museum, New Orleans LA
Louisiana Museum of Modern Art, Humlebaek
Loveland Museum/Gallery, Loveland CO
Loyola University Chicago, Loyola University Museum of Art, Chicago IL
Lyme Historical Society, Florence Griswold Museum, Old Lyme CT
Lyon College Kresge Gallery, Batesville AR
Mabee-Gerrer Museum of Art, Shawnee OK
Madison Museum of Contemporary Art, Madison WI
Madison Museum of Fine Art, Madison GA
Maine College of Art, The Institute of Contemporary Art, Portland ME
Maison Saint-Gabriel Museum, Montreal QC
Maricopa County Historical Society, Desert Caballeros Western Museum, Wickenburg AZ
Marietta College, Grover M Hermann Fine Arts Center, Marietta OH
Marietta-Cobb Museum of Art, Marietta GA
The Mariners' Museum, Newport News VA
Mark Twain, Hartford CT
Maryhill Museum of Art, Goldendale WA
Maryland Hall for the Creative Arts, Chaney Gallery, Annapolis MD
Marylhurst University, The Art Gym, Marylhurst OR
Mathaf: Arab Museum of Modern Art, Doha
McLean County Historical Society, McLean County Museum of History, Bloomington IL
McNay Art Museum, San Antonio TX
Meem Gallery, Dubai
Memphis Brooks Museum of Art, Memphis TN
Mennello Museum of American Art, Orlando FL
Meredith College, Frankie G Weems Gallery & Rotunda Gallery, Raleigh NC
Meridian Museum of Art, Meridian MS
Mesa Arts Center, Mesa Contemporary Arts Museum, Mesa AZ
The Metropolitan Museum of Art, New York NY
The Mexican Museum, San Francisco CA
Mhiripiri Gallery, Bloomington MN
Middle Border Museum & Oscar Howe Art Center, Mitchell SD
Midwest Museum of American Art, Elkhart IN
Miles B Carpenter Folk Art Museum, Waverly VA
Millicent Rogers Museum, Taos NM
Millikin University, Perkinson Gallery, Decatur IL
Minneapolis Institute of Art, Minneapolis MN
Minnesota Museum of American Art, Saint Paul MN
The Mint Museum, Mint Museum of Craft & Design, Charlotte NC
Mississippi Museum of Art, Jackson MS
Mississippi Valley Conservation Authority, R Tait McKenzie Memorial Museum, Almonte ON
Missoula Art Museum, Missoula MT
Mobile Museum of Art, Mobile AL
Moderna Galerija, Modern Gallery - National Museum of Modern Art, Zagreb
Modernism, San Francisco CA
Montana State University, Helen E Copeland Gallery, Bozeman MT
Montclair Art Museum, Montclair NJ
Montgomery Museum of Fine Arts, Montgomery AL
Moore College of Art & Design, The Galleries at Moore, Philadelphia PA
Moravska Galerie v Brne, Moravian Gallery in Brno, Brno
Morehead State University, Kentucky Folk Art Center, Morehead KY
Morris Museum, Morristown NJ
Morris Museum of Art, Augusta GA
Moscow Museum of Modern Art, Moscow
Mount Allison University, Owens Art Gallery, Sackville NB
MTG Hawkes Bay, Napier
Muhlenberg College, Martin Art Gallery, Allentown PA
Muscatine Art Center, Muscatine IA
Musee Cognacq-Jay, Cognacq-Jay Museum, Paris
Musee des Beaux-Arts d'Orleans, Museum of Fine Arts, Orleans
Musee des Beaux-Arts de Tours, Museum of Fine Arts, Tours
Musee National des Beaux Arts du Quebec, Quebec QC
Musee Regional de lu Cote-Nord, Sept-Iles QC
Musee Regional de Vaudreuil-Soulanges, Vaudreuil-Dorion QC
Museen der Stadt Koln, Museum Ludwig - Ludwig Museum, Cologne
Museen der Stadt Koln, Wallraf-Richartz-Museum & Fondation Corboud - Wallraf-Richartz Museum & Corboud Foundation, Cologne
Museo de Arte de Ponce, The Luis A Ferre Foundation Inc, Ponce PR
Museo De Las Americas, Denver CO
Museo di Palazzo Ducale, Ducale Palace Museum, Mantua
Museo Italo Americano, San Francisco CA
Museo Nacional de Bellas Artes, National Museum of Fine Arts, Santiago
Museu Nacional D'Art De Catalunya, Catalona National Museum of Art, Barcelona
Museu Nacional de Arte Contemporanea do Chiado, National Museum of Contemporary Art, Museu Do Chiado, Lisbon
The Museum, Greenwood SC
Museum De Lakenhal, Leiden
Museum of Art & History, Santa Cruz, Santa Cruz CA
Museum of Art - Deland FL, Inc, Deland FL
Museum of Art, Fort Lauderdale, Fort Lauderdale FL
Museum of Arts & Design, New York NY
The Museum of Arts & Sciences Inc, Daytona Beach FL
Museum of Arts & Sciences, Inc, Macon GA
Museum of Contemporary Art Chicago, Chicago IL
Museum of Contemporary Art Jacksonville, Jacksonville FL
Museum of Contemporary Art San Diego, San Diego CA
Museum of Contemporary Canadian Art, Toronto ON
Museum of Fine Arts, Boston MA
Museum of Fine Arts, Saint Petersburg, Florida, Inc, Saint Petersburg FL
Museum of Latin American Art, Long Beach CA
Museum of Modern Art, New York NY
Museum of Modern Art, Ibaraki, Mito Ibaraki
Museum of Northern Arizona, Flagstaff AZ
Museum of Northwest Art, La Conner WA
Museum of the Plains Indian & Crafts Center, Browning MT
Museum of the Southwest, Midland TX
Museum of Wisconsin Art, West Bend WI
Museum of York County, Rock Hill SC
Museum Plantin-Moretus, Antwerp
Museum zu Allerheiligen, Schaffhausen
Muzej Moderne I Suvremene Umjetnosti, Museum of Modern and Contemporary Art, Rijeka
Muzej za Umjetnost i Obrt, Museum of Arts & Crafts, Zagreb
Muzeul de Istorie Nationala Si Arheologie Constanta, National History & Archaeology Museum, Constanta
Muzeul National de Arta al Romaniei, National Museum of Art of Romania, Bucharest
Muzeum Narodowe W Kielcach, National Museum in Kielce, Kielce
Muzeum Narodowe w Poznaniu, National Museum in Poznan, Poznan

Nara Kokuritsu Hakubutsu-Kan, Nara National Museum, Nara
Narodna Galerija, National Gallery of Slovenia, Ljubljana
Nassau Community College, Firehouse Art Gallery, Garden City NY
Nassau County Museum of Art, Roslyn Harbor NY
National Archaeological Museum, Athens
The National Art Center, Tokyo, Tokyo
National Art Museum of Moldova, Chisinau
National Baseball Hall of Fame & Museum, Cooperstown NY
National Museum & Art Gallery of Trinidad and Tobago, Port of Spain
The National Museum of Modern Art, Tokyo, Tokyo
The National Museum of Puerto Rican Arts & Culture, Chicago IL
National Museum of the American Indian, George Gustav Heye Center, New York NY
National Museum of the Philippines, Manila
The National Museum of Western Art, Tokyo
National Museum of Wildlife Art of the Unites States, Jackson WY
National Museums Scotland, National Museum of Scotland, Edinburgh
National Portrait Gallery, London
National Trust for Historic Preservation, Chesterwood, Stockbridge MA
National Veterans Art Museum, Chicago IL
Naval Historical Center, National Museum of the US Navy, Washington DC
Nebraska Game and Parks Commission, Arbor Lodge State Historical Park & Morton Mansion, Nebraska City NE
Nebraska State Capitol, Lincoln NE
Nebraska Wesleyan University, Elder Gallery, Lincoln NE
Nelson Mandela Metropolitan Art Museum, Port Elizabeth
The Nelson-Atkins Museum of Art, Kansas City MO
Neue Galerie New York, New York NY
Nevada Museum of Art, Reno NV
Neville Public Museum of Brown County, Green Bay WI
New Britain Museum of American Art, New Britain CT
New Brunswick Museum, Saint John NB
New Canaan Historical Society, New Canaan CT
New Gallery of Modern Art, Charlotte NC
New Orleans Artworks at New Orleans Glassworks & Printmaking Studio, New Orleans LA
New Orleans Museum of Art, New Orleans LA
New Visions Gallery, Inc, Marshfield WI
New York State Military Museum and Veterans Research Center, Saratoga Springs NY
New York State Office of Parks Recreation & Historic Preservation, John Jay Homestead State Historic Site, Katonah NY
Newport Art Museum and Association, Newport RI
Niagara University, Castellani Art Museum, Niagara NY
Niigata Prefectural Museum of Modern Art, Nagaoka
Norsk Maritimt Museum, Norwegian Maritime Museum, Oslo
North Carolina Central University, NCCU Art Museum, Durham NC
North Carolina Museum of Art, Raleigh NC
North End Gallery, Leonardtown MD
Norton Simon Museum, Pasadena CA
Norwich Free Academy, Slater Memorial Museum, Norwich CT
Nova Scotia College of Art and Design, Anna Leonowens Gallery, Halifax NS
Noyes Art Gallery, Lincoln NE
Oberlin College, Allen Memorial Art Museum, Oberlin OH
Ogden Museum of Southern Art, University of New Orleans, New Orleans LA
Ogunquit Museum of American Art, Ogunquit ME
Ohio History Connection, National Afro-American Museum & Cultural Center, Wilberforce OH
Ohio University, Kennedy Museum of Art, Athens OH
Oklahoma City Museum of Art, Oklahoma City OK
Olana State Historic Site, Hudson NY
Old Dartmouth Historical Society, New Bedford Whaling Museum, New Bedford MA
The Old Jail Art Center, Albany TX
Olivet College, Armstrong Collection, Olivet MI
Omenka Gallery, Lagos
Oshkosh Public Museum & Library, Oshkosh WI
Osterreichische Galerie Belvedere Vienna, Belvedere Museum Vienna, Vienna
Owensboro Museum of Fine Art, Owensboro KY
Page-Walker Arts & History Center, Cary NC
Palm Springs Art Museum, Palm Springs CA
Panhandle-Plains Historical Museum, Canyon TX
Parrish Art Museum, Water Mill NY
Patrick Henry, Red Hill National Memorial, Brookneal VA
Peabody Essex Museum, Salem MA
Pearson Lakes Art Center, Okoboji IA
Pennsylvania Academy of the Fine Arts, Philadelphia PA
Pennsylvania Historical & Museum Commission, Railroad Museum of Pennsylvania, Strasburg PA
Philadelphia History Museum, Philadelphia PA
Philadelphia Museum of Art, Rodin Museum of Philadelphia, Philadelphia PA
Philbrook Museum of Art, Tulsa OK
Phillips Academy, Addison Gallery of American Art, Andover MA
Phoenix Art Museum, Phoenix AZ
Piedmont Arts Association, Martinsville VA
Pioneer Town, Pioneer Museum of Western Art, Wimberley TX
Plains Art Museum, Fargo ND
Polish Museum of America (PMA), Chicago IL
Polk Museum of Art, Lakeland FL
The Pomona College, Claremont CA
Ponca City Cultural Center & Museum, Ponca City OK
Portland Art Museum, Portland OR
Portland Museum of Art, Portland ME
Preservation Virginia, John Marshall House, Richmond VA
PS1 Contemporary Art Center, Long Island City NY
Pueblo Museum, Desert Hot Springs CA
Pump House Center for the Arts, Chillicothe OH
Purchase College, Neuberger Museum of Art, Purchase NY
Pyramid Hill Sculpture Park & Museum, Hamilton OH
Queen Victoria Museum and Art Gallery, Launceston TAS
Queen's University, Agnes Etherington Art Centre, Kingston ON
Queens College, City University of New York, Godwin-Ternbach Museum, Flushing NY
Radio-Canada SRC CBC, Georges Goguen CBC Art Gallery, Moncton NB
Reading Public Museum, Reading PA
Real Art Ways (RAW), Hartford CT
Red River Valley Museum, Vernon TX
Regina Public Library, Dunlop Art Gallery, Regina SK
Rensselaer County Historical Society, Hart-Cluett Mansion, 1827, Troy NY
Reynolda House Museum of American Art, Winston-Salem NC
The Robert McLaughlin Gallery, Oshawa ON
Robischon Gallery, Denver CO
Rogue Community College, Wiseman Gallery - FireHouse Gallery, Grants Pass OR
Rollins College, George D & Harriet W Cornell Fine Arts Museum, Winter Park FL
Roswell Museum & Art Center, Roswell NM
Royal Arts Foundation, Belcourt Castle, Newport RI
Rubin Museum of Art, New York NY
Rutgers University, Stedman Art Gallery, Camden NJ
Ryerss Victorian Museum & Library, Philadelphia PA
Saco Museum, Saco ME
Saginaw Art Museum, Saginaw MI
Saint Anselm College, Alva de Mars Megan Chapel Art Center, Manchester NH
Saint Bonaventure University, Regina A Quick Center for the Arts, Saint Bonaventure NY
Saint Clair County Community College, Jack R Hennesey Art Galleries, Port Huron MI
Saint Johnsbury Athenaeum, Saint Johnsbury VT
Saint Mary's College of California, Museum of Art, Moraga CA
Saint Olaf College, Flaten Art Museum, Northfield MN
Saint-Gaudens National Historic Site, Cornish NH
Salisbury University, Ward Museum of Wildfowl Art, Salisbury MD
Sammlung Boros, Berlin
San Angelo Museum of Fine Arts, San Angelo TX
San Antonio Museum of Art, San Antonio TX
San Carlos Cathedral, Monterey CA
San Diego Museum of Art, San Diego CA
San Francisco Museum of Modern Art, San Francisco CA
San Jose Museum of Art, San Jose CA
Santa Barbara Museum of Art, Santa Barbara CA
Santa Clara University, de Saisset Museum, Santa Clara CA
Santarella Museum & Gardens, Tyringham MA
Schweinfurth Art Center, Auburn NY
Scripps College, Ruth Chandler Williamson Gallery, Claremont CA
Scripps College, Clark Humanities Museum, Claremont CA
Sculpture Space, Inc, Utica NY
Seneca-Iroquois National Museum, Salamanca NY
Shanghai Museum, Shanghai
Sheldon Art Galleries, Saint Louis MO
Slovenska Narodna Galeria, Slovak National Gallery, Bratislava
Soap Factory, Minneapolis MN
The Society of the Cincinnati at Anderson House, Washington DC
Socrates Sculpture Park, Long Island City NY
Solomon R Guggenheim Museum, New York NY
South Carolina Artisans Center, Walterboro SC
South Carolina State Museum, Columbia SC
South Dakota State University, South Dakota Art Museum, Brookings SD
South Shore Arts, Munster IN
Southeastern Center for Contemporary Art, Winston-Salem NC
Southern Baptist Theological Seminary, Joseph A Callaway Archaeological Museum, Louisville KY
Southern Methodist University, Meadows Museum, Dallas TX
Spark Gallery, Denver CO
Spartanburg Art Museum, Spartanburg SC
The Speed Art Museum, Louisville KY
Spertus Institute of Jewish Studies, Chicago IL
Springfield Art Museum, Springfield MO
Spruce Forest Artisan Village, Grantsville MD
St Mary's College of Maryland, The Dwight Frederick Boyden Gallery, St Mary's City MD
Staatliche Museen zu Berlin Stiftung Preussischer Kulturbesitz, National Museums in Berlin, Prussian Cultural Heritage Foundation, Berlin
Stamford Museum & Nature Center, Stamford CT
Stanford University, Cantor Arts Center at Stanford University, Stanford CA
The State Museum of Fine Arts of Tatarstan Republic, Kazan
State University of New York at Geneseo, Bertha V B Lederer Gallery, Geneseo NY
State University of New York at Oswego, Tyler Art Gallery, Oswego NY
The State University of New York at Potsdam, The Art Museum, Potsdam NY
State University of New York at Ulster, Muroff-Kotler Visual Arts Gallery, Stone Ridge NY
State University of New York College at Cortland, Dowd Fine Arts Gallery, Cortland NY
State University of New York College at Fredonia, Cathy and Jesse Marion Art Gallery, Fredonia NY
Staten Island Museum, Staten Island NY
Stedelijk Museum Alkmaar, Alkmaar Municipal Museum, Alkmaar
Stephens College, Lewis James & Nellie Stratton Davis Art Gallery, Columbia MO
Stone Quarry Hill Art Park, Winner Gallery, Cazenovia NY
Storm King Art Center, New Windsor NY
The Studio Museum in Harlem, New York NY
Suan Pakkad Palace Museum, Bangkok
Surrey Art Gallery, Surrey BC
Swetcharnik Art Studio, Mount Airy MD
Swope Art Museum, Terre Haute IN
Szepmuveszeti Muzeum, Museum of Fine Arts, Budapest
Tacoma Art Museum, Tacoma WA
Tampa Museum of Art, Tampa FL
Temiskaming Art Gallery, Haileybury ON
Texas Christian University, Fort Worth Contemporary Art, Fort Worth TX
Texas Ranger Hall of Fame & Museum, Waco TX
Thomas Jefferson Foundation, Inc, Monticello, Charlottesville VA
Thomas More College, Eva G Farris Art Gallery, Crestview KY
Timken Museum of Art, San Diego CA
Tinkertown Museum, Sandia Park NM
Tohono Chul Park, Tucson AZ
Tokyo National Museum, Tokyo
Toledo Museum of Art, Toledo OH
Traffic Zone Center for Visual Art, Minneapolis MN

Triton Museum of Art, Santa Clara CA
Tubac Center of the Arts, Santa Cruz Valley Art Association, Tubac AZ
Tubman African American Museum, Macon GA
Tucson Museum of Art and Historic Block, Tucson AZ
Turtle Bay Exploration Park, Redding CA
Tver Regional Art Gallery, Tver
Twin City Art Foundation, Masur Museum of Art, Monroe LA
Two Rivers Art Gallery, Prince George BC
Tyler Museum of Art, Tyler TX
Ucross Foundation, Big Red Barn Gallery, Clearmont WY
Ukrainian Institute of Modern Art, Chicago IL
The Ukrainian Museum, New York NY
UMLAUF Sculpture Garden & Museum, Austin TX
United States Capitol, Architect of the Capitol, Washington DC
United States Figure Skating Association, World Figure Skating Museum & Hall of Fame, Colorado Springs CO
University of Arkansas at Little Rock, Art Galleries, Little Rock AR
University of Calgary, Nickle Galleries, Calgary AB
University of California, Berkeley, Phoebe Apperson Hearst Museum of Anthropology, Berkeley CA
University of California, Davis, Jan Shrem and Maria Manetti Shrem Museum of Art, Davis CA
University of California, Los Angeles, Hammer Museum, Los Angeles CA
University of California, San Diego, Stuart Collection, La Jolla CA
University of Chicago, Smart Museum of Art, Chicago IL
University of Florida, Samuel P Harn Museum of Art, Gainesville FL
University of Georgia, Georgia Museum of Art, Athens GA
University of Illinois at Urbana-Champaign, Krannert Art Museum and Kinkead Pavilion, Champaign IL
University of Indianapolis, Christel DeHaan Fine Arts Gallery, Indianapolis IN
University of Kansas, Spencer Museum of Art, Lawrence KS
The University of Kentucky Art Museum, Lexington KY
University of Miami, Lowe Art Museum, Coral Gables FL
University of Michigan, Kelsey Museum of Archaeology, Ann Arbor MI
University of Minnesota, Katherine E Nash Gallery, Minneapolis MN
University of Minnesota Duluth, Tweed Museum of Art, Duluth MN
University of Nebraska-Lincoln, Great Plains Art Museum, Lincoln NE
University of Nevada, Reno, Sheppard Contemporary & University Galleries, Reno NV
University of New Mexico, The Harwood Museum of Art, Taos NM
University of North Carolina at Greensboro, Weatherspoon Art Museum, Greensboro NC
University of North Dakota, Hughes Fine Arts Center-Col Eugene Myers Art Gallery, Grand Forks ND
University of Notre Dame, Snite Museum of Art, Notre Dame IN
University of Pennsylvania, Arthur Ross Gallery, Philadelphia PA
University of Richmond, University Museums, Richmond VA
University of Saskatchewan, Diefenbaker Canada Centre, Saskatoon SK
University of Texas at Austin, Blanton Museum of Art, Austin TX
University of Utah, Utah Museum of Fine Arts, Salt Lake City UT
University of Wisconsin-Eau Claire, Foster Gallery, Eau Claire WI
University of Wisconsin-Madison, Chazen Museum of Art, Madison WI
University of Wisconsin-Stout, J Furlong Gallery, Menomonie WI
Ursinus College, Philip & Muriel Berman Museum of Art, Collegeville PA
Utah Arts Council, Chase Home Museum of Utah Folk Arts, Salt Lake City UT
The Valentine, Richmond VA
Valley Art Gallery, Forest Grove OR
Van Gogh Museum, Amsterdam
Vancouver Art Gallery, Vancouver BC
Vassar College, The Frances Lehman Loeb Art Center, Poughkeepsie NY
Venice Art Center, Venice FL
Vero Beach Museum of Art, Vero Beach FL
Vesterheim Norwegian-American Museum, Decorah IA
Victoria Mansion - Morse Libby House, Portland ME
Villa Terrace Decorative Arts Museum, Milwaukee WI
Virginia Museum of Fine Arts, Richmond VA
Viridian Artists Inc, New York NY
Vizcaya Museum & Gardens, Miami FL
Volcano Art Center Gallery, Hawaii Volcanoes National Park HI
Wadsworth Atheneum Museum of Art, Hartford CT
Walker Art Center, Minneapolis MN
Walker Art Gallery, Liverpool
Walker Fine Art, Denver CO
The Wallace Collection, London
Walter Anderson Museum of Art, Ocean Springs MS
Walters Art Museum, Baltimore MD
Washburn University, Mulvane Art Museum, Topeka KS
Washington County Museum of Fine Arts, Hagerstown MD
Waterloo Center of the Arts, Waterloo IA
Waterworks Visual Arts Center, Salisbury NC
Westmoreland Museum of American Art, Greensburg PA
Whalers Village Museum, Lahaina HI
Wharton Esherick Museum, Paoli PA
Whatcom Museum, Bellingham WA
Wheaton College, Beard and Weil Galleries, Norton MA
Wheelwright Museum of the American Indian, Santa Fe NM
White House, Washington DC
Whitney Museum of American Art, New York NY
Wichita Art Museum, Wichita KS
Wichita State University, Ulrich Museum of Art, Wichita KS
Wildling Art Museum, Solvang CA
Wilfrid Laurier University, Robert Langen Art Gallery, Waterloo ON
Wilkes Art Gallery, North Wilkesboro NC
Wilkes University, Sordoni Art Gallery, Wilkes-Barre PA
William Paterson University, University Galleries, Wayne NJ
Winkler Gallery of Fine Art, DuBois PA
The Winnipeg Art Gallery, Winnipeg MB
Winston-Salem State University, Diggs Gallery, Winston-Salem NC
Wiregrass Museum of Art, Dothan AL
Woodlawn/The Pope-Leighey, Alexandria VA
Woodmere Art Museum Inc, Philadelphia PA
Worcester Art Museum, Worcester MA
World Erotic Art Museum, Miami Beach FL
Wyoming State Museum, Cheyenne WY
Yale University, Yale Center for British Art, New Haven CT
Yerba Buena Center for the Arts, San Francisco CA
Yeshiva University Museum, New York NY
Yokohama Museum of Art, Yokohama
Zigler Art Museum, Jennings LA

SILVER

Adams County Historical Society, Gettysburg PA
Alaska State Museum, Juneau AK
Albany Institute of History & Art, Albany NY
Albuquerque Museum of Art & History, Albuquerque NM
Allentown Art Museum, Allentown PA
Americas Society Art Gallery, New York NY
Amherst College, Mead Art Museum, Amherst MA
Amsterdam Museum, Amsterdam
Arnot Art Museum, Elmira NY
Art Gallery of South Australia, Adelaide
Art Without Walls Inc, Sayville NY
The Baltimore Museum of Art, Baltimore MD
Bangladesh National Museum, Dhaka
Baroda Museum and Picture Gallery, Vadodara
The Bartlett Museum, Amesbury MA
Bayerisches Nationalmuseum, Bavarian National Museum, Munich
Biggs Museum of American Art, Dover DE
Birmingham Museum of Art, Birmingham AL
Bob Jones University Museum & Gallery Inc, Greenville SC
Canadian Museum of History, Gatineau QC
Cape Ann Museum, Gloucester MA
Casa-Museu Medeiros e Almeida, Lisbon
Charleston Museum, Joseph Manigault House, Charleston SC
Chatillon-DeMenil House Foundation, Chatillon-DeMenil Mansion, Saint Louis MO
The Children's Museum of Indianapolis, Indianapolis IN
Cincinnati Art Museum, Cincinnati Art Museum, Cincinnati OH
The City of Petersburg Museums, Petersburg VA
Clark Art Institute, Williamstown MA
College of William & Mary, Muscarelle Museum of Art, Williamsburg VA
The Columbus Museum, Columbus GA
Concord Museum, Concord MA
Congregation Beth Israel's Plotkin Judaica Museum, Scottsdale AZ
The Courtauld Institute of Art, The Courtauld Gallery, London
Craft and Folk Art Museum (CAFAM), Los Angeles CA
Cranbrook Art Museum, Bloomfield Hills MI
Crocker Art Museum, Sacramento CA
The Currier Museum of Art, Manchester NH
DAR Museum, National Society Daughters of the American Revolution, Washington DC
Dartmouth College, Hood Museum of Art, Hanover NH
Delaware Division of Historical & Cultural Affairs, Dover DE
Delphi Archaeological Museum, Delphi
Denver Art Museum, Denver CO
Designmuseum Danmark, Danish Design Museum, Copenhagen
Detroit Institute of Arts, Detroit MI
Doncaster Museum and Art Gallery, Doncaster Yorks
Ellen Noel Art Museum of the Permian Basin, Odessa TX
Elverhoj Museum of History and Art, Solvang CA
Environment Canada - Parks Canada, Laurier House, National Historic Site, Ottawa ON
Erie Art Museum, Erie PA
Erie County Historical Society, Erie PA
Evanston Historical Society, Charles Gates Dawes House, Evanston IL
Fetherston Foundation, Packwood House Museum, Lewisburg PA
Fishkill Historical Society, Van Wyck Homestead Museum, Fishkill NY
Fitton Center for Creative Arts, Hamilton OH
Flint Institute of Arts, Flint MI
Florence County Museum, Florence SC
Fondazione Musei Civici Di Venezia, Museo Correr - Correr Museum, Venice
Forest Lawn Museum, Glendale CA
Frederic Remington, Ogdensburg NY
The Frick Art & Historical Center, Inc, Frick Art Museum, Pittsburgh PA
Fuller Craft Museum, Brockton MA
Gadsden Museum of Art, Gadsden AL
Gallery One Visual Arts Center, Ellensburg WA
Germantown Historical Society, Philadelphia PA
Girard College, Stephen Girard Collection, Philadelphia PA
Glanmore National Historic Site of Canada, Belleville ON
Glasgow University, The Hunterian, Glasgow
Glessner House Museum, Chicago IL
Haystack Mountain School of Crafts, Deer Isle ME
Headley-Whitney Museum, Lexington KY
Headquarters Fort Monroe, Dept of Army, Casemate Museum, Hampton VA
Heard Museum, Phoenix AZ
Hecht Museum, Haifa
Henry Morrison Flagler Museum, Palm Beach FL
Henry Sheldon Museum of Vermont History and Research Center, Middlebury VT
Heritage Center, Inc, Pine Ridge SD
Het Noordbrabants Museum, s-Hertogenbosch
Hill-Stead Museum, Farmington CT
Hillwood Museum & Gardens Foundation, Hillwood Estate Museum & Gardens, Washington DC
Historic Cherry Hill, Albany NY
Historic Deerfield, Inc, Deerfield MA
Historic Newton, Newton MA
Historical Society of Cheshire County, Keene NH
History Colorado Center Museum, Denver CO
History Museum of Mobile, Mobile AL

Hunter Museum of American Art, Chattanooga TN
Illinois State Museum, ISM Lockport Gallery, Chicago Gallery & Southern Illinois Art Gallery, Springfield IL
Independence Seaport Museum, Philadelphia PA
Indiana Landmarks, Morris-Butler House, Indianapolis IN
Indiana State Museum, Indianapolis IN
Iroquois Indian Museum, Howes Cave NY
Jacques Marchais Museum of Tibetan Art, Staten Island NY
James Monroe Museum, Fredericksburg VA
John B Aird Gallery, Toronto ON
Johns Hopkins University, Evergreen Museum & Library, Baltimore MD
Johns Hopkins University, Homewood Museum, Baltimore MD
Kenosha Public Museums, Kenosha WI
Kentucky Museum of Art and Craft, Louisville KY
Kereszteny Muzeum, Christian Museum, Esztergom
Kimbell Art Foundation, Kimbell Art Museum, Fort Worth TX
Kings County Historical Society & Museum, Hampton NB
Kirkland Museum of Fine & Decorative Art, Denver CO
Kunsthistorisches Museum Wien, Museum of Fine Arts, Vienna
Latino Art Museum, Pomona CA
Lauren Rogers, Laurel MS
Le Grand Curtius, The Grand Curtius, Liege
Liberty Hall Historic Site, Liberty Hall Museum, Frankfort KY
Lightner Museum, Saint Augustine FL
Lincoln County Historical Association, Inc, 1811 Old Lincoln County Jail & Lincoln County Museum, Wiscasset ME
Lincolnshire County Council, The Collection: Art & Archaeology in Lincolnshire, Lincoln
Livingston County Historical Society, Museum, Geneseo NY
The Long Island Museum of American Art, History & Carriages, Stony Brook NY
Longue Vue House & Gardens, New Orleans LA
Los Angeles County Museum of Natural History, William S Hart Museum, Newhall CA
Louisiana Department of Culture, Recreation & Tourism, Louisiana State Museum, New Orleans LA
Loyola University Chicago, Loyola University Museum of Art, Chicago IL
Lyman Allyn Art Museum, New London CT
Marblehead Museum & Historical Society, Marblehead MA
Marblehead Museum & Historical Society, Jeremiah Lee Mansion, Marblehead MA
Mark Twain, Hartford CT
Maryland Historical Society, Museum of Maryland History, Baltimore MD
McDowell House & Apothecary Shop, Danville KY
Mennello Museum of American Art, Orlando FL
Millicent Rogers Museum, Taos NM
Mobile Museum of Art, Mobile AL
Montclair Art Museum, Montclair NJ
Mount Vernon Hotel Museum & Garden, New York NY
Musee des Beaux-Arts d'Orleans, Museum of Fine Arts, Orleans
Musee des Beaux-Arts de Tours, Museum of Fine Arts, Tours
Musee des Maitres et Artisans du Quebec, Montreal QC
Musees Royaux d'Art et d'Histoire, Royal Museums of Art and History, Brussels
Museo De Las Americas, Denver CO
Museo di Palazzo Ducale, Ducale Palace Museum, Mantua
Museu Nacional D'Art De Catalunya, Catalona National Museum of Art, Barcelona
Museum De Lakenhal, Leiden
Museum of Arts & Design, New York NY
The Museum of Arts & Sciences Inc, Daytona Beach FL
Museum of Fine Arts, Boston MA
Museum of Fine Arts, Saint Petersburg, Florida, Inc, Saint Petersburg FL
Museum of Northern Arizona, Flagstaff AZ
Museum Prinsenhof Delft, Delft
Museum zu Allerheiligen, Schaffhausen
Muzej za Umjetnost i Obrt, Museum of Arts & Crafts, Zagreb
Muzeul de Istorie Nationala Si Arheologie Constanta, National History & Archaeology Museum, Constanta
Muzeul National de Arta al Romaniei, National Museum of Art of Romania, Bucharest
Muzeum Narodowe W Kielcach, National Museum in Kielce, Kielce
Muzeum Narodowe w Poznaniu, National Museum in Poznan, Poznan
National Archaeological Museum, Athens
National Art Museum of Moldova, Chisinau
National Baseball Hall of Fame & Museum, Cooperstown NY
National Museums Scotland, National Museum of Scotland, Edinburgh
National Society of Colonial Dames of America in the State of Maryland, Mount Clare Museum House, Baltimore MD
National Society of the Colonial Dames of America in The Commonwealth of Virginia, Wilton House Museum, Richmond VA
Naval Historical Center, National Museum of the US Navy, Washington DC
Neue Galerie New York, New York NY
New Orleans Museum of Art, New Orleans LA
New York State Military Museum and Veterans Research Center, Saratoga Springs NY
New York State Office of Parks Recreation & Historic Preservation, John Jay Homestead State Historic Site, Katonah NY
Norwich Free Academy, Slater Memorial Museum, Norwich CT
Noyes Art Gallery, Lincoln NE
The Ohio Historical Society, Inc, Campus Martius Museum & Ohio River Museum, Marietta OH
Ohio University, Kennedy Museum of Art, Athens OH
Okanagan Heritage Museum, Kelowna BC
Olana State Historic Site, Hudson NY
Owensboro Museum of Fine Art, Owensboro KY
Panhandle-Plains Historical Museum, Canyon TX
Pasadena Museum of History, Pasadena CA
Patrick Henry, Red Hill National Memorial, Brookneal VA
Philadelphia History Museum, Philadelphia PA
Phillips Academy, Addison Gallery of American Art, Andover MA
Phoenix Art Museum, Phoenix AZ
Piedmont Arts Association, Martinsville VA
Plumas County Museum, Quincy CA
Polish Museum of America (PMA), Chicago IL
Polk Museum of Art, Lakeland FL
Port Huron Museum, Port Huron MI
Portland Art Museum, Portland OR
Pump House Center for the Arts, Chillicothe OH
Putnam Museum of History and Natural Science, Davenport IA
Queen Victoria Museum and Art Gallery, Launceston TAS
Rawls Museum Arts, Courtland VA
Reading Public Museum, Reading PA
Rensselaer County Historical Society, Hart-Cluett Mansion, 1827, Troy NY
Rhode Island Historical Society, John Brown House, Providence RI
The Rosenbach Museum & Library, Philadelphia PA
Royal Arts Foundation, Belcourt Castle, Newport RI
Saco Museum, Saco ME
San Antonio Museum of Art, San Antonio TX
San Diego Museum of Art, San Diego CA
Santa Clara University, de Saisset Museum, Santa Clara CA
Seneca-Iroquois National Museum, Salamanca NY
Shirley Plantation Foundation, Charles City VA
Slovenska Narodna Galeria, Slovak National Gallery, Bratislava
The Society of the Cincinnati at Anderson House, Washington DC
The Speed Art Museum, Louisville KY
Spertus Institute of Jewish Studies, Chicago IL
Staatliche Museen zu Berlin Stiftung Preussischer Kulturbesitz, National Museums in Berlin, Prussian Cultural Heritage Foundation, Berlin
The State Museum of Fine Arts of Tatarstan Republic, Kazan
State University of New York at Geneseo, Bertha V B Lederer Gallery, Geneseo NY
State University of New York at New Paltz, Samuel Dorsky Museum of Art, New Paltz NY
Staten Island Museum, Staten Island NY
Stedelijk Museum Alkmaar, Alkmaar Municipal Museum, Alkmaar
Stratford Historical Society, Catharine B Mitchell Museum, Stratford CT
Suan Pakkad Palace Museum, Bangkok
The Summit County Historical Society of Akron, OH, Akron OH
Suomen Kansallismuseo, National Museum of Finland, Helsinki
Tohono Chul Park, Tucson AZ
Tokyo National Museum, Tokyo
Tver Regional Art Gallery, Tver
Tyne and Wear Archives & Museums, Sunderland Museum & Winter Gardens, Sunderland
University of Chicago, Smart Museum of Art, Chicago IL
University of Georgia, Georgia Museum of Art, Athens GA
University of Illinois at Urbana-Champaign, Krannert Art Museum and Kinkead Pavilion, Champaign IL
University of Kansas, Spencer Museum of Art, Lawrence KS
The University of Kentucky Art Museum, Lexington KY
University of Miami, Lowe Art Museum, Coral Gables FL
University of Minnesota, Goldstein Museum of Design, Saint Paul MN
University of Notre Dame, Snite Museum of Art, Notre Dame IN
University of Richmond, University Museums, Richmond VA
University of Saskatchewan, Diefenbaker Canada Centre, Saskatoon SK
University of South Carolina, McKissick Museum, Columbia SC
University of Utah, Utah Museum of Fine Arts, Salt Lake City UT
University of Wisconsin-Madison, Chazen Museum of Art, Madison WI
USS Constitution Museum, Boston MA
The Valentine, Richmond VA
Vesterheim Norwegian-American Museum, Decorah IA
Victoria Mansion - Morse Libby House, Portland ME
Villa Terrace Decorative Arts Museum, Milwaukee WI
Virginia Museum of Fine Arts, Richmond VA
Volcano Art Center Gallery, Hawaii Volcanoes National Park HI
Wadsworth Atheneum Museum of Art, Hartford CT
Walker Art Gallery, Liverpool
The Wallace Collection, London
Waterworks Visual Arts Center, Salisbury NC
Westfries Museum, Hoorn
Westmoreland Museum of American Art, Greensburg PA
Wheelwright Museum of the American Indian, Santa Fe NM
Wilkes Art Gallery, North Wilkesboro NC
Willard House & Clock Museum, Inc, North Grafton MA
Wiregrass Museum of Art, Dothan AL
Wisconsin Historical Society, Wisconsin Historical Museum, Madison WI
Witte Museum, San Antonio TX
Woodlawn/The Pope-Leighey, Alexandria VA
Worcester Art Museum, Worcester MA
World Erotic Art Museum, Miami Beach FL

SILVERSMITHING

Eula Mae Edwards Museum & Gallery, Clovis NM
Norwich Free Academy, Slater Memorial Museum, Norwich CT
Society for Contemporary Craft, Pittsburgh PA
Springfield Art Museum, Springfield MO
Wyoming Trails Gallery, Wheatland WY

SOUTHWESTERN ART

Albion College, Bobbitt Visual Arts Center, Albion MI
Albuquerque Museum of Art & History, Albuquerque NM
Amon Carter Museum of American Art, Fort Worth TX
Arnot Art Museum, Elmira NY
Art Museum of Greater Lafayette, Lafayette IN
Art Without Walls Inc, Sayville NY

Artesia Historical Museum and Art Center, Artesia NM
Aurora University, Schingoethe Center for Native American Cultures & The Schingoethe Art Gallery, Aurora IL
Bangladesh National Museum, Dhaka
Barnes Foundation, Merion PA
Blauvelt Demarest Foundation, Hiram Blauvelt Art Museum, Oradell NJ
Bone Creek Museum of Agrarian Art, David City NE
Booth Western Art Museum, Cartersville GA
Brown University, Haffenreffer Museum of Anthropology, Providence RI
C M Russell Museum, Great Falls MT
California State University, East Bay, C E Smith Museum of Anthropology, Hayward CA
Carlsbad Museum & Art Center, Carlsbad NM
Cincinnati Art Museum, Cincinnati Art Museum, Cincinnati OH
City of El Paso, El Paso TX
Clark County Historical Society, Pioneer - Krier Museum, Ashland KS
College of William & Mary, Muscarelle Museum of Art, Williamsburg VA
Coutts Museum of Art, Inc, El Dorado KS
Craft and Folk Art Museum (CAFAM), Los Angeles CA
Cripple Creek District Museum, Cripple Creek CO
Crocker Art Museum, Sacramento CA
Denver Art Museum, Denver CO
Dickinson College, The Trout Gallery, Carlisle PA
Eiteljorg Museum of American Indians & Western Art, Indianapolis IN
Ellen Noel Art Museum of the Permian Basin, Odessa TX
Erie Art Museum, Erie PA
Florence County Museum, Florence SC
Folk Art Society of America, Richmond VA
The Frank Phillips Foundation Inc, Woolaroc Museum, Bartlesville OK
Gadsden Museum, Mesilla NM
George Phippen, Phippen Museum - Art of the American West, Prescott AZ
Haystack Mountain School of Crafts, Deer Isle ME
Heard Museum, Phoenix AZ
Heritage Center, Inc, Pine Ridge SD
Hermitage Museum & Gardens, Norfolk VA
History Colorado Center Museum, Denver CO
i.d.e.a. Museum, Mesa AZ
Illinois State Museum, ISM Lockport Gallery, Chicago Gallery & Southern Illinois Art Gallery, Springfield IL
Independence Historical Museum & Art Center, Independence KS
Indian Pueblo Cultural Center, Albuquerque NM
INTAR Gallery, New York NY
International Museum of Art, El Paso TX
James Dick Foundation, Festival - Institute, Round Top TX
Jefferson County Open Space, Hiwan Homestead Museum, Evergreen CO
Kenosha Public Museums, Kenosha WI
Kentucky Museum of Art and Craft, Louisville KY
L D Brinkman, Kerrville TX
LA County Museum of Art, Los Angeles CA
Lalit Kala Akademi Rabindra Bhavan Art Galleries, National Academy of Art, New Delhi, New Delhi
Leanin' Tree Museum & Sculpture Garden of Western Art, Boulder CO
Louise Hopkins Underwood Center for the Arts, Lubbock TX
Mabee-Gerrer Museum of Art, Shawnee OK
Maricopa County Historical Society, Desert Caballeros Western Museum, Wickenburg AZ
Mennello Museum of American Art, Orlando FL
Mesa Arts Center, Mesa Contemporary Arts Museum, Mesa AZ
The Mexican Museum, San Francisco CA
Midwest Museum of American Art, Elkhart IN
Millicent Rogers Museum, Taos NM
Mills College Art Museum, Oakland CA
Montana State University, Helen E Copeland Gallery, Bozeman MT
Museo De Las Americas, Denver CO
Museum of Northern Arizona, Flagstaff AZ
Museum of the Southwest, Midland TX
National Museum of Wildlife Art of the Unites States, Jackson WY
National Park Service, Hubbell Trading Post National Historic Site, Ganado AZ
Nelda C & H J Lutcher Stark Foundation, Stark Museum of Art, Orange TX
New Mexico Department of Cultural Affairs, Palace of Governors, Santa Fe NM
New Visions Gallery, Inc, Marshfield WI
Ohio History Connection, National Road-Zane Grey Museum, Norwich OH
Ohio University, Kennedy Museum of Art, Athens OH
Owensboro Museum of Fine Art, Owensboro KY
Panhandle-Plains Historical Museum, Canyon TX
Peoria Riverfront Museum, Peoria IL
Piedmont Arts Association, Martinsville VA
Pueblo Museum, Desert Hot Springs CA
Red Rock Park, Red Rock Park, Church Rock NM
Riverside Metropolitan Museum, Riverside CA
Roswell Museum & Art Center, Roswell NM
Royal Ontario Museum, Toronto ON
Saginaw Art Museum, Saginaw MI
Saint Joseph Museum, Inc., Saint Joseph MO
San Antonio Museum of Art, San Antonio TX
South Dakota State University, South Dakota Art Museum, Brookings SD
Springfield Art Museum, Springfield MO
Springville Museum of Art, Springville UT
Stone Quarry Hill Art Park, Winner Gallery, Cazenovia NY
Taos Historic Museums, Ernest Blumenschein Home & Studio, Taos NM
Texas Ranger Hall of Fame & Museum, Waco TX
Tohono Chul Park, Tucson AZ
Trust Authority, Museum of the Great Plains, Lawton OK
Tucson Museum of Art and Historic Block, Tucson AZ
University of California, Berkeley, Phoebe Apperson Hearst Museum of Anthropology, Berkeley CA
University of Georgia, Georgia Museum of Art, Athens GA
University of Illinois at Urbana-Champaign, Krannert Art Museum and Kinkead Pavilion, Champaign IL
University of Miami, Lowe Art Museum, Coral Gables FL
University of Nevada, Reno, Sheppard Contemporary & University Galleries, Reno NV
University of New Mexico, The Harwood Museum of Art, Taos NM
University of Texas at Austin, Blanton Museum of Art, Austin TX
University of Utah, Utah Museum of Fine Arts, Salt Lake City UT
University of Wisconsin-Madison, Chazen Museum of Art, Madison WI
Washburn University, Mulvane Art Museum, Topeka KS
Wichita Art Museum, Wichita KS

STAINED GLASS

1890 House-Museum & Center for the Arts, Cortland NY
Academy of the New Church, Glencairn Museum, Bryn Athyn PA
Adams County Historical Society, Gettysburg PA
Alaska State Museum, Juneau AK
Albin Polasek Museum & Sculpture Gardens, Winter Park FL
Albuquerque Museum of Art & History, Albuquerque NM
Amherst College, Mead Art Museum, Amherst MA
Ancient Spanish Monastery, North Miami Beach FL
The Art Center of Waco, Waco TX
Art Community Center, Art Center of Corpus Christi, Corpus Christi TX
Art Gallery of Bancroft Inc, Bancroft ON
Art Without Walls Inc, Sayville NY
Balzekas Museum of Lithuanian Culture, Chicago IL
Baroda Museum and Picture Gallery, Vadodara
Bob Jones University Museum & Gallery Inc, Greenville SC
Bronx Community College (CUNY), Hall of Fame for Great Americans, Bronx NY
Cameron Art Museum, Wilmington NC
Canadian Clay and Glass Gallery, Waterloo ON
Canadian Museum of History, Gatineau QC
Cayuga Museum of History & Art, Auburn NY
Chatham Historical Society, The Atwood House Museum, Chatham MA
The Children's Museum of Indianapolis, Indianapolis IN
The City of Petersburg Museums, Petersburg VA
Corcoran Gallery of Art, Washington DC
Craigdarroch Castle Historical Museum Society, Victoria BC
Cripple Creek District Museum, Cripple Creek CO
Detroit Institute of Arts, Detroit MI
Erie County Historical Society, Erie PA
Evanston Historical Society, Charles Gates Dawes House, Evanston IL
Fairbanks Museum & Planetarium, Saint Johnsbury VT
Fetherston Foundation, Packwood House Museum, Lewisburg PA
Forest Lawn Museum, Glendale CA
Frederic Remington, Ogdensburg NY
Fuller Craft Museum, Brockton MA
Galleria Nazionale dell'Umbria, Umbrian National Gallery, Perugia
Gallery One Visual Arts Center, Ellensburg WA
General Board of Discipleship, The United Methodist Church, The Upper Room Chapel & Museum, Nashville TN
Headquarters Fort Monroe, Dept of Army, Casemate Museum, Hampton VA
Hebrew Union College - Jewish Institute of Religion, Skirball Museum Cincinnati, Cincinnati OH
Henry County Museum & Cultural Arts Center, Clinton MO
Hermitage Museum & Gardens, Norfolk VA
Historic Holyoke at Wistariahurst & City of Holyoke, Holyoke MA
Historic Hudson Valley, Pocantico Hills NY
The History Center in Tompkins County, Ithaca NY
Hot Shops Art Center, Omaha NE
Hunter Museum of American Art, Chattanooga TN
Illinois State Museum, ISM Lockport Gallery, Chicago Gallery & Southern Illinois Art Gallery, Springfield IL
International Museum of Art, El Paso TX
Iredell Museums, Statesville NC
Jekyll Island Museum, Jekyll Island GA
John B Aird Gallery, Toronto ON
Johns Hopkins University, Evergreen Museum & Library, Baltimore MD
Kenosha Public Museums, Kenosha WI
Kereszteny Muzeum, Christian Museum, Esztergom
LaGrange Art Museum, LaGrange GA
Latino Art Museum, Pomona CA
Le Grand Curtius, The Grand Curtius, Liege
Lightner Museum, Saint Augustine FL
Lillian & Coleman Taube Museum of Art, Minot ND
Louise Hopkins Underwood Center for the Arts, Lubbock TX
Loyola University Chicago, Loyola University Museum of Art, Chicago IL
Madison & Main Gallery, Greeley CO
Madison Museum of Fine Art, Madison GA
The Mariners' Museum, Newport News VA
Mark Twain, Hartford CT
Musees Royaux d'Art et d'Histoire, Royal Museums of Art and History, Brussels
Museu Nacional D'Art De Catalunya, Catalona National Museum of Art, Barcelona
Museum De Lakenhal, Leiden
Museum of Arts & Design, New York NY
The Museum of Arts & Sciences Inc, Daytona Beach FL
Museum of the Plains Indian & Crafts Center, Browning MT
Museum zu Allerheiligen, Schaffhausen
Muzej za Umjetnost i Obrt, Museum of Arts & Crafts, Zagreb
Nebraska Game and Parks Commission, Arbor Lodge State Historical Park & Morton Mansion, Nebraska City NE
Nelson Mandela Metropolitan Art Museum, Port Elizabeth
Neustadt Collection of Tiffany Glass, Long Island City NY
North End Gallery, Leonardtown MD
Norwich Free Academy, Slater Memorial Museum, Norwich CT
Noyes Art Gallery, Lincoln NE
Oshkosh Public Museum & Library, Oshkosh WI
Owensboro Museum of Fine Art, Owensboro KY
Panhandle-Plains Historical Museum, Canyon TX
Piedmont Arts Association, Martinsville VA
Pioneer Historical Museum of South Dakota, Hot Springs SD
Plumas County Museum, Quincy CA
Pump House Center for the Arts, Chillicothe OH
Queens College, City University of New York, Godwin-Ternbach Museum, Flushing NY

Reading Public Museum, Reading PA
Rosemount Museum, Inc, Pueblo CO
Royal Arts Foundation, Belcourt Castle, Newport RI
Saint Anselm College, Alva de Mars Megan Chapel Art Center, Manchester NH
Saint Joseph Museum, Inc., Saint Joseph MO
South Carolina Artisans Center, Walterboro SC
South Dakota State University, South Dakota Art Museum, Brookings SD
The Speed Art Museum, Louisville KY
Spertus Institute of Jewish Studies, Chicago IL
The State Museum of Fine Arts of Tatarstan Republic, Kazan
Strasburg Museum, Strasburg VA
Suan Pakkad Palace Museum, Bangkok
Suomen Kansallismuseo, National Museum of Finland, Helsinki
Swedish American Museum, Chicago IL
Tver Regional Art Gallery, Tver
United States Capitol, Architect of the Capitol, Washington DC
University of Georgia, Georgia Museum of Art, Athens GA
University of Illinois at Urbana-Champaign, Krannert Art Museum and Kinkead Pavilion, Champaign IL
University of Notre Dame, Snite Museum of Art, Notre Dame IN
University of Pennsylvania, Arthur Ross Gallery, Philadelphia PA
University of Wisconsin-Madison, Chazen Museum of Art, Madison WI
Victoria Mansion - Morse Libby House, Portland ME
Villa Terrace Decorative Arts Museum, Milwaukee WI
Volcano Art Center Gallery, Hawaii Volcanoes National Park HI
Wadsworth Atheneum Museum of Art, Hartford CT
Walker Art Gallery, Liverpool
Waterworks Visual Arts Center, Salisbury NC
Wheaton College, Beard and Weil Galleries, Norton MA
Wilkes Art Gallery, North Wilkesboro NC
William Morris Gallery, London
Wiregrass Museum of Art, Dothan AL
Workman & Temple Family Homestead Museum, City of Industry CA
World Erotic Art Museum, Miami Beach FL

TAPESTRIES

Academy of the New Church, Glencairn Museum, Bryn Athyn PA
African American Atelier, Greensboro NC
Alaska State Museum, Juneau AK
Albany Institute of History & Art, Albany NY
American Swedish Institute, Minneapolis MN
Arizona Historical Society-Yuma, Sanguinetti House Museum & Garden, Yuma AZ
Arnot Art Museum, Elmira NY
Art Gallery of Nova Scotia, Halifax NS
Art Without Walls Inc, Sayville NY
Balzekas Museum of Lithuanian Culture, Chicago IL
Bangladesh National Museum, Dhaka
Barnes Foundation, Merion PA
Baroda Museum and Picture Gallery, Vadodara
Bayerisches Nationalmuseum, Bavarian National Museum, Munich
Beaverbrook Art Gallery, Fredericton NB
Bob Jones University Museum & Gallery Inc, Greenville SC
Botswana National Museum, Gaborone
Bucknell University, Edward & Marthann Samek Art Gallery, Lewisburg PA
Byzantine & Christian Museum, Athens, Athens
Cameron Art Museum, Wilmington NC
Canadian Museum of History, Gatineau QC
Casa-Museu Medeiros e Almeida, Lisbon
Chateau de Versailles, Palace of Versailles, Versailles
The Children's Museum of Indianapolis, Indianapolis IN
City of Pittsfield Office of Cultural Development, Lichtenstein Center for the Arts, Pittsfield MA
Clark County Historical Society, Pioneer - Krier Museum, Ashland KS
Colonial Williamsburg Foundation, DeWitt Wallace Decorative Arts Museum, Williamsburg VA
The Columbus Museum, Columbus GA
Congregation Beth Israel's Plotkin Judaica Museum, Scottsdale AZ
Corcoran Gallery of Art, Washington DC
Craft and Folk Art Museum (CAFAM), Los Angeles CA
Cranbrook Art Museum, Bloomfield Hills MI
Cripple Creek District Museum, Cripple Creek CO
Cuneo Mansion & Gardens, Vernon Hills IL
The Currier Museum of Art, Manchester NH
Danville Museum of Fine Arts & History, Danville VA
Dartmouth College, Hood Museum of Art, Hanover NH
Denver Art Museum, Denver CO
Designmuseum Danmark, Danish Design Museum, Copenhagen
Detroit Institute of Arts, Detroit MI
Detroit Zoological Institute, Wildlife Interpretive Gallery, Royal Oak MI
Doncaster Museum and Art Gallery, Doncaster Yorks
The Ethel Wright Mohamed Stitchery Museum, Belzoni MS
Evansville Museum of Arts, History & Science, Evansville IN
Everhart Museum, Scranton PA
Flint Institute of Arts, Flint MI
Florence County Museum, Florence SC
Fondazione Musei Civici Di Venezia, Museo Correr - Correr Museum, Venice
Fondazione Musei Civici Di Venezia, Ca' Rezzonico, Venice
The Frick Art & Historical Center, Inc, Frick Art Museum, Pittsburgh PA
Fuller Craft Museum, Brockton MA
General Board of Discipleship, The United Methodist Church, The Upper Room Chapel & Museum, Nashville TN
Heard Museum, Phoenix AZ
Henry Sheldon Museum of Vermont History and Research Center, Middlebury VT
Hermitage Museum & Gardens, Norfolk VA
Het Noordbrabants Museum, s-Hertogenbosch
Hillwood Museum & Gardens Foundation, Hillwood Estate Museum & Gardens, Washington DC
Hunter Museum of American Art, Chattanooga TN
The Hyde Collection, Glens Falls NY
Illinois State Museum, ISM Lockport Gallery, Chicago Gallery & Southern Illinois Art Gallery, Springfield IL
Independence Historical Museum & Art Center, Independence KS
International Museum of Art, El Paso TX
Iredell Museums, Statesville NC
John B Aird Gallery, Toronto ON
Jordan National Gallery of Fine Arts, Amman
Kentucky Museum of Art and Craft, Louisville KY
Kereszteny Muzeum, Christian Museum, Esztergom
Kings County Historical Society & Museum, Hampton NB
Kirchner Museum Davos, Davos
Kunsthistorisches Museum Wien, Museum of Fine Arts, Vienna
Lafayette Science Museum & Planetarium, Lafayette LA
The Long Island Museum of American Art, History & Carriages, Stony Brook NY
Louise Hopkins Underwood Center for the Arts, Lubbock TX
Loyola University Chicago, Loyola University Museum of Art, Chicago IL
Moderna Galerija, Modern Gallery - National Museum of Modern Art, Zagreb
Montana State University, Helen E Copeland Gallery, Bozeman MT
Moravska Galerie v Brne, Moravian Gallery in Brno, Brno
MTG Hawkes Bay, Napier
Musee Cognacq-Jay, Cognacq-Jay Museum, Paris
Musee des Beaux-Arts de Tours, Museum of Fine Arts, Tours
Musees Royaux d'Art et d'Histoire, Royal Museums of Art and History, Brussels
Museo De Las Americas, Denver CO
Museo di Palazzo Ducale, Ducale Palace Museum, Mantua
Museu Nacional D'Art De Catalunya, Catalona National Museum of Art, Barcelona
Museum De Lakenhal, Leiden
Museum of Arts & Design, New York NY
Museum Plantin-Moretus, Antwerp
Museum Prinsenhof Delft, Delft
Museum zu Allerheiligen, Schaffhausen
Muzej za Umjetnost i Obrt, Museum of Arts & Crafts, Zagreb
Muzeul National de Arta al Romaniei, National Museum of Art of Romania, Bucharest
Muzeum Narodowe W Kielcach, National Museum in Kielce, Kielce
National Art Museum of Moldova, Chisinau
The National Museum of Western Art, Tokyo
National Palace Museum, Taipei
The National Shrine of the North American Martyrs, Fultonville NY
National Silk Art Museum, Weston MO
National Society of Colonial Dames of America in the State of Maryland, Mount Clare Museum House, Baltimore MD
Nebraska State Capitol, Lincoln NE
New Brunswick Museum, Saint John NB
New York State Office of Parks, Recreation & Historic Preservation, Staatsburgh State Historic Site, Staatsburg NY
Nichols House Museum, Inc, Boston MA
Norton Simon Museum, Pasadena CA
Norwich Free Academy, Slater Memorial Museum, Norwich CT
Oshkosh Public Museum & Library, Oshkosh WI
Panhandle-Plains Historical Museum, Canyon TX
Pennsylvania Academy of the Fine Arts, Philadelphia PA
Peoria Riverfront Museum, Peoria IL
Pioneer Historical Museum of South Dakota, Hot Springs SD
Polish Museum of America (PMA), Chicago IL
Reading Public Museum, Reading PA
Royal Arts Foundation, Belcourt Castle, Newport RI
Saginaw Art Museum, Saginaw MI
Saint Olaf College, Flaten Art Museum, Northfield MN
Santa Barbara Museum of Art, Santa Barbara CA
Santa Clara University, de Saisset Museum, Santa Clara CA
Scripps College, Ruth Chandler Williamson Gallery, Claremont CA
The Society of the Cincinnati at Anderson House, Washington DC
South Dakota State University, South Dakota Art Museum, Brookings SD
The Speed Art Museum, Louisville KY
Spertus Institute of Jewish Studies, Chicago IL
Staatliche Museen zu Berlin Stiftung Preussischer Kulturbesitz, National Museums in Berlin, Prussian Cultural Heritage Foundation, Berlin
Staten Island Museum, Staten Island NY
The Summit County Historical Society of Akron, OH, Akron OH
Taos Historic Museums, Ernest Blumenschein Home & Studio, Taos NM
Timken Museum of Art, San Diego CA
Tokyo National Museum, Tokyo
Tver Regional Art Gallery, Tver
Ukrainian Institute of Modern Art, Chicago IL
University of Georgia, Georgia Museum of Art, Athens GA
University of Illinois at Urbana-Champaign, Krannert Art Museum and Kinkead Pavilion, Champaign IL
The University of Kentucky Art Museum, Lexington KY
University of Minnesota, Goldstein Museum of Design, Saint Paul MN
University of Utah, Utah Museum of Fine Arts, Salt Lake City UT
Ursinus College, Philip & Muriel Berman Museum of Art, Collegeville PA
Vesterheim Norwegian-American Museum, Decorah IA
Virginia Museum of Fine Arts, Richmond VA
Vizcaya Museum & Gardens, Miami FL
Volcano Art Center Gallery, Hawaii Volcanoes National Park HI
Walker Art Gallery, Liverpool
Wayne Center for the Arts, Wooster OH
Wilfrid Laurier University, Robert Langen Art Gallery, Waterloo ON
William Morris Gallery, London
World Erotic Art Museum, Miami Beach FL
Yokohama Museum of Art, Yokohama

TEXTILES

Abington Art Center, Jenkintown PA
Academy of the New Church, Glencairn Museum, Bryn Athyn PA
Adams County Historical Society, Gettysburg PA

African American Museum in Philadelphia, Philadelphia PA
African Art Museum of Maryland, Columbia MD
Alaska State Museum, Juneau AK
Albany Institute of History & Art, Albany NY
Albion College, Bobbitt Visual Arts Center, Albion MI
Albuquerque Museum of Art & History, Albuquerque NM
Alexandria Museum of Art, Alexandria LA
American Folk Art Museum, New York NY
American Swedish Institute, Minneapolis MN
American Textile History Museum, Lowell MA
Americas Society Art Gallery, New York NY
Amherst College, Mead Art Museum, Amherst MA
Amsterdam Museum, Amsterdam
Anchorage Museum at Rasmuson Center, Anchorage AK
Arizona Historical Society-Yuma, Sanguinetti House Museum & Garden, Yuma AZ
Arnot Art Museum, Elmira NY
Art Center of Battle Creek, Battle Creek MI
Art Gallery of Bancroft Inc, Bancroft ON
Art Gallery of Nova Scotia, Halifax NS
Art Gallery of South Australia, Adelaide
Art Museum of Greater Lafayette, Lafayette IN
Art Without Walls Inc, Sayville NY
Artesia Historical Museum and Art Center, Artesia NM
Asian Art Museum of San Francisco, Chong-Moon Lee Ctr for Asian Art and Culture, San Francisco CA
Atlanta Historical Society Inc, Atlanta History Center, Atlanta GA
Aurora University, Schingoethe Center for Native American Cultures & The Schingoethe Art Gallery, Aurora IL
The Baltimore Museum of Art, Baltimore MD
Balzekas Museum of Lithuanian Culture, Chicago IL
Bangladesh National Museum, Dhaka
Barnes Foundation, Merion PA
Baroda Museum and Picture Gallery, Vadodara
Bay County Historical Society, Historical Museum of Bay County, Bay City MI
Bellevue Arts Museum, Bellevue WA
Bennington Museum, Bennington VT
Berea College, Doris Ulmann Galleries, Berea KY
Besser Museum for Northeast Michigan, Alpena MI
Beverly Historical Society, Cabot, Hale & Balch House Museums, Beverly MA
Biggs Museum of American Art, Dover DE
Birmingham Museum of Art, Birmingham AL
Blanden Memorial Art Museum, Fort Dodge IA
Bob Jones University Museum & Gallery Inc, Greenville SC
Botswana National Museum, Gaborone
Brick Store Museum, Kennebunk ME
Brooklyn Historical Society, Brooklyn OH
Brown University, Haffenreffer Museum of Anthropology, Providence RI
Bruce Museum, Inc, Greenwich CT
Buffalo Niagara Heritage Village, Amherst NY
Burke Arts Council, Jailhouse Galleries, Morganton NC
Bush-Holley Historic Site & Storehouse Gallery, Greenwich Historical Society, Cos Cob CT
Byzantine & Christian Museum, Athens, Athens
C W Post Campus of Long Island University, Hillwood Art Museum, Brookville NY
California State University, East Bay, C E Smith Museum of Anthropology, Hayward CA
Cameron Art Museum, Wilmington NC
Canadian Museum of History, Gatineau QC
Cape Ann Museum, Gloucester MA
Carnegie Center for Art & History, New Albany IN
Centenary College of Louisiana, Meadows Museum of Art, Shreveport LA
Charleston Museum, Charleston SC
Chatham Historical Society, The Atwood House Museum, Chatham MA
Chatillon-DeMenil House Foundation, Chatillon-DeMenil Mansion, Saint Louis MO
Chicago Athenaeum, Museum of Architecture & Design, Galena IL
The Children's Museum of Indianapolis, Indianapolis IN
Cincinnati Art Museum, Cincinnati Art Museum, Cincinnati OH
City of Austin Parks & Recreation, O Henry Museum, Austin TX
City of Fayette, Alabama, Fayette Art Museum, Fayette AL
City of Fremont, Olive Hyde Art Gallery, Fremont CA
City of Gainesville, Thomas Center Galleries - Cultural Affairs, Gainesville FL
City of Pittsfield Office of Cultural Development, Lichtenstein Center for the Arts, Pittsfield MA
City of Springdale, Shiloh Museum of Ozark History, Springdale AR
Clark County Historical Society, Pioneer - Krier Museum, Ashland KS
The Cleveland Museum of Art, Cleveland OH
Cohasset Historical Society, Pratt Building (Society Headquarters), Cohasset MA
Colonial Williamsburg Foundation, Abby Aldrich Rockefeller Folk Art Museum, Williamsburg VA
Columbia Museum of Art, Columbia SC
The Columbus Museum, Columbus GA
Columbus Museum of Art, Columbus OH
Concord Museum, Concord MA
Congregation Beth Israel's Plotkin Judaica Museum, Scottsdale AZ
Craft and Folk Art Museum (CAFAM), Los Angeles CA
Craigdarroch Castle Historical Museum Society, Victoria BC
Cranbrook Art Museum, Bloomfield Hills MI
Cranford Historical Society, Cranford NJ
Crocker Art Museum, Sacramento CA
Crook County Museum & Art Gallery, Sundance WY
The Currier Museum of Art, Manchester NH
Danbury Scott-Fanton Museum & Historical Society, Inc, Danbury CT
Danville Museum of Fine Arts & History, Danville VA
DAR Museum, National Society Daughters of the American Revolution, Washington DC
Dartmouth Heritage Museum, Dartmouth NS
Daum Museum of Contemporary Art, Sedalia MO
Davidson College, William H Van Every Jr & Edward M Smith Galleries, Davidson NC
Delaware Division of Historical & Cultural Affairs, Dover DE
Denver Art Museum, Denver CO
Designmuseum Danmark, Danish Design Museum, Copenhagen
Detroit Institute of Arts, Detroit MI
Detroit Repertory Theatre Gallery, Detroit MI
Detroit Zoological Institute, Wildlife Interpretive Gallery, Royal Oak MI
Doncaster Museum and Art Gallery, Doncaster Yorks
Dublin Arts Council, Dublin OH
Dumbarton Oaks, Dumbarton Oaks Museum, Washington DC
Durham Art Guild, Durham NC
Edgecombe County Cultural Arts Council, Inc, Blount-Bridgers House, Hobson Pittman Memorial Gallery, Tarboro NC
Eiteljorg Museum of American Indians & Western Art, Indianapolis IN
Environment Canada - Parks Canada, Laurier House, National Historic Site, Ottawa ON
Erie Art Museum, Erie PA
Erie County Historical Society, Erie PA
Evanston Historical Society, Charles Gates Dawes House, Evanston IL
Evansville Museum of Arts, History & Science, Evansville IN
Fairbanks Museum & Planetarium, Saint Johnsbury VT
Fetherston Foundation, Packwood House Museum, Lewisburg PA
Fine Arts Museums of San Francisco, Legion of Honor, San Francisco CA
Fishkill Historical Society, Van Wyck Homestead Museum, Fishkill NY
Fitton Center for Creative Arts, Hamilton OH
Flint Institute of Arts, Flint MI
Florence County Museum, Florence SC
Florida State University and Central Florida Community College, The Appleton Museum of Art, Ocala FL
Folk Art Society of America, Richmond VA
Fondazione Musei Civici Di Venezia, Museo Correr - Correr Museum, Venice
Fondazione Musei Civici Di Venezia, Ca' Rezzonico, Venice
Fort George G Meade Museum, Fort Meade MD
Fort Smith Regional Art Museum, Fort Smith AR
The Frank Phillips Foundation Inc, Woolaroc Museum, Bartlesville OK
Frontier Times Museum, Bandera TX
Fuller Craft Museum, Brockton MA
Fulton County Historical Society Inc, Fulton County Museum (Tetzlaff Reference Room), Rochester IN
Gadsden Museum, Mesilla NM
Galerie Montcalm, Gatineau QC
Galleria Nazionale dell'Umbria, Umbrian National Gallery, Perugia
Gaston County Museum of Art & History, Dallas NC
General Board of Discipleship, The United Methodist Church, The Upper Room Chapel & Museum, Nashville TN
Genesee Country Village & Museum, John L Wehle Art Gallery, Mumford NY
George Phippen, Phippen Museum - Art of the American West, Prescott AZ
Germantown Historical Society, Philadelphia PA
Girard College, Stephen Girard Collection, Philadelphia PA
Glanmore National Historic Site of Canada, Belleville ON
Glessner House Museum, Chicago IL
Grand Rapids Public Museum, Grand Rapids MI
Grassroots Art Center, Lucas KS
Greene County Historical Society, Bronck Museum, Coxsackie NY
Hancock Shaker Village, Inc, Pittsfield MA
Harness Racing Museum & Hall of Fame, Goshen NY
Haystack Mountain School of Crafts, Deer Isle ME
Headley-Whitney Museum, Lexington KY
Heard Museum, Phoenix AZ
Hebrew Union College - Jewish Institute of Religion, Skirball Museum Cincinnati, Cincinnati OH
Henry County Museum & Cultural Arts Center, Clinton MO
Henry Morrison Flagler Museum, Palm Beach FL
Henry Sheldon Museum of Vermont History and Research Center, Middlebury VT
Heritage Center, Inc, Pine Ridge SD
Hermitage Museum & Gardens, Norfolk VA
Hershey Museum, Hershey PA
High Desert Museum, Bend OR
Hill-Stead Museum, Farmington CT
Hillwood Museum & Gardens Foundation, Hillwood Estate Museum & Gardens, Washington DC
Historic Cherry Hill, Albany NY
Historic Deerfield, Inc, Deerfield MA
Historic Holyoke at Wistariahurst & City of Holyoke, Holyoke MA
Historic Hudson Valley, Pocantico Hills NY
Historic Newton, Newton MA
Historic Northampton Museum & Education Center, Northampton MA
Historical Society of Cheshire County, Keene NH
Historical Society of Old Newbury, Cushing House Museum, Newburyport MA
Historisches und Volkerkundemuseum, Museum of History and Ethnology, St Gallen
The History Center in Tompkins County, Ithaca NY
History Colorado Center Museum, Denver CO
Holter Museum of Art, Helena MT
Honolulu Museum of Art, Honolulu HI
Hui No'eau Visual Arts Center, Gallery and Gift Shop, Makawao Maui HI
Hunter Museum of American Art, Chattanooga TN
The Hyde Collection, Glens Falls NY
Hyde Park Art Center, Chicago IL
i.d.e.a. Museum, Mesa AZ
Idaho Historical Museum, Boise ID
Illinois Historic Preservation Agency, Bishop Hill State Historic Site, Bishop Hill IL
Independence Historical Museum & Art Center, Independence KS
Independence Seaport Museum, Philadelphia PA
Indiana Landmarks, Morris-Butler House, Indianapolis IN
Indiana State Museum, Indianapolis IN
International Museum of Art & Science, McAllen TX
Iredell Museums, Statesville NC
Iroquois Indian Museum, Howes Cave NY
Jacksonville University, Alexander Brest Museum & Gallery, Jacksonville FL
Jacques Marchais Museum of Tibetan Art, Staten Island NY
Jefferson County Historical Society, Watertown NY
Jefferson County Open Space, Hiwan Homestead Museum, Evergreen CO
The Jewish Museum, New York NY
Joe Gish's Old West Museum, Fredericksburg TX
John B Aird Gallery, Toronto ON
Johns Hopkins University, Homewood Museum, Baltimore MD
Jordan National Gallery of Fine Arts, Amman
Joslyn Art Museum, Omaha NE

Karakalpak State Art Museum, Nukus Republic of Karakalpakstan
Kelly-Griggs House Museum, Red Bluff CA
Kenosha Public Museums, Kenosha WI
Kentucky Museum of Art and Craft, Louisville KY
Keresztény Muzeum, Christian Museum, Esztergom
Kings County Historical Society & Museum, Hampton NB
Kirchner Museum Davos, Davos
Koochiching Museums, International Falls MN
Koshare Indian Museum, Inc, La Junta CO
Kunsthistorisches Museum Wien, Museum of Fine Arts, Vienna
LA County Museum of Art, Los Angeles CA
Lac du Flambeau Band of Lake Superior Chippewa Indians, George W Brown Jr Ojibwe Museum & Cultural Center, Lac Du Flambeau WI
Lafayette College, Lafayette College Art Galleries, Easton PA
Lafayette Science Museum & Planetarium, Lafayette LA
LaGrange Art Museum, LaGrange GA
Lahore Museum, Lahore
Lalit Kala Akademi Rabindra Bhavan Art Galleries, National Academy of Art, New Delhi, New Delhi
Latino Art Museum, Pomona CA
Lehigh Valley Heritage Center, Allentown PA
Liberty Hall Historic Site, Liberty Hall Museum, Frankfort KY
Lightner Museum, Saint Augustine FL
Lillian & Coleman Taube Museum of Art, Minot ND
Lincoln County Historical Association, Inc, 1811 Old Lincoln County Jail & Lincoln County Museum, Wiscasset ME
Livingston County Historical Society, Museum, Geneseo NY
The Long Island Museum of American Art, History & Carriages, Stony Brook NY
Longfellow-Evangeline State Commemorative Area, Saint Martinville LA
Longue Vue House & Gardens, New Orleans LA
Los Angeles County Museum of Art, Los Angeles CA
Los Angeles County Museum of Natural History, William S Hart Museum, Newhall CA
Louise Hopkins Underwood Center for the Arts, Lubbock TX
Louisiana Arts & Science Museum, Baton Rouge LA
Louisiana Department of Culture, Recreation & Tourism, Louisiana State Museum, New Orleans LA
Loveland Museum/Gallery, Loveland CO
Loyola University Chicago, Loyola University Museum of Art, Chicago IL
Madison & Main Gallery, Greeley CO
Marblehead Museum & Historical Society, Marblehead MA
Marblehead Museum & Historical Society, Jeremiah Lee Mansion, Marblehead MA
Maricopa County Historical Society, Desert Caballeros Western Museum, Wickenburg AZ
Mark Twain, Hartford CT
Maryhill Museum of Art, Goldendale WA
Maryland Historical Society, Museum of Maryland History, Baltimore MD
Massillon Museum, Massillon OH
McLean County Historical Society, McLean County Museum of History, Bloomington IL
McPherson Museum and Arts Foundation, McPherson KS
Memphis Brooks Museum of Art, Memphis TN
Mennello Museum of American Art, Orlando FL
Mesa Arts Center, Mesa Contemporary Arts Museum, Mesa AZ
Middle Border Museum & Oscar Howe Art Center, Mitchell SD
Millicent Rogers Museum, Taos NM
Mills College Art Museum, Oakland CA
Mission San Luis Rey de Francia, Mission San Luis Rey Museum, Oceanside CA
Mississippi Museum of Art, Jackson MS
Mobile Museum of Art, Mobile AL
Monroe County Historical Association, Elizabeth D Walters Library, Stroudsburg PA
Montana State University, Helen E Copeland Gallery, Bozeman MT
Moore College of Art & Design, The Galleries at Moore, Philadelphia PA
Moravian Historical Society, Nazareth PA
Moravska Galerie v Brne, Moravian Gallery in Brno, Brno
Morehead State University, Kentucky Folk Art Center, Morehead KY
Morris Museum of Art, Augusta GA
Morris-Jumel Mansion, Inc, New York NY
Mount Vernon Hotel Museum & Garden, New York NY
MTG Hawkes Bay, Napier
Muscatine Art Center, Muscatine IA
Musee des Beaux-Arts de Tours, Museum of Fine Arts, Tours
Musee des Maitres et Artisans du Quebec, Montreal QC
Musee Regional de lu Cote-Nord, Sept-Iles QC
Musees Royaux d'Art et d'Histoire, Royal Museums of Art and History, Brussels
Museo De Las Americas, Denver CO
The Museum, Greenwood SC
Museum De Lakenhal, Leiden
Museum of Art & History, Santa Cruz, Santa Cruz CA
Museum of Art - Deland FL, Inc, Deland FL
Museum of Arts & Design, New York NY
The Museum of Arts & Sciences Inc, Daytona Beach FL
Museum of Chinese in America, New York NY
Museum of Islamic Art, Doha
Museum of Northern Arizona, Flagstaff AZ
Museum of Northern British Columbia, Ruth Harvey Art Gallery, Prince Rupert BC
Museum of Northwest Art, La Conner WA
Museum of the Plains Indian & Crafts Center, Browning MT
Museum of the Southwest, Midland TX
Museum of York County, Rock Hill SC
Museum Prinsenhof Delft, Delft
Museum zu Allerheiligen, Schaffhausen
Muzej za Umjetnost i Obrt, Museum of Arts & Crafts, Zagreb
Muzeul National de Arta al Romaniei, National Museum of Art of Romania, Bucharest
Muzeum Narodowe W Kielcach, National Museum in Kielce, Kielce
Nathan Hale Homestead Museum, Coventry CT
National Art Museum of Moldova, Chisinau
National Baseball Hall of Fame & Museum, Cooperstown NY
National Museum of the American Indian, George Gustav Heye Center, New York NY
National Museum of the Philippines, Manila
National Museums Scotland, National Museum of Scotland, Edinburgh
The National Quilt Museum, Paducah KY
The National Shrine of the North American Martyrs, Fultonville NY
National Silk Art Museum, Weston MO
National Society of Colonial Dames of America in the State of Maryland, Mount Clare Museum House, Baltimore MD
National Society of the Colonial Dames of America in The Commonwealth of Virginia, Wilton House Museum, Richmond VA
National Trust for Historic Preservation, Shadows-on-the-Teche, New Iberia LA
National Trust for Historic Preservation, Chesterwood, Stockbridge MA
Nelson Mandela Metropolitan Art Museum, Port Elizabeth
Neue Galerie New York, New York NY
Nevada Museum of Art, Reno NV
New Brunswick Museum, Saint John NB
New Canaan Historical Society, New Canaan CT
New York State Military Museum and Veterans Research Center, Saratoga Springs NY
New York State Office of Parks Recreation & Historic Preservation, John Jay Homestead State Historic Site, Katonah NY
New York State Office of Parks, Recreation & Historic Preservation, Staatsburgh State Historic Site, Staatsburg NY
Newfields, Indianapolis IN
Nichols House Museum, Inc, Boston MA
North Carolina Museum of Art, Raleigh NC
Norwich Free Academy, Slater Memorial Museum, Norwich CT
Nova Scotia College of Art and Design, Anna Leonowens Gallery, Halifax NS
Noyes Art Gallery, Lincoln NE
Ogden Museum of Southern Art, University of New Orleans, New Orleans LA
Ohara Museum of Art, Kurashiki
The Ohio Historical Society, Inc, Campus Martius Museum & Ohio River Museum, Marietta OH
Ohio University, Kennedy Museum of Art, Athens OH
Okanagan Heritage Museum, Kelowna BC
Olana State Historic Site, Hudson NY
Old Island Restoration Foundation Inc, Oldest House in Key West, Key West FL
Oshkosh Public Museum & Library, Oshkosh WI
Owensboro Museum of Fine Art, Owensboro KY
Pacific Island Ethnic Art Museum, Long Beach CA
Page-Walker Arts & History Center, Cary NC
Panhandle-Plains Historical Museum, Canyon TX
Pasadena Museum of History, Pasadena CA
Peabody Essex Museum, Salem MA
Pennsylvania Historical & Museum Commission, Railroad Museum of Pennsylvania, Strasburg PA
Peoria Riverfront Museum, Peoria IL
Philadelphia History Museum, Philadelphia PA
Philadelphia University, Paley Design Center, Philadelphia PA
Phoenix Art Museum, Phoenix AZ
Piedmont Arts Association, Martinsville VA
Plainsman Museum, Aurora NE
Polk Museum of Art, Lakeland FL
Port Huron Museum, Port Huron MI
Preservation Virginia, John Marshall House, Richmond VA
Principia College, School of Nations Museum, Elsah IL
Pueblo Museum, Desert Hot Springs CA
Putnam Museum of History and Natural Science, Davenport IA
Quapaw Quarter Association, Inc, Villa Marre, Little Rock AR
Queen Victoria Museum and Art Gallery, Launceston TAS
Queens College, City University of New York, Godwin-Ternbach Museum, Flushing NY
Randolph College, Maier Museum of Art, Lynchburg VA
Reading Public Museum, Reading PA
Red Deer & District Museum & Archives, Red Deer AB
Rensselaer County Historical Society, Hart-Cluett Mansion, 1827, Troy NY
Rhode Island Historical Society, John Brown House, Providence RI
Rhodes College, Clough-Hanson Gallery, Memphis TN
Riverside Metropolitan Museum, Riverside CA
Rollins College, George D & Harriet W Cornell Fine Arts Museum, Winter Park FL
Roswell Museum & Art Center, Roswell NM
Royal Arts Foundation, Belcourt Castle, Newport RI
Saco Museum, Saco ME
Saginaw Art Museum, Saginaw MI
Saint Olaf College, Flaten Art Museum, Northfield MN
San Antonio Museum of Art, San Antonio TX
Schweinfurth Art Center, Auburn NY
Scripps College, Ruth Chandler Williamson Gallery, Claremont CA
Scripps College, Clark Humanities Museum, Claremont CA
Shaker Museum & Library, Old Chatham NY
Shaker Village of Pleasant Hill, Harrodsburg KY
Shirley Plantation Foundation, Charles City VA
Slater Mill, Old Slater Mill Association, Pawtucket RI
Slovenska Narodna Galeria, Slovak National Gallery, Bratislava
Society for Contemporary Craft, Pittsburgh PA
The Society of the Cincinnati at Anderson House, Washington DC
South Carolina Artisans Center, Walterboro SC
South Carolina State Museum, Columbia SC
South Dakota State University, South Dakota Art Museum, Brookings SD
Southern Baptist Theological Seminary, Joseph A Callaway Archaeological Museum, Louisville KY
Spartanburg Art Museum, Spartanburg SC
The Speed Art Museum, Louisville KY
Spertus Institute of Jewish Studies, Chicago IL
St Mary's College of Maryland, The Dwight Frederick Boyden Gallery, St Mary's City MD
Staatliche Museen zu Berlin Stiftung Preussischer Kulturbesitz, National Museums in Berlin, Prussian Cultural Heritage Foundation, Berlin
The State Museum of Fine Arts of Tatarstan Republic, Kazan
The State Museum of Oriental Art, Moscow
State University of New York College at Cortland, Dowd Fine Arts Gallery, Cortland NY

Staten Island Museum, Staten Island NY
Stone Quarry Hill Art Park, Winner Gallery, Cazenovia NY
Stratford Historical Society, Catharine B Mitchell Museum, Stratford CT
The Summit County Historical Society of Akron, OH, Akron OH
Suomen Kansallismuseo, National Museum of Finland, Helsinki
Swedish American Museum, Chicago IL
T C Steele State Historic Site, Nashville IN
Tampa Museum of Art, Tampa FL
Taos Historic Museums, Ernest Blumenschein Home & Studio, Taos NM
Taos Historic Museums, La Hacienda de Los Martinez, Taos NM
Textile Museum of Canada, Toronto ON
The Tokugawa Art Museum, Nagoya
Tokyo National Museum, Tokyo
Tubac Center of the Arts, Santa Cruz Valley Art Association, Tubac AZ
Tubman African American Museum, Macon GA
Tucson Museum of Art and Historic Block, Tucson AZ
Turtle Bay Exploration Park, Redding CA
Tver Regional Art Gallery, Tver
Tyne and Wear Archives & Museums, Sunderland Museum & Winter Gardens, Sunderland
Ucross Foundation, Big Red Barn Gallery, Clearmont WY
Ukrainian Canadian Archives & Museum of Alberta, Edmonton AB
Ukrainian Institute of Modern Art, Chicago IL
The Ukrainian Museum, New York NY
United Society of Shakers, Shaker Museum, New Gloucester ME
University of Calgary, Nickle Galleries, Calgary AB
University of California, Berkeley, Phoebe Apperson Hearst Museum of Anthropology, Berkeley CA
University of Florida, Samuel P Harn Museum of Art, Gainesville FL
University of Georgia, Georgia Museum of Art, Athens GA
University of Illinois at Urbana-Champaign, Krannert Art Museum and Kinkead Pavilion, Champaign IL
University of Kansas, Spencer Museum of Art, Lawrence KS
The University of Kentucky Art Museum, Lexington KY
University of Manchester, Whitworth Art Gallery, Manchester
University of Miami, Lowe Art Museum, Coral Gables FL
University of Michigan, Kelsey Museum of Archaeology, Ann Arbor MI
University of Minnesota, Goldstein Museum of Design, Saint Paul MN
University of Minnesota Duluth, Tweed Museum of Art, Duluth MN
University of Nevada, Reno, Sheppard Contemporary & University Galleries, Reno NV
University of New Mexico, The Harwood Museum of Art, Taos NM
University of North Dakota, Hughes Fine Arts Center-Col Eugene Myers Art Gallery, Grand Forks ND
University of Saskatchewan, Diefenbaker Canada Centre, Saskatoon SK
University of Texas at Austin, Blanton Museum of Art, Austin TX
University of Utah, Utah Museum of Fine Arts, Salt Lake City UT
University of Wisconsin-Madison, Chazen Museum of Art, Madison WI
Ursinus College, Philip & Muriel Berman Museum of Art, Collegeville PA
USS Constitution Museum, Boston MA
Vancouver Art Gallery, Vancouver BC
Vesterheim Norwegian-American Museum, Decorah IA
Victoria Mansion - Morse Libby House, Portland ME
Vizcaya Museum & Gardens, Miami FL
Volcano Art Center Gallery, Hawaii Volcanoes National Park HI
Vorarlberg Museum, Bregenz
Wadsworth Atheneum Museum of Art, Hartford CT
Waterworks Visual Arts Center, Salisbury NC
Westmoreland Museum of American Art, Greensburg PA
Whatcom Museum, Bellingham WA
Wheaton College, Beard and Weil Galleries, Norton MA
Wheelwright Museum of the American Indian, Santa Fe NM
Wichita Art Museum, Wichita KS
Wilfrid Laurier University, Robert Langen Art Gallery, Waterloo ON
Wilkes Art Gallery, North Wilkesboro NC
Willard House & Clock Museum, Inc, North Grafton MA
William Morris Gallery, London
Winston-Salem State University, Diggs Gallery, Winston-Salem NC
Witte Museum, San Antonio TX
Woodlawn/The Pope-Leighey, Alexandria VA
Wyoming State Museum, Cheyenne WY
Yellowstone County Museum, Billings MT
Yeshiva University Museum, New York NY

WATERCOLORS

A.E. Backus Museum & Gallery, Fort Pierce FL
Academy Art Museum, Easton MD
Academy of the New Church, Glencairn Museum, Bryn Athyn PA
African American Museum in Philadelphia, Philadelphia PA
Alaska Heritage Museum at Wells Fargo, Anchorage AK
Alaska State Museum, Juneau AK
Albertina Museum, Vienna
The Albrecht-Kemper Museum of Art, Saint Joseph MO
Albuquerque Museum of Art & History, Albuquerque NM
Alexandria Museum of Art, Alexandria LA
Alton Museum of History & Art, Inc, Alton IL
American University, Museum at the Katzen, Washington DC
Amherst College, Mead Art Museum, Amherst MA
Amon Carter Museum of American Art, Fort Worth TX
Anchorage Museum at Rasmuson Center, Anchorage AK
Arkansas Arts Center, Little Rock AR
Arnold Mikelson Mind & Matter Art Gallery, Surrey BC
Art and History Museums - Maitland, Maitland FL
The Art Center of Waco, Waco TX
Art Community Center, Art Center of Corpus Christi, Corpus Christi TX
Art Gallery of Alberta, Edmonton AB
Art Gallery of Bancroft Inc, Bancroft ON
The Art Gallery of Cornwall, Cornwall ON
Art Gallery of Nova Scotia, Halifax NS
Art Gallery of South Australia, Adelaide
The Art Museum of Eastern Idaho, Idaho Falls ID
Art Museum of Greater Lafayette, Lafayette IN
Art Without Walls Inc, Sayville NY
Artesia Historical Museum and Art Center, Artesia NM
Asheville Art Museum, Asheville NC
Baker Arts Center, Liberal KS
Balzekas Museum of Lithuanian Culture, Chicago IL
Bangladesh National Museum, Dhaka
Barnes Foundation, Merion PA
Baroda Museum and Picture Gallery, Vadodara
Baruch College of the City University of New York, Sidney Mishkin Gallery, New York NY
Baton Rouge Gallery, Center For Contemporary Art, Baton Rouge LA
Bayerische Staatsgemaldesammlungen, Bavarian State Painting Collections, Munich
Bennington Museum, Bennington VT
Bethany College, Mingenback Art Center, Lindsborg KS
Biggs Museum of American Art, Dover DE
Billie Trimble Chandler, Texas State Museum of Asian Cultures, Corpus Christi TX
Birger Sandzen Memorial Gallery, Lindsborg KS
Blauvelt Demarest Foundation, Hiram Blauvelt Art Museum, Oradell NJ
Blowing Rock Art and History Museum, Blowing Rock NC
Boise Art Museum, Boise ID
Bone Creek Museum of Agrarian Art, David City NE
Booth Western Art Museum, Cartersville GA
Boston Public Library, Albert H Wiggin Gallery & Print Department, Boston MA
The Bostonian Society, Old State House Museum, Boston MA
Botswana National Museum, Gaborone
Brevard College, Spiers Gallery, Brevard NC
Brickton Art Center, Park Ridge IL
Bucknell University, Edward & Marthann Samek Art Gallery, Lewisburg PA
Burchfield Penney Art Center, Buffalo NY
Burke Arts Council, Jailhouse Galleries, Morganton NC
The California Historical Society, San Francisco CA
Calvert Marine Museum, Solomons MD
Cameron Art Museum, Wilmington NC
Canadian Museum of History, Gatineau QC
Canadian Museum of Nature, Musee Canadien de la Nature, Ottawa ON
Canton Museum of Art, Canton OH
Cape Ann Museum, Gloucester MA
Cape Cod Museum of Art Inc, Dennis MA
Capital University, Schumacher Gallery, Columbus OH
Carlsbad Museum & Art Center, Carlsbad NM
Carnegie Mellon University, Hunt Institute for Botanical Documentation, Pittsburgh PA
Cartoon Art Museum, San Francisco CA
Cayuga Museum of History & Art, Auburn NY
Cedar Rapids Museum of Art, Cedar Rapids IA
Centenary College of Louisiana, Meadows Museum of Art, Shreveport LA
Central Methodist University, Ashby-Hodge Gallery of American Art, Fayette MO
Channel Islands Maritime Museum, Oxnard CA
Chatham Historical Society, The Atwood House Museum, Chatham MA
Chesapeake Bay Maritime Museum, Saint Michaels MD
Cincinnati Art Museum, Cincinnati Art Museum, Cincinnati OH
City of El Paso, El Paso TX
City of Fayette, Alabama, Fayette Art Museum, Fayette AL
City of Fremont, Olive Hyde Art Gallery, Fremont CA
City of Gainesville, Thomas Center Galleries - Cultural Affairs, Gainesville FL
The City of Petersburg Museums, Petersburg VA
City of Pittsfield Office of Cultural Development, Lichtenstein Center for the Arts, Pittsfield MA
Clark Art Institute, Williamstown MA
Coastal Arts League Museum, Half Moon Bay CA
Colgate University, Picker Art Gallery, Hamilton NY
College of William & Mary, Muscarelle Museum of Art, Williamsburg VA
Colonial Williamsburg Foundation, Abby Aldrich Rockefeller Folk Art Museum, Williamsburg VA
Colonial Williamsburg Foundation, DeWitt Wallace Decorative Arts Museum, Williamsburg VA
The Columbus Museum, Columbus GA
Corcoran Gallery of Art, Washington DC
Cornell University, Herbert F Johnson Museum of Art, Ithaca NY
Coutts Museum of Art, Inc, El Dorado KS
Crary Art Gallery, Warren PA
Cripple Creek District Museum, Cripple Creek CO
Crocker Art Museum, Sacramento CA
Crook County Museum & Art Gallery, Sundance WY
The Currier Museum of Art, Manchester NH
Dahesh Museum of Art, Greenwich CT
Danville Museum of Fine Arts & History, Danville VA
Dartmouth College, Hood Museum of Art, Hanover NH
Dartmouth Heritage Museum, Dartmouth NS
Daum Museum of Contemporary Art, Sedalia MO
Davidson College, William H Van Every Jr & Edward M Smith Galleries, Davidson NC
Deines Cultural Center, Russell KS
DeLeon White Gallery, Toronto ON
Detroit Institute of Arts, Detroit MI
Detroit Repertory Theatre Gallery, Detroit MI
Dixie State University, Sears Art Museum Gallery, Saint George UT
The Dixon Gallery & Gardens, Memphis TN
Doncaster Museum and Art Gallery, Doncaster Yorks
Dublin Arts Council, Dublin OH
Eastern Illinois University, Tarble Arts Center, Charleston IL
Eiteljorg Museum of American Indians & Western Art, Indianapolis IN
Ellen Noel Art Museum of the Permian Basin, Odessa TX
Elmhurst Art Museum, Elmhurst IL
Emory University, Michael C Carlos Museum, Atlanta GA

Erie County Historical Society, Erie PA
Eula Mae Edwards Museum & Gallery, Clovis NM
Evansville Museum of Arts, History & Science, Evansville IN
Everhart Museum, Scranton PA
Fairbanks Museum & Planetarium, Saint Johnsbury VT
Fetherston Foundation, Packwood House Museum, Lewisburg PA
Flint Institute of Arts, Flint MI
Florence County Museum, Florence SC
Florida State University and Central Florida Community College, The Appleton Museum of Art, Ocala FL
Fort Smith Regional Art Museum, Fort Smith AR
The Frank Phillips Foundation Inc, Woolaroc Museum, Bartlesville OK
Frederic Remington, Ogdensburg NY
The Frick Art & Historical Center, Inc, Frick Art Museum, Pittsburgh PA
Frye Art Museum, Seattle WA
Fuller Craft Museum, Brockton MA
Gadsden Museum of Art, Gadsden AL
Galerie Montcalm, Gatineau QC
Genesee Country Village & Museum, John L Wehle Art Gallery, Mumford NY
George Phippen, Phippen Museum - Art of the American West, Prescott AZ
Georgia O'Keeffe Museum, Santa Fe NM
Girard College, Stephen Girard Collection, Philadelphia PA
Glanmore National Historic Site of Canada, Belleville ON
Hamilton College, Emerson Gallery, Clinton NY
Headquarters Fort Monroe, Dept of Army, Casemate Museum, Hampton VA
Heard Museum, Phoenix AZ
Hecht Museum, Haifa
Henry County Museum & Cultural Arts Center, Clinton MO
Henry Sheldon Museum of Vermont History and Research Center, Middlebury VT
Heritage Center, Inc, Pine Ridge SD
Hickory Museum of Art, Inc, Hickory NC
Hill-Stead Museum, Farmington CT
Hillwood Museum & Gardens Foundation, Hillwood Estate Museum & Gardens, Washington DC
Historical Society of Cheshire County, Keene NH
The History Center in Tompkins County, Ithaca NY
Holter Museum of Art, Helena MT
Hui No'eau Visual Arts Center, Gallery and Gift Shop, Makawao Maui HI
Hunter Museum of American Art, Chattanooga TN
Huntsville Museum of Art, Huntsville AL
The Hyde Collection, Glens Falls NY
Hyde Park Art Center, Chicago IL
i.d.e.a. Museum, Mesa AZ
Illinois State Museum, ISM Lockport Gallery, Chicago Gallery & Southern Illinois Art Gallery, Springfield IL
Independence Historical Museum & Art Center, Independence KS
Independence Seaport Museum, Philadelphia PA
Indiana Landmarks, Morris-Butler House, Indianapolis IN
Institute of Contemporary Art, Los Angeles, Los Angeles CA
Institute of Puerto Rican Culture, Museo Fuerte Conde de Mirasol, Vieques PR
International Museum of Art, El Paso TX
International Museum of Art & Science, McAllen TX
Iredell Museums, Statesville NC
The Israel Museum, Jerusalem, Jerusalem
Jacksonville University, Alexander Brest Museum & Gallery, Jacksonville FL
James A Michener Art Museum, Doylestown PA
JMW Turner Museum, Sarasota FL
John B Aird Gallery, Toronto ON
The John L. Clarke Western Art Gallery & Memorial Museum, East Glacier Park MT
Jordan National Gallery of Fine Arts, Amman
Joslyn Art Museum, Omaha NE
Juniata College Museum of Art, Huntingdon PA
Kalamazoo Institute of Arts, Kalamazoo MI
Kamloops Art Gallery, Kamloops BC
Karakalpak State Art Museum, Nukus Republic of Karakalpakstan
Kenosha Public Museums, Kenosha WI
Kentucky Museum of Art and Craft, Louisville KY
Kereszteny Muzeum, Christian Museum, Esztergom
Kimbell Art Foundation, Kimbell Art Museum, Fort Worth TX
Kings County Historical Society & Museum, Hampton NB
Kirchner Museum Davos, Davos
Kirkland Museum of Fine & Decorative Art, Denver CO
Kitchener-Waterloo Art Gallery, Kitchener ON
Knoxville Museum of Art, Knoxville TN
Koshare Indian Museum, Inc, La Junta CO
Kunstmuseum Solothurn, Solothurn Art Museum, Solothurn
Kyiv Museum of Russian Art, Kyiv Ukrainian
L D Brinkman, Kerrville TX
La Salle University Art Museum, Philadelphia PA
Lafayette College, Lafayette College Art Galleries, Easton PA
LaGrange Art Museum, LaGrange GA
Lahore Museum, Lahore
Latino Art Museum, Pomona CA
Leanin' Tree Museum & Sculpture Garden of Western Art, Boulder CO
Lehigh Valley Heritage Center, Allentown PA
Leigh Yawkey Woodson Art Museum, Wausau WI
Liberty Hall Historic Site, Liberty Hall Museum, Frankfort KY
Lighthouse ArtCenter Museum & School of Art, Tequesta FL
Lightner Museum, Saint Augustine FL
Lillian & Coleman Taube Museum of Art, Minot ND
Lincoln County Historical Association, Inc, 1811 Old Lincoln County Jail & Lincoln County Museum, Wiscasset ME
Lincolnshire County Council, Library & Heritage Services, Lincoln
Lincolnshire County Council, The Collection: Art & Archaeology in Lincolnshire, Lincoln
The Long Island Museum of American Art, History & Carriages, Stony Brook NY
Longview Museum of Fine Art, Longview TX
Los Angeles County Museum of Natural History, William S Hart Museum, Newhall CA
Louise Hopkins Underwood Center for the Arts, Lubbock TX
Louisiana Department of Culture, Recreation & Tourism, Louisiana State Museum, New Orleans LA
Macau Museum of Art, NAPE
Madison & Main Gallery, Greeley CO
Marblehead Museum & Historical Society, Marblehead MA
Marblehead Museum & Historical Society, Jeremiah Lee Mansion, Marblehead MA
Maricopa County Historical Society, Desert Caballeros Western Museum, Wickenburg AZ
The Mariners' Museum, Newport News VA
Maryland Hall for the Creative Arts, Chaney Gallery, Annapolis MD
Massachusetts Institute of Technology, MIT Museum, Cambridge MA
Massillon Museum, Massillon OH
McPherson College Gallery, McPherson KS
Meem Gallery, Dubai
Mennello Museum of American Art, Orlando FL
Meridian Museum of Art, Meridian MS
Mesa Arts Center, Mesa Contemporary Arts Museum, Mesa AZ
Michelson Museum of Art, Marshall TX
Middle Border Museum & Oscar Howe Art Center, Mitchell SD
Midwest Museum of American Art, Elkhart IN
Miller Art Center Foundation Inc, Miller Art Museum, Sturgeon Bay WI
Millicent Rogers Museum, Taos NM
Millikin University, Perkinson Gallery, Decatur IL
Minnesota Museum of American Art, Saint Paul MN
Minot State University, Northwest Art Center, Minot ND
Mississippi Museum of Art, Jackson MS
Mobile Museum of Art, Mobile AL
Moderna Galerija, Modern Gallery - National Museum of Modern Art, Zagreb
Montana State University, Helen E Copeland Gallery, Bozeman MT
Montgomery Museum of Fine Arts, Montgomery AL
Moore College of Art & Design, The Galleries at Moore, Philadelphia PA
Moravian College, Payne Gallery, Bethlehem PA
Moravian Historical Society, Nazareth PA
Moravska Galerie v Brne, Moravian Gallery in Brno, Brno
Morehead State University, Kentucky Folk Art Center, Morehead KY
Morris Museum, Morristown NJ
Morris Museum of Art, Augusta GA
Muscatine Art Center, Muscatine IA
Musee Cognacq-Jay, Cognacq-Jay Museum, Paris
Musee des Beaux-Arts d'Orleans, Museum of Fine Arts, Orleans
Musee des Beaux-Arts de Tours, Museum of Fine Arts, Tours
Musee Regional de lu Cote-Nord, Sept-Iles QC
Museen der Stadt Koln, Wallraf-Richartz-Museum & Fondation Corboud - Wallraf-Richartz Museum & Corboud Foundation, Cologne
Museo De Bellas Artes, Museum of Fine Arts, Caracas
Museo De Las Americas, Denver CO
Museo di Palazzo Ducale, Ducale Palace Museum, Mantua
Museo Italo Americano, San Francisco CA
Museu Nacional D'Art De Catalunya, Catalona National Museum of Art, Barcelona
Museum of Art & History, Santa Cruz, Santa Cruz CA
Museum of Art - Deland FL, Inc, Deland FL
The Museum of Arts & Sciences Inc, Daytona Beach FL
Museum of Fine Arts, Saint Petersburg, Florida, Inc, Saint Petersburg FL
Museum of Latin American Art, Long Beach CA
Museum of Modern Art, Ibaraki, Mito Ibaraki
Museum of Northwest Art, La Conner WA
Museum of the Southwest, Midland TX
Museum of Wisconsin Art, West Bend WI
Museum Plantin-Moretus, Antwerp
Museum zu Allerheiligen, Schaffhausen
Muzej za Umjetnost i Obrt, Museum of Arts & Crafts, Zagreb
Muzeul National de Arta al Romaniei, National Museum of Art of Romania, Bucharest
Napa Valley Museum, Yountville CA
Narodna Galerija, National Gallery of Slovenia, Ljubljana
Nassau County Museum of Art, Roslyn Harbor NY
National Art Museum of Moldova, Chisinau
National Baseball Hall of Fame & Museum, Cooperstown NY
National Museum & Art Gallery of Trinidad and Tobago, Port of Spain
The National Museum of Modern Art, Tokyo, Tokyo
The National Museum of Western Art, Tokyo
National Museum of Wildlife Art of the Unites States, Jackson WY
National Park Service, Weir Farm National Historic Site, Wilton CT
National Society of Colonial Dames of America in the State of Maryland, Mount Clare Museum House, Baltimore MD
National Veterans Art Museum, Chicago IL
Naval Historical Center, National Museum of the US Navy, Washington DC
Nelson Mandela Metropolitan Art Museum, Port Elizabeth
Neue Galerie New York, New York NY
Nevada Museum of Art, Reno NV
Neville Public Museum of Brown County, Green Bay WI
New Britain Museum of American Art, New Britain CT
New Brunswick Museum, Saint John NB
New Visions Gallery, Inc, Marshfield WI
New York State Military Museum and Veterans Research Center, Saratoga Springs NY
Newfields, Indianapolis IN
Newport Art Museum and Association, Newport RI
Niagara University, Castellani Art Museum, Niagara NY
Nihon Mingeikan, Japan Folk Crafts Museum, Tokyo
The Noble Maritime Collection, Staten Island NY
North End Gallery, Leonardtown MD
Northeastern Nevada Museum, Elko NV
Norwich Free Academy, Slater Memorial Museum, Norwich CT
Noyes Art Gallery, Lincoln NE
Ogden Museum of Southern Art, University of New Orleans, New Orleans LA
Ohio University, Kennedy Museum of Art, Athens OH
Oklahoma City Museum of Art, Oklahoma City OK
The Old Jail Art Center, Albany TX
Oshkosh Public Museum & Library, Oshkosh WI

Osterreichische Galerie Belvedere Vienna, Belvedere Museum Vienna, Vienna
Owensboro Museum of Fine Art, Owensboro KY
Panhandle-Plains Historical Museum, Canyon TX
Pasadena Museum of History, Pasadena CA
Passaic County Community College, Broadway, LRC, and Hamilton Club Galleries, Paterson NJ
Pennsylvania Historical & Museum Commission, Railroad Museum of Pennsylvania, Strasburg PA
Pensacola Museum of Art, Pensacola FL
Philadelphia History Museum, Philadelphia PA
Philbrook Museum of Art, Tulsa OK
Phillips Academy, Addison Gallery of American Art, Andover MA
The Phillips Collection, Washington DC
Phoenix Art Museum, Phoenix AZ
Piedmont Arts Association, Martinsville VA
Pioneer Historical Museum of South Dakota, Hot Springs SD
Plains Art Museum, Fargo ND
Polish Museum of America (PMA), Chicago IL
The Pomona College, Claremont CA
Port Huron Museum, Port Huron MI
Pump House Center for the Arts, Chillicothe OH
Putnam County Historical Society, Foundry School Museum, Cold Spring NY
Putnam Museum of History and Natural Science, Davenport IA
Queen Victoria Museum and Art Gallery, Launceston TAS
Queens College, City University of New York, Godwin-Ternbach Museum, Flushing NY
Radio-Canada SRC CBC, Georges Goguen CBC Art Gallery, Moncton NB
Rahr-West Art Museum, Manitowoc WI
Rapid City Arts Council, Dahl Arts Center, Rapid City SD
Rawls Museum Arts, Courtland VA
Reading Public Museum, Reading PA
Rhode Island Historical Society, John Brown House, Providence RI
Riverside County Museum, Edward-Dean Museum & Gardens, Cherry Valley CA
Robert Louis Stevenson Museum, Saint Helena CA
The Robert McLaughlin Gallery, Oshawa ON
Ross Memorial Museum, Saint Andrews NB
Roswell Museum & Art Center, Roswell NM
Rutgers University, Stedman Art Gallery, Camden NJ
Saco Museum, Saco ME
Saginaw Art Museum, Saginaw MI
Saint Anselm College, Alva de Mars Megan Chapel Art Center, Manchester NH
Saint Bonaventure University, Regina A Quick Center for the Arts, Saint Bonaventure NY
Saint Joseph College, Art Gallery, University of Saint Joseph, West Hartford CT
Saint Olaf College, Flaten Art Museum, Northfield MN
Salisbury University, Ward Museum of Wildfowl Art, Salisbury MD
San Antonio Museum of Art, San Antonio TX
The San Joaquin Pioneer & Historical Society, The Haggin Museum, Stockton CA
Santa Barbara Museum of Art, Santa Barbara CA
Schweinfurth Art Center, Auburn NY
Scripps College, Ruth Chandler Williamson Gallery, Claremont CA
Seneca-Iroquois National Museum, Salamanca NY
Shaker Museum & Library, Old Chatham NY
Slovenska Narodna Galeria, Slovak National Gallery, Bratislava
The Society of the Cincinnati at Anderson House, Washington DC
Solomon R Guggenheim Museum, New York NY
South Carolina Artisans Center, Walterboro SC
South Dakota State University, South Dakota Art Museum, Brookings SD
Spartanburg Art Museum, Spartanburg SC
The Speed Art Museum, Louisville KY
Spertus Institute of Jewish Studies, Chicago IL
Springfield Art Museum, Springfield MO
Springville Museum of Art, Springville UT
St Mary's College of Maryland, The Dwight Frederick Boyden Gallery, St Mary's City MD
Staatliche Museen zu Berlin Stiftung Preussischer Kulturbesitz, National Museums in Berlin, Prussian Cultural Heritage Foundation, Berlin
Stanford University, Cantor Arts Center at Stanford University, Stanford CA
The State Museum of Fine Arts of Tatarstan Republic, Kazan
State University of New York at Geneseo, Bertha V B Lederer Gallery, Geneseo NY
The State University of New York at Potsdam, The Art Museum, Potsdam NY
Stratford Historical Society, Catharine B Mitchell Museum, Stratford CT
Swedish American Museum, Chicago IL
Tampa Museum of Art, Tampa FL
Temiskaming Art Gallery, Haileybury ON
Tohono Chul Park, Tucson AZ
Topeka & Shawnee County Public Library, Alice C Sabatini Gallery, Topeka KS
Tubac Center of the Arts, Santa Cruz Valley Art Association, Tubac AZ
Tucson Museum of Art and Historic Block, Tucson AZ
Turtle Bay Exploration Park, Redding CA
Tver Regional Art Gallery, Tver
Twin City Art Foundation, Masur Museum of Art, Monroe LA
Tyne and Wear Archives & Museums, Sunderland Museum & Winter Gardens, Sunderland
Ucross Foundation, Big Red Barn Gallery, Clearmont WY
Ukrainian Canadian Archives & Museum of Alberta, Edmonton AB
Ukrainian Institute of Modern Art, Chicago IL
The Ukrainian Museum, New York NY
UMLAUF Sculpture Garden & Museum, Austin TX
United Society of Shakers, Shaker Museum, New Gloucester ME
United States Capitol, Architect of the Capitol, Washington DC
United States Military Academy, West Point Museum, West Point NY
University of Calgary, Nickle Galleries, Calgary AB
University of California, Davis, Jan Shrem and Maria Manetti Shrem Museum of Art, Davis CA
University of Chicago, Smart Museum of Art, Chicago IL
University of Florida, Samuel P Harn Museum of Art, Gainesville FL
University of Georgia, Georgia Museum of Art, Athens GA
University of Illinois at Urbana-Champaign, Krannert Art Museum and Kinkead Pavilion, Champaign IL
University of Indianapolis, Christel DeHaan Fine Arts Gallery, Indianapolis IN
University of Kansas, Spencer Museum of Art, Lawrence KS
The University of Kentucky Art Museum, Lexington KY
University of Manchester, Whitworth Art Gallery, Manchester
University of Mary Washington, University of Mary Washington Galleries, Fredericksburg VA
University of Minnesota, The Bell Museum of Natural History, Minneapolis MN
University of Minnesota Duluth, Tweed Museum of Art, Duluth MN
University of Nebraska-Lincoln, Great Plains Art Museum, Lincoln NE
University of Nevada, Reno, Sheppard Contemporary & University Galleries, Reno NV
University of New Mexico, The Harwood Museum of Art, Taos NM
University of Notre Dame, Snite Museum of Art, Notre Dame IN
University of Richmond, University Museums, Richmond VA
University of Saskatchewan, Diefenbaker Canada Centre, Saskatoon SK
University of Texas at Austin, Blanton Museum of Art, Austin TX
University of Utah, Utah Museum of Fine Arts, Salt Lake City UT
University of Wisconsin-Eau Claire, Foster Gallery, Eau Claire WI
University of Wisconsin-Madison, Chazen Museum of Art, Madison WI
Ursinus College, Philip & Muriel Berman Museum of Art, Collegeville PA
USS Constitution Museum, Boston MA
The Valentine, Richmond VA
Van Gogh Museum, Amsterdam
Vassar College, The Frances Lehman Loeb Art Center, Poughkeepsie NY
Venice Art Center, Venice FL
Vero Beach Museum of Art, Vero Beach FL
Vesterheim Norwegian-American Museum, Decorah IA
Volcano Art Center Gallery, Hawaii Volcanoes National Park HI
Walker Art Gallery, Liverpool
Walker Fine Art, Denver CO
The Wallace Collection, London
Walter Anderson Museum of Art, Ocean Springs MS
Washburn University, Mulvane Art Museum, Topeka KS
Waterworks Visual Arts Center, Salisbury NC
Westmoreland Museum of American Art, Greensburg PA
Wharton Esherick Museum, Paoli PA
Whatcom Museum, Bellingham WA
Wheaton College, Beard and Weil Galleries, Norton MA
Wichita Art Museum, Wichita KS
Wichita State University, Ulrich Museum of Art, Wichita KS
Wildling Art Museum, Solvang CA
Wilfrid Laurier University, Robert Langen Art Gallery, Waterloo ON
Wilkes Art Gallery, North Wilkesboro NC
Winston-Salem State University, Diggs Gallery, Winston-Salem NC
Wiregrass Museum of Art, Dothan AL
Woodlawn/The Pope-Leighey, Alexandria VA
Woodmere Art Museum Inc, Philadelphia PA
Worcester Art Museum, Worcester MA
World Erotic Art Museum, Miami Beach FL
Wustum Museum Art Association, Charles A Wustum Museum of Fine Arts, Racine WI
Wyoming State Museum, Cheyenne WY
Wyoming Trails Gallery, Wheatland WY
Yale University, Yale Center for British Art, New Haven CT
Yokohama Museum of Art, Yokohama

WOODCARVINGS

A.E. Backus Museum & Gallery, Fort Pierce FL
A.I.R. Gallery, Brooklyn NY
Academy of the New Church, Glencairn Museum, Bryn Athyn PA
African American Museum in Philadelphia, Philadelphia PA
Alaska Department of Education, Division of Libraries, Archives & Museums, Sheldon Jackson Museum, Sitka AK
Albany Institute of History & Art, Albany NY
Albin Polasek Museum & Sculpture Gardens, Winter Park FL
Albuquerque Museum of Art & History, Albuquerque NM
Alton Museum of History & Art, Inc, Alton IL
American Swedish Institute, Minneapolis MN
Amherst College, Mead Art Museum, Amherst MA
Arkansas Arts Center, Little Rock AR
Arnold Mikelson Mind & Matter Art Gallery, Surrey BC
Arnot Art Museum, Elmira NY
Art and History Museums - Maitland, Maitland FL
Art Gallery of Hamilton, Hamilton ON
Art Gallery of Nova Scotia, Halifax NS
Art Museum of Greater Lafayette, Lafayette IN
Art Without Walls Inc, Sayville NY
Asian Art Museum of San Francisco, Chong-Moon Lee Ctr for Asian Art and Culture, San Francisco CA
Balzekas Museum of Lithuanian Culture, Chicago IL
Bangladesh National Museum, Dhaka
Baroda Museum and Picture Gallery, Vadodara
Beaumont Art League, Beaumont TX
Bellevue Arts Museum, Bellevue WA
Billie Trimble Chandler, Texas State Museum of Asian Cultures, Corpus Christi TX
Blanden Memorial Art Museum, Fort Dodge IA
Blauvelt Demarest Foundation, Hiram Blauvelt Art Museum, Oradell NJ
Bob Jones University Museum & Gallery Inc, Greenville SC
Bucknell University, Edward & Marthann Samek Art Gallery, Lewisburg PA
Calvert Marine Museum, Solomons MD
Canadian Museum of History, Gatineau QC
Canadian Museum of Nature, Musee Canadien de la Nature, Ottawa ON
Cape Cod Museum of Art Inc, Dennis MA
Carlsbad Museum & Art Center, Carlsbad NM
Center for Puppetry Arts, Atlanta GA
Central United Methodist Church, Swords Into Plowshares Peace Center & Gallery, Detroit MI

Chateau de Versailles, Palace of Versailles, Versailles
Chatham Historical Society, The Atwood House Museum, Chatham MA
Chesapeake Bay Maritime Museum, Saint Michaels MD
The Children's Museum of Indianapolis, Indianapolis IN
Cincinnati Art Museum, Cincinnati Art Museum, Cincinnati OH
City of Fayette, Alabama, Fayette Art Museum, Fayette AL
City of Gainesville, Thomas Center Galleries - Cultural Affairs, Gainesville FL
City of Springdale, Shiloh Museum of Ozark History, Springdale AR
Clark County Historical Society, Pioneer - Krier Museum, Ashland KS
Clinton Art Association, River Arts Center, Clinton IA
The Columbus Museum, Columbus GA
Craft and Folk Art Museum (CAFAM), Los Angeles CA
Cripple Creek District Museum, Cripple Creek CO
Crook County Museum & Art Gallery, Sundance WY
The Currier Museum of Art, Manchester NH
Danville Museum of Fine Arts & History, Danville VA
Davidson College, William H Van Every Jr & Edward M Smith Galleries, Davidson NC
Detroit Institute of Arts, Detroit MI
Detroit Repertory Theatre Gallery, Detroit MI
Doncaster Museum and Art Gallery, Doncaster Yorks
Dublin Arts Council, Dublin OH
Eastern Washington State Historical Society, Northwest Museum of Arts & Culture, Spokane WA
Ella Sharp Museum, Jackson MI
Ellen Noel Art Museum of the Permian Basin, Odessa TX
Elmhurst Art Museum, Elmhurst IL
Emory University, Michael C Carlos Museum, Atlanta GA
Essex Historical Society and Shipbuilding Museum, Essex MA
Eula Mae Edwards Museum & Gallery, Clovis NM
Fetherston Foundation, Packwood House Museum, Lewisburg PA
Five Civilized Tribes Museum, Muskogee OK
Flint Institute of Arts, Flint MI
Florence County Museum, Florence SC
Florida CraftArt, Saint Petersburg FL
Folk Art Society of America, Richmond VA
Fuller Craft Museum, Brockton MA
Fulton County Historical Society Inc, Fulton County Museum (Tetzlaff Reference Room), Rochester IN
Gadsden Museum, Mesilla NM
Gadsden Museum of Art, Gadsden AL
Galerie Montcalm, Gatineau QC
General Board of Discipleship, The United Methodist Church, The Upper Room Chapel & Museum, Nashville TN
George Phippen, Phippen Museum - Art of the American West, Prescott AZ
Glessner House Museum, Chicago IL
Gloridale Partnership, National Museum of Woodcarving, Custer SD
Grassroots Art Center, Lucas KS
Haystack Mountain School of Crafts, Deer Isle ME
Heard Museum, Phoenix AZ
Hecht Museum, Haifa
Henry County Museum & Cultural Arts Center, Clinton MO
Henry Sheldon Museum of Vermont History and Research Center, Middlebury VT
Heritage Center, Inc, Pine Ridge SD
Hermitage Museum & Gardens, Norfolk VA
Hershey Museum, Hershey PA
Het Noordbrabants Museum, s-Hertogenbosch
Hillwood Museum & Gardens Foundation, Hillwood Estate Museum & Gardens, Washington DC
Holter Museum of Art, Helena MT
Hunter Museum of American Art, Chattanooga TN
The Hyde Collection, Glens Falls NY
i.d.e.a. Museum, Mesa AZ
Illinois State Museum, ISM Lockport Gallery, Chicago Gallery & Southern Illinois Art Gallery, Springfield IL
Independence Historical Museum & Art Center, Independence KS
Independence Seaport Museum, Philadelphia PA
International Museum of Art, El Paso TX
International Museum of Art & Science, McAllen TX
Iredell Museums, Statesville NC
Iroquois Indian Museum, Howes Cave NY
The Israel Museum, Jerusalem, Jerusalem
Jacksonville University, Alexander Brest Museum & Gallery, Jacksonville FL
John B Aird Gallery, Toronto ON
The John L. Clarke Western Art Gallery & Memorial Museum, East Glacier Park MT
Jordan National Gallery of Fine Arts, Amman
Kalamazoo Institute of Arts, Kalamazoo MI
Kenosha Public Museums, Kenosha WI
Kentucky Museum of Art and Craft, Louisville KY
Kereszteny Muzeum, Christian Museum, Esztergom
Kimbell Art Foundation, Kimbell Art Museum, Fort Worth TX
Kirkland Museum of Fine & Decorative Art, Denver CO
Koshare Indian Museum, Inc, La Junta CO
Lac du Flambeau Band of Lake Superior Chippewa Indians, George W Brown Jr Ojibwe Museum & Cultural Center, Lac Du Flambeau WI
Lafayette Science Museum & Planetarium, Lafayette LA
LaGrange Art Museum, LaGrange GA
Lalit Kala Akademi Rabindra Bhavan Art Galleries, National Academy of Art, New Delhi, New Delhi
Latino Art Museum, Pomona CA
Leigh Yawkey Woodson Art Museum, Wausau WI
Lightner Museum, Saint Augustine FL
Lillian & Coleman Taube Museum of Art, Minot ND
Lincoln County Historical Association, Inc, 1811 Old Lincoln County Jail & Lincoln County Museum, Wiscasset ME
The Long Island Museum of American Art, History & Carriages, Stony Brook NY
Los Angeles County Museum of Natural History, William S Hart Museum, Newhall CA
Louise Hopkins Underwood Center for the Arts, Lubbock TX
Louisiana Department of Culture, Recreation & Tourism, Louisiana State Museum, New Orleans LA
Lusaka National Museum, Lusaka
The Mariners' Museum, Newport News VA
Mark Twain, Hartford CT
Maryland Hall for the Creative Arts, Chaney Gallery, Annapolis MD
McPherson Museum and Arts Foundation, McPherson KS
Mennello Museum of American Art, Orlando FL
Meredith College, Frankie G Weems Gallery & Rotunda Gallery, Raleigh NC
Miles B Carpenter Folk Art Museum, Waverly VA
Mills College Art Museum, Oakland CA
The Mint Museum, Mint Museum of Craft & Design, Charlotte NC
Missoula Art Museum, Missoula MT
Mobile Museum of Art, Mobile AL
Moderna Galerija, Modern Gallery - National Museum of Modern Art, Zagreb
Moravska Galerie v Brne, Moravian Gallery in Brno, Brno
Morehead State University, Kentucky Folk Art Center, Morehead KY
Morris Museum of Art, Augusta GA
Musee des Beaux-Arts de Tours, Museum of Fine Arts, Tours
Musee des Maitres et Artisans du Quebec, Montreal QC
Musee National des Beaux Arts du Quebec, Quebec QC
Musee Regional de lu Cote-Nord, Sept-Iles QC
Museo De Las Americas, Denver CO
Museo di Palazzo Ducale, Ducale Palace Museum, Mantua
Museu Nacional D'Art De Catalunya, Catalona National Museum of Art, Barcelona
The Museum, Greenwood SC
Museum of Arts & Design, New York NY
Museum of Latin American Art, Long Beach CA
Museum of Northern Arizona, Flagstaff AZ
Museum of Northern British Columbia, Ruth Harvey Art Gallery, Prince Rupert BC
Museum of Northwest Art, La Conner WA
Museum of the Plains Indian & Crafts Center, Browning MT
Museum of York County, Rock Hill SC
Museum Plantin-Moretus, Antwerp
Museum zu Allerheiligen, Schaffhausen
Muzeul National de Arta al Romaniei, National Museum of Art of Romania, Bucharest
Nanticoke Indian Museum, Millsboro DE
Narodna Galerija, National Gallery of Slovenia, Ljubljana
National Art Museum of Moldova, Chisinau
National Baseball Hall of Fame & Museum, Cooperstown NY
National Museum & Art Gallery of Trinidad and Tobago, Port of Spain
National Palace Museum, Taipei
The National Shrine of the North American Martyrs, Fultonville NY
Nebraska Game and Parks Commission, Arbor Lodge State Historical Park & Morton Mansion, Nebraska City NE
Nebraska State Capitol, Lincoln NE
Nelson Mandela Metropolitan Art Museum, Port Elizabeth
Neue Galerie New York, New York NY
Nevada Museum of Art, Reno NV
New Brunswick Museum, Saint John NB
New England Maple Museum, Pittsford VT
Norwich Free Academy, Slater Memorial Museum, Norwich CT
Noyes Art Gallery, Lincoln NE
Ogden Museum of Southern Art, University of New Orleans, New Orleans LA
Ohrmann Museum and Gallery, Drummond MT
Olana State Historic Site, Hudson NY
Old Island Restoration Foundation Inc, Oldest House in Key West, Key West FL
Oshkosh Public Museum & Library, Oshkosh WI
Ouachita River Art Gallery, Monroe LA
Owensboro Museum of Fine Art, Owensboro KY
Panhandle-Plains Historical Museum, Canyon TX
Pennsylvania Academy of the Fine Arts, Philadelphia PA
Peoria Riverfront Museum, Peoria IL
Plains Art Museum, Fargo ND
Plainsman Museum, Aurora NE
Pueblo Museum, Desert Hot Springs CA
Pump House Center for the Arts, Chillicothe OH
Queens College, City University of New York, Godwin-Ternbach Museum, Flushing NY
Radio-Canada SRC CBC, Georges Goguen CBC Art Gallery, Moncton NB
Randolph College, Maier Museum of Art, Lynchburg VA
Reading Public Museum, Reading PA
Rhodes College, Clough-Hanson Gallery, Memphis TN
Roswell Museum & Art Center, Roswell NM
Saginaw Art Museum, Saginaw MI
Saint Clair County Community College, Jack R Hennesey Art Galleries, Port Huron MI
Salisbury University, Ward Museum of Wildfowl Art, Salisbury MD
San Antonio Museum of Art, San Antonio TX
Schweinfurth Art Center, Auburn NY
Seneca-Iroquois National Museum, Salamanca NY
Sheldon Museum & Cultural Center, Inc, Sheldon Museum & Cultural Center, Haines AK
Shirley Plantation Foundation, Charles City VA
South Carolina Artisans Center, Walterboro SC
South Dakota State University, South Dakota Art Museum, Brookings SD
South Street Seaport Museum, New York NY
Spartanburg Art Museum, Spartanburg SC
The Speed Art Museum, Louisville KY
Spertus Institute of Jewish Studies, Chicago IL
Springfield Art Museum, Springfield MO
St Mary's College of Maryland, The Dwight Frederick Boyden Gallery, St Mary's City MD
The State Museum of Fine Arts of Tatarstan Republic, Kazan
Stone Quarry Hill Art Park, Winner Gallery, Cazenovia NY
Suan Pakkad Palace Museum, Bangkok
SVACA - Sheyenne Valley Arts & Crafts Association, Bjarne Ness Gallery at Bear Creek Hall, Fort Ransom ND
Swedish American Museum, Chicago IL
Tacoma Art Museum, Tacoma WA
Taos Historic Museums, La Hacienda de Los Martinez, Taos NM
Tinkertown Museum, Sandia Park NM
Tohono Chul Park, Tucson AZ
Tokyo National Museum, Tokyo
Topeka & Shawnee County Public Library, Alice C Sabatini Gallery, Topeka KS

Tubman African American Museum, Macon GA
Tver Regional Art Gallery, Tver
Ukrainian Institute of Modern Art, Chicago IL
The Ukrainian Museum, New York NY
UMLAUF Sculpture Garden & Museum, Austin TX
University of California, Berkeley, Phoebe Apperson Hearst Museum of Anthropology, Berkeley CA
University of California, Davis, Jan Shrem and Maria Manetti Shrem Museum of Art, Davis CA
University of Florida, Samuel P Harn Museum of Art, Gainesville FL
University of Georgia, Georgia Museum of Art, Athens GA
University of Illinois at Urbana-Champaign, Krannert Art Museum and Kinkead Pavilion, Champaign IL
University of Indianapolis, Christel DeHaan Fine Arts Gallery, Indianapolis IN
The University of Kentucky Art Museum, Lexington KY
University of Miami, Lowe Art Museum, Coral Gables FL
University of Nevada, Reno, Sheppard Contemporary & University Galleries, Reno NV
University of New Mexico, The Harwood Museum of Art, Taos NM
University of Texas at Austin, Blanton Museum of Art, Austin TX
University of Utah, Utah Museum of Fine Arts, Salt Lake City UT
University of Washington, Burke Museum of Natural History and Culture, Seattle WA
USS Constitution Museum, Boston MA
Vesterheim Norwegian-American Museum, Decorah IA
Volcano Art Center Gallery, Hawaii Volcanoes National Park HI
Wadsworth Atheneum Museum of Art, Hartford CT
Walker Fine Art, Denver CO
Walter Anderson Museum of Art, Ocean Springs MS
Warther Museum Inc, Dover OH
Waterfront Museum, Brooklyn NY
Waterloo Center of the Arts, Waterloo IA
Waterworks Visual Arts Center, Salisbury NC
Wendell Gilley, Southwest Harbor ME
Wharton Esherick Museum, Paoli PA
Whatcom Museum, Bellingham WA
Wheaton College, Beard and Weil Galleries, Norton MA
Wichita Art Museum, Wichita KS
Wilfrid Laurier University, Robert Langen Art Gallery, Waterloo ON
Winston-Salem State University, Diggs Gallery, Winston-Salem NC
Wiregrass Museum of Art, Dothan AL
Wisconsin Historical Society, Wisconsin Historical Museum, Madison WI
Wyoming Trails Gallery, Wheatland WY
Yokohama Museum of Art, Yokohama
Zigler Art Museum, Jennings LA

WOODCUTS

A.E. Backus Museum & Gallery, Fort Pierce FL
A.I.R. Gallery, Brooklyn NY
Academy Art Museum, Easton MD
African American Museum in Philadelphia, Philadelphia PA
Alaska Heritage Museum at Wells Fargo, Anchorage AK
Albany Institute of History & Art, Albany NY
Albion College, Bobbitt Visual Arts Center, Albion MI
The Albrecht-Kemper Museum of Art, Saint Joseph MO
Albuquerque Museum of Art & History, Albuquerque NM
American University, Museum at the Katzen, Washington DC
Amherst College, Mead Art Museum, Amherst MA
Amon Carter Museum of American Art, Fort Worth TX
Arnot Art Museum, Elmira NY
Art and History Museums - Maitland, Maitland FL
Art Gallery of Alberta, Edmonton AB
Art Gallery of Nova Scotia, Halifax NS
Art Gallery of South Australia, Adelaide
The Art Museum of Eastern Idaho, Idaho Falls ID
Art Museum of Greater Lafayette, Lafayette IN
Art Without Walls Inc, Sayville NY
ArtSpace/Lima, Lima OH
Balzekas Museum of Lithuanian Culture, Chicago IL
Bangladesh National Museum, Dhaka
Baruch College of the City University of New York, Sidney Mishkin Gallery, New York NY
Billie Trimble Chandler, Texas State Museum of Asian Cultures, Corpus Christi TX
Birger Sandzen Memorial Gallery, Lindsborg KS
Blanden Memorial Art Museum, Fort Dodge IA
Boise Art Museum, Boise ID
Bone Creek Museum of Agrarian Art, David City NE
Boston Public Library, Albert H Wiggin Gallery & Print Department, Boston MA
Bucknell University, Edward & Marthann Samek Art Gallery, Lewisburg PA
Burchfield Penney Art Center, Buffalo NY
Canadian Museum of History, Gatineau QC
Cape Cod Museum of Art Inc, Dennis MA
Carleton College, Art Gallery, Northfield MN
Carnegie Mellon University, Hunt Institute for Botanical Documentation, Pittsburgh PA
Carnegie Museums of Pittsburgh, Carnegie Museum of Art, Pittsburgh PA
Carolina Art Association, Gibbes Museum of Art, Charleston SC
Centenary College of Louisiana, Meadows Museum of Art, Shreveport LA
The Children's Museum of Indianapolis, Indianapolis IN
Cincinnati Art Museum, Cincinnati Art Museum, Cincinnati OH
City of Cedar Falls, Iowa, James & Meryl Hearst Center for the Arts & Sculpture Garden, Cedar Falls IA
City of El Paso, El Paso TX
City of Fayette, Alabama, Fayette Art Museum, Fayette AL
City of Gainesville, Thomas Center Galleries - Cultural Affairs, Gainesville FL
City of Pittsfield Office of Cultural Development, Lichtenstein Center for the Arts, Pittsfield MA
Clark Art Institute, Williamstown MA
Clinton Art Association, River Arts Center, Clinton IA
Colgate University, Picker Art Gallery, Hamilton NY
College of William & Mary, Muscarelle Museum of Art, Williamsburg VA
The Columbus Museum, Columbus GA
Coos Art Museum, Coos Bay OR
Cornell University, Herbert F Johnson Museum of Art, Ithaca NY
Craft and Folk Art Museum (CAFAM), Los Angeles CA
Crary Art Gallery, Warren PA
Cripple Creek District Museum, Cripple Creek CO
Crocker Art Museum, Sacramento CA
Danville Museum of Fine Arts & History, Danville VA
Dartmouth College, Hood Museum of Art, Hanover NH
Daum Museum of Contemporary Art, Sedalia MO
Davidson College, William H Van Every Jr & Edward M Smith Galleries, Davidson NC
deCordova Sculpture Park & Museum, Lincoln MA
Deines Cultural Center, Russell KS
DeLeon White Gallery, Toronto ON
Detroit Institute of Arts, Detroit MI
Detroit Repertory Theatre Gallery, Detroit MI
Dickinson College, The Trout Gallery, Carlisle PA
Dixie State University, Sears Art Museum Gallery, Saint George UT
Doncaster Museum and Art Gallery, Doncaster Yorks
Eastern Illinois University, Tarble Arts Center, Charleston IL
Elmhurst Art Museum, Elmhurst IL
Eula Mae Edwards Museum & Gallery, Clovis NM
Evansville Museum of Arts, History & Science, Evansville IN
Everhart Museum, Scranton PA
Flint Institute of Arts, Flint MI
Florence County Museum, Florence SC
Fort Ticonderoga Association, Ticonderoga NY
Fuller Craft Museum, Brockton MA
Gadsden Museum of Art, Gadsden AL
Galerie Montcalm, Gatineau QC
Hammonds House Museum, Atlanta GA
Haystack Mountain School of Crafts, Deer Isle ME
Hebrew Union College - Jewish Institute of Religion, Skirball Museum Cincinnati, Cincinnati OH
Henry County Museum & Cultural Arts Center, Clinton MO
Hickory Museum of Art, Inc, Hickory NC
Hill-Stead Museum, Farmington CT
Hillwood Museum & Gardens Foundation, Hillwood Estate Museum & Gardens, Washington DC
The Hyde Collection, Glens Falls NY
i.d.e.a. Museum, Mesa AZ
Illinois State Museum, ISM Lockport Gallery, Chicago Gallery & Southern Illinois Art Gallery, Springfield IL
Independence Seaport Museum, Philadelphia PA
International Museum of Art & Science, McAllen TX
Iredell Museums, Statesville NC
The Israel Museum, Jerusalem, Jerusalem
Jacksonville University, Alexander Brest Museum & Gallery, Jacksonville FL
John B Aird Gallery, Toronto ON
The John L. Clarke Western Art Gallery & Memorial Museum, East Glacier Park MT
Jordan National Gallery of Fine Arts, Amman
Joslyn Art Museum, Omaha NE
Juniata College Museum of Art, Huntingdon PA
Kalamazoo Institute of Arts, Kalamazoo MI
Kenosha Public Museums, Kenosha WI
Kereszteny Muzeum, Christian Museum, Esztergom
Kings County Historical Society & Museum, Hampton NB
Kirchner Museum Davos, Davos
Knoxville Museum of Art, Knoxville TN
Kunsthistorisches Museum Wien, Museum of Fine Arts, Vienna
La Salle University Art Museum, Philadelphia PA
Lafayette College, Lafayette College Art Galleries, Easton PA
LaGrange Art Museum, LaGrange GA
Lalit Kala Akademi Rabindra Bhavan Art Galleries, National Academy of Art, New Delhi, New Delhi
Latino Art Museum, Pomona CA
Leigh Yawkey Woodson Art Museum, Wausau WI
The Long Island Museum of American Art, History & Carriages, Stony Brook NY
Longview Museum of Fine Art, Longview TX
Louise Hopkins Underwood Center for the Arts, Lubbock TX
Loyola University Chicago, Loyola University Museum of Art, Chicago IL
The Mariners' Museum, Newport News VA
Maryland Hall for the Creative Arts, Chaney Gallery, Annapolis MD
Mennello Museum of American Art, Orlando FL
Mesa Arts Center, Mesa Contemporary Arts Museum, Mesa AZ
Michelson Museum of Art, Marshall TX
Midwest Museum of American Art, Elkhart IN
Miller Art Center Foundation Inc, Miller Art Museum, Sturgeon Bay WI
Mills College Art Museum, Oakland CA
Minot State University, Northwest Art Center, Minot ND
Mississippi Museum of Art, Jackson MS
Missoula Art Museum, Missoula MT
Mobile Museum of Art, Mobile AL
Moderna Galerija, Modern Gallery - National Museum of Modern Art, Zagreb
Montgomery Museum of Fine Arts, Montgomery AL
Moravian College, Payne Gallery, Bethlehem PA
Moravska Galerie v Brne, Moravian Gallery in Brno, Brno
Morris Museum of Art, Augusta GA
Muhlenberg College, Martin Art Gallery, Allentown PA
Musee des Beaux-Arts d'Orleans, Museum of Fine Arts, Orleans
Musee Regional de lu Cote-Nord, Sept-Iles QC
Museo De Las Americas, Denver CO
Museum of Art - Deland FL, Inc, Deland FL
The Museum of Arts & Sciences Inc, Daytona Beach FL
Museum of Fine Arts, Saint Petersburg, Florida, Inc, Saint Petersburg FL
Museum of Latin American Art, Long Beach CA
Museum of Modern Art, Ibaraki, Mito Ibaraki
Museum of Northwest Art, La Conner WA
Museum of the Plains Indian & Crafts Center, Browning MT
Museum Plantin-Moretus, Antwerp
Museum zu Allerheiligen, Schaffhausen
Muzeul National de Arta al Romaniei, National Museum of Art of Romania, Bucharest
Narodna Galerija, National Gallery of Slovenia, Ljubljana
National Museum & Art Gallery of Trinidad and Tobago, Port of Spain

Naval Historical Center, National Museum of the US Navy, Washington DC
Nelson Mandela Metropolitan Art Museum, Port Elizabeth
The Nelson-Atkins Museum of Art, Kansas City MO
Nevada Museum of Art, Reno NV
New Britain Museum of American Art, New Britain CT
New Brunswick Museum, Saint John NB
New Gallery of Modern Art, Charlotte NC
New Visions Gallery, Inc, Marshfield WI
Newport Art Museum and Association, Newport RI
Niagara University, Castellani Art Museum, Niagara NY
Niigata Prefectural Museum of Modern Art, Nagaoka
Norton Simon Museum, Pasadena CA
Norwich Free Academy, Slater Memorial Museum, Norwich CT
Ogden Museum of Southern Art, University of New Orleans, New Orleans LA
Ohio University, Kennedy Museum of Art, Athens OH
Oklahoma City Museum of Art, Oklahoma City OK
The Old Jail Art Center, Albany TX
Owensboro Museum of Fine Art, Owensboro KY
Palm Beach County Parks & Recreation Department, Morikami Museum & Japanese Gardens, Delray Beach FL
Panhandle-Plains Historical Museum, Canyon TX
Pennsylvania Academy of the Fine Arts, Philadelphia PA
Pensacola Museum of Art, Pensacola FL
Phillips Academy, Addison Gallery of American Art, Andover MA
The Phillips Collection, Washington DC
Phoenix Art Museum, Phoenix AZ
Plains Art Museum, Fargo ND
The Pomona College, Claremont CA
Pump House Center for the Arts, Chillicothe OH
Purdue University Galleries, West Lafayette IN
Queen Victoria Museum and Art Gallery, Launceston TAS
Queens College, City University of New York, Godwin-Ternbach Museum, Flushing NY
Radio-Canada SRC CBC, Georges Goguen CBC Art Gallery, Moncton NB
Reading Public Museum, Reading PA
The Robert McLaughlin Gallery, Oshawa ON
Roswell Museum & Art Center, Roswell NM
Saginaw Art Museum, Saginaw MI
Saint Anselm College, Alva de Mars Megan Chapel Art Center, Manchester NH
Saint Bonaventure University, Regina A Quick Center for the Arts, Saint Bonaventure NY
Saint Joseph College, Art Gallery, University of Saint Joseph, West Hartford CT
Saint Olaf College, Flaten Art Museum, Northfield MN
Santa Barbara Museum of Art, Santa Barbara CA
Schweinfurth Art Center, Auburn NY
Scripps College, Ruth Chandler Williamson Gallery, Claremont CA
Shirley Plantation Foundation, Charles City VA
South Carolina Artisans Center, Walterboro SC
South Dakota State University, South Dakota Art Museum, Brookings SD
The Speed Art Museum, Louisville KY
Spertus Institute of Jewish Studies, Chicago IL
Springfield Art Museum, Springfield MO
St Mary's College of Maryland, The Dwight Frederick Boyden Gallery, St Mary's City MD
Staatliche Museen zu Berlin Stiftung Preussischer Kulturbesitz, National Museums in Berlin, Prussian Cultural Heritage Foundation, Berlin
Stanford University, Cantor Arts Center at Stanford University, Stanford CA
State Capital Museum, Olympia WA
State University of New York at Geneseo, Bertha V B Lederer Gallery, Geneseo NY
The State University of New York at Potsdam, The Art Museum, Potsdam NY
State University of New York College at Cortland, Dowd Fine Arts Gallery, Cortland NY
Staten Island Museum, Staten Island NY
Stone Quarry Hill Art Park, Winner Gallery, Cazenovia NY
T W Wood Gallery, Montpelier VT
Tacoma Art Museum, Tacoma WA
Tampa Museum of Art, Tampa FL
Tohono Chul Park, Tucson AZ
Tubman African American Museum, Macon GA
Turk ve Islam Eserleri Muzesi, Museum of Turkish and Islamic Art, Istanbul
Tver Regional Art Gallery, Tver
Twin City Art Foundation, Masur Museum of Art, Monroe LA
Tyne and Wear Archives & Museums, Sunderland Museum & Winter Gardens, Sunderland
Ukrainian Canadian Archives & Museum of Alberta, Edmonton AB
Ukrainian Institute of Modern Art, Chicago IL
The Ukrainian Museum, New York NY
University of Arkansas at Little Rock, Art Galleries, Little Rock AR
University of California, Davis, Jan Shrem and Maria Manetti Shrem Museum of Art, Davis CA
University of Chicago, Smart Museum of Art, Chicago IL
University of Georgia, Georgia Museum of Art, Athens GA
University of Illinois at Urbana-Champaign, Krannert Art Museum and Kinkead Pavilion, Champaign IL
University of Kansas, Spencer Museum of Art, Lawrence KS
The University of Kentucky Art Museum, Lexington KY
University of Mary Washington, University of Mary Washington Galleries, Fredericksburg VA
University of Minnesota Duluth, Tweed Museum of Art, Duluth MN
University of Nebraska-Lincoln, Great Plains Art Museum, Lincoln NE
University of Nevada, Reno, Sheppard Contemporary & University Galleries, Reno NV
University of Notre Dame, Snite Museum of Art, Notre Dame IN
University of Richmond, University Museums, Richmond VA
University of Texas at Austin, Blanton Museum of Art, Austin TX
University of Utah, Utah Museum of Fine Arts, Salt Lake City UT
University of Wisconsin-Eau Claire, Foster Gallery, Eau Claire WI
Ursinus College, Philip & Muriel Berman Museum of Art, Collegeville PA
Van Gogh Museum, Amsterdam
Vero Beach Museum of Art, Vero Beach FL
Vesterheim Norwegian-American Museum, Decorah IA
Volcano Art Center Gallery, Hawaii Volcanoes National Park HI
Wadsworth Atheneum Museum of Art, Hartford CT
Walker Art Gallery, Liverpool
Walker Fine Art, Denver CO
Walter Anderson Museum of Art, Ocean Springs MS
Washburn University, Mulvane Art Museum, Topeka KS
Waterworks Visual Arts Center, Salisbury NC
Wesleyan University, Davison Art Center, Middletown CT
Wharton Esherick Museum, Paoli PA
Wheaton College, Beard and Weil Galleries, Norton MA
Wichita State University, Ulrich Museum of Art, Wichita KS
Wildling Art Museum, Solvang CA
Wilfrid Laurier University, Robert Langen Art Gallery, Waterloo ON
William Morris Gallery, London
Winston-Salem State University, Diggs Gallery, Winston-Salem NC
Wiregrass Museum of Art, Dothan AL
Worcester Art Museum, Worcester MA
World Erotic Art Museum, Miami Beach FL
Yokohama Museum of Art, Yokohama
Zigler Art Museum, Jennings LA

Collections

A S Palmer Film Collection
San Francisco Maritime National Historical Park, Maritime Museum San Francisco CA

Aaron Pyle Collection
Chappell Memorial Library and Art Gallery, Chappell NE

Addison Mizner Collection
The Society of the Four Arts, Gioconda & Joseph King Library Palm Beach FL

Admiral Raphael Semmes Collection
History Museum of Mobile, Mobile AL

Adolph D & Wilkins C Williams Collection
Virginia Museum of Fine Arts, Richmond VA

Ailsa Mellon Bruce Collection of Decorative Arts
Virginia Museum of Fine Arts, Richmond VA

Alan Chasanoff Ceramic Collection
The Mint Museum, Mint Museum of Craft & Design Charlotte NC

Albert H Wiggin Collection
Boston Public Library, Albert H Wiggin Gallery & Print Department Boston MA

Alexander M Craighead Collection of European & American Military Art
United States Military Academy, West Point Museum West Point NY

Alfred H & Eva Underhill Holbrook Collection of American Art
University of Georgia, Georgia Museum of Art Athens GA

Alfred I Barton Collection
University of Miami, Lowe Art Museum Coral Gables FL

Algur H Meadows Collection of Spanish Paintings
Southern Methodist University, Meadows Museum Dallas TX

Alice B Nunn Silver Collection
Portland Art Museum, Portland OR

Alice Baber Collection of Contemporary American Art
Art Museum of Greater Lafayette, Lafayette IN

Alice F Schott Doll Collection
Santa Barbara Museum of Art, Santa Barbara CA

Andrew McClelland Collection of World Curiosities
Rosemount Museum, Inc, Pueblo CO

Anita Pohndorff Yates Collection of Saratoga History
Skidmore College, Lucy Scribner Library Saratoga Springs NY

Anka Gvozdanovic Collection
Muzej za Umjetnost i Obrt, Museum of Arts & Crafts Zagreb

Anna Russell Jones Collection
African American Museum in Philadelphia, Philadelphia PA

Armand Hammer Collection
University of Southern California, USC Fisher Museum of Art Los Angeles CA

Arnotts Biscuits Collection
Museum of Contemporary Art, Sydney NSW

Arthur & Margaret Glasgow Collection of Renaissance Art
Virginia Museum of Fine Arts, Richmond VA

Arthur M Sackler Collection
Freer Gallery of Art & Arthur M Sackler Gallery, Arthur M Sackler Gallery Washington DC

Arthur Rubloff Paperweight Collection
The Art Institute of Chicago, Chicago IL

Ashby Collection of American Art
Central Methodist University, Ashby-Hodge Gallery of American Art Fayette MO

Austen D Warburton Native American Art & Artifacts Collection
Triton Museum of Art, Santa Clara CA

B R Davis Southey Collection
University of Waterloo, Dana Porter Library Waterloo ON

Bancroft Collection of English Pre-Raphaelite Paintings
Delaware Art Museum, Wilmington DE

Barbara Johnson Whaling Collection
San Francisco Maritime National Historical Park, Maritime Museum San Francisco CA

Barry M Goldwater Katsina Doll & Photograph Collection
Heard Museum, Phoenix AZ

Bartlett Wicks Collection
University of Utah, Utah Museum of Fine Arts Salt Lake City UT

Beeson Wedgewood Collection
Birmingham Museum of Art, Clarence B Hanson Jr Library Birmingham AL

Benjamin A & Julia M Trustman Collection of Honore Daumier Prints
Brandeis University, Leonard L Farber Library Waltham MA

Berghammer Art Collection
Lloydminster Cultural & Science Centre, Lloydminster SK

Bernard Baruch Silver Collection
University of South Carolina, McKissick Museum Columbia SC

Bert Piso Collection
New Orleans Museum of Art, New Orleans LA

Bertie Lord Collection
Ravalli County Museum, Hamilton MT

Biggs Collection
Biggs Museum of American Art, Dover DE

Bill & Polly Nordeen Collection of Western Art
University of Montana, Montana Museum of Art & Culture Missoula MT

Bloomsbury Collection of Kenneth Curry
Rollins College, George D & Harriet W Cornell Fine Arts Museum Winter Park FL

Boehm Collection
Bellingrath Gardens & Home, Theodore AL

Bowen Collection of Antiquities
Bob Jones University Museum & Gallery Inc, Greenville SC

Bower Collection
Red Deer & District Museum & Archives, Red Deer AB

Boyd Martin Collection
University of Louisville, Ekstrom Library Photographic Archives Louisville KY

Bradley Collection
Milwaukee Art Museum, Milwaukee WI

Branch Collection of Renaissance Art
Virginia Museum of Fine Arts, Richmond VA

Bresler Collection
The Mint Museum, Mint Museum of Craft & Design Charlotte NC

Broder Collection
University of Nebraska-Lincoln, Great Plains Art Museum Lincoln NE

Burnap Collection
The Nelson-Atkins Museum of Art, Kansas City MO

Burrison Folklife Collection
Atlanta Historical Society Inc, Atlanta History Center Atlanta GA

C G Wallace Collection
Heard Museum, Phoenix AZ

C R Savage Collection
Brigham Young University, Harold B Lee Library Provo UT

C R Smith Collection of Western American Art
University of Texas at Austin, Blanton Museum of Art Austin TX

Candace Wheeler Collection
Mark Twain, Hartford CT

Caplan Collection
The Children's Museum of Indianapolis, Indianapolis IN

Cappadocia Collection of Southeast Asian Textiles
University of Montana, Montana Museum of Art & Culture Missoula MT

Cargo Collection of American Quilts
Birmingham Museum of Art, Clarence B Hanson Jr Library Birmingham AL

Carnegie Collection of Prints
Dickinson College, The Trout Gallery Carlisle PA

Carrington Collection of Chinese Export Objects
Rhode Island Historical Society, John Brown House Providence RI

Carter & Eustis Collection of Furniture
Oatlands Plantation, Leesburg VA

Catherine Van Rensselaer Bonney Collection of Oriental Decorative Art
Historic Cherry Hill, Albany NY

Cesnola Collection
Stanford University, Cantor Arts Center at Stanford University Stanford CA

Chambon (Raymond) Collection
Corning Museum of Glass, Juliette K and Leonard S Rakow Research Library Corning NY

Chapman H Hyams Collection
New Orleans Museum of Art, New Orleans LA

Charles A Greenfield Collection
The Metropolitan Museum of Art, New York NY

Charles Cutts Collection
Nevada Museum of Art, Reno NV

Charles Nelson Spinks Collection of Japanese Prints
American University, Jack I & Dorothy G Bender Library & Learning Resources Center New York NY

Charles Pratt Collection of Chinese Jades
Vassar College, The Frances Lehman Loeb Art Center Poughkeepsie NY

Charles Small Puzzle Collection
Fresno Metropolitan Museum, Fresno CA

Charles W Guildman Collection
University of Nebraska-Lincoln, Great Plains Art Museum Lincoln NE

Chase Collection
Foosaner Art Museum, Melbourne FL

Cintas Foundation Collection
University of Miami, Lowe Art Museum Coral Gables FL

Clara Champlain Griswold Toy Collection
Lyme Historical Society, Florence Griswold Museum Old Lyme CT

Clark European Collection
Corcoran Gallery of Art, Washington DC

Clark Field Collection of American Indian Crafts
Philbrook Museum of Art, Tulsa OK

Cleanth Brooks Collection
University of Southern Mississippi, McCain Library & Archives Hattiesburg MS

Clewell Pottery Collection
Besser Museum for Northeast Michigan, Alpena MI

Clifford M Clarke Collection
Agnes Scott College, Dalton Art Gallery Decatur GA

Cloud Wampler Collection of Oriental Art
Everson Museum of Art, Syracuse NY

Clowes Fund Collection
Newfields, Indianapolis IN

Cluny Collection
Harvard University, Frances Loeb Library Cambridge MA

Cochran Collection of Windsor Chairs
Philipse Manor Hall State Historic Site, Yonkers NY

Cochrane Collection of American Art
Virginia Museum of Fine Arts, Richmond VA

Coe Collection
Coe College, Eaton-Buchan Gallery & Marvin Cone Gallery Cedar Rapids IA

Colburn Gemstone Collection
University of South Carolina, McKissick Museum Columbia SC

Cole Collection of Oriental & Decorative Arts
Dickinson College, The Trout Gallery Carlisle PA

Collins Archive
The Art Institute of Chicago, Ryerson & Burnham Libraries Chicago IL

Collins Collection of English Ceramics
Birmingham Museum of Art, Clarence B Hanson Jr Library Birmingham AL

Cone Collection
The Baltimore Museum of Art, Baltimore MD
University of North Carolina at Greensboro, Weatherspoon Art Museum Greensboro NC

Conger Metcalf Collection of Paintings
Coe College, Eaton-Buchan Gallery & Marvin Cone Gallery Cedar Rapids IA

Cooper Collection
University of Louisville, Ekstrom Library Photographic Archives Louisville KY

Cooper Collection of Rugs
Birmingham Museum of Art, Clarence B Hanson Jr Library Birmingham AL

Copeland Collection
Delaware Art Museum, Wilmington DE

Cotter Collection
Saint Mary's College, Moreau Galleries Notre Dame IN

Couldery European Art Collection
Glanmore National Historic Site of Canada, Belleville ON

Cowan Collection
Board of Parks & Recreation, The Parthenon Nashville TN

Cyrus Dallin Bronze Collection
Springville Museum of Art, Springville UT

Czartoryski Collection
Muzeum Narodowe w Krakowie, National Museum in Kracow Krakow

Dana Collection of American Impressionists
University of Montana, Montana Museum of Art & Culture Missoula MT

Daschle Career papers
South Dakota State University, Hilton M. Briggs Library Brookings SD

David Belasco Collection
Neville Public Museum of Brown County, Green Bay WI

David Roberts Collection
Riverside County Museum, Edward-Dean Museum & Gardens Cherry Valley CA

David T Vernon Indian Arts Collection
Grand Teton National Park Service, Moose WY

De Beer Collection
Dunedin Public Art Gallery, Dunedin

de Grummond Collection
University of Southern Mississippi, McCain Library & Archives Hattiesburg MS

Dexter M Ferry Collection
Vassar College, The Frances Lehman Loeb Art Center Poughkeepsie NY

Dicke Collection
University of Evansville, Krannert Gallery & Peterson Gallery Evansville IN

Dillard Collection: Works on Paper
University of North Carolina at Greensboro, Weatherspoon Art Museum Greensboro NC

Donald Buchanan Art Collection
Southern Alberta Art Gallery, Lethbridge AB

Donald Deskey Archive
Cooper Hewitt, Smithsonian Design Museum, Library New York NY

Donenberg Collection
Quincy Art Center, Quincy IL

Dorothy & Herbert Vogel Collection
Yellowstone Art Museum, Billings MT

Dorothy Adler Routh Collection of Cloisonne
Scripps College, Ruth Chandler Williamson Gallery Claremont CA

Dorothy Stevens Collection
United States Figure Skating Association, World Figure Skating Museum & Hall of Fame Colorado Springs CO

Dr & Mrs William E Ballard Collection of Japanese Prints
Scripps College, Ruth Chandler Williamson Gallery Claremont CA

Dr Bern Dibner Collection of Leonardo Da Vinci Books
Brandeis University, Leonard L Farber Library Waltham MA

Dr C Ford Collection
National Museum of Beirut, Beirut

Dr Louis Levy Collection of American Prints
Memphis Brooks Museum of Art, Memphis TN

Dr Paul Lamp Collection
Glanmore National Historic Site of Canada, Belleville ON

Dr Ruth Wright Hayre Collection
African American Museum in Philadelphia, Philadelphia PA

DuBose Civil War Collection
Atlanta Historical Society Inc, Atlanta History Center Atlanta GA

Dunbarton Collection of Prints
Saint Mary's College, Moreau Galleries Notre Dame IN

Dunnigan Collection of 19th Century Etchings
Parrish Art Museum, Water Mill NY

Duveneck Collection
Triton Museum of Art, Santa Clara CA

E L Wiegand Art Collection
Nevada Museum of Art, Reno NV

Eadweard Muybridge Photography Collection
Stanford University, Cantor Arts Center at Stanford University Stanford CA

Earl Bailey Meldrum Collection
Lunenburg Art Gallery Society, Lunenburg NS

Earnest A Walen Collection
University of Southern Mississippi, McCain Library & Archives Hattiesburg MS

Ebnother Collection
Museum zu Allerheiligen, Schaffhausen

Edith H K Fetherston Collection
Fetherston Foundation, Packwood House Museum Lewisburg PA

Edmond R Ruben Film Study Collection
Walker Art Center, Minneapolis MN

Edward Ayer Collection, Manuscripts & Maps
The Newberry, Chicago IL

Edward Virginius Valentine Sculpture Collection
The Valentine, Richmond VA

Edwin M Blake Memorial Collection
Trinity College, Austin Arts Center, Widener Gallery Hartford CT

Elder Collection - Artist Self-Portraits, Prints, Drawings, Watercolors, Paintings, c 1925-1975
Georgetown University, Lauinger Library - Special Collections Division Washington DC

Eli Lilly Collection of Chinese Art
Newfields, Indianapolis IN

Elizabeth Cole Butler Collection of Native American Art
Portland Art Museum, Portland OR

Elizabeth Holmes Fisher Collection
University of Southern California, USC Fisher Museum of Art Los Angeles CA

Elizabeth Parke Firestone Collection of 18th Century Silver
Detroit Institute of Arts, Detroit MI

Elizabeth S Navas Papers
Wichita Art Museum, Wichita KS

Elkins Collection
Casa Amesti, Monterey CA

Ellis Collection
Western Kentucky University, Kentucky Library & Museum Bowling Green KY

Emerick Arts Collection
The University of Montana - Western, Lucy Carson Memorial Library Dillon MT

Emily Woodward Collection
Eastern Shore Art Association, Inc, Eastern Shore Art Center Fairhope AL

Eric F Menke Collection - Prints, Drawings, Watercolors, Paintings
Georgetown University, Lauinger Library - Special Collections Division Washington DC

Eric Smith Collection - Original Editorial Cartoon
Georgetown University, Lauinger Library - Special Collections Division Washington DC

Ernest C & Jane Werner Watson Collection of Indian Miniatures
University of Wisconsin-Madison, Chazen Museum of Art Madison WI

Ernest L Blumenschein & Family Collection
Taos Historic Museums, Ernest Blumenschein Home & Studio Taos NM

Ernie Simon Collection of Photographs & Newspapers
Port Washington Public Library, Port Washington NY

Ernst Mahler Collection of Germanic Glass
Bergstrom-Mahler Museum of Glass, Neenah WI

Esso Collection
University of Miami, Lowe Art Museum Coral Gables FL

Eteljorg Collection of African Art
Newfields, Indianapolis IN

Eugene B Adkins Collection of Native American & Western Art
Philbrook Museum of Art, Tulsa OK

Eugene Fuller Memorial Collection of Chinese Jades
Seattle Art Museum, Seattle WA

Evan H Roberts Sculpture Collection
Portland Art Museum, Portland OR

Evelyn McCurdy Salisbury Ceramic Collection
Lyme Historical Society, Florence Griswold Museum Old Lyme CT

Everett D Graff Collection of Western Americana books & manuscripts
The Newberry, Chicago IL

Everett Shinn Archives
Delaware Art Museum, Helen Farr Sloan Library Wilmington DE

F B Doane Collection of Western American Art
Frontier Times Museum, Bandera TX

F B Housser Memorial Collection
Museum London, London ON

F. Price Cossman Collection of Steuben Glass
Wichita Art Museum, Wichita KS

Fedderson Collection of Rembrandt Collections
University of Notre Dame, Snite Museum of Art Notre Dame IN

Feinberg Collection of Masks from Around the World
Octagon Center for the Arts, Ames IA

Felix M Warburg Collection of Medieval Sculpture
Vassar College, The Frances Lehman Loeb Art Center Poughkeepsie NY

Fischer Collection of Expressionism
Virginia Museum of Fine Arts, Richmond VA

Fisher Collection
Central Iowa Art Association, Inc, Marshalltown IA

Fisher Memorial Collection
Beloit College, Wright Museum of Art Beloit WI

Flagg Collection of Haitian Art
Milwaukee Art Museum, Milwaukee WI

Flexner Slide Collection
University of Louisville, Ekstrom Library Photographic Archives Louisville KY

Florence Naftzger Evans Collection of Porcelain
Wichita Art Museum, Wichita KS

Floyd & Josephine Segel Collection of Photography
Milwaukee Art Museum, Milwaukee WI

Forbes Family Collection
Captain Forbes House Museum, Milton MA

Fowler Collection
Gadsden Museum of Art, Gadsden AL

Francis King Collection of Western Art
Sangre de Cristo Arts & Conference Center, Pueblo CO

Frank & Mary Alice Diener Collection
Fresno Metropolitan Museum, Fresno CA

Frank deBellis Collection on Italian Culture
San Francisco State University, J Paul Leonard Library San Francisco CA

Frank Schoonover Archives
Delaware Art Museum, Helen Farr Sloan Library Wilmington DE

Fred & Estelle Marer Contemporary Ceramics Collection
Scripps College, Ruth Chandler Williamson Gallery Claremont CA

Fred Harvey Fine Arts Collection
Heard Museum, Phoenix AZ

Frederick K & Margaret R Barbour Furniture Collection
Connecticut Historical Society, Hartford CT

Galen Biary Photograph Collection
Whatcom Museum, Bellingham WA

Garrow Collection of British Illustrated Books & Wood Engravings of the 1860s
Art Gallery of Ontario, Edward P Taylor Research Library & Archives Toronto ON

Gary M Hoffer '74 Memorial Photography Collection
Colgate University, Picker Art Gallery Hamilton NY

Gascoigne Collection
Leeds Museums & Galleries, Lotherton Hall Leeds

Gebauer Collection of Cameroon Art
Portland Art Museum, Portland OR

Gene Kloss Collection
Sangre de Cristo Arts & Conference Center, Pueblo CO

General Edward Young Collection of American Paintings
Scripps College, Ruth Chandler Williamson Gallery Claremont CA

George A Lucas Collection
The Baltimore Museum of Art, Baltimore MD

George Anderson Collection of Early Utah Photographs
Brigham Young University, Harold B Lee Library Provo UT

George Chaplin Collection
Trinity College, Austin Arts Center, Widener Gallery Hartford CT

George Costakis Collection
State Museum of Contemporary Art, Thessaloniki

George Dudley Seymour Collection of Furniture
Connecticut Historical Society, Hartford CT

George Eastman Legacy Collection
George Eastman Museum, Rochester NY

George F McMurray Collection
Trinity College, Austin Arts Center, Widener Gallery Hartford CT

George P Tweed Memorial Collection of American & European Paintings
University of Minnesota Duluth, Tweed Museum of Art Duluth MN

George Phippen Memorial Western Bronze Collection
Maricopa County Historical Society, Desert Caballeros Western Museum Wickenburg AZ

George Swinton Collection on Eskimo & North American Indian Art & Culture
The Winnipeg Art Gallery, Clara Lander Library & Archives Winnipeg MB

Gerard Collection of Bowling Green Photographs
Western Kentucky University, Kentucky Library & Museum Bowling Green KY

Gerofsky Collection of African Art
Dickinson College, The Trout Gallery Carlisle PA

Gillert Collection of Ceramics
Philbrook Museum of Art, Tulsa OK

Gillis Grafstrom Collection
United States Figure Skating Association, World Figure Skating Museum & Hall of Fame Colorado Springs CO

Gladys McFerron Collection
United States Figure Skating Association, World Figure Skating Museum & Hall of Fame Colorado Springs CO

Golda & Meyer B Marks Cobra Art Collection
Museum of Art, Fort Lauderdale, Fort Lauderdale FL

Gordon Kuntz Collection
Will Rogers Memorial Museum & Birthplace Ranch, Claremore OK

Grace & Abigail French Collection
Rapid City Arts Council, Dahl Arts Center Rapid City SD

Grace Whitney-Hoff Collection of Fine Bindings
Detroit Institute of Arts, Detroit MI

Grant Wood Collection
Coe College, Eaton-Buchan Gallery & Marvin Cone Gallery Cedar Rapids IA

Grice Native American Ceramic Collection
The Mint Museum, Mint Museum of Craft & Design Charlotte NC

Griiswold Collections
University of Louisville, Ekstrom Library Photographic Archives Louisville KY

Gritchenko Foundation Collection
Ukrainian Institute of America, Inc, New York NY

Gurley Korean Pottery Collection
Beloit College, Wright Museum of Art Beloit WI

Gussman Collection of African Sculpture
Philbrook Museum of Art, Tulsa OK

Guy Rowe Wax Drawings Collection
Angelo State University, Houston Harte University Center San Angelo TX

Gwen Houston Naftzger Collection of Porcelain
Wichita Art Museum, Wichita KS

H Kress Collection of European Paintings
Seattle Art Museum, Seattle WA

Hall Collection of American Folk Art
Milwaukee Art Museum, Milwaukee WI

Hallmark Photographic Collection
The Nelson-Atkins Museum of Art, Kansas City MO

Hamilton Collection
Fort Wayne Museum of Art, Inc, Fort Wayne IN

Hamilton King Meek Memorial Collection
Museum London, London ON

Hammer Collections
University of California, Los Angeles, Hammer Museum Los Angeles CA

Hammer Honore Daumier Collection
University of California, Los Angeles, Grunwald Center for the Graphic Arts at Hammer Museum Los Angeles CA

Harry C Goebel Collection
Saint John's University, Dr. M.T. Geoffrey Yeh Art Gallery Queens NY

Harry G Friedman Collection of Ceremonial Objects
The Jewish Museum, New York NY

Harry J Stein-Samuel Friedenberg Collection
The Jewish Museum, New York NY

Harry L Dalton Collection
Agnes Scott College, Dalton Art Gallery Decatur GA

Harry Mueller Philately Book Collection
Wichita Public Library, Wichita KS

Harry Neigher Collection of Political Cartoons, 1928-1975
Colgate University, Picker Art Gallery Hamilton NY

Harry T Norton Collection of Ancient Glass
Montreal Museum of Fine Arts, Montreal QC

Hartford Steam Boiler Collection of America
Lyme Historical Society, Florence Griswold Museum Old Lyme CT

Haynes Collection of Art, Photographs & Artifacts
Montana Historical Society, Helena MT

Hazel Schwentker Collection
Rapid City Arts Council, Dahl Arts Center Rapid City SD

Hazel Smith Collection
Austin Peay State University, Mabel Larsen Fine Arts Gallery Clarksville TN

Heeramaneck Collection of Asian Art
Virginia Museum of Fine Arts, Richmond VA

Heeramaneck Collection of Primitive Art
Seattle Art Museum, Seattle WA

Helen & Paul Covert Collection
Montana State University at Billings, Northcutt Steele Gallery Billings MT

Helen S Slosberg Collection
Brandeis University, Rose Art Museum Waltham MA

Henry & Martha Issacson Collection of 18th Century European Porcelain
Seattle Art Museum, Seattle WA

Henry Dreyfuss Archive
Cooper Hewitt, Smithsonian Design Museum, Library New York NY

Henry Eichheim Collection
Santa Barbara Museum of Art, Santa Barbara CA

Henry P McIntosh Collection
The Society of the Four Arts, Gioconda & Joseph King Library Palm Beach FL

Henry Pearson Collection-donations of works by Henry Pearson and other leading artists
Community Council for the Arts, Kinston NC

Herman Collection of Modern Chinese Woodcuts
Colgate University, Picker Art Gallery Hamilton NY

Hinkhouse Collection of Contemporary Art
Coe College, Eaton-Buchan Gallery & Marvin Cone Gallery Cedar Rapids IA

Hirschberg Collection of West African Arts
Topeka & Shawnee County Public Library, Alice C Sabatini Gallery Topeka KS

Hirsh Collection of Oriental Rugs
Portland Art Museum, Portland OR

Hitt Collection of 19th Century French Furniture
Birmingham Museum of Art, Clarence B Hanson Jr Library Birmingham AL

Hogsett Collection
Fort Morgan Heritage Foundation, Fort Morgan CO

Honda Collection of Southeast Asian Ceramics
Fukuoka Art Museum, Fukuoka

Hope Collection of Engraved Portraits
Oxford University, Ashmolean Museum Oxford

Hosmer-Pillow-Vaughan Collection
Beaverbrook Art Gallery, Fredericton NB

Howard E Wooden Papers
Wichita Art Museum, Wichita KS

Howard Pyle Archives and Library
Delaware Art Museum, Helen Farr Sloan Library Wilmington DE

Hudson & Carpenter Family Collection
City of Ukiah, Grace Hudson Museum & The Sun House Ukiah CA

I Webb Surratt Jr Print Collection
University of Richmond, University Museums Richmond VA

Ike Parker Collection: Callie Hart
Henry County Museum & Cultural Arts Center, Clinton MO

Isaac Scott Collection
Glessner House Museum, Chicago IL

J C Coovert Collection
Arts & Science Center for Southeast Arkansas, Pine Bluff AR

J Chester Armstrong Collection
Zigler Art Museum, Jennings LA

J Harry Howard Gemstone Collection
University of South Carolina, McKissick Museum Columbia SC

J Henry Ray American Indian Artifacts Collection
Red River Valley Museum, Vernon TX

J M W Turner Collection
Newfields, Indianapolis IN

J Marvin Hunter Western Americana Collection
Frontier Times Museum, Bandera TX

J W Power Collection
Museum of Contemporary Art, Sydney NSW

Jack Woods Collection
Pioneer Town, Pioneer Museum of Western Art Wimberley TX

James & Mari Michener Collection of American Paintings
University of Texas at Austin, Blanton Museum of Art Austin TX

James F Byrnes Collection
University of South Carolina, McKissick Museum Columbia SC

James I Merrill Collection
The Society of the Four Arts, Gioconda & Joseph King Library Palm Beach FL

James Shettel Collection
York County Heritage Trust, York PA

James Townes Medal Collection
Delta State University, Fielding L Wright Art Center Cleveland MS

Jane & Arthur Mason Collection
The Mint Museum, Mint Museum of Craft & Design Charlotte NC

Jay Gould Collection
The National Trust for Historic Preservation, Lyndhurst Tarrytown NY

Jean & Marie Erikson Rug & Textile Collection
University of Calgary, Nickle Galleries Calgary AB

Jeffersonian Collection
Thomas Jefferson Foundation, Inc, Monticello Charlottesville VA

Jenny Lind Collection of Photos
The Barnum Museum, Bridgeport CT

Jesuit Collection - American fine prints, c 1900-1950
Georgetown University, Lauinger Library - Special Collections Division Washington DC

JJ Lankes Collection
Buffalo & Erie County Public Library, Buffalo NY

Joans Lie Collection of Panama Canal Oils
United States Military Academy, West Point Museum West Point NY

Joe & Lucy Howorth Collection
Delta State University, Fielding L Wright Art Center Cleveland MS

Joey and Toby Tanenbaum Collection
Art Gallery of Hamilton, Hamilton ON

John Barrow Collection
John D Barrow, Skaneateles NY

John Barton Payne Collection
Virginia Museum of Fine Arts, Richmond VA

John C Jessup Collection
The Society of the Four Arts, Gioconda & Joseph King Library Palm Beach FL

John Chandler Bancroft Collection of Japanese Prints
Worcester Art Museum, Worcester MA

John J Mayers Collection
Boca Raton Museum of Art, Boca Raton FL

John M Howard Collection
Arts & Science Center for Southeast Arkansas, Pine Bluff AR

John M Wing Foundation Collection on history of printing & aesthetics of book design
The Newberry, Chicago IL

John Magnani Collection of Arts & Crafts
San Francisco State University, J Paul Leonard Library San Francisco CA

John Sloan Archives and Library
Delaware Art Museum, Helen Farr Sloan Library Wilmington DE

Johnson Collection
Topeka & Shawnee County Public Library, Alice C Sabatini Gallery Topeka KS

Jonathan Sax Print Collection
University of Minnesota Duluth, Tweed Museum of Art Duluth MN

Joseph Bonaparte Collection
Athenaeum of Philadelphia, Philadelphia PA

Joseph E Coleman Collection
African American Museum in Philadelphia, Philadelphia PA

Joseph E Davies Collection of Russian Icons & Paintings
University of Wisconsin-Madison, Chazen Museum of Art Madison WI

Joseph Henry Sharp Collection of Indian Photographs
C M Russell Museum, Frederic G Renner Memorial Library Great Falls MT

Joseph Pennell Collection
The George Washington University, Luther W Brady Art Gallery Washington DC

Justin K Thannhauser Collection of Impressionist & Post-Impressionist Paintings
Solomon R Guggenheim Museum, New York NY

Katherine C White Collection of African Art
Seattle Art Museum, Seattle WA

Kenan Ozbel Private Collections
Topkapi Palace Museum, Istanbul

Keyser Art of the Greater West Coll
Nevada Museum of Art, Reno NV

Kimura Teizo Collection
Aichi Prefectural Museum of Art, Nagoya

Kinne Water Turbine Collection
Jefferson County Historical Society, Watertown NY

Kloss Photo Collection
United States Figure Skating Association, World Figure Skating Museum & Hall of Fame Colorado Springs CO

Kowalsky Collection
Ukrainian Institute of Modern Art, Chicago IL

Krannert Memorial Collection
University of Indianapolis, Christel DeHaan Fine Arts Gallery Indianapolis IN

Kraus II Collection of Modern & Contemporary Design
Philbrook Museum of Art, Tulsa OK

Kress Collection of Italian Renaissance Art
Birmingham Museum of Art, Clarence B Hanson Jr Library Birmingham AL

Kress Collection of Italian Renaissance Painting
Honolulu Museum of Art, Honolulu HI

Kress Collection of Renaissance & Baroque Periods
City of El Paso, El Paso TX

Kress Foundation Study Collection
Baylor University, Armstrong Browning Library Waco TX

Kress Study Collection
University of Notre Dame, Snite Museum of Art Notre Dame IN

Krone Collection
California State University, East Bay, C E Smith Museum of Anthropology Hayward CA

Kurdian Collection of Pre-Columbian & Mexican Art
Wichita Art Museum, Wichita KS

Kusuma Collection of Textiles
Fukuoka Art Museum, Fukuoka

L S & Ida L Naftzger Collection of Prints & Drawings
Wichita Art Museum, Wichita KS

Ladislav Sutnar Archive
Cooper Hewitt, Smithsonian Design Museum, Library New York NY

Lady Nancy Astor Collection of English China
Virginia Museum of Fine Arts, Richmond VA

Lamprecht Collection of Cast Iron Art
Birmingham Museum of Art, Clarence B Hanson Jr Library Birmingham AL

Larson Drawing Collection
Austin Peay State University, Mabel Larsen Fine Arts Gallery Clarksville TN

Latter-Schlesinger Miniature Collection
New Orleans Museum of Art, New Orleans LA

Laura A Clubb Collection of Paintings
Philbrook Museum of Art, Tulsa OK

Lawther Collection of Ethiopian Crosses
Portland Art Museum, Portland OR

Layman Glass Collection in Annie Pfeiffer Chapel
Florida Southern College, Melvin Art Gallery Lakeland FL

Layton Collection
Milwaukee Art Museum, Milwaukee WI

Lee Archives
Washington & Lee University, Lee Chapel & Museum Lexington VA

Lee Collection
California State University, East Bay, C E Smith Museum of Anthropology Hayward CA

Lehman Collection, Medieval Art & The Cloisters
The Metropolitan Museum of Art, New York NY

Lenoir C Wright Collection of Japanese Woodblock Prints
University of North Carolina at Greensboro, Weatherspoon Art Museum Greensboro NC

LeRoy M Backus Collection of Drawings & Paintings
Seattle Art Museum, Seattle WA

Lewis Collection of Classical Antiquities
Portland Art Museum, Portland OR

Liedesdorf Collection of European Armor
United States Military Academy, West Point Museum West Point NY

Lillian Thomas Pratt Collection of Czarist Jewels
Virginia Museum of Fine Arts, Richmond VA

Locke Collection of Indian Artifacts
Roberts County Museum, Miami TX

Lockwood deForest Collection
Mark Twain, Hartford CT

Loomis Wildlife Collection of Northeastern Birds and Mammals
Roberson Museum & Science Center, Binghamton NY

Loti & Victor Smorgon Collection of Contemporary Australian Art
Museum of Contemporary Art, Sydney NSW

Louisa Gordon Collection of Antiques
Frontier Times Museum, Bandera TX

Louise Norton Classic Design Collection
State University of New York at Plattsburgh, Art Museum Plattsburgh NY

Lucile Pillow Porcelain Collection
Montreal Museum of Fine Arts, Montreal QC

Luis De Hoyos Collection of Pre-Columbian Art
Colgate University, Picker Art Gallery Hamilton NY

Luther W. Brady Collection
Colgate University, Picker Art Gallery Hamilton NY

Lyle Tuttle Collection
Tattoo Art Museum, San Francisco CA

Lynd Ward Collection - Prints, Drawings, Watercolors, Paintings, c 1925-1980
Georgetown University, Lauinger Library - Special Collections Division Washington DC

M C Naftzger Collection of Charles M Russell Paintings
Wichita Art Museum, Wichita KS

Mackay Collection of C M Russell Art
Montana Historical Society, Helena MT

Madden Arnholz Collection
Irish Museum of Modern Art, Dublin

Maltwood Collection of Decorative Art
University of Victoria, The Legacy Art Gallery Victoria BC

Maningrida Collection of Aboriginal Art
Museum of Contemporary Art, Sydney NSW

Manson F Backus Collection of Prints
Seattle Art Museum, Seattle WA

Manvell Collection of Film Stills
University of Louisville, Ekstrom Library Photographic Archives Louisville KY

Marcia & Granvil Specks Collection
Milwaukee Art Museum, Milwaukee WI

Marghab Linens Collection
South Dakota State University, South Dakota Art Museum Brookings SD

Marianne Moore Papers Collection
The Rosenbach Museum & Library, Philadelphia PA

Marianne Young World Costume Collection
Owatonna Arts Center, Owatonna MN

Marion Sharp Robinson Collection
University of Utah, Utah Museum of Fine Arts Salt Lake City UT

Marvin Cone Alumni Collection
Coe College, Eaton-Buchan Gallery & Marvin Cone Gallery Cedar Rapids IA

Mary Andrews Ladd Collection of Japanese Prints
Portland Art Museum, Portland OR

Mary Louise Reynolds Collection
The Art Institute of Chicago, Ryerson & Burnham Libraries Chicago IL

Matsunaga Collection
Fukuoka Art Museum, Fukuoka

Matthew Vassar Collection
Vassar College, The Frances Lehman Loeb Art Center Poughkeepsie NY

Matthias H Arnot Collection
Arnot Art Museum, Elmira NY

Maurice & Esther Leah Ritz Collection
Milwaukee Art Museum, Milwaukee WI

Maurice Sendak Archive
The Rosenbach Museum & Library, Philadelphia PA

Maurice Wertheim Collection
Harvard University, William Hayes Fogg Art Museum Cambridge MA

Max Simon Comic Book Collection
The Children's Museum of Indianapolis, Indianapolis IN

McCrillis Collection of Antique Dolls
Rhode Island Historical Society, John Brown House Providence RI

McGregor Collection of Rare Books
Western Kentucky University, Kentucky Library & Museum Bowling Green KY

McIntosh Collection of Books on Sepulchral Monuments
Art Gallery of Ontario, Edward P Taylor Research Library & Archives Toronto ON

Mead Collection of Mammoth Bones & Fossils
Roberts County Museum, Miami TX

Melvin P Billups Glass Collection
New Orleans Museum of Art, New Orleans LA

Mestrovich Collection
Fondazione Musei Civici Di Venezia, Ca' Rezzonico Venice

Mildred Manty Memorial Collection
Mid-America All-Indian Center, Indian Center Museum Wichita KS

Miles B Carpenter Collection
Miles B Carpenter Folk Art Museum, Waverly VA

Miriam Cowger Allen Doll Collection
The Art Association of Jacksonville, The David Strawn Art Gallery Jacksonville IL

Monrad Collection of Early European Graphics
Museum of New Zealand Te Papa Tongarewa, Wellington

Moore Collection
Museum London, London ON
University of Illinois at Urbana-Champaign, Krannert Art Museum and Kinkead Pavilion Champaign IL

Morgan-Whitney Collection of Chinese Jades
New Orleans Museum of Art, New Orleans LA

Morrison Collection
University of Minnesota Duluth, Tweed Museum of Art Duluth MN

Morse Collection
Beloit College, Wright Museum of Art Beloit WI

Mount Family Artwork 19th, 20th & 21st century landscape paintings
The Long Island Museum of American Art, History & Carriages, Library Stony Brook NY

Mourot Collection of Meissen Porcelain
Virginia Museum of Fine Arts, Richmond VA

Mr & Mrs Edward Rose Collection
Brandeis University, Rose Art Museum Waltham MA

Mr & Mrs John D Rockefeller 3rd Collection of Asian Art
Asia Society Museum, New York NY

Mrs Arthur Kelly Evans Collection of Pottery & Porcelain
Virginia Museum of Fine Arts, Richmond VA

Mrs James Johnson Collection of Contemporary American, British, Korean, Mexican & Japanese Ceramics
Scripps College, Ruth Chandler Williamson Gallery Claremont CA

Mrs Leslie Fenton Netsuke Collection
Hartnell College Gallery, Salinas CA

Mrs Virginia Bacher Haichol Artifact Collection
Hartnell College Gallery, Salinas CA

Muldoon Collection of Aesop Editions
Art Gallery of Ontario, Edward P Taylor Research Library & Archives Toronto ON

Munras Memorial Collection
Carmel Mission & Gift Shop, Carmel CA

Murphy Collection
University of California, Los Angeles, Hammer Museum Los Angeles CA

Murphy Collection - American Fine Prints, c 1900-1950
Georgetown University, Lauinger Library - Special Collections Division Washington DC

Musgrave Kinley Outsider Art Collection
Irish Museum of Modern Art, Dublin

Nagel Collection of Chinese & Tibetan Sculpture & Textiles
Scripps College, Clark Humanities Museum Claremont CA

Nan Kivell Collection of British Original Prints
Museum of New Zealand Te Papa Tongarewa, Wellington

Natacha Rambova Egyptian Collection
University of Utah, Utah Museum of Fine Arts Salt Lake City UT

Neal Collection of Utopian Materials
Western Kentucky University, Kentucky Library & Museum Bowling Green KY

Neese Fund Collection of Contemporary Art
Beloit College, Wright Museum of Art Beloit WI

Nelson International Ceramics
University of Minnesota Duluth, Tweed Museum of Art Duluth MN

Nelson Maritime Arts Foundation Collection
Channel Islands Maritime Museum, Oxnard CA

Nezu Kaichiro Sr Collection
Nezu Bijutsukan, Nezu Museum Tokyo

Norman Davis Collection of Classical Art
Seattle Art Museum, Seattle WA

Olga Hasbrouck Collection of Chinese Ceramics
Vassar College, The Frances Lehman Loeb Art Center Poughkeepsie NY

Oliver Collection of English Porcelain
Birmingham Museum of Art, Clarence B Hanson Jr Library Birmingham AL

Olsen Collection
University of Illinois at Urbana-Champaign, Krannert Art Museum and Kinkead Pavilion Champaign IL

Opal Leonard Collection of Chinese & Japanese Art
Montana State University at Billings, Northcutt Steele Gallery Billings MT

Oppenheimer Collection of Late Medieval & Early Renaissance Sculpture & Paintings
McNay Art Museum, San Antonio TX

Osborn Collection
Yale University, New Haven CT

Oscar & Maria Salzer Collection of 16th & 17th Century Dutch & Flemish Paintings
Fresno Metropolitan Museum, Fresno CA

Oscar & Maria Salzer Collection of Still Life & Trompe l'oeil Paintings
Fresno Metropolitan Museum, Fresno CA

Ottilia Buerger Collection of Ancient Coins
Lawrence University, Wriston Art Center Galleries Appleton WI

Overmyer Civil War Collection
Fulton County Historical Society Inc, Fulton County Museum (Tetzlaff Reference Room) Rochester IN

Owen & Edith Dodson Memorial Collection
Hatch-Billops Collection, Inc, New York NY

Owen T Gromme Collection
University of Minnesota, The Bell Museum of Natural History Minneapolis MN

Parish Collection of Belter Furniture
Frederic Remington, Ogdensburg NY

Parker Lace Collection
Montreal Museum of Fine Arts, Montreal QC

Paul M Hahn Collection of 18th Century English & American Silver
Berkshire Museum, Pittsfield MA

Paul McPharlin Collection of Theatre & Graphic Arts
Detroit Institute of Arts, Detroit MI

Paul Strand Archive
Aperture Foundation, New York NY

Pearce Western Art Collection
Navarro College, Gaston T Gooch Library & Learning Resource Center Corsicana TX

Percier & Fontaine Collection
The Art Institute of Chicago, Ryerson & Burnham Libraries Chicago IL

Percival DeLuce Memorial Collection
Northwest Missouri State University, DeLuce Art Gallery Maryville MO

Peter Carl Faberge Collection of Czarist Jewels
Virginia Museum of Fine Arts, Richmond VA

Phelps Collection of Andrew Wyeth Works
Delaware Art Museum, Wilmington DE

Philip & Muriel Berman Collection
Ursinus College, Philip & Muriel Berman Museum of Art Collegeville PA

Philip Trammell Shutze Collection of Decorative Arts
Atlanta Historical Society Inc, Atlanta History Center Atlanta GA

Pierre Brunet Collection
United States Figure Skating Association, World Figure Skating Museum & Hall of Fame Colorado Springs CO

Pitkin Asian Art Collection
Beloit College, Wright Museum of Art Beloit WI

Pittman Collection of Oil, Watercolors, and Drawings
Edgecombe County Cultural Arts Council, Inc, Blount-Bridgers House, Hobson Pittman Memorial Gallery Tarboro NC

Pohl Collection - German Expressionism
Lawrence University, Wriston Art Center Galleries Appleton WI

Poindexter Collection of Abstract Art
Montana Historical Society, Helena MT

Poindexter Collection of Abstract Expressionism
Yellowstone Art Museum, Billings MT

Pope & Leighey Family Collections
Frank Lloyd Wright's, Alexandria VA

Potamkin Collection of 19th & 20th Century Work
Dickinson College, The Trout Gallery Carlisle PA

Potlatch Collection of Royal Canadian Mounted Police Illustrations
University of Minnesota Duluth, Tweed Museum of Art Duluth MN

Powers Ceramics Collection
Cornell College, Peter Paul Luce Gallery Mount Vernon IA

Preston Morton Collection of American Art
Santa Barbara Museum of Art, Santa Barbara CA

Putnam Collection
Timken Museum of Art, San Diego CA

RA Young Collection
Oklahoma City Museum of Art, Oklahoma City OK

Ramingining Collection of Aboriginal Art
Museum of Contemporary Art, Sydney NSW

Rasmussen Collection of Eskimo Art
Portland Art Museum, Portland OR

Rawlings Nelson Collection
University of Minnesota Duluth, Tweed Museum of Art Duluth MN

Ray Meadows Collection
Mid-America All-Indian Center, Indian Center Museum Wichita KS

Raymond Jonson Reserved Retrospective Collection of Paintings
University of New Mexico, Raymond Jonson Collection & Archive Albuquerque NM

Reid Bill Collection
Bill Reid Gallery of Northwest Coast Art, Vancouver BC

Reilly Collection of Old Master Drawings
University of Notre Dame, Snite Museum of Art Notre Dame IN

Rene von Schleintz Collection
Milwaukee Art Museum, Milwaukee WI

Rentschler Collection of Last Supper Art
Lutheran Theological Seminary, Krauth Memorial Library Philadelphia PA

Reynolds Collection of Paintings
Tennessee Valley Art Association, Tuscumbia AL

Rich Collection: Rare Books & Manuscripts
The Huntington Library, Art Collections & Botanical Gardens, San Marino CA

Richard Mandell Collection
University of South Carolina, McKissick Museum Columbia SC

Ricker Papers
University of Illinois at Urbana-Champaign, Ricker Library of Architecture & Art Champaign IL

Robert E Wilson Collection of Paintings & Sculpture
Huntington University, Robert E Wilson Art Gallery Huntington IN

Robert F Rockwell Foundation Collection
The Rockwell Museum, Corning NY

Robert Frank Photography Collection
Stanford University, Cantor Arts Center at Stanford University Stanford CA

Robert Gumbiner Foundation Collection
Museum of Latin American Art, Long Beach CA

Robert H Tannahill Collection of Impressionist & Post Impressionist Paintings
Detroit Institute of Arts, Detroit MI

Roberta C Lawson Collection of Indian Costumes & Artifacts
Philbrook Museum of Art, Tulsa OK

Rodman Collection of Popular Art
The Art Galleries of Ramapo College, Mahwah NJ

Roland P Murdock Collection of American Art
Wichita Art Museum, Wichita KS

Rosa Breithhaupt Clark Architectural History Collection
University of Waterloo, Dana Porter Library Waterloo ON

Rose & Benjamin Mintz Collection of Eastern European Art
The Jewish Museum, New York NY

Roy C Leventritt Collection
Asian Art Museum of San Francisco, Chong-Moon Lee Ctr for Asian Art and Culture San Francisco CA

Roycroft Collection
Burchfield Penney Art Center, Buffalo NY

Ruesch Collection of Whistler Lithographs
University of California, Davis, Jan Shrem and Maria Manetti Shrem Museum of Art Davis CA

Sackler Collection
The Metropolitan Museum of Art, New York NY

Saidye and Samuel Bronfman Collection of Contemporary Canadian Art
Montreal Museum of Fine Arts, Montreal QC

Sami Ozgiritli Furniture Collection
Topkapi Palace Museum, Istanbul

Samuel Courtauld Collection of Impressionist & Post-Impressionist Art
The Courtauld Institute of Art, The Courtauld Gallery London

Samuel Friedenberg Collection of Plaques & Medals
The Jewish Museum, New York NY

Samuel H Kress Collection
Allentown Art Museum, Allentown PA
City of El Paso, El Paso TX
Memphis Brooks Museum of Art, Memphis TN
New Orleans Museum of Art, New Orleans LA
Philbrook Museum of Art, Tulsa OK
University of Miami, Lowe Art Museum Coral Gables FL

Samuel H Kress Collection of European Paintings & Sculpture
University of Wisconsin-Madison, Chazen Museum of Art Madison WI

Samuel H Kress Collection of Renaissance Painting & Sculpture
Portland Art Museum, Portland OR

Samuel H Kress Collection of Renaissance Paintings
Columbia Museum of Art, Columbia SC
The Pomona College, Claremont CA

Samuel H Kress Study Collection
Trinity College, Austin Arts Center, Widener Gallery Hartford CT
University of Georgia, Georgia Museum of Art Athens GA

Samuel K Lathrop Collection
University of Miami, Lowe Art Museum Coral Gables FL

Samuel Parrish Collection of Renaissance Art
Parrish Art Museum, Water Mill NY

Samuels Hobbitt Collection, woodcarvings
Navarro College, Gaston T Gooch Library & Learning Resource Center Corsicana TX

Sang Collection of Fine Bindings
North Central College, Oesterle Library Naperville IL

Santo Collection
Sangre de Cristo Arts & Conference Center, Pueblo CO

Schiller Collection of Social Commentary Art 1930-1970
Columbus Museum of Art, Columbus OH

Schreiber Collection of Numismatic Art on Martin Luther & the Reformation
Lutheran Theological Seminary, Krauth Memorial Library Philadelphia PA

Schuette Woodland Indian Collection
Rahr-West Art Museum, Manitowoc WI

Schwartz Collection of Chinese Ivories
Rahr-West Art Museum, Manitowoc WI

Scotese Collection of Graphics
Columbia Museum of Art, Columbia SC

Seibels Collection of Renaissance Art
Columbia Museum of Art, Columbia SC

Sharp Collection of Period Glass, China, Silver & Cameos
Frederic Remington, Ogdensburg NY

Shuey Collection
Cranbrook Art Museum, Bloomfield Hills MI

Simon Collection of Art of the American West
Birmingham Museum of Art, Clarence B Hanson Jr Library Birmingham AL

Simon Fraser Collection
Simon Fraser University, Simon Fraser University Gallery Burnaby BC

Sinclair Lewis Collection of Books, Manuscripts, Photographs, & Ephemera
Port Washington Public Library, Port Washington NY

Sir Harold Beauchamp Collection
Museum of New Zealand Te Papa Tongarewa, Wellington

Sir Hugh Lane Collection
Dublin City Gallery The Hugh Lane, Dublin

Sir John Ilott Collection of Prints
Museum of New Zealand Te Papa Tongarewa, Wellington

Sir Mackenzie Bowell Collection
Glanmore National Historic Site of Canada, Belleville ON

Slathin Collection
State University of New York at Plattsburgh, Art Museum Plattsburgh NY

Sloan Collection
Valparaiso University, Brauer Museum of Art Valparaiso IN

Smith Collection of European & American Paintings
Woodmere Art Museum Inc, Philadelphia PA

Smith Watch Key Collection
Rollins College, George D & Harriet W Cornell Fine Arts Museum Winter Park FL

Smith-Patterson Memorial Collection
Delta State University, Fielding L Wright Art Center Cleveland MS

Snelgrove Historical Collection
Gadsden Museum of Art, Gadsden AL

Sonnenschein Collection of European Drawings
Cornell College, Peter Paul Luce Gallery Mount Vernon IA

Stanford Family Collection
Stanford University, Cantor Arts Center at Stanford University Stanford CA

Staples Collection of Indonesian Art
James Madison University, Duke Hall Gallery of Fine Art Harrisonburg VA

Stegeman Collection of Japanese Woodcut Prints
Northwestern College, Te Paske Gallery Orange City IA

Steinberg Collection
University of Texas at Austin, Blanton Museum of Art Austin TX

Stella Duncan Collection of European Paintings
University of Montana, Montana Museum of Art & Culture Missoula MT

Stemmler Collection
Museum zu Allerheiligen, Schaffhausen

Stephen S Wise Manuscripts Collection
American Jewish Historical Society, Lee M Friedman Memorial Library Boston MA

Stern-Davis Collection of Peruvian Painting
New Orleans Museum of Art, New Orleans LA

Sturzenegger Collection
Museum zu Allerheiligen, Schaffhausen

Suida-Manning Collection
University of Texas at Austin, Blanton Museum of Art Austin TX

Swallow Collection of Inuit and Indian Art
Red Deer & District Museum & Archives, Red Deer AB

T Catesby Jones Collection of 20th Century European Art
Virginia Museum of Fine Arts, Richmond VA

Tabor Collection of Oriental Art
Philbrook Museum of Art, Tulsa OK

Tamassy Collection of Old Masterworks on Paper
Northwood University, Jeannette Hare Art Gallery West Palm Beach FL

Taos Society of Artists Collection
Taos Historic Museums, Ernest Blumenschein Home & Studio Taos NM

Teresa Jackson Weill Collection
Brandeis University, Rose Art Museum Waltham MA

Thanos Zintilis Cypriot Art Collection
Museum of Cycladic Art, Athens

Thatcher Family Collection
Rosemount Museum, Inc, Pueblo CO

The Adler Pewter Collection
The Dixon Gallery & Gardens, Memphis TN

The Batlinger Collection
Albertina Museum, Vienna

The Bob & Mary Ernst Collection
Buena Vista Museum of Natural History, Bakersfield CA

The Charlotte Stuart Hooker Collection
The Dixon Gallery & Gardens, Memphis TN

The Clarendon Collection of Portraits
Plymouth City Museum and Art Gallery, Plymouth Devon

The Cottonian Collection
Plymouth City Museum and Art Gallery, Plymouth Devon

The Edmond de Rothschild Collection
Musee du Louvre, The Louvre Paris

The Edwin L & Ruth E Kennedy Southwest Native American Collection
Ohio University, Kennedy Museum of Art Athens OH

The Gonor Collection
Allen Sapp, North Battleford SK

The Lee Goodman Collection
Texas A&M University-Corpus Christi, Weil Art Gallery Corpus Christi TX

The Mary & Alden Gomez Collection
Oak Ridge Art Center, Oak Ridge TN

The Matilda Geddings Gray Foundation Collection
New Orleans Museum of Art, New Orleans LA

The Nagel Collection of Oriental Ceramics & Sculpture
University of California, Davis, Jan Shrem and Maria Manetti Shrem Museum of Art Davis CA

The Paulson Collection of Ancient Near Eastern Coins
University of Georgia, Georgia Museum of Art Athens GA

The Rudolf L Baumfeld Collection of Landscape Drawings & Prints
University of California, Los Angeles, Grunwald Center for the Graphic Arts at Hammer Museum Los Angeles CA

The Walt Disney-Tishman African Art Collection
National Museum of African Art, Smithsonian Institution Washington DC

Theodore M Brown - Robert J Doherty Collection
University of Louisville, Ekstrom Library Photographic Archives Louisville KY

Theodore Wores Collection
Triton Museum of Art, Santa Clara CA

Thieme Collection
Fort Wayne Museum of Art, Inc, Fort Wayne IN

Thomas D Stimson Memorial Collection of Far Eastern Art
Seattle Art Museum, Seattle WA

Thomas S Dickey Civil War Ordnance Collection
Atlanta Historical Society Inc, Atlanta History Center Atlanta GA

Tobias Collection of African and Oceanic Art and Artifacts
William Paterson University, University Galleries Wayne NJ

Tobin Theatre Arts Collection
McNay Art Museum, San Antonio TX

Tokugawa Family Collection
The Tokugawa Art Museum, Nagoya

Tolliver Collection
Zigler Art Museum, Jennings LA

Tombaugh World War II Collection
Fulton County Historical Society Inc, Fulton County Museum (Tetzlaff Reference Room) Rochester IN

Trees Collection of European & American Painting
University of Illinois at Urbana-Champaign, Krannert Art Museum and Kinkead Pavilion Champaign IL

Turner Collection of Asian Art
Columbia Museum of Art, Columbia SC

Tyler Coverlet Collection
Jefferson County Historical Society, Watertown NY

U S Grant Collection
The George Washington University, Luther W Brady Art Gallery Washington DC

Van Vleck Collection of Japanese Prints
University of Wisconsin-Madison, Chazen Museum of Art Madison WI

Vanderpoel Collection of Asian Art
Norwich Free Academy, Slater Memorial Museum Norwich CT

Vernon Hall Collection of European Medals
University of Wisconsin-Madison, Chazen Museum of Art Madison WI

Vever Collection
Freer Gallery of Art & Arthur M Sackler Gallery, Arthur M Sackler Gallery Washington DC

Victor Kiam Painting Collection
New Orleans Museum of Art, New Orleans LA

Virgil Barker Collection
University of Miami, Lowe Art Museum Coral Gables FL

Virginia & George Ablah Collection of British Watercolors
Wichita Art Museum, Wichita KS

Vivian & Gordon Gilkey Graphics Art Collection
Portland Art Museum, Portland OR

Vogel Collection
University of Nevada, Las Vegas, Donna Beam Fine Art Gallery Las Vegas NV

Vyvyan Blackford Collection
Fort Hays State University, Moss-Thorns Gallery of Arts Hays KS

W C Bryant Collection
Brockton Public Library, Joseph A Driscoll Art Gallery Brockton MA

W J Holliday Collection
Newfields, Indianapolis IN

W Lloyd Wright Collection
The George Washington University, Luther W Brady Art Gallery Washington DC

Wachovia Permanent Collection
Burke Arts Council, Jailhouse Galleries Morganton NC

Wagner Collection of African Sculpture
Scripps College, Ruth Chandler Williamson Gallery Claremont CA
Scripps College, Clark Humanities Museum Claremont CA

Walker Collection of French Impressionists
Corcoran Gallery of Art, Washington DC

Wally Findlay Collection
Northwood University, Jeannette Hare Art Gallery West Palm Beach FL

Walter E Corbin Collection of Photographic Prints & Slides
Forbes Library, Northampton MA

Warda Stevens Stout Collection of 18th Century German Porcelain
The Dixon Gallery & Gardens, Memphis TN

Washington Allston Trust Collection
University of Miami, Lowe Art Museum Coral Gables FL

Washington-Custis-Lee Art Collection
Washington & Lee University, Lee Chapel & Museum Lexington VA

Watkins Collection of Artist's Books
American University, Jack I & Dorothy G Bender Library & Learning Resources Center New York NY

Watskinson Collection of Pre-1917 Art Reference
Wadsworth Atheneum Museum of Art, Auerbach Art Library Hartford CT

Watts Tower Collection
Saving & Preserving Arts & Cultural Environments, Spaces Library & Archive Aptos CA

Wayne State Foundation Print Collection
Wayne State College, Nordstrand Visual Arts Gallery Wayne NE

Weatherhead Collection
Fort Wayne Museum of Art, Inc, Fort Wayne IN

Wellington Collection of Wood Engravings
Mobile Museum of Art, Mobile AL

Weltkunst Foundation Collection
Irish Museum of Modern Art, Dublin

Westheimer Family Collection
Oklahoma City Museum of Art, Oklahoma City OK

Whiting Collection of Phoenician Glass
Cornell College, Peter Paul Luce Gallery Mount Vernon IA

Whittington Memorial Collection
Delta State University, Fielding L Wright Art Center Cleveland MS

Wiiken Contemporary Glass Collection
University of Minnesota Duluth, Tweed Museum of Art Duluth MN

Wilder Collection of Art Nouveau Glass & Ceramics
Topeka & Shawnee County Public Library, Alice C Sabatini Gallery Topeka KS

William H Jackson Photo Collection
History Colorado Center Museum, Denver CO

William Henry Jackson Glass Plate Negatives of Views West of the Mississippi
History Colorado Center Museum, Stephen H Hart Library Denver CO

William Henry Price Memorial Collection of Oil Paintings
Oregon State University, Memorial Union Art Gallery Corvallis OR

William Inge Memorabilia Collection
Independence Historical Museum & Art Center, Independence KS

William J Hubbard Drawings & Oils
The Valentine, Richmond VA

William Keith Paintings Collection
Saint Mary's College of California, Museum of Art Moraga CA

William McKendree Snyder Collection
Jefferson County Historical Society Museum, Madison IN

William Merritt Chase Collection
Parrish Art Museum, Water Mill NY

William Randolph Hearst Collection of Arms & Armor & Flemish Tapestries
Detroit Institute of Arts, Detroit MI

William S Ladd Collection of Pre-Columbian Art
Portland Art Museum, Portland OR

William Schwanekamp Collection
Buffalo & Erie County Public Library, Buffalo NY

Willitts J Hole Collection
University of California, Los Angeles, Hammer Museum Los Angeles CA

Willoughby Collection
University of Chicago, Max Epstein Archive Chicago IL

Winifred Kimball Hudnut Collection
University of Utah, Utah Museum of Fine Arts Salt Lake City UT

Winston Churchill Oil Painting Collection
National Churchill Museum, Fulton MO

Zundel Collection of Oriental Materials
Southern Oregon University, Schneider Museum of Art Ashland OR

Personnel Index

Individuals affiliated with art schools are indicated by "S".

Aaberg, Patricia, *Dir,* Liberty Village Arts Center & Gallery, Chester MT
Aakhus, Michael, *Prof Emeritus,* University of Southern Indiana, Art & Design Dept, Evansville IN (S)
Aalgaand, Morgan, *Dir Visual Arts,* Pearson Lakes Art Center, Okoboji IA
Aaron, Billye, *Chmn Emeritus,* The APEX Museum, Atlanta GA
Aarons, Philip, *Pres,* Printed Matter, Inc, New York NY
Aaronson, Lawrence R, *Dean Arts & Sciences,* Utica College of Syracuse University, Division of Art & Science, Utica NY (S)
Abbarno, Elizabeth, *Head Registrar,* The American Federation of Arts, New York NY
Abbatiello, Darcie, *Registrar,* University at Albany, State University of New York, University Art Museum, Albany NY
Abbe, Ronald, *Prog Coordr,* Housatonic Community College, Art Dept, Bridgeport CT (S)
Abbott, John, *Asst Prof,* Western New Mexico University, Expressive Arts Dept, Silver City NM (S)
Abbott, Randy, *Head Reference Librn,* University of Evansville, University Library, Evansville IN
Abbott, Sandra, *Cur Colls & Outreach,* University of Maryland, Baltimore County, Center for Art Design and Visual Culture, Baltimore MD
Abbott, Terrence, *Adminr,* Brown University, David Winton Bell Gallery, Providence RI
Abdo, George, *VPres Advancement,* The Huntington Library, Art Collections & Botanical Gardens, Library, San Marino CA
Abdu'Allah, Faisal, *Asst Prof,* University of Wisconsin, Madison, Dept of Art, Madison WI (S)
Abdul-Musawwir, Najjar, *Assoc Prof & Head Undergrad Studies,* Southern Illinois University, School of Art & Design, Carbondale IL (S)
Abdur-Rahman, Uthman, *Head Dept Art,* Tuskegee University, Liberal Arts & Education, Tuskegee AL (S)
Abel, Charles, *Instr,* Springfield College, Dept of Visual & Performing Arts, Springfield MA (S)
Abel, Mickey, *Assoc Prof Art History,* University of North Texas, College of Visual Arts & Design, Denton TX (S)
Abel, Timothy J, *Dir,* Jefferson County Historical Society, Watertown NY
Abell, E J, *Educ,* River Heritage Museum, Paducah KY
Abell, Marin, *Catron Prof of Art,* Washburn University of Topeka, Dept of Art, Topeka KS (S)
Abell, Mary, *Assoc Prof,* Dowling College, Dept of Visual Arts, Oakdale NY (S)
Abelman, Arthur, *Treas,* SculptureCenter, Long Island City NY
Abercrombie, Bea, *Chief Admin Officer,* Witte Museum, San Antonio TX
Abercrombie, Karin Moen, *Exec Dir,* Swedish American Museum, Chicago IL
Abia-Smith, Lisa, *Dir Education/Outreach,* University of Oregon, Jordan Schnitzer Museum of Art, Eugene OR
Abide, Joseph, *Assoc Prof,* Delta State University, Dept of Art, Cleveland MS (S)
Abiodun, Rowland O, *John C Newton Prof of Art & History of Art & Black Studies,* Amherst College, Dept of Art & the History of Art, Amherst MA (S)
Abler, Timothy, *Asst Prof,* Cardinal Stritch University, Art Dept, Milwaukee WI (S)
Abler, Timothy, *Chmn Art Dept,* Cardinal Stritch University, Northwestern Mutual Gallery, Milwaukee WI
Abraham, Guenet, *Assoc Prof,* University of Maryland, Baltimore County, Intermedia & Digital Arts (IMDA), Dept of Visual Arts, Baltimore MD (S)
Abraham, MJ, *Dir,* Riverside Art Museum, Library, Riverside CA
Abraham, Richard, *Instr,* Central Community College - Columbus Campus, Business & Arts Cluster, Columbus NE (S)
Abrahamson, Elizabeth, *Progs & Communs Mgr,* Judd Foundation, Marfa TX
Abram, Ronald, *Assoc Prof,* Denison University, Studio Art Program, Granville OH (S)
Abram, Trudi, *Instr Art History,* Glendale Community College, Visual & Performing Arts Div, Glendale CA (S)
Abrams, Daniel, *Co-Dir,* Prince Street Gallery, New York NY
Abrams, Jan, *VPres,* SculptureCenter, Long Island City NY
Abrams, Leslie, *Asst Prof,* Springfield College, Dept of Visual & Performing Arts, Springfield MA (S)
Abshoff, Lynda, *Dir Develop,* Canadian Clay and Glass Gallery, Waterloo ON
Abusharkh, Grace, *Vol Coordr,* Palo Alto Art Center, Palo Alto CA
Accurso, Li Ching, *Instr,* Columbia College, Fine Arts, Sonora CA (S)
Aceti, Lanfranco, *Program Director,* Boston University, Graduate Program - Arts Administration, Boston MA (S)
Acevedo-Yates, Carla, *Assoc Cur,* Michigan State University, Eli & Edythe Broad Art Museum, East Lansing MI
Acita, Marcia, *Dir Exhibs & Opers,* Bard College, Center for Curatorial Studies and the Hessel Museum of Art, Annandale-on-Hudson NY
Acita, Marcia, *Dir Exhibs and Opers,* Bard College, Center for Curatorial Studies Graduate Program, Annandale-on-Hudson NY (S)
Acker, George, *Security Mgr,* Bard College, Center for Curatorial Studies and the Hessel Museum of Art, Annandale-on-Hudson NY
Ackerman, Andrew, *Exec Dir,* Children's Museum of Manhattan, New York NY
Ackermann, Paul, *Mus Specialist,* United States Military Academy, West Point Museum, West Point NY
Ackner, John, *Preparator,* Schenectady County Historical Society, Schenectady NY
Acock, Anthony, *Asst Prof,* California State Polytechnic University, Pomona, Department of Art, Pomona CA (S)
Acompanado, Gay, *Art Library Supervisor,* Old Dominion University, Elise N Hofheimer Art Library, Norfolk VA
Acosta, Marie, *Exec Dir,* Latino Center of Art and Culture, Sacramento CA
Acres, Al, *Asst Prof,* Georgetown University, Dept of Art & Art History, Washington DC (S)
Acs, Alajos, *Midwest Representative,* American Society of Artists, Inc, Palatine IL
Acuff, Michelle, *Asst Prof Art,* Whitman College, Art Dept, Walla Walla WA (S)
Acuna-Hansen, Chris, *Prof Photog,* Rio Hondo College, Arts & Cultural Programs Dept, Whittier CA (S)
Acus-Smith, Jenn, *Educ Coordr,* Fitton Center for Creative Arts, Hamilton OH
Adae, Joellen, *Dir Communs,* Yale University, Yale University Art Gallery, New Haven CT
Adains, Mac, *Chmn,* State University of New York College at Old Westbury, Visual Arts Dept, Old Westbury NY (S)
Adair, Cindy, *Office Mgr,* Pennsylvania Historical & Museum Commission, Railroad Museum of Pennsylvania, Strasburg PA
Adair, Everl, *Dir Research & Rare Coll,* R W Norton Art Foundation, R W Norton Art Gallery, Shreveport LA
Adair, Macra, *Mus Shop Mgr,* Booth Western Art Museum, Cartersville GA
Adam, Mazih, *Asst Prof,* Community College of Rhode Island, Dept of Art, Warwick RI (S)
Adamcik-Huettel, Patricia, *Multimedia & Web Design,* Art Institute of Pittsburgh, Pittsburgh PA (S)
Adams, Andrew, *Educ & Events Dir,* Erie County Historical Society, Erie PA
Adams, Ashley, *Cur Educ,* Museum of Art & History, Santa Cruz, Santa Cruz CA
Adams, Betsy, *Cur,* Concord Art Association, Concord MA
Adams, Brad, *Assoc Prof,* Berry College, Art Dept, Mount Berry GA (S)
Adams, Branden, *Asst Dir & Dir Exhib,* Piedmont Arts Association, Martinsville VA
Adams, Cecil, *Head Mus Design,* Wadsworth Atheneum Museum of Art, Hartford CT
Adams, Chris, *Asst Prof,* South Plains College, Fine Arts Dept, Levelland TX (S)
Adams, Daniel, *Chmn Dept,* Harding University, Dept of Art & Design, Searcy AR (S)
Adams, Dean, *Asst Prof - Foundation,* Montana State University, School of Art, Bozeman MT (S)
Adams, Donna, *Assoc Prof,* University of Indianapolis, Dept Art & Design, Indianapolis IN (S)
Adams, Doug, *Chief Digital Officer,* Anchorage Museum at Rasmuson Center, Anchorage AK
Adams, Edward, *Instr,* Milwaukee Area Technical College, School of Media & Creative Arts, Milwaukee WI (S)
Adams, Gina, *Development,* Museum of Latin American Art, Long Beach CA
Adams, Gloria Rejune, *Dir,* Cornell Museum of Art and American Culture, Delray Beach FL
Adams, Helen, *Dir Visitor Services,* Clemson University, Fort Hill Plantation, Clemson SC
Adams, Henry, *Prof,* Case Western Reserve University, Dept of Art History & Art, Cleveland OH (S)
Adams, Holly, *Adjunct Instr,* Davis & Elkins College, Dept of Art, Elkins WV (S)
Adams, Idie, *Chmn & Ceramic Coordr,* Butte College, Dept of Fine Arts and Communication Tech, Oroville CA (S)

Adams, J Marshall, *Dir Educ,* Vero Beach Museum of Art, Vero Beach FL
Adams, Jackie, *Dir Educ & Engagement,* Columbia Museum of Art, Columbia SC
Adams, Jacqueline, *Supv Librn,* San Diego Public Library, Art, Music & Recreation, San Diego CA
Adams, James, *Asst Prof of Art,* Thomas University, Humanities Division, Thomasville GA (S)
Adams, Jamie, *Dept Head,* Judson College, Division of Fine and Performing Arts, Marion AL (S)
Adams, Jean, *Adjunct Prof,* Wilkes University, Dept of Art, Wilkes-Barre PA (S)
Adams, Jeffrey, *Chair,* Idaho State University, John B Davis Gallery of Fine Art, Pocatello ID
Adams, Jeffrey, *Chmn,* Idaho State University, Dept of Art, Pocatello ID (S)
Adams, Kathryn, *Exec Dir,* Audrain County Historical Society, Graceland Museum & American Saddlehorse Museum & Fire Brick Industry Museum, Mexico MO
Adams, Kathy, *Exec Dir,* Ponca City Cultural Center & Museum, Library, Ponca City OK
Adams, Kathy, *Exec Dir,* Ponca City Cultural Center & Museum, Ponca City OK
Adams, Keith, *Asst Chair,* Rowan University, Dept of Art, Glassboro NJ (S)
Adams, Kelly, *Dir,* East Carolina University, Media Center, Greenville NC
Adams, Lee Ann, *Prog & Operations Mgr,* Association of Independent Colleges of Art & Design, Providence RI
Adams, Madge B, *Pres & CEO,* Shaker Village of Pleasant Hill, Harrodsburg KY
Adams, Marlin, *Instr,* Gordon College, Dept of Fine Arts, Barnesville GA (S)
Adams, Naomi, *Faculty,* Idaho State University, Dept of Art, Pocatello ID (S)
Adams, Nicholas, *Prof,* Vassar College, Art Dept, Poughkeepsie NY (S)
Adams, Nixon, *CEO & Dir,* Lake Pontchartrain Basin Maritime Museum, Madisonville LA
Adams, Pam, *Instr,* Bob Jones University, School of Fine Arts, Div of Art & Design, Greenville SC (S)
Adams, Patsy Baker, *Gallery Dir & Adminr,* New Orleans Academy of Fine Arts, Academy Gallery, New Orleans LA
Adams, Renee, *Arts Programmer,* Gallery One Visual Arts Center, Ellensburg WA
Adams, Stephanie, *Mktg Mgr,* Biggs Museum of American Art, Dover DE
Adams, William R, *Chmn,* City of Saint Augustine, Saint Augustine FL
Adams-Ramsey, Susan, *Chmn,* Clinch Valley College of the University of Virginia, Visual & Performing Arts Dept, Wise VA (S)
Adamson, John, *VPres,* Strasburg Museum, Strasburg VA
Adamson, Rob, *Prof,* Salt Lake Community College, Graphic Design Dept, Salt Lake City UT (S)
Adamy, George E, *Dir,* Polyadam Concrete System Workshops, Ossining NY (S)
Adan, Elizabeth, *Asst Prof Art History,* California Polytechnic State University at San Luis Obispo, Dept of Art & Design, San Luis Obispo CA (S)
Adan, Joan, *Exhib Designer,* Forest Lawn Museum, Glendale CA
Adato, Linda, *Pres,* Society of American Graphic Artists, New York NY
Addamo, Daniela, *Educ & Outreach Coordinator,* Queens Historical Society, Kingsland Homestead, Flushing NY
Addison, Christopher, *Owner,* Addison/Ripley Fine Art, Washington DC
Addison, E W, *Dir,* Brewton-Parker College, Visual Arts, Mount Vernon GA (S)
Addison, Laura, *Cur Contemporary,* New Mexico Department of Cultural Affairs, New Mexico Museum of Art, Unit of NM Dept of Cultural Affairs, Santa Fe NM
Addison, Lynne, *Registrar,* Yale University, Yale University Art Gallery, New Haven CT
Addiss, Stephen, *Prof,* University of Richmond, Dept of Art and Art History, Richmond VA (S)
Ade, Ken, *Coordr Opers,* Kenosha Public Museums, Kenosha WI
Adejumo, Christopher, *Asst Chair - Visual Art Studies,* University of Texas, Dept of Art & Art History, Austin TX (S)
Adelman, Charles, *Prof,* University of Northern Iowa, Dept of Art, Cedar Falls IA (S)
Adelman, Everett Mayo, *Instr,* North Carolina Wesleyan College, Dept of Visual & Performing Arts, Rocky Mount NC (S)
Adelson, Fred, *Chair,* Rowan University, Dept of Art, Glassboro NJ (S)
Adgate, Brian, *Adj Instruc,* Quincy College, Art Dept, Quincy MA (S)
Adger, Jalissa, *Exec Asst,* The Museum, Greenwood SC
Adkins, Barb, *Mgr, Bloomington - Normal Vis Center,* McLean County Historical Society, McLean County Museum of History, Bloomington IL
Adkins, Gary, *Pres,* American Numismatic Association, Edward C. Rochette Money Museum, Colorado Springs CO
Adkins, Shaina, *Event Dir,* Salisbury University, Ward Museum of Wildfowl Art, Salisbury MD
Adler Abramson, Karen, *Dir Archives,* National Archives & Records Administration, John F Kennedy Presidential Library & Museum, Boston MA
Adler, Amy, *Prof & Chair,* University of California, San Diego, Dept of Visual Arts, La Jolla CA (S)
Adler, Marlene, *Bd Mem,* American Color Print Society, Narberth PA
Adler, Marlene, *Instr,* Wayne Art Center, Wayne PA (S)
Adler, Michelle, *Develop Asst,* Swope Art Museum, Terre Haute IN
Adler, Michelle, *Develop Asst,* Swope Art Museum, Research Library, Terre Haute IN
Adler, Pam, *Store Mgr,* South Dakota State University, South Dakota Art Museum, Brookings SD
Adler, Rachel, *Coll Mgr & Registrar,* Tucson Museum of Art and Historic Block, Tucson AZ
Adler, Rachel, *Colls Mgr & Registrar,* Tucson Museum of Art and Historic Block, Tucson AZ
Adlestein, Gary, *Assoc Prof,* Albright College, Dept of Art, Reading PA (S)
Adley, Allyson, *Coll & Educ Asst,* York University, Art Gallery of York University, Toronto ON
Adolph, Cheryl, *Chief Operating Officer,* Staten Island Museum, Archives Library, Staten Island NY
Adolph, Cheryl, *Pres & CEO,* Staten Island Museum, Staten Island NY
Adoquei, Sam, *Sec,* Portrait Society of America, Tallahassee FL
Adrean, Louis, *Head Research Pub Progs,* The Cleveland Museum of Art, Ingalls Library, Cleveland OH
Adrian, Barbara, *Prof Theatre,* Marymount Manhattan College, Fine & Performing Arts Div, New York NY (S)
Adrian, Donna, *Instr,* La Sierra University, Art Dept, Riverside CA (S)
Adrian, Liz, *Dir Retail,* Institute of Contemporary Art/Boston, Boston MA
Adrienne, Karen, *Dir,* University of Maine at Augusta, The Danforth Gallery, Augusta ME
Adrio, Michael, *Dir Develop,* Washington University, Mildred Lane Kemper Art Museum, Saint Louis MO
Aesoph, Jill, *Dir Develop,* Washington State University, Museum of Art, Pullman WA
Aesoph, Stacy, *Marketing & Develop,* South Dakota State University, South Dakota Art Museum, Brookings SD
Affleck, Arthur, *VPres Devel,* American Alliance of Museums, Arlington VA
Aframe, Debby, *Librn,* Worcester Art Museum, Library, Worcester MA
Aframe, Deborah, *Librn,* Worcester Art Museum, Worcester MA
Agamedia, Allan, *Technology,* Art Institute of Pittsburgh, Pittsburgh PA (S)
Agamy, Susan J, *Dir Develop,* The Barnum Museum, Bridgeport CT
Agar, Will, *Dir,* North Hennepin Community College, Joseph Gazzuolo Fine Arts Gallery, Brooklyn Park MN
Agar, Will, *Instr,* North Hennepin Community College, Art Dept, Brooklyn Park MN (S)
Agard, James, *Assoc Prof,* Gettysburg College, Dept of Visual Arts, Gettysburg PA (S)
Agarwal, Neha, *Asst Prof,* La Roche College, Division of Design, Pittsburgh PA (S)
Ageh, Tony, *Chief Digital Officer,* The New York Public Library, New York NY
Ageloff, Scott, *Dean,* New York School of Interior Design, New York NY (S)
Aghiarian, Michelle, *Coordr Mem & Develop,* American Textile History Museum, Lowell MA
Agnew, Charlie, *Assoc Prof of Art, Art Prog Coordr, Gallery Dir Peacock Gallery,* Middle Georgia State University, College of Arts & Sciences, Media, Culture & the Arts, Cochran GA (S)
Agramonte-Gomez, Maria, *Bus Mgr,* Harriet Beecher Stowe Center, Hartford CT
Agre-Kippenhan, Susan, *Assoc Prof,* Portland State University, Dept of Art, Portland OR (S)
Agrella, Ellen, *Fiscal Officer,* Florida State University, Museum of Fine Arts, Tallahassee FL
Aguinaga-Martinez, Raquel, *Assoc Dir, Registrar,* National Museum of Mexican Art, Chicago IL
Aguirre, Joe, *Director,* McGroarty Cultural Art Center, Tujunga CA (S)
Aguis, Liliana, *Contact & Admin Asst,* Vassar College, Art Dept, Poughkeepsie NY (S)
Ahern, Emilie, *Outreach Coord,* Center for Book Arts, New York NY
Ahern, Jack, *Dept Head,* University of Massachusetts, Amherst, Dept of Landscape Architecture & Regional Planning, Amherst MA (S)
Ahern, Nathan, *Chief Preparator,* Williams College, Museum of Art, Williamstown MA
Ahl, Diane Cole, *Dept Head,* Lafayette College, Dept of Art, Easton PA (S)
Ahlberg, Joanna, *Mng Ed,* The Drawing Center, New York NY
Ahlersmeyer, Amy, *Chief Mktg Officer,* Indiana State Museum, Indianapolis IN
Ahnen, Phillip, *Facility Dir/Exhib Preparator,* Rochester Art Center, Rochester MN
Aho, Arnold, *Prof,* Norwich University, Dept of Architecture and Art, Northfield VT (S)
Ahola-Young, Laura, *Faculty,* Idaho State University, Dept of Art, Pocatello ID (S)
Ahrens, Liz, *Dir,* Crooked Tree Arts Council, Virginia M McCune Community Arts Center, Petoskey MI
Ahrens, Liz, *Pres,* Crooked Tree Arts Center - Traverse City, Gallery, Traverse City MI
Ahrens, Todd, *Dir Develop,* Toledo Museum of Art, Toledo OH
Aidman, Eva, *Gift Shop Mgr & Fin Advisor,* Seneca-Iroquois National Museum, Salamanca NY
Aiello, Rose, *Data Mgr,* National Air and Space Museum, Regional Planetary Image Facility, Washington DC
Aiken, Jane, *Prof Emerita,* Virginia Polytechnic Institute & State University, Dept of Art & Art History, Blacksburg VA (S)
Aikey, Michael, *CEO & Dir,* New York State Military Museum and Veterans Research Center, Saratoga Springs NY
Aikin, Roger, *Instr Art History,* Creighton University, Fine & Performing Arts Dept, Omaha NE (S)
Aikman, John, *Instr,* Linn Benton Community College, Fine & Applied Art Dept, Albany OR (S)
Airhart, Chad, *Assoc Prof,* Carson-Newman University, Art Dept, Jefferson City TN (S)
Airulla, Barbara, *Asst Prof,* University of Texas at Tyler, Department of Art, School of Visual & Performing Arts, Tyler TX (S)
Aistars, John, *Dir,* Cazenovia College, Chapman Art Center Gallery, Cazenovia NY
Aitali, Erin, *Exhib Mgr,* Pasadena Museum of California Art, Pasadena CA

Aitken, Molly, *Asst Prof,* City College of New York, Art Dept, New York NY (S)
Aja, Adam, *Asst Cur,* Harvard University, Semitic Museum, Cambridge MA
Aje, Jide, *International Project,* National Conference of Artists, Michigan Chapter Gallery, Detroit MI
Ajootian, Aileen, *Prof,* University of Mississippi, Department of Art, University MS (S)
Akeley-Charron, Kim, *Mktg Coordr,* Loveland Museum/Gallery, Loveland CO
Akers, Norman, *Assoc Prof,* University of Kansas, The School of the Arts, Dept of Visual Art, Lawrence KS (S)
Akers, Rich, *Dept Head,* Contra Costa Community College, Dept of Art, San Pablo CA (S)
Akilah, Oni, *Emerging Arts Prog,* National Conference of Artists, Michigan Chapter Gallery, Detroit MI
Akin-Kivanc, Esra, *Asst Prof,* University of South Florida, School of Art & Art History, Tampa FL (S)
Akiyama, Sachiko, *Asst Prof,* University of New Hampshire, Dept of Art & Art History, Durham NH (S)
Akmon, Devon, *Dir,* ACCESS, Arab American National Museum, Dearborn MI
Al-Khudhairi, Wassan, *Chief Cur,* Contemporary Art Museum St Louis, Saint Louis MO
Alafat, Gary, *Security & Bldg Mgr,* Dartmouth College, Hood Museum of Art, Hanover NH
Alaimo, Holly, *VPres,* Martha's Vineyard Center for the Visual Arts, Oak Bluffs MA
Alanary, Lisa, *Assoc Prof,* Carson-Newman University, Art Dept, Jefferson City TN (S)
Alanen, Marie, *Prof,* East Los Angeles College, Art Dept, Monterey Park CA (S)
Albacete, M J, *Exec Dir,* Canton Museum of Art, Art Library, Canton OH
Albacete, Manuel J, *Exec Dir,* Canton Museum of Art, Canton OH (S)
Albacete, Manuel J, *Exec Dir,* Canton Museum of Art, Canton OH
Albano Lambrecht, Nancy, *Acting Exec Dir,* Robert & Mary Montgomery Armory Art Center, Armory Art Center, West Palm Beach FL
Albano, John, *Dean,* Merced College, Arts Division, Merced CA (S)
Albee, Becca, *Assoc Prof,* City College of New York, Art Dept, New York NY (S)
Alberico, Sarah, *Cur, Educ Prog Coordr & Vol Coordr,* Rock Ford Foundation, Inc, Rock Ford Plantation, Lancaster PA
Albert, Karen, *Assoc Dir Exhibs & Coll,* Hofstra University, Hofstra University Museum, Hempstead NY
Albert, Mary, *Registrar,* Loyola University Chicago, Loyola University Museum of Art, Chicago IL
Albert, Meg, *Develop Mgr,* New Bedford Art Museum/ Artworks!, New Bedford MA
Alberti, Janet, *Deputy Dir,* Museum of Contemporary Art Chicago, Chicago IL
Alberti, Janet, *Deputy Dir Admin & Finance,* San Francisco Museum of Modern Art, San Francisco CA
Albertson, Constant, *Assoc Prof,* University of Maine, Dept of Art, Orono ME (S)
Albiston, Renee, *Mktg & Outreach Mgr,* Kirkland Museum of Fine & Decorative Art, Denver CO
Albrecht, Ivan, *Asst Prof,* University of Miami, Dept of Art & Art History, Coral Gables FL (S)
Albrecht, Mary, *Sr Dir Devel,* Milwaukee Art Museum, Milwaukee WI
Albritton, Marty, *Develop Dir,* Eastern Shore Art Association, Inc, Eastern Shore Art Center, Fairhope AL
Alcaide, Myrna, *Develop & Admin Assoc,* The California Historical Society, San Francisco CA
Alden Russell, Ian, *Cur,* Brown University, David Winton Bell Gallery, Providence RI
Alden, Donna, *Asst Prof,* University of Nebraska, Kearney, Dept of Art & Art History, Kearney NE (S)
Alderedge, Amy, *Exec Dir,* Dallas Historical Society, Hall of State, Dallas TX
Alderson, Julia, *Assoc Prof,* Humboldt State University, College of Arts & Humanities, Art Dept, Arcata CA (S)
Aldrich, Ginger, *Develop,* Haystack Mountain School of Crafts, Deer Isle ME
Aldrich, Ginger, *Develop Dir,* Haystack Mountain School of Crafts, Center for Community Programs Gallery, Deer Isle ME
Aldrich, Marvette, *Asst Prof,* Winston-Salem State University, Art Dept, Winston-Salem NC (S)
Aleci, Linda, *Assoc Prof,* Franklin & Marshall College, Art & Art History Dept, Lancaster PA (S)
Aleckson, Luke, *Dir,* Northwestern College, Denler Art Gallery, Saint Paul MN
Alegria, Christina, *Educ Asst,* California State University, Long Beach, University Art Museum, Long Beach CA
Aleo, Nancy, *Pres Bd Trustees,* Attleboro Arts Museum, Attleboro MA
Alex, Kathleen, *Dir Fin,* Cultural Council of Palm Beach County, Lake Worth FL
Alexander, Aaron, *New Media Design,* Florida School of the Arts, Visual Arts, Palatka FL (S)
Alexander, Carolyn, *Chmn Art,* Mount San Antonio College, Art Dept, Walnut CA (S)
Alexander, Catherine, *Gallery Dir,* Salem Art Association, Bush Barn Art Center, Salem OR
Alexander, Darsie, *Exec Dir,* Katonah Museum of Art, Katonah NY
Alexander, David, *Pres,* British Columbia Museums Association, Victoria BC
Alexander, Elizabeth, *Admin,* Dartmouth College, Dept of Art History, Hanover NH (S)
Alexander, Hope P, *Secy,* Newport Historical Society & Museum of Newport History, Newport RI
Alexander, Irene, *Cur,* Stephens College, Lewis James & Nellie Stratton Davis Art Gallery, Columbia MO
Alexander, James, *Prof,* University of Alabama at Birmingham, Dept of Art & Art History, Birmingham AL (S)
Alexander, Jane, *Chief Digital Information Officer,* The Cleveland Museum of Art, Cleveland OH
Alexander, Janet, *Asst Dir,* Sarah Lawrence College Library, Esther Raushenbush Library, Bronxville NY
Alexander, Jean, *Head of Hunt Reference,* Carnegie Mellon University, Hunt Library, Pittsburgh PA
Alexander, Julie, *Dir Finance,* Lighthouse ArtCenter Museum & School of Art, Tequesta FL
Alexander, Kathy, *In Charge Art Coll,* First Tennessee Bank, Memphis TN
Alexander, Melanie, *Dir,* Muscatine Art Center, Muscatine IA
Alexander, Pat, *Mus Educ,* Napa Valley Museum, Yountville CA
Alexander, Rebecca, *Media Asst,* San Francisco Art Institute, Anne Bremer Memorial Library, San Francisco CA
Alexander, Robbyn, *Faculty,* John F Kennedy, Department of Arts & Consciousness, Pleasant Hill CA (S)
Alexander, Ronald J, *Head Dept,* University of Louisiana at Monroe, Dept of Art, Monroe LA (S)
Alexick, David, *Prof,* Christopher Newport University, Dept of Fine Performing Arts, Newport News VA (S)
Alferio, K, *Pres & Dir Programming,* The Cultural Arts Center at Glen Allen, Glen Allen VA
Alfonso, Cristie, *Front Desk Associate + Tour Coordinator,* Miami-Dade College, MDC Museum of Art & Design, Miami FL
Alfonso, Lina, *Progs & Opers Mgr,* Art in General, Brooklyn NY
Alford, John, *Asst Prof,* Mississippi University for Women, Division of Fine & Performing Arts, Columbus MS (S)
Alford, Keith, *VPres,* Mississippi Art Colony, Stoneville MS
Alger, Erin, *Colls Mgr,* Museum of Northern British Columbia, Ruth Harvey Art Gallery, Prince Rupert BC
Alger, Erin, *Colls Mgr,* Museum of Northern British Columbia, Library, Prince Rupert BC
Alger, Jeff, *Librn,* Kansas State University, Paul Weigel Library of Architecture Planning & Design, Manhattan KS
Ali, Sasha, *Mgr Exhibitions & Communications,* Craft and Folk Art Museum (CAFAM), Los Angeles CA
Aliriza, Gulgun, *Treas,* Blue Mountain Gallery, New York NY
Alisanne, Laura, *Gallery and Program Manager,* City of Port Angeles, Port Angeles Fine Arts Center & Webster Woods Art Park, Port Angeles WA
Alix, Sylvie, *Librn,* Musee d'art Contemporain de Montreal, Mediatheque/ Media Centre, Centre for Research & Documentation on Contemporary Art, Montreal QC
Allaben, Craig, *Gallery Mgr,* University of Massachusetts, Amherst, University Gallery, Amherst MA
Allaik, Khalil, *Asst Preparator,* Lehigh University Art Galleries, Museum Operation, Bethlehem PA
Allan, Elizabeth, *Cur Colls & Exhibits,* Morven Museum & Garden, Princeton NJ
Allan, Ken, *Assoc Prof,* Seattle University, Dept of Art & Art History, Seattle WA (S)
Allan, Margaret, *Chair,* The Rooms Provincial Art Gallery, Saint John's NF
Allegood, Aelin, *Devel Coord,* University of Alaska, Museum of the North, Fairbanks AK
Alleman, Karen, *Educ Coordr,* The Art Center of Waco, Waco TX
Allen, Andra, *Dir Accounting & HR,* Tucson Museum of Art and Historic Block, Tucson AZ
Allen, Angelo, *Instr,* Pierce College, Art Dept, Woodland Hills CA (S)
Allen, Anne, *Coordr of Fine Arts,* Indiana University-Southeast, Fine Arts Dept, New Albany IN (S)
Allen, Bambi, *Cur,* Southern Plains Indian Museum, Anadarko OK
Allen, Bob, *Pres,* Allied Arts Association, Allied Arts Center & Gallery, Richland WA
Allen, Brad, *Assoc Prof,* University of Montana, School of Art, Missoula MT (S)
Allen, Brianna, *Develop Coordr,* Bunnell Street Arts Center, Homer AK
Allen, Bruce, *Chmn Dept & Prof,* Centenary College of Louisiana, Dept of Art, Shreveport LA (S)
Allen, Carl M, *Prof,* Ashland University, Art Dept, Ashland OH (S)
Allen, Casey, *Registrar,* Utah State University, Nora Eccles Harrison Museum of Art, Logan UT
Allen, David, *VPres,* Allied Arts of Seattle, Seattle WA
Allen, Douglas, *Assoc Dean,* Georgia Institute of Technology, College of Architecture, Atlanta GA (S)
Allen, Frank R, *Assoc Dir Admin,* University of Central Florida Libraries, Orlando FL
Allen, Greg, *Dir Finance & Admin,* American Craft Council, Minneapolis MN
Allen, Heidi, *Asst Prof,* Concordia College, Art Dept, Moorhead MN (S)
Allen, Jacqueline, *Dir Libraries,* Dallas Museum of Art, Mildred R & Frederick M Mayer Library, Dallas TX
Allen, James, *Prof,* Daemen College, Art Dept, Amherst NY (S)
Allen, Jan, *Dir,* Queen's University, Agnes Etherington Art Centre, Kingston ON
Allen, Janice, *Financial Admin,* Auburn University, Jule Collins Smith Museum of Fine Art, Auburn AL
Allen, Jeff, *Chief Preparator & Exhib Design,* The Currier Museum of Art, Manchester NH
Allen, Jennifer, *Dir Colls Management,* Harvard University, Harvard Art Museums, Cambridge MA
Allen, Jim, *Instr,* Springfield College in Illinois, Dept of Art, Springfield IL (S)
Allen, Jules, *Asst Prof,* Queensborough Community College, Dept of Art & Photography, Bayside Hills NY (S)
Allen, Katy, *VP Human Resources & Organizational Devel,* The Children's Museum of Indianapolis, Indianapolis IN

Allen, Kay, *Assoc Dir,* University of Southern California, USC Fisher Museum of Art, Los Angeles CA

Allen, Kelly, *Dir Educ,* Academy of Fine Arts, Lynchburg VA

Allen, Kristie, *Museum Store Mgr,* Birmingham Museum of Art, Birmingham AL

Allen, Laura, *Cur Japanese Art,* Asian Art Museum of San Francisco, Chong-Moon Lee Ctr for Asian Art and Culture, San Francisco CA

Allen, Linda, *Admin Asst,* Shasta College, Arts, Communications & Social Sciences Division, Redding CA (S)

Allen, Lynne, *Dir School of Visual Arts,* Boston University, School for the Arts, Boston MA (S)

Allen, Michael, *Preparator,* Washburn University, Mulvane Art Museum, Topeka KS

Allen, Nash, *Chief Financial Officer,* BanCorp South, Art Collection, Tupelo MS

Allen, Nathaniel, *Asst Prof,* Alabama State University, Dept of Visual Arts, Montgomery AL (S)

Allen, Pam, *Dir Finance & Facility,* Piedmont Arts Association, Martinsville VA

Allen, Pamela, *Asst Prof,* Troy State University, Dept of Art & Classics, Troy AL (S)

Allen, Robert, *VPres,* South Arkansas Arts Center, El Dorado AR

Allen, Robyn, *Exec Dir,* Prescott Fine Arts Association, Gallery, Prescott AZ

Allen, Walter, *Div Chmn of Art,* James H Faulkner, Art Dept, Bay Minette AL (S)

Allen, William, *Prof,* Arkansas State University, Dept of Art, State University AR (S)

Alley, Jon, *Instr,* Bucks County Community College, Fine Arts Dept, Newtown PA (S)

Alley-Bavaes, Royal, *Instr,* Seattle Central Community College, Humanities - Social Sciences Division, Seattle WA (S)

Allgor, Catherine, *Pres,* Massachusetts Historical Society, Boston MA

Allison, Andrea, *Librn,* Quetico Park, John B Ridley Research Library, Atikokan ON

Allison, Joseph, *Studio Mgr,* Austin College, Art Dept, Sherman TX (S)

Allison, Wayne, *Instr & Chair,* North Iowa Area Community College, Dept of Art, Mason City IA (S)

Allman, Anne, *Prof,* College of the Ozarks, Dept of Art, Point Lookout MO (S)

Allman, Marion, *CEO,* AIC College of Design, Cincinnati OH (S)

Allmendinger, Carolyn, *Dir Acad Progs,* University of North Carolina at Chapel Hill, Ackland Art Museum, Chapel Hill NC

Allred, Ry, *Head Opers,* Pier 24 Photography, San Francisco CA

Allyn, Anita, *Dept Chair,* The College of New Jersey, School of Arts & Sciences, Ewing NJ (S)

Alm, Rebecca, *Prof,* Minneapolis College of Art & Design, Minneapolis MN (S)

Almas, Bryan, *Asst,* Gallery Moos Ltd, Toronto ON

Almasi, Jesse, *Adjunct Prof,* Community College of Allegheny County, Boyce Campus, Art Dept, Monroeville PA (S)

Alonso, Elisa, *Admin Asst to Exec Dir,* Bass Museum of Art, Miami Beach FL

Alonzo, Juan, *Facilities Coordr,* Museum of Fine Arts, Houston, Rienzi Center for European Decorative Arts, Houston TX

Alonzo, Pedro, *Adjunct Cur,* Dallas Contemporary, Dallas Visual Art Center, Dallas TX

Alpert, Gary J, *VPres Publs,* Old Salem Museums & Gardens, Museum of Early Southern Decorative Arts, Winston-Salem NC

Alpert, L, *Assoc Prof,* University of Oregon, Dept of Fine & Applied Arts, Eugene OR (S)

Alphonso, Christina, *Mgr Admin,* The Metropolitan Museum of Art, The Met Cloisters, New York NY

Alsobrook, Robert, *Asst Prof,* Taylor University, Visual Art Dept, Upland IN (S)

Alston, Littleton, *Instr Sculpture,* Creighton University, Fine & Performing Arts Dept, Omaha NE (S)

Alswang, Hope, *Exec Dir & CEO,* Norton Museum of Art, West Palm Beach FL

Alt, Kasie, *Affiliate Faculty,* Brenau University, Art & Design Dept, Gainesville GA (S)

Altamura, Mauro, *Asst Prof,* New Jersey City University, Art Dept, Jersey City NJ (S)

Altemus, Anne R, *Asst Prof,* Johns Hopkins University, School of Medicine, Dept of Art as Applied to Medicine, Baltimore MD (S)

Alten, Helen, *Dir,* Sheldon Museum & Cultural Center, Inc, Sheldon Museum & Cultural Center, Haines AK

Alter-Muri, Simone, *Asst Prof,* Springfield College, Dept of Visual & Performing Arts, Springfield MA (S)

Althaver, Burt, *Chmn,* Artrain, Inc, Ann Arbor MI

Althoff, Sarah, *Dir Annual Giving,* University of Virginia, The Fralin Museum of Art at the University of Virginia, Charlottesville VA

Altman, Phyllis, *Art Gallery Mgr,* Jewish Community Center of Greater Washington, Jane L & Robert H Weiner Judaic Museum, Rockville MD

Altmann, Helen, *Cur,* Chalet of the Golden Fleece, New Glarus WI

Altschul, Mark, *Secy,* National Association of Women Artists, Inc, NAWA Gallery, New York NY

Alvarado, Alex, *Dir Opers,* National Museum of Mexican Art, Chicago IL

Alvare, Gigi, *Dir Educ,* The Rockwell Museum, Corning NY

Alvarez, Julio, *Bldg Opers Mgr,* Florida International University, The Patricia & Phillip Frost Art Museum, Miami FL

Alvarez, Sarah, *Dir Teacher Progs,* The Art Institute of Chicago, Crown Family Educator Resource Center, Chicago IL

Alvarez, Yetzenia, *Pub Rels Mgr,* Museo de Arte de Puerto Rico, San Juan PR

Alvarez-Mathies, Carolina, *Sr Mgr Pub Rels,* El Museo del Barrio, New York NY

Alves, Brian, *Assoc Prof,* Salem State University, Art & Design Department, Salem MA (S)

Alves, Bruce, *Gallery Asst,* Foundry Art Centre, Saint Charles MO

Alves, C Douglass, *Dir,* Calvert Marine Museum, Solomons MD

Alvord, Ellen, *Coordr Acad Affairs,* Mount Holyoke College, Art Museum, South Hadley MA

Amato, Helen C, *Asst to Dir,* Lightner Museum, Saint Augustine FL

Amato, Micaela, *Prof Art & Women's Studies (Drawing/Painting),* Pennsylvania State University, University Park, Penn State School of Visual Arts, University Park PA (S)

Ambroge, Patti, *Assoc Prof,* Rochester Institute of Technology, School of Photographic Arts & Sciences, Rochester NY (S)

Ambrose, Andy, *Exec Dir,* Tubman African American Museum, Macon GA

Ambrose, Kate, *Membership & Devel Officer,* Laguna Art Museum, Laguna Beach CA

Ambrose, Kirk, *Chmn,* University of Colorado, Boulder, Dept of Art & Art History, Boulder CO (S)

Ambrose, Ric, *Exec Dir,* The Richmond Art Center, Richmond CA

Ambroselli, Cristina, *Asst Mgr Mus Experience,* The Metropolitan Museum of Art, The Met Breuer, New York NY

Ambrosini, Lynne, *Deputy Dir Curatorial Affairs & Chief Cur,* Taft Museum of Art, Cincinnati OH

Amburgy, Patricia, *Assoc Prof Art Educ,* Pennsylvania State University, University Park, Penn State School of Visual Arts, University Park PA (S)

Amemasor, James, *Library Specialist,* New Jersey Historical Society, Library, Newark NJ

Amendola, Julianne, *Chief Advancement Officer,* Minneapolis Institute of Art, Minneapolis MN

Ament, Elizabeth, *Asst Prof,* University of Wisconsin-Green Bay, Arts Dept, Green Bay WI (S)

Ames-Bell, Linda, *Prof,* University of Toledo, Dept of Art, Toledo OH (S)

Amick, Alison, *Sr Mgr Exhibs & Devel & Chief Cur,* Intuit: The Center for Intuitive & Outsider Art, Chicago IL

Amidon, Catherine, *Dir,* Plymouth State University, Karl Drerup Art Gallery, Plymouth NH

Amies, Marian, *Assoc Prof,* University of Missouri, Saint Louis, Dept of Art & Art History, Saint Louis MO (S)

Amin, Natessa, *Vis Artist,* Moravian College, Dept of Art, Bethlehem PA (S)

Amling, Diana, *Pres,* Coquille Valley Art Association, Library, Coquille OR

Ammirata, Kerri, *Devel Gallery Mgr,* White Columns, White Columns Curated Artist Registry, New York NY

Ammons, Betty, *Asst Librn,* United Methodist Historical Society, Library, Baltimore MD

Ammons, John, *Adjunct Prof,* Louisiana College, Dept of Art, Pineville LA (S)

Ammons, Wendi, *Develop & Visitor Servs Mgr,* Gibbes Museum of Art, Charleston SC (S)

Ammons, Wendi, *Develop & Visitor Servs Mgr & Bd Liason,* Carolina Art Association, Gibbes Museum of Art, Charleston SC

Amneus, Cynthia, *Chief Cur & Cur Fashion & Textile,* Cincinnati Art Museum, Cincinnati Art Museum, Cincinnati OH

Amoroso, Kathy, *Dir Digital Engagement,* Maine Historical Society, Portland ME

Amorous, Martin, *Dept Head,* Sam Houston State University, Art Dept, Huntsville TX (S)

Amory, Dita, *Cur in Charge & Admin, Robert Lehman Coll,* The Metropolitan Museum of Art, New York NY

Amos, Autumn, *Membership Manager,* The Columbus Museum, Columbus GA

Amoudi, Kassem, *Instr,* Wayne Art Center, Wayne PA (S)

Amphlett, Don, *Bd Dir,* Monroe Arts Center, Monroe WI

Ams, Charles M, *Pres,* Southern Vermont Art Center, Manchester VT

Amsler, Cory, *Cur Coll,* Bucks County Historical Society, Mercer Museum, Doylestown PA

Amsterdam, Susan, *Young People's Theatre Coordr,* Passaic County Community College, Broadway, LRC, and Hamilton Club Galleries, Paterson NJ

Amundson, David, *Instr,* Judson University, School of Art, Design & Architecture, Elgin IL (S)

Amundson, Jacob, *Asst Prof,* Greenville College, Art Dept, Greenville IL (S)

Amundson, Jhennifer, *Interim Dean,* Judson University, School of Art, Design & Architecture, Elgin IL (S)

Amussen, Laura, *Exec Dir & Cur,* Goucher College, Rosenberg & Silber Art Gallery, Baltimore MD

Amyx, Guyla, *Instr,* Cuesta College, Art Dept, San Luis Obispo CA (S)

Ananian, Michael, *Prof,* University of North Carolina at Greensboro, School of Art, Greensboro NC (S)

Anciani, Floribeth, *Dir Finance & Admin,* Museo de Arte de Ponce, The Luis A Ferre Foundation Inc, Ponce PR

Andersen, Amber, *Cur,* Estevan National Exhibition Centre Inc, Estevan Art Gallery & Museum, Estevan SK

Andersen, David, *Designer/Preparator,* Willamette University, Hallie Ford Museum of Art, Salem OR

Andersen, Douglas, *Asst Prof,* University of Hartford, Hartford Art School, West Hartford CT (S)

Andersen, Jeffrey, *Dir,* Lyme Historical Society, Library, Old Lyme CT

Andersen, Patricia, *Asst Admin,* Washington Art Association, Washington Depot CT

Andersen, Rachel Klees, *Cur Exhibits,* Kenosha Public Museums, Kenosha WI

Anderson Butler, Kent, *Prof,* Azusa Pacific University, College of Music & the Arts, Dept of Art & Design, Azusa CA (S)

Anderson, Arthur, *Assoc Prof,* York College of the City University of New York, Fine & Performing Arts, Jamaica NY (S)

Anderson, Austin, *Facility & Grounds,* Wassenberg Art Center, Van Wert OH
Anderson, Bea, *Fine & Performing Arts Support Coordr,* Cuesta College, Harold J Miossi Art Gallery, San Luis Obispo CA
Anderson, Bjorn, *Asst Prof,* Minnesota State University-Moorhead, Dept of Art & Design, Moorhead MN (S)
Anderson, Blue, *Mus Shop Mgr,* Columbia River Maritime Museum, Astoria OR
Anderson, Bonnie, *VPres,* Crary Art Gallery, Warren PA
Anderson, Bradley, *Children's Theatre,* Arkansas Arts Center, Little Rock AR (S)
Anderson, Brett, *Asst Prof Art,* University of Southern Indiana, Art & Design Dept, Evansville IN (S)
Anderson, Brooke, *Dir,* Pennsylvania Academy of the Fine Arts, Philadelphia PA
Anderson, Catie, *Cur Educ,* Leigh Yawkey Woodson Art Museum, Wausau WI
Anderson, Cy, *Digital Media Production/Video Production,* Art Institute of Pittsburgh, Pittsburgh PA (S)
Anderson, Daniel J, *Head Ceramic,* Southern Illinois University at Edwardsville, Dept of Art & Design, Edwardsville IL (S)
Anderson, David, *Dir,* Creek Council House Museum, Okmulgee OK
Anderson, David, *Dir,* Creek Council House Museum, Library, Okmulgee OK
Anderson, Donald, *CEO & Pres,* Roswell Artist-in-Residence Foundation, Anderson Museum of Contemporary Art, Roswell NM
Anderson, Donald, *Prof Emeritus,* University of Louisville, Allen R Hite Art Institute, Louisville KY (S)
Anderson, Donna, *Exec Dir,* The Exhibition Alliance, Hamilton NY
Anderson, Emily, *Exec Mgr,* Arts Midwest, Minneapolis MN
Anderson, Eric, *Educ & Asst Dir,* Blanden Memorial Art Museum, Fort Dodge IA
Anderson, Francine M, *Chief Arts Educ,* South Florida Cultural Consortium, Miami Dade County Dept of Cultural Affairs, Miami FL
Anderson, Glaire, *Asst Prof,* University of North Carolina at Chapel Hill, Art Dept, Chapel Hill NC (S)
Anderson, Hilary, *Dir Exhibits,* National Heritage Museum, Lexington MA
Anderson, Hugh B, *Dean of Arts,* Polk Community College, Art, Letters & Social Sciences, Winter Haven FL (S)
Anderson, Jennifer, *Admin Asst,* Scripps College, Ruth Chandler Williamson Gallery, Claremont CA
Anderson, Joanna, *Pres,* Daum Museum of Contemporary Art, Sedalia MO
Anderson, John, *Prof,* Framingham State College, Art Dept, Framingham MA (S)
Anderson, Jon, *Prof,* Utah State University, Dept of Art, Logan UT (S)
Anderson, Jonathan, *Assoc Prof,* Biola University, Department of Art, La Mirada CA (S)
Anderson, Joseph, *Librn,* Southern Alberta Art Gallery, Library, Lethbridge AB
Anderson, Josh, *Dir Gallery,* Mount Mary College, Marian Gallery, Milwaukee WI
Anderson, Kayla, *Spec Coll Mgr,* School of the Art Institute of Chicago, John M Flaxman Library, Chicago IL
Anderson, Ken, *Adjunct,* North Iowa Area Community College, Dept of Art, Mason City IA (S)
Anderson, Ken, *Prof,* University of Missouri, Saint Louis, Dept of Art & Art History, Saint Louis MO (S)
Anderson, Kenneth, *Prof,* Peru State College, Art Dept, Peru NE (S)
Anderson, Kimberly, *Dir Visual Arts,* Arts Place, Inc, Hugh N Ronald Memorial Gallery, Portland IN
Anderson, Kirsten, *Deputy Dir & Chief Cur,* Anchorage Museum at Rasmuson Center, Anchorage AK
Anderson, Kristian, *Exec Dir,* Salt Lake Art Center, Utah Museum of Contemporary Art, Salt Lake City UT
Anderson, Kristin, *Chmn,* Augsburg College, Art Dept, Minneapolis MN (S)
Anderson, Larry, *Dir Performing Arts & Pub Progs,* Snug Harbor Cultural Center, Newhouse Center for Contemporary Art, Staten Island NY
Anderson, Lawrence P, *Prof & Chmn,* Francis Marion University, Fine Arts Dept, Florence SC (S)
Anderson, Leslie, *Arts Libr,* California State University, Long Beach, University Library, Long Beach CA
Anderson, Linda, *Exec Dir,* Rapid City Arts Council, Dahl Arts Center, Rapid City SD
Anderson, Lisa, *HR,* Henry Gallery Association, Henry Art Gallery, Seattle WA
Anderson, Lisa, *Human Resources,* University of Washington, Henry Art Gallery, Seattle WA
Anderson, Maggie, *Dir Educ,* Newport Art Museum, Coleman Center for Creative Studies, Newport RI (S)
Anderson, Marge, *Sales Assoc,* Gene Roncka Willow Point Gallery/Museum, Ashland NE
Anderson, Mark R, *Chmn,* Presbyterian College, Visual & Theater Arts, Clinton SC (S)
Anderson, Mark W, *Chmn,* Baylor University - College of Arts and Sciences, Dept of Art, Waco TX (S)
Anderson, Martin, *Dept Head,* Henry Ford Community College, McKenzie Fine Art Ctr, Dearborn MI (S)
Anderson, Mary Ann, *Admin Asst,* Purdue University Galleries, West Lafayette IN
Anderson, Mary, *Gallery Asst & Educator,* Koffler Center of the Arts, Toronto ON (S)
Anderson, Naura, *Pub Programs Dir,* Rochester Art Center, Rochester MN
Anderson, Neil, *Prof,* Bucknell University, Dept of Art, Lewisburg PA (S)
Anderson, Patricia, *Dir,* Maryland Historical Society, Museum of Maryland History, Baltimore MD
Anderson, Paul, *Asst Dir Library Admin Servs,* University of Delaware, Morris Library, Newark DE
Anderson, Peter, *Treas,* South County Art Association, Kingston RI
Anderson, Richita, *Librn,* Aesthetic Realism Foundation, Eli Siegel Collection, New York NY
Anderson, Robert S, *Cur,* Safety Harbor Museum and Cultural Arts Center, Safety Harbor FL
Anderson, Robert, *Foundations Dir,* University of Texas, Dept of Art & Art History, Austin TX (S)
Anderson, Stacey, *Dir Public Progs,* Municipal Art Society of New York, New York NY
Anderson, Stacie, *Board Dirs Pres,* Sioux City Art Center, Sioux City IA
Anderson, Stacie, *Develop Coordr,* Sioux City Art Center, Sioux City IA (S)
Anderson, Stanford, *Head Dept,* Massachusetts Institute of Technology, School of Architecture and Planning, Cambridge MA (S)
Anderson, Steve A, *Exec Dir,* Carteret County Historical Society, The History Place, Morehead City NC
Anderson, Steve, *Exec Dir,* Catfish Capital Visitors Center and Museum, Belzoni MS
Anderson, Steven R, *CEO & Dir,* Iowa Great Lakes Maritime Museum, Arnolds Park IA
Anderson, Susan B, *Treas,* Madison & Main Gallery, Greeley CO
Anderson, Susan K, *Archivist,* Philadelphia Museum of Art, Library & Archives, Philadelphia PA
Anderson, Susan, *Dir Finance & Admin,* South Shore Arts, Munster IN
Anderson, Sven, *Assoc Prof,* State University of New York College at Oneonta, Dept of Art, Oneonta NY (S)
Anderson, Taylor, *Art Adv Bd Fellow,* Mount Holyoke College, Art Museum, South Hadley MA
Anderson, Ted, *Design Dir,* The Exhibition Alliance, Hamilton NY
Anderson, Terri, *Dir Mus Coll,* National Trust for Historic Preservation, Washington DC
Anderson, Terry, *Instr,* Northeast Mississippi Junior College, Art Dept, Booneville MS (S)
Anderson, Todd, *Asst Designer,* University of California, Santa Barbara, Art, Design & Architecture Museum, Santa Barbara CA
Anderson, Tom, *Prof,* Florida State University, Art Education Dept, Tallahassee FL (S)
Anderson, Tom, *Team Leader Private Records,* Royal Alberta Museum, Provincial Archives of Alberta, Edmonton AB
Anderson, Virginia, *Cur American Art,* The Baltimore Museum of Art, Baltimore MD
Anderson, Wayne, *Dept Chair,* Wayne State College, Dept Art & Design, Wayne NE (S)
Anderson, Wayne, *Prof,* Wayne State College, Nordstrand Visual Arts Gallery, Wayne NE
Anderson, Whitney, *Computer Instr,* Ames Free-Easton's Public Library, North Easton MA
Anderson, Wyatt, *Dean,* University of Georgia, Franklin College of Arts & Sciences, Lamar Dodd School of Art, Athens GA (S)
Andersson, Christiane, *Prof,* Bucknell University, Dept of Art, Lewisburg PA (S)
Ando, Erica, *Assoc Cur Educ,* Norton Museum of Art, West Palm Beach FL
Andraos, Amale, *Dean,* Columbia University, Graduate School of Architecture, Planning & Preservation, New York NY (S)
Andreasen, Jason, *Exec Dir,* Baton Rouge Gallery, Center For Contemporary Art, Baton Rouge LA
Andres, Glenn, *Prof,* Middlebury College, History of Art & Architecture Dept, Middlebury VT (S)
Andres, Hilda, *Dir Community Engagement,* Swope Art Museum, Terre Haute IN
Andress, Thomas, *Pres Print Selection Comt Chmn,* Print Club of Albany, Schenectady NY
Andrews, Bill, *Instr,* Mississippi State University, Dept of Art, Starville MS (S)
Andrews, Charmagne, *Assoc Prof,* Alabama State University, Dept of Visual Arts, Montgomery AL (S)
Andrews, Debbie, *Educ Coordr,* Farmington Village Green & Library Association, Stanley-Whitman House, Farmington CT
Andrews, Edwin, *Assoc Prof,* Northeastern University, Dept of Art & Architecture, Boston MA (S)
Andrews, G Aseneth, *Instr Visual Arts Educ,* Madonna University, College of Arts & Humanities, Livonia MI (S)
Andrews, Jim, *Instr,* Seton Hill University, Art Program, Greensburg PA (S)
Andrews, Scott, *Communs Dir,* Palos Verdes Art Center/Beverly G. Alpay Center for Arts Education, Rancho Palos Verdes CA
Andrews, William, *Dir,* Ogden Museum of Southern Art, University of New Orleans, New Orleans LA
Andrick, Annita, *Dir Library & Archives,* Erie County Historical Society, Erie PA
Andrieux, Beatrice, *Artistic Dir,* The Association of International Photography Art Dealers, Washington DC
Andriulli, Robert, *Prof Drawing, Painting & Watercolor,* Millersville University, Dept of Art & Design, Millersville PA (S)
Andro, Ginger, *VPres,* Sculptors Guild, Inc, Brooklyn NY
Andrus, Lynda, *Prof,* Kansas State University, Art Dept, Manhattan KS (S)
Andrus, Maryanne, *Dir Educ,* Buffalo Bill Memorial Association, Buffalo Bill Historical Center, Cody WY
Andrzejewski, Anna V, *Asst Prof,* University of Wisconsin, Madison, Dept of Art History, Madison WI (S)
Andyshak, Sarah, *Asst Prof,* University of Mary Hardin-Baylor, College of Visual & Performing Arts, Belton TX (S)
Angel, Catherine, *Prof,* University of Nevada, Las Vegas, Dept of Art, Las Vegas NV (S)
Angelo, Kate, *Librn,* City of Long Branch, Long Branch Free Public Library, Long Branch NJ
Angeloch, Eric, *Instr,* Woodstock School of Art, Inc, Woodstock NY (S)

Angert, Joe C, *Instr,* Saint Louis Community College at Forest Park, Art Dept, Saint Louis MO (S)
Anglin, B, *Asst Prof,* Christopher Newport University, Dept of Fine Performing Arts, Newport News VA (S)
Anglin, Barbara, *Technical Servs Librn,* Lee County Library, Tupelo MS
Angus, Scott, *Asst Prof Art,* Maryville University of Saint Louis, Art & Design Program, Saint Louis MO (S)
Anielski, Jennifer, *Librn, Tech Svcs,* The Mariners' Museum, Library, Newport News VA
Anixter, Julie, *Exec Dir,* American Institute of Graphic Arts, National Design Center, New York NY
Anke, Douglas, *Gen Educ,* Art Institute of Pittsburgh, Pittsburgh PA (S)
Anoushian, Suzanne E, *Chmn Commun Design,* Fashion Institute of Technology, School of Art & Design, New York NY (S)
Anreus, Alejandro, *Art Dept Chmn,* William Paterson University, Dept Arts, Wayne NJ (S)
Anstine, Michele, *Asst CEO,* Delaware Historical Society, Library, Wilmington DE
Anthony, Carolyn, *Dir,* Skokie Public Library, Skokie IL
Anthony, David, *Cur Anthropology,* Hartwick College, The Yager Museum, Oneonta NY
Anthony, David, *Dean,* Golden West College, Visual Art Dept, Huntington Beach CA (S)
Anthony, David, *Dean,* Golden West College, Visual Art Dept, Huntington Beach CA (S)
Anthony, Kristin, *Admin Coordr,* Laguna Art Museum, Laguna Beach CA
Anthony, Kristina, *Exhibs Mgr,* Hickory Museum of Art, Inc, Hickory NC
Antico, Danielle, *Exhibs Mgr,* New Hampshire Art Association, Inc, Portsmouth NH
Anton, Don, *Prof,* Humboldt State University, College of Arts & Humanities, Art Dept, Arcata CA (S)
Anton, Dorothy, *Secy,* Kelly-Griggs House Museum, Red Bluff CA
Anton, Janis K, *Dir Admis,* The Illinois Institute of Art - Chicago, Chicago IL (S)
Antonakis, Nick, *Dept Head Visual Arts,* Grand Rapids Community College, Visual Art Dept, Grand Rapids MI (S)
Antonelli, Karen, *Photog,* Art Institute of Pittsburgh, Pittsburgh PA (S)
Antonelli, Melanie, *Coll Mgr,* University of Mississippi, University Museum & Historic Houses, Oxford MS
Antoniades, Andrew, *Pres,* New York Society of Architects, New York NY
Antonio, Sheril, *Sr Assoc Dean,* New York University, Tisch School of the Arts, New York NY (S)
Antonoff, Jeff, *Exec Dir,* Barbara & Ray Alpert Jewish Community Center, Pauline & Zena Gatov Gallery, Long Beach CA
Antonsen, Lasse, *Coordr Gallery,* University of Massachusetts Dartmouth, College of Visual & Performing Arts, North Dartmouth MA (S)
Anyah, Eric, *CFO,* Museum of Fine Arts, Houston, Houston TX
Aoki, Katherine, *Assoc Prof,* Santa Clara University, Dept of Art & Art History, Santa Clara CA (S)
Aoki, Miho, *Assoc Prof,* University of Alaska Fairbanks, Art Department, Fairbanks AK (S)
Apchin, Nathalie, *CFO,* Peabody Essex Museum, Salem MA
Apgar, Jennifer, *Educ Dir,* Peters Valley School of Craft, Layton NJ
Aponte, Sandra, *Prof,* University of Puerto Rico, Mayaguez, Dept of Humanities, College of Fine Arts & Theory of Art Programs, Mayaguez PR (S)
Aponte, Sarah, *Chief Librn,* City College of the City University of New York, Morris Raphael Cohen Library, New York NY
Appel, Janet L, *Dir,* Shirley Plantation Foundation, Charles City VA
Appel, Kevin, *Prof Painting,* University of California, Irvine, Studio Art Dept, Irvine CA (S)
Appiah, Krystal, *Cur African American History,* Library Company of Philadelphia, Philadelphia PA
Appiah, Kwame, *VPres Literature,* American Academy of Arts & Letters, New York NY
Applegate, Barbara, *Treas,* Pemaquid Group of Artists, Pemaquid Art Gallery, Pemaquid Point ME
Applegate, Jared, *Instr,* University of Saint Francis, School of Creative Arts, Fort Wayne IN (S)
Applegate, Reed, *Resource Mgr,* California State University, Chico, Janet Turner Print Museum, CSU, Chicago, Chico CA
Aprea, Jennifer, *Mus Servs & Opers Mgr,* Southern Methodist University, Meadows Museum, Dallas TX
Aquin, Stephane, *Chief Cur,* Hirshhorn Museum & Sculpture Garden, Smithsonian Institution, Washington DC
Aquirre, Carlos, *Assoc Prof,* University of Miami, Dept of Art & Art History, Coral Gables FL (S)
Aranda-Alvarado, Rocio, *Assoc Cur, Special Projects,* El Museo del Barrio, New York NY
Arat, Serdar, *Dir Art Dept,* Concordia College, Art Dept, Bronxville NY (S)
Aravena, Lidia, *Conservator of Paintings,* Museo de Arte de Ponce, The Luis A Ferre Foundation Inc, Ponce PR
Arbino, Larry, *Adjunct,* College of the Canyons, Art Dept, Santa Clarita CA (S)
Arbolino, Jamie, *Assoc Registrar,* United States Senate Commission on Art, Washington DC
Arbuckle, Linda, *Prof,* University of Florida, School of Art & Art History, Gainesville FL (S)
Arbury, Steve, *Chmn,* Radford University, Art Dept, Radford VA (S)
Arceneaux, Pamela D, *Senior Librn,* The Historic New Orleans Collection, Williams Research Center, New Orleans LA
Arch, Xan, *Dean,* University of Portland, Wilson W Clark Memorial Library, Portland OR
Archer, Phil, *Director of Program & Interpretation,* Reynolda House Museum of American Art, Winston-Salem NC
Archias, Elise, *Asst Prof,* California State University, Chico, Department of Art & Art History, Chico CA (S)
Archibald, Courtney, *Accnt,* Willard Arts Center, Carr Gallery, Colonial Theater, Idaho Falls ID
Arena, Annie, *Instr,* Ocean City Arts Center, Ocean City NJ (S)
Arford, Kate, *Gallery Dir,* Soap Factory, Minneapolis MN
Argabrite, Diana, *Dir Arts & Schools Prog,* De Anza College, Euphrat Museum of Art, Cupertino CA
Argall, Quinn, *Asst Cur,* City of Austin Parks & Recreation, O Henry Museum, Austin TX
Argent, Lawrence, *Prof Sculpture,* University of Denver, School of Art & Art History, Denver CO (S)
Arias, Catherine, *Dir Visitor Engagement,* The Museum of Contemporary Art (MOCA), MOCA Grand Avenue, Los Angeles CA
Arifin, Roni, *Mus Accnt,* Southern Methodist University, Meadows Museum, Dallas TX
Arike, Michael, *VPres,* Society of American Graphic Artists, New York NY
Aristarkhova, Irina, *Asst Prof Women's Studies & Art (Art Criticism),* Pennsylvania State University, University Park, Penn State School of Visual Arts, University Park PA (S)
Arit, Abbey, *Administrative Manager,* Walker Fine Art, Denver CO
Arkin, Cynthia, *1st VPres,* Plastic Club, Art Club, Philadelphia PA
Arleth, Kimberly, *Registrar,* Hamline University Studio Arts & Art History Depts, Gallery, Saint Paul MN
Armborst, Tobias, *Asst Prof,* Vassar College, Art Dept, Poughkeepsie NY (S)
Armbrister, Clarence, *Pres,* Girard College, Stephen Girard Collection, Philadelphia PA
Armbruster, James, *Mgr Mus Design,* Colonial Williamsburg Foundation, DeWitt Wallace Decorative Arts Museum, Williamsburg VA
Armel, Don, *Prod,* Georgia Southern University, Betty Foy Sanders Dept of Art, Statesboro GA (S)
Armendariz, Richard, *Assoc Prof,* University of Texas at San Antonio, Dept of Art & Art History, San Antonio TX (S)
Armendariz, Yvette, *Mktg Dir,* i.d.e.a. Museum, Mesa AZ
Arminio, Roberta Y, *Dir,* Museum of Ossining Historical Society, Ossining NY
Armor, Kelly, *Dir Educ & Folk Art,* Erie Art Museum, Erie PA
Arms, Anneli, *Pres,* Federation of Modern Painters & Sculptors, New York NY
Armstead, Ray, *Mgr Mus Security,* Colonial Williamsburg Foundation, DeWitt Wallace Decorative Arts Museum, Williamsburg VA
Armstrong, Christopher Drew, *Asst Prof,* University of Pittsburgh, Henry Clay Frick Dept History of Art & Architecture, Pittsburgh PA (S)
Armstrong, David, *Pres & Founder,* American Museum of Ceramic Art, Pomona CA
Armstrong, Joy, *Cur Modern & Contemporary Art,* Colorado Springs Fine Arts Center, Taylor Museum, Colorado Springs CO
Armstrong, Lilian, *Prof,* Wellesley College, Art Dept, Wellesley MA (S)
Armstrong, Richard, *Dir Mus & Foundation,* Solomon R Guggenheim Museum, New York NY
Armstrong, Steve, *Exhibs Cur,* Imperial Centre's Maria V Howard Arts Center, Rocky Mount NC
Armstrong, Summer, *Admin Support,* California State University, Chico, Department of Art & Art History, Chico CA (S)
Armstutz, Bruce, *Prof,* Shoreline Community College, Humanities Division, Seattle WA (S)
Arnar, Anna, *Asst Prof,* Minnesota State University-Moorhead, Dept of Art & Design, Moorhead MN (S)
Arnett, Dana, *Pres,* American Institute of Graphic Arts, National Design Center, New York NY
Arnholm, Ron, *Prof Graphic Design,* University of Georgia, Franklin College of Arts & Sciences, Lamar Dodd School of Art, Athens GA (S)
Arning, Bill, *Dir,* Contemporary Arts Museum Houston, Houston TX
Arnison, Steve, *Prof,* Munson-Williams-Proctor Arts Institute, Pratt MWP College of Art, Utica NY (S)
Arnold, Chester, *Chmn,* College of Marin, Dept of Art, Kentfield CA (S)
Arnold, Jan, *Library Dir,* Springfield Art Association of Edwards Place, Michael Victor II Art Library, Springfield IL
Arnold, Jan, *Library Dir,* Springfield Art Association of Edwards Place, Springfield IL
Arnold, Kathy, *Prof & Dept Chair,* West Valley College, Art Dept, Saratoga CA (S)
Arnold, Kristina, *Gallery Dir,* Western Kentucky University, University Gallery, Bowling Green KY
Arnold, Lee, *Dir Library & Colls & COO,* Historical Society of Pennsylvania, Philadelphia PA
Arnold, Mark, *Exec Dir,* The Art Center of Waco, Library, Waco TX
Arnold, Pat, *Office Mgr,* Lehigh Valley Heritage Center, Allentown PA
Arnold, Patrick, *Instr,* Main Line Art Center, Haverford PA (S)
Arnold, Peter, *Pres & CEO,* Genesee Country Village & Museum, John L Wehle Art Gallery, Mumford NY
Arnold, Ramona, *Admin & Finance,* Institute of American Indian Arts, Museum of Contemporary Native Arts, Santa Fe NM (S)
Arnold, Robert, *Prof,* Ohio State University, Dept of Art Education, Columbus OH (S)
Arnold, Sara, *Dir Cur Affairs,* Gibbes Museum of Art, Charleston SC (S)
Arocho, Felix, *Performing Arts Mgr,* Hostos Center for the Arts & Culture, Bronx NY
Aron, Beth, *Deputy Dir Finance & Admin,* Newark Museum Association, The Newark Museum, Newark NJ
Aronoff, Mindy, *Sr Dir Engagement,* Bay Area Video Coalition, Inc, San Francisco CA
Aronowitz, Richard, *Dean Grad & Continuing Educ,* Massachusetts College of Art, Boston MA (S)

Aronson, Barbara, *Pres,* Association for Public Art, Philadelphia PA
Aronson, Julie, *Cur American Painting & Sculpture,* Cincinnati Art Museum, Cincinnati Art Museum, Cincinnati OH
Arp, Kimberly, *Prof,* Louisiana State University, School of Art, Baton Rouge LA (S)
Arpad, Tori, *Assoc Prof,* Florida International University, School of Art & Art History, Miami FL (S)
Arpadi, Allen, *Instr,* Saint Louis Community College at Forest Park, Art Dept, Saint Louis MO (S)
Arpin, Pierre, *Dir & CEO,* Contemporary Calgary, Calgary AB
Arquello, Lori, *Dir Mktg,* Putnam Museum of History and Natural Science, Davenport IA
Arquillos, Joel, *Exec Dir,* Social & Public Art Resource Center, (SPARC), Venice CA
Arrasmith, Lynnda, *Cur & Registrar,* Canton Museum of Art, Art Library, Canton OH
Arrasmith, Lynnda, *Cur Coll & Registrar,* Canton Museum of Art, Canton OH
Arrasmith, Lynnda, *Cur Exhibits & Registrar,* Canton Museum of Art, Canton OH (S)
Arredondo, Richard, *Chmn,* San Antonio College, Visual Arts & Technology, San Antonio TX (S)
Arredondo, Zaira, *Coordinator of Exhibitions,* Utah State University, Nora Eccles Harrison Museum of Art, Logan UT
Arrington, Gerald C, *Prof,* Concord College, Fine Art Division, Athens WV (S)
Arroyo, Alexa, *Vis Lectr,* University of New Orleans-Lake Front, Dept of Fine Arts, New Orleans LA (S)
Arroyo, Rafael, *Office Mgr,* University of Oregon, Aperture Photo Gallery - EMU Art Gallery, Eugene OR
Arsenault, Todd, *Asst Prof,* Dickinson College, Dept of Art & Art History, Carlisle PA (S)
Arseneau, Jennifer, *Educ & Public Programs Mgr,* University of Alaska, Museum of the North, Fairbanks AK
Arseneault, Jacques, *Dir,* Universite de Moncton, Dept of Visual Arts, Moncton NB (S)
Arteaga, Agustin, *Dir,* Dallas Museum of Art, Dallas TX
Arthur, Charmion, *Instr,* Fort Hays State University, Dept of Art & Design, Hays KS (S)
Arthur, Ellen, *Mus Mgr,* Biggs Museum of American Art, Dover DE
Arthur, Emily, *Asst Prof,* University of Wisconsin, Madison, Dept of Art, Madison WI (S)
Arthur, Kathleen, *Prof,* James Madison University, School of Art & Art History, Harrisonburg VA (S)
Arthur, Martin, *Supervisor,* City of Cedar Falls, Iowa, James & Meryl Hearst Center for the Arts & Sculpture Garden, Cedar Falls IA
Artimovich, Vicki, *Art History Instr,* Bellevue Community College, Art Dept, Bellevue WA (S)
Artz, Steve, *Mus Store Mgr,* The Pennsylvania State University, Palmer Museum of Art, University Park PA
Asaro, Janet, *Mktg & Pub Rels Dir,* Anchorage Museum at Rasmuson Center, Anchorage AK
Asbridge, Delaney, *Gallery Asst,* Shiawassee Arts Center, Owosso MI
Asbury, Jane, *Assoc Prof,* University of Kansas, The School of the Arts, Dept of Visual Art, Lawrence KS (S)
Ascencio, Mario, *College Libr and Mng Dir, ArtCenter Library,* ArtCenter College of Design, Pasadena CA (S)
Ascenio, Mario, *Libr Dir,* Corcoran Gallery of Art, Corcoran Library, Washington DC
Aschkenes, Anna M, *Exec Dir,* Middlesex County Cultural & Heritage Commission, New Brunswick NJ
Asdell, Brian, *Exhib Technician,* i.d.e.a. Museum, Mesa AZ
Asebedo, Anna, *Dept Chair,* City College of San Francisco, Art Dept, San Francisco CA (S)
Ash, Carol, *Chair & NHT Commissioner,* New York Office of Parks, Recreation & Historic Preservation, Natural Heritage Trust, Albany NY
Ashby, Andrea, *Librn Technician,* Independence National Historical Park, Library, Philadelphia PA
Ashby, Gil, *Chmn Illustration,* College for Creative Studies, Detroit MI (S)
Asher, Catherine, *Prof,* University of Minnesota, Minneapolis, Art History, Minneapolis MN (S)
Asher, Dorothy, *Dir,* Lizzadro Museum of Lapidary Art, Elmhurst IL
Asher, Frederick, *Prof,* University of Minnesota, Minneapolis, Art History, Minneapolis MN (S)
Ashkin, Michael, *Dept Chair,* Cornell University, Dept of Art, Ithaca NY (S)
Ashley, Carrie, *Educ Coordr,* National Audubon Society, John James Audubon Center at Mill Grove, Audubon PA
Ashley, Janis, *Adminr,* Los Angeles County Museum of Natural History, William S Hart Museum, Newhall CA
Ashley, Raymond, *Pres & CEO,* Maritime Museum of San Diego, San Diego CA
Ashman, Stuart, *Exec Dir,* Munoz Waxman Gallery - Center for Contemporary Arts, Santa Fe NM
Ashman, Stuart, *Exec Dir & Chief Cur,* The Center for Contemporary Arts of Santa Fe, Santa Fe NM
Ashton Fisher, Helen, *Coll Cur,* William A Farnsworth, Library, Rockland ME
Ashury, Kimberly, *Prof,* Saint Anselm College, Dept of Fine Arts, Manchester NH (S)
Asian, Ines, *VPres Communs,* New-York Historical Society, Museum, New York NY
Asihene, Emmanuel, *Prof,* Clark-Atlanta University, School of Arts & Sciences, Atlanta GA (S)
Asikis, Nikolas, *Preparator,* Smith College, Museum of Art, Northampton MA
Askew, Dan, *Lectr,* University of Texas of Permian Basin, Dept of Art, Odessa TX (S)
Askew, Dan, *Studio Art,* Florida School of the Arts, Visual Arts, Palatka FL (S)
Askren, David, *Interim Co-Chmn,* Queen Sofia Spanish Institute, New York NY
Asmus, Collin, *Assoc Prof,* Bridgewater State College, Art Dept, Bridgewater MA (S)
Asmus, Collin, *Asst Prof,* Millsaps College, Dept of Art, Jackson MS (S)
Asmuth, Thomas, *Asst Prof,* University of West Florida, Dept of Art, Pensacola FL (S)
Aspness, Mary, *Instr,* Century College, Humanities Dept, White Bear Lake MN (S)
Asprodites, Gail, *Deputy Dir Admin & Fin,* New Orleans Museum of Art, New Orleans LA
Assad, Alan, *Industrial Design Technology,* Art Institute of Pittsburgh, Pittsburgh PA (S)
Assad, Cyril, *Industrial Design Technology,* Art Institute of Pittsburgh, Pittsburgh PA (S)
Asselin Van Coppenolle, Orianne, *Exhib Coordr,* La Centrale Powerhouse Gallery, Montreal QC
Assner, Robin, *Assoc Prof,* Webster University, Department of Art, Design & Art History, Webster Groves MO (S)
Aste, Richard, *Dir,* McNay Art Museum, San Antonio TX
Ataoguz, Kirsten, *Asst Prof,* Indiana-Purdue University, Dept of Fine Arts, Fort Wayne IN (S)
Atchison, Alicia, *Mktg & Design Coordr,* Fort Collins Museum of Art, Inc, Fort Collins CO
Atchison, Sandra, *Asst Dean,* University of North Texas, Libraries, Denton TX
Atencio, Thomas, *Chief Security,* Institute of American Indian Arts, Museum of Contemporary Native Arts, Santa Fe NM (S)
Atencio, Thomas, *Facilities & Security Mgr,* Institute of American Indian Arts, IAIA Museum of Contemporary Native Arts, Santa Fe NM
Atheron, Cynthia, *Prof,* Middlebury College, History of Art & Architecture Dept, Middlebury VT (S)
Atkins, Christopher, *The Agnes and Jack Mulroney Associate Curator of European Painting and Sculpture before 1900,* Philadelphia Museum of Art, John G Johnson Collection, Philadelphia PA
Atkins, Jennifer, *Subject Librn for Art & Architecture,* Washington University, Kenneth & Nancy Kranzberg Art & Architecture Library, Saint Louis MO
Atkins, Sharon Matt, *Dir Curatorial Affairs,* Brooklyn Museum, Brooklyn NY
Atkinson, Becky, *Dir,* Murray State University, Art Galleries, Murray KY
Atkinson, Beth, *Librn,* Ryerss Victorian Museum & Library, Philadelphia PA
Atkinson, Conrad, *Prof Painting & Mixed Media,* University of California, Davis, Dept of Art & Art History, Davis CA (S)
Atkinson, Daniel, *Jazz Coordr,* Library Association of La Jolla, Athenaeum Music & Arts Library, La Jolla CA
Atkinson, Dianne, *Instr,* Mount Mary College, Art & Design Division, Milwaukee WI (S)
Atkinson, Lane, *Controller,* New Brunswick Museum, Saint John NB
Atkinson, Martha, *Educ Coordr,* The City of Petersburg Museums, Petersburg VA
Atkinson, Melanie, *Instr,* Hinds Community College, Dept of Art, Raymond MS (S)
Atkinson, Nora, *Cur of Craft,* American Art Museum, Renwick Gallery, Washington DC
Atkinson, Peter, *Dir Facilities Planning & Mgmt,* Harvard University, Harvard Art Museums, Cambridge MA
Attenborough, Debra, *Librn,* Rodman Hall Arts Centre, Library, Saint Catharines ON
Atterberry, Giselle, *Prof Art,* Joliet Junior College, Laura A Sprague Art Gallery, Joliet IL
Attie, Diana, *Prof,* University of Toledo, Dept of Art, Toledo OH (S)
Attyah, David, *Instr,* Glendale Community College, Visual & Performing Arts Div, Glendale CA (S)
Atwell, Michael, *Asst Dir,* Purdue University Galleries, West Lafayette IN
Atwell, Michael, *Cur,* Art Museum of Greater Lafayette, Lafayette IN
Atwell, Patty, *Treas,* Frontier Gateway Museum, Glendive MT
Atwood, Stephanie, *Finance Mgr,* Diverse Works, Houston TX
Atzbach, Nicole, *Cur,* Southern Methodist University, Meadows Museum, Dallas TX
Au, Jeri, *Assoc Prof,* Webster University, Department of Art, Design & Art History, Webster Groves MO (S)
Aubin, Rebeca, *Cur of Educ,* University of New Mexico, The Harwood Museum of Art, Taos NM
Aubin, Rebecca, *Head Educ & Visitor Servs,* New Mexico Department of Cultural Affairs, New Mexico Museum of Art, Santa Fe NM
Aubourg, Vickie, *Asst Dir,* California Polytechnic State University, College of Architecture & Environmental Design-Architecture Collection, San Luis Obispo CA
Audeh, Aida, *Dept Chair, Assoc Prof,* Hamline University, Dept of Studio Arts & Art History, Saint Paul MN (S)
Audette, Curie, *Coll Manager,* Bates College, Museum of Art, Lewiston ME
Audley, Paul, *Pres,* Discovery Museum, Bridgeport CT
Auellar, Linda, *Dir Develop & Communs,* Ferguson Library, Stamford CT
Augelli, John, *CEO, Exec Dir,* Rosenberg Library, Galveston TX
Augustin, Hazel, *Asst Gallery Coordr,* University of Indianapolis, Christel DeHaan Fine Arts Gallery, Indianapolis IN
Augustine, Nathan, *Colls Mgr,* Deere & Company, Moline IL
Augustine, Sylvia, *Mus Coordr,* Independence Historical Museum & Art Center, Independence KS
Aulisi, Joe, *Dir,* National Museum of Racing, National Museum of Racing & Hall of Fame, Saratoga Springs NY
Aulisi, Joseph E, *Acting Dir,* National Museum of Racing, Reference Library, Saratoga Springs NY
Aulisio, Terry, *Visitor Servs & Retail Mgr,* Polk Museum of Art, Lakeland FL

Aumann, Karen, *Assoc Prof,* Philadelphia Community College, Dept of Art, Philadelphia PA (S)
Aune, Alison, *Asst Prof,* University of Minnesota, Duluth, Art Dept, Duluth MN (S)
Aunspaugh, Richard, *Chmn,* Young Harris College, Dept of Art, Young Harris GA (S)
Aurbach, Michael, *Prof,* Vanderbilt University, Dept of Art, Nashville TN (S)
Aureden, Deidre, *Dir Progs & Special Projects,* Schweinfurth Art Center, Auburn NY
Ausfeld, Margaret Lynne, *Sr Cur Art,* Montgomery Museum of Fine Arts, Montgomery AL
Ausfeld, Margaret Lynne, *Sr Cur Art,* Montgomery Museum of Fine Arts, Library, Montgomery AL
Austin, Betty, *Contact,* Arkansas State University, Dept of Art, State University AR (S)
Austin, Beverly, *Asst Prof,* Harding University, Dept of Art & Design, Searcy AR (S)
Austin, David, *Co-owner,* Imago Galleries, Palm Desert CA
Austin, Debbie, *Mgr Retail Operations,* The Adirondack Historical Association, The Adirondack Museum, Blue Mountain Lake NY
Austin, Howard, *Instr,* Milwaukee Area Technical College, School of Media & Creative Arts, Milwaukee WI (S)
Austin, Jerry, *Assoc Dean,* University of North Texas, College of Visual Arts & Design, Denton TX (S)
Austin, Leisa, *Co-owner,* Imago Galleries, Palm Desert CA
Austin, Marvin, *Div Chm,* Columbia State Community College, Dept of Art, Columbia TN (S)
Austin, Megan, *Office Asst,* Hamilton College, Emerson Gallery, Clinton NY
Austin, Ramona, *Senior Curator,* Old Dominion University, The College of Arts and Letters, Norfolk VA
Austrian, Sarah, *Gen Counsel,* Solomon R Guggenheim Museum, New York NY
Auten, Madison, *Asst Gallery Mgr,* University of Wisconsin, Union Art Gallery, Milwaukee WI
Autenreith, Amy, *Mus Exec Dir,* Houston Museum of Decorative Arts, Chattanooga TN
Auther, Elissa, *Assoc Prof Visual Arts,* University of Colorado-Colorado Springs, Visual & Performing Arts Dept (VAPA), Colorado Springs CO (S)
Autry, Carolyn, *Assoc Prof,* University of Toledo, Dept of Art, Toledo OH (S)
Avery, Alyson, *Information Mgmt Specialist,* James A Michener Art Museum, Doylestown PA
Avery, Elizabeth, *Vis Asst Prof,* Hamline University, Dept of Studio Arts & Art History, Saint Paul MN (S)
Avila, Betty, *Co Dir Advancement & Admin,* Self Help Graphics, Los Angeles CA
Avila, Nicole, *Proj Mgr,* United States General Services Administration, Art in Architecture and Fine Arts, Washington DC
Aviles, Victoria, *Graphic/Production Mgr,* University of Texas at El Paso, Stanlee & Gerald Rubin Center for the Visual Arts, El Paso TX
Avilla, Audre, *1st VPres,* Frontier Gateway Museum, Glendive MT
Avina, Maya, *Asst Prof,* University of Southern Colorado, Dept of Art, Pueblo CO (S)
Avitia, Rebecca, *Exec Dir,* National Hispanic Cultural Center, Art Museum, Albuquerque NM
Avril, Ellen, *Interim Co-Dir, Chief Cur & Cur Asian Art,* Cornell University, Herbert F Johnson Museum of Art, Ithaca NY
Awotona, Adenrele, *Dean,* Southern University A & M College, School of Architecture, Baton Rouge LA (S)
Axtman, Seb, *Cur,* South Dakota National Guard Museum, Pierre SD
Ayars, Lee, *Adjunct Asst Prof,* Spokane Falls Community College, Fine Arts Dept, Spokane WA (S)
Ayer, Elizabeth, *Asst Prof,* Hartwick College, Art Dept, Oneonta NY (S)
Ayers, Lucie, *Exhibit Coordr,* Tennessee Valley Art Association, Tuscumbia AL
Aygarn-Kowalski, Sue, *Preparator,* Art Complex Museum, Carl A Weyerhaeuser Library, Duxbury MA
Aylmer, Annabelle, *Instr,* Glendale Community College, Visual & Performing Arts Div, Glendale CA (S)
Aylsworth, David, *Colls Registrar,* Menil Foundation, Inc, The Menil Collection, Houston TX
Aylward, Marci, *Gallery Dir,* Avila University, Thornhill Art Gallery, Kansas City MO
Aylward, Marci, *Instr,* Avila College, Art Division, Dept of Humanities, Kansas City MO (S)
Azanza, Katie, *Opers Mgr,* Museums Sonoma County, Art Museum of Sonoma County & History Museum of Sonoma County, Santa Rosa CA
Azar, John, *Philosophy,* Henry Ford Community College, McKenzie Fine Art Ctr, Dearborn MI (S)
Azzaria, Georges, *Dir,* L'Universite Laval, Ecole des Arts Visuels, Quebec QC
Baba, Ronald, *Assoc Prof,* University of Wisconsin-Green Bay, Arts Dept, Green Bay WI (S)
Babb, Pamela, *Exec Dir,* Children's Art Carnival, New York NY
Babbitt, Steve, *Prof,* Black Hills State University, Art Dept, Spearfish SD (S)
Babcock, David, *Assoc Prof,* University of Central Missouri, Dept of Art & Design, Warrensburg MO (S)
Babcock, Ryan, *Asst Lectr,* Idaho State University, Dept of Art, Pocatello ID (S)
Babcock, Ryan, *Dir Gallery,* Idaho State University, John B Davis Gallery of Fine Art, Pocatello ID
Babcock, Sidney, *Cur & Dept Head Seals & Tablets,* The Morgan Library & Museum, Museum, New York NY
Babcox, Wendy, *Assoc Prof,* University of South Florida, School of Art & Art History, Tampa FL (S)
Baber, Larry, *Treas,* American Numismatic Association, Edward C. Rochette Money Museum, Colorado Springs CO
Babila, Susan, *Prog Coordr,* Edna Hibel Art Foundation, Hibel Museum of Art, Jupiter FL
Baboula, Evanthia, *Assoc Dean,* University of Victoria, Faculty of Arts, Victoria BC (S)
Baca, Judith F, *Artistic Dir,* Social & Public Art Resource Center, (SPARC), Venice CA
Bacchus, Lauren, *Mus Shop,* Asheville Art Museum, Asheville NC
Bach, Beverly, *Museum Registrar,* Miami University, Art Museum, Oxford OH
Bach, Penny Balkin, *Exec Dir,* Association for Public Art, Philadelphia PA
Bachman, Dona, *Dir,* Southern Illinois University Carbondale, University Museum, Carbondale IL
Bachman, Donna N, *Chmn,* Park University, Dept of Art & Design, Parkville MO (S)
Bachmeier, Brad, *Asst Prof,* Minnesota State University-Moorhead, Dept of Art & Design, Moorhead MN (S)
Backlund, Leslie, *Instr & Board of Dirs & Co-Pres,* Guild of Creative Art, Shrewsbury NJ (S)
Backus, Irene, *Asst Prof,* Oklahoma State University, Department of Art, Graphic Design and Art History, Stillwater OK (S)
Backus, Josephine, *Curatorial & Facilities Asst,* Boise Art Museum, Boise ID
Bacon, Larry, *Mem,* Newport Art Museum and Association, Newport RI
Bacon, Mardges, *Prof,* Northeastern University, Dept of Art & Architecture, Boston MA (S)
Bacot, Parrott, *Asst Prof,* Louisiana State University, School of Art, Baton Rouge LA (S)
Baczkowski, Steve, *Music Dir,* Hallwalls Contemporary Arts Center, Buffalo NY
Badder, Susan, *Cur Educ,* Corcoran Gallery of Art, Washington DC
Badeaux, Brynne, *Deputy Dir,* North Fourth Art Center & Gallery, Albuquerque NM
Badel, Julio, *Admin Asst,* San Francisco Museum of Modern Art, Artist Gallery, San Francisco CA
Bader, Emily, *Dir,* Springfield City Library, Springfield MA
Bader, Jason, *Dept Chair,* Mt San Jacinto College, Art Dept, San Jacinto CA (S)
Badgett, Barry, *Interim Dir,* Wichita State University, School of Art & Design, Wichita KS (S)
Badham, Aaron, *Prof,* Hastings College, Department of Visual Arts, Hastings NE (S)
Badoud, Jamie, *Exec Dir,* Hambidge Center for Creative Arts & Sciences, Rabun Gap GA
Badran, Nadine, *Mgr Pub Progs,* Canadian Clay and Glass Gallery, Waterloo ON
Badt, Pat, *Prof,* Cedar Crest College, Art Dept, Allentown PA (S)
Bae, Jaehan, *Asst Prof,* University of Wisconsin Oshkosh, Dept of Art, Oshkosh WI (S)
Bae, Justine, *Mus Coordr,* The Pomona College, Claremont CA
Bae, Min, *Prof, Film & Media Arts,* University of Windsor, School of Creative Arts, Windsor ON (S)
Baer, Mark, *Exec Dir,* Monterey History & Art Association, Maritime Museum of Monterey, Monterey CA
Baerg, Rachel, *Head Educ,* The Winnipeg Art Gallery, Winnipeg MB
Baerman, Brooke, *Mgr Curatorial Services,* Lowell Art Association, Inc, Whistler House Museum of Art, Lowell MA
Bafford, Rebecca, *Art Dir,* Howard Community College, The Rouse Company Foundation Gallery, Columbia MD
Baganz, Bruce P, *Co-Chair,* George Washington University, The George Washington Museum and The Textile Museum, Washington DC
Baggett, Lynne, *Asst,* Louisiana State University, School of Art, Baton Rouge LA (S)
Baggs, Stephanie Robison, *Instr,* Marylhurst University, Art Dept, Marylhurst OR (S)
Bagley, Cricket, *Admin Secy,* Jekyll Island Museum, Jekyll Island GA
Bagnall, Mindi, *Registrar,* Western Michigan University Gwen Frostic School of Art, Richmond Center for Visual Arts, Kalamazoo MI
Bagnatori, Paola, *Mng Dir,* Museo Italo Americano, San Francisco CA
Bah, Macky, *Treas,* YMI Cultural Center, Asheville NC
Bahe, Norman, *Educ Cur,* Navajo Nation, Navajo Nation Museum, Window Rock AZ
Bahr, David, *Assoc Prof,* Baltimore City Community College, Dept of Fine Arts, Baltimore MD (S)
Bahrin, Adliana, *Prog & Web Mgr,* Asian American Arts Centre, New York NY
Bahus, Jen, *Dir Mktg,* North Carolina Museum of Art, Raleigh NC
Baie, Sarah Kate, *Dir Programming & Chief of Fictions,* Museum of Contemporary Art Denver, Denver CO
Bailey Cox, Andrea, *CEO,* Art and History Museums - Maitland, Maitland Art Center, Maitland FL
Bailey, Barry, *Prof,* Tulane University, Sophie H Newcomb Memorial College, New Orleans LA (S)
Bailey, Carol, *Instr,* Midland College, Art Dept, Midland TX (S)
Bailey, Dan, *Prof & Dir Imaging Research Ctr,* University of Maryland, Baltimore County, Intermedia & Digital Arts (IMDA), Dept of Visual Arts, Baltimore MD (S)
Bailey, David, *Cur History,* Museum of Western Colorado, Museum of the West, Grand Junction CO
Bailey, Elizabeth, *Dept Head,* Virginia Western Community College, Communication Design, Fine Art & Photography, Roanoke VA (S)
Bailey, Hilton, *Archivist,* Caramoor Center for Music & the Arts, Inc, Rosen House at Caramoor, Katonah NY
Bailey, James, *Prof,* University of Montana, School of Art, Missoula MT (S)
Bailey, Jeff, *Art Instr,* Burlington County College, Humanities & Fine Art Div, Pemberton NJ (S)
Bailey, Jeff, *Reference Librn,* Arkansas State University-Art Department, Jonesboro, Library, Jonesboro AR

Bailey, Laura W, *Exec Asst to Boards,* Jamestown-Yorktown Foundation, Jamestown Settlement, Williamsburg VA
Bailey, Lebe, *Asst Prof,* Wesleyan College, Art Dept, Macon GA (S)
Bailey, Lisbit, *Supervisory Archivist,* San Francisco Maritime National Historical Park, Maritime Museum, San Francisco CA
Bailey, Radcliffe, *Asst Prof Drawing & Painting,* University of Georgia, Franklin College of Arts & Sciences, Lamar Dodd School of Art, Athens GA (S)
Bailey, Rebecca, *Chmn,* Meredith College, Art Dept, Raleigh NC (S)
Bailey, Scott, *Prof,* Wenatchee Valley College, Art Dept, Wenatchee WA (S)
Bailey, Shannon, *Dir,* Stephen F Austin State University, SFA Galleries, Nacogdoches TX
Baillargeon, Annie, *Pres,* VU Centre De Diffusion Et De Production De La Photographie, Quebec QC
Baillargeon, Claude, *Assoc Prof,* Oakland University, Dept of Art & Art History, Rochester MI (S)
Baines, Lauren, *Coordr Family Progs & Outreach,* Palo Alto Art Center, Palo Alto CA
Bains, Sneh, *Library Dir,* Bayonne Free Public Library, Cultural Center, Bayonne NJ
Baird, Jill, *Cur of Educ & Pub Prog,* University of British Columbia, Museum of Anthropology, Vancouver BC
Baird, Lily, *Librn,* Kirkland Museum of Fine & Decorative Art, Denver CO
Baird, M Duncan, *Asst Prof,* Delta State University, Dept of Art, Cleveland MS (S)
Baird, Nancy, *KY Spec,* Western Kentucky University, Kentucky Library & Museum, Bowling Green KY
Bajko, Daria, *Admin Dir,* The Ukrainian Museum, New York NY
Bak, Susan K, *Sr Dir Mktg & Retail Opers,* Jamestown-Yorktown Foundation, Jamestown Settlement, Williamsburg VA
Baker Horsey, Ann, *Cur Coll,* Delaware Division of Historical & Cultural Affairs, Dover DE
Baker Prindle, Paul, *Dir, Univ Galleries,* University of Nevada, Reno, Sheppard Contemporary & University Galleries, Reno NV
Baker, Aaron, *Cur & Bus Develop Dir,* Playboy Enterprises, Inc, Beverly Hills CA
Baker, Alyson, *Dir,* Aldrich Museum of Contemporary Art, Ridgefield CT
Baker, Barry B, *Dir,* University of Central Florida Libraries, Orlando FL
Baker, Bernard, *Prof Emeritus,* California State University, Dominguez Hills, Art & Design Dept, Carson CA (S)
Baker, Bob, *Dir,* Art Community Center, Art Center of Corpus Christi, Corpus Christi TX
Baker, Cindy, *Program Coordr,* AKA Artist Run Centre, Library, Saskatoon SK
Baker, Damika, *Director of Advancement,* Academy Art Museum, Easton MD
Baker, David R, *Instr,* Southwestern Michigan College, Fine & Performing Arts Dept, Dowagiac MI (S)
Baker, David, *Pres,* Canton Museum of Art, Canton OH
Baker, Donna, *Bd Mbr,* Valley Art Center Inc, Clarkston WA
Baker, Doug, *Adjunct Prof Fine Art,* Johnson County Community College, Fine Arts Dept & Art History Dept, Overland Park KS (S)
Baker, Gary, *Prof,* Polk Community College, Art, Letters & Social Sciences, Winter Haven FL (S)
Baker, Gretchen, *VPres Exhibitions,* Natural History Museum of Los Angeles County, Los Angeles CA
Baker, Helen, *Adminr,* University of Michigan, Kelsey Museum of Archaeology, Ann Arbor MI
Baker, James, *Exec Dir,* Pilchuck Glass School, Stanwood WA (S)
Baker, James, *Prof,* Providence College, Art & Art History Dept, Providence RI (S)
Baker, Janet, *Cur Asian Art,* Phoenix Art Museum, Phoenix AZ
Baker, Joanna, *Head Coll Mgmnt, Visitor Svcs & Pvt Events,* The Kreeger Museum, Washington DC
Baker, Joe, *Exec Dir,* Palos Verdes Art Center/Beverly G. Alpay Center for Arts Education, Rancho Palos Verdes CA
Baker, Judith, *Prof,* University of Wisconsin College - Marinette, Art Dept, Marinette WI (S)
Baker, Katie, *Exhib Coordr,* Manifest Gallery, Cincinnati OH
Baker, Kendall, *Dir,* Caldwell College, The Visceglia Art Gallery, Caldwell NJ
Baker, Kendall, *Prof,* Caldwell College, Dept of Fine Arts, Caldwell NJ (S)
Baker, Kevin, *Studio Mgr,* Noyes Art Gallery, Lincoln NE
Baker, Kim, *Project Mgr,* United States General Services Administration, Art in Architecture and Fine Arts, Washington DC
Baker, Malcolm, *Prof,* University of California, Riverside, Dept of the History of Art, Riverside CA (S)
Baker, Malissa Kay, *Admin Asst,* Art Community Center, Art Center of Corpus Christi, Corpus Christi TX
Baker, Mark, *Preparator,* Cranbrook Art Museum, Bloomfield Hills MI
Baker, Michael, *Director,* Almond Historical Society, Inc, Hagadorn House, The 1800-37 Museum, Almond NY
Baker, Nash, *Photographer,* Rice University, Rice Gallery, Houston TX
Baker, Ray, *Dir,* Miami-Dade Public Library, Miami FL
Baker, Richard, *Conservation Specialist,* Tryon Palace, Library & Museum, New Bern NC
Baker, Sarah, *Cur Asst,* Denison University, Art Gallery, Granville OH
Baker, Scott, *Asst Dir,* Howard University, Gallery of Art, Washington DC
Baker, Sharon, *Pub Servs Asst,* Lutheran Theological Seminary, Krauth Memorial Library, Philadelphia PA
Baker, Wendy, *Exec Dir,* California State University, Los Angeles, Luckman Gallery, Los Angeles CA
Bakke, Buck, *Information Technology,* Menil Foundation, Inc, The Menil Collection, Houston TX
Bakken, Mike, *Dir Comm Sch Arts,* Mayville State University, Northern Lights Art Gallery, Mayville ND
Bakker, Conrad, *Asst Dir Grad Studies, Assoc Prof,* University of Illinois, Urbana-Champaign, School of Art & Design, Champaign IL (S)
Bakkom, Matthew, *Asst Prof,* University of Wisconsin, Madison, Dept of Art, Madison WI (S)
Bakos, Stephanie, *Dir,* Berkeley Heights Free Public Library, Berkeley Heights NJ
Balachandran, Sanchita, *Cur & Conservator,* Johns Hopkins University, Archaeological Museum, Baltimore MD
Balakier, Ann, *Assoc Prof,* University of South Dakota, Department of Art, College of Fine Arts, Vermillion SD (S)
Balboni, Kathleen, *Coordr Finance Servs,* College of Central Florida, Appleton Museum of Art, Ocala FL
Balch, Inge, *Prof Art,* Baker University, Dept of Mass Media & Visual Arts, Baldwin City KS (S)
Baldaia, Peter J, *Curatorial Affairs Dir,* Huntsville Museum of Art, Reference Library, Huntsville AL
Baldaia, Peter J, *Dir Cur Affairs,* Huntsville Museum of Art, Huntsville AL
Baldassano, Alison, *Museum Asst,* Jacques Marchais Museum of Tibetan Art, Staten Island NY
Balderson, Patricia, *Mgr Mus Educ,* Colonial Williamsburg Foundation, Abby Aldrich Rockefeller Folk Art Museum, Williamsburg VA
Baldi, Marilyn, *Board of Dirs & VPres,* Guild of Creative Art, Shrewsbury NJ (S)
Baldini, Don, *Deputy Dir,* The New York Public Library, The New York Public Library for the Performing Arts, New York NY
Baldino, Patt, *Treas,* Catharine Lorillard Wolfe, New York NY
Baldissera, Lisa, *Sr Cur,* Contemporary Calgary, Calgary AB
Baldonieri, Amy, *Dir Develop & Finance,* Westmoreland Museum of American Art, Art Reference Library, Greensburg PA
Baldridge, Mark, *Prof,* Longwood University, Dept of Art, Farmville VA (S)
Balducci, Francis J, *Rec Secy,* Baldwin Historical Society Museum, Baldwin NY
Baldus, Jeff, *Lectr,* Briar Cliff University, Art Dept, Sioux City IA (S)
Baldwin, Adam, *Dir Community Partnerships & Outreach,* Anchorage Museum at Rasmuson Center, Anchorage AK
Baldwin, Fred, *Chmn & Co-Founder,* Foto Fest International, Houston TX
Baldwin, Guy, *Assoc Prof,* University of Minnesota, Minneapolis, Dept of Art, Minneapolis MN (S)
Baldwin, K Read, *Assoc Prof,* Kenyon College, Art Dept, Gambier OH (S)
Baldwin, Lauren, *Dir Educ,* Mary R Koch Arts Center, Mark Arts, Wichita KS
Baldwin, Tom, *Instr,* Cuyahoga Valley Art Center, Cuyahoga Falls OH (S)
Bale, Andrew, *Adjunct Faculty,* Dickinson College, Dept of Art & Art History, Carlisle PA (S)
Balenovic, Tay, *Events Coordr,* New Mexico Department of Cultural Affairs, Palace of Governors, Santa Fe NM
Balestrieri Kohn, Beret, *Audio Visual Librn,* Milwaukee Art Museum, George Peckham Miller Art Research Library, Milwaukee WI
Baley, Susan, *Exec Dir & Cur Exhibs,* Swope Art Museum, Terre Haute IN
Balfour, Alan, *Dean,* Rensselaer Polytechnic Institute, School of Architecture, Troy NY (S)
Balint, Valerie, *Assoc Cur,* Olana State Historic Site, Hudson NY
Balint, Valerie, *Cur,* Olana State Historic Site, Library, Hudson NY
Balise, Sett, *Technical Dir,* Davistown Museum, Liberty Location, Liberty ME
Baljon, Caroline, *Asst Dir,* Bowdoin College, Museum of Art, Brunswick ME
Balk, Moon-he, *Assoc Prof,* University of Louisville, Allen R Hite Art Institute, Louisville KY (S)
Balkin, Ellen, *Educ,* Ogden Museum of Southern Art, University of New Orleans, New Orleans LA
Ball, Amanda, *Dir Pub Rels,* The National Quilt Museum, Paducah KY
Ball, Deena, *Instr,* Wayne Art Center, Wayne PA (S)
Ball, Fiona, *Asst Dir,* LACE (Los Angeles Contemporary Exhibitions), Los Angeles CA
Ball, Heather, *Librn,* Virginia Polytechnic Institute & State University, Art & Architecture Library, Blacksburg VA
Ball, Helena, *Exec Dir,* Homer Watson, Kitchener ON
Ball, Hiram, *Treas,* National Sculpture Society, New York NY
Ball, Isabel, *Dean,* Our Lady of the Lake University, Dept of Art, San Antonio TX (S)
Ball, Jeffrey, *Assoc Prof Art,* Harford Community College, Visual, Performing and Applied Arts Division, Bel Air MD (S)
Ball, Jennifer, *Prof,* City University of New York, PhD Program in Art History, New York NY (S)
Ball, Larry, *Prof,* University of Wisconsin-Stevens Point, Dept of Art & Design, Stevens Point WI (S)
Ball, Melissa, *Pub Progs Mgr,* Hermitage Museum & Gardens, Museum, Norfolk VA
Ball, Stefanie, *Public Relations Mgr,* Amon Carter Museum of American Art, Fort Worth TX
Ball, Susan, *Deputy Dir,* Bruce Museum, Inc, Greenwich CT
Balla, Wesley, *Dir Coll & Exhibs,* New Hampshire Historical Society, New Hampshire Historical Society Museum, Concord NH
Balla, Wesley, *Dir Colls & Exhibs,* New Hampshire Historical Society, New Hampshire Historical Society Library, Concord NH
Ballangee-Morris, Christine, *Asst Prof,* Ohio State University, Dept of Art Education, Columbus OH (S)

Ballard, Helen, *Visitors Svcs,* Lightner Museum, Saint Augustine FL
Ballard, Jan, *Archivist,* Lehigh Valley Heritage Center, Allentown PA
Ballard, Jan, *Librn & Archivist,* Lehigh Valley Heritage Center, Scott Andrew Trexler II Library, Allentown PA
Ballard, Rachel, *Project Coordr,* City of Atlanta, Chastain Arts Center & Gallery, Atlanta GA
Ballard-Ryan, Kitty, *Gallery Attendant,* Carl & Marilynn Thoma Art Foundation, Art House Santa Fe, Santa Fe NM
Ballew Neff, Emily, *Dir,* Memphis Brooks Museum of Art, Memphis TN
Ballew Neff, Emily, *Executive Director,* Memphis Brooks Museum of Art, Library, Memphis TN
Balli, Cristina, *Exec Dir,* Guadalupe Cultural Arts Center, San Antonio TX
Ballinger, Patricia, *Gallery Dir,* University of Texas Pan American, Charles & Dorothy Clark Gallery; University Gallery, Edinburg TX
Ballinger, Patricia, *Gallery Dir,* University of Texas Pan American, UTPA Art Galleries, Edinburg TX
Ballou, Matthew, *Asst Tchg Prof,* University of Missouri - Columbia, Dept of Art, Columbia MO (S)
Baloyra, Bibi, *Exec Dir,* Bakehouse Art Complex, Inc, Miami FL
Balter, Renee, *Secy, Treas,* Martha's Vineyard Center for the Visual Arts, Oak Bluffs MA
Baltmanis, George, *Dir Finance & Personnel,* Kalamazoo Institute of Arts, The Mary & Edwin Meader Fine Arts Library, Kalamazoo MI
Baltmanis, George, *Dir Finance & Personnel,* Kalamazoo Institute of Arts, Kalamazoo MI
Baltrushunas, John, *Assoc Prof Art & Prog Dir Studio Art,* Maryville University of Saint Louis, Art & Design Program, Saint Louis MO (S)
Baltrushunas, John, *Gallery Dir,* Maryville University Saint Louis, Morton J May Foundation Gallery, Saint Louis MO
Balzekas, Robert A, *Librn,* Balzekas Museum of Lithuanian Culture, Research Library, Chicago IL
Balzekas, Robert, *Dir Genealogy Dept,* Balzekas Museum of Lithuanian Culture, Chicago IL
Balzekas, Stanley, *Exec Dir & Pres,* Balzekas Museum of Lithuanian Culture, Chicago IL
Balzekas, Stanley, *Pres,* Balzekas Museum of Lithuanian Culture, Research Library, Chicago IL
Balzer, David, *Ed-in-Chf & Co-Publr,* Canadian Art Foundation, Toronto ON
Bambo-Kocze, Peter, *Bibliographer,* Corning Museum of Glass, Juliette K and Leonard S Rakow Research Library, Corning NY
Bamburak, Michele, *Media Arts & Animation,* Art Institute of Pittsburgh, Pittsburgh PA (S)
Bambury, Jill, *Instr,* Southern University A & M College, School of Architecture, Baton Rouge LA (S)
Banasiak, John, *Prof,* University of South Dakota, Department of Art, College of Fine Arts, Vermillion SD (S)
Bancroft, Alex, *Pres,* Mystic Art Association, Inc, Mystic Museum of Art, Mystic CT
Bancroft, Katherine, *Dir Educ, Coll & Exhibs,* Port Huron Museum, Port Huron MI
Bancroft, Sarah, *Cur,* Orange County Museum of Art, Newport Beach CA
Banduric, Pamela, *Instr Interior Design,* Henry Ford Community College, McKenzie Fine Art Ctr, Dearborn MI (S)
Banerji, Naseem, *Asst Prof,* Weber State University, Dept of Visual Arts, Ogden UT (S)
Bang, Peggy, *Adjunct Emer,* North Iowa Area Community College, Dept of Art, Mason City IA (S)
Bangert, Shaun, *Asst Prof,* Saginaw Valley State University, Dept of Art & Design, University Center MI (S)
Banister, Kim, *Cur,* Rose Lehrman Art Gallery, Harrisburg PA
Bank, Larissa, *Instr,* Pierce College, Art Dept, Woodland Hills CA (S)
Banker, Cindy, *Director,* Almond Historical Society, Inc, Hagadorn House, The 1800-37 Museum, Almond NY
Bankerd, Carol, *Assoc Prof,* Purchase College, State University of New York, School of Art+Design, Purchase NY (S)
Banko, Bernadette, *Dir Develop,* Edsel & Eleanor Ford House, Grosse Pointe Shores MI
Banks Sutherland, Nora, *Develop Mgr,* Association for Public Art, Philadelphia PA
Banks, Blair, *Educ Coordr,* Atlanta International Museum of Art & Design, Museum of Design Atlanta, Atlanta GA
Banks, Carol, *Mgr,* Edgecombe County Cultural Arts Council, Inc, Blount-Bridgers House, Hobson Pittman Memorial Gallery, Tarboro NC
Bannard, Darby, *Prof,* University of Miami, Dept of Art & Art History, Coral Gables FL (S)
Bannon, Anthony L, *Exec Dir,* Burchfield Penney Art Center, Buffalo NY
Bannon, Anthony, *Exec Dir,* Burchfield Penney Art Center, Library, Buffalo NY
Bannon, Brian, *Commissioner,* Chicago Public Library, Harold Washington Library Center, Chicago IL
Bannos, Pamela, *Lectr,* Northwestern University, Evanston, Dept of Art Theory & Practice, Evanston IL (S)
Banocy-Payne, Marge, *Dean,* Tallahassee Community College, Art Dept, Tallahassee FL (S)
Banta, Andaleeb, *Cur American & European Art,* Oberlin College, Allen Memorial Art Museum, Oberlin OH
Banta, Andaleeb, *Sr Cur Prints, Drawings and Photographs,* The Baltimore Museum of Art, Baltimore MD
Bantens, Robert, *Art Historian,* University of South Alabama, Dept of Art & Art History, Mobile AL (S)
Banz, Martha, *Dean Arts & Sciences,* Southern Nazarene University, Art & Design Department, Bethany OK (S)
Bao, Li-ying, *Prof Art & Design,* University of Wisconsin-Eau Claire, Dept of Art & Design, Eau Claire WI (S)
Barajas, Ana, *Dir,* YYZ Artists' Outlet, Toronto ON
Baral, Jody, *Chmn & Prof,* Mount Saint Mary's College, Art Dept, Los Angeles CA (S)
Baral, Jody, *Gallery Dir,* Mount Saint Mary's College, Jose-Drudis-Biada Art Gallery, Los Angeles CA
Barant, Jim, *Documentary Art & Photo Acquisition,* National Archives of Canada, Art & Photography Archives, Ottawa ON
Baratta, Jill, *Pres,* National Association of Women Artists, Inc, NAWA Gallery, New York NY
Baratto, Brenda, *Dir,* Aiken County Historical Museum, Aiken SC
Barba, Melissa, *Asst Dir,* University of Texas at El Paso, Stanlee & Gerald Rubin Center for the Visual Arts, El Paso TX
Barbash, Yekaterina, *Assoc Cur Egyptian Art,* Brooklyn Museum, Brooklyn NY
Barbee, Rebecca, *Operations Mgr,* Palo Alto Art Center, Palo Alto CA
Barber, Heather, *Mus Shop Mgr,* Nevada Northern Railway Museum, Ely NV
Barber, Lisa, *Asst Prof,* University of Wisconsin-Parkside, Art Dept, Kenosha WI (S)
Barber, Peter, *Board Pres,* Landis Valley Village and Farm Museum, PA Historical & Museum Commission, Lancaster PA
Barber, Rehema, *Dir & Chief Cur,* Eastern Illinois University, Tarble Arts Center, Charleston IL
Barber, Robbie, *Assoc Prof,* Baylor University - College of Arts and Sciences, Dept of Art, Waco TX (S)
Barber, Tom, *Secy,* Huronia Museum, Gallery of Historic Huronia, Midland ON
Barbieri, Frances J, *Educ Dir,* Seneca Falls Historical Society Museum, Seneca Falls NY
Barbour, Cody, *Assoc Coordr Mus Experience,* The Metropolitan Museum of Art, The Met Breuer, New York NY
Barcellona Kidd, Nina, *Advertising, Exhibs & Design,* Society for Photographic Education (SPE), SPE Gallery, Cleveland OH
Barclay, Neil A, *Dir & CEI,* Contemporary Arts Center, New Orleans LA
Barclay, Stacy, *Visual Resources Cur,* San Jose State University, Dr. Martin Luther King Jr. Library, San Jose CA
Bard, Sue, *Pres,* Beaumont Art League, Beaumont TX
Bardhan, Gail, *Reference Librn,* Corning Museum of Glass, Juliette K and Leonard S Rakow Research Library, Corning NY
Bardi, Gina, *Reference,* San Francisco Maritime National Historical Park, Maritime Library, San Francisco CA
Bardolph, Paige, *Asst Cur,* Autry National Center, Southwest Museum of the American Indian, Mt. Washington Campus, Los Angeles CA
Bareis, Arbe, *Instr,* Kirkwood Community College, Dept of Arts & Humanities, Cedar Rapids IA (S)
Barello, Julia, *Assoc Prof,* New Mexico State University, Art Dept, Las Cruces NM (S)
Barhaug, Shirley, *Pres,* Cody Country Art League, Cody WY
Barilleaux, Rene Paul, *Deputy Dir Prog,* Mississippi Museum of Art, Howorth Library, Jackson MS
Barilleaux, Rene Paul, *Head Cur Affairs,* McNay Art Museum, San Antonio TX
Barke, Rande, *Artist,* Walker's Point Artists Assoc Inc, Gallery 218, Milwaukee WI
Barkee, Ken, *Co-Pres,* Klamath Art Association, Klamath Falls OR
Barker, Alex, *Dir,* University of Missouri, Museum of Art & Archaeology, Columbia MO
Barker, Angela, *Reg & Cur Permanent Coll,* California State University, Long Beach, University Art Museum, Long Beach CA
Barker, Anne, *Music,* University of Missouri, Art, Archaeology & Music Collection, Columbia MO
Barker, Bill, *Asst Archivist,* The Mariners' Museum, Library, Newport News VA
Barker, Elaine, *Pres Elect,* Arts Council of Greater Kingsport, Renaissance Center Main Gallery, Kingsport TN
Barker, Elizabeth, *Stanford Calderwood Dir,* Boston Athenaeum, Boston MA
Barker, Gloria, *Co-Founder,* Barker Character, Comic and Cartoon Museum, Cheshire CT
Barker, Herbert, *Co-Founder,* Barker Character, Comic and Cartoon Museum, Cheshire CT
Barker, James, *Pres,* Clemson University, College of Architecture, Arts & Humanities, Art Dept, Clemson SC (S)
Barker, Jimmy, *Prof,* Sam Houston State University, Art Dept, Huntsville TX (S)
Barker, Kandis, *Cur Educ,* Washburn University, Mulvane Art Museum, Topeka KS
Barker, Katherine, *Field Svcs Dir,* Textile Conservation Workshop Inc, South Salem NY
Barker, Keith, *Art Dept Chair, Instr,* Asbury University, Art Dept, Wilmore KY (S)
Barker, Keith, *Photography & Graphic Arts, Dept Chair,* Asbury College, Student Center Gallery, Wilmore KY
Barker, Lance, *Adjunct,* Feather River Community College, Art Dept, Quincy CA (S)
Barker, Marcia, *VPres,* Goshen Historical Society, Goshen CT
Barker, Norman, *Assoc Prof,* Johns Hopkins University, School of Medicine, Dept of Art as Applied to Medicine, Baltimore MD (S)
Barkley, Jack, *Events Coordr,* Longview Museum of Fine Art, Longview TX
Barkley, Tim, *Registrar,* Contemporary Arts Museum Houston, Houston TX
Barleben, Christa, *Registrar,* Eiteljorg Museum of American Indians & Western Art, Indianapolis IN
Barletta, Barbara, *Prof,* University of Florida, School of Art & Art History, Gainesville FL (S)
Barley, Gerlinde, *Coll Develop,* State University of New York at New Paltz, Sojourner Truth Library, New Paltz NY

Barlow Smedstad, Deborah, *Head Librn,* Museum of Fine Arts, William Morris Hunt Memorial Library, Boston MA

Barlow, Christy, *Community Programs Coordinator,* The Columbus Museum, Columbus GA

Barlow, Debra, *Chair,* Dartmouth Heritage Museum, Dartmouth NS

Barna, Ginger, *Head Librn,* Leo Baeck, Library, New York NY

Barnaby, Martine, *Asst Prof,* State University of New York, College at Cortland, Dept Art & Art History, Cortland NY (S)

Barnard, Anne-Marie, *Dir Communs, Mktg & Foundation,* Musee d'art Contemporain de Montreal, Montreal QC

Barnard, Kathy, *Pres,* The Stained Glass Association of America, Raytown MO

Barnard, Katie, *Cur Educ,* Westmoreland Museum of American Art, Art Reference Library, Greensburg PA

Barnard, Megan, *Assoc Dir,* University of Texas at Austin, Harry Ransom Humanities Research Center, Austin TX

Barnard, Melissa, *Dir,* Grace A Dow, Fine Arts Dept, Midland MI

Barner, David L, *Chmn,* Westminster College, Art Dept, New Wilmington PA (S)

Barnes, Bernadine, *Prof,* Wake Forest University, Dept of Art, Winston-Salem NC (S)

Barnes, Bruce, *Dir,* George Eastman Museum, Rochester NY

Barnes, Gail, *Assoc Adminr,* Presidential Museum & Leadership Library, Odessa TX

Barnes, Imani, *Guest Servs Coordr,* Green Hill Center for North Carolina Art, Greenhill, Greensboro NC

Barnes, James, *Gallery Dir,* Rhode Island School of Design, Bayard Ewing Building Gallery, Providence RI

Barnes, Jonathan, *Dept Chmn,* Saint Petersburg College, Fine & Applied Arts at Clearwater Campus, Clearwater FL (S)

Barnes, Laurie, *Cur Chinese Art,* Norton Museum of Art, West Palm Beach FL

Barnes, Raymond S, *Asst Prof,* Muhlenberg College, Dept of Art, Allentown PA (S)

Barnes, Reinaldo, *Mgr,* Longfellow-Evangeline State Commemorative Area, Saint Martinville LA

Barnes, Ruth, *Cur Indo-Pacific Art,* Yale University, Yale University Art Gallery, New Haven CT

Barnes, Sharron, *Assoc Prof,* Gulf Coast Community College, Division of Visual & Performing Arts, Panama City FL (S)

Barnes, Ted, *Dean,* University of Mary Hardin-Baylor, College of Visual & Performing Arts, Belton TX (S)

Barnes, William, *Assoc Prof,* College of William & Mary, Dept of Fine Arts, Williamsburg VA (S)

Barnes, William, *Prof,* University of St Thomas, Deptartment of Art History, Saint Paul MN (S)

Barnett, Cheryl, *Prof 3-D Prog,* Merced College, Arts Division, Merced CA (S)

Barnett, Erin, *Dir Exhibs & Colls,* International Center of Photography, Museum, New York NY

Barnett, John, *Prof,* California State University, Art Dept, Turlock CA (S)

Barnett, Loretta, *Prof,* Colby-Sawyer College, Dept of Fine & Performing Arts, New London NH (S)

Barnett, Mary, *Mus Store Mgr,* City of High Point, High Point Museum, High Point NC

Barnett, Philip, *Reference Librn,* City College of the City University of New York, Morris Raphael Cohen Library, New York NY

Barnett, Redmond, *Cur Exhib,* State Capital Museum, Olympia WA

Barnett, Richard, *Prof,* College of Mount Saint Vincent, Fine Arts Dept, Riverdale NY (S)

Barnett, Susan, *Cur,* Erie Art Museum, Erie PA

Barney, Cheryl, *Sr Dir Human Resources,* Genesee Country Village & Museum, John L Wehle Art Gallery, Mumford NY

Barney, Emily, *Asst Cur,* Elmhurst Art Museum, Elmhurst IL

Barney, Sean, *Executive Director,* Five Civilized Tribes Museum, Muskogee OK

Barney, Win, *Cur,* Kanab Heritage Museum & Juniper Fine Arts Gallery, Kanab UT

Barnhart, Chris, *Design Dept Head,* Bob Jones University, School of Fine Arts, Div of Art & Design, Greenville SC (S)

Barnhart, Chris, *Instr,* Bob Jones University, School of Fine Arts, Div of Art & Design, Greenville SC (S)

Barnhart, Jeff, *Chief Mus Officer,* Omaha Children's Museum, Omaha NE

Barnhart, Tom, *Mem Chmn,* Blacksburg Regional Art Association, Blacksburg VA

Barnhill, Emily, *Dir Develop,* Virginia Museum of Contemporary Art, Virginia Beach VA

Barnow, Penny, *Develop Co-Exec Dir,* Boulder Museum of Contemporary Art, Boulder CO

Baroff, Deborah, *Cur Spec Coll,* Trust Authority, Research Library, Lawton OK

Baroff, Deborah, *Head Cur,* Trust Authority, Museum of the Great Plains, Lawton OK

Barolsky, Paul, *Prof,* University of Virginia, McIntire Dept of Art, Charlottesville VA (S)

Baron, Alice, *Catalog & Reference Librn,* Becker College, William F Ruska Library, Worcester MA

Baron, Meaghan, *VPres Communs & Public Affairs,* Municipal Art Society of New York, New York NY

Baron-Horn, Rachel, *Deputy Dir,* The Andy Warhol Museum, Pittsburgh PA

Baronne, Geriod, *Pres,* New Orleans Artworks at New Orleans Glassworks & Printmaking Studio, New Orleans LA

Baroody, Julie, *Art Coordr,* Tallahassee Community College, Art Dept, Tallahassee FL (S)

Barr, Anne Q, *Coordr,* Greenville County Museum of Art Center for Museum Education, Greenville SC (S)

Barr, Brian, *Dir Horticulture,* Hillwood Museum & Gardens Foundation, Hillwood Estate Museum & Gardens, Washington DC

Barr, Peter, *Assoc Prof Art History,* Siena Heights University, Studio Angelico-Art Dept, Adrian MI (S)

Barr, Peter, *Dir,* Siena Heights College, Klemm Gallery, Studio Angelico, Adrian MI

Barr, Zemie, *Exhibs Mgr,* Blue Sky Gallery, Oregon Center for the Photographic Arts, Portland OR

Barraclough, Dennis, *Assoc Prof,* Daemen College, Art Dept, Amherst NY (S)

Barraclough, Jeffrey, *Asst Exec Dir,* Manchester Historic Association, Millyard Museum, Manchester NH

Barraclough, Jeffrey, *Asst Exec Dir,* Manchester Historic Association, Library, Manchester NH

Barraza, Santa, *Chmn,* Texas A&M University-Kingsville, Art Dept, Kingsville TX (S)

Barraza, Santa, *Dir,* Texas A&M University, Art Gallery, Kingsville TX

Barre, Monica, *Security,* Ogden Museum of Southern Art, University of New Orleans, New Orleans LA

Barrera, Lisa Hsu, *Coll Mgr,* School for Advanced Research (SAR), Indian Arts Research Center, Santa Fe NM

Barrera, Tim, *Gallery Asst,* Pence Gallery, Davis CA

Barret, Heidi, *Opers Mgr,* Ascension Lutheran Church Library, Milwaukee WI

Barrett, Doug, *Asst Prof,* University of Alabama at Birmingham, Dept of Art & Art History, Birmingham AL (S)

Barrett, Justina, *Site Mgr Historic Houses,* Philadelphia Museum of Art, Mount Pleasant, Philadelphia PA

Barrett, Justina, *Site Mgr Historic Houses & Educ,* Philadelphia Museum of Art, Cedar Grove, Philadelphia PA

Barrett, Michael, *CEO & Gen Dir,* Caramoor Center for Music & the Arts, Inc, Rosen House at Caramoor, Katonah NY

Barrett, Ned, *Humanities Chmn,* Idyllwild Arts Academy, Idyllwild CA (S)

Barrett, Sue, *Bd Dir,* Monroe Arts Center, Monroe WI

Barrett, Terry, *Prof,* Ohio State University, Dept of Art Education, Columbus OH (S)

Barrett, Terry, *Prof Art Educ,* University of North Texas, College of Visual Arts & Design, Denton TX (S)

Barrick, William E, *Exec Dir,* Bellingrath Gardens & Home, Theodore AL

Barrie, Don, *Asst Prof,* Seattle Central Community College, Humanities - Social Sciences Division, Seattle WA (S)

Barringer, Tim, *Chmn & Dir Grad Studies,* Yale University, Dept of the History of Art, New Haven CT (S)

Barron, Robert, *Facilities Coordr,* Workman & Temple Family Homestead Museum, City of Industry CA

Barrow, Dennis, *Librn,* Fairfield Historical Society, Library, Fairfield CT

Barrow, Jake, *Tech Dir Ritz Theater,* Tennessee Valley Art Association, Tuscumbia AL

Barrow, Jane, *Head Painting,* Southern Illinois University at Edwardsville, Dept of Art & Design, Edwardsville IL (S)

Barrow, Lee, *Dept Head,* North Georgia College & State University, Fine Arts Dept, Dahlonega GA (S)

Barrow, VA, *Registrar,* Society of Scribes, Ltd, New York NY

Barrows, Jennifer, *Instr,* San Joaquin Delta College, Arts & Communication, Stockton CA (S)

Barrows, Scott, *Prog Coordr,* University of Illinois at Chicago, Biomedical Visualization, Chicago IL (S)

Barry, Alisa, *VPres Experience & Engagement,* Canadian Museum of Nature, Musee Canadien de la Nature, Ottawa ON

Barry, Bob, *Chmn,* Long Island University, Brooklyn Campus, Art Dept, Brooklyn NY (S)

Barry, Claire M, *Dir Conservation,* Kimbell Art Foundation, Kimbell Art Museum, Fort Worth TX

Barry, Jill, *Deputy Dir Develop,* Montgomery Museum of Fine Arts, Library, Montgomery AL

Barry, Jill, *Develop Officer,* Montgomery Museum of Fine Arts, Montgomery AL

Barry, Jill, *Exec Dir,* Morven Museum & Garden, Princeton NJ

Barry, Joseph, *VPres,* Historical Society of Bloomfield, Bloomfield NJ

Barry, Lynda, *Asst Prof,* University of Wisconsin, Madison, Dept of Art, Madison WI (S)

Barry, Sandra, *VPres Operations,* New Hampshire Institute of Art, Manchester NH

Barry, Tim, *Bldg Mgr,* Hot Shops Art Center, Omaha NE

Barry, William D, *Reference Historian,* Maine Historical Society, Library and Museum, Portland ME

Barsdate, Kelly J, *Chief Prog & Planning Officer,* National Assembly of State Arts Agencies, Washington DC

Barsness, Jim, *Asst Prof Drawing & Painting,* University of Georgia, Franklin College of Arts & Sciences, Lamar Dodd School of Art, Athens GA (S)

Bart, Lenny, *Exec Dir,* Quincy Society of Fine Arts, Quincy IL

Barta, David, *Technician,* California State University, Chico, Department of Art & Art History, Chico CA (S)

Barta, Joy, *Pres,* Independence Historical Museum & Art Center, Independence KS

Bartel, Tom, *Asst Prof,* Viterbo University, Art Dept, La Crosse WI (S)

Bartels, Kathleen, *Dir,* Vancouver Art Gallery, Vancouver BC

Bartelt, Bill, *Pres Bd Dir,* Evansville Museum of Arts, History & Science, Evansville IN

Bartelt, Deborah, *Instr,* Marian University, Art Dept, Fond Du Lac WI (S)

Barten, Julie, *Conservator Colls & Exhibs,* Solomon R Guggenheim Museum, New York NY

Bartenhagen, Lynn, *Office Coordr,* Muscatine Art Center, Muscatine IA

Barth, Charles, *Prof,* Mount Mercy University, Art Dept, Cedar Rapids IA (S)

Barth, Uta, *Prof,* University of California, Riverside, Dept of Art, Riverside CA (S)
Bartlett, Alex, *Librn & Archivist,* Germantown Historical Society, Philadelphia PA
Bartlett, Brian, *Dir Installations & Facilities,* Madison Museum of Contemporary Art, Madison WI
Bartlett, Carly, *Pres,* National Society of Mural Painters, Inc, New York NY
Bartlett, Noah, *Dir Opers, Facilities & Security,* San Francisco Museum of Modern Art, San Francisco CA
Bartlett, Selina, *Asst Registrar,* Oberlin College, Allen Memorial Art Museum, Oberlin OH
Bartling, Mary, *Instr,* Mount Mary College, Art & Design Division, Milwaukee WI (S)
Bartner, Howard C, *Assoc Prof,* Johns Hopkins University, School of Medicine, Dept of Art as Applied to Medicine, Baltimore MD (S)
Barton Miller, Michael, *Prof Studio Art,* California Polytechnic State University at San Luis Obispo, Dept of Art & Design, San Luis Obispo CA (S)
Barton, Althea, *Dir Outreach & Develop,* Kimball Jenkins Estate, Concord NH
Barton, Dave, *Finance Dir,* Dunedin Fine Art Center, Dunedin FL (S)
Barton, David, *Multimedia & Web Design,* Art Institute of Pittsburgh, Pittsburgh PA (S)
Barton, Diane, *Fin Secy,* Graphic Artists Guild, New York NY
Barton, Gary, *Assoc Chmn,* Brigham Young University, Dept of Visual Arts, Provo UT (S)
Barton, James, *Pres,* Johnson Atelier Technical Institute of Sculpture, Trenton NJ (S)
Barton, Jeni, *Dir Prog & Admin,* Pyramid Hill Sculpture Park & Museum, Hamilton OH
Barton, Kathryn, *Cur,* Yellowstone County Museum, Billings MT
Barton, Matt, *Asst Prof Visual Arts,* University of Colorado-Colorado Springs, Visual & Performing Arts Dept (VAPA), Colorado Springs CO (S)
Barton, Max, *Mktg Dir,* Canton Museum of Art, Art Library, Canton OH
Barton-Navitsky, Elizabeth, *Dir,* Marcella Sembrich Memorial Association Inc, Marcella Sembrich Opera Museum, Bolton Landing NY
Bartos, Armand, *Pres,* SculptureCenter, Long Island City NY
Barulich, Frances, *Cur Mary Flagler Cary Music Manuscripts & Dept Head,* The Morgan Library & Museum, Museum, New York NY
Barzman, Karen, *Assoc Prof,* Binghamton University, Art History Department, Binghamton NY (S)
Basbas, Sarah, *Branch Mgr,* Manchester City Library, Manchester NH
Basgall, Janet, *Office Asst,* Fort Hays State University, Forsyth Library, Hays KS
Basham, Kathleen, *COO,* Walters Art Museum, Baltimore MD
Bashkoff, Tracy, *Cur Colls & Exhibs,* Solomon R Guggenheim Museum, New York NY
Basic, Julie W, *Senior Develop Officer,* Jamestown-Yorktown Foundation, Jamestown Settlement, Williamsburg VA
Basil, John, *Asst Prof Theatre,* Marymount Manhattan College, Fine & Performing Arts Div, New York NY (S)
Basile, Jennifer, *Instr,* Miami-Dade Community College, Arts & Philosophy Dept, Miami FL (S)
Basinger, Amy, *Events Coordr,* Bob Jones University Museum & Gallery Inc, Greenville SC
Baskin, Gene, *Co-Dir,* Detroit Focus, Royal Oak MI
Baskin, Kenneth, *Assoc Prof,* McNeese State University, Dept of Visual Arts, Lake Charles LA (S)
Baskino, Samantha, *Prod,* Cleveland State University, Art Dept, Cleveland OH (S)
Baskins, Cristelle, *Assoc Prof,* Tufts University, Dept of Art & Art History, Medford MA (S)
Basmadjian, Terry, *Instr,* Saginaw Valley State University, Dept of Art & Design, University Center MI (S)
Bass, Clayton, *Pres & CEO,* Huntsville Museum of Art, Huntsville AL
Bass, Judy, *Prof,* Marymount University, School of Arts & Sciences Div, Arlington VA (S)
Bass, Marisa, *Dir Undergrad Studies,* Yale University, Dept of the History of Art, New Haven CT (S)
Bass, Ruth, *Chmn,* Bronx Community College, Music & Art Dept, Bronx NY (S)
Bassanese, Lynn, *Deputy Dir,* National Archives & Records Administration, Franklin D Roosevelt Library, Hyde Park NY
Basseches, Josh, *Dir & CEO,* Royal Ontario Museum, Toronto ON
Bassett, Joan, *Cur,* Nevada Northern Railway Museum, Ely NV
Bassett, Mark S, *CEO & Exec Dir,* Nevada Northern Railway Museum, Ely NV
Bassett, Ruth, *Librn,* Brandywine Conservancy, Library, Chadds Ford PA
Bassi, George, *Dir,* Lauren Rogers, Laurel MS
Bassolos, Arturo, *Art Dept Chmn,* Delaware State College, Dept of Art & Art Education, Dover DE (S)
Bassuk, Jane, *Instr,* North Hennepin Community College, Art Dept, Brooklyn Park MN (S)
Bastidas, Hugo, *MFA,* New Jersey City University, Art Dept, Jersey City NJ (S)
Bastos, Flavia, *Dir Art Educ Prog & Asst Prof Art Educ,* University of Cincinnati, School of Art, Cincinnati OH (S)
Basu, Chandreyi, *Assoc Prof,* St Lawrence University, Dept of Fine Arts, Canton NY (S)
Batchelor, Anthony, *Prof,* Art Academy of Cincinnati, Cincinnati OH (S)
Batchelor, Betsey, *Assoc Prof,* Arcadia University, Dept of Fine Arts, Glenside PA (S)
Batdorff, Jon, *Head,* Goddard College, Dept of Art, Plainfield VT (S)
Bateman, Edward, *Asst Prof,* University of Utah, Dept of Art & Art History, Salt Lake City UT (S)
Bater, John, *Area Head,* Kentucky State University, Jackson Hall Gallery, Frankfort KY
Bates, Bob, *Co-Founder & Artistic Dir,* Inner-City Arts, Los Angeles CA (S)
Bates, Evelyne, *Visitor & Vol Relations,* Lighthouse ArtCenter Museum & School of Art, Tequesta FL
Bates, Thomas, *Assoc Prof,* La Roche College, Division of Design, Pittsburgh PA (S)
Bates-McArthur, Rebecca, *Historian,* Cohasset Historical Society, Pratt Building (Society Headquarters), Cohasset MA
Bates-McArthur, Rebecca, *Historian,* Cohasset Historical Society, Cohasset Maritime Museum, Cohasset MA
Batey, Dorothy, *Asst Prof,* Clark-Atlanta University, School of Arts & Sciences, Atlanta GA (S)
Bath, Jon, *Asst Prof,* University of Saskatchewan, Art & Art History Dept, Saskatoon SK (S)
Batista, Kenneth, *Assoc Prof,* University of Pittsburgh, Dept of Studio Arts, Pittsburgh PA (S)
Batkin, Jonathan, *Dir,* Wheelwright Museum of the American Indian, Mary Cabot Wheelwright Research Library, Santa Fe NM
Batkin, Jonathan, *Dir,* Wheelwright Museum of the American Indian, Santa Fe NM
Batt, Ted, *Exhib Cur,* Academy of Fine Arts, Lynchburg VA
Battaglia, Steven, *Sr Opers Mgr,* Rubin Museum of Art, New York NY
Battis, Abby, *Exec Dir,* Rockport Art Association, Rockport MA
Battle, Kendra, *Visual Libr Tech,* Wake Forest University, A Lewis Aycock Visual Resource Library, Winston-Salem NC
Battle, Stephanie, *Coll Mgr,* Santa Clara University, de Saisset Museum, Santa Clara CA
Batzloff, Gary, *Asst Prof,* East Central University, School of Fine Arts, Ada OK (S)
Bauer, Jessica, *Officer Mgr & Program Coordr,* Paint Creek Center for the Arts, Rochester MI
Bauer, Marjorie, *Publications,* Historical Society of Rockland County, New City NY
Bauer, Marlene, *Instr,* Marylhurst University, Art Dept, Marylhurst OR (S)
Bauer, Sarah, *Assoc Prof,* University of Minnesota, Duluth, Art Dept, Duluth MN (S)
Baugh, Brian, *Asst Prof Art,* Monmouth College, Dept of Art, Monmouth IL (S)
Baugh, Chera, *Gallery Coordr,* Atlanta-Fulton Public Library, Central Library Art Gallery, Atlanta GA
Baugham, Matthew, *Instr Design,* AIC College of Design, Cincinnati OH (S)
Baulos, Doug, *Asst,* University of Alabama at Birmingham, Dept of Art & Art History, Birmingham AL (S)
Baum, Katy, *Sec,* Guild of Book Workers, New York NY
Bauman, Janet, *2nd VPres,* Salmagundi Club, New York NY
Bauman, Lisa, *Asst Prof,* George Mason University, College of Humanities & Social Sciences, Dept of History & Art History, Fairfax VA (S)
Baumann, Caroline, *Dir,* Cooper Hewitt, Smithsonian Design Museum, Smithsonian Institution, New York NY
Baumann, Richard, *Instr,* Columbia College, Art Dept, Columbia MO (S)
Baumann, Timothy, *Cur Archaeology,* University of Tennessee, McClung Museum of Natural History & Culture, Knoxville TN
Baume, Nicholas, *Dir & Chief Cur,* Public Art Fund, Inc, New York NY
Baume, Nicholas, *Dir & Chief Cur,* Public Art Fund, Inc, Visual Archive, New York NY
Baumgartner, Aretta, *Educ Progs,* Center for Puppetry Arts, Atlanta GA
Baumgartner, Nolan, *Instr,* University of Utah, Dept of Art & Art History, Salt Lake City UT (S)
Baumler, Christine Arle, *Asst Prof,* University of Minnesota, Minneapolis, Dept of Art, Minneapolis MN (S)
Baumler, Mark, *Preservation Officer,* Montana Historical Society, Helena MT
Bauske, Clay, *Mus Cur,* National Archives & Records Administration, Harry S Truman Museum and Library, Independence MO
Bautista, Preston, *Deputy Dir Public Progs & Audience Engagement,* Newfields, Indianapolis IN
Bavar, Ann, *Head Dept,* Manhattanville College, Art Dept, Purchase NY (S)
Bawel, Andy, *CFO,* The Children's Museum of Indianapolis, Indianapolis IN
Baxter, Denise, *Chair, Dept Art Educ,* University of North Texas, College of Visual Arts & Design, Denton TX (S)
Baxter, Ellen, *Chief Conservator,* Carnegie Museums of Pittsburgh, Carnegie Museum of Art, Pittsburgh PA
Baxter, Gary, *Head Art Dept,* Houghton College, Art Dept, Houghton NY (S)
Baxter, Karen, *Visual Arts Librn,* California Institute of the Arts Library, Santa Clarita CA
Baxter, Kristin, *Prof,* Moravian College, Dept of Art, Bethlehem PA (S)
Baxter, Tiffany, *Video Game Art & Animation,* Holland College, School of Visual Arts & Journalism, Charlottetown PE (S)
Baxter, William, *Head, History & Culture Dept,* National Museum of American History, Library, Washington DC
Bay, Lee, *VPres Planning, Educ & Mus Experience,* DuSable Museum of African American History, Chicago IL
Bay, Richard, *Asst Prof,* Radford University, Art Dept, Radford VA (S)
Bayer, Andrea, *Interim Deputy Dir Colls & Admin,* The Metropolitan Museum of Art, New York NY
Bayles, Jennifer, *Interim Head Develop,* The Buffalo Fine Arts Academy, Albright-Knox Art Gallery, Buffalo NY
Bayless, Jonathan, *Chief Cur,* Yosemite Museum, Research Library, Yosemite National Park CA
Baylor, Trenton, *Asst Prof,* University of Wisconsin-Parkside, Art Dept, Kenosha WI (S)
Baymiller, Paula, *Art Library Asst,* Oberlin College, Clarence Ward Art Library, Oberlin OH

Bayuzick, Dennis, *Assoc Prof,* University of Wisconsin-Parkside, Art Dept, Kenosha WI (S)

Beach, Gleny, *Dir Art,* Southeastern Oklahoma State University, Dept of Art, Communication & Theatre, Durant OK (S)

Beach, Ray, *Tech Dir,* Ashtabula Arts Center, Ashtabula OH

Beachley, Patricia, *Assoc Prof,* Seton Hill University, Art Program, Greensburg PA (S)

Beadle, Kristine, *Instr,* John C Calhoun, Department of Fine Arts, Tanner AL (S)

Beal, Stephen, *Pres,* California College of the Arts, San Francisco CA (S)

Beall-Fofana, Barbara, *Assoc Prof,* Assumption College, Dept of Art, Music & Theatre, Worcester MA (S)

Beals, Ruth, *Assoc Prof & Coordr Interior Design,* Converse College, School of the Arts, Dept of Art & Design, Spartanburg SC (S)

Beam, Michael J, *Cur Colls & Exhibs,* Niagara University, Castellani Art Museum, Niagara NY

Beamish, Rollin, *Asst Prof - Painting & Drawing,* Montana State University, School of Art, Bozeman MT (S)

Bean, Phoebe, *Librn,* Rhode Island Historical Society, Library, Providence RI

Bean, Roger, *Prof,* Illinois Central College, Arts & Communication Dept, East Peoria IL (S)

Beane, Frances A, *Deputy Dir,* Harvard University, Arthur M Sackler Museum, Cambridge MA

Beane, Frances A, *Deputy Dir,* Harvard University, William Hayes Fogg Art Museum, Cambridge MA

Beanland, Rachel, *Dir Opers,* Visual Arts Center of Richmond, Richmond VA

Beard, Bethany, *Gallery Adminr,* Allied Arts Association, Allied Arts Center & Gallery, Richland WA

Beard, Deborah, *Chmn Technical Design,* Fashion Institute of Technology, School of Art & Design, New York NY (S)

Beard, Dena, *Dir,* The Lab, San Francisco CA

Beard, Teri, *Adin,* Old Island Restoration Foundation Inc, Oldest House in Key West, Key West FL

Beardsley, Kelcey, *Dir,* Marylhurst University, Art Dept, Marylhurst OR (S)

Bearor, Karen, *Assoc Prof,* Florida State University, Art History Dept, Tallahassee FL (S)

Beasley, Todd, *Creative Dir,* Morris Museum of Art, Augusta GA

Beatly, Michael, *Assoc Prof,* College of the Holy Cross, Dept of Visual Arts, Worcester MA (S)

Beatty, Frances, *VPres,* Art Dealers Association of America, Inc, New York NY

Beatty, Nicole, *Branch Coordr,* Indiana University, Fine Arts Library, Bloomington IN

Beatty, Tracy, *Exhibs Coordr,* Northeastern Nevada Museum, Elko NV

Beauchard, Sabina, *Reproductions Coordr,* Massachusetts Historical Society, Library, Boston MA

Beauchesne, Dawn, *Events Coordr,* Kimball Jenkins Estate, Concord NH

Beaudry, Marie-Christine, *Librn,* Universite du Quebec, Bibliotheque des Arts, Montreal QC

Beaulieu, Allyson, *Gallery Asst,* Modernism, San Francisco CA

Beaulieu, Danielle, *Dir,* Modernism, San Francisco CA

Beaulieu, Nancy, *Registrar,* New Brunswick College of Craft & Design, Fredericton NB (S)

Beaulieu, Rebekah, *Dir,* Lyme Historical Society, Florence Griswold Museum, Old Lyme CT

Beaupre, Marie-Eve, *Cur of the Coll,* Musee d'art Contemporain de Montreal, Montreal QC

Beausoleil, Deanne, *Adjunct,* Chemeketa Community College, Dept of Humanities & Communications, Art Program, Salem OR (S)

Beaver, Frank, *Assoc Chair,* University of Hawaii at Manoa, Dept of Art, Honolulu HI (S)

Beaver, Jeanne, *Asst Prof,* Murray State University, Dept of Art, Murray KY (S)

Beben, Sylvia, *Asst Mus Dir,* Jordan Historical Museum of The Twenty, Jordan ON

Becenti, Pete, *Park Supv,* Red Rock Park, Red Rock Park, Church Rock NM

Becerra, Andrea, *Youth Prog Coordr,* City of Irvine, Irvine Fine Arts Center, Irvine CA

Bechand, Elizabeth, *Mus Shop Mgr,* Albany Institute of History & Art, Albany NY

Becher, Melissa, *Reference Team Leader,* American University, Jack I & Dorothy G Bender Library & Learning Resources Center, New York NY

Becherer, Joseph, *Prof,* Aquinas College, Art Dept, Grand Rapids MI (S)

Bechet, Ron, *Chmn,* Xavier University of Louisiana, Dept of Fine Arts, New Orleans LA (S)

Bechtell, MC, *Chmn,* Madison Museum of Fine Art, Madison GA

Bechtell, Michele, *CEO, Pres & Dir,* Madison Museum of Fine Art, Madison GA

Beck, Amy, *Mktg & Communs Mgr,* Leigh Yawkey Woodson Art Museum, Wausau WI

Beck, Boyde, *Cur History,* Prince Edward Island Museum & Heritage Foundation, Charlottetown PE

Beck, Dawn, *Controller,* Seattle Art Museum, Seattle WA

Beck, Jacqueline, *Dir Educ,* Headley-Whitney Museum, Lexington KY

Beck, Jessica, *Milton Fine Cur of Art,* The Andy Warhol Museum, Pittsburgh PA

Beck, Kimberly, *Deputy Director for Operations,* The Columbus Museum, Columbus GA

Beck, Lesley Ann, *Dir Commun,* Berkshire Museum, Pittsfield MA

Beck, Megan, *Curator,* The Noble Maritime Collection, Staten Island NY

Beck, Sheila, *Coordr Technical Svcs,* Queensborough Community College Library, Kurt R Schmeller Library, Flushing NY

Beck, Susan Gilbert, *Dir,* Siena Heights College, Art Library, Adrian MI

Beck, Tom, *Affiliate Assoc Prof, Chief Cur AOK Libr & Dir CBSA,* University of Maryland, Baltimore County, Intermedia & Digital Arts (IMDA), Dept of Visual Arts, Baltimore MD (S)

Beck, Tracey, *Exec Dir,* American Swedish Historical Foundation & Museum, American Swedish Historical Museum, Philadelphia PA

Beck, Tracey, *Exec Dir,* American Swedish Historical Foundation & Museum, Nord Library, Philadelphia PA

Beckel, Meg, *Pres & CEO,* Canadian Museum of Nature, Musee Canadien de la Nature, Ottawa ON

Beckelman, John, *Chmn Art Dept,* Coe College, Eaton-Buchan Gallery & Marvin Cone Gallery, Cedar Rapids IA

Beckelman, John, *Prof,* Coe College, Dept of Art, Cedar Rapids IA (S)

Becker Nelson, Jane, *Dir,* Saint Olaf College, Flaten Art Museum, Northfield MN

Becker, Barry, *Chief Staff,* Please Touch Museum, Philadelphia PA

Becker, Carol, *Dean of Faculty,* Columbia University, School of the Arts, New York NY (S)

Becker, Chuck, *1st Vice Pres,* Cumberland Art Society Inc, Cookeville Art Gallery, Cookeville TN

Becker, David, *Emer Prof,* University of Wisconsin, Madison, Dept of Art, Madison WI (S)

Becker, Elizabeth, *Cur Educ,* Albuquerque Museum of Art & History, Albuquerque NM

Becker, Jack F, *Exec Dir & CEO,* Joslyn Art Museum, Omaha NE

Becker, Janis, *Educ Coordr,* Mamie McFaddin Ward, Beaumont TX

Becker, Jim, *COO,* Taubman Museum of Art, Roanoke VA

Becker, Julia, *Prof Art,* University of Great Falls, Art Dept, Great Falls MT (S)

Becker, Lisa Tamiris, *Dir,* University of Colorado, CU Art Museum, Boulder CO

Becker, Max, *Dir Technical & Facilities Opers,* FilmNorth, Saint Paul MN

Becker, Thomas, *Pres,* Chautauqua Center for the Visual Arts, Chautauqua NY

Beckerman, Richard, *COO,* Seattle Art Museum, Seattle WA

Becket, Charlotte, *Prof,* Pace University, Dyson College of Arts & Sciences, Pleasantville NY (S)

Beckham, Donita, *Library & Archives Liaison,* Heard Museum, Billie Jane Baguley Library and Archives, Phoenix AZ

Beckham, Peggy, *Adjunct Prof,* Missouri Southern State University, Dept of Art, Joplin MO (S)

Beckham, Terry, *Exhibs Designer,* Birmingham Museum of Art, Birmingham AL

Beckman, Jean, *Dean Arts & Sciences,* University of Evansville, Krannert Gallery & Peterson Gallery, Evansville IN

Beckman, Joy, *Dir,* Beloit College, Wright Museum of Art, Beloit WI

Beckstrom, Robert, *Chmn,* Lorain County Community College, Art Dept, Elyria OH (S)

Beckwith, Alice, *Assoc Prof,* Providence College, Art & Art History Dept, Providence RI (S)

Beckwith, Claudia, *Registrar Pub Rels,* Greenville County Museum of Art, Greenville SC

Beckwith, Patterson, *Lectr,* City College of New York, Art Dept, New York NY (S)

Bedard, Robert J, *Treas,* Art PAC, Washington DC

Beddow, Julie Ann, *Fine & Performing Arts,* University of Northern Iowa, Fine & Performing Arts Collection Rod Library, Cedar Falls IA

Beder, Louise, *Mem Coordr,* James A Michener Art Museum, Doylestown PA

Bedford, Christopher, *Dir,* The Baltimore Museum of Art, Baltimore MD

Bedford, Laura, *Treas,* Guild of Book Workers, New York NY

Bee, Martin, *Prof,* McNeese State University, Dept of Visual Arts, Lake Charles LA (S)

Beebe, Mary Livingstone, *Dir,* University of California, San Diego, Stuart Collection, La Jolla CA

Beeching, Lynne, *Develop Officer,* Hidalgo County Historical Museum, Edinburg TX

Beegan, Gerry, *Chair, Art & Design Dept, Assoc Prof,* Rutgers, The State University of New Jersey, Mason Gross School of the Arts, New Brunswick NJ (S)

Beegles, Anna, *Site Mgr,* County of Henrico, Library, Glen Allen VA

Beegles, Anna, *Site Mgr,* County of Henrico, Meadow Farm Museum, Glen Allen VA

Beeler, Kristin, *Assoc Prof Jewelry & Metalwork, Program Coordr Applied Design,* Long Beach City College, Art & Photography Dept, Long Beach CA (S)

Beerman, Doug, *Dir Operations,* South Carolina State Museum, Columbia SC

Beers, Debra, *Instr,* Lewis & Clark College, Dept of Art, Portland OR (S)

Beesch, Ruth, *Deputy Dir Prog Admin,* The Jewish Museum, New York NY

Beeson, Alison, *Assoc Cur,* Wiregrass Museum of Art, Dothan AL

Beeson, Nick, *Cur Colls,* History Museum of Mobile, Mobile AL

Begay, Clarenda, *Cur,* Navajo Nation, Navajo Nation Museum, Window Rock AZ

Begay, Lorenzo J, *Exec Dir,* Atlatl, Phoenix AZ

Beggs, Sarah, *Educ Dir,* Kirkland Arts Center, KAC Gallery, Kirkland WA

Begland, Mary Anne, *Chmn Graphic Design,* Rochester Institute of Technology, School of Design, Rochester NY (S)

Begley, Christine, *VPres Develop,* American Academy in Rome, New York NY (S)

Begley, John, *Gallery Dir,* University of Louisville, Hite Art Institute, Louisville KY

Begley, John, *Gallery Dir & Adjunct Assoc Prof,* University of Louisville, Allen R Hite Art Institute, Louisville KY (S)

Beglin, Patricia, *Instr,* Cazenovia College, Center for Art & Design Studies, Cazenovia NY (S)

Begnaud, Joseph, *Assoc Prof,* University of North Carolina at Pembroke, Art Dept, Pembroke NC (S)

Begonia, Jennifer, *Exec Dir,* Long Beach Island Foundation of the Arts & Sciences, Loveladies NJ

Behar, Ionit, *Cur Colls & Exhibs,* Spertus Institute of Jewish Studies, Chicago IL
Behl, Diana, *Asst Prof,* South Dakota State University, Dept of Visual Arts, Brookings SD (S)
Behm, Anthea, *Asst Prof,* University of Florida, School of Art & Art History, Gainesville FL (S)
Behnke, Betsy, *Secy,* Dillman's Creative Arts Foundation, Tom Lynch Resource Center, Lac du Flambeau WI
Behnke, Henry, *VPres Mktg & External Affairs,* Staten Island Museum, Staten Island NY
Behrend, Rene, *Prof,* Saint Louis Community College at Meramec, Art Dept, Saint Louis MO (S)
Behrends, Huck, *Dir Exhibits,* South Carolina State Museum, Columbia SC
Behrens, Fred, *Prof,* Columbia State Community College, Dept of Art, Columbia TN (S)
Behrens, Roy, *Prof,* University of Northern Iowa, Dept of Art, Cedar Falls IA (S)
Behrens, Todd, *Cur,* Sioux City Art Center, Sioux City IA (S)
Behrens, Todd, *Cur,* Sioux City Art Center, Sioux City IA
Beibers, Sam, *Instr,* Belhaven College, Art Dept, Jackson MS (S)
Beidler, Anne, *Chmn,* Agnes Scott College, Dept of Art, Decatur GA (S)
Beidler, Anne, *Printmaker,* Agnes Scott College, Dalton Art Gallery, Decatur GA
Beidler, Brien, *VPres,* Guild of Book Workers, New York NY
Beim, David O, *VChmn,* Wave Hill, Bronx NY
Beiner, Susan, *Instr,* California State University, San Bernardino, Dept of Art, San Bernardino CA (S)
Beinhardt, Tracy, *Secy,* Cardinal Stritch University, Art Dept, Milwaukee WI (S)
Beiswanger, Bert, *Dir Mktg & Communs,* Eiteljorg Museum of American Indians & Western Art, Indianapolis IN
Beiter, Michael, *VPres,* Historic Cherry Hill, Albany NY
Beitz, Michael, *Asst Prof,* University of Wisconsin Oshkosh, Dept of Art, Oshkosh WI (S)
Bekedam, Kathy, *Exec Dir,* Livingston Center for Art & Culture, Livingston MT
Belan, Kyra, *Gallery Dir,* Broward Community College - South Campus, Art Gallery, Pembroke Pines FL
Belanger, Gentiane, *Dir & Cur,* Bishop's University, Foreman Art Gallery, Sherbrooke QC
Belanger, Lyne, *Chief Librn,* Universite de Montreal, Bibliotheque d'Amenagement, Montreal QC
Belanger, Pamela, *Cur 19th & 20th Century,* William A Farnsworth, Library, Rockland ME
Belanger-Turner, Tammy, *Dir Finance,* Caramoor Center for Music & the Arts, Inc, Rosen House at Caramoor, Katonah NY
Belardo, John, *Treas,* Hudson Valley Art Association, Brooklyn NY
Belasco, Ruth, *Prof,* Spring Hill College, Department of Fine & Performing Arts, Mobile AL (S)
Belcher, Patty, *Reference Librn,* Bernice Pauahi Bishop, Library & Archives, Honolulu HI
Belger, Evelyn Craft, *Dir,* Belger Crane Yard Studios, Kansas City MO
Belin, Jenny, *Asst to Dir,* Viridian Artists Inc, New York NY
Belisle Kurtin, Lyn, *Pres,* San Antonio Art League, San Antonio Art League Museum, San Antonio TX
Belisle, Jean-Francois, *Exec Dir & Cur,* Musee d'art de Joliette, Joliette QC
Belisle, Patt, *Dir,* Middletown Arts Center, Middletown OH
Belknap, Beth, *Assoc,* Mount Saint Joseph University, Department of Art and Design, Cincinnati OH (S)
Bell Yank, Sue, *Dir Communs & Outreach,* 18th Street Arts Complex, Santa Monica CA
Bell, Adrienne, *Asst Prof Art History,* Marymount Manhattan College, Fine & Performing Arts Div, New York NY (S)
Bell, Caleb, *Pub Rels & Mktg,* Tyler Museum of Art, Tyler TX
Bell, Christine, *Lectr,* Northwestern University, Evanston, Dept of Art History, Evanston IL (S)
Bell, Denise, *Dir Grants & Contracts,* California State University, Long Beach Foundation, Long Beach CA
Bell, Doug, *Preparator & Registrar,* Tufts University, Tufts University Art Gallery, Medford MA
Bell, Jennifer, *Instr,* Morehead State University, Art & Design Dept, Morehead KY (S)
Bell, Jude, *Admin Asst,* University of California, Berkeley, College of Letters & Sciences-Art Practice Dept, Berkeley CA (S)
Bell, Judith, *Instr,* San Jose City College, School of Fine Arts, San Jose CA (S)
Bell, Karen, *Dept Secy,* California State University, Fullerton, Art Dept, Fullerton CA (S)
Bell, Keith, *Prof,* University of Saskatchewan, Art & Art History Dept, Saskatoon SK (S)
Bell, Kelley, *Asst Prof & Assoc Chair,* University of Maryland, Baltimore County, Intermedia & Digital Arts (IMDA), Dept of Visual Arts, Baltimore MD (S)
Bell, Kevin, *Assoc Prof,* University of Montana, School of Art, Missoula MT (S)
Bell, Kurt, *Librn & Archivist,* Pennsylvania Historical & Museum Commission, Railroad Museum of Pennsylvania, Strasburg PA
Bell, Leslie, *Prof Art,* Saint Ambrose University, Art Dept, Davenport IA (S)
Bell, Lynne, *Prof,* University of Saskatchewan, Art & Art History Dept, Saskatoon SK (S)
Bell, Maaji, *Prof,* Concordia University, Division of Performing & Visual Arts, Mequon WI (S)
Bell, Malcolm, *Prof,* University of Virginia, McIntire Dept of Art, Charlottesville VA (S)
Bell, Marybeth, *Dir,* State University of New York at Oswego, Penfield Library, Oswego NY
Bell, Nicole, *Professor of Media Arts,* Los Angeles City College, School of Visual & Media Arts, Los Angeles CA (S)
Bell, Tom, *Dir Finance & HR,* New Britain Museum of American Art, New Britain CT
Bell, Trevor, *Prof Emeritus,* Florida State University, Art Dept, Tallahassee FL (S)
Bellabia, Kim, *Dir,* Klamath County Museum, Baldwin Hotel Museum Annex, Klamath Falls OR
Bellabia, Kim, *Dir,* Klamath County Museum, Research Library, Klamath Falls OR
Bellabia, Kim, *Dir,* Klamath County Museum, Klamath Falls OR
Bellah, Suzzane, *Cultural Arts Supv,* Carnegie Art Museum, Oxnard CA
Bellais, Leslie, *Cur Social History,* Wisconsin Historical Society, Wisconsin Historical Museum, Madison WI
Bellamy, Steve, *Dean,* Humber College, School of Creative & Performing Arts, Toronto ON (S)
Belletire, Steve, *Prof & Design Area Head,* Southern Illinois University, School of Art & Design, Carbondale IL (S)
Belleville, Patricia, *Prof,* Eastern Illinois University, Art Dept, Charleston IL (S)
Belli, Melia, *Asst Prof,* University of Texas at Arlington, Art & Art History Department, Arlington TX (S)
Bellisio, Nina, *Asst Prof,* Saint Thomas Aquinas College, Art Dept, Sparkill NY (S)
Bellows, Joseph, *Dir,* Joseph Bellows Gallery, La Jolla CA
Bellum, Slade, *Dir Fin & Opers,* Armory Center for the Arts, Pasadena CA
Belluscio, Lynne, *Dir,* LeRoy Historical Society, The Jell-O Gallery, LeRoy NY
Belmont-Earl, Jennifer, *Progs Coordr,* The National Society of The Colonial Dames of America in the State of New Hampshire, Moffatt-Ladd House & Garden, Portsmouth NH
Belnap, Jeffrey, *Chmn,* Brigham Young University, Hawaii Campus, Division of Fine Arts, Laie HI (S)
Belson, Anne, *Corresp Secy,* New England Watercolor Society, Boston MA
Belson, Janer Danforth, *Pres,* Cleveland Institute of Art, Cleveland Art Association, Cleveland OH
Beltemacchi, Peter, *Assoc Prof,* Illinois Institute of Technology, College of Architecture, Chicago IL (S)
Beltke, Bridget, *Finance Mgr,* Pelham Art Center, Pelham NY
Belville, Scott, *Assoc Prof Drawing & Painting,* University of Georgia, Franklin College of Arts & Sciences, Lamar Dodd School of Art, Athens GA (S)
Belvo, Hazel, *Faculty,* Grand Marais Art Colony, Grand Marais MN (S)
Belz, Suzanne, *Membership Mgr,* Burchfield Penney Art Center, Buffalo NY
Belzile, Gervais, *Material Resources Tech,* Le Musee Regional de Rimouski, Centre National d'Exposition, Rimouski QC
Bemonister, Theresa, *Associate Curator,* Akron Art Museum, Akron OH
Ben-Horin, Barbara, *Dir Develop,* Santa Barbara Museum of Art, Library, Santa Barbara CA
Benally, Ailema, *Educ Dir & Chief Interpreter,* National Park Service, Hubbell Trading Post National Historic Site, Ganado AZ
Benarde, Scott, *Dir Communs,* Norton Museum of Art, West Palm Beach FL
Benavides, Stacy, *Admin,* Ellen Noel Art Museum of the Permian Basin, Odessa TX
Benay, Erin, *Asst Prof,* Case Western Reserve University, Dept of Art History & Art, Cleveland OH (S)
Benbow, Ann, *Exec Dir,* Archaeological Institute of America, Boston MA
Benbow, Joyce, *Secy,* Switzerland County Historical Society Inc, Switzerland County Historical Museum, Vevay IN
Benbow, Joyce, *Secy,* Switzerland County Historical Society Inc, Life on the Ohio: River History Museum, Vevay IN
Benchabane, Manel, *Gallery Asst,* Pointe Claire Cultural Centre, Stewart Hall Art Gallery, Pointe Claire QC
Bender, Christine, *Admin Asst,* Hayward Area Forum for the Arts, Sun Gallery, Hayward CA
Bender, Heather, *Master Teacher,* University of Wyoming, University of Wyoming Art Museum, Laramie WY
Bender, Mark, *Graphic Design,* Art Institute of Pittsburgh, Pittsburgh PA (S)
Bender, Nathan, *House Cur,* Buffalo Bill Memorial Association, Harold McCracken Research Library, Cody WY
Bender, Neil, *Assoc Prof,* University of South Florida, School of Art & Art History, Tampa FL (S)
Bender, Phil, *Dir,* Pirate-Contemporary Art, Denver CO
Benedetti, Joan M, *Librn,* LA County Museum of Art, Edith R Wyle Research Library of The Craft & Folk Art Museum, Los Angeles CA
Benedetto, Mark, *Pres,* University of Sioux Falls, Dept of Art, Sioux Falls SD (S)
Benedict, Dow, *Dean,* Shepherd University, Dept of Contemporary Art & Theater, Shepherdstown WV (S)
Benedict, Jim, *Asst Prof Sculpture,* Jacksonville University, Jacksonville FL (S)
Benedict, Jim, *Dir,* Jacksonville University, Alexander Brest Museum & Gallery, Jacksonville FL
Benedict, Karl, *Dir,* University of New Mexico, Fine Arts Library, Albuquerque NM
Benedict, Sean, *Media Arts & Animation,* Art Institute of Pittsburgh, Pittsburgh PA (S)
Benedict, Sophia, *Sales & Mktg,* Arts Place, Inc, Hugh N Ronald Memorial Gallery, Portland IN
Benedict-Johnson, Jennifer, *Gallery Dir,* Colorado Mountain Art Gallery, Georgetown CO
Beneditti, Joan, *Librn,* LA County Museum of Art, Los Angeles CA
Benefiel, Christian, *Coordr Sculpture,* Shepherd University, Dept of Contemporary Art & Theater, Shepherdstown WV (S)
Benero, Paul, *Adjunct Prof,* University of Texas at Arlington, Art & Art History Department, Arlington TX (S)

Benesh, Coina, *Dir Devel,* Santa Barbara Museum of Art, Santa Barbara CA

Benesh, Joseph, *Dir,* Phoenix Center for the Arts, Phoenix AZ

Benezra, Neal, *Dir ISS,* San Francisco Museum of Modern Art, San Francisco CA

Benezra, Neal, *Helen and Charles Schwab Dir,* San Francisco Museum of Modern Art, San Francisco CA

Benford, Benjamin, *Dean Liberal Arts,* Tuskegee University, Liberal Arts & Education, Tuskegee AL (S)

Bengston, Carl, *Dean Library Serv,* California State University Stanislaus, Vasche Library, Turlock CA

Bengston, Monee, *Registrar & Prep,* Virginia Museum of Contemporary Art, Virginia Beach VA

Bengston, Rod, *Dir,* University of Hawaii at Manoa, The Art Gallery & The John Young Museum of Art, Honolulu HI

Benhisen, Louisa, *Prof 2-D Prog,* Merced College, Arts Division, Merced CA (S)

Benicaso, Jesse, *Gallery Asst,* Seton Hall University, Walsh Gallery & Library, South Orange NJ

Benington-Kozlowski, Eliza, *Dir Communs & Audience Develop,* George Eastman Museum, Rochester NY

Benini, Lorraine, *Pres,* The Benini Foundation & Sculpture Ranch, Johnson City TX

Benini, Sara, *Admin Asst,* St Mary's University, Art Gallery, Halifax NS

Benio, Pauleve, *Prof,* Adrian College, Art & Design Dept, Adrian MI (S)

Benitez, Marimar, *Dir,* Escuela de Artes Plasticas, Biblioteca Francisco Oller, San Juan PR

Benitz, Megan, *Registrar & Exhibs Mgr,* The Albrecht-Kemper Museum of Art, Saint Joseph MO

Benjamin, Brent, *Dir,* Saint Louis Art Museum, Saint Louis MO

Benjamin, Jack, *Chmn,* University of South Carolina at Aiken, Dept of Visual & Performing Arts, Aiken SC (S)

Benjamin, Jess, *Gallery Dir,* Creighton University, Lied Art Gallery, Omaha NE

Benjamin, Susan, *Chmn,* Pickens County Museum of Art & History, Pickens SC

Benner, Karl, *Gallery Mgr,* Cooperstown Art Association, Cooperstown NY

Bennett Easterson, Toni, *Visual Arts Specialist,* Northfield Arts Guild, Northfield MN

Bennett Simorella, Michelle, *Head Coll Mgmt & Registration,* Rubin Museum of Art, New York NY

Bennett, Astrid, *Pres,* Surface Design Association, Inc, Las Vegas NM

Bennett, Bob, *Head Dept,* Miles Community College, Dept of Fine Arts & Humanities, Miles City MT (S)

Bennett, Callie, *Asst Mus Educ,* University of Tennessee, McClung Museum of Natural History & Culture, Knoxville TN

Bennett, Fernanda, *Registrar,* Nassau County Museum of Art, Roslyn Harbor NY

Bennett, Frank, *Exec Dir,* The National Quilt Museum, Paducah KY

Bennett, Hannah, *Dir Fine Arts & Museum Librares,* University of Pennsylvania, Fisher Fine Arts Library, Philadelphia PA

Bennett, Jack, *Pres,* Drew County Historical Society, Museum, Monticello AR

Bennett, Kate, *Dir Develop,* Wildling Art Museum, Solvang CA

Bennett, Scot, *Prof,* Roberts Wesleyan College, Department of Visual Art, Rochester NY (S)

Bennett, Shannon, *Dir Mktg & Communs,* Indianapolis Art Center, Marilyn K. Glick School of Art, Indianapolis IN

Bennett, Susan, *Exec Dir,* Port Huron Museum, Port Huron MI

Bennett, Swannee, *Cur,* Historic Arkansas Museum, Library, Little Rock AR

Bennett, Swannee, *Cur Research,* Historic Arkansas Museum, Little Rock AR

Bennett, William, *Studio Faculty,* University of Virginia, McIntire Dept of Art, Charlottesville VA (S)

Bennewitz, Kathleen Motes, *Cur,* Lockwood-Mathews Mansion Museum, Norwalk CT

Benoit, Aimee, *Cur,* City of Lethbridge, Sir Alexander Galt Museum, Lethbridge AB

Benso, Helen, *VPres Mktg,* Brookgreen Gardens, Murrells Inlet SC

Benson Linek, Robin, *Special Events Mgr,* Southern Methodist University, Meadows Museum, Dallas TX

Benson, Aaron Lee, *Chmn,* Union University, Dept of Art, Jackson TN (S)

Benson, Claire, *Dir,* Lyndon House Art, Athens GA

Benson, Ilana, *Educator,* Yeshiva University Museum, New York NY

Benson, Mark, *Dept Head,* Auburn University Montgomery, Dept of Fine Arts, Montgomery AL (S)

Benson, Nicole, *Gallery Dir,* Portlock Galleries at SoNo, Chesapeake VA

Benson, Timothy, *Cur,* Los Angeles County Museum of Art, Robert Gore Rifkind Center for German Expressionist Studies, Los Angeles CA

Bensur, Barbara J, *Assoc Prof Art Educ,* Millersville University, Dept of Art & Design, Millersville PA (S)

Bent, George, *Head,* Washington and Lee University, Div of Art, Lexington VA (S)

Bent, Nila, *Art Reference Librn,* The Society of the Four Arts, Gioconda & Joseph King Library, Palm Beach FL

Bentley, Anne E, *Cur Art & Artifacts,* Massachusetts Historical Society, Boston MA

Bentley, Eden R, *Librn,* Johnson Atelier Technical Institute of Sculpture, Johnson Atelier Library, Mercerville NJ

Bently, Christine, *Asst Prof,* University of Indianapolis, Dept Art & Design, Indianapolis IN (S)

Benton, Janetta, *Prof,* Pace University, Dyson College of Arts & Sciences, Pleasantville NY (S)

Benton, Jared, *Asst Prof,* Old Dominion University, Art Dept, Norfolk VA (S)

Benton, Steve, *Dir,* Massachusetts Institute of Technology, Center for Advanced Visual Studies, Cambridge MA (S)

Bentor, Eli, *Asst Prof,* Appalachian State University, Dept of Art, Boone NC (S)

Bentz, Kate, *Prof,* Saint Anselm College, Dept of Fine Arts, Manchester NH (S)

Bentz, Laura, *Asst Prof,* Chadron State College, Dept of Art, Chadron NE (S)

Benzow, Jeff, *Assoc Prof,* University of Wisconsin-Green Bay, Arts Dept, Green Bay WI (S)

Beono, Tom, *Assoc Prof,* Texas State University - San Marcos, Dept of Art and Design, San Marcos TX (S)

Berben, Silvan, *Dir,* Owatonna Arts Center, Library, Owatonna MN

Berber, Sidney, *Dir Phillips Libr,* Peabody Essex Museum, Phillips Library, Salem MA

Berelowitz, Jo-Anne, *Art History Grad Coordr,* San Diego State University, School of Art, Design & Art History, San Diego CA (S)

Berens, Stephen, *Prof,* Chapman University, Art Dept, Orange CA (S)

Berezansky, Tracey, *Asst Dir Government Records,* Alabama Department of Archives & History, Museum of Alabama, Montgomery AL

Berg, Kathy, *Admin Asst,* Sangre de Cristo Arts & Conference Center, Pueblo CO

Berg, Niels, *Sub Dir,* Ages of Man Foundation, Amenia NY

Berg-Gilbert, Tempy, *Instr,* Dallas Baptist University, Dept of Art, Dallas TX (S)

Bergeman, Rich, *Instr,* Linn Benton Community College, Fine & Applied Art Dept, Albany OR (S)

Berger, Carol, *Acting Chmn Div,* Saint Louis Community College at Florissant Valley, Liberal Arts Division, Ferguson MO (S)

Berger, Emily, *VPres,* American Abstract Artists, Brooklyn NY

Berger, Evelyn Craft, *Exec Dir,* Belger Arts Center, Kansas City MO

Berger, Jerry A, *Dir,* Springfield Art Museum, Springfield MO

Berger, Jerry, *Dir,* Southwest Missouri Museum Associates Inc, Springfield Art Museum, Springfield MO

Berger, Lisa, *Develop & Commun,* Art Center Sarasota, Sarasota FL

Berger, Maurice, *Research Prof & Chief Cur,* University of Maryland, Baltimore County, Center for Art Design and Visual Culture, Baltimore MD

Berger, Quindi, *Librn II, Prog Mgr,* San Francisco Public Library, Art, Music & Recreation Center, San Francisco CA

Bergerin, Catena, *Deputy Dir & Dir Devel,* Westmoreland Museum of American Art, Greensburg PA

Bergeron, Kim, *Exec Dir,* St Tammany Art Association, Covington LA

Bergeron, Sylvie, *Treas,* Institut des Arts au Saguenay, Centre National D'Exposition a Jonquiere, Jonquiere QC

Bergeron, Tom, *Chmn Creative Arts,* Western Oregon State College, Creative Arts Division, Visual Arts, Monmouth OR (S)

Bergess, Nancy, *Treas,* Clinton Art Association, River Arts Center, Clinton IA

Bergfeld, Mary Ann, *Assoc Prof,* Saint Xavier University, Dept of Art & Design, Chicago IL (S)

Bergh, Susan, *Cur Pre-Columbian & Native North American Art,* The Cleveland Museum of Art, Cleveland OH

Bergman, Joseph, *Prof,* Siena Heights University, Studio Angelico-Art Dept, Adrian MI (S)

Bergman, Sky, *Dept Chmn, Prof Photog,* California Polytechnic State University at San Luis Obispo, Dept of Art & Design, San Luis Obispo CA (S)

Bergmann, Malena, *Coordr Undergrad Educ,* University of North Carolina at Charlotte, Dept Art, Charlotte NC (S)

Bergquist, Dick, *Treas,* Snake River Heritage Center, Weiser ID

Bergsieker, David, *Instr,* Illinois Valley Community College, Division of Humanities & Fine Arts, Oglesby IL (S)

Bergstrom, Christopher (Kip), *Deputy Commissioner,* Department of Economic & Community Development, State of Connecticut DECD Eric Sloane Museum, Kent CT

Bergstrom, Doug, *Exhib Technician,* University of Kansas, Spencer Museum of Art, Lawrence KS

Berhard, Dianne B, *1st VPres,* Pastel Society of America, National Arts Club, Grand Gallery, New York NY

Berke, Deborah, *Dean,* Yale University, School of Architecture, New Haven CT (S)

Berke, Joanne, *Prof,* Humboldt State University, College of Arts & Humanities, Art Dept, Arcata CA (S)

Berkeley, Sydney, *Prog Dir,* Anderson County Arts Council, Anderson Arts Center, Anderson SC

Berko, Linda, *Cur Colls,* Prince Edward Island Museum & Heritage Foundation, Charlottetown PE

Berley, Tanya, *VPres Educ & Pres Emeritus,* DuPage Art League School & Gallery, Wheaton IL

Berliant, Susan, *Develop Dir,* Contemporary Arts Center, Cincinnati OH

Berliner, Laura, *Dir of Visitor Experience,* Norman Rockwell Museum, Stockbridge MA

Berlyn, Judith, *Librn,* Chateau Ramezay Museum, Library, Montreal QC

Berman, Donna, *Exec Dir,* Charter Oak Cultural Center, Hartford CT

Berman, Patricia, *Chmn,* Wellesley College, Art Dept, Wellesley MA (S)

Bernal, Monica, *Treas,* Centro Cultural De La Raza, San Diego CA

Bernal, Rudy, *Chief Preparator,* University of Chicago, Smart Museum of Art, Chicago IL

Bernard, Ellen, *Chair Bd Trustees,* Walters Art Museum, Baltimore MD

Bernard, Geneive, *Cur Educ,* Mennello Museum of American Art, Orlando FL

Bernberg, Bruce, *Pres,* Racine Art Museum, Racine WI

Berndt-Morris, Liz, *Cur Music,* Boston Public Library, Arts Reference Department, Boston MA

Berner, Andrew, *Dir & Cur Collections,* University Club Library, New York NY

Berner, Christopher, *Acting Registrar,* Allentown Art Museum, Allentown PA

Berner, Cynthia, *Dir,* Wichita Public Library, Wichita KS

Berner, Tracy, *Reg,* Illinois State University, University Galleries, Normal IL

Bernhard, Robin, *Coll Mgr & Registrar,* University of California, Davis, Jan Shrem and Maria Manetti Shrem Museum of Art, Davis CA

Bernhard, Robin, *Registrar,* Saint Mary's College of California, Museum of Art, Moraga CA

Bernhardt-Lowdon, Margaret, *Exec Dir,* Portage and District Arts Council, Portage Arts Centre, Portage la Prairie MB

Bernier, Elizabeth, *Asst to Dir,* Old Colony Historical Society, Museum, Taunton MA

Bernis, Terry, *VPres,* Creek Council House Museum, Okmulgee OK

Berns, Marla C, *Dir,* University of California, Los Angeles, Fowler Museum at UCLA, Los Angeles CA

Bernson, Julie, *Dep Dir Learning & Engagement,* deCordova Sculpture Park & Museum, Lincoln MA

Bernstein, Jill, *Dir Communs & Pub Affairs,* Dallas Museum of Art, Dallas TX

Bernstein, Roberta, *Prof,* State University of New York at Albany, Art Dept, Albany NY (S)

Bernstein, Sheri, *Dir Music & Educ,* Hebrew Union College, Skirball Cultural Center, Los Angeles CA

Bero, Meg, *Dir,* Aurora University, Schingoethe Center for Native American Cultures & The Schingoethe Art Gallery, Aurora IL

Beroza, Barbara, *Chief Cur,* Yosemite Museum, Yosemite National Park CA

Beroza, Barbara, *Coll Cur,* Yosemite Museum, Research Library, Yosemite National Park CA

Berreth, David, *Dir,* University of Mary Washington, Gari Melchers Home and Studio, Fredericksburg VA

Berrios, Eduardo, *Dean of Admin,* Escuela de Artes Plasticas, Biblioteca Francisco Oller, San Juan PR

Berry, Ann, *Dir,* Pilgrim Society, Library, Plymouth MA

Berry, Christopher, *Assoc Prof,* Lakeland Community College, Fine Arts Department, Kirtland OH (S)

Berry, E Raymond, *Chmn,* Randolph-Macon College, Dept of the Arts, Ashland VA (S)

Berry, Ian, *Consulting Dir,* Hamilton College, Emerson Gallery, Clinton NY

Berry, Judith, *Lectr,* Wayne State College, Dept Art & Design, Wayne NE (S)

Berry, Linda, *Security Supvr,* Huntsville Museum of Art, Huntsville AL

Berry, Matthew, *Mktg & PR Assoc,* Rhode Island School of Design, Museum of Art, Providence RI

Berry, Megan, *Fine Arts Events Coordr,* Friends University, Riney Fine Arts Center Gallery, Wichita KS

Berry, Melanie, *Undergrad Prog Dir,* University of Maryland, Baltimore County, Intermedia & Digital Arts (IMDA), Dept of Visual Arts, Baltimore MD (S)

Berry, Nina, *Admin Asst,* Art Gallery of Guelph, Guelph ON

Berry, Paul, *Librn,* Calvert Marine Museum, Library, Solomons MD

Berry, Shawn, *Mgr Arts & Cultural Educ,* Cultural Council of Palm Beach County, Lake Worth FL

Berson, Jordan, *Dir Colls,* Old Dartmouth Historical Society, New Bedford Whaling Museum, New Bedford MA

Berson, Ruth, *Deputy Dir Curatorial Affairs,* San Francisco Museum of Modern Art, San Francisco CA

Berthiaume, Guy, *Librn & Archivist,* National Archives of Canada, Art & Photography Archives, Ottawa ON

Bertoletti, Isabella, *Chmn Modern Languages & Cultures,* Fashion Institute of Technology, School of Art & Design, New York NY (S)

Bertrand, Crystal, *Instr,* West Texas A&M University, Art, Theatre & Dance Dept, Canyon TX (S)

Berube, Holly, *Head Visitor Svcs,* deCordova Sculpture Park & Museum, Lincoln MA

Berube, Matt, *Reference,* Jones Library, Inc, Amherst MA

Berz, Wiliam, *Dir Music Dept,* Rutgers, The State University of New Jersey, Mason Gross School of the Arts, New Brunswick NJ (S)

Berzock, Kathleen, *Assoc Dir Cur Affairs,* Northwestern University, Mary & Leigh Block Museum of Art, Evanston IL

Beschi, Leonore-Namkha, *Curatorial Admin & Interpretation,* Art Gallery of Alberta, Edmonton AB

Besemer, Linda, *Prof,* Occidental College, Dept of Art History & Visual Arts, Los Angeles CA (S)

Bess, Joshlyn, *Devel Coord,* Auburn University, Jule Collins Smith Museum of Fine Art, Auburn AL

Bessa, Antonio Sergio, *Dir Progs,* Bronx Museum of the Arts, Bronx NY

Besselsen, Sandra, *Head Librn,* Interlochen Center for the Arts, Interlochen MI

Bessey, Richard B, *Dir,* The Rockwell Museum, Library, Corning NY

Bessire, Mark, *Dir,* Portland Museum of Art, Portland ME

Best, Jonathan W, *Prof,* Wesleyan University, Dept of Art & Art History, Middletown CT (S)

Best, Linda Delone, *Coll Mgr,* Mount Holyoke College, Art Museum, South Hadley MA

Best, Mickey D, *Dean,* New Mexico Junior College, Arts & Sciences, Hobbs NM (S)

Best, Sherry L, *Art Coll Cur,* Topeka & Shawnee County Public Library, Alice C Sabatini Gallery, Topeka KS

Bethany, Adeline, *Chmn Dept,* Cabrini College, Dept of Fine Arts, Radnor PA (S)

Bethel, Suzanne, *Exec Dir,* The Art League Gallery & School, Alexandria VA

Bething, Dan, *Lectr,* University of Tennessee at Chattanooga, Dept of Art, Chattanooga TN (S)

Bethke, Karl, *Prof,* University of Minnesota, Minneapolis, Dept of Art, Minneapolis MN (S)

Betsch, William, *Asst Prof,* University of Miami, Dept of Art & Art History, Coral Gables FL (S)

Betthauser, Tom, *Cur Jones Gallery,* Bakersfield College, Art Dept, Bakersfield CA (S)

Bettison-Varga, Lori, *Pres & Dir,* Natural History Museum of Los Angeles County, Los Angeles CA

Betty, Claudia Michelle, *Reference & Pub Servs Librn,* Art Center College of Design, James Lemont Fogg Memorial Library, Pasadena CA

Betzen, R Eileen, *Co-Owner,* Gadsden Museum, Mesilla NM

Betzer, Sarah, *Assoc Prof Art History,* University of Virginia, McIntire Dept of Art, Charlottesville VA (S)

Beuhler, Sara, *Registrar,* James A Michener Art Museum, Doylestown PA

Beutell, Jackie, *Visual Arts Comt Chair,* University of Minnesota, The Studio/Larson Gallery, Saint Paul MN

Bevan, Julie, *Exec Dir,* Nanaimo Art Gallery, Nanaimo BC

Beverly, Roberta, *Exec Dir,* Ogden Union Station, Union Station Museums, Ogden UT

Beverly, Roberta, *Exec Dir,* Ogden Union Station, Myra Powell Art Gallery & Gallery at the Station, Ogden UT

Bevers Ellison, Chayla, *Dir Office Events & Vol,* The Newberry, Chicago IL

Beyer, Albin, *Prof,* University of South Carolina at Aiken, Dept of Visual & Performing Arts, Aiken SC (S)

Bhogal, Surinder, *Chief Librn,* Surrey Art Gallery, Library, Surrey BC

Biada, Charles, *Dir Operations,* National Academy Museum & School, Archives, New York NY

Bialy, Mark G, *Prof,* Passaic County Community College, Division of Humanities, Paterson NJ (S)

Bianco, Juliette, *Deputy Dir,* Dartmouth College, Hood Museum of Art, Hanover NH

Bibas, David, *Technology Cur,* California Science Center, Los Angeles CA

Bibler, Carol, *Instr,* Chemeketa Community College, Dept of Humanities & Communications, Art Program, Salem OR (S)

Bickel, Barbara, *Asst Prof,* Southern Illinois University, School of Art & Design, Carbondale IL (S)

Bickley, Steve, *Prof,* Virginia Polytechnic Institute & State University, Dept of Art & Art History, Blacksburg VA (S)

Bicknell, Sarah Lou, *Mus Gift Shop Mgr & Historian,* Cedarhurst Center for the Arts, Mitchell Museum, Mount Vernon IL

Biddiscombe, Jennae, *Registrar,* Louisiana Department of Culture, Recreation & Tourism, Louisiana State Museum, New Orleans LA

Biddle, Mark, *Prof,* Weber State University, Dept of Visual Arts, Ogden UT (S)

Bidstrup, Wendy, *Dir,* Marion Art Center, Cecil Clark Davis Gallery, Marion MA

Bidwell, John, *Astor Cur & Dept Head Printed Books & Bindings,* The Morgan Library & Museum, Museum, New York NY

Bidzinski, Heather, *Head Colls,* Canadian Museum for Human Rights, Winnipeg MB

Biecker, Matthew, *CFO,* Chicago Architecture Foundation, Chicago IL

Bielak, Susy, *Dir of Engagment/ Cur Public Practice,* Northwestern University, Mary & Leigh Block Museum of Art, Evanston IL

Bieling, Cathleen, *Asst to the Chair,* The Sage Colleges, Dept Visual Arts, Albany NY (S)

Bieloh, David, *Instr,* Texas Woman's University, School of the Arts, Dept of Visual Arts, Denton TX (S)

Bielski, Sarah, *Asst Prod,* Georgia Southern University, Betty Foy Sanders Dept of Art, Statesboro GA (S)

Bien, Josh, *Technical Dir, Theatre Mgr & IT Mgr,* North Fourth Art Center & Gallery, Albuquerque NM

Biers, William R, *Prof Emeritus,* University of Missouri - Columbia, Art History & Archaeology Dept, Columbia MO (S)

Bieth, Ted, *Adjunct,* North Iowa Area Community College, Dept of Art, Mason City IA (S)

Biferie, Dan, *Prof,* Daytona Beach Community College, Dept of Fine Arts & Visual Arts, Daytona Beach FL (S)

Bigazzi, Anna, *Art Reference Librn,* University of Hartford, Anne Bunce Cheney Art Collection, West Hartford CT

Bigazzi, Anna, *Art Reference Librn,* University of Hartford, Mortensen Library, West Hartford CT

Bigbee, Shawn, *Project Mgr,* Quint Projects, La Jolla CA

Bigelow, Brad, *Mgr Retail Opers,* Seattle Art Museum, Dorothy Stimson Bullitt Library, Seattle WA

Bigelow, Rod, *Exec Dir,* Crystal Bridges Museum of American Art, Bentonville AR

Biggs, George, *Instr,* New Mexico Junior College, Arts & Sciences, Hobbs NM (S)

Bigley, Heather A, *Dir Gen Educ,* Art Institute of Pittsburgh, Pittsburgh PA (S)

Bilbo, Rebecca, *Chmn,* Thomas More College, Art Dept, Crestview Hills KY (S)

Bilello, Michelle, *Operations Asst,* Quapaw Quarter Association, Inc, Villa Marre, Little Rock AR

Bilello, Michelle, *Operations Asst,* Quapaw Quarter Association, Inc, Preservation Resource Center/ Historic Cannon Hall, Little Rock AR

Bilimek, Kendra, *Gallery/Event Coord,* Wassenberg Art Center, Van Wert OH

Billeaudeaux, Brigitte, *Special Colls Librarian & Archivist,* University of Memphis, Visual Resource Collection, Memphis TN

Billig, Victoria, *Asst Dir,* College of Central Florida, Appleton Museum of Art, Ocala FL

Billings, Cathy, *Sr Library Supvr,* Glendale Public Library, Brand Library & Art Center, Glendale CA
Billingslea, Renee, *Lectr,* Santa Clara University, Dept of Art & Art History, Santa Clara CA (S)
Billops, Camille, *Pres,* Hatch-Billops Collection, Inc, New York NY
Bills, Danny, *Cur Coll & Exhib,* Wichita Falls Museum & Art Center, Wichita Falls TX
Bilodeau, Jean-Francois, *Deputy Dir Advancement & Pub Engagement,* National Gallery of Canada, Ottawa ON
Bilsky, Angela, *Mem & Registrar,* Cape Cod Museum of Art Inc, Dennis MA
Bimber, Leyna, *Treas,* Crary Art Gallery, Warren PA
Binder-Klein, Hillary, *Instr,* Guild of Creative Art, Shrewsbury NJ (S)
Bindseil, Kenneth, *Chmn Humanities,* Quincy College, Art Dept, Quincy MA (S)
Bingham, Susan, *Dir,* Thunderbird Foundation for the Arts, Mount Carmel UT
Bingley, Angela, *Opers Mgr & Educ Coordr,* Fairbanks Arts Association, Bear Gallery, Fairbanks AK
Bingman, Beth, *Mng Dir & Gallery Dir,* Appalshop Inc, Appalshop, Whitesburg KY
Binkard, Daniel, *Instr,* Chadron State College, Dept of Art, Chadron NE (S)
Binkowski, Kraig, *Chief Librn,* Yale University, Yale Center for British Art, New Haven CT
Binks, Ronald, *Prof,* University of Texas at San Antonio, Dept of Art & Art History, San Antonio TX (S)
Binnington, Georgia, *Assoc Dean School,* Washington University, School of Art, Saint Louis MO (S)
Binstock, Jonathan P, *Dir,* University of Rochester, Memorial Art Gallery, Rochester NY
Biondi, Priscilla, *Head Librn Access & Organization,* Wentworth Institute of Technology, Douglas D Schumann Library & Learning Commons, Boston MA
Biondo-Gemmell, Susannah, *Dept Chair,* Cornell College, Peter Paul Luce Gallery, Mount Vernon IA
Bippes, Bill, *Div Dir Music Arts,* Spring Arbor College, Art Dept, Spring Arbor MI (S)
Bippes, Will, *Instr,* Hillsdale College, Art Dept, Hillsdale MI (S)
Birch, Eugenie, *Prof,* University of Pennsylvania, School of Design (PennDesign), Philadelphia PA (S)
Birch, Jesse, *Cur,* Nanaimo Art Gallery, Nanaimo BC
Birch, Jill, *Exec Dir,* Galerie Montcalm, Gatineau QC
Birckhead, Janet, *Adult Servs Dept Head,* City of Long Branch, Long Branch Free Public Library, Long Branch NJ
Bird, Anne, *Dir Mem,* Society of Architectural Historians, Chicago IL
Bird, Gwen, *Univ Librn & Dean of Libraries,* Simon Fraser University, W A C Bennett Library, Burnaby BC
Bird, John, *Mgr Gen Servs,* Rothmans, Benson & Hedges, Art Collection, Don Mills ON
Bird, Leslie, *Assoc Dir Mus & Fin Ops,* Bowdoin College, Museum of Art, Brunswick ME
Bird, Mary F, *Owner & Cur,* Gadsden Museum, Mesilla NM
Bird, Matthew, *Newsletter Editor,* National Watercolor Society, San Pedro CA
Bird, Richard, *Chair Performing & Visual Arts,* Chadron State College, Memorial Hall Main Gallery & Memorial Hall Gallery 239, Chadron NE
Bird, Richard, *Chmn,* Chadron State College, Dept of Art, Chadron NE (S)
Birdsong, Daniel, *Instr,* Weatherford College, Dept of Speech Fine Arts, Weatherford TX (S)
Birdsong, Heather, *Gallery Mgr,* Upfor Gallery, Portland OR
Birdsong, Sherri, *Cur Coll,* Mamie McFaddin Ward, Beaumont TX
Birk, Sherry, *Cur Coll,* American Architectural Foundation, The Octagon Museum, Washington DC
Birkett, Barbara, *Prof,* Rochester Institute of Technology, School of Printing Management & Sciences, Rochester NY (S)
Birkett, Whitney, *Colls Mgr,* Hartwick College, The Yager Museum, Oneonta NY
Birkett, William H, *Assoc Prof,* Rochester Institute of Technology, School of Printing Management & Sciences, Rochester NY (S)
Birkholz, Kathleen, *VPres,* Mesquite Fine Arts Center & Gallery, Mesquite NV
Birkle, Eric, *Assoc Cur,* Saginaw Art Museum, Saginaw MI
Birkmaier, Ulrich, *Chief Conservator,* Wadsworth Atheneum Museum of Art, Hartford CT
Birkner, Tom, *Adjunct Asst Prof,* Drew University, Art Dept, Madison NJ (S)
Birmingham, Mary, *Cur,* Visual Arts Center of New Jersey, Summit NJ
Birnbaum, Nathan, *Exec Dir,* Angels Gate Cultural Center, Gallery A & Gallery G, San Pedro CA
Birnie, Jenny, *Exec Dir,* Center for the Arts Piper Gallery, Crested Butte CO
Bisbee, John, *Lectr,* Bowdoin College, Art Dept, Brunswick ME (S)
Bisbing, Roger, *Technician,* State University of New York at Albany, Art Dept, Albany NY (S)
Bisch, Jennifer, *Chief Prog Officer & Cur,* Dalnavert Museum, Winnipeg MB
Bisenius, Jim, *Instr,* Morningside College, Art Dept, Sioux City IA (S)
Bishop, Allen, *Art Instr,* Crowder College, Longwell Museum/Art Department, Neosho MO (S)
Bishop, Barbara, *Mktg & Communs Dir,* Bush-Holley Historic Site & Storehouse Gallery, Greenwich Historical Society, Cos Cob CT
Bishop, Bob, *Admin Asst,* Santa Cruz Art League, Center for the Arts, Santa Cruz CA
Bishop, Brian, *Asst Prof,* Framingham State College, Art Dept, Framingham MA (S)
Bishop, Brian, *Prof,* Lansing Community College, Visual Arts & Media Dept, Lansing MI (S)
Bishop, Claire, *Prof,* City University of New York, PhD Program in Art History, New York NY (S)
Bishop, Joe, *Dir Facility & Security,* National Museum of Wildlife Art of the Unites States, Jackson WY
Bishop, John C, *Chair Bd Trustees,* Santa Barbara Museum of Art, Library, Santa Barbara CA
Bishop, Michael, *Prof,* California State University, Chico, Department of Art & Art History, Chico CA (S)
Bishop, Ron, *Cur & Dir,* Edison State College, Bob Rauschenberg Gallery at Edison State College, Fort Myers FL
Bishop, Scott, *Cur of Education,* Auburn University, Jule Collins Smith Museum of Fine Art, Auburn AL
Bishop, Steve, *Assoc Prof,* Murray State University, Dept of Art, Murray KY (S)
Bishop, Suznne, *Develop & Pub Info Officer,* University of Alaska, Elmer E Rasmuson Library, Fairbanks AK
Bissett, George Ann, *Pres & CEO,* Dunedin Fine Art Center, Dunedin FL (S)
Bissonette, John, *Faculty,* Yakima Valley Community College, Dept of Visual Arts, Yakima WA (S)
Bissonnette, Daniel, *Dir,* Musee Regional de Vaudreuil-Soulanges, Vaudreuil-Dorion QC
Bissonnette, Daniel, *Dir,* Musee Regional de Vaudreuil-Soulanges, Centre d'Histoire d'la Presqu'ile, Vaudreuil QC
Bitetti, Bronwen, *Librn,* Bard College, Center for Curatorial Studies and the Hessel Museum of Art, Annandale-on-Hudson NY
Bithell, David, *Asst Prof Art,* Southern Oregon University, Art & Art History Dept, Ashland OR (S)
Bittel, Erica, *Instr,* Fort Hays State University, Dept of Art & Design, Hays KS (S)
Bitters, Shawn (Daina), *Asst Prof,* University of Kansas, The School of the Arts, Dept of Visual Art, Lawrence KS (S)
Bittick, Ann, *Instr,* Southern Arkansas University at Magnolia, Dept of Art & Design, Magnolia AR (S)
Bittman, Lana, *Elec Resources & Serials,* Fashion Institute of Technology - SUNY, Gladys Marcus Library, New York NY
Bixler, Nancy, *Admin Asst,* Kennebec Valley Art Association, Harlow Gallery, Hallowell ME
Bizzarro, Tina Walduier, *Chmn Div,* Rosemont College, Art Program, Rosemont PA (S)
Bjarke, Amy, *Gallery Shop Mgr,* Fuller Lodge Art Center, Los Alamos NM
Bjarnson, Corey, *Dean Students,* Antonelli College, Cincinnati OH (S)
Bjelajac, David, *Prof,* George Washington University, Dept of Art of Fine Arts & Art History, Washington DC (S)
Bjorklund, Dana, *Technical Svcs Librn,* Cleveland Institute of Art, Jessica Gund Memorial Library, Cleveland OH
Bjornseth, Dick, *Cur,* Valdosta State University, Art Gallery, Valdosta GA
Bjurlin, Marvin, *Prof,* State University of New York at Fredonia, Dept of Art, Fredonia NY (S)
Black, Allison, *Assoc Prof,* South Plains College, Fine Arts Dept, Levelland TX (S)
Black, Amy, *Pub Rels & Mktg,* Worcester Center for Crafts, Krikorian Gallery, Worcester MA
Black, Bettye, *Dir Library,* Langston University, Melvin B Tolson Black Heritage Center, Langston OK
Black, Brea, *Special Colls/Art Librn,* Topeka & Shawnee County Public Library, Alice C Sabatini Gallery, Topeka KS
Black, Diana, *Asst Prof,* University of Wisconsin-Stevens Point, Dept of Art & Design, Stevens Point WI (S)
Black, Jack, *Bd Chmn & Cur,* City of Fayette, Alabama, Fayette Art Museum, Fayette AL
Black, Janet, *Prof, Art History,* College of San Mateo, Creative Arts Dept, San Mateo CA (S)
Black, Jerry, *Exec Officer Finance,* American Homing Pigeon Museum & Library, Oklahoma City OK
Black, Jessi, *Community Arts Dir,* Quad City Arts Inc, Rock Island IL
Black, Kathy, *Prog Dir,* Vermont Studio Center, The Red Mill, Johnson VT
Black, Kell, *Assoc Prof,* Austin Peay State University, Dept of Art, Clarksville TN (S)
Black, Sandra, *Dir Admin,* Appalachian State University, Turchin Center for the Visual Arts, Boone NC
Black, Steve O, *Dept Head,* Grayson County College, Art Dept, Denison TX (S)
Black, Steve, *Assoc Prof,* Vincennes University Junior College, Humanities Art Dept, Vincennes IN (S)
Black, Sue, *Visitors Svcs Mgr,* Southern Alberta Art Gallery, Library, Lethbridge AB
Black, Susan, *Exec Dir,* Erie Art Museum, Erie PA
Blackborn, Theresa, *Exec Dir,* Brickton Art Center, Park Ridge IL
Blackburn, Bob, *Exec Dir,* Oklahoma Historical Society, Research Center, Oklahoma City OK
Blackburn, Gary L, *Assoc Prof,* Mercer University, Art Dept, Macon GA (S)
Blackely, Colin, *Dept Head,* Eastern Michigan University, Ford Gallery, Ypsilanti MI
Blackhurst, Phillip, *Prof Emer,* University of Kansas, The School of the Arts, Dept of Visual Art, Lawrence KS (S)
Blackman, Ivy, *Mng Librn,* Whitney Museum of American Art, Frances Mulhall Achilles Library, New York NY
Blackmon, Mary Collins, *Dir,* Elisabet Ney, Library, Austin TX
Blackmon, Mary Collins, *Dir,* Elisabet Ney, Austin TX
Blackmore, Eric, *Adjunct Instr Art,* Florida Southern College, Melvin Art Gallery, Lakeland FL
Blackmore, Eric, *Adjunct Instr Art,* Florida Southern College, Department of Art & Art History, Lakeland FL (S)
Blackmun, Barbara, *Instr,* San Diego Mesa College, Fine Arts Dept, San Diego CA (S)
Blackport, Mary Jo, *Library Dir,* Olivet College, Library, Olivet MI

Blackson, Robert, *Dir Exhibs,* Temple University, Temple Contemporary, Philadelphia PA
Blackstone, Julie, *Asst Prof,* Oklahoma Baptist University, Art & Design Dept, Shawnee OK (S)
Blackwell Pence, Cat, *Cur Galleries,* Memphis College of Art, Memphis TN (S)
Blackwell, Mary, *Production Mgr,* City of Hampton, Hampton Arts Commission, Hampton VA
Blackwell, Tyler, *School Progs Asst,* The Art Institute of Chicago, Crown Family Educator Resource Center, Chicago IL
Blackwood, C Roy, *Art History,* Southeastern Louisiana University, Art & Design, Hammond LA (S)
Bladen, Martha, *Exec Dir,* Switzerland County Historical Society Inc, Life on the Ohio: River History Museum, Vevay IN
Bladen, Martha, *Exec Dir,* Switzerland County Historical Society Inc, Switzerland County Historical Museum, Vevay IN
Blades, John, *Dir,* Henry Morrison Flagler Museum, Palm Beach FL
Blades, Rena, *Pres & CEO,* Cultural Council of Palm Beach County, Lake Worth FL
Blaine, Becky, *Pres,* Illinois Alliance for Arts Education (IAAE), DeKalb IL
Blaine-Cher, Cidney, *Registrar & Social Media Mgr,* Page Bond Gallery, Richmond VA
Blair, Brent, *Instr,* Gettysburg College, Dept of Visual Arts, Gettysburg PA (S)
Blair, Cindy, *Artist in Res,* Alexandria Museum of Art, Alexandria LA
Blair, David, *Deputy Dir,* University of California, Los Angeles, Fowler Museum at UCLA, Los Angeles CA
Blair, Nikki, *Prof,* University of North Carolina at Greensboro, School of Art, Greensboro NC (S)
Blair, Steve, *Asst Prof Music-Jazz,* Johnson State College, Dept Fine & Performing Arts, Dibden Center for the Arts, Johnson VT (S)
Blair, Terri, *Instr,* Grayson County College, Art Dept, Denison TX (S)
Blake, Casey, *Pub Rels Dir,* Mesa Arts Center, Mesa Contemporary Arts Museum, Mesa AZ
Blake, Edward, *Chmn,* Dayton Art Institute, Dayton OH
Blake, Erin, *Head Coll Info Servs,* Folger Shakespeare, Washington DC
Blake, Holly, *Residency Mgr,* Headlands Center for the Arts, Sausalito CA
Blake, Janet, *Cur Historical Art,* Laguna Art Museum, Laguna Beach CA
Blake, Jody, *Prof,* Bucknell University, Dept of Art, Lewisburg PA (S)
Blake, Joy, *Accounting & HR,* Virginia Museum of Contemporary Art, Virginia Beach VA
Blake, Judy, *Grants,* Newport Art Museum and Association, Newport RI
Blakeley, Karel, *Chmn & Asst. Prof,* Le Moyne College, Visual & Performing Arts Dept, Syracuse NY (S)
Blakeley, Loretta, *Library Admin Support Coordr,* California State University Stanislaus, Vasche Library, Turlock CA
Blakely, David, *Dir Theater Dept,* North Carolina Wesleyan College, Dept of Visual & Performing Arts, Rocky Mount NC (S)
Blakely, George, *Prof,* Florida State University, Art Dept, Tallahassee FL (S)
Blakely, Glen, *Prof,* Dixie College, Art Dept, Saint George UT (S)
Blakely, Larry, *Asst Prof,* Taylor University, Visual Art Dept, Upland IN (S)
Blakeslee-Collin, Carol, *Dir & Cur,* Clinton County Historical Association, Clinton County Historical Museum, Plattsburgh NY
Blalock Jones, Ruth, *Commissioner,* United States Department of the Interior, Indian Arts & Crafts Board, Washington DC
Blamos, Donald C, *Dir,* McLennan Community College, Visual Arts Dept, Waco TX (S)
Blancas, Elizabeth, *Volunteer & Intern Coordr,* Galeria de la Raza, Studio 24, San Francisco CA
Blanchard Gross, Diana, *Cur,* Peninsula Fine Arts Center, Newport News VA
Blanchard, Andrew, *Assoc Prof Studio Art,* Converse College, School of the Arts, Dept of Art & Design, Spartanburg SC (S)
Blanchard, Edith M, *Dir,* City of Mason City, Charles H MacNider Art Museum, Mason City IA
Blanchard, Edward V, *Pres,* American Folk Art Museum, New York NY
Blanchard, Julie, *VPres,* New England Watercolor Society, Boston MA
Blanchard, Marianne, *Pres,* Schenectady County Historical Society, Schenectady NY
Blanchard, Mary, *Cur, Mgr & Purchasing,* New England Maple Museum, Pittsford VT
Blanchard, Michael, *Pres,* New England Maple Museum, Pittsford VT
Blanchard, Paula, *Operations & Communs Mgr,* CMCA-Center for Maine Contemporary Art, Art Gallery, Rockport ME
Blanchet, Jacques, *VP,* La Chambre Blanche, Quebec QC
Blanchette, Manon, *Pres,* Canadian Museums Association, Association des Musees Canadiens, Ottawa ON
Blanco, Ivanete, *Assoc Prof,* Old Dominion University, Art Dept, Norfolk VA (S)
Bland, Bartholomew, *Cur Exhibs,* The Hudson River Museum, Yonkers NY
Bland, Donna, *1st VPres,* Coppini Academy of Fine Arts, Library, San Antonio TX
Bland, Sharon, *Owner,* Tabor Opera House Museum, Leadville CO
Bland, Tom, *Asst Dean,* California Institute of the Arts, School of Art, Valencia CA (S)
Blanding, Amber, *Art Adminr,* Stone Quarry Hill Art Park, Winner Gallery, Cazenovia NY
Blank, Peter, *Deputy Librn,* Stanford University, Art & Architecture Library, Stanford CA
Blankemeyer, Gary, *COO & CFO,* The Mint Museum, Charlotte NC
Blankenbaker, Jeremiah, *Registrar,* Rockford Art Museum, Rockford IL
Blankenmeyer, Gary, *COO & CFO,* The Mint Museum, Art Organization & Library, Charlotte NC
Blankenship, Angela, *Bus Mgr,* Lightner Museum, Saint Augustine FL
Blankenship, Cory, *Cur,* Charles B Goddard, Ardmore OK
Blankenship, Jody, *CEO & Exec Dir,* Connecticut Historical Society, Hartford CT
Blanton, Linnis, *Instr,* Lamar University, Art Dept, Beaumont TX (S)
Blatchley, Jeremy, *Reference Librn,* Bryn Mawr College, Rhys Carpenter Library for Art, Archaeology, Classics & Cities, Bryn Mawr PA
Blatchley, Ronald, *Pres,* Clinton Art Association, River Arts Center, Clinton IA
Blaugher, Kurt, *Art Faculty,* Mount Saint Mary's University, Visual & Performing Arts Dept, Emmitsburg MD (S)
Blauvelt, Andrew, *Mus Dir,* Cranbrook Academy of Art, Bloomfield Hills MI (S)
Blayton, Anitra, *Assoc Prof,* Tarrant County College, Art Dept, Hurst TX (S)
Blazek, Sonya, *Cur Asst,* Thames Art Gallery, Chatham ON
Bleeke, Marian, *Assoc Prod,* Cleveland State University, Art Dept, Cleveland OH (S)
Bleiberg, Edward, *Sr Cur Egyptian, Classical & Ancient Near Eastern Art,* Brooklyn Museum, Brooklyn NY
Bleiweis, Maxine, *Dir,* Westport Public Library, Westport CT
Blereau, Laura, *Cur,* University of Louisiana at Lafayette, Paul and Lulu Hilliard University Art Museum, Lafayette LA
Blessing, Jennifer, *Cur Photography,* Solomon R Guggenheim Museum, New York NY
Bletter, Rosemarie Haag, *Prof Emerita,* City University of New York, PhD Program in Art History, New York NY (S)
Blevins, Tedd, *Instr,* Virginia Intermont College, Fine Arts Div, Bristol VA (S)
Blew, Gregory, *Clinical Asst Prof,* University of Illinois at Chicago, Biomedical Visualization, Chicago IL (S)
Blick, Sarah, *Prof,* Kenyon College, Art Dept, Gambier OH (S)
Blinderman, Barry, *Dir,* Illinois State University, University Galleries, Normal IL
Blinn, Ken, *Educ Progs,* The Barnum Museum, Bridgeport CT
Bliss, Harry E, *Assoc Prof & Dir,* Palomar Community College, Art Dept, San Marcos CA (S)
Bliss, Kelly, *Cataloger,* Corning Museum of Glass, Juliette K and Leonard S Rakow Research Library, Corning NY
Bliss, Sara, *Asst to Dir,* American Civilization Foundation, National Museum of American Illustration, Newport RI
Blitch, Jenna, *Mem Svcs Coord,* Morris Museum of Art, Augusta GA
Blizard, Christine, *Asst Prof,* University of Texas at San Antonio, Dept of Art & Art History, San Antonio TX (S)
Bloch, Kathy, *Colls Mgr,* Spertus Institute of Jewish Studies, Chicago IL
Bloch, Laura, *Accounting Mgr,* San Francisco Arts Education Project, San Francisco CA
Blochmann, George, *Dir,* Goethe-Institut New York, New York NY
Block, Alex, *Artist,* Walker's Point Artists Assoc Inc, Gallery 218, Milwaukee WI
Block, Diana, *Gallery Dir,* University of North Texas, Art Gallery, Denton TX
Block, Holly, *Exec Dir,* Bronx Museum of the Arts, Bronx NY
Block, Jane, *Librn,* University of Illinois at Urbana-Champaign, Ricker Library of Architecture & Art, Champaign IL
Block, Judy, *Assoc Prof,* Wellesley College, Art Dept, Wellesley MA (S)
Block, Lora, *Pres,* Pastel Society of Oregon, Roseburg OR
Block, Sarah, *Asst to Chair,* Mount Royal College, Dept of Interior Design, Calgary AB (S)
Blocker, Jane, *Assoc Prof,* University of Minnesota, Minneapolis, Art History, Minneapolis MN (S)
Blocton, Lulu, *Chmn,* Eastern Connecticut State University, Fine Arts Dept, Willimantic CT (S)
Bloess, Elizabeth, *Mus Opers Supv,* Forest Lawn Museum, Glendale CA
Blomquist, Shastyn, *Asst Cur & Exhibitions Coordr,* The Center for Contemporary Arts of Santa Fe, Santa Fe NM
Blomstrom, Stacey, *Director,* Studio Gallery, Washington DC
Blondin, Bruce, *Instr,* Solano Community College, Division of Fine & Applied Art & Behavioral Science, Fairfield CA (S)
Blondin, Jill, *Asst Prof,* University of Texas at Tyler, Department of Art, School of Visual & Performing Arts, Tyler TX (S)
Blood, Peggy, *Dir,* Savannah State University, Dept of Fine Arts, Savannah GA (S)
Bloodgood, Craig, *Contemporary Cur,* Art Complex Museum, Carl A Weyerhaeuser Library, Duxbury MA
Bloodgood, Josephine, *Exec Dir & Cur Permanent Coll,* Woodstock Artists Association & Museum, Woodstock NY
Bloodgood, Josephine, *Executive Director,* Historic Huguenot Street, New Paltz NY
Bloom, Charles, *VP Corp Svcs,* Canadian Museum of Nature, Musee Canadien de la Nature, Ottawa ON
Bloom, Ken, *Dir,* University of Minnesota Duluth, Tweed Museum of Art, Duluth MN
Bloom, Sharon, *Chmn,* West Shore Community College, Division of Humanities & Fine Arts, Scottville MI (S)
Bloom, Sue, *Dept Head,* Western Maryland College, Dept of Art & Art History, Westminster MD (S)
Bloomer, Harlan, *Dir,* Minnesota State University, Mankato, Mankato MN

Bloomer, Jerry, *Secy-Treas,* R W Norton Art Foundation, Library, Shreveport LA
Bloomfield, Debra, *Instr,* Solano Community College, Division of Fine & Applied Art & Behavioral Science, Fairfield CA (S)
Bloomquist, Charly, *Instr,* Whitman College, Art Dept, Walla Walla WA (S)
Bloomquist, Laura, *Website Admin,* Culture Capital, Washington DC
Blosser, John, *Chmn,* Goshen College, Art Dept, Goshen IN (S)
Blount, Amy, *Instr,* Pierce College, Art Dept, Woodland Hills CA (S)
Blue, Carol, *Cur Educ,* Branigan Cultural Center, Las Cruces NM
Blum, Andrea, *Assoc Chair, Studio Art,* Hunter College, Dept of Art & Art History, New York NY (S)
Blum, Martin, *Dept Head Critical Studies,* University of British Columbia Okanagan, Faculty of Creative & Critical Studies, Kelowna BC (S)
Blum-Cumming, Nancy, *Lectr,* University of Wisconsin-Stout, Dept of Art & Design, Menomonie WI (S)
Blumberg, Adam, *Exhibs Technician,* Temple University, Temple Contemporary, Philadelphia PA
Blumberg, Linda, *Exec Dir,* Art Dealers Association of America, Inc, New York NY
Blundell, Harry, *Dir Theatre,* Arts Center of the Ozarks, Springdale AR
Blundell, Kathi, *Dir,* Arts Center of the Ozarks, Springdale AR
Blunt, Hannah, *Curatorial Asst,* Mount Holyoke College, Art Museum, South Hadley MA
Boada, Maria, *Gen Educ,* Art Institute of Pittsburgh, Pittsburgh PA (S)
Board, Aaron, *Instr,* Mohawk Valley Community College, Utica NY (S)
Bober, Jacqueline, *Cur,* City of Lubbock, Buddy Holly Center, Lubbock TX
Bobick, Bruce, *Chmn,* State University of West Georgia, Art Dept, Carrollton GA (S)
Bobo, Susan, *Architecture Librn,* Oklahoma State University, Architecture Library, Stillwater OK
Bobrow, Niclk, *Deputy Dir Opers & CFO,* Royal Ontario Museum, Toronto ON
Boccardo-Dubay, Genny, *Deputy Dir,* Laguna Art Museum, Laguna Beach CA
Bocci, Roberto, *Prof,* Georgetown University, Dept of Art & Art History, Washington DC (S)
Bochicchio, Nicholas, *Dir Admin Servs,* Ferguson Library, Stamford CT
Bochnowski, Jean, *Dir,* National Audubon Society, John James Audubon Center at Mill Grove, Audubon PA
Bock, Elaine, *Exec Sec,* Jefferson County Historical Society, Watertown NY
Bockbrader, Nancy, *Prof, Chairperson,* Rhode Island College, Art Dept, Providence RI (S)
Bockelman, James, *Dir,* Concordia University, Marxhausen Art Gallery, Seward NE
Bockelman, Jim, *Prof,* Concordia University, Art Dept, Seward NE (S)
Bockelman, Josie, *Dir Educ,* The Clay Studio, Philadelphia PA
Bocz, George, *Assoc Prof,* Florida State University, Art Dept, Tallahassee FL (S)
Boden, Jim, *Prof Painting & Drawing,* Coker College, Art Dept, Hartsville SC (S)
Bodenheimer, Louise, *Asst Prof,* Southeast Missouri State University, Dept of Art, Cape Girardeau MO (S)
Bodily, Vince, *Instr,* Ricks College, Dept of Art, Rexburg ID (S)
Bodine, William, *Dir,* The Frick Art & Historical Center, Inc, Frick Art Museum, Pittsburgh PA
Bodle, Kelli, *Asst Cur,* Boca Raton Museum of Art, Boca Raton FL
Boehine, Sarah E, *Cur,* Nelda C & H J Lutcher Stark Foundation, Stark Museum of Art, Orange TX
Boehm, Barbara, *Sr Cur,* The Metropolitan Museum of Art, The Met Cloisters, New York NY
Boehme, Anne-Dorothee, *Spec Col Librn,* School of the Art Institute of Chicago, John M Flaxman Library, Chicago IL
Boehr, Kay M, *Asst Prof,* Park University, Dept of Art & Design, Parkville MO (S)
Boerner, Steve, *Librn & Archivist,* East Hampton Library, Long Island Collection, East Hampton NY
Boettcher, Chris, *Exec Dir,* Randall Junior Museum, San Francisco CA
Boettcher, Graham, *Dir,* Birmingham Museum of Art, Birmingham AL
Boettcher, Graham, *Mus Dir,* Birmingham Museum of Art, Clarence B Hanson Jr Library, Birmingham AL
Bogart, Heath, *Coordr Coll Analysis & Develop,* Fort Hays State University, Forsyth Library, Hays KS
Bogart, Michele H, *Prof,* Stony Brook University, College of Arts & Sciences, Dept of Art, Stony Brook NY (S)
Bogdanov, Kristina, *Asst Prof,* Ohio Wesleyan University, Fine Arts Dept, Delaware OH (S)
Boger, Christyl, *Asst Prof,* Indiana University, Bloomington, Henry Radford Hope School of Fine Arts, Bloomington IN (S)
Boggess, Evan, *Dir Exhib,* Shepherd University, Dept of Contemporary Art & Theater, Shepherdstown WV (S)
Boggess, Lynn, *Prof,* Fairmont State College, Div of Fine Arts, Fairmont WV (S)
Boggs, David, *Assoc Prof,* Concordia College, Art Dept, Moorhead MN (S)
Bogle, Bridgett, *Instr,* Sinclair Community College, Division of Fine & Performing Arts, Dayton OH (S)
Bognar, Pat, *Dir,* University of Portland, Buckley Center Gallery, Portland OR
Bogoniewski, Scott, *Chmn Entertainment Arts,* College for Creative Studies, Detroit MI (S)
Bogosian, David, *Chief Preparator,* Purchase College, Neuberger Museum of Art, Purchase NY
Bogosian, Sara, *President/Executive Dir.,* Lowell Art Association, Inc, Whistler House Museum of Art, Lowell MA
Bohan, Ruth, *Assoc Prof,* University of Missouri, Saint Louis, Dept of Art & Art History, Saint Louis MO (S)
Bohannon, Jordan, *Marketing & Digital Content Coordr,* Tucson Museum of Art and Historic Block, Tucson AZ
Bohannon, Kenneth, *Exec Dir,* Charles B Goddard, Ardmore OK
Bohlinger, Karen, *Exec Dir,* Holter Museum of Art, Helena MT
Bohlk, Laurie, *Assoc Dir Communs & Mktg,* Cooper Hewitt, Smithsonian Design Museum, Smithsonian Institution, New York NY
Bohls, Margaret, *Asst Prof,* University of Minnesota, Minneapolis, Dept of Art, Minneapolis MN (S)
Bohmann, Emma, *Develop Mgr,* Arts Midwest, Minneapolis MN
Bohnert, Thomas, *Prof,* Mott Community College, Fine Arts & Social Sciences Division, Flint MI (S)
Bohr, Ted, *Gallery Dir,* Creighton University, Fine & Performing Arts Dept, Omaha NE (S)
Bohrer, Fred, *Assoc Prof,* Hood College, Dept of Art, Frederick MD (S)
Bokamba, Eyenga, *Exec Dir,* Intermedia Arts, Minneapolis MN
Bokelman, Dorothy, *Dir,* Nazareth College of Rochester, Art Dept, Rochester NY (S)
Boland, Lynn, *Cur Pierre Daura,* University of Georgia, Georgia Museum of Art, Athens GA
Bolanos, Susan, *Registrar,* Museum of Latin American Art, Long Beach CA
Bolcer, John, *Univ Archivist,* University of Washington, Univ of Washington Libraries, Special Collections, Seattle WA
Bolden, Joyce, *Chmn,* Alcorn State University, Dept of Fine Arts, Lorman MS (S)
Boldenow, John, *Theatre Develop,* Wichita Center for the Arts, Mary R Koch School of Visual Arts, Wichita KS (S)
Bolding, Gary, *Prof,* Stetson University, Department of Creative Arts, Deland FL (S)
Bolduc, Sara, *Treas,* Marblehead Arts Association, Inc, Marblehead MA
Bolen, Jerry, *Dept Head,* Southwestern Illinois College, Art Dept, Belleville IL (S)
Bolge, George, *CEO,* Museum of Art - Deland FL, Inc, Deland FL
Bolger, Laurie, *Conservation Librn,* University Club Library, New York NY
Bolker, Mare, *Vis Asst Prof Art,* Whitman College, Art Dept, Walla Walla WA (S)
Bollinger, Ben, *Dean of Faculty,* Citrus College, Art Dept, Glendora CA (S)
Bollmann, Marc, *Library Asst,* University of Rochester, Art/Music Library, Rochester NY
Bolser, Barbara, *Asst Prof,* University of Illinois at Springfield, Visual Arts Program, Springfield IL (S)
Bolt, Ed, *Mill Site Mgr,* Pickens County Museum of Art & History, Pickens SC
Bolt, Macyn, *Preparator,* Fried, Frank, Harris, Shriver & Jacobson, Art Collection, New York NY
Bolt, Marvin, *Cur Science & Technology,* Corning Museum of Glass, Museum, Corning NY
Bolton, Andrew, *Cur in Charge, The Costume Inst,* The Metropolitan Museum of Art, New York NY
Bolton, David, *Ceramics,* College of Lake County, Art Dept, Grayslake IL (S)
Bomberger, Bruce D, *Cur,* Landis Valley Village and Farm Museum, PA Historical & Museum Commission, Landis Collections Gallery, Lancaster PA
Bomberger, Bruce, *Cur,* Landis Valley Village and Farm Museum, PA Historical & Museum Commission, Lancaster PA
Bonario, Bernard, *Chmn Art History,* University of Saint Thomas, Fine and Performing Arts Dept, Houston TX (S)
Bonas, Rebecca, *Dir Prog,* Morgan County Foundation, Inc, Madison-Morgan Cultural Center, Madison GA
Bond, Deborah, *Librn,* Pensacola Museum of Art, Harry Thornton Library, Pensacola FL
Bond, Janet, *Reference Librn,* Kutztown University, Rohrbach Library, Kutztown PA
Bond, Kener E, *Prof,* Rochester Institute of Technology, School of Design, Rochester NY (S)
Bondarchuk, Karen, *Foundation Area Coordr,* Western Michigan University, Frostic School of Art, Kalamazoo MI (S)
Bonde, Sheila, *Prof & Chair,* Brown University, Dept of History of Art & Architecture, Providence RI (S)
Bondil, Nathalie, *Chief Cur & Cur European Art,* Montreal Museum of Fine Arts, Montreal QC
Bondil, Nathalie, *Dir, Chief Cur & Cur European Art,* Montreal Museum of Fine Arts, Montreal QC
Bone, Lloyd E, *Chmn,* Glenville State College, Dept of Fine Arts, Glenville WV (S)
Bonilla, Ileana, *Mgr,* Wells Fargo & Co, History Museum, Los Angeles CA
Bonjorni, Mary Ann, *Prof,* University of Montana, School of Art, Missoula MT (S)
Bonn, Claudia, *Dir Exec/Pres,* Wave Hill, Bronx NY
Bonnelly, Claude, *Dir Gen Library System,* L'Universite Laval, Library, Quebec QC
Bonnemaison, Susan, *Prof & Grad Coordr,* Dalhousie University, School of Architecture, Halifax NS (S)
Bonner, Charles, *Artist,* Keystone Gallery, Scott City KS
Bonner, Jean, *Dean Art Dept,* Schoolcraft College, Dept of Art & Design, Livonia MI (S)
Bonner, Judith H, *Sr Cur,* The Historic New Orleans Collection, Royal Street Galleries, New Orleans LA
Bonner, Logan, *Web Designer,* Keystone Gallery, Scott City KS
Bonner, Peter, *Adj Prof,* Saint Joseph's University, Art Dept, Philadelphia PA (S)
Bonzelaar, Helen, *Prof,* Calvin College, Art Dept, Grand Rapids MI (S)
Book, Michael, *Assoc Prof,* Louisiana State University, School of Art, Baton Rouge LA (S)

Booker, Mary Ames, *Cur,* State of North Carolina, Battleship North Carolina, Wilmington NC
Booker, Robert, *Chief Security,* Brandywine Conservancy, Brandywine River Museum, Chadds Ford PA
Bookwalter, Thomas, *Asst Prof,* Kansas State University, Art Dept, Manhattan KS (S)
Boomhower, Daniel, *Dir Libr,* Dumbarton Oaks, Dumbarton Oaks Research Library, Washington DC
Boone, Allyn, *Develop Dir,* Lauren Rogers, Laurel MS
Boone, Elizabeth, *Prof,* Tulane University, Sophie H Newcomb Memorial College, New Orleans LA (S)
Boord, Charlotte, *Mus Supv,* City of San Antonio, Spanish Governor's Palace, San Antonio TX
Boot, Chris, *Exec Dir,* Aperture Foundation, New York NY
Boot, Lee, *Affiliate Assoc Prof & Assoc Dir Imaging Research Ctr,* University of Maryland, Baltimore County, Intermedia & Digital Arts (IMDA), Dept of Visual Arts, Baltimore MD (S)
Booth, Annette, *Dir Exhibitions,* Aperture Foundation, New York NY
Booth, Cynthia, *Interim Library Dir,* Maryland Institute, Decker Library, Baltimore MD
Booth, Helen, *Mus Dir,* Jordan Historical Museum of The Twenty, Jordan ON
Booth, Michael, *Chmn,* Blue Mountain Community College, Fine Arts Dept, Pendleton OR (S)
Booth, Paul, *Asst Prof,* Fort Lewis College, Art Dept, Durango CO (S)
Booth, Paula, *Dir Gallery,* Western Oregon University, Dan & Gail Cannon Gallery of Art, Monmouth OR
Booth, Peter, *Dir,* Museum of Western Colorado, Museum of the West, Grand Junction CO
Booth, Robert, *Prof,* State University of New York at Fredonia, Dept of Art, Fredonia NY (S)
Boothby, Ron, *Dir Facilities,* Kalamazoo Institute of Arts, Kalamazoo MI
Boothe, Berrisford, *Assoc Prof,* Lehigh University, Dept of Art, Architecture & Design, Bethlehem PA (S)
Boothe, Constance, *Instr,* Clark-Atlanta University, School of Arts & Sciences, Atlanta GA (S)
Boothe, Power, *Dir,* Ohio University, School of Art, Athens OH (S)
Bopp, Jay, *Chmn,* Bob Jones University, School of Fine Arts, Div of Art & Design, Greenville SC (S)
Boppel, Todd, *Prof,* University of Wisconsin-Stout, Dept of Art & Design, Menomonie WI (S)
Borchardt, Susan A, *Asst Dir,* Gunston Hall Plantation, Mason Neck VA
Borchardt, Susan, *Cur,* Gunston Hall Plantation, Library, Mason Neck VA
Borcherbing, Kate, *Asst Prof,* Sam Houston State University, Art Dept, Huntsville TX (S)
Bordeaux, Mary, *Cur,* Heritage Center, Inc, Pine Ridge SD
Borden, Lee, *Events & Commun,* Western Colorado Center for the Arts, The Art Center, Grand Junction CO
Borderud, Jennifer, *Access & Outreach Librn,* Baylor University, Armstrong Browning Library, Waco TX
Boreen, Jean, *Assoc Dean,* Northern Arizona University, College of Arts & Letters, Flagstaff AZ (S)
Boresen, Gloria, *Gen Mgr,* Fort Collins Museum of Art, Inc, Fort Collins CO
Borey, Erica, *Colls Mgr,* National Society of the Colonial Dames of America in The Commonwealth of Virginia, Wilton House Museum, Richmond VA
Borg, Victoria, *Communs Coordr,* Oakville Galleries, Centennial Square and Gairloch Gardens, Oakville ON
Borge, John, *Instr,* Concordia College, Art Dept, Moorhead MN (S)
Borges, Seb, *Gen Mgr,* Providence Art Club, Providence RI
Borgeson Zimmer, Jacquelyn L, *Cur,* Martin and Osa Johnson, Chanute KS
Borgeson, Jacquelyn, *Cur,* Martin and Osa Johnson, Imperato Collection of West African Artifacts, Chanute KS
Borgeson, Jacquelyn, *Cur,* Martin and Osa Johnson, Selsor Art Gallery, Chanute KS
Borgeson, Jacquelyn, *Cur,* Martin and Osa Johnson, Johnson Collection of Photographs, Movies & Memorabilia, Chanute KS
Borgeson, Jacquelyn, *Cur,* Martin and Osa Johnson, Scott Explorers Library, Chanute KS
Borick, Carl, *Dir & CEO,* Charleston Museum, Charleston SC
Boring, Christine, *Exec Dir,* Arts on the Park, Lakeland Center for Creative Arts, Lakeland FL
Boris, Staci, *Assoc Dir & Cur Contemporary Art,* Carl & Marilynn Thoma Art Foundation, Art House Santa Fe, Santa Fe NM
Borja, Sheena, *Gift & Develop,* Stanford University, Cantor Arts Center at Stanford University, Stanford CA
Borland, Jennifer, *Assoc Prof,* Oklahoma State University, Department of Art, Graphic Design and Art History, Stillwater OK (S)
Born, Richard A, *Sr Cur,* University of Chicago, Smart Museum of Art, Chicago IL
Bornarth, Philip W, *Prof,* Rochester Institute of Technology, School of Design, Rochester NY (S)
Borrego, Andrew, *Instr,* Bakersfield College, Art Dept, Bakersfield CA (S)
Borromeo, Gina, *Cur Ancient Art,* Rhode Island School of Design, Museum of Art, Providence RI
Borsberry, Joe, *Pres,* Contemporary Art Center, Peoria IL
Borst, Kim, *Lectr,* University of Wisconsin-Superior, Programs in the Visual Arts, Superior WI (S)
Bortoli, Natalie, *VPres Educ Prog & Experience Devel,* Chicago Children's Museum, Chicago IL
Borys, Stephen D, *Dir & CEO,* The Winnipeg Art Gallery, Winnipeg MB
Bos, Rosanne, *2nd VPres,* Frontier Gateway Museum, Glendive MT
Bosch, Doug, *Assoc Prof, Found Coordr,* Rhode Island College, Art Dept, Providence RI (S)
Bosch, Lindsay, *Snr Mgmt Mktg & Comm,* Northwestern University, Mary & Leigh Block Museum of Art, Evanston IL
Bosch, Stephen, *Librn,* University of Arizona, Library, Tucson AZ
Bosco, Bob, *Instr,* Creighton University, Fine & Performing Arts Dept, Omaha NE (S)
Bosco, Christine, *Dir Spec Events & Facility Rental,* Caramoor Center for Music & the Arts, Inc, Rosen House at Caramoor, Katonah NY
Bose, Arvn, *Assoc Prof,* Herbert H Lehman, Art Dept, Bronx NY (S)
Boshart, Jeff, *Prof,* Eastern Illinois University, Art Dept, Charleston IL (S)
Boshart, Jon D, *Chmn,* Saint Peter's College, Fine Arts Dept, Jersey City NJ (S)
Bosiak, Amanda, *Mem Svcs Coordr,* Saskatchewan Craft Council & Affinity Gallery, Saskatoon SK
Bosket, Jamie, *Pres & CEO,* Virginia Historical Society, Richmond VA
Bosse, David C, *Librn,* Historic Deerfield, Inc, Henry N Flynt Library, Deerfield MA
Bosse, David, *Libr,* Pocumtuck Valley Memorial Association, Memorial Hall Museum, Deerfield MA
Bosselmann, Peter, *Prof Urban Design in Architecture, Head Grad Adviser & Head Master Urban Design Prog,* University of California, Berkeley, College of Environmental Design, Berkeley CA (S)
Bostock, Bret, *Colls Mgr,* Academy of the New Church, Glencairn Museum, Bryn Athyn PA
Bostrom, Jane, *Spec Events,* Eastern Shore Art Association, Inc, Eastern Shore Art Center, Fairhope AL
Bostrom, Leslie, *Prof & Chair,* Brown University, Dept of Visual Art, Providence RI (S)
Boswell, Tracy, *Adjunct Prof Art History,* Johnson County Community College, Fine Arts Dept & Art History Dept, Overland Park KS (S)
Bosworth, Barbara, *Chmn Media,* Massachusetts College of Art, Boston MA (S)
Bosworth, Earl F, *Dir,* Broward County Board of Commissioners, Broward Cultural Div, Fort Lauderdale FL
Botier, Saul, *Student Employee,* Manhattanville College, Brownson Gallery, Purchase NY
Botier, Saul, *Student Employee,* Manhattanville College, Arthur M Berger Gallery, Purchase NY
Botti-Salitsky, Rose, *Lectr,* Mount Ida College, Chamberlayne School of Design & Merchandising, Boston MA (S)
Bottinelli, Lora, *Exec Dir,* Salisbury University, Ward Museum of Wildfowl Art, Salisbury MD
Bottomley, Kristina, *Snr Registrar,* Northwestern University, Mary & Leigh Block Museum of Art, Evanston IL
Bottonly-O'looney, Jennifer, *Sr Cur,* Montana Historical Society, Helena MT
Botwinick, Michael, *Dir,* The Hudson River Museum, Yonkers NY
Bouasavanh, Kheuavanh, *Sr Admin Asst,* Santa Clara University, de Saisset Museum, Santa Clara CA
Bouc, Rod, *Executive Deputy Dir Oper & Chief Registrar,* Columbus Museum of Art, Columbus OH
Boucher, Alanna, *Educ Prog Asst,* New Bedford Art Museum/Artworks!, New Bedford MA
Boucher, Barbara, *Dir,* Mohawk Valley Center for the Arts Inc, Little Falls NY
Boucher, Kathryn, *Dir,* Converse College, Milliken Art Gallery, Spartanburg SC
Boudet, Daniel, *Web & eMktg Mgr,* Cultural Council of Palm Beach County, Lake Worth FL
Boudreau, Donna, *Dir Admin,* New Brunswick College of Craft & Design, Fredericton NB (S)
Boudrot, Christopher, *Dir Bus Opers & Augusta Thomas Dir Finance,* Boston Athenaeum, Boston MA
Bouffard, Karen, *Pres,* Portsmouth Athenaeum, Joseph Copley Research Library, Portsmouth NH
Boughton, Douglas, *Div Head Art Educ,* Northern Illinois University, School of Art & Design, DeKalb IL (S)
Bouin, Thierry, *Supt,* Forges du Saint-Maurice National Historic Site, Trois Rivieres QC
Boulanger, Jennifer, *Dean,* Herkimer County Community College, Humanities Social Services, Herkimer NY (S)
Boulton, Anna, *Community Outreach Mgr,* Utah Arts Council, Chase Home Museum of Utah Folk Arts, Salt Lake City UT
Boulware, Jonathan, *Exec Dir,* South Street Seaport Museum, Melville Gallery, New York NY
Boulware, Jonathan, *Exec Dir,* South Street Seaport Museum, New York NY
Bourassa, Linda, *Prof,* Hiram College, Art Dept, Hiram OH (S)
Bourbeau, Melanie, *Cur,* Hill-Stead Museum, Farmington CT
Bourbon, Matthew, *Assoc Prof Drawing & Painting,* University of North Texas, College of Visual Arts & Design, Denton TX (S)
Bourdon, Alison, *Visual Content Mgr,* The One Club for Creativity, New York NY
Bourgault, Therese, *Tech Svcs Librarian,* Montreal Museum of Fine Arts, Library, Montreal QC
Bourgeau, Jef, *Creative Dir,* Museum of New Art, Troy MI
Bourgeois, Angi, *Asst Prof,* Mississippi State University, Dept of Art, Starville MS (S)
Bourgeois, John, *Prog Dir, Film & TV Acting,* Humber College, School of Creative & Performing Arts, Toronto ON (S)
Bourne, Sandy, *Chief Mktg & Communs Officer,* Royal Ontario Museum, Toronto ON
Bourque, Paul, *Technician,* Galerie d'art de l'Universite de Moncton, Moncton NB
Bourque, Susan, *Exhibits Coordr,* Oregon State University, Memorial Union Art Gallery, Corvallis OR
Bousson, Susie, *Admin,* Lannan Foundation, Santa Fe NM

Bouton, Cassie, *Gallery Manager,* Kennebec Valley Art Association, Harlow Gallery, Hallowell ME
Bouw, Jonathan, *Assoc Prof,* Taylor University, Visual Art Dept, Upland IN (S)
Bouw, Jonathan, *Chmn,* Taylor University, Metcalf Art Gallery, Upland IN
Bowar, Sharon, *Assoc Prof,* Wilkes University, Dept of Art, Wilkes-Barre PA (S)
Bowditch, Lucy, *Prof,* The College of Saint Rose, The Center For Art and Design, Albany NY (S)
Bowen, Kasuya, *Assoc Prof,* Florida State University, Art Dept, Tallahassee FL (S)
Bowen, Kate, *Video Prog Coordr,* Museum of Contemporary Photography, Columbia College Chicago, Chicago IL
Bowen, Katrina, *Reference,* Mason City Public Library, Mason City IA
Bowen, Ken, *Adjunct Instr,* Virginia Wesleyan College, Art Dept of the Humanities Div, Norfolk VA (S)
Bowen, Linnell R, *Exec Dir,* Maryland Hall for the Creative Arts, Chaney Gallery, Annapolis MD
Bowen, Nancy, *Assoc Prof,* Purchase College, State University of New York, School of Art+Design, Purchase NY (S)
Bowen, Robert, *CFO,* Detroit Institute of Arts, Detroit MI
Bower, Bob, *Div Dir,* Southwestern Oregon Community College, Visual Arts Dept, Coos Bay OR (S)
Bower, Gerald, *Prof,* Louisiana State University, School of Art, Baton Rouge LA (S)
Bower, Joe, *Dir Develop,* Kalamazoo Institute of Arts, The Mary & Edwin Meader Fine Arts Library, Kalamazoo MI
Bower, Mary, *Cur Coll,* Evansville Museum of Arts, History & Science, Evansville IN
Bower-Peterson, Kathi, *Librn,* Library Association of La Jolla, Athenaeum Music & Arts Library, La Jolla CA
Bowers, Emma, *Dir,* Roberts County Museum, Miami TX
Bowers, John, *Asst Prof,* Oregon State University, Dept of Art, Corvallis OR (S)
Bowers, Paul, *Prof,* State University of New York at Fredonia, Dept of Art, Fredonia NY (S)
Bowers, Tiffini, *Cur History,* California African-American Museum, Los Angeles CA
Bowie, Jaclyn, *Gallery Educ,* CAM Contemporary Art Museum, Raleigh NC
Bowitz, John, *Chmn,* Morningside College, Art Dept, Sioux City IA (S)
Bowker, Jeanette, *Treas,* Blacksburg Regional Art Association, Blacksburg VA
Bowles, Johnson, *Asst Prof,* Longwood University, Dept of Art, Farmville VA (S)
Bowles, Kay Johnson, *Dir,* Longwood Center for the Visual Arts, Farmville VA
Bowles, Ron, *Dean Fine Arts,* Dallas Baptist University, Dept of Art, Dallas TX (S)
Bowles, Vickery, *City Librn,* Toronto Public Library Board, Library, Toronto ON
Bowling, Karen, *Designer,* Noyes Art Gallery, Lincoln NE
Bowling, Marilyn, *Design Coordr,* Ritz-Carlton Hotel Company, Art Collection, Chevy Chase MD
Bowman, Amy, *Adj Instr,* University of West Florida, Dept of Art, Pensacola FL (S)
Bowman, Amy, *Dir,* University of West Florida, Art Gallery, Pensacola FL
Bowman, Anthony, *Educ Outreach Coordr,* McLean County Historical Society, McLean County Museum of History, Bloomington IL
Bowman, Donna, *Vis Arts Librn,* University of Regina, Education/Fine Arts Library, Regina SK
Bowman, James, *Registrar & Exhib Preparator,* Dickinson College, The Trout Gallery, Carlisle PA
Bowman, Jessi, *Exhibitions Coord,* Houston Center For Photography, Houston TX
Bowman, JoAnn, *Cur,* Schuyler-Hamilton House, Morristown NJ
Bowman, John, *Assoc Prof Art (Drawing/Painting),* Pennsylvania State University, University Park, Penn State School of Visual Arts, University Park PA (S)
Bowman, Karmien, *Assoc Prof,* Tarrant County College, Art Dept, Hurst TX (S)
Bowman, Lee, *Instr,* Dallas Baptist University, Dept of Art, Dallas TX (S)
Bowman, Liz, *Public Art Administrator,* Kansas City Municipal Art Commission, Kansas City MO
Bowman, Portico K, *Prof,* Pittsburg State University, Art Dept, Pittsburg KS (S)
Bowman, Robert, *Exhibs Dir & Retail Mgr,* Minnetonka Center for the Arts, Wayzata MN
Bowman, Ruth, *Assoc Prof & Undergrad Coordr,* University of Kansas, The School of the Arts, Dept of Visual Art, Lawrence KS (S)
Bowman, Travis, *Supervising Cur,* New York State Office of Parks, Recreation and Historic Preservation, Bureau of Historic Sites, Waterford NY
Bowne, Kristine, *Vice Pres, Profl Develop & Industry Engagement,* ArtCenter College of Design, Pasadena CA (S)
Bowser, Diane, *Gen Educ,* Art Institute of Pittsburgh, Pittsburgh PA (S)
Bowzer, Melanie J, *Exec Dir,* Association of Medical Illustrators, Lexington KY
Boyadjian, Ani, *Dept Mgr,* Los Angeles Public Library, Art, Music, Recreation & Rare Books, Los Angeles CA
Boyajian, Ani, *Dir,* Pearl Fincher Museum of Fine Arts, Spring TX
Boyan, Elise, *Chair,* Southwest School of Art, San Antonio TX
Boyce, David, *Mgr,* Oatlands Plantation, Leesburg VA
Boyd Hinojosa, Ally, *Venue & Event Mgr,* UMLAUF Sculpture Garden & Museum, Austin TX
Boyd, Jamie, *Adjunct Prof,* Community College of Allegheny County, Boyce Campus, Art Dept, Monroeville PA (S)
Boyd, Steve, *Exhibits Mgr,* Oklahoma Contemporary Arts Center, Oklahoma City OK
Boyd-Pollack, Grace, *Dir Admin,* Art Dealers Association of America, Inc, New York NY
Boyer Ferhat, Caroline, *Div Chair,* William Woods University, Cox Gallery, Fulton MO
Boyer, Charles, *Liberal Arts Chair,* Montserrat College of Art, Beverly MA (S)
Boyer, Cindy, *Dir Public Progs,* Landmark Society of Western New York, Inc, The Campbell-Whittlesey House Museum, Rochester NY
Boyer, John, *Pres & CEO,* Bechtler Museum of Modern Art, Charlotte NC
Boyer, Nathan P, *Assoc Prof (Painting & Drawing),* University of Missouri - Columbia, Dept of Art, Columbia MO (S)
Boyer, Ron, *Dir,* Kateri Tekakwitha Shrine/St. Francis Xavier Mission, Kahnawake QC
Boyer-Reehlin, Nancy, *Cur,* Principia College, School of Nations Museum, Elsah IL
Boyes, Janet W, *Financial Adminr,* Newport Historical Society & Museum of Newport History, Newport RI
Boykin, Emily, *Educ Dir,* R W Norton Art Foundation, R W Norton Art Gallery, Shreveport LA
Boyko, Lee, *Exec Dir,* Sooke Region Museum & Art Gallery, Sooke BC
Boyle, Bernadette, *VPres,* Burlington County Historical Society, Burlington NJ
Boyle, Carol Anne, *Treas,* Frontier Times Museum, Bandera TX
Boyle, Jeremy, *Asst Prof,* Clarion University of Pennsylvania, Dept of Art, Clarion PA (S)
Boyle-Clapp, Dee, *Dir,* Arts Extension Service, Amherst MA
Boyles, Zoey, *Office Mgr,* Southern Oregon University, Art & Art History Dept, Ashland OR (S)
Boylston, Kristen, *Dir Mktg & Pub Rels,* Telfair Museums, Telfair Academy of Arts & Sciences Library, Savannah GA
Bozek, Iwona, *Head Librn,* Polish Museum of America (PMA), Chicago IL
Bozek, Iwona, *Head Librn Spec Cols,* Polish Museum of America (PMA), The Polish Museum of America Library (PMAL), Chicago IL
Braaten, Duane, *Dir Art & Philanthropy,* C M Russell Museum, Great Falls MT
Brabham, Heather, *Mgr Operations & Mem,* University of Tampa, Henry B Plant Museum, Tampa FL
Bracchi, Jennifer, *Librn,* Cooper Hewitt, Smithsonian Design Museum, Library, New York NY
Bracht, Kathryn, *Assoc Prof & Head, Theatre Dept,* University of Regina, Faculty of Media, Art & Performance, Regina SK (S)
Brack, HG Skip, *Cur,* Davistown Museum, Liberty Location, Liberty ME
Brack, Lillie, *Dir Central Libr,* Kansas City Public Library, Kansas City MO
Brackbill, Eleanor, *Head Mus Educ,* Purchase College, Neuberger Museum of Art, Purchase NY
Brackett, David, *Asst Prof,* University of Kansas, The School of the Arts, Dept of Visual Art, Lawrence KS (S)
Brackman, Bob, *Dir Botanical Gardens,* Cheekwood Nashville's Home of Art & Gardens, Education Dept, Nashville TN (S)
Bradberry, Richard, *Dir,* Morgan State University, Library, Baltimore MD
Bradburn, Douglas, *Libr Dir,* George Washington's Mount Vernon, The Fred W Smith National Library for the Study of George Washington, Mount Vernon VA
Bradbury, Leonie, *Gallery Dir,* Montserrat College of Art, Beverly MA (S)
Braddock, Alan, *Prof,* Syracuse University, Dept of Fine Arts (Art History), Syracuse NY (S)
Bradeen, N J, *Dir & Head Research & Instructional Servs,* Fashion Institute of Technology - SUNY, Gladys Marcus Library, New York NY
Bradfield, Nancy, *Office Mgr,* First Tennessee Bank, Memphis TN
Bradford, Barry, *Head of Dept,* Chattanooga-Hamilton County Bicentennial Library, Fine Arts Dept, Chattanooga TN
Bradham, Sharon, *Exec Dir,* Cedarhurst Center for the Arts, Mitchell Museum, Mount Vernon IL
Bradley, Alisa, *Mus & Park Opers Mgr,* Mississippi River Museum at Mud-Island River Park, Memphis TN
Bradley, Betsy, *Dir,* Mississippi Museum of Art, Jackson MS
Bradley, Betsy, *Dir,* Mississippi Museum of Art, Howorth Library, Jackson MS
Bradley, Bob, *Cur Colls,* Alabama Department of Archives & History, Museum of Alabama, Montgomery AL
Bradley, Diane, *Pres,* Saint Augustine Art Association and Art Gallery, Saint Augustine FL
Bradley, Jennifer, *Dean,* Kirkwood Community College, Dept of Arts & Humanities, Cedar Rapids IA (S)
Bradley, Laurel, *Dir & Cur,* Carleton College, Art Gallery, Northfield MN
Bradley, Nancy, *Asst to Dir,* Rock Ford Foundation, Inc, Rock Ford Plantation, Lancaster PA
Bradley, Ray, *Pres Bd,* Rock Ford Foundation, Inc, Rock Ford Plantation, Lancaster PA
Bradley, Steve, *Assoc Prof,* University of Maryland, Baltimore County, Intermedia & Digital Arts (IMDA), Dept of Visual Arts, Baltimore MD (S)
Bradley, Thomas, *Assoc Dean,* University of Hartford, Hartford Art School, West Hartford CT (S)
Bradshaw, Barbara, *Admin Asst,* Piedmont Arts Association, Martinsville VA
Bradshaw, Mark, *Gallery Asst,* Art Association of Harrisburg, School & Galleries, Harrisburg PA
Bradsher, Kelly, *Social Media & Mem Coordr,* Paint Creek Center for the Arts, Rochester MI
Bradt, Laurie, *Registrar,* Lyme Historical Society, Library, Old Lyme CT
Bradway, Rich, *Dir Digital Learning & Engagement,* Norman Rockwell Museum, Stockbridge MA
Brady, Allie, *Events & Rental Mgr,* Burchfield Penney Art Center, Buffalo NY

Brady, Carol, *Treas,* National Association of Women Artists, Inc, NAWA Gallery, New York NY
Brady, Denise, *Coordr,* University of Nebraska at Omaha, UNO Art Gallery, Omaha NE
Brady, Edith, *Exec Dir,* City of High Point, High Point Museum, High Point NC
Brady, Elyse, *Exec Dir,* Saint Augustine Art Association and Art Gallery, Saint Augustine FL
Brady, John, *CEO & Pres,* Independence Seaport Museum, Philadelphia PA
Brady, Meghan, *Vis Asst Prof,* Bowdoin College, Art Dept, Brunswick ME (S)
Braemer, Dorothea, *Acting Dir,* Locust Street Neighborhood Art Classes, Inc, Buffalo NY (S)
Braff, Arnold, *Co-Treas,* Greenwich Art Society Inc, Greenwich CT
Bragg, Cheryl, *Dir,* Anniston Museum of Natural History, Anniston AL
Bragg, Terry A, *Exec Dir,* State of North Carolina, Battleship North Carolina, Wilmington NC
Braggins, Donna, *Assoc Dean Design Illustration & Photography,* Sheridan College, Faculty of Animation, Arts & Design, Oakville ON (S)
Braide, Carol, *Publs Mgr,* The Africa Center, New York NY
Brake, Karl, *Dir,* Rogue Community College, Wiseman Gallery - FireHouse Gallery, Grants Pass OR
Braman, Andrew, *Controller,* The Rockwell Museum, Corning NY
Brammer, Mark, *Dir,* Wyoming State Museum, Cheyenne WY
Branaff, Cis, *Prog Mgr,* Pacific Northwest Art School, Gallery at the Wharf, Coupeville WA
Branagan, Carmine, *Dir,* National Academy Museum & School, Archives, New York NY
Branch, Harrison, *Prof,* Oregon State University, Dept of Art, Corvallis OR (S)
Branch, Robert, *CFO & COO,* Grand Rapids Art Museum, Grand Rapids MI
Branch-Rice, Gweneth, *Fundamental Arts,* Holland College, School of Visual Arts & Journalism, Charlottetown PE (S)
Branchick, Thomas J, *Dir,* Williamstown Art Conservation Center, Williamstown MA
Branco, Susan, *Instr,* Wayne Art Center, Wayne PA (S)
Brand, Jonathan, *Pres,* Cornell College, Peter Paul Luce Gallery, Mount Vernon IA
Branden, Mack, *Chmn,* California Baptist University, Art Dept, Riverside CA (S)
Branden, Shirley, *Head Reference Dept,* University of Delaware, Morris Library, Newark DE
Brander, Susan, *Admin Dir,* Museum of the Hudson Highlands, Cornwall On Hudson NY
Brandrup, Jessica, *Head Mktg & Pub Rels,* Kimbell Art Foundation, Kimbell Art Museum, Fort Worth TX
Brands, Lyn, *Assoc Prof,* Arkansas Tech University, Dept of Art, Russellville AR (S)
Brandson, Lorraine, *Cur,* Eskimo Museum, Churchill MB
Brandson, Lorraine, *Cur,* Eskimo Museum, Library, Churchill MB
Brandt, Elaine, *Instr,* California State University, Dominguez Hills, Art & Design Dept, Carson CA (S)
Brandt, Peter, *Area Coordr,* New York School of Interior Design, New York NY (S)
Brandt, Thomas, *Dir,* Highland Community College, Art Dept, Freeport IL (S)
Brandt, Trevor, *Cur,* American Swedish Historical Foundation & Museum, American Swedish Historical Museum, Philadelphia PA
Brandt, Trevor, *Cur,* American Swedish Historical Foundation & Museum, Nord Library, Philadelphia PA
Branham, Joan, *Prof,* Providence College, Art & Art History Dept, Providence RI (S)
Branning, Katherine, *VPres Library,* French Institute-Alliance Francaise, Library, New York NY
Brannon, Patrick, *Dept Head,* University of Saint Francis, Fine Arts Dept, Joliet IL (S)
Bransbourg, Gilles, *Assoc Cur,* American Numismatic Society, New York NY
Bransfield, Kevin, *Photog Instr,* Monterey Peninsula College, Art Dept/Art Gallery, Monterey CA (S)
Bransford, Pam, *Registrar,* Montgomery Museum of Fine Arts, Library, Montgomery AL
Bransford, Pamela, *Registrar,* Montgomery Museum of Fine Arts, Montgomery AL
Branston, Stuart, *Chmn,* Oral Roberts University, Art Dept, Tulsa OK (S)
Brant, Allison, *Dir,* The Brant Foundation Art Study Center, Greenwich CT
Brant, Nikki, *Exec Dir,* Burke Arts Council, Jailhouse Galleries, Morganton NC
Brant, Pip, *Assoc Prof,* Florida International University, School of Art & Art History, Miami FL (S)
Brantley, Royal, *Prof,* West Texas A&M University, Art, Theatre & Dance Dept, Canyon TX (S)
Braren, Lesley, *Admin Dir,* Essex Art Association, Inc, Essex CT
Brasch, Jean, *Bookkeeper,* Cultural Council of Palm Beach County, Lake Worth FL
Braschnewitz, Victor, *Head Security,* Hillwood Museum & Gardens Foundation, Hillwood Estate Museum & Gardens, Washington DC
Brase, Don, *Dir,* Chemeketa Community College, Dept of Humanities & Communications, Art Program, Salem OR (S)
Brashear, Jim, *Prof,* University of Alaska Fairbanks, Art Department, Fairbanks AK (S)
Brasier, Robert, *Deputy Dir Educ & Pub Progs,* Palm Springs Art Museum, Palm Springs CA
Brasile, Jeanne, *Gallery Dir,* Seton Hall University, Walsh Gallery & Library, South Orange NJ
Brask Hutchinson, Rachel, *Educ & Outreach Mgr,* Rhode Island Historical Society, John Brown House, Providence RI
Brassard, Lionel, *Pres,* Institut des Arts au Saguenay, Centre National D'Exposition a Jonquiere, Jonquiere QC
Braswell, Tom, *Dir,* East Carolina University, Wellington B Gray Gallery, Greenville NC
Brauer, Daniel R, *Dir Publications,* University of California, Los Angeles, Fowler Museum at UCLA, Los Angeles CA
Brauhn, Molly I, *Asst Prof,* Brazosport College, Communications & Fine Art, Lake Jackson TX (S)
Brault, Simon, *Dir & CEO,* Canada Council for the Arts, Conseil des Arts du Canada, Ottawa ON
Braun, Emily, *Prof,* City University of New York, PhD Program in Art History, New York NY (S)
Braun, Laura, *CCA Communs Assoc,* California College of the Arts, CCAC Wattis Institute for Contemporary Arts, San Francisco CA
Braun, Lon R, *Dir Bus & Fin,* Fort Wayne Museum of Art, Inc, Fort Wayne IN
Braun, Mary E, *Dir,* St Mary's College of Maryland, The Dwight Frederick Boyden Gallery, St Mary's City MD
Braun, Matt, *Dir Develop,* Cornell University, Herbert F Johnson Museum of Art, Ithaca NY
Braunstein, Susan, *Sr Cur,* The Jewish Museum, New York NY
Bravo, Joseph, *Exec Dir,* International Museum of Art & Science, McAllen TX
Brawner, Dan, *Assoc Prof & Chair,* Watkins College of Art, Design & Film, Nashville TN (S)
Brawning-Mullis, Shannon, *Cur Decorative Arts & Historic Sites,* Telfair Museums, Savannah GA
Bray, Carmen, *Dir Communs,* Western Pennsylvania Conservancy, Fallingwater, Mill Run PA
Bray, Kimberly D, *Librn, Archivist,* The San Joaquin Pioneer & Historical Society, Petzinger Memorial Library & Earl Rowland Art Library, Stockton CA
Bray, Kimberly, *Librn & Archivist,* The San Joaquin Pioneer & Historical Society, The Haggin Museum, Stockton CA
Brayham, Angela, *Dir & Cur,* Gallery Stratford, Stratford ON
Brayman, Ruby, *Visual Arts Comt Chair,* University of Minnesota, The Studio/Larson Gallery, Saint Paul MN
Braysmith, Hilary, *Prof,* University of Southern Indiana, Art & Design Dept, Evansville IN (S)
Brazel, Jennifer, *Dir Educ,* Hunterdon Art Museum, Clinton NJ
Brazell, Danielle, *Gen Mgr,* City of Los Angeles, Cultural Affairs Dept, Los Angeles CA
Brazil, Sally, *Chief Archives & Records Mgmt,* The Frick Collection, Frick Art Reference Library, New York NY
Brazile, Orella R, *Dir,* Southern University Library, Shreveport LA
Breault, Christina, *Mus Dir,* Lac du Flambeau Band of Lake Superior Chippewa Indians, George W Brown Jr Ojibwe Museum & Cultural Center, Lac Du Flambeau WI
Breaux, Pam, *CEO,* National Assembly of State Arts Agencies, Washington DC
Breaux, Robbie, *Pres,* Western Colorado Center for the Arts, Library, Grand Junction CO
Breaux, Steven, *Prof,* University of Louisiana at Lafayette, Dept of Visual Arts, Lafayette LA (S)
Breaznell, Ann, *Assoc Prof,* The College of Saint Rose, The Center For Art and Design, Albany NY (S)
Brechter, Bart, *Cur Gardens,* Museum of Fine Arts Houston, Bayou Bend Collection & Gardens, Houston TX
Brecken, Bradford A, *Pres Emeritus,* Newport Historical Society & Museum of Newport History, Newport RI
Breckenridge Barrett, Anne, *Dir Cols & Exhibs,* Museum of Contemporary Art Chicago, Chicago IL
Breckenridge, Bruce, *Emer Prof,* University of Wisconsin, Madison, Dept of Art, Madison WI (S)
Breckenridge, Martha, *Asst Prof,* Northwest Missouri State University, Dept of Fine & Performing Arts, Maryville MO (S)
Bredhoff, Stacey, *Cur,* National Archives & Records Administration, John F Kennedy Presidential Library & Museum, Boston MA
Breen, Ivy, *Treas,* Valley Art Center Inc, Clarkston WA
Bregande, Michele, *Communs & Special Events Mgr,* The Print Center, Philadelphia PA
Bregman, Matt, *VPres Devel,* New-York Historical Society, Museum, New York NY
Brehm, Georgia L, *Dir,* Black River Academy Museum & Historical Society, Black River Academy Museum, Ludlow VT
Brehm, Susan, *Dir Special Events Sales,* Columbus Museum of Art, Columbus OH
Breiling, Roy, *Instr,* Yavapai College, Visual & Performing Arts Div, Prescott AZ (S)
Breimayer, Mary Phyllis, *Assoc Prof,* Georgian Court University, Dept of Art, Lakewood NJ (S)
Breitenbach, Eric, *Prof,* Daytona Beach Community College, Dept of Fine Arts & Visual Arts, Daytona Beach FL (S)
Breitner, Michael, *Dir,* University of Wisconsin - Platteville, Harry & Laura Nohr Gallery, Platteville WI
Breland, Evelyn, *Treas,* Mississippi Art Colony, Stoneville MS
Breneman, David W, *Pres,* The Society of the Four Arts, Palm Beach FL
Brener, Art, *Bd Mem,* American Color Print Society, Narberth PA
Brennan, Anne, *Asst Dir,* Cameron Art Museum, Wilmington NC
Brennan, Chris, *Asst Prof,* Lewis & Clark Community College, Art Dept, Godfrey IL (S)
Brennan, Joan, *Photo,* University of Colorado at Denver, College of Arts & Media Visual Arts Dept, Denver CO (S)
Brennan, Marnie, *Chmn Theatre,* Harrisburg Area Community College, Division of Communications, Humanities & the Arts, Harrisburg PA (S)
Brennan, Sandy, *Research Secy,* Livingston County Historical Society, Museum, Geneseo NY
Brennan, Tom, *Chair, Assoc Prof,* Chowan College, Dept. of Communication Arts, Fine and Applied Arts, Murfreesboro NC (S)
Brenneman, David, *Dir,* Indiana University, Eskenazi Museum of Art, Bloomington IN

Brenneman, Jina, *Cur,* University of New Mexico, The Harwood Museum of Art, Taos NM
Brenner, Keith, *Bd Chair,* Colorado Photographic Arts Center, Denver CO
Brenner, Susan, *Assoc Prof,* University of North Carolina at Charlotte, Dept Art, Charlotte NC (S)
Brenner-Leonard, Hannah, *Educ Cur,* Lehman College Art Gallery, Bronx NY
Brenningmeyer, Todd, *Assoc Prof Art History,* Maryville University of Saint Louis, Art & Design Program, Saint Louis MO (S)
Brenny, Barbara, *Visual Resources Librn,* North Carolina State University, Harrye Lyons Design Library, Raleigh NC
Breslauer, George, *Dir,* University of California, Berkeley, The Magnes Collection of Jewish Art & Life, Berkeley CA
Breslauer, Lori, *Gen Counsel,* Field Museum, Chicago IL
Bresnahan, Edith, *Chmn,* Dominican College of San Rafael, Art Dept, San Rafael CA (S)
Breth, Renata, *Dir,* Santa Rosa Junior College, Art Gallery, Santa Rosa CA
Brett, Hillary, *Exec Dir,* LeMoyne Art Foundation, Center for the Visual Arts, Tallahassee FL
Breuer, Nancy, *Secy & Gen Counsel,* National Gallery of Art, Washington DC
Brewer, Chris, *Gallery Mgr,* Washington County Arts Council, Gallery, Hagerstown MD
Brewer, Esther Vivian, *Gallery Dir,* National Conference of Artists, Michigan Chapter Gallery, Detroit MI
Brewer, Laurie, *Assoc Cur Costumes & Textiles,* Rhode Island School of Design, Museum of Art, Providence RI
Brewer, Nan, *Cur Works on Paper,* Indiana University, Eskenazi Museum of Art, Bloomington IN
Brewer, Piper, *Exec Dir,* Shiawassee Arts Center, Owosso MI
Brewer, William, *Chmn,* Hutchinson Community College, Visual Arts Dept, Hutchinson KS (S)
Brewster, Twania, *VPres Mktg,* Chicago Children's Museum, Chicago IL
Brey, Natalie, *Artist,* Walker's Point Artists Assoc Inc, Gallery 218, Milwaukee WI
Breza, Michael, *Asst Dir,* Oshkosh Public Museum & Library, Oshkosh WI
Brian, Cameron, *Instr,* Bakersfield College, Art Dept, Bakersfield CA (S)
Brian, Nancy K, *Chmn,* California State University, Fresno, Art & Design, Fresno CA (S)
Bricher, Naya, *Admin Coordr,* Fine Arts Work Center, Hudson D. Walker Gallery, Provincetown MA
Bridegam, Nathalie, *Cur Visual Coll,* University of Massachusetts, Amherst, Dorothy W Perkins Slide Library, Amherst MA
Bridges, Don, *Bookstore Mgr,* Irvine Museum, Irvine CA
Bridges, Steven, *Assoc Cur,* Michigan State University, Eli & Edythe Broad Art Museum, East Lansing MI
Brief, Martin, *Asst Prof,* Longwood University, Dept of Art, Farmville VA (S)
Brienen, Rebecca, *Dept Head Art & Art History,* Oklahoma State University, Department of Art, Graphic Design and Art History, Stillwater OK (S)
Brier, Ida, *Archivist & Librn,* Olana State Historic Site, Hudson NY
Brier, Ida, *Librn & Archivist,* Olana State Historic Site, Library, Hudson NY
Briggs, Alicia, *Admin Specialist,* Benedict College, School of Humanities, Arts & Social Sciences, Columbia SC (S)
Briggs, Jo, *Asst Cur 18th-19thc Art,* Walters Art Museum, Baltimore MD
Briggs, Karen, *Exec Dir,* LaGrange Art Museum, LaGrange GA
Briggs, Peter S, *Cur Art,* Texas Tech University, Museum of Texas Tech University, Lubbock TX
Briggs, Stephen R, *Pres,* Berry College, Moon Gallery, Mount Berry GA
Brigham, David R, *CEO,* Pennsylvania Academy of the Fine Arts, Office of Admission, Philadelphia PA (S)
Brigham, David, *Pres & CEO,* Pennsylvania Academy of the Fine Arts, Philadelphia PA
Bright, Karen, *Assoc Prof,* Monmouth University, Dept of Art & Design, West Long Branch NJ (S)
Bright, Paul, *Asst Dir,* Wake Forest University, Charlotte & Philip Hanes Art Gallery, Winston-Salem NC
Bright, Paul, *Gallery Dir,* Wake Forest University, Dept of Art, Winston-Salem NC (S)
Briley, Jeff, *Deputy Dir,* Oklahoma Historical Society, State Museum of History, Oklahoma City OK
Brill, Margaret, *Prof,* Corning Community College, Division of Humanities, Corning NY (S)
Brilla, Maureen, *Assoc Prof,* Nazareth College of Rochester, Art Dept, Rochester NY (S)
Brindle, Tracy, *Chief Cur,* Mark Twain, Research Library, Hartford CT
Brindle, Tracy, *Chief Cur,* Mark Twain, Hartford CT
Brindley, Liz, *Educ,* Georgia O'Keeffe Museum, Santa Fe NM
Brindza, Christine, *Glasser Cur Art American West,* Tucson Museum of Art and Historic Block, Tucson AZ
Brine, Linda, *Retail Mgr,* Canadian Clay and Glass Gallery, Waterloo ON
Brink, Annette, *Dir,* Tubac Center of the Arts, Library, Tubac AZ
Brink, Deborah, *Community Outreach Dir,* North Fourth Art Center & Gallery, Albuquerque NM
Brink, Vicki, *Contact,* Northwest Pastel Society (NPS), Dallas OR
Brinkerhoff, Dericksen M, *Prof Emeriti,* University of California, Riverside, Dept of the History of Art, Riverside CA (S)
Brinkman, Don, *Trustee,* L D Brinkman, Kerrville TX
Brinkman, Lynn, *Instr,* Lourdes University, Art Dept, Sylvania OH (S)
Brinkman, Stacy, *Librn,* Miami University, Wertz Art & Architecture Library, Oxford OH
Brinson, Ericah, *Rental Coordr,* Historical Society of Martin County, Elliott Museum, Stuart FL
Brinson, Katherine, *Cur Contemporary Art,* Solomon R Guggenheim Museum, New York NY
Brinton, Dean, *CEO,* The Rooms Provincial Art Gallery, Saint John's NF
Brinton, Jeff, *Exec Dir,* Alberta Foundation for the Arts, Edmonton AB
Briones, Thomas, *Chmn,* National Hispanic Cultural Center, Art Museum, Albuquerque NM
Britschgi, Jorrit, *Dir Exhibs, Colls & Research,* Rubin Museum of Art, New York NY
Brittingham, John, *Interim Assoc Dir,* Montana State University, School of Architecture, Bozeman MT (S)
Britton, Benjamin, *Assoc Prof Fine Arts,* University of Cincinnati, School of Art, Cincinnati OH (S)
Britton, Peter, *Asst Prof,* Missouri Western State University, School of Fine Arts, Saint Joseph MO (S)
Britton, Sandy, *Dean of Student Serv,* Kendall College of Art & Design of Ferris State University, Grand Rapids MI (S)
Brixey, Shawn, *Chair,* University of California, Berkeley, College of Letters & Sciences-Art Practice Dept, Berkeley CA (S)
Brixey, Shawn, *Dean,* Virginia Commonwealth University, School of the Arts, Richmond VA (S)
Brixey, Shawn, *Dean,* York University, School of the Arts, Media, Performance & Design, Toronto ON (S)
Broad, David, *Dean,* Elgin Community College, Fine Arts Dept, Elgin IL (S)
Broadsky, Jessica, *Director of Campus Galleries,* Miami-Dade College, MDC Museum of Art & Design, Miami FL
Brochhauren, Philip, *Program Head,* Western Wisconsin Technical College, Graphics Division, La Crosse WI (S)
Brock, Emily, *Photo Archivist,* New Mexico Department of Cultural Affairs, Palace of Governors, Santa Fe NM
Brockington, Lynn, *Librn,* Vancouver Art Gallery, Library, Vancouver BC
Brockman, Eric, *Mktg & Communs Mgr,* Dayton Art Institute, Dayton OH
Brockmann, J Nicholas, *Media Arts & Animation/Gen Educ,* Art Institute of Pittsburgh, Pittsburgh PA (S)
Brockway, Ken, *Dir,* Redwood Library & Athenaeum, Newport RI
Broda, Alysan, *Dir Visual & Performing Arts,* Aims Community College, Visual & Performing Arts, Greeley CO (S)
Brodar, Valerie, *Assoc Prof Visual Arts & Dir,* University of Colorado-Colorado Springs, Visual & Performing Arts Dept (VAPA), Colorado Springs CO (S)
Brode, Carol, *Dir Gallery & Asst Prof,* Seton Hill University, Art Program, Greensburg PA (S)
Broderick, Amy, *Assoc Prof Art, Foundations, Drawing & Painting,* Florida Atlantic University, D F Schmidt College of Arts & Letters Dept of Visual Arts & Art History, Boca Raton FL (S)
Broderick, Geoff, *Prof,* Abilene Christian University, Dept of Art & Design, Abilene TX (S)
Broderick, Herbert R, *Chmn,* Herbert H Lehman, Art Dept, Bronx NY (S)
Broderick, James, *Prof Emeritus,* University of Texas at San Antonio, Dept of Art & Art History, San Antonio TX (S)
Brodeur, David, *Asst Prof,* University of North Carolina at Charlotte, Dept Art, Charlotte NC (S)
Brodhead, Heather, *Librn,* Santa Barbara Museum of Art, Library, Santa Barbara CA
Brodie, Scott, *Prof,* The College of Saint Rose, The Center For Art and Design, Albany NY (S)
Brodsky, Michael, *Prof,* Loyola Marymount University, Dept of Art & Art History, Los Angeles CA (S)
Brody, David, *Faculty,* Maryland Institute, Mount Royal School of Art, Baltimore MD (S)
Brody, Jeanne, *Adj Prof,* Saint Joseph's University, Art Dept, Philadelphia PA (S)
Broggi, Judith, *Dept Coord,* The Art Institute of Chicago, Dept of Prints & Drawings, Chicago IL
Broidy, Barbara, *Cur & Asst to Dir,* Lighthouse ArtCenter Museum & School of Art, Tequesta FL
Broker, Karin, *Prof,* Rice University, Visual & Dramatic Arts, Houston TX (S)
Broker, Kim, *Assoc Registrar Colls,* Washington University, Mildred Lane Kemper Art Museum, Saint Louis MO
Brokken, Robbie, *Gallery Dir,* Lanesboro Arts Center, Lanesboro MN
Bromage, Stephen, *Exec Dir,* Maine Historical Society, Portland ME
Bromage, Steve, *Exec Dir,* Maine Historical Society, Wadsworth-Longfellow House, Portland ME
Bromage, Steve, *Exec Dir,* Maine Historical Society, MHS Museum, Portland ME
Broman, Elizabeth, *Ref Librn,* Cooper Hewitt, Smithsonian Design Museum, Library, New York NY
Bromberg, Nicolette, *Cur Visual Materials,* University of Washington, Univ of Washington Libraries, Special Collections, Seattle WA
Bromberg, Peter, *Dir,* Salt Lake City Public Library, Nonfiction & Audiovisual Dept & Gallery at Library Square, Salt Lake City UT
Bromley, Kimble, *Asst Prof,* North Dakota State University, Division of Fine Arts, Fargo ND (S)
Bronnar, Lorran, *Special Events,* Stanford University, Cantor Arts Center at Stanford University, Stanford CA
Bronner, Simon J, *Dir Humanities,* Penn State Harrisburg, School of Humanities, Middletown PA (S)
Bronson, Julie, *Collections Admin,* McMaster University, McMaster Museum of Art, Hamilton ON
Bronson, Marcie, *Dir,* Rodman Hall Arts Centre, Saint Catharines ON
Broocks, Steven, *Exec Dir,* Coos Art Museum, Coos Bay OR
Broocks, Steven, *Exec Dir,* Coos Art Museum, Coos Bay OR (S)

Broodwell, Carolyn, *Prof,* Napa Valley College, Art Dept, Napa CA (S)
Brooke, Sandra Ludig, *Librn,* Princeton University, Marquand Library of Art & Archaeology, Princeton NJ
Brooke, Sandra, *Dir Library,* The Huntington Library, Art Collections & Botanical Gardens, San Marino CA
Brooker, Moe, *Chmn Basic Arts,* Moore College of Art & Design, Philadelphia PA (S)
Brookman, Philip, *Cur Photo & Media Arts,* Corcoran Gallery of Art, Washington DC
Brooks Lavallee, Susanna, *Cur Japanese Art,* Palm Beach County Parks & Recreation Department, Morikami Museum & Japanese Gardens, Delray Beach FL
Brooks, Aimee, *Collections Manager,* The Columbus Museum, Columbus GA
Brooks, Arnold, *Instr,* Manhattan Graphics Center, New York NY (S)
Brooks, Carol, *Cur,* Arizona Historical Society-Yuma, Sanguinetti House Museum & Garden, Yuma AZ
Brooks, Caroline, *Asst Dir,* Roswell Museum & Art Center, Roswell NM
Brooks, Charles, *Dir Theatre Ensemble,* Benedict College, School of Humanities, Arts & Social Sciences, Columbia SC (S)
Brooks, Eric, *Galleries Cur Assoc,* Sierra Arts Foundation, Sierra Arts Gallery, Reno NV
Brooks, George, *Chief Preparator,* Philbrook Museum of Art, Tulsa OK
Brooks, Hebe, *Dir of Publicity,* National Oil & Acrylic Painters Society, Houston TX
Brooks, Lori, *Dir Communs,* Oklahoma Contemporary Arts Center, Oklahoma City OK
Brooks, Reena, *Bd Mem,* American Color Print Society, Narberth PA
Brooks, Regan, *Registrar,* Gaston County Museum of Art & History, Dallas NC
Brooks, Steven, *Photographer,* University of California, Berkeley, Architecture Visual Resources Library, Berkeley CA
Brooks, Susanna, *Dir Learning Innovation,* Whatcom Museum, Bellingham WA
Brooks, Valerie, *Undergrad Acad Adv,* Southern Illinois University, School of Art & Design, Carbondale IL (S)
Brooks, Wendell, *Assoc Prof,* The College of New Jersey, School of Arts & Sciences, Ewing NJ (S)
Brooks, William F, *Exec Dir,* Henry Sheldon Museum of Vermont History and Research Center, Middlebury VT
Broome, Skooker, *Exhib Designer,* University of British Columbia, Museum of Anthropology, Vancouver BC
Brose, Lawrence F, *Exec Dir,* Center for Exploratory & Perceptual Art, CEPA Library, Buffalo NY
Brosie, Vanessa, *Office Mgr,* Zanesville Museum of Art, Zanesville OH
Broske, Janet G, *Colls Mgr,* University of Delaware, University Museums, Newark DE
Brosrven, Lori, *Technical Servs,* Redwood Library & Athenaeum, Newport RI
Bross, John, *Prof,* Greenfield Community College, Art Dept, Greenfield MA (S)
Brosseau, Carol, *Special Projects,* Joseph Bellows Gallery, La Jolla CA
Brothers, Clayton, *Dir,* New Image Art, West Hollywood CA
Brotherton, Marianna, *Commun Chmn,* Guild of Book Workers, New York NY
Brouch, Virginia, *Coordr Computer Graphics,* Phoenix College, Dept of Art & Photography, Phoenix AZ (S)
Broucke, Peter, *Chmn,* Middlebury College, History of Art & Architecture Dept, Middlebury VT (S)
Broude, Norma, *Prof,* American University, Dept of Art, New York NY (S)
Brought, Katye, *Dir Communs,* Witte Museum, San Antonio TX
Brouillette, Jackie, *Educ Prog,* Kern County Museum, Library, Bakersfield CA
Brousseau, Hélène, *Libr,* Artexte Information Centre, Documentation Centre, Montreal QC
Brouwer, Charles, *Prof,* Radford University, Art Dept, Radford VA (S)
Browdo, Bar, *Cur,* Wenham Museum, Wenham MA
Brower, Mary, *Music Librn,* Rice University, Brown Fine Arts Library, Houston TX
Brower, Paul, *Mus Spec,* Western Washington University, Western Gallery, Bellingham WA
Brown, Angela, *Assoc DIr of Devel,* University of Mississippi, University Museum & Historic Houses, Oxford MS
Brown, Anne, *Sr Dir Communications & Mktg,* The Baltimore Museum of Art, Baltimore MD
Brown, Autumn, *Jewelry/Metals Area Coordr,* Western Michigan University, Frostic School of Art, Kalamazoo MI (S)
Brown, Bill, *Chmn Illustration,* Moore College of Art & Design, Philadelphia PA (S)
Brown, Brad, *Exhibit Designer,* City of Lethbridge, Sir Alexander Galt Museum, Lethbridge AB
Brown, Bruce, *Prof,* Monroe Community College, Art Dept, Rochester NY (S)
Brown, Calvin, *Assoc Cur Prints & Drawings,* Princeton University, Princeton University Art Museum, Princeton NJ
Brown, Carlin, *Co-Curator,* Portland State University, White Gallery, Portland OR
Brown, Carlin, *Visual Arts Cur,* Portland State University, Littman Gallery, Portland OR
Brown, Cassie, *Mktg & Communs,* Daytona State College, Southeast Museum of Photography, Daytona Beach FL
Brown, Chad, *Gen Educ,* Art Institute of Pittsburgh, Pittsburgh PA (S)
Brown, Chad, *VPres,* Zanesville Museum of Art, Zanesville OH
Brown, Claudia, *Asst Prof Mass Communs,* Harford Community College, Visual, Performing and Applied Arts Division, Bel Air MD (S)
Brown, Clinton, *Prof,* Oregon State University, Dept of Art, Corvallis OR (S)
Brown, Darren, *Cur,* Beverly Historical Society, Library, Beverly MA
Brown, David, *Cur Renaissance Painting,* National Gallery of Art, Washington DC
Brown, David, *Vice Pres,* Essex Historical Society and Shipbuilding Museum, Essex MA
Brown, DeSoto, *Archivist,* Bernice Pauahi Bishop, Library & Archives, Honolulu HI
Brown, Dolita, *Mem Mgr,* Arts Council Of New Orleans, New Orleans LA
Brown, Donald W, *Bibliographer,* Carnegie Mellon University, Hunt Institute for Botanical Documentation, Pittsburgh PA
Brown, Doris, *Exec Dir,* Arts United for Davidson County, The Arts Center, Lexington NC
Brown, Dorothy D, *Chmn,* Georgia College & State University, Art Dept, Milledgeville GA (S)
Brown, Dottie, *Instr,* Sierra Community College, Art Dept, Rocklin CA (S)
Brown, Ellsworth, *Dir,* Wisconsin Historical Society, Wisconsin Historical Museum, Madison WI
Brown, Erika, *Registrar,* City of Ketchikan Museum Department, Totem Heritage Center, Ketchikan AK
Brown, Geoffrey I, *Dir,* Navajo Nation, Navajo Nation Museum, Window Rock AZ
Brown, Glen R, *Prof,* Kansas State University, Art Dept, Manhattan KS (S)
Brown, Hillary, *Dir Communs,* University of Georgia, Georgia Museum of Art, Athens GA
Brown, James, *Assoc Prof,* William Paterson University, Dept Arts, Wayne NJ (S)
Brown, Jana, *Educator Cur,* Trust Authority, Museum of the Great Plains, Lawton OK
Brown, Jason, *Assoc Prof,* Eastern Oregon University, School of Arts & Science, La Grande OR (S)
Brown, Jeff, *Chmn Fine Arts,* Jones County Junior College, Art Dept, Ellisville MS (S)
Brown, Jeff, *VPres,* Kappa Pi International Honorary Art Fraternity, Cleveland MS
Brown, Jill, *Dir Human Resources,* Alberta College of Art & Design, Calgary AB (S)
Brown, Jill, *Sales Mgr,* Stephen Huneck Gallery at Dog Mountain, Saint Johnsbury VT
Brown, Joe, *Dean, Theater Arts,* Texas Wesleyan University, Dept of Art, Fort Worth TX (S)
Brown, John, *Interim Dean,* University of Calgary, Faculty of Environmental Design, Calgary AB
Brown, Judith, *Dir Educ,* Davistown Museum, Liberty Location, Liberty ME
Brown, Judy, *Foundation Dept,* Montserrat College of Art, Beverly MA (S)
Brown, Julia, *Asst Prof,* George Washington University, Dept of Art of Fine Arts & Art History, Washington DC (S)
Brown, Julia, *Bd Chair,* American Association of University Women, Washington DC
Brown, Karen F, *Libr Technician,* National Museum of African Art, Warren M Robbins Library, Washington DC
Brown, Kimberly, *Dir,* Morgan County Foundation, Inc, Madison-Morgan Cultural Center, Madison GA
Brown, Laura, *Asst Admin,* Morgan State University, James E Lewis Museum of Art, Baltimore MD
Brown, Lenard, *Asst Prof Painting & Printmaking,* University of Texas Pan American, Art Dept, Edinburg TX (S)
Brown, Leslie E, *Instr Drawing,* Millersville University, Dept of Art & Design, Millersville PA (S)
Brown, Likassina, *Receptionist,* Lafayette Science Museum & Planetarium, Lafayette LA
Brown, Lindie K, *Dir Develop,* Anniston Museum of Natural History, Anniston AL
Brown, Lisa, *Instr Art Educ,* Eastern Oregon University, School of Arts & Science, La Grande OR (S)
Brown, Lorna, *Dir & Cur,* University of British Columbia, Morris & Helen Belkin Art Gallery, Vancouver BC
Brown, Louise Freshman, *Prof,* University of North Florida, Dept of Communications & Visual Arts, Jacksonville FL (S)
Brown, Maggie, *Cur,* Museum of Southern History, Joella & Stewart Morris Cultural Arts Center, Houston TX
Brown, Margaret, *Branch Librn,* Arlington County Department of Public Libraries, Fine Arts Section, Arlington VA
Brown, Marilyn R, *Prof,* Tulane University, Sophie H Newcomb Memorial College, New Orleans LA (S)
Brown, Michael, *Assoc Cur European Art,* San Diego Museum of Art, San Diego CA
Brown, Michael, *Develop Officer Grant Funding,* Contemporary Arts Center, Cincinnati OH
Brown, Michael, *Pres & CEO,* School for Advanced Research (SAR), Indian Arts Research Center, Santa Fe NM
Brown, Monica, *Assoc Dir Devel,* ARC Gallery and Educational Foundation, Chicago IL
Brown, Nancy F, *Exec Dir & Cur,* Lillian & Coleman Taube Museum of Art, Minot ND
Brown, Pam, *Cur Pacific Northwest,* University of British Columbia, Museum of Anthropology, Vancouver BC
Brown, Patricia, *Exhib Chmn,* Delta State University, Fielding L Wright Art Center, Cleveland MS
Brown, Patricia, *Prof,* Delta State University, Dept of Art, Cleveland MS (S)
Brown, Patrick, *Chief Preparator & Exhib Designer,* Worcester Art Museum, Worcester MA
Brown, Rachel, *Educ,* Hidalgo County Historical Museum, Edinburg TX
Brown, Randy, *Admin Asst,* Wichita Center for the Arts, Mary R Koch School of Visual Arts, Wichita KS (S)
Brown, Rebecca, *Asst Prof,* Saint Mary's College of Maryland, Art & Art History Dept, Saint Mary's City MD (S)
Brown, Robert B, *Secy & Treas,* National Museum of Ceramic Art, Baltimore MD
Brown, Roderick, *Museum Manager,* Middle Border Museum & Oscar Howe Art Center, Mitchell SD

Brown, Scott, *Color & Graphic Instr,* Hutchinson Community College, Visual Arts Dept, Hutchinson KS (S)

Brown, Sharon, *Co-Chair,* Santa Ana College, Art Dept, Santa Ana CA (S)

Brown, Shirley B, *Adminr,* National Museum of Ceramic Art, Baltimore MD

Brown, Sienna, *Cur Modern & Contemp Art,* Philbrook Museum of Art, Tulsa OK

Brown, Sonia, *Cur Educ,* California African-American Museum, Los Angeles CA

Brown, Stephen, *Assoc Prof,* University of Hartford, Hartford Art School, West Hartford CT (S)

Brown, Steven, *Photog & Graphic Design,* Southern Illinois University at Edwardsville, Dept of Art & Design, Edwardsville IL (S)

Brown, Steven, *Prof,* University of Science & Arts of Oklahoma, Art Dept, Chickasha OK (S)

Brown, Teresa, *Dir,* Pacific Grove Art Center, Pacific Grove CA

Brown, Tim, *Cur Educ,* Montgomery Museum of Fine Arts, Library, Montgomery AL

Brown, Trina, *Head Librn,* National Museum of American History, Library, Washington DC

Brown, Vida, *Cur Visual Arts & Prog Mgr.,* California African-American Museum, Los Angeles CA

Brown, Wendell, *Asst Prof,* Benedict College, School of Humanities, Arts & Social Sciences, Columbia SC (S)

Brown, William, *Chief Conservator,* North Carolina Museum of Art, Raleigh NC

Brown, William, *Dept Head, Prof,* University of Evansville, Art Dept, Evansville IN (S)

Brown, William, *Gallery Dir,* University of Evansville, Krannert Gallery & Peterson Gallery, Evansville IN

Brown-Urso, Rian, *Asst Prof,* Oberlin College, Dept of Art, Oberlin OH (S)

Browne, Christopher, *Deputy Dir,* National Air and Space Museum, Smithsonian Institution, Washington DC

Browne, Christopher, *Deputy Dir,* National Air And Space Museum, Steven F Udvar-Hazy Center, Chantilly VA

Browne, Georgia, *Prog & Outreach Dir,* Bainbridge Arts & Crafts Gallery, Bainbridge Island WA

Browne, Kelvin, *Exec Dir,* George R Gardiner Museum of Ceramic Art, Toronto ON

Browne, William, *Chmn Bd Trustees,* Indiana State Museum, Indianapolis IN

Brownfield, Gail, *Pres,* Redlands Art Association, Redlands Art Association Gallery & Art Center, Redlands CA

Brownfield, John, *Chmn,* University of Redlands, Dept of Art, Redlands CA (S)

Browning, Alan, *Dir Develop,* Boulder History Museum, Museum of History, Boulder CO

Browning, Dawn C, *Dir,* Maysville, Kentucky Gateway Museum Center, Maysville KY

Browning, Kaye, *Cur Miniatures,* Maysville, Kentucky Gateway Museum Center, Maysville KY

Browning, Marion, *Receptionist,* Maysville, Kentucky Gateway Museum Center, Maysville KY

Browning, Terry, *Gallery Dir,* Ann Arbor Art Center, Art Center, Ann Arbor MI

Brozovich, Tom J, *Instr,* American River College, Dept of Art/Art New Media, Sacramento CA (S)

Brozynski, Dennis, *Coordr Fashion Design,* Columbia College, Art Dept, Chicago IL (S)

Bruce, Chris, *Dir,* Washington State University, Museum of Art, Pullman WA

Bruce, Jeff, *Dir Exhib,* Tubman African American Museum, Macon GA

Bruce, Tobi, *Dir Exhib & Coll & Sr Cur,* Art Gallery of Hamilton, Hamilton ON

Brucker, Jane, *Prof,* Loyola Marymount University, Dept of Art & Art History, Los Angeles CA (S)

Bruegeman, Nancy, *Coll Mgr,* University of British Columbia, Museum of Anthropology, Vancouver BC

Brueggeman, Mark, *Sr Lectr,* University of Wisconsin-Stevens Point, Dept of Art & Design, Stevens Point WI (S)

Brueggenhohann, Jean, *Prof (Graphic Design),* University of Missouri - Columbia, Dept of Art, Columbia MO (S)

Bruin, Joan, *Dir,* LA County Museum of Art, Los Angeles CA

Brumagen, Regan, *Reference & Emerging Tech Librn,* Corning Museum of Glass, Juliette K and Leonard S Rakow Research Library, Corning NY

Brumley, Lizabeth, *Visitor Svcs Coordr,* Lauren Rogers, Laurel MS

Brumm, Tina, *Colls Asst,* Texas Ranger Hall of Fame & Museum, Waco TX

Brummett, Bill, *Pres,* Livingston County Historical Society, Museum, Geneseo NY

Brune Sigler, Danielle, *Assoc Dir,* University of Texas at Austin, Harry Ransom Humanities Research Center, Austin TX

Bruner, Rich, *Coordr Photog,* Shepherd University, Dept of Contemporary Art & Theater, Shepherdstown WV (S)

Bruner, Richard, *Mus Store Mgr,* Oklahoma City Museum of Art, Oklahoma City OK

Brunett, Keven, *Assoc Lect,* University of Wisconsin-Stevens Point, Dept of Art & Design, Stevens Point WI (S)

Brungardt, Kevin, *Chmn Human & Fine Arts,* Garden City Community College, Art Dept, Garden City KS (S)

Brunner, Christal, *Head Librn,* Mexico-Audrain County Library, Mexico MO

Brunner, Helen M, *Dir Spec Projects,* Art Resources International, Washington DC

Brunner, Ludwig, *Asst Dir,* Saint Bonaventure University, Regina A Quick Center for the Arts, Saint Bonaventure NY

Brunner, Wilfred, *Art Chair Tacoma Park,* Montgomery College, Dept of Art, Rockville MD (S)

Brunning, Dennis, *Art Specialist,* Arizona State University, ASU Library, Tempe AZ

Bruno, Lugene, *Cur Art,* Carnegie Mellon University, Hunt Institute for Botanical Documentation, Pittsburgh PA

Bruns, Craig, *Chief Cur,* Independence Seaport Museum, Philadelphia PA

Bruns, Jim, *Dir,* Naval Historical Center, National Museum of the US Navy, Washington DC

Brunson, Drew, *Educ Coordr,* Craftsmen's Guild of Mississippi, Inc, Mississippi Craft Center, Ridgeland MS

Brunson, Ty, *Assoc Prof,* Arkansas Tech University, Dept of Art, Russellville AR (S)

Brunsting, Karen, *Librarian,* Memphis Brooks Museum of Art, Library, Memphis TN

Brunt, Bonnie, *Dean,* Spokane Falls Community College, Fine Arts Dept, Spokane WA (S)

Bruntse, Line, *Asst Prof 2D & 3D Design, Drawing & Sculpture,* Millersville University, Dept of Art & Design, Millersville PA (S)

Brunvand, Sandy, *Instr,* University of Utah, Dept of Art & Art History, Salt Lake City UT (S)

Brusati, Celeste, *Prof & Assoc Chair,* University of Michigan, Ann Arbor, Dept of History of Art, Ann Arbor MI (S)

Brush, Gloria D, *Prof, Head Dept,* University of Minnesota, Duluth, Art Dept, Duluth MN (S)

Bruso, Arthur, *Dir,* Curious Matter, Jersey City NJ

Brutschy, Sarah, *Dir Mem Svcs,* Henry Morrison Flagler Museum, Palm Beach FL

Bruttomesso, Patty, *Cur,* Louisa May Alcott Memorial Association, Orchard House, Concord MA

Brutvan, Cheryl, *Dir Curatorial Affairs, Cur Contemporary Art,* Norton Museum of Art, West Palm Beach FL

Bruya, Chris, *Assoc Dean,* Mount Hood Community College, Visual Arts Center, Gresham OR (S)

Bryan, Betsy, *Dir Near Eastern & Egyptian Art,* Johns Hopkins University, Archaeological Museum, Baltimore MD

Bryan, Jerry, *Chmn,* Western Oklahoma State College, Art Dept, Altus OK (S)

Bryan, John, *Chmn Art History,* University of South Carolina, Dept of Art, Columbia SC (S)

Bryan, Kailey, *Gallery Dir,* Craft Council of Newfoundland & Labrador, Saint John's NF

Bryan, Paul, *Asst Guest Servs & Opers Mgr,* University of Chicago, Smart Museum of Art, Chicago IL

Bryan, Tracy, *Dir of Facilities,* Virginia Historical Society, Library, Richmond VA

Bryant, David, *Dir,* New Canaan Library, H. Pelham Curtis Gallery, New Canaan CT

Bryant, Jim, *Chmn,* Eastern New Mexico University, Dept of Art, Portales NM (S)

Bryant, Keith, *Lectr,* University of North Carolina at Charlotte, Dept Art, Charlotte NC (S)

Bryant, Khaliq, *Mgr Finance & Admin,* African American Museum, Dallas TX

Bryant, Kim, *Arts Admin Asst,* Baker Arts Center, Liberal KS

Bryant, Rhonda, *VPres,* Drew County Historical Society, Museum, Monticello AR

Bryant, Sampson, *Performance Coordr,* Museum of Northern British Columbia, Ruth Harvey Art Gallery, Prince Rupert BC

Bryant, Sampson, *Performance Coordr,* Museum of Northern British Columbia, Library, Prince Rupert BC

Bryne, Bruce, *Workshop Supv & Master Carpenter,* Grenfell Campus, Memorial University of Newfoundland, Division of Fine Arts, Visual Arts Program, Corner Brook NF (S)

Brynolf, Anita, *Instr,* San Diego Mesa College, Fine Arts Dept, San Diego CA (S)

Brynteson, Susan, *Vice Provost & May Morris Dir Libraries,* University of Delaware, Morris Library, Newark DE

Bryson, Gregg, *Prof,* Virginia Polytechnic Institute & State University, Dept of Art & Art History, Blacksburg VA (S)

Brzozowski, Carole, *Dean,* Syracuse University, College of Visual & Performing Arts, Syracuse NY (S)

Bucci, Jonathan, *Coll Cur,* Willamette University, Hallie Ford Museum of Art, Salem OR

Buch, Wayna, *Dir Arts Based Pre-School,* Wichita Center for the Arts, Mary R Koch School of Visual Arts, Wichita KS (S)

Buchanan, Donna, *Group Tour Sales Dir,* Edsel & Eleanor Ford House, Grosse Pointe Shores MI

Buchanan, Jacque, *Treas,* Woodburn Art Center, Glatt House Gallery, Woodburn OR

Buchanan, John, *Instr,* Alcorn State University, Dept of Fine Arts, Lorman MS (S)

Buchanan, Mandy, *Cur Educ,* Lauren Rogers, Laurel MS

Buchanan, Mel, *Cur Decorative Arts & Design,* New Orleans Museum of Art, New Orleans LA

Buchanan, Serena, *Potter,* Thousand Islands Arts Center - Home of the Handweaving Museum, Clayton NY (S)

Bucheit, Chris, *Instr,* Western Wisconsin Technical College, Graphics Division, La Crosse WI (S)

Bucher, Burt, *Prof,* Missouri Southern State University, Dept of Art, Joplin MO (S)

Buchholz, Rylan, *Exhibs Mgr,* Japan Society, Inc, Japan Society Gallery, New York NY

Buchi, Kevin, *Treas,* American Craft Council, Minneapolis MN

Buchli, Ines, *Assoc Prof & Chair, Dept of Theatre,* York University, School of the Arts, Media, Performance & Design, Toronto ON (S)

Buchman, Bill, *Instr,* Art Center Sarasota, Sarasota FL (S)

Buchman, Lorne, *Pres,* ArtCenter College of Design, Pasadena CA (S)

Buchtel, John, *Spec Coll Librn,* Georgetown University, Lauinger Library - Special Collections Division, Washington DC

Bucino, Erika G, *Mus Shop Mgr,* Brandywine Conservancy, Brandywine River Museum, Chadds Ford PA

Buck, Christine, *Treas,* Cortland County Historical Society, Suggett House Museum, Cortland NY

Buck, Paper, *Print Studio Mgr,* Kala Institute, Kala Art Institute, Berkeley CA

Buckingham, Daniel, *Prof,* Munson-Williams-Proctor Arts Institute, Pratt MWP College of Art, Utica NY (S)
Buckingham, Jim, *Pres,* Carteret County Historical Society, The History Place, Morehead City NC
Buckingham, Lark, *Registrar,* Historic Arkansas Museum, Little Rock AR
Buckland, Alex, *Instr,* Lincoln Memorial University, Division of Humanities, Harrogate TN (S)
Buckley, David, *Exec Dir,* California State University, Chico, Associated Students, 3rd Floor Art Gallery, Chico CA
Buckley, Donald G, *Asst Dir,* Westfield Athenaeum, Jasper Rand Art Museum, Westfield MA
Buckley, Kerry, *Exec Dir,* Historic Northampton Museum & Education Center, Northampton MA
Buckley, Laurene, *Asst Dir,* State University of New York at Oswego, Tyler Art Gallery, Oswego NY
Buckley, R F, *Prof,* Florida International University, School of Art & Art History, Miami FL (S)
Buckman, Barbara, *Dept Coordr MFA,* Niagara County Community College, Fine Arts Division, Sanborn NY (S)
Buckman, Pamela, *Sculpture Garden Mgr,* New Orleans Museum of Art, New Orleans LA
Buckner, Cindy, *Assoc Cur,* Grand Rapids Art Museum, Reference Library, Grand Rapids MI
Buckner, Virginia, *Exec Advisor,* Halifax Historical Society, Inc, Halifax Historical Museum, Daytona Beach FL
Buckno, Josh, *Mng Dir,* Boston University Art Galleries, The Faye G, Jo & James Stone Gallery, Boston MA
Buckwalter, Linda, *Contact,* Ohio History Connection, National Afro-American Museum & Cultural Center, Wilberforce OH
Bucsis, Andrew, *Cur Asst,* Canadian Clay and Glass Gallery, Waterloo ON
Bucuvalas, Tina, *Folk Arts Coordr,* Florida Folklife Programs, Tallahassee FL
Buczynski, Erin, *Gallery Dir,* Bradley University, Heuser Art Center, Peoria IL
Budahl, Lee P, *Assoc Prof,* Western Carolina University, Dept of Art/College of Arts & Science, Cullowhee NC (S)
Budde, Diana, *Prof,* University of Wisconsin College - Marinette, Art Dept, Marinette WI (S)
Budhinata, Linda, *Finance Mgr,* American Institute for Conservation of Historic & Artistic Works, Washington DC
Budish, Ian, *Preparator,* Brown University, David Winton Bell Gallery, Providence RI
Budrovich, Tony, *Deputy Dir Opers,* California Science Center, Los Angeles CA
Budzyna, John, *Exec Dir,* Essex Art Center, Lawrence MA
Buechley, Mary, *Reference Technical Assoc,* Indiana University, Fine Arts Library, Bloomington IN
Buege, Elizabeth, *Membership + Events Coordinator,* Miami-Dade College, MDC Museum of Art & Design, Miami FL
Buenger, Barbara C, *Prof Art History,* University of Wisconsin, Madison, Dept of Art History, Madison WI (S)
Buentello, Mia Marisol, *Programming Officer,* Hidalgo County Historical Museum, Edinburg TX
Buerker, Sandy, *Gallery Mgr & Admin Dir,* Farmington Valley Arts Center, Avon CT
Buescher, Jean, *Instr,* Siena Heights University, Studio Angelico-Art Dept, Adrian MI (S)
Buesgen, Linda, *Mem Coordr,* Lehigh Valley Heritage Center, Allentown PA
Buettner, Brigitte, *Prof,* Smith College, Art Dept, Northampton MA (S)
Bufano, Michelle, *Exec Dir,* City Art Works, Pratt Fine Arts Center, Seattle WA (S)
Buffalo, Jo, *Prof,* Cazenovia College, Center for Art & Design Studies, Cazenovia NY (S)
Buffington, Mel, *Instr Photog,* Eastern Oregon University, School of Arts & Science, La Grande OR (S)
Buffington, Ron, *Prof,* University of Tennessee at Chattanooga, Dept of Art, Chattanooga TN (S)
Buffington, Sean T, *Pres,* University of the Arts, Philadelphia Colleges of Art & Design, Performing Arts & Media & Communication, Philadelphia PA (S)
Buford, Bonita, *COO,* Harvey B Gantt Center for African American Arts + Culture, Charlotte NC
Bugler, Pam, *Dir Educ,* Wichita Center for the Arts, Mary R Koch School of Visual Arts, Wichita KS (S)
Buhl, Gudrun, *Cur & Mus Dir,* Dumbarton Oaks, Dumbarton Oaks Museum, Washington DC
Buhr, Margaret, *Dir Educ,* Dubuque Museum of Art, Dubuque IA
Buhr, Michelle, *Dir Advancement,* National Postal Museum, Smithsonian Institution, Washington DC
Buhr, Sarah, *Cur Exhibs,* Springfield Art Museum, Springfield MO
Buick, Kirsten Pai, *Dir,* University of New Mexico, Department of Fine Arts & Art History, Albuquerque NM (S)
Buie Niewyk, Ellen, *Head Bywaters Spec Coll,* Southern Methodist University, Hamon Arts Library, Dallas TX
Buie, Sarah, *Dir,* Clark University, The Schiltkamp Gallery/Traina Center for the Arts, Worcester MA
Buis, Ed, *Lib Dir,* Southeast Missouri State University, Kent Library, Cape Girardeau MO
Buisch, Derrick, *Prof,* University of Wisconsin, Madison, Dept of Art, Madison WI (S)
Buizy, Michele, *Prof & Chair,* California State University, Dominguez Hills, Art & Design Dept, Carson CA (S)
Bukar, Nat, *VPres,* The National Art League, Douglaston NY
Bukowski, Lucy, *Deputy Dir Admin,* Heritage Museums & Gardens, Sandwich MA
Bukowski, William, *Head of Dept,* Bethany Lutheran College, Art Dept, Mankato MN (S)
Bul-Burton, Kim, *Dir,* Monterey Public Library, Art & Architecture Dept, Monterey CA
Bulaich, Angie, *Head Develop,* Kimbell Art Foundation, Kimbell Art Museum, Fort Worth TX
Bule, Sarah, *Prof,* Clark University, Dept of Visual & Performing Arts, Worcester MA (S)
Bulger, Stephen, *Pres,* Stephen Bulger Gallery, Toronto ON
Bulla, John, *COO & Deputy Dir,* Heard Museum, Phoenix AZ
Buller, Rob, *Assistant Prof, Art,* Chowan College, Dept. of Communication Arts, Fine and Applied Arts, Murfreesboro NC (S)
Bullock, Katherine, *Discovery Educ Dir,* Living Arts & Science Center, Inc, Lexington KY
Bulow, Harry, *Head of School (upa),* Purdue University, West Lafayette, Patti and Rusty Rueff School of Visual & Performing Arts, Art & Design Dept, West Lafayette IN (S)
Bumpass, Terry, *Cur,* Museum of New Mexico, Office of Cultural Affairs of New Mexico, The Governor's Gallery, Santa Fe NM
Bunch, Lisa, *Office Mgr & Bookkeeper,* Green Hill Center for North Carolina Art, Greenhill, Greensboro NC
Bunch, Lonnie, *Co-Chair,* United States National Committee of the International Council of Museums, Washington DC
Bunch, Lonnie, *Founding Dir,* National Museum of African American History and Culture, Smithsonian Institution, Washington DC
Bundy, Annalee, *Exec Dir,* Ames Free-Easton's Public Library, North Easton MA
Bundy-Jost, Barbara, *Dir,* Rahr-West Art Museum, Manitowoc WI
Bunge, Jean, *Co-Dir,* Nobles County Art Center, Worthington MN
Bunge, Martin, *Co-Dir,* Nobles County Art Center, Worthington MN
Bunger, Janet, *Bd Finance Vice Chair,* American Association of University Women, Washington DC
Bunkin, Robert, *Cur Art,* Staten Island Museum, Staten Island NY
Bunkin, Robert, *Cur Art,* Staten Island Museum, Archives Library, Staten Island NY
Bunn, Steven, *Exhib Technician,* Bowdoin College, Peary-MacMillan Arctic Museum, Brunswick ME
Bunnenberg-Boehmer, Kay, *Instr,* Chemeketa Community College, Dept of Humanities & Communications, Art Program, Salem OR (S)
Bunner, Patty, *Instr,* Southwestern Michigan College, Fine & Performing Arts Dept, Dowagiac MI (S)
Bunzick, John, *Pres,* Photographic Resource Center, Inc, Cambridge MA
Buonaccorsi, Jim, *Assoc Prof Sculpture,* University of Georgia, Franklin College of Arts & Sciences, Lamar Dodd School of Art, Athens GA (S)
Buonagurio, Toby, *Prof,* Stony Brook University, College of Arts & Sciences, Dept of Art, Stony Brook NY (S)
Buonpastore, Andrew, *VPres Opers,* New-York Historical Society, Museum, New York NY
Buranakorn, Wanrudee, *Asst Prof,* University of Wisconsin-Eau Claire, Dept of Art & Design, Eau Claire WI (S)
Burbach, Sarah, *Chmn Bd,* Morgan County Foundation, Inc, Madison-Morgan Cultural Center, Madison GA
Burback, Bill, *VPres,* Garrison Art Center, Garrison NY
Burbank, Jennifer, *Gallery Manager,* Silvermine Arts Center, Silvermine Galleries, New Canaan CT
Burbul, Derrick, *Asst Prof,* University of Nebraska, Kearney, Dept of Art & Art History, Kearney NE (S)
Burchby, Casey, *Mng Dir Mus Advancement,* Nevada Museum of Art, Reno NV
Burchett, Jayme, *Prof,* College of the Ozarks, Dept of Art, Point Lookout MO (S)
Burchett, Kenneth, *Prof,* University of Central Arkansas, Department of Art, Conway AR (S)
Burchfield, Janelle, *Dir Mktg & Community Engagement,* Peninsula Fine Arts Center, Newport News VA
Burden, Jeff, *Chmn,* Columbus State University, Dept of Art, Fine Arts Hall, Columbus GA (S)
Burden, Jeffrey, *Prof,* University of Nevada, Las Vegas, Dept of Art, Las Vegas NV (S)
Burden, Rhonda, *Shop Mgr,* Comox Valley Art Gallery, Courtenay BC
Burdette, Raven, *Pres,* Cuyahoga Valley Art Center, Cuyahoga Falls OH (S)
Burge, Denise, *Foundations Coordr, Undergrad Adv & Assoc Prof Fine Arts,* University of Cincinnati, School of Art, Cincinnati OH (S)
Burge, Nolina, *Circ Supv,* Art Center College of Design, James Lemont Fogg Memorial Library, Pasadena CA
Burger, Thomas Julius, *Dir,* University of Bridgeport, Shintaro Akatsu School of Design, Bridgeport CT (S)
Burger, Thomas Julius, *Dir,* University of Bridgeport, Shintaro Akatsu School of Design, Bridgeport CT (S)
Burgess, Cynthia A, *Cur Books & Printed Material,* Baylor University, Armstrong Browning Library, Waco TX
Burgess, Elizabeth, *Coll Mgr,* Harriet Beecher Stowe Center, Library, Hartford CT
Burgess, Elizabeth, *Colls Mgr,* Harriet Beecher Stowe Center, Hartford CT
Burgess, Julie, *Registrar,* Grand Rapids Art Museum, Grand Rapids MI
Burgess, Kimberly, *Dir,* Page Bond Gallery, Richmond VA
Burggraf, Ray, *Prof & Assoc Chair,* Florida State University, Art Dept, Tallahassee FL (S)
Burgiss-Hill, Bee, *Guest Servs,* The Albrecht-Kemper Museum of Art, Saint Joseph MO
Burgner, Kelly, *Chmn,* Ricks College, Dept of Art, Rexburg ID (S)
Burk, Teresa, *Head Librn,* Savannah College of Art & Design - Atlanta, ACA Library of Atlanta, Atlanta GA
Burke, Christina, *Cur Native American & Non-Western Art,* Philbrook Museum of Art, Tulsa OK
Burke, Daniel, *Prof,* Mercyhurst University, Dept of Art, Erie PA (S)

Burke, Gregory, *Exec Dir & CEO,* Remai Modern, Saskatoon SK
Burke, James, *VPres Finance & Admin,* The Newberry, Chicago IL
Burke, Jessica, *Asst Prod,* Georgia Southern University, Betty Foy Sanders Dept of Art, Statesboro GA (S)
Burke, Jo, *Dir,* Northern Illinois University, NIU Art Museum, DeKalb IL
Burke, John SJ, *Prof,* Longwood University, Dept of Art, Farmville VA (S)
Burke, Jonathan, *Dean Visual Commun,* Art Institute of Southern California, Laguna Beach CA (S)
Burke, Ken, *Prof,* Mills College, Art Dept, Oakland CA (S)
Burke, Marcus, *Sr Cur Paintings & Metalwork,* The Hispanic Society of America, Hispanic Society Museum & Library, New York NY
Burke, Mary Anne, *Exec Dir,* Washington County Arts Council, Gallery, Hagerstown MD
Burke, Mary Beth, *Develop Coordr,* Springfield Art Association of Edwards Place, Springfield IL
Burke, Mary, *Dir,* Sid W Richardson Foundation, Sid Richardson Museum, Fort Worth TX
Burke, Matt, *Asst Prof,* University of Kansas, The School of the Arts, Dept of Visual Art, Lawrence KS (S)
Burke, Peggy, *Exec Dir,* Concord Museum, Concord MA
Burke, Penny, *Exec Dir,* Northampton Center for the Arts, Northampton MA
Burke, Ren, *Progs Asst,* Center for Fine Art Photography, Fort Collins CO
Burke, Shannon, *Dir Educ & Visitor Servs,* Harriet Beecher Stowe Center, Hartford CT
Burke, Shannon, *Educ & Visitor Svcs,* Harriet Beecher Stowe Center, Library, Hartford CT
Burke, William J, *Exec Dir,* Philadelphia Art Commission, Philadelphia PA
Burke, William J, *Prof,* Florida International University, School of Art & Art History, Miami FL (S)
Burkhalter, Laura, *Cur,* Edmundson Art Foundation, Inc, Des Moines Art Center, Des Moines IA
Burkhauser, Elizabeth, *Instr,* Keystone College, Fine Arts Dept, LaPlume PA (S)
Burks, Sarah L, *Preservation Planner,* Cambridge Historical Commission, City of Cambridge, Research Library on Architectural and Social History of Cambridge, Mass, Cambridge MA
Burleigh, Kimberly, *Dir MFA Prog, Chair & Prof Fine Arts,* University of Cincinnati, School of Art, Cincinnati OH (S)
Burlingame, Steve, *Chmn,* Chatham Historical Society, The Atwood House Museum, Chatham MA
Burlingham, Cynthia, *Dir,* University of California, Los Angeles, Grunwald Center for the Graphic Arts at Hammer Museum, Los Angeles CA
Burman, Jenny, *Prof & Dept Chair,* McGill University, Dept of Art History & Communication Studies, Montreal QC (S)
Burmeister, Alice, *Asst Prof,* Winthrop University, Dept of Art & Design, Rock Hill SC (S)
Burnay, Diogo, *Assoc Prof & Dir School of Architecture,* Dalhousie University, School of Architecture, Halifax NS (S)
Burnett, Ronald, *Pres & Vice Chancellor,* Emily Carr University of Art + Design, Vancouver BC (S)
Burnett, Sandra, *Exec Dir,* Salem Art Association, Bush Barn Art Center, Salem OR
Burnett, Vernon, *Customer Svcs Mgr,* Light Work, Robert B Menschel Photography Gallery, Syracuse NY
Burnette, Karin, *Dir Fin & Opers,* Southeastern Center for Contemporary Art, Winston-Salem NC
Burnette, Marshall, *Mus Aid,* Indian Arts & Crafts Board, US Dept of the Interior, Sioux Indian Museum, Rapid City SD
Burnette, Scott, *Instr,* Guilford Technical Community College, Commercial Art Dept, Jamestown NC (S)
Burnham, Jenny, *Cur Educ,* Twin City Art Foundation, Masur Museum of Art, Monroe LA
Burnham, Laura E, *Exec Dir,* Abington Art Center, Jenkintown PA
Burnham, Lauren, *Educ & Public Progs Mgr,* American Swedish Historical Foundation & Museum, American Swedish Historical Museum, Philadelphia PA
Burnham, Lauren, *Educ & Public Progs Mgr,* American Swedish Historical Foundation & Museum, Nord Library, Philadelphia PA
Burnham, Richard, *2nd VPres,* Newport Historical Society & Museum of Newport History, Newport RI
Burnhan, Harold, *Pres,* Essex Historical Society and Shipbuilding Museum, Essex MA
Burns, Barry, *Asst Prof,* California Lutheran University, Art Dept, Thousand Oaks CA (S)
Burns, Courtney, *Chief Cur,* New York State Military Museum and Veterans Research Center, Saratoga Springs NY
Burns, Erin, *Digital Photog,* North Seattle College, North Seattle College Dept of Art, Seattle WA (S)
Burns, Kathy, *Coord,* LeSueur Museum, Le Sueur MN
Burns, Laura, *Library Support Specialist,* Ohio University, Fine Arts Library, Athens OH
Burns, Mark, *Prof & Chmn,* University of Nevada, Las Vegas, Dept of Art, Las Vegas NV (S)
Burns, Millie, *Asst Prof Art Dir Hewitt Gallery,* Marymount Manhattan College, Fine & Performing Arts Div, New York NY (S)
Burns, Nancy, *Asst Chief Cur Prints, Drawings & Photography,* Worcester Art Museum, Worcester MA
Burns, Robert, *Exec Dir,* Mattatuck Historical Society, Mattatuck Museum, Waterbury CT
Burns, Roxanne M, *Pres,* Jefferson County Historical Society, Watertown NY
Burns, Todd, *Asst Prof,* University of Louisville, Allen R Hite Art Institute, Louisville KY (S)
Burns, W James, *Exec Dir,* Maricopa County Historical Society, Desert Caballeros Western Museum, Wickenburg AZ
Burr, Josephine, *Studio Mgr,* Greenwich House Inc, Greenwich House Pottery, New York NY (S)
Burrell, Debra, *Arts Coordr,* City of Hampton, Hampton Arts Commission, Hampton VA
Burrell, Jane, *VP Educ & Pub Progs,* Los Angeles County Museum of Art, Los Angeles CA
Burriesci, Matt, *Exec Dir,* Providence Athenaeum, Providence RI
Burros, Julie, *Chief, Arts & Culture,* City of Boston Arts & Culture, City Hall Galleries, Boston MA
Burroughs, Brody, *Instr,* Ithaca College, Fine Art Dept, Ithaca NY (S)
Burrows, Geoff, *Pres,* Sandwich Historical Society, Center Sandwich NH
Burrows-Johnson, Susan, *Exec Dir & CEO,* City of Lethbridge, Sir Alexander Galt Museum, Lethbridge AB
Burrus, Bobby, *VPres,* Red River Valley Museum, Vernon TX
Burson, Max M, *Library Dir,* Friends University, Edmund Stanley Library, Wichita KS
Burson, Nancy, *Admin Asst,* Scripps College, Clark Humanities Museum, Claremont CA
Burt, Ann, *Dir,* Ormond Memorial Art Museum and Gardens, Ormond Beach FL
Burt, Emily Wilson, *Cur,* C M Russell Museum, Frederic G Renner Memorial Library, Great Falls MT
Burt, Helene, *Exec Dir,* Toronto Art Therapy Institute, Toronto ON (S)
Burt, Patricia, *Asst Prof Music,* Harford Community College, Visual, Performing and Applied Arts Division, Bel Air MD (S)
Burton, Anne, *Gallery Dir,* BlackRock Center for the Arts, Germantown MD
Burton, Douglas, *Asst Prof,* Lenoir Rhyne College, Dept of Art, Hickory NC (S)
Burton, Jenera, *Supvr Librn, Branches,* Oakland Public Library, Art, Music, History & Literature Section, Oakland CA
Burton, Joseph, *President,* Museum of Ossining Historical Society, Library, Ossining NY
Burton, Melody, *Deputy Univ Librn,* University of British Columbia, Art & Architecture Planning, UBC Library, Vancouver BC
Burton, Michelle, *Registrar,* Marquette University, Haggerty Museum of Art, Milwaukee WI
Burton, Patrick, *Exhibs Coordr,* University of Virginia, The Fralin Museum of Art at the University of Virginia, Charlottesville VA
Burton, Troy, *Artistic Dir,* Eubie Blake National Jazz Institute and Cultural Center, Baltimore MD
Burtscher, Sarah, *Gallery Dir,* Stephen Bulger Gallery, Toronto ON
Burwell, Joan, *Mem Chairperson,* Three Forks Area Historical Society, Headwaters Heritage Museum, Three Forks MT
Bury, Stephen, *Andrew W Mellon Chief Librn,* The Frick Collection, Frick Art Reference Library, New York NY
Bury, Stephen, *Chief Librarian,* Frick Collection, New York NY
Burzcyk, Monika, *Instr,* Springfield College, Dept of Visual & Performing Arts, Springfield MA (S)
Busby, James, *Chmn,* Houston Baptist University, Dept of Art, Houston TX (S)
Busceme, Greg, *Dir,* The Art Studio Inc, Beaumont TX
Busceme, Greg, *Instr,* Lamar University, Art Dept, Beaumont TX (S)
Busch, Ellen Cone, *Dir,* Planting Fields Foundation, Coe Hall at Planting Fields Arboretum, Oyster Bay NY
Buschor, Elizabeth, *Sr Paper Conservator,* Midwest Art Conservation Center, Minneapolis MN
Buser, Tom, *Assoc Prof,* University of Louisville, Allen R Hite Art Institute, Louisville KY (S)
Bush, Harold, *Head of Security,* University of Illinois at Urbana-Champaign, Spurlock Museum, Urbana IL
Bush, Jennifer, *Registrar,* Johnson-Humrickhouse Museum, Coshocton OH
Bush, Kathy, *VPres Devel,* Avampato Discovery Museum, The Clay Center for Arts & Sciences, Charleston WV
Bush, Rebecca, *Curator of History/Exhibition Coordinator,* The Columbus Museum, Columbus GA
Bush, Robert, *Pres,* Arts & Science Council, Charlotte NC
Bush, Sarah, *Treas,* Surface Design Association, Inc, Las Vegas NM
Bushara, Leslie, *Deputy Dir Educ & Guest Servs,* Children's Museum of Manhattan, New York NY
Bushara, Leslie, *Deputy Dir Educ & Guest Svcs,* Children's Museum of Manhattan, New York NY
Bushelle, Renee, *Visitor Svcs Mgr,* Staten Island Museum, Staten Island NY
Bushman, Mark, *Educ Dir,* Salisbury University, Ward Museum of Wildfowl Art, Salisbury MD
Bushuev, Marina, *Accnt,* Women's Art Association of Canada, Dignam Gallery, Toronto ON
Businelli, David, *Chmn Board,* Staten Island Museum, Staten Island NY
Bussard, Kate, *Peter C. Bumell Cur Photog,* Princeton University, Princeton University Art Museum, Princeton NJ
Bussmann, Tom, *Co-Owner,* Philip Slein Gallery, Saint Louis MO
Busta, Vicki, *Prog Coordr,* SVACA - Sheyenne Valley Arts & Crafts Association, Organization, Fort Ransom ND
Bustamante, Cody A, *Prof,* Southern Oregon University, Art & Art History Dept, Ashland OR (S)
Butckovitz, Dean, *Gallery Mgr,* University of North Carolina at Charlotte, Dept Art, Charlotte NC (S)
Buthod, Craig, *Pres & CEO,* The Filson Historical Society, Louisville KY
Butler, Ann, *Dir Library & Archives,* Bard College, Center for Curatorial Studies Graduate Program, Annandale-on-Hudson NY (S)
Butler, Ann, *Dir Library & Archives,* Bard College, Center for Curatorial Studies and the Hessel Museum of Art, Annandale-on-Hudson NY

Butler, Carol, *Asst Dir Colls,* National Museum of Natural History, Smithsonian Institution, Washington DC
Butler, David, *Exec Dir,* Knoxville Museum of Art, Knoxville TN
Butler, Diane, *Dir,* State University of New York at Binghamton, Binghamton University Art Museum, Binghamton NY
Butler, Erin, *Information Resources,* Municipal Art Society of New York, Greenacre Reference Library, New York NY
Butler, Erin, *Newsletter Ed & Bd Mem,* Women in the Arts Foundation, Inc, Staten Island NY
Butler, Jan, *VPres,* Gallery XII, Wichita KS
Butler, Janine, *Librn,* Art Gallery of Windsor, Reference Library, Windsor ON
Butler, Jerry E, *Chmn,* Madison Area Technical College, Art Dept, Madison WI (S)
Butler, Joshua, *Assoc Prof,* Colorado Mesa University, Art Dept, Grand Junction CO (S)
Butler, Larry, *Instr,* George Mason University, College of Humanities & Social Sciences, Dept of History & Art History, Fairfax VA (S)
Butler, Linda, *Dir Mktg, Commun & Visitor Experience,* Fine Arts Museums of San Francisco, Legion of Honor, San Francisco CA
Butler, Maria, *Exec Dir,* Pensacola Museum of Art, Harry Thornton Library, Pensacola FL
Butler, Owen, *Assoc Prof,* Rochester Institute of Technology, School of Photographic Arts & Sciences, Rochester NY (S)
Butler, Stephen M, *Graphic Design,* Art Institute of Pittsburgh, Pittsburgh PA (S)
Butler, Susan, *Prog Coordr Photog Dept,* Pine Manor College, Visual Arts Dept, Chestnut Hill MA (S)
Butler, William, *Exec Dir,* Contemporary Art Center, Peoria IL
Butler-Ludwig, John L, *Cur,* University of Chicago, Visual Resources Collection, Chicago IL
Butt, Christopher, *Opers Mgr,* Okanagan Heritage Museum, Kelowna BC
Butt, Harlan, *Regents Prof Metals,* University of North Texas, College of Visual Arts & Design, Denton TX (S)
Buttacavoli, Eva, *Exec Dir,* Dayton Visual Arts Center, Dayton OH
Butterfield, Tom, *Art Dir,* Virginia Polytechnic Institute & State University, Perspective Gallery, Blacksburg VA
Butterill, Dale, *Pres,* Women's Art Association of Canada, Dignam Gallery, Toronto ON
Butts, H Daniel, *Art Dir,* Mansfield Fine Arts Guild, Library, Mansfield OH
Butts, H Daniel, *Dir,* Mansfield Fine Arts Guild, Mansfield Art Center, Mansfield OH
Butts, Patricia, *Asst to Dir,* The Columbus Museum, Columbus GA
Butts, Vicki, *Dir Finance,* Grace Museum, Inc, The Grace Museum, Abilene TX
Buttwinick, Edward, *Dir,* Brentwood Art Center, Los Angeles CA (S)
Butz, Bob, *Pres,* Phelps County Historical Society, Nebraska Prairie Museum, Holdrege NE
Butz, Lane, *Instr,* Western Wisconsin Technical College, Graphics Division, La Crosse WI (S)
Butz, Robert, *Pres,* Phelps County Historical Society, Donald O. Lindgren Library, Holdrege NE
Buvoli, Luca, *Dir,* Maryland Institute, Mount Royal School of Art, Baltimore MD (S)
Buxbaum, Elyse, *Deputy Dir Devel,* The Jewish Museum, New York NY
Buxbaum, Melba, *Chmn,* Blackburn College, Dept of Art, Carlinville IL (S)
Buxkamper, Barry, *Instr,* Middle Tennessee State University, Art Dept, Murfreesboro TN (S)
Buyer, Sarah, *Dir Educ & Prog,* Arlington Center for the Arts, Arlington MA
Buzzard, Colleen, *VPres,* Rochester Contemporary, Art Center, Rochester NY
Byam, David, *VPres,* Springfield Art & Historical Society, Springfield VT
Byam, Kathi, *Secy,* Springfield Art & Historical Society, Springfield VT
Byce, Joane, *Instr,* Pierce College, Art Dept, Woodland Hills CA (S)
Bychinski, Jan, *Mus Receptionist,* Washburn University, Mulvane Art Museum, Topeka KS
Bye, Elizabeth, *Head Dept,* University of Minnesota, Dept of Design, Housing & Apparel, Saint Paul MN (S)
Byers, Bill, *Dir,* Brevard College, Spiers Gallery, Brevard NC
Byers, Bill, *Prof,* Brevard College, Department of Art, Brevard NC (S)
Byers, Larry, *Assoc Prof,* Saint Louis Community College at Florissant Valley, Liberal Arts Division, Ferguson MO (S)
Byford, Bruce, *VPres & CFO,* Banff Centre, Banff AB (S)
Byford, Bruce, *VPres Admin & CFO,* Banff Centre, Walter Phillips Gallery, Banff AB
Byler, Cynthia, *Asst Prof,* Lincoln University, Dept Visual and Performing Arts, Jefferson City MO (S)
Bylsma, Megan, *Assoc Dir,* Kendall College of Art & Design, Urban Institute for Contemporary Arts, Grand Rapids MI
Bynum, Delois, *Guest Servs Coord,* Green Hill Center for North Carolina Art, Greenhill, Greensboro NC
Byrd, Jeff, *Prof, Art Dept Head,* University of Northern Iowa, Dept of Art, Cedar Falls IA (S)
Byrd, Joan, *Prof,* Western Carolina University, Dept of Art/College of Arts & Science, Cullowhee NC (S)
Byrd, John, *Assoc Prof,* University of South Florida, School of Art & Art History, Tampa FL (S)
Byrd, Trenda, *Dir Educ,* Tubman African American Museum, Macon GA
Byrn, Brian D, *Cur Exhib & Educ,* Midwest Museum of American Art, Elkhart IN
Byrne, Alison, *Cur Educ,* Virginia Museum of Contemporary Art, Virginia Beach VA
Byrne, Alison, *Dir Exhibs & Educ,* Virginia Museum of Contemporary Art, Virginia Beach VA
Byrne, Elizabeth, *Head,* University of California, Berkeley, Environmental Design Library, Berkeley CA
Byrne, Joseph, *Chmn, Prof Fine Arts,* Trinity College, Dept of Studio Arts, Hartford CT (S)
Byrne, Peter, *Design Chair,* Rochester Institute of Technology, College of Imaging Arts & Sciences, Rochester NY (S)
Byrnes, Sheila, *Second VPres,* National League of American Pen Women, Washington DC
Byron, Michael, *Assoc Dean,* Washington University, School of Art, Saint Louis MO (S)
Bytof, Corey, *Pub Rels,* City of San Rafael, Falkirk Cultural Center, San Rafael CA
Bywaters, Diane, *Prof,* University of Wisconsin-Stevens Point, Dept of Art & Design, Stevens Point WI (S)
Bzura, Katherine, *Prof,* State College of Florida Manatee - Sarasota, Art, Design, Humanities, Bradenton FL (S)
Cabellero-Perez, Juan Carlos, *School for American Crafts Chair,* Rochester Institute of Technology, College of Imaging Arts & Sciences, Rochester NY (S)
Cabezas, Thomas, *Cur,* University of Wisconsin - Platteville, Harry & Laura Nohr Gallery, Platteville WI
Cable, Annette, *Education Coordinator,* Louisville Visual Art, Louisville KY
Cabrera, Yvette, *Prof,* University of Puerto Rico, Mayaguez, Dept of Humanities, College of Fine Arts & Theory of Art Programs, Mayaguez PR (S)
Caceres, Pedro, *Preparator,* University of Colorado, CU Art Museum, Boulder CO
Cadaret, Marge, *VPres,* Spectrum Gallery, Toledo OH
Cadby-Sorensen, Robin, *Vol Dir, Cur & Mus Shop Mgr,* Three Forks Area Historical Society, Headwaters Heritage Museum, Three Forks MT
Caddell, Flo, *Arts Dir,* Frankfort Community Public Library, Anna & Harlan Hubbard Gallery, Frankfort IN
Cade, Leslie, *Interim Director of Library & Museum Archives, Museum Archivist & Records Manager,* The Cleveland Museum of Art, Ingalls Library, Cleveland OH
Cadez, Robert, *Mgr Enrichment,* Henry Ford Community College, McKenzie Fine Art Ctr, Dearborn MI (S)
Cadora, Francis, *Instr,* University of Evansville, Art Dept, Evansville IN (S)
Cadou, Carol, *Sr Cur & VPres,* George Washington's Mount Vernon, Mount Vernon VA
Cadwell, Michael B, *Dir,* Ohio State University, Austin E Knowlton School of Architecture, Columbus OH (S)
Cagenello, Cynthia, *Dir Communs,* Hill-Stead Museum, Farmington CT
Cagley, Eric, *Registrar & Exhibs Coordr,* University of Tennessee, Ewing Gallery of Art and Architecture, Knoxville TN
Cahalan, Joseph M, *VPres Xerox Foundation,* Xerox Corporation, Art Collection, Norwalk CT
Cahan, Susan, *Assoc Prof,* University of Missouri, Saint Louis, Dept of Art & Art History, Saint Louis MO (S)
Cahan, Susan, *Dean,* Temple University, Tyler School of Art, Philadelphia PA (S)
Cahill, Holly, *Finance & HR Manager,* Contemporary Arts Center, Cincinnati OH
Cahill, Kristen, *Mus Store & Cafe Mgr,* Henry Morrison Flagler Museum, Palm Beach FL
Cahill, Nicholas D, *Prof,* University of Wisconsin, Madison, Dept of Art History, Madison WI (S)
Cahill, Stephen, *Photog,* Pitzer College, Dept of Art, Claremont CA (S)
Cahill, Theresa, *Bus & Vocations Librn,* Long Beach Public Library, Long Beach NY
Cain, Asante, *Reference & Adult Svcs Coordr,* Grand Rapids Public Library, Grand Rapids MI
Cain, John, *Exec Dir,* South Shore Arts, Munster IN
Cain, Marcus, *Cur,* Kansas City Jewish Museum of Contemporary Art - Epsten Gallery, Overland Park KS
Cain, Paula, *Head Technical Svcs,* Ponca City Library, Art Dept, Ponca City OK
Cain, Peggy, *Asst to the Dean,* Massachusetts Institute of Technology, School of Architecture and Planning, Cambridge MA (S)
Cain, Roger, *Maintenance,* Rosemount Museum, Inc, Pueblo CO
Caine, William, *Proj Mgr,* United States General Services Administration, Art in Architecture and Fine Arts, Washington DC
Cairns, R Christopher, *Prof,* Haverford College, Fine Arts Dept, Haverford PA (S)
Cairns, Roger, *Assoc Prof,* Montgomery County Community College, Art Center, Blue Bell PA (S)
Caivano, Felice, *Cur,* Trinity College, Austin Arts Center, Widener Gallery, Hartford CT
Caivano, Nicholas, *Lectr,* Georgian Court University, Dept of Art, Lakewood NJ (S)
Cakmak, Burak, *Dean School of Fashion,* The New School, Parsons School of Design, New York NY (S)
Calabrese, John A, *Prof,* Texas Woman's University, School of the Arts, Dept of Visual Arts, Denton TX (S)
Calabria, Debbie, *Mem & Special Events Mgr,* Cultural Council of Palm Beach County, Lake Worth FL
Calabrigo, David, *Chair,* Vancouver Art Gallery, Vancouver BC
Calabro, Richard, *Prof,* University of Rhode Island, Dept of Art & Art History, Kingston RI (S)
Calafiore, Robert, *Asst Dean,* University of Hartford, Hartford Art School, West Hartford CT (S)
Calamia, Libby, *Bd Mem,* American Color Print Society, Narberth PA
Caldeira, Phillippa, *Ref,* Laney College Library, Art Section, Oakland CA
Caldemeyer, Charles D, *Assoc Prof,* Ashland University, Art Dept, Ashland OH (S)
Calden, Lisa, *Dir Registration,* University of California, Berkeley, Berkeley Art Museum & Pacific Film Archive, Berkeley CA
Calderon, Beatriz, *Opers Mgr,* Bakehouse Art Complex, Inc, Miami FL

Calderon, Christopher, *Gallery Mgr,* Eastern New Mexico University, Golden Library/Runnels Gallery, Portales NM
Calderon, Diana, *Educ & Engagement Mgr,* Xico Inc, Phoenix AZ
Calderon-Rosado, Vanessa, *CEO,* Inquilinos Boricuas en Accion (IBA), Villa Victoria Center for the Arts, Boston MA
Calderwood, Jessica, *Asst Prof,* University of Wisconsin Oshkosh, Dept of Art, Oshkosh WI (S)
Calderwood, Kathy, *Assoc Prof,* Nazareth College of Rochester, Art Dept, Rochester NY (S)
Caldwell, Blaine, *Gallery Dir,* University of the Ozarks, Stephens Gallery, Clarksville AR
Caldwell, Blaine, *Prof,* University of the Ozarks, Dept of Art, Clarksville AR (S)
Caldwell, Brian, *Instr,* Oklahoma State University Institute of Technology, School of Visual Communications, Okmulgee OK (S)
Caldwell, Joan G, *Cur,* Tulane University, University Art Collection, New Orleans LA
Caldwell, Margaret M, *Admin Secy,* Johnson Atelier Technical Institute of Sculpture, Trenton NJ (S)
Caldwell, Melissa, *Chief Cur,* Philadelphia Art Alliance, Philadelphia PA
Caldwell, Michael, *Prof,* Seattle Pacific University, Art Dept, Seattle WA (S)
Caldwell, Peter, *Dir & CEO,* Ontario Crafts Council, Artists in Stained Glass, Toronto ON
Calhoun, Laura, *Exhibs & Colls Mgr,* University of New Hampshire, Museum of Art, Durham NH
Calhoun, Marc, *Catalog/Reference Librn,* Rhode Island School of Design, Fleet Library at RISD, Providence RI
Califano, Cheryl, *Mem & Box Office Mgr,* Sangre de Cristo Arts & Conference Center, Pueblo CO
Calisch, Doug, *Prof,* Wabash College, Art Dept, Crawfordsville IN (S)
Call, J Randolph, *Asst Dir for Tech Servs,* Detroit Public Library, Art & Literature Dept, Detroit MI
Callaghan, Karen, *Dean,* Barry University, Dept of Fine Arts, Miami Shores FL (S)
Callahan, Barbara, *Museum Asst,* Gibson Society, Inc, Gibson House Museum, Boston MA
Callahan, Betty, *Vis Coordr,* Okefenokee Heritage Center, Inc, Waycross GA
Callahan, Colin J, *Dir Art Center,* Saint Paul's School, Art Center in Hargate, Concord NH
Callahan, David, *Chief Librn Circ Coll Mgr,* The New York Public Library, The New York Public Library for the Performing Arts, New York NY
Callahan, Debra, *Educ,* Birmingham Bloomfield Art Center, Art Center, Birmingham MI
Callahan, Diane, *Adjunct Prof,* Southwest Baptist University, Art Dept, Bolivar MO (S)
Callahan, Nancy, *Prof,* State University of New York College at Oneonta, Dept of Art, Oneonta NY (S)
Callahan, Patrick, *Dir,* Purchase College, Library, Purchase NY
Callan, Borislava, *Dir,* Callan Contemporary, New Orleans LA
Callan, Ginny, *Exec Dir,* T W Wood Gallery, Montpelier VT
Callan, Meaghan, *Prof Art,* Joliet Junior College, Laura A Sprague Art Gallery, Joliet IL
Callan, Scott, *Exec Dir,* The History Center in Tompkins County, Ithaca NY
Callan, Steven, *Owner,* Callan Contemporary, New Orleans LA
Callander, Miranda, *Registrar,* University of Oregon, Jordan Schnitzer Museum of Art, Eugene OR
Callans, Jennifer, *Exec Dir,* Anton Art Center, Mount Clemens MI
Callanta, Bryan, *Preparator,* Triton Museum of Art, Santa Clara CA
Callaway, Cathy, *Cur Educ,* University of Missouri, Museum of Art & Archaeology, Columbia MO
Calleja, Dan, *Grants Mgr,* Orlando Museum of Art, Orlando FL
Calleja, Dan, *Grants Mgr,* Orlando Museum of Art, Orlando Sentinel Library, Orlando FL
Callender, Alexis, *Asst Tchg Prof,* University of Missouri - Columbia, Dept of Art, Columbia MO (S)
Callewaert, Megan, *Colls Mgr,* Edsel & Eleanor Ford House, Grosse Pointe Shores MI
Callis, Daniel, *Assoc Prof,* Biola University, Department of Art, La Mirada CA (S)
Calloway, Edwin, *Chmn,* Truett-McConnell College, Fine Arts Dept & Arts Dept, Cleveland GA (S)
Calloway, William, *Exec Dir,* South Carolina State Museum, Columbia SC
Calluori Holcombe, Anna, *Prof,* University of Florida, School of Art & Art History, Gainesville FL (S)
Calo, Mary Ann, *Asst Prof,* Colgate University, Dept of Art & Art History, Hamilton NY (S)
Calsbeek, John, *Assoc Cur,* Missoula Art Museum, Missoula MT
Calvert, Toby, *Pres,* McNay Art Museum, San Antonio TX
Calvin, Christine, *Dir Mktg,* Crocker Art Museum, Sacramento CA
Calvin, James, *Assoc Prof (Sculpture),* University of Missouri - Columbia, Dept of Art, Columbia MO (S)
Calvin, Suzanne, *Admin Asst,* Ursinus College, Philip & Muriel Berman Museum of Art, Collegeville PA
Calvit, Jeanne, *Artistic/Exec Dir,* Interact Center for the Visual & Performing Arts, Interact Gallery, Minneapolis MN
Calza, Susan, *Prof Sculpture,* Johnson State College, Dept Fine & Performing Arts, Dibden Center for the Arts, Johnson VT (S)
Calzada-Charma, Antonio, *Dir Security & Opers,* Delaware Center for the Contemporary Arts, Wilmington DE
Calzonetti, Jo Ann, *Head Librn,* West Virginia University, Evansdale Library, Morgantown WV
Camara, Esperanca, *Asst Prof,* University of Saint Francis, School of Creative Arts, Fort Wayne IN (S)
Cambre, Javier, *Asst Prof,* Queensborough Community College, Dept of Art & Photography, Bayside Hills NY (S)
Cameron, Ainsley, *Cur South Asian Art,* Cincinnati Art Museum, Cincinnati Art Museum, Cincinnati OH
Cameron, Ben, *Instr,* Columbia College, Art Dept, Columbia MO (S)
Cameron, Linda, *Prog Mgr,* Minnesota Historical Society, Minnesota State Capitol Historic Site, Saint Paul MN
Cameron, Robert, *Sr Assoc Dean,* New York University, Tisch School of the Arts, New York NY (S)
Cameron, Sandy, *Acting Dir & Librn,* Regina Public Library, Art Dept, Regina SK
Cammuso, Philomena M, *Exec Dir,* Seneca Falls Historical Society Museum, Seneca Falls NY
Camp, Ann, *Asst Cur Educ,* City of El Paso, El Paso TX
Camp, Carl, *Cur,* Utah Department of Natural Resources, Division of Parks & Recreation, Territorial Statehouse State Park Museum, Fillmore UT
Camp, Roger, *Chmn & Instr,* Golden West College, Visual Art Dept, Huntington Beach CA (S)
Camp, Susan, *Adjunct Asst Prof,* University of Maine, Dept of Art, Orono ME (S)
Campagna, Barbara, *Architect,* National Trust for Historic Preservation, Washington DC
Campbell, Anita, *Dir,* Dartmouth Heritage Museum, Dartmouth NS
Campbell, Anna, *Asst Prof,* Grand Valley State University, Art & Design Dept, Allendale MI (S)
Campbell, Barbara, *Prof,* University of North Carolina at Greensboro, School of Art, Greensboro NC (S)
Campbell, Bonnie, *Dir,* Museum of Fine Arts Houston, Bayou Bend Collection & Gardens, Houston TX
Campbell, C Jean, *Prof,* Emory University, Art History Dept, Atlanta GA (S)
Campbell, Charles, *Instr,* Saint Mary's University of Minnesota, Art & Design Dept, Winona MN (S)
Campbell, Critz, *Asst Prof,* Mississippi State University, Dept of Art, Starville MS (S)
Campbell, Cyndie, *Library, Archives & Research Fels Prog,* National Gallery of Canada, Library, Ottawa ON
Campbell, Deborah, *Instr,* Adrian College, Art & Design Dept, Adrian MI (S)
Campbell, Dennis, *Bldg & Grounds Supv,* Belle Grove Inc, Belle Grove Plantation, Middletown VA
Campbell, Graham, *Chmn,* Brandeis University, Dept of Fine Arts, Waltham MA (S)
Campbell, Heather, *Cur Mus Progs,* University of Richmond, University Museums, Richmond VA
Campbell, Ian, *Asst Prof Art,* Lyon College Kresge Gallery, Batesville AR
Campbell, Janet, *Bus Mgr,* Woodrow Wilson, Woodrow Wilson Presidential Library, Staunton VA
Campbell, Janet, *Business Mgr,* Woodrow Wilson, Staunton VA
Campbell, Jayne, *Instr,* Glendale Community College, Visual & Performing Arts Div, Glendale CA (S)
Campbell, Jessica, *Educ Coordr,* Southern Alleghenies Museum of Art, Loretto Facility, Loretto PA
Campbell, Kamilah, *Adjunct Prof,* Brazosport College, Communications & Fine Art, Lake Jackson TX (S)
Campbell, Katharine, *Exec Dir,* The Sandwich Historical Society, Inc & Sandwich Glass Museum, Sandwich Glass Museum, Sandwich MA
Campbell, Kay, *Assoc Prof,* Oregon State University, Dept of Art, Corvallis OR (S)
Campbell, L Kathleen, *Asst Prof,* Appalachian State University, Dept of Art, Boone NC (S)
Campbell, Laurel, *Asst Prof,* Indiana-Purdue University, Dept of Fine Arts, Fort Wayne IN (S)
Campbell, Lecy, *Mus Shop Mgr,* University of Tennessee, McClung Museum of Natural History & Culture, Knoxville TN
Campbell, Mary, *Prof,* New Jersey City University, Art Dept, Jersey City NJ (S)
Campbell, Michael, *Asst Prof,* Shippensburg University, Art Dept, Shippensburg PA (S)
Campbell, Mona, *Admin Mgr,* The Arts Council of Winston-Salem & Forsyth County, Winston-Salem NC
Campbell, Nancy, *Dir,* Wayne Art Center, Wayne PA
Campbell, Sally, *Asst Prof,* University of Texas at Tyler, Department of Art, School of Visual & Performing Arts, Tyler TX (S)
Campbell, Sarah, *Dir,* Portland Public Library, Art - Audiovisual Dept, Portland ME
Campbell, Shearon, *Dir,* Montgomery Museum & Lewis Miller Regional Art Center, Christianburg VA
Campbell, Stephen, *Chmn,* Spring Hill College, Department of Fine & Performing Arts, Mobile AL (S)
Campbell, Stephen, *Chmn,* Johns Hopkins University, Dept of the History of Art, Baltimore MD (S)
Campbell, Susan, *Adjunct Faculty,* University of Maryland, Baltimore County, Intermedia & Digital Arts (IMDA), Dept of Visual Arts, Baltimore MD (S)
Campbell, Tony, *Vis Artist,* University of New Orleans-Lake Front, Dept of Fine Arts, New Orleans LA (S)
Campbell-Miller, Megan, *Production Coordr,* Cornish College of the Arts, Fisher Gallery, Seattle WA
Campbell-Shoaf, Heidi, *Dir & Chief Cur,* DAR Museum, National Society Daughters of the American Revolution, Washington DC
Campbell-Shoaf, Heidi, *Dir & Chief Cur,* DAR Museum, Library, Washington DC
Campognone, Andi, *Assoc Dir,* Riverside Art Museum, Riverside CA
Campos, Alexander, *Exec Dir & Cur,* Center for Book Arts, New York NY
Campos, Alexander, *Sec,* Morris-Jumel Mansion, Inc, New York NY
Campos, Martin, *Instr,* Wayne Art Center, Wayne PA (S)
Canaves, Marie, *Prof,* Cape Cod Community College, Art Dept, West Barnstable MA (S)
Canby, Sheila, *Cur in Charge, Islamic Art,* The Metropolitan Museum of Art, New York NY

Canepa, Sofia, *Chief Librn,* Museo de Arte de Ponce, Library, Ponce PR
Canepa, Sofia, *Librn,* Museo de Arte de Ponce, The Luis A Ferre Foundation Inc, Ponce PR
Canes, Mary Pat, *Recording Secy,* National League of American Pen Women, Washington DC
Canfield, Megan, *Educ Coordr,* Liberty Hall Historic Site, Library, Frankfort KY
Canfield, Michael, *Pres & CEO,* Indian Pueblo Cultural Center, Albuquerque NM
Cangelosi, Keith, *Chmn Memorial Hall Comt,* Confederate Memorial Hall, Confederate Museum, New Orleans LA
Caniff, Al, *Chmn,* Western State College of Colorado, Quigley Hall Art Gallery, Gunnison CO
Cann, Tyler, *Cur Contemp Art,* Columbus Museum of Art, Columbus OH
Canna, Jacqueline, *Pres,* Rhode Island Watercolor Society, Pawtucket RI
Cannady, Shelly, *CFO,* Telfair Museums, Telfair Academy of Arts & Sciences Library, Savannah GA
Cannestra, Amy, *Secy,* Kappa Pi International Honorary Art Fraternity, Cleveland MS
Canniffe, Bernard, *Chair Design Dept,* Minneapolis College of Art & Design, Minneapolis MN (S)
Canning, Jonathan, *Director of Cur Affairs & Programming,* The Hyde Collection, Glens Falls NY
Canning, Scott, *Dir Horticulture,* Wave Hill, Bronx NY
Canning, Stephanie, *Exhib & Educ Coordr,* Saskatchewan Craft Council & Affinity Gallery, Saskatoon SK
Canning, Susan, *Prof,* The College of New Rochelle, School of Arts & Sciences Art Dept, New Rochelle NY (S)
Cannizzo, Anna, *Cur Colls,* Denison University, Art Gallery, Granville OH
Cannon, Caley, *Librn,* Glendale Public Library, Brand Library & Art Center, Glendale CA
Cannon, Caley, *Ref Librn,* Savannah College of Art & Design - Atlanta, ACA Library of Atlanta, Atlanta GA
Cannuli, Richard, *Chmn,* Villanova University, Dept of Theater, Villanova PA (S)
Cannuli, Richard, *Dir,* Villanova University Art Gallery, The Art Gallery, Villanova PA
Canright, Steve, *Cur Maritime History,* San Francisco Maritime National Historical Park, Maritime Museum, San Francisco CA
Cansler, Sue, *Pres,* Glynn Visual Arts, Inc, Saint Simons Island GA
Canson, Eric, *Opers,* Henry Gallery Association, Henry Art Gallery, Seattle WA
Cantella, Michael, *Multimedia & Web Design,* Art Institute of Pittsburgh, Pittsburgh PA (S)
Canter, Nancy, *Dean Creative Arts,* De Anza College, Creative Arts Division, Cupertino CA (S)
Canter, Stacy, *Bus Mgr,* The National Quilt Museum, Paducah KY
Cantley, John, *Dir,* County of Los Angeles, Century Gallery, Sylmar CA
Cantley, Lee Musgrave, *Dir,* County of Los Angeles, Century Gallery, Sylmar CA
Cantone, Amy, *Archivist/Cur,* National Churchill Museum, Fulton MO
Cantor, Mira, *Assoc Prof,* Northeastern University, Dept of Art & Architecture, Boston MA (S)
Cantor, Sarah, *Kress Interpretive Fellow,* Fairfield University, Art Museum, Fairfield CT
Cantrell, Jimmy, *Instr,* John C Calhoun, Department of Fine Arts, Tanner AL (S)
Cantu, Anthony, *Dean,* Fresno City College, Art Dept, Fresno CA (S)
Cantwell, Kyley, *Cur Coll,* Museum of East Texas, Lufkin TX
Cantwell, Louise, *Pres,* San Antonio Art League, Library, San Antonio TX
Canty-Jones, Eliza, *Ed,* Oregon Historical Society, Oregon History Museum, Portland OR
Canuel, Robin, *Head Librn,* McGill University, Blackader-Lauterman Library of Architecture and Art, Montreal QC
Canwell, Jeremy, *Registrar,* University of Montana, Montana Museum of Art & Culture, Missoula MT
Cao, Jordan, *Asst Registrar,* North Carolina State University, Gregg Museum of Art & Design, Raleigh NC
Cao, Nancy, *Donor Rels Mgr,* Museum of African American History, Boston MA
Capaldi, Patricia, *Asst Prof,* Ithaca College, Fine Art Dept, Ithaca NY (S)
Capasso, Nick, *Dir,* Fitchburg Art Museum, Fitchburg MA
Caperton y Montoya, Will, *Dir Mktg & Devel,* City of Los Angeles, Cultural Affairs Dept, Los Angeles CA
Caperton, John, *Cur,* The Print Center, Philadelphia PA
Caplan, Alison, *Dir Educ,* Akron Art Museum, Akron OH
Caplan, Cindy, *Chief Counsel & Talent Officer,* The Jewish Museum, New York NY
Caplan, Margi, *Mem & Mktg Dir,* Smith College, Museum of Art, Northampton MA
Capobianco, John, *Dir Opers,* Society of Illustrators, Museum of American Illustration, New York NY
Capone, Truman, *Prof,* Virginia Polytechnic Institute & State University, Dept of Art & Art History, Blacksburg VA (S)
Caporale, Wende, *Corresp Secy,* Pastel Society of America, National Arts Club, Grand Gallery, New York NY
Capote, Melody, *Deputy Dir,* Caribbean Cultural Center African Diaspora Institute, Cultural Arts Organization & Resource Center, New York NY
Cappelli, Stephen, *Chmn,* Alabama State University, Dept of Visual Arts, Montgomery AL (S)
Capper, Karen, *Trustee,* Merrick Art Gallery, New Brighton PA
Capps, John, *Interim Chmn Div Human,* Virginia Western Community College, Communication Design, Fine Art & Photography, Roanoke VA (S)
Capps, Terry, *Cur,* Pearl Fincher Museum of Fine Arts, Spring TX
Cappuccio, Guy, *Brd Treas,* Mohawk Valley Heritage Association, Inc, Walter Elwood Museum, Amsterdam NY
Cappuccio, Thomas, *Prof,* Northern Michigan University, Dept of Art & Design, Marquette MI (S)
Capshaw, William, *Pres,* Oak Ridge Art Center, Oak Ridge TN
Capuano, James, *Supvr,* Newark Public Library, Reference, Newark NJ
Caputo, Robert, *Instr,* Kirkwood Community College, Dept of Arts & Humanities, Cedar Rapids IA (S)
Caputo, Victor, *Coordr Progs & Pub Rels,* Bryant Library, Roslyn NY
Caracciolo, Jessie, *Office Assistant,* Kirkland Art Center, Clinton NY
Caratzola, Kristy L, *Colls Mgr,* Hofstra University, Hofstra University Museum, Hempstead NY
Carbone, David, *Assoc Prof,* State University of New York at Albany, Art Dept, Albany NY (S)
Carbone, Kathy, *Performing Arts Librn,* California Institute of the Arts Library, Santa Clarita CA
Carbonell, Marilyn, *Head Lib Svcs,* The Nelson-Atkins Museum of Art, Spencer Art Reference Library, Kansas City MO
Cardell, Victor, *Music Librn,* San Diego Public Library, Art, Music & Recreation, San Diego CA
Cardenas, Carolyn, *Head Dept,* Missouri State University, Dept of Art & Design, Springfield MO (S)
Cardinale, Carrie, *Exec Dir,* Sam Bass Gallery, Concord NC
Cardoni, Edmund, *Dir,* Hallwalls Contemporary Arts Center, Buffalo NY
Cardonsky, Darby, *MFA Coordr,* Western Connecticut State University, School of Visual & Performing Arts, Danbury CT (S)
Cardot, Gary, *Asst Prof,* Mercyhurst University, Dept of Art, Erie PA (S)
Cardozo, Irene, *Mem Mgr,* Orlando Museum of Art, Orlando Sentinel Library, Orlando FL
Cardozo, Irene, *Mem Mgr,* Orlando Museum of Art, Orlando FL
Carey, Ellen, *Assoc Prof,* University of Hartford, Hartford Art School, West Hartford CT (S)
Carey, Frank, *Asst Head Librn,* Daemen College, Marian Library, Amherst NY
Carey, Ian, *Project Coordr,* McLean County Art Association, McLean County Arts Center, Bloomington IL
Carey, Katherine, *Head Educ,* McNay Art Museum, San Antonio TX
Carey, Linda, *Accounting Mgr,* Lannan Foundation, Santa Fe NM
Cargill, Jim, *Chmn,* Black Hills State University, Art Dept, Spearfish SD (S)
Cargill, Kelly, *Event Sales Manager,* The Columbus Museum, Columbus GA
Cariens, Benjamin, *Assoc Prof,* University of New Hampshire, Dept of Art & Art History, Durham NH (S)
Cariglia, Andrew, *Head Bldgs & Grounds,* American Antiquarian Society, Worcester MA
Cariolano, Jody, *Assoc Prof,* Our Lady of the Lake University, Dept of Art, San Antonio TX (S)
Carl, Jeffery, *Chmn Dept Art & Design & Gallery Dir,* Judson University, School of Art, Design & Architecture, Elgin IL (S)
Carlano, Annie, *Dir,* The Mint Museum, Mint Museum of Craft & Design, Charlotte NC
Carlano, Annie, *Dir Craft Design,* The Mint Museum, Art Organization & Library, Charlotte NC
Carlano, Annie, *Dir Craft, Design & Fashion,* The Mint Museum, Charlotte NC
Carle, Richard, *Pres,* Toledo Artists' Club, Toledo Artists' Club & Gallery, Toledo OH
Carley, Brian, *Preparator,* Longwood Center for the Visual Arts, Farmville VA
Carley, Michal Ann, *Instr,* Cardinal Stritch University, Art Dept, Milwaukee WI (S)
Carlin Fogarty, Karen, *Instr,* Wayne Art Center, Wayne PA (S)
Carlisle, Roger, *Assoc Prof,* Arkansas State University, Dept of Art, State University AR (S)
Carlisle, Terry, *Pres,* Hancock County Trustees of Public Reservations, Woodlawn: Museum, Gardens & Park, Ellsworth ME
Carlos, Gary, *Instr,* San Joaquin Delta College, Arts & Communication, Stockton CA (S)
Carlson, Arnold, *Prof Sculpture,* Northwestern College, Te Paske Gallery, Orange City IA
Carlson, Brian, *Assoc Dean,* Milwaukee Area Technical College, School of Media & Creative Arts, Milwaukee WI (S)
Carlson, Eleanor, *Chmn Music Dept,* University of Massachusetts Dartmouth, College of Visual & Performing Arts, North Dartmouth MA (S)
Carlson, Elizabeth, *Chair & Assoc Prof,* Lawrence University, Dept of Art & Art History, Appleton WI (S)
Carlson, Eric, *Asst Prof,* University of Saint Francis, School of Creative Arts, Fort Wayne IN (S)
Carlson, Ginger, *Exec Dir,* Truck Contemporary Art in Calgary, Calgary AB
Carlson, Helen, *Pres,* Legacy Ltd, Bellevue WA
Carlson, J David, *Prof,* Azusa Pacific University, College of Music & the Arts, Dept of Art & Design, Azusa CA (S)
Carlson, Kristi, *Chair,* Waldorf College, Art Dept, Forest City IA (S)
Carlson, M Teresa, *Acting Dir,* University of Saskatchewan, Diefenbaker Canada Centre, Saskatoon SK
Carlson, Warner, *Secy,* Phelps County Historical Society, Nebraska Prairie Museum, Holdrege NE
Carlson, Wayne E, *Chmn,* Ohio State University, Dept of Industrial Interior & Visual Communication Design, Columbus OH (S)
Carlson, William D., *Prof,* University of Miami, Dept of Art & Art History, Coral Gables FL (S)
Carlson, William, *Secy,* Wellfleet Historical Society & Museum, Inc, Wellfleet MA

Carman, Marsha, *Instr Art Ed,* Southwestern Oklahoma State University, Art, Communication & Theatre, Weatherford OK (S)

Carmer, Brie, *Exec Dir,* Glenwood Center for the Arts, Glenwood Springs CO

Carmichael, Amber, *Office Mgr,* Willard Arts Center, Carr Gallery, Colonial Theater, Idaho Falls ID

Carmichael, Kris, *Supv,* Page-Walker Arts & History Center, Cary NC

Carnahan, Paul, *Librn,* Vermont Historical Society, Library, Montpelier VT

Carney Smith, Jessie, *Dir,* Fisk University, Library, North Nashville TN

Carney, Hoarce, *Chmn,* Alabama A & M University, Dept of Visual Performing & Communication Arts, Normal AL (S)

Carney, Joseph T, *Sr Dir, Prin & Major Gifts,* University of Rochester, Memorial Art Gallery, Rochester NY

Carney, Liz, *Assistant Curator,* Akron Art Museum, Akron OH

Carns, Janet, *Asst to Dir,* Westmoreland Museum of American Art, Art Reference Library, Greensburg PA

Carnwath, Squeak, *Undergrad faculty adv,* University of California, Berkeley, College of Letters & Sciences-Art Practice Dept, Berkeley CA (S)

Carothers, Mary, *Assoc Prof,* University of Louisville, Allen R Hite Art Institute, Louisville KY (S)

Carpenter Meyers, Laura, *Dir,* Van Cortlandt House Museum, Bronx NY

Carpenter, Barbara, *Mem Coordr,* Spark Gallery, Denver CO

Carpenter, Cathy, *Head Librn,* Georgia Institute of Technology, College of Architecture Library, Atlanta GA

Carpenter, Edie, *Dir Curatorial & Artistic Progs,* Green Hill Center for North Carolina Art, Greenhill, Greensboro NC

Carpenter, Margot, *Exec Dir,* Aesthetic Realism Foundation, New York NY (S)

Carpenter, Margot, *Exec Dir,* Aesthetic Realism Foundation, New York NY

Carpenter, Mari, *Chief Registrar,* Florida State University, John & Mable Ringling Museum of Art, Sarasota FL

Carpenter, Nadine, *Secy,* University of Vermont, Francis Colburn Gallery, Burlington VT

Carpenter, Richard, *Pres,* John C Calhoun, Art Gallery, Decatur AL

Carpenter, Syd, *Prof,* Swarthmore College, Dept of Art & Art History, Swarthmore PA (S)

Carpenter, William, *Assoc Prof,* Indiana Wesleyan University, School of Arts & Humanities, Division of Art, Marion IN (S)

Carpio, Cece, *Gallery Mgr,* San Francisco Arts Commission, Gallery, San Francisco CA

Carr, Carol, *Mgr Library Servs,* Hallmark Cards, Inc, Creative Library, Kemo MO

Carr, Christopher, *Perparator,* Auburn University, Jule Collins Smith Museum of Fine Art, Auburn AL

Carr, Jeffrey, *Prof,* Saint Mary's College of Maryland, Art & Art History Dept, Saint Mary's City MD (S)

Carr, Jeffrey, *Registrar,* Ohio University, Kennedy Museum of Art, Athens OH

Carr, Mary Margaret, *Colls Mgr,* United States General Services Administration, Art in Architecture and Fine Arts, Washington DC

Carr, Michael, *Assoc Mus Librn,* The Metropolitan Museum of Art, The Cloisters Library & Archives, New York NY

Carracio, Kathleen, *Lectr,* Coe College, Dept of Art, Cedar Rapids IA (S)

Carrageorge, Adrianne, *Asst Prof,* Rochester Institute of Technology, School of Photographic Arts & Sciences, Rochester NY (S)

Carraro, Francine, *Dir,* National Museum of Wildlife Art of the Unites States, Library, Jackson WY

Carrasco-Zanini, Adrian, *Instr,* Butte College, Dept of Fine Arts and Communication Tech, Oroville CA (S)

Carraway, Charles W, *Assoc Prof,* Jackson State University, Dept of Art, Jackson MS (S)

Carrell, Dan, *Chmn,* Benedictine College, Art Dept, Atchison KS (S)

Carrell, Kayla, *Assoc Dir,* New London County Historical Society, Shaw Mansion, New London CT

Carrico, Anita, *Head,* University of Maryland, College Park, Architecture Library, College Park MD

Carrico, Shane, *Preparator,* University of North Carolina at Greensboro, Weatherspoon Art Museum, Greensboro NC

Carriel, Pedro, *Dep Dir & Head Finance & Admin,* Art Gallery of Alberta, Edmonton AB

Carrier, Jacynthe, *Co-Dir,* VU Centre De Diffusion Et De Production De La Photographie, Quebec QC

Carriere, Paul, *COO,* Atlanta Historical Society Inc, Atlanta History Center, Atlanta GA

Carrigan, Patricia, *Prof Drawing,* Manchester Community College, Visual Fine Art Dept, Manchester CT (S)

Carrillo, Alex, *Instr,* Pierce College, Art Dept, Woodland Hills CA (S)

Carrillo, Maria, *Assoc Archivist,* Lincoln Memorial Shrine, Redlands CA

Carrillo, Mariah, *Colls Asst,* University of New Mexico, University of New Mexico Art Museum, Albuquerque NM

Carrion, Gwendolyn, *Tour Coord,* Glessner House Museum, Chicago IL

Carrlee, Ellen, *Conservator,* Alaska State Museum, Juneau AK

Carrlee, Scott, *Cur Mus Svcs,* Alaska State Museum, Juneau AK

Carrol, Eric, *Instr,* Macalester College, Art & Art History Dept, Saint Paul MN (S)

Carroll, David, *Dir Coll & Exhibs,* University of Utah, Utah Museum of Fine Arts, Salt Lake City UT

Carroll, Holly, *Interim Dir,* Cleveland Public Library, Fine Arts & Special Collections Dept, Cleveland OH

Carroll, James F L, *Dir,* New Arts Program, Inc, NAP Museum, NAP Main Gallery, William Zimmer Reference Library, Kutztown PA

Carroll, Jaret, *Accountant,* Montgomery Museum of Fine Arts, Library, Montgomery AL

Carroll, Jennifer, *Educ Dir,* Historical Society of Cheshire County, Keene NH

Carroll, Joanne, *Admin Asst,* New Arts Program, Inc, NAP Museum, NAP Main Gallery, William Zimmer Reference Library, Kutztown PA

Carroll, John, *Adjunct Prof Fine Art,* Johnson County Community College, Fine Arts Dept & Art History Dept, Overland Park KS (S)

Carroll, Margaret, *Prof,* Wellesley College, Art Dept, Wellesley MA (S)

Carroll, Maureen, *Dir Admissions,* Cornell University, College of Architecture, Art, and Planning, Ithaca NY (S)

Carroll, Mike, *Owner & Dir,* The Schoolhouse Gallery, Provincetown MA

Carroll, Richard, *Mgr Mus Experience,* The Metropolitan Museum of Art, The Met Breuer, New York NY

Carros, Briony, *Exec Dir,* Visual Arts Nova Scotia, Halifax NS

Carroway, Rosemary, *Lectr,* Lambuth University, Dept of Human Ecology & Visual Arts, Jackson TN (S)

Carry, Melissa, *Marketing Asst,* Fort Smith Regional Art Museum, Fort Smith AR

Carscallen, Janie, *Colls Mgr,* York County Heritage Trust, York PA

Carson Pastan, Elizabeth, *Assoc Prof,* Emory University, Art History Dept, Atlanta GA (S)

Carson, David, *Pub Affairs Dir,* Henry Morrison Flagler Museum, Palm Beach FL

Carson, Denise, *Dir,* Bethany College, Wallerstedt Library, Lindsborg KS

Carson, Jade, *Grants Specialist,* Idaho Commission on the Arts, Boise ID

Carson, JoAnne, *Dept Chair & Prof,* State University of New York at Albany, Art Dept, Albany NY (S)

Carson, Juli, *Assoc Prof Art History & Cur Studies,* University of California, Irvine, Studio Art Dept, Irvine CA (S)

Carsten, Robert, *Instr,* Woodstock School of Art, Inc, Woodstock NY (S)

Cart, Doran L, *Cur,* Liberty Memorial Museum & Archives, The National Museum of World War I, Kansas City MO

Cartagena, Jose, *Exhib Designer,* United States Military Academy, West Point Museum, West Point NY

Carte, Suzanne, *Asst Cur,* York University, Art Gallery of York University, Toronto ON

Carter Martine, Margaret, *Instr,* Appalachian State University, Dept of Art, Boone NC (S)

Carter Southard, Edna, *Cur Coll,* Miami University, Art Museum, Oxford OH

Carter, Alice, *Pres,* Norman Rockwell Museum, Stockbridge MA

Carter, Beth, *Cur,* Bill Reid Gallery of Northwest Coast Art, Vancouver BC

Carter, Brian, *Pres,* Association of African American Museums, Washington DC

Carter, Carol Ann, *Prof,* University of Kansas, The School of the Arts, Dept of Visual Art, Lawrence KS (S)

Carter, Charles Hill, *Owner,* Shirley Plantation Foundation, Charles City VA

Carter, Claire, *Asst Cur,* Scottsdale Cultural Council, Scottsdale Museum of Contemporary Art, Scottsdale AZ

Carter, Frances, *Secy,* Philadelphia Sketch Club, Philadelphia PA

Carter, Joseph, *Dir,* Will Rogers Memorial Museum & Birthplace Ranch, Media Center Library, Claremore OK

Carter, Keith, *Prof,* Lamar University, Art Dept, Beaumont TX (S)

Carter, Lisa R, *Photographic Archivist,* The University of Kentucky Art Museum, Photographic Archives, Lexington KY

Carter, Lynn, *Sr Advisor,* The American-Scandinavian Foundation, Scandinavia House: The Nordic Center in America, New York NY

Carter, Nathan, *Fine Arts Dept Chmn,* Morgan State University, Dept of Art, Baltimore MD (S)

Carter, Patricia, *Prod,* Georgia Southern University, Betty Foy Sanders Dept of Art, Statesboro GA (S)

Carter, Randy, *Deputy Dir,* Shirley Plantation Foundation, Charles City VA

Carter, Susan, *Cur & Registrar,* University of Tampa, Henry B Plant Museum, Tampa FL

Carter, Suzanne, *Gift Shop Coordr,* Lewistown Art Center, Lewistown MT

Carter, Tara Y, *Dean, Arts, Communs & Social Sciences,* Kishwaukee College, Art Dept, Malta IL (S)

Carter, Val, *Sr Instr,* University of Idaho College of Art & Architecture, Dept of Art & Design, Moscow ID (S)

Carthel, Cindy, *Instr,* Wayland Baptist University, Dept of Art, School of Fine Art, Plainview TX (S)

Carton, Anthony, *Asst Prof,* South Dakota State University, Dept of Visual Arts, Brookings SD (S)

Carton, Deborah, *Librn,* Berkeley Public Library, Art & Music Department, Berkeley CA

Cartwright, Derrick, *Gallery Dir,* University of San Diego, Founders' Gallery, San Diego CA

Cartwright, Guenther, *Assoc Prof,* Rochester Institute of Technology, School of Photographic Arts & Sciences, Rochester NY (S)

Cartwright, Rick, *Dean,* University of Saint Francis, School of Creative Arts, Fort Wayne IN (S)

Cartwright, Rick, *Dean,* University of Saint Francis, School of Creative Arts, John P Weatherhead Gallery & Lupke Gallery, Fort Wayne IN

Cartwright, Roy, *Prof Fine Arts,* University of Cincinnati, School of Art, Cincinnati OH (S)

Carusi, Laura, *Curatorial & Coll Coordr,* Art Gallery of Mississauga, Mississauga ON

Caruso, Dominic, *Design, Marketing & Communications Coordinator,* Akron Art Museum, Akron OH

Caruthers, Rochelle, *Univ Acad Prog Coordr,* Washington University, Mildred Lane Kemper Art Museum, Saint Louis MO

Carvajal, Rina, *Exec Dir & Chief Cur,* Miami-Dade College, Kendal Campus, Art Gallery, Miami FL

Carvajal, Rina, *Executive Director and Chief Curator,* Miami-Dade College, MDC Museum of Art & Design, Miami FL

Carvalho, Cheryl, *Admin Asst,* Newport Historical Society & Museum of Newport History, Newport RI

Carvalho, Joseph, *Exec Dir & Pres,* Springfield Museums, George Walker Vincent Smith Art Museum, Springfield MA

Carvalho, Joseph, *Pres & Exec Dir,* Springfield Museums, Connecticut Valley Historical Society,

Carver, Dan, *Mus Educ,* Springfield Art Museum, Springfield MO

Carver, Melvin, *Prof,* North Carolina Central University, Art Dept, Durham NC (S)

Cary, Susan, *Registrar,* Archives of American Art, Smithsonian Institution, Washington DC

Caryn, Laurel, *Asst Prof Lectr,* University of Utah, Dept of Art & Art History, Salt Lake City UT (S)

Casaletto, Kristin, *Assoc Prof,* Augusta State University, Dept of Art, Augusta GA (S)

Casbarro, Shawn, *Instr,* Taylor University, Visual Art Dept, Upland IN (S)

Casebeer, Doug, *Assoc Dir & Artistic Dir Ceramics,* Anderson Ranch Arts Center, Snowmass Village CO

Casebier, Lindy, *Executive Director,* Louisville Visual Art, Louisville KY

Casely-Hayford, Gus, *Dir,* National Museum of African Art, Smithsonian Institution, Washington DC

Casey, Candace, *Gallery Store,* Worcester Center for Crafts, Worcester MA (S)

Casey, John, *Chair Animation,* Lesley University, College of Art & Design, Cambridge MA (S)

Casey, Jonathan, *Archivist,* Liberty Memorial Museum & Archives, The National Museum of World War I, Kansas City MO

Casey, Michael, *Chmn Fashion Design,* Fashion Institute of Technology, School of Art & Design, New York NY (S)

Casey, Sean, *Reference Librn,* Boston Public Library, Rare Book & Manuscripts Dept, Boston MA

Cash, G Gerald, *Chmn Fine Arts Div,* Florida Keys Community College, Fine Arts Div, Key West FL (S)

Cash, Sarah, *Bechhoefer Cur American Art,* Corcoran Gallery of Art, Washington DC

Cash, Susan, *Assoc Prof & Chair, Dept of Dance,* York University, School of the Arts, Media, Performance & Design, Toronto ON (S)

Cashman, Carol, *Instr,* Bismarck State College, Fine Arts Dept, Bismarck ND (S)

Casid, Jill H, *Asst Prof,* University of Wisconsin, Madison, Dept of Art History, Madison WI (S)

Casillas, Marlene Hernandez, *Exhib Designer,* Museo de las Americas, Viejo San Juan PR

Caslin, Jean, *Exec Dir,* Louise Hopkins Underwood Center for the Arts, Lubbock TX

Casolary, Terri, *Admin Asst,* Shasta College, Arts, Communications & Social Sciences Division, Redding CA (S)

Cason, Christine, *Visual Fine Arts Coordr,* Hill College, Fine Arts Dept, Hillsboro TX (S)

Casper, Joseph, *CEO,* Caspers, Inc, Art Collection, Tampa FL

Cass, Doug, *Archivist,* Glenbow Museum, Library, Calgary AB

Cass, William, *Lectr,* Northwestern University, Evanston, Dept of Art Theory & Practice, Evanston IL (S)

Cassara, Tina, *Dept Head Sculpture & Expanded Media,* Cleveland Institute of Art, Cleveland OH (S)

Cassaro, James P, *Head Librn,* University of Pittsburgh, Henry Clay Frick Fine Arts Library, Pittsburgh PA

Casselman, Carol Ann, *Portfolio of Makers Mgr,* Ontario Crafts Council, Craft Resource Centre, Toronto ON

Cassidy, Christopher, *Director,* University of North Carolina at Greensboro, School of Art, Greensboro NC (S)

Cassidy, Donna, *Prof Art Hist,* University of Southern Maine, Dept of Art, Gorham ME (S)

Cassidy, Emerald, *Dir Mktg & Pub Rels,* Grace Museum, Inc, The Grace Museum, Abilene TX

Cassidy, Laurie, *Admin Asst,* Lynchburg College, Daura Gallery, Lynchburg VA

Cassidy, Stephanie, *Archivist,* Art Students League of New York, New York NY

Cassie, Angela, *VPres Pub Affairs & Progs,* Canadian Museum for Human Rights, Winnipeg MB

Cassin, Michael, *Cur Educ,* Clark Art Institute, Williamstown MA

Cassone, John, *Assoc Prof,* Los Angeles Harbor College, Art Dept, Wilmington CA (S)

Casstevens, Margot, *Adjunct Asst Prof,* Spokane Falls Community College, Fine Arts Dept, Spokane WA (S)

Castagna, Peg, *Bookkeeper,* Ocean City Arts Center, Ocean City NJ (S)

Castaldi, Mary Louise, *Reference Librn,* The University of the Arts, University Libraries, Philadelphia PA

Castaldo, Nicole, *Appraisal Dept Coord,* Art Dealers Association of America, Inc, New York NY

Castaneda, Emily, *Office Mgr,* Baker Arts Center, Liberal KS

Castellani, Carla, *Asst Mus Shop Mgr,* Niagara University, Castellani Art Museum, Niagara NY

Castellani, Margaret, *Cataloging Librarian,* The Cleveland Museum of Art, Ingalls Library, Cleveland OH

Castellucci, Dale, *Adj Instr,* University of West Florida, Dept of Art, Pensacola FL (S)

Castelnuovo, Sheri, *Cur Educ,* Madison Museum of Contemporary Art, Madison WI

Castets, Simon, *Dir,* Swiss Institute, New York NY

Castillo, Christie, *Mem Svcs Mgr & Database Opers Mgr,* National Art Education Association, Alexandria VA

Castle, Charles, *Deputy Dir,* Museum of Contemporary Art, San Diego, Geisel Library, La Jolla CA

Castle, Charles, *Deputy Dir & CFO,* Museum of Contemporary Art San Diego, La Jolla CA

Castle, Charles, *Deputy Dir & CFO,* Museum of Contemporary Art San Diego, San Diego CA

Castle, Lynn, *Exec Dir,* Art Museum of Southeast Texas, Beaumont TX

Castle, Wendell, *Prof,* Rochester Institute of Technology, School of Design, Rochester NY (S)

Casto, S Michele, *Librn,* Public Library of the District of Columbia, Art Division, Washington DC

Casto, Shelly, *Dir Educ,* Ohio State University, Wexner Center for the Arts, Columbus OH

Castonguay, Renee, *Student & Events Coordr,* Toronto School of Art, Toronto ON (S)

Castorano, Kerry, *Dir Develop,* Fruitlands Museum, Inc, Harvard MA

Castricone, Al, *Dir Facilities & IT,* Municipal Art Society of New York, New York NY

Castriota, David, *Faculty,* Sarah Lawrence College, Dept of Art History, Bronxville NY (S)

Castro, Andrew, *Dir,* Mount Mercy University, White Gallery, Cedar Rapids IA

Castro, Milagros, *Dir,* Institute of Puerto Rican Culture, Parque Ceremonial Indigena de Caguana, Utuado PR

Castro, Susannah, *Co-Dir,* Tubac Center of the Arts, Santa Cruz Valley Art Association, Tubac AZ

Caswell, Ben, *Preparator & Bldg Mgr,* Woodstock Artists Association & Museum, Woodstock NY

Caswell, Bexx, *Pres,* Guild of Book Workers, New York NY

Caswell, Tasha, *Research & Colls Assoc,* Connecticut Historical Society, Library, Hartford CT

Cataldo, Samantha, *Asst Cur,* The Currier Museum of Art, Manchester NH

Catalfo, Jayne, *Bookkeeper,* Jacques Marchais Museum of Tibetan Art, Staten Island NY

Catchi, Benice, *Exec VPres,* New York Society of Women Artists, Inc, Westport CT

Cate, Barbara, *Prof,* Seton Hall University, College of Arts & Sciences, South Orange NJ (S)

Cateforts, David, *Assoc Prof,* University of Kansas, Kress Foundation Dept of Art History, Lawrence KS (S)

Catherall, Virginia, *Cur Educ, Family Progs, Visitor Experience & Community Outreach,* University of Utah, Utah Museum of Fine Arts, Salt Lake City UT

Cathey, Ellen, *Assoc Dir,* National Architectural Accrediting Board, Inc, Washington DC

Cathey, Jerry, *Dir,* Ponca City Art Association, Ponca City OK

Catizone, Richard, *Media Arts & Animation,* Art Institute of Pittsburgh, Pittsburgh PA (S)

Catlin, Jane, *Asst Prof,* Utah State University, Dept of Art, Logan UT (S)

Catling, William, *Dept Chair, Prof,* Azusa Pacific University, College of Music & the Arts, Dept of Art & Design, Azusa CA (S)

Cato, Tom, *Chmn,* Armstrong Atlantic State University, Department of Art, Music & Theatre, Savannah GA (S)

Caton, Mary Anne, *Dir,* Mount Vernon Hotel Museum & Garden, New York NY

Catron, Joanna D, *Cur,* University of Mary Washington, Gari Melchers Home and Studio, Fredericksburg VA

Cattan, Dani, *Prog Dir,* En Foco, Inc, Bronx NY

Catterall, Kate, *Asst Chair - Design,* University of Texas, Dept of Art & Art History, Austin TX (S)

Caulfield, Sean, *Assoc Chair Undergrad Studies & Coordr Printmaking,* University of Alberta, Dept of Art & Design, Edmonton AB (S)

Caulk, Meg, *Assoc Dir,* National Air and Space Museum, Smithsonian Institution, Washington DC

Caulkins, Beth, *Co-Owner & Creative Dir,* Frank Lloyd Wright Museum, AD German Warehouse, Richland Center WI

Causey, Adera, *Cur Educ,* Hunter Museum of American Art, Chattanooga TN

Causey, Adera, *Cur Educ,* Hunter Museum of American Art, Reference Library, Chattanooga TN

Cauthen, Gene, *Chmn Dept Art,* Mount Wachusett Community College, East Wing Gallery, Gardner MA

Cavallaro, David, *Assoc Chair,* State University of New York at New Paltz, Art Education Program, New Paltz NY (S)

Cavallaro, Marie, *Assoc Prof,* Salisbury State University, Art Dept, Salisbury MD (S)

Cavallo, Steven, *Children's Librn,* Palisades Park Public Library, Palisades Park NJ

Cavanagh, Lynn, *Asst Prof & Head, Music Dept,* University of Regina, Faculty of Media, Art & Performance, Regina SK (S)

Cavanaugh, Alden, *Chmn,* Indiana State University, Dept of Art, Terre Haute IN (S)

Cavanaugh, Marianne L, *Head Librn,* Saint Louis Art Museum, Richardson Memorial Library, Saint Louis MO

Cavanaugh, Megan, *Dir Exhibs Mgmt,* Ohio State University, Wexner Center for the Arts, Columbus OH

Cave, Mark, *Manuscripts,* The Historic New Orleans Collection, Williams Research Center, New Orleans LA

Cavendish, Kim L, *Pres,* Museum of Discovery & Science, Fort Lauderdale FL

Cavicchi, Daniel, *Provost,* Rhode Island School of Design, Providence RI (S)

Cawley, David, *Dir, Rapid Prototyping & Model Shops,* ArtCenter College of Design, Pasadena CA (S)

Cawthorne, Bonnie, *Library Technical Asst,* University of Maryland, College Park, Art Library, College Park MD

Cazabon, Lynn, *Assoc Prof,* University of Maryland, Baltimore County, Intermedia & Digital Arts (IMDA), Dept of Visual Arts, Baltimore MD (S)

Cease, Bleu, *Exec Dir & Cur,* Rochester Contemporary, Art Center, Rochester NY

Cebulash, Glen, *Chair & Prof,* Wright State University, Dept of Art & Art History, Dayton OH (S)
Cecil, Andrew John, *Cur Coll,* Roswell Museum & Art Center, Roswell NM
Cecil, Rocky, *Edu Coordr,* Owensboro Museum of Fine Art, Owensboro KY
Cederna, Ann, *Asst Prof,* Catholic University of America, School of Architecture & Planning, Washington DC (S)
Celentano, Denyce, *Asst Prof,* Louisiana State University, School of Art, Baton Rouge LA (S)
Celestino, Vincent, *Vpres,* Saint Augustine Art Association and Art Gallery, Saint Augustine FL
Cembrola, Robert, *Cur,* Naval War College Museum, Newport RI
Cempellin, Leda, *Assoc Prof,* South Dakota State University, Dept of Visual Arts, Brookings SD (S)
Censky, Ellen, *Sr VPres & Academic Dean,* Milwaukee Public Museum, Milwaukee WI
Cepero, Roxanne, *Instr,* Inter American University of Puerto Rico, Fine Arts Dept -Art Program, San German PR (S)
Cepluch, Henry, *Arts in Common Dir,* Fitton Center for Creative Arts, Hamilton OH (S)
Cepluch, Henry, *Arts in Common Dir,* Fitton Center for Creative Arts, Hamilton OH
Certo, Alberta Patella, *Gen Educ,* Art Institute of Pittsburgh, Pittsburgh PA (S)
Ceruti, Mary, *Exec Dir,* SculptureCenter, Long Island City NY
Ceruti, Mary, *Exec Dir,* SculptureCenter, Gallery, Long Island City NY
Cerutti, Jessi, *Registrar,* Contemporary Art Museum St Louis, Saint Louis MO
Cervantes, James, *Cur Military History,* Heritage Museums & Gardens, Sandwich MA
Cervenka, Barbara, *Assoc Prof,* Siena Heights University, Studio Angelico-Art Dept, Adrian MI (S)
Cervino, Anthony, *Asst Prof,* Dickinson College, Dept of Art & Art History, Carlisle PA (S)
Cestaro, Gina, *Adj Instr,* University of West Florida, Dept of Art, Pensacola FL (S)
Cetlin, Cynthia, *Prof,* Ohio Wesleyan University, Fine Arts Dept, Delaware OH (S)
Cezanne, Danielle, *Prog Dir,* White Bear Center for the Arts, Gallery, White Bear Lake MN
Cha, Jae, *Instr,* Judson University, School of Art, Design & Architecture, Elgin IL (S)
Chace, Stephanie, *Adminr,* Jay I Kislak Foundation, Miami Lakes FL
Chacon, Rafael, *Prof,* University of Montana, School of Art, Missoula MT (S)
Chadwick-Reid, Ann, *Chmn,* Skagit Valley College, Dept of Art, Mount Vernon WA (S)
Chaffee, Cathleen, *Chief Cur,* Albright-Knox Art Gallery, Buffalo NY
Chaffee, Tom, *Prof,* Arkansas State University, Dept of Art, State University AR (S)
Chaffey, Charlotte, *Archivist & Records Mgr,* Royal Ontario Museum, Library & Archives, Toronto ON
Chaffin, Cortney, *Prof,* University of Wisconsin-Stevens Point, Dept of Art & Design, Stevens Point WI (S)
Chagnon, Stéphane, *Exec Dir,* Societe des Musees Quebecois, Montreal QC
Chaichian, Camyar, *Arts Coordr,* Richmond Arts Centre, Richmond BC
Chait, Steven, *Treas,* National Antique & Art Dealers Association of America, Inc, New York NY
Chalif, Lisa, *Cur,* The Heckscher Museum of Art, Huntington NY
Chalmers, Kim, *Dept Head,* Western Kentucky University, Art Dept, Bowling Green KY (S)
Chalmers, Kim, *Dept Head,* Western Kentucky University, University Gallery, Bowling Green KY
Chalmers, Pattie, *Asst Prof,* Southern Illinois University, School of Art & Design, Carbondale IL (S)
Chamberlain, Barbara, *VPres,* Madison County Historical Society, Cottage Lawn, Oneida NY
Chamberlin, Marsha, *CEO & Pres,* Ann Arbor Art Center, Art Center, Ann Arbor MI
Chambers, Barbara, *Treas,* Napoleonic Society of America, Museum & Library, Saint Helena CA
Chambers, Bryon, *Mgr Tours & Adult Learning,* Oklahoma City Museum of Art, Oklahoma City OK
Chambers, Christine D, *Dir Fin & Admin,* The Frick Art & Historical Center, Inc, Frick Art Museum, Pittsburgh PA
Chambers, Hayley, *Sr Cur Colls,* City of Ketchikan Museum Department, Totem Heritage Center, Ketchikan AK
Chambers, Hayley, *Sr Cur Colls,* City of Ketchikan Museum Department, Tongass Historical Museum, Ketchikan AK
Chambers, Jackie, *Dir Develop & Communs,* Craft Alliance Center of Art & Design, Saint Louis MO
Chambers, Julia, *Exec Dir,* Channel Islands Maritime Museum, Oxnard CA
Chambers, Sheila, *Prof,* Salt Lake Community College, Graphic Design Dept, Salt Lake City UT (S)
Chametzky, Peter, *Dir & Prof,* Southern Illinois University, School of Art & Design, Carbondale IL (S)
Chamness, Cay, *Libr Asst,* Maysville, Kentucky Gateway Museum Center, Maysville KY
Champagne, Anne, *Head Technical Svcs,* The Art Institute of Chicago, Ryerson & Burnham Libraries, Chicago IL
Champion, Karin, *Develop Mgr,* Southern Alberta Art Gallery, Library, Lethbridge AB
Chan, Amy, *Dir,* City of Nome Alaska, Carrie M McLain Memorial Museum, Nome AK
Chan, Elise, *Cur Coll,* Jefferson County Historical Society, Watertown NY
Chan, Frances, *Admin Asst,* Queens College, City University of New York, Art Library, Flushing NY
Chan, Gaye, *Dept Chair,* University of Hawaii at Manoa, Dept of Art, Honolulu HI (S)
Chan, Irene, *Assoc Prof,* University of Maryland, Baltimore County, Intermedia & Digital Arts (IMDA), Dept of Visual Arts, Baltimore MD (S)
Chan, Ying Kit, *Prof,* University of Louisville, Allen R Hite Art Institute, Louisville KY (S)
Chance, Delores, *Gallery Dir,* Coe College, Eaton-Buchan Gallery & Marvin Cone Gallery, Cedar Rapids IA
Chancey, Jill, *Cur,* Lauren Rogers, Laurel MS
Chand, Rakashi, *Sr Library Asst,* Massachusetts Historical Society, Library, Boston MA
Chandler, Christine, *Cur Natural Science,* Putnam Museum of History and Natural Science, Davenport IA
Chandler, Karen, *Dir, Arts Management,* College of Charleston, School of the Arts, Charleston SC (S)
Chandler, Roger A, *Assoc Prof,* Northwestern State University of Louisiana, School of Creative & Performing Arts - Dept of Fine & Graphic Arts, Natchitoches LA (S)
Chandler-Mills, Leah, *Instr Theatre,* University of Colorado-Colorado Springs, Visual & Performing Arts Dept (VAPA), Colorado Springs CO (S)
Chaney, Robert, *Dir Cur Affairs,* University of Pennsylvania, Institute of Contemporary Art, Philadelphia PA
Chang Jantz, Leslie, *Cur Educ,* University of Tennessee, McClung Museum of Natural History & Culture, Knoxville TN
Chang, Lauren, *Conservator,* The Art Institute of Chicago, Department of Textiles, Textile Society, Chicago IL
Chang, Li Fen, *Assoc Prof Fashion Design,* University of North Texas, College of Visual Arts & Design, Denton TX (S)
Chang, Patty, *Faculty,* Maryland Institute, Mount Royal School of Art, Baltimore MD (S)
Chanlatte, Luis A, *Archaeologist,* University of Puerto Rico, Museum of Anthropology, History & Art, Rio Piedras PR
Chanzit, Gwen, *Sr Lectr Art History & Dir Mus Studies,* University of Denver, School of Art & Art History, Denver CO (S)
Chapel, Robert, *Exhibit Specialist,* United States Naval Academy, USNA Museum, Annapolis MD
Chapin, Anne, *Chmn Art,* Brevard College, James A Jones Library, Brevard NC
Chapin, Anne, *Coordr Fine Arts,* Brevard College, Department of Art, Brevard NC (S)
Chapin, Chris, *Prof,* Kansas City Art Institute, Kansas City MO (S)
Chapin, Mary Weaver, *Cur Prints & Drawings,* Portland Art Museum, Portland OR
Chaplin, Carol A, *Mktg & Pub Rels,* University of Southern California, USC Pacific Asia Museum, Pasadena CA
Chapman, Amelia, *Educ Cur,* University of Southern California, USC Pacific Asia Museum, Pasadena CA
Chapman, Amy, *Chief of Staff,* American Institute of Graphic Arts, National Design Center, New York NY
Chapman, Betsy, *Exec Dir,* Belton Center for the Arts, Belton SC
Chapman, Christopher, *Media Resources Cur,* Clemson University, Emery A Gunnin Architectural Library, Clemson SC
Chapman, Duane, *Assoc Prof,* Glenville State College, Dept of Fine Arts, Glenville WV (S)
Chapman, Gary, *Prof,* University of Alabama at Birmingham, Dept of Art & Art History, Birmingham AL (S)
Chapman, Jefferson, *Dir,* University of Tennessee, McClung Museum of Natural History & Culture, Knoxville TN
Chapman, Stow, *Assoc Prof,* University of Louisville, Allen R Hite Art Institute, Louisville KY (S)
Chapman, Susan, *Instr,* Truett-McConnell College, Fine Arts Dept & Arts Dept, Cleveland GA (S)
Chapman, Tia, *Deputy Dir Extern Affairs,* Frick Collection, New York NY
Chapman, Tracy, *Library Technician,* University of Oklahoma, Architecture Library, Norman OK
Chappell, Barbara, *Instr,* Mount Mary College, Art & Design Division, Milwaukee WI (S)
Charette, Luc, *Dir,* Galerie d'art de l'Universite de Moncton, Moncton NB
Charette, Nancy, *Admin Asst,* Thomas College, Art Gallery, Waterville ME
Charland, Bill, *Art Educ Area Coordr,* Western Michigan University, Frostic School of Art, Kalamazoo MI (S)
Charlap, Peter, *Chair & Assoc Prof,* Vassar College, Art Dept, Poughkeepsie NY (S)
Charles, Jim, *Visual Art Mgr,* Sharon Lynne Wilson Center for the Arts, Ploch Art Gallery, Brookfield WI
Charles, Laura, *Devel Asst,* The ARTS Council of the Southern Finger Lakes, Corning NY
Charles, Peter, *Prof,* Georgetown University, Dept of Art & Art History, Washington DC (S)
Charles, Susan, *Dir,* Nova Scotia Centre for Craft & Design, Mary E Black Gallery, Halifax NS
Charleville, Leslie, *Events Coordr,* Louisiana Arts & Science Museum, Baton Rouge LA
Charmin, Lee, *Asst Prof,* Portland State University, Dept of Art, Portland OR (S)
Charney, Ed, *Assoc Prof,* Wittenberg University, Art Dept, Springfield OH (S)
Charney, Hallie, *Instr,* Rhodes College, Dept of Art, Memphis TN (S)
Charpenel, Patrick, *Exec Dir,* El Museo del Barrio, New York NY
Chartier, Isabelle, *Cur,* University of Pittsburgh, University Art Gallery, Pittsburgh PA
Chartrand, Rheanne, *Cur Indigenous Art,* McMaster University, McMaster Museum of Art, Hamilton ON
Chase, Alisia, *Asst Prof,* State University of New York College at Brockport, Dept of Art, Brockport NY (S)
Chase, Amy, *Dir Creative Design,* Louisville Visual Art, Louisville KY
Chase, Carol Lee, *Assoc Prof,* St Catherine University, Art & Art History Dept, Saint Paul MN (S)
Chase, Colin, *Prof,* City College of New York, Art Dept, New York NY (S)

Chase, Shara, *Asst Cur,* City of Providence Parks Department, Roger Williams Park Museum of Natural History, Providence RI

Chasen, Andrew, *Pres,* Chasen Galleries of Fine Art, Richmond VA

Chasin, Noah, *Exec Ed,* The Drawing Center, New York NY

Chason, Helen, *Dir,* The Kreeger Museum, Washington DC

Chastain, CM, *Assoc Prof,* North Georgia College & State University, Fine Arts Dept, Dahlonega GA (S)

Chastain, Ellen, *Educ Mgr,* Polk Museum of Art, Lakeland FL

Chastain-Elliott, Catherine, *Prof,* University of Tampa, College of Arts & Letters, Tampa FL (S)

Chatelain, Gary, *Prof,* James Madison University, School of Art & Art History, Harrisonburg VA (S)

Chatham, Walter, *Co-Chair,* National Academy Museum & School, New York NY

Chatman, Aaron, *Asst Mgr of Visitor Svcs,* Northwestern University, Mary & Leigh Block Museum of Art, Evanston IL

Chauda, Jagdish, *Dept Adv,* University of Central Florida, Art Dept, Orlando FL (S)

Chauveaux, Tony, *Dir,* Longue Vue House & Gardens, New Orleans LA

Chauvin, Catherine, *Assoc Prof Drawing & Printmaking,* University of Denver, School of Art & Art History, Denver CO (S)

Chauvin, Tom, *Registrar,* The Art Institute of Dallas, Dallas TX (S)

Chave, Anna, *Prof,* City University of New York, PhD Program in Art History, New York NY (S)

Chaves, Caesar, *Creative Dir,* Heard Museum, Billie Jane Baguley Library and Archives, Phoenix AZ

Chavez, Anja, *Dir,* Colgate University, Picker Art Gallery, Hamilton NY

Chavez, Michael, *Cur,* Foothills Art Center, Inc, Golden CO

Chavez, Nicolasa, *Cur Latino, Hispano ,Spanish Colonial Colls,* New Mexico Department of Cultural Affairs, Museum of International Folk Art, Santa Fe NM

Chavis, Virginia, *Assoc Prof,* University of Mississippi, Department of Art, University MS (S)

Chears, Benita, *Secy,* Alabama A & M University, Dept of Visual Performing & Communication Arts, Normal AL (S)

Cheasley Paterson, Elaine, *Chair, Art History,* Concordia University, Faculty of Fine Arts, Montreal QC (S)

Checefsky, Bruce, *Gallery Dir,* Cleveland Institute of Art, Reinberger Galleries, Cleveland OH

Chedester, Mike, *Board Pres,* Pueblo Museum, Desert Hot Springs CA

Chee, Yeonsoo, *Asst Cur,* University of Southern California, USC Pacific Asia Museum, Pasadena CA

Cheek, Belinda, *Technician,* North Central College, Oesterle Library, Naperville IL

Cheek, Edwin, *Technical Svcs Asst,* Indiana University, Fine Arts Library, Bloomington IN

Cheeney, Andrea, *Develop Coordr,* Historical Society of Cheshire County, Keene NH

Cheetham, Mark, *Assoc Chmn Grad Studies,* University of Toronto, Dept of Fine Art, Toronto ON (S)

Cheevers, James W, *Sr Cur,* United States Naval Academy, USNA Museum, Annapolis MD

Cheli, Ami, *Dean's Asst,* University of Victoria, Faculty of Arts, Victoria BC (S)

Chemello, Claudia, *Conservator,* University of Michigan, Kelsey Museum of Archaeology, Ann Arbor MI

Chemevych, Andrew, *Archivist,* City of Lethbridge, Sir Alexander Galt Museum, Lethbridge AB

Chen Lou, Sandra, *Chief Develop Officer,* University of Southern California, USC Pacific Asia Museum, Pasadena CA

Chen, Abby, *Cur & Artistic Dir,* Chinese Culture Foundation, Center Gallery, San Francisco CA

Chen, Abre, *Prog Dir,* Westchester Community College, Westchester Art Workshop, White Plains NY (S)

Chen, Beatrice, *VPres Progs & Mus Experience,* Museum of Chinese in America, New York NY

Chen, Ching-Jung, *Art/Architecture Visual Resources Librn,* City College of the City University of New York, Morris Raphael Cohen Library, New York NY

Chen, Chiong-Yiao, *Prof,* University of North Alabama, Dept of Art, Florence AL (S)

Chen, George, *Audience Devel Coordr,* Museum of Contemporary Photography, Columbia College Chicago, Chicago IL

Chen, Hsiao-ping, *Asst Prof,* Grand Valley State University, Art & Design Dept, Allendale MI (S)

Chen, Julie, *Dir,* New World Art Center, T F Chen Cultural Center, New York NY

Chen, Lucia, *Pres & Exec Dir,* New World Art Center, T F Chen Cultural Center, New York NY

Chen, Michael, *Instr,* Joe Kubert, Dover NJ (S)

Chen, Millie, *Intermedia,* University at Buffalo, State University of New York, Dept of Visual Studies, Buffalo NY (S)

Chen, Tao, *Asst Prof,* University of Wisconsin-Parkside, Art Dept, Kenosha WI (S)

Chen, Ted, *VPres,* New World Art Center, T F Chen Cultural Center, New York NY

Chen, Yilin, *Admin. Asst.,* New York University, Grey Art Gallery, New York NY

Chenchar Hanus, Paual, *Exec Dir,* Clear Lake Arts Center, Clear Lake IA

Chenery, Helen, *Treas,* Liberty Hall Historic Site, Library, Frankfort KY

Cheng, Yu-San, *Finance Mgr,* Society for Contemporary Craft, Pittsburgh PA

Chepp, Mark, *Dir,* Springfield Museum of Art, Library, Springfield OH

Chepp, Mark, *Exec Dir,* Southern Ohio Museum Corporation, Southern Ohio Museum, Portsmouth OH

Cherin, Margaret, *Cur,* Bard College at Simon's Rock, Hillman-Jackson Gallery, Great Barrington MA

Chermonte, Debra, *Dean Admissions,* Oberlin College, Dept of Art, Oberlin OH (S)

Chernow, Allison, *Dir Develop,* Bronx Museum of the Arts, Bronx NY

Cherry, Kate, *Dir,* Meridian Museum of Art, Meridian MS

Cherry, Matthew, *Sr Assoc Dean Acad Affairs,* Lesley University, College of Art & Design, Cambridge MA (S)

Chesla, Joe, *Prof,* Saint Louis Community College at Meramec, Art Dept, Saint Louis MO (S)

Chesloff, Susan, *Mus Admin,* Bartow-Pell Mansion Museum & Gardens, Bronx NY

Chesney, Lee, *Assoc Chair,* University of Texas, Dept of Art & Art History, Austin TX (S)

Chesser, Ward, *Museum Shop Mgr,* Montgomery Museum of Fine Arts, Montgomery AL

Chester, Stacey, *Mus Mgr,* Riverside County Museum, Edward-Dean Museum & Gardens, Cherry Valley CA

Chesterfield, Lee, *Dir,* University of Florida, Samuel P Harn Museum of Art, Gainesville FL

Chestler, Jeremy T, *Prog Mgr,* Museum of Contemporary Art, North Miami FL

Cheuk, Beth, *Prog Mgr,* Longwood Center for the Visual Arts, Farmville VA

Chevalier, Andrea, *Sr Paintings Conservator,* Intermuseum Conservation Association, Cleveland OH

Chhangur, Emelie, *Asst Dir & Cur,* York University, Art Gallery of York University, Toronto ON

Chi, Ke-Hsin, *Assoc Prof,* Eastern Illinois University, Art Dept, Charleston IL (S)

Chiang, Jennifer, *Dir Finance & Admin,* Jamaica Center for Arts & Learning (JCAL), Jamaica NY

Chiang, Olivia, *Prof Art History,* Manchester Community College, Visual Fine Art Dept, Manchester CT (S)

Chiappe, Luis, *Sr. VPres Research,* Natural History Museum of Los Angeles County, Los Angeles CA

Chiba Smith, Judith, *Registrar Colls Mgr,* Georgia O'Keeffe Museum, Santa Fe NM

Chibnik, Kitty, *Assoc Dir & Head Access Servs,* Columbia University, Avery Architectural & Fine Arts Library, New York NY

Chidester, Paul, *Assoc Prof Art (Core Prog & Drawing/Painting),* Pennsylvania State University, University Park, Penn State School of Visual Arts, University Park PA (S)

Chieffo, Beverly, *Chmn & Assoc Prof Art,* Albertus Magnus College, Visual and Performing Arts, New Haven CT (S)

Chiesa, Wilfredo, *Prof,* University of Massachusetts - Boston, Art Dept, Boston MA (S)

Chigounis, Karen, *Exec Dir,* Perkins Center for the Arts, Moorestown NJ

Chilberg, Hans, *Videography Coordr,* Nossi College of Art, Nashville TN (S)

Child, Kent, *Gallery Adv & Humanities Div Dir,* Gavilan Community College, Art Gallery, Gilroy CA

Childers, Ann, *Southern Illinois Representative,* American Society of Artists, Inc, Palatine IL

Childs, Carl, *Deputy Director,* Colonial Williamsburg Foundation, John D Rockefeller, Jr Library, Williamsburg VA

Childs, John, *Chief Coll Svcs & Library Dir,* Peabody Essex Museum, Salem MA

Childs, Peter, *Concert Coordr & Oper Mgr,* Academy of the New Church, Glencairn Museum, Bryn Athyn PA

Childs, Stephen, *Asst Prof,* Azusa Pacific University, College of Music & the Arts, Dept of Art & Design, Azusa CA (S)

Chiles, Chantilly, *Develop & Engagement Mgr,* Corporate Council for the Arts/Arts Fund, Seattle WA

Chiles, Michelle, *Robinson Research Center Mgr,* Rhode Island Historical Society, Library, Providence RI

Chilla, Benigna, *Instr,* Berkshire Community College, Dept of Fine Arts, Pittsfield MA (S)

Chilton, Meredith, *Chief Cur,* George R Gardiner Museum of Ceramic Art, Toronto ON

Chin, Caroline, *Assoc Dir Finance & Opers,* The American Federation of Arts, New York NY

Chin, Christina, *Art Edu,* Western Michigan University, Frostic School of Art, Kalamazoo MI (S)

Chin, Susan, *Assoc Registrar,* University of California, Los Angeles, Grunwald Center for the Graphic Arts at Hammer Museum, Los Angeles CA

Chinda, Dan-Horia, *Industrial Design Technology,* Art Institute of Pittsburgh, Pittsburgh PA (S)

Chindlund, Jan, *Dean of Lib,* Columbia College Chicago, Library, Chicago IL

Chinn, Cassie, *Deputy Exec Dir,* Wing Luke Asian Museum, Governor Gary Locke Library and Community Heritage Center, Seattle WA

Chinn, Jennie, *Exec Dir,* Kansas State Historical Society, Kansas Museum of History, Topeka KS

Chinov, Stefan, *Assoc Prof,* Wright State University, Dept of Art & Art History, Dayton OH (S)

Chioffi, David, *Div Chair Design Arts,* Memphis College of Art, Memphis TN (S)

Chipley, Sheila M, *Asst Prof,* Concord College, Fine Art Division, Athens WV (S)

Chisholm, Deirdre, *Dir & Cur,* Lynnwood Arts Centre, Simcoe ON

Chism, Sandy, *Assoc Prof,* Tulane University, Sophie H Newcomb Memorial College, New Orleans LA (S)

Chisolm, Sallie, *Museum Store Mgr,* Palm Beach County Parks & Recreation Department, Morikami Museum & Japanese Gardens, Delray Beach FL

Chiu, Melissa, *Dir,* Hirshhorn Museum & Sculpture Garden, Smithsonian Institution, Washington DC

Chmiel, Mary Faith, *Dir,* Free Public Library of Elizabeth, Elizabeth NJ

Chmielewski, Wendy, *Cur Peace Coll,* Swarthmore College, Friends Historical Library of Swarthmore College, Swarthmore PA

Cho, Charlie, *Lectr,* Northwestern University, Evanston, Dept of Art Theory & Practice, Evanston IL (S)
Cho, Kyoung Ae, *Chair,* University of Wisconsin-Milwaukee, Peck School of the Arts, Dept of Art & Design, Milwaukee WI (S)
Cho, Mika, *Dir,* California State University, Los Angeles, Fine Arts Gallery, Los Angeles CA
Choate, Jerry, *Instr,* Northeastern State University, College of Arts & Letters, Tahlequah OK (S)
Choate, Steven B, *Assoc Prof Art,* Harding University, Dept of Art & Design, Searcy AR (S)
Choberka, Matthew, *Chair & Assoc Prof,* Weber State University, Dept of Visual Arts, Ogden UT (S)
Chock, Mike, *Dir Security,* Honolulu Museum of Art, Honolulu HI
Chodkowski, Henry, *Prof Emeritus,* University of Louisville, Allen R Hite Art Institute, Louisville KY (S)
Chodos, Elizabeth, *Dir Regina Gouger Miller Gallery,* Carnegie Mellon University, College of Fine Arts, Pittsburgh PA (S)
Choen, Lewis, *Asst Prof,* College of William & Mary, Dept of Fine Arts, Williamsburg VA (S)
Choi, Bo, *Digital Art,* North Seattle College, North Seattle College Dept of Art, Seattle WA (S)
Choi, Myongsin, *Prof,* North Carolina Central University, Art Dept, Durham NC (S)
Choi, Sohyung, *Designer,* Pence Gallery, Davis CA
Choi, Sylvia, *Col Management Librn,* School of the Art Institute of Chicago, John M Flaxman Library, Chicago IL
Choice, Thomas L, *Pres,* Kishwaukee College, Art Dept, Malta IL (S)
Chojecki, Randolph, *Ref Librn,* Daemen College, Marian Library, Amherst NY
Choma, Julie, *Coll Mgr,* Ursinus College, Philip & Muriel Berman Museum of Art, Collegeville PA
Chong Kim, Hyun, *Assoc Prof,* Jackson State University, Dept of Art, Jackson MS (S)
Chong, Alan, *Dir & CEO,* The Currier Museum of Art, Manchester NH
Chong, Elaine, *Adjunct Prof,* College of Saint Elizabeth, Art Dept, Morristown NJ (S)
Choo, Chunghi, *Prof Metalsmithing & Jewelry,* University of Iowa, School of Art & Art History, Iowa City IA (S)
Choo, Phil, *Assoc Prof,* Oklahoma State University, Department of Art, Graphic Design and Art History, Stillwater OK (S)
Choo, Philip, *Asst Prof,* University of Minnesota, Duluth, Art Dept, Duluth MN (S)
Choquette, Keith, *Asst Dir,* Brockton Public Library, Joseph A Driscoll Art Gallery, Brockton MA
Chou, Diana, *Assoc Cur East Asian Art,* San Diego Museum of Art, San Diego CA
Chou, Wang-Ling, *Asst Prof,* Louisiana College, Dept of Art, Pineville LA (S)
Chouinard, Gary, *Devel Mgr,* New Brunswick Museum, Saint John NB
Chouris, Vicki, *VPres & COO,* South Florida Fair, Yesteryear Village, West Palm Beach FL
Chouteau, Suzanne, *Prof,* Xavier University, Dept of Art, Cincinnati OH (S)
Chow, Alan, *Exec Dir,* Chinese-American Arts Council, New York NY
Choy, Lillian, *Asst Pub Prog Mgr,* Workman & Temple Family Homestead Museum, City of Industry CA
Chrismas, Douglas, *Dir,* Ace Gallery, Los Angeles CA (S)
Christ, Ronald, *Grad Coordr,* Wichita State University, School of Art & Design, Wichita KS (S)
Christakos, Demetra, *Dir & Cur,* Laurentian University, Art Centre Library, Sudbury ON
Christakos, Demetra, *Dir & Cur,* Laurentian University, Museum & Art Centre, Sudbury ON
Christen, Derrick, *Asst Prof,* Northern Michigan University, Dept of Art & Design, Marquette MI (S)
Christensen, Candice, *Tour Registrar,* Minnesota Historical Society, Minnesota State Capitol Historic Site, Saint Paul MN
Christensen, Dan, *Treas & Exec Dir,* Phelps County Historical Society, Nebraska Prairie Museum, Holdrege NE
Christensen, Katie, *Cur Educ,* University of Wyoming, University of Wyoming Art Museum, Laramie WY
Christensen, Mary, *Board of Dirs,* Guild of Creative Art, Shrewsbury NJ (S)
Christensen, Michelle, *Visitor Svcs Coord,* City of Lethbridge, Sir Alexander Galt Museum, Lethbridge AB
Christensen, Susan, *Pres,* Octagon Center for the Arts, Ames IA
Christensen, V A, *Prof,* Missouri Southern State University, Dept of Art, Joplin MO (S)
Christi, John, *Chmn,* Capitol Community Technical College, Humanities Division & Art Dept, Hartford CT (S)
Christian, Ann, *Coordr Cultural Progs,* City of Scarborough, Cedar Ridge Creative Centre, Scarborough ON
Christian, Kendall, *Head Preparator,* Oberlin College, Allen Memorial Art Museum, Oberlin OH
Christian, Kurt, *Chief Preparator,* Carnegie Museums of Pittsburgh, Carnegie Museum of Art, Pittsburgh PA
Christian, Michele, *Univ Archivist,* South Dakota State University, Hilton M. Briggs Library, Brookings SD
Christiano, Melissa, *Instr,* Williams Baptist College, Dept of Art, Walnut Ridge AR (S)
Christiano, Michael, *Dir Educ & Interpretation,* University of Chicago, Smart Museum of Art, Chicago IL
Christiansen, Karen, *COO,* The Nelson-Atkins Museum of Art, Kansas City MO
Christiansen, Keith, *Chmn, European Paintings,* The Metropolitan Museum of Art, New York NY
Christianson, Denny, *Prog Dir, Music,* Humber College, School of Creative & Performing Arts, Toronto ON (S)
Christianson, Karen, *Dir Dept Pub Engagement,* The Newberry, Chicago IL
Christie, Leona, *Asst Prof,* State University of New York at Albany, Art Dept, Albany NY (S)
Christie, Marshall, *Metal Arts,* Sloss Furnaces National Historic Landmark, Birmingham AL
Christman, Linda, *Exec Dir,* Bismarck Art & Galleries Association, Bismarck ND
Christodoulou, Marilena, *Dir Finance & Admin,* Rubin Museum of Art, New York NY
Christofferson, Doris, *Receptionist,* Sweetwater County Library System and School District #1, Community Fine Arts Center, Rock Springs WY
Christoforou, Tony, *Dir Opers & Maintenance,* New-York Historical Society, Museum, New York NY
Christopher, Nicholas J, *Registrar & Preparator,* Pensacola Museum of Art, Pensacola FL
Christovich, Mary Louise, *Chmn,* The Historic New Orleans Collection, Williams Research Center, New Orleans LA
Christy, Cory, *Dir Develop,* Walter Anderson Museum of Art, Ocean Springs MS
Chrumka, Margaret, *Exec Dir,* Kamloops Art Gallery, Kamloops BC
Chrysler, Christina, *Cur,* St Lawrence College, Art Gallery, Kingston ON
Chrysler, Christina, *Prog Contact & Gallery Cur,* St Lawrence College, Visual & Creative Arts Program, Brockville ON (S)
Chu, Brian, *Prof,* University of New Hampshire, Dept of Art & Art History, Durham NH (S)
Chu, Jane, *Chmn,* National Endowment for the Arts, Washington DC
Chu, Kevin, *Colls Mgr,* Museum of Chinese in America, New York NY
Chubb, Taryn, *Asst Prof,* East Central University, School of Fine Arts, Ada OK (S)
Chudzik, Theresa, *Instr,* Hibbing Community College, Art Dept, Hibbing MN (S)
Chuk, Aileen, *Chief Registrar,* The Metropolitan Museum of Art, New York NY
Chumley, Jere, *Head,* Cleveland State Community College, Dept of Art, Cleveland TN (S)
Chun, Susan, *Chief Content Officer,* Museum of Contemporary Art Chicago, Chicago IL
Chung, Estella, *Dir Collections & Co-Chair Exhibs,* Hillwood Museum & Gardens Foundation, Hillwood Estate Museum & Gardens, Washington DC
Chung, Nogin, *Asst Prof,* Bloomsburg University, Dept of Art & Art History, Bloomsburg PA (S)
Chung, Robert Y, *Asst Prof,* Rochester Institute of Technology, School of Printing Management & Sciences, Rochester NY (S)
Chung, Sam, *Asst Prof,* Northern Michigan University, Dept of Art & Design, Marquette MI (S)
Chung, Vincent, *Instr,* Oklahoma State University Institute of Technology, School of Visual Communications, Okmulgee OK (S)
Chung, Youngmin, *Registrar,* University of Houston, Blaffer Art Museum, Houston TX
Chunko, Shelby, *Mus Shop Mgr,* Landis Valley Village and Farm Museum, PA Historical & Museum Commission, Lancaster PA
Chupa, Anna, *Assoc Prof,* Lehigh University, Dept of Art, Architecture & Design, Bethlehem PA (S)
Church, Sharyn L, *Deputy Dir,* Inner-City Arts, Los Angeles CA (S)
Churches, Kimberly, *CEO,* American Association of University Women, Washington DC
Chytilo, Lynne, *Prof,* Albion College, Bobbitt Visual Arts Center, Albion MI
Ciampa, John, *Chmn American Video Institute,* Rochester Institute of Technology, School of Photographic Arts & Sciences, Rochester NY (S)
Ciampa, Nicholas, *Dir,* Fleetwood Museum, North Plainfield NJ
Ciccarelli, Debby, *Coordr,* Community College of Baltimore County, School of Technology, Art & Design, Catonsville MD (S)
Cichy, Barbara, *Instr,* Bismarck State College, Fine Arts Dept, Bismarck ND (S)
Cicutto, Gail, *Pres,* Cumberland Art Society Inc, Cookeville Art Gallery, Cookeville TN
Cid, Christina, *Dir Progs,* High Desert Museum, Bend OR
Ciesielski, Alex, *Gallery Dir,* The Guild of Boston Artists, Boston MA
Cieslewicz, Kathy C, *Cur & Collections Mgr,* Dixie State University, Sears Art Museum Gallery, Saint George UT
Ciganick, Jan, *Instr,* Moravian College, Dept of Art, Bethlehem PA (S)
Cinelli, Michael J, *Head Dept,* Northern Michigan University, Dept of Art & Design, Marquette MI (S)
Cinquino, David, *Instr,* Daemen College, Art Dept, Amherst NY (S)
Cintello, Joe, *Chief Preparator,* Contemporary Arts Center, Cincinnati OH
Cioffoletti, Jessica, *Prog Mgr,* Pelham Art Center, Pelham NY
Ciolek, Nancy, *Chmn Fine Arts,* Rochester Institute of Technology, School of Design, Rochester NY (S)
Ciotti, Angelo L, *Gen Educ, Graphic Design,* Art Institute of Pittsburgh, Pittsburgh PA (S)
Cipriani-Willis, Janice, *Exec Dir,* Dorland Mountain Arts Colony, Art Residency Program, Temecula CA (S)
Cipriano, M, *Chmn Dept,* Central Connecticut State University, Dept of Art, New Britain CT (S)
Ciravolo, Jeanne, *Pres,* New Haven Paint & Clay Club, Inc, Whitneyville CT
Cisar, Liz, *Colls Asst,* Augustana University, Center for Western Studies, Sioux Falls SD
Citron, Harvey, *Chmn,* New York Academy of Art, Graduate School of Figurative Art, New York NY (S)
Ciufo, Jody, *Exec Dir,* Royal Architectural Institute of Canada, Ottawa ON
Claassen, Christina, *Mktg & PR Mgr,* Whatcom Museum, Bellingham WA
Claassen, Garth, *Dir,* The College of Idaho, Rosenthal Art Gallery, Caldwell ID

Claffen-Sullivan, Susan, *Prof Ceramics,* Manchester Community College, Visual Fine Art Dept, Manchester CT (S)
Claflin, Caroline, *Comm Coord,* Northwestern University, Mary & Leigh Block Museum of Art, Evanston IL
Claire, Michael, *Pres,* College of San Mateo, Creative Arts Dept, San Mateo CA (S)
Claire, William H, *Pres,* Coachella Valley History Museum, Indio CA
Clancey, Erin, *Sr Cur,* Hebrew Union College, Skirball Cultural Center, Los Angeles CA
Clancy, Brian, *Chair & Asst Prof,* Colby-Sawyer College, Dept of Fine & Performing Arts, New London NH (S)
Clancy, Jeff, *Asst Prof,* University of Wisconsin, Madison, Dept of Art, Madison WI (S)
Clancy, Megan, *Registrar,* University of Arizona, Center for Creative Photography, Tucson AZ
Clancy, Steven, *Chmn Art History,* Ithaca College, Handwerker Gallery of Art, Ithaca NY
Clapper, Michael, *Assoc Prof,* Franklin & Marshall College, Art & Art History Dept, Lancaster PA (S)
Clapper, Peter, *Instr,* Woodstock School of Art, Inc, Woodstock NY (S)
Clark, Andrew, *Prog Dir, Comedy,* Humber College, School of Creative & Performing Arts, Toronto ON (S)
Clark, Benjamin L, *Exec Dir,* MonDak Heritage Center, History Library, Sidney MT
Clark, Beth, *Instr,* Wayne Art Center, Wayne PA (S)
Clark, Bob, *Chief Archivist,* National Archives & Records Administration, Franklin D Roosevelt Museum, Hyde Park NY
Clark, Bob, *Head Librn,* Montana Historical Society, Library, Helena MT
Clark, Bob, *Instr,* Southwestern Community College, Advertising & Graphic Design, Sylva NC (S)
Clark, Brandi, *Dir Progs,* City Art Works, Pratt Fine Arts Center, Seattle WA (S)
Clark, Brian, *Pres,* Restigouche Gallery, Campbellton NB
Clark, Christian, *Dir Educ & Interpretation,* The University of Texas at San Antonio, Institute of Texan Cultures, San Antonio TX
Clark, Cynthia, *Chief Registrar & Cur History,* The New Museum at the Bradford Brinton Ranch, The Brinton Museum, Big Horn WY
Clark, Don, *Bd Dir, Chmn,* Plumas County Museum, Museum Archives, Quincy CA
Clark, Donald, *Assoc Prof,* Minnesota State University-Moorhead, Dept of Art & Design, Moorhead MN (S)
Clark, Dwayne, *Exhibition Designer & Preparator,* Morris Museum of Art, Augusta GA
Clark, Eleanor, *Museum Cur,* Rosenberg Library, Galveston TX
Clark, Fred, *Prof,* Lansing Community College, Visual Arts & Media Dept, Lansing MI (S)
Clark, Gary, *Pres,* Vermont Studio Center, The Red Mill, Johnson VT
Clark, Ginenne, *Events & Publs Coordr,* Society for Photographic Education (SPE), SPE Gallery, Cleveland OH
Clark, Gregory, *Chmn Dept,* University of the South, Dept of Fine Arts, Sewanee TN (S)
Clark, James M, *Prof,* Blackburn College, Dept of Art, Carlinville IL (S)
Clark, Joan, *Head Main Library,* Cleveland Public Library, Fine Arts & Special Collections Dept, Cleveland OH
Clark, John, *Head Adult Information Svcs,* Springfield City Library, Springfield MA
Clark, Judy, *Grad Coordr - Art Educ, Design, Studio Art,* University of Texas, Dept of Art & Art History, Austin TX (S)
Clark, Juleigh, *Pub Svcs Librn,* Colonial Williamsburg Foundation, John D Rockefeller, Jr Library, Williamsburg VA
Clark, Karen, *Sr Conservator,* Textile Conservation Workshop Inc, South Salem NY
Clark, Katreena, *Opers Mgr,* University of Richmond, University Museums, Richmond VA
Clark, Kimball, *Cataloger,* Dumbarton Oaks, Image Collections and Fieldwork Archives, Washington DC
Clark, Laurie Beth, *Prof,* University of Wisconsin, Madison, Dept of Art, Madison WI (S)
Clark, Marcia, *Dir,* Blue Mountain Gallery, New York NY
Clark, Marsha, *Bus Mgr,* Historic Pensacola Preservation Board, T.T. Wentworth Jr. Florida State Museum, Pensacola FL
Clark, Martha Fuller, *VPres,* Portsmouth Historical Society, John Paul Jones House & Discover Portsmouth, Portsmouth NH
Clark, Mary D, *Registrar,* Maysville, Kentucky Gateway Museum Center, Maysville KY
Clark, Marylou, *Adj Prof,* Quincy College, Art Dept, Quincy MA (S)
Clark, Rebecca, *Assoc Dir Library,* Visual Arts Library, New York NY
Clark, Robert, *Supervisory Archivist,* National Archives & Records Administration, Franklin D Roosevelt Library, Hyde Park NY
Clark, Sara B, *Adjunct Instr,* Saginaw Valley State University, Dept of Art & Design, University Center MI (S)
Clark, Sharon, *Asst to Dir,* University of Rhode Island, Fine Arts Center Galleries, Kingston RI
Clark, Stephanie, *Adj Asst Prof,* University of Texas at Arlington, Art & Art History Department, Arlington TX (S)
Clark, Sussanne, *Secy,* Coppini Academy of Fine Arts, Library, San Antonio TX
Clark, Wendy, *Dir Mus, Visual Arts & Indemnity,* National Endowment for the Arts, Washington DC
Clark, William, *Asst Prof,* Cedar Crest College, Art Dept, Allentown PA (S)
Clark-Binder, Miranda, *Cur Educ & Public Progs,* La Salle University Art Museum, Philadelphia PA
Clark-Langager, Sarah, *Dir,* Western Washington University, Western Gallery, Bellingham WA
Clarke, Adrienne, *Dept Admin,* Bryn Mawr College, Dept of the History of Art, Bryn Mawr PA (S)
Clarke, Alaina, *Conf & Prog Mgr,* Society of North American Goldsmiths, Eugene OR
Clarke, Bede, *Prof (Ceramics),* University of Missouri - Columbia, Dept of Art, Columbia MO (S)
Clarke, Candace, *Deputy Dir,* James A Michener Art Museum, Doylestown PA
Clarke, Cindy, *Secy,* Women's Art Association of Canada, Dignam Gallery, Toronto ON
Clarke, J Grier, *Pres & Dir,* Clarke Galleries, Stowe VT
Clarke, Jason, *Gen Mgr,* Arts and Letters Club of Toronto, Library, Toronto ON
Clarke, Robert, *Assoc Prof,* Mohawk Valley Community College, Utica NY (S)
Clarkin, Michelle, *Chief Adv Officer,* Norman Rockwell Museum, Stockbridge MA
Clarkson, Larry, *Asst Prof,* Weber State University, Dept of Visual Arts, Ogden UT (S)
Clary, Owen, *Commission Chair,* Aiken County Historical Museum, Aiken SC
Clause, Matthew, *Registrar,* Daum Museum of Contemporary Art, Sedalia MO
Claussen, Louise Keith, *Fine Art Mgr,* Morris Communications Co. LLC, Corporate Collection, Augusta GA
Claxton, Ronald, *Assoc Prof,* Central State University, Dept of Art, Wilberforce OH (S)
Clay, Joe, *Dir Progs,* Koshare Indian Museum, Inc, Library, La Junta CO
Claybourn, Bradford, *Mus Cur,* Mission San Luis Rey de Francia, Mission San Luis Rey Museum, Oceanside CA
Clayden, Stephen, *Head Botany & Mycology Sect & Research Cur,* New Brunswick Museum, Saint John NB
Claypool, Lisa, *Coordr History of Art, Design & Visual Culture Honours Advisor,* University of Alberta, Dept of Art & Design, Edmonton AB (S)
Clayson, Hollis, *Prof,* Northwestern University, Evanston, Dept of Art History, Evanston IL (S)
Clayton, Christine, *Asst Librn,* Worcester Art Museum, Library, Worcester MA
Clayton, Debra, *Exec Dir,* Michigan Guild of Artists & Artisans, Michigan Guild Gallery, Ann Arbor MI
Clayton, Greg, *Assoc Prof Art,* Harding University, Dept of Art & Design, Searcy AR (S)
Clayton, Ron, *Prof & Interim Chmn,* Southeast Missouri State University, Dept of Art, Cape Girardeau MO (S)
Clearwater, Bonnie, *Dir,* Museum of Contemporary Art, North Miami FL
Clearwaters, Deb, *Dir Educ,* Asian Art Museum of San Francisco, Chong-Moon Lee Ctr for Asian Art and Culture, San Francisco CA
Cleary, John R, *Assoc Prof,* Salisbury State University, Art Dept, Salisbury MD (S)
Cleary, Manon, *Prof,* University of the District of Columbia, Dept of Mass Media, Visual & Performing Arts, Washington DC (S)
Cleary, Tim, *Lectr,* University of Wisconsin-Superior, Programs in the Visual Arts, Superior WI (S)
Clem, Amanda, *Mem & Gallery Mgr,* Blue Sky Gallery, Oregon Center for the Photographic Arts, Portland OR
Clem, Debra, *Assoc Prof,* Indiana University-Southeast, Fine Arts Dept, New Albany IN (S)
Clem, Jena, *Special Events Mgr,* Gibbes Museum of Art, Charleston SC (S)
Cleman, Rebecca, *Distribution Dir,* Electronic Arts Intermix (EAI), New York NY
Clemens Pedersen, Deanna, *Dir Opers,* Cedar Rapids Museum of Art, Cedar Rapids IA
Clemens, Nori, *Spec Projects Mgr,* Arts Council Of New Orleans, New Orleans LA
Clement, Constance, *Deputy Dir,* Yale University, Yale Center for British Art, New Haven CT
Clement, Paul, *Chmn Social Science,* Fashion Institute of Technology, School of Art & Design, New York NY (S)
Clement, Russell T, *Head Art Coll,* Northwestern University, Art Collection, University Library, Evanston IL
Clementi, Bobbie, *Prof,* Daytona Beach Community College, Dept of Fine Arts & Visual Arts, Daytona Beach FL (S)
Clements, Bob, *Digital Design,* Art Institute of Pittsburgh, Pittsburgh PA (S)
Clements, Dawn, *Faculty,* Maryland Institute, Mount Royal School of Art, Baltimore MD (S)
Clements, Elaine, *Exec Dir,* Andover Historical Society, Andover MA
Clements, Emmett, *Gallery Mgr,* Pasadena Museum of California Art, Pasadena CA
Clements, Lisa, *Asst Dir Educ, Pub Progs & Interpretive Media,* The Getty Center, The J Paul Getty Museum, Los Angeles CA
Clements, Lisa, *Chief Communs & Brand,* Art Gallery of Ontario, Toronto ON
Clements, Martin, *Adjunct Instr,* New York Institute of Technology, Fine Arts Dept, Old Westbury NY (S)
Clements, Rodney, *Asst Dir,* Secretary of State Museum Division, Louisiana State Exhibit Museum, Shreveport LA
Cleminshaw, Doug, *Asst Prof,* Rochester Institute of Technology, School of Design, Rochester NY (S)
Clemmons, Sarah, *VPres Instr,* Chipola College, Dept of Fine & Performing Arts, Marianna FL (S)
Clemons, G Scott, *Pres,* Grolier Club Library, New York NY
Clendenin, Juliana, *Asst Prof,* Adrian College, Art & Design Dept, Adrian MI (S)
Clendenin, Paula, *Asst Prof,* West Virginia State University, Art Dept, Institute WV (S)
Clercx, Byron, *Chmn,* Marshall University, Dept of Art & Design, Huntington WV (S)
Cleveland, Felice, *Educ & Pub Progs Mgr,* Contemporary Arts Museum Houston, Houston TX
Clevenger, Jessica, *Lectr,* Georgia Southern University, Betty Foy Sanders Dept of Art, Statesboro GA (S)
Clews, Christina, *Chair Pub Rels Comt,* La Napoule Art Foundation, Chateau de la Napoule, Denver CO

Clews, Christopher S, *Pres,* La Napoule Art Foundation, Chateau de la Napoule, Denver CO
Clews, Noele M, *Exec Dir,* La Napoule Art Foundation, Chateau de la Napoule, Denver CO
Clift, Vicki, *Instr,* Appalachian State University, Dept of Art, Boone NC (S)
Clifton, Deborah, *Colls Cur,* Lafayette Science Museum & Planetarium, Lafayette LA
Clifton, Tom, *Chmn,* University of Arkansas at Little Rock, Art Library and Galleries, Little Rock AR
Cline, Holly, *Asst to Dir,* Wildling Art Museum, Solvang CA
Cline, Tricia, *Instr,* Woodstock School of Art, Inc, Woodstock NY (S)
Clinger, Melinda, *Dir Museum,* Fulton County Historical Society Inc, Fulton County Museum (Tetzlaff Reference Room), Rochester IN
Clive, Mark, *Sr Lectr,* University of Texas at Arlington, Art & Art History Department, Arlington TX (S)
Cloer, Garrett, *Park Ranger,* Longfellow National Historic Site, Longfellow House - Washington's Headquarters, Cambridge MA
Cloeter, Netha, *Dir,* North Dakota State University, Memorial Union Gallery, Fargo ND
Cloeter, Netha, *Dir Educ & Social Engagement,* Plains Art Museum, Fargo ND
Clontz, Lauren, *Asst Dir & Educ Dir,* McDowell House & Apothecary Shop, Danville KY
Clothier, Anne, *Dir Educ,* Saratoga County Historical Society, Brookside Museum, Ballston Spa NY
Cloud, Jasmine, *Asst Prof,* University of Central Missouri, Dept of Art & Design, Warrensburg MO (S)
Clough, Jan, *Prof,* Western Illinois University, Department of Art, Macomb IL (S)
Clough, Sebastian, *Dir Exhibs,* University of California, Los Angeles, Fowler Museum at UCLA, Los Angeles CA
Clouser, Lynn C, *Dir,* Drexel University, Drexel Collection, Philadelphia PA
Clouten, Neville H, *Dean,* Lawrence Technological University, College of Architecture, Southfield MI (S)
Clovis, John, *Prof,* Fairmont State College, Div of Fine Arts, Fairmont WV (S)
Clowe, Jeremy, *Mgr Media Svcs,* Norman Rockwell Museum, Stockbridge MA
Clowes, Jody, *Dir,* Wisconsin Academy of Sciences, Arts & Letters, James Watrous Gallery, Madison WI
Clucas, Deanna, *Instr,* Cuyahoga Valley Art Center, Cuyahoga Falls OH (S)
Clum, Claire, *Cur Educ,* Boca Raton Museum of Art, Library, Boca Raton FL
Clum, Claire, *Dir Educ,* Boca Raton Museum of Art, Boca Raton FL
Cluster, Julie, *Asst Dir,* Santa Paula Art Museum, Santa Paula CA
Clymer, Frances, *Librn,* Buffalo Bill Memorial Association, Harold McCracken Research Library, Cody WY
Clyne, Corey, *Facilities Mgr & Preparator,* Boise Art Museum, Boise ID
Coates, James, *Chmn Dept,* University of Massachusetts Lowell, Dept of Art, Lowell MA (S)
Coates, Joseph, *Asst Prof,* California Polytechnic State University at San Luis Obispo, Dept of Art & Design, San Luis Obispo CA (S)
Coates, Robert, *Asst Prof,* Sinclair Community College, Division of Fine & Performing Arts, Dayton OH (S)
Coates, Trisha, *Co-Dir,* Butler Community College, Erman B. White Gallery, El Dorado KS
Cobarruvias, Gerardo, *Assoc Prof,* Del Mar College, Art Dept, Corpus Christi TX (S)
Cobb, Donna, *Finance Mgr,* Walter Anderson Museum of Art, Ocean Springs MS
Cobb, Gary, *Chmn Fine Art,* Pepperdine University, Seaver College, Dept of Art, Malibu CA (S)
Cobb, Henry N, *VPres Art,* American Academy of Arts & Letters, New York NY
Cobb, June, *Dir Admin & Finance,* National Heritage Museum, Lexington MA
Cobb, Rebekah, *Guest Svcs,* Bob Jones University Museum & Gallery Inc, Greenville SC
Cobble, Kelly, *Cur,* Adams National Historic Park, Quincy MA
Cober Gentry, Leslie, *Secy,* Society of Illustrators, New York NY
Coblentz, Cassandra, *Assoc Cur,* Scottsdale Cultural Council, Scottsdale Museum of Contemporary Art, Scottsdale AZ
Coburn, Carol, *Chmn Humanities,* Avila College, Art Division, Dept of Humanities, Kansas City MO (S)
Coburn, Oakley H, *Dir,* Wofford College, Sandor Teszler Library Gallery, Spartanburg SC
Cocanougher, Robert L, *Assoc Prof,* University of North Florida, Dept of Communications & Visual Arts, Jacksonville FL (S)
Cochran, Dorothy, *Dir & Cur,* The Interchurch Center, Galleries at the Interchurch Center, New York NY
Cochran, Dorothy, *Dir & Cur Galleries,* The Interchurch Center, Library, New York NY
Cochran, Jessica, *Dir Finance & Opers,* The Renaissance Society, Chicago IL
Cochran, Michelle, *Instr,* Saint Mary's University of Minnesota, Art & Design Dept, Winona MN (S)
Cochrane, George, *Faculty,* Fairleigh Dickinson University, Fine Arts Dept, Madison NJ (S)
Cochrane, Mike, *COO,* Confederation Centre Art Gallery and Museum, Charlottetown PE
Cocke, Dudley, *Theater Dir,* Appalshop Inc, Appalshop, Whitesburg KY
Cockerell, Priscilla, *2nd VChmn,* Art and History Museums - Maitland, Maitland FL
Coconaur, SC, *Chmn,* Barnard's Mill Art Museum, Glen Rose TX
Codding, Mitchell A, *Exec Dir & Pres,* The Hispanic Society of America, Hispanic Society Museum & Library, New York NY
Coddington Rast, Ann, *Assoc Prof,* Eastern Illinois University, Art Dept, Charleston IL (S)
Codispot, Lawrence, *VPres,* Historical Society of Rockland County, New City NY
Codling, Mattie, *Dir Colls & Exhibs,* Walter Anderson Museum of Art, Ocean Springs MS
Codney, Jean, *Pres (V),* Cottonlandia Museum, Greenwood MS
Coerver, Chad, *Chief Content Officer,* San Francisco Museum of Modern Art, San Francisco CA
Coester, Dan, *Exhib Technician,* University of Kansas, Spencer Museum of Art, Lawrence KS
Coffey, John, *Dep Dir Art Coll,* North Carolina Museum of Art, Raleigh NC
Coffey, Marylyn, *Staff Asst,* University of Alabama at Huntsville, Union Grove Gallery & University Center Gallery, Huntsville AL
Coffman, Pam, *Educ Cur,* Museum of Art - Deland FL, Inc, Deland FL
Coffman, Rebecca L, *Asst Prof,* Huntington College, Art Dept, Huntington IN (S)
Cofi, Dario, *Prof Emeritus,* University of Louisville, Allen R Hite Art Institute, Louisville KY (S)
Cofield, Carol, *Bookkeeper,* Creative Arts Guild, Dalton GA
Cofrancesco, Brian, *Head Educ,* Old State House, Hartford CT
Cogan, Andrew, *Pres,* Chinati Foundation, Marfa TX
Cogan, Kathryn, *Dir,* Knights of Columbus Supreme Council, Knights of Columbus Museum, New Haven CT
Coggeshall, Jan, *Pres,* Rosenberg Library, Galveston TX
Coggins, Sonnet K, *Assoc Dir Academic & Public Engagement,* Williams College, Museum of Art, Williamstown MA
Cognato, Karen, *Librn,* New York Institute of Technology, Art & Architectural Library, Old Westbury NY
Cohen, Ada, *Chair,* Dartmouth College, Dept of Art History, Hanover NH (S)
Cohen, Doug, *Dir Finance,* The Heckscher Museum of Art, Huntington NY
Cohen, Hallie, *Assoc Prof Art & Chair Art Dept,* Marymount Manhattan College, Fine & Performing Arts Div, New York NY (S)
Cohen, Hallie, *Dir,* Marymount Manhattan College Hewitt Gallery, New York NY
Cohen, Janie, *Dir,* University of Vermont, Robert Hull Fleming Museum, Burlington VT
Cohen, Kathi, *Dir School,* The Art League Gallery & School, Alexandria VA
Cohen, Landon, *Program Dir,* Hillel Foundation, Hillel Jewish Student Center Gallery, Cincinnati OH
Cohen, Martin, *Chmn,* Guild Hall of East Hampton, Inc, Guild Hall Museum, East Hampton NY
Cohen, Michele, *Cur,* United States Capitol, Architect of the Capitol, Washington DC
Cohen, Michele, *Exec Dir,* The Art Center of Highland Park - TAC, Highland Park IL
Cohen, Olivia, *Spec Events Mgr,* Rubin Museum of Art, New York NY
Cohen, Sandy, *Dir,* North Central Washington Museum, Wenatchee Valley Museum & Cultural Center, Wenatchee WA
Cohen, Sarah, *Assoc Prof,* State University of New York at Albany, Art Dept, Albany NY (S)
Cohen, Seth, *Proj Mgr,* Public Art Fund, Inc, New York NY
Cohen, Seth, *Project Mgr,* Public Art Fund, Inc, Visual Archive, New York NY
Cohen, Stan, *VPres,* Rocky Mountain Museum of Military History, Missoula MT
Cohen-Stratyner, Barbara, *Cur Exhib,* The New York Public Library, The New York Public Library for the Performing Arts, New York NY
Cohn, Marjorie B, *Cur Prints,* Harvard University, William Hayes Fogg Art Museum, Cambridge MA
Cohn, Melanie, *Exec Dir,* Visual Arts Center of New Jersey, Summit NJ
Cohn, Michael, *CFO,* The Historic New Orleans Collection, Royal Street Galleries, New Orleans LA
Cohn, Peter, *Librn Urban Studies, Planning & Real Estate,* Massachusetts Institute of Technology, Rotch Library of Architecture & Planning, Cambridge MA
Coker, Alyce, *Assoc Prof,* University of Minnesota, Duluth, Art Dept, Duluth MN (S)
Coker, Crystal, *Admin Asst & Rental Coordr,* Creative Arts Guild, Dalton GA
Coker, Rachel, *Dir Develop,* Storm King Art Center, New Windsor NY
Colagross, John T, *Dept Chmn,* John C Calhoun, Department of Fine Arts, Tanner AL (S)
Colagross, John, *Dept Chair,* John C Calhoun, Art Gallery, Decatur AL
Colan, John, *Graphic Design,* Montserrat College of Art, Beverly MA (S)
Colangelo, Carmon, *Dir,* University of Georgia, Franklin College of Arts & Sciences, Lamar Dodd School of Art, Athens GA (S)
Colangelo, Carmon, *Dir,* University of Georgia, Dept of Art Lamar Dodd School of Art, Athens GA
Colangelo, Carmon, *Dir,* University of Georgia, Franklin College of Arts & Sciences, Lamar Dodd School of Art, Athens GA (S)
Colarusso, Stefanie, *Dir Progs,* Everhart Museum, Scranton PA
Colasurdo, Donna, *Board of Dirs,* Guild of Creative Art, Shrewsbury NJ (S)
Colazzi, Vittorio, *Asst Prof,* Old Dominion University, Art Dept, Norfolk VA (S)
Colbert, Charles, *Asst Prof,* Portland State University, Dept of Art, Portland OR (S)
Colbert, Cynthia, *Chmn Art Educ,* University of South Carolina, Dept of Art, Columbia SC (S)
Colbert, Tom, *Treas,* Wayne County Historical Society, Museum, Honesdale PA
Colborne, Allison, *Librn,* New Mexico Department of Cultural Affairs, Laboratory of Anthropology Library, Santa Fe NM
Colburn, Cynthia, *Assoc Prof,* Pepperdine University, Seaver College, Dept of Art, Malibu CA (S)
Colburn, Richard, *Prof,* University of Northern Iowa, Dept of Art, Cedar Falls IA (S)

Colby, Chad, *Assoc Prof,* Fort Lewis College, Art Dept, Durango CO (S)
Colby, Gary, *Prof Photog,* University of La Verne, Dept of Art, La Verne CA (S)
Colby, James, *Dir,* Jamestown Community College, The Weeks, Jamestown NY
Coldiron, Barbara, *Admin Asst,* The Pomona College, Claremont CA
Coldiron, Lisa M, *Spec Projects Specialist,* National Gallery of Art, Department of Image Collections, Washington DC
Cole, Carol, *Instr,* Main Line Art Center, Haverford PA (S)
Cole, Caroline, *Curatorial Asst,* Museum of Fine Arts, Houston, Rienzi Center for European Decorative Arts, Houston TX
Cole, Charlene, *Dir Library Svcs,* Tougaloo College, Coleman Library, Tougaloo MS
Cole, Don, *Dir Photog,* University of California, Los Angeles, Fowler Museum at UCLA, Los Angeles CA
Cole, Elizabeth, *Cur Collections,* RedMill Museum Village, Clinton NJ
Cole, Harold D, *Prof Art History,* Baldwin-Wallace College, Dept of Art, Berea OH (S)
Cole, Jennie, *Mgr Collections Access,* The Filson Historical Society, Louisville KY
Cole, Katherine, *Pres,* Mesquite Fine Arts Center & Gallery, Mesquite NV
Cole, Michael, *Dept Chair,* Columbia University, Dept of Art History & Archaeology, New York NY (S)
Cole, Michael, *Dept Chair,* Columbia University, Dept of Art History & Archaeology, New York NY
Cole, Michael, *Instr,* De Anza College, Creative Arts Division, Cupertino CA (S)
Cole, Nancy, *Instr,* Dallas Baptist University, Dept of Art, Dallas TX (S)
Cole, Nita, *Cur,* Secretary of State Museum Division, Louisiana State Exhibit Museum, Shreveport LA
Cole, Robert A, *Prof,* Rochester Institute of Technology, School of Design, Rochester NY (S)
Cole, Steve, *Prof,* Birmingham Southern College, Doris Wainwright Kennedy Art Center, Birmingham AL
Cole, Steve, *Prof,* Birmingham-Southern College, Art & Art History, Birmingham AL (S)
Cole, Susan A, *Pres,* Montclair State University, Art Galleries, Upper Montclair NJ
Cole, Theresa, *Assoc,* Tulane University, Sophie H Newcomb Memorial College, New Orleans LA (S)
Cole, Thomas, *Asst Dean for Admin,* Cornell University, College of Architecture, Art, and Planning, Ithaca NY (S)
Cole-Zielanski, Trudy, *Assoc Prof,* James Madison University, School of Art & Art History, Harrisonburg VA (S)
Colegrove, Ted, *Instr,* Moravian College, Dept of Art, Bethlehem PA (S)
Coleman, C Allen, *Exec Dir,* Pickens County Museum of Art & History, Pickens SC
Coleman, David, *Caretaker,* Jefferson County Historical Society, Library, Watertown NY
Coleman, Dorothy J, *Pres,* New Orleans Academy of Fine Arts, Academy Gallery, New Orleans LA
Coleman, Dorothy, *Exec Dir,* Oil Pastel Association, Stockholm NJ
Coleman, Elizabeth, *Pres,* Bennington College, Visual Arts Division, Bennington VT (S)
Coleman, Gabriella, *Prof & Undergrad Dir, Commun Studies,* McGill University, Dept of Art History & Communication Studies, Montreal QC (S)
Coleman, Holly, *Dir HR,* Norman Rockwell Museum, Stockbridge MA
Coleman, Johnny, *Assoc Prof,* Oberlin College, Dept of Art, Oberlin OH (S)
Coleman, Kathleen, *Cur,* Saratoga County Historical Society, Brookside Museum, Ballston Spa NY
Coleman, Laura, *Pub Rels & Mktg,* Kentucky Historical Society, Old State Capitol & Annex, Frankfort KY
Coleman, Michelle, *Dir Community Develop,* Idaho Commission on the Arts, Boise ID
Coleman, Myrlan, *Head Visual Arts & Instr,* Weatherford College, Dept of Speech Fine Arts, Weatherford TX (S)
Coleman, Rebekah, *Cur Educ,* San Angelo Museum of Fine Arts, San Angelo TX
Coleman, Richard, *Instr,* Glendale Community College, Visual & Performing Arts Div, Glendale CA (S)
Coleman, Susan, *Coord Exhibs,* Cornell College, Peter Paul Luce Gallery, Mount Vernon IA
Colenda, Marianne, *Dir Spec Events,* Thiel College, Weyers-Sampson Art Gallery, Greenville PA
Coles, Sarah, *Dir Mktg & Communs,* Ruder Finn Arts & Communications, Inc, New York NY
Coletta, Natalie, *Prof,* Community College of Rhode Island, Dept of Art, Warwick RI (S)
Colford, Michael, *Director of Library Svcs.,* Boston Public Library, Central Library, Boston MA
Colgrove, Clare, *Staff Asst,* United States Senate Commission on Art, Washington DC
Colkitt, Brian, *Photog,* Art Institute of Pittsburgh, Pittsburgh PA (S)
Collamore, Tracy, *Pres,* First Street Gallery, New York NY
Collens, David R, *Chief Cur,* Storm King Art Center, New Windsor NY
Colley, Binta, *Educ Dir,* T W Wood Gallery, Montpelier VT
Colley, Brett, *Asst Prof,* Grand Valley State University, Art & Design Dept, Allendale MI (S)
Colley, Christine, *Prof,* Shorter College, Art Dept, Rome GA (S)
Colley, Tom, *Archive & Coll Mgr,* School of the Art Institute of Chicago, Video Data Bank, Chicago IL
Collier, Brian, *Asst Prof,* St Michael's College, Fine Arts Dept, Colchester VT (S)
Collier, Brian, *Dir & Assoc Prof Fine Arts,* McCarthy Gallery, Colchester VT
Collier, Martin, *Contact,* University of Rochester, Dept of Art & Art History, Rochester NY (S)
Collier, Sidney, *Accounting Mgr,* Fort Ticonderoga Association, Ticonderoga NY
Collings, Ed, *Instr Photog & Ceramics,* Columbia College, Art Dept, Columbia MO (S)
Collins, Austin, *Chmn,* University of Notre Dame, Dept of Art, Art History & Design, Notre Dame IN (S)
Collins, D Cheryl, *Dir,* Riley County Historical Society & Museum, Seaton Library, Manhattan KS
Collins, D Cheryl, *Dir & Cur,* Riley County Historical Society & Museum, Riley County Historical Museum, Manhattan KS
Collins, Dana, *Instr,* Illinois Valley Community College, Division of Humanities & Fine Arts, Oglesby IL (S)
Collins, David, *Chmn Filmmaking,* Woodbury University, School of Media, Culture & Design, Burbank CA (S)
Collins, Doris, *Community Coordr,* Art Complex Museum, Carl A Weyerhaeuser Library, Duxbury MA
Collins, Dylan, *Asst Prof,* West Virginia University, College of Creative Arts, School of Art & Design, Morgantown WV (S)
Collins, Gregory, *Communs Dir,* Minnetonka Center for the Arts, Wayzata MN
Collins, Joel, *Chmn,* Mount Union College, Dept of Art, Alliance OH (S)
Collins, John, *Dean,* Surry Community College, Art Dept, Dobson NC (S)
Collins, Kenlyn, *Librn,* The Winnipeg Art Gallery, Clara Lander Library & Archives, Winnipeg MB
Collins, Kristin, *Instr,* Marylhurst University, Art Dept, Marylhurst OR (S)
Collins, Kurt, *Instr,* California State University, San Bernardino, Dept of Art, San Bernardino CA (S)
Collins, Lisa, *Prof,* Vassar College, Art Dept, Poughkeepsie NY (S)
Collins, Ruth, *Asst Deputy Dir Pub Svcs,* Buffalo & Erie County Public Library, Buffalo NY
Collins, Thomas, *Exec Dir,* Barnes Foundation, Merion PA
Collins, Toni, *Adminr,* Pennsylvania Historical & Museum Commission, Brandywine Battlefield Park, Chadds Ford PA
Collinsworth, Matt, *Dir,* Morehead State University, Kentucky Folk Art Center, Morehead KY
Collison, Nicholas, *Treas,* Special Libraries Association, Mc Lean VA
Collura, Bonnie, *Asst Prof Art (Sculpture),* Pennsylvania State University, University Park, Penn State School of Visual Arts, University Park PA (S)
Colombe, Vic, *Commissioner,* United States Department of the Interior, Indian Arts & Crafts Board, Washington DC
Colombik, Roger Bruce, *Prof,* Texas State University - San Marcos, Dept of Art and Design, San Marcos TX (S)
Colombo, Meg, *Pub Rels Mgr, Social Media & Webmaster,* University of Rochester, Memorial Art Gallery, Rochester NY
Colon, Carmen N, *Head Librn,* Escuela de Artes Plasticas, Biblioteca Francisco Oller, San Juan PR
Colon, Doreen, *Educ,* Museo de Arte de Puerto Rico, San Juan PR
Colon, Nancy, *Human Resources Manager,* Museo de Arte de Ponce, The Luis A Ferre Foundation Inc, Ponce PR
Colosimo, Melanie, *Gallery Dir,* Nova Scotia College of Art and Design, Anna Leonowens Gallery, Halifax NS
Colpitts, GE, *Instr,* Judson University, School of Art, Design & Architecture, Elgin IL (S)
Colt Rogers, Jessie, *Develop Dir,* Historical Museum at Fort Missoula, Missoula MT
Colton, Helen, *Progs Coordr,* Carl & Marilynn Thoma Art Foundation, Art House Santa Fe, Santa Fe NM
Coltrin, Chris, *Coordr Art History,* Shepherd University, Dept of Contemporary Art & Theater, Shepherdstown WV (S)
Colvard, Jane, *Asst Librn,* American Numismatic Association, Library, Colorado Springs CO
Colvert, Nancy, *Store Mgr,* Millicent Rogers Museum, Taos NM
Colvin, Kaersten, *Assoc Prof,* Clarion University of Pennsylvania, Dept of Art, Clarion PA (S)
Colvin, Richard D, *Cur Coll,* Art and History Museums - Maitland, Maitland FL
Colyar, Pat, *Sr Ceramics Technician,* Kirkland Arts Center, KAC Gallery, Kirkland WA
Comanda, Bridgette, *Public Servs Librn,* Trinity College Library, Washington DC
Comba, Steve, *Assoc Dir & Registrar,* The Pomona College, Claremont CA
Combe, Jennifer, *Asst Prof,* University of Montana, School of Art, Missoula MT (S)
Combs Dreiling, Helene, *Interim Exec Dir,* National Architectural Accrediting Board, Inc, Washington DC
Combs, Brad, *Researcher/Editor,* Alton Museum of History & Art, Inc, Alton IL
Combs, Brian, *Pres,* Alton Museum of History & Art, Inc, Alton IL
Combs, Glenna, *Prog Admin Mgr,* Kentucky Guild of Artists & Craftsmen Inc, Berea KY
Combs, Nicky, *Head Major Gifts & Fundraising Events,* Rubin Museum of Art, New York NY
Combs, Thomas, *Operations & Finance,* George Eastman Museum, Rochester NY
Comer, Julia, *Shop Sales Mgr,* Kentucky Museum of Art and Craft, Louisville KY
Comley, Ruth, *Computer Animation,* Art Institute of Pittsburgh, Pittsburgh PA (S)
Como, Thomas, *Prof, Chmn,* Slippery Rock University of Pennsylvania, Dept of Art, Slippery Rock PA (S)
Compton, Douglas, *Instr,* Joe Kubert, Dover NJ (S)
Compton, Mary, *Advisor,* Texas A&M University, MSC Visual Arts Committee, College Station TX
Comstock, Allyson, *Chair & Prof,* Auburn University, Dept of Art & Art History, Auburn AL (S)
Comte, Gabrielle, *Colls Mgr & Office Mgr,* Bone Creek Museum of Agrarian Art, David City NE

Conard, Susannah, *Facilities Coordr,* National Audubon Society, John James Audubon Center at Mill Grove, Audubon PA
Conaway, Stephanie, *Head Opers,* Museum of Contemporary Photography, Columbia College Chicago, Chicago IL
Concholar, Dan, *Pres & Dir,* Art Information Center, Inc, New York NY
Conciatori, Christine, *Dir Exhibitions & Mediation,* Musee National des Beaux Arts du Quebec, Quebec QC
Condict, Amanda, *Newsletter Ed,* Berks Art Alliance, Reading PA
Condon, Lorna, *Cur Library & Archives,* Historic New England, Library and Archives, Boston MA
Cone, Leslie, *Registrar & Collections Mgr,* Rollins College, George D & Harriet W Cornell Fine Arts Museum, Winter Park FL
Conelli, Maria, *Dir,* American Folk Art Museum, Shirley K. Schlafer Library, New York NY
Confessore, Lisa-Marie, *Exec Dir,* Art Center Sarasota, Sarasota FL (S)
Conforti, Michael, *Director,* Clark Art Institute, Williamstown MA
Cong, Zhiyuan, *Assoc Prof,* William Paterson University, Dept Arts, Wayne NJ (S)
Conger, Bill, *Cur,* Illinois State University, University Galleries, Normal IL
Conger, Jeffrey, *Prof Graphic Design,* Montana State University, School of Art, Bozeman MT (S)
Conger, William, *Prof,* Northwestern University, Evanston, Dept of Art Theory & Practice, Evanston IL (S)
Conine, Libby, *Dir Develop,* Contemporary Arts Museum Houston, Houston TX
Conklin, Donnelle, *Head Librn,* Lauren Rogers, Library, Laurel MS
Conklin, Jo-Ann, *Dir,* Brown University, David Winton Bell Gallery, Providence RI
Conklin, Julie, *Cur Asst,* Grand Rapids Art Museum, Reference Library, Grand Rapids MI
Conklin-Wingfield, Cara, *Dir Educ,* Parrish Art Museum, Water Mill NY
Conlan, Teressa, *Asst Librn,* Toledo Museum of Art, Art Reference Library, Toledo OH
Conley, B, *Instr,* Golden West College, Visual Art Dept, Huntington Beach CA (S)
Conley, Kyren, *Administrative Assistant,* Carnegie Arts Center, Alliance NE
Conley, Lisa, *Bus Mgr,* University of Georgia, Georgia Museum of Art, Athens GA
Conley, Mary, *Admin,* The Summit County Historical Society of Akron, OH, Akron OH
Conlon, William, *Div Chmn,* Fordham University, Art Dept, New York NY (S)
Conn, Peter, *Exec Dir,* Athenaeum of Philadelphia, Philadelphia PA
Connaghan, Stephen, *Librn,* Catholic University of America, Humanities Library, Mullen Library, Washington DC
Connell, Anne, *Dir School,* Silvermine Arts Center, School of Art, New Canaan CT (S)
Connell, Anne, *Dir School,* Silvermine Arts Center, Silvermine Galleries, New Canaan CT
Connell, Jim, *Assoc Prof,* Winthrop University, Dept of Art & Design, Rock Hill SC (S)
Connell, John, *Librn,* Yonkers Public Library, Fine Arts Dept, Yonkers NY
Connell, John, *Librn,* Yonkers Public Library, Will Library, Yonkers NY
Connell, Kevin, *Assoc Prof Theatre,* Marymount Manhattan College, Fine & Performing Arts Div, New York NY (S)
Connelly, David, *Dir Pub Rels,* Museum of Fine Arts, Saint Petersburg, Florida, Inc, Saint Petersburg FL
Connelly, Michael, *Asst Prof,* Montgomery County Community College, Art Center, Blue Bell PA (S)
Connelly, Trinity, *Curatorial Asst,* California State University, Chico, Janet Turner Print Museum, CSU, Chicago, Chico CA
Conner, Ann, *Prof,* University of North Carolina at Wilmington, Dept of Fine Arts - Division of Art, Wilmington NC (S)
Conner, Anne, *Chmn,* The Mariners' Museum, Newport News VA
Conner, Jeanne, *Dir Develop,* Bennington Museum, Bennington VT
Conner, Margie, *Dir Mktg,* Anniston Museum of Natural History, Anniston AL
Conner, Nadiya, *Sr Develop Assoc,* University of Southern California, USC Pacific Asia Museum, Pasadena CA
Connett, Christina, *Chief Cur,* Old Dartmouth Historical Society, New Bedford Whaling Museum, New Bedford MA
Conniff-O'Shea, Christine, *Conservation Tech,* The Art Institute of Chicago, Dept of Prints & Drawings, Chicago IL
Connolly, Dan, *Asst Prof,* Alma College, Clack Art Center, Dept of Art & Design, Alma MI (S)
Connolly, Felicia, *Office Admin,* Wenham Museum, Wenham MA
Connolly, Patrick, *Asst Prof,* La Roche College, Division of Design, Pittsburgh PA (S)
Connor, Kathy, *House Cur,* George Eastman Museum, Rochester NY
Connor, Scot, *Instr,* Mohawk Valley Community College, Utica NY (S)
Connor-Talasek, Catherine, *Assoc Prof,* Fontbonne University, Fine Art Dept, Saint Louis MO (S)
Connors McQuade, Margaret, *Asst Dir & Cur Decorative Arts,* The Hispanic Society of America, Hispanic Society Museum & Library, New York NY
Connors, Andrew, *Cur Art,* Albuquerque Museum of Art & History, Albuquerque NM
Connors, Michael, *Prof,* University of Wisconsin, Madison, Dept of Art, Madison WI (S)
Connors, Sarah, *Asst Dir,* International Preservation Studies Center, Mount Carroll IL (S)
Connorton, Judy, *Architecture Librn,* City College of the City University of New York, Morris Raphael Cohen Library, New York NY
Conrad Russen, Frank, *Dir,* Principle Gallery, Charleston, Charleston SC
Conrad, Eric, *Asst,* Emporia State University, Dept of Art, Emporia KS (S)
Conrad, Geoffrey W, *Dir,* Indiana University, The Mathers Museum of World Cultures, Bloomington IN
Conrad, Jennifer, *Mus Coordr,* University of Colorado, CU Art Museum, Boulder CO
Conrad, John, *Instr,* San Diego Mesa College, Fine Arts Dept, San Diego CA (S)
Conrad, Linda, *Pres & CEO,* Stan Hywet, Akron OH
Conradi, Jan, *Asst Prof,* State University of New York at Fredonia, Dept of Art, Fredonia NY (S)
Conrads, Margaret, *Dir Curatorial Affairs,* Crystal Bridges Museum of American Art, Bentonville AR
Conrey, Joseph, *Coordr,* Ocean County College, Humanities Dept, Toms River NJ (S)
Conroy, Michel, *Prof,* Texas State University - San Marcos, Dept of Art and Design, San Marcos TX (S)
Conroy, Shaun, *Exhibs Coordr,* George A Spiva, Joplin MO
Consales, Judy, *Interim Head,* University of California, Los Angeles, Arts Library, Los Angeles CA
Considine, Raymond, *Asst Dean Arts & Sciences,* Indian River Community College, Fine Arts Dept, Fort Pierce FL (S)
Constantine, Gregory, *Chmn,* Andrews University, Dept of Art, Art History & Design, Berrien Springs MI (S)
Constantinou, Meghan R, *Librn,* Grolier Club Library, New York NY
Conte, Christine, *Exec Dir,* Tohono Chul Park, Tucson AZ
Conte, Phil, *Exec VPres & CFO,* The Africa Center, New York NY
Conti, Nick, *Dir Information Technology,* American Antiquarian Society, Worcester MA
Contreras-Koterbay, Karlota, *Gallery Dir,* East Tennessee State University, College of Arts and Sciences, Dept of Art & Design, Johnson City TN (S)
Conway, Brenda, *Mem Asst,* Southern Oregon Historical Society, Library, Medford OR
Conway, Jan, *Adjunct Prof,* Wilkes University, Dept of Art, Wilkes-Barre PA (S)
Conway, Kelly, *Cur American Glass,* Corning Museum of Glass, Museum, Corning NY
Conway, Kerry, *Facilities Rental Manager,* Museum of Wisconsin Art, West Bend WI
Conway, Matthew, *Registrar,* Cornell University, Herbert F Johnson Museum of Art, Ithaca NY
Conyers, Wayne, *Chmn,* McPherson College, Art Dept, McPherson KS (S)
Conyers, Wayne, *Dir,* McPherson College Gallery, McPherson KS
Coogan, Jay, *Chmn,* Association of Independent Colleges of Art & Design, Providence RI
Coogan, Michael, *Dir Publ,* Harvard University, Semitic Museum, Cambridge MA
Cooianne, Jenelle, *Mktg Dir,* The Museum of Arts & Sciences Inc, Daytona Beach FL
Cook, Arthur, *Asst Prof,* Seton Hall University, College of Arts & Sciences, South Orange NJ (S)
Cook, Barbara, *Pub Rels,* Winterset Art Center, Winterset IA
Cook, Cathy, *Assoc Prof,* University of Maryland, Baltimore County, Intermedia & Digital Arts (IMDA), Dept of Visual Arts, Baltimore MD (S)
Cook, Heidi, *Gallery Dir,* Truman College Art Gallery, Chicago IL
Cook, Hope, *Gallery Coordr,* Mankato Area Arts Council, Carnegie Art Center, Mankato MN
Cook, J. English, *Graduate Curatorial Asst.,* New York University, Grey Art Gallery, New York NY
Cook, James, *Prof,* Elmira College, Art Dept, Elmira NY (S)
Cook, Jon, *Exec Dir,* Peggy R McConnell Arts Center of Worthington, Columbus OH
Cook, Kim, *Pres & CEO,* Arts Council Of New Orleans, New Orleans LA
Cook, Linda, *Supt,* National Park Service, Weir Farm National Historic Site, Wilton CT
Cook, Marlana L, *Cur Art,* United States Military Academy, West Point Museum, West Point NY
Cook, Meg, *Mem & Develop Assoc,* Portland Art Museum, Northwest Film Center, Portland OR
Cook, Michael D, *Prof,* University of New Mexico, Department of Fine Arts & Art History, Albuquerque NM (S)
Cook, Rachel, *Cur,* Diverse Works, Houston TX
Cook, Richard L, *Emeritus,* College of Santa Fe, Art Dept, Santa Fe NM (S)
Cook, Steve, *Asst Dir,* Indiana University, Eskenazi Museum of Art, Bloomington IN
Cook, Tom, *Pub Rels,* Montana Historical Society, Helena MT
Cooke, Judy, *Instr,* Pacific Northwest College of Art, Portland OR (S)
Cooke, S Tucker, *Chmn,* University of North Carolina at Asheville, Dept of Art, Asheville NC (S)
Cooke, Thomas, *Admin Asst,* Chaffey Community College, Art Dept, Rancho Cucamonga CA (S)
Cooksey, Susan, *Cur African Art,* University of Florida, Samuel P Harn Museum of Art, Gainesville FL
Coolidge, Miles, *Chair & Assoc Prof Photog,* University of California, Irvine, Studio Art Dept, Irvine CA (S)
Coombe, JoAnne, *Exec Dir,* Saint Louis County Historical Society, St. Louis County Historical Society, Duluth MN
Coombe, Kaye, *Gallery Dir,* The Fine Arts Center of Hot Springs, Hot Springs AR
Coombs, Nancy, *Communs Coordr,* Fuller Lodge Art Center, Los Alamos NM
Coon, Alexandra Nicholis, *Exec,* Massillon Museum, Massillon OH
Coones, R C, *Instr,* Northeastern State University, College of Arts & Letters, Tahlequah OK (S)
Cooney Frelinghuysen, Alice, *Cur in Charge, American Decorative Arts,* The Metropolitan Museum of Art, New York NY
Cooney, Anita, *Dean,* Pratt Institute, School of Design, Brooklyn NY (S)

Cooney, Lynne, *Artistic Dir,* Boston University Art Galleries, The Faye G, Jo & James Stone Gallery, Boston MA
Cooney, Nerissa, *Creative Dir,* Mana Contemporary, Jersey City NJ
Coonin, Victor, *Chmn, Asst Prof,* Rhodes College, Dept of Art, Memphis TN (S)
Cooper Wright, Carolyn, *Pub Relations,* Miles B Carpenter Folk Art Museum, Waverly VA
Cooper, Charisse, *Facility & Special Events Coordr,* Philbrook Museum of Art, Tulsa OK
Cooper, David, *Instr,* Butte College, Dept of Fine Arts and Communication Tech, Oroville CA (S)
Cooper, Frederick A, *Prof,* University of Minnesota, Minneapolis, Art History, Minneapolis MN (S)
Cooper, Gina, *Mus Store Mgr,* Anniston Museum of Natural History, Anniston AL
Cooper, Janet, *Mktg Dir,* Dublin Arts Council, Dublin OH
Cooper, Kate, *Head Librn,* Montgomery College of Art & Design Library, Takoma Park MD
Cooper, Lane, *Dept Head Painting,* Cleveland Institute of Art, Cleveland OH (S)
Cooper, Marisa, *Dir Educ,* Nevada Museum of Art, Reno NV
Cooper, Melody, *Instr,* Pierce College, Art Dept, Woodland Hills CA (S)
Cooper, Michael, *Instr,* De Anza College, Creative Arts Division, Cupertino CA (S)
Cooper, Nickki, *Publ Cur,* Fort Morgan Heritage Foundation, Fort Morgan CO
Cooper, Rhea, *Bookkeeper,* George A Spiva, Joplin MO
Cooper, Rhonda, *Dir,* State University of New York at Stony Brook, University Art Gallery, Stony Brook NY
Cooper, Simon, *Pres & CEO,* Ritz-Carlton Hotel Company, Art Collection, Chevy Chase MD
Cooper, Tara, *Asst Prof & Assoc Chair, Grad Studies,* University of Waterloo, Dept of Fine Arts, Waterloo ON (S)
Cooper, Tim, *Adjunct,* Howard Payne University, School of Fine Arts, Brownwood TX (S)
Cooper, Victoria, *Develop & Opers Mgr,* Ukrainian Institute of Modern Art, Chicago IL
Cooper, Virginia, *Registrar,* Muscatine Art Center, Muscatine IA
Cooperman, Andrew, *Dir,* Chatillon-DeMenil House Foundation, Chatillon-DeMenil Mansion, Saint Louis MO
Cooperman, Lisa, *Cur Educ,* The San Joaquin Pioneer & Historical Society, The Haggin Museum, Stockton CA
Copas, Susan, *Dept Chair,* Seward County Community College, Art Dept, Liberal KS (S)
Cope, Abner, *Assoc Prof,* Central State University, Dept of Art, Wilberforce OH (S)
Cope, Steve, *Prof Painting,* Saint Joseph's University, Art Dept, Philadelphia PA (S)
Copeland, Huey, *Asst Prof,* Northwestern University, Evanston, Dept of Art History, Evanston IL (S)
Copeley, Douglas, *Colls Mgr,* New Hampshire Historical Society, New Hampshire Historical Society Museum, Concord NH
Coppin, Kerry, *Assoc Prof,* Rochester Institute of Technology, School of Photographic Arts & Sciences, Rochester NY (S)
Copping, Lisette, *Chmn Fine Arts,* Delgado College, Dept of Fine Arts, New Orleans LA (S)
Copple, Carolyn, *Mem & Special Events Mgr,* Wichita State University, Ulrich Museum of Art, Wichita KS
Corbett, M Timothy, *Vol Pres,* Hill-Stead Museum, Farmington CT
Corbin, George, *Prof Emeritus,* City University of New York, PhD Program in Art History, New York NY (S)
Corbin, Tarrence, *Assoc Prof Fine Arts,* University of Cincinnati, School of Art, Cincinnati OH (S)
Corbus, Lili, *Prof Emeritus,* University of North Carolina at Charlotte, Dept Art, Charlotte NC (S)
Corcoran, Kathryn L, *Dir Library Svcs,* Munson-Williams-Proctor Arts Institute, Art Reference Library, Utica NY
Corcoran, Kathryn, *Librn,* Munson-Williams-Proctor Arts Institute, Museum of Art, Utica NY
Corcoran, Scott, *Asst Cur,* History Museum of Mobile, Mobile AL
Cordell, Douglas, *Serials & Electronic Resources Librn,* Los Angeles County Museum of Art, Allan C Balch Art Research Library, Los Angeles CA
Cordero, Edwin, *Prof,* University of Puerto Rico, Mayaguez, Dept of Humanities, College of Fine Arts & Theory of Art Programs, Mayaguez PR (S)
Cordova, Sasha, *Bd VPres,* Centro Cultural De La Raza, San Diego CA
Cordova, Viviana, *Asst Prof,* University of Maryland, Baltimore County, Intermedia & Digital Arts (IMDA), Dept of Visual Arts, Baltimore MD (S)
Cordrey, Brandon, *Exec Dir,* Visual Art Exchange, Raleigh NC
Core, Jennifer, *Dir Mem,* Tennessee Historical Society, Nashville TN
Core, Lyndell, *Mgr,* Bluemont Historical Railroad Junction, Arlington VA
Corea, Ellen, *Dir,* South Peace Art Society, Dawson Creek Art Gallery, Dawson Creek BC
Corell, Pam, *Asst Cur,* St Mary's University, Art Gallery, Halifax NS
Corey, Erika, *Bus Dir,* Visual Art Exchange, Raleigh NC
Corey, Karen M, *Interim Libr Dir,* Purdue University Calumet, Library Gallery, Hammond IN
Corey, Maureen, *Cur Art,* Loveland Museum/Gallery, Loveland CO
Corey, Sharon, *Prof,* Chapman University, Art Dept, Orange CA (S)
Cork, Sheila, *Librn,* New Orleans Museum of Art, New Orleans LA
Cork, Sheila, *Librn,* New Orleans Museum of Art, Felix J Dreyfous Library, New Orleans LA
Corle, Ed, *Dir,* University of Findlay, Dudley & Mary Marks Lea Gallery, Findlay OH
Corle, Jack (Ed), *Assoc Prof,* University of Findlay, Art Program, Findlay OH (S)
Corlett-Stahl, Claudia, *Assoc Dir,* University of Illinois at Urbana-Champaign, Krannert Art Museum and Kinkead Pavilion, Champaign IL
Corley, Erin, *Opers Mgr,* Manifest Gallery, Cincinnati OH
Cormier, Cynthia, *Project Cur,* Harriet Beecher Stowe Center, Hartford CT
Cornejo, Cesar, *Asst Prof,* University of South Florida, School of Art & Art History, Tampa FL (S)
Cornelius, Camille, *Instr,* Pierce College, Art Dept, Woodland Hills CA (S)
Cornelius, Kim, *Treas,* Brown County Art Gallery Foundation, Nashville IN
Cornelius, Sally, *Prof,* Virginia Polytechnic Institute & State University, Dept of Art & Art History, Blacksburg VA (S)
Cornell, Anne, *Artistic Dir & Community Studio Artist,* Pomerene Center for the Arts, Coshocton OH
Cornell, Daniell, *Deputy Dir Art, Sr Cur,* Palm Springs Art Museum, Palm Springs CA
Cornell, Thomas B, *Prof,* Bowdoin College, Art Dept, Brunswick ME (S)
Corner, Francie, *Pres,* The Art Institute of Chicago, The Woman's Board of the Art Institute of Chicago, Chicago IL
Cornish, Glenn, *Music Instr,* Edison Community College, Gallery of Fine Arts, Fort Myers FL (S)
Cornish, Jack, *Chmn,* Kean University, Fine Arts Dept, Union NJ (S)
Corrales, Brittany, *Cur Coord,* Arizona State University, ASU Art Museum, Tempe AZ
Corrie, Rebecca W, *Prof,* Bates College, Art & Visual Culture, Lewiston ME (S)
Corrigan, Caroline, *Educ & Exhibs Mgr,* The Arts Center of the Capital Region, Troy NY
Corrigan, David J, *Cur,* Connecticut State Library, Museum of Connecticut History, Hartford CT
Corris, Michael, *Prof,* Southern Methodist University, Meadows School of the Arts - Division of Art, Dallas TX (S)
Corry, Dan, *Director of Finance,* Museum of Wisconsin Art, West Bend WI
Corso, Anne, *Dir Educ,* Reading Public Museum, Reading PA
Corso, Anne, *Dir Educ & Pub Progs,* Chrysler Museum of Art, Norfolk VA
Corso, John, *Asst Prof,* Oakland University, Dept of Art & Art History, Rochester MI (S)
Cortes, Tess, *Galleries Coordr,* Wright State University, Robert and Elaine Stein Galleries, Dayton OH
Cortez, Mike, *IT Specialist,* Auburn University, Jule Collins Smith Museum of Fine Art, Auburn AL
Cortinas, Miguel, *Asst Prof,* University of the Incarnate Word, Art Dept, San Antonio TX (S)
Corwin, Mark, *Chair, Music,* Concordia University, Faculty of Fine Arts, Montreal QC (S)
Corwin, Sharon, *Cur,* Colby College, Museum of Art, Waterville ME
Cosentino, Cira, *Instr,* Indian River Community College, Fine Arts Dept, Fort Pierce FL (S)
Cosentino, Geraldine, *Dir,* Organization of Independent Artists, Inc, Brooklyn NY
Cosgrove, Tracy, *Dir Finance & Admin,* Missoula Art Museum, Missoula MT
Coslit, Rod, *Mus Shop Mgr,* Montana Historical Society, Helena MT
Cosner, Chris, *Assoc Prof,* Glenville State College, Dept of Fine Arts, Glenville WV (S)
Cossaboon, Claire, *Mgr Membership,* Grounds for Sculpture, Hamilton NJ
Cost, Steven, *Asst Prof,* Amarillo College, Visual Art Dept, Amarillo TX (S)
Costa, Jennifer, *Prof, Dept Chair & Cur,* Illinois Central College, Arts & Communication Dept, East Peoria IL (S)
Costa, Jorge, *Instr,* Springfield College, Dept of Visual & Performing Arts, Springfield MA (S)
Costa, Lenora, *Cur,* Longue Vue House & Gardens, New Orleans LA
Costa, Mary Len, *Major Gifts & Foundation Officer,* Arts Council Of New Orleans, New Orleans LA
Costanzo, Nancy, *Chmn Dept,* Our Lady of Elms College, Dept of Fine Arts, Chicopee MA (S)
Costello, Christy, *Dir Devel,* Museo De Las Americas, Denver CO
Costello, Judy, *Educ Mgr,* City of Springdale, Shiloh Museum of Ozark History, Springdale AR
Costello, Kim, *Director,* Almond Historical Society, Inc, Hagadorn House, The 1800-37 Museum, Almond NY
Costello, Lisa, *Gallery Dir,* Parkland College, Parkland Art Gallery, Champaign IL
Costello, Mary Jay, *Sec,* Hudson Valley Art Association, Brooklyn NY
Costilow, Walt, *Pres Elect,* Watercolor Society of Alabama, Town Creek AL
Cote, Jean-Francois, *Librn,* Quickdraw Animation Society, Calgary AB
Cote, Marc, *Chmn,* Framingham State College, Art Dept, Framingham MA (S)
Cothren, Michael, *Chmn & Prof,* Swarthmore College, Dept of Art & Art History, Swarthmore PA (S)
Cotner, Cynthia, *Reference Desk Coordr,* University of Missouri, Art, Archaeology & Music Collection, Columbia MO
Cotner, Teresa, *Chmn & Assoc Prof,* California State University, Chico, Department of Art & Art History, Chico CA (S)
Cotten, Charles, *Adminr,* Presidential Museum & Leadership Library, Odessa TX
Cotter, Anita, *CSPWC Adminr,* Canadian Society of Painters In Watercolour, Toronto ON
Cotton, Martha, *Pres,* Licking County Arts, Art Gallery, Newark OH
Cotton, Nancy, *Pres. Emeritus,* Allegany County Historical Society, Gordon-Roberts House, Cumberland MD
Cottong, Kathy, *Dir,* The Arts Club of Chicago, Reference Library, Chicago IL

Cottrill, Mary, *Mgr Mus Operations & Hennage Auditorium,* Colonial Williamsburg Foundation, Abby Aldrich Rockefeller Folk Art Museum, Williamsburg VA

Cottrill, Mary, *Mgr Mus Opers & Hennage Auditorium,* Colonial Williamsburg Foundation, DeWitt Wallace Decorative Arts Museum, Williamsburg VA

Couch, Dale, *Cur Decorative Art,* University of Georgia, Georgia Museum of Art, Athens GA

Couch, Kirsten, *Instr,* Northeastern Oklahoma A & M College, Art Dept, Miami OK (S)

Couchon, Marie-Paule, *Archivist,* Musee des Augustines de l'Hotel Dieu de Quebec, Archive, Quebec QC

Coucke, Hester, *Cur,* The Arts Center, Corvallis OR

Coughlin, Joan Hopkins, *Cur,* Wellfleet Historical Society & Museum, Inc, Wellfleet MA

Coughlin, Michelle, *Museum Admin,* Gibson Society, Inc, Gibson House Museum, Boston MA

Couillard, Martine, *Sr Officer, Government & Institutional Relations,* McCord Museum of Canadian History, Montreal QC

Coulomb, Andrew, *Dir Opers & Facility Mgmt,* Virginia Museum of Contemporary Art, Virginia Beach VA

Council, Dorothy, *VPres,* Rawls Museum Arts, Courtland VA

Council, Floyd, *Exec Dir,* Birmingham Public Library, Arts, Literature & Sports Department, Birmingham AL

Coupolos-Selle, Stephanie, *Prof,* University of Wisconsin College - Marinette, Art Dept, Marinette WI (S)

Courchaine, Rocky, *Dir,* Crook County Museum & Art Gallery, Sundance WY

Courtmanche, Elizabeth, *Assoc Dir Develop,* Johns Hopkins University, Homewood Museum, Baltimore MD

Courtney, Janice, *Arts Advisor & Asst Dir,* Saint Cloud State University, Atwood Memorial Center Gallery, Saint Cloud MN

Courtney, Matthew, *Instr,* Wayne Art Center, Wayne PA (S)

Courtright, Nicola M, *Prof of Art & History of Art,* Amherst College, Dept of Art & the History of Art, Amherst MA (S)

Courts, Garland, *Mgr,* Branigan Cultural Center, Las Cruces NM

Cousino, Jennifer, *Cur History,* Loveland Museum/ Gallery, Loveland CO

Cousino, Mike, *Sir Graphic Designer,* University of Minnesota Duluth, Tweed Museum of Art, Duluth MN

Coutre, Jacquelyn N., *Bader Cur European Art,* Queen's University, Agnes Etherington Art Centre, Kingston ON

Couture, Theresa, *Co-Chairperson Dept Music & Art,* Rivier College, Art Dept, Nashua NH (S)

Covalucci, Renee, *Pres,* The Boston Printmakers, at Lesley University, Boston MA

Covell, Heike, *2nd VPres,* Watercolor Society of Alabama, Town Creek AL

Cover, Karen, *Archivist,* United States Figure Skating Association, World Figure Skating Museum & Hall of Fame, Colorado Springs CO

Covert, Claudia, *Spec Coll Librn,* Rhode Island School of Design, Fleet Library at RISD, Providence RI

Covert, Nan, *Dept Head,* Bridgewater College, Art Dept, Bridgewater VA (S)

Covertino, Karen, *Registrar,* Everson Museum of Art, Syracuse NY

Coviello, Liz, *Pres,* Redlands Art Association, Redlands Art Association Gallery & Art Center, Redlands CA

Cowan, Aaron J, *Dir,* University of Cincinnati, DAAP Galleries-College of Design Architecture, Art & Planning, Cincinnati OH

Cowan, Aaron, *Cur,* Swine Gallery, Chattanooga TN

Cowan, Elaine, *Registrar,* Worcester Center for Crafts, Worcester MA (S)

Cowan, Kathy, *Sr Reference Librn,* Maryland Institute, Decker Library, Baltimore MD

Cowardin, Mark, *Asst Prof Fine Art & Sculpture Dept Coordr,* Johnson County Community College, Fine Arts Dept & Art History Dept, Overland Park KS (S)

Cowart, Jack, *Deputy Dir & Chief Cur,* Corcoran Gallery of Art, Washington DC

Cowden, Chris, *Exec Dir,* Women & Their Work, Austin TX

Cowden, Dorothy, *Dir Gallery,* University of Tampa, College of Arts & Letters, Tampa FL (S)

Cowden, Dorothy, *Dir of Galleries,* University of Tampa, Scarfone/Hartley Gallery, Tampa FL

Cowen, James, *Music Reference Librn,* The University of the Arts, University Libraries, Philadelphia PA

Cowette, Thomas, *Assoc Prof,* University of Minnesota, Minneapolis, Dept of Art, Minneapolis MN (S)

Cox, Amanda, *Art Educ Dir,* Sumter Gallery of Art, Sumter SC

Cox, Amy, *Dir Interior Design & Assoc Prof,* Harding University, Dept of Art & Design, Searcy AR (S)

Cox, Anna, *Asst Prof,* Longwood University, Dept of Art, Farmville VA (S)

Cox, Bruce, *Asst Dir,* University of Missouri, Museum of Art & Archaeology, Columbia MO

Cox, Carolyn, *VPres,* Sturdivant Museum Association, Sturdivant Museum, Selma AL

Cox, Christopher, *Dean of Library Svcs,* University of Northern Iowa, Fine & Performing Arts Collection Rod Library, Cedar Falls IA

Cox, Cindy, *Membership Officer,* Auburn University, Jule Collins Smith Museum of Fine Art, Auburn AL

Cox, Dennis, *Assoc Prof,* Pacific Lutheran University, Dept of Art, Tacoma WA (S)

Cox, Greg, *Cur Collections,* Yosemite Museum, Yosemite National Park CA

Cox, Jennifer, *Librn,* Art Institutes International at Portland, Portland OR

Cox, Joshua, *Dir,* Peoria Art Guild, Peoria IL

Cox, Julian, *Deputy Dir & Chief Cur,* Art Gallery of Ontario, Toronto ON

Cox, Kathleen, *Controller,* American Institute of Graphic Arts, National Design Center, New York NY

Cox, Lynn, *Prof,* Hastings College, Department of Visual Arts, Hastings NE (S)

Cox, Michael, *Co-Dir,* University of Manitoba, Faculty of Architecture Exhibition Centre, Winnipeg MB

Cox, Richard, *Prof,* Louisiana State University, School of Art, Baton Rouge LA (S)

Cox, Robert, *Lectr,* University of Tennessee at Chattanooga, Dept of Art, Chattanooga TN (S)

Cox, Samuel, *Cur,* United States Navy, Art Gallery, Washington DC

Cox, Sharon, *Chmn,* University of Jamestown, Art Dept, Jamestown ND (S)

Cox, Sheri, *Gallery Mgr,* Craftsmen's Guild of Mississippi, Inc, Mississippi Craft Center, Ridgeland MS

Cox, Sheri, *Opers Mgr,* Craftsmen's Guild of Mississippi, Inc, Mississippi Craft Center, Ridgeland MS

Coyle, Heather Campbell, *Chief Cur & Cur American Art,* Delaware Art Museum, Wilmington DE

Coyle, Kathryn, *Technical Svcs,* The University of the Arts, University Libraries, Philadelphia PA

Coyne, Catherine, *Children's Librn,* Ames Free-Easton's Public Library, North Easton MA

Coyne, Janine, *Adj Assoc Prof,* College of Staten Island, Performing & Creative Arts Dept, Staten Island NY (S)

Coyne, Michael, *Prof,* Grenfell Campus, Memorial University of Newfoundland, Division of Fine Arts, Visual Arts Program, Corner Brook NF (S)

Cozad Feehan, Jennifer, *Coordr Mem & Pub Rels,* The Pennsylvania State University, Palmer Museum of Art, University Park PA

Cozzi, Leslie, *Cur Assoc,* University of California, Los Angeles, Grunwald Center for the Graphic Arts at Hammer Museum, Los Angeles CA

Crabb, Patrick S, *Ceramics,* Santa Ana College, Art Dept, Santa Ana CA (S)

Crable, James, *Prof,* James Madison University, School of Art & Art History, Harrisonburg VA (S)

Cracco, Derek, *Assoc Prof,* University of Alabama at Birmingham, Dept of Art & Art History, Birmingham AL (S)

Craft, Jeff, *Chief Admin,* University of Michigan, Ann Arbor, Dept of History of Art, Ann Arbor MI (S)

Craig, Debbie, *Pottery Dir,* Glynn Visual Arts, Inc, Saint Simons Island GA

Craig, Gerry, *Cur Educ,* Detroit Zoological Institute, Wildlife Interpretive Gallery, Royal Oak MI

Craig, James, *Art Dept Lead & Instr,* Columbia Basin College, Esvelt Gallery, Pasco WA (S)

Craig, Leah W, *Exec Dir,* Historic Paris - Bourbon County, Inc, Hopewell Museum, Paris KY

Craig, Rita, *CFO,* Oklahoma City Museum of Art, Oklahoma City OK

Craig, Rob, *Mgr Family Events,* Newark Museum Association, Junior Museum, Newark NJ

Craig, Susan V, *Librn,* University of Kansas, Murphy Library of Art & Architecture, Lawrence KS

Craighill, Marcee F, *Dir,* United States Department of State, Diplomatic Reception Rooms, Washington DC

Crain, Brian, *Asst Prof Art,* Marian University, Visual Arts Dept, Indianapolis IN (S)

Crall, Steven, *Asst Prof,* South Carolina State University, Dept of Visual & Performing Arts, Orangeburg SC (S)

Cramer, George, *Emer Prof,* University of Wisconsin, Madison, Dept of Art, Madison WI (S)

Cramer, Lissa, *Exhib Coordr,* Tufts University, Tufts University Art Gallery, Medford MA

Cramer, Patricia T, *Dir,* Westfield Athenaeum, Jasper Rand Art Museum, Westfield MA

Cramer, Sam, *Instr & Coordr,* Luzerne County Community College, Commercial Art Dept, Nanticoke PA (S)

Crandell, Stephen, *Asst Prof,* West Texas A&M University, Art, Theatre & Dance Dept, Canyon TX (S)

Crane, Bonnie L, *Owner, Dir & Pres,* Crane Collection, Gallery of American Painting and Sculpture, Magnolia MA

Crane, Carey, *Exhib Designer,* Calvert Marine Museum, Solomons MD

Crane, David, *Prof,* Virginia Polytechnic Institute & State University, Dept of Art & Art History, Blacksburg VA (S)

Crane, Diane, *Instr,* Viterbo University, Art Dept, La Crosse WI (S)

Crane, Jennifer, *Assoc Prof,* University of Saskatchewan, Art & Art History Dept, Saskatoon SK (S)

Crane, Kenneth, *Security Officer,* University of North Carolina at Greensboro, Weatherspoon Art Museum, Greensboro NC

Crane, Kevin, *Warehouse Opers Mgr,* The Names Project Foundation AIDS Memorial Quilt, Atlanta GA

Cranin, Tonya, *Mktg Dir,* Architects Design Group Inc, Winter Park FL

Cranston, Donald, *Chair,* City of Toronto Museum Services, Historic Fort York, Toronto ON

Cranston, Meg, *Chmn,* Otis College of Art & Design, Fine Arts, Los Angeles CA (S)

Craven Fernandez, Happy, *Pres,* Moore College of Art & Design, Philadelphia PA (S)

Craven, Allen, *Assoc Prof,* Fort Hays State University, Dept of Art & Design, Hays KS (S)

Craven, Leigh, *Asst Prof,* Bridgewater State College, Art Dept, Bridgewater MA (S)

Cravens, Kate, *Cur Hall of Fame,* National Museum of Racing, National Museum of Racing & Hall of Fame, Saratoga Springs NY

Crawford, Barbara, *Head Dept,* Southern Virginia College, Division of Arts and Humanities, Buena Vista VA (S)

Crawford, Cameron, *Grad Adv & Prof,* California State University, Chico, Department of Art & Art History, Chico CA (S)

Crawford, Denton, *Lectr,* Humboldt State University, College of Arts & Humanities, Art Dept, Arcata CA (S)
Crawford, Gretchen, *Instr,* Capital University, Fine Arts Dept, Columbus OH (S)
Crawford, James, *Cur,* Canajoharie Library & Art Gallery, Library, Canajoharie NY
Crawford, Katelyn, *William Cary Hulsey Cur American Art,* Birmingham Museum of Art, Birmingham AL
Crawford, Nicole, *Cur Coll,* University of Wyoming, University of Wyoming Art Museum, Laramie WY
Crawford, Pam, *Gallery Mgr,* Brown County Art Gallery Foundation, Nashville IN
Crawford, Paul, *Dir & Cur,* The Penticton Art Gallery, Penticton BC
Crawford, Randal, *Prof,* Delta College, Art Dept, University Center MI (S)
Creasy, June, *Assoc Prof,* Lambuth University, Dept of Human Ecology & Visual Arts, Jackson TN (S)
Creech, Jenny, *Mgr Galleries & Digital Media,* Paint Creek Center for the Arts, Rochester MI
Creed Barros, Margaret, *Exec Dir,* Rutland Area Art Association, Chaffee Art Center & Chaffee Downtown Galleries, Rutland VT
Cremer, Ryan, *Develop Dir,* Yellowstone Art Museum, Billings MT
Cresson, Pat, *Prof,* Monmouth University, Dept of Art & Design, West Long Branch NJ (S)
Creston, Bill, *Dir Emeritus,* eMediaLoft.org, New York NY
Crew, John, *Pres,* Wenatchee Valley College, Robert Graves Gallery, Wenatchee WA
Crew, Morgan, *Exec Asst,* Orlando Museum of Art, Orlando Sentinel Library, Orlando FL
Crew, Morgan, *Exec Asst,* Orlando Museum of Art, Orlando FL
Crewdson, Gregory, *Dir Graduate Studies in Photog,* Yale University, School of Art, New Haven CT (S)
Creyts, Katie, *Assoc Prof,* Whitworth University, Art Dept, Spokane WA (S)
Cribb Curran, Tonya, *Dir,* Stetson University, Hand Art Center, Deland FL
Cribelli, Susan, *Acad Dean Communs & Humanities,* Aims Community College, Visual & Performing Arts, Greeley CO (S)
Crimmins, Jaynie, *Pres,* Garrison Art Center, Garrison NY
Crisman, Beth, *Technical Dir,* Maryland-National Capital Park & Planning Commission, Montpelier Arts Center, Laurel MD
Crisman, Richard, *Gift Shop Mgr,* Delta Blues Museum, Clarksdale MS
Crismon, David, *Asst Prof,* Oklahoma Christian University of Science & Arts, Dept of Art & Design, Oklahoma City OK (S)
Crispe, Joanna, *Dir Community Engagement & Educ,* Municipal Art Society of New York, New York NY
Crist, Andi, *Preparator,* Hyde Park Art Center, Chicago IL
Cristal, Melissa, *Assoc Dir, Advancement,* Archives of American Art, Smithsonian Institution, Washington DC
Crites, Gary, *Cur Paleoethnobotany,* University of Tennessee, McClung Museum of Natural History & Culture, Knoxville TN
Crittendon, Shelly, *Colls Mgr,* Texas Ranger Hall of Fame & Museum, Waco TX
Croce, Charles, *Exec Dir & CEO,* Philadelphia History Museum, Philadelphia PA
Croce, Judith, *Chmn,* Caldwell College, Dept of Fine Arts, Caldwell NJ (S)
Croce, Marianne Della, *Coll Mgr,* Planting Fields Foundation, Coe Hall at Planting Fields Arboretum, Oyster Bay NY
Crocker, Elli, *Dir Studio Art Prog,* Clark University, Dept of Visual & Performing Arts, Worcester MA (S)
Crocker, Kyle, *Prof,* Bemidji State University, Visual Arts Dept, Bemidji MN (S)
Crockett, Candace, *Chmn,* San Francisco State University, Art Dept, San Francisco CA (S)
Crockett-Green, Mary, *Deputy Dir,* Tennessee State Museum, Nashville TN
Croft, Parker, *Vis Asst Prof,* Middlebury College, History of Art & Architecture Dept, Middlebury VT (S)
Croghan, Nicholas, *Gallery Dir,* University of West Florida, Dept of Art, Pensacola FL (S)
Croins, Sonya, *Office Mgr,* Mississippi Museum of Art, Howorth Library, Jackson MS
Cromley, Elizabeth, *Chmn,* Northeastern University, Dept of Art & Architecture, Boston MA (S)
Cromwell, Sara, *Asst Dir,* Wake Forest University, Museum of Anthropology, Winston-Salem NC
Cromwell, Sue, *Accnt,* Touchstone Center for Crafts, Hart Moore Museum, Farmington PA
Cronan, Todd, *Asst Prof,* Emory University, Art History Dept, Atlanta GA (S)
Cronin, Betsy, *Prog Coordr for the Arts,* Wheaton College, Beard and Weil Galleries, Norton MA
Cronin, Elizabeth, *Miriam & Ira D Wallach Asst Cur, Prints & Photographs,* The New York Public Library, Art & Architecture Collection, New York NY
Cronin, Jennifer, *Assoc Dir,* Museum of Fine Arts, Houston, Glassell School of Art, Houston TX (S)
Cronin, Mary W, *Supv Educ,* Brandywine Conservancy, Brandywine River Museum, Chadds Ford PA
Crook, Lillian, *Librn Dir,* Dickinson State University, Stoxen Library, Dickinson ND
Crooks, Julian, *Assistant Professor,* Harcum College, Fashion Design, Bryn Mawr PA (S)
Cropper, Elizabeth, *Dean, Center for Advanced Study in Visual Arts,* National Gallery of Art, Washington DC
Croquer, Luis, *Dir & Chief Cur,* Brandeis University, Rose Art Museum, Waltham MA
Crosby, Anna, *Bd Mem (Past Pres),* Coquille Valley Art Association, Coquille OR
Crosby, Eric, *Cur Contemp Art,* Carnegie Museums of Pittsburgh, Carnegie Museum of Art, Pittsburgh PA
Crosby, Suzanne, *Dir,* Hillsborough Community College, Fine Arts Dept, Tampa FL (S)
Crosby-Hinds, Patricia, *Prof,* Antelope Valley College, Art Dept, Division of Fine Arts, Lancaster CA (S)
Crosman, Christopher B, *Dir,* William A Farnsworth, Museum, Rockland ME
Crosman, Christopher B, *Dir,* William A Farnsworth, Library, Rockland ME
Cross, Scott, *Archivist,* Oshkosh Public Museum & Library, Oshkosh WI
Crossman, Rodney, *Chair, Prof,* Indiana Wesleyan University, School of Arts & Humanities, Division of Art, Marion IN (S)
Crotchett, Cat, *Art Appreciation,* Western Michigan University, Frostic School of Art, Kalamazoo MI (S)
Croteau, Ginette, *Libr Supv,* University of Manitoba, Architecture & Fine Arts Library, Winnipeg MB
Croteau, Jeffrey, *Mgr Lib,* National Heritage Museum, Lexington MA
Croton, Lynn, *Dean Visual & Performing Arts,* C W Post Campus of Long Island University, School of Visual & Performing Arts, Brookville NY (S)
Crotteau, Katie, *Contact,* Center for the Visual Arts, Gallery, Wausau WI
Crotty, John, *Dir Library,* Union for Reformed Judaism, Synagogue Art & Architectural Library, New York NY
Crouse, Kate, *Cur Arts,* Channel Islands Maritime Museum, Oxnard CA
Crouse, Michael, *Chmn Art & Art History Dept,* University of Alabama in Huntsville, Dept of Art and Art History, Huntsville AL (S)
Crouther, Betty, *Assoc Prof,* University of Mississippi, Department of Art, University MS (S)
Crow, Amanda, *Educator for Early Childhood, Family & Youth Engagement,* Akron Art Museum, Akron OH
Crow, James, *Asst Prof,* Lincoln University, Dept Visual and Performing Arts, Jefferson City MO (S)
Crow, Lance, *Educ Dir,* Richmond Art Museum, Richmond IN
Crow, Lance, *Educ Dir,* Richmond Art Museum, Israel D. Edelman Library, Richmond IN
Crow, Paul, *Asst Prof,* Weber State University, Dept of Visual Arts, Ogden UT (S)
Crowe, Edith, *Art Reference Librn,* San Jose State University, Dr. Martin Luther King Jr. Library, San Jose CA
Crowe, Gregg, *Pres,* Art Institutes International at Portland, Portland OR
Crowe, John, *Chair Art Educ,* Massachusetts College of Art, Boston MA (S)
Crowell, Aron, *Arctic Studies Center Dir,* Anchorage Museum at Rasmuson Center, Anchorage AK
Crowell, Doug, *Pres,* Kings County Historical Society & Museum, Hampton NB
Crowell, Megan, *Sales Mgr,* Society for Contemporary Craft, Pittsburgh PA
Crowley, Evan, *Instr,* University of Evansville, Art Dept, Evansville IN (S)
Crowley, John, *Exhibs Dir & Cur,* City of Boston Arts & Culture, City Hall Galleries, Boston MA
Crowley, Michael, *Chief of User Servs,* City College of the City University of New York, Morris Raphael Cohen Library, New York NY
Crowley, Tony, *Chmn,* Grinnell College, Dept of Art, Grinnell IA (S)
Crown, Cathleen, *Develop Coordr,* Old Barracks Museum, Trenton NJ
Crown, Patricia, *Prof Emeritus,* University of Missouri - Columbia, Art History & Archaeology Dept, Columbia MO (S)
Crowston, Catherine, *Exec Dir & Chief Cur,* Art Gallery of Alberta, Edmonton AB
Croy, Mike, *Security Supv,* Historic Arkansas Museum, Little Rock AR
Croyle, Arthur, *Coordr Integrated Arts,* Iowa State University, Dept of Art & Design, Ames IA (S)
Crozier, Monica, *Research Resources Asst,* Whitney Museum of American Art, Frances Mulhall Achilles Library, New York NY
Crozier, Richard, *Studio Faculty,* University of Virginia, McIntire Dept of Art, Charlottesville VA (S)
Crum, Roger, *Assoc Prof,* University of Dayton, Visual Arts Dept, Dayton OH (S)
Crumby, F Todd, *Dir Archives & Libr,* Reynolda House Museum of American Art, Library, Winston-Salem NC
Crutchfield, Margo, *Sr Adjunct Cur,* Museum of Contemporary Art Cleveland, Cleveland OH
Cruz, Alfredo, *Chmn,* Our Lady of the Lake University, Dept of Art, San Antonio TX (S)
Cruz, Amanda, *Dir,* Phoenix Art Museum, Phoenix AZ
Cruz, Michele A, *Instr,* North Carolina Wesleyan College, Dept of Visual & Performing Arts, Rocky Mount NC (S)
Crystal, Kris, *Chief Revenue Officer,* Toledo Museum of Art, Toledo OH
Cubbage, John, *Prof Music,* University of Great Falls, Art Dept, Great Falls MT (S)
Cubina, Silvia Karmen, *Exec Dir & Chief Cur,* Bass Museum of Art, Miami Beach FL
Cudianat, Brian, *Spec Events Coordr & Vol Coordr,* University of Illinois at Urbana-Champaign, Spurlock Museum, Urbana IL
Cuesta, Maggy, *Dean Visual Arts,* New World School of the Arts, Gallery, Miami FL
Cuffaro, Daniel, *Dept Head Industrial Design,* Cleveland Institute of Art, Cleveland OH (S)
Cui, Jian, *Asst Prof,* State University of New York College at Oneonta, Dept of Art, Oneonta NY (S)
Cui, Shanshan, *Asst Prof,* Bridgewater State College, Art Dept, Bridgewater MA (S)
Culbert, Caroline, *Director of Digital Communication and Engagement,* Kenyon College, Gund Gallery, Gambier OH
Culbertson, Ben, *Coordr,* Hagerstown Junior College, Art Dept, Hagerstown MD (S)
Culbertson, Margaret, *Dir BB Library,* Museum of Fine Arts Houston, Bayou Bend Collection & Gardens, Houston TX
Culbertson, Robert, *Security,* Saint Joseph Museum, Inc., Saint Joseph MO

Culbreth, Kelvin, *Exhibits Coordr,* Arts Council of Fayetteville-Cumberland County, The Arts Center, Fayetteville NC
Culen, Lubos, *Curator,* Vernon Public Art Gallery, Vernon BC
Cullen, Cecily, *Mng Dir & Cur,* Metropolitan State University of Denver, Center for Visual Art, Denver CO
Cullen, Charles, *Pres & CEO,* Historical Society of Pennsylvania, Philadelphia PA
Cullen, Deborah, *Dir & Chief Cur,* Columbia University, Miriam & Ira D Wallach Art Gallery, New York NY
Cullen, Kevin M, *Deputy Dir,* Neville Public Museum of Brown County, Green Bay WI
Culligan, Jenine, *Sr Cur,* Huntington Museum of Art, Huntington WV
Cullimore, Cheryl, *Mus Properties VChmn,* The National Society of The Colonial Dames of America in the State of New Hampshire, Moffatt-Ladd House & Garden, Portsmouth NH
Cullimore, Joanne, *Asst Prof,* Dominican College of San Rafael, Art Dept, San Rafael CA (S)
Cullinan, Deborah, *CEO,* Yerba Buena Center for the Arts, San Francisco CA
Cullivan, Lynn, *Mgmt Asst,* San Francisco Maritime National Historical Park, Maritime Museum, San Francisco CA
Cullum, Marguerite, *Head Librn,* Crazy Horse Memorial, Indian Museum of North America, Native American Educational & Cultural Center & Crazy Horse Memorial Library (Reference), Crazy Horse SD
Culp, Patti, *VPres & Hostess,* Alton Museum of History & Art, Inc, Alton IL
Culver, Michael, *Dir & Cur,* Ogunquit Museum of American Art, Reference Library, Ogunquit ME
Culver, Michael, *Dir & Cur,* Ogunquit Museum of American Art, Ogunquit ME
Cumbo, Laurie, *Exec Dir,* MoCADA - The Museum of Contemporary African Diasporan Arts, Brooklyn NY
Cumming, Doug, *Prof,* University of Wisconsin-Stout, Dept of Art & Design, Menomonie WI (S)
Cummings, Allison, *Mgr Civic Art Coll,* San Francisco City & County Arts Commission, San Francisco CA
Cummings, Alyson Amendola, *Exec Dir,* Erie County Historical Society, Erie PA
Cummings, Cathleen, *Assoc Prof,* University of Alabama at Birmingham, Dept of Art & Art History, Birmingham AL (S)
Cummings, DeAnna, *CEO,* Juxtaposition Arts, Minneapolis MN
Cummings, Richard, *Assoc Prof,* College of the Ozarks, Dept of Art, Point Lookout MO (S)
Cummings, Roger, *Chief Cultural Producter,* Juxtaposition Arts, Minneapolis MN
Cummings, Sandy, *Dir Communs,* High Desert Museum, Bend OR
Cummings, Twyla, *Sr Assoc Dean,* Rochester Institute of Technology, College of Imaging Arts & Sciences, Rochester NY (S)
Cummins, Joan, *Lisa & Bernard Selz Sr Cur Asian Art,* Brooklyn Museum, Brooklyn NY
Cundiff, Linda, *Prof of Art,* Campbellsville University, Art & Design Department, Campbellsville KY (S)
Cunningham, Ben J, *Asst Prof 2D Design & Drawing,* Millersville University, Dept of Art & Design, Millersville PA (S)
Cunningham, Dennis, *Instr,* Marylhurst University, Art Dept, Marylhurst OR (S)
Cunningham, John, *Pres,* Cape Ann Museum, Gloucester MA
Cunningham, Laura, *Progs & Colls Coordr,* Nichols House Museum, Inc, Boston MA
Cunningham, Richard, *Instr,* North Central Michigan College, Art Dept, Petoskey MI (S)
Cunningham, Stephanie, *Prof Art, Graphic Design,* Florida Atlantic University, D F Schmidt College of Arts & Letters Dept of Visual Arts & Art History, Boca Raton FL (S)
Cunningham-Kruppa, Ellen, *Assoc Dir,* University of Texas at Austin, Harry Ransom Humanities Research Center, Austin TX
Cupo, Steven, *Treas,* Culture Capital, Washington DC
Curley, John J, *Asst Prof,* Wake Forest University, Dept of Art, Winston-Salem NC (S)
Curnow, Kathy, *Assoc Prof,* Cleveland State University, Art Dept, Cleveland OH (S)
Curran, Annabelle, *Archivist,* Moore College of Art & Design, Library, Philadelphia PA
Curran, Brian, *Assoc Prof,* Pennsylvania State University, University Park, Dept of Art History, University Park PA (S)
Curran, Judy, *Pres,* Klein Museum, Mobridge SD
Curran, Kit, *Executive Director,* Salisbury House Foundation, Salisbury House and Garden, Des Moines IA
Curran, Mary, *Asst to Dir,* Art Complex Museum, Carl A Weyerhaeuser Library, Duxbury MA
Curran-Gawron, Marguerite, *Communs, Pub Rels & Vol Coordr,* Muskegon Museum of Art Foundation, Muskegon Museum of Art, Muskegon MI
Curren, Kerry, *Registrar,* Maine Photographic Workshops, The International T.V. & Film Workshops & Rockport College, Rockport ME (S)
Currie Jones, Amanda, *Mem & Develop Assoc,* Second Street Gallery, Charlottesville VA
Currie, Doug, *VPres Natural History,* Royal Ontario Museum, Toronto ON
Currier, Richard, *Pres,* Willard House & Clock Museum, Inc, North Grafton MA
Currier, Tara, *Pub Rels,* Booth Western Art Museum, Cartersville GA
Curry, Alexis, *Head Librn,* Los Angeles County Museum of Art, Allan C Balch Art Research Library, Los Angeles CA
Curry, De Nice, *Admin Asst,* WaterWorks Art Museum, Miles City MT
Curry, Michael P, *Dir,* City of Hampton, Hampton Arts Commission, Hampton VA
Curry-Evans, Kim, *Pub Art Coordr,* City of Raleigh Arts Commission, Miriam Preston Block Gallery, Raleigh NC
Curt, Lisa, *Asst Dir Colls,* Salt Lake City Public Library, Nonfiction & Audiovisual Dept & Gallery at Library Square, Salt Lake City UT
Curtin, Christopher, *Asst Prof,* Appalachian State University, Dept of Art, Boone NC (S)
Curtin, Donna, *Dir & Librn,* Pilgrim Society, Pilgrim Hall Museum, Plymouth MA
Curtin, Donna, *Exec Dir,* Plymouth Antiquarian Society, Plymouth MA
Curtin, Nancy, *Dir,* Port Washington Public Library, Port Washington NY
Curtis, Brian, *Assoc Prof,* University of Miami, Dept of Art & Art History, Coral Gables FL (S)
Curtis, Chad, *Assoc Dean & Grad Prog Dir,* Temple University, Tyler School of Art, Philadelphia PA (S)
Curtis, David, *Pres,* Rockport Art Association, Rockport MA
Curtis, Julie, *Assoc Prof,* Northeastern University, Dept of Art & Architecture, Boston MA (S)
Curtis, Kerry, *Visual Arts Dir,* Gunnison Arts Center, Gunnison CO
Curtis, Marvin, *Dean,* Indiana University South Bend, Fine Arts Dept, South Bend IN (S)
Curtis, Winifred, *Dir,* Harcum College, Fashion Design, Bryn Mawr PA (S)
Curtright, Drew, *Designer,* Noyes Art Gallery, Lincoln NE
Cusack, Mary, *Dean,* Mott Community College, Fine Arts & Social Sciences Division, Flint MI (S)
Cusack, Mary, *Pres,* Lansing Art Gallery, Lansing MI
Cuscaden, Rebecca, *Cur Visual Arts,* Dairy Arts Center, Boulder CO
Cuscadew, Rebecca, *Visual Art Cur,* Dairy Arts Center, Boulder CO
Cushing, Al, *Chief Exec Officer,* Yukon Arts Centre Gallery, Whitehorse YT
Cushing, Stanley, *Ann C and David J Brober Curator of Rare Books, Manuscripts & Maps,* Boston Athenaeum, Boston MA
Cushing-Davis, Lisa, *Dir,* Cuneo Mansion & Gardens, Vernon Hills IL
Cushman, Brad, *Gallery Cur,* University of Arkansas at Little Rock, Art Library and Galleries, Little Rock AR
Cushman, Brad, *Gallery Dir,* University of Arkansas at Little Rock, Art Galleries, Little Rock AR
Cushner, Steven, *Instr,* American University, Dept of Art, New York NY (S)
Cushnie, John Edward, *Exec Dir,* Organization for the Development of Artists, Gallery Connexion, Fredericton NB
Custance, Jayne, *Dir Bus Opers,* Royal Alberta Museum, Royal Alberta Museum, Edmonton AB
Cuthbert, Sara, *Vis Serv,* City of Woodstock, Woodstock Art Gallery, Woodstock ON
Cutler, Anthony, *Evan Pugh Prof,* Pennsylvania State University, University Park, Dept of Art History, University Park PA (S)
Cutler, Christian H, *Gallery Dir,* University of Central Missouri, Gallery of Art & Design, Warrensburg MO
Cutler, Judy AG, *Dir,* American Civilization Foundation, National Museum of American Illustration, Newport RI
Cutler, Laurence S, *Chmn,* American Civilization Foundation, National Museum of American Illustration, Newport RI
Cutler-Lake, Karina, *Assoc Prof,* University of Wisconsin Oshkosh, Dept of Art, Oshkosh WI (S)
Cutrona, Robert, *Registrar,* Burchfield Penney Art Center, Buffalo NY
Cyhers Wright, Jeffrey, *Creative Projects Resident,* eMediaLoft.org, New York NY
Cypriano, David, *Asst Educ Specialist,* King Kamehameha V Judiciary History Center, Honolulu HI
Cyril, Jasmin, *Assoc Prof,* Benedict College, School of Humanities, Arts & Social Sciences, Columbia SC (S)
Czajkowski, Jennifer, *Dir Educ,* Detroit Institute of Arts, Detroit MI
Czaplinski, Lane, *Dir Performing Arts,* Ohio State University, Wexner Center for the Arts, Columbus OH
Czarnecki, Emma-Lou, *Treas,* Historical Society of Bloomfield, Bloomfield NJ
Czechowski, Susan, *Asst Prof,* Western Illinois University, Department of Art, Macomb IL (S)
Czerkowicz, John, *Chmn,* Montclair State University, Fine Arts Dept, Montclair NJ (S)
Czichos, C L, *Dir Video,* Pioneer Town, Pioneer Museum of Western Art, Wimberley TX
Czichos, Raymond L, *Dir,* Pioneer Town, Pioneer Museum of Western Art, Wimberley TX
Czubinski, Grant, *Registrar,* Anacostia Community Museum, Smithsonian Institution, Washington DC
D'Agostino, Elizabeth, *Mng Dir,* Toronto School of Art, Toronto ON (S)
D'Agostino, Rachel, *Cur Printed Books,* Library Company of Philadelphia, Philadelphia PA
D'Alessandro, Laura, *Head of Conservation,* University of Chicago, Oriental Institute, Chicago IL
D'Alessandro, Michael, *Exec Dir,* Northwind Arts Center, Port Townsend WA
D'Amato, Laura, *Dir Develop,* Racine Art Museum, Racine WI
D'Ambra, Eve, *Prof,* Vassar College, Art Dept, Poughkeepsie NY (S)
D'Ambrosio, Anna T, *Dir & Chief Cur,* Munson-Williams-Proctor Arts Institute, Museum of Art, Utica NY
D'Ambrosio, Paul, *Pres,* New York State Historical Association, Research Library, Cooperstown NY
D'Anbrosio, Paul S, *Pres & CEO,* New York State Historical Association, Fenimore Art Museum, Cooperstown NY
D'Angelo, Starlyn, *Cur,* Shaker Museum & Library, Old Chatham NY
D'Arc, James, *Cur Arts, Communs & Film,* Brigham Young University, Harold B Lee Library, Provo UT
Da Costa Nunes, Jadviga, *Chmn,* Muhlenberg College, Dept of Art, Allentown PA (S)

da Costa, Beatriz, *Assoc Prof Interactive Installation, & Programming,* University of California, Irvine, Studio Art Dept, Irvine CA (S)
Dabakis, Melissa, *Prof,* Kenyon College, Art Dept, Gambier OH (S)
Dabash, Adrian G, *Assoc Prof,* Providence College, Art & Art History Dept, Providence RI (S)
Dabb, Jean Ann, *Chair & Assoc Prof,* University of Mary Washington, Dept of Art & Art History, Fredericksburg VA (S)
Dablow, Dean, *Dir,* Louisiana Tech, School of Art, Ruston LA (S)
Dabrowski, Gina, *Instr,* North Hennepin Community College, Art Dept, Brooklyn Park MN (S)
Dackerman, Susan, *Dir,* Stanford University, Cantor Arts Center at Stanford University, Stanford CA
Daddona, Laurie, *Instr,* Wayne Art Center, Wayne PA (S)
Daderko, Dean, *Cur,* Contemporary Arts Museum Houston, Houston TX
Dagdigian, Jamie, *Graphics Instr,* Monterey Peninsula College, Art Dept/Art Gallery, Monterey CA (S)
Dagen, Michael, *Director,* Nemeth Art Center, Park Rapids MN
Dahl, Barrett, *Director,* Robert Louis Stevenson Museum, Museum, Saint Helena CA
Dahlgren, De, *Resource Devel Dir,* Fort Collins Museum of Art, Inc, Fort Collins CO
Dahm, Kristi, *Assoc Paper Conservator,* The Art Institute of Chicago, Dept of Prints & Drawings, Chicago IL
Dahms, David, *Gallery Technician,* Mount Saint Vincent University, MSVU Art Gallery, Halifax NS
Dahms, Rose, *Treas,* Cumberland Art Society Inc, Cookeville Art Gallery, Cookeville TN
Dai-Yu, Han, *Asst Prof,* Loyola Marymount University, Dept of Art & Art History, Los Angeles CA (S)
Daigle-Orians, Neil, *Visual Arts Coordr,* Real Art Ways (RAW), Hartford CT
Dailey, Velma, *Dir,* College of Mount Saint Joseph, Studio San Giuseppe, Cincinnati OH
Dainty, Linda, *Dir Art Dept,* Southwestern Community College, Art Dept, Creston IA (S)
Daix Westcoat, Bonna, *Assoc Prof,* Emory University, Art History Dept, Atlanta GA (S)
Dake, Jason, *Educ Cur,* Northwestern Michigan College, Dennos Museum Center, Traverse City MI
Dakwar, Mohammad, *Dean,* Milwaukee Area Technical College, School of Media & Creative Arts, Milwaukee WI (S)
Dal Poggetto, Newton, *VPres,* Sonoma Valley Historical Society, Depot Park Museum, Sonoma CA
Dale, Alison, *Assoc Prof,* Seton Hall University, College of Arts & Sciences, South Orange NJ (S)
Dale, Kerstin, *Asst Prof,* Del Mar College, Art Dept, Corpus Christi TX (S)
Dale, Maria Saffiotti, *Cur Paintings, Sculpture & Decorative Arts,* University of Wisconsin-Madison, Chazen Museum of Art, Madison WI
Dale, Thomas E A, *Prof,* University of Wisconsin, Madison, Dept of Art History, Madison WI (S)
Daley, Ginny, *Archivist,* Southern Highland Craft Guild, Folk Art Center, Asheville NC
Daley, Sheila, *Asst Cur/Archivist,* Noah Webster House, Inc, Noah Webster House & West Hartford Historical Society, West Hartford CT
Dalkey, F, *Instr,* Sacramento City College, Art Dept, Sacramento CA (S)
Dallow, Jessica, *Assoc Prof,* University of Alabama at Birmingham, Dept of Art & Art History, Birmingham AL (S)
Dally, Lynn, *Assoc Prof & Coordr Graphic Commun,* Tarrant County College, Art Dept, Hurst TX (S)
Dalton, Dennis, *Asst Prof,* University of Southern Colorado, Dept of Art, Pueblo CO (S)
Dalton, Laurie, *Dir/Cur,* Acadia University Art Gallery, Wolfville NS
Dalton, Laurie, *Gallery Dir & Cur,* Acadia University, Faculty of Arts, Wolfville NS (S)
Dalton, Stephanie, *VPres Activities,* DuPage Art League School & Gallery, Wheaton IL
Daly, Amy, *Assoc Prof,* Azusa Pacific University, College of Music & the Arts, Dept of Art & Design, Azusa CA (S)
Daly, Brenda, *Vol Coordr,* Montgomery Museum of Fine Arts, Montgomery AL
Daly, David, *Coll Mgr,* Longfellow National Historic Site, Longfellow House - Washington's Headquarters, Cambridge MA
Daly, Rachel, *Visual Arts Dir,* Artistry, Inez Greenberg Gallery, Bloomington MN
Daly, Robert A., *Chmn Bd Dirs,* American Film Institute (AFI), Los Angeles CA (S)
Daly, Terri, *Pub Rels,* Mount Vernon Hotel Museum & Garden, New York NY
Daly, Thomas, *Cur Educ,* Norman Rockwell Museum, Stockbridge MA
Dalzell, Justin, *Tech Asst,* North Dakota Museum of Art, Grand Forks ND
Damast, Rafael, *Exhibs Prog Mgr & Cur,* Taller Puertorriqueno Inc, Lorenzo Homar Gallery, Philadelphia PA
Dambach, Cathy, *Ceramics,* Henry Ford Community College, McKenzie Fine Art Ctr, Dearborn MI (S)
Damer, Jack, *Prof,* University of Wisconsin, Madison, Dept of Art, Madison WI (S)
Damian, Carol, *Prof Dir, Mus Studies,* Florida International University, School of Art & Art History, Miami FL (S)
Damiani, Christopher, *Dir Public Progs,* Historical Society of Pennsylvania, Philadelphia PA
Damkoehler, David, *Prof,* University of Wisconsin-Green Bay, Arts Dept, Green Bay WI (S)
Damm, Nancy, *Information Resources Supv,* University of Michigan, Fine Arts Library, Ann Arbor MI
Damon, Erin, *Registrar,* Portland Museum of Art, Portland ME
Damon, William, *Artist & Owner,* Gallery 4, Ltd, Fargo ND
Dampier, Elizabeth, *Dir,* Gaston County Museum of Art & History, Dallas NC
Damron, J, *Asst Prof,* Sierra Nevada College, Fine Arts Dept, Incline Village NV (S)
Dana, Robin, *Gallery Coordr,* University of Georgia, Franklin College of Arts & Sciences, Lamar Dodd School of Art, Athens GA (S)
Dane, Kasarian, *Asst Prof,* St Lawrence University, Dept of Fine Arts, Canton NY (S)
Danford, Gerald, *VPres,* Fort Morgan Heritage Foundation, Fort Morgan CO
Daniel, Amanda, *Asst Cur,* Yellowstone Art Museum, Billings MT
Daniel, Clifton, *Interim Dean,* Cathedral of Saint John the Divine, New York NY
Daniel, Dwayne, *Asst Prof,* Central State University, Dept of Art, Wilberforce OH (S)
Daniel, Jenni, *Dir Develop,* New Orleans Museum of Art, New Orleans LA
Daniel, Mike, *Instr,* Long Beach City College, Art & Photography Dept, Long Beach CA (S)
Daniel, Vesta, *Assoc Prof,* Ohio State University, Dept of Art Education, Columbus OH (S)
Daniels, Brad, *Instructor,* Concordia University, Art and Design Department, Saint Paul MN (S)
Daniels, Dawn, *Program Director,* The Noble Maritime Collection, Staten Island NY
Daniels, Diane, *Exec Dir,* Historical Society of Kent County, Chestertown MD
Daniels, Eric, *Chmn Interior Design,* Fashion Institute of Technology, School of Art & Design, New York NY (S)
Daniels, Eric, *Chmn Interior Design,* Fashion Institute of Technology, School of Art & Design, New York NY (S)
Daniels, Eve, *Cur & Registrar,* Roberson Museum & Science Center, Binghamton NY
Daniels, Michelle, *Instructor,* Concordia University, Art and Design Department, Saint Paul MN (S)
Daniels, Ray, *Instr,* Lamar University, Art Dept, Beaumont TX (S)
Daniels, Risa, *Exhibs & Progs Mgr,* FLAG Art Foundation, New York NY
Danielson, Deborah, *Prof,* Siena Heights University, Studio Angelico-Art Dept, Adrian MI (S)
Danielson, Sigrid, *Asst Prof,* Grand Valley State University, Art & Design Dept, Allendale MI (S)
Daniggelis, Chris, *Asst Prof,* University of Missouri - Columbia, Dept of Art, Columbia MO (S)
Dankel, Jason, *Preparator,* The Robert McLaughlin Gallery, Oshawa ON
Dankert, Rachel, *Project Coord,* Folger Shakespeare, Washington DC
Danko, Selina, *Education Dir,* North Central Washington Museum, Wenatchee Valley Museum & Cultural Center, Wenatchee WA
Dannahower, Robin, *Mktg Dir,* A.E. Backus Museum & Gallery, Fort Pierce FL
Danner, Anita, *Treas,* Switzerland County Historical Society Inc, Switzerland County Historical Museum, Vevay IN
Danner, Anita, *Treas,* Switzerland County Historical Society Inc, Life on the Ohio: River History Museum, Vevay IN
Dansberger, Dorothy, *Dir Finance & Opers,* Museum of Art - Deland FL, Inc, Deland FL
Dantzic, Cynthia, *Prof,* Long Island University, Brooklyn Campus, Art Dept, Brooklyn NY (S)
Dantzic, Cynthia, *VPres,* Society of Scribes, Ltd, New York NY
Danziger, Maria, *Exec Dir,* The Art School at Old Church, Demarest NJ (S)
Dao, Jennifer, *Mktg/Design Assoc,* Triton Museum of Art, Santa Clara CA
Darbandi, Shiva, *Library Dir,* Maine College of Art, Joanne Waxman Library, Portland ME
Dargo Caplan, Jessica, *Dir Pub Progs & Engagement,* Koffler Center of the Arts, Toronto ON (S)
Darish, Patricia, *Asst Prof,* University of Kansas, Kress Foundation Dept of Art History, Lawrence KS (S)
Darland, Carmen, *Exec Dir,* Quad City Arts Inc, Rock Island IL
Darley, Claire, *Chmn Foundation Dept,* Art Academy of Cincinnati, Cincinnati OH (S)
Darling Pigat, Heather, *Coll Mgr,* University of Toronto, Art Centre, Toronto ON
Darling, Michael, *James W Alsdorf Chief Cur,* Museum of Contemporary Art Chicago, Chicago IL
Darlington, Cathy, *Instr,* Wayne Art Center, Wayne PA (S)
Darr, Alan, *Sr Cur European Paintings, Sculpture & Decorative Arts,* Detroit Institute of Arts, Detroit MI
Darr, William, *Vol Coordr,* Bellingrath Gardens & Home, Theodore AL
Darroch, Michael, *Undergrad Coordr,* University of Windsor, School of Creative Arts, Windsor ON (S)
Darrow, Deb, *Exec Dir,* Rosemount Museum, Inc, Pueblo CO
Dart, Donald, *Sr VPres Fin Corp Srvc,* Alberta College of Art & Design, Calgary AB (S)
Darway, Chris, *Instr,* Wayne Art Center, Wayne PA (S)
Dasch Houuhton, Rowena, *Instr,* Southwestern University, Sarofim School of Fine Art, Dept of Art & Art History, Georgetown TX (S)
Daschle, Thomas A, *VChmn,* United States Senate Commission on Art, Washington DC
Dasher, Glenn, *Prof,* University of Alabama in Huntsville, Dept of Art and Art History, Huntsville AL (S)
Dashnaw, Tom, *Mus Aide,* Village of Potsdam, Potsdam Public Museum, Potsdam NY
Daskam, Rick, *Pres Oil,* Hudson Valley Art Association, Brooklyn NY
Dass, Carol, *Instr Visual Arts,* University of Colorado-Colorado Springs, Visual & Performing Arts Dept (VAPA), Colorado Springs CO (S)
Dass, Dean, *Studio Faculty,* University of Virginia, McIntire Dept of Art, Charlottesville VA (S)
Dasti, Haroon, *Asst. Operations Manager,* 18th Street Arts Complex, Santa Monica CA
Daubert, Debra, *Cur,* Oshkosh Public Museum & Library, Oshkosh WI

Daugherty, John, *Clinical Asst Prof,* University of Illinois at Chicago, Biomedical Visualization, Chicago IL (S)

Daugherty, Michael, *Dir,* Louisiana State University, School of Art, Baton Rouge LA (S)

Dauphin, Sylvie, *Cur, Head of Colls,* The Stewart Museum, Library, Montreal QC

Dauphin, Sylvie, *Cur, Head of Colls,* The Stewart Museum, Montreal QC

Dauphinee, Margo, *Exec Dir,* Nova Scotia Association of Architects, Halifax NS

Davalos, Christopher, *Co-Exec Dir,* Morris-Jumel Mansion, Inc, New York NY

Dave, Alfonzo, *VPres,* Museum of African American Art, Los Angeles CA

Davenny, Ward, *Assoc Prof,* Dickinson College, Dept of Art & Art History, Carlisle PA (S)

Davi, Susan A, *Subject Librn (Art & Art History),* University of Delaware, Morris Library, Newark DE

David, Lynn, *Dir Pub Rels,* Maysville, Kentucky Gateway Museum Center, Maysville KY

David, Michael, *Chair Fine Arts,* Lesley University, College of Art & Design, Cambridge MA (S)

David, Roy, *Exec Dir,* Farmington Valley Arts Center, Avon CT

David-Weill, Michel, *Cur in Charge,* The Metropolitan Museum of Art, The Met Cloisters, New York NY

Davidhazy, Andrew, *Chmn Imaging & Photographic Technology,* Rochester Institute of Technology, School of Photographic Arts & Sciences, Rochester NY (S)

Davidoff, Naomi, *Prog Mgr & Registry Coordr,* Maryland Art Place, Baltimore MD

Davidowitz, Anthony, *Dir Opers,* Storm King Art Center, New Windsor NY

Davidson, Amanda, *Communs & Mktg Mgr,* Headlands Center for the Arts, Sausalito CA

Davidson, Andrea, *Dir & Librn,* The Temple-Tifereth Israel, Lee & Dolores Hartzmark Library, Beachwood OH

Davidson, Ben, *Dir,* Americans for the Arts, Library, New York NY

Davidson, Conrad, *Chmn Div Humanities,* Minot State University, Dept of Art, Division of Humanities, Minot ND (S)

Davidson, Deborah, *Dir & Cur,* Suffolk University, Gallery, Boston MA

Davidson, Jacqueline, *Dir,* Charles City Arts Center, Charles City IA

Davidson, Jeanne, *Head of Pub Servs,* South Dakota State University, Hilton M. Briggs Library, Brookings SD

Davidson, Joshua M, *Sr Rabbi,* Congregation Emanu-El, Bernard Judaica Museum, New York NY

Davidson, Julie, *Chief Devel Officer,* International Center of Photography, Museum, New York NY

Davidson, Richard, *Chmn Trustees,* Longfellow's Wayside Inn Museum, Sudbury MA

Davidson, Susan, *Sr Cur Colls & Exhibs,* Solomon R Guggenheim Museum, New York NY

Davidson, Thomas E, *Curatorial Servs Mgr,* Jamestown-Yorktown Foundation, Jamestown Settlement, Williamsburg VA

Davidson, Vanessa, *Cur Latin American Art,* Phoenix Art Museum, Phoenix AZ

Davies, Caroline, *Pres,* Sunbury Shores Arts & Nature Centre, Inc, Gallery, Saint Andrews NB

Davies, Harry, *Chmn,* Adelphi University, Dept of Art & Art History, Garden City NY (S)

Davies, Hugh M, *Dir,* Museum of Contemporary Art, San Diego, Geisel Library, La Jolla CA

Davies, Hugh M, *Dir Expansion & Capital Campaign,* Museum of Contemporary Art San Diego, San Diego CA

Davies, Hugh, *David C Copley Dir,* Museum of Contemporary Art San Diego, La Jolla CA

Davies, Irene, *Asst to Dir,* Southern Methodist University, Meadows Museum, Dallas TX

Davies, Leigh, *Chmn & Dir Creative Arts,* Russell Sage College, Visual & Performing Arts Dept, Troy NY (S)

Davies, Melissa, *Educ,* Colgate University, Picker Art Gallery, Hamilton NY

Davies, Sandy, *Publicity,* Redlands Art Association, Redlands Art Association Gallery & Art Center, Redlands CA

Davini, Mark, *Visual Com Instr,* Western Wisconsin Technical College, Graphics Division, La Crosse WI (S)

Davis Brown, Susan, *Contact,* Alabama Southern Community College, Art Dept, Monroeville AL (S)

Davis, Adria Crossen, *Coll Mgr,* California State University, Chico, Janet Turner Print Museum, CSU, Chicago, Chico CA

Davis, Amanda, *Exec Dir,* Star-Spangled Banner Flag House Association, Flag House & 1812 Museum, Baltimore MD

Davis, Arcenia, *Prof,* Winston-Salem State University, Art Dept, Winston-Salem NC (S)

Davis, Art, *Head Dept,* Grace College, Dept of Art, Winona Lake IN (S)

Davis, Ashlyn, *Executive Director,* Houston Center For Photography, Houston TX

Davis, Bill, *Asst Prof,* Shippensburg University, Art Dept, Shippensburg PA (S)

Davis, Bill, *Photo/Intermedia,* Western Michigan University, Frostic School of Art, Kalamazoo MI (S)

Davis, Blair, *PT Instr,* Middle Georgia State University, College of Arts & Sciences, Media, Culture & the Arts, Cochran GA (S)

Davis, Brandon, *Bd Pres,* George A Spiva, Joplin MO

Davis, Bruce, *Cur,* Craigdarroch Castle Historical Museum Society, Victoria BC

Davis, Carla, *Mktg Dir,* Akron-Summit County Public Library, Fine Arts Division, Akron OH

Davis, Carol, *Dir Educ,* Edna Hibel Art Foundation, Hibel Museum Gallery, Jupiter FL

Davis, Carol, *Dir Educ,* Edna Hibel Art Foundation, Hibel Museum of Art, Jupiter FL

Davis, Charles, *Asst Prof Art,* Mississippi Valley State University, Fine Arts Dept, Itta Bena MS (S)

Davis, Christie, *Prog Dir,* Lannan Foundation, Santa Fe NM

Davis, Danita, *Visual Resource Specialist,* Indiana University - Purdue University at Indianapolis, Herron School of Art Library, Indianapolis IN

Davis, Debbie, *Bus & Events Mgr,* Mount Holyoke College, Art Museum, South Hadley MA

Davis, Don, *Assoc Prof,* East Tennessee State University, College of Arts and Sciences, Dept of Art & Design, Johnson City TN (S)

Davis, Doreen, *Admin Dir,* Santa Cruz Art League, Center for the Arts, Santa Cruz CA

Davis, Dustin P, *Chair,* Frostburg State University, The Stephanie Ann Roper Gallery, Frostburg MD

Davis, Dustin P, *Head Dept,* Frostburg State University, Dept of Visual Arts, Frostburg MD (S)

Davis, E Holmes, *Treas,* Halifax Historical Society, Inc, Halifax Historical Museum, Daytona Beach FL

Davis, Eli, *Assoc Prof,* Illinois Central College, Arts & Communication Dept, East Peoria IL (S)

Davis, Gainor B, *Pres & CEO,* Western Reserve Historical Society, Cleveland OH

Davis, George O, *Exec Dir,* California African-American Museum, Research Library, Los Angeles CA

Davis, George, *Exec Dir,* California African-American Museum, Los Angeles CA

Davis, Glenn Herbert, *Asst Prof, Photog,* University of Tulsa, School of Art, Tulsa OK (S)

Davis, Gordon, *Mem Bd Dir,* Hatch-Billops Collection, Inc, New York NY

Davis, Gordon, *Publicity,* Wiscasset, Waterville & Farmington Railway Museum (WW&F), Alna ME

Davis, Jacqueline Z, *Dir,* The New York Public Library, The New York Public Library for the Performing Arts, New York NY

Davis, James, *Asst Prof,* Mississippi State University, Dept of Art, Starville MS (S)

Davis, Jeff, *Assoc Prof,* Texas State University - San Marcos, Dept of Art and Design, San Marcos TX (S)

Davis, Jeff, *Graphic Design,* Art Institute of Pittsburgh, Pittsburgh PA (S)

Davis, Jeremiah, *Artistic Dir,* Oklahoma Contemporary Arts Center, Oklahoma City OK

Davis, John, *Exec Dir,* Lanesboro Arts Center, Lanesboro MN

Davis, John, *Prof,* Smith College, Art Dept, Northampton MA (S)

Davis, John, *Provost & Under Secy for Museums Educ & Research,* Smithsonian Institution, Smithsonian Institution Building (The Castle), Washington DC

Davis, Julie, *Asst Prof,* Oberlin College, Dept of Art, Oberlin OH (S)

Davis, Kasey, *Gallery Asst,* The Art Spirit Gallery, Coeur D Alene ID

Davis, Kate, *Dir,* University of Regina, MacKenzie Art Gallery Resource Centre, Regina SK

Davis, Katherine M, *VPres,* Liberty Hall Historic Site, Library, Frankfort KY

Davis, Keahe, *Educ Specialist,* King Kamehameha V Judiciary History Center, Honolulu HI

Davis, Larry, *Faculty Coordr Fine Arts,* Florida Community College at Jacksonville, South Campus, Art Dept, Jacksonville FL (S)

Davis, Lauren, *Cur,* West Baton Rouge Parish, West Baton Rouge Museum, Port Allen LA

Davis, Lawrence A, *Chancellor,* University of Arkansas at Pine Bluff, Art Dept, Pine Bluff AR (S)

Davis, Lee Baxter, *Instr Printmaking,* Texas A&M University Commerce, Dept of Art, Commerce TX (S)

Davis, Lilly, *Develop Mgr,* UMLAUF Sculpture Garden & Museum, Austin TX

Davis, Lisa, *Prog & Events Coordr,* University of California, Berkeley, The Magnes Collection of Jewish Art & Life, Berkeley CA

Davis, Lynn, *Admin Asst,* Patrick Henry, Red Hill National Memorial, Brookneal VA

Davis, Marsh, *Pres,* Indiana Landmarks, Information Center Library, Indianapolis IN

Davis, Marsh, *Pres,* Indiana Landmarks, Morris-Butler House, Indianapolis IN

Davis, Meg, *Dir & Cur,* Gem County Historical Society and Museum, Gem County Historical Village Museum, Emmett ID

Davis, Meredith, *Assoc Prof Art History,* Ramapo College of New Jersey, School of Contemporary Arts, Mahwah NJ (S)

Davis, Michael, *Architecture,* Mount Holyoke College, Art Dept, South Hadley MA (S)

Davis, Paula, *Art Education Director,* Longview Museum of Fine Art, Longview TX

Davis, Rebecca, *Asst Prof,* Mississippi State University, Dept of Art, Starville MS (S)

Davis, Rhonda, *Instr,* Tulsa Community College, Center for Creativity, Tulsa OK (S)

Davis, Richard, *Assoc Prof,* Monmouth University, Dept of Art & Design, West Long Branch NJ (S)

Davis, Richard, *Chmn,* Potomac State College, Dept of Art, Keyser WV (S)

Davis, Richard, *Prof Sculpture,* University of North Texas, College of Visual Arts & Design, Denton TX (S)

Davis, Robert, *Dir Develop,* Winterthur Museum, Winterthur Museum, Garden & Library, Winterthur DE

Davis, Rodrecas, *Assoc Prof,* Grambling State University, Art Dept, Grambling LA (S)

Davis, Sandy, *Registrar,* Santa Barbara Museum of Art, Library, Santa Barbara CA

Davis, Sasha, *Cur Colls,* The Renee & Chaim Gross Foundation, Chaim Gross Studio, New York NY

Davis, Shane, *Bldg & Tech Opers Asst,* University of Minnesota, Frederick R Weisman Art Museum, Minneapolis MN

Davis, Sharon, *Librn,* Greenville College, The Richard W Bock Sculpture Collection & Art Library, Greenville IL

Davis, Sonya, *Exec Dir,* Pensacola Museum of Art, Pensacola FL

Davis, Stewart D, *Pres,* Rochester Contemporary, Art Center, Rochester NY

Davis, Suzanne, *Conservator,* University of Michigan, Kelsey Museum of Archaeology, Ann Arbor MI
Davis, Tracey, *Account,* Joseph Bellows Gallery, La Jolla CA
Davis, William J, *Dir,* MacArthur Memorial, Norfolk VA
Davis, Zina, *Dir,* University of Hartford, Joseloff Gallery, West Hartford CT
Davis-Rosenbaum, Kate, *Instr,* Midway College, Art Dept, Midway KY (S)
Davis-Rosenbaum, Steve, *Chmn,* Midway College, Art Dept, Midway KY (S)
Davish, Peggy, *Adminr,* Middletown Arts Center, Library, Middletown OH
Davison, Claudine, *Dir Baltimore Jewish Film Festival,* Norman and Sarah Brown Art Gallery, Baltimore MD
Davison, Darlene, *Assoc Prof & Prog Dir, Interior Design,* Maryville University of Saint Louis, Art & Design Program, Saint Louis MO (S)
Davison, Liane, *Dir,* Surrey Art Gallery, Surrey BC
Davison, Liane, *Dir,* Surrey Art Gallery, Library, Surrey BC
Davison, Mark, *Chmn,* Clinton Community College, Art Dept, Plattsburgh NY (S)
Davison, Nancy R, *Treas,* Barn Gallery, Ogunquit ME
Davison, Susan, *VPres Mktg & Develop,* Springfield Museums, Connecticut Valley Historical Society,
Davson, Victor, *Exec Dir,* Aljira Center for Contemporary Art, Newark NJ
Davy, Mark, *Preparator,* Pacific Grove Art Center, Pacific Grove CA
Dawes, Gordon, *Special Collections,* Brigham Young University, Harold B Lee Library, Provo UT
Dawes, John, *Asst Prof,* University of the Incarnate Word, Art Dept, San Antonio TX (S)
Dawes, Roy, *Head Prep,* Brandeis University, Rose Art Museum, Waltham MA
Dawes, Roy, *Head Preparator,* Brandeis University, Rose Art Museum, Waltham MA
Dawnson, Jim, *Facilities Mgr,* Swope Art Museum, Terre Haute IN
Daws, Russell S, *CEO & Exec Dir,* Tallahassee Museum of History & Natural Science, Museum, Tallahassee FL
Daws, Russell S, *Dir,* Tallahassee Museum of History & Natural Science, Tallahassee FL
Dawsari, Elizabeth, *Dir of Library,* Frank Lloyd Wright School, William Wesley Peters Library, Scottsdale AZ
Dawson, David, *Instr Animation,* Rio Hondo College, Arts & Cultural Programs Dept, Whittier CA (S)
Dawson, Kathleen, *Quilt Natl Dir,* The Dairy Barn Arts Center, Athens OH
Dawson, Will, *Pres,* Klamath Art Association, Klamath Falls OR
Day, Alfred, *Gen Sec,* United Methodist Church General Commission on Archives & History, Madison NJ
Day, Brenda, *Dir,* Baker University, Old Castle Museum, Baldwin City KS
Day, Christopher, *Digital Servs Librn,* School of the Art Institute of Chicago, John M Flaxman Library, Chicago IL
Day, Fran, *Development Director,* Arrowmont School of Arts & Crafts, Gatlinburg TN (S)
Day, Homer, *Pres,* Abraham Baldwin Agricultural College, Art & Humanities Dept, Tifton GA (S)
Day, Janet, *Pres,* Art Institute of Atlanta, Atlanta GA (S)
Day, Jennifer, *Registrar,* School for Advanced Research (SAR), Indian Arts Research Center, Santa Fe NM
Day, Jessica, *Guest Svcs Coordr,* Neville Public Museum of Brown County, Green Bay WI
Day, John, *Chmn & Dean,* University of South Dakota, Department of Art, College of Fine Arts, Vermillion SD (S)
Day, John, *Dir,* Fryeburg Academy, The Palmina F & Stephen S Pace Galleries of Art, Fryeburg ME
Day, Robyn, *Communs Mgr,* Carl & Marilynn Thoma Art Foundation, Art House Santa Fe, Santa Fe NM
Day, Russell, *Dept Chair,* Penn Foster College, School of Interior Design, Scranton PA (S)
Days, Russell, *Coordr Facilities,* College of Central Florida, Appleton Museum of Art, Ocala FL
Days, Russell, *Facilities Dir,* Florida State University and Central Florida Community College, The Appleton Museum of Art, Ocala FL
De Cocker, Dean, *Gallery Dir,* California State University Stanislaus, University Art Gallery, Turlock CA
de Fato, Elizabeth, *Librn,* Seattle Art Museum, Dorothy Stimson Bullitt Library, Seattle WA
De Fronzo, Stephen, *Artistic Dir,* Gateway Arts, Gateway Gallery, Brookline MA
De Garie-Lamanque, Ève, *Cur Contemporary Art,* Le Musee Regional de Rimouski, Centre National d'Exposition, Rimouski QC
De Groft, Aaron H, *Dir,* College of William & Mary, Muscarelle Museum of Art, Williamsburg VA
De Hoff, William, *Asst Prof,* University of Wisconsin-Stout, Dept of Art & Design, Menomonie WI (S)
De Jong, Paul, *Prog Dir, Theatre Performance,* Humber College, School of Creative & Performing Arts, Toronto ON (S)
De Koning, Marion, *Dept Chair,* Grossmont Community College, Hyde Art Gallery, El Cajon CA
de La Rosa, Francise, *Asst Prof,* Wesleyan College, Art Dept, Macon GA (S)
De Long, Paul, *Prof,* University of Wisconsin-Stout, Dept of Art & Design, Menomonie WI (S)
De Los Santos, Ofelia, *Chief Financial Officer,* Inner-City Arts, Los Angeles CA (S)
de Luise, Alexandra, *Cur,* Queens College, City University of New York, Queens College Art Center, Flushing NY
De Marcos, Sally, *Asst Prof,* Baltimore City Community College, Dept of Fine Arts, Baltimore MD (S)
de Maria, Blake, *Chair, Assoc Prof,* Santa Clara University, Dept of Art & Art History, Santa Clara CA (S)
de Mos, Mark, *Pres,* New Jersey Watercolor Society, Parsippany NJ
De Nunzio, John, *Chmn,* Lackawanna College, Fine Arts Dept, Scranton PA (S)
De Rosa, Elizabeth, *Sec,* Neustadt Collection of Tiffany Glass, Long Island City NY
de Sales Dinneen, Marie, *Chmn,* Regis College, Dept of Art, Weston MA (S)
De Salvo, Donna, *Deputy Dir International Initiatives & Sr Cur,* Whitney Museum of American Art, New York NY
de Silva, Kauka, *Chmn,* University of Hawaii, Kapiolani Community College, Honolulu HI (S)
De Silvo, Verneal, *Prof,* Compton Community College, Art Dept, Compton CA (S)
de Smet, Lorraine, *Secretary,* Art Centre of New Jersey, Livingston NJ (S)
de Smet, Louis, *Treas,* Art Centre of New Jersey, Livingston NJ (S)
De Sola, Edgar, *CEO,* The Mexican Museum, San Francisco CA
de Troy Miller, Stephanie, *Asst Cur & Registrar,* Guild Hall of East Hampton, Inc, Guild Hall Museum, East Hampton NY
de Verges, Jolene, *Dir & Head Reserach Servs,* Southern Methodist University, Hamon Arts Library, Dallas TX
De Verges, Jolene, *Librn Architecture & Visual Arts,* Massachusetts Institute of Technology, Rotch Library of Architecture & Planning, Cambridge MA
de Ville, Roy V, *Dir University Gallery,* Louisiana State University at Alexandria, University Gallery, Alexandria LA
De Young, Jim, *Sr Conservator,* Milwaukee Art Museum, Milwaukee WI
De Zorzi, Vanessa, *Graphic Design & Social Media Specialist,* The Currier Museum of Art, Manchester NH
de-Cossio, Renee, *Technical/Art Specialist,* San Francisco Museum of Modern Art, Artist Gallery, San Francisco CA
Deacy-Quinn, Christa, *Collections Mgr,* University of Illinois at Urbana-Champaign, Spurlock Museum, Urbana IL
Deadman, Pat, *Instr,* Art Center Sarasota, Sarasota FL (S)
Deal, David, *Asst Prof Art & Graphic Design,* Eastern New Mexico University, Runnels Gallery, Golden Library, Portales NM
Deal, Ryan, *Sr VP Cultural & Community Investment,* Arts & Science Council, Charlotte NC
DeAlmeida, Claudia, *Circ Supv,* Roger Williams University, Architecture Library, Bristol RI
Dean McCauley, Emily, *Educ Cur,* University of Mississippi, University Museum & Historic Houses, Oxford MS
Dean, Amy, *Circ Asst,* Ames Free-Easton's Public Library, North Easton MA
Dean, Angel, *Events Planning & Mem Servs,* Providence Art Club, Providence RI
Dean, Jim, *Dean Admis,* Ringling School of Art & Design, Sarasota FL (S)
Dean, Paul, *Asst Prof,* Louisiana State University, School of Art, Baton Rouge LA (S)
Deane, Bridget, *Dir Develop,* Clark County Historical Society, Heritage Center of Clark County, Springfield OH
Deane, Dennis, *Assoc Prof,* Ohio University-Chillicothe Campus, Fine Arts & Humanities Division, Chillicothe OH (S)
Deane, Robert, *Instr,* Wayne Art Center, Wayne PA (S)
DeAngelis, Anita, *Prof,* East Tennessee State University, College of Arts and Sciences, Dept of Art & Design, Johnson City TN (S)
DeAngelo, Darlene, *Dir Programming,* Huntington Beach Art Center, Huntington Beach CA
Deans, John, *Pres,* Jefferson Community College, Art Dept, Watertown NY (S)
Dearborn, Alan, *Asst Cur Physics,* Northern Maine Museum of Science, Presque Isle ME
Dearinger, David, *Susan Morse Hilles Sr Cur Paintings & Sculpture & Dir Exhibs,* Boston Athenaeum, Boston MA
DeArmendi, Nicole, *Instr,* George Mason University, College of Humanities & Social Sciences, Dept of History & Art History, Fairfax VA (S)
Dearth, Donna, *Assistant,* New Canaan Historical Society, New Canaan CT
Deaton, Judy, *Instr,* McMurry University, Art Dept, Abilene TX (S)
Deaton, Linda, *Chief Cur,* Tallahassee Museum of History & Natural Science, Museum, Tallahassee FL
Deaton, Linda, *Cur Coll & Exhib,* Tallahassee Museum of History & Natural Science, Tallahassee FL
Deaton, Susan, *Asst Prof Art,* Lander University, College of Arts & Humanities - Visual Arts, Greenwood SC (S)
Deaver, Loretta, *Library Servs Coordr,* San Diego Museum of Art, Art Library & Archives, San Diego CA
DeBardelaben, LaNesha, *Secy,* Association of African American Museums, Washington DC
Debardeleben, Patty, *Mus Shop Mgr,* Sturdivant Museum Association, Sturdivant Museum, Selma AL
Debarry, Christina, *Treas,* Allied Artists of America, Inc, Florham Park NJ
DeBartolo, Rob, *Pres,* Essex Art Association, Inc, Essex CT
Debauchy, Jane, *Rec Secy,* Berks Art Alliance, Reading PA
DeBeer, Jan, *Deputy Dir,* Nicolaysen Art Museum & Discovery Center, Children's Discovery Center, Casper WY
deBeixedon, Dianne, *Assoc Prof,* Old Dominion University, Art Dept, Norfolk VA (S)
Debela, Achameleh, *Prof,* North Carolina Central University, Art Dept, Durham NC (S)

DeBiase, Brad, *Opers & Spec Initiatives Coordr,* Arizona Commission on the Arts, Phoenix AZ
DeBolt, Dean, *Dir Spec Coll,* University of West Florida, Library, Pensacola FL
DeBord, Betty, *Assoc Prof Art,* Lincoln Memorial University, Division of Humanities, Harrogate TN (S)
deBrer, Christian, *Head Conservator,* University of California, Los Angeles, Fowler Museum at UCLA, Los Angeles CA
DeBruyne, Paul, *Co-Pres,* DeBruyne Fine Art, Naples FL
DeBruyne, Suzanne, *Co-Pres,* DeBruyne Fine Art, Naples FL
DeCaigny, Tom, *Dir Cultural Affairs,* San Francisco City & County Arts Commission, San Francisco CA
deCamargo, Luiza, *Assoc Cur,* The Society of Arts & Crafts, Boston MA
DeCaroli, Robert, *Instr,* George Mason University, College of Humanities & Social Sciences, Dept of History & Art History, Fairfax VA (S)
DeCarolis, Lisa, *Art Library Asst,* Smith College, Hillyer Art Library, Northampton MA
DeCat, Lisa, *Asst Prof Dance,* Lake Erie College, Fine Arts Dept, Painesville OH (S)
Decelestino, Blase, *Adjunct Instr,* New York Institute of Technology, Fine Arts Dept, Old Westbury NY (S)
Dechert, Caroline, *Librn & Archivist,* New Mexico Department of Cultural Affairs, Bartlett Library, Santa Fe NM
Deci, Edward L, *Pres,* Monhegan Museum, Monhegan Museum of Art & History, Monhegan ME
DeCicco, Deb, *School Dir,* Sharon Arts Center, Sharon Arts Center Exhibition Gallery, Peterborough NH
Decicco, Stephanie, *Chmn,* Waubonsee Community College, Art Dept, Sugar Grove IL (S)
Deck, Rhonda, *Mktg Mgr,* University of Virginia, The Fralin Museum of Art at the University of Virginia, Charlottesville VA
Decker, Adrienne, *Folk Arts Specialist,* Utah Arts Council, Chase Home Museum of Utah Folk Arts, Salt Lake City UT
Decker, Jillian, *Develop Mgr,* Delaware Center for the Contemporary Arts, Wilmington DE
Decker, John, *Grad Dir,* Georgia State University, Ernest G Welch School of Art & Design, Atlanta GA (S)
Decker, Juilee, *Prof Art History & Dept Chair,* Georgetown College, Art Dept, Georgetown KY (S)
Decker, Julie, *Dir & CEO,* Anchorage Museum at Rasmuson Center, Anchorage AK
Decker, Nick, *Visitor Services Representative,* The Columbus Museum, Columbus GA
Decker, Thomas, *Treas,* Japanese American National Museum, Los Angeles CA
Decklin, Tara, *Opers Mgr,* Society of North American Goldsmiths, Eugene OR
DeCocinis, Anthony, *CFO,* Pennsylvania Academy of the Fine Arts, Philadelphia PA
DeCoker, Dean, *Prof,* California State University, Art Dept, Turlock CA (S)
DeCosta, Alex, *Gallery Dir,* Grossmont Community College, Hyde Art Gallery, El Cajon CA
Decoteau, Pamela, *Head Art History,* Southern Illinois University at Edwardsville, Dept of Art & Design, Edwardsville IL (S)
deDeaux, Dick, *Painting,* Western Michigan University, Frostic School of Art, Kalamazoo MI (S)
Deegan, Denis, *Prof,* Daytona Beach Community College, Dept of Fine Arts & Visual Arts, Daytona Beach FL (S)
Deere, Bill, *Assoc Prof,* Purchase College, State University of New York, School of Art+Design, Purchase NY (S)
DeEsch, Vasti, *Coll Asst,* Lehigh University Art Galleries, Museum Operation, Bethlehem PA
Deese, Martha, *Sr Admin Exhibs & International Affairs,* The Metropolitan Museum of Art, New York NY
Deetsch, Mike, *Dir Educ & Engagement,* Toledo Museum of Art, Toledo OH
DeFee, F Brooks, *Asst Prof,* Northwestern State University of Louisiana, School of Creative & Performing Arts - Dept of Fine & Graphic Arts, Natchitoches LA (S)
Defenbaugh, Deni, *Asst Prof,* Rochester Institute of Technology, School of Photographic Arts & Sciences, Rochester NY (S)
Defoor, T, *Music Instr,* Edison Community College, Gallery of Fine Arts, Fort Myers FL (S)
DeFord, Matt, *Asst Prof,* Northwestern State University of Louisiana, School of Creative & Performing Arts - Dept of Fine & Graphic Arts, Natchitoches LA (S)
DeFord, Nick, *Prog Dir,* Arrowmont School of Arts & Crafts, Gatlinburg TN (S)
deGennaro, Cristina, *Assoc Prof,* The College of New Rochelle, School of Arts & Sciences Art Dept, New Rochelle NY (S)
DeGennaro, Frank J, *Graphic Design,* Art Institute of Pittsburgh, Pittsburgh PA (S)
DeGennaro, Mark, *Preparator,* Miami University, Art Museum, Oxford OH
DeGiacomo, Lynne, *Exec Admin,* Cohasset Historical Society, Captain John Wilson Historical House, Cohasset MA
DeGiacomo, Lynne, *Exec Dir,* Cohasset Historical Society, Pratt Building (Society Headquarters), Cohasset MA
DeGiacomo, Lynne, *Exec Dir,* Cohasset Historical Society, Cohasset Maritime Museum, Cohasset MA
DeGraaf, Lee, *Treas,* Canton Museum of Art, Canton OH
DeGrace, Lisa, *Exec Dir,* Blue Sky Gallery, Oregon Center for the Photographic Arts, Portland OR
DeGraffenried, Judith, *Head Dept, Prof,* Middlesex Community College, Fine Arts Div, Middletown CT (S)
DeGroat, Mary, *Dir Mktg Communs,* Monterey Museum of Art, Monterey Museum of Art -Pacific Street, Monterey Museum of Art - La Mirada, Monterey CA
Degutis, Alan N, *Head Cataloging Svcs,* American Antiquarian Society, Worcester MA
DeHaan, Andrea, *Admin Coordr,* Utah State University, Nora Eccles Harrison Museum of Art, Logan UT
Dehan, Amy, *Cur Decorative Arts & Design,* Cincinnati Art Museum, Cincinnati Art Museum, Cincinnati OH
Dehart, Gail, *Pres LMA,* Lafayette Museum Association, Lafayette Museum-Alexandre Mouton House, Lafayette LA
Dehn, Brenda, *Dir,* Henry County Museum & Cultural Arts Center, Clinton MO
Dehne, Christine, *Faculty Cur,* Manhattanville College, Brownson Gallery, Purchase NY
Dehne, Christine, *Faculty Cur,* Manhattanville College, Arthur M Berger Gallery, Purchase NY
Dehner, Elke, *Head Mktg & Communs,* Rubin Museum of Art, New York NY
DeHut, Rose, *Exec Dir,* Center for the Visual Arts, Gallery, Wausau WI
Deibler, Cora-Lynn, *Head Dept,* University of Connecticut, Dept of Art & Art History, Storrs CT (S)
Deily, Dave, *VPres MCG Youth & Arts,* Manchester Bidwell Corporation, Manchester Craftsmen's Guild Youth & Arts Program, Pittsburgh PA
Deines, Craig, *Chmn Art,* Mount San Antonio College, Art Dept, Walnut CA (S)
Deits, Katie, *Exec Dir,* Florida CraftArt, Saint Petersburg FL
Deits, Katie, *Exec Dir,* Lighthouse ArtCenter Museum & School of Art, Not Profit Art Center, Tequesta FL
Deits, Katie, *Exec Dir & School of Art Interim Dir,* Lighthouse ArtCenter Museum & School of Art, Tequesta FL
Dejardin, Fiona, *Assoc Prof,* Hartwick College, Art Dept, Oneonta NY (S)
Dejardin, Ian, *Exec Dir,* McMichael Canadian Art Collection, Kleinburg ON
DeJong, Constance, *Prof,* University of New Mexico, Department of Fine Arts & Art History, Albuquerque NM (S)
del Alamo, Constancio, *Cur Archaeology & Sculpture,* The Hispanic Society of America, Hispanic Society Museum & Library, New York NY
del Amo, Yolanda, *Assoc Prof Photo,* Ramapo College of New Jersey, School of Contemporary Arts, Mahwah NJ (S)
Del Nero, Constance, *Director of ArtReach & Community Programs,* Academy Art Museum, Easton MD
del Valle, Ed, *Prof,* Florida International University, School of Art & Art History, Miami FL (S)
Del Vecchio, Carolina, *Gift Shop Mgr,* Ancient Spanish Monastery, North Miami Beach FL
dela Houssaye, Isabella, *Pres,* Crowley Art Association, The Gallery, Crowley LA
Delahanty, Patricia, *Exhibitions Coord,* National Sculpture Society, New York NY
DeLamater, Peg, *Assoc Prof,* Winthrop University, Dept of Art & Design, Rock Hill SC (S)
Delaney, Esmeralda, *Asst Prof Art,* Grand Canyon University, Art Dept, Phoenix AZ (S)
Delaney, Susan, *Art History Instr,* Miracosta College, Art Dept, Oceanside CA (S)
DeLang, Val, *Dir Educ,* San Jose Museum of Art, Library, San Jose CA
Delano, Pablo, *Asst Prof,* Trinity College, Dept of Studio Arts, Hartford CT (S)
Delanoy, Geoff, *Assoc Prof,* College of Notre Dame of Maryland, Art Dept, Baltimore MD (S)
DeLap, Amy, *Prof,* Vincennes University Junior College, Humanities Art Dept, Vincennes IN (S)
Delatte, Cara, *Cur History,* Staten Island Museum, Staten Island NY
DeLaura, Angela, *Asst Prof,* William Paterson University, Dept Arts, Wayne NJ (S)
Delavaux, Denise, *Adjunct,* College of the Canyons, Art Dept, Santa Clarita CA (S)
DeLay, Matthew, *Educ Coordr,* Iowa State University, Brunnier Art Museum, Ames IA
Delbo, Jose, *Instr,* Joe Kubert, Dover NJ (S)
Deleary, Mary, *Primitive Edge Gallery Coordr,* Institute of American Indian Arts, Museum of Contemporary Native Arts, Santa Fe NM (S)
Delgado, Elaine, *Develop Officer,* The Hispanic Society of America, Hispanic Society Museum & Library, New York NY
Delgado, Ivan, *Opers Mgr,* The Kreeger Museum, Washington DC
Delgado, John, *Instr,* Southern University A & M College, School of Architecture, Baton Rouge LA (S)
Delgado, Sally, *Cur Educ,* Ohio University, Kennedy Museum of Art, Athens OH
Delgado, Steve, *VPres,* Second Street Gallery, Charlottesville VA
Delgreco, Kate, *Dir Develop,* Birmingham Museum of Art, Birmingham AL
Delikat, Dawn, *Assoc Dir,* Pen & Brush, Inc, New York NY
Delisle, Andre, *Exec Dir & Cur,* Chateau Ramezay Museum, Montreal QC
Delker, Kathy, *Reference Librn,* Friends University, Edmund Stanley Library, Wichita KS
Dell'Olio, L, *Prof,* Camden County College, Visual & Performing Arts Dept, Blackwood NJ (S)
Dell, Deborah, *Asst Ceramics Instr,* Red Rocks Community College, Arts Dept, Lakewood CO (S)
Dell, Jeff, *Assoc Prof,* Texas State University - San Marcos, Dept of Art and Design, San Marcos TX (S)
Dell, Jery, *Prof,* University of Wisconsin-Green Bay, Arts Dept, Green Bay WI (S)
Della Valle, Jared, *Chair,* Van Alen Institute, New York NY
Dellapina, Ardath, *Dir Educ & Progs,* Clark County Historical Society, Heritage Center of Clark County, Springfield OH
Dellatte, Cara, *Archivist,* Staten Island Museum, Archives Library, Staten Island NY

Dellavalle, Jacques A, *Prof,* Daytona Beach Community College, Dept of Fine Arts & Visual Arts, Daytona Beach FL (S)
Deller, Harris, *Prof,* Southern Illinois University, School of Art & Design, Carbondale IL (S)
Dellinger, Adrienne, *Exec Dir,* Clayworks Gallery, Charlotte NC
Dellosso, Gabrielle, *VPres,* Allied Artists of America, Inc, Florham Park NJ
Delman, Kirk, *Coll Mgr, Registrar,* Scripps College, Ruth Chandler Williamson Gallery, Claremont CA
Delois, Patti, *AV Mgr,* Portland Public Library, Art - Audiovisual Dept, Portland ME
DeLorme, Harry, *Cur Educ,* Telfair Museums, Telfair Academy of Arts & Sciences Library, Savannah GA
DeLorme, Harry, *Senior Cur Educ,* Telfair Museums, Savannah GA
Delos, Kate, *Instr,* Solano Community College, Division of Fine & Applied Art & Behavioral Science, Fairfield CA (S)
Delphia, Rachel, *Cur Decorative Arts,* Carnegie Museums of Pittsburgh, Carnegie Museum of Art, Pittsburgh PA
Delto, Byron, *Instr,* Glendale Community College, Visual & Performing Arts Div, Glendale CA (S)
DeLuca, Daniel S, *Dir,* Mobius Inc, Cambridge MA
Delucca, Sharon, *Assoc Prof,* Roger Williams University, Visual Art Dept, Bristol RI (S)
DeLucia, Angela, *Interim Dir,* Youngstown State University, The John J McDonough Museum of Art, Youngstown OH
DeLura, Mark, *Prep,* Bard College, Center for Curatorial Studies and the Hessel Museum of Art, Annandale-on-Hudson NY
DelValle, Helen, *VPres,* American Society of Artists, Inc, Palatine IL
Delvin, Robert C, *Fine Arts Librn,* Illinois Wesleyan University, Sheean Library, Bloomington IL
DeMarco-Logue, Mary, *Coordr,* Mattawoman Creek Art Center, Marbury MD
DeMaria, Shelley, *Curatorial Asst,* Southern Methodist University, Meadows Museum, Dallas TX
Demarjian, Haig, *Prof,* Salem State University, Art & Design Department, Salem MA (S)
DeMarsche, Kay, *Head,* Mississippi State University, Dept of Art, Starville MS (S)
DeMarte, Jason, *Asst Prof,* Mississippi State University, Dept of Art, Starville MS (S)
DeMartino, Lisa, *Dir Human Resources,* Milwaukee Public Museum, Milwaukee WI
Demas, Sara, *Instr,* Mohawk Valley Community College, Utica NY (S)
DeMay, Susan, *Sr Lectr,* Vanderbilt University, Dept of Art, Nashville TN (S)
DeMent, Nichole, *Exec Dir,* CoCA Center on Contemporary Art, Seattle WA
Demeroukas, Marie, *Librn,* City of Springdale, Shiloh Museum of Ozark History, Springdale AR
Demers, Sheryl, *Bus Mgr,* Fitchburg Art Museum, Fitchburg MA
Demeter, Frank, *Sales,* Gene Roncka Willow Point Gallery/Museum, Ashland NE
Demetri, Justin, *Director of Tours,* Essex Historical Society and Shipbuilding Museum, Essex MA
Demlow, Jacob, *Educ Dir,* Golden Isles Arts & Humanities Association, Brunswick GA
DeMong, Temesa Ann, *Office & Progs Mgr,* University of Saskatchewan, Diefenbaker Canada Centre, Saskatoon SK
Demore, Carissa, *Team Leader, Preservation Svcs,* Historic New England, Boston MA
DeMots, Lois, *Instr,* Siena Heights University, Studio Angelico-Art Dept, Adrian MI (S)
Dempsey, Connie, *Chief Certification Officer,* Penn Foster College, School of Interior Design, Scranton PA (S)
Dempsey, Jaime, *Exec Dir,* Arizona Commission on the Arts, Reference Library, Phoenix AZ
Dempsey, Jaime, *Exec Dir,* Arizona Commission on the Arts, Phoenix AZ
Dempsey, John, *Prof,* Mott Community College, Fine Arts & Social Sciences Division, Flint MI (S)
Demulder, Kim, *Instr,* Joe Kubert, Dover NJ (S)
den Hartog, Jacci, *Prog Dir Sculpture/New Genres,* Otis College of Art & Design, Fine Arts, Los Angeles CA (S)
Denaci, Mark, *Asst Prof,* St Lawrence University, Dept of Fine Arts, Canton NY (S)
DeNatale, Douglas, *Senior Lecturer,* Boston University, Graduate Program - Arts Administration, Boston MA (S)
Dene English, Donna, *Area Coordr,* Saint Mary-of-the-Woods College, Art Dept, Saint Mary of the Woods IN (S)
Denenberg, Tom, *Dir,* Shelburne Museum, Museum, Shelburne VT
Denis, Paul, *Asst Cur,* Royal Ontario Museum, Dept of Western Art & Culture, Toronto ON
Denison, Dirk, *Studio Prof,* Illinois Institute of Technology, College of Architecture, Chicago IL (S)
Denk, Leslie, *Dir External Affairs,* Norton Simon Museum, Pasadena CA
Denk-Leigh, Margaret, *Dept Head Printmaking,* Cleveland Institute of Art, Cleveland OH (S)
Denlsnap, Susan, *Lectr,* Bates College, Art & Visual Culture, Lewiston ME (S)
Denney, Gaylon, *Sr Admin,* Rice University, Visual & Dramatic Arts, Houston TX (S)
Denning, Elizabeth, *Pres,* Fall River Historical Society, Fall River MA
Denning, Kylee, *Cur Coll,* The San Joaquin Pioneer & Historical Society, The Haggin Museum, Stockton CA
Denninger, Nina, *Assoc Prof,* Seton Hill University, Art Program, Greensburg PA (S)
Dennis, Linda, *Exec Dir,* Rockford Art Museum, Rockford IL
Dennis, Mac, *Asst Prof,* Elmira College, Art Dept, Elmira NY (S)
Dennis, Terry, *Instr,* Rochester Community & Technical College, Art Dept, Rochester MN (S)
Dennis, Tom, *Assoc Prof,* University of Nebraska, Kearney, Dept of Art & Art History, Kearney NE (S)
Dennison, Logan, *Education & Community Engagement Dir,* Lexington Art League, Inc, Lexington KY
Denniston, Susan, *Treas,* The Boston Printmakers, at Lesley University, Boston MA
Denny, Katie, *Dir Develop & Communs,* Socrates Sculpture Park, Long Island City NY
Denny, Walter B, *Prof,* University of Massachusetts, Amherst, Art History Program, Amherst MA (S)
Densmore, Christopher, *Cur,* Swarthmore College, Friends Historical Library of Swarthmore College, Swarthmore PA
Dent, Danielle, *Dir Mem & Mktg,* Association of Collegiate Schools of Architecture, Washington DC
Denton, Elaine, *First VPres,* Art Centre of New Jersey, Livingston NJ (S)
Denton, Judy, *Chief Cur,* Grace Museum, Inc, The Grace Museum, Abilene TX
Denton, Margaret, *Assoc Prof,* University of Richmond, Dept of Art and Art History, Richmond VA (S)
Denton, Tanya, *Dir Admin & Operations,* University of Oklahoma, Fred Jones Jr Museum of Art, Norman OK
Denyer, Alison, *Asst Prof,* University of Utah, Dept of Art & Art History, Salt Lake City UT (S)
Denyes, Kaaren, *Dept Head,* Ferris State University, Visual Communication Dept, Big Rapids MI (S)
Depaty, Annik, *Dir Events & Vols,* Madison Museum of Contemporary Art, Madison WI
DePrisco, Michael, *Pres,* Art Institute of Philadelphia, Philadelphia PA (S)
Deragon, Rick, *Exec Dir,* Napa Valley Museum, Yountville CA
Derbes, Anne, *Chmn,* Hood College, Dept of Art, Frederick MD (S)
Derby, John, *Asst Prof,* University of Kansas, The School of the Arts, Dept of Visual Art, Lawrence KS (S)
Derezinski, Matthew, *Asst Prof,* Emporia State University, Dept of Art, Emporia KS (S)
Derksen, Karen, *Dir,* Winthrop University Galleries, Rock Hill SC
Dernehl, Maggie, *Exhib Technician,* Neville Public Museum of Brown County, Green Bay WI
DeRosa, Donald, *Pres,* University of the Pacific, Jeannette Powell Art Center, Stockton CA
DeRosa, Michael, *Head Dept,* Coffeyville Community College, Art Dept, Coffeyville KS (S)
DeRose, Julia, *Devel Assoc,* The Renaissance Society, Chicago IL
Derrevere, William, *Instr,* Tulsa Community College, Center for Creativity, Tulsa OK (S)
Derry, Bill, *Asst Dir Innovation & User Experience,* Westport Public Library, Westport CT
Derstine, Andria, *Dir,* Oberlin College, Allen Memorial Art Museum, Oberlin OH
Deruosi, Jessica, *Mus Shop Mgr,* Virginia Historical Society, Library, Richmond VA
Dery, Joanne, *Library Dept Head,* Montreal Museum of Fine Arts, Library, Montreal QC
Des Roches, Anne-Marie, *Assoc Dir & Sr Policy Advisor,* Canadian Conference of the Arts, Ottawa ON
Desabritas, Elizabeth, *Instr,* Centenary College, Humanities Dept, Hackettstown NJ (S)
Desai, Madhuri, *Asst Prof,* Pennsylvania State University, University Park, Dept of Art History, University Park PA (S)
Desai, Smita, *Sec,* Passaic County Community College, Broadway, LRC, and Hamilton Club Galleries, Paterson NJ
Descoteaux, Ann, *Dir Docents,* Fitchburg Art Museum, Fitchburg MA
DeSeve, Teresa, *Instr,* Wayne Art Center, Wayne PA (S)
DeSiano, Michael, *Coordr Art Educ,* Kean University, Fine Arts Dept, Union NJ (S)
Desiderio, Vincent, *Instr,* New York Academy of Art, Graduate School of Figurative Art, New York NY (S)
Desimone, Jaime, *Cur,* Museum of Contemporary Art Jacksonville, Jacksonville FL
DesJardins, Peggy, *Art House Coordr,* St Tammany Art Association, Covington LA
Deslis, Konstantine, *Develop Dir,* Kimball Art Center, Park City UT
DesMeules, Hadley, *Interim Mgr Student & Visitor Engagement,* Williams College, Museum of Art, Williamstown MA
DesMeules, Hadley, *Visitor Services Coordinator,* Williams College, Museum of Art, Williamstown MA
Desmond, Kathleen, *Prof,* University of Central Missouri, Dept of Art & Design, Warrensburg MO (S)
Desormeau, Monique, *Cur Educ,* Flint Institute of Arts, Flint MI
Desormeau, Monique, *Cur Educ,* Flint Institute of Arts, Library, Flint MI
Desormeaux, Monique, *Deputy CEO,* Ottawa Public Library, Fine Arts Dept, Ottawa ON
Dessornes, Maria, *CEO & VPres,* Conejo Valley Art Museum, Thousand Oaks CA
Deters, Alexandra, *Gallery Administrator,* First Street Gallery, New York NY
Detrich, David, *Grad Coordr,* Clemson University, College of Architecture, Arts & Humanities, Art Dept, Clemson SC (S)
DeTurk, Sabrina, *Adj Prof,* Saint Joseph's University, Art Dept, Philadelphia PA (S)
Detweiler, Kelly, *Prof,* Santa Clara University, Dept of Art & Art History, Santa Clara CA (S)
Deupi, Jill, *Dir,* University of Miami, Lowe Art Museum, Coral Gables FL
Deutsch, Alexandra, *Chief Cur,* Maryland Historical Society, Museum of Maryland History, Baltimore MD
Deutsch, Todd, *Chmn & Assoc Prof,* St Catherine University, Art & Art History Dept, Saint Paul MN (S)

Devening, Dan, *Lectr,* Northwestern University, Evanston, Dept of Art Theory & Practice, Evanston IL (S)

Devereaux Lewis, Caitlain, *Visual Resources Cur,* University at Albany, State University of New York, Visual Resources Library, Albany NY

Devereaux, Kent, *Dept Chair,* Cornish College of the Arts, Fisher Gallery, Seattle WA

deVille, Roy V, *Prof Art,* Louisiana State University at Alexandria, Dept of Fine Arts & Design, Alexandria LA (S)

Devine, Jack, *Bd Pres,* Ocean City Arts Center, Ocean City NJ

Devine, Jerry, *Security Officer,* Amherst College, Mead Art Museum, Amherst MA

Devine, Michael, *Acting Dir,* National Archives & Records Administration, Harry S Truman Museum and Library, Independence MO

Devinney, Rosemary A, *Mgr & Coordr,* Shoshone Bannock Tribes, Shoshone Bannock Tribal Museum, Fort Hall ID

DeVinny, Douglas, *Prof,* University of Wisconsin-Parkside, Art Dept, Kenosha WI (S)

Devlin, Kate, *Vis Servs Coordr,* Historical Society of Pennsylvania, Philadelphia PA

Devlin, Peter, *Tour Interpreter,* Farmington Village Green & Library Association, Stanley-Whitman House, Farmington CT

Devlin, Teresa, *Pub Rel Dir,* The Historic New Orleans Collection, Williams Research Center, New Orleans LA

DeVoe, Patty, *Registrar,* Lyme Academy College of Fine Arts, Old Lyme CT (S)

Devon, Marjorie, *Dir,* University of New Mexico, Tamarind Institute, Albuquerque NM (S)

Devono, Lanny, *Chmn,* Eastern Washington University, Dept of Art, Cheney WA (S)

DeVries, Karl, *Asst Dir,* Ships of the Sea Maritime Museum, Savannah GA

Dew, Patti, *VPres Finance & Opers,* Milwaukee Public Museum, Milwaukee WI

Dewald, Ann, *Dir,* Archaeological Society of Ohio, Indian Museum of Lake County Library, Willoughby OH

Dewald, Ann, *Dir,* Archaeological Society of Ohio, Indian Museum of Lake County, Ohio, Willoughby OH

DeWalt, James D, *Head,* Free Library of Philadelphia, Rare Book Dept, Philadelphia PA

DeWeese, Josh, *Asst Prof Ceramics,* Montana State University, School of Art, Bozeman MT (S)

Dewey II, Tom, *Assoc Prof,* University of Mississippi, Department of Art, University MS (S)

Dewey, Jennifer, *Develop Dir,* Baton Rouge Gallery, Center For Contemporary Art, Baton Rouge LA

Dewey, Kevin, *Music,* Henry Ford Community College, McKenzie Fine Art Ctr, Dearborn MI (S)

Dewey, Toby, *Dir,* Charles River School, Creative Arts Program, Dover MA (S)

Dewhurst, Marit, *Dir,* City College of New York, Art Dept, New York NY (S)

Dewhurst, Marit, *Prog Dir Art Ed Asst Prof,* City College of New York, Art Dept, New York NY (S)

DeWitt, Karen, *Head Design Library,* North Carolina State University, Harrye Lyons Design Library, Raleigh NC

DeWitt, Lloyd, *Chief Cur,* Chrysler Museum of Art, Norfolk VA

DeWitt, Marci, *Pres,* Hillwood Museum & Gardens Foundation, Hillwood Estate Museum & Gardens, Washington DC

Dewitt, Marcia, *Chm (V),* Biggs Museum of American Art, Dover DE

DeWitt, Marcia, *Pres Board,* Rehoboth Art League, Inc, Rehoboth Beach DE

Dewitte, Debra, *Adj Asst Prof,* University of Texas at Arlington, Art & Art History Department, Arlington TX (S)

DeWitte, Elizabeth, *Instr,* University of Utah, Dept of Art & Art History, Salt Lake City UT (S)

Dey, Barbara, *Ref Librn,* History Colorado Center Museum, Stephen H Hart Library, Denver CO

Dey, Hendrik, *Assoc Chair, Art History,* Hunter College, Dept of Art & Art History, New York NY (S)

Deyasi, Marco, *Asst Prof,* University of Idaho College of Art & Architecture, Dept of Art & Design, Moscow ID (S)

Deyhie, David, *VPres External Rels,* Chicago History Museum, Chicago IL

DeYoe, Mary, *Dir Strategic Partnerships & Spec Projects,* Chicago Artists Coalition, Chicago IL

DeYoung Kohler, Ruth, *Exec Dir,* Sheboygan Arts Foundation, Inc, John Michael Kohler Arts Center, Sheboygan WI

DeYoung, Mark, *Instr,* Kalamazoo Valley Community College, Center for New Media, Kalamazoo MI (S)

Dhayatker, Kali, *Vol & Event Coordr,* Fort Collins Museum of Art, Inc, Fort Collins CO

di Maria, Tom, *Dir,* Creative Growth Art Center, Oakland CA

Diamato, Paul, *Instr,* Maine College of Art, Portland ME (S)

Diamond, Drew, *Exec Dir,* The Sherwin Miller Museum of Jewish Art, Tulsa OK

Diamond, Jennifer, *Exec Dir,* Arts Council of White Lake, Gallery, Whitehall MI

Diamond, Julie, *Dir Pub Rels,* The Long Island Museum of American Art, History & Carriages, Stony Brook NY

Diamond, Pamela, *Dir Mktg & Communs,* American Craft Council, Minneapolis MN

Diamond, Sara, *Pres,* OCAD University, Toronto ON (S)

Diamond, Tom, *Colls & Materials Selector Librn,* Louisiana State University, Middleton Library, Baton Rouge LA

Diamond-Nigh, John, *Asst,* Elmira College, Art Dept, Elmira NY (S)

Diaz, Alfred, *Student Aid Coordr,* Escuela de Artes Plasticas de Puerto Rico, San Juan PR (S)

Diaz, Dorsi, *Exec Dir,* Hayward Area Forum for the Arts, Sun Gallery, Hayward CA

Diaz, Jose, *Chief Cur,* The Andy Warhol Museum, Pittsburgh PA

Diaz, Josef, *Cur Southwest & Mexican Colonial Art & History Colls,* New Mexico Department of Cultural Affairs, Palace of Governors, Santa Fe NM

Diaz, Julius, *Dir Educ,* Social & Public Art Resource Center, (SPARC), Venice CA

Diaz, Lynette, *Jr Mus Supv,* Newark Museum Association, Junior Museum, Newark NJ

Diaz, Melissa, *Museum Studies Program Coordinator,* Miami-Dade College, MDC Museum of Art & Design, Miami FL

Dibble, Valerie, *Community Coordr,* American Print Alliance, Peachtree City GA

DiBella, Joseph, *Chair,* University of Mary Washington, Dept of Art & Art History, Fredericksburg VA (S)

Dibella-Olson, Suzanne, *Pub Rels & Events Coordr,* Charleston Museum, Charleston SC

DiCicco, John, *Slide Librn,* Providence College, Art & Art History Dept, Providence RI (S)

Dick, James, *Founder & Dir,* James Dick Foundation, Festival - Institute, Round Top TX

Dick, Jeanette, *Pres,* Catharine Lorillard Wolfe, New York NY

Dick, Stephen, *Mgr Protection Servs,* The Robert McLaughlin Gallery, Oshawa ON

Dick, Sylvia, *Co Dir Art Ed,* Mount Saint Joseph University, Department of Art and Design, Cincinnati OH (S)

Dickens, Marie, *COO,* Vancouver Art Gallery, Vancouver BC

Dickerson, C.D., *Cur Sculpture & Decorative Arts,* National Gallery of Art, Washington DC

Dickerson, Cindy, *Dir Educ,* Hancock Shaker Village, Inc, Pittsfield MA

Dickerson, Jennifer, *Curator History,* San Bernardino County Museum, Redlands CA

Dickerson, Roger, *Music,* Southern University in New Orleans, Fine Arts & Philosophy Dept, New Orleans LA (S)

Dickes, Rodger, *MFA,* Glendale Community College, Visual & Performing Arts Div, Glendale CA (S)

Dickey, Mike, *Adminr,* Arrow Rock State Historic Site, Arrow Rock MO

Dickey, Shawn, *Recorder,* Mississippi University for Women, Fine Arts Gallery, Columbus MS

Dickins, Michael, *Dir,* Austin Peay State University, Margaret Fort Trahern Gallery, Clarksville TN

Dickinson, Brent Everett, *Asst Prof,* Azusa Pacific University, College of Music & the Arts, Dept of Art & Design, Azusa CA (S)

Dickinson, John, *Asst Prof,* Wright State University, Dept of Art & Art History, Dayton OH (S)

Dickinson, Pat, *Coordr,* Baycrest Centre for Geriatric Care, The Morris & Sally Justein of Baycrest Heritage Museum, Toronto ON

Dickinson, Theresa, *Dir Mktg,* Morgan County Foundation, Inc, Madison-Morgan Cultural Center, Madison GA

Dickson, Sally, *Develop Mgr,* Eiteljorg Museum of American Indians & Western Art, Indianapolis IN

DiCola Matos, Jennifer, *Dir Educ,* Noah Webster House, Inc, Noah Webster House & West Hartford Historical Society, West Hartford CT

DiCosola, Angela, *Prof Art, Ceramics,* Florida Atlantic University, D F Schmidt College of Arts & Letters Dept of Visual Arts & Art History, Boca Raton FL (S)

DiDiego, Charles, *Adjunct Asst Prof,* New York Institute of Technology, Fine Arts Dept, Old Westbury NY (S)

Diduk, Barbara, *Prof,* Dickinson College, Dept of Art & Art History, Carlisle PA (S)

Diebold, William J, *Chmn Art History & Humanities,* Reed College, Dept of Art, Portland OR (S)

Diedrich, Norah, *Exec Dir,* Evanston Art Center, Evanston IL

Diehl, Lindsay, *Exec Dir,* Wenham Museum, Timothy Pickering Library, Wenham MA

Diehl, Steve, *Assoc Prof,* Rochester Institute of Technology, School of Photographic Arts & Sciences, Rochester NY (S)

Dieker, Joseph, *Dean,* Cornell College, Peter Paul Luce Gallery, Mount Vernon IA

DiEleuterio, Rachael, *Head Librn,* Delaware Art Museum, Helen Farr Sloan Library, Wilmington DE

Diemente, Deborah, *Registrar & Coll Mgr,* Smith College, Museum of Art, Northampton MA

Diercks, Robert, *Co-Chmn,* Franklin Pierce College, Dept of Fine Arts & Graphic Communications, Rindge NH (S)

Dierdorf, Amy, *Develop Asst,* Dallas Contemporary, Dallas Visual Art Center, Dallas TX

Dierdorf, Amy, *Visitor Servs & Learning Assoc,* Dallas Contemporary, Dallas Visual Art Center, Dallas TX

Dierdorff, Brooks, *Adjunct Faculty,* Southern Oregon University, Art & Art History Dept, Ashland OR (S)

Dierdorff, Jo, *Dance Chmn,* Riverside Community College, Dept of Art & Mass Media, Riverside CA (S)

Diersen, Jenny, *Art Educ Coordr,* Kimball Art Center, Park City UT

Dieter, Joseph, *Lectr,* Johns Hopkins University, School of Medicine, Dept of Art as Applied to Medicine, Baltimore MD (S)

Dieterich, Danielle, *Director,* Cuyahoga Valley Art Center, Cuyahoga Falls OH (S)

Diethorn, Karie, *Chief Cur,* Independence National Historical Park, Library, Philadelphia PA

Diethorn, Karie, *Chief Mus Branch,* Independence National Historical Park, Philadelphia PA

Dietrich, Gretchen, *Exec Dir,* University of Utah, Utah Museum of Fine Arts, Salt Lake City UT

Dietrick, Joelle, *Prof,* Davidson College, Art Dept, Davidson NC (S)

Dietz, Joanne, *Mem,* Berks Art Alliance, Reading PA

Dietz, Ulysses, *Interim Co-Dir, Chief Cur & Cur Decorative Arts,* Newark Museum Association, The Newark Museum, Newark NJ

Dietze, Christine, *COO,* The Baltimore Museum of Art, Baltimore MD

Dietzel, Tracy Doreen, *Dir Exhibs,* St Johns University, Alice R Rogers/Target Galleries, Collegeville MN
Dietzel, Tracy, *Instr,* Edgewood College, Art Dept, Madison WI (S)
Difee, Nancy, *Chmn,* GumTree Museum of Art, Tupelo MS
Digby, Linda, *Exec Dir,* Okanagan Heritage Museum, Kelowna Public Archives, Kelowna BC
Digby, Linda, *Exec Dir,* Okanagan Heritage Museum, Kelowna BC
DiGenova, Kathy, *Mus Store Mgr,* University of California, Los Angeles, Fowler Museum at UCLA, Los Angeles CA
Diggle, Justin, *Assoc Prof,* University of Utah, Dept of Art & Art History, Salt Lake City UT (S)
Digney, Kathleen, *Art School Dir,* Spartanburg Art Museum, Spartanburg SC
Dillaway, Brandelyn, *Gallery Dir,* Mt San Jacinto College, Art Dept, San Jacinto CA (S)
Dillon, David, *Exhib Coordr,* Contemporary Arts Center, Cincinnati OH
Dillon, Diane, *Dir Dept Exhibs & Maj Projects,* The Newberry, Chicago IL
Dillon, Heather, *Cur Educ,* Florence County Museum, Florence SC
Dillon, Sheila, *Assoc Prof & Dir Undergrad Studies,* Duke University, Dept of Art, Art History & Visual Studies, Durham NC (S)
Dillon, Tambra, *Dir,* Bard College, Fisher Art Center, Annandale-on-Hudson NY
Dills, Keith, *Prof,* California Polytechnic State University at San Luis Obispo, Dept of Art & Design, San Luis Obispo CA (S)
DiLorenzo, Marie, *Gallery Mgr,* Cooperstown Art Association, Cooperstown NY
DiLuzio, Raphael, *Assoc Prof - Digital,* University of Southern Maine, Dept of Art, Gorham ME (S)
Dilworth, Robert, *Interim Chair Art & Art History,* University of Rhode Island, Fine Arts Center Galleries, Kingston RI
Dilworth, Robert, *Prof,* University of Rhode Island, Dept of Art & Art History, Kingston RI (S)
DiMarco, Dominic, *Pres,* Cranbrook Academy of Art, Bloomfield Hills MI (S)
DiMarzo, Michelle, *Cur of Education & Academic Engagment,* Fairfield University, Art Museum, Fairfield CT
Dimas, Jerald, *Pres,* Inter-Society Color Council, Frederick MD
DiMattia, Ernest A, *Pres,* Ferguson Library, Stamford CT
Dimattio, Vincent, *Chmn,* Monmouth University, Dept of Art & Design, West Long Branch NJ (S)
Diminich, Jason, *Educ Dir,* Think 360 Art Complete Education, Colo Chapter, Denver CO
Dimock, George, *Prof,* University of North Carolina at Greensboro, School of Art, Greensboro NC (S)
Dimock, Margaret, *Asst Cur,* Saint Anselm College, Alva de Mars Megan Chapel Art Center, Manchester NH
Dimond, Thomas, *Prof Art,* Eastern Oregon University, School of Arts & Science, La Grande OR (S)
Dimond, V Scott, *Cur Visual Arts,* Southern Alleghenies Museum of Art, Loretto Facility, Loretto PA
DiNardo, Matt, *Campus Mgr,* Touchstone Center for Crafts, Hart Moore Museum, Farmington PA
Dingwerth, Shaun T, *Exec Dir,* Richmond Art Museum, Richmond IN
Dingwerth, Shaun T, *Exec Dir,* Richmond Art Museum, Israel D. Edelman Library, Richmond IN
Dinkins, Gerald, *Cur Malacology,* University of Tennessee, McClung Museum of Natural History & Culture, Knoxville TN
Dinkins, Stephanie, *Assoc Prof,* Stony Brook University, College of Arts & Sciences, Dept of Art, Stony Brook NY (S)
Dinschel, Elizabeth, *Educ Specialist,* National Archives & Records Administration, Herbert Hoover Presidential Library - Museum, West Branch IA
DiNucci, Celeste, *Dir Develop,* Painted Bride Art Center Gallery, Philadelphia PA
Dion, Lizabeth, *Devel Coord,* Arizona State University, ASU Art Museum, Tempe AZ
Dion, Phil, *Preparator,* Contemporary Art Gallery Society of British Columbia, Vancouver BC
Dionisio, Max, *Librarian, H.H. Mu Far Eastern Library,* Royal Ontario Museum, Library & Archives, Toronto ON
Diope, Corinne, *Asst Prof,* James Madison University, School of Art & Art History, Harrisonburg VA (S)
DiPietro, David, *Assoc Prof Art (Fayette Campus),* Pennsylvania State University, University Park, Penn State School of Visual Arts, University Park PA (S)
Dirado, Stephen, *Instr,* Clark University, Dept of Visual & Performing Arts, Worcester MA (S)
Diresta, Kathleen, *Mus Shop Mgr,* Sea Cliff Village Museum, Sea Cliff NY
Diring, Connie, *Admin Asst,* University of Wisconsin-Madison, Chazen Museum of Art, Madison WI
Dirishenko, Peter, *Exec Dir,* Dallas Contemporary, Dallas Visual Art Center, Dallas TX
DiRito, Ron, *Photog,* Montserrat College of Art, Beverly MA (S)
Dirocco, Rose, *Dir,* Lycoming College Gallery, Williamsport PA
Disbro, Bill, *Art Coordr,* Jamestown Community College, Arts, Humanities & Health Sciences Division, Jamestown NY (S)
Disney, Betty, *Dir,* Cypress College, Fine Arts Gallery, Cypress CA
DiSpigna, Antonio, *Adjunct Assoc Prof,* New York Institute of Technology, Fine Arts Dept, Old Westbury NY (S)
Disston, Debbie, *Gallery Dir,* Southern New Hampshire University, McIninch Art Gallery, Hooksett NH
Ditner, Judy, *Cur Photography,* Yale University, Yale University Art Gallery, New Haven CT
DiTommaso, Francis, *Dir & Cur,* School of Visual Arts, Chelsea Gallery, New York NY
Dittman, Emily, *Coll & Exhib Coordr,* Syracuse University, SUArt Galleries, Syracuse NY
Dittmer, Donna, *Secy,* Independence Historical Museum & Art Center, Independence KS
Dittrich, Dennis, *MFA,* New Jersey City University, Art Dept, Jersey City NJ (S)
Diviney, David, *Asst Cur,* Southern Alberta Art Gallery, Library, Lethbridge AB
Divis, Sunshine, *Progs Mgr,* Center for Fine Art Photography, Fort Collins CO
Divola, John, *Prof,* University of California, Riverside, Dept of Art, Riverside CA (S)
Divola, John, *Prof,* University of California, Riverside, Dept of Art, Riverside CA (S)
Dixie, Gwen, *Art Librn,* J Eric Johnson, Fine Arts Division, Dallas TX
Dixon, Bob, *Assoc Prof,* University of Illinois at Springfield, Visual Arts Program, Springfield IL (S)
Dixon, David, *Assoc Prof,* East Tennessee State University, College of Arts and Sciences, Dept of Art & Design, Johnson City TN (S)
Dixon, David, *Communs Coordr,* Rockford Art Museum, Rockford IL
Dixon, Elsabé, *VPres,* Washington Sculptors Group, Washington DC
Dixon, Jenny, *Exec Dir,* Isamu Noguchi, Isamu Noguchi Garden Museum, Long Island City NY
Dixon, Keith, *Dir Develop & Communs,* Louisiana Arts & Science Museum, Baton Rouge LA
Dixon, Laurinda, *Prof,* Syracuse University, Dept of Fine Arts (Art History), Syracuse NY (S)
Dixon, Melanie, *COO,* National Art Education Association, Alexandria VA
Dixon, Michael, *Assoc Prof & Dept Chair,* Albion College, Bobbitt Visual Arts Center, Albion MI
Dixon, Sierra, *Research & Colls Assoc,* Connecticut Historical Society, Library, Hartford CT
Dixon, Susan M, *Asst Prof, Art Hist,* University of Tulsa, School of Art, Tulsa OK (S)
Dixon, Terry, *Computer Art,* College of Lake County, Art Dept, Grayslake IL (S)
Dixon, Yvonne, *Prof,* Trinity College, Fine Arts Program, Washington DC (S)
Dixson, Ronna, *Coll Mgr,* New York State Office of Parks, Recreation and Historic Preservation, Bureau of Historic Sites, Waterford NY
Dizik, Elizabeth, *Library Asst,* Cranbrook Art Museum, Library, Bloomfield Hills MI
Djoka, Mimi, *Lectr,* Humboldt State University, College of Arts & Humanities, Art Dept, Arcata CA (S)
Dlouhy, Linda, *Educ Coordr,* Clear Lake Arts Center, Clear Lake IA
Dluhy, Deborah H, *Dean,* School of the Museum of Fine Arts, Boston MA (S)
Dmytriw, Charles, *Prof,* Northwestern Connecticut Community College, Fine Arts Dept, Winsted CT (S)
Do, Anh, *Instr,* Virginia State University, Department of Art & Design, Petersburg VA (S)
Dobbins, Harriet, *Treas,* Huntsville Art League, Lowe Mill Arts & Entertainment, Huntsville AL
Dobbins, John, *Prof,* University of Virginia, McIntire Dept of Art, Charlottesville VA (S)
Dobbs, Christopher, *Dir,* Noah Webster House, Inc, Noah Webster House & West Hartford Historical Society, West Hartford CT
Dobrowitsky, Catherine, *Bd Chair,* Pewabic Society Inc, Pewabic, Detroit MI
Dobson, Jenni, *Coordr Educ,* Loveland Museum/Gallery, Loveland CO
Dobson, Mike, *Pres,* Lunenburg Art Gallery Society, Lunenburg NS
Dobson, Terry, *Asst Prof,* Azusa Pacific University, College of Music & the Arts, Dept of Art & Design, Azusa CA (S)
Docherty, Linda, *Prof,* Bowdoin College, Art Dept, Brunswick ME (S)
Docktor, Mali, *Pres,* Alberta Society of Artists, Calgary AB
Dodd, Beth, *Head Librn & Cur Alexander Architectural Archive,* University of Texas at Austin, Architecture & Planning Library, Austin TX
Dodd, Jerry, *Instr Sculpture,* Texas A&M University Commerce, Dept of Art, Commerce TX (S)
Dodd, Marie, *Treas,* Glynn Visual Arts, Inc, Saint Simons Island GA
Dodds, Jerrilynn, *Dean,* Sarah Lawrence College, Dept of Art History, Bronxville NY (S)
Dodds, Richard J, *Cur Maritime History,* Calvert Marine Museum, Solomons MD
Dodez, Paul, *Asst Lectr,* Idaho State University, Dept of Art, Pocatello ID (S)
Dodge, Robert, *Instr,* Bucks County Community College, Fine Arts Dept, Newtown PA (S)
Dodson, Drew, *Asst Prof,* Radford University, Art Dept, Radford VA (S)
Dodson, Linda, *Registrar,* Washington County Museum of Fine Arts, Hagerstown MD
Dody, Diane, *Instr, Online,* Wayland Baptist University, Dept of Art, School of Fine Art, Plainview TX (S)
Doe, Rachel, *Faculty of Arts Academic Advisor,* Mount Royal College, Dept of Interior Design, Calgary AB (S)
Doell, Margaret, *Head Chair & Prof Art,* Adams State College, Dept of Visual Arts, Alamosa CO (S)
Doering, James, *Instr Music,* Randolph-Macon College, Dept of the Arts, Ashland VA (S)
Doern-Danko, Maura, *Gen Educ,* Art Institute of Pittsburgh, Pittsburgh PA (S)
Doerner, Richard L, *Museum Specialist,* United States Senate Commission on Art, Washington DC
Dogu, Mehmet, *Designer,* University of California, Santa Barbara, Art, Design & Architecture Museum, Santa Barbara CA
Doherty, Caitlin, *Dir,* Museum of Contemporary Art Jacksonville, Jacksonville FL
Doherty, Deirdre, *Dir Develop,* The Long Island Museum of American Art, History & Carriages, Stony Brook NY

Doherty, Dornith, *Prof Photog,* University of North Texas, College of Visual Arts & Design, Denton TX (S)
Doherty, Laura, *Communs Coordr,* Art Complex Museum, Carl A Weyerhaeuser Library, Duxbury MA
Doherty, Meghan C, *Dir & Asst Prof,* Berea College, Art & Art History Program, Berea KY (S)
Doherty, Meghan C, *Dir & Cur,* Berea College, Doris Ulmann Galleries, Berea KY
Doherty, Richard, *Assoc Prof Photog,* Tarrant County College, Art Dept, Hurst TX (S)
Doherty, Ryan, *Dir & Cur,* Southern Alberta Art Gallery, Lethbridge AB
Doktorski, Eileen, *Dept Chair,* Mt San Jacinto College, Art Dept, San Jacinto CA (S)
Dolan, Anne R, *Dir,* Lincoln County Historical Association, Inc, Library, Wiscasset ME
Dolan, Douglas, *Exec Dir,* Bucks County Historical Society, Mercer Museum, Doylestown PA
Dolbin, Steve, *Dir,* Shippensburg University, Kauffman Gallery, Shippensburg PA
Dolbin, Steven, *Asst Prof,* Shippensburg University, Art Dept, Shippensburg PA (S)
Dole, Nadia, *Shaker Mercantile Buyer,* Hancock Shaker Village, Inc, Pittsfield MA
Dolembo, Marie, *Adjunct Asst Prof Art History,* Johnson County Community College, Fine Arts Dept & Art History Dept, Overland Park KS (S)
Dolgos, Charles, *Prof,* Miami-Dade Community College, Arts & Philosophy Dept, Miami FL (S)
Dolkart, Judith F, *Dir,* Phillips Academy, Addison Gallery of American Art, Andover MA
Doll, Don, *Instr,* Creighton University, Fine & Performing Arts Dept, Omaha NE (S)
Doll, Nancy, *Dir,* University of North Carolina at Greensboro, Weatherspoon Art Museum, Greensboro NC
Dollar, Betsy, *Exec Dir,* Springfield Art Association of Edwards Place, Springfield IL
Dolman, Marjorie, *Admin Asst,* Charles B Goddard, Ardmore OK
Dolton, Dennis, *Dir Gallery,* University of Southern Colorado, College of Liberal & Fine Arts, Pueblo CO
Dombrowski, Mark, *Cataloging,* Siena Heights College, Art Library, Adrian MI
Domel, August, *Instr,* Judson University, School of Art, Design & Architecture, Elgin IL (S)
Domencil, Laura, *Dir,* Pittsburgh Center for the Arts, Pittsburgh PA
Domine, Doug, *Chmn Dept,* Northwestern Michigan College, Art Dept, Traverse City MI (S)
Domingo, Beatrice Santo, *VChmn,* Queen Sofia Spanish Institute, New York NY
Dominguez, Frank, *Chmn,* Bucks County Community College, Hicks Art Center, Newtown PA
Dominguez, Frank, *Chmn Dept,* Bucks County Community College, Fine Arts Dept, Newtown PA (S)
Dominguez, Jose, *Dir,* Pyramid Atlantic, Hyattsville MD
Dominique, Gina, *Assoc Prof & Dept Chmn,* Delta College, Art Dept, University Center MI (S)
Domino, Dusty, *Dir Art Dept,* North Arkansas Community-Technical College, Art Dept, Harrison AR (S)
Domkowski, Dorothy, *Graphics Design & Editor,* The National Shrine of the North American Martyrs, Fultonville NY
Donabedian, Meg, *Librn,* New York School of Interior Design, New York School of Interior Design Library, New York NY
Donadio, Emmie, *Chief Cur,* Middlebury College, Museum of Art, Middlebury VT
Donaghey, Ellen, *Chief Financial Officer,* Boston Public Library, Central Library, Boston MA
Donaghy, Kieran, *Dean,* Cornell University, College of Architecture, Art, and Planning, Ithaca NY (S)
Donaher, Sean, *Artistic Dir,* Center for Exploratory & Perceptual Art, CEPA Library, Buffalo NY
Donaher, Sean, *interim Exec & Artistic Dir,* Center for Exploratory & Perceptual Art, CEPA Gallery, Buffalo NY
Donahue, Deirdre, *Librn,* International Center of Photography, Research Center, New York NY
Donahue, Gail, *Asst Dir,* Woodlawn/The Pope-Leighey, Alexandria VA
Donahue, Kevin, *Drawing,* Henry Ford Community College, McKenzie Fine Art Ctr, Dearborn MI (S)
Donahue, Marsha, *Founder,* North Light Gallery, Millinocket ME
Donahue, Mary, *Asst Prof,* Chadron State College, Dept of Art, Chadron NE (S)
Donahue, Michael, *Chmn,* Temple College, Art Dept, Temple TX (S)
Donahue-Semenza, Stacey, *Art Dept Coordr,* Keystone College, Fine Arts Dept, LaPlume PA (S)
Donahue-Wallace, Kelly, *Assoc Prof Art History,* University of North Texas, College of Visual Arts & Design, Denton TX (S)
Donaldson, David, *Chief Tech Officer,* The Children's Museum of Indianapolis, Indianapolis IN
Donaldson, Jeff, *Cur,* Booth Western Art Museum, Cartersville GA
Donaldson, P, *Instr,* Golden West College, Visual Art Dept, Huntington Beach CA (S)
Donatelli, Kara, *Assoc Prof,* South Plains College, Fine Arts Dept, Levelland TX (S)
Donbeck, John, *Business Mgr,* Bainbridge Arts & Crafts Gallery, Bainbridge Island WA
Dondero, Mary, *Asst Prof,* Bridgewater State College, Art Dept, Bridgewater MA (S)
Donesky, Grant, *Design Dept Chair,* Cornish College of the Arts, Art Dept, Seattle WA (S)
Doney, Todd, *Adjunct Prof,* College of Saint Elizabeth, Art Dept, Morristown NJ (S)
Donjuan, Carlos, *Adj Asst Prof,* University of Texas at Arlington, Art & Art History Department, Arlington TX (S)
Donley, Robert, *Prof,* DePaul University, Dept of Art, Chicago IL (S)
Donley, Thomas, *Photog,* Art Institute of Pittsburgh, Pittsburgh PA (S)
Donnelly, Cathy, *Exhib Develop,* Indiana State Museum, Indianapolis IN
Donnelly, Daniel, *Co-Chair ADAD Dept,* Butte College, Art Gallery, Oroville CA
Donnelly, John, *Instr,* Mount Vernon Nazarene University, Art Dept, Mount Vernon OH (S)
Donohue, Adrienne, *Coll Mgr,* Concord Museum, Concord MA
Donohue, Andrew, *Bookkeeper,* Buffalo Niagara Heritage Village, Amherst NY
Donohue, Bill, *Exec Dir Jekyll Island,* Jekyll Island Museum, Jekyll Island GA
Donovan Fisher, Jeanne, *Chair,* Bard College, Fisher Art Center, Annandale-on-Hudson NY
Donovan, Jeremiah, *Prof,* State University of New York, College at Cortland, Dept Art & Art History, Cortland NY (S)
Donovan, Margaret, *Dir Pub Rels,* Southern Vermont Art Center, Manchester VT
Donovan, Maureen, *Deputy Dir,* Harvard University, Harvard Art Museums, Cambridge MA
Donovan, Missy, *Dir Progs & Outreach,* Peggy R McConnell Arts Center of Worthington, Columbus OH
Dooley Fairchild, Sira, *Colls Mgr,* The Bostonian Society, Library, Boston MA
Dooley, Beth, *Treas,* Kent Art Association, Gallery, Kent CT
Dooley, Michael, *Instr,* University of Utah, Dept of Art & Art History, Salt Lake City UT (S)
Dooley, Tim, *Assoc Prof,* University of Northern Iowa, Dept of Art, Cedar Falls IA (S)
Dooley, William, *Dir,* University of Alabama, Sarah Moody Gallery of Art, Tuscaloosa AL
Dooling, Daniella, *Asst Prof,* Colgate University, Dept of Art & Art History, Hamilton NY (S)
Dooner, Steve, *Asst Prof,* Quincy College, Art Dept, Quincy MA (S)
Dooney, Karen, *Instr,* Guild of Creative Art, Shrewsbury NJ (S)
Doran, Camille, *Registrar,* University of Minnesota Duluth, Tweed Museum of Art, Duluth MN
Doran, Faye, *Prof,* Harding University, Dept of Art & Design, Searcy AR (S)
Doran, Jennifer, *Owner & Dir,* Robischon Gallery, Denver CO
Dorazewski-Smouse, Kimberly, *Colls Mgr & Registrar,* University of Colorado, CU Art Museum, Boulder CO
Dorethy, Rex, *Prof,* University of Wisconsin-Stevens Point, Dept of Art & Design, Stevens Point WI (S)
Dorfman, Geoffrey, *Adj Assoc Prof,* College of Staten Island, Performing & Creative Arts Dept, Staten Island NY (S)
Dorfmann, Tracey, *Prog Dir,* Jewish Community Center of Greater Washington, Jane L & Robert H Weiner Judaic Museum, Rockville MD
Dorin, Lisa, *Dep Dur Curatorial Affairs,* Williams College, Museum of Art, Williamstown MA
Dorman, Dana, *Dir,* Beaumont Art League, Beaumont TX
Dorman, Nicholas, *Conservator,* Seattle Art Museum, Dorothy Stimson Bullitt Library, Seattle WA
Dorman, Nicholas, *Conservator,* Seattle Art Museum, Seattle WA
Dormon, Jessica, *Dir Publications,* The Historic New Orleans Collection, Williams Research Center, New Orleans LA
Dorn, Rachel, *Dir,* Yakima Valley Community College, Dept of Visual Arts, Yakima WA (S)
Dornbush, Talya, *Educ Dir,* Metropolitan State University of Denver, Center for Visual Art, Denver CO
Dornfeld, Mary, *Communs Asst,* Marquette University, Haggerty Museum of Art, Milwaukee WI
Dorrah, Katy, *Exec Dir,* Kansas Watercolor Society, Mark Arts, Wichita KS
Dorrah, Katy, *Exec Dir,* Mary R Koch Arts Center, Mark Arts, Wichita KS
Dorrien, Carlos, *Prof,* Wellesley College, Art Dept, Wellesley MA (S)
Dorrill, Lisa, *Adjunct Faculty,* Dickinson College, Dept of Art & Art History, Carlisle PA (S)
Dorrill, Lisa, *Instr,* Gettysburg College, Dept of Visual Arts, Gettysburg PA (S)
Dorsett, Wendy, *Publs & Mem,* Anthology Film Archives, New York NY
Dorsey, Doug, *Corresponding Secy,* Gilpin County Arts Association, Central City CO
Dorsey, Henry, *Chmn,* Coahoma Community College, Art Education & Fine Arts Dept, Clarksdale MS (S)
Dorsey, Rachael, *Assoc Dir Press & Mktg,* PS1 Contemporary Art Center, Long Island City NY
Dorsky, David, *Dir,* Dorsky Gallery, Dorsky Gallery Curatorial Programs, Long Island City NY
Dosik, Jeff, *Library Technician,* The National Park Service, United States Department of the Interior, Statue of Liberty National Monument & The Ellis Island Immigration Museum, Washington DC
Dostal, Matt, *Studio Mgr,* Creative Growth Art Center, Oakland CA
Dougan, Jay, *Asst Prof,* Fort Lewis College, Art Dept, Durango CO (S)
Dougherty, Dan, *Finance Dir,* Orlando Museum of Art, Orlando Sentinel Library, Orlando FL
Dougherty, Dana, *Finance Dir,* Orlando Museum of Art, Orlando FL
Dougherty, John, *Asst Prof,* East Central University, School of Fine Arts, Ada OK (S)
Dougherty, Linda, *Chief Cur,* North Carolina Museum of Art, Raleigh NC
Dougherty, Richard, *Chmn,* Murray State University, Dept of Art, Murray KY (S)
Doughty, Sonia, *Director of Development,* Bellevue Arts Museum, Bellevue WA
Douglas, Andrew, *Dir Ticketing,* Mesa Arts Center, Mesa Contemporary Arts Museum, Mesa AZ
Douglas, Deanna, *Prof,* University of Southern Mississippi, Dept of Art & Design, Hattiesburg MS (S)
Douglas, Deborah, *Cur Science & Technology,* Massachusetts Institute of Technology, MIT Museum, Cambridge MA

Douglas, Kendra, *Educ & Prog Coordr,* Franconia Sculpture Park, Franconia MN
Douglas, Kris, *Chief Cur,* Rochester Art Center, Rochester MN
Douglas, Mark, *Asst Prof & Chair,* Fontbonne University, Fine Art Dept, Saint Louis MO (S)
Douglas, Robert, *Prof,* University of Louisville, Allen R Hite Art Institute, Louisville KY (S)
Douley, Scott, *Asst Prof,* Wittenberg University, Art Dept, Springfield OH (S)
Doumato, Lamia, *Head Reader Svcs,* National Gallery of Art, Library, Washington DC
Doutriaux, Miriam, *Coll Mgr,* Anacostia Community Museum, Smithsonian Institution, Washington DC
Doutrick, Reba, *Vol Chmn,* Riverside, the Farnsley-Moremen Landing, Louisville KY
Dove, Christy, *Store Mgr & Buyer,* Morris Museum of Art, Augusta GA
Dove, Daniel, *Asst Prof Studio Art,* California Polytechnic State University at San Luis Obispo, Dept of Art & Design, San Luis Obispo CA (S)
Dove, Elizabeth, *Prof,* University of Montana, School of Art, Missoula MT (S)
Dove, Judy, *Member,* Gallery XII, Wichita KS
Dover, Conilia, *Guest Svcs,* Tellus Northwest Georgia Science Museum, Cartersville GA
Dowbenka, Michael, *Exhib & Outreach Technician,* City of Toronto Culture, The Market Gallery, Toronto ON
Dowdle, Paul, *VPres Information Technology,* Bowers Museum, Santa Ana CA
Dowds, Lesa, *Dir Conservation Servs Dept,* The Newberry, Chicago IL
Dowdy, William, *Chmn Dept,* Blue Mountain College, Art Dept, Blue Mountain MS (S)
Dowell, Kathy, *Dir Art & Humanities Programming,* Mid-America Arts Alliance & Exhibits USA, Kansas City MO
Dowell-Dennis, Terri, *Assoc Cur of Educ,* University of North Carolina at Greensboro, Weatherspoon Art Museum, Greensboro NC
Dowhie, Jr, Leonard, *Prof Emeritus,* University of Southern Indiana, Art & Design Dept, Evansville IN (S)
Dowling, Carole, *Secy,* Rancho Santa Fe Art Guild, Rancho Santa Fe CA
Dowling, Russell, *Chmn Bd,* High Plains Museum, McCook NE
Dowling, Teri, *Assoc Dir Libraries,* California College of the Arts, Libraries, Oakland CA
Dowling, Tom, *Prof Drawing & Painting,* Orange Coast College, Visual & Performing Arts Division, Costa Mesa CA (S)
Down, Chris, *Assoc Prof,* Mount Allison University, Dept of Fine Arts, Sackville NB (S)
Downes-Le Guin, Theo, *Prin,* Upfor Gallery, Portland OR
Downey, Martha J, *Site Mgr,* Illinois Historic Preservation Agency, Bishop Hill State Historic Site, Bishop Hill IL
Downey, Paige, *Dir Educ & Pub Progs,* Homer Watson, Kitchener ON
Downing, Ariel, *Curator of Museum Education,* The New Museum at the Bradford Brinton Ranch, The Brinton Museum, Big Horn WY
Downing, Caroline, *Prof, Chair,* State University of New York College at Potsdam, Dept of Fine Arts, Potsdam NY (S)
Downing, Milton, *Visual Arts,* Christina Cultural Arts Center, Inc, Wilmington DE
Downs, Clyde, *Prof,* Northwestern State University of Louisiana, School of Creative & Performing Arts - Dept of Fine & Graphic Arts, Natchitoches LA (S)
Downs, Stuart, *Instr,* James Madison University, School of Art & Art History, Harrisonburg VA (S)
Downward, Pat, *Museum Store Mgr,* San Jose Museum of Art, San Jose CA
Doxzen, Duane, *Dir Develop & Communs,* Delaplaine Visual Arts Education Center, Frederick MD
Doyle, Allan, *Dir Technology,* Massachusetts Institute of Technology, MIT Museum, Cambridge MA
Doyle, Brendan, *Pres,* Organization for the Development of Artists, Gallery Connexion, Fredericton NB
Doyle, Casey, *Asst Prof,* University of Idaho College of Art & Architecture, Dept of Art & Design, Moscow ID (S)
Doyle, Christopher, *Facilities Mgr,* Headlands Center for the Arts, Sausalito CA
Doyle, Kerry, *Dir,* University of Texas at El Paso, Stanlee & Gerald Rubin Center for the Visual Arts, El Paso TX
Doyle, Leo, *Instr,* California State University, San Bernardino, Dept of Art, San Bernardino CA (S)
Doyle, Michael, *Instr,* Wayne Art Center, Wayne PA (S)
Doyle, Michele, *Librn,* Old Salem Museums & Gardens, Library and Research Center, Winston-Salem NC
Doyle, Richard, *Pres & Cur,* San Fernando Valley Historical Society, Mark Harrington Library, Mission Hills CA
Doyle, Richard, *VPres & Cur,* San Fernando Valley Historical Society, Mission Hills CA
Doyle, Wanda, *Interim Dept Sec,* Millersville University, Dept of Art & Design, Millersville PA (S)
Doyon, Lina, *Documentation Tech,* Musee National des Beaux Arts du Quebec, Bibliotheque, Quebec QC
Doyon, Suzette J, *Assoc Prof,* University of West Florida, Dept of Art, Pensacola FL (S)
Doz, Daniel, *Pres & CEO,* Alberta College of Art & Design, Calgary AB (S)
Dozier, Kelly, *Pres,* LeMoyne Art Foundation, Center for the Visual Arts, Tallahassee FL
Dozois, Paula, *Interior Design Acad Advisor,* Mount Royal College, Dept of Interior Design, Calgary AB (S)
Dragisic, Stephan, *Dir of Development,* Reynolda House Museum of American Art, Winston-Salem NC
Dragonfly, David, *Cur,* Museum of the Plains Indian & Crafts Center, Browning MT
Drake, Amy, *Cur Special Projects,* Southern Oregon Historical Society, Library, Medford OR
Drake, Chantal, *Dir Communs,* The Dixon Gallery & Gardens, Memphis TN
Drake, Susan R, *Deputy Dir Finance & Admin,* Kimbell Art Foundation, Kimbell Art Museum, Fort Worth TX
Drakes, Aqua, *Enterprise & Sales Mgr,* Harriet Beecher Stowe Center, Hartford CT
Drapeau, Judy, *Asst Librn,* Saint Augustine Historical Society, Library, Saint Augustine FL
Draper, Jerry L, *Dean School Visual Arts,* Florida State University, Art History Dept, Tallahassee FL (S)
Drdak, Maureen, *Pres,* Pennsylvania Academy of the Fine Arts, Fellowship of the Pennsylvania Academy of the Fine Arts, New Philadelphia PA
Dreher, Derick, *Dir,* The Rosenbach Museum & Library, Philadelphia PA
Dreishpoon, Douglas, *Chief Cur,* The Buffalo Fine Arts Academy, Albright-Knox Art Gallery, Buffalo NY
Dreiss, Joseph, *Prof,* University of Mary Washington, Dept of Art & Art History, Fredericksburg VA (S)
Dreith, Corey, *Asst Prof Visual Arts,* University of Colorado-Colorado Springs, Visual & Performing Arts Dept (VAPA), Colorado Springs CO (S)
Drennan, Cohn, *Dir,* Wichita Falls Museum & Art Center, Wichita Falls TX
Drennan, Emily, *Cur, Registrar,* City of Cedar Falls, Iowa, James & Meryl Hearst Center for the Arts & Sculpture Garden, Cedar Falls IA
Drennen, Barbara, *Prof,* Malone University, Dept of Art, Canton OH (S)
Dresbach, Chad, *Asst Prof,* Winthrop University, Dept of Art & Design, Rock Hill SC (S)
Drescher, William, *Assoc Prof,* Elizabeth City State University, School of Arts & Humanities, Dept of Art, Elizabeth City NC (S)
Dresner Sadaka, Jane, *Co Chmn,* The Drawing Center, New York NY
Dressler, Rachel, *Asst Prof,* State University of New York at Albany, Art Dept, Albany NY (S)
Drewal, Henry J, *Prof,* University of Wisconsin, Madison, Dept of Art History, Madison WI (S)
Dreyer, Chris, *Pres,* Martha's Vineyard Center for the Visual Arts, Oak Bluffs MA
Dreyfuss, Elizabeth K, *Treas,* John D Barrow, Skaneateles NY
Driesbach, Janice, *Chief Cur,* Akron Art Museum, Akron OH
Driggers, Marci, *Head of Collections & Registrar,* Amon Carter Museum of American Art, Fort Worth TX
Drinan, Patricia, *Chmn,* University of San Diego, Art Dept, San Diego CA (S)
Drinkard, Nisha, *Asst Prof,* William Paterson University, Dept Arts, Wayne NJ (S)
Driscoll, David, *Cur Economic History,* Wisconsin Historical Society, Wisconsin Historical Museum, Madison WI
Driscoll, Tim, *Treas,* Portsmouth Historical Society, John Paul Jones House & Discover Portsmouth, Portsmouth NH
Driver, David, *Coll Mgr,* State University of New York at Plattsburgh, Art Museum, Plattsburgh NY
Drix, Pamela, *Instr,* Ithaca College, Fine Art Dept, Ithaca NY (S)
Drogoul, Laure, *Adjunct,* York College of Pennsylvania, Dept of Music, Art & Speech Communications, York PA (S)
Drolsum, Chris, *Reference Librn,* Maryland Institute, Decker Library, Baltimore MD
Dronen, Marcy, *Artist & Owner,* Gallery 4, Ltd, Fargo ND
Drost, Lise, *Chair, Assoc Prof,* University of Miami, Dept of Art & Art History, Coral Gables FL (S)
Droth, Martina, *Deputy Dir Research & Educ and Cur Sculpture,* Yale University, Yale Center for British Art, New Haven CT
Drought, Michael H, *Dir,* East Carolina University, School of Art & Design, Greenville NC (S)
Druckenmiller, Pat, *Dir,* University of Alaska, Museum of the North, Fairbanks AK
Druckrey, Timothy, *Dir,* Maryland Institute, Graduate Photographic & Electronic Media, Baltimore MD (S)
Drumheller, Grant, *Prof,* University of New Hampshire, Dept of Art & Art History, Durham NH (S)
Drumm, Charlotte, *Asst Prof,* Sam Houston State University, Art Dept, Huntsville TX (S)
Drummey, Peter, *Stephen T Riley Librn,* Massachusetts Historical Society, Library, Boston MA
Drusian, Lory, *VPres Exhib Devel & Project Mgmqt,* Royal Ontario Museum, Toronto ON
Dryburgh, Mary, *Dir Gallery & Instr,* Columbia Basin College, Esvelt Gallery, Pasco WA (S)
Dryfhout, John H, *Supt & Cur,* Saint-Gaudens National Historic Site, Cornish NH
Duany, Patricia, *Collection Specialist,* Miami-Dade College, MDC Museum of Art & Design, Miami FL
Duarte, Dora, *Rentals,* Brownsville Art League, Brownsville Museum of Fine Art, Brownsville TX
Dubansky, Mindell, *Mus Librn, Sherman Fairchild Ctr for Book Conservation,* The Metropolitan Museum of Art, Museum Libraries, New York NY
Dubbeldam, Winka, *Prof & Chair, Architecture,* University of Pennsylvania, School of Design (PennDesign), Philadelphia PA (S)
Dube, Ilene, *Dir Mktg,* James A Michener Art Museum, Doylestown PA
Dube, Manon, *Admin Asst,* Musee des Maitres et Artisans du Quebec, Montreal QC
DuBois, William, *Dir,* Rochester Institute of Technology, School of Photographic Arts & Sciences, Rochester NY (S)
Dubreuil, Steve, *Conservateur,* Musee Regional de lu Cote-Nord, Sept-Iles QC
Dubrevil, Patrick, *Instr,* Lourdes University, Art Dept, Sylvania OH (S)

Dubrulle, Elizabeth, *Dir Educ & Pub Progs,* New Hampshire Historical Society, New Hampshire Historical Society Museum, Concord NH
Dubsky, Shelagh, *Dance Dir,* Ashtabula Arts Center, Ashtabula OH
Ducady, Geralyn, *Dir Educ & Public Progs,* Brown University, Haffenreffer Museum of Anthropology, Providence RI
Ducady, Geralyn, *Dir Goff Center,* Rhode Island Historical Society, John Brown House, Providence RI
Ducceschi, Laura, *Instr,* Wayne Art Center, Wayne PA (S)
Duchesne, Jean, *Photography & Digital Imaging,* Holland College, School of Visual Arts & Journalism, Charlottetown PE (S)
Duckett, Dejay, *Dir Curatorial Svcs,* African American Museum in Philadelphia, Philadelphia PA
Duckworth, Harry W, *Pres,* Dalnavert Museum, Winnipeg MB
Duclos, Rebecca, *Dean, Fine Arts,* Concordia University, Faculty of Fine Arts, Montreal QC (S)
Duda, Jana, *Library Tech Servs,* Fashion Institute of Technology - SUNY, Gladys Marcus Library, New York NY
Duddingston, Chuck, *Vice Chair,* American Craft Council, Minneapolis MN
Duddy, David A, *Dep Dir Opers,* deCordova Sculpture Park & Museum, Lincoln MA
Dudek, Steve, *Dir,* Barton County Community College, Fine Arts Dept, Great Bend KS (S)
Dudich, Michael, *Dir Opers & HR,* Hillwood Museum & Gardens Foundation, Hillwood Estate Museum & Gardens, Washington DC
Dudley, Janice Stafford, *Admin Asst,* MacArthur Memorial, Norfolk VA
Dudley, Mary, *Prof,* Howard College, Art Dept, Big Spring TX (S)
Dudley, Nancy, *Dir Educ,* Essex Historical Society and Shipbuilding Museum, Essex MA
Dudley, Russell, *Dir Gallery,* Sierra Nevada College, Fine Arts Dept, Incline Village NV (S)
Duehr, Gary, *Gallery Dir,* Bromfield Art Gallery, Boston MA
Duesing, James, *Prof & Dir, Ctr for the Arts in Society,* Carnegie Mellon University, School of Art, Pittsburgh PA (S)
Duff, Barb, *Coordr Library Svcs,* The Robert McLaughlin Gallery, Library, Oshawa ON
Duff, Charles, *Act Dept Head,* Ancilla College, Art Dept, Donaldson IN (S)
Duff, Penny, *Dir Educ,* Chicago Artists Coalition, Chicago IL
Duffy, Brian R, *Gallery Cur,* Villa Maria College of Buffalo, Art Dept, Buffalo NY (S)
Duffy, Brian, *Dir Library & Info Servs,* Pennsylvania Academy of the Fine Arts, Library, Philadelphia PA
Duffy, Heather, *Exhibs Cur,* Kendall College of Art & Design, Urban Institute for Contemporary Arts, Grand Rapids MI
Duffy, Henry J, *Cur & Div Chief,* Saint-Gaudens National Historic Site, Library, Cornish NH
Duffy, Henry, *Cur,* Saint-Gaudens National Historic Site, Cornish NH
Duffy, Jim, *Cur & Caretaker,* South County Art Association, Kingston RI
Duffy, Michael, *Merchandise Sales Mgr.,* Norman Rockwell Museum, Stockbridge MA
Duffy, Shauna, *Mng Dir, Co-Dir,* AS220, Main Gallery, Providence RI
Duffy-Zeballos, Lisa, *Dir Art Research,* International Foundation for Art Research, Inc (IFAR), New York NY
Dufilho, Diane, *Instr,* Centenary College of Louisiana, Dept of Art, Shreveport LA (S)
DuFresne, John, *Term Professor,* Concordia University, Art and Design Department, Saint Paul MN (S)
Dufresne, Laura, *Assoc Prof,* Winthrop University, Dept of Art & Design, Rock Hill SC (S)
Dugal, Rod, *Prog Chair,* Sheridan College, Art Dept, Sheridan WY (S)
Dugan, Joel, *Prof,* Fort Hays State University, Dept of Art & Design, Hays KS (S)
Dugan, Steve, *Vol Coordr,* Workman & Temple Family Homestead Museum, City of Industry CA
Dugaune, Erica, *Asst Prof,* Texas State University - San Marcos, Dept of Art and Design, San Marcos TX (S)
Dugdale, James, *Instr,* Joliet Junior College, Fine Arts Dept, Joliet IL (S)
Duggal, Elizabeth, *Deputy Dir & COO,* Solomon R Guggenheim Museum, New York NY
Duggan, Lynn, *Prof,* Nazareth College of Rochester, Art Dept, Rochester NY (S)
Duggins, Steve, *Mus Preparator,* University of Richmond, University Museums, Richmond VA
Duguense, Chuck, *AV Specialist,* Moore College of Art & Design, Library, Philadelphia PA
Duillo, John, *Pres,* Society of American Historical Artists, Oyster Bay NY
Dujin, Veljko, *Coll Cur,* Palm Beach County Parks & Recreation Department, Morikami Museum & Japanese Gardens, Delray Beach FL
Duke, Amy, *Assoc Dir Public Engagement,* University of Kansas, Spencer Museum of Art, Lawrence KS
Duke, Laurie, *Head of Finance & Admin.,* New York University, Grey Art Gallery, New York NY
Dukhic, Branica, *Executive Director,* Queens Historical Society, Kingsland Homestead, Flushing NY
Dull, Keith A, *Asst Prof,* Ashland University, Art Dept, Ashland OH (S)
Dullum, David, *Treas,* The Art League Gallery & School, Alexandria VA
Dumbadze, Alexander, *Asst Prof,* George Washington University, Dept of Art of Fine Arts & Art History, Washington DC (S)
Dumohoo, Andrew, *Educ,* Fort Morgan Heritage Foundation, Fort Morgan CO
Dunbar, Elizabeth, *Director & CEO,* Everson Museum of Art, Syracuse NY
Dunbar, Richard, *Vice Pres Finance,* Springfield Museums, Connecticut Valley Historical Society,
Duncan, Chris, *Chmn Visual Arts,* Union College, Dept of Visual Arts, Schenectady NY (S)
Duncan, Concetta, *Head Communs,* National Portrait Gallery, Smithsonian Institution, Washington DC
Duncan, Donald, *Asst Prof,* Capital University, Fine Arts Dept, Columbus OH (S)
Duncan, Jen, *Exec Dir,* Hermitage Museum & Gardens, Norfolk VA
Duncan, Jen, *Exec Dir,* Hermitage Museum & Gardens, Museum, Norfolk VA
Duncan, Joyce, *Treas,* Hendricks Hill Museum, Southport ME
Duncan, Richard, *Pres Bd Trustees,* Zanesville Museum of Art, Zanesville OH
Duncan, Samuel, *Head of Library,* Amon Carter Museum of American Art, Fort Worth TX
Duncan, Samuel, *Head of Library & Archives,* Amon Carter Museum of American Art, Research Library, Fort Worth TX
Duncan, Tim, *Head Preparator,* Loyola University Chicago, Loyola University Museum of Art, Chicago IL
Duncan, Warren, *Chmn Fine & Performing Arts,* Tuskegee University, Liberal Arts & Education, Tuskegee AL (S)
Dunfey, Patrick, *Exhibitions Designer,* Dartmouth College, Hood Museum of Art, Hanover NH
Dunham, John, *Registrar,* Owensboro Museum of Fine Art, Owensboro KY
Dunham, Nancy, *Fin Dir,* Prescott Fine Arts Association, Gallery, Prescott AZ
Dunham, Rebecca, *Cur of Collections & Exhibitions,* Utah State University, Nora Eccles Harrison Museum of Art, Logan UT
Dunkelberger, Michelle, *Assistant to Executive Director,* Art Center of Battle Creek, Battle Creek MI
Dunkelberger, Michelle, *Asst to Exec Dir,* Art Center of Battle Creek, Michigan Art & Artist Archives, Battle Creek MI
Dunkelman, Arthur, *Dir,* Jay I Kislak Foundation, Miami Lakes FL
Dunlap, Chance, *Prof,* Tyler Junior College, Art Program, Tyler TX (S)
Dunlap, Ellen S, *Pres,* American Antiquarian Society, Worcester MA
Dunlap, William H, *Pres,* New Hampshire Historical Society, New Hampshire Historical Society Library, Concord NH
Dunn Marsh, Michelle, *Exec Dir & Cur,* Photo Center NW, Seattle WA
Dunn, Andrew, *Chair,* McMichael Canadian Art Collection, Kleinburg ON
Dunn, BJ, *Deputy Superintendent,* Independence National Historical Park, Philadelphia PA
Dunn, Chuck, *VChmn,* Mississippi Museum of Art, Howorth Library, Jackson MS
Dunn, David W, *Dir,* Pennsylvania Historical & Museum Commission, Railroad Museum of Pennsylvania, Strasburg PA
Dunn, David W, *Mus Dir,* Pennsylvania Historical & Museum Commission, The State Museum of Pennsylvania, Harrisburg PA
Dunn, David, *Mus Dir,* Pennsylvania Historical & Museum Commission, The State Museum of Pennsylvania, Harrisburg PA
Dunn, Elizabeth C, *Gen Educ,* Art Institute of Pittsburgh, Pittsburgh PA (S)
Dunn, Jamila, *Youth Art Progs Mgr,* Kala Institute, Kala Art Institute, Berkeley CA
Dunn, Jodi, *Instr,* Keystone College, Fine Arts Dept, LaPlume PA (S)
Dunn, Kirsten, *Community Outreach and Volunteer Coordinator,* The Columbus Museum, Columbus GA
Dunn, Laura, *Office Mgr,* Glynn Visual Arts, Inc, Saint Simons Island GA
Dunn, Madeline, *Cur Educ,* Delaware Division of Historical & Cultural Affairs, Dover DE
Dunn, Michael, *Photo Branch,* United States Capitol, Architect of the Capitol, Washington DC
Dunn, Nancy, *Mus Mgr,* Artesia Historical Museum and Art Center, Artesia NM
Dunn, Robert, *VPres,* National Society of Painters in Casein & Acrylic, Inc, Whitehall PA
Dunn, Roger, *Prof,* Bridgewater State College, Art Dept, Bridgewater MA (S)
Dunnahoe, Donna, *Exec Dir,* The Fine Arts Center of Hot Springs, Hot Springs AR
Dunne, Susan, *Treas,* Art Dealers Association of America, Inc, New York NY
Dunnell, Molly, *Mktg Assoc,* University of Wyoming, University of Wyoming Art Museum, Laramie WY
Dunning, Jeanne, *Assoc Prof,* Northwestern University, Evanston, Dept of Art Theory & Practice, Evanston IL (S)
Dunstan, Graham, *VPres Mktg & Communs,* Americans for the Arts, New York NY
Dupere, Daniel, *Head Opers,* The Stewart Museum, Montreal QC
Duperon, Summer, *Mktg & Commun,* Longue Vue House & Gardens, New Orleans LA
Duperry, Robin, *Library Coordr,* Colby College, Bixler Art & Music Library, Waterville ME
Dupre, Kelly, *Faculty,* Grand Marais Art Colony, Grand Marais MN (S)
DuPrey, Michelle, *Admin Asst,* Ames Free-Easton's Public Library, North Easton MA
DuPuy, David, *Asst Head, Art,* Free Library of Philadelphia, Art Dept, Philadelphia PA
Duran, Adrian, *Asst Prof,* University of Nebraska at Omaha, School of the Arts, Omaha NE (S)
Duran, Grace, *Admin Asst,* Queensborough Community College, Art Gallery, Bayside NY
Durand, Mark, *Librn,* Playboy Enterprises, Inc, Library, Beverly Hills CA
Durant, John, *Dir,* Massachusetts Institute of Technology, MIT Museum, Cambridge MA
Durant, Mark Alice, *Prof,* University of Maryland, Baltimore County, Intermedia & Digital Arts (IMDA), Dept of Visual Arts, Baltimore MD (S)
Durben, Silvan A, *Dir & Cur,* Owatonna Arts Center, Owatonna MN

Durden, Bob, *Senior Cur,* Yellowstone Art Museum, Billings MT

Durden, Joan, *Asst Prof,* Appalachian State University, Dept of Art, Boone NC (S)

Durham, Marty, *Bldg Maintenance Supvr,* Charleston Museum, Charleston SC

Durham, Robert, *Lectr,* Vanderbilt University, Dept of Art, Nashville TN (S)

During, Helen Klisser, *Dir Visual Arts,* Westport Arts Center, Westport CT

Durkin, Brigid, *Cur Specialist,* Danbury Scott-Fanton Museum & Historical Society, Inc, Danbury CT

Durkin, Brigid, *Cur Specialist,* Danbury Scott-Fanton Museum & Historical Society, Inc, Library, Danbury CT

Durnin, Nathan, *Instr,* Wayne Art Center, Wayne PA (S)

Durocher, Kristina, *Dir,* University of New Hampshire, Museum of Art, Durham NH

Durrant, Doug, *Chmn,* Palomar Community College, Art Dept, San Marcos CA (S)

Duse, Kathy, *Convention & Progs Coordr,* National Art Education Association, Alexandria VA

Dusenbury, Carolyn, *Dir,* California State University, Chico, Meriam Library, Chico CA

Duson, Virginia, *VPres,* Crowley Art Association, The Gallery, Crowley LA

Dussart, Christel, *Cur Visual Arts,* Sangre de Cristo Arts & Conference Center, Pueblo CO

Dustin, Ko, *Facilities Mgr,* Kimball Jenkins Estate, Concord NH

Dutiel, Robert, *Assoc Prof Theatre,* Marymount Manhattan College, Fine & Performing Arts Div, New York NY (S)

Dutremaine, James, *Art Educ,* University of Texas Pan American, Art Dept, Edinburg TX (S)

Dutschke, Alithia, *Mgr Annual Giving,* Caramoor Center for Music & the Arts, Inc, Rosen House at Caramoor, Katonah NY

Dutton, Jeff, *Preparator & Designer,* Montgomery Museum of Fine Arts, Montgomery AL

Dutton, Matthew, *Cur,* Swine Gallery, Chattanooga TN

Duval, Douglas P, *Facilities Mgr,* Jamestown-Yorktown Foundation, Jamestown Settlement, Williamsburg VA

DuVerneay, Jessica, *Information Resources Specialist,* University of Michigan, Fine Arts Library, Ann Arbor MI

Duychak, Linda, *Reference Librn,* University of Wisconsin-Madison, Kohler Art Library, Madison WI

Dvorchak, David, *Communs Dir,* AS220, Main Gallery, Providence RI

Dwiggins, David, *IT Officer,* Historic New England, Library and Archives, Boston MA

Dwyer, Eugene J, *Prof,* Kenyon College, Art Dept, Gambier OH (S)

Dwyer, William, *Exec Dir,* Creative Art Center-North Oakland County, Pontiac Creative Arts Center, Pontiac MI (S)

Dyangani Ose, Elvira, *Sr Cur,* Creative Time, New York NY

Dybdahl, Tammy, *Financial Aid,* Rocky Mountain College of Art & Design, Lakewood CO (S)

Dye Sherpe, Chloe, *Assoc Cur,* Museum of Northwest Art, La Conner WA

Dye, Joseph, *Lectr,* College of William & Mary, Dept of Fine Arts, Williamsburg VA (S)

Dyer, Cecily, *Reference Libr,* Brooklyn Historical Society, Othmer Library, Brooklyn NY

Dyer, Deb, *Exec Dir,* National Institute of Art & Disabilities (NIAD), Florence Ludins-Katz Gallery, Richmond CA

Dyer, Eric, *Assoc Prof,* University of Maryland, Baltimore County, Intermedia & Digital Arts (IMDA), Dept of Visual Arts, Baltimore MD (S)

Dyer, M Wayne, *Prof,* East Tennessee State University, College of Arts and Sciences, Dept of Art & Design, Johnson City TN (S)

Dyer, Suzy, *Develop Asst,* Museum of Ventura County, Ventura CA

Dykhuis, Peter, *Dir & Cur,* Dalhousie University, Dalhousie Art Gallery, Halifax NS

Dyki, Judy, *Dir Library,* Cranbrook Art Museum, Library, Bloomfield Hills MI

Dyki, Judy, *Libr Dir,* Cranbrook Academy of Art, Bloomfield Hills MI (S)

Dykuis, Claire, *Prog Coordr,* Mount Saint Vincent University, MSVU Art Gallery, Halifax NS

Dynak, Sharon, *Exec Dir,* Ucross Foundation, Big Red Barn Gallery, Clearmont WY

Dyrhaug, Kurt, *Assoc Prof,* Lamar University, Art Dept, Beaumont TX (S)

Eachus, Lee, *Develop Dir,* Lexington Art League, Inc, Lexington KY

Eacret-Simmons, Carol, *Dir,* Dickinson State University, Art Gallery, Dickinson ND

Eacret-Simmons, Carol, *Gallery Dir & Assoc Prof Art,* Dickinson State University, Dept of Art, Dickinson ND (S)

Eagle, Rachel, *Secy,* Monroe County Community College, Humanities Division, Monroe MI (S)

Eagle, Scott, *Asst Dir,* East Carolina University, School of Art & Design, Greenville NC (S)

Eagleton, Tod, *Registrar,* McLean County Historical Society, McLean County Museum of History, Bloomington IL

Earenfight, Phillip, *Dir,* Dickinson College, The Trout Gallery, Carlisle PA

Earle, Susan, *Cur European & American Art,* University of Kansas, Spencer Museum of Art, Lawrence KS

Earls, Mollie, *Prog Coordr,* CAM Contemporary Art Museum, Raleigh NC

Earnest, Greta K, *Assoc Dir,* Fashion Institute of Technology - SUNY, Gladys Marcus Library, New York NY

Earnest, Royce, *Grad Coordr,* Judson University, School of Art, Design & Architecture, Elgin IL (S)

Earp, Lisa C, *Office Mgr,* Jefferson County Historical Society, Library, Watertown NY

Easby, Rebecca, *Chmn & Assoc Prof,* Trinity College, Fine Arts Program, Washington DC (S)

Easter, Earl, *Graphic Design,* Art Institute of Pittsburgh, Pittsburgh PA (S)

Easto, Elizabeth, *Cur Coll,* Aurora University, Schingoethe Center for Native American Cultures & The Schingoethe Art Gallery, Aurora IL

Easton-Moore, Barbara, *Exec Dir,* Rawls Museum Arts, Courtland VA

Eastwood, Jane, *Library Dir,* Saint Paul Public Library, Central Adult Public Services, Saint Paul MN

Eaton, Aurore, *Exec Dir,* Manchester Historic Association, Millyard Museum, Manchester NH

Eaton, Aurore, *Exec Dir,* Manchester Historic Association, Library, Manchester NH

Eaton, Linda, *Dir Colls,* Winterthur Museum, Winterthur Museum, Garden & Library, Winterthur DE

Eaton, Lynn, *Reference Archivist,* Duke University Library, Hartman Center for Sales, Advertising & Marketing History, Durham NC

Ebel, Malia, *Reference Librn/Archivist,* New Hampshire Historical Society, New Hampshire Historical Society Library, Concord NH

Ebeling, Jeffrey, *Exec Dir,* Banfill-Locke Center for the Arts, Fridley MN

Eberhardt, Brett, *Assoc Prof Art,* Western Illinois University, Department of Art, Macomb IL (S)

Eberhardt, Herman, *Cur,* National Archives & Records Administration, Franklin D Roosevelt Library, Hyde Park NY

Eberhardt, Herman, *Cur,* National Archives & Records Administration, Franklin D Roosevelt Museum, Hyde Park NY

Eberle-Nielander, Lilith, *Instr,* Appalachian State University, Dept of Art, Boone NC (S)

Ebert, D, *Instr,* Golden West College, Visual Art Dept, Huntington Beach CA (S)

Ebert, Howard, *Dir,* Saint Norbert College, Div of Humanities & Fine Arts, De Pere WI (S)

Ebitz, David, *Assoc Prof Art & Art Educ,* Pennsylvania State University, University Park, Penn State School of Visual Arts, University Park PA (S)

Ebner, Christian-Joseph, *Deputy Dir,* Austrian Cultural Forum Gallery, New York NY

Ebner, Martha, *Communs Coord,* Smith College, Museum of Art, Northampton MA

Ebner, Michaela, *Head Admin,* Austrian Cultural Forum Gallery, New York NY

Ebner, Stella, *Assoc Prof,* Purchase College, State University of New York, School of Art+Design, Purchase NY (S)

Eccles, Tom, *Exec Dir,* Bard College, Center for Curatorial Studies Graduate Program, Annandale-on-Hudson NY (S)

Eccles, Tom, *Exec Dir,* Bard College, Center for Curatorial Studies and the Hessel Museum of Art, Annandale-on-Hudson NY

Ecdao, Paul, *Co-Owner,* Thumbprint Gallery, La Jolla CA

Echevery, Santiago, *Prof,* University of Tampa, College of Arts & Letters, Tampa FL (S)

Echtner, Mark, *Prof,* Sinclair Community College, Division of Fine & Performing Arts, Dayton OH (S)

Eckersley, Robyn D, *Educ Coordr,* Lighthouse ArtCenter Museum & School of Art, Tequesta FL

Eckert, Cathy Lee, *Treas,* Booth Western Art Museum, Cartersville GA

Eckert, John, *Preparator,* Gertrude Herbert Institute of Art, Augusta GA

Eckert, Mitch, *Assoc Prof,* University of Louisville, Allen R Hite Art Institute, Louisville KY (S)

Eckhardt, Marcus, *Cur Mus,* National Archives & Records Administration, Herbert Hoover Presidential Library - Museum, West Branch IA

Eckhardt, Susan, *Dir Mus Educ,* Kalamazoo Institute of Arts, Kalamazoo MI

Eckhardt, Susan, *Dir Museum Educ,* Kalamazoo Institute of Arts, The Mary & Edwin Meader Fine Arts Library, Kalamazoo MI

Eckhaus, Karen, *Sr Dir Opers & Vis Engagement,* International Center of Photography, Museum, New York NY

Eckle, Cliff, *Sr History Cur,* Ohio History Connection, Columbus OH

Eckley, Laura, *Dir Library,* Bronxville Public Library, Bronxville NY

Eckmann, Dorothy, *Educ Dir,* Gertrude Herbert Institute of Art, Augusta GA

Eckmann, Sabine, *Dir & Chief Cur,* Washington University, Mildred Lane Kemper Art Museum, Saint Louis MO

Eckmann, Teresa, *Asst Prof,* University of Texas at San Antonio, Dept of Art & Art History, San Antonio TX (S)

Eckstein, Eileen, *Corresp Secy,* Plastic Club, Art Club, Philadelphia PA

Economon, Barbara, *Visual Resources Librn,* Walker Art Center, Library and Archives, Minneapolis MN

Edberg, Jane, *Chmn & Prof,* Gavilan College, Art Dept, Gilroy CA (S)

Edberg, Jane, *Prof Art & New Technology,* Gavilan Community College, Art Gallery, Gilroy CA

Edborg, Judy A, *American Artisans Dir,* American Society of Artists, Inc, Palatine IL

Eddings, Melissa, *Assoc Prof Art,* Ohio Northern University, Dept of Art & Design, Ada OH (S)

Eddins, Rebecca, *Dir Colls Management,* Reynolda House Museum of American Art, Winston-Salem NC

Eddy, Cheri, *Facilities Mgr,* Bank One Wisconsin, Milwaukee WI

Eddy, Chrisine, *Dir Devel,* Erie Art Museum, Erie PA

Eddy, Christine, *Dir Develop,* Erie Art Museum, Erie PA

Eddy, Dave, *Asst Prof Lectr,* University of Utah, Dept of Art & Art History, Salt Lake City UT (S)

Edelson, Gilbert S, *Admin VPres & Counsel,* Art Dealers Association of America, Inc, New York NY

Edelson, Rae, *Dir,* Gateway Arts, Gateway Gallery, Brookline MA

Edelstein, Susan, *ArtLab Gallery Dir,* University of Western Ontario, Dept of Visual Arts, London ON (S)

Eden, John, *Adjunct Prof,* University of Maine, Dept of Art, Orono ME (S)

Eden, Xandra, *Exec Dir & Chief Cur,* Diverse Works, Houston TX
Edens, Abbie, *Director of Education,* The Columbus Museum, Columbus GA
Eder, Elizabeth, *Asst Dir,* SculptureCenter, Long Island City NY
Edgar, David, *Chmn,* Ashland University, Art Dept, Ashland OH (S)
Edgar, David, *Prof,* University of North Carolina at Charlotte, Dept Art, Charlotte NC (S)
Edgar, Rana, *Dir Educ,* Arkansas Arts Center, Little Rock AR
Edgar, William R, *Dir Interior Design, Industrial Design Tech,* The Art Institutes, The Art Institute of Seattle, Seattle WA (S)
Edge, Rhea, *Dir,* Burgess Hall Art Gallery - Eureka College,
Edge, Tom, *Bldg Operations Mgr,* Allentown Art Museum, Allentown PA
Edinberg, Lucinda, *Outreach Coordr,* St John's College, Elizabeth Myers Mitchell Art Gallery, Annapolis MD
Edinger, Faye, *Treas,* Toledo Artists' Club, Toledo Artists' Club & Gallery, Toledo OH
Edison, Diane, *Assoc Prof Drawing & Painting,* University of Georgia, Franklin College of Arts & Sciences, Lamar Dodd School of Art, Athens GA (S)
Edizel, Gerar, *Dean,* New York State College of Ceramics at Alfred University, School of Art & Design, Alfred NY (S)
Edlow, Kenneth, *Treas & Asst Secy,* American Numismatic Society, New York NY
Edmondson, Carol, *CFO,* Cincinnati Art Museum, Cincinnati Art Museum, Cincinnati OH
Edmondson, Jo, *Educ Coordr,* Tubac Center of the Arts, Santa Cruz Valley Art Association, Tubac AZ
Edmonson, Adrienne, *Dir Mktg & Communs,* Tacoma Art Museum, Tacoma WA
Edmonson, Christine, *Reference Librn,* The Cleveland Museum of Art, Ingalls Library, Cleveland OH
Edmonson, Randall W, *Prof,* Longwood University, Dept of Art, Farmville VA (S)
Edmunds, Allan L, *Pres & Exec Dir,* Brandywine Workshop, Center for the Visual Arts, Philadelphia PA
Edson, Erik, *Prof,* Mount Allison University, Dept of Fine Arts, Sackville NB (S)
Edward, Laurie, *Prog Mgr,* Banff Centre, Paul D Fleck Library & Archives, Banff AB
Edwards, Brendan, *Head Library & Archives,* Royal Ontario Museum, Library & Archives, Toronto ON
Edwards, Brooke, *Theatre Mgr,* Imperial Centre's Maria V Howard Arts Center, Rocky Mount NC
Edwards, Bruce, *Residency Coordr,* SPACES, Cleveland OH
Edwards, Byron, *VPres Acad Affairs,* Nossi College of Art, Nashville TN (S)
Edwards, Christian, *Treas,* North Carolina Museums Council, Raleigh NC
Edwards, Elizabeth, *Exec Dir,* Art Dealers Association of Canada, Toronto ON
Edwards, Geoffrey, *Archivist,* Cincinnati Art Museum, Mary R Schiff Library & Archives, Cincinnati OH
Edwards, Glen, *Prof,* Utah State University, Dept of Art, Logan UT (S)
Edwards, JoAnn, *Exec Dir,* San Francisco Museum of Craft and Design, San Francisco CA
Edwards, June, *Prof,* Slippery Rock University of Pennsylvania, Dept of Art, Slippery Rock PA (S)
Edwards, Kathleen, *Sr Cur,* University of Iowa, University of Iowa Museum of Art, Iowa City IA
Edwards, Kathy, *Ref Librn,* Clemson University, Emery A Gunnin Architectural Library, Clemson SC
Edwards, Katie, *Cur,* UMLAUF Sculpture Garden & Museum, Austin TX
Edwards, Mary, *Assoc Dean,* University of Illinois, Urbana-Champaign, College of Fine & Applied Arts, Champaign IL (S)
Edwards, Nancy, *Cur European Art & Head Acad Svcs,* Kimbell Art Foundation, Kimbell Art Museum, Fort Worth TX
Edwards, Pam, *Dir Retail Opers,* Columbus Museum of Art, Columbus OH
Edwards, Patricia, *Lect Sr,* Old Dominion University, Art Dept, Norfolk VA (S)
Edwards, Rebecca, *Adjunct,* College of the Canyons, Art Dept, Santa Clarita CA (S)
Edwards, Richard, *Dir,* Baldwin Gallery, Aspen CO
Edwards, Sandi, *Pres,* Rancho Santa Fe Art Guild, Rancho Santa Fe CA
Edwards, Sara Foley, *Pub Progs Mgr,* Museum of Fine Arts, Houston, Rienzi Center for European Decorative Arts, Houston TX
Edwards, Sarah, *Develop Coordr,* Latitude 53 Contemporary Visual Culture, Edmonton AB
Edwards, Skip, *Master Woodcarver,* Calvert Marine Museum, Solomons MD
Edwards, Susan C S, *Dir Historic Resources,* The Trustees of Reservations, The Mission House, Ipswich MA
Edwards, Susan, *Executive Director,* Historical Society of Old Newbury, Cushing House Museum, Newburyport MA
Edwards, Tammi, *Dir Spec Projects,* Tennessee State Museum, Nashville TN
Edwards, Taryn, *Partnerships Librn,* Mechanics' Institute, San Francisco CA
Edwards, Wanda, *Chief Cur,* Historic Pensacola Preservation Board, T.T. Wentworth Jr. Florida State Museum, Pensacola FL
Edwards, Wendy, *Prof,* Brown University, Dept of Visual Art, Providence RI (S)
Effler, Jim, *Instr Foundation/Illustration,* AIC College of Design, Cincinnati OH (S)
Efland, Arthur, *Prof Emeritus,* Ohio State University, Dept of Art Education, Columbus OH (S)
Egami, Yash, *VP, Content and Marketing,* The One Club, New York NY
Egami, Yash, *VPres Content & Mktg,* The One Club for Creativity, New York NY
Egan Stalfort, Heather, *Assoc Dir Communs & Mktg,* Johns Hopkins University, Homewood Museum, Baltimore MD
Egan, Natasha, *Exec Dir,* Museum of Contemporary Photography, Columbia College Chicago, Chicago IL
Egbert, Elizabeth, *CEO & Pres,* Staten Island Museum, Archives Library, Staten Island NY
Egelston, Rachel, *Children's Progs Mgr,* Western Colorado Center for the Arts, The Art Center, Grand Junction CO
Eggebrecht, David, *Acad Dean,* Concordia University Wisconsin, Fine Art Gallery, Mequon WI
Eggener, Keith, *Assoc Prof,* University of Missouri - Columbia, Art History & Archaeology Dept, Columbia MO (S)
Eggers, Jill, *Assoc Prof,* Grand Valley State University, Art & Design Dept, Allendale MI (S)
Eggers, Rachel, *Pub Relations Mgr,* Seattle Art Museum, Seattle WA
Eggleston, Robert, *Dean pro tem,* University of British Columbia Okanagan, Faculty of Creative & Critical Studies, Kelowna BC (S)
Eglinski, Edmund, *Assoc Prof,* University of Kansas, Kress Foundation Dept of Art History, Lawrence KS (S)
Egnoski, Christine, *Exec Dir,* Portrait Society of America, Tallahassee FL
Ehlers, Marla, *Asst Library Dir,* Grand Rapids Public Library, Grand Rapids MI
Ehnbom, Daniel, *Art History Instr,* University of Virginia, McIntire Dept of Art, Charlottesville VA (S)
Ehrgott, Sarina, *Mktg & Communs Mgr,* Utah Arts Council, Chase Home Museum of Utah Folk Arts, Salt Lake City UT
Ehrhardt, Ursula M, *Asst Prof,* Salisbury State University, Art Dept, Salisbury MD (S)
Ehringer, Martha, *Events Coordr,* Mingei International, Inc, Mingei International Museum - Balboa Park & Mingei International Museum - Escondido, San Diego CA
Ehrman, Deborah, *Deputy Dir,* Salt Lake City Public Library, Nonfiction & Audiovisual Dept & Gallery at Library Square, Salt Lake City UT
Ehrnst, Elizabeth, *Digital Initiatives Librn,* Georgia O'Keeffe Museum, Research Center, Santa Fe NM
Eiben, Charles, *Art Transport Mgr & Preparator,* Intermuseum Conservation Association, Cleveland OH
Eichenberg, Roberta, *Assoc Prof of Art & Galleries Dir,* Emporia State University, Norman R Eppink Art Gallery, Emporia KS
Eichenberg, Roberta, *Asst,* Emporia State University, Dept of Art, Emporia KS (S)
Eichensehr, Kasey, *Cur,* Clark County Historical Society, Heritage Center of Clark County, Springfield OH
Eichhorn, Virginia, *Dir & Chief Cur,* Tom Thomson Memorial Art Gallery, Owen Sound ON
Eichner, Timothy, *Graphic Design Chmn,* Palm Beach Community College, Dept of Art, Lake Worth FL (S)
Eickmeier, Valerie, *Dean,* Indiana University-Purdue University, Indianapolis, Herron School of Art & Design, Indianapolis IN (S)
Eide, John, *Instr,* Maine College of Art, Portland ME (S)
Eifler, David, *Planning & Instruction Librn,* University of California, Berkeley, Environmental Design Library, Berkeley CA
Eike, Claire, *Exec Dir,* School of the Art Institute of Chicago, John M Flaxman Library, Chicago IL
Eikmeier, Linda, *Asst Site Mgr,* County of Henrico, Meadow Farm Museum, Glen Allen VA
Eiland, William, *Museum Dir,* University of Georgia, Georgia Museum of Art, Athens GA
Eilertsen, Kate, *Exec Dir,* Sonoma Valley Museum of Art, Sonoma CA
Einfalt, Linda, *Assoc Prof Fine Arts,* University of Cincinnati, School of Art, Cincinnati OH (S)
Eis, Andrea, *Chmn Dept & Spec Instr,* Oakland University, Dept of Art & Art History, Rochester MI (S)
Eisenbach, Diane, *Ceramics Instr,* Monterey Peninsula College, Art Dept/Art Gallery, Monterey CA (S)
Eisenbach-Bush, Laurie, *Instr Graphic Design,* Maryville University of Saint Louis, Art & Design Program, Saint Louis MO (S)
Eisenberg, Michelle, *Deputy Dir,* Conservation Center for Art & Historic Artifacts, Philadelphia PA
Eisenhauer, Paul, *Exec Dir & Cur,* Wharton Esherick Museum, Paoli PA
Eisenman, Stephen, *Prof,* Northwestern University, Evanston, Dept of Art History, Evanston IL (S)
Eisinger, Marguerite, *Docent Coordr,* State University of New York at Plattsburgh, Art Museum, Plattsburgh NY
Eisman, Hy, *Instr,* Joe Kubert, Dover NJ (S)
Eitel, Sydney, *Pres,* Colorado Watercolor Society, Denver CO
Eitzmann, Jennifer, *Develop Asst,* Montgomery Museum of Fine Arts, Montgomery AL
Ekechi, Lawrence, *Community Outreach Liaison,* The Africa Center, New York NY
Eklund, Brian, *Commun & Mktg Dir,* Hockaday Museum of Art, Kalispell MT
Elarfi, Meredith, *Mktg,* Tampa Museum of Art, Tampa FL
Elder, Dennis, *CFO,* Maryland Historical Society, Library, Baltimore MD
Elder, Donald, *Instr,* Woodstock School of Art, Inc, Woodstock NY (S)
Elder, Douglas Shaw, *Exec Dir,* Firehouse Art Center, Norman OK
Elder, Marianne, *Assoc VPres Student Affairs,* Alberta College of Art & Design, Calgary AB (S)
Elder, Sarah, *Cur,* Saint Joseph Museum, Inc., Saint Joseph MO
Elder, Tanya, *Sr Archivist,* American Jewish Historical Society, The Center for Jewish History, New York NY
Eldin, Marie, *Adj Prof,* Saint Joseph's University, Art Dept, Philadelphia PA (S)

Eldredge, Charles, *Prof,* University of Kansas, Kress Foundation Dept of Art History, Lawrence KS (S)
Eldridge, Jan, *Instr,* Solano Community College, Division of Fine & Applied Art & Behavioral Science, Fairfield CA (S)
Eldridge, Todd, *Art Instr,* East Central Community College, Art Dept, Decatur MS (S)
Elefante, Carl, *Pres,* American Institute of Architects, The Octagon Museum, Washington DC
Elet, Yvonne, *Asst Prof,* Vassar College, Art Dept, Poughkeepsie NY (S)
Eley, Shirley, *Pres,* Miles B Carpenter Folk Art Museum, Waverly VA
Elhenny, James, *Painting & Drawing,* University of Colorado at Denver, College of Arts & Media Visual Arts Dept, Denver CO (S)
Elias, Arthur, *Treas,* Prince Street Gallery, New York NY
Elias, Dan, *Exec Dir,* New Art Center in Newton, Newtonville MA
Eliason, Craig, *Prof,* University of St Thomas, Deptartment of Art History, Saint Paul MN (S)
Elkington, Richard, *Asst Prof,* Providence College, Art & Art History Dept, Providence RI (S)
Elkins, Nathan, *Asst Prof,* Baylor University - College of Arts and Sciences, Dept of Art, Waco TX (S)
Ellenbogen, Josh, *Asst Prof,* University of Pittsburgh, Henry Clay Frick Dept History of Art & Architecture, Pittsburgh PA (S)
Ellerbee, Genevieve, *Assoc Registar,* University of Nebraska, Lincoln, Sheldon Memorial Art Gallery & Sculpture Garden, Lincoln NE
Ellerbroek, Betsey, *Educ Dir,* Columbia River Maritime Museum, Astoria OR
Ellerby, Laura, *Mus Shop Mgr,* Institute of American Indian Arts, Museum of Contemporary Native Arts, Santa Fe NM (S)
Ellett, Tommy, *Pres,* Cottonlandia Museum, Greenwood MS
Elligott, Michelle, *Chief Library & Mus Archives,* Museum of Modern Art, Library and Museum Archives, New York NY
Elliman, George, *Pres,* MEXIC-ARTE Museum, Austin TX
Ellingson, Bruce, *VPres,* Witter Gallery, Storm Lake IA
Ellington, Howard W, *Exec Dir,* Wichita Center for the Arts, Mary R Koch School of Visual Arts, Wichita KS (S)
Elliot Shaw, Catherine, *Cur,* University of Western Ontario, McIntosh Gallery, London ON
Elliot, Elizabet, *Cur Progs,* Mobile Museum of Art, Mobile AL
Elliot, Gregory, *Asst Prof,* Louisiana State University, School of Art, Baton Rouge LA (S)
Elliot, John, *Asst Prof,* University of South Carolina at Aiken, Dept of Visual & Performing Arts, Aiken SC (S)
Elliot, Sandy, *Secy,* Western Art Association, Ellensburg WA
Elliot, Steve, *Prof,* Wayne State College, Dept Art & Design, Wayne NE (S)
Elliott, Andrea, *Instructor & Coordr Educ,* Converse College, School of the Arts, Dept of Art & Design, Spartanburg SC (S)
Elliott, Bill, *Deputy Dir Fin & Admin,* The Winnipeg Art Gallery, Winnipeg MB
Elliott, Diann, *Asst Cur,* Eskimo Museum, Library, Churchill MB
Elliott, Emmeline, *Library Operations Manager,* South Dakota State University, Hilton M. Briggs Library, Brookings SD
Elliott, Eric, *Asst Prof,* Colorado Mesa University, Art Dept, Grand Junction CO (S)
Elliott, Gregory, *Dept Chair,* University of Texas at San Antonio, Dept of Art & Art History, San Antonio TX (S)
Elliott, Jessica, *Administrative Director,* City of Port Angeles, Port Angeles Fine Arts Center & Webster Woods Art Park, Port Angeles WA
Elliott, John, *Pres,* Oil Pastel Association, Stockholm NJ
Elliott, Joseph, *Asst Prof,* Muhlenberg College, Dept of Art, Allentown PA (S)
Elliott, Joslyn, *Assoc Cur Exhibs,* Fort Wayne Museum of Art, Inc, Fort Wayne IN
Elliott, Kate, *Cur,* Luther College, Fine Arts Collection, Decorah IA
Elliott, Vanessa, *Admin Asst,* Ormond Memorial Art Museum and Gardens, Ormond Beach FL
Ellis, Bryan, *Lectr,* University of North Carolina at Greensboro, School of Art, Greensboro NC (S)
Ellis, Eric, *Dir Operations & Prog,* Association of Collegiate Schools of Architecture, Washington DC
Ellis, Erica, *Community Engagement,* San Luis Obispo Museum of Art, San Luis Obispo CA
Ellis, Jack, *Co-Chmn Theater,* Western New Mexico University, Expressive Arts Dept, Silver City NM (S)
Ellis, Jesika, *Instr,* University of Evansville, Art Dept, Evansville IN (S)
Ellis, Joe, *Dir,* Nicolaysen Art Museum & Discovery Center, Museum, Casper WY
Ellis, Lori, *Chmn & Prof,* State University of New York, College at Cortland, Dept Art & Art History, Cortland NY (S)
Ellis, Mac, *Custodian,* Glanmore National Historic Site of Canada, Belleville ON
Ellis, Peggy, *Res & Instr Srvcs Lib,* University of Western Ontario, The D B Weldon Library, London ON
Ellis, Rex, *Assoc Dir Curatorial Affairs,* National Museum of African American History and Culture, Smithsonian Institution, Washington DC
Ellis, Rhianna, *Asst Cur,* Nassau County Museum of Art, Roslyn Harbor NY
Ellis, Timothy, *Bd Pres,* Ogunquit Museum of American Art, Reference Library, Ogunquit ME
Ellison, Scott, *VPres Exec Comt,* Bank of Oklahoma NA, Art Collection, Tulsa OK
Elloian, Peter, *Prof,* University of Toledo, Dept of Art, Toledo OH (S)
Ellzy-Wright, Leatrice, *Interim Exec Dir,* Hammonds House Museum, Atlanta GA
Elmendorf, Dana, *Asst,* Seton Hill University, Art Program, Greensburg PA (S)
Elmore, Aaron, *Exhibits Designer,* Alaska State Museum, Juneau AK
Elms, Anthony, *Chief Cur,* University of Pennsylvania, Institute of Contemporary Art, Philadelphia PA
Elnimeiri, Mahjoub, *Prof,* Illinois Institute of Technology, College of Architecture, Chicago IL (S)
Elsmo, Nancy, *Librn,* Wustum Museum Art Association, Wustum Art Library, Racine WI
Elsner, Linda, *Pres,* Kelly-Griggs House Museum, Red Bluff CA
Elston, Ashley, *Asst Prof,* Berea College, Art & Art History Program, Berea KY (S)
Elton, Stephanie, *Communs Dir,* Toledo Museum of Art, Toledo OH
Elwell, Louann, *Secy to Dir,* Southern Illinois University, School of Art & Design, Carbondale IL (S)
Ely, Marcia, *VP Programs & External Affairs,* Brooklyn Historical Society, Brooklyn NY
Emberlin, Barbara, *Adjunct Instr, Art History,* Montana State University, School of Art, Bozeman MT (S)
Embree, Anna, *Guild Librn,* Guild of Book Workers, Library, Iowa City IA
Emerson, Bert, *Asst Prof,* Salve Regina University, Art Dept, Newport RI (S)
Emerson, Philip G, *Exec Dir,* Jamestown-Yorktown Foundation, Jamestown Settlement, Williamsburg VA
Emery, Lea, *Acting Dir,* Purchase College, Neuberger Museum of Art, Purchase NY
Emery, Marty, *Mgr Pub Rels & Internet Affairs,* National Postal Museum, Smithsonian Institution, Washington DC
Emery, Megan, *Chief Conservator & Sr Objects Conservator,* Midwest Art Conservation Center, Minneapolis MN
Emig, Emilia, *Cur Colls,* Marblehead Museum & Historical Society, Jeremiah Lee Mansion, Marblehead MA
Emison, Patricia, *Prof,* University of New Hampshire, Dept of Art & Art History, Durham NH (S)
Emlen, Robert, *Univ Cur,* Brown University, Annmary Brown Memorial, Providence RI
Emma, Sheena, *Vis Ctr Mgr,* Norwich Free Academy, Slater Memorial Museum, Norwich CT
Emme, Mary-Jane, *Secy Gen,* Canadian Society for Education Through Art, Victoria BC
Emmet, Andrew, *Develop & Outreach Assoc,* Storefront for Art & Architecture, New York NY
Emmons, Carol, *Prof,* University of Wisconsin-Green Bay, Arts Dept, Green Bay WI (S)
Emmons, Deborah, *Cur,* Historic Cherry Hill, Albany NY
Emmons-Andarawl, Deborah, *Interpreter,* Schuyler Mansion State Historic Site, Albany NY
Emond, Lauren, *Mgr Community Engagement,* Columbus Museum of Art, Columbus OH
Enabnit, Kenneth, *Art Librn,* Mason City Public Library, Mason City IA
Encina, Sebastian, *Mus Coll Mgr,* University of Michigan, Kelsey Museum of Archaeology, Ann Arbor MI
Endersby, Linda, *Asst Dir,* Missouri Department of Natural Resources, Elizabeth Rozier Gallery, Jefferson City MO
Endersby, Linda, *Asst Dir,* Missouri Department of Natural Resources, Missouri State Museum, Jefferson City MO
Endslow, Ellen, *Dir Coll & Cur,* Chester County Historical Society, West Chester PA
Endter, Laureen, *Shop Mgr,* Bergstrom-Mahler Museum of Glass, Library, Neenah WI
Engel, Scott, *Chmn,* Arapahoe Community College, Colorado Gallery of the Arts, Littleton CO
Engelbert, John P, *Pres,* First State Bank, They Also Ran Gallery, Norton KS
Engelmann, Lothar K, *Prof,* Rochester Institute of Technology, School of Photographic Arts & Sciences, Rochester NY (S)
Engelskirchen, Barbara, *Chief Devel Officer,* National Museum of Mexican Art, Chicago IL
Engglezos, Yvonne, *Dir,* Bowne House Historical Society, Flushing NY
Engh, Michael, *Acad Pres,* Santa Clara University, de Saisset Museum, Santa Clara CA
England, Ann, *Cur,* Georgia State University, School of Art & Design, Visual Resource Center, Atlanta GA
England, Susan, *Prog Asst,* Kentucky Guild of Artists & Craftsmen Inc, Berea KY
Engle, Karen, *Dir, School of Creative Arts,* University of Windsor, School of Creative Arts, Windsor ON (S)
Engler, Dara, *Asst Gallery Dir,* University of Louisiana at Monroe, Bry Gallery, Monroe LA
Engler, Dora, *Asst Prof,* Ithaca College, Fine Art Dept, Ithaca NY (S)
English, Anderson B, *Photog,* Art Institute of Pittsburgh, Pittsburgh PA (S)
English, Margaret, *Librn,* University of Toronto, Fine Art Library, Toronto ON
English, Sara, *Event Coordr,* Historic Holyoke at Wistariahurst & City of Holyoke, Holyoke MA
Engman, Berin, *Assoc Prof,* Colby College, Art Dept, Waterville ME (S)
Engman, Kerstin, *Adjunct Asst Prof,* University of Maine, Dept of Art, Orono ME (S)
Engstrom, Dustin, *Exec Asst,* Henry Gallery Association, Henry Art Gallery, Seattle WA
Engstrom, Mark, *Deputy Dir Colls & Research,* Royal Ontario Museum, Toronto ON
Enguet, Aurore, *Exec Dir,* Everhart Museum, Scranton PA
Ennen, Rita, *Dir Acquisition & Cataloging,* Dickinson State University, Stoxen Library, Dickinson ND
Ennis, Ciara, *Dir,* Pitzer College, Pitzer Art Galleries, Claremont CA (S)

Enniss, Stephen, *Dir,* University of Texas at Austin, Harry Ransom Humanities Research Center, Austin TX
Eno, Kristin, *Community Educ,* Education Alliance, Art School & Gallery, New York NY (S)
Enriquez, Alyssa, *Visual Arts & Literary Arts Prog Coordr,* Fairbanks Arts Association, Bear Gallery, Fairbanks AK
Enriquez, Carola Rupert, *Dir,* Kern County Museum, Bakersfield CA
Enriquez, Carola Rupert, *Dir,* Kern County Museum, Library, Bakersfield CA
Enroth, Tessa, *Develop & Communs Mgr,* Franconia Sculpture Park, Franconia MN
Ensign, Nancy, *Cur,* Patterson Library & Octagon Art Gallery, Westfield NY
Enstice, Wayne, *Prof Fine Arts,* University of Cincinnati, School of Art, Cincinnati OH (S)
Entin, Daniel, *Exec Dir,* Nicholas Roerich, New York NY
Entrekin, Donovan, *Art School Dir,* Flint Institute of Arts, Flint MI
Enyeart, James, *Asst Prof,* College of Santa Fe, Art Dept, Santa Fe NM (S)
Enzenaurer, Julie, *Admin Asst,* Owatonna Arts Center, Library, Owatonna MN
Epley Sheets, Elizabeth, *CAO,* Cheekwood-Tennessee Botanical Garden & Museum of Art, Nashville TN
Epley Sheets, Elizabeth, *CAO,* Cheekwood-Tennessee Botanical Garden & Museum of Art, Museum of Art, Nashville TN
Epley, Brad, *Chief Conservator,* Menil Foundation, Inc, The Menil Collection, Houston TX
Eppley, Brenda, *Instr,* Harrisburg Area Community College, Division of Communications, Humanities & the Arts, Harrisburg PA (S)
Epps, Lane, *Development Coordinator,* Albin Polasek Museum & Sculpture Gardens, Winter Park FL
Epps, Michelle, *Community Engagement Mgr,* SPACES, Cleveland OH
Erard, Mary Jane, *1st VPres,* Spectrum Gallery, Toledo OH
Erazmus, Alison, *Cur Exhibs,* Southern Illinois University Carbondale, University Museum, Carbondale IL
Erazmus, Alison, *Dir,* University of South Dakota, University Art Galleries, Vermillion SD
Erbach, Jeff, *Exec Dir,* The Art Gallery of Grand Prairie, Grande Prairie AB
Erbes, Scott, *Cur Decorative Arts & Design,* The Speed Art Museum, Louisville KY
Erbl, Claire, *Dir Mktg & Pub Rels,* Westmoreland Museum of American Art, Greensburg PA
Erbolato-Ramsey, Christiane, *Fine Arts Librn,* Brigham Young University, Harold B Lee Library, Provo UT
Erchak, Wyatt, *Programs & Operations Manager,* Shaker Museum & Library, Emma B King Library, New Lebanon NY
Ercums, Kris, *Cur Global Cont & Asian Art,* University of Kansas, Spencer Museum of Art, Lawrence KS
Erda, Andrea F, *Mgr,* Westover Plantation, Charles City VA
Erdelsky, Pat, *Asst Pub & Finance,* Westmoreland Museum of American Art, Art Reference Library, Greensburg PA
Erdman, Selena, *Gallery Mgr,* University of Wisconsin, Union Art Gallery, Milwaukee WI
Erdmann, Mariella, *Prof, Chmn,* Silver Lake College, Art Dept, Manitowoc WI (S)
Erf, Greg, *Asst Prof,* Eastern New Mexico University, Dept of Art, Portales NM (S)
Erf, Greg, *Prof Art & Animation,* Eastern New Mexico University, Runnels Gallery, Golden Library, Portales NM
Erf, Lisa K, *Exec Dir & Chief Cur,* The JPMorgan Chase, Art Collection, New York NY
Erhard, Peter, *Prof,* La Sierra University, Art Dept, Riverside CA (S)
Erickson, Christa, *Assoc Prof,* Stony Brook University, College of Arts & Sciences, Dept of Art, Stony Brook NY (S)
Erickson, Clark, *Cur in Charge,* University of Pennsylvania, Museum of Archaeology & Anthropology, Philadelphia PA
Erickson, Edmund, *Dir Library,* Black Hills State University, Library, Spearfish SD
Erickson, Elizabeth, *Prof,* Minneapolis College of Art & Design, Minneapolis MN (S)
Erickson, Gary, *Instr,* Macalester College, Art & Art History Dept, Saint Paul MN (S)
Erickson, Jeffrey, *Visual Resources Cur,* Davidson College, Katherine & Tom Belk Visual Arts Center, Davidson NC
Erickson, John, *Asst Prof Lectr,* University of Utah, Dept of Art & Art History, Salt Lake City UT (S)
Erickson, Joyce, *Dean Col Arts & Sciences,* Seattle Pacific University, Art Dept, Seattle WA (S)
Erickson, Pam, *Bookkeeper,* Fuller Lodge Art Center, Los Alamos NM
Erickson, Robert, *Prof,* University of Wisconsin-Stevens Point, Dept of Art & Design, Stevens Point WI (S)
Erickson, Robyn, *Rentals Mgr,* Villa Terrace Decorative Arts Museum, Milwaukee WI
Erickson, Russanne, *Educ,* Hastings Museum of Natural & Cultural History, Hastings NE
Ericson, Margaret, *Librn,* Colby College, Bixler Art & Music Library, Waterville ME
Eriksen, Roger, *Assoc Prof Art,* Adams State College, Dept of Visual Arts, Alamosa CO (S)
Erikson, Bruce, *Assoc Prof,* Xavier University, Dept of Art, Cincinnati OH (S)
Erlandson, Molly, *Asst Prof,* West Virginia State University, Art Dept, Institute WV (S)
Erlebacher, Martha Mayer, *Instr,* New York Academy of Art, Graduate School of Figurative Art, New York NY (S)
Ermansons, Taiga, *Assoc Educ,* Smith College, Museum of Art, Northampton MA
Ernst Croskrey, Wendy, *Prof,* University of Alaska Fairbanks, Art Department, Fairbanks AK (S)
Erskins, Eleanor, *Assoc Prof,* Portland State University, Dept of Art, Portland OR (S)
Ertelt, Victoria, *Admin,* Mount Angel Abbey Library, Saint Benedict OR
Erway, Janet, *Dir,* Cooperstown Art Association, Cooperstown NY
Erwin, Bobbie, *Dir,* New Visions Gallery, Inc, Marshfield WI
Erwin, Sarah, *Cur Archival Coll,* University of Tulsa, Library, Tulsa OK
Escalante, Jim, *Prof,* University of Wisconsin, Madison, Dept of Art, Madison WI (S)
Eschapasse, Anne, *Deputy Dir Exhibs & Outreach,* National Gallery of Canada, Ottawa ON
Escobar, Gloria, *Chmn,* Hartwick College, Art Dept, Oneonta NY (S)
Escobar, Jesus, *Assoc Prof,* Northwestern University, Evanston, Dept of Art History, Evanston IL (S)
Escobar, Laurie, *CINTAS Coordinator,* Miami-Dade College, MDC Museum of Art & Design, Miami FL
Escobedo, Valerie, *Assoc Prof,* University of Findlay, Art Program, Findlay OH (S)
Eskildsen, Noreen, *Lectr,* Briar Cliff University, Art Dept, Sioux City IA (S)
Eskilson, Stephen, *Prof,* Eastern Illinois University, Art Dept, Charleston IL (S)
Eskridge, Robert, *Dir Museum Educ,* The Art Institute of Chicago, Kraft Education Center/Museum Education, Chicago IL
Esler, Jennifer, *Pres & CEO,* Historical Society of Martin County, Elliott Museum, Stuart FL
Esmaye, Rodayne, *Prof,* Salt Lake Community College, Graphic Design Dept, Salt Lake City UT (S)
Esmond, Judi, *Educ Coordr,* State University of New York at New Paltz, Samuel Dorsky Museum of Art, New Paltz NY
Esmonde, Gary, *Librn,* Cleveland Botanical Garden, Eleanor Squire Library, Cleveland OH
Espey, Jule Adele, *Assoc Prof,* Our Lady of the Lake University, Dept of Art, San Antonio TX (S)
Espinosa, Christopher, *Gen Mgr,* El Pueblo de Los Angeles Historical Monument, Los Angeles CA
Espinosa, Fred, *Maintenance,* Museum of Western Colorado, Museum of the West, Grand Junction CO
Esposito, Cecilia, *Dir,* State University of New York at Plattsburgh, Art Museum, Plattsburgh NY
Esposito, Dan, *Asst Security & Facility Mgr,* The Pennsylvania State University, Palmer Museum of Art, University Park PA
Esquibel, George A, *Instr,* Sacramento City College, Art Dept, Sacramento CA (S)
Esselman, Paul, *COO,* The Speed Art Museum, Louisville KY
Esser, Cary, *The Kathleen Collins Chair & Prof,* Kansas City Art Institute, Kansas City MO (S)
Esser, Hillary, *Dir Develop,* Cedarhurst Center for the Arts, Mitchell Museum, Mount Vernon IL
Esser, Joe, *Designer & Preparator,* The Long Island Museum of American Art, History & Carriages, Stony Brook NY
Esser, Joseph, *Exhib Designer,* The Long Island Museum of American Art, History & Carriages, Library, Stony Brook NY
Essig, Joseph, *Treas,* Society of American Graphic Artists, New York NY
Essinger, Catherine, *Libr Coordr,* University of Houston, William R Jenkins Architecture & Art Library, Houston TX
Essl, Mike, *Acting Dean,* Cooper Union, School of Art, New York NY (S)
Esslinger, Claudia, *Prof,* Kenyon College, Art Dept, Gambier OH (S)
Estep, Connie, *Instr,* Illinois Wesleyan University, School of Art, Bloomington IL (S)
Estes, Jessica M, *Registrar,* Telfair Museums, Savannah GA
Estomin, B Lynn, *Chmn,* Lycoming College, Art Dept, Williamsport PA (S)
Estrella, Lori, *Gallery Dir,* Rhode Island Watercolor Society, Pawtucket RI
Etchieson, David, *Historic Site Specialist,* Historic Arkansas Museum, Little Rock AR
Etemad, Jaleh, *Pres,* The Society of Layerists in Multi-Media (SLMM), Albuquerque NM
Etherington, Nathan, *Prog & Community Coordr,* Brant Historical Society, Brant Museum & Archives, Brantford ON
Ethier, Nicole, *Art Dept Mgr,* University of Calgary, Dept of Art, Calgary AB (S)
Ethington, Bob, *Mgr History & Humanities Div,* Akron-Summit County Public Library, Fine Arts Division, Akron OH
Etling, Russell, *Cultural Affairs Progs Coordr,* City of Gainesville, Thomas Center Galleries - Cultural Affairs, Gainesville FL
Ettema, Michael, *Dir,* Maricopa County Historical Society, Eleanor Blossom Memorial Library, Wickenburg AZ
Etter, Ann, *Theater Specialist,* Northfield Arts Guild, Northfield MN
Eubank, Danielle, *VPres,* Women's Caucus For Art, New York NY
Eubank, Larry, *Opers Mgr,* Kimbell Art Foundation, Kimbell Art Museum, Fort Worth TX
Eudenbach, Peter, *Assoc Prof & Chair,* Old Dominion University, Art Dept, Norfolk VA (S)
Eva Raehse, Amy, *Exec Dir & Cur,* Goya Contemporary, Baltimore MD
Evalenko, Suzi, *Treas,* First Street Gallery, New York NY
Evangelista, Kristen, *Dir,* William Paterson University, University Galleries, Wayne NJ
Evanisko, Sonya, *Coordr Painting,* Shepherd University, Dept of Contemporary Art & Theater, Shepherdstown WV (S)
Evans Warren, Helen, *Chmn,* Mount Royal College, Dept of Interior Design, Calgary AB (S)
Evans, Allison, *Collections Mgr & Registrar,* Nelda C & H J Lutcher Stark Foundation, Stark Museum of Art, Orange TX
Evans, Barbara, *Dir Develop,* Telfair Museums, Telfair Academy of Arts & Sciences Library, Savannah GA

Evans, Catherine, *Chief Cur,* Carnegie Museums of Pittsburgh, Carnegie Museum of Art, Pittsburgh PA
Evans, Donald H, *Prof Emeritus,* Vanderbilt University, Dept of Art, Nashville TN (S)
Evans, Douglas R, *Registrar,* Westmoreland Museum of American Art, Art Reference Library, Greensburg PA
Evans, Douglas W, *Mgr Colls,* Westmoreland Museum of American Art, Greensburg PA
Evans, Elizabeth, *Mus Shop Mgr,* Palo Alto Art Center, Palo Alto CA
Evans, Helen, *Pres,* International Center of Medieval Art, New York NY
Evans, Jon, *Chief Dir,* Museum of Fine Arts, Houston, Hirsch Library, Houston TX
Evans, Julie, *Instr,* Guilford Technical Community College, Commercial Art Dept, Jamestown NC (S)
Evans, Kenya, *Gallery Supervisor,* Contemporary Arts Museum Houston, Houston TX
Evans, Kevin, *Controller,* Salisbury University, Ward Museum of Wildfowl Art, Salisbury MD
Evans, Laura, *Dir Advancement,* Canadian Museum of Nature, Musee Canadien de la Nature, Ottawa ON
Evans, Lee, *Chmn,* Pace University, Theatre & Fine Arts Dept, New York NY (S)
Evans, Libba, *Secy,* American Craft Council, Minneapolis MN
Evans, Lois, *Librn,* J T & E J Crumbaugh, Le Roy IL
Evans, Megan, *Administrative Assistant,* Kenyon College, Gund Gallery, Gambier OH
Evans, Oliver H, *Interim Pres,* Kendall College of Art & Design of Ferris State University, Grand Rapids MI (S)
Evans, Pat, *Registrar,* Scottsdale Cultural Council, Scottsdale Museum of Contemporary Art, Scottsdale AZ
Evans, Paula, *Accounting Specialist II,* The Columbus Museum, Columbus GA
Evans, Peggy, *Bd Mem,* French Art Colony, Gallipolis OH
Evans, Ron, *Chmn,* Cartoon Art Museum, San Francisco CA
Evans, Ryan, *Archivist,* Bard College, Center for Curatorial Studies and the Hessel Museum of Art, Annandale-on-Hudson NY
Evans, Scott, *Faculty,* Idaho State University, Dept of Art, Pocatello ID (S)
Evans, Sharon, *Interim Dean Fine Arts & Commun,* Western Illinois University, Department of Art, Macomb IL (S)
Evans, Steven, *Exec Dir,* Foto Fest International, Houston TX
Evans, Susan, *Asst Prof,* Oakland University, Dept of Art & Art History, Rochester MI (S)
Evans-Cantrell, Deborah, *Catalog/Reference Librn,* Newfields, Stout Reference Library, Indianapolis IN
Evanson, Barbara, *Community Serv Dir,* Rapid City Arts Council, Dahl Arts Center, Rapid City SD
Evarts, Wilbur, *Cur,* Paint 'N Palette Club, Grant Wood Memorial Park & Gallery, Anamosa IA
Eveillard, Elizabeth, *Chmn,* Frick Collection, New York NY
Eveler, Amanda, *Asst Librn,* York County Heritage Trust, Library and Archives, York PA
Evelyn, Douglas, *Co-Chair,* George Washington University, The George Washington Museum and The Textile Museum, Washington DC
Even, Megan, *Develop Coord,* Plains Art Museum, Fargo ND
Even, Yael, *Prof,* University of Missouri, Saint Louis, Dept of Art & Art History, Saint Louis MO (S)
Evenhaugen, Anne, *Head Librn,* American Art Museum, Library, Washington DC
Evenhaugen, Anne, *Head Librn,* National Portrait Gallery, Library, Washington DC
Evenhouse, Raymond, *Clinical Asst Prof,* University of Illinois at Chicago, Biomedical Visualization, Chicago IL (S)
Everett Zamora, Kristie, *Exhib Coordr,* Flint Institute of Arts, Library, Flint MI
Everett, Eileen, *Dir Liberal Arts & Grad Studies,* Academy of Art University, Fine Arts Dept, San Francisco CA (S)
Everett, Gwendolyn, *Assoc Dir,* Howard University, Gallery of Art, Washington DC
Everett, Terry, *Educ,* Tellus Northwest Georgia Science Museum, Cartersville GA
Everetts, Amy, *Dir Development,* Everhart Museum, Scranton PA
Everhart, Sarah, *Photo Librn,* History Colorado Center Museum, Stephen H Hart Library, Denver CO
Evers, Hans, *Dir Exhibs,* Robert & Mary Montgomery Armory Art Center, Armory Art Center, West Palm Beach FL
Eversole, Elizabeth, *Creative Assistant,* Pyramid Hill Sculpture Park & Museum, Hamilton OH
Everson, Kevin, *Studio Faculty,* University of Virginia, McIntire Dept of Art, Charlottesville VA (S)
Evins, Jennifer, *Pres & COO,* Arts Partnership of Greater Spartanburg, Inc, Chapman Cultural Center, Spartanburg SC
Evnin, Judy, *Chmn Bd Trustees,* Caramoor Center for Music & the Arts, Inc, Rosen House at Caramoor, Katonah NY
Ewan, Janette Cousins, *Registrar,* Museum London, London ON
Ewen, Anne, *Cur Art & Heritage,* Peter & Catharine Whyte Foundation, Whyte Museum of the Canadian Rockies, Banff AB
Ewers, Don, *Lectr,* University of the Incarnate Word, Art Dept, San Antonio TX (S)
Ewers, William, *Exec Dir,* Palette & Chisel Academy of Fine Arts, Chicago IL
Ewing, Rick, *Main Library Gen Mgr,* Akron-Summit County Public Library, Fine Arts Division, Akron OH
Ewing, Rosemary, *Chmn,* Louisiana Department of Culture, Recreation & Tourism, Louisiana State Museum, New Orleans LA
Ewing, Susan, *Dir,* Cranbrook Academy of Art, Bloomfield Hills MI (S)
Exxon, Randall L, *Prof,* Swarthmore College, Dept of Art & Art History, Swarthmore PA (S)
Eyer, Shawn, *Dir Communs & Develop,* The George Washington Masonic National Memorial Association, The George Washington Masonic National Memorial, Alexandria VA
Eyerdam, Pamela J, *Mgr,* Cleveland Public Library, Fine Arts & Special Collections Dept, Cleveland OH
Eyermann, Linda, *Dir Educ,* South Shore Arts, Munster IN
Eyjolfsson, Kristjana, *Dir Educ,* Historical Museum at Fort Missoula, Missoula MT
Eyler, Carolyn, *Dir Exhibs,* University of Southern Maine, Dept of Art, Gorham ME (S)
Ezell, Liz, *Mus Dir,* Marine Corps University, National Museum of the Marine Corps, Triangle VA
Ezell, Lynn, *Publications Mgr,* National Art Education Association, Alexandria VA
Ezell-Gilson, Carol, *Cur,* City of Charleston, City Hall Council Chamber Gallery, Charleston SC
Fabbri Butera, Virginia, *Chmn Dept,* College of Saint Elizabeth, Art Dept, Morristown NJ (S)
Faber, Carolyn, *Media Preservation & Digitization Librn,* School of the Art Institute of Chicago, John M Flaxman Library, Chicago IL
Faber, David, *Assoc Prof,* Wake Forest University, Dept of Art, Winston-Salem NC (S)
Fabian, Carole Ann, *Dir,* Columbia University, Avery Architectural & Fine Arts Library, New York NY
Fabiszak, Dennis, *Dir,* East Hampton Library, Long Island Collection, East Hampton NY
Fabius, Roxana, *Exec Dir,* A.I.R. Gallery, Brooklyn NY
Fabozzi, Paul, *Chmn,* Saint John's University, Dept of Fine Arts, Jamaica NY (S)
Fabricand-Person, Nicole, *Japanese Art Specialist,* Princeton University, Marquand Library of Art & Archaeology, Princeton NJ
Fabrick, Lane, *Assoc Prof,* Southeast Missouri State University, Dept of Art, Cape Girardeau MO (S)
Faccinto, Victor, *Dir,* Wake Forest University, Charlotte & Philip Hanes Art Gallery, Winston-Salem NC
Facio, Isaac, *Dept Specialist,* The Art Institute of Chicago, Department of Textiles, Textile Society, Chicago IL
Fadler, Matthew, *First VPres,* Rome Historical Society, Museum & Archives, Rome NY
Fagan Affleck, Diane, *Exhib Consultant,* American Textile History Museum, Lowell MA
Fagan, Barry, *Financial Coordr,* Queen's University, Agnes Etherington Art Centre, Kingston ON
Fagan, Sha, *Dir Lib & Acad Computing,* Sarah Lawrence College Library, Esther Raushenbush Library, Bronxville NY
Fagan, Tricia, *Cur,* Mercer County Community College, Arts, Communication & Engineering Technology, West Windsor NJ (S)
Faggioli, Renzo, *Instr,* Moravian College, Dept of Art, Bethlehem PA (S)
Fahey-Flynn, Anna, *Central Library Mgr.,* Boston Public Library, Central Library, Boston MA
Fahlman, Betsy, *Cur American Art,* Phoenix Art Museum, Phoenix AZ
Fahnestock, Jon, *Assoc Prof Interactive Design,* Maryville University of Saint Louis, Art & Design Program, Saint Louis MO (S)
Fahrney, Cassie, *CFO,* Cheekwood-Tennessee Botanical Garden & Museum of Art, Nashville TN
Fahrney, Cassie, *CFO,* Cheekwood-Tennessee Botanical Garden & Museum of Art, Museum of Art, Nashville TN
Fahy, Deborah, *Exec Dir,* Kennebec Valley Art Association, Harlow Gallery, Hallowell ME
Failing, Brian, *Executive Director,* Aurora Regional Fire Museum, Aurora IL
Faillace, Rachael, *Dir Gallery,* The Art School at Old Church, Demarest NJ (S)
Fairall, Tiffany, *Cur Exhibs,* Mesa Arts Center, Mesa Contemporary Arts Museum, Mesa AZ
Fairbanks, Natalie, *Communs Coordr,* Milwaukee Public Museum, Milwaukee WI
Fairchild, Sira, *Coll Mgr,* The Bostonian Society, Old State House Museum, Boston MA
Fairley, Judy, *VPres,* Valley Art Center Inc, Clarkston WA
Fairlie, Carol, *Asst Prof,* Sul Ross State University, Dept of Fine Arts & Communications, Alpine TX (S)
Fairlie, Holly, *Chief Security & Special Events Coordr,* Cornell University, Herbert F Johnson Museum of Art, Ithaca NY
Fairman, Elisabeth, *Chief Cur Rare Books & Manuscripts,* Yale University, Yale Center for British Art, New Haven CT
Fairweather, Paula, *Dir Mktg,* Bill Reid Gallery of Northwest Coast Art, Vancouver BC
Faison, Michael, *Exec Dir,* Idaho Commission on the Arts, Boise ID
Faist, Jennifer, *Photo Research Cur,* Art Center College of Design, James Lemont Fogg Memorial Library, Pasadena CA
Fajardo, Carlos, *Prof,* University of Puerto Rico, Mayaguez, Dept of Humanities, College of Fine Arts & Theory of Art Programs, Mayaguez PR (S)
Fajardo, Juliana, *Develop & Mktg Coordr,* Think 360 Art Complete Education, Colo Chapter, Denver CO
Fajardo, Rafael, *Assoc Prof Electronic Media Arts & Design,* University of Denver, School of Art & Art History, Denver CO (S)
Fajzi-DeGroot, Ester, *Gallery Asst,* Lawrence University, Wriston Art Center Galleries, Appleton WI
Fakundiny, Robert, *Chief Geological Survey,* New York State Museum, Albany NY
Falanga, Neal, *Exhibit Preparator,* St John's College, Elizabeth Myers Mitchell Art Gallery, Annapolis MD
Falcaro, Millie, *Assoc Prof Art,* Marymount Manhattan College, Fine & Performing Arts Div, New York NY (S)
Falco, Jaci, *Registrar,* Cedar Rapids Museum of Art, Cedar Rapids IA

Falcone-Hall, Kelly, *Vice Pres,* Western Reserve Historical Society, Cleveland OH

Falconer, Shelley, *Pres & CEO,* Art Gallery of Hamilton, Hamilton ON

Fales, Christine, *Acad Affairs Asst,* New Hampshire Institute of Art, Manchester NH

Fales, Melanie, *Exec Dir,* Boise Art Museum, Boise ID

Falgner, Susan M, *Head Pub Svcs,* College of Mount Saint Joseph, Archbishop Alter Library, Cincinnati OH

Falk, Karen, *Gallery Dir,* Jewish Community Center of Greater Washington, Jane L & Robert H Weiner Judaic Museum, Rockville MD

Falk, Lorne, *Dean Faculty,* School of the Museum of Fine Arts, Boston MA (S)

Falke, Emily, *Cur,* Bakersfield Art Foundation, Bakersfield Museum of Art, Bakersfield CA

Falkenstien-Doyle, Cheri, *Cur,* Wheelwright Museum of the American Indian, Mary Cabot Wheelwright Research Library, Santa Fe NM

Falkenstien-Doyle, Cheri, *Cur,* Wheelwright Museum of the American Indian, Santa Fe NM

Falkner, Avery, *Prof,* Pepperdine University, Seaver College, Dept of Art, Malibu CA (S)

Falkner, Lorett, *Asst Prof,* Rochester Institute of Technology, School of Photographic Arts & Sciences, Rochester NY (S)

Fallacaro, Bill, *Facilities Mgr,* Henry Morrison Flagler Museum, Palm Beach FL

Fallon, Roberta, *Adj Prof,* Saint Joseph's University, Art Dept, Philadelphia PA (S)

Falls, Jo, *Dir Educ & Visitor Servs,* Tohono Chul Park, Tucson AZ

Faloon, Ronda, *Dir,* Cape Ann Museum, Gloucester MA

Faloon, Ronda, *Dir,* Cape Ann Museum, Library, Gloucester MA

Falsetta, Vincent, *Prof Drawing & Painting,* University of North Texas, College of Visual Arts & Design, Denton TX (S)

Falvey, Tom, *Dir Educ,* South Carolina State Museum, Columbia SC

Falzon, Patricia, *Dir Develop,* Orange County Museum of Art, Newport Beach CA

Famighetti, Michael, *Magazine Ed,* Aperture Foundation, New York NY

Familian, David, *Asst Dir,* University of California, Irvine, Beall Center for Art + Technology, and University Art Gallery, Irvine CA

Fancher, Ollie, *Instr,* Middle Tennessee State University, Art Dept, Murfreesboro TN (S)

Fanelli, Doris, *Chief Cultural Resources,* Independence National Historical Park, Library, Philadelphia PA

Fanelli, Doris, *Chief, Division of Cultural Resources Management,* Independence National Historical Park, Philadelphia PA

Fankhauser, Teresa, *Exec Dir,* Allied Arts Council of St Joseph, Saint Joseph MO

Fannon, Megan, *VPres,* Rensselaer Newman Foundation Chapel + Cultural Center, The Gallery at the Chapel & Cultural Center, Troy NY

Fantasia, Kari, *Deputy Dir External Affairs,* National Museum of American History, Smithsonian Institution, Washington DC

Faraci, Carolyn, *Deputy Dir,* Huntsville Museum of Art, Huntsville AL

Farago, Andrew, *Cur,* Cartoon Art Museum, San Francisco CA

Farber, Ellen, *Prof,* State University of New York College at Oneonta, Dept of Art, Oneonta NY (S)

Farber, Leslie, *Assoc Prof,* William Paterson University, Dept Arts, Wayne NJ (S)

Farber, Robert, *Head Dept Prod,* Georgia Southern University, Betty Foy Sanders Dept of Art, Statesboro GA (S)

Farbstein, Tracy, *Library Asst,* University of California, Berkeley, Architecture Visual Resources Library, Berkeley CA

Farhad, Massumeh, *Chief Cur,* Freer Gallery of Art & Arthur M Sackler Gallery, Arthur M Sackler Gallery, Washington DC

Farhad, Massumeh, *Chief Cur,* Freer Gallery of Art & Arthur M Sackler Gallery, Freer Gallery of Art, Washington DC

Farina, John, *Dir Develop,* Beck Center for the Arts, Lakewood OH

Farina, Michele, *Controller,* Municipal Art Society of New York, New York NY

Faris, Anthony, *Asst Prod,* Georgia Southern University, Betty Foy Sanders Dept of Art, Statesboro GA (S)

Farkas, Alex, *Co-Founder,* U Gallery, San Francisco CA

Farkash, Gary, *Pres,* Baldwin Historical Society Museum, Baldwin NY

Farley Harger, Sara, *Exec Dir,* Liberty Hall Historic Site, Library, Frankfort KY

Farley, Gale, *Asst Prof,* Herkimer County Community College, Humanities Social Services, Herkimer NY (S)

Farley, Janice, *Prof,* Kingsborough Community College, Dept of Art, Brooklyn NY (S)

Farley, Joy, *Registrar,* Institute of American Indian Arts, Museum of Contemporary Native Arts, Santa Fe NM (S)

Farlow, Shannon, *Dir Mktg,* Waterloo Center of the Arts, Waterloo IA

Farlowe, Allie, *Asst Cur,* The Mint Museum, Mint Museum of Craft & Design, Charlotte NC

Farm, Linda Lee Kuuleilani, *Interim Pres & CEO,* Bernice Pauahi Bishop, Honolulu HI

Farmar, Angela, *Head Info & Reference,* Public Library of Cincinnati & Hamilton County, Info & Reference Dept, Cincinnati OH

Farmer, Dustin, *Art Instr,* Seward County Community College, Art Dept, Liberal KS (S)

Farmer, Lorraine, *Human Resources Dir,* Canadian Museum for Human Rights, Winnipeg MB

Farmer, Nancy, *Museum Shop Mgr,* Hammond-Harwood House Association, Inc, Hammond-Harwood House, Annapolis MD

Farn, George, *Treas,* Bowne House Historical Society, Flushing NY

Farnell, Cynthia, *Gallery Dir,* Georgia State University, Ernest G Welch Gallery, Atlanta GA

Farnia, Ahmad, *Mus Cafe Gen Mgr,* Oklahoma City Museum of Art, Oklahoma City OK

Farnsworth, Craig, *Instr,* Judson University, School of Art, Design & Architecture, Elgin IL (S)

Farr, Jeanette, *Instr,* Glendale Community College, Visual & Performing Arts Div, Glendale CA (S)

Farr, Joshua, *Exec Dir,* Vermont Center for Photography, Brattleboro VT

Farr, Libby, *Instr,* Marylhurst University, Art Dept, Marylhurst OR (S)

Farrar, Helene, *VPres,* Kennebec Valley Art Association, Harlow Gallery, Hallowell ME

Farrar-Wegener, Louise, *Instr,* Marylhurst University, Art Dept, Marylhurst OR (S)

Farrell, Anne, *Dir External Affairs,* Museum of Contemporary Art, San Diego, Geisel Library, La Jolla CA

Farrell, Cynthia, *Admin Asst,* University of New Hampshire, Museum of Art, Durham NH

Farrell, David, *Colls Registrar, Mus Colls,* Art Gallery of Peel, Peel Heritage Complex, Brampton ON

Farrell, Karolyn, *Secy,* National Oil & Acrylic Painters Society, Houston TX

Farrell, Laurie, *Cur & Department Head Contemporary Art,* Detroit Institute of Arts, Detroit MI

Farrell, Mary, *Prof,* Gonzaga University, Dept of Art, Spokane WA (S)

Farrell, Michael, *Prof, Media Art Histories & Visual Culture,* University of Windsor, School of Creative Arts, Windsor ON (S)

Farrell, Peggy, *Secy,* Pemaquid Group of Artists, Pemaquid Art Gallery, Pemaquid Point ME

Farrell, William, *Industrial Design Technology,* Art Institute of Pittsburgh, Pittsburgh PA (S)

Farrier, Sanford, *Chmn, Visual Communs,* Endicott College, School of Visual & Performing Arts, Beverly MA (S)

Farrington, Jennifer, *Pres & CEO,* Chicago Children's Museum, Chicago IL

Farrington, Rusty, *Chmn,* Iowa Central Community College, Dept of Art, Fort Dodge IA (S)

Farris, Mark, *Asst Prof,* University of Central Missouri, Dept of Art & Design, Warrensburg MO (S)

Farriss, Adra, *Prog Coordr,* Edna Hibel Art Foundation, Hibel Museum Gallery, Jupiter FL

Farrokhi, Abdollah, *Instr,* Black Hills State University, Art Dept, Spearfish SD (S)

Farthing, Stephen, *Exec Dir,* New York Academy of Art, Graduate School of Figurative Art, New York NY (S)

Farugee, Anoka, *Dir Graduate Studies in Painting & Printmaking,* Yale University, School of Art, New Haven CT (S)

Farynyk, Diane, *Chief Registrar & Exhibs Mgr,* Frick Collection, New York NY

Farzaneh-Far, Angelica, *Commun Mgr,* Swedish American Museum, Chicago IL

Fasoldt, Staats, *Instr,* Woodstock School of Art, Inc, Woodstock NY (S)

Fass, Philip, *Prof,* University of Northern Iowa, Dept of Art, Cedar Falls IA (S)

Fasse, Jane, *Instr,* Edgewood College, Art Dept, Madison WI (S)

Fassett, Brian, *Instr,* University of Louisiana at Monroe, Dept of Art, Monroe LA (S)

Fassnacht, Claire, *Devel Coordr,* Intuit: The Center for Intuitive & Outsider Art, Chicago IL

Fathman, Melissa, *Exec Dir,* Dairy Arts Center, Boulder CO

Fauconnet, Laurance, *Mgr Communs,* Municipal Art Society of New York, New York NY

Faudie, Fred, *Prof,* University of Massachusetts Lowell, Dept of Art, Lowell MA (S)

Faulds, W Rod, *Dir University Galleries,* Florida Atlantic University, University Galleries/Ritter Art Gallery/Schmidt Center Gallery, Boca Raton FL

Faulkes, Eve, *Prof,* West Virginia University, College of Creative Arts, School of Art & Design, Morgantown WV (S)

Faulkner, Phillip, *Asst Prof,* Finlandia Univ, International School of Art and Design, Hancock MI (S)

Faurot, Carlis, *Bldg Suprv,* Cedar Rapids Museum of Art, Cedar Rapids IA

Fauske, Ben, *Bus Dir,* Bergstrom-Mahler Museum of Glass, Library, Neenah WI

Fausone, Lynn G, *Adjunct Asst Prof,* Oakland University, Dept of Art & Art History, Rochester MI (S)

Faust, Kate, *Corresp Secy,* Catharine Lorillard Wolfe, New York NY

Fausz, Jeanette, *Asst Dir,* Saint Louis Art Museum, Saint Louis MO

Fauteux, Amanda, *Prog Mgr,* Struts Gallery, Sackville NB

Favata, Alexa A, *Deputy Dir,* University of South Florida, Contemporary Art Museum, Tampa FL

Favela, Maria, *Security,* Institute of American Indian Arts, IAIA Museum of Contemporary Native Arts, Santa Fe NM

Favella, Maria, *Dep Security Office,* Institute of American Indian Arts, Museum of Contemporary Native Arts, Santa Fe NM (S)

Favier, Pieter, *Sculptor,* University of South Alabama, Dept of Art & Art History, Mobile AL (S)

Favila, Allegra, *Asst. to the Dir. & Press Officer,* New York University, Grey Art Gallery, New York NY

Favis, Roberta, *Cur of the Vera Bluemner Kouba Coll,* Stetson University, Hand Art Center, Deland FL

Favret, John, *Faculty,* Housatonic Community College, Art Dept, Bridgeport CT (S)

Fawcett, Linda D, *Prof,* Hardin-Simmons University, Art Dept, Abilene TX (S)

Fawcett, Mim Brooks, *Exec Dir,* Attleboro Arts Museum, Attleboro MA

Fawkes, Tom, *Instr,* Pacific Northwest College of Art, Portland OR (S)

Faxon, Susan, *Assoc Dir & Cur,* Phillips Academy, Addison Gallery of American Art, Andover MA

Fay, Bob, *VPres,* The San Joaquin Pioneer & Historical Society, The Haggin Museum, Stockton CA
Fay, Ming, *Prof,* William Paterson University, Dept Arts, Wayne NJ (S)
Fay, Rebecca, *Head Mus Progs,* Delaware Historical Society, Delaware History Museum and Center for African American Heritage, Wilmington DE
Faye, Chris, *Cur,* Kauai Museum Association, Ltd, Lihue HI
Fayerman, Faye, *Prof,* New York Institute of Technology, Fine Arts Dept, Old Westbury NY (S)
Fazio, Karla, *Bd Pres,* Mary R Koch Arts Center, Mark Arts, Wichita KS
Feagin, Ashley, *Asst Prof,* Albion College, Bobbitt Visual Arts Center, Albion MI
Feagin, Susan, *VPres,* American Society for Aesthetics, Denver CO
Feagins, J R, *Chief Security,* Birmingham Museum of Art, Birmingham AL
Fealy, Rose, *VPres Fin & Adminstrn, CFO,* Museum of Science & Industry, Chicago IL
Fearson-Boone, Margaret, *Admin Asst,* California Institute of the Arts Library, Santa Clarita CA
Feast, Terra, *Cur Educ,* Boise Art Museum, Boise ID
Feather, Meghan, *Admin Asst,* Touchstone Center for Crafts, Hart Moore Museum, Farmington PA
Featherstone, Jull, *Dir Educ,* Edmundson Art Foundation, Inc, Des Moines Art Center, Des Moines IA
Feavyour, Dawn, *Prog Coordr,* Art and History Museums - Maitland, Maitland FL
Feazel, Emily, *Events Designer,* R W Norton Art Foundation, R W Norton Art Gallery, Shreveport LA
FeBland, Harriet, *Dir & Instr,* Harriet FeBland, New York NY (S)
FeBland, Harriet, *Pres Emerita,* American Society of Contemporary Artists (ASCA), Yorktown Heights NY
Febo, Samuel, *Dir,* Institute of Puerto Rican Culture, Dr Jose C Barbosa Museum, Bayamon PR
Febo-Cotto, Samuel D, *Dir,* Institute of Puerto Rican Culture, Museo y Parque Historico Ruinas de Caparra, Guaynabo PR
Febre, Ricardo, *Asst Prof,* Humboldt State University, College of Arts & Humanities, Art Dept, Arcata CA (S)
Fecho, Susan C, *Dean,* Barton College, School of Visual, Performing & Communication Arts, Wilson NC (S)
Fecho, Susan, *Dir,* Barton College, Barton Museum - Virginia Graves Gallery - Lula E Rackley Gallery, Wilson NC
Fechter, Earl, *Prof,* Norwich University, Dept of Architecture and Art, Northfield VT (S)
Fedders, Kristin, *Convener,* Earlham College, Art Dept, Richmond IN (S)
Fedeler, Barbara, *Asst Prof,* Wartburg College, Dept of Art, Waverly IA (S)
Federici, Mario, *Chmn Production Mgmt,* Fashion Institute of Technology, School of Art & Design, New York NY (S)
Fedor, Stefanie, *Exec Dir,* Visual Arts Center of Richmond, Richmond VA
Fedor, Stefanie, *Exec Dir,* Arlington Arts Center (AAC), Arlington VA
Fedorak, Lisa, *Prog Coordr,* Contemporary Art Gallery Society of British Columbia, Vancouver BC
Fedorchenko, Xenia, *Asst Prof,* Lamar University, Art Dept, Beaumont TX (S)
Feeler, William, *Dean,* Midland College, Art Dept, Midland TX (S)
Fefee, Claudette, *Secy,* The State University of New York at Potsdam, The Art Museum, Potsdam NY
Feher-Simonelli, Brenda, *Gallery Coordr,* Texas A&M University Commerce, Dept of Art, Commerce TX (S)
Feig, Randy, *Asst Prof,* Edgewood College, Art Dept, Madison WI (S)
Feige, Juliet, *Adjunct,* Idaho State University, Dept of Art, Pocatello ID (S)
Feik, J J, *VChmn,* Witte Museum, San Antonio TX
Fein, Ruth, *Asst Cur,* National Gallery of Art, Index of American Design, Washington DC
Feinberg, David, *Assoc Prof,* University of Minnesota, Minneapolis, Dept of Art, Minneapolis MN (S)
Feinberg, Larry J, *Dir,* Santa Barbara Museum of Art, Library, Santa Barbara CA
Feinberg, Larry J, *Dir,* Santa Barbara Museum of Art, Santa Barbara CA
Feinberg, Rachel, *Dir Develop,* UrbanGlass, Robert Lehman Gallery, Brooklyn NY
Feinburg, Daniel, *Asst Prof,* Berea College, Art & Art History Program, Berea KY (S)
Feingold, Eric, *History Cur,* Ohio History Connection, Columbus OH
Feinstein, Marta, *Mus Educator,* Cultural Affairs Department, Los Angeles Municipal Art Gallery, Los Angeles CA
Feinstein, Michael, *Chief Operating Officer,* Jewish Community Center of Greater Washington, Jane L & Robert H Weiner Judaic Museum, Rockville MD
Feintuch, Robert, *Senior Lectr,* Bates College, Art & Visual Culture, Lewiston ME (S)
Feiro, Christopher, *Asst Prof & Head Art Dept,* Philadelphia Community College, Dept of Art, Philadelphia PA (S)
Feisal, Marcia M, *Dept Chair,* Southern Nazarene University, Art & Design Department, Bethany OK (S)
Fejes, Yolande, *Owner,* Alaska House Art Gallery, Fairbanks AK
Fekete-Shukla, Alexis, *Dir Advancement & Planning,* University of Kansas, Spencer Museum of Art, Lawrence KS
Feklman, Bruce, *Chmn Photog,* College for Creative Studies, Detroit MI (S)
Fekner, John, *Asst Prof,* C W Post Campus of Long Island University, School of Visual & Performing Arts, Brookville NY (S)
Felder, Wendy, *Coordr Traveling Exhibs & Registrar,* Ohio History Connection, National Afro-American Museum & Cultural Center, Wilberforce OH
Feldman, Anita, *Deputy Dir, Curatorial Affairs & Education,* San Diego Museum of Art, San Diego CA
Feldman, Bob, *Pres,* Key West Art & Historical Society, East Martello Museum & Gallery, Key West FL
Feldman, Hannah, *Asst Prof,* Northwestern University, Evanston, Dept of Art History, Evanston IL (S)
Feldman, Joan, *Adjunct Faculty,* University of Maryland, Baltimore County, Intermedia & Digital Arts (IMDA), Dept of Visual Arts, Baltimore MD (S)
Feldman, Kaywin, *Dir & Pres,* Minneapolis Institute of Art, Minneapolis MN
Feldman, Sari, *Exec Dir,* Cuyahoga County Public Library, Parma OH
Feliciano, Awilda, *Instr,* Guilford Technical Community College, Commercial Art Dept, Jamestown NC (S)
Feliciano, Lares, *Program Director,* Think 360 Art Complete Education, Colo Chapter, Denver CO
Feliciano, Melissa, *Manager, Museum Services,* Lockwood-Mathews Mansion Museum, Norwalk CT
Felix, Amanda, *Mus Mgr,* Ogden Union Station, Union Station Museums, Ogden UT
Feller, Andrea, *Cur of Education,* Arizona State University, ASU Art Museum, Tempe AZ
Fellows, Leslie, *Gallery Mgr,* University of California at Santa Cruz, Eloise Pickard Smith Gallery, Santa Cruz CA
Fellows, Susan, *Member,* Gallery XII, Wichita KS
Felos, Charlene, *Chairperson,* Cypress College, Cypress CA (S)
Felshin, Nina, *Cur Exhib,* Wesleyan University, Ezra & Cecile Zilkha Gallery, Middletown CT
Felt, Tom, *Archivist,* Museum of American Glass in WV, Weston WV
Felton, Craig, *Prof,* Smith College, Art Dept, Northampton MA (S)
Fencl, Brian, *Asst Prof,* West Liberty State College, Div Art, West Liberty WV (S)
Fender, Kimber L, *Dir,* Public Library of Cincinnati & Hamilton County, Info & Reference Dept, Cincinnati OH
Fenety, Lois, *Dir,* Sunbury Shores Arts & Nature Centre, Inc, Library, Saint Andrews NB
Feng, ZL, *MFA,* Radford University, Art Dept, Radford VA (S)
Fengin, Christle, *Events Coordr,* Art Museum of Southeast Texas, Beaumont TX
Fenichel, Emily, *Asst Prof Art History,* Florida Atlantic University, D F Schmidt College of Arts & Letters Dept of Visual Arts & Art History, Boca Raton FL (S)
Fenkart-Froeschl, Dieter, *COO,* San Diego Museum of Art, San Diego CA
Fennell, Patricia, *Emer Prof,* University of Wisconsin, Madison, Dept of Art, Madison WI (S)
Fens, Emily, *Gallery Attendant,* Lawndale Art Center, Houston TX
Fenske, Hannah, *Dir,* Western Washington University, Viking Union Gallery, Bellingham WA
Fenski, Daniel, *Chmn,* Monmouth Museum & Cultural Center, Lincroft NJ
Fenster, Fred, *Emer Prof,* University of Wisconsin, Madison, Dept of Art, Madison WI (S)
Fenton, Susan, *Photog,* Saint Joseph's University, Art Dept, Philadelphia PA (S)
Fenton, Wendell, *VPres,* Brandywine Conservancy, Brandywine River Museum, Chadds Ford PA
Ferber, Andrea, *Faculty,* Idaho State University, Dept of Art, Pocatello ID (S)
Feren, Steve, *Emer Prof,* University of Wisconsin, Madison, Dept of Art, Madison WI (S)
Ference, Bill, *Dir Finance,* Bruce Museum, Inc, Greenwich CT
Fergus, Victoria, *Assoc Prof Emeritus,* West Virginia University, College of Creative Arts, School of Art & Design, Morgantown WV (S)
Ferguson DiMarco, Alexis, *Dir Devel,* Katonah Museum of Art, Katonah NY
Ferguson, Barbara, *Admin Asst,* Dunedin Fine Art Center, Dunedin FL (S)
Ferguson, David, *Pres,* Art Gallery of Bancroft Inc, Bancroft ON
Ferguson, Judy, *Pres,* Witter Gallery, Storm Lake IA
Ferguson, Kathleen, *Asst to Dir,* International Foundation for Art Research, Inc (IFAR), New York NY
Ferguson, Kristin, *Chief Director's Office,* Museum of Fine Arts, Boston MA
Ferguson, Melissa, *Dir Mktg & Communs,* Columbus Museum of Art, Columbus OH
Fergusson, Mary E D'Aquin, *Asst Dir,* Longue Vue House & Gardens, New Orleans LA
Fergusson, Peter J, *Prof,* Wellesley College, Art Dept, Wellesley MA (S)
Feria, Alexis, *Develop Coordr,* Preservation Virginia, Richmond VA
Fernandes, Irene, *Gift Shop Mgr,* Museum of Northern British Columbia, Ruth Harvey Art Gallery, Prince Rupert BC
Fernandes, Irene, *Gift Shop Mgr,* Museum of Northern British Columbia, Library, Prince Rupert BC
Fernandez, Alexandra, *Cur Asst,* University of Tampa, Henry B Plant Museum, Tampa FL
Fernandez, George, *Asst Prof,* State University of New York at Farmingdale, Visual Communications, Farmingdale NY (S)
Fernandez, Maria Ester, *Cur Educ,* Triton Museum of Art, Santa Clara CA
Fernandez-Keys, Alba, *Head of Lib & Archives,* Newfields, Stout Reference Library, Indianapolis IN
Ferrald, Caroline Jean, *Executive Director,* Millicent Rogers Museum, Taos NM
Ferrante, Virginia, *Instr,* Johns Hopkins University, School of Medicine, Dept of Art as Applied to Medicine, Baltimore MD (S)
Ferrara, Greg, *Dir Retail Operations,* The Baltimore Museum of Art, Baltimore MD
Ferrara, Luigi, *Dean, School of Design,* George Brown College of Applied Arts & Technology, Centre for

Arts, Design & Information Technology, Toronto ON (S)

Ferrari, Roberto, *Cur Art Properties,* Columbia University, Avery Architectural & Fine Arts Library, New York NY

Ferree, Cathy, *CEO & Pres,* Indiana State Museum, Indianapolis IN

Ferreira, Jose, *Artistic Dir, Sculpture,* Anderson Ranch Arts Center, Snowmass Village CO

Ferreira, Nick, *Reference & Instruction Librn,* School of the Art Institute of Chicago, John M Flaxman Library, Chicago IL

Ferrell, Brian, *Instr,* Seton Hill University, Art Program, Greensburg PA (S)

Ferrer, Arlene, *Col Asst,* Hostos Center for the Arts & Culture, Bronx NY

Ferrer, Elizabeth, *VPres Contemporary Art,* BRIC - Brooklyn Information & Culture, BRIC House, Brooklyn NY

Ferri, Rita, *Asst Dir,* Santa Barbara Contemporary Arts Forum, Santa Barbara CA

Ferrill, Elizabeth, *Artistic Dir, Painting, Drawing & Printmaking,* Anderson Ranch Arts Center, Snowmass Village CO

Ferris, Alison, *Cur,* Sheboygan Arts Foundation, Inc, John Michael Kohler Arts Center, Sheboygan WI

Ferris, Alison, *Sr Cur,* Edmundson Art Foundation, Inc, Des Moines Art Center, Des Moines IA

Ferris, Robert, *Pres,* Cortland County Historical Society, Suggett House Museum, Cortland NY

Ferriso, Brian, *Dir & Chief Cur,* Portland Art Museum, Portland OR

Ferro, Anthony, *Assoc Prof Dance,* Marymount Manhattan College, Fine & Performing Arts Div, New York NY (S)

Ferro, William, *Dir,* Hewlett-Woodmere Public Library, Hewlett NY

Ferry, Jane, *Cur of Educ,* Orlando Museum of Art, Orlando FL

Ferry, Jane, *Cur of Educ,* Orlando Museum of Art, Orlando Sentinel Library, Orlando FL

Fersuson, Sara, *Instr,* Ithaca College, Fine Art Dept, Ithaca NY (S)

Fertitta, Becky, *Mgr Visitor Center,* Mamie McFaddin Ward, Beaumont TX

Feser, Edward, *Dean,* University of Illinois, Urbana-Champaign, College of Fine & Applied Arts, Champaign IL (S)

Festa, Joseph, *Special Colls Librn,* New York State Historical Association, Research Library, Cooperstown NY

Festa, Lisa, *Asst Prof,* Georgian Court University, Dept of Art, Lakewood NJ (S)

Fetig, Kathy, *Admin Asst,* Bismarck Art & Galleries Association, Bismarck ND

Fetterman-Mulvey, Mia, *Assoc Prof,* University of Denver, School of Art & Art History, Denver CO (S)

Fettes, John, *Head Dept,* Magnum Opus, Sterling VA (S)

Feye, Cornelia, *School Dir,* Library Association of La Jolla, Athenaeum Music & Arts Library, La Jolla CA

Ffrench, Courtney, *Gen Mgr, JPAC,* Jamaica Center for Arts & Learning (JCAL), Jamaica NY

Fiak, Jose, *Interim Dir,* Wethersfield Historical Society Inc, Old Academy Library, Wethersfield CT

Ficarra, Marianne, *VChmn,* Monmouth Museum & Cultural Center, Lincroft NJ

Fich, Dean K, *IMAX Theater Mgr,* Putnam Museum of History and Natural Science, Davenport IA

Fichner-Rathus, Lois, *Chmn Dept,* The College of New Jersey, School of Arts & Sciences, Ewing NJ (S)

Fichter, Mary, *Dir Communs,* National Academy Museum & School, Archives, New York NY

Fichter, Robert, *Prof,* Florida State University, Art Dept, Tallahassee FL (S)

Ficke, Bob, *Treas,* Iroquois County Historical Society Museum, Old Courthouse Museum, Watseka IL

Ficke, Judy, *Office Mgr,* Iroquois County Historical Society Museum, Old Courthouse Museum, Watseka IL

Fidler, Spencer, *Dept Head,* New Mexico State University, Art Dept, Las Cruces NM (S)

Fiegel, Kay, *Asst Dir Opers & Pub Rels, Cur Cross Orchard, Gift Shop Mgr,* Museum of Western Colorado, Museum of the West, Grand Junction CO

Field, Addison, *Chief Cur,* Alaska State Museum, Juneau AK

Field, Charles, *Prof Emeritus,* University of Texas at San Antonio, Dept of Art & Art History, San Antonio TX (S)

Field, Christopher, *Asst Prof,* Morehead State University, Art & Design Dept, Morehead KY (S)

Field, John, *Dean of Humanities & Fine Arts,* Holyoke Community College, Dept of Art, Holyoke MA (S)

Field, Philip S, *Prof Painting,* University of Texas Pan American, Art Dept, Edinburg TX (S)

Field, Richard, *Dir Gallery,* Indiana University of Pennsylvania, Kipp Gallery, Indiana PA

Fielder, Daniel, *Head Dept,* Eastern Wyoming College, Art Dept, Torrington WY (S)

Fielding, Ariel, *Dir Communs,* University of North Carolina at Chapel Hill, Ackland Art Museum, Chapel Hill NC

Fielding, Peter, *Assoc Dean,* Red Deer College, School of Creative Arts, Red Deer AB (S)

Fields, Carl, *Interim Exec Dir,* Jamaica Center for Arts & Learning (JCAL), Jamaica NY

Fields, Catherine Keene, *Dir,* Litchfield History Museum, Litchfield CT

Fields, Catherine Keene, *Dir,* Litchfield History Museum, Ingraham Memorial Research Library, Litchfield CT

Fields, John, *Cur,* University of Alabama at Birmingham, Abroms-Engel Institute for the Visual Arts, Birmingham AL

Fields, Robert, *Prof,* Virginia Polytechnic Institute & State University, Dept of Art & Art History, Blacksburg VA (S)

Fields-Kuehl, Susanne, *Asst Dir,* Maryland-National Capital Park & Planning Commission, Montpelier Arts Center, Laurel MD

Fierst, Eva, *Educ Cur,* University of Massachusetts, Amherst, University Gallery, Amherst MA

Fiese, Richard, *Dean,* Howard Payne University, School of Fine Arts, Brownwood TX (S)

Fife Harbert, Laurie G, *Cur,* North Canton Public Library, The Little Art Gallery, North Canton OH

Figarelle, Thomas, *Exec Dir,* C M Russell Museum, Great Falls MT

Figenshow Koss, Pamela, *Exec Dir,* Glass Art Society, Seattle WA

Figueroa, Adrian, *Secy,* New York Society of Architects, New York NY

Figueroa, Mencia, *Dir Pub Relations, Progs & Special Events,* The Hispanic Society of America, Hispanic Society Museum & Library, New York NY

Filbert, Anna, *Instr,* Judson University, School of Art, Design & Architecture, Elgin IL (S)

Filer, Felicia, *Pub Art Dir,* City of Los Angeles, Cultural Affairs Dept, Los Angeles CA

Filip, Mona, *Dir & Cur,* Koffler Centre of the Arts, Koffler Gallery, Toronto ON

Filip, Mona, *Gallery Dir & Cur,* Koffler Center of the Arts, Toronto ON (S)

Filippo, Susan, *Asst Mng Dir,* Museo Italo Americano, San Francisco CA

Filippone, Christine, *Asst Prof Art History,* Millersville University, Dept of Art & Design, Millersville PA (S)

Fillebrown, Tom, *Instr,* Sierra Community College, Art Dept, Rocklin CA (S)

Fillmore, Sarah, *Chief Cur,* Art Gallery of Nova Scotia, Halifax NS

Finberg, Ben, *Dir IT & Opers,* Georgia O'Keeffe Museum, Santa Fe NM

Finch, Julia, *Asst Prof,* Morehead State University, Art & Design Dept, Morehead KY (S)

Finch, Robert, *Instr,* Main Line Art Center, Haverford PA (S)

Finch, Warren, *Dir,* National Archives & Records Administration, John F Kennedy Presidential Library & Museum, Boston MA

Findikoglu, Ziki, *Art Chair Germantown,* Montgomery College, Dept of Art, Rockville MD (S)

Findlay, Kimberly, *Pres & CEO,* Putnam Museum of History and Natural Science, Davenport IA

Findling, Shoshana, *VPres,* Long Beach Art League, Long Beach Library, Long Beach NY

Fine, Dina, *Pres,* Long Beach Art League, Long Beach Library, Long Beach NY

Fine, Peter, *Asst Prof,* New Mexico State University, Art Dept, Las Cruces NM (S)

Fineman, Richard, *Prof,* Northwestern Connecticut Community College, Fine Arts Dept, Winsted CT (S)

Fink, Charles, *Prof,* Miami-Dade Community College, Arts & Philosophy Dept, Miami FL (S)

Fink, Sue, *Dir Educ,* North Dakota Museum of Art, Grand Forks ND

Finlay, Dennis, *Treas,* Rhode Island Watercolor Society, Pawtucket RI

Finley, Greg, *Asst,* Plymouth State University, Karl Drerup Art Gallery, Plymouth NH

Finley, Kristi, *Commun Mgr,* Swope Art Museum, Research Library, Terre Haute IN

Finley, Kristi, *Office & Publ Mgr,* Swope Art Museum, Terre Haute IN

Finley, Lisa, *Instr,* Tidewater Community College, Visual Arts Center, Portsmouth VA (S)

Finley, Patrick, *Asst Prof,* Oklahoma State University, Department of Art, Graphic Design and Art History, Stillwater OK (S)

Finn, Candice, *Website/Communs,* National Council on Education for the Ceramic Arts (NCECA), Boulder CO

Finn, Courtney, *Cur,* Aspen Art Museum, Aspen CO

Finn, David, *Prof,* Wake Forest University, Dept of Art, Winston-Salem NC (S)

Finn, Matthew, *Asst Prof,* Saint Thomas Aquinas College, Art Dept, Sparkill NY (S)

Finnegan, Jacqueline, *Mus Technician,* Mount Holyoke College, Art Museum, South Hadley MA

Finnegan, Kate, *Exec Dir,* Kaji Aso Studio, Gallery Nature & Temptation, Boston MA

Finnegan, Maggie, *Senior Admin Asst,* Mount Holyoke College, Art Museum, South Hadley MA

Finnegan, Patrick, *Vol Treas,* Three Forks Area Historical Society, Headwaters Heritage Museum, Three Forks MT

Finnell, Patrick, *Mgr Progs & Graphic Design,* African American Museum, Dallas TX

Finnemore, Bonny, *Resident Custodian,* Waterville Historical Society, Redington Museum, Waterville ME

Finnemore, Bryan, *Resident Custodian,* Waterville Historical Society, Redington Museum, Waterville ME

Finner, Leigh, *Admin Asst,* Halifax Historical Society, Inc, Halifax Historical Museum, Daytona Beach FL

Finneran, Mary, *Asst Prof,* Eastern New Mexico University, Dept of Art, Portales NM (S)

Finnerty-Pyne, Sinead, *Gallery Progs Mgr,* Armory Center for the Arts, Pasadena CA

Finney, Jay, *Chief Mktg Officer,* Peabody Essex Museum, Salem MA

Fiorani, Francesca, *Assoc Prof & Chair,* University of Virginia, McIntire Dept of Art, Charlottesville VA (S)

Fiorenza, Giancarlo, *Asst Prof Art History,* California Polytechnic State University at San Luis Obispo, Dept of Art & Design, San Luis Obispo CA (S)

Fiorenza, Lily, *Kateria Media Center Mgr,* The National Shrine of the North American Martyrs, Fultonville NY

Fiorese, Lisa, *Dir Admin,* Dutchess County Arts Council, Poughkeepsie NY

Firestone Rosen, Amy, *Exhibs & Educ Asst,* St Louis Artists' Guild & Galleries, Clayton MO

Firestone, Evan, *Prof Art History,* University of Georgia, Franklin College of Arts & Sciences, Lamar Dodd School of Art, Athens GA (S)

Firestone, Laura, *Mus Shop Mgr,* Akron Art Museum, Akron OH

Firmani, Domenico, *Chmn Prof,* College of Notre Dame of Maryland, Art Dept, Baltimore MD (S)

Fischel, Sharo, *Instr,* American University, Dept of Art, New York NY (S)
Fischer, Andrea, *Dir,* Transylvania University, Morlan Gallery, Lexington KY
Fischer, Barb, *Instr,* Western Wisconsin Technical College, Graphics Division, La Crosse WI (S)
Fischer, Barbara, *Exec Dir & Chief Cur,* University of Toronto, Art Centre, Toronto ON
Fischer, Barbara, *Exec Dir & Chief Cur,* University of Toronto, Justina M Barnicke Gallery, Toronto ON
Fischer, Joshua, *Asst Cur,* Rice University, Rice Gallery, Houston TX
Fischer-Carlson, Lynn, *Prof,* Rock Valley College, Humanities and Fine Arts Division, Rockford IL (S)
Fischli, Ron, *Dean College of Fine Arts,* Midwestern State University, Lamar D. Fain College of Fine Arts, Wichita Falls TX (S)
Fiser, Daniel, *Staff Artist,* Oshkosh Public Museum & Library, Oshkosh WI
Fish, Adrian, *Assoc Prof & Chair, Media Arts Div,* Nova Scotia College of Art & Design, Halifax NS (S)
Fish, Alida, *Interim Dean, College of Art & Design,* University of the Arts, Philadelphia Colleges of Art & Design, Performing Arts & Media & Communication, Philadelphia PA (S)
Fish, Belinda, *Dir & Educ Coordr,* Belz Museum of Asian & Judaic Art, Memphis TN
Fishel, Teresa, *Dir Library,* Macalester College, DeWitt Wallace Library, Saint Paul MN
Fisher, Aaron, *Order Fulfillment,* Printed Matter, Inc, New York NY
Fisher, Alan, *Assoc Prof,* Dakota State University, College of Liberal Arts, Madison SD (S)
Fisher, Andrea, *Gallery Dir,* Transylvania University, Art Program, Lexington KY (S)
Fisher, Beth, *Museum Shop Mgr,* Museum of Arts & Sciences, Inc, Macon GA
Fisher, Beverly, *Adj Prof,* Saint Joseph's University, Art Dept, Philadelphia PA (S)
Fisher, Carolyn, *Pres,* Kent Art Association, Gallery, Kent CT
Fisher, Dale William, *Cur Educ,* University of Iowa, University of Iowa Museum of Art, Iowa City IA
Fisher, Debra, *Chmn,* State University of New York College at Brockport, Dept of Art, Brockport NY (S)
Fisher, Ellen, *Assoc Dean,* New York School of Interior Design, New York NY (S)
Fisher, Helen Ashton, *Coll Cur,* William A Farnsworth, Museum, Rockland ME
Fisher, Joshua, *Asst Prof,* Arkansas Tech University, Dept of Art, Russellville AR (S)
Fisher, June, *Dir Fashion Design,* Art Institute of Fort Lauderdale, Fort Lauderdale FL (S)
Fisher, Kate, *Vis Asst Prof,* Hamline University, Dept of Studio Arts & Art History, Saint Paul MN (S)
Fisher, Kristina, *Exec Dir,* Marblehead Arts Association, Inc, Marblehead MA
Fisher, Lawrence A, *Exec Dir,* The Barnum Museum, Bridgeport CT
Fisher, Linda, *Coordr Interior Design,* Kean University, Fine Arts Dept, Union NJ (S)
Fisher, Melissa, *Pres,* Marblehead Arts Association, Inc, Marblehead MA
Fisher, Paul, *Cur Science,* Museum of Arts & Sciences, Inc, Macon GA
Fisher, Richard, *Asst Prof,* College of Santa Fe, Art Dept, Santa Fe NM (S)
Fisher, Robert, *Coll Mgr,* Wing Luke Asian Museum, Governor Gary Locke Library and Community Heritage Center, Seattle WA
Fisher, Stephen, *Colls Mgr,* Amherst College, Mead Art Museum, Amherst MA
Fisher, Stephen, *Prof,* Rhode Island College, Art Dept, Providence RI (S)
Fisher, Steven M, *Prof Art,* The College of Idaho, Rosenthal Art Gallery, Caldwell ID
Fisher, Tim, *Assoc Prof,* Grand Valley State University, Art & Design Dept, Allendale MI (S)
Fisher, Will, *Instr,* Yavapai College, Visual & Performing Arts Div, Prescott AZ (S)
Fisk, Lars, *Studio Mgr,* Socrates Sculpture Park, Long Island City NY
Fisler, Ben, *Assoc Prof Theatre,* Harford Community College, Visual, Performing and Applied Arts Division, Bel Air MD (S)
Fitch, Carlana, *Dir,* Kemp Center for the Arts, Wichita Falls TX
Fitch, Kenneth W, *Librn,* Salmagundi Club, Library, New York NY
Fitch, Steve, *Adjunct Assoc,* College of Santa Fe, Art Dept, Santa Fe NM (S)
Fitch, Wendy, *Exec Dir,* Museums Association of Saskatchewan, Regina SK
Fithian, Charles, *Cur Archaeology,* Delaware Division of Historical & Cultural Affairs, Dover DE
Fithian, David, *Exhibitions,* Museum of Art - Deland FL, Inc, Deland FL
Fitts, Catherine E, *Cur,* Supreme Court of the United States, Office of the Curator, Washington DC
Fitzgerald, Barnaby, *Prof,* Southern Methodist University, Meadows School of the Arts - Division of Art, Dallas TX (S)
Fitzgerald, Jason, *Finance Mgr,* Beaverbrook Art Gallery, Fredericton NB
Fitzgerald, Kenneth, *Prof,* Old Dominion University, Art Dept, Norfolk VA (S)
Fitzgerald, Sally, *Chmn,* Chabot College, Humanities Division, Hayward CA (S)
Fitzgerald, Shannon, *Exec Dir,* Mennello Museum of American Art, Orlando FL
Fitzgerald, Shannon, *Exec Dir,* Rochester Art Center, Rochester MN
Fitzgerald, Sharon, *Cur Mineralogical Mus,* University of Delaware, University Museums, Newark DE
Fitzgibbons, Leslee, *Visitor Svcs,* Irvine Museum, Irvine CA
FitzGibbons, Sean, *Dir,* Centenary College of Louisiana, Meadows Museum of Art, Shreveport LA
Fitzpatrick, Amy, *Dir Develop,* Montclair Art Museum, Montclair NJ
Fitzpatrick, Ann, *VPres Communs,* Edsel & Eleanor Ford House, Grosse Pointe Shores MI
Fitzpatrick, Tracy, *Cur & Asst Prof Art History,* Purchase College, Neuberger Museum of Art, Purchase NY
Fitzsimmons, Christine, *Dir Finance & Operations,* Children's Creativity Museum, San Francisco CA
Fitzsimmons, Julie, *College Asst Prof,* New Mexico State University, Art Dept, Las Cruces NM (S)
Fitzsimmons, Mary, *Board of Dirs,* Guild of Creative Art, Shrewsbury NJ (S)
Fitzsimons, Constance, *Dean Div,* El Camino College, Division of Fine Arts, Torrance CA (S)
Fitzsimons, Sarah, *Asst Prof,* University of Wisconsin, Madison, Dept of Art, Madison WI (S)
Flack, Melanie, *Dir Develop,* Frederic Remington, Ogdensburg NY
Flagel, Deb, *Exec Dir,* Woman Made Gallery, Chicago IL
Flahaven, Jim, *Lectr Painting & Drawing,* University of Southern Maine, Dept of Art, Gorham ME (S)
Flaherty, Barbara, *Chair,* University of the Pacific, Jeannette Powell Art Center, Stockton CA
Flaherty, Barbara, *Chmn,* University of the Pacific, College of the Pacific, Dept of Art & Art History, Stockton CA (S)
Flaherty, Kirsten, *Prog & Communs Mgr,* Dieu Donne Papermill, Inc, Gallery, Brooklyn NY
Flaherty, Patrick, *Pres & Exec Dir,* Indianapolis Art Center, Marilyn K. Glick School of Art, Indianapolis IN
Flahive, Ryan, *Archivist,* Institute of American Indian Arts, College of Contemporary Native Arts Library and Archives, Santa Fe NM
Flam, Jack, *Prof Emeritus,* City University of New York, PhD Program in Art History, New York NY (S)
Flanagan, Daly, *Dir School,* Rockland Center for the Arts, West Nyack NY (S)
Flanagan, Daly, *School Dir,* Rockland Center for the Arts, West Nyack NY
Flanagan, Jeanne, *Dir,* College of Saint Rose, Art Gallery, Albany NY
Flanagan, Maureen, *Adminr,* Hussian School of Art, Commercial Art Dept, Philadelphia PA (S)
Flanagan, Michael, *Asst Dir,* State University of New York at Oswego, Tyler Art Gallery, Oswego NY
Flanagan, Michael, *Dir,* University of Wisconsin-Whitewater, Crossman Gallery, Whitewater WI
Flanigan, Theresa, *Assoc Prof,* The College of Saint Rose, The Center For Art and Design, Albany NY (S)
Flannery Ericson, Treena, *Gallery Dir,* The Scarab Club, Gallery, Detroit MI
Flannery, Anne, *Head Archivist,* University of Chicago, Oriental Institute, Chicago IL
Flannery, Marina, *Educ Coordr,* Slater Mill, Old Slater Mill Association, Pawtucket RI
Flansburg, Rick, *Assoc Dir,* National Air and Space Museum, Smithsonian Institution, Washington DC
Flashner, Dale, *Asst Prof,* Adelphi University, Dept of Art & Art History, Garden City NY (S)
Flathu, Ryan, *Art Instr,* Kellogg Community College, Arts & Communication Dept, Battle Creek MI (S)
Flax, Lehze, *Bd Chair,* Artworks Trenton, Trenton NJ
Fleck, Rudolf, *Prof,* Loyola Marymount University, Dept of Art & Art History, Los Angeles CA (S)
Flecky, Michael, *Assoc Chair,* Creighton University, Fine & Performing Arts Dept, Omaha NE (S)
Fleeher, Kathy, *Asst Cur & Mus Guild Coordr,* Canton Museum of Art, Canton OH
Fleischer, Arthur, *Chmn,* Fried, Frank, Harris, Shriver & Jacobson, Art Collection, New York NY
Fleischer, Mary, *Prof & Chair Theatre,* Marymount Manhattan College, Fine & Performing Arts Div, New York NY (S)
Fleischer, Roland E, *Prof Emeritus,* Pennsylvania State University, University Park, Dept of Art History, University Park PA (S)
Fleischman, Martha, *Pres,* Kennedy Galleries, Kennedy Galleries, Inc, New York NY
Fleischman, Stephen, *Dir,* Madison Museum of Contemporary Art, Madison WI
Fleischmann, Jo, *Admin Asst,* The Arts Council of Wayne County, Goldsboro NC (S)
Fleischmann, Laura, *Sr Registrar,* The Buffalo Fine Arts Academy, Albright-Knox Art Gallery, Buffalo NY
Fleming, Alison, *Asst Prof,* College of the Holy Cross, Dept of Visual Arts, Worcester MA (S)
Fleming, Elizabeth, *Cur of Coll,* C W Post Campus of Long Island University, Hillwood Art Museum, Brookville NY
Fleming, Elma, *Prin HS,* Forest Hills Adult and Youth Center, Forest Hills NY (S)
Fleming, Erika, *Pres College,* International Fine Arts College, Miami FL (S)
Fleming, Jeff, *Dir,* Edmundson Art Foundation, Inc, Des Moines Art Center, Des Moines IA
Fleming, Jeff, *Treas,* Association of Art Museum Directors, New York NY
Fleming, Kelly, *Develop Dir,* Arkansas Arts Center, Little Rock AR (S)
Fleming, Kelly, *Dir Develop,* Arkansas Arts Center, Little Rock AR
Fleming, Lauren, *Assistant Collections Manager,* The Columbus Museum, Columbus GA
Fleming, Mark, *Illustration Coordr,* Nossi College of Art, Nashville TN (S)
Fleming, Meghan, *Assoc Prof,* McNeese State University, Dept of Visual Arts, Lake Charles LA (S)
Fleming, Nancy, *Mus Co-Dir,* Roswell Artist-in-Residence Foundation, Anderson Museum of Contemporary Art, Roswell NM
Fleming, Stephen, *Residency Dir,* Roswell Artist-in-Residence Foundation, Anderson Museum of Contemporary Art, Roswell NM
Fleming, Tom, *Prof,* University of Wisconsin College - Marinette, Art Dept, Marinette WI (S)
Fleming, Tricia, *Dir Educ,* Antonelli Institute, Professional Photography & Commercial Art, Erdenheim PA (S)

Flescher, Sharon, *Dir,* International Foundation for Art Research, Inc (IFAR), Authentication Service, New York NY
Flescher, Sharon, *Exec Dir, Ed in Chief,* International Foundation for Art Research, Inc (IFAR), New York NY
Flesher, Karen, *Prog Coordr,* University of Illinois at Urbana-Champaign, Spurlock Museum, Urbana IL
Flester, Inge, *Office Mgr,* Colonial Williamsburg Foundation, John D Rockefeller, Jr Library, Williamsburg VA
Fletcher, Carrol, *CEO,* Harrison County Historical Museum, Marshall TX
Fletcher, Dorothy, *Dir Undergrad Studies & Sr Lectr,* Emory University, Art History Dept, Atlanta GA (S)
Fletcher, Marylynn, *Head Dept,* Victoria College, Fine Arts Dept, Victoria TX (S)
Fletcher, Nicole, *Colls Mgr,* The Winnipeg Art Gallery, Winnipeg MB
Fletcher, Pamela, *Asst Prof,* Bowdoin College, Art Dept, Brunswick ME (S)
Fletcher, Peter, *Prof,* Viterbo University, Art Dept, La Crosse WI (S)
Fletcher-Garrett, Traci, *Pres,* Antonelli College, Cincinnati OH (S)
Fleurov, Ellen, *Exec Dir,* Silver Eye Center for Photography, Pittsburgh PA
Fleury, Michel, *Dir, School of Design,* Universite Laval, Faculty of Planning, Architecture, Arts & Design, Quebec QC (S)
Flexner, Paul, *Chmn,* Salisbury State University, Art Dept, Salisbury MD (S)
Flicker, Melissa, *Assoc Prof,* California State Polytechnic University, Pomona, Department of Art, Pomona CA (S)
Fliegel, Stephen, *Cur Medieval Art,* The Cleveland Museum of Art, Cleveland OH
Flink, Chris, *Exec Dir,* Exploratorium, San Francisco CA
Flint, Jean, *Instr,* Arkansas State University, Dept of Art, State University AR (S)
Flint, Matt, *Prof 2-D,* Central Wyoming College, Art Center, Riverton WY (S)
Flint, Russ, *Adjunct,* Feather River Community College, Art Dept, Quincy CA (S)
Flint, Suzanne, *Cur,* Pocumtuck Valley Memorial Association, Memorial Hall Museum, Deerfield MA
Fliss, Roberta Behrendt, *Dir Productions,* National YoungArts Foundation, Miami FL
Flitcroft, Holly, *Office Mgr,* Sculpture Space, Inc, Utica NY
Flitner, Jane V, *Asst Educ,* Brandywine Conservancy, Brandywine River Museum, Chadds Ford PA
Flom, Veronica, *Coordr Exhibs & Pub Progs,* Americas Society Art Gallery, New York NY
Flood, James, *Dept Chmn,* Towson State University, Dept of Art, Towson MD (S)
Flood, Mike, *2nd VPres,* Independence Historical Museum & Art Center, Independence KS
Flook, Kimberly, *Historic Site Mgr,* Olana State Historic Site, Library, Hudson NY
Flook, Kimberly, *Historic Site Mgr,* Philipse Manor Hall State Historic Site, Yonkers NY
Flora, Judith, *Dir Finance,* Mystic Art Association, Inc, Mystic Museum of Art, Mystic CT
Flora, Karen, *Instr,* Bob Jones University, School of Fine Arts, Div of Art & Design, Greenville SC (S)
Florentin, Bryan, *Sr Lectr,* University of Texas at Arlington, Art & Art History Department, Arlington TX (S)
Flores, Richard, *Instr,* College of the Sequoias, Art Dept, Visalia CA (S)
Flores, Tia, *Prog Mgr,* Sierra Arts Foundation, Sierra Arts Gallery, Reno NV
Flores, Tobias, *Asst Prof,* Fort Hays State University, Dept of Art & Design, Hays KS (S)
Florez, Lyndsey, *Progs Specialist,* Bay Area Video Coalition, Inc, San Francisco CA
Florin, Sharon, *VPres Historian,* Catharine Lorillard Wolfe, New York NY
Flowers, Randolph, *Prof,* Del Mar College, Art Dept, Corpus Christi TX (S)
Flowers, Randy, *Gallery Dir,* Del Mar College, Joseph A Cain Memorial Art Gallery, Corpus Christi TX
Floyd, Connie M, *Chmn,* North Carolina Central University, Art Dept, Durham NC (S)
Flug, Janice, *Acting Asst University Librn,* American University, Jack I & Dorothy G Bender Library & Learning Resources Center, New York NY
Flusche, Laura, *Exec Dir,* Atlanta International Museum of Art & Design, Museum of Design Atlanta, Atlanta GA
Flynn, Christopher, *Instr Graphic Commun,* Tarrant County College, Art Dept, Hurst TX (S)
Flynn, Kathleen, *Exec Dir,* Dieu Donne Papermill, Inc, Gallery, Brooklyn NY
Flynn, Michael, *VPres Interpretation & Visitor Experience,* Independence Seaport Museum, Philadelphia PA
Flynn, Pamela, *Pres,* Phoenix Gallery, New York NY
Focht, Brenda, *Cur Coll & Exhib,* Riverside Metropolitan Museum, Riverside CA
Fogarty, Lori, *Exec Dir,* Oakland Museum of California, Art Dept, Oakland CA
Fogarty, Lori, *Pres,* Association of Art Museum Directors, New York NY
Fogel, Dan, *Instr,* Mesa Community College, Dept of Art, Mesa AZ (S)
Fogelman, Peggy, *Norma Jean Calderwood Dir,* Isabella Stewart Gardner Museum, Boston MA
Fogerty, Lee, *Asst Dir,* Springfield City Library, Springfield MA
Fogher, Valentina, *Cur,* Museo Italo Americano, Library, San Francisco CA
Fogt, Rex, *Assoc Prof,* University of Toledo, Dept of Art, Toledo OH (S)
Folda, Jaroslav, *Prof,* University of North Carolina at Chapel Hill, Art Dept, Chapel Hill NC (S)
Foldes, Lance, *Dir,* Berry College, Memorial Library, Mount Berry GA
Foley, Bridget, *VPres Admin,* The Africa Center, New York NY
Foley, Cindy, *Exec Asst Dir & Dir Learning & Experience,* Columbus Museum of Art, Columbus OH
Foley, Jim, *Pres,* Long Branch Historical Association Church of the Presidents Museum, Long Branch NJ
Foley, Jodie, *Archivist,* Montana Historical Society, Helena MT
Foley, Kathy Kelsey, *Dir,* Leigh Yawkey Woodson Art Museum, Wausau WI
Foley, Mike, *Design Ctr Adjunct,* Iowa Wesleyan College, Art Dept, Mount Pleasant IA (S)
Foley, Priscilla, *Dir. of Neighborhood Svcs.,* Boston Public Library, Central Library, Boston MA
Foley, Rebecca, *Assoc Prof,* Missouri Western State University, School of Fine Arts, Saint Joseph MO (S)
Foley, Rebecca, *Gallery Director,* Missouri Western State University, Gallery 206 Foyer Gallery, Saint Joseph MO
Foley, Shannon, *Mgr Educ,* Mingei International, Inc, Mingei International Museum - Balboa Park & Mingei International Museum - Escondido, San Diego CA
Foley, Tate, *Asst Prof,* Webster University, Department of Art, Design & Art History, Webster Groves MO (S)
Foley, William, *Asst Prof Art,* Marian University, Visual Arts Dept, Indianapolis IN (S)
Folk, Amy, *Colls Mgr,* Oysterponds Historical Society, Museum, Orient NY
Folkerts, Jason, *Visual Arts Center Dir,* Washington Pavilion of Arts & Science, Visual Arts Center, Sioux Falls SD
Folsom, James, *Dir Botanical Gardens,* The Huntington Library, Art Collections & Botanical Gardens, San Marino CA
Folsom, James, *Dir Botanical Gardens,* The Huntington Library, Art Collections & Botanical Gardens, Library, San Marino CA
Folts, James, *Chmn,* Oregon State University, Dept of Art, Corvallis OR (S)
Folts, James, *Chmn & Gallery Dir,* Oregon State University, Dept of Art, Corvallis OR (S)
Foltz, Amy, *Instr,* Morningside College, Art Dept, Sioux City IA (S)
Folwell, Sue, *Mus Shop Mgr,* Putnam Museum of History and Natural Science, Davenport IA
Fombella, Trinidad, *Exhib Mgr & Asst Cur,* El Museo del Barrio, New York NY
Fomin, Elizabeth, *Asst Prof,* Rochester Institute of Technology, School of Design, Rochester NY (S)
Fondas, Michelle, *Registrar,* National Gallery of Art, Washington DC
Fonfara, Chad, *Asst Prof,* University of Nebraska, Kearney, Dept of Art & Art History, Kearney NE (S)
Fong, Mimi, *Instr,* Sacramento City College, Art Dept, Sacramento CA (S)
Fong, Yem, *Art & Architecture Librn,* University of Colorado, Art & Architecture Library, Boulder CO
Fontaine-White, Barbar, *Prof,* University of Mary Hardin-Baylor, College of Visual & Performing Arts, Belton TX (S)
Fontana, Jeffrey, *Prof,* Austin College, Art Dept, Sherman TX (S)
Fontana, Leslie, *Adjunct Prof Art,* University of Great Falls, Art Dept, Great Falls MT (S)
Fontanella, Megan, *Asst Cur Colls,* Solomon R Guggenheim Museum, New York NY
Fontenot-Jamerson, Berlinda, *Pres,* Museum of African American Art, Los Angeles CA
Foornier, Stephanie, *Bus Asst,* Dartmouth College, Hood Museum of Art, Hanover NH
Forbes, Dawn, *Instr,* Whitman College, Art Dept, Walla Walla WA (S)
Forbes, Kim, *Events Svcs Dir,* Mesa Arts Center, Mesa Contemporary Arts Museum, Mesa AZ
Forbes, Lyles, *VPres Colls & Chief Cur,* The Mariners' Museum, Newport News VA
Forbes, Susan, *Div Chmn,* Wells College, Dept of Art, Aurora NY (S)
Forbush, Sebastian, *Educ Coordr,* City of Lubbock, Buddy Holly Center, Lubbock TX
Force, Leah, *Lectr,* Baylor University - College of Arts and Sciences, Dept of Art, Waco TX (S)
Ford, Ann, *Asst Prof,* Virginia State University, Department of Art & Design, Petersburg VA (S)
Ford, Beth, *Prof Emerita,* Florida Southern College, Melvin Art Gallery, Lakeland FL
Ford, Beth, *Prof Emerita,* Florida Southern College, Department of Art & Art History, Lakeland FL (S)
Ford, Carolyn, *Chair & Prof of Art,* Limestone College, Art Dept, Gaffney SC (S)
Ford, Cindi, *Cur, Contact,* Van Singel Fine Arts Center, Van Singel Art Gallery, Byron Center MI
Ford, Inga, *Communs Coordr,* Boca Raton Museum of Art, Boca Raton FL
Ford, Inga, *Dir Innovations, Mktg & Communications,* Boca Raton Museum of Art, Library, Boca Raton FL
Ford, Janice, *Gallery Dir,* Pikeville College, Humanities Division, Pikeville KY (S)
Ford, John, *Asst Prof,* University of North Carolina at Charlotte, Dept Art, Charlotte NC (S)
Ford, Maury, *Registrar,* Oklahoma City Museum of Art, Oklahoma City OK
Ford, Ryan, *Treas,* Second Street Gallery, Charlottesville VA
Ford, Sarah, *COO,* Art Center Sarasota, Sarasota FL
Ford, Tim, *Instr,* Appalachian State University, Dept of Art, Boone NC (S)
Forde, Ed, *Chmn Dept,* University of Nebraska-Lincoln, Dept of Art & Art History, Lincoln NE (S)
Fordham, Amy, *Cur Visual Resources,* University of Louisville, Visual Resources Center, Louisville KY
Fordham, Douglas, *Assoc Prof Art History,* University of Virginia, McIntire Dept of Art, Charlottesville VA (S)
Fordham, Leslie, *Pub Art Admin,* Broward County Board of Commissioners, Broward Cultural Div, Fort Lauderdale FL
Foreman, Brian, *Asst Cur,* Surrey Art Gallery, Library, Surrey BC

Foreman, Hank T, *Associate Vice Chancellor for Arts Engagement,* Appalachian State University, Turchin Center for the Visual Arts, Boone NC

Foreman, Henry T, *Instr,* Appalachian State University, Dept of Art, Boone NC (S)

Forer, Taj, *Dir,* Durham Art Guild, Durham NC

Forest Wilson, Ernest, *Prof,* Catholic University of America, School of Architecture & Planning, Washington DC (S)

Forgit, Susan, *Finance Dir,* American Antiquarian Society, Worcester MA

Forino, Belle, *Spec Events & Vols,* Boca Raton Museum of Art, Boca Raton FL

Fornandez, Fabio J, *Exec Dir,* The Society of Arts & Crafts, Boston MA

Forne Thomas, Nette, *Pres,* Pen & Brush, Inc, New York NY

Forney, Darrell, *Instr,* Sacramento City College, Art Dept, Sacramento CA (S)

Fornwald, Blair, *Cur Asst,* Regina Public Library, Dunlop Art Gallery, Regina SK

Foronda, Diego, *Develop Officer,* Fraunces Tavern Museum, New York NY

Forsberg, Diane, *Chief Cur,* Canajoharie Library & Art Gallery, Arkell Museum of Canajoharie, Canajoharie NY

Forschler-Tarrasch, Anne, *Chief Cur & Cur Decorative Arts,* Birmingham Museum of Art, Birmingham AL

Forshay, Patrick, *Instr,* Hillsdale College, Art Dept, Hillsdale MI (S)

Forst, Bill, *Instr,* Barton County Community College, Fine Arts Dept, Great Bend KS (S)

Forster-Hahn, Francoise, *Prof Emeriti,* University of California, Riverside, Dept of the History of Art, Riverside CA (S)

Forsyth, Alex, *Instr,* Guilford Technical Community College, Commercial Art Dept, Jamestown NC (S)

Forsyth, Amy, *Assoc Prof,* Lehigh University, Dept of Art, Architecture & Design, Bethlehem PA (S)

Fort, Bernadette, *Adjunct Prof,* Northwestern University, Evanston, Dept of Art History, Evanston IL (S)

Fort, Lifran, *Chmn & Instr,* Fisk University, Art Dept, Nashville TN (S)

Fort, Thomas A, *Asst Dir & Cur Exhibits,* Hidalgo County Historical Museum, Edinburg TX

Forte, Joseph C, *Faculty,* Sarah Lawrence College, Dept of Art History, Bronxville NY (S)

Forte, Larry, *Art Handler,* University of Georgia, Georgia Museum of Art, Athens GA

Fortenberry, Tobin, *Registrar,* Mississippi Museum of Art, Howorth Library, Jackson MS

Fortenot, Michelle, *Mus Coll Mgr,* University of Michigan, Kelsey Museum of Archaeology, Ann Arbor MI

Fortescue, Ann, *Dir,* Springfield Museum of Art, Springfield OH (S)

Fortescue, Ann, *Exec Dir,* Springfield Museum of Art, Springfield OH

Fortriede, Steven, *Assoc Dir,* Allen County Public Library, Art, Music & Audiovisual Services, Fort Wayne IN

Fortune, Janice, *Gallery Opers Asst,* Art Gallery of Peterborough, Peterborough ON

Fortushniak, Ivan, *Asst Prof,* Indiana University of Pennsylvania, College of Fine Arts, Indiana PA (S)

Fortwengler, Nancy, *Pres,* The Art League Gallery & School, Alexandria VA

Fosdick, Rose, *Commissioner,* United States Department of the Interior, Indian Arts & Crafts Board, Washington DC

Fosque, William, *Prof,* Portland State University, Dept of Art, Portland OR (S)

Foss, Brian, *Dir, School for Studies in Art & Culture,* Carleton University, School for Studies in Art & Culture, Ottawa ON (S)

Foss, Matt, *Project Mgr,* Leigh Yawkey Woodson Art Museum, Wausau WI

Foss, Pauline, *Instr Visual Arts,* University of Colorado-Colorado Springs, Visual & Performing Arts Dept (VAPA), Colorado Springs CO (S)

Fostel, Clarissa, *Head Registar,* National Museum of African Art, Smithsonian Institution, Washington DC

Foster Jones, Julienne, *Dir,* Liberty Hall Historic Site, Orlando Brown House, Frankfort KY

Foster Jones, Julienne, *Exec Dir,* Liberty Hall Historic Site, Liberty Hall Museum, Frankfort KY

Foster, April, *Instr,* Art Academy of Cincinnati, Cincinnati OH (S)

Foster, Bill, *Dir,* Portland Art Museum, Northwest Film Center, Portland OR

Foster, Brendan, *Exec Dir,* National Veterans Art Museum, Chicago IL

Foster, Carter, *Deputy Dir Curatorial Affairs & Cur Prints & Drawings,* University of Texas at Austin, Blanton Museum of Art, Austin TX

Foster, Daniel, *Exec Dir,* Riverside Art Museum, Riverside CA

Foster, David, *Chmn Art Dept,* Lake Tahoe Community College, Art Dept, South Lake Tahoe CA (S)

Foster, Dick, *IT Website,* Sonoma Valley Historical Society, Depot Park Museum, Sonoma CA

Foster, Emily, *Librn,* Berkeley Public Library, Art & Music Department, Berkeley CA

Foster, Frank, *Chmn,* Victor Valley Community College, Art Dept, Victorville CA (S)

Foster, H Eugene, *Facilities Supv,* International Center of Photography, School, New York NY (S)

Foster, Jill, *Admin Staff,* Greenwich Art Society Inc, Greenwich CT

Foster, Laura, *Dir & Cur,* Frederic Remington, Ogdensburg NY

Foster, Marlon, *Vis Servs Coordr,* Cultural Council of Palm Beach County, Lake Worth FL

Foster, Mary, *Office Coordr,* University of Notre Dame, Dept of Art, Art History & Design, Notre Dame IN (S)

Foster, Robert, *Gallery Dir,* Artists Association of Nantucket, Nantucket MA

Foster, Scott, *Asst Prof Painting & Drawing,* Siena College, Dept of Creative Arts, Loudonville NY (S)

Foster, Selene, *Coordr Exhib,* Palo Alto Art Center, Palo Alto CA

Foster, Stephen, *Assoc Dean Research & Grad Studies,* University of British Columbia Okanagan, Faculty of Creative & Critical Studies, Kelowna BC (S)

Foster, Thomas, *Exec Dir,* Bullion Plaza Cultural Center & Museum, Miami AZ

Foster-Campbell, Megan, *Asst Prof,* Illinois Central College, Arts & Communication Dept, East Peoria IL (S)

Foti, Silvana, *Chmn,* Methodist College, Art Dept, Fayetteville NC (S)

Fought, Rick, *Librn,* Art Institute of Fort Lauderdale, Technical Library, Fort Lauderdale FL

Foumberg, Jason, *Cur Digital Art,* Carl & Marilynn Thoma Art Foundation, Art House Santa Fe, Santa Fe NM

Fountain, Benny, *Asst Prof,* Baylor University - College of Arts and Sciences, Dept of Art, Waco TX (S)

Fourhman-Shaull, Lila, *Dir Libr & Archives,* York County Heritage Trust, York PA

Fourhman-Shaull, Lila, *Librn,* York County Heritage Trust, Library and Archives, York PA

Foushee, Sean, *Instr Graphic Commun,* Tarrant County College, Art Dept, Hurst TX (S)

Foust, Andrea, *Mem/Pub Rels Mgr,* Willamette University, Hallie Ford Museum of Art, Salem OR

Fouts, Kaci, *Director of Strategic Planning,* The Frank Phillips Foundation Inc, Woolaroc Museum, Bartlesville OK

Fowle, Bruce, *Pres,* National Academy Museum & School, New York NY

Fowle, Kate, *Exec Dir,* Independent Curators International, New York NY

Fowler, Erin, *Dir Strategic Initiatives,* Carl & Marilynn Thoma Art Foundation, Art House Santa Fe, Santa Fe NM

Fowler, Sherry, *Asst Prof,* Lewis & Clark College, Dept of Art, Portland OR (S)

Fox, Broderick, *Prof,* Occidental College, Dept of Art History & Visual Arts, Los Angeles CA (S)

Fox, Carson, *Instr,* Main Line Art Center, Haverford PA (S)

Fox, Christopher D, *Cur,* Fort Ticonderoga Association, Ticonderoga NY

Fox, Craig Burns, *Chief Cur,* Independence Seaport Museum, Library, Philadelphia PA

Fox, Edward, *Prof,* Nassau Community College, Art Dept, Garden City NY (S)

Fox, Elizabeth, *Educational Outreach Coordr,* Rawls Museum Arts, Courtland VA

Fox, Hugh R, *Asst Prof,* Rochester Institute of Technology, School of Printing Management & Sciences, Rochester NY (S)

Fox, Jennifer, *Dir Fin & Opers,* Marietta-Cobb Museum of Art, Marietta GA

Fox, John, *Asst Prof,* Finger Lakes Community College, Visual & Performing Arts Dept, Canandaigua NY (S)

Fox, Kate, *Mus Shop Mgr,* Cleveland Botanical Garden, Eleanor Squire Library, Cleveland OH

Fox, Marisa, *Mgr Mktg & Community Engagement,* Museum of Contemporary Photography, Columbia College Chicago, Chicago IL

Fox, Michael, *Cur History,* Montana State University, Museum of the Rockies, Bozeman MT

Fox, Pamela, *Dean School Fine Arts,* Miami University, Art Dept, Oxford OH (S)

Fox, Paulette, *Dir Pub Rels,* Tennessee State Museum, Nashville TN

Fox, Randall, *Supt,* Nebraska Game and Parks Commission, Arbor Lodge State Historical Park & Morton Mansion, Nebraska City NE

Fox, Stacey, *Lectr,* University of Kansas, The School of the Arts, Dept of Visual Art, Lawrence KS (S)

Fox, Terri, *Exhibs Designer & Mgr,* Nelda C & H J Lutcher Stark Foundation, Stark Museum of Art, Orange TX

Fox, William L, *Dir Center for Art & Environ,* Nevada Museum of Art, Reno NV

Fox-Pfeiffer, Lisa, *Exec Dir,* Burlington County Historical Society, Burlington NJ

Foxman, Sheryl, *Registrar,* C M Russell Museum, Frederic G Renner Memorial Library, Great Falls MT

Foxworth, Judith, *Assoc Librn,* Saint Augustine Historical Society, Library, Saint Augustine FL

Foye, Noelle, *Dir Educ,* Fuller Craft Museum, Brockton MA

Fraas, Kathleen, *Registrar,* Niagara University, Castellani Art Museum, Niagara NY

Fraccareta, Dylan, *Design Dir,* Museum of Contemporary Art Chicago, Chicago IL

Fragua, Monique, *Acting Mus Dir,* Indian Pueblo Cultural Center, Albuquerque NM

Fraker, Pat, *Cataloger,* History Colorado Center Museum, Stephen H Hart Library, Denver CO

Frakes, Jim, *Asst Prof,* University of North Carolina at Charlotte, Dept Art, Charlotte NC (S)

Fraleigh, Angela, *Chmn,* Moravian College, Dept of Art, Bethlehem PA (S)

Fraleigh, Angela, *Chmn Art Dept,* Moravian College, Payne Gallery, Bethlehem PA

Fraley, Stacie, *Vol Srvcs Coordr,* Port Huron Museum, Port Huron MI

Frame, Susan, *Faculty,* Grand Marais Art Colony, Grand Marais MN (S)

Franc, Julie, *Opers Mgr,* Walter Anderson Museum of Art, Ocean Springs MS

Francez, Mimi, *VPres,* Lafayette Museum Association, Lafayette Museum-Alexandre Mouton House, Lafayette LA

Franchino, Mark, *Prof,* Clarion University of Pennsylvania, Dept of Art, Clarion PA (S)

Franchino, Patricia, *Interim Director,* Printmaking Center of New Jersey, Branchburg NJ

Francik, Jeff, *Visitor Svcs Coordr,* Elmhurst Art Museum, Elmhurst IL

Francis Pelkey, Brenda, *Prof, Photography & Studio Art,* University of Windsor, School of Creative Arts, Windsor ON (S)

Francis, Ed, *Asst Prof,* Tidewater Community College, Visual Arts Center, Portsmouth VA (S)
Francis, Kate, *VPres Devel,* Arts & Education Council of Greater Saint Louis, Saint Louis MO
Franco, Andi, *Pres,* Art Center Manatee, Bradenton FL
Franco, Leo, *Co-Dir,* Spark Gallery, Denver CO
Franco, Pamela, *Asst Prof,* Tulane University, Sophie H Newcomb Memorial College, New Orleans LA (S)
Franco, Rebecca, *Youth Progs Coordr,* Philadelphia Museum of Art, Samuel S Fleisher Art Memorial, Philadelphia PA
Franczak, John, *Lectr,* University of Nebraska, Kearney, Dept of Art & Art History, Kearney NE (S)
Frandrup, Dennis, *Chmn,* College of Saint Benedict, Art Dept, Saint Joseph MN (S)
Frandrup, Dennis, *Prof,* Saint John's University, Art Dept, Collegeville MN (S)
Franits, Wayne, *Chmn, Prof,* Syracuse University, Dept of Fine Arts (Art History), Syracuse NY (S)
Frank, Barbara, *Prof,* Stony Brook University, College of Arts & Sciences, Dept of Art, Stony Brook NY (S)
Frank, David, *Prof,* Mississippi University for Women, Division of Fine & Performing Arts, Columbus MS (S)
Frank, Denise, *Dir Fine Arts,* Chattanooga State Technical Community College, Advertising Arts Dept, Chattanooga TN (S)
Frank, Eric, *Prof,* Occidental College, Dept of Art History & Visual Arts, Los Angeles CA (S)
Frank, Ilene, *Art Reference Librn,* University of South Florida, Library, Tampa FL
Frank, Ilene, *Chief Cur,* Connecticut Historical Society, Hartford CT
Frank, Jacqueline, *Assoc Prof,* C W Post Campus of Long Island University, School of Visual & Performing Arts, Brookville NY (S)
Frank, Jean, *Gift Gallery Mgr,* Delaplaine Visual Arts Education Center, Frederick MD
Frank, Patrick, *Asst Prof,* University of Kansas, Kress Foundation Dept of Art History, Lawrence KS (S)
Frank, Peter, *Sr Cur,* Riverside Art Museum, Riverside CA
Franke, John C, *Gen Educ,* Art Institute of Pittsburgh, Pittsburgh PA (S)
Frankenberg, Susan, *Dir,* University of Illinois at Urbana-Champaign, Spurlock Museum, Urbana IL
Franki, Jamie, *Assoc Prof,* University of North Carolina at Charlotte, Dept Art, Charlotte NC (S)
Franklin Campbell, Virginia, *National Pres,* National League of American Pen Women, Washington DC
Franklin, Dick, *VPres,* State Historical Society of Missouri, Gallery and Library, Columbia MO
Franklin, Jamie, *Cur,* Bennington Museum, Bennington VT
Franklin, Julia, *Dept Coordr & Assoc Prof,* Graceland University, Fine Arts Div, Lamoni IA (S)
Franklin, Julie, *Registrar, Exhib Coordr & Rights Mgr,* University of California, Berkeley, The Magnes Collection of Jewish Art & Life, Berkeley CA
Franklin, Laura L, *Chair Div Fine Arts,* Brevard College, Department of Art, Brevard NC (S)
Franklin, Marjorie, *Assoc Prof,* University of Minnesota, Minneapolis, Dept of Art, Minneapolis MN (S)
Franklin-David, Amy, *Cur Educ,* University of Tampa, Henry B Plant Museum, Tampa FL
Franko, Joseph, *Assoc Dean Arts & Science,* Pace University, Dyson College of Arts & Sciences, Pleasantville NY (S)
Franks, Pamela, *Cur Modern & Contemporary Art,* Yale University, Yale University Art Gallery, New Haven CT
Franks, Tina, *Head Librn,* Ohio State University, Fine Arts Library, Columbus OH
Franson, Scott, *Instr,* Ricks College, Dept of Art, Rexburg ID (S)
Frantz, April, *Interpretation Supvr,* Landis Valley Village and Farm Museum, PA Historical & Museum Commission, Lancaster PA
Frantz, Barry, *Instr,* Cuesta College, Art Dept, San Luis Obispo CA (S)
Frantz, Paul, *Pres Bd Trustees,* Taubman Museum of Art, Roanoke VA
Franz, Jason, *Founding Exec Dir & Chief Cur,* Manifest Gallery, Cincinnati OH
Franzini, Robert, *Chmn,* Morehead State University, Art & Design Dept, Morehead KY (S)
Franzoni, Richelle, *Gallery & Educ Coord,* Rutland Area Art Association, Chaffee Art Center & Chaffee Downtown Galleries, Rutland VT
Frasco, Michael, *CFO,* Montclair Art Museum, Montclair NJ
Fraser, Andrea, *Dept Chair,* University of California, Los Angeles, Dept of Art, Los Angeles CA (S)
Fraser, Bob, *CEO,* The Frank Phillips Foundation Inc, Woolaroc Museum, Bartlesville OK
Fraser, Elisabeth, *Prof,* University of South Florida, School of Art & Art History, Tampa FL (S)
Fraser, John, *Chmn Advertising & Mktg Communs,* Fashion Institute of Technology, School of Art & Design, New York NY (S)
Fraser, Karen, *Asst Prof,* Santa Clara University, Dept of Art & Art History, Santa Clara CA (S)
Fraser, Patricia, *Dir Visitor Experience,* Museum of Contemporary Art Chicago, Chicago IL
Fraser, Sandra, *Cur Colls,* Remai Modern, Saskatoon SK
Fraser, Sarah E, *Chmn & Assoc Prof,* Northwestern University, Evanston, Dept of Art History, Evanston IL (S)
Frasier, Stephanie, *Assoc Prof,* University of Evansville, Art Dept, Evansville IN (S)
Fratello, Bradley, *Prof,* Saint Louis Community College at Meramec, Art Dept, Saint Louis MO (S)
Frater, Sally, *Cur Modern & Contemporary Art,* Wichita State University, Ulrich Museum of Art, Wichita KS
Fratzke, Rachelle, *Dir Performing Arts,* Pearson Lakes Art Center, Okoboji IA
Frauenberger, Michelle, *Coll Mgr,* National Archives & Records Administration, Franklin D Roosevelt Library, Hyde Park NY
Frauenberger, Michelle, *Registrar,* National Archives & Records Administration, Franklin D Roosevelt Museum, Hyde Park NY
Frauenholtz, Judy, *Preparator,* Cedar Rapids Museum of Art, Cedar Rapids IA
Fraver, Kellie, *Pub Rel Mgr,* George Eastman Museum, Rochester NY
Frazier, Amanda, *Mktg & Pub Rels Dir,* Ashtabula Arts Center, Ashtabula OH
Frazier, Clifton T, *Assoc Prof,* Rochester Institute of Technology, School of Printing Management & Sciences, Rochester NY (S)
Frazier, L'Merchie, *Dir Educ,* Museum of African American History, Boston MA
Frazier, Nancy, *Lectr,* Humboldt State University, College of Arts & Humanities, Art Dept, Arcata CA (S)
Frazier, Niki, *Admin Svcs Mgr,* Sloss Furnaces National Historic Landmark, Birmingham AL
Frechette, Mary Enns, *Mgr Fine Arts Dept,* Saint Louis Public Library, Saint Louis MO
Fredendall, Phyllis, *Prof,* Finlandia Univ, International School of Art and Design, Hancock MI (S)
Frederick, Jennie, *Head Dept,* Maple Woods Community College, Dept of Art & Art History, Kansas City MO (S)
Frederick, Karen, *Cur & Exhib Coordr,* Bush-Holley Historic Site & Storehouse Gallery, Greenwich Historical Society, Cos Cob CT
Frederick, Margaretta S, *Cur Bancroft Coll,* Delaware Art Museum, Wilmington DE
Fredrick, Charles, *Prof Emer,* California State Polytechnic University, Pomona, Department of Art, Pomona CA (S)
Fredrick, Corinne, *Social Media & Comms,* A.E. Backus Museum & Gallery, Fort Pierce FL
Fredrick, Kathleen P, *Dir,* A.E. Backus Museum & Gallery, Fort Pierce FL
Fredrickson, Kathy, *Chief Cur Affairs,* Peabody Essex Museum, Salem MA
Freeburg, Gary, *Gallery Dir,* James Madison University, Duke Hall Gallery of Fine Art, Harrisonburg VA
Freed, Tanya, *Educ Coordr,* Quickdraw Animation Society, Calgary AB
Freed, Wayne, *Assoc Prof,* Mohawk Valley Community College, Utica NY (S)
Freedman, Jacqueline, *Assoc Prof,* Cuyahoga Community College, Dept of Art, Cleveland OH (S)
Freedman, Joan A, *Lectr,* Johns Hopkins University, School of Medicine, Dept of Art as Applied to Medicine, Baltimore MD (S)
Freedman, Susan K, *Pres,* Public Art Fund, Inc, New York NY
Freedman, Susan K, *Pres,* Public Art Fund, Inc, Visual Archive, New York NY
Freel, Robert, *Regional Manager,* University of California, Los Angeles, Arts Library, Los Angeles CA
Freeman, Amy, *Vis Asst Prof,* University of Florida, School of Art & Art History, Gainesville FL (S)
Freeman, Andrew, *Assoc Dean,* California Institute of the Arts, School of Art, Valencia CA (S)
Freeman, Asia, *Exec & Artistic Dir,* Bunnell Street Arts Center, Homer AK
Freeman, Dana, *Assoc Prof & Dir Exhibs,* Aquinas College, Art Dept, Grand Rapids MI (S)
Freeman, Dave, *Interim Dir,* Cottonlandia Museum, Greenwood MS
Freeman, David, *Prof,* Winthrop University, Dept of Art & Design, Rock Hill SC (S)
Freeman, Deborah, *Finance,* Fusion: The Ontario Clay & Glass Association, Fusion Clay & Glass Association, Toronto ON
Freeman, Dorothy, *Publ & Pub Rels,* The University of Kentucky Art Museum, Lexington KY
Freeman, Gary, *Dept Chmn,* Gaston College, Art Dept, Dallas NC (S)
Freeman, Heather, *Asst Prof,* University of North Carolina at Charlotte, Dept Art, Charlotte NC (S)
Freeman, Jeff, *Prof,* University of South Dakota, Department of Art, College of Fine Arts, Vermillion SD (S)
Freeman, Joanne, *Information Systems,* The National Shrine of the North American Martyrs, Fultonville NY
Freeman, John C, *Assoc Prof,* University of Massachusetts Lowell, Dept of Art, Lowell MA (S)
Freeman, K Genevieve, *Asst Prof,* Pepperdine University, Seaver College, Dept of Art, Malibu CA (S)
Freeman, Kirk, *Prof,* Bethel University, Dept of Art & Design, Saint Paul MN (S)
Freeman, McArthur, *Asst Prof,* University of South Florida, School of Art & Art History, Tampa FL (S)
Freeman, Rusty, *Dir Visual Arts,* Cedarhurst Center for the Arts, Mitchell Museum, Mount Vernon IL
Freeman, Sandi, *Dir Opers,* University of Tulsa, Gilcrease Museum, Tulsa OK
Freeman, Sarah, *Exhibitions Mgr,* Brattleboro Museum & Art Center, Brattleboro VT
Freeman, Suzanne H, *Head Fine Arts Librn,* Virginia Museum of Fine Arts, Margaret R & Robert M Freeman Library, Richmond VA
Freeman, Turner, *Film & Video Librn,* Public Library of the District of Columbia, Audiovisual Division, Washington DC
Freer, Elene J, *Exec Dir,* Muskoka Arts & Crafts Inc, Chapel Gallery, Bracebridge ON
Freese, David, *Adj Prof,* Saint Joseph's University, Art Dept, Philadelphia PA (S)
Fregin, Nancy J, *Pres,* American Society of Artists, Inc, Palatine IL
Freiberg, Jack, *Asst Prof,* Florida State University, Art History Dept, Tallahassee FL (S)
Freilach, David, *Admin Officer,* Massachusetts Institute of Technology, List Visual Arts Center, Cambridge MA
Freilach, David, *Dir Devel,* Phillips Academy, Addison Gallery of American Art, Andover MA

Frembling, Jon, *Archivist & reference Servs Mgr,* Amon Carter Museum of American Art, Research Library, Fort Worth TX
French, Amanda, *Mgr,* Mississauga Library System, Mississauga ON
French, Amanda, *Mgr,* Mississauga Library System, Central Library, Arts Dept, Mississauga ON
French, Annette, *Visitor Info Center,* Mississippi Museum of Art, Howorth Library, Jackson MS
French, Elizabeth, *Admin Asst,* The Art Studio Inc, Beaumont TX
French, Eva, *Exec Dir & Chief Cur,* Storefront for Art & Architecture, New York NY
French, Heather, *Mus Shop Mgr,* Riverside, the Farnsley-Moremen Landing, Louisville KY
French, Hugh, *Dir,* Tides Institute & Museum of Art, Eastport ME
French, Jeannie, *Prof,* South Dakota State University, Dept of Visual Arts, Brookings SD (S)
French, John, *Chair,* Huronia Museum, Gallery of Historic Huronia, Midland ON
French, Kate Pearson, *Pres,* Wave Hill, Bronx NY
French, Katherine, *Dir,* Danforth Museum of Art, Danforth Museum of Art, Framingham MA
French, Katherine, *Dir,* Danforth Museum of Art, Library, Framingham MA
French, Lexie, *Pres,* The Art Museum of Eastern Idaho, Idaho Falls ID
French, Susanne, *Gallery Dir,* Merced College, Arts Division, Merced CA (S)
Freudenberg, Kit, *Asst Dir,* National Churchill Museum, Fulton MO
Freund, Louise, *Publicity,* Gallery 9, Los Altos CA
Frew, Craig, *Chmn (V),* The Barnum Museum, Bridgeport CT
Frewaldt, Shannon, *Instr,* South Dakota State University, Dept of Visual Arts, Brookings SD (S)
Frewerd, Sherry, *Secy,* Junction City Arts Council Gallery, Junction City KS
Frey, Barbara, *Dir,* Texas A&M University - Commerce, University Gallery, Commerce TX
Frey, Barbara, *Instr Ceramics,* Texas A&M University Commerce, Dept of Art, Commerce TX (S)
Frey, Erick, *Treas,* Kelly-Griggs House Museum, Red Bluff CA
Frey, Julie, *Dir Mus Services,* Stan Hywet, Akron OH
Frey, Mary, *Assoc Prof,* University of Hartford, Hartford Art School, West Hartford CT (S)
Frey, Michael, *Gen Mgr,* Edina Art Center, Margaret Foss Gallery, Edina MN
Frias, Jennifer, *Gallery Mgr,* UCR ARTSblock, Sweeney Art Gallery, Riverside CA
Fricke, Michele, *The Ray Beagle Chair & Prof,* Kansas City Art Institute, Kansas City MO (S)
Fricker, Geoff, *Instr,* Butte College, Dept of Fine Arts and Communication Tech, Oroville CA (S)
Frickey, Paula, *Acctg,* Ravalli County Museum, Hamilton MT
Frickman, Andrea, *Corp Rels & Events Mgr,* Mystic Art Association, Inc, Mystic Museum of Art, Mystic CT
Fridgen, Alyssa, *Cur/Registrar,* Alexandria Museum of Art, Alexandria LA
Fridh, Beth, *Communs Mgr,* Oregon College of Art & Craft, Hoffman Gallery, Portland OR
Friebel, Todd, *Dir Fin & Opers,* The Adirondack Historical Association, The Adirondack Museum, Blue Mountain Lake NY
Fried, Rob, *Exec Dir,* Kimball Jenkins Estate, Concord NH
Friedman, Alice T, *Prof,* Wellesley College, Art Dept, Wellesley MA (S)
Friedman, Ann, *Dir,* Evergreen State College, Evergreen Gallery, Olympia WA
Friedman, Barbara, *Prof,* Pace University, Dyson College of Arts & Sciences, Pleasantville NY (S)
Friedman, Betty, *Art Dept Chair,* Notre Dame de Namur University, Wiegand Gallery, Belmont CA (S)
Friedman, Jennifer, *Librn Architecture & Visual Arts,* Massachusetts Institute of Technology, Rotch Library of Architecture & Planning, Cambridge MA
Friedman, Joel, *Asst Prof,* Seton Hall University, College of Arts & Sciences, South Orange NJ (S)
Friedman, Rebecca K, *Asst Librn,* Princeton University, Marquand Library of Art & Archaeology, Princeton NJ
Friedman, Robert, *Dir,* Stephens College, Lewis James & Nellie Stratton Davis Art Gallery, Columbia MO
Friedman, Robert, *Instr,* Stephens College, Art Dept, Columbia MO (S)
Friel, Tom, *Coord Interpretation & Pub Engagement,* Tulane University, Newcomb Art Museum, New Orleans LA
Frieling, Rudolf, *Cur Media Arts,* San Francisco Museum of Modern Art, San Francisco CA
Friere, Andrew, *Operations Manager,* LACE (Los Angeles Contemporary Exhibitions), Los Angeles CA
Friesen, Leslie, *Power Creative Designer-in-Residence,* University of Louisville, Allen R Hite Art Institute, Louisville KY (S)
Friesen, Paul, *Faculty Emeritus,* Hesston College, Art Dept, Hesston KS (S)
Frieser, Hannah, *Dir,* Light Work, Robert B Menschel Photography Gallery, Syracuse NY
Frieseu, Jacqueline, *Chief Admin Officer,* Dalnavert Museum, Winnipeg MB
Frigard, Kelly, *Asst Prof,* McPherson College, Art Dept, McPherson KS (S)
Friis-Hansen, Dana, *Dir & CEO,* Grand Rapids Art Museum, Grand Rapids MI
Frisbee Johnson, Mary, *Prof,* University of Northern Iowa, Dept of Art, Cedar Falls IA (S)
Frisby, Rachel, *Cur,* Albin Polasek Museum & Sculpture Gardens, Winter Park FL
Frischkorn, Shauna L, *Assoc Prof Photog,* Millersville University, Dept of Art & Design, Millersville PA (S)
Frish, Scott, *Assoc Prof,* West Texas A&M University, Art, Theatre & Dance Dept, Canyon TX (S)
Frisinger, Ryan, *Admin,* International Center of Medieval Art, New York NY
Frith, Deidre, *Dir Community Rels,* Wiregrass Museum of Art, Dothan AL
Fritsch, Jodi, *Dir Pub Rel and Mktg,* Fitton Center for Creative Arts, Hamilton OH
Fritz, Don, *Assoc Prof,* Santa Clara University, Dept of Art & Art History, Santa Clara CA (S)
Fritz, James, *Prof,* Southwestern Oregon Community College, Visual Arts Dept, Coos Bay OR (S)
Fritz, Kelsey, *Cur Exhibs,* Center for Puppetry Arts, Atlanta GA
Fritz, Kelsey, *Exhibs Dir,* Center for Puppetry Arts, Museum & Library, Atlanta GA
Fritz, Lisa, *Instr,* Indian Hills Community College, Ottumwa Campus, Dept of Art, Ottumwa IA (S)
Fritz, Nancy, *Treas,* ARC Gallery and Educational Foundation, Chicago IL
Fritz, Natalie, *Asst Cur,* Clark County Historical Society, Heritage Center of Clark County, Springfield OH
Fritz-Bonar, Hillaurie, *Communs Dir,* Art Guild of Burlington, Art Center of Burlington, Burlington IA
Frizzell, Deborah, *Asst Prof,* William Paterson University, Dept Arts, Wayne NJ (S)
Frizzell, Jason, *Dean,* Red Deer College, School of Creative Arts, Red Deer AB (S)
Frocheur, Nicole, *Adj Asst Prof,* College of Staten Island, Performing & Creative Arts Dept, Staten Island NY (S)
Froehlich, Conrad G, *Dir,* Martin and Osa Johnson, Johnson Collection of Photographs, Movies & Memorabilia, Chanute KS
Froehlich, Conrad G, *Dir,* Martin and Osa Johnson, Selsor Art Gallery, Chanute KS
Froehlich, Conrad G, *Dir,* Martin and Osa Johnson, Imperato Collection of West African Artifacts, Chanute KS
Froehlich, Conrad G, *Dir,* Martin and Osa Johnson, Chanute KS
Froehlich, Conrad G, *Dir,* Martin and Osa Johnson, Scott Explorers Library, Chanute KS
Froehlich, Kristen, *Dir Colls & Exhibs,* Philadelphia History Museum, Philadelphia PA
Froeschle, Ann, *Prog Coordr,* City of Ketchikan Museum Department, Totem Heritage Center, Ketchikan AK
From, Kristy, *Gallery Adminr,* University of Alabama at Huntsville, Union Grove Gallery & University Center Gallery, Huntsville AL
Froman, David, *Chmn,* Northeastern Oklahoma A & M College, Art Dept, Miami OK (S)
Frontz, Stephanie J, *Librn,* University of Rochester, Art/Music Library, Rochester NY
Frorup, Kendra, *Prof,* University of Tampa, College of Arts & Letters, Tampa FL (S)
Frost, Alan, *Instr,* Judson University, School of Art, Design & Architecture, Elgin IL (S)
Frost, Anne, *Prog Dir, Arts Admin,* Humber College, School of Creative & Performing Arts, Toronto ON (S)
Frostick, Dana, *Pres,* Artspace, Richmond VA
Fruchter, Susan, *Interim Dir,* National Museum of American History, Smithsonian Institution, Washington DC
Frudakis, Jennifer, *Instr,* Wayne Art Center, Wayne PA (S)
Frudakis, Tony, *Asst Prof,* Hillsdale College, Art Dept, Hillsdale MI (S)
Frus, Brian, *Vis Asst Prof of Glass,* Jacksonville University, Jacksonville FL (S)
Frusier, Stephanie, *Chmn Art Dept,* University of Evansville, Krannert Gallery & Peterson Gallery, Evansville IN
Fry, Amy, *Exec Dir,* Lahaina Arts Society, Art Organization, Lahaina HI
Fry, Kate, *Treas,* New Mexico Art League, Gallery & School, Albuquerque NM
Fry, Laura, *Sr Cur & Cur Art,* University of Tulsa, Gilcrease Museum, Tulsa OK
Frye, Bella, *Staff Mem,* Santa Cruz Art League, Center for the Arts, Santa Cruz CA
Frye, Todd, *Gallery Dir,* Brigham Young University, B F Larsen Gallery, Provo UT
Frykman, Sharon, *Faculty,* Grand Marais Art Colony, Grand Marais MN (S)
Frykman, Steve, *Faculty,* Grand Marais Art Colony, Grand Marais MN (S)
Fuchs, Angelee, *Prof,* Mount Mary College, Art & Design Division, Milwaukee WI (S)
Fuentes, Leo, *Chair,* City College of New York, Art Dept, New York NY (S)
Fuentes, Tina, *Dir & Prof,* Texas Tech University, Dept of Art, Lubbock TX (S)
Fuerhoff, Hannah, *Research Dir,* Environic Foundation International Library, Glen Allen VA
Fuerst, Judy, *Cur,* Barker Character, Comic and Cartoon Museum, Cheshire CT
Fuhrman Bragg, Elizabeth, *Registrar,* Evansville Museum of Arts, History & Science, Evansville IN
Fuhro, Laura, *Dept. Head,* Berkeley Heights Free Public Library, Berkeley Heights NJ
Fukawa, Hirokazu, *Asst Prof,* University of Hartford, Hartford Art School, West Hartford CT (S)
Fulda, Caryn, *Exec Asst,* Museum of Fine Arts Houston, Bayou Bend Collection & Gardens, Houston TX
Fulda, Paul, *2nd VPres,* Huntsville Art League, Lowe Mill Arts & Entertainment, Huntsville AL
Fuller Wildt, Angi, *Chief Develop Officer,* Columbia Museum of Art, Columbia SC
Fuller, Charles, *Dean School Fine Arts,* Ouachita Baptist University, Dept of Visual Art, Arkadelphia AR (S)
Fuller, Cindy, *Bd Pres,* North Shore Art League, Winnetka IL (S)
Fuller, Corey, *Asst Prof,* Oklahoma Baptist University, Art & Design Dept, Shawnee OK (S)
Fuller, Dan, *Instr,* University of Wisconsin, Madison, Dept of Art History, Madison WI (S)
Fuller, Daniel, *Cur,* Atlanta Contemporary Art Center, Atlanta GA

Fuller, Danny, *Sr. Libr Specialist,* University of Houston, William R Jenkins Architecture & Art Library, Houston TX
Fuller, Elizabeth E, *Librn,* The Rosenbach Museum & Library, Philadelphia PA
Fuller, Lori, *Assoc Librn Coll Mgmt,* Corning Museum of Glass, Juliette K and Leonard S Rakow Research Library, Corning NY
Fullerton, Deborah, *Cur,* South Texas Institute for the Arts Affiliated with Texas A&M University - Corpus Christi, Art Museum of South Texas, Corpus Christi TX
Fullerton, Deborah, *Cur Exhibs,* South Texas Institute for the Arts Affiliated with Texas A&M University - Corpus Christi, Library, Corpus Christi TX
Fullerton, Monica, *Vis Instr,* Kenyon College, Art Dept, Gambier OH (S)
Fulmer, Mara, *Prof,* Mott Community College, Fine Arts & Social Sciences Division, Flint MI (S)
Fulton, Brianne, *Art Faculty,* Cottey College, Art Dept, Nevada MO (S)
Fulton, Christopher, *Assoc Prof,* University of Louisville, Allen R Hite Art Institute, Louisville KY (S)
Funchess, Atiim, *Asst Dir Mktg,* Detroit Public Library, Art & Literature Dept, Detroit MI
Funderburk, Brent, *Prof,* Mississippi State University, Dept of Art, Starville MS (S)
Funderburk, Danielle, *Registrar,* Auburn University, Jule Collins Smith Museum of Fine Art, Auburn AL
Fung, Ming, *Grad Dir,* Southern California Institute of Architecture, Los Angeles CA (S)
Funk, Carla, *Dir Univ Mus,* Foosaner Art Museum, Melbourne FL
Funkenstein, Susan, *Asst Prof,* University of Wisconsin-Parkside, Art Dept, Kenosha WI (S)
Funkhouser, Kate, *Fine Arts Dept Chmn,* Brazosport College, Communications & Fine Art, Lake Jackson TX (S)
Fuong, Ping, *Foster Foundation Curator of Chinese Art,* Seattle Art Museum, Seattle Asian Art Museum, Seattle WA
Fuqua, Dana, *Dir Opers & CFO,* Chrysler Museum of Art, Norfolk VA
Furber, Rich, *Dir,* Chief Plenty Coups Museum State Park, Pryor MT
Furgol, Edward, *Cur,* Naval Historical Center, National Museum of the US Navy, Washington DC
Furlong, Jim, *Gallery Dir,* Hudson Guild, Hudson Guild Gallery, New York NY
Furman, David, *Prof Ceramics,* Pitzer College, Dept of Art, Claremont CA (S)
Furqueron, Reagan, *Asst Prof, Dir Foundation,* Indiana University-Purdue University, Indianapolis, Herron School of Art & Design, Indianapolis IN (S)
Furry, Stephanie, *Instr,* John C Calhoun, Department of Fine Arts, Tanner AL (S)
Furst, Donald, *Prof,* University of North Carolina at Wilmington, Dept of Fine Arts - Division of Art, Wilmington NC (S)
Furtkamp, Darryl, *Asst Prof,* New England College, Art & Art History, Henniker NH (S)
Fusco, Joy, *Office Mgr,* Franconia Sculpture Park, Franconia MN
Fusey, Jean-Francois, *Gen Dir,* Musee National des Beaux Arts du Quebec, Quebec QC
Fuson, Eric, *Artist in Res,* Missouri Western State University, School of Fine Arts, Saint Joseph MO (S)
Fuster, Valentin, *Interim Co-Chmn,* Queen Sofia Spanish Institute, New York NY
Futter, Catherine, *Dir Cur Affairs,* The Nelson-Atkins Museum of Art, Kansas City MO
Futtner, Joseph, *Acting Area Head History,* Pasadena City College, Visual Arts and Media Studies Division, Pasadena CA (S)
Gaa, David, *Exec Dir,* Mission San Luis Rey de Francia, Mission San Luis Rey Museum, Oceanside CA
Gaard, Eric, *Exhibs Dir,* CAM Contemporary Art Museum, Raleigh NC
Gaasch, Cynnie, *Exec & Artistic Dir,* Chautauqua Center for the Visual Arts, Chautauqua NY
Gabany, Donald, *Video Production,* Art Institute of Pittsburgh, Pittsburgh PA (S)
Gabarra, Ed, *Admin,* Mission San Luis Rey de Francia, Mission San Luis Rey Museum, Oceanside CA
Gabbard, Paula, *Fine Arts Librn,* Columbia University, Avery Architectural & Fine Arts Library, New York NY
Gabbard, Tomn, *Pres,* Spirit Square Center for Arts & Education, Charlotte NC
Gabbert, Tammy, *Art at Work,* Eastern Washington State Historical Society, Northwest Museum of Arts & Culture, Spokane WA
Gabel, Sarah, *Chair,* Loyola University of Chicago, Dept of Fine and Performing Arts, Chicago IL (S)
Gabriele, Sandra, *Assoc Prof & Chair, Dept of Design,* York University, School of the Arts, Media, Performance & Design, Toronto ON (S)
Gach Peelle, Susie, *Rec Secy,* American Artists Professional League, Inc, New York NY
Gacummo, Beth, *Mus Exhibs Dir,* Islip Art Museum, East Islip NY
Gadd, Sarah, *Reg,* University of Wyoming, University of Wyoming Art Museum, Laramie WY
Gadzia, Jimi, *VPres,* Roswell Museum & Art Center, Roswell NM
Gaffin, Harold, *Dir,* Rochester Institute of Technology, School of Printing Management & Sciences, Rochester NY (S)
Gaffken, Kara, *Director of Public Programming,* Historic Huguenot Street, New Paltz NY
Gaffney, Gary, *Instr,* Art Academy of Cincinnati, Cincinnati OH (S)
Gaffney, Nicholas, *Asst Prof,* Colby-Sawyer College, Dept of Fine & Performing Arts, New London NH (S)
Gagler, Mary, *Dir,* Amos Eno Gallery, Brooklyn NY
Gagne, Prudence, *Finance Dir,* League of New Hampshire Craftsmen, Grodin Permanent Collection Museum, Concord NH
Gagne, Tami, *Financial Dir,* Riverside Arts Center, Riverside IL (S)
Gahagan, Sean, *VPres Retail Mktg & Licensing,* National Baseball Hall of Fame & Museum, Cooperstown NY
Gaines Pritchett, Vicki, *Exec Dir,* Troy-Pike Cultural Arts Center, Troy AL
Gaines, Ann, *Dean School of Art, Media & Tech,* The New School, Parsons School of Design, New York NY (S)
Gaines, Anne, *Adjunct Asst Prof,* Drew University, Art Dept, Madison NJ (S)
Gaither, Edmund B, *Dir & Cur,* Museum of the National Center of Afro-American Artists, Boston MA
Gajewski, Cezary, *Chair,* University of Alberta, Dept of Art & Design, Edmonton AB (S)
Galante, Peter, *Asst Prof,* Cardinal Stritch University, Art Dept, Milwaukee WI (S)
Galante, Thomas, *Lib Dir,* Queens Borough Public Library, Fine Arts & Recreation Division, Jamaica NY
Galanti, Tera, *Asst Prof Studio Art,* California Polytechnic State University at San Luis Obispo, Dept of Art & Design, San Luis Obispo CA (S)
Galassi, Susan Grace, *Sr Cur,* Frick Collection, New York NY
Galatro, Steve, *Exec Dir,* Pratt Fine Arts Center, Gallery, Seattle WA
Galazka, Suzanne, *Gallery Asst,* Artlink, Inc, Auer Center for Arts & Culture, Fort Wayne IN
Galbraith, James, *Chief Librn,* Corning Museum of Glass, Juliette K and Leonard S Rakow Research Library, Corning NY
Galbraith, Jeanne, *Research Sec,* Livingston County Historical Society, Museum, Geneseo NY
Galbreath, Joseph, *Asst Prof,* West Virginia University, College of Creative Arts, School of Art & Design, Morgantown WV (S)
Galczenski, Marian, *Instr,* Cuesta College, Art Dept, San Luis Obispo CA (S)
Galembo, Phyllis, *Prof,* State University of New York at Albany, Art Dept, Albany NY (S)
Galender Meyer, Sarah, *Gallery Mgr,* Creative Growth Art Center, Oakland CA
Galeno, Ciro, *Asst Dir,* The Noble Maritime Collection, Staten Island NY
Galey, Chuck, *Lectr,* Mississippi State University, Dept of Art, Starville MS (S)
Galizia, Ed, *Dir Music & Video Bus,* Art Institute of Fort Lauderdale, Fort Lauderdale FL (S)
Gallagher Landis, Gary, *Deputy Dir of Extended Affairs,* San Jose Museum of Art, Library, San Jose CA
Gallagher, Brian, *Cur Decorative Arts,* The Mint Museum, Charlotte NC
Gallagher, Brian, *Treas,* Berks Art Alliance, Reading PA
Gallagher, Edward, *Dir Educ,* Beck Center for the Arts, Lakewood OH
Gallagher, Edward, *Pres & CEO,* The American-Scandinavian Foundation, Scandinavia House: The Nordic Center in America, New York NY
Gallagher, Jean, *Prof,* California State University, Chico, Department of Art & Art History, Chico CA (S)
Gallagher, Jerry, *COO,* Museum of the City of New York, Research Room, New York NY
Gallagher, Kate, *Registrar & Colls Mgr,* Johns Hopkins University, Archaeological Museum, Baltimore MD
Gallagher, Laraine, *Fiscal Officer,* Visual Studies Workshop, Rochester NY (S)
Gallagher, Michael, *Conservator in Charge, Paintings,* The Metropolitan Museum of Art, New York NY
Gallagher, Sean, *Instr,* Judson University, School of Art, Design & Architecture, Elgin IL (S)
Gallagher, Sean, *Secy,* Madison Museum of Fine Art, Madison GA
Gallagher, Tara, *Cur,* Ravalli County Museum, Hamilton MT
Gallagher, Tim, *VPres,* Arts on the Park, Lakeland Center for Creative Arts, Lakeland FL
Gallagher, Will, *Secy,* Glynn Visual Arts, Inc, Saint Simons Island GA
Gallaher, Ben, *Webmaster,* JMW Turner Museum, Sarasota FL
Gallaher, Debbie, *Vis Servs Mgr,* Chelan County Public Utility District, Rocky Reach Dam, Wenatchee WA
Gallant, Aprile, *Cur Prints, Drawings & Photographs,* Smith College, Museum of Art, Northampton MA
Gallant, Michele, *Registrar & Preparator,* Dalhousie University, Dalhousie Art Gallery, Halifax NS
Gallaway, Natasha, *Chair Residency Comt,* La Napoule Art Foundation, Chateau de la Napoule, Denver CO
Gallenberger, Rose, *Dir,* National Society of Colonial Dames of America in the State of Maryland, Library, Baltimore MD
Gallenberger, Rose, *Dir,* National Society of Colonial Dames of America in the State of Maryland, Mount Clare Museum House, Baltimore MD
Gallent, Jenny, *Vixitor Svcs,* Alexandria Museum of Art, Alexandria LA
Gallerani, Elizabeth, *Cur Acad Progs,* Williams College, Museum of Art, Williamstown MA
Gallery, Julie, *Accounting Asst,* Sangre de Cristo Arts & Conference Center, Pueblo CO
Galliardt, Jan, *Chief Preparator/Exhib Technician,* Bass Museum of Art, Miami Beach FL
Galliera, Izabel, *Cur,* McDaniel College, Esther Prangley Rice Gallery, Westminster MD
Galligan, Avan, *Jewelry,* North Seattle College, North Seattle College Dept of Art, Seattle WA (S)
Gallini, Karen, *Head Circulation Dept,* Springfield Free Public Library, Donald B Palmer Museum, Springfield NJ
Galloway, Angel, *Dir Mktg,* Arkansas Arts Center, Little Rock AR (S)
Galloway, Curtis, *Sales & Events Mgr,* Chatillon-DeMenil House Foundation, Chatillon-DeMenil Mansion, Saint Louis MO

Galloway, Elizabeth, *VPres & Dir,* Art Center College of Design, James Lemont Fogg Memorial Library, Pasadena CA

Galloway, Julia, *Prof,* University of Montana, School of Art, Missoula MT (S)

Galloway, Kat, *Prof Art,* Eastern Oregon University, School of Arts & Science, La Grande OR (S)

Galloway, Robert, *Instr,* Mesa Community College, Dept of Art, Mesa AZ (S)

Galloway, Thomas D, *Dean,* Georgia Institute of Technology, College of Architecture, Atlanta GA (S)

Galpern, Jennifer, *Research Assoc,* Rhode Island Historical Society, Library, Providence RI

Galpin, Amy, *Chief Curator,* Florida International University, The Patricia & Phillip Frost Art Museum, Miami FL

Galvin, Jeanne, *Chief Librn,* Queensborough Community College Library, Kurt R Schmeller Library, Flushing NY

Gamble, Shweta, *Exec Dir,* Kentuck Museum Association, Inc, Kentuck Art Center & Festival of the Arts, Northport AL

Gamble, Steven G, *Pres,* Southern Arkansas University, Art Dept Gallery & Magale Art Gallery, Magnolia AR

Gammell, Brad, *Chap Prog Coord,* The Names Project Foundation AIDS Memorial Quilt, Atlanta GA

Gancz, Sheri, *Visitor Relations,* Lighthouse ArtCenter Museum & School of Art, Tequesta FL

Gandara, Nancy, *Asst Dir,* Central Library, Dept of Fine Arts, San Antonio TX

Gandee, Cynthia, *Dir,* University of Tampa, Henry B Plant Museum, Tampa FL

Gander, Chris, *Instr,* Pacific Northwest College of Art, Portland OR (S)

Gandy, Janice, *Art Historian,* University of South Alabama, Dept of Art & Art History, Mobile AL (S)

Gandy, Jim, *Archivist,* New York State Military Museum and Veterans Research Center, Saratoga Springs NY

Gandy, Shawna, *Library Dir,* Oregon Historical Society, Oregon History Museum, Portland OR

Gandy, Shawna, *Library Dir,* Oregon Historical Society, Research Library, Portland OR

Ganger, Jessica, *Dir Grad Studies,* University of Wisconsin-Milwaukee, Peck School of the Arts, Dept of Art & Design, Milwaukee WI (S)

Gann, Amanda, *Commun Mgr,* Association of Collegiate Schools of Architecture, Washington DC

Gann-Smith, Lori, *Art & Design Chair,* Brenau University, Art & Design Dept, Gainesville GA (S)

Gannon, Stacey, *Exec Dir,* Saginaw Art Museum, Saginaw MI

Gans, Lucy, *Prof,* Lehigh University, Dept of Art, Architecture & Design, Bethlehem PA (S)

Ganstrom, Linda, *Asst Prof,* Fort Hays State University, Dept of Art & Design, Hays KS (S)

Gant Fisher, Lisa, *Opers Dir,* Museum of Arts & Sciences, Inc, Macon GA

Gant, Ella, *Prof Art,* Hamilton College, Art Dept, Clinton NY (S)

Gant, Sally, *Dir Educ & Spec Progs,* Old Salem Museums & Gardens, Museum of Early Southern Decorative Arts, Winston-Salem NC

Ganter, Sara, *Chief Operating Officer,* Rehoboth Art League, Inc, Rehoboth Beach DE (S)

Ganther, Becky, *Mktg & Pub Rels Mgr,* Golden State Mutual Life Insurance Company, Afro-American Art Collection, Los Angeles CA

Gantner, Robert, *Treas,* Essex Art Association, Inc, Essex CT

Gantt, Nancy, *Cur,* Sturdivant Museum Association, Sturdivant Museum, Selma AL

Gantt, Richard, *Lectr,* University of North Carolina at Greensboro, School of Art, Greensboro NC (S)

Ganz, Christopher, *Assoc Prof,* Indiana-Purdue University, Dept of Fine Arts, Fort Wayne IN (S)

Ganz, James, *Cur Prints, Drawings & Photog,* Clark Art Institute, Williamstown MA

Ganz, Sarah, *Deputy Dir Exhibs, Educ & Progs,* Rhode Island School of Design, Museum of Art, Providence RI

Gappmayer, Sam, *Exec Dir,* Sun Valley Center for the Arts, Dept of Fine Art, Sun Valley ID (S)

Gappmayer, Sam, *Pres & CEO,* Peoria Riverfront Museum, Peoria IL

Gara, James, *COO & Asst Treas,* Museum of Modern Art, New York NY

Garand, Betsey, *Sr Resident Artist,* Amherst College, Dept of Art & the History of Art, Amherst MA (S)

Garber, Kari, *External Relations & Events Coordr,* Touchstone Center for Crafts, Hart Moore Museum, Farmington PA

Garber, Kate, *Mktg & Communs Coordr,* Visual Arts Center of Richmond, Richmond VA

Garbow, Karen, *Fashion Merchandising Prog Dir,* Brenau University, Art & Design Dept, Gainesville GA (S)

Garcelon-Hart, Eva, *Archivist,* Henry Sheldon Museum of Vermont History and Research Center, Middlebury VT

Garcia Sayaram, Carolina, *Pres & CEO,* National YoungArts Foundation, Miami FL

Garcia, Alex, *Opers Dir,* Orlando Museum of Art, Orlando FL

Garcia, Alex, *Opers Dir,* Orlando Museum of Art, Orlando Sentinel Library, Orlando FL

Garcia, Christopher, *Prof,* Antioch College, Visual Arts Dept, Yellow Springs OH (S)

Garcia, Edward, *Exhib Supv,* California African-American Museum, Los Angeles CA

Garcia, Ernie, *Contact,* San Bernardino Art Association, National Orange Show Art Gallery, San Bernardino CA

Garcia, Gustavo, *Assoc Dir,* Brandywine Workshop, Center for the Visual Arts, Philadelphia PA

Garcia, Jen, *Art History,* North Seattle College, North Seattle College Dept of Art, Seattle WA (S)

Garcia, Joel, *Co Dir Prog & Operations,* Self Help Graphics, Los Angeles CA

Garcia, Jose Ramon, *President,* Pimeria Alta Historical Society, Library, Nogales AZ

Garcia, Jose, *Pres,* Pimeria Alta Historical Society, Nogales AZ

Garcia, Juan R, *Asst Prof,* Johns Hopkins University, School of Medicine, Dept of Art as Applied to Medicine, Baltimore MD (S)

Garcia, Layza, *Relationship Mktg Coordr,* En Foco, Inc, Bronx NY

Garcia, Lety, *Asst to Dir & Outrreach Coordr,* University of California, Santa Barbara, Art, Design & Architecture Museum, Santa Barbara CA

Garcia, Louie, *Asst to Dir,* International Museum of Art, El Paso TX

Garcia, Marcela, *Exec Dir,* Walker's Point Center for the Arts, Milwaukee WI

Garcia, Marina, *Finance & HR Mgr,* Florida International University, The Patricia & Phillip Frost Art Museum, Miami FL

Garcia, Miki, *Dir,* Arizona State University, ASU Art Museum, Tempe AZ

Garcia, Miki, *Exec Dir,* Santa Barbara Contemporary Arts Forum, Santa Barbara CA

Garcia, Ofelia, *Prof,* William Paterson University, Dept Arts, Wayne NJ (S)

Garcia, Pam, *Dir Fin,* The California Historical Society, San Francisco CA

Garcia, Robert, *Coll & Exhib,* Hidalgo County Historical Museum, Edinburg TX

Garcia, Tonya, *Dir,* City of Long Branch, Long Branch Free Public Library, Long Branch NJ

Garcia-Nuthmann, Andre, *Chmn,* New Mexico Highlands University, Dept of Communications & Fine Arts, Las Vegas NM (S)

Garcia-Roil, Lilian, *Assoc Prof,* Florida State University, Art Dept, Tallahassee FL (S)

Garcia-Sola, Arturo, *Vol Pres Bd Trustees,* Museo de Arte de Puerto Rico, San Juan PR

Gardiner, Diana, *Instr,* University of Utah, Dept of Art & Art History, Salt Lake City UT (S)

Gardner, Andrea, *Dir Collections,* Toledo Museum of Art, Toledo OH

Gardner, Benjamin, *Asscc Prof Art & Dept Chmn,* Drake University, Dept Art & Design, Des Moines IA (S)

Gardner, Courtney, *Exec Dir,* Peninsula Fine Arts Center, Newport News VA

Gardner, Jacquie, *Gallery Clerk,* City of Toronto Culture, The Market Gallery, Toronto ON

Gardner, James, *Library Assoc,* Washington University, Kenneth & Nancy Kranzberg Art & Architecture Library, Saint Louis MO

Gardner, Jennifer, *Deputy Dir,* Diverse Works, Houston TX

Gardner, Josie, *Gift Shop Mgr,* Walter Anderson Museum of Art, Ocean Springs MS

Gardner, Karleen, *Dir Learning Innovation,* Minneapolis Institute of Art, Minneapolis MN

Gardner, Kevin N, *Asst Prof,* Berea College, Art & Art History Program, Berea KY (S)

Gardner, Symmes, *Affiliate Assoc Prof & Dir Ctr for Art Design & Visual Culture,* University of Maryland, Baltimore County, Intermedia & Digital Arts (IMDA), Dept of Visual Arts, Baltimore MD (S)

Gardner, Symmes, *Exec Dir,* University of Maryland, Baltimore County, Center for Art Design and Visual Culture, Baltimore MD

Gardner, William F, *Instr,* North Florida Community College, Dept Humanities & Art, Madison FL (S)

Garey, Phyllis, *Visual Arts Coordr,* Hill Country Arts Foundation, Duncan-McAshan Visual Arts Center, Ingram TX

Garfield, Ellen, *Assoc Prof,* Monmouth University, Dept of Art & Design, West Long Branch NJ (S)

Gargano, John, *Prof,* University of Louisiana at Lafayette, Dept of Visual Arts, Lafayette LA (S)

Gargasz, Joseph, *Dir Exhib & Collections,* Emory University, Michael C Carlos Museum, Atlanta GA

Gariff, David, *Asst Prof,* University of Wisconsin-Stout, Dept of Art & Design, Menomonie WI (S)

Garis, Jane, *Archival Records Coordr & Cur,* North Tonawanda History Museum, North Tonawanda NY

Garka, Scott, *Pres,* CultureWorks, Richmond VA

Garland, James, *Assoc VPres of Univ Rels,* University of Bridgeport Gallery, Bridgeport CT

Garland, Jeff, *Head Dept,* Springfield College in Illinois, Dept of Art, Springfield IL (S)

Garlando, Jenee, *Development Officer,* Akron Art Museum, Akron OH

Garlington, Nina, *Dir Develop,* Berkshire Museum, Pittsfield MA

Garmendia, Tatiana, *Prof,* Seattle Central Community College, Humanities - Social Sciences Division, Seattle WA (S)

Garmon, Carole, *Sr Lectr,* University of Mary Washington, Dept of Art & Art History, Fredericksburg VA (S)

Garneau, Neil, *Cur,* Owen Sound Historical Society, Marine & Rail Heritage Museum, Owen Sound ON

Garner, Jackie, *Visitor & Mem Serv,* Appalachian State University, Turchin Center for the Visual Arts, Boone NC

Garner, Judy, *Dir,* American Jewish Historical Society, Lee M Friedman Memorial Library, Boston MA

Garner, Sharon, *Mus Aide,* Historical Museum at Fort Missoula, Missoula MT

Garner, Teresa S, *Dept Head,* Colorado Mesa University, Art Dept, Grand Junction CO (S)

Garnett, Carla, *Exec Dir & Cur,* John B Aird Gallery, Toronto ON

Garnett, Leah, *Assoc Prof,* Mount Allison University, Dept of Fine Arts, Sackville NB (S)

Garoian, Charles, *Dir & Prof Art Educ,* Pennsylvania State University, University Park, Penn State School of Visual Arts, University Park PA (S)

Garon, Libby, *Gallery Mgr,* Walker Fine Art, Denver CO

Garoutte, Claire, *Assoc Prof,* Seattle University, Dept of Art & Art History, Seattle WA (S)

Garoza, Valdis, *Chmn,* Marietta College, Grover M Hermann Fine Arts Center, Marietta OH

Garoza, Valdis, *Chmn,* Marietta College, Art Dept, Marietta OH (S)
Garrard, Mary, *Prof,* American University, Dept of Art, New York NY (S)
Garrels, Gary, *Cur Painting & Sculpture,* San Francisco Museum of Modern Art, San Francisco CA
Garrels, Gary, *Sr Cur Painting & Sculpture,* San Francisco Museum of Modern Art, San Francisco CA
Garrepy, Ken, *Dir Admin & Fin,* Providence Athenaeum, Providence RI
Garrera, Joseph, *Exec Dir,* Lehigh Valley Heritage Center, Allentown PA
Garrett Moore, Justin, *Exec Dir,* Design Commission of the City of New York, New York NY
Garrett, Aaron, *Bd Mem,* Utah Lawyers for the Arts, Salt Lake City UT
Garrett, Michael, *Head Dept,* Mississippi University for Women, Division of Fine & Performing Arts, Columbus MS (S)
Garrett, Tom, *Prof Design Dept,* Minneapolis College of Art & Design, Minneapolis MN (S)
Garrido Schneider, Gary, *Exec Dir,* Grounds for Sculpture, Hamilton NJ
Garrison, Elizabeth, *Educ Cur,* Willamette University, Hallie Ford Museum of Art, Salem OR
Garrison, Helen, *Dean Liberal Arts,* Art Institute of Southern California, Laguna Beach CA (S)
Garrison, Jodie, *Head Art Dept,* Western Oregon University, Dan & Gail Cannon Gallery of Art, Monmouth OR
Garrison, Laura, *Asst Dir,* Rensselaer Polytechnic Institute, Eye Ear Studio Dept of Art, Troy NY (S)
Garrison, Nan, *Deputy Dir External Rels,* Henry Gallery Association, Henry Art Gallery, Seattle WA
Garrity, Noreen Scott, *Assoc Dir Educ,* Rutgers University, Stedman Art Gallery, Camden NJ
Garry, Eileen, *Exec Dir,* Kansas City Jewish Museum of Contemporary Art - Epsten Gallery, Overland Park KS
Garside, Heather, *Historic Site Mgr & Cur,* Passaic County Historical Society, Lambert Castle Museum & Library, Paterson NJ
Gartenmann, Donna, *City of Boulder Arts Commission & Dir Cultural Programs,* Boulder Public Library & Gallery, Arts Gallery, Boulder CO
Garthwaite, Ernest, *Assoc Prof,* York College of the City University of New York, Fine & Performing Arts, Jamaica NY (S)
Gartrell, William, *Registrar & Dir, Enrollment Svcs,* ArtCenter College of Design, Pasadena CA (S)
Garven, Leah, *Cur & Mgr,* Allen Sapp, North Battleford SK
Garver, Grace, *Deputy Dir Finance,* Museum of Contemporary Art Cleveland, Cleveland OH
Gary, Anne-Bridget, *Prof,* University of Wisconsin-Stevens Point, Dept of Art & Design, Stevens Point WI (S)
Gary, Susan, *Sr VP & COO,* Arts & Science Council, Charlotte NC
Garza, Amorette, *Assoc Prof,* Del Mar College, Art Dept, Corpus Christi TX (S)
Garza, David, *Exec Dir,* Henry Street Settlement, Abrons Art Center, New York NY
Garza, Monica, *Dir Educ,* Institute of Contemporary Art/Boston, Boston MA
Garzillo, Robert, *Technical Servs Librn,* Rhode Island School of Design, Fleet Library at RISD, Providence RI
Garzon, Gerry, *Dir Library Svcs,* Oakland Public Library, Art, Music, History & Literature Section, Oakland CA
Gasbarre, Jessica, *Engagement Specialist,* University of Rochester, Memorial Art Gallery, Rochester NY
Gascogne, Laura-Harris, *Assoc Prof Fine Art & Ceramic Dept Coordr,* Johnson County Community College, Fine Arts Dept & Art History Dept, Overland Park KS (S)
Gasiowski, Joanne, *Vis Servs & Mem Mgr,* Philadelphia History Museum, Philadelphia PA
Gaske, Fred, *Bureau Chief,* Florida Folklife Programs, Tallahassee FL
Gaskell, Ivan, *Cur Painting,* Harvard University, William Hayes Fogg Art Museum, Cambridge MA
Gaskil, Darlene, *Adj Prof,* Oral Roberts University, Art Dept, Tulsa OK (S)
Gaston, Elizabeth, *Asst Prof,* Mount Mary College, Art & Design Division, Milwaukee WI (S)
Gastonguay, Nicole, *Documentation Tech,* Musee National des Beaux Arts du Quebec, Bibliotheque, Quebec QC
Gatchalian, Raphael, *Admin Coord & Business Specialist,* University of Southern California, USC Fisher Museum of Art, Los Angeles CA
Gates, James L, *Library Dir,* National Baseball Hall of Fame & Museum, Cooperstown NY
Gates, Jordene, *Interior Design,* Art Institute of Pittsburgh, Pittsburgh PA (S)
Gates, Lindsay, *Devel Dir,* Peters Valley School of Craft, Layton NJ
Gates, Nadine, *Cur/Dir,* Yarmouth County Historical Society, Yarmouth County Museum & Archives, Yarmouth NS
Gates, Rebecca, *Colls Mgr,* Kirkland Museum of Fine & Decorative Art, Denver CO
Gates, Sue, *Dir,* Dacotah Prairie Museum, Lamont Art Gallery, Aberdeen SD
Gates, Sue, *Dir,* Dacotah Prairie Museum, Ruth Bunker Memorial Library, Aberdeen SD
Gatewood, Caterine, *Events Coordr,* The Buffalo Fine Arts Academy, Albright-Knox Art Gallery, Buffalo NY
Gatlin, Janice, *Dir Progs,* The Multicultural Center of the South, Shreveport LA
Gatten, Jeff, *Dean,* California Institute of the Arts Library, Santa Clarita CA
Gattle, Kim, *Deputy Dir Institutional Advancement,* Newfields, Indianapolis IN
Gatzke, Donald, *Dean,* Tulane University, School of Architecture, New Orleans LA (S)
Gaucher, Jeremy, *Pub Arts Admin,* Cambridge Arts Council, CAC Gallery, Cambridge MA
Gaucher, Karine, *Programming & Communs Coordr,* Guilde canadienne des metiers d'art, Canadian Guild of Crafts, Montreal QC
Gaudelius, Yvonne, *Prof Art Educ,* Pennsylvania State University, University Park, Penn State School of Visual Arts, University Park PA (S)
Gaudet, Deborah, *Cur Film & Theater,* Wadsworth Atheneum Museum of Art, Hartford CT
Gaudet, Lisette, *Archivist,* Yarmouth County Historical Society, Yarmouth County Museum & Archives, Yarmouth NS
Gaudette, Mary, *Gallery Asst,* Saint Paul's School, Art Center in Hargate, Concord NH
Gaudin, Susanne, *Grants & Fund-raising Adv to Bd,* Brown County Art Gallery Foundation, Nashville IN
Gaudio, Michael, *Asst Prof,* University of Minnesota, Minneapolis, Art History, Minneapolis MN (S)
Gaugler, Jonathan, *Media Rel Mgr,* Carnegie Museums of Pittsburgh, Carnegie Museum of Art, Pittsburgh PA
Gauigan, Sarah, *Library Dir,* New Hampshire Historical Society, New Hampshire Historical Society Library, Concord NH
Gaul, Elaine, *Co-Cur Exhibs,* Indiana University, The Mathers Museum of World Cultures, Bloomington IN
Gaumond, Lisa, *Gallery Mgr,* University of Hartford, Joseloff Gallery, West Hartford CT
Gauntt, Stan, *Treas,* Junction City Arts Council Gallery, Junction City KS
Gause, Conni, *Admin Asst,* Grinnell College, Faulconer Gallery, Grinnell IA
Gausepohl, Jane, *Sec,* Southern Illinois University at Edwardsville, Dept of Art & Design, Edwardsville IL (S)
Gauthier, Annie, *Dir Collections & Research,* Musee National des Beaux Arts du Quebec, Quebec QC
Gauthier, Caroline, *Documentation Tech,* Musee National des Beaux Arts du Quebec, Bibliotheque, Quebec QC
Gauthier, Sue, *Museum Store Mgr,* University of Tampa, Henry B Plant Museum, Tampa FL
Gautreaux, Hurley, *Secy,* Crowley Art Association, The Gallery, Crowley LA
Gavagan, Kevin, *Bd Chmn,* George Eastman Museum, Rochester NY
Gawronski, Bryan, *Interim Head Opers,* The Buffalo Fine Arts Academy, Albright-Knox Art Gallery, Buffalo NY
Gawronski, Jenny, *Asst Prof,* Adams State College, Dept of Visual Arts, Alamosa CO (S)
Gay, Julie, *Exec Dir,* Bonita Historical Society, Bonita Museum and Cultural Center, Bonita CA
Gay, Matt, *Art Preparator,* North Carolina State University, Gregg Museum of Art & Design, Raleigh NC
Gay, Richard, *Chair,* University of North Carolina at Pembroke, Art Dept, Pembroke NC (S)
Gay, Scott, *Instr,* Kirkwood Community College, Dept of Arts & Humanities, Cedar Rapids IA (S)
Gazda, Elaine K, *Cur,* University of Michigan, Kelsey Museum of Archaeology, Ann Arbor MI
Gazda, Elaine K, *Prof & Cur, Kelsey Mus of Archaeology,* University of Michigan, Ann Arbor, Dept of History of Art, Ann Arbor MI (S)
Gazzo, Bridget, *Pre-Columbian Studies Librn,* Dumbarton Oaks, Dumbarton Oaks Research Library, Washington DC
Gazzole, Bob, *Pres & CEO,* American Film Institute (AFI), Los Angeles CA (S)
Gearding, Dave, *Facility Dir,* Contemporary Arts Center, Cincinnati OH
Gebb, Wayne, *Instr Music & Choir,* Midway College, Art Dept, Midway KY (S)
Gebhardt, Denise, *Cur,* Central Methodist University, Ashby-Hodge Gallery of American Art, Fayette MO
Gebhart, Bradley, *VPres,* Lancaster County Art Association, Inc, Strasburg PA
Geddes, Mathew, *Instr,* Ricks College, Dept of Art, Rexburg ID (S)
Gedeon, Lucinda H, *Exec Dir,* Vero Beach Museum of Art, Vero Beach FL
Gee, Norman, *Prof Emer,* University of Kansas, The School of the Arts, Dept of Visual Art, Lawrence KS (S)
Gee, Regina, *Asst Prof - Art History,* Montana State University, School of Art, Bozeman MT (S)
Geelhood, Lisa, *Dir Educ,* Huntington Museum of Art, Huntington WV
Geffen, Amara, *Chair Art Dept,* Allegheny College, Art Dept, Meadville PA (S)
Gehnrich, Babette, *Chief Conservator,* American Antiquarian Society, Worcester MA
Gehringer, Barbara, *Exec Dir,* Gallery 92 West / Fremont Area Art Association, Fremont NE
Gehrm, Barbara, *Registrar,* Salisbury University, Ward Museum of Wildfowl Art, Salisbury MD
Geidel, Ed, *Building Operations,* Museum of Wisconsin Art, West Bend WI
Geiger, Deborah, *Cur,* Muchnic Foundation & Atchison Art Association, Muchnic Gallery, Atchison KS
Geiger, Gail L, *Prof, Dept Chmn,* University of Wisconsin, Madison, Dept of Art History, Madison WI (S)
Geiger, Justin, *Vis Svcs Coordr,* University of Mary Washington, University of Mary Washington Galleries, Fredericksburg VA
Geiger, Karin, *Exec Dir,* Studio Channel Islands Art Center, Camarillo CA
Geiger, Mark, *Pres,* Frontier Gateway Museum, Glendive MT
Geiger, Philip, *Studio Faculty,* University of Virginia, McIntire Dept of Art, Charlottesville VA (S)
Geis, Terri, *Cur Acad Progs,* The Pomona College, Claremont CA
Geis, Terri, *Dir Educa & Interpretation,* University of California, Los Angeles, Fowler Museum at UCLA, Los Angeles CA
Geisbrecht, Miles, *Technician,* Open Space, Victoria BC

Geisinger, William, *Instr,* De Anza College, Creative Arts Division, Cupertino CA (S)
Geisler, Carol, *Fiscal Officer & Admin Assoc,* University of Missouri, Museum of Art & Archaeology, Columbia MO
Geisser, Gail, *Access Servs Mgr,* Rhode Island School of Design, Fleet Library at RISD, Providence RI
Geist, Joe, *Registrar,* Central Methodist University, Ashby-Hodge Gallery of American Art, Fayette MO
Geist, Ronnie, *Dir Programming,* Women's Interart Center, Inc, Interart Gallery, New York NY
Gelardi Holmes, Meghan, *Cur,* Gibson Society, Inc, Gibson House Museum, Boston MA
Geldin, Sherri, *Dir,* Ohio State University, Wexner Center for the Arts, Columbus OH
Geller, Beatrice, *Assoc Prof,* Pacific Lutheran University, Dept of Art, Tacoma WA (S)
Gellert, Jill, *COO,* Norman Rockwell Museum, Stockbridge MA
Gelover, Cheryl, *Asst Prof,* Montgomery County Community College, Art Center, Blue Bell PA (S)
Gendreau, Anne, *Registrar & Curatorial Team,* Bainbridge Arts & Crafts Gallery, Bainbridge Island WA
Gendron, Heather, *Art Librn,* University of North Carolina at Chapel Hill, Joseph Curtis Sloane Art Library, Chapel Hill NC
Gendron, Heather, *Dir,* Yale University, The Robert B. Haas Family Arts Library, New Haven CT
Genevro, Rosalie, *Exec Dir,* Architectural League of New York, New York NY
Gengler, Matthew, *Head Access Servs,* The Cleveland Museum of Art, Ingalls Library, Cleveland OH
Gengler, Tom, *Colls Asst,* Spertus Institute of Jewish Studies, Chicago IL
Genik, Chris, *Undergrad Dir,* Southern California Institute of Architecture, Los Angeles CA (S)
Gennis, Emmalyn, *Asst Prof,* Pittsburg State University, Art Dept, Pittsburg KS (S)
Genshaft, Carole, *Cur-at-Large,* Columbus Museum of Art, Columbus OH
Genszler, Leslie, *Dir Retail Opers,* Madison Museum of Contemporary Art, Madison WI
Gentele, Glen, *Dir,* Orlando Museum of Art, Orlando FL
Gentele, Glen, *Dir,* Orlando Museum of Art, Orlando Sentinel Library, Orlando FL
Genteman, Sheila, *Gallery Dir,* Saint Mary-of-the-Woods College, Art Dept, Saint Mary of the Woods IN (S)
Gentilini, David, *Dir,* Capital University, Schumacher Gallery, Columbus OH
Gentis, Thierry, *Cur,* Brown University, Haffenreffer Museum of Anthropology, Providence RI
Gentle, Drew, *Co-owner,* Eureka Fine Art Gallery, Eureka Springs AR
Gentry, David, *Instr & Gallery Dir,* Shasta College, Arts, Communications & Social Sciences Division, Redding CA (S)
Gentry, James, *Instr,* Eastern Arizona College, Art Dept, Thatcher AZ (S)
Gentry, Liz, *Librn & Archivist,* Booth Western Art Museum, Cartersville GA
Gentry, Sandra J, *Exec Asst,* Pensacola Museum of Art, Harry Thornton Library, Pensacola FL
Gentzler, Lynn W, *Assoc Dir,* State Historical Society of Missouri, Columbia MO
Gentzler, Lynn W, *Assoc Dir,* State Historical Society of Missouri, Gallery and Library, Columbia MO
Geoffino, Tom, *Dir,* New Rochelle Public Library, Art Section, New Rochelle NY
George, Chastity, *Assistant,* Mohawk Valley Heritage Association, Inc, Walter Elwood Museum, Amsterdam NY
George, Christy, *Mktg & Communs Mgr,* The Albrecht-Kemper Museum of Art, Saint Joseph MO
George, David N, *Prof,* Truett-McConnell College, Fine Arts Dept & Arts Dept, Cleveland GA (S)
George, Ivana, *Asst Prof,* Bridgewater State College, Art Dept, Bridgewater MA (S)
George, Judith N, *Progs & Chmn,* Jefferson County Historical Society, Watertown NY
George, Kate, *Tour Coordr,* Dartmouth College, Hood Museum of Art, Hanover NH
George, Valerie, *Asst Prof,* University of West Florida, Dept of Art, Pensacola FL (S)
George-Shengo, David, *Dir,* Seneca-Iroquois National Museum, Salamanca NY
Georgeadis, Socrates J, *Treas,* Reading Public Museum, Reading PA
Georger, Lauren, *Archivist, Spec Colls Librn,* Manhattanville College, Library, Purchase NY
Georgiades, Aristotle, *Prof,* University of Wisconsin, Madison, Dept of Art, Madison WI (S)
Geppert, Melissa, *Asst Prof,* Southern Oregon University, Art & Art History Dept, Ashland OR (S)
Geraci, Phil, *Asst Prof,* Eastern New Mexico University, Dept of Art, Portales NM (S)
Geralds, John, *VPres,* Brooklyn Historical Society, Brooklyn OH
Gerard, Mira, *Assoc Prof,* East Tennessee State University, College of Arts and Sciences, Dept of Art & Design, Johnson City TN (S)
Gerbaulet-Vanasse, Caroline, *Mem & Community Engagement Mgr,* Swedish American Museum, Chicago IL
Gerber, Linda, *Dir Retail Svcs,* Witte Museum, San Antonio TX
Gerber, Steve, *Gallery Mgr,* City Lights Gallery, Bridgeport CT
Gerbracht, Grady, *Asst Prof,* Stony Brook University, College of Arts & Sciences, Dept of Art, Stony Brook NY (S)
Gerdes, Kirsten, *Assoc Cur,* Boulder Museum of Contemporary Art, Boulder CO
Gerety, Lorraine, *Visual Resources Cur,* Visual Arts Library, New York NY
Geritz, Kathy, *Assoc Film Cur,* University of California, Berkeley, Pacific Film Archive, Berkeley CA
Geritz, Kathy, *Cur Film,* University of California, Berkeley, Berkeley Art Museum & Pacific Film Archive, Berkeley CA
Gerlach, Monte, *Assoc Prof,* Saint Xavier University, Dept of Art & Design, Chicago IL (S)
Germain, Justin, *Retail Mgr,* Tucson Museum of Art and Historic Block, Tucson AZ
Germano, Thomas, *Assoc Prof,* State University of New York at Farmingdale, Visual Communications, Farmingdale NY (S)
Gerrard, Susan, *Dir Mktg,* Museum of Ventura County, Ventura CA
Gerring, Andrea, *Instr,* North Central Michigan College, Art Dept, Petoskey MI (S)
Gerring, Todd, *Coordr of Mus Visitor Programs,* University of Michigan, Kelsey Museum of Archaeology, Ann Arbor MI
Gerrits, Hendrik, *Dir Exhibs,* Museum of Arts & Design, New York NY
Gerry, Rip, *Exhib Designer & Photo Archivist,* Brown University, Haffenreffer Museum of Anthropology, Providence RI
Gershman, Richard, *Assoc Prof & Chair Film School,* Watkins College of Art, Design & Film, Nashville TN (S)
Gerson, Frances, *Chmn,* The Print Center, Philadelphia PA
Gerson, Paula, *Chmn,* Florida State University, Art History Dept, Tallahassee FL (S)
Gerstein, Beth Ann, *Exec Dir,* American Museum of Ceramic Art, Pomona CA
Gerstein, Marc, *Assoc Prof,* University of Toledo, Dept of Art, Toledo OH (S)
Gerth, Troy, *Asst Prof,* Mount Mary College, Art & Design Division, Milwaukee WI (S)
Gertjejansen, Doyle J, *Prof Emeritus,* University of New Orleans-Lake Front, Dept of Fine Arts, New Orleans LA (S)
Gertjejansen, Doyle, *Gallery Dir,* University of New Orleans, Fine Arts Gallery, New Orleans LA
Gertsman, Elina, *Assoc Prof,* Case Western Reserve University, Dept of Art History & Art, Cleveland OH (S)
Gervais, Christine, *Assoc Cur Decorative Arts,* Museum of Fine Arts, Houston, Rienzi Center for European Decorative Arts, Houston TX
Gervase, Keith, *Collections Mgr,* New Britain Museum of American Art, New Britain CT
Gervits, Maya, *Dir,* New Jersey Institute of Technology, Littman Architecture & Design Library, Newark NJ
Getchell, Katie, *CBO & Deputy Dir,* Museum of Fine Arts, Boston MA
Getek, Lauren Marie, *Dir,* Rome Art & Community Center, Rome NY
Geter, Tyrone, *Prof Art & Dir Ponder Gallery,* Benedict College, School of Humanities, Arts & Social Sciences, Columbia SC (S)
Getty, Cassandra, *Cur Art,* Museum London, London ON
Getzels, Julia E, *Exec VPres, Gen Coun, Secy,* The Art Institute of Chicago, Chicago IL
Gevas, Sophia, *Dir,* Sacred Heart University, Gallery of Contemporary Art, Fairfield CT
Gever, Martha, *Assoc Prof Media Histories,* University of California, Irvine, Studio Art Dept, Irvine CA (S)
Gevins, Jack, *Instr,* Bucks County Community College, Fine Arts Dept, Newtown PA (S)
Gevni, Heather, *Gallery Coordr,* The ArtsCenter, The Nicholson Gallery at the Arts Center, Carrboro NC
Gevurtz, Sara, *Adj Instr,* University of West Florida, Dept of Art, Pensacola FL (S)
Geyer, Nancy, *Exec Dir,* Boulder History Museum, Museum of History, Boulder CO
Gffis, Damian, *Griffis Sculpture Park Manager,* Ashford Hollow Foundation for Visual & Performing Arts, Griffis Sculpture Park & Essex Arts Center, East Otto NY
Gherardi, Beth, *Educ Coordr,* Fort Collins Museum of Art, Inc, Fort Collins CO
Ghevaurd, Emily, *Painting & Drawing,* North Seattle College, North Seattle College Dept of Art, Seattle WA (S)
Ghimire, Deepa, *Staff Accountant,* Oklahoma Contemporary Arts Center, Oklahoma City OK
Ghirardo, Raymond, *Prof,* Ithaca College, Fine Art Dept, Ithaca NY (S)
Ghize, Shannon, *Admin Aid,* Frederic Remington, Ogdensburg NY
Ghose, Madhuvanti, *Assoc Cur Indian, SE Asian, Himalayan & Islamic Art,* The Art Institute of Chicago, Department of Asian Art, Chicago IL
Ghosh, Pika, *Assoc Prof,* University of North Carolina at Chapel Hill, Art Dept, Chapel Hill NC (S)
Giacopuzzi, Michelle, *Exhib Coordr,* California State University, Northridge, Art Galleries, Northridge CA
Giambi, M Dina, *Asst Dir Library Technical Servs,* University of Delaware, Morris Library, Newark DE
Giancola, Deborah, *Graphic Design,* Art Institute of Pittsburgh, Pittsburgh PA (S)
Giangaspero, Maric, *Chief of Staff,* Jack Richard Gallery, Almond Tea Museum & Jane Williams Galleries, Divisions of Studios of Jack Richard, Cuyahoga Falls OH
Giannelli, Gary, *Dir Computer Svcs,* Ferguson Library, Stamford CT
Giannotti, John, *Chmn,* Rutgers University, Camden, Art Dept, Camden NJ (S)
Giaquinto, Michael, *Mgr Exhib,* Cape Cod Museum of Art Inc, Dennis MA
Giarritta, Shirley, *Dir,* Cumberland Theatre, Lobby for the Arts Gallery, Cumberland MD
Giarrizzo, John, *Assoc Prof,* Northwest Community College, Dept of Art, Powell WY (S)
Giasson, Patrice, *Cur Art of the Americas,* Purchase College, Neuberger Museum of Art, Purchase NY
Gibbons, Arthur, *Dir,* Bard College, Milton Avery Graduate School of the Arts, Annandale-on-Hudson NY (S)
Gibbons, Bud, *Assoc Prof Art,* Pennsylvania State University at New Kensington, Depts of Art & Architecture, Upper Burrell PA (S)

Gibbons, Connie, *Dir,* Washburn University, Mulvane Art Museum, Topeka KS
Gibbons, Lari, *Asst Prof,* University of Dayton, Visual Arts Dept, Dayton OH (S)
Gibbons, Larry, *Assoc Prof Printmaking,* University of North Texas, College of Visual Arts & Design, Denton TX (S)
Gibbons, Michael, *Cur,* Yaquina River Museum of Art, Toledo OR
Gibbs, Andrea, *Dep Chief & Architecture Specialist,* National Gallery of Art, Department of Image Collections, Washington DC
Gibbs, Carrie, *Dir Shrode Art Center,* Cedarhurst Center for the Arts, Mitchell Museum, Mount Vernon IL
Gibbs, Ed, *Dir,* Tidewater Community College, Visual Arts Center, Portsmouth VA (S)
Gibbs, Gary, *Pres,* National Assembly of State Arts Agencies, Washington DC
Gibbs, Jason, *Librn II, Prog Mgr,* San Francisco Public Library, Art, Music & Recreation Center, San Francisco CA
Gibbs, Jocelyn, *Cur Architectural Drawings,* University of California, Santa Barbara, Art, Design & Architecture Museum, Santa Barbara CA
Gibbs, Judith, *Dep Dir Develop,* The Baltimore Museum of Art, Baltimore MD
Gibbs, Owen, *Library Asst,* Rhode Island Historical Society, Library, Providence RI
Gibbs, Steve, *Owner,* The Art Spirit Gallery, Coeur D Alene ID
Gibbs, Tom, *Instr,* Loras College, Dept of Art, Dubuque IA (S)
Gibbs-Riley, Brandy, *Asst Prof,* Colby-Sawyer College, Dept of Fine & Performing Arts, New London NH (S)
Giberga, Ovidio, *Assoc Prof,* University of Texas at San Antonio, Dept of Art & Art History, San Antonio TX (S)
Gibney, Kate, *VPres Develop,* Americans for the Arts, New York NY
Gibson Moqtaderi, Heather, *Asst Dir & Assoc Cur,* University of Pennsylvania, Arthur Ross Gallery, Philadelphia PA
Gibson, Barbara, *Pres Bd & Dir,* Associates for Community Development, The Arts Center, Inc, Martinsburg WV
Gibson, Ben, *Fine Arts Representative,* Edinboro University of Pennsylvania, Art Dept, Edinboro PA (S)
Gibson, Christine, *Educ Mgr,* Oklahoma Contemporary Arts Center, Oklahoma City OK
Gibson, Edward, *Dir,* Jones Memorial Library, Lynchburg VA
Gibson, Ingrid, *Interlibrary Loan Librn,* Dumbarton Oaks, Dumbarton Oaks Research Library, Washington DC
Gibson, Jay, *Asst Dir,* SculptureCenter, Long Island City NY
Gibson, Jen, *Database Coordr,* Glanmore National Historic Site of Canada, Belleville ON
Gibson, Jennifer, *Dir,* United States General Services Administration, Art in Architecture and Fine Arts, Washington DC
Gibson, Jonathan, *Assoc Prof,* Xavier University, Dept of Art, Cincinnati OH (S)
Gibson, Julia, *Faculty,* Florida College, Division of Art, Temple Terrace FL (S)
Gibson, Michael, *Assoc Prof Communs Design,* University of North Texas, College of Visual Arts & Design, Denton TX (S)
Gibson, Michael, *Treas,* Society of Architectural Historians, Chicago IL
Gibson, Robert, *Asst Prof,* Mississippi University for Women, Division of Fine & Performing Arts, Columbus MS (S)
Gibson, Robin, *Assoc Prof Art (Printmaking),* Pennsylvania State University, University Park, Penn State School of Visual Arts, University Park PA (S)
Gibson, Stacy, *Prof,* Harding University, Dept of Art & Design, Searcy AR (S)
Giddens, Phyllis, *Dir External Affairs,* Morris Museum of Art, Augusta GA
Giduz, Lee Carol, *Exec Dir,* Blowing Rock Art and History Museum, Blowing Rock NC
Giebel, Douglas, *Dir Art,* Roberts Wesleyan College, Department of Visual Art, Rochester NY (S)
Gieber, Terry, *Prof Emeritus,* Gonzaga University, Dept of Art, Spokane WA (S)
Giersdorf, Jens, *Assoc Prof Dance,* Marymount Manhattan College, Fine & Performing Arts Div, New York NY (S)
Gierster, Patrick, *Dean Humanities,* San Jose City College, School of Fine Arts, San Jose CA (S)
Gierster, Patrick, *Dean Humanities & Social Science,* San Jose City College, School of Fine Arts, San Jose CA (S)
Giffuni Wellner, JoAnn, *Treas,* Pastel Society of America, National Arts Club, Grand Gallery, New York NY
Giffuni, Flora B, *Founder & Hon Chair,* Pastel Society of America, National Arts Club, Grand Gallery, New York NY
Gigante, Linda, *Art History Prog Head,* University of Louisville, Hite Art Institute, Louisville KY
Gigante, Linda, *Assoc Prof,* University of Louisville, Allen R Hite Art Institute, Louisville KY (S)
Gikas, Carol S, *Exec Dir,* Louisiana Arts & Science Museum, Library, Baton Rouge LA
Gikas, Carol S, *Pres & Exec Dir,* Louisiana Arts & Science Museum, Baton Rouge LA
Gilats, Andrea, *Dir,* University of Minnesota, Minneapolis, Split Rock Arts Program, St Paul MN (S)
Gilbert, Claire, *Archives Mgr,* Royal British Columbia Museum, BC Archives, Victoria BC
Gilbert, Courtney, *Cur Visual Arts,* Sun Valley Center for the Arts, Dept of Fine Art, Sun Valley ID (S)
Gilbert, Edi, *Tour Scheduling,* Lafayette Science Museum & Planetarium, Lafayette LA
Gilbert, Gail R, *Dir Art Library,* University of Louisville, Margaret M Bridwell Art Library, Louisville KY
Gilbert, Kathy, *Adjunct Prof,* Community College of Allegheny County, Boyce Campus, Art Dept, Monroeville PA (S)
Gilbert, Meg, *Exec Dir,* The Art Center of Waco, Waco TX
Gilbert, Paula, *Dir Operations,* Martin Memorial Library, York PA
Gilbert, Peg, *Staff Asst,* Grassroots Art Center, Lucas KS
Gilbert, Suzanne, *Gallery Dir,* North Shore Arts Association, Inc, Gloucester MA
Gilbert, William T, *Prof,* University of New Mexico, Department of Fine Arts & Art History, Albuquerque NM (S)
Gilbertson, Claire, *Library Asst,* Vermont Historical Society, Library, Montpelier VT
Gilbertson, Greg, *Instr,* Pierce College, Art Dept, Woodland Hills CA (S)
Gilbertson, Lauran, *Chief Cur,* Vesterheim Norwegian-American Museum, Decorah IA
Gilbertson, Leanne, *Gallery Dir,* Montana State University at Billings, Northcutt Steele Gallery, Billings MT
Gilboe, Roberta Frey, *Registrar,* Cranbrook Art Museum, Bloomfield Hills MI
Gilchrist, Preston, *Adjunct Prof,* Louisiana College, Dept of Art, Pineville LA (S)
Gilchrist, Ron, *Dir Engineering Svcs,* New-York Historical Society, Museum, New York NY
Giles, Laura, *Cur Prints & Drawings,* Princeton University, Princeton University Art Museum, Princeton NJ
Gilfillan, Timothy, *Preparator,* Amherst College, Mead Art Museum, Amherst MA
Gilg, Karen, *Prof,* University of Maine at Augusta, College of Arts & Humanities, Augusta ME (S)
Gilgore, Susan, *Exec Dir,* Lockwood-Mathews Mansion Museum, Norwalk CT
Gill, Cecil, *Exec Dir,* Roberts County Museum, Miami TX
Gill, Edward A, *VPres, Dean Educ,* Art Institute of Pittsburgh, Pittsburgh PA (S)
Gill, Jennifer, *Develop Dir,* Kirkland Arts Center, KAC Gallery, Kirkland WA
Gill, Lyn, *3rd VPres,* Watercolor Society of Alabama, Town Creek AL
Gill, Vanessa, *Develop Dir,* Calvert Marine Museum, Solomons MD
Gillan, Maria Mazziotti, *Exec Dir Cultural Affairs,* Passaic County Community College, Broadway, LRC, and Hamilton Club Galleries, Paterson NJ
Gillcrist, Christopher, *Exec Dir,* Great Lakes Historical Society, Inland Seas Maritime Museum, Vermilion OH
Gillenwater, Karen, *Museum Mgr,* 21c Museum, Louisville KY
Gillepsie, Marilyn, *Exec Dir,* Las Vegas Natural History Museum, Las Vegas NV
Gillespie, Ashley, *Dir,* Coker College, Cecelia Coker Bell Gallery, Hartsville SC
Gillespie, Clark, *Asst Cur,* Knoxville Museum of Art, Knoxville TN
Gillespie, Dan, *Coordr Opers,* The Drawing Center, New York NY
Gillespie, Kristine, *Sales + Tours Manager,* Historic Huguenot Street, New Paltz NY
Gillespie, Sarah Kate, *Cur American Art,* University of Georgia, Georgia Museum of Art, Athens GA
Gillette, Allison, *Archives & Library Manager,* Shelburne Museum, Library, Shelburne VT
Gillette, Allison, *Librn,* The Speed Art Museum, Art Reference Library, Louisville KY
Gillette, David D, *Cur Geology,* Museum of Northern Arizona, Flagstaff AZ
Gillette, Jonathan, *Instr,* Union University, Dept of Art, Jackson TN (S)
Gillette-Woodard, Helene, *Objects Conservator & Dept Head,* Williamstown Art Conservation Center, Williamstown MA
Gillham, Andrew, *Assoc Prof,* Indiana University of Pennsylvania, College of Fine Arts, Indiana PA (S)
Gillham, Will, *Head of Publications,* Amon Carter Museum of American Art, Fort Worth TX
Gilliam, Georgen, *Cur Library & Archives,* Nantucket Historical Association, Historic Nantucket, Nantucket MA
Gilliam, Gina, *Pub Affairs Officer,* Independence National Historical Park, Library, Philadelphia PA
Gilliam, Jan, *Mgr Exhibit Planning,* Colonial Williamsburg Foundation, Abby Aldrich Rockefeller Folk Art Museum, Williamsburg VA
Gilliland, Cynthia, *Assoc Registrar,* Dartmouth College, Hood Museum of Art, Hanover NH
Gillis Bruni, Margaret, *Interim Dir Public Servs,* Detroit Public Library, Art & Literature Dept, Detroit MI
Gillis, Jeanie, *Cur Botanical Science,* Heritage Museums & Gardens, Sandwich MA
Gillis, Kathy, *Conservator,* Asian Art Museum of San Francisco, Chong-Moon Lee Ctr for Asian Art and Culture, San Francisco CA
Gillison, David, *Asst Prof,* Herbert H Lehman, Art Dept, Bronx NY (S)
Gillispie, John, *Pub Rels,* Huntington Museum of Art, Huntington WV
Gilman, Amy, *Dir,* University of Wisconsin-Madison, Chazen Museum of Art, Madison WI
Gilman, Claire, *Chief Cur,* The Drawing Center, New York NY
Gilmor, Jane, *Prof,* Mount Mercy University, Art Dept, Cedar Rapids IA (S)
Gilmore, Barton, *Asst Prof,* Saint Petersburg College, Fine & Applied Arts at Clearwater Campus, Clearwater FL (S)
Gilmore, Jean A, *Registrar,* Brandywine Conservancy, Brandywine River Museum, Chadds Ford PA
Gilmore, Kate, *Assoc Prof,* Purchase College, State University of New York, School of Art+Design, Purchase NY (S)
Gilmore, R, *Prof,* Gonzaga University, Dept of Art, Spokane WA (S)
Gilo, Anthony, *Dept Tech Dir,* Sierra Community College, Art Dept, Rocklin CA (S)

Giltrop, Jennifer, *Interim Dir,* Jacksonville Public Library, Fine Arts & Recreation Dept, Jacksonville FL

Gilwood, Deborah, *Asst Prof,* Seton Hall University, College of Arts & Sciences, South Orange NJ (S)

Gimeson, Dewayne, *Instr,* Chadron State College, Dept of Art, Chadron NE (S)

Giminez, JoAnn, *Registrar,* International Council for Cultural Exchange (ICCE), Brookhaven NY (S)

Gindhart, Maria, *Assoc Dir,* Georgia State University, Ernest G Welch School of Art & Design, Atlanta GA (S)

Gingerich, Ron, *Chmn,* Dickinson State University, Dept of Art, Dickinson ND (S)

Gingles, Mack, *Asst Prof,* Baylor University - College of Arts and Sciences, Dept of Art, Waco TX (S)

Ginkins, Terry, *Pres,* Carnegie Center for Art & History, New Albany IN

Ginoza, Tania, *Dir Fin,* Honolulu Museum of Art, Honolulu HI

Ginther, Gary, *Art Librn,* Ohio University, Fine Arts Library, Athens OH

Giobbia, Teri, *Asst Prof,* West Virginia University, College of Creative Arts, School of Art & Design, Morgantown WV (S)

Gioffre, Dolores, *Chmn,* Woodbridge Township Cultural Arts Commission, Barron Arts Center, Woodbridge NJ

Gionet, Bruce, *Asst Prof,* William Paterson University, Dept Arts, Wayne NJ (S)

Gioni, Massimiliano, *Artistic Dir,* New Museum of Contemporary Art, New Museum, New York NY

Giordana, Enrico, *Chmn & Prof,* College of Mount Saint Vincent, Fine Arts Dept, Riverdale NY (S)

Giordano, David, *Graphic Designer,* California College of the Arts, CCAC Wattis Institute for Contemporary Arts, San Francisco CA

Giordano, Molly, *Dir Devel & External Affairs,* Delaware Art Museum, Wilmington DE

Giordano, Patti, *COO & Deputy Dir,* University of Rochester, Memorial Art Gallery, Rochester NY

Giordano, Susan, *Mus Shop Mgr,* Worcester Art Museum, Worcester MA

Giovanetti, Suzanne, *Pres,* Pilgrim Society, Pilgrim Hall Museum, Plymouth MA

Gipe, Thomas D, *Head Sculpture,* Southern Illinois University at Edwardsville, Dept of Art & Design, Edwardsville IL (S)

Girard, Jack, *Prof, Div Chair,* Transylvania University, Art Program, Lexington KY (S)

Girard, Kathryn, *Chief of Staff,* Hebrew Union College, Skirball Cultural Center, Los Angeles CA

Girmschied, Mary Kay, *Mus Shop Mgr,* Trenton City Museum, Trenton NJ

Giroir Luckett, Jeannie, *Educ Cur,* West Baton Rouge Parish, West Baton Rouge Museum, Port Allen LA

Gish, Joe, *Owner,* Joe Gish's Old West Museum, Fredericksburg TX

Gittleman, Peter, *Team Leader, Visitor Experience,* Historic New England, Boston MA

Giuel, Rosanne, *Dir Visual Communs,* Art Institute of Fort Lauderdale, Fort Lauderdale FL (S)

Giuffrida, Noelle, *Asst Prof,* Case Western Reserve University, Dept of Art History & Art, Cleveland OH (S)

Giuliani, David S, *Graphic Design,* Art Institute of Pittsburgh, Pittsburgh PA (S)

Giuliano, Marie, *Bus Office Supv,* Ferguson Library, Stamford CT

Giunio-Zorkin, Deborah, *Pres,* Nanaimo Art Gallery, Nanaimo BC

Giuntini, Gilles, *Assoc Prof,* University of Hartford, Hartford Art School, West Hartford CT (S)

Giuntini, Trey, *Gen Mgr,* Mississippi River Museum at Mud-Island River Park, Memphis TN

Giuriceo, Judy, *Cur Exhibs & Media,* The National Park Service, United States Department of the Interior, Statue of Liberty National Monument & The Ellis Island Immigration Museum, Washington DC

Giurini, John, *Asst Dir Pub Affairs,* The Getty Center, The J Paul Getty Museum, Los Angeles CA

Givens, Lisa, *Arts Secy,* Merced College, Arts Division, Merced CA (S)

Giviskos, Christine, *Cur Prints, Drawings & European Art,* Rutgers, The State University of New Jersey, Zimmerli Art Museum at Rutgers University, New Brunswick NJ

Gjertson, Sarah, *Dir, Assoc Prof Foundations,* University of Denver, School of Art & Art History, Denver CO (S)

Gjovick, Peder, *Asst Prof,* Northwest Community College, Dept of Art, Powell WY (S)

Glab, Tracee, *Cur Colls & Exhibs,* Flint Institute of Arts, Flint MI

Glabicki, Paul, *Prof,* University of Pittsburgh, Dept of Studio Arts, Pittsburgh PA (S)

Gladdys, Katerie, *Assoc Prof,* University of Florida, School of Art & Art History, Gainesville FL (S)

Glanville, Gayle, *Vol Coordr,* The Summit County Historical Society of Akron, OH, Akron OH

Glanzer, Harvey W, *Co-Owner, Mgr & Dir,* Frank Lloyd Wright Museum, AD German Warehouse, Richland Center WI

Glasby, Becky, *Cur Educ,* The National Quilt Museum, Paducah KY

Glaser, Marie-Catherine, *Dir,* French Institute-Alliance Francaise, Library, New York NY

Glaser-Weiss, Samantha, *Dir & Ptnr,* Kohn Gallery, Los Angeles CA

Glasgow, Hamidah, *Exec Dir,* Center for Fine Art Photography, Fort Collins CO

Glasgow, Isti Haroh, *Dir,* Cultural Affairs Department City of Los Angeles, Barnsdall Art Center & Junior Arts Center, Los Angeles CA

Glasgow, Linda, *Cur Archives & Libr,* Riley County Historical Society & Museum, Riley County Historical Museum, Manhattan KS

Glasgow, Linda, *Library Archivist,* Riley County Historical Society & Museum, Seaton Library, Manhattan KS

Glaske, Sheila, *Cur Horticulture,* Paine Art Center & Gardens, Oshkosh WI

Glass, Michelle, *Prog Dir,* Side Street Projects, Pasadena CA

Glasscock, Megan, *Develop & Progs,* CoCA Center on Contemporary Art, Seattle WA

Glasser, Dale, *Dir, Synagogue Mgr,* Union for Reformed Judaism, Synagogue Art & Architectural Library, New York NY

Glassford, C, *Instr,* Golden West College, Visual Art Dept, Huntington Beach CA (S)

Glassman, Avery, *Cur & Adult Educ,* Western Colorado Center for the Arts, The Art Center, Grand Junction CO

Glasson, Lloyd, *Prof,* University of Hartford, Hartford Art School, West Hartford CT (S)

Glatz, Lindsey, *Mktg & Communs Dir,* Arts Council Of New Orleans, New Orleans LA

Glaubinger, Jane, *Cur Prints & Mem,* The Cleveland Museum of Art, Print Club of Cleveland, Cleveland OH

Glavin, Ellen, *Prof,* Emmanuel College, Art Dept, Boston MA (S)

Glazer, Steve, *Asst Prof,* Concord College, Fine Art Division, Athens WV (S)

Gleason, Laura, *Dir Advancement,* National Air and Space Museum, Smithsonian Institution, Washington DC

Gleason, Leigh, *Cur Colls,* UCR ARTSblock, California Museum of Photography, Riverside CA

Gleaves, Spray, *Instr,* Dallas Baptist University, Dept of Art, Dallas TX (S)

Glenn, Allyson, *Asst Prof,* University of Saskatchewan, Art & Art History Dept, Saskatoon SK (S)

Glenn, Barbara, *Head Art Prog,* J Sargeant Reynolds Community College, Humanities & Social Science Division, Richmond VA (S)

Glenn, Bridgett, *Chmn,* Lock Haven University, Dept of Fine Arts, Lock Haven PA (S)

Glenn, Jim, *Pub Arts & Design Arts Mgr,* Utah Arts Council, Chase Home Museum of Utah Folk Arts, Salt Lake City UT

Glenn, Jim, *Visual Arts Mgr,* Utah Arts Council, Chase Home Museum of Utah Folk Arts, Salt Lake City UT

Glenn, Joralyn, *Mktg & Pub Rels Coordr,* Academy of the New Church, Glencairn Museum, Bryn Athyn PA

Glenn, Ralph F, *Instr Art History,* Madonna University, College of Arts & Humanities, Livonia MI (S)

Glenn, Rebecca, *Asst Prof,* Southern Arkansas University at Magnolia, Dept of Art & Design, Magnolia AR (S)

Glennon, Michael L, *Chairperson,* Northport-East Northport Public Library, Northport NY

Glennon, Sharon, *Dir Corp Rel & Art Loan Prog,* deCordova Sculpture Park & Museum, Lincoln MA

Glick, Jen, *Dir Develop,* Longue Vue House & Gardens, New Orleans LA

Glidden, Craig, *Chmn Fine Arts Prog,* Westminster College of Salt Lake City, Dept of Arts, Salt Lake City UT (S)

Gliniecki, Anita, *Dean,* Saint Clair County Community College, Jack R Hennesey Art Dept, Port Huron MI (S)

Gliniecki, Anita, *VPres Acad Svcs,* Saint Clair County Community College, Jack R Hennesey Art Dept, Port Huron MI (S)

Glockner, Jennifer, *Dir,* City of Pittsfield Office of Cultural Development, Lichtenstein Center for the Arts, Pittsfield MA

Gloeckler, Terry, *Assoc Prof,* Eastern Oregon University, School of Arts & Science, La Grande OR (S)

Gloman, David I, *Sr Resident Artist,* Amherst College, Dept of Art & the History of Art, Amherst MA (S)

Glover, Cherie, *Co-Owner,* Joe Gish's Old West Museum, Fredericksburg TX

Glover, David, *Instr,* Pierce College, Art Dept, Woodland Hills CA (S)

Glover, Hugh, *Furniture Conservator & Dept Head,* Williamstown Art Conservation Center, Williamstown MA

Glover, Jack, *Owner & Cur,* Joe Gish's Old West Museum, Fredericksburg TX

Glover, Stephanie, *Opers Dir,* Touchstone Center for Crafts, Hart Moore Museum, Farmington PA

Glowacki, Michael, *Instr,* Delta College, Art Dept, University Center MI (S)

Gluck, Nahan, *VPres,* Japanese American National Museum, Los Angeles CA

Gluk, Hallie, *Educ Asst,* Houston Center For Photography, Houston TX

Glushien, Scott, *Asst Prof,* Assumption College, Dept of Art, Music & Theatre, Worcester MA (S)

Gluszek, Magda, *Faculty & Gallery Director,* Northland Pioneer College, Art Dept, Show Low AZ (S)

Gmyrek, Marsha, *Special Events Coordr,* The National Society of The Colonial Dames of America in the State of New Hampshire, Moffatt-Ladd House & Garden, Portsmouth NH

Gochenour, Anne, *Gallery Dir,* Central Michigan University, University Art Gallery, Mount Pleasant MI

Gochman, Julie, *International Planning Dir,* International Council for Cultural Exchange (ICCE), Brookhaven NY (S)

Gochman, Stanley I, *Prog Coordr,* International Council for Cultural Exchange (ICCE), Brookhaven NY (S)

Godbout, Helene, *Reference Agent,* Musee National des Beaux Arts du Quebec, Bibliotheque, Quebec QC

Goddard, Elizabeth, *Exec Dir,* Spartanburg Art Museum, Spartanburg SC

Goddard, Elizabeth, *Exec Dir,* Newport Art Museum and Association, Newport RI

Goddard, Elizabeth, *Exec Dir,* Newport Art Museum, Coleman Center for Creative Studies, Newport RI (S)

Goddard, Janet D, *Museum Store Mgr,* McNay Art Museum, San Antonio TX

Goddard, Leslie, *Educ Officer,* Evanston Historical Society, Charles Gates Dawes House, Evanston IL

Goddard, Stephen, *Assoc Dir,* University of Kansas, Spencer Museum of Art, Lawrence KS

Goddard, Stephen, *IPCR Proj Coordr,* Print Council of America, Chicago IL

Goddard, Stephen, *Prof,* University of Kansas, Kress Foundation Dept of Art History, Lawrence KS (S)

Godeke, Jason, *Assoc Prof,* Bloomsburg University, Dept of Art & Art History, Bloomsburg PA (S)

Goders, John, *Prof Emeritus,* California State University, Dominguez Hills, Art & Design Dept, Carson CA (S)

Godfrey, Kimberly, *Theater & Music Dir,* Ashtabula Arts Center, Ashtabula OH

Godfrey, Robert, *Head Dept,* Western Carolina University, Dept of Art/College of Arts & Science, Cullowhee NC (S)

Godfrey, Stephen, *Cur Paleontology,* Calvert Marine Museum, Solomons MD

Godfrey, William R, *Pres,* Environic Foundation International Library, Glen Allen VA

Godlewska, Maja, *Asst Prof,* University of North Carolina at Charlotte, Dept Art, Charlotte NC (S)

Godlewski, Henry, *Assoc Prof,* Mohawk Valley Community College, Utica NY (S)

Godollei, Ruthann, *Chair & Prof,* Macalester College, Art & Art History Dept, Saint Paul MN (S)

Godsey, William, *Instr,* John C Calhoun, Department of Fine Arts, Tanner AL (S)

Godwin, Stan, *Asst Prof,* Texas A&M University Commerce, Dept of Art, Commerce TX (S)

Godwin, Sybil, *Dir,* Shain Gallery, Charlotte NC

Goebel, Deedee, *Bus Mgr,* Southern Vermont Art Center, Gallery, Manchester VT

Goeckler, Holly, *Instr,* Trinity University, Department of Art & Art History, San Antonio TX (S)

Goedde, Lawrence, *Art History Instr,* University of Virginia, McIntire Dept of Art, Charlottesville VA (S)

Goeddeke, Jayne, *Mgr Exhibs & Opers,* Michigan State University, Eli & Edythe Broad Art Museum, East Lansing MI

Goering, Douglas, *Prof Emeritus,* Albion College, Bobbitt Visual Arts Center, Albion MI

Goering, Karen M, *Mng Dir Admin & Opers,* Missouri Historical Society, Missouri History Museum, Saint Louis MO

Goetz, Mary Anna, *Instr,* Woodstock School of Art, Inc, Woodstock NY (S)

Goetz, Nancy, *Mus Shop Mgr,* Aiken County Historical Museum, Aiken SC

Goff, Allison, *Educ Dir,* Henry Morrison Flagler Museum, Palm Beach FL

Goff, Mary, *Information Assistant,* The Columbus Museum, Columbus GA

Goff, Terri, *Communs Dir,* Associated Artists of Winston-Salem, Winston-Salem NC

Goffin, Jordan, *Head Cur Colls,* Providence Public Library, Art & Music Services, Providence RI

Goganian, Susan J, *Dir & Cur,* Beverly Historical Society, Cabot, Hale & Balch House Museums, Beverly MA

Goganian, Susan, *Dir,* Beverly Historical Society, Library, Beverly MA

Goggin, Nan, *Dir, Prof,* University of Illinois, Urbana-Champaign, School of Art & Design, Champaign IL (S)

Goguen, George, *Dir,* Radio-Canada SRC CBC, Georges Goguen CBC Art Gallery, Moncton NB

Goh, Xenna, *Gallery Coordr,* China Institute in America, China Institute Gallery, New York NY

Gohde, Kurt, *Assoc Prof, Prog Dir,* Transylvania University, Art Program, Lexington KY (S)

Gohman, Melissa, *Dir,* Paramount Gallery, Saint Cloud MN

Golahny, Amy, *Prof,* Lycoming College, Art Dept, Williamsport PA (S)

Golan, Romy, *Prof,* City University of New York, PhD Program in Art History, New York NY (S)

Gold, Allyssa, *Asst Prof Fine Arts Metals,* Millersville University, Dept of Art & Design, Millersville PA (S)

Gold, Dawn, *Instr,* Dallas Baptist University, Dept of Art, Dallas TX (S)

Gold, Elaine, *Dir,* York University, Glendon Gallery, Toronto ON

Gold, Elise, *Dir Communs,* Cornell University, College of Architecture, Art, and Planning, Ithaca NY (S)

Gold, Lawrence, *Assoc Prof,* Pacific Lutheran University, Dept of Art, Tacoma WA (S)

Gold, Umber, *Interpreter,* Schuyler Mansion State Historic Site, Albany NY

Goldberg, Beth, *Cur,* City of San Rafael, Falkirk Cultural Center, San Rafael CA

Goldberg, Carol, *Instr,* American University, Dept of Art, New York NY (S)

Goldberg, David, *Chief of Staff,* The Jewish Museum, New York NY

Goldberg, Gail, *Librn,* Spertus Institute of Jewish Studies, Asher Library, Chicago IL

Goldberg, Glenn, *Instr,* American University, Dept of Art, New York NY (S)

Goldberg, Joan, *Instr,* Daemen College, Art Dept, Amherst NY (S)

Goldberg, Kenneth P, *Librn,* Northeast Ohio Areawide Coordinating Agency (NOACA), Information Resource Center, Cleveland OH

Goldberg, Liz, *Instr,* Main Line Art Center, Haverford PA (S)

Goldberg, Margery, *Dir,* Zenith Gallery, Washington DC

Goldberg, Marsea, *Dir,* New Image Art, West Hollywood CA

Goldberg, Sara, *Cur Manuscripts,* Historic Newton, Newton MA

Goldblatt, Mark, *Chmn Educational Skills,* Fashion Institute of Technology, School of Art & Design, New York NY (S)

Golden, Andrew, *Program, Advocacy & Opers Mgr,* Corporate Council for the Arts/Arts Fund, Seattle WA

Golden, Jacqueline, *Assoc Prof,* University of Arkansas, Art Dept, Fayetteville AR (S)

Golden, Jennifer, *Dir Educ,* Tallahassee Museum of History & Natural Science, Tallahassee FL

Golden, Kenneth, *Assoc Prof,* Queensborough Community College, Dept of Art & Photography, Bayside Hills NY (S)

Golden, Nancy, *Cur,* Hartwick College, Foreman Gallery, Oneonta NY

Golden, Patricia, *Dir,* Culberson County Historical Museum, Clark Hotel Historical Museum, Van Horn TX

Golden, Susan, *Director PR/Media,* Museum of Latin American Art, Long Beach CA

Golden, Thelma, *Dir & Chief Cur,* The Studio Museum in Harlem, New York NY

Golden, Vincent L, *Cur Newspapers & Periodicals,* American Antiquarian Society, Worcester MA

Goldenberg, Helyn, *Pres,* The Arts Club of Chicago, Chicago IL

Goldfarb, Alvin, *Pres,* Western Illinois University, Western Illinois University Art Gallery, Macomb IL

Goldfarb, Hilliard T, *Sr Cur Colls & Old Masters,* Montreal Museum of Fine Arts, Montreal QC

Golding, Deeno, *Assoc Prof,* Morehead State University, Art & Design Dept, Morehead KY (S)

Goldman, Casey, *Assoc Cur Educ,* Orlando Museum of Art, Orlando Sentinel Library, Orlando FL

Goldman, Casey, *Assoc Cur Educ,* Orlando Museum of Art, Orlando FL

Goldman, Ken, *Pres,* National Watercolor Society, San Pedro CA

Goldman, Nancy, *Library Head,* University of California, Berkeley, Pacific Film Archive, Berkeley CA

Goldman, Stephanie, *Recording Secy,* National Watercolor Society, San Pedro CA

Goldowsky, Alexander, *Dir Exhibs,* Massachusetts Institute of Technology, MIT Museum, Cambridge MA

Goldsby, Kay, *Office Mgr,* Crossroads Art Center Gallery, Richmond VA

Goldsleger, Cheryl, *Dept Head,* Piedmont College, Art Dept, Demorest GA (S)

Goldsmith, Alan, *Assoc Prof,* University of Wisconsin-Parkside, Art Dept, Kenosha WI (S)

Goldstein, Alan, *Instr,* Bucks County Community College, Fine Arts Dept, Newtown PA (S)

Goldstein, Elizabeth, *Pres,* Municipal Art Society of New York, New York NY

Goldstein, Fred, *VP & Gen Counsel,* Los Angeles County Museum of Art, Los Angeles CA

Goldstein, Marilyn, *Prof,* C W Post Campus of Long Island University, School of Visual & Performing Arts, Brookville NY (S)

Goldstein, Mark, *Library Technician,* San Francisco Maritime National Historical Park, Maritime Library, San Francisco CA

Goldstein, Norma, *Dean,* Shoreline Community College, Humanities Division, Seattle WA (S)

Goldstein, Renee, *Coord Visitor Servs,* Old State House, Hartford CT

Goldstein, Sara June, *Dir Literary Arts,* South Carolina Arts Commission, Columbia SC

Goldstone, Elissa, *Exhibs Prog Mgr,* Socrates Sculpture Park, Long Island City NY

Golik, Jay, *Prof,* Napa Valley College, Art Dept, Napa CA (S)

Goliti, Susie, *Dir Opers,* Inner-City Arts, Los Angeles CA (S)

Gollini, Michael, *Dept Head Interior Architecture,* Cleveland Institute of Art, Cleveland OH (S)

Golomb, Alison, *Educ,* University of Connecticut, William Benton Museum of Art, Storrs CT

Golub, Mike, *Chmn,* Regional Arts & Culture Council, Metropolitan Center for Public Arts, Portland OR

Golubov, Nicholas, *Dir Research,* Historical Society of Palm Beach County, The Richard and Pat Johnson Palm Beach County History Museum, West Palm Beach FL

Golzalez, Sally, *1st VPres,* Arizona Watercolor Association, Phoenix AZ

Gombert, Carl, *Asst Prof,* Maryville College, Dept of Fine Arts, Maryville TN (S)

Gomes, Lyle, *Prof Photog,* College of San Mateo, Creative Arts Dept, San Mateo CA (S)

Gomez Marrero, Mercedes, *Exec Dir Institute of Culture,* Institute of Puerto Rican Culture, National Gallery, San Juan PR

Gomez, David, *Pres,* Hostos Center for the Arts & Culture, Bronx NY

Gomez, Drake, *Assoc Prof,* Keystone College, Fine Arts Dept, LaPlume PA (S)

Gomez, Maya, *Artists in Educ Prog Dir,* Southern Exposure, San Francisco CA

Gomez, Mercedes, *Dir,* Institute of Puerto Rican Culture, Instituto de Cultura Puertorriquena, San Juan PR

Gomez, Mirta, *Prof,* Florida International University, School of Art & Art History, Miami FL (S)

Gomez, Sergio, *Exhib Designer,* Pasadena Museum of California Art, Pasadena CA

Gomez-Ibanez, Miguel, *Treas,* Haystack Mountain School of Crafts, Deer Isle ME

Gomula, Jessica, *Prof,* California State University, Art Dept, Turlock CA (S)

Goncharov, Kathleen, *Cur,* Boca Raton Museum of Art, Boca Raton FL

Goncharov, Kathy, *Cur Exhibs & Audience Engagement,* Boca Raton Museum of Art, Library, Boca Raton FL

Gonsalves, Priscilla, *Exec Dir Lahaina Arts Assoc,* Lahaina Arts Society, Art Organization, Lahaina HI

Gonzales, Elyse A, *Cur Exhibs & Asst Dir,* University of California, Santa Barbara, Art, Design & Architecture Museum, Santa Barbara CA

Gonzales, Marie, *Recording Secy,* Pastel Society of the West Coast, Sacramento Fine Arts Center, Fresno CA

Gonzales, Nathan, *Cur,* Lincoln Memorial Shrine, Redlands CA

Gonzales, Quinton, *Painting & Drawing,* University of Colorado at Denver, College of Arts & Media Visual Arts Dept, Denver CO (S)

Gonzalez, Alfred James, *Acting Area Head Ceramics,* Pasadena City College, Visual Arts and Media Studies Division, Pasadena CA (S)

Gonzalez, Christie, *Gallery Mgr,* Bronx River Art Center Inc, Bronx NY

Gonzalez, Cristina, *Assoc Prof,* Oklahoma State University, Department of Art, Graphic Design and Art History, Stillwater OK (S)

Gonzalez, Emily, *Archivist,* Cambridge Historical Commission, City of Cambridge, Research Library on Architectural and Social History of Cambridge, Mass, Cambridge MA

Gonzalez, Geovanni, *Gen Mgr,* World Erotic Art Museum, Miami Beach FL

Gonzalez, Gerardo, *Pres,* Brownsville Art League, Brownsville Museum of Fine Art, Brownsville TX

Gonzalez, Jorge, *Adjunct Asst Prof,* University of Maine, Dept of Art, Orono ME (S)

Gonzalez, Pedro, *Instr,* Amarillo College, Visual Art Dept, Amarillo TX (S)

Gonzalez, Raymond, *Asst Prof,* Berea College, Art & Art History Program, Berea KY (S)

Gonzalez, Tamarah, *Intake Coordr,* North Fourth Art Center & Gallery, Albuquerque NM

Gonzalez, Vanessa, *Gallery Asst,* Bronx Council on the Arts, Longwood Arts Gallery @ Hostos, Bronx NY

Gonzalez-Cid, Malena, *Exec Dir,* Centro Cultural Aztlan, San Antonio TX

Gonzelez, Joseph, *Exec Dir,* Delaware Center for the Contemporary Arts, Wilmington DE

Gooch, Peter, *Assoc Prof,* University of Dayton, Visual Arts Dept, Dayton OH (S)

Good, Aimee, *Dir Educ & Community Progs,* The Drawing Center, New York NY

Good, Cipperly, *Colls Mgr,* Penobscot Marine Museum, Stephen Phillips Memorial Library, Searsport ME

Good, Kristin, *Asst Registrar,* Washington University, Mildred Lane Kemper Art Museum, Saint Louis MO

Good, Sara C, *Colls Mgr,* Bucks County Historical Society, Mercer Museum Research Library, Doylestown PA

Goodale, R, *Instr,* University of Southern Maine, Dept of Art, Gorham ME (S)

Goodarzi, Shoki, *Lectr,* Stony Brook University, College of Arts & Sciences, Dept of Art, Stony Brook NY (S)

Goodbar, Paula, *Gallery Dir,* Emerald Empire Art Association, Emerald Art Center, Springfield OR

Goode, Jamie, *Instr,* Siena Heights University, Studio Angelico-Art Dept, Adrian MI (S)

Goodfellow, Charmyne, *Deputy Dir Fin & Admin,* Rhode Island Historical Society, Providence RI

Goodkind, Joan, *Librn,* Bard College at Simon's Rock, Library, Great Barrington MA

Goodlett, V, *Instr,* University of Southern Maine, Dept of Art, Gorham ME (S)

Goodman, Bill, *Instr,* Hibbing Community College, Art Dept, Hibbing MN (S)

Goodman, Dan, *Registrar,* New Mexico Department of Cultural Affairs, New Mexico Museum of Art, Unit of NM Dept of Cultural Affairs, Santa Fe NM

Goodman, Dana, *Chmn,* Indiana-Purdue University, Dept of Fine Arts, Fort Wayne IN (S)

Goodman, Frances, *Chmn Bd,* Cameron Art Museum, Wilmington NC

Goodman, Herb, *Asst Prof,* Louisiana State University, School of Art, Baton Rouge LA (S)

Goodman, Jodi, *Head Spec Colls,* New Bedford Free Public Library, Special Collections Dept: Art Collection, New Bedford MA

Goodman, Michael, *Dir Information Technology,* College Art Association, New York NY

Goodman, Paul, *Security & Maintenance,* Blanden Memorial Art Museum, Fort Dodge IA

Goodman, Rhonna, *Dir,* Manhattanville College, Library, Purchase NY

Goodman, Robin, *Collections Manager and Registrar,* Kenyon College, Gund Gallery, Gambier OH

Goodman, Seth, *Prof,* Lycoming College, Art Dept, Williamsport PA (S)

Goodman, Sherry, *Dir Educ & Academic Relations,* University of California, Berkeley, Berkeley Art Museum & Pacific Film Archive, Berkeley CA

Goodman, Ted, *Avery Index & Communs Coordr,* Columbia University, Avery Architectural & Fine Arts Library, New York NY

Goodman, Toni, *CEO,* Jewish Community Center of Greater Washington, Jane L & Robert H Weiner Judaic Museum, Rockville MD

Goodman, Wayne, *Exec Dir,* Landmark Society of Western New York, Inc, The Campbell-Whittlesey House Museum, Rochester NY

Goodmundson, Susan, *Pres & Exhibits Chair,* Pastel Society of the West Coast, Sacramento Fine Arts Center, Fresno CA

Goodrich, Jonathan, *Registrar,* Northeast Document Conservation Center, Inc, Andover MA

Goodrich, Laura, *Asst Mgr,* New England Maple Museum, Pittsford VT

Goodrow, Christopher, *Mus Technician,* United States Military Academy, West Point Museum, West Point NY

Goodrum, Becca, *Registrar,* Kirkland Museum of Fine & Decorative Art, Denver CO

Goodson, Lucy, *Asst Prof,* Coe College, Dept of Art, Cedar Rapids IA (S)

Goodstein, Richard E (Rick), *Dean, CAAH,* Clemson University, College of Architecture, Arts & Humanities, Art Dept, Clemson SC (S)

Goodwin, Anna, *Coll Mgr,* Maryhill Museum of Art, Goldendale WA

Goodwin, Daniel, *Asst Prof,* State University of New York at Albany, Art Dept, Albany NY (S)

Goodwin, Stewart, *Dir,* Heritage Museums & Gardens, Sandwich MA

Goody, Dick, *Dir,* Oakland University, Oakland University Art Gallery, Rochester MI

Goody, Stephen, *Gallery Dir & Spec Instr,* Oakland University, Dept of Art & Art History, Rochester MI (S)

Goodyear, Anne Collins, *Pres,* College Art Association, New York NY

Goodyear, Anne, *Co-Dir,* Bowdoin College, Museum of Art, Brunswick ME

Goodyear, Frank, *Co-Dir,* Bowdoin College, Museum of Art, Brunswick ME

Gootee, Marita, *Prof,* Mississippi State University, Dept of Art, Starville MS (S)

Gorbelt, Mandi, *Gallery Coordr,* Spectrum Gallery, Toledo OH

Gorcica, Bill, *Gallery Dir,* Saint Cloud State University, Kiehle Gallery, Saint Cloud MN

Gorder, Eric, *Assoc Prof Art,* Joliet Junior College, Laura A Sprague Art Gallery, Joliet IL

Gordon, Charlotte, *Artistic Dir,* Southern Ohio Museum Corporation, Southern Ohio Museum, Portsmouth OH

Gordon, Charlotte, *Cur,* Springfield Museum of Art, Springfield OH (S)

Gordon, Cheryl, *Prog Coordr,* Arts Midland Galleries & School, Midland MI

Gordon, Christopher, *CFO,* Tucson Museum of Art and Historic Block, Tucson AZ

Gordon, Dave, *Interim Provost,* State University of New York at Geneseo, Bertha V B Lederer Gallery, Geneseo NY

Gordon, David, *Asst Dir,* Bakersfield Art Foundation, Bakersfield Museum of Art, Bakersfield CA

Gordon, Heather M, *City Archivist,* Vancouver City Archives, Vancouver BC

Gordon, J, *Cur Coordr,* Delaware Center for the Contemporary Arts, Wilmington DE

Gordon, Lauren, *Mktg & Design Specialist,* Green Hill Center for North Carolina Art, Greenhill, Greensboro NC

Gordon, Lida, *Prof,* University of Louisville, Allen R Hite Art Institute, Louisville KY (S)

Gordon, Lola, *Cur,* Pine Bluff/Jefferson County Historical Museum, Pine Bluff AR

Gordon, Mark, *Assoc Prof,* Barton College, School of Visual, Performing & Communication Arts, Wilson NC (S)

Gordon, Martha, *Chair & Assoc Prof,* Tarrant County College, Art Dept, Hurst TX (S)

Gordon, Robert, *Assoc Prof Film,* Watkins College of Art, Design & Film, Nashville TN (S)

Gordon, Steve, *Pres,* Barbara & Ray Alpert Jewish Community Center, Pauline & Zena Gatov Gallery, Long Beach CA

Gordon, Wendy, *Assoc Dir,* Boulder History Museum, Museum of History, Boulder CO

Gore, Allison, *Mus Shop Mgr,* Alabama Department of Archives & History, Museum of Alabama, Montgomery AL

Gore, Robert, *Librn for Art,* University of California, Los Angeles, Arts Library, Los Angeles CA

Gorenbergh, Elizabeth, *Social Media & Mktg Asst,* Lockwood-Mathews Mansion Museum, Norwalk CT

Gorewitz, Shalom, *Prof, Video Art & New Media,* Ramapo College of New Jersey, School of Contemporary Arts, Mahwah NJ (S)

Gorham-Smith, Karen, *Assoc Cur,* Patrick Henry, Red Hill National Memorial, Brookneal VA

Goring, Rich, *Historic Site Mgr,* New York State Office of Parks: Recreation and Historic Preservation, Senate House State Historic Site, Kingston NY

Goring, Rich, *Historic Site Mgr,* New York State Office of Parks: Recreation and Historic Preservation, Reference Library, Kingston NY

Gorman, Albartus, *Coordr Pub Progs & Engagement,* Carnegie Center for Art & History, New Albany IN

Gorman, Carma, *Assoc Prof & Acad Area Head,* Southern Illinois University, School of Art & Design, Carbondale IL (S)

Gorman, Joshua, *Head, Colls Mgmnt & Registrar,* National Museum of American History, Smithsonian Institution, Washington DC

Gormel, Donna M, *Vol Coordr,* Brandywine Conservancy, Brandywine River Museum, Chadds Ford PA

Gormley, Jim, *Assoc Prof,* Saint Louis Community College at Florissant Valley, Liberal Arts Division, Ferguson MO (S)

Gormley, Nina Z, *Exec Dir,* Wendell Gilley, Southwest Harbor ME

Goro-Rapoport, Victoria, *Asst Prof,* University of Nebraska, Kearney, Dept of Art & Art History, Kearney NE (S)

Goroff, Nancy, *Pres & Chmn,* Gallery North, Setauket NY

Gorse, George, *Prof,* Pomona College, Dept of Art History, Claremont CA (S)

Gort, Gene, *Asst Prof,* University of Hartford, Hartford Art School, West Hartford CT (S)

Gorzegno, Janet, *Prof,* University of Southern Mississippi, Dept of Art & Design, Hattiesburg MS (S)

Gosack Fleming, Elizabeth, *Opers & Rental Mgr,* National Society of the Colonial Dames of America in The Commonwealth of Virginia, Wilton House Museum, Richmond VA

Gosar, Kris, *PT Instr,* Adams State College, Dept of Visual Arts, Alamosa CO (S)

Gose, Robin, *Dir Educ,* Thinkery, Austin TX

Goss, Charles, *Prof & Chmn,* Cazenovia College, Center for Art & Design Studies, Cazenovia NY (S)

Gossel, Deborah, *Develop Dir,* Flint Institute of Arts, Library, Flint MI

Gothard, Paul, *Prof,* Lake Erie College, Fine Arts Dept, Painesville OH (S)

Gotlieb, Albert, *Graphic Design,* Art Institute of Pittsburgh, Pittsburgh PA (S)

Gotlieb, Marc, *Chmn,* University of Toronto, Dept of Fine Art, Toronto ON (S)

Gott, Wesley A, *Chmn,* Southwest Baptist University, Art Dept, Bolivar MO (S)

Gottesfeld, Linda, *Prof,* Pace University, Dyson College of Arts & Sciences, Pleasantville NY (S)

Gottfried, Benna, *PR & Mktg,* Portland Art Museum, Northwest Film Center, Portland OR

Gottlieb, Dan, *Dir Planning & Design,* North Carolina Museum of Art, Raleigh NC

Gottlieb, Donna, *Chair,* Fellows of Contemporary Art, Los Angeles CA

Gottlieb-Miller, Lauren, *Librn,* Menil Foundation, Inc, The Menil Collection, Houston TX

Gottwald, Dave, *Asst Prof,* University of Idaho College of Art & Architecture, Dept of Art & Design, Moscow ID (S)
Gould, Claudia, *Dir,* The Jewish Museum, Library, New York NY
Gould, Claudia, *Dir,* The Jewish Museum, New York NY
Gould, Elsy, *Mem Coordr,* The Robert McLaughlin Gallery, Oshawa ON
Gould, Meggan, *Vis Asst Prof,* Bowdoin College, Art Dept, Brunswick ME (S)
Gould, Peter, *Interim Co-Dir, Deputy Dir & Dir Fin & Admin,* Cornell University, Herbert F Johnson Museum of Art, Ithaca NY
Gould, Rosemary, *Instr,* North Central Michigan College, Art Dept, Petoskey MI (S)
Gould, Sarah, *Lead Curatorial Research,* The University of Texas at San Antonio, Institute of Texan Cultures, San Antonio TX
Gould, Thomas, *Chmn,* Newburyport Maritime Society, Inc, Custom House Maritime Museum, Newburyport MA
Goulding, Daniel, *Chmn,* Oberlin College, Dept of Art, Oberlin OH (S)
Gourley, Julia, *Exec Dir,* Krasl Art Center, Saint Joseph MI
Govan, Michael, *CEO & Wallis Annenberg Dir,* Los Angeles County Museum of Art, Los Angeles CA
Gove, Wayne, *Treas (V),* The Bartlett Museum, Amesbury MA
Gover, Kevin, *Dir,* National Museum of the American Indian, Smithsonian Institution, Washington DC
Govlya, Joann, *Dir Opers,* California Institute of the Arts, School of Art, Valencia CA (S)
Gow, David, *Conservator,* Willard House & Clock Museum, Inc, North Grafton MA
Goward, Rick, *Div Dir,* Henry Ford Community College, McKenzie Fine Art Ctr, Dearborn MI (S)
Gowen, John R, *Prof,* Ocean County College, Humanities Dept, Toms River NJ (S)
Grabbe, Kaye, *Admin Librn,* Lake Forest Library, Fine Arts Dept, Lake Forest IL
Graber, Kristina, *Gallery Mgr,* San Francisco Camerawork, San Francisco CA
Grabiec, Alex, *Exhib Mgr,* Longwood Center for the Visual Arts, Farmville VA
Grabill, Vin, *Assoc Prof,* University of Maryland, Baltimore County, Intermedia & Digital Arts (IMDA), Dept of Visual Arts, Baltimore MD (S)
Grabow, Nicole, *Objects Conservator,* Midwest Art Conservation Center, Minneapolis MN
Grabowski, Beth, *Asst Chm & Prof,* University of North Carolina at Chapel Hill, Art Dept, Chapel Hill NC (S)
Grabowski, John, *Dir Research,* Western Reserve Historical Society, Library, Cleveland OH
Grace, Alfred, *Pres & CEO,* Polynesian Cultural Center, Laie HI
Grace, James F, *Exec Dir,* Arts & Business Council of Greater Boston, Inc, Volunteer Lawyers for the Arts of MA, Boston MA
Grace, Kathy, *Admin Officer,* National Archives & Records Administration, Herbert Hoover Presidential Library - Museum, West Branch IA
Grace, Laura, *Visual Resources Cur,* University of Arkansas at Little Rock, Art Library and Galleries, Little Rock AR
Gracey, Patty, *Operations Mgr,* Rose Center & Council for the Arts, Morristown TN
Grachos, Louis, *Dir,* The Buffalo Fine Arts Academy, Albright-Knox Art Gallery, Buffalo NY
Gracie, David, *Asst Prof,* Nebraska Wesleyan University, Art Dept, Lincoln NE (S)
Gradle, Sally, *Assoc Prof,* Southern Illinois University, School of Art & Design, Carbondale IL (S)
Grady, Ann, *Collections Mgr,* Pope County Historical Society, Pope County Museum, Glenwood MN
Grady, Edward, *Asst Cur Tolson Ctr,* Langston University, Melvin B Tolson Black Heritage Center, Langston OK
Grady, John, *Instr,* Elgin Community College, Fine Arts Dept, Elgin IL (S)
Grady, Thomas, *Vis Asst Prof,* Assumption College, Dept of Art, Music & Theatre, Worcester MA (S)
Graf, Dean, *Prof,* Concordia University, Division of Performing & Visual Arts, Mequon WI (S)
Graf, Jaz, *VPres,* Manhattan Graphics Center, New York NY (S)
Grafe, Steven L., *Cur Art,* Maryhill Museum of Art, Goldendale WA
Grafelman, Glenn, *Instr,* North Hennepin Community College, Art Dept, Brooklyn Park MN (S)
Graff, Ann-Barbara, *VPres Acad & Research,* Nova Scotia College of Art & Design, Halifax NS (S)
Graff, Terry, *Dir & CEO,* Beaverbrook Art Gallery, Fredericton NB
Gragert, Steven, *Library & Colls,* Will Rogers Memorial Museum & Birthplace Ranch, Claremore OK
Graham, Amy, *Head Gardener,* Longue Vue House & Gardens, New Orleans LA
Graham, Ann, *Visual Resources Cur,* University of North Texas, Visual Resources Collection, Denton TX
Graham, Anne, *Instr,* Wayne Art Center, Wayne PA (S)
Graham, Brenda, *Asst Prof,* Oakland City University, Division of Fine Arts, Oakland City IN (S)
Graham, Cathy, *Secy,* Shippensburg University, Kauffman Gallery, Shippensburg PA
Graham, Daniel, *Art Dept Chair,* Georgetown College, Georgetown College Fine Art Galleries, Georgetown KY
Graham, Isis, *Dir, Stockholm, Sweden,* JMW Turner Museum, Sarasota FL
Graham, Jan, *Reg & Prog Dir,* Pacific Northwest Art School, Gallery at the Wharf, Coupeville WA
Graham, John David, *Asst Prof,* University of Saskatchewan, Art & Art History Dept, Saskatoon SK (S)
Graham, John R, *Cur Exhib,* Western Illinois University, Western Illinois University Art Gallery, Macomb IL
Graham, Juliet, *Registrar,* University of Lethbridge, Art Gallery, Lethbridge AB
Graham, Kim, *Educ Dir,* Christina Cultural Arts Center, Inc, Wilmington DE
Graham, Kurt, *Cur McCracken Research Library,* Buffalo Bill Memorial Association, Buffalo Bill Historical Center, Cody WY
Graham, Lisa, *Assoc Prof,* University of Texas at Arlington, Art & Art History Department, Arlington TX (S)
Graham, Lonnie, *Asst Prof Art (Photog),* Pennsylvania State University, University Park, Penn State School of Visual Arts, University Park PA (S)
Graham, Mark, *VPres Research & Collections,* Canadian Museum of Nature, Musee Canadien de la Nature, Ottawa ON
Graham, Michael S, *Dir & Cur,* United Society of Shakers, Shaker Museum, New Gloucester ME
Graham, Michael, *Assoc Prof,* American University, Dept of Art, New York NY (S)
Graham, Michael, *Dir & Cur,* United Society of Shakers, The Shaker Library, New Gloucester ME
Graham, Richard, *Instr,* Salt Lake Community College, Graphic Design Dept, Salt Lake City UT (S)
Graham, Robert, *Prof,* Virginia Polytechnic Institute & State University, Dept of Art & Art History, Blacksburg VA (S)
Graham, Sandra, *Dean Acad Affairs,* The Illinois Institute of Art - Chicago, Chicago IL (S)
Graham, Shelby, *Dir,* University of California at Santa Cruz, Mary Porter Sesnon Art Gallery, Santa Cruz CA
Graham, Susan, *Spec Coll Librn,* Albin O Kuhn Library & Gallery, Baltimore MD
Graham, Tracy, *Asst Registrar,* Bucknell University, Edward & Marthann Samek Art Gallery, Lewisburg PA
Grainger, Nessa, *Corresp Secy,* American Watercolor Society, Inc, New York NY
Gralewski, Tim, *Asst Prof,* Marygrove College, Department of Art, Detroit MI (S)
Gralnick, Lisa, *Prof,* University of Wisconsin, Madison, Dept of Art, Madison WI (S)
Gramma, Remus, *Dir,* Saint Mary's Romanian Orthodox Cathedral, Romanian Ethnic Art Museum, Cleveland OH
Granado, Laura, *VPres Public Affairs,* MEXIC-ARTE Museum, Austin TX
Grand, Stanley I, *Dir,* Lancaster Museum of Art, Lancaster PA
Granda, Margaret, *Grants Coordr,* Cultural Council of Palm Beach County, Lake Worth FL
Grandmaitre, Robert, *Chief Coll Consultation,* National Archives of Canada, Art & Photography Archives, Ottawa ON
Graney, Carol H, *Library Dir,* The University of the Arts, University Libraries, Philadelphia PA
Granger, Bryan, *Mgr Exhibs & Public Programs,* College of Charleston School of Arts, Halsey Institute of Contemporary Art, Charleston SC
Granger, Steven T, *Archivist,* Archives of the Archdiocese of St Paul & Minneapolis, Saint Paul MN
Grannan, Kurt, *Asst Prof,* Mount Saint Joseph University, Department of Art and Design, Cincinnati OH (S)
Grannis, Pete, *Commissioner Dept Environmental Conservation,* New York Office of Parks, Recreation & Historic Preservation, Natural Heritage Trust, Albany NY
Grannis, Sue Ellen, *Cur Books & Art,* Maysville, Kentucky Gateway Museum Center, Maysville KY
Granquist, Paula, *Literary Arts Specialist,* Northfield Arts Guild, Northfield MN
Granson, Robert, *Dir Finance,* Museum of Art, Fort Lauderdale, Library, Fort Lauderdale FL
Grant, Hugh, *Dir,* Kirkland Museum of Fine & Decorative Art, Denver CO
Grant, Jacqueline, *Dir,* Museum of the Hudson Highlands, Cornwall On Hudson NY
Grant, Jerry, *Director of Collections and Research,* Shaker Museum & Library, Emma B King Library, New Lebanon NY
Grant, Kim, *Chmn & Assoc Prof Art Hist,* University of Southern Maine, Dept of Art, Gorham ME (S)
Grant, Susan Kae, *Prof,* Texas Woman's University, School of the Arts, Dept of Visual Arts, Denton TX (S)
Grantham, Shirlyn, *Bus Mgr,* Carson County Square House Museum, Panhandle TX
Granzke, Leah, *Educ Dir,* Lewistown Art Center, Lewistown MT
Grash, Valerie, *Dept Head,* University of Pittsburgh at Johnstown, Dept of Fine Arts, Johnstown PA (S)
Grass, Kevin, *Assoc Prof,* Saint Petersburg College, Fine & Applied Arts at Clearwater Campus, Clearwater FL (S)
Grauer, Michael R, *Art Cur,* Panhandle-Plains Historical Museum, Canyon TX
Graves, Beverly, *Operations Mgr,* Portraits South, Raleigh NC
Graves, Chris, *Asst Prof,* Northwest Missouri State University, Dept of Fine & Performing Arts, Maryville MO (S)
Graves, Jane, *Acting Chmn,* Skidmore College, Lucy Scribner Library, Saratoga Springs NY
Graves, Jerrold, *Acting Area Head Design,* Pasadena City College, Visual Arts and Media Studies Division, Pasadena CA (S)
Graves, Kathy, *Contact,* Saint Paul's Western Sculpture Park, Saint Paul MN
Graves, Maurice, *Foundations,* Art Institute of Pittsburgh, Pittsburgh PA (S)
Graves, Travis, *Asst Prof,* East Tennessee State University, College of Arts and Sciences, Dept of Art & Design, Johnson City TN (S)
Gray, Amy, *Program Admin,* Wesley Theological Seminary, Henry Luce III Center for the Arts & Religion, Dadian Gallery, Washington DC
Gray, Ashley, *Mus Shop Mgr,* Brookgreen Gardens, Murrells Inlet SC
Gray, Chris, *Assoc Dean,* Illinois Central College, Arts & Communication Dept, East Peoria IL (S)

Gray, Debi, *Exec Dir,* Virginia Museum of Contemporary Art, Virginia Beach VA

Gray, Jane, *Exec Dir,* Kauai Museum Association, Ltd, Lihue HI

Gray, Jim, *Adminr,* University of South Florida, Library, Tampa FL

Gray, Johnnie, *Chmn Fine Arts Dept,* Mississippi Gulf Coast Community College-Jackson County Campus, Art Dept, Gautier MS (S)

Gray, Julia, *Director of Member Services,* Museum of Wisconsin Art, West Bend WI

Gray, Lynn, *Assoc Prof,* University of Minnesota, Minneapolis, Dept of Art, Minneapolis MN (S)

Gray, Mary Ann, *Head Archivist,* Chatham Historical Society, The Atwood House Museum, Chatham MA

Gray, Mary Kathryn, *Treas,* North Shore Arts Association, Inc, Gloucester MA

Gray, Meredith, *Director of Communs,* Chrysler Museum of Art, Norfolk VA

Gray, Meridith, *Chief Registrar,* Museum of Contemporary Art Chicago, Chicago IL

Gray, Richard, *Grad Dir,* University of Notre Dame, Dept of Art, Art History & Design, Notre Dame IN (S)

Gray, Sharon, *Admin Asst,* Frostburg State University, The Stephanie Ann Roper Gallery, Frostburg MD

Gray, Thomas, *Dir,* Drew County Historical Society, Museum, Monticello AR

Gray-Young, Rhonda, *Fine Arts Prog Asst,* Federal Reserve Board, Art Gallery, Washington DC

Graybill, Lela, *Asst Prof,* University of Utah, Dept of Art & Art History, Salt Lake City UT (S)

Graybill, Maribeth, *Arlene & Harold Schnitzer Cur Asian Art,* Portland Art Museum, Portland OR

Graydon Smith, John, *Dir & CEO,* Reading Public Museum, Reading PA

Graydon, Elisa, *Cataloging Librn,* Moore College of Art & Design, Library, Philadelphia PA

Graziose Corrin, Lisa, *Dir,* Northwestern University, Mary & Leigh Block Museum of Art, Evanston IL

Grazzini, Patricia J, *Deputy Dir & COO,* Minneapolis Institute of Art, Minneapolis MN

Greaser, KP, *Pub Rels Dir,* The Barnum Museum, Bridgeport CT

Greco, Anna, *Educ Cur,* Bush-Holley Historic Site & Storehouse Gallery, Greenwich Historical Society, Cos Cob CT

Gredinger, Martin, *CFO,* Fuller Craft Museum, Brockton MA

Greeley, Andrew M, *Gallery Opers & Outreach,* Second Street Gallery, Charlottesville VA

Greeley, Anne, *Asst Prof,* Indiana Wesleyan University, School of Arts & Humanities, Division of Art, Marion IN (S)

Green, Allyson, *Dean,* New York University, Tisch School of the Arts, New York NY (S)

Green, Amanda, *Asst Prof Photog & Video,* Siena College, Dept of Creative Arts, Loudonville NY (S)

Green, Amy, *Adjunct,* College of the Canyons, Art Dept, Santa Clarita CA (S)

Green, Bill, *Interim Dir,* Carson County Square House Museum, Panhandle TX

Green, Cameron, *Military Progs Supervisor,* Fort Ticonderoga Association, Ticonderoga NY

Green, Gregory, *Assoc Prof,* University of South Florida, School of Art & Art History, Tampa FL (S)

Green, Harriett, *Dir Visual Arts,* South Carolina Arts Commission, Columbia SC

Green, Heather, *Gallery Coordr,* Rogue Community College, Wiseman Gallery - FireHouse Gallery, Grants Pass OR

Green, Holly, *Mktg Dir,* Lauren Rogers, Laurel MS

Green, Jack, *Research Assoc,* University of Chicago, Oriental Institute, Chicago IL

Green, James N, *Librn,* Library Company of Philadelphia, Philadelphia PA

Green, Jonathan W, *Prof,* University of California, Riverside, Dept of the History of Art, Riverside CA (S)

Green, Jonathan, *Exec Dir,* UCR ARTSblock, California Museum of Photography, Riverside CA

Green, Joshua, *Exec Dir,* National Council on Education for the Ceramic Arts (NCECA), Boulder CO

Green, Julie, *Asst Prof,* Oregon State University, Dept of Art, Corvallis OR (S)

Green, Karen, *Gallery Coordr,* College of Eastern Utah, Gallery East, Price UT

Green, Karen, *VPres,* Society of Illustrators, New York NY

Green, Kate, *Cur,* City of El Paso, El Paso Museum of Art, El Paso TX

Green, Krista, *Asst Dir Cultural Affairs,* School 33 Art Center, Baltimore MD

Green, Leamon, *Assoc Prof,* Texas Southern University, College of Liberal Arts & Behavioral Sciences, Houston TX (S)

Green, Louise, *Reference Librn,* University of Maryland, College Park, Art Library, College Park MD

Green, Maggie, *Dir Educ,* Fruitlands Museum, Inc, Harvard MA

Green, Mike, *Chmn,* College of Southern Idaho, Art Dept, Twin Falls ID (S)

Green, Nancy E, *Cur European & American Art, Prints & Drawings,* Cornell University, Herbert F Johnson Museum of Art, Ithaca NY

Green, Nancy W, *Interim Librn,* American Numismatic Association, Library, Colorado Springs CO

Green, Nancy, *Chief Develop Officer,* Please Touch Museum, Philadelphia PA

Green, Peter, *Instr Music,* Glendale Community College, Visual & Performing Arts Div, Glendale CA (S)

Green, Rebecca, *Communs Mgr,* Quad City Arts Inc, Rock Island IL

Green, Richard, *Instr,* Eastern Arizona College, Art Dept, Thatcher AZ (S)

Green, Robert, *Prof,* Abilene Christian University, Dept of Art & Design, Abilene TX (S)

Green, Seth, *Art Instr,* Morehead State University, Art & Design Dept, Morehead KY (S)

Green, Virginia, *Asst Prof,* Baylor University - College of Arts and Sciences, Dept of Art, Waco TX (S)

Green, William, *Assoc Prof,* New Mexico State University, Art Dept, Las Cruces NM (S)

Green-Price, Tina, *Gallery Cur,* Oregon State University, Giustina Gallery, Corvallis OR

Greenberg, Elizabeth, *Dir,* Sage College of Albany, Opalka Gallery, Albany NY

Greenberg, Gary, *Asst Prof,* Clarion University of Pennsylvania, Dept of Art, Clarion PA (S)

Greenberg, Hannah, *Develop Assoc & Mem,* Anthology Film Archives, New York NY

Greenberg, Ira, *Asst Prof,* Seton Hall University, College of Arts & Sciences, South Orange NJ (S)

Greenberger, John, *Fin & Admin Dir,* Yellowstone Art Museum, Billings MT

Greene Bowman, Leslie, *Pres,* Thomas Jefferson Foundation, Inc, Monticello, Charlottesville VA

Greene, Amy Gundrum, *Dir & Cur,* Headley-Whitney Museum, Lexington KY

Greene, Casey, *Head Spec Coll,* Rosenberg Library, Galveston TX

Greene, Jane, *Admin Asst,* Jacksonville State University, Art Dept, Jacksonville AL (S)

Greene, Joseph A, *Asst Dir,* Harvard University, Semitic Museum, Cambridge MA

Greene, Lois, *Chmn,* University of Kansas, Dept of Design, Lawrence KS (S)

Greene, Lois, *Chmn Dept,* University of Kansas, Dept of Art & Music Education & Music Therapy, Lawrence KS (S)

Greene, Marjorie, *Instr,* Saint Petersburg College, Fine & Applied Arts at Clearwater Campus, Clearwater FL (S)

Greene, Mary Lou, *Chair,* Marygrove College, Department of Art, Detroit MI (S)

Greene, Rhonda, *Co-Site Supv,* Fort Totten State Historic Site, Pioneer Daughters Museum, Fort Totten ND

Greene, Sanford, *Instr,* Benedict College, School of Humanities, Arts & Social Sciences, Columbia SC (S)

Greene, Vivian, *Cur 19th & Early 20th c Art,* Solomon R Guggenheim Museum, New York NY

Greene, Warren, *Gallery Dir,* Austin Peay State University, Art Dept Library, Clarksville TN

Greenleaf, Heather, *Registrar,* Art Services International, Alexandria VA

Greenman, Christopher, *Assoc Prof,* Alabama State University, Dept of Visual Arts, Montgomery AL (S)

Greennagle, Dave, *Dir Coral Act,* Randolph-Macon College, Dept of the Arts, Ashland VA (S)

Greenough, Sarah, *Chief Photographic Svcs,* National Gallery of Art, Washington DC

Greenwald, Lou Anne, *Dir,* University of Louisiana at Lafayette, Paul and Lulu Hilliard University Art Museum, Lafayette LA

Greenwall, Steven R, *Dept Head,* Allen County Community College, Art Dept, Iola KS (S)

Greenwell, Matt, *Head & Prof,* University of Tennessee at Chattanooga, Dept of Art, Chattanooga TN (S)

Greenwold, Mark, *Assoc Prof,* State University of New York at Albany, Art Dept, Albany NY (S)

Greenwood, Jill, *Cur Educ,* Oberlin College, Allen Memorial Art Museum, Oberlin OH

Greenwood, Jill, *Vis Asst Prof,* Kenyon College, Art Dept, Gambier OH (S)

Greenwood, Kevin, *Cur Asian Art,* Oberlin College, Allen Memorial Art Museum, Oberlin OH

Greenwood, Wynne, *Lectr,* Seattle University, Dept of Art & Art History, Seattle WA (S)

Greer, Chad, *2nd Bd VPres,* George A Spiva, Joplin MO

Greer, Glenn, *Asst Colls Mgr & Office Mgr,* Academy of the New Church, Glencairn Museum, Bryn Athyn PA

Greer, Jasmine, *Asst Prof,* Arkansas Tech University, Dept of Art, Russellville AR (S)

Greet, Michele, *Dir Art History Prog,* George Mason University, College of Humanities & Social Sciences, Dept of History & Art History, Fairfax VA (S)

Grefe, C Morgan, *Exec Dir,* Rhode Island Historical Society, Providence RI

Grefe, C Morgan, *Exec Dir,* Rhode Island Historical Society, John Brown House, Providence RI

Grefe, Dick, *Sr Reference Librn,* Washington & Lee University, Leyburn Library, Lexington VA

Gregersen, Thomas, *Cultural Dir,* Palm Beach County Parks & Recreation Department, Morikami Museum & Japanese Gardens, Delray Beach FL

Gregg, Chris, *Asst Prof,* George Mason University, College of Humanities & Social Sciences, Dept of History & Art History, Fairfax VA (S)

Gregg, Gail, *Asst Treas,* American Abstract Artists, Brooklyn NY

Gregg, Rebecca, *Instr,* Sierra Community College, Art Dept, Rocklin CA (S)

Gregg, Ryan, *Asst Prof,* Webster University, Department of Art, Design & Art History, Webster Groves MO (S)

Gregoire, Mathieu, *Project Dir,* University of California, San Diego, Stuart Collection, La Jolla CA

Gregorio, Teresa, *Educ Officer,* McMaster University, McMaster Museum of Art, Hamilton ON

Gregorski, Peggy, *Deputy Dir,* Kenosha Public Museums, Kenosha WI

Gregory, Dale, *VPres Pub Prog,* New-York Historical Society, Museum, New York NY

Gregory, Elaine, *Secy,* Toledo Artists' Club, Toledo Artists' Club & Gallery, Toledo OH

Gregory, Maggie, *Registrar,* North Carolina Museum of Art, Raleigh NC

Gregory, Sharon, *Chmn & Assoc Prof Art History,* St Francis Xavier University, Art Dept, Antigonish NS (S)

Gregory, Shirley, *Dir,* Barton College, Library, Wilson NC

Gregson, Chris, *Historic Preservation Supv,* County of Henrico, Meadow Farm Museum, Glen Allen VA

Greig, Charmayne, *Bookkeeper,* Canadian Clay and Glass Gallery, Waterloo ON

Greig, Rick E, *Dir Prog,* Angelo State University, Houston Harte University Center, San Angelo TX
Greiner, William, *Prof & Chair,* Olivet Nazarene University, Dept of Art, Bourbonnais IL (S)
Grell, Krystyna, *Librarian,* Polish Museum of America (PMA), The Polish Museum of America Library (PMAL), Chicago IL
Greminger, Gretchen, *Cur Educ,* Jekyll Island Museum, Jekyll Island GA
Grenda, C, *Prof,* City Colleges of Chicago, Daley College, Chicago IL (S)
Gresham, Jodi Hays, *Asst to Dir,* Cambridge Art Association, Cambridge MA
Greshem, Emily, *Cur Educ,* Longwood Center for the Visual Arts, Farmville VA
Grey, Emily, *Cur Annual Exhibs,* Monhegan Museum, Monhegan Museum of Art & History, Monhegan ME
Grey, Wilma, *Dir,* Newark Public Library, Reference, Newark NJ
Grief, Kathy, *Mktg,* Salvador Dali, Library, Saint Petersburg FL
Grieger, Scott, *Prog Dir Painting,* Otis College of Art & Design, Fine Arts, Los Angeles CA (S)
Griesheimer, Martha, *Vol Coordr,* Vesterheim Norwegian-American Museum, Decorah IA
Griesinger, Pamela, *Prof,* Daytona Beach Community College, Dept of Fine Arts & Visual Arts, Daytona Beach FL (S)
Griffen, Sara, *Pres Olana Partnership,* Olana State Historic Site, Library, Hudson NY
Griffen, Sara, *Pres The Olana,* Olana State Historic Site, Hudson NY
Griffin, Cathryn, *Assoc Prof,* Western Carolina University, Dept of Art/College of Arts & Science, Cullowhee NC (S)
Griffin, David, *Prof,* Eastern Illinois University, Art Dept, Charleston IL (S)
Griffin, Erica, *Assoc Dir Membership & Vol Servs,* DuSable Museum of African American History, Chicago IL
Griffin, Eve, *Cur Fine Arts,* Boston Public Library, Arts Reference Department, Boston MA
Griffin, Gerald, *Instr,* Ricks College, Dept of Art, Rexburg ID (S)
Griffin, Henry, *Facilities Mgr,* Pearl Fincher Museum of Fine Arts, Spring TX
Griffin, Jacqueline, *Chief Admin Officer,* University of California, San Diego, Dept of Visual Arts, La Jolla CA (S)
Griffin, Jennifer, *Instr,* Sacramento City College, Art Dept, Sacramento CA (S)
Griffin, Jerri, *Ceramics & Sculpture Instr,* Hutchinson Community College, Visual Arts Dept, Hutchinson KS (S)
Griffin, Joanne, *Secy,* Bluff Country Artists Gallery, Spring Grove MN
Griffin, Julie, *Bookkeeper,* Springfield Museum of Art, Springfield OH (S)
Griffin, Kathy, *Gen Educ,* Art Institute of Pittsburgh, Pittsburgh PA (S)
Griffin, Kristy, *Cur,* Sitka Historical Society, Sitka History Museum, Sitka AK
Griffin, Leah, *Assoc Cur,* Pensacola Museum of Art, Pensacola FL
Griffin, Linda Smith, *Head Resource Description & Metadata Servs,* Louisiana State University, Middleton Library, Baton Rouge LA
Griffin, Paul, *Lectr & Sculpture Tech,* Mount Allison University, Dept of Fine Arts, Sackville NB (S)
Griffin, Penny, *Asst Prof,* Salem Academy & College, Art Dept, Winston-Salem NC (S)
Griffin, Shirley, *Treas,* Crowley Art Association, The Gallery, Crowley LA
Griffin, Steve, *Assoc Prof,* University of Mary Washington, Dept of Art & Art History, Fredericksburg VA (S)
Griffin, Tim, *Exec Dir & Chief Cur,* The Kitchen, New York NY
Griffis Lampman, Nila, *Exec Dir,* Ashford Hollow Foundation for Visual & Performing Arts, Griffis Sculpture Park & Essex Arts Center, East Otto NY
Griffis, Tyler, *Essex Arts Center Mgr,* Ashford Hollow Foundation for Visual & Performing Arts, Griffis Sculpture Park & Essex Arts Center, East Otto NY
Griffith, Glenn, *Sr Interpreter,* Schuyler Mansion State Historic Site, Albany NY
Griffith, John, *Chmn & Dept Chair,* Mount Saint Joseph University, Department of Art and Design, Cincinnati OH (S)
Griffith, Karlyn, *Asst Prof,* California State Polytechnic University, Pomona, Department of Art, Pomona CA (S)
Griffith, Laura S, *Asst Dir,* Association for Public Art, Philadelphia PA
Griffith, Margaret, *Asst Prof Painting & Drawing,* Rio Hondo College, Arts & Cultural Programs Dept, Whittier CA (S)
Griffith, Roberta, *Prof,* Hartwick College, Art Dept, Oneonta NY (S)
Griffith, William, *Cur,* University of Mississippi, Rowan Oak, Home of William Faulkner, Oxford MS
Griffith, William, *Rowan Oak Cur,* University of Mississippi, University Museum & Historic Houses, Oxford MS
Griffiths, Caitlin, *Communs & Mktg,* New Brunswick Museum, Saint John NB
Griggs, Jacob, *Visual Com Instr,* Western Wisconsin Technical College, Graphics Division, La Crosse WI (S)
Griggs, Miyai Abe, *Dir,* The Art Museum of Eastern Idaho, Idaho Falls ID
Griggs, Richard, *COO,* Judd Foundation, Marfa TX
Grigsby, Eddy, *Asst Dir,* City of Lubbock, Buddy Holly Center, Lubbock TX
Grill, J Brett, *Assoc Prof, Dir Grad Studies (Painting & Drawing),* University of Missouri - Columbia, Dept of Art, Columbia MO (S)
Grillo, Janet, *Educ Dir,* Order Sons of Italy in America, Garibaldi & Meucci Museum, Staten Island NY
Grillo, Michael, *Assoc Prof & Chair,* University of Maine, Dept of Art, Orono ME (S)
Grillo, Michael, *Mus Educator,* Van Cortlandt House Museum, Bronx NY
Grim, Ruth, *Chief Cur,* The Museum of Arts & Sciences Inc, Daytona Beach FL
Grimaldi, Ann, *Cur Educ,* University of North Carolina at Greensboro, Weatherspoon Art Museum, Greensboro NC
Grimaldi, Elizabeth, *Exec Dir,* Fleisher Art Memorial, Philadelphia PA (S)
Grimaldi, Elizabeth, *Exec Dir,* Philadelphia Museum of Art, Samuel S Fleisher Art Memorial, Philadelphia PA
Grimaldi, Peter, *VPres Gardens & Horticulture,* Cheekwood-Tennessee Botanical Garden & Museum of Art, Museum of Art, Nashville TN
Grimaldi, Peter, *VPres Gardens and Horticulture,* Cheekwood-Tennessee Botanical Garden & Museum of Art, Nashville TN
Grimes Rand, Anne, *Pres,* USS Constitution Museum, Boston MA
Grimes, Ann, *Bookmobile Librn,* Lee County Library, Tupelo MS
Grimes, Sharon, *Dir,* Greenville College, Art Dept, Greenville IL (S)
Grimes, Sharon, *Dir & Cur,* Greenville College, Richard W Bock Sculpture Collection, Almira College House, Greenville IL
Grimm, Gerit, *Asst Prof,* University of Wisconsin, Madison, Dept of Art, Madison WI (S)
Grimmer, Jean, *Dir Develop,* Nantucket Historical Association, Historic Nantucket, Nantucket MA
Grimsley, Meredith, *Asst Prof,* Bloomsburg University, Dept of Art & Art History, Bloomsburg PA (S)
Grinage, Jeanine, *Head Educ,* New York State Museum, Albany NY
Gring, Heather, *Archivist,* Burchfield Penney Art Center, Buffalo NY
Grinnell, Nancy, *Cur,* Newport Art Museum and Association, Newport RI
Grinstead, Steve, *Publications Ed,* History Colorado Center Museum, Denver CO
Grishin, Cheri, *Asst Dir,* Marblehead Museum & Historical Society, Jeremiah Lee Mansion, Marblehead MA
Grissano, Joan, *Reference Coordr,* New York City Technical College, Ursula C Schwerin Library, Brooklyn NY
Grissim, Mary, *Dir Educ,* Cheekwood Nashville's Home of Art & Gardens, Education Dept, Nashville TN (S)
Griswold, Justin, *Coll Registrar,* University of Massachusetts, Amherst, University Gallery, Amherst MA
Griswold, William M, *Dir, Pres & CEO,* The Cleveland Museum of Art, Cleveland OH
Gritt, Stephen, *Dir Conservation & Tech Research,* National Gallery of Canada, Ottawa ON
Grittner, James, *Chmn,* University of Wisconsin-Superior, Programs in the Visual Arts, Superior WI (S)
Gritton, Joy, *Assoc Prof,* Morehead State University, Art & Design Dept, Morehead KY (S)
Grivetti, Al, *Assoc Prof,* Clarke College, Dept of Art, Dubuque IA (S)
Grobes, Thelma, *Bd Mem,* American Color Print Society, Narberth PA
Groble, Dan, *Dean,* Western Connecticut State University, School of Visual & Performing Arts, Danbury CT (S)
Groce, Susan, *Prof,* University of Maine, Dept of Art, Orono ME (S)
Grodenchik, Barly, *VPres,* Bowne House Historical Society, Flushing NY
Groenert, Diane, *Gallery Receptionist,* Artlink, Inc, Auer Center for Arts & Culture, Fort Wayne IN
Groeninger, Scott, *Asst Prof,* Florida State University, Art Dept, Tallahassee FL (S)
Groff, Jeff, *Estate Historian & Cur Garden Objects,* Winterthur Museum, Winterthur Museum, Garden & Library, Winterthur DE
Groft, Tammis K, *Deputy Dir Coll & Exhibs,* Albany Institute of History & Art, Albany NY
Grogan, Carolyn, *Mgr Visitor Svcs,* Norman Rockwell Museum, Stockbridge MA
Grogan, Cynthia, *Pub Info Officer,* Secretary of State Museum Division, Louisiana State Exhibit Museum, Shreveport LA
Grogan, Geoffrey, *Asst Prof,* Adelphi University, Dept of Art & Art History, Garden City NY (S)
Grogan, Kevin, *Exec Dir & Chief Cur,* Morris Museum of Art, Augusta GA
Groleau, Amy, *Cur Latin American & Caribbean Colls,* New Mexico Department of Cultural Affairs, Museum of International Folk Art, Santa Fe NM
Grom, Brenton, *Dir Library Progs,* Delaware Historical Society, Read House and Gardens, New Castle DE
Gron, Jack, *Chmn,* University of Kentucky, Dept of Art, Lexington KY (S)
Gronsdahl, Troy, *Admin Coordr,* AKA Artist Run Centre, Library, Saskatoon SK
Groover, Charles, *Head,* Jacksonville State University, Art Dept, Jacksonville AL (S)
Grosch, Carolyn, *Asst Cur,* Asheville Art Museum, Asheville NC
Grose, Donald, *Dean,* University of North Texas, Libraries, Denton TX
Groshong, Mae, *Sec,* Cambridge Museum, Cambridge NE
Grosland, Roberta, *Registrar,* City of Woodstock, Woodstock Art Gallery, Woodstock ON
Grosner, Tracy, *Educ Coordr,* Imperial Centre's Maria V Howard Arts Center, Rocky Mount NC
Grosowsky, Vera, *Instr,* Solano Community College, Division of Fine & Applied Art & Behavioral Science, Fairfield CA (S)
Gross, Benjamin, *Professor,* Salem State University, Art & Design Department, Salem MA (S)
Gross, Betsy, *Coordr Bd Mem,* Women in the Arts Foundation, Inc, Staten Island NY
Gross, Corey, *Registrar,* Kalamazoo Institute of Arts, Kalamazoo MI
Gross, Erik, *VPres Finance,* New Hampshire Institute of Art, Manchester NH

Gross, Jennifer, *Sr Cur,* deCordova Sculpture Park & Museum, Lincoln MA
Gross, Kelly M, *Dir,* The Art Association of Jacksonville, The David Strawn Art Gallery, Jacksonville IL
Gross, Mimi, *Pres,* The Renee & Chaim Gross Foundation, Chaim Gross Studio, New York NY
Gross, Molly, *Communs Dir,* The Drawing Center, New York NY
Gross, Naomi, *Chmn Fashion Business Mgmt,* Fashion Institute of Technology, School of Art & Design, New York NY (S)
Gross, Roberta, *Communications,* Plastic Club, Art Club, Philadelphia PA
Grosse, Russell, *Exec Dir,* Society for the Protection & Preservation of Black Culture in Nova Scotia, Black Cultural Center for Nova Scotia, Cherry Brook NS
Grosser, Jean, *Prof Art, Chair,* Coker College, Art Dept, Hartsville SC (S)
Grossman, Arlene, *Chair Foundation,* Lesley University, College of Art & Design, Cambridge MA (S)
Groth, Chuck, *Prof,* Saint Louis Community College at Meramec, Art Dept, Saint Louis MO (S)
Groth, William, *Bd Pres,* Pyramid Hill Sculpture Park & Museum, Hamilton OH
Grou, Claude, *Oratory Rector,* Saint Joseph's Oratory, Museum, Montreal QC
Groube, Prudence, *Creative Projects Resident,* eMediaLoft.org, New York NY
Grove, Lisa, *Dir & CEO,* Telfair Museums, Savannah GA
Grove, Nancy, *Prof,* Long Island University, Brooklyn Campus, Art Dept, Brooklyn NY (S)
Grover, Kevin, *Dir,* National Museum of the American Indian, George Gustav Heye Center, New York NY
Grover, Ruth, *Dir & Cur,* University of Tennessee at Chattanooga, Cress Gallery of Art, Chattanooga TN
Grover, Ryan, *Cur,* Biggs Museum of American Art, Dover DE
Groves, Anne K, *Chair,* Historic Deerfield, Inc, Deerfield MA
Groves, Jennifer, *Assistant Prof, Graphics,* Chowan College, Dept. of Communication Arts, Fine and Applied Arts, Murfreesboro NC (S)
Groves, Matthew, *Dir, Fine Arts,* Loyola University of Chicago, Dept of Fine and Performing Arts, Chicago IL (S)
Grow, Charlie, *Dep Dir,* Marine Corps University, National Museum of the Marine Corps, Triangle VA
Grow, Stephanie, *Asst Exec Dir,* Elmhurst Art Museum, Elmhurst IL
Growborg, Erik, *Instr,* Miracosta College, Art Dept, Oceanside CA (S)
Groyl, Frank, *Instr,* Keystone College, Fine Arts Dept, LaPlume PA (S)
Grozio, Jennifer, *Development Director,* Art and History Museums - Maitland, Maitland Art Center, Maitland FL
Grubb, Troy, *Asst Educ,* Pennsylvania Historical & Museum Commission, Railroad Museum of Pennsylvania, Strasburg PA
Grubbs, Rhonda, *Instr,* Ohio Northern University, Dept of Art & Design, Ada OH (S)
Grube, Sue, *Secy,* Virginia Museum of Contemporary Art, Virginia Beach VA
Gruber, Elliot, *Dir,* National Postal Museum, Smithsonian Institution, Washington DC
Gruber, John, *Asst Prof,* Southwest Baptist University, Art Dept, Bolivar MO (S)
Grubola, James T, *Chmn Dept Fine Arts, Dir Hite Art Institute,* University of Louisville, Allen R Hite Art Institute, Louisville KY (S)
Grubola, James, *Chmn,* University of Louisville, Hite Art Institute, Louisville KY
Gruendell, Lana, *Instr,* Salt Lake Community College, Graphic Design Dept, Salt Lake City UT (S)
Gruener, Mark, *Instr,* Wayne Art Center, Wayne PA (S)
Gruenwald, Helen, *Prof,* Kirkwood Community College, Dept of Arts & Humanities, Cedar Rapids IA (S)
Grumbine-Hornock, Penelope, *Adjunct,* York College of Pennsylvania, Dept of Music, Art & Speech Communications, York PA (S)
Grundy, Jane, *Asst Prof,* New York Institute of Technology, Fine Arts Dept, Old Westbury NY (S)
Gruner, Charles J, *Dir Lect & Demonstration Serv,* American Society of Artists, Inc, Palatine IL
Gruninger, Sandi, *Pres,* Wood Tobe-Coburn School, New York NY (S)
Grupp, Carl A, *Chmn,* Augustana College, Art Dept, Sioux Falls SD (S)
Grutzeck, Laura, *Visual Resources & Special Colls Librn,* The University of the Arts, University Libraries, Philadelphia PA
Grynsztejn, Madeleine, *Pritzker Dir,* Museum of Contemporary Art Chicago, Chicago IL
Grynsztejn, Madeleine, *VPres & Secy,* Association of Art Museum Directors, New York NY
Grzyb, Paul, *Mgr Facility & Security,* New Britain Museum of American Art, New Britain CT
Grzybek, Heather, *Horticulture Supv,* Palm Beach County Parks & Recreation Department, Morikami Museum & Japanese Gardens, Delray Beach FL
Guadamuz, Susan, *Registrar Colls,* California African-American Museum, Los Angeles CA
Guajardo, Ruth M., *Arts Prog Dir,* Centro Cultural Aztlan, San Antonio TX
Gualtieri, Rose, *Cur Educ,* Historical Society of Palm Beach County, The Richard and Pat Johnson Palm Beach County History Museum, West Palm Beach FL
Guan, Zhimin, *Assoc Prof,* Minnesota State University-Moorhead, Dept of Art & Design, Moorhead MN (S)
Guarneiri, Sarisha, *Registrar,* Colgate University, Picker Art Gallery, Hamilton NY
Guay, Gisele, *Librn,* Universite du Quebec, Bibliotheque des Arts, Montreal QC
Gubser, Rose Mary, *Exec Asst,* Manchester Bidwell Corporation, Manchester Craftsmen's Guild Youth & Arts Program, Pittsburgh PA
Guckes, Patty, *Instr,* Ocean City Arts Center, Ocean City NJ (S)
Gudenrath, William, *RA,* Corning Museum of Glass, The Studio, Corning NY
Gudmundsen, Tor, *Instr,* Woodstock School of Art, Inc, Woodstock NY (S)
Gue, Randy, *Board Chair,* Atlanta Contemporary Art Center, Atlanta GA
Guenthler, John R, *Assoc Prof,* Indiana University-Southeast, Fine Arts Dept, New Albany IN (S)
Guerdat, Chelsea, *Registrar & Exhib Mgr,* Bass Museum of Art, Miami Beach FL
Guerhin, Michelle, *Bus Mgr,* Concord Museum, Concord MA
Guerin, Charles A, *Dir,* Biggs Museum of American Art, Dover DE
Guerin, Francesca Schuler, *Dir,* Schuler School of Fine Arts, Baltimore MD (S)
Guerin, Hans Schuler, *Asst Dir,* Schuler School of Fine Arts, Baltimore MD (S)
Guerin, Manon, *Dir,* Institut des Arts au Saguenay, Centre National D'Exposition a Jonquiere, Jonquiere QC
Guernsey, Dan, *Assoc Prof,* Florida International University, School of Art & Art History, Miami FL (S)
Guernsey, Dawn, *Prof,* University of Kansas, The School of the Arts, Dept of Visual Art, Lawrence KS (S)
Guerra, Alyssabeth, *Mus Asst,* Lamar University, Dishman Art Museum, Beaumont TX
Guerra, Emily, *Community Engagement Dir,* Pearl Fincher Museum of Fine Arts, Spring TX
Guerrero, Francheska, *Interim Chair, Undergrad Design,* Corcoran School of Art, Washington DC (S)
Guerrero, Francisco, *Assoc Prof,* Seattle University, Dept of Art & Art History, Seattle WA (S)
Guerrero, Tony, *Dir Operations,* PS1 Contemporary Art Center, Long Island City NY
Guess, Rhonda, *Professor of Journalism,* Los Angeles City College, School of Visual & Media Arts, Los Angeles CA (S)
Guest, Gerald, *Chmn,* John Carroll University, Dept of Art History & Humanities, University Heights OH (S)
Guffin, R L, *Prof,* Stillman College, Stillman Art Gallery & Art Dept, Tuscaloosa AL (S)
Guheen, Elizabeth, *Pres,* Ucross Foundation, Big Red Barn Gallery, Clearmont WY
Guichet, Melody, *Prof,* Louisiana State University, School of Art, Baton Rouge LA (S)
Guido, Jeannine, *Dir Mus Opers,* The Broad, Los Angeles CA
Guidry, Keith J, *Cur,* Opelousas Museum of Art, Inc (OMA), Opelousas LA
Guigmon, Norah, *Marketing Mgr,* Society for Contemporary Craft, Pittsburgh PA
Guild, Bridgette, *Cur,* Grand Teton National Park Service, Moose WY
Guild, Henley, *Mus Preparator,* University of Richmond, University Museums, Richmond VA
Guillot, Charlotte, *Asst Cur,* Lafayette Science Museum & Planetarium, Lafayette LA
Guilmette, Joanne, *Dir Commun,* New York State Museum, Albany NY
Guimaraes, Sandra, *Chief Cur,* Remai Modern, Saskatoon SK
Guinn, Michael, *3rd VPres,* Plastic Club, Art Club, Philadelphia PA
Guion, David S, *Exec Dir,* Dublin Arts Council, Dublin OH
Guip, David, *Chmn,* University of Toledo, Dept of Art, Toledo OH (S)
Guip, David, *Chmn,* University of Toledo, Dept of Art, Toledo OH (S)
Guleranson, Jim, *VPres,* San Fernando Valley Historical Society, Mark Harrington Library, Mission Hills CA
Gulley, Cheryl, *Chair & Assoc Prof Interior Design,* Watkins College of Art, Design & Film, Nashville TN (S)
Gulsvig, Brent, *Archivist,* Pope County Historical Society, Pope County Museum, Glenwood MN
Gumbiner, Robert, *Founder,* Pacific Island Ethnic Art Museum, Long Beach CA
Gummel, Rob, *Instr Guitar,* Ocean City Arts Center, Ocean City NJ (S)
Gumpert, Julie, *Gallery Mgr,* Academy of Motion Picture Arts & Sciences, The Academy Gallery, Beverly Hills CA
Gumpert, Lynn, *Dir,* New York University, Grey Art Gallery, New York NY
Gunderson, Chad, *Prof Art,* University of Puget Sound, Dept of Art & Art History, Tacoma WA (S)
Gunderson, Dan, *Prof,* Stetson University, Department of Creative Arts, Deland FL (S)
Gunderson, Jeff, *Librn,* San Francisco Art Institute, Anne Bremer Memorial Library, San Francisco CA
Gunderson, Keith, *Instr,* Woodstock School of Art, Inc, Woodstock NY (S)
Gundlach, Cory, *Cur Arts of African, Oceania & Americas,* University of Iowa, University of Iowa Museum of Art, Iowa City IA
Gunn, Nancy, *Dir Museum Develop & Mem,* Wellesley College, Davis Museum & Cultural Center, Wellesley MA
Gunter, Rebecca, *Gallery Coordinator and Education Manager,* Sheldon Art Galleries, Saint Louis MO
Gunter, Susanne, *Asst Prof & Dept Chmn,* Converse College, School of the Arts, Dept of Art & Design, Spartanburg SC (S)
Guptill, Chris, *Dean,* Rio Hondo College, Arts & Cultural Programs Dept, Whittier CA (S)
Guptill, Chris, *Div Dean,* Rio Hondo College Art Gallery, Whittier CA
Gura, Judith, *Area Coordr,* New York School of Interior Design, New York NY (S)
Guraedy, J Bruce, *Head Dept,* East Central Community College, Art Dept, Decatur MS (S)

Gureckas, Vytenis A, *Assoc Prof,* Catholic University of America, School of Architecture & Planning, Washington DC (S)

Gurgel-Seefeldt, Nicole, *Communs Mgr,* Alternate ROOTS, Inc, Atlanta GA

Gurley, Hezron, *COO & CFO,* American Institute of Graphic Arts, National Design Center, New York NY

Gurstelle, Andrew, *Acad Dir,* Wake Forest University, Museum of Anthropology, Winston-Salem NC

Gurwitz, Danny, *Chmn Board Trustees,* Hidalgo County Historical Museum, Edinburg TX

Gury, Al, *Painting Dept Chair,* Pennsylvania Academy of the Fine Arts, Office of Admission, Philadelphia PA (S)

Gus, Wendy, *Dir Finance,* Historic New England, Boston MA

Gusler, Cyndi, *Professor of Visual and Communication Arts,* Eastern Mennonite University, Visual and Communication Arts, Harrisonburg VA (S)

Gussak, David, *Chmn Art Educ Dept,* Florida State University, Art Education Dept, Tallahassee FL (S)

Gustafson, Brian, *MFA,* New Jersey City University, Art Dept, Jersey City NJ (S)

Gustafson, Donna, *Cur American Art & Mellon Dir Academic Programs,* Rutgers, The State University of New Jersey, Zimmerli Art Museum at Rutgers University, New Brunswick NJ

Gustafson, Elaine D, *Cur Coll,* University of North Carolina at Greensboro, Weatherspoon Art Museum, Greensboro NC

Gustafson, Elaine, *Chief Cur,* Tampa Museum of Art, Tampa FL

Gustafson, Julie, *Dir,* College of Marin, Art Gallery, Kentfield CA

Gustafson, Lisa, *IT,* Noyes Art Gallery, Lincoln NE

Gustafson, Paul, *Assoc Prof,* State University of New York at Farmingdale, Visual Communications, Farmingdale NY (S)

Gustafson, Peter, *Develop Coord,* See Science Center, Manchester NH

Gustafson, Rachel, *Asst Curatorial,* Norton Museum of Art, West Palm Beach FL

Gustafson, Roger, *Instr,* Elgin Community College, Fine Arts Dept, Elgin IL (S)

Gustavson, Carrie, *Dir,* Bisbee Arts & Humanities Council, Lemuel Shattuck Memorial Library, Bisbee AZ

Gustavson, Todd, *Cur Technology Coll,* George Eastman Museum, Rochester NY

Gustin, Amanda, *Public Prog Mgr,* Vermont Historical Society, Museum, Montpelier VT

Guston, Judith M, *Cur & Dir Colls,* The Rosenbach Museum & Library, Philadelphia PA

Guth, Kristin, *School Admin,* Carleton University, School for Studies in Art & Culture, Ottawa ON (S)

Guthier, Amy, *Develop Specialist,* University of Wisconsin-Madison, Chazen Museum of Art, Madison WI

Guthier, Mark, *Union Dir,* University of Wisconsin-Madison, Wisconsin Union Galleries, Madison WI

Guthrie, Anabeth, *Chief of Communicaitons,* National Gallery of Art, Washington DC

Guthrie, Mareca, *Asst Prof,* University of Alaska Fairbanks, Art Department, Fairbanks AK (S)

Guthworth, Sarah, *Asst Prof,* Murray State University, Dept of Art, Murray KY (S)

Gutierrez, Carlos, *Chmn,* Meridian International Center, Cafritz Galleries, Washington DC

Gutierrez, Diego, *Instr,* Bakersfield College, Art Dept, Bakersfield CA (S)

Gutman, Bertha, *Prof,* Delaware County Community College, Communications, Art & Humanities, Media PA (S)

Guy, Jody, *Instr Art Educ,* Pennsylvania State University, University Park, Penn State School of Visual Arts, University Park PA (S)

Guyer, Rod, *Instr,* Solano Community College, Division of Fine & Applied Art & Behavioral Science, Fairfield CA (S)

Guynes, Jason, *Chmn,* University of West Alabama, Division of Fine Arts, Livingston AL (S)

Guynn, Tod, *Asst Prof,* Cazenovia College, Center for Art & Design Studies, Cazenovia NY (S)

Guzman, Alessandra, *Exhibs Mgr,* Amon Carter Museum of American Art, Fort Worth TX

Gwynne, James, *Chmn & Prof,* County College of Morris, Art Dept, Randolph NJ (S)

Gylfe, Per, *Digital Media Labs,* International Center of Photography, School, New York NY (S)

Gylfe, Per, *Facilities Supv,* International Center of Photography, Rita K Hillman Education Gallery, New York NY

Gyllenhaal, C Edward, *Cur,* Academy of the New Church, Glencairn Museum, Bryn Athyn PA

Gyorody, Ninette, *Exec Dir,* Orillia Museum of Art & History, Orillia ON

Gyuk, Drin, *Dir IT,* The Newberry, Chicago IL

Ha, Paul C, *Dir,* Massachusetts Institute of Technology, List Visual Arts Center, Cambridge MA

Haag, Pat, *Asst Dean,* Herkimer County Community College, Humanities Social Services, Herkimer NY (S)

Haag, Patty, *Asst Prof,* Spokane Falls Community College, Fine Arts Dept, Spokane WA (S)

Haakanson, Sven, *Cur Native Amer Ethnology,* University of Washington, Burke Museum of Natural History and Culture, Seattle WA

Haapanen, Lawrence, *Prof,* Lewis-Clark State College, Art Dept, Lewiston ID (S)

Haar, Annemarie, *Dir Libraries,* California College of the Arts, Libraries, Oakland CA

Haarer, Anne, *Assoc Prof,* College of Saint Elizabeth, Art Dept, Morristown NJ (S)

Haas, David, *Instr,* Muhlenberg College, Dept of Art, Allentown PA (S)

Haas, Kathy, *Dir Historical Resources,* Girard College, Stephen Girard Collection, Philadelphia PA

Haas, Kristin, *Gallery Dir,* Brickton Art Center, Park Ridge IL

Haas, Tara, *Visual Resources Librn,* Columbus College of Art & Design, Packard Library, Columbus OH

Haas, V Heidi, *Dir Research Servs,* The Morgan Library & Museum, Library, New York NY

Haavik, Benjamin, *Team Leader, Property Care,* Historic New England, Boston MA

Habarth, Gerald, *Assoc Prof,* West Virginia University, College of Creative Arts, School of Art & Design, Morgantown WV (S)

Habeger, Hans, *Drawing & Design,* College of Lake County, Art Dept, Grayslake IL (S)

Haberman, Pattty, *Mesa Contemp Arts Chief Cur,* Mesa Arts Center, Mesa Contemporary Arts Museum, Mesa AZ

Habermehl, Lisa, *Dir Mktg,* Museum of Art - Deland FL, Inc, Deland FL

Hachey, Michael C, *Assoc Prof,* Worcester State College, Visual & Performing Arts Dept, Worcester MA (S)

Hachiyanagi, Rie, *Studio Chmn,* Mount Holyoke College, Art Dept, South Hadley MA (S)

Hachmeister, John, *Assoc Prof,* University of Kansas, The School of the Arts, Dept of Visual Art, Lawrence KS (S)

Hackbardt, Marcella M, *Prof,* Kenyon College, Art Dept, Gambier OH (S)

Hacker, Kathy, *Exec Asst to Pres,* The Huntington Library, Art Collections & Botanical Gardens, Library, San Marino CA

Hacker, Robert G, *Paul & Louise Miller Prof,* Rochester Institute of Technology, School of Printing Management & Sciences, Rochester NY (S)

Hackler, Paige, *Colls & Exhibs Mgr,* Greenville Museum of Art, Inc, Greenville NC

Hackney, Stan, *Mgr External Affairs,* Mobile Museum of Art, Mobile AL

Hackstatter, Rene, *V-Chair,* Huronia Museum, Gallery of Historic Huronia, Midland ON

Hadacek, Lori, *Adjunct,* Waldorf College, Art Dept, Forest City IA (S)

Hadaway, Sandra S, *Admin,* Telfair Museums, Telfair Academy of Arts & Sciences Library, Savannah GA

Haddad, Farid A, *Prof,* New England College, Art & Art History, Henniker NH (S)

Haddaway, Wade, *Library Tech Head,* University of Washington, Art Slide Library, Seattle WA

Hadden, Helen, *Librn,* Art Gallery of Hamilton, Muriel Isabel Bostwick Library, Hamilton ON

Haddon, Maurice, *IT Dir,* Institute of Contemporary Art/Boston, Boston MA

Hadler, Mona, *Prof,* City University of New York, PhD Program in Art History, New York NY (S)

Hadley, Richard, *Dir Mus Exhibs & Operations,* Colonial Williamsburg Foundation, Abby Aldrich Rockefeller Folk Art Museum, Williamsburg VA

Haeusslein, Allie, *Assoc Dir,* Pier 24 Photography, San Francisco CA

Hafeli, Mary, *Prog Dir,* Columbia University, Art & Art Education Program at Teachers College, New York NY (S)

Hafer, Mark K, *Pres,* Victor Heritage Museum, Victor MT

Hafermann, Amy, *Graphic Designer,* Museum of Wisconsin Art, West Bend WI

Haffar, Nadra E, *Educ Cur,* Utah State University, Nora Eccles Harrison Museum of Art, Logan UT

Hafner, Andre, *Dir IT Solutions,* Cornell University, College of Architecture, Art, and Planning, Ithaca NY (S)

Hagan, Kathy, *Chmn 3-D Studies,* Bowling Green State University, School of Art, Bowling Green OH (S)

Hagan, Sarah, *Sr Fine Arts Reference Librn,* Boston Public Library, Arts Reference Department, Boston MA

Hage, Emily, *Prof Art History,* Saint Joseph's University, Art Dept, Philadelphia PA (S)

Hagedorn, Bernard, *Assoc Prof,* Vincennes University Junior College, Humanities Art Dept, Vincennes IN (S)

Hagedorn, Deborah, *Assoc Prof,* Vincennes University Junior College, Humanities Art Dept, Vincennes IN (S)

Hageman, George, *Prof,* Sinclair Community College, Division of Fine & Performing Arts, Dayton OH (S)

Hagemeyer, Jim, *Chmn,* Heidelberg College, Dept of Art, Tiffin OH (S)

Hagen, Annemarie, *Cur & Supv Mus Servs,* Art Gallery of Peel, Peel Heritage Complex, Brampton ON

Hagen, Kay, *Chmn,* Saint Louis Community College at Forest Park, Art Dept, Saint Louis MO (S)

Hager, Bradley, *Director,* Almond Historical Society, Inc, Hagadorn House, The 1800-37 Museum, Almond NY

Hager, Greg, *Dir,* Willard Library, Dept of Fine Arts, Evansville IN

Hager, Hellmut, *Evan Pugh Prof Emeritus,* Pennsylvania State University, University Park, Dept of Art History, University Park PA (S)

Hager, Michael, *Asst Prof,* Washburn University of Topeka, Dept of Art, Topeka KS (S)

Hagerman, Sharon, *Admin Asst,* Owensboro Museum of Fine Art, Owensboro KY

Hagerty, Dan, *Dir Strategic Devel & Programming,* Heard Museum, Phoenix AZ

Haggerty, Christine, *Prof,* Marymount University, School of Arts & Sciences Div, Arlington VA (S)

Hagood, John, *Reference Librn,* National Gallery of Art, Library, Washington DC

Hagstrom, Lorna Jean, *First VPres,* National League of American Pen Women, Washington DC

Hague, Erica, *Colls Mgr,* Atlanta Historical Society Inc, Atlanta History Center, Atlanta GA

Hahn, Alex, *Secy & Office Coordr,* Syracuse University, SUArt Galleries, Syracuse NY

Hahn, Bryan, *Gallery Mgr,* Eastern New Mexico University, Runnels Gallery, Golden Library, Portales NM

Hahn, Cynthia J, *Prof,* Florida State University, Art History Dept, Tallahassee FL (S)

Hahn, Danielle, *Music Dept Specialist,* National Gallery of Art, Washington DC

Hahn, Dorothy, *Instr,* Hannibal La Grange College, Art Dept, Hannibal MO (S)

Hahn, Elizabeth, *Librn,* American Numismatic Society, Library, New York NY
Hahn, Eric, *Industrial Design Technology,* Art Institute of Pittsburgh, Pittsburgh PA (S)
Hahn, Mary, *Pres & Dance Specialist,* Northfield Arts Guild, Northfield MN
Hahn, Suzan, *Interim Dean Libraries,* University of Alaska, Elmer E Rasmuson Library, Fairbanks AK
Haien, Gretchen, *Instr,* Belhaven College, Art Dept, Jackson MS (S)
Haigh, Katie, *COO,* Newfields, Indianapolis IN
Haik, Claire, *Instr,* Wayne Art Center, Wayne PA (S)
Hailey, Dabney, *Cur,* Wellesley College, Davis Museum & Cultural Center, Wellesley MA
Haiman, Kurt, *Pres,* Belskie Museum, Closter NJ
Haines, Annette, *Art & Design Field Librn,* University of Michigan, Media Union Library, Ann Arbor MI
Haines, Lee, *Dir Pub Rels,* Buffalo Bill Memorial Association, Buffalo Bill Historical Center, Cody WY
Haizlett, Jim, *Assoc Prof,* West Liberty State College, Div Art, West Liberty WV (S)
Haizlett, Karen, *Outreach & Vol Coordr,* Belle Grove Inc, Belle Grove Plantation, Middletown VA
Hajian, Paul, *Chair Environmental Design,* Massachusetts College of Art, Boston MA (S)
Hakala, Ken, *Pres,* Buckham Fine Arts Project, Buckham Gallery, Flint MI
Hake, Carol, *Exhibits Chmn,* Gallery 9, Los Altos CA
Hakim, Sy, *Pub Chmn,* American Color Print Society, Narberth PA
Hakimzadeh, Heather, *Cur,* Virginia Museum of Contemporary Art, Virginia Beach VA
Halaby, Raouf, *Prof,* Ouachita Baptist University, Dept of Visual Art, Arkadelphia AR (S)
Halbreich, Kathy, *Assoc Dir and Cur,* Museum of Modern Art, New York NY
Hale, Alma, *Asst Prof,* Murray State University, Dept of Art, Murray KY (S)
Hale, Ann, *Chief Devel Officer,* Anchorage Museum at Rasmuson Center, Anchorage AK
Hale, Chris, *Treas,* New England Watercolor Society, Boston MA
Hale, David, *Instr,* Goddard College, Dept of Art, Plainfield VT (S)
Hale, Eddie, *Instr,* Western Wisconsin Technical College, Graphics Division, La Crosse WI (S)
Hale, Jack, *1st VPres,* Fishkill Historical Society, Van Wyck Homestead Museum, Fishkill NY
Hale, Linda, *Adjunct,* Feather River Community College, Art Dept, Quincy CA (S)
Hale, Mike, *Pres,* Copper Village Museum & Arts Center, Anaconda MT
Hale, Nathan Cabot, *Pres,* Ages of Man Foundation, Amenia NY
Hale, Sheffield, *Pres & CEO,* Atlanta Historical Society Inc, Atlanta History Center, Atlanta GA
Hale, Sheffield, *Pres & CEO,* City of Atlanta, Atlanta Cyclorama & Civil War Museum, Atlanta GA
Hale, Wendy, *Pres,* New England Watercolor Society, Boston MA
Hales, Andrea, *Librn,* Museum of Contemporary Art, San Diego, Geisel Library, La Jolla CA
Halevy, Richard, *Dir Community Devel,* The Hudson River Museum, Yonkers NY
Haley, Laura, *Vol Treas,* Rangeley Lakes Region Logging Museum, Rangeley ME
Haley, Pat, *VPres,* Coquille Valley Art Association, Coquille OR
Hall, Alana, *Gift Shop Mgr & Admin Asst,* South Peace Art Society, Dawson Creek Art Gallery, Dawson Creek BC
Hall, Andrew, *Owner,* Hall Art Foundation, Reading VT
Hall, Casey, *Facility Rental Mgr,* Orlando Museum of Art, Orlando Sentinel Library, Orlando FL
Hall, Casey, *Facility Rental Mgr,* Orlando Museum of Art, Orlando FL
Hall, Christine, *Owner,* Hall Art Foundation, Reading VT
Hall, Christopher, *Cur,* Maine Maritime Museum, Bath ME
Hall, Daniel, *Asst Prof,* Indiana Wesleyan University, School of Arts & Humanities, Division of Art, Marion IN (S)
Hall, Eli M, *Asst Prof,* Colorado Mesa University, Art Dept, Grand Junction CO (S)
Hall, Gail, *Pres,* Dawson County Historical Society, Museum, Lexington NE
Hall, Gina, *Assoc Educator School & Family Progs,* Smith College, Museum of Art, Northampton MA
Hall, Harry, *Pres,* Wiregrass Museum of Art, Dothan AL
Hall, Joe, *Instr,* Kirkwood Community College, Dept of Arts & Humanities, Cedar Rapids IA (S)
Hall, Katherine, *Admin,* Utah Valley University, Woodbury Art Museum, Orem UT
Hall, Katie, *Registrar,* Arkansas Arts Center, Little Rock AR
Hall, Katie, *Registrar,* Arkansas Arts Center, Little Rock AR (S)
Hall, Katy, *VPres Develop,* The Newberry, Chicago IL
Hall, Kit, *Dean Art Dept,* Texas Wesleyan University, Dept of Art, Fort Worth TX (S)
Hall, Lauren, *Visual Arts Mgr,* The Cultural Arts Center at Glen Allen, Glen Allen VA
Hall, Laurilyn, *Instr,* Bob Jones University, School of Fine Arts, Div of Art & Design, Greenville SC (S)
Hall, Lisa H, *VPres,* Marcella Sembrich Memorial Association Inc, Marcella Sembrich Opera Museum, Bolton Landing NY
Hall, Mark, *Chmn,* Maryville College, Fine Arts Center Gallery, Maryville TN
Hall, Mark, *Instr,* Butte College, Dept of Fine Arts and Communication Tech, Oroville CA (S)
Hall, Mark, *Mgr Art, Music, Bus & Technical Science,* San Francisco Public Library, Art, Music & Recreation Center, San Francisco CA
Hall, Mia, *Chmn,* University of Arkansas at Little Rock, Dept of Art & Design, Little Rock AR (S)
Hall, Priscilla, *VPres,* Association of Hawaii Artists, Honolulu HI
Hall, Ray, *Dir,* Mexico-Audrain County Library, Mexico MO
Hall, Richard, *Sr Preparator,* The Pennsylvania State University, Palmer Museum of Art, University Park PA
Hall, Sarah, *Dir Cur Affairs,* The Frick Art & Historical Center, Inc, Frick Art Museum, Pittsburgh PA
Hall, Stephanie L, *Pub Servs Mgr,* Topeka & Shawnee County Public Library, Alice C Sabatini Gallery, Topeka KS
Hall, Steven B, *Dir,* Regis College, Carney Gallery, Weston MA
Hall, Thomas, *Chmn Fine Arts,* York College of Pennsylvania, Dept of Music, Art & Speech Communications, York PA (S)
Hall, Verna, *Pres,* Tyler Museum of Art, Tyler TX
Hall, Walter, *Assoc Prof,* University of Hartford, Hartford Art School, West Hartford CT (S)
Hall, Wanda, *Asst Librn,* United Methodist Historical Society, Lovely Lane Museum, Baltimore MD
Hall, Wayne, *Adjunct Asst Prof,* University of Maine, Dept of Art, Orono ME (S)
Hall-Cheathan, Tomeka, *CFO,* Craftsmen's Guild of Mississippi, Inc, Mississippi Craft Center, Ridgeland MS
Hallagan, Anna Mana, *Brd Pres,* Brickton Art Center, Park Ridge IL
Hallam, John, *Chmn,* Pacific Lutheran University, Dept of Art, Tacoma WA (S)
Halleck, Charles W, *Treas,* Gallery 9, Los Altos CA
Haller, Robert A, *Dir Emeritus Colls & Spec Projs,* Anthology Film Archives, New York NY
Hallet, Stanley I, *Prof,* Catholic University of America, School of Architecture & Planning, Washington DC (S)
Hallett, Phyllis, *Secy,* Moncur Gallery, Boissevain MB
Hallman, Gary, *Assoc Prof,* University of Minnesota, Minneapolis, Dept of Art, Minneapolis MN (S)
Hallman, Kirk, *Develop Officer,* Muskegon Museum of Art Foundation, Muskegon Museum of Art, Muskegon MI
Hallman, Tim, *Dir Communs & Bus Develop,* Asian Art Museum of San Francisco, Chong-Moon Lee Ctr for Asian Art and Culture, San Francisco CA
Hallmark, Kellye, *Asst Librn,* Dallas Museum of Art, Mildred R & Frederick M Mayer Library, Dallas TX
Hallock, Robert, *Pres,* Greene County Historical Society, Bronck Museum, Coxsackie NY
Halonen, Jessica, *Assoc Prof,* Trinity University, Department of Art & Art History, San Antonio TX (S)
Halsted, Kye, *Mgr,* Noyes Art Gallery, Lincoln NE
Halter, Susan, *Contact,* Lynn Arts, Lynn MA
Haltman, Kenneth, *Prog Head,* Michigan State University, Dept of Art & Art History, East Lansing MI (S)
Halverson, Jackie, *Instr,* Mount Mary College, Art & Design Division, Milwaukee WI (S)
Halvorson, Richard, *Museum Coordr,* Brown County Art Gallery Foundation, Nashville IN
Hamanaka, Mayumi, *Gallery Cur & Communs Dir,* Kala Institute, Kala Art Institute, Berkeley CA
Hamanaka, Takuji, *Instr,* Manhattan Graphics Center, New York NY (S)
Hamann, Brad, *Chair Art, Asst Prof Art & Graphic Design,* Eastern New Mexico University, Runnels Gallery, Golden Library, Portales NM
Hamann, Thomas, *Dir Ctr for New Media,* Kalamazoo Valley Community College, Center for New Media, Kalamazoo MI (S)
Hamberg, Jackie, *Cur Colls,* Alaska Department of Education, Division of Libraries, Archives & Museums, Sheldon Jackson Museum, Sitka AK
Hamblen, Mary Anne, *Special Colls & Archives Librn,* Corning Museum of Glass, Juliette K and Leonard S Rakow Research Library, Corning NY
Hambleton, Judy, *Dir Educ,* Newport Art Museum and Association, Newport RI
Hamblin, Diane, *Doll Cur,* Wenham Museum, Wenham MA
Hamel, Teresa, *Treas,* Warwick Museum of Art, Warwick RI
Hamer, Linnea, *Cur Exhibits,* American Architectural Foundation, The Octagon Museum, Washington DC
Hamilton Baker, Kelia, *Proj Mgr,* Manifest Gallery, Cincinnati OH
Hamilton French, Leah, *Exhibs Coordr,* New Art Center in Newton, Newtonville MA
Hamilton, Amanda, *Assoc Prof,* Bethel University, Dept of Art & Design, Saint Paul MN (S)
Hamilton, J Hank, *Fine Arts Dept Chmn,* Cheyney University of Pennsylvania, Dept of Art, Cheyney PA (S)
Hamilton, Jeanne, *Gallery Asst,* Pacific Grove Art Center, Pacific Grove CA
Hamilton, Jennifer, *Dir,* Appaloosa Museum and Heritage Center, Moscow ID
Hamilton, Kevin, *Assoc Dean,* University of Illinois, Urbana-Champaign, College of Fine & Applied Arts, Champaign IL (S)
Hamilton, Linda, *Develop Dir,* Dunedin Fine Art Center, Dunedin FL (S)
Hamilton, Lynn, *Dir Admin,* Discovery Museum, Bridgeport CT
Hamilton, Whitney, *Visitor Svcs Mgr,* DuSable Museum of African American History, Chicago IL
Hamlin, Amy, *Asst Prof,* St Catherine University, Art & Art History Dept, Saint Paul MN (S)
Hamm Walsh, Dawna, *Head Art Dept,* Dallas Baptist University, Dept of Art, Dallas TX (S)
Hamm, Beccy, *Educ & Special Events,* Rose Center & Council for the Arts, Morristown TN
Hamm, Monte, *Acting Chmn,* Kentucky Wesleyan College, Dept Art, Owensboro KY (S)
Hammatt, Dawn, *Dir Curatorial Svcs,* Louisiana Department of Culture, Recreation & Tourism, Louisiana State Museum,
Hammett, Beverly, *Dir,* Webster Parish Library, Minden LA
Hammett, Kevin, *Prog Management Specialist,* University of Maryland, College Park, National

Trust for Historic Preservation Library Collection, College Park MD
Hammock, Margo, *Gift Shop Mgr,* Strasburg Museum, Strasburg VA
Hammond Group, Lou, *Media & PR,* Carolina Art Association, Gibbes Museum of Art, Charleston SC
Hammond, Carol, *VPres & CFO,* South Florida Fair, Yesteryear Village, West Palm Beach FL
Hammond, Jennifer, *Dir Educ,* Museum of Fine Arts Houston, Bayou Bend Collection & Gardens, Houston TX
Hammond, Lauren, *Pres,* Ashtabula Arts Center, Ashtabula OH
Hammond, Leslie, *Dir Curatorial Affairs,* Florida State University and Central Florida Community College, The Appleton Museum of Art, Ocala FL
Hammond, Susan G, *Exec Dir,* National Association of Women Artists, Inc, NAWA Gallery, New York NY
Hammond, Theresa, *Dir & Cur,* Guilford College, Guilford College Art Gallery, Greensboro NC
Hammond, Wayne G, *Librn,* Williams College, Chapin Library, Williamstown MA
Hammond-Hagman, Hannah, *Dir Educ,* Munroe Center for the Arts, Lexington MA (S)
Hammontree, Eddie, *Librn,* Webster Parish Library, Minden LA
Hamnel, Lindsey, *Mgr Vis & Vol Servs,* Birmingham Museum of Art, Birmingham AL
Hamon, Amanda Martin, *Assoc Dir Schools & Educ Engagement,* University of Kansas, Spencer Museum of Art, Lawrence KS
Hamon, Matt, *Assoc Prof,* University of Montana, School of Art, Missoula MT (S)
Hamon, Rodney, *Educ Dir,* University of New Mexico, Tamarind Institute, Albuquerque NM (S)
Hampton, Eric, *Instr Video,* AIC College of Design, Cincinnati OH (S)
Hampton, John, *Exec Dir,* The Art Gallery of Southwestern Manitoba, Brandon MB
Hampton, Sandra, *Bookkeeper,* Southern Alleghenies Museum of Art, Loretto Facility, Loretto PA
Hamrick Ferrara, Dana, *Instr,* Dallas Baptist University, Dept of Art, Dallas TX (S)
Hamwi, Richard, *Asst Prof,* Albright College, Dept of Art, Reading PA (S)
Hanahan, Martin, *Chief Registrar,* Boca Raton Museum of Art, Library, Boca Raton FL
Hanahan, Martin, *Registrar,* Boca Raton Museum of Art, Boca Raton FL
Hanami, Clement, *Dir Support Svcs,* Japanese American National Museum, Los Angeles CA
Hance, Jennifer, *Mgr Collections & Technical Servs,* Sheridan College of Applied Arts and Technology, Trafalgar Campus Library, Oakville ON
Hancock, Blair, *Dir,* Wilkes Community College, Arts & Science Division, Wilkesboro NC (S)
Hancock, John, *Prof,* University of Mary Hardin-Baylor, College of Visual & Performing Arts, Belton TX (S)
Hancock, Kathleen, *Asst Prof,* Roger Williams University, Visual Art Dept, Bristol RI (S)
Hancock, Mariko, *Coordr,* Castleton State College, Art Dept, Castleton VT (S)
Hand, Diana, *Office Mgr,* Jefferson County Historical Society Museum, Madison IN
Handel, Cynthia, *Asst Prof,* Louisiana State University, School of Art, Baton Rouge LA (S)
Handsloser, Diane, *Chmn,* Santa Barbara City College, Fine Arts Dept, Santa Barbara CA (S)
Handy, Christopher, *Technical Servs Librn,* Saint Louis Art Museum, Richardson Memorial Library, Saint Louis MO
Handy, Ellen, *Assoc Prof,* City College of New York, Art Dept, New York NY (S)
Handysides, Barb, *Pres,* South Peace Art Society, Dawson Creek Art Gallery, Dawson Creek BC
Hane, Maria, *Pres,* Museum of Science & History, Jacksonville FL
Hanel, Jodi, *Dir Devel,* The Queens Museum of Art, Flushing NY
Haney, Kristine, *Assoc Prof,* University of Massachusetts, Amherst, Art History Program, Amherst MA (S)
Haney, Lou, *Asst Prof,* University of Mississippi, Department of Art, University MS (S)
Haney, Nick, *Adjunct Assoc Prof Fine Art,* Johnson County Community College, Fine Arts Dept & Art History Dept, Overland Park KS (S)
Haney, Rich, *VPres Educ Affairs,* College of Lake County, Art Dept, Grayslake IL (S)
Haney, Sarah, *Mem Dir,* Core, New Art Space, Denver CO
Hanger, Anne, *Vis Artist,* Mary Baldwin College, Dept of Art & Art History, Staunton VA (S)
Hanger, Barbara, *Assoc Prof,* University of Louisville, Allen R Hite Art Institute, Louisville KY (S)
Hanks, Christina, *Chmn & Pres,* Iroquois Indian Museum, Howes Cave NY
Hanley, Andrea R, *Mem & Prog Mgr,* Institute of American Indian Arts, IAIA Museum of Contemporary Native Arts, Santa Fe NM
Hanlon, David, *Prof,* Saint Louis Community College at Meramec, Art Dept, Saint Louis MO (S)
Hanlon, Whitney, *Mktg Mgr,* American Museum of Ceramic Art, Pomona CA
Hanna, Emily, *Sr Cur & Cur Arts of Africa & Americas,* Birmingham Museum of Art, Birmingham AL
Hannaford, Joey, *Acad Professional Graphic Design,* University of Georgia, Franklin College of Arts & Sciences, Lamar Dodd School of Art, Athens GA (S)
Hannah, Cassie, *Instr,* Weatherford College, Dept of Speech Fine Arts, Weatherford TX (S)
Hannah, Kimberly, *Libr Asst,* New York University, Stephen Chan Library of Fine Arts, New York NY
Hannan, Catalina, *Librn,* Historic Hudson Valley, Pocantico Hills NY
Hannan, Sarah, *Dir,* South Shore Art Center, Cohasset MA
Hanni, Jane, *Asst Cur Educ,* Washburn University, Mulvane Art Museum, Topeka KS
Hannibal, Joe, *Prof,* California State Polytechnic University, Pomona, Department of Art, Pomona CA (S)
Hanninen, Kim, *Registrar,* Northwestern Michigan College, Dennos Museum Center, Traverse City MI
Hannon, Ken, *VPres & COO,* Dunedin Fine Art Center, Dunedin FL (S)
Hanor, Stephanie, *Dir,* Mills College Art Museum, Oakland CA
Hanover, Lisa Tremper, *Dir,* James A Michener Art Museum, Doylestown PA
Hanrahan, Thomas, *Dean,* Pratt Institute, School of Architecture, Brooklyn NY (S)
Hansel, Debbie, *Asst,* North Canton Public Library, The Little Art Gallery, North Canton OH
Hansen, Al, *Instr Pottery,* Bay De Noc Community College, Art Dept, Escanaba MI (S)
Hansen, Chris, *Exec Dir,* Craft Alliance Center of Art & Design, The Kranzberg Arts Center, Saint Louis MO
Hansen, Cindy, *Exec Asst Leadership Support,* University of Chicago, Smart Museum of Art, Chicago IL
Hansen, Diana, *Dir Gallery,* Craft Alliance Center of Art & Design, The Kranzberg Arts Center, Saint Louis MO
Hansen, Elaine, *Pres,* Bates College, Art & Visual Culture, Lewiston ME (S)
Hansen, Gregory, *Folklife Adminr,* Florida Folklife Programs, Tallahassee FL
Hansen, Harry, *Asst Chmn,* University of South Carolina, Dept of Art, Columbia SC (S)
Hansen, Hugh, *Accounting Mgr,* The Winnipeg Art Gallery, Winnipeg MB
Hansen, Lorraine, *Exec Dir,* Ocean City Arts Center, Ocean City NJ (S)
Hansen, Pearl, *Chmn Art,* Wayne State College, Nordstrand Visual Arts Gallery, Wayne NE
Hansen, Pearl, *Prof,* Wayne State College, Dept Art & Design, Wayne NE (S)
Hansen, Richard, *Assoc Prof,* University of Southern Colorado, Dept of Art, Pueblo CO (S)
Hansen, Sandi, *Dir,* Sonoma Valley Historical Society, Depot Park Museum, Sonoma CA
Hansen, Steve, *Prof,* Andrews University, Dept of Art, Art History & Design, Berrien Springs MI (S)
Hansen, Victoria, *Assoc Prof,* University of Southern Colorado, Dept of Art, Pueblo CO (S)
Hansen, Will, *Dir Reader Servs Dept,* The Newberry, Chicago IL
Hanson Forsyth, Barbara, *Sr Mgr Colls & Registration,* Mingei International, Inc, Mingei International Museum - Balboa Park & Mingei International Museum - Escondido, San Diego CA
Hanson, Brent, *Chmn,* Dixie College, Art Dept, Saint George UT (S)
Hanson, Elizabeth, *Asst Cur,* California State University, Long Beach, University Art Museum, Long Beach CA
Hanson, Emma, *Cur Plains Indian Museum,* Buffalo Bill Memorial Association, Buffalo Bill Historical Center, Cody WY
Hanson, Jacquelyn, *Adjunct Asst Prof Art Educ,* Florida Southern College, Melvin Art Gallery, Lakeland FL
Hanson, Jacquelyn, *Adjunct Asst Prof Art Educ,* Florida Southern College, Department of Art & Art History, Lakeland FL (S)
Hanson, Jody, *Sr Art Preparator,* The Buffalo Fine Arts Academy, Albright-Knox Art Gallery, Buffalo NY
Hanson, Lars, *VPres,* Wayne County Historical Society, Museum, Honesdale PA
Hanson, Lowell, *Instr Art,* Everett Community College, Art Dept, Everett WA (S)
Hanson, Robert, *Instr,* Pacific Northwest College of Art, Portland OR (S)
Hanspach-Bernal, Ellen, *Head Conservator,* Detroit Institute of Arts, Detroit MI
Hanssen, Heidi, *Secy,* Cincinnati Art Club, Cincinnati OH
Hantman, Alan M, *Architect of the Capitol,* United States Capitol, Architect of the Capitol, Washington DC
Hanzel, Yvette A, *Dir Mktg,* Beck Center for the Arts, Lakewood OH
Hapgood, Thomas, *Asst Prof,* University of Arkansas, Art Dept, Fayetteville AR (S)
Happer, Todd, *Dir Mktg,* The Adirondack Historical Association, The Adirondack Museum, Blue Mountain Lake NY
Haqberg, Amy, *Internship Coordr,* University of Southern Maine, Dept of Art, Gorham ME (S)
Harbage-Page, Susan, *Instr,* University of North Carolina at Chapel Hill, Art Dept, Chapel Hill NC (S)
Harber, Laine, *CFO,* Arkansas Arts Center, Little Rock AR
Harber, Laine, *Dept Dir & CFO,* Arkansas Arts Center, Little Rock AR (S)
Harbison, Craig, *Prof,* University of Massachusetts, Amherst, Art History Program, Amherst MA (S)
Harbour, Robert, *Mktg,* World Erotic Art Museum, Miami Beach FL
Harcourt, Carolyn, *Asst to Dir,* Willamette University, Hallie Ford Museum of Art, Salem OR
Hard, Nicole, *Asst Prof,* Murray State University, Dept of Art, Murray KY (S)
Hardaway, Aubrey, *ANM Chair,* Kalamazoo Valley Community College, Center for New Media, Kalamazoo MI (S)
Harde, Grace, *Trustee & Dir,* Aidron Duckworth Art Preservation Trust, Aidron Duckworth Art Museum, Meriden NH
Harden, Andrea Griffa, *HR Mgr,* The Buffalo Fine Arts Academy, Albright-Knox Art Gallery, Buffalo NY
Harden, Richard, *Prof Painting,* Manchester Community College, Visual Fine Art Dept, Manchester CT (S)
Harders, Faith, *Librn,* University of Kentucky, Hunter M Adams Architecture Library, Lexington KY
Hardesty, Susan, *Dir,* Norwalk Community College, Art Galleries & Collection, Norwalk CT

Hardiman, Tom, *Keeper,* Portsmouth Athenaeum, Joseph Copley Research Library, Portsmouth NH

Hardin, Cable, *Assoc Prof,* South Dakota State University, Dept of Visual Arts, Brookings SD (S)

Hardin, Jennifer, *Asst Librn,* Cincinnati Art Museum, Mary R Schiff Library & Archives, Cincinnati OH

Hardin, Jennifer, *Chief Cur,* Museum of Fine Arts, Saint Petersburg, Florida, Inc, Saint Petersburg FL

Harding, Hana, *Gallery Mgr,* Barn Gallery, Ogunquit ME

Harding, Jonathan, *Historian,* Artists' Fellowship, Inc, New York NY

Harding, Megan, *Publications, Mem & Media Mgr,* Oberlin College, Allen Memorial Art Museum, Oberlin OH

Harding, Meredith, *Mus Properties Chmn,* The National Society of The Colonial Dames of America in the State of New Hampshire, Moffatt-Ladd House & Garden, Portsmouth NH

Hardison, Horace, *Bus Mgr,* Owensboro Museum of Fine Art, Owensboro KY

Hardmon, Frank, *Assoc Prof Art,* Mississippi Valley State University, Fine Arts Dept, Itta Bena MS (S)

Hardwick, Hillary, *VPres Mktg & Communs,* City of Atlanta, Atlanta Cyclorama & Civil War Museum, Atlanta GA

Hardwig, Scott, *Prof,* Roanoke College, Fine Arts Dept-Art, Salem VA (S)

Hardwood, Edward S, *Assoc Prof,* Bates College, Art & Visual Culture, Lewiston ME (S)

Hardy, Beatriz, *Dean of Libraries & Instructional Resources,* Salisbury University, SU Libraries Guerreri Academic Commons, Salisbury MD

Hardy, Jacqueline, *Office Mgr,* National Council on Education for the Ceramic Arts (NCECA), Boulder CO

Hardy, Linda, *Museum Store Mgr,* Key West Art & Historical Society, East Martello Museum & Gallery, Key West FL

Hardy, Mary, *Instr (2-D),* Mississippi Gulf Coast Community College-Jackson County Campus, Art Dept, Gautier MS (S)

Hardy, Michele, *Cur,* University of Calgary, Nickle Galleries, Calgary AB

Hardy, Myra, *Librn,* Maysville, Kentucky Gateway Museum Center, Maysville KY

Hardy, Saralyn Reece, *Dir,* University of Kansas, Spencer Museum of Art, Lawrence KS

Hargett, Brian, *Reference Librn,* Lee County Library, Tupelo MS

Hargraves, Matthew, *Chief Cur Art Collections,* Yale University, Yale Center for British Art, New Haven CT

Hargreaves, Eddie, *Webmaster, Publicity,* The San Joaquin Pioneer & Historical Society, The Haggin Museum, Stockton CA

Hargrove, James, *Asst Prof,* Roanoke College, Fine Arts Dept-Art, Salem VA (S)

Hargrove, June, *Chmn,* University of Maryland, Dept of Art History & Archaeology, College Park MD (S)

Hargrove, Kristi, *Assoc Prof & Chair of Fine Art,* Watkins College of Art, Design & Film, Nashville TN (S)

Harham, Ashraf, *Develop Assoc,* Henry Gallery Association, Henry Art Gallery, Seattle WA

Haring, Valerie, *Co-Dir,* Butler Community College, Erman B. White Gallery, El Dorado KS

Haring, Valerie, *Instr,* Butler Community College, Art Dept, El Dorado KS (S)

Harkness, Ed, *Ceramics Area Coordr,* Western Michigan University, Frostic School of Art, Kalamazoo MI (S)

Harlacher, Sherry, *Dir,* Denison University, Art Gallery, Granville OH

Harlan, Susan, *Assoc Prof,* Portland State University, Dept of Art, Portland OR (S)

Harle, Matt, *Vis Asst Prof,* Connecticut College, Dept of Art, New London CT (S)

Harley-Wilson, Theresa, *Registrar,* Indiana University, The Mathers Museum of World Cultures, Bloomington IN

Harlow, Andy, *Treas,* Charles B Goddard, Ardmore OK

Harlow, Rebecca, *Curatorial Asst,* University of California, Santa Barbara, Art, Design & Architecture Museum, Santa Barbara CA

Harmelink, Daniel, *Exec Dir,* Concordia Historical Institute, Saint Louis MO

Harmon, Darla, *Exec Dir,* Center for Contemporary Arts, Abilene TX

Harmon, David, *Chmn Dept Art,* Howard Payne University, School of Fine Arts, Brownwood TX (S)

Harmon, J Scott, *Dir,* United States Naval Academy, USNA Museum, Annapolis MD

Harmon, Nathan, *Instr,* Oklahoma State University Institute of Technology, School of Visual Communications, Okmulgee OK (S)

Harms, Kim, *Pub Rels Coordr,* The Children's Museum of Indianapolis, Indianapolis IN

Harp, Chris, *Mktg & Spec Events Coordr,* Liberty Hall Historic Site, Liberty Hall Museum, Frankfort KY

Harpaz, Nathan, *Cur Gallery,* Oakton Community College, Language Humanities & Art Divisions, Des Plaines IL (S)

Harper, Amber, *Asst Cur,* The Drawing Center, New York NY

Harper, Colleen, *Coordr,* Florida State University and Central Florida Community College, The Appleton Museum of Art, Ocala FL

Harper, Colleen, *Mgr Mem, Events & Fundraisers,* College of Central Florida, Appleton Museum of Art, Ocala FL

Harper, Dennis, *Cur of Collections & Exhibitions,* Auburn University, Jule Collins Smith Museum of Fine Art, Auburn AL

Harper, Donna, *Adj Instr,* University of West Florida, Dept of Art, Pensacola FL (S)

Harper, Gordon, *Dir,* Alaska Museum of Science & Nature, Anchorage AK

Harper, Katherine, *Assoc Prof,* Loyola Marymount University, Dept of Art & Art History, Los Angeles CA (S)

Harper, Lu, *Librn,* University of Rochester, Charlotte W Allen Library-Memorial Art Gallery, Rochester NY

Harper, Natisha, *Instruction Librn,* Ringling College of Art & Design, Verman Kimbrough Memorial Library, Sarasota FL

Harper, Pat, *Library Mgr,* Southern Oregon Historical Society, Library, Medford OR

Harper, Paula, *Assoc Prof,* University of Miami, Dept of Art & Art History, Coral Gables FL (S)

Harper, Robert W, *Exec Dir,* Lightner Museum, Saint Augustine FL

Harper, Wallace G, *1st VChmn,* Art and History Museums - Maitland, Maitland FL

Harr, Jemima, *Exec Dir & Cur,* Humboldt Arts Council, Morris Graves Museum of Art, Eureka CA

Harrell, Liliana, *Visitor Services Representative,* The Columbus Museum, Columbus GA

Harrington, Bernadette, *Library Asst,* Vermont Historical Society, Library, Montpelier VT

Harrington, Christi, *Instr,* Mohawk Valley Community College, Utica NY (S)

Harrington, Ellen, *Gallery Dir,* Academy of Motion Picture Arts & Sciences, The Academy Gallery, Beverly Hills CA

Harrington, Heather, *Asst Librn,* Historic Deerfield, Inc, Henry N Flynt Library, Deerfield MA

Harrington, Leslie, *Exec Dir,* Color Association of the United States, New York NY

Harrington, Neal, *Assoc Prof,* Arkansas Tech University, Dept of Art, Russellville AR (S)

Harrington, Richard A, *VPres,* Philadelphia Sketch Club, Philadelphia PA

Harris MacKay, Susan, *Dir Teaching & Learning,* Portland Children's Museum, Portland OR

Harris, Adam D, *Cur Art & Reserach,* National Museum of Wildlife Art of the Unites States, Jackson WY

Harris, Alison, *Asst Prof,* Colorado Mesa University, Art Dept, Grand Junction CO (S)

Harris, Althea, *Develop & Membership Mgr,* Whatcom Museum, Bellingham WA

Harris, Beth R, *Dir Library,* Paier College of Art, Inc, Library, Hamden CT

Harris, Caroline, *Assoc Dir Educ,* Princeton University, Princeton University Art Museum, Princeton NJ

Harris, Chad, *Theater Mgr,* Art & Culture Center of Hollywood, Art Gallery/Multidisciplinary Cultural Center, Hollywood FL

Harris, David, *Assoc Prof,* Missouri Western State University, School of Fine Arts, Saint Joseph MO (S)

Harris, Elizabeth, *Instr,* Walla Walla Community College, Fine Arts Dept, Walla Walla WA (S)

Harris, George, *Cur,* Two Rivers Art Gallery, Prince George BC

Harris, Gregory, *Asst Cur Photography,* High Museum of Art, Atlanta GA

Harris, Julie, *Exec Dir & Mus Shop Mgr,* River Heritage Museum, Paducah KY

Harris, Kevin, *Assoc Prof,* Sinclair Community College, Division of Fine & Performing Arts, Dayton OH (S)

Harris, Kyle, *Coordr Educ,* Los Angeles County Museum of Natural History, William S Hart Museum, Newhall CA

Harris, Lew, *Prof,* University of Tampa, College of Arts & Letters, Tampa FL (S)

Harris, Lois, *Provost,* Cornish College of the Arts, Art Dept, Seattle WA (S)

Harris, Mara, *Communs Mgr,* Georgia O'Keeffe Museum, Santa Fe NM

Harris, Mark, *Dir, School of Art & Prof Fine Arts,* University of Cincinnati, School of Art, Cincinnati OH (S)

Harris, Monroe, *Pres,* Virginia Museum of Fine Arts, Richmond VA

Harris, Nancy, *COO,* American Film Institute (AFI), Los Angeles CA (S)

Harris, Pamela, *Communs Coordr,* Salina Art Center, Salina KS

Harris, Rene, *Colls & Educ Progs Mgr,* New Mexico Department of Cultural Affairs, Palace of Governors, Santa Fe NM

Harris, Robert A, *Dir,* Helen M Plum, Lombard IL

Harris, Ronna, *Assoc Prof,* Tulane University, Sophie H Newcomb Memorial College, New Orleans LA (S)

Harris, Scott, *Dir,* James Monroe Museum, Fredericksburg VA

Harris, Shawnya, *Larry D & Brenda A Thompson Cur of African American & African Diasporic Art,* University of Georgia, Georgia Museum of Art, Athens GA

Harris, Stephanie, *Exec Dir,* Lexington Art League, Inc, Lexington KY

Harris, Sue, *Pres,* Quincy College, Art Dept, Quincy MA (S)

Harris, Teresa, *Assoc Prof,* Missouri Western State University, School of Fine Arts, Saint Joseph MO (S)

Harris, Teresa, *Cur Classics,* Columbia University, Avery Architectural & Fine Arts Library, New York NY

Harris, Thomas N, *Pres,* Porter-Phelps-Huntington Foundation, Inc, Historic House Museum, Hadley MA

Harris, William, *Sr VPres Develop & Mktg,* California Science Center, Los Angeles CA

Harris-Fernandez, Al, *Dir,* Sioux City Art Center, Sioux City IA (S)

Harris-Fernandez, Al, *Dir,* Sioux City Art Center, Sioux City IA

Harrison, Eugene, *Prof,* Eastern Illinois University, Art Dept, Charleston IL (S)

Harrison, Helen, *Lectr,* Stony Brook University, College of Arts & Sciences, Dept of Art, Stony Brook NY (S)

Harrison, Myra, *Supt,* Longfellow National Historic Site, Longfellow House - Washington's Headquarters, Cambridge MA

Harrison, Ronda, *Security Chief,* Montana State University, Museum of the Rockies, Bozeman MT

Harrison, Verne, *Gallery Coordr,* Art Gallery of Guelph, Guelph ON
Harriss, Martin, *Pres & Dir,* The New England Museum of Telephony, Inc, The Telephone Museum, Ellsworth ME
Harrity, Gail, *Pres & COO,* Philadelphia Museum of Art, Main Building, Philadelphia PA
Harrop, Patrick, *Co-Dir & Prof,* University of Manitoba, Faculty of Architecture Exhibition Centre, Winnipeg MB
Harrow, Del, *Asst Prof Art (Ceramics),* Pennsylvania State University, University Park, Penn State School of Visual Arts, University Park PA (S)
Harry, Christine, *Marketing & Pub Rels,* Ocean City Arts Center, Ocean City NJ (S)
Harry, Elizabeth, *Shop Mgr & Registrar,* Green Hill Center for North Carolina Art, Greenhill, Greensboro NC
Harsch, Janna, *Cur,* Noyes Art Gallery, Lincoln NE
Harsh, Vera, *Dir External Affairs,* Lyman Allyn Art Museum, New London CT
Harsh, Vera, *Director of External Affairs,* Haystack Mountain School of Crafts, Deer Isle ME (S)
Harshman, Melissa, *Assoc Prof Printmaking,* University of Georgia, Franklin College of Arts & Sciences, Lamar Dodd School of Art, Athens GA (S)
Hart, Dana, *Mgr Library Admin,* The Metropolitan Museum of Art, Museum Libraries, New York NY
Hart, Diane, *Sr Mus Registrar Colls & Exhibs,* Williams College, Museum of Art, Williamstown MA
Hart, Erdell, *Mus Shop Mgr,* Mississippi Museum of Art, Howorth Library, Jackson MS
Hart, John, *Dir Research & Coll,* New York State Museum, Albany NY
Hart, Katherine, *Senior Cur Colls & Acad Programming,* Dartmouth College, Hood Museum of Art, Hanover NH
Hart, Kerry, *Dean,* Laramie County Community College, Division of Arts & Humanities, Cheyenne WY (S)
Hart, Margaret, *Assoc Prof,* University of Massachusetts - Boston, Art Dept, Boston MA (S)
Hart, Naomi, *Faculty,* Grand Marais Art Colony, Grand Marais MN (S)
Hart, Nicki, *Mktg Specialist,* Sangre de Cristo Arts & Conference Center, Pueblo CO
Hart, Sharon, *Asst Prof Art & Photography,* Florida Atlantic University, D F Schmidt College of Arts & Letters Dept of Visual Arts & Art History, Boca Raton FL (S)
Hart, Steve, *Treas,* Cincinnati Art Club, Cincinnati OH
Hart, Tara, *Archives Mgr,* Whitney Museum of American Art, Frances Mulhall Achilles Library, New York NY
Harter, Jeff, *Dept Head Illustration,* Cleveland Institute of Art, Cleveland OH (S)
Hartig, Anthea, *Exec Dir & CEO,* The California Historical Society, San Francisco CA
Hartley, Cody, *Sr Director Colls & Interpretation,* Georgia O'Keeffe Museum, Santa Fe NM
Hartley, Melissa, *Managing Dir,* Multicultural Heritage Centre, Public Art Gallery, Stony Plain AB
Hartman, Joanne, *Adjunct Asst Prof,* New York Institute of Technology, Fine Arts Dept, Old Westbury NY (S)
Hartman, Mark, *Prof,* University of Nebraska, Kearney, Dept of Art & Art History, Kearney NE (S)
Hartman, Nick, *Film Coordr,* Kendall College of Art & Design, Urban Institute for Contemporary Arts, Grand Rapids MI
Hartman, Tanya, *Assoc Prof & Grad Dir,* University of Kansas, The School of the Arts, Dept of Visual Art, Lawrence KS (S)
Hartman, Terry L, *Instr,* Modesto Junior College, Arts Humanities & Communications Division, Modesto CA (S)
Hartman, Vladmir, *Photog,* Antonelli Institute, Professional Photography & Commercial Art, Erdenheim PA (S)
Hartranft, Janet, *Asst Prof Art,* Pennsylvania State University, University Park, Penn State School of Visual Arts, University Park PA (S)
Hartshorn, Mark, *Asst Prof,* Community College of Rhode Island, Dept of Art, Warwick RI (S)
Hartt, Jodan, *Dir Progs,* Centrum Arts & Creative Education, Port Townsend WA
Hartwell, Janice E, *Assoc Prof,* Florida State University, Art Dept, Tallahassee FL (S)
Hartz, Jill, *Exec Dir,* University of Oregon, Jordan Schnitzer Museum of Art, Eugene OR
Hartzold, Susan, *Cur,* McLean County Historical Society, McLean County Museum of History, Bloomington IL
Harvath, John, *Mgr Fine Arts & Recreation,* Houston Public Library, Houston TX
Harvey, Alan, *Dean,* Foothill College, Fine Arts & Communications Div, Los Altos Hills CA (S)
Harvey, Ben, *Asst Prof,* Mississippi State University, Dept of Art, Starville MS (S)
Harvey, Bruce, *Dir,* Housatonic Community College, Library, Bridgeport CT
Harvey, Bunny, *Prof,* Wellesley College, Art Dept, Wellesley MA (S)
Harvey, Dale, *Prof Art,* Rio Hondo College, Arts & Cultural Programs Dept, Whittier CA (S)
Harvey, Emily, *Discipline Coordr,* Rockland Community College, Graphic Arts & Advertising Tech Dept, Suffern NY (S)
Harvey, Kate, *Chief Develop Officer,* Indiana State Museum, Indianapolis IN
Harvey, Kelly, *Dir Develop,* University of Florida, Samuel P Harn Museum of Art, Gainesville FL
Harvey, Robin, *Dir,* Valley Art Center Inc, Clarkston WA
Harvey, Ruth, *Develop Dir,* AS220, Main Gallery, Providence RI
Harvey, Tobe, *Adjunct Asst Prof,* Spokane Falls Community College, Fine Arts Dept, Spokane WA (S)
Harvin, Nancy, *Interim Dir Develop,* Wadsworth Atheneum Museum of Art, Hartford CT
Harwood, Barry R, *Cur Decorative Arts,* Brooklyn Museum, Brooklyn NY
Harwood, Charles, *Commissioner,* United States Department of the Interior, Indian Arts & Crafts Board, Washington DC
Harwood, David, *Bus Mgr,* Blowing Rock Art and History Museum, Blowing Rock NC
Harwood, Roger, *Pres,* Clinton County Historical Association, Clinton County Historical Museum, Plattsburgh NY
Hasbun, Muriel, *Chair Fine Art Photog,* Corcoran School of Art, Washington DC (S)
Hasegawa, John, *Lectr,* Emporia State University, Dept of Art, Emporia KS (S)
Hasen, Irwin, *Instr,* Joe Kubert, Dover NJ (S)
Hasenberg, Tina, *Educ Dir,* City of Brea, Art Gallery, Brea CA
Hash, Mike, *Security,* University of Mississippi, University Museum & Historic Houses, Oxford MS
Hashimoto, Alan, *Asst Prof,* Utah State University, Dept of Art, Logan UT (S)
Haskel, Diane, *Mus Shop Mgr & Facilities Rentals Mgr,* Dayton Art Institute, Dayton OH
Haskell, Eric, *Dir,* Scripps College, Clark Humanities Museum, Claremont CA
Haskell, Heather, *Dir,* Springfield Museums, Michele & Donald D'Amour Museum of Fine Arts, Springfield MA
Haskins, Jay, *Gallery Mgr,* Northwind Arts Center, Port Townsend WA
Hassan, Thomas E, *Prin,* Phillips Exeter Academy, Frederick R. Mayer Art Center, Lamont Gallery, Exeter NH
Hasselbalch, Kurt, *Cur,* Massachusetts Institute of Technology, Hart Nautical Galleries & Collections, Cambridge MA
Hasselbalch, Kurt, *Cur Hart Nautical Coll,* Massachusetts Institute of Technology, MIT Museum, Cambridge MA
Hassen, Carol, *Exec Dir,* Gallery One Visual Arts Center, Ellensburg WA
Hassenteuffel, Andrea, *Dir Tour Progs,* Sid W Richardson Foundation, Sid Richardson Museum, Fort Worth TX
Hassinger, John L, *Graphic Design,* Art Institute of Pittsburgh, Pittsburgh PA (S)
Hassler, Donna, *Exec Dir,* National Trust for Historic Preservation, Chesterwood, Stockbridge MA
Hassler, Hilda, *Treas,* Phillips County Museum, Holyoke CO
Hastedt, Catherine A, *Dir,* Texas A&M University, J Wayne Stark University Center Galleries, College Station TX
Hastings, Bill, *Instr,* Ithaca College, Fine Art Dept, Ithaca NY (S)
Hastings, Tina, *Dir,* State University of New York College at Fredonia, Cathy and Jesse Marion Art Gallery, Fredonia NY
Haston, Brady, *Asst Prof Fine Art & Studio Facilities Mgr,* Watkins College of Art, Design & Film, Nashville TN (S)
Haswell, Sharon, *Shop Mgr Retail,* University of British Columbia, Museum of Anthropology, Vancouver BC
Hatalski, Jon-Chris, *Dir Institutional Develop & Grants Mgmt,* Historical Society of Pennsylvania, Philadelphia PA
Hatch Aguilar, Teri, *Exhibs Admin Assit,* Southwest School of Art, San Antonio TX
Hatch, Bill, *Dept Chmn,* San Juan College, Art Dept, Farmington NM (S)
Hatch, Carla, *Bus Mgr,* Museum of Western Colorado, Museum of the West, Grand Junction CO
Hatch, Greg, *Head Fine Arts,* University of Utah, Katherine W Dumke Architecture Library, Marriott Library, Salt Lake City UT
Hatch, James V, *Mem Bd Dir,* Hatch-Billops Collection, Inc, New York NY
Hatch, Jeremy, *Assoc Prof Ceramics,* Montana State University, School of Art, Bozeman MT (S)
Hatch, Kevin, *Asst Prof,* Binghamton University, Art History Department, Binghamton NY (S)
Hatchadoorian, Lisa, *Exec Dir,* Fort Collins Museum of Art, Inc, Fort Collins CO
Hatcher, Alison, *Registrar,* Massachusetts Institute of Technology, List Visual Arts Center, Cambridge MA
Hatcher, Alison, *Sr Registrar,* Institute of Contemporary Art/Boston, Boston MA
Hatcher, Ben, *Exhibs Coordr,* New York University, Washington Square East Galleries, New York NY
Hatcher, Gary C, *Assoc Prof & Chmn,* University of Texas at Tyler, Department of Art, School of Visual & Performing Arts, Tyler TX (S)
Hatcher, Steven, *Dir Folk & Traditional Arts,* Idaho Commission on the Arts, Boise ID
Hatchett, Dana, *Instr,* Daemen College, Art Dept, Amherst NY (S)
Hatfield, John, *Exec Dir,* Socrates Sculpture Park, Long Island City NY
Hathaway, Jane, *CFO,* Washington Pavilion of Arts & Science, Visual Arts Center, Sioux Falls SD
Hatheway, Holly, *Head Librn,* Princeton University, Dept of Art & Archaeology, Princeton NJ (S)
Hathorn, John, *Prof,* University of Louisiana at Lafayette, Dept of Visual Arts, Lafayette LA (S)
Hatley, Pam, *Head Publs,* The Buffalo Fine Arts Academy, Albright-Knox Art Gallery, Buffalo NY
Hattendorf, John B., *Dir,* Naval War College Museum, Newport RI
Hattersley, Pat, *Secy,* Searchlight Historic Museum & Mining Park, Searchlight NV
Hau, Amy, *Admin Dir,* Isamu Noguchi, Isamu Noguchi Garden Museum, Long Island City NY
Haubach, Janna L, *Gen Educ,* Art Institute of Pittsburgh, Pittsburgh PA (S)
Hauber, Amy, *Asst Prof,* St Lawrence University, Dept of Fine Arts, Canton NY (S)
Haubold, Susan, *Lectr,* Lambuth University, Dept of Human Ecology & Visual Arts, Jackson TN (S)
Hauenstein, Erin, *Dir,* Patterson Library & Octagon Art Gallery, Westfield NY
Hauerstein, Suzanne, *Vol Coordr,* Newport Art Museum and Association, Newport RI

Haugaard, David, *Dir Research,* Historical Society of Pennsylvania, Philadelphia PA
Haugen, Eunice, *Registrar,* University of Minnesota, Goldstein Museum of Design, Saint Paul MN
Haughland, Alyson, *Mem & Donor Coordr,* Hunter Museum of American Art, Chattanooga TN
Haught, Roy, *Chmn & Prof,* Loras College, Dept of Art, Dubuque IA (S)
Haught, Teri, *VPres Opers & CFO,* ArtsWave, Cincinnati OH
Haupt, Jeffrey, *Assoc Prof,* Mississippi State University, Dept of Art, Starville MS (S)
Hauptmann, Hank, *Dir,* Robert Klein Gallery, Boston MA
Hause, Melissa, *Asst Prof Art History,* Belhaven College, Art Dept, Jackson MS (S)
Hauser, Mary, *Registrar & Assoc Dir,* North Carolina State University, Gregg Museum of Art & Design, Raleigh NC
Hausey, Robert, *Prof,* Louisiana State University, School of Art, Baton Rouge LA (S)
Hausman, Mariah, *Instr,* University of Miami, Dept of Art & Art History, Coral Gables FL (S)
Haust, Bill, *Head Dept,* Plymouth State College, Art Dept, Plymouth NH (S)
Hauus, Paula, *Adjunct,* North Iowa Area Community College, Dept of Art, Mason City IA (S)
Hauver, Emily, *Cur Exhibs,* Albin O Kuhn Library & Gallery, Baltimore MD
Havekost, Niki, *Instr,* Siena Heights University, Studio Angelico-Art Dept, Adrian MI (S)
Havekotte, Sara, *Gallery Asst,* Goya Contemporary, Baltimore MD
Havel, Anne, *Treas,* Society of North American Goldsmiths, Eugene OR
Havel, Joseph, *Dir,* Museum of Fine Arts, Houston, Glassell School of Art, Houston TX (S)
Havelak, Sharon, *Instr,* Lourdes University, Art Dept, Sylvania OH (S)
Havemeyer, Ann, *Cur,* Norfolk Historical Society Inc, Museum, Norfolk CT
Haven, Mark, *Assoc Prof,* Rochester Institute of Technology, School of Photographic Arts & Sciences, Rochester NY (S)
Haven, Sarah, *Retail Mgr,* Gallery One Visual Arts Center, Ellensburg WA
Havener, Jon, *Prof,* University of Kansas, The School of the Arts, Dept of Visual Art, Lawrence KS (S)
Havens, Sue, *Asst Prof,* University of South Florida, School of Art & Art History, Tampa FL (S)
Havenstein, Kenneth, *Lectr,* State University of New York College at Oneonta, Dept of Art, Oneonta NY (S)
Havice, Christine, *Dir,* Kent State University, School of Art, Kent OH (S)
Havice, Christine, *School of Art Dir,* Kent State University, School of Art Galleries, Kent OH
Haviland, Sarah, *Secy,* Sculptors Guild, Inc, Brooklyn NY
Havlena, Janice M, *Asst Prof,* Edgewood College, Art Dept, Madison WI (S)
Havv, Jane, *Cur Gallery,* Passaic County Community College, Division of Humanities, Paterson NJ (S)
Haw, Jane, *Gallery Cur,* Passaic County Community College, Broadway, LRC, and Hamilton Club Galleries, Paterson NJ
Haw, Kate, *Dir,* Archives of American Art, Smithsonian Institution, Washington DC
Haw, Kate, *Exec Dir Develop & Admin,* Skowhegan School of Painting & Sculpture, New York NY (S)
Hawes, Libbie, *Preservation Dir,* Cliveden, Philadelphia PA
Hawk, Mikaela, *Dir Asst,* The Print Center, Philadelphia PA
Hawk, William, *Assoc Prof (Painting & Drawing),* University of Missouri - Columbia, Dept of Art, Columbia MO (S)
Hawke, Nadine, *Instr,* Arkansas State University, Dept of Art, State University AR (S)
Hawke, Shannon, *Communs Coordr,* Orillia Museum of Art & History, Orillia ON
Hawken, George, *Undergrad Coordr Visual Studies,* University of Toronto, Dept of Fine Art, Toronto ON (S)
Hawkes, Rob, *Prof,* Tidewater Community College, Visual Arts Center, Portsmouth VA (S)
Hawkins, Amy Harris, *Asst Cur,* The Ethel Wright Mohamed Stitchery Museum, Belzoni MS
Hawkins, Cynthia, *Dir Galleries,* Bertha V B Lederer Fine Arts Gallery-Suny Geneseo, Bertha V B Lederer Fine Arts Gallery, Geneseo NY
Hawkins, Cynthia, *Dir Galleries,* State University of New York at Geneseo, Lockhart Gallery, Geneseo NY
Hawkins, Cynthia, *Dir of Galleries,* State University of New York at Geneseo, Bertha V B Lederer Gallery, Geneseo NY
Hawkins, David, *Head Educ,* The Kreeger Museum, Washington DC
Hawkins, Juarez, *Co-Cur,* Chicago State University, President's Gallery, Chicago IL
Hawkins, Laurie, *Deputy Dir Develop & Endowments,* Timken Museum of Art, San Diego CA
Hawkins, Pamela, *Coordr Bd Mem,* Women in the Arts Foundation, Inc, Staten Island NY
Hawkins, Todd Eric, *Exec Dir,* Irving Arts Center, Galleries & Sculpture Garden, Irving TX
Haworth, Marina, *Instr,* North Hennepin Community College, Art Dept, Brooklyn Park MN (S)
Hawthorne, Frances, *Lectr,* University of North Carolina at Charlotte, Dept Art, Charlotte NC (S)
Hawthorne, Jeff, *Communs Assoc,* Regional Arts & Culture Council, Metropolitan Center for Public Arts, Portland OR
Hawthorne, Jeff, *Interim Exec Dir,* Regional Arts & Culture Council, Metropolitan Center for Public Arts, Portland OR
Hay, Michael, *Dir Youth Develop,* Intermedia Arts, Minneapolis MN
Hay, Peter, *Exhibits Dir,* Durango Arts Center, Barbara Conrad Art Gallery, Durango CO
Hay, Sara, *Reg,* Yosemite Museum, Yosemite National Park CA
Hayashi-Smith, Donna, *Coll Mgr,* White House, Washington DC
Hayden, Carla, *Dir,* Enoch Pratt, Baltimore MD
Hayden, Carla, *Librn of Congress,* Library of Congress, Prints & Photographs Division, Washington DC
Hayden, Caroline, *Digital Servs Mgr,* Historical Society of Pennsylvania, Philadelphia PA
Hayden, Casey, *Adv,* Western Washington University, Viking Union Gallery, Bellingham WA
Hayden, Diane, *Financial Admin,* Sharon Arts Center, Sharon Arts Center Exhibition Gallery, Peterborough NH
Hayden, Jason, *Director of Development & Marketing,* Owensboro Museum of Fine Art, Owensboro KY
Hayden, John, *Pres,* Antonelli Institute, Professional Photography & Commercial Art, Erdenheim PA (S)
Hayden, Leanne, *Colls Mgr,* Brick Store Museum, Kennebunk ME
Hayden, William, *Dir & Pres,* Hayden Museum of American Art, Paris TX
Hayes, Ann Marie, *Dir Educ,* Figge Art Museum, Art Reference Library, Davenport IA
Hayes, Bonnie, *Asst Prof,* Arcadia University, Dept of Fine Arts, Glenside PA (S)
Hayes, Cheryl A, *Chair & Assoc Prof,* University of New Orleans-Lake Front, Dept of Fine Arts, New Orleans LA (S)
Hayes, Daniel T, *Pres,* Finger Lakes Community College, Visual & Performing Arts Dept, Canandaigua NY (S)
Hayes, Edward, *Cur,* Museum of Latin American Art, Long Beach CA
Hayes, Elisa, *Lead Registrar,* Arizona State University, ASU Art Museum, Tempe AZ
Hayes, Greg, *Supv Ranger,* Jack London, House of Happy Walls, Glen Ellen CA
Hayes, Jonny, *Dir Design,* Anchorage Museum at Rasmuson Center, Anchorage AK
Hayes, Julia Chytil, *Instr,* Lourdes University, Art Dept, Sylvania OH (S)
Hayes, Karen, *Asst Cur Exhibs & Colls Mgr,* Tohono Chul Park, Tucson AZ
Hayes, Kathleen, *Deputy Dir Admin & CFO,* American Folk Art Museum, New York NY
Hayes, Martha, *VPres & Publicity,* Clinton Art Association, River Arts Center, Clinton IA
Hayes, Mike, *Pres,* Midland Center for the Arts, Alden B Dow Museum of Science & Art, Midland MI
Hayes, Nicole, *Cur,* The Fields Sculpture Park at Omi International Arts Center, Ghent NY
Hayes, Richard, *Instr,* University of Louisiana at Monroe, Dept of Art, Monroe LA (S)
Hayes, Sharon, *VPres,* The Boston Printmakers, at Lesley University, Boston MA
Hayes-Thumann, Karen, *Asst Dir Undergrad,* University of Oklahoma, School of Art, Norman OK (S)
Haymaker, James, *Dir,* Pfeiffer University, Art Program, Misenheimer NC (S)
Hayman, Marc, *Chief Interpretation,* San Francisco Maritime National Historical Park, Maritime Museum, San Francisco CA
Haymond, Lizzy, *Tours,* First Horizon National Corp, First Tennessee Heritage Collection, Memphis TN
Hayner, Judith, *Exec Dir,* Muskegon Museum of Art Foundation, Muskegon Museum of Art, Muskegon MI
Haynes, Carol, *Pres,* Phillips County Museum, Holyoke CO
Haynes, Chris, *Asst Prof,* Springfield College, Dept of Visual & Performing Arts, Springfield MA (S)
Haynes, Deborah, *Data Mgr,* Dartmouth College, Hood Museum of Art, Hanover NH
Haynes, Elizabeth, *Comptroller,* State of North Carolina, Battleship North Carolina, Wilmington NC
Haynes, Peggy, *Mktg,* Art Center Manatee, Bradenton FL
Haynes, Sandra, *Acting Area Head History,* Pasadena City College, Visual Arts and Media Studies Division, Pasadena CA (S)
Hays, James, *Dir Devel,* Houston Center For Photography, Houston TX
Hays, Michelle, *Asst Prof,* Texas State University - San Marcos, Dept of Art and Design, San Marcos TX (S)
Hays, Trudy, *Program Coordinator,* Scottsdale Artists' School, Scottsdale AZ (S)
Hays-Gilpin, Kelley, *Danson Cur Anthropology,* Museum of Northern Arizona, Flagstaff AZ
Hayward, Justin, *Instr,* Casper College, Dept of Visual Arts, Casper WY (S)
Hazard, Kyle, *Dir Exhibs,* Visual Art Exchange, Raleigh NC
Hazelwood, Donna, *Prof,* Oakland City University, Division of Fine Arts, Oakland City IN (S)
Hazen, Wayne, *Chmn,* Southern Adventist University, Art Dept, Collegedale TN (S)
Heaberlin, Tim, *Corporate Art Admin,* Ashland Inc, Ashland KY
Head, Danielle, *Asst Prof,* Washburn University of Topeka, Dept of Art, Topeka KS (S)
Head, Greg, *Dir,* Public Library of Des Moines, Central Library Information Services, Des Moines IA
Headrick, Annabeth, *Assoc Prof Art History,* University of Denver, School of Art & Art History, Denver CO (S)
Heagy, Anderson, *Preparator,* deCordova Sculpture Park & Museum, Lincoln MA
Healey, Marilyn, *Art Librn,* University of Georgia, University of Georgia Libraries, Athens GA
Healy, Anne, *Undergrad faculty adv,* University of California, Berkeley, College of Letters & Sciences-Art Practice Dept, Berkeley CA (S)
Healy, Caitlin, *Dir Educ,* Lyman Allyn Art Museum, New London CT
Healy, Caitlyn, *Director of Education,* Haystack Mountain School of Crafts, Deer Isle ME (S)
Healy, Jessica, *Vice Chair,* Van Alen Institute, New York NY
Healy, Patricia, *Asst Cur,* University of Texas at Arlington, Gallery at UTA, Arlington TX

Heaps, Douglas N, *Prog Chmn Digital Media Production,* Art Institute of Pittsburgh, Pittsburgh PA (S)
Heard, Carol, *Circulation & Interlibrary Loan Tech,* Anacostia Community Museum, Library, Washington DC
Hearn, Maxwell, *Chmn Asian Art,* The Metropolitan Museum of Art, New York NY
Hearn, Skyla, *Archivist & Spec Cols Librn,* DuSable Museum of African American History, Chicago IL
Hearn, Tricia, *Archival Asst,* Ozark Folk Center, Arkansas State Park, Ozark Cultural Resource Center, Mountain View AR
Hearne, Pardee, *Prof Painting,* University of California, Davis, Dept of Art & Art History, Davis CA (S)
Hearst, George R, *Chair Bd Trustees,* Albany Institute of History & Art, Albany NY
Hearst-Woods, Tracey, *Dir Develop & Progs,* The Sherwin Miller Museum of Jewish Art, Tulsa OK
Heasley, Charles, *Prof,* State University of New York, College at Cortland, Dept Art & Art History, Cortland NY (S)
Heath, Angela, *Assoc Prof,* South Plains College, Fine Arts Dept, Levelland TX (S)
Heath, Heather, *Exec Dir,* Golden Isles Arts & Humanities Association, Brunswick GA
Heath, Margo, *Auxiliary VPres,* Mississippi Museum of Art, Howorth Library, Jackson MS
Heath-Wiersma, Anne, *Asst Prof,* Hope College, Dept of Art & Art History, Holland MI (S)
Heathcott, Mary, *Exec Dir,* Blue Star Contemporary Art Center, San Antonio TX
Heathington, Mary Dell, *Chmn,* North Central Texas College, Division of Communications & Fine Arts, Gainesville TX (S)
Heatly, Stanley, *Pres Bd Dirs,* Red River Valley Museum, Vernon TX
Heaton, Nancy, *Dir,* Bay Arts, Inc, Bay Village OH
Heaton, Roxanne, *Exec Dir,* Minnetonka Center for the Arts, Wayzata MN
Heator, Megan, *Opers Mgr,* Northwestern Michigan College, Dennos Museum Center, Traverse City MI
Heavey, Elaine, *Dir Library,* Massachusetts Historical Society, Library, Boston MA
Hebermehl, Tom, *Chmn & Pres (V),* Bicentennial Art Center & Museum, Paris IL
Hebert, Melissa, *Instr,* Black Hawk College, Art Dept, Moline IL (S)
Hebert, Stephanie, *Registrar,* American Textile History Museum, Lowell MA
Heck, Joey, *Exhibits Mgr,* Herrett Center for Arts & Sciences, Jean B King Art Gallery, Twin Falls ID
Heckel, Inge, *Pres,* New York School of Interior Design, New York NY (S)
Hecker, Daren, *Dir Finance,* Henry Gallery Association, Henry Art Gallery, Seattle WA
Hecker, Daren, *Dir Finance & Admin,* University of Washington, Henry Art Gallery, Seattle WA
Heckerman, Maureen, *Exec Dir,* Institute for Arts & Humanities Education, New Jersey Summer Arts Institute, Staten Island NY (S)
Hedden, Claire, *Cur,* McLean County Art Association, McLean County Arts Center, Bloomington IL
Hedges, Tracy, *Exec,* San Angelo Museum of Fine Arts, San Angelo TX
Hedin, Thomas F, *Prof,* University of Minnesota, Duluth, Art Dept, Duluth MN (S)
Hedquist, Valerie, *Prof,* University of Montana, School of Art, Missoula MT (S)
Hedquist, Valerie, *Treas,* Midwest Art History Society, Waco TX
Hedspeth, Clinee, *Dir Pub Prog & Educ,* DuSable Museum of African American History, Chicago IL
Heep-Coll, Priscilla, *VPres Sculpture,* Catharine Lorillard Wolfe, New York NY
Heermans, Debra, *Asst Prof,* Mount Mary College, Art & Design Division, Milwaukee WI (S)
Heermans, Debra, *Prog Dir Fine Art,* Mount Mary College, Marian Gallery, Milwaukee WI
Heezen, Ronald, *Exec Dir,* Las Vegas-Clark County Library District, Las Vegas NV
Heffernan, Mary Beth, *Prof,* Occidental College, Dept of Art History & Visual Arts, Los Angeles CA (S)
Heffner, Jinger, *Exhib Coordr & Gallery Registrar,* Otis College of Art & Design, Ben Maltz Gallery, Los Angeles CA
Heft, Caren, *Dir,* University of Wisconsin-Stevens Point, Carlsten Art Gallery, Stevens Point WI
Heft, Caren, *Dir Gallery,* University of Wisconsin-Stevens Point, Dept of Art & Design, Stevens Point WI (S)
Heft, Carol, *Instr,* Muhlenberg College, Dept of Art, Allentown PA (S)
Hegarty, Carol, *Chmn Dept Humanities,* Imperial Valley College, Humanities Department, Imperial CA (S)
Heggemeyer, Amy, *Asst Registrar,* University of Illinois at Urbana-Champaign, Spurlock Museum, Urbana IL
Hegley, Douglas, *Chief Digital Officer,* Minneapolis Institute of Art, Minneapolis MN
Heher, Jody, *Assoc Dir Museum Admin,* Yeshiva University Museum, New York NY
Heidel, Gail, *Programs Coordr,* Greenwich House Inc, Greenwich House Pottery, New York NY (S)
Heider, Nate, *Develop Mem & Pub Rels,* River Heritage Museum, Paducah KY
Heighton, Jennifer, *Exec Dir,* Santa Paula Art Museum, Santa Paula CA
Heikens, Joan A, *Sr Sales & Promotions Mgr,* Jamestown-Yorktown Foundation, Jamestown Settlement, Williamsburg VA
Heil, Elizabeth, *Assoc Prof,* Roanoke College, Fine Arts Dept-Art, Salem VA (S)
Heil, Harry, *Dir Gallery,* Western State College of Colorado, Quigley Hall Art Gallery, Gunnison CO
Heil, Mary Colleen, *Pres,* Pennsylvania School of Art & Design, Lancaster PA (S)
Heilmer, Steve, *Dept Head,* Greenville College, Art Dept, Greenville IL (S)
Heiman, Ken, *Mktg Coordr,* Palo Alto Art Center, Palo Alto CA
Heiman, Richard SV, *CFO,* Virginia Historical Society, Library, Richmond VA
Heimann, Nora, *Asst Prof,* Catholic University of America, Dept of Art, Washington DC (S)
Heimerdinger, Barbara, *Exec Dir,* Illinois Alliance for Arts Education (IAAE), DeKalb IL
Heimowitz, James, *Pres,* China Institute in America, China Institute Gallery, New York NY
Heinbaugh, Allison, *Access Services,* Colonial Williamsburg Foundation, John D Rockefeller, Jr Library, Williamsburg VA
Heine, Yvonne, *Office Mgr,* Santa Barbara Contemporary Arts Forum, Santa Barbara CA
Heineman, Stephanie, *Dir,* Northport-East Northport Public Library, Northport NY
Heinlein, Douglas, *Dir Graphic Design, Web Design & Interactive Media, Digital Design,* The Art Institutes, The Art Institute of Seattle, Seattle WA (S)
Heinrich, Christoph, *Frederick & Jan Mayer Dir,* Denver Art Museum, Denver CO
Heinritz, Ryan, *Exec Dir,* Paradise Center for the Arts, Faribault MN
Heipp, Richard, *Prof & Dir,* University of Florida, School of Art & Art History, Gainesville FL (S)
Heischman, Robert, *Prof,* Rochester Institute of Technology, School of Design, Rochester NY (S)
Heisler, Virginia, *Prof,* Saint Louis Community College at Meramec, Art Dept, Saint Louis MO (S)
Heiss, Alanna, *Exec Dir,* PS1 Contemporary Art Center, Long Island City NY
Heiss, Wesley, *Assoc Prof,* Lehigh University, Dept of Art, Architecture & Design, Bethlehem PA (S)
Heist, Eric, *Co Dir,* Momenta Art, Brooklyn NY
Held, John, *Curator,* Museum of Conceptual Art, Society of Independent Artists (SIA), San Francisco CA
Helfrich, Richard, *Asst Prof,* La Roche College, Division of Design, Pittsburgh PA (S)
Helgesen, Brita, *Research Asst,* Queens College, City University of New York, Godwin-Ternbach Museum, Flushing NY
Heller, Dulcey, *Libr Asst,* American Craft Council, Library, Minneapolis MN
Heller, Ena, *Dir,* Rollins College, George D & Harriet W Cornell Fine Arts Museum, Winter Park FL
Hellier, Bob, *Preparator,* Tampa Museum of Art, Tampa FL
Helling, David, *Facility Mgr,* Foundry Art Centre, Saint Charles MO
Hellings, Benjamin, *Cur Numismatics,* Yale University, Yale University Art Gallery, New Haven CT
Helm, Alison, *Prof & Dir of Art,* West Virginia University, College of Creative Arts, School of Art & Design, Morgantown WV (S)
Helm, Dannie, *Dir,* Saint Augustine Historical Society, Oldest House Museum Complex, Saint Augustine FL
Helm, David, *Prof,* University of Nebraska at Omaha, School of the Arts, Omaha NE (S)
Helm, Elizabeth, *Prog & Circulation Dir,* National Sculpture Society, New York NY
Helmer, Matthew S, *Dir,* Colorado State University, Curfman Gallery, Fort Collins CO
Helmke, George E., *Cur,* Fleetwood Museum, North Plainfield NJ
Helms, Hilary, *Dir,* Central Iowa Art Association, Inc, Marshalltown IA
Helton, Jo-Lyn, *Bus Mgr,* Lauren Rogers, Laurel MS
Helzberg, Shirley, *Chair Board of Trustees,* The Nelson-Atkins Museum of Art, Kansas City MO
Hembroff, Nicole, *Communs Coordr,* Southern Alberta Art Gallery, Lethbridge AB
Hemmelgarn, Elaine, *Dir Develop,* Fitton Center for Creative Arts, Hamilton OH
Hemminger, Pete, *Exec Dir,* Quickdraw Animation Society, Calgary AB
Hempel, Melissa, *Interim Dir,* Utah Valley University, Woodbury Art Museum, Orem UT
Hemzik, Pamela, *Coordr Div Arts,* York College of Pennsylvania, Dept of Music, Art & Speech Communications, York PA (S)
Hendee, Stephen, *Asst Prof,* University of Nevada, Las Vegas, Dept of Art, Las Vegas NV (S)
Hendershot, James, *Assoc Prof,* College of Saint Benedict, Art Dept, Saint Joseph MN (S)
Hendershot, James, *Assoc Prof,* Saint John's University, Art Dept, Collegeville MN (S)
Hendershot, Leann, *Secy,* The Ohio Historical Society, Inc, Campus Martius Museum & Ohio River Museum, Marietta OH
Hendershot, Susan, *Lectr,* Saint John's University, Art Dept, Collegeville MN (S)
Henderson, Adele, *Print Media,* University at Buffalo, State University of New York, Dept of Visual Studies, Buffalo NY (S)
Henderson, Avis, *Exec Dir,* Monmouth Museum & Cultural Center, Lincroft NJ
Henderson, Barry, *Librn,* Beaverbrook Art Gallery, Library, Fredericton NB
Henderson, Brian, *Dir,* Academy of the New Church, Glencairn Museum, Bryn Athyn PA
Henderson, Brooke, *Art Librn,* Wellesley College, Art Library, Wellesley MA
Henderson, Bruce, *Photog,* Art Institute of Pittsburgh, Pittsburgh PA (S)
Henderson, Cathy, *Assoc Dir,* University of Texas at Austin, Harry Ransom Humanities Research Center, Austin TX
Henderson, Douglas, *Dir Entertainment Technology Center,* Art Institute of Pittsburgh, Pittsburgh PA (S)
Henderson, Garry, *Gallery Cur,* Riverside Arts Center, Riverside IL (S)
Henderson, Jackie, *Cur Educ,* Sangre de Cristo Arts & Conference Center, Pueblo CO
Henderson, Jamie, *Archivist & Digital Archivist,* The California Historical Society, North Baker Research Library, San Francisco CA
Henderson, Jessica, *Asst Prof,* Bethel University, Dept of Art & Design, Saint Paul MN (S)
Henderson, Jill, *Gallery Coordr,* Contemporary Art Gallery Society of British Columbia, Vancouver BC

Henderson, Jim, *Pres,* Owen Sound Historical Society, Marine & Rail Heritage Museum, Owen Sound ON

Henderson, Maren, *Prof Emer,* California State Polytechnic University, Pomona, Department of Art, Pomona CA (S)

Henderson, Mike, *Prof Painting,* University of California, Davis, Dept of Art & Art History, Davis CA (S)

Hendin, David, *Assoc Cur,* American Numismatic Society, New York NY

Hendon, Karen Crews, *Cur,* Monterey Museum of Art, Monterey Museum of Art -Pacific Street, Monterey Museum of Art - La Mirada, Monterey CA

Hendren, Eileen, *Asst Dir,* Pence Gallery, Davis CA

Hendrick, Joe, *Assoc Prof,* Monroe Community College, Art Dept, Rochester NY (S)

Hendricks, Barkley L, *Prof,* Connecticut College, Dept of Art, New London CT (S)

Hendricks, Becky, *Finance Dir,* Hill-Stead Museum, Farmington CT

Hendricks, Janet, *Director of Programs & Design,* Academy Art Museum, Easton MD

Hendricks, Kevin, *Supt,* San Francisco Maritime National Historical Park, Maritime Library, San Francisco CA

Hendrickson, George, *Studio Mgr,* Sculpture Space, Inc, Utica NY

Hendrickson, Ted, *Assoc Prof,* Connecticut College, Dept of Art, New London CT (S)

Hendrickx, Jim, *Chmn,* Mount Vernon Nazarene University, Art Dept, Mount Vernon OH (S)

Hendrix, Charlotte, *Comm & Mktg Specialist,* Auburn University, Jule Collins Smith Museum of Fine Art, Auburn AL

Hendrix, Janel, *Cur,* Historical Society of Martin County, Elliott Museum, Stuart FL

Heneghan, Marguerite, *Maintainer,* Osborne Homestead Museum, Derby CT

Henessey, Colleen, *Archives Asst,* The Phillips Collection, Library, Washington DC

Henige, Chris, *Chmn,* University of Wisconsin-Whitewater, Art Dept, Whitewater WI (S)

Henke, Carol, *Gallery Director,* Fullerton College, Division of Fine Arts, Fullerton CA (S)

Henke, Dellas, *Prof,* Grand Valley State University, Art & Design Dept, Allendale MI (S)

Henke, Mitch, *Assistant Prof, Graphics,* Chowan College, Dept. of Communication Arts, Fine and Applied Arts, Murfreesboro NC (S)

Henkel, James, *Assoc Prof,* University of Minnesota, Minneapolis, Dept of Art, Minneapolis MN (S)

Henley, David, *Assoc Prof,* C W Post Campus of Long Island University, School of Visual & Performing Arts, Brookville NY (S)

Henn, Rick, *Pres,* Medina Railroad Museum, Medina NY

Henn, Stuart W, *Develop Mktg Coordr,* Elmhurst Art Museum, Elmhurst IL

Henn, Stuart, *Coordinator, Marketing + Education,* Northern Illinois University, NIU Art Museum, DeKalb IL

Henna, Fredrick, *Music Coordr,* Creighton University, Fine & Performing Arts Dept, Omaha NE (S)

Hennessey, Todd, *Dean School of Fine Arts,* Grenfell Campus, Memorial University of Newfoundland, Division of Fine Arts, Visual Arts Program, Corner Brook NF (S)

Hennessy, Jeffrey, *Interim Dean of Arts,* Acadia University, Faculty of Arts, Wolfville NS (S)

Hennessy, Tricia, *Dir,* Western Michigan University, Frostic School of Art, Kalamazoo MI (S)

Henninger, Michael, *Interim Chmn,* California State University, Hayward, Art Dept, Hayward CA (S)

Hennings, Tyler, *Lectr,* Monmouth College, Dept of Art, Monmouth IL (S)

Hennlich, Andrew, *Art History,* Western Michigan University, Frostic School of Art, Kalamazoo MI (S)

Henri Robinson, Joyce, *Cur,* The Pennsylvania State University, Palmer Museum of Art, University Park PA

Henri, Janine, *Architecture/Design Librn,* University of California, Los Angeles, Arts Library, Los Angeles CA

Henrich, Sarah E, *Exec Dir,* Historical Society of Rockland County, New City NY

Henrickson, Shirley A, *Dir,* Dane G Hansen, Logan KS

Henrikson, Steve, *Cur Coll,* Alaska State Museum, Juneau AK

Henrotte, Yann, *Gen Mgr,* Arts Club of Washington, James Monroe House, Washington DC

Henry, Alicia, *Asst Prof,* Fisk University, Art Dept, Nashville TN (S)

Henry, Barbara, *Dir OMCA Lab,* Oakland Museum of California, Library & Archives, Oakland CA

Henry, Betsy, *Office Mgr,* Maharishi University of Management, Department of Art, Fairfield IA

Henry, Carole, *Assoc Prof Art Educ,* University of Georgia, Franklin College of Arts & Sciences, Lamar Dodd School of Art, Athens GA (S)

Henry, Chris, *Head of Library,* Walters Art Museum, Library, Baltimore MD

Henry, David, *Bill T Jones Dir Performing & Media Arts,* Institute of Contemporary Art/Boston, Boston MA

Henry, Elaine, *Chair,* Emporia State University, Dept of Art, Emporia KS (S)

Henry, Elena, *Deputy Dir & CFO,* Portland Museum of Art, Portland ME

Henry, Greg, *Assoc Prof,* Christopher Newport University, Dept of Fine Performing Arts, Newport News VA (S)

Henry, Helen, *Chmn Art Dept,* Washington & Jefferson College, Art Dept, Washington PA (S)

Henry, John B, *Dir,* Flint Institute of Arts, Library, Flint MI

Henry, John B, *Exec Dir,* Flint Institute of Arts, Flint MI

Henry, John, *Advertising Design Faculty,* Saint Clair County Community College, Jack R Hennesey Art Dept, Port Huron MI (S)

Henry, Kevin, *Coordr Pkg Designs,* Columbia College, Art Dept, Chicago IL (S)

Henry, Sarah, *Deputy Dir & Chief Cur,* Museum of the City of New York, Research Room, New York NY

Henry-Corrington, Sara, *Prof,* Drew University, Art Dept, Madison NJ (S)

Henschen, Lauren, *Deputy Dir,* Phoenix Center for the Arts, Phoenix AZ

Hensel, Jacqueline, *Bulletin Ed,* Marin County Watercolor Society, Corte Madera CA

Henshaw Jones, Susan, *Dir,* Museum of the City of New York, Museum, New York NY

Hensley, Fred Owen, *Prof,* University of North Alabama, Dept of Art, Florence AL (S)

Hentisz, Chryzanta, *Pres,* The Ukrainian Museum, New York NY

Hentschel, Alain, *Dean,* Florida School of the Arts, Visual Arts, Palatka FL (S)

Hentz, Christopher, *Prof,* Louisiana State University, School of Art, Baton Rouge LA (S)

Henzy, John, *Head,* Gloucester County College, Liberal Arts Dept, Sewell NJ (S)

Hepler, Anna, *Vis Asst Prof,* Bowdoin College, Art Dept, Brunswick ME (S)

Hepler, Wayne, *Assoc Prof Mass Communs,* Harford Community College, Visual, Performing and Applied Arts Division, Bel Air MD (S)

Heppner, Leianne Neff, *President & CEO,* The Summit County Historical Society of Akron, OH, Akron OH

Hepworth, Matt, *Asst Prof,* Missouri Western State University, School of Fine Arts, Saint Joseph MO (S)

Hepworth, Russell, *Assoc Prof,* College of Southern Idaho, Art Dept, Twin Falls ID (S)

Herbaugh, Karen, *Cur,* American Textile History Museum, Lowell MA

Herber, Artemis, *Pres,* Washington Sculptors Group, Washington DC

Herbert, James, *Distinguished Research Prof Drawing & Painting,* University of Georgia, Franklin College of Arts & Sciences, Lamar Dodd School of Art, Athens GA (S)

Herbert, Nell, *Gallery Mgr,* The University of San Francisco Thacher Gallery, San Francisco CA

Herbert, Sharon C, *Dir,* University of Michigan, Kelsey Museum of Archaeology, Ann Arbor MI

Herbst, Fred, *Assoc Prof,* Corning Community College, Division of Humanities, Corning NY (S)

Herceg, Trevor, *Instr,* Keystone College, Fine Arts Dept, LaPlume PA (S)

Herden, Nicole, *Cur Art,* Boise Art Museum, Boise ID

Herdter, Mark, *VPres,* Ward-Nasse Gallery, Home of the Year-Round Salon, Sussex NJ

Herendeen, Ed, *Coordr Theater,* Shepherd University, Dept of Contemporary Art & Theater, Shepherdstown WV (S)

Herhusky, Robert, *Assoc Prof,* California State University, Chico, Department of Art & Art History, Chico CA (S)

Heriard, Robert T, *Chmn Reference Svcs,* University of New Orleans, Earl K Long Library, New Orleans LA

Herlinger, Sara, *Coll Mgr,* Susquehanna University, Lore Degenstein Gallery, Selinsgrove PA

Herman, Bernard J, *Exec Dir/CEO,* Bakersfield Art Foundation, Bakersfield Museum of Art, Bakersfield CA

Herman, Brenda, *Dir Finance,* Museums Association of Saskatchewan, Regina SK

Herman, Bruce, *Dir Mktg & Pub Rels,* Boca Raton Museum of Art, Boca Raton FL

Herman, Judy S, *Admin Exec Dir,* Main Line Art Center, Haverford PA (S)

Herman, Judy S, *Admin Exec Dir,* Main Line Art Center, Haverford PA (S)

Herman, Judy, *Exec Dir,* Main Line Art Center, Haverford PA

Herman, Nancy, *Secy,* Lewis & Clark College, Dept of Art, Portland OR (S)

Herman, Todd A, *Exec Dir,* Arkansas Arts Center, Little Rock AR (S)

Herman, Todd A, *Exec Dir,* Arkansas Arts Center, Little Rock AR

Herman, Todd, *Exec Dir,* Arkansas Arts Center, Elizabeth Prewitt Taylor Memorial Library, Little Rock AR

Herman, Todd, *Pres & CEO,* The Mint Museum, Charlotte NC

Hermann Traub, Lynn, *Registrar,* deCordova Sculpture Park & Museum, Lincoln MA

Hermann, Kathy, *Asst Prof,* Taylor University, Visual Art Dept, Upland IN (S)

Hermanson, Carole, *Instr,* Marylhurst University, Art Dept, Marylhurst OR (S)

Hermo, Carmen, *Asst Cur Elizabeth A Sackler Center for Feminist Art,* Brooklyn Museum, Brooklyn NY

Hernandez, Ana M, *Chief Educ,* Museo de Arte de Ponce, The Luis A Ferre Foundation Inc, Ponce PR

Hernandez, Frances, *Mem Chmn,* Wiscasset, Waterville & Farmington Railway Museum (WW&F), Alna ME

Hernandez, Heather, *Technical Svcs,* San Francisco Maritime National Historical Park, Maritime Library, San Francisco CA

Hernandez, Jo Farb, *Dir,* Saving & Preserving Arts & Cultural Environments, Aptos CA

Hernandez, Jo Farb, *Dir,* Saving & Preserving Arts & Cultural Environments, Spaces Library & Archive, Aptos CA

Hernandez, Jo Farb, *Dir,* San Jose State University, Natalie & James Thompson Art Gallery, San Jose CA

Hernandez, John, *Dir,* Trust Authority, Research Library, Lawton OK

Hernandez, John, *Exec Dir,* Trust Authority, Museum of the Great Plains, Lawton OK

Hernandez, Lorna, *Asst Chmn Advertising Design,* Art Institute of Fort Lauderdale, Fort Lauderdale FL (S)

Hernandez, Lucy, *Art Coll Registrar,* California State University, Northridge, Art Galleries, Northridge CA

Hernandez, Patricia, *Dir Fellowship,* A.I.R. Gallery, Brooklyn NY

Hernandez, Sam, *Prof Emeritus,* Santa Clara University, Dept of Art & Art History, Santa Clara CA (S)
Hernandez, Susan, *Digital Archivist & Systems Librn,* The Cleveland Museum of Art, Ingalls Library, Cleveland OH
Hernandez, T Paul, *Assoc Prof,* Texas Lutheran University, Dept of Visual Arts, Seguin TX (S)
Hernandez, Tricia, *Dir Mktg & Develop,* South Shore Arts, Munster IN
Herne, Shawn, *Exec Dir,* Hammond-Harwood House Association, Inc, Hammond-Harwood House, Annapolis MD
Herold, Christian, *Exec Dir,* Munroe Center for the Arts, Lexington MA (S)
Herr, Carol, *Gallery Dir,* Lancaster County Art Association, Inc, Strasburg PA
Herre, Anneka, *Technical Producer,* Light Work, Robert B Menschel Photography Gallery, Syracuse NY
Herren, Angela, *Asst Prof,* University of North Carolina at Charlotte, Dept Art, Charlotte NC (S)
Herrera, Gina, *Instr,* Bakersfield College, Art Dept, Bakersfield CA (S)
Herrera, Luis, *City Librn,* San Francisco Public Library, Art, Music & Recreation Center, San Francisco CA
Herrick, Julie, *Exhibitions Coordinator,* Southern Methodist University, Meadows Museum, Dallas TX
Herrick, Rachel, *Prog Dir,* Visual Art Exchange, Raleigh NC
Herrin, Mindy, *Asst Prof,* East Tennessee State University, College of Arts and Sciences, Dept of Art & Design, Johnson City TN (S)
Herring, Joseph, *Asst Prof,* University of West Florida, Dept of Art, Pensacola FL (S)
Herrity, Carol M, *Reference Librn,* Lehigh Valley Heritage Center, Scott Andrew Trexler II Library, Allentown PA
Herrity, Carol, *Research Librn,* Lehigh Valley Heritage Center, Allentown PA
Herrmann, Frank, *Prof Fine Arts,* University of Cincinnati, School of Art, Cincinnati OH (S)
Herrnstadt, Steve, *Assoc Chair,* Iowa State University, Dept of Art & Design, Ames IA (S)
Herro, Daniel, *Head Designer & Preparator,* Marquette University, Haggerty Museum of Art, Milwaukee WI
Herrold, David, *Prof,* DePauw University, Art Dept, Greencastle IN (S)
Herron, Andy, *Dir Opers,* Peggy R McConnell Arts Center of Worthington, Columbus OH
Herron, Christopher, *Deputy Cur,* Kirkland Museum of Fine & Decorative Art, Denver CO
Herron, Cynthia, *Adjunct,* Chemeketa Community College, Dept of Humanities & Communications, Art Program, Salem OR (S)
Herron, Joseph, *Media Arts & Animation,* Art Institute of Pittsburgh, Pittsburgh PA (S)
Herron, Margaret, *Interior Design,* Art Institute of Pittsburgh, Pittsburgh PA (S)
Hershberger, Abner, *Prof,* Goshen College, Art Dept, Goshen IN (S)
Hershberger, April, *Contact,* Spruce Forest Artisan Village, Grantsville MD
Hershey, David, *Asst Coll Mgr,* University of Richmond, University Museums, Richmond VA
Hershman, Lynn, *Prof Electronic & Digital Arts,* University of California, Davis, Dept of Art & Art History, Davis CA (S)
Hershour, Jenny, *Mng Dir,* Citizens for the Arts in Pennsylvania, Harrisburg PA
Hertel, Heather, *Prof,* Slippery Rock University of Pennsylvania, Dept of Art, Slippery Rock PA (S)
Hertz, Carrie, *Cur Textiles & Dress,* New Mexico Department of Cultural Affairs, Museum of International Folk Art, Santa Fe NM
Hertzlieb, Gregg, *Dir & Cur,* Valparaiso University, Brauer Museum of Art, Valparaiso IN
Hertzson, Joyce, *Chmn Foundation Studies,* Rochester Institute of Technology, School of Design, Rochester NY (S)
Herz, Rebecca, *Head Educ,* Isamu Noguchi, Isamu Noguchi Garden Museum, Long Island City NY
Herzberg, Lesley, *Cur Coll,* Hancock Shaker Village, Inc, Pittsfield MA
Herzog, Elaine, *Pres,* Wayne County Historical Society, Museum, Honesdale PA
Herzog, Erin, *Vis Resource Specialist,* California State University, Chico, Department of Art & Art History, Chico CA (S)
Herzog, Melanie, *Assoc Prof,* Edgewood College, Art Dept, Madison WI (S)
Herzog, Melinda, *Exec Dir,* Iredell Museums, Statesville NC
Heslin, Linda, *Branch Dir,* New York Institute of Technology, Art & Architectural Library, Old Westbury NY
Hess, Catherine, *Acting Dir Art Coll,* The Huntington Library, Art Collections & Botanical Gardens, San Marino CA
Hess, Donnalynn, *Dir Educ,* Bob Jones University Museum & Gallery Inc, Greenville SC
Hess, Honee A, *Exec Dir,* Worcester Center for Crafts, Worcester MA (S)
Hess, Lali, *Gallery Dir,* Wabash College, Art Dept, Crawfordsville IN (S)
Hess, Paul, *Dir,* University of Manitoba, School of Art, Winnipeg MB (S)
Hess, Paul, *School of Art Dir,* University of Manitoba, School of Art Gallery, Winnipeg MB
Hess, Richard, *Secy,* Brown County Art Gallery Foundation, Nashville IN
Hess, Sara, *VPres,* Brown County Art Gallery Foundation, Nashville IN
Hess, Teresa, *Prof,* Lakeland Community College, Fine Arts Department, Kirtland OH (S)
Hessburg, Aloyse, *Assoc Prof,* Mount Mary College, Art & Design Division, Milwaukee WI (S)
Hesseldenz, Kate, *Cur,* Liberty Hall Historic Site, Orlando Brown House, Frankfort KY
Hesseldenz, Kate, *Cur,* Liberty Hall Historic Site, Liberty Hall Museum, Frankfort KY
Hesselgrave, Joyce, *Lectr,* California State Polytechnic University, Pomona, Department of Art, Pomona CA (S)
Hessemer, Peter, *Assoc Prof,* Oakton Community College, Language Humanities & Art Divisions, Des Plaines IL (S)
Hessling, Joanie, *Co-Dir,* Arthur Roy Mitchell, A.R. Mitchell Museum, Trinidad CO
Heston, Sally, *Instr,* Cuyahoga Valley Art Center, Cuyahoga Falls OH (S)
Hethorn, Janet, *Chair,* University of Delaware, Dept of Art, Newark DE (S)
Hetro, Amanda, *Cur Educ & Colls,* Bisbee Arts & Humanities Council, Lemuel Shattuck Memorial Library, Bisbee AZ
Hetruc, Mihaela, *Secretary,* Saint Mary's Romanian Orthodox Cathedral, Romanian Ethnic Art Museum, Cleveland OH
Heuck, Roger, *Cur Colls,* Cincinnati Art Club, Cincinnati OH
Heuer, Curt, *Chmn,* University of Wisconsin-Green Bay, Arts Dept, Green Bay WI (S)
Heuker, Jennifer, *Prof,* State University of New York College at Brockport, Dept of Art, Brockport NY (S)
Heurtin, Paige, *Opers Mgr,* Alternate ROOTS, Inc, Atlanta GA
Heuser, Douglas, *Dir,* See Science Center, Manchester NH
Hever, Amy, *Dir Advancement,* Palm Beach County Parks & Recreation Department, Morikami Museum & Japanese Gardens, Delray Beach FL
Hewes, Lauren B, *Andrew W Mellon Cur Graphic Arts,* American Antiquarian Society, Worcester MA
Hewitt, David, *Studio Grad Coordr,* San Diego State University, School of Art, Design & Art History, San Diego CA (S)
Hewitt, Patricia, *Librn,* New Mexico Department of Cultural Affairs, Palace of Governors, Santa Fe NM
Hewitt, Patricia, *Sr Cataloguer,* New Mexico Department of Cultural Affairs, Fray Angelico Chavez History Library, Santa Fe NM
Hewlett, Kristen, *CFO,* Special Libraries Association, Mc Lean VA
Hext, Charles R, *Prof,* Sul Ross State University, Dept of Fine Arts & Communications, Alpine TX (S)
Hextall, Loren, *Student Asst,* Hamline University Studio Arts & Art History Depts, Gallery, Saint Paul MN
Hey, Ken, *Instr,* Western Wisconsin Technical College, Graphics Division, La Crosse WI (S)
Heydt, Beth, *Colls Mgr,* National Postal Museum, Smithsonian Institution, Washington DC
Heydt, Stephanie, *Cur American Art,* High Museum of Art, Atlanta GA
Heying, Philip, *Adjunct Asst Prof Photog,* Johnson County Community College, Fine Arts Dept & Art History Dept, Overland Park KS (S)
Heyler, Joanne, *Dir & Chief Cur,* The Broad, Los Angeles CA
Heyman, Joy, *Deputy Dir Mus Advancement,* Walters Art Museum, Baltimore MD
Heywood, Stephen, *Prof,* Florida Community College at Jacksonville, South Campus, Art Dept, Jacksonville FL (S)
Heyworth, Kathleen, *Dir Mktg & Pub Rels,* Burchfield Penney Art Center, Buffalo NY
Hiam, Jonathan, *Cur Recordings,* The New York Public Library, The New York Public Library for the Performing Arts, New York NY
Hiatt, Akemi, *Prog Assoc,* Center for Photography at Woodstock Inc, Woodstock NY
Hickerson, Robert, *Database Mgr & Archivist,* University of Kansas, Spencer Museum of Art, Lawrence KS
Hickey, Benjamin, *Cur Colls & Exhibs,* Twin City Art Foundation, Masur Museum of Art, Monroe LA
Hickey, Christopher, *Assoc Prof,* Clark-Atlanta University, School of Arts & Sciences, Atlanta GA (S)
Hickey, Julia, *Develop Dir,* Women's Studio Workshop, Inc, Rosendale NY
Hickey, Nichole, *Mgr Artist Servs,* Cultural Council of Palm Beach County, Lake Worth FL
Hickman, Paul, *Asst Prof,* Arkansas State University, Dept of Art, State University AR (S)
Hickman, Wanda, *Rec Secy,* Northwest Watercolor Society, Woodinville WA
Hicks, Audrey, *Treas,* Moncur Gallery, Boissevain MB
Hicks, Bill, *CEO,* New Brunswick Museum, Saint John NB
Hicks, David, *Asst Prof,* University of North Carolina at Pembroke, Art Dept, Pembroke NC (S)
Hicks, Laurie E, *Prof,* University of Maine, Dept of Art, Orono ME (S)
Hicks, Patsy, *Cur Educ,* Santa Barbara Museum of Art, Santa Barbara CA
Hicks, Patsy, *Dir Educ,* Santa Barbara Museum of Art, Library, Santa Barbara CA
Hicks, Steve, *Chmn,* Oklahoma Baptist University, Art & Design Dept, Shawnee OK (S)
Hickson, Patricia, *Cur Contemporary Art,* Wadsworth Atheneum Museum of Art, Hartford CT
Hickson, Sally, *Dir,* University of Guelph, School of Fine Art & Music, Guelph ON (S)
Hickson-Stevenson, Pam, *Asst Dir,* Akron-Summit County Public Library, Fine Arts Division, Akron OH
Hidalgo, Sara, *Sidell Gallery Dir & Registrar,* Essex Art Center, Lawrence MA
Hide, Peter, *Coordr Sculpture,* University of Alberta, Dept of Art & Design, Edmonton AB (S)
Hider, Kelly, *Gallery Manager,* Arrowmont School of Arts & Crafts, Gatlinburg TN (S)
Hieblinger, Faith, *Exec Cur,* Homer Watson, Kitchener ON
Hiemstra, Janna, *Interim CEO & Cur,* Ontario Crafts Council, OCC Gallery, Toronto ON
Hiester, Becca, *Assoc Cur Educ,* Gibbes Museum of Art, Charleston SC (S)
Hiester, Jan, *Cur Textiles,* Charleston Museum, Charleston SC
Hietter, Paul, *Board CFO,* Pueblo Museum, Desert Hot Springs CA

Higbee, Brad, *Technical Dir,* Willard Arts Center, Carr Gallery, Colonial Theater, Idaho Falls ID
Higby, Sue, *Exec Dir,* Studio Place Arts, Barre VT
Higby-Flowers, Morgan, *Asst Prof Fine Art,* Watkins College of Art, Design & Film, Nashville TN (S)
Higdon, Debbie, *CFO,* Huntsville Museum of Art, Huntsville AL
Higginbotham, Carmenita, *Assoc Prof,* University of Virginia, McIntire Dept of Art, Charlottesville VA (S)
Higginbotham, Colleen, *Dir Visitor Servs,* Chrysler Museum of Art, Norfolk VA
Higgins, David, *Prof,* Corning Community College, Division of Humanities, Corning NY (S)
Higgins, Janet, *Instr,* Middle Tennessee State University, Art Dept, Murfreesboro TN (S)
Higgins, Kathleen, *Pres,* American Society for Aesthetics, Denver CO
Higgins, Larkin, *Prof,* California Lutheran University, Art Dept, Thousand Oaks CA (S)
Higgins, Padraig, *Staff Asst,* Delaplaine Visual Arts Education Center, Frederick MD
Higgins, Sarah, *Grad Program Coordr,* Bard College, Center for Curatorial Studies and the Hessel Museum of Art, Annandale-on-Hudson NY
Higgins, Shaun, *Dir Park Opers,* Pyramid Hill Sculpture Park & Museum, Hamilton OH
Higgins, Wesley, *VPres,* Snake River Heritage Center, Weiser ID
Higgs, Jamie, *Chmn,* Marian University, Visual Arts Dept, Indianapolis IN (S)
Higgs, Matthew, *Dir & Chief Cur,* White Columns, White Columns Curated Artist Registry, New York NY
High, Steven, *Exec Dir,* Florida State University, John & Mable Ringling Museum of Art, Sarasota FL
Highet, Alan, *Dir Fin,* Bronx Museum of the Arts, Bronx NY
Hightower, Chris, *Dir,* Arlington Museum of Art, Arlington TX
Higonnet, Anne, *Assoc Prof,* Wellesley College, Art Dept, Wellesley MA (S)
Hilbig, Valeska, *Deputy Dir Commun & Mktg,* National Museum of American History, Smithsonian Institution, Washington DC
Hild, Glenn, *Dept Chmn,* Eastern Illinois University, Art Dept, Charleston IL (S)
Hildebrandt, A Thomas, *Chair, Bd Trustees,* Genesee Country Village & Museum, John L Wehle Art Gallery, Mumford NY
Hile, Jeanette, *Prof,* Seton Hall University, College of Arts & Sciences, South Orange NJ (S)
Hileman, Jayne, *Chmn,* Saint Xavier University, Dept of Art & Design, Chicago IL (S)
Hileman, Kristen, *Sr Cur Contemp Art,* The Baltimore Museum of Art, Baltimore MD
Hiles, Jean, *VPres,* Iroquois County Historical Society Museum, Old Courthouse Museum, Watseka IL
Hiles, Tim, *Assoc Dir,* University of Tennessee, Knoxville, School of Art, Knoxville TN (S)
Hilgers, Ross, *Asst Prof,* Concordia College, Art Dept, Moorhead MN (S)
Hill, Amelia, *Develop Asst,* McLean County Historical Society, McLean County Museum of History, Bloomington IL
Hill, Annegreth, *Chief Cur,* Museum of Art, Fort Lauderdale, Fort Lauderdale FL
Hill, Beth, *Pres & CEO,* Fort Ticonderoga Association, Ticonderoga NY
Hill, Bill, *Assoc Prof Electronic Art,* Jacksonville University, Jacksonville FL (S)
Hill, Bonnie, *Instr,* North Central Michigan College, Art Dept, Petoskey MI (S)
Hill, Craig, *Asst Prof,* Kenyon College, Art Dept, Gambier OH (S)
Hill, Dan C, *Dir,* Hill Gallery and Sculpture Park, Sandy UT
Hill, Daniel G, *Pres,* American Abstract Artists, Brooklyn NY
Hill, David, *Asst Pro,* University of Mary Hardin-Baylor, College of Visual & Performing Arts, Belton TX (S)
Hill, Dennis, *Music Instr,* Edison Community College, Gallery of Fine Arts, Fort Myers FL (S)
Hill, Eric, *Registrar,* Regina Public Library, Dunlop Art Gallery, Regina SK
Hill, Jake, *Asst Dept Chair,* Langara College, Dept of Fine Arts, Vancouver BC (S)
Hill, Kaisa, *Coordr Educ & Outreach,* Pendleton Center for the Arts, Pendleton OR
Hill, Lisa, *Spec Progs Coordr,* Santa Barbara Museum of Art, Library, Santa Barbara CA
Hill, Lynn, *Asst Prof,* Elmhurst College, Art Dept, Elmhurst IL (S)
Hill, Martha L, *VPres Pub Progs & Vis Experience,* Eiteljorg Museum of American Indians & Western Art, Indianapolis IN
Hill, Michael, *Instr,* University of South Dakota, Department of Art, College of Fine Arts, Vermillion SD (S)
Hill, Michele, *Admin Officer,* United States Department of the Interior, Indian Arts & Crafts Board, Washington DC
Hill, Nicole Jean, *Assoc Prof,* Humboldt State University, College of Arts & Humanities, Art Dept, Arcata CA (S)
Hill, Phyllis, *Asst Prof Art Educ,* Elizabeth City State University, School of Arts & Humanities, Dept of Art, Elizabeth City NC (S)
Hill, Rosemary, *Assoc Prof,* Tidewater Community College, Visual Arts Center, Portsmouth VA (S)
Hill, Ryan, *Cur Educ,* Yale University, Yale University Art Gallery, New Haven CT
Hill, Sherri, *Prof, Graphic Design,* State College of Florida Manatee - Sarasota, Art, Design, Humanities, Bradenton FL (S)
Hill, Steve, *Pub Rels,* Shakespeare Ghost Town, Lordsburg NM
Hill, Thomas, *Librn,* Vassar College, Art Library, Poughkeepsie NY
Hill, Trey, *Assoc Prof,* University of Montana, School of Art, Missoula MT (S)
Hillard, Caroline, *Asst Prof,* Wright State University, Dept of Art & Art History, Dayton OH (S)
Hilles, Stefanie, *Library & Archives Manager,* Akron Art Museum, Akron OH
Hilles, Stefanie, *Librn & Archives Mgr,* Akron Art Museum, Martha Stecher Reed Art Library, Akron OH
Hillhouse, Susan, *Cur Exhib,* Museum of Art & History, Santa Cruz, Santa Cruz CA
Hilliard, Greg, *Dir Operations,* Cedarhurst Center for the Arts, Mitchell Museum, Mount Vernon IL
Hilliard, Mark, *Assoc Prof,* Wayland Baptist University, Dept of Art, School of Fine Art, Plainview TX (S)
Hilliard, Scott, *Exec Dir,* Touchstone Center for Crafts, Hart Moore Museum, Farmington PA
Hillier, John, *Chmn,* Kilgore College, Visual Arts Dept, Kilgore TX (S)
Hillings, Valerie, *Cur & Mgr Curatorial Affairs,* Solomon R Guggenheim Museum, New York NY
Hillman, Arthur, *Prof,* Simon's Rock College of Bard, Visual Arts Dept, Great Barrington MA (S)
Hillmann, Elizabeth, *Educ Coordr,* Art Center Sarasota, Sarasota FL
Hillquist, Rebecca, *Instr,* Glendale Community College, Visual & Performing Arts Div, Glendale CA (S)
Hilsdale, Cecily J, *Asst Prof,* Northwestern University, Evanston, Dept of Art History, Evanston IL (S)
Hilson, Douglas, *Chmn,* Hofstra University, Department of Fine Arts, Hempstead NY (S)
Hiltner, Alison, *Assoc Dir,* Soo Visual Arts Center, Minneapolis MN
Hilton, Alison, *Chmn & Prof,* Georgetown University, Dept of Art & Art History, Washington DC (S)
Hilty, Thomas, *Instr,* Lourdes University, Art Dept, Sylvania OH (S)
Hilyard, Stephen, *Prof,* University of Wisconsin, Madison, Dept of Art, Madison WI (S)
Himada, Nasrin, *Cur,* Art Metropole, Toronto ON
Himes, Gary, *Develop Dir,* Caramoor Center for Music & the Arts, Inc, Rosen House at Caramoor, Katonah NY
Himmelman, Ken, *Dean Admissions & Fin Aid,* Bennington College, Visual Arts Division, Bennington VT (S)
Hinckley, Bunny, *Head Docent,* The Historic New Orleans Collection, Royal Street Galleries, New Orleans LA
Hinckley, Robert L, *Exec VPres,* Wendell Gilley, Southwest Harbor ME
Hindmarch, Sara, *Head Registrar,* University of Chicago, Smart Museum of Art, Chicago IL
Hinds, Jill, *Instr,* Northwestern Michigan College, Art Dept, Traverse City MI (S)
Hindson, Bradley T, *Assoc Prof,* Rochester Institute of Technology, School of Photographic Arts & Sciences, Rochester NY (S)
Hine, Charles, *Dir,* Salvador Dali, Library, Saint Petersburg FL
Hine, Charles, *Exec Dir,* Salvador Dali, Saint Petersburg FL
Hiner, Thomas, *Secy,* Virginia Center for the Creative Arts, Amherst VA
Hines, Jessica, *Prof,* Georgia Southern University, Betty Foy Sanders Dept of Art, Statesboro GA (S)
Hines, Sally, *VPres Publicity & Promotion,* DuPage Art League School & Gallery, Wheaton IL
Hines, Sarah, *Head Pub Rels & Mem,* The Kreeger Museum, Washington DC
Hines, Sondra, *Cur Educ,* Holter Museum of Art, Helena MT
Hinken, Susan, *Head Colls Servs,* University of Portland, Wilson W Clark Memorial Library, Portland OR
Hinkle, Brian, *Dir Gallery,* Wichita Center for the Arts, Mary R Koch School of Visual Arts, Wichita KS (S)
Hinkson, Lauren, *Asst Cur Colls,* Solomon R Guggenheim Museum, New York NY
Hinojos, Erica, *Mus Shop Mgr,* Kern County Museum, Library, Bakersfield CA
Hinojosa, Marcela, *Artist Dir,* Brownsville Art League, Brownsville Museum of Fine Art, Brownsville TX
Hinson, Mary Joan, *Prof,* Florida Community College at Jacksonville, South Campus, Art Dept, Jacksonville FL (S)
Hinson, Peggy S, *Prof,* Methodist College, Art Dept, Fayetteville NC (S)
Hinton, Chloe, *Dir Educ & Prog Plng,* Albany Museum of Art, Albany GA
Hinton, William, *Dir & Cur,* Louisburg College, Art Gallery, Louisburg NC
Hintz, Glen, *Art Chair,* Rochester Institute of Technology, College of Imaging Arts & Sciences, Rochester NY (S)
Hintz, Glen, *Asst Prof,* Rochester Institute of Technology, School of Design, Rochester NY (S)
Hinze, Roxanne, *Adjunct Instr,* Northern State University, Art Dept, Aberdeen SD (S)
Hiott, Will, *Dir Historic Houses & Cur,* Clemson University, Fort Hill Plantation, Clemson SC
Hipp, Francis M, *Pres,* Liberty Life Insurance Company, Greenville SC
Hiramoto, Judy, *Instr,* American River College, Dept of Art/Art New Media, Sacramento CA (S)
Hiratsuka, Yuji, *Asst Prof,* Oregon State University, Dept of Art, Corvallis OR (S)
Hirayama, Mikiko, *Asst Prof Art History,* University of Cincinnati, School of Art, Cincinnati OH (S)
Hirbour, Kathy, *Educ Coordr,* American Textile History Museum, Lowell MA
Hires, Ben, *Dir. of Strategic Partnerships,* Boston Public Library, Central Library, Boston MA
Hirsch, Barron, *Prof,* Saginaw Valley State University, Dept of Art & Design, University Center MI (S)
Hirsch, Edward, *Pres,* John Simon Guggenheim, New York NY
Hirsch, Marjorie, *Dir,* Clark College, Archer Gallery/Gaiser Hall, Vancouver WA
Hirsch, Michael, *VPres,* Society for Commercial Archeology, Little Rock AR
Hirsch, Richard, *Prof,* Rochester Institute of Technology, School of Design, Rochester NY (S)
Hirsch, Robin, *Assoc Dir,* Art Saint Louis, Saint Louis MO

Hirschel, Anthony G, *Dana Feitler Dir,* University of Chicago, Smart Museum of Art, Chicago IL
Hirschfeld, Barbara, *Exec Dir,* Paine Art Center & Gardens, Oshkosh WI
Hirschfield, Jim, *Prof,* University of North Carolina at Chapel Hill, Art Dept, Chapel Hill NC (S)
Hirshon, Stephen, *Asst Prof,* Shippensburg University, Art Dept, Shippensburg PA (S)
Hirt, Brian, *Chair Ceramics,* Kalamazoo Institute of Arts, KIA School, Kalamazoo MI (S)
Hisa, Asuka, *Dir Educ,* Institute of Contemporary Art, Los Angeles, Los Angeles CA
Hisiger, Rebecca, *Asst Registrar,* University of California, Berkeley, The Magnes Collection of Jewish Art & Life, Berkeley CA
Hiss, Nancy, *Instr,* Marylhurst University, Art Dept, Marylhurst OR (S)
Hissey, Carey, *Assoc Prof,* Oklahoma State University, Department of Art, Graphic Design and Art History, Stillwater OK (S)
Hitchcock, Alix, *Instr,* Wake Forest University, Dept of Art, Winston-Salem NC (S)
Hitchcock, John, *Prof,* University of Wisconsin, Madison, Dept of Art, Madison WI (S)
Hitchcock, Julia, *Assoc Prof,* Baylor University - College of Arts and Sciences, Dept of Art, Waco TX (S)
Hites, Thomas, *Treas,* Brooklyn Historical Society, Brooklyn OH
Hittinger, Lauren, *Mktg & Develop Mgr,* The Arts Center of the Capital Region, Troy NY
Hlowatzki, William, *Pub Rels,* Canadian Clay and Glass Gallery, Waterloo ON
Ho, Angela, *Instr,* George Mason University, College of Humanities & Social Sciences, Dept of History & Art History, Fairfax VA (S)
Hoag, Marilyn, *Prog Coordr,* California State University, Chico, Associated Students, 3rd Floor Art Gallery, Chico CA
Hoagland, Eleanor T M, *Pres,* Wendell Gilley, Southwest Harbor ME
Hoanes, Tracy, *Exec Asst,* Dartmouth College, Hood Museum of Art, Hanover NH
Hoar, Bill, *Prof,* Northern State University, Art Dept, Aberdeen SD (S)
Hoard, Curtis, *Prof,* University of Minnesota, Minneapolis, Dept of Art, Minneapolis MN (S)
Hobbs, Frank, *Asst Prof,* Ohio Wesleyan University, Fine Arts Dept, Delaware OH (S)
Hobbs, Mary Alice, *Publicity & Heritage Writer,* Brigham City Corporation, Brigham City Museum of Art & History, Brigham City UT
Hobbs, Patricia, *Dir,* Washington & Lee University, Lee Chapel & Museum, Lexington VA
Hobbs, Toni, *Instr,* Morehead State University, Art & Design Dept, Morehead KY (S)
Hobgood, Wade, *Dean,* California State University, Long Beach, Design Dept, Long Beach CA (S)
Hobin, Timothy J, *Admin Asst,* Center for Exploratory & Perceptual Art, CEPA Library, Buffalo NY
Hoblitzell, Taylor, *Exhibition & Prog Coord,* Diverse Works, Houston TX
Hobruecker, Uli, *Bookkeeper,* Contemporary Art Gallery Society of British Columbia, Vancouver BC
Hobson, Hallie, *Deputy Dir Institutional Advancement,* The Studio Museum in Harlem, New York NY
Hobson, Marlena, *Assoc Prof,* Mary Baldwin College, Dept of Art & Art History, Staunton VA (S)
Hochhalter, Lindsay, *Develop Mgr,* i.d.e.a. Museum, Mesa AZ
Hochner, Kate, *Instr,* Wayne Art Center, Wayne PA (S)
Hochradel, Rebecca, *Fiscal Mgr,* Historic Arkansas Museum, Little Rock AR
Hock, John, *Artistic Dir & CEO,* Franconia Sculpture Park, Franconia MN
Hock, Rick, *Exhibs Coordr,* Visual Studies Workshop, Rochester NY (S)
Hockenberry, Alyssa, *Registrar,* Museum of Contemporary Art Jacksonville, Jacksonville FL
Hockensmith, Josh, *Libr Technical Asst,* University of North Carolina at Chapel Hill, Joseph Curtis Sloane Art Library, Chapel Hill NC
Hockensmith, Laura, *Educ & Pub Progs,* Naval Historical Center, National Museum of the US Navy, Washington DC
Hockett, Carol, *Coordr School & Family Progs,* Cornell University, Herbert F Johnson Museum of Art, Ithaca NY
Hockett, Roland L, *Assoc Prof,* Gulf Coast Community College, Division of Visual & Performing Arts, Panama City FL (S)
Hockhousen, Jim, *Dir Finance & Admin,* Newport Art Museum and Association, Newport RI
Hocking, Christopher, *Assoc Prof Foundations,* University of Georgia, Franklin College of Arts & Sciences, Lamar Dodd School of Art, Athens GA (S)
Hockwelt, Helen, *Cur,* Pickens County Museum of Art & History, Pickens SC
Hodge, Andrew, *Bd Chmn,* Virginia Museum of Contemporary Art, Virginia Beach VA
Hodge, Beth, *Exec Dir,* Stauton Augusta Art Center, Staunton VA
Hodgens, Mary Lee, *Prog Mgr,* Light Work, Robert B Menschel Photography Gallery, Syracuse NY
Hodges, Jeanne, *Admin Asst,* Two Rivers Art Gallery, Prince George BC
Hodges, Pat, *Manuscript Librn,* Western Kentucky University, Kentucky Library & Museum, Bowling Green KY
Hodgson, Jeffrey, *Provost,* New World School of the Arts, Miami FL (S)
Hodgson, Terri, *Admin Asst,* University of Redlands, Peppers Art Gallery, Redlands CA
Hodik, Barbara, *Prof,* Rochester Institute of Technology, School of Design, Rochester NY (S)
Hodson, Carol, *Prof,* Webster University, Department of Art, Design & Art History, Webster Groves MO (S)
Hodson, Janice, *Cur Art,* New Bedford Free Public Library, Special Collections Dept: Art Collection, New Bedford MA
Hoefferie, Mary, *Asst Prof,* University of Wisconsin Oshkosh, Dept of Art, Oshkosh WI (S)
Hoefle, Krista, *Gallery Dir,* Saint Mary's College, Moreau Galleries, Notre Dame IN
Hoege, Howard, *Pres,* The Mariners' Museum, Newport News VA
Hoeh, Michael, *Treas,* Aperture Foundation, New York NY
Hoeltzel, Susan, *Dir,* Lehman College Art Gallery, Bronx NY
Hoelzeman, George, *Gallery Dir,* Rialto Community Arts Center, The Gallery, Morrilton AR
Hofacket, Katy, *Coordr,* Deming-Luna Mimbres Museum, Deming NM
Hofelt, Miranda, *Assoc Cur,* Hunter Museum of American Art, Reference Library, Chattanooga TN
Hofer, Margi, *VPres & Mus Dir,* New-York Historical Society, Museum, New York NY
Hoff, April, *Educ,* Valley Art Gallery, Forest Grove OR
Hoffman, Angela, *Dir School of Art,* Palos Verdes Art Center/Beverly G. Alpay Center for Arts Education, Rancho Palos Verdes CA
Hoffman, Diane, *Assoc Prof,* Rhodes College, Dept of Art, Memphis TN (S)
Hoffman, Erin, *Prog Coordr,* Muskegon Community College, Dept of Creative & Performing Arts, Muskegon MI (S)
Hoffman, Eva, *Asst Prof,* Tufts University, Dept of Art & Art History, Medford MA (S)
Hoffman, Ian, *Chmn Dept Architecture,* Judson University, School of Art, Design & Architecture, Elgin IL (S)
Hoffman, Ian, *Instr,* Judson University, School of Art, Design & Architecture, Elgin IL (S)
Hoffman, Joel M, *Exec Dir,* Vizcaya Museum & Gardens, Miami FL
Hoffman, Kate, *Dir,* Huntington Beach Art Center, Huntington Beach CA
Hoffman, Katherine, *Chmn,* Saint Anselm College, Dept of Fine Arts, Manchester NH (S)
Hoffman, Kim, *Prof,* Western Oregon State College, Creative Arts Division, Visual Arts, Monmouth OR (S)
Hoffman, Lisa, *Cur Educ,* Leigh Yawkey Woodson Art Museum, Wausau WI
Hoffman, Mark, *COO,* The Buffalo Fine Arts Academy, Albright-Knox Art Gallery, Buffalo NY
Hoffman, Michael, *Div Head & Assoc Prof,* Norwich University, Dept of Architecture and Art, Northfield VT (S)
Hoffman, Randy, *Treas,* Independence Historical Museum & Art Center, Independence KS
Hoffman, Tom, *Instr,* University of Utah, Dept of Art & Art History, Salt Lake City UT (S)
Hoffman, Tom, *Prof,* University of Maine at Augusta, College of Arts & Humanities, Augusta ME (S)
Hoffmann, Mark, *Illustration,* Montserrat College of Art, Beverly MA (S)
Hofhiens, Mike, *Dir Opers,* National Museum of Wildlife Art of the Unites States, Jackson WY
Hofmann, Irene, *Phillips Dir & Chief Cur,* SITE Santa Fe, Santa Fe NM
Hofmann, Sally, *Visual Arts Coordr,* Beaufort County Arts Council, Washington NC
Hofstedt, Matthew, *Assoc Cur,* Supreme Court of the United States, Office of the Curator, Washington DC
Hofstetter, Philip, *Dir,* California State University, East Bay, University Art Gallery, Hayward CA
Hogan, Christopher, *Chmn, Buffalo Soc Natural Sci Bd Dirs,* Buffalo Society of Natural Sciences, Buffalo Museum of Science, Buffalo NY
Hogan, Jacqueline, *Asst Dir,* State University of New York at Binghamton, Binghamton University Art Museum, Binghamton NY
Hogan, John, *Opers Mgr,* Museum of Photographic Arts, Edmund L. and Nancy K Dubois Library, San Diego CA
Hogan, John, *Studio & Gallery Mgr,* California Institute of the Arts, School of Art, Valencia CA (S)
Hogan-Schofield, Dorothy, *Cur,* The Sandwich Historical Society, Inc & Sandwich Glass Museum, Sandwich Glass Museum, Sandwich MA
Hogarth, Brian, *Adjunct Asst Prof Art History,* Johnson County Community College, Fine Arts Dept & Art History Dept, Overland Park KS (S)
Hoggle, Matt, *Assoc Dir,* The Contemporary Austin, Austin TX
Hogu, Barbara J, *Asst Prof,* City Colleges of Chicago, Malcolm X College, Chicago IL (S)
Hohmann, Glynys, *Team Leader Government Records,* Royal Alberta Museum, Provincial Archives of Alberta, Edmonton AB
Hohmann, Kathryn, *Dir Philantrhopy,* Montana State University, Museum of the Rockies, Bozeman MT
Hoi, Sammy, *Secy,* Association of Independent Colleges of Art & Design, Providence RI
Hoi, Samuel, *Pres,* Maryland Institute, College of Art, Baltimore MD (S)
Hoinski, Michael, *Educ Coordr,* City of Austin Parks & Recreation, O Henry Museum, Austin TX
Hojonsky, Patrick, *Assoc Prof,* Southwestern University, Sarofim School of Fine Art, Dept of Art & Art History, Georgetown TX (S)
Hokanson, Taylor, *Asst Prof,* Oakland University, Dept of Art & Art History, Rochester MI (S)
Holahan, Mary F, *Cur Illustrations & Outlook Exhibs,* Delaware Art Museum, Wilmington DE
Holbert, Kelly, *Exhib Coordr,* Smith College, Museum of Art, Northampton MA
Holbrook-Shaw, Chanelle, *Contact,* Monarch Contemporary Art Center & Sculpture Park, Olympia WA
Holbrow, Dan, *Professional Develop Coordr,* Museums Association of Saskatchewan, Regina SK
Holcomb, Mark, *Interim Exec Dir,* Tacoma Art Museum, Tacoma WA
Holcombe, Anna Calluori, *Prof,* Kansas State University, Art Dept, Manhattan KS (S)

Holcombe, Julee, *Assoc Prof,* University of New Hampshire, Dept of Art & Art History, Durham NH (S)

Holden, Daniel, *Gallery Asst,* St Mary's College of Maryland, The Dwight Frederick Boyden Gallery, St Mary's City MD

Holden, John, *Asst Prof,* Bemidji State University, Visual Arts Dept, Bemidji MN (S)

Holden, Wendy, *Sr Assoc Cur,* University of Michigan, Asian Art Archives, Ann Arbor MI

Holder, Teresa, *Lectr,* Oklahoma State University, Department of Art, Graphic Design and Art History, Stillwater OK (S)

Holder, Thomas J, *Prof,* University of Nevada, Las Vegas, Dept of Art, Las Vegas NV (S)

Holder-Jones, Peggy, *Dir Admin,* Queen Sofia Spanish Institute, New York NY

Holderbaum, Linda, *Exec Dir,* Art Center of Battle Creek, Battle Creek MI

Holderbaum, Linda, *Exec Dir,* Art Center of Battle Creek, Michigan Art & Artist Archives, Battle Creek MI

Holen, Alisa, *Asst Prof Art,* University of Southern Indiana, Art & Design Dept, Evansville IN (S)

Holian, Heather, *Prof,* University of North Carolina at Greensboro, School of Art, Greensboro NC (S)

Holl, James, *Assoc Prof Art,* Marymount Manhattan College, Fine & Performing Arts Div, New York NY (S)

Holland, David, *Assoc Dir,* Arts & Business Council of Greater Boston, Inc, Volunteer Lawyers for the Arts of MA, Boston MA

Holland, Hillary, *Dir Pub Rels,* Brandywine Conservancy, Brandywine River Museum, Chadds Ford PA

Holland, Joy, *Adj Instr,* University of West Florida, Dept of Art, Pensacola FL (S)

Holland, Raymond, *VPres,* Lehigh Valley Heritage Center, Allentown PA

Holland, Rose, *Community Learning Center Dir,* Washington Pavilion of Arts & Science, Visual Arts Center, Sioux Falls SD

Hollander, Barbara J, *Altoona Coordr,* Southern Alleghenies Museum of Art, Altoona Facility, Altoona PA

Hollander, Joel, *Instr,* University of Miami, Dept of Art & Art History, Coral Gables FL (S)

Hollander, Stacy C, *Deputy Dir Curatorial Affairs, Chief Cur & Dir Exhibs,* American Folk Art Museum, New York NY

Hollein, Max, *Dir,* Fine Arts Museums of San Francisco, M H de Young Museum, San Francisco CA

Hollein, Max, *Dir,* Fine Arts Museums of San Francisco, Legion of Honor, San Francisco CA

Hollern, Matthew, *Dept Head Jewelry & Metals,* Cleveland Institute of Art, Cleveland OH (S)

Holley, Eva, *Graduate Prog Coordr,* University of Maryland, Baltimore County, Intermedia & Digital Arts (IMDA), Dept of Visual Arts, Baltimore MD (S)

Holliday, Chad, *Assoc Prof,* West Texas A&M University, Art, Theatre & Dance Dept, Canyon TX (S)

Holliday, Paul, *Acad Prog Asst,* Southern California Institute of Architecture, Los Angeles CA (S)

Holliday, Stuart, *Pres & CEO,* Meridian International Center, Cafritz Galleries, Washington DC

Hollingsworth, Mar, *Cur Visual Arts & Prog Mgr,* California African-American Museum, Los Angeles CA

Hollingsworth, Priscilla, *Prof,* Augusta State University, Dept of Art, Augusta GA (S)

Hollingwood, Keith, *Adjunct Faculty,* Mount Wachusett Community College, East Wing Gallery, Gardner MA

Hollins, Hunter, *COO,* University of Virginia, The Fralin Museum of Art at the University of Virginia, Charlottesville VA

Hollinshead, Mary, *Assoc Prof,* University of Rhode Island, Dept of Art & Art History, Kingston RI (S)

Hollis, Lucy, *Dir,* Tullahoma Fine Arts Center Regional Museum of Art, Tullahoma TN

Hollis, Sara, *Chmn,* Southern University in New Orleans, Fine Arts & Philosophy Dept, New Orleans LA (S)

Hollosy, E Gyuri, *Acad Asst,* Johnson Atelier Technical Institute of Sculpture, Trenton NJ (S)

Hollosy, Gyuri, *Dir Gallery,* Johnson Atelier Technical Institute of Sculpture, Johnson Atelier Library, Mercerville NJ

Holloway, James S, *Dir Mus Educ,* Jamestown-Yorktown Foundation, Jamestown Settlement, Williamsburg VA

Holloway, Jon, *Assoc Prof Art,* Lander University, College of Arts & Humanities - Visual Arts, Greenwood SC (S)

Holloway, Kay, *Instr,* Millsaps College, Dept of Art, Jackson MS (S)

Hollowell, David, *Prof Painting & Drawing,* University of California, Davis, Dept of Art & Art History, Davis CA (S)

Holly, Michael, *Dir Research & Academic Prog,* Clark Art Institute, Williamstown MA

Holm, Jack, *Asst Prof,* Rochester Institute of Technology, School of Photographic Arts & Sciences, Rochester NY (S)

Holm, Sharon, *Dir Commun & Mktg,* Bechtler Museum of Modern Art, Charlotte NC

Holman Conwill, Kinshasha, *Deputy Dir,* National Museum of African American History and Culture, Smithsonian Institution, Washington DC

Holman, Brian, *Quilt Opers Mgr,* The Names Project Foundation AIDS Memorial Quilt, Atlanta GA

Holman, L Bruce, *Art Faculty,* Cottey College, Art Dept, Nevada MO (S)

Holmberg, Jim, *Cur Coll,* The Filson Historical Society, Louisville KY

Holmes, Carolyn, *Mng Dir,* Two Rivers Art Gallery, Prince George BC

Holmes, Daphne, *Cur Pub Programs,* Cameron Art Museum, Wilmington NC

Holmes, David, *Prof,* University of Wisconsin-Parkside, Art Dept, Kenosha WI (S)

Holmes, Elizabeth, *Registrar,* Buffalo Bill Memorial Association, Buffalo Bill Historical Center, Cody WY

Holmes, Heather, *Digital Ed & Communs,* University of Pennsylvania, Institute of Contemporary Art, Philadelphia PA

Holmes, Karen, *Cur,* City of Ukiah, Grace Hudson Museum & The Sun House, Ukiah CA

Holmes, Kristy, *Asst Prof & Chair,* Lakehead University, Dept of Visual Arts, Thunder Bay ON (S)

Holmes, Lisa, *CFO,* National Museum of Wildlife Art of the Unites States, Jackson WY

Holmes, Meaghan, *Dir Promotions,* State of North Carolina, Battleship North Carolina, Wilmington NC

Holmes, Wendy B, *Prof,* University of Rhode Island, Dept of Art & Art History, Kingston RI (S)

Holmes, Willard, *COO,* Museum of Fine Arts, Houston, Houston TX

Holmgren, John C, *Asst Prof,* Franklin & Marshall College, Art & Art History Dept, Lancaster PA (S)

Holmquist, Anthony, *Asst Prof,* Fort Lewis College, Art Dept, Durango CO (S)

Holo, Selma, *Dir & Cur,* University of Southern California, USC Fisher Museum of Art, Los Angeles CA

Holoday, Carol, *Adjunct,* Monterey Peninsula College, Art Dept/Art Gallery, Monterey CA (S)

Holowacz, Eric V, *Exec Dir,* University of South Carolina Beaufort Art Gallery, Beaufort SC

Holownia, Thaddeus, *Dept Head,* Mount Allison University, Dept of Fine Arts, Sackville NB (S)

HOlsopple, Jerry, *Professor of Visual and Communication Arts,* Eastern Mennonite University, Visual and Communication Arts, Harrisonburg VA (S)

Holst, Erika, *Coll Cur,* Springfield Art Association of Edwards Place, Springfield IL

Holsten, Anna, *Instr Art,* Pearl River Community College, Visual Arts, Dept of Fine Arts & Communication, Poplarville MS (S)

Holt, Alexandra, *Exec VPres, Finance,* The Art Institute of Chicago, Chicago IL

Holt, Alison, *Catalog Librn,* Art Center College of Design, James Lemont Fogg Memorial Library, Pasadena CA

Holt, Bonnie, *Book Librn,* University of California, Davis, Art Dept Library, Davis CA

Holte, Bettye S, *Dir,* Austin Peay State University, Mabel Larsen Fine Arts Gallery, Clarksville TN

Holtgrewe, Doug, *Chmn,* Elmira College, Art Dept, Elmira NY (S)

Holton, John, *Asst Coll Mgr,* University of Illinois at Urbana-Champaign, Spurlock Museum, Urbana IL

Holton-Thomas, Henrietta, *Pres,* Lancaster County Art Association, Inc, Strasburg PA

Holtrop, Emily, *Dir Learning & Interpretation,* Cincinnati Art Museum, Cincinnati Art Museum, Cincinnati OH

Holtry, Elizabeth, *Prof,* Mount Saint Mary's University, Visual & Performing Arts Dept, Emmitsburg MD (S)

Holtzhauser, John, *CFO,* Western Reserve Historical Society, Library, Cleveland OH

Holz, Keith, *Asst Prof,* Western Illinois University, Department of Art, Macomb IL (S)

Holz, Molly, *Publ Mgr,* Montana Historical Society, Helena MT

Holzenberg, Eric, *Dir,* Grolier Club Library, New York NY

Homanchuk, Alex, *Head E-Reserves & E-Learning Support,* OCAD University, Dorothy H Hoover Library, Toronto ON

Homann, Joachim, *Cur,* Bowdoin College, Museum of Art, Brunswick ME

Homchick, Kent, *Multi-Media Study,* University of Colorado at Denver, College of Arts & Media Visual Arts Dept, Denver CO (S)

Honer, Michael, *Photog,* Pitzer College, Dept of Art, Claremont CA (S)

Hong, Ming, *Asst Prof,* Old Dominion University, Art Dept, Norfolk VA (S)

Hong, Zaixin, *Prof of Art History,* University of Puget Sound, Dept of Art & Art History, Tacoma WA (S)

Hood Morgan, Katie, *Cur Exhibs & Public Progs,* San Francisco Art Institute, Walter and McBean Galleries, San Francisco CA

Hood, Craig, *Chmn,* University of New Hampshire, Dept of Art & Art History, Durham NH (S)

Hood, Eugene, *Prof,* University of Wisconsin-Eau Claire, Dept of Art & Design, Eau Claire WI (S)

Hood, Mary Bryan, *Dir,* Owensboro Museum of Fine Art, Owensboro KY

Hood, Walter J, *Chair,* University of California, Berkeley, College of Environmental Design, Berkeley CA (S)

Hood, William, *Chmn,* Oberlin College, Dept of Art, Oberlin OH (S)

Hoofman, Kittie S, *Treas,* Drew County Historical Society, Museum, Monticello AR

Hoogerwerf, Katherine, *Dir Develop Events,* Atlanta Historical Society Inc, Atlanta History Center, Atlanta GA

Hook, Charles E, *Assoc Prof,* Florida State University, Art Dept, Tallahassee FL (S)

Hooker, John, *Asst Prof,* Bridgewater State College, Art Dept, Bridgewater MA (S)

Hooks, Judith, *Artist & Pres,* Walker's Point Artists Assoc Inc, Gallery 218, Milwaukee WI

Hoone, Jeffrey, *Exec Dir,* Light Work, Robert B Menschel Photography Gallery, Syracuse NY

Hooper, Cassandra, *Prof,* Purchase College, State University of New York, School of Art+Design, Purchase NY (S)

Hooper, Letha, *Collection Mgr,* Ellen Noel Art Museum of the Permian Basin, Odessa TX

Hoot, Cynthia, *Office Adminr,* Toledo Artists' Club, Toledo Artists' Club & Gallery, Toledo OH

Hoot, Robert, *Registrar,* Loveland Museum/Gallery, Loveland CO

Hooten, Joseph, *Educ Coordr,* McLean County Art Association, McLean County Arts Center, Bloomington IL

Hoover, Brian P, *Chmn,* Southern Utah State University, Dept of Art, Cedar City UT (S)
Hoover, Heather, *Prof Emeritus,* University of North Carolina at Charlotte, Dept Art, Charlotte NC (S)
Hope, Dan, *Lyndon House Art Foundation,* Lyndon House Art, Athens GA
Hopfensperger, Jim, *Foundation,* Western Michigan University, Frostic School of Art, Kalamazoo MI (S)
Hopkins, Dave, *Chief Bldg, Grounds & Security,* Tucson Museum of Art and Historic Block, Tucson AZ
Hopkins, Emily, *Dir,* Side Street Projects, Pasadena CA
Hopkins, Jessica, *Cur,* Museum of New Art, Troy MI
Hopkins, Randi, *Dir Visual Arts,* Boston Center for the Arts, Mills Gallery, Boston MA
Hopkins, Seth, *Exec Dir,* Booth Western Art Museum, Cartersville GA
Hopkins, Sharon, *Senior Instr,* Penn Foster College, School of Interior Design, Scranton PA (S)
Hopkins, Sharon, *Sr Instr,* Penn Foster College, Art/ Graphic Design, Scottsdale AZ (S)
Hopkins, Terri M, *Dir,* Marylhurst University, The Art Gym, Marylhurst OR
Hopkins, Terri, *Instr,* Marylhurst University, Art Dept, Marylhurst OR (S)
Hopkins-Benton, Ashley, *Educator,* Columbia County Historical Society, Luykas Van Alen House, Kinderhook NY
Hopkinson, Dana, *Mus Servs Coordr,* Okanagan Heritage Museum, Kelowna BC
Hopman, Rebecca, *Outreach Librn,* Corning Museum of Glass, Juliette K and Leonard S Rakow Research Library, Corning NY
Hoppe, David, *Prof Emeritus,* California State University, Chico, Department of Art & Art History, Chico CA (S)
Hopper, Gail, *Controller,* The Dixon Gallery & Gardens, Memphis TN
Hopper, Jeffrey, *Dir,* Warner House Association, MacPheadris-Warner House, Portsmouth NH
Hopper, W Kenneth, *Asst Prof,* Huntington College, Art Dept, Huntington IN (S)
Hore-Pabst, Susan, *Prof,* Black Hills State University, Art Dept, Spearfish SD (S)
Horita, Mari, *Pres & CEO,* Corporate Council for the Arts/Arts Fund, Seattle WA
Horn Johnson, Heather, *Dir Art Gallery,* Central Washington University, Sarah Spurgeon Gallery, Ellensburg WA
Horn, Amanda, *Dir Communs,* Nevada Museum of Art, Reno NV
Horn, Gerri, *Chair,* Morris Museum, Morristown NJ
Horn, Jason, *Dir,* Gordon College, Dept of Fine Arts, Barnesville GA (S)
Horn, Lawrence, *Acting Head,* Mississippi Valley State University, Fine Arts Dept, Itta Bena MS (S)
Horn, Susan, *Adjunct Prof Art,* Nebraska Wesleyan University, Art Dept, Lincoln NE (S)
Hornbeck, Elizabeth, *Instr,* University of Missouri - Columbia, Art History & Archaeology Dept, Columbia MO (S)
Hornbrook, Jessie, *Asst Prof,* University of Central Arkansas, Department of Art, Conway AR (S)
Horne Garland, Traci, *Gallery Coordr,* Virginia Commonwealth University, Anderson Gallery, Richmond VA
Horne-Leshinsky, Jody, *Community Develop Dir,* Broward County Board of Commissioners, Broward Cultural Div, Fort Lauderdale FL
Horner, Garin, *Asst Prof,* Adrian College, Art & Design Dept, Adrian MI (S)
Horner, Gerald, *Deputy Dir,* Kirkland Museum of Fine & Decorative Art, Denver CO
Horner, Marge, *Educ Dir,* Abington Art Center, Jenkintown PA
Hornik, Heidi J, *Prof,* Baylor University - College of Arts and Sciences, Dept of Art, Waco TX (S)
Hornik, Heidi, *Dir,* Baylor University, Martin Museum of Art, Waco TX
Hornik, Heidi, *Pres,* Midwest Art History Society, Waco TX
Horning, Jerry, *Instr,* Creighton University, Fine & Performing Arts Dept, Omaha NE (S)
Horning, Lisa, *Prof,* Ocean County College, Humanities Dept, Toms River NJ (S)
Hornor, Elizabeth S, *Dir Educ,* Emory University, Michael C Carlos Museum, Atlanta GA
Hornsby, Mike, *Sr VPres,* Museum of Science & History, Jacksonville FL
Horodner, Stuart, *Dir,* The University of Kentucky Art Museum, Lexington KY
Horoschak, Lynne, *Chmn Art Educ,* Moore College of Art & Design, Philadelphia PA (S)
Horovitz, Ellen, *Assoc Prof,* Nazareth College of Rochester, Art Dept, Rochester NY (S)
Horowitz, Amy, *Clerk Specialist,* Rensselaer Polytechnic Institute, Eye Ear Studio Dept of Art, Troy NY (S)
Horowitz, Sarah, *Curatorial Asst,* Colgate University, Picker Art Gallery, Hamilton NY
Horst, Randy, *Chmn Dept,* The University of Montana Western, Art Program, Dillon MT (S)
Horst, Randy, *Dir,* The University of Montana - Western, Art Gallery Museum, Dillon MT
Horsting, Archana, *Exec Dir,* Kala Institute, Kala Art Institute, Berkeley CA
Horstmann, Joy, *VPres,* Marion Art Center, Cecil Clark Davis Gallery, Marion MA
Horton, Christopher, *Assoc Prof,* University of Hartford, Hartford Art School, West Hartford CT (S)
Horton, David, *Assoc Prof,* William Paterson University, Dept Arts, Wayne NJ (S)
Horton, Malinda, *Interim Exec Dir,* Historic Pensacola Preservation Board, T.T. Wentworth Jr. Florida State Museum, Pensacola FL
Horton-Lopez, Ann, *Assoc Prof & Dir Grad Art Educ,* University of North Carolina at Pembroke, Art Dept, Pembroke NC (S)
Hortz Stanton, Laura, *Exec Dir,* Conservation Center for Art & Historic Artifacts, Philadelphia PA
Horvat, Krisjohn O, *Prof,* Rhode Island College, Art Dept, Providence RI (S)
Horvath, Albert, *COO & Under Secy Finance & Admin,* Smithsonian Institution, Smithsonian Institution Building (The Castle), Washington DC
Horvath, Annette, *Mem Services Coordr,* Saskatchewan Association of Architects, Saskatoon SK
Horvath, Robert, *Chmn,* Norman Rockwell Museum, Stockbridge MA
Horvath, Sharon, *Prof,* Purchase College, State University of New York, School of Art+Design, Purchase NY (S)
Horvay, Henrietta C, *Pres & Cur,* Goshen Historical Society, Goshen CT
Horvitz, Michael, *Secy,* Frick Collection, New York NY
Horwitz, Andrew, *Prog Dir,* Hebrew Union College, Skirball Cultural Center, Los Angeles CA
Hosey, Terrie, *Cur,* Art Association of Harrisburg, School & Galleries, Harrisburg PA
Hosford, John, *Visual Resources Cur,* New York State College of Ceramics at Alfred University, Scholes Library of Ceramics, Alfred NY
Hosford, Romy, *Asst Prof,* Roberts Wesleyan College, Department of Visual Art, Rochester NY (S)
Hoskins, W E, *Exec Dir,* San Francisco African-American Historical & Cultural Society, San Francisco CA
Hosterman, Bill, *Assoc Prof,* Grand Valley State University, Art & Design Dept, Allendale MI (S)
Hostetler, Lisa, *Cur Photog,* George Eastman Museum, Rochester NY
Hostetler, Soo, *Asst Prof,* University of Northern Iowa, Dept of Art, Cedar Falls IA (S)
Hostetter, David, *Cur Planetarium,* Lafayette Science Museum & Planetarium, Lafayette LA
Hotchkiss, Margit, *Deputy Dir Audience & Bus Devel,* Norman Rockwell Museum, Stockbridge MA
Hott, Carrie, *Prog Mgr Artists Residencies,* Kala Institute, Kala Art Institute, Berkeley CA
Hottle, Andrew, *Archivist,* SOHO20 Gallery, Brooklyn NY
Hottle, Max, *Guardian,* Mission San Miguel Museum, San Miguel CA
Houben, Anden, *Opers Mgr,* Kentuck Museum Association, Inc, Kentuck Art Center & Festival of the Arts, Northport AL
Houck, Jeremiah, *Asst Dir,* Colorado Springs Fine Arts Center, Bemis School of Art, Colorado Springs CO
Houck, Tracy, *Exec Dir,* Paris Gibson Square, Museum of Art, Great Falls MT
Houdek, Alesh, *Mktg Dir,* Art & Culture Center of Hollywood, Art Gallery/Multidisciplinary Cultural Center, Hollywood FL
Hough, Emanuel D, *Dir & Pres,* Shakespeare Ghost Town, Lordsburg NM
Hough, Katherine, *Chief Cur,* Palm Springs Art Museum, Palm Springs CA
Houghtaling, Kim, *Dir & Cur,* Art Gallery of Swift Current, Swift Current SK
Houghton, Charlotte, *Assoc Prof,* Pennsylvania State University, University Park, Dept of Art History, University Park PA (S)
Houghton, Melissa, *VPres,* American Architectural Foundation, Museum, Washington DC
Houle, Joy, *Exec Dir,* Saratoga County Historical Society, Brookside Museum, Ballston Spa NY
Houle, Matthew, *Cur Mus Coll,* University of Richmond, University Museums, Richmond VA
Hourahan, Richard, *Coll Mgr,* Queens Historical Society, Kingsland Homestead, Flushing NY
House, John, *Chair Prof,* University of Southern Mississippi, Dept of Art & Design, Hattiesburg MS (S)
House, Rowena, *Exec Dir,* Craft Council of Newfoundland & Labrador, Saint John's NF
Housefield, James, *Assoc Prof,* Texas State University - San Marcos, Dept of Art and Design, San Marcos TX (S)
Houser Barker, Kristen, *Pres,* Danville Museum of Fine Arts & History, Danville VA
Houser, Craig, *Lectr & Co-Dir Art History,* City College of New York, Art Dept, New York NY (S)
Houser, John, *Chief Info Officer,* Historical Society of Pennsylvania, Philadelphia PA
Houser, Thom, *Assoc Prof Interior Design,* University of Georgia, Franklin College of Arts & Sciences, Lamar Dodd School of Art, Athens GA (S)
Housh, Deb, *Art Educator,* Springfield Museum of Art, Springfield OH
Houston, Gay, *Pres,* Heart of West Texas Museum, Colorado City TX
Houston, Joe, *Cur,* Hallmark Cards, Inc, Hallmark Art Collection, Kansas City MO
Houston, Katie, *Coordr Mktg,* Kalamazoo Institute of Arts, Kalamazoo MI
Hovde, Amy, *Bus Mgr,* North Dakota Museum of Art, Grand Forks ND
Hoversten, Mark, *Dean,* North Carolina State University, College of Design, Raleigh NC (S)
Hovey, David, *Assoc Prof,* Illinois Institute of Technology, College of Architecture, Chicago IL (S)
Hovins, Kristen, *Prof,* Middlebury College, History of Art & Architecture Dept, Middlebury VT (S)
Howard, Andrew, *Chmn Dept,* Wheaton College, Art Dept, Norton MA (S)
Howard, Debbie, *Bus Mgr,* LaGrange Art Museum, LaGrange GA
Howard, Deborah, *Assoc Prof Drawing & Painting,* University of Denver, School of Art & Art History, Denver CO (S)
Howard, Hali, *Adjunct Instr,* Oklahoma State University Institute of Technology, School of Visual Communications, Okmulgee OK (S)
Howard, Jan, *Cur Prints, Drawings & Photos,* Rhode Island School of Design, Museum of Art, Providence RI
Howard, Joan, *Secy,* Pioneer Historical Museum of South Dakota, Hot Springs SD
Howard, Mallory, *Asst Cur,* Mark Twain, Research Library, Hartford CT
Howard, Nina, *Mktg,* Quint Projects, La Jolla CA
Howard, Robin, *Assoc Dir,* Morgan State University, James E Lewis Museum of Art, Baltimore MD

Howard, William, *Asst Prof,* Western Illinois University, Department of Art, Macomb IL (S)

Howard-Rogers, Kathryn, *Asst Prof,* Oakton Community College, Language Humanities & Art Divisions, Des Plaines IL (S)

Howe, Katherine S, *Dir,* Museum of Fine Arts, Houston, Rienzi Center for European Decorative Arts, Houston TX

Howe, Kathleen, *Dir,* The Pomona College, Claremont CA

Howe, Thomas, *Chair Art History,* Southwestern University, Sarofim School of Fine Art, Dept of Art & Art History, Georgetown TX (S)

Howell, Ashley, *Exec Dir,* Tennessee State Museum, Nashville TN

Howell, Elise, *Office Mgr,* Indianapolis Art Center, Marilyn K. Glick School of Art, Indianapolis IN

Howell, Jason, *Asst Prof,* Oral Roberts University, Art Dept, Tulsa OK (S)

Howell, Joyce B, *Assoc Prof,* Virginia Wesleyan College, Art Dept of the Humanities Div, Norfolk VA (S)

Howell, Marta, *Exec Dir,* Hershey Museum, Hershey PA

Howell, Maureen, *Grad Coordr - Art History,* University of Texas, Dept of Art & Art History, Austin TX (S)

Howell, Michael, *Collections Mgr & Registrar,* Colorado Springs Fine Arts Center, Taylor Museum, Colorado Springs CO

Howell, Michael, *Dir,* Albright College, Freedman Gallery, Reading PA

Howell, Robert, *Prof Photog,* California Polytechnic State University at San Luis Obispo, Dept of Art & Design, San Luis Obispo CA (S)

Howell, Tom, *Chmn,* Porterville College, Dept of Fine Arts, Porterville CA (S)

Hower, Robert, *Chmn,* University of Texas at Arlington, Art & Art History Department, Arlington TX (S)

Howes, Stephen, *Chmn,* Town of Cummington Historical Commission, Kingman Tavern Historical Museum, Cummington MA

Howick, Laura, *Dir Educ,* Fitchburg Art Museum, Fitchburg MA

Howk, Cynthia, *Res Coordr,* Landmark Society of Western New York, Inc, Wenrich Memorial Library, Rochester NY

Howkins, Mary Ball, *Prof,* Rhode Island College, Art Dept, Providence RI (S)

Howlett, Libby, *Coll Mgr,* Agecroft Association, Museum, Richmond VA

Hownion, Morris, *Chief Cataloguer,* New York City Technical College, Ursula C Schwerin Library, Brooklyn NY

Howorth-Bouman, Katherine, *Dir Educ,* Roberson Museum & Science Center, Binghamton NY

Hoydysh, Walter, *Dir Prog,* Ukrainian Institute of America, Inc, New York NY

Hoyer, Lindy, *Exec Dir,* Omaha Children's Museum, Omaha NE

Hoyt, Edward, *Pres,* Museum of the Hudson Highlands, Cornwall On Hudson NY

Hrehov, John, *Prof,* Indiana-Purdue University, Dept of Fine Arts, Fort Wayne IN (S)

Hrenko, Kelly, *Assoc Prof Art Educ,* University of Southern Maine, Dept of Art, Gorham ME (S)

Hriso, Peter, *Chmn Dept Art,* Missouri Western State University, Gallery 206 Foyer Gallery, Saint Joseph MO

Hriso, Peter, *Dept Chair, Assoc Prof,* Missouri Western State University, School of Fine Arts, Saint Joseph MO (S)

Hrivnak, Tom, *Dir Horticulture,* Stan Hywet, Akron OH

Hron, Vincent, *Assoc Prof,* Bloomsburg University, Dept of Art & Art History, Bloomsburg PA (S)

Hruba, Miloslava, *Study Room Supv & European Print Specialist,* Amherst College, Mead Art Museum, Amherst MA

Hsu, Lillian, *Dir Pub Art,* Cambridge Arts Council, CAC Gallery, Cambridge MA

Hu, Li, *Prof,* University of Wisconsin Oshkosh, Dept of Art, Oshkosh WI (S)

Hu, Xinran, *Assoc Prof,* University of Southern Indiana, Art & Design Dept, Evansville IN (S)

Hu, Zheng, *Exhib Designer,* University at Albany, State University of New York, University Art Museum, Albany NY

Huacuja-Person, Judith, *Asst Prof,* University of Dayton, Visual Arts Dept, Dayton OH (S)

Huang, Tien, *Dir,* Bau-Xi Gallery, Toronto ON

Hubbard, John D, *Prof,* Northern Michigan University, Dept of Art & Design, Marquette MI (S)

Hubbard, Marcia, *Treas,* Essex Historical Society and Shipbuilding Museum, Essex MA

Hubbard, Michael, *Instr,* Midland College, Art Dept, Midland TX (S)

Hubbard, Paul, *Chmn Fine Arts,* Moore College of Art & Design, Philadelphia PA (S)

Hubbard, Quatro, *Archivist,* Virginia Dept Historic Resources, Research Library, Richmond VA

Huber, Don, *Dir,* American Artists Professional League, Inc, New York NY

Huber, Fran, *Asst Dir Coll,* Louisiana State University, Museum of Art, Baton Rouge LA

Huberman, Anthony, *Dir & Chief Cur,* Capp Street Project, Wattis Institute, San Francisco CA

Huberman, Anthony, *Dir & Chief Cur,* California College of the Arts, CCAC Wattis Institute for Contemporary Arts, San Francisco CA

Huberman, Brian, *Assoc Prof,* Rice University, Visual & Dramatic Arts, Houston TX (S)

Hubert, Thomas, *Assoc Prof,* Mercyhurst University, Dept of Art, Erie PA (S)

Hubert, William Post, *Assoc Pres,* Marcella Sembrich Memorial Association Inc, Marcella Sembrich Opera Museum, Bolton Landing NY

Hubschmitt, Presley, *Admin Assistant,* Robert Louis Stevenson Museum, Museum, Saint Helena CA

Huckaby, Sedrick, *Vis Asst Prof,* University of Texas at Arlington, Art & Art History Department, Arlington TX (S)

Huddleson, Colleen, *Asst Dean,* University of Saint Francis, School of Creative Arts, Fort Wayne IN (S)

Hudson, Ayanna N, *Arts Educ Dir,* National Endowment for the Arts, Washington DC

Hudson, Eldred, *Assoc Prof,* University of North Carolina at Charlotte, Dept Art, Charlotte NC (S)

Hudson, James, *Video Production,* Art Institute of Pittsburgh, Pittsburgh PA (S)

Hudson, Kelly, *Deputy Dir,* Montalvo Center for the Arts, Saratoga CA

Hudson, Myrtle, *Information Resources Asst,* University of Michigan, Fine Arts Library, Ann Arbor MI

Hudson, Susan, *Dir Colls & Exhibitions,* Cincinnati Art Museum, Cincinnati Art Museum, Cincinnati OH

Hudson, Suzi, *Exec Dir,* White Bear Center for the Arts, Gallery, White Bear Lake MN

Hudson-Connors, Jenniffer, *Library and Archive Mgr,* Nelda C & H J Lutcher Stark Foundation, Stark Museum of Art, Orange TX

Huebler, Darcy, *Assoc Dean,* California Institute of the Arts, School of Art, Valencia CA (S)

Huebner, Carla, *Assoc Prof,* Mount Mary College, Art & Design Division, Milwaukee WI (S)

Huebner, Gregory, *Chmn,* Wabash College, Art Dept, Crawfordsville IN (S)

Huebner, Karla, *Assoc Prof,* Wright State University, Dept of Art & Art History, Dayton OH (S)

Huebner, Rosemarita, *Prof,* Mount Mary College, Art & Design Division, Milwaukee WI (S)

Huebner-Venezia, Carol, *Asst Prof,* C W Post Campus of Long Island University, School of Visual & Performing Arts, Brookville NY (S)

Huelsbergen, Deborah, *Prof, Dir Undergrad Studies (Graphic Design),* University of Missouri - Columbia, Dept of Art, Columbia MO (S)

Huelsmann, Mary, *Prof,* Saint Louis Community College at Meramec, Art Dept, Saint Louis MO (S)

Huerta, Benito, *Assoc Prof,* University of Texas at Arlington, Art & Art History Department, Arlington TX (S)

Huerta, Benito, *Dir & Cur,* University of Texas at Arlington, Gallery at UTA, Arlington TX

Hufbauer, Ben, *Assoc Prof,* University of Louisville, Allen R Hite Art Institute, Louisville KY (S)

Huff, David, *Educ,* Tom Thomson Memorial Art Gallery, Library/Archives, Owen Sound ON

Huff, Laura, *Deputy Dir,* Museum of Contemporary Art Denver, Denver CO

Huff, Robert, *Chmn,* Miami-Dade Community College, Arts & Philosophy Dept, Miami FL (S)

Huffman, Joan, *Park Supt,* Old Fort Harrod State Park Mansion Museum, Harrodsburg KY

Huffman, Leslie, *Admin Mgr,* CultureWorks, Richmond VA

Huffstutler Norton, Rebecca, *Exec Dir,* Frontier Times Museum, Bandera TX

Huftalen, Alison L, *Head Librn,* Toledo Museum of Art, Art Reference Library, Toledo OH

Huggett, Gretchen, *Head Weaving Dept,* Kalamazoo Institute of Arts, KIA School, Kalamazoo MI (S)

Huggins, Anita, *Admin Asst,* University of Memphis, Art Museum, Memphis TN

Huggins, Tavia, *Deputy Dir Fin,* ArtsConnection Inc, New York NY

Hughes, Ava, *Dir Arts Educ,* Arts Partnership of Greater Spartanburg, Inc, Chapman Cultural Center, Spartanburg SC

Hughes, Bailey, *Visitor Servs,* National Society of the Colonial Dames of America in The Commonwealth of Virginia, Wilton House Museum, Richmond VA

Hughes, Chad M, *Prof,* North Carolina Central University, Art Dept, Durham NC (S)

Hughes, Colleen, *2nd Vice Pres,* Cumberland Art Society Inc, Cookeville Art Gallery, Cookeville TN

Hughes, Dewane, *Asst Prof,* University of Texas at Tyler, Department of Art, School of Visual & Performing Arts, Tyler TX (S)

Hughes, Elaine, *Dir Colls,* Museum of Northern Arizona, Flagstaff AZ

Hughes, Gary, *History & Technology Cur,* New Brunswick Museum, Saint John NB

Hughes, George, *Painting,* University at Buffalo, State University of New York, Dept of Visual Studies, Buffalo NY (S)

Hughes, Hillary, *Asst to Dir,* Pensacola Museum of Art, Pensacola FL

Hughes, Holly E, *Coll Cur,* The Buffalo Fine Arts Academy, Albright-Knox Art Gallery, Buffalo NY

Hughes, Jane, *Asst Prof Interior Design,* Converse College, School of the Arts, Dept of Art & Design, Spartanburg SC (S)

Hughes, Jayne, *Educ Coordr,* Buffalo Arts Studio, Art Gallery, Buffalo NY

Hughes, Jeffrey, *Prof,* Webster University, Department of Art, Design & Art History, Webster Groves MO (S)

Hughes, Jessica, *Cur Asst,* Auburn University, Jule Collins Smith Museum of Fine Art, Auburn AL

Hughes, John, *Exec Dir,* Craigdarroch Castle Historical Museum Society, Victoria BC

Hughes, Julie, *Lectr,* Santa Clara University, Dept of Art & Art History, Santa Clara CA (S)

Hughes, Kevin, *Chief Admin Officer,* Connecticut Historical Society, Hartford CT

Hughes, Margaret, *Head Dept,* Butte College, Dept of Performing Arts, Oroville CA (S)

Hughes, Mary Jo, *Dir,* University of Victoria, The Legacy Art Gallery, Victoria BC

Hughes, Meg, *Cur Archives,* The Valentine, Richmond VA

Hughes, Michael, *Counsel,* American Artists Professional League, Inc, New York NY

Hughes, Michael, *Ref Libn,* New York University, Stephen Chan Library of Fine Arts, New York NY

Hughes, Savannah, *Special Events Mgr,* Albany Museum of Art, Albany GA

Hughes, Tarin, *Exec Dir,* AKA Artist Run Centre, Saskatoon SK

Hughes, Tonia, *Sr Lectr,* Georgia Southwestern State University, JEC Gallery & FAB Gallery, Americus GA
Hughley, John, *Prof,* North Carolina Central University, Art Dept, Durham NC (S)
Hughson, John, *Prof,* State University of New York at Fredonia, Dept of Art, Fredonia NY (S)
Hugo, Corina, *Cur Coll & Registrar,* Riley County Historical Society & Museum, Riley County Historical Museum, Manhattan KS
Hugo, Corina, *Registrar,* Riley County Historical Society & Museum, Seaton Library, Manhattan KS
Hugo, Kim, *Dir Mktg,* Wadsworth Atheneum Museum of Art, Hartford CT
Hui Tan, Boon, *Museum Dir,* Asia Society Museum, New York NY
Huisman, Carl, *Chmn Dept,* Calvin College, Art Dept, Grand Rapids MI (S)
Huldisch, Henriette, *Cur,* Massachusetts Institute of Technology, List Visual Arts Center, Cambridge MA
Hulen, Jeannie, *Dept Chair & Assoc Prof,* University of Arkansas, Art Dept, Fayetteville AR (S)
Hull, David, *Prin Librn,* San Francisco Maritime National Historical Park, Maritime Museum, San Francisco CA
Hull, John, *Chmn,* University of Colorado at Denver, College of Arts & Media Visual Arts Dept, Denver CO (S)
Hull, Lynne, *Jewelry & Metal Design,* North Seattle College, North Seattle College Dept of Art, Seattle WA (S)
Hull, Samantha, *Vis & Vol Coordr,* Sonoma Valley Museum of Art, Sonoma CA
Hull, Sarah, *Archivist,* Plainfield Public Library, Plainfield NJ
Hull, Vida, *Prof,* East Tennessee State University, College of Arts and Sciences, Dept of Art & Design, Johnson City TN (S)
Hulser, Richard, *Chief Librn,* Natural History Museum of Los Angeles County, Research Library, Los Angeles CA
Hulst, Connie, *Office Mgr,* North Dakota Museum of Art, Grand Forks ND
Humber, Sarah, *Cur,* Howard University, Architecture & Planning Library, Washington DC
Humbert, Gretchen, *CFO,* Natural History Museum of Los Angeles County, Los Angeles CA
Humbert, Marte, *Registrar,* New Art Center in Newton, Newtonville MA
Humbertson, Margaret, *Head Library & Archive Coll,* Springfield Museums, Connecticut Valley Historical Society,
Hume, Karen, *Exec Dir,* Capitol Arts Alliance, Houchens Gallery, Bowling Green KY
Hume, Naomi, *Assoc Prof & Chair,* Seattle University, Dept of Art & Art History, Seattle WA (S)
Humphrey, Beth, *Educ Cur,* Woodstock Artists Association & Museum, Woodstock NY
Humphrey, Charlie, *Exec Dir,* Pittsburgh Center for the Arts, Pittsburgh PA
Humphrey, Corinne, *Pub Rels,* Kimball Art Center, Park City UT
Humphrey, G Watts, *VChmn Bd,* Shaker Village of Pleasant Hill, Harrodsburg KY
Humphrey, Judy, *Prof,* Appalachian State University, Dept of Art, Boone NC (S)
Humphrey, Meaghan, *Exec Dir,* Ashtabula Arts Center, Ashtabula OH
Humphries, Jessica, *Admin Coordr,* Southern Alberta Art Gallery, Lethbridge AB
Humphries, Linda, *Secy, Fine Arts Div,* Grenfell Campus, Memorial University of Newfoundland, Division of Fine Arts, Visual Arts Program, Corner Brook NF (S)
Hundahl, Betsy, *Asst Dir,* Marblehead Arts Association, Inc, Marblehead MA
Hunder, Stephanie, *Prof,* Concordia University, Art and Design Department, Saint Paul MN (S)
Huneck, Gwendolyn, *Art Dir,* Stephen Huneck Gallery at Dog Mountain, Saint Johnsbury VT
Hung, Wu, *Consulting Cur,* University of Chicago, Smart Museum of Art, Chicago IL
Hungerford, Constance Cain, *Prof,* Swarthmore College, Dept of Art & Art History, Swarthmore PA (S)
Hunisak, John, *Prof,* Middlebury College, History of Art & Architecture Dept, Middlebury VT (S)
Hunsinger, Pat, *Instr,* Ithaca College, Fine Art Dept, Ithaca NY (S)
Hunt, Aimee, *Assoc Acad Cur,* University of Virginia, The Fralin Museum of Art at the University of Virginia, Charlottesville VA
Hunt, Amy, *Educator,* Washington County Museum of Fine Arts, Hagerstown MD
Hunt, Barbara, *Dir,* Artists Space, Irving Sandler Artists File, New York NY
Hunt, D Bradford, *VPres Research & Acad Progs,* The Newberry, Chicago IL
Hunt, Daniel, *Assoc Prof,* Kansas State University, Art Dept, Manhattan KS (S)
Hunt, Deborah, *Library Director,* Mechanics' Institute, San Francisco CA
Hunt, Gregory K, *Dean,* Catholic University of America, School of Architecture & Planning, Washington DC (S)
Hunt, Janice, *Bd Pres (V),* The Trustees of Reservations, The Mission House, Ipswich MA
Hunt, Jeffrey, *Bd Mem,* Utah Lawyers for the Arts, Salt Lake City UT
Hunt, Rebecca, *Educ Progs Coordr,* Krasl Art Center, Saint Joseph MI
Hunt, Susan, *Prof,* University of Wisconsin-Stout, Dept of Art & Design, Menomonie WI (S)
Hunter, Andrew, *Sr Cur,* Art Gallery of Guelph, Guelph ON
Hunter, David, *Head Librn & Music Librn,* University of Texas at Austin, Fine Arts Library, Austin TX
Hunter, Debora, *Asst Prof,* Southern Methodist University, Meadows School of the Arts - Division of Art, Dallas TX (S)
Hunter, Emily, *Dir Develop,* Indianapolis Art Center, Marilyn K. Glick School of Art, Indianapolis IN
Hunter, John, *Chief Cur,* Jekyll Island Museum, Jekyll Island GA
Hunter, Larry, *Security Deputy,* The Columbus Museum, Columbus GA
Hunter, Matthew, *Prof & Grad Prog Dir,* McGill University, Dept of Art History & Communication Studies, Montreal QC (S)
Hunter, Rob, *Exec Dir,* Vermont State Craft Center at Frog Hollow, Burlington VT
Huntington Fenn, Dan, *VPres,* Porter-Phelps-Huntington Foundation, Inc, Historic House Museum, Hadley MA
Huntley, Patty, *Mus Store Mgr,* The San Joaquin Pioneer & Historical Society, The Haggin Museum, Stockton CA
Huntley, Sondra, *Archivist,* Town of Cummington Historical Commission, Kingman Tavern Historical Museum, Cummington MA
Huntting, Nancy, *Contact,* Aesthetic Realism Foundation, New York NY (S)
Huntting, Nancy, *Listings Dept,* Aesthetic Realism Foundation, New York NY
Huntting, Nancy, *Listings Dept,* Aesthetic Realism Foundation, Eli Siegel Collection, New York NY
Huntting, Nancy, *Listings Dept,* Aesthetic Realism Foundation, Aesthetic Realism Foundation Library, New York NY
Hupfel, Gretchen, *Asst Prof Foundations,* University of Georgia, Franklin College of Arts & Sciences, Lamar Dodd School of Art, Athens GA (S)
Hurlburt, Roger, *Vis Instr Art History,* Florida Atlantic University, D F Schmidt College of Arts & Letters Dept of Visual Arts & Art History, Boca Raton FL (S)
Hurlbut, Geri, *Assoc Prof & Coordr Art Therapy,* Converse College, School of the Arts, Dept of Art & Design, Spartanburg SC (S)
Hurley, Tara, *Community Archivist,* Okanagan Heritage Museum, Kelowna Public Archives, Kelowna BC
Hurry, Robert J, *Registrar,* Calvert Marine Museum, Library, Solomons MD
Hurry, Robert J, *Registrar,* Calvert Marine Museum, Solomons MD
Hurst Wender, Jennifer, *Dir Mus Opers & Educ,* Preservation Virginia, Richmond VA
Hurst, K.C., *Dir Mktg & Commun,* Dallas Museum of Art, Dallas TX
Hurst, Larry, *Adjunct,* College of the Canyons, Art Dept, Santa Clarita CA (S)
Hurst, Ronald, *VPres Colls, Conservation & Museums,* Colonial Williamsburg Foundation, Abby Aldrich Rockefeller Folk Art Museum, Williamsburg VA
Hurst, Wendell, *Facilities Mgr & Security,* Hammonds House Museum, Atlanta GA
Hurst, William, *Dir Dept Arts & Science,* Dominican College of Blauvelt, Art Dept, Orangeburg NY (S)
Hurst-Wender, Jennifer, *Dir Mus Operations & Educ,* Preservation Virginia, John Marshall House, Richmond VA
Hurston, Robin, *Bd Mem,* Coquille Valley Art Association, Coquille OR
Hurt Chesterfield, Lee, *Ancient American Art,* Virginia Museum of Fine Arts, Richmond VA
Hurt, Cynthia, *Assoc Prof,* Tarrant County College, Art Dept, Hurst TX (S)
Hurt, Shannon L, *Activities & Communs Dir,* Arts Council of Southwestern Indiana, The Bower-Suhrheinrich Foundation Gallery, Evansville IN
Hurwitz, Jeffrey, *Instr,* Moravian College, Dept of Art, Bethlehem PA (S)
Husar, Janet, *Gift Shop Coordr,* Mankato Area Arts Council, Carnegie Art Center, Mankato MN
Husband, Timothy, *Cur Emeritus,* The Metropolitan Museum of Art, The Met Cloisters, New York NY
Husch, Gail, *Prof,* Goucher College, Art & Art History Dept, Baltimore MD (S)
Hushka, Rock, *Deputy Dir & Chief Cur,* Tacoma Art Museum, Tacoma WA
Hushka, Rock, *Deputy Dir & Chief Cur,* Tacoma Art Museum, Tacoma WA
Hussey, Kathryn, *Registrar,* Brick Store Museum, Kennebunk ME
Hussman, Dale, *Chmn Dept of Art,* Carlow College, Art Dept, Pittsburgh PA (S)
Huston, Alan, *Assoc Prof,* Winthrop University, Dept of Art & Design, Rock Hill SC (S)
Huston, John, *Assoc Prof Theater,* Lake Erie College, Fine Arts Dept, Painesville OH (S)
Hutchens, James, *Chmn Dept,* Ohio State University, Dept of Art Education, Columbus OH (S)
Hutcheson, Kay, *PT Instr,* Middle Georgia State University, College of Arts & Sciences, Media, Culture & the Arts, Cochran GA (S)
Hutchins, Grover M, *Prof Pathology,* Johns Hopkins University, School of Medicine, Dept of Art as Applied to Medicine, Baltimore MD (S)
Hutchins, Meg, *Mus Coordr,* 1890 House-Museum & Center for the Arts, Cortland NY
Hutchins, Rebecca, *Cur Colls,* Whatcom Museum, Bellingham WA
Hutchinson, Becka, *Mus Shop Mgr,* Creek Council House Museum, Okmulgee OK
Hutchinson, Brittany, *Community Engagement Manager,* City of El Paso, El Paso Museum of Archaeology, El Paso TX
Hutchinson, James, *CFO,* Santa Barbara Museum of Art, Library, Santa Barbara CA
Hutchinson, Jim, *Asst Prof,* Dallas Baptist University, Dept of Art, Dallas TX (S)
Hutchinson, Linda, *Instr,* Cuyahoga Valley Art Center, Cuyahoga Falls OH (S)
Hutchison, Jane C, *Prof,* University of Wisconsin, Madison, Dept of Art History, Madison WI (S)
Hutchison, Johannah, *Exec Dir,* International Sculpture Center, Hamilton NJ
Hutlova-Foy, Zora, *Deputy Dir Art Admin,* Seattle Art Museum, Seattle WA
Hutlova-Foy, Zora, *Mgr Exhibitions,* Seattle Art Museum, Dorothy Stimson Bullitt Library, Seattle WA
Hutson, Bill, *Instr,* Creighton University, Fine & Performing Arts Dept, Omaha NE (S)

Hutt, Ron, *Asst Prof,* University of Rhode Island, Dept of Art & Art History, Kingston RI (S)
Hutter, Cherie, *Chair,* Grace A Dow, Fine Arts Dept, Midland MI
Hutterer, Maile, *Asst Prof Art,* Western Illinois University, Department of Art, Macomb IL (S)
Hutto, Cary, *Dir Archives,* Historical Society of Pennsylvania, Philadelphia PA
Hutton, Brett, *Secy,* Rensselaer Newman Foundation Chapel + Cultural Center, The Gallery at the Chapel & Cultural Center, Troy NY
Hutton, Erin, *Dir,* Maine College of Art, The Institute of Contemporary Art, Portland ME
Hutton, John, *Prof,* Salem Academy & College, Art Dept, Winston-Salem NC (S)
Hutton, Kathleen, *Dir Educ,* Reynolda House Museum of American Art, Winston-Salem NC
Hutton, Matt, *Pres,* Haystack Mountain School of Crafts, Deer Isle ME
Hutzel, Jennifer, *Communs & Outreach Asst,* The American-Scandinavian Foundation, Scandinavia House: The Nordic Center in America, New York NY
Hutzel, Renaie, *Bd Pres,* Central Iowa Art Association, Inc, Art Reference Library, Marshalltown IA
Huun, Kathleen, *Instr,* Marylhurst University, Art Dept, Marylhurst OR (S)
Huxhold, Stacey, *Art, Music & Av Mgr,* Allen County Public Library, Art, Music & Audiovisual Services, Fort Wayne IN
Huynh, Phung, *Gallery Mgr,* Los Angeles Valley College, Art Gallery, Valley Glen CA
Hwangho, Imi, *Assoc Prof Sculpture,* University of Georgia, Franklin College of Arts & Sciences, Lamar Dodd School of Art, Athens GA (S)
Hyams, L Collier, *Asst Prof,* Georgetown University, Dept of Art & Art History, Washington DC (S)
Hyche, Jessica, *Dir Finance,* Pensacola Museum of Art, Pensacola FL
Hyde, Budge, *Prof,* Greenfield Community College, Art Dept, Greenfield MA (S)
Hyde, Marion, *Assoc Prof,* Utah State University, Dept of Art, Logan UT (S)
Hyde, Melissa, *Prof,* University of Florida, School of Art & Art History, Gainesville FL (S)
Hyde, Robb, *Exec Dir,* Wayne Center for the Arts, Wooster OH
Hyland, Alice R M, *Consulting Cur,* Art Complex Museum, Carl A Weyerhaeuser Library, Duxbury MA
Hyland, Matthew, *Dir,* Oakville Galleries, Centennial Square and Gairloch Gardens, Oakville ON
Hylen, Beth, *Reference & Educ Librn,* Corning Museum of Glass, Juliette K and Leonard S Rakow Research Library, Corning NY
Hylton, David, *Prof,* California State Polytechnic University, Pomona, Department of Art, Pomona CA (S)
Hyman, Wendy, *Librn,* Berkeley Public Library, Art & Music Department, Berkeley CA
Hynes, William, *Chmn Art Dept,* Shippensburg University, Art Dept, Shippensburg PA (S)
Hyslin, Richard P, *Prof Sculpture,* University of Texas Pan American, Art Dept, Edinburg TX (S)
Hyun, Kim, *Prof, Religion & Philosophy,* State College of Florida Manatee - Sarasota, Art, Design, Humanities, Bradenton FL (S)
Hébert, Jessica, *Libr,* Artexte Information Centre, Documentation Centre, Montreal QC
Iacono, Domenic J, *Dir,* Syracuse University, Art Collection, Syracuse NY
Iacono, Domenic J, *Dir,* Syracuse University, SUArt Galleries, Syracuse NY
Iannucci, Heather, *Historic Site Mgr,* New York State Office of Parks Recreation & Historic Preservation, John Jay Homestead State Historic Site, Katonah NY
Ianuzelli, Nicole, *Contact,* Rutgers, The State University of New Jersey, Mary H. Dana Women Artists Series, a Partnership of the Center for Women in the Arts & Humanities and Rutgers University Libraries, New Brunswick NJ
Iavicoli, Vincenzo, *Chair Product Design,* College for Creative Studies, Detroit MI (S)
Ibbitson, Roxie, *Registrar/Preparator,* Mount Allison University, Owens Art Gallery, Sackville NB
Ibrahim, Janet, *Instruction Mgr,* Delaplaine Visual Arts Education Center, Frederick MD
Ibur, James, *Prof,* Saint Louis Community College at Meramec, Art Dept, Saint Louis MO (S)
Ickes, Jennifer, *Head Registrar,* New Orleans Museum of Art, New Orleans LA
Ida, Richard, *Div Dean,* Solano Community College, Division of Fine & Applied Art & Behavioral Science, Fairfield CA (S)
Idelson, Jeffrey L, *Pres,* National Baseball Hall of Fame & Museum, Cooperstown NY
Iglesias, Lisa, *Asst Prof,* University of Florida, School of Art & Art History, Gainesville FL (S)
Igna, Mary Ann, *Cur,* Maricopa County Historical Society, Desert Caballeros Western Museum, Wickenburg AZ
Ignat, Lavinia, *Visitor Servs Mgr,* Museum of Fine Arts Houston, Bayou Bend Collection & Gardens, Houston TX
Ignatowich, William, *CFO,* Dahesh Museum of Art, Greenwich CT
Igwe, Kod, *Assoc Prof,* Claflin College, Dept of Art, Orangeburg SC (S)
Ikeda, Seiji, *Asst Prof,* University of Texas at Arlington, Art & Art History Department, Arlington TX (S)
Ikeda, Yoshiro, *Prof,* Kansas State University, Art Dept, Manhattan KS (S)
Ikemiya, Cheryl, *Dir Develop,* Japanese American National Museum, Los Angeles CA
Iki, Mari, *Guest Servs Mgr,* Pier 24 Photography, San Francisco CA
Iliescu, Sanda, *Studio Faculty,* University of Virginia, McIntire Dept of Art, Charlottesville VA (S)
Im, Sooyum, *Asst Prof,* California State Polytechnic University, Pomona, Department of Art, Pomona CA (S)
Im, Sooyun, *Asst Prof,* University of Wisconsin-Eau Claire, Dept of Art & Design, Eau Claire WI (S)
Imboden, Elis, *Dir Opers,* Stanford University, Dept of Art & Art History, Stanford CA (S)
Imeson, Katie, *Sec,* Florida Southern College, Department of Art & Art History, Lakeland FL (S)
Imm-Stroukoff, Eumie, *Dir Research Ctr,* Georgia O'Keeffe Museum, Research Center, Santa Fe NM
Immerman, Stephen D, *Pres,* Montserrat College of Art, Beverly MA (S)
Inabinett, Marian, *Cur Colls,* City of High Point, High Point Museum, High Point NC
Inada, Miles, *Prof,* Southern Oregon University, Art & Art History Dept, Ashland OR (S)
Incer, Eugenia, *Asst Dir Collections & Exhibitions,* University of Miami, Lowe Art Museum, Coral Gables FL
Indych-Lopez, Anna, *Assoc Prof & Chair,* City College of New York, Art Dept, New York NY (S)
Infinger, Jennifer, *Educ Dir,* LeMoyne Art Foundation, Center for the Visual Arts, Tallahassee FL
Ingalls, Sherrill, *Dir Communs,* San Jose Museum of Art, San Jose CA
Ingelright, Kelly, *Vis Asst Prof,* University of Texas at Arlington, Art & Art History Department, Arlington TX (S)
Inglis, Erik, *Asst Prof,* Oberlin College, Dept of Art, Oberlin OH (S)
Inglot, Joanne, *Assoc Prof,* Macalester College, Art & Art History Dept, Saint Paul MN (S)
Ingraham, Margaret, *Pres,* Virginia Center for the Creative Arts, Amherst VA
Inkster, Dana, *Media & Communs,* City of Lethbridge, Sir Alexander Galt Museum, Lethbridge AB
Inlow, Terry, *Prof,* Wilmington College, Art Dept, Wilmington OH (S)
Inman, Jan, *Instr,* La Sierra University, Art Dept, Riverside CA (S)
Inman, Jessie, *CEO,* Confederation Centre Art Gallery and Museum, Charlottetown PE
Inman, Marcie J, *Dir Exhibs & Educ Progs,* Irving Arts Center, Galleries & Sculpture Garden, Irving TX
Innella, Valerie, *Instr,* Casper College, Dept of Visual Arts, Casper WY (S)
Inselmann, Andrea, *Cur Modern & Contemp Art,* Cornell University, Herbert F Johnson Museum of Art, Ithaca NY
Iolascon, Filomena, *Educ & Outreach Mgr,* Pelham Art Center, Pelham NY
Ipson, Daniel A, *Dean Fine Arts,* Hartnell College, Art & Photography Dept, Salinas CA (S)
Irby, Frank, *Instr,* Pacific Northwest College of Art, Portland OR (S)
Irick, Chris, *Prof,* Munson-Williams-Proctor Arts Institute, Pratt MWP College of Art, Utica NY (S)
Irizarry Vizcarrondo, Jorge, *Exec Dir ICP,* Institute of Puerto Rican Culture, Museo de Arte Religioso Porta Coeli, San German PR
Irmer, Perri, *Pres & CEO,* DuSable Museum of African American History, Chicago IL
Irmscher, Laura, *Chief of Collections,* Boston Public Library, Central Library, Boston MA
Irvin, Kate, *Cur Costumes & Textiles,* Rhode Island School of Design, Museum of Art, Providence RI
Irvine, Karen, *Deputy Dir & Chief Cur,* Museum of Contemporary Photography, Columbia College Chicago, Chicago IL
Irvine, Mary, *Mus Protection & Vis Svcs Coordr,* Alaska State Museum, Juneau AK
Irvine-Stiver, Debra, *Instr,* Adrian College, Art & Design Dept, Adrian MI (S)
Irwin, Terry, *Prof & Head,* Carnegie Mellon University, School of Design, Pittsburgh PA (S)
Isaac, Joanne, *Mus Admin,* American Numismatic Society, New York NY
Isaac, Susan, *Pres,* Hutchinson Art Association, Hutchinson Art Center, Hutchinson KS
Isaacs, J Susan, *Cur,* Towson University, Center for the Arts Gallery, Towson MD
Isaacs, Judy, *Office Mgr & Bookkeeper,* Liberty Hall Historic Site, Liberty Hall Museum, Frankfort KY
Isaacson, Lynn, *Pres,* Snake River Heritage Center, Weiser ID
Isenbarger, Stacy, *Asst Prof,* University of Idaho College of Art & Architecture, Dept of Art & Design, Moscow ID (S)
Isenberg, E Duane, *Assoc Prof,* Mohawk Valley Community College, Utica NY (S)
Isenstadt, Sandy, *First VPres,* Society of Architectural Historians, Chicago IL
Isgett, Kevin, *Instr,* Bob Jones University, School of Fine Arts, Div of Art & Design, Greenville SC (S)
Isgett, Kevin, *Studio Dept Head,* Bob Jones University, School of Fine Arts, Div of Art & Design, Greenville SC (S)
Isham, Nina, *Colls Technician,* Lac du Flambeau Band of Lake Superior Chippewa Indians, George W Brown Jr Ojibwe Museum & Cultural Center, Lac Du Flambeau WI
Ishaque, Joan, *Admin,* Hawaii Pacific University, Art Gallery, Kaneohe HI
Ishikawa, Chiyo, *Cur European Painting,* Seattle Art Museum, Dorothy Stimson Bullitt Library, Seattle WA
Ishino, Catherine, *Asst Prof,* University of Minnesota, Duluth, Art Dept, Duluth MN (S)
Isken, Suzanne, *Exec Dir,* Craft and Folk Art Museum (CAFAM), Los Angeles CA
Ison, Susan, *Dir Cultural Svcs,* Loveland Museum/ Gallery, Loveland CO
Israel, Hannah, *Gallery Dir,* Columbus State University, Norman Shannon and Emmy Lou P Illges Gallery, Columbus GA
Istrabadi, Juliet, *Cur Ancient Art,* Indiana University, Eskenazi Museum of Art, Bloomington IN
Ivankine, Alex, *Finance Dir,* Canadian Art Foundation, Toronto ON
Ivanova, Silvia, *Registrar & Cur Educ,* State University of New York at Binghamton, Binghamton University Art Museum, Binghamton NY
Ivers, Louise, *Prof Emeritus,* California State University, Dominguez Hills, Art & Design Dept, Carson CA (S)

Iverson, Marsha, *Educ Dir,* Meridian Museum of Art, Meridian MS
Iverson, William, *Museum Exhibition Coordinator,* Miami-Dade College, MDC Museum of Art & Design, Miami FL
Ives, Laura, *Chmn,* Appalachian State University, Dept of Art, Boone NC (S)
Ivey, Marlene, *Assoc Prof & Chair, Design Div,* Nova Scotia College of Art & Design, Halifax NS (S)
Ivins, Jerry, *Acting Div Chmn & Dean Fine Arts,* San Jacinto Junior College, Division of Fine Arts, Pasadena TX (S)
Ivy, Carol Mohamed, *Cur,* The Ethel Wright Mohamed Stitchery Museum, Belzoni MS
Ivy, Krista, *Art Selector,* UCR ARTSblock, Tomas Rivera Library, Riverside CA
Ivy, Martin, *Gallery Assoc,* Houston Center For Photography, Houston TX
Ivy, Meredith, *Spec Events Mgr,* Mobile Museum of Art, Mobile AL
Ivy, Robert, *Exec VP & CEO,* American Institute of Architects, The Octagon Museum, Washington DC
Iwata, Chris, *Dir Humanities & Fine Arts,* Sacramento City College, Art Dept, Sacramento CA (S)
Izzo, Michele, *Treas,* American Watercolor Society, Inc, New York NY
J'Arbeloff, PA, *Dir Cambridge Science Festival,* Massachusetts Institute of Technology, MIT Museum, Cambridge MA
Jaber, George, *Chmn,* Community College of Allegheny County, Fine Arts Dept, West Mifflin PA (S)
Jablonski, Joyce, *Prof,* University of Central Missouri, Dept of Art & Design, Warrensburg MO (S)
Jablonski, Keith, *Cur,* Federal Reserve Bank of Minneapolis, Minneapolis MN
Jablonski, Mary Kathryn, *Asst Dir,* Skidmore College, Schick Art Gallery, Saratoga Springs NY
Jablow, Lisa, *Assoc Prof,* Johnson State College, Dept Fine & Performing Arts, Dibden Center for the Arts, Johnson VT (S)
Jabra, Lina, *Exec Dir,* Royal Canadian Academy of Arts, Toronto ON
Jack, Deborah, *MFA,* New Jersey City University, Art Dept, Jersey City NJ (S)
Jack, Jill, *Dir Library Svcs,* Coe College, Stewart Memorial Library & Gallery, Cedar Rapids IA
Jack, Marlene, *Assoc Prof,* College of William & Mary, Dept of Fine Arts, Williamsburg VA (S)
Jack, Meredith M, *Prof,* Lamar University, Art Dept, Beaumont TX (S)
Jacklitch, Paul, *Dir,* Baldwin-Wallace College, Fawick Art Gallery, Berea OH
Jacks, Philip, *Assoc Prof,* George Washington University, Dept of Art of Fine Arts & Art History, Washington DC (S)
Jackson, Anke, *Asst Dir,* Parrish Art Museum, Water Mill NY
Jackson, Arnold, *Dir Promotional Svcs,* American Society of Artists, Inc, Palatine IL
Jackson, Barbara, *Asst Librn & Pub Services,* University of Virginia, Fiske Kimball Fine Arts Library, Charlottesville VA
Jackson, Craig, *Colls Mgr,* Mechanics' Institute, San Francisco CA
Jackson, Duke, *Chmn,* Georgia Southwestern State University, Dept of Fine Arts, Americus GA (S)
Jackson, Emily, *Mus Opers & Communs Coord,* Brown University, Haffenreffer Museum of Anthropology, Providence RI
Jackson, Greg, *Archivist,* Academy of the New Church, Glencairn Museum, Bryn Athyn PA
Jackson, James, *Dir Security & Plant Operations,* Bob Jones University Museum & Gallery Inc, Greenville SC
Jackson, Jo Anne, *Dir Fin,* Christina Cultural Arts Center, Inc, Wilmington DE
Jackson, Joe, *Dir,* New Image Art, West Hollywood CA
Jackson, Julia, *MOWA Shop Manager,* Museum of Wisconsin Art, West Bend WI
Jackson, Kelli, *Head Jewelry Dept,* Kalamazoo Institute of Arts, KIA School, Kalamazoo MI (S)
Jackson, Kyle, *Audience Serv Mgr,* Painted Bride Art Center Gallery, Philadelphia PA
Jackson, Marcie, *Dir Educ & Curatorial Svcs,* Hill-Stead Museum, Farmington CT
Jackson, Margo, *Exec Asst,* Telfair Museums, Savannah GA
Jackson, Marian, *Chmn,* Wayne State University, Dept of Art & Art History, Detroit MI (S)
Jackson, Mark, *Grant Mgr,* Asheville Art Museum, Asheville NC
Jackson, Philip, *Asst Prof,* University of Mississippi, Department of Art, University MS (S)
Jackson, Phyllis, *Assoc Prof,* Pomona College, Dept of Art History, Claremont CA (S)
Jackson, Rafael, *Dir,* University of Puerto Rico, Mayaguez, Dept of Humanities, College of Fine Arts & Theory of Art Programs, Mayaguez PR (S)
Jackson, Robbyn, *Chief of Cultural Resources,* San Francisco Maritime National Historical Park, Maritime Library, San Francisco CA
Jackson, Robert, *Asst Prof Jewelry & Metalwork,* University of Georgia, Franklin College of Arts & Sciences, Lamar Dodd School of Art, Athens GA (S)
Jackson, Robin, *Chmn,* Treasure Valley Community College, Art Dept, Ontario OR (S)
Jackson, Stefanie, *Assoc Prof Drawing & Painting,* University of Georgia, Franklin College of Arts & Sciences, Lamar Dodd School of Art, Athens GA (S)
Jackson, Steve, *Cur Art & Photog,* Montana State University, Museum of the Rockies, Bozeman MT
Jackson, Steven, *Dir Finance & Admin,* American Textile History Museum, Lowell MA
Jackson, Tara, *Event Coordr,* The Columbian Theatre Foundation, Inc, Columbian Theatre Museum & Art Center, Wamego KS
Jackson, W Herbert, *Emeritus Prof,* Davidson College, Art Dept, Davidson NC (S)
Jackson, William D, *Prof,* Simon's Rock College of Bard, Visual Arts Dept, Great Barrington MA (S)
Jackson-Dumont, Sandra, *Chmn, Educ,* The Metropolitan Museum of Art, New York NY
Jackson-Reese, Carla, *Instr,* Tuskegee University, Liberal Arts & Education, Tuskegee AL (S)
Jacob, George, *Dir,* Ellen Noel Art Museum of the Permian Basin, Odessa TX
Jacob, Preminda, *Assoc Prof & Assoc Chair,* University of Maryland, Baltimore County, Intermedia & Digital Arts (IMDA), Dept of Visual Arts, Baltimore MD (S)
Jacobelli, Liz, *Board of Dirs Secy,* Guild of Creative Art, Shrewsbury NJ (S)
Jacobs, Amy, *Studio Collaborator & Educ Mgr,* Dieu Donne Papermill, Inc, Gallery, Brooklyn NY
Jacobs, Anita, *Dir Pub Progs,* Brooklyn Botanic Garden, Steinhardt Conservatory Gallery, Brooklyn NY
Jacobs, Bud, *Prof,* Niagara County Community College, Fine Arts Division, Sanborn NY (S)
Jacobs, Dan, *Dir Gallery,* University of Denver, School of Art & Art History, Denver CO (S)
Jacobs, Del, *Prof, Film,* State College of Florida Manatee - Sarasota, Art, Design, Humanities, Bradenton FL (S)
Jacobs, Jack, *Production Mgr,* Hostos Center for the Arts & Culture, Bronx NY
Jacobs, James, *Prof,* Weber State University, Dept of Visual Arts, Ogden UT (S)
Jacobs, Joyce, *Asst Prof,* Georgian Court University, Dept of Art, Lakewood NJ (S)
Jacobs, Lynn, *Prof,* University of Arkansas, Art Dept, Fayetteville AR (S)
Jacobs, Rich, *Dir,* New Image Art, West Hollywood CA
Jacobs, Steve, *Registration & Bldg Opers Mgr,* Plains Art Museum, Fargo ND
Jacobsen Bates, Esther, *CEO,* Elverhoj Museum of History and Art, Solvang CA
Jacobsen, Terry D, *Dir,* Carnegie Mellon University, Hunt Institute for Botanical Documentation, Pittsburgh PA
Jacobson, Cody, *Graphics & Communs Mgr,* Plains Art Museum, Fargo ND
Jacobson, Jake, *Assoc Prof,* University of Nebraska, Kearney, Dept of Art & Art History, Kearney NE (S)
Jacobson, Ken, *Head Div Arts,* Memorial University of Newfoundland, Sir Wilfred Grenfell College Art Gallery, Corner Brook NF
Jacobson, Lee, *Instr,* Chemeketa Community College, Dept of Humanities & Communications, Art Program, Salem OR (S)
Jacobson, Paul, *Chmn Div Language,* Western Nebraska Community College, Division of Language & Arts, Scottsbluff NE (S)
Jacobson, Shannon, *Admin Asst,* Pearl Fincher Museum of Fine Arts, Spring TX
Jacobson, Thora, *Exec Dir,* Philadelphia Art Alliance, Philadelphia PA
Jacobson, Tom, *Sr VPres Advancement,* Natural History Museum of Los Angeles County, Los Angeles CA
Jacobson-Sive, Emma, *Pub Rels,* Pasadena Museum of California Art, Pasadena CA
Jacoby, Mark, *1st VPres,* National Antique & Art Dealers Association of America, Inc, New York NY
Jacoby, Thomas J, *Art & Design Librn,* University of Connecticut, Art & Design Library, Storrs CT
Jacquemain, Patti, *Pres,* Wildling Art Museum, Solvang CA
Jacques, Michelle, *Chief Cur,* Art Gallery of Greater Victoria, Victoria BC
Jacques, Rhonda, *Box Office Coordr,* The Columbian Theatre Foundation, Inc, Columbian Theatre Museum & Art Center, Wamego KS
Jaeger, Tom, *Instr,* Judson University, School of Art, Design & Architecture, Elgin IL (S)
Jaffe, Amanda, *Dir Ceramics,* New Mexico State University, Art Dept, Las Cruces NM (S)
Jaffe, John G, *Dir,* Sweet Briar College, Mary Helen Cochran Library, Sweet Briar VA
Jager, Edwin, *Chmn,* University of Wisconsin Oshkosh, Dept of Art, Oshkosh WI (S)
Jagger, Emily, *Outreach Develop Coordr,* Cuesta College, Harold J Miossi Art Gallery, San Luis Obispo CA
Jagoda, Peter, *Adjunct Asst Prof,* Spokane Falls Community College, Fine Arts Dept, Spokane WA (S)
Jahns, Tim, *Educ Coordr,* City of Irvine, Irvine Fine Arts Center, Irvine CA (S)
Jakab, Peter, *Chief Cur,* National Air and Space Museum, Smithsonian Institution, Washington DC
Jakos, Aaron, *Preparator,* Colgate University, Picker Art Gallery, Hamilton NY
Jakubek, Frances, *Assoc Dir,* Arthur Griffin Center for Photographic Art, Griffin Museum of Photography, Winchester MA
James, Beth, *Exec Dir,* South Arkansas Arts Center, El Dorado AR
James, Dan, *Dean Fine & Liberal Arts,* Rocky Mountain College of Art & Design, Lakewood CO (S)
James, Dora, *Cur Educ,* Irvine Museum, Irvine CA
James, Hugh, *Treas,* Medina Railroad Museum, Medina NY
James, Joy, *Dept Chmn,* University of Western Ontario, Dept of Visual Arts, London ON (S)
James, Louise, *Dir & Cur,* Plains Indians & Pioneers Historical Foundation, Museum & Art Center, Woodward OK
James, Paige, *Mus Shop Mgr,* Historic Arkansas Museum, Little Rock AR
James, Pat, *Chief Interpretation,* Independence National Historical Park, Library, Philadelphia PA
James, Ray, *Facilities Mgr,* Rose Center & Council for the Arts, Morristown TN
James, Sara N, *Assoc Prof,* Mary Baldwin College, Dept of Art & Art History, Staunton VA (S)
James, Tasha, *Office Mgr,* Susquehanna Art Museum, Harrisburg PA

James, Virginia, *Admin Asst,* North Arkansas Community-Technical College, Art Dept, Harrison AR (S)
Jamison, Chelsea, *Finance Mgr,* United Indians of All Tribes Foundation, Daybreak Star Center Gallery, Seattle WA
Jamison, Margaret, *Instr,* Walla Walla Community College, Fine Arts Dept, Walla Walla WA (S)
Jammes, Michelle, *Mgr,* College of New Rochelle, Castle Gallery, New Rochelle NY
Jamra, Mark, *Instr,* Maine College of Art, Portland ME (S)
Jamro, Ron, *Dir,* History Museum of Mobile, Mobile AL
Jancosek, Pat, *Asst Prof,* Saint Mary-of-the-Woods College, Art Dept, Saint Mary of the Woods IN (S)
Jancourt, Jan, *Prof,* Minneapolis College of Art & Design, Minneapolis MN (S)
Janecek, James, *Asst Prof,* Providence College, Art & Art History Dept, Providence RI (S)
Janes, Todd, *Exec Dir,* Latitude 53 Contemporary Visual Culture, Edmonton AB
Janian, Christopher, *Pres,* Maryland Art Place, Baltimore MD
Janick, Richard, *Art Hist Instr,* Monterey Peninsula College, Art Dept/Art Gallery, Monterey CA (S)
Jankauskas, Jennifer, *Cur Art,* Montgomery Museum of Fine Arts, Montgomery AL
Jankauskas, Jennifer, *Cur Art,* Montgomery Museum of Fine Arts, Library, Montgomery AL
Jankawski, Andrew, *Publicity Coordinator,* Portland State University, White Gallery, Portland OR
Janke, James, *Assoc Prof,* Dakota State University, College of Liberal Arts, Madison SD (S)
Janken, Amy, *Educ Coordr,* Elmhurst Art Museum, Elmhurst IL
Jankowski, Andrew, *Publicity Coordinator,* Portland State University, Littman Gallery, Portland OR
Jankowski, Edward, *Asst Prof,* Monmouth University, Dept of Art & Design, West Long Branch NJ (S)
Jankowski, Leslie, *Dir Library Servs,* Columbus College of Art & Design, Packard Library, Columbus OH
Jankowski, Leslie, *Tech Svcs Librn,* Columbus College of Art & Design, Packard Library, Columbus OH
Jannotte, Nicole, *Foundation Exec Dir,* New Jersey State Museum, Fine Art Bureau, Trenton NJ
Janoskey, Pam, *Treas,* Carteret County Historical Society, The History Place, Morehead City NC
Janosy, Mimi, *Photog,* Antonelli Institute, Professional Photography & Commercial Art, Erdenheim PA (S)
Janov, Danie, *VPres,* Blacksburg Regional Art Association, Blacksburg VA
Janowich, Ron, *Assoc Prof,* University of Florida, School of Art & Art History, Gainesville FL (S)
Jans-Duffy, Kathleen, *Colls Mgr,* Seneca Falls Historical Society Museum, Seneca Falls NY
Jansen, Catherine, *Instr,* Bucks County Community College, Fine Arts Dept, Newtown PA (S)
Jansen, Charles, *Instr,* Middle Tennessee State University, Art Dept, Murfreesboro TN (S)
Jansen, Spencer, *Mgr Mem,* Arkansas Arts Center, Little Rock AR (S)
Jansma, Linda, *Sr Cur,* The Robert McLaughlin Gallery, Oshawa ON
Janssen, Suzanne, *Bus Svcs,* Loveland Museum/ Gallery, Loveland CO
Janz, Rita, *Art Dir,* Balzekas Museum of Lithuanian Culture, Chicago IL
Janzen, Gesine, *Asst Prof Printmaking,* Montana State University, School of Art, Bozeman MT (S)
Jaojoco, Patrick, *Asst Cur,* Art in General, Brooklyn NY
Jaramillo, Karla, *CFO,* Inquilinos Boricuas en Accion (IBA), Villa Victoria Center for the Arts, Boston MA
Jardine, Pam, *Cur Native American Art,* Montclair Art Museum, Montclair NJ
Jardine, Sally, *Pres,* Junction City Arts Council Gallery, Junction City KS
Jarnot, Jenn, *Instr Art,* Baker University, Dept of Mass Media & Visual Arts, Baldwin City KS (S)
Jarosi, Susan, *Asst Prof,* University of Louisville, Allen R Hite Art Institute, Louisville KY (S)
Jarvis, Doug, *Guest Cur,* Open Space, Victoria BC
Jarvis, Dwayne, *Dir Finance,* Storm King Art Center, New Windsor NY
Jarvis, John, *Dir,* Bay Path College, Dept of Art, Longmeadow MA (S)
Jaskot, Paul, *Asst Prof,* DePaul University, Dept of Art, Chicago IL (S)
Jaskulski, Faith, *Research Coordr,* North Tonawanda History Museum, North Tonawanda NY
Jason, Christine, *Operations Manager,* Hambidge Center for Creative Arts & Sciences, Rabun Gap GA
Jaster, Monica, *Finance Mgr,* Houston Center For Photography, Houston TX
Jauch, Patricia, *Treas,* Shores Memorial Museum, Lyndon Center VT
Jaus, Bonme, *Gift Shop Mgr,* Tubac Center of the Arts, Santa Cruz Valley Art Association, Tubac AZ
Javier, Joel, *Educ Mgr,* Intuit: The Center for Intuitive & Outsider Art, Chicago IL
Javorski, Susanne, *Art Librn,* Wesleyan University, OLIN Memorial Library, Middletown CT
Jay, Rebel, *Dir,* Colby Community College, Art Dept, Colby KS (S)
Jay, Tonya, *Sales Assoc,* Providence Gallery, Charlotte NC
Jean, Anne-Marie, *Exec Dir,* Conseil des Arts du Quebec (CATQ), Diagonale, Centre des arts et des fibres du Quebec, Montreal QC
Jeanbz, Danielle, *Exec Dir,* Chatham Historical Society, The Atwood House Museum, Chatham MA
Jebsen, Mary, *Asst Dir,* New Mexico Department of Cultural Affairs, New Mexico Museum of Art, Unit of NM Dept of Cultural Affairs, Santa Fe NM
Jech, Christa, *Library Services Specialist,* Laguna College of Art & Design, Dennis & Leslie Power Library, Laguna Beach CA
Jedda McNab, Barbara, *Cur,* American Kennel Club, Reference Library, Saint Louis MO
Jedda McNab, Barbara, *Cur & Mgr,* American Kennel Club, Museum of the Dog, Saint Louis MO
Jeffcoat, Kristy, *Sr Paintings Conservator,* Midwest Art Conservation Center, Minneapolis MN
Jeffecoat, Kristy, *Sr Paintings Conservator,* Midwest Art Conservation Center, Minneapolis MN
Jefferies, Eric, *Head Dept,* Atlanta Technical Institute, Visual Communications Class, Atlanta GA (S)
Jeffers, Jim, *Adjunct Asst Prof,* Drew University, Art Dept, Madison NJ (S)
Jeffers, Susan, *Gallery Coordr,* State University of New York at Ulster, Muroff-Kotler Visual Arts Gallery, Stone Ridge NY
Jeffery, Jonathan, *Librn,* Western Kentucky University, Kentucky Library & Museum, Bowling Green KY
Jeffett, William, *Cur Exhibs,* Salvador Dali, Library, Saint Petersburg FL
Jehle, Michael, *CEO,* Fairfield Historical Society, Fairfield Museum & History Center, Fairfield CT
Jemmson-Pollard, Dianne, *Chmn,* Texas Southern University, College of Liberal Arts & Behavioral Sciences, Houston TX (S)
Jendrzejewski, Andrew, *Chmn,* Vincennes University Junior College, Humanities Art Dept, Vincennes IN (S)
Jenkins, Delanie, *Assoc Prof,* University of Pittsburgh, Dept of Studio Arts, Pittsburgh PA (S)
Jenkins, Erik, *Asst Dean/Asst Prof,* Catholic University of America, School of Architecture & Planning, Washington DC (S)
Jenkins, Erin, *Opers Mgr,* Brattleboro Museum & Art Center, Brattleboro VT
Jenkins, Greg, *Opers Mgr & Chief Prep,* Gibbes Museum of Art, Charleston SC (S)
Jenkins, Hugh, *Brd Chmn,* Volcano Art Center Gallery, Hawaii Volcanoes National Park HI
Jenkins, John, *Pres,* The Illinois Institute of Art - Chicago, Chicago IL (S)
Jenkins, Sabrina, *Gallery Asst,* Cuesta College, Harold J Miossi Art Gallery, San Luis Obispo CA
Jenkins, Sydney, *Gallery Dir,* The Art Galleries of Ramapo College, Mahwah NJ
Jenkins, Ulysses, *Assoc Prof Video, African American Studies,* University of California, Irvine, Studio Art Dept, Irvine CA (S)
Jenkins, Virginia, *Chmn,* Grand Valley State University, Art & Design Dept, Allendale MI (S)
Jenkner, Ingrid, *Dir Art Gallery,* Mount Saint Vincent University, MSVU Art Gallery, Halifax NS
Jenneman, Eugene A, *Dir Mus,* Northwestern Michigan College, Dennos Museum Center, Traverse City MI
Jenner, Anne, *Pacific Northwest Cur,* University of Washington, Univ of Washington Libraries, Special Collections, Seattle WA
Jennings, Corrine, *Dir,* Kenkeleba House, Inc, Kenkeleba Gallery, New York NY
Jennings, David, *Dir,* Akron-Summit County Public Library, Fine Arts Division, Akron OH
Jennings, DeAnn, *Instr,* Los Angeles Harbor College, Art Dept, Wilmington CA (S)
Jennings, Patrick, *Educ Coordr,* Pensacola Museum of Art, Pensacola FL
Jensen, Carl, *Asst Prof,* University of Southern Colorado, Dept of Art, Pueblo CO (S)
Jensen, Elisa, *Dir Prog,* New York Studio School of Drawing, Painting & Sculpture, New York NY (S)
Jensen, Heidi, *Prof,* University of Wisconsin College - Marinette, Art Dept, Marinette WI (S)
Jensen, Hilbert J, *Mus Asst,* The Agricultural Memories Museum, Penn Yan NY
Jensen, Jan, *Exec Admin,* Hillwood Museum & Gardens Foundation, Hillwood Estate Museum & Gardens, Washington DC
Jensen, Jennifer R, *Owner & Operator,* The Agricultural Memories Museum, Penn Yan NY
Jensen, Karen, *Dir Visitor Experience,* Royal Alberta Museum, Royal Alberta Museum, Edmonton AB
Jensen, Leslie D, *Cur Weapons,* United States Military Academy, West Point Museum, West Point NY
Jensen, Natalia, *Instr,* Clarion University of Pennsylvania, Dept of Art, Clarion PA (S)
Jensen, Pam, *Site Supervisor,* Jeffers Petroglyphs Historic Site, Comfrey MN
Jensen-Inman, Leslie, *Lectr,* University of Tennessee at Chattanooga, Dept of Art, Chattanooga TN (S)
Jent, Deanna, *Assoc Prof,* Fontbonne University, Fine Art Dept, Saint Louis MO (S)
Jentleson, Katherine, *Cur Folk & Self-Taught Art,* High Museum of Art, Atlanta GA
Jeong, E K, *Assoc Prof,* Southwestern Oklahoma State University, Art, Communication & Theatre, Weatherford OK (S)
Jercich, George, *Prof Studio Art,* California Polytechnic State University at San Luis Obispo, Dept of Art & Design, San Luis Obispo CA (S)
Jerger, Holly, *Cur Exhib,* Craft and Folk Art Museum (CAFAM), Los Angeles CA
Jernegan, Jeremy, *Assoc Prof,* Tulane University, Sophie H Newcomb Memorial College, New Orleans LA (S)
Jerolmon, Linda, *Mem,* Yale University, Yale University Art Gallery, New Haven CT
Jerry, Jane, *Pres,* Cheekwood Nashville's Home of Art & Gardens, Education Dept, Nashville TN (S)
Jery, Jane, *Dir,* The Bascomb, Highlands NC
Jessop, F Bradley, *Chair,* East Central University, School of Fine Arts, Ada OK (S)
Jessup, Robert, *Prof Drawing & Painting,* University of North Texas, College of Visual Arts & Design, Denton TX (S)
Jette, Carol, *Dir,* Copper Village Museum & Arts Center, Library, Anaconda MT
Jevack, Lisa, *Asst to Dir,* University of Virginia, The Fralin Museum of Art at the University of Virginia, Charlottesville VA
Jewell, Christine, *Dir Educ,* Fairfield Historical Society, Fairfield Museum & History Center, Fairfield CT
Jewell, Jeff, *Photo Archives Historian,* Whatcom Museum, Bellingham WA
Jewell, Linda, *Chair, Dept Landscape Architecture & Environmental Planning & Prof Landscape*

Architecture & Urban Design, University of California, Berkeley, College of Environmental Design, Berkeley CA (S)
Jewell, Robert, *CEO & Pres,* Brookgreen Gardens, Murrells Inlet SC
Jhashi, Tamara, *Assoc Prof,* Oakland University, Dept of Art & Art History, Rochester MI (S)
Jian, Li, *Cur East Asian Art,* Virginia Museum of Fine Arts, Richmond VA
Jiang, Lin Xia, *Interim Chair,* State University of New York College at Buffalo, Fine Arts Dept, Buffalo NY (S)
JianXin, Xue, *Cur Chinese Art,* New England Center for Contemporary Art, Brooklyn CT
Jicha, Jon, *Prof,* Western Carolina University, Dept of Art/College of Arts & Science, Cullowhee NC (S)
Jilg, Joyce, *Instr,* Fort Hays State University, Dept of Art & Design, Hays KS (S)
Jimenez, Dan'etta, *Dir Educ,* Caribbean Cultural Center African Diaspora Institute, Cultural Arts Organization & Resource Center, New York NY
Jimenez, Pancho, *Sr Lectr,* Santa Clara University, Dept of Art & Art History, Santa Clara CA (S)
Jimenez-Torres, Maria, *Exec Dir,* Plaza de la Raza Cultural Center, Los Angeles CA
Jiminez, Gabriel, *Admin Office Asst,* Plaza de la Raza Cultural Center, Los Angeles CA
Jiminez, Ingrid M, *Pres,* La Casa del Libro Museum, San Juan PR
Jiminez, Jill Berk, *CEO & Dir,* Berkeley Art Center, Berkeley CA
Jimison, Tom, *Cur,* Middle Tennessee State University, Baldwin Photographic Gallery, Murfreesboro TN
Jipson, Jim, *Assoc Prof,* University of West Florida, Dept of Art, Pensacola FL (S)
Jirges, Barbara, *Dir,* Bismarck State College, The Else Forde Gallery, Bismarck ND (S)
Jo-Smith, Tyler, *Assoc Prof Art History,* University of Virginia, McIntire Dept of Art, Charlottesville VA (S)
Joannette, Michelle, *Exec Dir,* Guilde canadienne des metiers d'art, Canadian Guild of Crafts, Montreal QC
Joassin, Odile, *Asst Cur,* The Art Institute of Chicago, Department of Textiles, Textile Society, Chicago IL
Johaneman, Elaine, *Bookkeeper,* Lehigh Valley Heritage Center, Allentown PA
Johanning, Jared, *IT Support Technician,* University of Kansas, Spencer Museum of Art, Lawrence KS
Johansen, Chris, *Dir,* New Image Art, West Hollywood CA
Johanson, David, *Asst Prof,* North Park University, Art Dept, Chicago IL (S)
Johanson, Melanie, *Mus Asst,* Cornell Museum of Art and American Culture, Delray Beach FL
Johanssen, Betty, *Art Instr,* Big Bend Community College, Art Dept, Moses Lake WA (S)
John, Deborah, *Asst Prof,* Mercyhurst University, Dept of Art, Erie PA (S)
John, Jessy, *Chmn,* Troy State University, Dept of Art & Classics, Troy AL (S)
Johns, Jennifer, *Cur,* Ruthmere Museum, Robert B. Beardsley Arts Reference Library, Elkhart IN
Johns, Shellie, *Coordr Conf,* Chadron State College, Memorial Hall Main Gallery & Memorial Hall Gallery 239, Chadron NE
Johnsen, Emily, *Gallery Mgr,* William Paterson University, University Galleries, Wayne NJ
Johnson Jr, Charles W, *Chmn,* University of Richmond, Dept of Art and Art History, Richmond VA (S)
Johnson, Al, *Security Deputy,* The Columbus Museum, Columbus GA
Johnson, Alan, *Dir,* Church of Jesus Christ of Latter-Day Saints, Church History Museum, Salt Lake City UT
Johnson, Alex, *Dir Digital Progs,* Koffler Center of the Arts, Toronto ON (S)
Johnson, Alford, *Pres,* Taos Center for the Arts, Stables Gallery, Taos NM
Johnson, Amber, *Graphic Design & Mktg Coordr,* Pensacola Museum of Art, Pensacola FL
Johnson, Amy, *Librn,* Montgomery Museum of Fine Arts, Montgomery AL
Johnson, Amy, *Librn,* Montgomery Museum of Fine Arts, Library, Montgomery AL
Johnson, Angela, *Exhibitions Coordinator,* Wisconsin Academy of Sciences, Arts & Letters, James Watrous Gallery, Madison WI
Johnson, Anne, *Instr,* Pacific Northwest College of Art, Portland OR (S)
Johnson, Anne-Marie, *Visitor Experience Mgr,* Environment Canada - Parks Canada, Laurier House, National Historic Site, Ottawa ON
Johnson, Audrey, *Exec Asst,* Hammonds House Museum, Atlanta GA
Johnson, Bob, *Trustee, Sarasota, FL,* JMW Turner Museum, Sarasota FL
Johnson, Brad, *Exhibs Dir,* Oglebay Institute, Stifel Fine Arts Center, Wheeling WV
Johnson, Brad, *Instr,* West Liberty State College, Div Art, West Liberty WV (S)
Johnson, Brett John, *Dir Visual Arts,* Lorton Arts Foundation, Workhouse Arts Center, Lorton VA
Johnson, Byron, *Exec Dir,* Texas Ranger Hall of Fame & Museum, Waco TX
Johnson, Carla C, *Dir,* New York State College of Ceramics at Alfred University, Scholes Library of Ceramics, Alfred NY
Johnson, Carlyle, *Instr,* Middle Tennessee State University, Art Dept, Murfreesboro TN (S)
Johnson, Charlene, *Researcher,* Alton Museum of History & Art, Inc, Alton IL
Johnson, Charles, *Res Librn,* Museum of Ventura County, Ventura CA
Johnson, Charlie, *Instr,* Southern University in New Orleans, Fine Arts & Philosophy Dept, New Orleans LA (S)
Johnson, Cherry, *Registrar & Archivist,* Tellus Northwest Georgia Science Museum, Cartersville GA
Johnson, Chris, *Exec Dir,* Vesterheim Norwegian-American Museum, Decorah IA
Johnson, Cleveland, *Exec Dir,* Morris Museum, Morristown NJ
Johnson, Colleen, *Admin Asst,* Keene State College, Thorne-Sagendorph Art Gallery, Keene NH
Johnson, Craig, *Acting Head,* Utah State University, Dept of Landscape Architecture Environmental Planning, Logan UT (S)
Johnson, David J, *Mus Specialist,* Headquarters Fort Monroe, Dept of Army, Casemate Museum, Hampton VA
Johnson, David, *Ed Mus Publications,* New Orleans Museum of Art, New Orleans LA
Johnson, David, *Instr,* Indian Hills Community College, Dept of Art, Centerville IA (S)
Johnson, Dawn, *Cur Educ,* Tampa Museum of Art, Judith Rozier Blanchard Library, Tampa FL
Johnson, Dawn, *Cur Educ,* Tampa Museum of Art, Tampa FL
Johnson, Deborah J, *Dir Develop,* The Heckscher Museum of Art, Huntington NY
Johnson, Deborah, *Asst Prof,* Providence College, Art & Art History Dept, Providence RI (S)
Johnson, Diane, *Chmn Art History,* College of Charleston, School of the Arts, Charleston SC (S)
Johnson, Dorothy, *Cur,* Historical Society of Bloomfield, Bloomfield NJ
Johnson, Dorothy, *Dir,* University of Iowa, School of Art & Art History, Iowa City IA (S)
Johnson, Douglas C, *Exec Dir,* McLean County Art Association, McLean County Arts Center, Bloomington IL
Johnson, Eileen, *Exec Dir,* Texas Tech University, Museum of Texas Tech University, Lubbock TX
Johnson, Eric, *Dean,* Dakota State University, College of Liberal Arts, Madison SD (S)
Johnson, Eric, *Prof Photog,* California Polytechnic State University at San Luis Obispo, Dept of Art & Design, San Luis Obispo CA (S)
Johnson, Ezra, *Asst Prof,* University of South Florida, School of Art & Art History, Tampa FL (S)
Johnson, Frederic P, *Pres Historical Society,* Waterville Historical Society, Redington Museum, Waterville ME
Johnson, Gary, *Pres,* Chicago History Museum, Chicago IL
Johnson, Gloria J, *Security Chief,* United States Military Academy, West Point Museum, West Point NY
Johnson, Hannah, *Educ Prog Coordr,* McLean County Historical Society, McLean County Museum of History, Bloomington IL
Johnson, Harvey, *Art Coordr & Assoc Prof,* Texas Southern University, College of Liberal Arts & Behavioral Sciences, Houston TX (S)
Johnson, Herbert H, *Assoc Prof,* Rochester Institute of Technology, School of Printing Management & Sciences, Rochester NY (S)
Johnson, Isabelle, *Librn,* Women's Art Association of Canada, Library, Toronto ON
Johnson, James, *Chmn Photog & Digital Arts,* Moore College of Art & Design, Philadelphia PA (S)
Johnson, Jane, *Community Svcs,* Westerly Public Library, Hoxie Gallery, Westerly RI
Johnson, Jeremy L, *Asst Prof,* University of Nebraska at Omaha, School of the Arts, Omaha NE (S)
Johnson, Jeremy W, *Pres & CEO,* Historical Society of Palm Beach County, The Richard and Pat Johnson Palm Beach County History Museum, West Palm Beach FL
Johnson, Jessica, *Visitor Servs Coordr,* University of Pennsylvania, Institute of Contemporary Art, Philadelphia PA
Johnson, Jim, *Dean Div,* Modesto Junior College, Arts Humanities & Communications Division, Modesto CA (S)
Johnson, Joan, *Dir Central Library Svcs,* Milwaukee Public Library, Art, Music & Recreation Dept, Milwaukee WI
Johnson, Joe, *Asst Prof (Photog),* University of Missouri - Columbia, Dept of Art, Columbia MO (S)
Johnson, Jolie, *Mgr Mktg & Mem,* University of Louisiana at Lafayette, Paul and Lulu Hilliard University Art Museum, Lafayette LA
Johnson, Julie, *Asst Prof,* Utah State University, Dept of Art, Logan UT (S)
Johnson, Julie, *Asst Prof,* University of Texas at San Antonio, Dept of Art & Art History, San Antonio TX (S)
Johnson, Julie, *Director/Interim & Instr,* Illinois Wesleyan University, School of Art, Bloomington IL (S)
Johnson, Justin, *Gallery Dir,* University of Saint Francis, School of Creative Arts, John P Weatherhead Gallery & Lupke Gallery, Fort Wayne IN
Johnson, Kat, *Educ Coordr,* University of Maine, Museum of Art, Bangor ME
Johnson, Kirk, *Sant Dir,* National Museum of Natural History, Smithsonian Institution, Washington DC
Johnson, Kris, *Photographer,* City of Springdale, Shiloh Museum of Ozark History, Springdale AR
Johnson, Kristen, *Pres (V),* Art League of Houston, Houston TX
Johnson, Larry, *Chmn Dept,* California State University, Fullerton, Art Dept, Fullerton CA (S)
Johnson, Laura, *Instr,* Linfield College, Department of Art & Visual Culture, McMinnville OR (S)
Johnson, Lee, *Art Area Coordr,* Western State College of Colorado, Quigley Hall Art Gallery, Gunnison CO
Johnson, Lia, *Assoc Prof,* University of Wisconsin-Eau Claire, Dept of Art & Design, Eau Claire WI (S)
Johnson, Linda, *Chair, Prof Art, Graphic Design,* Florida Atlantic University, D F Schmidt College of Arts & Letters Dept of Visual Arts & Art History, Boca Raton FL (S)
Johnson, Lisa, *Dir,* Farmington Village Green & Library Association, Stanley-Whitman House, Farmington CT
Johnson, Liz, *Edu Asst,* The Art Museum of Eastern Idaho, Idaho Falls ID
Johnson, Lorna, *Exec Dir,* Red Deer & District Museum & Archives, Red Deer AB

Johnson, Lydia, *Dir,* Southern Utah University, Braithwaite Fine Arts Gallery, Cedar City UT
Johnson, Margaret, *Assoc Prof,* Winthrop University, Dept of Art & Design, Rock Hill SC (S)
Johnson, Margaret, *Prog Dir Art Educ,* State University of New York at New Paltz, Art Education Program, New Paltz NY (S)
Johnson, Mark M, *Dir,* Montgomery Museum of Fine Arts, Montgomery AL
Johnson, Mark M, *Dir,* Montgomery Museum of Fine Arts, Library, Montgomery AL
Johnson, Mark, *Board Pres,* Peoria Historical Society, Peoria IL
Johnson, Mark, *Instr,* Maine College of Art, Portland ME (S)
Johnson, Martha K, *Dir,* Randolph College, Maier Museum of Art, Lynchburg VA
Johnson, Mary, *Bookkeeper,* Hickory Museum of Art, Inc, Hickory NC
Johnson, Mary, *Registrar,* California Center for the Arts, Escondido Museum, Escondido CA
Johnson, Melvin, *Asst Preparator,* Mississippi Museum of Art, Howorth Library, Jackson MS
Johnson, Michael, *Assoc Prof,* Murray State University, Dept of Art, Murray KY (S)
Johnson, Michael, *Prof Art,* University of Puget Sound, Dept of Art & Art History, Tacoma WA (S)
Johnson, Mike, *Interim Executive Director,* Think 360 Art Complete Education, Colo Chapter, Denver CO
Johnson, Mimi, *Acad Dept Assoc,* University of Wisconsin-Stevens Point, Dept of Art & Design, Stevens Point WI (S)
Johnson, Neil, *Lectr,* Centenary College of Louisiana, Dept of Art, Shreveport LA (S)
Johnson, Neil, *VPres Develop,* Banff Centre, Banff AB (S)
Johnson, Pam, *Instr,* Sierra Community College, Art Dept, Rocklin CA (S)
Johnson, Pamela, *Assoc Prof,* Bates College, Art & Visual Culture, Lewiston ME (S)
Johnson, Patricia, *Assoc Div Chmn,* J Sargeant Reynolds Community College, Humanities & Social Science Division, Richmond VA (S)
Johnson, Paul, *Interim Dir Develop,* American Craft Council, Minneapolis MN
Johnson, Paul, *VPres Exhibit Design, Fabrication & Installation,* Bowers Museum, Santa Ana CA
Johnson, Quinn, *Exhibs Preparator,* Loveland Museum/Gallery, Loveland CO
Johnson, Richard A, *Prof,* University of New Orleans-Lake Front, Dept of Fine Arts, New Orleans LA (S)
Johnson, Richard, *Assoc Dir,* University of Georgia, Franklin College of Arts & Sciences, Lamar Dodd School of Art, Athens GA (S)
Johnson, Rick, *Chmn,* Iowa Great Lakes Maritime Museum, Arnolds Park IA
Johnson, Robert S, *Cur,* Fort George G Meade Museum, Fort Meade MD
Johnson, Sam, *CEO & Dir,* Columbia River Maritime Museum, Astoria OR
Johnson, Steven, *Associate Professor of Visual and Communication Arts, Department Chair,* Eastern Mennonite University, Visual and Communication Arts, Harrisonburg VA (S)
Johnson, Sue, *Dept Chmn,* Saint Mary's College of Maryland, Art & Art History Dept, Saint Mary's City MD (S)
Johnson, Suni, *Librn,* United Methodist Historical Society, Library, Baltimore MD
Johnson, Susan, *Dir Planned Giving,* The Dixon Gallery & Gardens, Memphis TN
Johnson, Tama, *Admin Asst to Dir Univ Mus,* Foosaner Art Museum, Melbourne FL
Johnson, Teresa, *Treas,* Almond Historical Society, Inc, Hagadorn House, The 1800-37 Museum, Almond NY
Johnson, Thomas B, *Dir,* Victoria Mansion - Morse Libby House, Portland ME
Johnson, Tony, *Instr,* Oklahoma State University Institute of Technology, School of Visual Communications, Okmulgee OK (S)
Johnson, Tora, *Pres,* Watercolor Society of Alabama, Town Creek AL
Johnson, Tracy, *Exec Dir,* Hockaday Museum of Art, Kalispell MT
Johnson, Tullis, *Cur & Mgr Archives,* Burchfield Penney Art Center, Buffalo NY
Johnson, Valerie, *Asst Exec Dir,* Boca Raton Museum of Art, Boca Raton FL
Johnson, Victoria, *Visitor Experience & Research Assoc,* Nichols House Museum, Inc, Boston MA
Johnson, Wanda, *Dir,* Beaufort County Arts Council, Washington NC
Johnson-Dibb, Rebecca, *Conservator,* Textile Conservation Workshop Inc, South Salem NY
Johnston, Amanda, *Gallery Asst,* Pointe Claire Cultural Centre, Stewart Hall Art Gallery, Pointe Claire QC
Johnston, Angel, *Program Dir,* Iredell Museums, Statesville NC
Johnston, Ben, *Art Installer/Driver,* San Francisco Museum of Modern Art, Artist Gallery, San Francisco CA
Johnston, Benjamin, *Asst Prof,* Delta State University, Dept of Art, Cleveland MS (S)
Johnston, Eileen, *Registrar,* Howard University, Gallery of Art, Washington DC
Johnston, Jeff, *Prof,* College of the Ozarks, Dept of Art, Point Lookout MO (S)
Johnston, Joe, *Bd Pres,* Wilkes Art Gallery, North Wilkesboro NC
Johnston, Ky, *Treas,* Kappa Pi International Honorary Art Fraternity, Cleveland MS
Johnston, Lisa N, *Pub Svcs,* Sweet Briar College, Mary Helen Cochran Library, Sweet Briar VA
Johnston, Matthew, *Asst Prof,* Radford University, Art Dept, Radford VA (S)
Johnston, Megan, *Instructor,* Concordia University, Art and Design Department, Saint Paul MN (S)
Johnston, Rebecca, *Paper Conservator,* Williamstown Art Conservation Center, Williamstown MA
Johnston, Robert C, *Library Dir,* Le Moyne College, Wilson Art Gallery, Syracuse NY
Johnston, Samantha, *Exec Dir,* Colorado Photographic Arts Center, Denver CO
Johnston, Sue, *Dir Mem,* California Watercolor Association, Gallery Concord, Concord CA
Johnston, Thomas, *Chmn Dept Art,* Western Washington University, Art Dept, Bellingham WA (S)
Johnstone, Lesley, *Cur & Head Exhibs & Educ,* Musee d'art Contemporain de Montreal, Montreal QC
Joice, Gail, *Sr Deputy Dir,* Seattle Art Museum, Dorothy Stimson Bullitt Library, Seattle WA
Jokl, Todd, *Campus Dean,* Lyme Academy College of Fine Arts, Old Lyme CT (S)
Jolly, Ernest, *Preparator,* University of California, Berkeley, The Magnes Collection of Jewish Art & Life, Berkeley CA
Jolly, Marilyn, *Assoc Prof,* University of Texas at Arlington, Art & Art History Department, Arlington TX (S)
Joly, Melanie, *Minister Canadian Heritage,* Department of Canadian Heritage, Canadian Conservation Institute, Ottawa ON
Jonas, Edward, *Chmn,* Portrait Society of America, Tallahassee FL
Jonason, Maureen Kelly, *Exec Dir,* Historical and Cultural Society of Clay County, Hjemkomst Center, Moorhead MN
Jonasson, Cathy, *Exec Dir,* Koffler Centre of the Arts, Koffler Gallery, Toronto ON
Jonasson, Cathy, *Exec Dir,* Koffler Center of the Arts, Toronto ON (S)
Jones Hamberg, Cheryl, *Info Literacy Librn,* Fisk University, Library, North Nashville TN
Jones, Allan, *Prof,* University of Louisiana at Lafayette, Dept of Visual Arts, Lafayette LA (S)
Jones, Anita, *Cur Textiles,* The Baltimore Museum of Art, Baltimore MD
Jones, Ann, *Librn,* McNay Art Museum, San Antonio TX
Jones, Ann, *Librn,* McNay Art Museum, McNay Art Museum Library & Archives, San Antonio TX
Jones, Anna Bell, *Operations & Sales,* Longue Vue House & Gardens, New Orleans LA
Jones, Art, *Dir,* University of North Dakota, Hughes Fine Arts Center-Col Eugene Myers Art Gallery, Grand Forks ND
Jones, Ashley, *Vis Asst Prof,* University of Florida, School of Art & Art History, Gainesville FL (S)
Jones, Barbara L, *Chief Cur,* Westmoreland Museum of American Art, Greensburg PA
Jones, Barbara L, *Cur,* Westmoreland Museum of American Art, Art Reference Library, Greensburg PA
Jones, Ben, *Prof,* New Jersey City University, Art Dept, Jersey City NJ (S)
Jones, Billy, *Educ Dir, Studio Progs,* Mesa Arts Center, Mesa Contemporary Arts Museum, Mesa AZ
Jones, Bob, *Chmn Bd,* Bob Jones University Museum & Gallery Inc, Greenville SC
Jones, Bob, *Prof,* Delaware County Community College, Communications, Art & Humanities, Media PA (S)
Jones, Catherine, *Educ Fellow,* Bates College, Museum of Art, Lewiston ME
Jones, Chad, *Exec Dir,* San Francisco Arts Education Project, San Francisco CA
Jones, Charles E, *Librn,* University of Chicago, Oriental Institute Research Archives, Chicago IL
Jones, Charlotte, *Art Gallery Dir,* Grenfell Campus, Memorial University of Newfoundland, Division of Fine Arts, Visual Arts Program, Corner Brook NF (S)
Jones, Dana, *Asst Dir Artists' Servs,* Virginia Center for the Creative Arts, Amherst VA
Jones, David, *Dir,* Dartmouth Heritage Museum, Dartmouth NS
Jones, Dennis, *Dir,* University of Arizona, Dept of Art, Tucson AZ (S)
Jones, Don R, *Chmn,* Iowa Wesleyan College, Art Dept, Mount Pleasant IA (S)
Jones, Donna, *Gallery Admin Asst,* University of Manitoba, School of Art Gallery, Winnipeg MB
Jones, Douglas, *Dir Museum Logistics,* American Homing Pigeon Museum & Library, Oklahoma City OK
Jones, Elliott, *Assoc Prof & Chief Dept Advisor,* Old Dominion University, Art Dept, Norfolk VA (S)
Jones, Emily, *Archivist,* Woodstock Artists Association & Museum, Woodstock NY
Jones, Erica, *Cur African Arts,* University of California, Los Angeles, Fowler Museum at UCLA, Los Angeles CA
Jones, Erin, *Dir,* Bob Jones University Museum & Gallery Inc, Greenville SC
Jones, Frederick N, *Instr,* Guilford Technical Community College, Commercial Art Dept, Jamestown NC (S)
Jones, Gregory, *Bd Trustees,* Sioux City Art Center, Sioux City IA
Jones, Gregory, *Instr,* Adrian College, Art & Design Dept, Adrian MI (S)
Jones, Jane, *VPres,* African American Museum, Dallas TX
Jones, Jeff, *VPres,* National Baseball Hall of Fame & Museum, Cooperstown NY
Jones, Jennifer, *Dir Colls & Research,* Minnesota Historical Society, Library, Saint Paul MN
Jones, Jessimi, *Dir Educ & Pub Prog,* Philbrook Museum of Art, Tulsa OK
Jones, Jo Ann, *Gift Shop Mgr,* Koshare Indian Museum, Inc, La Junta CO
Jones, Joanne, *Instr,* University of Arkansas, Art Dept, Fayetteville AR (S)
Jones, Joyce, *Dir Finance & Opers,* Knoxville Museum of Art, Knoxville TN
Jones, Kay, *Admin Asst,* University of Central Oklahoma, Dept of Art & Design, Edmond OK (S)
Jones, Keith, *Asst Prof,* University of Alabama in Huntsville, Dept of Art and Art History, Huntsville AL (S)
Jones, Kenneth, *Assoc Prof Art,* Harford Community College, Visual, Performing and Applied Arts Division, Bel Air MD (S)

Jones, Kenneth, *Treas,* Virginia Center for the Creative Arts, Amherst VA
Jones, Kent, *Visual Arts,* Memorial University of Newfoundland, Sir Wilfred Grenfell College Art Gallery, Corner Brook NF
Jones, Kent, *VPres Retail Opers,* California Science Center, Los Angeles CA
Jones, Kim, *Library Dir,* Charles City Library, Mooney Art Collection, Charles City IA
Jones, Kimberly Koller, *Exec Dir,* Hoyt Center for the Arts, Arts & Education of the Hoyt, New Castle PA
Jones, Kimberly, *Instr,* Southwestern University, Sarofim School of Fine Art, Dept of Art & Art History, Georgetown TX (S)
Jones, Kristopher, *Dir of Talent Acquisition & Recruitment,* Kendall College of Art & Design of Ferris State University, Grand Rapids MI (S)
Jones, Leonard, *Secy,* YMI Cultural Center, Asheville NC
Jones, Leslie, *VPres Museum Affairs & Cur Decorative Arts,* Cheekwood-Tennessee Botanical Garden & Museum of Art, Nashville TN
Jones, Leslie, *VPres Museum Affairs & Cur Decorative Arts,* Cheekwood-Tennessee Botanical Garden & Museum of Art, Museum of Art, Nashville TN
Jones, Lilyan, *Colls Asst,* School for Advanced Research (SAR), Indian Arts Research Center, Santa Fe NM
Jones, Lisa, *Visual Resource Cur,* East Tennessee State University, College of Arts and Sciences, Dept of Art & Design, Johnson City TN (S)
Jones, Lynda, *Dir Human Resources,* Historic Hudson Valley, Pocantico Hills NY
Jones, Marilyn, *Assoc Prof,* Lehigh University, Dept of Art, Architecture & Design, Bethlehem PA (S)
Jones, Mary, *Chmn,* American Academy in Rome, New York NY (S)
Jones, Michael, *Animal Cur,* Tallahassee Museum of History & Natural Science, Tallahassee FL
Jones, Michael, *CEO,* Saskatchewan Arts Board, Regina SK
Jones, Mike, *Prof & Chmn,* Hardin-Simmons University, Art Dept, Abilene TX (S)
Jones, Patty Sue, *International Child Art Coordr,* Cultural Affairs Department City of Los Angeles, Barnsdall Art Center & Junior Arts Center, Los Angeles CA
Jones, Paul, *Prof,* Tyler Junior College, Art Program, Tyler TX (S)
Jones, Peggy, *Instr Digital Art,* Miracosta College, Art Dept, Oceanside CA (S)
Jones, Phillip J, *Librn,* University of Arkansas, Fine Arts Library, Fayetteville AR
Jones, Rachel, *Library Mgr,* Rockport College, Carter-Haas Library, Rockport ME
Jones, Reba, *Coll Mgr,* Amarillo Art Association, Amarillo Museum of Art, Amarillo TX
Jones, Rick H, *Exec Dir,* Fitton Center for Creative Arts, Hamilton OH (S)
Jones, Rick H, *Exec Dir,* Fitton Center for Creative Arts, Hamilton OH
Jones, Robert L, *Head Div Fine Arts,* Truman State University, Art Dept, Kirksville MO (S)
Jones, Robin, *Chair,* Southwestern Oklahoma State University, Art, Communication & Theatre, Weatherford OK (S)
Jones, Ron, *Pres,* Memphis College of Art, Memphis TN (S)
Jones, Sasha, *Admin Coordr,* Portland State University, Littman Gallery, Portland OR
Jones, Sasha, *Gallery Dir,* Portland State University, White Gallery, Portland OR
Jones, Sonja, *Asst Curator,* The Robert McLaughlin Gallery, Library, Oshawa ON
Jones, Steve, *Asst Prof,* Florida State University, Art Dept, Tallahassee FL (S)
Jones, Steven, *Instr,* Millsaps College, Dept of Art, Jackson MS (S)
Jones, Susan Henshaw, *Pres & Dir,* Museum of the City of New York, Research Room, New York NY
Jones, Tate, *Exec Dir,* Rocky Mountain Museum of Military History, Missoula MT
Jones, Tisidra, *Dir Creative Leadership Opers & Policy,* Intermedia Arts, Minneapolis MN
Jones, Tom, *Assoc Prof,* University of Wisconsin, Madison, Dept of Art, Madison WI (S)
Jones, Tony, *The Nerman Family President,* Kansas City Art Institute, Kansas City MO (S)
Jones, Tracey, *Asst Prof,* College of Staten Island, Performing & Creative Arts Dept, Staten Island NY (S)
Jones, Tsitsi, *Treas,* Association of African American Museums, Washington DC
Jones, Win, *Instr,* Art Center Sarasota, Sarasota FL (S)
Jones-Avery, H Raye, *Exec Dir,* Christina Cultural Arts Center, Inc, Wilmington DE
Jonte-Pace, Diane, *Sr Vice Provost for Acad Affairs,* Santa Clara University, de Saisset Museum, Santa Clara CA
Jordan, Brenda, *Asst Prof,* Florida State University, Art History Dept, Tallahassee FL (S)
Jordan, Bryan, *CEO,* First Horizon National Corp, First Tennessee Heritage Collection, Memphis TN
Jordan, Candace, *Librn & Mus Library Cataloger,* Roswell Museum & Art Center, Library, Roswell NM
Jordan, Edward, *Instr,* Southern University in New Orleans, Fine Arts & Philosophy Dept, New Orleans LA (S)
Jordan, Krista, *Lead Vis Svcs,* Nova Scotia Museum, Maritime Museum of the Atlantic, Halifax NS
Jordan, Mary Anne, *Prof & Chair,* University of Kansas, The School of the Arts, Dept of Visual Art, Lawrence KS (S)
Jordan, Patricia, *Instr,* Wayne Art Center, Wayne PA (S)
Jordan, Shirley, *VPres,* Northwest Watercolor Society, Woodinville WA
Jordon, Shelley, *Assoc Prof,* Oregon State University, Dept of Art, Corvallis OR (S)
Jorgensen, Joseph, *Assoc Prof,* Culver-Stockton College, Art Dept, Canton MO (S)
Jorgensen, Roy, *Librn,* Fishkill Historical Society, Van Wyck Homestead Museum, Fishkill NY
Jorgenson, Tim, *Events Coordr,* Historical and Cultural Society of Clay County, Hjemkomst Center, Moorhead MN
Joselit, David, *Prof,* City University of New York, PhD Program in Art History, New York NY (S)
Joseph, Cami, *Asst Dir,* University of Louisiana at Lafayette, Paul and Lulu Hilliard University Art Museum, Lafayette LA
Joseph, Ellis, *Treas,* San Francisco African-American Historical & Cultural Society, Library, San Francisco CA
Joseph, Ellis, *Treasurer,* San Francisco African-American Historical & Cultural Society, San Francisco CA
Joseph, Emily, *Dir Individual Giving,* Virginia Center for the Creative Arts, Amherst VA
Joseph, Phil, *Art Coordr,* Miami University, Dept Fine Arts, Hamilton OH (S)
Joseph, Sarah, *Dir Exhibitions,* Kendall College of Art & Design, Kendall Gallery, Grand Rapids MI
Joslin, Kelly, *Chair Arts & Asst Prof,* Sinclair Community College, Division of Fine & Performing Arts, Dayton OH (S)
Jost, Stephan, *Michael & Sonja Koerner Dir & CEO,* Art Gallery of Ontario, Toronto ON
Jovanelli, Kathryn, *Asst Mus Coordr & Mem Mgr,* University of Maine, Museum of Art, Bangor ME
Joy, Carol, *Chmn,* Laney College, Art Dept, Oakland CA (S)
Joy, Diane Chisnall, *Dir,* Osborne Homestead Museum, Derby CT
Joy, Jason, *Gen Educ,* Art Institute of Pittsburgh, Pittsburgh PA (S)
Joy-Abney, Chiwishi, *Instr,* Wayne Art Center, Wayne PA (S)
Joyal, France, *Prog Dir,* Universite du Quebec, Trois-Rivieres, Department of Philosophy & the Arts, Trois-Rivieres QC (S)
Joyce, Daniel, *Dir,* Kenosha Public Museums, Kenosha WI
Joyce, Julie, *Cur Contemporary Art,* Santa Barbara Museum of Art, Library, Santa Barbara CA
Joyce, Julie, *Cur Contemporary Art,* Santa Barbara Museum of Art, Santa Barbara CA
Joyce, Lillian, *Asst Prof,* University of Alabama in Huntsville, Dept of Art and Art History, Huntsville AL (S)
Joyce, Lisa, *Visual Resources Cur,* State University of New York College at Cortland, Visual Resources Collection, Cortland NY
Joyner, Alexis, *Chair,* Elizabeth City State University, School of Arts & Humanities, Dept of Art, Elizabeth City NC (S)
Joyner, Gary T, *Sr Retail Opers Mgr,* Jamestown-Yorktown Foundation, Jamestown Settlement, Williamsburg VA
Juba, Krystal, *Dir Vis Svcs,* Anchorage Museum at Rasmuson Center, Anchorage AK
Juchniewich, Daniel, *Asst Dir,* Rahr-West Art Museum, Manitowoc WI
Judd, Flavin, *Artistic Dir,* Judd Foundation, Marfa TX
Judd, Rainer, *Pres,* Judd Foundation, Marfa TX
Judge, Vaughan, *Dir School of Art,* Montana State University, Helen E Copeland Gallery, Bozeman MT
Judge, Vaughan, *Dir School of Art,* Montana State University, School of Art, Bozeman MT (S)
Judson, David, *1st VPres,* The Stained Glass Association of America, Raytown MO
Juergens, Karyn, *Gallery Shop Mgr,* Kalamazoo Institute of Arts, Kalamazoo MI
Juhasz, Victor, *Exec VPres,* Society of Illustrators, New York NY
Juliusburger, Thomas, *Art Dept Chmn,* University of Bridgeport Gallery, Bridgeport CT
Junco, Jenille, *Asst Cur & Colls Mgr,* Villa Terrace Decorative Arts Museum, Milwaukee WI
Juneau, Madeleine, *Exec Dir,* Maison Saint-Gabriel Museum, Montreal QC
Jung, Hyun Tae, *Asst Prof,* Lehigh University, Dept of Art, Architecture & Design, Bethlehem PA (S)
Jung, Kathleen, *Pres,* Association of Medical Illustrators, Lexington KY
Jung, Nancy, *Office Mgr,* Cultural Affairs Department City of Los Angeles, Library, Los Angeles CA
Jung, Stephanie, *Instr,* Amarillo College, Visual Art Dept, Amarillo TX (S)
Junker, Patti, *Cur, Ann M. Barwick American Art,* Seattle Art Museum, Seattle WA
Juorio, Alex, *Dir,* John M Cuelenaere, Grace Campbell Gallery, Prince Albert SK
Jurakic, Ivan, *Dir & Cur,* University of Waterloo, University of Waterloo Art Gallery, Waterloo ON
Jurakic, Ivan, *Dir & Cur, Univ of Waterloo Art Gallery,* University of Waterloo, Dept of Fine Arts, Waterloo ON (S)
Jurgemeyer, Marne, *Dir,* Fort Morgan Heritage Foundation, Fort Morgan CO
Jurgensmeier, Charles, *Instr Music,* Creighton University, Fine & Performing Arts Dept, Omaha NE (S)
Jurkowski, Edward, *Dean,* University of Lethbridge, Faculty of Fine Arts, Lethbridge AB (S)
Juroszek, Steven, *Interim Dir,* Montana State University, School of Architecture, Bozeman MT (S)
Jurovics, Toby, *Chief Cur,* Joslyn Art Museum, Omaha NE
Jurus, Richard, *Prof,* Sinclair Community College, Division of Fine & Performing Arts, Dayton OH (S)
Jusino-Iturralde, Maribel, *Educ Specialist,* New Jersey Historical Society, Newark NJ
Just, Bryan, *Cur & Lectr Art of Ancient Americas,* Princeton University, Princeton University Art Museum, Princeton NJ
Justice, Lorraine, *Dean Col,* Rochester Institute of Technology, College of Imaging Arts & Sciences, Rochester NY (S)
Justice, Sarah, *Dir Educ,* Paris Gibson Square, Museum of Art, Great Falls MT
Juszczyk, James, *Treas,* American Abstract Artists, Brooklyn NY

Kabala, Irene, *Assoc Prof,* Indiana University of Pennsylvania, College of Fine Arts, Indiana PA (S)
Kabot, Sarah, *Head Drawing,* Cleveland Institute of Art, Cleveland OH (S)
Kabriel, J Ronald, *Asst Prof,* Catholic University of America, School of Architecture & Planning, Washington DC (S)
Kacerguis, Ed, *Treas,* Rensselaer Newman Foundation Chapel + Cultural Center, The Gallery at the Chapel & Cultural Center, Troy NY
Kachmar, Suzanne, *Exec Dir,* City Lights Gallery, Bridgeport CT
Kachur, Louis, *Coordr Art History,* Kean University, Fine Arts Dept, Union NJ (S)
Kaczman, James, *Graphic Designer,* Mystic Art Association, Inc, Mystic Museum of Art, Mystic CT
Kaczmarczyk, Madeline, *Adjunct Instr Ceramics,* Aquinas College, Art Dept, Grand Rapids MI (S)
Kaczmarek, Sheila, *VPres,* New Haven Paint & Clay Club, Inc, Whitneyville CT
Kadish, Skip, *Adjunct,* Monterey Peninsula College, Art Dept/Art Gallery, Monterey CA (S)
Kadoche, Salomon, *Second VPres,* Art Centre of New Jersey, Livingston NJ (S)
Kadow, Joan, *Instr,* Mount Mary College, Art & Design Division, Milwaukee WI (S)
Kagan, J, *Instr,* University of Southern Maine, Dept of Art, Gorham ME (S)
Kagan, Judy, *Asst Dir,* Wooster Community Art Center, Danbury CT
Kagin, Donald, *VPres,* American Numismatic Association, Edward C. Rochette Money Museum, Colorado Springs CO
Kahle, David, *Dept Head,* Mount Marty College, Fine Arts Dept, Yankton SD (S)
Kahle, David, *Dir,* Bede Art Gallery, Yankton SD
Kahle, Patricia, *Dir,* National Trust for Historic Preservation, Shadows-on-the-Teche, New Iberia LA
Kahler, Bruce, *Dr,* Bethany College, Art Dept, Lindsborg KS (S)
Kahler, Bruce, *Prof,* Bethany College, Mingenback Art Center, Lindsborg KS
Kahler, Caroline, *Head Art Dept,* Bethany College, Art Dept, Lindsborg KS (S)
Kahler, Caroline, *Prof,* Bethany College, Mingenback Art Center, Lindsborg KS
Kahler, Chris, *Prof,* Eastern Illinois University, Art Dept, Charleston IL (S)
Kahn, David M, *Dir,* The Adirondack Historical Association, The Adirondack Museum, Blue Mountain Lake NY
Kahn, Deborah, *Assoc Prof,* American University, Dept of Art, New York NY (S)
Kahn, Eunice, *Archivist,* Navajo Nation, Navajo Nation Museum, Window Rock AZ
Kahn, Johanna, *Develop Assoc,* Triton Museum of Art, Santa Clara CA
Kahn, Leslie, *Supvr,* Newark Public Library, Reference, Newark NJ
Kahng, Eik, *Chief Cur,* Santa Barbara Museum of Art, Library, Santa Barbara CA
Kahng, Eik, *Chief Cur,* Santa Barbara Museum of Art, Santa Barbara CA
Kahoun, Cindy, *Mus Shop Mgr,* Grants Pass Museum of Art, Grants Pass OR
Kahute, Robert M, *Assoc Prof,* Rochester Institute of Technology, School of Design, Rochester NY (S)
Kaier, Dale A, *Office Mgr,* Rome Art & Community Center, Rome NY
Kaigler, Doug, *Prof Art,* Eastern Oregon University, School of Arts & Science, La Grande OR (S)
Kaimal, Padma, *Asst Prof,* Colgate University, Dept of Art & Art History, Hamilton NY (S)
Kain, Alice, *Study Rm Supvr & Campus Art Coordr,* University of Chicago, Smart Museum of Art, Chicago IL
Kain, Evelyn, *Prof,* Ripon College, Art Dept, Ripon WI (S)
Kain, Kaylee, *Dir Communs,* University of Oklahoma, Fred Jones Jr Museum of Art, Norman OK
Kain, Lisa, *Cur,* Neville Public Museum of Brown County, Green Bay WI
Kaineg, Kristin, *Coordr Computer Labs,* Shepherd University, Dept of Contemporary Art & Theater, Shepherdstown WV (S)
Kaineg, Kristin, *Coordr Design,* Shepherd University, Dept of Contemporary Art & Theater, Shepherdstown WV (S)
Kaiser, Karen, *Cur Educ,* Gonzaga University, Jundt Art Museum, Spokane WA
Kaiser, Keelan, *Instr,* Judson University, School of Art, Design & Architecture, Elgin IL (S)
Kaiser, Kurt, *Assoc Prof,* Aquinas College, Art Dept, Grand Rapids MI (S)
Kaiser, Michel, *Instr Commercial Art,* Honolulu Community College, Commercial Art Dept, Honolulu HI (S)
Kakas, Karen, *Chmn Art Educ,* Bowling Green State University, School of Art, Bowling Green OH (S)
Kalasky, Matt, *Educ & Pub Engagement Coordr,* Moore College of Art & Design, The Galleries at Moore, Philadelphia PA
Kalavrezou, Ioli, *Chmn Dept,* Harvard University, Dept of History of Art & Architecture, Cambridge MA (S)
Kalb, Kent, *VPres,* Maysville, Kentucky Gateway Museum Center, Maysville KY
Kalba, Laura, *Assoc Prof,* Smith College, Art Dept, Northampton MA (S)
Kaldahl, Eric, *Chief Cur,* Amerind Foundation, Inc, Amerind Museum, Fulton-Hayden Memorial Art Gallery, Dragoon AZ
Kaldahl, Eric, *Chief Cur,* Amerind Foundation, Inc, Fulton-Hayden Memorial Library & Art Gallery, Dragoon AZ
Kaldany, Mary, *Sr Conservator,* Textile Conservation Workshop Inc, South Salem NY
Kaldor, Cynthia, *Dir,* Mayville State University, Northern Lights Art Gallery, Mayville ND
Kalin, Amelia, *Library Dir,* Valley Cottage Library, Gallery, Valley Cottage NY
Kalivas Fulton, Andrea, *Deputy Dir & Chief Mktg Offier,* Denver Art Museum, Denver CO
Kalke, Ed, *Chmn,* Carthage College, Art Dept, Kenosha WI (S)
Kallan, Linda, *Dept Chmn,* East Los Angeles College, Art Dept, Monterey Park CA (S)
Kallenberger, Klaus, *Instr,* Middle Tennessee State University, Art Dept, Murfreesboro TN (S)
Kallsen, Mark, *Asst Prof,* University of Wisconsin-Stout, Dept of Art & Design, Menomonie WI (S)
Kalmbach, Ann, *Exec Dir,* Women's Studio Workshop, Inc, Rosendale NY
Kalogeros-Chattan, Charles, *Dir,* Mesa Public Library Art Gallery, Los Alamos NM
Kaloyanides, Michael G, *Chmn,* University of New Haven, Dept of Visual & Performing Arts & Philosophy, West Haven CT (S)
Kalter, Jennifer, *Dir Educ,* Please Touch Museum, Philadelphia PA
Kama-Drake, Lyah, *Mem Mgr/Admin,* Kauai Museum Association, Ltd, Lihue HI
Kamalipour, Yahya R, *Head,* Purdue University Calumet, Dept of Communication & Creative Arts, Hammond IN (S)
Kamas, Louise, *Prof Art,* Clarke College, Dept of Art, Dubuque IA (S)
Kamen, Brian, *Preparator & Facilities Coordr,* University of Delaware, University Museums, Newark DE
Kamenev, Ruth, *Secy,* Manitoba Society of Artists, Winnipeg MB
Kamerer, Tracy, *Chief Cur,* Henry Morrison Flagler Museum, Palm Beach FL
Kamerling, Leonard, *Cur,* University of Alaska, Museum of the North, Fairbanks AK
Kaminishi, Ikumi, *Assoc Prof,* Tufts University, Dept of Art & Art History, Medford MA (S)
Kamiya, Yukie, *Gallery Dir,* Japan Society, Inc, Japan Society Gallery, New York NY
Kamm, David, *Gallery Coordr,* Luther College, Fine Arts Collection, Decorah IA
Kammer, Greg, *Dir,* Everett Community College, Art Dept, Everett WA (S)
Kammerman, Amy, *Librn,* Watkins College of Art, Design & Film, Library, Nashville TN
Kammerzell, Kay, *Dir,* Westcott Bay Institute, Island Museum of Art & Westcott Bay Sculpture Park, Friday Harbor WA
Kampf, Ray, *Chair/Assoc Prof,* California State Polytechnic University, Pomona, Department of Art, Pomona CA (S)
Kamphaus, Lisa, *Asst Prof,* La Roche College, Division of Design, Pittsburgh PA (S)
Kamphuis, Mark, *IT Mgr,* Contemporary Arts Center, Cincinnati OH
Kamps, Toby, *Dir & Chief Cur,* University of Houston, Blaffer Art Museum, Houston TX
Kamrath, Nicole, *Program Coordinator,* Art Guild of Burlington, Art Center of Burlington, Burlington IA
Kandianis, Patricia, *Ed,* Lehigh University Art Galleries, Museum Operation, Bethlehem PA
Kane, Adam, *Exec Dir,* Fairbanks Museum & Planetarium, Saint Johnsbury VT
Kane, Charlotte, *Office Mgr,* Springfield Art Association of Edwards Place, Springfield IL
Kane, Daniel, *Operations & Sales,* Longue Vue House & Gardens, New Orleans LA
Kane, John, *Operations Manager,* Akron Art Museum, Akron OH
Kane, Julie, *Technical Svcs,* Sweet Briar College, Mary Helen Cochran Library, Sweet Briar VA
Kane, Katherine, *Exec Dir,* Harriet Beecher Stowe Center, Library, Hartford CT
Kane, Katherine, *Exec Dir,* Harriet Beecher Stowe Center, Hartford CT
Kane, Mary Ann, *Dir,* Cortland County Historical Society, Kellogg Memorial Research Library, Cortland NY
Kane, Mary Ann, *Dir,* Cortland County Historical Society, Suggett House Museum, Cortland NY
Kane, Nocolas, *Leadership Ann Giving Officer,* deCordova Sculpture Park & Museum, Lincoln MA
Kane, Patricia, *Cur American Decorative Arts,* Yale University, Yale University Art Gallery, New Haven CT
Kane, Susan, *Assoc Prof,* Oberlin College, Dept of Art, Oberlin OH (S)
Kane, Virginia Rose, *Dir Educ,* Delaplaine Visual Arts Education Center, Frederick MD
Kaneshiro, Alexis, *Mktg & Outreach Coordr,* Pasadena Museum of California Art, Pasadena CA
Kang, Sung Yung, *Coordr Graphic Design,* Iowa State University, Dept of Art & Design, Ames IA (S)
Kanjo, Kathryn, *Chief Cur,* Museum of Contemporary Art San Diego, La Jolla CA
Kanjo, Kathryn, *Dir & CEO,* Museum of Contemporary Art San Diego, San Diego CA
Kann, Amy, *1st VPres,* National Sculpture Society, New York NY
Kann, Andrea, *Assoc Prof,* Coe College, Dept of Art, Cedar Rapids IA (S)
Kanost, Elizabeth, *Communs Mgr,* University of Kansas, Spencer Museum of Art, Lawrence KS
Kanotz, Sheila, *Dir Horticulture,* Philbrook Museum of Art, Tulsa OK
Kanter, Joshua S, *Chmn Bd,* International Sculpture Center, Hamilton NJ
Kanter, Laurence, *Cur European Art,* Yale University, Yale University Art Gallery, New Haven CT
Kantgias, Amy, *Exhib,* Birmingham Bloomfield Art Center, Art Center, Birmingham MI
Kantilal Patel, Alpesh, *Asst Prof, Grad Dir,* Florida International University, School of Art & Art History, Miami FL (S)
Kanwischer, Charlie, *Dir Grad Studies,* Bowling Green State University, School of Art, Bowling Green OH (S)
Kao, James, *Asst Prof of Art,* Aurora University, Art Dept, Aurora IL (S)
Kapitan, Lynn, *Chmn,* Mount Mary College, Art & Design Division, Milwaukee WI (S)
Kaplan, Carol, *Dir Educ,* Farmington Valley Arts Center, Avon CT

Kaplan, Cathy, *Chmn,* Aperture Foundation, New York NY

Kaplan, Flora, *Dir,* Dahesh Museum of Art, Greenwich CT

Kaplan, Frances, *Reference Librn,* The California Historical Society, North Baker Research Library, San Francisco CA

Kaplan, Ilee, *Assoc Dir,* California State University, Long Beach, University Art Museum, Long Beach CA

Kaplan, Julius, *Instr,* California State University, San Bernardino, Dept of Art, San Bernardino CA (S)

Kaplan, Susan A, *Dir,* Bowdoin College, Peary-MacMillan Arctic Museum, Brunswick ME

Kapler, Joseph, *Cur Art Coll,* Wisconsin Historical Society, Wisconsin Historical Museum, Madison WI

Kaplin, Judith, *Recording Secy,* South County Art Association, Kingston RI

Kaplowitz, Kenneth, *Assoc Prof,* The College of New Jersey, School of Arts & Sciences, Ewing NJ (S)

Kapplinger, Kent, *Lectr,* North Dakota State University, Division of Fine Arts, Fargo ND (S)

Karagheusian-Murphy, Marsha, *Prof,* Xavier University, Dept of Art, Cincinnati OH (S)

Karakalos, Ariane, *Asst Cur,* Museum of Ventura County, Ventura CA

Karalias, Ioannis, *VPres,* Chicago Athenaeum, Museum of Architecture & Design, Galena IL

Karasiuk, Caroline, *Undergrad Admin, Art History & Film Studies,* Carleton University, School for Studies in Art & Culture, Ottawa ON (S)

Karberg, Richard, *Assoc Prof,* Cuyahoga Community College, Dept of Art, Cleveland OH (S)

Karbowski, Kayle, *Mgr Mktg,* Charles Allis Art Museum, Milwaukee WI

Kardon, Carol, *Instr,* Main Line Art Center, Haverford PA (S)

Kardon, Carol, *Instr,* Wayne Art Center, Wayne PA (S)

Karellas, Heather, *Dir Devel,* Center for Puppetry Arts, Atlanta GA

Karibo, Lou, *Cur,* Kentucky New State Capitol, Division of Historic Properties, Frankfort KY

Karimi-Hakak, Mahmood, *Prof Theatre,* Siena College, Dept of Creative Arts, Loudonville NY (S)

Karlotski, William, *Instr,* Luzerne County Community College, Commercial Art Dept, Nanticoke PA (S)

Karnes, Andrea, *Cur,* Modern Art Museum, Fort Worth TX

Karns, Lynn, *Art Instr,* Grand Canyon University, Art Dept, Phoenix AZ (S)

Karp, Diane R, *Dir,* Santa Fe Arts Institute, Santa Fe NM (S)

Karp, Marty, *Rental Manager,* Contemporary Arts Center, Cincinnati OH

Karp, Rebecca, *Asst Cur Educ,* Dartmouth College, Hood Museum of Art, Hanover NH

Karpen, John E, *Prof,* Rochester Institute of Technology, School of Photographic Arts & Sciences, Rochester NY (S)

Karpman, Estie, *Develop Dir,* Abraham Lincoln Presidential Library & Museum, Springfield IL

Karr, Kaitlyn, *Vol Coordr,* Hastings Museum of Natural & Cultural History, Hastings NE

Karson, Richard, *Chief Design & Installations,* San Jose Museum of Art, Library, San Jose CA

Karstadt, Bruce, *Pres & CEO,* American Swedish Institute, Minneapolis MN

Karsten, Sharon, *Exec Dir,* Comox Valley Art Gallery, Courtenay BC

Karszewski, Jim, *VPres Buildings & Grounds,* DuPage Art League School & Gallery, Wheaton IL

Kart, Susan, *Asst Prof,* Lehigh University, Dept of Art, Architecture & Design, Bethlehem PA (S)

Kart, Susan, *Faculty,* Sarah Lawrence College, Dept of Art History, Bronxville NY (S)

Kasfir, Sidney L, *Prof,* Emory University, Art History Dept, Atlanta GA (S)

Kashar, Summerlea, *Exec Dir,* Cartoon Art Museum, San Francisco CA

Kasindorf, Deborah, *Interim Co-Dir, Deputy Dir Institutional Advancement,* Newark Museum Association, The Newark Museum, Newark NJ

Kaspar, Thomas L, *Preservation Architect,* Nebraska State Capitol, Lincoln NE

Kasper, Jamie, *State Advisor,* Pennsylvania Department of Education, Arts in Education Program, Harrisburg PA

Kasper, Michael, *Reference & Fine Arts Librn,* Amherst College, Robert Frost Library, Amherst MA

Kass, Ray, *Prof,* Virginia Polytechnic Institute & State University, Dept of Art & Art History, Blacksburg VA (S)

Kastell, Christina, *Cur Hist & Anthropology,* Putnam Museum of History and Natural Science, Davenport IA

Kastner, Carolyn, *Cur,* Georgia O'Keeffe Museum, Santa Fe NM

Kasumi, Naomi, *Assoc Prof,* Seattle University, Dept of Art & Art History, Seattle WA (S)

Kaszubski, Lynda, *Exec Asst,* Center for Exploratory & Perceptual Art, CEPA Gallery, Buffalo NY

Katchen, Michael, *Sr Archivist,* Franklin Furnace Archive, Inc, Brooklyn NY

Kates, Michael, *Dir,* African American Museum of Iowa, Cedar Rapids IA

Kather, Jan, *Asst,* Elmira College, Art Dept, Elmira NY (S)

Katich, Lorraine, *Mgr, Supervisor,* Rosicrucian Egyptian Museum & Planetarium, Rosicrucian Order, AMORC, San Jose CA

Katrib, Ruba, *Cur,* SculptureCenter, Gallery, Long Island City NY

Katsiaficas, Mary Diane, *Prof,* University of Minnesota, Minneapolis, Dept of Art, Minneapolis MN (S)

Katsolis, Christina, *Educ Dept,* Daytona State College, Southeast Museum of Photography, Daytona Beach FL

Katz, Cima, *Prof,* University of Kansas, The School of the Arts, Dept of Visual Art, Lawrence KS (S)

Katz, Janice, *Assoc Cur Japanese Art,* The Art Institute of Chicago, Department of Asian Art, Chicago IL

Katz, Jill, *Dir Mktg & Communs,* University of Pennsylvania, Institute of Contemporary Art, Philadelphia PA

Katz, Robert, *Prof,* University of Maine at Augusta, College of Arts & Humanities, Augusta ME (S)

Katz-Harris, Felicia, *Sr Cur & Cur Asian & Oceanic Folk Art,* New Mexico Department of Cultural Affairs, Museum of International Folk Art, Santa Fe NM

Katzenmeyer, Charles, *VPres Institutional Advancement,* Field Museum, Chicago IL

Kauffman, Elizabeth, *Dir of Galleries,* Salisbury University, Salisbury University Art Galleries, Salisbury MD

Kauffman, Ingrid, *Head Art Prog,* Arlington County Department of Public Libraries, Fine Arts Section, Arlington VA

Kauffman, Sandra, *Dir, Dance,* Loyola University of Chicago, Dept of Fine and Performing Arts, Chicago IL (S)

Kaufman, Amy, *Bus Mgr,* The Butler Institute of American Art, Art Museum, Youngstown OH

Kaufman, Claudia, *Pres,* Marblehead Arts Association, Inc, Marblehead MA

Kaufman, Glen, *Prof Fabric Design,* University of Georgia, Franklin College of Arts & Sciences, Lamar Dodd School of Art, Athens GA (S)

Kaufman, Jolene, *Bus Mgr,* Oregon Trail Museum Association, Scotts Bluff National Monument, Gering NE

Kaufman, Kristina, *Asst Dir,* The New School Parsons School of Design, Sheila C Johnson Design Center, New York NY (S)

Kaufman, Linda, *Pres,* Evanston Art Center, Evanston IL

Kaufman, Molly, *Dir Develop,* The Cultural Arts Center at Glen Allen, Glen Allen VA

Kaufmann, Cynthia, *Chief Horticulture,* National Gallery of Art, Washington DC

Kaufmann, Faith, *Arts & Music Librn,* Forbes Library, Northampton MA

Kaur, Amrita, *Library Asst,* University of Maryland, College Park, Art Library, College Park MD

Kaur, Ina, *Prof,* University of Tampa, College of Arts & Letters, Tampa FL (S)

Kauten, Heather, *Adjunct Asst Prof Art History,* Johnson County Community College, Fine Arts Dept & Art History Dept, Overland Park KS (S)

Kavalier, Jonathan, *Dir Gardens & Grounds,* Dumbarton Oaks, Dumbarton Oaks Museum, Washington DC

Kaveeshwar, Jaya, *Deputy Dir,* Hirshhorn Museum & Sculpture Garden, Smithsonian Institution, Washington DC

Kaven, Dennis, *Dept Head,* Grand View College, Art Dept, Des Moines IA (S)

Kawaiaea, Sachiyo, *Librn,* Honolulu Museum of Art, Robert Allerton Art Library, Honolulu HI

Kawalez, Marlene, *Secy,* Sculptor's Society of Canada, Canadian Sculpture Centre, Toronto ON

Kawamoto, Wayne, *Design Asst,* University of Hawaii at Manoa, The Art Gallery & The John Young Museum of Art, Honolulu HI

Kay, Ceyrona, *Dir,* Maharishi University of Management, Department of Art, Fairfield IA

Kay, Jaeson, *Assoc Dir,* American Museum of Cartoon Art, Inc, Sunland CA

Kay, Jeremy, *Dir & Cur,* American Museum of Cartoon Art, Inc, Sunland CA

Kay, Liz, *Treas,* American Museum of Cartoon Art, Inc, Sunland CA

Kay, Mary, *Assoc Prof,* Bethany College, Mingenback Art Center, Lindsborg KS

Kay, Mary, *Prof,* Bethany College, Art Dept, Lindsborg KS (S)

Kay, Pamela, *Bus Office,* Blanden Memorial Art Museum, Fort Dodge IA

Kayali, Francis, *Prof,* Saint Anselm College, Dept of Fine Arts, Manchester NH (S)

Kays, Elena, *Asst Prof Interior Design,* Centenary College, Humanities Dept, Hackettstown NJ (S)

Kays, Kym, *1st VPres,* Independence Historical Museum & Art Center, Independence KS

Kayser, Robert, *Assoc Prof,* Rochester Institute of Technology, School of Photographic Arts & Sciences, Rochester NY (S)

Kayuha, Alice, *Treas,* National Watercolor Society, San Pedro CA

Kazimi, Ali, *Assoc Prof & Chair, Dept of Cinema & Media Arts,* York University, School of the Arts, Media, Performance & Design, Toronto ON (S)

Kear, Andrew, *Chief Cur,* The Winnipeg Art Gallery, Winnipeg MB

Kearnan, Kathleen, *Assoc Dir,* Center for Exploratory & Perceptual Art, CEPA Library, Buffalo NY

Kearney, Jarod, *Cur,* James Monroe Museum, Fredericksburg VA

Kearney, Judy, *Reference Archivist,* Bernice Pauahi Bishop, Library & Archives, Honolulu HI

Kearns, Martha, *Instr,* Moravian College, Dept of Art, Bethlehem PA (S)

Kearny, Susanna, *Visual Arts Outreach Dir,* North Fourth Art Center & Gallery, Albuquerque NM

Kearse, Mary Boyd, *VPres Bd Dir,* Associates for Community Development, The Arts Center, Inc, Martinsburg WV

Keasler, Carrie, *Exhibs & Educ,* St Louis Artists' Guild & Galleries, Clayton MO

Keats, Robert, *CEO,* Patton Museum Foundation, General George Patton Museum and Center of Leadership, Fort Knox KY

Kee, Cynthia, *Instr,* University of Louisiana at Monroe, Dept of Art, Monroe LA (S)

Keech, John, *Prof,* Arkansas State University, Dept of Art, State University AR (S)

Keefe, Anne, *Publications Coord,* Southern Methodist University, Meadows Museum, Dallas TX

Keefe, Tara, *Artist,* Walker's Point Artists Assoc Inc, Gallery 218, Milwaukee WI

Keegan, Larry, *Prof,* Rensselaer Polytechnic Institute, Eye Ear Studio Dept of Art, Troy NY (S)

Keeler, Bruce, *Dir Devel,* Archaeological Institute of America, Boston MA

Keeler, Emily, *Artistic Dir,* San Francisco Arts Education Project, San Francisco CA

Keeler, William, *Librn & Archivist,* Rochester Historical Society, Rochester NY

Keeling, Bob, *Instr,* Southwestern Community College, Advertising & Graphic Design, Sylva NC (S)

Keenan, James P, *Dir,* American Society of Bookplate Collectors & Designers, Tucson AZ

Keenan, Jon, *Prof,* Colby-Sawyer College, Dept of Fine & Performing Arts, New London NH (S)

Keenan, Patrick, *Dir,* Willard House & Clock Museum, Inc, North Grafton MA

Keene Muhlert, Jan, *Dir,* The Pennsylvania State University, Palmer Museum of Art, University Park PA

Keenlyside, David, *Exec Dir,* Prince Edward Island Museum & Heritage Foundation, Charlottetown PE

Keens, David, *Prof,* University of Texas at Arlington, Art & Art History Department, Arlington TX (S)

Keesee, Tom, *Instr,* University of Saint Francis, School of Creative Arts, Fort Wayne IN (S)

Keeton, Darra, *Assoc Prof,* Rice University, Visual & Dramatic Arts, Houston TX (S)

Kefauver, Will, *VPres,* Kent Art Association, Gallery, Kent CT

Kefner, Chrystine, *Asst Prof Art,* Lander University, College of Arts & Humanities - Visual Arts, Greenwood SC (S)

Kegler, Kevin, *Asst Prof,* Daemen College, Art Dept, Amherst NY (S)

Kegler, Kevin, *Dir,* Daemen College, Fanette Goldman & Carolyn Greenfield Gallery, Amherst NY

Kehoe, Nita, *Chair Dept,* Central Wyoming College, Art Center, Riverton WY (S)

Kehoe, Tonua, *Asst Prof,* Kirkwood Community College, Dept of Arts & Humanities, Cedar Rapids IA (S)

Keidel, Michael, *Instr Design,* AIC College of Design, Cincinnati OH (S)

Keifer, Stephanie, *Admin Asst,* Dickinson College, The Trout Gallery, Carlisle PA

Keifer-Boyd, Karen, *Prof Art Educ & Women's Studies,* Pennsylvania State University, University Park, Penn State School of Visual Arts, University Park PA (S)

Keil, Kate, *Cur Collections,* Missouri Department of Natural Resources, Missouri State Museum, Jefferson City MO

Keiley, Michael, *Events Mgr,* Charles Allis Art Museum, Milwaukee WI

Keiley, Michael, *Events Mgr,* Villa Terrace Decorative Arts Museum, Milwaukee WI

Keim, Barbara, *Chmn,* Westfield State College, Art Dept, Westfield MA (S)

Keim, Delphine, *Assoc Prof,* University of Idaho College of Art & Architecture, Dept of Art & Design, Moscow ID (S)

Keiser Edwards, Sandra, *Deputy Dir,* Crystal Bridges Museum of American Art, Bentonville AR

Keiser, Sandra, *Assoc Prof,* Mount Mary College, Art & Design Division, Milwaukee WI (S)

Keisling, Bruce, *Librn,* Southern Baptist Theological Seminary, Joseph A Callaway Archaeological Museum, Louisville KY

Keister, Ann, *Assoc Prof,* Grand Valley State University, Art & Design Dept, Allendale MI (S)

Keith, Herman, *Chmn,* Claflin College, Dept of Art, Orangeburg SC (S)

Keith, Morrison, *Dean,* San Francisco State University, Art Dept, San Francisco CA (S)

Keith, Naima, *Deputy Dir & Chief Cur,* California African-American Museum, Los Angeles CA

Keith, Rachel, *Dir Colls & Exhibs,* Philbrook Museum of Art, Tulsa OK

Keith, Sallie, *Educ Coordr,* LaGrange Art Museum, LaGrange GA

Kelder, Diane, *Prof Emerita,* City University of New York, PhD Program in Art History, New York NY (S)

Keliher, Brian, *Assoc Dir Develop,* The American Federation of Arts, New York NY

Kelker, Nancy, *Instr,* Middle Tennessee State University, Art Dept, Murfreesboro TN (S)

Kell, Patricia, *Dir Gen & COO,* Department of Canadian Heritage, Canadian Conservation Institute, Ottawa ON

Kellar, Jane, *Dir,* Friends of Historic Kingston, Fred J Johnston House Museum, Kingston NY

Kelleher, Susan, *Events Coordr,* Landis Valley Village and Farm Museum, PA Historical & Museum Commission, Lancaster PA

Keller, Candace, *Prof,* Wayland Baptist University, Dept of Art, School of Fine Art, Plainview TX (S)

Keller, Carol, *Prof Art,* Amherst College, Dept of Art & the History of Art, Amherst MA (S)

Keller, Corey, *Cur Photog,* San Francisco Museum of Modern Art, San Francisco CA

Keller, Dorothy Bosch, *Chmn Dept,* University of Saint Joseph, Connecticut, Dept of Fine Arts, West Hartford CT (S)

Keller, John, *Prof,* Harding University, Dept of Art & Design, Searcy AR (S)

Keller, Katie, *Ref Librn,* Stanford University, Art & Architecture Library, Stanford CA

Keller, Margaret, *Prof,* Saint Louis Community College at Meramec, Art Dept, Saint Louis MO (S)

Keller, Mariah, *Editorial,* Indiana University, Eskenazi Museum of Art, Bloomington IN

Keller, Peter, *Pres,* Bowers Museum, Santa Ana CA

Kellerman, Edd, *Mtkg & Communs Mgr,* George Phippen, Phippen Museum - Art of the American West, Prescott AZ

Kellerman, Moritz, *Prof,* Oakton Community College, Language Humanities & Art Divisions, Des Plaines IL (S)

Kelley, Carol, *Spec Events Officer,* National Gallery of Art, Washington DC

Kelley, Cherie, *Visitor Serv Assoc,* University of Wyoming, University of Wyoming Art Museum, Laramie WY

Kelley, Don, *Prof Fine Arts,* University of Cincinnati, School of Art, Cincinnati OH (S)

Kelley, Heather, *Prof,* McNeese State University, Dept of Visual Arts, Lake Charles LA (S)

Kelley, Judy, *Mem Secy,* Newport Historical Society & Museum of Newport History, Newport RI

Kelley, Jyl, *Asst Prof,* University of Wisconsin-Eau Claire, Dept of Art & Design, Eau Claire WI (S)

Kelley, Karen, *Mgr Reference,* Denver Public Library, Reference, Denver CO

Kellner, Tana, *Artistic Dir,* Women's Studio Workshop, Inc, Rosendale NY

Kellogg, Jasmine, *Admin Asst,* Colgate University, Picker Art Gallery, Hamilton NY

Kellum, Barbara, *Prof,* Smith College, Art Dept, Northampton MA (S)

Kelly Trombly, Margaret, *Dir,* Forbes Magazine, Inc, Forbes Collection, Jersey City NJ

Kelly, Amy, *Registrar,* The Old Jail Art Center, Albany TX

Kelly, Amy, *Registrar,* The Old Jail Art Center, Green Research Library, Albany TX

Kelly, Audra, *Head Interpretation,* Hillwood Museum & Gardens Foundation, Hillwood Estate Museum & Gardens, Washington DC

Kelly, Brian, *Prof,* University of Louisiana at Lafayette, Dept of Visual Arts, Lafayette LA (S)

Kelly, Cathie, *Assoc Prof,* University of Nevada, Las Vegas, Dept of Art, Las Vegas NV (S)

Kelly, Colleen, *Dir Devel,* The Renaissance Society, Chicago IL

Kelly, Danielle, *Exec Dir,* Surface Design Association, Inc, Las Vegas NM

Kelly, Donna, *Assoc Prof,* Rhode Island College, Art Dept, Providence RI (S)

Kelly, Franklin, *Deputy Dir,* National Gallery of Art, Washington DC

Kelly, Gemey, *Adjunct Prof & Dir Owens Art Gallery,* Mount Allison University, Dept of Fine Arts, Sackville NB (S)

Kelly, Gemey, *Dir & Cur,* Mount Allison University, Owens Art Gallery, Sackville NB

Kelly, Gerard, *Chief Financial Officer,* Snug Harbor Cultural Center, Newhouse Center for Contemporary Art, Staten Island NY

Kelly, Jim, *Exec Dir,* 4 Culture, Seattle WA

Kelly, Kate, *Guest Servs & Opers Mgr,* University of Chicago, Smart Museum of Art, Chicago IL

Kelly, Kristin, *Grants Officer,* Laguna Art Museum, Laguna Beach CA

Kelly, Lisa, *Mktg & Outreach Mgr,* City of Long Branch, Long Branch Free Public Library, Long Branch NJ

Kelly, Lyn, *Dir Pub Rels,* North Central Washington Museum, Wenatchee Valley Museum & Cultural Center, Wenatchee WA

Kelly, Madeline, *Supv Reference,* Berkshire Athenaeum, Reference Dept, Pittsfield MA

Kelly, Meghan, *Dir,* Buckham Fine Arts Project, Buckham Gallery, Flint MI

Kelly, Michelle, *Drawing & Painting,* North Seattle College, North Seattle College Dept of Art, Seattle WA (S)

Kelly, Mikkel, *Chief Exec Officer,* Western Colorado Center for the Arts, Library, Grand Junction CO

Kelly, Nannette, *Prof Art,* Imperial Valley College, Humanities Department, Imperial CA (S)

Kelly, Patrick E, *Exec Dir,* Saint John Paul II National Shrine, Washington DC

Kelly, Patrick, *Cur Exhibs,* The Old Jail Art Center, Green Research Library, Albany TX

Kelly, Patrick, *Exec Dir,* The Old Jail Art Center, Albany TX

Kelly, Robert E, *Coll Develop,* Redwood Library & Athenaeum, Newport RI

Kelly, Samantha, *Dir Educ,* Tacoma Art Museum, Tacoma WA

Kelly, Wendy, *Acting Cur,* Discovery Museum, Bridgeport CT

Kelly, William, *Chmn,* John Simon Guggenheim, New York NY

Kelman, M, *Prof,* Community College of Rhode Island, Dept of Art, Warwick RI (S)

Kelto, Megan, *Assoc Dir,* Crooked Tree Arts Center - Traverse City, Gallery, Traverse City MI

Kemp, Flo, *VPres Painting,* Catharine Lorillard Wolfe, New York NY

Kemp, Jenny, *Mktg Asst,* Sangre de Cristo Arts & Conference Center, Pueblo CO

Kemp, Weston D, *Prof,* Rochester Institute of Technology, School of Photographic Arts & Sciences, Rochester NY (S)

Kemp, William, *Librn,* McLean County Historical Society, McLean County Museum of History, Bloomington IL

Kempe, Deborah, *Chief Coll Mgmt & Access,* The Frick Collection, Frick Art Reference Library, New York NY

Kemper, David W, *CEO & Pres,* Commerce Bancshares, Inc, Fine Art Collection, Kansas City MO

Kemper, Julie, *Cur,* Missouri Department of Natural Resources, Elizabeth Rozier Gallery, Jefferson City MO

Kemper, Julie, *Cur Exhibs,* Missouri Department of Natural Resources, Missouri State Museum, Jefferson City MO

Kemper, Mariner, *Chmn,* UMB Financial Corporation, Kansas City MO

Kemper, Mark, *Asst Supt,* Nebraska Game and Parks Commission, Arbor Lodge State Historical Park & Morton Mansion, Nebraska City NE

Kemper, R Crosby, *Exec Dir,* Kansas City Public Library, Kansas City MO

Kempf de Jong, Joan, *Assoc Prof,* University of Southern Indiana, Art & Design Dept, Evansville IN (S)

Kempler, Cheryl, *Curatorial Consultant,* B'nai B'rith International, B'nai B'rith Klutznick National Jewish Museum, Washington DC

Kendall, Andrew, *Exec Dir,* The Trustees of Reservations, The Mission House, Ipswich MA

Kendall, Donald M, *Former Chmn & CEO,* PepsiCo Inc, Donald M Kendall Sculpture Garden, Purchase NY

Kendall, Douglas, *Coordr,* Hartwick College, The Yager Museum, Oneonta NY

Kendall, Gail, *Chmn Grad Comt,* University of Nebraska-Lincoln, Dept of Art & Art History, Lincoln NE (S)
Kendall, Ginny, *Instr,* Main Line Art Center, Haverford PA (S)
Kendall, Rick, *Supt,* Saint-Gaudens National Historic Site, Library, Cornish NH
Kender, Ronald C, *Exec Dean,* Philadelphia University, Philadelphia PA (S)
Kendrick, Allison, *Chair,* Ogden Museum of Southern Art, University of New Orleans, New Orleans LA
Kendrick, Diane, *Coordr,* Averett College, Art Dept, Danville VA (S)
Kennan, Tracy, *Cur Educ,* New Orleans Museum of Art, New Orleans LA
Kennard, Amy, *Mktg Coordr,* Fraunces Tavern Museum, New York NY
Kenneally, Rebecca, *Chmn Performing Arts,* Endicott College, School of Visual & Performing Arts, Beverly MA (S)
Kennedy Grant, Dauna, *Exec Dir,* Vernon Public Art Gallery, Vernon BC
Kennedy III, John, *VPres & Bd of Trustees,* Telfair Museums, Telfair Academy of Arts & Sciences Library, Savannah GA
Kennedy, Amy, *Instr,* Muskingum College, Art Department, New Concord OH (S)
Kennedy, Brian P, *Pres, Dir & CEO,* Toledo Museum of Art, Toledo OH
Kennedy, Corinne, *Info Assoc,* Georgia Institute of Technology, College of Architecture Library, Atlanta GA
Kennedy, Dan, *Exhib & Graphic Design Mgr,* Independence Seaport Museum, Philadelphia PA
Kennedy, Douglas R, *Video Production,* Art Institute of Pittsburgh, Pittsburgh PA (S)
Kennedy, Frank, *Mgr IT,* Norman Rockwell Museum, Stockbridge MA
Kennedy, Gail, *Dir,* The University of Kentucky Art Museum, Lucille Little Fine Arts Library, Lexington KY
Kennedy, Greg, *Visual Arts Chmn,* Idyllwild Arts Academy, Idyllwild CA (S)
Kennedy, Joyce, *Div Chmn,* Governors State University, College of Arts & Science, Art Dept, University Park IL (S)
Kennedy, Kimberly, *Cur,* Historical Society of Rockland County, New City NY
Kennedy, Linda, *Adjunct Instr,* Wayland Baptist University, Dept of Art, School of Fine Art, Plainview TX (S)
Kennedy, Mary, *Cur,* Iowa Great Lakes Maritime Museum, Arnolds Park IA
Kennedy, Patricia, *Prof,* Ocean County College, Humanities Dept, Toms River NJ (S)
Kennedy, Philip, *Preparator,* Illinois State Museum, ISM Lockport Gallery, Chicago Gallery & Southern Illinois Art Gallery, Springfield IL
Kennedy, Robyn, *Chief Admin,* American Art Museum, Renwick Gallery, Washington DC
Kenner, Samantha, *Communs Dir,* National Archives and Records Administration, Eisenhower Presidential Library, Abilene KS
Kennerk, Emily, *Asst Prof,* University of Nevada, Las Vegas, Dept of Art, Las Vegas NV (S)
Kenney, Christopher, *Cur Educ,* Historical Society of Rockland County, New City NY
Kenney, Lianne, *Dir Fin,* Mobile Museum of Art, Mobile AL
Kenny, Mary, *Asst Prof,* Sierra Nevada College, Fine Arts Dept, Incline Village NV (S)
Kenny, Ryan, *Dir Exhibs,* Anchorage Museum at Rasmuson Center, Anchorage AK
Kenny-Urban, Anne, *Exec Dir,* Agecroft Association, Museum, Richmond VA
Kenny-Urban, Anne, *Exec Dir,* Agecroft Association, Agecroft Hall, Richmond VA
Kent, Heather, *Prog Dir, Theatre Production,* Humber College, School of Creative & Performing Arts, Toronto ON (S)
Kent, James, *Instr,* Guild of Creative Art, Shrewsbury NJ (S)
Kent, Jennifer, *VPres Advancement,* Historic New England, Boston MA
Kent, Jo Anne, *Coll Mgr,* Koshare Indian Museum, Inc, La Junta CO
Kent, Liz, *Serials Librn,* Sweet Briar College, Mary Helen Cochran Library, Sweet Briar VA
Kent, Richard K, *Prof,* Franklin & Marshall College, Art & Art History Dept, Lancaster PA (S)
Kenton, Carlie, *Dir Opers,* Gunnison Arts Center, Gunnison CO
Kenyon, Matthew, *Asst Prof Art (New Media),* Pennsylvania State University, University Park, Penn State School of Visual Arts, University Park PA (S)
Kenyon, Paula, *Interim Exec Dir,* Museum of Art & History, Santa Cruz, Santa Cruz CA
Kenzie, Monica, *Archit Librn,* New Jersey Institute of Technology, Littman Architecture & Design Library, Newark NJ
Keogh, Michael, *Instr,* Casper College, Dept of Visual Arts, Casper WY (S)
Keough, Jane, *Dir Corporate Mem Svcs,* Fitchburg Art Museum, Fitchburg MA
Keough, Margaret, *Dir Mktg & Communs,* Mid-America Arts Alliance & Exhibits USA, Kansas City MO
Keough, Tracey, *Dir,* City of Providence Parks Department, Roger Williams Park Museum of Natural History, Providence RI
Keown, Gary, *Graphic Design,* Southeastern Louisiana University, Art & Design, Hammond LA (S)
Kerber, Gwen, *Instr,* Bucks County Community College, Fine Arts Dept, Newtown PA (S)
Kereszi, Lisa, *Dir Undergraduate Studies in Art,* Yale University, School of Art, New Haven CT (S)
Keris, Holly, *Acting Dir,* Cummer Museum of Art & Gardens, Museum & Library, Jacksonville FL
Kern, Amy, *Graphic Design,* Art Institute of Pittsburgh, Pittsburgh PA (S)
Kerns, Ed, *Prof Art,* Lafayette College, Dept of Art, Easton PA (S)
Kerr, Beth, *Theatre & Dance Librn,* University of Texas at Austin, Fine Arts Library, Austin TX
Kerr, Debra, *Exec Dir,* Intuit: The Center for Intuitive & Outsider Art, Chicago IL
Kerr, Don, *Adjunct Prof,* Aquinas College, Art Dept, Grand Rapids MI (S)
Kerr, Joellen, *Dir,* University of Charleston, Carleton Varney Dept of Art & Design, Charleston WV (S)
Kerratti, Jennifer, *Digital Media Librn,* Maryland Institute, Decker Library, Baltimore MD
Kersels, Martin, *Dir Graduate Studies in Sculpture,* Yale University, School of Art, New Haven CT (S)
Kersey, Barbara, *Pres,* Crary Art Gallery, Warren PA
Kersh, Joanne, *Asst Dir Research,* Association of Independent Colleges of Art & Design, Providence RI
Kershaw, Mary, *Dir,* New Mexico Department of Cultural Affairs, New Mexico Museum of Art, Unit of NM Dept of Cultural Affairs, Santa Fe NM
Kershaw, Mary, *Dir,* New Mexico Department of Cultural Affairs, New Mexico Museum of Art, Santa Fe NM
Kershaw, Mary, *Dir,* New Mexico Department of Cultural Affairs, New Mexico Museum of Art, Santa Fe NM
Kertes, Natalie, *Dir Literary & Theatre Progs,* Koffler Center of the Arts, Toronto ON (S)
Kerven, Don, *Facilities Mgr,* Museum of Western Colorado, Museum of the West, Grand Junction CO
Kerwin, Mark, *CFO & Deputy Dir,* Museum of Fine Arts, Boston MA
Kessel, Courtney, *Gallery Dir,* Ohio University, Ohio University Art Gallery, Athens OH
Kessel, Suzan, *Dir,* Fairfield Art Association, Fairfield IA
Kessell, Kelley, *Alumni Community Coord,* National YoungArts Foundation, Miami FL
Kessenich, Veronica, *Exec Dir,* Atlanta Contemporary Art Center, Atlanta GA
Kessler, Jamie Paul, *Instr,* Lamar University, Art Dept, Beaumont TX (S)
Kessmann, Dean, *Assoc Prof,* George Washington University, Dept of Art of Fine Arts & Art History, Washington DC (S)
Kestenbaum, Stuart, *Bd Chair,* American Craft Council, Minneapolis MN
Kester, Marilyn, *Pres,* Cambridge Museum, Cambridge NE
Ketcham, Maria, *Dept Head,* Detroit Institute of Arts, Research Library & Archives, Detroit MI
Ketchum, Cavaliere, *Emer Prof,* University of Wisconsin, Madison, Dept of Art, Madison WI (S)
Ketter, Cathy, *Opers Mgr,* Allied Arts Council of St Joseph, Saint Joseph MO
Kettering, Alison, *Chmn,* Carleton College, Dept of Art & Art History, Northfield MN (S)
Kettler, Kim, *Pres,* Truro Center for the Arts at Castle Hill, Inc, Truro MA (S)
Keusch, Bruno, *Book Store Dir,* Neue Galerie New York, New York NY
Keville, Jim, *Assoc Prof,* California State University, Dominguez Hills, Art & Design Dept, Carson CA (S)
Kewl-Durfey, Grace, *Community Develop Arts Educ,* Broward County Board of Commissioners, Broward Cultural Div, Fort Lauderdale FL
Key, Bonnie, *Office Mgr,* Embroiderers Guild of America, Dorothy Babcock Memorial Library, Louisville KY
Key, Lisa, *Dir Devel,* Museum of Contemporary Art Chicago, Chicago IL
Keyes, David, *Prof,* Pacific Lutheran University, Dept of Art, Tacoma WA (S)
Keyes, Shelby, *Instr,* Dallas Baptist University, Dept of Art, Dallas TX (S)
Keys, Den, *Mus Shop Mgr,* Pickens County Museum of Art & History, Pickens SC
Keys, Kathleen, *Chmn,* Boise State University, Art Dept, Boise ID (S)
Keyse Rudolph, William, *Chief Cur,* San Antonio Museum of Art, San Antonio TX
Keyser, William, *Prof,* Rochester Institute of Technology, School of Design, Rochester NY (S)
Khaki, Shirin, *Libr Asst,* New York University, Stephen Chan Library of Fine Arts, New York NY
Khalidi, Omar, *Librn Aga Khan Prog,* Massachusetts Institute of Technology, Rotch Library of Architecture & Planning, Cambridge MA
Khalili, Meena, *Asst Prof,* Virginia State University, Department of Art & Design, Petersburg VA (S)
Khalsa, Sant, *Instr,* California State University, San Bernardino, Dept of Art, San Bernardino CA (S)
Khan, Arif, *Dir,* University of New Mexico, University of New Mexico Art Museum, Albuquerque NM
Khan, Beverly, *Acting Dean,* Fairfield University, Visual & Performing Arts, Fairfield CT (S)
Khan, Osman, *Assoc Prof & Dir MFA Program,* University of Michigan, Ann Arbor, Penny W Stamps School of Art & Design, Ann Arbor MI (S)
Khan, Sabir, *Assoc Dean,* Georgia Institute of Technology, College of Architecture, Atlanta GA (S)
Khanam, Ferdousi, *Sec,* United States Department of the Interior, Indian Arts & Crafts Board, Washington DC
Khandekar, Narayan, *Dir Center for the Technical Study of Modern Art,* Harvard University, Harvard Art Museums, Cambridge MA
Khewhok, Sanit, *Cur,* Hawaii Pacific University, Art Gallery, Kaneohe HI
Kholeif, Omar, *Manilow Sr Cur & Dir Global Initiatives,* Museum of Contemporary Art Chicago, Chicago IL
Kiaer, Christina, *Assoc Prof,* Northwestern University, Evanston, Dept of Art History, Evanston IL (S)
Kianka, Hope, *CFO,* Buffalo Society of Natural Sciences, Buffalo Museum of Science, Buffalo NY
Kibler, Brian, *Dir Opers,* UrbanGlass, Robert Lehman Gallery, Brooklyn NY
Kibler, Robert, *Prof of Art,* Glendale Community College, Visual & Performing Arts Div, Glendale CA (S)

Kidd, J Benton, *Cur Ancient Art,* University of Missouri, Museum of Art & Archaeology, Columbia MO

Kidd, Kevin, *Dir,* Wentworth Institute of Technology, Douglas D Schumann Library & Learning Commons, Boston MA

Kidd, Mark, *Communs Dir,* Appalshop Inc, Appalshop, Whitesburg KY

Kidd, Mark, *Instr,* Wayne Art Center, Wayne PA (S)

Kidder, Karin, *Dir Mktg & Communs,* Bellevue Arts Museum, Bellevue WA

Kiddie, David, *Chmn,* Chapman University, Art Dept, Orange CA (S)

Kiel, Dennis, *Dir,* Lamar University, Dishman Art Museum, Beaumont TX

Kiel, Martha, *Prof,* Hardin-Simmons University, Art Dept, Abilene TX (S)

Kiely, Declan, *Robert H Taylor Cur & Dept Head,* The Morgan Library & Museum, Museum, New York NY

Kiely, Mary, *Dir Fin & Opers,* Danforth Museum of Art, Danforth Museum of Art, Framingham MA

Kiely, Paula, *Library Dir,* Milwaukee Public Library, Art, Music & Recreation Dept, Milwaukee WI

Kiendl, Anthony, *Dir,* University of Regina, MacKenzie Art Gallery, Regina SK

Kienzle, Karen, *Dir,* Palo Alto Art Center, Palo Alto CA

Kiernan, Scott, *Gallery Mgr,* Swiss Institute, New York NY

Kiesel, Izumi, *Bookkeeper,* Museum of Ventura County, Ventura CA

Kieselburg, James, *Dir,* Grohmann Museum, Milwaukee WI

Kihata, Hideki, *Chmn Dept, Prof,* Saginaw Valley State University, Dept of Art & Design, University Center MI (S)

Kiick, Kim, *Exec Dir,* American Numismatic Association, Edward C. Rochette Money Museum, Colorado Springs CO

Kiihne, Robert, *Dir Exhibits,* USS Constitution Museum, Boston MA

Kilburn, Jan, *Vice Pres,* Pemaquid Group of Artists, Pemaquid Art Gallery, Pemaquid Point ME

Kilby, Lorraine, *Office Admin,* Arlington Center for the Arts, Arlington MA

Kile, Karen M, *Exec Dir,* San Luis Obispo Museum of Art, San Luis Obispo CA

Kilgallen, Caitlin, *Dir Library,* Visual Arts Library, New York NY

Kilgore, Sydney, *Media Coordr, Images,* University of Texas at Austin, Fine Arts Library, Austin TX

Kilian, Peter, *Prof & Coordr,* Northern State University, Art Dept, Aberdeen SD (S)

Kilkenny, Amy, *Head Library & Archives,* Wadsworth Atheneum Museum of Art, Auerbach Art Library, Hartford CT

Killeen, Maureen, *Dept Mgr,* Princeton University, Dept of Art & Archaeology, Princeton NJ (S)

Killhour, Caroline, *Exec Dir,* Hui No'eau Visual Arts Center, Gallery and Gift Shop, Makawao Maui HI

Killion, Robert, *Coll Mgr,* Peoria Historical Society, Peoria IL

Kilman, Ernie, *Co-owner,* Eureka Fine Art Gallery, Eureka Springs AR

Kilmer, Jennifer, *Dir,* Washington State Historical Society, Washington History Museum, Tacoma WA

Kim Han, Hyonjeong, *Cur Korean Art,* Asian Art Museum of San Francisco, Chong-Moon Lee Ctr for Asian Art and Culture, San Francisco CA

Kim, Alexa, *Prog Coord,* Self Help Graphics, Los Angeles CA

Kim, Gloria, *Gallery Cur & Recreation Supvr,* City of Fremont, Olive Hyde Art Gallery, Fremont CA

Kim, Heemong, *Prof,* Rhode Island College, Art Dept, Providence RI (S)

Kim, Julia, *Librn,* Los Angeles County Museum of Art, Robert Gore Rifkind Center for German Expressionist Studies, Los Angeles CA

Kim, Kai, *Instr,* Mesa Community College, Dept of Art, Mesa AZ (S)

Kim, Michelle, *Gallery Mgr,* Pro Arts, Oakland CA

Kim, Min Jung, *Dir & CEO,* New Britain Museum of American Art, New Britain CT

Kim, Nanhee, *Asst Prof,* University of North Alabama, Dept of Art, Florence AL (S)

Kim, Sarah, *Deputy Dir,* The Valentine, Richmond VA

Kim, Sei Young, *Progs Dir,* Lower East Side Printshop Inc, New York NY (S)

Kim, Soo, *Prog Dir Photog,* Otis College of Art & Design, Fine Arts, Los Angeles CA (S)

Kim, Stephen, *Assoc Dir Information & Technology,* Princeton University, Princeton University Art Museum, Princeton NJ

Kimball, Cathy, *Dir,* San Jose Institute of Contemporary Art, San Jose CA

Kimball, Justin, *Prof,* Amherst College, Dept of Art & the History of Art, Amherst MA (S)

Kimball, Kathryn, *Upper Room Cur,* General Board of Discipleship, The United Methodist Church, The Upper Room Chapel & Museum, Nashville TN

Kimball, Laura, *Interior Design Coordr,* Community College of Baltimore County, School of Technology, Art & Design, Catonsville MD (S)

Kimball, Richard, *Cur Mathematics,* Northern Maine Museum of Science, Presque Isle ME

Kimberling, Kristen, *Registrar,* The Dixon Gallery & Gardens, Memphis TN

Kimes, Diane, *Dir Develop,* Historical Society of Martin County, Elliott Museum, Stuart FL

Kimes, Don, *Chmn Dept & Prof,* American University, Dept of Art, New York NY (S)

Kimes, Don, *Dir Art School,* Chautauqua Institution, School of Art, Chautauqua NY (S)

Kincaid, Kayte, *Dir Educ,* Avampato Discovery Museum, The Clay Center for Arts & Sciences, Charleston WV

Kincaid, Merna, *Treas,* Big Horn County Historical Museum, Hardin MT

Kincaid, Sage, *Assoc Cur Educ,* University of Georgia, Georgia Museum of Art, Athens GA

Kincannon, Ronald, *Pres,* No Man's Land Historical Society, No Man's Land Museum, Goodwell OK

Kindall, Elizabeth, *Prof,* University of St Thomas, Deptartment of Art History, Saint Paul MN (S)

Kinder, Ben, *Preparator,* Confederation Centre Art Gallery and Museum, Charlottetown PE

Kindred, Ann, *Assoc Dir,* Robert Louis Stevenson Museum, Saint Helena CA

Kindstedt, Susan, *Archivist,* Portsmouth Athenaeum, Joseph Copley Research Library, Portsmouth NH

Kindt, Diane, *Cur & Mus Shop Mgr,* Klein Museum, Mobridge SD

King, Angie, *Cur Adult Educ,* Mobile Museum of Art, Mobile AL

King, Angie, *Outreach Educ Coordr,* Lauren Rogers, Laurel MS

King, Carolyne, *Pres,* ARC Gallery and Educational Foundation, Chicago IL

King, Codie, *CEO & Dir,* Wailoa Arts & Cultural Center, Hilo HI

King, Cornelia S, *Chief Ref & Cur Women's History,* Library Company of Philadelphia, Philadelphia PA

King, Danielle, *VPres,* Manitoba Society of Artists, Winnipeg MB

King, Deborah, *Registrar,* New Mexico Department of Cultural Affairs, Palace of Governors, Santa Fe NM

King, Denise, *Central Servs Adminr,* Montana Historical Society, Helena MT

King, Diana, *Librn for Film, TV & Theater,* University of California, Los Angeles, Arts Library, Los Angeles CA

King, George G, *Exec Dir,* Mystic Art Association, Inc, Mystic Museum of Art, Mystic CT

King, Jack, *Prof,* University of Tampa, College of Arts & Letters, Tampa FL (S)

King, Jeanne, *Prof,* Cazenovia College, Center for Art & Design Studies, Cazenovia NY (S)

King, Juliet, *Asst Prof, Dir Art Therapy,* Indiana University-Purdue University, Indianapolis, Herron School of Art & Design, Indianapolis IN (S)

King, Karlene, *Admin & Develop Coordr,* Bard College, Center for Curatorial Studies and the Hessel Museum of Art, Annandale-on-Hudson NY

King, Kathleen, *Assoc Prof,* Kansas State University, Art Dept, Manhattan KS (S)

King, Kristina, *Gallery Dir,* Pyramid Atlantic, Hyattsville MD

King, Landa, *Asst Prof,* Texas Lutheran University, Dept of Visual Arts, Seguin TX (S)

King, Linda, *Instr,* Long Beach City College, Art & Photography Dept, Long Beach CA (S)

King, Lindsay, *Pub Svcs Librn,* Northwestern University, Art Collection, University Library, Evanston IL

King, Lyndel, *Dir & Chief Cur,* University of Minnesota, Frederick R Weisman Art Museum, Minneapolis MN

King, Margery, *Cur,* The American Federation of Arts, New York NY

King, Maureen, *Secy,* Cypress College, Fine Arts Gallery, Cypress CA

King, Morgana, *Spec Projects & Pub Art Dir,* Arts Council Of New Orleans, New Orleans LA

King, Sam, *Gallery Dir,* University of Arkansas, Fine Arts Center Gallery, Fayetteville AR

King, Sharon, *Prof,* Sam Houston State University, Art Dept, Huntsville TX (S)

King, Susan, *Pres,* Women's Caucus For Art, New York NY

King, Valeria, *Music,* Southern University in New Orleans, Fine Arts & Philosophy Dept, New Orleans LA (S)

King-Nero, Sally, *Cur Drawings & Photography,* Andy Warhol Foundation for the Visual Arts, New York NY

Kinghorn, George, *Dir,* University of Maine, Museum of Art, Bangor ME

Kingston, Donna, *Office Mgr,* Osborne Homestead Museum, Derby CT

Kingston, John, *Prof Ceramics,* Simon's Rock College of Bard, Visual Arts Dept, Great Barrington MA (S)

Kingston, Kitty, *Prof & Chmn,* University of Wisconsin College - Marinette, Art Dept, Marinette WI (S)

Kingston, Robert, *Instr,* Pierce College, Art Dept, Woodland Hills CA (S)

Kinhart, Erin, *Head, Colls Processing,* Archives of American Art, Smithsonian Institution, Washington DC

Kinlaw, Hilary, *Opers Mgr,* North Carolina State University, Gregg Museum of Art & Design, Raleigh NC

Kinnard, Judith, National Architectural Accrediting Board, Inc, Washington DC

Kinne, Carol, *Asst Prof,* Colgate University, Dept of Art & Art History, Hamilton NY (S)

Kinsman, Betty, *Treas,* Springfield Art & Historical Society, Springfield VT

Kinsolving, Lucie, *Chief Conservator,* National Academy Museum & School, Archives, New York NY

Kintner, Alecia, *Pres & CEO,* ArtsWave, Cincinnati OH

Kip Siler, Beth, *CFO,* Taft Museum of Art, Cincinnati OH

Kira, Keiko, *Adjunct Prof Fine Art,* Johnson County Community College, Fine Arts Dept & Art History Dept, Overland Park KS (S)

Kirbabas, Christopher, *Dir Progs,* Society of Architectural Historians, Chicago IL

Kirby Gibbs, Lis, *Pres,* Worcester Art Museum, Worcester MA

Kirby, Adam, *Cur,* Swine Gallery, Chattanooga TN

Kirby, Carol, *Treas,* Art Gallery of Bancroft Inc, Bancroft ON

Kirby, Catherine, *Asst Prof,* Nazareth College of Rochester, Art Dept, Rochester NY (S)

Kirby, Jennifer, *Owner & Exhibs Dir,* Crossroads Art Center Gallery, Richmond VA

Kirch, Lisa, *Asst Prof,* University of North Alabama, Dept of Art, Florence AL (S)

Kirchhefer, Dan R, *Prof,* Emporia State University, Dept of Art, Emporia KS (S)

Kirchman, Kim, *Asst Prof,* Saint Petersburg College, Fine & Applied Arts at Clearwater Campus, Clearwater FL (S)

Kirchner, Joy, *Librn,* York University, Fine Arts Phase II Slide Library, North York ON

Kirin, Asen, *Asst Prof Art History,* University of Georgia, Franklin College of Arts & Sciences, Lamar Dodd School of Art, Athens GA (S)

Kirjakovic, Dusica, *Exec Dir,* Lower East Side Printshop Inc, New York NY (S)

Kirk, Judith, *Asst Dir,* Indiana University, The Mathers Museum of World Cultures, Bloomington IN

Kirk, Michele, *Treas,* Mystic Art Association, Inc, Mystic Museum of Art, Mystic CT

Kirk, Paula, *Accnt,* Embroiderers Guild of America, Margaret Parshall Gallery, Louisville KY

Kirkbride, Robert, *Dean School of Constructed Environments,* The New School, Parsons School of Design, New York NY (S)

Kirkeby, Gary, *Chmn,* Prince George's Community College, Art Dept, Largo MD (S)

Kirkland, Stefanie, *Dir Exhibs,* Craft Alliance Center of Art & Design, Saint Louis MO

Kirkpatrick, Doug, *VPres & Dir,* The New England Museum of Telephony, Inc, The Telephone Museum, Ellsworth ME

Kirkpatrick, Garland, *Asst Prof,* Loyola Marymount University, Dept of Art & Art History, Los Angeles CA (S)

Kirkwood, Heather, *Art Librn,* Purchase College, Library, Purchase NY

Kirkwood, Jane, *Gallery Dir,* East End Arts & Humanities Council, Riverhead NY

Kirkwood, Jeffrey, *Asst Prof,* Binghamton University, Art History Department, Binghamton NY (S)

Kirsch, Edith, *Assoc Prof,* Colorado College, Dept of Art, Colorado Springs CO (S)

Kirsch, Eva, *Dir Gallery,* California State University, San Bernardino, San Bernardino CA

Kirsch, Eva, *Dir Mus,* California State University, San Bernardino, Dept of Art, San Bernardino CA (S)

Kirschbaum, Robert, *Prof Fine Arts,* Trinity College, Dept of Studio Arts, Hartford CT (S)

Kirschensteiner, Brian, *Chief Preparator,* Michigan State University, Eli & Edythe Broad Art Museum, East Lansing MI

Kirschtel-Taylor, Debbye, *Chief Registrar,* Florida International University, The Patricia & Phillip Frost Art Museum, Miami FL

Kirshenbaum, Esther, *Gallery Coordr,* Michigan Guild of Artists & Artisans, Michigan Guild Gallery, Ann Arbor MI

Kirton, Doug, *Assoc Prof & Chair, Dept Fine Arts,* University of Waterloo, Dept of Fine Arts, Waterloo ON (S)

Kirwin, Liza, *Deputy Dir,* Archives of American Art, Smithsonian Institution, Washington DC

Kisielewska, Lara, *Pres,* Graphic Artists Guild, New York NY

Kisiow, Karen, *Colls Mgr,* The Winnipeg Art Gallery, Winnipeg MB

Kisor, Doug, *Chmn Graphic Design,* College for Creative Studies, Detroit MI (S)

Kistner, Lauren, *Mktg/Commun Mgr,* Laumeier Sculpture Park, Saint Louis MO

Kitagawa, Anne, *Chief Cur of Collections,* University of Oregon, Jordan Schnitzer Museum of Art, Eugene OR

Kitchen, Larry, *Instr,* Kilgore College, Visual Arts Dept, Kilgore TX (S)

Kitchens, Sonya, *Dir,* Maryland-National Capital Park & Planning Commission, Montpelier Arts Center, Laurel MD

Kitchin, Cameron, *Dir,* Cincinnati Art Museum, Cincinnati Art Museum, Cincinnati OH

Kitteredge, Frank, *Asst Cur Mathematics,* Northern Maine Museum of Science, Presque Isle ME

Kittinger, Susan, *Colls Mgr,* Rosemount Museum, Inc, Pueblo CO

Kittleson, Michelle, *Commun Coordr,* Historical and Cultural Society of Clay County, Hjemkomst Center, Moorhead MN

Kizer, Katie, *Colls & Exhibs Asst,* The Dixon Gallery & Gardens, Library, Memphis TN

Kjaer, Lise, *Lectr,* City College of New York, Art Dept, New York NY (S)

Kjaer, Merete, *Asst Dir,* University of California-San Diego, University Art Gallery, La Jolla CA

Kjelgaard, Roberta, *Dir Develop,* Boca Raton Museum of Art, Library, Boca Raton FL

Kjellgren, Eric, *Prof,* University of St Thomas, Deptartment of Art History, Saint Paul MN (S)

Kjellman-Chapin, Monica, *Asst,* Emporia State University, Dept of Art, Emporia KS (S)

Kjera, Ann, *Chief HR Officer,* Anchorage Museum at Rasmuson Center, Anchorage AK

Klaff, Len, *Pres,* Ojai Art Center, Ojai CA

Klages, Ricki, *Head Dept,* University of Wyoming, Dept of Art, Laramie WY (S)

Klaneski Reisner, Mariah, *Pres,* Wesleyan University, Friends of the Davison Art Center, Middletown CT

Klapperich, Leah, *Instr,* Marian University, Art Dept, Fond Du Lac WI (S)

Klare, Tom, *Instr,* Mesa Community College, Dept of Art, Mesa AZ (S)

Klatt, Lori, *Vol Coordr,* Nicolaysen Art Museum & Discovery Center, Children's Discovery Center, Casper WY

Klaus, Marianne, *Archives,* Maui Historical Society, Hale Hoike ike at the Bailey House, Wailuku HI

Klawans, Alan J, *2nd VPres,* Plastic Club, Art Club, Philadelphia PA

Klawans, Alan J, *Bd Mem,* American Color Print Society, Narberth PA

Klawuhn, Cole, *Cur,* Saint Joseph Museum, Inc., Saint Joseph MO

Klee, Susan, *Pres (V),* Berkeley Art Center, Berkeley CA

Kleespies, Gavin, *Dir Progs,* Massachusetts Historical Society, Boston MA

Klein Longmire, Tyler, *Production Coordr,* Quickdraw Animation Society, Calgary AB

Klein, Caroline, *Instr,* Guild of Creative Art, Shrewsbury NJ (S)

Klein, Emanuel, *Pres,* Brown County Art Gallery Foundation, Nashville IN

Klein, Joy, *Prog Coordr,* Arizona State University, Memorial Union Gallery, Tempe AZ

Klein, Mary Anne, *Correspondence Secy,* The National Art League, Douglaston NY

Klein, Michelle, *Asst Dir Develop,* University of California, Los Angeles, Fowler Museum at UCLA, Los Angeles CA

Klein, Nancy, *Cur Villa Philmont,* Philmont Scout Ranch, Philmont Museum - Seton Memorial Library, Cimarron NM

Klein, Richard, *Exhib Dir,* Aldrich Museum of Contemporary Art, Ridgefield CT

Klein, Robert, *Owner,* Robert Klein Gallery, Boston MA

Klein, Ron, *Prof Sculpture/3D,* Saint Joseph's University, Art Dept, Philadelphia PA (S)

Klein, Terry M, *Pres,* Fairfield Art Association, Fairfield IA

Klein, Warren, *Cur,* Congregation Emanu-El, Bernard Judaica Museum, New York NY

Kleiner, Diana, *Pres,* Berks Art Alliance, Reading PA

Kleinfelder, Arthur, *Dept Head,* Suffolk County Community College, Art Dept, Selden NY (S)

Klem, Alan, *Assoc Chair Performing Arts,* Creighton University, Fine & Performing Arts Dept, Omaha NE (S)

Klema, Stephen A, *Graphic Design Coordr,* Tunxis Community Technical College, Graphic Design Dept, Farmington CT (S)

Klemens, Courtney, *Outreach Coordr,* Massachusetts Institute of Technology, List Visual Arts Center, Cambridge MA

Klenk, William, *Prof,* University of Rhode Island, Dept of Art & Art History, Kingston RI (S)

Klepacz, Kristina, *Archivist,* Dayton Art Institute, Library, Dayton OH

Kleppin, Jeri, *Secy,* Snake River Heritage Center, Weiser ID

Kleppinger, Kathleen, *Chmn,* Reading Public Museum, Reading PA

Kletchka, Dana Carlisle, *Cur Educ,* The Pennsylvania State University, Palmer Museum of Art, University Park PA

Klicka, John, *Cur Birds,* University of Washington, Burke Museum of Natural History and Culture, Seattle WA

Kliewer, Joy, *Director of Development,* 18th Street Arts Complex, Santa Monica CA

Kligensmith, Ann, *Chmn Fine Arts Div,* Iowa Wesleyan College, Art Dept, Mount Pleasant IA (S)

Kligman, Misha, *Adjunct Asst Prof Fine Art,* Johnson County Community College, Fine Arts Dept & Art History Dept, Overland Park KS (S)

Klihdt, Steve, *Dev,* Tampa Museum of Art, Tampa FL

Klimaszewski, Cathy, *Ames Assoc Dir & Cur Educ,* Cornell University, Herbert F Johnson Museum of Art, Ithaca NY

Klimchak, Maria, *Cur,* Ukrainian National Museum & Library, Chicago IL

Klimiades, Mario Nick, *Library Archives Dir,* Heard Museum, Billie Jane Baguley Library and Archives, Phoenix AZ

Klimiades, Mario, *Dir Library & Archives,* Heard Museum, Phoenix AZ

Kline, J, *Pres,* Watkins College of Art, Design & Film, Brownlee O Currey Gallery, Nashville TN

Kline, Mary, *Vol Coordr,* Salisbury University, Ward Museum of Wildfowl Art, Salisbury MD

Klingemann, John, *VPres,* San Angelo Museum of Fine Arts, San Angelo TX

Klinger, Marsha, *2nd VPres Shows,* Scottsdale Artists' League, Scottsdale AZ

Klingler, Ashley, *Adminstr,* Carl & Marilynn Thoma Art Foundation, Art House Santa Fe, Santa Fe NM

Klingman, Berry J, *Prof,* Baylor University - College of Arts and Sciences, Dept of Art, Waco TX (S)

Klink, Peter J, *Pres,* Heritage Center, Inc, Pine Ridge SD

Klinkon, Heinz, *Asst Prof,* Rochester Institute of Technology, School of Design, Rochester NY (S)

Klinkow, Meg, *Cur,* University of Chicago, Max Epstein Archive, Chicago IL

Klobe, Tom, *Dir Gallery,* University of Hawaii at Manoa, Dept of Art, Honolulu HI (S)

Klochko, Deborah, *Exec Dir,* Museum of Photographic Arts, Edmund L. and Nancy K Dubois Library, San Diego CA

Klocke, Richard, *Exhib Designer,* University of Kansas, Spencer Museum of Art, Lawrence KS

Kloner, Jay, *Assoc Prof,* University of Louisville, Allen R Hite Art Institute, Louisville KY (S)

Klooz, Donan, *Cur Exhibs,* Mobile Museum of Art, Library, Mobile AL

Klooz, Donan, *Cur Exhibs,* Mobile Museum of Art, Mobile AL

Klopfer, Dennis, *Assoc Prof,* Mount Mary College, Art & Design Division, Milwaukee WI (S)

Klopfer, Mary, *Assoc Prof,* University of Saint Francis, School of Creative Arts, Fort Wayne IN (S)

Klopsch, Bill, *Financial Secy,* The Stained Glass Association of America, Raytown MO

Klosky, Peter, *Dir Exhibits,* Roberson Museum & Science Center, Binghamton NY

Klotzbach, Janien, *VPres,* Medina Railroad Museum, Medina NY

Kluba, William, *Assoc Prof,* Tunxis Community Technical College, Graphic Design Dept, Farmington CT (S)

Klueg, James, *Prof,* University of Minnesota, Duluth, Art Dept, Duluth MN (S)

Kluttz, Ann, *Lectr,* University of North Carolina at Charlotte, Dept Art, Charlotte NC (S)

Kmelnitsky, Dmitry, *Asst Prof,* Loyola Marymount University, Dept of Art & Art History, Los Angeles CA (S)

Kmetz, Janice, *Assoc Prof,* University of Minnesota, Duluth, Art Dept, Duluth MN (S)

Knaack, Beth, *Dir Visitor Svcs,* Putnam Museum of History and Natural Science, Davenport IA

Knapp, Alice, *Dir User Servs,* Ferguson Library, Stamford CT

Knapp, Cynthia, *Dir Opers,* Regional Arts & Culture Council, Metropolitan Center for Public Arts, Portland OR

Knapp, Jacquelyn, *Chmn, Assoc Prof Art,* University of Science & Arts of Oklahoma, Art Dept, Chickasha OK (S)

Knapp, M Jason, *Chmn,* Anderson University, Art Dept, Anderson IN (S)

Knapp, Tim, *Asst Dir,* Cleveland State University, The Galleries at CSU, Cleveland OH

Knappe, Brett, *Chair & Asst Prof Art History,* Baker University, Dept of Mass Media & Visual Arts, Baldwin City KS (S)

Knappe, Brett, *Exec Dir,* The Albrecht-Kemper Museum of Art, Saint Joseph MO

Knapple, Barb, *Sec,* Dawson County Historical Society, Museum, Lexington NE

Knauff, Carol, *Dir Communs,* Massachusetts Historical Society, Boston MA

Knavel, Jenny, *Prof,* Western Illinois University, Department of Art, Macomb IL (S)

Knebelsberger, Caroline, *Asst Dir,* Roswell Museum & Art Center, Library, Roswell NM

Knecht, Champ, *Deputy Dir Admin,* The Drawing Center, New York NY

Knecht, John, *Chmn,* Colgate University, Dept of Art & Art History, Hamilton NY (S)

Knecht, Michael S, *Dir,* Laurel Arts, Somerset PA

Knecht, Samuel, *Dir,* Hillsdale College, Art Dept, Hillsdale MI (S)

Knechtel, Nancy, *Prof,* Niagara County Community College, Fine Arts Division, Sanborn NY (S)

Knepper, Alice, *Adjunct Prof,* Missouri Southern State University, Dept of Art, Joplin MO (S)

Knibb, Nicole, *Sr Educ Officer,* McMaster University, McMaster Museum of Art, Hamilton ON

Knicely, Bryan W, *Dir,* Evansville Museum of Arts, History & Science, Evansville IN

Knicely, Bryan W, *Exec Dir,* Coral Springs Museum of Art, Coral Springs FL

Knicely, Jo-Ann, *Treas,* Huronia Museum, Gallery of Historic Huronia, Midland ON

Knickmeyer, Hank, *Prof,* Fontbonne University, Fine Art Dept, Saint Louis MO (S)

Knight, Anne, *Pres,* Sturdivant Museum Association, Sturdivant Museum, Selma AL

Knight, Clarence, *Chmn,* Bowie State University, Fine & Performing Arts Dept, Bowie MD (S)

Knight, Cynthia, *Dir,* Woodbridge Township Cultural Arts Commission, Barron Arts Center, Woodbridge NJ

Knight, David, *Dir Exhib & Colls,* Northern Kentucky University, Galleries, Highland Heights KY

Knight, Lynn, *Dir of Events Coordr,* Earlham College, Leeds Gallery, Richmond IN

Knight, Mary Ann, *Music & Arts Specialist,* Berkshire Athenaeum, Reference Dept, Pittsfield MA

Knight, Robert, *Asst Prof,* Hamilton College, Art Dept, Clinton NY (S)

Knight, Russell, *Pres,* Dubuque Museum of Art, Dubuque IA

Knight, Wanda, *Assoc Prof Art Educ,* Pennsylvania State University, University Park, Penn State School of Visual Arts, University Park PA (S)

Knipp, Tammy, *Assoc Prof Art, Graphic Design,* Florida Atlantic University, D F Schmidt College of Arts & Letters Dept of Visual Arts & Art History, Boca Raton FL (S)

Knittel, K D, *Asst Prof,* Seton Hall University, College of Arts & Sciences, South Orange NJ (S)

Knoblauch, Ann-Marie, *Prof,* Virginia Polytechnic Institute & State University, Dept of Art & Art History, Blacksburg VA (S)

Knoedler, J, *Educ Dir,* The Barnum Museum, Bridgeport CT

Knoles, Thomas G, *Marcus A McCorison Librn & Cur Manuscripts,* American Antiquarian Society, Worcester MA

Knoll, Ann M, *Interim Dir,* University of Notre Dame, Snite Museum of Art, Notre Dame IN

Knopke, Liz, *Membership Coordinator,* Museum of Wisconsin Art, West Bend WI

Knopp, Michael, *Cur Chemistry,* Northern Maine Museum of Science, Presque Isle ME

Knott, Stephanie, *Reference & Special Colls,* Providence Athenaeum, Library, Providence RI

Knowles, Amanda, *Gallery Cur,* North Seattle College, North Seattle College Dept of Art, Seattle WA (S)

Knowles, Amanda, *Printmaking & Drawing,* North Seattle College, North Seattle College Dept of Art, Seattle WA (S)

Knowles, Craig, *Caretaker Bldgs & Grounds,* American Civilization Foundation, National Museum of American Illustration, Newport RI

Knowles, Elizabeth, *Exec Dir,* Wildling Art Museum, Solvang CA

Knowlton, Kenn, *Instr,* Art Academy of Cincinnati, Cincinnati OH (S)

Knowton, Ken, *Instr Photography,* AIC College of Design, Cincinnati OH (S)

Knox, John, *Dir Opers,* North Carolina Museum of Art, Raleigh NC

Knox, Tyra, *Exec Secy,* Springfield Art Museum, Springfield MO

Knudsen, Dean, *Historian,* Oregon Trail Museum Association, Scotts Bluff National Monument, Gering NE

Knudson, Ellen, *Assoc Prof,* University of Florida, School of Art & Art History, Gainesville FL (S)

Knuth, John, *Gallery Cur,* Mt San Jacinto College, Fine Art Gallery, San Jacinto CA

Knutson, James, *Prof,* Black Hills State University, Art Dept, Spearfish SD (S)

Knutson, Karen, *Faculty,* Grand Marais Art Colony, Grand Marais MN (S)

Knutson, Michael, *Prof Art,* Reed College, Dept of Art, Portland OR (S)

Koatsis, Kriszta, *Prof of Art History,* University of Puget Sound, Dept of Art & Art History, Tacoma WA (S)

Kobik, Steven, *Pres,* The Huntington Library, Art Collections & Botanical Gardens, Library, San Marino CA

Kobrynich, Bill, *Dir Interior Design,* Art Institute of Fort Lauderdale, Fort Lauderdale FL (S)

Koch, Beth, *Asst Prof,* West Virginia Wesleyan College, Art Dept, Buckhannon WV (S)

Koch, Cynthia M, *Dir,* National Archives & Records Administration, Franklin D Roosevelt Library, Hyde Park NY

Koch, Cynthia, *Dir,* National Archives & Records Administration, Franklin D Roosevelt Museum, Hyde Park NY

Koch, Peter, *Pres,* North Carolina Museums Council, Raleigh NC

Koch, Richard, *Performing Arts Mgr & Technical Dir,* The Cultural Arts Center at Glen Allen, Glen Allen VA

Kochan, Roman V, *Dean Lib & Acad Tech,* California State University, Long Beach, University Library, Long Beach CA

Kochavi, Shir, *Asst Cur,* University of California, Berkeley, The Magnes Collection of Jewish Art & Life, Berkeley CA

Kochman, Adrienne, *Cur,* Ukrainian Institute of Modern Art, Chicago IL

Kocot, Marion, *Museum Deputy Director,* Asia Society Museum, New York NY

Kocs, Constance, *Instr,* Pierce College, Art Dept, Woodland Hills CA (S)

Koebel, Jenifer, *Youth Program Coordinator,* Museum of Wisconsin Art, West Bend WI

Koedel, Nikki, *Event Coordinator,* Pyramid Hill Sculpture Park & Museum, Hamilton OH

Koefoed, Lori, *Instr,* Pierce College, Art Dept, Woodland Hills CA (S)

Koehler, Keri, *Colls Mgr,* San Francisco Maritime National Historical Park, Maritime Library, San Francisco CA

Koehler, Ron, *Chmn,* Delta State University, Dept of Art, Cleveland MS (S)

Koehler, Ronald G, *Chmn Dept,* Delta State University, Fielding L Wright Art Center, Cleveland MS

Koen, Michael, *Pres,* Kemp Center for the Arts, Wichita Falls TX

Koenig, Richard, *Prof,* Kalamazoo College, Art Dept, Kalamazoo MI (S)

Koeninger, Kay, *Asst Prof,* Sinclair Community College, Division of Fine & Performing Arts, Dayton OH (S)

Koernig, Marie, *Exec Dir,* Nicolaysen Art Museum & Discovery Center, Children's Discovery Center, Casper WY

Koeth, David M, *Chair, Prof Art,* Bakersfield College, Art Dept, Bakersfield CA (S)

Koetting, Mickey, *Pres,* Ste Genevieve Museum, Sainte Genevieve MO

Koga, Kim, *Exec Dir,* Museum of Neon Art, Glendale CA

Kogn, Lee, *Cur Spec Projects,* American Folk Art Museum, Shirley K. Schlafer Library, New York NY

Kohl, Allan, *Visual Resources Librn,* Minneapolis College of Art & Design, Library, Minneapolis MN

Kohl, Amelia, *Coordr Acad Prog,* Dartmouth College, Hood Museum of Art, Hanover NH

Kohl, Jeanette, *Assoc Prof,* University of California, Riverside, Dept of the History of Art, Riverside CA (S)

Kohl, Kurt C, *Treas,* The Art Cafe, Davisburg MI

Kohl, Laura, *Admin,* New Mexico Department of Cultural Affairs, New Mexico Museum of Art, Unit of NM Dept of Cultural Affairs, Santa Fe NM

Kohl, Laura, *Prin Cataloger,* University of New Mexico, Fine Arts Library, Albuquerque NM

Kohler, Olivia, *Asst Dir,* The George Washington University, Luther W Brady Art Gallery, Washington DC

Kohler, Ruth, *Dir,* Kohler Co, John Michael Kohler Arts Center - Arts/Industry Program, Sheboygan WI

Kohli, Michael, *Bd Pres,* Rome Historical Society, Museum & Archives, Rome NY

Kohut, Khrystia, *2nd VP,* Ukrainian Canadian Archives & Museum of Alberta, Edmonton AB

Kois, Dennis, *Mus Dir,* deCordova Sculpture Park & Museum, Sculpture Park, Lincoln MA

Kois, Dennis, *Pres & CEO,* Milwaukee Public Museum, Milwaukee WI

Koivisto, Chris, *Instr,* Vermilion Community College, Art Dept, Ely MN (S)

Kokoris, Eva, *Corresp Secy,* Society of Scribes, Ltd, New York NY

Kolasinski, Jacek, *Assoc Prof, Dept Chair,* Florida International University, School of Art & Art History, Miami FL (S)

Kolb, Jennifer, *Deputy Division Admin,* Wisconsin Historical Society, Wisconsin Historical Museum, Madison WI

Kolb, Leah, *Cur Exhibs,* Madison Museum of Contemporary Art, Madison WI

Kolb, Robin, *Asst Mgr,* The Schepis, Louisiana Artists Museum, Columbia LA

Kolber, Georgina, *Mng Dir,* Mizel Museum, Denver CO

Kolbo, John, *Instr,* Morningside College, Art Dept, Sioux City IA (S)

Kolczynski, Charlotte, *Sr Music Reference Librn,* Boston Public Library, Arts Reference Department, Boston MA

Kole, Cindy, *Dir Develop,* Kalamazoo Institute of Arts, Kalamazoo MI

Koles, Jeanne, *Publs Coordr,* Tufts University, Tufts University Art Gallery, Medford MA

Koletsky, Susan, *Dir Mus,* The Temple-Tifereth Israel, The Temple Museum of Religious Art, Beachwood OH

Kollmeyer, Mary, *1st VPres,* San Angelo Art Club, Helen King Kendall Memorial Art Gallery, San Angelo TX

Kolster, Michael, *Asst Prof,* Bowdoin College, Art Dept, Brunswick ME (S)

Kolsters, Stephanie, *Cur,* Mississippi Valley Conservation Authority, R Tait McKenzie Memorial Museum, Almonte ON

Kolt, Ingrid, *Cur Prog,* Surrey Art Gallery, Library, Surrey BC

Komanski, Debbie, *Exec Dir,* Albin Polasek Museum & Sculpture Gardens, Winter Park FL

Komatsuka, Carol, *VPres External,* Japanese American National Museum, Los Angeles CA

Kominos, Nicolette, *Sunday Coordr,* Cultural Affairs Department City of Los Angeles, Barnsdall Art Center & Junior Arts Center, Los Angeles CA

Kondrup, Gloria, *Exec Dir, Hoffmitz Milken Center for Typography,* ArtCenter College of Design, Pasadena CA (S)

Kong, Praseth, *Circ Mgr,* Indiana University - Purdue University at Indianapolis, Herron School of Art Library, Indianapolis IN

Konrad, Michael, *Information Svc Asst,* New York University, Institute of Fine Arts Visual Resources Collection, New York NY

Kontar, Diane, *Assoc Prof,* University of Findlay, Art Program, Findlay OH (S)

Konya, Seiko, *Corresp Secy,* Northwest Watercolor Society, Woodinville WA

Koons McCullough, Hollis, *Cur Fine Arts & Exhibits,* Telfair Museums, Telfair Academy of Arts & Sciences Library, Savannah GA

Koop, Kathy, *Dir,* Westminster College, Art Gallery, New Wilmington PA

Koop, Ken, *Dir Retail Svcs,* Vesterheim Norwegian-American Museum, Decorah IA

Koop, Rebecca, *Instr,* William Jewell College, Art Dept, Liberty MO (S)

Koortbojian, Michael, *Chair & Prof Art & Archaeology,* Princeton University, Dept of Art & Archaeology, Princeton NJ (S)

Koos, Greg, *Exec Dir,* McLean County Historical Society, McLean County Museum of History, Bloomington IL

Koosmann, Chuck, *Bd Pres,* The Phipps Center for the Arts, Galleries, Hudson WI

Koostra, Barbara, *Dir,* University of Montana, Montana Museum of Art & Culture, Missoula MT

Kopczak, Chuck, *Cur World Ecology,* California Science Center, Los Angeles CA

Kopczynski, Carol, *Admin & Colls Asst,* North Tonawanda History Museum, North Tonawanda NY

Kopelman, Arie, *VPres,* Nantucket Historical Association, Historic Nantucket, Nantucket MA

Koperski, Kate, *Dir,* Niagara University, Castellani Art Museum, Niagara NY

Kopet, Donna, *Tour Coordr,* Anniston Museum of Natural History, Anniston AL

Kopp, Maggie, *Cur European Books,* Brigham Young University, Harold B Lee Library, Provo UT

Kopren, Eileen, *Dir Pub Svcs,* Dickinson State University, Stoxen Library, Dickinson ND

Korchinski, Kevin, *Exec Dir,* Organization of Saskatchewan Arts Councils (OSAC), Regina SK

Kordich, Diane D, *Prof,* Northern Michigan University, Dept of Art & Design, Marquette MI (S)

Kordos, Richard S, *Exec Dir,* Academy of Fine Arts, Lynchburg VA

Koren, Cynthia, *Assoc Prof,* Munson-Williams-Proctor Arts Institute, Pratt MWP College of Art, Utica NY (S)

Korenblat, Ellen, *Communs Dir,* Historic Arkansas Museum, Library, Little Rock AR

Korenblat, Ellen, *Dir Community Engagement,* Historic Arkansas Museum, Little Rock AR

Korenic, Lyn, *Dir,* University of Wisconsin-Madison, Kohler Art Library, Madison WI

Korff, David, *Coordr Galleries & Exhibits,* Saint Clair County Community College, Jack R Hennesey Art Galleries, Port Huron MI

Korff, David, *Dept Chmn,* Saint Clair County Community College, Jack R Hennesey Art Dept, Port Huron MI (S)

Korisheli, Margaret, *Chair Fine Arts,* Cuesta College, Harold J Miossi Art Gallery, San Luis Obispo CA

Korkow, Cory, *Assoc Cur European Art,* The Cleveland Museum of Art, Cleveland OH

Korman, Jaymie, *Site Supv,* Minnesota Historical Society, Minnesota State Capitol Historic Site, Saint Paul MN

Korn, Emily, *Event Coordr,* Saginaw Art Museum, Saginaw MI

Kornek, Jay, *Radio,* Henry Ford Community College, McKenzie Fine Art Ctr, Dearborn MI (S)

Kornfeld, Abby, *Asst Prof,* City College of New York, Art Dept, New York NY (S)

Kornfeld, Fran, *Asst Dir,* Holland Tunnel Art Projects, Brooklyn NY

Korns, Jenny, *Prog Coordr,* Franklin Furnace Archive, Inc, Brooklyn NY

Koroscik, Judith, *Dean Col,* Ohio State University, College of the Arts, Columbus OH (S)

Koroscik, Judith, *Prof,* Ohio State University, Dept of Art Education, Columbus OH (S)

Korow, Elinore, *Instr,* Cuyahoga Valley Art Center, Cuyahoga Falls OH (S)

Korzon, John, *Chmn & Instr,* Southwestern Michigan College, Fine & Performing Arts Dept, Dowagiac MI (S)

Koshinsky, Deborah, *Adminr & Asc Librn,* Arizona State University, Architecture & Environmental Design Library, Tempe AZ

Koshinsky, Deborah, *Architecture Librn,* Arizona State University, ASU Library, Tempe AZ

Kosinski, Dorothy M, *Dir & CEO,* The Phillips Collection, Washington DC

Koski, Kasey, *Exhibits Curator,* North Central Washington Museum, Wenatchee Valley Museum & Cultural Center, Wenatchee WA

Kosmere, Ellen, *Prof,* Worcester State College, Visual & Performing Arts Dept, Worcester MA (S)

Koss, Gene H, *Prof,* Tulane University, Sophie H Newcomb Memorial College, New Orleans LA (S)

Kossar, Carolyn, *Gallery Dir,* Hillsborough Community College, Fine Arts Dept, Tampa FL (S)

Kostelny, Elizabeth, *CEO,* Preservation Virginia, John Marshall House, Richmond VA

Kostelny, Elizabeth, *CEO,* Preservation Virginia, Richmond VA

Kostes, Stephen, *Facility Coordr,* Lockwood-Mathews Mansion Museum, Norwalk CT

Kostopoulos, Kate, *Dir,* Chase Young Gallery, Boston MA

Kosuge, Michihiro, *Dept Chmn, Prof,* Portland State University, Dept of Art, Portland OR (S)

Kot, Malgorzata, *Mng Dir,* Polish Museum of America (PMA), Chicago IL

Koterbay, Scott, *Assoc Prof,* East Tennessee State University, College of Arts and Sciences, Dept of Art & Design, Johnson City TN (S)

Kotoulas, Sotirios, *Pres,* Plug In, Institute of Contemporary Art, Winnipeg MB

Kotsch, Kristine, *Instr,* Moravian College, Dept of Art, Bethlehem PA (S)

Kotting, Joey, *Dir,* California State University, Bakersfield, Todd Madigan Gallery, Bakersfield CA

Kotz, Liz, *Assoc Prof,* University of California, Riverside, Dept of the History of Art, Riverside CA (S)

Kouba, Don, *Dept Chmn,* Prairie State College, Art Dept, Chicago Heights IL (S)

Koumijian, Jeanette, *Recording Secy,* Catharine Lorillard Wolfe, New York NY

Kourasis, Betty, *Dean Student Affairs,* The Illinois Institute of Art - Chicago, Chicago IL (S)

Kourbatov, Orysia, *Admin,* Ukrainian National Museum & Library, Chicago IL

Kourelis, Kostis, *Asst Prof,* Franklin & Marshall College, Art & Art History Dept, Lancaster PA (S)

Kovach, Jodi, *Curator of Academic Programs,* Kenyon College, Gund Gallery, Gambier OH

Koval, Anne, *Assoc Prof,* Mount Allison University, Dept of Fine Arts, Sackville NB (S)

Kovarik, Jennifer, *Registrar & Librn,* Vesterheim Norwegian-American Museum, Decorah IA

Koven, Katie Lee, *Exec Dir & Chief Cur,* Utah State University, Nora Eccles Harrison Museum of Art, Logan UT

Kowal, Calvin, *Instr,* Art Academy of Cincinnati, Cincinnati OH (S)

Kowal, Jill, *Educ Coordr,* Art Center Sarasota, Sarasota FL (S)

Kowalchuk, Anna, *Mus Admin,* Livingston County Historical Society, Museum, Geneseo NY

Kowalchuk, Elizabeth, *Assoc Prof & Assoc Dean,* University of Kansas, The School of the Arts, Dept of Visual Art, Lawrence KS (S)

Kowalchuk, Elizabeth, *Asst Prof,* University of Kansas, Dept of Art & Music Education & Music Therapy, Lawrence KS (S)

Kowalewski, Phoebe, *Cataloger/Processing Archivist,* The University of the Arts, University Libraries, Philadelphia PA

Kowalick, Stephanie, *Coll Mgr & Registrar,* University of Southern California, USC Fisher Museum of Art, Los Angeles CA

Kowski, Robert, *Prof,* Greensboro College, Dept of Art, Division of Fine Arts, Greensboro NC (S)

Koyne, Paul, *Assoc Prof Music,* Siena College, Dept of Creative Arts, Loudonville NY (S)

Kozionnyi, Alexander, *Dir Exhib Installation & Architect,* Chicago Athenaeum, Museum of Architecture & Design, Galena IL

Kozlowski, John, *VPres,* Canadian Museum for Human Rights, Winnipeg MB

Kozokoff, Neil, *Chmn,* Chicago Athenaeum, Museum of Architecture & Design, Galena IL

Kraball, Merrill, *Chmn,* Bethel College, Dept of Art, North Newton KS (S)

Kraeger, Markus, *Dir Visitor Svcs,* Historical and Cultural Society of Clay County, Hjemkomst Center, Moorhead MN

Kraemer, Pat, *Instr,* Rochester Community & Technical College, Art Dept, Rochester MN (S)

Kraft, Michelle, *Chmn & Instr,* Lubbock Christian University, Dept of Communication & Fine Art, Lubbock TX (S)

Kraft, Toni Lee, *Registrar,* Tyler Museum of Art, Reference Library, Tyler TX

Krajniak, Miranda, *Exec Dir,* Kendall College of Art & Design, Urban Institute for Contemporary Arts, Grand Rapids MI

Kralickova, Petra, *Cur,* Ohio University, Kennedy Museum of Art, Athens OH

Kralisz, Victor, *Mgr Fine Art Div,* J Eric Johnson, Fine Arts Division, Dallas TX

Kramer, Berri, *Pres,* Heartwood College of Art, Main Gallery, Biddeford ME

Kramer, Cheryl, *Gallery Dir,* Ithaca College, Handwerker Gallery of Art, Ithaca NY

Kramer, Don, *Art Educ Adjunct,* Iowa Wesleyan College, Art Dept, Mount Pleasant IA (S)

Kramer, Edith, *Cur Film,* University of California, Berkeley, Pacific Film Archive, Berkeley CA

Kramer, Gerald, *Coordr Fine Art Prog,* Cuyahoga Community College, Dept of Art, Cleveland OH (S)

Kramer, Hjunjee, *Graphic Design, Web & PR Coordinator,* College of Central Florida, Appleton Museum of Art, Ocala FL

Kramer, Jane, *Prog Mgr,* Lansing Art Gallery, Lansing MI

Kramer, Kathryn, *Assoc Prof,* State University of New York, College at Cortland, Dept Art & Art History, Cortland NY (S)

Kramer, Kathyrn, *Librn,* C M Russell Museum, Frederic G Renner Memorial Library, Great Falls MT

Kramer, Leslie, *Asst Prof,* Elmira College, Art Dept, Elmira NY (S)

Kramer, Leslie, *Dir,* Elmira College, George Waters Gallery, Elmira NY

Kramer, Steve, *Head Dept South Campus,* Austin Community College, Dept of Commercial Art, North Ridge Campus, Austin TX (S)

Kramer, William, *Preparator,* Syracuse University, Art Collection, Syracuse NY

Kramer-Johnson, Jean, *Asset Mgr,* Traffic Zone Center for Visual Art, Minneapolis MN

Krammes, Barry, *Prof,* Biola University, Department of Art, La Mirada CA (S)

Krane, Susan, *Exec Dir,* San Jose Museum of Art, San Jose CA

Kranker, Holly, *Residency Prog Mgr,* Bemis Center for Contemporary Arts, Omaha NE

Krannig, Dora, *Instr Dance,* Glendale Community College, Visual & Performing Arts Div, Glendale CA (S)
Krantz, Kevin, *Dir,* Lafayette Science Museum & Planetarium, Lafayette LA
Krantzler, Robert, *Prof,* Miami-Dade Community College, Arts & Philosophy Dept, Miami FL (S)
Krasevac-Lenz, Karin, *Dir,* Rensselaer County Historical Society, Museum & Library, Troy NY
Krasevac-Lenz, Karin, *Dir,* Rensselaer County Historical Society, Hart-Cluett Mansion, 1827, Troy NY
Kraskin, Sandra, *Dir,* Baruch College of the City University of New York, Sidney Mishkin Gallery, New York NY
Kraus, Corrine, *Instr,* Milwaukee Area Technical College, School of Media & Creative Arts, Milwaukee WI (S)
Kraus, Heidi, *Dir,* Hope College, DePree Art Center & Gallery, Holland MI
Kraus, Heidi, *Gallery Dir,* Hope College, Dept of Art & Art History, Holland MI (S)
Kraus, Russell C, *Prof,* Rochester Institute of Technology, School of Photographic Arts & Sciences, Rochester NY (S)
Krause, Joann, *Instr,* Grand Marais Art Colony, Grand Marais MN (S)
Krause, Kim, *Instr,* Art Academy of Cincinnati, Cincinnati OH (S)
Kraushaar, Andy, *Cur Visual Materials,* Wisconsin Historical Society, Wisconsin Historical Museum, Madison WI
Krauss, James A, *Chmn & Prof,* Oakton Community College, Language Humanities & Art Divisions, Des Plaines IL (S)
Krauss, Sharon, *Asst Dir,* Becker College, William F Ruska Library, Worcester MA
Kravitz, Susan, *Chmn,* Nassau Community College, Art Dept, Garden City NY (S)
Kravitz, Walter, *Dir,* George Mason University, College of Visual & Performing Arts, Fine Arts Gallery, Fairfax VA (S)
Kray, Hazele, *Cur,* The Bartlett Museum, Amesbury MA
Krazer, Kim A, *Registrar,* Newport Historical Society & Museum of Newport History, Newport RI
Krazmien, Mindy, *Exec Dir,* Putnam County Historical Society, Foundry School Museum, Cold Spring NY
Kreager, Tom, *Chmn,* Hastings College, Department of Visual Arts, Hastings NE (S)
Kreager, Tom, *Prof,* Hastings College, Department of Visual Arts, Hastings NE (S)
Krehbiel, Bryce, *Pres,* Maude Kerns Art Center, Eugene OR
Krehbiel, James, *Chmn,* Ohio Wesleyan University, Fine Arts Dept, Delaware OH (S)
Krehmeier, Bill, *Instr,* Hannibal La Grange College, Art Dept, Hannibal MO (S)
Kreidler, Nicole Bieak, *Asst Prof & Dept Chair Interior Design,* La Roche College, Division of Design, Pittsburgh PA (S)
Kreimer, Julian, *Assoc Prof,* Purchase College, State University of New York, School of Art+Design, Purchase NY (S)
Kreindel, Mary Jo, *Art Div,* Lane Community College, Art & Applied Design Dept, Eugene OR (S)
Kreiner, Mary Beth, *Librn,* Cranbrook Art Museum, Library, Bloomfield Hills MI
Kreizinger, Joe, *Chmn Dept Fine & Performing Arts,* Northwest Missouri State University, DeLuce Art Gallery, Maryville MO
Krejcarek, Philip, *Assoc Prof,* Carroll College, Art Dept, Waukesha WI (S)
Krejci, Mark, *Instr Set Design,* Creighton University, Fine & Performing Arts Dept, Omaha NE (S)
Krell, Rebekah, *Deputy Dir,* San Francisco City & County Arts Commission, San Francisco CA
Kremenik, Andrea, *Cur Asst,* University of Lethbridge, Art Gallery, Lethbridge AB
Kremer, Gary R, *Exec Dir,* State Historical Society of Missouri, Columbia MO
Kremer, Gary R, *Exec Dir,* State Historical Society of Missouri, Gallery and Library, Columbia MO
Kremers, Michele, *Instr,* Marylhurst University, Art Dept, Marylhurst OR (S)
Krempel, Sara, *Prof,* Central Oregon Community College, Dept of Art, Bend OR (S)
Krenos, Elizabeth, *Instr,* Moravian College, Dept of Art, Bethlehem PA (S)
Krensky, Beth, *Asst Prof,* University of Utah, Dept of Art & Art History, Salt Lake City UT (S)
Krepps, Jerald, *Assoc Prof,* University of Minnesota, Minneapolis, Dept of Art, Minneapolis MN (S)
Kress, Julia, *Libr Specialist,* University of Houston, William R Jenkins Architecture & Art Library, Houston TX
Kress, Katherine, *Mus Shop Mgr,* Northwood University, Jeannette Hare Art Gallery, West Palm Beach FL
Kret, Robert A, *Dir,* Georgia O'Keeffe Museum, Santa Fe NM
Kreutzer-Hodson, Teresa, *Cur & Coll,* Hastings Museum of Natural & Cultural History, Hastings NE
Krevens, Frank, *Asst Prof Art,* Brescia University, Art Dept, Owensboro KY (S)
Krevens, Frank, *Asst Prof of Art,* Brescia University, Anna Eaton Stout Memorial Art Gallery, Owensboro KY
Krezel, Cindy, *Dir Develop,* Planting Fields Foundation, Coe Hall at Planting Fields Arboretum, Oyster Bay NY
Krick, Jessa J, *Colls Mgr,* Historic Hudson Valley, Pocantico Hills NY
Krieger, Louise, *Dir Asst,* Smith College, Museum of Art, Northampton MA
Kriff, Leslie, *Registrar,* Rutgers, The State University of New Jersey, Zimmerli Art Museum at Rutgers University, New Brunswick NJ
Krill, Hanya, *Mktg & Pub Relations,* The Ukrainian Museum, New York NY
Kriner, Lisa L, *Chmn,* Berea College, Art & Art History Program, Berea KY (S)
Krinock, Mary, *VPres Educ & Guest Servs,* Museum of Science & Industry, Chicago IL
Kristof, Jane, *Assoc Prof,* Portland State University, Dept of Art, Portland OR (S)
Kritselis, Alexander, *Div Dean,* Pasadena City College, Visual Arts and Media Studies Division, Pasadena CA (S)
Krivak, Andrea, *Sr Designer,* Erie Art Museum, Erie PA
Krody, Sumru Belger, *Sr Cur,* George Washington University, The George Washington Museum and The Textile Museum, Washington DC
Kroeff-Streng, Kay, *Technical Svcs Librn,* Minneapolis College of Art & Design, Library, Minneapolis MN
Kroemer, Angela, *Secy,* University of Northern Iowa, Dept of Art, Cedar Falls IA (S)
Kroft, David, *Chmn,* Concordia University, Dept of Fine Arts, Austin TX (S)
Krohn, Laurie, *Cafe Mgr,* Worcester Art Museum, Worcester MA
Krol, Penne, *Prof,* Greenfield Community College, Art Dept, Greenfield MA (S)
Krolak, K Malia, *Dir,* Louisiana State University School of Art, Alfred C Glassell Jr Exhibition Gallery, Baton Rouge LA
Krolak, Kristin Malia, *Dir Galleries,* Louisiana State University, School of Art - Glassell Gallery, Baton Rouge LA
Kroll, Jim, *Mgr Western History & Genealogy,* Denver Public Library, Reference, Denver CO
Kromer, Lindsay, *Media Productions Coordr,* University of Tennessee, McClung Museum of Natural History & Culture, Knoxville TN
Krone, Ted, *Chmn,* Friends University, Art Dept, Wichita KS (S)
Kronewetter, Justin, *Dir,* Richard M Ross Art Museum at Wesleyan University, Delaware OH
Kronkright, Dale, *Head Conservation,* Georgia O'Keeffe Museum, Santa Fe NM
Kropf, Joan R, *Deputy Dir & Cur,* Salvador Dali, Library, Saint Petersburg FL
Kropp, Kaitlin, *Assoc Dir Mem Engagement,* Madison Museum of Contemporary Art, Madison WI
Kroupa, Sandra, *Book Arts & Rare Books Cur,* University of Washington, Univ of Washington Libraries, Special Collections, Seattle WA
Kruck, Martin, *Printmaking Prof,* New Jersey City University, Art Dept, Jersey City NJ (S)
Kruckenberg, Molly, *Research Center Dir,* Montana Historical Society, Helena MT
Krueger, Dana, *Registrar,* Hamilton College, Emerson Gallery, Clinton NY
Krueger, David, *Preparator,* Rice University, Rice Gallery, Houston TX
Krueger, Michael, *Assoc Prof,* University of Kansas, The School of the Arts, Dept of Visual Art, Lawrence KS (S)
Krueger, September, *Instr, Chair,* Southeastern Community College, Dept of Art, Whiteville NC (S)
Krueger-Corrado, Kristen, *Mktg & Communs Mgr,* Grand Rapids Public Library, Grand Rapids MI
Krug, Don, *Assoc Prof,* Ohio State University, Dept of Art Education, Columbus OH (S)
Kruger, Betty, *Cur,* Cambridge Museum, Cambridge NE
Kruger, Laura, *Cur,* Hebrew Union College - Jewish Institute of Religion Museum, Jewish Institute of Religion, New York NY
Krule, Bernard K, *Assoc Prof,* Oakton Community College, Language Humanities & Art Divisions, Des Plaines IL (S)
Krull, Dennis, *Artist & Owner,* Gallery 4, Ltd, Fargo ND
Krull, Jeffrey R, *Dir,* Allen County Public Library, Art, Music & Audiovisual Services, Fort Wayne IN
Krumm, Beverly, *Instr,* South Dakota State University, Dept of Visual Arts, Brookings SD (S)
Krush, Wayne, *Dept Chmn,* State University of New York at Farmingdale, Visual Communications, Farmingdale NY (S)
Krutak, Lars, *Prog Specialist,* United States Department of the Interior, Indian Arts & Crafts Board, Washington DC
Ksepka, Daniel, *Cur Sci,* Bruce Museum, Inc, Greenwich CT
Kuan, Baulu, *Assoc Prof,* College of Saint Benedict, Art Dept, Saint Joseph MN (S)
Kuan, Baulu, *Assoc Prof,* Saint John's University, Art Dept, Collegeville MN (S)
Kubert, Joe, *Pres,* Joe Kubert, Dover NJ (S)
Kubesh, Tasha, *Assoc Cur Colls & Exhibs,* Plains Art Museum, Fargo ND
Kubieka, Rhiarnon, *Co Chmn,* The Drawing Center, New York NY
Kubiski, Joyce, *Art History,* Western Michigan University, Frostic School of Art, Kalamazoo MI (S)
Kucharski, Malcolm E, *Assoc Prof,* Pittsburg State University, Art Dept, Pittsburg KS (S)
Kuchler, Lee, *Instr,* Ocean City Arts Center, Ocean City NJ (S)
Kucker, Patricia, *Provost,* The University of the Arts, Rosenwald-Wolf Gallery, Philadelphia PA
Kuder, Nicholas, *Graphic Design,* Western Michigan University, Frostic School of Art, Kalamazoo MI (S)
Kuderle, Chris, *Admin Dir,* Nanaimo Art Gallery, Nanaimo BC
Kudryavtseva, Ekaterina, *Asst Prof,* Stetson University, Department of Creative Arts, Deland FL (S)
Kuebel-Stanky, Melanie, *Dir Visitor & Mem Svcs,* Erie County Historical Society, Erie PA
Kueber, Rita, *Dir Mktg & Communs,* Western Reserve Historical Society, Library, Cleveland OH
Kuebler-Wolf, Beth, *Asst Prof,* University of Saint Francis, School of Creative Arts, Fort Wayne IN (S)
Kuehn, David, *Dir,* Cotuit Center for the Arts, Cotuit MA
Kuehn, Trena, *Asst Cur,* Frontier Gateway Museum, Glendive MT
Kuenstner, Molli E, *Northern & Central Europe Specialist,* National Gallery of Art, Department of Image Collections, Washington DC

Kuentzel, Peter, *Prof,* Miami-Dade Community College, Arts & Philosophy Dept, Miami FL (S)
Kufahl, Kim, *Pub Rels,* Wichita Center for the Arts, Mary R Koch School of Visual Arts, Wichita KS (S)
Kugat, Sanja, *Dir Vis Servs,* Harvard University, Harvard Art Museums, Cambridge MA
Kugo, Eduardo, *Instr,* Inter American University of Puerto Rico, Fine Arts Dept -Art Program, San German PR (S)
Kuharic, Katharine, *Kevin Kennedy Assoc Prof Art,* Hamilton College, Art Dept, Clinton NY (S)
Kuhlman, Anna, *Exec Dir,* Gulf Beach Art Center, Indian Rocks Beach FL
Kuhlman, Gayle, *FOCUS Chair,* Noyes Art Gallery, Lincoln NE
Kuhn, Ashley, *Instr,* Moravian College, Dept of Art, Bethlehem PA (S)
Kuhn, Terry, *Maintenance Dir,* State of North Carolina, Battleship North Carolina, Wilmington NC
Kuhr, Alexis, *Assoc Prof,* University of Minnesota, Minneapolis, Dept of Art, Minneapolis MN (S)
Kuiper, Adriana, *Assoc Prof,* Mount Allison University, Dept of Fine Arts, Sackville NB (S)
Kuiper, James, *Prof,* California State University, Chico, Department of Art & Art History, Chico CA (S)
Kukella, Joseph, *Asst Prof & Chmn,* Daemen College, Art Dept, Amherst NY (S)
Kukla, Jon, *Exec Dir,* Patrick Henry, Red Hill National Memorial, Brookneal VA
Kulak-Harris, Alyssa, *Outreach Dir,* Brickton Art Center, Park Ridge IL
Kumar, Susan, *Dir,* Palisades Park Public Library, Palisades Park NJ
Kumar, Vijay, *Instr,* Manhattan Graphics Center, New York NY (S)
Kumata, Michelle, *Exhib Dir,* Wing Luke Asian Museum, Seattle WA
Kumle, Aden, *Dir Grad Studies,* University of Chicago, Dept of Art History, Chicago IL (S)
Kumnick, Charles, *Assoc Prof,* The College of New Jersey, School of Arts & Sciences, Ewing NJ (S)
Kunau, Kate, *Assoc Cur,* Cedar Rapids Museum of Art, Cedar Rapids IA
Kunce, Craig, *Instr,* Western Wisconsin Technical College, Graphics Division, La Crosse WI (S)
Kundar, Cynthia A, *Dir & Educ Dir,* Merrick Art Gallery, New Brighton PA
Kuntz, Margaret, *Asst Prof,* Drew University, Art Dept, Madison NJ (S)
Kuntz, Melissa, *Prof,* Clarion University of Pennsylvania, Dept of Art, Clarion PA (S)
Kuntzman, Lauren, *Coordr Educ,* Canton Museum of Art, Canton OH
Kuntzman, Lauren, *Cur Educ,* Canton Museum of Art, Canton OH (S)
Kunzendorf, Eric, *Assoc Prof of Animation,* Jacksonville University, Jacksonville FL (S)
Kuonen, Lily, *Asst Prof Art & Foundations Coordr,* Jacksonville University, Jacksonville FL (S)
Kupper, Ketti, *Asst Prof,* University of Bridgeport, Shintaro Akatsu School of Design, Bridgeport CT (S)
Kuras, Jean, *Pres,* Historical Society of Bloomfield, Bloomfield NJ
Kuretsky, Susan D, *Prof,* Vassar College, Art Dept, Poughkeepsie NY (S)
Kurin, Richard, *Acting Dir,* Freer Gallery of Art & Arthur M Sackler Gallery, Freer Gallery of Art, Washington DC
Kurin, Richard, *Acting Dir,* Freer Gallery of Art & Arthur M Sackler Gallery, Arthur M Sackler Gallery, Washington DC
Kurnit, Daniel, *Admin Asst,* School for Advanced Research (SAR), Indian Arts Research Center, Santa Fe NM
Kurot, Renee, *School and Youth Programs,* Hofstra University, Hofstra University Museum, Hempstead NY
Kurtin, William, *Exec Dir,* San Antonio Art League, San Antonio Art League Museum, San Antonio TX
Kurtz, Carla, *Office & Accts Mgr,* Society for Photographic Education (SPE), SPE Gallery, Cleveland OH
Kurtz, Debra, *Dir Mem Experiences,* Edmundson Art Foundation, Inc, Des Moines Art Center, Des Moines IA
Kurtz, Howard, *Asst Cur Costumes & Textiles,* Hillwood Museum & Gardens Foundation, Hillwood Estate Museum & Gardens, Washington DC
Kusaba, Yoshio, *Prof Emeritus,* California State University, Chico, Department of Art & Art History, Chico CA (S)
Kusaba, Yoshio, *Prof Emeritus Art History Research,* California State University, Chico, Janet Turner Print Museum, CSU, Chicago, Chico CA
Kushner, Sam, *Acting Branch Mgr,* Las Vegas-Clark County Library District, Flamingo Gallery, Las Vegas NV
Kusik, James, *Assoc Librn,* Saint Xavier University, Robert and Mary Rita Murphy Stump Library, Chicago IL
Kuspit, Donald B, *Prof,* Stony Brook University, College of Arts & Sciences, Dept of Art, Stony Brook NY (S)
Kussack, John, *Admin Mgr,* Oregon Trail Museum Association, Scotts Bluff National Monument, Gering NE
Kusser, Robert L, *Dir,* South Dakota National Guard Museum, Pierre SD
Kusserow, Karl, *Cur American Art,* Princeton University, Princeton University Art Museum, Princeton NJ
Kussow, Timothy, *Prof Sculpture,* Manchester Community College, Visual Fine Art Dept, Manchester CT (S)
Kuster, Deborah, *Prof,* University of Central Arkansas, Department of Art, Conway AR (S)
Kuster, Diane, *Archivist,* Art Gallery of Peel, Archives, Brampton ON
Kutbay, Bonnie, *Asst Prof & Chmn Dept,* Mansfield University, Art Dept, Mansfield PA (S)
Kuwabara, Kelly, *Develop Mgr,* Allens Lane Art Center, Carolyn-Fielder-Alber Gallery, Philadelphia PA
Kuzma, Marta, *Dean,* Yale University, School of Art, New Haven CT (S)
Kvapi, Jay, *Chmn,* California State University, Long Beach, Art Dept, Long Beach CA (S)
Kvarnstrom, Arthur, *Co-Dir,* Prince Street Gallery, New York NY
Kwan, Billy, *Library Dir,* New York School of Interior Design, New York School of Interior Design Library, New York NY
Kwas, Amy, *Chief Devel Officer,* The Children's Museum of Indianapolis, Indianapolis IN
Kwiatkowski, Helen, *Prof,* University of Mary Hardin-Baylor, College of Visual & Performing Arts, Belton TX (S)
Kwilecki, Gerard, *Admin Dir,* Firehouse Center for the Arts, Institution for Savings Art Gallery, Bainbridge GA
Kwok, Zoe, *Asst Cur Asian Art,* Princeton University, Princeton University Art Museum, Princeton NJ
Kwon, Miwon, *Dept Chair,* University of California, Los Angeles, Dept of Art History, Los Angeles CA (S)
Kwong, Maria, *Dir Retail & Visitors,* Japanese American National Museum, Los Angeles CA
Kyle, Nick, *Dept Head,* Missouri Southern State University, Dept of Art, Joplin MO (S)
Kyoung Kim, Sun, *Asst Prof,* Southern Illinois University, School of Art & Design, Carbondale IL (S)
Kyriakodis, Harry, *Librn,* Ryerss Victorian Museum & Library, Philadelphia PA
L'Engle, Madeleine, *Librn,* Cathedral of Saint John the Divine, Library, New York NY
La Follette, Laetitia, *Assoc Prof,* University of Massachusetts, Amherst, Art History Program, Amherst MA (S)
La Marca, Jeane, *Develop Mem,* Shakespeare Ghost Town, Lordsburg NM
La Pierre, Randy, *Program Manager,* Yakima Valley Community College, Larson Gallery, Yakima WA
La Roche, Stephan, *Exec Dir,* Musee de l'Amerique Francophone, Quebec QC
Labadie, John Antoine, *Prof,* University of North Carolina at Pembroke, Art Dept, Pembroke NC (S)
LaBarbera, Anne, *Museum Shop Mgr,* Niagara University, Castellani Art Museum, Niagara NY
LaBarre, Becky, *Cur,* City of Chicago Dept. of Cultural Affairs & Special Events, Clarke House Museum, Chicago IL
LaBarrett, Joye, *Mng Dir,* Billie Trimble Chandler, Texas State Museum of Asian Cultures, Corpus Christi TX
Labe, Paul, *Dean,* Harford Community College, Visual, Performing and Applied Arts Division, Bel Air MD (S)
Laber, Phil, *Prof,* Northwest Missouri State University, Dept of Fine & Performing Arts, Maryville MO (S)
Laber, Philip, *Olive DeLuce Art Gallery Coll Cur,* Northwest Missouri State University, DeLuce Art Gallery, Maryville MO
LaBlanc, Necol, *Secy,* Galerie d'art de l'Universite de Moncton, Moncton NB
LaBossiere, Holly, *Dir,* Ponca City Library, Art Dept, Ponca City OK
Labuz, Ronald, *Prof,* Mohawk Valley Community College, Utica NY (S)
Lacasse, Brigitte, *Educ & Culture,* Le Musee Regional de Rimouski, Centre National d'Exposition, Rimouski QC
Lachowski, Michael, *Pub Rels Coordr,* University of Georgia, Georgia Museum of Art, Athens GA
Lacina, Ray, *Pres,* Owatonna Arts Center, Owatonna MN
Lacis, Indra, *Exhib Dir,* Western Michigan University Gwen Frostic School of Art, Richmond Center for Visual Arts, Kalamazoo MI
LaCouture, Jay, *Assoc Prof,* Salve Regina University, Art Dept, Newport RI (S)
Lacy, Laura, *Develop Asst,* McLean County Historical Society, McLean County Museum of History, Bloomington IL
Ladd, Spencer, *Chmn Design,* University of Massachusetts Dartmouth, College of Visual & Performing Arts, North Dartmouth MA (S)
Ladd-Simmons, Marilyn, *Gallery Mgr,* SPACES, Cleveland OH
Ladis, Andrew, *Franklin Prof Art History,* University of Georgia, Franklin College of Arts & Sciences, Lamar Dodd School of Art, Athens GA (S)
Ladislas Derr, Robert, *Dept Dir,* University of Nebraska, Lincoln, Eisentrager Howard Gallery, Lincoln NE
Ladnier, Paul, *Assoc Prof,* University of North Florida, Dept of Communications & Visual Arts, Jacksonville FL (S)
Ladu, Jen, *Coordr Outreach Educ,* Hebrew Union College - Jewish Institute of Religion, Skirball Museum Cincinnati, Cincinnati OH
LaFarge, Antoinette, *Assoc Prof Digital Media,* University of California, Irvine, Studio Art Dept, Irvine CA (S)
Lafferty, Susan, *Dir Educ,* The Huntington Library, Art Collections & Botanical Gardens, Library, San Marino CA
Laffin, Angeline, *Dir Visitor Experience,* Canadian Museum of Nature, Musee Canadien de la Nature, Ottawa ON
Lafis, Zoie, *Treas,* Washington Sculptors Group, Washington DC
Laflin, John, *Prof,* Dakota State University, College of Liberal Arts, Madison SD (S)
LaFrance, Liselle, *CEO & Dir,* Historic Cherry Hill, Albany NY
LaFrance, Robert, *Dir,* Ball State University, David Owsley Museum of Art, Muncie IN
LaGamma, Alisa, *Cur in Charge, Arts of Africa, Oceania & the Americas,* The Metropolitan Museum of Art, New York NY
Lagattuta, Bill, *Tamarind Master Printer & Studio Mgr,* University of New Mexico, Tamarind Institute, Albuquerque NM (S)

Lagneaux, Blake, *Cur Exhibs,* Lafayette Science Museum & Planetarium, Lafayette LA

LaGrassa, Stephan J, *Assoc Dean,* University of Detroit Mercy, School of Architecture, Detroit MI (S)

LaGrone, Libra, *Deputy Dir/Music Cur,* Ogden Museum of Southern Art, University of New Orleans, New Orleans LA

Lagsteid, Carol, *Asst Prof,* Saint Thomas Aquinas College, Art Dept, Sparkill NY (S)

Laguerre, JoAnn, *Office Sec,* Hofstra University, Department of Fine Arts, Hempstead NY (S)

Lahikainen, Dean, *Cur,* Peabody Essex Museum, Andrew-Safford House, Salem MA

Lahs-Gonzales, Olivia, *Dir,* Sheldon Art Galleries, Saint Louis MO

Lai, Diane, *Archivist,* Mechanics' Institute, San Francisco CA

Lai, Guolong, *Assoc Prof,* University of Florida, School of Art & Art History, Gainesville FL (S)

Lai, Waihang, *Faculty,* Kauai Community College, Dept of Art, Lihue HI (S)

Laidlaw, Ann, *Secy,* Inter-Society Color Council, Frederick MD

Laidlaw, Christy, *Mem Coordr,* Cahoon Museum of American Art, Cotuit MA

Laidlaw, Stephen, *Gallery Asst & Cur Tech,* Nanaimo Art Gallery, Nanaimo BC

Laing, Aileen H, *Prof,* Sweet Briar College, Art History Dept, Sweet Briar VA (S)

Laing, Beverly, *Site Adminstr,* Delaware Division of Historical & Cultural Affairs, Dover DE

Laing, Greg, *Cur Spec Coll,* Haverhill Public Library, Special Collections, Haverhill MA

Laing, Sue, *Instr,* Jefferson Davis Community College, Art Dept, Brewton AL (S)

Lainhoff, Thomas A, *Dir,* Gunston Hall Plantation, Mason Neck VA

Laise, Kristen, *Exec Dir,* Belle Grove Inc, Belle Grove Plantation, Middletown VA

LaJeunesse, Monique, *Business Mgr,* Little River Hotglass Studio & Gallery, Moscow VT

Lajoie, Paul, *Evening Access Servs & ILL,* Fashion Institute of Technology - SUNY, Gladys Marcus Library, New York NY

Lake, Ellen, *Dir Develop,* Kala Institute, Kala Art Institute, Berkeley CA

Lake, Ellen, *Head Dept,* Central Community College - Columbus Campus, Business & Arts Cluster, Columbus NE (S)

Lake, Lauren, *Assoc Prof & Chmn,* University of Alabama at Birmingham, Dept of Art & Art History, Birmingham AL (S)

Lake-Farm, Naomi, *Exec Dir,* Maui Historical Society, Hale Hoike ike at the Bailey House, Wailuku HI

Laken, Lorraine, *Dir,* Hammond Museum & Japanese Stroll Garden, Cross-Cultural Center, North Salem NY

Lallande, Becky, *Office Mgr,* District of Columbia Arts Center (DCAC), Washington DC

Lalonde, Jerome, *Assoc Prof,* Mohawk Valley Community College, Utica NY (S)

LaMalfa, James, *Prof,* University of Wisconsin College - Marinette, Art Dept, Marinette WI (S)

Laman, Jean, *Prof,* Texas State University - San Marcos, Dept of Art and Design, San Marcos TX (S)

Lamar, Deanna, *Dir Visual Arts,* Morgan County Foundation, Inc, Madison-Morgan Cultural Center, Madison GA

LaMarcz, Howard, *Prof,* C W Post Campus of Long Island University, School of Visual & Performing Arts, Brookville NY (S)

LaMark, Michael W, *Graphic Design,* Art Institute of Pittsburgh, Pittsburgh PA (S)

Lamb, Corey, *Asst Prof Painting,* Florida Atlantic University, D F Schmidt College of Arts & Letters Dept of Visual Arts & Art History, Boca Raton FL (S)

Lamb, Donna, *Dir,* Schweinfurth Art Center, Auburn NY

Lamb, Patricia, *Adjunct Prof Art,* Florida Southern College, Melvin Art Gallery, Lakeland FL

Lambe, Claire, *Instr,* Woodstock School of Art, Inc, Woodstock NY (S)

Lamberger, Ed, *Chief HR Officer,* San Francisco Museum of Modern Art, San Francisco CA

Lamberger, Nancy, *Dir Publicity,* Artistry, Inez Greenberg Gallery, Bloomington MN

Lambert, Alice, *Chmn Art Dept,* Anna Maria College, Saint Luke's Gallery, Paxton MA

Lambert, Alice, *Chmn Dept,* Anna Maria College, Dept of Art, Paxton MA (S)

Lambert, Ashley, *Develop Coordr,* Virginia Museum of Contemporary Art, Virginia Beach VA

Lambert, Brian, *Collections Mgr,* University of Western Ontario, McIntosh Gallery, London ON

Lambert, Ed, *Prof Fabric Design,* University of Georgia, Franklin College of Arts & Sciences, Lamar Dodd School of Art, Athens GA (S)

Lambert, Kirby, *Cur Coll,* Montana Historical Society, Library, Helena MT

Lambert, Phyllis, *Dir Emeritus,* Canadian Centre for Architecture, Library, Montreal QC

Lamberton, John, *Adjunct Prof Photog,* Johnson County Community College, Fine Arts Dept & Art History Dept, Overland Park KS (S)

Lamberton, Michelle, *Assoc Dir,* National Air and Space Museum, Smithsonian Institution, Washington DC

Lambertson, John, *Chmn Art Dept & Assoc Prof,* Washington & Jefferson College, Art Dept, Washington PA (S)

Lambousey, Greg, *Dir Coll,* Louisiana Department of Culture, Recreation & Tourism, Louisiana State Museum, New Orleans LA

Lambson, Jeff, *Dir & Cur,* Emmanuel Gallery, Denver CO

LaMere, Kate, *Asst Dir,* East Carolina University, School of Art & Design, Greenville NC (S)

Lamers, Nancy, *Chmn,* Alverno College, Art Dept, Milwaukee WI (S)

Lamia, Stephen, *Dept Chair, Assoc Prof & Gallery Dir,* Dowling College, Dept of Visual Arts, Oakdale NY (S)

Lamm, Jay, *Planetarium Producer,* Louisiana Arts & Science Museum, Baton Rouge LA

Lammers, Heather, *Coll Mgr,* McNay Art Museum, San Antonio TX

Lamothe, Donat, *Prof,* Assumption College, Dept of Art, Music & Theatre, Worcester MA (S)

Lamothe, Sue, *Finance Dir,* Canadian Museums Association, Association des Musees Canadiens, Ottawa ON

Lamoureux, Marie E, *Colls Mgr,* American Antiquarian Society, Worcester MA

Lampe, Lauren, *Prof,* La Roche College, Division of Design, Pittsburgh PA (S)

Lampe, Ted, *Prog Dir,* Gateway Arts, Gateway Gallery, Brookline MA

Lampela, Laurel, *Prof,* University of New Mexico, Department of Fine Arts & Art History, Albuquerque NM (S)

Lancaster, Gary R, *Pres,* Rocky Mountain Museum of Military History, Missoula MT

Lancaster, Kate, *Communs Coordr,* Place des Arts at Heritage Square, Coquitlam BC

Lancet, Marc, *Instr,* Solano Community College, Division of Fine & Applied Art & Behavioral Science, Fairfield CA (S)

Lanctot, Marc, *Cur,* Musee d'art Contemporain de Montreal, Montreal QC

Land, Brian, *Chief Cur,* Arkansas Arts Center, Little Rock AR (S)

Land, Doylene, *Cur Educ,* Ellen Noel Art Museum of the Permian Basin, Odessa TX

Land, Norman, *Prof,* University of Missouri - Columbia, Art History & Archaeology Dept, Columbia MO (S)

Land, Peter, *Prof,* Illinois Institute of Technology, College of Architecture, Chicago IL (S)

Landau, Laureen, *Instr,* Sacramento City College, Art Dept, Sacramento CA (S)

Landauer, Susan, *Chief Cur,* San Jose Museum of Art, Library, San Jose CA

Landefeld, Stewart, *Chmn Bd,* Seattle Art Museum, Seattle WA

Lander Burke, Adele, *Learning for Life,* Hebrew Union College, Skirball Cultural Center, Los Angeles CA

Landes, Eric, *Chair, Prof Art, Graphic Design,* Florida Atlantic University, D F Schmidt College of Arts & Letters Dept of Visual Arts & Art History, Boca Raton FL (S)

Landfield, Noad, *Preparator,* New York University, Grey Art Gallery, New York NY

Landgraff, Dionne, *Assoc Prof,* Silver Lake College, Art Dept, Manitowoc WI (S)

Landis, Ann, *Div Chmn,* Thomas University, Humanities Division, Thomasville GA (S)

Landis, Connie M, *Chair,* Montana State University-Billings, Art Dept, Billings MT (S)

Landis, Dick, *Pres,* Southern Lorain County Historical Society, Spirit of '76 Museum, Elyria OH

Landis, Kevin, *Asst Prof & Dir Theatre,* University of Colorado-Colorado Springs, Visual & Performing Arts Dept (VAPA), Colorado Springs CO (S)

Landis, Mark, *Chmn Theatre Dept,* College of Charleston, School of the Arts, Charleston SC (S)

Landis, Sandy, *Exec Dir,* Community Council for the Arts, Kinston NC

Landman, Brenda, *Chmn Asst,* University of Memphis, Art Dept, Memphis TN (S)

Landon, John, *Prof,* West Texas A&M University, Art, Theatre & Dance Dept, Canyon TX (S)

Landon, Kaia, *Dir,* Brigham City Corporation, Brigham City Museum of Art & History, Brigham City UT

Landrey, Greg, *Dir Library, Colls Management & Acad Progs,* Winterthur Museum, Winterthur Museum, Garden & Library, Winterthur DE

Landry, Craig, *Lead Interpreter,* St Mary Chapter Louisiana Landmarks Society, Grevemberg House Museum, Franklin LA

Landry, Pierre, *Dir Colls Mngmt & Info,* Musee National des Beaux Arts du Quebec, Bibliotheque, Quebec QC

Landwer, Kerstin, *Asst Dir,* George A Spiva, Joplin MO

Landy, Paul, *Design Shop Dir,* Neue Galerie New York, New York NY

Lane, Anne, *Cur Coll,* Museum of York County, Staff Research Library, Rock Hill SC

Lane, Barbara, *Prof,* City University of New York, PhD Program in Art History, New York NY (S)

Lane, Bruce, *Asst Prof,* Rochester Institute of Technology, School of Photographic Arts & Sciences, Rochester NY (S)

Lane, Jeff, *Facilities Manager,* Essex Historical Society and Shipbuilding Museum, Essex MA

Lane, Jennifer, *Pub Rels & Mktg Mgr,* Wichita State University, Ulrich Museum of Art, Wichita KS

Lane, Jenny, *Communs Mgr,* Huntsville Museum of Art, Huntsville AL

Lane, Joshua, *Cur Furniture,* Historic Deerfield, Inc, Deerfield MA

Lane, Lisa, *Develop Dir/Mem,* Beyond Baroque Foundation, Beyond Baroque Literary Arts Center, Venice CA

Lane, Mikki, *Events Outreach Coordr,* Middlebury College, Museum of Art, Middlebury VT

Lane, Thomas, *Assoc Prof,* University of Minnesota, Minneapolis, Dept of Art, Minneapolis MN (S)

Lanes, Susan, *Grant Writer,* Copper Village Museum & Arts Center, Anaconda MT

Lang, Alexandria, *Admin Asst,* Philadelphia History Museum, Philadelphia PA

Lang, Alyssa, *Assoc Chair/Assoc Prof,* California State Polytechnic University, Pomona, Department of Art, Pomona CA (S)

Lang, Brian J, *Art Dir,* Bank of NY Mellon Corporation, Pittsburgh PA

Lang, Brian, *Chief Cur,* Arkansas Arts Center, Elizabeth Prewitt Taylor Memorial Library, Little Rock AR

Lang, Brian, *Chief Cur,* Arkansas Arts Center, Little Rock AR

Lang, Tom, *Chmn,* Webster University, Department of Art, Design & Art History, Webster Groves MO (S)

Lang, Tom, *Dept Chair,* Webster University, Cecille R Hunt Gallery, Webster Groves MO
Langa, Helen, *Asst Prof,* American University, Dept of Art, New York NY (S)
Langan, Katie, *Assoc Prof & Chair Dance,* Marymount Manhattan College, Fine & Performing Arts Div, New York NY (S)
Langan, Sarah, *Sr Opers Coordr,* The Association of International Photography Art Dealers, Washington DC
Langdale, Shelley, *Pres,* Print Council of America, Chicago IL
Langdon, Rita, *Pub Rels,* C W Post Campus of Long Island University, Hillwood Art Museum, Brookville NY
Langdon, Susan, *Assoc Prof,* University of Missouri - Columbia, Art History & Archaeology Dept, Columbia MO (S)
Lange, Amanda E, *Cur Chair,* Historic Deerfield, Inc, Deerfield MA
Lange, Gerard, *Assoc Prof,* Barton College, School of Visual, Performing & Communication Arts, Wilson NC (S)
Lange, Jane, *Dir,* City of San Rafael, Falkirk Cultural Center, San Rafael CA
Lange, Michael, *Exec Dir,* Department of Commerce, Wyoming Arts Council Gallery, Cheyenne WY
Langelier, Nathalie, *Coll Archivist,* Le Musee Regional de Rimouski, Centre National d'Exposition, Rimouski QC
Langeneckert, Mark, *Asst Tchs Prof & Dir Florence Prog,* University of Missouri - Columbia, Dept of Art, Columbia MO (S)
Langer, James V, *Gallery Cur & Chmn Dept Art,* Greensboro College, Irene Cullis Gallery, Greensboro NC
Langer, James V, *Instr,* Greensboro College, Dept of Art, Division of Fine Arts, Greensboro NC (S)
Langer-Holt, Una Charlene, *Prof Foundations Studies,* Art Institute of Pittsburgh, Pittsburgh PA (S)
Langham, Eleanor, *Dir Events & Progs,* Slater Mill, Old Slater Mill Association, Pawtucket RI
Langill, Caroline, *Dean, Faculty of Liberal Arts & Sciences,* OCAD University, Toronto ON (S)
Langlais, Michel, *Pres,* National Sculpture Society, New York NY
Langley, John, *Secy,* Alton Museum of History & Art, Inc, Alton IL
Langley, Judy, *Secy,* Birger Sandzen Memorial Gallery, Lindsborg KS
Langlois, Craig, *Dir Educ & Progs,* Berkshire Museum, Pittsfield MA
Langnas, Bob, *Assoc Prof,* Saint Louis Community College at Florissant Valley, Liberal Arts Division, Ferguson MO (S)
langshaw, pk, *Chair, Design & Computational Arts,* Concordia University, Faculty of Fine Arts, Montreal QC (S)
Langston, Judy, *Coord & Asst Prof,* Oakton Community College, Language Humanities & Art Divisions, Des Plaines IL (S)
Langton, Charlie, *Ed,* Vesterheim Norwegian-American Museum, Decorah IA
Lanier, Chris, *Asst Prof,* Sierra Nevada College, Fine Arts Dept, Incline Village NV (S)
Lanieri, Edna, *Dir Programs,* Longue Vue House & Gardens, New Orleans LA
Lanka, Jason, *Asst Prof,* University of Wisconsin-Eau Claire, Dept of Art & Design, Eau Claire WI (S)
Lanka, Jason, *Prof,* Sheridan College, Art Dept, Sheridan WY (S)
Lankford, E Louis, *Des Lee Foundation Prof Art Educ,* University of Missouri, Saint Louis, Dept of Art & Art History, Saint Louis MO (S)
Lanman, Jennifer, *Coll Mgr,* Swope Art Museum, Research Library, Terre Haute IN
Lannan, Patrick, *Pres,* Lannan Foundation, Santa Fe NM
Lanning, Anne, *VPres Mus Affairs,* Historic Deerfield, Inc, Deerfield MA
Lanning, Regan, *Cur,* Weyburn Arts Council, Allie Griffin Art Gallery, Weyburn SK
LaNore, Ruth, *Registrar,* New Mexico Department of Cultural Affairs, Museum of International Folk Art, Santa Fe NM
Lansbury, Edgar, *Pres,* Nicholas Roerich, New York NY
Lansdown, Robert R, *Dir,* The Frank Phillips Foundation Inc, Library, Bartlesville OK
Lansing, Amy Kurtz, *Cur,* Lyme Historical Society, Florence Griswold Museum, Old Lyme CT
Lantz, Dona, *Acad Dean,* Moore College of Art & Design, Philadelphia PA (S)
Lantz, Michael, *Instr,* Moravian College, Dept of Art, Bethlehem PA (S)
Lantzas, Jennifer, *Cur,* City of New York Parks & Recreation, Arsenal Gallery, New York NY
Lanzo, Juanita, *Dir & Cur,* Bronx Council on the Arts, Longwood Arts Gallery @ Hostos, Bronx NY
Lapaeva, Olga, *Gift Shop Mgr,* Knights of Columbus Supreme Council, Knights of Columbus Museum, New Haven CT
Lapaite, Livija, *Dir BAC Educ,* Cultural Affairs Department City of Los Angeles, Library, Los Angeles CA
LaPalombara, David, *Dir,* Ohio University, Ohio University Art Gallery, Athens OH
Lapalombara, David, *Prof,* Antioch College, Visual Arts Dept, Yellow Springs OH (S)
Lape, Peter, *Cur Archaeology,* University of Washington, Burke Museum of Natural History and Culture, Seattle WA
LaPerla, Susan, *Liaison Librn,* New Canaan Library, H. Pelham Curtis Gallery, New Canaan CT
LaPlante, Dave, *Supvr Exhibit Production,* New York State Museum, Albany NY
Lapointe, Jon, *Dir Communs,* Armory Center for the Arts, Pasadena CA
Lapointe, Jon, *Pres Bd Dir,* Side Street Projects, Pasadena CA
LaPorte, Angela M, *Assoc Prof,* University of Arkansas, Art Dept, Fayetteville AR (S)
LaPorte, Chris, *Adjunct Assoc Prof,* Aquinas College, Art Dept, Grand Rapids MI (S)
Laporte, Claire, *Dir Communs,* Museum of Arts & Design, New York NY
LaPorte, Mary, *Prof Graphic Design,* California Polytechnic State University at San Luis Obispo, Dept of Art & Design, San Luis Obispo CA (S)
Lappie, Joseph, *Asst Prof Art,* Saint Ambrose University, Art Dept, Davenport IA (S)
Lapres, Geoff, *CFO,* Please Touch Museum, Philadelphia PA
Lapthisophon, Stephen, *Vis Asst Prof,* University of Texas at Arlington, Art & Art History Department, Arlington TX (S)
Laputka, Dolores A, *Chmn,* Allentown Art Museum, Allentown PA
Lard, Jim, *Instr,* Harrisburg Area Community College, Division of Communications, Humanities & the Arts, Harrisburg PA (S)
Large, Anne Marie, *Cataloger,* Ames Free-Easton's Public Library, North Easton MA
Large, David, *Pres,* International Society of Marine Painters, Puryear TN
LaRiccia, S., *Treas & Gallery Coodr,* New Zone Virtual Gallery, Eugene OR
Laris, Elisa, *Dir Devel,* Armory Center for the Arts, Pasadena CA
Laris, Jeorgia, *Instr,* San Diego Mesa College, Fine Arts Dept, San Diego CA (S)
Lariviere, Richard, *Pres & CEO,* Field Museum, Chicago IL
Larken, Dan, *Lectr,* Rochester Institute of Technology, School of Photographic Arts & Sciences, Rochester NY (S)
Larkin, Todd, *Prof Art History,* Montana State University, School of Art, Bozeman MT (S)
Larmann, Ralph, *Assoc Prof,* University of Evansville, Art Dept, Evansville IN (S)
Larned, Ron, *Chmn,* Rollins College, Dept of Art, Main Campus, Winter Park FL (S)
LaRoche, Lynda, *Asst Prof,* Indiana University of Pennsylvania, College of Fine Arts, Indiana PA (S)
Larochelle, Steven, *Librn,* Thomas College, Mariner Library, Waterville ME
Larocque, Peter, *Cur New Brunswick Cultural History & Art,* New Brunswick Museum, Saint John NB
LaRose, Matthew, *Dept Head, Assoc Prof,* University of Louisiana at Lafayette, Dept of Visual Arts, Lafayette LA (S)
LaRose, Matthew, *Head, Assoc Prof,* Davis & Elkins College, Dept of Art, Elkins WV (S)
Larose, Thomas, *Chmn & Dir,* Virginia State University, Department of Art & Design, Petersburg VA (S)
LaRou, George, *Instr,* Maine College of Art, Portland ME (S)
Larowe, Bruce, *Interim Pres & CEO,* The Mint Museum, Art Organization & Library, Charlotte NC
Larry, Charles, *Arts Librn,* Northern Illinois University, The University Libraries, DeKalb IL
Larsen, Adam, *Dir,* Snow College Art Gallery, Ephraim UT
Larsen, Devon, *Registrar,* Tampa Museum of Art, Tampa FL
Larsen, Diana, *Exhib Design, Coll Mgmt & Curatorial Affairs,* Boston College, McMullen Museum of Art, Chestnut Hill MA
Larsen, Kim, *Admin Mgr,* Cranbrook Art Museum, Bloomfield Hills MI
Larsen, Peik, *Instr,* Woodstock School of Art, Inc, Woodstock NY (S)
Larson, Avis, *Asst Cur,* Purchase College, Neuberger Museum of Art, Purchase NY
Larson, Barbara, *Assoc Prof,* University of West Florida, Dept of Art, Pensacola FL (S)
Larson, Barbara, *Prof,* Syracuse University, Dept of Fine Arts (Art History), Syracuse NY (S)
Larson, Bradley, *Dir,* Oshkosh Public Museum & Library, Oshkosh WI
Larson, Derek, *Asst Prof,* Georgia Southern University, Betty Foy Sanders Dept of Art, Statesboro GA (S)
Larson, Ian, *Chief Art Servs & Installation,* The Mint Museum, Charlotte NC
Larson, Janeen, *Prof,* Black Hills State University, Art Dept, Spearfish SD (S)
Larson, Jeanne, *Instr,* Grand Marais Art Colony, Grand Marais MN (S)
Larson, Lucy, *Dir Edu,* Palo Alto Art Center, Palo Alto CA
Larson, Lucy, *Dir Educ,* San Jose Museum of Art, San Jose CA
Larson, Nathan, *Asst Gallery Cur,* University of Arkansas at Little Rock, Art Library and Galleries, Little Rock AR
Larson, Nathan, *Cur Asst,* University of Arkansas at Little Rock, Art Galleries, Little Rock AR
Larson, Phoebe, *Communs & Digital Servs Dir,* Saint Paul Public Library, Central Adult Public Services, Saint Paul MN
Larson, Shannon, *Graphic Designer,* Quincy Art Center, Quincy IL
Larson, Sidney, *Instr,* Columbia College, Art Dept, Columbia MO (S)
Larson, Stephan, *Asst Prof,* Northern Michigan University, Dept of Art & Design, Marquette MI (S)
Larson, Tina, *Exec Dir,* Plainsman Museum, Aurora NE
Larson, Zoe, *Assoc Dir,* The Brant Foundation Art Study Center, Greenwich CT
Lasansky, Leonardo, *Artist-in-Residence,* Hamline University, Dept of Studio Arts & Art History, Saint Paul MN (S)
Lasater, Sandra, *1st VPres,* Huntsville Art League, Lowe Mill Arts & Entertainment, Huntsville AL
Lash, Jean, *Instr,* Siena Heights University, Studio Angelico-Art Dept, Adrian MI (S)
Lasiter, Leslie, *Bibliographer & Inventory Mgr,* Printed Matter, Inc, New York NY
Laskowski, Eileen, *Educ & Progs Mgr,* C M Russell Museum, Frederic G Renner Memorial Library, Great Falls MT
Lasser, Howard, *Exec Dir,* Brookfield Craft Center, Inc, Gallery, Brookfield CT

Latham, Ron, *Dir,* Berkshire Athenaeum, Reference Dept, Pittsfield MA
Lathrop, Allison, *Public Programs Mgr,* University of North Carolina at Chapel Hill, Ackland Art Museum, Chapel Hill NC
Latimore, Lindsay, *Prog Dir,* Bainbridge Island Arts Council, Bainbridge Island WA
Latman, Laura, *Registrar & Colls Mgr,* Bowdoin College, Museum of Art, Brunswick ME
LaTocha, Athena, *Registrar,* National Academy Museum & School, Archives, New York NY
Latour, Terry S, *Dir Library Svcs,* Delta State University, Roberts LaForge Library, Cleveland MS
LaTrespo, Brigitte, *Chmn,* Pikeville College, Humanities Division, Pikeville KY (S)
Lattardo, Craig, *Finance Dir,* Contemporary Arts Center, Cincinnati OH
Laudeman, Sue, *Cur Educ,* The Historic New Orleans Collection, Royal Street Galleries, New Orleans LA
Laudenslager, Evan, *Sls & Prog Mgr,* The Print Center, Philadelphia PA
Lauder, Ronald, *Hon Chmn,* Museum of Modern Art, New York NY
Laughlin, Page, *Prof,* Wake Forest University, Dept of Art, Winston-Salem NC (S)
Laughman, Thomas, *Dir & CEO,* Wadsworth Atheneum Museum of Art, Hartford CT
Laughton, John, *Dean,* University of Massachusetts Dartmouth, College of Visual & Performing Arts, North Dartmouth MA (S)
Laurent, Elizabeth, *Pres,* Chester County Historical Society, West Chester PA
Laurents, Terry, *Dir Educ,* Monterey Museum of Art, Monterey Museum of Art -Pacific Street, Monterey Museum of Art - La Mirada, Monterey CA
Laurette, Sandra, *Cur Educ,* Art Museum of Southeast Texas, Beaumont TX
Laury, Brenda, *Security Supv,* Southern Methodist University, Meadows Museum, Dallas TX
Lauster, Darryl, *Asst Prof,* University of Texas at Arlington, Art & Art History Department, Arlington TX (S)
Lauter, Max, *Gallery Mgr & Progs Producer,* Storefront for Art & Architecture, New York NY
Lauter, Nancy A, *Pres,* The Art Institute of Chicago, Society for Contemporary Art, Chicago IL
Lautzenheiser, Matt, *Exec Dir,* Historical Museum at Fort Missoula, Missoula MT
Lavadour, Roberta, *Exec Dir,* Pendleton Center for the Arts, Pendleton OR
LaVallee, Melissa, *Appraisal Coordr,* Art Dealers Association of Canada, Toronto ON
LaValley, Dennis, *Chmn,* Alvin Community College, Art Dept, Alvin TX (S)
Lavanger, Anna, *Administrative Assoc,* Minnesota Museum of American Art, Saint Paul MN
LaVelle, Lori, *Mem Coordr,* University of California, Los Angeles, Fowler Museum at UCLA, Los Angeles CA
Laver, Tara, *Archives Asst,* The Nelson-Atkins Museum of Art, Spencer Art Reference Library, Kansas City MO
Lavergne, Jacques, *VPres Visitor Experience & Engagement,* Canadian Museum for Human Rights, Winnipeg MB
Laverty, Bruce, *Cur Architecture,* Athenaeum of Philadelphia, Library, Philadelphia PA
Laverty, Bruce, *Cur Architecture,* Athenaeum of Philadelphia, Philadelphia PA
Lavery, Ariel, *Asst Prof Fine Art,* Watkins College of Art, Design & Film, Nashville TN (S)
Lavery, Barry, *Photog,* Art Institute of Pittsburgh, Pittsburgh PA (S)
Lavezzi, John, *Chmn Art History,* Bowling Green State University, School of Art, Bowling Green OH (S)
Lavin, Gabrielle, *Gallery Dir,* Moore College of Art & Design, The Galleries at Moore, Philadelphia PA
Lavino, Jane, *Cur Educ & Exhibs,* National Museum of Wildlife Art of the Unites States, Jackson WY
Laviolette, Suzanna, *Site & Cur Mus,* Longfellow-Evangeline State Commemorative Area, Saint Martinville LA
Lavitt, Susan, *Head Develop & Communs,* Contemporary Art Gallery Society of British Columbia, Vancouver BC
Lavoie, Claude, *Prof & Dir, School of Land Management & Regional Planning,* Universite Laval, Faculty of Planning, Architecture, Arts & Design, Quebec QC (S)
Lavoy, Carl, *Dir & Cur,* Thames Art Gallery, Chatham ON
Law, Beth, *Site Mgr,* Longfellow National Historic Site, Longfellow House - Washington's Headquarters, Cambridge MA
Law, Charles "Chuck", *Ex Dir,* Grand Prairie Arts Council, Inc, Arts Center of the Grand Prairie, Stuttgart AR
Law, Craig, *Prof,* Utah State University, Dept of Art, Logan UT (S)
Law, Dennis, *Dean,* Kansas State University, College of Architecture Planning & Design, Manhattan KS (S)
Law, Horatio, *Instr,* Pacific Northwest College of Art, Portland OR (S)
Law, Polly M, *Instr,* Woodstock School of Art, Inc, Woodstock NY (S)
Lawing, Preston, *Chair,* Saint Mary's University of Minnesota, Art & Design Dept, Winona MN (S)
Lawler, Greg, *Prof,* Munson-Williams-Proctor Arts Institute, Pratt MWP College of Art, Utica NY (S)
Lawler, Patrick, *Asst Prof,* Sam Houston State University, Art Dept, Huntsville TX (S)
Lawley, Neil, *Asst Prof,* Missouri Western State University, School of Fine Arts, Saint Joseph MO (S)
Lawley, Neil, *Asst Prof,* Missouri Western State University, School of Fine Arts, Saint Joseph MO (S)
Lawlor, Susan, *Chmn Art & Design,* Avila College, Art Division, Dept of Humanities, Kansas City MO (S)
Lawn, Patti, *Exec Dir,* Chilliwack Community Arts Council, Community Arts Centre, Chilliwack BC
Lawn, Richard J, *Dean, College of Performing Arts,* University of the Arts, Philadelphia Colleges of Art & Design, Performing Arts & Media & Communication, Philadelphia PA (S)
Lawn, Robert, *Prof,* Nassau Community College, Art Dept, Garden City NY (S)
Lawrence, Annette, *Chair, Dept Studio,* University of North Texas, College of Visual Arts & Design, Denton TX (S)
Lawrence, Bob, *Pres,* Arts Council of Greater Kingsport, Renaissance Center Main Gallery, Kingsport TN
Lawrence, Charles D, *Exec Dir,* Fine Arts Association, School of Fine Arts, Willoughby OH
Lawrence, Charles, *Dir,* Willoughby School of Fine Arts, Visual Arts Dept, Willoughby OH (S)
Lawrence, Clara, *Dir,* Central United Methodist Church, Swords Into Plowshares Peace Center & Gallery, Detroit MI
Lawrence, David, *Head Dept,* San Bernardino Valley College, Art Dept, San Bernardino CA (S)
Lawrence, Deirdre E, *Prin Librn Libraries & Archives,* Brooklyn Museum, Libraries Archives, Brooklyn NY
Lawrence, John D, *Dept Head,* LaGrange College, Lamar Dodd Art Center Museum, LaGrange GA (S)
Lawrence, John D, *Dir,* LaGrange College, Lamar Dodd Art Center Museum, LaGrange GA
Lawrence, John H, *Dir Mus Progs,* The Historic New Orleans Collection, Royal Street Galleries, New Orleans LA
Lawrence, John, *Dir Mus Prog,* The Historic New Orleans Collection, Williams Research Center, New Orleans LA
Lawrence, Lisa, *Instr,* Kirkwood Community College, Dept of Arts & Humanities, Cedar Rapids IA (S)
Lawrence, Mike, *Asst Dir Exhibs,* National Museum of Natural History, Smithsonian Institution, Washington DC
Lawrence, Nora, *Cur,* Storm King Art Center, New Windsor NY
Lawrence, Pat, *Show Dir,* Marin County Watercolor Society, Corte Madera CA
Lawrence, Patricia, *Prof,* Louisiana State University, School of Art, Baton Rouge LA (S)
Lawrence, Priscilla, *Dir The Historic New Orleans Collection,* The Historic New Orleans Collection, Williams Research Center, New Orleans LA
Lawrence, Priscilla, *Exec Dir,* The Historic New Orleans Collection, Royal Street Galleries, New Orleans LA
Lawrence, Randy, *Dir,* Olympic College, Social Sciences & Humanities Div, Bremerton WA (S)
Lawrence, Robert, *Assoc Prof,* University of South Florida, School of Art & Art History, Tampa FL (S)
Lawrence, Sally, *Pres,* Pacific Northwest College of Art, Portland OR (S)
Lawrence, Sarah, *Dean School of Art & Design,* The New School, Parsons School of Design, New York NY (S)
Lawrence, Susan, *Co Dir Art Ed,* Mount Saint Joseph University, Department of Art and Design, Cincinnati OH (S)
Lawrie, Irene L, *Registrar,* Lightner Museum, Saint Augustine FL
Lawrimore, Katrina P, *Historic House Admin,* Charleston Museum, Heyward-Washington House, Charleston SC
Lawrimore, Katrina P, *Historic House Admin,* Charleston Museum, Joseph Manigault House, Charleston SC
Laws, Holly, *Assoc Prof,* University of Central Arkansas, Department of Art, Conway AR (S)
Lawson, Brenda, *VPres Colls,* Massachusetts Historical Society, Boston MA
Lawson, Darren, *Dean,* Bob Jones University, School of Fine Arts, Div of Art & Design, Greenville SC (S)
Lawson, Karol, *Dir,* Sweet Briar College, Art Collection & Galleries, Sweet Briar VA
Lawson, Laura, *Dir Special Events,* The Albrecht-Kemper Museum of Art, Saint Joseph MO
Lawson, Mary, *Develop,* Greenville County Museum of Art, Greenville SC
Lawson, Roger, *Admin Librn,* National Gallery of Art, Library, Washington DC
Lawson, Scott, *CEO,* Plumas County Museum, Museum Archives, Quincy CA
Lawson, Scott, *Dir,* Plumas County Museum, Quincy CA
Lawson, Shawn, *Vol & Festivals Dir,* Mesa Arts Center, Mesa Contemporary Arts Museum, Mesa AZ
Lawson, Thomas, *Dean,* California Institute of the Arts, School of Art, Valencia CA (S)
Lawson, Trent, *Chief Preparator,* Oklahoma City Museum of Art, Oklahoma City OK
Lawton, Carol, *Prof,* Lawrence University, Dept of Art & Art History, Appleton WI (S)
Lawton, Cheryl, *Ranger,* Jack London, House of Happy Walls, Glen Ellen CA
Lawton, Mary, *Lectr,* Lake Forest College, Dept of Art, Lake Forest IL (S)
Lawton, Pamela, *Asst Prof,* University of North Carolina at Charlotte, Dept Art, Charlotte NC (S)
Laxman, Eric, *Treas,* Sculptors Guild, Inc, Brooklyn NY
Laxton, Susan, *Asst Prof,* University of California, Riverside, Dept of the History of Art, Riverside CA (S)
Lay, Bill, *Security Officer,* Morris Museum of Art, Augusta GA
Lay, Daniel, *Preparator,* Mabee-Gerrer Museum of Art, Shawnee OK
Lay, Gary, *Media Coordr, Audio Visual,* University of Texas at Austin, Fine Arts Library, Austin TX
Layden, Donald, *Pres Bd Trustees,* Milwaukee Art Museum, Milwaukee WI
Layne, Margaret Mary, *Dir Develop,* Huntington Museum of Art, Huntington WV
Layne, Scott, *Special Events Mgr,* Laumeier Sculpture Park, Saint Louis MO
Lazar, Howard, *Dir Street Artist Prog,* San Francisco City & County Arts Commission, San Francisco CA

Lazaro, Emily, *Docent Coordr,* University of Virginia, The Fralin Museum of Art at the University of Virginia, Charlottesville VA
Lazarus, Jason, *Asst Prof,* University of South Florida, School of Art & Art History, Tampa FL (S)
Lazarus, Lisa, *Asst Dir & Cur,* Egan Maritime Institute, Shipwreck & Lifesaving Museum, Nantucket MA
Laziza, Kathleen, *Artistic Dir, Exec Dir,* Promote Art Works Inc (PAWI), The MicroMuseum, Brooklyn NY
Laziza, Kathleen, *Exec Dir,* Promote Art Works Inc (PAWI), Laziza Electrique Dance Co, Brooklyn NY
Laziza, Kathleen, *Exec Dir,* Promote Art Works Inc (PAWI), Job Readiness in the Arts-Media-Communication, Brooklyn NY (S)
Laziza, William, *Tech Dir,* Promote Art Works Inc (PAWI), The MicroMuseum, Brooklyn NY
Laziza, William, *Technical Dir,* Promote Art Works Inc (PAWI), Job Readiness in the Arts-Media-Communication, Brooklyn NY (S)
Laziza, William, *Technical Dir,* Promote Art Works Inc (PAWI), Laziza Electrique Dance Co, Brooklyn NY
Le Mense, Montserrat, *Paintings Conservator,* Williamstown Art Conservation Center, Williamstown MA
Lea, Ike, *Prof,* Lansing Community College, Visual Arts & Media Dept, Lansing MI (S)
Leach, David, *Develop,* Worcester Center for Crafts, Krikorian Gallery, Worcester MA
Leach, David, *Dir Facilities & Security,* Columbus Museum of Art, Columbus OH
Leach, Jessica, *Educ Dir,* Oglebay Institute, Stifel Fine Arts Center, Wheeling WV
Leach, Jim, *Interim Dir,* University of Iowa, University of Iowa Museum of Art, Iowa City IA
Leach, Mark R, *Exec Dir,* Southeastern Center for Contemporary Art, Winston-Salem NC
Leach, Patricia, *Dir,* Whatcom Museum, Bellingham WA
Leach, Robert, *Instr,* Sacramento City College, Art Dept, Sacramento CA (S)
Leach, Tiffany, *Asst Prof Ceramics,* Jacksonville University, Jacksonville FL (S)
Leache, Adam, *Cur Genetic Resources,* University of Washington, Burke Museum of Natural History and Culture, Seattle WA
Leacock, Kathryn, *Cur Coll,* Buffalo Society of Natural Sciences, Buffalo Museum of Science, Buffalo NY
Leader, Karen, *Assoc Prof Art History,* Florida Atlantic University, D F Schmidt College of Arts & Letters Dept of Visual Arts & Art History, Boca Raton FL (S)
Leadon, Denise, *Gen Asst,* Black American West Museum & Heritage Center, Denver CO
Leahy, Debby, *Exec Dir,* Salem Art Association, Salem OR
Leahy, Elaine, *Develop Mgr,* Blue Star Contemporary Art Center, San Antonio TX
Leahy, Margaret, *Chmn Interior Design,* Moore College of Art & Design, Philadelphia PA (S)
Leak, Carol, *Chmn,* Loyola University of New Orleans, Dept of Visual Arts, New Orleans LA (S)
Lean, Larry, *Chmn,* Mount Olive College, Dept of Art, Mount Olive NC (S)
Learmonth, Stephanie, *Registrar,* Triton Museum of Art, Santa Clara CA
Lease, Michael, *Exhib Mgr,* Virginia Commonwealth University, Anderson Gallery, Richmond VA
Leavens, Ileana, *Prof,* Seattle Central Community College, Humanities - Social Sciences Division, Seattle WA (S)
LeBaron, Robin, *Treas,* Morris-Jumel Mansion, Inc, New York NY
Lebedinskaia, Natalia, *Cur,* The Art Gallery of Southwestern Manitoba, Brandon MB
LeBlanc, Alice, *Admin Asst,* West Baton Rouge Parish, West Baton Rouge Museum, Port Allen LA
LeBlanc, Janine, *Collections Asst,* North Carolina State University, Gregg Museum of Art & Design, Raleigh NC
LeBlanc, Lajla, *Dir Communs,* Sharon Arts Center, Sharon Arts Center Exhibition Gallery, Peterborough NH
Leblond, Helene, *Archiviste,* Saint Joseph's Oratory, Centre d'archives et de Documentation Roland-Guthier, Montreal QC
Lebordais, Elise, *Admin Officer,* Universite du Quebec, Trois-Rivieres, Department of Philosophy & the Arts, Trois-Rivieres QC (S)
LeBras, Carol, *Art Reference Librn,* Chicago Public Library, Harold Washington Library Center, Chicago IL
Lechner, Anat, *Dir Data & Educ,* Color Association of the United States, New York NY
Leckey, Colun, *Chmn Humanities,* Lincoln Memorial University, Division of Humanities, Harrogate TN (S)
LeClair, Laura, *Pres,* Arts & Crafts Association of Meriden Inc, Gallery 53, Meriden CT
Leclerc, Erin, *Prof,* Saint Louis Community College at Meramec, Art Dept, Saint Louis MO (S)
Leclere, Mary, *Assoc Dir Core Residency Prog,* Museum of Fine Arts, Houston, Glassell School of Art, Houston TX (S)
LeCount, Chuck, *Sr Dir Progs & Colls,* Genesee Country Village & Museum, John L Wehle Art Gallery, Mumford NY
Ledbury, Mark, *Assoc Dir Research & Academic Prog,* Clark Art Institute, Williamstown MA
Ledee, Kimberly, *Asst Prof,* South Carolina State University, Dept of Visual & Performing Arts, Orangeburg SC (S)
Lederer, Carrie, *Cur,* Dean Lesher, Bedford Gallery, Walnut Creek CA
Lederer, Robert, *Coordr Industrial Design,* University of Alberta, Dept of Art & Design, Edmonton AB (S)
Ledford, Victoria, *Visual Art Educ,* Rapid City Arts Council, Dahl Arts Center, Rapid City SD
Ledgerwood, Judy, *Assoc Prof,* Northwestern University, Evanston, Dept of Art Theory & Practice, Evanston IL (S)
Leduc, Rebecca, *Press Relations,* San Luis Obispo Museum of Art, San Luis Obispo CA
Lee, Annie, *Registrar,* University of Southern California, USC Pacific Asia Museum, Pasadena CA
Lee, Anthony, *Bus Mgr,* University of Southern California, USC Pacific Asia Museum, Pasadena CA
Lee, Barbara Brown, *Chief Educ,* Milwaukee Art Museum, Milwaukee WI
Lee, Beverly, *Prog Asst,* Piatt Castles, West Liberty OH
Lee, Billy, *Prof,* University of North Carolina at Greensboro, School of Art, Greensboro NC (S)
Lee, Bovey, *Asst Prof,* University of Pittsburgh, Dept of Studio Arts, Pittsburgh PA (S)
Lee, Brent, *Prof, Music & Sound, Sonic Art,* University of Windsor, School of Creative Arts, Windsor ON (S)
Lee, Christopher, *CEO,* Columbus Chapel & Boal Mansion Museum, Boalsburg PA
Lee, Chui-Chun, *Dir,* State University of New York at New Paltz, Sojourner Truth Library, New Paltz NY
Lee, Cody, *Director of Communication,* Laguna Art Museum, Laguna Beach CA
Lee, De-Nin, *Asst Prof,* Bowdoin College, Art Dept, Brunswick ME (S)
Lee, Elizabeth, *Asst Prof,* Dickinson College, Dept of Art & Art History, Carlisle PA (S)
Lee, Eric M, *Dir,* Kimbell Art Foundation, Kimbell Art Museum, Fort Worth TX
Lee, Esther, *Div Mgr,* Queens Borough Public Library, Fine Arts & Recreation Division, Jamaica NY
Lee, Helen, *Asst Prof,* University of Wisconsin, Madison, Dept of Art, Madison WI (S)
Lee, Hoon, *Asst Prof,* Grand Valley State University, Art & Design Dept, Allendale MI (S)
Lee, Jack, *Dir,* Taipei Economic & Cultural Office, Chinese Information & Culture Center Library, New York NY
Lee, Jason, *Assoc Prof,* West Virginia University, College of Creative Arts, School of Art & Design, Morgantown WV (S)
Lee, Jenny, *Develop Mktg Mgr,* Kirkland Arts Center, KAC Gallery, Kirkland WA
Lee, Jill L, *Librn,* Athenaeum of Philadelphia, Philadelphia PA
Lee, Jim, *Assoc Prof,* University of Hartford, Hartford Art School, West Hartford CT (S)
Lee, Jiyong, *Assoc Prof,* Southern Illinois University, School of Art & Design, Carbondale IL (S)
Lee, Jon, *Assoc Prof,* Trinity University, Department of Art & Art History, San Antonio TX (S)
Lee, Junghee, *Assoc Prof,* Portland State University, Dept of Art, Portland OR (S)
Lee, Katelin, *Membership & Mktg Assoc,* American Institute for Conservation of Historic & Artistic Works, Washington DC
Lee, Kerry, *Opers Assoc,* Alternate ROOTS, Inc, Atlanta GA
Lee, Kristie, *Graphic Designer,* University of Missouri, Museum of Art & Archaeology, Columbia MO
Lee, Liz, *Prof,* State University of New York at Fredonia, Dept of Art, Fredonia NY (S)
Lee, Margaret, *Educ Coordr,* Lillian & Coleman Taube Museum of Art, Minot ND
Lee, Marilyn, *Assoc Prof,* Dickinson State University, Dept of Art, Dickinson ND (S)
Lee, Paul, *Chmn,* Washington State University, Fine Arts Dept, Pullman WA (S)
Lee, Paul, *Dir School of Art,* University of Tennessee, Knoxville, School of Art, Knoxville TN (S)
Lee, Robert, *Exec Dir,* Asian American Arts Centre, New York NY
Lee, Rodney, *Dir,* Mount Vernon Public Library, Fine Art Dept, Mount Vernon NY
Lee, Sandra, *Asst Prof,* Kenyon College, Art Dept, Gambier OH (S)
Lee, Shirley, *Bd Mem,* Coquille Valley Art Association, Coquille OR
Lee, Steph D, *CAS Gen,* Columbus Historic Foundation, Blewett-Harrison-Lee Museum, Columbus MS
Lee, Stephen, *Prof & Head,* Carnegie Mellon University, School of Architecture, Pittsburgh PA (S)
Lee, Talice, *Archivist & Develop Assoc,* Asian American Arts Centre, New York NY
Lee, Thom, *Instr Art,* Everett Community College, Art Dept, Everett WA (S)
Lee, Tracy, *Student Gallery Coordr,* College of New Jersey, Art Gallery, Ewing NJ
Lee, Yachin Crystal, *Prof,* California State Polytechnic University, Pomona, Department of Art, Pomona CA (S)
Lee-Warren, S, *Instr,* Golden West College, Visual Art Dept, Huntington Beach CA (S)
Leech, Tom, *Dir Palace Press,* New Mexico Department of Cultural Affairs, Palace of Governors, Santa Fe NM
Leedy, James, *Exec Dir,* Leedy-Voulkos Art Center, Kansas City MO
Leen, Mary, *Assoc Dir,* Massachusetts Institute of Technology, MIT Museum, Cambridge MA
Leers, Don, *Cur Photography,* Carnegie Museums of Pittsburgh, Carnegie Museum of Art, Pittsburgh PA
Lees, Gary P, *Dir Dept,* Johns Hopkins University, School of Medicine, Dept of Art as Applied to Medicine, Baltimore MD (S)
Lees, Nicola, *Dir,* New York University, Washington Square East Galleries, New York NY
Lees, Sarah, *Asst Cur Paintings,* Clark Art Institute, Williamstown MA
Lees, Sarah, *Cur European Art,* Philbrook Museum of Art, Tulsa OK
Leete Smith, Avery, *Pres Bd,* Friends of Historic Kingston, Fred J Johnston House Museum, Kingston NY

Leete, William C, *Prof,* Northern Michigan University, Dept of Art & Design, Marquette MI (S)

Leeuwrik, Linda, *Affiliate Faculty,* Idaho State University, Dept of Art, Pocatello ID (S)

Lefebvre-Carter, Michelle, *Dir,* Will Rogers Memorial Museum & Birthplace Ranch, Claremore OK

Lefevre, Shawn, *Registrar/Preparator,* University of Maine, Museum of Art, Bangor ME

Leffel, Joann, *Instr Art History,* Bay De Noc Community College, Art Dept, Escanaba MI (S)

Leffler, Laura, *Social Media & Pub Rels,* Robischon Gallery, Denver CO

LeFlore, Gail, *Sr Svcs Coordr,* City of Cedar Falls, Iowa, James & Meryl Hearst Center for the Arts & Sculpture Garden, Cedar Falls IA

Legault, Marianne, *Assoc Dean Undergrad Studies,* University of British Columbia Okanagan, Faculty of Creative & Critical Studies, Kelowna BC (S)

Legband, Megan, *Prog Coordr,* The Art Center of Waco, Waco TX

LeGear Hartsfield, Yvette, *Mng Dir Develop,* Missouri Historical Society, Missouri History Museum, Saint Louis MO

Legette, Lee David, *Interim Chmn,* Winston-Salem State University, Art Dept, Winston-Salem NC (S)

Legge, Katie Frinkle, *Pres (V),* Artists Association of Nantucket, Nantucket MA

Legleiter, Kim, *Dir & Financial Dir,* Stauth Foundation & Museum, Stauth Memorial Museum, Montezuma KS

LeGrow, Jane, *Director of Exhibitions & Registrar,* Haystack Mountain School of Crafts, Deer Isle ME (S)

LeGrow, Jane, *Registrar & Dir Exhibs,* Lyman Allyn Art Museum, New London CT

Leguillow-Torres, Gloria, *Exec Admin Asst,* Harvey B Gantt Center for African American Arts + Culture, Charlotte NC

Lehman, Erin, *Dir,* Towson University, Center for the Arts Gallery, Towson MD

Lehman, Linda, *Instr,* Ohio Northern University, Dept of Art & Design, Ada OH (S)

Lehman, Paul, *Gen Mgr,* Mississippi Valley Conservation Authority, R Tait McKenzie Memorial Museum, Almonte ON

Lehman, Tina, *Johnstown Coordr,* Southern Alleghenies Museum of Art, Johnstown Gallery, Johnstown PA

Lehner, Warren, *Prof,* Purchase College, State University of New York, School of Art+Design, Purchase NY (S)

Lehr, Lydia, *Instr,* Main Line Art Center, Haverford PA (S)

Lehrecke, Barbara, *Conservator,* Textile Conservation Workshop Inc, South Salem NY

Leibel, Jane, *VPres,* Klein Museum, Mobridge SD

Leibert, Peter, *Prof,* Connecticut College, Dept of Art, New London CT (S)

Leibsohn, Dana, *Prof,* Smith College, Art Dept, Northampton MA (S)

Leidich, David, *Asst to Dir,* Moravian College, Payne Gallery, Bethlehem PA

Leidl, Judith, *Art Instr,* Acadia University, Faculty of Arts, Wolfville NS (S)

Leidy, Susan, *Deputy Dir Colls & Exhibs,* Chrysler Museum of Art, Norfolk VA

Leif, Laura, *Programming Dir,* Quickdraw Animation Society, Calgary AB

Leiggi, Patrick, *Exhibs & Paleo Dir,* Montana State University, Museum of the Rockies, Bozeman MT

Leigh, Emily, *Asst Dir,* Kentuck Museum Association, Inc, Kentuck Art Center & Festival of the Arts, Northport AL

Leigh, Karon, *Weekend Supv,* Tubac Center of the Arts, Santa Cruz Valley Art Association, Tubac AZ

Leigh, Sheri, *Dir Summer Arts,* Sierra Nevada College, Fine Arts Dept, Incline Village NV (S)

Lein, Sharon, *Dir,* Deming-Luna Mimbres Museum, Deming NM

Leinbach, Charles, *Chmn,* California State University, Long Beach, Design Dept, Long Beach CA (S)

Leiner, Virginia, *Mus Shop Mgr,* Westmoreland Museum of American Art, Art Reference Library, Greensburg PA

Leininger, Jill, *Deputy Dir External Relations,* University of Washington, Henry Art Gallery, Seattle WA

Leininger-Miller, Theresa, *Dir Art Hist Prog & Asst Prof Art Educ,* University of Cincinnati, School of Art, Cincinnati OH (S)

Leinroth, Martha, *Asst Prof,* Rochester Institute of Technology, School of Photographic Arts & Sciences, Rochester NY (S)

Leipzig, Mel, *Prof,* Mercer County Community College, Arts, Communication & Engineering Technology, West Windsor NJ (S)

Leiser, Amy, *Exec Dir,* Monroe County Historical Association, Elizabeth D Walters Library, Stroudsburg PA

Leiser, Lee, *Exhib Tech,* Buffalo Niagara Heritage Village, Amherst NY

Leister, Claudia, *Coll Mgr,* Delaware Division of Historical & Cultural Affairs, Dover DE

Leitch, Flynn, *Cur,* Art Gallery of Peterborough, Peterborough ON

Leite, Dawn, *Asst to Dir,* Allied Arts Council of Lethbridge, Bowman Arts Center, Lethbridge AB

Leithauser, Mark, *Chief Design & Installation,* National Gallery of Art, Washington DC

Leither, Luke, *Fine Arts Librn,* University of Utah, Katherine W Dumke Architecture Library, Marriott Library, Salt Lake City UT

Leitzes, Jacqueline, *Dir Develop,* American Jewish Historical Society, The Center for Jewish History, New York NY

Lemay, Bonnie White, *Adminr,* Palm Beach County Parks & Recreation Department, Morikami Museum & Japanese Gardens, Delray Beach FL

Lemay, Eugene, *Artistic Dir,* Mana Contemporary, Jersey City NJ

Lemieux, Andrea, *Art Center Coordinator,* Williamsburg Contemporary Art Center, Williamsburg VA

Lemke, Beth A, *Mus Dir,* Neville Public Museum of Brown County, Green Bay WI

Lemke, Melissa Beck, *Italian Specialist,* National Gallery of Art, Department of Image Collections, Washington DC

Lemme, Shiobbean, *Admin Asst,* City of Pittsfield Office of Cultural Development, Lichtenstein Center for the Arts, Pittsfield MA

Lemmon, Alfred, *Dir Williams Research Ctr,* The Historic New Orleans Collection, Williams Research Center, New Orleans LA

LeMoine, Genevieve, *Cur & Registrar,* Bowdoin College, Peary-MacMillan Arctic Museum, Brunswick ME

Lemon, Christina, *Prod,* Georgia Southern University, Betty Foy Sanders Dept of Art, Statesboro GA (S)

Lemonedes, Heather, *Chief Curator,* The Cleveland Museum of Art, Cleveland OH

Lemonedes, Heather, *Dep Dir and Chief Curator,* The Cleveland Museum of Art, Cleveland OH

Lemp, Frank J, *Chmn,* Ottawa University, Dept of Art, Ottawa KS (S)

Lempka, Wayne, *Coll Mgr,* State University of New York at New Paltz, Samuel Dorsky Museum of Art, New Paltz NY

Lenaghan, Patrick, *Cur Prints & Photographs,* The Hispanic Society of America, Hispanic Society Museum & Library, New York NY

Lenahan, Colleen, *Exhib Prog Mgr,* Kirkland Arts Center, KAC Gallery, Kirkland WA

Lenderman, Max, *Prof,* Rochester Institute of Technology, School of Design, Rochester NY (S)

Lenhart, Anne, *Collections Mgr,* Southern Methodist University, Meadows Museum, Dallas TX

Lenihan, Teresa, *Asst Prof,* Loyola Marymount University, Dept of Art & Art History, Los Angeles CA (S)

Lenoir, Susan, *Dir Workshops,* California Watercolor Association, Gallery Concord, Concord CA

Lenssen, Georganna, *Instr,* Wayne Art Center, Wayne PA (S)

Lent, Amy, *Exec Dir,* Maine Maritime Museum, Bath ME

Lentz, Craig, *VPres,* Hammond Castle Museum, Gloucester MA

Lentz, Lamar, *Dir Library & Mus,* James Dick Foundation, Festival - Institute, Round Top TX

Lentz, Stephanie, *Dir Devel,* Chicago Artists Coalition, Chicago IL

Lenz, William, *Dir Fine & Performing Arts,* Chatham College, Art Gallery, Pittsburgh PA

Lenzi, Kristina, *Instr,* University of Utah, Dept of Art & Art History, Salt Lake City UT (S)

Leo, Samantha, *Interim Dir Develop,* San Francisco Museum of Modern Art, San Francisco CA

Leo, Sue, *Asst Prof,* Roberts Wesleyan College, Department of Visual Art, Rochester NY (S)

Leon, Janet, *Assistant Professor,* Inter American University of Puerto Rico, Fine Arts Dept -Art Program, San German PR (S)

Leona, Marco, *Scientist in Charge,* The Metropolitan Museum of Art, New York NY

Leonard, Anne, *Cur & Assoc Dir Academic Initiatives,* University of Chicago, Smart Museum of Art, Chicago IL

Leonard, Brandie, *Develop Dir,* Willard Arts Center, Carr Gallery, Colonial Theater, Idaho Falls ID

Leonard, Craig, *Asst Prof & Chair, Foundation Studies Div,* Nova Scotia College of Art & Design, Halifax NS (S)

Leonard, David, *Pres,* Boston Public Library, Central Library, Boston MA

Leonard, Donald, *Registrar,* United States Naval Academy, USNA Museum, Annapolis MD

Leonard, Rebecca, *Asst Librn,* Japan Society, Inc, C.V. Starr Library, New York NY

Leonard, Susan, *Dir,* South Carolina Arts Commission, Media Center, Columbia SC

Leonard, Susan, *Librn,* Bard College, Center For Curatorial Studies Library,

Leonard, Yvonne, *Asst Prof,* Community College of Rhode Island, Dept of Art, Warwick RI (S)

Leonard-Cravens, Mary, *Prof,* Eastern Illinois University, Art Dept, Charleston IL (S)

Leonardo, Shaun, *Dir of Pub Progs & Community Rels,* Socrates Sculpture Park, Long Island City NY

Leone, Giacomo R, *Chmn,* Illinois Valley Community College, Division of Humanities & Fine Arts, Oglesby IL (S)

Leong, Lampo, *Prof (Painting & Drawing),* University of Missouri - Columbia, Dept of Art, Columbia MO (S)

Leopold, Alan, *Dir Col Servs,* The Newberry, Chicago IL

Leow, Jacqueline, *Registrar,* Oakland University, Oakland University Art Gallery, Rochester MI

LePore, Ann, *Assoc Prof 3D Design & Animation,* Ramapo College of New Jersey, School of Contemporary Arts, Mahwah NJ (S)

LePore, William, *Asst Prof,* Portland State University, Dept of Art, Portland OR (S)

Lepper, Sandra, *Dir,* Russell Day Gallery, Everett WA

Lepper, Sandra, *Instr Art,* Everett Community College, Art Dept, Everett WA (S)

Leppla, Heather, *Mem Relations Mgr,* Dayton Art Institute, Dayton OH

Leppmann, Erika, *Prof,* Southern Oregon University, Art & Art History Dept, Ashland OR (S)

Lere, Dan, *Exec Dir,* Sangre de Cristo Arts & Conference Center, Pueblo CO

Lerer, Marisa, *Asst Prof,* Manhattan College, Visual & Performing Arts Dept, Bronx NY (S)

Lerner, A, *Prof,* City Colleges of Chicago, Daley College, Chicago IL (S)

Lerner, Adam, *Dir & Chief Animator,* Museum of Contemporary Art Denver, Denver CO

Lerner, Lynne, *Asst Dir,* Greenwich House Inc, Greenwich House Pottery, New York NY (S)

LeRoy, Glen, *Pres,* Boston Architectural College, McCormick Gallery, Boston MA

Lesher, Pete, *Cur,* Chesapeake Bay Maritime Museum, Howard I Chapelle Memorial Library, Saint Michaels MD

Lesher, Pete, *Cur,* Chesapeake Bay Maritime Museum, Saint Michaels MD
Leshnoff, Susan, *Asst Prof,* Seton Hall University, College of Arts & Sciences, South Orange NJ (S)
LeShock, Ed, *Asst Prof,* Radford University, Art Dept, Radford VA (S)
Lesinski, Peg, *Head Acquisitions,* American Antiquarian Society, Worcester MA
Lesko, Jim, *Assoc Prof,* University of Bridgeport, Shintaro Akatsu School of Design, Bridgeport CT (S)
Lesley, Kimberly, *Access Servs Librn,* The University of the Arts, University Libraries, Philadelphia PA
Leslie, Ken, *Dept Painting,* Johnson State College, Dept Fine & Performing Arts, Dibden Center for the Arts, Johnson VT (S)
Leslie, Matt, *Exhib & Educ Adminr,* Muckenthaler Cultural Center, Fullerton CA
Leslie, Richard, *Vis Assoc Prof,* Stony Brook University, College of Arts & Sciences, Dept of Art, Stony Brook NY (S)
Lessley, Chris, *Instr,* Bakersfield College, Art Dept, Bakersfield CA (S)
Lester, Audra, *Treas,* Saint Augustine Art Association and Art Gallery, Saint Augustine FL
Lester, Barri, *Asst Prof,* Kansas State University, Art Dept, Manhattan KS (S)
Lester, Howard, *Chmn Film/Video,* Rochester Institute of Technology, School of Photographic Arts & Sciences, Rochester NY (S)
Lester, Laurie, *Gift Shop & Mem Mgr,* Western Colorado Center for the Arts, The Art Center, Grand Junction CO
Lester, William Carey, *Prof,* Delta State University, Dept of Art, Cleveland MS (S)
Lestition Burke, Amy, *Exec Dir,* Special Libraries Association, Mc Lean VA
LeSuer, Sharon, *Acad Dean,* Tunxis Community Technical College, Graphic Design Dept, Farmington CT (S)
Lethbridge, York, *Exec Dir,* Mercer Union, A Centre for Contemporary Art, Toronto ON
Lethen, Paulien, *Dir,* Holland Tunnel Art Projects, Brooklyn NY
Lethen, Roy, *Graphic Designer,* Holland Tunnel Art Projects, Brooklyn NY
Letizia, Christopher, *Chief Conservator,* Boston Public Library, Rare Book & Manuscripts Dept, Boston MA
LeTourneux, Francois, *Assoc Cur,* Musee d'art Contemporain de Montreal, Montreal QC
Letson, Carol, *Pres,* Pocumtuck Valley Memorial Association, Memorial Hall Museum, Deerfield MA
Lettenstrom, Dean R, *Prof,* University of Minnesota, Duluth, Art Dept, Duluth MN (S)
Lettieri, Robert, *Chair,* Citizens for the Arts in Pennsylvania, Harrisburg PA
Lettieri, Robin, *Dir,* Port Chester-Rye Brook Public Library, Port Chester NY
Letzer, Mark, *Pres & CEO,* Maryland Historical Society, Library, Baltimore MD
Leubke, Thomas, *Secy,* United States Commission of Fine Arts, Washington DC
Leuchak, Rebecca, *Asst Prof,* Roger Williams University, Visual Art Dept, Bristol RI (S)
Leung, Christina, *Archivist/Curation Assistant,* White Columns, White Columns Curated Artist Registry, New York NY
Leung, Cynthia, *Dir Pub Progs & Tours,* Museums Sonoma County, Art Museum of Sonoma County & History Museum of Sonoma County, Santa Rosa CA
Leung, Simon, *Assoc Prof Contemporary Art History,* University of California, Irvine, Studio Art Dept, Irvine CA (S)
Leuthold, Steve, *Asst Prof,* Northern Michigan University, Dept of Art & Design, Marquette MI (S)
LeVan, Susan, *Chair Illustration,* Lesley University, College of Art & Design, Cambridge MA (S)
LeVant, Howard, *Assoc Prof,* Rochester Institute of Technology, School of Photographic Arts & Sciences, Rochester NY (S)
Levasseur, Marie-Andree, *Dir,* Maison de la Culture, Centre d'exposition Raymond-Lasnier, Trois Rivieres QC
LeVeille, Fayn (no e), *Mus Dir,* Halifax Historical Society, Inc, Halifax Historical Museum, Daytona Beach FL
Levenson, Cyra, *Dep Dir & Head of Public and Academic Engagement,* The Cleveland Museum of Art, Cleveland OH
Leverette, Carlton, *Coordr Arts,* Baltimore City Community College, Art Gallery, Baltimore MD
Levesque, Richard, *VPres,* International Society of Marine Painters, Puryear TN
Levesque, Sophie, *Boutique Mgr,* Musee Regional de lu Cote-Nord, Sept-Iles QC
Levi, Pavle, *Assoc Prof & Dir Film/Media Studies,* Stanford University, Dept of Art & Art History, Stanford CA (S)
Levin Martinez, Jessica, *Head Div Acad & Pub Progs,* Harvard University, Harvard Art Museums, Cambridge MA
Levin, Gail, *Prof,* City University of New York, PhD Program in Art History, New York NY (S)
Levin, Golan, *Prof & Dir, Frank-Ratchye STUDIO for Creative Inquiry,* Carnegie Mellon University, School of Art, Pittsburgh PA (S)
Levin, Jed, *Chief Historian,* Independence National Historical Park, Library, Philadelphia PA
Levin, John, *Treas,* Birger Sandzen Memorial Gallery, Lindsborg KS
Levine, Adam, *Dep Dir,* Toledo Museum of Art, Toledo OH
Levine, Adam, *Vis Asst Prof Art, Film & Media Studies,* Amherst College, Dept of Art & the History of Art, Amherst MA (S)
Levine, Cary, *Asst Prof,* University of North Carolina at Chapel Hill, Art Dept, Chapel Hill NC (S)
Levine, Frances, *Pres,* Missouri Historical Society, Missouri History Museum, Saint Louis MO
Levine, Julius S, *Assoc Prof,* Catholic University of America, School of Architecture & Planning, Washington DC (S)
Levine, Martin, *Asst Prof,* Stony Brook University, College of Arts & Sciences, Dept of Art, Stony Brook NY (S)
Levinthal, Beth E, *Exec Dir,* Hofstra University, Hofstra University Museum, Hempstead NY
Levinthal, Beth E, *Exec Dir,* The Heckscher Museum of Art, Library, Huntington NY
Levister, Delores, *Grad & undergrad advising asst,* University of California, Berkeley, College of Letters & Sciences-Art Practice Dept, Berkeley CA (S)
Levitt, Emma, *Design & Drawing,* North Seattle College, North Seattle College Dept of Art, Seattle WA (S)
Levitt, Viera, *Dir,* Community College of Rhode Island, Knight Campus Art Gallery, Warwick RI
Levitz, Dale R, *Asst Prof,* Johns Hopkins University, School of Medicine, Dept of Art as Applied to Medicine, Baltimore MD (S)
Levrant-Bretteville, Sheila, *Dir Graduate Studies Graphic Design,* Yale University, School of Art, New Haven CT (S)
Levy, David C, *Pres & Dir,* Corcoran Gallery of Art, Washington DC
Levy, David, *Board of Dirs & Co-Pres,* Guild of Creative Art, Shrewsbury NJ (S)
Levy, Diane, *Dir Educ,* The Mexican Museum, San Francisco CA
Levy, Elinor, *Folk Arts Prog Mgr,* Dutchess County Arts Council, Poughkeepsie NY
Levy, Gady, *Dir,* University of Judaism, Dept of Continuing Education, Los Angeles CA (S)
Levy, Judith, *Dir Cur,* Gallery North, Setauket NY
Levy, Miranda, *Director of Cultural Relations,* Museum of Wisconsin Art, West Bend WI
Levy, Robert, *Chmn Bd Trustees,* The Art Institute of Chicago, Chicago IL
Levy, Tracey, *Opers Mgr Gallery Shop,* The Buffalo Fine Arts Academy, Albright-Knox Art Gallery, Buffalo NY
Levy, Wendy, *Exec Dir,* National Alliance for Media Arts & Culture, San Francisco CA
Lewandowicz, Galina, *Head Librn,* Cincinnati Art Museum, Mary R Schiff Library & Archives, Cincinnati OH
Lewars, James, *Dir,* Landis Valley Village and Farm Museum, PA Historical & Museum Commission, Landis Collections Gallery, Lancaster PA
Lewellyn, Michaela, *Prog Mgr,* Kentuck Museum Association, Inc, Kentuck Art Center & Festival of the Arts, Northport AL
Lewin, Ralph, *Exec Dir,* Mechanics' Institute, San Francisco CA
Lewin, Zoe, *Asst Cur,* University of California, Berkeley, The Magnes Collection of Jewish Art & Life, Berkeley CA
Lewis, Andrea, *Exec Dir,* The Dairy Barn Arts Center, Athens OH
Lewis, Andrew, *Asst Prof,* West Texas A&M University, Art, Theatre & Dance Dept, Canyon TX (S)
Lewis, Ann-Eliza, *Exec Dir,* Columbia County Historical Society, Luykas Van Alen House, Kinderhook NY
Lewis, Audrey, *Assoc Cur,* Brandywine Conservancy, Brandywine River Museum, Chadds Ford PA
Lewis, Barbara, *Prof,* James Madison University, School of Art & Art History, Harrisonburg VA (S)
Lewis, C Stanley, *Prof,* American University, Dept of Art, New York NY (S)
Lewis, Cathleen, *Dir Educ & Progs,* Museum of Arts & Design, New York NY
Lewis, Cheryl, *Dir Progs,* Space One Eleven, Inc, Birmingham AL
Lewis, Chris, *Media Librn,* American University, Jack I & Dorothy G Bender Library & Learning Resources Center, New York NY
Lewis, Cindi, *VPres,* The Art League Gallery & School, Alexandria VA
Lewis, Clara, *Dir Develop,* Pearl Fincher Museum of Fine Arts, Spring TX
Lewis, Cynthia, *Asst Prof Art History,* Rio Hondo College, Arts & Cultural Programs Dept, Whittier CA (S)
Lewis, David, *Chair,* Hampden-Sydney College, Fine Arts Dept, Hampden Sydney VA (S)
Lewis, Eileen, *Gift Shop Mgr,* Ships of the Sea Maritime Museum, Savannah GA
Lewis, Frank, *Cur & Dir,* Lawrence University, Wriston Art Center Galleries, Appleton WI
Lewis, Hal M, *Pres & CEO,* Spertus Institute of Jewish Studies, Chicago IL
Lewis, Janet, *Instr,* Pittsburg State University, Art Dept, Pittsburg KS (S)
Lewis, Janice, *Chmn Fashion Design,* Moore College of Art & Design, Philadelphia PA (S)
Lewis, Jerry, *Chmn Dept,* Joliet Junior College, Fine Arts Dept, Joliet IL (S)
Lewis, Joe, *Dept Chmn,* California State University, Northridge, Dept of Art, Northridge CA (S)
Lewis, Joseph S, *Dir,* University of California, Irvine, Beall Center for Art + Technology, and University Art Gallery, Irvine CA
Lewis, Katherine, *Va House Site Mgr,* Virginia Historical Society, Library, Richmond VA
Lewis, Kelli, *Develop Dir,* Maritime Museum of San Diego, San Diego CA
Lewis, Lawrence R, *Opers Mgr,* Center for Photography at Woodstock Inc, Woodstock NY
Lewis, Lynn, *Gallery Coordr,* Florida State College at Jacksonville, South Gallery, Jacksonville FL
Lewis, Mark, *Contact,* University of Tulsa, Alexandre Hogue Gallery, Tulsa OK
Lewis, Mary, *Dir Develop,* Cultural Council of Palm Beach County, Lake Worth FL
Lewis, Michael H, *Prof,* University of Maine, Dept of Art, Orono ME (S)
Lewis, Morgan, *Arts Adminr,* Florida Department of State, Division of Cultural Affairs, Florida Council on Arts & Culture, Tallahassee FL

Lewis, Naomi, *Outreach Coordr,* University at Albany, State University of New York, University Art Museum, Albany NY
Lewis, Paul, *Assoc Dean,* Princeton University, School of Architecture, Princeton NJ (S)
Lewis, Richard, *Prof,* Salem State University, Art & Design Department, Salem MA (S)
Lewis, Ron, *Instr,* University of Saint Francis, School of Creative Arts, Fort Wayne IN (S)
Lewis, Russell, *Exec VP & Chief Historian,* Chicago History Museum, Chicago IL
Lewis, Ryan, *Graphic Design,* Western Michigan University, Frostic School of Art, Kalamazoo MI (S)
Lewis, Samella, *Founder,* Museum of African American Art, Los Angeles CA
Lewis, Stacy, *Office Mgr,* Toronto School of Art, Toronto ON (S)
Lewis, Steve, *Head,* Allan Hancock College, Fine Arts Dept, Santa Maria CA (S)
Lewis, Susan, *Acting Dean,* University of Victoria, Faculty of Arts, Victoria BC (S)
Lewis, Susan, *Library Dir,* Boston Architectural College, Library, Boston MA
Lewis, Sylvia, *Recording Secy,* Association of Hawaii Artists, Honolulu HI
Lewis, Tim, *Facilities Supv,* Buffalo Niagara Heritage Village, Amherst NY
Lewiston, Cal, *Head Speech & Fine Arts,* Weatherford College, Dept of Speech Fine Arts, Weatherford TX (S)
Lewitin, Margot, *Artistic Dir,* Women's Interart Center, Inc, Interart Gallery, New York NY
Lewthwaite, Barbara-Jayne, *Pres,* Centenary College, Humanities Dept, Hackettstown NJ (S)
Leyendecker, Gingher, *Chair,* Mesa Community College, Dept of Art, Mesa AZ (S)
Leys, Dale, *Prof,* Murray State University, Dept of Art, Murray KY (S)
Li, Chu-tsing, *Prof Emeritus,* University of Kansas, Kress Foundation Dept of Art History, Lawrence KS (S)
Li, Dougfeng, *Asst Prof,* Morehead State University, Art & Design Dept, Morehead KY (S)
Li, Vivian, *Cur Asian Art,* Worcester Art Museum, Worcester MA
Lianarducci, Barbara, *Dir of Operations,* Silvermine Arts Center, Silvermine Galleries, New Canaan CT
Liao, Jing, *Asst Librn,* University of Illinois at Urbana-Champaign, Ricker Library of Architecture & Art, Champaign IL
Liao, Kathy, *Asst Prof,* Missouri Western State University, School of Fine Arts, Saint Joseph MO (S)
Libbey, Lizabeth, *Prof,* University of Maine at Augusta, College of Arts & Humanities, Augusta ME (S)
Libby, Eileen, *VPres,* California Watercolor Association, Gallery Concord, Concord CA
Liberman, Jack, *Instr,* Cuyahoga Valley Art Center, Cuyahoga Falls OH (S)
Liberman, Kristen, *Assoc Library Dir,* Boston Architectural College, Library, Boston MA
Libke, Audrey, *Receptionist,* Michigan Guild of Artists & Artisans, Michigan Guild Gallery, Ann Arbor MI
Licata, Chris, *Assoc Prof,* Saint Louis Community College at Florissant Valley, Liberal Arts Division, Ferguson MO (S)
Liccardo, Andrew, *Dir,* University of Northern Colorado, School of Art & Design, Greeley CO (S)
Lichtendorf, Victoria, *Dir Edu & Pub Progs,* Storm King Art Center, New Windsor NY
Lichtenfeld, Danny, *Dir,* Brattleboro Museum & Art Center, Brattleboro VT
Licka, Sean, *Chmn,* University of Alaska Anchorage, Dept of Art, Anchorage AK (S)
Liddle, Matt, *Asst Prof,* Western Carolina University, Dept of Art/College of Arts & Science, Cullowhee NC (S)
Liddy, Tim, *Assoc Prof,* Fontbonne University, Fine Art Dept, Saint Louis MO (S)
Lie, Heather, *Event Coordr,* Boise Art Museum, Boise ID
Lieber Mays, Jane, *Adjunct,* Chemeketa Community College, Dept of Humanities & Communications, Art Program, Salem OR (S)
Lieber, Stephanie, *VPres Devel,* Chicago Children's Museum, Chicago IL
Lieberman, Freddie, *Pres,* Scottsdale Artists' League, Scottsdale AZ
Lieberth, Dave, *Board Chair,* The Summit County Historical Society of Akron, OH, Akron OH
Liebling, Alex, *Pres,* Harrison County Historical Museum, Marshall TX
Liebman, Stuart, *Prof Emeritus,* City University of New York, PhD Program in Art History, New York NY (S)
Lieja Quintanar, Daniela, *Cur,* LACE (Los Angeles Contemporary Exhibitions), Los Angeles CA
Lien, Fu-Chia-Wen, *Asst Prof,* Lamar University, Art Dept, Beaumont TX (S)
Lien, Kim, *VPres,* Dacotah Prairie Museum, Lamont Art Gallery, Aberdeen SD
Lien, Krist, *Head Dept,* Pensacola State College, Visual Arts Dept, Pensacola FL (S)
Liester, Eric, *Treas,* The Art Museum of Eastern Idaho, Idaho Falls ID
Liford, Melissa, *Instr Visual Arts Educ,* Madonna University, College of Arts & Humanities, Livonia MI (S)
Lifshin, Rosalyn, *Exec Dir,* Ocean City Arts Center, Ocean City NJ
Ligan, Eric, *Assoc Dean & Distinguished Teaching Prof,* University of North Texas, College of Visual Arts & Design, Denton TX (S)
Light, Flash, *IT Dir,* Artists Talk on Art (ATOA), New York NY
Light, Rolland, *Pres & Chmn Mgmt Comt,* Iroquois County Historical Society Museum, Old Courthouse Museum, Watseka IL
Lightfoot, Thomas, *Asst Prof,* Rochester Institute of Technology, School of Design, Rochester NY (S)
Lightfoot, Tulla, *Prof & Coordr Undergrad Art Educ,* University of North Carolina at Pembroke, Art Dept, Pembroke NC (S)
Lightman, Jean, *Pres,* The Guild of Boston Artists, Boston MA
Lightner, Karen, *Acting Head,* Free Library of Philadelphia, Print & Picture Collection, Philadelphia PA
Lightner, Karen, *Head Librn Art, Dept,* Free Library of Philadelphia, Art Dept, Philadelphia PA
Ligo, Larry L, *Prof,* Davidson College, Art Dept, Davidson NC (S)
Ligon, Doris Hillian, *Dir,* African Art Museum of Maryland, Columbia MD
Ligon, Eric, *Assoc Dean,* University of North Texas, College of Visual Arts & Design, Denton TX (S)
Lilie, Stuart, *Dir Interpretation,* Fort Ticonderoga Association, Ticonderoga NY
Lillehoj, Elizabeth, *Assoc Prof,* DePaul University, Dept of Art, Chicago IL (S)
Lilley, Kristin, *Art Dir,* Children's Museum of Manhattan, New York NY
Lillich, Meredith, *Prof,* Syracuse University, Dept of Fine Arts (Art History), Syracuse NY (S)
Lilly, Tina, *Interim Dir,* Morgan County Foundation, Inc, Madison-Morgan Cultural Center, Madison GA
Lillywhite, Kimberley, *Social Media Coordr,* Toronto School of Art, Toronto ON (S)
Lily, Jane, *Asst Prof Interior Design,* University of Georgia, Franklin College of Arts & Sciences, Lamar Dodd School of Art, Athens GA (S)
Lilyard-Mitchell, Corinne, *Asst Prof,* Tidewater Community College, Visual Arts Center, Portsmouth VA (S)
Lim, Andrea, *Project Mgr,* CoCA Center on Contemporary Art, Seattle WA
Lim, Eun-Hee, *Prof,* University of North Carolina at Greensboro, School of Art, Greensboro NC (S)
Lima, Benjamin, *Asst Prof,* University of Texas at Arlington, Art & Art History Department, Arlington TX (S)
Limbaugh, Stephen N, *Vol Pres,* State Historical Society of Missouri, Columbia MO
Limouze, Dorothy, *Assoc Prof,* St Lawrence University, Dept of Fine Arts, Canton NY (S)
Lin, Cynthia, *Asst Prof,* Purchase College, State University of New York, School of Art+Design, Purchase NY (S)
Lin, Jasper, *Graphics Lab,* Fashion Institute of Technology - SUNY, Gladys Marcus Library, New York NY
Linabury, Sandy, *Vol Coordr,* Kalamazoo Institute of Arts, Kalamazoo MI
Lincoln, Evelyn, *Prof & Dir Grad Studies,* Brown University, Dept of History of Art & Architecture, Providence RI (S)
Lincoln, Justin, *Asst Prof Art,* Whitman College, Art Dept, Walla Walla WA (S)
Lincoln, Paula, *Gallery Visitor Servs,* Sheldon Art Galleries, Saint Louis MO
Lind Newey, Maggie, *Assoc Dir Acad Progs & Public Educ,* Smith College, Museum of Art, Northampton MA
Lindale, Paul, *Dept Chair,* Greenfield Community College, Art Dept, Greenfield MA (S)
Lindall, Terrance, *Pres & Treas,* Williamsburg Art & Historical Center, Brooklyn NY
Lindblom, Michelle, *Instr,* Bismarck State College, Fine Arts Dept, Bismarck ND (S)
Lindblom, Ronald Allan, *Chmn,* Point Park College, Performing Arts Dept, Pittsburgh PA (S)
Lindbloom, Terri, *Assoc Prof,* Florida State University, Art Dept, Tallahassee FL (S)
Linde, Leonard, *Treas,* Klein Museum, Mobridge SD
Lindeen, Rachel, *Pres Bd Dirs,* Art Guild of Burlington, Art Center of Burlington, Burlington IA
Lindell, Ann, *Architecture Fine Arts Bibliographer & Head Librn,* University of Florida, Architecture & Fine Arts Library, Gainesville FL
Lindell, Byron, *Prof,* Iowa Lakes Community College, Dept of Art, Estherville IA (S)
Lindelow, Miranda, *Visual Resources Coordr,* Academy of Art, University Library, San Francisco CA
Lindeman, Leslie, *Dir Mktg,* Newport Historical Society & Museum of Newport History, Newport RI
Lindenbach, Jackie, *Dir Finance & Opers,* University of Regina, MacKenzie Art Gallery, Regina SK
Lindenberger, Beth, *Instr,* Cuyahoga Valley Art Center, Cuyahoga Falls OH (S)
Lindenheim, Diane, *Instr,* Bucks County Community College, Fine Arts Dept, Newtown PA (S)
Linder, Erin, *Exhib Coordr,* Kimball Art Center, Park City UT
Linder, Joan, *Drawing Chair,* University at Buffalo, State University of New York, Dept of Visual Studies, Buffalo NY (S)
Linder, Timothy, *Prof,* Saint Louis Community College at Meramec, Art Dept, Saint Louis MO (S)
Lindner, Harry, *Instr,* Northeast Community College, Dept of Liberal Arts, Norfolk NE (S)
Lindou, Angela, *Foundation & Corp Giving Mgr,* Henry Gallery Association, Henry Art Gallery, Seattle WA
Lindquist, Evan, *Prof,* Arkansas State University, Dept of Art, State University AR (S)
Lindsay, Betsy, *Instr,* Pacific Northwest College of Art, Portland OR (S)
Lindsay, Lindsay, *Assistant Director,* Allegany County Historical Society, Gordon-Roberts House, Cumberland MD
Lindsay, Opal, *Acting Dir,* Mount Vernon Public Library, Fine Art Dept, Mount Vernon NY
Lindsey, Anne, *Prof,* University of Tennessee at Chattanooga, Dept of Art, Chattanooga TN (S)
Lindsey, George, *Deputy Dir Finance & Opers,* University of Utah, Utah Museum of Fine Arts, Salt Lake City UT
Lindsey, Jeremy, *Instr,* Judson University, School of Art, Design & Architecture, Elgin IL (S)
Lindstrom, Janet, *Exec Dir,* New Canaan Historical Society, New Canaan CT

Linehan, Chaitra, *Adj Asst Prof,* University of Texas at Arlington, Art & Art History Department, Arlington TX (S)
Linehan, James, *Prof,* University of Maine, Dept of Art, Orono ME (S)
Linehan, Karen, *Adjunct Asst Prof,* University of Maine, Dept of Art, Orono ME (S)
Linehan, Monika, *Asst Prof,* Cameron University, Art Dept, Lawton OK (S)
Linehan, Ryan, *Mng Dir,* Kimball Jenkins Estate, Concord NH
Linehan, Thomas E, *Pres,* Ringling School of Art & Design, Sarasota FL (S)
Linforth, Jennifer, *Educator,* Wendell Gilley, Southwest Harbor ME
Linga, Mark, *Mktg,* Massachusetts Institute of Technology, List Visual Arts Center, Cambridge MA
Lingen, Joan, *Chmn & Prof Art,* Clarke College, Dept of Art, Dubuque IA (S)
Link, Michael, *VPres,* Halifax Historical Society, Inc, Halifax Historical Museum, Daytona Beach FL
Linker, Amy, *Registrar,* Bard College, Center for Curatorial Studies and the Hessel Museum of Art, Annandale-on-Hudson NY
Linn, Judith, *Adjunct Asst Prof,* Vassar College, Art Dept, Poughkeepsie NY (S)
Linn, Patti, *CEO & Dir,* Riverside, the Farnsley-Moremen Landing, Louisville KY
Linnehan, Genevieve, *Institutional Advancement Assoc,* Guild Hall of East Hampton, Inc, Guild Hall Museum, East Hampton NY
Linnell, Eric, *Pres,* Parson Fisher House, Jonathan Fisher Memorial, Inc, Blue Hill ME
Linnell, Sandra, *Adminr,* Parson Fisher House, Jonathan Fisher Memorial, Inc, Blue Hill ME
Linnenberg, David, *Chief Admin Officer,* Cincinnati Art Museum, Cincinnati Art Museum, Cincinnati OH
Linskey-Deegan, Mara, *Assoc Cur & Registrar,* City of Mason City, Charles H MacNider Art Museum, Mason City IA
Linson, Marty, *Chief Preparator,* Laumeier Sculpture Park, Saint Louis MO
Lint, Suzanne, *Exec Dir,* Allied Arts Council of Lethbridge, Bowman Arts Center, Lethbridge AB
Linton, Henri, *Dept Chmn,* University of Arkansas at Pine Bluff, Art Dept, Pine Bluff AR (S)
Lintz, Rachel, *Asst Processing Archivist,* American Jewish Historical Society, The Center for Jewish History, New York NY
Linz Ross, Judy, *Dir Mktg & Pub Rels,* Westmoreland Museum of American Art, Art Reference Library, Greensburg PA
Liontas-Warren, Kathy, *Assoc Prof,* Cameron University, Art Dept, Lawton OK (S)
Lipfert, Nathan, *Dir Library,* Maine Maritime Museum, Bath ME
Lipfert, Nathan, *Senior Cur,* Maine Maritime Museum, Archives Library, Bath ME
Lipinski, Lisa, *Interim Chair, Arts & Humanities,* Corcoran School of Art, Washington DC (S)
Lipinski, Marlene, *Coordr Graphics,* Columbia College, Art Dept, Chicago IL (S)
Lipp, Frederick, *Prof,* Rochester Institute of Technology, School of Design, Rochester NY (S)
Lippe, Jean, *Dir Mktg & Communs,* Musee National des Beaux Arts du Quebec, Quebec QC
Lippincott III, Bert, *Reference Librn & Genealogist,* Newport Historical Society & Museum of Newport History, Newport RI
Lippincott, Bertram, *Librn,* Newport Historical Society & Museum of Newport History, Library, Newport RI
Lippincott, Louise W, *Cur Fine Art,* Carnegie Museums of Pittsburgh, Carnegie Museum of Art, Pittsburgh PA
Lippman, Irvin, *Exec Dir,* Boca Raton Museum of Art, Library, Boca Raton FL
Lippman, Irvin, *Exec Dir & Pres,* Museum of Art, Fort Lauderdale, Fort Lauderdale FL
Lippman, Paula, *Representative,* Art Without Walls Inc, Sayville NY
Lippman, Sharon, *Exec Dir,* Art Without Walls Inc, Sayville NY
Lipschutz, Jeff, *Prof,* University of Wisconsin Oshkosh, Dept of Art, Oshkosh WI (S)
Lipscomb, Diane, *Chmn,* Feather River Community College, Art Dept, Quincy CA (S)
Lipsey, Ellen, *Secy,* Culberson County Historical Museum, Clark Hotel Historical Museum, Van Horn TX
Lipsey, Joe (Buddy), *Pres (V),* Alexandria Museum of Art, Alexandria LA
Lipsky, Patricia, *Assoc Prof,* University of Hartford, Hartford Art School, West Hartford CT (S)
Lipson, Hyla, *Exec Dir,* Grants Pass Museum of Art, Grants Pass OR
Liriano, Maria, *Assoc Chief Librn,* The New York Public Library, Print Room, New York NY
Lisak, Pamela A, *Interior Design,* Art Institute of Pittsburgh, Pittsburgh PA (S)
Lisberger, L, *Instr,* University of Southern Maine, Dept of Art, Gorham ME (S)
Lisiecki, Denise, *Dir KIA School,* Kalamazoo Institute of Arts, KIA School, Kalamazoo MI (S)
Lisiecki, Denise, *Dir of School,* Kalamazoo Institute of Arts, The Mary & Edwin Meader Fine Arts Library, Kalamazoo MI
Lisiecki, Denise, *School Dir,* Kalamazoo Institute of Arts, Kalamazoo MI
Lisk, Susan J, *Exec Dir,* Porter-Phelps-Huntington Foundation, Inc, Historic House Museum, Hadley MA
Liss, Kay, *Gallery Mgr,* Lincoln County Historical Association, Inc, Maine Art Gallery, Wiscasset ME
Liss, Laurence A, *Pres,* Wharton Esherick Museum, Paoli PA
Lissoway, Brenna, *Archivist,* Yosemite Museum, Research Library, Yosemite National Park CA
List, Kara, *Reference Librn,* University of Oregon, Architecture & Allied Arts Library, Eugene OR
Listamann, Lyle, *Publs Coordr,* Sioux City Art Center, Sioux City IA (S)
Lister, Doris A, *Treas,* Baldwin Historical Society Museum, Baldwin NY
Litchfield, Jennifer, *VPres,* Boothbay Region Art Foundation Inc, Boothbay Harbor ME
Lithgow, Rachel, *Exec Dir,* American Jewish Historical Society, The Center for Jewish History, New York NY
Litow, Joseph, *Asst Prof Arts & Communs,* Orange County Community College, Arts & Communication, Middletown NY (S)
Littell, David, *Instr,* Saginaw Valley State University, Dept of Art & Design, University Center MI (S)
Littell-Herrick, Dori, *Chair Animation,* Woodbury University, School of Media, Culture & Design, Burbank CA (S)
Little Bert, Catherine, *Dir & Owner,* Bert Gallery, Providence RI
Little, Adriane, *Digital Media Photog Area Coordr,* Western Michigan University, Frostic School of Art, Kalamazoo MI (S)
Little, Adriane, *Photo/Intermedia,* Western Michigan University, Frostic School of Art, Kalamazoo MI (S)
Little, Cynthia, *Historian,* Philadelphia History Museum, Philadelphia PA
Little, David E, *Dir & Chief Cur,* Amherst College, Mead Art Museum, Amherst MA
Little, Ken, *Prof,* University of Texas at San Antonio, Dept of Art & Art History, San Antonio TX (S)
Little, Mark A, *Proj Dir,* Atlatl, Phoenix AZ
Little, Melanie, *Show Dir,* American Craft Council, Minneapolis MN
Little, Nancy, *School Dir,* National Academy Museum & School, Archives, New York NY
Little, Paula, *Co-Dir,* Arthur Roy Mitchell, A.R. Mitchell Museum, Trinidad CO
Little, Polly, *Dir Develop,* Hallwalls Contemporary Arts Center, Buffalo NY
Little, Ted, *Chair, Theatre,* Concordia University, Faculty of Fine Arts, Montreal QC (S)
Little, Tess, *Prof Reach Coordr,* Sinclair Community College, Division of Fine & Performing Arts, Dayton OH (S)
Littlefield, Robert, *Adj Instr,* Quincy College, Art Dept, Quincy MA (S)
Littleton, Harvey K, *Dir,* Maurine Littleton Gallery, Washington DC
Littman, Brett, *Exec Dir,* The Drawing Center, New York NY
Littman, Mara, *Dir Mktg & Pub Rels,* Cambridge Arts Council, CAC Gallery, Cambridge MA
Litts, Douglas, *Exec Dir,* The Art Institute of Chicago, Ryerson & Burnham Libraries, Chicago IL
Litvak, Vita, *Mgr Adult Progs,* Philadelphia Museum of Art, Samuel S Fleisher Art Memorial, Philadelphia PA
Litzer, Doris, *Chmn,* Linn Benton Community College, Fine & Applied Art Dept, Albany OR (S)
Liu, Cary, *Cur Asian Art,* Princeton University, Princeton University Art Museum, Princeton NJ
Liu, Heping, *Asst Prof,* Wellesley College, Art Dept, Wellesley MA (S)
Liu, Hung, *Prof,* Mills College, Art Dept, Oakland CA (S)
Liu, Jun-Cheng, *Assoc Prof,* Franklin & Marshall College, Art & Art History Dept, Lancaster PA (S)
Liu, Lily, *Lectr,* Emporia State University, Dept of Art, Emporia KS (S)
Liu, Sofia Galarza, *Head Coll Mgmt,* University of Kansas, Spencer Museum of Art, Lawrence KS
Livaudais, Larry, *Asst,* Louisiana State University, School of Art, Baton Rouge LA (S)
Livesay, Jessica, *Bus Mgr,* The Art Museum of Eastern Idaho, Idaho Falls ID
Livesay, Robert S, *Section Head,* Ohio State University, Austin E Knowlton School of Architecture, Columbus OH (S)
Livesay, Thomas A, *Exec. Dir,* Biscoe Western Art Museum, San Antonio TX
Livingstone, Donna, *Pres & CEO,* Glenbow Museum, Calgary AB
Lizak, Andrew Mann, *VPres,* Fall River Historical Society, Fall River MA
Lizama, Silvia, *Chair Fine Arts Dept,* Barry University, Dept of Fine Arts, Miami Shores FL (S)
Lizotte, Sylvie, *Exec Dir,* The Art Gallery of Cornwall, Cornwall ON
Lizzadro, John S, *Exec Dir,* Lizzadro Museum of Lapidary Art, Elmhurst IL
Lloyd, Craig, *Assoc Prof,* Mount Saint Joseph University, Department of Art and Design, Cincinnati OH (S)
Lloyd, Jan, *Div Chair Fine Art & Commun,* Eula Mae Edwards Museum & Gallery, Clovis NM
Lloyd, Joan, *Registrar,* Oshkosh Public Museum & Library, Oshkosh WI
Lloyd, Scott, *Dir,* College of Mount Saint Joseph, Archbishop Alter Library, Cincinnati OH
Lloyd, Tim, *Gallery Mgr,* Massachusetts Institute of Technology, List Visual Arts Center, Cambridge MA
Lloyd, Wendy, *Mgr Communs,* Bergstrom-Mahler Museum of Glass, Neenah WI
Lloyd-Miller, Daniel, *Asst Dir,* The Guild of Boston Artists, Boston MA
Lmus, Valerie, *Projects & Exhibs Prog Dir,* Southern Exposure, San Francisco CA
Lo, Beth, *Prof,* University of Montana, School of Art, Missoula MT (S)
Loar, Steve, *Assoc Prof,* Rochester Institute of Technology, School of Design, Rochester NY (S)
Loar, Steve, *Dir, Turning & Furniture Design Ctr,* Indiana University of Pennsylvania, College of Fine Arts, Indiana PA (S)
Lobbig, Lois, *Gift Shop Chmn,* Alton Museum of History & Art, Inc, Alton IL
Lockamy, Michelle, *Gallery Mgr,* Philadelphia Sketch Club, Philadelphia PA
Lockard, Ray Anne, *Bibliographer & Pub Svcs Librn,* University of Pittsburgh, Henry Clay Frick Fine Arts Library, Pittsburgh PA
Locke, Linda, *Dir Pub Rels,* The Hudson River Museum, Yonkers NY

Locke, Nancy, *Assoc Prof,* Pennsylvania State University, University Park, Dept of Art History, University Park PA (S)

Lockerman, Leslie B, *Graphic Design,* Art Institute of Pittsburgh, Pittsburgh PA (S)

Lockhart, Claire, *Gallery Staff,* Academy of Motion Picture Arts & Sciences, The Academy Gallery, Beverly Hills CA

Lockhart, Sarah, *Assoc Dir,* Pro Arts, Oakland CA

Locklear, Hayes A, *Mus Educ Prog Coordr,* Institute of American Indian Arts, Museum of Contemporary Native Arts, Santa Fe NM (S)

Lockman, Lisa, *Assoc Prof,* Nebraska Wesleyan University, Art Dept, Lincoln NE (S)

Locks, Norman, *Chmn,* University of California, Santa Cruz, Art Dept, Santa Cruz CA (S)

Lockwood, Stephen, *Coll Mgr,* University of New Mexico, University of New Mexico Art Museum, Albuquerque NM

Lococo, Mark, *Dir, Theatre,* Loyola University of Chicago, Dept of Fine and Performing Arts, Chicago IL (S)

Loder, Bryce, *Sandzen Foundation Pres & CEO,* Birger Sandzen Memorial Gallery, Lindsborg KS

Loder, Chad, *Cur Outdoor Areas,* Northern Maine Museum of Science, Presque Isle ME

Lodge, Liz, *Exec Dir,* Penobscot Marine Museum, Searsport ME

Loeb, Barbara, *Assoc Prof,* Oregon State University, Dept of Art, Corvallis OR (S)

Loeb, Heidi, *Dir Special Projects,* Nevada Museum of Art, Reno NV

Loeffler, Frances, *Cur,* Oakville Galleries, Centennial Square and Gairloch Gardens, Oakville ON

Loehr, Scott W, *CEO,* Delaware Historical Society, Delaware History Museum and Center for African American Heritage, Wilmington DE

Loehr, Scott W, *CEO,* Delaware Historical Society, Library, Wilmington DE

Loehr, Thomas, *Prof, Chmn Communs Div,* Spring Hill College, Department of Fine & Performing Arts, Mobile AL (S)

Loehudorf, Aaron, *Educ Colls Asst,* City of Springdale, Shiloh Museum of Ozark History, Springdale AR

Loeser, Tom, *Prof,* University of Wisconsin, Madison, Dept of Art, Madison WI (S)

Loesl, Sue, *Instr,* Mount Mary College, Art & Design Division, Milwaukee WI (S)

LoFaso, Christine, *Div Head FA Studio,* Northern Illinois University, School of Art & Design, DeKalb IL (S)

Loflin, Teresa, *Community Rels,* City of High Point, High Point Museum, High Point NC

Lofthus, Brian, *Asst to Dir,* North Dakota Museum of Art, Grand Forks ND

Loftis, Elsa, *Dir Library Servs,* Oregon College of Art & Craft, Library, Portland OR

Loftus, Sydney, *Exec Dir,* Madison County Historical Society, Cottage Lawn, Oneida NY

Logan, Darcy, *Gallery Svcs Coordr,* Allied Arts Council of Lethbridge, Bowman Arts Center, Lethbridge AB

Logan, Juan, *Assoc Prof,* University of North Carolina at Chapel Hill, Art Dept, Chapel Hill NC (S)

Logan, Virginia A, *Brandywine Conservancy Exec Dir,* Brandywine Conservancy, Brandywine River Museum, Chadds Ford PA

Logan-Peters, Kay, *Prof & Digital Arts Coordr,* University of Nebraska, Lincoln, Architecture Library, Lincoln NE

LoGrippo, Bob, *Dir,* Spartanburg County Museum of Art, The Art School, Spartanburg SC (S)

Logsdon, Heather, *Art Director & Prof of Art,* Kentucky Wesleyan College, Dept Art, Owensboro KY (S)

Loh Anokye, Akua-Ak, *Sr Prog & Develop Dir,* Jamaica Center for Arts & Learning (JCAL), Jamaica NY

Lohman, Jack, *CEO,* Royal BC Museum, Victoria BC

Lohman, Lauren, *Controller,* Lawndale Art Center, Houston TX

Lohmiller, Nancy, *Asst Prof,* Mount Mary College, Art & Design Division, Milwaukee WI (S)

Lohnes, Dan, *Pres,* Beverly Historical Society, Cabot, Hale & Balch House Museums, Beverly MA

Lohnes, Dan, *Pres,* Beverly Historical Society, Library, Beverly MA

Lohr, Kathleen, *Instr,* Central Community College - Columbus Campus, Business & Arts Cluster, Columbus NE (S)

Lokensgard, Lynne, *Prof,* Lamar University, Art Dept, Beaumont TX (S)

Lomahaftew-Singer, Tatiana, *Cur Coll,* Institute of American Indian Arts, Museum of Contemporary Native Arts, Santa Fe NM (S)

Lomahaftewa-Singer, Tatiana, *Cur Colls,* Institute of American Indian Arts, IAIA Museum of Contemporary Native Arts, Santa Fe NM

Lomas, Esteban, *Archival Asst,* Hidalgo County Historical Museum, Edinburg TX

Lombard, Lynette, *Asst Prof,* Knox College, Dept of Art, Galesburg IL (S)

Lombardo, Cindy, *Library Admin,* Cleveland Public Library, Fine Arts & Special Collections Dept, Cleveland OH

Lombino, Mary-Kay, *Cur & Asst Dir Strategic Planning,* Vassar College, The Frances Lehman Loeb Art Center, Poughkeepsie NY

Lonchyna, Natalia, *Librn,* North Carolina Museum of Art, Art Reference Library, Raleigh NC

Lonchyna, Natalia, *Librn,* North Carolina Museum of Art, Raleigh NC

Long, Adam, *Adjunct Assoc Prof Photog,* Johnson County Community College, Fine Arts Dept & Art History Dept, Overland Park KS (S)

Long, Andrea, *Registrar,* Orlando Museum of Art, Orlando FL

Long, Andrea, *Registrar,* Orlando Museum of Art, Orlando Sentinel Library, Orlando FL

Long, Barry, *Prof,* Mount Saint Mary's University, Visual & Performing Arts Dept, Emmitsburg MD (S)

Long, J, *Cur History,* Charleston Museum, Charleston SC

Long, Jane, *Assoc Prof,* Roanoke College, Fine Arts Dept-Art, Salem VA (S)

Long, Jeremy, *Assoc Prof,* Wright State University, Dept of Art & Art History, Dayton OH (S)

Long, Jeremy, *Vis Asst Prof,* Assumption College, Dept of Art, Music & Theatre, Worcester MA (S)

Long, John M, *Dean,* Troy State University, Dept of Art & Classics, Troy AL (S)

Long, Matt, *Assoc Prof,* University of Mississippi, Department of Art, University MS (S)

Long, Nancy, *Prof,* Munson-Williams-Proctor Arts Institute, Pratt MWP College of Art, Utica NY (S)

Long, Richard, *Emer Prof,* University of Wisconsin, Madison, Dept of Art, Madison WI (S)

Long, Robert, *Prof,* Mississippi State University, Dept of Art, Starville MS (S)

Long, Sheila, *Prog Supv,* Imperial Centre's Maria V Howard Arts Center, Rocky Mount NC

Long, TImothy, *Head Cur,* University of Regina, MacKenzie Art Gallery, Regina SK

Longchamps, Denis, *Artistic Dir & Chief Cur,* Art Gallery of Burlington, Burlington ON

Longfellow, Holly, *Admin Asst,* Ohio State University, Dept of Art Education, Columbus OH (S)

Longhauser, Elsa, *Exec Dir,* Institute of Contemporary Art, Los Angeles, Los Angeles CA

Longhenry, Susan, *Dir,* University of New Mexico, The Harwood Museum of Art, Taos NM

Longhenry, Susan, *Dir & Chief Cur,* Marquette University, Haggerty Museum of Art, Milwaukee WI

Longinotti, Katie, *Youth Coordr,* Sawtooth Center for Visual Art, Winston-Salem NC (S)

Longley, Annie, *Mem Coordr,* Provincetown Art Association & Museum, Provincetown MA

Longley-Cook, Tracy, *Assoc Prof,* Wright State University, Dept of Art & Art History, Dayton OH (S)

Longman, Jenanne, *Office Adminr,* Fusion: The Ontario Clay & Glass Association, Fusion Clay & Glass Association, Toronto ON

Longman, Mary, *Assoc Prof,* University of Saskatchewan, Art & Art History Dept, Saskatoon SK (S)

Longo, Julie, *Chmn Liberal Arts,* College for Creative Studies, Detroit MI (S)

Longshore, Jennifer, *Instr,* Southern Oregon University, Art & Art History Dept, Ashland OR (S)

Longwell, Alicia, *Lewis B & Dorothy Cullman Chief Cur Art & Educ,* Parrish Art Museum, Water Mill NY

Longwell, David, *Preparator,* Tucson Museum of Art and Historic Block, Tucson AZ

Lonnberg, Tom, *Cur History,* Evansville Museum of Arts, History & Science, Evansville IN

Loo, Violet, *Chmn,* Honolulu Museum of Art, Honolulu HI

Loomis, Tom, *Assoc Prof,* Mansfield University, Art Dept, Mansfield PA (S)

Loonsk, Susan, *Assoc Prof,* University of Wisconsin-Superior, Programs in the Visual Arts, Superior WI (S)

Looper, Matt, *Prof,* California State University, Chico, Department of Art & Art History, Chico CA (S)

Lopata, Renee, *Devel Dir,* Mesa Arts Center, Mesa Contemporary Arts Museum, Mesa AZ

Lopez Travez, Lucila, *Dir Events & Membership,* The One Club for Creativity, New York NY

Lopez, Jr, Albert, *Opers Dir,* Orange County Museum of Art, Newport Beach CA

Lopez, Agapita Judy, *Director Historic Properties,* Georgia O'Keeffe Museum, Santa Fe NM

Lopez, Alex, *Asst Prof,* Southern Illinois University, School of Art & Design, Carbondale IL (S)

Lopez, Ana, *Assoc Prof Metals,* University of North Texas, College of Visual Arts & Design, Denton TX (S)

Lopez, Armando, *Dir IT,* New-York Historical Society, Museum, New York NY

Lopez, Elizabeth, *Professor of Art History,* Los Angeles City College, School of Visual & Media Arts, Los Angeles CA (S)

Lopez, Frank, *Librn,* Palm Springs Art Museum, Palm Springs CA

Lopez, J Tomas, *Prof,* University of Miami, Dept of Art & Art History, Coral Gables FL (S)

Lopez, John, *Bd Dir,* Grand River Museum, Lemmon SD

Lopez, Marines, *Acad Dean,* Escuela de Artes Plasticas, Biblioteca Francisco Oller, San Juan PR

Lopez, Mario Gee, *Treas,* Latino Art Museum, Pomona CA

Lopez, Ramon, *Prof,* University of Puerto Rico, Mayaguez, Dept of Humanities, College of Fine Arts & Theory of Art Programs, Mayaguez PR (S)

Lopez, Robert A, *Asst Prof,* Southern Illinois University, School of Art & Design, Carbondale IL (S)

Lopez, Teresa, *Acting Dean Acad/Study Affairs,* Escuela de Artes Plasticas de Puerto Rico, San Juan PR (S)

Lopez, Teresa, *CFO,* College Art Association, New York NY

Lopez, Tom, *Asst Prof,* Rochester Institute of Technology, School of Photographic Arts & Sciences, Rochester NY (S)

Lopez-Isnardi, C Sandy, *Prof,* Alma College, Clack Art Center, Dept of Art & Design, Alma MI (S)

Lord, Allyn, *Dir,* City of Springdale, Shiloh Museum of Ozark History, Springdale AR

Lord, Catherine, *Prof Critical Theory, Feminism, Photog,* University of California, Irvine, Studio Art Dept, Irvine CA (S)

Lord, Evelyn, *Head Librn,* Laney College Library, Art Section, Oakland CA

Lord, Keith, *Asst Prof Art,* University of La Verne, Dept of Art, La Verne CA (S)

Lord, Richard, *Vol Treas,* Macartney House Museum, Oakland ME

Lord, Russell, *Cur Photog, Prints & Drawings,* New Orleans Museum of Art, New Orleans LA

Lord, S., *Film & Media Dir,* Queen's University, Faculty of Arts & Sciences, Creative Arts Program, Kingston ON (S)
Lord, Shelley, *Dir,* Cando Arts Center, Cando ND
Lord, Trudy, *Secy-Treas,* Laurens County Historical Society, Dublin-Laurens Museum, Dublin GA
Lorence, Marian, *Adjunct,* York College of Pennsylvania, Dept of Music, Art & Speech Communications, York PA (S)
Lorenson, Rob, *Assoc Prof,* Bridgewater State College, Art Dept, Bridgewater MA (S)
Lorenz, Elaine, *Asst Prof,* William Paterson University, Dept Arts, Wayne NJ (S)
Lorenz, Elaine, *Pres,* Sculptors Guild, Inc, Brooklyn NY
Lorenz, Hilary, *Prof,* Long Island University, Brooklyn Campus, Art Dept, Brooklyn NY (S)
Lorenz, Janie, *Bus Mgr,* Florida CraftArt, Saint Petersburg FL
Lorenz, Kate, *Exec Dir,* Hyde Park Art Center, Chicago IL
Lorenz, Michael, *Prof,* Saint Louis Community College at Meramec, Art Dept, Saint Louis MO (S)
Lorieo, Jacqueline, *Pres Sculpture,* Hudson Valley Art Association, Brooklyn NY
Lorigan, Jim, *Chair,* College of the Canyons, Art Dept, Santa Clarita CA (S)
Lorimer, Cal, *Office Mgr,* Women's Art Association of Canada, Dignam Gallery, Toronto ON
Lorini, Frederick, *Gen Educ,* Art Institute of Pittsburgh, Pittsburgh PA (S)
Lorren, Margaret N, *VPres,* Pensacola Museum of Art, Harry Thornton Library, Pensacola FL
Lorys, Jan M, *Historian,* Polish Museum of America (PMA), Chicago IL
Losavio, Sam, *Asst Dir,* Louisiana Arts & Science Museum, Library, Baton Rouge LA
Losavio, Sam, *Asst Dir,* Louisiana Arts & Science Museum, Baton Rouge LA
Losch, Michael, *Assoc Prof,* Western Maryland College, Dept of Art & Art History, Westminster MD (S)
LoSchiavo, Joseph A, *Exec Dir,* Saint Bonaventure University, Regina A Quick Center for the Arts, Saint Bonaventure NY
Losinski, Patrick, *CEO,* Columbus Metropolitan Library, Arts & Media Division Carnegie Gallery, Columbus OH
Lossi, Christina, *Mus Shop Mgr,* New Orleans Museum of Art, New Orleans LA
Lossmann, Robert, *Painting & Watercolor,* College of Lake County, Art Dept, Grayslake IL (S)
Loto, Judith, *Cur,* Litchfield History Museum, Litchfield CT
Lott, Laura L., *Pres & CEO,* American Alliance of Museums, Arlington VA
Lott, Linda, *Rare Book Librn,* Dumbarton Oaks, Dumbarton Oaks Research Library, Washington DC
Lott, Robin, *Dir Retail & Vis Servs,* Genesee Country Village & Museum, John L Wehle Art Gallery, Mumford NY
Lotz, Stacy, *Dept Chair & Assoc Prof Art,* Monmouth College, Dept of Art, Monmouth IL (S)
Lou, Julie, *Dir Fin,* The Queens Museum of Art, Flushing NY
Lou, Richard, *Chmn,* San Diego Mesa College, Fine Arts Dept, San Diego CA (S)
Louckes, Theresa, *Mktg Coordr,* Cultural Council of Palm Beach County, Lake Worth FL
Louden, William F, *Librn,* University of Evansville, University Library, Evansville IN
Loudenback, Brad, *Prof,* Webster University, Department of Art, Design & Art History, Webster Groves MO (S)
Louder, John, *Prof,* University of Central Missouri, Dept of Art & Design, Warrensburg MO (S)
Loudon, Sarah, *Dir Garden Center Asian Art & Ideas,* Seattle Art Museum, Dorothy Stimson Bullitt Library, Seattle WA
Loudon, Sarah, *Dir, Gardner Center Asian Art & Ideas,* Seattle Art Museum, Seattle WA
Loughheed, Claire, *Exec Dir,* Dundas Valley School of Art, Dundas ON (S)
Loughman, Thomas, *Dir & CEO,* United States National Committee of the International Council of Museums, Washington DC
Loughridge Bush, Sally, *Bd Pres,* Lincoln County Historical Association, Inc, Maine Art Gallery, Wiscasset ME
Loughridge, Martha, *Develop Dir,* SPACES, Cleveland OH
Loughridge, Sally, *Pres,* Pemaquid Group of Artists, Pemaquid Art Gallery, Pemaquid Point ME
Louis, Elizabeth, *Gallery Coordr,* Florida Community College at Jacksonville, South Campus, Art Dept, Jacksonville FL (S)
Lourse, Margaret, *Communs Ed,* University of Michigan, Kelsey Museum of Archaeology, Ann Arbor MI
Lousplain, Mary, *Coordr,* Middlebury College, History of Art & Architecture Dept, Middlebury VT (S)
Lovaglio Costello, Enrica, *Asst Prof Digital Media,* California Polytechnic State University at San Luis Obispo, Dept of Art & Design, San Luis Obispo CA (S)
Love, Angela, *Media Arts & Animation,* Art Institute of Pittsburgh, Pittsburgh PA (S)
Love, Camille, *Exec Dir,* City of Atlanta, Public Art Program, Atlanta GA
Love, Ed, *Prof Emeritus,* Florida State University, Art Dept, Tallahassee FL (S)
Love, Georgina, *Exhib Coordr,* A.E. Backus Museum & Gallery, Fort Pierce FL
Love, Jeff, *Brd Pres,* Art Museum of Greater Lafayette, Lafayette IN
Love, M Jordan, *Acad Cur,* University of Virginia, The Fralin Museum of Art at the University of Virginia, Charlottesville VA
Love, Tyler, *Archivist,* Independence National Historical Park, Library, Philadelphia PA
Lovejoy, Barbara, *Registrar,* The University of Kentucky Art Museum, Lexington KY
Lovejoy, Claudine, *Admin Asst,* Museum of East Texas, Lufkin TX
Lovelace, Joan, *Admin Opers Dir,* Rochester Art Center, Rochester MN
Loveland, Richard, *Exec Dir,* Danville Museum of Fine Arts & History, Danville VA
Loveless, Jim, *Prof,* Colgate University, Dept of Art & Art History, Hamilton NY (S)
Loveless, Natalie, *Coordr History of Art, Design & Visual Culture,* University of Alberta, Dept of Art & Design, Edmonton AB (S)
Lovell, Carol W, *Cur,* Stratford Historical Society, Genealogical Library, Stratford CT
Lovell, Carol, *Cur,* Stratford Historical Society, Catharine B Mitchell Museum, Stratford CT
Loven, Del Rey, *Dept Head,* University of Akron, Myers School of Art, Akron OH (S)
Lovering-Brown, Theresa, *Jewelry & Metals Instr,* Monterey Peninsula College, Art Dept/Art Gallery, Monterey CA (S)
Lovett, Beverly, *Park Specialist,* Red Rock Park, Red Rock Park, Church Rock NM
Lovett, O Rufus, *Instr,* Kilgore College, Visual Arts Dept, Kilgore TX (S)
Lovett, Rachel, *Asst Dir,* Hammond-Harwood House Association, Inc, Hammond-Harwood House, Annapolis MD
Lovingood, Melissa, *Instr,* North Iowa Area Community College, Dept of Art, Mason City IA (S)
Lovington, Nan, *Dir of Outreach,* California Watercolor Association, Gallery Concord, Concord CA
Lovinguth, Sandra, *Assoc Dir Devel,* National Museum of Natural History, Smithsonian Institution, Washington DC
Low, Bill, *Cur Coll,* Bates College, Museum of Art, Lewiston ME
Lowe, Arline, *Asst Prof,* Seton Hall University, College of Arts & Sciences, South Orange NJ (S)
Lowe, Constance, *Prof,* University of Texas at San Antonio, Dept of Art & Art History, San Antonio TX (S)
Lowe, Karen, *Facility Mgr,* City of Atlanta, Chastain Arts Center & Gallery, Atlanta GA
Lowe, Patricia, *Librn,* Will Rogers Memorial Museum & Birthplace Ranch, Media Center Library, Claremore OK
Lowe, Phillip, *Coordr Fine Arts,* Hill College, Fine Arts Dept, Hillsboro TX (S)
Lowe, Truman, *Emer Prof,* University of Wisconsin, Madison, Dept of Art, Madison WI (S)
Lowe-Stockwell, Susie, *Dir,* League of New Hampshire Craftsmen, Grodin Permanent Collection Museum, Concord NH
Lowe-Stockwell, Susie, *Dir,* League of New Hampshire Craftsmen, Kira Fournier Resource Library Center, Concord NH
Lowenberg, Susan, *Info Resources Librn,* California Institute of the Arts Library, Santa Clarita CA
Lowery, Liz, *Dept Chair,* Howard College, Art Dept, Big Spring TX (S)
Lowley, Scott, *Chmn,* Mars Hill College, Art Dept, Mars Hill NC (S)
Lowly, Tim, *Dir Gallery,* North Park University, Carlson Tower Art Gallery, Chicago IL
Lowrance, Melanie, *Assoc Prof,* University of Central Missouri, Dept of Art & Design, Warrensburg MO (S)
Lowrance, Sandy, *Acting Chmn,* University of Memphis, Art Dept, Memphis TN (S)
Lowry, Connor, *Comm & Mktg Specialist,* Auburn University, Jule Collins Smith Museum of Fine Art, Auburn AL
Lowther, Andrea, *Deputy Dir Experience Design,* National Museum of American History, Smithsonian Institution, Washington DC
Loy, Jessica, *Prof,* The College of Saint Rose, The Center For Art and Design, Albany NY (S)
Loyola, Walter, *Assoc Prof,* Mount Saint Joseph University, Department of Art and Design, Cincinnati OH (S)
Lozano, Yadhira, *Communs & Special Projects Dir,* Guadalupe Cultural Arts Center, San Antonio TX
Lozar, Carmen, *Adjunct Instr,* Illinois Wesleyan University, School of Art, Bloomington IL (S)
Lozar, Carmen, *Dir,* Illinois Wesleyan University, Merwin & Wakeley Galleries, Bloomington IL
Lu, Lilly, *Asst Prof,* University of Nebraska at Omaha, School of the Arts, Omaha NE (S)
Luark, Carolyn, *Dept Chmn,* Bellevue Community College, Art Dept, Bellevue WA (S)
Luay, Jennifer, *Mktg Mgr,* Hermitage Museum & Gardens, Museum, Norfolk VA
Lubell, Mark, *Exec Dir,* International Center of Photography, Museum, New York NY
Lubensky, Gerald, *Prof,* University of Kansas, The School of the Arts, Dept of Visual Art, Lawrence KS (S)
Luber, Katherine, *Dir,* San Antonio Museum of Art, San Antonio TX
Luber, Patrick, *Chmn,* University of North Dakota, Art Department, Grand Forks ND (S)
Lubin, David M, *Charlotte C Weber Prof Art,* Wake Forest University, Dept of Art, Winston-Salem NC (S)
Lubowsky Talbott, Susan, *Exec Dir,* The Fabric Workshop & Museum, Philadelphia PA
Lucarelli, Vincent, *Instr,* Illinois Benedictine University, Department of Fine Arts, Lisle IL (S)
Lucas Hardy, Linda, *Dir,* National Oil & Acrylic Painters Society, Houston TX
Lucas, Barb, *Dir Finance & Admin,* Art Gallery of Greater Victoria, Victoria BC
Lucas, Barbara, *Regent,* George Washington's Mount Vernon, Mount Vernon VA
Lucas, Christina, *Contact,* Canada Science & Technology Museums Corporation, Canada Aviation Museum, Ottawa ON
Lucas, Cindy, *Asst to Dir,* College of William & Mary, Muscarelle Museum of Art, Williamsburg VA
Lucas, Claire, *Educ Coordr,* The Summit County Historical Society of Akron, OH, Akron OH

Lucas, June, *Dir Research,* Old Salem Museums & Gardens, Library and Research Center, Winston-Salem NC

Lucas, June, *Librn & Cur Research Coll,* Old Salem Museums & Gardens, Museum of Early Southern Decorative Arts, Winston-Salem NC

Lucas, Paula, *Instr,* West Liberty State College, Div Art, West Liberty WV (S)

Lucas, Robert, *Pres,* Ohio History Connection, National Road-Zane Grey Museum, Norwich OH

Lucas, Thomas, *Co-Cur,* Chicago State University, President's Gallery, Chicago IL

Lucchesi, Joe, *Asst Prof,* Saint Mary's College of Maryland, Art & Art History Dept, Saint Mary's City MD (S)

Luce, Ken, *Instr,* San Jacinto College-North, Art Dept, Houston TX (S)

Lucey, Susan, *Assoc Prof,* University of Minnesota, Minneapolis, Dept of Art, Minneapolis MN (S)

Luchans, Miriam, *Registrar,* Yosemite Museum, Research Library, Yosemite National Park CA

Luchanski, Michael, *Dir Coll Servs,* Royal Alberta Museum, Royal Alberta Museum, Edmonton AB

Luck, Andy, *Asst Dir,* Free Public Library of Elizabeth, Elizabeth NJ

Lucke, Susan, *Registrar,* University of California, Santa Barbara, Art, Design & Architecture Museum, Santa Barbara CA

Lucker, Amy, *Head Librn,* New York University, Stephen Chan Library of Fine Arts, New York NY

Luckett, Sandra, *Asst Prof,* University of Central Arkansas, Department of Art, Conway AR (S)

Lucy, Martha, *Deputy Dir Research, Interpretation & Educ,* Barnes Foundation, Merion PA

Luderowski, Barbara, *Bd Mem, Co-Dir,* The Mattress Factory, Pittsburgh PA

Ludwig, Daniel, *Assoc Prof,* Salve Regina University, Art Dept, Newport RI (S)

Ludwig, Deborah, *Dean,* Fort Hays State University, Forsyth Library, Hays KS

Ludwig, Jeffrey, *Preparator,* Lehigh University Art Galleries, Museum Operation, Bethlehem PA

Ludwig, Robert, *Adj Asst Prof,* College of Staten Island, Performing & Creative Arts Dept, Staten Island NY (S)

Lue, Joanne, *Admin Asst,* University at Albany, State University of New York, University Art Museum, Albany NY

Luebbers, Leslie L, *Dir,* University of Memphis, Art Museum, Memphis TN

Luecking, Stephen, *Chmn Dept,* DePaul University, Dept of Art, Chicago IL (S)

Luedke, Jill, *Librn,* Temple University, Tyler School of Art Library, Philadelphia PA

Luehrman, Mick, *Chair Dept,* University of Central Missouri, Dept of Art & Design, Warrensburg MO (S)

Luft, Alan, *Asst Prof,* Edgewood College, Art Dept, Madison WI (S)

Luginbuhl, Gregg, *Chair,* Bluffton University, Art Dept, Bluffton OH (S)

Luhikhuizen, Henry, *Prof,* Calvin College, Art Dept, Grand Rapids MI (S)

Lujan, Melisa, *Registrar,* El Museo del Barrio, New York NY

Lujan, Vernon, *Dir,* Pueblo of Pojoaque, Poeh Museum, Santa Fe NM

Luk, Cynthia, *Paintings Conservator & Internatl Projs Specialist,* Williamstown Art Conservation Center, Williamstown MA

Lukacher, Brian, *Prof,* Vassar College, Art Dept, Poughkeepsie NY (S)

Lukasiewicz, Jenni, *Educ Coordr,* Greenwich House Pottery, Jane Hartsook Gallery, New York NY

Lukasiewicz, Nancy, *Cur,* Lyndon House Art, Athens GA

Luke, Margie L, *Archivist,* St Mary Chapter Louisiana Landmarks Society, Grevemberg House Museum, Franklin LA

Luke, Suzanne, *Cur,* Wilfrid Laurier University, Robert Langen Art Gallery, Waterloo ON

Luker, Amanda, *Graphic Designer,* Utah Valley University, Woodbury Art Museum, Orem UT

Lukins, Cat, *Sec,* Washington Sculptors Group, Washington DC

Lukkas, Lynn, *Asst Prof,* University of Minnesota, Minneapolis, Dept of Art, Minneapolis MN (S)

Lum, Ken, *Prof & Chair, Fine Arts,* University of Pennsylvania, School of Design (PennDesign), Philadelphia PA (S)

Luman, Mitch, *Dir Science Experiences,* Evansville Museum of Arts, History & Science, Evansville IN

Lumpkin, Olivia L, *Prof,* University of New Mexico, Department of Fine Arts & Art History, Albuquerque NM (S)

Luna, Sandra, *Receptionist,* Hidalgo County Historical Museum, Edinburg TX

Lund, Karsten, *Asst Cur,* The Renaissance Society, Chicago IL

Lundberg, Nozomi, *Admin Asst,* Billie Trimble Chandler, Texas State Museum of Asian Cultures, Corpus Christi TX

Lunde, Mary Lee, *Chmn,* State University of New York at Fredonia, Dept of Art, Fredonia NY (S)

Lundegard, Stephanie, *Admin Asst,* Order Sons of Italy in America, Garibaldi & Meucci Museum, Staten Island NY

Lundgren, Jodi, *Cur Exhibs,* South Dakota State University, South Dakota Art Museum, Brookings SD

Lundin, Laurie, *Admin Coord,* Allens Lane Art Center, Carolyn-Fielder-Alber Gallery, Philadelphia PA

Lundskow, Pete, *Cur Coll,* Boulder History Museum, Museum of History, Boulder CO

Luner, Karin, *Dir Opers,* Women's Caucus For Art, New York NY

Lunsford, John J, *Deputy Dir Admin,* Jamestown-Yorktown Foundation, Jamestown Settlement, Williamsburg VA

Lunt, Eve, *Gallery Dir,* Barbara & Ray Alpert Jewish Community Center, Pauline & Zena Gatov Gallery, Long Beach CA

Luo, Jian, *Assoc Prof,* University of Wisconsin-Eau Claire, Dept of Art & Design, Eau Claire WI (S)

Luong, Natasha, *Educ Asst,* Fort Smith Regional Art Museum, Fort Smith AR

Lupher, Vance, *Registrar,* Erie Art Museum, Erie PA

Lupo, Joseph, *Assoc Prof,* West Virginia University, College of Creative Arts, School of Art & Design, Morgantown WV (S)

Lurie, Deirdre, *Dir Strategic Communs,* Children's Museum of Manhattan, New York NY

Lurie, Evan, *Dir,* Evan Lurie Fine Art Gallery, Carmel IN

Lurie, Janice Lea, *Head Librn,* Minneapolis Institute of Art, Art Research & Reference Library, Minneapolis MN

Lursen, Mary Beth, *Media Mktg Specialist,* Mobile Museum of Art, Mobile AL

Lushington, Nancy, *Artist in Res, Dance,* Marymount Manhattan College, Fine & Performing Arts Div, New York NY (S)

Lusk, Kendell, *Admin Asst, Graphic Designer & Instructor,* Belton Center for the Arts, Belton SC

Lusk, Kyle, *Assoc Prof,* Brevard College, Department of Art, Brevard NC (S)

Lustig, John, *Gallery Mgr Lockport,* Illinois State Museum, ISM Lockport Gallery, Chicago Gallery & Southern Illinois Art Gallery, Springfield IL

Lustig, Steven, *Pres,* Jewish Community Center of Greater Washington, Jane L & Robert H Weiner Judaic Museum, Rockville MD

Luther, Kathryn, *Artist & Owner,* Gallery 4, Ltd, Fargo ND

Luther, Olivia, *Mus Dir,* California Center for the Arts, Escondido Museum, Escondido CA

Luther, Sherry, *Exec Dir,* Saskatchewan Craft Council & Affinity Gallery, Saskatoon SK

Lutiger, Jim, *Bd Treas,* The Phipps Center for the Arts, Galleries, Hudson WI

Lutsch, Gail, *Assoc Prof,* Bethel College, Dept of Art, North Newton KS (S)

Lutterodt, Isabelle, *Dir,* Cultural Affairs Department, Los Angeles Municipal Art Gallery, Los Angeles CA

Lutz, Barbara, *Admin Asst,* University of Minnesota, Goldstein Museum of Design, Saint Paul MN

Lutz, Jim, *Prof,* Rhodes College, Dept of Art, Memphis TN (S)

Lutz, Penny, *Gallery Director,* Pennsylvania College of Technology, The Gallery at Penn College, Williamsport PA (S)

Lutz, Tina, *Exec Dir & Pub Rels,* GumTree Museum of Art, Tupelo MS

Luukkonen, John, *School of Design,* Art Institute of Houston, Houston TX (S)

Luxenberg, Alisa, *Asst Prof Art History,* University of Georgia, Franklin College of Arts & Sciences, Lamar Dodd School of Art, Athens GA (S)

Lybarger, Mary, *Instr,* Edgewood College, Art Dept, Madison WI (S)

Lyders, Laurie S, *Treas,* Liberty Village Arts Center & Gallery, Chester MT

Lydon, Catherine, *Instr,* Springfield College, Dept of Visual & Performing Arts, Springfield MA (S)

Lydon, Kate, *Dir Exhibs,* Society for Contemporary Craft, Pittsburgh PA

Lyford, Amy, *Prof,* Occidental College, Dept of Art History & Visual Arts, Los Angeles CA (S)

Lyke, Linda, *Prof,* Occidental College, Dept of Art History & Visual Arts, Los Angeles CA (S)

Lykins, Jere, *Assoc Prof,* Berry College, Art Dept, Mount Berry GA (S)

Lykins, Jere, *Dir,* Berry College, Moon Gallery, Mount Berry GA

Lyles, Cornelia, *Dr,* Compton Community College, Art Dept, Compton CA (S)

Lyman, Christy, *Mktg Mgr,* Museum of Northwest Art, La Conner WA

Lyman, Daniel, *Interim Pres,* New Hampshire Institute of Art, Manchester NH

Lyman, Daniel, *Interim Pres,* New Hampshire Institute of Art, Manchester NH (S)

Lyman, David H, *Founder & Dir,* Rockport College, Maine Photographic Workshops, Rockport ME

Lyman, David H, *Founder & Dir,* Maine Photographic Workshops, The International T.V. & Film Workshops & Rockport College, Rockport ME (S)

Lynch, Beth, *Martyrs Mus Mgr,* The National Shrine of the North American Martyrs, Fultonville NY

Lynch, Cynthia D, *Dir Library Servs,* Milwaukee Institute of Art & Design, Library, Milwaukee WI

Lynch, Jacqueline, *Exhib Coordr,* Sage College of Albany, Opalka Gallery, Albany NY

Lynch, James, *Asst Archivist,* Bethel College, Mennonite Library & Archives, North Newton KS

Lynch, Jo, *Lectr,* Oklahoma State University, Department of Art, Graphic Design and Art History, Stillwater OK (S)

Lynch, Laura, *Dir Educ,* Nassau County Museum of Art, Roslyn Harbor NY

Lynch, Matthew, *Asst Prof Fine Arts,* University of Cincinnati, School of Art, Cincinnati OH (S)

Lynch, Robert L, *Pres & CEO,* Americans for the Arts, Washington DC

Lynch, Robert, *Pres & CEO,* Americans for the Arts, New York NY

Lynch, Robin, *Assoc Prof,* Purchase College, State University of New York, School of Art+Design, Purchase NY (S)

Lynch, Shelia, *Prof Art & Art History,* Rio Hondo College, Arts & Cultural Programs Dept, Whittier CA (S)

Lynch, Steve, *Pres,* Fishkill Historical Society, Van Wyck Homestead Museum, Fishkill NY

Lynch-Maas, Rebecca, *Capital Campaign Coordr,* Asheville Art Museum, Asheville NC

Lynch-McWhite, Wyona, *Dir,* Fuller Craft Museum, Brockton MA

Lynch-McWhite, Wyona, *Exec Dir,* Fuller Craft Museum, Library, Brockton MA

Lynch-McWhite, Wyona, *Exec Dir,* Fruitlands Museum, Inc, Harvard MA

Lynde, Richard, *VPres,* Montclair State University, Art Galleries, Upper Montclair NJ

Lynes, Lisa, *Instr,* North Idaho College, Art Dept, Coeur D'Alene ID (S)

Lynn, Billie G, *Asst Prof,* University of Miami, Dept of Art & Art History, Coral Gables FL (S)
Lynn, Judy G, *Exec Dir,* Pacific Northwest Art School, Gallery at the Wharf, Coupeville WA
Lynne, Michael, *2nd VChmn,* Guild Hall of East Hampton, Inc, Guild Hall Museum, East Hampton NY
Lynx, David, *Dir,* Yakima Valley Community College, Larson Gallery, Yakima WA
Lyon, Gabrielle, *VPres Educ & Experiences,* Chicago Architecture Foundation, Chicago IL
Lyon, Jen, *Preparator,* City of Ukiah, Grace Hudson Museum & The Sun House, Ukiah CA
Lyon, Joyce, *Assoc Prof,* University of Minnesota, Minneapolis, Dept of Art, Minneapolis MN (S)
Lyon, Robert F, *Chmn,* University of South Carolina, Dept of Art, Columbia SC (S)
Lyons, Heather, *Exec Dir,* Living Arts & Science Center, Inc, Lexington KY
Lyons, Kelly S., *Cur. Education,* Cranbrook Art Museum, Bloomfield Hills MI
Lyons, Kenneth H, *Pres Emeritus,* Newport Historical Society & Museum of Newport History, Newport RI
Lyttle, Sue, *VPres,* Marin Society of Artists Inc, San Rafael CA
Ma, Yue, *Dir Colls & Research,* Museum of Chinese in America, New York NY
Maas, Bernard, *Chmn Crafts,* Edinboro University of Pennsylvania, Art Dept, Edinboro PA (S)
Mabee, Laura, *Front End Develop,* Homer Watson, Kitchener ON
Maberry, Johnnie Mae, *Dir, Cur,* Tougaloo College, Tougaloo Art Collection, Tougaloo MS
Maberry, Sue, *Dir,* Otis College of Art & Design, Millard Sheets Library, Los Angeles CA
Mac Low, Mordecai-Mark, *Chair Dept Physical Sciences,* American Museum of Natural History, Rose Center for Earth & Space, New York NY
MacAdam, Barbara J, *Cur American Art,* Dartmouth College, Hood Museum of Art, Hanover NH
Macapia, Paul, *Mus Photography,* Seattle Art Museum, Dorothy Stimson Bullitt Library, Seattle WA
Macara, Peter, *Registrar,* Provincetown Art Association & Museum, Provincetown MA
Macaulay, Lorinda, *Educ Asst,* Lehigh Valley Heritage Center, Allentown PA
Macaulay, Sally, *Exec Dir,* Marietta-Cobb Museum of Art, Marietta GA
MacAulay, Suzanne, *Chair, Visual & Performing Arts,* University of Colorado-Colorado Springs, Visual & Performing Arts Dept (VAPA), Colorado Springs CO (S)
MacBain, Ken, *Jewelry & Metals Prof,* New Jersey City University, Art Dept, Jersey City NJ (S)
MacDonald, Cheryl, *Admin Mgr,* Acadia University, Faculty of Arts, Wolfville NS (S)
MacDonald, Connie, *VPres Programs Events & Comml Svcs,* Royal Ontario Museum, Toronto ON
Macdonald, Eileen, *Assoc Prof,* California State University, Chico, Department of Art & Art History, Chico CA (S)
MacDonald, Elizabeth H, *VPres & Treas,* American Color Print Society, Narberth PA
MacDonald, Katherine, *Dir,* Old Colony Historical Society, Museum, Taunton MA
MacDonald, Kevin, *Cur,* Newburyport Maritime Society, Inc, Custom House Maritime Museum, Newburyport MA
MacDonald, Lucy, *Cur Educ,* Mount Allison University, Owens Art Gallery, Sackville NB
MacDonald, Norm, *Curator,* Museum of Ossining Historical Society, Library, Ossining NY
MacDonald, Sara, *Pub Services Librn,* The University of the Arts, University Libraries, Philadelphia PA
MacDowell, Cyndra, *Prof, Photography,* University of Windsor, School of Creative Arts, Windsor ON (S)
Macechak, Jeffrey, *Educ Dir,* Burlington County Historical Society, Burlington NJ
MacElwee, John A, *Exec Dir,* Centrum Arts & Creative Education, Port Townsend WA
MacElwee, John, *Dir,* Hostos Center for the Arts & Culture, Bronx NY
MacGuffie, Larry, *VPres,* Western Art Association, Ellensburg WA
Machado, Miriam, *Educ Cur,* Florida International University, The Patricia & Phillip Frost Art Museum, Miami FL
Machead, Cynthia, *Superintendent,* Independence National Historical Park, Philadelphia PA
Machead, Cynthia, *Supt,* Independence National Historical Park, Library, Philadelphia PA
Machek, Frank, *Prof Emer,* Albion College, Bobbitt Visual Arts Center, Albion MI
Machell, Iain, *Chmn,* Ulster County Community College/SUNY Ulster, Dept of Art, Design, Music, Theatre, Communication & Fashion, Stone Ridge NY (S)
Machin, Jana, *Dir Mus Store,* San Francisco Museum of Modern Art, San Francisco CA
Machlin, Daniel, *Exec Dir,* Segue Foundation, Reading Room-Archive, New York NY
Machlis, Sally, *Prof & Dept Chair,* University of Idaho College of Art & Architecture, Dept of Art & Design, Moscow ID (S)
Machtan, James, *Asst Dir,* New Visions Gallery, Inc, Marshfield WI
Maciarello, Sarah, *Gift & Mem Coordr,* Salisbury University, Ward Museum of Wildfowl Art, Salisbury MD
Macias, Irene, *Lib Dir,* Santa Barbara Public Central Library, Faulkner Memorial Art Wing, Santa Barbara CA
Macias, Maria Elena, *Cur,* International Museum of Art & Science, McAllen TX
Macias, Nanette Yannuzzi, *Assoc Prof,* Oberlin College, Dept of Art, Oberlin OH (S)
Maciejunes, Nannette V, *Exec Dir,* Columbus Museum of Art, Columbus OH
MacInnes, Roddy, *Assoc Prof Photog,* University of Denver, School of Art & Art History, Denver CO (S)
MacInnis, Karen, *Cur,* Marblehead Museum & Historical Society, Marblehead MA
MacInnis, Karen, *Cur,* Marblehead Museum & Historical Society, Archives, Marblehead MA
MacInnis, Karen, *Cur,* Marblehead Museum & Historical Society, John Orne Johnson Frost Gallery, Marblehead MA
MacIvor, Mike, *Technician,* Promote Art Works Inc (PAWI), Laziza Electrique Dance Co, Brooklyn NY
Mack Weber, Carey, *Asst Dir,* Fairfield University, Art Museum, Fairfield CT
Mack, Angela D, *Exec Dir & Chief Cur,* Carolina Art Association, Gibbes Museum of Art, Charleston SC
Mack, Angela, *Dir,* Carolina Art Association, Library, Charleston SC
Mack, Angela, *Exec Dir & Chief Cur,* Gibbes Museum of Art, Charleston SC (S)
Mack, Anissa, *Asst Prof,* Queensborough Community College, Dept of Art & Photography, Bayside Hills NY (S)
Mack, Honour, *Instr,* Maine College of Art, Portland ME (S)
Mack, James, *Chmn,* City Colleges of Chicago, Wright College, Chicago IL (S)
Mack, Laurce, *Instr,* Chemeketa Community College, Dept of Humanities & Communications, Art Program, Salem OR (S)
Mack, Rita, *Office Mgr,* Nassau County Museum of Art, Roslyn Harbor NY
MacKay, Camilla, *Head Librn,* Bryn Mawr College, Rhys Carpenter Library for Art, Archaeology, Classics & Cities, Bryn Mawr PA
MacKay, Carrie, *Prog Coordr,* Visual Arts Nova Scotia, Halifax NS
Mackay, Chris, *Pres (2013),* Emerald Empire Art Association, Emerald Art Center, Springfield OR
MacKay, Keith, *Exec Dir,* National Society of the Colonial Dames of America in The Commonwealth of Virginia, Wilton House Museum, Richmond VA
Mackay-Collins, Dorothy, *Cur,* Robert Louis Stevenson Museum, Saint Helena CA
MacKay-Lyons, Brian, *Prof,* Dalhousie University, School of Architecture, Halifax NS (S)
Mackenzie, Colin, *Robert P Youngman Cur Asian Art,* Middlebury College, History of Art & Architecture Dept, Middlebury VT (S)
Mackey, David, *Pres,* Hopewell Museum, Hopewell NJ
Mackey, Judith, *Artist,* Flint Hills Gallery, Cottonwood Falls KS
Mackie, Elizabeth, *Assoc Prof,* The College of New Jersey, School of Arts & Sciences, Ewing NJ (S)
Mackie, Lisa, *Instr,* Woodstock School of Art, Inc, Woodstock NY (S)
Macko, Nancy, *Chmn Dept,* Scripps College, Millard Sheets Art Center-Williamson Gallery, Claremont CA (S)
Macks-Kahn, Martha, *Founder,* Goya Contemporary, Baltimore MD
MacLaren, Shelly, *Gallery Dir,* University of the South, University Art Gallery, Sewanee TN
Maclean, Alison, *Prog Dir, Publishing,* Humber College, School of Creative & Performing Arts, Toronto ON (S)
MacLean, George A., *Dean,* University of New Brunswick, Faculty of Arts, Fredericton NB (S)
MacLean, Rick, *Journalism,* Holland College, School of Visual Arts & Journalism, Charlottetown PE (S)
MacLellan, Iain, *Dir,* Saint Anselm College, Alva de Mars Megan Chapel Art Center, Manchester NH
MacLeod, Jane, *Pres & CEO,* Cheekwood-Tennessee Botanical Garden & Museum of Art, Nashville TN
MacLeod, Jane, *Pres & CEO,* Cheekwood-Tennessee Botanical Garden & Museum of Art, Museum of Art, Nashville TN
MacInnes-Adams, Kate, *Office Mgr,* Kings County Historical Society & Museum, Hampton NB
MacMillan, Sean, *Prof,* Slippery Rock University of Pennsylvania, Dept of Art, Slippery Rock PA (S)
MacNulty, Thomas, *Assoc Prof,* Adelphi University, Dept of Art & Art History, Garden City NY (S)
Macpherson, Kate, *Dir Mktg & Fundraising,* Homer Watson, Kitchener ON
MacPherson, Kathy, *Gallery Mgr & Outreach Coordr,* Otis College of Art & Design, Ben Maltz Gallery, Los Angeles CA
MacPherson, Susan, *Bd President,* Kennebec Valley Art Association, Harlow Gallery, Hallowell ME
MacQueen, Christopher, *Day Arts Dir,* North Fourth Art Center & Gallery, Albuquerque NM
Macrae, Laurie, *Librn,* Taos Public Library, Fine Art Collection, Taos NM
MacRae, Nancy, *CFO,* Confederation Centre Art Gallery and Museum, Charlottetown PE
Macro, Maggie, *VPres,* Redlands Art Association, Redlands Art Association Gallery & Art Center, Redlands CA
MacTaggart, Alan, *Chair,* Augusta State University, Dept of Art, Augusta GA (S)
Macy, Christine, *Prof & Dean, Faculty of Architecture & Planning,* Dalhousie University, School of Architecture, Halifax NS (S)
Madacs, David, *Secy,* Mystic Art Association, Inc, Mystic Museum of Art, Mystic CT
Madar, Heather, *Assoc Prof,* Humboldt State University, College of Arts & Humanities, Art Dept, Arcata CA (S)
Madden, Jack, *Facility Opers Dir,* Oklahoma City Museum of Art, Oklahoma City OK
Madden, Julie, *Dir Community Arts,* Cambridge Arts Council, CAC Gallery, Cambridge MA
Madden, Mary W, *Dir Mus,* Kansas State Historical Society, Kansas Museum of History, Topeka KS
Madden, Mimi, *Dir Poetry Festival,* Hill-Stead Museum, Farmington CT
Madden, Tom, *Chmn Crafts,* College for Creative Studies, Detroit MI (S)
Maddigan, Emily, *Instr,* Bakersfield College, Art Dept, Bakersfield CA (S)
Maddock, Pam, *Spokesperson,* American River College, Dept of Art/Art New Media, Sacramento CA (S)
Maddox, CB, *Museum Shop Mgr,* Danville Museum of Fine Arts & History, Danville VA
Maddox, Gene, *Instr,* College of the Sequoias, Art Dept, Visalia CA (S)

Maddox, Jerrold, *Prof Art (Gen Educ),* Pennsylvania State University, University Park, Penn State School of Visual Arts, University Park PA (S)
Mader, Daniel, *Prof,* Mount Saint Joseph University, Department of Art and Design, Cincinnati OH (S)
Madill, Shirley, *Exec Dir,* Kitchener-Waterloo Art Gallery, Kitchener ON
Madison, Kurt, *Adjunct Asst Prof,* Spokane Falls Community College, Fine Arts Dept, Spokane WA (S)
Madison, Nina, *Dir Special Events,* Parrish Art Museum, Water Mill NY
Madkour, Christopher, *Dir,* Southern Vermont Art Center, Manchester VT
Madkour, Christopher, *Dir,* Huntsville Museum of Art, Reference Library, Huntsville AL
Madson, Barbara, *Reference,* Mason City Public Library, Mason City IA
Madura, Nancy, *Instr,* Casper College, Dept of Visual Arts, Casper WY (S)
Madyun, Nashid, *Dir,* Hampton University, University Museum, Hampton VA
Madzy, Leonard, *Chmn Dept,* Berkshire Community College, Dept of Fine Arts, Pittsfield MA (S)
Maeckelbergh, Kenneth, *Chmn,* Century College, Humanities Dept, White Bear Lake MN (S)
Maeglin, William, *Chmn,* Bucks County Historical Society, Mercer Museum, Doylestown PA
Maegowan, Ciaran, *Instr,* San Jose City College, School of Fine Arts, San Jose CA (S)
Maeson Yang, Jessica, *Educ Dir,* Angels Gate Cultural Center, Gallery A & Gallery G, San Pedro CA
Magee, Carol, *Asst Prof,* University of North Carolina at Chapel Hill, Art Dept, Chapel Hill NC (S)
Maggio, John, *Prof,* University of North Carolina at Greensboro, School of Art, Greensboro NC (S)
Maggio, Ronald, *Chmn,* Springfield College, William Blizard Gallery, Springfield MA
Maggio, Ronald, *Chmn,* Springfield College, Dept of Visual & Performing Arts, Springfield MA (S)
Magill, John, *Historian & Cur,* The Historic New Orleans Collection, Williams Research Center, New Orleans LA
Maginnis, Ken, *Assoc Prof Design,* Coker College, Art Dept, Hartsville SC (S)
Magistro, Charles, *Prof,* William Paterson University, Dept Arts, Wayne NJ (S)
Magleby, Mark, *Dir,* Brigham Young University, Museum of Art, Provo UT
Magliocco, Stephen, *Design Consultant,* The Schoolhouse Gallery, Provincetown MA
Magnan, Oscar, *Dir,* Saint Peter's College, Art Gallery, Jersey City NJ
Magnani, Patricia, *Registrar,* Purchase College, Neuberger Museum of Art, Purchase NY
Magner, Nancy, *Prof Art,* Bakersfield College, Art Dept, Bakersfield CA (S)
Magnusson, Mishell, *Pres,* Madison County Historical Society, Cottage Lawn, Oneida NY
Magrath, Lauren, *Dir Admissions,* Bennington College, Visual Arts Division, Bennington VT (S)
Magri, Ken, *Instr,* American River College, Dept of Art/Art New Media, Sacramento CA (S)
Magrin, Roger, *Sr Dir Facilities & Grounds,* Genesee Country Village & Museum, John L Wehle Art Gallery, Mumford NY
Magruder, Janet, *Bus Mgr,* University of Maryland, Baltimore County, Center for Art Design and Visual Culture, Baltimore MD
Mague, Bill, *Exec Dir,* Soap Factory, Minneapolis MN
Maguire, Catherine, *Asst Dir,* National Museum of Racing, Reference Library, Saratoga Springs NY
Maguire, George, *Pres,* South Arkansas Arts Center, El Dorado AR
Maguire, Michelle, *Cur,* Ohio State University, Visual Resources Library, Columbus OH
Maguire, Nancy, *Assoc Dir Exhibitions,* Rutgers University, Stedman Art Gallery, Camden NJ
Maguire, William, *Prof,* Florida International University, School of Art & Art History, Miami FL (S)
Mahaffey, Richard, *Art Dept Chmn,* Tacoma Community College, Art Dept, Tacoma WA (S)
Mahaney, Nancy, *Cur,* National Park Service, Hubbell Trading Post National Historic Site, Ganado AZ
Maher, Kathleen, *Cur,* The Barnum Museum, Bridgeport CT
Maher, Tim, *Pres,* Art Centre of New Jersey, Livingston NJ (S)
Mahin, Michael, *Prog & Mktg Coordr,* Arlington Center for the Arts, Arlington MA
Mahitas, Frank, *Dept Head,* Fort Valley State College, H A Hunt Memorial Library, Fort Valley GA
Mahnke, Helen, *Mus Educ,* Pennsylvania Historical & Museum Commission, Brandywine Battlefield Park, Chadds Ford PA
Mahon, Patrick, *Grad Chair,* University of Western Ontario, Dept of Visual Arts, London ON (S)
Mahoney, James, *Affiliate Assoc Prof,* University of Maryland, Baltimore County, Intermedia & Digital Arts (IMDA), Dept of Visual Arts, Baltimore MD (S)
Mahoney, John, *Board VPres,* Pueblo Museum, Desert Hot Springs CA
Mahoney, Julie, *Prof,* Western Illinois University, Department of Art, Macomb IL (S)
Mahoney, Martin, *Dir Colls & Registration,* Norman Rockwell Museum, Stockbridge MA
Mahoney, Mike, *Exec Dir Corp Spec Projects & Dir Opers,* Art Gallery of Ontario, Toronto ON
Mahoparn, Irin, *Asst Cur of Educ,* Laguna Art Museum, Laguna Beach CA
Mahowald, Kari, *Office Coordr,* Augustana University, Center for Western Studies, Sioux Falls SD
Mai, Josie, *Asst Prof,* Pittsburg State University, Art Dept, Pittsburg KS (S)
Mai, Josie, *Prof,* Missouri Southern State University, Dept of Art, Joplin MO (S)
Maidenberg, Sharon, *Exec Dir,* Headlands Center for the Arts, Sausalito CA
Maiella, Melissa, *Mktg Dir,* Hoyt Center for the Arts, Arts & Education of the Hoyt, New Castle PA
Maier, Joan, *Admin Dir,* Moose Jaw Art Museum, Inc, Art & History Museum, Moose Jaw SK
Maietta, Andrew, *Video Production,* Art Institute of Pittsburgh, Pittsburgh PA (S)
Mainardi, Patricia, *Prof Emerita,* City University of New York, PhD Program in Art History, New York NY (S)
Maines, Clark, *Prof,* Wesleyan University, Dept of Art & Art History, Middletown CT (S)
Mainland, Timothy, *Dean,* Concord College, Fine Art Division, Athens WV (S)
Majewski, David, *Chmn,* Richard Bland College, Art Dept, Petersburg VA (S)
Majoli, Monica, *Assoc Prof Painting,* University of California, Irvine, Studio Art Dept, Irvine CA (S)
Major, James, *Dean,* Illinois State University, College of Fine Arts, Normal IL (S)
Majumdar, Santanu, *Asst Prod,* Georgia Southern University, Betty Foy Sanders Dept of Art, Statesboro GA (S)
Mak, Jennifer, *Daytime Access Servs Mgr,* Fashion Institute of Technology - SUNY, Gladys Marcus Library, New York NY
Mak, Kam, *Chmn Fashion Illustrations,* Fashion Institute of Technology, School of Art & Design, New York NY (S)
Mak-Shahbazi, Sonia, *Mgr Devel,* Craft and Folk Art Museum (CAFAM), Los Angeles CA
Makholm, Kristin, *Exec Dir,* Minnesota Museum of American Art, Saint Paul MN
Maklansky, Steven, *Exec Dir,* Boca Raton Museum of Art, Boca Raton FL
Makov, Susan, *Prof,* Weber State University, Dept of Visual Arts, Ogden UT (S)
Makrandi, Nandini, *Chief Cur,* Hunter Museum of American Art, Chattanooga TN
Makrandi, Nandini, *Chief Cur,* Hunter Museum of American Art, Reference Library, Chattanooga TN
Makrandi, Nandini, *Clinical Prof,* University of Tennessee at Chattanooga, Dept of Art, Chattanooga TN (S)
Maksymiuk, Catherine, *Mgr Media & Mktg,* The Winnipeg Art Gallery, Winnipeg MB
Maksymowicz, Virginia A, *Dept Chair,* Franklin & Marshall College, Art & Art History Dept, Lancaster PA (S)
Makuch, Nestor, *1st VP,* Ukrainian Canadian Archives & Museum of Alberta, Edmonton AB
Malak, Gregory, *Cur,* Will Rogers Memorial Museum & Birthplace Ranch, Media Center Library, Claremore OK
Malak, Gregory, *Cur,* Will Rogers Memorial Museum & Birthplace Ranch, Claremore OK
Malak, Michael, *VPres Opers & Bus Strategy,* Chicago Architecture Foundation, Chicago IL
Malbaurn, Scott, *Dir,* Southern Oregon University, Schneider Museum of Art, Ashland OR
Malbin, Susan, *Dir Library & Archives,* American Jewish Historical Society, The Center for Jewish History, New York NY
Malcolm, Heather, *Dir Devel,* University of Georgia, Georgia Museum of Art, Athens GA
Malcolm, Pamela, *Historic Site Mgr,* New York State Office of Parks, Recreation & Historic Preservation, Staatsburgh State Historic Site, Staatsburg NY
Malec, Jacek, *Exec Dir,* Where Edmonton Community Artists Network Society, Harcourt House Arts Centre, Edmonton AB
Malenke, Patti, *Dir,* Johnson-Humrickhouse Museum, Coshocton OH
Malgeri, Dina G, *Dir & Librn,* Malden Public Library, Art Dept & Gallery, Malden MA
Malik Demosthenes, Debra, *Registrar & Gallery Mgr,* Robischon Gallery, Denver CO
Malinowski, Monica, *Sr Librn,* Newark Public Library, Reference, Newark NJ
Malkovich, Mark P, *Pres,* Royal Arts Foundation, Belcourt Castle, Newport RI
Mallard, Michael, *Interim Exhibs Mgr,* Albany Museum of Art, Albany GA
Malle, Michael, *Graphic Design,* Art Institute of Pittsburgh, Pittsburgh PA (S)
Mallen, Mike, *Acting CEO,* Museum of Vancouver, Vancouver BC
Mallen, Mike, *Acting CEO,* Museum of Vancouver, Museum of Vancouver Library, Vancouver BC
Mallette, Carol S, *Admin Asst,* City of Raleigh Arts Commission, Miriam Preston Block Gallery, Raleigh NC
Mallette, Wallace, *Coordr,* Mississippi Delta Community College, Dept of Fine Arts, Moorhead MS (S)
Malley, Diane, *Dir,* Clarion University, Hazel Sandford Gallery, Clarion PA
Malliarakis, Rallou, *Chmn,* First Street Gallery, New York NY
Mallison, Theodore, *Curator,* The Summit County Historical Society of Akron, OH, Akron OH
Mallon, Edward, *Pres,* Portsmouth Historical Society, John Paul Jones House & Discover Portsmouth, Portsmouth NH
Mallory, Cathryn, *Prof,* University of Montana, School of Art, Missoula MT (S)
Mallory, Deana, *Dir Pub & Educ Progs, Vol,* Bennington Museum, Bennington VT
Mallory, Michael, *Chmn,* Brooklyn College, Art Dept, Brooklyn NY (S)
Malloy, Greg, *Asst Dir,* Cumberland Theatre, Lobby for the Arts Gallery, Cumberland MD
Malloy, Jeanne, *Educ Specialist,* Ormond Memorial Art Museum and Gardens, Ormond Beach FL
Malloy, Joe, *Bibliographic Instruction & Branch Librn,* Sweet Briar College, Mary Helen Cochran Library, Sweet Briar VA
Malloy, Kip, *Exec Asst,* James A Michener Art Museum, Doylestown PA
Malloy, Mark, *Prof,* Salem State University, Art & Design Department, Salem MA (S)
Malloy, Nancy, *Dir Artist Mem,* National Academy Museum & School, Archives, New York NY
Malloy, Vanja, *Cur American Art,* Amherst College, Mead Art Museum, Amherst MA
Malone, Carolyn, *Chair,* University of Southern California, College of Letters, Arts & Sciences, Los Angeles CA (S)

Malone, Jewel, *COO,* National YoungArts Foundation, Miami FL
Malone, Karen, *Cur Educ,* Evansville Museum of Arts, History & Science, Evansville IN
Malone, Meredith, *Assoc Cur,* Washington University, Mildred Lane Kemper Art Museum, Saint Louis MO
Malone, Robert R, *Head Printmaking,* Southern Illinois University at Edwardsville, Dept of Art & Design, Edwardsville IL (S)
Malone, Roxanne, *Asst Prof,* College of Santa Fe, Art Dept, Santa Fe NM (S)
Maloney, Agnes, *Bus Mgr,* Cahoon Museum of American Art, Cotuit MA
Maloney, Judy, *Dir,* Juniata College Museum of Art, Huntingdon PA
Maloney, Kara, *Advancement Dir,* Lanesboro Arts Center, Lanesboro MN
Maloney, Michael, *Librn/Archivist,* Schenectady County Historical Society, Grems-Dolittle Library, Schenectady NY
Maloney, Patricia, *Dir,* Southern Exposure, San Francisco CA
Maloney, Stephanie, *Prof,* University of Louisville, Allen R Hite Art Institute, Louisville KY (S)
Maloof, George, *Cur,* City of El Paso, El Paso Museum of Archaeology, El Paso TX
Malshibini, Deborah, *Dir,* VSA Arts of New Mexico, Enabled Arts Center, Albuquerque NM (S)
Malta, John, *Asst Prof,* University of Central Missouri, Dept of Art & Design, Warrensburg MO (S)
Maltais, Marie, *Dir,* University of New Brunswick, Art Centre, Fredericton NB
Maltese, Vinnie, *Dean,* Monroe County Community College, Fine Arts Council, Monroe MI
Malugani, Ty, *Educ,* Sloss Furnaces National Historic Landmark, Birmingham AL
Malus, Mary June, *Coordr,* Imperial Calcasieu Museum, Gibson-Barham Gallery, Lake Charles LA
Malus, Mary June, *Coordr,* Imperial Calcasieu Museum, Gibson Library, Lake Charles LA
Malvern, Fred, *Coordr Interior Design,* Iowa State University, Dept of Art & Design, Ames IA (S)
Malyk, Mike, *Human Resources Mgr,* The Winnipeg Art Gallery, Winnipeg MB
Mambo, Marjorie, *Assoc Prof,* Indiana University of Pennsylvania, College of Fine Arts, Indiana PA (S)
Mana, Moishe, *Chmn,* Mana Contemporary, Jersey City NJ
Manaffey, Ellen, *Instr,* Lake Tahoe Community College, Art Dept, South Lake Tahoe CA (S)
Manchanda, Catharina, *Cur Modern & Contemporary Art,* Seattle Art Museum, Seattle WA
Manchester, Carri, *Head Educ,* Olana State Historic Site, Hudson NY
Mancinelli, Diane, *Dance,* Henry Ford Community College, McKenzie Fine Art Ctr, Dearborn MI (S)
Mancini, Nick, *Dir Visitor Svcs,* New-York Historical Society, Museum, New York NY
Mancuso, William, *Asst Prof Art,* Ohio Northern University, Dept of Art & Design, Ada OH (S)
Manderen, Elizabeth, *Exec Dir,* Firelands Association for the Visual Arts, Oberlin OH
Mandeville, Lynn, *Dir of Develop,* Museum of Art, Fort Lauderdale, Library, Fort Lauderdale FL
Mandeville-Gamble, Steven, *Univ Librn,* UCR ARTSblock, Tomas Rivera Library, Riverside CA
Maneen, Thomas, *Instr,* Mohawk Valley Community College, Utica NY (S)
Manega, Antonio, *Designer,* Rice University, Rice Gallery, Houston TX
Manfredi, John, *Chmn (V),* Creative Arts Center, Pontiac MI
Mangan, Kelly, *Fin Asst / DBA,* Historical Society of Martin County, Elliott Museum, Stuart FL
Mangat, Lisa, *Dir California State Parks,* California State Parks, State Indian Museum, Sacramento CA
Mangubi, Marina, *Assoc Prof,* The College of Wooster, Dept of Art and Art History, Wooster OH (S)
Maniscalco, Nelson, *Prof,* Cedar Crest College, Art Dept, Allentown PA (S)
Manister, Craig, *Adj Asst Prof,* College of Staten Island, Performing & Creative Arts Dept, Staten Island NY (S)
Mankin, Diane, *Assoc Prof Fine Arts,* University of Cincinnati, School of Art, Cincinnati OH (S)
Manley, Christopher, *Admin Asst,* Longview Museum of Fine Art, Longview TX
Manley, Jason, *Asst Prof,* Weber State University, Dept of Visual Arts, Ogden UT (S)
Manley, Juniper, *Develop Officer,* University of New Mexico, The Harwood Museum of Art, Taos NM
Manley, Mary, *Assoc Dir,* Henry Sheldon Museum of Vermont History and Research Center, Middlebury VT
Manley, Roger, *Dir,* North Carolina State University, Gregg Museum of Art & Design, Raleigh NC
Manly, Nancy, *Board Dirs,* Lake County Civic Center Association, Inc, Heritage Museum & Gallery, Leadville CO
Mann, C. Griffith, *Cur in Charge, Medieval Art & The Cloisters,* The Metropolitan Museum of Art, New York NY
Mann, Jack, *Prof,* Wittenberg University, Art Dept, Springfield OH (S)
Mann, Janice, *Prof,* Bucknell University, Dept of Art, Lewisburg PA (S)
Mann, Katrina, *Admin,* Fremont Center for the Arts, Canon City CO
Mannarino, Amy, *Dir Communs & Mktg,* National Museum of Women in the Arts, Washington DC
Mannell, Steven, *Prof & Dir Col of Sustainability,* Dalhousie University, School of Architecture, Halifax NS (S)
Manning, Albina, *Dir,* School of the Art Institute of Chicago, Video Data Bank, Chicago IL
Manning, Cynthia, *Develop,* Discovery Museum, Bridgeport CT
Manning, David, *Museum History Specialist,* Fort George G Meade Museum, Fort Meade MD
Manning, Jackie, *Cur Exhibs,* Alaska State Museum, Juneau AK
Manning, Maureen, *Librn,* University Club Library, New York NY
Manning, Patrick, *Assoc Chair & Assoc Prof,* University of New Mexico, Department of Fine Arts & Art History, Albuquerque NM (S)
Mannion, John, *Digital Lab Mgr,* Light Work, Robert B Menschel Photography Gallery, Syracuse NY
Mannix, Christine, *Instruction Librn,* Columbus College of Art & Design, Packard Library, Columbus OH
Mannix, Christine, *Pub Svcs Librn,* Columbus College of Art & Design, Packard Library, Columbus OH
Manno, Sierra, *Museum Front Desk Associate + Volunteer Coordinator,* Miami-Dade College, MDC Museum of Art & Design, Miami FL
Manns, Suzanne, *Chmn Studio Arts,* University of Saint Thomas, Fine and Performing Arts Dept, Houston TX (S)
Manoguerra, Paul, *Dir & Cur,* Gonzaga University, Jundt Art Museum, Spokane WA
Manoogian, Daron, *Dir Communs,* Harvard University, Harvard Art Museums, Cambridge MA
Manring, Lynne, *Dir Youth Progs,* Pocumtuck Valley Memorial Association, Memorial Hall Museum, Deerfield MA
Mansell, Brandon, *Facilities Mgr,* San Angelo Museum of Fine Arts, San Angelo TX
Mansfield, Gregory, *Cur,* Ancient Spanish Monastery, North Miami Beach FL
Mansfield, Marcia, *Treas,* Lincoln County Historical Association, Inc, Maine Art Gallery, Wiscasset ME
Mansfield, Phil, *Digital Lab Mgr,* Center for Photography at Woodstock Inc, Woodstock NY
Mansfield, Steve, *Div & Dept Chair,* Salt Lake Community College, Graphic Design Dept, Salt Lake City UT (S)
Mansker, Larry, *Co-owner,* Eureka Fine Art Gallery, Eureka Springs AR
Manthorne, Katherine, *Prof,* City University of New York, PhD Program in Art History, New York NY (S)
Manuel, Chuck, *Instr,* Graceland University, Fine Arts Div, Lamoni IA (S)
Manuel, Steve, *Exec Dir,* New London County Historical Society, Shaw Mansion, New London CT
Manuele, Lisa, *Instr,* Springfield College in Illinois, Dept of Art, Springfield IL (S)
Manwaring, Beth, *Mktg Dir,* The Rockwell Museum, Corning NY
Maphet, Tony, *Dir,* Clark County Historical Society, Pioneer - Krier Museum, Ashland KS
Maple, Amanda, *Head Arts & Humanities Library,* The Pennsylvania State University, Arts & Humanities Library, University Park PA
Mar, Louis, *Art Dir,* Coppini Academy of Fine Arts, Library, San Antonio TX
Maranci, Christina, *Prof & Dept Chair,* Tufts University, Dept of Art & Art History, Medford MA (S)
Maranda, Michael, *Asst Cur,* York University, Art Gallery of York University, Toronto ON
Marantz, Kenneth, *Prof Emeritus,* Ohio State University, Dept of Art Education, Columbus OH (S)
Marblo, Christopher, *Pres,* The Arts Center of the Capital Region, Troy NY
Marcanage, Janet, *Prof Art,* University of Puget Sound, Dept of Art & Art History, Tacoma WA (S)
Marcantel, Gregory, *Pres Bd Trustees,* Zigler Art Museum, Jennings LA
Marcet, David, *Instr,* Illinois Benedictine University, Department of Fine Arts, Lisle IL (S)
Marchant, Barbara, *Interim Chair, Theater Dept, Head of Acting,* Rutgers, The State University of New Jersey, Mason Gross School of the Arts, New Brunswick NJ (S)
Marche, Theresa, *Emer Prof,* University of Wisconsin, Madison, Dept of Art, Madison WI (S)
Marchessault, Lesley, *Cur,* LeMoyne Art Foundation, Center for the Visual Arts, Tallahassee FL
Marchi, Riccardo, *Assoc Prof,* University of South Florida, School of Art & Art History, Tampa FL (S)
Marchione, Ken, *Prof,* Munson-Williams-Proctor Arts Institute, Pratt MWP College of Art, Utica NY (S)
Marciari, John, *Engelhard Cur & Dept Head,* The Morgan Library & Museum, Museum, New York NY
Marciari-Alexander, Julia, *Exec Dir,* Walters Art Museum, Baltimore MD
Marcincowski, David, *Dir,* Pratt Institute, Pratt Manhattan, New York NY (S)
Marciniak, Wendy, *Exec Dir,* Chesterton Art Center, Chesterton IN
Marcinowski, Gary, *Assoc Prof,* University of Dayton, Visual Arts Dept, Dayton OH (S)
Marcotte, Christian, *Dir,* Musee Regional de lu Cote-Nord, Sept-Iles QC
Marcou, George T, *Prof,* Catholic University of America, School of Architecture & Planning, Washington DC (S)
Marcoux, Johanie, *Dir Mktg, Communs & Pub Affairs,* Vancouver Art Gallery, Vancouver BC
Marcovy, Aaron, *Exec Dir,* Intermuseum Conservation Association, Cleveland OH
Marcum-Estes, Leah, *Dir,* Oak Ridge Art Center, Oak Ridge TN
Marcum-Estes, Leah, *Dir,* Oak Ridge Art Center, Library, Oak Ridge TN
Marcus, Elizabeth A., *Dir,* Brockton Public Library, Joseph A Driscoll Art Gallery, Brockton MA
Marcus, Louis, *Prof,* University of South Florida, School of Art & Art History, Tampa FL (S)
Marcy, Christie, *Mktg & Communs Dir,* Salt Lake Art Center, Utah Museum of Contemporary Art, Salt Lake City UT
Marcy, Jane, *Adj Prof,* Saint Thomas Aquinas College, Art Dept, Sparkill NY (S)
Mardikos, JoAnn, *Acting Pres & CEO,* Snug Harbor Cultural Center, Newhouse Center for Contemporary Art, Staten Island NY
Mardilovich, Galina, *Cur Russian & European Art,* Amherst College, Mead Art Museum, Amherst MA

Margalit, Nathan, *Vis Assoc Prof,* Trinity College, Dept of Studio Arts, Hartford CT (S)
Margeson, Hank, *Asst Prof,* North Georgia College & State University, Fine Arts Dept, Dahlonega GA (S)
Margol, Deborah J, *Deputy Dir,* South Florida Cultural Consortium, Miami Dade County Dept of Cultural Affairs, Miami FL
Marichal, Flavia, *Dir,* University of Puerto Rico, Museum of Anthropology, History & Art, Rio Piedras PR
Marien, Mary, *Prof,* Syracuse University, Dept of Fine Arts (Art History), Syracuse NY (S)
Marinangeli, Dan, *Treas,* Peter & Catharine Whyte Foundation, Whyte Museum of the Canadian Rockies, Banff AB
Marini, Gina, *Adminr Mgr,* Heritage Museum Association, Inc, The Heritage Museum of Northwest Florida, Valparaiso FL
Mariniello, Silvestra, *Prof & Dept Dir,* Universite de Montreal, Dept of Art History & Film Studies, Montreal QC (S)
Marinsky, Jane, *Instr,* Daemen College, Art Dept, Amherst NY (S)
Marion, Joanne, *Cur Art,* Esplanade Arts & Heritage Centre, Medicine Hat AB
Marion, Nancy, *Treas,* Octagon Center for the Arts, Ames IA
Mariona, Myrna, *Mgr Human Resources,* Japanese American National Museum, Los Angeles CA
Marioni, Tom, *Dir,* Museum of Conceptual Art, Society of Independent Artists (SIA), San Francisco CA
Marioni, Tom, *Dir,* Museum of Conceptual Art, Library, San Francisco CA
Marios, Daniel, *Professor of Media Arts,* Los Angeles City College, School of Visual & Media Arts, Los Angeles CA (S)
Maris-Wolf, Edward, *Dir,* Colonial Williamsburg Foundation, John D Rockefeller, Jr Library, Williamsburg VA
Mariscal, Joe, *Instr,* San Joaquin Delta College, Arts & Communication, Stockton CA (S)
Mark, Monette, *Lectr,* Washburn University of Topeka, Dept of Art, Topeka KS (S)
Mark, Peter, *Prof,* Wesleyan University, Dept of Art & Art History, Middletown CT (S)
Markert, Kate, *Exec Dir & CEO,* Hillwood Museum & Gardens Foundation, Hillwood Estate Museum & Gardens, Washington DC
Markey, Mike, *Instr Arts Mgmt,* Creighton University, Fine & Performing Arts Dept, Omaha NE (S)
Markin, Linda, *Sr VPres,* Discovery Museum, Bridgeport CT
Markle, Gary, *Asst Prof & Chair Crafts Div,* Nova Scotia College of Art & Design, Halifax NS (S)
Markle, Leslie, *Cur Pub Art,* Washington University, Mildred Lane Kemper Art Museum, Saint Louis MO
Markov, Tavon, *Facility Opers & Event Mgr,* Erie Art Museum, Erie PA
Markowitz, Joan, *Sr Cur,* Boulder Museum of Contemporary Art, Boulder CO
Markowitz, John, *Program Dir,* University of West Florida, Dept of Art, Pensacola FL (S)
Markowski, Eugene D, *Lectr,* Trinity College, Fine Arts Program, Washington DC (S)
Marks, Andrea, *Asst Prof,* Oregon State University, Dept of Art, Corvallis OR (S)
Marks, Claire, *Instr,* Cuyahoga Valley Art Center, Cuyahoga Falls OH (S)
Marks, Pamela, *Assoc Prof,* Connecticut College, Dept of Art, New London CT (S)
Marks, Steven, *Treas,* Studio Gallery, Washington DC
Markwalter, Mary, *Dir,* Mason City Public Library, Mason City IA
Markwith, Jillian, *Dir Mktg & Special Events,* Historical Society of Palm Beach County, The Richard and Pat Johnson Palm Beach County History Museum, West Palm Beach FL
Marlais, Michael, *Prof,* Colby College, Art Dept, Waterville ME (S)
Marlatt, Megan, *Studio Faculty,* University of Virginia, McIntire Dept of Art, Charlottesville VA (S)
Marler, Vickie, *CFO,* Turtle Bay Exploration Park, Redding CA
Marling de Cuellar, Michael, *Asst Prof,* North Georgia College & State University, Fine Arts Dept, Dahlonega GA (S)
Marling, Karal Ann, *Prof,* University of Minnesota, Minneapolis, Art History, Minneapolis MN (S)
Marlowe, Claudia, *Catalog Asst,* San Francisco Art Institute, Anne Bremer Memorial Library, San Francisco CA
Marnel, Alexis, *Co Exec Dir,* Morris-Jumel Mansion, Inc, New York NY
Marotta, Joseph, *Prof,* University of Utah, Dept of Art & Art History, Salt Lake City UT (S)
Maroulis, Nora, *Dir Strategic Initiatives,* Worcester Art Museum, Worcester MA
Marquardt-Cherry, Janet, *Prof,* Eastern Illinois University, Art Dept, Charleston IL (S)
Marquet, Cynthia, *Librn,* Historical Society of the Cocalico Valley, Ephrata PA
Marquez, Jose, *Coll Mgr,* Foosaner Art Museum, Melbourne FL
Marquez, Lorrie, *Facilities & Beverage Mgr,* Sangre de Cristo Arts & Conference Center, Pueblo CO
Marquez, Phillip, *Interim Gallery Dir,* Santa Ana College, Art Gallery, Santa Ana CA
Marqusec, Debra, *Educ Specialist,* Sioux City Art Center, Sioux City IA
Marqusee, Debra, *Interim Studio Prog Coordr,* Sioux City Art Center, Sioux City IA (S)
Marran, Elizabeth, *Assoc Prof,* University of Massachusetts - Boston, Art Dept, Boston MA (S)
Marriott, Bill, *Assoc Prof Drawing & Painting,* University of Georgia, Franklin College of Arts & Sciences, Lamar Dodd School of Art, Athens GA (S)
Marsalis, Nelson, *Asst Prof,* Xavier University of Louisiana, Dept of Fine Arts, New Orleans LA (S)
Marschalek, Doug, *Emer Prof,* University of Wisconsin, Madison, Dept of Art, Madison WI (S)
Marsden, Susan, *Cur,* Museum of Northern British Columbia, Ruth Harvey Art Gallery, Prince Rupert BC
Marsden, Susan, *Cur,* Museum of Northern British Columbia, Library, Prince Rupert BC
Marsden-Atlass, Lynn, *Dir & Univ Cur,* University of Pennsylvania, Arthur Ross Gallery, Philadelphia PA
Marsden-Smith, Carolyn, *Assoc Dir Exhibs,* The Getty Center, The J Paul Getty Museum, Los Angeles CA
Marsee, Todd, *Instr,* Siena Heights University, Studio Angelico-Art Dept, Adrian MI (S)
Marsh, Charles, *Studio Art,* Florida School of the Arts, Visual Arts, Palatka FL (S)
Marsh, Cindy, *Chair,* Austin Peay State University, Dept of Art, Clarksville TN (S)
Marsh, Jeanne, *Comptroller,* Greenville County Museum of Art, Greenville SC
Marsh, Jim, *Pres,* Art Gallery of Windsor, Windsor ON
Marsh, Lisa, *Dir Educ & Visitor Svcs,* Long Beach Museum of Art Foundation, Long Beach Museum of Art, Long Beach CA
Marsh, Natalie, *Director,* Kenyon College, Gund Gallery, Gambier OH
Marsh, Robert, *Prof,* Averett College, Art Dept, Danville VA (S)
Marshall Furness, Amy, *Rosamond Ivey Spec Colls Archivist & Head Library & Archives,* Art Gallery of Ontario, Edward P Taylor Research Library & Archives, Toronto ON
Marshall, Heidi, *Head Archives & Colls,* Columbia College Chicago, Library, Chicago IL
Marshall, Howard, *Prof Emeritus,* University of Missouri - Columbia, Art History & Archaeology Dept, Columbia MO (S)
Marshall, Janet, *Admin Asst, BB,* Museum of Fine Arts Houston, Bayou Bend Collection & Gardens, Houston TX
Marshall, John Dudley, *Projectionist & Film Asst,* Oklahoma City Museum of Art, Oklahoma City OK
Marshall, John, *Assoc Prof & Dir MDes Integrative Design,* University of Michigan, Ann Arbor, Penny W Stamps School of Art & Design, Ann Arbor MI (S)
Marshall, Keny, *Dir Exhibs,* The Andy Warhol Museum, Pittsburgh PA
Marshall, Linda, *Exec Dir,* Nichols House Museum, Inc, Boston MA
Marshall, Michael, *Asst Prof Photog,* University of Georgia, Franklin College of Arts & Sciences, Lamar Dodd School of Art, Athens GA (S)
Marshall, Mike, *Exec Dir,* East Hawaii Cultural Center, Hawaii Museum of Contemporary Art, Hilo HI
Marshall, Nancy R, *Assoc Prof,* University of Wisconsin, Madison, Dept of Art History, Madison WI (S)
Marshall, Sarah S, *Dir Communications,* Katonah Museum of Art, Katonah NY
Marshall, Tom, *Asst,* Noyes Art Gallery, Lincoln NE
Marshall, William J, *Dir Spec Coll & Archives,* The University of Kentucky Art Museum, Photographic Archives, Lexington KY
Marsters, Rogers, *Cur Marine History,* Nova Scotia Museum, Maritime Museum of the Atlantic, Halifax NS
Marston-Reid, Linda, *Exec Dir,* Dutchess County Arts Council, Poughkeepsie NY
Martel, Ralph, *Prof,* College of Staten Island, Performing & Creative Arts Dept, Staten Island NY (S)
Martel, Richard, *Dir,* Les Editions Intervention, Inter-Le Lieu, Documentation Center, Quebec QC
Martell, Danielle, *Mem Asst,* Museum of Ventura County, Ventura CA
Marten, Jess, *Cur,* University of Rochester, Memorial Art Gallery, Rochester NY
Marten, Robert, *Interim Chmn,* Wayne State University, Dept of Art & Art History, Detroit MI (S)
Martens-Haworth, Megan, *Asst Prof,* Spokane Falls Community College, Fine Arts Dept, Spokane WA (S)
Martensen, Kelda, *Drawing, Painting, Design & Printmaking,* North Seattle College, North Seattle College Dept of Art, Seattle WA (S)
Martin, Allan, *Restoration Mgr,* Pennsylvania Historical & Museum Commission, Railroad Museum of Pennsylvania, Strasburg PA
Martin, Amanda, *Deputy Dir Admin & Communs,* Fort Wayne Museum of Art, Inc, Fort Wayne IN
Martin, Amy, *Dir Fin,* Historical Society of Martin County, Elliott Museum, Stuart FL
Martin, Andrew, *Assoc Dir & Assoc Prof,* Texas Tech University, Dept of Art, Lubbock TX (S)
Martin, Annie, *Chair Art Dept,* University of Lethbridge, Faculty of Fine Arts, Lethbridge AB (S)
Martin, Anya, *Vis Artist,* University of New Orleans-Lake Front, Dept of Fine Arts, New Orleans LA (S)
Martin, Art, *Sr Cur & Dir Colls & Exhib,* Muskegon Museum of Art Foundation, Muskegon Museum of Art, Muskegon MI
Martin, Bobby, *Instr,* Northeastern State University, College of Arts & Letters, Tahlequah OK (S)
Martin, Brigitte, *Pres,* Society of North American Goldsmiths, Eugene OR
Martin, Caitlin, *Media & Communs Mgr,* Association for Public Art, Philadelphia PA
Martin, Craig, *Dir Gallery,* Purdue University Galleries, West Lafayette IN
Martin, Dan, *Dean & Prof,* Carnegie Mellon University, College of Fine Arts, Pittsburgh PA (S)
Martin, Darlene Fossum, *Educ Specialist-Folk Art,* Vesterheim Norwegian-American Museum, Decorah IA
Martin, David, *VPres Academic Affairs,* Milwaukee Institute of Art & Design, Milwaukee WI (S)
Martin, Don, *Chmn,* Flagler College, Visual Arts Dept, Saint Augustine FL (S)
Martin, Erin L, *CEO,* Historical Society of Rockland County, New City NY

Martin, Frank, *Instr,* South Carolina State University, Dept of Visual & Performing Arts, Orangeburg SC (S)

Martin, Geoffrey, *Arts Adminr,* Columbus Cultural Arts Center, Columbus OH

Martin, George, *Pres,* North Shore Arts Association, Inc, Gloucester MA

Martin, George-McKinley, *Chief Art Div,* Public Library of the District of Columbia, Art Division, Washington DC

Martin, Hal, *Pres,* Coppini Academy of Fine Arts, Library, San Antonio TX

Martin, J Landis, *Chmn,* Denver Art Museum, Denver CO

Martin, Jack, *Exec Dir,* Providence Public Library, Art & Music Services, Providence RI

Martin, Jane, *Assoc Prof,* University of Saint Francis, School of Creative Arts, Fort Wayne IN (S)

Martin, Jane, *Librn,* Martin and Osa Johnson, Scott Explorers Library, Chanute KS

Martin, Jeanne, *Dir Mktg,* Robert & Mary Montgomery Armory Art Center, Armory Art Center, West Palm Beach FL

Martin, Jennifer, *VPres,* The Clay Studio, Philadelphia PA

Martin, Jesse, *Museum Coordinator,* The Art Museum of Eastern Idaho, Idaho Falls ID

Martin, Julie, *Develop & Pub Rels Coordr,* Northeast Document Conservation Center, Inc, Andover MA

Martin, Kate, *Dir Gallery,* Ventura College, Art Galleries, Ventura CA

Martin, Kate, *Head Colls & Mus,* University of Northern Iowa, Fine & Performing Arts Collection Rod Library, Cedar Falls IA

Martin, Kathy, *Dir Educ,* Hockaday Museum of Art, Kalispell MT

Martin, Lesley, *Book Publisher,* Aperture Foundation, New York NY

Martin, Linda L, *Dir,* Montgomery Museum & Lewis Miller Regional Art Center, Library, Christianburg VA

Martin, Lisa, *Communs & Outreach Dir,* Southern Exposure, San Francisco CA

Martin, Lisa, *Exec Asst,* Blue Lake Fine Arts Camp, Art Dept, Twin Lake MI (S)

Martin, Lyn, *Spec Coll,* Willard Library, Dept of Fine Arts, Evansville IN

Martin, Margaret, *Admin,* Chatham Historical Society, The Atwood House Museum, Chatham MA

Martin, Marianne, *Visual Resources Editorial Librn,* Colonial Williamsburg Foundation, John D Rockefeller, Jr Library, Williamsburg VA

Martin, Martha Kent, *Instr,* Main Line Art Center, Haverford PA (S)

Martin, Mary, *Asst Prof Art History,* Johnson State College, Dept Fine & Performing Arts, Dibden Center for the Arts, Johnson VT (S)

Martin, Michele, *VPres,* Marblehead Arts Association, Inc, Marblehead MA

Martin, Nicholas A, *French Specialist,* National Gallery of Art, Department of Image Collections, Washington DC

Martin, Patrick, *Asst Prof,* Emporia State University, Dept of Art, Emporia KS (S)

Martin, Ray, *Assoc Prof,* Greensboro College, Dept of Art, Division of Fine Arts, Greensboro NC (S)

Martin, Rebecca, *Educ Coordr,* Litchfield History Museum, Litchfield CT

Martin, Rene, *Librn,* Alberta College of Art & Design, Luke Lindoe Library, Calgary AB

Martin, Roland, *Asst Prof,* Lakehead University, Dept of Visual Arts, Thunder Bay ON (S)

Martin, Sarah, *Cur Educ & Pub Progs,* University of Notre Dame, Snite Museum of Art, Notre Dame IN

Martin, Scott, *Cur Asst,* Southern Methodist University, Hamon Arts Library, Dallas TX

Martin, Sydney, *Pres,* American Numismatic Society, New York NY

Martin, Terry, *Instr,* Salt Lake Community College, Graphic Design Dept, Salt Lake City UT (S)

Martin, Victoria, *Acting Area Head Photog,* Pasadena City College, Visual Arts and Media Studies Division, Pasadena CA (S)

Martin, Victoria, *Guest Svcs Asst,* Belz Museum of Asian & Judaic Art, Memphis TN

Martin, Wilbert R, *Prof Printmaking & Drawing,* University of Texas Pan American, Art Dept, Edinburg TX (S)

Martin, William, *Dir,* The Valentine, Richmond VA

Martin, William, *Prof,* Rhode Island College, Art Dept, Providence RI (S)

Martinage, Daniel, *Exec Dir,* Industrial Designers Society of America, Herndon VA

Martindale, Robin, *Prof,* Appalachian State University, Dept of Art, Boone NC (S)

Martinez Wormser, Jennifer, *Head Librn,* Laguna College of Art & Design, Dennis & Leslie Power Library, Laguna Beach CA

Martinez, Andrew, *Archivist,* Rhode Island School of Design, Fleet Library at RISD, Providence RI

Martinez, Charmaine, *Asst Prof Graphic Design,* California Polytechnic State University at San Luis Obispo, Dept of Art & Design, San Luis Obispo CA (S)

Martinez, Cindy, *CFO,* Wadsworth Atheneum Museum of Art, Hartford CT

Martinez, Colonia, *Registrar,* Santa Barbara Museum of Art, Santa Barbara CA

Martinez, Dan, *Chmn,* Cabrillo College, Visual & Performing Arts Division, Aptos CA (S)

Martinez, Daniel, *Prof Pub Art, Sculpture,* University of California, Irvine, Studio Art Dept, Irvine CA (S)

Martinez, Dennis, *Asst Prof,* Dixie College, Art Dept, Saint George UT (S)

Martinez, Diana, *Asst Prof,* Tufts University, Dept of Art & Art History, Medford MA (S)

Martinez, Ed W, *Chmn Dept,* University of Nevada, Reno, Art Dept, Reno NV (S)

Martinez, Joyce, *Mus Tech,* Fort Morgan Heritage Foundation, Fort Morgan CO

Martinez, Juan, *Prof Emeritus,* Florida International University, School of Art & Art History, Miami FL (S)

Martinez, Kim, *Assoc Prof,* University of Utah, Dept of Art & Art History, Salt Lake City UT (S)

Martinez, Laudelina, *Pres,* Rensselaer County Historical Society, Hart-Cluett Mansion, 1827, Troy NY

Martinez, Magda, *Dir Progs,* Philadelphia Museum of Art, Samuel S Fleisher Art Memorial, Philadelphia PA

Martinez, Manual, *Instr,* Cochise College, Art Dept, Douglas AZ (S)

Martinez, Patricia, *Coordr,* California State Polytechnic University, Pomona, Department of Art, Pomona CA (S)

Martinez, Peggy Halbig, *Instr,* Lourdes University, Art Dept, Sylvania OH (S)

Martinez, Reuben, *Colls Mgr,* Pueblo of Pojoaque, Poeh Museum, Santa Fe NM

Martinez, Val, *Discovery Center Coordr,* Nicolaysen Art Museum & Discovery Center, Museum, Casper WY

Martinez, Witnie, *Dir Develop,* Harvey B Gantt Center for African American Arts + Culture, Charlotte NC

Martins, Michael, *Cur,* Fall River Historical Society, Fall River MA

Martinson, Kate, *Head Dept,* Luther College, Art Dept, Decorah IA (S)

Martiny, Sandy, *Cur Educ,* National Academy Museum & School, Archives, New York NY

Martis, Susan, *Cur Educ,* Dayton Art Institute, Dayton OH

Martonis, Stephen, *Exhibs, Facilities & Securities Mgr,* University of Colorado, CU Art Museum, Boulder CO

Martorell, Penni, *Cur & City Hist,* Historic Holyoke at Wistariahurst & City of Holyoke, Holyoke MA

Martyka, Paul, *Assoc Prof,* Winthrop University, Dept of Art & Design, Rock Hill SC (S)

Martz, Genie, *Weekend Mgr,* Walter Anderson Museum of Art, Ocean Springs MS

Martz, Jean-Marie, *Chmn Dance,* Idyllwild Arts Academy, Idyllwild CA (S)

Martz, Mary J, *Coordr Handicapped Svcs,* Cultural Affairs Department City of Los Angeles, Barnsdall Art Center & Junior Arts Center, Los Angeles CA

Marumoto, Karen, *Exhibs Dir,* Shiawassee Arts Center, Owosso MI

Marusin, Dawn, *Visitor Servs Coordr,* Nanaimo Art Gallery, Nanaimo BC

Maruzella, Laura, *Art Educator & Volunteer Coordr,* Green Hill Center for North Carolina Art, Greenhill, Greensboro NC

Marvel, Kate, *Secy,* Marion Art Center, Cecil Clark Davis Gallery, Marion MA

Marvin, Carolyn, *Research Librn,* Portsmouth Athenaeum, Joseph Copley Research Library, Portsmouth NH

Marvin, Judy, *Registrar,* Susquehanna University, Lore Degenstein Gallery, Selinsgrove PA

Marvin, Miranda, *Prof,* Wellesley College, Art Dept, Wellesley MA (S)

Marx, Bridget, *Assoc Dir & Cur Exhibs,* Southern Methodist University, Meadows Museum, Dallas TX

Marx, Colin, *Bldg Mgr,* Soap Factory, Minneapolis MN

Marx, Tony, *Pres. & CEO,* The New York Public Library, New York NY

Marzan, Mario, *Asst Prof,* University of North Carolina at Chapel Hill, Art Dept, Chapel Hill NC (S)

Marzanno, Christine, *Curatorial Asst,* The Long Island Museum of American Art, History & Carriages, Library, Stony Brook NY

Marzano, Christine, *Coll Mgr,* The Long Island Museum of American Art, History & Carriages, Stony Brook NY

Marzolf, Helen, *Exec Dir,* Open Space, Victoria BC

Mas, Deborah, *Dean Acad Affairs,* International Fine Arts College, Miami FL (S)

Masayamptewa, Lloyd, *Park Supt,* National Park Service, Hubbell Trading Post National Historic Site, Ganado AZ

Masengarb, Jen, *Dir Interpretation & Research,* Chicago Architecture Foundation, Chicago IL

Masi, Antonio, *Pres,* American Watercolor Society, Inc, New York NY

Masich, Andrew, *PHMC Chmn,* Pennsylvania Historical & Museum Commission, The State Museum of Pennsylvania, Harrisburg PA

Mason, Bonnie C, *Cur Educ,* Miami University, Art Museum, Oxford OH

Mason, Hal, *Pres,* Valley Art Association, Mansion House Art Center, Hagerstown MD

Mason, Joel, *Chmn,* New York City College of Technology of the City University of New York, Dept of Advertising Design & Graphic Arts, Brooklyn NY (S)

Mason, John, *Pres & CEO,* Lorton Arts Foundation, Workhouse Arts Center, Lorton VA

Mason, Kelvin, *Assoc Prof,* Augustana College, Art Dept, Rock Island IL (S)

Mason, Melissa, *Visual Arts Prog Dir,* Center for the Arts Piper Gallery, Crested Butte CO

Mason, Noelle, *Assoc Prof,* University of South Florida, School of Art & Art History, Tampa FL (S)

Mason, Robert, *Instr,* Andrews University, Dept of Art, Art History & Design, Berrien Springs MI (S)

Mason, Wally, *Dir & Chief Cur,* University of Nebraska, Lincoln, Sheldon Memorial Art Gallery & Sculpture Garden, Lincoln NE

Mason-Teague, Stephanie, *Director of Development,* The Museum of Arts & Sciences Inc, Daytona Beach FL

Massaia, Judy, *VPres,* Woodburn Art Center, Glatt House Gallery, Woodburn OR

Massari, Caren, *Fin Mgr,* Boise Art Museum, Boise ID

Massaro, Marilyn R, *Cur,* City of Providence Parks Department, Roger Williams Park Museum of Natural History, Providence RI

Massaroni, Dino, *Instr,* Cuyahoga Valley Art Center, Cuyahoga Falls OH (S)

Masse, Joanne, *Mgr Financial Servs,* Northeast Document Conservation Center, Inc, Andover MA

Massen, Suzannah, *Chief Pub Servs,* The Frick Collection, Frick Art Reference Library, New York NY

Massey, Allyn, *Prof, Chair,* Goucher College, Art & Art History Dept, Baltimore MD (S)

Massey, Bryan, *Prof,* University of Central Arkansas, Department of Art, Conway AR (S)

Massey, Lew, *Property Mgr,* Bank One Fort Worth, Fort Worth TX

Massey, Scott, *Asst Prof,* University of Louisville, Allen R Hite Art Institute, Louisville KY (S)

Massey, Scott, *Sculpture,* University of Colorado at Denver, College of Arts & Media Visual Arts Dept, Denver CO (S)

Massey, Tim, *Asst Prof,* State University of New York College at Brockport, Dept of Art, Brockport NY (S)

Massey, Walter, *Chancellor,* School of the Art Institute of Chicago, Chicago IL (S)

Massie Lane, Rebecca, *Dir,* Washington County Museum of Fine Arts, Hagerstown MD

Massie, Amanda, *Assoc Cur,* New York State Office of Parks, Recreation and Historic Preservation, Bureau of Historic Sites, Waterford NY

Massier, John, *Visual Arts Cur,* Hallwalls Contemporary Arts Center, Buffalo NY

Massman, Denise, *Asst Prof Theatre Design,* Siena College, Dept of Creative Arts, Loudonville NY (S)

Mast, Bill, *VPres,* Coos County Historical Society Museum, Coos Bay OR

Mast, Sarah, *Asst Prof Painting,* Montana State University, School of Art, Bozeman MT (S)

Mastandrea, Eva, *Prof,* The University of Montana Western, Art Program, Dillon MT (S)

Masters, Bonnie, *Sec,* Cumberland Art Society Inc, Cookeville Art Gallery, Cookeville TN

Masters, Jonelle, *Chmn,* Bismarck State College, Fine Arts Dept, Bismarck ND (S)

Masters, Lindsay, *Exec Dir,* Bainbridge Arts & Crafts Gallery, Bainbridge Island WA

Masters, Richard, *Prof,* University of Wisconsin Oshkosh, Dept of Art, Oshkosh WI (S)

Masterson, Dan, *Asst Mem & Box Office Mgr,* Sangre de Cristo Arts & Conference Center, Pueblo CO

Masterson, Mike, *Chmn,* Northwest Community College, Dept of Art, Powell WY (S)

Mastin, Catherine M., *Dir,* Art Gallery of Windsor, Windsor ON

Mastin, Lauren, *Mus Shop Mgr,* Historic Cherry Hill, Albany NY

Mastroeini, Georgia, *Cur Educ,* Cameron Art Museum, Wilmington NC

Masuoka, Mark, *Dir & CEO,* Akron Art Museum, Akron OH

Mata, Nancy R, *Assoc Prof Graphic Design,* Millersville University, Dept of Art & Design, Millersville PA (S)

Matero, Frank, *Chair, Historic Preservation,* University of Pennsylvania, School of Design (PennDesign), Philadelphia PA (S)

Mates, Judy, *Instr,* Joe Kubert, Dover NJ (S)

Matheny, Paul, *Dir Collections,* South Carolina State Museum, Columbia SC

Mather, Autumn, *Head Reader Servs,* The Art Institute of Chicago, Ryerson & Burnham Libraries, Chicago IL

Mather, Tim, *Dir, Assoc Prof,* Indiana University, Bloomington, Henry Radford Hope School of Fine Arts, Bloomington IN (S)

Mathers, Mary Ellen, *Exec Dir,* Sager Creek Arts Center, Siloam Springs AR

Matheson, Pat, *Cur,* University of Regina, Visual Resource Center, Regina SK

Matheson, Susan, *Cur Ancient Art,* Yale University, Yale University Art Gallery, New Haven CT

Mathews, John, *Instr,* Bucks County Community College, Fine Arts Dept, Newtown PA (S)

Mathews, Karen, *Asst Prof,* University of Colorado at Denver, College of Arts & Media Visual Arts Dept, Denver CO (S)

Mathews, Patricia, *Assoc Prof,* Oberlin College, Dept of Art, Oberlin OH (S)

Mathews, Roger, *Instr,* Butler Community College, Art Dept, El Dorado KS (S)

Mathias, Eve Page, *Coordr Fine Arts,* San Jose City College, School of Fine Arts, San Jose CA (S)

Mathiason, Jerry, *Instr,* North Hennepin Community College, Art Dept, Brooklyn Park MN (S)

Mathie, William, *Dir Gallery,* Edinboro University of Pennsylvania, Art Dept, Edinboro PA (S)

Mathies, Linda, *Tour Coordr,* Old Barracks Museum, Trenton NJ

Mathis, Jaci, *Instr,* Northeastern Junior College, Art Department, Sterling CO (S)

Mathison, Tara, *Asst Cur,* Queens College, City University of New York, Queens College Art Center, Flushing NY

Mathur, Ashok, *Dept Head Creative Studies,* University of British Columbia Okanagan, Faculty of Creative & Critical Studies, Kelowna BC (S)

Matijcio, Steven, *Cur Contemporary Art,* Southeastern Center for Contemporary Art, Winston-Salem NC

Matijcio, Steven, *Curator,* Contemporary Arts Center, Cincinnati OH

Matilsky, Barbara, *Cur Art,* Whatcom Museum, Bellingham WA

Matin, Marty, *Sr Cur & Dir Exhibs,* Abraham Lincoln Presidential Library & Museum, Springfield IL

Matis, Walter, *Prog & Vol Coordr,* Fairfield Historical Society, Fairfield Museum & History Center, Fairfield CT

Matlock, Ann, *Assoc Prof,* Lamar University, Art Dept, Beaumont TX (S)

Mato, Nancy, *Exec VPres,* The Society of the Four Arts, Palm Beach FL

Matotek, Jennifer, *Dir & Cur,* Regina Public Library, Dunlop Art Gallery, Regina SK

Matsubara, Fuyuko, *Assoc Prof,* Indiana University of Pennsylvania, College of Fine Arts, Indiana PA (S)

Matt, Bill, *Deputy Dir Admin,* Michigan State University, Eli & Edythe Broad Art Museum, East Lansing MI

Mattason, Michael, *Gallery Mgr,* District of Columbia Arts Center (DCAC), Washington DC

Mattei, Edwin J, *Head Dept,* Pontifical Catholic University of Puerto Rico, Dept of Fine Arts, Ponce PR (S)

Mattern, Tom, *C+CC Dir,* Rensselaer Newman Foundation Chapel + Cultural Center, The Gallery at the Chapel & Cultural Center, Troy NY

Mattern, Yvette, *Asst Prof,* State University of New York at Albany, Art Dept, Albany NY (S)

Matteson, Charles C, *Chmn,* State University of New York, Cobleskill, Art Dept, Cobleskill NY (S)

Matthews, Harriett, *Prof,* Colby College, Art Dept, Waterville ME (S)

Matthews, Nancy, *Sr Cur Educ,* Kenosha Public Museums, Kenosha WI

Matthie, Paige, *Registrar,* Confederation Centre Art Gallery and Museum, Charlottetown PE

Matthis, Rose, *Instr,* Lamar University, Art Dept, Beaumont TX (S)

Mattice, Matt, *Exec Dir,* King Kamehameha V Judiciary History Center, Honolulu HI

Mattice, Shelby, *Mus Mgr,* Greene County Historical Society, Bronck Museum, Coxsackie NY

Mattleson, Tisa, *Plateau Curator,* Eastern Washington State Historical Society, Northwest Museum of Arts & Culture, Spokane WA

Matto, Elizabeth, *Bd Pres,* Hunterdon Art Museum, Clinton NJ

Mattox, Diane, *Instr,* Bob Jones University, School of Fine Arts, Div of Art & Design, Greenville SC (S)

Mattson, John, *Co-Site Supvr,* Fort Totten State Historic Site, Pioneer Daughters Museum, Fort Totten ND

Mattson, Robert, *Chmn Art Dept & Coordr Art Gallery,* Ridgewater College, Art Dept, Willmar MN (S)

Mattys, Joe, *Assoc Prof,* Randolph-Macon College, Dept of the Arts, Ashland VA (S)

Matus, Edward M, *Gen Educ,* Art Institute of Pittsburgh, Pittsburgh PA (S)

Matuscak, Melissa, *Mus Dir & Cur,* Northern Michigan University, De Vos Art Museum, Marquette MI

Matvey, Richard, *Gen Educ,* Art Institute of Pittsburgh, Pittsburgh PA (S)

Matyas, Diane, *Dir Exhibs & Programs,* Staten Island Museum, Archives Library, Staten Island NY

Matyas, Diane, *VPres Exhibs & Progs,* Staten Island Museum, Staten Island NY

Maude, Marshall, *Asst Prof,* University of Kansas, The School of the Arts, Dept of Visual Art, Lawrence KS (S)

Mauersberger, George, *Prof,* Cleveland State University, Art Dept, Cleveland OH (S)

Mauk, Patrick, *Gallery Mgr,* Dayton Visual Arts Center, Dayton OH

Maul, John, *Asst Prof,* Oregon State University, Dept of Art, Corvallis OR (S)

Mauldin, Stephen L, *Instr,* Saint Gregory's University, Dept of Art, Shawnee OK (S)

Maune, Ramsey, *Chmn Bd Trustees,* Laumeier Sculpture Park, Saint Louis MO

Maupin, Sandra, *Adjunct Prof,* Southwest Baptist University, Art Dept, Bolivar MO (S)

Maurelli, Erin, *Instructor,* Concordia University, Art and Design Department, Saint Paul MN (S)

Mauren, Paul, *Prof,* The College of Saint Rose, The Center For Art and Design, Albany NY (S)

Maurer, KC, *CFO & Treas,* Andy Warhol Foundation for the Visual Arts, New York NY

Maurer, Renée, *Museum Shop Mgr.,* Auburn University, Jule Collins Smith Museum of Fine Art, Auburn AL

Maurer, Tracy, *Instr,* University of Evansville, Art Dept, Evansville IN (S)

Maurier, Adele, *Opers & Design,* See Science Center, Manchester NH

Mauro, Robert, *Chmn,* Arcadia University, Dept of Fine Arts, Glenside PA (S)

Maury, Kate, *Asst Prof,* University of Wisconsin-Stout, Dept of Art & Design, Menomonie WI (S)

Maury, Nichole, *Print Media Area Coordr,* Western Michigan University, Frostic School of Art, Kalamazoo MI (S)

Maus, Andrew, *Dir & CEO,* Plains Art Museum, Fargo ND

Maute, Mary Jo, *Educ,* Whatcom Museum, Bellingham WA

Mavers, Steve, *Cur Educ,* Museum London, London ON

Mavery, Andy, *Assoc Prof,* University of Maine, Dept of Art, Orono ME (S)

Mavis, Morgan, *Comm Coord,* OCAD University, Ignite Gallery, Toronto ON

Mawani, Salma, *Mgr Admin/Shop Wholesale,* University of British Columbia, Museum of Anthropology, Vancouver BC

Maxon, Jennifer, *Assoc Librn & Archivist,* Museum of Ventura County, Ventura CA

Maxon, Mary, *Cur,* Rapid City Arts Council, Dahl Arts Center, Rapid City SD

Maxville, Karen, *Registrar,* National Archives & Records Administration, Herbert Hoover Presidential Library - Museum, West Branch IA

Maxwell, Anita, *Acting Dir & Sr Cur Progs,* City of Ketchikan Museum Department, Totem Heritage Center, Ketchikan AK

Maxwell, Anita, *Acting Dir & Sr Cur Progs,* City of Ketchikan Museum Department, Tongass Historical Museum, Ketchikan AK

Maxwell, Betty, *Asst Dir,* Henry County Museum & Cultural Arts Center, Clinton MO

Maxwell, Christoper, *Cur European Glass,* Corning Museum of Glass, Museum, Corning NY

Maxwell, Deborah, *Lectr,* Emporia State University, Dept of Art, Emporia KS (S)

Maxwell, Jack, *Head Dept & Chmn,* Abilene Christian University, Dept of Art & Design, Abilene TX (S)

Maxwell, Kathleen, *Assoc Prof,* Santa Clara University, Dept of Art & Art History, Santa Clara CA (S)

Maxwell, Kathryn, *Assoc Dean & Prof,* Arizona State University, Herberger Institute for Design and the Arts, Tempe AZ (S)

Maxwell, Stephanie, *Asst Prof,* Rochester Institute of Technology, School of Photographic Arts & Sciences, Rochester NY (S)

Maxwell, Susan, *Assoc Prof,* University of Wisconsin Oshkosh, Dept of Art, Oshkosh WI (S)

Maxwell, William C, *Prof,* The College of New Rochelle, School of Arts & Sciences Art Dept, New Rochelle NY (S)

May, Bill, *Dir,* Arrowmont School of Arts & Crafts, Gatlinburg TN (S)

May, Dan, *Chair,* Southern Arkansas University at Magnolia, Dept of Art & Design, Magnolia AR (S)

May, Jessica, *Chief Cur,* Portland Museum of Art, Portland ME

May, Jim, *Exec Dir,* Hoosier Salon Patrons Association, Inc, Art Gallery & Membership Organization, Indianapolis IN

May, Joyce, *Instr,* Northeastern Junior College, Art Department, Sterling CO (S)

May, Julia, *Cur,* Earlham College, Ronald Gallery, Richmond IN

May, Julie L, *Mng Dir Library & Archives,* Brooklyn Historical Society, Othmer Library, Brooklyn NY

May, Ken, *Exec Dir,* South Carolina Arts Commission, Columbia SC

May, Keshema, *Store Mgr,* Museum of Northwest Art, La Conner WA

May, Larry, *Instr,* Art Academy of Cincinnati, Cincinnati OH (S)

Mayberry, Rodney, *Pres,* San Angelo Museum of Fine Arts, San Angelo TX

Maycock, Susan E, *Dir Survey,* Cambridge Historical Commission, City of Cambridge, Research Library on Architectural and Social History of Cambridge, Mass, Cambridge MA

Mayer, Carol, *Cur Africa Pacific,* University of British Columbia, Museum of Anthropology, Vancouver BC

Mayer, Daniel, *Exec Dir,* The ArtsCenter, The Nicholson Gallery at the Arts Center, Carrboro NC

Mayer, Edward, *Prof,* State University of New York at Albany, Art Dept, Albany NY (S)

Mayer, Marc, *Dir & CEO,* National Gallery of Canada, Ottawa ON

Mayer, Randy, *Instr,* Guild of Creative Art, Shrewsbury NJ (S)

Mayer, William A, *University Librn,* American University, Jack I & Dorothy G Bender Library & Learning Resources Center, New York NY

Mayer, William, *Prof,* Hope College, Dept of Art & Art History, Holland MI (S)

Mayes, Dewey, *Instr,* Wilkes Community College, Arts & Science Division, Wilkesboro NC (S)

Mayes, Michele, *Vice Pres., Gen. Counsel & Sec.,* The New York Public Library, New York NY

Mayes, Steven L, *Prof,* Arkansas State University, Dept of Art, State University AR (S)

Mayes, Steven, *Dir,* Arkansas State University-Art Department, Jonesboro, Fine Arts Center Gallery, Jonesboro AR

Mayhew, Rebecca, *Educ & Mem,* See Science Center, Manchester NH

Mayhugh, Cathy, *Exhib,* Fitton Center for Creative Arts, Hamilton OH (S)

Mayhugh, Cathy, *Exhib,* Fitton Center for Creative Arts, Hamilton OH

Maylone, Cybele, *Exec Dir,* UrbanGlass, Robert Lehman Gallery, Brooklyn NY

Maynard, George, *Asst,* GumTree Museum of Art, Tupelo MS

Maynard, Margaret, *Dir Visitor Experience & Interpreter,* San Jose Museum of Art, Library, San Jose CA

Maynard, Margie, *Educ & Pub Progs Dir,* Sonoma Valley Museum of Art, Sonoma CA

Maynard, Marianne, *Pres,* Grand Prairie Arts Council, Inc, Arts Center of the Grand Prairie, Stuttgart AR

Maynes, Bill, *Dir,* The Fields Sculpture Park at Omi International Arts Center, Ghent NY

Mayo, Ann, *Mgr Security & Guest Servs,* Smith College, Museum of Art, Northampton MA

Mayo, Doug, *Special Collections,* Colonial Williamsburg Foundation, John D Rockefeller, Jr Library, Williamsburg VA

Mayo, Seth, *Director of Astronomy,* The Museum of Arts & Sciences Inc, Daytona Beach FL

Mayocole, Lynne, *Pres,* Artists Talk on Art (ATOA), New York NY

Mayor, Babette, *Prof Emeritus,* California State Polytechnic University, Pomona, Department of Art, Pomona CA (S)

Mays, Amber, *Admin Mgr & Asst to Pres,* African American Museum in Philadelphia, Philadelphia PA

Mays, Brian, *Adjunct Prof,* Southern Nazarene University, Art & Design Department, Bethany OK (S)

Mays, Gayle, *Libr Asst,* Fort Worth Public Library Arts & Humanities, Fine Arts Section, Fort Worth TX

Mays, Margaret, *Financial Mgr,* Mingei International, Inc, Mingei International Museum - Balboa Park & Mingei International Museum - Escondido, San Diego CA

Mays, Peter, *Exec Dir,* Gallery 825/Los Angeles Art Association, Gallery 825, Los Angeles CA

Mays, Susan, *Cur Educ,* Museum of Arts & Sciences, Inc, Macon GA

Mayse, Kevin, *Chmn Performing Arts & Media,* Riverside Community College, Dept of Art & Mass Media, Riverside CA (S)

Mayshak, Katie, *Dir Develop,* Institute of Contemporary Art/Boston, Boston MA

Mayson, Trapeta, *Exec Dir,* Germantown Historical Society, Philadelphia PA

Mazellen, Ron, *Prof,* Indiana Wesleyan University, School of Arts & Humanities, Division of Art, Marion IN (S)

Maziar, Paul, *Co-Curator,* Portland State University, White Gallery, Portland OR

Maziar, Paul, *Visual Arts Cur,* Portland State University, Littman Gallery, Portland OR

Mazonowicz, Douglas, *Dir,* Gallery of Prehistoric Paintings, Library, New York NY

Mazow, Alissa, *Asst Prof,* University of Arkansas, Art Dept, Fayetteville AR (S)

Mazow, Leo, *Assoc Prof,* University of Arkansas, Art Dept, Fayetteville AR (S)

Mazur, Michael, *Exec Dir,* Fresno Arts Center & Museum, Fresno CA

Mazur, Zachary, *Asst Cur,* Washington State University, Museum of Art, Pullman WA

Mazzaccaro, Paul R, *Asst Dir & COO,* Westport Public Library, Westport CT

Mazzei, Cara, *Dir Develop,* Honolulu Museum of Art, Honolulu HI

Mazzei, Justin, *Dir MCG Youth & Arts,* Manchester Bidwell Corporation, Manchester Craftsmen's Guild Youth & Arts Program, Pittsburgh PA

Mazziotti Gillan, Maria, *Exec Dir Cultural Arts,* Passaic County Community College, Division of Humanities, Paterson NJ (S)

McAbee, Doug, *Asst Prof Art,* Lander University, College of Arts & Humanities - Visual Arts, Greenwood SC (S)

McAdams Olson, Holly, *Dir,* Kimmel-Harding-Nelson Center for the Arts, Nebraska City NE

McAdams, Margaret, *Assoc Prof,* Ohio University-Chillicothe Campus, Fine Arts & Humanities Division, Chillicothe OH (S)

McAdams, Shane, *Instr,* Marian University, Art Dept, Fond Du Lac WI (S)

Mcafee, Michael, *Cur History,* United States Military Academy, West Point Museum, West Point NY

McAleer-Keeler, Kerry, *Dir Art & The Book,* Corcoran School of Art, Washington DC (S)

McAlister, Lori, *Office & Prog Mgr,* Lincoln Arts Council, Lincoln NE

McAlister, Richard A, *Assoc Prof,* Providence College, Art & Art History Dept, Providence RI (S)

McAllister, Kay, *Bus Mgr,* Canton Museum of Art, Canton OH (S)

McAllister, Kay, *Bus, Admin & Mus Shop Mgr,* Canton Museum of Art, Canton OH

McAllister, Michael F, *Gen Counsel,* Art Services International, Alexandria VA

McAlpine, Donald, *Chmn Dept Natural Science, Head Zoology Sect & Research Cur,* New Brunswick Museum, Saint John NB

McAlpine, Keith, *Dir,* New Brunswick College of Craft & Design, Fredericton NB (S)

McAlpine, Keith, *Dir Admin,* New Brunswick College of Craft & Design, Library, Fredericton NB

McAn, Robert, *Mem & Spec Events Mgr,* Kimbell Art Foundation, Kimbell Art Museum, Fort Worth TX

McAndrews, Mick, *Instr,* Wayne Art Center, Wayne PA (S)

McArt, Craig, *Prof,* Rochester Institute of Technology, School of Design, Rochester NY (S)

McArthur, Andrew, *Pres Bd Dir,* Boulder Museum of Contemporary Art, Boulder CO

McArthur, Damon, *Asst Prof,* Western Illinois University, Department of Art, Macomb IL (S)

McAsey, Veronica, *Lib Dir,* Southwestern College, Deets Library - Art Dept, Winfield KS

McAvity, John G, *Exec Dir & CEO,* Canadian Museums Association, Association des Musees Canadiens, Ottawa ON

McAvoy, Suzette, *Dir,* CMCA-Center for Maine Contemporary Art, Art Gallery, Rockport ME

McBain, Rhona, *Chairperson & Assoc Prof,* Pittsburg State University, Art Dept, Pittsburg KS (S)

McBratney-Stapleton, Deborah, *Exec Dir,* Anderson Fine Arts Center, The Anderson Center for the Arts, Anderson IN

McBride, Carolyn N, *Secy,* National Hall of Fame for Famous American Indians, Anadarko OK

McBride, Joe, *Dir & Exec VPres,* National Hall of Fame for Famous American Indians, Anadarko OK

McBride, Steve, *Exec Dir,* Pewabic Society Inc, Pewabic, Detroit MI

McBrien, Kate, *Chief Cur,* Maine Historical Society, Portland ME

McBrien, Kate, *Mus Cur,* Maine Historical Society, Library and Museum, Portland ME

McBryde, Malcolm, *Head Librn,* Kalamazoo Institute of Arts, The Mary & Edwin Meader Fine Arts Library, Kalamazoo MI

McBryde, Malcolm, *Librn,* Kalamazoo Institute of Arts, Kalamazoo MI

McCabe, Caroline, *Gallery Coordr,* Santa Ana College, Art Gallery, Santa Ana CA

McCabe, Dan, *Instr,* Kirkwood Community College, Dept of Arts & Humanities, Cedar Rapids IA (S)

McCabe, Maureen, *Prof,* Connecticut College, Dept of Art, New London CT (S)

McCabe, Michael M, *Library Dir,* Brevard College, James A Jones Library, Brevard NC

McCabe, Michael M, *Library Dir,* Brevard College, Spiers Gallery, Brevard NC

McCabe, Shauna, *Exec Dir,* Art Gallery of Guelph, Guelph ON

McCafferty, Jay, *Instr,* Los Angeles Harbor College, Art Dept, Wilmington CA (S)

McCall, Christopher, *Dir,* Pier 24 Photography, San Francisco CA

McCall, Ida, *Mgr Mktg, Communs & Visitor Servs,* Washington University, Mildred Lane Kemper Art Museum, Saint Louis MO

McCall, Janet, *Exec Dir,* Society for Contemporary Craft, Pittsburgh PA

McCall, Robert, *Prof,* Saint Mary's University of Minnesota, Art & Design Dept, Winona MN (S)

McCall, William, *Treas,* Association for Public Art, Philadelphia PA

McCalla, Mary Bea, *Dir,* French Art Colony, Library, Gallipolis OH

McCallister Clark, Ellen, *Dir Library,* The Society of the Cincinnati at Anderson House, Washington DC

McCampbell, Jerry, *Chmn Math & Science,* Idyllwild Arts Academy, Idyllwild CA (S)

McCance, Josh, *Coll & Admin Clerk,* American Museum of Ceramic Art, Pomona CA

McCandaless, Michael, *Theater Instr,* Creighton University, Fine & Performing Arts Dept, Omaha NE (S)
McCann, Ashleigh, *Colls Admin,* Cascade County Historical Society, The History Museum, Great Falls MT
McCann, Don, *Pres,* Lahaina Arts Society, Art Organization, Lahaina HI
McCann, Heather, *Librn Urban Studies & Planning,* Massachusetts Institute of Technology, Rotch Library of Architecture & Planning, Cambridge MA
McCarroll Cutshaw, Stacey, *Exposure Ed,* Society for Photographic Education (SPE), SPE Gallery, Cleveland OH
McCarron, Tom, *Secy,* Portsmouth Historical Society, John Paul Jones House & Discover Portsmouth, Portsmouth NH
McCarthy, Christine, *Exec Dir,* Provincetown Art Association & Museum, Library, Provincetown MA
McCarthy, Christine, *Exec Dir,* Provincetown Art Association & Museum, Provincetown MA
McCarthy, David, *Assoc Prof,* Rhodes College, Dept of Art, Memphis TN (S)
McCarthy, Mary, *Pub Rels,* Greenville County Museum of Art, Greenville SC
McCarthy, Miluzka, *Visual Arts Comt Chair,* University of Minnesota, The Studio/Larson Gallery, Saint Paul MN
McCarthy, Ted, *Treas,* Pasadena Museum of California Art, Pasadena CA
McCartney, Kevin, *Dir,* Northern Maine Museum of Science, Presque Isle ME
McCarty, Laura, *Colls Registrar,* Tufts University, Tufts University Art Gallery, Medford MA
McCarty, Lee, *Instr,* Hinds Community College, Dept of Art, Raymond MS (S)
McCasland, Paul, *Museum & Planetarium Tech,* Lafayette Science Museum & Planetarium, Lafayette LA
McCaslin, Jack, *Prof,* James Madison University, School of Art & Art History, Harrisonburg VA (S)
McCauley, Anne, *Prof,* Albion College, Bobbitt Visual Arts Center, Albion MI
McCauley, Barbara, *Chmn,* North Florida Community College, Dept Humanities & Art, Madison FL (S)
McCauley, Frank, *Asst Dir & Cur,* Sumter Gallery of Art, Sumter SC
McCauley, Joan, *Exec Dir,* Place des Arts at Heritage Square, Coquitlam BC
McCauley, Robert N, *Chmn Dept Fine Arts,* Rockford University, Dept of Fine Arts, Rockford IL (S)
McCaw, Shana, *Gallery Dir,* Cardinal Stritch University, Northwestern Mutual Gallery, Milwaukee WI
McCaw, Shana, *Sr Cur,* Charles Allis Art Museum, Milwaukee WI
McClain, Stephanie, *Asst Park Mgr,* Florida Department of Environmental Protection, Stephen Foster Folk Culture Center State Park, White Springs FL
McClanan, Anne, *Asst Prof,* Portland State University, Dept of Art, Portland OR (S)
McCleary, Jill, *Interim Dir,* University of Arizona, Museum of Art & Archive of Visual Arts, Tucson AZ
McCleary, Stephen, *Pres,* Ocean County College, Humanities Dept, Toms River NJ (S)
McClellan, Andrew, *Prof,* Tufts University, Dept of Art & Art History, Medford MA (S)
McClellan, Bethany, *Cur Support Group Mgr,* Birmingham Museum of Art, Birmingham AL
McClellan, Christina, *Colls Mgr & Coordr Exhibs & Progs,* University of Alabama at Birmingham, Abroms-Engel Institute for the Visual Arts, Birmingham AL
McClellan, Kiara, *Social Media and Online Coordinator,* The Columbus Museum, Columbus GA
McClelland, Mary, *Gallery Mgr,* South Shore Arts, Munster IN
McClenny, Bart, *Dir Develop,* Trust Authority, Museum of the Great Plains, Lawton OK
McCloskey, Barbara, *Assoc Prof,* University of Pittsburgh, Henry Clay Frick Dept History of Art & Architecture, Pittsburgh PA (S)
McCloskey, Martha, *Gift Shop Mgr,* San Angelo Museum of Fine Arts, San Angelo TX
McCloud, Kathryn, *Cur Colls,* The University of Texas at San Antonio, Institute of Texan Cultures, San Antonio TX
McCloy, Keenon, *Dir Libraries,* Memphis-Shelby County Public Library & Information Center, Humanities Department, Memphis TN
McClsokey, Barbara, *Dir,* University of Pittsburgh, University Art Gallery, Pittsburgh PA
McClure, John, *Dir Lib Services,* Virginia Historical Society, Library, Richmond VA
McClure, William, *Treas,* National Gallery of Art, Washington DC
McCluskey, Holly, *Dir,* Oglebay Institute, Mansion Museum, Wheeling WV
McClusky, Pamela, *Cur African Art,* Seattle Art Museum, Dorothy Stimson Bullitt Library, Seattle WA
McClusky, Pamela, *Cur African Art,* Seattle Art Museum, Seattle WA
Mccoin, Mark, *Asst Prof,* University of Texas at San Antonio, Dept of Art & Art History, San Antonio TX (S)
McColl, Bruce, *Dir Art Educ,* The Currier Museum of Art, Manchester NH
McColl, Donald, *Contact,* Washington College, Kohl Gallery, Chestertown MD
McCollam, Phil, *Asst Prof,* West Virginia Wesleyan College, Art Dept, Buckhannon WV (S)
McCollough, Pam, *Pres,* Casa Amesti, Monterey CA
McCollum, Ken, *Asst Prof,* Muskingum College, Art Department, New Concord OH (S)
McComas, Jenny, *Cur 19th & 20th Century Art,* Indiana University, Eskenazi Museum of Art, Bloomington IN
McCombs, Bruce, *Prof,* Hope College, Dept of Art & Art History, Holland MI (S)
McCone, John, *Pres,* The Bartlett Museum, Amesbury MA
McConnachie, Darlene, *Dir,* Southampton Art Centre, Art School & Gallery, Southampton ON (S)
McConnaughy, James, *Pres,* National Antique & Art Dealers Association of America, Inc, New York NY
McConnell, Angela, *Exec Dir,* Montalvo Center for the Arts, Saratoga CA
McConnell, Brian, *Assoc Prof Art History & Classical Archaeology,* Florida Atlantic University, D F Schmidt College of Arts & Letters Dept of Visual Arts & Art History, Boca Raton FL (S)
McConnell, Valerie, *Accnt,* University of North Carolina at Greensboro, Weatherspoon Art Museum, Greensboro NC
McConnor, Sean, *Dir Permanent Coll,* Thiel College, Weyers-Sampson Art Gallery, Greenville PA
McConville, Matthew, *Prof,* Goucher College, Art & Art History Dept, Baltimore MD (S)
McCool, Karl, *Distribution Mgr,* Electronic Arts Intermix (EAI), New York NY
McCormack, John, *Dir,* INTAR Gallery, New York NY
McCormick, Jennifer, *Archivist & Colls Mgr,* Charleston Museum, Charleston SC
McCormick, Jennifer, *Colls Mgr,* Charleston Museum, Library & Archives, Charleston SC
McCormick, Karen, *Asst Prof,* Mount Mary College, Art & Design Division, Milwaukee WI (S)
McCormick, Kathryn, *Asst Prof Graphic Design,* California Polytechnic State University at San Luis Obispo, Dept of Art & Design, San Luis Obispo CA (S)
McCormick, Sooa, *Assistant Curator of Korean Art,* The Cleveland Museum of Art, Cleveland OH
McCourt, Bonnie, *Publicity Coordr,* Order Sons of Italy in America, Garibaldi & Meucci Museum, Staten Island NY
McCourt, Emer, *Dir Mktg & PR,* Concord Museum, Concord MA
McCourt, Tim, *Assoc Prof,* Mississippi State University, Dept of Art, Starville MS (S)
McCoy, Claire B, *Asst Prof,* Longwood University, Dept of Art, Farmville VA (S)
McCoy, Dennis, *1st VPres,* Newport Historical Society & Museum of Newport History, Newport RI
McCoy, John, *Multimedia & Design Serv,* Boston College, McMullen Museum of Art, Chestnut Hill MA
McCoy, Mary, *Sr Librn,* Los Angeles Public Library, Art, Music, Recreation & Rare Books, Los Angeles CA
McCoy, Nancy, *Dir Educ & Pub Progs,* National Archives & Records Administration, John F Kennedy Presidential Library & Museum, Boston MA
McCoy, Paul A, *Prof & Ceramic in Res,* Baylor University - College of Arts and Sciences, Dept of Art, Waco TX (S)
McCoy, Tammy, *Exec Dir,* Art Guild of Burlington, Art Center of Burlington, Burlington IA
McCracken, Patrick, *Dir & Cur,* Amarillo Art Association, Amarillo Museum of Art, Amarillo TX
McCrady, Brian, *Chief Facilities Officer, Capital Devel & Facilities,* Royal Ontario Museum, Toronto ON
McCrane, John, *Dir Finance & Admin,* The Trustees of Reservations, The Mission House, Ipswich MA
McCrea, Judith, *Chmn,* University of Kansas, Dept of Art, Lawrence KS (S)
McCrea, Judith, *Prof,* University of Kansas, The School of the Arts, Dept of Visual Art, Lawrence KS (S)
McCreary, Kim, *Fiscal Office Mgr,* Arizona Commission on the Arts, Phoenix AZ
McCreary, Robert, *Instr,* University of South Carolina at Aiken, Dept of Visual & Performing Arts, Aiken SC (S)
McCreery, Jen, *Library Dir,* Alice Curtis Desmond, Hudson River Reference Collection, Garrison NY
McCrohan, Kay, *Art Chair Rockville,* Montgomery College, Dept of Art, Rockville MD (S)
McCroskey, Nancy, *Assoc Prof,* Indiana-Purdue University, Dept of Fine Arts, Fort Wayne IN (S)
McCue, Becky, *Vis Servs & Mus Store Mgr,* National Churchill Museum, Fulton MO
McCue, Don, *Dir,* Lincoln Memorial Shrine, Redlands CA
McCullough, Gloria, *Librn,* Wayne County Historical Society, Museum, Honesdale PA
McCullough, James, *Dean,* Oklahoma State University Institute of Technology, School of Visual Communications, Okmulgee OK (S)
McCumber, Barbara, *Gift Shop Mgr,* McDowell House & Apothecary Shop, Danville KY
McCusker Boehm, Cate, *Dir Mktg & Commun,* Birmingham Museum of Art, Birmingham AL
McCusker, Carol, *Cur Photography,* University of Florida, Samuel P Harn Museum of Art, Gainesville FL
McDade, Carrie L, *Head Librn,* Lesley University, College of Art & Design Library, Boston MA
McDade, Elizabeth, *Dir,* State University of New York, College at Brockport, Tower Fine Arts Gallery, Brockport NY
McDade, Marci, *Ed Surface Design Journal,* Surface Design Association, Inc, Las Vegas NM
McDaniel, Anita, *Colls Mgr,* Taos Historic Museums, E.L. Blumenschein Home & Museum & La Hacienda de los Martinez, Taos NM
McDaniel, Anne, *Gallery Monitor,* Randolph College, Maier Museum of Art, Lynchburg VA
McDaniel, Bridget, *Asst Prof,* McNeese State University, Dept of Visual Arts, Lake Charles LA (S)
McDaniel, Joann, *Asst Dean,* University of Michigan, Ann Arbor, Penny W Stamps School of Art & Design, Ann Arbor MI (S)
McDaniel, Kennedy, *Admin Asst,* Eubie Blake National Jazz Institute and Cultural Center, Baltimore MD
McDaniel, Sheila, *Deputy Dir, Finance & Admin,* The Studio Museum in Harlem, New York NY

McDaniel, Sue Lynn, *Univ Archivist,* Western Kentucky University, Kentucky Library & Museum, Bowling Green KY
McDaniels, Frank, *Mus Preparator,* Plains Art Museum, Fargo ND
McDavid, Charlotte, *Treas,* Watercolor Society of Alabama, Town Creek AL
McDavid, Stephanie, *Chmn Art Dept & Instr,* Saint Andrews Presbyterian College, Art Program, Laurinburg NC (S)
McDearmon, Nancy, *Registrarial Asst,* Sweet Briar College, Art Collection & Galleries, Sweet Briar VA
McDermott, Amanda, *Gallery Mgr,* Stephen Huneck Gallery at Dog Mountain, Saint Johnsbury VT
McDermott, Carole, *VPres,* American Watercolor Society, Inc, New York NY
McDermott, Inez, *Assoc Prof,* New England College, Art & Art History, Henniker NH (S)
McDermott, J, *Instr,* University of Southern Maine, Dept of Art, Gorham ME (S)
McDermott, Kathleen, *Sr Assoc Dean,* New York University, Tisch School of the Arts, New York NY (S)
McDermott, Marise, *Pres & CEO,* Witte Museum, San Antonio TX
McDevitt, Jeannette, *Asst Librn,* Carnegie Mellon University, Hunt Institute for Botanical Documentation, Pittsburgh PA
McDivitt, Dawn, *Chief Deputy Dir,* Natural History Museum of Los Angeles County, Los Angeles CA
McDole, Amber, *Instr,* Graceland University, Fine Arts Div, Lamoni IA (S)
McDonah, Becky, *Secy,* Society of North American Goldsmiths, Eugene OR
McDonald, Ann, *Asst Prof,* Northeastern University, Dept of Art & Architecture, Boston MA (S)
McDonald, Christine, *Educ Coordr,* Academy of the New Church, Glencairn Museum, Bryn Athyn PA
McDonald, Claire, *Dept Chmn,* University of Saint Thomas, Fine and Performing Arts Dept, Houston TX (S)
McDonald, Danielle, *CEO,* Ottawa Public Library, Fine Arts Dept, Ottawa ON
McDonald, Evelyn, *Admin Secy & Sales Asst,* City of Hampton, Hampton Arts Commission, Hampton VA
McDonald, Helen, *Registrar,* University of Chicago, Oriental Institute, Chicago IL
McDonald, J P, *Exec Dir,* Museum of East Texas, Lufkin TX
McDonald, Jessica, *Cur Colls,* Visual Studies Workshop, Research Center, Rochester NY (S)
McDonald, Jillian, *Prof,* Pace University, Dyson College of Arts & Sciences, Pleasantville NY (S)
McDonald, Julie, *Library Coordr,* New Brunswick College of Craft & Design, Library, Fredericton NB
McDonald, Larry, *Theatre Librn,* University of Regina, Education/Fine Arts Library, Regina SK
McDonald, Louisa, *Asst Prof,* University of Nevada, Las Vegas, Dept of Art, Las Vegas NV (S)
McDonald, Mary, *VPres,* Folk Art Society of America, Richmond VA
McDonald, Mercedes, *Adjunct,* College of the Canyons, Art Dept, Santa Clarita CA (S)
McDonald, Norman D, *Pres,* Museum of Ossining Historical Society, Ossining NY
McDonald, Robert, *Coordr Art,* Cape Cod Community College, Art Dept, West Barnstable MA (S)
McDonald, Shirley, *Project Coordr,* Frederic Remington, Ogdensburg NY
McDonald, Terry, *Exec Dir,* Roberson Museum & Science Center, Binghamton NY
McDonald, Timothy, *Asst Prof,* Framingham State College, Art Dept, Framingham MA (S)
McDonald-Bell, Sheila, *Dir Events,* Lighthouse ArtCenter Museum & School of Art, Tequesta FL
McDonnell, Patricia, *Dir,* Wichita Art Museum, Emprise Bank Research Library, Wichita KS
McDonnell, Patricia, *Dir,* Wichita Art Museum, Wichita KS
McDonough, Anne, *Dir Library & Colls,* Historical Society of Washington DC, The City Museum of Washington DC, Washington DC
McDonough, Anne, *Dir Library & Colls,* Historical Society of Washington DC, Library, Washington DC
McDonough, Kaitlin, *Program Coordinator,* New York Studio School of Drawing, Painting & Sculpture, Gallery, New York NY
McDonough, Tom, *Assoc Prof,* Binghamton University, Art History Department, Binghamton NY (S)
McDowell, Bill, *Prof Photog,* Texas A&M University Commerce, Dept of Art, Commerce TX (S)
McDowell, David, *Bookkeeper,* Fairbanks Arts Association, Bear Gallery, Fairbanks AK
McDowell, Tim, *Prof,* Connecticut College, Dept of Art, New London CT (S)
McDuffie, Dorian, *Pub Art Mgr,* City of Atlanta, Gallery 72, Atlanta GA
McEiwan, Marilyn, *Instr,* University of Indianapolis, Dept Art & Design, Indianapolis IN (S)
McElnea, Patrick, *Adjunct Instr,* Vassar College, Art Dept, Poughkeepsie NY (S)
McElrath, Susan, *Archives & Spec Coll,* American University, Jack I & Dorothy G Bender Library & Learning Resources Center, New York NY
McElroy, Penny, *Chair Art Dept,* University of Redlands, Peppers Art Gallery, Redlands CA
McElvain, Jean, *Asst Cur,* University of Minnesota, Goldstein Museum of Design, Saint Paul MN
McEntee, Nancy, *Dept Head Photog,* Cleveland Institute of Art, Cleveland OH (S)
McEwen, Neal, *Education Coordinator,* George Phippen, Phippen Museum - Art of the American West, Prescott AZ
McEwin, Florence, *Dir,* Western Wyoming Community College Art Gallery, Rock Springs WY
McEwin, Florence, *Head Dept,* Western Wyoming Community College, Art Dept, Rock Springs WY (S)
McFadden, Dennis, *Assoc Dir,* Wellesley College, Davis Museum & Cultural Center, Wellesley MA
McFadden, Dennis, *Director,* Academy Art Museum, Easton MD
McFadden, Martin, *Treas,* Artspace, Richmond VA
McFadden, Robert, *Educ,* Pennsylvania Historical & Museum Commission, State Archives Div, Harrisburg PA
McFadden, Theresa, *Asst Prof,* Northern Virginia Community College, Art Dept, Annandale VA (S)
McFalls, Sarah, *Colls Mgr,* University of Tennessee, Ewing Gallery of Art and Architecture, Knoxville TN
McFarland, Felix, *Buildings & Grounds Supv,* Mamie McFaddin Ward, Beaumont TX
McFarland, James, *Prof Art,* Harford Community College, Visual, Performing and Applied Arts Division, Bel Air MD (S)
McFarland, Seth, *Opers Mgr,* New Mexico Department of Cultural Affairs, Palace of Governors, Santa Fe NM
McFarland, Thomas, *Chmn,* Union College, Music and Fine Arts Dept, Barbourville KY (S)
McFarlane, Joe, *Assoc Prof,* Lewis & Clark Community College, Art Dept, Godfrey IL (S)
McFarlane, Leesa, *Dir Sales,* State of North Carolina, Battleship North Carolina, Wilmington NC
McFee, Doris, *Asst Librn,* Chappell Memorial Library and Art Gallery, Chappell NE
McGaffin, Terri, *Asst Prof,* Morningside College, Art Dept, Sioux City IA (S)
McGahey, Laurie, *Dir Advanc,* James A Michener Art Museum, Doylestown PA
McGarry Bartlet, Jessica, *Secy,* First Street Gallery, New York NY
McGarry, Joan, *Dir Educ & Vis Svcs,* Westmoreland Museum of American Art, Greensburg PA
McGeachy, Heather, *Faculty,* Green River Community College, Art Dept, Auburn WA (S)
McGee, Barry, *Dir,* New Image Art, West Hollywood CA
McGee, Donna, *Prof,* Grambling State University, Art Dept, Grambling LA (S)
McGee, Gigi, *Chmn Graphic Design,* Moore College of Art & Design, Philadelphia PA (S)
McGee, Mike, *Cur,* California State University, Fullerton, Visual Arts Galleries, Fullerton CA
McGehee, Thomas C, *Dir Mus,* Bellingrath Gardens & Home, Theodore AL
McGehee, Turner, *Chmn Dept,* Hastings College, Department of Visual Arts, Hastings NE (S)
McGehee, Turner, *Prof,* Hastings College, Department of Visual Arts, Hastings NE (S)
McGeough, Michelle, *Mus Studies Dept Faculty,* Institute of American Indian Arts, Museum of Contemporary Native Arts, Santa Fe NM (S)
McGibbon, Phyllis, *Assoc Prof,* Wellesley College, Art Dept, Wellesley MA (S)
McGill, Charles, *Gallery Dir,* Manhattanville College, Brownson Gallery, Purchase NY
McGill, Charles, *Gallery Dir,* Manhattanville College, Arthur M Berger Gallery, Purchase NY
McGill, David, *Prof,* Azusa Pacific University, College of Music & the Arts, Dept of Art & Design, Azusa CA (S)
McGill, Forrest, *Chief Cur,* Asian Art Museum of San Francisco, Chong-Moon Lee Ctr for Asian Art and Culture, San Francisco CA
McGilly Mitchell, Hope, *Registrar,* Orillia Museum of Art & History, Orillia ON
McGilvray, Jacqueline, *Exhib & Prog Mgr,* Blue Star Contemporary Art Center, San Antonio TX
McGinness, Karin, *Instr,* Century College, Humanities Dept, White Bear Lake MN (S)
McGinnis, George, *Instr,* California State University, San Bernardino, Dept of Art, San Bernardino CA (S)
McGinnis, Helen F, *Slide Cur,* Moore College of Art & Design, Library, Philadelphia PA
McGinnis, Mark, *Gallery Dir,* Northern State University, Northern Galleries, Aberdeen SD
McGinnis, Mark, *Prof,* Northern State University, Art Dept, Aberdeen SD (S)
McGinnis, Robin, *Admin,* University of Guelph, School of Fine Art & Music, Guelph ON (S)
McGivern, Andy, *Cur Exhibs,* Leigh Yawkey Woodson Art Museum, Wausau WI
McGloughlin, Kate, *Pres,* Woodstock School of Art, Inc, Woodstock NY (S)
McGlown, Misha, *Prog Dir,* Children's Art Carnival, New York NY
McGlumphy, Douglas, *Preparator,* The College of Wooster, The College of Wooster Art Museum, Wooster OH
McGovern, Robert M, *VChmn,* Lehigh Valley Heritage Center, Allentown PA
McGovern, Thomas F, *Chmn,* Northern Kentucky University, Dept of Visual Arts, Highland Heights KY (S)
McGovern, Thomas, *Instr,* California State University, San Bernardino, Dept of Art, San Bernardino CA (S)
McGowan, Cara, *Dir Mktg & Communs,* Hunter Museum of American Art, Chattanooga TN
McGowan, Courtney, *Asst Cur,* Telfair Museums, Telfair Academy of Arts & Sciences Library, Savannah GA
McGowan, Elizabeth, *Chair & Prof,* Williams College, Dept of Art History & Studio Art, Williamstown MA (S)
McGowan, Jeanie, *Cur Colls,* Northern Maine Museum of Science, Presque Isle ME
McGowan, Rebecca, *Exec Dir,* A Space, Toronto ON
McGowan, Rick, *Security Chief,* The Columbus Museum, Columbus GA
McGowen, Courtney, *Chair,* Mingei International, Inc, Mingei International Museum - Balboa Park & Mingei International Museum - Escondido, San Diego CA
McGowen, Molly, *Coordr,* University of Saint Francis, School of Creative Arts, John P Weatherhead Gallery & Lupke Gallery, Fort Wayne IN

McGowin, William, *Prof,* State University of New York College at Old Westbury, Visual Arts Dept, Old Westbury NY (S)
McGrady, Patrick J, *Cur,* The Pennsylvania State University, Palmer Museum of Art, University Park PA
McGrath, Bryan, *Prof,* Munson-Williams-Proctor Arts Institute, Pratt MWP College of Art, Utica NY (S)
McGrath, Carla, *Exec Dir,* Highpoint Center for Printmaking, Minneapolis MN
McGrath, Elaine, *Event Coordr,* Florida Department of Environmental Protection, Stephen Foster Folk Culture Center State Park, White Springs FL
McGrath, Kiki, *Cur,* Wesley Theological Seminary, Henry Luce III Center for the Arts & Religion, Dadian Gallery, Washington DC
McGrath, Maggie, *Registration Coord,* The Contemporary Austin, Austin TX
McGrath, Michelle, *Secy,* Artspace, Richmond VA
McGraw, Marvin, *Dir Mktg & Pub Rels,* Louisiana Department of Culture, Recreation & Tourism, Louisiana State Museum,
McGraw, Stephen R, *VPres,* Waterville Historical Society, Redington Museum, Waterville ME
McGregor, Dan, *Prof,* Abilene Christian University, Dept of Art & Design, Abilene TX (S)
McGrew, Rebecca, *Cur,* The Pomona College, Claremont CA
McGuinn, Martin, *CMOA Bd,* Carnegie Museums of Pittsburgh, Carnegie Museum of Art, Pittsburgh PA
McGuinness, Kate, *Co-Dir,* Spark Gallery, Denver CO
McGuire, Abigael, *Gallery Dir,* Hera Educational Foundation, Hera Gallery, Wakefield RI
McGuire, Dennis, *Head Technical Serv & Coll Mgr,* Columbia College Chicago, Library, Chicago IL
McGuire, Galina, *Asst Prof,* Eastern New Mexico University, Dept of Art, Portales NM (S)
McGuire, Kara, *Circ & ILL Librn,* Daemen College, Marian Library, Amherst NY
McGuire, Sharon, *Chair Multimedia & Design,* Art Institute of Pittsburgh, Pittsburgh PA (S)
McHenry, Tim, *Dir Progs & Engagement,* Rubin Museum of Art, New York NY
McHollin, Mattie, *Archivist,* Fisk University, Library, North Nashville TN
McHugh, Eileen, *Dir,* Cayuga Museum of History & Art, Auburn NY
McHugh, Julia, *Cur Paleontology,* Museum of Western Colorado, Museum of the West, Grand Junction CO
McInerney, Gay, *Exec Dir,* Bay County Historical Society, Historical Museum of Bay County, Bay City MI
McInnis, Beth, *Assoc Dir & Chief Fin Officer,* Vancouver Art Gallery, Vancouver BC
McInnis, Maurie, *Prof,* University of Virginia, McIntire Dept of Art, Charlottesville VA (S)
McIntosh, Johnny, *CFO,* Birmingham Museum of Art, Birmingham AL
McIntyre, Donald, *Assoc Prof,* University of Bridgeport, Shintaro Akatsu School of Design, Bridgeport CT (S)
McIntyre, Genny, *VPres Institutional Advancement,* Western Pennsylvania Conservancy, Fallingwater, Mill Run PA
McIntyre, Jessica, *Asst Librn,* Minneapolis Institute of Art, Art Research & Reference Library, Minneapolis MN
McIver, Denise L, *Librn,* California African-American Museum, Research Library, Los Angeles CA
McKamey, Sheldon, *Exec Dir,* Montana State University, Museum of the Rockies, Bozeman MT
McKay, Alison, *Exec Dir,* Bartow-Pell Mansion Museum & Gardens, Bronx NY
McKay, Barrie G, *Dir,* Church of Jesus Christ of Latter-Day Saints, Independence Visitors' Center, Independence MO
McKay, Behnoush, *Chmn Graphic Design,* Woodbury University, School of Media, Culture & Design, Burbank CA (S)
McKay, Bill, *Dean Arts & Humanities,* Columbia Basin College, Esvelt Gallery, Pasco WA (S)
McKay, Gayle H, *Bus Mgr,* Maysville, Kentucky Gateway Museum Center, Maysville KY
McKay, Michael, *Dir Finance & Human Resources,* National Academy Museum & School, Archives, New York NY
McKeand, Barbara, *Cur,* Imhoff Art Gallery, St. Walburg SK
McKee, Claire, *Mem & Mktg Mgr,* Mingei International, Inc, Mingei International Museum - Balboa Park & Mingei International Museum - Escondido, San Diego CA
McKee, Fred, *Instr,* Miles Community College, Dept of Fine Arts & Humanities, Miles City MT (S)
Mckee, Jeffrey, *Graphic Designer,* University of Kansas, Spencer Museum of Art, Lawrence KS
McKee, Kristi, *Dir Mktg,* Purchase College, Neuberger Museum of Art, Purchase NY
McKee, Linda R, *Head Librn,* Florida State University, The John and Mable Ringling Museum of Art Library, Sarasota FL
McKee, Maria, *Pres,* Hoyt Center for the Arts, Arts & Education of the Hoyt, New Castle PA
McKee, Michael, *Dir,* Gallery 25, Art Gallery, Fresno CA
McKee, William, *Assoc Lectr,* University of Wisconsin-Stevens Point, Dept of Art & Design, Stevens Point WI (S)
McKeen, Allison, *PR & Documentation Specialist,* Kennebec Valley Art Association, Harlow Gallery, Hallowell ME
McKellar, Susan, *Chief Mus Opers,* Charleston Museum, Charleston SC
McKelvey, Marcia, *Dir Admin,* Vesterheim Norwegian-American Museum, Decorah IA
McKenna, Mary Lynn, *Dir,* Copper Village Museum & Arts Center, Anaconda MT
McKenzie, Brett, *Creative Mgr,* The One Club for Creativity, New York NY
McKenzie, Joy, *VPres Acad Affairs,* Watkins College of Art, Design & Film, Nashville TN (S)
McKenzie, Tom, *Exec Dir,* Fellows of Contemporary Art, Los Angeles CA
McKeown, Fiona, *Mgr,* Arts and Letters Club of Toronto, Toronto ON
McKernin, Mark P, *Chmn,* Northeastern Illinois University, Art Dept, Chicago IL (S)
McKibbin, Bobbie, *Interim Dir,* Grinnell College, Dept of Art, Grinnell IA (S)
McKiernan Gonzalez, Eileen, *Assoc Prof & Prog Chair,* Berea College, Art & Art History Program, Berea KY (S)
McKiernan, Monica, *Asst Cur,* White House, Washington DC
McKiernan, Patricia, *Exec Dir,* Graphic Artists Guild, New York NY
McKinley, Cara, *Instruction & Youth Progs,* Lighthouse ArtCenter Museum & School of Art, Tequesta FL
McKinley, Kimberly, *Educ Coordr,* South Shore Arts, Munster IN
McKinney Burket, Ruth, *Clay Prog Coordr,* Women's Studio Workshop, Inc, Rosendale NY
McKinney, Art, *Assoc Dir,* Art Institute of Fort Lauderdale, Technical Library, Fort Lauderdale FL
McKinney, Joel, *Asst Prof & Adjunct,* Northern State University, Art Dept, Aberdeen SD (S)
McKinney, Ruth, *Asst Prof,* Northern State University, Art Dept, Aberdeen SD (S)
McKinsey, Kristan, *Cur,* Peoria Riverfront Museum, Peoria IL
McKinstry, Skip, *Adjunct Prof,* Oklahoma Christian University of Science & Arts, Dept of Art & Design, Oklahoma City OK (S)
McKirahan, John, *Lectr,* University of Nebraska, Kearney, Dept of Art & Art History, Kearney NE (S)
McKnight, Jennifer, *Asst Prof,* University of Missouri, Saint Louis, Dept of Art & Art History, Saint Louis MO (S)
McKone, Jim, *Pub Rels Officer,* Hidalgo County Historical Museum, Edinburg TX
McLain, Dell, *Chmn,* Southeastern Oklahoma State University, Dept of Art, Communication & Theatre, Durant OK (S)
McLain, Kimowan, *Asst Prof,* University of North Carolina at Chapel Hill, Art Dept, Chapel Hill NC (S)
McLain, Nancy A, *Bus Mgr,* Dartmouth College, Hood Museum of Art, Hanover NH
McLallen, Helen M, *Cur,* Columbia County Historical Society, 1820 James Vanderpoel House, Kinderhook NY
McLane, Kelly, *Instr,* Bakersfield College, Art Dept, Bakersfield CA (S)
McLatchy, Patricia, *Exhib Coordr,* Hoyt Center for the Arts, Arts & Education of the Hoyt, New Castle PA
McLaughlin, Beth, *Contract Textile Conservator,* Midwest Art Conservation Center, Minneapolis MN
McLaughlin, Bryne, *Mng Ed,* Canadian Art Foundation, Toronto ON
McLaughlin, Kevin, *Instr,* South Central Technical College, Commercial & Technical Art Dept, North Mankato MN (S)
McLaughlin, Patricia, *Chmn Art Dept,* State University of New York College at Old Westbury, Amelie A Wallace Gallery, Old Westbury NY
McLaurin, Cathy, *Beland Gallery Dir & Special Projects,* Essex Art Center, Lawrence MA
McLaurin, Melanie, *Devel Assoc,* New Jersey Historical Society, Newark NJ
McLean Ward, Barbara, *Dir & Cur,* The National Society of The Colonial Dames of America in the State of New Hampshire, Moffatt-Ladd House & Garden, Portsmouth NH
McLean, Carlos, *Asst Dean,* Laney College, Art Dept, Oakland CA (S)
McLean, Dollie, *Founding Exec Dir,* Artists Collective Inc, Hartford CT
McLean, Jackie, *Founder,* Artists Collective Inc, Hartford CT
McLean, Linda, *Historic Site Mgr,* Olana State Historic Site, Hudson NY
McLean-Cowan, Evelyn, *Instr,* Marian University, Art Dept, Fond Du Lac WI (S)
McLean-Parker, Pam, *Gallery Dir,* Montgomery County Guild of Professional Artists, King of Prussia PA
McLellan, Bryan T, *Finance Dir,* The New England Museum of Telephony, Inc, The Telephone Museum, Ellsworth ME
McLemore, Mary, *Dean,* Motlow State Community College, Art Dept, Tullahoma TN (S)
McLendon, Kirk, *Graphic Design,* Henry Ford Community College, McKenzie Fine Art Ctr, Dearborn MI (S)
McLendon, Liz, *Communs Coordr,* Florida State University, Museum of Fine Arts, Tallahassee FL
McLendon, Marty, *Chair Visual Arts,* Northeast Mississippi Junior College, Art Dept, Booneville MS (S)
McLendon, Matthew, *Family Dir,* University of Virginia, The Fralin Museum of Art at the University of Virginia, Charlottesville VA
McLeod, Laurie, *COO & CFO,* International Center of Photography, Museum, New York NY
McLeod, Nicole, *Dir Mktg & Pub Rels,* Morris Museum of Art, Augusta GA
McLorn, Anne, *Secy,* State University of New York, College at Cortland, Dept Art & Art History, Cortland NY (S)
McMahan, Robert, *Prof,* Antelope Valley College, Art Dept, Division of Fine Arts, Lancaster CA (S)
McMahon, Cliff, *Prof,* Delta State University, Dept of Art, Cleveland MS (S)
McMahon, Colleen, *Shop Mgr,* Moravian Historical Society, Nazareth PA
McMahon, Diane, *Mus Shop Mgr,* Wenham Museum, Timothy Pickering Library, Wenham MA
McMahon, John, *Dir Artist Svcs,* Idaho Commission on the Arts, Boise ID
McMahon, Maggie, *Prof,* University of Tennessee at Chattanooga, Dept of Art, Chattanooga TN (S)
McMahon, Sharon, *Chmn,* Saint Mary's University, Dept of Fine Arts, San Antonio TX (S)
McManus Zurko, Kitty, *Dir,* The College of Wooster, The College of Wooster Art Museum, Wooster OH

McManus, James, *Prof Emeritus,* California State University, Chico, Department of Art & Art History, Chico CA (S)
McManus, James, *Prof Emeritus Art History Research,* California State University, Chico, Janet Turner Print Museum, CSU, Chicago, Chico CA
McManus, Laura, *Curator of Education,* Randolph College, Maier Museum of Art, Lynchburg VA
McManvs, Dee, *Assoc Dir,* Newburyport Maritime Society, Inc, Custom House Maritime Museum, Newburyport MA
McMath, Sheila, *Cur,* Canadian Clay and Glass Gallery, Waterloo ON
McMathon, Janet, *Admin Spec,* Iowa State University, Brunnier Art Museum, Ames IA
McMichael, Luci, *Instr,* University of Missouri, Saint Louis, Dept of Art & Art History, Saint Louis MO (S)
McMillan, David, *Security Mgr,* Kimbell Art Foundation, Kimbell Art Museum, Fort Worth TX
McMillan, Edna, *Chmn,* Cameron University, Art Dept, Lawton OK (S)
McMillan, Gillian, *Assoc Chief Conservator Colls,* Solomon R Guggenheim Museum, New York NY
McMillan, Julie, *Artistic Dir,* Eye Level Gallery, Halifax NS
McMillan, Kristi, *Progs Mgr,* Asheville Art Museum, Asheville NC
McMillan, Morgan, *Coll Mgr,* Lehigh Valley Heritage Center, Allentown PA
McMullan, Kirk, *Pres,* Frontier Times Museum, Bandera TX
McMullen, Paul, *Asst Prof,* Siena Heights University, Studio Angelico-Art Dept, Adrian MI (S)
McMullin, Gert, *Quilt Production Mgr,* The Names Project Foundation AIDS Memorial Quilt, Atlanta GA
McMurrey, Enfys, *Instr,* Indian Hills Community College, Dept of Art, Centerville IA (S)
McNab, Barbara, *Curator of Exhibitions,* The New Museum at the Bradford Brinton Ranch, The Brinton Museum, Big Horn WY
McNair, Amy, *Assoc Prof,* University of Kansas, Kress Foundation Dept of Art History, Lawrence KS (S)
McNally, Dennis, *Chmn & Prof Painting,* Saint Joseph's University, Art Dept, Philadelphia PA (S)
McNally, Joanne, *Dir Exhib,* Valley Cottage Library, Gallery, Valley Cottage NY
McNally, Samantha, *Dir Communs,* California Watercolor Association, Gallery Concord, Concord CA
McNally, Sheila J, *Prof,* University of Minnesota, Minneapolis, Art History, Minneapolis MN (S)
McNally, Susan, *Gallery Dir,* Valley Art Association, Mansion House Art Center, Hagerstown MD
McNamara, Chris, *Registrar,* Parrish Art Museum, Water Mill NY
McNamara, Doug, *Coordr,* Community College of Baltimore County, School of Technology, Art & Design, Catonsville MD (S)
McNamara, Jennifer, *Asst Prof,* State University of New York, College at Cortland, Dept Art & Art History, Cortland NY (S)
McNamara, Kate, *Dir Galleries & Exhibitions,* Otis College of Art & Design, Ben Maltz Gallery, Los Angeles CA
McNamara, Mary, *Pres & Exec Dir,* The Interchurch Center, Library, New York NY
McNamara, Sarah, *Pub Rels & Spec Events,* Rockford Art Museum, Rockford IL
McNamee, Aaron, *Vis Artist,* University of New Orleans-Lake Front, Dept of Fine Arts, New Orleans LA (S)
McNaught, William, *Cur,* Oysterponds Historical Society, Museum, Orient NY
McNaughton, John, *Prof Emeritus,* University of Southern Indiana, Art & Design Dept, Evansville IN (S)
McNaughton, Mary Davis, *Dir,* Scripps College, Ruth Chandler Williamson Gallery, Claremont CA
McNeely, Merritt, *Dir Mktg,* South Carolina State Museum, Columbia SC
McNeer, James B, *Pres,* Richard Bland College, Art Dept, Petersburg VA (S)
McNeil, Courtney, *Cur Fine Arts & Exhibit,* Telfair Museums, Savannah GA
McNeil, Sherry, *Dir Finance,* The Currier Museum of Art, Manchester NH
McNeill, Michael, *Assoc Dir Devel & Chief Matchmaker,* Museum of Contemporary Art Denver, Denver CO
McNeill, Richard, *VPres & Gallery Co Dir,* Sculptor's Society of Canada, Canadian Sculpture Centre, Toronto ON
McNeill, Winifred, *Asst Prof,* New Jersey City University, Art Dept, Jersey City NJ (S)
McNulty, Mary, *Curatorial Asst,* The Long Island Museum of American Art, History & Carriages, Library, Stony Brook NY
McNulty, Neely, *School & Family Programs Coordr,* Dartmouth College, Hood Museum of Art, Hanover NH
McNutt, James, *Adjunct Prof,* Washington & Jefferson College, Art Dept, Washington PA (S)
McPhail, John, *Pres,* Community Council for the Arts, Kinston NC
McPhee, Maureen, *Adjunct,* Feather River Community College, Art Dept, Quincy CA (S)
McPhee, Sarah Collyer, *Prof,* Emory University, Art History Dept, Atlanta GA (S)
McPherson, Heather, *Prof,* University of Alabama at Birmingham, Dept of Art & Art History, Birmingham AL (S)
McPherson, Rachel, *Digital Projects Librarian,* The Cleveland Museum of Art, Ingalls Library, Cleveland OH
McQueen, Alison, *Dir,* McMaster University, School of the Arts, Hamilton ON (S)
McQuillen, Troy, *Adjunct Instr,* Northern State University, Art Dept, Aberdeen SD (S)
McRorie, Jennifer, *Cur Dir,* Moose Jaw Art Museum, Inc, Art & History Museum, Moose Jaw SK
McRorie, Sharon, *Educ Progs Mgr,* Asheville Art Museum, Asheville NC
McSweeney, Emmett, *Dir,* Silas Bronson, Waterbury CT
McTavish, Lianne, *Assoc Chair Grad Studies & Research,* University of Alberta, Dept of Art & Design, Edmonton AB (S)
McTavish-Wisden, Oliver, *Fine & Performing Arts Prog,* Place des Arts at Heritage Square, Coquitlam BC
McTighe, Lake, *Dir Gallery,* College of Santa Fe, Art Dept, Santa Fe NM (S)
McTique, Mary, *Exec Dir,* Boston Center for Adult Education, Boston MA (S)
McTyre, Robert, *Interim Chmn,* Middle Georgia State University, College of Arts & Sciences, Media, Culture & the Arts, Cochran GA (S)
McVaugh, Robert, *Assoc Prof,* Colgate University, Dept of Art & Art History, Hamilton NY (S)
McVicker, Charles, *Asst Prof,* The College of New Jersey, School of Arts & Sciences, Ewing NJ (S)
McWeeney, Jim, *Instr,* Joe Kubert, Dover NJ (S)
McWhorter, Mark, *Dept Head,* Indian Hills Community College, Ottumwa Campus, Dept of Art, Ottumwa IA (S)
McWhorter, Mark, *Head Dept,* Indian Hills Community College, Dept of Art, Centerville IA (S)
McWilliams, Leighton, *Assoc Prof,* University of Texas at Arlington, Art & Art History Department, Arlington TX (S)
McWillie, Judy, *Prof Drawing & Painting,* University of Georgia, Franklin College of Arts & Sciences, Lamar Dodd School of Art, Athens GA (S)
Meacham, Sue, *Secy,* San Angelo Art Club, Helen King Kendall Memorial Art Gallery, San Angelo TX
Mead, Elizabeth, *Assoc Prof,* Portland State University, Dept of Art, Portland OR (S)
Meade, Jr, James, *Prof,* University of Southern Mississippi, Dept of Art & Design, Hattiesburg MS (S)
Meador, Kate, *Exec Dir,* Conrad-Caldwell House Museum, Louisville KY
Meadows, Nina, *Dir,* Union County Public Library Union Room, Monroe NC
Meadows, Ted, *Adjunct Assoc Prof Art History/ Architecture,* Johnson County Community College, Fine Arts Dept & Art History Dept, Overland Park KS (S)
Meadows, Teresa, *Assoc Prof, Film Studies & Visual & Performing Arts,* University of Colorado-Colorado Springs, Visual & Performing Arts Dept (VAPA), Colorado Springs CO (S)
Mealing, Cathleen, *Dir,* Bryant Library, Roslyn NY
Meanley, Jennifer, *Prof,* University of North Carolina at Greensboro, School of Art, Greensboro NC (S)
Means, Leland, *Sculpture,* Orange Coast College, Visual & Performing Arts Division, Costa Mesa CA (S)
Mear, Margaret, *Prof,* Saint Mary's University of Minnesota, Art & Design Dept, Winona MN (S)
Mearns, Travis, *Pub Rels Coordr,* Southern Alleghenies Museum of Art, Ligonier Valley Facility, Ligonier PA
Mears, Lee, *Contact,* Island Gallery West, Holmes Beach FL
Mecklenburg, Virginia, *Chief Cur,* American Art Museum, Smithsonian Institution, Washington DC
Mecky, Debra L, *Exec Dir,* Bush-Holley Historic Site & Storehouse Gallery, Greenwich Historical Society, Cos Cob CT
Meddick, Bill, *VPres,* New Haven Paint & Clay Club, Inc, Whitneyville CT
Meder, Brenda K., *Exec Dir,* Hays Arts Center, Hays KS
Medina, Rafael, *Sr Prog Dir,* Inquilinos Boricuas en Accion (IBA), Villa Victoria Center for the Arts, Boston MA
Medina, Ron, *Instr,* Laramie County Community College, Division of Arts & Humanities, Cheyenne WY (S)
Medley, Chris, *Asst Prof,* Maryland College of Art & Design, Silver Spring MD (S)
Medlock, Anne, *Assoc Prof,* West Texas A&M University, Art, Theatre & Dance Dept, Canyon TX (S)
Medlock, Rudy, *Prof Emeritus,* Asbury University, Art Dept, Wilmore KY (S)
Medrano, Jerry, *Asst Cur,* City of El Paso, El Paso TX
Medua, Maria, *Corporate Art Coordr,* San Francisco Museum of Modern Art, Artist Gallery, San Francisco CA
Medvedow, Jill, *Ellen Matilda Poss Dir,* Institute of Contemporary Art/Boston, Boston MA
Meech, Marc, *CFO,* Charleston Museum, Charleston SC
Meehan, Brian, *Exec Dir,* Museum London, London ON
Meek, A J, *Prof,* Louisiana State University, School of Art, Baton Rouge LA (S)
Meek, William, *Prof,* Texas State University - San Marcos, Dept of Art and Design, San Marcos TX (S)
Meeker, Cheryl, *Prof Art,* Monmouth College, Dept of Art, Monmouth IL (S)
Meeks, Donna M, *Chmn & Prof,* Lamar University, Art Dept, Beaumont TX (S)
Meeks, Stephanie, *Pres,* National Trust for Historic Preservation, Washington DC
Meghelli, Samir, *Chief Cur,* Anacostia Community Museum, Smithsonian Institution, Washington DC
Mehalakes, Elaine, *Cur,* Wellesley College, Davis Museum & Cultural Center, Wellesley MA
Mehalakes, Elaine, *VPres Curatorial Affairs,* Allentown Art Museum, Allentown PA
Mehlferber, Jon, *Chmn,* Virginia Intermont College, Fine Arts Div, Bristol VA (S)
Mehling, Beth, *Pres,* Big Horn County Historical Museum, Hardin MT
Mehner, Da-ka-xeen, *Asst Prof,* University of Alaska Fairbanks, Art Department, Fairbanks AK (S)
Mehnng, Christine, *Chair,* University of Chicago, Dept of Art History, Chicago IL (S)

Mehran, Laleh, *Assoc Prof Electronic Media Arts & Design,* University of Denver, School of Art & Art History, Denver CO (S)
Mehrhoff, Arthur, *Academic Coordr,* University of Missouri, Museum of Art & Archaeology, Columbia MO
Mei, Ingrid, *Office Mgr,* China Institute in America, China Institute Gallery, New York NY
Meier, Anthony, *VPres,* Art Dealers Association of America, Inc, New York NY
Meier, Carsten, *Asst Prof,* University of Miami, Dept of Art & Art History, Coral Gables FL (S)
Meier, Jan, *Mgr,* Maritz, Inc, Library, Fenton MO
Meier, Mary Elizabeth, *Asst Prof,* Mercyhurst University, Dept of Art, Erie PA (S)
Meier, Scott, *Exhibit Preparator,* University of Michigan, Kelsey Museum of Archaeology, Ann Arbor MI
Meiers, Susanna, *Dir,* El Camino College Art Gallery, Torrance CA
Meifert, Ken, *VPres Sponsorship & Develop,* National Baseball Hall of Fame & Museum, Cooperstown NY
Meighan, Tom, *Assoc Dir & Dir Opers & Mus Svcs,* Vancouver Art Gallery, Vancouver BC
Meijer, Lena, *Prof Art History,* Aquinas College, Art Dept, Grand Rapids MI (S)
Meine, Carol, *Dir,* Mesa Public Library Art Gallery, Los Alamos NM
Meinert, Jim, *Exec Dir,* Cascade County Historical Society, The History Museum, Great Falls MT
Meinzer, Melissa, *Admin Coordr,* Washington University, Mildred Lane Kemper Art Museum, Saint Louis MO
Meissner-Gigstead, Elizabeth, *Dir,* Miller Art Center Foundation Inc, Miller Art Museum, Sturgeon Bay WI
Mejchar, James D, *Exec Dir,* International Clown Hall of Fame & Research Center, Inc, West Allis WI
Mejer, Robert Lee, *Dir Gallery,* Quincy University, The Gray Gallery, Quincy IL
Mejer, Robert Lee, *Prof Art,* Quincy University, Dept of Art, Quincy IL (S)
Mejia, Jane Devine, *Chief Librn,* Vancouver Art Gallery, Library, Vancouver BC
Mejia-Krumbein, Beatriz, *Prof,* La Sierra University, Art Dept, Riverside CA (S)
Mekas, Jonas, *Artistic Dir,* Anthology Film Archives, New York NY
Melamed, Carmen, *Dir Finance,* High Desert Museum, Bend OR
Melancon, Joseph, *Instr,* Art Center Sarasota, Sarasota FL (S)
Melandri, Lisa, *Exec Dir,* Contemporary Art Museum St Louis, Saint Louis MO
Melberg, Jerald, *Dir,* Jerald Melberg Gallery, Charlotte NC
Melching, Sarah, *Adj Faculty Conservation,* University of Denver, School of Art & Art History, Denver CO (S)
Melenbrink, Michael, *Bus Mgr,* Flint Institute of Arts, Library, Flint MI
Melenbrink, Michael, *Dir Finance & Admin,* Flint Institute of Arts, Flint MI
Melhem, Yahya, *Aga Khan Cataloger,* Massachusetts Institute of Technology, Rotch Library of Architecture & Planning, Cambridge MA
Melick, Randolph, *Instr,* New York Academy of Art, Graduate School of Figurative Art, New York NY (S)
Melion, Walter S, *Prof,* Emory University, Art History Dept, Atlanta GA (S)
Melis, Rachel, *Asst Prof,* Kansas State University, Art Dept, Manhattan KS (S)
Melius, Jeremy, *Asst Prof,* Tufts University, Dept of Art & Art History, Medford MA (S)
Melius, Mary, *Mgr Traveling Exhibs,* Norman Rockwell Museum, Stockbridge MA
Mella, Joseph S, *Dir,* Vanderbilt University, Vanderbilt University Fine Arts Gallery, Nashville TN
Mellili, Mary, *Prof Chairperson,* Salem State University, Art & Design Department, Salem MA (S)
Mello, Emily, *Cur Educ,* Purchase College, Neuberger Museum of Art, Purchase NY
Mello, Sally Dean, *Coordr Educ,* Art Complex Museum, Carl A Weyerhaeuser Library, Duxbury MA
Mellon, Andrew, *Dir. of the Research Libraries,* The New York Public Library, New York NY
Mellone, Allyson, *Colls Mgr,* Queens College, City University of New York, Godwin-Ternbach Museum, Flushing NY
Melmer, Janeen, *Mus Registrar,* Crazy Horse Memorial, Indian Museum of North America, Native American Educational & Cultural Center & Crazy Horse Memorial Library (Reference), Crazy Horse SD
Meloche, Jaclyn, *Cur Contemporary Art,* Art Gallery of Windsor, Windsor ON
Melton, Allison, *Asst Prof,* Delta State University, Dept of Art, Cleveland MS (S)
Melton, Laura, *Chmn Music,* Idyllwild Arts Academy, Idyllwild CA (S)
Melton, Marcus, *Assoc Prof,* West Texas A&M University, Art, Theatre & Dance Dept, Canyon TX (S)
Melton, Matthew, *Chmn,* Lee University, Dept of Communication & the Arts, Cleveland TN (S)
Melton, Maureen, *Susan Morse Hilles Dir Library & Archives and Museum Historian,* Museum of Fine Arts, William Morris Hunt Memorial Library, Boston MA
Melvin, Meg, *Modern Specialist,* National Gallery of Art, Department of Image Collections, Washington DC
Menard, Lloyd, *Prof,* University of South Dakota, Department of Art, College of Fine Arts, Vermillion SD (S)
Menard, Michael J, *Cur Archives & Librn,* Museum of Western Colorado, Museum of the West, Grand Junction CO
Menchaca, Belinda, *Educ Dir,* Guadalupe Cultural Arts Center, San Antonio TX
Mencini, Susan, *Instr,* Cuyahoga Valley Art Center, Cuyahoga Falls OH (S)
Mendell, Cyndi, *Instr Foundation 1st yr,* AIC College of Design, Cincinnati OH (S)
Mendell, Sean M, *Pres,* AIC College of Design, Cincinnati OH (S)
Mendenhall, Kathleen, *Adjunct Assoc Prof Art History,* Johnson County Community College, Fine Arts Dept & Art History Dept, Overland Park KS (S)
Mendenhall, Susan, *Dir Resource Develop,* Arts United of Greater Fort Wayne, Fort Wayne IN
Mendive, Toni, *Archivist,* Northeastern Nevada Museum, Elko NV
Mendoza, Cora Myers, *Mem Bd Dir,* Hatch-Billops Collection, Inc, New York NY
Mendoza, Mary, *Treas,* Long Beach Art League, Long Beach Library, Long Beach NY
Menefee Gau, Terry, *Prog Assoc,* CultureWorks, Richmond VA
Menefee, Amanda, *VPres,* Pacific Grove Art Center, Pacific Grove CA
Menendez, Sheila, *Board of Dirs & Treas,* Guild of Creative Art, Shrewsbury NJ (S)
Meneray, Gene, *Artist Servs Dir,* Arts Council Of New Orleans, New Orleans LA
Meng, Sara F, *Chmn Art Dept,* Harrisburg Area Community College, Division of Communications, Humanities & the Arts, Harrisburg PA (S)
Menn, Richard J, *Cur,* Carmel Mission & Gift Shop, Carmel CA
Menocal, Narcisco G, *Prof,* University of Wisconsin, Madison, Dept of Art History, Madison WI (S)
Menschel, Robert B, *Chmn Emeritus,* Museum of Modern Art, New York NY
Mensching, Bill, *Vice Pres,* National Society of Mural Painters, Inc, New York NY
Menser, Shirley, *Chmn,* Dawson Springs Museum and Art Center, Dawson Springs KY
Mentor, Will, *Assoc Prof,* St Michael's College, Fine Arts Dept, Colchester VT (S)
Meranda, Lauren, *Instr,* Judson University, School of Art, Design & Architecture, Elgin IL (S)
Mercede, Nevin, *Prof,* Antioch College, Visual Arts Dept, Yellow Springs OH (S)
Mercer, Cydna, *Head Admin,* Museum London, London ON
Mercer, Deborah O, *Pres,* Warwick Museum of Art, Warwick RI
Mercer, John, *Coordr, Photograph Dept,* Phoenix College, Dept of Art & Photography, Phoenix AZ (S)
Mercer, Valerie, *Cur African American Art,* Detroit Institute of Arts, Detroit MI
Merchant, Linda, *Visual Art Dir,* Ashtabula Arts Center, Ashtabula OH
Merchant, Susan, *Dir,* Dartmouth Heritage Museum, Dartmouth NS
Mercier, Dominic, *Dir Communs,* Philadelphia Museum of Art, Samuel S Fleisher Art Memorial, Philadelphia PA
Meredith, Pamela, *Sr Cur,* Toronto Dominion Bank, Toronto ON
Meredo-Burich, John, *Exec Dir,* Eastern Washington State Historical Society, Northwest Museum of Arts & Culture, Spokane WA
Merger, Adrien, *Gallery Director,* Hera Educational Foundation, Hera Gallery, Wakefield RI
Merker, Mary Ann, *Civic Arts Coordr,* Berkeley Civic Arts Program, Berkeley CA
Merkt, Donna, *Cur Educ,* Mabee-Gerrer Museum of Art, Shawnee OK
Merle, Michel D, *Prof,* Worcester State College, Visual & Performing Arts Dept, Worcester MA (S)
Merline, Mark, *Chair Art Dept,* Marian University, Art Dept, Fond Du Lac WI (S)
Merling, Mitchell, *Paul Mellon Cur & Head Dept European Art,* Virginia Museum of Fine Arts, Richmond VA
Merrick, Jim, *Archivist,* Stanley Museum, Inc, Kingfield ME
Merrill, Yolanda, *Art Librn,* Washington & Lee University, Leyburn Library, Lexington VA
Merriman, Larry, *Asst Prof & Gallery Dir,* Coker College, Art Dept, Hartsville SC (S)
Merritt, David, *Undergrad Chair,* University of Western Ontario, Dept of Visual Arts, London ON (S)
Merritt, Elizabeth, *VPres Strategic Foresight,* American Alliance of Museums, Arlington VA
Merritt, Keely, *Head Photographer,* The Historic New Orleans Collection, Royal Street Galleries, New Orleans LA
Merritt, Sarah, *Exec Dir,* The Arts Council of Wayne County, Goldsboro NC (S)
Merryday, Michaela, *Asst Prof, Art Hist & Visual Cult,* University of Tulsa, School of Art, Tulsa OK (S)
Mershimer, Frederick, *Instr,* Manhattan Graphics Center, New York NY (S)
Mershon, Tom, *Mus Shop Mgr,* Pocumtuck Valley Memorial Association, Memorial Hall Museum, Deerfield MA
Mersmann, Armin, *Mus School Mgr,* Alden B. Dow Museum of Science & Art, Alden B. Dow Museum School, Midland MI (S)
Mersmann, Armin, *Museum School Mgr,* Midland Center for the Arts, Alden B Dow Museum of Science & Art, Midland MI
Mersmann, Armin, *Studio School Coordr & Registrar,* Arts Midland Galleries & School, Midland MI
Mesa-Gaido, Elisabeth, *Prof,* Morehead State University, Art & Design Dept, Morehead KY (S)
Mesa-Gaido, Gary, *Prof,* Morehead State University, Art & Design Dept, Morehead KY (S)
Meserve, Lauren, *Sr VPres & Chief Investment Officer,* The Metropolitan Museum of Art, New York NY
Mesquita, Thomas, *Registrar & Image Svcs,* Norman Rockwell Museum, Stockbridge MA
Messec, Don, *Asst Prof,* College of Santa Fe, Art Dept, Santa Fe NM (S)
Messer, James, *Instr,* Mitchell Community College, Visual Art Dept, Statesville NC (S)
Messer, Jennifer, *Asst to Dir,* Sweetwater County Library System and School District #1, Community Fine Arts Center, Rock Springs WY

Messersmith, Mark, *Prof,* Florida State University, Art Dept, Tallahassee FL (S)
Messimer, Susan, *Cur Community Life,* Landis Valley Village and Farm Museum, PA Historical & Museum Commission, Lancaster PA
Messina, Mitchell, *Assoc Prof,* Nazareth College of Rochester, Art Dept, Rochester NY (S)
Messinger, Faye, *Librn,* Monterey History & Art Association, Library, Monterey CA
Messman-Mandicott, Lea, *Dir,* Frostburg State University, Lewis J Ort Library, Frostburg MD
Metcalf, D, *Librn Asst,* Fort Worth Public Library Arts & Humanities, Fine Arts Section, Fort Worth TX
Metcalf, Jack, *Dir,* University of Montana, Gallery of Visual Arts, Missoula MT
Metcalf, Michael, *Prof,* Western New Mexico University, Expressive Arts Dept, Silver City NM (S)
Metcalf, Preston, *Chief Cur,* Triton Museum of Art, Santa Clara CA
Metcalf, Susan E, *Cur,* Miracle at Pentecost Foundation, Biblical Arts Center, Dallas TX
Metcalfe, Robin, *Dir & Cur,* St Mary's University, Art Gallery, Halifax NS
Metcoff, Donald, *Chicago Representative,* American Society of Artists, Inc, Palatine IL
Metcoff, Donald, *Librn,* American Society of Artists, Inc, Library Organization, Palatine IL
Metoyer, Priscilla, *Curriculum Specialist,* The Multicultural Center of the South, Shreveport LA
Metrou, Wendy, *Dir Media & Film Relations,* Ford Motor Company, Henry Ford Museum & Greenfield Village, Dearborn MI
Mettala, Teri, *Dir,* Ojai Art Center, Ojai CA
Mette, Alan T, *Exec Assoc Dir, Prof,* University of Illinois, Urbana-Champaign, School of Art & Design, Champaign IL (S)
Mettler, Bonnie, *Instr,* Main Line Art Center, Haverford PA (S)
Mettler, Bonnie, *Instr,* Wayne Art Center, Wayne PA (S)
Metz, Diane, *Secy,* San Bernardino Valley College, Art Dept, San Bernardino CA (S)
Metz, Don, *Assoc Dir,* Burchfield Penney Art Center, Buffalo NY
Metz, Katy, *Adult Prog Coordr,* City of Irvine, Irvine Fine Arts Center, Irvine CA
Metzen, Greg, *Chmn,* Ellsworth Community College, Dept of Fine Arts, Iowa Falls IA (S)
Metzler, Sue, *Dir Develop,* Oregon Historical Society, Oregon History Museum, Portland OR
Meunier, Brian A, *Prof,* Swarthmore College, Dept of Art & Art History, Swarthmore PA (S)
Meunier, Élisabeth, *Cur,* Musee des Maitres et Artisans du Quebec, Montreal QC
Meurer, John, *VPres Admis,* Rocky Mountain College of Art & Design, Lakewood CO (S)
Mew, T J, *Prof Art,* Berry College, Memorial Library, Mount Berry GA
Mey, Andree, *Cur Coll,* Lehigh Valley Heritage Center, Allentown PA
Meyer Ernst, Renee, *Asst Prof Art,* Saint Ambrose University, Art Dept, Davenport IA (S)
Meyer, Diane, *Asst Prof,* Loyola Marymount University, Dept of Art & Art History, Los Angeles CA (S)
Meyer, Elizabeth, *Vis Reference Librn,* University of Cincinnati, Visual Resource Center, Cincinnati OH
Meyer, Elizabeth, *Visual Resources Librn,* University of Cincinnati, Robert A. Deshon and Karl J. Schlachter Library for Design, Architecture, Art, and Planning, Cincinnati OH
Meyer, Ellen L, *Pres,* Watkins College of Art, Design & Film, Nashville TN (S)
Meyer, Ellen, *Instr,* Edgewood College, Art Dept, Madison WI (S)
Meyer, Jaymie, *Dir Educ,* Green Hill Center for North Carolina Art, Greenhill, Greensboro NC
Meyer, Joseph, *Farm & Garden Mgr,* Landis Valley Village and Farm Museum, PA Historical & Museum Commission, Lancaster PA
Meyer, Kate, *Cur, Works on Paper,* University of Kansas, Spencer Museum of Art, Lawrence KS
Meyer, Nancy, *Instr,* California State University, Chico, Department of Art & Art History, Chico CA (S)
Meyer, Norman, *Instr,* Clark-Atlanta University, School of Arts & Sciences, Atlanta GA (S)
Meyer, Rachel, *Dir,* Palo Alto Junior Museum & Zoo, Palo Alto CA
Meyer, Sarah, *Prof,* California State Polytechnic University, Pomona, Department of Art, Pomona CA (S)
Meyer, Susan, *Asst Prof,* The College of Saint Rose, The Center For Art and Design, Albany NY (S)
Meyer, Susan, *Dir Finance,* Indianapolis Art Center, Marilyn K. Glick School of Art, Indianapolis IN
Meyer, Susan, *Lectr Foundations,* University of Denver, School of Art & Art History, Denver CO (S)
Meyerer, Kim, *Designer & Digital Facility,* Center for Exploratory & Perceptual Art, CEPA Library, Buffalo NY
Meyers, Amy, *Dir,* Yale University, Yale Center for British Art, New Haven CT
Meyers, Buzz, *Pres,* Spectrum Gallery, Toledo OH
Meyers, Carole J, *Pres,* American Color Print Society, Narberth PA
Meyers, Christine, *Chief Develop & Corporate Rels Officer,* National Gallery of Art, Washington DC
Meyers, Gifford C, *Prof Ceramic Sculpture,* University of California, Irvine, Studio Art Dept, Irvine CA (S)
Meyers, Jill, *Exec Dir,* Triton Museum of Art, Santa Clara CA
Meyers, Kenneth, *Cur American Art,* Detroit Institute of Arts, Detroit MI
Meyers, Peggy, *Treas,* Northwest Watercolor Society, Woodinville WA
Meyers, Rebecca, *Permanent Coll Cur,* National Museum of Mexican Art, Chicago IL
Meyrick, Charles, *Instr,* Art Center Sarasota, Sarasota FL (S)
Meza, Alberto, *Prof,* Miami-Dade Community College, Arts & Philosophy Dept, Miami FL (S)
Mezguida, Pavlova, *Supvr Educ Guides,* Museo de las Americas, Viejo San Juan PR
Mhiripiri, John, *Dir,* Anthology Film Archives, New York NY
Mhiripiri, Julie, *Co-Owner,* Mhiripiri Gallery, Bloomington MN
Mhiripiri, Rex, *Co-Owner,* Mhiripiri Gallery, Bloomington MN
Micas, Nieves, *Assoc Prof,* New York Institute of Technology, Fine Arts Dept, Old Westbury NY (S)
Michael, Ronald, *Dir,* Birger Sandzen Memorial Gallery, Lindsborg KS
Michael, Simon, *Head Dept,* Simon Michael, Lena MS (S)
Michaels, Bonni-Dara, *Cur & Registrar,* Yeshiva University Museum, New York NY
Michaels, Kathleen, *Office Mgr,* Millicent Rogers Museum, Taos NM
Michaelson, Alan, *Librn,* University of Washington, Architecture-Urban Planning Library, Seattle WA
Michalak, Kyle, *Dir Gallery,* Firelands Association for the Visual Arts, Oberlin OH
Michalak, Shannon, *Visual Resource Cur,* Wright State University, Visual Resources Center, Department of Art & Art History, Dayton OH
Michalczyk, John, *Chmn,* Boston College, Fine Arts Dept, Chestnut Hill MA (S)
Michaud, Bronson, *Cur Colls,* Old Colony Historical Society, Museum, Taunton MA
Michaud, Ronald, *Chmn Dept,* University of Massachusetts, Amherst, College of Arts & Sciences, Fine Arts Center, Amherst MA (S)
Michaud, Ronald, *Dir,* University of Massachusetts, Amherst, Art History Program, Amherst MA (S)
Michel, Barbara, *Gallery Dir,* Huntington University, Robert E Wilson Art Gallery, Huntington IN
Michel, Bill, *Dir,* University of Chicago, Reva and David Logan Center for the Arts, Chicago IL
Michels, Dana, *Assoc Cur,* Iowa State University, Brunnier Art Museum, Ames IA
Michels, Tatiana, *Mktg,* Delaware Center for the Contemporary Arts, Wilmington DE
Mickelson, Duane, *Prof,* Concordia College, Art Dept, Moorhead MN (S)
Mickenberg, David, *Dir,* Wellesley College, Davis Museum & Cultural Center, Wellesley MA
Mickenberg, David, *Exec Dir,* Taubman Museum of Art, Roanoke VA
Mickenberg, David, *Pres & CEO,* Allentown Art Museum, Allentown PA
Mickey, Hollis, *Dir Learning & Engagement,* Anchorage Museum at Rasmuson Center, Anchorage AK
Mickie, Jima, *Instr,* Williams Baptist College, Dept of Art, Walnut Ridge AR (S)
Mickle, Katherine, *Prof,* Slippery Rock University of Pennsylvania, Dept of Art, Slippery Rock PA (S)
Middlemas, Vicki, *Exec Dir,* Visual Arts Center of Northwest Florida, Panama City FL
Middleswarth, Vicky, *Educ,* Liberty Hall Historic Site, Liberty Hall Museum, Frankfort KY
Middleton, Alexandra, *Director of Sales & Special Events,* The Museum of Arts & Sciences Inc, Daytona Beach FL
Midgett, Corinne, *Registrar,* City of High Point, High Point Museum, High Point NC
Midgett, Ed, *Assoc Prof,* Appalachian State University, Dept of Art, Boone NC (S)
Midgette, Dameron, *Exec Dir,* Roswell Artist-in-Residence Foundation, Anderson Museum of Contemporary Art, Roswell NM
Midkiff, David, *Chmn,* Williams Baptist College, Dept of Art, Walnut Ridge AR (S)
Mieczinkowski, Richard, *Chmn Dept,* California University of Pennsylvania, Dept of Art, California PA (S)
Miele Holt, Madeline, *Asst Dir,* Ames Free-Easton's Public Library, North Easton MA
Mierse, William E, *Chmn,* University of Vermont, Dept of Art, Burlington VT (S)
Migliaccio, Tony, *Board of Dirs & VPres,* Guild of Creative Art, Shrewsbury NJ (S)
Migliori, Larry, *Head Dept,* Mohawk Valley Community College, Utica NY (S)
Mihaly, Sara, *Circ & Student Supvr,* University of Cincinnati, Robert A. Deshon and Karl J. Schlachter Library for Design, Architecture, Art, and Planning, Cincinnati OH
Mika, Megan, *Dir Special Events,* Delaware Center for the Contemporary Arts, Wilmington DE
Mikami, Lynn, *VPres,* The Society of Layerists in Multi-Media (SLMM), Albuquerque NM
Mikelson, Arnold, *Mgr,* Arnold Mikelson Mind & Matter Art Gallery, Surrey BC
Mikelson, Mary, *Pres,* Arnold Mikelson Mind & Matter Art Gallery, Surrey BC
Mikelson, Myra, *Asst Dir,* Arnold Mikelson Mind & Matter Art Gallery, Surrey BC
Mikelson, Sapphire, *Asst Mgr,* Arnold Mikelson Mind & Matter Art Gallery, Surrey BC
Mikkelson, Rick, *Chmn,* State University of New York at Plattsburgh, Art Dept, Plattsburgh NY (S)
Miklas, Lois, *Pub Programs Mgr,* Hershey Museum, Hershey PA
Mikle, Tricia, *Pres,* Nobles County Art Center, Worthington MN
Mikolajczak, Jeremy, *CEO,* Tucson Museum of Art and Historic Block, Tucson AZ
Mikos, Adam, *Facilities & Gallery Mgr,* The Arts Club of Chicago, Chicago IL
Milad, Jackie, *Cur & Coordr,* University of Maryland, College Park, Stamp Gallery, College Park MD
Milakovich, Jeannie, *Chmn,* Gogebic Community College, Fine Arts Dept, Ironwood MI (S)
Milanesi, Betty, *Asst Librn,* Williams College, Sawyer Library, Williamstown MA
Milanowski, Stephanie, *Asst Prof,* Hope College, Dept of Art & Art History, Holland MI (S)
Mileaf, Janine, *Assoc Prof,* Swarthmore College, Dept of Art & Art History, Swarthmore PA (S)
Mileaf, Janine, *Exec Dir,* The Arts Club of Chicago, Chicago IL
Miles, Carolyn, *Dir,* Atrium Gallery, Saint Louis MO

Miles, Christine M, *Dir,* Albany Institute of History & Art, Albany NY
Miles, David, *Prof,* Ohio University-Eastern Campus, Dept Comparative Arts, Saint Clairsville OH (S)
Miles, Emily, *Communs Mgr,* Kentucky Museum of Art and Craft, Louisville KY
Miles, Jenna, *Gallery Mgr,* Metropolitan State University of Denver, Center for Visual Art, Denver CO
Miles, Kim, *Admin Asst,* Frontier Times Museum, Bandera TX
Miles, Michaela, *Vis Servs Mgr,* The University of Kentucky Art Museum, Lexington KY
Miletic-Vejzovic, Laila, *Head Spec Coll,* University of Central Florida Libraries, Orlando FL
Miley, E J, *Chmn,* Lincoln College, Art Dept, Lincoln IL (S)
Miley, Karen, *Instr Painting & Design,* Lincoln College, Art Dept, Lincoln IL (S)
Miley, Randy B, *Head Art Dept,* Mississippi College, Art Dept, Clinton MS (S)
Milford, Mary-Ann, *Prof,* Mills College, Art Dept, Oakland CA (S)
Milholland, Valerie, *Instr,* University of Evansville, Art Dept, Evansville IN (S)
Milillu, Joey, *Prog Mgr,* Museum of Fine Arts Houston, Bayou Bend Collection & Gardens, Houston TX
Milio, Marcella, *Cur Textile & Costume Coll,* Philadelphia University, Paley Design Center, Philadelphia PA
Milkie, Jane, *Asst Prof,* Northern Michigan University, Dept of Art & Design, Marquette MI (S)
Milkofsky, Brenda, *Dir,* Wethersfield Historical Society Inc, Museum, Wethersfield CT
Milkova, Liliana, *Cur Acad Progs,* Oberlin College, Allen Memorial Art Museum, Oberlin OH
Mill, Cheryl, *Office Mgr,* Phelps County Historical Society, Donald O. Lindgren Library, Holdrege NE
Millan, Bruce E, *Dir,* Detroit Repertory Theatre Gallery, Detroit MI
Millan, Jacqueline R, *Dir Art Prog,* PepsiCo Inc, Donald M Kendall Sculpture Garden, Purchase NY
Millar, Joyce, *Dir Art Gallery,* Pointe Claire Cultural Centre, Stewart Hall Art Gallery, Pointe Claire QC
Millar, Sara, *VPres Horticulture & Conservation,* Brookgreen Gardens, Murrells Inlet SC
Millard, Larry, *Prof Sculpture,* University of Georgia, Franklin College of Arts & Sciences, Lamar Dodd School of Art, Athens GA (S)
Millard, Lee S, *Gallery Assoc,* Bloomsburg University of Pennsylvania, Haas Gallery of Art, Bloomsburg PA
Millard, Sandra, *Asst Dir Library Pub Serv,* University of Delaware, Morris Library, Newark DE
Millard-Mendez, Robert, *Assoc Prof,* University of Southern Indiana, Art & Design Dept, Evansville IN (S)
Millarson, Lucille, *Mus Shop Mgr,* New York State Military Museum and Veterans Research Center, Saratoga Springs NY
Milledge, Cynthia, *Dir Mktg & Pub Rels,* Montgomery Museum of Fine Arts, Montgomery AL
Milledge, Cynthia, *Dirk Mktg & Pub Relations,* Montgomery Museum of Fine Arts, Library, Montgomery AL
Miller Altman, Apryl, *VPres & Artistic Dir,* Williamsburg Contemporary Art Center, Williamsburg VA
Miller, Aaron, *Asst Cur Visual & Material Culture,* Mount Holyoke College, Art Museum, South Hadley MA
Miller, Adria, *Develop Dir,* Galerie Montcalm, Gatineau QC
Miller, Alexis, *Chief Paintings Conservator,* Balboa Art Conservation Center, San Diego CA
Miller, Allison, *Asst Prof,* Southwestern University, Sarofim School of Fine Art, Dept of Art & Art History, Georgetown TX (S)
Miller, Amy, *Museum Shop Mgr,* University of Georgia, Georgia Museum of Art, Athens GA
Miller, Andrea, *Asst Mus Shop Mgr,* South Shore Arts, Munster IN
Miller, Anelle, *Dir,* Society of Illustrators, Museum of American Illustration, New York NY
Miller, Barbara, *Prof Art History,* Eastern Washington University, Dept of Art, Cheney WA (S)
Miller, C Cameron, *Treas,* Inter-Society Color Council, Frederick MD
Miller, Cary Beth, *Instr & Dir Gen Educ & BA Prog,* Watkins College of Art, Design & Film, Nashville TN (S)
Miller, Chris, *Assoc Prof,* Judson University, School of Art, Design & Architecture, Elgin IL (S)
Miller, Christine, *Assoc Prof,* Mohawk Valley Community College, Utica NY (S)
Miller, Darren Lee, *Gallery Dir,* Allegheny College, Bowman, Megahan & Penelec Galleries, Meadville PA
Miller, Deanna, *VPres,* Searchlight Historic Museum & Mining Park, Searchlight NV
Miller, Debra, *Dir Visual Art & Educ,* ArtsQuest, Bethlehem PA
Miller, Dennis, *Prof,* University of Wisconsin, Madison, Dept of Art, Madison WI (S)
Miller, Edward C, *Assoc Prof,* Rochester Institute of Technology, School of Design, Rochester NY (S)
Miller, Eric Rhys, *Exec Dir,* Community Arts Council of Vancouver, Vancouver BC
Miller, Ethelbert, *Pres,* Provisions Library, Provisions Research Center for Arts & Social Change, Fairfax VA
Miller, Fayette, *Cur,* Frontier Gateway Museum, Glendive MT
Miller, Fred, *Vis Asst Prof,* University of Texas at Arlington, Art & Art History Department, Arlington TX (S)
Miller, G Chris, *Photog,* Art Institute of Pittsburgh, Pittsburgh PA (S)
Miller, George, *Dir,* California State University, East Bay, C E Smith Museum of Anthropology, Hayward CA
Miller, Glen, *Asst Prof,* Rochester Institute of Technology, School of Photographic Arts & Sciences, Rochester NY (S)
Miller, Greg, *Asst Prof,* Mount Mary College, Art & Design Division, Milwaukee WI (S)
Miller, Gregory, *Pres,* White Columns, White Columns Curated Artist Registry, New York NY
Miller, Gretchen, *Exec Dir,* Butte Silver Bow Arts Foundation, Butte MT
Miller, J Robert, *Prof,* McMurry University, Art Dept, Abilene TX (S)
Miller, James, *Studio Dir & Master Printer,* Lower East Side Printshop Inc, New York NY (S)
Miller, Jason, *Mus Media Specialist,* University of Memphis, Art Museum, Memphis TN
Miller, Jean, *Secy,* Sonoma Valley Historical Society, Depot Park Museum, Sonoma CA
Miller, Jo Anne, *Mus Store Mgr,* Vero Beach Museum of Art, Vero Beach FL
Miller, Jo, *Treas,* Sonoma Valley Historical Society, Depot Park Museum, Sonoma CA
Miller, Joan, *Mus Shop Mgr & Mus Asst,* Big Horn County Historical Museum, Hardin MT
Miller, Joanna, *Educ,* Kentucky Museum of Art and Craft, Louisville KY
Miller, Joanna, *Membership & Events,* Asheville Art Museum, Asheville NC
Miller, John M, *Photog Dept Head,* Johnson State College, Dept Fine & Performing Arts, Dibden Center for the Arts, Johnson VT (S)
Miller, John, *Dir,* North Dakota State University, Division of Fine Arts, Fargo ND (S)
Miller, Joseph E, *Dir,* Viterbo University, Art Gallery, La Crosse WI
Miller, Joyce, *Ceramics Prof,* Mount Wachusett Community College, East Wing Gallery, Gardner MA
Miller, Karen, *Admin Asst,* Lafayette Science Museum & Planetarium, Lafayette LA
Miller, Kathryn, *Drawing,* Pitzer College, Dept of Art, Claremont CA (S)
Miller, Kevin R, *Dir,* Daytona State College, Southeast Museum of Photography, Daytona Beach FL
Miller, Kevin, *Exec Dir,* Thelma Sadoff Center for the Arts, Fond Du Lac WI
Miller, Kimberly, *Asst Prof,* Transylvania University, Art Program, Lexington KY (S)
Miller, Kitty, *Asst Prof,* Graceland University, Fine Arts Div, Lamoni IA (S)
Miller, Laurette, *FOIP Officer,* Royal Alberta Museum, Provincial Archives of Alberta, Edmonton AB
Miller, Lenore D, *Dir & Chief Cur,* The George Washington University, Luther W Brady Art Gallery, Washington DC
Miller, Linda, *Graphic Design,* Art Institute of Pittsburgh, Pittsburgh PA (S)
Miller, Linda, *VPres,* Contemporary Art Center, Peoria IL
Miller, Lynda, *Lectr,* Washburn University of Topeka, Dept of Art, Topeka KS (S)
Miller, Lynette, *Cur Art,* Washington State Historical Society, Research Center, Tacoma WA
Miller, Lynn, *Office Mgr,* Galesburg Civic Art Center, Galesburg IL
Miller, Marcus, *Dir,* University of Saskatchewan, Gordon Snelgrove Art Gallery, Saskatoon SK
Miller, Margaret A, *Dir,* University of South Florida, Contemporary Art Museum, Tampa FL
Miller, Marie Celeste, *Prof,* Aquinas College, Art Dept, Grand Rapids MI (S)
Miller, Marilyn, *Dir Budget,* California Watercolor Association, Gallery Concord, Concord CA
Miller, Marlene, *Instr,* Bucks County Community College, Fine Arts Dept, Newtown PA (S)
Miller, Mary Jane, *Acting Registrar,* Pennsylvania Historical & Museum Commission, The State Museum of Pennsylvania, Harrisburg PA
Miller, Mary Jane, *Colls Mgr,* Pennsylvania Historical & Museum Commission, The State Museum of Pennsylvania, Harrisburg PA
Miller, Mary, *Instr,* Oklahoma State University Institute of Technology, School of Visual Communications, Okmulgee OK (S)
Miller, Mathew, *Cur,* Deines Cultural Center, Russell KS
Miller, Merceds Santos, *Mus Mgr,* Caramoor Center for Music & the Arts, Inc, Rosen House at Caramoor, Katonah NY
Miller, Michael D, *Head Librn & Dir Arts & Engineering Librs,* University of Michigan, Media Union Library, Ann Arbor MI
Miller, Michael, *Coordr Grad Progs & Instr Painting,* Texas A&M University Commerce, Dept of Art, Commerce TX (S)
Miller, Monica, *Asst Dir,* Gallery One Visual Arts Center, Ellensburg WA
Miller, Olivia, *Cur Exhibs & Educ,* University of Arizona, Museum of Art & Archive of Visual Arts, Tucson AZ
Miller, Pamela, *Dir Programs,* California Watercolor Association, Gallery Concord, Concord CA
Miller, Patrick, *Assoc Prof,* Mississippi State University, Dept of Art, Starville MS (S)
Miller, Patrick, *Graphic Design,* University of South Alabama, Dept of Art & Art History, Mobile AL (S)
Miller, Penelope, *Art Adjunct,* Des Moines Area Community College, Art Dept, Boone IA (S)
Miller, Randall, *Webmaster,* Art Association of Harrisburg, School & Galleries, Harrisburg PA
Miller, Remy, *Acad Dean & Div Chair Foundation,* Memphis College of Art, Memphis TN (S)
Miller, Remy, *Div Chair Foundations,* Memphis College of Art, Memphis TN (S)
Miller, Richard H, *Preparator,* Williams College, Museum of Art, Williamstown MA
Miller, Rob, *Lectr,* University of Wisconsin-Parkside, Art Dept, Kenosha WI (S)
Miller, Robert A, *Gallery Dir,* Rio Hondo College Art Gallery, Whittier CA
Miller, Robert B, *Vis Lect,* Lewis & Clark College, Dept of Art, Portland OR (S)
Miller, Robert, *Instr Ceramics & Gallery Dir,* Rio Hondo College, Arts & Cultural Programs Dept, Whittier CA (S)

Miller, Roland, *Photog,* College of Lake County, Art Dept, Grayslake IL (S)
Miller, Ronald A, *Graphic Design,* Art Institute of Pittsburgh, Pittsburgh PA (S)
Miller, Sally, *Adj Instr,* University of West Florida, Dept of Art, Pensacola FL (S)
Miller, Sean, *Asst Prof,* University of Florida, School of Art & Art History, Gainesville FL (S)
Miller, Stephen S, *Dir,* Landis Valley Village and Farm Museum, PA Historical & Museum Commission, Lancaster PA
Miller, Steve, *Assoc Prof,* Palomar Community College, Art Dept, San Marcos CA (S)
Miller, Tami, *Dir Exhibs & Colls,* Krasl Art Center, Saint Joseph MI
Miller, Tricia, *Head Registrar,* University of Georgia, Georgia Museum of Art, Athens GA
Miller, Ty, *Sr Curatorial Specialist,* Northern Arizona University, Art Museum & Galleries, Flagstaff AZ
Miller, Valerie, *Cur of Colls,* Red Deer & District Museum & Archives, Red Deer AB
Miller, Wendell, *VPres,* Zigler Art Museum, Jennings LA
Millet, Cristin, *Asst Prof Art (Sculpture),* Pennsylvania State University, University Park, Penn State School of Visual Arts, University Park PA (S)
Millette, Andrea, *Acad Dean,* Antonelli College, Cincinnati OH (S)
Milligan, Frank D, *CEO,* Nantucket Historical Association, Historic Nantucket, Nantucket MA
Milligan, Kayla, *Registrar,* Society for Photographic Education (SPE), SPE Gallery, Cleveland OH
Milliken, Aldy, *Exec Dir,* Kentucky Museum of Art and Craft, Louisville KY
Millin, Laura, *Exec Dir,* Missoula Art Museum, Missoula MT
Milliron, Dena, *Cur Educ,* i.d.e.a. Museum, Mesa AZ
Mills, Beth, *Head Reference,* New Rochelle Public Library, Art Section, New Rochelle NY
Mills, Connie, *Libr Coordr,* Western Kentucky University, Kentucky Library & Museum, Bowling Green KY
Mills, Cynthia K, *VP Progs,* Birmingham Bloomfield Art Center, Art Center, Birmingham MI
Mills, Cynthia, *VPres Programs,* Birmingham Bloomfield Art Center, Birmingham MI (S)
Mills, Dan, *Dir,* Bates College, Museum of Art, Lewiston ME
Mills, Emmy, *Admin Asst,* Arts Midland Galleries & School, Midland MI
Mills, Emmy, *Bus & Opers Mgr,* Midland Center for the Arts, Alden B Dow Museum of Science & Art, Midland MI
Mills, Josephine, *Dir & Cur,* University of Lethbridge, Art Gallery, Lethbridge AB
Mills, Kelly, *Instr,* Avila College, Art Division, Dept of Humanities, Kansas City MO (S)
Mills, Kristi, *Dir Finance,* Montana State University, Museum of the Rockies, Bozeman MT
Mills, Lea, *Dean,* College of the Redwoods, Arts & Languages Dept Division, Eureka CA (S)
Mills, Mary Cheek, *Educ Progs Mgr,* Corning Museum of Glass, The Studio, Corning NY
Mills, Richard, *Asst Prof,* C W Post Campus of Long Island University, School of Visual & Performing Arts, Brookville NY (S)
Mills, Ron, *Prof,* Linfield College, Department of Art & Visual Culture, McMinnville OR (S)
Millsap, Gina, *Exec Dir,* Topeka & Shawnee County Public Library, Alice C Sabatini Gallery, Topeka KS
Milne, Joseph W, *Graphic Design & Digital Design,* Art Institute of Pittsburgh, Pittsburgh PA (S)
Milner, Jay, *Mus Preparator,* Asheville Art Museum, Asheville NC
Milosevich, Joe B, *Prof of Art Gallery Dir,* Joliet Junior College, Laura A Sprague Art Gallery, Joliet IL
Milosevich, Joe, *Instr,* Joliet Junior College, Fine Arts Dept, Joliet IL (S)
Milot, Barbara, *Prof,* Framingham State College, Art Dept, Framingham MA (S)
Milroy, Elizabeth, *Assoc Prof, Dir,* Wesleyan University, Dept of Art & Art History, Middletown CT (S)
Milstead, Leslie, *Exec Asst,* Grand Rapids Public Museum, Grand Rapids MI
Milukas, Kelly, *Pres,* Providence Art Club, Providence RI
Mimlitsch-Gray, Myra, *Chmn Art Studio & Art Educ,* State University of New York at New Paltz, Art Education Program, New Paltz NY (S)
Min, Yong Soon, *Prof Asian American Studies,* University of California, Irvine, Studio Art Dept, Irvine CA (S)
Minchin, Edward, *Instr,* Art Center Sarasota, Sarasota FL (S)
Mindlin, Beth, *Recording Secy,* Halifax Historical Society, Inc, Halifax Historical Museum, Daytona Beach FL
Mineau, Ted, *Dir Tours Prog,* Municipal Art Society of New York, New York NY
Minegar, Dawn, *Registrar,* Laguna Art Museum, Laguna Beach CA
Miner, Curt, *Acting Cur,* Pennsylvania Historical & Museum Commission, The State Museum of Pennsylvania, Harrisburg PA
Minet, Cynthia, *Asst Prof,* Antelope Valley College, Art Dept, Division of Fine Arts, Lancaster CA (S)
Minglu, Gao, *Assoc Prof,* University of Pittsburgh, Henry Clay Frick Dept History of Art & Architecture, Pittsburgh PA (S)
Mingst, Raymond E, *Dir,* Curious Matter, Jersey City NJ
Minikes, Cheryl, *1st VChmn,* Guild Hall of East Hampton, Inc, Guild Hall Museum, East Hampton NY
Mink, Pat, *Assoc Prof,* East Tennessee State University, College of Arts and Sciences, Dept of Art & Design, Johnson City TN (S)
Minkkinen, Arno, *Prof,* University of Massachusetts Lowell, Dept of Art, Lowell MA (S)
Minkowski, Lenka, *Bookstore/Archive Mgr,* Beyond Baroque Foundation, Beyond Baroque Literary Arts Center, Venice CA
Minks, Ronald, *Co-Dir Gallery,* Mississippi Valley State University, Fine Arts Dept, Itta Bena MS (S)
Minnaert, Sarah, *Deputy Dir,* Carnegie Museums of Pittsburgh, Carnegie Museum of Art, Pittsburgh PA
Minogue, Eileen, *Asst Dir,* Northport-East Northport Public Library, Northport NY
Minogue, Nancy, *Admin & Prog Specialist,* Northern Virginia Community College, Art Dept, Annandale VA (S)
Minor Harris, DeLisa, *Reference Librn Spec Colls,* Fisk University, Library, North Nashville TN
Mintich, Mary, *Prof,* Winthrop University, Dept of Art & Design, Rock Hill SC (S)
Minton, Randy, *Instr,* Hinds Community College, Dept of Art, Raymond MS (S)
Mintz, Ally, *Exhibitions & Publications Mgr.,* New York University, Grey Art Gallery, New York NY
Mintz, Deborah, *Exec Dir,* Arts Council of Fayetteville-Cumberland County, The Arts Center, Fayetteville NC
Miraglia, Anthony J, *Chmn Fine Art,* University of Massachusetts Dartmouth, College of Visual & Performing Arts, North Dartmouth MA (S)
Miranda, Valeria, *Exec Dir,* Santa Cruz Art League, Center for the Arts, Santa Cruz CA
Mirch, Kijeong Jeon, *Prof,* California State University, Chico, Department of Art & Art History, Chico CA (S)
Mirensky, Gabriela, *Dir Awards & Design,* The One Club for Creativity, New York NY
Mirkovic, Zeljko, *Instructor of Visual and Communication Arts,* Eastern Mennonite University, Visual and Communication Arts, Harrisonburg VA (S)
Mirrer, Louise, *Pres & CEO,* New-York Historical Society, Museum, New York NY
Misegadis, Lois, *Head Dept,* Hesston College, Art Dept, Hesston KS (S)
Mishler, John, *Asst Prof,* Goshen College, Art Dept, Goshen IN (S)
Mishne, Merle, *Pres & Dir,* Portholes Into the Past, Medina OH
Misite, Phyllis, *School Dir,* Mount Ida College, Chamberlayne School of Design & Merchandising, Boston MA (S)
Missal, Paul, *Instr,* Pacific Northwest College of Art, Portland OR (S)
Misterka, Halina, *Head Archivist,* Polish Museum of America (PMA), Chicago IL
Mistick, Barbara K, *Pres & Dir,* Carnegie Museums of Pittsburgh, Carnegie Library of Pittsburgh, Pittsburgh PA
Mistrovich, Joyce, *Dir Educ,* The Butler Institute of American Art, Art Museum, Youngstown OH
Mitas, William R, *Industrial Design Technology,* Art Institute of Pittsburgh, Pittsburgh PA (S)
Mitchell, Andrew, *Music Counsellor,* McMaster University, School of the Arts, Hamilton ON (S)
Mitchell, Ann, *Dept Chmn,* Long Beach City College, Art & Photography Dept, Long Beach CA (S)
Mitchell, Beverly, *Art Librn,* Southern Methodist University, Hamon Arts Library, Dallas TX
Mitchell, Brenda, *Assoc Prof,* Indiana University of Pennsylvania, College of Fine Arts, Indiana PA (S)
Mitchell, Cheryl, *Admin Asst,* Anderson Fine Arts Center, The Anderson Center for the Arts, Anderson IN
Mitchell, Cynthia, *Asst Librn,* Thomas College, Mariner Library, Waterville ME
Mitchell, Deb, *Educ,* Montana Historical Society, Helena MT
Mitchell, Diana, *Pres,* DuPage Art League School & Gallery, Wheaton IL
Mitchell, Dori, *Dir Communs & Mktg,* Colorado Springs Fine Arts Center, Taylor Museum, Colorado Springs CO
Mitchell, Elliott, *Instr,* Greenfield Community College, Art Dept, Greenfield MA (S)
Mitchell, Heather, *Exec Dir,* New Hampshire Antiquarian Society, Hopkinton Historical Society, Hopkinton NH
Mitchell, Joseph, *Adjunct Prof Art,* Florida Southern College, Melvin Art Gallery, Lakeland FL
Mitchell, Joseph, *Adjunct Prof Art,* Florida Southern College, Department of Art & Art History, Lakeland FL (S)
Mitchell, Kathryn, *Cur Educ,* Grace Museum, Inc, The Grace Museum, Abilene TX
Mitchell, Lois, *Treas,* Alton Museum of History & Art, Inc, Alton IL
Mitchell, Mark, *Cur American Painting & Sculpture,* Yale University, Yale University Art Gallery, New Haven CT
Mitchell, Meg, *Asst Prof,* University of Wisconsin, Madison, Dept of Art, Madison WI (S)
Mitchell, Michelle, *Gallery Coordr,* The APEX Museum, Atlanta GA
Mitchell, Nancy, *Instr,* Sinclair Community College, Division of Fine & Performing Arts, Dayton OH (S)
Mitchell, Shannon, *Instr,* University of Arkansas, Art Dept, Fayetteville AR (S)
Mitchell, Starr, *Dir Educ,* Historic Arkansas Museum, Little Rock AR
Mitchell, Starr, *Educ Dir,* Historic Arkansas Museum, Library, Little Rock AR
Mitchell, Suzanne, *Prof Emeritus,* University of Louisville, Allen R Hite Art Institute, Louisville KY (S)
Mitchell, Teresa, *Mus Mgr,* Lac du Flambeau Band of Lake Superior Chippewa Indians, George W Brown Jr Ojibwe Museum & Cultural Center, Lac Du Flambeau WI
Mitchell, William J, *Dean,* Massachusetts Institute of Technology, School of Architecture and Planning, Cambridge MA (S)
Mitro, Catherine, *Prog Dir, Jazz & Community Music,* Humber College, School of Creative & Performing Arts, Toronto ON (S)
Mitsu Shiba, Kristin, *Chmn Bd,* Haystack Mountain School of Crafts, Deer Isle ME

Mitten, David Gordon, *Cur Ancient Art,* Harvard University, Arthur M Sackler Museum, Cambridge MA

Mittenberg, Valerie, *Information Access,* State University of New York at New Paltz, Sojourner Truth Library, New Paltz NY

Mittenthal, Cherie, *Exec Dir,* Truro Center for the Arts at Castle Hill, Inc, Truro MA (S)

Mittman, Asa, *Assoc Prof,* California State University, Chico, Department of Art & Art History, Chico CA (S)

Mitton, Maureen, *Asst Prof,* University of Wisconsin-Stout, Dept of Art & Design, Menomonie WI (S)

Mixon, Jamie, *Prof,* Mississippi State University, Dept of Art, Starville MS (S)

Miyata, Masako, *Prof,* James Madison University, School of Art & Art History, Harrisonburg VA (S)

Miyata, Shigeto, *Remote Preparator,* Joseph Bellows Gallery, La Jolla CA

Miyata, Wayne A, *Faculty,* Kauai Community College, Dept of Art, Lihue HI (S)

Miyauchi, Alison, *Assoc VPres Research & Academic Affairs,* Alberta College of Art & Design, Calgary AB (S)

Mize, Julie, *Adjunct,* Howard Payne University, School of Fine Arts, Brownwood TX (S)

Mizel, Larry, *Chmn Bd,* Mizel Museum, Denver CO

Mladenoff, Nancy, *Prof,* University of Wisconsin, Madison, Dept of Art, Madison WI (S)

Mlotkowski, Jessica, *Librn Public Servs & Catalog,* Institute of American Indian Arts, College of Contemporary Native Arts Library and Archives, Santa Fe NM

Moak, Mark, *Chmn,* Rocky Mountain College, Art Dept, Billings MT (S)

Moazami, Emily, *Asst Head Archivist,* National Museum of the American Indian, Archive Center, Suitland MD

Mobbs, Leslie, *Dir,* Vancouver City Archives, Vancouver BC

Moberg, David, *Chmn Fine Arts,* Indian River Community College, Fine Arts Dept, Fort Pierce FL (S)

Moberly, Juanita, *Gallery Mgr,* Brown County Art Gallery Foundation, Nashville IN

Mobley Guenther, Amanda, *Cur,* Bone Creek Museum of Agrarian Art, David City NE

Mocilnikar, Gregory, *Instructional Support Technician,* University Art Gallery at California State University, Dominguez Hills, Carson CA

Mocko, Sarah, *Coordr Pub Programs,* Noah Webster House, Inc, Noah Webster House & West Hartford Historical Society, West Hartford CT

Moderegger, Hajoe, *DIAP MFA Prog Dir,* City College of New York, Art Dept, New York NY (S)

Modiano, Richard, *Exec Dir,* Beyond Baroque Foundation, Beyond Baroque Literary Arts Center, Venice CA

Modine, Austin, *Mktg & Pub Rels Assoc,* Boca Raton Museum of Art, Boca Raton FL

Modler, David, *Coordr Art Educ,* Shepherd University, Dept of Contemporary Art & Theater, Shepherdstown WV (S)

Modlin, Ruti, *Secy,* ARC Gallery and Educational Foundation, Chicago IL

Moe, Dawn, *Communs,* Plainsman Museum, Aurora NE

Moeller, Christian, *Dept Chmn,* University of California, Los Angeles, Dept of Design Media Arts, Los Angeles CA (S)

Moeller, Gary E, *Dir,* Rogers State College, Art Dept, Claremore OK (S)

Moffat, Constance, *Prof,* Pierce College, Art Dept, Woodland Hills CA (S)

Moffat, Martha, *Site Supvr,* Ryerss Victorian Museum & Library, Philadelphia PA

Moffatt, Bonnie, *Dir Admin,* South Carolina State Museum, Columbia SC

Moffit, Judy, *Art Hist Instr,* Grand Canyon University, Art Dept, Phoenix AZ (S)

Moffitt, Sally, *Admin Asst,* Oberlin College, Allen Memorial Art Museum, Oberlin OH

Mohan, Rajee, *Adjunct Prof Art History,* Johnson County Community College, Fine Arts Dept & Art History Dept, Overland Park KS (S)

Mohar, Karen, *Asst Librn,* Lourdes College, Duns Scotus Library, Sylvania OH

Mohivddin, Rouben, *Asst Prof,* California State University, Chico, Department of Art & Art History, Chico CA (S)

Mohr, Cynthia, *Chair, Dept Design,* University of North Texas, College of Visual Arts & Design, Denton TX (S)

Mohr, Lisa, *Art Coordr & Instr,* Carl Sandburg College, Galesburg IL (S)

Mohr, Melissa, *Dir Educ,* Figge Art Museum, Davenport IA

Mohsin, Mohammad, *Gallery Dir,* Saint John's University, Dept of Fine Arts, Jamaica NY (S)

Mohsin, Parvez, *Dir Gallery,* Saint John's University, Dr. M.T. Geoffrey Yeh Art Gallery, Queens NY

Moir, Lindsay, *Librn,* Glenbow Museum, Library, Calgary AB

Mojica, Francis J, *Dir,* Centro de Estudios Avanzados, Art Library, Old San Juan PR

Mokren, Jennifer, *Asst Prof,* University of Wisconsin-Green Bay, Arts Dept, Green Bay WI (S)

Molanphy, Brian, *Asst Prof,* Southern Methodist University, Meadows School of the Arts - Division of Art, Dallas TX (S)

Mold, David, *Prof Theatre & Chair Fine & Performing Arts,* Marymount Manhattan College, Fine & Performing Arts Div, New York NY (S)

Moldenhauer, Susan, *Dir & Chief Cur,* University of Wyoming, University of Wyoming Art Museum, Laramie WY

Molen, Jan, *Chmn & Dir,* Napa Valley College, Art Dept, Napa CA (S)

Moles, Kathleen, *Cur,* Museum of Northwest Art, La Conner WA

Moley, Mary Beth, *Art Instr,* Metropolitan Community College - Penn Valley, Art Dept, Kansas City MO (S)

Molife, Brenda, *Chmn,* Bridgewater State College, Art Dept, Bridgewater MA (S)

Molinaro, Anthony, *Dir, Music,* Loyola University of Chicago, Dept of Fine and Performing Arts, Chicago IL (S)

Mollett, David, *Dept Chmn & Assoc Prof,* University of Alaska Fairbanks, Art Department, Fairbanks AK (S)

Mollo, Arlene, *Chmn Art Educ,* University of Massachusetts Dartmouth, College of Visual & Performing Arts, North Dartmouth MA (S)

Molloy, Bryan, *Gallery Asst,* Art Association of Harrisburg, School & Galleries, Harrisburg PA

Molnar, Imre, *Acad Dean,* College for Creative Studies, Detroit MI (S)

Molnar, Mike, *Instr,* Luzerne County Community College, Commercial Art Dept, Nanticoke PA (S)

Molon, Dominic, *Cur Contemporary Art,* Rhode Island School of Design, Museum of Art, Providence RI

Moloney, Kate, *Exec Asst,* Pensacola Museum of Art, Pensacola FL

Moloshok, Rachel, *Ed,* Historical Society of Pennsylvania, Philadelphia PA

Mompho, Bo, *Registrar,* Wellesley College, Davis Museum & Cultural Center, Wellesley MA

Monaco, Theresa, *Chmn Art Dept,* Emmanuel College, Art Dept, Boston MA (S)

Monaco, Theresa, *Chmn Art Dept,* Emmanuel College, Art Dept, Boston MA (S)

Monahan, Casey, *Educ Asst,* Museum of Fine Arts, Houston, Rienzi Center for European Decorative Arts, Houston TX

Monahan, Rebekah, *Registrar,* Utah Valley University, Woodbury Art Museum, Orem UT

Monath, Marilyn, *Mktg & Develop,* Landis Valley Village and Farm Museum, PA Historical & Museum Commission, Lancaster PA

Monau, Steve, *Assoc Prof,* East Los Angeles College, Art Dept, Monterey Park CA (S)

Moncada, Cuauhtemoc, *Access Servs Asst,* University of California, Los Angeles, Arts Library, Los Angeles CA

Moncur, Shannon, *Chmn,* Moncur Gallery, Boissevain MB

Monday, Elden, *Pres,* The Art Institutes, The Art Institute of Seattle, Seattle WA (S)

Mondi, Annelies, *Deputy Dir,* University of Georgia, Georgia Museum of Art, Athens GA

Mondowney, Jo Anne, *Exec Dir,* Detroit Public Library, Art & Literature Dept, Detroit MI

Mondro, Anne, *Assoc Prof & Undergrad Prog Co-Dir,* University of Michigan, Ann Arbor, Penny W Stamps School of Art & Design, Ann Arbor MI (S)

Monenerkit, Marcus, *Dir Community Engagement,* Heard Museum, Phoenix AZ

Monfils, Nicole, *Gallery Asst,* Rhode Island Watercolor Society, Pawtucket RI

Monge, Janet, *Physical Anthropology Cur,* University of Pennsylvania, Museum of Archaeology & Anthropology, Philadelphia PA

Monhollen, Kyle, *Preparator,* University of California, Davis, Jan Shrem and Maria Manetti Shrem Museum of Art, Davis CA

Moning, Zach, *Communs Mgr,* ArtsWave, Cincinnati OH

Monk, Philip, *Dir & Cur,* York University, Art Gallery of York University, Toronto ON

Monk-Hilty, Tamara, *Instr,* Lourdes University, Art Dept, Sylvania OH (S)

Monkhouse, Christopher, *Cur & Chair,* The Art Institute of Chicago, Department of Textiles, Textile Society, Chicago IL

Monkoff, Daphne, *Drawing & Painting,* North Seattle College, North Seattle College Dept of Art, Seattle WA (S)

Monroe, Dan L, *Exec Dir,* Peabody Essex Museum, Salem MA

Monroe, Dan L, *Exec Dir,* Peabody Essex Museum, Cotting-Smith-Assembly House, Salem MA

Monroe, Erin, *Assoc Cur American Paintings & Sculpture,* Wadsworth Atheneum Museum of Art, Hartford CT

Monroe, Gary, *Prof,* Daytona Beach Community College, Dept of Fine Arts & Visual Arts, Daytona Beach FL (S)

Monroe, Mark, *Chair,* Austin College, Ida Green Gallery, Sherman TX

Monroe, Mark, *Prof,* Austin College, Art Dept, Sherman TX (S)

Monroe, Rose, *Chmn,* Baltimore City Community College, Dept of Fine Arts, Baltimore MD (S)

Monroe-Kane, Erika, *Dir Communs,* Madison Museum of Contemporary Art, Madison WI

Monson, Sarah, *Graphic Design & Mktg,* Ravalli County Museum, Hamilton MT

Montag, Ann, *Finance Mgr,* Shaker Museum & Library, Old Chatham NY

Montague, Benjamin, *Assoc Prof,* Wright State University, Dept of Art & Art History, Dayton OH (S)

Montague, Matthew, *Studio Mgr,* Kimball Jenkins Estate, Concord NH

Montalbano, Karen, *VPres & Cur,* Baldwin Historical Society Museum, Baldwin NY

Montali, Amy, *Asst Prof,* Rhode Island College, Art Dept, Providence RI (S)

Montan, Tom, *Dir,* Sculpture Space, Inc, Utica NY

Monteiro, Eileen, *Mem Chair,* National Conference of Artists, Michigan Chapter Gallery, Detroit MI

Monteiro, Lorrie, *Exec Officer Mus Opers,* American Homing Pigeon Museum & Library, Oklahoma City OK

Monteith, Jerry, *Prof, Head Grad Studies & Studio Area Head,* Southern Illinois University, School of Art & Design, Carbondale IL (S)

Montenegro, Diane, *Office Mgr,* Newport Art Museum and Association, Newport RI

Montes, Chemi, *Assoc Prof,* American University, Dept of Art, New York NY (S)

Montes, Tracy, *Mktg & Communs Coordr,* Hyde Park Art Center, Chicago IL

Montford, James, *Gallery Dir,* Rhode Island College, Edward M Bannister Gallery, Providence RI
Montgomery, Alexandra, *Dir & CEO,* Bill Reid Gallery of Northwest Coast Art, Vancouver BC
Montgomery, Andrea, *Dean Humanities,* Tougaloo College, Art Dept, Tougaloo MS (S)
Montgomery, Bill, *Dir Security,* New-York Historical Society, Museum, New York NY
Montgomery, Brandon, *Prod, Humanities,* State College of Florida Manatee - Sarasota, Art, Design, Humanities, Bradenton FL (S)
Montgomery, David, *Prof,* Saint Louis Community College at Meramec, Art Dept, Saint Louis MO (S)
Montgomery, Doris, *Archivist,* Almond Historical Society, Inc, Hagadorn House, The 1800-37 Museum, Almond NY
Montgomery, Edward, *Prof,* Miami University, Dept Fine Arts, Hamilton OH (S)
Montgomery, Janet, *Instr,* Appalachian State University, Dept of Art, Boone NC (S)
Montgomery, Scott, *Assoc Prof Art History,* University of Denver, School of Art & Art History, Denver CO (S)
Montgomery, Susan, *Adjunct Faculty,* Mount Wachusett Community College, East Wing Gallery, Gardner MA
Montgomery, Tennielle, *Admin Asst,* Coutts Museum of Art, Inc, El Dorado KS
Montgomery, Tom, *Pres,* Gallery XII, Wichita KS
Monti, Lia, *Gallery Assoc,* Japan Society, Inc, Japan Society Gallery, New York NY
Monti, Michael J, *Exec Dir,* Association of Collegiate Schools of Architecture, Washington DC
Montileaux, Paulette, *Interim Cur,* Indian Arts & Crafts Board, US Dept of the Interior, Sioux Indian Museum, Rapid City SD
Montley, Pat, *Chmn,* Chatham College, Fine & Performing Arts, Pittsburgh PA (S)
Montoya, Malaquias, *Cooperating Faculty Dept of Art,* University of California, Davis, Dept of Art & Art History, Davis CA (S)
Montrose-Graem, Douglass, *Treas, Sarasota, FL,* JMW Turner Museum, Sarasota FL
Montross, Sarah, *Assoc Cur Contemporary Art,* deCordova Sculpture Park & Museum, Lincoln MA
Moody, Marge, *Asst Prof,* Winthrop University, Dept of Art & Design, Rock Hill SC (S)
Moody, Phil, *Assoc Prof,* Winthrop University, Dept of Art & Design, Rock Hill SC (S)
Moon, Bruce, *Prof,* Mount Mary College, Art & Design Division, Milwaukee WI (S)
Moon, Susan, *Head Arts Library,* University of California, Santa Barbara, Arts Library, Santa Barbara CA
Moonelis, Judy, *Faculty,* Fairleigh Dickinson University, Fine Arts Dept, Madison NJ (S)
Mooney, Tom, *Archivist & Cur,* Cherokee Heritage Center, Library & Archives, Tahlequah OK
Moore, Allison, *Asst Prof,* University of South Florida, School of Art & Art History, Tampa FL (S)
Moore, Bernadette, *Dir Mktg,* Piedmont Arts Association, Martinsville VA
Moore, Beth, *Asst Cur,* Telfair Museums, Savannah GA
Moore, Bob, *Publicity,* Plastic Club, Art Club, Philadelphia PA
Moore, Bobby J, *Coll Mgr,* Southern Alleghenies Museum of Art, Loretto Facility, Loretto PA
Moore, Connie, *Graphic Design,* Art Institute of Pittsburgh, Pittsburgh PA (S)
Moore, Craig, *Assoc Prof,* Taylor University, Visual Art Dept, Upland IN (S)
Moore, Cynthia, *Mktg & Pub Rels,* Virginia Historical Society, Library, Richmond VA
Moore, Dan, *Pres, Dir & Founder,* The APEX Museum, Atlanta GA
Moore, Daryl, *Chmn Art Dept,* Montclair State University, Art Galleries, Upper Montclair NJ
Moore, David G, *Area Dir Visual Arts Prog & Adj Asst Prof,* Le Moyne College, Visual & Performing Arts Dept, Syracuse NY (S)
Moore, Donald Everett, *Chmn,* Mitchell Community College, Visual Art Dept, Statesville NC (S)
Moore, Elizabeth, *Asst Cur,* Telfair Museums, Telfair Academy of Arts & Sciences Library, Savannah GA
Moore, Elizabeth, *Asst Prof,* Cazenovia College, Center for Art & Design Studies, Cazenovia NY (S)
Moore, Ellen, *Cur Educ,* Roswell Museum & Art Center, Roswell NM
Moore, Gina, *Prof,* Benedict College, School of Humanities, Arts & Social Sciences, Columbia SC (S)
Moore, J. Kenneth, *Cur in Charge, Musical Instruments,* The Metropolitan Museum of Art, New York NY
Moore, Janice, *Recording Secy,* Plastic Club, Art Club, Philadelphia PA
Moore, Jeanne, *Instr Art History,* Madonna University, College of Arts & Humanities, Livonia MI (S)
Moore, Jenny, *Dir,* Chinati Foundation, Marfa TX
Moore, Joe, *Asst Prof,* City College of New York, Art Dept, New York NY (S)
Moore, John, *Prof,* Smith College, Art Dept, Northampton MA (S)
Moore, Justin, *Exec Dir,* Design Commission of the City of New York, Associates of the Art Commission, Inc, New York NY
Moore, Kate, *VPres Mktg & Pub Rels,* Grand Rapids Public Museum, Grand Rapids MI
Moore, Kathleen, *Admin Coord,* San Francisco Arts Education Project, San Francisco CA
Moore, Kathleen, *Visual Arts Coordr,* Endicott College, School of Visual & Performing Arts, Beverly MA (S)
Moore, Kathy, *VPres,* North Shore Arts Association, Inc, Gloucester MA
Moore, Kemille, *Prof, Chmn,* University of North Carolina at Wilmington, Dept of Fine Arts - Division of Art, Wilmington NC (S)
Moore, Kyle, *Friends of Lovejoy Librn,* Southern Illinois University, Lovejoy Library, Edwardsville IL
Moore, Laura, *Pres & CEO,* Grace Museum, Inc, The Grace Museum, Abilene TX
Moore, Lynda, *Dir California Shows,* California Watercolor Association, Gallery Concord, Concord CA
Moore, Mary Ruth, *Lectr Photog,* University of Georgia, Franklin College of Arts & Sciences, Lamar Dodd School of Art, Athens GA (S)
Moore, Mary, *Dean,* Arkansas State University-Art Department, Jonesboro, Library, Jonesboro AR
Moore, Patrick, *Dir,* The Andy Warhol Museum, Pittsburgh PA
Moore, Richard, *Dir,* Barnard's Mill Art Museum, Glen Rose TX
Moore, Robert, *Assoc Prof,* West Virginia University, College of Creative Arts, School of Art & Design, Morgantown WV (S)
Moore, Robyn, *Asst Prof,* Delta State University, Dept of Art, Cleveland MS (S)
Moore, Stanley, *Speech,* Henry Ford Community College, McKenzie Fine Art Ctr, Dearborn MI (S)
Moore, Susan, *Instr & Exhib Dir,* Paris Junior College, Visual Art Dept, Paris TX (S)
Moore, Sylvia, *Educ,* Midmarch Associates/Midmarch Arts Press, Midmarch Arts Press and Library, New York NY
Moore, Teri, *Exec Dir,* Yeiser Art Center Inc, Paducah KY
Moore, Tina, *VPres,* Pastel Society of the West Coast, Sacramento Fine Arts Center, Fresno CA
Moore, Tracey, *Progs Dir,* Aldrich Museum of Contemporary Art, Ridgefield CT
Moore, William, *Instr,* Pacific Northwest College of Art, Portland OR (S)
Moorji, Aliza, *Gallery Asst,* Saint John's University, Dr. M.T. Geoffrey Yeh Art Gallery, Queens NY
Moorman, Evette, *Inst,* Grayson County College, Art Dept, Denison TX (S)
Moorman, Jay, *Dean,* Butler Community College, Art Dept, El Dorado KS (S)
Moos, Walter A, *Pres,* Gallery Moos Ltd, Toronto ON
Moose, Nancy, *Assoc Prof,* Dakota State University, College of Liberal Arts, Madison SD (S)
Moover, Lindsay, *Dir Visual Arts,* Arts Center of the Ozarks, Springdale AR
Moquino, Denise, *Tourism Dir,* Pueblo of San Ildefonso, Maria Martinez Museum, Santa Fe NM
Morales, Raymond, *Prof,* University of Utah, Dept of Art & Art History, Salt Lake City UT (S)
Morales, Reinaldo, *Assoc Prof,* University of Central Arkansas, Department of Art, Conway AR (S)
Morales-Coll, Eduardo, *Pres,* Ateneo Puertorriqueno, Ateneo Gallery, San Juan PR
Morales-Coll, Eduardo, *Pres,* Ateneo Puertorriqueno, Library, San Juan PR
Moran, Arturo, *Groundskeeper,* Plaza de la Raza Cultural Center, Los Angeles CA
Moran, Claudia, *Opers Mgr,* Museo De Las Americas, Denver CO
Moran, Diane D, *Prof,* Sweet Briar College, Art History Dept, Sweet Briar VA (S)
Moran, George F, *Treas,* National Hall of Fame for Famous American Indians, Anadarko OK
Moran, James David, *VPres Prog & Outreach,* American Antiquarian Society, Worcester MA
Moran, Joe, *Chmn Art Dept,* California State University, San Bernardino, San Bernardino CA
Moran, Joe, *Chmn Dept & Instr,* California State University, San Bernardino, Dept of Art, San Bernardino CA (S)
Moran, Lynda A, *Exec Dir,* Islip Art Museum, East Islip NY
Moran, Susan, *Dir Resource Center,* Art Institute of Pittsburgh, John P. Barclay Memorial Gallery, Pittsburgh PA
Moran, Tom, *Chief Cur & Artistic Dir,* Grounds for Sculpture, Hamilton NJ
Morandi, Thomas, *Prof,* Oregon State University, Dept of Art, Corvallis OR (S)
Moraru, Ortansa, *Pres,* Society of Canadian Artists, Toronto ON
More, Marilyn, *Dir,* Dartmouth Heritage Museum, Dartmouth NS
More, Susan L, *Assoc Prof, Chair,* Indiana University South Bend, Fine Arts Dept, South Bend IN (S)
More, Torii, *Cur Digital Humanities,* McLean County Historical Society, McLean County Museum of History, Bloomington IL
Moreau, Robert, *Asst Prof,* Northwestern State University of Louisiana, School of Creative & Performing Arts - Dept of Fine & Graphic Arts, Natchitoches LA (S)
Morehouse, John, *Treas,* Salmagundi Club, New York NY
Moreland, Catherine, *Exec Dir & CEO,* Delaplaine Visual Arts Education Center, Frederick MD
Morello, Sr VPres Educ & Public Progs, *VP Devel,* Los Angeles County Museum of Art, Los Angeles CA
Moren, Lisa, *Prof,* University of Maryland, Baltimore County, Intermedia & Digital Arts (IMDA), Dept of Visual Arts, Baltimore MD (S)
Moreno Vega, Dr Marta, *Founder & Bd Pres,* Caribbean Cultural Center African Diaspora Institute, Cultural Arts Organization & Resource Center, New York NY
Moreno, AnaMaria, *Program Asst,* Lannan Foundation, Santa Fe NM
Moreno, Barry, *Library Technician,* The National Park Service, United States Department of the Interior, Statue of Liberty National Monument & The Ellis Island Immigration Museum, Washington DC
Moreno, Ceareo, *Dir Visual Arts & Chief Cur,* National Museum of Mexican Art, Chicago IL
Moreno, Mario, *Instr,* San Joaquin Delta College, Arts & Communication, Stockton CA (S)
Moreno, Michelle, *Dir.,* Japanese American Cultural & Community Center, George J Doizaki Gallery, Los Angeles CA
Moreno, Vanessa, *Mus Opers Mgr,* The Mexican Museum, San Francisco CA
Moretti, GianPiero, *Assoc Prof & Dir, School of Architecture,* Universite Laval, Faculty of Planning, Architecture, Arts & Design, Quebec QC (S)
Morey, Gina, *Dir Prog & Educ,* Anniston Museum of Natural History, Anniston AL

Morey, Mark, *Cur Educ,* Amarillo Art Association, Amarillo Museum of Art, Amarillo TX

Morgan Taylor, Robert, *Adjunct Asst Prof,* College of Staten Island, Performing & Creative Arts Dept, Staten Island NY (S)

Morgan, Amber, *Dir Colls & Registration,* The Andy Warhol Museum, Pittsburgh PA

Morgan, Blake, *Asst Prof,* University of Science & Arts of Oklahoma, Art Dept, Chickasha OK (S)

Morgan, Carol, *Deputy Dir Education,* ArtsConnection Inc, New York NY

Morgan, Cheryl, *Dir Institutional Giving,* New-York Historical Society, Museum, New York NY

Morgan, Clarence, *Chmn Dept,* University of Minnesota, Minneapolis, Dept of Art, Minneapolis MN (S)

Morgan, Dave W, *Mus Dir,* Carlsbad Museum & Art Center, Carlsbad NM

Morgan, David, *Asst Prof,* University of Wisconsin-Stout, Dept of Art & Design, Menomonie WI (S)

Morgan, Donna, *Adjunct Instr,* Davis & Elkins College, Dept of Art, Elkins WV (S)

Morgan, Jessica, *Dir,* Dia Art Foundation, Beacon NY

Morgan, Julie, *Mem & Develop Mgr,* Hermitage Museum & Gardens, Museum, Norfolk VA

Morgan, Julie, *Registrar,* Sawtooth Center for Visual Art, Winston-Salem NC (S)

Morgan, Kenn, *Instr Photo,* Locust Street Neighborhood Art Classes, Inc, Buffalo NY (S)

Morgan, Kenneth, *Chair & Prof Fine Arts,* Bethany College, Visual & Performing Arts Dept, Bethany WV (S)

Morgan, Mary, *Instr,* Dallas Baptist University, Dept of Art, Dallas TX (S)

Morgan, Melissa, *Dean Acad Affairs,* Hussian School of Art, Commercial Art Dept, Philadelphia PA (S)

Morgan, Melissa, *Exec Dir,* Pensacola Museum of Art, Pensacola FL

Morgan, Olivia, *Educator,* University of Louisiana at Lafayette, Paul and Lulu Hilliard University Art Museum, Lafayette LA

Morgan, Rick, *Dir,* Oglebay Institute, Stifel Fine Arts Center, Wheeling WV

Morgan, Robert C, *Prof,* Rochester Institute of Technology, School of Design, Rochester NY (S)

Morgan, Sara, *Assoc Dir,* South Texas Institute for the Arts Affiliated with Texas A&M University - Corpus Christi, Art Museum of South Texas, Corpus Christi TX

Morgan, Spencer, *Develop Dir,* Buffalo Niagara Heritage Village, Amherst NY

Morgan, Sue, *Pres,* Allegany County Historical Society, Gordon-Roberts House, Cumberland MD

Morgan, William, *Prof,* University of Wisconsin-Superior, Programs in the Visual Arts, Superior WI (S)

Morgan, William, *Prof Emeritus,* University of Louisville, Allen R Hite Art Institute, Louisville KY (S)

Morhouse, Sanford W, *Chmn,* Fort Ticonderoga Association, Ticonderoga NY

Moriarity, Lyn, *Admin Dir,* National Trust for Historic Preservation, Washington DC

Moriarty, John, *Instr,* Springfield College, Dept of Visual & Performing Arts, Springfield MA (S)

Morihara, Chizu, *Art Librn,* University of California, Santa Barbara, Arts Library, Santa Barbara CA

Morin, Jeffrey, *Pres,* Milwaukee Institute of Art & Design, Milwaukee WI (S)

Morin, Mark, *Treas,* Westfield Athenaeum, Jasper Rand Art Museum, Westfield MA

Morin, Thomas, *Dir,* Rochester Institute of Technology, School for American Craft, Rochester NY (S)

Moriority, Kaleen, *Asst Prof,* Rochester Institute of Technology, School of Photographic Arts & Sciences, Rochester NY (S)

Morita, Linda, *Librn & Archivist,* McMichael Canadian Art Collection, Library & Archives, Kleinburg ON

Moritz, Tom, *Dir Library Servs,* American Museum of Natural History, Library, New York NY

Morlan, Jenny, *Asst Prof,* DePaul University, Dept of Art, Chicago IL (S)

Morley, Alison, *Chair Photog & Photojournalism Prog,* International Center of Photography, School, New York NY (S)

Morley, Gabriel, *Dir,* Atlanta-Fulton Public Library, Central Library Art Gallery, Atlanta GA

Morley, Stephen, *Dir Emeritus,* Academy of the New Church, Glencairn Museum, Bryn Athyn PA

Moro, Takeshi, *Asst Prof,* Santa Clara University, Dept of Art & Art History, Santa Clara CA (S)

Morrell, John, *Asst Prof,* Georgetown University, Dept of Art & Art History, Washington DC (S)

Morrill, Michael, *Assoc Prof,* University of Pittsburgh, Dept of Studio Arts, Pittsburgh PA (S)

Morrin, Peter, *Adjunct Assoc Prof,* University of Louisville, Allen R Hite Art Institute, Louisville KY (S)

Morris, Amy, *Instr,* Wittenberg University, Art Dept, Springfield OH (S)

Morris, Amy, *Prof, Unit Coordr,* University of Nebraska at Omaha, School of the Arts, Omaha NE (S)

Morris, Betsy, *Prof,* Saint Louis Community College at Meramec, Art Dept, Saint Louis MO (S)

Morris, Catherine J, *Cur Elizabeth A Sackler Center for Feminist Art,* Brooklyn Museum, Brooklyn NY

Morris, Curtis, *Exhib Designer,* City of Springdale, Shiloh Museum of Ozark History, Springdale AR

Morris, Elke, *Senior Lectr,* Bates College, Art & Visual Culture, Lewiston ME (S)

Morris, Fae, *Circ,* J T & E J Crumbaugh, Le Roy IL

Morris, James, *Assoc Prof,* State University of New York College at Brockport, Dept of Art, Brockport NY (S)

Morris, Jeffory, *Cur,* i.d.e.a. Museum, Mesa AZ

Morris, Jerry W, *Chmn,* Miami University, Art Dept, Oxford OH (S)

Morris, Juliana, *Exec Dir,* Associated Artists of Pittsburgh, Pittsburgh PA

Morris, Katherine, *Assoc Prof,* Santa Clara University, Dept of Art & Art History, Santa Clara CA (S)

Morris, Kathleen, *Dir Exhibs & Colls & Cur Decorative Arts,* Clark Art Institute, Williamstown MA

Morris, Krist, *Fin Dir,* Ashtabula Arts Center, Ashtabula OH

Morris, Laura, *Prog Coordr,* University of Oregon, Aperture Photo Gallery - EMU Art Gallery, Eugene OR

Morris, Nikki, *Registrar,* Booth Western Art Museum, Cartersville GA

Morris, Stuart, *Asst Prof,* University of Wisconsin-Stevens Point, Dept of Art & Design, Stevens Point WI (S)

Morris, Valerie B, *Dean,* College of Charleston, School of the Arts, Charleston SC (S)

Morris, W S, *Chmn & CEO,* Morris Communications Co. LLC, Corporate Collection, Augusta GA

Morris-Cafiero, Haley, *Dir Grad Studies,* Memphis College of Art, Memphis TN (S)

Morris-Hunt, Carolyn, *COO,* Burchfield Penney Art Center, Library, Buffalo NY

Morris-Hunt, Carolyn, *COO,* Burchfield Penney Art Center, Buffalo NY

Morrisey, Bob, *Prof,* Polk Community College, Art, Letters & Social Sciences, Winter Haven FL (S)

Morrison, Bill, *Pres,* National Cartoonists Society, Orlando FL

Morrison, Cindi, *Dir,* College of Central Florida, Appleton Museum of Art, Ocala FL

Morrison, Ian, *Asst Prof Art, Chair,* Grand Canyon University, Art Dept, Phoenix AZ (S)

Morrison, Jeff, *Asst Prof Theatre,* Marymount Manhattan College, Fine & Performing Arts Div, New York NY (S)

Morrison, Patrick, *Educ,* Pennsylvania Historical & Museum Commission, Railroad Museum of Pennsylvania, Strasburg PA

Morrison, Susan, *Prof,* University of Wisconsin-Stevens Point, Dept of Art & Design, Stevens Point WI (S)

Morrisroe, Julia, *Assoc Prof,* University of Florida, School of Art & Art History, Gainesville FL (S)

Morrissey, T, *Prof,* Community College of Rhode Island, Dept of Art, Warwick RI (S)

Morrissey, Tom, *Dir & Librn,* Community College of Rhode Island, Flanagan Valley Campus Art Gallery, Lincoln RI

Morrow, David, *Treas,* Barnard's Mill Art Museum, Glen Rose TX

Morrow, Delores, *Photograph Cur,* Montana Historical Society, Library, Helena MT

Morrow, Kara, *Asst Prof,* The College of Wooster, Dept of Art and Art History, Wooster OH (S)

Morrow, Nancy, *Asst Prof,* Kansas State University, Art Dept, Manhattan KS (S)

Morsch, Lori, *Sec,* State University of New York at Geneseo, Bertha V B Lederer Gallery, Geneseo NY

Morsch, Lori, *Sec,* State University of New York at Geneseo, Lockhart Gallery, Geneseo NY

Morsch, Lori, *Secy,* Bertha V B Lederer Fine Arts Gallery-Suny Geneseo, Bertha V B Lederer Fine Arts Gallery, Geneseo NY

Morse, Bill, *Rec Secy,* Graphic Artists Guild, New York NY

Morse, Karen W, *Archivist,* Historic Hudson Valley, Pocantico Hills NY

Morse, Mary Jane, *Contact Admin,* Aidron Duckworth Art Preservation Trust, Aidron Duckworth Art Museum, Meriden NH

Morse, Samuel C, *Howard M & Martha P Mitchell Prof of History of Art & Asian Languages/ Civilizations,* Amherst College, Dept of Art & the History of Art, Amherst MA (S)

Morse, William, *Asst Prof Art,* Belhaven College, Art Dept, Jackson MS (S)

Morse, William, *Asst Prof of Art,* Campbellsville University, Art & Design Department, Campbellsville KY (S)

Mort, Rhonda, *Children's Librn,* Willard Library, Dept of Fine Arts, Evansville IN

Mort, Trian, *Admin Asst,* Bard College, Center for Curatorial Studies and the Hessel Museum of Art, Annandale-on-Hudson NY

Morten, Meredith, *Sculpture Chair,* Montserrat College of Art, Beverly MA (S)

Mortensen, Hans, *Asst Prod,* Georgia Southern University, Betty Foy Sanders Dept of Art, Statesboro GA (S)

Mortensen, Loring, *Pub & Community Relations,* University of North Carolina at Greensboro, Weatherspoon Art Museum, Greensboro NC

Mortensen, Shelley, *Chief Librn,* The Art Gallery of Southwestern Manitoba, Brandon Public Library, Brandon MB

Mortenson, Chris, *Instr,* Kirkwood Community College, Dept of Arts & Humanities, Cedar Rapids IA (S)

Mortenson, Christian, *Adj Prof,* Augustana College, Art Dept, Rock Island IL (S)

Morton, Christopher, *Registrar,* New York State Military Museum and Veterans Research Center, Saratoga Springs NY

Morton, Elizabeth, *Asst Prof Art History,* Wabash College, Art Dept, Crawfordsville IN (S)

Morton, Ennette, *Dir Mus,* Riverside Metropolitan Museum, Riverside CA

Morton, Jean Pell, *Staff,* Gallery 9, Los Altos CA

Morton, Patricia M, *Chmn & Assoc Prof,* University of California, Riverside, Dept of the History of Art, Riverside CA (S)

Morton-Bentley, Kaitlin, *Asst Cur,* Schenectady County Historical Society, Schenectady NY

Morusma, Ron, *Assoc Prof,* Indiana University South Bend, Fine Arts Dept, South Bend IN (S)

Mosca, Gus, *Pres,* Burlington County Historical Society, Burlington NJ

Moscardini, Gina, *Mus Shop Mgr,* The Bartlett Museum, Amesbury MA

Moscarillo, Mark, *Assoc Prof,* State University of New York at Farmingdale, Visual Communications, Farmingdale NY (S)

Moscatelli, Mary, *Exec Dir,* Venice Art Center, Venice FL

Moschella, Jay, *Cur Rare Books,* Boston Public Library, Rare Book & Manuscripts Dept, Boston MA
Moscovitch, Ruth, *Pres,* Manhattan Graphics Center, New York NY (S)
Moseley, Bill, *Prof,* University of Maine at Augusta, College of Arts & Humanities, Augusta ME (S)
Moseley, W L Tim, *Cur,* Alice Moseley Folk Art and Antique Museum, Bay Saint Louis MS
Mosena, David, *Pres & CEO,* Museum of Science & Industry, Chicago IL
Moser, Christine, *Dir,* Austrian Cultural Forum Gallery, New York NY
Moser, Jeffrey, *Teaching Asst Prof,* West Virginia University, College of Creative Arts, School of Art & Design, Morgantown WV (S)
Moser, Nikki, *Instr,* Keystone College, Fine Arts Dept, LaPlume PA (S)
Moser, Suzy, *Assoc VPres Advancement,* The Huntington Library, Art Collections & Botanical Gardens, Library, San Marino CA
Moses, Jennifer, *Prof,* University of New Hampshire, Dept of Art & Art History, Durham NH (S)
Moses, Kerry, *Accnt & HR Mgr,* Tyler Museum of Art, Tyler TX
Moses, Monica, *Editor in Chief American Craft Mag,* American Craft Council, Minneapolis MN
Mosher Long, Daniel, *Prof Photog,* Manchester Community College, Visual Fine Art Dept, Manchester CT (S)
Mosher, Mike, *Asst Prof,* Saginaw Valley State University, Dept of Art & Design, University Center MI (S)
Moshier, Wendy, *Dir Community Develop,* Salina Art Center, Salina KS
Moske, James, *Mng Archivist,* The Metropolitan Museum of Art, New York NY
Mosko Scheren, Tess, *Pres,* Arizona Artists Guild, Phoenix AZ
Moskowitz, Anita, *Chair & Prof,* Stony Brook University, College of Arts & Sciences, Dept of Art, Stony Brook NY (S)
Moskowitz, Mollie, *Admin Asst,* Queens College, City University of New York, Queens College Art Center, Flushing NY
Mosley, Kim, *Prof,* Saint Louis Community College at Florissant Valley, Liberal Arts Division, Ferguson MO (S)
Moss, Barry, *Exec Dir,* Alberta Craft Council, Edmonton AB
Moss, Jessica, *Assoc Cur Contemp Art,* University of Chicago, Smart Museum of Art, Chicago IL
Moss, Kent, *Prof,* Midland College, Art Dept, Midland TX (S)
Moss, Nina, *Asst to Dir,* Mississippi Museum of Art, Howorth Library, Jackson MS
Moss, Susan, *Prof, chmn dept,* Fort Lewis College, Art Dept, Durango CO (S)
Mossaides Strassfield, Christina, *Mus Dir & Chief Cur,* Guild Hall of East Hampton, Inc, Guild Hall Museum, East Hampton NY
Mosser, Dennis, *Library Technician III,* University of Oklahoma, Fine Arts Library, Norman OK
Most, Gregory P J, *Chief,* National Gallery of Art, Department of Image Collections, Washington DC
Most, Gregory P J, *Chief, Library Image Coll,* National Gallery of Art, Library, Washington DC
Moster, Hilary, *Exec Dir,* Maude Kerns Art Center, Eugene OR
Mosyjowski, Maryann, *Instr,* Cuyahoga Valley Art Center, Cuyahoga Falls OH (S)
Mote, Cindy, *Admin Asst,* Amarillo Art Association, Amarillo Museum of Art, Amarillo TX
Motes, J Barry, *Fine Art Dept Head,* Jefferson Community College & Technical College, Fine Arts, Louisville KY (S)
Motley, Caitlin, *Registrar,* Upfor Gallery, Portland OR
Mott, Beth, *Youth Educ,* San Luis Obispo Museum of Art, San Luis Obispo CA
Mott, Cathy, *Cur Educ,* Muskegon Museum of Art Foundation, Muskegon Museum of Art, Muskegon MI
Mott, Laura, *Cur. Art & Design,* Cranbrook Art Museum, Bloomfield Hills MI
Mott, Margie, *Vol Coordr,* Delaplaine Visual Arts Education Center, Frederick MD
Mott, Rebecca, *Assoc Prof,* West Shore Community College, Division of Humanities & Fine Arts, Scottville MI (S)
Motte, Stephen, *Cur Coll,* Florence County Museum, Florence SC
Motts, Wayne E, *Exec Dir,* Adams County Historical Society, Gettysburg PA
Motyka, Judith, *Develop Officer,* Ellen Noel Art Museum of the Permian Basin, Odessa TX
Moudry, Mary Lou, *Exec Dir,* Crow Wing County Historical Society, Brainerd MN
Moufawad-Paul, Vicky, *Dir & Cur,* A Space, Toronto ON
Moulton, Marc, *Asst Prod,* Georgia Southern University, Betty Foy Sanders Dept of Art, Statesboro GA (S)
Mount, Allison, *Dir,* State University of New York College at Cortland, Dowd Fine Arts Gallery, Cortland NY
Mount, Natalia, *Exec Dir,* Pro Arts, Oakland CA
Mouton, Alexander, *Assoc Prof,* Seattle University, Dept of Art & Art History, Seattle WA (S)
Movahedi-Lankarani, Stephanie, *Library Supv,* The Pennsylvania State University, Architecture & Landscape Architecture Library, University Park PA
Mowder, William, *Dean,* Kutztown University, College of Visual & Performing Arts, Kutztown PA (S)
Mowery, Lynn, *Treas,* Cody Country Art League, Cody WY
Mowry, Elizabeth, *Instr,* Woodstock School of Art, Inc, Woodstock NY (S)
Mowry, Robert, *Cur Chinese Art,* Harvard University, Arthur M Sackler Museum, Cambridge MA
Moxley, Elizabeth, *Dir & Custodian Holdings,* National Archives of Canada, Art & Photography Archives, Ottawa ON
Moye, Holly, *Dir School Visual Arts,* Oklahoma City University, Hulsey Gallery-Norick Art Center, Oklahoma City OK
Moyer, Ashleigh, *Prog Dir,* University of Tennessee, Visual Arts Committee, Knoxville TN
Moyer, David, *Cur Estuarine Biology,* Calvert Marine Museum, Solomons MD
Moyer, G Gary, *Exec Dir,* Southern Alleghenies Museum of Art, Altoona Facility, Altoona PA
Moyer, G Gary, *Exec Dir,* Southern Alleghenies Museum of Art, Ligonier Valley Facility, Ligonier PA
Moyer, G Gary, *Exec Dir,* Southern Alleghenies Museum of Art, Loretto Facility, Loretto PA
Moyer, G Gary, *Exec Dir,* Southern Alleghenies Museum of Art, Johnstown Gallery, Johnstown PA
Moyer, Lydia, *Asst Prof Studio Art,* University of Virginia, McIntire Dept of Art, Charlottesville VA (S)
Moyer, Nancy, *Chmn Dept,* University of Texas Pan American, Art Dept, Edinburg TX (S)
Moyers, Michael, *Assoc Dean,* Yuba College, Fine Arts Division, Marysville CA (S)
Moynahan, Karen, *Exec Dir,* National Association of Schools of Art & Design, Reston VA
Moyse, Katherine, *Assoc Prof,* Hillsborough Community College, Fine Arts Dept, Tampa FL (S)
Mozingo, Mark, *Events & Mem Dir,* Lexington Art League, Inc, Lexington KY
Mroczak, Andrew, *Assoc Dir,* Lesley University, Roberts Gallery, Cambridge MA
Mroz, Michael, *Exec Dir,* Newburyport Maritime Society, Inc, Custom House Maritime Museum, Newburyport MA
Mualler, Stacy, *Archivist,* Saving & Preserving Arts & Cultural Environments, Spaces Library & Archive, Aptos CA
Muchanic, Paris, *Instr,* Wayne Art Center, Wayne PA (S)
Muchow, Michael, *Librn,* University of Missouri, Art, Archaeology & Music Collection, Columbia MO
Mudd, Douglas, *Museum Dir & Cur,* American Numismatic Association, Edward C. Rochette Money Museum, Colorado Springs CO
Mudd, Peter, *Exec Dir,* C G Jung Center, Evanston IL
Muder, Craig, *Dir Communications,* National Baseball Hall of Fame & Museum, Cooperstown NY
Mudrinich, David, *Prof,* Arkansas Tech University, Dept of Art, Russellville AR (S)
Muehlemann, Kathy, *Acting Chmn,* Randolph-Macon Woman's College, Dept of Art, Lynchburg VA (S)
Mueller, Ellen, *Asst Prof,* West Virginia Wesleyan College, Art Dept, Buckhannon WV (S)
Mueller, Greg, *Asst Prof Studio Art,* Converse College, School of the Arts, Dept of Art & Design, Spartanburg SC (S)
Mueller, Jeffrey, *Gallery Dir,* Silvermine Arts Center, Silvermine Galleries, New Canaan CT
Mueller, John C, *Prof,* University of Detroit Mercy, School of Architecture, Detroit MI (S)
Mueller, Lyn, *Instr,* Wayne Art Center, Wayne PA (S)
Mueller, Margaret, *Librn,* Riverside County Museum, Library, Cherry Valley CA
Mueller, Mark, *Adj Asst Prof,* University of Texas at Arlington, Art & Art History Department, Arlington TX (S)
Mueller, Marlene, *Prof,* Wayne State College, Dept Art & Design, Wayne NE (S)
Mueller, Marlene, *Prof,* Wayne State College, Nordstrand Visual Arts Gallery, Wayne NE
Mueller, Mitzi, *Mus Serv Coordr,* Paine Art Center & Gardens, Oshkosh WI
Mueller, Robert, *Assoc Prof,* University of Florida, School of Art & Art History, Gainesville FL (S)
Muente, Tamera, *Assoc Cur,* Taft Museum of Art, Cincinnati OH
Mugavero, C J, *Owner,* The Artful Deposit, Inc, The Artful Deposit Gallery, Bordentown NJ
Muhlbauer, Mic, *Asst Prof,* Eastern New Mexico University, Dept of Art, Portales NM (S)
Muhlbauer, Mic, *Prof Art,* Eastern New Mexico University, Runnels Gallery, Golden Library, Portales NM
Muhm, LouAnn, *Chair of the Board,* Nemeth Art Center, Park Rapids MN
Muhn, B G, *Assoc Prof,* Georgetown University, Dept of Art & Art History, Washington DC (S)
Muhsam, Armin, *Assoc Prof,* Northwest Missouri State University, Dept of Fine & Performing Arts, Maryville MO (S)
Muir, Linda, *Acting Cur,* Harvard University, Busch-Reisinger Museum, Cambridge MA
Muir, Paul, *Exec Dir,* RedMill Museum Village, Clinton NJ
Muirawski, Michael, *Dir Educ & Pub Rels,* Portland Art Museum, Portland OR
Muirhead, Robert, *Prof,* Hamilton College, Art Dept, Clinton NY (S)
Mulberry, Rebecca, *Coordr Mem,* Boise Art Museum, Boise ID
Mulcahy, Fran, *Cur Educ,* Museum of Art, Fort Lauderdale, Library, Fort Lauderdale FL
Muldowney, Jacob, *Assistant Prof, Art,* Chowan College, Dept. of Communication Arts, Fine and Applied Arts, Murfreesboro NC (S)
Muldrow, Ralph, *Dir, Historic Preservation,* College of Charleston, School of the Arts, Charleston SC (S)
Mulford, Hansen, *Cur,* Orlando Museum of Art, Orlando FL
Mulford, Hansen, *Cur,* Orlando Museum of Art, Orlando Sentinel Library, Orlando FL
Mulgrew, John, *Chmn,* Pace University, Dyson College of Arts & Sciences, Pleasantville NY (S)
Mulgrew, John, *Dept Chair,* Pace University Gallery, Art Gallery in Choate House, Pleasantville NY
Mulhollen, Jack, *Instr,* Cuyahoga Valley Art Center, Cuyahoga Falls OH (S)
Mulkey, Elly, *Treas/Secy,* Roswell Museum & Art Center, Roswell NM
Mulkey, Jan, *Office Mgr,* San Angelo Museum of Fine Arts, San Angelo TX
Mullally, Susan, *Asst Prof,* Baylor University - College of Arts and Sciences, Dept of Art, Waco TX (S)

Mullane, Sarah, *Dir Mem & Guest Relations,* Flint Institute of Arts, Flint MI
Mullen Kreamer, Christine, *Deputy Dir & Chief Cur,* National Museum of African Art, Smithsonian Institution, Washington DC
Mullen, Conor, *Prep,* University of Wyoming, University of Wyoming Art Museum, Laramie WY
Mullen, Denise, *Pres,* National Association of Schools of Art & Design, Reston VA
Mullen, Denise, *Pres,* Oregon College of Art & Craft, Hoffman Gallery, Portland OR
Mullen, Denise, *Vice Chmn,* Association of Independent Colleges of Art & Design, Providence RI
Mullen, Jim, *Prof,* Bowdoin College, Art Dept, Brunswick ME (S)
Mullen, Karen, *Cur Educ,* Laumeier Sculpture Park, Saint Louis MO
Muller, Debra, *Asst Dir,* Eccles Community Art Center, Ogden UT
Muller, Jeffrey, *Prof,* Brown University, Dept of History of Art & Architecture, Providence RI (S)
Muller, Kristin, *Exec Dir,* Peters Valley School of Craft, Layton NJ
Muller, Maria, *Deputy Dir,* Museum of Fine Arts, Boston MA
Muller, Martin, *Pres,* Modernism, San Francisco CA
Muller, Priscilla E, *Cur Emeritus,* The Hispanic Society of America, Hispanic Society Museum & Library, New York NY
Muller, Sheila, *Prof,* University of Utah, Dept of Art & Art History, Salt Lake City UT (S)
Muller, William, *VPres,* Society of American Historical Artists, Oyster Bay NY
Mullery, Tracey, *Visitor Services Manager,* Academy Art Museum, Easton MD
Mullin, Diane, *Cur,* University of Minnesota, Frederick R Weisman Art Museum, Minneapolis MN
Mullin, Timothy, *Dept Head,* Western Kentucky University, Kentucky Library & Museum, Bowling Green KY
Mullineaux, Connie, *Chairperson,* Edinboro University of Pennsylvania, Art Dept, Edinboro PA (S)
Mullings, Ted, *VPres,* Lake County Civic Center Association, Inc, Heritage Museum & Gallery, Leadville CO
Mullins, Corey, *Sr Preparator,* Nova Scotia Museum, Maritime Museum of the Atlantic, Halifax NS
Mullins, Derek, *Mktg & Sales,* Appalshop Inc, Appalshop, Whitesburg KY
Mullins, Kara, *Deputy Dir Develop & Opers,* The Phillips Collection, Washington DC
Mulno, Mike, *Dir,* Joseph Bellows Gallery, La Jolla CA
Mulrooney, Melissa, *Dir,* Stamford Museum & Nature Center, Stamford CT
Mulvaney, Kathy, *Dir Educ & Exhibs,* The Bostonian Society, Old State House Museum, Boston MA
Mulvaney, Rebecca, *Dir Gallery,* Northern State University, Northern Galleries, Aberdeen SD
Mumford, Jessica, *Registrar,* Telfair Museums, Telfair Academy of Arts & Sciences Library, Savannah GA
Mumm, Susan, *Dean,* Queen's University, Faculty of Arts & Sciences, Creative Arts Program, Kingston ON (S)
Mummert, Joan J, *Pres & CEO,* York County Heritage Trust, York PA
Mundy, James, *Dir,* Vassar College, The Frances Lehman Loeb Art Center, Poughkeepsie NY
Munger, Kari, *Head Librn,* Canajoharie Library & Art Gallery, Arkell Museum of Canajoharie, Canajoharie NY
Muniappan, Brindha, *Dir Programs,* Massachusetts Institute of Technology, MIT Museum, Cambridge MA
Munns, Judith, *Dir,* Skagway City Museum & Archives, Skagway AK
Munoz, Gabriela, *Artist Progs Mgr,* Arizona Commission on the Arts, Phoenix AZ
Munoz, Nick, *Preparator,* City of El Paso, El Paso Museum of Art, El Paso TX
Munoz, Steven, *Dir,* Lee Arts Center, Arlington VA
Munoz, Terresa, *Prof,* Loyola Marymount University, Dept of Art & Art History, Los Angeles CA (S)
Munro, Gale, *Art Coll Cur,* Naval Historical Center, National Museum of the US Navy, Washington DC
Munroe, Alexandra, *Cur Asian Art,* Solomon R Guggenheim Museum, New York NY
Munroe, Dana, *Registrar,* Rhode Island Historical Society, Library, Providence RI
Munson, Susannah, *Cur Anthro,* Southern Illinois University Carbondale, University Museum, Carbondale IL
Muntges, Anne, *Educ & Studio Mgr,* Center for Book Arts, New York NY
Murad, Andrew, *Coordr,* McLennan Community College, Visual Arts Dept, Waco TX (S)
Muraoka, Anne, *Asst Prof,* Old Dominion University, Art Dept, Norfolk VA (S)
Murawski, Alex, *Asst Prof Graphic Design,* University of Georgia, Franklin College of Arts & Sciences, Lamar Dodd School of Art, Athens GA (S)
Murback, Mitch, *Prof Chmn,* DePauw University, Art Dept, Greencastle IN (S)
Murch, Anna Valentina, *Prof,* Mills College, Art Dept, Oakland CA (S)
Murchison, Alex, *Photography & Digital Imaging,* Holland College, School of Visual Arts & Journalism, Charlottetown PE (S)
Murdoch, Carol, *Reference Librn,* North Central College, Oesterle Library, Naperville IL
Murdoch, John, *Dir Colls,* The Huntington Library, Art Collections & Botanical Gardens, Library, San Marino CA
Murdock, Debralynn, *Controller,* Independence Seaport Museum, Philadelphia PA
Murdock, Elizabeth, *COO,* Cheekwood-Tennessee Botanical Garden & Museum of Art, Nashville TN
Murdock, Elizabeth, *COO,* Cheekwood-Tennessee Botanical Garden & Museum of Art, Museum of Art, Nashville TN
Muro, Michelle, *Colls Coordr,* Workman & Temple Family Homestead Museum, City of Industry CA
Murphey, F Warren, *Dir Mus & Historic Preservation,* Jekyll Island Museum, Jekyll Island GA
Murphy Milligan, Bridget, *Assoc Prof,* The College of Wooster, Dept of Art and Art History, Wooster OH (S)
Murphy, Betty, *Librn,* Heard Museum, Billie Jane Baguley Library and Archives, Phoenix AZ
Murphy, Bridget, *Assoc Prof,* Marymount University, School of Arts & Sciences Div, Arlington VA (S)
Murphy, Camille, *Prof,* Moravian College, Dept of Art, Bethlehem PA (S)
Murphy, Christopher, *Dir Mktg & Pub Rels,* The Cultural Arts Center at Glen Allen, Glen Allen VA
Murphy, Debra E, *Asst Prof,* University of North Florida, Dept of Communications & Visual Arts, Jacksonville FL (S)
Murphy, Greg, *Dean,* Maine College of Art, Portland ME (S)
Murphy, Jeff, *Assoc Prof,* University of North Carolina at Charlotte, Dept Art, Charlotte NC (S)
Murphy, Kelly, *Dir External Relations & Special Events,* Philadelphia History Museum, Philadelphia PA
Murphy, Kevin, *Senior Curator of American Art,* Williams College, Museum of Art, Williamstown MA
Murphy, Laura, *PT Instr,* Adams State College, Dept of Visual Arts, Alamosa CO (S)
Murphy, Margaret H, *Chmn,* Alabama Southern Community College, Art Dept, Monroeville AL (S)
Murphy, Marilyn, *Chair,* Vanderbilt University, Dept of Art, Nashville TN (S)
Murphy, Marilyn, *Dir Lib Srvs,* Mount Mercy University, Library, Cedar Rapids IA
Murphy, Mary, *Vis Resources Librn,* Savannah College of Art & Design - Atlanta, ACA Library of Atlanta, Atlanta GA
Murphy, Michael, *Assistant,* New Canaan Historical Society, New Canaan CT
Murphy, Michael, *Exhibits Mgr,* Putnam Museum of History and Natural Science, Davenport IA
Murphy, Michael, *Instr,* California State University, Chico, Department of Art & Art History, Chico CA (S)
Murphy, Patricia, *Pub Rels,* Friends of Historic Kingston, Fred J Johnston House Museum, Kingston NY
Murrah, Molly, *Pres,* Northwest Watercolor Society, Woodinville WA
Murray Adams, Claire, *Prof,* Malone University, Dept of Art, Canton OH (S)
Murray, Ann H, *Dir,* Wheaton College, Beard and Weil Galleries, Norton MA
Murray, Carol, *Asst to the Dir,* Museum of the National Center of Afro-American Artists, Boston MA
Murray, Catherine, *Prof, Interim Chair,* East Tennessee State University, College of Arts and Sciences, Dept of Art & Design, Johnson City TN (S)
Murray, David, *Assoc Prof,* Black Hawk College, Art Dept, Moline IL (S)
Murray, Debi, *Dir Research & Archives,* Historical Society of Palm Beach County, The Richard and Pat Johnson Palm Beach County History Museum, West Palm Beach FL
Murray, Donna, *Dir Educ,* Putnam Museum of History and Natural Science, Davenport IA
Murray, Gale, *Assoc Prof,* Colorado College, Dept of Art, Colorado Springs CO (S)
Murray, Holly, *Dir Gallery,* Springfield College, William Blizard Gallery, Springfield MA
Murray, Holly, *Instr,* Springfield College, Dept of Visual & Performing Arts, Springfield MA (S)
Murray, Jan, *Prof,* University of Mississippi, Department of Art, University MS (S)
Murray, Julia K, *Prof,* University of Wisconsin, Madison, Dept of Art History, Madison WI (S)
Murray, Karin, *Dir Gallery,* Valdosta State University, Art Gallery, Valdosta GA
Murray, Mary E, *Cur Modern & Contemporary Art,* Munson-Williams-Proctor Arts Institute, Museum of Art, Utica NY
Murray, Mary M, *Secy,* Second Street Gallery, Charlottesville VA
Murray, Michelle, *Pres,* National Oil & Acrylic Painters Society, Houston TX
Murray, Neale, *Chmn Dept,* North Park University, Art Dept, Chicago IL (S)
Murray, Peter J, *Dir,* The National Shrine of the North American Martyrs, Fultonville NY
Murray, Rich, *Dir Fin,* Georgia O'Keeffe Museum, Santa Fe NM
Murray, Steve, *Dir,* Alabama Department of Archives & History, Museum of Alabama, Montgomery AL
Murray, Tina, *Mgr Vis Servs,* Foosaner Art Museum, Melbourne FL
Murray, Todd, *Photog,* Antonelli Institute, Professional Photography & Commercial Art, Erdenheim PA (S)
Murtaugh, Rebecca, *Assoc Prof,* Hamilton College, Art Dept, Clinton NY (S)
Musgnug, Kristin, *Assoc Prof,* University of Arkansas, Art Dept, Fayetteville AR (S)
Mussallem, Edward G, *VChmn,* Lightner Museum, Saint Augustine FL
Musto, Linda, *Gen Educ,* Art Institute of Pittsburgh, Pittsburgh PA (S)
Muther, Erik, *Board Chmn,* American Swedish Historical Foundation & Museum, American Swedish Historical Museum, Philadelphia PA
Muto, Iya, *Intern,* New Image Art, West Hollywood CA
Muto, Margot, *Exhib Coord,* University of Rochester, Memorial Art Gallery, Rochester NY
Mutter, William, *Adjunct Asst Prof,* Drew University, Art Dept, Madison NJ (S)
Mutza, Amy, *Opers Mgr,* Wildling Art Museum, Solvang CA
Muzikar, Debra, *Exec Dir,* Red Brick Center for the Arts, Aspen CO
Myall, Hanna, *Registrar,* Art Metropole, Toronto ON
Myatt, Adam, *Gallery Asst,* St Mary's University, Art Gallery, Halifax NS
Mycue, David J, *Cur Archives & Coll,* Hidalgo County Historical Museum, Edinburg TX

Myeroff, Chris, *Pres (V),* Akron Art Museum, Akron OH
Myers, Barry W, *Cur,* Lightner Museum, Saint Augustine FL
Myers, Derek, *Prof,* Virginia Polytechnic Institute & State University, Dept of Art & Art History, Blacksburg VA (S)
Myers, Frances, *Emer Prof,* University of Wisconsin, Madison, Dept of Art, Madison WI (S)
Myers, Glen, *Cur,* Wells Fargo Bank, Wells Fargo History Museum, San Francisco CA
Myers, Julia, *Cur,* Washburn University, Mulvane Art Museum, Topeka KS
Myers, Kat, *Assoc Prof,* Western Illinois University, Department of Art, Macomb IL (S)
Myers, Kevin, *Prof Ceramics,* Orange Coast College, Visual & Performing Arts Division, Costa Mesa CA (S)
Myers, Mickey, *Exec Dir,* Bryan Memorial Gallery, Cambridge VT
Myers, Mike, *Develop Coord,* Corporate Council for the Arts/Arts Fund, Seattle WA
Myers, Pamela L, *Exec Dir,* Asheville Art Museum, Asheville NC
Myers, Rachel, *Opers Mgr,* Women's Studio Workshop, Inc, Rosendale NY
Myers, Susan, *Asst Cur & Project Mgr,* Association for Public Art, Philadelphia PA
Myers, Susan, *Instr,* Ocean City Arts Center, Ocean City NJ (S)
Myers, Virginia, *Prof Foil Stamping,* University of Iowa, School of Art & Art History, Iowa City IA (S)
Mynes, Jess, *Coordr, Library Svcs,* Mount Wachusett Community College, La Chance Library, Gardner MA
Myren, Bruce, *Acting Exec Dir,* Photographic Resource Center, Inc, Cambridge MA
Myrick, Bryon, *Pres,* Mississippi Art Colony, Stoneville MS
Myrick, Tommy, *Instr,* Southern University in New Orleans, Fine Arts & Philosophy Dept, New Orleans LA (S)
Mysock, Adam, *Drawing Center Coordr,* Manifest Gallery, Cincinnati OH
Naar, Harry I, *Prof Art & Dir,* Rider University, Art Gallery, Lawrenceville NJ
Nabeta, Vivian, *Dir Mktg,* Harriet Beecher Stowe Center, Hartford CT
Nacke, Bruce, *Assoc Prof Interior Design,* University of North Texas, College of Visual Arts & Design, Denton TX (S)
Nadarajan, Gunalan, *Dean,* University of Michigan, Ann Arbor, Penny W Stamps School of Art & Design, Ann Arbor MI (S)
Nadaskay, Chris, *Prof,* Union University, Dept of Art, Jackson TN (S)
Nadeau, Ed, *Adjunct Asst Prof,* University of Maine, Dept of Art, Orono ME (S)
Nadeau, Nils, *Head Publishing & Communs,* Dartmouth College, Hood Museum of Art, Hanover NH
Nadel, Joshua, *Chmn,* University of Maine at Augusta, College of Arts & Humanities, Augusta ME (S)
Nadkarni, Priya, *Admin Asst,* Arts Extension Service, Amherst MA
Naeem, Asma, *Chief Cur,* The Baltimore Museum of Art, Baltimore MD
Naficy, Hamid, *Adjunct Prof,* Northwestern University, Evanston, Dept of Art History, Evanston IL (S)
Nagai, Mona, *Film Coll Mgr,* University of California, Berkeley, Pacific Film Archive, Berkeley CA
Nagai, Mona, *Film Coll Mgr,* University of California, Berkeley, Berkeley Art Museum & Pacific Film Archive, Berkeley CA
Nagar, Deeksha, *Cur Coll,* Indiana University, The Mathers Museum of World Cultures, Bloomington IN
Nagar, Devvrat, *Prof,* La Roche College, Division of Design, Pittsburgh PA (S)
Nagasawa, Nobuho, *Assoc Prof,* Stony Brook University, College of Arts & Sciences, Dept of Art, Stony Brook NY (S)
Nagata, Helen, *Div Head Art History,* Northern Illinois University, School of Art & Design, DeKalb IL (S)
Nagawiecki, Mia, *VPres Educ,* New-York Historical Society, Museum, New York NY
Nagel Spinner, Tiffany, *Dir Develop,* Edmundson Art Foundation, Inc, Des Moines Art Center, Des Moines IA
Nagel, Alexander, *Undergrad Coordr Art History,* University of Toronto, Dept of Fine Art, Toronto ON (S)
Nagel, Brian, *Dir Interpretation,* Genesee Country Village & Museum, John L Wehle Art Gallery, Mumford NY
Nagelberg, Seth, *Dept Head Ceramics,* Cleveland Institute of Art, Cleveland OH (S)
Nagle, Barbara, *Artist & Owner,* Gallery 4, Ltd, Fargo ND
Nagy, Jean, *Instr,* Middle Tennessee State University, Art Dept, Murfreesboro TN (S)
Nahorski, Kathryn, *Exec Dir,* St Louis Artists' Guild & Galleries, Clayton MO
Najjar, Al, *CEO/Pres,* Avampato Discovery Museum, The Clay Center for Arts & Sciences, Charleston WV
Nakamura, Cayleen, *Dir National Program,* Japanese American National Museum, Los Angeles CA
Nakamura, Kotaro, *Dir,* San Diego State University, University Art Gallery, San Diego CA
Nakano, Yuzo, *Artistic Dir,* Kala Institute, Kala Art Institute, Berkeley CA
Nakao, Susan, *Lectr,* Emporia State University, Dept of Art, Emporia KS (S)
Nakashima, Thomas, *Prof,* Catholic University of America, Dept of Art, Washington DC (S)
Nakata, Rory, *Prof 3D Sculpture & Ceramics,* College of San Mateo, Creative Arts Dept, San Mateo CA (S)
Nakoneczny, Michael, *Assoc Prof,* University of Alaska Fairbanks, Art Department, Fairbanks AK (S)
Nam, Yoomi, *Assoc Prof,* University of Kansas, The School of the Arts, Dept of Visual Art, Lawrence KS (S)
Nam, Yun-Dong, *Prof,* University of North Carolina at Chapel Hill, Art Dept, Chapel Hill NC (S)
Namkung, Michael, *Asst Prof,* Florida International University, School of Art & Art History, Miami FL (S)
Nancarrow, Mindy, *Dir Grad Studies Art History,* University of Alabama, Dept of Art, Tuscaloosa AL (S)
Nance, Glenn, *Sec,* San Francisco African-American Historical & Cultural Society, Library, San Francisco CA
Nanney, Brittany, *Asst to the Dir,* University of Kansas, Spencer Museum of Art, Lawrence KS
Naos, Theodore, *Prof,* Catholic University of America, School of Architecture & Planning, Washington DC (S)
Napier, Louise, *Chmn Div,* Wingate University, Art Department, Wingate NC (S)
Napoli, Marie, *Mus Shop Mgr,* Taubman Museum of Art, Roanoke VA
Naragon, Dwain, *Prof,* Eastern Illinois University, Art Dept, Charleston IL (S)
Narcum-Perez, Patricia, *Bush House Coordr,* Salem Art Association, Archives, Salem OR
Nardi, Brenda, *Sr Dir Advancement,* University of Illinois at Urbana-Champaign, Krannert Art Museum and Kinkead Pavilion, Champaign IL
Nardi, Graciela H, *Pres & Founder,* Latino Art Museum, Pomona CA
Narkiewicz-Laine, Christian K, *Dir & Pres,* Chicago Athenaeum, Museum of Architecture & Design, Galena IL
Narr, Laura, *Development Assistant,* The Columbus Museum, Columbus GA
Naselli, Cheri Reif, *VPres,* ARC Gallery and Educational Foundation, Chicago IL
Nasgaard, Roald, *Chmn Studio Art,* Florida State University, Art Dept, Tallahassee FL (S)
Nash, Maureen, *Chief Devel Officer,* Museum of Arts & Design, New York NY
Nash, Steven A, *Exec Dir,* Palm Springs Art Museum, Palm Springs CA
Nasisse, Andy, *Grad Coordr,* University of Georgia, Franklin College of Arts & Sciences, Lamar Dodd School of Art, Athens GA (S)
Nasse, Harry, *Pres,* Ward-Nasse Gallery, Home of the Year-Round Salon, Sussex NJ
Nasse, Leda, *Outreach,* Ward-Nasse Gallery, Home of the Year-Round Salon, Sussex NJ
Nasser, Matt, *Gallery Dir,* La MaMa La Galleria, New York NY
Nassif, Monica, *Pres,* Walker Art Center, Minneapolis MN
Nastri, Sarah, *Mem Data Mgt,* Lighthouse ArtCenter Museum & School of Art, Tequesta FL
Natale, Marie, *Instr,* Ocean City Arts Center, Ocean City NJ (S)
Natale, Vince, *Instr,* Woodstock School of Art, Inc, Woodstock NY (S)
Natanson, Barbara, *Head Reference Section,* Library of Congress, Prints & Photographs Division, Washington DC
Natella, Dora, *Assoc Prof,* Indiana University South Bend, Fine Arts Dept, South Bend IN (S)
Nathan, Gail, *Exec Dir,* Bronx River Art Center Inc, Bronx NY
Nathan, Jacqueline S, *Dir Galleries,* Bowling Green State University, Fine Arts Center Galleries, Bowling Green OH
Nathan, Jacqueline, *Dir Gallery,* Bowling Green State University, School of Art, Bowling Green OH (S)
Nathanson, Jeff, *Exec Dir,* Museums Sonoma County, Art Museum of Sonoma County & History Museum of Sonoma County, Santa Rosa CA
Nathanson, Marjorie Frankel, *Exec Dir,* Hunterdon Art Museum, Clinton NJ
Natif, Mika, *Asst Prof,* George Washington University, Dept of Art of Fine Arts & Art History, Washington DC (S)
Naughton Becker, Amy, *Dir,* Minneapolis College of Art & Design, Library, Minneapolis MN
Naugle, Bonnie, *Commun & Membership Dir,* American Institute for Conservation of Historic & Artistic Works, Washington DC
Naujoks, Robert, *Instr,* Kirkwood Community College, Dept of Arts & Humanities, Cedar Rapids IA (S)
Naulin, Melissa, *Asst Cur,* White House, Washington DC
Nauts, Alan, *Instr,* University of Saint Francis, School of Creative Arts, Fort Wayne IN (S)
Navaretta, Cynthia, *Exec Dir,* Midmarch Associates/ Midmarch Arts Press, Midmarch Arts Press and Library, New York NY
Navas, Eduardo, *Instr,* Pierce College, Art Dept, Woodland Hills CA (S)
Navlty, Rosemary, *Develop Dir,* Springfield Museum of Art, Library, Springfield OH
Nawrocki, Thomas, *Prof,* Mississippi University for Women, Division of Fine & Performing Arts, Columbus MS (S)
Nay, Barbara, *Admin Asst,* Sharon Arts Center, Sharon Arts Center Exhibition Gallery, Peterborough NH
Naylor, Pamela, *Library Specialist,* Cornish College of the Arts, Cornish Library, Seattle WA
Naylor, Valerie J, *Supt,* Oregon Trail Museum Association, Scotts Bluff National Monument, Gering NE
Nazim-Starnes, Asma, *Asst Prof Art,* Lander University, College of Arts & Humanities - Visual Arts, Greenwood SC (S)
Nazionale, Nina, *Dir Library Opers,* New-York Historical Society, Museum, New York NY
Nazworth, Daniel, *Chmn,* South Plains College, Fine Arts Dept, Levelland TX (S)
Neaderland, Louise, *Dir,* International Society of Copier Artists (ISCA), Brooklyn NY
Neal, Dan, *Reference & Instruction Coordr,* Wentworth Institute of Technology, Douglas D Schumann Library & Learning Commons, Boston MA
Neal, Lindsay, *Cur Colls,* Hermitage Museum & Gardens, Norfolk VA

Neal, Lindsay, *Cur Colls,* Hermitage Museum & Gardens, Museum, Norfolk VA
Neal, Michael, *Treas,* Portrait Society of America, Tallahassee FL
Neal, Pat, *Opers Mgr,* Textile Museum of Canada, Toronto ON
Neal, Sheri, *CFO,* Oregon Historical Society, Oregon History Museum, Portland OR
Neal, Susan, *Exec Dir,* University of Tulsa, Gilcrease Museum, Tulsa OK
Neale, Maria, *Dir Educ Servs,* Genesee Country Village & Museum, John L Wehle Art Gallery, Mumford NY
Near, Andrew, *Temp Opers Mgr,* Zanesville Museum of Art, Zanesville OH
Near, Hollis, *Dir Library Svcs,* Cornish College of the Arts, Cornish Library, Seattle WA
Near, Rebecca, *Tech Svcs & Circ Coordr,* Grand Rapids Public Library, Grand Rapids MI
Near, Susan, *Devel Officer,* Montana Historical Society, Helena MT
Neault, Carolyn, *Cur,* Columbus Historic Foundation, Blewett-Harrison-Lee Museum, Columbus MS
Nebel, Ken, *Dir,* Fuller Lodge Art Center, Los Alamos NM
Necarsulmer, Robert, *Dir & CFO,* Winterthur Museum, Winterthur Museum, Garden & Library, Winterthur DE
Nechis, Barbara, *Instr,* Art Center Sarasota, Sarasota FL (S)
Necowitz, Joel E., *Dir Fin & Admin,* Brandywine Conservancy, Brandywine River Museum, Chadds Ford PA
Nedd, Patrick, *Dir Finance,* Longue Vue House & Gardens, New Orleans LA
Neel, Jim, *Art Chair Prof,* Birmingham-Southern College, Art & Art History, Birmingham AL (S)
Neel, Jim, *Prof,* Birmingham Southern College, Doris Wainwright Kennedy Art Center, Birmingham AL
Neely, John, *Assoc Prof,* Utah State University, Dept of Art, Logan UT (S)
Neenan, Erika, *Asst to the Dir & Exhibs Coordr,* Mystic Art Association, Inc, Mystic Museum of Art, Mystic CT
Neese, Megan, *Chmn,* Industrial Designers Society of America, Herndon VA
Neff, Heidi, *Assoc Prof Art,* Harford Community College, Visual, Performing and Applied Arts Division, Bel Air MD (S)
Neff, Mary Kay, *Prog Dir & Assoc Prof,* Seton Hill University, Art Program, Greensburg PA (S)
Negret, Marcel, *Proj Mgr Preservation & Planning,* Municipal Art Society of New York, New York NY
Negron-Rivera, Mayra, *COO,* Inquilinos Boricuas en Accion (IBA), Villa Victoria Center for the Arts, Boston MA
Nehls, Edie, *Advancement Dir,* Museum of Contemporary Art San Diego, La Jolla CA
Neidhardt, Jane, *Head of Publications,* Washington University, Mildred Lane Kemper Art Museum, Saint Louis MO
Neil, Erik, *Dir,* Chrysler Museum of Art, Norfolk VA
Neill, Nancy, *Dir,* Muse Art Gallery, Philadelphia PA
Neilson, Robert, *Assoc Prof,* Lawrence University, Dept of Art & Art History, Appleton WI (S)
Nell-Smith, Bruce, *Head Dept,* Newberry College, Dept of Art, Newberry SC (S)
Nellermoe, J, *Chmn,* Texas Lutheran University, Dept of Visual Arts, Seguin TX (S)
Nelly, Benjamin F, *Coll Mgr,* Adams County Historical Society, Gettysburg PA
Nelsen, Betty, *Spokesperson,* American River College, Dept of Art/Art New Media, Sacramento CA (S)
Nelsen, Ginger, *Admin,* Washington Art Association, Washington Depot CT
Nelson Thomas, Trina, *Dir Stark Art & History Venues,* Nelda C & H J Lutcher Stark Foundation, Stark Museum of Art, Orange TX
Nelson, Alex, *Deputy Dir,* Arizona Commission on the Arts, Phoenix AZ
Nelson, Amelia, *Sr Librn & Pub Svcs,* The Nelson-Atkins Museum of Art, Spencer Art Reference Library, Kansas City MO
Nelson, Carol, *Staff Asst,* Dawson County Historical Society, Museum, Lexington NE
Nelson, Charmaine, *Prof & Undergrad Dir, Art History,* McGill University, Dept of Art History & Communication Studies, Montreal QC (S)
Nelson, Crystal, *Dir & Cur,* Yankton County Historical Society, Dakota Territorial Museum, Yankton SD
Nelson, Dean, *Mus Adminr,* Connecticut State Library, Museum of Connecticut History, Hartford CT
Nelson, Erik, *Head Admin Serv,* University of California, Berkeley, The Magnes Collection of Jewish Art and Life, Berkeley CA
Nelson, Fred, *Coordr Illustration,* Columbia College, Art Dept, Chicago IL (S)
Nelson, Harold, *Dir,* Long Beach Museum of Art Foundation, Long Beach Museum of Art, Long Beach CA
Nelson, Irving, *Librn,* Navajo Nation Library System, Window Rock AZ
Nelson, Jenny, *Instr,* Woodstock School of Art, Inc, Woodstock NY (S)
Nelson, John, *Interim CEO,* Virginia Historical Society, Library, Richmond VA
Nelson, Julie D, *Exec Dir,* Quincy Art Center, Quincy IL
Nelson, Kelly, *Asst Prof,* Longwood University, Dept of Art, Farmville VA (S)
Nelson, Kim, *Prof, Film & Media Arts,* University of Windsor, School of Creative Arts, Windsor ON (S)
Nelson, Kristi, *Prof Art History,* University of Cincinnati, School of Art, Cincinnati OH (S)
Nelson, Kristin, *Develop Mgr,* Independent Curators International, New York NY
Nelson, Kyle, *Library Information Specialist,* University of New Mexico, Fine Arts Library, Albuquerque NM
Nelson, Leona, *Asst Prof,* Mount Mary College, Art & Design Division, Milwaukee WI (S)
Nelson, Leslee, *Emer Prof,* University of Wisconsin, Madison, Dept of Art, Madison WI (S)
Nelson, Linda, *Exec Dir,* North Shore Art League, Winnetka IL
Nelson, Lucie, *Cur,* State University of New York at Binghamton, Binghamton University Art Museum, Binghamton NY
Nelson, Marilyn, *Assoc Prof,* University of Arkansas, Art Dept, Fayetteville AR (S)
Nelson, Marshall, *Gen Mgr,* Harold Warp, Minden NE
Nelson, Mary Carroll, *Founder,* The Society of Layerists in Multi-Media (SLMM), Albuquerque NM
Nelson, Mary Elizabeth, *Instr,* Wayne Art Center, Wayne PA (S)
Nelson, Michael A, *Exec Dir,* Volcano Art Center Gallery, Hawaii Volcanoes National Park HI
Nelson, Natalie, *Dir & Cur,* Pence Gallery, Davis CA
Nelson, Nathan, *Dept Chair,* Evangel University, Humanities-Art Dept, Springfield MO (S)
Nelson, Norman L, *Chmn,* First State Bank, They Also Ran Gallery, Norton KS
Nelson, Ron, *Exec Dir,* Long Beach Museum of Art Foundation, Long Beach Museum of Art, Long Beach CA
Nelson, Sarah, *Cur Educ,* Lehigh Valley Heritage Center, Allentown PA
Nelson, Sharon, *Exec Dir,* Associated Artists of Winston-Salem, Winston-Salem NC
Nelson, Steve, *Assoc Prof & Chmn,* Hope College, Dept of Art & Art History, Holland MI (S)
Nelson, Steve, *Mgr,* Hope College, DePree Art Center & Gallery, Holland MI
Nelson, Susan, *Assoc Prof,* University of Saint Mary, Fine Arts Dept, Leavenworth KS (S)
Nelson, Traci, *Events & Publicity Coordr,* Cheltenham Center for the Arts, Cheltenham PA (S)
Nelson, Vance, *Site Supv I,* Fort Totten State Historic Site, Pioneer Daughters Museum, Fort Totten ND
Nelson-Mayson, Lin, *Dir,* University of Minnesota, Paul Whitney Larson Gallery, Saint Paul MN
Nelson-Mayson, Lin, *Dir,* University of Minnesota, Goldstein Museum of Design, Saint Paul MN
Nemcosky, Gary, *Assoc Prof,* Appalachian State University, Dept of Art, Boone NC (S)
Nemec, Vernita, *Dir,* Viridian Artists Inc, New York NY
Nemec, Vernita, *Founder & Exec Dir,* Earthfire, Art from Detritus: Recycling with Imagination, New York NY
Nemerov, Alexander, *Prof, Dept Chmn & Dir Art History,* Stanford University, Dept of Art & Art History, Stanford CA (S)
Nemzoff, Judy, *Dir Community Investments,* San Francisco City & County Arts Commission, San Francisco CA
Nenno, Mardis, *Asst Prof,* Spokane Falls Community College, Fine Arts Dept, Spokane WA (S)
Nero, Irene, *Art History,* Southeastern Louisiana University, Art & Design, Hammond LA (S)
Nersesian, Abigail, *Librn,* Phoenix Art Museum, Lemon Art Research Library, Phoenix AZ
Nerstad Kemp, Linda, *Treas,* Bluff Country Artists Gallery, Spring Grove MN
Nesbit, Molly, *Prof,* Vassar College, Art Dept, Poughkeepsie NY (S)
Nesbitt, Bill, *Cur,* Dundurn National Historic Site, Dundurn Castle, Hamilton ON
Nesbitt, Elizabeth, *Cur Invertebrate Paleontology,* University of Washington, Burke Museum of Natural History and Culture, Seattle WA
Nesbitt, Sarah, *Asst Prof,* Marygrove College, Department of Art, Detroit MI (S)
Neset, Marjorie, *Exec Dir,* North Fourth Art Center & Gallery, Albuquerque NM
Nesmith, Joseph, *Progs Mgr,* National YoungArts Foundation, Miami FL
Nesser-Chu, Janice, *Instr II,* Saint Louis Community College at Florissant Valley, Liberal Arts Division, Ferguson MO (S)
Nesser-Chu, Janice, *Treas & Secy,* Women's Caucus For Art, New York NY
Nesteruk, Janet, *Prof,* Northwestern Connecticut Community College, Fine Arts Dept, Winsted CT (S)
Neszpaul, Susan, *Dir External Affairs,* The Frick Art & Historical Center, Inc, Frick Art Museum, Pittsburgh PA
Netsky, Ron, *Head Dept,* Nazareth College of Rochester, Art Dept, Rochester NY (S)
Netsky, Ron, *Head Dept,* Nazareth College of Rochester, Art Dept, Rochester NY (S)
Netsky, Ron, *Instr,* Woodstock School of Art, Inc, Woodstock NY (S)
Nettleton, John, *Asst Prof,* Oregon State University, Dept of Art, Corvallis OR (S)
Netzer, Nancy, *Dir,* Boston College, McMullen Museum of Art, Chestnut Hill MA
Netzer, Sylvia, *Prof,* City College of New York, Art Dept, New York NY (S)
Neu, Wendy, *Bus Mgr,* Kala Institute, Kala Art Institute, Berkeley CA
Neubauer, Joan, *Pres,* Yankton County Historical Society, Dakota Territorial Museum, Yankton SD
Neubauer, Joseph, *Chair,* Barnes Foundation, Merion PA
Neugebauer, Kurt, *Assoc Dir Admin & Exhibitions,* University of Oregon, Jordan Schnitzer Museum of Art, Eugene OR
Neuhaus, Margie, *Assoc Prof,* The College of New Rochelle, School of Arts & Sciences Art Dept, New Rochelle NY (S)
Neuman de Vegvar, Carol, *Prof,* Ohio Wesleyan University, Fine Arts Dept, Delaware OH (S)
Neuman, Robert M, *Prof,* Florida State University, Art History Dept, Tallahassee FL (S)
Neumann, Dietrich, *Prof,* Brown University, Dept of History of Art & Architecture, Providence RI (S)
Neumann, Orian, *Dir Colls & Registration,* Carnegie Museums of Pittsburgh, Carnegie Museum of Art, Pittsburgh PA
Neumann, Timothy C, *Dir & CEO,* Pocumtuck Valley Memorial Association, Memorial Hall Museum, Deerfield MA
Neve, Erin, *Co-Coordr Photog,* Shepherd University, Dept of Contemporary Art & Theater, Shepherdstown WV (S)

Neves, Steve, *Assoc Prof,* Hardin-Simmons University, Art Dept, Abilene TX (S)

Neville, Kristoffer, *Asst Prof,* University of California, Riverside, Dept of the History of Art, Riverside CA (S)

Nevins, Jerome, *Prof Art,* Albertus Magnus College, Visual and Performing Arts, New Haven CT (S)

Nevitt, Stephen, *Chmn,* Columbia College, Dept of Art, Columbia SC (S)

Newberry, Susette, *Art Librarian,* Cornell University, Fine Arts Library, Ithaca NY

Newberry-Mills, Ashleigh, *Tour Coordr,* R W Norton Art Foundation, R W Norton Art Gallery, Shreveport LA

Newbold, Abby, *Dir Exhibs,* Institute of Contemporary Art/Boston, Boston MA

Newby, Kirsten, *CFO,* Anchorage Museum at Rasmuson Center, Anchorage AK

Newcomb, Mary, *Co-VP Dir of Classes & Office Mgr,* Greenwich Art Society Inc, Greenwich CT

Newell, Aimee, *Dir Coll,* National Heritage Museum, Lexington MA

Newhouse, Meta, *Asst Prof Graphic Design,* Montana State University, School of Art, Bozeman MT (S)

Newkirk, Sally, *Dir,* Carnegie Center for Art & History, New Albany IN

Newland, Sally, *Librn,* Amerind Foundation, Inc, Fulton-Hayden Memorial Library & Art Gallery, Dragoon AZ

Newlands, Jennifer, *Adjunct Asst Prof Art History,* Johnson County Community College, Fine Arts Dept & Art History Dept, Overland Park KS (S)

Newman, Bernie, *Artist,* Walker's Point Artists Assoc Inc, Gallery 218, Milwaukee WI

Newman, Geoffrey, *Dean,* Montclair State University, Fine Arts Dept, Montclair NJ (S)

Newman, Geoffrey, *Dean,* Montclair State University, Art Galleries, Upper Montclair NJ

Newman, Jessica, *Educ Coordr,* MonDak Heritage Center, Museum, Sidney MT

Newman, John, *Assoc Prof,* University of Arkansas, Art Dept, Fayetteville AR (S)

Newman, Joseph, *Exec Dir,* Lyme Art Association, Inc, Old Lyme CT

Newman, Laura, *Assoc Prof,* Vassar College, Art Dept, Poughkeepsie NY (S)

Newman, Lia, *Dir,* Davidson College, William H Van Every Jr & Edward M Smith Galleries, Davidson NC

Newman, Rebecca, *VPres Mktg,* Rocky Mountain College of Art & Design, Lakewood CO (S)

Newman, Stephanie, *Prof Graphic Design,* Montana State University, School of Art, Bozeman MT (S)

Newman-Goins, Diane, *2nd VPres,* Warwick Museum of Art, Warwick RI

Newquist, Ruth, *Second VPres,* Kent Art Association, Gallery, Kent CT

Newsom, Carol, *3rd VPres,* National Watercolor Society, San Pedro CA

Newsom, Thomas W, *Pres,* The Art Institute of Dallas, Dallas TX (S)

Newsome, Levi, *Dir,* Danbury Scott-Fanton Museum & Historical Society, Inc, Library, Danbury CT

Newsome, Levi, *Dir,* Danbury Scott-Fanton Museum & Historical Society, Inc, Danbury CT

Newton, Brandi, *Exec Dir,* Willard Arts Center, Carr Gallery, Colonial Theater, Idaho Falls ID

Newton, David, *Prof of Art,* Guilford College, Art Dept, Greensboro NC (S)

Newton, Janet, *Prof,* Illinois Central College, Arts & Communication Dept, East Peoria IL (S)

Newton, Savannah, *Mktg & Curatorial Coordr,* Bainbridge Arts & Crafts Gallery, Bainbridge Island WA

Newton, Tim, *Bd Chmn,* Salmagundi Club, New York NY

Newton, Travis, *Dir Music & Arts Admin,* Le Moyne College, Visual & Performing Arts Dept, Syracuse NY (S)

Neyen, Chris, *Assistant Prof of Art,* Limestone College, Art Dept, Gaffney SC (S)

Ng, Petrina, *Exhib Coordr,* University of Toronto at Mississauga, Blackwood Gallery, Mississauga ON

Ngoc Bich, Nguyen, *Pres,* VICANA (Vietnamese Cultural Association in North America) Library, Springfield VA

Ngoh, Soon Ee, *Assoc Prof,* Mississippi State University, Dept of Art, Starville MS (S)

Nguyen, Chi, *Co-Pres,* Society of Scribes, Ltd, New York NY

Nguyen, Jessica, *Dir,* American Homing Pigeon Museum & Library, Oklahoma City OK

Nguyen, Kim, *Cur & Head Progs,* Capp Street Project, Wattis Institute, San Francisco CA

Nguyen, Kim, *Cur & Head Progs,* California College of the Arts, CCAC Wattis Institute for Contemporary Arts, San Francisco CA

Nguyen, Thuy, *CFO,* Bowers Museum, Santa Ana CA

Nguyen, Trian, *Asst Prof, Chmn,* Bates College, Art & Visual Culture, Lewiston ME (S)

Nguyen-Duy, Pipo, *Asst Prof,* Oberlin College, Dept of Art, Oberlin OH (S)

Nicastro, Kathleen, *Libr Asst,* University of Rochester, Charlotte W Allen Library-Memorial Art Gallery, Rochester NY

Nicholas, Grace, *Admin Asst,* 1890 House-Museum & Center for the Arts, Kellogg Library & Reading Room, Cortland NY

Nicholas, Jamar, *Cur Asst,* Arcadia University Art Gallery, Spruance Fine Arts Center, Glenside PA

Nicholas, Leslee, *Front Desk Clerk,* Longfellow's Wayside Inn Museum, Sudbury MA

Nicholl, Robert, *Visitor Servs & Volunteer Coordr,* American Swedish Institute, Minneapolis MN

Nicholl-Lynam, Marie, *Branch Mgr,* Las Vegas-Clark County Library District, Las Vegas NV

Nicholls, Susan, *Admin Asst,* East Carolina University, Wellington B Gray Gallery, Greenville NC

Nichols, Angela, *Dir Visual Arts,* Morgan County Foundation, Inc, Madison-Morgan Cultural Center, Madison GA

Nichols, Bill, *Dir Opers & Vis Servs,* The Frick Art & Historical Center, Inc, Frick Art Museum, Pittsburgh PA

Nichols, Charlotte, *Chmn,* Seton Hall University, College of Arts & Sciences, South Orange NJ (S)

Nichols, Charlotte, *Chmn,* Seton Hall University, College of Arts & Sciences, South Orange NJ (S)

Nichols, Charlotte, *Dir,* Seton Hall University, South Orange NJ

Nichols, Cherie, *Dir Budgeting & Reporting,* The Phillips Collection, Washington DC

Nichols, George, *Dir Human Resources & General Counsel,* Ferguson Library, Stamford CT

Nichols, Jeff, *Adjunct Prof Photog,* Johnson County Community College, Fine Arts Dept & Art History Dept, Overland Park KS (S)

Nichols, Jeffrey, *Art Gallery Dir,* Living Arts & Science Center, Inc, Lexington KY

Nichols, Kerrie, *Dir,* Wornall Majors House Museums, John Wornall House Museum, Kansas City MO

Nichols, Kerrie, *Exec Dir,* Wornall Majors House Museums, Research Library & Archives, Kansas City MO

Nichols, Lawrence, *Sr Cur,* Toledo Museum of Art, Toledo OH

Nichols, Meghan, *Adjunct Prof Photog,* Johnson County Community College, Fine Arts Dept & Art History Dept, Overland Park KS (S)

Nichols, Michele, *Chief of Staff,* Minneapolis Institute of Art, Minneapolis MN

Nicholson, Cheryl, *Adminr,* Dauphin & District Allied Arts Council, Watson Art Centre, Dauphin MB

Nicholson, Paul, *Dir,* Muhlenberg College, Martin Art Gallery, Allentown PA

Nicholson, Paul, *VPres,* Legacy Ltd, Bellevue WA

Nickard, Gary, *Photog & Visual Studies,* University at Buffalo, State University of New York, Dept of Visual Studies, Buffalo NY (S)

Nickel, Douglas, *Prof,* Brown University, Dept of History of Art & Architecture, Providence RI (S)

Nickel, Lorene, *Prof,* University of Mary Washington, Dept of Art & Art History, Fredericksburg VA (S)

Nickel, Richard, *Assoc Prof,* Old Dominion University, Art Dept, Norfolk VA (S)

Nickel, Richard, *Instr,* Valley City State College, Art Dept, Valley City ND (S)

Nickell, Jeff, *Asst Dir,* Kern County Museum, Bakersfield CA

Nickell, Jeff, *Cur,* Kern County Museum, Library, Bakersfield CA

Nickels, Kim, *Dir Finance,* Putnam Museum of History and Natural Science, Davenport IA

Nickerson, Samantha, *CFO,* Genesee Country Village & Museum, John L Wehle Art Gallery, Mumford NY

Nickle, Elspeth, *Librn,* Southern Alberta Art Gallery, Library, Lethbridge AB

Nicknish, Michael, *CFO,* Menil Foundation, Inc, The Menil Collection, Houston TX

Nickson, Graham, *Dean,* New York Studio School of Drawing, Painting & Sculpture, New York NY (S)

Nickson, Graham, *Dean,* New York Studio School of Drawing, Painting & Sculpture, Library, New York NY

Nickson, Graham, *Dean,* New York Studio School of Drawing, Painting & Sculpture, Gallery, New York NY

Nicolescu, Alec, *Dir Gallery,* Kean University, Fine Arts Dept, Union NJ (S)

Nicoletti, Lisa, *Vis Asst Prof,* Centenary College of Louisiana, Dept of Art, Shreveport LA (S)

Nicoll, Gayle, *Dean, Faculty of Design,* OCAD University, Toronto ON (S)

Nicoll, Jennifer, *Coll Mgr & Exhib Coordr,* Queen's University, Agnes Etherington Art Centre, Kingston ON

Nicoll, Jessica, *Dir & Chief Cur,* Smith College, Museum of Art, Northampton MA

Nideffer, Robert, *Prof Elec Intermedia, Tech & Culture,* University of California, Irvine, Studio Art Dept, Irvine CA (S)

Niederstadt, Leah, *Asst Prof Mus Studies/Art History & Cur Permanent Coll,* Wheaton College, Beard and Weil Galleries, Norton MA

Nielsen, Dori, *Conf Mgr,* National Council on Education for the Ceramic Arts (NCECA), Boulder CO

Nielsen, Erik, *Chmn,* Texas State University - San Marcos, Dept of Art and Design, San Marcos TX (S)

Nielsen, Kristine, *Instr,* Illinois Wesleyan University, School of Art, Bloomington IL (S)

Nielsen, Mark, *Dir,* University of Michigan, Jean Paul Slusser Gallery, Ann Arbor MI

Nielsen, Signe, *Pres,* Design Commission of the City of New York, New York NY

Nielson, Nancy, *Coll Access,* State University of New York at New Paltz, Sojourner Truth Library, New Paltz NY

Nielson, Sherri, *Exec Dir,* Sawtooth Center for Visual Art, Winston-Salem NC (S)

Nieman, Lynne, *VPres Devel,* Chicago Architecture Foundation, Chicago IL

Niemeyer, Donna, *Dean,* Northeast Community College, Dept of Liberal Arts, Norfolk NE (S)

Niemeyer, Stephanie, *Docent Prog Mgr,* Museum of Fine Arts, Houston, Rienzi Center for European Decorative Arts, Houston TX

Niesar, Sherry, *Program Dir,* Bismarck Art & Galleries Association, Bismarck ND

Nieson, Audrey, *Interpretation Supv,* New York State Office of Parks, Recreation and Historic Preservation, Bureau of Historic Sites, Waterford NY

Nietcr, Gary, *Assoc Prof,* Grace College, Dept of Art, Winona Lake IN (S)

Nieto, Sharah, *Dir Educ,* Heard Museum, Phoenix AZ

Niewald, Janet, *Prof,* Virginia Polytechnic Institute & State University, Dept of Art & Art History, Blacksburg VA (S)

Nigh, Robin, *Admin,* City of Tampa, Public Art Program, Tampa FL

Nigro, Christie, *Chmn,* Worcester State College, Visual & Performing Arts Dept, Worcester MA (S)

Nii, Yuko, *Founder & Chmn,* Williamsburg Art & Historical Center, Brooklyn NY

Niki, Kenji, *Librn,* Saint John's University, Asian Collection, Queens NY

Nikolov, Nikolai, *Asst Prof,* Lehigh University, Dept of Art, Architecture & Design, Bethlehem PA (S)

Nilan, Jeffrey, *Asst Prof,* Ohio Wesleyan University, Fine Arts Dept, Delaware OH (S)

Niles, Fred, *Prof, Chmn Dept,* University of Dayton, Visual Arts Dept, Dayton OH (S)

Niles, Richard, *Prof Theatre,* Marymount Manhattan College, Fine & Performing Arts Div, New York NY (S)

Nilson, Craig, *Prof,* Tidewater Community College, Visual Arts Center, Portsmouth VA (S)

Nilson, Robert, *Dir Facilities,* Albany Institute of History & Art, Albany NY

Nisbet, Peter, *Deputy Dir Cur Affairs,* University of North Carolina at Chapel Hill, Ackland Art Museum, Chapel Hill NC

Nishioka, Reiko, *Dir Educ,* Palm Beach County Parks & Recreation Department, Morikami Museum & Japanese Gardens, Delray Beach FL

Nissenholt, Mark, *Prof Emeritus,* Lakehead University, Dept of Visual Arts, Thunder Bay ON (S)

Nisson, Penny, *Dir Educ,* Mizel Museum, Denver CO

Nitchun, Alyssa, *Acting Exec Dir,* Creative Time, New York NY

Nitsch, Michael, *Mus Asst,* Miller Art Center Foundation Inc, Miller Art Museum, Sturgeon Bay WI

Nivens, Charles, *Prof,* Eastern Illinois University, Art Dept, Charleston IL (S)

Nix, Jody, *Asst Prof,* University of Saint Francis, School of Creative Arts, Fort Wayne IN (S)

Nixon, Erin, *Asst Dir,* University of Illinois at Chicago, Gallery 400, Chicago IL

Nixon, John W, *Exec Dir,* Sloss Furnaces National Historic Landmark, Birmingham AL

Nixon, Nancy H, *Arts Specialist,* Patterson Library & Octagon Art Gallery, Westfield NY

Nixon, Sean, *Assoc Prof,* University of Bridgeport, Shintaro Akatsu School of Design, Bridgeport CT (S)

Nixon, Sean, *Prof,* Ulster County Community College/ SUNY Ulster, Dept of Art, Design, Music, Theatre, Communication & Fashion, Stone Ridge NY (S)

Nixon, Wally, *Pres,* Historic Arkansas Museum, Little Rock AR

Nixx, Tanja, *Mgr,* Tattoo Art Museum, San Francisco CA

Noble, Bonnie, *Asst Prof,* University of North Carolina at Charlotte, Dept Art, Charlotte NC (S)

Noble, Cynthia, *Asst Prof,* Springfield College, Dept of Visual & Performing Arts, Springfield MA (S)

Noble, Jillian, *Prof,* University of Wisconsin-Stevens Point, Dept of Art & Design, Stevens Point WI (S)

Noble, Joni, *Instr,* University of Louisiana at Monroe, Dept of Art, Monroe LA (S)

Noble, Karen, *Exhibs Coordr,* Museum of Photographic Arts, Edmund L. and Nancy K Dubois Library, San Diego CA

Noble, Nancy, *Archivist & Cataloger,* Maine Historical Society, Library and Museum, Portland ME

Noble, Nancy, *Dir & CEO,* Art Gallery of Nova Scotia, Halifax NS

Noble, Sandra, *Owner & Mgr,* Green Mountain Fine Art Gallery, Stowe VT

Noble, Scott, *Owner,* Green Mountain Fine Art Gallery, Stowe VT

Noblett, David, *Prof,* Missouri Southern State University, Dept of Art, Joplin MO (S)

Noblett, Duane, *Head Dept & Prof,* Kansas State University, Art Dept, Manhattan KS (S)

Noblick, Martha, *Asst Librn,* Historic Deerfield, Inc, Henry N Flynt Library, Deerfield MA

Nochberg, Edwin, *VPres,* SculptureCenter, Long Island City NY

Nocom, Rowena, *Admin Asst,* Broward County Board of Commissioners, Broward Cultural Div, Fort Lauderdale FL

Noda, Masaaki, *VPres,* Society of American Graphic Artists, New York NY

Nodelman, Jenny, *Mktg & Events Officer,* Nova Scotia Museum, Maritime Museum of the Atlantic, Halifax NS

Nodine, Cassie, *Dir Holocaust Educ,* The Sherwin Miller Museum of Jewish Art, Tulsa OK

Nodine, Jane, *Dir Gallery,* University of South Carolina at Spartanburg, Art Gallery, Spartanburg SC

Noe, Lendon H, *Asst Prof,* Lambuth University, Dept of Human Ecology & Visual Arts, Jackson TN (S)

Noeding, Thomas, *Owner,* Bent Museum & Gallery, Taos NM

Noga, Joseph L, *Coordr Grad Prog,* Rochester Institute of Technology, School of Printing Management & Sciences, Rochester NY (S)

Nogrady, Elizabeth, *Cur Academic Progs,* Vassar College, The Frances Lehman Loeb Art Center, Poughkeepsie NY

Nohe, Timothy, *Prof,* University of Maryland, Baltimore County, Intermedia & Digital Arts (IMDA), Dept of Visual Arts, Baltimore MD (S)

Nolan Jehorek, Tiffany, *Exec Director,* Longview Museum of Fine Art, Longview TX

Nolan Warren, Gwen, *Mus Shop Mgr,* Harrison County Historical Museum, Marshall TX

Nolan, Carrie, *Mgr,* Ford Motor Company, Henry Ford Museum & Greenfield Village, Dearborn MI

Nolan, Ed, *Cur Spec Coll,* Washington State Historical Society, Research Center, Tacoma WA

Nolan, John, *Instr,* Bob Jones University, School of Fine Arts, Div of Art & Design, Greenville SC (S)

Nolan, Mary, *Asst Dir & Ed,* C G Jung Center, Evanston IL

Nolan, Patricia E, *Spec Arts Services Dir,* American Society of Artists, Inc, Palatine IL

Noland, Katherine, *Exec Asst,* University of San Diego, Founders' Gallery, San Diego CA

Nold, Carl R, *Pres & CEO,* Historic New England, Boston MA

Nolen, Lori, *Instr,* Union University, Dept of Art, Jackson TN (S)

Noll, Steve, *Exec Dir,* Wornall Majors House Museums, The 1859 Jail, Marshal's Home & Museum, Independence MO

Noonan, Jennifer, *Asst Prof,* Caldwell College, Dept of Fine Arts, Caldwell NJ (S)

Norberg, Deborah, *Deputy Dir,* San Jose Museum of Art, San Jose CA

Norbert, Deborah, *Deputy Dir,* San Jose Museum of Art, Library, San Jose CA

Norbut, Irene, *Dir Periodicals Coll,* Balzekas Museum of Lithuanian Culture, Chicago IL

Nordlund, Benjamin, *Dir,* Yellowstone County Museum, Billings MT

Nordman, Russ, *Assoc Prod,* University of Nebraska at Omaha, School of the Arts, Omaha NE (S)

Nordquist, Caroline, *Sr Develop Mgr,* Mingei International, Inc, Mingei International Museum - Balboa Park & Mingei International Museum - Escondido, San Diego CA

Nordtorp-Madson, Shelly, *Prof,* University of St Thomas, Deptartment of Art History, Saint Paul MN (S)

Nordyke, John, *Asst Prof,* University of Hartford, Hartford Art School, West Hartford CT (S)

Nore, Nano, *Chmn,* William Jewell College, Art Dept, Liberty MO (S)

Noreen, Kirsten, *Asst,* Louisiana State University, School of Art, Baton Rouge LA (S)

Noreen, Kirstin, *Assoc Prof,* Loyola Marymount University, Dept of Art & Art History, Los Angeles CA (S)

Norganes, Yvonne, *Archaeologist,* University of Puerto Rico, Museum of Anthropology, History & Art, Rio Piedras PR

Noriega, Ed, *Prof,* Troy State University, Dept of Art & Classics, Troy AL (S)

Norlen, Alison, *Prof,* University of Saskatchewan, Art & Art History Dept, Saskatoon SK (S)

Norley, Mark, *Advising Cur,* Hockaday Museum of Art, Kalispell MT

Norman, Heather L, *CEO & Archivist,* Galesburg Civic Art Center, Galesburg IL

Norman, Joe, *Assoc Prof Drawing & Painting,* University of Georgia, Franklin College of Arts & Sciences, Lamar Dodd School of Art, Athens GA (S)

Norman, Karl, *Chmn,* Grambling State University, Art Dept, Grambling LA (S)

Normandin, Pascal, *Head Exhibs Mgmnt,* Montreal Museum of Fine Arts, Montreal QC

Norris, Andrea, *Dir Mus,* University of Kansas, Kress Foundation Dept of Art History, Lawrence KS (S)

Norris, Deann, *Instr,* Pittsburg State University, Art Dept, Pittsburg KS (S)

Norris, Joyce, *Librn,* Wichita Art Museum, Emprise Bank Research Library, Wichita KS

Norris, Sarah, *Rental Coordr,* Art Community Center, Art Center of Corpus Christi, Corpus Christi TX

Norris, Tim, *Prog Coordr,* Muskegon Community College, Dept of Creative & Performing Arts, Muskegon MI (S)

North, Cori, *Cur,* Birger Sandzen Memorial Gallery, Lindsborg KS

North, Kenda, *Prof,* University of Texas at Arlington, Art & Art History Department, Arlington TX (S)

Northerner, Sara, *Assoc Prof,* Utah State University, Dept of Art, Logan UT (S)

Northrop, Eileen, *Dir Admis,* Art Institute of Fort Lauderdale, Fort Lauderdale FL (S)

Northrop, Eileen, *Dir Admissions,* Art Institute of Fort Lauderdale, Fort Lauderdale FL (S)

Northrop, Jennifer, *Dir Mktg & Communs,* San Francisco Museum of Modern Art, San Francisco CA

Northrup, JoAnne, *Sr Cur,* San Jose Museum of Art, Library, San Jose CA

Norton, Ann Wood, *Chmn,* Providence College, Art & Art History Dept, Providence RI (S)

Norton, Chris, *Collections Manager, Registrar, Preparator,* Old Dominion University, The College of Arts and Letters, Norfolk VA

Norton, Heidi, *Guest Experience & Retail Mgr,* The Currier Museum of Art, Manchester NH

Norton, James, *Instr,* University of Louisiana at Monroe, Dept of Art, Monroe LA (S)

Norton, Julia, *Admin & Volunteer Coordr,* Laumeier Sculpture Park, Saint Louis MO

Norton, M Lewis, *Pres Bd,* R W Norton Art Foundation, R W Norton Art Gallery, Shreveport LA

Norton, Nancy, *VPres,* Blacksburg Regional Art Association, Blacksburg VA

Norton, Ruth, *Secy-Treas & Dir Pub Rels,* R W Norton Art Foundation, R W Norton Art Gallery, Shreveport LA

Norton-Westbrook, Halona, *Dir Cur Affairs,* Toledo Museum of Art, Toledo OH

Norville, Anna, *VPres Develop & External Relations,* The Mariners' Museum, Newport News VA

Noss, Maggie, *Acting Dir, School of Art + Design,* Montgomery College, Dept of Art, Rockville MD (S)

Nostrala, Justin, *Asst Prof,* Simpson College, Farnham Gallery, Indianola IA

Nottage, James H, *VPres & Chief Curatorial Officer,* Eiteljorg Museum of American Indians & Western Art, Indianapolis IN

Nouril, Bruno, *Develop Dir,* The Drawing Center, New York NY

Nourse, Mike, *Dir Educ,* Hyde Park Art Center, Chicago IL

Nova, Olga, *Asst Dir,* Academy of Art, University Library, San Francisco CA

Novak, Alice, *Asst Cur Educ,* Montgomery Museum of Fine Arts, Library, Montgomery AL

Novak, Allen, *Visual Resources Librn,* Ringling College of Art & Design, Verman Kimbrough Memorial Library, Sarasota FL

Novak, Amy, *Assoc Coordr Mus Experience,* The Metropolitan Museum of Art, The Met Breuer, New York NY

Novak, Celeste, *Treas,* National Architectural Accrediting Board, Inc, Washington DC

Novak, Constance, *Supervising Librn,* The New York Public Library, Mid-Manhattan Library, Picture Collection, New York NY

Novak, Ellie, *Devel Dir,* Bemis Center for Contemporary Arts, Omaha NE

Novak, Martin, *Instr,* University of Utah, Dept of Art & Art History, Salt Lake City UT (S)

Novak, William, *Chmn Graphic Arts & Design,* Woodbury University, School of Media, Culture & Design, Burbank CA (S)

Novelli, Martin, *Dean Humanities,* Ocean County College, Humanities Dept, Toms River NJ (S)

Novikova, Svetlana, *Adminr,* Gallery Moos Ltd, Toronto ON

Nowacki, Thomas, *Dept Head Biomedical Art,* Cleveland Institute of Art, Cleveland OH (S)

Nowak, Rhea, *Assoc Prof,* State University of New York College at Oneonta, Dept of Art, Oneonta NY (S)

Nowicki, Angie, *Ranger,* Jack London, House of Happy Walls, Glen Ellen CA

Nowicki, Joshua, *Dir Community Rels,* Krasl Art Center, Saint Joseph MI

Nowlan, Gillian, *Music Librn & Film Librn,* University of Regina, Education/Fine Arts Library, Regina SK

Nowlin, Brian, *COO,* California State University, Long Beach Foundation, Long Beach CA

Nowlin, Bridget, *Visual Arts Librn,* Cornish College of the Arts, Cornish Library, Seattle WA

Nowlin, Devon, *Dir,* Texas Christian University, Moudy Gallery, Fort Worth TX

Nowlin, Stephen, *Dir,* Art Center College of Design, Alyce de Roulet Williamson Gallery, Pasadena CA

Nowlin, Stephen, *Dir Alyce de Roulet Williamson Gallery,* ArtCenter College of Design, Pasadena CA (S)

Nowlin, Tim, *Dept Head, Art & Art History,* University of Saskatchewan, Art & Art History Dept, Saskatoon SK (S)

Nowling, Bobbie, *Admin Dir,* Palos Verdes Art Center/ Beverly G. Alpay Center for Arts Education, Rancho Palos Verdes CA

Noworyta, Rachelynn, *Educ Dir,* Locust Street Neighborhood Art Classes, Inc, Buffalo NY (S)

Nowosielski, Rodney, *Assoc Prof,* Saginaw Valley State University, Dept of Art & Design, University Center MI (S)

Noyes, Cecilia, *Instr,* Bakersfield College, Art Dept, Bakersfield CA (S)

Noyes, Julia, *Dir,* Noyes Art Gallery, Lincoln NE

Noyes, Julie, *Instr,* Northeast Community College, Dept of Liberal Arts, Norfolk NE (S)

Noyes, Nicholas, *Cur Library Colls,* Maine Historical Society, Library and Museum, Portland ME

Noyes, Nicholas, *Cur Library Colls,* Maine Historical Society, Portland ME

Nucci Kelly, Julia, *Coordr Communs & Mktg,* University of Illinois at Urbana-Champaign, Krannert Art Museum and Kinkead Pavilion, Champaign IL

Nuell, Christie, *Instr,* Middle Tennessee State University, Art Dept, Murfreesboro TN (S)

Nuell, Lon, *Instr,* Middle Tennessee State University, Art Dept, Murfreesboro TN (S)

Nugent, Patricia, *Assoc Prof & Dir Gallery,* Rosemont College, Art Program, Rosemont PA (S)

Null, Charleen A, *Instr,* Pearl River Community College, Visual Arts, Dept of Fine Arts & Communication, Poplarville MS (S)

Null, Matthew, *Writing Coordr,* Fine Arts Work Center, Hudson D. Walker Gallery, Provincetown MA

Nunes, Grafton, *Pres,* Cleveland Institute of Art, Cleveland OH (S)

Nunes, Grafton, *Pres,* Cleveland Institute of Art, Reinberger Galleries, Cleveland OH

Nunez, Mercedes, *Prof,* Bridgewater State College, Art Dept, Bridgewater MA (S)

Nunn, Julie, *Dir Mktg, Communs, Frontline & Mem,* Exploratorium, San Francisco CA

Nussbaum, Margaret, *Instr,* Manhattan Graphics Center, New York NY (S)

Nutter, Robin, *Develop Dir,* Pilgrim Society, Pilgrim Hall Museum, Plymouth MA

Nuvayestewa, Grace, *Library Specialist,* Institute of American Indian Arts, College of Contemporary Native Arts Library and Archives, Santa Fe NM

Nyberg, John, *Dir,* Jefferson County Historical Society Museum, Madison IN

Nydorf, Roy, *Prof of Art,* Guilford College, Art Dept, Greensboro NC (S)

Nye, Jelinda, *Sales Manager of Sales Gallery,* Carnegie Arts Center, Alliance NE

Nye, Lauren, *Dir Exhibs,* Susquehanna Art Museum, Harrisburg PA

Nye, Michelle, *Gallery Coordr,* San Francisco Museum of Modern Art, Artist Gallery, San Francisco CA

Nye, Valerie, *Library Dir,* Institute of American Indian Arts, College of Contemporary Native Arts Library and Archives, Santa Fe NM

Nyerges, Alex, *Dir & CEO,* Virginia Museum of Fine Arts, Richmond VA

Nygard, Travis, *Asst Prof,* Ripon College, Art Dept, Ripon WI (S)

Nyman, Stacey, *Educ Mgr,* Swedish American Museum, Chicago IL

Nyman, William, *Asst Prof,* The College of New Jersey, School of Arts & Sciences, Ewing NJ (S)

Nyquist, Lars, *Industrial Design,* Art Institute of Pittsburgh, Pittsburgh PA (S)

NyQuist, Michelle, *Pres,* Dauphin & District Allied Arts Council, Watson Art Centre, Dauphin MB

Nystrom, Gwendolen, *Dir Volunteers & Heritage Experiences,* Indiana Landmarks, Morris-Butler House, Indianapolis IN

Nytes, Jackie, *CEO,* Indianapolis Marion County Public Library, Central Library, Indianapolis IN

O'Bourke, Rosemarie, *Dir,* Gulf Coast Community College, Division of Visual & Performing Arts, Panama City FL (S)

O'Brian, Melanie, *Dir & Cur,* Simon Fraser University, Simon Fraser University Gallery, Burnaby BC

O'Brien, Alden, *Cur Costumes & Textiles,* DAR Museum, Library, Washington DC

O'Brien, Ann, *VPres,* ARC Gallery and Educational Foundation, Chicago IL

O'Brien, Derek, *Instr,* Lakeland Community College, Fine Arts Department, Kirtland OH (S)

O'Brien, Flynn, *Exhibs & Mem Mgr,* Sonoma Valley Museum of Art, Sonoma CA

O'Brien, James, *Instructor,* Concordia University, Art and Design Department, Saint Paul MN (S)

O'Brien, Jennifer, *Data Asst,* National Air and Space Museum, Regional Planetary Image Facility, Washington DC

O'Brien, Lilian, *Bus Mgr,* Cape Cod Museum of Art Inc, Dennis MA

O'Brien, Liz Hunt, *Dir Arts Prog,* Artists Association of Nantucket, Nantucket MA

O'Brien, Maureen, *Cur Painting & Sculpture,* Rhode Island School of Design, Museum of Art, Providence RI

O'Brien, Neil, *Exhib Specialist & Preparator,* University of Memphis, Art Museum, Memphis TN

O'Brien, Susan, *Assoc Prof,* University of Wisconsin-Eau Claire, Dept of Art & Design, Eau Claire WI (S)

O'Brien, Susan, *Asst Prof,* Murray State University, Dept of Art, Murray KY (S)

O'Brien, Tara, *Dir Conservation,* Historical Society of Pennsylvania, Philadelphia PA

O'Brien, Tim, *Pres,* Society of Illustrators, New York NY

O'Brien, Tim, *Pres,* Society of Illustrators, Museum of American Illustration, New York NY

O'Callaghan, Thomas A, *Spanish Specialist,* National Gallery of Art, Department of Image Collections, Washington DC

O'Connell, Bethany, *Mktg & Communs,* Missoula Art Museum, Missoula MT

O'Connell, Bonnie, *Prof,* University of Nebraska at Omaha, School of the Arts, Omaha NE (S)

O'Connell, John, *Asst Prof,* University of Utah, Dept of Art & Art History, Salt Lake City UT (S)

O'Connell, John, *Instr,* Middle Tennessee State University, Art Dept, Murfreesboro TN (S)

O'Connell, Karen, *Accounting Mgr,* Portraits South, Raleigh NC

O'Connell, Meg, *Pres,* Skaneateles Library Association, Skaneateles NY

O'Connor, Harold, *Head,* Dunconor Workshops, Salida CO (S)

O'Connor, John, *Asst Prof,* Radford University, Art Dept, Radford VA (S)

O'Connor, Margaret, *Exec Dir,* Gilbert Stuart Memorial Association, Inc, Gilbert Stuart Birthplace & Museum, Saunderstown RI

O'Connor, Rachel, *Asst Cur,* Art Association of Harrisburg, School & Galleries, Harrisburg PA

O'Day, Karen, *Assoc Prof,* University of Wisconsin-Eau Claire, Dept of Art & Design, Eau Claire WI (S)

O'Day, Tom, *Asst Prof,* Spokane Falls Community College, Fine Arts Dept, Spokane WA (S)

O'Dell, Kathy, *Assoc Prof,* University of Maryland, Baltimore County, Intermedia & Digital Arts (IMDA), Dept of Visual Arts, Baltimore MD (S)

O'Donnell, Hugh, *Prof,* Boston University, School for the Arts, Boston MA (S)

O'Donnell, Patrick, *Educ & Outreach Mgr,* Norman Rockwell Museum, Stockbridge MA

O'Donnell, Patrick, *Education & Outreach Manager,* Norman Rockwell Museum, Stockbridge MA

O'Donnell, Sue, *Asst Prof,* Bloomsburg University, Dept of Art & Art History, Bloomsburg PA (S)

O'Dwyer, Deirdre, *Managing Ed,* University of California, Los Angeles, Fowler Museum at UCLA, Los Angeles CA

O'Flaherty, Deirdre, *Pres,* Barn Gallery, Ogunquit ME

O'Gorman, James F, *Chmn,* Wellesley College, Art Dept, Wellesley MA (S)

O'Grady, Jennifer Nsocky, *Prof & Chair,* Cleveland State University, Art Dept, Cleveland OH (S)

O'Grady, Sarah, *Educ Coordr,* Mississippi Valley Conservation Authority, R Tait McKenzie Memorial Museum, Almonte ON

O'Halloran, Kate, *Secy,* Waterville Historical Society, Redington Museum, Waterville ME

O'Hanian, Hunter, *Exec Dir,* College Art Association, New York NY

O'Hara, Virginia, *Cur Collections,* Brandywine Conservancy, Brandywine River Museum, Chadds Ford PA

O'Hare, Joanne, *Artist,* Walker's Point Artists Assoc Inc, Gallery 218, Milwaukee WI

O'Harrow, Sean, *Dir,* Honolulu Museum of Art, Honolulu HI

O'Keefe, Doris N, *Sr Cataloger Rare Books,* American Antiquarian Society, Worcester MA

O'Keefe, Michael J, *Chmn,* Oklahoma Christian University of Science & Arts, Dept of Art & Design, Oklahoma City OK (S)

O'Keeffe, Timothy, *Asst Prof,* University of Wisconsin-Stout, Dept of Art & Design, Menomonie WI (S)

O'Leary, Helen, *Prof Art (Drawing/Painting),* Pennsylvania State University, University Park, Penn State School of Visual Arts, University Park PA (S)

O'Loughlin, Meghan, *Cur Educ,* Arnot Art Museum, Elmira NY

O'Malley, Jeannette, *Exec Dir,* Pasadena Museum of History, Pasadena CA

O'Malley, Kathleen L, *Pres,* Cohasset Historical Society, Cohasset Maritime Museum, Cohasset MA

O'Malley, Kathleen L, *Pres,* Cohasset Historical Society, Pratt Building (Society Headquarters), Cohasset MA

O'Malley, Kathleen L, *Pres,* Cohasset Historical Society, Captain John Wilson Historical House, Cohasset MA

O'Malley, Kathleen, *Registrar,* Dartmouth College, Hood Museum of Art, Hanover NH

O'Malley, Tom, *Ceramics & Photog Dept Head,* Worcester Center for Crafts, Worcester MA (S)

O'Mara, Joan, *Assoc Prof,* Washington and Lee University, Div of Art, Lexington VA (S)

O'Mara, Shawn, *Digital Design,* Art Institute of Pittsburgh, Pittsburgh PA (S)
O'Meara, Nancy G, *Exec Dir,* Philadelphia Museum of Art, Women's Committee, Philadelphia PA
O'Neal, Jeremy, *Interim Exec Dir,* Bay Area Video Coalition, Inc, San Francisco CA
O'Neal, Larry, *Dept Head Graphic Design,* Cleveland Institute of Art, Cleveland OH (S)
O'Neil, Alexandra, *Co-Chair ADAD Dept,* Butte College, Art Gallery, Oroville CA
O'Neil, Karen, *Instr,* Woodstock School of Art, Inc, Woodstock NY (S)
O'Neil, Kevin, *Instr,* Keystone College, Fine Arts Dept, LaPlume PA (S)
O'Neil, Mary Lovelace, *Chair,* University of California, Berkeley, College of Letters & Sciences-Art Practice Dept, Berkeley CA (S)
O'Neil, Maureen, *Instr,* Flagler College, Visual Arts Dept, Saint Augustine FL (S)
O'Neil, Robert, *Asst Prof,* The College of Saint Rose, The Center For Art and Design, Albany NY (S)
O'Neill, Cheryl, *Librn,* Art Complex Museum, Carl A Weyerhaeuser Library, Duxbury MA
O'Neill, Cheryl, *Librn,* Art Complex Museum, Library, Duxbury MA
O'Neill, Ed, *Chmn,* Brookdale Community College, Center for the Visual Arts, Lincroft NJ (S)
O'Neill, Francis, *Sr Reference Librn,* Maryland Historical Society, Library, Baltimore MD
O'Neill, John, *Cur Rare Books,* The Hispanic Society of America, Hispanic Society Museum & Library, New York NY
O'Neill, Joseph, *Treas,* Phoenix Gallery, New York NY
O'Neill, Kevin, *Facilities Mgr,* Chatillon-DeMenil House Foundation, Chatillon-DeMenil Mansion, Saint Louis MO
O'Neill, Mark, *Pres & CEO,* Canadian War Museum, Ottawa ON
O'Neill, Mark, *Pres & CEO,* Canadian Museum of History, Gatineau QC
O'Neill, Morna, *Asst Prof,* Wake Forest University, Dept of Art, Winston-Salem NC (S)
O'Neill, Paul, *Dir Grad Prog,* Bard College, Center for Curatorial Studies and the Hessel Museum of Art, Annandale-on-Hudson NY
O'Neill, Paul, *Grad Prog Dir,* Bard College, Center for Curatorial Studies Graduate Program, Annandale-on-Hudson NY (S)
O'Neill, Stephen, *Assoc Dir & Cur,* Pilgrim Society, Library, Plymouth MA
O'Neill, Walter, *Dir The Art School,* Boca Raton Museum of Art, Library, Boca Raton FL
O'Neill, Yvette, *Instr,* Lower Columbia College, Art Dept, Longview WA (S)
O'Reere, Regina, *Gallery Preparator,* Nebraska Wesleyan University, Elder Gallery, Lincoln NE
O'Reilly, Margaret, *Exec Dir,* New Jersey State Museum, Fine Art Bureau, Trenton NJ
O'Rork, Sunnee D, *Exec Dir,* i.d.e.a. Museum, Mesa AZ
O'Rouke, Hugh, *Gallery Mgr,* New York University, Washington Square East Galleries, New York NY
O'Rourke, Kathryn, *Secy,* Society of Architectural Historians, Chicago IL
O'Rourke, Michael, *Exec Dir, ADC,* The One Club for Creativity, New York NY
O'Rourke-Kaplan, Marian, *Assoc Prof Fashion Design,* University of North Texas, College of Visual Arts & Design, Denton TX (S)
O'Shaughnessy, David, *Chmn,* Los Angeles Harbor College, Art Dept, Wilmington CA (S)
O'Toole, Judith H, *CEO & The Richard H Scaife Dir,* Westmoreland Museum of American Art, Greensburg PA
O'Toole, Judith H, *Dir & CEO,* Westmoreland Museum of American Art, Art Reference Library, Greensburg PA
Oakley, Lucy, *Head of Education and Programs,* New York University, Grey Art Gallery, New York NY
Oakley, Rochelle L R, *Coll Mgr, Registrar,* Saint Joseph College, Art Gallery, University of Saint Joseph, West Hartford CT
Oakley, Ron, *Chmn,* Davidson County Community College, Humanities Div, Lexington NC (S)
Oaks, Gary, *Asst Prof,* Southern University in New Orleans, Fine Arts & Philosophy Dept, New Orleans LA (S)
Oats, Joclyn, *Architectural-Grad Studies & Coordr Interior Design,* Columbia College, Art Dept, Chicago IL (S)
Obalil, Deborah, *Pres & Exec Dir,* Association of Independent Colleges of Art & Design, Providence RI
Ober, Abigail, *Instr,* Wayne Art Center, Wayne PA (S)
Ober, Ingram, *Gallery Dir,* Palomar Community College, Boehm Gallery, San Marcos CA
Ober, Kathy, *Dir Libr Svcs,* Art Institute of Pittsburgh, Resource Center, Pittsburgh PA
Obermeyer, Cheryl, *VPres Finance,* Chicago History Museum, Chicago IL
Obert, Liz, *Assoc Prof,* Linfield College, Department of Art & Visual Culture, McMinnville OR (S)
Obert, Susan, *Develop Officer,* The San Joaquin Pioneer & Historical Society, The Haggin Museum, Stockton CA
Obetz, Tim, *Chief Preparator,* Institute of Contemporary Art/Boston, Boston MA
Obler, Bibiana, *Asst Prof,* George Washington University, Dept of Art of Fine Arts & Art History, Washington DC (S)
Oblinger, Mollie, *Asst Prof,* Ripon College, Art Dept, Ripon WI (S)
Obrochta, William, *Dir Educ,* Virginia Historical Society, Library, Richmond VA
Ocampo, Lisa, *Mus Shop Mgr,* Telfair Museums, Telfair Academy of Arts & Sciences Library, Savannah GA
Ocasio, Billy, *CEO & Pres,* The National Museum of Puerto Rican Arts & Culture, Chicago IL
Occhiogrosso, Gina, *Assoc Prof,* The College of Saint Rose, The Center For Art and Design, Albany NY (S)
Och, Marjorie, *Asst Prof,* University of Mary Washington, Dept of Art & Art History, Fredericksburg VA (S)
Ochoa, Jody, *Registrar,* Idaho Historical Museum, Boise ID
Ochs, Steven, *Prof,* Southern Arkansas University, Art Dept Gallery & Magale Art Gallery, Magnolia AR
Ochs, Steven, *Prof,* Southern Arkansas University at Magnolia, Dept of Art & Design, Magnolia AR (S)
Oddi, Benedict, *Instr,* Clarion University of Pennsylvania, Dept of Art, Clarion PA (S)
Oddo, Shawn, *Culinary Arts & Management,* Art Institute of Pittsburgh, Pittsburgh PA (S)
Odegaard, Jill, *Asst Prof,* Cedar Crest College, Art Dept, Allentown PA (S)
Odel, Bill, *Prof,* University of Massachusetts, Amherst, Art History Program, Amherst MA (S)
Oden, Fred, *Pres,* Fulton County Historical Society Inc, Fulton County Museum (Tetzlaff Reference Room), Rochester IN
Odencrantz, Susan, *Library Dir,* Tacoma Public Library, Handforth Gallery, Tacoma WA
Odita, Donald, *Assoc Prof,* Florida State University, Art Dept, Tallahassee FL (S)
Oduyoye, Carole L, *Events Coordr,* African Art Museum of Maryland, Columbia MD
Oehler, David, *Assoc Prof/Chair,* Northwest Missouri State University, Dept of Fine & Performing Arts, Maryville MO (S)
Oehlke, Vailey, *Multnomah County Libr Dir,* Multnomah County Library, Henry Failing Art & Music Dept, Portland OR
Oehm, John, *Instr,* Butler Community College, Art Dept, El Dorado KS (S)
Oelkers, Karl, *IT Mgr,* New Orleans Museum of Art, New Orleans LA
Oerichbauer, Edgar, *Exec Dir,* Koochiching Museums, International Falls MN
Oertling, Sewall, *Chmn,* State University of New York College at Oswego, Art Dept, Oswego NY (S)
Oettinger, Marion, *Cur Emeritus Latin American Art,* San Antonio Museum of Art, San Antonio TX
Offutt, Jon, *Artist & Owner,* Gallery 4, Ltd, Fargo ND
Ogar, Ray, *Assoc Prof,* University of Central Arkansas, Department of Art, Conway AR (S)
Ogden, Dale, *Chief Cur Cultural History,* Indiana State Museum, Indianapolis IN
Ogden, Vivian, *Cur,* Kelly-Griggs House Museum, Red Bluff CA
Ogilvie, Cheryl, *Cur,* McDonald's Corporation, Art Collection, Oak Brook IL
Ogilvie, Michael, *Coordr,* Kohler Co, John Michael Kohler Arts Center - Arts/Industry Program, Sheboygan WI
Ogle, Drew, *Exec Dir,* Rose Center & Council for the Arts, Morristown TN
Oglesby, Janet, *Electronic Imaging & Print Instr,* Western Wisconsin Technical College, Graphics Division, La Crosse WI (S)
Oglesby, Lizzie, *Media Rel Spec,* Virginia Historical Society, Library, Richmond VA
Ogoli, David M, *Asst Prof,* Judson University, School of Art, Design & Architecture, Elgin IL (S)
Oguz, Cetin, *Asst Prof,* Delta State University, Dept of Art, Cleveland MS (S)
Oh, Lili, *Dir,* Concord Art Association, Concord MA
Oh, Su, *VPres Educ & Prog,* Natural History Museum of Los Angeles County, Los Angeles CA
Ohira-Rollando, Akemi, *Studio Faculty,* University of Virginia, McIntire Dept of Art, Charlottesville VA (S)
Ohland, Karen, *Assoc Dir Finance & Opers,* Princeton University, Princeton University Art Museum, Princeton NJ
Ohnigian, Robert, *Instr,* Woodstock School of Art, Inc, Woodstock NY (S)
Ohrmann, Bill, *Artist & Owner,* Ohrmann Museum and Gallery, Drummond MT
Ohta, Heather, *Advancement Officer,* Oregon College of Art & Craft, Hoffman Gallery, Portland OR
Oiler, Bradley, *Assoc Prof,* Whitworth University, Art Dept, Spokane WA (S)
Oishei, Judith, *Prog Dir,* Library Association of La Jolla, Athenaeum Music & Arts Library, La Jolla CA
Oitzinger, Destinee, *Gallery Coordr,* National Veterans Art Museum, Chicago IL
Oja, Vivien, *Prog Assoc,* University of Minnesota, Minneapolis, Split Rock Arts Program, St Paul MN (S)
Okamura, Linda, *Professor of Media Arts,* Los Angeles City College, School of Visual & Media Arts, Los Angeles CA (S)
Okaya, Michiko, *Dir Gallery,* Lafayette College, Lafayette College Art Galleries, Easton PA
Okazaki, Arthur, *Chmn,* Tulane University, Sophie H Newcomb Memorial College, New Orleans LA (S)
Oke, Ejenobo, *Assoc Prof,* Manchester College, Dept of Art, North Manchester IN (S)
Okeke-Agulu, Chika, *Asst Prof,* Pennsylvania State University, University Park, Dept of Art History, University Park PA (S)
Okoruwa, Vassandra, *Sales & Mktg,* City of Lubbock, Buddy Holly Center, Lubbock TX
Okshteyn, Sasha, *Co Dir & Cur,* Black & White Gallery, Brooklyn NY
Okshteyn, Tatyana, *Founder & Co Dir,* Black & White Gallery, Brooklyn NY
Olbrantz, John, *Dir,* Willamette University, Hallie Ford Museum of Art, Salem OR
Older, Caroline, *Exec Dir,* Chicago Artists Coalition, Chicago IL
Oldfield, Erin, *Dir Educ & Public Programming,* Oklahoma Contemporary Arts Center, Oklahoma City OK
Oldham, Terry, *Dir,* The Albrecht-Kemper Museum of Art, Bradley Art Library, Saint Joseph MO
Olds, Clifton, *Prof,* Bowdoin College, Art Dept, Brunswick ME (S)
Olijnyk, Michael, *Bd Mem, Co-Dir,* The Mattress Factory, Pittsburgh PA
Olivant, David, *Prof,* California State University, Art Dept, Turlock CA (S)
Olivares, Corie, *Mktg & Develop Dir,* Brownsville Art League, Brownsville Museum of Fine Art, Brownsville TX

Olive, Nancy, *Chmn,* University of Sioux Falls, Dept of Art, Sioux Falls SD (S)
Oliver, Christopher, *Asst Cur American Art,* Virginia Museum of Fine Arts, Richmond VA
Oliver, Debbie, *Registrar,* Nicolaysen Art Museum & Discovery Center, Museum, Casper WY
Oliver, Dorothy, *Dept Secy,* West Virginia Institute of Technology, Creative Arts Dept, Montgomery WV (S)
Oliver, James M, *Prof,* Pittsburg State University, Art Dept, Pittsburg KS (S)
Oliver, Judith, *Assoc Prof,* Colgate University, Dept of Art & Art History, Hamilton NY (S)
Oliver, Kurt, *Cataloger,* Wentworth Institute of Technology, Douglas D Schumann Library & Learning Commons, Boston MA
Oliver, Lauren, *Mem Coordr,* LaGrange Art Museum, LaGrange GA
Oliver, Megan, *Asst Librn,* Florida State University, The John and Mable Ringling Museum of Art Library, Sarasota FL
Oliver, Tracey, *Exec Dir,* Sierra Arts Foundation, Sierra Arts Gallery, Reno NV
Oliver, Wendy, *Dir Workshops,* California Watercolor Association, Gallery Concord, Concord CA
Oliver-Smith, Kerry, *Cur Contemporary Art,* University of Florida, Samuel P Harn Museum of Art, Gainesville FL
Oliveras, Autumn, *Admin Asst,* Cultural Council of Palm Beach County, Lake Worth FL
Oliveri, Meg, *Cur,* Nassau Community College, Firehouse Art Gallery, Garden City NY
Oliveri, Michael, *Asst Prof Digital Media,* University of Georgia, Franklin College of Arts & Sciences, Lamar Dodd School of Art, Athens GA (S)
Olivette, Daniel, *Dir,* Susquehanna University, Lore Degenstein Gallery, Selinsgrove PA
Olivier, Christine, *Prog Dir,* Garner Arts Center, Garnerville NY
Olivier-Salmon, Camille, *Prog Dir,* San Francisco Arts Education Project, San Francisco CA
Ollman, Arthur, *Dir,* San Diego State University, School of Art, Design & Art History, San Diego CA (S)
Olmstead, Richard, *Cur Herbarium,* University of Washington, Burke Museum of Natural History and Culture, Seattle WA
Olon, Gill, *Asst Prof,* University of Wisconsin-Eau Claire, Dept of Art & Design, Eau Claire WI (S)
Olsen, Charles, *Chmn,* St Francis College, Fine Arts Dept, Loretto PA (S)
Olsen, Christina, *Dir,* University of Michigan, Museum of Art, Ann Arbor MI
Olsen, Dennis, *Prof,* University of Texas at San Antonio, Dept of Art & Art History, San Antonio TX (S)
Olsen, Deric, *Chair New Media Dept,* University of Lethbridge, Faculty of Fine Arts, Lethbridge AB (S)
Olsen, Haylee, *Registrar,* Yakima Valley Community College, Larson Gallery, Yakima WA
Olsen, John, *Interim Store Mgr & Buyer,* Montana State University, Museum of the Rockies, Bozeman MT
Olsen, Kathleen, *Dir,* Washington & Lee University, Gallery of DuPont Hall, Lexington VA
Olsen, Mel, *Prof,* University of Wisconsin-Superior, Programs in the Visual Arts, Superior WI (S)
Olson, A J, *Prof,* Troy State University, Dept of Art & Classics, Troy AL (S)
Olson, Alan, *Dir Colls,* Dallas Historical Society, Research Center Library, Dallas TX
Olson, Alan, *Dir Colls,* Dallas Historical Society, Hall of State, Dallas TX
Olson, Ana, *Dir,* Glenhyrst Art Gallery of Brant, Brantford ON
Olson, Cameron, *Vol Pres,* Kenosha Public Museums, Kenosha WI
Olson, Carrie, *Assoc Prof & Chair,* Denison University, Studio Art Program, Granville OH (S)
Olson, Dennis, *Asst Prof,* Amarillo College, Visual Art Dept, Amarillo TX (S)
Olson, Kristina, *Assoc Prof,* West Virginia University, College of Creative Arts, School of Art & Design, Morgantown WV (S)
Olson, Kristina, *Cur,* West Virginia University, Laura & Paul Mesaros Galleries, Morgantown WV
Olson, Michael, *Instr,* Casper College, Dept of Visual Arts, Casper WY (S)
Olson, Pat, *Assoc Prof,* St Catherine University, Art & Art History Dept, Saint Paul MN (S)
Olson, Peter, *Assistant Director,* Northern Illinois University, NIU Art Museum, DeKalb IL
Olson, Phillis, *Board President,* City of Port Angeles, Port Angeles Fine Arts Center & Webster Woods Art Park, Port Angeles WA
Olson, Roger, *Bd VPres,* The Phipps Center for the Arts, Galleries, Hudson WI
Olson, Sarah, *Supt,* Roosevelt-Vanderbilt National Historic Sites, Hyde Park NY
Olson, Susan, *Develop Secy,* Iowa State University, Brunnier Art Museum, Ames IA
Olson-Clark, Kim, *Develop Officer,* Evanston Historical Society, Charles Gates Dawes House, Evanston IL
Olson-Janjic, Kathleen, *Assoc Prof,* Washington and Lee University, Div of Art, Lexington VA (S)
Olt, Frank, *Assoc Prof,* C W Post Campus of Long Island University, School of Visual & Performing Arts, Brookville NY (S)
Oltjenbruns, Leona, *Secy,* Phillips County Museum, Holyoke CO
Oltvedt, Carl, *Prof,* Minnesota State University-Moorhead, Dept of Art & Design, Moorhead MN (S)
Olvera, John, *Prof,* Winthrop University, Dept of Art & Design, Rock Hill SC (S)
Oman, Earl, *Cur Colls (Emeritus),* Northern Maine Museum of Science, Presque Isle ME
Omann, Britt, *Gallery Asst,* Soo Visual Arts Center, Minneapolis MN
Ondo, Greg, *Adjunct Asst Prof,* University of Maine, Dept of Art, Orono ME (S)
Ondrizek, Geraldine, *Asst Prof Art,* Reed College, Dept of Art, Portland OR (S)
Oney, Danielle, *Events Coord,* North Tonawanda History Museum, North Tonawanda NY
Onli, Meg, *Asst Cur,* University of Pennsylvania, Institute of Contemporary Art, Philadelphia PA
Onofrio, Jennifer, *Prof,* Augusta State University, Dept of Art, Augusta GA (S)
Onorato, Ronald, *Prof,* University of Rhode Island, Dept of Art & Art History, Kingston RI (S)
Ontiveros, Salvador, *Dir Fin,* Oklahoma Contemporary Arts Center, Oklahoma City OK
Onyile, Onyile B, *Prod,* Georgia Southern University, Betty Foy Sanders Dept of Art, Statesboro GA (S)
Opalko, Michael N, *Graphic Design,* Art Institute of Pittsburgh, Pittsburgh PA (S)
Ophime, Jeff, *Dir,* Colquitt County Arts Center, Moultrie GA
Opoku, Kofi, *Asst Prof,* West Virginia University, College of Creative Arts, School of Art & Design, Morgantown WV (S)
Opp, Nathan, *Instr,* Oral Roberts University, Art Dept, Tulsa OK (S)
Oppenheim, Phyllis, *Colls Mgr,* Herrett Center for Arts & Sciences, Jean B King Art Gallery, Twin Falls ID
Oppenhimer, Ann, *Dir,* Folk Art Society of America, Richmond VA
Oppenhimer, William, *C.F.O.,* Folk Art Society of America, Richmond VA
Oppio, Amy, *Deputy Dir & COO,* Nevada Museum of Art, Reno NV
Orcutt, Kimberly, *Andrew W Mellon Cur American Art,* Brooklyn Museum, Brooklyn NY
Ordon, Maggie, *Cur History,* Montana Historical Society, Helena MT
Ore, Joyce, *Dir Pub Rels,* Hastings College, Department of Visual Arts, Hastings NE (S)
Orenstein, Ellen, *Assoc Prof Theatre,* Marymount Manhattan College, Fine & Performing Arts Div, New York NY (S)
Orenstein, Nadine, *Cur in Charge, Drawings & Prints,* The Metropolitan Museum of Art, New York NY
Orgren, Sally, *Ed,* Handweavers Guild of America, Suwanee GA
Oring, Sheryl, *Prof,* University of North Carolina at Greensboro, School of Art, Greensboro NC (S)
Oritsky, Mimi, *Instr,* Main Line Art Center, Haverford PA (S)
Orlando, Fran, *Dir Exhib,* Bucks County Community College, Hicks Art Center, Newtown PA
Orlando, Joe, *Dir Educ,* Art Institute of Houston, Houston TX (S)
Orlofsky, Patsy, *Exec Dir,* Textile Conservation Workshop Inc, South Salem NY
Orlovski, Stas, *Instr,* Long Beach City College, Art & Photography Dept, Long Beach CA (S)
Ormai, Ted, *Vice Pres,* New Arts Program, Inc, NAP Museum, NAP Main Gallery, William Zimmer Reference Library, Kutztown PA
Ormasen, Debbie, *Accnt Mgr,* Frederic Remington, Ogdensburg NY
Orme, Joyce, *Staff Asst III,* College of Central Florida, Appleton Museum of Art, Ocala FL
Ormerod-Glynn, Barbara, *Acting Dir,* Greenwich Library, Greenwich CT
Ornstein, Cindy, *Exec Dir,* Mesa Arts Center, Mesa Contemporary Arts Museum, Mesa AZ
Orologas, Claire, *Exec Dir & Chief Cur,* Polk Museum of Art, Lakeland FL
Orozco, Sylvia, *Exec Dir,* MEXIC-ARTE Museum, Austin TX
Orr, Amy, *Asst Prof,* Rosemont College, Art Program, Rosemont PA (S)
Orr, Clint, *Assoc Prof,* University of Central Missouri, Dept of Art & Design, Warrensburg MO (S)
Orr, Estelle, *Painting,* Santa Ana College, Art Dept, Santa Ana CA (S)
Orr, Fred, *Opers Tech,* Zanesville Museum of Art, Zanesville OH
Orr, Heather, *Dept Chair,* Western State College of Colorado, Dept of Art & Industrial Technology, Gunnison CO (S)
Orr, Rebecca, *Mem Adminr,* Southern Highland Craft Guild, Folk Art Center, Asheville NC
Orr, Vivian, *Communs Coordr,* Saskatchewan Craft Council & Affinity Gallery, Saskatoon SK
Orrell, Theresa, *Vol Coordr,* Mobile Museum of Art, Mobile AL
Orsinger, Marilyn, *Dir Opers,* Delaplaine Visual Arts Education Center, Frederick MD
Ortbals, John, *Assoc Prof,* Saint Louis Community College at Florissant Valley, Liberal Arts Division, Ferguson MO (S)
Ortega, Jean, *Asst Dir,* Bass Museum of Art, Miami Beach FL
Ortega, Lisa, *Edu,* University of Puerto Rico, Museum of Anthropology, History & Art, Rio Piedras PR
Ortega, Rina, *Communs Mgr,* ArtsConnection Inc, New York NY
Ortega, Vickie, *Admin Asst,* New Mexico Department of Cultural Affairs, Palace of Governors, Santa Fe NM
Orthmann, Lucas, *Cur,* Clymer Museum of Art, The Clymer Museum & Gallery, Ellensburg WA
Ortiz Declet, Bianca, *Dir Exhibs & Educ Prog,* The National Museum of Puerto Rican Arts & Culture, Chicago IL
Ortiz, Alfredo, *Prof,* University of Puerto Rico, Mayaguez, Dept of Humanities, College of Fine Arts & Theory of Art Programs, Mayaguez PR (S)
Ortiz, Andrew, *Assoc Prof,* University of Texas at Arlington, Art & Art History Department, Arlington TX (S)
Ortiz, Jose, *Exhib Mgr,* Philadelphia Museum of Art, Samuel S Fleisher Art Memorial, Philadelphia PA
Ortiz, Lionel, *Designer,* University of Puerto Rico, Museum of Anthropology, History & Art, Rio Piedras PR
Ortner, Frederick, *Chmn,* Knox College, Dept of Art, Galesburg IL (S)
Orzel, Robyn P, *Dir Develop,* Vero Beach Museum of Art, Vero Beach FL

Osberg, Kerry K, *Exec Dir,* Visual Arts Minnesota, Saint Cloud MN

Osborn, Nancy, *Theater,* Saint Clair County Community College, Jack R Hennesey Art Dept, Port Huron MI (S)

Osborne, Josie, *Dir Foundations,* University of Wisconsin-Milwaukee, Peck School of the Arts, Dept of Art & Design, Milwaukee WI (S)

Osborne, Zachary, *Librn,* Textile Museum of Canada, Toronto ON

Osbourne, Ginger, *Office Mgr,* Association for Public Art, Philadelphia PA

Osby, Kayla, *Opers Mgr,* Pearl Fincher Museum of Fine Arts, Spring TX

Osepchook, Felicity, *Head, Archives & Research Library,* New Brunswick Museum, Archives & Research Library, Saint John NB

Oshana, Christopher, *Production,* monOrchid Gallery, Phoenix AZ

Oshima, David, *Art Dept Chmn,* Pierce College, Art Dept, Woodland Hills CA (S)

Osman, Jim, *Secy,* American Abstract Artists, Brooklyn NY

Osmond, Lynn J, *Pres & CEO,* Chicago Architecture Foundation, Chicago IL

Ospina, Adriana, *Cur,* Art Museum of the Americas, Archive of Contemporary Latin American Art, Washington DC

Ospina, Adriana, *Cur Permanent Coll & Educ,* Art Museum of the Americas, Washington DC

Oste-Alexander, Pia, *Instr,* Woodstock School of Art, Inc, Woodstock NY (S)

Ostendarp, Carl, *Dir Grad Studies,* Cornell University, Dept of Art, Ithaca NY (S)

Ostendorf, Eleanor, *Cur Historic House,* Iowa State University, Brunnier Art Museum, Ames IA

Osterman, William, *Asst Prof,* Rochester Institute of Technology, School of Photographic Arts & Sciences, Rochester NY (S)

Osthoff, Simone, *Assoc Prof Art (Art Criticism),* Pennsylvania State University, University Park, Penn State School of Visual Arts, University Park PA (S)

Ostman, Jessica, *Prog Dir,* Saint Cloud State University, Atwood Memorial Center Gallery, Saint Cloud MN

Ostrow, Steven, *Chmn & Prof,* University of Minnesota, Minneapolis, Art History, Minneapolis MN (S)

Osttinger, April, *Prof,* Goucher College, Art & Art History Dept, Baltimore MD (S)

Ostwald, Don, *Pres Heritage Foundation,* Fort Morgan Heritage Foundation, Fort Morgan CO

Ostwind, Marcia, *Coordr Bd Mem,* Women in the Arts Foundation, Inc, Staten Island NY

Oswald, April, *Educ Dir,* Munson-Williams-Proctor Arts Institute, Museum of Art, Utica NY

Oszuscik, Philippe, *Art Historian,* University of South Alabama, Dept of Art & Art History, Mobile AL (S)

Othman, Hadeel, *Gallery Servs Adminr,* Where Edmonton Community Artists Network Society, Harcourt House Arts Centre, Edmonton AB

Otis, Michaelin, *Faculty,* Grand Marais Art Colony, Grand Marais MN (S)

Otoupalik, Hayes, *VPres,* Rocky Mountain Museum of Military History, Missoula MT

Otremsky, William, *Assoc Prof Art, Chmn Dept Art & Art History, Dir Studio Prog,* Florida Southern College, Melvin Art Gallery, Lakeland FL

Otremsky, William, *Assoc Prof Art, Dept Art & Art History Chair, Dir Studio Programming,* Florida Southern College, Department of Art & Art History, Lakeland FL (S)

Otrs, Julie Ann, *Develop Mem Coordr,* Dartmouth College, Hood Museum of Art, Hanover NH

Otsuka, Ron, *Adj Faculty Art History,* University of Denver, School of Art & Art History, Denver CO (S)

Ott, Lili, *Dir,* Shaker Museum & Library, Old Chatham NY

Ott, Rachel, *Dir Develop Mktg,* Neville Public Museum of Brown County, Green Bay WI

Ott, William, *Info Sys Mgr,* Grand Rapids Public Library, Grand Rapids MI

Ottaviano, Lillian, *Prof,* Cazenovia College, Center for Art & Design Studies, Cazenovia NY (S)

Otterson, Nathan, *Sr Conservator Objects,* Solomon R Guggenheim Museum, New York NY

Ottinger, Matt, *Dir Facilities & Historic Preservation,* The Bostonian Society, Old State House Museum, Boston MA

Ottman, Rebecca, *Dir Mktg & Communs,* University of Wisconsin, Arts Center Gallery, Milwaukee WI

Ottmann, Klaus, *Cur, Robert Lehman,* Parrish Art Museum, Water Mill NY

Ottmann, Klaus, *Deputy Dir Curatorial & Academic Affairs,* The Phillips Collection, Washington DC

Otto, Charlotte, *Visitor Servs Mgr,* Kirkland Museum of Fine & Decorative Art, Denver CO

Otto, Elizabeth, *Art History & Visual Studies,* University at Buffalo, State University of New York, Dept of Visual Studies, Buffalo NY (S)

Otto, Richard H, *Pres,* American Academy of Art, Chicago IL (S)

Otto-Miller, Jackie, *Dir,* Valencia Community College - East Campus, Art Dept, Orlando FL (S)

Otts, Dylan, *Site Mgr,* Stone Quarry Hill Art Park, Winner Gallery, Cazenovia NY

Ouellet, Kathi, *Bd Pres,* Indian Arts & Crafts Association, Albuquerque NM

Ouellet, Therese, *VPres,* Institut des Arts au Saguenay, Centre National D'Exposition a Jonquiere, Jonquiere QC

Ouellette, Jonathan, *Dir Finance & Admin,* Royal Architectural Institute of Canada, Ottawa ON

Ouellette, Julia, *Chair,* Museum of Contemporary Canadian Art, Toronto ON

Oursler, Henry Charles, *Asst Prof Art,* Western Illinois University, Department of Art, Macomb IL (S)

Ousey, Jack, *Instr,* Southeastern Oklahoma State University, Dept of Art, Communication & Theatre, Durant OK (S)

Overall, Scott, *Assoc Dir & Cur,* University Club Library, New York NY

Overbeck, John, *Prof,* State University of New York at Albany, Art Dept, Albany NY (S)

Overbey, Karen, *Assoc Prof & Dir Grad Studies,* Tufts University, Dept of Art & Art History, Medford MA (S)

Overby, Osmund, *Prof Emeritus,* University of Missouri - Columbia, Art History & Archaeology Dept, Columbia MO (S)

Overstreet, Joe, *Art Dir,* Kenkeleba House, Inc, Kenkeleba Gallery, New York NY

Overton, Carmen, *Director of Development,* The Columbus Museum, Columbus GA

Overy, Jane Bunker, *Founder,* Searchlight Historic Museum & Mining Park, Searchlight NV

Ovesia, Steluta, *Information Specialist,* Jardin Botanique de Montreal, Bibliotheque, Montreal QC

Oviedo, Rebecca, *Colls Mgr & Registrar,* La Salle University Art Museum, Philadelphia PA

Ovrebo, Reidun, *Chair,* West Virginia State University, Art Dept, Institute WV (S)

Ovstebo, Solvieg, *Exec Dir & Chief Cur,* The Renaissance Society, Chicago IL

Ow-Wing, Darin, *Dir Educ & Engagement,* Chinese Culture Foundation, Center Gallery, San Francisco CA

Owcvark, Bob, *Div Chmn,* Pine Manor College, Visual Arts Dept, Chestnut Hill MA (S)

Owczarski, Marian, *Dir,* St Mary's Galeria, Orchard Lake MI

Owen Moss, Eric, *Dir,* Southern California Institute of Architecture, Los Angeles CA (S)

Owen, Evelyn, *Curatorial Fellow,* The Africa Center, New York NY

Owen, Ginger, *Photo/Intermedia,* Western Michigan University, Frostic School of Art, Kalamazoo MI (S)

Owen, Jane, *Exec Dir,* Center for Art & Education, Van Buren AR

Owen, Lisa, *Assoc Prof Art History,* University of North Texas, College of Visual Arts & Design, Denton TX (S)

Owen, Robert, *Facilities & Spec Events,* Tyler Museum of Art, Tyler TX

Owen, Robert, *Spec Events & Facilities Mgr,* Tyler Museum of Art, Reference Library, Tyler TX

Owens, Beth, *Patron Svcs Librn,* Cleveland Institute of Art, Jessica Gund Memorial Library, Cleveland OH

Owens, Carlotta, *Asst Cur,* National Gallery of Art, Index of American Design, Washington DC

Owens, Chris, *Part-Time Instr,* Oklahoma Baptist University, Art & Design Dept, Shawnee OK (S)

Owens, Heather, *CFO,* Cedarhurst Center for the Arts, Mitchell Museum, Mount Vernon IL

Owens, Keith, *Assoc Prof Commun Design,* University of North Texas, College of Visual Arts & Design, Denton TX (S)

Owens, Mike, *Prof,* East Los Angeles College, Art Dept, Monterey Park CA (S)

Owens, Quintin, *Adj Instr,* University of West Florida, Dept of Art, Pensacola FL (S)

Owens, Robert G, *Head Div of Fine Arts & Humanities,* Fayetteville State University, Performing & Fine Arts, Fayetteville NC (S)

Owens, Susan, *Youth Prog Dir,* Birmingham Bloomfield Art Center, Birmingham MI (S)

Owens, Valerie, *Prof,* Texarkana College, Art Dept, Texarkana TX (S)

Owens-Pelton, Lesley, *Mgr,* Stone Quarry Hill Art Park, John & Virginia Winner Memorial Art Gallery, Cazenovia NY

Owensby, Mary, *Exec Asst,* Trust Authority, Museum of the Great Plains, Lawton OK

Owinell, Kim, *Instr,* Art Institute of Southern California, Laguna Beach CA (S)

Owsiany, Richard, *Pres,* Polish Museum of America (PMA), Chicago IL

Oxley, Jon, *Admin Mgr,* University of Lethbridge, Art Gallery, Lethbridge AB

Oxman, M, *Prof,* American University, Dept of Art, New York NY (S)

Oxman, Ron Haynie, *Assoc Prof,* American University, Dept of Art, New York NY (S)

Oxtoby, Susan, *Sr Film Cur,* University of California, Berkeley, Berkeley Art Museum & Pacific Film Archive, Berkeley CA

Oye, Deanna, *Chair Music Dept,* University of Lethbridge, Faculty of Fine Arts, Lethbridge AB (S)

Ozdogan, Turker, *Prof,* George Washington University, Dept of Art of Fine Arts & Art History, Washington DC (S)

Ozolis, Auseklis, *Dir Academy,* New Orleans Academy of Fine Arts, Academy Gallery, New Orleans LA

Ozubko, Christopher, *Dir,* University of Washington, School of Art, Seattle WA (S)

Pacaud, Margaret, *Treas,* Revelstoke Visual Arts Centre, Revelstoke BC

Pace, James R, *Prof,* University of Texas at Tyler, Department of Art, School of Visual & Performing Arts, Tyler TX (S)

Pace, Philana, *Prof,* Tyler Junior College, Art Program, Tyler TX (S)

Pace-Robinson, Jennifer, *VP Experience Development & Family Learning,* The Children's Museum of Indianapolis, Indianapolis IN

Pacheco, John, *Painting Prof,* Mount Wachusett Community College, East Wing Gallery, Gardner MA

Pacheco, Raoul, *Prof,* Augusta State University, Dept of Art, Augusta GA (S)

Packard, Sally, *Dir School of Art,* Texas Christian University, Fort Worth Contemporary Art, Fort Worth TX

Padgett Griffin, Amy, *Exec Dir,* Leesburg Center for the Arts, Leesburg FL

Padgett, Deborah L, *Media Relations Mgr,* Jamestown-Yorktown Foundation, Jamestown Settlement, Williamsburg VA

Padgett, J Michael, *Cur Ancient Art,* Princeton University, Princeton University Art Museum, Princeton NJ

Padgett, James, *Adv,* Wilberforce University, Art Dept, Wilberforce OH (S)

Padgett, Michael, *Chmn,* University of Wisconsin-River Falls, Art Dept, River Falls WI (S)
Padgett, Michael, *Dir Gallery,* University of Wisconsin, Gallery 101, River Falls WI
Padilla Virola, Shirley, *Educ Coordr,* Museo de las Americas, Viejo San Juan PR
Padon, Thomas, *Brandywine River Mus Dir,* Brandywine Conservancy, Brandywine River Museum, Chadds Ford PA
Padulo, Louis, *Exec Dean College & Architecture,* Philadelphia University, Philadelphia PA (S)
Pagani, Catherine, *Chair,* University of Alabama, Dept of Art, Tuscaloosa AL (S)
Pagano, Donna, *Mgr Exhibs,* Staten Island Museum, Archives Library, Staten Island NY
Pagano, Donna, *Mgr Exhibs,* Staten Island Museum, Staten Island NY
Page, Carol, *Pres,* Sonoma Valley Historical Society, Depot Park Museum, Sonoma CA
Page, Helen, *Assoc Dir Admin,* Delaware Center for the Contemporary Arts, Wilmington DE
Page, Joe, *Vis Asst Prof Art,* Whitman College, Art Dept, Walla Walla WA (S)
Page, Kacey, *Coll Mgr,* Buffalo Society of Natural Sciences, Buffalo Museum of Science, Buffalo NY
Page, Katherine, *Interim Cur Contemporary Art,* Delaware Center for the Contemporary Arts, Wilmington DE
Page, Kelly, *Registrar,* Maine Maritime Museum, Archives Library, Bath ME
Page, Mary, *Head of Acquisitions,* University of Central Florida Libraries, Orlando FL
Page, Sylvia, *Head Librn,* Memphis College of Art, G Pillow Lewis Memorial Library, Memphis TN
Pagel, Angelika, *Assoc Prof,* Weber State University, Dept of Visual Arts, Ogden UT (S)
Pagel, David, *Chair,* Claremont Graduate University, Art Department, Claremont CA (S)
Paggie, Michael, *Bus Mgr,* Madison Museum of Contemporary Art, Madison WI
Pagh, Barbara, *Prof,* University of Rhode Island, Dept of Art & Art History, Kingston RI (S)
Pagnucci, Anna, *Head Dept,* Ashford University, Art Dept, Clinton IA (S)
Pahn, Michael, *Head Archivist,* National Museum of the American Indian, Archive Center, Suitland MD
Paice, Kimberly, *Asst Prof Art History,* University of Cincinnati, School of Art, Cincinnati OH (S)
Paier, Daniel, *VPres,* Paier College of Art, Inc, Library, Hamden CT
Paier, Jonathan E, *Pres,* Paier College of Art, Inc, Hamden CT (S)
Paier, Jonathan E, *Pres,* Paier College of Art, Inc, Library, Hamden CT
Pain, Eric, *Supt,* Ringwood Manor House Museum, Ringwood NJ
Paine, Howard, *Div Chair Fine Arts,* Memphis College of Art, Memphis TN (S)
Paine, Wesley M, *Dir,* Board of Parks & Recreation, The Parthenon, Nashville TN
Paisley, Leslie, *Paper Conservator & Dept Head,* Williamstown Art Conservation Center, Williamstown MA
Paitz, Kendra, *Cur,* Illinois State University, University Galleries, Normal IL
Palado, Stacy, *Assoc Dir External Relations,* University of Tennessee, McClung Museum of Natural History & Culture, Knoxville TN
Palakunnathu Matthew, Annu, *Asst Prof,* University of Rhode Island, Dept of Art & Art History, Kingston RI (S)
Palanque North, Pamela, *Pres,* Morris-Jumel Mansion, Inc, New York NY
Palatucci, Ernie, *Dir Opers,* Visual Arts Center of New Jersey, Summit NJ
Palazzolo, T, *Prof,* City Colleges of Chicago, Daley College, Chicago IL (S)
Palermo, Lou, *Dir Educ,* Arkansas Arts Center, Little Rock AR (S)
Palermo, Louise, *Cur Educ,* Maryhill Museum of Art, Goldendale WA
Paletz, Susan, *Prog Dir,* Barbara & Ray Alpert Jewish Community Center, Pauline & Zena Gatov Gallery, Long Beach CA
Palevitz, Robert, *Corresp Secy,* Allied Artists of America, Inc, Florham Park NJ
Paley, Albert, *Prof,* Rochester Institute of Technology, School of Design, Rochester NY (S)
Paley, Laurel, *Professor of Art,* Los Angeles City College, School of Visual & Media Arts, Los Angeles CA (S)
Paley, Valerie, *Historian & VPres Scholarly Progs,* New-York Historical Society, Museum, New York NY
Palijczuk, Wasyl, *Prof,* Western Maryland College, Dept of Art & Art History, Westminster MD (S)
Palisin, B, *Instr,* Sacramento City College, Art Dept, Sacramento CA (S)
Palkovic, Francis, *Art Instr,* Big Bend Community College, Art Dept, Moses Lake WA (S)
Palkovic, Rie, *Dir,* Big Bend Community College, Art Dept, Moses Lake WA (S)
Palladino-Craig, Allys, *Dir & Ed-in-Chief,* Florida State University, Museum of Fine Arts, Tallahassee FL
Pallesen, Jackie, *Dir Educ & Outreach,* Louisville Visual Art, Louisville KY
Palm, Nancy, *Asst Prof,* University of North Carolina at Pembroke, Art Dept, Pembroke NC (S)
Palmer Schwind, Arlene, *Cur,* Victoria Mansion - Morse Libby House, Portland ME
Palmer, Barbara, *Assoc Dir Mus Budget & Opers,* Williams College, Museum of Art, Williamstown MA
Palmer, Bob E, *Chmn,* University of Central Oklahoma, Dept of Art & Design, Edmond OK (S)
Palmer, Briana, *Art Counsellor,* McMaster University, School of the Arts, Hamilton ON (S)
Palmer, Doug, *Chair,* Sioux City Art Center, Sioux City IA (S)
Palmer, Erin, *Assoc Prof,* Southern Illinois University, School of Art & Design, Carbondale IL (S)
Palmer, Patricia, *Art Educ,* Montserrat College of Art, Beverly MA (S)
Palmer, Patrick, *Faculty Chair & Studio School Dean,* Museum of Fine Arts, Houston, Glassell School of Art, Houston TX (S)
Palmer, Sharon S, *Exec Dir,* Columbia County Historical Society, 1820 James Vanderpoel House, Kinderhook NY
Palmer, Stephen, *2nd VPres,* South County Art Association, Kingston RI
Palmer, Teri Evans, *Asst Prof,* Texas State University - San Marcos, Dept of Art and Design, San Marcos TX (S)
Palmeri, Mark, *Asst Prof,* Oakton Community College, Language Humanities & Art Divisions, Des Plaines IL (S)
Palmeri, Nancy, *Assoc Prof,* University of Texas at Arlington, Art & Art History Department, Arlington TX (S)
Palmisano, Susan, *Prof,* Indiana University of Pennsylvania, College of Fine Arts, Indiana PA (S)
Pan, Insher, *Asst Dir,* China Institute in America, China Institute Gallery, New York NY
Pancost, Rose, *Gallery Dir,* Carnegie Arts Center, Alliance NE
Pandelis, Judy E, *Office Mgr,* Birmingham-Southern College, Art & Art History, Birmingham AL (S)
Panella Bourns, Victoria, *Dir,* Utah Arts Council, Chase Home Museum of Utah Folk Arts, Salt Lake City UT
Panella, Rachel, *Technical Services Librarian & Archivist,* Amon Carter Museum of American Art, Research Library, Fort Worth TX
Panet-Raymond, Silvy, *Chair, Contemporary Dance,* Concordia University, Faculty of Fine Arts, Montreal QC (S)
Pang, Toni, *Supv,* City of Irvine, Irvine Fine Arts Center, Irvine CA (S)
Panhorst, Michael, *Cur Art,* Montgomery Museum of Fine Arts, Montgomery AL
Panhorst, Michael, *Cur Art,* Montgomery Museum of Fine Arts, Library, Montgomery AL
Panitz, Zimra, *Head Tech Servs,* Visual Arts Library, New York NY
Pankin, Jared, *Instr,* Bakersfield College, Art Dept, Bakersfield CA (S)
Pankow, David P, *Asst Prof,* Rochester Institute of Technology, School of Printing Management & Sciences, Rochester NY (S)
Pannafino, James, *Asst Prof Graphic & Interactive Design,* Millersville University, Dept of Art & Design, Millersville PA (S)
Pannebaker, William, *Secy,* Frontier Times Museum, Bandera TX
Pannen, Richard, *Chmn,* Rochester Institute of Technology, School for American Craft, Rochester NY (S)
Panske, Gail, *Dir,* University of Wisconsin Oshkosh, Allen Priebe Gallery, Oshkosh WI
Panske, Gail, *Prof,* University of Wisconsin Oshkosh, Dept of Art, Oshkosh WI (S)
Pantano, Nadine, *Adjunct Asst Prof Art History,* Florida Southern College, Department of Art & Art History, Lakeland FL (S)
Pantano, Nadine, *Adjunct Asst Prof Art History,* Florida Southern College, Melvin Art Gallery, Lakeland FL
Panzer, Robert, *Exec Dir,* Visual Artists & Galleries Association (VAGA), New York NY
Paoletta, Donald, *Dept Chair, Prof Art History,* Nebraska Wesleyan University, Art Dept, Lincoln NE (S)
Paoletta, Donald, *Dir,* Nebraska Wesleyan University, Elder Gallery, Lincoln NE
Paoli, Julia, *Dir Exhibs & Progs,* Mercer Union, A Centre for Contemporary Art, Toronto ON
Papa-Tudor, Nicole, *Education Coordr,* Gadsden Museum of Art, Gadsden AL
Papacz, Andrea, *Dir Exhibs & Colls,* Connecticut Historical Society, Library, Hartford CT
Papajani, Sara, *Retail Mgr & Art Rental Mgr, Curatorial Team,* Bainbridge Arts & Crafts Gallery, Bainbridge Island WA
Papanek-Miller, MaryAnn, *Chmn,* Bemidji State University, Visual Arts Dept, Bemidji MN (S)
Papararo, Jenifer, *Cur,* Contemporary Art Gallery Society of British Columbia, Vancouver BC
Papararo, Jenifer, *Exec Dir,* Plug In, Institute of Contemporary Art, Winnipeg MB
Papavero, Emily, *Assoc Dir,* UCR ARTSblock, California Museum of Photography, Riverside CA
Papazian, Aline, *Asst Dir,* Passaic County Community College, Division of Humanities, Paterson NJ (S)
Pape, Whitney, *Spec Coll Librn,* Redwood Library & Athenaeum, Newport RI
Papenfoth, Mary, *1st VPres,* South County Art Association, Kingston RI
Papenfus, Esther, *Opers Mgr,* Foothills Art Center, Inc, Golden CO
Papineau, Karen, *Registrar,* The Currier Museum of Art, Manchester NH
Pappalardo, Anna, *Asst Dir,* University of British Columbia, Museum of Anthropology, Vancouver BC
Pappas, Andrea, *Assoc Prof,* Santa Clara University, Dept of Art & Art History, Santa Clara CA (S)
Pappas, Matthew, *Mem Mgr,* Villa Terrace Decorative Arts Museum, Milwaukee WI
Pappenheimer, William, *Prof,* Pace University, Dyson College of Arts & Sciences, Pleasantville NY (S)
Papson, Don, *Interim Dir,* Hershey Museum, Hershey PA
Paraham, Wesley, *Guest Servs Admin,* Belz Museum of Asian & Judaic Art, Memphis TN
Parasiuk, Halyna, *Tour Guide,* Ukrainian National Museum & Library, Chicago IL
Paratore, Philip, *Prof,* University of Maine at Augusta, College of Arts & Humanities, Augusta ME (S)
Parcon, Dana, *Dir Capital Improvements of Facility Opers,* Museum of African American History, Boston MA
Pardee, Pattie, *Dir Develop,* Museum of Art - Deland FL, Inc, Deland FL
Pardo, Mary, *Assoc Prof,* University of North Carolina at Chapel Hill, Art Dept, Chapel Hill NC (S)

Pardue, Cindy, *Exec Dir,* Wilkes Art Gallery, North Wilkesboro NC

Pardue, Diana, *Chief Cur,* The National Park Service, United States Department of the Interior, Statue of Liberty National Monument & The Ellis Island Immigration Museum, Washington DC

Parenteau-Lebeuf, Marie-Claude, *Exec Dir,* Association professionnelle des designers d'interieur du Quebec, Montreal QC

Paret, Paul, *Asst Prof,* University of Utah, Dept of Art & Art History, Salt Lake City UT (S)

Pargeter, Karri, *Business Mgr,* University of Oregon, Jordan Schnitzer Museum of Art, Eugene OR

Parham, Annette, *Acquisitions Librn,* Colonial Williamsburg Foundation, John D Rockefeller, Jr Library, Williamsburg VA

Parham, Mercedes, *Marketing and Media Manager,* The Columbus Museum, Columbus GA

Paris Ott, Bonnie, *Historian,* Shores Memorial Museum, Lyndon Center VT

Paris, Brad, *Chmn Photog,* Fashion Institute of Technology, School of Art & Design, New York NY (S)

Paris, Eric, *Pres,* Shores Memorial Museum, Lyndon Center VT

Paris, Laura, *Devel Asst,* Erie Art Museum, Erie PA

Paris, Marguerite, *Secy,* DuPage Art League School & Gallery, Wheaton IL

Paris, Robin, *Assoc Prof & Chair Photog,* Watkins College of Art, Design & Film, Nashville TN (S)

Paris, Tiara L, *Dir Exhibs,* North Carolina Museum of Art, Raleigh NC

Pariser, David, *Chair, Art Educ,* Concordia University, Faculty of Fine Arts, Montreal QC (S)

Parish, Frank, *Dir Facilities,* Cornell University, College of Architecture, Art, and Planning, Ithaca NY (S)

Park, Jim, *Asst Prof,* Minnesota State University-Moorhead, Dept of Art & Design, Moorhead MN (S)

Park, JP, *Asst Prof,* University of California, Riverside, Dept of the History of Art, Riverside CA (S)

Park, Kyong, *Founder,* Storefront for Art & Architecture, New York NY

Park, Penny, *Assoc Prof,* Wright State University, Dept of Art & Art History, Dayton OH (S)

Park, So Yeon, *Assoc Prof,* University of Kansas, The School of the Arts, Dept of Visual Art, Lawrence KS (S)

Park, Sunyoung, *Catalog Librn,* Museum of Fine Arts, Houston, Hirsch Library, Houston TX

Parke-Harrison, Robert, *Assoc Prof,* College of the Holy Cross, Dept of Visual Arts, Worcester MA (S)

Parker Smith, Bettye, *VPres Acad Affairs,* Tougaloo College, Tougaloo Art Collection, Tougaloo MS

Parker, Ann, *Dir Develop,* Washington Pavilion of Arts & Science, Visual Arts Center, Sioux Falls SD

Parker, Barbara, *Dir Programs,* Piedmont Arts Association, Martinsville VA

Parker, Beula, *Arts Prog Coordr,* City of Raleigh Arts Commission, Miriam Preston Block Gallery, Raleigh NC

Parker, Bradford, *Dir of Finance & Operations,* Corporate Council for the Arts/Arts Fund, Seattle WA

Parker, Carolyn, *Head Dept,* Peace College, Art Dept, Raleigh NC (S)

Parker, Donna, *Exhib Cur,* Western Kentucky University, Kentucky Library & Museum, Bowling Green KY

Parker, Hannah, *Dir Develop,* Judd Foundation, Marfa TX

Parker, Jennifer, *Architecture Librn,* University of Notre Dame, Architecture Library, Notre Dame IN

Parker, Laura, *Instr,* American River College, Dept of Art/Art New Media, Sacramento CA (S)

Parker, Lynne, *Adjunct,* Idaho State University, Dept of Art, Pocatello ID (S)

Parker, Marsha H, *Dean Fine Arts & Performing Arts,* Lindenwood University, Harry D Hendren Gallery, Saint Charles MO

Parker, Martha, *Mem Coordr,* Historical Society of Martin County, Elliott Museum, Stuart FL

Parker, Mary Jo, *Pub Rels & Mem,* Tennessee Valley Art Association, Tuscumbia AL

Parker, Niles, *Chief Cur,* Nantucket Historical Association, Historic Nantucket, Nantucket MA

Parker, Richard (Scott), *Assoc Prof,* Tarrant County College, Art Dept, Hurst TX (S)

Parker, Shalon, *Chmn,* Gonzaga University, Dept of Art, Spokane WA (S)

Parker, Shannon, *Cur Colls,* Art Gallery of Nova Scotia, Halifax NS

Parker, Stephen, *Prof,* Black Hills State University, Art Dept, Spearfish SD (S)

Parker, Susan R, *Exec Dir,* Saint Augustine Historical Society, Library, Saint Augustine FL

Parker, Susan, *Univ Librn,* University of British Columbia, Art & Architecture Planning, UBC Library, Vancouver BC

Parker, Teresa J, *Cur,* Illinois Benedictine University, Department of Fine Arts, Lisle IL (S)

Parker, Todd, *Asst Prof,* Southwestern Oklahoma State University, Art, Communication & Theatre, Weatherford OK (S)

Parkinson, Carol, *Exec Dir,* Harvestworks, Inc, New York NY

Parkinson, Trude, *Instr,* Marylhurst University, Art Dept, Marylhurst OR (S)

Parks Smith, Margaret, *Prof Ceramics Sculpture,* Asbury College, Student Center Gallery, Wilmore KY

Parks, Carrie Frances, *Prof & Graduate Prog Dir,* University of Maryland, Baltimore County, Intermedia & Digital Arts (IMDA), Dept of Visual Arts, Baltimore MD (S)

Parks, Nancy, *Asst Prof Art Educ,* University of Cincinnati, School of Art, Cincinnati OH (S)

Parks, Tonya, *Mem Coordr,* Embroiderers Guild of America, Margaret Parshall Gallery, Louisville KY

Parks-Kirby, Carrie Anne, *Prof,* Alma College, Clack Art Center, Dept of Art & Design, Alma MI (S)

Parmenter, Becky, *Educ Coordr,* Gallery One Visual Arts Center, Ellensburg WA

Parmenter, Marian, *Dir,* San Francisco Museum of Modern Art, Artist Gallery, San Francisco CA

Parnes, Laura, *Co Dir,* Momenta Art, Brooklyn NY

Parr, Doug, *VPres,* Owatonna Arts Center, Owatonna MN

Parr, Sean, *Prof,* Saint Anselm College, Dept of Fine Arts, Manchester NH (S)

Parra, Victor, *Musuem Preparator & Dir Asst,* East Los Angeles College, Vincent Price Art Museum, Monterey Park CA

Parrington, Gary, *Dir Develop,* Lyme Art Association, Inc, Old Lyme CT

Parris, Melissa, *Head Colls & Exhibs,* College of William & Mary, Muscarelle Museum of Art, Williamsburg VA

Parrish, Veronica, *Mem & Fin Mgr,* Albany Museum of Art, Albany GA

Parrott, Frances, *Chmn,* Iowa Western Community College, Art Dept, Council Bluffs IA (S)

Parrott, Lindsy R, *Dir & Cur,* Neustadt Collection of Tiffany Glass, Long Island City NY

Parsley, Tim, *Asst Prof,* University of Saint Francis, School of Creative Arts, Fort Wayne IN (S)

Parson, Del, *Asst Prof,* Dixie College, Art Dept, Saint George UT (S)

Parson, Leon, *Instr,* Ricks College, Dept of Art, Rexburg ID (S)

Parsons Roy, Carolyn, *Coll Mgr,* Saco Museum, Saco ME

Parsons, David, *Dir Finance,* Historic Hudson Valley, Pocantico Hills NY

Parsons, David, *Instr,* California State University, Dominguez Hills, Art & Design Dept, Carson CA (S)

Parsons, Joel, *Gallery Dir,* Rhodes College, Clough-Hanson Gallery, Memphis TN

Parsons, Laura, *Chmn,* American Folk Art Museum, New York NY

Parsons, Michael, *Prof,* Ohio State University, Dept of Art Education, Columbus OH (S)

Parsons, Sara-Jayne, *Cur,* Texas Christian University, Fort Worth Contemporary Art, Fort Worth TX

Parsons, Sara-Jayne, *Cur,* Texas Christian University, Moudy Gallery, Fort Worth TX

Parsons-O'Keefe, Colby, *Asst Prof,* Texas Woman's University, School of the Arts, Dept of Visual Arts, Denton TX (S)

Partin, Bruce, *Chmn,* Roanoke College, Fine Arts Dept-Art, Salem VA (S)

Partington, Judith, *Librn,* The Filson Historical Society, Reference & Research Library, Louisville KY

Partovi, Pat, *Dir,* Spokane Public Library, Spokane WA

Partridge, David, *Chmn,* Pasadena Museum of California Art, Pasadena CA

Partridge, Kathleen, *Instr,* Mohawk Valley Community College, Utica NY (S)

Parzanese, Frances, *Pres Elect,* Berks Art Alliance, Reading PA

Pasas, Anna Liza, *Head Librn & Archivist,* Autry National Center, Braun Research Library, Los Angeles CA

Pascale, Mark, *Cur,* The Art Institute of Chicago, Dept of Prints & Drawings, Chicago IL

Pasch, Anne, *Dir,* Alaska Museum of Science & Nature, Anchorage AK

Paschal, Mary Lou, *Chmn,* Central Piedmont Community College, Visual & Performing Arts, Charlotte NC (S)

Paschke, Ed, *Prof,* Northwestern University, Evanston, Dept of Art Theory & Practice, Evanston IL (S)

Pascual, Carmen, *Facility Rental Mgr,* Triton Museum of Art, Santa Clara CA

Pascucci, Marisa J, *Cur,* Boca Raton Museum of Art, Boca Raton FL

Pascucci, Marisa, *Cur 20th Century & Contemporary Art,* Boca Raton Museum of Art, Library, Boca Raton FL

Paska, Judith, *Dir Develop,* Hillwood Museum & Gardens Foundation, Hillwood Estate Museum & Gardens, Washington DC

Pasquina, Lavinia, *Asst Prof,* Catholic University of America, School of Architecture & Planning, Washington DC (S)

Pass, Dewayne, *Instr,* Tulsa Community College, Center for Creativity, Tulsa OK (S)

Passanise, Gary, *Prof,* Webster University, Department of Art, Design & Art History, Webster Groves MO (S)

Passarello, Rebecca, *Coordr Child Art,* Palo Alto Art Center, Palo Alto CA

Passic, Frank, *Chmn Numismatic,* Balzekas Museum of Lithuanian Culture, Chicago IL

Passlof, Pat, *Coordr Art Prog,* College of Staten Island, Performing & Creative Arts Dept, Staten Island NY (S)

Paster, Carol, *Exec Dir,* Creative Arts Center, Pontiac MI

Pasternak, Anne, *Dir,* Brooklyn Museum, Brooklyn NY

Pasternak, Stephanie, *Secy,* Town of Cummington Historical Commission, Kingman Tavern Historical Museum, Cummington MA

Pasti, Sara, *Interim Dir,* State University of New York at New Paltz, Samuel Dorsky Museum of Art, New Paltz NY

Pastore, Heather, *Controller,* Elmhurst Art Museum, Elmhurst IL

Pastore, Jay, *Artistic Director,* Rehoboth Art League, Inc, Rehoboth Beach DE (S)

Patalano, Anna, *Pres & Co-VP Dir of Classes,* Greenwich Art Society Inc, Greenwich CT

Patch, Diana, *Cur in Charge, Egyptian Art,* The Metropolitan Museum of Art, New York NY

Patchell, Chris, *Graphic Design,* Antonelli Institute, Professional Photography & Commercial Art, Erdenheim PA (S)

Patchen, Jeffrey, *Pres & CEO,* The Children's Museum of Indianapolis, Indianapolis IN

Pate, Annette, *Med Adjunct Prof,* Oklahoma Christian University of Science & Arts, Dept of Art & Design, Oklahoma City OK (S)

Patel, Hilesh, *Deputy Dir,* Hyde Park Art Center, Chicago IL

Patel, Tarjani, *Acctg Specialist,* i.d.e.a. Museum, Mesa AZ
Paterson, James C, *Assoc Prof,* Franklin & Marshall College, Art & Art History Dept, Lancaster PA (S)
Paton, Jennifer, *Exec Dir,* Edward Hopper, Nyack NY
Patrick, Jehra, *Gallery Dir & Cur,* Macalester College, Macalester College Art Gallery, Saint Paul MN
Patrick, Jill, *Dir Library Svcs,* OCAD University, Dorothy H Hoover Library, Toronto ON
Patrick, Vernon, *Prof Emeritus,* California State University, Chico, Department of Art & Art History, Chico CA (S)
Patry Leidy, Denise, *Cur Asian Art,* Yale University, Yale University Art Gallery, New Haven CT
Patt, Annie, *Rec Secy,* Allied Artists of America, Inc, Florham Park NJ
Patt, Stephne, *Instr,* La Sierra University, Art Dept, Riverside CA (S)
Patt, Susan, *Chmn,* La Sierra University, Art Dept, Riverside CA (S)
Patten, James, *Dir & Chief Cur,* University of Western Ontario, McIntosh Gallery, London ON
Patten, James, *Finance Dir,* Wiscasset, Waterville & Farmington Railway Museum (WW&F), Alna ME
Patterson, Aubrey B, *Pres,* BanCorp South, Art Collection, Tupelo MS
Patterson, Belinda A, *Lectr,* Lambuth University, Dept of Human Ecology & Visual Arts, Jackson TN (S)
Patterson, Carl, *Adj Faculty Conservation,* University of Denver, School of Art & Art History, Denver CO (S)
Patterson, Charlene, *Pub Rels Coordr,* Eastern Shore Art Association, Inc, Eastern Shore Art Center, Fairhope AL
Patterson, Jeremiah, *Asst Prof,* University of Hartford, Hartford Art School, West Hartford CT (S)
Patterson, Josie, *Dir Pub Rels & Mktg,* Massachusetts Institute of Technology, MIT Museum, Cambridge MA
Patterson, Karen, *Assoc Cur,* Sheboygan Arts Foundation, Inc, John Michael Kohler Arts Center, Sheboygan WI
Patterson, Kate, *Pres,* San Francisco City & County Arts Commission, San Francisco CA
Patterson, L., *Archivist & Records Admin,* United Methodist Church General Commission on Archives & History, Madison NJ
Patterson, Michelle, *Prof,* North Carolina Central University, Art Dept, Durham NC (S)
Patterson, Oscar, *Chmn,* University of North Florida, Dept of Communications & Visual Arts, Jacksonville FL (S)
Patterson, Oscar, *Chmn,* University of North Florida, Dept of Communications & Visual Arts, Jacksonville FL (S)
Patterson, Richard, *Dir,* Old Barracks Museum, Trenton NJ
Patterson, Roy, *Board Mem,* Cambridge Museum, Cambridge NE
Patterson, Theolyn, *Mem & Visitor Servs Mgr.,* Loyola University Chicago, Loyola University Museum of Art, Chicago IL
Patterson, William C, *Pres,* Philadelphia Sketch Club, Philadelphia PA
Patterson, William, *Treas,* Philadelphia Sketch Club, Philadelphia PA
Patterson, Zabet, *Asst Prof,* Stony Brook University, College of Arts & Sciences, Dept of Art, Stony Brook NY (S)
Patterson-Tutschka, Andrew, *Instr,* Shasta College, Arts, Communications & Social Sciences Division, Redding CA (S)
Patteson, Rita S, *Dir & Cur Manuscripts,* Baylor University, Armstrong Browning Library, Waco TX
Patton, Kayle, *Educ Coordr,* Southern Methodist University, Meadows Museum, Dallas TX
Patton, Pamela, *Dir,* Princeton University, Index of Christian Art, Princeton NJ
Patton, Rachel, *Mus Shop Mgr,* Olana State Historic Site, Hudson NY
Patton, Tom, *Prof,* California State University, Chico, Department of Art & Art History, Chico CA (S)
Patula, Timothy A, *Dir of Design,* Chicago Athenaeum, Museum of Architecture & Design, Galena IL
Paty, Karen, *Exec Dir,* Georgia Council for the Arts, Georgia's State Art Collection, Atlanta GA
Patyk, Catherine, *VPres HR,* Chicago Children's Museum, Chicago IL
Patzlaff, Kris, *Prof,* Humboldt State University, College of Arts & Humanities, Art Dept, Arcata CA (S)
Pauckner, Jenny, *Asst Prof Art History,* Marian University, Visual Arts Dept, Indianapolis IN (S)
Paul, Cassandra, *Acad Admin Coord,* Alberta College of Art & Design, Illingworth Kerr Gallery, Calgary AB
Paul, Gayle, *Cur,* Portsmouth Museums, Courthouse Galleries, Portsmouth VA
Paul, Rob, *Archivist,* University of Saskatchewan, Diefenbaker Canada Centre, Saskatoon SK
Paul, Sarah, *Dept Head Sculpture & Expanded Media,* Cleveland Institute of Art, Cleveland OH (S)
Pauley, Caren, *Mus Vis Svcs Coordr,* The Society of the Cincinnati at Anderson House, Washington DC
Pauley, Ed, *CEO & Exec Dir,* The Cultural Center of Fine Arts, Art Gallery, Parkersburg WV
Pauley, Edward E, *Dir,* Ohio University, Kennedy Museum of Art, Athens OH
Pauley, Steve, *Instr,* North Hennepin Community College, Art Dept, Brooklyn Park MN (S)
Paulk, Ann, *Vis Asst Prof,* Hamline University, Dept of Studio Arts & Art History, Saint Paul MN (S)
Paull, Samantha, *Preservation Adminr,* Cambridge Historical Commission, City of Cambridge, Research Library on Architectural and Social History of Cambridge, Mass, Cambridge MA
Paulsen, Richard, *Chmn,* Elmhurst College, Art Dept, Elmhurst IL (S)
Paulson, Alan, *Prof,* Gettysburg College, Dept of Visual Arts, Gettysburg PA (S)
Paulson, Lexi, *Gallery Asst,* Modernism, San Francisco CA
Paulson, Wesley E, *Pres,* Maryland College of Art & Design, Silver Spring MD (S)
Pauly, Nancy, *Prof,* University of New Mexico, Department of Fine Arts & Art History, Albuquerque NM (S)
Paustenbaugh, Jennifer, *Dir Libraries,* Brigham Young University, Harold B Lee Library, Provo UT
Pautler, Charles D, *Historic Site Mgr,* Charles A Lindbergh Historic Site, Little Falls MN
Pavelec, Karen Marie, *Exec Dir,* Maude Kerns, Eugene OR (S)
Pavlock, Paul, *Instr,* Marylhurst University, Art Dept, Marylhurst OR (S)
Pavlos, Laurie, *Bus Mgr,* Lyme Art Association, Inc, Old Lyme CT
Pavlovic, Milutin, *Designer & Preparator,* Telfair Museums, Telfair Academy of Arts & Sciences Library, Savannah GA
Pavone, Julia, *Dir & Cur,* Alexey von Schlippe Gallery of Art, Groton CT
Pawloski, Carole, *Visual Resource Librn,* Eastern Michigan University, Art Dept Slide Collection, Ypsilanti MI
Pawlowicz, Peter, *Assoc Prof,* East Tennessee State University, College of Arts and Sciences, Dept of Art & Design, Johnson City TN (S)
Pawson, Linda, *Exec Dir,* Bellevue Arts Museum, Bellevue WA
Payan, Andres, *Cur Public Engagement,* Craft and Folk Art Museum (CAFAM), Los Angeles CA
Payne, Ashleigh, *Exhibs Coordr,* Spartanburg Art Museum, Spartanburg SC
Payne, Carolyn, *Exec Dir,* Soo Visual Arts Center, Minneapolis MN
Payne, Cheryl, *Tech Svcs Librn,* Museum of Fine Arts, Houston, Hirsch Library, Houston TX
Payne, Christopher, *Chmn,* Huntingdon College, Dept of Art, Montgomery AL (S)
Payne, Daniel, *Head Instructional Svcs,* OCAD University, Dorothy H Hoover Library, Toronto ON
Payne, Darien, *Graphics Instr,* Monterey Peninsula College, Art Dept/Art Gallery, Monterey CA (S)
Payne, Jennifer Cover, *Pres,* Culture Capital, Washington DC
Payne, Marian, *Admin Asst,* University of Arkansas at Little Rock, Dept of Art & Design, Little Rock AR (S)
Payne, Suzanne, *Pres,* Minneapolis Institute of Art, Friends of the Institute, Minneapolis MN
Payne, Thomas, *Dept Head,* Wartburg College, Dept of Art, Waverly IA (S)
Paynter, Lee Ann, *Vis Asst Prof,* Morehead State University, Art & Design Dept, Morehead KY (S)
Pazar, Emily, *Cur Asst,* The Mint Museum, Mint Museum of Craft & Design, Charlotte NC
Pazcoguin, Melissa, *Exec Asst,* The Art School at Old Church, Demarest NJ (S)
Peague, Ed, *Head Librn,* University of Oregon, Architecture & Allied Arts Library, Eugene OR
Peak, Marianne, *Supt,* Adams National Historic Park, Quincy MA
Peak, Pamela, *Chmn,* Charleston Southern University, Dept of Language & Visual Art, Charleston SC (S)
Peake, James, *Educ Coordr,* Firelands Association for the Visual Arts, Oberlin OH
Pearce, A Blake, *Acting Head Art Dept,* Valdosta State University, Art Gallery, Valdosta GA
Pearce, A Blake, *Dept Head,* Valdosta State University, Dept of Art, Valdosta GA (S)
Pearce, Anne, *Gallery Dir,* Rockhurst University, Dept of Communication & Fine Arts, Kansas City MO (S)
Pearce, Donald, *VChmn,* Town of Cummington Historical Commission, Kingman Tavern Historical Museum, Cummington MA
Pearce, John N, *Dir,* James Monroe Museum, James Monroe Memorial Library, Fredericksburg VA
Pearce, Lisa, *Dir,* Meredith College, Frankie G Weems Gallery & Rotunda Gallery, Raleigh NC
Pearce, Michael, *Asst Prof,* California Lutheran University, Art Dept, Thousand Oaks CA (S)
Pearl, Sandy, *Secy,* American Numismatic Association, Edward C. Rochette Money Museum, Colorado Springs CO
Pearlman, Alison, *Prof,* California State Polytechnic University, Pomona, Department of Art, Pomona CA (S)
Pearlman, Eden Juron, *Cur,* Evanston Historical Society, Charles Gates Dawes House, Evanston IL
Pearlstein, Elinor, *Assoc Cur Chinese Art,* The Art Institute of Chicago, Department of Asian Art, Chicago IL
Pears, Catherine M, *Exec Dir,* Alexandria Museum of Art, Alexandria LA
Pearson, Arla Mae, *Board Mem,* Cambridge Museum, Cambridge NE
Pearson, Dana, *Dir Library Svcs,* North Central Texas College, Library, Gainesville TX
Pearson, David, *Dep Dir,* Columbia River Maritime Museum, Library, Astoria OR
Pearson, David, *Deputy Dir,* Columbia River Maritime Museum, Astoria OR
Pearson, Gary, *Instr,* Ricks College, Dept of Art, Rexburg ID (S)
Pearson, James, *Coll Mgr,* Beloit College, Wright Museum of Art, Beloit WI
Pearson, James, *Frame Shop Mgr,* Erie Art Museum, Erie PA
Pearson, Jason, *Educ Coordr,* Rochester Art Center, Rochester MN
Pearson, Jim, *Prof,* Vincennes University Junior College, Humanities Art Dept, Vincennes IN (S)
Pearson, John, *Prof,* Oberlin College, Dept of Art, Oberlin OH (S)
Pearson, Paul, *Dir Arts Servs,* Alberta Foundation for the Arts, Edmonton AB
Pearson, Steven, *Dir,* McDaniel College, Esther Prangley Rice Gallery, Westminster MD
Pease, Brian, *Historic Site Mgr,* Minnesota Historical Society, Minnesota State Capitol Historic Site, Saint Paul MN
Pease, Mark, *Asst Prof,* Southern Illinois University, School of Art & Design, Carbondale IL (S)

Pec, Steve, *Librn,* Greene County Historical Society, Bronck Museum, Coxsackie NY

Pecchio, Pamela, *Asst Prof Studio Art,* University of Virginia, McIntire Dept of Art, Charlottesville VA (S)

Pecimon, Sandy, *Bus Mgr,* The Summit County Historical Society of Akron, OH, Akron OH

Peck, James, *Exec Dir,* The Old Jail Art Center, Green Research Library, Albany TX

Peck, Nathan, *Instr,* Saint Xavier University, Dept of Art & Design, Chicago IL (S)

Peckham, Cynthia, *Cur,* Sandy Bay Historical Society & Museums, Sewall Scripture House-Old Castle, Rockport MA

Peckham, Julie, *Deputy Dir Admin & CFO,* National Gallery of Canada, Ottawa ON

Peckham, Mark, *Dir,* New York State Office of Parks, Recreation and Historic Preservation, Bureau of Historic Sites, Waterford NY

Peckman, Beth, *Asst Cur,* Temple University, Slide Library, Elkins PA

Pecore, Joanna, *Dir,* Towson University, Asian Arts & Culture Center, Towson MD

Pedersen, Morrie, *Chmn,* Fort Steilacoom Community College, Fine Arts Dept, Lakewood WA (S)

Pederson, Curt, *Cur Exhibs & Colls,* American Swedish Institute, Minneapolis MN

Pederson, Lindsey, *Instr,* Mesa Community College, Dept of Art, Mesa AZ (S)

Pederson, Ron, *Chmn Dept & Prof,* Aquinas College, Art Dept, Grand Rapids MI (S)

Pedone, Francis, *Dir Operations,* Worcester Art Museum, Worcester MA

Pedros, Natasha, *Minister Communs,* Niagara Artists Centre, Saint Catharines ON

Peeler, Diedre, *Mus Store Mgr,* Art and History Museums - Maitland, Maitland FL

Peer, Charles, *Head Dept,* John Brown University, Art Dept, Siloam Springs AR (S)

Peers, Douglas, *Dean of Arts,* University of Waterloo, Dept of Fine Arts, Waterloo ON (S)

Peffer, John, *Assoc Prof Art History,* Ramapo College of New Jersey, School of Contemporary Arts, Mahwah NJ (S)

Peglau, Michael, *Dept Chmn,* Drew University, Art Dept, Madison NJ (S)

Pegno, Marianna, *Cur Community Engagement,* Tucson Museum of Art and Historic Block, Tucson AZ

Peihl, Mark, *Archivist,* Historical and Cultural Society of Clay County, Hjemkomst Center, Moorhead MN

Peiser, Judy, *Exec Dir,* Center for Southern Folklore, Memphis TN

Peitz, Doris, *Financial Bus Mgr,* Paine Art Center & Gardens, Oshkosh WI

Pekarsky, Melvin H, *Prof,* Stony Brook University, College of Arts & Sciences, Dept of Art, Stony Brook NY (S)

Pelasky Hout, Jacqueline, *Art Image Cur & Developer,* Denison University, Slide Library, Granville OH

Pelfrey, Bob, *Chmn Fine Arts Div & Instr,* Cuesta College, Art Dept, San Luis Obispo CA (S)

Pelizzari, M Antonella, *Prof,* City University of New York, PhD Program in Art History, New York NY (S)

Pellathy, Elisabeth, *Asst Prof,* University of Alabama at Birmingham, Dept of Art & Art History, Birmingham AL (S)

Pellcrito, Marlene, *Instr,* Saginaw Valley State University, Dept of Art & Design, University Center MI (S)

Pellegrin, Maurizio, *Dean,* National Academy Museum & School, New York NY

Pellegrin, Maurizio, *Dir School,* National Academy School, New York NY (S)

Pelletier, Carol, *Chair, Fine Arts,* Endicott College, School of Visual & Performing Arts, Beverly MA (S)

Pelletier, Denise, *Vis Asst Prof,* Connecticut College, Dept of Art, New London CT (S)

Pellum, Frederick, *Assoc Prof,* Alabama State University, Dept of Visual Arts, Montgomery AL (S)

Pelrine, Christopher, *Opers Mgr,* Intermuseum Conservation Association, Cleveland OH

Pelrine, Diane, *Assoc Dir Curatorial Services & Cur African & Oceanic Pre-Columbian Art,* Indiana University, Eskenazi Museum of Art, Bloomington IN

Peltier, Cynthia, *Operations Mgr,* Bucknell University, Edward & Marthann Samek Art Gallery, Lewisburg PA

Peluso, Robert, *Gen Educ,* Art Institute of Pittsburgh, Pittsburgh PA (S)

Pelvit, Leann, *Admin Asst,* MonDak Heritage Center, Museum, Sidney MT

Pelvit, Leann, *Admin Asst,* MonDak Heritage Center, History Library, Sidney MT

Pena, Alejandra, *Exec Dir,* Museo de Arte de Ponce, Library, Ponce PR

Pena, Alejandra, *Exec Dir,* Museo de Arte de Ponce, The Luis A Ferre Foundation Inc, Ponce PR

Pena, Jess, *Exec Dir,* Fairbanks Arts Association, Bear Gallery, Fairbanks AK

Penafiel, Guillermo, *Prof,* University of Wisconsin-Stevens Point, Dept of Art & Design, Stevens Point WI (S)

Pence, David, *Industrial Design Technology,* Art Institute of Pittsburgh, Pittsburgh PA (S)

Pendell, David, *Prof,* University of Utah, Dept of Art & Art History, Salt Lake City UT (S)

Pender, Michael R, *Trustee,* JMW Turner Museum, Sarasota FL

Pendergast, Jim, *Asst Prof,* Western New Mexico University, Expressive Arts Dept, Silver City NM (S)

Pendergrass, Candice, *Dir Mktg & Mem,* Fresno Metropolitan Museum, Fresno CA

Pendergrass, Gayle, *Instr,* Arkansas State University, Dept of Art, State University AR (S)

Pendleton, Belle, *Prof,* Christopher Newport University, Dept of Fine Performing Arts, Newport News VA (S)

Pendleton, Debbie, *Asst Dir Pub Svcs,* Alabama Department of Archives & History, Museum of Alabama, Montgomery AL

Pendleton, Edith, *Head Dept Fine & Performing Arts,* Edison Community College, Gallery of Fine Arts, Fort Myers FL (S)

Pendoley, Meg, *Admin Asst,* University of Pennsylvania, Arthur Ross Gallery, Philadelphia PA

Pener, Syndey, *Adjunct Prof Fine Art,* Johnson County Community College, Fine Arts Dept & Art History Dept, Overland Park KS (S)

Peniston, David, *Registrar,* Modernism, San Francisco CA

Penman, Evelyn, *Cur,* Saint Bonaventure University, Regina A Quick Center for the Arts, Saint Bonaventure NY

Penn, Beverley, *Prof,* Texas State University - San Marcos, Dept of Art and Design, San Marcos TX (S)

Pennington, Claudia, *Exec Dir,* Key West Art & Historical Society, East Martello Museum & Gallery, Key West FL

Pennington, Julia, *Cur,* Turtle Bay Exploration Park, Redding CA

Penny, Simon, *Prof Robotic Sculpture, Critical Theory,* University of California, Irvine, Studio Art Dept, Irvine CA (S)

Penuel, Jaime, *Lectr,* North Dakota State University, Division of Fine Arts, Fargo ND (S)

Peonie, Ann M, *Exec Dir,* Mohawk Valley Heritage Association, Inc, Walter Elwood Museum, Amsterdam NY

Pepich, Bruce W, *Dir,* Wustum Museum Art Association, Charles A Wustum Museum of Fine Arts, Racine WI

Pepich, Bruce W, *Dir,* Wustum Museum Art Association, Racine WI

Pepich, Bruce W, *Dir,* Wustum Museum Art Association, Wustum Art Library, Racine WI

Pepich, Bruce, *CEO,* Racine Art Museum, Racine WI

Pepin, Leah, *Cur,* Shoreline Historical Museum, Shoreline WA

Pepos, Noellynn, *Exhibits,* Ravalli County Museum, Hamilton MT

Peppe, Dee, *Vis Asst Prof,* Colby College, Art Dept, Waterville ME (S)

Pepper, Jerold L, *Library Dir,* The Adirondack Historical Association, Library, Blue Mountain Lake NY

Perakis, Stephen, *Gallery Asst,* Richard M Ross Art Museum at Wesleyan University, Delaware OH

Peraza, Nilda, *Contact,* Institute of Puerto Rican Culture, Museo del Grabado Latinoamericano, Viejo San Juan PR

Perbeck, David, *Dir Opers,* Hill-Stead Museum, Farmington CT

Percy, Ingrid Mary, *Prog Chair & Asst Prof,* Grenfell Campus, Memorial University of Newfoundland, Division of Fine Arts, Visual Arts Program, Corner Brook NF (S)

Pereira, Caitlin, *Visual Resources Dir,* Massachusetts College of Art and Design, Library, Boston MA

Peres, Michael, *Chmn Biomedical Photo Communs,* Rochester Institute of Technology, School of Photographic Arts & Sciences, Rochester NY (S)

Perez, Jackelyn, *Media Engagement Specialist,* Bay Area Video Coalition, Inc, San Francisco CA

Perez, Jamie, *Art Dept Chair,* Fullerton College, Division of Fine Arts, Fullerton CA (S)

Perez, Katrina, *Office Asst,* Hostos Center for the Arts & Culture, Bronx NY

Perez, Manny, *Park Mgr,* Florida Department of Environmental Protection, Stephen Foster Folk Culture Center State Park, White Springs FL

Perez, Myrna Z, *Develop Mem,* Museo de Arte de Puerto Rico, San Juan PR

Perez, Pablo, *European Art Asst Cur,* Museo de Arte de Ponce, The Luis A Ferre Foundation Inc, Ponce PR

Perez, Pamela, *Admin Dean, Junior School,* Museum of Fine Arts, Houston, Glassell School of Art, Houston TX (S)

Perez, Robert, *Lead Preparator,* Miami-Dade College, MDC Museum of Art & Design, Miami FL

Perez, Suzanne, *Instr,* Tarrant County College, Art Dept, Hurst TX (S)

Perin, Dorothee, *Educ Outreach Coordr,* Tufts University, Tufts University Art Gallery, Medford MA

Perkins, Abigail, *Office Mgr,* Noah Webster House, Inc, Noah Webster House & West Hartford Historical Society, West Hartford CT

Perkins, Allison C, *Exec Dir,* Reynolda House Museum of American Art, Winston-Salem NC

Perkins, Cynthia, *Prof,* Del Mar College, Art Dept, Corpus Christi TX (S)

Perkins, Douglas, *Admin Opers Mgr,* Middlebury College, Museum of Art, Middlebury VT

Perkins, Frank, *Facilities Mgr,* Staten Island Museum, Staten Island NY

Perkins, George, *Archivist,* McLean County Historical Society, McLean County Museum of History, Bloomington IL

Perkins, Jill, *Interiors Admin,* American Civilization Foundation, National Museum of American Illustration, Newport RI

Perkins, Jon, *Treas,* Livingston County Historical Society, Museum, Geneseo NY

Perkins, Nancy, *Exec Dir,* Craftsmen's Guild of Mississippi, Inc, Mississippi Craft Center, Ridgeland MS

Perkins, Phyllis, *VPres,* Southern Lorain County Historical Society, Spirit of '76 Museum, Elyria OH

Perkins, Scott, *Dir Preservation,* Western Pennsylvania Conservancy, Fallingwater, Mill Run PA

Perkins, Stephen, *Acad Cur Art,* University of Wisconsin, Green Bay, Lawton Gallery, Green Bay WI

Perkinson, Stephen, *Asst Prof,* Bowdoin College, Art Dept, Brunswick ME (S)

Perlin, Alana, *Digital Media Prof,* Merced College, Arts Division, Merced CA (S)

Perlman, Bill, *VPres,* Women's Interart Center, Inc, Interart Gallery, New York NY

Perloneo, Marie, *Instr,* Mount Mary College, Art & Design Division, Milwaukee WI (S)
Perlov, Diane, *Deputy Dir Exhib,* California Science Center, Los Angeles CA
Peronace, Nikki, *Visitor Prog Mgr,* Supreme Court of the United States, Office of the Curator, Washington DC
Perrault, Joseph, *Production Mgr,* Adirondack Lakes Center for the Arts, Blue Mountain Lake NY
Perreault, Bryan, *Gen Dir,* Shawinigan Art Center, Shawinigan QC
Perret, Marguerite, *Assoc Prof, Interim Chair,* Washburn University of Topeka, Dept of Art, Topeka KS (S)
Perrill, Elizabeth, *Prof,* University of North Carolina at Greensboro, School of Art, Greensboro NC (S)
Perrin, Ralph W, *Dean Div Arts, Commun & Soc Sciences,* Shasta College, Arts, Communications & Social Sciences Division, Redding CA (S)
Perron, Luc, *Chief Finance,* Musee d'art Contemporain de Montreal, Montreal QC
Perron, Margot, *Dir Educ,* Wave Hill, Bronx NY
Perron, Nicole, *Dir Mus,* Musee des Augustines de l'Hotel Dieu de Quebec, Archive, Quebec QC
Perron, Nicole, *Dir Mus,* Musee des Augustines de l'Hotel Dieu de Quebec, Quebec QC
Perry, Adam, *VPres Strategy & Prog,* Arts Midwest, Minneapolis MN
Perry, Beth, *Exec Dir,* Arts Council of the Mid-Columbia Region, Kennewick WA
Perry, Carole, *Artistic Dir,* Edward Hopper, Nyack NY
Perry, Elizabeth, *Assoc Prof,* Framingham State College, Art Dept, Framingham MA (S)
Perry, Mary, *Instr,* Appalachian State University, Dept of Art, Boone NC (S)
Perry, Michelle, *Fin & Admin Mgr,* University of Mississippi, University Museum & Historic Houses, Oxford MS
Perry, Nancy S, *Dir,* Portsmouth Museums, Courthouse Galleries, Portsmouth VA
Perry, Stephanie, *Gen Educ,* Art Institute of Pittsburgh, Pittsburgh PA (S)
Perry, Steven, *Dean,* Ramapo College of New Jersey, School of Contemporary Arts, Mahwah NJ (S)
Perry, Susan L, *Dir,* Mount Holyoke College, Art Library, South Hadley MA
Perry, Wendy, *Dir Devel,* Heritage Museums & Gardens, Sandwich MA
Perryman, Tom, *Instr,* Lenoir Rhyne College, Dept of Art, Hickory NC (S)
Pershey, Ed, *Dir Mus Servs,* Western Reserve Historical Society, Library, Cleveland OH
Person, Adele, *Asst Dir,* Bunnell Street Arts Center, Homer AK
Person, Robin Seage, *Exec Dir,* Cottonlandia Museum, Greenwood MS
Pertl, Susan, *Cur,* McDonald's Corporation, Art Collection, Oak Brook IL
Perusha, Allison, *Develop Dir,* SculptureCenter, Gallery, Long Island City NY
Pesanti, Heather, *Cur,* The Buffalo Fine Arts Academy, Albright-Knox Art Gallery, Buffalo NY
Pesesky, Jill, *Cur Educ,* Agecroft Association, Museum, Richmond VA
Pesesky, Jill, *Cur Educ,* Agecroft Association, Agecroft Hall, Richmond VA
Pesetti, Pam, *Mus Store Mgr,* Crocker Art Museum, Sacramento CA
Peshek, Brian, *Instr,* Pierce College, Art Dept, Woodland Hills CA (S)
Pestel, Michael, *Asst Prof,* Chatham College, Fine & Performing Arts, Pittsburgh PA (S)
Pestel, Michael, *Dir,* Chatham College, Art Gallery, Pittsburgh PA
Pestrak, Judy, *Exec Dir,* Manitoba Association of Architects, Winnipeg MB
Peter, August, *Preparator & Exhibit Director,* Museum of Wisconsin Art, West Bend WI
Peterman, Aaron, *Assoc Dir,* Providence Public Library, Art & Music Services, Providence RI
Peters Quinn, Allison, *Dir Exhibs & Residency,* Hyde Park Art Center, Chicago IL
Peters, Belinda A, *Chmn Dept,* Clark-Atlanta University, School of Arts & Sciences, Atlanta GA (S)
Peters, John, *Gallery Coordr,* Augustana University, Eide-Dalrymple Gallery, Sioux Falls SD
Peters, John, *Instr,* Augustana College, Art Dept, Sioux Falls SD (S)
Peters, Judy, *Instr,* West Shore Community College, Division of Humanities & Fine Arts, Scottville MI (S)
Peters, Laura, *Registrar,* Touchstone Center for Crafts, Farmington PA (S)
Peters, Martha, *Art in Pub Places Mgr,* City of Austin Parks & Recreation Department, Julia C Butridge Gallery, Austin TX
Peters, Siriporn, *Asst Prof Graphic Design,* Southwestern Oklahoma State University, Art, Communication & Theatre, Weatherford OK (S)
Peters, Steven, *Dean,* University of Montevallo, College of Fine Arts, Montevallo AL (S)
Petersen, Elizabeth, *Adj Instr,* University of West Florida, Dept of Art, Pensacola FL (S)
Petersen, Meghan, *Librn & Archivist,* The Currier Museum of Art, Manchester NH
Petersen, Natalie, *Assoc Dir,* Springville Museum of Art, Springville UT
Petersen, Natalie, *Asst Dir,* Utah Arts Council, Chase Home Museum of Utah Folk Arts, Salt Lake City UT
Petersen, Robert, *Assoc Prof,* Eastern Illinois University, Art Dept, Charleston IL (S)
Petersen, Stacie, *Registrar,* Roswell Museum & Art Center, Roswell NM
Peterson Heyrman, Joy, *Exec Dir,* Virginia Center for the Creative Arts, Amherst VA
Peterson Mason, Dayna, *Chmn Art Dept,* Riverside Community College, Dept of Art & Mass Media, Riverside CA (S)
Peterson Riley, Jenna, *Educator,* Schenectady County Historical Society, Grems-Dolittle Library, Schenectady NY
Peterson, Andrew, *Exec Dir,* FilmNorth, Saint Paul MN
Peterson, Brian, *Cur Exhib & Sr Cur,* James A Michener Art Museum, Doylestown PA
Peterson, Bryan, *Adjunct Instr Metalsmithing,* Montana State University, School of Art, Bozeman MT (S)
Peterson, Chuck, *Pres,* Caspers, Inc, Art Collection, Tampa FL
Peterson, Constance, *Prof,* Lansing Community College, Visual Arts & Media Dept, Lansing MI (S)
Peterson, D R, *Instr,* Normandale Community College, Art Dept, Bloomington MN (S)
Peterson, Dean A, *Asst Prof,* Salisbury State University, Art Dept, Salisbury MD (S)
Peterson, Dwight, *Dir Information Technology,* Oregon Historical Society, Oregon History Museum, Portland OR
Peterson, Elizabeth, *Chair & Assoc Prof,* University of Utah, Dept of Art & Art History, Salt Lake City UT (S)
Peterson, Eric, *Coordr Visual Resources/Facilitator Web Enhanced Curriculum,* Southern Illinois University, School of Art & Design, Carbondale IL (S)
Peterson, Frederick, *Chmn,* University of Minnesota, Morris, Humanities Division, Morris MN (S)
Peterson, Glen L, *Instr,* Yavapai College, Visual & Performing Arts Div, Prescott AZ (S)
Peterson, Herb, *Asst Prof,* Indiana Wesleyan University, School of Arts & Humanities, Division of Art, Marion IN (S)
Peterson, Jenna, *Educ & Asst Cur,* Schenectady County Historical Society, Schenectady NY
Peterson, Jim, *Treas,* Guild Hall of East Hampton, Inc, Guild Hall Museum, East Hampton NY
Peterson, Karin, *Dir Mus,* Department of Economic & Community Development, State of Connecticut DECD Eric Sloane Museum, Kent CT
Peterson, Kirk, *Chmn Art,* Mount San Antonio College, Art Dept, Walnut CA (S)
Peterson, Mark, *VPres,* Octagon Center for the Arts, Ames IA
Peterson, Merlin, *Cur,* Pope County Historical Society, Pope County Museum, Glenwood MN
Peterson, Nedra, *Art Subject Librn,* State University of New York at Oswego, Penfield Library, Oswego NY
Peterson, Nick, *Display Technician,* Herrett Center for Arts & Sciences, Jean B King Art Gallery, Twin Falls ID
Peterson, Pam, *Dir,* Marblehead Museum & Historical Society, Jeremiah Lee Mansion, Marblehead MA
Peterson, Pam, *Dir,* Marblehead Museum & Historical Society, John Orne Johnson Frost Gallery, Marblehead MA
Peterson, Pam, *Dir,* Marblehead Museum & Historical Society, Marblehead MA
Peterson, Robyn G, *Exec Dir,* Yellowstone Art Museum, Billings MT
Peterson, Stacy, *Assoc Cur & Registrar,* Dubuque Museum of Art, Dubuque IA
Peterson, Tessa Rose, *Finance Dir,* Museum of Northwest Art, La Conner WA
Pethel, Stan, *Dept Chair,* Berry College, Moon Gallery, Mount Berry GA
Petican, Laura, *Galleries Dir,* Texas A&M University-Corpus Christi, Weil Art Gallery, Corpus Christi TX
Petik, Jim, *Bd Dir,* Grand River Museum, Lemmon SD
Petik, Kim, *Bd Dir,* Grand River Museum, Lemmon SD
Petraits, Ellen, *Research & Instruction Librn,* Rhode Island School of Design, Fleet Library at RISD, Providence RI
Petre, Tracy, *Instr,* Columbia Basin College, Esvelt Gallery, Pasco WA (S)
Petrescu, Nicole, *Gallery coordr,* William Woods University, Cox Gallery, Fulton MO
Petriaccia, Mikael, *Instr,* Greenfield Community College, Art Dept, Greenfield MA (S)
Petrone, Chris, *Studio Mgr,* Women's Studio Workshop, Inc, Rosendale NY
Petros, Michael, *Assoc Prof of Media Art,* Glendale Community College, Visual & Performing Arts Div, Glendale CA (S)
Petrosky, Ron, *Adjunct,* College of the Canyons, Art Dept, Santa Clarita CA (S)
Petrosky, Sara, *Cur Educ,* Foosaner Art Museum, Melbourne FL
Petrouie, Marc, *Dept Head Glass,* Cleveland Institute of Art, Cleveland OH (S)
Petrovich-Mwaniki, Louis, *Assoc Prof,* Western Carolina University, Dept of Art/College of Arts & Science, Cullowhee NC (S)
Petrulis, Elizabeth (Lisa), *Cur Colls & Exhibs,* Swope Art Museum, Research Library, Terre Haute IN
Petsch, Jean, *Asst Prof,* Morehead State University, Art & Design Dept, Morehead KY (S)
Petsch, Jean, *Chmn,* Morehead State University, Claypool-Young Art Gallery, Morehead KY
Pettengel, Pamela J, *OESS Dir Educ,* Jamestown-Yorktown Foundation, Jamestown Settlement, Williamsburg VA
Petteplace, Jennifer, *Installation & Preservation Officer,* McMaster University, McMaster Museum of Art, Hamilton ON
Petteplace, Jennifer, *Installation & Preservation Officer,* McMaster University, McMaster Museum of Art, Hamilton ON
Petterson, Erika, *Associate Curator,* Museum of Wisconsin Art, West Bend WI
Petterson, Leslie, *Art Librn,* Chicago Public Library, Harold Washington Library Center, Chicago IL
Pettibone, John W, *Acting Dir & Cur,* Hammond Castle Museum, Gloucester MA
Pettis, Shari, *Admin Asst,* South Shore Arts, Munster IN
Peven, Michael, *Prof,* University of Arkansas, Art Dept, Fayetteville AR (S)
Pevitts, Bob, *Dir Art Dept,* Texas Wesleyan University, Dept of Art, Fort Worth TX (S)
Pezalla-Granlund, Margaret, *Art Dir,* College of New Jersey, Art Gallery, Ewing NJ

Pfaff, Larry, *Head Reader Svcs,* Art Gallery of Ontario, Edward P Taylor Research Library & Archives, Toronto ON
Pfalzgraf, Daniel, *Cur,* Carnegie Center for Art & History, New Albany IN
Pfanschmidt, Martha, *Instr,* Marylhurst University, Art Dept, Marylhurst OR (S)
Pfeifer, Nezka, *Cur,* Everhart Museum, Scranton PA
Pfeifer, William, *Dir,* Colonial Williamsburg Foundation, Visitor Center, Williamsburg VA
Pfeiffer, Cheryl, *Dir,* University of the South, Jessie Ball duPont Library, Sewanee TN
Pfeiffer, Sonya, *Owner & Creative Dir,* Elder Gallery, Charlotte NC
Pfliger, Doug, *Gallery Mgr,* Lillian & Coleman Taube Museum of Art, Minot ND
Pflueger, Beth, *Assoc Prof Music,* Glendale Community College, Visual & Performing Arts Div, Glendale CA (S)
Pfohl, Katie, *Cur Contemporary & Modern Art,* New Orleans Museum of Art, New Orleans LA
Pforte, Patty, *Progs & Visitor Experience Mgr,* The California Historical Society, San Francisco CA
Pfotenhauer, Louise, *Colls Mgr,* Neville Public Museum of Brown County, Research Library, Photo & Film Collection, Green Bay WI
Pfotenhauer, Louise, *Colls Mgr,* Neville Public Museum of Brown County, Green Bay WI
Phagan, Patricia, *Cur Prints & Drawings,* Vassar College, The Frances Lehman Loeb Art Center, Poughkeepsie NY
Pham, Trung, *Asst Prof,* Seattle University, Dept of Art & Art History, Seattle WA (S)
Phares, Robert, *Treas,* Pioneer Historical Museum of South Dakota, Hot Springs SD
Pharis, Patty, *Dir,* Heart of West Texas Museum, Colorado City TX
Phegley, Melissa, *Dir Develop,* Philadelphia Museum of Art, Samuel S Fleisher Art Memorial, Philadelphia PA
Phelan, Andrew, *Dir,* University of Oklahoma, School of Art, Norman OK (S)
Phelan, Janice, *Mus Shop Mgr,* Lightner Museum, Saint Augustine FL
Phelps, Carol, *Pres,* San Fernando Valley Historical Society, Mission Hills CA
Phelps, Holly, *Chief Cataloguer,* Library Company of Philadelphia, Philadelphia PA
Phelps, Judith, *Asst Secy,* Reading Public Museum, Reading PA
Phelps, Kelly, *Chair & Assoc Prof,* Xavier University, Dept of Art, Cincinnati OH (S)
Phelps, Martin, *Founder & Cur,* Medina Railroad Museum, Medina NY
Phelps, Meg, *Mus Educ,* Santa Paula Art Museum, Santa Paula CA
Phelps, Timothy H, *Assoc Prof,* Johns Hopkins University, School of Medicine, Dept of Art as Applied to Medicine, Baltimore MD (S)
Phifer, Glenn, *Prof,* Appalachian State University, Dept of Art, Boone NC (S)
Phifer, William G, *Prof,* Appalachian State University, Dept of Art, Boone NC (S)
Philbin, Ann, *Dir,* University of California, Los Angeles, Hammer Museum, Los Angeles CA
Philliben, Ruth, *Pres,* Arizona Watercolor Association, Phoenix AZ
Phillip, Bill, *Pres,* Western Art Association, Ellensburg WA
Phillips, Amanda, *Dir Site Interpretation & Partnerships,* Frank Lloyd Wright's, Alexandria VA
Phillips, Anthony, *Users Svcs Mgr,* Arkansas State University-Art Department, Jonesboro, Library, Jonesboro AR
Phillips, Carolyn, *Instr,* Eastern Iowa Community College, Clinton Community College, Clinton IA (S)
Phillips, Chalen, *Cur Coll,* Springfield Art Museum, Springfield MO
Phillips, Debbie, *Mktg Coord,* National Museum of Wildlife Art of the Unites States, Jackson WY
Phillips, Holly, *Assoc Mgr Colls,* The Metropolitan Museum of Art, Museum Libraries, New York NY
Phillips, Jackie, *Pres,* Middletown Arts Center, Middletown OH
Phillips, Janna, *Arts Educ Coordr,* Space One Eleven, Inc, Birmingham AL
Phillips, Jessica, *Exec Dir,* Fraunces Tavern Museum, New York NY
Phillips, Joan A, *Registrar,* Taos Historic Museums, La Hacienda de Los Martinez, Taos NM
Phillips, Joan A, *Registrar,* Taos Historic Museums, Ernest Blumenschein Home & Studio, Taos NM
Phillips, Joan, *Educ Dir,* Cheltenham Center for the Arts, Cheltenham PA (S)
Phillips, Joanna, *Sr Conservator Time-Based Media,* Solomon R Guggenheim Museum, New York NY
Phillips, John, *Owner,* Willet Hauser Architectural Glass Inc, Winona MN
Phillips, Kathryn D, *Librn,* Freer Gallery of Art & Arthur M Sackler Gallery, Library, Washington DC
Phillips, Kathy, *Pres,* Coquille Valley Art Association, Coquille OR
Phillips, Kenneth E, *Aerospace Cur,* California Science Center, Los Angeles CA
Phillips, Kimberly, *Cur,* Contemporary Art Gallery, Vancouver BC
Phillips, Larry, *Spec Proj & Community Relations,* Institute of American Indian Arts, Museum of Contemporary Native Arts, Santa Fe NM (S)
Phillips, Lisa, *Dir,* New Museum of Contemporary Art, The Soho Center Library, New York NY
Phillips, Lisa, *Toby Devan Lewis Dir,* New Museum of Contemporary Art, New Museum, New York NY
Phillips, Lynne, *Coll Mgr,* Chesapeake Bay Maritime Museum, Howard I Chapelle Memorial Library, Saint Michaels MD
Phillips, Michele, *Chief Conservator,* New York State Office of Parks, Recreation and Historic Preservation, Bureau of Historic Sites, Waterford NY
Phillips, Patsy, *Dir,* Institute of American Indian Arts, IAIA Museum of Contemporary Native Arts, Santa Fe NM
Phillips, Patsy, *Dir,* Institute of American Indian Arts, Museum of Contemporary Native Arts, Santa Fe NM (S)
Phillips, Patti, *Develop Dir,* University of Minnesota, Frederick R Weisman Art Museum, Minneapolis MN
Phillips, Quitman E, *Prof,* University of Wisconsin, Madison, Dept of Art History, Madison WI (S)
Phillips, Rebecca, *Registrar,* Pine Bluff/Jefferson County Historical Museum, Pine Bluff AR
Phillips, Richard, *Asst Prof Art History,* University of Texas Pan American, Art Dept, Edinburg TX (S)
Phillips, Robert, *Pres Board Trustees,* Roswell Museum & Art Center, Roswell NM
Phillips, Stephen Bennett, *Dir,* Federal Reserve Board, Art Gallery, Washington DC
Phillips, Susan, *Prof,* Waynesburg College, Dept of Fine Arts, Waynesburg PA (S)
Philpot, Eloise, *Asst Prof,* Radford University, Art Dept, Radford VA (S)
Phinney, Gail, *Dir Educ Progs,* Palos Verdes Art Center/Beverly G. Alpay Center for Arts Education, Rancho Palos Verdes CA
Phinney, Jessica, *Cur,* Thousand Islands Arts Center - Home of the Handweaving Museum, Clayton NY (S)
Phipps, Vickie, *Asst Prof,* Augustana College, Art Dept, Rock Island IL (S)
Phoenix, Masyn, *Coordr Research & Teaching,* Fort Hays State University, Forsyth Library, Hays KS
Phong, Ann, *Lectr,* California State Polytechnic University, Pomona, Department of Art, Pomona CA (S)
Phounsavat, Taeng, *Admin Asst,* Manitoba Association of Architects, Winnipeg MB
Piasecki, Sara, *Archivist,* Anchorage Museum at Rasmuson Center, Atwood Alaska Resource Center, Anchorage AK
Piasentin, Joe, *Prof,* Pepperdine University, Seaver College, Dept of Art, Malibu CA (S)
Piastuck, Gina, *Dept Head,* East Hampton Library, Long Island Collection, East Hampton NY
Piatek, Eva, *Events & Mktg Coord,* The Clay Studio, Philadelphia PA
Piatt, Margaret, *Pres & CEO,* Piatt Castles, West Liberty OH
Piccirillo, Rebecca, *Archivist,* Pilgrim Society, Pilgrim Hall Museum, Plymouth MA
Picco, Ronald, *Prof,* College of Santa Fe, Art Dept, Santa Fe NM (S)
Piccolo, Ellen, *Sec,* Prince Street Gallery, New York NY
Piccone, James, *Dean,* Cumberland County College, Arts & Humanities, Vineland NJ (S)
Piccuirro, Jeneen, *Instr,* American University, Dept of Art, New York NY (S)
Picha, Allie, *Develop & Special Events Mgr,* University of Washington, Henry Art Gallery, Seattle WA
Piche, Thomas, *Dir,* Daum Museum of Contemporary Art, Sedalia MO
Pichnarcik, Lisa, *Sr Admin,* Farmington Valley Arts Center, Avon CT
Pickard, Carey, *Exec Dir,* Tubman African American Museum, Keil Resource Center, Macon GA
Pickel, John, *Assoc Prof,* Wake Forest University, Dept of Art, Winston-Salem NC (S)
Pickens, Donna, *Asst Cur Educ,* Montgomery Museum of Fine Arts, Library, Montgomery AL
Pickens, Donna, *Asst Cur Educ,* Montgomery Museum of Fine Arts, Montgomery AL
Picker, Tobias, *VPres Music,* American Academy of Arts & Letters, New York NY
Pickering, Amy, *Visitor Svcs,* State University of New York at New Paltz, Samuel Dorsky Museum of Art, New Paltz NY
Pickering-Carter, Yvonne, *Chairperson & Prof,* University of the District of Columbia, Dept of Mass Media, Visual & Performing Arts, Washington DC (S)
Pickford, Melissa, *Art Gallery Dir,* Monterey Peninsula College, Art Dept/Art Gallery, Monterey CA (S)
Piehl, Angela, *Assoc Prof,* Oklahoma State University, Department of Art, Graphic Design and Art History, Stillwater OK (S)
Piehl, Walter, *Art Dept Coordr,* Minot State University, Dept of Art, Division of Humanities, Minot ND (S)
Piejko, Alex, *Asst Prof,* Mohawk Valley Community College, Utica NY (S)
Piepenburg, Robert, *Chmn,* Oakland Community College, Art Dept, Farmington Hills MI (S)
Pier, Gwen P, *Exec Dir,* National Sculpture Society, New York NY
Pierce Meyer, Katie, *Archit & Planning Librn,* University of Texas at Austin, Architecture & Planning Library, Austin TX
Pierce, Charles, *Co-owner,* Eureka Fine Art Gallery, Eureka Springs AR
Pierce, Greg, *Instr,* Columbia Basin College, Esvelt Gallery, Pasco WA (S)
Pierce, Judy, *Mktg Dir,* Cherokee Heritage Center, Park Hill OK
Pierce, Kristen, *Organizational Grants & Svcs Mgr,* Arizona Commission on the Arts, Phoenix AZ
Pierce, Michael A, *VPres Mem,* Artspace, Richmond VA
Piercey, James, *Recording Secy,* The Stained Glass Association of America, Raytown MO
Pierotti, Julie, *Cur,* The Dixon Gallery & Gardens, Memphis TN
Pierozzi, Lou, *Chmn & Prof,* Oakton Community College, Language Humanities & Art Divisions, Des Plaines IL (S)
Pierre, Vickie, *Registrar,* Miami-Dade College, MDC Museum of Art & Design, Miami FL
Pierson Ellingson, Susan, *Asst Prof,* Concordia College, Art Dept, Moorhead MN (S)
Pietrangeli, Jason, *Dir Fin & Opers,* Brooklyn Historical Society, Brooklyn NY
Piispanen, Ruth, *Dir Arts Educ,* Idaho Commission on the Arts, Boise ID

Pike, Jeffrey C, *Dean School,* Washington University, School of Art, Saint Louis MO (S)
Pike, Kermit J, *COO,* Western Reserve Historical Society, Library, Cleveland OH
Pike, Kermit J, *COO,* Western Reserve Historical Society, Cleveland OH
Pike, Paulita, *Pres,* The Art Institute of Chicago, Auxiliary Board of the Art Institute of Chicago, Chicago IL
Pilachowski, David, *Librn,* Williams College, Sawyer Library, Williamstown MA
Pilar, Jacqueline, *Cur,* Fresno Arts Center & Museum, Fresno CA
Pilgram, Suzanne, *Assoc Prof,* Georgian Court University, Dept of Art, Lakewood NJ (S)
Pili, Leala E, *Exec Dir & Cur,* Jean P Haydon, Pago Pago, American Samoa PI
Pilic, Patty, *Secy,* Mississippi Art Colony, Stoneville MS
Pillod, Elizabeth, *Prof,* Oregon State University, Dept of Art, Corvallis OR (S)
Pillote, Lauren, *Dean Design & Communs Art,* Rocky Mountain College of Art & Design, Lakewood CO (S)
Pillow, Kirk E, *Provost,* University of the Arts, Philadelphia Colleges of Art & Design, Performing Arts & Media & Communication, Philadelphia PA (S)
Pillsbury, Robert, *Pres,* Salmagundi Club, New York NY
Pilosi, Lisa, *Conservator in Charge, Objects,* The Metropolitan Museum of Art, New York NY
Pinales, Deena, *Mus Educ,* Springfield Museum of Art, Library, Springfield OH
Pinardi, Brenda, *Prof,* University of Massachusetts Lowell, Dept of Art, Lowell MA (S)
Pinckley, Donna, *Prof,* University of Central Arkansas, Department of Art, Conway AR (S)
Pindell, Howardena, *Prof,* Stony Brook University, College of Arts & Sciences, Dept of Art, Stony Brook NY (S)
Pindle, Arthur, *Instr,* Southern University in New Orleans, Fine Arts & Philosophy Dept, New Orleans LA (S)
Pine, Steven, *Conservator,* Museum of Fine Arts Houston, Bayou Bend Collection & Gardens, Houston TX
Pineau, Alain, *Nat Dir,* Canadian Conference of the Arts, Ottawa ON
Pinette, Robert J, *Cur Herbarium,* Northern Maine Museum of Science, Presque Isle ME
Pingree, Nichole, *Finance Mgr,* Riverside Art Museum, Library, Riverside CA
Pingrey, Bradley, *Pres,* Washington County Museum of Fine Arts, Hagerstown MD
Pinholster, Jacob, *Assoc Dean Policy & Initiatives & Assoc Prof,* Arizona State University, Herberger Institute for Design and the Arts, Tempe AZ (S)
Pinkston, David, *Adjunct Prof,* University of Texas at Arlington, Art & Art History Department, Arlington TX (S)
Pinkston, Dorothy, *Dir Fin & Admin,* Staten Island Museum, Staten Island NY
Pinkston, Heidi, *Educ Coordr,* Piedmont Arts Association, Martinsville VA
Pinkston, Howell, *Instr,* Pierce College, Art Dept, Woodland Hills CA (S)
Pintado, Vanessa, *Asst Cur Rare Books & US,* The Hispanic Society of America, Hispanic Society Museum & Library, New York NY
Pinto, Vincent, *VPres & Sec,* Federation of Modern Painters & Sculptors, New York NY
Pintz, Joe, *Asst Prof,* University of Missouri - Columbia, Dept of Art, Columbia MO (S)
Pinyol, Ysabel, *Curatorial Dir,* Mana Contemporary, Jersey City NJ
Piombino, Dante, *Multimedia & Web Design,* Art Institute of Pittsburgh, Pittsburgh PA (S)
Pion-Berlin, David, *Secy,* Latino Art Museum, Pomona CA
Pionati, Francis A, *Media Arts & Animation,* Art Institute of Pittsburgh, Pittsburgh PA (S)
Piper, Andre, *Asst Prof,* Emporia State University, Dept of Art, Emporia KS (S)
Piper, Clinton, *Mus Prog Asst,* Western Pennsylvania Conservancy, Fallingwater, Mill Run PA
Piper, Elise, *Dir Devel,* The Dixon Gallery & Gardens, Memphis TN
Pipman, Mor, *Adj Assoc Prof,* College of Staten Island, Performing & Creative Arts Dept, Staten Island NY (S)
Pires, Kristin, *Editor,* University of Wisconsin-Madison, Chazen Museum of Art, Madison WI
Pires, Wendy, *Cur Educ,* Dickinson College, The Trout Gallery, Carlisle PA
Piribeck, Jan, *Prof Digital & Foundation,* University of Southern Maine, Dept of Art, Gorham ME (S)
Pirone, Jane, *Dean School of Design Strategies,* The New School, Parsons School of Design, New York NY (S)
Pirosky, Daniel, *Assoc Prof,* Portland State University, Dept of Art, Portland OR (S)
Pirozzolo, Rick, *Exec Dir,* Arnot Art Museum, Elmira NY
Pirraglia, Diane, *Asst Educ Cur,* Sangre de Cristo Arts & Conference Center, Pueblo CO
Pisciotta, Henry, *Arts & Architecture Librn,* The Pennsylvania State University, Architecture & Landscape Architecture Library, University Park PA
Pisciotta, Henry, *Arts & Architecture Librn,* The Pennsylvania State University, Arts & Humanities Library, University Park PA
Pisha, Nikki, *Fine Arts Prog Asst,* Federal Reserve Board, Art Gallery, Washington DC
Pishkur, Frank, *Prof,* Missouri Southern State University, Dept of Art, Joplin MO (S)
Piskel, Annette, *Vis Instr Graphic Design,* Florida Atlantic University, D F Schmidt College of Arts & Letters Dept of Visual Arts & Art History, Boca Raton FL (S)
Pissarro, Joachim, *Prof & Galleries Dir,* Hunter College, Dept of Art & Art History, New York NY (S)
Pisto, Ann, *Sec,* New Mexico Art League, Gallery & School, Albuquerque NM
Pitluga, Kurt, *Prof,* Slippery Rock University of Pennsylvania, Dept of Art, Slippery Rock PA (S)
Pitman, Brian, *Instr,* Adrian College, Art & Design Dept, Adrian MI (S)
Pitre, Frederic, *Botanist & Librn,* Jardin Botanique de Montreal, Bibliotheque, Montreal QC
Pitt, Paul, *Prof,* Harding University, Dept of Art & Design, Searcy AR (S)
Pittman, John, *Chmn,* John Jay College of Criminal Justice, Dept of Art, Music & Philosophy, New York NY (S)
Pittman, Jude, *Prof 2D Art,* College of San Mateo, Creative Arts Dept, San Mateo CA (S)
Pitts, Angela, *Instr,* Dallas Baptist University, Dept of Art, Dallas TX (S)
Pivovar, Ronald A, *Chmn Dept,* Thiel College, Dept of Art, Greenville PA (S)
Pixley, Mary, *Cur European & American Art,* University of Missouri, Museum of Art & Archaeology, Columbia MO
Pizer, Alan, *Asst Prof,* Texas State University - San Marcos, Dept of Art and Design, San Marcos TX (S)
Pizzo, Tony, *Exec Dir,* Ships of the Sea Maritime Museum, Savannah GA
Place-Gleason, Michelle, *Secy,* Warwick Museum of Art, Warwick RI
Plankensteiner, Barbara, *Cur African Art,* Yale University, Yale University Art Gallery, New Haven CT
Plante, Michael, *Assoc Prof,* Tulane University, Sophie H Newcomb Memorial College, New Orleans LA (S)
Plascencia, Gustavo, *Asst Prof,* Lycoming College, Art Dept, Williamsport PA (S)
Platanis, Liz, *Key Mktg & Event Planner,* Principle Gallery, Charleston, Charleston SC
Platow, Raphaela, *Dir & Chief Cur,* Contemporary Arts Center, Cincinnati OH
Platt, Christopher, *Chief Branch Library Officer,* The New York Public Library, New York NY
Platt, Melvin, *Dept Chmn & Prof,* University of Missouri - Columbia, Dept of Art, Columbia MO (S)
Platt, Ron, *Chief Cur,* Grand Rapids Art Museum, Grand Rapids MI
Plavsa, Manda, *Head Coll Devel & Access Svcs,* OCAD University, Dorothy H Hoover Library, Toronto ON
Pleasants, Sheila Gully, *Deputy Dir & Dir Artists' Servs,* Virginia Center for the Creative Arts, Amherst VA
Pleau, Jean-Christian, *Dean,* Universite du Quebec a Montreal, Faculty of Arts, Montreal QC (S)
Plesch, Veronique, *Assoc Prof,* Colby College, Art Dept, Waterville ME (S)
Ploeger, Dick, *VPres,* Fremont Center for the Arts, Canon City CO
Plosky, Charles, *Prof,* New Jersey City University, Art Dept, Jersey City NJ (S)
Plotek, Ariel, *Curator of Modern & Contemporary Art,* San Diego Museum of Art, San Diego CA
Plotkin, Edna Hibel, *Exec Trustee,* Edna Hibel Art Foundation, Hibel Museum of Art, Jupiter FL
Plotkin, Helene, *Dir Sales,* Edna Hibel Art Foundation, Hibel Museum of Art, Jupiter FL
Plume, Kathy, *Secy,* City of Springdale, Shiloh Museum of Ozark History, Springdale AR
Plumlee, Janie, *Admin Asst & Mus Store Mgr,* Carson County Square House Museum, Panhandle TX
Plummer Rohloff, Rebecca, *Asst Prof,* Salem State University, Art & Design Department, Salem MA (S)
Plummer, Ann, *Chmn,* Winona State University, Dept of Art, Winona MN (S)
Plummer, Bruce, *Dean Library,* Becker College, William F Ruska Library, Worcester MA
Plummer, Jack, *Prof Emeritus,* University of Texas at Arlington, Art & Art History Department, Arlington TX (S)
Plunkett, Stephanie Haboush, *Deputy Dir & Chief Cur,* Norman Rockwell Museum, Stockbridge MA
Plybon, Amanda, *Educ Cur,* National Churchill Museum, Fulton MO
Plyler, Anne, *Gallery Coordr,* James Prendergast, Jamestown NY
Poce, Patrick E, *Dir,* Eccles Community Art Center, Ogden UT
Pocius, Edward, *Cur Cartography,* Balzekas Museum of Lithuanian Culture, Chicago IL
Pockriss, Peter, *Dir Devel,* Historic Hudson Valley, Pocantico Hills NY
Podedworny, Carol, *Dir & Chief Cur,* McMaster University, McMaster Museum of Art, Hamilton ON
Podmaniczky, Christine B, *Assoc Cur NC Wyeth Collections,* Brandywine Conservancy, Brandywine River Museum, Chadds Ford PA
Poe, Michelle, *Educ Dir,* African American Museum of Iowa, Cedar Rapids IA
Poggioli, Emma, *Registrar & Admin Asst,* Balboa Art Conservation Center, San Diego CA
Pogue, Ed, *Prof,* Bethany College, Art Dept, Lindsborg KS (S)
Pogue, Ed, *Prof,* Bethany College, Mingenback Art Center, Lindsborg KS
Pogue, Megan, *Exec Dir,* Timken Museum of Art, San Diego CA
Pohl, Frances, *Chmn & Prof,* Pomona College, Dept of Art History, Claremont CA (S)
Pohl, Lyn, *Admin Mgr & Dir of Spec Projects,* Cornell University, College of Architecture, Art, and Planning, Ithaca NY (S)
Pohlad, Mark, *Asst Prof,* DePaul University, Dept of Art, Chicago IL (S)
Pohle, Peter, *Asst Prof,* John Brown University, Art Dept, Siloam Springs AR (S)
Pohlkamp, Mark, *Lect,* University of Wisconsin-Stevens Point, Dept of Art & Design, Stevens Point WI (S)

Pohlman, Ken, *Designer,* Middlebury College, Museum of Art, Middlebury VT

Pohlman, Lynette, *Dir,* Iowa State University, Brunnier Art Museum, Ames IA

Poindexter, David, *Asst Prof,* University of Texas of Permian Basin, Dept of Art, Odessa TX (S)

Poindexter, Edith, *Cur,* Patrick Henry, Red Hill National Memorial, Brookneal VA

Poirier, Francine, *Dir,* Canada Science & Technology Museums Corporation, Canada Aviation Museum, Ottawa ON

Poland, Barbara, *Research Librn,* Warner Bros Studio Research Library, Burbank CA

Polednik, Marcelle, *Exec Dir,* Milwaukee Art Museum, Milwaukee WI

Polesnak, Ronald, *Technical Support & Installation,* State University of New York at Binghamton, Binghamton University Art Museum, Binghamton NY

Poliakov, Lev, *Asst Prof,* New York Institute of Technology, Fine Arts Dept, Old Westbury NY (S)

Polich, Debra, *Exec Dir,* Artrain, Inc, Ann Arbor MI

Polillo, Jennifer, *Dir Educ,* Delaware Center for the Contemporary Arts, Wilmington DE

Poling, Jenna, *Music Dir,* The National Shrine of the North American Martyrs, Fultonville NY

Polinsky, Alyssa, *Interim Exec Dir,* British Columbia Museums Association, Victoria BC

Polirer, Sarah A, *Mgr,* CIGNA Corporation, CIGNA Art Collection, Bloomfield CT

Polisar, Sierra, *Colls Mgr & Exhibs Registrar,* Tulane University, Newcomb Art Museum, New Orleans LA

Polishook, Mark, *Prof,* University of Maine at Augusta, College of Arts & Humanities, Augusta ME (S)

Polizzotti, Mark, *Publr & Ed in Chief,* The Metropolitan Museum of Art, New York NY

Polk, Tom, *Assoc Prof Art History,* University of Georgia, Franklin College of Arts & Sciences, Lamar Dodd School of Art, Athens GA (S)

Poll, MandiAnne, *Cur of Educ,* Eccles Community Art Center, Ogden UT

Pollack, Anat, *Assoc Prof,* University of South Florida, School of Art & Art History, Tampa FL (S)

Pollack, Lisa, *Chief of Communications,* Boston Public Library, Central Library, Boston MA

Pollan, Ellen, *Develop,* Bronx Council on the Arts, Longwood Arts Gallery @ Hostos, Bronx NY

Pollei, Dane, *Dir and Chief Cur,* Mabee-Gerrer Museum of Art, Shawnee OK

Polli, Andrea, *Prof,* University of New Mexico, Department of Fine Arts & Art History, Albuquerque NM (S)

Pollman, Howard, *Dir External Affairs,* Pennsylvania Historical & Museum Commission, The State Museum of Pennsylvania, Harrisburg PA

Pollock, Janine, *Asst Head,* Free Library of Philadelphia, Rare Book Dept, Philadelphia PA

Pollock, Kelly, *Exec Dir,* Center of Creative Arts (COCA), Millstone Gallery, Saint Louis MO

Pollock, Tracy, *Dir Admin & Devel,* Bard College, Center for Curatorial Studies and the Hessel Museum of Art, Annandale-on-Hudson NY

Poloukhine, Olga, *Recording Sec,* New York Society of Women Artists, Inc, Westport CT

Polowy, Barbara, *Librn,* Smith College, Hillyer Art Library, Northampton MA

Pomeroy Draper, Stacy F, *Cur,* Rensselaer County Historical Society, Hart-Cluett Mansion, 1827, Troy NY

Pomeroy Draper, Stacy, *Cur,* Rensselaer County Historical Society, Museum & Library, Troy NY

Pomeroy, Dan, *Chief Cur & Dir Colls,* Tennessee State Museum, Nashville TN

Pomeroy, Jordana, *Dir,* Florida International University, The Patricia & Phillip Frost Art Museum, Miami FL

Pommer, Joyce, *Treas,* New York Society of Women Artists, Inc, Westport CT

Pompelia, Mark, *Visual & Material Resource Librn,* Rhode Island School of Design, Fleet Library at RISD, Providence RI

Pon, Steve, *Exhib Supv,* San Francisco Museum of Modern Art, Artist Gallery, San Francisco CA

Ponce de Leon, Monica, *Dean,* Princeton University, School of Architecture, Princeton NJ (S)

Ponce, Magaly, *Asst Prof,* Bridgewater State College, Art Dept, Bridgewater MA (S)

Pond, Mandy, *Archivist,* Massillon Museum, Massillon OH

Pondone, Marc, *Instr,* Solano Community College, Division of Fine & Applied Art & Behavioral Science, Fairfield CA (S)

Pongetti, Rachael, *Adj Instr,* University of West Florida, Dept of Art, Pensacola FL (S)

Ponikvar, Laura, *Image & Instruc Srvcs Librn,* Cleveland Institute of Art, Jessica Gund Memorial Library, Cleveland OH

Pontious, Susan, *Dir Pub Art Prog,* San Francisco City & County Arts Commission, San Francisco CA

Pontynen, Arthur, *Prof,* University of Wisconsin Oshkosh, Dept of Art, Oshkosh WI (S)

Poole, Kristin, *Artistic Dir,* Sun Valley Center for the Arts, Dept of Fine Art, Sun Valley ID (S)

Poole, Mary, *Exec Dir,* Artspace Inc, Raleigh NC

Poole, William D, *Exec Dir,* Canadian Clay and Glass Gallery, Waterloo ON

Poon, Elysia, *Cur Educ,* School for Advanced Research (SAR), Indian Arts Research Center, Santa Fe NM

Poor, Robert, *Prof,* University of Minnesota, Minneapolis, Art History, Minneapolis MN (S)

Poore, Mark, *Instr,* Glendale Community College, Visual & Performing Arts Div, Glendale CA (S)

Popa, Amy Jo, *Assoc Lectr,* Idaho State University, Dept of Art, Pocatello ID (S)

Popadics, Joel, *VPres,* American Watercolor Society, Inc, New York NY

Pope, Karen, *Sr Lectr,* Baylor University - College of Arts and Sciences, Dept of Art, Waco TX (S)

Pope, Linda, *Dir,* University of California at Santa Cruz, Eloise Pickard Smith Gallery, Santa Cruz CA

Pope, Louise, *Assoc Prof,* Dakota State University, College of Liberal Arts, Madison SD (S)

Pope, Nancy, *Head Cur, History Dept,* National Postal Museum, Smithsonian Institution, Washington DC

Popkin, Maggie, *Asst Prof,* Case Western Reserve University, Dept of Art History & Art, Cleveland OH (S)

Poplack, Robert, *Gallery Dir,* Notre Dame de Namur University, Wiegand Gallery, Belmont CA (S)

Popovic, Milica, *Art Gallery Mgr,* Herrett Center for Arts & Sciences, Jean B King Art Gallery, Twin Falls ID

Popovich, George, *Dir Theater,* Henry Ford Community College, McKenzie Fine Art Ctr, Dearborn MI (S)

Popp, Zan, *Art Exhibit Cur,* Topeka & Shawnee County Public Library, Alice C Sabatini Gallery, Topeka KS

Poras, E Linda, *Exec Dir,* The Brush Art Gallery & Studios, Lowell MA

Porcari, George, *Acquisitions Librn,* Art Center College of Design, James Lemont Fogg Memorial Library, Pasadena CA

Porch, Whitney, *Assoc Professional Specialist,* Southern Nazarene University, Art & Design Department, Bethany OK (S)

Porobic, Damir, *Lectr Printmaking and Digital Photo,* University of Southern Maine, Dept of Art, Gorham ME (S)

Porps, Ernest O, *Prof,* University of Colorado at Denver, College of Arts & Media Visual Arts Dept, Denver CO (S)

Porsild, Charlene, *Head Librn & Archivist,* Montana Historical Society, Library, Helena MT

Porta, Giogio, *Asst Prof,* Northern Virginia Community College, Art Dept, Annandale VA (S)

Porteous, Densil, *Dir Mktg & Communs,* Ohio State University, Wexner Center for the Arts, Columbus OH

Porter, Alberta, *Pres,* Macartney House Museum, Oakland ME

Porter, Ann, *Prof,* Black Hills State University, Ruddell Gallery, Spearfish SD

Porter, Austin, *Asst Prof,* Kenyon College, Art Dept, Gambier OH (S)

Porter, Benjamin, *Dir,* University of California, Berkeley, Phoebe Apperson Hearst Museum of Anthropology, Berkeley CA

Porter, Carolyn, *Asst Dir Develop,* University of Texas, Dept of Art & Art History, Austin TX (S)

Porter, David S, *Assoc Prof,* University of North Florida, Dept of Communications & Visual Arts, Jacksonville FL (S)

Porter, James, *Designer & Preparator,* Wichita State University, Ulrich Museum of Art, Wichita KS

Porter, Jeanne Chenault, *Assoc Prof Emeritus,* Pennsylvania State University, University Park, Dept of Art History, University Park PA (S)

Porter, Larry, *Assoc Prof,* Central State University, Dept of Art, Wilberforce OH (S)

Porter, Liz, *VPres,* Livingston County Historical Society, Museum, Geneseo NY

Porter, Matt, *Cur Educ,* Morris Museum of Art, Augusta GA

Porter, Michele, *Cur Coll,* Dacotah Prairie Museum, Ruth Bunker Memorial Library, Aberdeen SD

Porter, Richard, *Instr,* Wayland Baptist University, Dept of Art, School of Fine Art, Plainview TX (S)

Porter, Robert F, *Fine Arts Chmn,* Queens College, Fine Arts Dept, Charlotte NC (S)

Porter, Ron, *Sr Lectr,* Vanderbilt University, Dept of Art, Nashville TN (S)

Porter, Stephanie, *Educ Officer,* City of Woodstock, Woodstock Art Gallery, Woodstock ON

Porter, Tom, *Instr,* Bismarck State College, Fine Arts Dept, Bismarck ND (S)

Porterfield, Jimmy, *Chief Security Officer,* Nelda C & H J Lutcher Stark Foundation, Stark Museum of Art, Orange TX

Portnoy, Deidre, *VPres,* Wellfleet Historical Society & Museum, Inc, Wellfleet MA

Portwood, Rick, *VChair,* Pewabic Society Inc, Pewabic, Detroit MI

Posey, Laurel, *Mgr Grants & Communications,* South Carolina Arts Commission, Columbia SC

Poshek, Joe, *Div Dean,* Orange Coast College, Visual & Performing Arts Division, Costa Mesa CA (S)

Posner, Helaine, *Chief Cur & Deputy Dir Cur Affairs,* Purchase College, Neuberger Museum of Art, Purchase NY

Poss, Sharon, *Office Mgr,* Historical Society of Palm Beach County, The Richard and Pat Johnson Palm Beach County History Museum, West Palm Beach FL

Post, Greg, *Dir Information Servs & Electronic Systems,* Milwaukee Public Museum, Milwaukee WI

Post, Linda, *Grad Asst,* Stephen F Austin State University, School of Art, Nacogdoches TX (S)

Posther, David, *Art Chair,* Kalamazoo Valley Community College, Center for New Media, Kalamazoo MI (S)

Posthumus, Mike, *VPres Educ,* Grand Rapids Public Museum, Grand Rapids MI

Poston, Virginia, *Instr,* University of Southern Indiana, Art & Design Dept, Evansville IN (S)

Potance, Rebecca, *Head Educ & Visitor Experience,* New Mexico Department of Cultural Affairs, New Mexico Museum of Art, Santa Fe NM

Potance, Rebecca, *Librn, Archivist & Webmaster,* New Mexico Department of Cultural Affairs, New Mexico Museum of Art, Santa Fe NM

Potash, Chris, *Mgr Mktg & PR,* Allentown Art Museum, Allentown PA

Pote, Judy, *Pres,* Philadelphia Museum of Art, Women's Committee, Philadelphia PA

Poteel, Daniel, *Provost,* School of the Museum of Fine Arts, Boston MA (S)

Potochniak, Andrea, *Editorial Mgr,* Cornell University, Herbert F Johnson Museum of Art, Ithaca NY

Potochnik, Sherry, *Educational Specialist,* The Ohio Historical Society, Inc, Campus Martius Museum & Ohio River Museum, Marietta OH

Potratz, Wayne, *Assoc Prof,* University of Minnesota, Minneapolis, Dept of Art, Minneapolis MN (S)

Potter, Dave, *Assoc Prof,* Keystone College, Fine Arts Dept, LaPlume PA (S)
Potter, Donna, *Admin Asst,* Saskatchewan Craft Council & Affinity Gallery, Saskatoon SK
Potter, Edmund, *Dir Coll,* Woodrow Wilson, Woodrow Wilson Presidential Library, Staunton VA
Potter, Edmund, *Dir Coll,* Woodrow Wilson, Staunton VA
Potter, Janice, *Special Events Mgr,* Worcester Art Museum, Worcester MA
Potter, Leslie, *Exhib & Educ Coordr,* Saskatchewan Craft Council & Affinity Gallery, Saskatoon SK
Potter, Susan, *Librn,* Springfield Art Museum, Library, Springfield MO
Potter, Susan, *Librn,* Springfield Art Museum, Springfield MO
Potter, Terry, *Library Dir,* Independence Seaport Museum, Library, Philadelphia PA
Potter-Ndiaye, Emily, *Dir Educ,* Brooklyn Historical Society, Brooklyn NY
Pottie, John, *Cur,* National Silk Art Museum, Weston MO
Pottie, Venessa, *Cur,* National Silk Art Museum, Weston MO
Pottinger, Mark, *Assoc Prof,* Manhattan College, Visual & Performing Arts Dept, Bronx NY (S)
Potts, Jennifer, *Cur Objects,* Delaware Historical Society, Delaware History Museum and Center for African American Heritage, Wilmington DE
Potts, Timothy, *Dir,* The Getty Center, The J Paul Getty Museum, Los Angeles CA
Potts, Timothy, *Dir,* Getty Center, The J Paul Getty Museum - Getty Villa, Malibu CA
Potts, Timothy, *Dir.,* The Getty Center, Trust Museum, Los Angeles CA
Poulin, Carmen, *Assoc Dean,* University of New Brunswick, Faculty of Arts, Fredericton NB (S)
Poulos, Basilios N, *Prof Emeritus,* Rice University, Visual & Dramatic Arts, Houston TX (S)
Poulter, Jennifer, *Special Facility Mgr,* Baton Rouge Gallery, Center For Contemporary Art, Baton Rouge LA
Poulter, Melissa, *Sales Assoc,* Gene Roncka Willow Point Gallery/Museum, Ashland NE
Pourchot, Eric, *Institutional Advancement Dir,* American Institute for Conservation of Historic & Artistic Works, Washington DC
Pourtemour, Peggy, *Registrar,* Pueblo Museum, Desert Hot Springs CA
Pouwels, J, *Instr,* California State University, Chico, Department of Art & Art History, Chico CA (S)
Povlsen-Jones, Malunda, *Instr,* Whitman College, Art Dept, Walla Walla WA (S)
Povse, Matt, *Chmn,* Marywood University, Art Dept, Scranton PA (S)
Powell, Amy, *Cur Modern & Contemp Art,* University of Illinois at Urbana-Champaign, Krannert Art Museum and Kinkead Pavilion, Champaign IL
Powell, Ann, *Dir Devel,* The Trustees of Reservations, The Mission House, Ipswich MA
Powell, Brandon, *Program Coordr,* Woodbridge Township Cultural Arts Commission, Barron Arts Center, Woodbridge NJ
Powell, Carl, *Chief Info Officer,* Columbus Metropolitan Library, Arts & Media Division Carnegie Gallery, Columbus OH
Powell, Daniel, *Dir Fine & Performing Arts,* Chipola College, Dept of Fine & Performing Arts, Marianna FL (S)
Powell, Earl A, *Dir,* National Gallery of Art, Washington DC
Powell, Edward, *Assoc Prof,* University of Pittsburgh, Dept of Studio Arts, Pittsburgh PA (S)
Powell, Isaac, *Asst Prof,* Northwestern State University of Louisiana, School of Creative & Performing Arts - Dept of Fine & Graphic Arts, Natchitoches LA (S)
Powell, Jennifer, *Business Office Mgr,* Birmingham Museum of Art, Birmingham AL
Powell, John, *Cur,* City of Saint Augustine, Saint Augustine FL
Powell, Kimberly, *Asst Prof Art Educ & Curriculum & Instruction,* Pennsylvania State University, University Park, Penn State School of Visual Arts, University Park PA (S)
Powell, Lalana, *Library Technician,* University of Kentucky, Hunter M Adams Architecture Library, Lexington KY
Powell, Mary Ellen, *Registrar,* Frederick R Weisman Art Foundation, Los Angeles CA
Powell, Nancy, *Senior Cur,* National Audubon Society, John James Audubon Center at Mill Grove, Audubon PA
Powell, Pamela, *Photo Archivist,* Chester County Historical Society, West Chester PA
Powelson, Rosemary, *Chmn,* Lower Columbia College, Art Dept, Longview WA (S)
Powers, Carol, *Instr,* Mount Mary College, Art & Design Division, Milwaukee WI (S)
Powers, Jessica, *Cur Ancient Mediterranean Art,* San Antonio Museum of Art, San Antonio TX
Powers, Joan, *Assoc Prof,* C W Post Campus of Long Island University, School of Visual & Performing Arts, Brookville NY (S)
Powers, Leland, *Chmn,* Fort Hays State University, Dept of Art & Design, Hays KS (S)
Powers, Leland, *Chmn,* Fort Hays State University, Moss-Thorns Gallery of Arts, Hays KS
Powers, Linda, *Develop Dir,* Koshare Indian Museum, Inc, La Junta CO
Powers, Linda, *Exec Dir,* Koshare Indian Museum, Inc, Library, La Junta CO
Powers, Marty, *Maintenance,* City of Springdale, Shiloh Museum of Ozark History, Springdale AR
Powers, Mathew, *Exec Dir,* Saint Johnsbury Athenaeum, Saint Johnsbury VT
Powers, Michelle, *VPres,* Carteret County Historical Society, The History Place, Morehead City NC
Powers, Nancy, *Visitor Servs Coordr,* Johns Hopkins University, Evergreen Museum & Library, Baltimore MD
Poynor, Robin, *Prof,* University of Florida, School of Art & Art History, Gainesville FL (S)
Poyourow, Jill, *Instr,* Pierce College, Art Dept, Woodland Hills CA (S)
Pozzi, Clelia, *Cur Intern,* Harvard University, Busch-Reisinger Museum, Cambridge MA
Pozzi, Tessa, *Annual Giving Coord,* Figge Art Museum, Davenport IA
Pradel, Chari, *Assoc Prof,* California State Polytechnic University, Pomona, Department of Art, Pomona CA (S)
Prainito-Wisczaer, Maria, *Adjunct,* Marygrove College, Department of Art, Detroit MI (S)
Prasil, S Renee, *Secy,* Huntsville Art League, Lowe Mill Arts & Entertainment, Huntsville AL
Pratesi, Angela, *Fine & performing Arts,* University of Northern Iowa, Fine & Performing Arts Collection Rod Library, Cedar Falls IA
Prather, Mary, *Instr,* Appalachian State University, Dept of Art, Boone NC (S)
Prats, Laurel, *VPres Mem,* MEXIC-ARTE Museum, Austin TX
Pratt, Barry, *Artistic Assoc,* Adirondack Lakes Center for the Arts, Blue Mountain Lake NY
Pratt, Benjamin, *Asst Prof,* University of Wisconsin-Stout, Dept of Art & Design, Menomonie WI (S)
Pratt, Greta, *Assoc Prof,* Old Dominion University, Art Dept, Norfolk VA (S)
Pratt, Harvey, *Chmn,* United States Department of the Interior, Indian Arts & Crafts Board, Washington DC
Pratt, Lori, *Exec Dir,* Audrain County Historical Society, Graceland Museum & American Saddlehorse Museum & Fire Brick Industry Museum, Mexico MO
Praytor, Blake, *Dept Head,* Greenville Technical College, Visual Arts Dept, Greenville SC (S)
Preiss Odom, Becky, *History Cur,* Ohio History Connection, Columbus OH
Preissler, Kate, *Dir,* Historic Holyoke at Wistariahurst & City of Holyoke, Holyoke MA
Prelinger, Elizabeth, *Prof,* Georgetown University, Dept of Art & Art History, Washington DC (S)
Premo, Kate, *Dir Mktg & Commun,* Montclair Art Museum, Montclair NJ
Prendergast, Erin, *Chief of Staff & Corp Secy,* Art Gallery of Ontario, Toronto ON
Prendergast, Whitney, *Develop Dir,* Rutgers, The State University of New Jersey, Zimmerli Art Museum at Rutgers University, New Brunswick NJ
Prendeville, Jet M, *Art & Architecture Librn,* Rice University, Brown Fine Arts Library, Houston TX
Presciutti, Diana, *Asst Prof,* The College of Wooster, Dept of Art and Art History, Wooster OH (S)
Present, Susan, *Bus Mgr,* Henry Morrison Flagler Museum, Palm Beach FL
Presgrave, Trevor, *Instr Math,* AIC College of Design, Cincinnati OH (S)
Presnar, Robert, *Prog Dir,* Hoyt Center for the Arts, Arts & Education of the Hoyt, New Castle PA
Presneill, Max, *Dir & Cur,* Torrance Art Museum, Torrance CA
Prestegaard, Kristin, *Chief Engagement Officer,* Minneapolis Institute of Art, Minneapolis MN
Preston Blier, Suzanne, *Pres,* College Art Association, New York NY
Preston, Charles, *Cur Draper Mus of Natural History,* Buffalo Bill Memorial Association, Buffalo Bill Historical Center, Cody WY
Preston, Deborah, *Dean Arts,* Montgomery College, Dept of Art, Rockville MD (S)
Preston, Lesley, *Asst Prof,* Presbyterian College, Visual & Theater Arts, Clinton SC (S)
Preston, Leslie, *Head Acquisitions & Metadata servs,* Fashion Institute of Technology - SUNY, Gladys Marcus Library, New York NY
Preston, Teresa, *Art History Instr,* Hutchinson Community College, Visual Arts Dept, Hutchinson KS (S)
Prestwich, Larry B, *Prof,* Northeastern Junior College, Art Department, Sterling CO (S)
Preucel, Robert, *Dir,* Brown University, Haffenreffer Museum of Anthropology, Providence RI
Preuss, Sandy, *VPres,* First State Bank, They Also Ran Gallery, Norton KS
Prevec, Rose Anne, *Communs Officer,* McMaster University, McMaster Museum of Art, Hamilton ON
Price Shimp, Robert, *Exec Dir,* Buffalo Bill Memorial Association, Buffalo Bill Historical Center, Cody WY
Price, Amber, *Mem Coordr,* deCordova Sculpture Park & Museum, Lincoln MA
Price, Annalisa, *Resource Manager,* Marin Society of Artists Inc, San Rafael CA
Price, Brad, *Part-Time Instr,* Oklahoma Baptist University, Art & Design Dept, Shawnee OK (S)
Price, Dustin, *Instr,* Mott Community College, Fine Arts & Social Sciences Division, Flint MI (S)
Price, Gary, *Chair,* Cambridge Public Library and Gallery, Idea Exchange, Cambridge ON
Price, Janice, *Pres,* Banff Centre, Banff AB (S)
Price, Janice, *Pres & CEO,* Banff Centre, Walter Phillips Gallery, Banff AB
Price, Jennifer Casler, *Cur of Asian & non-Western Art,* Kimbell Art Foundation, Kimbell Art Museum, Fort Worth TX
Price, Kelly, *Registrar,* Yellowstone Art Museum, Billings MT
Price, Linda, *Instr,* Ithaca College, Fine Art Dept, Ithaca NY (S)
Price, Mark, *Chmn Art Dept,* Middle Tennessee State University, Art Dept, Murfreesboro TN (S)
Price, Marla, *Dir,* Modern Art Museum, Fort Worth TX
Price, Marshall, *Asst Cur Contemporary Art,* National Academy Museum & School, Archives, New York NY
Price, Mary Jo, *Exhib Librn,* Frostburg State University, Lewis J Ort Library, Frostburg MD
Price, Pam, *Chmn,* University of Texas of Permian Basin, Dept of Art, Odessa TX (S)
Price, Pam, *Library Dir,* Mercer County Community College, Library, West Windsor NJ

Price, Peggy, *Librn,* University of Southern Mississippi, McCain Library & Archives, Hattiesburg MS

Price, Rebecca, *Visual Resources Librn & Selector Art & Design, Architecture & Urban Planning Librn,* University of Michigan, Media Union Library, Ann Arbor MI

Price, Renee, *Director,* Neue Galerie New York, New York NY

Price, Rob, *Prof,* University of Wisconsin-Stout, Dept of Art & Design, Menomonie WI (S)

Price, Stephanie, *Mktg Mgr,* Panhandle-Plains Historical Museum, Canyon TX

Prickett, Sylvia, *COO,* National Assembly of State Arts Agencies, Washington DC

Pridal, Cathryn, *VPres,* Cottey College, Art Dept, Nevada MO (S)

Priest, Al, *2nd VPres,* The Stained Glass Association of America, Raytown MO

Priest, Brian James, *Lectr Studio Art,* California Polytechnic State University at San Luis Obispo, Dept of Art & Design, San Luis Obispo CA (S)

Priest, Mark, *Assoc Prof,* University of Louisville, Allen R Hite Art Institute, Louisville KY (S)

Prime, Craig, *Instr,* Saginaw Valley State University, Dept of Art & Design, University Center MI (S)

Primer, Jesse, *Chair,* Tougaloo College, Tougaloo Art Collection, Tougaloo MS

Prince, David, *Assoc Dir,* Syracuse University, SUArt Galleries, Syracuse NY

Prince, David, *Cur,* Syracuse University, Art Collection, Syracuse NY

Prince, Lily, *Asst Prof,* William Paterson University, Dept Arts, Wayne NJ (S)

Prince, Nigel, *Exec Dir,* Contemporary Art Gallery, Vancouver BC

Prince, Nigel, *Exec Dir,* Contemporary Art Gallery Society of British Columbia, Vancouver BC

Prindaville, Shelby, *Asst Prof & Prog Dir,* University of Saint Mary, Fine Arts Dept, Leavenworth KS (S)

Prindle, Beth, *Head Spec Colls,* Boston Public Library, Albert H Wiggin Gallery & Print Department, Boston MA

Prindle, Elizabeth, *Head Spec Colls,* Boston Public Library, Rare Book & Manuscripts Dept, Boston MA

Pringle, Cynthia, *Acting Deputy Dir Opers & Fin,* Creative Time, New York NY

Prinz, Peter, *Co-Founder & CEO,* Space One Eleven, Inc, Birmingham AL

Prior, Barbara Q, *Art Librn,* Oberlin College, Clarence Ward Art Library, Oberlin OH

Prior, Gail, *Sales Shop Mgr,* Jericho Historical Society, Jericho VT

Pritchard, David, *Dir Opers,* Please Touch Museum, Philadelphia PA

Pritchard, Shannon, *Asst Prof,* University of Southern Indiana, Art & Design Dept, Evansville IN (S)

Pritchard, William, *Cur Center for So Craft & Design,* Ogden Museum of Southern Art, University of New Orleans, New Orleans LA

Pritchett, Mark, *Fine Arts Program Dir,* San Antonio College, Visual Arts & Technology, San Antonio TX (S)

Pritikin, Renny, *Dir,* University of California, Davis, Jan Shrem and Maria Manetti Shrem Museum of Art, Davis CA

Pritzker, Elisa, *VPres,* New York Society of Women Artists, Inc, Westport CT

Pro, Regan, *Deputy Dir Educ,* Seattle Art Museum, Seattle WA

Probes, Anna Greidanus, *Assoc Prof,* Calvin College, Art Dept, Grand Rapids MI (S)

Probst, Peter, *Prof,* Tufts University, Dept of Art & Art History, Medford MA (S)

Proch, Pauline, *Exec Dir,* Egan Maritime Institute, Shipwreck & Lifesaving Museum, Nantucket MA

Prochaska, David, *Instr,* Cuesta College, Art Dept, San Luis Obispo CA (S)

Proctor, Grover B, *Exec Dir,* Northwood University, Alden B Dow Creativity Center, Midland MI (S)

Proctor, Tammy, *VPres Mem,* DuPage Art League School & Gallery, Wheaton IL

Proffitt, Judith, *Programs Coordr,* Johns Hopkins University, Homewood Museum, Baltimore MD

Proft, Megan, *Develop & Bus Dir,* Owatonna Arts Center, Owatonna MN

Prohaska, Albert, *Adjunct Prof,* New York Institute of Technology, Fine Arts Dept, Old Westbury NY (S)

Proios, Victoria, *Sr Accnt,* The American Federation of Arts, New York NY

Prokop, Clifton, *Chmn Fine Arts,* Keystone College, Fine Arts Dept, LaPlume PA (S)

Propeack, Scott, *Assoc Dir & Chief Cur,* Burchfield Penney Art Center, Library, Buffalo NY

Propeack, Scott, *Assoc Dir & Chief Cur,* Burchfield Penney Art Center, Buffalo NY

Proper, Donna, *Asst Prof,* State University of New York at Farmingdale, Visual Communications, Farmingdale NY (S)

Proper, Joann, *Circ Library Asst,* Colonial Williamsburg Foundation, John D Rockefeller, Jr Library, Williamsburg VA

Prophet, Jane, *Assoc Dean,* University of Michigan, Ann Arbor, Penny W Stamps School of Art & Design, Ann Arbor MI (S)

Proser, Adriana, *John H. Foster Senior Curator for Traditional Asian Art,* Asia Society Museum, New York NY

Prost, Cynthia, *Pres & CEO,* Arts & Education Council of Greater Saint Louis, Saint Louis MO

Prothro, Monica, *Art Prog Mgr,* City of Atlanta, Office of Cultural Affairs, Atlanta GA

Protka, Jacqueline, *Digital Assets & Media Librn,* Corcoran Gallery of Art, Corcoran Library, Washington DC

Protka, Jacqueline, *Librn,* Hirshhorn Museum & Sculpture Garden, Library, Washington DC

Proulx, Anne-Marie, *Co-Dir,* VU Centre De Diffusion Et De Production De La Photographie, Quebec QC

Provan, Archibald D, *Assoc Prof,* Rochester Institute of Technology, School of Printing Management & Sciences, Rochester NY (S)

Provan, Jill E, *Librn,* Tucson Museum of Art and Historic Block, Library, Tucson AZ

Provence, Dana, *Prof Art,* Adams State College, Dept of Visual Arts, Alamosa CO (S)

Provenzano, Sandra Parker, *Head Cataloger,* Dumbarton Oaks, Dumbarton Oaks Research Library, Washington DC

Provine, William, *Instr,* John C Calhoun, Department of Fine Arts, Tanner AL (S)

Provo, Dan, *Dir,* Oklahoma Historical Society, State Museum of History, Oklahoma City OK

Provost, Jon C, *Dir Finance & Admin,* Berkshire Museum, Pittsfield MA

Provost, Thomas, *Asst Dir,* Principle Gallery, Charleston, Charleston SC

Pruchniewski, Mary, *Dir Fin,* Erie Art Museum, Erie PA

Pruden, Sue, *Retail Operations Dir,* Contemporary Arts Museum Houston, Houston TX

Prudic, Nancy, *Asst Prof Visual Art,* Lake Erie College, Fine Arts Dept, Painesville OH (S)

Pruett, Jeff, *Progs Coordr,* Gaston County Museum of Art & History, Dallas NC

Pruitt, Jack, *Dir Develop & External Affairs,* The Historic New Orleans Collection, Royal Street Galleries, New Orleans LA

Pruner, Gary, *Instr,* American River College, Dept of Art/Art New Media, Sacramento CA (S)

Prusa, Carol, *Prof Art, Painting/Drawing,* Florida Atlantic University, D F Schmidt College of Arts & Letters Dept of Visual Arts & Art History, Boca Raton FL (S)

Prut, Dmitry, *Founder & Dir,* Avant Gallery, Miami FL

Pry, George, *Pres,* Art Institute of Pittsburgh, Pittsburgh PA (S)

Przybysz, Jane, *Exec Dir,* University of South Carolina, McKissick Museum, Columbia SC

Psomas, Tim, *Exploratory Arts Dir,* North Fourth Art Center & Gallery, Albuquerque NM

Ptacek, Bill, *CEO,* Calgary Public Library, Arts & Recreation Dept, Calgary AB

Ptak, Laurel, *Exec Dir & Cur,* Art in General, Brooklyn NY

Puccinelli, Keith, *VPres,* Santa Barbara Contemporary Arts Forum, Santa Barbara CA

Pucher, John, *Mgr Bus & Opers,* Woodrow Wilson, Washington DC

Puckett, Jean L, *Dir Finance,* Jamestown-Yorktown Foundation, Jamestown Settlement, Williamsburg VA

Puckett, Lee, *Preparator,* Robischon Gallery, Denver CO

Puckett, Paula, *Chmn,* Kellogg Community College, Arts & Communication Dept, Battle Creek MI (S)

Puckitt, Sarah, *Colls Information Specialist,* Montgomery Museum of Fine Arts, Library, Montgomery AL

Puff, Allison, *Assoc Prof,* State University of New York at Farmingdale, Visual Communications, Farmingdale NY (S)

Puff, Robert L, *Pres (Vol),* Montgomery Museum & Lewis Miller Regional Art Center, Christianburg VA

Puffer, John, *Assoc Prof,* Vincennes University Junior College, Humanities Art Dept, Vincennes IN (S)

Puffer, Wendy, *Asst Prof,* Indiana Wesleyan University, School of Arts & Humanities, Division of Art, Marion IN (S)

Pugh, Barbara, *President,* Hera Educational Foundation, Hera Gallery, Wakefield RI

Pugsley, Marsha, *VChmn,* Palo Alto Art Center, Palo Alto CA

Puhner, Ned, *Exec Dir,* Greenville Museum of Art, Inc, Greenville NC

Pujol, Elliott, *Prof,* Kansas State University, Art Dept, Manhattan KS (S)

Pulin, Carol, *Dir,* American Print Alliance, Peachtree City GA

Pulivarti, Shejal, *Pub Affairs Officer,* Naval Historical Center, National Museum of the US Navy, Washington DC

Pullen, Raelene, *Dir Develop,* Figge Art Museum, Davenport IA

Pullini Brown, Ada, *Assoc Prof Painting & Drawing,* Rio Hondo College, Arts & Cultural Programs Dept, Whittier CA (S)

Puls, Jonathan, *Interim Chair,* Biola University, Department of Art, La Mirada CA (S)

Puls, Lucy, *Prof Sculpture,* University of California, Davis, Dept of Art & Art History, Davis CA (S)

Pulsifer, Dorothy, *Prof,* Bridgewater State College, Art Dept, Bridgewater MA (S)

Pultz, John, *Assoc Prof,* University of Kansas, Kress Foundation Dept of Art History, Lawrence KS (S)

Pulver, Sara, *Gallery Coordr,* Lansing Art Gallery, Lansing MI

Pumphrey, M Jo, *Prof,* Brevard College, Department of Art, Brevard NC (S)

Pumphrey, Richard, *Prof,* Lynchburg College, Art Dept, Lynchburg VA (S)

Pumputiene, Irena, *Librn,* Balzekas Museum of Lithuanian Culture, Chicago IL

Punt, Gerry, *Instr,* Augustana College, Art Dept, Sioux Falls SD (S)

Purcell, Amy Lixi, *Prof,* University of North Carolina at Greensboro, School of Art, Greensboro NC (S)

Purcell, Carl, *Chmn,* Snow College, Art Dept, Ephraim UT (S)

Purcell, Marilu, *Dir Visual Arts & National Gallery,* Institute of Puerto Rican Culture, National Gallery, San Juan PR

Purdy, Beth, *Instr,* Kalamazoo Valley Community College, Center for New Media, Kalamazoo MI (S)

Purinton, William, *Treas,* Portsmouth Athenaeum, Joseph Copley Research Library, Portsmouth NH

Purkiss, Christine, *Library Asst,* Bryn Mawr College, Rhys Carpenter Library for Art, Archaeology, Classics & Cities, Bryn Mawr PA

Purpura, Allyson, *Sr Cur & Cur Global African Art,* University of Illinois at Urbana-Champaign, Krannert Art Museum and Kinkead Pavilion, Champaign IL

Purrington, Robert H, *Innkeeper,* Longfellow's Wayside Inn Museum, Sudbury MA

Purves, Eric, *Assoc Prof,* Appalachian State University, Dept of Art, Boone NC (S)
Purvis, Alston, *Chmn Graphic Design,* Boston University, School for the Arts, Boston MA (S)
Purvis, Amy, *Chief Develop Officer,* Museum of Fine Arts, Houston, Houston TX
Putman, Sumi, *Printmaker,* University of South Alabama, Dept of Art & Art History, Mobile AL (S)
Putnam, Carol, *Mng Dir,* Grass Roots Art & Community Effort (GRACE), Firehouse Gallery, Hardwick VT
Putnam, Dee, *Librn,* The Museum of Western Art, Museum of Western Art & Research Library, Kerrville TX
Putnam, Rosane, *Pres,* Springfield Art & Historical Society, Springfield VT
Puzziferro, Maria, *Pres & Provost,* Rocky Mountain College of Art & Design, Lakewood CO (S)
Pye, Jennifer, *Chief Cur,* Monhegan Museum, Monhegan Museum of Art & History, Monhegan ME
Pygin, Cynthia, *CFO,* California Science Center, Los Angeles CA
Pyle, Aaron, *Mus Tech,* University of Maine, Museum of Art, Bangor ME
Pyle, Dorothy, *Div Chmn,* Maui Community College, Art Program, Kahului HI (S)
Pyrke, Dougla, *Dir Develop,* Hill-Stead Museum, Farmington CT
Pyrzewski, Thomas, *Dir Galleries & Special Prog,* Wayne State University, Community Arts Gallery, Detroit MI
Pytlinski, Deanne, *Exec Dir,* Metropolitan State University of Denver, Center for Visual Art, Denver CO
Périnet, Francine, *Gen Mgr,* Le Musee Regional de Rimouski, Centre National d'Exposition, Rimouski QC
Qibgirne, Joan, *Instr,* Greenfield Community College, Art Dept, Greenfield MA (S)
Quackenbush, Elizabeth, *Assoc Prof Art (Ceramics),* Pennsylvania State University, University Park, Penn State School of Visual Arts, University Park PA (S)
Quackenbush, Laura, *Cur,* Leelanau Historical Museum, Leland MI
Qualls, Kristin, *Exec Dir,* Wheaton Arts & Cultural Center, Museum of American Glass, Millville NJ
Qualman, Roger, *VPres,* Columbia River Maritime Museum, Astoria OR
Quandt, Renae, *Gift Shop Mgr,* Clear Lake Arts Center, Clear Lake IA
Quaranta, Thomas G, *Dir Exhibits & Bldg Opers,* Children's Museum of Manhattan, New York NY
Quarcoopome, Nii, *Co-Chief Cur,* Detroit Institute of Arts, Detroit MI
Quella, Hillary, *Instr,* Marian University, Art Dept, Fond Du Lac WI (S)
Quick, Jonathan, *Asst Prof,* Ohio Wesleyan University, Fine Arts Dept, Delaware OH (S)
Quigley, D. Samuel, *Director,* Haystack Mountain School of Crafts, Deer Isle ME (S)
Quigley, Samuel, *Dir,* Lyman Allyn Art Museum, New London CT
Quimby, Sara, *Instruction & Reference Librn,* Institute of American Indian Arts, College of Contemporary Native Arts Library and Archives, Santa Fe NM
Quin, Emma, *Exec Dir,* Textile Museum of Canada, Toronto ON
Quincy, Susan, *Environmental Educ,* Osborne Homestead Museum, Derby CT
Quinlan-Brown, Susan, *Mus Store Mgr,* Cahoon Museum of American Art, Cotuit MA
Quinn, Alana, *Sr Prog Assoc,* National Academy of Sciences, Arts in the Academy, Washington DC
Quinn, Chris, *Asst Librn,* University of Illinois at Urbana-Champaign, Ricker Library of Architecture & Art, Champaign IL
Quinn, Ellen, *Asst Prof,* New Jersey City University, Art Dept, Jersey City NJ (S)
Quinn, Kate, *Co-Chair,* United States National Committee of the International Council of Museums, Washington DC
Quinn, Kristin, *Prof Art,* Saint Ambrose University, Art Dept, Davenport IA (S)
Quinn, Megan, *Prof,* Augustana College, Art Dept, Rock Island IL (S)
Quinn, Raymond, *Treas,* Van Alen Institute, New York NY
Quinn-Cary, Bridget, *Dir,* Buffalo & Erie County Public Library, Buffalo NY
Quinn-Hensley, Carolyn I, *Prof,* Colorado Mesa University, Art Dept, Grand Junction CO (S)
Quinones, Victor, *Controller,* International Center of Photography, Museum, New York NY
Quinones-Keber, Eloise, *Prof Emerita,* City University of New York, PhD Program in Art History, New York NY (S)
Quinonez, Gary, *Sculpture Instr,* Monterey Peninsula College, Art Dept/Art Gallery, Monterey CA (S)
Quint, Mark, *Owner,* Quint Projects, La Jolla CA
Quintana, Frances, *Gift Shop Mgr,* Pueblo of Pojoaque, Poeh Museum, Santa Fe NM
Quintanilla, Faustino, *Adj Asst Prof,* College of Staten Island, Performing & Creative Arts Dept, Staten Island NY (S)
Quintanilla, Faustino, *Executive Director,* Queensborough Community College, Art Gallery, Bayside NY
Quintella, Joel, *Maintenance Chief/Security,* San Angelo Museum of Fine Arts, San Angelo TX
Quinto, Carmela, *Cur,* Millicent Rogers Museum, Taos NM
Quinton, Sarah, *Cur Dir,* Textile Museum of Canada, Toronto ON
Quirarte, Mitzi, *Dir,* International Museum of Art, El Paso TX
Quirolgico, Ray, *Dean Students,* ArtCenter College of Design, Pasadena CA (S)
Qureshi, Diana, *Art Librn,* Hewlett-Woodmere Public Library, Hewlett NY
Rabe, Lana, *Asst Direct Publ Coordr,* Quincy Art Center, Quincy IL
Rabe, Michael, *Assoc Prof,* Saint Xavier University, Dept of Art & Design, Chicago IL (S)
Rabenold, Christine, *Asst Prof Art,* North Central College, Dept of Art, Naperville IL (S)
Rabiner, Mollie, *Art Educ Coordr,* Living Arts & Science Center, Inc, Lexington KY
Rabinow, Rebecca, *Dir,* Menil Foundation, Inc, The Menil Collection, Houston TX
Rabun, Julie, *Assoc Prof & Dept Chmn,* Carson-Newman University, Art Dept, Jefferson City TN (S)
Raby, Megan G, *Dir Educ,* Tryon Palace, New Bern NC
Rackow, Marcia, *Coordr,* Aesthetic Realism Foundation, Terrain Gallery, New York NY
Raczka, Laurel, *Exec Dir,* Painted Bride Art Center Gallery, Philadelphia PA
Radan, George, *Prof,* Villanova University, Dept of Theater, Villanova PA (S)
Radandt, Gina, *Cur Collections,* Kenosha Public Museums, Kenosha WI
Radcliffe, Tony, *VPres,* Redlands Art Association, Redlands Art Association Gallery & Art Center, Redlands CA
Radford, Michelle Berg, *Instr,* Bob Jones University, School of Fine Arts, Div of Art & Design, Greenville SC (S)
Radice, Anne-Imelda, *Exec Dir,* American Folk Art Museum, New York NY
Radke, Don, *Adjunct Assoc Prof,* Texas Woman's University, School of the Arts, Dept of Visual Arts, Denton TX (S)
Radke, Gary, *Prof,* Syracuse University, Dept of Fine Arts (Art History), Syracuse NY (S)
Radulovlic, Radovan, *Head Mus Servs,* The Winnipeg Art Gallery, Winnipeg MB
Radusky, Jan, *Dir Grants,* Cultural Council of Palm Beach County, Lake Worth FL
Radycki, Diane, *Dir,* Moravian College, Payne Gallery, Bethlehem PA
Radycki, Diane, *Dir of Payne Gallery & Prof,* Moravian College, Dept of Art, Bethlehem PA (S)
Radyk, Michael, *Dir Educ,* American Craft Council, Minneapolis MN
Raen-Mendez, Nancy, *Instr,* University of Southern Indiana, Art & Design Dept, Evansville IN (S)
Raetsen-Kemp, Donna, *CEO,* The Robert McLaughlin Gallery, Oshawa ON
Rafat, Pasha, *Assoc Prof,* University of Nevada, Las Vegas, Dept of Art, Las Vegas NV (S)
Raffaele, Piera, *Instr,* Wayne Art Center, Wayne PA (S)
Rafferty, Emily, *Head Librn & Archivist,* The Baltimore Museum of Art, E Kirkbride Miller Art Library, Baltimore MD
Rafferty, Emily, *Librn,* The Baltimore Museum of Art, Baltimore MD
Rafferty-Weinisch, Jill, *Dir Performing Arts & Outreach,* The Arts Center of the Capital Region, Troy NY
Ragain, Melissa, *Assoc Prof Art History,* Montana State University, School of Art, Bozeman MT (S)
Ragains, Meredith, *Exec Dir,* Georgia Lawyers for the Arts, Atlanta GA
Rager, Andrea, *Asst Prof,* Case Western Reserve University, Dept of Art History & Art, Cleveland OH (S)
Raguin, Virginia C, *Prof,* College of the Holy Cross, Dept of Visual Arts, Worcester MA (S)
Rahaim, Margaret, *Prof,* Mount Saint Mary's University, Visual & Performing Arts Dept, Emmitsburg MD (S)
Rahe, Diane, *VPres,* Phillips County Museum, Holyoke CO
Raia, Nancy, *ABC Project Dir,* Eastern Shore Art Association, Inc, Eastern Shore Art Center, Fairhope AL
Raine, Vicki, *Div Chmn Humanities,* Metropolitan Community College - Penn Valley, Art Dept, Kansas City MO (S)
Rainer, Yvonne, *Prof & Bren Chair,* University of California, Irvine, Studio Art Dept, Irvine CA (S)
Raines, Kevin, *Prof,* College of Notre Dame of Maryland, Art Dept, Baltimore MD (S)
Rains, Jerry, *Chmn,* Northeast Mississippi Junior College, Art Dept, Booneville MS (S)
Raiselis, Tara, *Mus Dir,* Saco Museum, Saco ME
Raithel, Jan, *Dept Chmn,* Chaffey Community College, Art Dept, Rancho Cucamonga CA (S)
Raizman, David, *Treas,* International Center of Medieval Art, New York NY
Rakes, Susan, *Asst Dir,* Art & Culture Center of Hollywood, Art Gallery/Multidisciplinary Cultural Center, Hollywood FL
Ralph, Fran, *Dir Mktg,* The National Shrine of the North American Martyrs, Fultonville NY
Ralph, Thomas F, *Dir Opers,* The National Shrine of the North American Martyrs, Fultonville NY
Rama, Ronnie, *Prof,* Abilene Christian University, Dept of Art & Design, Abilene TX (S)
Ramage, Priscilla, *Mus Shop Mgr,* Hill-Stead Museum, Farmington CT
Ramage, William, *Prof,* Castleton State College, Art Dept, Castleton VT (S)
Ramberg, W Dodd, *Prof,* Catholic University of America, School of Architecture & Planning, Washington DC (S)
Ramey, Ashley, *Site Coordr,* Preservation Virginia, John Marshall House, Richmond VA
Ramey, Craig, *Mktg Mgr,* Tryon Palace, New Bern NC
Ramirez, Cynthia, *Instr,* Southern University in New Orleans, Fine Arts & Philosophy Dept, New Orleans LA (S)
Ramirez, Dee, *Bookkeeper,* Brownsville Art League, Brownsville Museum of Fine Art, Brownsville TX
Ramirez, Maryanna, *Mgr Strategic Initiatives,* Florida International University, The Patricia & Phillip Frost Art Museum, Miami FL
Ramirez, Tommy, *Bd Pres,* Centro Cultural De La Raza, San Diego CA
Ramirez, Victoria, *Dir,* City of El Paso, El Paso Museum of Art, El Paso TX

Ramirez-Montagut, Monica, *Dir,* Tulane University, Newcomb Art Museum, New Orleans LA

Ramirez-Weaver, Eric, *Asst Prof, Art History,* University of Virginia, McIntire Dept of Art, Charlottesville VA (S)

Ramljak, Suzanne, *Cur,* The American Federation of Arts, New York NY

Ramon, Art, *Archives,* Deming-Luna Mimbres Museum, Deming NM

Ramoran, Edwin, *Dir Exhibs & Progs,* Aljira Center for Contemporary Art, Newark NJ

Ramos, E. Carmen, *Deputy Chief Cur,* American Art Museum, Smithsonian Institution, Washington DC

Ramos, Jim, *Instr,* Gettysburg College, Dept of Visual Arts, Gettysburg PA (S)

Ramos, Julianne, *Exec Dir,* Rockland Center for the Arts, West Nyack NY (S)

Ramos, Julianne, *Exec Dir,* Rockland Center for the Arts, West Nyack NY

Ramos, Liliane, *Exec Dir,* Institute of Puerto Rican Culture, Dr Jose C Barbosa Museum, Bayamon PR

Ramos, Ora, *Exec Dir,* Institute of Puerto Rican Culture, Museo y Parque Historico Ruinas de Caparra, Guaynabo PR

Ramos, Rosa, *Mus Adminr,* Islip Art Museum, East Islip NY

Ramos-Rivas, Lourdes, *Dir,* Museo de Arte de Puerto Rico, San Juan PR

Ramsaran, Helen, *Assoc Prof,* John Jay College of Criminal Justice, Dept of Art, Music & Philosophy, New York NY (S)

Ramsay, Chris, *Prof,* Oklahoma State University, Department of Art, Graphic Design and Art History, Stillwater OK (S)

Ramsey, Chuck, *Coordr,* Clark College, Art Dept, Vancouver WA (S)

Rancourt, Lichen, *Head of Info Svcs,* Manchester City Library, Manchester NH

Rand, Charles E, *Archivist & Librn,* United Society of Shakers, The Shaker Library, New Gloucester ME

Rand, Charles, *Librn/Archivist,* United Society of Shakers, Shaker Museum, New Gloucester ME

Rand, Erica, *Prof,* Bates College, Art & Visual Culture, Lewiston ME (S)

Rand, Richard, *Assoc Dir Colls,* The Getty Center, The J Paul Getty Museum, Los Angeles CA

Rand, Richard, *Cur Mathematics,* Northern Maine Museum of Science, Presque Isle ME

Rand, Richard, *Sr Cur of Paintings & Sculpture,* Clark Art Institute, Williamstown MA

Rand, Valerie, *Dir Housing,* The Illinois Institute of Art - Chicago, Chicago IL (S)

Randall, Colette, *Dir Mktg, Research & Communs,* Institute of Contemporary Art/Boston, Boston MA

Randall, Laura, *Archivist & Assoc Registrar,* Rubell Family Collection and Contemporary Arts Foundation, Miami FL

Randall, Ross, *Dir,* Woodlawn/The Pope-Leighey, Alexandria VA

Randall, Susan, *Instr,* Midland College, Art Dept, Midland TX (S)

Randall, Vaughn, *Asst Prof,* State University of New York, College at Cortland, Dept Art & Art History, Cortland NY (S)

Randel, Melissa, *Instr,* Glendale Community College, Visual & Performing Arts Div, Glendale CA (S)

Randolph, Deborah, *Cur Educ,* Southeastern Center for Contemporary Art, Winston-Salem NC

Randolph, Irene, *Owner,* Fireweed Gallery, Homer AK

Randolph, Karen, *Prof,* Lubbock Christian University, Dept of Communication & Fine Art, Lubbock TX (S)

Randolph, Olivia, *Educ Coordr,* City of Cedar Falls, Iowa, James & Meryl Hearst Center for the Arts & Sculpture Garden, Cedar Falls IA

Rangel, Gabriela, *Dir Visual Arts,* Americas Society Art Gallery, New York NY

Rank-Beauchamp, Beth, *CEO, Pres,* Sharon Arts Center, Sharon Arts Center Exhibition Gallery, Peterborough NH

Rankin, Robin, *Dir,* Kimball Art Center, Park City UT

Rankin, Shan, *Exec Dir,* Hidalgo County Historical Museum, Edinburg TX

Rankine, John, *Co-owner,* Eureka Fine Art Gallery, Eureka Springs AR

Ranne, Jessica, *Assoc Mgr Circulation & Tech Servs,* The Metropolitan Museum of Art, Museum Libraries, New York NY

Ransom, Brian, *Prof,* Eckerd College, Art Dept, Saint Petersburg FL (S)

Ransom, Brittany, *Asst Prof,* Southern Methodist University, Meadows School of the Arts - Division of Art, Dallas TX (S)

Ransom, Marzia, *Adj Instr,* University of West Florida, Dept of Art, Pensacola FL (S)

Ranta, Michelle, *Instr,* North Hennepin Community College, Art Dept, Brooklyn Park MN (S)

Rante, Danielle, *Assoc Prof,* Wright State University, Dept of Art & Art History, Dayton OH (S)

Rantoul, T Neal, *Assoc Prof,* Northeastern University, Dept of Art & Architecture, Boston MA (S)

Rappaport, Deborah, *Pres,* San Jose Museum of Art, Library, San Jose CA

Rappaport, Matt, *Asst Prof,* University of Dayton, Visual Arts Dept, Dayton OH (S)

Rappoport, Eileen, *VPres,* Culture Capital, Washington DC

Rappoport, Eve, *Mgr Cultural Servs,* Torrance Art Museum, Torrance CA

Rasic, Alexandra, *Pub Prog Mgr,* Workman & Temple Family Homestead Museum, City of Industry CA

Rasmussen, Jack, *Dir & Cur,* American University, Museum at the Katzen, Washington DC

Rasmussen, Lisa Anne, *Coordr & Instr,* Walla Walla Community College, Fine Arts Dept, Walla Walla WA (S)

Rasmussen, Mary, *Res Asst Prof,* University of Illinois at Chicago, Biomedical Visualization, Chicago IL (S)

Rasmussen, Shelli, *Asst Dir,* Kimmel-Harding-Nelson Center for the Arts, Nebraska City NE

Rasmussen, William, *Cur Art,* Virginia Historical Society, Library, Richmond VA

Rasmussen, William, *Cur of Virginia Art,* Virginia Historical Society, Richmond VA

Rass, Patty, *Instr,* Mount Mary College, Art & Design Division, Milwaukee WI (S)

Rassetti, Mark L, *Dir,* Hutchinson Art Association, Hutchinson Art Center, Hutchinson KS

Ratcliff, Douglas, *Dir of Retail,* Museum of Art, Fort Lauderdale, Fort Lauderdale FL

Ratcliff, Gary, *Head,* University of Louisiana at Monroe, Bry Gallery, Monroe LA

Ratcliff, Gary, *Instr,* University of Louisiana at Monroe, Dept of Art, Monroe LA (S)

Ratcliffe, Megan, *Executive Director,* Kirkland Art Center, Clinton NY

Rathburn, Linda, *Gen Educ,* Art Institute of Pittsburgh, Pittsburgh PA (S)

Rathburn, Nichole, *Commun Dir,* 911 Media Arts Center, Seattle WA

Rather, Susan, *Asst Chair - Art History,* University of Texas, Dept of Art & Art History, Austin TX (S)

Rathje, Terry, *Asst Prof,* Western Illinois University, Department of Art, Macomb IL (S)

Ratliff, Troy, *COO,* DuSable Museum of African American History, Chicago IL

Ratner, Peter, *Asst Prof,* James Madison University, School of Art & Art History, Harrisonburg VA (S)

Ratte, Christopher, *Assoc Prof,* University of Michigan, Kelsey Museum of Archaeology, Ann Arbor MI

Ratterree, Scott, *Head Preparator,* The Historic New Orleans Collection, Royal Street Galleries, New Orleans LA

Rattner, Carl, *Prof,* Saint Thomas Aquinas College, Art Dept, Sparkill NY (S)

Rau, Sue, *Instr Painting,* Ocean City Arts Center, Ocean City NJ (S)

Rauf, Barb, *Dir,* Thomas More College, Eva G Farris Art Gallery, Crestview KY

Rauf, Barbara, *Assoc Prof,* Thomas More College, Art Dept, Crestview Hills KY (S)

Rauhauser, Andrew, *VPres,* Ages of Man Foundation, Amenia NY

Rauschenbusch, Stephanie, *Pres,* New York Society of Women Artists, Inc, Westport CT

Rauser, Amelia, *Assoc Prof,* Franklin & Marshall College, Art & Art History Dept, Lancaster PA (S)

Rautman, Marcus, *Prof,* University of Missouri - Columbia, Art History & Archaeology Dept, Columbia MO (S)

Ravago, Rachel, *Guest Servs,* Buffalo Niagara Heritage Village, Amherst NY

Ravago, Rachel, *Librn,* Buffalo Niagara Heritage Village, Niederlander Research Library, Amherst NY

Ravenal, John, *Mus Dir,* deCordova Sculpture Park & Museum, Lincoln MA

Ravenwood, Gregory, *Exhib Coordr,* Boulder Public Library & Gallery, Arts Gallery, Boulder CO

Raverty, Dennis, *Prof,* New Jersey City University, Art Dept, Jersey City NJ (S)

Ravnitzky Silberglied, Gail, *VPres Govt Rels & Communs,* American Alliance of Museums, Arlington VA

Rawles, Susan J, *Cur American Painting & Decorative Art,* Virginia Museum of Fine Arts, Richmond VA

Rawlings, Nichole, *Gallery Dir,* Brenau University, Art & Design Dept, Gainesville GA (S)

Rawlins, Dori, *Cur,* City of Irvine, Irvine Fine Arts Center, Irvine CA (S)

Rawlins, Gary, *Adjunct,* Chemeketa Community College, Dept of Humanities & Communications, Art Program, Salem OR (S)

Rawlins, Kathleen L, *Asst Dir,* Cambridge Historical Commission, City of Cambridge, Research Library on Architectural and Social History of Cambridge, Mass, Cambridge MA

Rawlins, W Scott, *Asst Prof,* Arcadia University, Dept of Fine Arts, Glenside PA (S)

Rawls, James A, *Chmn,* Pearl River Community College, Visual Arts, Dept of Fine Arts & Communication, Poplarville MS (S)

Rawstern, Sherri, *Cur Educ,* Dacotah Prairie Museum, Lamont Art Gallery, Aberdeen SD

Ray, Alan, *CFO,* California State University, Long Beach Foundation, Long Beach CA

Ray, Cindy, *Coordr,* Mississippi Delta Community College, Dept of Fine Arts, Moorhead MS (S)

Ray, Kristofer, *Editor, TN Historical Quarterly,* Tennessee Historical Society, Nashville TN

Ray, Lawrence A, *Chmn,* Lambuth University, Dept of Human Ecology & Visual Arts, Jackson TN (S)

Rayborn, Judy, *Dir HR,* The Newberry, Chicago IL

Rayburn, Nikki, *Exhibs Coord,* Maine College of Art, The Institute of Contemporary Art, Portland ME

Rayca, Brian, *Registrar,* United States Military Academy, West Point Museum, West Point NY

Rayen, James W, *Prof,* Wellesley College, Art Dept, Wellesley MA (S)

Rayme, Mary, *Adjunct Instr,* Davis & Elkins College, Dept of Art, Elkins WV (S)

Raymond, Christopher, *Cur,* Shores Memorial Museum, Lyndon Center VT

Raymond, Yasmil, *Cur,* Dia Art Foundation, Beacon NY

Raynor, Rachel, *Dir Registration & Collections Mgr,* University of California, Los Angeles, Fowler Museum at UCLA, Los Angeles CA

Razzore, Lauren, *Asst Prof,* William Paterson University, Dept Arts, Wayne NJ (S)

Re, Peggy, *Assoc Prof,* University of Maryland, Baltimore County, Intermedia & Digital Arts (IMDA), Dept of Visual Arts, Baltimore MD (S)

Rea, Douglas F, *Assoc Prof,* Rochester Institute of Technology, School of Photographic Arts & Sciences, Rochester NY (S)

Read, Bob, *Art Dir,* New Mexico Highlands University, The Ray Drew Gallery, Las Vegas NM

Read, Brittney, *Inter-Library Loan Librn,* Bethany College, Wallerstedt Library, Lindsborg KS

Read, Cindy, *Asst Prof,* Marygrove College, Department of Art, Detroit MI (S)

Read, Edith, *Vis Asst Prof,* Assumption College, Dept of Art, Music & Theatre, Worcester MA (S)

Reading, Christine, *Instr,* Sacramento City College, Art Dept, Sacramento CA (S)

Ready, John, *Gallery Dir,* University of Wisconsin-La Crosse, Center for the Arts, La Crosse WI (S)
Reagan, Pat, *Assoc Prof,* Southeast Missouri State University, Dept of Art, Cape Girardeau MO (S)
Reamer, Melissa, *Colls Mgr,* Daytona State College, Southeast Museum of Photography, Daytona Beach FL
Reardon, Siobhan A, *Library Pres & Dir,* Free Library of Philadelphia, Art Dept, Philadelphia PA
Reaven, Marci, *VPres History Exhibs,* New-York Historical Society, Museum, New York NY
Reaves, James, *Dir of Librn,* United Methodist Historical Society, Lovely Lane Museum, Baltimore MD
Rebac, Laurie, *Asst Gallery Mgr,* Sharon Arts Center, Sharon Arts Center Exhibition Gallery, Peterborough NH
Reber, Paul, *Exec Dir,* National Trust for Historic Preservation, Decatur House, Washington DC
Reber, Wally, *Assoc Dir,* Buffalo Bill Memorial Association, Buffalo Bill Historical Center, Cody WY
Reboli, SJ, Father John, *Assoc Prof,* College of the Holy Cross, Dept of Visual Arts, Worcester MA (S)
Rebsamen, Werner, *Assoc Prof,* Rochester Institute of Technology, School of Printing Management & Sciences, Rochester NY (S)
Rebsom, Paula, *Sculpture,* North Seattle College, North Seattle College Dept of Art, Seattle WA (S)
Recchia, Marissa, *Instr,* Middle Tennessee State University, Art Dept, Murfreesboro TN (S)
Rech, Leslie, *Asst Prof,* South Carolina State University, Dept of Visual & Performing Arts, Orangeburg SC (S)
Recht, Ray, *Prof Theatre,* Marymount Manhattan College, Fine & Performing Arts Div, New York NY (S)
Reck, Eve, *Mus Opers Mgr,* Springfield Museum of Art, Springfield OH
Rector, Renee, *Arts in Educ Dir,* Creative Arts Guild, Dalton GA
Recuparo, Joan, *Admin Specialist,* Syracuse University, SUArt Galleries, Syracuse NY
Redden, Debbie, *Instr,* Guild of Creative Art, Shrewsbury NJ (S)
Reddig, Deborah, *Dir Mus Advancement,* Pennsylvania Historical & Museum Commission, Railroad Museum of Pennsylvania, Strasburg PA
Reddin, Jim, *Prof,* Shoreline Community College, Humanities Division, Seattle WA (S)
Redding, Jim, *Prof,* Lansing Community College, Visual Arts & Media Dept, Lansing MI (S)
Redding, Mary Anne, *Cur,* Appalachian State University, Turchin Center for the Visual Arts, Boone NC
Redgate Favorito, Nacy, *Treas & Acting Secy,* Society of Scribes, Ltd, New York NY
Redington, Andrew, *Assoc Prof,* University of Wisconsin Oshkosh, Dept of Art, Oshkosh WI (S)
Redman, Elisa, *Dir Preservation Svcs,* Midwest Art Conservation Center, Minneapolis MN
Redman, Paul, *Exec Asst Dean,* University of Illinois, Urbana-Champaign, College of Fine & Applied Arts, Champaign IL (S)
Redman, Scott, *Instr,* Springfield College, Dept of Visual & Performing Arts, Springfield MA (S)
Redmond, Jon, *Instr,* Wayne Art Center, Wayne PA (S)
Redmond, Malissa, *Library Admin Servs Coordr,* Wentworth Institute of Technology, Douglas D Schumann Library & Learning Commons, Boston MA
Redmond, Michael, *Dean Art & Humanities,* Bergen Community College, Visual Art Dept, Paramus NJ (S)
Redwine, Julie, *Colls Mgr,* United States General Services Administration, Art in Architecture and Fine Arts, Washington DC
Reece-Hughes, Shirley, *Cur Paintings & Sculpture,* Amon Carter Museum of American Art, Fort Worth TX
Reed, Alan, *Assoc Prof,* Saint John's University, Art Dept, Collegeville MN (S)
Reed, Barbara E, *Librn,* Dartmouth College, Sherman Art Library, Hanover NH
Reed, Carl, *Chmn,* Colorado College, Dept of Art, Colorado Springs CO (S)
Reed, Dana, *Interim C.E.O.,* The Africa Center, New York NY
Reed, Dennis, *Chmn,* Los Angeles Valley College, Art Dept, Van Nuys CA (S)
Reed, Dennis, *Dean,* Los Angeles Valley College, Art Gallery, Valley Glen CA
Reed, Ehren, *Outreach Prog Mgr,* Louisville Visual Art, Louisville KY
Reed, Evan, *Dir Gallery,* Georgetown University, Dept of Art & Art History, Washington DC (S)
Reed, Jeffrey, *Asst Prof,* Philadelphia Community College, Dept of Art, Philadelphia PA (S)
Reed, Jessica, *Promotions Coordr,* Light Work, Robert B Menschel Photography Gallery, Syracuse NY
Reed, Mike, *Asst Dir Facilities & Risk Management,* Contemporary Arts Museum Houston, Houston TX
Reed, Pamela, *Art History,* Phoenix College, Dept of Art & Photography, Phoenix AZ (S)
Reed, Peter, *Sr Dep Dir Cur Affairs,* Museum of Modern Art, New York NY
Reed, Richard, *Chmn Humanities,* City Colleges of Chicago, Olive-Harvey College, Chicago IL (S)
Reed, Roger, *Prof,* Dakota State University, College of Liberal Arts, Madison SD (S)
Reed, Scott, *Assoc Prof,* Colby College, Art Dept, Waterville ME (S)
Reed, Sharon, *Prog & Exec Coordr,* Dartmouth College, Hood Museum of Art, Hanover NH
Reed, Stan, *Tech Dir,* Prescott Fine Arts Association, Gallery, Prescott AZ
Reed, Susan H, *Dir,* Imperial Calcasieu Museum, Lake Charles LA
Reeder, Deborah, *Dir,* St George Art Museum, Saint George UT
Reeder, Leah, *Registrar,* Fort Wayne Museum of Art, Inc, Fort Wayne IN
Reeder, Ron, *Asst Prof 3D & 2D Design,* Rio Hondo College, Arts & Cultural Programs Dept, Whittier CA (S)
Reel, David M, *Dir,* United States Military Academy, West Point Museum, West Point NY
Reese, Brandon, *Assoc Prof,* Oklahoma State University, Department of Art, Graphic Design and Art History, Stillwater OK (S)
Reese, David, *Dir,* Gunston Hall Plantation, Library, Mason Neck VA
Reese, Laura, *Exec Dir,* Individual Artists of Oklahoma, Oklahoma City OK
Reeve, Deborah B, *Exec Dir,* National Art Education Association, Alexandria VA
Reeves V, I S K, *Pres,* Architects Design Group Inc, Winter Park FL
Reeves, Alvin, *Asst Cur Agriculture (Emeritus),* Northern Maine Museum of Science, Presque Isle ME
Reeves, Linda, *Secy,* Woodburn Art Center, Glatt House Gallery, Woodburn OR
Reeves, Stockton, *VChmn,* Art and History Museums - Maitland, Maitland FL
Reff, Yvonne, *Reference Librn,* Roswell P Flower, Watertown NY
Regan, David, *Prof,* The University of Montana Western, Art Program, Dillon MT (S)
Regan, Tom, *Dean,* Texas A&M University, College of Architecture, College Station TX (S)
Regan-Dalzell, Kathie, *Instr,* Main Line Art Center, Haverford PA (S)
Regina, Kristen, *Arcadia Dir Libr & Archives,* Philadelphia Museum of Art, Library & Archives, Philadelphia PA
Register, Christopher M, *Assoc Prof,* Longwood University, Dept of Art, Farmville VA (S)
Regnier, Suzanne M, *Dir Develop,* Brandywine Conservancy, Brandywine River Museum, Chadds Ford PA
Rego, Brian, *Instr,* Benedict College, School of Humanities, Arts & Social Sciences, Columbia SC (S)
Rehm-Mott, Denise, *Prof,* Eastern Illinois University, Art Dept, Charleston IL (S)
Rehman, Sadia, *Dir,* Bose Pacia, Brooklyn NY
Rehrig, Jeanne, *Program Coordr,* Berkeley Art Center, Berkeley CA
Reibe, Denise, *Adjunct Instr Foundations,* Montana State University, School of Art, Bozeman MT (S)
Reich, Dindy, *Gallery Dir,* University of Texas Pan American, Art Dept, Edinburg TX (S)
Reich, Marsha, *Educ Coordr,* Southern Alberta Art Gallery, Library, Lethbridge AB
Reichardt, Peter, *Instr,* South Dakota State University, Dept of Visual Arts, Brookings SD (S)
Reiche, Christopher, *New Music Coordr,* Open Space, Victoria BC
Reichert, Barbara, *Sr Dir, External Relations,* United States Figure Skating Association, World Figure Skating Museum & Hall of Fame, Colorado Springs CO
Reichertz, Mathew, *Chair, Fine Arts Div,* Nova Scotia College of Art & Design, Halifax NS (S)
Reid, Anne, *Art Educ,* Alexandria Museum of Art, Alexandria LA
Reid, Dolores Erikson, *VPres,* North Shore Arts Association, Inc, Gloucester MA
Reid, Graeme, *Director of Collections and Exhibitions,* Museum of Wisconsin Art, West Bend WI
Reid, Jacqueline, *Dir,* Duke University Library, Hartman Center for Sales, Advertising & Marketing History, Durham NC
Reid, Kim, *Educ Coordr,* Wilkes Art Gallery, North Wilkesboro NC
Reid, Margaret, *Head,* Guilford Technical Community College, Commercial Art Dept, Jamestown NC (S)
Reid, Mary, *Cur/Dir,* City of Woodstock, Woodstock Art Gallery, Woodstock ON
Reid, Mary, *Gallery Dir,* University of Manitoba, School of Art Gallery, Winnipeg MB
Reid, Patricia L, *Tech Svcs Assoc,* Corcoran Gallery of Art, Corcoran Library, Washington DC
Reid, Randal, *Prof,* Texas State University - San Marcos, Dept of Art and Design, San Marcos TX (S)
Reid, Shannon, *Shop Mgr,* Craft Council of Newfoundland & Labrador, Saint John's NF
Reid, Stuart, *Dir,* Tom Thomson Memorial Art Gallery, Library/Archives, Owen Sound ON
Reidel, Caroline, *Cur,* University of Victoria, The Legacy Art Gallery, Victoria BC
Reiff, Daniel, *Prof,* State University of New York at Fredonia, Dept of Art, Fredonia NY (S)
Reifsneider, Jennifer, *Registrar,* Missoula Art Museum, Missoula MT
Reigle, Alexandra, *Reference Librn,* National Portrait Gallery, Library, Washington DC
Reigle, Alexandra, *Reference Librn,* American Art Museum, Library, Washington DC
Reiland, Neal, *Prof,* Salt Lake Community College, Graphic Design Dept, Salt Lake City UT (S)
Reiling Lindell, Joanna, *Cur,* Thrivent Financial for Lutherans, Gallery of Religious Art, Minneapolis MN
Reilly, James, *Assoc Prof,* Rochester Institute of Technology, School of Photographic Arts & Sciences, Rochester NY (S)
Reilly, Jerry M, *Instr,* Modesto Junior College, Arts Humanities & Communications Division, Modesto CA (S)
Reilly, John, *Mus Store Mgr,* Santa Barbara Museum of Art, Library, Santa Barbara CA
Reilly, Karen, *Assoc Dir,* College of the Holy Cross, Dinand Library, Worcester MA
Reilly, Karen, *Director,* College of the Holy Cross, Dinand Library, Worcester MA
Reilly, Maura, *Exec Dir,* National Academy Museum & School, New York NY
REilly, Meg, *Recording Secretary,* Marin Society of Artists Inc, San Rafael CA
Reilly, Nora, *Archivist & Asst Librn,* New York School of Interior Design, New York School of Interior Design Library, New York NY

Reilly, Patricia L, *Assoc Provost & Assoc Prof,* Swarthmore College, Dept of Art & Art History, Swarthmore PA (S)
Reily, Stephen, *Dir,* The Speed Art Museum, Louisville KY
Reimann, Amy, *Exec Dir,* Ella Sharp Museum, Jackson MI
Reimer, Karen, *Dir Publs & Registrar,* The Renaissance Society, Chicago IL
Reinauer, Lisa, *Prof,* McNeese State University, Dept of Visual Arts, Lake Charles LA (S)
Reinckens, Sharon, *Deputy Dir,* Anacostia Community Museum, Smithsonian Institution, Washington DC
Reinert, Elaine, *VPres Prog,* Berks Art Alliance, Reading PA
Reinhardt, Beatrix, *Asst Prof,* College of Staten Island, Performing & Creative Arts Dept, Staten Island NY (S)
Reinhardt, Janine, *Admin Asst,* University of Wyoming, University of Wyoming Art Museum, Laramie WY
Reinhardt, Kim, *Gen Mgr,* Nova Scotia Museum, Maritime Museum of the Atlantic, Halifax NS
Reins Schweer, Lorie, *Chair,* Vesterheim Norwegian-American Museum, Decorah IA
Reinsel, Joe, *Adjunct Faculty,* University of Maryland, Baltimore County, Intermedia & Digital Arts (IMDA), Dept of Visual Arts, Baltimore MD (S)
Reintjes, Brandon, *Sr Cur,* Missoula Art Museum, Missoula MT
Reis, Jennifer, *Asst Prof,* Morehead State University, Art & Design Dept, Morehead KY (S)
Reis, Jennifer, *Dir,* Morehead State University, Claypool-Young Art Gallery, Morehead KY
Reischmann, Monica, *Dir Develop,* Nassau County Museum of Art, Roslyn Harbor NY
Reising, Christine, *Prof & Chmn,* Siena Heights University, Studio Angelico-Art Dept, Adrian MI (S)
Reiss, Ellen, *Chmn Educ,* Aesthetic Realism Foundation, New York NY (S)
Reiss, Ellen, *Chmn Educ,* Aesthetic Realism Foundation, New York NY
Reiss, Michell, *Pres & CEO,* Colonial Williamsburg Foundation, Williamsburg VA
Reist, Inge, *Dir Center for the History of Collecting,* The Frick Collection, Frick Art Reference Library, New York NY
Reitmaier, Heidi, *Exec Dir & Cur,* Museum of Contemporary Canadian Art, Toronto ON
Reitzenstein, Reinhard, *Sculpture & Undergraduate Director,* University at Buffalo, State University of New York, Dept of Visual Studies, Buffalo NY (S)
Rejholec, Joe, *Chmn,* South Suburban College, Art Dept, South Holland IL (S)
Rekedal, Jane, *Instr,* Gavilan College, Art Dept, Gilroy CA (S)
Reker, Ken, *Prof,* Salem State University, Art & Design Department, Salem MA (S)
Reller, Tracy, *Assoc Prof,* Hillsborough Community College, Fine Arts Dept, Tampa FL (S)
Relyea, Lane, *Asst Prof,* Northwestern University, Evanston, Dept of Art Theory & Practice, Evanston IL (S)
Relyea, Linda, *PT Instr,* Adams State College, Dept of Visual Arts, Alamosa CO (S)
Rembold, Pamela, *Exec Dir,* Kirkland Arts Center, KAC Gallery, Kirkland WA
Remeczki, Paul, *Asst Librn,* Queens College, City University of New York, Art Library, Flushing NY
Remington, R Roger, *Prof,* Rochester Institute of Technology, School of Design, Rochester NY (S)
Remley, David, *Museum Opers Asst,* Pearl Fincher Museum of Fine Arts, Spring TX
Rempel, Heidi, *Visual Resources Cur,* William Paterson University, University Galleries, Wayne NJ
Remus, Stephen, *Minister of Energy, Minds & Resources,* Niagara Artists Centre, Saint Catharines ON
Renaldi, Beverly, *Properties Mgr,* Lehigh Valley Heritage Center, Allentown PA
Renc-Carter, Christine, *Dir Adult Educ,* Dunedin Fine Art Center, Dunedin FL (S)
Rendon, Joanne, *Librn,* The Society of the Four Arts, Gioconda & Joseph King Library, Palm Beach FL
Reneau, Davie, *Assoc Prof Art,* Campbellsville University, Art & Design Department, Campbellsville KY (S)
Renfro, Charles, *Pres,* Storefront for Art & Architecture, New York NY
Renfro, Cora, *Instr,* Campbellsville University, Art & Design Department, Campbellsville KY (S)
Renfro, William, *Prof,* Texas A&M University-Kingsville, Art Dept, Kingsville TX (S)
Renneker, Holly, *Educ Coordr,* Anderson Fine Arts Center, The Anderson Center for the Arts, Anderson IN
Rennie, Renate, *Secy,* Queen Sofia Spanish Institute, New York NY
Reno, Carolyn, *Coll Mgr,* City of Springdale, Shiloh Museum of Ozark History, Springdale AR
Reno, Kathy, *Mktg,* Saint Joseph Museum, Inc., Saint Joseph MO
Reno, Timothy, *Asst Prof Music,* Siena College, Dept of Creative Arts, Loudonville NY (S)
Renskers, Kim, *Lib Asst,* New York Institute of Technology, Art & Architectural Library, Old Westbury NY
Renz, Kevin, *Assoc Dean Interior Design,* Endicott College, School of Visual & Performing Arts, Beverly MA (S)
Repinski, Robert, *Asst Prof,* University of Minnesota, Duluth, Art Dept, Duluth MN (S)
Reres, Sara, *Dir, Treas & Cur,* Sea Cliff Village Museum, Sea Cliff NY
Reside, Doug, *Theatre Cur,* The New York Public Library, The New York Public Library for the Performing Arts, New York NY
Resnick, Elizabeth, *Chair Commun Design,* Massachusetts College of Art, Boston MA (S)
Resnik, Kim, *Pub Rels Media Contact,* International Fine Arts College, Miami FL (S)
Respini, Eva, *Barbara Lee Chief Cur,* Institute of Contemporary Art/Boston, Boston MA
Ressler, Jay, *Publicity,* Berks Art Alliance, Reading PA
Ressler, Tony, *Co-Chair,* Los Angeles County Museum of Art, Los Angeles CA
Restauri, Jennifer, *Cur Educ,* Nelda C & H J Lutcher Stark Foundation, Stark Museum of Art, Orange TX
Retallack, John, *Assoc Prof,* Rochester Institute of Technology, School of Photographic Arts & Sciences, Rochester NY (S)
Retsek, Fanny, *Studio Supv,* Palo Alto Art Center, Palo Alto CA
Rettew, Robert H, *Librn,* Saint Paul's School, Ohrstrom Library, Concord NH
Rettich, Jon, *Treas,* Federation of Modern Painters & Sculptors, New York NY
Reuss, David, *Treas,* Society of Illustrators, New York NY
Reuter, Laurel J, *Dir & Chief Cur,* North Dakota Museum of Art, Grand Forks ND
Reutter, David, *Registrar,* College of Central Florida, Appleton Museum of Art, Ocala FL
Revett, Jon, *Asst Prof,* West Texas A&M University, Art, Theatre & Dance Dept, Canyon TX (S)
ReVille, Stephen W, *Owner & CEO,* Portraits South, Raleigh NC
Revock, Ross, *Asst Prod,* Cleveland State University, Art Dept, Cleveland OH (S)
Rexroat, DeeAnn, *Dir Pub Info,* Cornell College, Peter Paul Luce Gallery, Mount Vernon IA
Rey, Alberto, *Prof,* State University of New York at Fredonia, Dept of Art, Fredonia NY (S)
Reyes, Ann N, *Cur Educ,* Museum of East Texas, Lufkin TX
Reyes, Danny, *Asst Prof,* Western New Mexico University, Expressive Arts Dept, Silver City NM (S)
Reyes, David, *Cur Colls & Exhibs,* Huntsville Museum of Art, Huntsville AL
Reyes, Marissa, *Polk Bros Assoc Dir Educ,* Museum of Contemporary Art Chicago, Chicago IL
Reyes, Roman, *Chmn,* Phoenix College, Dept of Art & Photography, Phoenix AZ (S)
Reymann, Patrick H, *VPres,* Western Reserve Historical Society, Library, Cleveland OH
Reymond, Rhonda, *Assoc Prof,* West Virginia University, College of Creative Arts, School of Art & Design, Morgantown WV (S)
Reyna, Nazario, *Maintenance,* Hidalgo County Historical Museum, Edinburg TX
Reyner, Justen, *Asst Prof,* Oklahoma State University, Department of Art, Graphic Design and Art History, Stillwater OK (S)
Reynolds, Ben, *Acad Professional Photog,* University of Georgia, Franklin College of Arts & Sciences, Lamar Dodd School of Art, Athens GA (S)
Reynolds, Carol, *Dir,* Congregation Beth Israel's Plotkin Judaica Museum, Scottsdale AZ
Reynolds, Carol, *Museum Shop Manager,* Pilgrim Society, Pilgrim Hall Museum, Plymouth MA
Reynolds, Ed, *Interim Cur,* Robert Louis Stevenson Museum, Saint Helena CA
Reynolds, Edmond, *Dir,* Robert Louis Stevenson Museum, Saint Helena CA
Reynolds, John, *Lead Preparator,* Dartmouth College, Hood Museum of Art, Hanover NH
Reynolds, Joycelyn, *Artist Servs Mgr,* Arts Council Of New Orleans, New Orleans LA
Reynolds, Katie, *Mgr Tour Svcs,* Agecroft Association, Museum, Richmond VA
Reynolds, Kimberly, *Cur Manuscripts,* Boston Public Library, Rare Book & Manuscripts Dept, Boston MA
Reynolds, Lisa I, *Office Mgr,* National Trust for Historic Preservation, Chesterwood, Stockbridge MA
Reynolds, Lynn, *Assoc Prof & Dept Head,* McNeese State University, Dept of Visual Arts, Lake Charles LA (S)
Reynolds, Lynn, *Chmn,* McNeese State University, Dept of Visual Arts, Lake Charles LA (S)
Reynolds, Lynn, *Dir,* McNeese State University, Dept of Visual Arts, Abercrombie Gallery and Grand Gallery, Lake Charles LA
Reynolds, Michael, *Asst Preparator,* Oberlin College, Allen Memorial Art Museum, Oberlin OH
Reynolds, Rebecca, *Asst Prof,* University of New Orleans-Lake Front, Dept of Fine Arts, New Orleans LA (S)
Reynolds, Ryan, *Asst Prof,* Santa Clara University, Dept of Art & Art History, Santa Clara CA (S)
Reynolds, Sarah, *Exec Dir,* Adirondack Lakes Center for the Arts, Blue Mountain Lake NY
Reynolds, Vic, *Prof,* Wayne State College, Dept Art & Design, Wayne NE (S)
Reynoso, Rondall, *Dept Coordr,* Louisiana College, Dept of Art, Pineville LA (S)
Reznicek, Laura, *Develop Dir,* University of Nebraska, Lincoln, Sheldon Memorial Art Gallery & Sculpture Garden, Lincoln NE
Rhea, Patty, *Cur,* Rockford Art Museum, Rockford IL
Rheault, Karman, *Artist & Owner,* Gallery 4, Ltd, Fargo ND
Rhein, Katrina, *Dir,* College of New Rochelle, Castle Gallery, New Rochelle NY
Rhinehart, Benjamin, *Assoc Prof,* Lawrence University, Dept of Art & Art History, Appleton WI (S)
Rhoad, Julie, *Pres & CEO,* The Names Project Foundation AIDS Memorial Quilt, Atlanta GA
Rhoades, Sara, *Asst Dir,* University of Southern Indiana, New Harmony Gallery of Contemporary Art, New Harmony IN
Rhoads, Beverly, *Prof,* Lynchburg College, Art Dept, Lynchburg VA (S)
Rhodes, C T, *Acting Dir,* eMediaLoft.org, New York NY
Rhodes, Che, *Asst Prof,* University of Louisville, Allen R Hite Art Institute, Louisville KY (S)
Rhodes, David, *Pres,* School of Visual Arts, New York NY (S)

Rhodes, Mark, *Assoc Prof,* University of Richmond, Dept of Art and Art History, Richmond VA (S)

Rhodes, Milton, *Pres & CEO,* The Arts Council of Winston-Salem & Forsyth County, Winston-Salem NC

Rhodes, Silas H, *Chmn,* School of Visual Arts, New York NY (S)

Rhodes, Tisha, *Dir Servs,* Montgomery Museum of Fine Arts, Library, Montgomery AL

Rhodes-Murphy, Alyson, *Cur Colls,* Tryon Palace, New Bern NC

Rhodes-Ousley, Marjorie, *Assoc Dir,* California State University, East Bay, C E Smith Museum of Anthropology, Hayward CA

Rhone, Kim, *Instr,* Lycoming College, Art Dept, Williamsport PA (S)

Rhyne, Grace, *Exec Dir,* WomanKraft Art Center, Tucson AZ

Rhyne, Zoe, *Dir Exhibs,* WomanKraft Art Center, Tucson AZ

Rial, Vicki, *Exhib Coordr,* University of Alabama, Sarah Moody Gallery of Art, Tuscaloosa AL

Ribas, Jose, *Preparator,* Bowdoin College, Museum of Art, Brunswick ME

Ribaudo, Maria, *Coll Mgr,* Morris Museum, Morristown NJ

Ribner, Naomi, *Instr,* College of the Holy Cross, Dept of Visual Arts, Worcester MA (S)

Riccardi, Lee-Ann, *Prof Art History,* The College of New Jersey, School of Arts & Sciences, Ewing NJ (S)

Ricci, Pat, *Cur,* Confederate Memorial Hall, Confederate Museum, New Orleans LA

Ricci, Steve, *Pub Rels & Mktg Mgr,* Albany Institute of History & Art, Albany NY

Rice, Anne, *Dir Educ,* Wadsworth Atheneum Museum of Art, Hartford CT

Rice, Dani, *Head Preparator,* Art Gallery of Alberta, Edmonton AB

Rice, Donovan, *COO,* Pomerene Center for the Arts, Coshocton OH

Rice, James, *Chmn Photographic Processing & Finishing Management,* Rochester Institute of Technology, School of Photographic Arts & Sciences, Rochester NY (S)

Rice, Jamie K, *Dir Library Servs,* Maine Historical Society, Library and Museum, Portland ME

Rice, Jane, *Dir Institutional Advancement,* Museum of Contemporary Art, San Diego, Geisel Library, La Jolla CA

Rice, Jenna, *Gallery Coordr,* Florida Southern College, Melvin Art Gallery, Lakeland FL

Rice, John, *Cur South Asian & Islamic Art,* Virginia Museum of Fine Arts, Richmond VA

Rice, Kevin, *Dir,* Confederation Centre Art Gallery and Museum, Charlottetown PE

Rice, Laura, *Chief Cur,* The Adirondack Historical Association, The Adirondack Museum, Blue Mountain Lake NY

Rice, Laura, *Visitor Svcs Facility Mgr,* Oklahoma Contemporary Arts Center, Oklahoma City OK

Rice, Noelle, *Curatorial Asst,* Columbia Museum of Art, Lee Alexander Lorick Library, Columbia SC

Rice, Ryan, *Chief Cur,* Institute of American Indian Arts, Museum of Contemporary Native Arts, Santa Fe NM (S)

Rice, Tom, *Chmn,* Kalamazoo College, Art Dept, Kalamazoo MI (S)

Rice, Yael, *Vis Asst Prof & RE Keiter '57 Post-Doc Fellow,* Amherst College, Dept of Art & the History of Art, Amherst MA (S)

Rice-Allen, Daphne, *Chmn,* Black American West Museum & Heritage Center, Denver CO

Ricetti, Valentina, *Cur,* Raccolte Artistiche Del Castello Sforzesco, Museo degli Strumenti Musicali - Museum of Musical Instruments, Milan

Rich, Adrienne, *Visitor Services Associate,* University of Wisconsin-Madison, Chazen Museum of Art, Madison WI

Rich, Sarah, *Assoc Prof,* Pennsylvania State University, University Park, Dept of Art History, University Park PA (S)

Richard, Charles, *Media Chmn,* Riverside Community College, Dept of Art & Mass Media, Riverside CA (S)

Richard, Jack, *Dir,* Studios of Jack Richard, Professional School of Painting & Design, Cuyahoga Falls OH (S)

Richard, John-Thomas, *Instr,* Kirkwood Community College, Dept of Arts & Humanities, Cedar Rapids IA (S)

Richard, Lucille, *Vol Secy,* Rangeley Lakes Region Logging Museum, Rangeley ME

Richard, Lynn-Marie, *Registrar,* Nova Scotia Museum, Maritime Museum of the Atlantic, Halifax NS

Richard, Mervin, *Chief Conservation,* National Gallery of Art, Washington DC

Richard, Nicole, *Cur Drawings & Archives,* Columbia University, Avery Architectural & Fine Arts Library, New York NY

Richard, Rodney C, *Vol Pres & Dir,* Rangeley Lakes Region Logging Museum, Rangeley ME

Richard, Stephen A, *Festival Coordr,* Rangeley Lakes Region Logging Museum, Rangeley ME

Richard, Tom, *Chmn,* University of Arkansas at Monticello, Fine Arts Dept, Monticello AR (S)

Richards, Earl, *Admin Asst,* Headquarters Fort Monroe, Dept of Army, Casemate Museum, Hampton VA

Richards, Evann, *Asst Prof,* Saint Louis Community College at Forest Park, Art Dept, Saint Louis MO (S)

Richards, Janet, *Assoc Cur,* University of Michigan, Kelsey Museum of Archaeology, Ann Arbor MI

Richards, Karen, *Accnt,* The San Joaquin Pioneer & Historical Society, The Haggin Museum, Stockton CA

Richards, Kathleen, *Exhibs Mgr & Progs Coord,* Carl & Marilynn Thoma Art Foundation, Art House Santa Fe, Santa Fe NM

Richards, Kathy, *House Mgr,* Van Singel Fine Arts Center, Van Singel Art Gallery, Byron Center MI

Richards, Kevin, *Liberal Arts Dept Chair,* Pennsylvania Academy of the Fine Arts, Office of Admission, Philadelphia PA (S)

Richards, Patricia, *Assoc Prof Photog,* Tarrant County College, Art Dept, Hurst TX (S)

Richards, Ron, *Admin Mgr,* Sonoma Valley Museum of Art, Sonoma CA

Richards, Ron, *Chief Cur Nat History,* Indiana State Museum, Indianapolis IN

Richards, Rosalyn, *Head Dept,* Bucknell University, Dept of Art, Lewisburg PA (S)

Richardson, Carl, *Asst Prof,* Spokane Falls Community College, Fine Arts Dept, Spokane WA (S)

Richardson, Cassandra, *Gallery Dir,* Elder Gallery, Charlotte NC

Richardson, Dave, *Asst Prof,* Eastern Illinois University, Art Dept, Charleston IL (S)

Richardson, Debra, *Exec Dir,* Fillmore County Historical Society, Fillmore County History Center, Fountain MN

Richardson, Erin, *Dir Colls,* New York State Historical Association, Research Library, Cooperstown NY

Richardson, Mary, *Library Dir,* Museum of Contemporary Art, Library, Chicago IL

Richardson, Pam, *Dean,* Pennsylvania School of Art & Design, Lancaster PA (S)

Richardson, Terry, *Instr,* Rochester Community & Technical College, Art Dept, Rochester MN (S)

Richardson, Tracey, *Assoc Prof,* Silver Lake College, Art Dept, Manitowoc WI (S)

Richardson, Trevor, *Contact,* University of Massachusetts, Amherst, Herter Art Gallery, Amherst MA

Richardson, Vicki, *Dir,* Left of Center Art Gallery & Studio, North Las Vegas NV

Richey-Ward, Diane, *Instr,* American River College, Dept of Art/Art New Media, Sacramento CA (S)

Richman, Arlene, *Recording Secy,* Pastel Society of America, National Arts Club, Grand Gallery, New York NY

Richman, Elise, *Chmn (until 2019), Prof Art,* University of Puget Sound, Dept of Art & Art History, Tacoma WA (S)

Richman, Gary, *Prof,* University of Rhode Island, Dept of Art & Art History, Kingston RI (S)

Richman, Irwin, *Prof,* Penn State Harrisburg, School of Humanities, Middletown PA (S)

Richman, Roger, *Prof,* University of Maine at Augusta, College of Arts & Humanities, Augusta ME (S)

Richmond, David, *Head Art Dept,* Simpson College, Farnham Gallery, Indianola IA

Richmond, Jennifer, *Asst Cur,* University of North Texas, Visual Resources Collection, Denton TX

Richner, Nancy, *Mus Educ Dir,* Hofstra University, Hofstra University Museum, Hempstead NY

Richter, Donald, *Pres,* Vermilion County Museum Society, Danville IL

Richter, Donald, *Pres,* Vermilion County Museum Society, Library, Danville IL

Richter, Marianne, *Director,* The Columbus Museum, Columbus GA

Richter, Marianne, *Exec Dir,* Swope Art Museum, Research Library, Terre Haute IN

Richter, Susan E, *Dir,* Vermilion County Museum Society, Library, Danville IL

Richter, Susan, *Dir,* Vermilion County Museum Society, Danville IL

Richwine, Holly, *Preparator,* Portland State University, Littman Gallery, Portland OR

Rickerson, Irini, *Art History,* Orange Coast College, Visual & Performing Arts Division, Costa Mesa CA (S)

Rickert, Rachel, *Gallery Coordinator,* New York Studio School of Drawing, Painting & Sculpture, Gallery, New York NY

Ricketts, Vicki, *Dir,* James D Veatch Camp Breckinridge Museum & Arts Center, Morganfield KY

Ricklin, Elaine, *Sec,* Spark Gallery, Denver CO

Ricks, Tonya, *Dir Develop,* Mabee-Gerrer Museum of Art, Shawnee OK

Riddle, Lola, *Treas,* Fulton County Historical Society Inc, Fulton County Museum (Tetzlaff Reference Room), Rochester IN

Riddle, Shannon, *Lectr,* Middle Georgia State University, College of Arts & Sciences, Media, Culture & the Arts, Cochran GA (S)

Ridel, Robert, *Dean Educ,* Art Institutes International at Portland, Portland OR

Rideout, Alan, *Preparator,* The University of Kentucky Art Museum, Lexington KY

Rider, Diane, *Library-LRC Dir,* Art Institute of Fort Lauderdale, Technical Library, Fort Lauderdale FL

Rider, Jonathan, *Assoc Dir,* FLAG Art Foundation, New York NY

Ridgway, Ginger, *Dir,* Pueblo Museum, Desert Hot Springs CA

Ridgway, Linda, *Admin Coordr,* National Audubon Society, John James Audubon Center at Mill Grove, Audubon PA

Riedel, Walter, *Pres & CEO Stark Foundation,* Nelda C & H J Lutcher Stark Foundation, Stark Museum of Art, Orange TX

Rieder, Andrew, *Instr,* Delta College, Art Dept, University Center MI (S)

Riedman, Connie, *Artist & Owner,* Gallery 4, Ltd, Fargo ND

Rieger, Dixie, *Exec Dir,* WaterWorks Art Museum, Miles City MT

Rieger, Sonja, *Prof,* University of Alabama at Birmingham, Dept of Art & Art History, Birmingham AL (S)

Rierson, Charlotte, *Art Coordr,* North Central Arkansas Art Gallery, Fairfield Bay AR

Riesby, Mark, *Mus Dir,* University of Southern Mississippi, Dept of Art & Design, Hattiesburg MS (S)

Riese, Tara, *Asst Librn,* The Buffalo Fine Arts Academy, G Robert Strauss Jr Memorial Library, Buffalo NY

Riess, Jonathan, *Prof Art History,* University of Cincinnati, School of Art, Cincinnati OH (S)

Rieth, Sheri, *Chair & Prof,* University of Mississippi, Department of Art, University MS (S)

Rietveld, Rickard, *Chmn,* Valencia Community College - East Campus, Art Dept, Orlando FL (S)

Rife, Jerry, *Chmn,* Rider University, Dept of Fine Arts, Lawrenceville NJ (S)
Rifenburg, Leigh, *Chief Cur,* Delaware Historical Society, Delaware History Museum and Center for African American Heritage, Wilmington DE
Rifenburg, Leigh, *Chief Cur,* Delaware Historical Society, Library, Wilmington DE
Riffee, Steve, *Asst Dir,* Lynchburg College, Daura Gallery, Lynchburg VA
Riffle, Brenda, *Librn,* Hampshire County Public Library, Romney WV
Rigby, Bruce, *Prof,* The College of New Jersey, School of Arts & Sciences, Ewing NJ (S)
Rigby, Mary Ellen, *Gift Shop Mgr,* Dartmouth College, Hood Museum of Art, Hanover NH
Rigg, Siobhan, *Asst Prof,* George Washington University, Dept of Art of Fine Arts & Art History, Washington DC (S)
Riggs, Ed, *Chair Commun Art Technology,* Montgomery College, Dept of Art, Rockville MD (S)
Rigoulot, Lisa, *Board Member,* Kennebec Valley Art Association, Harlow Gallery, Hallowell ME
Rigsby, Mark, *Asst Dir,* University of Southern Mississippi, Museum of Art, Hattiesburg MS
Riker, Janet, *Dir,* University at Albany, State University of New York, University Art Museum, Albany NY
Riley, Caroline, *Cur,* Gunston Hall Plantation, Library, Mason Neck VA
Riley, Christine, *Artist in Res, Musical Theatre,* Marymount Manhattan College, Fine & Performing Arts Div, New York NY (S)
Riley, Cynthia, *Staff Asst,* State University of New York at Binghamton, Binghamton University Art Museum, Binghamton NY
Riley, Dixie, *Head Librn,* Chappell Memorial Library and Art Gallery, Chappell NE
Riley, Jill St Clair, *Asst Prof,* Catholic University of America, School of Architecture & Planning, Washington DC (S)
Riley, Lynn, *Mgr,* Delaware Division of Historical & Cultural Affairs, Dover DE
Riley, Megan, *Dir External Affairs,* Bass Museum of Art, Miami Beach FL
Riley, Wendy, *Instr,* Casper College, Dept of Visual Arts, Casper WY (S)
Rime, Robyn, *Exposure Copyeditor,* Society for Photographic Education (SPE), SPE Gallery, Cleveland OH
Rimel, Luanne, *Educ Dir,* Craft Alliance Center of Art & Design, Saint Louis MO
Rimmer, Cate, *Cur,* Emily Carr Institute of Art & Design, The Charles H Scott Gallery, Vancouver BC
Rinaldi, Tina, *Gallery Dir,* Lane Arts Council, Jacobs Gallery, Eugene OR
Rinder, Lawrence, *Dir & Chief Cur,* University of California, Berkeley, Berkeley Art Museum & Pacific Film Archive, Berkeley CA
Rindfleisch, Jan, *Dir,* De Anza College, Euphrat Museum of Art, Cupertino CA
Rine, Henry, *Dean,* Jacksonville University, Jacksonville FL (S)
Rinehart, Jeff, *Instr,* University of New Orleans-Lake Front, Dept of Fine Arts, New Orleans LA (S)
Rinehart-Keever, Donna, *Exec Dir,* Oklahoma Contemporary Arts Center, Oklahoma City OK
Riner, Amanda, *Chair,* 1078 Gallery, Chico CA
Riner, Kimberly, *Temp Asst Prof,* Georgia Southern University, Betty Foy Sanders Dept of Art, Statesboro GA (S)
Ringer, Mark, *Prof Theatre,* Marymount Manhattan College, Fine & Performing Arts Div, New York NY (S)
Ringering, Dennis L, *Head Drawing,* Southern Illinois University at Edwardsville, Dept of Art & Design, Edwardsville IL (S)
Ringler, Denise, *Director of Arts & Cultural Programs,* Appalachian State University, Turchin Center for the Visual Arts, Boone NC
Ringler, Sara, *Prof,* Cape Cod Community College, Art Dept, West Barnstable MA (S)
Ringler, Tamsie, *Asst Prof,* St Catherine University, Art & Art History Dept, Saint Paul MN (S)
Rini, David, *Assoc Prof,* Johns Hopkins University, School of Medicine, Dept of Art as Applied to Medicine, Baltimore MD (S)
Rinklin, Cristi, *Asst Prof,* College of the Holy Cross, Dept of Visual Arts, Worcester MA (S)
Riordon, Bernard, *Dir Emeritus,* Beaverbrook Art Gallery, Fredericton NB
Rios, David, *Dir Public Progs,* Children's Museum of Manhattan, New York NY
Rios-Bermudez, Anna, *Cur Colls,* Museum of Ventura County, Ventura CA
Ripepi, Maria, *Asst Prof,* La Roche College, Division of Design, Pittsburgh PA (S)
Ripley, Richard, *Instructional Aide,* Victor Valley Community College, Art Dept, Victorville CA (S)
Ripley, Robert C, *Capitol Adminr,* Nebraska State Capitol, Lincoln NE
Rippe, Diane, *Dir Opers,* Key West Art & Historical Society, East Martello Museum & Gallery, Key West FL
Ripperger, Margaret, *Chmn,* Winterset Art Center, Winterset IA
Risbeck, Phil, *Chmn,* Colorado State University, Dept of Art, Fort Collins CO (S)
Risberg, Debra, *Cur,* Illinois State University, Museum Library, Normal IL
Riseman, Henry, *Dir,* New England Center for Contemporary Art, Brooklyn CT
Rishel, Joseph, *Curator Emeritus,* Philadelphia Museum of Art, John G Johnson Collection, Philadelphia PA
Riskin, Seth, *Emerging Technologies Coordr,* Massachusetts Institute of Technology, MIT Museum, Cambridge MA
Rislow, Madeline, *Asst Prof,* Missouri Western State University, School of Fine Arts, Saint Joseph MO (S)
Ritchie, Andrea, *Paints Coordr,* Visual Arts Nova Scotia, Halifax NS
Ritchie, Cathy, *Theater/Film Librn,* J Eric Johnson, Fine Arts Division, Dallas TX
Ritchie, David, *Instr,* Pacific Northwest College of Art, Portland OR (S)
Ritchie, Robert C, *Dir Research & Educ,* The Huntington Library, Art Collections & Botanical Gardens, Library, San Marino CA
Riter, David, *Chmn,* City Colleges of Chicago, Daley College, Chicago IL (S)
Ritger, Suzanne, *Gallery Dir,* Johnson State College, Dept Fine & Performing Arts, Dibden Center for the Arts, Johnson VT (S)
Ritiger, Scott, *Industrial Design Technology,* Art Institute of Pittsburgh, Pittsburgh PA (S)
Ritsma, Natasha, *Cur,* Loyola University Chicago, Loyola University Museum of Art, Chicago IL
Ritson, Kate, *Prof,* Trinity University, Department of Art & Art History, San Antonio TX (S)
Rittelmann, Leesa, *Assoc Prof,* Hartwick College, Art Dept, Oneonta NY (S)
Rittenhouse, Cherri, *Prof,* Rock Valley College, Humanities and Fine Arts Division, Rockford IL (S)
Ritter, Josef, *Prof,* Cazenovia College, Center for Art & Design Studies, Cazenovia NY (S)
Ritter, Julia, *Chair & Artistic Dir Dance Dept,* Rutgers, The State University of New Jersey, Mason Gross School of the Arts, New Brunswick NJ (S)
Ritter, Shelley, *Dir,* Delta Blues Museum, Clarksdale MS
Rittler, Steve, *Asst Prof,* William Paterson University, Dept Arts, Wayne NJ (S)
Rivard, TJ, *Chmn,* Indiana University-East, Humanities Dept, Richmond IN (S)
Riven, Stephanie, *Interim Dir,* Laumeier Sculpture Park, Saint Louis MO
Rivera, Adrian, *Coordr Exhib,* Escuela de Artes Plasticas, Biblioteca Francisco Oller, San Juan PR
Rivera, Ani, *Exec Dir,* Galeria de la Raza, Studio 24, San Francisco CA
Rivera, Frank, *Prof,* Mercer County Community College, Arts, Communication & Engineering Technology, West Windsor NJ (S)
Rivera, Maria Navedo, *Instr,* Inter American University of Puerto Rico, Fine Arts Dept -Art Program, San German PR (S)
Rivera, Shey, *Artistic Dir, Co-Dir,* AS220, Main Gallery, Providence RI
Rivero, Arturo, *Industrial Design Technology,* Art Institute of Pittsburgh, Pittsburgh PA (S)
Rivero, Marito, *Exec Dir,* Museum of African American History, Boston MA
Rivers Powell, Palemeschia "Pal", *Deputy Dir,* Polk Museum of Art, Lakeland FL
Rivers, Todd, *Chief Preparator,* University of Georgia, Georgia Museum of Art, Athens GA
Rives, Veda, *Interim Dir,* Illinois State University, Normal Editions Workshop, Normal IL
Rix, Marilu, *Store Mgr,* Maricopa County Historical Society, Desert Caballeros Western Museum, Wickenburg AZ
Rizzardi, Nancy, *Instr,* Pierce College, Art Dept, Woodland Hills CA (S)
Rizzo, Mike, *Designer,* National Heritage Museum, Lexington MA
Roach, Enid, *Art Instructor,* Kentucky Wesleyan College, Dept Art, Owensboro KY (S)
Roach, Stephanie, *Dir,* FLAG Art Foundation, New York NY
Roan, Joan, *Circ & Interlibrary Loan,* Ames Free-Easton's Public Library, North Easton MA
Robayo Sheridan, Sarah, *Cur,* University of Toronto, Art Centre, Toronto ON
Robayo Sheridan, Sarah, *Cur,* University of Toronto, Justina M Barnicke Gallery, Toronto ON
Robb, Jenny E, *Cur,* Ohio State University, Billy Ireland Cartoon Library & Museum, Columbus OH
Robb, Lisa, *Exec Dir,* Pelham Art Center, Pelham NY
Robb, Penny, *School of Art Admin Asst,* Lighthouse ArtCenter Museum & School of Art, Tequesta FL
Robbennolt, Linda, *Assoc Dean,* University of Illinois, Urbana-Champaign, College of Fine & Applied Arts, Champaign IL (S)
Robbin, C Roxanne, *Prof,* California State University, Art Dept, Turlock CA (S)
Robbins, Carolyn, *Cur Educ,* Scottsdale Cultural Council, Scottsdale Museum of Contemporary Art, Scottsdale AZ
Robbins, Christopher, *Dir & Assoc Prof,* Purchase College, State University of New York, School of Art+Design, Purchase NY (S)
Robbins, Gay, *Prof,* Emory University, Art History Dept, Atlanta GA (S)
Robbins, Jay, *Exec Dir,* Lincoln County Historical Association, Inc, Pownalborough Courthouse, Wiscasset ME
Robbins, Jay, *Exec Dir,* Lincoln County Historical Association, Inc, 1811 Old Lincoln County Jail & Lincoln County Museum, Wiscasset ME
Robbins, Mark, *Pres & CEO,* American Academy in Rome, New York NY (S)
Robbins, Noel, *Instr,* Southwestern University, Sarofim School of Fine Art, Dept of Art & Art History, Georgetown TX (S)
Robedee, Davana, *Prog Coord,* Schweinfurth Art Center, Auburn NY
Roberge, Michele, *Asst Mgr,* Lincoln County Historical Association, Inc, Maine Art Gallery, Wiscasset ME
Roberson, Keith, *Assoc Prof,* Florida State University, Art Dept, Tallahassee FL (S)
Roberson, Robert, *Dir Asst,* Plains Indians & Pioneers Historical Foundation, Museum & Art Center, Woodward OK
Roberson, Tana, *Asst Prof,* West Texas A&M University, Art, Theatre & Dance Dept, Canyon TX (S)
Roberson, Tom, *Devel,* Booth Western Art Museum, Cartersville GA
Robert, Brenda, *Dean,* Anoka Ramsey Community College, Art Dept, Coon Rapids MN (S)

Robert, Jocelyn, *Prof & Dir, School of Art,* Universite Laval, Faculty of Planning, Architecture, Arts & Design, Quebec QC (S)
Roberts, Anna, *Admin Asst,* Clark County Historical Society, Heritage Center of Clark County, Springfield OH
Roberts, Anne, *Chmn,* Lake Forest College, Dept of Art, Lake Forest IL (S)
Roberts, Diane, *Exec Dir,* Riverfront Renaissance Center for the Arts, Millville NJ
Roberts, Doren, *Mgr Events & Rentals,* The Winnipeg Art Gallery, Winnipeg MB
Roberts, Ellen, *Cur American Art,* Norton Museum of Art, West Palm Beach FL
Roberts, Eva, *Prof, Visual Communication Design,* Indiana University-Purdue University, Indianapolis, Herron School of Art & Design, Indianapolis IN (S)
Roberts, Holly, *Spec Events Mng,* Wiregrass Museum of Art, Dothan AL
Roberts, Jo, *Dir,* The Ella Carothers Dunnegan Gallery of Art, Bolivar MO
Roberts, Joshua, *Digital Initiatives & Systems Librn,* The University of the Arts, University Libraries, Philadelphia PA
Roberts, Kelley, *Instr,* Southern University A & M College, School of Architecture, Baton Rouge LA (S)
Roberts, Marilyn, *Chmn,* Waynesburg College, Dept of Fine Arts, Waynesburg PA (S)
Roberts, Matt, *Assoc Prof,* Stetson University, Department of Creative Arts, Deland FL (S)
Roberts, Michael, *Exec Dir,* Fine Arts Work Center, Hudson D. Walker Gallery, Provincetown MA
Roberts, Michelle, *Chief Registrar,* New Mexico Department of Cultural Affairs, New Mexico Museum of Art, Unit of NM Dept of Cultural Affairs, Santa Fe NM
Roberts, Nita, *Photographer,* New York University, Institute of Fine Arts Visual Resources Collection, New York NY
Roberts, Perri Lee, *Prof,* University of Miami, Dept of Art & Art History, Coral Gables FL (S)
Roberts, Randall, *Admin Gallery Coordr,* Midwest Museum of American Art, Elkhart IN
Roberts, Rhea, *Exec Dir,* Quapaw Quarter Association, Inc, Villa Marre, Little Rock AR
Roberts, Rhea, *Exec Dir,* Quapaw Quarter Association, Inc, Preservation Resource Center/ Historic Cannon Hall, Little Rock AR
Roberts, Samantha, *Events, Membership & Vis Svcs Coordr,* University of Alabama at Birmingham, Abroms-Engel Institute for the Visual Arts, Birmingham AL
Roberts, Susan, *Prof Graphic Design,* University of Georgia, Franklin College of Arts & Sciences, Lamar Dodd School of Art, Athens GA (S)
Roberts, Virginia, *Dir,* Rhinelander District Library, Rhinelander WI
Robertson, Bruce, *Dir,* University of California, Santa Barbara, Art, Design & Architecture Museum, Santa Barbara CA
Robertson, D Scott, *Prof,* University of Wisconsin-Eau Claire, Dept of Art & Design, Eau Claire WI (S)
Robertson, Dale, *Pres & CEO,* Grand Rapids Public Museum, Grand Rapids MI
Robertson, David J, *Prof,* Rochester Institute of Technology, School of Photographic Arts & Sciences, Rochester NY (S)
Robertson, Dennis, *Pres,* Dillman's Creative Arts Foundation, Lac Du Flambeau WI
Robertson, Dennis, *Pres,* Dillman's Creative Arts Foundation, Tom Lynch Resource Center, Lac du Flambeau WI
Robertson, Donna, *Dean,* Illinois Institute of Technology, College of Architecture, Chicago IL (S)
Robertson, Glenn, *Mgr Pub Rels,* Mobile Museum of Art, Mobile AL
Robertson, Jocelyn, *Dir Communs,* Idaho Commission on the Arts, Boise ID
Robertson, Lynn, *Gallery Dir,* Capitol Arts Alliance, Houchens Gallery, Bowling Green KY
Robertson, Meredith, *Exec Dir,* The Association of International Photography Art Dealers, Washington DC
Robertson, Phillip, *Dir,* Julian Scott Memorial Gallery, Johnson VT
Robertson, Roderick, *Prof,* Saint Mary's University of Minnesota, Art & Design Dept, Winona MN (S)
Robertson, Ruthanne, *Adjunct Assoc Prof Fine Art,* Johnson County Community College, Fine Arts Dept & Art History Dept, Overland Park KS (S)
Robertson, Scott, *Website/Brochure,* Dillman's Creative Arts Foundation, Lac Du Flambeau WI
Robertson, Sue, *VPres,* Dillman's Creative Arts Foundation, Lac Du Flambeau WI
Robertson, Sue, *VPres,* Dillman's Creative Arts Foundation, Tom Lynch Resource Center, Lac du Flambeau WI
Robertson, Susan, *Exec Dir,* Wiregrass Museum of Art, Dothan AL
Robertson, Susanne, *CFO,* Canadian Museum for Human Rights, Winnipeg MB
Robertson, Tony, *Bd Pres,* Audrain County Historical Society, Graceland Museum & American Saddlehorse Museum & Fire Brick Industry Museum, Mexico MO
Robideau, Patrick, *Sr Preparator,* Burchfield Penney Art Center, Buffalo NY
Robin, Madeleine, *Dir Art,* L'Universite Laval, Library, Quebec QC
Robinacci, Lorraine, *Serials Technician,* Ames Free-Easton's Public Library, North Easton MA
Robinson, Alex, *Contact,* Saint Edward's University, Fine Arts Gallery, Austin TX
Robinson, Barbara, *Co-owner,* Eureka Fine Art Gallery, Eureka Springs AR
Robinson, Bonnell, *Dir Gallery & Exhib,* Lesley University, Roberts Gallery, Cambridge MA
Robinson, Brian, *Art Teacher,* Motlow State Community College, Art Dept, Tullahoma TN (S)
Robinson, Bridget, *Trustee, Canada,* JMW Turner Museum, Sarasota FL
Robinson, Chris, *Exec Dir,* Royal Alberta Museum, Royal Alberta Museum, Edmonton AB
Robinson, Christie, *Mktg & Progs,* Skokie Public Library, Skokie IL
Robinson, Cory, *Assoc Prof, Chair Fine Arts,* Indiana University-Purdue University, Indianapolis, Herron School of Art & Design, Indianapolis IN (S)
Robinson, Edward, *Supervisor of Buildings & Grounds,* Academy Art Museum, Easton MD
Robinson, Harry, *Pres & CEO,* African American Museum, Dallas TX
Robinson, Jeri L, *Prof Drawing, 2D & Graphic Design,* Millersville University, Dept of Art & Design, Millersville PA (S)
Robinson, Kim, *Office Mgr,* Mennello Museum of American Art, Orlando FL
Robinson, Mary, *Dir,* Five Civilized Tribes Museum, Library, Muskogee OK
Robinson, Mary, *Librn,* Buffalo Bill Memorial Association, Buffalo Bill Historical Center, Cody WY
Robinson, Michelle, *Cur,* Figge Art Museum, Art Reference Library, Davenport IA
Robinson, Phillip, *Asst Prof,* University of Missouri, Saint Louis, Dept of Art & Art History, Saint Louis MO (S)
Robinson, Sally, *Pres,* Yukon Historical & Museums Association, Whitehorse YT
Robinson, Scott, *Prof,* North Central Texas College, Division of Communications & Fine Arts, Gainesville TX (S)
Robinson, Shanna, *Dept Contact,* North Central Michigan College, Art Dept, Petoskey MI (S)
Robinson, Susan, *Mus Educ,* Osborne Homestead Museum, Derby CT
Robinson, William W, *Cur Drawings,* Harvard University, William Hayes Fogg Art Museum, Cambridge MA
Robinson, William, *Sr Cur Modern Art,* The Cleveland Museum of Art, Cleveland OH
Robischon, Jim, *Owner & Dir,* Robischon Gallery, Denver CO
Robison, Janice, *Asst Dir,* Audrain County Historical Society, Graceland Museum & American Saddlehorse Museum & Fire Brick Industry Museum, Mexico MO
Robotham, Hugh, *VPres,* New York Society of Architects, New York NY
Robtoy, Tim, *Registrar,* Art Museum of Southeast Texas, Beaumont TX
Robu, Emil, *Rector & Pastor,* San Carlos Cathedral, Monterey CA
Roby, Thomas, *Chmn,* City Colleges of Chicago, Kennedy-King College, Chicago IL (S)
Roch, Manon, *Asst & Cur,* Maison Saint-Gabriel Museum, Montreal QC
Roche, David, *Dir,* Heard Museum, Billie Jane Baguley Library and Archives, Phoenix AZ
Roche, David, *Dir & CEO,* Heard Museum, Phoenix AZ
Roche, James, *Prof,* Florida State University, Art Dept, Tallahassee FL (S)
Roche, Joanne, *Librn,* Yonkers Public Library, Fine Arts Dept, Yonkers NY
Roche, Joanne, *Librn,* Yonkers Public Library, Will Library, Yonkers NY
Roche, Valerie, *Dance Coordr,* Creighton University, Fine & Performing Arts Dept, Omaha NE (S)
Rochester, Susan, *Dir Fine Arts,* Umpqua Community College, Fine & Performing Arts Dept, Roseburg OR (S)
Rochon, Alain, *Dean Planning, Architecture Art & Design,* Universite Laval, Faculty of Planning, Architecture, Arts & Design, Quebec QC (S)
Rock, Rodney, *Dir,* University of Connecticut, Jorgensen Auditorium, Storrs CT
Rock, Sheri, *Controller,* Taubman Museum of Art, Roanoke VA
Rock, Tracey, *Mus Shop Mgr,* Berkshire Museum, Pittsfield MA
Rockefeller, Sharon, *Chmn Board Trustees,* National Gallery of Art, Washington DC
Rockhill, King, *Pres,* Appaloosa Museum and Heritage Center, Moscow ID
Rockman, Dawn, *Treas,* Wellfleet Historical Society & Museum, Inc, Wellfleet MA
Rodda, Jenni, *Cur,* New York University, Institute of Fine Arts Visual Resources Collection, New York NY
Roddenberry, Heather, *Asst Cur & Registrar,* Pensacola Museum of Art, Harry Thornton Library, Pensacola FL
Rode, Meredith, *Prof,* University of the District of Columbia, Dept of Mass Media, Visual & Performing Arts, Washington DC (S)
Rode, Penny, *Assoc Prof,* Indiana University of Pennsylvania, College of Fine Arts, Indiana PA (S)
Rodeiro, Jose, *Prof,* New Jersey City University, Art Dept, Jersey City NJ (S)
Rodenbeck, Judith, *Faculty,* Sarah Lawrence College, Dept of Art History, Bronxville NY (S)
Rodenhauser, Debora, *Instr,* Bakersfield College, Art Dept, Bakersfield CA (S)
Rodgers, Aaron, *Dir Devel,* Hyde Park Art Center, Chicago IL
Rodgers, Coreen, *CFO,* The Huntington Library, Art Collections & Botanical Gardens, San Marino CA
Rodgers, Darlene, *Secy,* Glanmore National Historic Site of Canada, Belleville ON
Rodgers, Kenneth G, *Dir,* North Carolina Central University, NCCU Art Museum, Durham NC
Rodgers, Kenneth, *Prof, Dir Art Museum,* North Carolina Central University, Art Dept, Durham NC (S)
Rodgers, Natalie, *Access & Community Educ Coord,* Houston Center For Photography, Houston TX
Rodgers, Tim, *Dir,* The Wolfsonian-Florida International University, Miami Beach FL
Rodgers, Tim, *Dir,* Scottsdale Cultural Council, Scottsdale Museum of Contemporary Art, Scottsdale AZ
Rodgers, Tommie, *Registrar,* Lauren Rogers, Laurel MS

Rodney, Lee, *Prof, Media Art Histories & Visual Culture,* University of Windsor, School of Creative Arts, Windsor ON (S)
Rodning Bash, Sharon, *Prog Dir,* Arts Midwest, Minneapolis MN
Rodriguez A, Rommy, *Outreach Coordr,* Ontario Crafts Council, Craft Resource Centre, Toronto ON
Rodriguez, Ana, *Recording Secy,* Society of Scribes, Ltd, New York NY
Rodriguez, Angelica, *Gallery Coord,* Mission Cultural Center for Latino Arts, San Francisco CA
Rodriguez, Elizabeth, *Mus Technician,* Saint-Gaudens National Historic Site, Library, Cornish NH
Rodriguez, George, *Ceramics,* North Seattle College, North Seattle College Dept of Art, Seattle WA (S)
Rodriguez, Jennie, *Exec Dir,* Mission Cultural Center for Latino Arts, San Francisco CA
Rodriguez, Kathy, *Instr,* University of New Orleans-Lake Front, Dept of Fine Arts, New Orleans LA (S)
Rodriguez, Linda, *Cur Educ,* South Texas Institute for the Arts Affiliated with Texas A&M University - Corpus Christi, Art Museum of South Texas, Corpus Christi TX
Rodriguez, Luis, *Univ Librn,* Kean University, Nancy Thompson Library, Union NJ
Rodriguez, M Teresa Lapid, *Dir,* Montclair State University, Art Galleries, Upper Montclair NJ
Rodriguez, Maria del Carmen, *Coll Supvr,* Museo de las Americas, Viejo San Juan PR
Rodriguez, Nohemi, *Volunteer & Outreach Coord,* UMLAUF Sculpture Garden & Museum, Austin TX
Rodriguez, Ramiro, *Exhib Coordr,* University of Notre Dame, Snite Museum of Art, Notre Dame IN
Rodriguez-Mont, Jacquelina, *Exhibs Mgr,* Museo de Arte de Puerto Rico, San Juan PR
Roe, Beck, *Assoc Prof,* Azusa Pacific University, College of Music & the Arts, Dept of Art & Design, Azusa CA (S)
Roe, Betsy Knab, *Gallery Assoc,* Topeka & Shawnee County Public Library, Alice C Sabatini Gallery, Topeka KS
Roe, Bill, *Board Pres,* Pence Gallery, Davis CA
Roe, Daniel, *Dir Educ,* York County Heritage Trust, York PA
Roe, Linda, *Deputy Dir,* Public Library of Des Moines, Central Library Information Services, Des Moines IA
Roe, Ward V, *Prof,* Keystone College, Fine Arts Dept, LaPlume PA (S)
Roediger, Michael, *Dir & CEO,* Dayton Art Institute, Dayton OH
Roelofs, Jessie, *Develop & Communs Mgr,* Intermedia Arts, Minneapolis MN
Roeper, Susan, *Librn,* Clark Art Institute, Library, Williamstown MA
Roesch, Rob, *Sculpture Dept Chair,* Pennsylvania Academy of the Fine Arts, Office of Admission, Philadelphia PA (S)
Roese, Ronnie L, *Dir,* Miracle at Pentecost Foundation, Biblical Arts Center, Dallas TX
Roff, Mary, *Assoc Dir,* Art Center Manatee, Bradenton FL
Rogal, Maria, *Assoc Prof,* University of Florida, School of Art & Art History, Gainesville FL (S)
Rogan, Clare, *Cur,* Wesleyan University, Davison Art Center, Middletown CT
Rogan, Mary Ellen, *Dir,* Plainfield Public Library, Plainfield NJ
Rogerge, Celeste, *Prof,* University of Florida, School of Art & Art History, Gainesville FL (S)
Rogers, Alexis, *Lead Mus Technician,* Daytona State College, Southeast Museum of Photography, Daytona Beach FL
Rogers, Arthur, *Pres Bd,* Pacific Grove Art Center, Pacific Grove CA
Rogers, Cheryl, *Registrar & Preparator,* Fort Collins Museum of Art, Inc, Fort Collins CO
Rogers, Christine, *Asst Photog,* Watkins College of Art, Design & Film, Nashville TN (S)
Rogers, Cole, *Artistic Dir,* Highpoint Center for Printmaking, Minneapolis MN
Rogers, Dan, *Instr,* Bismarck State College, Fine Arts Dept, Bismarck ND (S)
Rogers, Darlene, *Interpretive Program Dir,* Schuyler Mansion State Historic Site, Albany NY
Rogers, Donald, *Dir Facilities Mgmt,* Hillwood Museum & Gardens Foundation, Hillwood Estate Museum & Gardens, Washington DC
Rogers, Eric, *Exec Dir,* Arts Place, Inc, Hugh N Ronald Memorial Gallery, Portland IN
Rogers, Geoffrey, *Chmn Science & Math,* Fashion Institute of Technology, School of Art & Design, New York NY (S)
Rogers, James, *Div Fine & Performing Arts Chair, Prof Art History,* Florida Southern College, Department of Art & Art History, Lakeland FL (S)
Rogers, James, *Pres,* Westfield Athenaeum, Jasper Rand Art Museum, Westfield MA
Rogers, James, *Prof Art History & Chmn Div Fine & Performing Arts,* Florida Southern College, Melvin Art Gallery, Lakeland FL
Rogers, Kathy, *Exec Dir,* Piedmont Arts Association, Martinsville VA
Rogers, Liz, *Gallery Mgr,* Florida CraftArt, Saint Petersburg FL
Rogers, Nancy M, *Exec Dir,* Wooster Community Art Center, Danbury CT
Rogers, Nancy M, *Exec Dir,* Wooster Community Art Center, Library, Danbury CT
Rogers, Paul, *Archivist,* Yosemite Museum, Yosemite National Park CA
Rogers, Richard L, *Pres,* College for Creative Studies, Detroit MI (S)
Rogers, Robert Meadows, *Chair,* Concordia College, Art Dept, Moorhead MN (S)
Rogers, Robert, *Assoc Prof,* Queensborough Community College, Dept of Art & Photography, Bayside Hills NY (S)
Rogers, Robert, *Cur Antique Auto Mus,* Heritage Museums & Gardens, Sandwich MA
Rogers, Robin, *Acting Mgr Glass Studio,* Chrysler Museum of Art, Norfolk VA
Rogers-Naff, Shirley, *Store & Office Mgr,* Martin and Osa Johnson, Chanute KS
Rogerson, Lynn K, *Dir & CEO,* Art Services International, Alexandria VA
Rogerson, Rachel, *Dir,* The McKinney Avenue Contemporary (The MAC), Dallas TX
Roglan, Mark, *Dir,* Southern Methodist University, Meadows Museum, Dallas TX
Rogstad, Mary Labate, *Registrar,* Vermont Historical Society, Museum, Montpelier VT
Roh, Michael, *Facility Project Advisor,* Columbia Museum of Art, Columbia SC
Rohkea, Seija, *Exhibs Preparator,* Long Beach Museum of Art Foundation, Long Beach Museum of Art, Long Beach CA
Rohlf, Logan, *Media Coordr,* Foundry Art Centre, Saint Charles MO
Rohmiller, Ellen, *Librn,* Dayton Art Institute, Library, Dayton OH
Rohn, Erick, *Asst Prof,* Oakton Community College, Language Humanities & Art Divisions, Des Plaines IL (S)
Rohovit, Ron, *Deputy Dir Educ,* California Science Center, Los Angeles CA
Rohrbach, John, *Sr Cur Photographs,* Amon Carter Museum of American Art, Fort Worth TX
Rohrer, Judith C, *Assoc Prof,* Emory University, Art History Dept, Atlanta GA (S)
Rohrer, Susan, *Cur Educ,* State Capital Museum, Olympia WA
Rohrer, Thelma S, *Chmn Dept,* Manchester College, Dept of Art, North Manchester IN (S)
Rojas, Juan, *Chief Preparator,* University of Southern California, USC Fisher Museum of Art, Los Angeles CA
Rojas-Sukkar, Alba, *Chief Develop Officer,* Tucson Museum of Art and Historic Block, Tucson AZ
Rokes, Carla, *Asst Prof & Gallery Dir,* University of North Carolina at Pembroke, Art Dept, Pembroke NC (S)
Roland, Craig, *Prof,* University of Florida, School of Art & Art History, Gainesville FL (S)
Roland, Marya, *Asst Prof,* Western Carolina University, Dept of Art/College of Arts & Science, Cullowhee NC (S)
Roldan, Deborah, *Asst Dir Exhibs,* Museum of Fine Arts, Houston, Houston TX
Roll, Susan, *Adminr,* William Bonifas, Escanaba MI
Rolle, James, *Lectr,* Saint John's University, Art Dept, Collegeville MN (S)
Roller, Terry M, *Prof,* Baylor University - College of Arts and Sciences, Dept of Art, Waco TX (S)
Rollinger, Jeffrey, *Photog Faculty,* Harford Community College, Visual, Performing and Applied Arts Division, Bel Air MD (S)
Rollins Stanis, Suzanne, *Dir Heritage Educ & Info,* Indiana Landmarks, Morris-Butler House, Indianapolis IN
Rollins, Eleanor, *Admin Asst,* Beaufort County Arts Council, Washington NC
Rollins, Fred, *Mus Aide,* Village of Potsdam, Potsdam Public Museum, Potsdam NY
Rollins, Ken, *Dir,* Tampa Museum of Art, Tampa FL
Rollins, Rich, *Instr,* Marylhurst University, Art Dept, Marylhurst OR (S)
Rollison, Randy, *Dir,* Intersection for the Arts, San Francisco CA
Rolnick, Neil, *Chmn,* Rensselaer Polytechnic Institute, Eye Ear Studio Dept of Art, Troy NY (S)
Rolon, Edwin, *Asst Cur Modern Books (1830-Present),* The Hispanic Society of America, Hispanic Society Museum & Library, New York NY
Rom, Cristine, *Library Dir,* Cleveland Institute of Art, Jessica Gund Memorial Library, Cleveland OH
Romaine, Paul, *Develop & Mem,* Center for Book Arts, New York NY
Romais, Miriam, *Exec Dir,* En Foco, Inc, Bronx NY
Roman, Dulce, *Chief Cur & Cur Modern Art,* University of Florida, Samuel P Harn Museum of Art, Gainesville FL
Romano, Lisa, *Asst Dir,* Riverfront Renaissance Center for the Arts, Millville NJ
Romer Huckaby, Laura, *Coll Mgr,* San Angelo Museum of Fine Arts, San Angelo TX
Romer, Teresa, *Admin Asst,* Pace University Gallery, Art Gallery in Choate House, Pleasantville NY
Romero, G, *Mgr School & Family Progs,* Morris-Jumel Mansion, Inc, New York NY
Romero, Lynda, *Admin Asst,* Pueblo of Pojoaque, Poeh Museum, Santa Fe NM
Romero, Samuel, *Asst Prof Art & Dir Graphic Design Prog,* Florida Southern College, Department of Art & Art History, Lakeland FL (S)
Romero, Samuel, *Asst Prof Art & Dir Graphic Design Prog,* Florida Southern College, Melvin Art Gallery, Lakeland FL
Romnes, Juliana, *Exhib Coordr,* Daytona State College, Southeast Museum of Photography, Daytona Beach FL
Romney, Jeff, *Dir,* City of El Paso, El Paso Museum of Archaeology, El Paso TX
Ron, Will, *Art Dept Chmn,* Montana State University-Northern, Humanities & Social Sciences, Havre MT (S)
Ronayne, Natalie, *Exec Dir,* Cleveland Botanical Garden, Eleanor Squire Library, Cleveland OH
Roncka, Gene, *Artist,* Gene Roncka Willow Point Gallery/Museum, Ashland NE
Roncka, Mary, *Gallery Dir,* Gene Roncka Willow Point Gallery/Museum, Ashland NE
Rondeau, James, *Pres & Eloise W Martin Dir,* The Art Institute of Chicago, Chicago IL
Rondon, Camila, *Co-Director,* Studio Gallery, Washington DC
Rone, Catherine, *Gift Shop Mgr,* Yuma Fine Arts Association, Yuma Art Center, Yuma AZ
Ronn, Emma, *Mktg Asst,* American Swedish Historical Foundation & Museum, American Swedish Historical Museum, Philadelphia PA
Ronzio, Katherine, *Admin, Mktg & Develop Asst,* Canadian Clay and Glass Gallery, Waterloo ON
Rood, Warren, *Instr,* Walla Walla Community College, Fine Arts Dept, Walla Walla WA (S)
Rooks, Michael, *Cur Modern & Contemporary,* High Museum of Art, Atlanta GA

Rooney, Khan, *Colls Asst,* The Stewart Museum, Library, Montreal QC
Rooney, Marsha, *Cur History,* Eastern Washington State Historical Society, Northwest Museum of Arts & Culture, Spokane WA
Roos, Pieter, *Exec Dir,* Mark Twain, Hartford CT
Roosa, Rosemary, *Exec Dir,* Walter Anderson Museum of Art, Ocean Springs MS
Roosa, Wayne L, *Prof,* Bethel University, Dept of Art & Design, Saint Paul MN (S)
Root, Linda, *Office Mgr,* Koshare Indian Museum, Inc, La Junta CO
Root, Margaret, *Cur,* University of Michigan, Kelsey Museum of Archaeology, Ann Arbor MI
Root, Patricia, *Head of Reference,* Bronxville Public Library, Bronxville NY
Roper, Tim, *Asst Prof,* Louisiana College, Dept of Art, Pineville LA (S)
Ropson, Jerry, *Asst Prof,* Mount Allison University, Dept of Fine Arts, Sackville NB (S)
Rorech, Joseph, *Deputy Dir Fin & Admin,* The Jewish Museum, New York NY
Rorschach, Kimberly, *Dir,* Seattle Art Museum, McCaw Foundation Asian Art Library, Seattle WA
Rorschach, Kimberly, *Dir,* Seattle Art Museum, Olympic Sculpture Park, Seattle WA
Rorschach, Kimberly, *Dir,* Seattle Art Museum, Ann P Wyckoff Teacher Resource Center, Seattle WA
Rorschach, Kimberly, *Dir,* Seattle Art Museum, Seattle Asian Art Museum, Seattle WA
Rorschach, Kimberly, *Dir & CEO, Illsley Ball Nordstrom,* Seattle Art Museum, Seattle WA
Ros, Andrea, *VPres,* New Zone Virtual Gallery, Eugene OR
Rosa, Joseph, *Dir,* Frye Art Museum, Seattle WA
Rosal, Marcia L, *Prof,* Florida State University, Art Education Dept, Tallahassee FL (S)
Rosales, Eimy, *Bus Dir,* National Museum of Mexican Art, Chicago IL
Rosales, Miguel, *Librn,* The New York Public Library, Art & Architecture Collection, New York NY
Rosandich, T J, *CEO,* American Sport Art Museum and Archives, Daphne AL
Rosario, Francisco, *Dir Security,* Bronx Museum of the Arts, Bronx NY
Rosas, Carlos, *Assoc Prof Art (New Media),* Pennsylvania State University, University Park, Penn State School of Visual Arts, University Park PA (S)
Rosasco, Betsy J, *Research Cur European Painting & Sculpture,* Princeton University, Princeton University Art Museum, Princeton NJ
Rosata, Nancy, *Assoc Dir,* Regis College, Carney Gallery, Weston MA
Rosati, Tony, *Printmaking Dept Chair,* Pennsylvania Academy of the Fine Arts, Office of Admission, Philadelphia PA (S)
Roschmann, Marlene, *Trustee,* Brooklyn Historical Society, Brooklyn OH
Roscoe Hartigan, Lynda, *Deputy Dir,* Peabody Essex Museum, Salem MA
Rose, Barbara, *Prof,* American University, Dept of Art, New York NY (S)
Rose, C, *Mediterranean Section Cur,* University of Pennsylvania, Museum of Archaeology & Anthropology, Philadelphia PA
Rose, Elizabeth, *Libr Dir,* Fairfield Historical Society, Fairfield Museum & History Center, Fairfield CT
Rose, Ellen, *Circ Librn,* Athenaeum of Philadelphia, Library, Philadelphia PA
Rose, Erin, *Asst Cur,* University of Wisconsin, Green Bay, Lawton Gallery, Green Bay WI
Rose, James, *Asst Prof,* Clarion University of Pennsylvania, Dept of Art, Clarion PA (S)
Rose, Joshua, *Prof,* New Mexico State University, Art Dept, Las Cruces NM (S)
Rose, Julia, *Dir,* West Baton Rouge Parish, West Baton Rouge Museum, Port Allen LA
Rose, Julia, *Dir & Cur,* Johns Hopkins University, Evergreen Museum & Library, Baltimore MD
Rose, June, *Gallery Mgr,* Boothbay Region Art Foundation Inc, Boothbay Harbor ME
Rose, Michael, *Gallery Mgr,* Providence Art Club, Providence RI
Rose, Patrice, *Dir Admin & Gift Shop Mgr,* Krasl Art Center, Saint Joseph MI
Rose, Rebecca, *Dir Mus Colls & Registration,* Virginia Historical Society, Richmond VA
Rose, Richard, *Chmn Studio,* University of South Carolina, Dept of Art, Columbia SC (S)
Rose, Steve, *Pres,* Passaic County Community College, Division of Humanities, Paterson NJ (S)
Rose, Thomas, *Prof,* University of Minnesota, Minneapolis, Dept of Art, Minneapolis MN (S)
Rosedale, Jeff, *Asst Library Dir,* Manhattanville College, Library, Purchase NY
Rosek, Mary, *Assoc Lect,* University of Wisconsin-Stevens Point, Dept of Art & Design, Stevens Point WI (S)
Roselione-Valadez, Juan, *Dir,* Rubell Family Collection and Contemporary Arts Foundation, Miami FL
Roselle, David P, *Dir,* Winterthur Museum, Winterthur Museum, Garden & Library, Winterthur DE
Roseman, Harry, *Prof,* Vassar College, Art Dept, Poughkeepsie NY (S)
Rosemurgy, Madeline, *Creative Content Coordr,* Michigan State University, Eli & Edythe Broad Art Museum, East Lansing MI
Rosen, Andrea, *Cur,* University of Vermont, Robert Hull Fleming Museum, Burlington VT
Rosen, Annabeth, *Prof,* University of California, Davis, Dept of Art & Art History, Davis CA (S)
Rosen, Blake, *Spec Events Coordr,* Montgomery Museum of Fine Arts, Montgomery AL
Rosen, Leila, *Librn,* Aesthetic Realism Foundation, Eli Siegel Collection, New York NY
Rosen, M, *Prof,* City Colleges of Chicago, Daley College, Chicago IL (S)
Rosen, Robert, *Dir,* University of Southern California, Cinema-Television Library & Archives of Performing Arts, Los Angeles CA
Rosen-Queralt, Jann, *Dir,* Maryland Institute, Rinehart School of Sculpture, Baltimore MD (S)
Rosenbaum, Arthur, *Wheatley Prof Drawing & Painting,* University of Georgia, Franklin College of Arts & Sciences, Lamar Dodd School of Art, Athens GA (S)
Rosenbaum, Dan, *Maintenance,* Museum of Western Colorado, Museum of the West, Grand Junction CO
Rosenberg, Deborah, *Dept Chair,* Southern Oregon University, Art & Art History Dept, Ashland OR (S)
Rosenberg, Doug, *Prof,* University of Wisconsin, Madison, Dept of Art, Madison WI (S)
Rosenberg, Eric, *Assoc Prof,* Tufts University, Dept of Art & Art History, Medford MA (S)
Rosenberg, Herbert, *Prof,* New Jersey City University, Art Dept, Jersey City NJ (S)
Rosenberg, Kristina, *Dir Educ,* Timken Museum of Art, San Diego CA
Rosenberg, Ramona, *Dir External Affairs,* Bard College, Center for Curatorial Studies and the Hessel Museum of Art, Annandale-on-Hudson NY
Rosenberg, Ronni, *Dean,* Sheridan College, Faculty of Animation, Arts & Design, Oakville ON (S)
Rosenberg, Steve, *Chmn Music Dept,* College of Charleston, School of the Arts, Charleston SC (S)
Rosenberg, Whitney Lucas, *Dir Institutional Advancement,* Bruce Museum, Inc, Greenwich CT
Rosenblum, Paul, *Mng Dir,* Caramoor Center for Music & the Arts, Inc, Rosen House at Caramoor, Katonah NY
Rosenfeld, Andrew, *Prof,* Mount Saint Mary's University, Visual & Performing Arts Dept, Emmitsburg MD (S)
Rosenfeld, Daniel, *Dir,* Colby College, Museum of Art, Waterville ME
Rosenfeld, Jason, *Assoc Prof Art History,* Marymount Manhattan College, Fine & Performing Arts Div, New York NY (S)
Rosenfeld, Susan, *Asst Cur,* University of California, Los Angeles, Visual Resource Collection, Los Angeles CA
Rosenfield, Saralyn, *Dir Educ,* Delaware Art Museum, Wilmington DE
Rosengren, Jim, *Deputy Dir Finance/Admin,* Florida State University and Central Florida Community College, The Appleton Museum of Art, Ocala FL
Rosenheim, Jeff, *Conservator in Charge, Photographs,* The Metropolitan Museum of Art, New York NY
Rosenheim, Jeff, *Cur in Charge, Photographs,* The Metropolitan Museum of Art, New York NY
Rosensaft, Jean Bloch, *Dir,* Hebrew Union College - Jewish Institute of Religion Museum, Jewish Institute of Religion, New York NY
Rosenstveicht, Lisa, *Lectr,* Humboldt State University, College of Arts & Humanities, Art Dept, Arcata CA (S)
Rosenthal, Barbara, *Artist in Residence,* eMediaLoft.org, New York NY
Rosenthal, Barbara, *FT,* University of Wisconsin Oshkosh, Dept of Art, Oshkosh WI (S)
Rosenthal, Deborah, *Cur,* Miller Art Center Foundation Inc, Miller Art Museum, Sturgeon Bay WI
Rosera, Kathy, *Office Mgr,* Neville Public Museum of Brown County, Green Bay WI
Rosichelli, Marco, *Asst Prof,* University of Central Missouri, Dept of Art & Design, Warrensburg MO (S)
Rosier, Ken, *Chair & Prof,* Del Mar College, Art Dept, Corpus Christi TX (S)
Rosier, Ken, *Chair Art & Drama Dept,* Del Mar College, Joseph A Cain Memorial Art Gallery, Corpus Christi TX
Rosier, Meredith, *Instr,* Woodstock School of Art, Inc, Woodstock NY (S)
Roslak, Robyn, *Assoc Prof,* University of Minnesota, Duluth, Art Dept, Duluth MN (S)
Roslonic, Dennis, *AV Technician,* Neville Public Museum of Brown County, Green Bay WI
Rosner, Brienne, *Gallery Dir,* Peters Valley School of Craft, Layton NJ
Rosoff, Nancy, *Andrew W Mellon Cur of the Arts of the Americas,* Brooklyn Museum, Brooklyn NY
Rospert, Jennifer, *Asst Prof,* University of Central Arkansas, Department of Art, Conway AR (S)
Ross, Alex, *Head Librn,* Stanford University, Art & Architecture Library, Stanford CA
Ross, Chris, *Preparator,* Akron Art Museum, Akron OH
Ross, Cynthia, *Instr,* Goddard College, Dept of Art, Plainfield VT (S)
Ross, Dan, *Dir Community Develop,* Arts United of Greater Fort Wayne, Fort Wayne IN
Ross, Dave, *Div Chmn,* Rock Valley College, Humanities and Fine Arts Division, Rockford IL (S)
Ross, Diane, *Archivist,* University of Southern Mississippi, McCain Library & Archives, Hattiesburg MS
Ross, Eliza, *Event Coordr,* Walker Fine Art, Denver CO
Ross, Elizabeth, *Assoc Prof,* University of Florida, School of Art & Art History, Gainesville FL (S)
Ross, Gary, *Chmn,* Capital University, Fine Arts Dept, Columbus OH (S)
Ross, Laine, *Pres,* Allied Arts of Seattle, Seattle WA
Ross, Linda, *Dir Humanities,* Penn State Harrisburg, School of Humanities, Middletown PA (S)
Ross, Margaret, *Dir,* Chatham College, Fine & Performing Arts, Pittsburgh PA (S)
Ross, Murray, *Instr Theater,* University of Colorado-Colorado Springs, Visual & Performing Arts Dept (VAPA), Colorado Springs CO (S)
Ross, Nancy, *Instr,* Mary Baldwin College, Dept of Art & Art History, Staunton VA (S)
Ross, Randy, *Mktg Dir,* Orlando Museum of Art, Orlando FL
Ross, Randy, *Mktg Dir,* Orlando Museum of Art, Orlando Sentinel Library, Orlando FL
Ross, Robert, *Prof Emeritus,* University of Arkansas, Art Dept, Fayetteville AR (S)
Ross, Scott, *Asst Prof,* Linfield College, Department of Art & Visual Culture, McMinnville OR (S)
Ross, Shelley, *Chief Librn,* Medicine Hat Public Library, Medicine Hat AB

Rosseau, Gwenn, *VP Fin,* Birmingham Bloomfield Art Center, Birmingham MI (S)

Rosseau, Gwenn, *VP Finance,* Birmingham Bloomfield Art Center, Art Center, Birmingham MI

Rosser, Kay, *Vol Coordr,* Plaza de la Raza Cultural Center, Los Angeles CA

Rossetti, John, *Colls Assoc Registrar,* Tufts University, Tufts University Art Gallery, Medford MA

Rossi, Peter, *Pres,* American Artists Professional League, Inc, New York NY

Rossiter, Shannon, *Dir,* Mohave Museum of History & Arts, Kingman AZ

Rossman, Val, *Instr,* Main Line Art Center, Haverford PA (S)

Rossnagel, Liz, *Dir,* Lethbridge Public Library, Art Gallery, Lethbridge AB

Rossol, Monona, *Pres,* Arts, Craft & Theater Safety, New York NY

Rosson, Lindsay G, *Financial Officer,* Asheville Art Museum, Asheville NC

Rossy, Caroline, *Communs & Opers Mgr,* American Swedish Historical Foundation & Museum, Nord Library, Philadelphia PA

Rostek, Philip, *Assoc Prof,* Seton Hill University, Art Program, Greensburg PA (S)

Roth, Dan, *Cur & Dir,* United States Navy Supply Corps School, US Navy Supply Corps Museum, Newport RI

Roth, James, *Deputy Dir,* National Archives & Records Administration, John F Kennedy Presidential Library & Museum, Boston MA

Roth, John, *Assoc Prof,* Old Dominion University, Art Dept, Norfolk VA (S)

Roth, Linda, *Cur European Decorate Arts,* Wadsworth Atheneum Museum of Art, Hartford CT

Roth, Liz, *Assoc Prof,* Oklahoma State University, Department of Art, Graphic Design and Art History, Stillwater OK (S)

Roth, Moira, *Prof,* Mills College, Art Dept, Oakland CA (S)

Roth, Theo, *Colls Mgr,* Center for Book Arts, New York NY

Rothermel, Barbara, *Dir,* Lynchburg College, Daura Gallery, Lynchburg VA

Rothermel, Barbara, *Lectr,* Lynchburg College, Art Dept, Lynchburg VA (S)

Rothkopf, Katherine, *Sr Cur European Painting & Sculpture,* The Baltimore Museum of Art, Baltimore MD

Rothkopf, Scott, *Deputy Dir Progs,* Whitney Museum of American Art, New York NY

Rothman, Roger, *Art Historian,* Agnes Scott College, Dalton Art Gallery, Decatur GA

Rothrock, Kristin, *Lectr,* University of North Carolina at Charlotte, Dept Art, Charlotte NC (S)

Rothweiler, David, *Adjunct Prof Art,* University of Great Falls, Art Dept, Great Falls MT (S)

Rotondo-McCord, Lisa, *Deputy Dir Curatorial Affairs & Cur Asian Art,* New Orleans Museum of Art, New Orleans LA

Rouleau, Edie, *Buyer/Merchandiser,* Clymer Museum of Art, The Clymer Museum & Gallery, Ellensburg WA

Rounds, Adam, *Bus Mgr,* Utah State University, Nora Eccles Harrison Museum of Art, Logan UT

Rouse, Jocelyn, *Communs Coordr,* Cliveden, Philadelphia PA

Rousseau, Valerie, *Cur, Art of the Self-Taught & Art Brut,* American Folk Art Museum, New York NY

Rousseaux, Mary, *Instr Studio Art,* Madonna University, College of Arts & Humanities, Livonia MI (S)

Rouston, Roger, *Asst Prof,* Kansas State University, Art Dept, Manhattan KS (S)

Rovet, Christine, *Sr Dir Guest Relations & Admin,* Genesee Country Village & Museum, John L Wehle Art Gallery, Mumford NY

Row, Brian, *Prof,* Texas State University - San Marcos, Dept of Art and Design, San Marcos TX (S)

Rowan, Gerald, *Prog Coordr,* Northampton Community College, Art Dept, Bethlehem PA (S)

Rowe Jennings, Susan, *VPres Opers,* Arts & Education Council of Greater Saint Louis, Saint Louis MO

Rowe, Aiden, *Coordr Art & Design Fundamentals,* University of Alberta, Dept of Art & Design, Edmonton AB (S)

Rowe, Donald, *Dir,* Olivet College, Armstrong Collection, Olivet MI

Rowe, Donald, *Prof,* Olivet College, Art Dept, Olivet MI (S)

Rowe, Jay, *Vol Mgr,* Brookgreen Gardens, Murrells Inlet SC

Rowe, Libby, *Assoc Prof,* University of Texas at San Antonio, Dept of Art & Art History, San Antonio TX (S)

Rowe, Libby, *Sr Lectr,* Vanderbilt University, Dept of Art, Nashville TN (S)

Rowe, Martha, *Admin Research Assoc,* Old Salem Museums & Gardens, Library and Research Center, Winston-Salem NC

Rowe, Martha, *Dir Research Center,* Old Salem Museums & Gardens, Museum of Early Southern Decorative Arts, Winston-Salem NC

Rowe, Nina, *VPres,* International Center of Medieval Art, New York NY

Rowe, Susan, *Instr,* Olivet College, Art Dept, Olivet MI (S)

Rowe, William Brit, *Chmn,* Ohio Northern University, Dept of Art & Design, Ada OH (S)

Rowe, William H, *Instr,* Arkansas State University, Dept of Art, State University AR (S)

Rowitz, Scott, *COO,* Yerba Buena Center for the Arts, San Francisco CA

Rowland, Ann, *CFO,* Los Angeles County Museum of Art, Los Angeles CA

Rowland, Chris, *Instr Marketing/Branding,* AIC College of Design, Cincinnati OH (S)

Rowland, Cynthia, *Pres,* New Mexico Art League, Gallery & School, Albuquerque NM

Rowland, Leslie W, *Exec Dir,* Thousand Islands Arts Center - Home of the Handweaving Museum, Clayton NY (S)

Rowlands, J, *Dean & Prof,* Camden County College, Visual & Performing Arts Dept, Blackwood NJ (S)

Rowlett, Jeannette, *Dir,* Kentucky Guild of Artists & Craftsmen Inc, Berea KY

Roworth, Wendy W, *Chair,* University of Rhode Island, Dept of Art & Art History, Kingston RI (S)

Roxberg, Val, *Treas,* Searchlight Historic Museum & Mining Park, Searchlight NV

Roy, Carolina, *Asst Cur Art,* Carnegie Mellon University, Hunt Institute for Botanical Documentation, Pittsburgh PA

Roy, Denise, *Instr,* Marylhurst University, Art Dept, Marylhurst OR (S)

Roy, Jan, *Pres,* Searchlight Historic Museum & Mining Park, Searchlight NV

Roy, Rob, *Painting,* Montserrat College of Art, Beverly MA (S)

Royall, Richard R, *Managing Dir,* James Dick Foundation, Festival - Institute, Round Top TX

Royce, Amy Cavanaugh, *Exec Dir,* Maryland Art Place, Baltimore MD

Royce, Linden, *Mgr Mus Store,* Museum of Ventura County, Ventura CA

Royce, Michael, *Exec Dir,* New York Foundation for the Arts, Brooklyn NY

Royer, Catherine M, *Chmn, Assoc Prof,* Adrian College, Art & Design Dept, Adrian MI (S)

Royer, Jennifer, *Cur,* Landis Valley Village and Farm Museum, PA Historical & Museum Commission, Landis Collections Gallery, Lancaster PA

Royer, Randall, *Prof,* Black Hills State University, Art Dept, Spearfish SD (S)

Royster, Kenneth, *Coordr Art Dept,* Morgan State University, Dept of Art, Baltimore MD (S)

Rozanc, Gary, *Asst Prof,* University of Maryland, Baltimore County, Intermedia & Digital Arts (IMDA), Dept of Visual Arts, Baltimore MD (S)

Rozdolsky, Olivia, *Asst Cur,* Ukrainian Institute of Modern Art, Chicago IL

Rozell, Sarah, *Events Dir,* Gunnison Arts Center, Gunnison CO

Rozier, Robert, *Assoc Prof,* Alma College, Clack Art Center, Dept of Art & Design, Alma MI (S)

Rozman, Joseph, *Prof,* Mount Mary College, Art & Design Division, Milwaukee WI (S)

Roznoy, Cynthia, *Cur,* Mattatuck Historical Society, Mattatuck Museum, Waterbury CT

Rozzi Casey, Lynn, *Dir & Cur,* Nassau Community College, Firehouse Art Gallery, Garden City NY

Rub, Timothy, *The George D Widener Dir & CEO,* Philadelphia Museum of Art, Main Building, Philadelphia PA

Rubenstein, David, *Chmn,* The John F Kennedy Center for the Performing Arts, Washington DC

Rubenstein, Elliott, *Assoc Prof,* Rochester Institute of Technology, School of Photographic Arts & Sciences, Rochester NY (S)

Rubin, James, *Prof,* Stony Brook University, College of Arts & Sciences, Dept of Art, Stony Brook NY (S)

Rubin, Jeff, *Dir Cur Serv,* Louisiana Department of Culture, Recreation & Tourism, Louisiana State Museum, New Orleans LA

Rubin, Michael, *VChmn,* Monmouth Museum & Cultural Center, Lincroft NJ

Rubin, Stephen, *Asst Prof Art (Photog),* Pennsylvania State University, University Park, Penn State School of Visual Arts, University Park PA (S)

Rubini, Gail, *Assoc Prof,* Florida State University, Art Dept, Tallahassee FL (S)

Rubinoff, Michael, *Assoc Dean Visual & Performing Arts,* Sheridan College, Faculty of Animation, Arts & Design, Oakville ON (S)

Rubinstein, Ernest, *Librn,* The Interchurch Center, Library, New York NY

Rubio, Adriana, *Exec Asst,* Museum of Fine Arts, Houston, Rienzi Center for European Decorative Arts, Houston TX

Rubio, Alex, *MOSAIC Artist-in-Res,* Blue Star Contemporary Art Center, San Antonio TX

Rubio, Armando, *Instr,* Bakersfield College, Art Dept, Bakersfield CA (S)

Ruble, Paula, *Reference Tech,* Maysville, Kentucky Gateway Museum Center, Maysville KY

Ruby, Janet, *Assoc Prof,* Shippensburg University, Art Dept, Shippensburg PA (S)

Ruckler, Eric, *Coll Specialist,* State University of New York at Plattsburgh, Art Museum, Plattsburgh NY

Ruda, Jeffrey, *Dir Art History,* University of California, Davis, Dept of Art & Art History, Davis CA (S)

Rudd, Jeremy, *Asst Prof Art,* Divine Word College, Father Weyland SVD Gallery, Epworth IA

Rudder, Joey, *Financial Officer,* Telfair Museums, Savannah GA

Rude, Mathew, *Asst Prof,* Gonzaga University, Dept of Art, Spokane WA (S)

Rudey, Liz, *Prof,* Long Island University, Brooklyn Campus, Art Dept, Brooklyn NY (S)

Rudick, Nancy, *Supv,* Skidmore College, Lucy Scribner Library, Saratoga Springs NY

Rudloff Stanton, Anne, *Secy,* International Center of Medieval Art, New York NY

Rudnick, Michele, *Admin,* Glessner House Museum, Chicago IL

Rudolf, Scooter, *Dir,* New Image Art, West Hollywood CA

Rudolph, Beth, *Exec Dir,* VSA Arts of New Mexico, Enabled Arts Center, Albuquerque NM (S)

Rudolph, Conrad, *Prof,* University of California, Riverside, Dept of the History of Art, Riverside CA (S)

Rudowski, Sharron, *Gallery Coordr,* Arts & Humanities Council of Tuscaloosa, Junior League Gallery, Dinah Washington Cultural Arts Center Galleries, Tuscaloosa AL

Rudy, Carl, *Asst Prof,* Indiana Wesleyan University, School of Arts & Humanities, Division of Art, Marion IN (S)

Rudzykte, Rasa, *Dir Intl Prog,* Balzekas Museum of Lithuanian Culture, Chicago IL

Ruedi, Katerina, *Dir School Archit,* University of Illinois at Chicago, College of Architecture, Chicago IL (S)

Ruedy, Don, *Prof,* University of Wisconsin, Center-Barron County, Dept of Art, Rice Lake WI (S)
Ruehle, Linda, *Arts Educ Dir,* Shiawassee Arts Center, Owosso MI
Ruesch, Andre, *Chair Photog,* Lesley University, College of Art & Design, Cambridge MA (S)
Ruet, Karen, *Gallery Coord,* New Brunswick College of Craft & Design, Gallery, Fredericton NB
Rufe, Laurie, *Dir,* Roswell Museum & Art Center, Roswell NM
Ruff, Elizabeth, *Asst Prof,* Newberry College, Dept of Art, Newberry SC (S)
Ruff, Gloria, *Assoc Cur & Registrar,* Valparaiso University, Brauer Museum of Art, Valparaiso IN
Ruff, Joshua, *Dir Coll & Interpretation,* The Long Island Museum of American Art, History & Carriages, Stony Brook NY
Ruff, Joshua, *Dir Colls & Interpretation,* The Long Island Museum of American Art, History & Carriages, Library, Stony Brook NY
Ruff, Morgen, *Exhib Prog Mgr,* Portland Art Museum, Northwest Film Center, Portland OR
Ruffer, Gregory, *Pres & CEO,* Boston Center for the Arts, Mills Gallery, Boston MA
Ruffin, Ellen, *Cur,* University of Southern Mississippi, McCain Library & Archives, Hattiesburg MS
Ruffini, Marco, *Adjunct Prof,* Northwestern University, Evanston, Dept of Art History, Evanston IL (S)
Ruffler, Kim, *Events Coordinator,* Albin Polasek Museum & Sculpture Gardens, Winter Park FL
Ruffolo, Joyce, *Treas,* Princeton Antiques Bookservice, Art Marketing Reference Library, Atlantic City NJ
Ruffolo, Robert A, *Secy,* Princeton Antiques Bookservice, Art Marketing Reference Library, Atlantic City NJ
Ruffolo, Robert E, *Pres,* Princeton Antiques Bookservice, Art Marketing Reference Library, Atlantic City NJ
Rufkahr, Abby, *Prog & Develop Asst,* Kansas City Jewish Museum of Contemporary Art - Epsten Gallery, Overland Park KS
Ruggerio, Marie, *Mus Shop Mgr,* Bergen County Historical Society, Steuben House Museum, River Edge NJ
Ruggie Saunders, Cathie, *Assoc Prof,* Saint Xavier University, Dept of Art & Design, Chicago IL (S)
Ruggiero, Laurence, *Dir,* Charles Morse, Charles Hosmer Morse Museum of American Art, Winter Park FL
Ruggio, Pamela, *Dir Communs,* Aldrich Museum of Contemporary Art, Ridgefield CT
Ruggles, Janet, *Chief Exec & Chief Paper Conservator,* Balboa Art Conservation Center, San Diego CA
Ruhberg, Regina, *Husby Performing Arts Center Dir,* Washington Pavilion of Arts & Science, Visual Arts Center, Sioux Falls SD
Ruhstaller, Tod, *Dir,* The San Joaquin Pioneer & Historical Society, Petzinger Memorial Library & Earl Rowland Art Library, Stockton CA
Ruhstaller, Tod, *Dir & Cur of History,* The San Joaquin Pioneer & Historical Society, The Haggin Museum, Stockton CA
Ruiz, Amber, *Acting Head, VRC,* Stanford University, Art & Architecture Library, Stanford CA
Rukenbrod Smith, Gwynne, *Exec Dir,* Society of North American Goldsmiths, Eugene OR
Rule, Dan, *Asst Prof,* University of New Orleans-Lake Front, Dept of Fine Arts, New Orleans LA (S)
Ruleaux, Don, *Instr,* Chadron State College, Dept of Art, Chadron NE (S)
Rumery, Caitlin, *Assoc Colls Mgr & Registrar,* University of Colorado, CU Art Museum, Boulder CO
Rumfelt, Heather, *Educ Dir,* Walter Anderson Museum of Art, Ocean Springs MS
Rummel, Hal, *Dept Chair,* Community College of Baltimore County, School of Technology, Art & Design, Catonsville MD (S)
Rummel, Lee, *Facilities Mgr,* Southern Alleghenies Museum of Art, Loretto Facility, Loretto PA
Rumrill, Alan, *Exec Dir,* Historical Society of Cheshire County, Keene NH
Runge, Christen, *Asst Cur,* Georgetown University, Art Collection, Washington DC
Runge, Christen, *Asst Cur,* Georgetown University, Lauinger Library - Special Collections Division, Washington DC
Runge, Teresa, *Gallery Asst,* The Art Spirit Gallery, Coeur D Alene ID
Runnells, Jamie, *Assoc Prof,* Mississippi State University, Dept of Art, Starville MS (S)
Ruppert, John, *Chmn,* University of Maryland, Department of Art, College Park MD (S)
Ruppman, Walter C, *Exec Dir,* Peoria Historical Society, Peoria IL
Rupsch, Christina, *Dean of School of Fine and Applied Arts, Professor of Art,* Chowan College, Dept. of Communication Arts, Fine and Applied Arts, Murfreesboro NC (S)
Ruschman, Mark, *Gallery Coordr,* University of Indianapolis, Christel DeHaan Fine Arts Gallery, Indianapolis IN
Rusfvold, Georgia, *Prog Coordr,* SVACA - Sheyenne Valley Arts & Crafts Association, Bjarne Ness Gallery at Bear Creek Hall, Fort Ransom ND
Rush, Kent, *Prof,* University of Texas at San Antonio, Dept of Art & Art History, San Antonio TX (S)
Rush, Sallee, *Instr,* Main Line Art Center, Haverford PA (S)
Rushing, Kim, *Prof,* Delta State University, Dept of Art, Cleveland MS (S)
Rushing, Mollie Rollins, *Instr,* Delta State University, Dept of Art, Cleveland MS (S)
Rushing, W Jackson, *Chmn,* University of Houston, Dept of Art, Houston TX (S)
Rushmore, RJ, *Digital Mktg Mgr,* Creative Time, New York NY
Rushton, Edward, *Assoc Prod,* Georgia Southern University, Betty Foy Sanders Dept of Art, Statesboro GA (S)
Rusnak, Jeff, *Dir Develop,* Art & Culture Center of Hollywood, Art Gallery/Multidisciplinary Cultural Center, Hollywood FL
Russ, Barbara, *Mus Asst,* Department of Economic & Community Development, State of Connecticut DECD Eric Sloane Museum, Kent CT
Russell Love, Camille, *Dir,* City of Atlanta, Gallery 72, Atlanta GA
Russell, Barry, *Instr Dean Fine Arts,* Cerritos Community College, Fine Arts & Communication Div, Norwalk CA (S)
Russell, Catherine, *Chair, Mel Hoppenheim School of Cinema,* Concordia University, Faculty of Fine Arts, Montreal QC (S)
Russell, Donald H, *Exec Dir,* Art Resources International, Washington DC
Russell, Donald, *Dir & Cur,* Provisions Library, Provisions Research Center for Arts & Social Change, Fairfax VA
Russell, Douglas, *Gallery Dir,* Oregon State University, Fairbanks Gallery, Corvallis OR
Russell, Douglas, *Sr Research Assoc,* Oregon State University, Dept of Art, Corvallis OR (S)
Russell, J Shepherd, *Pres,* Arkansas Arts Center, Little Rock AR (S)
Russell, John, *Chmn Critical Studies,* Massachusetts College of Art, Boston MA (S)
Russell, Katherine, *Dir of Vol Services,* Georgia Lawyers for the Arts, Atlanta GA
Russell, Lisa, *Assoc Prof,* Rhode Island College, Art Dept, Providence RI (S)
Russell, Lynn, *Educ Div Head,* National Gallery of Art, Washington DC
Russell, Marilyn M, *Cur Educ,* Carnegie Museums of Pittsburgh, Carnegie Museum of Art, Pittsburgh PA
Russell, Paul, *Asst Dir,* Plumas County Museum, Quincy CA
Russell, Robert, *Chmn & Assoc Prof Art Educ,* University of Cincinnati, School of Art, Cincinnati OH (S)
Russell, Robert, *Dir, Historic Preservation,* College of Charleston, School of the Arts, Charleston SC (S)
Russell, Sandra, *Dept Adminr,* University of Wisconsin, Madison, Dept of Art History, Madison WI (S)
Russi Kirshner, Judith, *Dean,* University of Illinois at Chicago, College of Architecture, Chicago IL (S)
Russick, John, *VPres Interpretation & Educ,* Chicago History Museum, Chicago IL
Russin, Sarah, *Exec Dir,* LACE (Los Angeles Contemporary Exhibitions), Los Angeles CA
Russo, Barbara, *Fine Arts Mgr,* Cypress College, Cypress CA (S)
Russo, Howard, *Instr,* Elgin Community College, Fine Arts Dept, Elgin IL (S)
Russo, Jillian, *Cur,* Art Students League of New York, New York NY
Russo, Melissa, *Dir,* San Bernardino County Museum, Redlands CA
Russo, Regina, *Dir Commun & Community Engagement,* Contemporary Arts Center, Cincinnati OH
Russo, Susan, *Chmn,* Youngstown State University, Dept of Art, Youngstown OH (S)
Russolo, Lloyd, *Assoc Provost,* Philadelphia University, Philadelphia PA (S)
Rust, Brian, *Prof,* Augusta State University, Dept of Art, Augusta GA (S)
Rusted, Brian, *Art Dept Head,* University of Calgary, Dept of Art, Calgary AB (S)
Rustige, Rona, *Cur,* Glanmore National Historic Site of Canada, Belleville ON
Ruta, Anne, *Colls Mgr,* DAR Museum, Library, Washington DC
Ruth, Nicholas, *Chair,* Hobart & William Smith Colleges, Art Dept, Geneva NY (S)
Rutherford, Sarah, *Asst Prof,* Cleveland State University, Art Dept, Cleveland OH (S)
Rutigliano, Vincenzo, *Librn,* The New York Public Library, Art & Architecture Collection, New York NY
Rutkovsky, Paul, *Assoc Prof,* Florida State University, Art Dept, Tallahassee FL (S)
Rutkowski, Sandra, *Dir Libr Svcs,* Lourdes College, Duns Scotus Library, Sylvania OH
Rutland, Beau, *Assoc Cur Contemporary Art,* The Cleveland Museum of Art, Cleveland OH
Rutter, Deborah, *Pres,* The John F Kennedy Center for the Performing Arts, Washington DC
Ruttner, Nancy, *Dir,* Art Institute of Pittsburgh, John P. Barclay Memorial Gallery, Pittsburgh PA
Ruxlow, Anna, *Dir,* McPherson Museum and Arts Foundation, McPherson KS
Ruzi, Gino, *Asst Cur,* American Museum of Ceramic Art, Pomona CA
Ryan Kelley, Heather, *Coordr,* McNeese State University, Dept of Visual Arts, Abercrombie Gallery and Grand Gallery, Lake Charles LA
Ryan, Barbara, *Contact Person,* Broward Community College - A. Hugh Adams Campus, Fine Arts Gallery, Davie FL
Ryan, Chris, *Assoc Prof, Dept Chair,* Hiram College, Art Dept, Hiram OH (S)
Ryan, David, *Chief Preparator & Bldg Coordr,* Cornell University, Herbert F Johnson Museum of Art, Ithaca NY
Ryan, Denise, *Co-owner,* Eureka Fine Art Gallery, Eureka Springs AR
Ryan, Donna B, *Newsletter Ed/Sec,* Almond Historical Society, Inc, Hagadorn House, The 1800-37 Museum, Almond NY
Ryan, Helen, *Admin Asst to the Arts,* Drew University, Art Dept Library, Madison NJ
Ryan, Joleen, *Asst Cur Children's Mus,* Sangre de Cristo Arts & Conference Center, Pueblo CO
Ryan, Linda Lee, *Prog Dir,* Casper College, Dept of Visual Arts, Casper WY (S)
Ryan, Mark, *Assistant Director for Collections & Exhibitions,* Washington University, Mildred Lane Kemper Art Museum, Saint Louis MO
Ryan, Michael, *VPres & Dir of Patricia D Klingstein Library,* New-York Historical Society, Library, New York NY
Ryan, Michael, *VPres & Library Dir,* New-York Historical Society, Museum, New York NY

Ryan, Paul, *Assoc Prof,* Mary Baldwin College, Dept of Art & Art History, Staunton VA (S)

Ryan, Raymond, *Cur Architecture,* Carnegie Museums of Pittsburgh, Carnegie Museum of Art, Pittsburgh PA

Ryan, Susan, *Asst,* Louisiana State University, School of Art, Baton Rouge LA (S)

Ryan, Tim, *Special Projects Mgr,* Delaplaine Visual Arts Education Center, Frederick MD

Ryan-Cook, Joelle, *Deputy Dir & Dir External Affairs,* Columbia Museum of Art, Columbia SC

Rychlak, Bonnie, *Cur,* Isamu Noguchi, Isamu Noguchi Garden Museum, Long Island City NY

Ryckbosch, Bart, *Institutional Archivist,* The Art Institute of Chicago, Ryerson & Burnham Libraries, Chicago IL

Rydell, Christine, *Instr,* Solano Community College, Division of Fine & Applied Art & Behavioral Science, Fairfield CA (S)

Ryder-O'Malley, Grace, *Educ Asst,* Provincetown Art Association & Museum, Provincetown MA

Rye, Leigh, *Sec,* Reading Public Museum, Reading PA

Rykels, Sam, *Mus Dir,* Louisiana Department of Culture, Recreation & Tourism, Louisiana State Museum, New Orleans LA

Ryker-Crawford, Jessie, *Mus Studies Dept Chair,* Institute of American Indian Arts, Museum of Contemporary Native Arts, Santa Fe NM (S)

Ryles, Susan, *Dir,* Glynn Visual Arts, Inc, Saint Simons Island GA

Rzoska, Linda, *Instr,* Kalamazoo Valley Community College, Center for New Media, Kalamazoo MI (S)

Saari, Maija, *Assoc Dean Film Television & Journalism,* Sheridan College, Faculty of Animation, Arts & Design, Oakville ON (S)

Saarnio, Robert, *Dir,* University of Mississippi, University Museum & Historic Houses, Oxford MS

Sabin, Jenny, *Dir Grad Studies,* Cornell University, Dept of Architecture, Ithaca NY (S)

Sabine, Kathleen, *Adjunct,* Sheridan College, Art Dept, Sheridan WY (S)

Sablow, Mark, *Prof,* Florida Community College at Jacksonville, South Campus, Art Dept, Jacksonville FL (S)

Sacaridiz, Paul, *Dir,* Haystack Mountain School of Crafts, Deer Isle ME (S)

Sacaridiz, Paul, *Dir,* Haystack Mountain School of Crafts, Center for Community Programs Gallery, Deer Isle ME

Sacaridiz, Paul, *Dir,* Haystack Mountain School of Crafts, Deer Isle ME

Saccone, Tony, *Facilities Mgr,* Mystic Art Association, Inc, Mystic Museum of Art, Mystic CT

Sachs, Sid, *Dir Exhibs,* The University of the Arts, Rosenwald-Wolf Gallery, Philadelphia PA

Sack, Bill, *Tech Dir,* Hallwalls Contemporary Arts Center, Buffalo NY

Sackel, Matthew, *Art Hist Librn,* University of Wisconsin-Stevens Point, Dept of Art & Design, Stevens Point WI (S)

Sackett, Margot Magee, *Dir,* Ross Memorial Museum, Saint Andrews NB

Sackey, Janet, *Communs & Social Media Coordr,* Caribbean Cultural Center African Diaspora Institute, Cultural Arts Organization & Resource Center, New York NY

Sackman, Elmer, *Librn,* Fort Worth Public Library Arts & Humanities, Fine Arts Section, Fort Worth TX

Sacks, Karen, *Instr,* Wayne Art Center, Wayne PA (S)

Sade, Marianne, *Instructional Librn,* Maryland Institute, Decker Library, Baltimore MD

Sadler Takach, Bonnie, *Coordr Visual Communs Design,* University of Alberta, Dept of Art & Design, Edmonton AB (S)

Sadler, Cody, *Co-Dir,* Canadian Wildlife & Wilderness Art Museum, Ottawa ON

Sadler, Cody, *Co-Dir,* Canadian Wildlife & Wilderness Art Museum, Library, Ottawa ON

Sadler, Donna, *Chmn Art Dept,* Agnes Scott College, Dalton Art Gallery, Decatur GA

Sadler, Ginna, *Prof,* Abilene Christian University, Dept of Art & Design, Abilene TX (S)

Saenger, Allana, *Cur Exhibits,* Riley County Historical Society & Museum, Riley County Historical Museum, Manhattan KS

Saenger, Allana, *Exhibits,* Riley County Historical Society & Museum, Seaton Library, Manhattan KS

Saenz, Marisela, *Admin Asst,* Hidalgo County Historical Museum, Edinburg TX

Safiran, Ed, *Asst Site Mgr,* Illinois Historic Preservation Agency, Bishop Hill State Historic Site, Bishop Hill IL

Saganic, Livio, *Prof,* Drew University, Art Dept, Madison NJ (S)

Sage, Colleen, *Human Resources Mgr,* The Adirondack Historical Association, The Adirondack Museum, Blue Mountain Lake NY

Sage, Marisa, *Dir,* New Mexico State University, Art Gallery, Las Cruces NM

Sager, Judy, *Owner,* Sager Studios, Fort Worth TX (S)

Sahdana-Melber, Soledad, *Educ Dir,* Pacific Northwest Art School, Gallery at the Wharf, Coupeville WA

Said, Tania, *Dir Educ,* Ball State University, David Owsley Museum of Art, Muncie IN

Saidel, Alice, *Ref Librn,* Dayton Art Institute, Library, Dayton OH

Saikai, Paul, *Coordr, Graphic Design,* York College of Pennsylvania, Dept of Music, Art & Speech Communications, York PA (S)

Saile, Anne, *Interim Dir,* The Hyde Collection, Glens Falls NY

Sailer, Stephanie, *Recruiter,* Northern Illinois University, School of Art & Design, DeKalb IL (S)

Sajet, Kim, *Dir,* National Portrait Gallery, Smithsonian Institution, Washington DC

Sakel, Keelin, *Exhibs,* Santa Cruz Art League, Center for the Arts, Santa Cruz CA

Sakoulas, Thomas, *Prof,* State University of New York College at Oneonta, Dept of Art, Oneonta NY (S)

Saks, Dawn, *Instr,* Century College, Humanities Dept, White Bear Lake MN (S)

Sakurai, Motoatsu, *Pres Japan Society,* Japan Society, Inc, Japan Society Gallery, New York NY

Sala Pomeranz, Christine, *Chmn International Trade,* Fashion Institute of Technology, School of Art & Design, New York NY (S)

Salam, Halide, *Prof,* Radford University, Art Dept, Radford VA (S)

Salart-Pans, Salvador, *Dir,* Detroit Institute of Arts, Detroit MI

Salas, Rafael, *Chmn,* Ripon College, Art Dept, Ripon WI (S)

Salas, Rafael, *Dir,* Ripon College Caestecker Art Gallery, Ripon WI

Salata, Benjamen, *Cur Colls,* Historical Society of Palm Beach County, The Richard and Pat Johnson Palm Beach County History Museum, West Palm Beach FL

Salazar, Carolina, *Executive Administrative Assistant,* Miami-Dade College, MDC Museum of Art & Design, Miami FL

Salazar, Jim Bob, *Asst Prof,* Sul Ross State University, Dept of Fine Arts & Communications, Alpine TX (S)

Salazar, Lauren, *Head Merchandising,* Hillwood Museum & Gardens Foundation, Hillwood Estate Museum & Gardens, Washington DC

Salazar, Ramiro, *Dir,* Central Library, Dept of Fine Arts, San Antonio TX

Salazar, Roberto, *HR Coordr,* University of California, Los Angeles, Fowler Museum at UCLA, Los Angeles CA

Salazar, Rosemarie, *Supv Ranger,* Mesa Verde National Park, Research Library, Mesa Verde National Park CO

Salazar, Stacey, *Dir,* Maryland Institute, Graduate Art Education, Baltimore MD (S)

Salberg, Lester, *Prof,* Rock Valley College, Humanities and Fine Arts Division, Rockford IL (S)

Sale, Tom, *Dir,* Navarro College, Art Dept, Corsicana TX (S)

Salerno, Dawn, *Deputy Dir Pub Engagement & Opers,* Mystic Art Association, Inc, Mystic Museum of Art, Mystic CT

Salesses, John J, *Pres,* Newport Historical Society & Museum of Newport History, Newport RI

Salgian, Mitzura, *Pres,* Allied Artists of America, Inc, Florham Park NJ

Salic, Patricia, *Develop Dir,* The Society of Arts & Crafts, Boston MA

Saliga, Pauline, *Exec Dir,* Society of Architectural Historians, Chicago IL

Saligumba, Roberta, *Fiscal Officer,* California African-American Museum, Los Angeles CA

Saliklis, Ruta, *Exhib & Develop Dir,* San Luis Obispo Museum of Art, San Luis Obispo CA

Salinas, Juan Carlos, *Educ Dir,* Jamaica Center for Arts & Learning (JCAL), Jamaica NY

Salinas, Vickie, *Pres,* Fusion: The Ontario Clay & Glass Association, Fusion Clay & Glass Association, Toronto ON

Salinger, Adrienne, *Regents Prof,* University of New Mexico, Department of Fine Arts & Art History, Albuquerque NM (S)

Salisbury, Anne, *Instr,* Saint John's University, Art Dept, Collegeville MN (S)

Salisbury, Mackenzie, *Reference & Instruction Librn,* School of the Art Institute of Chicago, John M Flaxman Library, Chicago IL

Salisbury, Tami, *Exec Dir,* Paint Creek Center for the Arts, Rochester MI

Sallee, Roberta, *Pres,* Blacksburg Regional Art Association, Blacksburg VA

Sallinger, Joan, *Foundations,* Orange Coast College, Visual & Performing Arts Division, Costa Mesa CA (S)

Sallozzo, Anne, *Bus Progs Mgr,* Hartwick College, The Yager Museum, Oneonta NY

Salmi, Lyle J, *Art Dept Chair,* Millikin University, Perkinson Gallery, Decatur IL

Salmi, Lyle, *Chmn Art Dept,* Millikin University, Art Dept, Decatur IL (S)

Salmon, Lori, *Librn,* The New York Public Library, Art & Architecture Collection, New York NY

Salmon, Ray, *Instr,* Solano Community College, Division of Fine & Applied Art & Behavioral Science, Fairfield CA (S)

Salmon, Robin, *VPres & Cur,* Brookgreen Gardens, Murrells Inlet SC

Salmon, Robin, *VPres Sculpture,* Brookgreen Gardens, Library, Murrells Inlet SC

Salmond, Wendy, *Chmn,* Chapman University, Art Dept, Orange CA (S)

Salmond, Wendy, *Prof,* Chapman University, Art Dept, Orange CA (S)

Salomon, Colleen, *Digital Specialist,* Scripps College, Ruth Chandler Williamson Gallery, Claremont CA

Salomon, Nanette, *Prof,* College of Staten Island, Performing & Creative Arts Dept, Staten Island NY (S)

Salomon, Peter, *Bus Mgr,* Laguna Art Museum, Laguna Beach CA

Salomon, Suzanne, *Chair Art Comt,* New Canaan Library, H. Pelham Curtis Gallery, New Canaan CT

Salomon, Xavier, *Chief Cur,* Frick Collection, New York NY

Salopek, Alexander, *Access Servs Librn,* Trinity College Library, Washington DC

Salsbury, Kathleen, *Asst Librn,* Munson-Williams-Proctor Arts Institute, Art Reference Library, Utica NY

Salter, Mandy, *Dir & Cur,* Art Gallery of Mississauga, Mississauga ON

Saltz, Ina, *Prof,* City College of New York, Art Dept, New York NY (S)

Saltz, Laura, *Asst Prof,* Colby College, Art Dept, Waterville ME (S)

Saluti, Andrew, *Asst Dir Mus Opers,* Syracuse University, SUArt Galleries, Syracuse NY

Salvator, Marilee, *Asst Prof,* Bloomsburg University, Dept of Art & Art History, Bloomsburg PA (S)

Salvayon, Leon L, *Multimedia & Web Design,* Art Institute of Pittsburgh, Pittsburgh PA (S)

Salvest, John J, *Assoc Prof,* Arkansas State University, Dept of Art, State University AR (S)

Salway, Gareth, *Chief Registrar,* Worcester Art Museum, Worcester MA

Salway, Randy, *Exhibs Designer Preparator,* Ball State University, David Owsley Museum of Art, Muncie IN
Salzillo, William, *Prof,* Hamilton College, Art Dept, Clinton NY (S)
Salzman, Kevin, *Asst Prof,* Wittenberg University, Art Dept, Springfield OH (S)
Samaras, Connie, *Prof Photog & Media Theory,* University of California, Irvine, Studio Art Dept, Irvine CA (S)
Samborska, Paulina, *Curatorial Programming Coord,* Otis College of Art & Design, Ben Maltz Gallery, Los Angeles CA
Samitz Cohen, Phyllis, *Dir Public Art,* Municipal Art Society of New York, New York NY
Sammons, Richard, *Assoc Prof,* Bismarck State College, Fine Arts Dept, Bismarck ND (S)
Samoylova, Anastasia, *Asst Prof,* Illinois Central College, Arts & Communication Dept, East Peoria IL (S)
Sampson, Cherie, *Assoc Prof (Environmental Sculpture, Video & Performance),* University of Missouri - Columbia, Dept of Art, Columbia MO (S)
Sampson, Debra, *Dir,* Academy of Art, University Library, San Francisco CA
Sampson, George, *Lectr Arts Admin,* University of Virginia, McIntire Dept of Art, Charlottesville VA (S)
Samuel-Siegel, Tamar, *Special Projects Coord,* The ARTS Council of the Southern Finger Lakes, Corning NY
Samuels, Clifford, *Dir,* Trova Foundation, Philip Samuels Fine Art, Saint Louis MO
Samuels, Philip, *Pres,* Trova Foundation, Philip Samuels Fine Art, Saint Louis MO
Samuelson, Claire, *Cur,* Headquarters Fort Monroe, Dept of Army, Casemate Museum, Hampton VA
Samuelson, Jerry, *Dean School of Arts,* California State University, Fullerton, Art Dept, Fullerton CA (S)
San Martin, Unai, *Custom Printing Mgr,* Kala Institute, Kala Art Institute, Berkeley CA
San Miguel, Carmen Febo, *Exec Dir,* Taller Puertorriqueno Inc, Lorenzo Homar Gallery, Philadelphia PA
Sanborn, Reilly, *Exec Dir,* Foothills Art Center, Inc, Golden CO
Sanborn, Rhonda, *Develop,* Florida CraftArt, Saint Petersburg FL
Sanchez Kouassi, Maria, *Educ Dir,* Essex Art Center, Lawrence MA
Sanchez Villarreal, Ernesto, *Head Design & Installation,* Oklahoma City Museum of Art, Oklahoma City OK
Sanchez, Jacquelyn Roesch, *Dir,* Montclair Art Museum, Yard School of Art, Montclair NJ (S)
Sanchez, Jesse, *Pres,* New Rochelle Public Library, New Rochelle Art Association, New Rochelle NY
Sanchez, Nereida, *Exec Sec,* New York Society of Architects, New York NY
Sanchez, Stephanie, *Chmn,* Santa Rosa Junior College, Art Dept, Santa Rosa CA (S)
Sanchez, Virginia, *Research Libr,* Yosemite Museum, Yosemite National Park CA
Sanchez, Yesenia, *Dir Finance & Organization Develop,* Intersection for the Arts, San Francisco CA
Sanchez-Dallam, Marta, *Adj Prof,* Saint Joseph's University, Art Dept, Philadelphia PA (S)
Sanchez-Rodriguez, Nilda, *Librn,* City College of the City University of New York, Architecture Library, New York NY
Sancho Lobis, Victoria, *Prince Trust Interim Chair & Cur Prints & Drawings,* The Art Institute of Chicago, Dept of Prints & Drawings, Chicago IL
Sandall, Andrew, *Dir,* The Museum of Arts & Sciences Inc, Daytona Beach FL
Sandals, Leah, *Assoc Ed,* Canadian Art Foundation, Toronto ON
Sandbeck, Derek, *Gallery Coord,* AKA Artist Run Centre, Saskatoon SK
Sandberg, Emmet, *Asst Prof,* University of Wisconsin Oshkosh, Dept of Art, Oshkosh WI (S)
Sandberg, Sharon, *Adjunct Assoc Prof Painting,* Aquinas College, Art Dept, Grand Rapids MI (S)
Sanders, Frank, *Facility Mgr,* American Swedish Historical Foundation & Museum, American Swedish Historical Museum, Philadelphia PA
Sanders, Jan, *Dir,* Pasadena Public Library, Fine Arts Dept, Pasadena CA
Sanders, Jay, *Exec Dir & Chief Cur,* Artists Space, New York NY
Sanders, Jay, *Exec Dir & Chief Cur,* Artists Space, Artists Space Gallery, New York NY
Sanders, Jean, *Assoc Prof Art (Printmaking & New Media),* Pennsylvania State University, University Park, Penn State School of Visual Arts, University Park PA (S)
Sanders, Joe, *Assoc Prof Printmaking,* University of Georgia, Franklin College of Arts & Sciences, Lamar Dodd School of Art, Athens GA (S)
Sanders, Joy, *Gift Shop,* Saint Joseph Museum, Inc., Saint Joseph MO
Sanders, Mark, *Educ Dir,* WaterWorks Art Museum, Miles City MT
Sanders, Philip, *Asst Prof,* The College of New Jersey, School of Arts & Sciences, Ewing NJ (S)
Sanders, Randy, *Dir,* East Tennessee State University, The Reece Museum, Johnson City TN
Sanders, Rebecca, *Dir Art School,* Boca Raton Museum of Art, Boca Raton FL
Sanders, Tom, *Site Mgr,* Jeffers Petroglyphs Historic Site, Comfrey MN
Sanders, William, *Instr,* Surry Community College, Art Dept, Dobson NC (S)
Sanderson, Brandon, *Asst Prof,* University of North Carolina at Pembroke, Art Dept, Pembroke NC (S)
Sanderson, Doug, *Asst Prof,* Oberlin College, Dept of Art, Oberlin OH (S)
Sanderson, Sheri, *Events, Gift Shop,* LeMoyne Art Foundation, Center for the Visual Arts, Tallahassee FL
Sandford, Debra, *Head Youth Svcs,* Springfield Free Public Library, Donald B Palmer Museum, Springfield NJ
Sandhoff, Bridget, *Asst Prof,* University of Nebraska at Omaha, School of the Arts, Omaha NE (S)
Sandino, Margarita, *Cur Educ,* The Dixon Gallery & Gardens, Memphis TN
Sandman, Keith, *Prof,* Munson-Williams-Proctor Arts Institute, Pratt MWP College of Art, Utica NY (S)
Sandone, Corinne, *Assoc Prof,* Johns Hopkins University, School of Medicine, Dept of Art as Applied to Medicine, Baltimore MD (S)
Sandore Namachchivay, Beth, *Univ Librn,* University of Waterloo, Dana Porter Library, Waterloo ON
Sandoval, Angelica, *Adjunct Assoc Prof Fine Art,* Johnson County Community College, Fine Arts Dept & Art History Dept, Overland Park KS (S)
Sandoval, Claudia, *Coordr,* City of Brea, Art Gallery, Brea CA
Sandoval, Jeanny, *Gallery Educ,* CAM Contemporary Art Museum, Raleigh NC
Sands, Craig, *Adjunct Asst Prof Photog,* Johnson County Community College, Fine Arts Dept & Art History Dept, Overland Park KS (S)
Sands, Janice, *Dir,* Pen & Brush, Inc, Library, New York NY
Sands, Janice, *Exec Dir,* Pen & Brush, Inc, New York NY
Sands, Melissa, *Exec Financial Officer,* Royal BC Museum, Victoria BC
Sandstedt, Kathy, *Store Mgr & Exec Sec.,* University of Minnesota Duluth, Tweed Museum of Art, Duluth MN
Sandulli, Justin M, *Visual Arts Comt Chair,* Duke University Union, Louise Jones Brown Gallery, Durham NC
Sanfilippo, Amanda, *Cur & Artist Mgr,* South Florida Cultural Consortium, Miami Dade County Dept of Cultural Affairs, Miami FL
Sanford, Eva, *Adult Librn,* Willard Library, Dept of Fine Arts, Evansville IN
Sangelo, Trish, *Gallery Coordr,* Arapahoe Community College, Colorado Gallery of the Arts, Littleton CO
Sanger, Carrie, *Mktg & Pub Rels Mgr,* Southern Methodist University, Meadows Museum, Dallas TX
Sanger, Erika, *Dir Educ,* Albany Institute of History & Art, Albany NY
Saniat, Christine, *Registrar & Exhib Dir,* University of Illinois at Urbana-Champaign, Krannert Art Museum and Kinkead Pavilion, Champaign IL
Sano, Emily, *Cur Asian Art,* San Antonio Museum of Art, San Antonio TX
Sanpei, Sandra, *Dept Head,* Honolulu Community College, Commercial Art Dept, Honolulu HI (S)
Sanso, Alex, *Chief Storyteller,* Bainbridge Arts & Crafts Gallery, Bainbridge Island WA
Sansone, Kristina Lamour, *Chair Design,* Lesley University, College of Art & Design, Cambridge MA (S)
Santamaria, Jose, *Dir & Cur,* Tellus Northwest Georgia Science Museum, Cartersville GA
Santana, Azela, *Assoc Cur,* Orlando Museum of Art, Orlando Sentinel Library, Orlando FL
Santana, Azela, *Assoc Cur,* Orlando Museum of Art, Orlando FL
Santana, Nil, *Prof,* Abilene Christian University, Dept of Art & Design, Abilene TX (S)
Santana, Sharlene, *Cur Mammals,* University of Washington, Burke Museum of Natural History and Culture, Seattle WA
Santangelo, Mark, *Chief Librn & Archivist,* George Washington's Mount Vernon, The Fred W Smith National Library for the Study of George Washington, Mount Vernon VA
Santee, Ruth, *Instr,* San Joaquin Delta College, Arts & Communication, Stockton CA (S)
Santelli, Thomas, *Assoc Prof,* The College of Saint Rose, The Center For Art and Design, Albany NY (S)
Santiago, Chakira, *Colls Registrar,* University of Puerto Rico, Museum of Anthropology, History & Art, Rio Piedras PR
Santiago, Fernando, *Assoc Prof,* Inter American University of Puerto Rico, Fine Arts Dept -Art Program, San German PR (S)
Santiago, Yashira, *Admin Coordr,* Charter Oak Cultural Center, Hartford CT
Santina, Adrianne, *Instr,* Linfield College, Department of Art & Visual Culture, McMinnville OR (S)
Santmyers, Stephanie, *Chmn,* North Carolina Agricultural & Technical State University, Visual Arts Dept, Greensboro NC (S)
Santorella, Julie, *Asst Dir,* Bowdoin College, Peary-MacMillan Arctic Museum, Brunswick ME
Santoro, Geraldine, *Cur Coll,* The National Park Service, United States Department of the Interior, Statue of Liberty National Monument & The Ellis Island Immigration Museum, Washington DC
Santos, Lori, *Prof,* University of Nebraska, Kearney, Dept of Art & Art History, Kearney NE (S)
Santos, Tammy, *Prog Coordr,* Allied Arts Council of St Joseph, Saint Joseph MO
Santoso, Dee, *Deputy Dir,* Manchester City Library, Manchester NH
Sanyal, Bish, *Urban Studies & Planning,* Massachusetts Institute of Technology, School of Architecture and Planning, Cambridge MA (S)
Sapienza, Ellen, *Registrar,* Lafayette College, Lafayette College Art Galleries, Easton PA
Sapp, David, *Prof Art,* Bowling Green State University, Firelands College, Humanities Dept, Huron OH (S)
Sapp, Kelly, *Show Mgr,* The Association of International Photography Art Dealers, Washington DC
Sapp, Rocky, *Assoc Prof Sculpture,* University of Georgia, Franklin College of Arts & Sciences, Lamar Dodd School of Art, Athens GA (S)
Saracino, Jennifer, *Faculty,* Yakima Valley Community College, Dept of Visual Arts, Yakima WA (S)
Sarault, Sylvie, *Dir Human Resources,* National Gallery of Canada, Ottawa ON
Sargent, Shannon, *Exhib & Coll Coordr,* Sioux City Art Center, Sioux City IA (S)

Sargent, Shannon, *Instr,* Morningside College, Art Dept, Sioux City IA (S)

Sarli, Kristin, *Mgr Special Events,* The American Federation of Arts, New York NY

Sarmiento, Leo, *Publ Relations & Community Partnership Mgr,* Art & Culture Center of Hollywood, Art Gallery/Multidisciplinary Cultural Center, Hollywood FL

Sarmiento, Roberto, *Pres,* Special Libraries Association, Mc Lean VA

Sarnacki, Michael, *Dir,* Detroit Focus, Royal Oak MI

Sarno, Lisa, *Asst Gen Mgr,* El Pueblo de Los Angeles Historical Monument, Los Angeles CA

Sarns, Mary, *Dept Chair,* Willoughby School of Fine Arts, Visual Arts Dept, Willoughby OH (S)

Sarofim, Louisa S, *Chmn,* Menil Foundation, Inc, The Menil Collection, Houston TX

Saroyan, Ione, *Dir Merchandis Opers,* New-York Historical Society, Museum, New York NY

Sarre, Camille, *Assoc Prof,* Murray State University, Dept of Art, Murray KY (S)

Sarris, Rita, *Dir,* Arts & Crafts Association of Meriden Inc, Gallery 53, Meriden CT

Sarris, Rita, *Gallery Dir,* Arts & Crafts Association of Meriden Inc, Gallery 53, Meriden CT

Sarser, Clair, *Admin Asst,* Northport-East Northport Public Library, Northport NY

Sartor, Curtis, *Instr,* Judson University, School of Art, Design & Architecture, Elgin IL (S)

Sartwell, Crispin, *Assoc Prof,* Dickinson College, Dept of Art & Art History, Carlisle PA (S)

Sarver, Jennifer, *Dir Educ,* Cedarhurst Center for the Arts, Mitchell Museum, Mount Vernon IL

Sarver, Jill, *Visual Arts Coordr,* Westport Arts Center, Westport CT

Sasaki, Lisa, *Interim Dir,* Anacostia Community Museum, Smithsonian Institution, Washington DC

Saslow, James M, *Prof,* City University of New York, PhD Program in Art History, New York NY (S)

Saslow, James, *Chmn,* Queens College, Art Dept, Flushing NY (S)

Sassa, Reiko, *Dir,* Japan Society, Inc, C.V. Starr Library, New York NY

Sasse, Julie, *Chief Cur & Cur Modern & Contemporary Art,* Tucson Museum of Art and Historic Block, Tucson AZ

Sasser, Morgan, *People & Community Practice Mgr,* Arts Council Of New Orleans, New Orleans LA

Sasser, Teiko, *Instr,* Sacramento City College, Art Dept, Sacramento CA (S)

Sasso, Paul, *Prof,* Murray State University, Dept of Art, Murray KY (S)

Satake, Shoji, *Assoc Prof,* West Virginia University, College of Creative Arts, School of Art & Design, Morgantown WV (S)

Satalino, Jennifer, *Dir Enrol,* Pacific Northwest College of Art, Portland OR (S)

Satchell, Ernest R, *Coordr Art Educ,* University of Maryland Eastern Shore, Art & Technology Dept, Princess Anne MD (S)

Sattar, Haroom, *Assoc Prof,* University of Central Missouri, Dept of Art & Design, Warrensburg MO (S)

Satterfield, Debra, *Assoc Prof,* Arkansas State University, Dept of Art, State University AR (S)

Satterfield, Debra, *Coordr Graphic Design,* Iowa State University, Dept of Art & Design, Ames IA (S)

Satterlee, Corinne, *Head Children's Prog,* Kalamazoo Institute of Arts, KIA School, Kalamazoo MI (S)

Satterlee, Craig, *Assoc Prof,* Northwest Community College, Dept of Art, Powell WY (S)

Satterlee, Joy, *Exec Dir,* Art & Culture Center of Hollywood, Art Gallery/Multidisciplinary Cultural Center, Hollywood FL

Sauder, Molly, *Archivist & Librn,* The Old Jail Art Center, Albany TX

Sauder, Molly, *Archivist/Librn,* The Old Jail Art Center, Green Research Library, Albany TX

Sauer, Nancy, *Office Mgr,* Rockford Art Museum, Rockford IL

Sauer, Stacy, *Educ Coordr & Mus Asst,* Rockford Art Museum, Rockford IL

Saul, Rachel, *Studio Prog Coordr,* Society for Contemporary Craft, Pittsburgh PA

Saumders, Gregory, *Adj Instr,* University of West Florida, Dept of Art, Pensacola FL (S)

Saunders, Jeanette, *Registrar,* University of California, Los Angeles, Fowler Museum at UCLA, Los Angeles CA

Saunders, Kathy, *Comp,* Huntington Museum of Art, Huntington WV

Saunders, Preston, *Asst Prof,* Bridgewater State College, Art Dept, Bridgewater MA (S)

Saunders, Richard, *Dir,* Middlebury College, Museum of Art, Middlebury VT

Saunders, Richard, *Dir College Museum,* Middlebury College, History of Art & Architecture Dept, Middlebury VT (S)

Saunders, Susanna T, *Instr,* Main Line Art Center, Haverford PA (S)

Saupe, Ted, *Assoc Prof Ceramics,* University of Georgia, Franklin College of Arts & Sciences, Lamar Dodd School of Art, Athens GA (S)

Sautman, Anne, *Dir Educ,* University of Illinois at Urbana-Champaign, Krannert Art Museum and Kinkead Pavilion, Champaign IL

Sauvage, Suzanne, *Pres & CEO,* McCord Museum of Canadian History, Montreal QC

Sauvage, Suzanne, *Pres & CEO,* The Stewart Museum, Montreal QC

Sauzer, Jennifer, *Head Access Serv & Assessment,* Columbia College Chicago, Library, Chicago IL

Savage, Cort, *Prof,* Davidson College, Art Dept, Davidson NC (S)

Savage, J Thomas, *Dir Museum Affairs,* Winterthur Museum, Winterthur Museum, Garden & Library, Winterthur DE

Savage, Kirk, *Chmn,* University of Pittsburgh, Henry Clay Frick Dept History of Art & Architecture, Pittsburgh PA (S)

Savage, Niall, *Assoc Prof & Undergrad Coordr,* Dalhousie University, School of Architecture, Halifax NS (S)

Saverino, Rocco, *CFO Fin & Info Tech,* Art Gallery of Ontario, Toronto ON

Saviello, Debbie, *Mus Shop Mgr,* The Barnum Museum, Bridgeport CT

Savig, Berndt, *Assoc Prof,* Red Rocks Community College, Arts Dept, Lakewood CO (S)

Savini, Richard, *Prof,* California State University, Art Dept, Turlock CA (S)

Savoy, Daniel, *Assoc Prof,* Manhattan College, Visual & Performing Arts Dept, Bronx NY (S)

Savu, Cristina, *Registrar,* Massillon Museum, Massillon OH

Saw, James T, *Assoc Prof,* Palomar Community College, Art Dept, San Marcos CA (S)

Sawada, Naomi, *Mgr Pub Progs,* University of British Columbia, Morris & Helen Belkin Art Gallery, Vancouver BC

Sawicki, Nicholas, *Assoc Prof,* Lehigh University, Dept of Art, Architecture & Design, Bethlehem PA (S)

Sawyer, Drew, *Head Exhibs & Assoc Cur Photog,* Columbus Museum of Art, Columbus OH

Sawyer, Janet, *Secy,* Blue Mountain Gallery, New York NY

Sawyer, Tamra, *Instr,* Dallas Baptist University, Dept of Art, Dallas TX (S)

Saxon, Mark, *Instr,* Milwaukee Area Technical College, School of Media & Creative Arts, Milwaukee WI (S)

Saxton, Nathan, *Sr Exhib Specialist,* University of Arizona, Museum of Art & Archive of Visual Arts, Tucson AZ

Sayre, Henry, *Prof,* Oregon State University, Dept of Art, Corvallis OR (S)

Sayre, Roger, *Prof,* Pace University, Dyson College of Arts & Sciences, Pleasantville NY (S)

Saywell, Edward, *Chief Exhibs Strategy,* Museum of Fine Arts, Boston MA

Sbarge, Suzanne, *Exec Dir,* 516 ARTS, Albuquerque NM

Scala, Laura, *Sr Dir Develop,* Genesee Country Village & Museum, John L Wehle Art Gallery, Mumford NY

Scallen, Catherine, *Assoc Prof, Dept Chmn,* Case Western Reserve University, Dept of Art History & Art, Cleveland OH (S)

Scalmato, Anthony, *Dept Head Admin & Int Dept Head Game Design,* Cleveland Institute of Art, Cleveland OH (S)

Scaltreto, Dawn, *Recording Secy,* New England Watercolor Society, Boston MA

Scamahorn, Dru, *Librn,* Amarillo Art Association, Library, Amarillo TX

Scandaliato, Lisa, *Asst Dir,* Queensborough Community College, Art Gallery, Bayside NY

Scanlan, Jennifer, *Curatorial & Exhibs Dir,* Oklahoma Contemporary Arts Center, Oklahoma City OK

Scannella, John, *Cur Paleontology,* Montana State University, Museum of the Rockies, Bozeman MT

Scaramella, Julie, *Dir,* Boston Sculptors at Chapel Gallery, West Newton MA

Scarborough, Don, *Pres,* Anson County Historical Society, Inc, Wadesboro NC

Scarborough, Klare, *Dir & Chief Cur,* La Salle University Art Museum, Philadelphia PA

Scarbrough, Karly, *Libr Dir,* Cochise College, Charles Di Peso Library, Douglas AZ

Scarlato, William, *Prof,* Illinois Benedictine University, Department of Fine Arts, Lisle IL (S)

Scary, Rocio, *Adjunct Prof,* College of Saint Elizabeth, Art Dept, Morristown NJ (S)

Scavone, Jennifer, *Instr,* Illinois Benedictine University, Department of Fine Arts, Lisle IL (S)

Scerbo, Drusiano, *Prof,* Elizabeth City State University, School of Arts & Humanities, Dept of Art, Elizabeth City NC (S)

Scerbo, Jean, *Mus Store Mgr,* Saint Augustine Historical Society, Oldest House Museum Complex, Saint Augustine FL

Schaad, Dee, *Chair,* University of Indianapolis, Dept Art & Design, Indianapolis IN (S)

Schaber, Ken, *Instr,* Lake Michigan College, Dept of Art & Science, Benton Harbor MI (S)

Schaber, Todd, *Mgr & Cur Traveling Exhibs,* The Art Gallery of Grand Prairie, Grande Prairie AB

Schachenmeyer, Norm, *Bldg Supvr,* Plainsman Museum, Aurora NE

Schachter, Ruth, *Libr Dir,* Art Institute of Philadelphia Library, Philadelphia PA

Schaefer, Matt, *Reference Archivist,* National Archives & Records Administration, Herbert Hoover Presidential Library - Museum, West Branch IA

Schaefer, Susan, *Asst Gallery Mgr,* Sharon Arts Center, Sharon Arts Center Exhibition Gallery, Peterborough NH

Schaeffer, Christine, *Dir Grad Adult Studies,* Seton Hill University, Art Program, Greensburg PA (S)

Schaeffer, Romana, *Collections Mgr,* Seton Hall University, Walsh Gallery & Library, South Orange NJ

Schaeffer, Ron, *Archivist,* Bernice Pauahi Bishop, Library & Archives, Honolulu HI

Schafer, Michael I, *Pres,* Mohawk Valley Community College, Utica NY (S)

Schaffer, Dale E, *Owner,* Gloridale Partnership, National Museum of Woodcarving, Custer SD

Schaffer, Marcy, *Historic Site Mgr,* Schuyler Mansion State Historic Site, Albany NY

Schaffer, Shannon, *Dir,* Safety Harbor Museum and Cultural Arts Center, Safety Harbor FL

Schaffner, Wesley, *Preparator,* Santa Ana College, Art Gallery, Santa Ana CA

Schafroth, Colleen, *Dir,* Maryhill Museum of Art, Goldendale WA

Schaller, Arthur, *Asst Prof,* Norwich University, Dept of Architecture and Art, Northfield VT (S)

Schaller, Hydee, *Dir,* St John's College, Elizabeth Myers Mitchell Art Gallery, Annapolis MD

Schaming, Corinna, *Assoc Dir,* University at Albany, State University of New York, University Art Museum, Albany NY

Schaming, Mark, *Dir Exhibits,* New York State Museum, Albany NY

Schanilec, Anicka, *Registrar,* Minnetonka Center for the Arts, Wayzata MN
Schantz, Jennifer, *Exec VPres & COO,* New-York Historical Society, Museum, New York NY
Schantz, Michael W, *Exec Dir & CEO,* The Heckscher Museum of Art, Huntington NY
Schapp, Rebecca M, *Dir,* Santa Clara University, de Saisset Museum, Santa Clara CA
Schar, Stuart, *Dean,* University of Hartford, Hartford Art School, West Hartford CT (S)
Scharf, Carrie, *Circ Asst,* National Gallery of Art, Department of Image Collections, Washington DC
Scharf, Emily, *Instruction & Liaison ServLibrn,* Webster University, Emerson Library, St Louis MO
Schartow, Christianna, *Asst Dir,* Northwood University, Alden B Dow Creativity Center, Midland MI (S)
Schatz, Charlotte, *Instr,* Bucks County Community College, Fine Arts Dept, Newtown PA (S)
Schatz, Doug, *Instr,* Middle Tennessee State University, Art Dept, Murfreesboro TN (S)
Schaub, James, *Cur Exhibis,* Tohono Chul Park, Tucson AZ
Schaunam, Lora, *Cur Exhib,* Dacotah Prairie Museum, Lamont Art Gallery, Aberdeen SD
Schechan, Kevin, *Colls Mgr,* Maritime Museum of San Diego, San Diego CA
Scheele, Christie, *Instr,* Woodstock School of Art, Inc, Woodstock NY (S)
Scheer, Elaine, *Prof,* University of Wisconsin, Madison, Dept of Art, Madison WI (S)
Scheer, Stephen, *Assoc Prof Photog,* University of Georgia, Franklin College of Arts & Sciences, Lamar Dodd School of Art, Athens GA (S)
Schefcik, Jerry, *Dir,* University of Nevada, Las Vegas, Donna Beam Fine Art Gallery, Las Vegas NV
Scheffler, Bethany, *Development Director,* The Summit County Historical Society of Akron, OH, Akron OH
Scheid, Ann, *Archivist,* University of Southern California/The Gamble House, Greene & Greene Archives, San Marino CA
Scheidt, Diana, *Dir,* Big Horn County Historical Museum, Hardin MT
Scheirer, Wendy, *Instr,* Wayne Art Center, Wayne PA (S)
Schelemanow, Amy, *Exposure Designer,* Society for Photographic Education (SPE), SPE Gallery, Cleveland OH
Schelemanow, Amy, *Mgr Publications,* George Eastman Museum, Rochester NY
Schell, Edwin, *Exec Secy,* United Methodist Historical Society, Lovely Lane Museum, Baltimore MD
Schell, William H, *Dir,* Martin Memorial Library, York PA
Schenk, Joe, *Dir,* South Texas Institute for the Arts Affiliated with Texas A&M University - Corpus Christi, Art Museum of South Texas, Corpus Christi TX
Schenk, Joe, *Dir,* South Texas Institute for the Arts Affiliated with Texas A&M University - Corpus Christi, Library, Corpus Christi TX
Schenk, Mary Jane, *Exec Dir,* Arts Council of Southwestern Indiana, The Bower-Suhrheinrich Foundation Gallery, Evansville IN
Schenning, Brett, *Instr,* Limestone College, Art Dept, Gaffney SC (S)
Scher, Zach, *Asst Prof,* Dowling College, Dept of Visual Arts, Oakdale NY (S)
Scherer, Brooke, *Prof,* University of Tampa, College of Arts & Letters, Tampa FL (S)
Scherer, Gwen, *Instr,* Alabama State University, Dept of Visual Arts, Montgomery AL (S)
Schermerhorn, Gretchen, *Artistic Dir,* Pyramid Atlantic, Hyattsville MD
Scherpereel, Richard, *Prof,* Texas A&M University-Kingsville, Art Dept, Kingsville TX (S)
Schertz, Peter, *Cur Ancient Art,* Virginia Museum of Fine Arts, Richmond VA
Schick, Marjorie K, *Prof,* Pittsburg State University, Art Dept, Pittsburg KS (S)
Schiemann, Larry, *Dir,* Ashland College Arts & Humanities Gallery, The Coburn Gallery, Ashland OH
Schienbaum, David, *Asst Prof,* College of Santa Fe, Art Dept, Santa Fe NM (S)
Schietinger, Jim, *Gallery Dir,* Millikin University, Perkinson Gallery, Decatur IL
Schiff, Andre, *Technical Dir,* Regis College, Carney Gallery, Weston MA
Schiff, Jeffrey, *Assoc Prof,* Wesleyan University, Dept of Art & Art History, Middletown CT (S)
Schiffer, Tim, *Exec Dir,* Museum of Ventura County, Ventura CA
Schiffer, Tim, *Exec Dir,* Figge Art Museum, Davenport IA
Schifferdecker, Patrick, *Site Mgr,* Minnesota Historical Society, North West Company Fur Post, Pine City MN
Schillemat, Katharine, *Admin Asst,* Historical Society of Cheshire County, Keene NH
Schiller, Barbara, *Pres,* American Society of Contemporary Artists (ASCA), Yorktown Heights NY
Schiller, Lauren, *Asst Prof,* Utah State University, Dept of Art, Logan UT (S)
Schilling, Eugene, *Prof Art,* Adams State College, Dept of Visual Arts, Alamosa CO (S)
Schillings, Chuck, *Exec Dir,* Omniplex Science Museum, Oklahoma City OK
Schillo, Deb, *Librn,* Southern Highland Craft Guild, Folk Art Center, Asheville NC
Schimke, Susan, *Instr & Gallery Dir,* Shasta College, Arts, Communications & Social Sciences Division, Redding CA (S)
Schimmelman, Janice, *Prof,* Oakland University, Dept of Art & Art History, Rochester MI (S)
Schindel, Terri, *Cur Costumes,* Boulder History Museum, Museum of History, Boulder CO
Schindler, Leona Lopez, *Adjunct Asst Prof,* Spokane Falls Community College, Fine Arts Dept, Spokane WA (S)
Schindler, Robert, *Cur European Art,* Birmingham Museum of Art, Birmingham AL
Schipporeit, George, *Assoc Prof,* Illinois Institute of Technology, College of Architecture, Chicago IL (S)
Schirm, David, *Painting,* University at Buffalo, State University of New York, Dept of Visual Studies, Buffalo NY (S)
Schisla, Gretchen, *Assoc Prof,* University of Missouri, Saint Louis, Dept of Art & Art History, Saint Louis MO (S)
Schissel, Amy, *Asst Prof,* West Virginia University, College of Creative Arts, School of Art & Design, Morgantown WV (S)
Schlanger, Gregg, *Chmn,* Central Washington University, Dept of Art, Ellensburg WA (S)
Schlanzky, Gerhard, *Dir Exhib & Creative Dir,* New-York Historical Society, Museum, New York NY
Schlatter, Elizabeth, *Deputy Dir,* University of Richmond, University Museums, Richmond VA
Schlawin, Judy, *Prof,* Winona State University, Dept of Art, Winona MN (S)
Schlegel, Allison, *Gallery Tech,* The New School Parsons School of Design, Sheila C Johnson Design Center, New York NY (S)
Schlegel, Amy Ingrid, *Dir,* Tufts University, Tufts University Art Gallery, Medford MA
Schleh, Karoline, *Gallery Dir,* Collins C. Diboll Art Gallery, New Orleans LA
Schlemowitz, Emily, *Asst Cur,* Sheboygan Arts Foundation, Inc, John Michael Kohler Arts Center, Sheboygan WI
Schlenzka, Jenny, *Exec Artistic Dir,* Performance Space 122, New York NY
Schlesier, Douglas, *Prof Art,* Clarke College, Dept of Art, Dubuque IA (S)
Schleuning, Sarah, *Cur Decorative Arts & Design,* High Museum of Art, Atlanta GA
Schleyer, Ray, *Office Asst,* Carnegie Arts Center, Alliance NE
Schlichting, Eunice, *Chief Cur,* Putnam Museum of History and Natural Science, Davenport IA
Schlimmer, Alexa, *Asst Prof,* High Point University, Fine Arts Dept, High Point NC (S)
Schlink, John-Mark T, *Dir Exhibs,* Hamline University Studio Arts & Art History Depts, Gallery, Saint Paul MN
Schlink, John-Mark, *Dir Soeffker Gallery & Permanent Coll, Lectr,* Hamline University, Dept of Studio Arts & Art History, Saint Paul MN (S)
Schlinke, John, *Architecture Art Librn,* Roger Williams University, Architecture Library, Bristol RI
Schlitt, Melinda, *Prof,* Dickinson College, Dept of Art & Art History, Carlisle PA (S)
Schloder, John E, *Interim Cur Educ,* Museum of Fine Arts, Saint Petersburg, Florida, Inc, Saint Petersburg FL
Schlosser, Herbert S, *Chmn Bd Trustees,* American Museum of the Moving Image, Astoria NY
Schlosser, Tom, *Chmn Dept,* College of Saint Mary, Art Dept, Omaha NE (S)
Schmalbach, Heidi, *Research Fellow,* Arts Council Of New Orleans, New Orleans LA
Schmedding, Karen, *Mus Shop Mgr,* Belle Grove Inc, Belle Grove Plantation, Middletown VA
Schmidd, Robert, *Prof,* Norwich University, Dept of Architecture and Art, Northfield VT (S)
Schmidlapp, Don, *Assoc Prof,* Winona State University, Dept of Art, Winona MN (S)
Schmidt, Araan, *Asst Prof,* Colorado Mesa University, Art Dept, Grand Junction CO (S)
Schmidt, Edward, *Bd Dir,* Grand River Museum, Lemmon SD
Schmidt, Edward, *Instr,* New York Academy of Art, Graduate School of Figurative Art, New York NY (S)
Schmidt, Elaine, *Trustee & Secy,* Brooklyn Historical Society, Brooklyn OH
Schmidt, Herb, *Exec Dir,* Buffalo Niagara Heritage Village, Niederlander Research Library, Amherst NY
Schmidt, Herb, *Exec Dir,* Buffalo Niagara Heritage Village, Amherst NY
Schmidt, Jan, *Cur Dance,* The New York Public Library, The New York Public Library for the Performing Arts, New York NY
Schmidt, Jan, *Dir Human Resources,* Milwaukee Art Museum, Milwaukee WI
Schmidt, Kenneth, *Prof,* Concordia University, Art Dept, Seward NE (S)
Schmidt, Kristen, *Registrar,* University of Arizona, Museum of Art & Archive of Visual Arts, Tucson AZ
Schmidt, Lisa, *Bd Dir,* Grand River Museum, Lemmon SD
Schmidt, Lorraine, *Assoc Chair,* Corcoran School of Art, Washington DC (S)
Schmidt, Maurice, *Prof,* Texas A&M University-Kingsville, Art Dept, Kingsville TX (S)
Schmidt, Patrick T, *Asst Prof,* Washington & Jefferson College, Art Dept, Washington PA (S)
Schmidt, Peter, *Opers Dir,* The Art School at Old Church, Demarest NJ (S)
Schmidt, Phyllis, *Bd Dir,* Grand River Museum, Lemmon SD
Schmidt, Rolf D, *Immediate Past Chair,* Reading Public Museum, Reading PA
Schmidt, Sherrie, *Univ Librn,* Arizona State University, ASU Library, Tempe AZ
Schmidt, Stuart, *Pres, Bd Dir,* Grand River Museum, Lemmon SD
Schmidt, Susan S, *Assoc Prof,* College of the Holy Cross, Dept of Visual Arts, Worcester MA (S)
Schmidt, Teresa Tempero, *Prof,* Kansas State University, Art Dept, Manhattan KS (S)
Schmierbach, Amy, *Assoc Prof,* Fort Hays State University, Dept of Art & Design, Hays KS (S)
Schmitt, Ann, *VPres Educ,* Peoria Riverfront Museum, Peoria IL
Schmitt, Helmut, *Dir,* Merritt College, Art Dept, Oakland CA (S)
Schmitt, Jenn, *Cur Dept Asst,* deCordova Sculpture Park & Museum, Sculpture Park, Lincoln MA

Schmitt, Jessie, *Exhibs Asst,* The Exhibition Alliance, Hamilton NY

Schmitt, Julia, *Asst Prof,* Stetson University, Department of Creative Arts, Deland FL (S)

Schmitz, David, *Exec Dir,* Dubuque Museum of Art, Dubuque IA

Schmitz, Robert, *Prof,* Rochester Institute of Technology, School of Design, Rochester NY (S)

Schmoldt, Robin, *Art Advisor & Art Coll Mgr,* University of Wisconsin-Madison, Wisconsin Union Galleries, Madison WI

Schmuki, Jeff, *Asst Prod,* Georgia Southern University, Betty Foy Sanders Dept of Art, Statesboro GA (S)

Schnabel, JoAnn, *Prof,* University of Northern Iowa, Dept of Art, Cedar Falls IA (S)

Schneider, D, *Instr,* University of Southern Maine, Dept of Art, Gorham ME (S)

Schneider, Emery E, *Chmn Design Composition Division,* Rochester Institute of Technology, School of Printing Management & Sciences, Rochester NY (S)

Schneider, Erika, *Asst Prof,* Framingham State College, Art Dept, Framingham MA (S)

Schneider, Gary, *Artist in Res,* Stony Brook University, College of Arts & Sciences, Dept of Art, Stony Brook NY (S)

Schneider, John, *Dir Opers,* Newport Art Museum and Association, Newport RI

Schneider, John, *Gallery Bus Mgr,* Saint Mary's College of California, Museum of Art, Moraga CA

Schneider, Karen, *Head Librn,* The Phillips Collection, Library, Washington DC

Schneider, Keith, *Prof,* Humboldt State University, College of Arts & Humanities, Art Dept, Arcata CA (S)

Schneider, Laurie, *Prof,* John Jay College of Criminal Justice, Dept of Art, Music & Philosophy, New York NY (S)

Schneider, Nicholas, *Asst Prof Art,* Marymount Manhattan College, Fine & Performing Arts Div, New York NY (S)

Schneider, Richard, *Assoc Prof,* Cleveland State University, Art Dept, Cleveland OH (S)

Schneider, Sabine, *Cur Learning,* The Art Gallery of Grand Prairie, Grande Prairie AB

Schneider, Zoe, *Visual & Media Arts Coordr,* Organization of Saskatchewan Arts Councils (OSAC), Regina SK

Schneidermann, Cheryl, *Instr,* Marylhurst University, Art Dept, Marylhurst OR (S)

Schnirring, Cheryl, *Colls Mgr,* Abraham Lincoln Presidential Library & Museum, Springfield IL

Schnupp, Amy, *Patrons' Serv & Vol Coordr,* Pensacola Museum of Art, Pensacola FL

Schoch, Jason, *Instr,* North Hennepin Community College, Art Dept, Brooklyn Park MN (S)

Schoeben, Jan, *Pres,* Tubac Center of the Arts, Santa Cruz Valley Art Association, Tubac AZ

Schoedinger, Christy, *Dir Develop,* Ohio State University, Wexner Center for the Arts, Columbus OH

Schoelwer, Susan, *Cur,* George Washington's Mount Vernon, Mount Vernon VA

Schoenbaum, Mark, *Instr,* University of Evansville, Art Dept, Evansville IN (S)

Schoenfielder, Lisa, *Chmn,* Viterbo University, Art Dept, La Crosse WI (S)

Schoenweis, Desy, *Asst Prof,* Black Hills State University, Ruddell Gallery, Spearfish SD

Schoff, Soren, *Circ/Reserves,* University of Wisconsin-Madison, Kohler Art Library, Madison WI

Scholes, Marc, *Assoc VPres Instruc Affairs,* Alberta College of Art & Design, Calgary AB (S)

Scholten, Lisa, *Cur Coll,* South Dakota State University, South Dakota Art Museum, Brookings SD

Scholten, Sarah, *Mgr,* Public Library of Des Moines, Central Library Information Services, Des Moines IA

Schon, Miguel A, *Asst Prof,* Johns Hopkins University, School of Medicine, Dept of Art as Applied to Medicine, Baltimore MD (S)

Schonholtz, Gleniss, *Interim CEO,* The Interchurch Center, Galleries at the Interchurch Center, New York NY

Schoonmaker, Trevor, *Chief Cur& Cur Contemporary Art,* Duke University, Nasher Museum of Art at Duke University, Durham NC

Schorr, Annalee, *Treas,* Spark Gallery, Denver CO

Schorr, David, *Prof,* Wesleyan University, Dept of Art & Art History, Middletown CT (S)

Schorr, Elizabeth A, *Registrar,* City of El Paso, El Paso TX

Schorr, Laurie, *Dir Educ,* The Light Factory, Charlotte NC

Schorske, Bonnie, *Finance,* Plastic Club, Art Club, Philadelphia PA

Schott, Gene A, *Dir,* Heritage Museums & Gardens, Sandwich MA

Schott, Joseph, *Heirloom Seed Project,* Landis Valley Village and Farm Museum, PA Historical & Museum Commission, Lancaster PA

Schousen, Steve, *Prof,* Aquinas College, Art Dept, Grand Rapids MI (S)

Schoyer, Elizabeth, *Studio Faculty,* University of Virginia, McIntire Dept of Art, Charlottesville VA (S)

Schramm, Catherine, *Cur Educ,* National Trust for Historic Preservation, Shadows-on-the-Teche, New Iberia LA

Schranom, Harry, *Pres (V),* The Cultural Center of Fine Arts, Art Gallery, Parkersburg WV

Schreffler, Danni L, *Office Mgr,* Randolph College, Maier Museum of Art, Lynchburg VA

Schreyer, Alice, *Roger & Julie Baskes VPres Cols & Library Svcs,* The Newberry, Chicago IL

Schrock, Eileen, *VPres,* Phelps County Historical Society, Nebraska Prairie Museum, Holdrege NE

Schrock, Peggy, *Asst Prof,* Murray State University, Dept of Art, Murray KY (S)

Schroeder, Beth, *Dir Devel,* The Arts Center of the Capital Region, Troy NY

Schroeder, Elaine, *Admin Asst,* Rahr-West Art Museum, Manitowoc WI

Schroeder, Eunice, *Music Librn,* University of California, Santa Barbara, Arts Library, Santa Barbara CA

Schroeder, George, *Prof,* Hiram College, Art Dept, Hiram OH (S)

Schroeder, Ivy, *Chmn Dept,* Southern Illinois University at Edwardsville, Dept of Art & Design, Edwardsville IL (S)

Schroeder, Shari, *Admin Mgr,* Leigh Yawkey Woodson Art Museum, Wausau WI

Schroepfer, Dave, *Financial Officer,* Rockford Art Museum, Rockford IL

Schroth, Sarah, *Dir,* Duke University, Nasher Museum of Art at Duke University, Durham NC

Schry, Virginia, *Secy,* Allegany County Historical Society, Gordon-Roberts House, Cumberland MD

Schube, Lee, *Develop Dir,* Social & Public Art Resource Center, (SPARC), Venice CA

Schuck, Jason, *Mus Cur Asst,* Islip Art Museum, East Islip NY

Schuessler, Richard, *Asst Prof,* University of Nebraska, Kearney, Dept of Art & Art History, Kearney NE (S)

Schuette, Jan, *Conservatory Dean,* American Film Institute (AFI), Los Angeles CA (S)

Schuetz, Michael, *Asst Dir,* Eastern Illinois University, Tarble Arts Center, Charleston IL

Schuh, Larry, *Assoc Prof,* McNeese State University, Dept of Visual Arts, Lake Charles LA (S)

Schulenberg, Melissa, *Assoc Prof,* St Lawrence University, Dept of Fine Arts, Canton NY (S)

Schuler, Jane, *Prof,* York College of the City University of New York, Fine & Performing Arts, Jamaica NY (S)

Schuller, Brant D, *Chair & Assoc Prof Printmaking,* Millersville University, Dept of Art & Design, Millersville PA (S)

Schulte, Greg, *Assoc Prof,* Utah State University, Dept of Art, Logan UT (S)

Schultz Kilduff, Pat, *Assoc Dir Mktg,* Children's Creativity Museum, San Francisco CA

Schultz, Adam, *Facilities Dir,* Salisbury University, Ward Museum of Wildfowl Art, Salisbury MD

Schultz, Anne, *Mgr Library Operations,* University of New Mexico, Fine Arts Library, Albuquerque NM

Schultz, Christina, *VPres Cultural Affairs & Develop,* Dixie State University, Sears Art Museum Gallery, Saint George UT

Schultz, Donna, *Admin Asst,* Queens College, City University of New York, Art Library, Flushing NY

Schultz, Kathryn, *Dir,* Cambridge Art Association, Cambridge MA

Schultz, Kurt, *Div Head Design,* Northern Illinois University, School of Art & Design, DeKalb IL (S)

Schultz, Kurt, *Grad Coordr,* Northern Illinois University, School of Art & Design, DeKalb IL (S)

Schultz, Leslie, *Pres,* BRIC - Brooklyn Information & Culture, BRIC House, Brooklyn NY

Schultz, Lisa, *VPres,* The Art Museum of Eastern Idaho, Idaho Falls ID

Schultz, Nick, *Pres,* Jefferson County Historical Society Museum, Madison IN

Schultz, Robert, *Asst Dir Educ & Visual Arts,* Mesa Arts Center, Mesa Contemporary Arts Museum, Mesa AZ

Schultz, Robert, *Instr,* Northwest Missouri State University, Dept of Fine & Performing Arts, Maryville MO (S)

Schultz, Rosslyn, *Exec Dir,* Grassroots Art Center, Lucas KS

Schultz, Susan, *Grants Financial Analyst,* Broward County Board of Commissioners, Broward Cultural Div, Fort Lauderdale FL

Schulz, Barbara, *Bldg Contact,* Brown University, Annmary Brown Memorial, Providence RI

Schulz, Cornelia, *Prof Painting,* University of California, Davis, Dept of Art & Art History, Davis CA (S)

Schulz, Emily L, *Deputy Dir & Cur,* The Society of the Cincinnati at Anderson House, Washington DC

Schulz, Gina, *VPres Devel,* Grand Rapids Public Museum, Grand Rapids MI

Schumacher, Brian, *Systems & Online Resources Librn,* Academy of Art, University Library, San Francisco CA

Schumacher, Sheila, *Asst Prof Art,* Grand Canyon University, Art Dept, Phoenix AZ (S)

Schumacher, Walt, *Pres,* Huntsville Art League, Lowe Mill Arts & Entertainment, Huntsville AL

Schumaker, Julie, *Prog Mgr,* Boulder History Museum, Museum of History, Boulder CO

Schumann Mitchell, Stephanie, *Exec Dir,* Lawndale Art Center, Houston TX

Schumann, Elka, *Mgr,* Bread & Puppet Theater, Bread & Puppet Museum, Glover VT

Schumann, Max, *Assoc Dir,* Printed Matter, Inc, New York NY

Schumann, Max, *Exec Dir,* Printed Matter, Inc, New York NY

Schumann, Peter, *Artist,* Bread & Puppet Theater, Bread & Puppet Museum, Glover VT

Schupbach, Jason, *Dir,* Arizona State University, The Design School, Tempe AZ (S)

Schurmacher, Judy, *Bus Mgr,* Hammond Museum & Japanese Stroll Garden, Cross-Cultural Center, North Salem NY

Schussheim-Anderson, Rowen, *Chair,* Augustana College, Art Dept, Rock Island IL (S)

Schuster, Barbara R, *Asst Dir & develop,* The New Museum at the Bradford Brinton Ranch, The Brinton Museum, Big Horn WY

Schuster, Don, *VPres,* Cincinnati Art Club, Cincinnati OH

Schuster, Helmut, *Art Dir,* World Erotic Art Museum, Miami Beach FL

Schuster, Kenneth L, *Dir & Chief Cur,* The New Museum at the Bradford Brinton Ranch, The Brinton Museum, Big Horn WY

Schuster, Sarah, *Assoc Prof,* Oberlin College, Dept of Art, Oberlin OH (S)

Schutt., Melissa, *Tech Svcs Librarian,* Colonial Williamsburg Foundation, John D Rockefeller, Jr Library, Williamsburg VA

Schutz, Lacy, *Executive Director,* Shaker Museum & Library, Emma B King Library, New Lebanon NY
Schuweiler, Suzanne, *Assoc Prof & Coordr Art History,* Converse College, School of the Arts, Dept of Art & Design, Spartanburg SC (S)
Schuyler, Robert L, *Historical Arch Assoc Cur,* University of Pennsylvania, Museum of Archaeology & Anthropology, Philadelphia PA
Schuyler-King, Lynn, *Financial Officer,* San Jose Museum of Art, Library, San Jose CA
Schwab, Alice Anne, *Exec Dir,* Susquehanna Art Museum, Harrisburg PA
Schwab, Ben, *Assoc Prof,* The College of Saint Rose, The Center For Art and Design, Albany NY (S)
Schwab, Katherine, *Cur of the Plaster Cast Collection,* Fairfield University, Art Museum, Fairfield CT
Schwab, Michael C, *Media Arts & Animation,* Art Institute of Pittsburgh, Pittsburgh PA (S)
Schwab, Steve, *Dir Educ,* Art Institute of Fort Lauderdale, Fort Lauderdale FL (S)
Schwab, Tim, *Director of Design and Installation,* Laguna Art Museum, Laguna Beach CA
Schwabach, James Bruce, *Assoc Prof,* Herkimer County Community College, Humanities Social Services, Herkimer NY (S)
Schwager, Michael, *Art Chmn,* Sonoma State University, Art & Art History Dept, Rohnert Park CA (S)
Schwager, Michael, *Dir,* Sonoma State University, University Art Gallery, Rohnert Park CA
Schwain, Kristin, *Assoc Prof,* University of Missouri - Columbia, Art History & Archaeology Dept, Columbia MO (S)
Schwander, AJ, *Opers Mgr,* Delaware Art Museum, Wilmington DE
Schwankl, Elizabeth, *Artist & Owner,* Gallery 4, Ltd, Fargo ND
Schwarm, Larry, *Prof,* Emporia State University, Dept of Art, Emporia KS (S)
Schwarting, Paulette, *Dir Tech Services,* Virginia Historical Society, Library, Richmond VA
Schwartz, Amy, *Dir Devel, Educ & The Studio,* Corning Museum of Glass, The Studio, Corning NY
Schwartz, Deanna, *Dir Exhibs,* The Dairy Barn Arts Center, Athens OH
Schwartz, Deborah, *Pres,* Brooklyn Historical Society, Brooklyn NY
Schwartz, Louise, *Pres,* Almond Historical Society, Inc, Hagadorn House, The 1800-37 Museum, Almond NY
Schwartz, Melanie, *Prof,* Southwestern Oregon Community College, Visual Arts Dept, Coos Bay OR (S)
Schwartz, Michael, *Prof,* Augusta State University, Dept of Art, Augusta GA (S)
Schwartz, Robert, *Director,* Almond Historical Society, Inc, Hagadorn House, The 1800-37 Museum, Almond NY
Schwartz, Robin, *Asst Prof,* William Paterson University, Dept Arts, Wayne NJ (S)
Schwartz, Tom, *Library Dir,* National Archives & Records Administration, Herbert Hoover Presidential Library - Museum, West Branch IA
Schwarz, Gregory C, *Supv Interpretation,* Saint-Gaudens National Historic Site, Library, Cornish NH
Schwarz, Gregory, *Chief Ranger,* Saint-Gaudens National Historic Site, Cornish NH
Schwarz, Susan, *Visual Arts & Humanities Dead,* Grossmont Community College, Hyde Art Gallery, El Cajon CA
Schwarzer, Lynn, *Assoc Prof,* Colgate University, Dept of Art & Art History, Hamilton NY (S)
Schweiger, Christy, *Educ Coordr,* Moose Jaw Art Museum, Inc, Art & History Museum, Moose Jaw SK
Schweiger, Pam, *Executive Assistant,* Museum of Wisconsin Art, West Bend WI
Schweiger, Rebecca, *Founder, Dir & Instr,* The Art Studio New York, New York NY (S)
Schweigert, Scott A, *Cur Arts & Civilization,* Reading Public Museum, Reading PA
Schweitzer, Rob, *Dir Pub Rels,* Historic Hudson Valley, Pocantico Hills NY
Schweitzer, Tricia, *Prog Dir,* University of Minnesota, The Studio/Larson Gallery, Saint Paul MN
Schweizer, Paul D, *Dir Emeritus,* Munson-Williams-Proctor Arts Institute, Museum of Art, Utica NY
Schwender, Judy, *Cur & Registrar,* The National Quilt Museum, Paducah KY
Schwenke, Megan, *Archivist,* Harvard University, Harvard Art Museums, Cambridge MA
Schwertley, Mark, *Chmn Humanities,* City Colleges of Chicago, Malcolm X College, Chicago IL (S)
Schwetman, Sondra, *Assoc Prof,* Humboldt State University, College of Arts & Humanities, Art Dept, Arcata CA (S)
Schwitzner, Ted, *Pub Servs Librn,* North Central College, Oesterle Library, Naperville IL
Sconyers, Jim, *Asst Prof,* Mary Baldwin College, Dept of Art & Art History, Staunton VA (S)
Scopelites, Celeste, *Dir,* Art Gallery of Peterborough, Peterborough ON
Scorso, Rebecca, *CFO & Mng Dir,* Charter Oak Cultural Center, Hartford CT
Scorza, Phil, *Chmn, Prof,* Northwestern College, Art Dept, Orange City CA (S)
Scorza, Phil, *Prof Graphic Design,* Northwestern College, Te Paske Gallery, Orange City IA
Scott Clement, Anne, *Exec Dir,* Waterworks Visual Arts Center, Salisbury NC
Scott Reynolds, Becca, *Gallery Dir,* The Arts Council of Wayne County, Goldsboro NC (S)
Scott, Aaron, *Asst Prof,* Southern Illinois University, School of Art & Design, Carbondale IL (S)
Scott, Ann, *Ref Librn,* Kansas State University, Paul Weigel Library of Architecture Planning & Design, Manhattan KS
Scott, April, *Exec Dir,* Mid-America All-Indian Center, Indian Center Museum, Wichita KS
Scott, Barb, *Treas,* Bonita Historical Society, Bonita Museum and Cultural Center, Bonita CA
Scott, Bobbie, *Vol/Educ,* Paine Art Center & Gardens, Oshkosh WI
Scott, Cristie, *Exec Dir,* Durango Arts Center, Barbara Conrad Art Gallery, Durango CO
Scott, Curtis, *Assoc Dir Publishing & Communs,* Princeton University, Princeton University Art Museum, Princeton NJ
Scott, Darwin, *Librn,* Brandeis University, Leonard L Farber Library, Waltham MA
Scott, Deborah Emont, *Pres & CEO,* Taft Museum of Art, Cincinnati OH
Scott, Deirdre, *Exec Dir,* Bronx Council on the Arts, Longwood Arts Gallery @ Hostos, Bronx NY
Scott, Gale, *Glass & Metals Dept Head,* Worcester Center for Crafts, Worcester MA (S)
Scott, Helga, *Treas,* Women's Art Association of Canada, Dignam Gallery, Toronto ON
Scott, Henrietta, *Instr,* Campbellsville University, Art & Design Department, Campbellsville KY (S)
Scott, Jeanne, *Opers Mgr,* Museum of Ventura County, Ventura CA
Scott, John T, *Prof,* Xavier University of Louisiana, Dept of Fine Arts, New Orleans LA (S)
Scott, Jonathon, *Head Dept,* Castleton State College, Art Dept, Castleton VT (S)
Scott, Judy, *Exec Asst,* Royal Architectural Institute of Canada, Library, Ottawa ON
Scott, Julie, *Dir,* Rosicrucian Egyptian Museum & Planetarium, Rosicrucian Order, AMORC, San Jose CA
Scott, Kristi, *Cur Art,* Paris Gibson Square, Museum of Art, Great Falls MT
Scott, Laurel, *Assoc Prof,* University of Wisconsin-Superior, Programs in the Visual Arts, Superior WI (S)
Scott, Linda, *Web & eCommuns Mgr,* National Art Education Association, Alexandria VA
Scott, Michael, *Cur Educ,* City of High Point, High Point Museum, High Point NC
Scott, Rebecca, *Adjunct Prof Art,* University of Great Falls, Art Dept, Great Falls MT (S)
Scott, Roger, *Instr Animation,* Locust Street Neighborhood Art Classes, Inc, Buffalo NY (S)
Scott, Shelly, *Assoc Dean,* University of Lethbridge, Faculty of Fine Arts, Lethbridge AB (S)
Scott, Stanley, *Dir,* Colorado State University, Curfman Gallery, Fort Collins CO
Scott, Steve, *Mktg Mgr,* Caspers, Inc, Art Collection, Tampa FL
Scott, Tina, *Exec Dir,* James Prendergast, Jamestown NY
Scott, William, *Chmn Theater,* Idyllwild Arts Academy, Idyllwild CA (S)
Scudier, Kathryn, *Web Communs Mgr,* Women's Studio Workshop, Inc, Rosendale NY
Scuilla, Jason, *Asst Prof,* Kansas State University, Art Dept, Manhattan KS (S)
Scully, Cammie V, *Dir,* Waterloo Center of the Arts, Waterloo IA
Scully, Diana, *Treasurer,* Kennebec Valley Art Association, Harlow Gallery, Hallowell ME
Scully, Merry, *Head Curatorial Affairs, Cur Contemporary Art,* New Mexico Department of Cultural Affairs, New Mexico Museum of Art, Santa Fe NM
Scully-Morreale, Maria, *Interim Head Mktg, Corp & Pub Rels,* The Buffalo Fine Arts Academy, Albright-Knox Art Gallery, Buffalo NY
Seabold, Thomas, *Dir,* Keokuk Art Center, Keokuk IA
Seabury, Linda, *Dir Communs,* New Hampshire Institute of Art, Manchester NH
Seals, Hershall, *Chmn,* University of Mary Hardin-Baylor, College of Visual & Performing Arts, Belton TX (S)
Seals, Katy, *Asst Prof,* East Central University, School of Fine Arts, Ada OK (S)
Seaman, Sally, *Dean,* Lyme Academy College of Fine Arts, Old Lyme CT (S)
Seaman, Sara, *Dir,* National Park Community College Library, Hot Springs AR
Seamans, Casey, *Gallery Mgr,* Fort Smith Regional Art Museum, Fort Smith AR
Seamons, Steve, *Dir,* National Museum of Wildlife Art of the Unites States, Jackson WY
Seamus Callinan, Matthew, *Campus Exhibit Coordr,* Haverford College, Cantor Fitzgerald Gallery, Haverford PA (S)
Searcy, Manera S, *Cur,* Sturdivant Museum Association, Sturdivant Museum, Selma AL
Searle Jones, Anne, *Dir Communs,* The Renaissance Society, Chicago IL
Sears Cox, Beth, *Prof,* West Virginia University at Parkersburg, Art Dept, Parkersburg WV (S)
Sears, Elizabeth, *Prof & Chair,* University of Michigan, Ann Arbor, Dept of History of Art, Ann Arbor MI (S)
Sears, Mardy, *Conservation Tech,* The Art Institute of Chicago, Dept of Prints & Drawings, Chicago IL
Sears, Patrick, *Exec Dir,* Rubin Museum of Art, New York NY
Sears, Stanton, *Assoc Prof,* Macalester College, Art & Art History Dept, Saint Paul MN (S)
Seaton, Melynda, *Cur,* University of Nebraska-Lincoln, Great Plains Art Museum, Lincoln NE
Seay, Pamela R, *Sr Vice Pres Advancement,* Virginia Historical Society, Library, Richmond VA
Sebald, Romi, *Colls Mgr,* The State University of New York at Potsdam, The Art Museum, Potsdam NY
Sebberson, David, *Chair,* Saint Cloud State University, Dept of Art, Saint Cloud MN (S)
Seckinger, Craig, *Instr Drawing & Design,* Bay De Noc Community College, Art Dept, Escanaba MI (S)
Seckinger, Linda, *Prof,* Mississippi State University, Dept of Art, Starville MS (S)
Secor, James, *Gallery Assoc,* Studio Place Arts, Barre VT
Secoy, Reid, *Facilities Mgr,* The Dairy Barn Arts Center, Athens OH
Sedgwick, Robin, *Mus Registrar,* Longwood Center for the Visual Arts, Farmville VA
Seed, John, *Dept Chair,* Mt San Jacinto College, Art Dept, San Jacinto CA (S)

Seel, Rod, *Exec Dir,* Coutts Museum of Art, Inc, El Dorado KS
Seely, Carol, *Chair,* Warner House Association, MacPheadris-Warner House, Portsmouth NH
Seely, Nina, *Exec Dir,* UMLAUF Sculpture Garden & Museum, Austin TX
Seely, Peter, *Chair,* Illinois Benedictine University, Department of Fine Arts, Lisle IL (S)
Seeman, Rebecca, *Instr,* Art Academy of Cincinnati, Cincinnati OH (S)
Seestadt, Robert, *VPres Finance & Admin,* Edsel & Eleanor Ford House, Grosse Pointe Shores MI
Segal, Eric, *Dir Educ & Cur Academic Progs,* University of Florida, Samuel P Harn Museum of Art, Gainesville FL
Segal, Mark, *Dir Pub Rels,* Parrish Art Museum, Water Mill NY
Segalman, Richard, *Instr,* Woodstock School of Art, Inc, Woodstock NY (S)
Seggerman, Karen, *Pres,* Arts on the Park, Lakeland Center for Creative Arts, Lakeland FL
Seghers, George, *Executive Director,* The George Washington Masonic National Memorial Association, The George Washington Masonic National Memorial, Alexandria VA
Segre-Lewis, Chris, *Instr,* Asbury University, Art Dept, Wilmore KY (S)
Seguin, Lucie, *Librn,* Universite du Quebec, Bibliotheque des Arts, Montreal QC
Segura, Reyes, *Public Progs & Special Events Coordr,* Galeria de la Raza, Studio 24, San Francisco CA
Sehlossberg-Wood, Caren, *Instr Graphic Design,* Maryville University of Saint Louis, Art & Design Program, Saint Louis MO (S)
Seiber, Valerie, *Coll Mgr,* Hershey Museum, Hershey PA
Seiden, Jane, *Prin Librn,* Newark Public Library, Reference, Newark NJ
Seidman, Lenny, *Music Cur,* Painted Bride Art Center Gallery, Philadelphia PA
Seiffert, Gregory, *Vis Instr,* Vassar College, Art Dept, Poughkeepsie NY (S)
Seigel, Judy, *Educ,* Midmarch Associates/Midmarch Arts Press, Midmarch Arts Press and Library, New York NY
Seiler, Scott, *Artist & Owner,* Gallery 4, Ltd, Fargo ND
Seim, Jenny, *Mktg Asst,* Neville Public Museum of Brown County, Green Bay WI
Seim, Katie, *Vol Pres,* St Mary Chapter Louisiana Landmarks Society, Grevemberg House Museum, Franklin LA
Seitz, Carole, *Instr,* Creighton University, Fine & Performing Arts Dept, Omaha NE (S)
Seitz, David, *Gift Shop Mgr,* City of Lubbock, Buddy Holly Center, Lubbock TX
Seitz, John, *COO,* Washington Pavilion of Arts & Science, Visual Arts Center, Sioux Falls SD
Seitzinger, Adele, *Past Pres,* Cumberland Art Society Inc, Cookeville Art Gallery, Cookeville TN
Seiz, John, *Instr,* Springfield College in Illinois, Dept of Art, Springfield IL (S)
Sekanick, Bruce, *Secy,* American Institute of Architects, The Octagon Museum, Washington DC
Selberg, John, *Assoc Prof,* Glenville State College, Dept of Fine Arts, Glenville WV (S)
Selbig, Andrea, *Registrar,* University of Wisconsin-Madison, Chazen Museum of Art, Madison WI
Selby, Robert, *Instr,* Pacific Northwest College of Art, Portland OR (S)
Selden, Scott, *Instr,* Mohawk Valley Community College, Utica NY (S)
Selenow, Deena, *Dir,* Occidental College, Weingart Galleries, Los Angeles CA
Seley, Beverly, *Prof,* Grand Valley State University, Art & Design Dept, Allendale MI (S)
Self, Debra, *Pres,* Marin Society of Artists Inc, San Rafael CA
Seliger, Liz, *Admin Asst,* Amarillo Art Association, Amarillo Museum of Art, Amarillo TX
Seling, Rose, *Admin Coordr,* The College of Wooster, Dept of Art and Art History, Wooster OH (S)
Seling, Rose, *Art Mus Admin Coordr,* The College of Wooster, The College of Wooster Art Museum, Wooster OH
Sell, Tina, *Dir Educ,* Susquehanna Art Museum, Harrisburg PA
Sellars, Steven, *Asst Prof,* Cardinal Stritch University, Art Dept, Milwaukee WI (S)
Selle, Thomas, *Co-Chairperson,* Carroll College, Art Dept, Waukesha WI (S)
Selle, Thomas, *Co-Chmn,* Carroll College, Art Dept, Waukesha WI (S)
Selleck, Laurie, *Asst Prof,* Cazenovia College, Center for Art & Design Studies, Cazenovia NY (S)
Sellin, Christine, *Asst Prof,* California Lutheran University, Art Dept, Thousand Oaks CA (S)
Sellman, Barbara, *Board Member,* Folk Art Society of America, Richmond VA
Sellman, James, *Pres,* Folk Art Society of America, Richmond VA
Selman, Robyn, *Gen Mgr,* New York Institute of Photography, New York NY (S)
Selter, Dan S, *Prof of Art,* Transylvania University, Art Program, Lexington KY (S)
Semerena, Wade, *Prof,* Miami-Dade Community College, Arts & Philosophy Dept, Miami FL (S)
Seminara, Patricia, *Gallery Assoc,* Woodstock Artists Association & Museum, Woodstock NY
Semivan, Douglas, *Chmn Art Dept,* Madonna University, College of Arts & Humanities, Livonia MI (S)
Senat, Simone, *Instr,* Butte College, Dept of Fine Arts and Communication Tech, Oroville CA (S)
Seneca, Michael, *Dir Regional Digital Imaging Ctr,* Athenaeum of Philadelphia, Philadelphia PA
Senf, Becky, *Cur Photog,* Phoenix Art Museum, Phoenix AZ
Senf, Rebecca, *Chief Cur,* University of Arizona, Center for Creative Photography, Tucson AZ
Seng, Yvonne, *Cur Art,* Holter Museum of Art, Helena MT
Sengoku, Noriko, *Mem Bd Dir,* Hatch-Billops Collection, Inc, New York NY
Senie, Harriet, *Dir Mus Studies,* City College of New York, Art Dept, New York NY (S)
Senie, Harriet, *Prof,* City University of New York, PhD Program in Art History, New York NY (S)
Senior, Gordon, *Chmn Dept,* California State University, Art Dept, Turlock CA (S)
Senior, Gordon, *Dept Chair,* California State University Stanislaus, University Art Gallery, Turlock CA
Senior, Heidi, *Reference Librn,* University of Portland, Wilson W Clark Memorial Library, Portland OR
Senn, Carol, *Dir,* McDowell House & Apothecary Shop, Danville KY
Senn, Greg, *Prof Art,* Eastern New Mexico University, Runnels Gallery, Golden Library, Portales NM
Senn, Kurt, *Dir,* Missouri Department of Natural Resources, Elizabeth Rozier Gallery, Jefferson City MO
Senn, Kurt, *Mus Dir,* Missouri Department of Natural Resources, Missouri State Museum, Jefferson City MO
Senne, Jessica, *Asst Prof Interior Design,* Maryville University of Saint Louis, Art & Design Program, Saint Louis MO (S)
Sennett, Menique, *Pub Rels,* Art Museum of Southeast Texas, Beaumont TX
Seo, Sang-Duok, *Asst Prof,* University of Nevada, Las Vegas, Dept of Art, Las Vegas NV (S)
Serbe, Mary, *Educ Dir,* Yellowstone Art Museum, Billings MT
Serdjenian, Tina, *Librn,* Waterville Historical Society, Redington Museum, Waterville ME
Serebrennikov, Nina, *Prof,* Davidson College, Art Dept, Davidson NC (S)
Sergejeff, Nadine, *Librn,* Newark Public Library, Reference, Newark NJ
Serie, Patrick, *1st VPres Progs,* Scottsdale Artists' League, Scottsdale AZ
Serio, Alexis, *Asst Prof,* University of Texas at Tyler, Department of Art, School of Visual & Performing Arts, Tyler TX (S)
Serio, Faye, *Assoc Prof,* St Lawrence University, Dept of Fine Arts, Canton NY (S)
Serrao-Leiua, Tamara, *Curator Anthropology,* San Bernardino County Museum, Redlands CA
Serratare, Nick, *Gallery Mgr,* Rehoboth Art League, Inc, Rehoboth Beach DE
Serroes, Richard, *Instr,* Modesto Junior College, Arts Humanities & Communications Division, Modesto CA (S)
Sersland, Peggy, *Mem Mgr,* Vesterheim Norwegian-American Museum, Decorah IA
Servant, Lise, *Cur Slide Library,* Jardin Botanique de Montreal, Bibliotheque, Montreal QC
Servantez, Leslie, *Registrar,* Wichita Art Museum, Emprise Bank Research Library, Wichita KS
Servantez, Leslie, *Registrar,* Wichita Art Museum, Wichita KS
Serventi Steiner, Mary, *Cur,* Museo Italo Americano, San Francisco CA
Servon, Lisa, *Prof & Chair, City/Regional Planning,* University of Pennsylvania, School of Design (PennDesign), Philadelphia PA (S)
Sessions, Billie, *Instr,* California State University, San Bernardino, Dept of Art, San Bernardino CA (S)
Sessions, David, *Dir Exhibs, Curatorial Team,* Bainbridge Arts & Crafts Gallery, Bainbridge Island WA
Sethem, Brian, *Asst Prof,* California Lutheran University, Art Dept, Thousand Oaks CA (S)
Setter, Suzanne, *Librn,* East Hampton Library, Long Island Collection, East Hampton NY
Settle-Cooney, Mary, *Exec Dir,* Tennessee Valley Art Association, Tuscumbia AL
Settles, Dana, *Educ,* Mount Vernon Hotel Museum & Garden, New York NY
Settles, Kathleen, *Dir,* Georgian Court University, M Christina Geis Gallery, Lakewood NJ
Seubert, Christopher, *Instr,* Woodstock School of Art, Inc, Woodstock NY (S)
Sevanne Thomas, Tara, *Dir,* Colorado Springs Fine Arts Center, Bemis School of Art, Colorado Springs CO
Sevening, Rebecca, *Dir Mktg & Pub Rels,* Washington Pavilion of Arts & Science, Visual Arts Center, Sioux Falls SD
Sever, Ziya, *Chmn Art,* Western Nebraska Community College, Division of Language & Arts, Scottsbluff NE (S)
Severe, Milton, *Exhib Designer,* Grinnell College, Faulconer Gallery, Grinnell IA
Severino, Michelle A, *Exec Dir,* Heritage Museum Association, Inc, The Heritage Museum of Northwest Florida, Valparaiso FL
Severn, Gail, *Owner & Dir,* Gail Severn Gallery, Ketchum ID
Severstad, Jami, *Cur,* Bergstrom-Mahler Museum of Glass, Neenah WI
Sewell, Dennita, *Cur Fashion Design,* Phoenix Art Museum, Phoenix AZ
Sexton Larson, Rebecca, *Chief Curator,* Art and History Museums - Maitland, Maitland Art Center, Maitland FL
Sexton, Natasha, *Coord,* Westminster College, Fine Arts Dept, Fulton MO (S)
Seydl, Jon, *Dir Curatorial Affairs & Cur European Art,* Worcester Art Museum, Worcester MA
Seydler-Hepworth, Betty Lee, *Asst Dean,* Lawrence Technological University, College of Architecture, Southfield MI (S)
Seyler, Ruth, *Meetings Dir,* American Institute for Conservation of Historic & Artistic Works, Washington DC
Seymour, Gayle, *Prof,* University of Central Arkansas, Department of Art, Conway AR (S)
Seymour, Griff, *Recording Secy,* Salmagundi Club, New York NY
Sfirri, Mark, *Instr,* Bucks County Community College, Fine Arts Dept, Newtown PA (S)
Shaarhan, Jeff, *Prof,* Concordia University, Division of Performing & Visual Arts, Mequon WI (S)
Shablerut, Stephanie, *Marketing,* Dillman's Creative Arts Foundation, Lac Du Flambeau WI

Shablerut, Todd, *Treasurer,* Dillman's Creative Arts Foundation, Lac Du Flambeau WI

Shabout, Nada, *Assoc Prof Art History,* University of North Texas, College of Visual Arts & Design, Denton TX (S)

Shackelford, George TM, *Deputy Dir,* Kimbell Art Foundation, Kimbell Art Museum, Fort Worth TX

Shada, Mary, *Office Support Specialist,* Loveland Museum/Gallery, Loveland CO

Shady, Ronald L, *Prof,* University of North Alabama, Dept of Art, Florence AL (S)

Shaefer, Julie, *VPres Mktg & Commun,* Indiana State Museum, Indianapolis IN

Shafer, Emily, *Assistant Director,* Historical Society of Old Newbury, Cushing House Museum, Newburyport MA

Shafer, Jason, *Serials & Electronic Resources Librarian,* The Cleveland Museum of Art, Ingalls Library, Cleveland OH

Shafer, Phyllis, *Painting Instr,* Lake Tahoe Community College, Art Dept, South Lake Tahoe CA (S)

Shaffer, Travis, *Asst Tchg Prof,* University of Missouri - Columbia, Dept of Art, Columbia MO (S)

Shafik, Adel, *Prof Art,* Bakersfield College, Art Dept, Bakersfield CA (S)

Shah, Bijal, *Dir Asst,* Southern California Institute of Architecture, Los Angeles CA (S)

Shah, Monica, *Dir Colls & Chief Conservator,* Anchorage Museum at Rasmuson Center, Anchorage AK

Shahsahabi, Sam, *Asst Prof,* Lakehead University, Dept of Visual Arts, Thunder Bay ON (S)

Shain-Bryson, Gabrielle, *Owner,* Shain Gallery, Charlotte NC

Shainin, Christopher, *Exec Dir,* Museum of Northwest Art, La Conner WA

Shaken, Andy, *Asst Prof,* Oberlin College, Dept of Art, Oberlin OH (S)

Shaker, Andrea, *Asst Prof,* College of Saint Benedict, Art Dept, Saint Joseph MN (S)

Shaker, Andrea, *Asst Prof,* Saint John's University, Art Dept, Collegeville MN (S)

Shakeri, Shiva, *Mktg & Outreach Librn,* Columbus College of Art & Design, Packard Library, Columbus OH

Shakespeare, Matthew, *Exec VPres External Affairs,* American Antiquarian Society, Worcester MA

Shalom, Karen, *Admin Dir,* The Art School at Old Church, Demarest NJ (S)

Sham, James, *Asst Prof,* George Washington University, Dept of Art of Fine Arts & Art History, Washington DC (S)

Shambarger, Sara, *Dir Krasl Art Fair on the Bluff & Special Events,* Krasl Art Center, Saint Joseph MI

Shambaugh, Margie, *Assoc Educ/Vol Coordr,* Florida State University and Central Florida Community College, The Appleton Museum of Art, Ocala FL

Shamblin, Barbara, *Chmn,* Salve Regina University, Art Dept, Newport RI (S)

Shames, Susan, *Decorative Arts Librn,* Colonial Williamsburg Foundation, John D Rockefeller, Jr Library, Williamsburg VA

Shamey, Renzo, *Pres Elect,* Inter-Society Color Council, Frederick MD

Shamro, Joyce, *Prof,* Bluefield State College, Division of Arts & Sciences, Bluefield WV (S)

Shanahan, Carl, *Chmn,* State University of New York College at Geneseo, Dept of Art, Geneseo NY (S)

Shanberg, Ariel, *Exec Dir,* Center for Photography at Woodstock Inc, Woodstock NY

Shane, Robert, *Asst Prof,* The College of Saint Rose, The Center For Art and Design, Albany NY (S)

Shanfeld, Raymond, *VPres,* American Society of Contemporary Artists (ASCA), Yorktown Heights NY

Shang, Xuhong, *Prof,* Southern Illinois University, School of Art & Design, Carbondale IL (S)

Shangle, Max S, *Pres,* Harrington College of Design, Chicago IL (S)

Shanis, Carole Price, *Pres & Brd Chmn Emeritas,* Philadelphia Art Alliance, Philadelphia PA

Shank, Marilyn, *Pres,* Hoosier Salon Patrons Association, Inc, Art Gallery & Membership Organization, Indianapolis IN

Shank, Nick, *Dir,* University of Minnesota, Katherine E Nash Gallery, Minneapolis MN

Shankle, Kent, *Cur,* Waterloo Center of the Arts, Waterloo IA

Shanks, Bradlee, *Assoc Prof,* University of South Florida, School of Art & Art History, Tampa FL (S)

Shanley, Pam, *Operations Mgr,* Arlington Center for the Arts, Arlington MA

Shannon, Anna-Maria, *Assoc. Dir,* Washington State University, Museum of Art, Pullman WA

Shannon, Barbara, *Grad Admin,* Carleton University, School for Studies in Art & Culture, Ottawa ON (S)

Shannon, Jenkins, *Exec Dir,* Pasadena Museum of California Art, Pasadena CA

Shannon, Lucia M, *Head Adult Serv,* Brockton Public Library, Joseph A Driscoll Art Gallery, Brockton MA

Shannon, Mary Kay, *Cur Educ,* Branigan Cultural Center, Las Cruces NM

Shannon-Miller, Joan, *Gallery Dir,* University of Northern Colorado, Mariani Gallery, Greeley CO

Shantz, Susan, *Prof,* University of Saskatchewan, Art & Art History Dept, Saskatoon SK (S)

Shapero, Janet, *Assoc Prof,* Utah State University, Dept of Art, Logan UT (S)

Shapiro, Cara, *Dir Educ,* Louisa May Alcott Memorial Association, Orchard House, Concord MA

Shapiro, Chaya, *Asst to Dir,* Howard Community College, The Rouse Company Foundation Gallery, Columbia MD

Shapiro, David, *Prof,* William Paterson University, Dept Arts, Wayne NJ (S)

Shapiro, Keith, *Asst Prof Integrative Art & Art (Photog),* Pennsylvania State University, University Park, Penn State School of Visual Arts, University Park PA (S)

Shapiro, Martin, *Coll Develop Librn,* American University, Jack I & Dorothy G Bender Library & Learning Resources Center, New York NY

Sharafy, Azyz, *Prof,* Washburn University of Topeka, Dept of Art, Topeka KS (S)

Sharber, Virginia Anne, *Dir,* Hunter Museum of American Art, Reference Library, Chattanooga TN

Sharber, Virginia, *Exec Dir,* Hunter Museum of American Art, Chattanooga TN

Sharma, Anita, *Dir Archives,* Bose Pacia, Brooklyn NY

Sharp, Alison, *Coordr Pub Rels,* Dartmouth College, Hood Museum of Art, Hanover NH

Sharp, Kevin, *Dir,* The Dixon Gallery & Gardens, Memphis TN

Sharp, Sarah, *Prof & Dir Ctr for Innovative Research in Creative Arts,* University of Maryland, Baltimore County, Intermedia & Digital Arts (IMDA), Dept of Visual Arts, Baltimore MD (S)

Sharpe, David, *Assoc Prof,* Illinois Institute of Technology, College of Architecture, Chicago IL (S)

Sharpe, Linda, *Librn,* Turtle Bay Exploration Park, Shasta Historical Society Research Library, Redding CA

Sharpe, Yolanda, *Prof,* State University of New York College at Oneonta, Dept of Art, Oneonta NY (S)

Sharpley, Chris, *Video Game Art & Animation,* Holland College, School of Visual Arts & Journalism, Charlottetown PE (S)

Sharps, David, *Pres,* Waterfront Museum, Brooklyn NY

Sharps, Nancy, *Instr,* Chadron State College, Dept of Art, Chadron NE (S)

Sharry, Sharon, *Dir,* Jones Library, Inc, Amherst MA

Shaskan, Isabel, *Instr,* Sacramento City College, Art Dept, Sacramento CA (S)

Shastal, Belinda, *Secy,* Chicago Athenaeum, Museum of Architecture & Design, Galena IL

Shauck, Barry, *Chmn Art Educ,* Boston University, School for the Arts, Boston MA (S)

Shaughnessy, Michael, *Prof Sculpture,* University of Southern Maine, Dept of Art, Gorham ME (S)

Shaughnessy, Sandy, *Dir,* Florida Department of State, Division of Cultural Affairs, Florida Council on Arts & Culture, Tallahassee FL

Shaul, David, *Instr,* Middle Tennessee State University, Art Dept, Murfreesboro TN (S)

Shaw Lima, Patricia, *Ed Color Proof,* American Color Print Society, Narberth PA

Shaw, Andrew, *Mgr Communs,* Salt Lake City Public Library, Nonfiction & Audiovisual Dept & Gallery at Library Square, Salt Lake City UT

Shaw, Christine, *Dir & Cur,* University of Toronto at Mississauga, Blackwood Gallery, Mississauga ON

Shaw, Collin, *Mktg Specialist,* National Churchill Museum, Fulton MO

Shaw, DeAnn, *Bd Mem,* Coquille Valley Art Association, Coquille OR

Shaw, Frank, *Asst Prof,* Bethany College, Art Dept, Lindsborg KS (S)

Shaw, Frank, *Asst Prof,* Bethany College, Mingenback Art Center, Lindsborg KS

Shaw, Jill, *Sr Cur Colls,* Colgate University, Picker Art Gallery, Hamilton NY

Shaw, Justin, *Asst Prof,* University of Central Missouri, Dept of Art & Design, Warrensburg MO (S)

Shaw, Meg, *Librn,* The University of Kentucky Art Museum, Lucille Little Fine Arts Library, Lexington KY

Shaw, Richard, *Grad & undergrad faculty adv,* University of California, Berkeley, College of Letters & Sciences-Art Practice Dept, Berkeley CA (S)

Shaw, Tate, *Dir,* Visual Studies Workshop, Rochester NY (S)

Shawhan, Jeffrey, *Gallery Dir,* Concordia University Wisconsin, Fine Art Gallery, Mequon WI

Shawn, Doug, *Deputy Dir Exhibs,* Art Services International, Alexandria VA

Shay, Robert, *Dean,* University of Kentucky, Dept of Art, Lexington KY (S)

Shaykett, Jessica, *Librn,* American Craft Council, Library, Minneapolis MN

Shea, Donna, *Cur & Art Project Mgr,* Atlantic City Arts Commission, Garden Pier Art Gallery, Atlantic City NJ

Shea, Josephine, *Cur,* Edsel & Eleanor Ford House, Grosse Pointe Shores MI

Shea, Laura, *Digitization Specialist,* Mount Holyoke College, Art Museum, South Hadley MA

Shea, Norman, *Pres,* Hagerstown Junior College, Art Dept, Hagerstown MD (S)

Shea, Sue, *Treas,* The Stained Glass Association of America, Raytown MO

Sheahan, Kim, *Asst Educator,* University of Illinois at Urbana-Champaign, Spurlock Museum, Urbana IL

Sheakoski, Renee, *Mus Shop Mgr,* The Butler Institute of American Art, Art Museum, Youngstown OH

Sheaks, Barclay, *Assoc Prof,* Virginia Wesleyan College, Art Dept of the Humanities Div, Norfolk VA (S)

Shealy, Sara, *PR & Mktg Coordr,* Spartanburg Art Museum, Spartanburg SC

Shearer, Christine, *Develop Dir,* Canton Museum of Art, Art Library, Canton OH

Shearer, Lee Ann, *Contact,* First State Bank, They Also Ran Gallery, Norton KS

Sheary, Patrick, *Cur Historic Furnishings,* DAR Museum, Library, Washington DC

Sheats, Jamaal, *Dir & Cur Fisk Univ Galleries,* Fisk University, Carl Van Vechten Gallery, Nashville TN

Sheats, Jamaal, *Dir & Cur Fisk Univ Galleries,* Fisk University, Aaron Douglas Gallery, Nashville TN

Sheehan Becker, Suzanne, *VPres,* Association for Public Art, Philadelphia PA

Sheehan, Jennifer K, *Exhibs Mgr,* Grolier Club Library, New York NY

Sheehan, Kathryn T, *Registrar,* Rensselaer County Historical Society, Museum & Library, Troy NY

Sheehan, Kathryn, *Registrar,* Rensselaer County Historical Society, Hart-Cluett Mansion, 1827, Troy NY

Sheehy, Carolyn A, *Dir,* North Central College, Oesterle Library, Naperville IL

Sheehy, Colleen, *Exec Dir,* Saint Paul's Western Sculpture Park, Saint Paul MN
Sheer, Doug, *Chmn & Treas,* Artists Talk on Art (ATOA), New York NY
Sheesley, Timothy, *Gallery Dir,* State University of New York College at Oneonta, Martin - Mullen Art Gallery, Oneonta NY
Sheets, Allen, *Prof,* Minnesota State University-Moorhead, Dept of Art & Design, Moorhead MN (S)
Sheets, Luke, *Asst Prof Art,* Ohio Northern University, Dept of Art & Design, Ada OH (S)
Sheffer, Adam, *Pres,* Art Dealers Association of America, Inc, New York NY
Sheffer, Beth, *Cur Coll,* National Museum of Racing, Reference Library, Saratoga Springs NY
Sheffer, Bethany, *Cur & Registrar,* Knights of Columbus Supreme Council, Knights of Columbus Museum, New Haven CT
Sheffera, Beth, *Cur Coll,* National Museum of Racing, National Museum of Racing & Hall of Fame, Saratoga Springs NY
Sheffield, Ellen, *Instr,* Kenyon College, Art Dept, Gambier OH (S)
Sheffield, Lin, *Asst Dir,* Colquitt County Arts Center, Moultrie GA
Shefner, Christine, *Prof,* Shoreline Community College, Humanities Division, Seattle WA (S)
Sheidley, Nathaniel, *Exec Dir,* The Bostonian Society, Old State House Museum, Boston MA
Sheih, Annie, *Adj Prof,* Saint Thomas Aquinas College, Art Dept, Sparkill NY (S)
Shein, Richard, *CFO,* New-York Historical Society, Museum, New York NY
Shekore, Mark, *Prof,* Northern State University, Art Dept, Aberdeen SD (S)
Shelburne, Brian, *Visual Resources Cur,* Virginia Polytechnic Institute & State University, Art & Architecture Library, Blacksburg VA
Shell, Andrew, *Adjunct Asst Prof Fine Art,* Johnson County Community College, Fine Arts Dept & Art History Dept, Overland Park KS (S)
Shell, Martin, *Asst Prof,* Springfield College, Dept of Visual & Performing Arts, Springfield MA (S)
Shelley, Marjorie, *Conservator in Charge, Paper,* The Metropolitan Museum of Art, New York NY
Shelly, Ruth, *Exec Dir,* Portland Children's Museum, Portland OR
Shelnut-Hendrick, Stacey, *Dir Educ,* Crocker Art Museum, Research Library, Sacramento CA
Shelnut-Hendrick, Stacy, *Educ Dir,* Crocker Art Museum, Sacramento CA
Shelnutt, Greg, *Chair, Art Dept,* Clemson University, College of Architecture, Arts & Humanities, Art Dept, Clemson SC (S)
Shelton, Andrew, *Chmn,* Ohio State University, Dept of the History of Art, Columbus OH (S)
Shelton, Anita, *Dean,* Eastern Illinois University, Tarble Arts Center, Charleston IL
Shelton, Anthony, *Dir,* University of British Columbia, Museum of Anthropology, Vancouver BC
Shelton, Barbara, *Photographer,* Keystone Gallery, Scott City KS
Shelton, Betty, *Dean Fine Arts,* Art Institute of Southern California, Laguna Beach CA (S)
Shelton, Eamon, *Dir. of Opers.,* Boston Public Library, Central Library, Boston MA
Shen, Chen, *VPres World Cultures,* Royal Ontario Museum, Toronto ON
Shen, Richard, *Adjunct Asst Prof,* New York Institute of Technology, Fine Arts Dept, Old Westbury NY (S)
Shenefelt, Wendy, *Progs Mgr,* Alternate ROOTS, Inc, Atlanta GA
Sheng, Angela, *Art History Counsellor,* McMaster University, School of the Arts, Hamilton ON (S)
Shepard, Charles A, *Dir,* Fort Wayne Museum of Art, Inc, Fort Wayne IN
Shepard, Heidi, *Acad Dept Asst,* Connecticut College, Dept of Art, New London CT (S)
Shepard, Jaceena, *1st VPres & Exhib Dir,* Watercolor Society of Alabama, Town Creek AL
Shepard, Lee, *VPres Coll,* Virginia Historical Society, Library, Richmond VA
Sheperd, Lindy, *Media Coordr,* Mennello Museum of American Art, Orlando FL
Shepherd, Anna, *Develop Mgr,* Tryon Palace, New Bern NC
Shepherd, Stephanie, *Pub Rels,* Library Association of La Jolla, Athenaeum Music & Arts Library, La Jolla CA
Shepherd, Terry, *Artist in Res,* Western Colorado Center for the Arts, The Art Center, Grand Junction CO
Shepherdson-Scott, Kari, *Asst Prof,* Macalester College, Art & Art History Dept, Saint Paul MN (S)
Shepp, James G, *CEO & Exec Dir,* Art and History Museums - Maitland, Maitland FL
Shepstone, Carol, *Chief Librn,* Ryerson University, Ryerson University Library, Toronto ON
Sherer, Aaron, *Exec Dir,* Paine Art Center & Gardens, George P Nevitt Library, Oshkosh WI
Sherer, Scott, *Assoc Prof,* University of Texas at San Antonio, Dept of Art & Art History, San Antonio TX (S)
Sheridan, Clare, *Consulting Libr,* American Textile History Museum, Lowell MA
Sheridan, Ginger, *Assoc Prof Photog,* Jacksonville University, Jacksonville FL (S)
Sheriff, Mary, *Chm & Prof,* University of North Carolina at Chapel Hill, Art Dept, Chapel Hill NC (S)
Sherin, Kathleen, *Dir Gallery,* Niagara County Community College, Art Gallery, Sanborn NY
Sherk, Scott, *Assoc Prof,* Muhlenberg College, Dept of Art, Allentown PA (S)
Sherman, Dagan, *Instr,* Midland College, Art Dept, Midland TX (S)
Sherman, Gordon, *Prof,* Fort Hays State University, Dept of Art & Design, Hays KS (S)
Sherman, Paul T, *Admin Svcs Librn,* New York City Technical College, Ursula C Schwerin Library, Brooklyn NY
Sherman, Todd, *Prof,* University of Alaska Fairbanks, Art Department, Fairbanks AK (S)
Shermantine, Ray, *Facilities Supt,* The San Joaquin Pioneer & Historical Society, The Haggin Museum, Stockton CA
Shermer, James, *Grants Admin,* Broward County Board of Commissioners, Broward Cultural Div, Fort Lauderdale FL
Sherrell, Steve, *Instr,* Joliet Junior College, Fine Arts Dept, Joliet IL (S)
Sherrill, Martine, *Visual Resources Librn,* Wake Forest University, A Lewis Aycock Visual Resource Library, Winston-Salem NC
Sherrock, Roger, *CEO,* Clark County Historical Society, Heritage Center of Clark County, Springfield OH
Sherry, James, *Pres,* Segue Foundation, Reading Room-Archive, New York NY
Sherwin, Michael, *Assoc Prof,* West Virginia University, College of Creative Arts, School of Art & Design, Morgantown WV (S)
Sherwood, Katherine, *Grad & undergrad faculty adv,* University of California, Berkeley, College of Letters & Sciences-Art Practice Dept, Berkeley CA (S)
Sherwood, Patricia B, *Bd Pres,* Queens Historical Society, Kingsland Homestead, Flushing NY
Shetler, Brian, *Head Spec Colls, Archives & Methodist Librn,* United Methodist Church General Commission on Archives & History, Archives & History Center, Madison NJ
Shewchuk, Diane, *Cur,* Columbia County Historical Society, Luykas Van Alen House, Kinderhook NY
Shields, Alissa, *Asst Dir,* Chautauqua Center for the Visual Arts, Chautauqua NY
Shields, Ann, *Dir,* The Pennsylvania State University, HUB Robeson Galleries, University Park PA
Shields, Christopher, *Archivist,* Bush-Holley Historic Site & Storehouse Gallery, Greenwich Historical Society, Cos Cob CT
Shields, David, *Asst Prof,* Old Dominion University, Art Dept, Norfolk VA (S)
Shields, David, *Prof,* Texas State University - San Marcos, Dept of Art and Design, San Marcos TX (S)
Shields, Holly, *Assoc Prof,* Texas State University - San Marcos, Dept of Art and Design, San Marcos TX (S)
Shields, Paul M, *Asst Prof,* York College, Art Dept, York NE (S)
Shields, Scott, *Chief Cur & Assoc Dir,* Crocker Art Museum, Sacramento CA
Shields, Tom, *Asst Prof,* Augustana College, Art Dept, Sioux Falls SD (S)
Shields, Van W, *Exec Dir,* Museum of York County, Rock Hill SC
Shields, Van, *Exec Dir,* Berkshire Museum, Pittsfield MA
Shields, Wendy, *Dir,* City of Irvine, Irvine Fine Arts Center, Irvine CA
Shier, Kara, *Dir Admin,* Putnam County Historical Society, Foundry School Museum, Cold Spring NY
Shiffler, Meg, *Gallery Dir,* San Francisco Arts Commission, Gallery, San Francisco CA
Shifman, Barry, *Cur Decorative Arts After 1890,* Virginia Museum of Fine Arts, Richmond VA
Shifrin, Susan, *Assoc Dir Educ,* Ursinus College, Philip & Muriel Berman Museum of Art, Collegeville PA
Shih, Chia-Chun, *Librn,* Kimbell Art Foundation, Kimbell Art Museum, Fort Worth TX
Shilkoff, Jacqueline, *Assoc Cur New Media & Digital Mus,* Purchase College, Neuberger Museum of Art, Purchase NY
Shillabeer, S L, *Asst Prof,* Troy State University, Dept of Art & Classics, Troy AL (S)
Shilliam, Nicola, *Western Bibliographer,* Princeton University, Marquand Library of Art & Archaeology, Princeton NJ
Shimano, Yoshiko, *Prof,* University of New Mexico, Department of Fine Arts & Art History, Albuquerque NM (S)
Shimasaki, Sarah, *Retail Opers Dir,* Edmundson Art Foundation, Inc, Des Moines Art Center, Des Moines IA
Shimizu, Meredith, *Assoc Prof,* Whitworth University, Art Dept, Spokane WA (S)
Shimon, J, *Assoc Prof,* Lawrence University, Dept of Art & Art History, Appleton WI (S)
Shin-tsu Tai, Susan, *Cur Asian Art,* Santa Barbara Museum of Art, Library, Santa Barbara CA
Shinn, Amy, *Library Assit,* Maine College of Art, Joanne Waxman Library, Portland ME
Shinn, Nancy, *Sec,* Coquille Valley Art Association, Coquille OR
Shinners, Jackie, *Art Historian,* Northwestern Michigan College, Art Dept, Traverse City MI (S)
Shiplett, Claire, *Exec Dir,* Sunbury Shores Arts & Nature Centre, Inc, Gallery, Saint Andrews NB
Shipley, Anne, *Chmn,* Sierra Nevada College, Fine Arts Dept, Incline Village NV (S)
Shipman, Jennifer, *Special Project Manager,* Akron Art Museum, Akron OH
Shipman, John, *Dir,* University of Maryland, College Park, The Art Gallery, College Park MD
Shipp, Rebecca, *Tour Admin,* Liberty Hall Historic Site, Liberty Hall Museum, Frankfort KY
Shipp, Tony, *Prof,* Sam Houston State University, Art Dept, Huntsville TX (S)
Shiras, Susan, *Librn,* Brooks Institute of Photography, Ventura CA (S)
Shires, Christopher, *Dir Interpretation & Progs,* Edsel & Eleanor Ford House, Grosse Pointe Shores MI
Shires, James, *Educ Coordr,* Maysville, Kentucky Gateway Museum Center, Maysville KY
Shires, Jeanette, *Dir,* Northwest Florida State College, Mattie Kelly Arts Center Galleries, Niceville FL (S)
Shirey, David, *Ceramic Studio Mgr,* The Art School at Old Church, Demarest NJ (S)
Shirey, Heather, *Prof,* University of St Thomas, Deptartment of Art History, Saint Paul MN (S)
Shirley, Donna, *Dir,* Science Fiction and Fantasy Hall of Fame, Seattle WA
Shirley, Margaret, *Instr,* Marylhurst University, Art Dept, Marylhurst OR (S)

Shivers, Brooke, *Vis Svcs & Educ Programs Coord,* Morris Museum of Art, Augusta GA
Shmalo, Marlene, *Gen Educ,* AIC College of Design, Cincinnati OH (S)
Shockley, Darlas, *Dean Arts & Sciences,* Indian Hills Community College, Ottumwa Campus, Dept of Art, Ottumwa IA (S)
Shockley, Evelyn, *Prog Mgr,* Xerox Corporation, Art Collection, Norwalk CT
Shockley, Theresa, *Exec Dir,* The Community Education Center, Philadelphia PA
Shoemaker, Linda, *Exec Dir,* Arlington Center for the Arts, Arlington MA
Shofner, Judy, *Librn,* Texas Ranger Hall of Fame & Museum, Texas Ranger Research Center, Waco TX
Shomale, Lu, *Exec Dir,* Schoolhouse History & Art Center, Colstrip MT
Shook, Kevin, *Asst Prof,* Birmingham-Southern College, Art & Art History, Birmingham AL (S)
Shook, Kevin, *Prof,* Birmingham Southern College, Doris Wainwright Kennedy Art Center, Birmingham AL
Shook, Langley, *Pres,* Chesapeake Bay Maritime Museum, Saint Michaels MD
Shore, Bob, *VChmn,* Kern County Museum, Library, Bakersfield CA
Shore, Bob, *VPres,* Manhattan Graphics Center, New York NY (S)
Shore, Don, *Chmn Animation,* Mount San Antonio College, Art Dept, Walnut CA (S)
Shore, Francine, *Instr,* Main Line Art Center, Haverford PA (S)
Shore, Jeff, *Preparator,* Contemporary Arts Museum Houston, Houston TX
Short, Frank, *Coordr,* Montgomery County Community College, Art Center, Blue Bell PA (S)
Short, Georgianna, *Asst Prof,* Ohio State University, Dept of Art Education, Columbus OH (S)
Short, Janet, *Librn,* Bernice Pauahi Bishop, Library & Archives, Honolulu HI
Short, Sherry, *Asst Prof,* Minnesota State University-Moorhead, Dept of Art & Design, Moorhead MN (S)
Shortridge, Katherine, *Asst Prof,* Roanoke College, Fine Arts Dept-Art, Salem VA (S)
Shortslef, Lisa M, *Admin Aide,* State University of New York at Oswego, Tyler Art Gallery, Oswego NY
Shortt, A J (Fred), *Cur,* Canada Science & Technology Museums Corporation, Canada Aviation Museum, Ottawa ON
Shostak, Anthony, *Educ Cur,* Bates College, Museum of Art, Lewiston ME
Shoults, Lenore, *Exec Dir,* Arts & Science Center for Southeast Arkansas, Pine Bluff AR
Shoup, Libby, *Comm Coordr,* Salina Art Center, Salina KS
Showers, Norman, *Pres Emeritus,* Alton Museum of History & Art, Inc, Alton IL
Shrack, Marsha, *Art Instr,* Pratt Community College, Art Dept, Pratt KS (S)
Shrenk, Lisa, *Architectural History,* Norwich University, Dept of Architecture and Art, Northfield VT (S)
Shrewder, Susan, *Mus Shop Mgr & Buyer,* Philbrook Museum of Art, Tulsa OK
Shriver, Totem, *Instr,* Linfield College, Department of Art & Visual Culture, McMinnville OR (S)
Shteynberg, Catherine, *Asst Dir, Cur Art & Cultural Colls, Head of Web & Media,* University of Tennessee, McClung Museum of Natural History & Culture, Knoxville TN
Shtromberg, Elena, *Asst Prof,* University of Utah, Dept of Art & Art History, Salt Lake City UT (S)
Shu, Yue, *Librn,* Freer Gallery of Art & Arthur M Sackler Gallery, Library, Washington DC
Shuemake, Steve, *Asst Dir Opers,* Montgomery Museum of Fine Arts, Montgomery AL
Shuemake, Steve, *Asst Dir Opers,* Montgomery Museum of Fine Arts, Library, Montgomery AL
Shuey Altamirano, Noelle, *Coll Cur,* Palm Beach County Parks & Recreation Department, Donald B Gordon Memorial Library, Delray Beach FL
Shuflat, Michael S, *Capital Projects Admin,* Jamestown-Yorktown Foundation, Jamestown Settlement, Williamsburg VA
Shuford, Lindsey, *Asst Dir,* Union County Public Library Union Room, Monroe NC
Shugart, Sanford, *Pres,* Valencia Community College, Art Gallery-East Campus, Orlando FL
Shugert, Kate, *Mgr Publications & Exhibs,* Boston College, McMullen Museum of Art, Chestnut Hill MA
Shuler, Tawni, *Prof,* Sheridan College, Art Dept, Sheridan WY (S)
Shulman, Randy, *Asst VPres Advancement,* The Huntington Library, Art Collections & Botanical Gardens, San Marino CA
Shulman, Randy, *VPres Advancement,* The Huntington Library, Art Collections & Botanical Gardens, San Marino CA
Shultes, Stephanie, *CEO & Dir,* Iroquois Indian Museum, Howes Cave NY
Shultis, Eric, *Assoc Prof,* Saint Louis Community College at Florissant Valley, Liberal Arts Division, Ferguson MO (S)
Shultz, Jay, *Assoc Prof,* Palomar Community College, Art Dept, San Marcos CA (S)
Shultz, Mike, *Library Dir,* The University of Montana - Western, Lucy Carson Memorial Library, Dillon MT
Shultz, Randy, *Exhibs Dir,* Besser Museum for Northeast Michigan, Philip M Park Library, Alpena MI
Shum Allen, Irene, *Cur & Colls Mgr,* Philip Johnson Glass House, National Trust for Historic Preservation, New Canaan CT
Shumaker, Rhonda, *Dir,* South County Art Association, Kingston RI
Shuman, Amanda, *Assoc Dir Develop,* New Britain Museum of American Art, New Britain CT
Shumar, Allison, *Program Coordr & Visual Arts Comt Advisor,* Duke University Union, Louise Jones Brown Gallery, Durham NC
Shumow, Lynne, *Cur Educ,* Marquette University, Haggerty Museum of Art, Milwaukee WI
Shumway, John, *Asst Prof,* Slippery Rock University of Pennsylvania, Dept of Art, Slippery Rock PA (S)
Shunk, Hal, *Chmn,* Wilmington College, Art Dept, Wilmington OH (S)
Shunney, Mark, *Asst Cur,* University of California at Santa Cruz, Mary Porter Sesnon Art Gallery, Santa Cruz CA
Shurley-Olivas, Laura, *Adjunct,* College of the Canyons, Art Dept, Santa Clarita CA (S)
Shurter, James, *Asst Prof,* Mott Community College, Fine Arts & Social Sciences Division, Flint MI (S)
Shurtleff, Carol B, *Staff Coordr,* Art and History Museums - Maitland, Maitland FL
Shust, Maria, *Dir,* The Ukrainian Museum, Library, New York NY
Shust, Maria, *Dir,* The Ukrainian Museum, New York NY
Shutte, Sue, *Historic Site Admin,* Ringwood Manor House Museum, Ringwood NJ
Shynkaruk, Wil, *Assoc Prof,* Minnesota State University-Moorhead, Dept of Art & Design, Moorhead MN (S)
Shypski, Kayla, *Cur,* Buffalo Niagara Heritage Village, Amherst NY
Siano, Mary Ann, *Grants Officer,* Lehman College Art Gallery, Bronx NY
Sias, James H, *Prof,* Rochester Institute of Technology, School of Design, Rochester NY (S)
Sibbison, Diane, *Exhibits Mgr,* Delaplaine Visual Arts Education Center, Frederick MD
Siblik, John, *Dir School of Art,* Northern Illinois University, School of Art & Design, DeKalb IL (S)
Sicat, Chris, *Exhib Project Coordr,* Santa Clara University, de Saisset Museum, Santa Clara CA
Sickles, Carolyn, *Dir Engagement & Visual Arts,* Henry Street Settlement, Abrons Art Center, New York NY
Sicko, Barbara, *Registrar,* Bob Jones University Museum & Gallery Inc, Greenville SC
Sicola, Kimberly, *Coll Mgr,* County of Henrico, Meadow Farm Museum, Glen Allen VA
Siddall, Gillian, *VPres Acad & Provost,* OCAD University, Toronto ON (S)
Siddons, Louise, *Asst Prof,* Oklahoma State University, Department of Art, Graphic Design and Art History, Stillwater OK (S)
Sides, Carol, *Pres,* Pioneer Historical Museum of South Dakota, Hot Springs SD
Sides, Wayne, *Prof,* University of North Alabama, Dept of Art, Florence AL (S)
Sidner, Rob, *Exec Dir & CEO,* Mingei International, Inc, Mingei International Museum - Balboa Park & Mingei International Museum - Escondido, San Diego CA
Sidor, Christian, *Cur Vertebrate Paleontology,* University of Washington, Burke Museum of Natural History and Culture, Seattle WA
Sieber, Ellen, *Cur Educ,* Indiana University, The Mathers Museum of World Cultures, Bloomington IN
Sieber, Matthew, *Co-cur of Exhibits,* Indiana University, The Mathers Museum of World Cultures, Bloomington IN
Sieber, Richard, *Reader Svc Librn,* Philadelphia Museum of Art, Library & Archives, Philadelphia PA
Sieboda, Sedor, *Adjunct Prof,* Wilkes University, Dept of Art, Wilkes-Barre PA (S)
Siefmund, Tom, *Asst Prof,* Tidewater Community College, Visual Arts Center, Portsmouth VA (S)
Siegal, Robert L Rabin, *Dir,* Institute of Puerto Rican Culture, Museo Fuerte Conde de Mirasol, Vieques PR
Siegel, Julita, *Photo Coll Cur,* Polish Museum of America (PMA), Chicago IL
Siegesmund, Richard, *Asst Prof Art Educ,* University of Georgia, Franklin College of Arts & Sciences, Lamar Dodd School of Art, Athens GA (S)
Siegfried, Clifford, *Dir & Asst Commissioner,* New York State Museum, Albany NY
Siegfried, Jay, *Chmn,* Middlesex County College, Visual Arts Dept, Edison NJ (S)
Siegler, Cory, *Dir Asst & Gen Mgr,* Printed Matter, Inc, New York NY
Sierpinski, Cort, *Dept Head,* Southern Connecticut State University, Dept of Art, New Haven CT (S)
Sierpinski, Cort, *Dir,* Southern Connecticut State University, Art Dept, New Haven CT
Sierzha, Alonso, *Instructor,* Concordia University, Art and Design Department, Saint Paul MN (S)
Siesling, Jan, *Dir,* University of Southern Mississippi, Museum of Art, Hattiesburg MS
Sievelaing, Brian, *Board Member,* Folk Art Society of America, Richmond VA
Sievers, Ann H, *Dir, Cur,* Saint Joseph College, Art Gallery, University of Saint Joseph, West Hartford CT
Siewert, John, *Chmn,* The College of Wooster, Dept of Art and Art History, Wooster OH (S)
Sigal, Lisa, *Cur Open Sessions,* The Drawing Center, New York NY
Sigala, Patricia, *Outreach Educator,* New Mexico Department of Cultural Affairs, Museum of International Folk Art, Santa Fe NM
Sigel, Deborah S, *Assoc Prof Ceramics,* Millersville University, Dept of Art & Design, Millersville PA (S)
Sigel, Milt, *Instr,* Bucks County Community College, Fine Arts Dept, Newtown PA (S)
Sigerson, Marge, *Librn,* The Museum of Arts & Sciences Inc, Library, Daytona Beach FL
Siggers, Julian, *Dir,* University of Pennsylvania, Museum of Archaeology & Anthropology, Philadelphia PA
Siggins, Teri, *Arts & Culture Fin Dir,* Mesa Arts Center, Mesa Contemporary Arts Museum, Mesa AZ
Sigler, Doug, *Prof,* Rochester Institute of Technology, School of Design, Rochester NY (S)
Sigman, David L, *Dept Chair (art & design),* Purdue University, West Lafayette, Patti and Rusty Rueff School of Visual & Performing Arts, Art & Design Dept, West Lafayette IN (S)

Sigre-Lewis, Chris, *Painting & Drawing,* Asbury College, Student Center Gallery, Wilmore KY
Sigurdson, Victoria, *Head Visual Resources & Spec Colls,* OCAD University, Dorothy H Hoover Library, Toronto ON
Siker, Nancy, *Asst Dir Library Servs,* Milwaukee Institute of Art & Design, Milwaukee WI (S)
Siker, Nancy, *Asst Dir, Library Serv,* Milwaukee Institute of Art & Design, Library, Milwaukee WI
Sikes, Diane, *Dir Progs,* UMLAUF Sculpture Garden & Museum, Austin TX
Sikes, Diane, *Prog Dir,* Women & Their Work, Austin TX
Sikora, Carol, *Prog Coordr,* Venice Art Center, Venice FL
Silagy Benedek, Nelly, *Dir Educ,* The Jewish Museum, New York NY
Silas, Anna, *Dir,* Hopi Cultural Center Museum, Second Mesa AZ
Silberg, Nicholas, *Asst Prof,* Savannah State University, Dept of Fine Arts, Savannah GA (S)
Silberman, Jeffrey, *Chmn Textile Develop & Mktg,* Fashion Institute of Technology, School of Art & Design, New York NY (S)
Silberman, Robert, *Prof,* University of Minnesota, Minneapolis, Art History, Minneapolis MN (S)
Silbert, Susie, *Cur Modern & Contemporary Glass,* Corning Museum of Glass, Museum, Corning NY
Silcox, Sharon, *Library Asst,* North Carolina State University, Harrye Lyons Design Library, Raleigh NC
Sileika, Antanas, *Prog Dir, Creative Writing,* Humber College, School of Creative & Performing Arts, Toronto ON (S)
Silet, Emily, *Cur Educ,* deCordova Sculpture Park & Museum, Lincoln MA
Sill, Diane, *Gallery Mgr,* Gilpin County Arts Association, Central City CO
Sill, Robert, *Interim Dir Art & History,* Illinois State Museum, ISM Lockport Gallery, Chicago Gallery & Southern Illinois Art Gallery, Springfield IL
Silliman, Mark, *Dean,* Leeward Community College, Arts & Humanities Division, Pearl City HI (S)
Silva, German, *Opers Mgr,* Orlando Museum of Art, Orlando FL
Silva, German, *Opers Mgr,* Orlando Museum of Art, Orlando Sentinel Library, Orlando FL
Silva, Luis, *Asst Prof,* American University, Dept of Art, New York NY (S)
Silva, Robin, *Librn,* Portsmouth Athenaeum, Joseph Copley Research Library, Portsmouth NH
Silva, Teresa, *Dir Exhibs & Residencies,* Chicago Artists Coalition, Chicago IL
Silva, Timothy, *Art History,* Southeastern Louisiana University, Art & Design, Hammond LA (S)
Silva, Tom, *Asst Prof Art,* Tusculum College, Fine Arts Dept, Greeneville TN (S)
Silver, Nancy, *Gen Mgr,* Arts Council of Fayetteville-Cumberland County, The Arts Center, Fayetteville NC
Silveria, Kristine, *Shop Mgr,* Carmel Mission & Gift Shop, Carmel CA
Silverio, Jo-Ann B, *Admin Asst,* Farmington Village Green & Library Association, Stanley-Whitman House, Farmington CT
Silverman, Camille, *Exec Dir,* Western Colorado Center for the Arts, The Art Center, Grand Junction CO
Silverman, David, *Egyptian Section Cur,* University of Pennsylvania, Museum of Archaeology & Anthropology, Philadelphia PA
Silverman, Jason, *Cinema Dir,* The Center for Contemporary Arts of Santa Fe, Santa Fe NM
Silverman, Peggy, *Mission Coordr,* Buehler Challenger & Science Center, Paramus NJ
Silverman, Robert, *Asst Prof,* Louisiana State University, School of Art, Baton Rouge LA (S)
Silverman, Yehudit, *Coordr, Creative Arts Therapies,* Concordia University, Faculty of Fine Arts, Montreal QC (S)
Silverstein, Romy, *Dir,* Addison/Ripley Fine Art, Washington DC
Silverthorne, Jeanette, *Assoc Dir,* Columbia University, Miriam & Ira D Wallach Art Gallery, New York NY
Silvis, Gregg, *Asst Dir Library Computing Systems,* University of Delaware, Morris Library, Newark DE
Sim, Richard, *Prof,* Antelope Valley College, Art Dept, Division of Fine Arts, Lancaster CA (S)
Simard, Claire, *Secy,* Institut des Arts au Saguenay, Centre National D'Exposition a Jonquiere, Jonquiere QC
Simard, Jim, *Librn, Head Historical Coll,* Alaska State Library, Alaska Historical Collections, Juneau AK
Simblist, Noah, *Chair,* Southern Methodist University, Meadows School of the Arts - Division of Art, Dallas TX (S)
Simcoe, Barbara, *Prof,* University of Nebraska at Omaha, School of the Arts, Omaha NE (S)
Simcox, Andrew, *Placement, Faculty,* Antonelli Institute, Professional Photography & Commercial Art, Erdenheim PA (S)
Siminoski, Rachel, *Curatorial Asst,* Green Hill Center for North Carolina Art, Greenhill, Greensboro NC
Simkin, Phillips, *Coordr Fine Arts,* York College of the City University of New York, Fine & Performing Arts, Jamaica NY (S)
Simkin, Steven, *VPres,* Dahesh Museum of Art, Greenwich CT
Simmonds, Kim, *Exec Dir,* MonDak Heritage Center, Museum, Sidney MT
Simmons, Arthur L, *Exec Dir,* Rome Historical Society, William E Scripture Memorial Library, Rome NY
Simmons, Arthur L, *Exec Dir,* Rome Historical Society, Museum & Archives, Rome NY
Simmons, Donald, *Asst Prof Art,* Middle Georgia State University, College of Arts & Sciences, Media, Culture & the Arts, Cochran GA (S)
Simmons, Glori, *Dir,* The University of San Francisco Thacher Gallery, San Francisco CA
Simmons, Katherine, *Pres,* Lyme Art Association, Inc, Old Lyme CT
Simmons, Michael, *Prof Emeritus,* California State University, Chico, Department of Art & Art History, Chico CA (S)
Simmons, Seymour, *Assoc Prof,* Winthrop University, Dept of Art & Design, Rock Hill SC (S)
Simms, Jennifer, *Instr,* Greenfield Community College, Art Dept, Greenfield MA (S)
Simon, Ann, *Instr,* Main Line Art Center, Haverford PA (S)
Simon, Anne, *Accounting Asst,* Buffalo Arts Studio, Art Gallery, Buffalo NY
Simon, David, *Prof,* Colby College, Art Dept, Waterville ME (S)
Simon, Eric, *Chair, Studio Arts,* Concordia University, Faculty of Fine Arts, Montreal QC (S)
Simon, Gladys, *Opers Mgr,* The Museum of Western Art, Kerrville TX
Simon, Janice, *Assoc Prof Art History,* University of Georgia, Franklin College of Arts & Sciences, Lamar Dodd School of Art, Athens GA (S)
Simon, Joshua, *Exec Dir,* East Bay Asian Local Development Corp (EBALDC), Asian Resource Gallery, Oakland CA
Simon, Lisa, *Asst Prof,* Jefferson Community College & Technical College, Fine Arts, Louisville KY (S)
Simon, Meryl, *Librn,* Aesthetic Realism Foundation, Eli Siegel Collection, New York NY
Simon, Patricia, *Assoc Prof Theatre,* Marymount Manhattan College, Fine & Performing Arts Div, New York NY (S)
Simon, Robert, *Chmn Dept,* Holy Names College, Art Dept, Oakland CA (S)
Simona, Lauti, *Chmn Board Trustees,* Jean P Haydon, Pago Pago, American Samoa PI
Simoneau, Christiane, *Exec Dir,* Galerie d'Art du Parc-Manoir de Tonnancour, Manoir de Tonnancour, Trois Rivieres QC
Simoneaux, Victoria, *VPres,* St Mary Chapter Louisiana Landmarks Society, Grevemberg House Museum, Franklin LA
Simonite, Patricia, *Prof,* Trinity University, Department of Art & Art History, San Antonio TX (S)
Simons, Chris, *Prof,* Shoreline Community College, Humanities Division, Seattle WA (S)
Simons, Rachel, *Instr,* American University, Dept of Art, New York NY (S)
Simons, Sheri, *Prof,* California State University, Chico, Department of Art & Art History, Chico CA (S)
Simonsen, Garric, *Asst Prof,* Spokane Falls Community College, Fine Arts Dept, Spokane WA (S)
Simonsen, Oliver, *Pres of Board,* Canajoharie Library & Art Gallery, Library, Canajoharie NY
Simonsen, Oliver, *Pres of Board,* Canajoharie Library & Art Gallery, Arkell Museum of Canajoharie, Canajoharie NY
Simonson, Kurt, *Assoc Prof,* Biola University, Department of Art, La Mirada CA (S)
Simor, Suzanna, *Dir,* Queens College, City University of New York, Queens College Art Center, Flushing NY
Simor, Suzanna, *Head,* Queens College, City University of New York, Art Library, Flushing NY
Simpkins, Wayne, *Chmn Asst,* University of Memphis, Art Dept, Memphis TN (S)
Simpson Darden, Barbara, *Dean Library Serv,* Kutztown University, Rohrbach Library, Kutztown PA
Simpson Voth, Karrie, *Prof,* Fort Hays State University, Dept of Art & Design, Hays KS (S)
Simpson, Jr, John, *Media Arts & Animation,* Art Institute of Pittsburgh, Pittsburgh PA (S)
Simpson, Alan, *Chmn,* Buffalo Bill Memorial Association, Buffalo Bill Historical Center, Cody WY
Simpson, Bennett, *Sr Cur,* The Museum of Contemporary Art (MOCA), MOCA Grand Avenue, Los Angeles CA
Simpson, Erion, *Exec Dir,* Taos Art Museum, Taos NM
Simpson, Gail, *Prof,* University of Wisconsin, Madison, Dept of Art, Madison WI (S)
Simpson, Jane, *Visual Arts Dir,* Colquitt County Arts Center, Moultrie GA
Simpson, Janet F, *Exec Dir,* Kansas City Artists Coalition, Kansas City MO
Simpson, Janice, *Dir Grad Prog,* Michigan State University, Dept of Art & Art History, East Lansing MI (S)
Simpson, Kathleen, *Dir Museum Educ & Institutional Advancement,* Springfield Museums, George Walker Vincent Smith Art Museum, Springfield MA
Simpson, Kathleen, *VPres,* Springfield Museums, Michele & Donald D'Amour Museum of Fine Arts, Springfield MA
Simpson, Larry, *Chmn,* University of South Alabama, Dept of Art & Art History, Mobile AL (S)
Simpson, Larry, *Chmn & Graphic Design,* University of South Alabama, Dept of Art & Art History, Mobile AL (S)
Simpson, Larry, *Pres,* Culberson County Historical Museum, Clark Hotel Historical Museum, Van Horn TX
Simpson, Leland, *Bd Mem,* Coquille Valley Art Association, Coquille OR
Simpson, Lisa A, *Dir,* Louisa May Alcott Memorial Association, Orchard House, Concord MA
Simpson, Marc, *Cur American Art,* Clark Art Institute, Williamstown MA
Simpson, Mary, *Asst Prof,* Eastern Illinois University, Art Dept, Charleston IL (S)
Simpson, Matthew, *VPres Mktg & Communs,* Museum of Science & Industry, Chicago IL
Simpson, Michael, *Lectr,* University of North Carolina at Charlotte, Dept Art, Charlotte NC (S)
Simpson, Milward, *Exec Dir,* Paramount Gallery, Saint Cloud MN
Simpson, Pamela H, *Prof,* Washington and Lee University, Div of Art, Lexington VA (S)

Simpson, Pamela, *Chmn Dept Art,* Washington & Lee University, Gallery of DuPont Hall, Lexington VA

Simpson, Samantha, *Gallery Director, Curator of Collections,* Georgetown College, Georgetown College Fine Art Galleries, Georgetown KY

Simpson, Shannon, *Cur,* Ellis County Museum Inc, Waxahachie TX

Sims, Arlie, *Head Ref & Instruction,* Columbia College Chicago, Library, Chicago IL

Sims, Nathan, *Instr,* Waynesburg College, Dept of Fine Arts, Waynesburg PA (S)

Sims, Theo, *Preparator,* Plug In, Institute of Contemporary Art, Winnipeg MB

Simtich, Andrea, *Dept Chair,* Cornell University, Dept of Architecture, Ithaca NY (S)

Sincavage, Heather, *Dir,* Wilkes University, Sordoni Art Gallery, Wilkes-Barre PA

Sinchak, Kenneth, *CFO,* Cleveland Botanical Garden, Eleanor Squire Library, Cleveland OH

Sinclair, Don, *Assoc Prof & Chair, Dept of Computational Arts,* York University, School of the Arts, Media, Performance & Design, Toronto ON (S)

Sinclair, Jane, *Prof,* Chapman University, Art Dept, Orange CA (S)

Sinclaire, Mahara T, *Gallery Dir,* Pasadena City College, Art Galleries, Pasadena CA

Sincox, Kim Robinson, *Cur,* State of North Carolina, Battleship North Carolina, Wilmington NC

Sindelar, Norma, *Archivist,* Saint Louis Art Museum, Richardson Memorial Library, Saint Louis MO

Sinfield, Ann, *Registrar,* University of Wisconsin-Madison, Chazen Museum of Art, Madison WI

Sing, Susan, *Instr,* Glendale Community College, Visual & Performing Arts Div, Glendale CA (S)

Singer, Marijane, *Dir,* Blauvelt Demarest Foundation, Hiram Blauvelt Art Museum, Oradell NJ

Singerman, Howard, *Chmn & Galleries Exec Dir,* Hunter College, Dept of Art & Art History, New York NY (S)

Singh, Juanita, *Admin Asst,* Northeast Document Conservation Center, Inc, Andover MA

Singh, Sandra, *Head Librarian,* Vancouver Public Library, Public Art Program, Vancouver BC

Singh, Somya, *Dir Exhibs,* Portland Children's Museum, Portland OR

Singh-Bischofberger, Surana, *Assoc Prof,* East Los Angeles College, Art Dept, Monterey Park CA (S)

Singletary, Sandy, *Asst Prof Art,* Lander University, College of Arts & Humanities - Visual Arts, Greenwood SC (S)

Singleton, Carolyn, *Dir,* Carnegie Arts Center, Leavenworth KS

Singleton, David, *Dir,* Public Library of Charlotte & Mecklenburg County, Charlotte NC

Singleton, Pamela, *Treas,* Artists' Fellowship, Inc, New York NY

Sinnett, Gretchen, *Asst Prof,* Salem State University, Art & Design Department, Salem MA (S)

Sinon, Michael, *Carmel Gallery Mgr,* Hoosier Salon Patrons Association, Inc, Art Gallery & Membership Organization, Indianapolis IN

Sio, Elizabeth M, *Sec,* John D Barrow, Skaneateles NY

Siokalo, Zorianne, *Cur Pub Progs,* James A Michener Art Museum, Doylestown PA

Sipiorski, Dennis, *Art Dept Head,* Nicholls State University, Dept of Art, Thibodaux LA (S)

Sipp, Kevin, *Gallery 72 Project Coordr,* City of Atlanta, Gallery 72, Atlanta GA

Sippel, Jeffrey, *Assoc Prof,* University of Missouri, Saint Louis, Dept of Art & Art History, Saint Louis MO (S)

Siracusa, Joseph, *VP Opers,* New York State Historical Association, Fenimore Art Museum, Cooperstown NY

Siren, Janne, *Peggy Pierce Elfvin Dir,* Albright-Knox Art Gallery, Buffalo NY

Sirmans, Franklin, *Dir,* Perez Art Museum Miami, Miami FL

Sirna, Jessie, *Prof,* Mott Community College, Fine Arts & Social Sciences Division, Flint MI (S)

Siry, Joseph, *Chair,* Wesleyan University, Dept of Art & Art History, Middletown CT (S)

Sissen, Melissa M, *Pub Servs Librn,* Siena Heights College, Art Library, Adrian MI

Sisson, Mark, *Prof,* Oklahoma State University, Department of Art, Graphic Design and Art History, Stillwater OK (S)

Sissons, Kimberly, *Collections Mgr,* University of Illinois at Urbana-Champaign, Krannert Art Museum and Kinkead Pavilion, Champaign IL

Siwecki, Barbara, *University Galleries Coordr,* Wright State University, Robert and Elaine Stein Galleries, Dayton OH

Six, Dean, *Exec Dir,* Museum of American Glass in WV, Weston WV

Six, Trudy, *Gallery Mgr,* Center for Contemporary Arts, Abilene TX

Sjogren, Margaret, *Dept Chmn,* Southern Oregon University, Art & Art History Dept, Ashland OR (S)

Sjogren, Margaret, *Prod,* Southern Oregon University, Art & Art History Dept, Ashland OR (S)

Sjoholm, Karen, *Chair,* John F Kennedy, Department of Arts & Consciousness, Pleasant Hill CA (S)

Sjovold, Erling, *Asst Prof,* University of Richmond, Dept of Art and Art History, Richmond VA (S)

Skaff, Stephanie, *Develop Assoc,* Dieu Donne Papermill, Inc, Gallery, Brooklyn NY

Skaggs, Dale, *Dir Horticulture,* The Dixon Gallery & Gardens, Memphis TN

Skaggs, Steve, *Prof,* University of Louisville, Allen R Hite Art Institute, Louisville KY (S)

Skeele, Devon, *Librn & Archivist,* New Mexico Department of Cultural Affairs, New Mexico Museum of Art, Unit of NM Dept of Cultural Affairs, Santa Fe NM

Skillman, Teri, *Program Specialist,* King Kamehameha V Judiciary History Center, Honolulu HI

Skinner, Arthur, *Prof,* Eckerd College, Art Dept, Saint Petersburg FL (S)

Skinner, Bill, *Chmn Div of Communs & Arts,* North Arkansas Community-Technical College, Art Dept, Harrison AR (S)

Skinner, Jaineth, *Asst Prof,* Bemidji State University, Visual Arts Dept, Bemidji MN (S)

Skinner, Steven A, *Dir,* Lewis County Historical Museum, Library, Chehalis WA

Sklar, Marilyn, *Cur Educ,* DAR Museum, Library, Washington DC

Skliris, Dimitris, *Dir Exhibs,* Mary R Koch Arts Center, Mark Arts, Wichita KS

Skoglund, Margaret, *Prof Emeritus,* University of Southern Indiana, Art & Design Dept, Evansville IN (S)

Skorton, David, *Secy,* Smithsonian Institution, Smithsonian Institution Building (The Castle), Washington DC

Skove, Margaret A, *Dir,* Huntington Museum of Art, Huntington WV

Skroch, Diana P, *Div Chair,* Valley City State College, Art Dept, Valley City ND (S)

Skrzynski, Jackie, *Assoc Prof Drawing & Painting,* Ramapo College of New Jersey, School of Contemporary Arts, Mahwah NJ (S)

Skubinna, Bradd, *Adjunct asst Prof,* Spokane Falls Community College, Fine Arts Dept, Spokane WA (S)

Skupin, Marinta, *Cur Educ,* Laguna Art Museum, Laguna Beach CA

Skuratofsky, Carol, *Mgr,* Prudential Art Program, Newark NJ

Skurkis, Barry, *Assoc Prof,* North Central College, Dept of Art, Naperville IL (S)

Skutvik, Keilayn, *Store Mgr,* University of North Carolina at Chapel Hill, Ackland Art Museum, Chapel Hill NC

Skvarla, Diane, *Cur,* United States Senate Commission on Art, Reference Library, Washington DC

Skwerski, Thomas, *Mus Cur,* Springfield Museum of Art, Library, Springfield OH

Slack, Joe, *Pres,* Coos County Historical Society Museum, Coos Bay OR

Slade, Alex, *Asst Chmn,* Otis College of Art & Design, Fine Arts, Los Angeles CA (S)

Slade, Kathy, *Cur Educ,* Buffalo Niagara Heritage Village, Amherst NY

Slade, Terry, *Asst Prof,* Hartwick College, Art Dept, Oneonta NY (S)

Slagell, Jeff H, *Asst Dir,* Delta State University, Roberts LaForge Library, Cleveland MS

Slagle, Jim, *Chair & Assoc Prof Art,* Lander University, College of Arts & Humanities - Visual Arts, Greenwood SC (S)

Slagle, Nancy, *Assoc Dir & Assoc Prof,* Texas Tech University, Dept of Art, Lubbock TX (S)

Slane, Kathleen, *Prof,* University of Missouri - Columbia, Art History & Archaeology Dept, Columbia MO (S)

Slaney, Deborah, *Cur History,* Albuquerque Museum of Art & History, Albuquerque NM

Slania, Heather, *Dir of Libr & Res Ctr,* National Museum of Women in the Arts, Library & Research Center, Washington DC

Slankard, Mark, *Assoc Prod,* Cleveland State University, Art Dept, Cleveland OH (S)

Slater, Kaiti, *Assoc Prof,* University of Utah, Dept of Art & Art History, Salt Lake City UT (S)

Slater, Lynn-Joy, *Finance Mgr,* Canadian Museum for Human Rights, Winnipeg MB

Slater, Sandra, *Genealogy Librn,* Phelps County Historical Society, Nebraska Prairie Museum, Holdrege NE

Slater, Sandra, *Genealogy Librn,* Phelps County Historical Society, Donald O. Lindgren Library, Holdrege NE

Slater-Tanner, Susan, *Asst Prof Arts & Communs,* Orange County Community College, Arts & Communication, Middletown NY (S)

Slatery, W Patrick, *Art Dept Chmn,* Palm Beach Community College, Dept of Art, Lake Worth FL (S)

Slatkin, Wendy E, *Lectr,* California State Polytechnic University, Pomona, Department of Art, Pomona CA (S)

Slatton, Ralph, *Prof,* East Tennessee State University, College of Arts and Sciences, Dept of Art & Design, Johnson City TN (S)

Slaughter, Rebecca, *Asst Mgr,* Branigan Cultural Center, Las Cruces NM

Slautterback, Catharina, *Cur Prints & Photos,* Boston Athenaeum, Boston MA

Slavick, Elin O, *Prof,* University of North Carolina at Chapel Hill, Art Dept, Chapel Hill NC (S)

Slavin, Ruth, *Deputy Dir Educ,* University of Michigan, Museum of Art, Ann Arbor MI

Slawson, Brian, *Assoc Prof,* University of Florida, School of Art & Art History, Gainesville FL (S)

Slaymaker, Samuel C, *Exec Dir,* Rock Ford Foundation, Inc, Rock Ford Plantation, Lancaster PA

Sledd, Michael, *Instr,* Columbia College, Art Dept, Columbia MO (S)

Sledge, Sarah, *Dir Commun,* Cedarhurst Center for the Arts, Mitchell Museum, Mount Vernon IL

Slein, Alison, *Prof,* Virginia Polytechnic Institute & State University, Dept of Art & Art History, Blacksburg VA (S)

Slein, Philip, *Co-Owner,* Philip Slein Gallery, Saint Louis MO

Slick, David, *Mgr Facilities,* Norman Rockwell Museum, Stockbridge MA

Slider, HJ, *Adjunct Asst Prof Art Educ,* Aquinas College, Art Dept, Grand Rapids MI (S)

Slimon, Gary, *Dir,* Canadian Wildlife & Wilderness Art Museum, Ottawa ON

Slimon, Gary, *Dir,* Canadian Wildlife & Wilderness Art Museum, Library, Ottawa ON

Sloan, David, *Chmn,* Whittier College, Dept of Art, Whittier CA (S)

Sloan, Geno, *Contact Person,* Mott Gallery of History & Art, Mott ND

Sloan, Katherine, *Pres,* Massachusetts College of Art, Boston MA (S)

Sloan, Laurie, *Assoc Head,* University of Connecticut, Dept of Art & Art History, Storrs CT (S)

Sloan, Mark, *Dir,* College of Charleston School of Arts, Halsey Institute of Contemporary Art, Charleston SC

Sloane, Kim, *Asst Prof,* Cedar Crest College, Art Dept, Allentown PA (S)

Sloane, Robert, *Librn & Head Art Dept,* Chicago Public Library, Harold Washington Library Center, Chicago IL

Slobe, Gennie, *Progs Coordr,* Workman & Temple Family Homestead Museum, City of Industry CA

Sloboda, Stacey, *Assoc Prof,* Southern Illinois University, School of Art & Design, Carbondale IL (S)

Slonaker, Evan, *Exec Dir,* Allegany County Historical Society, Gordon-Roberts House, Cumberland MD

Slorck, Lonnie, *Prof Photog,* Central Wyoming College, Art Center, Riverton WY (S)

Slovin, Rochelle, *Dir,* American Museum of the Moving Image, Astoria NY

Slyfield, Donna, *Adult Servs,* Helen M Plum, Lombard IL

Small, Carol, *Asst Prof,* Gettysburg College, Dept of Visual Arts, Gettysburg PA (S)

Small, Cindy, *Faculty,* Green River Community College, Art Dept, Auburn WA (S)

Small, Lisa, *Cur European Art,* Brooklyn Museum, Brooklyn NY

Small, Tempris, *Asst for Admin,* The Metropolitan Museum of Art, The Met Breuer, New York NY

Smalley, David, *Prof,* Connecticut College, Dept of Art, New London CT (S)

Smalls, James, *Prof,* University of Maryland, Baltimore County, Intermedia & Digital Arts (IMDA), Dept of Visual Arts, Baltimore MD (S)

Smallwood, Linda, *Library Asst,* Maine College of Art, Joanne Waxman Library, Portland ME

Smart Martin, Ann, *Assoc Prof,* University of Wisconsin, Madison, Dept of Art History, Madison WI (S)

Smart, Pamela, *Assoc Prof,* Binghamton University, Art History Department, Binghamton NY (S)

Smelko, James J, *Interior Design,* Art Institute of Pittsburgh, Pittsburgh PA (S)

Smetak, Robert, *Dir Financial Services,* The Illinois Institute of Art - Chicago, Chicago IL (S)

Smetana, David, *Chmn Art Comt,* North Canton Public Library, The Little Art Gallery, North Canton OH

Smetana, Zbynek, *Lectr,* Murray State University, Dept of Art, Murray KY (S)

Smigocki, Stephen, *Prof,* Fairmont State College, Div of Fine Arts, Fairmont WV (S)

Smiley, Kristen, *Develop Assoc,* Cultural Council of Palm Beach County, Lake Worth FL

Smilkovich, Cora, *Exec Dir,* The Art Cafe, Davisburg MI

Smit, David, *Assoc Prof,* Illinois Central College, Arts & Communication Dept, East Peoria IL (S)

Smith de Tarnowsky, Andrea, *Historic Site Mgr,* T C Steele State Historic Site, Nashville IN

Smith Lake, Kendal, *Pub Information Officer,* Modern Art Museum, Fort Worth TX

Smith, Jr, C Shaw, *Chmn,* Davidson College, Art Dept, Davidson NC (S)

Smith, Allison, *Assoc Prof Art History & Chair Art History,* Johnson County Community College, Fine Arts Dept & Art History Dept, Overland Park KS (S)

Smith, Allison, *Prog Mgr,* Association of Collegiate Schools of Architecture, Washington DC

Smith, Alyssa, *Mktg Asst,* The Columbian Theatre Foundation, Inc, Columbian Theatre Museum & Art Center, Wamego KS

Smith, Arthur, *Pub Rels Dir,* Louisiana Department of Culture, Recreation & Tourism, Louisiana State Museum, New Orleans LA

Smith, B J, *Dir,* Oklahoma State University, Gardiner Art Gallery, Stillwater OK

Smith, Barb, *Preparator,* University of Missouri, Museum of Art & Archaeology, Columbia MO

Smith, Bettina, *Mgr Image Coll & Fieldwork Archives,* Dumbarton Oaks, Image Collections and Fieldwork Archives, Washington DC

Smith, Bob, *Contact,* Buena Vista Museum of Natural History, Bakersfield CA

Smith, Bradley K, *Cur Adminr,* Pennsylvania Historical & Museum Commission, The State Museum of Pennsylvania, Harrisburg PA

Smith, Bradley, *Cur,* Pennsylvania Historical & Museum Commission, Railroad Museum of Pennsylvania, Strasburg PA

Smith, Brena, *Reference & Instruction Librn,* California Institute of the Arts Library, Santa Clarita CA

Smith, Brenda, *Gallery Manager,* George Phippen, Phippen Museum - Art of the American West, Prescott AZ

Smith, Brett, *Pub Progs,* The Rockwell Museum, Corning NY

Smith, Brian, *Photo Lab Technician,* Trust Authority, Museum of the Great Plains, Lawton OK

Smith, Bruce, *Deputy Dir External Affairs,* deCordova Sculpture Park & Museum, Lincoln MA

Smith, C, *Prof,* Community College of Rhode Island, Dept of Art, Warwick RI (S)

Smith, Carolyn, *Librn,* Johns Hopkins University, George Peabody Library, Baltimore MD

Smith, Catherine Howett, *Assoc Dir,* Emory University, Michael C Carlos Museum, Atlanta GA

Smith, Charles, *Instr,* Southern University A & M College, School of Architecture, Baton Rouge LA (S)

Smith, Christy, *Student Svcs,* Maine Photographic Workshops, The International T.V. & Film Workshops & Rockport College, Rockport ME (S)

Smith, Claudia, *Prof,* University of Wisconsin-Stout, Dept of Art & Design, Menomonie WI (S)

Smith, Conifer, *Prof,* Kirkwood Community College, Dept of Arts & Humanities, Cedar Rapids IA (S)

Smith, Corrine, *Adj Prof,* Augustana College, Art Dept, Rock Island IL (S)

Smith, Craig, *Assoc Prof,* University of Florida, School of Art & Art History, Gainesville FL (S)

Smith, Craig, *Instr,* American River College, Dept of Art/Art New Media, Sacramento CA (S)

Smith, Curtis, *Instr Music,* University of Colorado-Colorado Springs, Visual & Performing Arts Dept (VAPA), Colorado Springs CO (S)

Smith, Darrin, *Pres & CEO,* Washington Pavilion of Arts & Science, Visual Arts Center, Sioux Falls SD

Smith, David H., *Acting Exec Dir,* Columbia County Historical Society, Columbia County Museum and Library, Kinderhook NY

Smith, David, *Assoc Prof,* Edgewood College, Art Dept, Madison WI (S)

Smith, David, *Asst Prof Graphic Design,* Jacksonville University, Jacksonville FL (S)

Smith, David, *Preparator & Asst Cur,* University of Lethbridge, Art Gallery, Lethbridge AB

Smith, David, *Pres,* Brewton-Parker College, Visual Arts, Mount Vernon GA (S)

Smith, Debbie, *Comm Mgr,* University of Oregon, Jordan Schnitzer Museum of Art, Eugene OR

Smith, Debbie, *Dir,* Stanley Museum, Inc, Kingfield ME

Smith, Diane, *Chmn Acad Studies Dept,* Art Academy of Cincinnati, Cincinnati OH (S)

Smith, Dickson K, *Dean Arts & Scis,* Cardinal Stritch University, Art Dept, Milwaukee WI (S)

Smith, Don, *Dean,* Maryland College of Art & Design, Silver Spring MD (S)

Smith, Doretha, *Secy,* Miles B Carpenter Folk Art Museum, Waverly VA

Smith, Doug, *Instr,* Modesto Junior College, Arts Humanities & Communications Division, Modesto CA (S)

Smith, Edward, *Asst,* Louisiana State University, School of Art, Baton Rouge LA (S)

Smith, Elise, *Chmn,* Millsaps College, Dept of Art, Jackson MS (S)

Smith, Elizabeth B, *Assoc Prof,* Pennsylvania State University, University Park, Dept of Art History, University Park PA (S)

Smith, Elizabeth, *Exec Dir,* Sharon Arts Center, Sharon Arts Center Exhibition Gallery, Peterborough NH

Smith, Emily, *Cur Modern & Contemporary Art,* Virginia Museum of Fine Arts, Richmond VA

Smith, Emily, *Exec Dir,* 1708 Gallery, Richmond VA

Smith, G., *Fine Art Dir,* Queen's University, Faculty of Arts & Sciences, Creative Arts Program, Kingston ON (S)

Smith, Gab, *Exec Dir,* CAM Contemporary Art Museum, Raleigh NC

Smith, Gary T, *Dir,* Hartnell College Gallery, Salinas CA

Smith, George, *Asst Prof,* University of the District of Columbia, Dept of Mass Media, Visual & Performing Arts, Washington DC (S)

Smith, George, *Prof Emeritus,* Rice University, Visual & Dramatic Arts, Houston TX (S)

Smith, Gil R, *Chmn,* Eastern Kentucky University, Art Dept, Richmond KY (S)

Smith, Gregory A, *Pres,* Art Academy of Cincinnati, Cincinnati OH (S)

Smith, Greta, *Library Asst,* Old Colony Historical Society, Library, Taunton MA

Smith, Howard, *Adj Asst Prof,* College of Staten Island, Performing & Creative Arts Dept, Staten Island NY (S)

Smith, Ian, *Pres Bd Dir,* Santa Barbara Contemporary Arts Forum, Santa Barbara CA

Smith, Jack, *VPres,* Westmoreland Museum of American Art, Art Reference Library, Greensburg PA

Smith, James F, *Registrar,* Carleton College, Art Gallery, Northfield MN

Smith, Jan Mirenda, *Exec Dir,* Bergstrom-Mahler Museum of Glass, Library, Neenah WI

Smith, Jasmine, *Libr,* Chester County Historical Society, West Chester PA

Smith, JD, *Develop Dir,* Pendleton Center for the Arts, Pendleton OR

Smith, Jeff, *Cur,* Columbia River Maritime Museum, Astoria OR

Smith, Jeff, *Cur,* Columbia River Maritime Museum, Library, Astoria OR

Smith, Jennifer, *Assoc Cur,* Washington County Museum of Fine Arts, Hagerstown MD

Smith, Jerry, *Chief Cur,* Dayton Art Institute, Dayton OH

Smith, Jessica, *Publicity,* Ellen Noel Art Museum of the Permian Basin, Odessa TX

Smith, John O, *Prof,* University of Wisconsin-Stevens Point, Dept of Art & Design, Stevens Point WI (S)

Smith, John, *Dir,* Rhode Island School of Design, Museum of Art, Providence RI

Smith, John, *Dir Mus of Art,* Rhode Island School of Design, Providence RI (S)

Smith, Joseph E, *Prof,* Oakland City University, Division of Fine Arts, Oakland City IN (S)

Smith, Josh, *Asst Prof,* Asbury University, Art Dept, Wilmore KY (S)

Smith, Joshua, *Gallery Mgr,* Salina Art Center, Salina KS

Smith, Judith, *Dir,* The Contemporary Austin, Austin TX

Smith, Jury, *Prof Ceramics,* Saint Joseph's University, Art Dept, Philadelphia PA (S)

Smith, Karen Burgess, *VPres Acad Affairs,* New Hampshire Institute of Art, Manchester NH

Smith, Karyn, *Sec,* New Zone Virtual Gallery, Eugene OR

Smith, Katherine, *Facilities Coordr,* African American Museum of Iowa, Cedar Rapids IA

Smith, Kathy, *Admin Dir,* Riverside Art Museum, Library, Riverside CA

Smith, Katie, *Dir Special Events,* Marian University, Allison Mansion, Indianapolis IN

Smith, Kelly, *Develop Mgr,* Hickory Museum of Art, Inc, Hickory NC

Smith, Kendall, *Dir,* Art Museum of Greater Lafayette, Lafayette IN

Smith, Kerry, *Prep,* University of Connecticut, William Benton Museum of Art, Storrs CT

Smith, Kevin P, *Deputy Dir & Cur,* Brown University, Haffenreffer Museum of Anthropology, Providence RI

Smith, Kimberly, *Prof,* Southwestern University, Sarofim School of Fine Art, Dept of Art & Art History, Georgetown TX (S)
Smith, Laura E, *Dir Educ,* Huntsville Museum of Art, Reference Library, Huntsville AL
Smith, Laura S, *Chief Advancement Officer,* National Assembly of State Arts Agencies, Washington DC
Smith, Laura, *Mus Academy Dir,* Huntsville Museum of Art, Huntsville AL
Smith, Leah, *Tour Coordr,* Academy of the New Church, Glencairn Museum, Bryn Athyn PA
Smith, Leslie, *Asst Prof,* University of Wisconsin, Madison, Dept of Art, Madison WI (S)
Smith, Liz, *Assoc Prof,* University of Central Arkansas, Department of Art, Conway AR (S)
Smith, Lyn, *Dir Educ,* The Dairy Barn Arts Center, Athens OH
Smith, Lynn, *A/V Archivist,* National Archives & Records Administration, Herbert Hoover Presidential Library - Museum, West Branch IA
Smith, Maie, *Group Tour Mgr,* Delta Blues Museum, Clarksdale MS
Smith, Malcolm, *Assoc Prof,* Indiana University, Bloomington, Henry Radford Hope School of Fine Arts, Bloomington IN (S)
Smith, Margaret Park, *Instr,* Asbury University, Art Dept, Wilmore KY (S)
Smith, Mariann, *Cur Educ,* The Buffalo Fine Arts Academy, Albright-Knox Art Gallery, Buffalo NY
Smith, Marilyn, *Dir,* Southern Alberta Art Gallery, Library, Lethbridge AB
Smith, Marilyn, *Prof,* Appalachian State University, Dept of Art, Boone NC (S)
Smith, Mark Addison, *Asst Prof,* City College of New York, Art Dept, New York NY (S)
Smith, Mark, *Dir,* Portland Community College, North View Gallery, Portland OR
Smith, Mark, *Prof,* Austin College, Art Dept, Sherman TX (S)
Smith, Mary Ruth, *Prof,* Baylor University - College of Arts and Sciences, Dept of Art, Waco TX (S)
Smith, Matt, *Asst Prof,* University of Mary Hardin-Baylor, College of Visual & Performing Arts, Belton TX (S)
Smith, Matthew Ryan, *Cur,* Glenhyrst Art Gallery of Brant, Brantford ON
Smith, Maureen, *Bus & Progs Coordr,* University of Toronto, Art Centre, Toronto ON
Smith, Melinda K, *Cur,* United States Senate Commission on Art, Washington DC
Smith, Melissa, *Asst Cur Manuscripts,* Louisiana State University, Middleton Library, Baton Rouge LA
Smith, Melissa, *Sr Mgr Learning & Engagement,* Intuit: The Center for Intuitive & Outsider Art, Chicago IL
Smith, Michael, *Prof,* East Tennessee State University, College of Arts and Sciences, Dept of Art & Design, Johnson City TN (S)
Smith, Mike, *Librn,* Freer Gallery of Art & Arthur M Sackler Gallery, Library, Washington DC
Smith, Morgan, *Exec Dir,* Bainbridge Island Arts Council, Bainbridge Island WA
Smith, Nan, *Prof,* University of Florida, School of Art & Art History, Gainesville FL (S)
Smith, Patricia F, *Vol Chmn,* Sea Cliff Village Museum, Sea Cliff NY
Smith, Patrick, *Cur,* Connecticut State Library, Museum of Connecticut History, Hartford CT
Smith, Paul, *Project Dir,* Museum of New Art, Troy MI
Smith, Philip, *Asst Dir,* University of Tennessee, Visual Arts Committee, Knoxville TN
Smith, Rachel, *Assoc Prof, Gilkison Family Chair in Art History,* Taylor University, Visual Art Dept, Upland IN (S)
Smith, Rebecca, *Secy,* Marcella Sembrich Memorial Association Inc, Marcella Sembrich Opera Museum, Bolton Landing NY
Smith, Reeves, *Photog Coordr,* Nossi College of Art, Nashville TN (S)
Smith, Rene, *Adj Prof,* Saint Thomas Aquinas College, Art Dept, Sparkill NY (S)
Smith, Renee, *Asst Dir,* Louisiana State University School of Art, Alfred C Glassell Jr Exhibition Gallery, Baton Rouge LA
Smith, Renee, *Bd Pres,* Yuma Fine Arts Association, Yuma Art Center, Yuma AZ
Smith, Rhonda, *Admin Dir,* Morgan County Foundation, Inc, Madison-Morgan Cultural Center, Madison GA
Smith, Rhonda, *Chair & Coordr Non-Toxic Printmaking,* Shepherd University, Dept of Contemporary Art & Theater, Shepherdstown WV (S)
Smith, Richard E, *Prof & Studio Area Head,* Southern Illinois University, School of Art & Design, Carbondale IL (S)
Smith, Richard Norton, *Exec Dir,* Abraham Lincoln Presidential Library & Museum, Springfield IL
Smith, Rob, *Dir,* Lachenmeyer Arts Center, Art Resource Library, Cushing OK
Smith, Robynn, *Painting Instr,* Monterey Peninsula College, Art Dept/Art Gallery, Monterey CA (S)
Smith, Roxanne E, *Tourism Supvr,* Nebraska State Capitol, Lincoln NE
Smith, Samantha, *Visitor Servs & Museum Store,* University of Connecticut, William Benton Museum of Art, Storrs CT
Smith, Sarah G, *Pres,* Boothbay Region Art Foundation Inc, Boothbay Harbor ME
Smith, Sarah, *Dir Colls,* Foosaner Art Museum, Melbourne FL
Smith, Sarah, *External Relations,* Reynolda House Museum of American Art, Winston-Salem NC
Smith, Sharon, *Prof Emeritus,* California State University, Chico, Department of Art & Art History, Chico CA (S)
Smith, Stephanie, *Instr,* Ouachita Baptist University, Dept of Visual Art, Arkadelphia AR (S)
Smith, Sterling, *Chief Prep,* University of Wyoming, University of Wyoming Art Museum, Laramie WY
Smith, Susan, *Winton M Blount Research Chair,* National Postal Museum, Smithsonian Institution, Washington DC
Smith, Tara, *Cur Asst,* California Center for the Arts, Escondido Museum, Escondido CA
Smith, Terence, *Mellon Prof,* University of Pittsburgh, Henry Clay Frick Dept History of Art & Architecture, Pittsburgh PA (S)
Smith, Thomas H, *Asst Prof,* Park University, Dept of Art & Design, Parkville MO (S)
Smith, Timothy B, *Asst Prof,* Birmingham-Southern College, Art & Art History, Birmingham AL (S)
Smith, Timothy H, *Research Asst,* Adams County Historical Society, Gettysburg PA
Smith, Timothy, *Prof,* Birmingham Southern College, Doris Wainwright Kennedy Art Center, Birmingham AL
Smith, Tina, *Museum Educ,* Wake Forest University, Museum of Anthropology, Winston-Salem NC
Smith, Todd, *Dir Advancement,* American Textile History Museum, Lowell MA
Smith, Toni, *Dir,* Baker Arts Center, Liberal KS
Smith, Trisha, *Librn,* Trinity College Library, Washington DC
Smith, Ya'Ke, *Asst Prof,* University of Texas at Arlington, Art & Art History Department, Arlington TX (S)
Smith-Abbott, Katherine, *Vis Asst Prof,* Middlebury College, History of Art & Architecture Dept, Middlebury VT (S)
Smith-Bavtista, Susana, *Deputy Dir,* University of Southern California, USC Pacific Asia Museum, Pasadena CA
Smith-Bove, Holly, *CFO,* Springfield Museums, George Walker Vincent Smith Art Museum, Springfield MA
Smith-Bove, Holly, *Pres,* Springfield Museums, Michele & Donald D'Amour Museum of Fine Arts, Springfield MA
Smith-Ferri, Sherrie, *Dir,* City of Ukiah, Grace Hudson Museum & The Sun House, Ukiah CA
Smith-Hunter, Susan, *Chmn,* Green Mountain College, Dept of Art, Poultney VT (S)
Smith-Talbott, Monica, *Instr,* Harrisburg Area Community College, Division of Communications, Humanities & the Arts, Harrisburg PA (S)
Smithling, Megan, *Reference & Instruction Librn,* Cornish College of the Arts, Cornish Library, Seattle WA
Smithson, Sandra, *Instr,* Millsaps College, Dept of Art, Jackson MS (S)
Smoak, Janet, *Dir,* Besser Museum for Northeast Michigan, Alpena MI
Smoke, Joe, *Grants Administration Div Dir,* City of Los Angeles, Cultural Affairs Dept, Los Angeles CA
Smolinsky, Matthew, *Instr,* University of Maine, Dept of Art, Orono ME (S)
Smook, Deb, *Studio Educ & Outreach Dir,* New Bedford Art Museum/Artworks!, New Bedford MA
Smoot, Frank, *Dir,* Coos County Historical Society Museum, Coos Bay OR
Smotherman, Ann, *Art Teacher,* Motlow State Community College, Art Dept, Tullahoma TN (S)
Smotrich, Keri, *Comm Coord,* James A Michener Art Museum, Doylestown PA
Smul, Debra, *Chief Mktg Officer,* Discovery Place Inc, Nature Museum, Charlotte NC
Smutko, Polina, *Dir Colls,* New Mexico Department of Cultural Affairs, Museum of International Folk Art, Santa Fe NM
Smyth, Margaret, *Devel Coordr,* African American Museum in Philadelphia, Philadelphia PA
Smyth, Megan, *Mgr Publications,* Kimbell Art Foundation, Kimbell Art Museum, Fort Worth TX
Smyth, Mimi, *Develop Coordr,* Grass Roots Art & Community Effort (GRACE), Firehouse Gallery, Hardwick VT
Smythe, James E, *Prof,* Western Carolina University, Dept of Art/College of Arts & Science, Cullowhee NC (S)
Snapp, Brian, *Assoc Prof,* University of Utah, Dept of Art & Art History, Salt Lake City UT (S)
Snay, Cheryl K, *Cur European Art,* University of Notre Dame, Snite Museum of Art, Notre Dame IN
Sneddon, Heather, *Bd Mem,* Utah Lawyers for the Arts, Salt Lake City UT
Snee, Alicia, *Slide Librn, Arts Librn,* California State University, Sacramento, Library - Central Reference Dept, Sacramento CA
Snell, Shawana, *Circ Mgr,* Corcoran Gallery of Art, Corcoran Library, Washington DC
Snell, Walter, *VPres,* Halifax Historical Society, Inc, Halifax Historical Museum, Daytona Beach FL
Snibbe, Robert, *Pres,* Napoleonic Society of America, Museum & Library, Saint Helena CA
Snider, Heather, *Exec Dir,* San Francisco Camerawork, San Francisco CA
Snipes, Elizabeth, *Asst Prof Art,* Lander University, College of Arts & Humanities - Visual Arts, Greenwood SC (S)
Snoddy, Suzie, *Dir,* Houston Baptist University, Museum of American Architecture and Decorative Arts, Houston TX
Snoddy, Suzie, *Dir,* Museum of Southern History, Joella & Stewart Morris Cultural Arts Center, Houston TX
Snodgrass, Susan, *Pres,* Gilpin County Arts Association, Central City CO
Snook, Randy, *Instr,* Sierra Community College, Art Dept, Rocklin CA (S)
Snouffer, Karen, *Prof,* Kenyon College, Art Dept, Gambier OH (S)
Snow, Maryly, *Librn,* University of California, Berkeley, Architecture Visual Resources Library, Berkeley CA
Snowman, Tracy, *Instr,* Spoon River College, Art Dept, Canton IL (S)
Snyder, Amanda, *Curatorial Mgr,* Okanagan Heritage Museum, Kelowna BC
Snyder, Barry, *Prof,* Fairmont State College, Div of Fine Arts, Fairmont WV (S)
Snyder, Gerry, *Chmn,* College of Santa Fe, Art Dept, Santa Fe NM (S)
Snyder, Gerry, *Dean,* Pratt Institute, School of Art, Brooklyn NY (S)

Snyder, Janet, *Prof,* West Virginia University, College of Creative Arts, School of Art & Design, Morgantown WV (S)
Snyder, Jennifer, *Admin,* Fetherston Foundation, Packwood House Museum, Lewisburg PA
Snyder, Jill, *Dir,* Museum of Contemporary Art Cleveland, Library, Cleveland OH
Snyder, Jill, *Exec Dir,* Museum of Contemporary Art Cleveland, Cleveland OH
Snyder, Laine, *Exec Dir,* Zanesville Museum of Art, Zanesville OH
Snyder, Mark, *Asst Prof,* University of Hartford, Hartford Art School, West Hartford CT (S)
Snyder, Patricia, *Exec Dir,* East End Arts & Humanities Council, Riverhead NY
Snyder, Randy, *Chmn Fine Arts Dept,* San Jacinto College-North, Art Dept, Houston TX (S)
Snyder, Richard, *Pres,* Hendricks Hill Museum, Southport ME
Snyder, Robin D, *Chmn,* Samford University, Art Dept, Birmingham AL (S)
Snyder, Sheryl, *Admin Asst,* Adams County Historical Society, Gettysburg PA
Snyder, Stephanie, *Dir,* Reed College, Douglas F Cooley Memorial Art Gallery, Portland OR
Snyder, William, *Cur,* National Archives and Records Administration, Eisenhower Presidential Library, Abilene KS
Soave, Sergio, *Chmn,* Ohio State University, Dept of Art, Columbus OH (S)
Sobel, Ronald, *Pres,* Leo Baeck, New York NY
Sobie Goldstein, Harriet, *Secy,* Phoenix Gallery, New York NY
Sobiech-Munson, Ann, *Coordr Core Prog,* Iowa State University, Dept of Art & Design, Ames IA (S)
Sobolik, Bonnie, *Dir Develop,* North Dakota Museum of Art, Grand Forks ND
Sobre, Judith, *Prof,* University of Texas at San Antonio, Dept of Art & Art History, San Antonio TX (S)
Sobsey, Leah, *Prof,* University of North Carolina at Greensboro, School of Art, Greensboro NC (S)
Soderlund, Ann, *Prog Coordr,* Francis Hardy Gallery, Fish Creek WI
Soderstrom, Henrik, *Asst Prof,* Indiana Wesleyan University, School of Arts & Humanities, Division of Art, Marion IN (S)
Sodervick, Bruce, *Assoc Prof,* Rochester Institute of Technology, School of Design, Rochester NY (S)
Soehner, Kenneth, *Chief Librn, Thomas J. Watson Library,* The Metropolitan Museum of Art, Museum Libraries, New York NY
Softie, Tanja, *Assoc Prof,* University of Richmond, Dept of Art and Art History, Richmond VA (S)
Sogard, Carol, *Assoc Prof,* University of Utah, Dept of Art & Art History, Salt Lake City UT (S)
Sohi, Marilyn, *Head Registrar,* Madison Museum of Contemporary Art, Madison WI
Sokalski, Joseph, *Theatre & Film Studies Counsellor,* McMaster University, School of the Arts, Hamilton ON (S)
Sokol, David, *Chmn Dept Art & Art History,* University of Illinois at Chicago, College of Architecture, Chicago IL (S)
Sokolove, Deborah, *Dir,* Wesley Theological Seminary, Henry Luce III Center for the Arts & Religion, Dadian Gallery, Washington DC
Sokolove, Nancy, *Instr,* Appalachian State University, Dept of Art, Boone NC (S)
Sokolowski, Thomas, *Dir,* Rutgers, The State University of New Jersey, Zimmerli Art Museum at Rutgers University, New Brunswick NJ
Solari, Nicole, *Acctg Mgr,* deCordova Sculpture Park & Museum, Lincoln MA
Soldati, Kathleen, *Exec Dir,* Portsmouth Historical Society, John Paul Jones House & Discover Portsmouth, Portsmouth NH
Solek, Vivian Lea, *Archivist,* Knights of Columbus Supreme Council, Knights of Columbus Museum, New Haven CT
Soler, Courtney, *Dir Fin & Admin,* Gibbes Museum of Art, Charleston SC (S)
Soler, Courtney, *Dir Finance & Admi,* Carolina Art Association, Gibbes Museum of Art, Charleston SC
Soles, Kathleen A, *Assoc Prof,* Emmanuel College, Art Dept, Boston MA (S)
Soles, Teresa, *Instr,* West Shore Community College, Division of Humanities & Fine Arts, Scottville MI (S)
Solien, T L, *Prof,* University of Wisconsin, Madison, Dept of Art, Madison WI (S)
Solis, Alexa, *Pub Rels & Mktg Assoc,* Sierra Arts Foundation, Sierra Arts Gallery, Reno NV
Solko, Dave, *Interactive Instr, Computer Graphics 2nd yr,* AIC College of Design, Cincinnati OH (S)
Soller, Helaine, *Coordr Bd Mem,* Women in the Arts Foundation, Inc, Staten Island NY
Solodkaya, Alex, *Access Svcs Supvr,* University of California, Los Angeles, Arts Library, Los Angeles CA
Solomon Marino, Beth, *Gallery Dir & Art Instr,* Fullerton College Art Gallery, Fullerton CA
Solomon, Mary Karen, *Chair,* Colorado Northwestern Community College, Art Dept, Rangely CO (S)
Solomon, Paul, *Art Appreciation,* Western Michigan University, Frostic School of Art, Kalamazoo MI (S)
Solon, Lisa, *Adjunct Asst Prof,* Drew University, Art Dept, Madison NJ (S)
SoloRio, Rachel, *Special Events Specialist,* Auburn University, Jule Collins Smith Museum of Fine Art, Auburn AL
Solowan, Barbara, *Art Dir,* Galerie Montcalm, Gatineau QC
Solowan, Barbara, *Art Dir,* Canadian Art Foundation, Toronto ON
Soloway, Lynn, *Prof,* Concordia University, Art Dept, Seward NE (S)
Soltesz, Melissa, *Dir,* Upfor Gallery, Portland OR
Solz, Julie, *Team Leader, Coll Svcs,* Historic New England, Boston MA
Somaio, Theresa, *Visual Resource Assoc,* Skidmore College, Lucy Scribner Library, Saratoga Springs NY
Somerdin, Steven, *Reference Librn & Adult Svcs,* Ames Free-Easton's Public Library, North Easton MA
Somers, David, *Cur,* Art Gallery of Peel, Archives, Brampton ON
Somers, Eric, *Dir,* Dutchess Community College, Dept of Visual Arts, Poughkeepsie NY (S)
Somers, Lee, *Gallery Dir,* University of Montevallo, The Gallery, Montevallo AL
Somerset, Angela, *Cur,* Comox Valley Art Gallery, Courtenay BC
Somerson, Rosanne, *Pres,* Rhode Island School of Design, Providence RI (S)
Somerson, Roseanne, *Pres,* Rhode Island School of Design, Museum of Art, Providence RI
Somerville, Alex, *Exec Dir,* Dawson City Museum, Dawson City YT
Somerville, Erin, *Deputy Dir & Cur,* White Columns, White Columns Curated Artist Registry, New York NY
Somma, Rachel, *Communs Coordr,* Staten Island Museum, Staten Island NY
Sommer, Karen, *Opers & Progs,* University of Connecticut, William Benton Museum of Art, Storrs CT
Sommer, Lucia, *Assoc Ed Afterimage,* Visual Studies Workshop, Rochester NY (S)
Sommers, Lynda J, *Dir Gallery,* Alverno College Gallery, Alverno Art and Cultures Gallery, Milwaukee WI
Somowich, Charles, *Curator,* Print Club of Albany, Schenectady NY
Somple, Michael, *Registrar & Exhib Mgr,* Munson-Williams-Proctor Arts Institute, Museum of Art, Utica NY
Sondeijker, Pierre, *Chief Preparator,* The Renaissance Society, Chicago IL
Sonderman, Karen, *Library Dir,* North Canton Public Library, The Little Art Gallery, North Canton OH
Sonders, Carter S, *Chief Develop Officer,* Jamestown-Yorktown Foundation, Jamestown Settlement, Williamsburg VA
Song, Felicia, *Adult Svcs Coordr,* Lake Forest Library, Fine Arts Dept, Lake Forest IL
Songe, Greta, *Instr,* Kirkwood Community College, Dept of Arts & Humanities, Cedar Rapids IA (S)
Sonnema, Roy, *Art Dept Chmn,* University of Southern Colorado, College of Liberal & Fine Arts, Pueblo CO
Sonnema, Roy, *Chmn,* University of Southern Colorado, Dept of Art, Pueblo CO (S)
Sonnichsen, Michael, *Instr,* University of North Carolina at Chapel Hill, Art Dept, Chapel Hill NC (S)
Sonnichsen, Mike, *Asst Prof,* University of Idaho College of Art & Architecture, Dept of Art & Design, Moscow ID (S)
Sontheimer, Anita, *Bookkeeper,* Saint Joseph Museum, Inc., Saint Joseph MO
Soorikian, Diana, *Dir,* Fairleigh Dickinson University, Edward Williams Gallery, Hackensack NJ
Sopotiuk, Owen, *Mgr Technical & Design Servs,* University of British Columbia, Morris & Helen Belkin Art Gallery, Vancouver BC
Sorel, Paul, *Assoc Dir,* New England Center for Contemporary Art, Brooklyn CT
Sorensen, Lee, *Art Librn,* Duke University, Lilly Art Library, Durham NC
Soria, Aida, *Secy,* Centro Cultural De La Raza, San Diego CA
Soriano, Irene, *Co-Chair,* Santa Ana College, Art Dept, Santa Ana CA (S)
Sorkin, Liz, *Paper Conservator,* Midwest Art Conservation Center, Minneapolis MN
Sorokin, Cherly, *Bd Secy,* American Association of University Women, Washington DC
Sorrell, Robert, *Asst Prof,* College of Santa Fe, Art Dept, Santa Fe NM (S)
Sorrell, Sonia, *Assoc Prof,* Pepperdine University, Seaver College, Dept of Art, Malibu CA (S)
Sotelo, Melissa, *Coll Coordr,* University of Illinois at Urbana-Champaign, Spurlock Museum, Urbana IL
Soto, Vanessa, *Asst Cur,* Morris-Jumel Mansion, Inc, New York NY
Soule, Debora Thaxton, *Dir,* Sweetwater County Library System and School District #1, Community Fine Arts Center, Rock Springs WY
Sourakli, Judy, *Cur Coll,* Henry Gallery Association, Henry Art Gallery, Seattle WA
Sourakli, Judy, *Cur Colls,* University of Washington, Henry Art Gallery, Seattle WA
Sousa, James, *Registrar,* Phillips Academy, Addison Gallery of American Art, Andover MA
South, Jennifer, *Exec & Development Asst,* Plains Art Museum, Fargo ND
South, Jessamy, *Youth and Family Programs Coordinator,* The Columbus Museum, Columbus GA
Southern, Keith, *Preparator,* Palo Alto Art Center, Palo Alto CA
Southwick, Kim, *Secy,* The Art Museum of Eastern Idaho, Idaho Falls ID
Southworth, Michael, *Chmn City & Regional Planning,* University of California, Berkeley, College of Environmental Design, Berkeley CA (S)
Southworth, Miles F, *Prof,* Rochester Institute of Technology, School of Printing Management & Sciences, Rochester NY (S)
Souza, Gabriella, *Communs Mgr,* Walters Art Museum, Baltimore MD
Sowd, Laurie, *Assoc VPres Operations,* The Huntington Library, Art Collections & Botanical Gardens, Library, San Marino CA
Sowder, Cheryl, *Assoc Prof Art Hist,* Jacksonville University, Jacksonville FL (S)
Sowiak, Christine, *Chief Cur,* University of Calgary, Nickle Galleries, Calgary AB
Sowry, Nathan, *Reference Archivist,* National Museum of the American Indian, Archive Center, Suitland MD
Spackman, Hal, *Exec Dir,* Sitka Historical Society, Sitka History Museum, Sitka AK

Spadafora, David, *Pres & Librn,* The Newberry, Chicago IL
Spadafora, Tracy, *Adj Instruc,* Quincy College, Art Dept, Quincy MA (S)
Spaetgens, Jacob, *Security,* University of Louisiana at Lafayette, Paul and Lulu Hilliard University Art Museum, Lafayette LA
Spagnolo, Francesco, *Cur,* University of California, Berkeley, The Magnes Collection of Jewish Art and Life, Berkeley CA
Spagnolo, Francesco, *Cur,* University of California, Berkeley, The Magnes Collection of Jewish Art & Life, Berkeley CA
Spahr, Andrew, *Dir Colls & Exhibs,* The Currier Museum of Art, Manchester NH
Spahr, Stephanie, *Curatorial Asst,* El Museo del Barrio, New York NY
Spaid, Gregory P, *Prof,* Kenyon College, Art Dept, Gambier OH (S)
Spain, Roger, *Bd Pres,* Montgomery Museum of Fine Arts, Montgomery AL
Spalatin, Ivana, *Instr Art History,* Texas A&M University Commerce, Dept of Art, Commerce TX (S)
Spalding, Ann E, *Educ Coordr,* Art and History Museums - Maitland, Maitland FL
Spalding, Jeffrey, *Chief Cur,* Beaverbrook Art Gallery, Fredericton NB
Spallina, Emily, *Registrar,* Canajoharie Library & Art Gallery, Arkell Museum of Canajoharie, Canajoharie NY
Spangenberg, Kristin, *Cur Prints,* Cincinnati Art Museum, Cincinnati Art Museum, Cincinnati OH
Spangler, David R, *Pres,* St Martins College, Humanities Dept, Lacey WA (S)
Spangler, Gary, *Chmn Visual Arts,* Malone University, Dept of Art, Canton OH (S)
Spangler, Shawn, *Asst Prof Art,* Western Illinois University, Department of Art, Macomb IL (S)
Spanich, Deborah, *Registrar,* Randolph College, Maier Museum of Art, Lynchburg VA
Spanich, John, *Mus Preparator,* Randolph College, Maier Museum of Art, Lynchburg VA
Sparagana, John, *Prof,* Rice University, Visual & Dramatic Arts, Houston TX (S)
Sparklin, Sophia, *Adjunct Prof Art,* University of Great Falls, Art Dept, Great Falls MT (S)
Sparks, Jill, *Art Instructor,* Kentucky Wesleyan College, Dept Art, Owensboro KY (S)
Sparks, Rhonda, *Librn,* Cedarhurst Center for the Arts, Cedar Hurst Library, Mount Vernon IL
Sparrow, James, *Exec Dir,* Arts United of Greater Fort Wayne, Fort Wayne IN
Spataro, Peter, *Instr,* Art Center Sarasota, Sarasota FL (S)
Spatz-Rabinowitz, Elaine, *Assoc Prof,* Wellesley College, Art Dept, Wellesley MA (S)
Spaulding, Daniel, *Cur Collections,* Anniston Museum of Natural History, Anniston AL
Spaulding, Fred, *Adjunct Prof,* University of Texas at Arlington, Art & Art History Department, Arlington TX (S)
Spaulding, Fred, *Prof,* Victoria College, Fine Arts Dept, Victoria TX (S)
Spaulding, Karen Lee, *Deputy Dir,* The Buffalo Fine Arts Academy, Albright-Knox Art Gallery, Buffalo NY
Spears, Dolores, *Cur,* Zigler Art Museum, Jennings LA
Spears, Kimberly, *Exec Dir,* Anderson County Arts Council, Anderson Arts Center, Anderson SC
Spears, Susan, *Dir,* Michelson Museum of Art, Marshall TX
Specht, Andrea, *Exec Dir,* Artistry, Inez Greenberg Gallery, Bloomington MN
Speck, Erin, *Dept Chmn,* George Washington University, School of Interior Design, Washington DC (S)
Speck, Lawrence, *Dean,* University of Texas, School of Architecture, Austin TX (S)
Specter, Patricia, *Treas,* Neustadt Collection of Tiffany Glass, Long Island City NY
Spector, Nancy, *Artistic Dir & Chief Cur,* Solomon R Guggenheim Museum, New York NY
Speed, Bonnie, *Dir,* Emory University, Michael C Carlos Museum, Atlanta GA
Speer, George, *Dir,* Northern Arizona University, Art Museum & Galleries, Flagstaff AZ
Speers, Veronica, *Contact,* Paier College of Art, Inc, Hamden CT (S)
Speight, Jerry, *Prof,* Murray State University, Dept of Art, Murray KY (S)
Spellman, Catherine, *Assoc Dir,* Arizona State University, The Design School, Tempe AZ (S)
Spence, Margaret, *Librn,* Arts and Letters Club of Toronto, Library, Toronto ON
Spence, Muneera U, *Asst Prof,* Oregon State University, Dept of Art, Corvallis OR (S)
Spence, Rachel, *Educ & Outreach,* Beck Center for the Arts, Lakewood OH
Spence, Scott, *Artistic Dir,* Beck Center for the Arts, Lakewood OH
Spencer Forsythe, Laurel, *Cur Coll & Educ,* Paine Art Center & Gardens, Oshkosh WI
Spencer, Christina, *Educ Coordr,* Owatonna Arts Center, Owatonna MN
Spencer, Cynthia, *Exec Dir,* The Arts Center, Corvallis OR
Spencer, Deirdre, *Head Fine Arts Library, Head Librn,* University of Michigan, Fine Arts Library, Ann Arbor MI
Spencer, Elizabeth, *1st VPres,* Salmagundi Club, New York NY
Spencer, Helen, *VPres,* Almond Historical Society, Inc, Hagadorn House, The 1800-37 Museum, Almond NY
Spencer, Lori, *Admin Assoc,* Ohio University, Kennedy Museum of Art, Athens OH
Spencer, Sue, *Dir,* Spoon River College, Art Dept, Canton IL (S)
Spencer, Sunnee, *Deputy Dir Mus Prog & Svcs,* Heritage Museums & Gardens, Sandwich MA
Spencer, Vivian L, *Cur Educ,* Pensacola Museum of Art, Harry Thornton Library, Pensacola FL
Spencer, Vivian, *Dir,* Pensacola State College, Visual Arts Gallery, Anna Lamar Switzer Center for Visual Arts, Pensacola FL
Sperandio, Christopher, *Assoc Prof,* Rice University, Visual & Dramatic Arts, Houston TX (S)
Speranza, Linda, *Instr,* Mesa Community College, Dept of Art, Mesa AZ (S)
Sperath, Albert, *Gallery Dir,* Murray State University, Dept of Art, Murray KY (S)
Sperling, Christine, *Chmn,* Bloomsburg University, Dept of Art & Art History, Bloomsburg PA (S)
Sperling, Christine, *Chmn Dept of Art,* Bloomsburg University of Pennsylvania, Haas Gallery of Art, Bloomsburg PA
Spevers, Franklin, *Prof,* Calvin College, Art Dept, Grand Rapids MI (S)
Spewock, Kelly JK, *Interior Design,* Art Institute of Pittsburgh, Pittsburgh PA (S)
Speyerer, Jay W, *Multimedia & Web Design,* Art Institute of Pittsburgh, Pittsburgh PA (S)
Spicanovic, Vladimir, *Dean, Faculty of Art,* OCAD University, Toronto ON (S)
Spicer, Ann, *Chmn,* Wayne Community College, Liberal Arts Dept, Goldsboro NC (S)
Spicer, Joaneath, *Cur Renaissance & Baroque Art,* Walters Art Museum, Baltimore MD
Spies, Kathleen, *Assoc Prof,* Birmingham-Southern College, Art & Art History, Birmingham AL (S)
Spies, Kathleen, *Prof,* Birmingham Southern College, Doris Wainwright Kennedy Art Center, Birmingham AL
Spike, John, *Asst Dir & Chief Cur,* College of William & Mary, Muscarelle Museum of Art, Williamsburg VA
Spillane, Sunny, *Prof,* University of North Carolina at Greensboro, School of Art, Greensboro NC (S)
Spiller, Harley, *Deputy Dir,* Franklin Furnace Archive, Inc, Brooklyn NY
Spiller, Joanne, *Mus Educator,* Jefferson County Historical Society Museum, Madison IN
Spina, Lou, *VPres,* American Artists Professional League, Inc, New York NY
Spindel, Dale, *Dir,* Springfield Free Public Library, Donald B Palmer Museum, Springfield NJ
Spinell, Stephen, *Pres,* Philadelphia University, Philadelphia PA (S)
Spinelli, Elizabeth, *Treas,* Marcella Sembrich Memorial Association Inc, Marcella Sembrich Opera Museum, Bolton Landing NY
Spinner, Sandy, *Cur,* Hillel Foundation, Hillel Jewish Student Center Gallery, Cincinnati OH
Spinosa, Arwen, *Cataloguer,* Florida State University, The John and Mable Ringling Museum of Art Library, Sarasota FL
Spione, Tricia, *Coordr,* Historic Arkansas Museum, Little Rock AR
Spiro, Kledia, *Dir Mktg,* Fitchburg Art Museum, Fitchburg MA
Spiro-Allen, Debra, *Dept Chmn,* Emma Willard School, Dept of Visual & Performing Arts, Troy NY (S)
Spitler, Carol, *Assoc Prof,* Oakland City University, Division of Fine Arts, Oakland City IN (S)
Spitzhoff, Katherine, *Lectr,* State University of New York College at Oneonta, Dept of Art, Oneonta NY (S)
Spitzzeri, Paul, *Asst Dir,* Workman & Temple Family Homestead Museum, City of Industry CA
Spitzzeri, Paul, *Coll Mgr & Library Head,* Workman & Temple Family Homestead Museum, Research Library, City of Industry CA
Spivey, Cooper, *Art Instr,* Birmingham-Southern College, Art & Art History, Birmingham AL (S)
Spoerner, Thomas, *Chmn,* Ball State University, Dept of Art, Muncie IN (S)
Sponenberg, Susan, *Coordr,* Luzerne County Community College, Commercial Art Dept, Nanticoke PA (S)
Spoon, Jennifer, *Assoc Prof,* Radford University, Art Dept, Radford VA (S)
Spoone, Rochelle, *Controller,* Sangre de Cristo Arts & Conference Center, Pueblo CO
Spote, Richard T, *Pres,* Fine Arts Association, School of Fine Arts, Willoughby OH
Spousta, Courtney, *Cur Educ,* Wichita Art Museum, Emprise Bank Research Library, Wichita KS
Spousta, Courtney, *Educ Cur,* Wichita Art Museum, Wichita KS
Spradlin, Carmen, *Library Tech,* North Carolina State University, Harrye Lyons Design Library, Raleigh NC
Spradling, Kim, *Prof,* Northwest Missouri State University, Dept of Fine & Performing Arts, Maryville MO (S)
Spradun, Becky, *Instr,* Ouachita Baptist University, Dept of Visual Art, Arkadelphia AR (S)
Sprague, Tiffany, *Dir Publs,* Yale University, Yale University Art Gallery, New Haven CT
Spring, Michael, *Exec Dir,* South Florida Cultural Consortium, Miami Dade County Dept of Cultural Affairs, Miami FL
Springer, Bethany, *Asst Prof,* University of Arkansas, Art Dept, Fayetteville AR (S)
Springer, Carolyn, *Instr,* University of Indianapolis, Dept Art & Design, Indianapolis IN (S)
Springgay, Stephanie, *Asst Prof Art Educ & Women's Studies,* Pennsylvania State University, University Park, Penn State School of Visual Arts, University Park PA (S)
Sprout, Francis, *Instr,* Indian River Community College, Fine Arts Dept, Fort Pierce FL (S)
Sprung, Lowri, *Historian,* National Watercolor Society, San Pedro CA
Sprung, Sharon, *VPres,* Artists' Fellowship, Inc, New York NY
Spungen, Elizabeth F, *Exec Dir,* The Print Center, Philadelphia PA
Spurgeon, Elizabeth, *Instr,* Marylhurst University, Art Dept, Marylhurst OR (S)
Squadroni, Tony, *Instr,* Wayne Art Center, Wayne PA (S)
Squier, Joseph, *Assoc Dir, Prof,* University of Illinois, Urbana-Champaign, School of Art & Design, Champaign IL (S)

Squires, Ann, *Pres,* Jericho Historical Society, Jericho VT

Squyres, Carly, *Educ Asst,* City of Springdale, Shiloh Museum of Ozark History, Springdale AR

Squyres, Leslie, *Archivist,* University of Arizona, Center for Creative Photography, Tucson AZ

Sromek, Teresa, *Archivist & Librn,* Polish Museum of America (PMA), Chicago IL

Sromek, Teresa, *Archivist & Librn,* Polish Museum of America (PMA), The Polish Museum of America Library (PMAL), Chicago IL

St Ama, Caryl, *Instr,* Glendale Community College, Visual & Performing Arts Div, Glendale CA (S)

St Aubyn, Jacklyn, *College Asst Prof,* New Mexico State University, Art Dept, Las Cruces NM (S)

St Cyr, Chris, *Asst Prof,* The College of Saint Rose, The Center For Art and Design, Albany NY (S)

St John, Pam, *Dir Educ,* The Frick Art & Historical Center, Inc, Frick Art Museum, Pittsburgh PA

St Laurent, Beatrice, *Asst Prof,* Bridgewater State College, Art Dept, Bridgewater MA (S)

St Onge, Stan, *Secy & Dir,* The New England Museum of Telephony, Inc, The Telephone Museum, Ellsworth ME

St-Amour, Danielle, *Exec Dir,* Art Metropole, Toronto ON

St-Arnaud, Jacques, *Guide,* Musee des Augustines de l'Hotel Dieu de Quebec, Quebec QC

St-Cyr, Chantal, *Coordr Vis,* Musee d'art Contemporain de Montreal, Montreal QC

St. Clair, Katie, *Prof,* Davidson College, Art Dept, Davidson NC (S)

St. Claire, Jacqueline, *Educ Coordr,* Sheldon Museum & Cultural Center, Inc, Sheldon Museum & Cultural Center, Haines AK

St. Laurent, Stephen, *Dir Security,* Harvard University, Harvard Art Museums, Cambridge MA

Staats, Ann, *Treas,* Bicentennial Art Center & Museum, Paris IL

Stabila, Luciana, *Registrar,* The Illinois Institute of Art - Chicago, Chicago IL (S)

Stabile, Mary Jean, *Graphic Design,* Art Institute of Pittsburgh, Pittsburgh PA (S)

Stacey, Joanne, *Chmn,* Revelstoke Visual Arts Centre, Revelstoke BC

Stack, Joan, *Art Cur,* State Historical Society of Missouri, Columbia MO

Stadtmueller, Peter, *Instr,* Mercyhurst University, Dept of Art, Erie PA (S)

Staebell, Sandy, *Coll Cur,* Western Kentucky University, Kentucky Library & Museum, Bowling Green KY

Staffne, Dennis, *Prof,* Northern Michigan University, Dept of Art & Design, Marquette MI (S)

Stafford, Carol, *Accounts Supvr,* University of Minnesota, Frederick R Weisman Art Museum, Minneapolis MN

Stafford, John, *Mus Shop Mgr,* New Mexico Department of Cultural Affairs, New Mexico Museum of Art, Unit of NM Dept of Cultural Affairs, Santa Fe NM

Stafford, Lisa, *Prof,* Hiram College, Art Dept, Hiram OH (S)

Stafford, Susan, *Exec Dir,* Bicentennial Art Center & Museum, Paris IL

Stageman, Brett, *Preparator,* University of Wisconsin-Madison, Chazen Museum of Art, Madison WI

Stager, Lawrence, *Dir,* Harvard University, Semitic Museum, Cambridge MA

Staggs, Michelle, *Develop Dir,* Kentucky Museum of Art and Craft, Louisville KY

Stahl, Dirck, *Pres Bd Dir,* Arts Council of Southwestern Indiana, The Bower-Suhrheinrich Foundation Gallery, Evansville IN

Stahl, Judith R, *Gallery Dir,* Louisiana State University, Student Union Art Gallery, Baton Rouge LA

Stahl, Judy, *Dir,* Louisiana State University, Student Union Art Gallery, Baton Rouge LA (S)

Staiger, Whitney, *Gallery Dir,* The Art League Gallery & School, Alexandria VA

Staiti, Paul, *Art History,* Mount Holyoke College, Art Dept, South Hadley MA (S)

Stake, Peter, *Chmn,* Skidmore College, Dept of Art & Art History, Saratoga Springs NY (S)

Stalder, Andrew, *Assoc Prof,* Tarrant County College, Art Dept, Hurst TX (S)

Staley, Chris, *Pres,* National Council on Education for the Ceramic Arts (NCECA), Boulder CO

Staley, Christopher, *Prof Art (Ceramics),* Pennsylvania State University, University Park, Penn State School of Visual Arts, University Park PA (S)

Stalfort, Heather, *Assoc Dir Commun & Mktg,* Johns Hopkins University, Evergreen Museum & Library, Baltimore MD

Staller, Natasha, *Prof,* Amherst College, Dept of Art & the History of Art, Amherst MA (S)

Stallings, Tyler, *Dir Sweeney Art Gallery & Artistic Dir Culver Ctr,* UCR ARTSblock, California Museum of Photography, Riverside CA

Stallworth, Kristopher, *Assoc Prof Art,* Bakersfield College, Art Dept, Bakersfield CA (S)

Stambler, Peter, *Dean, Div Liberal Arts,* University of the Arts, Philadelphia Colleges of Art & Design, Performing Arts & Media & Communication, Philadelphia PA (S)

Stamey, Emily, *Cur of Exhib,* University of North Carolina at Greensboro, Weatherspoon Art Museum, Greensboro NC

Stammler, Ursula, *Dir,* University of Kansas, Architectural Resource Center, Lawrence KS

Stamps, Ray, *Pres Board Dirs,* Lake County Civic Center Association, Inc, Heritage Museum & Gallery, Leadville CO

Stancliffe, Thomas, *Prof,* University of Northern Iowa, Dept of Art, Cedar Falls IA (S)

Standiford, Michelle, *Graphic Design,* Loveland Museum/Gallery, Loveland CO

Standley, Linda, *Pres,* The Art Association of Jacksonville, The David Strawn Art Gallery, Jacksonville IL

Standring, Timothy, *Adjunct Faculty Mus Studies,* University of Denver, School of Art & Art History, Denver CO (S)

Stanec, Kris, *Dir Educ,* Colorado Springs Fine Arts Center, Taylor Museum, Colorado Springs CO

Stanfield-Mazzi, Maya, *Asst Prof,* University of Florida, School of Art & Art History, Gainesville FL (S)

Stanford, Karen, *Dir Univ Galleries & Community Outreach,* Kutztown University, The Martin & Regina Miller Gallery, Kutztown PA

Stangeland, Bruce, *Pres,* California Watercolor Association, Gallery Concord, Concord CA

Stanger, Alexa, *Educ Dir,* The Art Museum of Eastern Idaho, Idaho Falls ID

Stanger, David, *Instr,* Seton Hill University, Art Program, Greensburg PA (S)

Stangl, Denise, *Asst to Dir,* Lehigh University Art Galleries, Museum Operation, Bethlehem PA

Stanicky, Paul, *Brd Dirs,* Ukrainian Cultural & Educational Centre, Gallery, Winnipeg MB

Stanicky, Paul, *Pres Board Dirs,* Ukrainian Cultural & Educational Centre, Library & Archives, Winnipeg MB

Stanicky, Paul, *Pres Brd Dirs,* Ukrainian Cultural & Educational Centre, Winnipeg MB

Stanionis, Lin, *Prof,* University of Kansas, The School of the Arts, Dept of Visual Art, Lawrence KS (S)

Stanis, Suzanne, *Educ & Information Dir,* Indiana Landmarks, Information Center Library, Indianapolis IN

Stanish, Loretta, *Dir Develop,* Society for Contemporary Craft, Pittsburgh PA

Stanislow, Gail, *Coll Librn,* Brandywine Conservancy, Library, Chadds Ford PA

Stanitz, Mark, *Prof,* Rochester Institute of Technology, School of Design, Rochester NY (S)

Staniunas Hopper, Jodi, *Chair, Assoc Prof,* Mercyhurst University, Dept of Art, Erie PA (S)

Stankiewicz, Carlotta, *Dir Mktg & Comms,* University of Texas at Austin, Blanton Museum of Art, Austin TX

Stankiewicz, Mary Ann, *Prof Art Educ,* Pennsylvania State University, University Park, Penn State School of Visual Arts, University Park PA (S)

Stanko, John, *Asst Prof,* University of Nebraska, Kearney, Dept of Art & Art History, Kearney NE (S)

Stanley, Annie, *Educ Coordr,* Ellen Noel Art Museum of the Permian Basin, Odessa TX

Stanley, B, *Dir,* District of Columbia Arts Center (DCAC), Washington DC

Stanley, Bruce, *Graphic Design Coordr,* Nossi College of Art, Nashville TN (S)

Stanley, Chris, *Assoc Prof,* University of Texas of Permian Basin, Dept of Art, Odessa TX (S)

Stanley, Diane, *Cur,* Southern Lorain County Historical Society, Spirit of '76 Museum, Elyria OH

Stanley, Eric, *History Cur,* Museums Sonoma County, Art Museum of Sonoma County & History Museum of Sonoma County, Santa Rosa CA

Stanley, James, *Instr,* University of Southern Indiana, Art & Design Dept, Evansville IN (S)

Stanley, James, *Visual Coordr,* Fine Arts Work Center, Hudson D. Walker Gallery, Provincetown MA

Stanley, Janet L, *Librn,* National Museum of African Art, Warren M Robbins Library, Washington DC

Stanley, Jared, *Instr,* Bob Jones University, School of Fine Arts, Div of Art & Design, Greenville SC (S)

Stanley, John, *COO,* Whitney Museum of American Art, New York NY

Stanley, Kathi, *Assoc Librn,* New York State Library, Manuscripts & Special Collections, Albany NY

Stanley, Lynn, *Educ Coordr,* Provincetown Art Association & Museum, Provincetown MA

Stanley, Michael, *Pres,* Kappa Pi International Honorary Art Fraternity, Cleveland MS

Stanley, Peter, *Gallery Mgr,* University of Puget Sound, Kittredge Art Gallery, Tacoma WA

Stanley, R Brent, *VPres Finance,* Americans for the Arts, New York NY

Stanley, Robert A, *Asst Prof,* Ashland University, Art Dept, Ashland OH (S)

Stanley, Susie, *Prof,* Lansing Community College, Visual Arts & Media Dept, Lansing MI (S)

Stanley, Tamar, *Dir,* Ravalli County Museum, Hamilton MT

Stanley, Teresa, *Chmn,* Humboldt State University, College of Arts & Humanities, Art Dept, Arcata CA (S)

Stansberry, Tammy, *Mus Store Mgr,* Amerind Foundation, Inc, Amerind Museum, Fulton-Hayden Memorial Art Gallery, Dragoon AZ

Stansbury-O'Donnell, Mark, *Prof,* University of St Thomas, Deptartment of Art History, Saint Paul MN (S)

Stanton, Anne Rudloff, *Chmn,* University of Missouri - Columbia, Art History & Archaeology Dept, Columbia MO (S)

Stanton, Edward, *Mgr Soc Independent Artists,* Museum of Conceptual Art, Society of Independent Artists (SIA), San Francisco CA

Stanton, Meridith Z, *Dir,* United States Department of the Interior, Indian Arts & Crafts Board, Washington DC

Stapleton, Douglas, *Assoc Cur ISM Chicago Gallery,* Illinois State Museum, ISM Lockport Gallery, Chicago Gallery & Southern Illinois Art Gallery, Springfield IL

Star Varner, Victoria, *Chair Art,* Southwestern University, Sarofim School of Fine Art, Dept of Art & Art History, Georgetown TX (S)

Starck, Sandra, *Assoc Prof,* University of Wisconsin-Eau Claire, Dept of Art & Design, Eau Claire WI (S)

Stark Locher, Anne, *Secy,* Aperture Foundation, New York NY

Stark, Bonnie, *Asst Dir,* Big Horn County Historical Museum, Hardin MT

Stark, David, *Chief Cur,* Columbus Museum of Art, Columbus OH

Stark, Johnnie, *Assoc Prof Interior Design,* University of North Texas, College of Visual Arts & Design, Denton TX (S)

Stark, Kathy, *Exhib Dir,* Grass Roots Art & Community Effort (GRACE), Firehouse Gallery, Hardwick VT

Stark, Mary, *Fine Arts Librn,* Beverly Hills Public Library, Fine Arts Library, Beverly Hills CA

Stark, Robert, *Dir,* Susquehanna Studio, Union Dale PA

Stark, Sonia, *VPres,* National Association of Women Artists, Inc, NAWA Gallery, New York NY

Stark, William, *Admin/Deputy Dir,* Mamie McFaddin Ward, Beaumont TX

Starke, Marissa, *Asst Dir,* Kansas City Artists Coalition, Kansas City MO

Starkey, Willow, *Curatorial Asst,* California State University, Chico, Janet Turner Print Museum, CSU, Chicago, Chico CA

Starling, Zoe, *Cur Educ,* North Carolina State University, Gregg Museum of Art & Design, Raleigh NC

Starnes, Ashton, *Graphic Arts Designer & PR Mgr,* Sam Bass Gallery, Concord NC

Starnes, Clarissa, *Shop HMA/Collections Manager,* Hickory Museum of Art, Inc, Hickory NC

Starr, Barbara Patten, *Prof,* Spring Hill College, Department of Fine & Performing Arts, Mobile AL (S)

Starr, Daniel, *Assoc Chief Librn,* The Metropolitan Museum of Art, Museum Libraries, New York NY

Starr, Tom, *Assoc Prof,* Northeastern University, Dept of Art & Architecture, Boston MA (S)

Starr, Tyler, *Prof,* Davidson College, Art Dept, Davidson NC (S)

Starrett, Judy L, *Owner,* Louisiana Pottery, Sorrento LA

Staseson, Rae, *Prof & Dean,* University of Regina, Faculty of Media, Art & Performance, Regina SK (S)

Staso, Sharon, *Mgr of Museum Operations,* Hockaday Museum of Art, Kalispell MT

Statlander, Raymond, *Assoc Prof,* New Jersey City University, Art Dept, Jersey City NJ (S)

Statz, Brian, *VP Opers & Gen Counsel,* The Children's Museum of Indianapolis, Indianapolis IN

Statzer, Mary, *Cur Photographs & Prints,* University of New Mexico, University of New Mexico Art Museum, Albuquerque NM

Stauffer, George B, *Dean,* Rutgers, The State University of New Jersey, Mason Gross School of the Arts, New Brunswick NJ (S)

Stauffer, Sandra, *Sr Assoc Dean & Prof,* Arizona State University, Herberger Institute for Design and the Arts, Tempe AZ (S)

Staum, Sonja, *Dir,* Indiana University - Purdue University at Indianapolis, Herron School of Art Library, Indianapolis IN

Stausland, Lillian, *Instr,* Wagner College, Arts Administration Dept, Staten Island NY (S)

Staveloz, Auntaneshia, *VPres,* Association of African American Museums, Washington DC

Stavitsky, Gail, *Chief Cur,* Montclair Art Museum, Montclair NJ

Stealey, Jo, *Prof (Fibers),* University of Missouri - Columbia, Dept of Art, Columbia MO (S)

Stearns, Emily, *Dir,* Wenham Museum, Wenham MA

Stearns, Rose, *Pres,* Plymouth Antiquarian Society, Plymouth MA

Stebbins, Joan, *Cur,* Southern Alberta Art Gallery, Library, Lethbridge AB

Stebich, Stephanie, *Dir,* American Art Museum, Smithsonian Institution, Washington DC

Stec Dankert, Holly, *Research & Access Servs Librn,* School of the Art Institute of Chicago, John M Flaxman Library, Chicago IL

Stechschulte, Brian, *Gallery Dir,* National Institute of Art & Disabilities (NIAD), Florence Ludins-Katz Gallery, Richmond CA

Steck, Stuart, *Chair Art History,* Lesley University, College of Art & Design, Cambridge MA (S)

Steedle, Bill, *Assoc Prof,* State University of New York at Farmingdale, Visual Communications, Farmingdale NY (S)

Steel, Virginia Oberlin, *Dir & Cur,* Rutgers University, Stedman Art Gallery, Camden NJ

Steele, Brian, *Deputy Dir Facilities & Opers,* Anchorage Museum at Rasmuson Center, Anchorage AK

Steele, Curtis, *Assoc Prof,* Arkansas State University, Dept of Art, State University AR (S)

Steele, Curtis, *Chair Art Dept,* Arkansas State University-Art Department, Jonesboro, Fine Arts Center Gallery, Jonesboro AR

Steele, Jonathan, *Dean,* Saint Petersburg College, Fine & Applied Arts at Clearwater Campus, Clearwater FL (S)

Steele, Kelly, *Historic Preservation Off,* United States Senate Commission on Art, Washington DC

Steele, Lisa, *Assoc Chmn Visual Studies,* University of Toronto, Dept of Fine Art, Toronto ON (S)

Steele, Michael, *Prof Dir School of Design,* South Dakota State University, Dept of Visual Arts, Brookings SD (S)

Steele, Priscilla, *Adjunct,* Coe College, Dept of Art, Cedar Rapids IA (S)

Steele, Susan, *Advertising & Publicity,* Society of Scribes, Ltd, New York NY

Steele, Susan, *Co-Pres,* Society of Scribes, Ltd, New York NY

Steele, Valerie, *Dir,* Fashion Institute of Technology - SUNY, The Museum at FIT, New York NY

Steele-Hamme, Nancy, *Chair,* Midwestern State University, Lamar D. Fain College of Fine Arts, Wichita Falls TX (S)

Steen, Karen, *Assoc Prof,* Cazenovia College, Center for Art & Design Studies, Cazenovia NY (S)

Steenburg, Nancy, *Pres,* New London County Historical Society, Shaw Mansion, New London CT

Steere, Thomas, *Director,* Almond Historical Society, Inc, Hagadorn House, The 1800-37 Museum, Almond NY

Steever, Lasley, *Dir Progs & Digital Engagement,* Gibbes Museum of Art, Charleston SC (S)

Steeves, Dan, *Lectr & Printmaking Tech,* Mount Allison University, Dept of Fine Arts, Sackville NB (S)

Stefani, Robert, *Pres,* The National Art League, Douglaston NY

Stefanuk, Kyra, *Mgr,* Lloydminster Cultural & Science Centre, Lloydminster SK

Steffen, Pamela, *Assoc Prof,* Mount Mary College, Art & Design Division, Milwaukee WI (S)

Steffensen, Jared, *Cur Exhibs,* Salt Lake Art Center, Utah Museum of Contemporary Art, Salt Lake City UT

Stefl, Bob, *Assoc Prof,* Lincoln College, Art Dept, Lincoln IL (S)

Steggles, Mary Ann, *Assoc Dir,* University of Manitoba, School of Art, Winnipeg MB (S)

Stein, Joan, *Head of Access Services,* Carnegie Mellon University, Hunt Library, Pittsburgh PA

Stein, Julie, *Exec Dir,* University of Washington, Burke Museum of Natural History and Culture, Seattle WA

Stein, Lynn, *Artistic Dir,* Rockland Center for the Arts, West Nyack NY (S)

Stein, Lynn, *Artistic Dir,* Rockland Center for the Arts, West Nyack NY

Stein, Michael, *Faculty,* Housatonic Community College, Art Dept, Bridgeport CT (S)

Stein, Raymond, *Adjunct Asst Prof,* Drew University, Art Dept, Madison NJ (S)

Stein, Robert, *Exec VPres & CPO,* American Alliance of Museums, Arlington VA

Stein, Todd, *CEO,* Mid-America Arts Alliance & Exhibits USA, Kansas City MO

Steinbach, Ken, *Prof,* Bethel University, Dept of Art & Design, Saint Paul MN (S)

Steinberg, Barbara, *Slide Librn,* University of New Hampshire, Dept of the Arts Slide Library, Durham NH

Steinberg, Bryan E, *Assoc Prof,* Rhode Island College, Art Dept, Providence RI (S)

Steinberg, Judy, *Registrar,* American Folk Art Museum, New York NY

Steinberg, Rachel, *Gallery Dir,* SOHO20 Gallery, Brooklyn NY

Steinbrenner, Paul, *Treas,* Newport Historical Society & Museum of Newport History, Newport RI

Steiner, Frederick, *Dean & Prof,* University of Pennsylvania, School of Design (PennDesign), Philadelphia PA (S)

Steiner, Katherine, *Chief Registrar,* The Mint Museum, Charlotte NC

Steiner, Rochelle, *Assoc Dir & Chief Cur,* Vancouver Art Gallery, Vancouver BC

Steiner, Suzanne, *Assoc Chmn,* Carlow College, Art Dept, Pittsburgh PA (S)

Steinhauer, Lise, *Mem Assoc,* Historical Society of Palm Beach County, The Richard and Pat Johnson Palm Beach County History Museum, West Palm Beach FL

Steinkeller, Piotr, *Cur Cuneiform Coll,* Harvard University, Semitic Museum, Cambridge MA

Steinle, John, *Adminr,* Jefferson County Open Space, Hiwan Homestead Museum, Evergreen CO

Steinmann, Callan, *Assoc Cur Educ,* University of Georgia, Georgia Museum of Art, Athens GA

Steinmann, Danielle, *Asst Cur Educ,* Clark Art Institute, Williamstown MA

Steirnagle, Michael, *Assoc Prof,* Palomar Community College, Art Dept, San Marcos CA (S)

Stelick, Melinda, *Dir Business Svc Ctr,* Cornell University, College of Architecture, Art, and Planning, Ithaca NY (S)

Stelioeswills, Alex, *Cur,* Mississippi University for Women, Fine Arts Gallery, Columbus MS

Stelzer, Stuart, *Library Dir,* University of the Ozarks, Robson Library, Clarksville AR

Stemwedel, Mark, *Instr Prog Coordr Studio Art,* South Dakota State University, Dept of Visual Arts, Brookings SD (S)

Stene, Larry M, *Prof,* Washington and Lee University, Div of Art, Lexington VA (S)

Stenner, Jack, *Assoc Prof,* University of Florida, School of Art & Art History, Gainesville FL (S)

Stenstrom, Kurt, *Instr,* Oklahoma State University Institute of Technology, School of Visual Communications, Okmulgee OK (S)

Stentaford, Karen, *Lectr & Photog Tech,* Mount Allison University, Dept of Fine Arts, Sackville NB (S)

Stentson, Daniel, *Exec Dir,* Louisiana State University, Museum of Art, Baton Rouge LA

Stentzel, Allen, *Adjunct,* Feather River Community College, Art Dept, Quincy CA (S)

Stenzel, Steve, *Vis Asst Prof,* Hamline University, Dept of Studio Arts & Art History, Saint Paul MN (S)

Stephan, Mariam, *Prof,* University of North Carolina at Greensboro, School of Art, Greensboro NC (S)

Stephen, Tegan, *Admin,* Artspace, Richmond VA

Stephens, Carolyn, *Dept Chmn,* Spokane Falls Community College, Fine Arts Dept, Spokane WA (S)

Stephens, Mary, *CEO,* California State University, Long Beach Foundation, Long Beach CA

Stephens, Robert, *Assoc Prof,* Graceland University, Fine Arts Div, Lamoni IA (S)

Stephens, Sandra, *Asst Prof,* Munson-Williams-Proctor Arts Institute, Pratt MWP College of Art, Utica NY (S)

Stephens, Scott, *Chmn,* University of Montevallo, College of Fine Arts, Montevallo AL (S)

Stephenson Baty, Daphne, *Exec Asst,* African American Museum, Dallas TX

Stephenson, Brad, *Dir Mktg,* Carnegie Museums of Pittsburgh, Carnegie Museum of Art, Pittsburgh PA

Stephenson, Kay, *Shop Mgr,* Wayne County Historical Society, Museum, Honesdale PA

Stephenson, Warren, *Library Technical Asst,* University of Maryland, College Park, Art Library, College Park MD

Stepic, Barbara, *Pres,* Brooklyn Historical Society, Brooklyn OH

Stepler, Christopher, *Yard & Property Manager,* Essex Historical Society and Shipbuilding Museum, Essex MA

Sterling, Caron, *Develop & Mktg Assoc,* CultureWorks, Richmond VA

Sterling, LaVone, *Treas,* Pastel Society of the West Coast, Sacramento Fine Arts Center, Fresno CA
Sterling, Susan Fisher, *Dir,* National Museum of Women in the Arts, Washington DC
Sterman, Chris, *Interpretive Progs & Tours,* Missouri Department of Natural Resources, Missouri State Museum, Jefferson City MO
Stern, Barry, *Dir,* C W Post Campus of Long Island University, Hillwood Art Museum, Brookville NY
Stern, David, *Dir,* Saint Xavier University, Robert and Mary Rita Murphy Stump Library, Chicago IL
Stern, Emily, *Chair,* The College of New Rochelle, School of Arts & Sciences Art Dept, New Rochelle NY (S)
Stern, Jean, *Exec Dir,* Irvine Museum, Irvine CA
Stern, John P, *Pres,* Storm King Art Center, New Windsor NY
Stern, Lindsay A, *Educ Coordr,* Center for Photography at Woodstock Inc, Woodstock NY
Stern, Selma, *Program Dir,* Long Beach Art League, Long Beach Library, Long Beach NY
Stern, Sharon, *Exec Dir,* Hillel Foundation, Hillel Jewish Student Center Gallery, Cincinnati OH
Stern, Ted, *Prof Music,* Glendale Community College, Visual & Performing Arts Div, Glendale CA (S)
Sternberger, Paul, *Deputy Chair,* Rutgers University, Newark, Arts, Culture & Media, Newark NJ (S)
Sterngold, Katherine, *Instr,* Lycoming College, Art Dept, Williamsport PA (S)
Sterr, John, *Exec Dir,* Charles Allis Art Museum, Milwaukee WI
Sterr, John, *Exec Dir,* Villa Terrace Decorative Arts Museum, Milwaukee WI
Sterrett, Jill, *Dir Conservation & Colls,* San Francisco Museum of Modern Art, San Francisco CA
Sterritt, Colleen, *Instr,* Long Beach City College, Art & Photography Dept, Long Beach CA (S)
Stetson, Carla, *Assoc Prof,* Ithaca College, Fine Art Dept, Ithaca NY (S)
Stettner, Patrick, *Dir Rutgers Filmmaking Ctr,* Rutgers, The State University of New Jersey, Mason Gross School of the Arts, New Brunswick NJ (S)
Stetz, Robert J, *Instr,* Guild of Creative Art, Shrewsbury NJ (S)
Stevanov, Zoran, *Prof,* Fort Hays State University, Dept of Art & Design, Hays KS (S)
Steven, Robert, *Pres & CEO,* Art Gallery of Burlington, Burlington ON
Stevens, Andrew, *Cur Prints, Drawings & Photos,* University of Wisconsin-Madison, Chazen Museum of Art, Madison WI
Stevens, Brad, *Chief Preparator,* University of Oklahoma, Fred Jones Jr Museum of Art, Norman OK
Stevens, Clark, *Pres,* Cincinnati Art Club, Cincinnati OH
Stevens, Don, *IT Tech/Mem Secy,* Sonoma Valley Historical Society, Depot Park Museum, Sonoma CA
Stevens, Grant, *Develop Dir,* African American Museum of Iowa, Cedar Rapids IA
Stevens, Jamie, *Cur,* Artists Space, New York NY
Stevens, Jane Alden, *Prof Fine Arts,* University of Cincinnati, School of Art, Cincinnati OH (S)
Stevens, Jonathan, *Pres & CEO,* American Textile History Museum, Lowell MA
Stevens, Joslin, *Adjunct Faculty,* Mount Wachusett Community College, East Wing Gallery, Gardner MA
Stevens, Kathy, *Exec Dir,* Octagon Center for the Arts, Ames IA
Stevens, Linda, *Board Secy,* Pueblo Museum, Desert Hot Springs CA
Stevens, N Lee, *Sr Cur Art,* Pennsylvania Historical & Museum Commission, The State Museum of Pennsylvania, Harrisburg PA
Stevens, Rachel, *Assoc Prof,* New Mexico State University, Art Dept, Las Cruces NM (S)
Stevens, Rick, *Develop Mgr,* Susquehanna Art Museum, Harrisburg PA
Stevens, Scott, *Head of Security,* University of Minnesota Duluth, Tweed Museum of Art, Duluth MN
Stevenson, Alice, *Dir DiMenna Children's History Museum,* New-York Historical Society, Museum, New York NY
Stevenson, Ann, *Information Mgr Audrey Harry Hawthorn Libr & Archives,* University of British Columbia, Museum of Anthropology, Vancouver BC
Stevenson, Janelle, *Visitor Servs Mgr,* University of Nebraska, Lincoln, Sheldon Memorial Art Gallery & Sculpture Garden, Lincoln NE
Stevenson, Jill, *Asst Prof Theatre,* Marymount Manhattan College, Fine & Performing Arts Div, New York NY (S)
Stevenson, Kathleen, *Prof,* Weber State University, Dept of Visual Arts, Ogden UT (S)
Stevenson, Ron, *Dir,* Witter Gallery, Storm Lake IA
Stevenson, Sara, *Prog Cur,* Goethe-Institut New York, New York NY
Stevenson, Susan, *Assoc Prof,* University of Central Missouri, Dept of Art & Design, Warrensburg MO (S)
Steward, James, *Dir,* Princeton University, Princeton University Art Museum, Princeton NJ
Steward, James, *Dir, Princeton Univ Art Mus,* Princeton University, Dept of Art & Archaeology, Princeton NJ (S)
Steward, Jeff, *Dir Digital Infrastructure & Emerging Tech,* Harvard University, Harvard Art Museums, Cambridge MA
Steward, Maureen, *Exec Dir & Cur,* Temiskaming Art Gallery, Haileybury ON
Stewart, Allyn, *Asst Prof,* Cazenovia College, Center for Art & Design Studies, Cazenovia NY (S)
Stewart, Amy, *Prof,* Jefferson Community College & Technical College, Fine Arts, Louisville KY (S)
Stewart, Ann, *Div Chmn,* James H Faulkner, Art Dept, Bay Minette AL (S)
Stewart, Bridget, *Adjunct Assoc Prof Fine Art,* Johnson County Community College, Fine Arts Dept & Art History Dept, Overland Park KS (S)
Stewart, Callie, *Colls Mgr,* Bennington Museum, Bennington VT
Stewart, Charles Anthony, *Asst Prof,* University of Saint Thomas, Fine and Performing Arts Dept, Houston TX (S)
Stewart, Chris, *Chair,* Angelo State University, Visual and Performing Arts, San Angelo TX (S)
Stewart, Dan, *Adjunct Prof Art,* Monroe County Community College, Humanities Division, Monroe MI (S)
Stewart, David, *Prof,* University of Alabama in Huntsville, Dept of Art and Art History, Huntsville AL (S)
Stewart, Deborah, *Byzantine Studies Librn,* Dumbarton Oaks, Dumbarton Oaks Research Library, Washington DC
Stewart, Evelyn, *Dir,* Twin City Art Foundation, Masur Museum of Art, Monroe LA
Stewart, Gaylen, *Assoc Prof Art,* Grand Canyon University, Art Dept, Phoenix AZ (S)
Stewart, Gene, *Dept Chair,* Regis University, Fine Arts Dept, Denver CO (S)
Stewart, Janice, *Instr,* Mount Mary College, Art & Design Division, Milwaukee WI (S)
Stewart, John, *Prof Fine Arts,* University of Cincinnati, School of Art, Cincinnati OH (S)
Stewart, Karol, *Mktg Dir,* South Texas Institute for the Arts Affiliated with Texas A&M University - Corpus Christi, Art Museum of South Texas, Corpus Christi TX
Stewart, Laura, *Gallery Dir & Cur Coll,* Georgetown College, Art Dept, Georgetown KY (S)
Stewart, Lorelei, *Dir,* University of Illinois at Chicago, Gallery 400, Chicago IL
Stewart, Mary Lou, *Asst Prof,* Elmhurst College, Art Dept, Elmhurst IL (S)
Stewart, Nick, *Develop Officer,* Arts & Science Council, Charlotte NC
Stewart, Regina, *Exec Dir,* New York Artists Equity Association, Inc, New York NY
Stewart, Richard D, *Asst Prof Communs,* Barton College, School of Visual, Performing & Communication Arts, Wilson NC (S)
Stewart, Roberta, *Dir Admin,* Boca Raton Museum of Art, Boca Raton FL
Stewart, Sara, *Asst Dir Develop & Mktg,* University of Pennsylvania, Arthur Ross Gallery, Philadelphia PA
Stewart, Susan, *Dean Faculty of Culture & Community,* Emily Carr University of Art + Design, Vancouver BC (S)
Stewart, Tracey, *Develop Officer,* Flint Institute of Arts, Flint MI
Stewart-Halevy, Jacob, *Asst Prof,* Tufts University, Dept of Art & Art History, Medford MA (S)
Steyaert, John, *Assoc Prof,* University of Minnesota, Minneapolis, Art History, Minneapolis MN (S)
Steylen, Traci, *Admin Asst & Website Mgr,* Mount Saint Vincent University, MSVU Art Gallery, Halifax NS
Sticha, Denise, *Reference & Pub Servs Librn,* Seton Hill College, Reeves Memorial Library, Greensburg PA
Stickley, Gloria, *Pres,* Strasburg Museum, Strasburg VA
Stickney, Laura, *Teacher Outreach Coordr,* Cultural Affairs Department City of Los Angeles, Barnsdall Art Center & Junior Arts Center, Los Angeles CA
Stidham, Jane, *Assoc Prof Design,* University of North Texas, College of Visual Arts & Design, Denton TX (S)
Stidsen, Donald, *Mgr Exhibs,* Massachusetts Institute of Technology, MIT Museum, Cambridge MA
Stier, David, *Dir,* Springfield Museums, George Walker Vincent Smith Art Museum, Springfield MA
Stiffler, Kmberley, *Develop & Grants Asst,* Virginia Center for the Creative Arts, Amherst VA
Stifler, Sarah L, *Chief Communs Officer,* The Museum of Contemporary Art (MOCA), MOCA Grand Avenue, Los Angeles CA
Stiger, Lucille, *Registrar,* Oberlin College, Allen Memorial Art Museum, Oberlin OH
Stigora, Alison, *Adj Prof,* Saint Joseph's University, Art Dept, Philadelphia PA (S)
Stiles, Victoria, *Exec Dir & CEO,* Shoreline Historical Museum, Shoreline WA
Still, Todd, *Dir of Youth,* Dunedin Fine Art Center, Dunedin FL (S)
Stiller, Dalia, *Pres,* Boca Raton Museum of Art, Boca Raton FL
Stillions, Wanda, *Bus Mgr,* Scottsdale Artists' School, Scottsdale AZ (S)
Stillman, Nick, *Deputy Dir,* Arts Council Of New Orleans, New Orleans LA
Stillman, Sharon, *Dir Human Resources,* Honolulu Museum of Art, Honolulu HI
Stillman, Waddell, *Pres,* Historic Hudson Valley, Pocantico Hills NY
Stillwell, Kim, *Registrar,* Museum of Contemporary Art, North Miami FL
Stinchcomb, Donna, *Cur Children's Mus,* Sangre de Cristo Arts & Conference Center, Pueblo CO
Stindt, Henry, *Prof,* Lenoir Community College, Dept of Visual Art, Kinston NC (S)
Stinely, Alison, *Asst Prof,* Old Dominion University, Art Dept, Norfolk VA (S)
Stinnett, Hester, *Pres,* The Print Center, Philadelphia PA
Stinson, Debby, *Media/PR Mgr,* Washington State University, Museum of Art, Pullman WA
Stinson, Lisa, *Asst Prof,* Appalachian State University, Dept of Art, Boone NC (S)
Stirton-Broad, Carol, *Instr,* Main Line Art Center, Haverford PA (S)
Stiso Mullins, Kathleen, *Pres,* Edsel & Eleanor Ford House, Grosse Pointe Shores MI
Stock, Joan, *Art Cur,* State Historical Society of Missouri, Gallery and Library, Columbia MO
Stock, Matthew, *Fine & Applied Arts Librn,* University of Oklahoma, Architecture Library, Norman OK
Stock, Matthew, *Fine & Applied Arts Librn,* University of Oklahoma, Fine Arts Library, Norman OK
Stockard, Ladymon, *Instr,* Benedict College, School of Humanities, Arts & Social Sciences, Columbia SC (S)

Stockert, Rebecca, *Gallery & Educ Coordr,* Artlink, Inc, Auer Center for Arts & Culture, Fort Wayne IN
Stocki, Robert, *Instr,* Milwaukee Area Technical College, School of Media & Creative Arts, Milwaukee WI (S)
Stockwell, Ross, *Instr,* San Diego Mesa College, Fine Arts Dept, San Diego CA (S)
Stoddard, Brooks, *Assoc Prof,* University of Maine at Augusta, College of Arts & Humanities, Augusta ME (S)
Stoddard, Pamela, *Gallery Coordr,* Michigan Guild of Artists & Artisans, Michigan Guild Gallery, Ann Arbor MI
Stoddart, Emily, *Coordr Exhibs & Public Progs,* The American-Scandinavian Foundation, Scandinavia House: The Nordic Center in America, New York NY
Stoepel, Kathe, *Graphic Artist,* Lake Forest Library, Fine Arts Dept, Lake Forest IL
Stofan, Ellen, *John & Adrienne Mars Dir,* National Air and Space Museum, Smithsonian Institution, Washington DC
Stofan, Ellen, *John & Adrienne Mars Dir,* National Air And Space Museum, Steven F Udvar-Hazy Center, Chantilly VA
Stohn, Franz, *Asst Chmn of Art,* Edinboro University of Pennsylvania, Art Dept, Edinboro PA (S)
Stojanovic, Jelena, *Dir,* Ithaca College, Handwerker Gallery of Art, Ithaca NY
Stoker, E, *Prof,* University of the Incarnate Word, Art Dept, San Antonio TX (S)
Stokes, David, *Assoc Prof,* Winthrop University, Dept of Art & Design, Rock Hill SC (S)
Stokes, Deborah, *Cur Educ,* National Museum of African Art, Smithsonian Institution, Washington DC
Stokes, Hunter, *VChmn,* Florence County Museum, Florence SC
Stokes, Julie, *Treas,* Madison County Historical Society, Cottage Lawn, Oneida NY
Stokes, Sally Sims, *Librn,* University of Maryland, College Park, National Trust for Historic Preservation Library Collection, College Park MD
Stokes, Vicki, *VPres,* Florence County Museum, Florence SC
Stokesbury, Bria, *Cur,* Kings County Historical Society & Museum, Hampton NB
Stokstad, Marilyn, *Prof,* University of Kansas, Kress Foundation Dept of Art History, Lawrence KS (S)
Stollar, Thomas, *Asst Prof Ceramics,* Florida Atlantic University, D F Schmidt College of Arts & Letters Dept of Visual Arts & Art History, Boca Raton FL (S)
Stollhans, Cindy, *Chmn,* Saint Louis University, Fine & Performing Arts Dept, Saint Louis MO (S)
Stolzer, Rob, *Prof,* University of Wisconsin-Stevens Point, Dept of Art & Design, Stevens Point WI (S)
Stomberg, John, *Florence Finch Abbott Dir,* Mount Holyoke College, Art Museum, South Hadley MA
Stone, Ben, *Foundations Coordr,* Northern Illinois University, School of Art & Design, DeKalb IL (S)
Stone, Carla, *Exhib Coordr,* Sonoma State University, University Art Gallery, Rohnert Park CA
Stone, Cindy, *Dir,* Historic Newton, Newton MA
Stone, Denise, *Assoc Prof,* University of Kansas, The School of the Arts, Dept of Visual Art, Lawrence KS (S)
Stone, Denise, *Asst Prof,* University of Kansas, Dept of Art & Music Education & Music Therapy, Lawrence KS (S)
Stone, Elisabeth, *Dir Educ,* University of Illinois at Urbana-Champaign, Spurlock Museum, Urbana IL
Stone, Elizabeth, *Pres,* Wenham Museum, Wenham MA
Stone, Ellen, *Dir, Develop & Mem,* North Carolina Museum of Art, Raleigh NC
Stone, Gaylund, *Gallery Dir,* Concordia University Wisconsin, Fine Art Gallery, Mequon WI
Stone, Jenny, *Librn,* Dallas Museum of Art, Mildred R & Frederick M Mayer Library, Dallas TX
Stone, Jim, *Prof,* University of New Mexico, Department of Fine Arts & Art History, Albuquerque NM (S)
Stone, Joan, *Dean,* Rochester Institute of Technology, School of Printing Management & Sciences, Rochester NY (S)
Stone, Joan, *Dean,* Rochester Institute of Technology, School of Printing Management & Sciences, Rochester NY (S)
Stone, Joan, *Dean,* Rochester Institute of Technology, School for American Craft, Rochester NY (S)
Stone, Jon, *Treas,* Fremont Center for the Arts, Canon City CO
Stone, Kenneth H, *Deputy Dir Finance,* Buffalo & Erie County Public Library, Buffalo NY
Stone, Lawre, *Mng Dir,* Bard College, Milton Avery Graduate School of the Arts, Annandale-on-Hudson NY (S)
Stone, Linda, *Cur Art,* The Frank Phillips Foundation Inc, Woolaroc Museum, Bartlesville OK
Stone, Martha, *Gallery Monitor,* Arthur Griffin Center for Photographic Art, Griffin Museum of Photography, Winchester MA
Stone, Millard, *Treas,* Spectrum Gallery, Toledo OH
Stone, Pam, *Trustee,* L D Brinkman, Kerrville TX
Stone, Rebecca R, *Assoc Prof,* Emory University, Art History Dept, Atlanta GA (S)
Stone, Robin, *Chmn,* Hannibal La Grange College, Art Dept, Hannibal MO (S)
Stone, Sara, *Dir Develop,* Cleveland Botanical Garden, Eleanor Squire Library, Cleveland OH
Stone, Thelma, *Unit Mgr,* Fort Worth Public Library Arts & Humanities, Fine Arts Section, Fort Worth TX
Stone-Ferrier, Linda, *Dept Chair,* University of Kansas, Kress Foundation Dept of Art History, Lawrence KS (S)
Stone-Street, Nancy, *Instr,* Mississippi Delta Community College, Dept of Fine Arts, Moorhead MS (S)
Stonehouse, Fred, *Assoc Prof,* University of Wisconsin, Madison, Dept of Art, Madison WI (S)
Stoner, Kathy, *Asst Cur,* City of Fayette, Alabama, Fayette Art Museum, Fayette AL
Stoner, Kevin, *Interim Chair Visual Arts,* The Sage Colleges, Dept Visual Arts, Albany NY (S)
Stoner, Richard, *Instr,* Seton Hill University, Art Program, Greensburg PA (S)
Stonesanders, Rebecca, *Asst Prof,* Lincoln University, Dept Visual and Performing Arts, Jefferson City MO (S)
Stopka, Christina, *Deputy Dir Opers,* Texas Ranger Hall of Fame & Museum, Waco TX
Stopka, Christina, *Head,* Texas Ranger Hall of Fame & Museum, Texas Ranger Research Center, Waco TX
Stoppel, Joel, *Instr,* North Central Michigan College, Art Dept, Petoskey MI (S)
Stoppelman, Gary, *Deputy Dir Mktg & External Affairs,* Newfields, Indianapolis IN
Storer, Gail, *Library Dir,* Columbus College of Art & Design, Packard Library, Columbus OH
Storey, Kate, *Mgr,* Ford Motor Company, Henry Ford Museum & Greenfield Village, Dearborn MI
Storhoff, Timothy, *Arts Admin,* Florida Department of State, Division of Cultural Affairs, Florida Council on Arts & Culture, Tallahassee FL
Story Cunningham, Dianne, *Pres,* New Zone Virtual Gallery, Eugene OR
Story, Mollie, *Admin Mgr,* Gertrude Herbert Institute of Art, Augusta GA
Story, Nancy, *Library Support Specialist,* Ohio University, Fine Arts Library, Athens OH
Story, Sarah, *Pub Relations,* Ogden Museum of Southern Art, University of New Orleans, New Orleans LA
Stott, Annette, *Prof Art History,* University of Denver, School of Art & Art History, Denver CO (S)
Stout, Andrew R, *Dir,* Florence County Museum, Florence SC
Stout, Andrew, *Asst Dir Grad,* University of Oklahoma, School of Art, Norman OK (S)
Stout, Nancy, *Assoc Dir Institutional Advancement,* Princeton University, Princeton University Art Museum, Princeton NJ
Stout, Paul, *Asst Prof,* University of Utah, Dept of Art & Art History, Salt Lake City UT (S)
Stout, Scotland, *Assoc Prof,* Southern Arkansas University at Magnolia, Dept of Art & Design, Magnolia AR (S)
Stout, Scotland, *Chmn Art Dept,* Southern Arkansas University, Art Dept Gallery & Magale Art Gallery, Magnolia AR
Stover Quarles, Valorie, *Prof Film,* Watkins College of Art, Design & Film, Nashville TN (S)
Stover, Craig, *Exec Dir,* Allens Lane Art Center, Carolyn-Fielder-Alber Gallery, Philadelphia PA
Stowell, Daniel, *Dir,* Abraham Lincoln Presidential Library & Museum, Springfield IL
Stowers, Robert, *Prof,* University of Wisconsin-Stevens Point, Dept of Art & Design, Stevens Point WI (S)
Stowman, Annetta T, *Asst Dir,* Villanova University Art Gallery, The Art Gallery, Villanova PA
Strackbein, Davidde, *Chmn,* Bush-Holley Historic Site & Storehouse Gallery, Greenwich Historical Society, Cos Cob CT
Strain, David, *Chmn,* University of the Ozarks, Dept of Art, Clarksville AR (S)
Straka, Keri, *Asst Prof,* Framingham State College, Art Dept, Framingham MA (S)
Strand, Chris, *Dir Garden & Estate,* Winterthur Museum, Winterthur Museum, Garden & Library, Winterthur DE
Strand, Eric, *Treas,* Marion Art Center, Cecil Clark Davis Gallery, Marion MA
Strand, Laura, *Head Fiber & Fabric,* Southern Illinois University at Edwardsville, Dept of Art & Design, Edwardsville IL (S)
Strandberg, Kevin, *Instr,* Illinois Wesleyan University, School of Art, Bloomington IL (S)
Stranges, Robert, *Instr,* Siena Heights University, Studio Angelico-Art Dept, Adrian MI (S)
Stranges, Robert, *Instr,* Adrian College, Art & Design Dept, Adrian MI (S)
Strangfeld, Robin, *Asst Prof,* Southern Oregon University, Art & Art History Dept, Ashland OR (S)
Stranieri, Amanda, *Community Campaign Coord,* Staten Island Museum, Staten Island NY
Strano, Susan, *Dir Mktg & Pub Rels, Space Rentals & Grp Tours,* Bennington Museum, Bennington VT
Strassberg, Roy, *Prof & Chair,* University of North Carolina at Charlotte, Dept Art, Charlotte NC (S)
Straszheim, Heather, *Cur,* Octagon Center for the Arts, Ames IA
Stratford, Linda, *Instr,* Asbury University, Art Dept, Wilmore KY (S)
Stratford, Linda, *Prof Art History,* Asbury College, Student Center Gallery, Wilmore KY
Stratis, Harriet, *Paper Conservator,* The Art Institute of Chicago, Dept of Prints & Drawings, Chicago IL
Stratton, David, *Prof Fine Arts,* Brescia University, Art Dept, Owensboro KY (S)
Stratton, David, *Prof of Art & Gallery Dir,* Brescia University, Anna Eaton Stout Memorial Art Gallery, Owensboro KY
Stratton, Donald, *Prof,* University of Maine at Augusta, College of Arts & Humanities, Augusta ME (S)
Stratton, Libby, *Production Manager,* The Columbian Theatre Foundation, Inc, Columbian Theatre Museum & Art Center, Wamego KS
Stratton, Shannon R., *Chief Cur,* Museum of Arts & Design, New York NY
Stratton, Winnie, *Pres Bd,* Seattle Art Museum, Seattle WA
Straub, Jim, *Pres,* Galesburg Civic Art Center, Galesburg IL
Straub, Kara, *VPres,* Alberta Society of Artists, Calgary AB
Straub, Leah, *Communs & Mktg Mgr,* Museum of Contemporary Art San Diego, San Diego CA
Strauch-Nelson, Wendy, *Assoc Prof,* University of Wisconsin Oshkosh, Dept of Art, Oshkosh WI (S)

Straughn, Celka, *Outreach Coord,* University of Kansas, Spencer Museum of Art, Lawrence KS

Strauss, Bonnie, *Educ Dir,* Michelson Museum of Art, Marshall TX

Strauss, Cassie, *Director of Development,* Missoula Art Museum, Missoula MT

Strauss, David, *Dir External Affairs,* The Queens Museum of Art, Flushing NY

Strauss, Haila, *Assoc Prof Dance,* Marymount Manhattan College, Fine & Performing Arts Div, New York NY (S)

Strauss, Linda, *Instr,* St Lawrence University, Dept of Fine Arts, Canton NY (S)

Strauss, Matthew, *Pres Bd Trustees,* Museum of Contemporary Art San Diego, La Jolla CA

Strauss, Samara, *Arts Coordr,* Northwood University, Jeannette Hare Art Gallery, West Palm Beach FL

Strawbridge, Simone, *Chmn,* Mississippi Delta Community College, Dept of Fine Arts, Moorhead MS (S)

Strawn, Cullen, *Dir Gallery,* Old Dominion University, Art Dept, Norfolk VA (S)

Stream, Heidi, *Dir Exhibitions & Publications,* The Cleveland Museum of Art, Cleveland OH

Strean, Jeffrey, *Dir Design & Architecture,* The Cleveland Museum of Art, Cleveland OH

Streb, Jennifer, *Chmn Dept,* Juniata College, Dept of Art & Art History, Huntingdon PA (S)

Streb, Sherry, *CFO,* Akron Art Museum, Akron OH

Streeter, Anita, *Exec Dir,* Embroiderers Guild of America, Margaret Parshall Gallery, Louisville KY

Streetman, John W, *Dir Emeritus,* Evansville Museum of Arts, History & Science, Evansville IN

Strehlke, Carl, *Curator Emeritus,* Philadelphia Museum of Art, John G Johnson Collection, Philadelphia PA

Streich, Amy, *Mktg Dir,* Octagon Center for the Arts, Ames IA

Streicker, John, *Pres,* Congregation Emanu-El, Bernard Judaica Museum, New York NY

Streifler, Leesa, *Prof & Head, Visual Arts Dept,* University of Regina, Faculty of Media, Art & Performance, Regina SK (S)

Streit, Jessica, *Vis Asst Prof,* Hamline University, Dept of Studio Arts & Art History, Saint Paul MN (S)

Stremmel, Peter, *Exec Dir,* Stremmel Gallery, Reno NV

Stremmel, Turkey, *Gallery Dir,* Stremmel Gallery, Reno NV

Stremsterfer, Marianne, *Instr,* Springfield College in Illinois, Dept of Art, Springfield IL (S)

Stretz, Sidney, *Educ Coordr,* The Center for Visual Artists - Greensboro, Greensboro NC

Strevy, Samantha, *Admin Asst,* Saratoga County Historical Society, Brookside Museum, Ballston Spa NY

Stricker, Warren, *Archivist & Librn,* Panhandle-Plains Historical Museum, Research Center, Canyon TX

Strickland, Barbour, *Exec Dir,* Greenville Museum of Art, Inc, Reference Library, Greenville NC

Stricklin, Linda, *Asst Prof,* McMurry University, Art Dept, Abilene TX (S)

Striegel, Rita, *Office Mgr,* Balzekas Museum of Lithuanian Culture, Chicago IL

Stringari, Carol, *Deputy Dir & Chief Conservator,* Solomon R Guggenheim Museum, New York NY

Stringer, Howard, *Chmn Bd Trustees,* American Film Institute (AFI), Los Angeles CA (S)

Strobel, Tracy, *Deputy Dir,* Cuyahoga County Public Library, Parma OH

Strohl, Erik, *VPres Exhibs & Colls,* National Baseball Hall of Fame & Museum, Cooperstown NY

Strohm, Robert, *COO, Assoc Dir,* Virginia Historical Society, Richmond VA

Stroker, Robert, *Dean,* Temple University, Temple Contemporary, Philadelphia PA

Strom, Christine, *Communs Mgr,* University of Minnesota Duluth, Tweed Museum of Art, Duluth MN

Strom, Jordan, *Cur,* Surrey Art Gallery, Surrey BC

Strom, Jordan, *Cur Exhib & Coll,* Surrey Art Gallery, Library, Surrey BC

Strom, Kristen, *Assoc Prof,* Grand Valley State University, Art & Design Dept, Allendale MI (S)

Stromberg, Caroline, *Cur Paleobotany,* University of Washington, Burke Museum of Natural History and Culture, Seattle WA

Strombotne, James S, *Prof,* University of California, Riverside, Dept of Art, Riverside CA (S)

Stromquist, Susan, *Exhib Chair,* Plastic Club, Art Club, Philadelphia PA

Stronach, Tami, *Asst Prof Dance,* Marymount Manhattan College, Fine & Performing Arts Div, New York NY (S)

Strong, Barbara, *Instr,* College of the Sequoias, Art Dept, Visalia CA (S)

Strong, Dan, *Assoc Dir,* Grinnell College, Faulconer Gallery, Grinnell IA

Strong, John, *Dir,* Lake George Arts Project, Courthouse Gallery, Lake George NY

Strong, Marjorie, *Asst Librn,* Vermont Historical Society, Library, Montpelier VT

Strong, Peter, *Dir,* Heritage Center, Inc, Pine Ridge SD

Strong, Scott M, *Admin,* United States Senate Commission on Art, Washington DC

Stroukoff, Eumie Imm, *Director of Research Center,* Georgia O'Keeffe Museum, Santa Fe NM

Strozza, Sarah, *Dir Special Events,* Laguna Art Museum, Laguna Beach CA

Strum, Martha, *Dir Develop,* Fort Ticonderoga Association, Ticonderoga NY

Strunsky, Mark, *Chair,* Orange County Community College, Arts & Communication, Middletown NY (S)

Struss, Sonny, *Instr,* Appalachian State University, Dept of Art, Boone NC (S)

Struthers, Webster, *Assoc Prof Communs,* Barton College, School of Visual, Performing & Communication Arts, Wilson NC (S)

Struve, Carol, *Asst Prof,* Bemidji State University, Visual Arts Dept, Bemidji MN (S)

Struve, Sue, *Commun Mgr,* National Assembly of State Arts Agencies, Washington DC

Stuart, Daniel, *Adjunct Instr Art,* Monroe County Community College, Fine Arts Council, Monroe MI

Stuart, Nancy, *Assoc Dir,* Rochester Institute of Technology, School of Photographic Arts & Sciences, Rochester NY (S)

Stuart-Hill, Vickie, *Art Cur,* Marine Corps University, National Museum of the Marine Corps, Triangle VA

Stubbs, Judy, *Cur Asian Art,* Indiana University, Eskenazi Museum of Art, Bloomington IN

Stubbs-Lee, Dee, *Conservator,* New Brunswick Museum, Saint John NB

Stuckenbruck, Corky, *Dir,* Texas Woman's University Art Gallery, Denton TX

Stuckenbruck, Linda, *Prof,* Texas Woman's University, School of the Arts, Dept of Visual Arts, Denton TX (S)

Stuckey, Rachel, *Gallery Dir,* Women & Their Work, Austin TX

Stuckle, Doug, *Artist & Owner,* Gallery 4, Ltd, Fargo ND

Stucky, John Carl, *Librn,* Asian Art Museum of San Francisco, C Laan Chun Library, San Francisco CA

Stucky, John, *Librn,* Asian Art Museum of San Francisco, Chong-Moon Lee Ctr for Asian Art and Culture, San Francisco CA

Stueber, Casey, *Art Instr,* Crowder College, Longwell Museum/Art Department, Neosho MO (S)

Stueve, Clint, *Exec Dir,* The Columbian Theatre Foundation, Inc, Columbian Theatre Museum & Art Center, Wamego KS

Stuhlman, Jonathan, *Sr Cur American, Modern & Contemporary Art,* The Mint Museum, Art Organization & Library, Charlotte NC

Stuhlman, Theresa, *Site Supvr,* Ryerss Victorian Museum & Library, Philadelphia PA

Stuhr, Patricia, *Prof,* Ohio State University, Dept of Art Education, Columbus OH (S)

Stukator, Angela, *Assoc Dean Animation & Game Design,* Sheridan College, Faculty of Animation, Arts & Design, Oakville ON (S)

Stula, Nancy, *Exec Dir,* University of Connecticut, William Benton Museum of Art, Storrs CT

Stulen, Scott, *Dir & Pres,* Philbrook Museum of Art, Tulsa OK

Stull, Will, *Instr,* Butte College, Dept of Fine Arts and Communication Tech, Oroville CA (S)

Stulpz, Larry, *Dean,* Art Institute of Atlanta, Atlanta GA (S)

Stunes, Steve, *Dir,* Moody County Historical Society, Moody County Museum, Flandreau SD

Stupek, Bev, *Develop Officer,* Turtle Bay Exploration Park, Redding CA

Sturgeon, John, *Prof,* University of Maryland, Baltimore County, Intermedia & Digital Arts (IMDA), Dept of Visual Arts, Baltimore MD (S)

Sturgeon, Mary C, *Prof,* University of North Carolina at Chapel Hill, Art Dept, Chapel Hill NC (S)

Sturgeon, Willie, *Security/Facilities Technician,* Ellen Noel Art Museum of the Permian Basin, Odessa TX

Sturgess, Louise, *Exec Dir,* Pittsburgh History & Landmarks Foundation, James D Van Trump Library, Pittsburgh PA

Sturhahn, Kelly, *Asst Prof Art & Dir Foundation Prog,* Florida Southern College, Department of Art & Art History, Lakeland FL (S)

Sturhahn, Kelly, *Asst Prof Art & Dir Foundation Prog,* Florida Southern College, Melvin Art Gallery, Lakeland FL

Sturm, Nancy, *Pres,* Society for Commercial Archeology, Little Rock AR

Sturrock, Sherrod A, *Deputy Dir,* Calvert Marine Museum, Solomons MD

Sturtevant, Sue, *Dir & CEO,* Hill-Stead Museum, Farmington CT

Stwyer, Aurolyn, *Chmn,* Atlatl, Phoenix AZ

Styers, Jeffrey, *Media Arts & Animation,* Art Institute of Pittsburgh, Pittsburgh PA (S)

Stykel, Eric, *Asst Prof,* University of Central Missouri, Dept of Art & Design, Warrensburg MO (S)

Style, Christine, *Assoc Prof,* University of Wisconsin-Green Bay, Arts Dept, Green Bay WI (S)

Styron, Thomas W, *Dir,* Greenville County Museum of Art, Greenville SC

Su, Margaret, *Exec Dir,* Wing Luke Asian Museum, Seattle WA

Suarez, Will, *Adjunct Prof,* College of Saint Elizabeth, Art Dept, Morristown NJ (S)

Subler, Craig, *Dir,* University of Missouri-Kansas City, Gallery of Art, Kansas City MO

Subramaniam, Radhika, *Dir & Chief Cur,* The New School Parsons School of Design, Sheila C Johnson Design Center, New York NY (S)

Suchland, Craig, *Assoc Dir Media & Tech,* Anchorage Museum at Rasmuson Center, Anchorage AK

Suderburg, Erika, *Chmn,* University of California, Riverside, Dept of Art, Riverside CA (S)

Sudolcan, John, *Dir Opers,* Norton Simon Museum, Pasadena CA

Suehiro, Hiroshi, *Deputy Pres & Exec Officer,* The Nippon Gallery at the Nippon Club, New York NY

Suffolk, Randall, *Dir,* High Museum of Art, Atlanta GA

Sugarman, David, *Pres,* Durham Art Gallery, Durham ON

Sugawara-Beda, Nishiki, *Asst Prof,* University of Idaho College of Art & Architecture, Dept of Art & Design, Moscow ID (S)

Sugden, Sarah, *Cur,* Waterville Historical Society, Redington Museum, Waterville ME

Sugerman, Sonja, *Visual Resources & Art Coll Cur,* Goucher College, Rosenberg & Silber Art Gallery, Baltimore MD

Suggs, Marianne, *Prof,* Appalachian State University, Dept of Art, Boone NC (S)

Sugimoto, Lisa, *Instr,* Avila College, Art Division, Dept of Humanities, Kansas City MO (S)

Sugita, Lisa, *Shop Supervisor,* Museum of Fine Arts Houston, Bayou Bend Collection & Gardens, Houston TX

Suh, Eun-Kyung, *Asst Prof,* University of Minnesota, Duluth, Art Dept, Duluth MN (S)

Suhoza, Rebecca, *Gen Educ,* Art Institute of Pittsburgh, Pittsburgh PA (S)
Suhre, Terry, *Asst Prof,* University of Missouri, Saint Louis, Dept of Art & Art History, Saint Louis MO (S)
Suhre, Terry, *Dir,* University of Missouri, Saint Louis, Gallery 210, Saint Louis MO
Sujdak, Andrew, *Graphic Design, Media Arts & Animation,* Art Institute of Pittsburgh, Pittsburgh PA (S)
Suk, Ian, *Assoc Prof,* Johns Hopkins University, School of Medicine, Dept of Art as Applied to Medicine, Baltimore MD (S)
Sulazar, Maruca, *Exec Dir,* Museo De Las Americas, Denver CO
Sulka, Arlie, *Secy,* National Antique & Art Dealers Association of America, Inc, New York NY
Sulkin, Robert, *Prof & Chair,* Hollins University, Art Dept, Roanoke VA (S)
Sullivan, Andrea, *Reference Librn,* Daemen College, Marian Library, Amherst NY
Sullivan, Autumn, *Acquisition & Technical Svcs,* Laney College Library, Art Section, Oakland CA
Sullivan, Carol, *Mus Shop Mgr,* Westmoreland Museum of American Art, Greensburg PA
Sullivan, Catherine, *Cur, Head of Colls,* California State University, Chico, Janet Turner Print Museum, CSU, Chicago, Chico CA
Sullivan, Charles M, *Exec Dir,* Cambridge Historical Commission, City of Cambridge, Research Library on Architectural and Social History of Cambridge, Mass, Cambridge MA
Sullivan, Gary, *Chmn,* Wagner College, Arts Administration Dept, Staten Island NY (S)
Sullivan, Jay, *Prof,* Southern Methodist University, Meadows School of the Arts - Division of Art, Dallas TX (S)
Sullivan, Jill, *Dir,* Winfred L & Elizabeth C Post Foundation, Post Art Library, Joplin MO
Sullivan, John M, *Chmn,* Jackson State University, Dept of Art, Jackson MS (S)
Sullivan, Karen, *Lectr,* California State Polytechnic University, Pomona, Department of Art, Pomona CA (S)
Sullivan, Katherine, *Assoc Prof,* Hope College, Dept of Art & Art History, Holland MI (S)
Sullivan, Kristin, *Cur & Folklorist,* Salisbury University, Ward Museum of Wildfowl Art, Salisbury MD
Sullivan, Mark, *Asst Prof,* Villanova University, Dept of Theater, Villanova PA (S)
Sullivan, Megan, *Vol Prog Mgr,* Kirkland Museum of Fine & Decorative Art, Denver CO
Sullivan, Michael, *Asst Prof,* Fontbonne University, Fine Art Dept, Saint Louis MO (S)
Sullivan, Shane, *Undergrad Coordr,* University of Texas, Dept of Art & Art History, Austin TX (S)
Sullivan, Sheila, *Assoc Lectr,* University of Wisconsin-Stevens Point, Dept of Art & Design, Stevens Point WI (S)
Sullivan, William J, *Mgr Opers,* ArtSpace/Lima, Lima OH
Sullivan-Blum, Constance R, *Exec Dir,* The ARTS Council of the Southern Finger Lakes, Corning NY
Sultan, Terrie, *Cur Contemporary Art,* Corcoran Gallery of Art, Washington DC
Sultan, Terrie, *Dir,* Parrish Art Museum, Water Mill NY
Summer, Stephen, *Exec Dir,* Colorado Mountain Art Gallery, Georgetown CO
Summers, Candace, *Dir Educ,* McLean County Historical Society, McLean County Museum of History, Bloomington IL
Summers, David, *Prof,* University of Virginia, McIntire Dept of Art, Charlottesville VA (S)
Summers, George, *Gallery Mgr,* The Society of Arts & Crafts, Boston MA
Summers, Ruth, *Dir,* Southern Highland Craft Guild, Folk Art Center, Asheville NC
Summerville, Christie, *Coordr of Arts,* University of New Haven, Dept of Visual & Performing Arts & Philosophy, West Haven CT (S)
Sumner, Andrew, *Secy,* The Art Cafe, Davisburg MI
Sumner, Carol, *Corresp Secy,* Berks Art Alliance, Reading PA
Sumrall, Bradley, *Cur,* Ogden Museum of Southern Art, University of New Orleans, New Orleans LA
Sumrall, Robert F, *Cur Ship Models,* United States Naval Academy, USNA Museum, Annapolis MD
Sun, Bonnie, *Sr Mktg & Commun Mgr,* University of British Columbia, Museum of Anthropology, Vancouver BC
Sun, Leon, *Graphic Design,* Western Michigan University, Frostic School of Art, Kalamazoo MI (S)
Sun, Yan John, *Chmn,* Muskingum College, Art Department, New Concord OH (S)
Sund, Judy, *Prof,* City University of New York, PhD Program in Art History, New York NY (S)
Sundahl, Steve, *Asst Prof,* Bemidji State University, Visual Arts Dept, Bemidji MN (S)
Sundberg, Beth, *Web & Office Mgr,* Davistown Museum, Liberty Location, Liberty ME
Sundby, Mel, *Instr,* Century College, Humanities Dept, White Bear Lake MN (S)
Sunderland, Luke, *VPres & COO,* Banff Centre, Banff AB (S)
Sundstrom, K, *Cur,* The Currier Museum of Art, Manchester NH
Sundt, Christine L, *Visual Resources Cur,* University of Oregon, Architecture & Allied Arts Library, Eugene OR
Sung, Hou-Mei, *Cur Asian Art,* Cincinnati Art Museum, Cincinnati Art Museum, Cincinnati OH
Sung, Lillian, *Instr,* Stephens College, Art Dept, Columbia MO (S)
Suominen Guyas, Anniina, *Prof,* Florida State University, Art Education Dept, Tallahassee FL (S)
Supcoff, Sarah, *Deputy Dir Mktg & Communs,* The Jewish Museum, New York NY
Suppa, Stephen, *Pres,* Wiscasset, Waterville & Farmington Railway Museum (WW&F), Alna ME
Surerus, Michelle, *Prof, Graphics,* Chowan College, Dept. of Communication Arts, Fine and Applied Arts, Murfreesboro NC (S)
Sures, Lynn, *Interim Chair, Fine Art,* Corcoran School of Art, Washington DC (S)
Suridis, Nick, *Dir Patron Svcs,* Washington Pavilion of Arts & Science, Visual Arts Center, Sioux Falls SD
Surkin, Elliot M, *Chmn (V),* The Trustees of Reservations, The Mission House, Ipswich MA
Surkmer, Suzette, *Exec Dir,* South Carolina Arts Commission, Media Center, Columbia SC
Surratt, Monte, *Instr Dept Head,* Cochise College, Art Dept, Douglas AZ (S)
Sussman, Eric, *Asst Bldg Mgr,* Fraunces Tavern Museum, New York NY
Sussman, Leonard, *Deputy Chair Art,* Bernard M Baruch College of the City University of New York, Art Dept, New York NY (S)
Sussman, Wendy, *Grad & undergrad faculty adv,* University of California, Berkeley, College of Letters & Sciences-Art Practice Dept, Berkeley CA (S)
Susstrink, Sabrine, *Asst Prof,* Rochester Institute of Technology, School of Photographic Arts & Sciences, Rochester NY (S)
Sutcliffe, Nina, *Adjunct Assoc Prof,* University of Maine, Dept of Art, Orono ME (S)
Suter, Ryan, *Media Arts Mgr,* Struts Gallery, Sackville NB
Sutherland, Daniel, *Asst Chair - Studio Art,* University of Texas, Dept of Art & Art History, Austin TX (S)
Sutherland, Doug, *Prof,* University of Tampa, College of Arts & Letters, Tampa FL (S)
Sutherland, Lesley, *Bookkeeper,* Saskatchewan Craft Council & Affinity Gallery, Saskatoon SK
Sutherland, Ross, *Bush House Mus Dir,* Salem Art Association, Bush House Museum, Salem OR
Sutinen, Paul, *Dir,* Marylhurst University, Art Dept, Marylhurst OR (S)
Sutley, Beverly, *Registrar,* The Pennsylvania State University, Palmer Museum of Art, University Park PA
Sutley, Kate, *Develop Coordr,* Pensacola Museum of Art, Pensacola FL
Sutor, Nancy, *Asst Prof,* College of Santa Fe, Art Dept, Santa Fe NM (S)
Sutton, Alice, *Staff Asst,* Grassroots Art Center, Lucas KS
Sutton, Elizabeth, *Asst Prof,* University of Northern Iowa, Dept of Art, Cedar Falls IA (S)
Sutton, Peter C, *Exec Dir,* Bruce Museum, Inc, Greenwich CT
Sutton, Sarah, *Asst Prof,* Ithaca College, Fine Art Dept, Ithaca NY (S)
Suzio, Peggy, *Instr,* Marylhurst University, Art Dept, Marylhurst OR (S)
Svarckopf, Jennifer, *Descriptive Servs Section,* National Archives of Canada, Art & Photography Archives, Ottawa ON
Svendson, Erin, *Educ Coordr,* Springfield Art Association of Edwards Place, Springfield IL
Swadley, Ryan, *Educ Specialist,* Neville Public Museum of Brown County, Green Bay WI
Swail, Barbara, *Treas,* South Peace Art Society, Dawson Creek Art Gallery, Dawson Creek BC
Swaim, Dawn, *Instr,* North Central Michigan College, Art Dept, Petoskey MI (S)
Swain, Adrian, *Cur,* Morehead State University, Kentucky Folk Art Center, Morehead KY
Swain, Kristin A, *Dir,* The Rockwell Museum, Corning NY
Swain, Tim, *Exhib Cur,* Anderson Fine Arts Center, The Anderson Center for the Arts, Anderson IN
Swallow, Nancy, *Registrar,* Corcoran Gallery of Art, Washington DC
Swan Mazzer, Ellen, *Sls & Mktg Coord,* Norman Rockwell Museum, Stockbridge MA
Swan, Claudia, *Chmn, Assoc Prof,* Northwestern University, Evanston, Dept of Art History, Evanston IL (S)
Swan, Kathryn, *Instructor,* Concordia University, Art and Design Department, Saint Paul MN (S)
Swan, N, *Mem/Communs,* National Watercolor Society, San Pedro CA
Swanbeck, Gayle, *Dir School of Arts,* WomanKraft Art Center, Tucson AZ
Swanepoel, Kevin, *CEO,* The One Club, New York NY
Swanepoel, Kevin, *CEO, The One Club,* The One Club for Creativity, New York NY
Swangstu, Holly, *Managing Dir,* Leedy-Voulkos Art Center, Kansas City MO
Swanson, Catherine, *Archivist,* National Heritage Museum, Lexington MA
Swanson, Don, *Chief Coll Preservation & Graphic Designer,* The Frick Collection, Frick Art Reference Library, New York NY
Swanson, James, *Assoc Prof,* Dakota State University, College of Liberal Arts, Madison SD (S)
Swanson, Jennifer, *Communications Mgr,* Asheville Art Museum, Asheville NC
Swanson, Kenneth J, *Museum Adminr,* Idaho Historical Museum, Boise ID
Swanson, Kyra, *Asst Cur & Registrar,* University of Mary Washington, University of Mary Washington Galleries, Fredericksburg VA
Swanson, Lealan, *Assoc Prof,* Jackson State University, Dept of Art, Jackson MS (S)
Swanson, Linda, *Adjunct Assoc,* College of Santa Fe, Art Dept, Santa Fe NM (S)
Swanson, Lori, *Events & Mem Coordr,* White Bear Center for the Arts, Gallery, White Bear Lake MN
Swanson, Mark, *Librn & AV Production Mgr,* C G Jung Center, Evanston IL
Swanson, Michael, *Chmn Dept,* Franklin College, Art Dept, Franklin IN (S)
Swanson, Richard, *Develop Dir,* Historical Society of Cheshire County, Keene NH
Swanson, Roy, *Prof,* Hutchinson Community College, Visual Arts Dept, Hutchinson KS (S)
Swanton, Wendy, *Cur,* Gibson Society, Inc, Gibson House Museum, Boston MA
Swarez, Bibiana, *Assoc Prof,* DePaul University, Dept of Art, Chicago IL (S)
Swartwood, Larry, *Asst Prof,* University of Arkansas, Art Dept, Fayetteville AR (S)

Swartz, Anne, *Dept Chair,* Bernard M Baruch College of the City University of New York, Art Dept, New York NY (S)

Swartz, Daniel, *Chmn,* Sterling College, Art & Design Dept, Sterling KS (S)

Swartzman-Brosky, Jayna, *Prog Dir,* Mills College Art Museum, Oakland CA

Swarz, Priscilla, *Lectr,* Oklahoma State University, Department of Art, Graphic Design and Art History, Stillwater OK (S)

Sweeney Marsh, Joan, *Dir Library & Learning Svcs,* Sheridan College of Applied Arts and Technology, Trafalgar Campus Library, Oakville ON

Sweeney O'Bryan, Judith, *Assoc Prof Graphic Design,* Watkins College of Art, Design & Film, Nashville TN (S)

Sweeney, Joanne, *Pres,* 1890 House-Museum & Center for the Arts, Cortland NY

Sweeney, John, *Treas,* New York Society of Architects, New York NY

Sweeney, Lisa, *Head of GIS,* Massachusetts Institute of Technology, Rotch Library of Architecture & Planning, Cambridge MA

Sweeney, Maureen, *Office Mgr,* Napa Valley Museum, Yountville CA

Sweeney, Nora, *Mus Store Mgr,* Boise Art Museum, Boise ID

Sweeney, Robert T, *Wm R Mead Prof of Art, Chair,* Amherst College, Dept of Art & the History of Art, Amherst MA (S)

Sweeney, Saria, *Community Prog Coord,* Old Colony Historical Society, Museum, Taunton MA

Sweeny, Joseph, *Instr,* Wayne Art Center, Wayne PA (S)

Sweet, Samuel, *Exec Dir & CEO,* Delaware Art Museum, Wilmington DE

Sweet, Thalia, *Technical Servs,* City of Long Branch, Long Branch Free Public Library, Long Branch NJ

Sweeters, Jim, *Dir,* California State University, Northridge, Art Galleries, Northridge CA

Sweigart, Wendy, *Exhibs Coordr,* Pennsylvania Department of Education, Arts in Education Program, Harrisburg PA

Sweigert, Lawrence, *Dir,* Rehoboth Art League, Inc, Rehoboth Beach DE

Swenson, David, *Lectr,* North Dakota State University, Division of Fine Arts, Fargo ND (S)

Swenson, Dean, *Adjunct,* North Iowa Area Community College, Dept of Art, Mason City IA (S)

Swenson, Kirsten, *Asst Prof,* University of Nevada, Las Vegas, Dept of Art, Las Vegas NV (S)

Swenson-Wolsey, Sonja, *Chmn,* Taft College, Art Department, Taft CA (S)

Swensson, Lise C, *Exec Dir,* Hickory Museum of Art, Inc, Hickory NC

Swepson-Twitty, Stephanie, *Chair,* YMI Cultural Center, Asheville NC

Swetcharnik, Sara Morris, *Project Coordr & Artist,* Swetcharnik Art Studio, Mount Airy MD

Swetcharnik, William, *Dir & Artist,* Swetcharnik Art Studio, Mount Airy MD

Swettenham, John, *Dir Mktg,* Canadian Museum of Nature, Musee Canadien de la Nature, Ottawa ON

Swick, Deane, *Lectr,* California State Polytechnic University, Pomona, Department of Art, Pomona CA (S)

Swick, Wendy, *Dir Information,* The Butler Institute of American Art, Art Museum, Youngstown OH

Swickard, Kelly, *Catalog Librn,* Maryland Institute, Decker Library, Baltimore MD

Swider, Bougdon, *Prof,* Colorado College, Dept of Art, Colorado Springs CO (S)

Swierenga, Heidi, *Sr Conservator,* University of British Columbia, Museum of Anthropology, Vancouver BC

Swindell, Jon, *Prof,* University of Kansas, The School of the Arts, Dept of Visual Art, Lawrence KS (S)

Swindull, Laurie, *Instr,* American University, Dept of Art, New York NY (S)

Swing, Michael, *Instr,* Guilford Technical Community College, Commercial Art Dept, Jamestown NC (S)

Swisher, Kate, *Registrar,* DuSable Museum of African American History, Chicago IL

Swisher, Michael, *Chmn Humanities,* City Colleges of Chicago, Truman College, Chicago IL (S)

Switzer, Terri, *Chair Art Dept & Prof Art History,* Saint Ambrose University, Art Dept, Davenport IA (S)

Swoboda, Michael, *Prof,* Saint Louis Community College at Meramec, Art Dept, Saint Louis MO (S)

Swonger, Denny, *Dean Arts & Sciences,* Eastern Oregon University, School of Arts & Science, La Grande OR (S)

Swopes, Thomas, *Assoc Prof,* Saint Mary-of-the-Woods College, Art Dept, Saint Mary of the Woods IN (S)

Sword, Karen, *Treas,* Allegany County Historical Society, Gordon-Roberts House, Cumberland MD

Swoveland, Julie, *Dir Admin,* Arts Place, Inc, Hugh N Ronald Memorial Gallery, Portland IN

Syct, Sarah, *Mus Educ,* Andover Historical Society, Andover MA

Sydenstricker, Janet, *Pub Rels Specialist,* Tidewater Community College, Visual Arts Center, Portsmouth VA (S)

Sylvester, Beverly, *Dept Adminr Asst,* Williams College, Dept of Art History & Studio Art, Williamstown MA (S)

Sylvester, Bob, *Director of Public Operations,* Madison Museum of Contemporary Art, Madison WI

Sylvester, Cindy, *Dir,* San Jose Museum of Art, Library, San Jose CA

Sylvester, Judith, *Conservator,* Indiana University, The Mathers Museum of World Cultures, Bloomington IN

Sylwester, Laurie, *Instr,* Columbia College, Fine Arts, Sonora CA (S)

Symmes, Edwin C, *Pres,* Symmes Systems, Photographic Investments Gallery, Atlanta GA

Symonds, Matthew, *Dir Corporate Secretariat & Ministerial Liaison,* National Gallery of Canada, Ottawa ON

Synder, Fred, *Dir & Consultant,* National Native American Co-Operative, North American Indian Information & Trade Center, Tucson AZ

Sypher, Jodi, *Cur,* University of Miami, Lowe Art Museum, Coral Gables FL

Syson, Luke, *Chmn, European Sculpture & Decorative Drawings,* The Metropolitan Museum of Art, New York NY

Szabla, Joanne, *Prof,* Rochester Institute of Technology, School of Design, Rochester NY (S)

Szabo, Joyce M, *Regents Prof,* University of New Mexico, Department of Fine Arts & Art History, Albuquerque NM (S)

Szabo, Joyce, *Chmn,* University of New Mexico, Dept of Art & Art History, Albuquerque NM (S)

Szakacs, Dennis, *Dir,* Orange County Museum of Art, Newport Beach CA

Szalus, Veronica, *Exec Dir,* Northern Virginia Fine Arts Association, The Athenaeum, Alexandria VA

Szavuly, Erin Palmer, *Chmn Fine Arts & Assoc Prof,* Lourdes University, Art Dept, Sylvania OH (S)

Szeliga, Sarah, *Asst Visual Resource Mgr, Onassis Library for Hellenic & Roman Art,* The Metropolitan Museum of Art, Museum Libraries, New York NY

Szeluga, Christine, *Mgr Educ,* Staten Island Museum, Staten Island NY

Szepe, Helena, *Assoc Prof,* University of South Florida, School of Art & Art History, Tampa FL (S)

Szmagaj, Kenneth, *Prof,* James Madison University, School of Art & Art History, Harrisonburg VA (S)

Szoke, Andrew, *Asst Prof,* Northampton Community College, Art Dept, Bethlehem PA (S)

Szpila, Kathleen, *Slide Cur,* Temple University, Slide Library, Elkins PA

Szpot, Naomi, *Cur Asst,* University of Nebraska-Lincoln, Great Plains Art Museum, Lincoln NE

Szupinska-Myers, Joanna, *CMP Cur Exhibs,* UCR ARTSblock, California Museum of Photography, Riverside CA

Szuter, Christine, *Exec Dir,* Amerind Foundation, Inc, Amerind Museum, Fulton-Hayden Memorial Art Gallery, Dragoon AZ

Szuter, Christine, *Exec Dir,* Amerind Foundation, Inc, Fulton-Hayden Memorial Library & Art Gallery, Dragoon AZ

Szwaczkowski, Daniel, *Preparator,* University of Texas at El Paso, Stanlee & Gerald Rubin Center for the Visual Arts, El Paso TX

Szycher, Lawrence, *Prof,* Caldwell College, Dept of Fine Arts, Caldwell NJ (S)

Taaffe, Renee, *Educ Cur,* Missoula Art Museum, Missoula MT

Taaffe, Susan, *Preparator,* University of North Carolina at Greensboro, Weatherspoon Art Museum, Greensboro NC

Tab, Winston, *Dir,* Johns Hopkins University, Homewood Museum, Baltimore MD

Tabaha, Kathy, *Mus Tech,* National Park Service, Hubbell Trading Post National Historic Site, Ganado AZ

Tabbert, Mark, *Director Mus & Library Collections,* The George Washington Masonic National Memorial Association, The George Washington Masonic National Memorial, Alexandria VA

Tacang, Lee, *Instr,* De Anza College, Creative Arts Division, Cupertino CA (S)

Tachora, Jerry, *Interim Exec Dir,* Hendersonville Arts Council, Monthaven Mansion, Hendersonville TN

Tacke, Melissa, *Librn,* Schenectady County Historical Society, Schenectady NY

Tacke, Melissa, *Librn/Archivist,* Schenectady County Historical Society, Grems-Dolittle Library, Schenectady NY

Tadashi Oshima, Ken, *Pres,* Society of Architectural Historians, Chicago IL

Taddie, Dan, *Chmn,* Maryville College, Dept of Fine Arts, Maryville TN (S)

Tafoya, Adriane, *Registrar & Colls Mgr,* University of Tennessee, McClung Museum of Natural History & Culture, Knoxville TN

Taft, Kristi, *Exhibs Officer,* Birmingham Museum of Art, Birmingham AL

Tagg, John, *Dist Prof,* Binghamton University, Art History Department, Binghamton NY (S)

Taggart, Julie, *Dean,* Columbus College of Art & Design, Fine Arts Dept, Columbus OH (S)

Tai, Susan, *Cur Asian Art,* Santa Barbara Museum of Art, Santa Barbara CA

Tait Glover, Deanna, *Cur,* Kanab Heritage Museum & Juniper Fine Arts Gallery, Kanab UT

Tait, Danielle, *Assoc Dir,* Southern Alberta Art Gallery, Lethbridge AB

Takechi, K, *Prof,* Shoreline Community College, Humanities Division, Seattle WA (S)

Takei, George, *VChmn,* Japanese American National Museum, Los Angeles CA

Takekawa, Beth, *Exec Dir,* Wing Luke Asian Museum, Governor Gary Locke Library and Community Heritage Center, Seattle WA

Takemori, Lianne, *Asst Cur Educ,* Mississippi Museum of Art, Howorth Library, Jackson MS

Takeshita, Audrey, *Graphics,* Santa Cruz Art League, Center for the Arts, Santa Cruz CA

Takeuchi, Arthur, *Assoc Prof,* Illinois Institute of Technology, College of Architecture, Chicago IL (S)

Talaga, Sally, *Dir,* Wayne County Historical Society, Museum, Honesdale PA

Talalay, Lauren E, *Assoc Dir & Assoc Cur Educ,* University of Michigan, Kelsey Museum of Archaeology, Ann Arbor MI

Talarico, Sandra, *Assoc Dir,* Florida State University and Central Florida Community College, The Appleton Museum of Art, Ocala FL

Talasek, JD, *Dir,* National Academy of Sciences, Arts in the Academy, Washington DC

Talbert, Hope C, *Dir,* Santarella Museum & Gardens, Tyringham MA

Talbot, Christopher K, *Dir,* Stephen F Austin State University, School of Art, Nacogdoches TX (S)

Talbot, Damon, *Special Colls Archivist,* Maryland Historical Society, Library, Baltimore MD

Talbott, Jennifer, *Dir Internal Opers,* University of Kansas, Spencer Museum of Art, Lawrence KS

Talbott, Ronald, *Instr,* Harrisburg Area Community College, Division of Communications, Humanities & the Arts, Harrisburg PA (S)

Talebi, Marjaneh, *Instr,* Harrisburg Area Community College, Division of Communications, Humanities & the Arts, Harrisburg PA (S)

Taliaferro Hill, Elsie, *Asst Prod,* Georgia Southern University, Betty Foy Sanders Dept of Art, Statesboro GA (S)

Talkov, Andrew, *VPres Prog,* Virginia Historical Society, Library, Richmond VA

Tallent, Tony, *Dir Library,* Boulder Public Library & Gallery, Arts Gallery, Boulder CO

Tallon, Andrew, *Asst Prof,* Vassar College, Art Dept, Poughkeepsie NY (S)

Talmon, Renee, *Dir Admissions,* San Francisco Art Institute, San Francisco CA (S)

Tam, Herb, *Cur & Dir Exhib,* Museum of Chinese in America, New York NY

Tam, Tsun, *VPres,* Belskie Museum, Closter NJ

Tamir, Rotem, *Vis Asst Prof,* University of Florida, School of Art & Art History, Gainesville FL (S)

Tanber, Joel, *Asst Prof,* Wake Forest University, Dept of Art, Winston-Salem NC (S)

Tancin, Charlotte, *Librn,* Carnegie Mellon University, Hunt Institute for Botanical Documentation, Pittsburgh PA

Tander, David, *Adjunct Instr,* Quincy College, Art Dept, Quincy MA (S)

Tanenbaum, Stephen, *Co-Founder,* U Gallery, San Francisco CA

Tang, Carol, *Exec Dir,* Children's Creativity Museum, San Francisco CA

Tang, Michael, *Chmn,* Loyola Marymount University, Dept of Art & Art History, Los Angeles CA (S)

Tanglao, Fatima, *Circ & Reference Asst,* New York University, Institute of Fine Arts Visual Resources Collection, New York NY

Tannen, Jason, *Chmn,* California State University, Chico, University Art Gallery, Chico CA

Tannen, Jason, *Instr,* California State University, Chico, Department of Art & Art History, Chico CA (S)

Tannenbaum, Barbara, *Cur Photog,* The Cleveland Museum of Art, Cleveland OH

Tannenbaum, Marilyn, *Instr,* Solano Community College, Division of Fine & Applied Art & Behavioral Science, Fairfield CA (S)

Tanner, Richard, *Prof,* Rochester Institute of Technology, School of Design, Rochester NY (S)

Tanner, Suzi, *Mgr Special Events, Guest Servs & Mem,* Museum of Art - Deland FL, Inc, Deland FL

Tantoco, Monica, *Asst Educ Coordr,* National Veterans Art Museum, Chicago IL

Tanze, Don, *Asst Prof,* Seattle Central Community College, Humanities - Social Sciences Division, Seattle WA (S)

Tanzer, James, *Museum Outreach Coord,* Bowdoin College, Peary-MacMillan Arctic Museum, Brunswick ME

Tarallo, Donald, *Asst Prof,* Bridgewater State College, Art Dept, Bridgewater MA (S)

Tardella, Sally S, *Spec Instr,* Oakland University, Dept of Art & Art History, Rochester MI (S)

Tardif, Mark, *Pub Rels Dir,* Thomas College, Art Gallery, Waterville ME

Tarica, Daniel, *Asst Gen Mgr,* City of Los Angeles, Cultural Affairs Dept, Los Angeles CA

Tarnow, Terry, *Museum Shop Mgr,* Northwestern Michigan College, Dennos Museum Center, Traverse City MI

Tarnowski, Tom, *Prof Emeritus Photog,* Johnson County Community College, Fine Arts Dept & Art History Dept, Overland Park KS (S)

Tarr, Blair, *Cur of Decorative Art,* Kansas State Historical Society, Kansas Museum of History, Topeka KS

Tarr, Scott, *Dir Security & IT,* Fort Wayne Museum of Art, Inc, Fort Wayne IN

Tarrell, Robert, *Prof,* Edgewood College, Art Dept, Madison WI (S)

Tasaka, Sharon, *Assoc Dir,* University of Hawaii at Manoa, The Art Gallery & The John Young Museum of Art, Honolulu HI

Tassie, Whitney, *Sr Cur,* University of Utah, Utah Museum of Fine Arts, Salt Lake City UT

Tasso, Francesca, *Cur,* Raccolte Artistiche Del Castello Sforzesco, Museo degli Strumenti Musicali - Museum of Musical Instruments, Milan

Tassone, Rachel, *Assoc Registrar,* Williams College, Museum of Art, Williamstown MA

Tate, Barbara, *Dir,* Henry Street Settlement Arts for Living Center, New York NY (S)

Tate, Belinda, *Dir, Cur, Develop & Registrar,* Winston-Salem State University, Diggs Gallery, Winston-Salem NC

Tate, Belinda, *Exec Dir,* Kalamazoo Institute of Arts, The Mary & Edwin Meader Fine Arts Library, Kalamazoo MI

Tate, Belinda, *Exec Dir,* Kalamazoo Institute of Arts, Kalamazoo MI

Tate, Jami-Lynn, *Dir,* Clymer Museum of Art, The Clymer Museum & Gallery, Ellensburg WA

Tate, Jamie, *Dir,* Mississippi Art Colony, Stoneville MS

Tate, William, *Asst Prof,* James Madison University, School of Art & Art History, Harrisonburg VA (S)

Tateishi, Cheryl, *Deputy Dir Admin,* California Science Center, Los Angeles CA

Tatro, Amy, *Asst to Dir,* Williams College, Museum of Art, Williamstown MA

Tatum, James, *Prof,* Lincoln University, Dept Visual and Performing Arts, Jefferson City MO (S)

Tatum, Joel, *Tech Mgr,* Bay Area Video Coalition, Inc, San Francisco CA

Tatum, Marcolm, *Graphic Designer,* The Columbus Museum, Columbus GA

Taubenberger, Michael, *CFO & COO,* Institute of Contemporary Art/Boston, Boston MA

Taugner, Julia, *Asst Prof,* University of Indianapolis, Dept Art & Design, Indianapolis IN (S)

Taugner, Stephanie, *Instr,* Art Institute of Southern California, Laguna Beach CA (S)

Taulbee, Ann, *Dir,* Hiestand Galleries, Oxford OH

Tavani, Robert, *Gallery Dir,* DePaul University, Dept of Art, Chicago IL (S)

Tavares, Shirley A, *Institutional Researcher,* Escuela de Artes Plasticas de Puerto Rico, San Juan PR (S)

Tavoletti, Lena, *Admin & Fin Coord,* The Andy Warhol Museum, Pittsburgh PA

Taxgenson, Mark, *Instr,* Judson University, School of Art, Design & Architecture, Elgin IL (S)

Taylor Kester, Nina, *Program Coordinator,* Cartoon Art Museum, San Francisco CA

Taylor, Adams, *Historic Sites & Colls Mgr,* Newport Historical Society & Museum of Newport History, Newport RI

Taylor, Aletha, *Children's Librn,* Mexico-Audrain County Library, Mexico MO

Taylor, Alexys, *Colls & Exhibs Mgr,* Harvey B Gantt Center for African American Arts + Culture, Charlotte NC

Taylor, Allison, *Head of Educ & Community Engagement,* Washington University, Mildred Lane Kemper Art Museum, Saint Louis MO

Taylor, Andrew, *Dir,* University of Wisconsin, Madison, Graduate School of Business, Bolz Center for Arts Administration, Madison WI (S)

Taylor, Barbara, *Exhibits Specialist,* Fort George G Meade Museum, Fort Meade MD

Taylor, Beth, *Asst Cur Entomology,* Northern Maine Museum of Science, Presque Isle ME

Taylor, Bethany, *Asst Prof,* University of Florida, School of Art & Art History, Gainesville FL (S)

Taylor, Bob, *Librn,* Airpower Museum Library, Ottumwa IA

Taylor, Bonnie, *Pres,* Manitoba Society of Artists, Winnipeg MB

Taylor, Brian, *Chmn Dept of Art,* San Jose State University, Dept of Art & Art History, San Jose CA (S)

Taylor, Brian, *Co-Chair,* Shorter College, Art Dept, Rome GA (S)

Taylor, Brook, *Educ Prog Coordr,* University of Illinois at Urbana-Champaign, Spurlock Museum, Urbana IL

Taylor, Bruce T, *VPres,* National Museum of Ceramic Art, Baltimore MD

Taylor, Caleb, *Asst Prof,* Kansas City Art Institute, Kansas City MO (S)

Taylor, Charlene, *Instr,* Lourdes University, Art Dept, Sylvania OH (S)

Taylor, Charles, *Preparator,* The Sherwin Miller Museum of Jewish Art, Tulsa OK

Taylor, Chris, *Dean,* Drew University, Elizabeth P Korn Gallery, Madison NJ

Taylor, Chris, *Instr Leadership,* AIC College of Design, Cincinnati OH (S)

Taylor, Christopher, *Pres,* The Clay Studio, Philadelphia PA

Taylor, Colleen, *Secy,* Fort Hays State University, Moss-Thorns Gallery of Arts, Hays KS

Taylor, Courtney, *Cur,* Arts & Science Center for Southeast Arkansas, Pine Bluff AR

Taylor, Darrell, *Dir,* University of Northern Iowa, UNI Gallery of Art, Cedar Falls IA

Taylor, David, *Photo Dir,* New Mexico State University, Art Dept, Las Cruces NM (S)

Taylor, David, *Pres & CEO,* Harvey B Gantt Center for African American Arts + Culture, Charlotte NC

Taylor, Diane, *Exec Asst,* Birmingham Bloomfield Art Center, Birmingham MI (S)

Taylor, Ellen, *Pres,* Art Students League of New York, New York NY (S)

Taylor, Ellen, *Pres,* Art Students League of New York, New York NY

Taylor, Elmer, *Regents Prof,* University of North Texas, College of Visual Arts & Design, Denton TX (S)

Taylor, Harriet, *Academic Dean,* New Brunswick College of Craft & Design, Fredericton NB (S)

Taylor, Hollis, *Cur,* Barnard's Mill Art Museum, Glen Rose TX

Taylor, Howard J, *Dir,* San Angelo Museum of Fine Arts, San Angelo TX

Taylor, Judith, *Asst Prof,* Arcadia University, Dept of Fine Arts, Glenside PA (S)

Taylor, Kathryn T, *Dir,* Westerly Public Library, Hoxie Gallery, Westerly RI

Taylor, Katie, *Registrar,* Northeastern Nevada Museum, Elko NV

Taylor, Kristen, *Develop Officer,* Kendall College of Art & Design, Urban Institute for Contemporary Arts, Grand Rapids MI

Taylor, Kristin, *Cur Academic Progs & Cols,* Museum of Contemporary Photography, Columbia College Chicago, Chicago IL

Taylor, Lisa, *Admin,* United States Military Academy, West Point Museum, West Point NY

Taylor, Lyrica, *Asst Prof,* Azusa Pacific University, College of Music & the Arts, Dept of Art & Design, Azusa CA (S)

Taylor, Marc, *Planetarium Coordr,* The Hudson River Museum, Yonkers NY

Taylor, Marcia, *Assoc Prof,* The College of New Jersey, School of Arts & Sciences, Ewing NJ (S)

Taylor, Mary Diane, *Chair, Div Fine Art,* Brescia University, Anna Eaton Stout Memorial Art Gallery, Owensboro KY

Taylor, Mary Diane, *Chmn,* Brescia University, Art Dept, Owensboro KY (S)

Taylor, Mary Katherine, *Secretary,* Essex Historical Society and Shipbuilding Museum, Essex MA

Taylor, Mary, *Pres,* San Angelo Art Club, Helen King Kendall Memorial Art Gallery, San Angelo TX

Taylor, Michael, *Assoc Prof,* Lewis & Clark College, Dept of Art, Portland OR (S)

Taylor, Michael, *Chmn Art History,* University of Massachusetts Dartmouth, College of Visual & Performing Arts, North Dartmouth MA (S)

Taylor, Michael, *Dir,* Dartmouth College, Hood Museum of Art, Hanover NH

Taylor, Michael, *Prof,* Rochester Institute of Technology, School of Design, Rochester NY (S)

Taylor, Miriam, *External Affairs,* Tulane University, Newcomb Art Museum, New Orleans LA

Taylor, Misty, *Registrar,* University of Louisiana at Lafayette, Paul and Lulu Hilliard University Art Museum, Lafayette LA

Taylor, Molly, *Dir Develop,* Telfair Museums, Savannah GA

Taylor, Monique, *Vice Chair,* YMI Cultural Center, Asheville NC

Taylor, Pam, *Asst Prof Art Educ,* University of Georgia, Franklin College of Arts & Sciences, Lamar Dodd School of Art, Athens GA (S)

Taylor, Rebecca, *Asst Prof Journalism,* Siena College, Dept of Creative Arts, Loudonville NY (S)

Taylor, Richard, *Pres,* National Museum of Ceramic Art, Baltimore MD

Taylor, Robin, *Librn,* Philmont Scout Ranch, Philmont Museum - Seton Memorial Library, Cimarron NM

Taylor, Rod A, *Head Dept,* Norfolk State University, Fine Arts Dept, Norfolk VA (S)

Taylor, Rose, *Dir Outreach,* Salisbury University, Ward Museum of Wildfowl Art, Salisbury MD

Taylor, Ruth, *Acquisitions Librn,* Mexico-Audrain County Library, Mexico MO

Taylor, Saddler, *Cur Folk Art & Research,* University of South Carolina, McKissick Museum, Columbia SC

Taylor, Sandra L, *Supt,* Tuskegee Institute National Historic Site, George Washington Carver & The Oaks, Montgomery AL

Taylor, Skip, *Performing Arts Coordr,* Organization of Saskatchewan Arts Councils (OSAC), Regina SK

Taylor, Stephanie, *Asst Prof,* New Mexico State University, Art Dept, Las Cruces NM (S)

Taylor, Steve, *Pres,* Second Street Gallery, Charlottesville VA

Taylor, Sue, *Assoc Prof,* Portland State University, Dept of Art, Portland OR (S)

Taylor, Susan M, *Dir,* New Orleans Museum of Art, New Orleans LA

Taylor, Susan, *Pres,* The Lindsay Gallery Inc, Lindsay ON

Taylor, Tom, *Coordr Fine Arts,* Columbia College, Art Dept, Chicago IL (S)

Taylor-Gearing, Dianne, *Pres,* Nova Scotia College of Art & Design, Halifax NS (S)

Taylor-Gearing, Dianne, *Treas,* Association of Independent Colleges of Art & Design, Providence RI

Taylor-Gore, Victoria, *Dept Head,* Amarillo College, Visual Art Dept, Amarillo TX (S)

Teagle, Rachel, *Cur,* Museum of Contemporary Art, San Diego, Geisel Library, La Jolla CA

Teague, Gypsey, *Branch Head,* Clemson University, Emery A Gunnin Architectural Library, Clemson SC

Teague, Patrick G, *Human Resources Mgr,* Jamestown-Yorktown Foundation, Jamestown Settlement, Williamsburg VA

Teal, Randall, *Instr,* Southern University A & M College, School of Architecture, Baton Rouge LA (S)

Teasley, Sarah, *Chmn and Gallery Director,* Hinds Community College, Dept of Art, Raymond MS (S)

Teasley, Sarah, *Dept Chair and Gallery Director,* Hinds Community College District, Marie Hull Gallery, Raymond MS

Tebo, Ginger, *Children's Librn,* Roswell P Flower, Watertown NY

Tebon, Elizabeth, *Prof,* Northern Virginia Community College, Art Dept, Annandale VA (S)

Tebow, Duncan, *Chmn,* Northern Virginia Community College, Art Dept, Annandale VA (S)

Tederick, Lydia, *Asst Cur,* White House, Washington DC

Tedeschi, Martha, *Dir,* Harvard University, Harvard Art Museums, Cambridge MA

Tegel, Matthew, *Preparator,* Rodman Hall Arts Centre, Saint Catharines ON

Tegge, Susan, *Head Adult Svcs,* Springfield Free Public Library, Donald B Palmer Museum, Springfield NJ

Teifer, Hermann, *Head Archivist,* Leo Baeck, Library, New York NY

Teifer, Hermann, *Head Archivist,* Leo Baeck, New York NY

Teilhet-Fisk, Jehnne, *Prof,* Florida State University, Art History Dept, Tallahassee FL (S)

Teipel, Juliet S, *Librn,* The Illinois Institute of Art - Chicago, Chicago IL (S)

Teitelbaum, Matthew, *Ann & Graham Gund Dir,* Museum of Fine Arts, Boston MA

Teixeira, Jose, *Assoc Vis Prof,* Case Western Reserve University, Dept of Art History & Art, Cleveland OH (S)

Tejada, Susana, *Head Research Resources,* The Buffalo Fine Arts Academy, Albright-Knox Art Gallery, Buffalo NY

Telfair, Tula, *Assoc Prof, Dir,* Wesleyan University, Dept of Art & Art History, Middletown CT (S)

Telford, John, *Chmn,* Brigham Young University, Dept of Visual Arts, Provo UT (S)

Teller, Alex, *Dir Communs & Mktg,* The Newberry, Chicago IL

Temkin, Susanna, *Assoc Cur Visual Arts,* Americas Society Art Gallery, New York NY

Temple, Lewis, *Assoc Prof,* McNeese State University, Dept of Visual Arts, Lake Charles LA (S)

Temple, Matt, *Office Mgr,* Wassenberg Art Center, Van Wert OH

Temple, Paula, *Prof,* University of Mississippi, Department of Art, University MS (S)

Templer, Peggy, *Exec Dir,* Mendocino Art Center, Library, Mendocino CA

Templer, Peggy, *Exec Dir,* Mendocino Art Center, Gallery & School, Mendocino CA

Templer, Peggy, *Exec Dir,* Mendocino Art Center, Mendocino CA (S)

Templeton, Ed, *Dir,* New Image Art, West Hollywood CA

Templeton, Kimberly, *Dir External Affairs,* Taubman Museum of Art, Roanoke VA

Templeton, Rijn, *Head Librn,* University of Iowa, Art Library, Iowa City IA

Tenabe, Gabriel S, *Dir & Cur,* Morgan State University, James E Lewis Museum of Art, Baltimore MD

Teng, Mabel, *Exec Dir,* Chinese Culture Foundation, Center Gallery, San Francisco CA

Tennant, Andy, *Interim Museum Dir,* Auburn University, Jule Collins Smith Museum of Fine Art, Auburn AL

Tennant, Brad, *Dir,* Wein Gallery, Aberdeen SD

Tennant, Carolyn, *Media Cur,* Hallwalls Contemporary Arts Center, Buffalo NY

Tennen, Steve, *Exec Dir,* ArtsConnection Inc, New York NY

Tenney, Kim, *Cur Arts Dept,* Boston Public Library, Arts Reference Department, Boston MA

Tenney, Matt, *Bd Mem,* Utah Lawyers for the Arts, Salt Lake City UT

Tenny, Elissa, *Pres,* School of the Art Institute of Chicago, Chicago IL (S)

Tenny, Elissa, *Pres, School of the Art Inst,* The Art Institute of Chicago, Chicago IL

Tent, Lauren, *Educ Coordr,* Center for Exploratory & Perceptual Art, CEPA Library, Buffalo NY

Tent, Lauren, *Educ Dir,* Center for Exploratory & Perceptual Art, CEPA Gallery, Buffalo NY

Tepper, Steven, *Dean & Prof,* Arizona State University, Herberger Institute for Design and the Arts, Tempe AZ (S)

Teramoto, John, *Asst Prof,* University of Kansas, Kress Foundation Dept of Art History, Lawrence KS (S)

Terbush, Kim, *Registrar,* University of North Carolina at Greensboro, Weatherspoon Art Museum, Greensboro NC

Terhune, Janet T, *Dir,* Harness Racing Museum & Hall of Fame, Goshen NY

Terjanian, Pierre, *Cur in Charge, Arms & Armor,* The Metropolitan Museum of Art, New York NY

Terlecki, Lisa, *Mem Coordr & Graphic Designer,* Polish Museum of America (PMA), Chicago IL

Termine, Allison, *Dickson Librn,* Chrysler Museum of Art, Jean Outland Chrysler Library, Norfolk VA

Terpstra, Jennifer Williams, *Chmn,* University of Wisconsin-La Crosse, Center for the Arts, La Crosse WI (S)

Terrano, Robert A, *Dean,* Mercer County Community College, Arts, Communication & Engineering Technology, West Windsor NJ (S)

Terrasi, Tore, *Asst Prof,* University of Texas at Arlington, Art & Art History Department, Arlington TX (S)

Terrell, James, *Chmn,* Northeastern State University, College of Arts & Letters, Tahlequah OK (S)

Terrell, Krista, *VPres Mktg & Communs,* Arts & Science Council, Charlotte NC

Terrell, Paul, *Pres-Elect,* Artspace, Richmond VA

Terrell, Richard, *Head Dept,* Doane College, Dept of Art, Crete NE (S)

Terrenato, Nicholas, *Assoc Prof,* University of Michigan, Kelsey Museum of Archaeology, Ann Arbor MI

Terreri, Taylor, *Office Mgr,* Warwick Museum of Art, Warwick RI

Terrono, Evie, *Lectr,* Randolph-Macon College, Dept of the Arts, Ashland VA (S)

Terry, Christopher, *Assoc Prof,* Utah State University, Dept of Art, Logan UT (S)

Terry, James H, *Chair,* Stephens College, Art Dept, Columbia MO (S)

Terry, Meghan, *Grad Advisor,* University of Tennessee, Visual Arts Committee, Knoxville TN

Tersteeg, William, *Prof,* Keystone College, Fine Arts Dept, LaPlume PA (S)

Terzia, Louise, *Develop Dir,* Historic Arkansas Museum, Library, Little Rock AR

Tesner, Linda, *Dir,* Ronna and Eric Hoffman Gallery of Contemporary Art, Portland OR

Tesso, Jane B, *Consulting Cur,* Federal Reserve Bank of Cleveland, Cleveland OH

Teter, Jennifer, *Dir Educ,* Quincy Art Center, Quincy IL

Teter, Marcia, *Mus Coordr,* Daum Museum of Contemporary Art, Sedalia MO

Teterenko, Paul, *Pres,* Ukrainian Canadian Archives & Museum of Alberta, Edmonton AB

Tetkowski, Neil, *Dir Gallery,* Kean University, James Howe Gallery, Union NJ

Tetkowski, Olga, *Exhib Mgr,* The Drawing Center, New York NY

Tettamanti, Steven, *Exec Dir,* New Jersey Historical Society, Newark NJ

Tetzlaff, Jennifer, *Dir Mktg & Communs,* Milwaukee Public Museum, Milwaukee WI

Tewell, Tanya, *Instr,* Middle Tennessee State University, Art Dept, Murfreesboro TN (S)

Texon, Wanda, *Director of Campus Galleries,* Miami-Dade College, MDC Museum of Art & Design, Miami FL

Thacker, Tara, *Visual Arts Dir,* Vermont Studio Center, The Red Mill, Johnson VT

Thacker, Terry, *Prof Fine Art,* Watkins College of Art, Design & Film, Nashville TN (S)

Thaler, Janice M, *Bd Mem,* French Art Colony, Gallipolis OH

Thalhuber, Margaret, *Dept Mgr,* University of California, Berkeley, College of Letters & Sciences-Art Practice Dept, Berkeley CA (S)

Thames, Charles, *Cur, Art Coll,* 3M, Art Collection, Maplewood MN

Tharp, Stephanie, *Assoc Prof & Undergrad Prog Co-Dir,* University of Michigan, Ann Arbor, Penny W Stamps School of Art & Design, Ann Arbor MI (S)

Thau, Ed, *Dir,* Quietude Garden Gallery, East Brunswick NJ

Thau, Sheila, *Dir,* Quietude Garden Gallery, East Brunswick NJ

Thaxton-Ward, Vanessa, *Cur Colls,* Hampton University, University Museum, Hampton VA

Thayer, Preston, *Dir Gallery,* Augustana College, Augustana College Art Museum, Rock Island IL

Thayer, Tom, *Assoc Prof,* City College of New York, Art Dept, New York NY (S)

Theaker, Liz, *Devel Dir,* Museum of Northwest Art, La Conner WA

Theeck, Jennifer, *Cur Educ,* History Museum of Mobile, Mobile AL
Theilking, Kristin, *Asst Prof,* University of Wisconsin-Stevens Point, Dept of Art & Design, Stevens Point WI (S)
Thein, John, *Instr,* Creighton University, Fine & Performing Arts Dept, Omaha NE (S)
Theis, Leah, *Slide Librn,* University of California, Davis, Art Dept Library, Davis CA
Theisen, Nate, *Asst Prof of Art,* Belhaven College, Art Dept, Jackson MS (S)
Theo, Christos, *Chmn,* University of Wisconsin-Eau Claire, Dept of Art & Design, Eau Claire WI (S)
Theodore, Wiebke, *Vis Asst Prof,* Bowdoin College, Art Dept, Brunswick ME (S)
Theoret, Yves, *Dir Opers & Admin,* Musee d'art Contemporain de Montreal, Montreal QC
Theriault, Michele, *Dir,* Concordia University, Leonard & Bina Ellen Art Gallery, Montreal QC
Thi Hoi, Dao, *Librn,* VICANA (Vietnamese Cultural Association in North America) Library, Springfield VA
Thibault, Nathalie, *Documentary & Archives Mngmt,* Musee National des Beaux Arts du Quebec, Bibliotheque, Quebec QC
Thibodean, Marianne, *Head Reference & Instruction Librn,* Wentworth Institute of Technology, Douglas D Schumann Library & Learning Commons, Boston MA
Thiedeman, Edwin, *Pres,* Mattawoman Creek Art Center, Marbury MD
Thiesen, Barbara A, *Librn,* Bethel College, Mennonite Library & Archives, North Newton KS
Thiesen, John D, *Archivist,* Bethel College, Mennonite Library & Archives, North Newton KS
Thobe, Christopher, *Preparator,* University of New Mexico, University of New Mexico Art Museum, Albuquerque NM
Thom, Laine, *Naturalist,* Grand Teton National Park Service, Moose WY
Thomas, Abraham, *Cur-in-Charge,* American Art Museum, Renwick Gallery, Washington DC
Thomas, Adam, *Cur American Art,* The Pennsylvania State University, Palmer Museum of Art, University Park PA
Thomas, Ally, *Educ Coordr,* Erie Art Museum, Erie PA
Thomas, Andrea, *Park Svc Specialist,* Florida Department of Environmental Protection, Stephen Foster Folk Culture Center State Park, White Springs FL
Thomas, Andrew L, *American Specialist,* National Gallery of Art, Department of Image Collections, Washington DC
Thomas, Angela, *Dir Mktg,* Knoxville Museum of Art, Knoxville TN
Thomas, Ann, *Deputy Dir Colls & Research & Chief Cur,* National Gallery of Canada, Ottawa ON
Thomas, Ben, *Dir Programs,* Archaeological Institute of America, Boston MA
Thomas, Brett, *Instr,* Wayne Art Center, Wayne PA (S)
Thomas, Bruce, *Assoc,* Lehigh University, Dept of Art, Architecture & Design, Bethlehem PA (S)
Thomas, Bruce, *Vis Asst Prof,* Hamline University, Dept of Studio Arts & Art History, Saint Paul MN (S)
Thomas, C David, *Prof,* Emmanuel College, Art Dept, Boston MA (S)
Thomas, Charles, *Trustee,* L D Brinkman, Kerrville TX
Thomas, Christopher, *Lectr,* University of North Carolina at Greensboro, School of Art, Greensboro NC (S)
Thomas, Dana, *Donor & Guest Relations Liaison & Educ Cur,* Rollins College, George D & Harriet W Cornell Fine Arts Museum, Winter Park FL
Thomas, Danielle, *Operations Director,* Art and History Museums - Maitland, Maitland Art Center, Maitland FL
Thomas, Delesha, *Pub Rels,* Carnegie Center for Art & History, New Albany IN
Thomas, Devin, *Dir Finance,* Thinkery, Austin TX
Thomas, Erin, *Educ Dir,* Cedar Rapids Museum of Art, Cedar Rapids IA
Thomas, Floyd, *Acting Dir,* Ohio History Connection, National Afro-American Museum & Cultural Center, Wilberforce OH
Thomas, Gary, *Prof,* Culver-Stockton College, Art Dept, Canton MO (S)
Thomas, Jack, *Information Technology,* University of Illinois at Urbana-Champaign, Spurlock Museum, Urbana IL
Thomas, Jacob, *Dir Living Collections & Horticulture Progs,* Barnes Foundation, Merion PA
Thomas, James E, *Prof,* Rochester Institute of Technology, School of Design, Rochester NY (S)
Thomas, Janet, *Technical Servs Librn,* Ringling College of Art & Design, Verman Kimbrough Memorial Library, Sarasota FL
Thomas, Jena, *Asst Prof Studio Art,* Converse College, School of the Arts, Dept of Art & Design, Spartanburg SC (S)
Thomas, Jesse, *Coordr Painting, Drawing & Intermedia,* University of Alberta, Dept of Art & Design, Edmonton AB (S)
Thomas, Joan, *Senior Cur Art,* Marine Corps University, National Museum of the Marine Corps, Triangle VA
Thomas, Joe, *Chmn,* Clarion University, Hazel Sandford Gallery, Clarion PA
Thomas, Joseph, *Communs Develop,* Alternate ROOTS, Inc, Atlanta GA
Thomas, Justin, *Mus Store Mgr,* Smith College, Museum of Art, Northampton MA
Thomas, Kristi, *Educ Asst,* Augustana University, Center for Western Studies, Sioux Falls SD
Thomas, Kristy, *Gallery Cur,* The Center for Visual Artists - Greensboro, Greensboro NC
Thomas, Kurtis, *Mgr Curatorial Affairs,* Mobile Museum of Art, Library, Mobile AL
Thomas, Kurtis, *Mgr Curatorial Affairs,* Mobile Museum of Art, Mobile AL
Thomas, Larry, *Prof & Chair Fine Art,* Johnson County Community College, Fine Arts Dept & Art History Dept, Overland Park KS (S)
Thomas, Leigh, *Asst Dir,* Norwich Free Academy, Slater Memorial Museum, Norwich CT
Thomas, Les, *Pres,* Turtle Mountain Chippewa Historical Society, Turtle Mountain Heritage Center, Belcourt ND
Thomas, Lorelle, *Prof,* Grand Valley State University, Art & Design Dept, Allendale MI (S)
Thomas, Mark, *Prof,* Art Academy of Cincinnati, Cincinnati OH (S)
Thomas, Mark, *Prof,* Art Academy of Cincinnati, Cincinnati OH (S)
Thomas, Michele M, *Gen Educ,* Art Institute of Pittsburgh, Pittsburgh PA (S)
Thomas, Nancy, *Sr Deputy Dir Art Admin & Colls,* Los Angeles County Museum of Art, Los Angeles CA
Thomas, Owen, *CEO,* Boston Properties LLC, San Francisco CA
Thomas, Paul, *Assoc Prof,* Illinois Institute of Technology, College of Architecture, Chicago IL (S)
Thomas, Prince, *Assoc Prof,* Lamar University, Art Dept, Beaumont TX (S)
Thomas, Stephanie, *Chief Educ & Interpretation,* Charleston Museum, Charleston SC
Thomas, Steve, *Educ Cur,* Riverside Art Museum, Riverside CA
Thomas, Susan, *Adjunct Prof Art,* University of Great Falls, Art Dept, Great Falls MT (S)
Thomas, Sylvia Lynn, *Exec Dir,* Dawson Springs Museum and Art Center, Dawson Springs KY
Thomas, Troy, *Assoc Prof,* Penn State Harrisburg, School of Humanities, Middletown PA (S)
Thomas, William G, *Supt,* San Francisco Maritime National Historical Park, Maritime Museum, San Francisco CA
Thomas, William, *Assoc Prof & Chair, Dept of Music,* York University, School of the Arts, Media, Performance & Design, Toronto ON (S)
Thomas, William, *Grounds & Maint,* Art Complex Museum, Carl A Weyerhaeuser Library, Duxbury MA
Thomas, Zoe B, *Educ & Pro Mgr,* Saco Museum, Saco ME
Thomas-McGee, Gina, *Assoc Educator,* Akron Art Museum, Akron OH
Thomas-Vickory, Stacy, *Printmaking,* Montserrat College of Art, Beverly MA (S)
Thomason, Barbara, *Lectr,* California State Polytechnic University, Pomona, Department of Art, Pomona CA (S)
Thompson Wylder, Viki, *Cur Educ,* Florida State University, Museum of Fine Arts, Tallahassee FL
Thompson, Alicia, *Mktg Dir,* Montana State University, Museum of the Rockies, Bozeman MT
Thompson, Ann, *Instr,* Appalachian State University, Dept of Art, Boone NC (S)
Thompson, Calla, *Assoc Prof,* University of Maryland, Baltimore County, Intermedia & Digital Arts (IMDA), Dept of Visual Arts, Baltimore MD (S)
Thompson, Carol, *Cur African Art,* High Museum of Art, Atlanta GA
Thompson, Carolyn, *Asst Dir,* Historical Museum at Fort Missoula, Missoula MT
Thompson, Catherine, *Devel Officer,* Auburn University, Jule Collins Smith Museum of Fine Art, Auburn AL
Thompson, Cheryl, *Pres Bd Trustees,* Boise Art Museum, Boise ID
Thompson, Christine, *Prof Art Educ,* Pennsylvania State University, University Park, Penn State School of Visual Arts, University Park PA (S)
Thompson, Christy, *Chief Exhibs & Colls,* Art Gallery of Ontario, Toronto ON
Thompson, Cynthia, *Bd Chmn,* Toledo Museum of Art, Toledo OH
Thompson, Diana, *Dir Collections & Cur,* National Academy Museum & School, New York NY
Thompson, Dolie, *Instr,* Morningside College, Art Dept, Sioux City IA (S)
Thompson, Donna, *Contact,* West Nebraska Art Center, Gallery, Scottsbluff NE
Thompson, Durant, *Assoc Prof,* University of Mississippi, Department of Art, University MS (S)
Thompson, Francis, *Gallery Coordr,* Virginia Polytechnic Institute & State University, Armory Art Gallery, Blacksburg VA
Thompson, Greig, *Mus Preparator Chief,* State Historical Society of Missouri, Columbia MO
Thompson, Harry F, *Exec Dir,* Augustana University, Center for Western Studies, Sioux Falls SD
Thompson, Jaime, *Cur Educ,* Contemporary Arts Center, Cincinnati OH
Thompson, James, *Prof,* Azusa Pacific University, College of Music & the Arts, Dept of Art & Design, Azusa CA (S)
Thompson, James, *Prof,* Western Carolina University, Dept of Art/College of Arts & Science, Cullowhee NC (S)
Thompson, Jean, *Admin Asst,* CMCA-Center for Maine Contemporary Art, Art Gallery, Rockport ME
Thompson, Jennifer, *The Gloria and Jack Drosdick Curator of European Painting & Sculpture & Curator of the John G Johnson Collection,* Philadelphia Museum of Art, John G Johnson Collection, Philadelphia PA
Thompson, Jennifer, *The Gloria and Jack Drosdick Curator of European Painting and Sculpture and Curator of the John G Johnson Collection,* Philadelphia Museum of Art, Rodin Museum of Philadelphia, Philadelphia PA
Thompson, Krista, *Asst Prof,* Northwestern University, Evanston, Dept of Art History, Evanston IL (S)
Thompson, Larry, *Chmn,* Ouachita Baptist University, Dept of Visual Art, Arkadelphia AR (S)
Thompson, Laura, *Exec Dir,* Arts Center in Orange, Orange VA
Thompson, Leslie, *Dir Adult Progs,* Sid W Richardson Foundation, Sid Richardson Museum, Fort Worth TX
Thompson, Lex, *Prof,* Bethel University, Dept of Art & Design, Saint Paul MN (S)
Thompson, Linda, *Admissions & Gift Shop Mgr,* Dawson City Museum, Dawson City YT

Thompson, Loyd, *Board Mem,* Cambridge Museum, Cambridge NE
Thompson, Matthew, *Registrar,* National Archives and Records Administration, Eisenhower Presidential Library, Abilene KS
Thompson, Nato, *Artistic Dir,* Creative Time, New York NY
Thompson, Nora, *Instr,* Seton Hill University, Art Program, Greensburg PA (S)
Thompson, Patricia, *Prof,* Daytona Beach Community College, Dept of Fine Arts & Visual Arts, Daytona Beach FL (S)
Thompson, Peter, *Chmn,* Coe College, Dept of Art, Cedar Rapids IA (S)
Thompson, RJ, *Vis Prof,* La Roche College, Division of Design, Pittsburgh PA (S)
Thompson, Sandy, *Develop Dir,* Rochester Art Center, Rochester MN
Thompson, Sandy, *Develop Dir,* Plains Art Museum, Fargo ND
Thompson, Scott B, *Dir,* Laurens County Historical Society, Dublin-Laurens Museum, Dublin GA
Thompson, Stacey, *Exec Dir,* The Museum, Greenwood SC
Thompson, Stacey, *Registrar,* Morris Museum of Art, Augusta GA
Thompson, Steve, *Chief Safety & Security,* Oklahoma City Museum of Art, Oklahoma City OK
Thompson, Sue, *Coordr Art Educ,* Adrian College, Art & Design Dept, Adrian MI (S)
Thompson, Toby, *Chmn Industrial, Interior & Packaging Design,* Rochester Institute of Technology, School of Design, Rochester NY (S)
Thompson, William R, *Cur of Coll,* City of El Paso, El Paso TX
Thompson, Yvonne, *VPres Office Mgmt,* DuPage Art League School & Gallery, Wheaton IL
Thomson, Bill, *Asst Prof,* University of Hartford, Hartford Art School, West Hartford CT (S)
Thomson, Carole, *Trustee,* Brooklyn Historical Society, Brooklyn OH
Thoresen, Allegra, *Communs Mgr,* Public Art Fund, Inc, Visual Archive, New York NY
Thoresen, Allegra, *Communs Mgr,* Public Art Fund, Inc, New York NY
Thorn Dalzin, Jennifer, *Dir Dept Digital Initiatives & Servs,* The Newberry, Chicago IL
Thornock, Marriah, *Deputy Dir,* North Central Washington Museum, Wenatchee Valley Museum & Cultural Center, Wenatchee WA
Thornton, Corey, *Cur,* MacArthur Memorial, Norfolk VA
Thornton, Jessica, *Asst Prof,* University of Missouri - Columbia, Dept of Art, Columbia MO (S)
Thornton, Terri, *Cur Educ,* Modern Art Museum, Fort Worth TX
Thorpe, Dana, *Exec Dir,* Fresno Metropolitan Museum, Fresno CA
Thorpe, Gordon L, *Lectr,* University of California, Riverside, Dept of Art, Riverside CA (S)
Thorpe, Lynn, *Instr & Asst Prof,* Northwest Community College, Dept of Art, Powell WY (S)
Thorson, Zaiga, *Asst Prof & Co Chair Commun & Fine Arts,* Black Hawk College, Art Dept, Moline IL (S)
Thrale, Ann, *Technician,* Alberta College of Art & Design, Illingworth Kerr Gallery, Calgary AB
Thrall, Rosanne, *Art Dir,* Hill Country Arts Foundation, Duncan-McAshan Visual Arts Center, Ingram TX
Thrift, Layne, *Asst Prof,* University of Science & Arts of Oklahoma, Art Dept, Chickasha OK (S)
Throm, Carrie, *Deputy Dir Devel & External Relations,* University of Michigan, Museum of Art, Ann Arbor MI
Throop, Mary Jane, *Weekend Receptionist,* Glanmore National Historic Site of Canada, Belleville ON
Thrush, George, *Assoc Prof,* Northeastern University, Dept of Art & Architecture, Boston MA (S)
Thull, Jim, *Ref Librn,* Montana State University, Creative Arts Library, Bozeman MT
Thumsujarit, Chaiwat, *Prof,* Fort Hays State University, Dept of Art & Design, Hays KS (S)
Thurber, Bart, *Assoc Dir Colls & Exhibs,* Princeton University, Princeton University Art Museum, Princeton NJ
Thurgood, Emma, *Exec Coordr,* Art Center Sarasota, Sarasota FL
Thuring, Reto, *Cur Contemporary Art,* The Cleveland Museum of Art, Cleveland OH
Thurman, Christa, *Cur Emerita,* The Art Institute of Chicago, Department of Textiles, Textile Society, Chicago IL
Thurman, Henry, *Instr,* Southern University A & M College, School of Architecture, Baton Rouge LA (S)
Thurman, James, *Asst Prof Art (Metal Art & Technology),* Pennsylvania State University, University Park, Penn State School of Visual Arts, University Park PA (S)
Thurman, Jennifer, *Dir Develop,* Oklahoma Contemporary Arts Center, Oklahoma City OK
Thurman, Shiloh, *Dir,* The Frank Phillips Foundation Inc, Woolaroc Museum, Bartlesville OK
Thurmer, Robert, *Dir & Chief Cur,* Cleveland State University, The Galleries at CSU, Cleveland OH
Thurston, Tom, *Dir Capital Devel,* Royal Alberta Museum, Royal Alberta Museum, Edmonton AB
Thygesen, Linda, *Admin Asst,* McDowell House & Apothecary Shop, Danville KY
Tibbets, Roger, *Chmn Fine Arts 2D,* Massachusetts College of Art, Boston MA (S)
Tibbitts, Alvin, *VPres,* Heritage Center, Inc, Pine Ridge SD
Tice, Carol, *Chmn,* Blue Lake Fine Arts Camp, Art Dept, Twin Lake MI (S)
Tice, Patricia, *Cur John L Wehle Art Gallery,* Genesee Country Village & Museum, John L Wehle Art Gallery, Mumford NY
Tidd, Lindsey, *Admin Coordr,* Schweinfurth Art Center, Auburn NY
Tiefenbach, Mark, *Treas,* Dauphin & District Allied Arts Council, Watson Art Centre, Dauphin MB
Tierney, Nathan, *Chmn,* California Lutheran University, Art Dept, Thousand Oaks CA (S)
Tierno, Mark, *Pres,* Cazenovia College, Center for Art & Design Studies, Cazenovia NY (S)
Tieso, Tara, *Board Pres,* Women's Art Registry of Minnesota Gallery, Saint Paul MN
Tietje, Burt, *Treas,* Zigler Art Museum, Jennings LA
Tilak, Elizabeth, *Asst Prof,* Cameron University, Art Dept, Lawton OK (S)
Tilghman, Benjamin, *Asst Prof,* Lawrence University, Dept of Art & Art History, Appleton WI (S)
Till, Barry, *Cur Asian Art,* Art Gallery of Greater Victoria, Victoria BC
Tillander, Michelle, *Asst Prof,* University of Florida, School of Art & Art History, Gainesville FL (S)
Tilley, Carey, *Exec Dir,* Cherokee Heritage Center, Park Hill OK
Tillinger, Elaine, *Chmn,* Lindenwood University, Harry D Hendren Gallery, Saint Charles MO
Tillinger, Elaine, *Chmn Dept, Contact,* Lindenwood College, Art Dept, Saint Charles MO (S)
Tillman, Patricia, *Asst Prof,* Trinity College, Dept of Studio Arts, Hartford CT (S)
Tillman, Reilly, *Deputy Dir & Educ Dir,* FilmNorth, Saint Paul MN
Tillotson, Lisa, *Registrar,* University of Calgary, Nickle Galleries, Calgary AB
Tilney, John S, *Pres,* Concord Art Association, Concord MA
Tilton, Sumner, *VPres,* Willard House & Clock Museum, Inc, North Grafton MA
Timberlake, Samuel, *Instr,* John C Calhoun, Department of Fine Arts, Tanner AL (S)
Timm-Ballard, Charles, *Chmn,* Whitman College, Art Dept, Walla Walla WA (S)
Timmerman, Erik, *Assoc Prof,* Rochester Institute of Technology, School of Photographic Arts & Sciences, Rochester NY (S)
Timmers, Gwilyn, *Pub Servs Mgr,* University of British Columbia, Museum of Anthropology, Vancouver BC
Timoshuk, Walter W, *Pres,* Norton Simon Museum, Pasadena CA
Timothy, John, *Dir,* Ataloa Lodge Museum, Muskogee OK
Timpano, Anne, *Dir,* University of Mary Washington, University of Mary Washington Galleries, Fredericksburg VA
Timpson, Corey, *VPres Exhibs, Research & Design,* Canadian Museum for Human Rights, Winnipeg MB
Tinapple, David, *Instr,* University of North Carolina at Chapel Hill, Art Dept, Chapel Hill NC (S)
Tinch, Crystal, *Commun Educ,* Center for Exploratory & Perceptual Art, CEPA Library, Buffalo NY
Tindale, Jan, *Chmn,* Charles B Goddard, Ardmore OK
Tiner, Archie, *Instr,* Southern University A & M College, School of Architecture, Baton Rouge LA (S)
Tingley, Charles, *Library Dir,* Saint Augustine Historical Society, Library, Saint Augustine FL
Tingley, Charles, *Library Mgr,* Saint Augustine Historical Society, Oldest House Museum Complex, Saint Augustine FL
Tinker, William, *Treas,* Mary R Koch Arts Center, Mark Arts, Wichita KS
Tinney, Harle, *Exec Dir,* Royal Arts Foundation, Belcourt Castle, Newport RI
Tinney, Stephen, *Deputy Dir & Chief Cur,* University of Pennsylvania, Museum of Archaeology & Anthropology, Philadelphia PA
Tinterow, Gary, *Dir,* Museum of Fine Arts, Houston, Houston TX
Tinti, Mary, *Cur,* Fitchburg Art Museum, Fitchburg MA
Tisdale, James, *Ceramics Coord,* The Contemporary Austin, Austin TX
Tisdale, Jane, *Fine Art Conservator,* Mount Allison University, Owens Art Gallery, Sackville NB
Tisher, Kelcie, *Assoc Dir,* The Contemporary Austin, Austin TX
Tite, Winston, *Assoc Prof,* University of North Carolina at Charlotte, Dept Art, Charlotte NC (S)
Titmus, Wilma, *Office Mgr,* Herrett Center for Arts & Sciences, Jean B King Art Gallery, Twin Falls ID
Titus, Harry B, *Prof,* Wake Forest University, Dept of Art, Winston-Salem NC (S)
Titus, Jack, *Prof,* Oklahoma State University, Department of Art, Graphic Design and Art History, Stillwater OK (S)
Tkaczuk, Lydia, *Pres,* Ukrainian National Museum & Library, Chicago IL
Tobert, Mitch, *Instr,* South Dakota State University, Dept of Visual Arts, Brookings SD (S)
Tobias, Jennifer, *Librn, Collection Develop,* Museum of Modern Art, Library and Museum Archives, New York NY
Tobkin, Donna, *Dir Finance,* Triton Museum of Art, Santa Clara CA
Toborg, Linda, *Secy,* Shores Memorial Museum, Lyndon Center VT
Tocci, Alison, *Bd Pres,* Waterfront Museum, Brooklyn NY
Tocci, George, *Treas,* Waterfront Museum, Brooklyn NY
Tockarshewsky, Margaret Anne, *Exec Dir,* New Haven Museum, Whitney Library, New Haven CT
Todd, Andrea, *Mktg Dir,* Willard Arts Center, Carr Gallery, Colonial Theater, Idaho Falls ID
Todd, Chris, *Instr,* Mesa Community College, Dept of Art, Mesa AZ (S)
Todd, Gui, *Instr,* Modesto Junior College, Arts Humanities & Communications Division, Modesto CA (S)
Todd, Joni, *Finance & HR Mgr,* Public Art Fund, Inc, New York NY
Todd, Joni, *Mgr Finance & HR,* Public Art Fund, Inc, Visual Archive, New York NY
Todd, Margaret, *Pres,* Gilbert Stuart Memorial Association, Inc, Gilbert Stuart Birthplace & Museum, Saunderstown RI
Todd, Margaret, *Pub Rels & Treas,* St Mary Chapter Louisiana Landmarks Society, Grevemberg House Museum, Franklin LA

Todd, Mark, *Prof,* Texas State University - San Marcos, Dept of Art and Design, San Marcos TX (S)
Todd, Melody, *Asst Prof,* Mount Mary College, Art & Design Division, Milwaukee WI (S)
Todd, Ron, *Gallery Dir,* Central Connecticut State University, Art Dept Museum, New Britain CT
Todd, Sandy, *Exec Asst,* Rollins College, George D & Harriet W Cornell Fine Arts Museum, Winter Park FL
Todenhoff, Mary, *Adjunct,* York College of Pennsylvania, Dept of Music, Art & Speech Communications, York PA (S)
Todoroff, Rhonda, *Asst Prof,* Tidewater Community College, Visual Arts Center, Portsmouth VA (S)
Toensing, Robert E, *Instr,* Anoka Ramsey Community College, Art Dept, Coon Rapids MN (S)
Tofanelli, Lori, *Communs Coordr,* Cedar Rapids Museum of Art, Cedar Rapids IA
Toffle, Sommer, *Ligonier Valley Coordr,* Southern Alleghenies Museum of Art, Ligonier Valley Facility, Ligonier PA
Tognarelli, Paula, *Exec Dir,* Arthur Griffin Center for Photographic Art, Griffin Museum of Photography, Winchester MA
Togneri, Carol, *Chief Cur,* Norton Simon Museum, Pasadena CA
Toivaner, Kati, *Chmn,* University of Missouri-Kansas City, Dept of Art & Art History, Kansas City MO (S)
Toker, Franklin, *Prof,* University of Pittsburgh, Henry Clay Frick Dept History of Art & Architecture, Pittsburgh PA (S)
Toku, Masami, *Prof,* California State University, Chico, Department of Art & Art History, Chico CA (S)
Tokuda Irwin, Jean, *Arts Educ Mgr,* Utah Arts Council, Chase Home Museum of Utah Folk Arts, Salt Lake City UT
Toland, Matthew, *Exec Dir,* International Preservation Studies Center, Mount Carroll IL (S)
Tolbert, Javier, *Instr,* Clark-Atlanta University, School of Arts & Sciences, Atlanta GA (S)
Toler, Joey, *Prog Dir,* Beaufort County Arts Council, Washington NC
Tolk, Stephanie, *Dir External Relations,* Portland Children's Museum, Portland OR
Toll, Carmen, *Exec Dir,* The Dalles Art Association, The Dalles Art Center, The Dalles OR
Tolman, Allison, *Chief Registrar & Assoc Cur Fashion Archives,* Maryland Historical Society, Library, Baltimore MD
Tolman, Kenny, *Adjunct Instr,* University of Science & Arts of Oklahoma, Art Dept, Chickasha OK (S)
Tolmie, Kris, *Chmn, Assoc Prof,* The College of Saint Rose, The Center For Art and Design, Albany NY (S)
Tolnick, Judith, *Galleries Dir,* University of Rhode Island, Fine Arts Center Galleries, Kingston RI
Tolton, Mary-Louise, *Art History Area Coordr,* Western Michigan University, Frostic School of Art, Kalamazoo MI (S)
Toluse, Joe, *Cur,* Idaho Historical Museum, Boise ID
Tom, Gregory, *Dir Gallery,* Eastern Michigan University, Ford Gallery, Ypsilanti MI
Tomasch, Otto, *Asst Prof,* York College of Pennsylvania, Dept of Music, Art & Speech Communications, York PA (S)
Tomasello, Terry, *Exec Dir,* Creative Arts Guild, Dalton GA
Tombarge, John, *Head Librn,* Washington & Lee University, Leyburn Library, Lexington VA
Tomczak, Catherine, *Opers Coodr,* Organization of Saskatchewan Arts Councils (OSAC), Regina SK
Tomczak, Pat, *Dean of Library,* Quincy University, Brenner Library, Quincy IL
Tomio, Ken, *Cur & Head Educ,* Tyler Museum of Art, Reference Library, Tyler TX
Tomio, Ken, *Head Educ Cur,* Tyler Museum of Art, Tyler TX
Tomio, Kimberley Bush, *Dir,* Tyler Museum of Art, Tyler TX
Tomio, Kimberley Bush, *Dir,* Tyler Museum of Art, Reference Library, Tyler TX
Tomkins, Emma, *Mktg Specialist,* Shiawassee Arts Center, Owosso MI
Tomlin, Susan, *Conservator,* Neustadt Collection of Tiffany Glass, Long Island City NY
Tomlin, Terry, *Chmn Fine Arts,* University of Texas at Brownsville & Texas Southmost College, Fine Arts Dept, Brownsville TX (S)
Tomlinson, Glenn, *Cur Educ,* Norton Museum of Art, West Palm Beach FL
Tomlinson, Janis A, *Dir,* University of Delaware, University Museums, Newark DE
Tomolillo, Bob, *Secy,* The Boston Printmakers, at Lesley University, Boston MA
Tomor, Michael A, *Dir,* City of El Paso, El Paso TX
Tompkins Rivas, Pilar, *Dir,* East Los Angeles College, Vincent Price Art Museum, Monterey Park CA
Tompkins, Andi, *Mus School Mgr,* Arkansas Arts Center, Little Rock AR (S)
Tompkins, Jack D, *VPres,* Lincoln Memorial Shrine, Redlands CA
Tomsic, Walt, *Assoc Prof,* Pacific Lutheran University, Dept of Art, Tacoma WA (S)
Tonelli, Edith A, *Exec Dir,* Cape Cod Museum of Art Inc, Dennis MA
Tonelli, Laura, *Dean,* Montserrat College of Art, Beverly MA (S)
Toney, Kimberly, *Head Readers' Serv,* American Antiquarian Society, Worcester MA
Tong, Darlene, *Art Librn,* San Francisco State University, J Paul Leonard Library, San Francisco CA
Tonkovich, Jennifer, *Eugene & Clare Thaw Cur Drawings & Prints,* The Morgan Library & Museum, Museum, New York NY
Tonz, Sandra, *Instr,* Mount Mary College, Art & Design Division, Milwaukee WI (S)
Tooley, Billie, *Exec Dir,* New Hampshire Art Association, Portsmouth NH
Toomer, Jean W, *VChmn Bd Trustees,* African Art Museum of Maryland, Columbia MD
Toon, Richard, *Dir,* Arizona State University, Deer Valley Petroglyph Preserve, Phoenix AZ
Toone, Thomas, *Assoc Prof,* Utah State University, Dept of Art, Logan UT (S)
Topfer, Stephen, *Coll Mgr,* Art Gallery of Greater Victoria, Victoria BC
Toplovich, Ann, *Exec Dir,* Tennessee Historical Society, Nashville TN
Topolski, Allen C, *Chmn,* University of Rochester, Dept of Art & Art History, Rochester NY (S)
Topp, Roger, *Dir of Exhibits,* University of Alaska, Museum of the North, Fairbanks AK
Topping, Holly, *Instr Life Draw,* Orange Coast College, Visual & Performing Arts Division, Costa Mesa CA (S)
Topping, Karin, *Co-Dir,* Tubac Center of the Arts, Santa Cruz Valley Art Association, Tubac AZ
Torano, Vince, *Painting,* Western Michigan University, Frostic School of Art, Kalamazoo MI (S)
Torano, Vince, *Painting Area Coordr,* Western Michigan University, Frostic School of Art, Kalamazoo MI (S)
Torchia, Richard, *Gallery Dir,* Arcadia University Art Gallery, Spruance Fine Arts Center, Glenside PA
Torcoletti, Enzo, *Prof,* Flagler College, Visual Arts Dept, Saint Augustine FL (S)
Torinus, Sigi, *Prof, Integrated Media,* University of Windsor, School of Creative Arts, Windsor ON (S)
Torke, Ann, *Chair,* University of Massachusetts - Boston, Art Dept, Boston MA (S)
Tornabene, Luke, *Cur Fishes,* University of Washington, Burke Museum of Natural History and Culture, Seattle WA
Tornheim, N, *Instr,* Golden West College, Visual Art Dept, Huntington Beach CA (S)
Tornquist, Kristi, *Chief Univ Librn,* South Dakota State University, Hilton M. Briggs Library, Brookings SD
Toro, Kalia, *Instr,* Inter American University of Puerto Rico, Fine Arts Dept -Art Program, San German PR (S)
Torrance, Joshua C, *Exec Dir,* Hancock County Trustees of Public Reservations, Woodlawn: Museum, Gardens & Park, Ellsworth ME
Torre, Mike, *Instr,* Northwestern Michigan College, Art Dept, Traverse City MI (S)
Torres, Bernadette, *Art Instr/Gallery Dir,* Metropolitan Community College - Penn Valley, Art Dept, Kansas City MO (S)
Torres, Harold, *Tourism Asst,* Pueblo of San Ildefonso, Maria Martinez Museum, Santa Fe NM
Torres, Jennifer, *Assoc Prof,* University of Southern Mississippi, Dept of Art & Design, Hattiesburg MS (S)
Torres, Jennifer, *Colls Tech,* Johns Hopkins University, Archaeological Museum, Baltimore MD
Torres, Manuel, *Prof Emeritus,* Florida International University, School of Art & Art History, Miami FL (S)
Torrey, Charles, *Research Historian,* History Museum of Mobile, Reference Library, Mobile AL
Torrey, Charles, *Researcher,* History Museum of Mobile, Mobile AL
Torri, Erika, *Exec Dir,* Library Association of La Jolla, Athenaeum Music & Arts Library, La Jolla CA
Tortolero, Carlos, *Pres,* National Museum of Mexican Art, Chicago IL
Toshkova, Irina, *Dir,* New Gallery of Modern Art, Charlotte NC
Tosten, Erik, *Adjunct Prof,* University of Texas at Arlington, Art & Art History Department, Arlington TX (S)
Tosti, Sally, *Assoc Prof,* Keystone College, Fine Arts Dept, LaPlume PA (S)
Toth, John Michael, *Interior Design,* Art Institute of Pittsburgh, Pittsburgh PA (S)
Toth, Myra, *Chmn,* Ventura College, Fine Arts Dept, Ventura CA (S)
Totton, Mary-Louise, *Art History,* Western Michigan University, Frostic School of Art, Kalamazoo MI (S)
Toub, Jim, *Assoc Prof,* Appalachian State University, Dept of Art, Boone NC (S)
Tourdot, Kelly, *Tech Svcs,* University of Wisconsin-Madison, Kohler Art Library, Madison WI
Tournear, Libby, *Exhibs Prep,* Quincy Art Center, Quincy IL
Tourtillotte, Bill, *Chief Cur,* South Bend Regional Museum of Art, South Bend IN
Tourtillotte, Julie, *Chmn,* Saint Mary's College, Dept of Art, Notre Dame IN (S)
Tousignant, John, *Exec Dir,* Franco-American Centre, Manchester NH
Tousignant, Zoë, *Cur,* Artexte Information Centre, Documentation Centre, Montreal QC
Towers, Debbie, *Admin Assoc,* Palm Beach County Parks & Recreation Department, Morikami Museum & Japanese Gardens, Delray Beach FL
Towers, Joel, *Exec Dean,* The New School, Parsons School of Design, New York NY (S)
Towers, Matthew, *Asst Prof,* University of Hartford, Hartford Art School, West Hartford CT (S)
Towler, Patty, *Treas,* San Angelo Art Club, Helen King Kendall Memorial Art Gallery, San Angelo TX
Towne, Marian, *Asst Prof Art Therapy,* Albertus Magnus College, Visual and Performing Arts, New Haven CT (S)
Towner, Mark, *Dean,* Endicott College, School of Visual & Performing Arts, Beverly MA (S)
Townsend, Belinda, *Secy,* Art and History Museums - Maitland, Maitland FL
Townsend, Gavin, *Prof,* University of Tennessee at Chattanooga, Dept of Art, Chattanooga TN (S)
Townsend, Lisa, *VP Mktg & External Rels,* The Children's Museum of Indianapolis, Indianapolis IN
Townsend, Melanie, *Head Exhibitions & Collections,* Museum London, London ON

Townsend, Pat O'Brien, *Vol Pres,* Three Forks Area Historical Society, Headwaters Heritage Museum, Three Forks MT

Townsend, Rhys, *Chmn,* Clark University, Dept of Visual & Performing Arts, Worcester MA (S)

Townsend, Richard, *Vol Secy,* Three Forks Area Historical Society, Headwaters Heritage Museum, Three Forks MT

Townsend, Ron, *Acquisitions Asst,* Lutheran Theological Seminary, Krauth Memorial Library, Philadelphia PA

Townsend, Tiffanie, *Assoc Prof,* Georgia Southern University, Betty Foy Sanders Dept of Art, Statesboro GA (S)

Townsend, Tina, *Dir of Operations,* Arts Center of the Ozarks, Springdale AR

Toy, Lyda, *Adj Instr,* University of West Florida, Dept of Art, Pensacola FL (S)

Trachtenberg, Mara, *Pres,* Hera Educational Foundation, Hera Gallery, Wakefield RI

Tracy, Bob, *Prof,* University of Nevada, Las Vegas, Dept of Art, Las Vegas NV (S)

Tracy, Jamie, *Prof, Studio Art,* State College of Florida Manatee - Sarasota, Art, Design, Humanities, Bradenton FL (S)

Tracz, Tim, *Chmn,* Austin College, Art Dept, Sherman TX (S)

Traetto, Michela, *Dir,* Order Sons of Italy in America, Garibaldi & Meucci Museum, Staten Island NY

Trafton, Carolyn, *Asst Dir,* Red River Valley Museum, Vernon TX

Trafton, Robin, *Cur,* Commerce Bancshares, Inc, Fine Art Collection, Kansas City MO

Trager, Neil C, *Dir,* State University of New York at New Paltz, Samuel Dorsky Museum of Art, New Paltz NY

Trager, Ruth, *Pres,* Halifax Historical Society, Inc, Halifax Historical Museum, Daytona Beach FL

Trager, Warren, *VPres,* Halifax Historical Society, Inc, Halifax Historical Museum, Daytona Beach FL

Trahan, Cole, *Museum Shop Associate,* The Columbus Museum, Columbus GA

Trahan, Eric, *Dir,* Canajoharie Library & Art Gallery, Arkell Museum of Canajoharie, Canajoharie NY

Trahan, Eric, *Dir Library,* Canajoharie Library & Art Gallery, Library, Canajoharie NY

Trainer, Jennifer, *CEO,* Hancock Shaker Village, Inc, Pittsfield MA

Tran Le, Julie, *Asst Mus Librn, Irene Lewisohn Costume Reference Library,* The Metropolitan Museum of Art, Museum Libraries, New York NY

Tran, Hoang, *Director of Archives,* Pennsylvania Academy of the Fine Arts, The Dorothy and Kenneth Woodcock Archive, Philadelphia PA

Tran, Howard, *Asst Prof,* Lycoming College, Art Dept, Williamsport PA (S)

Tran, Johnny, *Co-Owner,* Thumbprint Gallery, La Jolla CA

Traugott, Joseph, *Cur 20th Century Painting,* New Mexico Department of Cultural Affairs, New Mexico Museum of Art, Unit of NM Dept of Cultural Affairs, Santa Fe NM

Trautman, Beatrice, *4th VPres,* National Watercolor Society, San Pedro CA

Trautman, Charlotte, *Cur,* Mount Vernon Hotel Museum & Garden, New York NY

Travers, Cindy, *VPres,* Fairfield Art Association, Fairfield IA

Travers, Jason, *Prof of Practice,* Lehigh University, Dept of Art, Architecture & Design, Bethlehem PA (S)

Travis, Richard V, *Exec Dir,* National Heritage Museum, Lexington MA

Traynor, Marian, *Mgr Library User Servs,* Sheridan College of Applied Arts and Technology, Trafalgar Campus Library, Oakville ON

Treadwell, Jaime, *Prof,* Delaware County Community College, Communications, Art & Humanities, Media PA (S)

Trebilcock, Evelyn, *Chief Cur,* Olana State Historic Site, Hudson NY

Trebilcock, Evelyn, *Cur,* Olana State Historic Site, Library, Hudson NY

Trebour, Todd, *Prog Coordr,* Arts Extension Service, Amherst MA

Trecker, Stan, *Dean,* Lesley University, College of Art & Design, Cambridge MA (S)

Tredway, Cherry, *Assoc Prof,* Oklahoma Christian University of Science & Arts, Dept of Art & Design, Oklahoma City OK (S)

Trejo Williams, Susie, *Instr of Art,* Campbellsville University, Art & Design Department, Campbellsville KY (S)

Tremayne, Richard, *Dir,* Cripple Creek District Museum, Cripple Creek CO

Tremblay, Manon, *Library Tech Acquisitions,* Montreal Museum of Fine Arts, Library, Montreal QC

Trend, David, *Prof Visual Studies, Culture,* University of California, Irvine, Studio Art Dept, Irvine CA (S)

Trendler, Amy, *Librn,* Ball State University, Architecture Library, Muncie IN

Trenholme, Anne, *Acquisitions & Collection Development Librarian,* The Cleveland Museum of Art, Ingalls Library, Cleveland OH

Trepp, George, *Dir,* Long Beach Public Library, Long Beach NY

Treslan, Shane, *Office Mgr,* Clear Lake Arts Center, Clear Lake IA

Tresner, Cliff, *Asst Prof,* University of Louisiana at Monroe, Dept of Art, Monroe LA (S)

Tresner, Cliff, *Gallery Dir,* University of Louisiana at Monroe, Bry Gallery, Monroe LA

Tresner, Cliff, *Historian,* Kappa Pi International Honorary Art Fraternity, Cleveland MS

Trevethan, Shannon, *Dir,* Deines Cultural Center, Russell KS

Trickey, Anne, *Contact,* San Francisco City & County Arts Commission, San Francisco CA

Trickey, Karen, *Prof,* Nazareth College of Rochester, Art Dept, Rochester NY (S)

Triff, Michael, *Communs,* The Trustees of Reservations, The Mission House, Ipswich MA

Triggs, Nicholas, *Circulation Supervisor,* Cornish College of the Arts, Cornish Library, Seattle WA

Trillin, Calvin, *Secy,* American Academy of Arts & Letters, New York NY

Trim, Delaynna, *Cur Collections,* Mabee-Gerrer Museum of Art, Shawnee OK

Trim, Delaynna, *Part-Time Instr,* Oklahoma Baptist University, Art & Design Dept, Shawnee OK (S)

Trim, Sheryl, *Dir Finance,* Mississippi Museum of Art, Howorth Library, Jackson MS

Trimble, Brian, *Interim Dir,* California State University, Long Beach, University Art Museum, Long Beach CA

Trimble, Sandy, *Instr,* Seton Hill University, Art Program, Greensburg PA (S)

Trimpol, Michael, *Owner,* Little River Hotglass Studio & Gallery, Moscow VT

Triplett, Jayson, *Lectr,* Mississippi State University, Dept of Art, Starville MS (S)

Tripman, Holly, *Registrar,* Cameron Art Museum, Wilmington NC

Tripoli, Mandy, *Dir Community Engaged Practice,* Mesa Arts Center, Mesa Contemporary Arts Museum, Mesa AZ

Tripp, Lauren, *Head Jewelry Dept,* Kalamazoo Institute of Arts, KIA School, Kalamazoo MI (S)

Trissel, James, *Prof,* Colorado College, Dept of Art, Colorado Springs CO (S)

Tritel, Lynette, *Cur, Colls Mgr & Museum Store,* George Phippen, Phippen Museum - Art of the American West, Prescott AZ

Trivette, Karen, *Spec Coll & FIT Archives,* Fashion Institute of Technology - SUNY, Gladys Marcus Library, New York NY

Troffkin, Eric, *Dir Grad Studies,* Washington University, School of Art, Saint Louis MO (S)

Tronzo, Bill, *Prof,* Tulane University, Sophie H Newcomb Memorial College, New Orleans LA (S)

Trosko, Mariella, *Dir Educ,* Hershey Museum, Hershey PA

Trotman, Nat, *Cur Performance & Media,* Solomon R Guggenheim Museum, New York NY

Trotter, Ruth, *Dept Chmn, Prof Art,* University of La Verne, Dept of Art, La Verne CA (S)

Trotty, Sarah, *Assoc Prof,* Texas Southern University, College of Liberal Arts & Behavioral Sciences, Houston TX (S)

Trousdale, Deborah, *Instr,* Chemeketa Community College, Dept of Humanities & Communications, Art Program, Salem OR (S)

Trouse, Marilyn, *Instr,* West Hills Community College, Fine Arts Dept, Coalinga CA (S)

Trout, Cindy, *Mem Coordr,* Kalamazoo Institute of Arts, Kalamazoo MI

Trout, Katherine, *Admin Asst,* Springfield Museum of Art, Springfield OH (S)

Trovell, Robert, *Instr,* Harrisburg Area Community College, Division of Communications, Humanities & the Arts, Harrisburg PA (S)

Trover, Edward, *Registrar & Preparator,* Swope Art Museum, Terre Haute IN

Trowbridge, Kyle, *Instr,* University of Miami, Dept of Art & Art History, Coral Gables FL (S)

Troy, John, *Instr,* Joe Kubert, Dover NJ (S)

Troy, V, *Assoc Prof,* Berry College, Art Dept, Mount Berry GA (S)

Trubridge, Mark, *Assoc Prof,* Marymount University, School of Arts & Sciences Div, Arlington VA (S)

True, Rich, *Chmn,* Clackamas Community College, Art Dept, Oregon City OR (S)

Truitt, Edward, *Assoc Prof,* West Texas A&M University, Art, Theatre & Dance Dept, Canyon TX (S)

Trujillo, Arthur, *Asst Prof,* New Mexico Highlands University, Dept of Communications & Fine Arts, Las Vegas NM (S)

Trujillo-Porter, Sarah, *Dir,* Quint Projects, La Jolla CA

Trulock, Sue, *Dir,* Pine Bluff/Jefferson County Historical Museum, Pine Bluff AR

Truly, Gabriella, *Cir Collections Mgmt,* Dallas Museum of Art, Dallas TX

Truman-McGlohon, Susan, *Temp Asst Prof,* University of Alabama in Huntsville, Dept of Art and Art History, Huntsville AL (S)

Trumble, Edward P, *Founder,* Leanin' Tree Museum & Sculpture Garden of Western Art, Boulder CO

Trumble, Tom, *Pres,* Leanin' Tree Museum & Sculpture Garden of Western Art, Boulder CO

Trumpy, Sigrid, *Cur Robinson Coll,* United States Naval Academy, USNA Museum, Annapolis MD

Trumpy, Sigrid, *Dir Exhibs,* Maryland Hall for the Creative Arts, Chaney Gallery, Annapolis MD

Trunn, Amanda, *Cur Colls,* Montana Historical Society, Helena MT

Truong, Eileen, *Finance & Opers Mgr,* Hyde Park Art Center, Chicago IL

Truong, Lien, *Lectr,* Humboldt State University, College of Arts & Humanities, Art Dept, Arcata CA (S)

Trutty-Coohill, Patricia, *Chair & Prof Art History,* Siena College, Dept of Creative Arts, Loudonville NY (S)

Trépanier, Mario, *CEO,* University of Sherbrooke, Art Gallery, Sherbrooke QC

Tsai, Eugenie, *John & Barbara Vogelstein Cur Contemporary Art,* Brooklyn Museum, Brooklyn NY

Tsai, Joyce, *Asst Prof,* University of Florida, School of Art & Art History, Gainesville FL (S)

Tsang, Chui L, *Interim Pres,* San Jose City College, School of Fine Arts, San Jose CA (S)

Tsatos, Irene, *Dir Gallery Progs,* Armory Center for the Arts, Pasadena CA

Tschernisch, Sergei, *Pres,* Cornish College of the Arts, Art Dept, Seattle WA (S)

Tschinkel, Paul, *Prof,* Queensborough Community College, Dept of Art & Photography, Bayside Hills NY (S)

Tselentis, Jason, *Lectr,* University of North Carolina at Charlotte, Dept Art, Charlotte NC (S)

Tselos, George, *Supervisory Archivist,* The National Park Service, United States Department of the Interior, Statue of Liberty National Monument & The Ellis Island Immigration Museum, Washington DC

Tseng, Li Li, *Assoc Prof,* Pittsburg State University, Art Dept, Pittsburg KS (S)
Tsien, Billie, *Pres,* Architectural League of New York, New York NY
Tsiongas, Mary, *Chair,* University of New Mexico, Department of Fine Arts & Art History, Albuquerque NM (S)
Tso, Kwok-Pong (Bobby), *Instr,* Northwest Missouri State University, Dept of Fine & Performing Arts, Maryville MO (S)
Tsolakis, Alkis, *Chmn,* Drury College, Art & Art History Dept, Springfield MO (S)
Tsoules, Will, *VPres & CFO,* Massachusetts Historical Society, Boston MA
Tsuji, Bill, *Dean Humanities,* Sierra Community College, Art Dept, Rocklin CA (S)
Tsuji, Bill, *Dean Humanities,* Sierra Community College, Art Dept, Rocklin CA (S)
Tsukamoto, Darlene, *Asst Dir,* Lee Arts Center, Arlington VA
Tsukashima, Rodney, *Instr,* Long Beach City College, Art & Photography Dept, Long Beach CA (S)
Tsuno, Devon, *Asst Prof,* California State University, Dominguez Hills, Art & Design Dept, Carson CA (S)
Tubbs, Lyllian, *Mus Shop Mgr,* Cottonlandia Museum, Greenwood MS
Tucci, Judy, *Instr,* Northeast Mississippi Junior College, Art Dept, Booneville MS (S)
Tuccillo, Anita, *Asst Prof,* Illinois Central College, Arts & Communication Dept, East Peoria IL (S)
Tuccillo, John, *Prof,* Illinois Central College, Arts & Communication Dept, East Peoria IL (S)
Tuck, David, *Co-Dir,* Wynick Tuck Gallery, Toronto ON
Tucker Craig, Sara, *Director of Operations,* The Museum of Arts & Sciences Inc, Daytona Beach FL
Tucker, Cassidy, *Vis Servs & Retail,* Missoula Art Museum, Missoula MT
Tucker, Elizabeth, *Dir Develop,* Madison Museum of Contemporary Art, Madison WI
Tucker, LC, *Chief Preparator,* Mississippi Museum of Art, Howorth Library, Jackson MS
Tucker, Linda L, *Asst,* Black River Academy Museum & Historical Society, Black River Academy Museum, Ludlow VT
Tucker, Rebecca, *Mus Dir,* Colorado Springs Fine Arts Center, Taylor Museum, Colorado Springs CO
Tucker, Susan, *Dir,* Ormond Memorial Art Museum and Gardens, Ormond Beach FL
Tuckes, Aliza, *Office Asst,* eMediaLoft.org, New York NY
Tudor, William-John, *Exhib & Tech Dir, Ctr for Art,* University of Maryland, Baltimore County, Intermedia & Digital Arts (IMDA), Dept of Visual Arts, Baltimore MD (S)
Tuele, Andrea, *Admin,* University of British Columbia, Dept of Art History, Visual Art & Theory, Vancouver BC (S)
Tuis Nesbit, Colin, *Gallery Dir,* Indiana University-Purdue University, Indianapolis, Herron School of Art & Design, Indianapolis IN (S)
Tukey, Phillip A, *VPres Pub Opers,* Brookgreen Gardens, Murrells Inlet SC
Tulee, Mike, *Exec Dir,* United Indians of All Tribes Foundation, Daybreak Star Center Gallery, Seattle WA
Tullis, Linda, *Exec Dir,* Lewistown Art Center, Lewistown MT
Tullos, Mark A, *Dir,* Louisiana Department of Culture, Recreation & Tourism, Louisiana State Museum,
Tulovsky, Julia, *Cur Russian & Soviet Nonconformist Art,* Rutgers, The State University of New Jersey, Zimmerli Art Museum at Rutgers University, New Brunswick NJ
Tuma, Mary, *Assoc Prof,* University of North Carolina at Charlotte, Dept Art, Charlotte NC (S)
Tuman, Donna, *Asst Prof,* C W Post Campus of Long Island University, School of Visual & Performing Arts, Brookville NY (S)
Tung, Lisa, *Dir & Cur,* Massachusetts College of Art and Design, Bakalar & Paine Galleries, Boston MA
Tunstall, Arnold, *Colls Mgr,* Akron Art Museum, Akron OH
Tupa, Dana, *Div Chair & Prof,* Jacksonville University, Jacksonville FL (S)
Tupper, Jon, *Dir,* Art Gallery of Greater Victoria, Victoria BC
Tupper, Jon, *Dir,* Art Gallery of Greater Victoria, Library, Victoria BC
Tura, Hunter, *Secy,* Van Alen Institute, New York NY
Turbak, Jamie, *Assoc Dir,* Oakland Public Library, Art, Music, History & Literature Section, Oakland CA
Turbide, Chantal, *Museum Cur,* Saint Joseph's Oratory, Museum, Montreal QC
Turchirollo, Betty, *Asst Vol Coordr,* McLean County Historical Society, McLean County Museum of History, Bloomington IL
Turel, Noa, *Asst Prof,* University of Alabama at Birmingham, Dept of Art & Art History, Birmingham AL (S)
Turk, Christopher, *Prof,* East Los Angeles College, Art Dept, Monterey Park CA (S)
Turk, Gloria, *Librn,* San Jose Museum of Art, Library, San Jose CA
Turkovic, Dana, *Cur Exhib,* Laumeier Sculpture Park, Saint Louis MO
Turley, G Pasha, *Gallery Dir,* Southwestern College, Art Gallery, Chula Vista CA
Turlington, Matthew, *Photog Instr,* Southwestern Community College, Advertising & Graphic Design, Sylva NC (S)
Turlington, Patricia, *Instr,* Wayne Community College, Liberal Arts Dept, Goldsboro NC (S)
Turner, Anderson, *Dir Galleries,* Kent State University, School of Art, Kent OH (S)
Turner, Anderson, *Galleries Dir,* Kent State University, School of Art Galleries, Kent OH
Turner, Carlton, *Exec Dir,* Alternate ROOTS, Inc, Atlanta GA
Turner, Cindy, *Visual Resources Cur,* Ball State University, Architecture Library, Muncie IN
Turner, Colin D, *Exec Dir,* Midwest Art Conservation Center, Minneapolis MN
Turner, Elizabeth, *Univ Prof,* University of Virginia, McIntire Dept of Art, Charlottesville VA (S)
Turner, James, *Instr,* Bethany College, Art Dept, Lindsborg KS (S)
Turner, Jeff, *Asst Prof,* Maryville College, Dept of Fine Arts, Maryville TN (S)
Turner, Jim, *Instr,* Bethany College, Mingenback Art Center, Lindsborg KS
Turner, John D, *Prof,* University of North Alabama, Dept of Art, Florence AL (S)
Turner, Judith, *Dir,* Art Instruction Schools, Education Dept, Minneapolis MN (S)
Turner, Kathy, *Exec Asst,* Art Services International, Alexandria VA
Turner, Kevin, *Assoc Prof,* Indiana University of Pennsylvania, College of Fine Arts, Indiana PA (S)
Turner, Kevin, *Instr (3-D),* Mississippi Gulf Coast Community College-Jackson County Campus, Art Dept, Gautier MS (S)
Turner, Kyle, *Colls Asst,* Art Complex Museum, Carl A Weyerhaeuser Library, Duxbury MA
Turner, Lauren, *Asst Cur for the Coll,* University of North Carolina at Chapel Hill, Ackland Art Museum, Chapel Hill NC
Turner, Lee Ann, *Chmn,* Boise State University, Art Dept, Boise ID (S)
Turner, Luke, *Mgr Exhibs & Colls,* Mills College Art Museum, Oakland CA
Turner, Marcellus, *Exec Dir & Chief Librn,* Seattle Public Library, Arts, Recreation & Literature Dept, Seattle WA
Turner, Marietta, *Instr,* Bismarck State College, Fine Arts Dept, Bismarck ND (S)
Turner, Michele, *Librn,* The Currier Museum of Art, Library, Manchester NH
Turner, Richard, *Prof,* Chapman University, Art Dept, Orange CA (S)
Turner, Steve, *Executive Director,* History Colorado Center Museum, Denver CO
Turner, Sylvia, *Dean of Fine & Performing Arts,* Santa Ana College, Art Dept, Santa Ana CA (S)
Turner, Tom, *Chmn,* Pacific Union College, Art Dept, Angwin CA (S)
Turner-Ingham, Dianne, *Educ Specialist,* Ohio History Connection, National Afro-American Museum & Cultural Center, Wilberforce OH
Turner-Lowe, Susan, *VPres Communs,* The Huntington Library, Art Collections & Botanical Gardens, San Marino CA
Turner-Lowe, Susan, *VPres Communs,* The Huntington Library, Art Collections & Botanical Gardens, Library, San Marino CA
Turner-Rahman, Greg, *Assoc Prof,* University of Idaho College of Art & Architecture, Dept of Art & Design, Moscow ID (S)
Turnham, Stephanie, *Exec Dir,* The Museum of Western Art, Kerrville TX
Turnock, Elizabeth, *Exec Dir,* Garrison Art Center, Garrison NY
Turnure, James, *Prof,* Bucknell University, Dept of Art, Lewisburg PA (S)
Turrill, Catherine, *Chmn,* California State University, Sacramento, Dept of Art, Sacramento CA (S)
Turschman, Rick, *Asst Mgr Security & Guest Servs,* Smith College, Museum of Art, Northampton MA
Turtell, Neal, *Chief Librn,* National Gallery of Art, Washington DC
Turtell, Neal, *Exec Librn,* National Gallery of Art, Library, Washington DC
Turvey, Dana, *Owner & Mgr,* The John L. Clarke Western Art Gallery & Memorial Museum, East Glacier Park MT
Turvey, Malcom, *Prof & Dir, Film & Media Studies,* Tufts University, Dept of Art & Art History, Medford MA (S)
Tuscano, *Prof,* Lynn University, Art & Design Dept, Boca Raton FL (S)
Tush, Peter, *Cur Educ,* Salvador Dali, Library, Saint Petersburg FL
Tusman, Lee, *Adult Educ Cur,* Riverside Art Museum, Library, Riverside CA
Tustin, Kerry, *Asst Prof,* Flagler College, Visual Arts Dept, Saint Augustine FL (S)
Tutt, Trevor, *Coll Mgr,* Saint Joseph Museum, Inc., Saint Joseph MO
Tuttle, Emily, *Instr,* Limestone College, Art Dept, Gaffney SC (S)
Tuttle, Judith, *Consultant,* Tattoo Art Museum, San Francisco CA
Tuttle, Kay, *Exec Dir,* The Light Factory, Charlotte NC
Tuttle, Kevin, *Instr,* Muhlenberg College, Dept of Art, Allentown PA (S)
Tuttle, Lyle, *Dir,* Tattoo Art Museum, San Francisco CA
Tuzzeo, Suzanne, *Adj Instr,* University of West Florida, Dept of Art, Pensacola FL (S)
Twa, Lindsay, *Dir,* Augustana University, Eide-Dalrymple Gallery, Sioux Falls SD
Twachtmann, Jeannette, *Museum Relations,* University of Tampa, Henry B Plant Museum, Tampa FL
Tweedy, Joan, *Asst Prof,* University of North Carolina at Charlotte, Dept Art, Charlotte NC (S)
Twersky, Dana, *Registrar,* Vero Beach Museum of Art, Vero Beach FL
Tweten, Emily, *Event Mgr,* Rochester Art Center, Rochester MN
Twidwell, Joe, *Pres,* Sioux City Art Center, Sioux City IA (S)
Twigg, Andrew, *Treas,* American Institute of Graphic Arts, National Design Center, New York NY
Twiss, Adam J, *Dir Theatre at Barton & Asst Prof Theatre,* Barton College, School of Visual, Performing & Communication Arts, Wilson NC (S)
Twiss-Houting, Beth, *Dir Progs & Servs,* Historical Society of Pennsylvania, Philadelphia PA
Tycko, Joan, *Sec,* Association of Medical Illustrators, Lexington KY
Tyger, Ross, *Events & Van Go,* Susquehanna Art Museum, Harrisburg PA
Tyler, James, *Exec Dir,* Garner Arts Center, Garnerville NY
Tymas-Jones, Raymond, *Dean,* University of Utah, Dept of Art & Art History, Salt Lake City UT (S)

Tymchuk, Dave, *VPres Finance,* Royal Ontario Museum, Toronto ON

Tymchuk, Dave, *VPres Finance,* Royal Ontario Museum, Toronto ON

Tymchuk, Kerry, *Exec Dir,* Oregon Historical Society, Oregon History Museum, Portland OR

Tynes, Kyla, *Community Relations,* Saint Mary's College of California, Museum of Art, Moraga CA

Tyre, William, *Exec Dir & Cur,* Glessner House Museum, Chicago IL

Tyree, Morgan, *Asst Prof,* Northwest Community College, Dept of Art, Powell WY (S)

Tyrer, Nancy, *Asst Dir,* Heritage Museums & Gardens, Sandwich MA

Tyrrell, Kimberly, *Studio Mgr,* Clayworks Gallery, Charlotte NC

Tyson, Rhonda R, *Exhib & Design Mgr,* Jamestown-Yorktown Foundation, Jamestown Settlement, Williamsburg VA

Tyzack, Michael, *Chmn Studio Art,* College of Charleston, School of the Arts, Charleston SC (S)

Udechukwu, Obiora, *Prof,* St Lawrence University, Dept of Fine Arts, Canton NY (S)

Udesen, Britt, *Dir Educ,* Sun Valley Center for the Arts, Dept of Fine Art, Sun Valley ID (S)

Udick, James, *Coll Admin,* Hockaday Museum of Art, Kalispell MT

Uduehi, Joseph, *Assoc Prof,* University of Southern Indiana, Art & Design Dept, Evansville IN (S)

Uetz, M Katherine, *Dir,* Xavier University, Art Gallery, Cincinnati OH

Ueukerman, Kristen, *Secy,* Marblehead Arts Association, Inc, Marblehead MA

Uhlein, Thomas, *Asst Prof,* William Paterson University, Dept Arts, Wayne NJ (S)

Uhlenbrock, Jaimee, *Assoc Cur of Coll,* State University of New York at New Paltz, Samuel Dorsky Museum of Art, New Paltz NY

Ujczo, Anne, *Facilities Planner,* Federal Reserve Bank of Cleveland, Cleveland OH

Ujjainwala, Tasneem, *Undergrad Admin, Music,* Carleton University, School for Studies in Art & Culture, Ottawa ON (S)

Ulibarri, Nadine, *Cur,* Pueblo of Pojoaque, Poeh Museum, Santa Fe NM

Ullery, Cathy, *Dir Employee & Organizational Develop,* Georgia O'Keeffe Museum, Santa Fe NM

Ulloa, Derby, *Prof,* Florida Community College at Jacksonville, South Campus, Art Dept, Jacksonville FL (S)

Ulmer, Sean, *Exec Dir,* Cedar Rapids Museum of Art, Cedar Rapids IA

Ulrich, David, *Art Dept Chair,* Cornish College of the Arts, Art Dept, Seattle WA (S)

Ulrich, Helen, *Asst Librn,* Ball State University, Architecture Library, Muncie IN

Ulrich, Keith, *Cur,* Swedish American Museum, Chicago IL

Ulry, James E, *Acad Dir,* Johnson Atelier Technical Institute of Sculpture, Trenton NJ (S)

Ultan, Deborah K, *Arts, Architecture & Landscape Architecture Librn,* University of Minnesota, Arts & Architecture Collections, Minneapolis MN

Ultan, Deborah, *Library Head,* University of Minnesota, Architecture & Landscape Library, Minneapolis MN

Um, Nancy, *Assoc Prof,* Binghamton University, Art History Department, Binghamton NY (S)

Umana, Pedro, *Pastor,* Mission San Miguel Museum, San Miguel CA

Umfleet, LeRae, *Asst Dir,* Tryon Palace, New Bern NC

Umlauf, Karl, *Prof & Artist in Res,* Baylor University - College of Arts and Sciences, Dept of Art, Waco TX (S)

Umstead, Linda, *Corresp Secy,* Association of Hawaii Artists, Honolulu HI

Unander, Lisa, *Dir Educ,* The Long Island Museum of American Art, History & Carriages, Stony Brook NY

Unchester, Robert, *Exhib Mgr,* Cameron Art Museum, Wilmington NC

Underhill, Jane, *2nd VPres,* Arizona Watercolor Association, Phoenix AZ

Underhill, Kristin, *Admin,* Hope College, DePree Art Center & Gallery, Holland MI

Underhill, Kristin, *Contact,* Hope College, Dept of Art & Art History, Holland MI (S)

Underwood, Candace, *Cur,* Colquitt County Arts Center, Moultrie GA

Underwood, David, *Prof,* Carson-Newman University, Art Dept, Jefferson City TN (S)

Unger, Fred, *Pres Bd Trustees,* Beck Center for the Arts, Lakewood OH

Unger, Geri, *Dir Educ,* Cleveland Botanical Garden, Eleanor Squire Library, Cleveland OH

Unger, Howard, *Prof,* Ocean County College, Humanities Dept, Toms River NJ (S)

Unrau, Janelle, *Exec Dir,* Saskatchewan Association of Architects, Saskatoon SK

Unruh, Allison, *Assoc Cur,* Washington University, Mildred Lane Kemper Art Museum, Saint Louis MO

Unterschulz, Cheryl, *Asst Prof,* Lincoln University, Dept Visual and Performing Arts, Jefferson City MO (S)

Unvir, Amira, *Dir Library,* College of Saint Elizabeth, Mahoney Library, Morristown NJ

Unwin-Barkley, Pam, *VPres,* Warwick Museum of Art, Warwick RI

Upham, Alison, *Develop & Mem,* Museums Sonoma County, Art Museum of Sonoma County & History Museum of Sonoma County, Santa Rosa CA

Uphoff, Joseph A, *Exec Dir (Arjuna Lib) & Ed in Chief, Journal of Regional Criticism,* Arjuna Library, Digital Visual Dream Laboratory & Acoustic Studio, Colorado Springs CO

Upitis, Alise, *Pub Art Cur,* Massachusetts Institute of Technology, List Visual Arts Center, Cambridge MA

Upton, Cody, *Exec Dir,* American Academy of Arts & Letters, New York NY

Uraneck, Joan, *Instr,* Maine College of Art, Portland ME (S)

Urban, Erin, *Dir,* The Noble Maritime Collection, Staten Island NY

Urbanelli, Lora, *Dir,* Montclair Art Museum, Montclair NJ

Urbanick, Paul, *Chmn Humanities,* City Colleges of Chicago, Harold Washington College, Chicago IL (S)

Urbanik, Markus, *Ceramics,* Central Wyoming College, Art Center, Riverton WY (S)

Urbanz, Angela, *Sr Prog Dir,* Arts Midwest, Minneapolis MN

Ure, Maureen O'Hara, *Asst Prof Lectr,* University of Utah, Dept of Art & Art History, Salt Lake City UT (S)

Uretsky, Jamie, *Acting Dir & Cur,* New Bedford Art Museum/Artworks!, New Bedford MA

Urian, Edward A, *Media Arts & Animation,* Art Institute of Pittsburgh, Pittsburgh PA (S)

Urness, Janine, *Office Mgr,* Avila University, Thornhill Art Gallery, Kansas City MO

Uroskie, Andrew, *Asst Prof,* Stony Brook University, College of Arts & Sciences, Dept of Art, Stony Brook NY (S)

Ursillo, Linda, *Dir Finance,* Boca Raton Museum of Art, Boca Raton FL

Ursillo, Linda, *Dir Finance,* Boca Raton Museum of Art, Library, Boca Raton FL

Urso, Len, *Prof,* Rochester Institute of Technology, School of Design, Rochester NY (S)

Urso, Lori, *Exec Dir,* Slater Mill, Old Slater Mill Association, Pawtucket RI

Usai, Paolo Cherchi, *Cur Motion Picture Coll,* George Eastman Museum, Rochester NY

Ushenko, Audrey, *Prof,* Indiana-Purdue University, Dept of Fine Arts, Fort Wayne IN (S)

Usher-Rankin, Paige, *Mem Coordr,* Real Art Ways (RAW), Hartford CT

Usherwood, Ron, *Exec Dir,* Taos Center for the Arts, Stables Gallery, Taos NM

Ussler, Christine, *Prof Practice,* Lehigh University, Dept of Art, Architecture & Design, Bethlehem PA (S)

Utter, Jodie, *Conservator, Works on Paper,* Amon Carter Museum of American Art, Fort Worth TX

Utz, Karen, *Cur & Historian,* Sloss Furnaces National Historic Landmark, Birmingham AL

Uyekawa, Jim, *Prof,* East Los Angeles College, Art Dept, Monterey Park CA (S)

Vaccaro, Kathleen, *Adj Prof,* Saint Joseph's University, Art Dept, Philadelphia PA (S)

Vaccaro, Mary, *Assoc Prof,* University of Texas at Arlington, Art & Art History Department, Arlington TX (S)

Vaccaro, Sal, *Mktg Mgr,* Caramoor Center for Music & the Arts, Inc, Rosen House at Caramoor, Katonah NY

Vaigardson, Val, *Asst Prof,* Rhodes College, Dept of Art, Memphis TN (S)

Vaitkute, Karile, *Dir Educ & Edit,* Balzekas Museum of Lithuanian Culture, Chicago IL

Vajracharya, Gautama, *Instr,* University of Wisconsin, Madison, Dept of Art History, Madison WI (S)

Valand, Roger, *Asst Prof,* Spring Arbor College, Art Dept, Spring Arbor MI (S)

Valandani, Jasmine, *Educ Dir,* Museum of Northwest Art, La Conner WA

Valavanis, Liz, *Pres,* South Shore Arts, Munster IN

Valderrama, Tonito, *Mus Educator,* C W Post Campus of Long Island University, Hillwood Art Museum, Brookville NY

Valdez, Julio, *Instr,* Woodstock School of Art, Inc, Woodstock NY (S)

Valdez, Ralph, *Exec Dir,* Dearborn Community Arts Council, Padzieski Art Gallery, Dearborn MI

Valdez, Zachary, *Administrative Assistant,* Columbia University, Miriam & Ira D Wallach Art Gallery, New York NY

Valencia, Romolo, *Instr Graphic Arts,* Honolulu Community College, Commercial Art Dept, Honolulu HI (S)

Valenti, Carlina, *VPres Catalog,* Catharine Lorillard Wolfe, New York NY

Valentin, Noel, *Permanent Coll Mgr,* El Museo del Barrio, New York NY

Valentin, Velky, *Controller,* The Africa Center, New York NY

Valentine, John, *New Media & Animation,* Southeastern Louisiana University, Art & Design, Hammond LA (S)

Valentine, Terry, *Prof,* Concordia University, Division of Performing & Visual Arts, Mequon WI (S)

Valenza, Ronile, *Treasurer,* Marin Society of Artists Inc, San Rafael CA

Valera, Philip J, *Asst Prof Communs,* Barton College, School of Visual, Performing & Communication Arts, Wilson NC (S)

Valerio, James, *Prof,* Northwestern University, Evanston, Dept of Art Theory & Practice, Evanston IL (S)

Valerio, William, *Dir & CEO,* Woodmere Art Museum Inc, Philadelphia PA

Valero, M Teresa, *Dir,* University of Tulsa, School of Art, Tulsa OK (S)

Valero, Meghan, *Admin,* Artists Association of Nantucket, Nantucket MA

Valiente, Jessica, *Librn,* University of Puerto Rico, Museum of Anthropology, History & Art, Rio Piedras PR

Valines, Ashlye, *Curatorial Asst,* Florida International University, The Patricia & Phillip Frost Art Museum, Miami FL

Valiquette, Sharon, *Pres,* Rensselaer Newman Foundation Chapel + Cultural Center, The Gallery at the Chapel & Cultural Center, Troy NY

Valladao, Roxanne, *Instr,* Feather River Community College, Art Dept, Quincy CA (S)

Valle, Chris, *Prof,* University of Tampa, College of Arts & Letters, Tampa FL (S)

Valleau, Steven, *Carver-in-Residence,* Wendell Gilley, Southwest Harbor ME

Vallee, Francois, *Coordr,* La Chambre Blanche, Quebec QC

Vallette, Marcie, *Graphics & Data Manager,* Bryan Memorial Gallery, Cambridge VT

Valley, Derek R, *Dir,* State Capital Museum, Olympia WA
Vallila, Marja, *Assoc Prof,* State University of New York at Albany, Art Dept, Albany NY (S)
Vallis, Beth, *Dir,* Dartmouth Heritage Museum, Dartmouth NS
Vallo, Brian, *Dir,* School for Advanced Research (SAR), Indian Arts Research Center, Santa Fe NM
Valmestad, Liv, *Art Librn,* University of Manitoba, Architecture & Fine Arts Library, Winnipeg MB
Valverde, Fernanda, *Conservator of Photography,* Amon Carter Museum of American Art, Fort Worth TX
van Aalst, Kirsten, *Asst Prof,* Norwich University, Dept of Architecture and Art, Northfield VT (S)
Van Aken, Annette, *Registrar,* University of Minnesota, Frederick R Weisman Art Museum, Minneapolis MN
van Alfen, Peter, *Cur,* American Numismatic Society, New York NY
Van Allen, Katherine, *Mng Dir Mus Svcs,* Missouri Historical Society, Missouri History Museum, Saint Louis MO
Van Ameyden, Vicki, *Head Printmaking,* Kalamazoo Institute of Arts, KIA School, Kalamazoo MI (S)
Van Auken, Michelle, *Information Serv Technologist,* Colgate University, Picker Art Gallery, Hamilton NY
Van Ausdall, Kristen, *Prof,* Kenyon College, Art Dept, Gambier OH (S)
Van Balgooy, Max, *Dir Interpretation,* National Trust for Historic Preservation, Washington DC
Van Benscheten, Elijah, *Instr,* Adrian College, Art & Design Dept, Adrian MI (S)
Van Benschoten, Elijah, *Instr,* South Dakota State University, Dept of Visual Arts, Brookings SD (S)
Van Bockel, Joni, *Mktg & Outreach Coord,* Soap Factory, Minneapolis MN
Van Brunt, Carl, *Gallery Dir,* Woodstock Artists Association & Museum, Woodstock NY
Van Buren, David, *Chmn,* University of Wisconsin-Platteville, Dept of Fine Art, Platteville WI (S)
Van Camp, Julie, *Secy & Treas,* American Society for Aesthetics, Denver CO
van der Graaff, Ivo, *Asst Prof,* University of New Hampshire, Dept of Art & Art History, Durham NH (S)
van der Leer, David, *Exec Dir,* Van Alen Institute, New York NY
van der Plas, Claire, *Asst Prof Art,* Adams State College, Dept of Visual Arts, Alamosa CO (S)
Van Deursen, Lyndi, *Mem Coordr,* The University of Kentucky Art Museum, Lexington KY
Van Deusen, Mimi, *Dir & Cur,* Village of Potsdam, Potsdam Public Museum, Potsdam NY
van Dijk, Ann, *Div Head Art History,* Northern Illinois University, School of Art & Design, DeKalb IL (S)
Van Dorp, Dale, *Mgr Performing Arts,* Henry Ford Community College, McKenzie Fine Art Ctr, Dearborn MI (S)
Van Duesen, Patrick, *Prof,* Daytona Beach Community College, Dept of Fine Arts & Visual Arts, Daytona Beach FL (S)
Van Duyne, Sue, *Instr,* Ocean City Arts Center, Ocean City NJ (S)
Van Dyk, Stephen H, *Dept Head, Librn,* Cooper Hewitt, Smithsonian Design Museum, Library, New York NY
Van Dyke, Dan R, *Exec Dir,* Phelps County Historical Society, Donald O. Lindgren Library, Holdrege NE
van Dyke, James, *Dean Arts, Humanities & Letters,* Marian University, Art Dept, Fond Du Lac WI (S)
Van Dyke, Lissa, *Librn,* Lyman Allyn Art Museum, Hendel Library, New London CT
van Eijnsbergen, Ellen, *Dir & Cur,* Burnaby Art Gallery, Burnaby BC
Van Gelderen, Annie, *Pres & CEO,* Birmingham Bloomfield Art Center, Art Center, Birmingham MI
Van Gelderen, Annie, *Pres & Ceo,* Birmingham Bloomfield Art Center, Birmingham MI (S)
Van Gent, Elona, *Assoc Dean,* University of Michigan, Ann Arbor, Penny W Stamps School of Art & Design, Ann Arbor MI (S)
Van Haaften, Rene, *Exec Dir,* Brownsville Art League, Brownsville Museum of Fine Art, Brownsville TX
Van Heerden, Peter, *Exec Dir,* Westport Arts Center, Westport CT
Van Hook, Bailey, *Art Chair & Interim Staff Dir,* Virginia Polytechnic Institute & State University, Armory Art Gallery, Blacksburg VA
Van Hook, L Bailey, *Head Dept,* Virginia Polytechnic Institute & State University, Dept of Art & Art History, Blacksburg VA (S)
Van Hooser, Karen, *Exec Admin,* The Society of Layerists in Multi-Media (SLMM), Albuquerque NM
Van Hooten, Joan, *Exec Dir,* Arts Council for Long Beach, Long Beach CA
Van Huffel, Hana, *Mus Resources Coordr,* Boise Art Museum, Boise ID
Van Keuren, Francis, *Prof Art History,* University of Georgia, Franklin College of Arts & Sciences, Lamar Dodd School of Art, Athens GA (S)
Van Lusk, Kyle, *Instr,* Appalachian State University, Dept of Art, Boone NC (S)
Van Meter, Kay, *Assoc Mgr,* ArtSpace/Lima, Lima OH
Van Meter, Peggy, *Cataloger,* Fulton County Historical Society Inc, Fulton County Museum (Tetzlaff Reference Room), Rochester IN
Van Miegroet, Hans J, *Chair & Prof,* Duke University, Dept of Art, Art History & Visual Studies, Durham NC (S)
Van Ness, Venus, *Archivist,* Norman Rockwell Museum, Library, Stockbridge MA
Van Nest, Dana, *Communs,* Henry Gallery Association, Henry Art Gallery, Seattle WA
Van Nort, Sydney, *Archivist,* City College of the City University of New York, Morris Raphael Cohen Library, New York NY
Van Nostrand, Jess, *Exhibition Cur,* Cornish College of the Arts, Fisher Gallery, Seattle WA
van Osnabrugge, William, *Pres,* Art Center Sarasota, Sarasota FL (S)
Van Patten, Kristen, *Instr,* Southwestern University, Sarofim School of Fine Art, Dept of Art & Art History, Georgetown TX (S)
van Rarenswaay, Megan, *Dir,* Moravian Historical Society, Nazareth PA
Van Rooyen, Robin, *Art Gallery Dir,* Grand Rapids Community College, Visual Art Dept, Grand Rapids MI (S)
Van Roy, Eugene, *Electronic Imag & Print Instr,* Western Wisconsin Technical College, Graphics Division, La Crosse WI (S)
Van Schaack, Eric, *Prof,* Colgate University, Dept of Art & Art History, Hamilton NY (S)
Van Sickle, Delene, *Admin Asst,* Washburn University, Mulvane Art Museum, Topeka KS
Van Strander, Kitren, *Dir,* Rochester Institute of Technology, Corporate Education & Training, Rochester NY
Van Suchtelen, Adrian, *Prof,* Utah State University, Dept of Art, Logan UT (S)
Van Tassel, Rhoda, *Instr,* Muskingum College, Art Department, New Concord OH (S)
Van Tomme, Niel, *Dir Arts & Media,* Provisions Library, Provisions Research Center for Arts & Social Change, Fairfax VA
Van Wagenberg, Anke, *Curator,* Academy Art Museum, Easton MD
Van Wey, Ken, *Program Specialist,* United States Department of the Interior, Indian Arts & Crafts Board, Washington DC
Van Winkle, Sarah, *Prog Coordr,* University of South Carolina Beaufort Art Gallery, Beaufort SC
Van Zante, Gary, *Cur Architecture & Design,* Massachusetts Institute of Technology, MIT Museum, Cambridge MA
Van Zanten, David, *Prof,* Northwestern University, Evanston, Dept of Art History, Evanston IL (S)
Van Zanten, Denise, *Lib Dir,* Manchester City Library, Manchester NH
VanAllen, David, *Asst Prof,* Mount Mercy University, Art Dept, Cedar Rapids IA (S)
VanAntwerp, Deb, *Dir Vols,* McLean County Historical Society, McLean County Museum of History, Bloomington IL
Vanaria, Cathy, *Chmn Art Dept,* Western Connecticut State University, School of Visual & Performing Arts, Danbury CT (S)
Vanausdall, John, *Pres & CEO,* Eiteljorg Museum of American Indians & Western Art, Indianapolis IN
VanBemmel, Liz, *Educ Project Mgr,* Kirkland Arts Center, KAC Gallery, Kirkland WA
Vance, Alex, *Exec Dir,* Bergstrom-Mahler Museum of Glass, Neenah WI
Vance, Steve, *Instr,* University of Wisconsin-Platteville, Dept of Fine Art, Platteville WI (S)
Vanche, Sheri, *Registrar,* Eastern Shore Art Association, Inc, Eastern Shore Art Center, Fairhope AL
Vancil, Colleen, *Bd Pres,* Woodburn Art Center, Glatt House Gallery, Woodburn OR
Vandenheuver, Alysa, *Educ Dir,* Gunnison Arts Center, Gunnison CO
Vander Kool, Yvonne, *Art Educ Coordr,* Nanaimo Art Gallery, Nanaimo BC
Vanderbrug, Kelly, *Asst Prof,* North Park University, Art Dept, Chicago IL (S)
Vanderburgh, Denise, *Admin Asst,* Ithaca College, Fine Art Dept, Ithaca NY (S)
Vanderhill, Rein, *Rotation Exhib Coordr,* Northwestern College, Te Paske Gallery, Orange City IA
Vanderhoff, Darci, *Chief Information Officer,* The Phillips Collection, Washington DC
VanderKaay, Cody, *Asst Prof,* Oakland University, Dept of Art & Art History, Rochester MI (S)
Vandermeer, Alicia, *Deputy Dir & Chief Advancement Officer,* Art Gallery of Ontario, Toronto ON
Vanderpool, Guy C, *Dir,* Panhandle-Plains Historical Museum, Canyon TX
Vanderpool, Guy, *Director of Development & Communications,* Amon Carter Museum of American Art, Fort Worth TX
VanDerpool, Karen, *Prof Emeritus,* California State University, Chico, Department of Art & Art History, Chico CA (S)
Vandersypen, Sarah Cortell, *Develop & Community Rels,* Alexandria Museum of Art, Alexandria LA
Vanderup, Sarah, *Chair & Assoc Prof,* California State University, Bakersfield, Dept of Art, Bakersfield CA (S)
Vanderwal, Anne, *Dir Spec Events,* New-York Historical Society, Museum, New York NY
Vandest, Bill, *Theater Coordr,* Creighton University, Fine & Performing Arts Dept, Omaha NE (S)
Vandeville, Denise, *Dean,* Finlandia Univ, International School of Art and Design, Hancock MI (S)
VanDyke, Fred, *Prof,* Salt Lake Community College, Graphic Design Dept, Salt Lake City UT (S)
VanHorn, Wendy, *Dir Educ,* Museum of Ventura County, Ventura CA
VanKeuren, Philip, *Prof,* Southern Methodist University, Meadows School of the Arts - Division of Art, Dallas TX (S)
vanMeenen, Karen, *Ed Afterimage,* Visual Studies Workshop, Rochester NY (S)
Vanouse, Paul, *Emerging Practices,* University at Buffalo, State University of New York, Dept of Visual Studies, Buffalo NY (S)
Vanover, Millie, *Research Assistant,* Panhandle-Plains Historical Museum, Research Center, Canyon TX
Vanscotter, Edward, *Cur Colls,* Carlsbad Museum & Art Center, Carlsbad NM
Vanture, Marnie, *Operations Coordinator,* Albin Polasek Museum & Sculpture Gardens, Winter Park FL
Vantz, Mickel, *Cur,* Cherokee Heritage Center, Park Hill OK
Vaquedano, Kimberly, *Gallery Coordr & Technology Adminr,* Bronx Council on the Arts, Longwood Arts Gallery @ Hostos, Bronx NY

Vardaro, Sherry, *Bldg Coordr,* Allegheny College, Bowman, Megahan & Penelec Galleries, Meadville PA
Varga, Darrell, *Chair, Art History & Critical Studies Div,* Nova Scotia College of Art & Design, Halifax NS (S)
Vargas, Kathy, *Chmn,* University of the Incarnate Word, Art Dept, San Antonio TX (S)
Vargas, William, *Colls Mgr,* Rubell Family Collection and Contemporary Arts Foundation, Miami FL
Vargo, Chris, *Asst Dir Opers,* State of North Carolina, Battleship North Carolina, Wilmington NC
Varnadoe, Kimberly, *Assoc Prof,* Salem Academy & College, Art Dept, Winston-Salem NC (S)
Varner, Eric, *Assoc Prof,* Emory University, Art History Dept, Atlanta GA (S)
Varone, Jason, *Info Serv,* New York University, Institute of Fine Arts Visual Resources Collection, New York NY
Varty, Anita, *Dir Bus Opers,* Port Huron Museum, Port Huron MI
Vasher-Dean, April, *Dir,* The State University of New York at Potsdam, The Art Museum, Potsdam NY
Vasiliauskiene, Regina, *Chmn Mem, Com Rels & Mus Shop Mgr,* Balzekas Museum of Lithuanian Culture, Chicago IL
Vasquez, Clare, *Pub Serv Librn,* Saint Louis Art Museum, Richardson Memorial Library, Saint Louis MO
Vasquez, Oneida, *Mus Mgr,* Van Cortlandt House Museum, Bronx NY
Vassallo, Christina, *Exec Dir,* SPACES, Cleveland OH
Vassar, Andrew, *Instr Art History,* Northeastern State University, College of Arts & Letters, Tahlequah OK (S)
Vassar, Theodore, *Asst Prof Art,* Monroe County Community College, Humanities Division, Monroe MI (S)
Vassar, Theodore, *Asst Prof Art,* Monroe County Community College, Fine Arts Council, Monroe MI
Vatandoost, Cyrus, *Exec VPres,* Nossi College of Art, Nashville TN (S)
Vatandoost, Nossi, *Founder, CEO & Pres,* Nossi College of Art, Nashville TN (S)
Vatsky, Sharon, *Dir Educ School & Family Progs,* Solomon R Guggenheim Museum, New York NY
Vaugeois, Heather, *Dir Advancement,* Dundas Valley School of Art, Dundas ON (S)
Vaughan, Daleana, *Educ Dir,* Fort Smith Regional Art Museum, Fort Smith AR
Vaughan, James M, *PHMC Exec Dir,* Pennsylvania Historical & Museum Commission, The State Museum of Pennsylvania, Harrisburg PA
Vaughan, James, *VPres,* National Trust for Historic Preservation, Washington DC
Vaughan, Janet, *VPres Memberships & Programs,* American Alliance of Museums, Arlington VA
Vaughn, Dorothy, *Co-Gallery Dir,* Mississippi Valley State University, Fine Arts Dept, Itta Bena MS (S)
Vaughn, Jeff, *Assoc Prof,* Lewis & Clark Community College, Art Dept, Godfrey IL (S)
Vaughn, Katherine, *Art Instr,* John C Calhoun, Art Gallery, Decatur AL
Vaughn, Melanie, *Program Assistant,* Iredell Museums, Statesville NC
Vaughn, Patti, *Dir Admin Operations,* Boston Architectural College, McCormick Gallery, Boston MA
Vaughn, Renae, *Treas,* Art and History Museums - Maitland, Maitland FL
Vaughn, Ron, *Pres of the Univ,* University of Tampa, Scarfone/Hartley Gallery, Tampa FL
Vaux, Richard, *Prof,* Adelphi University, Dept of Art & Art History, Garden City NY (S)
Vaz, Tina, *Deputy Dir & Chief Global Commun,* Solomon R Guggenheim Museum, New York NY
Vazquez Contreras, Ileamarie, *Reg,* Museo de las Americas, Viejo San Juan PR
Vazquez, Yoland, *Admin Asst,* University of Puerto Rico, Museum of Anthropology, History & Art, Rio Piedras PR
Veatch, James, *Assoc Prof,* University of Massachusetts Lowell, Dept of Art, Lowell MA (S)
Veazey, Shari, *Dir Develop,* Mississippi Museum of Art, Howorth Library, Jackson MS
Vecchiola, Rina, *Art & Architecture Librn,* Washington University, Kenneth & Nancy Kranzberg Art & Architecture Library, Saint Louis MO
Veda, Chris, *Instr,* Luzerne County Community College, Commercial Art Dept, Nanticoke PA (S)
Vedaa, Lisa, *Cur,* Historical and Cultural Society of Clay County, Hjemkomst Center, Moorhead MN
Veeder, Betty, *Secy,* St Mary Chapter Louisiana Landmarks Society, Grevemberg House Museum, Franklin LA
Vega Vega, Gloria A, *VPres,* La Casa del Libro Museum, San Juan PR
Vega, Aro Ivonne Maria Marcial, *Chancellor,* Escuela de Artes Plasticas de Puerto Rico, San Juan PR (S)
Vega, Randi, *Dir Cultural Affairs,* School 33 Art Center, Baltimore MD
Vega, Sergio, *Prof,* University of Florida, School of Art & Art History, Gainesville FL (S)
Veikley, Avis, *Dir,* Minot State University, Northwest Art Center, Minot ND
Veillon, Monica, *Admin Asst,* McNeese State University, Dept of Visual Arts, Lake Charles LA (S)
Veith, Gene Edward, *Dir,* Concordia University, Division of Performing & Visual Arts, Mequon WI (S)
Velasco, Maria, *Asst Prof,* University of Kansas, The School of the Arts, Dept of Visual Art, Lawrence KS (S)
Velasco, Zoot, *Center Adminr,* Muckenthaler Cultural Center, Fullerton CA
Velasquez, Alan, *Unit Supervisor,* Tulane University, Architecture Library, New Orleans LA
Velasquez, Geraldine, *Prof,* Georgian Court University, Dept of Art, Lakewood NJ (S)
Velasquez, Joseph, *Asst Prof Printmaking,* Florida Atlantic University, D F Schmidt College of Arts & Letters Dept of Visual Arts & Art History, Boca Raton FL (S)
Velasquez, Roxana, *Executive Director,* San Diego Museum of Art, San Diego CA
Velders, Deborah, *Dir,* Cameron Art Museum, Wilmington NC
Velders, Deborah, *Dir,* Mobile Museum of Art, Library, Mobile AL
Velders, Deborah, *Dir,* Mobile Museum of Art, Mobile AL
Veliz, Ron, *Owner,* Alaska House Art Gallery, Fairbanks AK
Velken, Jacquelyne, *Sr Vis Svcs Mgr,* Florida International University, The Patricia & Phillip Frost Art Museum, Miami FL
Venable, Charles, *Melvin and Bren Simon Dir & CEO,* Newfields, Indianapolis IN
Veneman, Katherine, *Cur Educ,* University of Houston, Blaffer Art Museum, Houston TX
Veneziano, Martina, *Gallery Educator,* Estevan National Exhibition Centre Inc, Estevan Art Gallery & Museum, Estevan SK
Venker, Josef, *Asst Prof,* Seattle University, Dept of Art & Art History, Seattle WA (S)
Venner, Tom, *Head Dept,* Eastern Michigan University, Dept of Art, Ypsilanti MI (S)
Vensel, William, *Dept Chmn,* Ohio Dominican College, Art Dept, Columbus OH (S)
Ventimiglia, John T, *Instr,* Maine College of Art, Portland ME (S)
Ventis, Summer, *Adjunct Faculty,* Southern Oregon University, Art & Art History Dept, Ashland OR (S)
Ventrudo, Meg, *CEO,* Jacques Marchais Museum of Tibetan Art, Staten Island NY
Venz, Pamela, *Art Chair Prof,* Birmingham-Southern College, Art & Art History, Birmingham AL (S)
Venz, Pamela, *Prof,* Birmingham Southern College, Doris Wainwright Kennedy Art Center, Birmingham AL
Ver Hague, James, *Prof,* Rochester Institute of Technology, School of Design, Rochester NY (S)
Vera, Maria Garcia, *Dir Prof,* Inter American University of Puerto Rico, Fine Arts Dept -Art Program, San German PR (S)
VerBrugghen, Kasandra, *Pres,* National Alliance for Media Arts & Culture, San Francisco CA
Verdon, Ron, *Head Dept,* University of Wisconsin-Stout, Dept of Art & Design, Menomonie WI (S)
Vergara, Lisa, *Prof Emerita,* City University of New York, PhD Program in Art History, New York NY (S)
Vergne, Philippe, *Dir,* The Museum of Contemporary Art (MOCA), MOCA Grand Avenue, Los Angeles CA
Verhoeven, Anneliese, *Preparator,* University of Minnesota Duluth, Tweed Museum of Art, Duluth MN
Verhoff, Andrew J, *Mgr,* The Ohio Historical Society, Inc, Campus Martius Museum & Ohio River Museum, Marietta OH
Verjee, Zainub, *Exec Dir,* Ontario Association of Art Galleries, Toronto ON
Verkerk, Dorothy, *Assoc Prof,* University of North Carolina at Chapel Hill, Art Dept, Chapel Hill NC (S)
Verlaan, Saskia, *Registrarial Asst.,* New York University, Grey Art Gallery, New York NY
Verlaque, Laura, *Colls Mgr,* Pasadena Museum of History, Pasadena CA
Vermelznd, Cate, *Term Professor,* Concordia University, Art and Design Department, Saint Paul MN (S)
Verna, Gaetane, *Dir,* Harbourfront Centre, The Power Plant Contemporary Art Gallery, Toronto ON
Vernon, Mary, *Prof,* Southern Methodist University, Meadows School of the Arts - Division of Art, Dallas TX (S)
Vernon, Samantha, *Adjunct Asst Prof,* Vassar College, Art Dept, Poughkeepsie NY (S)
Veros, Stacey, *Bd Secy,* Carteret County Historical Society, The History Place, Morehead City NC
Verschoor, Lynn, *Dir,* South Dakota State University, South Dakota Art Museum, Brookings SD
Vertacnik, David, *Assoc Prof,* University of Kansas, The School of the Arts, Dept of Visual Art, Lawrence KS (S)
Veshia, Lori, *Dir Finance & Admin,* Albany Institute of History & Art, Albany NY
Vessey, Alexis, *Studio Coordr,* Nova Scotia Centre for Craft & Design, Mary E Black Gallery, Halifax NS
Vetare, Margaret, *Cur Public Educ,* Vassar College, The Frances Lehman Loeb Art Center, Poughkeepsie NY
Vettel, Greg, *Exhib Coordr,* North Dakota Museum of Art, Grand Forks ND
Vicario, Gilbert, *Chief Cur,* Phoenix Art Museum, Phoenix AZ
Vicens, Nury, *Instr,* Main Line Art Center, Haverford PA (S)
Vicich, Gerald, *Instr,* Pierce College, Art Dept, Woodland Hills CA (S)
Vick-Knueiper, Mel, *Cur,* L D Brinkman, Kerrville TX
Vickerd, Brandon, *Assoc Prof & Chair, Dept Visual Art & Art History,* York University, School of the Arts, Media, Performance & Design, Toronto ON (S)
Vidarte, Juan Ignacio, *Deputy Dir & Chief Officer Global Strategies,* Solomon R Guggenheim Museum, New York NY
Videkanic, Bojana, *Asst Prof & Assoc Chair, Undergrad Studies,* University of Waterloo, Dept of Fine Arts, Waterloo ON (S)
Vidergar, Stephanie, *Assoc Mktg & Commun,* San Jose Museum of Art, Library, San Jose CA
Viditz-Ward, Vera, *Prof,* Bloomsburg University, Dept of Art & Art History, Bloomsburg PA (S)
Viebranz, Curt, *Pres & CEO,* George Washington's Mount Vernon, Mount Vernon VA
Viebranz, Curt, *Pres & CEO,* George Washington's Mount Vernon, The Fred W Smith National Library for the Study of George Washington, Mount Vernon VA

Vielbig, Bernadette, *Asst Prof,* Spokane Falls Community College, Fine Arts Dept, Spokane WA (S)

Vienneau, Larry, *Instr,* Century College, Humanities Dept, White Bear Lake MN (S)

Viens, Katheryn P, *Dir,* Old Colony Historical Society, Library, Taunton MA

Viens, Katheryn, *Dir Research,* Massachusetts Historical Society, Boston MA

Viera, Diane, *Exec VPres & COO,* Historic New England, Boston MA

Viera, Ricardo, *Dir Exhib & Coll,* Lehigh University Art Galleries, Museum Operation, Bethlehem PA

Viera, Ricardo, *Prof,* Lehigh University, Dept of Art, Architecture & Design, Bethlehem PA (S)

Vierus, Jenny, *Admin Asst,* Sandwich Historical Society, Center Sandwich NH

Vierya, Emily, *VPres,* Junction City Arts Council Gallery, Junction City KS

Vieter, Rosemary, *Pres,* Bowne House Historical Society, Flushing NY

Vietgen, Peter, *Pres,* Canadian Society for Education Through Art, Victoria BC

Viggers Nordin, Judith, *Pres,* Arts Club of Washington, James Monroe House, Washington DC

Vigilante, Amy, *Assoc Instr,* University of Florida, School of Art & Art History, Gainesville FL (S)

Vigilante, Amy, *Dir,* University of Florida, University Gallery, Gainesville FL

Vigiletti, Christine, *Asst Registrar,* Los Angeles County Museum of Art, Robert Gore Rifkind Center for German Expressionist Studies, Los Angeles CA

Vihstadt, Heather, *Dir Develop,* High Desert Museum, Bend OR

Vikram, Anuradha, *Artistic Director,* 18th Street Arts Complex, Santa Monica CA

Vilayphonh, Catzie, *Asst to Dir,* University of Pennsylvania, Institute of Contemporary Art, Philadelphia PA

Vilbar, Sinead, *Cur Japanese Art,* The Cleveland Museum of Art, Cleveland OH

Vilella, Maria Angela Lopez, *Exec Dir,* Museo de las Americas, Viejo San Juan PR

Viljoen, Madeleine, *Cur Prints & Photogs,* The New York Public Library, Print Room, New York NY

Villa, Michelle, *Registrar,* City of El Paso, El Paso Museum of Art, El Paso TX

Villalobos, Patricia, *Print Media,* Western Michigan University, Frostic School of Art, Kalamazoo MI (S)

Villalonga, Lionel, *Dir Gen,* ASTED Inc, Montreal QC

Villalonga, Yuneikys, *Asst Cur,* Lehman College Art Gallery, Bronx NY

Villalpando, Kim, *Dir,* George Phippen, Phippen Museum - Art of the American West, Prescott AZ

Villano, Steven, *Cur Exhibs,* City of Ketchikan Museum Department, Totem Heritage Center, Ketchikan AK

Villarreal, Raul, *Adjunct Prof,* College of Saint Elizabeth, Art Dept, Morristown NJ (S)

Villela, Khristaan, *Asst Prof,* College of Santa Fe, Art Dept, Santa Fe NM (S)

Villela, Khristaan, *Dir,* New Mexico Department of Cultural Affairs, Museum of International Folk Art, Santa Fe NM

Villeneuve, Pat, *Assoc Prof,* Florida State University, Art Education Dept, Tallahassee FL (S)

Villiquette, Michael, *Faculty Assoc,* University of Wisconsin, Madison, Dept of Art, Madison WI (S)

Villmagna, Robert, *Assoc Prof,* West Liberty State College, Div Art, West Liberty WV (S)

Vincent, Christine J, *Pres,* Maine College of Art, Portland ME (S)

Vincent, Haideh, *Accnt,* Creative Growth Art Center, Oakland CA

Vincent, Kim, *VPres Develop,* MEXIC-ARTE Museum, Austin TX

Vincent, Marc, *Chmn Div,* Baldwin-Wallace College, Dept of Art, Berea OH (S)

Vincent, Michael, *Dean,* Northern Arizona University, College of Arts & Letters, Flagstaff AZ (S)

Vinci, Sarah G, *Pub Relations Dir,* California State University, Long Beach, University Art Museum, Long Beach CA

Vincler, John, *Head Reader Svcs,* The Morgan Library & Museum, Library, New York NY

Vinokurov, Bryce, *Asst Prof,* Worcester State College, Visual & Performing Arts Dept, Worcester MA (S)

Vinovich, Jennifer, *Spec Projects Mgr,* South Shore Arts, Munster IN

Vinson, Mary, *Asst Dir,* Tellus Northwest Georgia Science Museum, Cartersville GA

Vinyard, Jordan, *Asst Prof,* University of Science & Arts of Oklahoma, Art Dept, Chickasha OK (S)

Violette, James, *Treas,* Waterville Historical Society, Redington Museum, Waterville ME

Virgint, Dwayne, *COO,* Indian Pueblo Cultural Center, Albuquerque NM

Virgo, Lauren, *Colls Mgr,* Aiken County Historical Museum, Aiken SC

Viscardi, Anthony, *Prof,* Lehigh University, Dept of Art, Architecture & Design, Bethlehem PA (S)

Visconti, Gianmarco, *Exec Admin,* Art Gallery of Alberta, Edmonton AB

Vissat, Maureen, *Asst Prof,* Seton Hill University, Art Program, Greensburg PA (S)

Visser, Mary, *Prof,* Southwestern University, Sarofim School of Fine Art, Dept of Art & Art History, Georgetown TX (S)

Visser, Susan R, *Exec Dir,* South Bend Regional Museum of Art, South Bend IN

Visser, Susan R, *Exec Dir,* South Bend Regional Museum of Art, Library, South Bend IN

Vitale, James, *Instr,* Mohawk Valley Community College, Utica NY (S)

Vitale, Thomas Jewell, *Assoc Prof,* Loras College, Dept of Art, Dubuque IA (S)

Vito, Kimberly, *Prof,* Wright State University, Dept of Art & Art History, Dayton OH (S)

Viverette, Lee B, *Reference Librn,* Virginia Museum of Fine Arts, Margaret R & Robert M Freeman Library, Richmond VA

Vivero, Michaela, *Assoc Prof,* Denison University, Studio Art Program, Granville OH (S)

Viviano, Norwood, *Asst Prof,* Grand Valley State University, Art & Design Dept, Allendale MI (S)

Vivoni, Paul, *Assoc Prof,* Inter American University of Puerto Rico, Fine Arts Dept -Art Program, San German PR (S)

Vizzutti, Jessica, *Program & Publ Coordr,* University of Montana, Montana Museum of Art & Culture, Missoula MT

Voci, Donna, *Adjunct Asst Prof,* New York Institute of Technology, Fine Arts Dept, Old Westbury NY (S)

Voci, Peter, *Chmn,* New York Institute of Technology, Gallery, Old Westbury NY

Voci, Peter, *Chmn & Assoc Prof,* New York Institute of Technology, Fine Arts Dept, Old Westbury NY (S)

Voelkel, David, *Cur,* James Monroe Museum, James Monroe Memorial Library, Fredericksburg VA

Voelker, Jim, *Head Dept,* Bluefield State College, Division of Arts & Sciences, Bluefield WV (S)

Voellinger, David, *Dir Develop,* Lehigh Valley Heritage Center, Allentown PA

Vogel, Alan, *Assoc Prof,* Rochester Institute of Technology, School of Photographic Arts & Sciences, Rochester NY (S)

Vogel, Randall, *Asst Dir Theaters & Opers,* Mesa Arts Center, Mesa Contemporary Arts Museum, Mesa AZ

Vogel, Stephan P, *Dean,* University of Detroit Mercy, School of Architecture, Detroit MI (S)

Vogel, Theodore, *Asst Prof,* Lewis & Clark College, Dept of Art, Portland OR (S)

Vogelsong, Diana, *Assoc University Librn,* American University, Jack I & Dorothy G Bender Library & Learning Resources Center, New York NY

Vogler, Lisa, *Dir Develop,* Arts Place, Inc, Hugh N Ronald Memorial Gallery, Portland IN

Vogt, Allie, *Dept Chmn,* North Idaho College, Art Dept, Coeur D'Alene ID (S)

Voinot, Andrea, *Art Sales Mgr,* Kala Institute, Kala Art Institute, Berkeley CA

Voisine, Don, *Asst Secy,* American Abstract Artists, Brooklyn NY

Vokt Ziemba, Emily, *Coll Mgr,* The Art Institute of Chicago, Dept of Prints & Drawings, Chicago IL

Volk, John, *Asst Prof,* Minnesota State University-Moorhead, Dept of Art & Design, Moorhead MN (S)

Vollbrecht, Andy, *Develop Coordr,* White Bear Center for the Arts, Gallery, White Bear Lake MN

Vollherbst, Emily, *Registrar,* Goya Contemporary, Baltimore MD

Volmar, Michael A, *Cur,* Fruitlands Museum, Inc, Library, Harvard MA

Volmar, Michael, *Cur,* Fruitlands Museum, Inc, Harvard MA

Volpacchio, John, *Prof,* Salem State University, Art & Design Department, Salem MA (S)

Volz, Linda, *New Harmony Gallery Mgr,* Hoosier Salon Patrons Association, Inc, Art Gallery & Membership Organization, Indianapolis IN

Von Barghahn, Barbara, *Prof,* George Washington University, Dept of Art of Fine Arts & Art History, Washington DC (S)

von Dassanowsky, Robert, *Prof & Dir Film Studies,* University of Colorado-Colorado Springs, Visual & Performing Arts Dept (VAPA), Colorado Springs CO (S)

Von Drasek, Lisa, *Cur,* University of Minnesota, Children's Literature Research Collections, Minneapolis MN

Von Kann, Lisa, *Library Dir,* Saint Johnsbury Athenaeum, Saint Johnsbury VT

von Lates, Adrienne, *Dir Educ,* Bass Museum of Art, Miami Beach FL

Von Lintel, Amy, *Asst Prof,* West Texas A&M University, Art, Theatre & Dance Dept, Canyon TX (S)

Von Martin, Christaan, *Sr Preparator,* Riverside Art Museum, Riverside CA

Von Rosk, Laura, *Gallery Dir,* Lake George Arts Project, Courthouse Gallery, Lake George NY

Von Schlegell, Mark, *Circ Supv,* Art Center College of Design, James Lemont Fogg Memorial Library, Pasadena CA

von Stuelpnagel, Anne, *Dir Exhibitions,* Bruce Museum, Inc, Greenwich CT

von Tsurikov, Vladimir, *Dir,* Museum of Russian Art, Minneapolis MN

Von Wolffersdorff, Joy, *Adjunct,* College of the Canyons, Art Dept, Santa Clarita CA (S)

Vonada, Wayne, *Sr Preparator,* Florida State University, Museum of Fine Arts, Tallahassee FL

Vondras, Barbara, *Dir,* Dawson County Historical Society, Museum, Lexington NE

Vong, Jennifer, *Gallery Adminr,* Redhead Gallery, Toronto ON

Vonkeman, Anine, *Head Pub Rels,* Southern Alberta Art Gallery, Library, Lethbridge AB

VonVoetcsch, Kurt, *Gallery Mgr,* Niagara University, Castellani Art Museum, Niagara NY

Vookles, Laura, *Chief Cur Collections,* The Hudson River Museum, Yonkers NY

Voorhees, Rebecca, *Design, Identity & Studio Mgr,* California State University, Sacramento, The University Union Gallery, Sacramento CA

Vorhaus, Kate, *Projects Mgr,* National Council on Education for the Ceramic Arts (NCECA), Boulder CO

Vossler, Megan, *Instr,* Macalester College, Art & Art History Dept, Saint Paul MN (S)

Vroom, Steven Michael, *Exec Dir,* 911 Media Arts Center, Seattle WA

Vrooman, Jason, *Cur Educ,* Middlebury College, Museum of Art, Middlebury VT

Vrotsus, Susan, *Dir Sales & Rental,* Cambridge Art Association, Cambridge MA

Vruwink, J, *Chmn,* Central College, Art Dept, Pella IA (S)

Vuchetich, Jill, *Archivist,* Walker Art Center, Library and Archives, Minneapolis MN

Vuwigh, James, *Assoc Prof,* University of Indianapolis, Dept Art & Design, Indianapolis IN (S)

Vymlatil, Rick, *CEO & Dir,* South Florida Fair, Yesteryear Village, West Palm Beach FL

Waala, Andrea, *Registrar,* Museum of Wisconsin Art, West Bend WI

Waale, Kim, *Assoc Prof,* Cazenovia College, Center for Art & Design Studies, Cazenovia NY (S)

Wabnitz, Robert, *Prof,* Rochester Institute of Technology, School of Design, Rochester NY (S)

Wachholder, Melanie, *CollectionsCur,* North Central Washington Museum, Wenatchee Valley Museum & Cultural Center, Wenatchee WA

Wachna, Pamela, *Cur,* City of Toronto Culture, The Market Gallery, Toronto ON

Wachs, Joel, *Pres,* Andy Warhol Foundation for the Visual Arts, New York NY

Wack, Ellen, *Admin Asst,* Portland State University, Dept of Art, Portland OR (S)

Wada, W, *Prof Painting,* Ramapo College of New Jersey, School of Contemporary Arts, Mahwah NJ (S)

Waddell, Wayne, *Dir,* Secretary of State Museum Division, Louisiana State Exhibit Museum, Shreveport LA

Waddington, Robert, *Instr,* Wayne Art Center, Wayne PA (S)

Wade Hogan, Beverly, *Pres,* Tougaloo College, Tougaloo Art Collection, Tougaloo MS

Wade, Bethany, *Progs Dir,* The Museum, Greenwood SC

Wade, Cara, *Asst Prof,* University of Saint Francis, School of Creative Arts, Fort Wayne IN (S)

Wade, Karen Graham, *Dir,* Workman & Temple Family Homestead Museum, City of Industry CA

Wade, Ken, *Security,* Booth Western Art Museum, Cartersville GA

Wadell, Arin, *Adjunct,* Sheridan College, Art Dept, Sheridan WY (S)

Wadley, William, *Head,* Texas A&M University Commerce, Dept of Art, Commerce TX (S)

Wadley, William, *Head,* Texas A&M University Commerce, Dept of Art, Commerce TX (S)

Wadsworth, David, *Historian,* Cohasset Historical Society, Captain John Wilson Historical House, Cohasset MA

Wagener, Thomas, *Dir,* University of Wisconsin-Eau Claire, Foster Gallery, Eau Claire WI

Wagener, Tom, *Dir Foster Gallery Woodshop Supv,* University of Wisconsin-Eau Claire, Dept of Art & Design, Eau Claire WI (S)

Wagenet, Hal, *Pres,* Arts Council of Mendocino County, Ukiah CA

Wager, Richard, *Chief Preparator,* New York University, Grey Art Gallery, New York NY

Wager, Susan, *Asst Prof,* University of New Hampshire, Dept of Art & Art History, Durham NH (S)

Waggoner, Jean, *Treas,* Coquille Valley Art Association, Coquille OR

Waggoner, Lynda, *Dir,* Western Pennsylvania Conservancy, Fallingwater, Mill Run PA

Waggoner, Ryan, *Creative Svcs Mgr,* University of Kansas, Spencer Museum of Art, Lawrence KS

Wagley, Sally, *Bd Mem,* Kennebec Valley Art Association, Harlow Gallery, Hallowell ME

Wagman, Evan, *Educ Mgr,* Foundry Art Centre, Saint Charles MO

Wagner, Ann P, *Cur Drawings,* Arkansas Arts Center, Little Rock AR (S)

Wagner, Ann Prentice, *Cur Drawings,* Arkansas Arts Center, Little Rock AR

Wagner, Ann, *Cur Drawings,* Arkansas Arts Center, Elizabeth Prewitt Taylor Memorial Library, Little Rock AR

Wagner, Beverly, *Admin Secy,* Texas A&M University, J Wayne Stark University Center Galleries, College Station TX

Wagner, Bob, *Preparator,* State University of New York at New Paltz, Samuel Dorsky Museum of Art, New Paltz NY

Wagner, Carolyn, *Dir Advancement,* American Museum of Ceramic Art, Pomona CA

Wagner, Catherine F, *Prof,* Mills College, Art Dept, Oakland CA (S)

Wagner, Jill, *Asst Prof Graphic Design,* Kansas Wesleyan University, Art Dept, Salina KS (S)

Wagner, Karen, *Archivist,* Nebraska State Capitol, Lincoln NE

Wagner, Lois, *Pres,* Lois Wagner Fine Arts, New York NY

Wagner, Mary, *Admin Asst,* Marquette University, Haggerty Museum of Art, Milwaukee WI

Wagner, Sarah, *Conserv,* National Gallery of Art, Department of Image Collections, Washington DC

Wagner, Shawna, *Develop Dir,* Vesterheim Norwegian-American Museum, Decorah IA

Wagner, Teri, *Asst Prof,* Cardinal Stritch University, Art Dept, Milwaukee WI (S)

Wagoner, Phillip, *Assoc Prof,* Wesleyan University, Dept of Art & Art History, Middletown CT (S)

Wagstaff, Sheena, *Chmn, Modern & Contemporary Art,* The Metropolitan Museum of Art, New York NY

Wahamaki, Sheila, *Dept Chmn,* Muskegon Community College, Dept of Creative & Performing Arts, Muskegon MI (S)

Wahbeh, Farris, *Dir Research,* Whitney Museum of American Art, Frances Mulhall Achilles Library, New York NY

Wahl, Sonja, *Cur Emeritus,* Thousand Islands Arts Center - Home of the Handweaving Museum, Clayton NY (S)

Wahl, Valerie, *Collection Mgr,* Eastern Washington State Historical Society, Northwest Museum of Arts & Culture, Spokane WA

Wahler, Marc-Olivier, *Dir,* Michigan State University, Eli & Edythe Broad Art Museum, East Lansing MI

Wahlgren, Bob, *VPres Finance,* DuPage Art League School & Gallery, Wheaton IL

Wahlgren, Kay, *VPres Exhibits,* DuPage Art League School & Gallery, Wheaton IL

Wahlmann, Susan, *Performing Arts & Arts in Educ Dir,* Quad City Arts Inc, Rock Island IL

Wahnee, B J, *Instr,* Haskell Indian Nations University, Art Dept, Lawrence KS (S)

Waide, Blaine, *Folk Arts Coordr,* Florida Folklife Programs, Library, Tallahassee FL

Wainright, Carolyn, *Office Mgr,* Rosemount Museum, Inc, Pueblo CO

Wainwright, Lindsey, *Coordr Academic Progs,* University of Tennessee, McClung Museum of Natural History & Culture, Knoxville TN

Wainwright, Lindsey, *Coordr Academic Progs,* University of Tennessee, McClung Museum of Natural History & Culture, Knoxville TN

Wainwright, Lisa, *Dean of Faculty,* School of the Art Institute of Chicago, Chicago IL (S)

Waits, Keith, *Facility & Gallery Mgr,* Louisville Visual Art, Louisville KY

Wakajima, Ryuta, *Asst Prof,* University of Minnesota, Minneapolis, Dept of Art, Minneapolis MN (S)

Wakefield, Donna, *Instr Student Sucess,* AIC College of Design, Cincinnati OH (S)

Wakeford, Elizabeth, *Cur Asst,* Dundurn National Historic Site, Dundurn Castle, Hamilton ON

Wakeford, Stacy, *Dir Content, Experience & Engagement,* Canadian Museum of Nature, Musee Canadien de la Nature, Ottawa ON

Wakeham, Duane, *2nd VPres,* Pastel Society of America, National Arts Club, Grand Gallery, New York NY

Wakeling, Melissa, *Educ,* Glanmore National Historic Site of Canada, Belleville ON

Walch, Tim, *Co-Chair,* National Academy Museum & School, New York NY

Walchuk, Kate, *Exhibs Coord,* Nova Scotia College of Art and Design, Anna Leonowens Gallery, Halifax NS

Walden Davis, Ashley, *Mng Dir,* Alternate ROOTS, Inc, Atlanta GA

Walden, Jerry, *Chmn,* Winthrop University, Dept of Art & Design, Rock Hill SC (S)

Walden, Olin, *Chmn Bd,* Hermitage Museum & Gardens, Norfolk VA

Waldman, Arthur, *Prof,* Ocean County College, Humanities Dept, Toms River NJ (S)

Waldrep, Lee W, *Asst Dean Student Affairs,* Illinois Institute of Technology, College of Architecture, Chicago IL (S)

Waldrop, Tim, *Asst Prof,* Western Illinois University, Department of Art, Macomb IL (S)

Walduier Bizzarro, Tina, *Chmn Div,* Rosemont College, Art Program, Rosemont PA (S)

Walen, Audrey, *Mgr Publs,* The American Federation of Arts, New York NY

Waletzky, Lucy R, *Chair State Council Parks, Recreation & Historic Preservation,* New York Office of Parks, Recreation & Historic Preservation, Natural Heritage Trust, Albany NY

Walford, E John, *Chmn,* Wheaton College, Dept of Art, Wheaton IL (S)

Walia, Christine, *Mgr Exhibs & Progs,* Aljira Center for Contemporary Art, Newark NJ

Walker, Andrew, *Director,* Amon Carter Museum of American Art, Fort Worth TX

Walker, Beth, *Dir,* College for Creative Studies, College of Art & Design Library, Detroit MI

Walker, Beth, *Prin Librn & Information Access Servs,* Pasadena Public Library, Fine Arts Dept, Pasadena CA

Walker, Betsy, *Interim Educ Coordr,* Pensacola Museum of Art, Pensacola FL

Walker, Bobbi, *Owner,* Walker Fine Art, Denver CO

Walker, Celia, *Cur Coll,* Cheekwood Nashville's Home of Art & Gardens, Education Dept, Nashville TN (S)

Walker, Craig, *Drama & Music Dir,* Queen's University, Faculty of Arts & Sciences, Creative Arts Program, Kingston ON (S)

Walker, Cynthia, *Exec Dir,* Brick Store Museum, Kennebunk ME

Walker, Dan, *Dean Instruction,* Butte College, Dept of Fine Arts and Communication Tech, Oroville CA (S)

Walker, Daniel, *Cur Islamic Art,* The Art Institute of Chicago, Department of Asian Art, Chicago IL

Walker, David B, *Exec Dir & CEO,* Nevada Museum of Art, CA & E Research Library, Reno NV

Walker, David B, *Exec Dir & CEO,* Nevada Museum of Art, Reno NV

Walker, Doug, *Chmn,* College of the Desert, Art Dept, Palm Desert CA (S)

Walker, Grant, *Research Assoc,* United States Naval Academy, USNA Museum, Annapolis MD

Walker, Gwendolyn, *Founder & Cur,* The Walker African American Museum & Research Center, Las Vegas NV

Walker, Jeffrey, *Instr,* Campbellsville University, Art & Design Department, Campbellsville KY (S)

Walker, John, *Prof,* Boston University, School for the Arts, Boston MA (S)

Walker, Julia, *Asst Prof,* Binghamton University, Art History Department, Binghamton NY (S)

Walker, Katy, *Artist Adminr,* Portraits South, Raleigh NC

Walker, Kenneth D, *Head Bldgs & Grounds,* The Buffalo Fine Arts Academy, Albright-Knox Art Gallery, Buffalo NY

Walker, Kristina, *Dir Educ,* University of Kansas, Spencer Museum of Art, Lawrence KS

Walker, Leah, *Site & Event Mgr,* Aiken County Historical Museum, Aiken SC

Walker, Lulen, *Art Coll Cur,* Georgetown University, Lauinger Library - Special Collections Division, Washington DC

Walker, Lulen, *Cur,* Georgetown University, Art Collection, Washington DC

Walker, Mara, *COO,* Americans for the Arts, New York NY

Walker, Margaret F.M., *Art Cur Asst,* Vanderbilt University, Vanderbilt University Fine Arts Gallery, Nashville TN

Walker, Martha, *Collections Librn,* Cornell University, Fine Arts Library, Ithaca NY

Walker, Mary, *Dir Develop,* Knoxville Museum of Art, Knoxville TN

Walker, Melveta, *Library Dir,* Eastern New Mexico University, Golden Library/Runnels Gallery, Portales NM

Walker, Myra, *Prof Fashion Design,* University of North Texas, College of Visual Arts & Design, Denton TX (S)

Walker, Natalie, *Communs & Facilities,* Alexandria Museum of Art, Alexandria LA

Walker, Pat, *Dir Educ,* Danforth Museum of Art, Danforth Museum of Art, Framingham MA

Walker, Pat, *Mus Educ,* Danforth Museum of Art, Library, Framingham MA

Walker, Patricia, *Dir,* Danforth Museum of Art School, Framingham MA (S)

Walker, Patricia, *Prod,* Georgia Southern University, Betty Foy Sanders Dept of Art, Statesboro GA (S)

Walker, Robert, *Instr,* College of the Canyons, Art Dept, Santa Clarita CA (S)

Walker, Roslyn A, *Sr Cur Arts of Africa, Pacific & Americas,* Dallas Museum of Art, Dallas TX

Walker, Sam, *Asst Prof,* Wayland Baptist University, Dept of Art, School of Fine Art, Plainview TX (S)

Walker, Sarah, *Assoc Prof,* Clark University, Dept of Visual & Performing Arts, Worcester MA (S)

Walker, Sydney, *Assoc Prof,* Ohio State University, Dept of Art Education, Columbus OH (S)

Walker, T. Mike, *Brd Pres,* Santa Cruz Art League, Center for the Arts, Santa Cruz CA

Walker-Millar, Kathy, *Head Dept,* McMurry University, Art Dept, Abilene TX (S)

Wall, Brent, *Assoc Prof,* Saint Xavier University, Dept of Art & Design, Chicago IL (S)

Wall, Deborah, *Lectr,* University of North Carolina at Charlotte, Dept Art, Charlotte NC (S)

Wall, Kay L, *Dir,* University of Southern Mississippi, McCain Library & Archives, Hattiesburg MS

Wall, Pam, *Exhibs Consultant,* Gibbes Museum of Art, Charleston SC (S)

Wall, Rick, *Chair, Foundation,* Corcoran School of Art, Washington DC (S)

Wallace, Alan, *Asst Prof,* Chattanooga State Technical Community College, Advertising Arts Dept, Chattanooga TN (S)

Wallace, Alan, *Instr,* Chattanooga State Technical Community College, Advertising Arts Dept, Chattanooga TN (S)

Wallace, Andrea, *Artistic Dir, Photog, New Media, Chair of Workshop & Artists-in-Residence Progs,* Anderson Ranch Arts Center, Snowmass Village CO

Wallace, Brian, *Cur,* State University of New York at New Paltz, Samuel Dorsky Museum of Art, New Paltz NY

Wallace, Brian, *Dir,* Keene State College, Thorne-Sagendorph Art Gallery, Keene NH

Wallace, Carolyn, *Educ Dir,* Cliveden, Philadelphia PA

Wallace, Charles, *Dir,* Pump House Center for the Arts, Chillicothe OH

Wallace, Danielle, *Prog Dir,* State of North Carolina, Battleship North Carolina, Wilmington NC

Wallace, Ellen, *Mktg & Pub Rels Mgr,* Southeastern Center for Contemporary Art, Winston-Salem NC

Wallace, Greg, *Librn,* Massachusetts College of Art and Design, Library, Boston MA

Wallace, Hope, *Exec Dir,* Wassenberg Art Center, Van Wert OH

Wallace, James, *Pres Board Trustees,* Edmundson Art Foundation, Inc, Des Moines Art Center, Des Moines IA

Wallace, Karen, *Deputy Director,* Buffalo Society of Natural Sciences, Buffalo Museum of Science, Buffalo NY

Wallace, Kate, *Mem, Events & Communs Coordr,* University of Mississippi, University Museum & Historic Houses, Oxford MS

Wallace, Kevin, *Dir,* Beatrice Wood Center for the Arts, Ojai CA

Wallace, Margaret, *Registrar,* Middlebury College, Museum of Art, Middlebury VT

Wallace, Margot, *VPres,* Rancho Santa Fe Art Guild, Rancho Santa Fe CA

Wallace, Mary, *Accnt,* Art Complex Museum, Carl A Weyerhaeuser Library, Duxbury MA

Wallace, Matt, *Asst Dir Educ,* North Dakota Museum of Art, Grand Forks ND

Wallace, Paula, *Pres,* Savannah College of Art & Design, (SCAD), Savannah GA (S)

Wallace, Randall, *Instr,* Trinity University, Department of Art & Art History, San Antonio TX (S)

Wallace, Richard W, *Prof,* Wellesley College, Art Dept, Wellesley MA (S)

Wallace, Scott, *Prof,* South Dakota State University, Dept of Visual Arts, Brookings SD (S)

Wallace, Sheila, *Library Dir,* Emily Carr Institute of Art & Design, Library, Vancouver BC

Wallace, Tammy, *Sr Asst,* Richard M Ross Art Museum at Wesleyan University, Delaware OH

Wallach, Alan, *Ralph H Wark Prof Art & Art History,* College of William & Mary, Dept of Fine Arts, Williamsburg VA (S)

Wallach, Ruth, *Reference Center,* University of Southern California, Helen Topping Architecture & Fine Arts Library, Los Angeles CA

Walldroff, Lenka, *Coll Mgr,* Jefferson County Historical Society, Library, Watertown NY

Waller, Diane, *Financial Coordr,* Women in the Arts Foundation, Inc, Staten Island NY

Waller, Richard, *Dir,* University of Richmond, University Museums, Richmond VA

Waller, Richard, *Exec Dir Univ Mus,* University of Richmond, Dept of Art and Art History, Richmond VA (S)

Waller, Susan, *Asst Prof,* University of Missouri, Saint Louis, Dept of Art & Art History, Saint Louis MO (S)

Wallestad, Tom, *Assoc Prof,* Marian University, Art Dept, Fond Du Lac WI (S)

Wallin, Scott, *Exhib Designer,* Whatcom Museum, Bellingham WA

Walline, Lucy, *Librn,* Bethany College, Wallerstedt Library, Lindsborg KS

Walling Blackburn, Mary, *Asst Prof,* Southern Methodist University, Meadows School of the Arts - Division of Art, Dallas TX (S)

Walling, Lauren V, *Deputy Exec Dir,* Women's Studio Workshop, Inc, Rosendale NY

Wallis, Jonathan, *Chmn Liberal Arts,* Moore College of Art & Design, Philadelphia PA (S)

Wallis, Scott, *Preparator,* Queen's University, Agnes Etherington Art Centre, Kingston ON

Walls, Adam, *Asst Prof,* University of North Carolina at Pembroke, Art Dept, Pembroke NC (S)

Walls, Lucinda, *Librn,* Queen's University, Stauffer Library Art Collection, Kingston ON

Walls, Nancy, *Dir,* Edna Hibel Art Foundation, Hibel Museum Gallery, Jupiter FL

Walls, Nancy, *Dir,* Edna Hibel Art Foundation, Hibel Museum of Art, Jupiter FL

Wallsmith, Matt, *VPres & COO,* South Florida Fair, Yesteryear Village, West Palm Beach FL

Walmsley, William, *Prof Emeritus,* Florida State University, Art Dept, Tallahassee FL (S)

Walsh, David, *Gallery Cur,* Valencia Community College, Art Gallery-East Campus, Orlando FL

Walsh, Johnathon, *Asst Prof,* South Carolina State University, Dept of Visual & Performing Arts, Orangeburg SC (S)

Walsh, Krista, *Vis Asst Prof,* Hamline University, Dept of Studio Arts & Art History, Saint Paul MN (S)

Walsh, Marguerite, *Prof,* New England College, Art & Art History, Henniker NH (S)

Walsh, Neal, *Gallery Dir,* AS220, Main Gallery, Providence RI

Walsh, Ryan, *Devel & Writing Dir,* Vermont Studio Center, The Red Mill, Johnson VT

Walsh, Stacey, *Registar,* University of Nebraska, Lincoln, Sheldon Memorial Art Gallery & Sculpture Garden, Lincoln NE

Walsh, Stephen, *Environmental & Studio Tech,* University of Southern Maine, Dept of Art, Gorham ME (S)

Walsh, Timothy F, *Head Dept,* Otero Junior College, Dept of Arts, La Junta CO (S)

Waltemath, Joan, *Dir,* Maryland Institute, Hoffberger School of Painting, Baltimore MD (S)

Walter, Barbara, *Interim Dir,* Syracuse University, College of Visual & Performing Arts, Syracuse NY (S)

Walter, Charles Thomas, *Assoc Prof,* Bloomsburg University, Dept of Art & Art History, Bloomsburg PA (S)

Walter, Wendy R, *Gallery Dir & Registrar,* San Luis Obispo Museum of Art, San Luis Obispo CA

Walter-Frojen, Rhonda, *Assoc Dir,* Dickinson State University, Art Gallery, Dickinson ND

Walters, Bruce, *Prof,* Western Illinois University, Department of Art, Macomb IL (S)

Walters, Chris, *Community Arts Mgr,* The ARTS Council of the Southern Finger Lakes, Corning NY

Walters, Dallas, *Prof,* Indiana Wesleyan University, School of Arts & Humanities, Division of Art, Marion IN (S)

Walters, David M, *Media Arts & Animation,* Art Institute of Pittsburgh, Pittsburgh PA (S)

Walters, Elizabeth J, *Assoc Prof,* Pennsylvania State University, University Park, Dept of Art History, University Park PA (S)

Walters, Jamie, *Co-Dir,* Carnegie Mellon University, The Frame, Pittsburgh PA

Walters, Jo Ann, *Assoc Prof,* Purchase College, State University of New York, School of Art+Design, Purchase NY (S)

Walters, Kim, *Ahmanson Cur of Native American History & Culture,* Autry National Center, Southwest Museum of the American Indian, Mt. Washington Campus, Los Angeles CA

Walters, Maura, *Asst to Dir,* Library Association of La Jolla, Athenaeum Music & Arts Library, La Jolla CA

Walters, Tania, *Membership,* Marin County Watercolor Society, Corte Madera CA

Walton, Jim, *Exec Dir,* Beck Center for the Arts, Lakewood OH

Walton, John, *Dir,* Palo Alto Junior Museum & Zoo, Palo Alto CA

Walton, Joseph, *Dir Design,* Akron Art Museum, Akron OH

Walton, Lee, *Prof,* University of North Carolina at Greensboro, School of Art, Greensboro NC (S)

Walton, Thomas, *Assoc Prof,* Catholic University of America, School of Architecture & Planning, Washington DC (S)

Walus, Dawn, *Chief Conservator,* Boston Athenaeum, Boston MA

Walz, Jonathan F, *Cur,* Rollins College, George D & Harriet W Cornell Fine Arts Museum, Winter Park FL

Walz, Jonathan, *Director of Curatorial Affairs & Curator of American Art,* The Columbus Museum, Columbus GA

Walzer, Barbara, *Exec Dir,* Worcester Center for Crafts, Krikorian Gallery, Worcester MA

Wamhoff, Meryl, *Fine Arts Div Dean,* San Joaquin Delta College, Arts & Communication, Stockton CA (S)

Wanamaker, Monty, *Southern Standard Staff Reporter,* Southern Museum & Galleries of Photography, Mc Minnville TN

Wanberg, Kate, *Preparator,* University of Wisconsin-Madison, Chazen Museum of Art, Madison WI

Wandtke, Terrence, *Instr,* Judson University, School of Art, Design & Architecture, Elgin IL (S)

Wang, Jenny, *Cataloging Librn,* Savannah College of Art & Design - Atlanta, ACA Library of Atlanta, Atlanta GA

Wang, Kirk, *Prof,* Eckerd College, Art Dept, Saint Petersburg FL (S)

Wang, Susan, *Mem & Bookstore Assoc,* Pasadena Museum of California Art, Pasadena CA

Wang, Tao, *Pritzker Chmn Asian Art & Cur Chinese Art,* The Art Institute of Chicago, Department of Asian Art, Chicago IL

Wang, Victor, *Assoc Prof,* Fontbonne University, Fine Art Dept, Saint Louis MO (S)

Wang, Ye, *Assoc Prof,* Washburn University of Topeka, Dept of Art, Topeka KS (S)

Wanserski, Martin, *Assoc Prof,* University of South Dakota, Department of Art, College of Fine Arts, Vermillion SD (S)

Warcup, Stacy, *Mem Coordr,* North Dakota Museum of Art, Grand Forks ND

Ward, Alf, *Prof,* Winthrop University, Dept of Art & Design, Rock Hill SC (S)
Ward, Carla, *Dir & Owner,* Tinkertown Museum, Sandia Park NM
Ward, Dawn, *Head Prof,* Arkansas Tech University, Dept of Art, Russellville AR (S)
Ward, Dawn, *Instr,* Northeastern State University, College of Arts & Letters, Tahlequah OK (S)
Ward, Elizabeth, *Chair & Prof,* Trinity University, Department of Art & Art History, San Antonio TX (S)
Ward, Erica M, *Archivist/Cur,* Coachella Valley History Museum, Indio CA
Ward, Frazer, *Assoc Prof,* Smith College, Art Dept, Northampton MA (S)
Ward, Gerry, *Bldg & Grounds Supt,* R W Norton Art Foundation, R W Norton Art Gallery, Shreveport LA
Ward, Gerry, *Cur & Colls,* Portsmouth Historical Society, John Paul Jones House & Discover Portsmouth, Portsmouth NH
Ward, Jane, *Librn,* American Textile History Museum, Lowell MA
Ward, Jane, *Librn,* American Textile History Museum, Osborne Library, Lowell MA
Ward, Jennifer, *Assoc Cur & Exhib Coordr,* Foto Fest International, Houston TX
Ward, Julie, *Asst Prof Sculpture,* Florida Atlantic University, D F Schmidt College of Arts & Letters Dept of Visual Arts & Art History, Boca Raton FL (S)
Ward, Karen, *Chmn,* Hampton University, Dept of Fine & Performing Arts, Hampton VA (S)
Ward, Linda, *Instr,* University of Louisiana at Monroe, Dept of Art, Monroe LA (S)
Ward, Michele, *Owner,* Principle Gallery, Charleston, Charleston SC
Ward, Neidra, *Progs Coordr,* National YoungArts Foundation, Miami FL
Ward, R D, *Prof,* Randolph-Macon College, Dept of the Arts, Ashland VA (S)
Ward, Rae, *Marketing Director,* Art and History Museums - Maitland, Maitland Art Center, Maitland FL
Ward, Robert Lee, *Retail Mgr,* The Sandwich Historical Society, Inc & Sandwich Glass Museum, Sandwich Glass Museum, Sandwich MA
Ward, Robert, *Coordr Gallery Dir,* Bowie State University, Fine & Performing Arts Dept, Bowie MD (S)
Ward, Robert, *Instr,* University of Louisiana at Monroe, Dept of Art, Monroe LA (S)
Ward, Robin, *Instr Graphic Design,* Madonna University, College of Arts & Humanities, Livonia MI (S)
Ward, Roger, *Lectr,* University of Kansas, Kress Foundation Dept of Art History, Lawrence KS (S)
Ward, Scott, *Exec Dir,* Armory Center for the Arts, Pasadena CA
Ward, Steve, *Div Dean,* Portland Community College, Visual & Performing Arts Division, Portland OR (S)
Ward, Wesley, *Dir Land Conservation,* The Trustees of Reservations, The Mission House, Ipswich MA
Warda, Jeffrey, *Conservator Paper & Photographs,* Solomon R Guggenheim Museum, New York NY
Warda, Rebecca, *Coll Mgr,* Widener University, Art Collection & Gallery, Chester PA
Wardell, Emily, *Accountant & Human Resources,* The New Museum at the Bradford Brinton Ranch, The Brinton Museum, Big Horn WY
Wardell, Joel, *Facilities Mgr,* The New Museum at the Bradford Brinton Ranch, The Brinton Museum, Big Horn WY
Wardlaw, Alvia, *Assoc Prof,* Texas Southern University, College of Liberal Arts & Behavioral Sciences, Houston TX (S)
Wardropper, Ian, *Dir,* Frick Collection, New York NY
Ware, Kate, *Cur Photog,* New Mexico Department of Cultural Affairs, New Mexico Museum of Art, Unit of NM Dept of Cultural Affairs, Santa Fe NM
Ware, Mike, *Instr,* Alice Lloyd College, Art Dept, Pippa Passes KY (S)
Wargo, Richard, *Artistic Dir,* Marcella Sembrich Memorial Association Inc, Marcella Sembrich Opera Museum, Bolton Landing NY
Warhola, Donald, *VP & Liaison to Andy Warhol Mus,* Andy Warhol Foundation for the Visual Arts, New York NY
Warlick, M E, *Prof Art History,* University of Denver, School of Art & Art History, Denver CO (S)
Warner, Brian, *Bldg & Security Mgr,* Berkshire Museum, Pittsfield MA
Warner, Craig, *Assoc Prof,* Northwest Missouri State University, Dept of Fine & Performing Arts, Maryville MO (S)
Warner, David, *Dir,* Wade House Historic Site-Wisconsin Historical Society, Wesley W. Jung Carriage Museum, Greenbush WI
Warner, Deborah, *Chmn Textile Design,* Moore College of Art & Design, Philadelphia PA (S)
Warner, Dona, *Dir,* Johnson Atelier Technical Institute of Sculpture, Trenton NJ (S)
Warner, Jeremy, *Mus Security & Facility Mgr,* The Pennsylvania State University, Palmer Museum of Art, University Park PA
Warner, Malcolm, *Exec Dir,* Laguna Art Museum, Laguna Beach CA
Warner, Marcia, *Library Dir,* Grand Rapids Public Library, Grand Rapids MI
Warner, Mary, *Assoc Prof,* University of Nevada, Las Vegas, Dept of Art, Las Vegas NV (S)
Warnock, Doug, *Faculty,* Idaho State University, Dept of Art, Pocatello ID (S)
Warp, Harold, *Pres,* Harold Warp, Minden NE
Warpole, Jenn, *Instr,* Wayne Art Center, Wayne PA (S)
Warren Perry, Edmund, *Asst Dir,* University of Memphis, Art Museum, Memphis TN
Warren, Benson, *Prof,* Cameron University, Art Dept, Lawton OK (S)
Warren, Carolyn, *VPres Arts,* Banff Centre, Banff AB (S)
Warren, Jack D, *Exec Dir,* The Society of the Cincinnati at Anderson House, Washington DC
Warren, James M "Butch", *Chmn,* Historic Arkansas Museum, Little Rock AR
Warren, Jennifer, *Bus Office Mgr,* The Art Center of Waco, Library, Waco TX
Warren, Kenneth, *VPres,* Birger Sandzen Memorial Gallery, Lindsborg KS
Warren, Mackenzie, *Develop Coordr,* Cliveden, Philadelphia PA
Warren, Maureen, *Cur European & American Art,* University of Illinois at Urbana-Champaign, Krannert Art Museum and Kinkead Pavilion, Champaign IL
Warren, Michael, *CEO,* Turtle Bay Exploration Park, Redding CA
Warren, Sandra, *Bus Mgr,* Indiana University, The Mathers Museum of World Cultures, Bloomington IN
Warren, Scott, *VPres,* North Carolina Museums Council, Raleigh NC
Warshaw, Andrew, *Assoc Prof Dance & Music,* Marymount Manhattan College, Fine & Performing Arts Div, New York NY (S)
Warshaw, Leila, *Mus Shop Mgr,* Maryland Historical Society, Library, Baltimore MD
Warstler, Pasgua, *Gallery Dir,* William Bonifas, Escanaba MI
Wartenberg Kagan, Ute, *Exec Dir & Secy,* American Numismatic Society, New York NY
Warther Moreland, Carol, *Pres & Gen Mgr,* Warther Museum Inc, Dover OH
Wartman, Bruce, *Pres,* Hussian School of Art, Commercial Art Dept, Philadelphia PA (S)
Warwick, Mark, *Chmn,* Gettysburg College, Dept of Visual Arts, Gettysburg PA (S)
Warwick, Wanda, *Board Mem,* Cambridge Museum, Cambridge NE
Warzecha, Christina, *Dir,* Rockford University, Art Gallery, Rockford IL
Waschek, Matthias, *The C. Jean and Myles McDonough Dir,* Worcester Art Museum, Worcester MA
Wasemiller, Kitty, *Prof,* Abilene Christian University, Dept of Art & Design, Abilene TX (S)
Wash, Charles, *Archivist,* Ohio History Connection, National Afro-American Museum & Cultural Center, Wilberforce OH
Washburn, Andrew, *Registrar,* Alaska State Museum, Juneau AK
Washburn, William, *Instr,* Marylhurst University, Art Dept, Marylhurst OR (S)
Washington, Angela, *Assoc Library Mgr,* The Metropolitan Museum of Art, Museum Libraries, New York NY
Washington, Benjamin, *CFO,* Missouri Historical Society, Missouri History Museum, Saint Louis MO
Washler, Deb, *Exec Dir,* Artlink, Inc, Auer Center for Arts & Culture, Fort Wayne IN
Washton Long, Rose Carol, *Prof,* City University of New York, PhD Program in Art History, New York NY (S)
Wasinger, Tracy, *Instr,* University of Charleston, Carleton Varney Dept of Art & Design, Charleston WV (S)
Wasman, Wendy, *Asst Librn,* The Temple-Tifereth Israel, Lee & Dolores Hartzmark Library, Beachwood OH
Wasowicz, Laura E, *Cur Children's Literature,* American Antiquarian Society, Worcester MA
Wasserboehr, Patricia, *Prof,* University of North Carolina at Greensboro, School of Art, Greensboro NC (S)
Wassermann, Mary S, *Librn Collection Develop,* Philadelphia Museum of Art, Library & Archives, Philadelphia PA
Watanabe, Joan, *Prof of Photog,* Glendale Community College, Visual & Performing Arts Div, Glendale CA (S)
Watcke, Tom, *Prof,* Albright College, Dept of Art, Reading PA (S)
Waterfield, Doug, *Chmn & Prof,* University of Nebraska, Kearney, Dept of Art & Art History, Kearney NE (S)
Waterhouse, Richard, *Dir & Cur,* Cahoon Museum of American Art, Cotuit MA
Waterloo, Candie, *Asst Cur Youth & Family Progs,* Kalamazoo Institute of Arts, Kalamazoo MI
Waterloo, Candie, *Cur Educ,* University of Wisconsin-Madison, Chazen Museum of Art, Madison WI
Waterman, Patricia, *3D Animation & Modeling,* Santa Ana College, Art Dept, Santa Ana CA (S)
Waters, Kathryn, *Prof,* University of Southern Indiana, Art & Design Dept, Evansville IN (S)
Waters, Moya, *Assoc Dir,* University of British Columbia, Museum of Anthropology, Vancouver BC
Waters, Tom, *Gallery Manager,* Bryan Memorial Gallery, Cambridge VT
Watkins, Adam, *Arts Program Coordr,* East Central College, Art Dept, Union MO (S)
Watkins, Beth, *Educ Coordr,* University of Illinois at Urbana-Champaign, Spurlock Museum, Urbana IL
Watkins, Della, *Exec Dir,* Columbia Museum of Art, Columbia SC
Watkins, Helga, *Asst Prof,* University of Nevada, Las Vegas, Dept of Art, Las Vegas NV (S)
Watkins, Paula, *Chm (V),* Anniston Museum of Natural History, Anniston AL
Watkins, Ron, *Treas,* Coppini Academy of Fine Arts, Library, San Antonio TX
Watkins, Sarah, *Dir Colls & Learning,* USS Constitution Museum, Boston MA
Watkins, Veronica, *Instr,* Northwest Missouri State University, Dept of Fine & Performing Arts, Maryville MO (S)
Watkins, W Anthony, *Asst Prof,* Northwestern State University of Louisiana, School of Creative & Performing Arts - Dept of Fine & Graphic Arts, Natchitoches LA (S)
Watkinson, Sharon, *Chmn,* Niagara University, Fine Arts Dept, Niagara Falls NY (S)
Watriss, Wendy, *Artistic Dir & Co-Founder,* Foto Fest International, Houston TX

Watrous, Livingston, *Art History & Visual Studies,* University at Buffalo, State University of New York, Dept of Visual Studies, Buffalo NY (S)
Watrous, Rebecca, *Educ Dir,* Historic Cherry Hill, Albany NY
Watson, Beth, *Dir Develop,* Redwood Library & Athenaeum, Newport RI
Watson, Donna, *Adjunct Prof,* Oklahoma Christian University of Science & Arts, Dept of Art & Design, Oklahoma City OK (S)
Watson, Ella, *Gallery Dir,* Montana State University, Helen E Copeland Gallery, Bozeman MT
Watson, Ian, *Chair,* Rutgers University, Newark, Arts, Culture & Media, Newark NJ (S)
Watson, Jewell, *Arts Admin Mgr,* University of Maryland, College Park, The Art Gallery, College Park MD
Watson, Joseph A, *Assoc Prof,* Rochester Institute of Technology, School of Design, Rochester NY (S)
Watson, Karen, *Exec Dir,* Sumter Gallery of Art, Sumter SC
Watson, Maya, *Instr,* Texas Southern University, College of Liberal Arts & Behavioral Sciences, Houston TX (S)
Watson, Neil, *Exec Dir,* The Long Island Museum of American Art, History & Carriages, Library, Stony Brook NY
Watson, Neil, *Exec Dir,* The Long Island Museum of American Art, History & Carriages, Stony Brook NY
Watson, Richard, *Exhibs Mgr & Artist in Res,* African American Museum in Philadelphia, Philadelphia PA
Watson, Sarah, *Gen Dir,* Artexte Information Centre, Documentation Centre, Montreal QC
Watson, Scott, *Prof & Dept Head,* University of British Columbia, Dept of Art History, Visual Art & Theory, Vancouver BC (S)
Watson, Shaydee, *Preparator,* San Angelo Museum of Fine Arts, San Angelo TX
Watson, Tom, *Chmn,* Columbia College, Art Dept, Columbia MO (S)
Watson-Mauro, Sharon, *Lib Dir,* Moore College of Art & Design, Library, Philadelphia PA
Watt, Kelly, *Asst Prof,* Washburn University of Topeka, Dept of Art, Topeka KS (S)
Watters, Ben, *Grants & Research Dir,* Arizona Commission on the Arts, Phoenix AZ
Watters, Tom, *Dir,* National Air and Space Museum, Regional Planetary Image Facility, Washington DC
Watts Pope, Elizabeth, *Cur Books,* American Antiquarian Society, Worcester MA
Watts, Allyson, *Treas,* Manitoba Society of Artists, Winnipeg MB
Watts, Angela, *Coll Mgr,* University of Kansas, Spencer Museum of Art, Lawrence KS
Watts, Barbara, *Assoc Prof,* Florida International University, School of Art & Art History, Miami FL (S)
Watts, Greg, *Chmn,* Metropolitan State University of Denver, Art Dept, Denver CO (S)
Watts, Mitra, *Dean Acad Affairs,* Art Institute of Colorado, Denver CO (S)
Watts, Rachel, *Dir Progs,* ArtsConnection Inc, New York NY
Watts, Steve, *Coordr,* University of Charleston, Carleton Varney Dept of Art & Design, Charleston WV (S)
Watts-Nunn, Donna, *Mem & Vol Coordr,* Hammonds House Museum, Atlanta GA
Waugaman, Linda, *Vis Arts Dir,* Indian River Community College, Fine Arts Dept, Fort Pierce FL (S)
Wavrat, Dennis, *Prof,* University of South Dakota, Department of Art, College of Fine Arts, Vermillion SD (S)
Wawruck, Kristin, *Dir Institutional Devel & Opers,* Swiss Institute, New York NY
Waxman, Adrianne, *Mgr Audience Engagement & Rentals,* Philadelphia Museum of Art, Samuel S Fleisher Art Memorial, Philadelphia PA
Way, Jennifer, *Assoc Prof Art History,* University of North Texas, College of Visual Arts & Design, Denton TX (S)
Way, Kaitlyn, *Mgr Visitor & Volunteer Experience,* New Britain Museum of American Art, New Britain CT
Way, Laura, *Exec Dir,* Green Hill Center for North Carolina Art, Greenhill, Greensboro NC
Wayman, Adele, *Prof of Art, Dept Chair,* Guilford College, Art Dept, Greensboro NC (S)
Wayne, Vikki, *Bd Mbr,* Valley Art Center Inc, Clarkston WA
Weand-Kilkenny, Betsy, *Develop Dir,* Abington Art Center, Jenkintown PA
Weander-Gaster, Kara, *Exec Dir,* Norfolk Arts Center, Norfolk NE
Weant, Nancy, *Grants Mgr,* Tucson Museum of Art and Historic Block, Tucson AZ
Wear, Lisa, *Dir,* Horizons Unlimited Supplementary Educational Center, Science Museum, Salisbury NC
Wear, Lori, *Cur,* Kern County Museum, Bakersfield CA
Wearth, Pat, *Mus Shop Mgr,* Kemp Center for the Arts, Wichita Falls TX
Weatherley, Glynn, *Lectr,* Lambuth University, Dept of Human Ecology & Visual Arts, Jackson TN (S)
Weathers, Dennis, *Area Dir,* College of the Siskiyous, Theatre Dept, Weed CA (S)
Weatherwax, Sarah, *Cur Prints & Photogs,* Library Company of Philadelphia, Philadelphia PA
Weaver, Angela, *Head Librn,* University of Washington, Art Slide Library, Seattle WA
Weaver, Angela, *Librn,* University of Washington, Art Library, Seattle WA
Weaver, James, *Dir Institutional Advancement Opers,* Heard Museum, Billie Jane Baguley Library and Archives, Phoenix AZ
Weaver, Joyce, *Dir Library & Archives,* The Mint Museum, Charlotte NC
Weaver, Patsy, *Bd Mem,* Coquille Valley Art Association, Coquille OR
Weaver, Ron, *Exhibs Preparator,* Washington University, Mildred Lane Kemper Art Museum, Saint Louis MO
Weaver, Suzanne, *Assoc Cur Contemporary Art,* Dallas Museum of Art, Dallas TX
Weaver, Suzanne, *Cur Contemporary Art,* San Antonio Museum of Art, San Antonio TX
Weaver, Timothy, *Assoc Prof Electronic Media Arts & Design,* University of Denver, School of Art & Art History, Denver CO (S)
Weaver, Victoria, *Asst Grad Prof Art Educ,* Millersville University, Dept of Art & Design, Millersville PA (S)
Weaver, Victoria, *Cur Educ,* Daum Museum of Contemporary Art, Sedalia MO
Webb, Ann, *Assoc Dir Engagement & Strategic Initiaves,* Vancouver Art Gallery, Vancouver BC
Webb, Ashley, *Colls Mgr,* Longwood Center for the Visual Arts, Farmville VA
Webb, Deborah, *Library Supv,* University of Notre Dame, Architecture Library, Notre Dame IN
Webb, Denise, *Vis Servs Rep,* American Textile History Museum, Lowell MA
Webb, Dixie, *Dean College Arts & Letters,* Austin Peay State University, Art Dept Library, Clarksville TN
Webb, Duncan J, *Dir Educ,* American Academy of Art, Chicago IL (S)
Webb, Frank, *Instr,* Art Center Sarasota, Sarasota FL (S)
Webb, Greg, *Instr,* Joe Kubert, Dover NJ (S)
Webb, Joel, *Head Tech Servs,* Mechanics' Institute, San Francisco CA
Webb, Lanny, *Prof Graphic Design,* University of Georgia, Franklin College of Arts & Sciences, Lamar Dodd School of Art, Athens GA (S)
Webb, Melissa, *Exhibs Mgr,* School 33 Art Center, Baltimore MD
Webb, Nicole, *Cur Colls,* Historical Museum at Fort Missoula, Missoula MT
Webb, Nikki, *Visiting Assoc Prof,* Old Dominion University, Art Dept, Norfolk VA (S)
Webb, Ron, *Dean,* Huntington College, Art Dept, Huntington IN (S)
Webb, Tom, *Dir,* Newport Visual Arts Center, Newport OR
Webber, Barry C, *Pres,* Norfolk Historical Society Inc, Museum, Norfolk CT
Webber, Cleve, *Assoc Prof,* Alabama State University, Dept of Visual Arts, Montgomery AL (S)
Webber, David, *Asst Prof,* Coe College, Dept of Art, Cedar Rapids IA (S)
Webber, Nancy E, *Asst Prof,* Los Angeles Harbor College, Art Dept, Wilmington CA (S)
Webber, Richard, *Events Coordr,* Northern Virginia Fine Arts Association, The Athenaeum, Alexandria VA
Webber, Sandra, *Paintings Conservator,* Williamstown Art Conservation Center, Williamstown MA
Webber-Dreeszen, Erin, *Develop Coordr,* Sioux City Art Center, Sioux City IA (S)
Weber, Bruce, *Sr Cur Nineteenth Century Art,* National Academy Museum & School, Archives, New York NY
Weber, Deborah, *Exec Dir,* Lincoln Arts Council, Lincoln NE
Weber, Heather, *Dir,* Northeastern Illinois University, Fine Arts Center Gallery, Chicago IL
Weber, Jean M, *Exec Dir,* Nantucket Historical Association, Historic Nantucket, Nantucket MA
Weber, John, *Prof,* Elmhurst College, Art Dept, Elmhurst IL (S)
Weber, Joseph A, *Art Educ,* Southern Illinois University at Edwardsville, Dept of Art & Design, Edwardsville IL (S)
Weber, Matthew, *Instr,* Middlesex Community College, Fine Arts Div, Middletown CT (S)
Weber, Robin, *Dir,* Museum of Northern British Columbia, Ruth Harvey Art Gallery, Prince Rupert BC
Weber, Robin, *Dir,* Museum of Northern British Columbia, Library, Prince Rupert BC
Webster Benwick, Suzi, *Dept Chair,* Langara College, Dept of Fine Arts, Vancouver BC (S)
Webster, Christine, *VPres,* Arts & Crafts Association of Meriden Inc, Gallery 53, Meriden CT
Webster, Drew, *Prof, Photog,* State College of Florida Manatee - Sarasota, Art, Design, Humanities, Bradenton FL (S)
Webster, Helen, *Graphic Design, Media Arts & Animation,* Art Institute of Pittsburgh, Pittsburgh PA (S)
Webster, Lynn, *Assoc Prof Art,* The College of Idaho, Rosenthal Art Gallery, Caldwell ID
Webster, Maryann, *Instr,* University of Utah, Dept of Art & Art History, Salt Lake City UT (S)
Webster, Sally, *Prof Emerita,* City University of New York, PhD Program in Art History, New York NY (S)
Weckel, Eric, *Chmn,* Abington Art Center, Jenkintown PA
Wedderspoon, Craig, *Dir Grad Studies Studio Art,* University of Alabama, Dept of Art, Tuscaloosa AL (S)
Weddig, Chris, *Exhib Preparator & Coordr,* University of Tennessee, McClung Museum of Natural History & Culture, Knoxville TN
Wedig, Dale, *Prof,* Northern Michigan University, Dept of Art & Design, Marquette MI (S)
Weech, Michael, *Curatorial Asst,* Heritage Museum Association, Inc, The Heritage Museum of Northwest Florida, Valparaiso FL
Weed, Rahila, *Assoc Prof,* University of Central Missouri, Dept of Art & Design, Warrensburg MO (S)
Weedman, Kenneth R, *Chmn,* Cumberland College, Dept of Art, Williamsburg KY (S)
Weekes, Monica, *Bd Secy,* The Phipps Center for the Arts, Galleries, Hudson WI
Weekly, Nancy, *Head Colls & Charles Cary Rumsey Cur,* Burchfield Penney Art Center, Buffalo NY
Weeks, Christopher W, *Assoc Prof,* Hillsborough Community College, Fine Arts Dept, Tampa FL (S)

Weeks, Dennis, *Prof Digital Photog,* Saint Joseph's University, Art Dept, Philadelphia PA (S)
Weeks, Jason, *Exec Dir,* Cambridge Arts Council, CAC Gallery, Cambridge MA
Weeks, John, *Dir,* University of Pennsylvania, Museum Library, Philadelphia PA
Weeks, Sarah, *Library Assoc,* Washington University, Kenneth & Nancy Kranzberg Art & Architecture Library, Saint Louis MO
Weems, Jason, *Asst Prof,* University of California, Riverside, Dept of the History of Art, Riverside CA (S)
Weese, Cynthia, *Dean,* Washington University, School of Architecture, Saint Louis MO (S)
Weese, Cynthia, *Dean School,* Washington University, School of Architecture, Saint Louis MO (S)
Weese, Judy, *Bus Mgr,* Landis Valley Village and Farm Museum, PA Historical & Museum Commission, Lancaster PA
Weg, Carol L, *VPres,* Wendell Gilley, Southwest Harbor ME
Wegner, Susan, *Dir Art History,* Bowdoin College, Art Dept, Brunswick ME (S)
Weider, Greg, *Media Arts & Animation,* Art Institute of Pittsburgh, Pittsburgh PA (S)
Weidman, Jim, *Interim Exec Dir,* Craft Alliance Center of Art & Design, Saint Louis MO
Weidner, Marsha, *Prof & Asian Grad Adv,* University of Kansas, Kress Foundation Dept of Art History, Lawrence KS (S)
Weiffenbach, Jeanie, *Exec Dir,* Roswell Museum & Art Center, Library, Roswell NM
Weigand, Herbert, *Chmn,* East Stroudsburg University, Fine Arts Center, East Stroudsburg PA (S)
Weigo, Norman, *Chmn,* Triton College, School of Arts & Sciences, River Grove IL (S)
Weigott, Joyce, *Accounting,* Maysville, Kentucky Gateway Museum Center, Maysville KY
Weiker, Anna, *Chmn Fashion Design,* Woodbury University, School of Media, Culture & Design, Burbank CA (S)
Weilan Hai, Willow, *Dir Galleries,* China Institute in America, China Institute Gallery, New York NY
Weiland, Kim, *Instr,* Ocean City Arts Center, Ocean City NJ (S)
Weiler, Megan, *Art in Pub Places Coordr,* City of Austin Parks & Recreation Department, Julia C Butridge Gallery, Austin TX
Weinberg, Adam, *Dir,* Whitney Museum of American Art, New York NY
Weiner, Howard, *Treas,* Mingei International, Inc, Mingei International Museum - Balboa Park & Mingei International Museum - Escondido, San Diego CA
Weiner, Joy L, *Dir Educ & Pub Progs,* The Heckscher Museum of Art, Huntington NY
Weingarden, Lauren, *Assoc Prof,* Florida State University, Art History Dept, Tallahassee FL (S)
Weinke, Jane, *Registrar & Cur Colls,* Leigh Yawkey Woodson Art Museum, Wausau WI
Weinkein, John L, *Chair,* Texas Woman's University Art Gallery, Denton TX
Weinkein, John, *Dir School of the Arts,* Texas Woman's University, School of the Arts, Dept of Visual Arts, Denton TX (S)
Weinreb, Allan M, *Interpretive Progs Asst,* New York State Office of Parks Recreation & Historic Preservation, John Jay Homestead State Historic Site, Katonah NY
Weinshall, Iris, *Chief Operating Officer, Chief Financial Officer, & Treasurer,* The New York Public Library, New York NY
Weinstein, Anne, *Asst Dir,* Hillel Foundation, Hillel Jewish Student Center Gallery, Cincinnati OH
Weinstein, Elizabeth, *Dir Interpretation & Museum Cur,* Louisiana Arts & Science Museum, Baton Rouge LA
Weinstein, Jennifer, *Exec Dir,* Southern Vermont Art Center, Gallery, Manchester VT
Weinstein, Kate, *Colls Mgr & Registrar,* Carl & Marilynn Thoma Art Foundation, Art House Santa Fe, Santa Fe NM
Weinstein, Raymond, *Chmn New Mem,* American Society of Contemporary Artists (ASCA), Yorktown Heights NY
Weinstein, Richard, *Prof,* Green Mountain College, Dept of Art, Poultney VT (S)
Weintraub, Max, *Gallery Dir & Cur,* Indiana University - Purdue University at Indianapolis, Herron Galleries, Indianapolis IN
Weir, Laura, *Asst Dir,* Long Beach Public Library, Long Beach NY
Weir, Marnie, *Dir Educ & Experience,* Worcester Art Museum, Worcester MA
Weis, Dick, *Prof,* Green Mountain College, Dept of Art, Poultney VT (S)
Weis, Richard, *Assoc Prof,* Grand Valley State University, Art & Design Dept, Allendale MI (S)
Weisberg, Gabriel P, *Prof,* University of Minnesota, Minneapolis, Art History, Minneapolis MN (S)
Weisbin, Kendra, *Asst Cur Educ,* Mount Holyoke College, Art Museum, South Hadley MA
Weise, Katrin, *Instr,* La Sierra University, Art Dept, Riverside CA (S)
Weise, Patricia, *Adj,* University of Saint Joseph, Connecticut, Dept of Fine Arts, West Hartford CT (S)
Weisenburger, Ray, *Assoc Dean,* Kansas State University, College of Architecture Planning & Design, Manhattan KS (S)
Weisend, Susan, *Chmn,* Ithaca College, Fine Art Dept, Ithaca NY (S)
Weisenfeld, Gennifer, *Assoc Prof & Dir Grad Studies,* Duke University, Dept of Art, Art History & Visual Studies, Durham NC (S)
Weiser, Stuart, *Deputy Dir,* Idaho Commission on the Arts, Boise ID
Weislogel, Andrew, *Cur Earlier Eur & Amer Art,* Cornell University, Herbert F Johnson Museum of Art, Ithaca NY
Weisman, Billie Milam, *Dir,* Frederick R Weisman Art Foundation, Los Angeles CA
Weiss Le, Jo, *Instr,* American University, Dept of Art, New York NY (S)
Weiss, Barton, *Assoc Prof,* University of Texas at Arlington, Art & Art History Department, Arlington TX (S)
Weiss, Daniel, *Acting Dir & CEO,* The Metropolitan Museum of Art, New York NY
Weiss, Emily C, *Gallery Mgr,* Volcano Art Center Gallery, Hawaii Volcanoes National Park HI
Weiss, Jeff, *Assoc Prof,* Rochester Institute of Technology, School of Photographic Arts & Sciences, Rochester NY (S)
Weiss, Jessica, *Head of Programs & Education,* Springville Museum of Art, Springville UT
Weiss, Karen, *Head, Digital Opers,* Archives of American Art, Smithsonian Institution, Washington DC
Weissberger, Robin, *Head Admin,* The Getty Center, The J Paul Getty Museum, Los Angeles CA
Weissenbach, Karl, *Dir,* National Archives and Records Administration, Eisenhower Presidential Library, Abilene KS
Weissinger, Sue, *Dir,* No Man's Land Historical Society, No Man's Land Museum, Goodwell OK
Weissman, Joel, *Asst Prof, Art Sculpture,* Ramapo College of New Jersey, School of Contemporary Arts, Mahwah NJ (S)
Weisz, Helen, *Instr,* Bucks County Community College, Fine Arts Dept, Newtown PA (S)
Weitan, Nelson, *Asst Prof,* University of Indianapolis, Dept Art & Design, Indianapolis IN (S)
Weitz, Ankeney, *Asst Prof,* Colby College, Art Dept, Waterville ME (S)
Weitz, Gayle, *Assoc Prof,* Appalachian State University, Dept of Art, Boone NC (S)
Weitzer, William, *Exec Dir,* Leo Baeck, Library, New York NY
Weitzer, William, *Exec Dir,* Leo Baeck, New York NY
Weitzman, Marty, *Pub Rels Dir,* Wave Hill, Bronx NY
Welch, Adam, *Cur,* Pittsburgh Center for the Arts, Pittsburgh PA
Welch, Adam, *Dir,* Greenwich House Pottery, First Floor Gallery, New York NY
Welch, Adam, *Dir,* Greenwich House Pottery, Library, New York NY
Welch, Adam, *Dir,* Greenwich House Pottery, Jane Hartsook Gallery, New York NY
Welch, Ben, *Park Dir,* Red Rock Park, Red Rock Park, Church Rock NM
Welch, Carrie, *Chief External Relations Officer,* The New York Public Library, New York NY
Welch, Elizabeth, *Executive Director,* Okefenokee Heritage Center, Inc, Waycross GA
Welch, Kjersten, *Admin Asst & Contact,* Sioux City Art Center, Sioux City IA
Welch, Kjersten, *Sec,* Sioux City Art Center, Sioux City IA (S)
Welch, Matthew, *Deputy Dir & Chief Cur,* Minneapolis Institute of Art, Minneapolis MN
Welch, Nancy, *Campus Dir,* Greenville Technical College, Visual Arts Dept, Greenville SC (S)
Welch, Roxie, *Bus Mgr,* Calvert Marine Museum, Solomons MD
Welch, Steven J, *Dir,* Corbit-Calloway Memorial Library, Odessa DE
Weldon, Scott, *Treas,* Association of Medical Illustrators, Lexington KY
Welker, Janie, *Cur Coll & Exhibs,* The University of Kentucky Art Museum, Lexington KY
Well-Off-Man, Manuela, *Chief Cur,* Institute of American Indian Arts, IAIA Museum of Contemporary Native Arts, Santa Fe NM
Wellenbach, Patricia, *Pres & CEO,* Please Touch Museum, Philadelphia PA
Weller, Eric, *Prof,* Texas State University - San Marcos, Dept of Art and Design, San Marcos TX (S)
Weller, Laurie, *Adjunct Assoc Prof,* Texas Woman's University, School of the Arts, Dept of Visual Arts, Denton TX (S)
Weller, Richard, *Prof & Chair, Landscape Architecture,* University of Pennsylvania, School of Design (PennDesign), Philadelphia PA (S)
Welliver, Michael, *Instr,* Mercer County Community College, Arts, Communication & Engineering Technology, West Windsor NJ (S)
Wellman, Lesley, *Cur Educ,* Dartmouth College, Hood Museum of Art, Hanover NH
Wellner, Laura, *Registrar,* Syracuse University, Art Collection, Syracuse NY
Wellner, Laura, *Registrar,* Syracuse University, SUArt Galleries, Syracuse NY
Wells, Annette, *Assoc Prof Sr,* Miami-Dade Community College, Arts & Philosophy Dept, Miami FL (S)
Wells, David, *Dir,* Edgewood College, DeRicci Gallery, Madison WI
Wells, Keith, *Cur,* Washington State University, Museum of Art, Pullman WA
Wells, Luther D, *Chmn,* Florida A & M University, Dept of Visual Arts, Humanities & Theatre, Tallahassee FL (S)
Wells, Morgan, *Cur Educ & Community Partnerships,* Tucson Museum of Art and Historic Block, Tucson AZ
Wells, Nicholas, *Bd Mem,* Utah Lawyers for the Arts, Salt Lake City UT
Wells, Pamela, *Community Relations,* Art and History Museums - Maitland, Maitland FL
Wells, Raymond, *Proj Dir,* National Conference of Artists, Michigan Chapter Gallery, Detroit MI
Wells, Rebecca, *Museum Cur,* Concordia Historical Institute, Saint Louis MO
Wells, Tom, *Photo Archivist,* Brigham Young University, Harold B Lee Library, Provo UT
Welnowska, Mira, *Instr,* Guild of Creative Art, Shrewsbury NJ (S)
Welsh, Rosemary, *Asst Prof,* Wells College, Dept of Art, Aurora NY (S)
Welsh, Susan, *Dir,* Museum of Arts & Sciences, Inc, Macon GA
Welter, Cole H, *Dir,* James Madison University, School of Art & Art History, Harrisonburg VA (S)
Welu, Judith A, *Assoc Prof,* Briar Cliff University, Art Dept, Sioux City IA (S)

Welu, William J, *Chairperson,* Briar Cliff University, Art Dept, Sioux City IA (S)
Welych, Anita, *Assoc Prof,* Cazenovia College, Center for Art & Design Studies, Cazenovia NY (S)
Wemmlinger, Raymond, *Cur & Librn,* Hampden-Booth Theatre Library, New York NY
Wendel, Joanna, *Cur Asst,* Harvard University, Busch-Reisinger Museum, Cambridge MA
Wendel, Lou, *Retail & Vis Svcs Mgr,* Cedar Rapids Museum of Art, Cedar Rapids IA
Wendland, Amy K, *Assoc Prof,* Fort Lewis College, Art Dept, Durango CO (S)
Wendt, Alex, *Visual Arts Comt Chair,* University of Minnesota, The Studio/Larson Gallery, Saint Paul MN
Wendt, Diane, *Bus Mgr,* Leigh Yawkey Woodson Art Museum, Wausau WI
Wendt, Doug, *Adjunct Prof Art,* University of Great Falls, Art Dept, Great Falls MT (S)
Wendt, Pan, *Cur,* Confederation Centre Art Gallery and Museum, Charlottetown PE
Wengler, Maureen, *Colls Mgr,* Art Complex Museum, Carl A Weyerhaeuser Library, Duxbury MA
Weninger, Beth, *Educ Dir,* Octagon Center for the Arts, Ames IA
Wenker, Jennifer, *Creative Dir,* Antioch College, Herndon Gallery, Yellow Springs OH
Wennerstrom, Brian, *Prog Coordr,* Truck Contemporary Art in Calgary, Calgary AB
Wentenhall, John, *Dir Museum,* Cheekwood Nashville's Home of Art & Gardens, Education Dept, Nashville TN (S)
Wentworth, Eryl J, *Dir,* American Architectural Foundation, The Octagon Museum, Washington DC
Wentworth, Eryl, *Exec Dir,* American Institute for Conservation of Historic & Artistic Works, Washington DC
Wentworth, Linda, *Head Borrower Servs,* Jones Library, Inc, Amherst MA
Wenz, Angharad, *Project Cur,* Dawson City Museum, Dawson City YT
Wenzel, Duane, *Head Librn,* Bernice Pauahi Bishop, Library & Archives, Honolulu HI
Werfel, Gina, *Chmn Art Studio,* University of California, Davis, Dept of Art & Art History, Davis CA (S)
Werhane, David, *Dir,* Philmont Scout Ranch, Philmont Museum - Seton Memorial Library, Cimarron NM
Werle, Thomas, *Prof,* Capitol Community Technical College, Humanities Division & Art Dept, Hartford CT (S)
Werline, Dee, *Pres,* Maysville, Kentucky Gateway Museum Center, Maysville KY
Werner, Lisa, *Dir Opers,* Centrum Arts & Creative Education, Port Townsend WA
Werner, Michael, *Assoc Prof,* State University of New York at Albany, Art Dept, Albany NY (S)
Werness, Hope, *Prof,* California State University, Art Dept, Turlock CA (S)
Werring, Joel, *Chmn Fine Arts,* Fashion Institute of Technology, School of Art & Design, New York NY (S)
Wertheimer, Gary, *Chmn,* Olivet College, Art Dept, Olivet MI (S)
Wertz, Sandra, *Chmn Media Arts,* University of South Carolina, Dept of Art, Columbia SC (S)
Wesaw Sloan, Sallie, *Graphic Designer,* Institute of American Indian Arts, IAIA Museum of Contemporary Native Arts, Santa Fe NM
Weselmann, Mona, *Registrar,* Saint Olaf College, Flaten Art Museum, Northfield MN
Wesley, John, *Photo Instr,* Bellevue Community College, Art Dept, Bellevue WA (S)
Wessel, Frederick, *Prof,* University of Hartford, Hartford Art School, West Hartford CT (S)
Wessel, Mary, *Adjunct Prof Photog,* Johnson County Community College, Fine Arts Dept & Art History Dept, Overland Park KS (S)
West, Amanda, *Instr,* Bob Jones University, School of Fine Arts, Div of Art & Design, Greenville SC (S)
West, Bruce, *Vis Lect,* Lewis & Clark College, Dept of Art, Portland OR (S)
West, Carolyn, *Prog Facilitator,* Central Florida Community College, Humanities Dept, Ocala FL (S)
West, Coleen, *Exec Dir,* Howard County Arts Council, Ellicott City MD
West, Mark, *Chmn Transportation Design,* College for Creative Studies, Detroit MI (S)
West, Matt, *Instr,* Laramie County Community College, Division of Arts & Humanities, Cheyenne WY (S)
West, Robert, *Dir Opers,* Boston Athenaeum, Boston MA
West, Ruth, *Instr,* Springfield College, Dept of Visual & Performing Arts, Springfield MA (S)
West, W., *Pres & CEO,* Autry National Center, Museum of the American West, Griffith Park, Los Angeles CA
Westbrook, Paul, *Asst Dean,* Northeastern State University, College of Arts & Letters, Tahlequah OK (S)
Westergard, Gina, *Assoc Prof,* University of Kansas, The School of the Arts, Dept of Visual Art, Lawrence KS (S)
Westerhaus, Sheree, *Planetarium Mgr,* Louisiana Arts & Science Museum, Baton Rouge LA
Westfall, Anna, *Assistant Professor of Visual and Communication Arts,* Eastern Mennonite University, Visual and Communication Arts, Harrisonburg VA (S)
Westfall, Chase, *Dir,* Virginia Commonwealth University, Anderson Gallery, Richmond VA
Westlake, Richard, *Theatre Arts Instr,* Edison Community College, Gallery of Fine Arts, Fort Myers FL (S)
Westman, Barbara, *Prof,* Slippery Rock University of Pennsylvania, Dept of Art, Slippery Rock PA (S)
Westman, Hans, *Media Arts & Animation,* Art Institute of Pittsburgh, Pittsburgh PA (S)
Westmark, Michelle, *Assoc Prof,* Bethel University, Dept of Art & Design, Saint Paul MN (S)
Weston, Victoria, *Assoc Prof,* University of Massachusetts - Boston, Art Dept, Boston MA (S)
Westpfahl, Richard, *Chmn,* Western Wisconsin Technical College, Graphics Division, La Crosse WI (S)
Westphal, Hayley, *Audience Engagement & PR Mgr,* Louisiana Arts & Science Museum, Baton Rouge LA
Wetenhall, John, *Dir,* George Washington University, The George Washington Museum and The Textile Museum, Washington DC
Wetherell, Leslie, *CFO,* Maryhill Museum of Art, Goldendale WA
Wethli, Mark, *Chair,* Bowdoin College, Art Dept, Brunswick ME (S)
Wetmore, Laura, *Cur Collections,* Arnot Art Museum, Elmira NY
Wetta, Frank, *Dean,* Daytona Beach Community College, Dept of Fine Arts & Visual Arts, Daytona Beach FL (S)
Wetzel, Annaleigh, *Mktg Coordr,* Intuit: The Center for Intuitive & Outsider Art, Chicago IL
Wetzel, Jean, *Assoc Prof Art History,* California Polytechnic State University at San Luis Obispo, Dept of Art & Design, San Luis Obispo CA (S)
Wetzel, Ray, *Cur,* Gadsden Museum of Art, Gadsden AL
Wetzig, Jeffrey, *Prof,* Bethel University, Dept of Art & Design, Saint Paul MN (S)
Wexler, Lynn, *Ref Librn,* Museum of Fine Arts, Houston, Hirsch Library, Houston TX
Weyer, Jeff, *Communications Specialist,* University of Wisconsin-Madison, Chazen Museum of Art, Madison WI
Weyerhaeuser, Charles A, *Dir & CEO,* Art Complex Museum, Carl A Weyerhaeuser Library, Duxbury MA
Weyerhaeuser, Charles, *Dir,* Art Complex Museum, Library, Duxbury MA
Weygandt, Virginia, *Dir Colls,* Clark County Historical Society, Heritage Center of Clark County, Springfield OH
Weyhrich, Denise, *Prof,* Chapman University, Art Dept, Orange CA (S)
Weymouth, George A, *Chmn (V),* Brandywine Conservancy, Brandywine River Museum, Chadds Ford PA
Whalen, Mary, *Chair Photog & Digital Media,* Kalamazoo Institute of Arts, KIA School, Kalamazoo MI (S)
Whalen, Wickie, *Prof,* Miami-Dade Community College, Arts & Philosophy Dept, Miami FL (S)
Whatford, Mark, *Librn,* Gunston Hall Plantation, Library, Mason Neck VA
Wheat, Robert, *Deputy Dir,* Louisiana Department of Culture, Recreation & Tourism, Louisiana State Museum,
Wheat, Steve, *Asst Dir Admin,* Alabama Department of Archives & History, Museum of Alabama, Montgomery AL
Wheeler, Alexadra, *Deputy Dir Advancement,* Whitney Museum of American Art, New York NY
Wheeler, Barbara, *Dir,* Roswell P Flower, Watertown NY
Wheeler, Bonnie, *Registrar,* Dundas Valley School of Art, Dundas ON (S)
Wheeler, Ken, *Vol Chmn,* River Heritage Museum, Paducah KY
Wheeler, Laura, *Vis Servs & Mus Shop Mgr,* Asheville Art Museum, Asheville NC
Wheeler, Lauren, *Pres,* Royal Alberta Museum, Provincial Archives of Alberta, Edmonton AB
Wheeler, Lawrence J, *Dir,* North Carolina Museum of Art, Raleigh NC
Wheeler, Linda, *Staff Coordr,* Cedarhurst Center for the Arts, Mitchell Museum, Mount Vernon IL
Wheeler, Lisa, *Educ,* Booth Western Art Museum, Cartersville GA
Wheeler, Stephen, *Fine Art,* San Diego Public Library, Art, Music & Recreation, San Diego CA
Wheelock, Arthur, *Cur Northern Baroque Painting,* National Gallery of Art, Washington DC
Wheelock, Scott, *Instr,* Main Line Art Center, Haverford PA (S)
Wheihan, Linda, *Museum Educator,* Brattleboro Museum & Art Center, Brattleboro VT
Whelan, Agnieszka, *Lect Sr,* Old Dominion University, Art Dept, Norfolk VA (S)
Whelan, Jeff, *Asst Prof,* Elizabeth City State University, School of Arts & Humanities, Dept of Art, Elizabeth City NC (S)
Whelan, John, *Instr,* Saint Mary's University of Minnesota, Art & Design Dept, Winona MN (S)
Wheless, Andrea, *Chmn,* High Point University, Fine Arts Dept, High Point NC (S)
Wherry, Martha, *Secy,* Gallery XII, Wichita KS
Whetstone, Jeff, *Asst Prof,* University of North Carolina at Chapel Hill, Art Dept, Chapel Hill NC (S)
Whetzel, Cate, *Prog Develop,* T C Steele State Historic Site, Nashville IN
Whiffen, Lorraine, *Grants & Membership Manager,* The Long Island Museum of American Art, History & Carriages, Stony Brook NY
Whine, Ben, *Assoc Dir,* SculptureCenter, Gallery, Long Island City NY
Whipple, Sally, *Exec Dir,* Old State House, Hartford CT
Whisenhunt, Brian Lee, *Exec Dir,* Museum of the Southwest, Midland TX
Whisler, Eddie, *Dir Planetarium & School Progs,* Museum of Science & History, Jacksonville FL
Whisman, Beth, *Dir Develop,* McLean County Historical Society, McLean County Museum of History, Bloomington IL
Whisonant, Brittney, *Adjunct,* Sheridan College, Art Dept, Sheridan WY (S)
Whistler, Debbie, *Interim Chmn Dept,* Hanover College, Dept of Art, Hanover IN (S)
Whitaker, Ashlee, *Head Cur,* Brigham Young University, Museum of Art, Provo UT
Whitaker, Jayne, *Asst Prof,* University of Dayton, Visual Arts Dept, Dayton OH (S)
Whitaker, Joel, *Asst Prof,* University of Dayton, Visual Arts Dept, Dayton OH (S)
White, Ali, *Artistic Dir,* Firehouse Center for the Arts, Institution for Savings Art Gallery, Bainbridge GA

White, Bethany, *Mus Educator,* New York State Office of Parks Recreation & Historic Preservation, John Jay Homestead State Historic Site, Katonah NY
White, Brooke, *Assoc Prof,* University of Mississippi, Department of Art, University MS (S)
White, Cara, *Mus Shop Mgr,* Cape Ann Museum, Gloucester MA
White, Carla, *Librn,* Martin and Osa Johnson, Scott Explorers Library, Chanute KS
White, Charles, *Chmn Dept Fine Arts,* La Salle University, Dept of Art, Philadelphia PA (S)
White, Charlie, *Prof & Head,* Carnegie Mellon University, School of Art, Pittsburgh PA (S)
White, Claire, *Gallery Shop Mgr,* The Dairy Barn Arts Center, Athens OH
White, David, *Prog Rep,* Southern Illinois University, Applied Arts, Carbondale IL (S)
White, Dennis, *Dean Fine & Performing Arts Div,* Antelope Valley College, Art Dept, Division of Fine Arts, Lancaster CA (S)
White, Derrick, *Prof & Art Dept Chair,* Tyler Junior College, Art Program, Tyler TX (S)
White, E Alan, *Prof,* University of Tennessee at Chattanooga, Dept of Art, Chattanooga TN (S)
White, Eric, *Chief,* Public Library of the District of Columbia, Audiovisual Division, Washington DC
White, Jake, *Develop Dir,* Orlando Museum of Art, Orlando Sentinel Library, Orlando FL
White, Jake, *Develop Dir,* Orlando Museum of Art, Orlando FL
White, James, *VPres,* Piatt Castles, West Liberty OH
White, Jennifer, *Registrar,* University of Illinois at Urbana-Champaign, Spurlock Museum, Urbana IL
White, John D, *Secy & Treas,* Pioneer Town, Pioneer Museum of Western Art, Wimberley TX
White, Kathy, *Deputy Dir,* Salvador Dali, Library, Saint Petersburg FL
White, Ken, *Chmn Fine Arts Photo,* Rochester Institute of Technology, School of Photographic Arts & Sciences, Rochester NY (S)
White, Kim, *Shop Mgr,* Arkansas Arts Center, Little Rock AR (S)
White, Larry, *Instr,* Long Beach City College, Art & Photography Dept, Long Beach CA (S)
White, Leigh, *Cur Educ,* Imperial Centre's Maria V Howard Arts Center, Rocky Mount NC
White, Leonard, *Events Mgr,* Socrates Sculpture Park, Long Island City NY
White, Mark, *Dir & Chief Cur,* University of Oklahoma, Fred Jones Jr Museum of Art, Norman OK
White, Matt, *Asst Prof,* University of Saint Francis, School of Creative Arts, Fort Wayne IN (S)
White, Matthew, *Dir,* Mamie McFaddin Ward, Beaumont TX
White, Matthew, *Dir,* Mamie McFaddin Ward, McFaddin-Ward House, Beaumont TX
White, Matthew, *Dir Education,* National Postal Museum, Smithsonian Institution, Washington DC
White, Michael, *Bd Chmn,* The Mattress Factory, Pittsburgh PA
White, Michael, *Chmn Crafts,* Rochester Institute of Technology, School of Design, Rochester NY (S)
White, Michael, *Dir,* Georgia State University, Ernest G Welch School of Art & Design, Atlanta GA (S)
White, Michelle, *Cur,* Menil Foundation, Inc, The Menil Collection, Houston TX
White, Patricia, *Pres,* Marion Art Center, Cecil Clark Davis Gallery, Marion MA
White, Rachel, *Asst Cur Educ,* Hunter Museum of American Art, Reference Library, Chattanooga TN
White, Rachel, *Cur Educ,* Birmingham Museum of Art, Birmingham AL
White, Stephen, *Founder,* DeLeon White Gallery, Toronto ON
White, Susanna, *Assoc Dir & Cur,* Hamilton College, Emerson Gallery, Clinton NY
White, Terri, *Object Conservator,* Milwaukee Art Museum, Milwaukee WI
White, Tommy, *Asst Prof,* Denison University, Studio Art Program, Granville OH (S)
White, Tony, *Assoc Chief Librn,* The Metropolitan Museum of Art, Museum Libraries, New York NY
White, Tony, *Head Librn,* Indiana University, Fine Arts Library, Bloomington IN
White, Wiley, *Develop Coord,* Troy-Pike Cultural Arts Center, Troy AL
Whitefield, Katharine, *Prog Dir,* Locust Street Neighborhood Art Classes, Inc, Buffalo NY (S)
Whitehead, Glen, *Asst Prof & Dir, Music,* University of Colorado-Colorado Springs, Visual & Performing Arts Dept (VAPA), Colorado Springs CO (S)
Whitehead, Jessie, *Franklin Fellow Asst Prof,* University of Georgia, Franklin College of Arts & Sciences, Lamar Dodd School of Art, Athens GA (S)
Whitehead, Vagner M, *Assoc Prof,* Oakland University, Dept of Art & Art History, Rochester MI (S)
Whitehouse, Margaret M, *Dir,* John D Barrow, Skaneateles NY
Whitelaw, Dana, *Exec Dir,* High Desert Museum, Bend OR
Whitelaw, Dawn, *VChmn,* Portrait Society of America, Tallahassee FL
Whites, Jennifer, *Educ & Art Coordr,* Cottonlandia Museum, Greenwood MS
Whitesell, John, *Prof,* University of Louisville, Allen R Hite Art Institute, Louisville KY (S)
Whitesell, Marilyn, *Asst Prof,* Indiana University-Southeast, Fine Arts Dept, New Albany IN (S)
Whiteside, Kathy, *Asst Prof,* South Plains College, Fine Arts Dept, Levelland TX (S)
Whiteside, Kirk, *Chmn Visual & Performing Arts,* Phillips Community College at The University of Arkansas, Dept of English & Fine Arts, Helena AR (S)
Whitfield, Bill, *Hist,* Ravalli County Museum, Hamilton MT
Whitfield, Herman, *Dir Concerts,* Ancient Spanish Monastery, North Miami Beach FL
Whitham, Sundra, *Pres,* Switzerland County Historical Society Inc, Life on the Ohio: River History Museum, Vevay IN
Whitham, Sundra, *Pres,* Switzerland County Historical Society Inc, Switzerland County Historical Museum, Vevay IN
Whiting, Janice, *Prof,* Augusta State University, Dept of Art, Augusta GA (S)
Whiting-Looze, Britney, *Develop Mgr,* Boise Art Museum, Boise ID
Whitley, Angela, *Office Mgr,* University of Mary Washington, University of Mary Washington Galleries, Fredericksburg VA
Whitlock, Jennifer, *Archivist,* Newfields, Stout Reference Library, Indianapolis IN
Whitlock, Veronica, *Area Coordr,* New York School of Interior Design, New York NY (S)
Whitlow, Joan, *Registrar,* Massachusetts Institute of Technology, MIT Museum, Cambridge MA
Whitmarsh, Lee, *Coordr New Media,* Texas A&M University Commerce, Dept of Art, Commerce TX (S)
Whitmore, Anthony, *Pres,* Potomac State College, Dept of Art, Keyser WV (S)
Whitmore, Erin, *Dir Educ,* The Old Jail Art Center, Albany TX
Whitmore, Stacia, *VPres Institutional Giving,* Chicago Children's Museum, Chicago IL
Whitmore, Sue, *Assoc Prof,* California State University, Chico, Department of Art & Art History, Chico CA (S)
Whitney, Barb, *Exec Dir,* Lansing Art Gallery, Lansing MI
Whitney, Catherine, *Chief Cur & Cur American Art,* Philbrook Museum of Art, Tulsa OK
Whitney, Judy, *Dir Devel,* Museum of Fine Arts, Saint Petersburg, Florida, Inc, Saint Petersburg FL
Whitney, Linda, *Dept Chair,* Valley City State College, Art Dept, Valley City ND (S)
Whitney, Lynn, *Chmn 2-D Studies,* Bowling Green State University, School of Art, Bowling Green OH (S)
Whitney, Patrick, *Dir,* Illinois Institute of Technology, Institute of Design, Chicago IL (S)
Whitridge, Roger, *Prof Drawing & Painting,* Orange Coast College, Visual & Performing Arts Division, Costa Mesa CA (S)
Whitsett, Darron, *Instr Children's d&p,* Locust Street Neighborhood Art Classes, Inc, Buffalo NY (S)
Whittel, Pattie, *Mus Shop Mgr,* Noah Webster House, Inc, Noah Webster House & West Hartford Historical Society, West Hartford CT
Whitten, Morris, *Educator,* Taos Historic Museums, Ernest Blumenschein Home & Studio, Taos NM
Whitten, Richard, *Asst Prof,* Rhode Island College, Art Dept, Providence RI (S)
Whittenberg, Bruce, *Dir,* Montana Historical Society, Helena MT
Whittingham, E Michael, *Pres & CEO,* Oklahoma City Museum of Art, Oklahoma City OK
Whittingham, Selby, *Trustee, London,* JMW Turner Museum, Sarasota FL
Whittington, Amelia, *Mem Coordr,* Ogden Museum of Southern Art, University of New Orleans, New Orleans LA
Whittington, Blair, *Librn,* Glendale Public Library, Brand Library & Art Center, Glendale CA
Whittington, Caitlin, *Designer,* The New York Public Library, The New York Public Library for the Performing Arts, New York NY
Whittington, E Michael, *Exec Dir,* Monterey Museum of Art, Monterey Museum of Art -Pacific Street, Monterey Museum of Art - La Mirada, Monterey CA
Whitton, Heather, *Assoc Dean Material, Art & Design,* Sheridan College, Faculty of Animation, Arts & Design, Oakville ON (S)
Whitty, Jeannie, *Events Coordr,* Oatlands Plantation, Leesburg VA
Whitwam, Melissa, *Exec Dir & Exhibs Mgr,* Foundry Art Centre, Saint Charles MO
Whitworth, Kent, *Exec Dir,* Kentucky Historical Society, Old State Capitol & Annex, Frankfort KY
Whorf, Sarah, *Assoc Prof,* Humboldt State University, College of Arts & Humanities, Art Dept, Arcata CA (S)
Wiant, Michael, *Interim Dir,* Illinois State Museum, ISM Lockport Gallery, Chicago Gallery & Southern Illinois Art Gallery, Springfield IL
Wicha, Simone, *Dir,* University of Texas at Austin, Blanton Museum of Art, Austin TX
Wick, Artis, *Assoc Librn,* Florida State University, The John and Mable Ringling Museum of Art Library, Sarasota FL
Wick, Bruce, *Chief Preparator,* American University, Museum at the Katzen, Washington DC
Wicker, Nancy L, *Chair & Prof,* University of Mississippi, University Gallery, University MS
Wicker, Nancy, *Prof,* University of Mississippi, Department of Art, University MS (S)
Wicklund, Jackie, *Mus Shop Mgr,* South Shore Arts, Munster IN
Wickre, Bille, *Prof,* Albion College, Bobbitt Visual Arts Center, Albion MI
Wicks, Molly, *Instr,* South Dakota State University, Dept of Visual Arts, Brookings SD (S)
Wicks, Richard, *Dir,* Miami University, Art Museum, Oxford OH
Wicks, Stephen, *Cur,* Knoxville Museum of Art, Knoxville TN
Widgery, Kristi, *Spec & Rental Events Coordr,* Museum of Contemporary Art Chicago, Chicago IL
Widmer, Jason, *Instr,* Linn Benton Community College, Fine & Applied Art Dept, Albany OR (S)
Widmer, Jess, *Instr Adult Drawing & Painting,* Locust Street Neighborhood Art Classes, Inc, Buffalo NY (S)
Widrick, Melissa, *Cur Educ,* Jefferson County Historical Society, Watertown NY
Wieck, Roger, *Cur & Dept Head Medieval & Renaissance Manuscripts,* The Morgan Library & Museum, Museum, New York NY

Wiedemann, D, *Prof,* City Colleges of Chicago, Daley College, Chicago IL (S)
Wiedemeyer, Ruth, *Shop Mgr,* Octagon Center for the Arts, Ames IA
Wiedenbaum, Marlene, *Recording Sec,* New York Society of Women Artists, Inc, Westport CT
Wiedenheft, Eileen, *Registrar,* Boise Art Museum, Boise ID
Wiederspahn, Peter, *Asst Prof,* Northeastern University, Dept of Art & Architecture, Boston MA (S)
Wiegmann, Richard, *Prof,* Concordia University, Art Dept, Seward NE (S)
Wier, Alyssum, *Exec Dir,* Arts Council of Mendocino County, Ukiah CA
Wierdrich, Alicyn, *Cur,* Imperial Centre's Maria V Howard Arts Center, Rocky Mount NC
Wierich, Jochen, *Interim Chief Cur,* Mississippi Museum of Art, Jackson MS
Wiersema, Juliet, *Asst Prof,* University of Texas at San Antonio, Dept of Art & Art History, San Antonio TX (S)
Wiersema, Susan, *Educ Coordr, Shipping Assoc & Art Rental,* Bainbridge Arts & Crafts Gallery, Bainbridge Island WA
Wiertz, Michael, *Dir Visitor Svcs,* Wave Hill, Bronx NY
Wiese, Vicki, *Colls Mgr,* Coos County Historical Society Museum, Coos Bay OR
Wiesenfeud, Alexandra, *Professor of Art,* Los Angeles City College, School of Visual & Media Arts, Los Angeles CA (S)
Wieske, Ellen, *Asst Dir,* Haystack Mountain School of Crafts, Center for Community Programs Gallery, Deer Isle ME
Wiggins, Denise, *Lab Coordr,* Wisconsin Historical Society, Wisconsin Historical Museum, Madison WI
Wiggins, Ginger, *Gallery Coordr,* Associated Artists of Winston-Salem, Winston-Salem NC
Wiggins, Mike, *Prof,* Abilene Christian University, Dept of Art & Design, Abilene TX (S)
Wigglesworth, Marisa, *Pres & CEO,* Buffalo Society of Natural Sciences, Buffalo Museum of Science, Buffalo NY
Wight, Darlene Coward, *Cur Inuit Art,* The Winnipeg Art Gallery, Winnipeg MB
Wight, Gail, *Assoc Prof & Dir Art Practice,* Stanford University, Dept of Art & Art History, Stanford CA (S)
Wight, Karol, *Pres & Exec Dir,* Corning Museum of Glass, Museum, Corning NY
Wightman, Jan, *Treas,* Dawson County Historical Society, Museum, Lexington NE
Wightman, Lisa Gregg, *Prof,* Munson-Williams-Proctor Arts Institute, Pratt MWP College of Art, Utica NY (S)
Wiklund, Ann, *Adjunct Prof Art History,* Johnson County Community College, Fine Arts Dept & Art History Dept, Overland Park KS (S)
Wilbers, Tim, *Assoc Prof,* University of Dayton, Visual Arts Dept, Dayton OH (S)
Wilbur, Kathy, *Bookkeeper,* Vesterheim Norwegian-American Museum, Decorah IA
Wilburn, Claudia, *Studio Arts Prog Dir,* Brenau University, Art & Design Dept, Gainesville GA (S)
Wilburn, Hugh, *Librn,* Harvard University, Frances Loeb Library, Cambridge MA
Wilburn, Karen, *CFO & VPres Admin,* Grand Rapids Public Museum, Grand Rapids MI
Wilcox, Christine, *Pres,* Lincoln Arts Council, Lincoln NE
Wilcox, Jeffrey, *Registrar,* University of Missouri, Museum of Art & Archaeology, Columbia MO
Wilcox, Lawrence, *Instr,* New Mexico Junior College, Arts & Sciences, Hobbs NM (S)
Wilcox, Scott, *COO,* Amon Carter Museum of American Art, Fort Worth TX
Wilcox, Scott, *Deputy Dir Collections,* Yale University, Yale Center for British Art, New Haven CT
Wilcox, Steve, *Communs Dir,* Arizona Commission on the Arts, Phoenix AZ
Wilcoxen, Jessa, *Asst Prof,* Greenville College, Art Dept, Greenville IL (S)
Wilcoxson, Shirlie Bowers, *Chmn & Prof Emerita,* Saint Gregory's University, Dept of Art, Shawnee OK (S)
Wilczek, Ronald, *Prof,* Roger Williams University, Visual Art Dept, Bristol RI (S)
Wild, Jane, *Educ & Prog Coordr,* Art Gallery of Peterborough, Peterborough ON
Wilde, Laura, *Exec Dir,* Xico Inc, Phoenix AZ
Wilde, Robert, *Instr,* College of Saint Benedict, Art Dept, Saint Joseph MN (S)
Wilde, Robert, *Lectr,* Saint John's University, Art Dept, Collegeville MN (S)
Wilder, Baasil, *Librn,* National Postal Museum, Library, Washington DC
Wilder, Baasil, *Librn,* Anacostia Community Museum, Library, Washington DC
Wilder, Michael, *Chmn,* Southwestern College, Art Dept, Winfield KS (S)
Wilder, Stanley, *Dean Libraries,* Louisiana State University, Middleton Library, Baton Rouge LA
Wilder, Stanley, *Dean LSU Libraries,* Louisiana State University, Library, Baton Rouge LA
Wilder, Susan, *Dean,* Heartwood College of Art, Main Gallery, Biddeford ME
Wilder, Wendy, *Bookkeeper,* Vermilion County Museum Society, Danville IL
Wilder, Wendy, *Bookkeeper,* Vermilion County Museum Society, Library, Danville IL
Wildey, Al, *Chmn Dept,* Central Michigan University, Dept of Art, Mount Pleasant MI (S)
Wildey, Sharon A, *Legal Affairs Adv to Bd,* Brown County Art Gallery Foundation, Nashville IN
Wiles, Stephanie, *Dir,* Yale University, Yale University Art Gallery, New Haven CT
Wiley, Francis, *Gallery Mgr,* Redlands Art Association, Redlands Art Association Gallery & Art Center, Redlands CA
Wilfong, Terry, *Assoc Cur,* University of Michigan, Kelsey Museum of Archaeology, Ann Arbor MI
Wilhelm, Elliot, *Cur Film,* Detroit Institute of Arts, Detroit MI
Wilhelms, Nancy, *Exec Dir,* Anderson Ranch Arts Center, Snowmass Village CO
Wilhoit, Sarah, *Asst Prof,* Harding University, Dept of Art & Design, Searcy AR (S)
Wilk, Elizabeth, *Registrar,* Wheaton Arts & Cultural Center, Museum of American Glass, Millville NJ
Wilk, Joseph, *Instr,* Antonelli Institute, Professional Photography & Commercial Art, Erdenheim PA (S)
Wilke, Amanda, *Educ Dir,* LeMoyne Art Foundation, Center for the Visual Arts, Tallahassee FL
Wilken, Marilyn, *Art Gallery Chmn & Secy,* Iroquois County Historical Society Museum, Old Courthouse Museum, Watseka IL
Wilkes, Peggy, *Lectr,* Texas A&M University-Kingsville, Art Dept, Kingsville TX (S)
Wilkie, Jane J, *Treas,* Plastic Club, Art Club, Philadelphia PA
Wilkins, Cary, *Librn & Archivist,* Morris Museum of Art, Augusta GA
Wilkins, David, *Prof Emeritus,* University of Pittsburgh, Henry Clay Frick Dept History of Art & Architecture, Pittsburgh PA (S)
Wilkins, Kristen, *Asst Prof,* University of Southern Indiana, Art & Design Dept, Evansville IN (S)
Wilkins, Nancy, *Instr,* Marylhurst University, Art Dept, Marylhurst OR (S)
Wilkins, Rebecca, *Asst Mgr,* Queens Borough Public Library, Fine Arts & Recreation Division, Jamaica NY
Wilkins, Will K, *Exec Dir,* Real Art Ways (RAW), Hartford CT
Wilkinson, Carlton, *Sr Lectr,* Vanderbilt University, Dept of Art, Nashville TN (S)
Wilkinson, John, *Dir Independent Studies,* Dundas Valley School of Art, Dundas ON (S)
Wilkinson, Lonnie, *Instr,* Southern University A & M College, School of Architecture, Baton Rouge LA (S)
Wilkinson, Sean, *Prof,* University of Dayton, Visual Arts Dept, Dayton OH (S)
Wilkinson, Steve, *Assoc Prof Graphic Design,* Watkins College of Art, Design & Film, Nashville TN (S)
Will, Gary, *Chair,* Bradley University, Dept of Art, Peoria IL (S)
Will, Gary, *Chmn Art Dept,* Bradley University, Heuser Art Center, Peoria IL
Willaert, James W., *Cur Interpretation,* Wade House Historic Site-Wisconsin Historical Society, Wesley W. Jung Carriage Museum, Greenbush WI
Willar, Carrie, *Interim Exec Dir,* Woodrow Wilson, Washington DC
Willard, David, *Dept Head,* West Texas A&M University, Art, Theatre & Dance Dept, Canyon TX (S)
Willard, Shirley, *Pres Emerita,* Fulton County Historical Society Inc, Fulton County Museum (Tetzlaff Reference Room), Rochester IN
Willcox, Christine, *Assoc Prof,* Macalester College, Art & Art History Dept, Saint Paul MN (S)
Willens, Michele, *Deputy Chief and Senior Archivist,* National Gallery of Art, Washington DC
Willer, John, *Co-owner,* Eureka Fine Art Gallery, Eureka Springs AR
Willers, Karl Emil, *Dir,* Nassau County Museum of Art, Roslyn Harbor NY
Willet, Jennifer, *Prof, Print & Bio Art,* University of Windsor, School of Creative Arts, Windsor ON (S)
Willett, Catherine, *Develop Officer,* Buffalo Arts Studio, Art Gallery, Buffalo NY
Willett, Erin, *Gallery Coordr & Opers Mgr,* 1708 Gallery, Richmond VA
Willett, John, *Board Member,* Folk Art Society of America, Richmond VA
Willetts, Khell, *Exec Dir,* Art League of Houston, Houston TX
William, Don, *Dean of Hancock Col of Liberal Arts,* Lubbock Christian University, Dept of Communication & Fine Art, Lubbock TX (S)
Williamon, Scott, *Facilities Mgr,* Anniston Museum of Natural History, Anniston AL
Williams, Al, *Pres,* San Francisco African-American Historical & Cultural Society, San Francisco CA
Williams, Alfred, *Pres,* San Francisco African-American Historical & Cultural Society, Library, San Francisco CA
Williams, Angela, *COO & Dep CEO Archives & Mus Opers,* Royal BC Museum, Victoria BC
Williams, Annette, *Instr,* Southern University A & M College, School of Architecture, Baton Rouge LA (S)
Williams, Anthony, *Chmn,* International Foundation for Art Research, Inc (IFAR), New York NY
Williams, Barbara, *Dir & Owner,* The Mather Homestead Museum, Library & Memorial Park, Wellsville NY
Williams, Benjamin, *Librn & Spec Coll Librn,* Field Museum, Library, Chicago IL
Williams, Blair, *Gallery Asst,* The Art Spirit Gallery, Coeur D Alene ID
Williams, Brad, *Pres,* Wellfleet Historical Society & Museum, Inc, Wellfleet MA
Williams, Brandon, *Lectr,* Savannah State University, Dept of Fine Arts, Savannah GA (S)
Williams, Caitlin, *Cur Art,* Art Museum of Southeast Texas, Beaumont TX
Williams, Carolyn, *Chair,* Academy Art Museum, Easton MD
Williams, Cecil, *Instr,* Claflin College, Dept of Art, Orangeburg SC (S)
Williams, Chad, *Dir,* Oklahoma Historical Society, Research Center, Oklahoma City OK
Williams, Cynthia, *Bd Pres,* Neustadt Collection of Tiffany Glass, Long Island City NY
Williams, Daniel, *Preparator,* Upfor Gallery, Portland OR
Williams, Deborah, *Develop Coordr,* Brick Store Museum, Kennebunk ME
Williams, Ed, *Dir Photo,* Art Institute of Fort Lauderdale, Fort Lauderdale FL (S)
Williams, Eliza, *Development Officer,* Akron Art Museum, Akron OH

Williams, Glen, *Assoc Prof,* Northwest Missouri State University, Dept of Fine & Performing Arts, Maryville MO (S)
Williams, Glenda, *Dir Libr Servs,* City of Long Beach, Long Beach Public Library, Long Beach CA
Williams, Glenn, *Olive DeLuce Art Gallery Coordr,* Northwest Missouri State University, DeLuce Art Gallery, Maryville MO
Williams, Greg, *Asst Dir,* Colby College, Museum of Art, Waterville ME
Williams, Heather, *Dir,* Gertrude Herbert Institute of Art, Augusta GA
Williams, J Dustin, *Archivist,* Carnegie Mellon University, Hunt Institute for Botanical Documentation, Pittsburgh PA
Williams, James, *Creative Dir,* Birmingham Museum of Art, Birmingham AL
Williams, Jane, *Agent,* Jack Richard Gallery, Almond Tea Museum & Jane Williams Galleries, Divisions of Studios of Jack Richard, Cuyahoga Falls OH
Williams, Jay, *Cur Coll & Exhibs,* Vero Beach Museum of Art, Vero Beach FL
Williams, Jim, *Prof Fine Arts,* University of Cincinnati, School of Art, Cincinnati OH (S)
Williams, Jim, *Ranch Mgr,* Will Rogers Memorial Museum & Birthplace Ranch, Claremore OK
Williams, John A, *Mem Bd Dir,* Hatch-Billops Collection, Inc, New York NY
Williams, John, *Lectr,* Longwood University, Dept of Art, Farmville VA (S)
Williams, Jordan, *Exhib Coordr,* Troy-Pike Cultural Arts Center, Troy AL
Williams, Jovani, *Cur Tolson Ctr,* Langston University, Melvin B Tolson Black Heritage Center, Langston OK
Williams, Katherine, *Community Prog Coordr,* Kendall College of Art & Design, Urban Institute for Contemporary Arts, Grand Rapids MI
Williams, KC, *Gallery Dir,* Northwest Florida State College, Mattie Kelly Arts Center Galleries, Niceville FL (S)
Williams, Keith, *Chmn,* Concordia University, Art and Design Department, Saint Paul MN (S)
Williams, Kelly, *Dir Mktg &Communs,* History Colorado Center Museum, Denver CO
Williams, Ken, *Prof Graphic Design,* University of Georgia, Franklin College of Arts & Sciences, Lamar Dodd School of Art, Athens GA (S)
Williams, Kevin, *Archivist,* Tulane University, Southeastern Architectural Archive, New Orleans LA
Williams, Lawrence, *Prof,* Rochester Institute of Technology, School of Design, Rochester NY (S)
Williams, Leslie, *Assoc Prof,* West Texas A&M University, Art, Theatre & Dance Dept, Canyon TX (S)
Williams, Linda, *Prof of Art History,* University of Puget Sound, Dept of Art & Art History, Tacoma WA (S)
Williams, Linda, *Secy,* Austin College, Art Dept, Sherman TX (S)
Williams, Lyle, *Cur Prints & Drawings,* McNay Art Museum, San Antonio TX
Williams, Lynda, *Bus Mgr,* Arnot Art Museum, Elmira NY
Williams, Lyneise, *Asst Prof,* University of North Carolina at Chapel Hill, Art Dept, Chapel Hill NC (S)
Williams, Lynora, *Dir of Library & Research Center,* National Museum of Women in the Arts, Washington DC
Williams, Lynora, *Librn,* George Washington University, Arthur D Jenkins Library, Washington DC
Williams, Mabel, *Director of Finance,* Academy Art Museum, Easton MD
Williams, Maggie, *Asst Prof,* William Paterson University, Dept Arts, Wayne NJ (S)
Williams, Mara, *Chief Cur,* Brattleboro Museum & Art Center, Brattleboro VT
Williams, Mark, *Chmn,* West Liberty State College, Div Art, West Liberty WV (S)
Williams, Mildred, *Box Office Mgr,* City of Hampton, Hampton Arts Commission, Hampton VA
Williams, Paige, *Instr,* Art Academy of Cincinnati, Cincinnati OH (S)
Williams, Pat Ward, *Prof,* Florida State University, Art Dept, Tallahassee FL (S)
Williams, Paula, *Exec Dir,* Albany Museum of Art, Albany GA
Williams, Peggy, *Bd Vice Chair,* American Association of University Women, Washington DC
Williams, Peter, *Art Instr,* Kellogg Community College, Arts & Communication Dept, Battle Creek MI (S)
Williams, Peter, *VPres Exhibits & Bldg Opers,* Chicago Children's Museum, Chicago IL
Williams, Phill, *Library Admin,* Warner Bros Studio Research Library, Burbank CA
Williams, Richard, *Prof,* Miami-Dade Community College, Arts & Philosophy Dept, Miami FL (S)
Williams, Robert, *Instr,* South Central Technical College, Commercial & Technical Art Dept, North Mankato MN (S)
Williams, Robert, *Instr,* Wagner College, Arts Administration Dept, Staten Island NY (S)
Williams, Roberta, *Instr,* Marian University, Visual Arts Dept, Indianapolis IN (S)
Williams, Roddy, *Dir Opers,* The Names Project Foundation AIDS Memorial Quilt, Atlanta GA
Williams, Roger D, *Exec Dir,* Quapaw Quarter Association, Inc, Preservation Resource Center/ Historic Cannon Hall, Little Rock AR
Williams, Teressa, *Resource Ctr Mgr/Librn,* Anchorage Museum at Rasmuson Center, Atwood Alaska Resource Center, Anchorage AK
Williams, Terrence, *Assoc Prof,* Catholic University of America, School of Architecture & Planning, Washington DC (S)
Williams, Thomas, *Asst Prof Art History,* Watkins College of Art, Design & Film, Nashville TN (S)
Williams, W Benjamin, *Librn,* Field Museum, Library, Chicago IL
Williams, Wayne, *Prof,* Finger Lakes Community College, Visual & Performing Arts Dept, Canandaigua NY (S)
Williamson, Calvin, *Chmn Science & Math,* Fashion Institute of Technology, School of Art & Design, New York NY (S)
Williamson, Elizabeth, *Exec Dir,* Handweavers Guild of America, Suwanee GA
Williamson, Ginger, *Instr,* Greensboro College, Dept of Art, Division of Fine Arts, Greensboro NC (S)
Williamson, Jacquelyn, *Asst Prof,* George Mason University, College of Humanities & Social Sciences, Dept of History & Art History, Fairfax VA (S)
Williamson, Jan, *Exec Dir,* 18th Street Arts Complex, Santa Monica CA
Williamson, Jane, *Dir,* Rokeby Museum, Ferrisburgh VT
Williamson, Janet, *Slide Librn,* University of Georgia, Dept of Art Lamar Dodd School of Art, Athens GA
Willick, Damon, *Asst Prof,* Loyola Marymount University, Dept of Art & Art History, Los Angeles CA (S)
Willing-Booher, Denise, *1st VPres,* National Watercolor Society, San Pedro CA
Willis, Jan, *Dir,* Lee County Library, Tupelo MS
Willis, Jim, *Art Head,* Northwest Nazarene College, Art Dept, Nampa ID (S)
Willis, Pauline, *Dir,* The American Federation of Arts, New York NY
Willis, William, *Morris Eminent Scholar in Art,* Augusta State University, Dept of Art, Augusta GA (S)
Willits, Zinnia, *Dir Coll & Opers,* Gibbes Museum of Art, Charleston SC (S)
Willits, Zinnia, *Dir Colls & Opers,* Carolina Art Association, Gibbes Museum of Art, Charleston SC
Willkom, Jan, *Grant Proj Dir,* Tucson Museum of Art and Historic Block, Library, Tucson AZ
Willman, Merle, *Asst Dept Head,* University of Massachusetts, Amherst, Dept of Landscape Architecture & Regional Planning, Amherst MA (S)
Willner, Judith, *Chmn,* Coppin State College, Dept Fine & Communication Arts, Baltimore MD (S)
Willoughby, Laura, *Coll Cur,* The City of Petersburg Museums, Petersburg VA
Wills, Misti, *HR Resources & Office Mgr,* The American Federation of Arts, New York NY
Wills, Sherri, *Assoc Prof,* University of Rhode Island, Dept of Art & Art History, Kingston RI (S)
Willse, Michael, *Assoc Prof,* Rosemont College, Art Program, Rosemont PA (S)
Willumson, Glenn, *Prof,* University of Florida, School of Art & Art History, Gainesville FL (S)
Willwerth, Ardis, *Dir Exhib,* Pasadena Museum of History, Pasadena CA
Wilmarth-Rabineau, Susan, *Asst Prof,* University of Hartford, Hartford Art School, West Hartford CT (S)
Wilsbach, Tom, *Art & AV Librn,* Portland Public Library, Art - Audiovisual Dept, Portland ME
Wilson Aden, Patricia, *Pres & CEO,* African American Museum in Philadelphia, Philadelphia PA
Wilson Horne, Catherine, *Pres & CEO,* Discovery Place Inc, Nature Museum, Charlotte NC
Wilson, Aaron, *Assoc Prof,* University of Northern Iowa, Dept of Art, Cedar Falls IA (S)
Wilson, Aaron, *Asst,* Beloit College, Wright Museum of Art, Beloit WI
Wilson, Alex, *Mgr Art Educ,* Paint Creek Center for the Arts, Rochester MI
Wilson, Bradley, *Visual Arts & Gallery Dir,* Creative Arts Guild, Dalton GA
Wilson, Bruce, *Archivist,* Wiscasset, Waterville & Farmington Railway Museum (WW&F), Alna ME
Wilson, Catherine, *Exec Dir,* Greene County Historical Society, Xenia OH
Wilson, Cathey, *Vol Tours Coordr,* The Sherwin Miller Museum of Jewish Art, Tulsa OK
Wilson, Cathryn, *Circ Coordr,* Milwaukee Institute of Art & Design, Library, Milwaukee WI
Wilson, Cathy, *Dir Grad Studies,* Memphis College of Art, Memphis TN (S)
Wilson, Cindy, *Adjunct Asst Prof,* Spokane Falls Community College, Fine Arts Dept, Spokane WA (S)
Wilson, Craig, *Asst Dir Library Collections,* University of Delaware, Morris Library, Newark DE
Wilson, Donny, *Dir,* Wallace State Community College, Evelyn Burrow Museum, Hanceville AL
Wilson, Gary, *Assoc Prof Art,* Monroe County Community College, Fine Arts Council, Monroe MI
Wilson, Gary, *Asst Prof Art,* Monroe County Community College, Humanities Division, Monroe MI (S)
Wilson, Gordon, *Dept Chair, Prof,* Whitworth University, Art Dept, Spokane WA (S)
Wilson, Hazel Mohamed, *Asst Cur & Webmaster,* The Ethel Wright Mohamed Stitchery Museum, Belzoni MS
Wilson, Heather, *Develop Officer,* Cameron Art Museum, Wilmington NC
Wilson, Jackie, *Educ Asst,* Iowa State University, Brunnier Art Museum, Ames IA
Wilson, Jennifer, *CFO,* Reading Public Museum, Reading PA
Wilson, Jessica, *Asst Prof,* Western New Mexico University, Expressive Arts Dept, Silver City NM (S)
Wilson, John, *Exec Dir,* Lakeside Studio, Lakeside MI
Wilson, John, *Instr,* Wayne Art Center, Wayne PA (S)
Wilson, Joyce, *Chmn,* Bellevue College, Art Dept, Bellevue NE (S)
Wilson, Kate, *Dir Devel,* Chrysler Museum of Art, Norfolk VA
Wilson, Katherine, *Mgr Exhibs & Collections,* University of Iowa, University of Iowa Museum of Art, Iowa City IA
Wilson, Kay, *Cur Coll,* Grinnell College, Faulconer Gallery, Grinnell IA
Wilson, Keyser, *Asst Prof,* Stillman College, Stillman Art Gallery & Art Dept, Tuscaloosa AL (S)

Wilson, Kristina, *Cur Asst,* Danforth Museum of Art, Danforth Museum of Art, Framingham MA

Wilson, Laura, *Exec Asst,* Kalamazoo Institute of Arts, Kalamazoo MI

Wilson, Letha, *Artists File Coordr,* Artists Space, Irving Sandler Artists File, New York NY

Wilson, Margit, *Librn,* Walker Art Center, Library and Archives, Minneapolis MN

Wilson, Marilyn, *Admin Mgr,* Polk Museum of Art, Lakeland FL

Wilson, Martha, *Founding Dir,* Franklin Furnace Archive, Inc, Brooklyn NY

Wilson, Neal, *Prof,* Texas State University - San Marcos, Dept of Art and Design, San Marcos TX (S)

Wilson, Pierre, *Dir,* Musee des Maitres et Artisans du Quebec, Montreal QC

Wilson, R, *Instr,* University of Southern Maine, Dept of Art, Gorham ME (S)

Wilson, Ric, *Assoc Prof (Graphic Design, Interactive Media),* University of Missouri - Columbia, Dept of Art, Columbia MO (S)

Wilson, Roger D (Sam), *Prof,* University of Utah, Dept of Art & Art History, Salt Lake City UT (S)

Wilson, Sara, *Dir,* Saint Joseph Museum, Inc., Saint Joseph MO

Wilson, Sheila, *Asst Prof,* Denison University, Studio Art Program, Granville OH (S)

Wilson, Sheilah, *Res Dir,* Santa Fe Arts Institute, Santa Fe NM (S)

Wilson, Siona, *Asst Prof,* College of Staten Island, Performing & Creative Arts Dept, Staten Island NY (S)

Wilson, Ted, *Registrar,* National Postal Museum, Smithsonian Institution, Washington DC

Wilson, Wallace, *Dir,* University of South Florida, School of Art & Art History, Tampa FL (S)

Wilson, Walter, *Design & Instillation Specailist,* University of Illinois at Urbana-Champaign, Krannert Art Museum and Kinkead Pavilion, Champaign IL

Wilson, Wesley, *Chief State Library Resource Center,* Enoch Pratt, Baltimore MD

Wilson, Will, *Asst Prof,* Oberlin College, Dept of Art, Oberlin OH (S)

Wilt, Matt, *Ceramics,* Sam Houston State University, Art Dept, Huntsville TX (S)

Wiltgen, Adam, *Prog Dir,* Lanesboro Arts Center, Lanesboro MN

Wilton, John, *Prof,* Daytona Beach Community College, Dept of Fine Arts & Visual Arts, Daytona Beach FL (S)

Wiltrout, Douglas, *Pres,* National Society of Painters in Casein & Acrylic, Inc, Whitehall PA

Wiltse, Terri, *Opers Mgr,* League of New Hampshire Craftsmen, Grodin Permanent Collection Museum, Concord NH

Wilzig, Naomi, *Owner, Cur,* World Erotic Art Museum, Miami Beach FL

Wimer, Rod, *Senior Design Consultant,* Providence Gallery, Charlotte NC

Wimmer, Mike, *Gallery Director,* Oklahoma City University, Norick Art Center, Oklahoma City OK (S)

Wimpfheimer, Debra, *Dir Strategic Partnerships,* The Queens Museum of Art, Flushing NY

Winchester, Flannery, *Cultural Affairs Assoc,* School 33 Art Center, Baltimore MD

Winchester, Juti, *Cur Buffalo Bill Mus,* Buffalo Bill Memorial Association, Buffalo Bill Historical Center, Cody WY

Winder, Kaye, *Instr,* University of Wisconsin-Platteville, Dept of Fine Art, Platteville WI (S)

Windham, Joshua, *Library Technician,* Tulane University, Architecture Library, New Orleans LA

Winegar, Joshua, *Asst Prof,* Weber State University, Dept of Visual Arts, Ogden UT (S)

Wines, Claudia, *Dir,* Northeastern Nevada Museum, Elko NV

Winfield, Charles, *Prof,* University of Maine at Augusta, College of Arts & Humanities, Augusta ME (S)

Wingert-Playdon, Kate, *Assoc Dean & Dir, Architecture & Environmental Design,* Temple University, Tyler School of Art, Philadelphia PA (S)

Wingertzahn, Marianne, *Head of Circ,* Bronxville Public Library, Bronxville NY

Wingood, Harold, *Dean Admissions,* Clark University, Dept of Visual & Performing Arts, Worcester MA (S)

Wink, Susan, *Mus Co-Dir,* Roswell Artist-in-Residence Foundation, Anderson Museum of Contemporary Art, Roswell NM

Winkelman, Michelle, *Dir Educ & Outreach,* Indianapolis Art Center, Marilyn K. Glick School of Art, Indianapolis IN

Winkenweder, Brian, *Chmn Dept,* Linfield College, Department of Art & Visual Culture, McMinnville OR (S)

Winkle, Jonathan, *Pres & CEO,* Sharon Lynne Wilson Center for the Arts, Ploch Art Gallery, Brookfield WI

Winkler, Alan, *Cur,* Wabaunsee County Historical Museum, Alma KS

Winninger, Bonnie, *Educ Dir,* Waterloo Center of the Arts, Waterloo IA

Winningham, Geoffrey, *Prof,* Rice University, Visual & Dramatic Arts, Houston TX (S)

Winship, Andrew, *Prof, Dir Grad Progs,* Indiana University-Purdue University, Indianapolis, Herron School of Art & Design, Indianapolis IN (S)

Winship, John, *Instr,* Gettysburg College, Dept of Visual Arts, Gettysburg PA (S)

Winslow, B B, *Dir,* Arts Midland Galleries & School, Midland MI

Winslow, B B, *Dir,* Alden B. Dow Museum of Science & Art, Alden B. Dow Museum School, Midland MI (S)

Winslow, Bruce, *Dir,* Midland Center for the Arts, Alden B Dow Museum of Science & Art, Midland MI

Winslow, John, *Chmn Dept,* Catholic University of America, Dept of Art, Washington DC (S)

Winslow, Margaret, *Cur Contemporary Art,* Delaware Art Museum, Wilmington DE

Winsryg, Marian, *Prof & Gallery Dir,* Santa Monica College Performing Arts Center, Pete & Susan Barrett Art Gallery, Santa Monica CA

Winston, Patrick, *Assoc Prof,* Montgomery County Community College, Art Center, Blue Bell PA (S)

Wintemberg, Timothy, *Deputy Dir Design & Exhibition,* Newark Museum Association, The Newark Museum, Newark NJ

Winter, Amy, *Dir & Cur,* Queens College, City University of New York, Godwin-Ternbach Museum, Flushing NY

Winter, Heather, *Archivist & Librn,* Milwaukee Art Museum, George Peckham Miller Art Research Library, Milwaukee WI

Winter, Heather, *Librn & Archivist,* Milwaukee Art Museum, Milwaukee WI

Winter, Heidi, *Director of Development,* Museum of Wisconsin Art, West Bend WI

Winter, Robert, *Chmn Dept,* Lenoir Rhyne College, Dept of Art, Hickory NC (S)

Winterrowd, Scott, *Dir Educ,* Southern Methodist University, Meadows Museum, Dallas TX

Winters, Laurie, *Exec Dir & CEO,* Museum of Wisconsin Art, West Bend WI

Winters, Susie, *Instr,* Appalachian State University, Dept of Art, Boone NC (S)

Winterton, Patricia, *Assoc Dir Develop,* Indiana University, Eskenazi Museum of Art, Bloomington IN

Winton, Georgina, *Museum Shop Mgr,* Nantucket Historical Association, Historic Nantucket, Nantucket MA

Winzenz, Karon, *Prof,* University of Wisconsin-Green Bay, Arts Dept, Green Bay WI (S)

Wirth, Chris, *Archives Specialist,* Longfellow National Historic Site, Longfellow House - Washington's Headquarters, Cambridge MA

Wirth, Harry, *Artist,* Walker's Point Artists Assoc Inc, Gallery 218, Milwaukee WI

Wisbey, Peter, *Cur Colls,* Genesee Country Village & Museum, John L Wehle Art Gallery, Mumford NY

Wisch, Barbara, *Prof,* State University of New York, College at Cortland, Dept Art & Art History, Cortland NY (S)

Wisdom, Monserrat, *Programming Asst,* National Veterans Art Museum, Chicago IL

Wise, Annette, *Cataloger,* Fulton County Historical Society Inc, Fulton County Museum (Tetzlaff Reference Room), Rochester IN

Wise, Jerry, *CFO,* Newfields, Indianapolis IN

Wise, JoAnn, *Treas & Exec Dir,* Western Art Association, Ellensburg WA

Wise, Kirsten, *Cur,* Cayuga Museum of History & Art, Auburn NY

Wise, Marie, *Hill Archive Proj Mgr,* Museum of Fine Arts Houston, Bayou Bend Collection & Gardens, Houston TX

Wish, Cyndi, *Summer Prog Dir,* Fine Arts Work Center, Hudson D. Walker Gallery, Provincetown MA

Wishart, Kimberly, *Chinese Art Specialist,* Princeton University, Marquand Library of Art & Archaeology, Princeton NJ

Wisotzki, Paula, *Secy,* Midwest Art History Society, Waco TX

Wisse, Jacob, *Asst Prof,* Adelphi University, Dept of Art & Art History, Garden City NY (S)

Wisse, Jacob, *Dir,* Yeshiva University Museum, New York NY

Wissinger, Charles, *Asst Prof Ceramics,* University of Texas Pan American, Art Dept, Edinburg TX (S)

Wissler-Thomas, Carrie, *Pres,* Art Association of Harrisburg, School & Galleries, Harrisburg PA

Wiswall, Wendy, *Asst Dir Science Prog Admin,* National Museum of Natural History, Smithsonian Institution, Washington DC

Witcher, Brooke, *Dir,* City of Lubbock, Buddy Holly Center, Lubbock TX

Witcombe, Christopher, *Chmn,* Sweet Briar College, Art History Dept, Sweet Briar VA (S)

Witek, Joseph, *Prof,* Stetson University, Department of Creative Arts, Deland FL (S)

Witherell, Mary, *Dir Library,* Englewood Library, Fine Arts Dept, Englewood NJ

Witkes, Michael, *Exec Dir,* Jewish Community Center of Greater Washington, Jane L & Robert H Weiner Judaic Museum, Rockville MD

Witmore, Michael, *Dir,* Folger Shakespeare, Washington DC

Witte, Rex, *Exhibs Designer,* i.d.e.a. Museum, Mesa AZ

Witten, Morris, *Educator,* Taos Historic Museums, La Hacienda de Los Martinez, Taos NM

Wittenbach, Tracy, *Opers Mgr Interim,* UMLAUF Sculpture Garden & Museum, Austin TX

Wittenbraker, Paul, *Assoc Prof,* Grand Valley State University, Art & Design Dept, Allendale MI (S)

Witter, Craig, *Preparator,* The Pennsylvania State University, Palmer Museum of Art, University Park PA

Wittershiem, John, *Prof,* Siena Heights University, Studio Angelico-Art Dept, Adrian MI (S)

Wittkopp, Greg, *Dir,* Cranbrook Art Museum, Bloomfield Hills MI

Wittmann, Charlotte, *Communs & Admin Assoc,* Nichols House Museum, Inc, Boston MA

Wittstruck, Martha, *Art Coordr,* Normandale Community College, Art Dept, Bloomington MN (S)

Witulski, Christine, *Dir,* Besser Museum for Northeast Michigan, Philip M Park Library, Alpena MI

Wix, Linney, *Prof,* University of New Mexico, Department of Fine Arts & Art History, Albuquerque NM (S)

Wodehouse, Kate, *Dir Colls & Library Servs,* Providence Athenaeum, Library, Providence RI

Wodek, Kristi, *Educ & Outreach Coord,* Crooked Tree Arts Center - Traverse City, Gallery, Traverse City MI

Woermke, Laura, *Exec Dir & Cur,* St Thomas-Elgin Public Art Centre, Saint Thomas ON

Woffard, Tobias, *Asst Prof,* Santa Clara University, Dept of Art & Art History, Santa Clara CA (S)
Wofford, Evelyn, *Treas,* National League of American Pen Women, Washington DC
Wofford, Kathy, *Colors Coordr,* Spartanburg Art Museum, Spartanburg SC
Wohlford-Metallo, Dawn, *Visual Arts Dir,* Quad City Arts Inc, Rock Island IL
Woike, Glenn V, *Head Librn,* Daemen College, Marian Library, Amherst NY
Wojtkowski, Kathi, *Pres,* Monterey History & Art Association, Monterey CA
Wolber, Paul, *Dir,* Spring Arbor College, Art Dept, Spring Arbor MI (S)
Wolek, Nathan, *Dept Chmn,* Stetson University, Department of Creative Arts, Deland FL (S)
Wolf, Henry, *Chm. of the Board,* Colonial Williamsburg Foundation, Williamsburg VA
Wolf, Rachel, *Dean,* Eastfield College, Humanities Division, Art Dept, Mesquite TX (S)
Wolf, Sylvia, *Dir,* University of Washington, Henry Art Gallery, Seattle WA
Wolf, Sylvia, *Dir,* Henry Gallery Association, Henry Art Gallery, Seattle WA
Wolfe, Anissa, *Bus Officer,* Cornell College, Peter Paul Luce Gallery, Mount Vernon IA
Wolfe, Ann M, *Sr Cur & Deputy Dir,* Nevada Museum of Art, Reno NV
Wolfe, Ann, *Asst Cur,* San Jose Museum of Art, Library, San Jose CA
Wolfe, Audrey, *Asst Dir Develop,* Massachusetts Historical Society, Boston MA
Wolfe, Dylan, *Gallery Dir,* Mercer County Community College, The Gallery at Mercer, West Windsor NJ
Wolfe, Linda, *Retail Mgr,* Tohono Chul Park, Tucson AZ
Wolfe, Richard, *Educ Coordr,* Pennsylvania Historical & Museum Commission, Brandywine Battlefield Park, Chadds Ford PA
Wolfe, Sandra, *Exec Dir,* Arts & Humanities Council of Tuscaloosa, Junior League Gallery, Dinah Washington Cultural Arts Center Galleries, Tuscaloosa AL
Wolfe, William W, *Asst Prof Art History,* Millersville University, Dept of Art & Design, Millersville PA (S)
Wolff, Cori, *Exec /Artistic Dir,* Buffalo Arts Studio, Art Gallery, Buffalo NY
Wolff, David, *Music Specialist,* Northfield Arts Guild, Northfield MN
Wolff, Eric, *Dir Operations,* Ann Arbor Art Center, Art Center, Ann Arbor MI
Wolff, Gabe, *Asst Cur Visual Arts & Colls Mgr,* Sangre de Cristo Arts & Conference Center, Pueblo CO
Wolff, Justin, *Assoc Prof,* University of Maine, Dept of Art, Orono ME (S)
Wolfram, William R, *Head Dept,* Concordia University, Art Dept, Seward NE (S)
Wolk-Simon, Linda, *Dir,* Fairfield University, Art Museum, Fairfield CT
Wollard, Lindsay, *Asst,* Edison State College, Bob Rauschenberg Gallery at Edison State College, Fort Myers FL
Wollensak, Andrea, *Assoc Prof,* Connecticut College, Dept of Art, New London CT (S)
Wollensak, Andrea, *Prof,* Connecticut College, Dept of Art History, Architectural Studies & Museum Studies, New London CT (S)
Wollman, Susan, *Brd Pres,* Mohawk Valley Heritage Association, Inc, Walter Elwood Museum, Amsterdam NY
Wollner, Jenny, *Office Mgr,* Midwest Art Conservation Center, Minneapolis MN
Wolochowicz, Stephen, *Asst Prof,* Weber State University, Dept of Visual Arts, Ogden UT (S)
Wolpert, Denise, *Dir Individual Giving & Special Events,* Bass Museum of Art, Miami Beach FL
Wolsk, Nancy, *Prof,* Transylvania University, Art Program, Lexington KY (S)
Wolstencroft, Pauline, *Sr Librn,* Los Angeles County Museum of Art, Allan C Balch Art Research Library, Los Angeles CA
Wolterstorff, Robert, *Exec Dir,* Bennington Museum, Bennington VT
Wolynetz, Lubow, *Cur Folk Art,* The Ukrainian Museum, New York NY
Womack, Steven, *Prof Film,* Watkins College of Art, Design & Film, Nashville TN (S)
Wonderlich, Jenee, *Pres,* Association of Hawaii Artists, Honolulu HI
Wong, Albert, *Head Dept,* University of Texas at El Paso, Dept of Art, El Paso TX (S)
Wong, Allison, *Deputy Dir Admin & Opers,* Honolulu Museum of Art, Honolulu HI
Wong, Chun-Hsi, *Asst Dir Facilities Opers,* National Museum of Natural History, Smithsonian Institution, Washington DC
Wong, Daisy, *Asst Dir,* The New School Parsons School of Design, Sheila C Johnson Design Center, New York NY (S)
Wong, Dorothy, *Assoc Prof,* University of Virginia, McIntire Dept of Art, Charlottesville VA (S)
Wong, Eddie, *Prof,* University of Wisconsin-Stout, Dept of Art & Design, Menomonie WI (S)
Wong, Karen, *Deputy Dir,* New Museum of Contemporary Art, New Museum, New York NY
Wong, Katrina, *Asst to Dir,* University of California, Davis, Jan Shrem and Maria Manetti Shrem Museum of Art, Davis CA
Wong, Michele, *Assoc Dir & Head Colls & Exhibs,* New York University, Grey Art Gallery, New York NY
Wong, Paul, *Artistic Dir,* Dieu Donne Papermill, Inc, Gallery, Brooklyn NY
Wong, Steve, *Mktg Dir,* Arts Partnership of Greater Spartanburg, Inc, Chapman Cultural Center, Spartanburg SC
Wong, Steven, *Cur,* Cultural Affairs Department, Los Angeles Municipal Art Gallery, Los Angeles CA
Wong-Ligda, Ed, *Prof,* Grand Valley State University, Art & Design Dept, Allendale MI (S)
Wonsidler, Mark, *Asst Dir,* Bard College, Milton Avery Graduate School of the Arts, Annandale-on-Hudson NY (S)
Wonsidler, Mark, *Coll Mgr,* Lehigh University Art Galleries, Museum Operation, Bethlehem PA
Woo, Joo, *Asst Prof,* University of South Florida, School of Art & Art History, Tampa FL (S)
Woo, Suzanne, *Mem & Spec Events,* Modern Art Museum, Fort Worth TX
Wood Jewett, Leah, *Exhibs Coordr,* Louisiana State University, Middleton Library, Baton Rouge LA
Wood, David, *Cur,* Concord Museum, Concord MA
Wood, Deborah, *Colls Mgr,* United States Senate Commission on Art, Washington DC
Wood, Dianne, *Curatorial Asst,* Wheaton Arts & Cultural Center, Museum of American Glass, Millville NJ
Wood, Janis, *Pres,* Williamsburg Contemporary Art Center, Williamsburg VA
Wood, Jim, *Asst. Dir Communs,* National Museum of Natural History, Smithsonian Institution, Washington DC
Wood, Joe, *Chmn Fine Arts 3D,* Massachusetts College of Art, Boston MA (S)
Wood, Ken, *Prof,* Saint Louis Community College at Meramec, Art Dept, Saint Louis MO (S)
Wood, Kerry, *Dir Advancement,* Crocker Art Museum, Sacramento CA
Wood, Kim, *Cur Educ,* Mobile Museum of Art, Library, Mobile AL
Wood, Kim, *Cur Educ,* Mobile Museum of Art, Mobile AL
Wood, Lawrence, *Chmn,* Christopher Newport University, Dept of Fine Performing Arts, Newport News VA (S)
Wood, Marilyn, *Instr,* Normandale Community College, Art Dept, Bloomington MN (S)
Wood, Nicholas, *Assoc Prof,* University of Texas at Arlington, Art & Art History Department, Arlington TX (S)
Wood, Patricia, *Librn,* Public Library of the District of Columbia, Art Division, Washington DC
Wood, Randy, *Bd Mem,* Utah Lawyers for the Arts, Salt Lake City UT
Wood, Richard, *Assoc Prof,* Centenary College, Humanities Dept, Hackettstown NJ (S)
Wood, Robert, *Photog,* Antonelli Institute, Professional Photography & Commercial Art, Erdenheim PA (S)
Wood, Rose, *Chief Registrar,* Birmingham Museum of Art, Birmingham AL
Wood, Ruth W, *Cur,* Macartney House Museum, Oakland ME
Wood, Sharon, *Prof,* Lansing Community College, Visual Arts & Media Dept, Lansing MI (S)
Wood, Sophie Bentham, *Dir Mktg & Communs,* Vero Beach Museum of Art, Vero Beach FL
Wood, Sue, *Accountant,* Paint Creek Center for the Arts, Rochester MI
Wood, Susan, *Prof,* Oakland University, Dept of Art & Art History, Rochester MI (S)
Wood, Thomas, *Secy,* National Architectural Accrediting Board, Inc, Washington DC
Wood, William G, *Exec Dir,* Jefferson County Historical Society, Library, Watertown NY
Woodard, Jeff, *Dir Mktg,* McLean County Historical Society, McLean County Museum of History, Bloomington IL
Woodard, Joel, *Head Security,* Laguna Art Museum, Laguna Beach CA
Woodard, Teresa, *Educ Cur,* Riverside Metropolitan Museum, Riverside CA
Woodburn, Steven, *Adjunct Asst Prof,* New York Institute of Technology, Fine Arts Dept, Old Westbury NY (S)
Woodford, Don, *Instr,* California State University, San Bernardino, Dept of Art, San Bernardino CA (S)
Woodhull, Margaret, *Asst Prof,* Rhodes College, Dept of Art, Memphis TN (S)
Woodhull, Victoria, *Assoc Dir,* William A Farnsworth, Museum, Rockland ME
Woodhull, Victoria, *Assoc Dir,* William A Farnsworth, Library, Rockland ME
Woodman, Charles, *Assoc Prof Fine Arts,* University of Cincinnati, School of Art, Cincinnati OH (S)
Woodruff, Lynne, *Head Art Library,* University of Maryland, College Park, Art Library, College Park MD
Woodruff, Robert, *Technician,* Women's Studio Workshop, Inc, Rosendale NY
Woodrum, Caterri, *Chief Deputy Dir & CFO,* North Carolina Museum of Art, Raleigh NC
Woods Rosner, Jennifer, *Chief Conservation,* Library Company of Philadelphia, Philadelphia PA
Woods, Christopher, *Dir,* University of Chicago, Oriental Institute, Chicago IL
Woods, James, *Dir,* Herrett Center for Arts & Sciences, Jean B King Art Gallery, Twin Falls ID
Woods, Leah, *Assoc Prof,* University of New Hampshire, Dept of Art & Art History, Durham NH (S)
Woods, Leon, *Gallery Asst,* Winston-Salem State University, Diggs Gallery, Winston-Salem NC
Woods, Marianne Berger, *Asst Prof,* University of Texas of Permian Basin, Dept of Art, Odessa TX (S)
Woods, Marinanne, *Coordr Jr Concerts & Mem Liaison,* Organization of Saskatchewan Arts Councils (OSAC), Regina SK
Woods, Molly, *Research & Colls Assoc,* Connecticut Historical Society, Library, Hartford CT
Woods, Shelley, *Mgr Tutoring Centres,* Sheridan College of Applied Arts and Technology, Trafalgar Campus Library, Oakville ON
Woods, Warren J, *Coll Mgr,* The Historic New Orleans Collection, Royal Street Galleries, New Orleans LA
Woodside, Janice, *Office Admin,* Coachella Valley History Museum, Indio CA
Woodside-Desire, Charmise, *Communications Director,* Hofstra University, Hofstra University Museum, Hempstead NY
Woodson, Shirley, *Museum Liaison,* National Conference of Artists, Michigan Chapter Gallery, Detroit MI
Woodul, Jasmine, *Gallery Mgr,* New Mexico State University, Art Gallery, Las Cruces NM

Woodward, David, *Dir,* Yuma Fine Arts Association, Yuma Art Center, Yuma AZ
Woodward, Kristen, *Chmn,* Albright College, Dept of Art, Reading PA (S)
Woodward, Richard B, *Cur African Art,* Virginia Museum of Fine Arts, Richmond VA
Woodward, Thomas, *Dir Institutional Advancement,* Harvard University, Harvard Art Museums, Cambridge MA
Woodward, Tilly, *Cur Acad & Community Outreach,* Grinnell College, Faulconer Gallery, Grinnell IA
Woodward-Detrich, Denise, *Dir,* Clemson University, Rudolph E Lee Gallery, Clemson SC
Woodworth, Robin, *Dir Develop,* Museum of Ventura County, Ventura CA
Wooff, Annette, *Adminr,* University of British Columbia, Morris & Helen Belkin Art Gallery, Vancouver BC
Woolf, David, *Assoc Prof,* Norwich University, Dept of Architecture and Art, Northfield VT (S)
Woolley, Lois, *Instr,* Woodstock School of Art, Inc, Woodstock NY (S)
Wootton-Forsyth, Tamara, *Dep Dir,* Dallas Museum of Art, Dallas TX
Word, Michelle, *Dir Educ,* Michigan State University, Eli & Edythe Broad Art Museum, East Lansing MI
Worden, Fred, *Assoc Prof,* University of Maryland, Baltimore County, Intermedia & Digital Arts (IMDA), Dept of Visual Arts, Baltimore MD (S)
Workman, Bob, *Dir,* Wichita State University, Ulrich Museum of Art, Wichita KS
Workneh, Sarah, *Exec Dir Prog,* Skowhegan School of Painting & Sculpture, New York NY (S)
Worrington, Susan, *Art Instr,* Phillips Community College at The University of Arkansas, Dept of English & Fine Arts, Helena AR (S)
Worteck, Ed, *Prof,* Goucher College, Art & Art History Dept, Baltimore MD (S)
Wortheimer, Gary, *Chmn Arts & Comm Depts,* Olivet College, Armstrong Collection, Olivet MI
Worthen, W B, *Dir,* Historic Arkansas Museum, Library, Little Rock AR
Worthen, William B, *Dir,* Historic Arkansas Museum, Little Rock AR
Worthley, Martha, *Young Artist Proj Prog Mgr,* Centrum Arts & Creative Education, Port Townsend WA
Wray, Jessica, *Library Assoc,* Miami University, Wertz Art & Architecture Library, Oxford OH
Wrega, Marek, *Mgr Finance & Admin,* Art Services International, Alexandria VA
Wren, Linnea, *Chmn,* Gustavus Adolphus College, Art & Art History Dept, Saint Peter MN (S)
Wride, Tim, *Cur Photography,* Norton Museum of Art, West Palm Beach FL
Wriedt, Laura, *Outreach Coordr,* Figge Art Museum, Davenport IA
Wright, Anita, *Coll Mgr,* Cortland County Historical Society, Suggett House Museum, Cortland NY
Wright, Audrey, *Chmn,* Seattle Central Community College, Humanities - Social Sciences Division, Seattle WA (S)
Wright, Ben, *Dir Educ,* UrbanGlass, Robert Lehman Gallery, Brooklyn NY
Wright, Beth, *Prof,* University of Texas at Arlington, Art & Art History Department, Arlington TX (S)
Wright, Briana, *Acctg,* Sheldon Museum & Cultural Center, Inc, Sheldon Museum & Cultural Center, Haines AK
Wright, Brianna, *Cur,* African American Museum of Iowa, Cedar Rapids IA
Wright, Cathy, *Dir,* Albuquerque Museum of Art & History, Albuquerque NM
Wright, Charles, *Chair Dept of Art & Prof,* Western Illinois University, Department of Art, Macomb IL (S)
Wright, Christina, *Director of Public Relations and Social Media,* Museum of Wisconsin Art, West Bend WI
Wright, Craig, *Archivist,* National Archives & Records Administration, Herbert Hoover Presidential Library - Museum, West Branch IA
Wright, Deborah, *VPres,* Glynn Visual Arts, Inc, Saint Simons Island GA
Wright, Elizabeth, *Dir Develop,* University of Virginia, The Fralin Museum of Art at the University of Virginia, Charlottesville VA
Wright, Erin, *Prof,* University of Alabama at Birmingham, Dept of Art & Art History, Birmingham AL (S)
Wright, Gene, *Asst Prof Scientific Illustration,* University of Georgia, Franklin College of Arts & Sciences, Lamar Dodd School of Art, Athens GA (S)
Wright, J Franklin, *Prof,* George Washington University, Dept of Art of Fine Arts & Art History, Washington DC (S)
Wright, Jana, *Dean of Academic Admin,* Columbia University, School of the Arts, New York NY (S)
Wright, Jennifer, *Mus Shop Mgr,* Sandwich Historical Society, Center Sandwich NH
Wright, Jessica, *State Svcs,* Arkansas Arts Center, Little Rock AR (S)
Wright, Jimmy, *Pres,* Pastel Society of America, National Arts Club, Grand Gallery, New York NY
Wright, Joanne, *Assoc Dean,* University of New Brunswick, Faculty of Arts, Fredericton NB (S)
Wright, Jonathan, *Deputy Dir Horticulture & Natural Resources,* Newfields, Indianapolis IN
Wright, Joseph, *Exec Dir,* French Art Colony, Gallipolis OH
Wright, Kortni, *Special Events Coordr,* Marian University, Allison Mansion, Indianapolis IN
Wright, Lesley, *Dir,* Grinnell College, Faulconer Gallery, Grinnell IA
Wright, Lori, *Asst Prof of Art Dept Chair,* Kansas Wesleyan University, Art Dept, Salina KS (S)
Wright, Lorri, *Museum Store Mgr,* Modern Art Museum, Fort Worth TX
Wright, Martha, *Coordr Mus Visitor & Tour Servs,* University of Richmond, University Museums, Richmond VA
Wright, Maya, *Educ Mgr & Historian,* Kirkland Museum of Fine & Decorative Art, Denver CO
Wright, Megan, *Assoc Prof Art,* Marian University, Visual Arts Dept, Indianapolis IN (S)
Wright, Pope, *Lectr,* University of Wisconsin-Superior, Programs in the Visual Arts, Superior WI (S)
Wright, Rebecca, *Dir Devel,* Fitchburg Art Museum, Fitchburg MA
Wright, Rick, *Pres,* Plastic Club, Art Club, Philadelphia PA
Wright, Rita, *Dir,* Springville Museum of Art, Springville UT
Wright, Robin, *Cur Native American Art,* University of Washington, Burke Museum of Natural History and Culture, Seattle WA
Wright, Ron, *Prof,* Marietta College, Art Dept, Marietta OH (S)
Wright, Sharyl, *Instr,* Avila College, Art Division, Dept of Humanities, Kansas City MO (S)
Wright, Steve, *Gen Mgr,* Chelan County Public Utility District, Rocky Reach Dam, Wenatchee WA
Wright, Suzanne, *Dir Budget & Fin,* Westmoreland Museum of American Art, Greensburg PA
Wright, Suzanne, *Dir Educ,* The Phillips Collection, Washington DC
Wright, Tony, *Head Design & Installation,* Modern Art Museum, Fort Worth TX
Wright, Vicki, *Dir Colls & Exhibs,* Kalamazoo Institute of Arts, The Mary & Edwin Meader Fine Arts Library, Kalamazoo MI
Wright, Vincent, *Asst Prof,* C W Post Campus of Long Island University, School of Visual & Performing Arts, Brookville NY (S)
Wright, Vonda, *Contact,* Ponder Fine Arts Gallery-Benedict College, Columbia SC
Wright, Welynda, *Asst Prof Interior Design,* University of Georgia, Franklin College of Arts & Sciences, Lamar Dodd School of Art, Athens GA (S)
Wright-Sedam, Jeffrey, *Preparator,* University at Albany, State University of New York, University Art Museum, Albany NY
Wrigley, LaVaine, *Coll Coordr,* Historical Society of Martin County, Elliott Museum, Stuart FL
Wrinn, Mariann, *Assoc Prof,* Herkimer County Community College, Humanities Social Services, Herkimer NY (S)
Wroath, Tami, *Dir Mktg & Public Relations,* University of Florida, Samuel P Harn Museum of Art, Gainesville FL
Wroble, Stephen, *Prof,* Schoolcraft College, Dept of Art & Design, Livonia MI (S)
Wu Giarratano, Frances, *Exhib Mgr,* Independent Curators International, New York NY
Wu, Ina, *Instr,* Olympic College, Social Sciences & Humanities Div, Bremerton WA (S)
Wu, Jialu, *Gen Educ,* Art Institute of Pittsburgh, Pittsburgh PA (S)
Wu, Xiaojin, *Cur Japanese & Korean Art,* Seattle Art Museum, Seattle Asian Art Museum, Seattle WA
Wu, Xiaojin, *Cur, Japanese & Korean Art,* Seattle Art Museum, Seattle WA
Wubben, Gerry, *Prof,* McNeese State University, Dept of Visual Arts, Lake Charles LA (S)
Wulf, Andrew, *Dir,* New Mexico Department of Cultural Affairs, Fray Angelico Chavez History Library, Santa Fe NM
Wunder, Amanda, *Prof,* City University of New York, PhD Program in Art History, New York NY (S)
Wuorinen, Charles, *Treas,* American Academy of Arts & Letters, New York NY
Wurzel, Linda, *Elberon Branch Head & Children's Dept Head,* City of Long Branch, Long Branch Free Public Library, Long Branch NJ
Wyar, Sue, *Prof,* State College of Florida Manatee - Sarasota, Art, Design, Humanities, Bradenton FL (S)
Wyatt, Greg, *Secy,* National Sculpture Society, New York NY
Wyatt, Jeffrey, *VPres,* Santa Barbara Contemporary Arts Forum, Santa Barbara CA
Wyatt, Judy, *Library Asst,* Kansas State University, Paul Weigel Library of Architecture Planning & Design, Manhattan KS
Wyatt, Thelma W, *Treas,* Miles B Carpenter Folk Art Museum, Waverly VA
Wyckoff, Elizabeth, *Cur,* Wellesley College, Davis Museum & Cultural Center, Wellesley MA
Wykes, Andrew, *Assoc Prof,* Hamline University, Dept of Studio Arts & Art History, Saint Paul MN (S)
Wylde, Nanette, *Assoc Prof,* California State University, Chico, Department of Art & Art History, Chico CA (S)
Wylie, Caroline, *Develop Officer,* Tyler Museum of Art, Reference Library, Tyler TX
Wylie, Charles, *Cur Contemporary Art,* Dallas Museum of Art, Dallas TX
Wylie, Charles, *Curator of Photography & New Media,* Santa Barbara Museum of Art, Santa Barbara CA
Wylie, Lyndsey, *Cur Asst,* San Jose Museum of Art, Library, San Jose CA
Wylie, Nick, *Assoc Dir,* Southern Exposure, San Francisco CA
Wylie, William, *Studio Faculty,* University of Virginia, McIntire Dept of Art, Charlottesville VA (S)
Wyllie, Nancy, *Prof,* Community College of Rhode Island, Dept of Art, Warwick RI (S)
Wylly, Barbara, *Exec Dir,* Center for Puppetry Arts, Museum & Library, Atlanta GA
Wylly, Barbara, *Exec Dir,* Center for Puppetry Arts, Atlanta GA
Wylly, Bill, *Exec Dir,* Center for Puppetry Arts, Atlanta GA
Wylly, Bill, *Exec Dir,* Center for Puppetry Arts, Museum & Library, Atlanta GA
Wyman, James, *Exec Dir,* Society for Photographic Education (SPE), SPE Gallery, Cleveland OH
Wyman, Sara, *Instr,* Walla Walla Community College, Fine Arts Dept, Walla Walla WA (S)
Wyner, Yehudi, *Pres,* American Academy of Arts & Letters, New York NY
Wynick, Lynne, *Co-Dir,* Wynick Tuck Gallery, Toronto ON
Wynn, Elaine, *Co-Chair,* Los Angeles County Museum of Art, Los Angeles CA

Wynn, Nancy, *Asst Prof,* University of Hartford, Hartford Art School, West Hartford CT (S)
Wynne, Alan, *Pres,* South County Art Association, Kingston RI
Wynne, David, *Secy & Treas,* Industrial Designers Society of America, Herndon VA
Wynne, Luke, *Instr,* Moravian College, Dept of Art, Bethlehem PA (S)
Wynne, Stephen, *Artistic Dir for School of Dance,* Sangre de Cristo Arts & Conference Center, Pueblo CO
Wyszomirski, Margaret, *Prof,* Ohio State University, Dept of Art Education, Columbus OH (S)
Wzontek, Joanne, *Develop,* Cedar Rapids Museum of Art, Cedar Rapids IA
Xiao, Peter, *Prof,* Augustana College, Art Dept, Rock Island IL (S)
Xu, Gan, *Instr,* Maine College of Art, Portland ME (S)
Xu, Jay, *Dir,* Asian Art Museum of San Francisco, Chong-Moon Lee Ctr for Asian Art and Culture, San Francisco CA
Yachik, Val, *Pres,* Palette & Chisel Academy of Fine Arts, Chicago IL
Yackulic, Evelyn, *Opers Mgr & Finance,* City of Lethbridge, Sir Alexander Galt Museum, Lethbridge AB
Yager, David, *Pres & CEO,* The University of the Arts, Rosenwald-Wolf Gallery, Philadelphia PA
Yahnke, David, *Instr,* Mohawk Valley Community College, Utica NY (S)
Yahr, Jayme, *Prof,* University of St Thomas, Deptartment of Art History, Saint Paul MN (S)
Yakstis, Gary, *Operations Dir,* University of Connecticut, Jorgensen Auditorium, Storrs CT
Yakubik, Lynn, *Interpretive Mgr,* The University of Texas at San Antonio, Institute of Texan Cultures, San Antonio TX
Yakunovich, Jennifer, *Mus Educator,* Manchester Historic Association, Millyard Museum, Manchester NH
Yakunovich, Jennifer, *Mus Educator,* Manchester Historic Association, Library, Manchester NH
Yale-Read, Barbara, *Assoc Prof,* Appalachian State University, Dept of Art, Boone NC (S)
Yamamoto, Koichi, *Asst Prof,* Utah State University, Dept of Art, Logan UT (S)
Yamanishi, Lailani, *Visitor Services Manager,* Laguna Art Museum, Laguna Beach CA
Yancey, John, *Chair,* University of Texas, Dept of Art & Art History, Austin TX (S)
Yanero, Susan, *Instr,* American University, Dept of Art, New York NY (S)
Yang, Christina, *Dir Educ Pub Progs,* Solomon R Guggenheim Museum, New York NY
Yang-Hellewell, Elizabeth, *Advancement Dir,* Museum of Contemporary Art San Diego, San Diego CA
Yanik, John V, *Prof,* Catholic University of America, School of Architecture & Planning, Washington DC (S)
Yank, Paul, *Art Dir,* Wisconsin Fine Arts Association, Inc, Ozaukee Art Center, Cedarburg WI
Yankavskas, Raye, *Library Asst,* Lesley University, College of Art & Design Library, Boston MA
Yankowski, Michael, *Prof,* Northwestern State University of Louisiana, School of Creative & Performing Arts - Dept of Fine & Graphic Arts, Natchitoches LA (S)
Yanto, Paul, *Asst Prof,* Oberlin College, Dept of Art, Oberlin OH (S)
Yantz, Jane, *Art Instr,* Burlington County College, Humanities & Fine Art Div, Pemberton NJ (S)
Yantz, Mickel, *Dir Colls & Exhibs,* The Sherwin Miller Museum of Jewish Art, Tulsa OK
Yao Maasbach, Nancy, *Pres,* Museum of Chinese in America, New York NY
Yapelli, Tina, *Gallery Dir,* San Diego State University, University Art Gallery, San Diego CA
Yarber, Robert, *Distinguished Prof Art (Drawing/ Painting),* Pennsylvania State University, University Park, Penn State School of Visual Arts, University Park PA (S)
Yarborough, Bert, *Assoc Prof,* Colby-Sawyer College, Dept of Fine & Performing Arts, New London NH (S)
Yarlow, Loretta, *Dir,* University of Massachusetts, Amherst, University Gallery, Amherst MA
Yarnall, James, *Newsletter Ed,* Newport Historical Society & Museum of Newport History, Newport RI
Yarrington, Kathryn Jo, *Prof, Chmn,* Fairfield University, Visual & Performing Arts, Fairfield CT (S)
Yasuda, Kim, *Chmn Dept,* University of California, Santa Barbara, Dept of Art Studio, Santa Barbara CA (S)
Yasuda, Robert, *Prof,* C W Post Campus of Long Island University, School of Visual & Performing Arts, Brookville NY (S)
Yates, Christopher, *Assistant Director,* Kenyon College, Gund Gallery, Gambier OH
Yates, Joey, *Cur,* Kentucky Museum of Art and Craft, Louisville KY
Yates, Sam, *Dir & Cur,* University of Tennessee, Ewing Gallery of Art and Architecture, Knoxville TN
Yatt, Barry D, *Assoc Prof,* Catholic University of America, School of Architecture & Planning, Washington DC (S)
Yau, Esther, *Prof,* Occidental College, Dept of Art History & Visual Arts, Los Angeles CA (S)
Yaukey, Margaret, *Asst Prof,* Appalachian State University, Dept of Art, Boone NC (S)
Yazzie, Peterson, *Faculty,* Northland Pioneer College, Art Dept, Show Low AZ (S)
Yeager, Paula, *Cur,* Texas Tech University, School of Art Visual Resource Center, Lubbock TX
Yeager, Raymond, *Chmn Art Dept,* MacMurray College, Art Dept, Jacksonville IL (S)
Yeager, Rebecca, *Sec,* Crary Art Gallery, Warren PA
Yedinak, James, *Industrial Design,* Art Institute of Pittsburgh, Pittsburgh PA (S)
Yee, Kay, *Acting Area Head Jewelry,* Pasadena City College, Visual Arts and Media Studies Division, Pasadena CA (S)
Yee, Shirley, *Graphic Design,* Art Institute of Pittsburgh, Pittsburgh PA (S)
Yelin Hirsch, Gilah, *Prof,* California State University, Dominguez Hills, Art & Design Dept, Carson CA (S)
Yes, Phyllis, *Prof,* Lewis & Clark College, Dept of Art, Portland OR (S)
Yevich, Courtney C, *Asst Librn,* Virginia Museum of Fine Arts, Margaret R & Robert M Freeman Library, Richmond VA
Yi, Hyewon, *Gallery Dir,* State University of New York College at Old Westbury, Amelie A Wallace Gallery, Old Westbury NY
Yi, Lidu, *Asst Prof,* Florida International University, School of Art & Art History, Miami FL (S)
Yildirm, Bahadir, *Expedition Admin,* Harvard University, Harvard Art Museums, Cambridge MA
Yingst, Dawn, *Admin,* The Art Institute of Chicago, Antiquarian Society of the Art Institute of Chicago, Chicago IL
Yoakum, Sherillyn, *Exec Dir,* Red River Valley Museum, Vernon TX
Yocom, Margaret, *Vol Mus Folklorist, Cur & Archivist,* Rangeley Lakes Region Logging Museum, Rangeley ME
Yoder, Charles, *Pres,* Artists' Fellowship, Inc, New York NY
Yokley, Shirley, *Instr,* Middle Tennessee State University, Art Dept, Murfreesboro TN (S)
Yoltar-Yildirim, Aysin, *Hagop Kevorkian Assoc Cur Islamic Art,* Brooklyn Museum, Brooklyn NY
Yonally-Coleman, Nancy, *Pres,* Grants Pass Museum of Art, Grants Pass OR
Yonan, Michael, *Asst Prof,* University of Missouri - Columbia, Art History & Archaeology Dept, Columbia MO (S)
Yonemoto, Bruce, *Prof Video, Film Theory, Exper Media,* University of California, Irvine, Studio Art Dept, Irvine CA (S)
Yontz, Terri, *Publicist,* Xavier University, Art Gallery, Cincinnati OH
Yonz, Barbara, *Assoc Prof,* Saint Thomas Aquinas College, Art Dept, Sparkill NY (S)
Yood, James, *Lectr,* Northwestern University, Evanston, Dept of Art Theory & Practice, Evanston IL (S)
Yoon, Jason, *Dir Educ,* The Queens Museum of Art, Flushing NY
Yoon, Sang, *Assoc Prof,* James Madison University, School of Art & Art History, Harrisonburg VA (S)
York, Bev, *Site Admin,* Nathan Hale Homestead Museum, Coventry CT
York, Robert, *Instr of Art,* Edison Community College, Gallery of Fine Arts, Fort Myers FL (S)
Yoshimine-Webster, Carol, *Assoc Prof,* Centenary College, Humanities Dept, Hackettstown NJ (S)
Yoshimoto, Jave, *Asst,* University of Nebraska at Omaha, School of the Arts, Omaha NE (S)
Yoshimoto, Midori, *Art History Prof,* New Jersey City University, Art Dept, Jersey City NJ (S)
Yoshimoto, Midori, *Dir,* New Jersey City University, Lemmerman Art Gallery, Jersey City NJ
Yoshimoto, Midori, *Dir,* New Jersey City University, Courtney Art Gallery & Lemmerman Gallery, Jersey City NJ
Yoshimura, Reiko, *Head Librn,* Freer Gallery of Art & Arthur M Sackler Gallery, Library, Washington DC
Yoshimura, Tera, *Instr,* Guild of Creative Art, Shrewsbury NJ (S)
Yost, Zane, *Instr,* Oklahoma State University Institute of Technology, School of Visual Communications, Okmulgee OK (S)
Yothers, Wendy, *Chmn Jewelry Design,* Fashion Institute of Technology, School of Art & Design, New York NY (S)
Young Brown, Patricia, *CEO,* Thinkery, Austin TX
Young Schoenthal, Rebecca, *Exec Dir,* Second Street Gallery, Charlottesville VA
Young, Anne, *Bd Secy,* Kennebec Valley Art Association, Harlow Gallery, Hallowell ME
Young, Beth, *Adjunct Instr,* Mary Baldwin College, Dept of Art & Art History, Staunton VA (S)
Young, Brad, *Chief Security,* University of North Carolina at Greensboro, Weatherspoon Art Museum, Greensboro NC
Young, Brian, *Lectr,* University of Central Arkansas, Department of Art, Conway AR (S)
Young, David, *Asst Prof,* University of Tennessee at Chattanooga, Dept of Art, Chattanooga TN (S)
Young, David, *Exec Dir,* Cliveden, Philadelphia PA
Young, J, *Treas,* Sculptor's Society of Canada, Canadian Sculpture Centre, Toronto ON
Young, Jane, *Dir,* Chase Young Gallery, Boston MA
Young, Jean, *Registrar & Book Designer,* Florida State University, Museum of Fine Arts, Tallahassee FL
Young, Jeff, *Chair, Prof,* University of Central Arkansas, Department of Art, Conway AR (S)
Young, Joan, *Assoc Cur Contemporary Art & Mgr Cur Affairs,* Solomon R Guggenheim Museum, New York NY
Young, John, *Pres & CEO,* Canadian Museum for Human Rights, Winnipeg MB
Young, Judi Michelle, *Pres,* Sculptor's Society of Canada, Canadian Sculpture Centre, Toronto ON
Young, Karen S, *Dir,* Taos Historic Museums, La Hacienda de Los Martinez, Taos NM
Young, Karen S, *Dir,* Taos Historic Museums, Taos NM
Young, Karen S, *Dir,* Taos Historic Museums, Ernest Blumenschein Home & Studio, Taos NM
Young, Kevin, *Dir,* The New York Public Library, Schomburg Center for Research in Black Culture, New York NY
Young, Kirk, *Adjunct,* Idaho State University, Dept of Art, Pocatello ID (S)
Young, Marjorie, *Team Leader Bibliographic Access,* State University of New York at New Paltz, Sojourner Truth Library, New Paltz NY
Young, Penelope, *Instr,* Bakersfield College, Art Dept, Bakersfield CA (S)
Young, Phil, *Prof,* Hartwick College, Art Dept, Oneonta NY (S)

Young, Rachel, *Business Mgr,* Kimball Jenkins Estate, Concord NH

Young, Rebecca, *Dir Library Servs,* Nova Scotia College of Art and Design, Library, Halifax NS

Young, Roy, *Cur Educ,* Western Pennsylvania Conservancy, Fallingwater, Mill Run PA

Young, Sarah, *Educator,* Boston University Art Galleries, Rubin-Frankel Gallery, Boston MA

Young, Shea Patterson, *Cur,* University of North Texas Health Science Center Fort Worth, Atrium Gallery, Fort Worth TX

Young, Susan, *Outreach Coordr,* City of Springdale, Shiloh Museum of Ozark History, Springdale AR

Young, Ted, *Assoc Provost, Faculty Affairs,* ArtCenter College of Design, Pasadena CA (S)

Young, Thomas E, *Librarian/Archivist,* Philbrook Museum of Art, H.A. & Mary K Chapman Library, Tulsa OK

Young, Thomas E, *Librarian/Archivist,* Philbrook Museum of Art, Eugene B Adkins Study Center, Tulsa OK

Young, Timothy, *Assoc Prof,* Grace College, Dept of Art, Winona Lake IN (S)

Young, Tom, *Prof,* Greenfield Community College, Art Dept, Greenfield MA (S)

Young, Victoria, *Chair, Prof,* University of St Thomas, Deptartment of Art History, Saint Paul MN (S)

Young, Victoria, *Second VPres,* Society of Architectural Historians, Chicago IL

Young, Wayne, *Journalism,* Holland College, School of Visual Arts & Journalism, Charlottetown PE (S)

Young, Zenida, *Architecture & Interior Design Chmn,* Palm Beach Community College, Dept of Art, Lake Worth FL (S)

Youngbird, Laura, *Dir Native American Progs,* Plains Art Museum, Fargo ND

Younger, Dan, *Chmn,* University of Missouri, Saint Louis, Dept of Art & Art History, Saint Louis MO (S)

Youngers, Peter L, *Instr,* Northeastern Junior College, Art Department, Sterling CO (S)

Younghans-Haug, Samantha, *Prog Dir,* University of California, Irvine, Beall Center for Art + Technology, and University Art Gallery, Irvine CA

Younginger, Jennifer, *Dir Exhib & Coll,* Heritage Museums & Gardens, Sandwich MA

Youngs, Christopher, *Lectr,* Albright College, Dept of Art, Reading PA (S)

Youngyeon, Anna, *Instr,* Berea College, Art & Art History Program, Berea KY (S)

Younker, Shirod, *Art Prog Mgr,* Oregon College of Art & Craft, Hoffman Gallery, Portland OR

Yourell, Karen, *Group Tour Coordinator,* Pilgrim Society, Pilgrim Hall Museum, Plymouth MA

Yow, Janice, *Pres,* Coppini Academy of Fine Arts, Elizabeth di Barbieri, San Antonio TX

Yox, David, *Prof,* Delaware County Community College, Communications, Art & Humanities, Media PA (S)

Yu Yu, Christina, *Dir,* University of Southern California, USC Pacific Asia Museum, Pasadena CA

Yu, Shuishan, *Asst Prof,* Oakland University, Dept of Art & Art History, Rochester MI (S)

Yuan, Juliana, *Sr Lectr,* University of Missouri, Saint Louis, Dept of Art & Art History, Saint Louis MO (S)

Yuars Petruccia, Breta, *Art Historian,* Greenfield Community College, Art Dept, Greenfield MA (S)

Yuasa, Noriko, *Assoc Prof,* Webster University, Department of Art, Design & Art History, Webster Groves MO (S)

Yuhas, Louise, *Chmn,* Occidental College, Dept of Art History & Visual Arts, Los Angeles CA (S)

Yuksel, Kate, *Admin Coordr,* Queen's University, Agnes Etherington Art Centre, Kingston ON

Yun, Michelle, *Senior Curator of Modern and Contemporary Art,* Asia Society Museum, New York NY

Yurkanin, Sharon, *Mus Store Mgr,* Allentown Art Museum, Allentown PA

Yust, Alex, *Chief Preparator,* Academy of Motion Picture Arts & Sciences, The Academy Gallery, Beverly Hills CA

Zabalotney, Bonne, *VPres Acad & Provost,* Emily Carr University of Art + Design, Vancouver BC (S)

Zabel, Craig, *Assoc Prof & Dept Head,* Pennsylvania State University, University Park, Dept of Art History, University Park PA (S)

Zaborowski, Dennis, *Prof,* University of North Carolina at Chapel Hill, Art Dept, Chapel Hill NC (S)

Zaccaro, Chris, *Mktg Mgr,* Old State House, Hartford CT

Zaccerras, Carmen, *Dir,* Taos Historic Museums, E.L. Blumenschein Home & Museum & La Hacienda de los Martinez, Taos NM

Zacharias, James, *Cur History & Science,* The Museum of Arts & Sciences Inc, Daytona Beach FL

Zacher, Melinda, *Dir Visual Arts,* Interlochen Center for the Arts, Interlochen Arts Academy, Dept of Visual Art, Interlochen MI (S)

Zaengle, Emily, *Exec Dir,* Stone Quarry Hill Art Park, Cazenovia NY

Zaffke, Mary, *Bd Pres,* Bluff Country Artists Gallery, Spring Grove MN

Zafren, Chris, *Pres,* Alaska Watercolor Society, Anchorage AK

Zahabl, Liese, *Asst Prof,* Weber State University, Dept of Visual Arts, Ogden UT (S)

Zaharia, Florence, *Conservator in Charge, Textiles,* The Metropolitan Museum of Art, New York NY

Zaharis, Kay, *Dir,* Cortland Free Library, Cortland NY

Zahid, Amira, *VPres, Sec & Treas,* Dahesh Museum of Art, Greenwich CT

Zahid, Mervat, *Pres,* Dahesh Museum of Art, Greenwich CT

Zahler, Mackenzie, *Outreach Progs,* The Cultural Arts Center at Glen Allen, Glen Allen VA

Zahner, Mary, *Assoc Prof,* University of Dayton, Visual Arts Dept, Dayton OH (S)

Zaibak, Marline, *Dir Public Progs & Professional Develop,* Intersection for the Arts, San Francisco CA

Zallinger, Jocelyn, *Gallery Mgr,* Lyme Art Association, Inc, Old Lyme CT

Zaloom, Carol, *Instr,* Woodstock School of Art, Inc, Woodstock NY (S)

Zaloom, Lorraine, *Communs,* The Art School at Old Church, Demarest NJ (S)

Zamagias, James D, *Chmn,* Allegany Community College, Art Dept, Cumberland MD (S)

Zambrano, Horacio, *Visitor Servs,* The Mexican Museum, San Francisco CA

Zamecnik, Sarah, *Exec Dir,* Francis Hardy Gallery, Fish Creek WI

Zamora, Frank, *Instr,* Sacramento City College, Art Dept, Sacramento CA (S)

Zanetti, Maria, *Office & Facilities Mgr,* Oakville Galleries, Centennial Square and Gairloch Gardens, Oakville ON

Zapata, Beverly, *Auxiliary Prof,* Pontifical Catholic University of Puerto Rico, Dept of Fine Arts, Ponce PR (S)

Zapata, Felix, *Prof,* University of Puerto Rico, Mayaguez, Dept of Humanities, College of Fine Arts & Theory of Art Programs, Mayaguez PR (S)

Zapico, Mark, *Chair Advertising Design,* College for Creative Studies, Detroit MI (S)

Zapolis, Frank, *Cur Folk Art,* Balzekas Museum of Lithuanian Culture, Chicago IL

Zapton, Steve, *Prof,* James Madison University, School of Art & Art History, Harrisonburg VA (S)

Zar, Howard, *Dir,* The National Trust for Historic Preservation, Lyndhurst, Tarrytown NY

Zaretsky, Barbara, *Exhibit Coordr,* C G Jung Center, Evanston IL

Zarkovich, Josephine, *Curator,* Linfield College, Department of Art & Visual Culture, McMinnville OR (S)

Zaros, Christa, *Colls Mgr,* The Long Island Museum of American Art, History & Carriages, Library, Stony Brook NY

Zarucchi, Jeanne Morgan, *Prof,* University of Missouri, Saint Louis, Dept of Art & Art History, Saint Louis MO (S)

Zarur, Elizabeth, *Assoc Prof,* New Mexico State University, Art Dept, Las Cruces NM (S)

Zaszlavik, Katalin, *Asst Prof,* Grand Valley State University, Art & Design Dept, Allendale MI (S)

Zaugg, Elwood, *Dean,* Salt Lake Community College, Graphic Design Dept, Salt Lake City UT (S)

Zavala, Adriana, *Assoc Prof,* Tufts University, Dept of Art & Art History, Medford MA (S)

Zavialova, Maria, *Cur,* Museum of Russian Art, Minneapolis MN

Zawacki, Andrew, *Conservator,* Historic Arkansas Museum, Little Rock AR

Zawacki, Mary, *Cur,* Schenectady County Historical Society, Grems-Dolittle Library, Schenectady NY

Zawacki, Mary, *Cur,* Schenectady County Historical Society, Schenectady NY

Zawada, Elizabeth, *Dir,* Greenwich House Inc, Greenwich House Pottery, New York NY (S)

Zawora, Ed, *Graphic Design,* Antonelli Institute, Professional Photography & Commercial Art, Erdenheim PA (S)

Zax, Jon, *Digital Media & Facilities Mgr,* Kala Institute, Kala Art Institute, Berkeley CA

Zayatz, Matthew, *Preparator,* Dartmouth College, Hood Museum of Art, Hanover NH

Zayed, Aime, *Prof & Dept Dir,* Universite du Quebec, Trois-Rivieres, Department of Philosophy & the Arts, Trois-Rivieres QC (S)

Zea, Philip, *Pres,* Historic Deerfield, Inc, Deerfield MA

Zebot, George, *Instr,* Art Institute of Southern California, Laguna Beach CA (S)

Zebrowski, Megan, *Mem & Communs,* National Alliance for Media Arts & Culture, San Francisco CA

Zeh, Roger, *Interim Mus Dir,* Museum of Fine Arts, Saint Petersburg, Florida, Inc, Saint Petersburg FL

Zehner, Jeffrey, *Media Arts & Animation,* Art Institute of Pittsburgh, Pittsburgh PA (S)

Zeidberg, David, *Dir Library,* The Huntington Library, Art Collections & Botanical Gardens, Library, San Marino CA

Zeiger, Aly, *Mus Asst, Colls,* Sheldon Museum & Cultural Center, Inc, Sheldon Museum & Cultural Center, Haines AK

Zeigler, Gordon, *Instr,* Wayland Baptist University, Dept of Art, School of Fine Art, Plainview TX (S)

Zeile, Kirche, *Asst Prof Theatre,* Marymount Manhattan College, Fine & Performing Arts Div, New York NY (S)

Zeisler, Wilfried, *Chief Cur & Co-Chair Exhibs,* Hillwood Museum & Gardens Foundation, Hillwood Estate Museum & Gardens, Washington DC

Zeiss, Kathleen, *CFO & VPres Fin,* Brookgreen Gardens, Murrells Inlet SC

Zela, Sara B, *Interim Dir,* Phillips Exeter Academy, Frederick R. Mayer Art Center, Lamont Gallery, Exeter NH

Zela, Sara, *Educ & Communs Mgr,* University of New Hampshire, Museum of Art, Durham NH

Zell, Valerie, *Adjunct Asst Prof Art History,* Johnson County Community College, Fine Arts Dept & Art History Dept, Overland Park KS (S)

Zella, Robbin, *Dir,* Housatonic Community College, Housatonic Museum of Art, Bridgeport CT

Zeller, Emily, *Vis Asst Prof,* Kenyon College, Art Dept, Gambier OH (S)

Zeller, Joyce, *Corresp Secy,* Artists' Fellowship, Inc, New York NY

Zeller, Linda, *Mus Gift Shop Mgr,* Wiscasset, Waterville & Farmington Railway Museum (WW&F), Alna ME

Zellers, Mark, *Dept Chmn & Asst Prof,* Community College of Rhode Island, Dept of Art, Warwick RI (S)

Zellmer, Benjamin, *Asst Prof,* Florida International University, School of Art & Art History, Miami FL (S)

Zellmer, Ginny, *Youth Educator,* Hickory Museum of Art, Inc, Hickory NC
Zellner Neal, Donna, *Dir,* North Tonawanda History Museum, North Tonawanda NY
Zemancik, Lisa, *Educ Coordr,* Wayne Center for the Arts, Wooster OH
Zempel, Glenis, *Dir Opers,* Interact Center for the Visual & Performing Arts, Interact Gallery, Minneapolis MN
Zeng, Li, *Asst Prof,* University of Central Arkansas, Department of Art, Conway AR (S)
Zenhari, Ellie, *Asst Prof,* California State University, Dominguez Hills, Art & Design Dept, Carson CA (S)
Zeppetelli, Anne-Marie, *Colls & Info Resources Mgr,* Musee d'art Contemporain de Montreal, Montreal QC
Zeppetelli, John, *Dir & Chief Cur,* Musee d'art Contemporain de Montreal, Montreal QC
Zerendow, Chris, *Cur,* University of Wisconsin-Stout, J Furlong Gallery, Menomonie WI
Zervigon, Andres, *Asst Prof Art History,* University of La Verne, Dept of Art, La Verne CA (S)
Zettle-Sterling, Renee, *Assoc Prof,* Grand Valley State University, Art & Design Dept, Allendale MI (S)
Zettler, Richard, *Assoc Cur in Charge,* University of Pennsylvania, Museum of Archaeology & Anthropology, Philadelphia PA
Zetzman, Frank, *Prof,* University of Wisconsin College - Marinette, Art Dept, Marinette WI (S)
Zevallos, Loretta, *Opers Dir,* Guadalupe Cultural Arts Center, San Antonio TX
Zhang, Fan, *Cur Exhibs,* Asian Art Museum of San Francisco, Chong-Moon Lee Ctr for Asian Art and Culture, San Francisco CA
Zhang, He, *Asst Prof,* William Paterson University, Dept Arts, Wayne NJ (S)
Zhang, Lu, *Asst Cur Chinese Art,* The Art Institute of Chicago, Department of Asian Art, Chicago IL
Zhang, Naijun, *Assoc Prof,* West Virginia University, College of Creative Arts, School of Art & Design, Morgantown WV (S)
Zhang, Shaoqian, *Asst Prof,* Oklahoma State University, Department of Art, Graphic Design and Art History, Stillwater OK (S)
Zhang, Yue, *Coordr,* University of Florida, University Gallery, Gainesville FL
Zhou, Yan, *Adjunct Asst Prof,* Kenyon College, Art Dept, Gambier OH (S)
Zhu, Tiffany, *Admin & Mem Mgr,* American Museum of Ceramic Art, Pomona CA
Zic, Virginia F, *Prof,* Sacred Heart University, Dept of Art, Fairfield CT (S)
Zichterman, Karen, *Secy,* Contemporary Art Center, Peoria IL
Zidek, Al, *Instr,* Solano Community College, Division of Fine & Applied Art & Behavioral Science, Fairfield CA (S)
Ziegler, Arthur P, *Pres,* Pittsburgh History & Landmarks Foundation, James D Van Trump Library, Pittsburgh PA
Ziegler, David, *Dir,* University of California, Los Angeles, Visual Resource Collection, Los Angeles CA
Ziegler, Janice, *Dir Educ,* Western Reserve Historical Society, Library, Cleveland OH
Ziegler, Joanna, *Prof,* College of the Holy Cross, Dept of Visual Arts, Worcester MA (S)
Zielke, Bridgitt, *Educ Specialist,* Wade House Historic Site-Wisconsin Historical Society, Wesley W. Jung Carriage Museum, Greenbush WI
Zierden, Martha, *Cur Historical Archaeology,* Charleston Museum, Charleston SC
Zies, Daniel, *Vis Servs Coordr,* Ellen Noel Art Museum of the Permian Basin, Odessa TX
Zietz, Stephen, *Head Spec Colls,* Cleveland Public Library, Fine Arts & Special Collections Dept, Cleveland OH
Ziglar, Katie, *Dir,* University of North Carolina at Chapel Hill, Ackland Art Museum, Chapel Hill NC
Zilinski, Rachel, *Registrar & Asst Cur,* University of Connecticut, William Benton Museum of Art, Storrs CT
Zill, Anne B, *Dir,* University of New England, Art Gallery, Portland ME
Zimmerer, Kathy, *Gallery Dir,* University Art Gallery at California State University, Dominguez Hills, Carson CA
Zimmerlink, PJ, *Preparator,* Westmoreland Museum of American Art, Art Reference Library, Greensburg PA
Zimmerman, Brian, *Asst Prof,* Webster University, Department of Art, Design & Art History, Webster Groves MO (S)
Zimmerman, Jerome, *Chmn & Prof,* C W Post Campus of Long Island University, School of Visual & Performing Arts, Brookville NY (S)
Zimmerman, Jim, *Archivist & Preparator,* Provincetown Art Association & Museum, Provincetown MA
Zimmerman, Randy, *Instr Computer Graphics 2nd yr,* AIC College of Design, Cincinnati OH (S)
Zimpel, Jim, *Assoc Prof Sculpture,* Montana State University, School of Art, Bozeman MT (S)
Zinke, Ryan, *Secy,* United States Department of the Interior, Interior Museum, Washington DC
Zinkham, Helena, *Dir Colls & Svcs and Chief of Prints & Photographs,* Library of Congress, Prints & Photographs Division, Washington DC
Zinn, Holly, *Dir Educ,* Pearson Lakes Art Center, Okoboji IA
Zinz, Kasia, *Secy,* Pioneer Town, Pioneer Museum of Western Art, Wimberley TX
Ziolkowski, Jan M, *Dir,* Dumbarton Oaks, Dumbarton Oaks Museum, Washington DC
Ziolkowski, Ruth, *CEO & Pres,* Crazy Horse Memorial, Indian Museum of North America, Native American Educational & Cultural Center & Crazy Horse Memorial Library (Reference), Crazy Horse SD
Zipay, Terry, *Chmn,* Wilkes University, Dept of Art, Wilkes-Barre PA (S)
Zippay, Lori, *Exec Dir,* Electronic Arts Intermix (EAI), New York NY
Zirkle, Merle W, *Prof,* Grinnell College, Dept of Art, Grinnell IA (S)
Zisk, Cathy, *Cataloger,* Dallas Museum of Art, Mildred R & Frederick M Mayer Library, Dallas TX
Zittlow, Todd, *Archivist,* Concordia Historical Institute, Saint Louis MO
Zivich, Matthew, *Prof,* Saginaw Valley State University, Dept of Art & Design, University Center MI (S)
Zivkovich, Kay M, *Asst Dir & Prof,* Southern Illinois University, School of Art & Design, Carbondale IL (S)
Zobel, James W, *Archivist,* MacArthur Memorial, Norfolk VA
Zobel, James W, *Archivist,* MacArthur Memorial, Library & Archives, Norfolk VA
Zoe, Vivian, *Dir,* Norwich Free Academy, Slater Memorial Museum, Norwich CT
Zoller, Guy, *Instr,* American University, Dept of Art, New York NY (S)
Zollinger, Wendy, *Exhib Coordr,* VSA Arts of New Mexico, Enabled Arts Center, Albuquerque NM (S)
Zona, Louis A, *Exec Dir & Chief Cur,* The Butler Institute of American Art, Art Museum, Youngstown OH
Zonker, Kenneth L, *Assoc Prof,* Sam Houston State University, Art Dept, Huntsville TX (S)
Zorn, David, *Pres,* Art Institute of Colorado, Denver CO (S)
Zorn, Jackson, *Instr,* Brazosport College, Communications & Fine Art, Lake Jackson TX (S)
Zortea, Flavia, *Graphic Design, Media Arts & Animation,* Art Institute of Pittsburgh, Pittsburgh PA (S)
Zotovich Phillips, Devon, *Prog Dir,* Bainbridge Island Arts Council, Bainbridge Island WA
Zouari, Ikram, *CFO & Dir Finance,* Canadian Museum of Nature, Musee Canadien de la Nature, Ottawa ON
Zsako, Julius, *Prof,* Seton Hall University, College of Arts & Sciences, South Orange NJ (S)
Zserdin, Carmelle, *Assoc Prof,* Clarke College, Dept of Art, Dubuque IA (S)
Zuberi, Sadaf, *Bus Opers Mgr,* Art Gallery of Mississauga, Mississauga ON
Zucco, Doug, *Instr,* Moravian College, Dept of Art, Bethlehem PA (S)
Zucker, Mark, *Prof,* Louisiana State University, School of Art, Baton Rouge LA (S)
Zuckerman Jacobson, Heidi, *Dir & Chief Cur,* Aspen Art Museum, Aspen CO
Zuckerman, Art, *Historian,* Bronx Community College (CUNY), Hall of Fame for Great Americans, Bronx NY
Zuckerman, Susan, *Dir & Historian,* Bronx Community College (CUNY), Hall of Fame for Great Americans, Bronx NY
Zugazagoitia, Julian, *CEO & Cur,* The Nelson-Atkins Museum of Art, Creative Arts Center, Kansas City MO
Zugazagoitia, Julian, *Dir & CEO,* The Nelson-Atkins Museum of Art, Kansas City MO
Zuhlke, Christy Lou, *Admin,* Rochester Historical Society, Rochester NY
Zuidema, Richard, *1st VChmn,* Reading Public Museum, Reading PA
Zumeta, Jay, *Instr,* Art Academy of Cincinnati, Cincinnati OH (S)
Zuniga, Pabol, *Dir,* Art Museum of the Americas, Washington DC
Zupnick, Matthew, *Prof,* University of Central Missouri, Dept of Art & Design, Warrensburg MO (S)
Zuraw, Shelley, *Assoc Dir,* University of Georgia, Franklin College of Arts & Sciences, Lamar Dodd School of Art, Athens GA (S)
Zurawski, Simone, *Assoc Prof,* DePaul University, Dept of Art, Chicago IL (S)
Zurinsky, Suzanne D, *Assoc Prof,* University of North Alabama, Dept of Art, Florence AL (S)
Zuris, Kathleen, *Research Specialist,* Danbury Scott-Fanton Museum & Historical Society, Inc, Danbury CT
Zuris, Kathleen, *Research Specialist,* Danbury Scott-Fanton Museum & Historical Society, Inc, Library, Danbury CT
Zurko, Walter, *Prof,* The College of Wooster, Dept of Art and Art History, Wooster OH (S)
Zust, Mark, *Chmn Design Studies,* Bowling Green State University, School of Art, Bowling Green OH (S)
Zwart, Joel, *Dir Exhibs,* Calvin College, Center Art Gallery, Grand Rapids MI
Zwerneman, Jane, *Prog Asst,* University of California, San Diego, Stuart Collection, La Jolla CA
Zwierciadlowski, Donna, *Librn,* Emily Carr Institute of Art & Design, Library, Vancouver BC
Zwilling, Jennifer, *Dir Devel U Cur Artistic Progs,* The Clay Studio, Philadelphia PA
Zwirner, David, *Owner,* David Zwirner Gallery, New York NY

Organization Index

Schools are indicated by "S".

1811 Old Lincoln County Jail & Lincoln County Museum, see Lincoln County Historical Association, Inc, Wiscasset ME
A.E. Backus Museum & Gallery, Fort Pierce FL (M)
A.I.R. Gallery, Brooklyn NY (M)
Aaron Douglas Gallery, see Fisk University, Nashville TN
Abby Aldrich Rockefeller Folk Art Museum, see Colonial Williamsburg Foundation, Williamsburg VA
Abilene Christian University, Dept of Art & Design, see Abilene TX (S)
Abington Art Center, Jenkintown PA (M)
Abraham Baldwin Agricultural College, Art & Humanities Dept, see Tifton GA (S)
Abraham Lincoln Presidential Library & Museum, Springfield IL (M)
Academy Art Museum, Easton MD (M)
Academy of Art University, Fine Arts Dept, see San Francisco CA (S)
Academy of Art, University Library, see San Francisco CA (L)
Academy of Fine Arts, Lynchburg VA (A)
Academy of Motion Picture Arts & Sciences, The Academy Gallery, see Beverly Hills CA (M)
Academy of the New Church, Glencairn Museum, see Bryn Athyn PA (M)
Acadia University Art Gallery, Wolfville NS (M)
Acadia University, Faculty of Arts, see Wolfville NS (S)
ACCESS, Arab American National Museum, see Dearborn MI (M)
Ace Gallery, Los Angeles CA (S)
Adams County Historical Society, Gettysburg PA (M)
Adams County Historical Society, Adams County Museum, see Brighton CO (M)
Adams National Historic Park, Quincy MA (M)
Adams State College, Dept of Visual Arts, see Alamosa CO (S)
Addison/Ripley Fine Art, Washington DC (M)
Adelphi University, Dept of Art & Art History, see Garden City NY (S)
The Adirondack Historical Association, The Adirondack Museum, see Blue Mountain Lake NY (M,L)
Adirondack Lakes Center for the Arts, Blue Mountain Lake NY (A)
Adrian College, Art & Design Dept, see Adrian MI (S)
Aesthetic Realism Foundation, New York NY (S)
Aesthetic Realism Foundation, New York NY (A,M,L)
The Africa Center, New York NY (M)
African American Atelier, Greensboro NC (M)
African American Museum, Dallas TX (M)
African American Museum in Philadelphia, Philadelphia PA (M)
African American Museum of Iowa, Cedar Rapids IA (M)
African Art Museum of Maryland, Columbia MD (M)
Agecroft Association, Agecroft Hall, see Richmond VA (A,M)
Ages of Man Foundation, Amenia NY (A)
Agnes Scott College, Dalton Art Gallery, see Decatur GA (M)
Agnes Scott College, Dept of Art, see Decatur GA (S)
The Agricultural Memories Museum, Penn Yan NY (M)
AIC College of Design, Cincinnati OH (S)
Aidron Duckworth Art Preservation Trust, Aidron Duckworth Art Museum, see Meriden NH (M)
Aiken County Historical Museum, Aiken SC (M)
Aims Community College, Visual & Performing Arts, see Greeley CO (S)
Airpower Museum Library, Ottumwa IA (L)
AKA Artist Run Centre, Saskatoon SK (M,L)
Akron-Summit County Public Library, Fine Arts Division, see Akron OH (L)
Akron Art Museum, Akron OH (M,L)
Alabama A & M University, Dept of Visual Performing & Communication Arts, see Normal AL (S)
Alabama Department of Archives & History, Museum of Alabama, see Montgomery AL (M)
Alabama Southern Community College, Art Dept, see Monroeville AL (S)
Alabama State University, Dept of Visual Arts, see Montgomery AL (S)
Alaska Department of Education, Division of Libraries, Archives & Museums, Sheldon Jackson Museum, see Sitka AK (M)
Alaska Heritage Museum at Wells Fargo, Anchorage AK (M)
Alaska House Art Gallery, Fairbanks AK (M)
Alaska Museum of Science & Nature, Anchorage AK (M)
Alaska State Library, Alaska Historical Collections, see Juneau AK (L)
Alaska State Museum, Juneau AK (M)
Alaska Watercolor Society, Anchorage AK (A)
Albany Institute of History & Art, Albany NY (M,L)
Albany Museum of Art, Albany GA (M)
Alberta College of Art & Design, Calgary AB (S)
Alberta College of Art & Design, Illingworth Kerr Gallery, see Calgary AB (M,L)
Alberta Craft Council, Edmonton AB (A)
Alberta Foundation for the Arts, Edmonton AB (A)
Alberta Society of Artists, Calgary AB (A)
Albert H Wiggin Gallery & Print Department, see Boston Public Library, Boston MA
Albertus Magnus College, Visual and Performing Arts, see New Haven CT (S)
Albin O Kuhn Library & Gallery, Baltimore MD (M)
Albin Polasek Museum & Sculpture Gardens, Winter Park FL (M)
Albion College, Bobbitt Visual Arts Center, see Albion MI (M)
The Albrecht-Kemper Museum of Art, Saint Joseph MO (M,L)
Albright-Knox Art Gallery, Buffalo NY (M)
Albright College, Dept of Art, see Reading PA (S)
Albright College, Freedman Gallery, see Reading PA (M)
Albuquerque Museum of Art & History, Albuquerque NM (M)
Alcorn State University, Dept of Fine Arts, see Lorman MS (S)
Alden B. Dow Museum of Science & Art, Alden B. Dow Museum School, see Midland MI (S)
Aldrich Museum of Contemporary Art, Ridgefield CT (M)
Alexandria Museum of Art, Alexandria LA (M)
Alexey von Schlippe Gallery of Art, Groton CT (M)
Alice Lloyd College, Art Dept, see Pippa Passes KY (S)
Alice Moseley Folk Art and Antique Museum, Bay Saint Louis MS (M)
Aljira Center for Contemporary Art, Newark NJ (A)
Allan Hancock College, Fine Arts Dept, see Santa Maria CA (S)
Allegany Arts Council The Saville Gallery, Cumberland MD (M)
Allegany Community College, Art Dept, see Cumberland MD (S)
Allegany County Historical Society, Gordon-Roberts House, see Cumberland MD (M)
Allegheny College, Art Dept, see Meadville PA (S)
Allegheny College, Bowman, Megahan & Penelec Galleries, see Meadville PA (M)
Charlotte W Allen Library-Memorial Art Gallery, see University of Rochester, Rochester NY
Allen County Community College, Art Dept, see Iola KS (S)
Allen County Public Library, Art, Music & Audiovisual Services, see Fort Wayne IN (L)
Allens Lane Art Center, Carolyn-Fielder-Alber Gallery, see Philadelphia PA (M)
Allentown Art Museum, Allentown PA (M)
Alliance Center Museum and Art Gallery, Abbeville LA (M)
Allied Artists of America, Inc, Florham Park NJ (O)
Allied Arts Association, Allied Arts Center & Gallery, see Richland WA (A)
Allied Arts Council of Lethbridge, Bowman Arts Center, see Lethbridge AB (A)
Allied Arts Council of St Joseph, Saint Joseph MO (A)
Allied Arts of Seattle, Seattle WA (A)
Alma College, Clack Art Center, Dept of Art & Design, see Alma MI (S)
Almond Historical Society, Inc, Hagadorn House, The 1800-37 Museum, see Almond NY (M)
Alternate ROOTS, Inc, Atlanta GA (M)
Alton Museum of History & Art, Inc, Alton IL (M)
Alverno College, Art Dept, see Milwaukee WI (S)
Alverno College Gallery, Alverno Art and Cultures Gallery, see Milwaukee WI (M)
Alvin Community College, Art Dept, see Alvin TX (S)
Amarillo Art Association, Amarillo Museum of Art, see Amarillo TX (A,L)
Amarillo College, Visual Art Dept, see Amarillo TX (S)
The American-Scandinavian Foundation, Scandinavia House: The Nordic Center in America, see New York NY (A)
American Abstract Artists, Brooklyn NY (O)
American Academy in Rome, New York NY (S)
American Academy of Art, Chicago IL (S)
American Academy of Arts & Letters, New York NY (O)
American Alliance of Museums, Arlington VA (O)
American Antiquarian Society, Worcester MA (O)
American Architectural Foundation, The Octagon Museum, see Washington DC (M)
American Artists Professional League, Inc, New York NY (O)
American Art Museum, Smithsonian Institution, see Washington DC (M,L)
American Association of University Women, Washington DC (O)

American Civilization Foundation, National Museum of American Illustration, see Newport RI (M)
American Color Print Society, Narberth PA (O)
American Craft Council, Minneapolis MN (O,L)
The American Federation of Arts, New York NY (O)
American Film Institute (AFI), Los Angeles CA (S)
American Folk Art Museum, New York NY (M,L)
American Homing Pigeon Museum & Library, Oklahoma City OK
American Institute for Conservation of Historic & Artistic Works, Washington DC (O)
American Institute of Architects, The Octagon Museum, see Washington DC (O)
American Institute of Graphic Arts, National Design Center, see New York NY (O)
American Jewish Historical Society, The Center for Jewish History, see New York NY (A,L)
American Kennel Club, Museum of the Dog, see Saint Louis MO (M,L)
American Museum of Cartoon Art, Inc, Sunland CA (M)
American Museum of Ceramic Art, Pomona CA (M)
American Museum of the Moving Image, Astoria NY (M)
American Numismatic Association, Edward C. Rochette Money Museum, see Colorado Springs CO (O,L)
American Numismatic Society, New York NY (O,L)
American Print Alliance, Peachtree City GA (M)
American River College, Dept of Art/Art New Media, see Sacramento CA (S)
Americans for the Arts, Washington DC (O)
Americans for the Arts, New York NY (O,L)
American Society for Aesthetics, Denver CO (O)
American Society of Artists, Inc, Palatine IL (O,L)
American Society of Bookplate Collectors & Designers, Tucson AZ (O)
American Society of Contemporary Artists (ASCA), Yorktown Heights NY (O)
American Sport Art Museum and Archives, Daphne AL (M)
American Swedish Historical Foundation & Museum, American Swedish Historical Museum, see Philadelphia PA (M,L)
American Swedish Institute, Minneapolis MN (M)
American Textile History Museum, Lowell MA (M,L)
American University, Dept of Art, see New York NY (S)
American University, Jack I & Dorothy G Bender Library & Learning Resources Center, see New York NY (L)
American University, Museum at the Katzen, see Washington DC (M)
American Watercolor Society, Inc, New York NY (O)
Americas Society Art Gallery, New York NY (M)
Amerind Foundation, Inc, Amerind Museum, Fulton-Hayden Memorial Art Gallery, see Dragoon AZ (A,L)
Ames Free-Easton's Public Library, North Easton MA (L)
Amherst College, Dept of Art & the History of Art, see Amherst MA (S)
Amherst College, Mead Art Museum, see Amherst MA (M,L)
Amon Carter Museum of American Art, Fort Worth TX (M,L)
Anacostia Community Museum, Smithsonian Institution, see Washington DC (M,L)
Anchorage Museum at Rasmuson Center, Anchorage AK (M,L)
Ancient Spanish Monastery, North Miami Beach FL (M)
Ancilla College, Art Dept, see Donaldson IN (S)
Anderson County Arts Council, Anderson Arts Center, see Anderson SC (A)
Anderson Fine Arts Center, The Anderson Center for the Arts, see Anderson IN (A)
Anderson Ranch Arts Center, Snowmass Village CO (A)
Anderson University, Art Dept, see Anderson IN (S)
Andover Historical Society, Andover MA (A)
Andrew-Safford House, see Peabody Essex Museum, Salem MA
Andrews University, Dept of Art, Art History & Design, see Berrien Springs MI (S)
Andy Warhol Foundation for the Visual Arts, New York NY (A)
The Andy Warhol Museum, Pittsburgh PA (M,L)
Angelo State University, Houston Harte University Center, see San Angelo TX (M)
Angelo State University, Visual and Performing Arts, see San Angelo TX (S)
Angels Gate Cultural Center, Gallery A & Gallery G, see San Pedro CA (M)
Anna Maria College, Dept of Art, see Paxton MA (S)
Anna Maria College, Saint Luke's Gallery, see Paxton MA (M)
Ann Arbor Art Center, Art Center, see Ann Arbor MI (A)
Anne Bunce Cheney Art Collection, see University of Hartford, West Hartford CT
Anniston Museum of Natural History, Anniston AL (M)
Anoka Ramsey Community College, Art Dept, see Coon Rapids MN (S)
Anson County Historical Society, Inc, Wadesboro NC (M)
Antelope Valley College, Art Dept, Division of Fine Arts, see Lancaster CA (S)
Anthology Film Archives, New York NY (M)
Antioch College, Herndon Gallery, see Yellow Springs OH (M)
Antioch College, Visual Arts Dept, see Yellow Springs OH (S)
Anton Art Center, Mount Clemens MI (A)
Antonelli College, Cincinnati OH (S)
Antonelli Institute, Professional Photography & Commercial Art, see Erdenheim PA (S)
Aperture Foundation, New York NY (O)
The APEX Museum, Atlanta GA (M)
Appalachian State University, Dept of Art, see Boone NC (S)
Appalachian State University, Turchin Center for the Visual Arts, see Boone NC (M)
Appaloosa Museum and Heritage Center, Moscow ID (M)
Appalshop Inc, Appalshop, see Whitesburg KY
Aquinas College, Art Dept, see Grand Rapids MI (S)
Arapahoe Community College, Colorado Gallery of the Arts, see Littleton CO (M)
Arcadia University Art Gallery, Spruance Fine Arts Center, see Glenside PA (M)
Arcadia University, Dept of Fine Arts, see Glenside PA (S)
ARC Gallery and Educational Foundation, Chicago IL (M)
Archaeological Institute of America, Boston MA (O)
Archaeological Society of Ohio, Indian Museum of Lake County, Ohio, see Willoughby OH (M,L)
Archbishop Alter Library, see College of Mount Saint Joseph, Cincinnati OH
Architects Design Group Inc, Winter Park FL (A)
Architectural League of New York, New York NY (A)
Archive of Contemporary Latin American Art, see Art Museum of the Americas, Washington DC
Archives of American Art, Smithsonian Institution, see Washington DC (M)
Archives of Manitoba, Winnipeg MB (L)
Archives of the Archdiocese of St Paul & Minneapolis, Saint Paul MN (M)
Arizona Artists Guild, Phoenix AZ (A)
Arizona Commission on the Arts, Phoenix AZ (A,L)
Arizona Historical Society-Yuma, Sanguinetti House Museum & Garden, see Yuma AZ (M)
Arizona State University, ASU Art Museum, see Tempe AZ (M,L)
Arizona State University, Deer Valley Petroglyph Preserve, see Phoenix AZ (M)
Arizona State University, Herberger Institute for Design and the Arts, see Tempe AZ (S)
Arizona Watercolor Association, Phoenix AZ (A)
Arjuna Library, Digital Visual Dream Laboratory & Acoustic Studio, see Colorado Springs CO (L)
Arkansas Arts Center, Little Rock AR (S)
Arkansas Arts Center, Little Rock AR (M,L)
Arkansas State University-Art Department, Jonesboro, Fine Arts Center Gallery, see Jonesboro AR (M,L)
Arkansas State University, Dept of Art, see State University AR (S)
Arkansas Tech University, Dept of Art, see Russellville AR (S)
Arlington Arts Center (AAC), Arlington VA (M)
Arlington Center for the Arts, Arlington MA (M)
Arlington County Department of Public Libraries, Fine Arts Section, see Arlington VA (L)
Arlington Museum of Art, Arlington TX (M)
Armory Center for the Arts, Pasadena CA (A)
Armstrong Atlantic State University, Department of Art, Music & Theatre, see Savannah GA (S)
Arnold Mikelson Mind & Matter Art Gallery, Surrey BC (M)
Arnot Art Museum, Elmira NY (M)
Aroostook County Historical & Art Museum, Houlton ME (M)
Arrowmont School of Arts & Crafts, Gatlinburg TN (S)
Arrow Rock State Historic Site, Arrow Rock MO (M)
Art & Culture Center of Hollywood, Art Gallery/ Multidisciplinary Cultural Center, see Hollywood FL (M)
Art Academy of Cincinnati, Cincinnati OH (S)
Art and History Museums - Maitland, Maitland FL (M, L)
Art Association of Harrisburg, School & Galleries, see Harrisburg PA (M)
The Art Association of Jacksonville, The David Strawn Art Gallery, see Jacksonville IL (M)
The Art Cafe, Davisburg MI (M)
ArtCenter College of Design, Pasadena CA (S)
Art Center College of Design, James Lemont Fogg Memorial Library, see Pasadena CA (L,M)
Art Center Manatee, Bradenton FL (A)
Art Center of Battle Creek, Battle Creek MI (M,L)
The Art Center of Highland Park - TAC, Highland Park IL (M)
The Art Center of Waco, Waco TX (M,L)
Art Center Sarasota, Sarasota FL (S)
Art Center Sarasota, Sarasota FL (A)
Art Centre of New Jersey, Livingston NJ (S)
Art Community Center, Art Center of Corpus Christi, see Corpus Christi TX (M)
Art Complex Museum, Carl A Weyerhaeuser Library, see Duxbury MA (M,L)
Art Dealers Association of America, Inc, New York NY (O)
Art Dealers Association of Canada, Toronto ON (O)
Artesia Historical Museum and Art Center, Artesia NM (M)
Artexte Information Centre, Documentation Centre, see Montreal QC (L)
The Artful Deposit, Inc, The Artful Deposit Gallery, see Bordentown NJ (M)
The Art Galleries of Ramapo College, Mahwah NJ (M)
Art Gallery of Alberta, Edmonton AB (M)
Art Gallery of Bancroft Inc, Bancroft ON (M)
Art Gallery of Burlington, Burlington ON (M)
The Art Gallery of Cornwall, Cornwall ON (M)
The Art Gallery of Grand Prairie, Grande Prairie AB (M)
Art Gallery of Greater Victoria, Victoria BC (M,L)
Art Gallery of Guelph, Guelph ON (M)
Art Gallery of Hamilton, Hamilton ON (M,L)
Art Gallery of Mississauga, Mississauga ON (M)
Art Gallery of Nova Scotia, Halifax NS (M)
Art Gallery of Ontario, Toronto ON (M)
Art Gallery of Peel, Peel Heritage Complex, see Brampton ON (M,L)
Art Gallery of Peterborough, Peterborough ON (M)
The Art Gallery of Southwestern Manitoba, Brandon MB (A,L)
Art Gallery of Swift Current, Swift Current SK (M)
Art Gallery of Windsor, Windsor ON (M,L)

Art Guild of Burlington, Art Center of Burlington, see Burlington IA (A)
Arthur D Jenkins Library, see George Washington University, Washington DC
Arthur Griffin Center for Photographic Art, Griffin Museum of Photography, see Winchester MA (M)
Art Information Center, Inc, New York NY (A)
Art in General, Brooklyn NY (A)
Art Institute of Atlanta, Atlanta GA (S)
The Art Institute of Chicago, Chicago IL (A,L,M)
Art Institute of Colorado, Denver CO (S)
The Art Institute of Dallas, Dallas TX (S)
Art Institute of Fort Lauderdale, Fort Lauderdale FL (S)
Art Institute of Fort Lauderdale, Technical Library, see Fort Lauderdale FL (L)
Art Institute of Houston, Houston TX (S)
Art Institute of Philadelphia, Philadelphia PA (S)
Art Institute of Philadelphia Library, Philadelphia PA (L)
Art Institute of Pittsburgh, Pittsburgh PA (S)
Art Institute of Pittsburgh, John P. Barclay Memorial Gallery, see Pittsburgh PA (M,L)
Art Institute of Southern California, Laguna Beach CA (S)
Art Institutes International at Portland, Portland OR (L)
The Art Institutes, The Art Institute of Seattle, see Seattle WA (S)
Art Instruction Schools, Education Dept, see Minneapolis MN (S)
Artistry, Inez Greenberg Gallery, see Bloomington MN (M)
Artists' Cooperative Gallery, Omaha NE (M)
Artists' Fellowship, Inc, New York NY (O)
Artists Association of Nantucket, Nantucket MA (A)
Artists Collective Inc, Hartford CT (A)
Artists in Stained Glass, see Ontario Crafts Council, Toronto ON
Artists Space, New York NY (A,M,L)
Artists Talk on Art (ATOA), New York NY (A)
The Art League Gallery & School, Alexandria VA (A)
Art League of Houston, Houston TX (A)
The Art League of Long Island, Stevenson Academy Program, see Dix Hills NY (S)
Artlink, Inc, Auer Center for Arts & Culture, see Fort Wayne IN (M)
Art Metropole, Toronto ON (M)
The Art Museum of Eastern Idaho, Idaho Falls ID (M)
Art Museum of Greater Lafayette, Lafayette IN (M)
Art Museum of Southeast Texas, Beaumont TX (M)
Art Museum of the Americas, Washington DC (M,L)
Art PAC, Washington DC (A)
Artrain, Inc, Ann Arbor MI (A)
Art Resources International, Washington DC (A)
Arts & Business Council of Greater Boston, Inc, Volunteer Lawyers for the Arts of MA, see Boston MA (A)
Arts & Crafts Association of Meriden Inc, Gallery 53, see Meriden CT (A,L)
Arts & Education Council of Greater Saint Louis, Saint Louis MO (A)
Arts & Humanities Council of Tuscaloosa, Junior League Gallery, Dinah Washington Cultural Arts Center Galleries, see Tuscaloosa AL (A)
Arts & Science Center for Southeast Arkansas, Pine Bluff AR (A)
Arts & Science Council, Charlotte NC (A)
Arts, Craft & Theater Safety, New York NY (A)
Art Saint Louis, Saint Louis MO (M)
Arts and Letters Club of Toronto, Toronto ON (A,L)
The Arts Center, Corvallis OR (M)
Arts Center in Orange, Orange VA (M)
The Arts Center of the Capital Region, Troy NY (A)
Arts Center of the Ozarks, Springdale AR (M)
The ArtsCenter, The Nicholson Gallery at the Arts Center, see Carrboro NC (M)
The Art School at Old Church, Demarest NJ (S)
The Arts Club of Chicago, Chicago IL (A,L)
Arts Club of Washington, James Monroe House, see Washington DC (M)
ArtsConnection Inc, New York NY (A)
Arts Council for Long Beach, Long Beach CA (A)
Arts Council of Fayetteville-Cumberland County, The Arts Center, see Fayetteville NC (M)
Arts Council of Greater Kingsport, Renaissance Center Main Gallery, see Kingsport TN (A)
Arts Council of Mendocino County, Ukiah CA (A)
Arts Council Of New Orleans, New Orleans LA (A)
Arts Council of Southwestern Indiana, The Bower-Suhrheinrich Foundation Gallery, see Evansville IN (A)
Arts Council of the Mid-Columbia Region, Kennewick WA (A)
The ARTS Council of the Southern Finger Lakes, Corning NY (A)
The Arts Council of Wayne County, Goldsboro NC (S)
Arts Council of White Lake, Gallery, see Whitehall MI (M)
The Arts Council of Winston-Salem & Forsyth County, Winston-Salem NC (A)
Art Services International, Alexandria VA (O)
Arts Extension Service, Amherst MA (O)
Arts Midland Galleries & School, Midland MI (A)
Arts Midwest, Minneapolis MN (A)
Arts on the Park, Lakeland Center for Creative Arts, see Lakeland FL (M)
Artspace, Richmond VA (M)
Artspace Inc, Raleigh NC (A)
ArtSpace/Lima, Lima OH (M)
Arts Partnership of Greater Spartanburg, Inc, Chapman Cultural Center, see Spartanburg SC (A)
The Art Spirit Gallery, Coeur D Alene ID (M)
Arts Place, Inc, Hugh N Ronald Memorial Gallery, see Portland IN (M)
ArtsQuest, Bethlehem PA (M)
Art Students League of New York, New York NY (S)
Art Students League of New York, New York NY (A,L)
The Art Studio Inc, Beaumont TX (A)
The Art Studio New York, New York NY (S)
Arts United for Davidson County, The Arts Center, see Lexington NC (M)
Arts United of Greater Fort Wayne, Fort Wayne IN (A)
ArtsWave, Cincinnati OH (A)
Art Without Walls Inc, Sayville NY (M)
Artworks Trenton, Trenton NJ (A,L)
Asbury College, Student Center Gallery, see Wilmore KY (M)
Asbury University, Art Dept, see Wilmore KY (S)
Ascension Lutheran Church Library, Milwaukee WI (L)
Asher Library, see Spertus Institute of Jewish Studies, Chicago IL
Asheville Art Museum, Asheville NC (M)
Ashford Hollow Foundation for Visual & Performing Arts, Griffis Sculpture Park & Essex Arts Center, see East Otto NY (A)
Ashford University, Art Dept, see Clinton IA (S)
The Ashland Academy of Art, Haiku HI (S)
Ashland College Arts & Humanities Gallery, The Coburn Gallery, see Ashland OH (M)
Ashland Inc, Ashland KY
Ashland University, Art Dept, see Ashland OH (S)
Ashtabula Arts Center, Ashtabula OH (A)
Asian American Arts Centre, New York NY (A)
Asian Art Museum of San Francisco, Chong-Moon Lee Ctr for Asian Art and Culture, see San Francisco CA (M,L)
Asian Collection, see Saint John's University, Queens NY
Asia Society Museum, New York NY (M)
A Space, Toronto ON (M)
Aspen Art Museum, Aspen CO (M)
Associated Artists of Pittsburgh, Pittsburgh PA (A)
Associated Artists of Winston-Salem, Winston-Salem NC (A)
Associates for Community Development, The Arts Center, Inc, see Martinsburg WV (M)
Associates of the Art Commission, Inc, see Design Commission of the City of New York, New York NY
Association for Public Art, Philadelphia PA (A)
Association of African American Museums, Washington DC (O)
Association of Art Museum Directors, New York NY (O)
Association of Collegiate Schools of Architecture, Washington DC (O)
Association of Hawaii Artists, Honolulu HI (A)
Association of Independent Colleges of Art & Design, Providence RI (O)
The Association of International Photography Art Dealers, Washington DC (A)
Association of Medical Illustrators, Lexington KY (O)
Association professionnelle des designers d'interieur du Quebec, Montreal QC (A)
Assumption College, Dept of Art, Music & Theatre, see Worcester MA (S)
ASTED Inc, Montreal QC (O)
AS220, Main Gallery, see Providence RI (M)
ASU Library, see Arizona State University, Tempe AZ
Ataloa Lodge Museum, Muskogee OK (M)
Ateneo Puertorriqueno, Ateneo Gallery, see San Juan PR (M,L)
Athenaeum of Philadelphia, Philadelphia PA (M,L)
Atlanta-Fulton Public Library, Central Library Art Gallery, see Atlanta GA (L)
Atlanta Contemporary Art Center, Atlanta GA (M)
Atlanta Cyclorama & Civil War Museum, see City of Atlanta, Atlanta GA
Atlanta Historical Society Inc, Atlanta History Center, see Atlanta GA (M)
Atlanta International Museum of Art & Design, Museum of Design Atlanta, see Atlanta GA (M)
Atlanta Technical Institute, Visual Communications Class, see Atlanta GA (S)
Atlantic City Arts Commission, Garden Pier Art Gallery, see Atlantic City NJ (M)
Atlantic Gallery, New York NY (M)
Atlatl, Phoenix AZ (O)
Atrium Gallery, Saint Louis MO (M)
Attleboro Arts Museum, Attleboro MA (M)
Auburn University, Dept of Art & Art History, see Auburn AL (S)
Auburn University, Jule Collins Smith Museum of Fine Art, see Auburn AL (M)
Auburn University Montgomery, Dept of Fine Arts, see Montgomery AL (S)
Audrain County Historical Society, Graceland Museum & American Saddlehorse Museum & Fire Brick Industry Museum, see Mexico MO (M)
Auerbach Art Library, see Wadsworth Atheneum Museum of Art, Hartford CT
Augsburg College, Art Dept, see Minneapolis MN (S)
Augustana College, Art Dept, see Sioux Falls SD (S)
Augustana College, Art Dept, see Rock Island IL (S)
Augustana College, Augustana College Art Museum, see Rock Island IL (M)
Augustana University, Center for Western Studies, see Sioux Falls SD (A)
Augustana University, Eide-Dalrymple Gallery, see Sioux Falls SD (M)
Augusta State University, Dept of Art, see Augusta GA (S)
Aurora Regional Fire Museum, Aurora IL (M)
Aurora University, Art Dept, see Aurora IL (S)
Aurora University, Schingoethe Center for Native American Cultures & The Schingoethe Art Gallery, see Aurora IL (M)
Austin College, Art Dept, see Sherman TX (S)
Austin College, Ida Green Gallery, see Sherman TX (M)
Austin Community College, Dept of Commercial Art, North Ridge Campus, see Austin TX (S)
Austin Peay State University, Dept of Art, see Clarksville TN (S)
Austin Peay State University, Margaret Fort Trahern Gallery, see Clarksville TN (M,L)
Austrian Cultural Forum Gallery, New York NY (M)
Autry National Center, Museum of the American West, Griffith Park, see Los Angeles CA (M,L)

Avampato Discovery Museum, The Clay Center for Arts & Sciences, see Charleston WV (M)
Avant Gallery, Miami FL (M)
Averett College, Art Dept, see Danville VA (S)
Avila College, Art Division, Dept of Humanities, see Kansas City MO (S)
Avila University, Thornhill Art Gallery, see Kansas City MO (M)
Azusa Pacific University, College of Music & the Arts, Dept of Art & Design, see Azusa CA (S)
B'nai B'rith International, B'nai B'rith Klutznick National Jewish Museum, see Washington DC (M)
Leo Baeck, New York NY (A,L)
Bainbridge Arts & Crafts Gallery, Bainbridge Island WA (M)
Bainbridge Island Arts Council, Bainbridge Island WA (A)
Bakehouse Art Complex, Inc, Miami FL (M)
Baker Arts Center, Liberal KS (M)
Bakersfield Art Foundation, Bakersfield Museum of Art, see Bakersfield CA (M)
Bakersfield College, Art Dept, see Bakersfield CA (S)
Baker University, Dept of Mass Media & Visual Arts, see Baldwin City KS (S)
Baker University, Old Castle Museum, see Baldwin City KS (M)
Balboa Art Conservation Center, San Diego CA (A)
Allan C Balch Art Research Library, see Los Angeles County Museum of Art, Los Angeles CA
Baldwin-Wallace College, Dept of Art, see Berea OH (S)
Baldwin-Wallace College, Fawick Art Gallery, see Berea OH (M)
Baldwin Gallery, Aspen CO (M)
Baldwin Historical Society Museum, Baldwin NY (M)
Baldwin Hotel Museum Annex, see Klamath County Museum, Klamath Falls OR
Ball State University, David Owsley Museum of Art, see Muncie IN (M,L)
Ball State University, Dept of Art, see Muncie IN (S)
Baltimore City Community College, Art Gallery, see Baltimore MD (M)
Baltimore City Community College, Dept of Fine Arts, see Baltimore MD (S)
The Baltimore Museum of Art, Baltimore MD (M,L)
Balzekas Museum of Lithuanian Culture, Chicago IL (M,L)
BanCorp South, Art Collection, see Tupelo MS
Banff Centre, Banff AB (S)
Banff Centre, Walter Phillips Gallery, see Banff AB (M, L)
Banfill-Locke Center for the Arts, Fridley MN (M)
Bank of NY Mellon Corporation, Pittsburgh PA
Bank of Oklahoma NA, Art Collection, see Tulsa OK
Bank One Fort Worth, Fort Worth TX
Bank One Wisconsin, Milwaukee WI
Barbara & Ray Alpert Jewish Community Center, Pauline & Zena Gatov Gallery, see Long Beach CA (M)
Bard College at Simon's Rock, Hillman-Jackson Gallery, see Great Barrington MA (M,L)
Bard College, Milton Avery Graduate School of the Arts, see Annandale-on-Hudson NY (S)
Bard College, Center for Curatorial Studies and the Hessel Museum of Art, see Annandale-on-Hudson NY (M,L)
Bard College, Center for Curatorial Studies Graduate Program, see Annandale-on-Hudson NY (S)
Bard College, Fisher Art Center, see Annandale-on-Hudson NY (M)
Barker Character, Comic and Cartoon Museum, Cheshire CT (M)
Barnard's Mill Art Museum, Glen Rose TX (M)
Barnes Foundation, Merion PA (M)
Barnes Museum, Southington CT (M)
Barn Gallery, Ogunquit ME (M)
The Barnum Museum, Bridgeport CT (M)
John D Barrow, Skaneateles NY (M)
Barry University, Dept of Fine Arts, see Miami Shores FL (S)
The Bartlett Museum, Amesbury MA (M)
Barton College, Barton Museum - Virginia Graves Gallery - Lula E Rackley Gallery, see Wilson NC (M,L)
Barton College, School of Visual, Performing & Communication Arts, see Wilson NC (S)
Barton County Community College, Fine Arts Dept, see Great Bend KS (S)
Bartow-Pell Mansion Museum & Gardens, Bronx NY (M)
Baruch College of the City University of New York, Sidney Mishkin Gallery, see New York NY (M)
The Bascomb, Highlands NC (M)
Bass Museum of Art, Miami Beach FL (M)
Bates College, Art & Visual Culture, see Lewiston ME (S)
Bates College, Museum of Art, see Lewiston ME (M)
Baton Rouge Gallery, Center For Contemporary Art, see Baton Rouge LA (M)
Bau-Xi Gallery, Toronto ON (M)
Bay Area Video Coalition, Inc, San Francisco CA (A)
Bay Arts, Inc, Bay Village OH (A)
Bay County Historical Society, Historical Museum of Bay County, see Bay City MI (M)
Baycrest Centre for Geriatric Care, The Morris & Sally Justein of Baycrest Heritage Museum, see Toronto ON (M)
Bay De Noc Community College, Art Dept, see Escanaba MI (S)
Baylor University - College of Arts and Sciences, Dept of Art, see Waco TX (S)
Baylor University, Martin Museum of Art, see Waco TX (M,L)
Bayonne Free Public Library, Cultural Center, see Bayonne NJ (L)
Bay Path College, Dept of Art, see Longmeadow MA (S)
Beaufort County Arts Council, Washington NC (A)
Beaumont Art League, Beaumont TX (M)
Beaverbrook Art Gallery, Fredericton NB (M,L)
Bechtler Museum of Modern Art, Charlotte NC (M)
Beck Center for the Arts, Lakewood OH (A)
Beck Cultural Exchange Center, Inc, Knoxville TN (M)
Becker College, William F Ruska Library, see Worcester MA (L)
Bede Art Gallery, Yankton SD (M)
Yale University, New Haven CT
Belger Arts Center, Kansas City MO (M)
Belger Crane Yard Studios, Kansas City MO (M)
Belhaven College, Art Dept, see Jackson MS (S)
Bellagio Resort & Casino, Bellagio Gallery of Fine Art, see Las Vegas NV (M)
Belle Grove Inc, Belle Grove Plantation, see Middletown VA (M)
Bellevue Arts Museum, Bellevue WA (M)
Bellevue College, Art Dept, see Bellevue NE (S)
Bellevue Community College, Art Dept, see Bellevue WA (S)
Bellingrath Gardens & Home, Theodore AL (M)
The Bell Museum of Natural History, see University of Minnesota, Minneapolis MN
Joseph Bellows Gallery, La Jolla CA (M)
Beloit College, Wright Museum of Art, see Beloit WI (M)
Belskie Museum, Closter NJ (M)
Belton Center for the Arts, Belton SC (M)
Belz Museum of Asian & Judaic Art, Memphis TN (M)
Bemidji State University, Visual Arts Dept, see Bemidji MN (S)
Bemis Center for Contemporary Arts, Omaha NE (M)
Benedict College, School of Humanities, Arts & Social Sciences, see Columbia SC (S)
Benedictine College, Art Dept, see Atchison KS (S)
The Benini Foundation & Sculpture Ranch, Johnson City TX (M)
W A C Bennett Library, see Simon Fraser University, Burnaby BC
Bennington College, Visual Arts Division, see Bennington VT (S)
Bennington Museum, Bennington VT (M)
Bent Museum & Gallery, Taos NM (M)
Berea College, Art & Art History Program, see Berea KY (S)
Berea College, Doris Ulmann Galleries, see Berea KY (M)
Bergen Community College, Visual Art Dept, see Paramus NJ (S)
Bergen County Historical Society, Steuben House Museum, see River Edge NJ (M)
Bergstrom-Mahler Museum of Glass, Neenah WI (M,L)
Berkeley Art Center, Berkeley CA (A)
Berkeley Civic Arts Program, Berkeley CA (A)
Berkeley Heights Free Public Library, Berkeley Heights NJ (L)
Berkeley Public Library, Art & Music Department, see Berkeley CA (L)
Berks Art Alliance, Reading PA (A)
Berkshire Athenaeum, Reference Dept, see Pittsfield MA (L)
Berkshire Community College, Dept of Fine Arts, see Pittsfield MA (S)
Berkshire Museum, Pittsfield MA (M)
Berman Museum, Anniston AL (M)
Bernard M Baruch College of the City University of New York, Art Dept, see New York NY (S)
Berry College, Art Dept, see Mount Berry GA (S)
Berry College, Moon Gallery, see Mount Berry GA (M, L)
Bert Gallery, Providence RI (M)
Bertha V B Lederer Fine Arts Gallery-Suny Geneseo, Bertha V B Lederer Fine Arts Gallery, see Geneseo NY (M)
Besser Museum for Northeast Michigan, Alpena MI (M, L)
Bethany College, Art Dept, see Lindsborg KS (S)
Bethany College, Mingenback Art Center, see Lindsborg KS (M,L)
Bethany College, Visual & Performing Arts Dept, see Bethany WV (S)
Bethany Lutheran College, Art Dept, see Mankato MN (S)
Bethel College, Dept of Art, see North Newton KS (S)
Bethel College, Mennonite Library & Archives, see North Newton KS (L)
Bethel University, Dept of Art & Design, see Saint Paul MN (S)
Beverly Hills Public Library, Fine Arts Library, see Beverly Hills CA (L)
Beverly Historical Society, Cabot, Hale & Balch House Museums, see Beverly MA (M,L)
Beyond Baroque Foundation, Beyond Baroque Literary Arts Center, see Venice CA (A)
Bicentennial Art Center & Museum, Paris IL (M)
Big Bend Community College, Art Dept, see Moses Lake WA (S)
Biggs Museum of American Art, Dover DE (M)
Big Horn County Historical Museum, Hardin MT (M)
Big Horn Galleries, Cody WY (M)
Binghamton University, Art History Department, see Binghamton NY (S)
Biola University, Department of Art, see La Mirada CA (S)
Birger Sandzen Memorial Gallery, Lindsborg KS (M)
Birmingham-Southern College, Art & Art History, see Birmingham AL (S)
Birmingham Bloomfield Art Center, Birmingham MI (S)
Birmingham Bloomfield Art Center, Art Center, see Birmingham MI (A)
Birmingham Museum of Art, Birmingham AL (M,L)
Birmingham Public Library, Arts, Literature & Sports Department, see Birmingham AL (L)
Birmingham Southern College, Doris Wainwright Kennedy Art Center, see Birmingham AL (M)
Bisbee Arts & Humanities Council, Lemuel Shattuck Memorial Library, see Bisbee AZ (L)
Biscoe Western Art Museum, San Antonio TX (M)
Bishop's University, Foreman Art Gallery, see Sherbrooke QC (M)
Bernice Pauahi Bishop, Honolulu HI (M,L)

Bismarck Art & Galleries Association, Bismarck ND (A)
Bismarck State College, Fine Arts Dept, see Bismarck ND (S)
Bixler Art & Music Library, see Colby College, Waterville ME
Black & White Gallery, Brooklyn NY (M)
Black American West Museum & Heritage Center, Denver CO (M)
Black Bear Bosin Resource Center, see Mid-America All-Indian Center, Wichita KS
Blackburn College, Dept of Art, see Carlinville IL (S)
Black Hawk College, Art Dept, see Moline IL (S)
Black Hills State University, Art Dept, see Spearfish SD (S)
Black Hills State University, Ruddell Gallery, see Spearfish SD (M,L)
Black River Academy Museum & Historical Society, Black River Academy Museum, see Ludlow VT (M)
BlackRock Center for the Arts, Germantown MD (M)
Blacksburg Regional Art Association, Blacksburg VA (A)
Blackwell Street Center for the Arts, Denville NJ (A)
Blanden Memorial Art Museum, Fort Dodge IA (M)
Blanton Museum of Art, see University of Texas at Austin, Austin TX
Blauvelt Demarest Foundation, Hiram Blauvelt Art Museum, see Oradell NJ (M)
Bloomsburg University, Dept of Art & Art History, see Bloomsburg PA (S)
Bloomsburg University of Pennsylvania, Haas Gallery of Art, see Bloomsburg PA (M)
Eleanor Blossom Memorial Library, see Maricopa County Historical Society, Wickenburg AZ
Blowing Rock Art and History Museum, Blowing Rock NC (M)
Bluefield State College, Division of Arts & Sciences, see Bluefield WV (S)
Blue Lake Fine Arts Camp, Art Dept, see Twin Lake MI (S)
Bluemont Historical Railroad Junction, Arlington VA (M)
Blue Mountain College, Art Dept, see Blue Mountain MS (S)
Blue Mountain Community College, Fine Arts Dept, see Pendleton OR (S)
Blue Mountain Gallery, New York NY (M)
Blue Sky Gallery, Oregon Center for the Photographic Arts, see Portland OR (M)
Blue Star Contemporary Art Center, San Antonio TX (M)
Bluff Country Artists Gallery, Spring Grove MN (M)
Bluffton University, Art Dept, see Bluffton OH (S)
Ernest Blumenschein Home & Studio, see Taos Historic Museums, Taos NM
Board of Parks & Recreation, The Parthenon, see Nashville TN (M)
Boca Raton Museum of Art, Boca Raton FL (A,L)
The Richard W Bock Sculpture Collection & Art Library, see Greenville College, Greenville IL
Bodley-Bullock House Museum, Lexington KY (M)
Boise Art Museum, Boise ID (M)
Boise State University, Art Dept, see Boise ID (S)
Bone Creek Museum of Agrarian Art, David City NE (M)
William Bonifas, Escanaba MI (M)
Bonita Historical Society, Bonita Museum and Cultural Center, see Bonita CA (M)
Boothbay Region Art Foundation Inc, Boothbay Harbor ME (A)
Booth Western Art Museum, Cartersville GA (M)
Bose Pacia, Brooklyn NY (M)
Boston Architectural College, McCormick Gallery, see Boston MA (A,L)
Boston Athenaeum, Boston MA (L)
Boston Center for Adult Education, Boston MA (S)
Boston Center for the Arts, Mills Gallery, see Boston MA (M)
Boston College, Fine Arts Dept, see Chestnut Hill MA (S)
Boston College, McMullen Museum of Art, see Chestnut Hill MA (M)
The Bostonian Society, Old State House Museum, see Boston MA (M,L)
The Boston Printmakers, at Lesley University, see Boston MA (A)
Boston Properties LLC, San Francisco CA
Boston Public Library, Central Library, see Boston MA (L,M)
Boston Sculptors at Chapel Gallery, West Newton MA (M)
Boston University Art Galleries, The Faye G, Jo & James Stone Gallery, see Boston MA (M)
Boston University, Graduate Program - Arts Administration, see Boston MA (S)
Boston University, School for the Arts, see Boston MA (S)
Muriel Isabel Bostwick Library, see Art Gallery of Hamilton, Hamilton ON
Botanic Hall Library, see Cheekwood-Tennessee Botanical Garden & Museum of Art, Nashville TN
Boulder History Museum, Museum of History, see Boulder CO (A)
Boulder Museum of Contemporary Art, Boulder CO (A)
Boulder Public Library & Gallery, Arts Gallery, see Boulder CO (L)
Bowdoin College, Art Dept, see Brunswick ME (S)
Bowdoin College, Peary-MacMillan Arctic Museum, see Brunswick ME (M)
Bowers Museum, Santa Ana CA (M)
Bowie Arts Center, Due West SC (M)
Bowie State University, Fine & Performing Arts Dept, see Bowie MD (S)
Bowling Green State University, Firelands College, Humanities Dept, see Huron OH (S)
Bowling Green State University, Fine Arts Center Galleries, see Bowling Green OH (M)
Bowling Green State University, School of Art, see Bowling Green OH (S)
Bowne House Historical Society, Flushing NY (A)
The Bradford Group, Niles IL (M)
Bradley University, Dept of Art, see Peoria IL (S)
Bradley University, Heuser Art Center, see Peoria IL (M)
Brandeis University, Dept of Fine Arts, see Waltham MA (S)
Brandeis University, Rose Art Museum, see Waltham MA (M,L)
Brandon Public Library, see The Art Gallery of Southwestern Manitoba, Brandon MB
Brandywine Battlefield Park, see Pennsylvania Historical & Museum Commission, Chadds Ford PA
Brandywine Conservancy, Brandywine River Museum, see Chadds Ford PA (M,L)
Brandywine Workshop, Center for the Visual Arts, see Philadelphia PA (A)
Branigan Cultural Center, Las Cruces NM (M)
The Brant Foundation Art Study Center, Greenwich CT (M)
Brant Historical Society, Brant Museum & Archives, see Brantford ON (M,L)
Brattleboro Museum & Art Center, Brattleboro VT (M)
Braun Research Library, see Autry National Center, Los Angeles CA
Brazosport College, Communications & Fine Art, see Lake Jackson TX (S)
Bread & Puppet Theater, Bread & Puppet Museum, see Glover VT (M)
Anne Bremer Memorial Library, see San Francisco Art Institute, San Francisco CA
Brenau University, Art & Design Dept, see Gainesville GA (S)
Brenner Library, see Quincy University, Quincy IL
Brentwood Art Center, Los Angeles CA (S)
Brescia University, Anna Eaton Stout Memorial Art Gallery, see Owensboro KY (M)
Brescia University, Art Dept, see Owensboro KY (S)
Brevard College, Department of Art, see Brevard NC (S)
Brevard College, Spiers Gallery, see Brevard NC (M,L)
Brewton-Parker College, Visual Arts, see Mount Vernon GA (S)
Briar Cliff University, Art Dept, see Sioux City IA (S)
BRIC - Brooklyn Information & Culture, BRIC House, see Brooklyn NY (M)
Brick Store Museum, Kennebunk ME (M)
Brickton Art Center, Park Ridge IL (M)
Bridgewater College, Art Dept, see Bridgewater VA (S)
Bridgewater State College, Art Dept, see Bridgewater MA (S)
Margaret M Bridwell Art Library, see University of Louisville, Louisville KY
Hilton M. Briggs Library, see South Dakota State University, Brookings SD
Brigham City Corporation, Brigham City Museum of Art & History, see Brigham City UT (M)
Brigham Young University, Hawaii Campus, Division of Fine Arts, see Laie HI (S)
Brigham Young University, Dept of Visual Arts, see Provo UT (S)
Brigham Young University, B F Larsen Gallery, see Provo UT (M,L)
L D Brinkman, Kerrville TX (M)
British Columbia Museums Association, Victoria BC (A)
The Broad, Los Angeles CA (M)
Brockton Public Library, Joseph A Driscoll Art Gallery, see Brockton MA (L)
Bromfield Art Gallery, Boston MA (M)
Silas Bronson, Waterbury CT (L)
Bronx Community College (CUNY), Hall of Fame for Great Americans, see Bronx NY (M)
Bronx Community College, Music & Art Dept, see Bronx NY (S)
Bronx Council on the Arts, Longwood Arts Gallery @ Hostos, see Bronx NY (M)
Bronx Museum of the Arts, Bronx NY (M)
Bronx River Art Center Inc, Bronx NY (M)
Bronxville Public Library, Bronxville NY (L)
Brookdale Community College, Center for the Visual Arts, see Lincroft NJ (S)
Brookfield Craft Center, Inc, Gallery, see Brookfield CT (M)
Brookgreen Gardens, Murrells Inlet SC (M,L)
Brooklyn Arts Council, BAC Gallery, see Brooklyn NY (A)
Brooklyn Botanic Garden, Steinhardt Conservatory Gallery, see Brooklyn NY (M)
Brooklyn College, Art Dept, see Brooklyn NY (S)
Brooklyn Historical Society, Brooklyn OH (M)
Brooklyn Historical Society, Brooklyn NY (A,L)
Brooklyn Museum, Brooklyn NY (M,L)
Brooklyn Public Library, Art & Music Division, see Brooklyn NY (L)
Brooks Institute of Photography, Ventura CA (L) (S)
Broward Community College - A. Hugh Adams Campus, Fine Arts Gallery, see Davie FL (M)
Broward Community College - South Campus, Art Gallery, see Pembroke Pines FL (M)
Broward County Board of Commissioners, Broward Cultural Div, see Fort Lauderdale FL (A)
Annmary Brown Memorial, see Brown University, Providence RI
Brown County Art Gallery Foundation, Nashville IN (A)
Armstrong Browning Library, see Baylor University, Waco TX
Browning Arts, Grand Forks ND (M)
John Brown House, see Rhode Island Historical Society, Providence RI
Orlando Brown House, see Liberty Hall Historic Site, Frankfort KY
Brownsville Art League, Brownsville Museum of Fine Art, see Brownsville TX (M)
Brown University, David Winton Bell Gallery, see Providence RI (M)
Brown University, Dept of History of Art & Architecture, see Providence RI (S)
Bruce Museum, Inc, Greenwich CT (M)
The Brush Art Gallery & Studios, Lowell MA (M)

Bryan Memorial Gallery, Cambridge VT (M)
Bryant Library, Roslyn NY (L)
Bryn Mawr College, Dept of the History of Art, see Bryn Mawr PA (S)
Bryn Mawr College, Rhys Carpenter Library for Art, Archaeology, Classics & Cities, see Bryn Mawr PA (L)
Buckham Fine Arts Project, Buckham Gallery, see Flint MI (M)
Bucknell University, Dept of Art, see Lewisburg PA (S)
Bucknell University, Edward & Marthann Samek Art Gallery, see Lewisburg PA (M)
Bucks County Community College, Fine Arts Dept, see Newtown PA (S)
Bucks County Community College, Hicks Art Center, see Newtown PA (M)
Bucks County Historical Society, Mercer Museum, see Doylestown PA (M,L)
Buehler Challenger & Science Center, Paramus NJ (M)
Buena Vista Museum of Natural History, Bakersfield CA (M)
Buffalo & Erie County Public Library, Buffalo NY (L)
Buffalo Arts Studio, Art Gallery, see Buffalo NY (M)
Buffalo Bill Memorial Association, Buffalo Bill Historical Center, see Cody WY (A,L)
The Buffalo Fine Arts Academy, Albright-Knox Art Gallery, see Buffalo NY (M,L)
Buffalo Niagara Heritage Village, Amherst NY (M,L)
Buffalo Society of Natural Sciences, Buffalo Museum of Science, see Buffalo NY (L)
Bullion Plaza Cultural Center & Museum, Miami AZ (M)
Ruth Bunker Memorial Library, see Dacotah Prairie Museum, Aberdeen SD
Bunnell Street Arts Center, Homer AK (M)
Burchfield Penney Art Center, Buffalo NY (M,L)
Burke Arts Council, Jailhouse Galleries, see Morganton NC (M)
Burke Museum of Natural History and Culture, see University of Washington, Seattle WA
Burlington County College, Humanities & Fine Art Div, see Pemberton NJ (S)
Burlington County Historical Society, Burlington NJ (A)
Burnaby Art Gallery, Burnaby BC (M)
Busch-Reisinger Museum, see Harvard University, Cambridge MA
Bush-Holley Historic Site & Storehouse Gallery, Greenwich Historical Society, see Cos Cob CT (M)
Bush Barn Art Center, see Salem Art Association, Salem OR
Bush House Museum, see Salem Art Association, Salem OR
Butler Community College, Art Dept, see El Dorado KS (S)
Butler Community College, Erman B. White Gallery, see El Dorado KS (M)
The Butler Institute of American Art, Art Museum, see Youngstown OH (M,L)
Butte College, Art Gallery, see Oroville CA (M)
Butte College, Dept of Fine Arts and Communication Tech, see Oroville CA (S)
Butte Silver Bow Arts Foundation, Butte MT (M)
Cabrillo College, Visual & Performing Arts Division, see Aptos CA (S)
Cabrini College, Dept of Fine Arts, see Radnor PA (S)
Cahoon Museum of American Art, Cotuit MA (M)
Caldwell College, Dept of Fine Arts, see Caldwell NJ (S)
Caldwell College, The Visceglia Art Gallery, see Caldwell NJ (M)
Calgary Public Library, Arts & Recreation Dept, see Calgary AB (L)
John C Calhoun, Art Gallery, see Decatur AL (M)
John C Calhoun, Department of Fine Arts, see Tanner AL (S)
California African-American Museum, Los Angeles CA (M,L)
California Baptist University, Art Dept, see Riverside CA (S)
California Center for the Arts, Escondido Museum, see Escondido CA (M)
California College of the Arts, San Francisco CA (S)
California College of the Arts, CCAC Wattis Institute for Contemporary Arts, see San Francisco CA (M)
California College of the Arts, Libraries, see Oakland CA (L)
The California Historical Society, San Francisco CA (M,L)
California Institute of the Arts Library, Santa Clarita CA (L)
California Institute of the Arts, School of Art, see Valencia CA (S)
California Lutheran University, Art Dept, see Thousand Oaks CA (S)
California Polytechnic State University at San Luis Obispo, Dept of Art & Design, see San Luis Obispo CA (S)
California Polytechnic State University, College of Architecture & Environmental Design-Architecture Collection, see San Luis Obispo CA (L)
California Science Center, Los Angeles CA (M)
California State Parks, State Indian Museum, see Sacramento CA (M)
California State Polytechnic University, Pomona, Department of Art, see Pomona CA (S)
California State University, Bakersfield, Dept of Art, see Bakersfield CA (S)
California State University, Bakersfield, Todd Madigan Gallery, see Bakersfield CA (M)
California State University, Chico, Department of Art & Art History, see Chico CA (S)
California State University, Chico, University Art Gallery, see Chico CA (M,L)
California State University, Dominguez Hills, Art & Design Dept, see Carson CA (S)
California State University, East Bay, University Art Gallery, see Hayward CA (M)
California State University, Fresno, Art & Design, see Fresno CA (S)
California State University, Fullerton, Art Dept, see Fullerton CA (S)
California State University, Fullerton, Visual Arts Galleries, see Fullerton CA (M)
California State University, Hayward, Art Dept, see Hayward CA (S)
California State University, Long Beach, Art Dept, see Long Beach CA (S)
California State University, Long Beach, University Art Museum, see Long Beach CA (M,L)
California State University, Los Angeles, Art Dept, see Los Angeles CA (S)
California State University, Los Angeles, Fine Arts Gallery, see Los Angeles CA (M)
California State University, Northridge, Art Galleries, see Northridge CA (M)
California State University, Northridge, Dept of Art, see Northridge CA (S)
California State University, Sacramento, Dept of Art, see Sacramento CA (S)
California State University, Sacramento, Library - Central Reference Dept, see Sacramento CA (M)
California State University, San Bernardino, San Bernardino CA (M)
California State University, San Bernardino, Dept of Art, see San Bernardino CA (S)
California State University, Art Dept, see Turlock CA (S)
California State University, Long Beach Foundation, see Long Beach CA (A)
California State University Stanislaus, University Art Gallery, see Turlock CA (M,L)
California University of Pennsylvania, Dept of Art, see California PA (S)
California Watercolor Association, Gallery Concord, see Concord CA (A)
Callan Contemporary, New Orleans LA (M)
Calvert Marine Museum, Solomons MD (M,L)
Calvin College, Art Dept, see Grand Rapids MI (S)
Calvin College, Center Art Gallery, see Grand Rapids MI (M)
Cambridge Art Association, Cambridge MA (A)
Cambridge Arts Council, CAC Gallery, see Cambridge MA (M)
Cambridge Historical Commission, City of Cambridge, Research Library on Architectural and Social History of Cambridge, Mass, see Cambridge MA (L)
Cambridge Museum, Cambridge NE (M)
Cambridge Public Library and Gallery, Idea Exchange, see Cambridge ON (L)
CAM Contemporary Art Museum, Raleigh NC (M)
Camden County College, Visual & Performing Arts Dept, see Blackwood NJ (S)
Cameron Art Museum, Wilmington NC (M)
Cameron University, Art Dept, see Lawton OK (S)
Cameron University Art Gallery, Lawton OK (M)
Campbellsville University, Art & Design Department, see Campbellsville KY (S)
Canada Council for the Arts, Conseil des Arts du Canada, see Ottawa ON (A)
Canada Science & Technology Museums Corporation, Canada Aviation Museum, see Ottawa ON (M)
Canadian Art Foundation, Toronto ON (O)
Canadian Centre for Architecture, Library, see Montreal QC (L)
Canadian Clay and Glass Gallery, Waterloo ON (M)
Canadian Conference of the Arts, Ottawa ON (O)
Canadian Museum for Human Rights, Winnipeg MB (M)
Canadian Museum of History, Gatineau QC (M)
Canadian Museum of Nature, Musee Canadien de la Nature, see Ottawa ON (M)
Canadian Museums Association, Association des Musees Canadiens, see Ottawa ON (O)
Canadian Society for Education Through Art, Victoria BC (O)
Canadian Society of Painters In Watercolour, Toronto ON (O)
Canadian War Museum, Ottawa ON (M)
Canadian Wildlife & Wilderness Art Museum, Ottawa ON (M,L)
Canajoharie Library & Art Gallery, Arkell Museum of Canajoharie, see Canajoharie NY (M,L)
Cando Arts Center, Cando ND (M)
Canton Museum of Art, Canton OH (S)
Canton Museum of Art, Canton OH (M,L)
Cape Ann Museum, Gloucester MA (M,L)
Cape Cod Community College, Art Dept, see West Barnstable MA (S)
Cape Cod Museum of Art Inc, Dennis MA (M)
Capital University, Fine Arts Dept, see Columbus OH (S)
Capital University, Schumacher Gallery, see Columbus OH (M,L)
Capitol Arts Alliance, Houchens Gallery, see Bowling Green KY (M)
Capitol Community Technical College, Humanities Division & Art Dept, see Hartford CT (S)
Capp Street Project, Wattis Institute, see San Francisco CA (M)
Captain Forbes House Museum, Milton MA (M)
Caramoor Center for Music & the Arts, Inc, Rosen House at Caramoor, see Katonah NY (M)
Cardinal Stritch University, Art Dept, see Milwaukee WI (S)
Cardinal Stritch University, Northwestern Mutual Gallery, see Milwaukee WI (M)
Caribbean Cultural Center African Diaspora Institute, Cultural Arts Organization & Resource Center, see New York NY (A)
Carl & Marilynn Thoma Art Foundation, Art House Santa Fe, see Santa Fe NM (M)
Carlen House, see History Museum of Mobile, Mobile AL
Carleton College, Art Gallery, see Northfield MN (M)
Carleton College, Dept of Art & Art History, see Northfield MN (S)
Carleton University, School for Studies in Art & Culture, see Ottawa ON (S)
Carlow College, Art Dept, see Pittsburgh PA (S)
Carl Sandburg College, Galesburg IL (S)
Carlsbad Museum & Art Center, Carlsbad NM (M)

Carmel Mission & Gift Shop, Carmel CA (M)
Carnegie Art Museum, Oxnard CA (M)
Carnegie Arts Center, Alliance NE (M)
Carnegie Arts Center, Leavenworth KS (M)
Carnegie Center for Art & History, New Albany IN (M)
Carnegie Mellon University, College of Fine Arts, see Pittsburgh PA (S)
Carnegie Mellon University, The Frame, see Pittsburgh PA (M,L)
Carnegie Museums of Pittsburgh, Carnegie Museum of Art, see Pittsburgh PA (M,L)
Carolina Art Association, Gibbes Museum of Art, see Charleston SC (M,L)
Carroll College, Art Dept, see Waukesha WI (S)
Carson-Newman University, Art Dept, see Jefferson City TN (S)
Carson County Square House Museum, Panhandle TX (M)
Lucy Carson Memorial Library, see The University of Montana - Western, Dillon MT
Carter-Haas Library, see Rockport College, Rockport ME
Carteret County Historical Society, The History Place, see Morehead City NC (M)
Carthage College, Art Dept, see Kenosha WI (S)
Cartoon Art Museum, San Francisco CA (M)
Carving Studio and Sculpture Center, West Rutland VT (M)
Casa Amesti, Monterey CA (M)
Cascade County Historical Society, The History Museum, see Great Falls MT (M)
Case Western Reserve University, Dept of Art History & Art, see Cleveland OH (S)
Casper College, Dept of Visual Arts, see Casper WY (S)
Caspers, Inc, Art Collection, see Tampa FL
Castleton State College, Art Dept, see Castleton VT (S)
Catfish Capital Visitors Center and Museum, Belzoni MS (M)
Cathedral of Saint John the Divine, New York NY (M, L)
Catholic University of America, Humanities Library, Mullen Library, see Washington DC (L)
Catholic University of America, School of Architecture & Planning, see Washington DC (S)
Cayuga Museum of History & Art, Auburn NY (M)
Cazenovia College, Center for Art & Design Studies, see Cazenovia NY (S)
Cazenovia College, Chapman Art Center Gallery, see Cazenovia NY (M)
Cedar Crest College, Art Dept, see Allentown PA (S)
Cedar Grove, see Philadelphia Museum of Art, Philadelphia PA
Cedarhurst Center for the Arts, Mitchell Museum, see Mount Vernon IL (M,L)
Cedar Hurst Library, see Cedarhurst Center for the Arts, Mount Vernon IL
Cedar Rapids Museum of Art, Cedar Rapids IA (M,L)
Centenary College, Humanities Dept, see Hackettstown NJ (S)
Centenary College of Louisiana, Dept of Art, see Shreveport LA (S)
Centenary College of Louisiana, Meadows Museum of Art, see Shreveport LA (M)
Center for Art & Education, Van Buren AR (M)
Center for Book Arts, New York NY (M)
Center for Contemporary Arts, Abilene TX (M)
The Center for Contemporary Arts of Santa Fe, Santa Fe NM (A)
Center for Creative Photography, see University of Arizona, Tucson AZ
Center for Exploratory & Perceptual Art, CEPA Gallery, see Buffalo NY (M,L)
Center for Fine Art Photography, Fort Collins CO (M)
Center for Photography at Woodstock Inc, Woodstock NY (A)
Center for Puppetry Arts, Atlanta GA (M,L)
Center for Southern Folklore, Memphis TN (A)
Center for the Arts Piper Gallery, Crested Butte CO (M)
Center for the Visual Arts, Gallery, see Wausau WI (M)
The Center for Visual Artists - Greensboro, Greensboro NC (A)
Center of Creative Arts (COCA), Millstone Gallery, see Saint Louis MO (M)
Central College, Art Dept, see Pella IA (S)
Central Community College - Columbus Campus, Business & Arts Cluster, see Columbus NE (S)
Central Connecticut State University, Art Dept Museum, see New Britain CT (M)
Central Connecticut State University, Dept of Art, see New Britain CT (S)
Central Florida Community College, Humanities Dept, see Ocala FL (S)
Central Iowa Art Association, Inc, Marshalltown IA (A, L)
Central Library, Dept of Fine Arts, see San Antonio TX (L)
Central Methodist University, Ashby-Hodge Gallery of American Art, see Fayette MO (M)
Central Michigan University, Dept of Art, see Mount Pleasant MI (S)
Central Michigan University, University Art Gallery, see Mount Pleasant MI (M)
Central Oregon Community College, Dept of Art, see Bend OR (S)
Central Piedmont Community College, Visual & Performing Arts, see Charlotte NC (S)
Central State University, Dept of Art, see Wilberforce OH (S)
Central United Methodist Church, Swords Into Plowshares Peace Center & Gallery, see Detroit MI (M)
Central Washington University, Dept of Art, see Ellensburg WA (S)
Central Washington University, Sarah Spurgeon Gallery, see Ellensburg WA (M)
Central Wyoming College, Art Center, see Riverton WY (S)
Centro Cultural Aztlan, San Antonio TX (A)
Centro Cultural De La Raza, San Diego CA (M)
Centro de Estudios Avanzados, Art Library, see Old San Juan PR (L)
Centrum Arts & Creative Education, Port Townsend WA (A)
Century College, Humanities Dept, see White Bear Lake MN (S)
Cerritos Community College, Fine Arts & Communication Div, see Norwalk CA (S)
C G Jung Center, Evanston IL (L)
Chabot College, Humanities Division, see Hayward CA (S)
Chadron State College, Dept of Art, see Chadron NE (S)
Chadron State College, Memorial Hall Main Gallery & Memorial Hall Gallery 239, see Chadron NE (M)
Chaffey Community College, Art Dept, see Rancho Cucamonga CA (S)
Chalet of the Golden Fleece, New Glarus WI (M)
Billie Trimble Chandler, Texas State Museum of Asian Cultures, see Corpus Christi TX (M)
Channel Islands Maritime Museum, Oxnard CA (M)
Stephen Chan Library of Fine Arts, see New York University, New York NY
Howard I Chapelle Memorial Library, see Chesapeake Bay Maritime Museum, Saint Michaels MD
Chapin Library, see Williams College, Williamstown MA
Chapman University, Art Dept, see Orange CA (S)
Chapman University Guggenheim Gallery, Orange CA (M)
Chappell Memorial Library and Art Gallery, Chappell NE (L)
Charles A Lindbergh Historic Site, Little Falls MN (M)
Charles Allis Art Museum, Milwaukee WI (M)
Charles Bruce Davis Museum of Art, History & Science, Yadkinville NC (M)
Charles City Arts Center, Charles City IA (M)
Charles City Library, Mooney Art Collection, see Charles City IA (M)
Charles River School, Creative Arts Program, see Dover MA (S)
Charleston Museum, Charleston SC (M,L)
Charleston Southern University, Dept of Language & Visual Art, see Charleston SC (S)
Charter Oak Cultural Center, Hartford CT (M)
Chasen Galleries of Fine Art, Richmond VA (M)
Chase Young Gallery, Boston MA (M)
Chastain Arts Center & Gallery, see City of Atlanta, Atlanta GA
Chateau Ramezay Museum, Montreal QC (M,L)
Chatham College, Art Gallery, see Pittsburgh PA (M)
Chatham College, Fine & Performing Arts, see Pittsburgh PA (S)
Chatham Historical Society, The Atwood House Museum, see Chatham MA (M)
Chatillon-DeMenil House Foundation, Chatillon-DeMenil Mansion, see Saint Louis MO (M)
Chattanooga-Hamilton County Bicentennial Library, Fine Arts Dept, see Chattanooga TN (L)
Chattanooga State Technical Community College, Advertising Arts Dept, see Chattanooga TN (S)
Chautauqua Center for the Visual Arts, Chautauqua NY (M)
Chautauqua Institution, School of Art, see Chautauqua NY (S)
Fray Angelico Chavez History Library, see New Mexico Department of Cultural Affairs, Santa Fe NM
Chazen Museum of Art, see University of Wisconsin-Madison, Madison WI
Cheekwood-Tennessee Botanical Garden & Museum of Art, Nashville TN (M,L)
Cheekwood Nashville's Home of Art & Gardens, Education Dept, see Nashville TN (S)
Chelan County Public Utility District, Rocky Reach Dam, see Wenatchee WA (M)
Cheltenham Center for the Arts, Cheltenham PA (S)
Chemeketa Community College, Dept of Humanities & Communications, Art Program, see Salem OR (S)
Cherokee Heritage Center, Park Hill OK (A,L)
Chesapeake Bay Maritime Museum, Saint Michaels MD (M,L)
Chester County Historical Society, West Chester PA (A)
Chesterton Art Center, Chesterton IN (M)
Cheyney University of Pennsylvania, Dept of Art, see Cheyney PA (S)
Chicago Architecture Foundation, Chicago IL (M)
Chicago Artists Coalition, Chicago IL (M)
Chicago Athenaeum, Museum of Architecture & Design, see Galena IL (M)
Chicago Children's Museum, Chicago IL (M)
Chicago History Museum, Chicago IL (A,L)
Chicago Public Library, Harold Washington Library Center, see Chicago IL (L)
Chicago State University, President's Gallery, see Chicago IL (M)
Chief Plenty Coups Museum State Park, Pryor MT (M)
Children's Art Carnival, New York NY (A)
Children's Creativity Museum, San Francisco CA (M)
The Children's Museum of Indianapolis, Indianapolis IN (M)
Children's Museum of Manhattan, New York NY (M)
Chilliwack Community Arts Council, Community Arts Centre, see Chilliwack BC (A)
China Institute in America, China Institute Gallery, see New York NY (M)
Chinati Foundation, Marfa TX (M)
Chinese-American Arts Council, New York NY (A)
Chinese Culture Foundation, Center Gallery, see San Francisco CA (M)
Chipola College, Dept of Fine & Performing Arts, see Marianna FL (S)
Chowan College, Dept. of Communication Arts, Fine and Applied Arts, see Murfreesboro NC (S)
Christina Cultural Arts Center, Inc, Wilmington DE (A)
Christopher Newport University, Dept of Fine Performing Arts, see Newport News VA (S)
Jean Outland Chrysler Library, see Chrysler Museum of Art, Norfolk VA
Chrysler Museum of Art, Norfolk VA (M,L)
Church of Jesus Christ of Latter-Day Saints, Church History Museum, see Salt Lake City UT (M)

Church of Jesus Christ of Latter-Day Saints, Independence Visitors' Center, see Independence MO (M)
CIGNA Corporation, CIGNA Art Collection, see Bloomfield CT
Cincinnati Art Club, Cincinnati OH (A)
Cincinnati Art Museum, Cincinnati Art Museum, see Cincinnati OH (M,L)
Citizens for the Arts in Pennsylvania, Harrisburg PA (A)
Citrus College, Art Dept, see Glendora CA (S)
City Art Works, Pratt Fine Arts Center, see Seattle WA (S)
City College of New York, Art Dept, see New York NY (S)
City College of San Francisco, Art Dept, see San Francisco CA (S)
City College of the City University of New York, Morris Raphael Cohen Library, see New York NY (L)
City Colleges of Chicago, Daley College, see Chicago IL (S)
City Lights Gallery, Bridgeport CT (M)
City of Atlanta, Office of Cultural Affairs, see Atlanta GA (A,M,L)
City of Austin Parks & Recreation Department, Julia C Butridge Gallery, see Austin TX (M)
City of Austin Parks & Recreation, O Henry Museum, see Austin TX (M)
City of Boston Arts & Culture, City Hall Galleries, see Boston MA (A)
City of Brea, Art Gallery, see Brea CA (M)
City of Cedar Falls, Iowa, James & Meryl Hearst Center for the Arts & Sculpture Garden, see Cedar Falls IA (M)
City of Charleston, City Hall Council Chamber Gallery, see Charleston SC (M)
City of Chicago Dept. of Cultural Affairs & Special Events, Clarke House Museum, see Chicago IL (M)
City of El Paso, El Paso TX (M,L)
City of Fayette, Alabama, Fayette Art Museum, see Fayette AL (M)
City of Fremont, Olive Hyde Art Gallery, see Fremont CA (M)
City of Gainesville, Thomas Center Galleries - Cultural Affairs, see Gainesville FL (M)
City of Hampton, Hampton Arts Commission, see Hampton VA (A)
City of High Point, High Point Museum, see High Point NC (M)
City of Irvine, Irvine Fine Arts Center, see Irvine CA (S)
City of Irvine, Irvine Fine Arts Center, see Irvine CA (M)
City of Ketchikan Museum Department, Tongass Historical Museum, see Ketchikan AK (M)
City of Ketchikan Museum Department, Totem Heritage Center, see Ketchikan AK (M)
City of Lethbridge, Sir Alexander Galt Museum, see Lethbridge AB (M)
City of Long Beach, Long Beach Public Library, see Long Beach CA (L)
City of Long Branch, Long Branch Free Public Library, see Long Branch NJ (L)
City of Los Angeles, Cultural Affairs Dept, see Los Angeles CA (M)
City of Lubbock, Buddy Holly Center, see Lubbock TX (M)
City of Mason City, Charles H MacNider Art Museum, see Mason City IA (M)
City of New York Parks & Recreation, Arsenal Gallery, see New York NY (M)
City of Nome Alaska, Carrie M McLain Memorial Museum, see Nome AK (M)
The City of Petersburg Museums, Petersburg VA (M)
City of Pittsfield Office of Cultural Development, Lichtenstein Center for the Arts, see Pittsfield MA (M)
City of Port Angeles, Port Angeles Fine Arts Center & Webster Woods Art Park, see Port Angeles WA (M)
City of Providence Parks Department, Roger Williams Park Museum of Natural History, see Providence RI (M,L)
City of Raleigh Arts Commission, Miriam Preston Block Gallery, see Raleigh NC (A)
City of Saint Augustine, Saint Augustine FL (A)
City of San Antonio, Spanish Governor's Palace, see San Antonio TX (M)
City of San Rafael, Falkirk Cultural Center, see San Rafael CA (M)
City of Scarborough, Cedar Ridge Creative Centre, see Scarborough ON (M)
City of Springdale, Shiloh Museum of Ozark History, see Springdale AR (M)
City of Tampa, Public Art Program, see Tampa FL (A)
City of Toronto Culture, The Market Gallery, see Toronto ON (M)
City of Toronto Museum Services, Historic Fort York, see Toronto ON (A)
City of Ukiah, Grace Hudson Museum & The Sun House, see Ukiah CA (M)
City of Woodstock, Woodstock Art Gallery, see Woodstock ON (M)
City University of New York, PhD Program in Art History, see New York NY (S)
Clackamas Community College, Art Dept, see Oregon City OR (S)
Claflin College, Dept of Art, see Orangeburg SC (S)
Claremont Graduate University, Art Department, see Claremont CA (S)
Clarion University of Pennsylvania, Dept of Art, see Clarion PA (S)
Clarion University, Hazel Sandford Gallery, see Clarion PA (M)
Clark-Atlanta University, School of Arts & Sciences, see Atlanta GA (S)
Clark Art Institute, Williamstown MA (M,L)
Clark College, Archer Gallery/Gaiser Hall, see Vancouver WA (M)
Clark College, Art Dept, see Vancouver WA (S)
Clark County Historical Society, Heritage Center of Clark County, see Springfield OH (M,L)
Clark County Historical Society, Pioneer - Krier Museum, see Ashland KS (M)
Clarke College, Dept of Art, see Dubuque IA (S)
Clarke Galleries, Stowe VT (M)
Clark University, Dept of Visual & Performing Arts, see Worcester MA (S)
Clark University, The Schiltkamp Gallery/Traina Center for the Arts, see Worcester MA (M)
Clay House Museum, Madison AL (M)
The Clay Studio, Philadelphia PA (M)
Clayworks Gallery, Charlotte NC (M)
Clear Creek History Park, Golden CO (M)
Clear Lake Arts Center, Clear Lake IA (M)
Clemson University, College of Architecture, Arts & Humanities, Art Dept, see Clemson SC (S)
Clemson University, Rudolph E Lee Gallery, see Clemson SC (M,L)
Cleveland Art Association, Cleveland OH (A)
Cleveland Art Association, see Cleveland Institute of Art, Cleveland OH
Cleveland Botanical Garden, Eleanor Squire Library, see Cleveland OH (L)
Cleveland Institute of Art, Cleveland OH (S)
Cleveland Institute of Art, Reinberger Galleries, see Cleveland OH (M,L,A)
The Cleveland Museum of Art, Cleveland OH (M,L,A)
Cleveland Public Library, Fine Arts & Special Collections Dept, see Cleveland OH (L)
Cleveland State Community College, Dept of Art, see Cleveland TN (S)
Cleveland State University, Art Dept, see Cleveland OH (S)
Clinch Valley College of the University of Virginia, Visual & Performing Arts Dept, see Wise VA (S)
Clinton Art Association, River Arts Center, see Clinton IA (M)
Clinton Community College, Art Dept, see Plattsburgh NY (S)
Clinton County Historical Association, Clinton County Historical Museum, see Plattsburgh NY (M)
Cliveden, Philadelphia PA (M)
Clymer Museum of Art, The Clymer Museum & Gallery, see Ellensburg WA (M)
CMCA-Center for Maine Contemporary Art, Art Gallery, see Rockport ME (A)
C M Russell Museum, Great Falls MT (M,L)
Coachella Valley History Museum, Indio CA (M)
Coahoma Community College, Art Education & Fine Arts Dept, see Clarksdale MS (S)
Coastal Arts League Museum, Half Moon Bay CA (M)
CoCA Center on Contemporary Art, Seattle WA (A)
Cochise College, Art Dept, see Douglas AZ (S)
Cochise College, Charles Di Peso Library, see Douglas AZ (L)
Cody Country Art League, Cody WY (A)
Coe College, Dept of Art, see Cedar Rapids IA (S)
Coe College, Eaton-Buchan Gallery & Marvin Cone Gallery, see Cedar Rapids IA (M)
Coffeyville Community College, Art Dept, see Coffeyville KS (S)
Cohasset Historical Society, Pratt Building (Society Headquarters), see Cohasset MA (M)
Cohasset Maritime Museum, see Cohasset Historical Society, Cohasset MA
Coker College, Art Dept, see Hartsville SC (S)
Coker College, Cecelia Coker Bell Gallery, see Hartsville SC (M)
Francis Colburn Gallery, see University of Vermont, Burlington VT
Colby-Sawyer College, Dept of Fine & Performing Arts, see New London NH (S)
Colby College, Art Dept, see Waterville ME (S)
Colby College, Museum of Art, see Waterville ME (M, L)
Colby Community College, Art Dept, see Colby KS (S)
Coleman Library, see Tougaloo College, Tougaloo MS
Colgate University, Dept of Art & Art History, see Hamilton NY (S)
Colgate University, Picker Art Gallery, see Hamilton NY (M)
College Art Association, New York NY (O)
College for Creative Studies, Detroit MI (S)
College for Creative Studies, College of Art & Design Library, see Detroit MI (L)
College of Central Florida, Appleton Museum of Art, see Ocala FL (M)
College of Charleston School of Arts, Halsey Institute of Contemporary Art, see Charleston SC (M)
College of Charleston, School of the Arts, see Charleston SC (S)
College of Eastern Utah, Gallery East, see Price UT (M)
The College of Idaho, Rosenthal Art Gallery, see Caldwell ID (M)
College of Lake County, Art Dept, see Grayslake IL (S)
College of Marin, Art Gallery, see Kentfield CA (M)
College of Marin, Dept of Art, see Kentfield CA (S)
College of Mount Saint Joseph, Studio San Giuseppe, see Cincinnati OH (M,L)
College of Mount Saint Vincent, Fine Arts Dept, see Riverdale NY (S)
College of New Jersey, Art Gallery, see Ewing NJ (M)
The College of New Jersey, School of Arts & Sciences, see Ewing NJ (S)
College of New Rochelle, Castle Gallery, see New Rochelle NY (M)
The College of New Rochelle, School of Arts & Sciences Art Dept, see New Rochelle NY (S)
College of Notre Dame of Maryland, Art Dept, see Baltimore MD (S)
College of Saint Benedict, Art Dept, see Saint Joseph MN (S)
College of Saint Benedict, Gorecki Gallery & Gallery Lounge, see Saint Joseph MN (M)
College of Saint Elizabeth, Art Dept, see Morristown NJ (S)
College of Saint Elizabeth, Mahoney Library, see Morristown NJ (L)
College of Saint Mary, Art Dept, see Omaha NE (S)
College of Saint Rose, Art Gallery, see Albany NY (M)
The College of Saint Rose, The Center For Art and Design, see Albany NY (S)

College of San Mateo, Creative Arts Dept, see San Mateo CA (S)
College of Santa Fe, Art Dept, see Santa Fe NM (S)
College of Southern Idaho, Art Dept, see Twin Falls ID (S)
College of Staten Island, Performing & Creative Arts Dept, see Staten Island NY (S)
College of the Canyons, Art Dept, see Santa Clarita CA (S)
College of the Desert, Art Dept, see Palm Desert CA (S)
College of the Holy Cross, Dept of Visual Arts, see Worcester MA (S)
College of the Holy Cross, Dinand Library, see Worcester MA (L)
College of the Ozarks, Dept of Art, see Point Lookout MO (S)
College of the Redwoods, Arts & Languages Dept Division, see Eureka CA (S)
College of the Sequoias, Art Dept, see Visalia CA (S)
College of the Siskiyous, Theatre Dept, see Weed CA (S)
College of William & Mary, Dept of Fine Arts, see Williamsburg VA (S)
College of William & Mary, Muscarelle Museum of Art, see Williamsburg VA (M)
The College of Wooster, Dept of Art and Art History, see Wooster OH (S)
The College of Wooster, The College of Wooster Art Museum, see Wooster OH (M)
Collins C. Diboll Art Gallery, New Orleans LA (M)
Colonial Williamsburg Foundation, Williamsburg VA (M,A,L)
Colorado College, Dept of Art, see Colorado Springs CO (S)
Colorado Mesa University, Art Dept, see Grand Junction CO (S)
Colorado Mountain Art Gallery, Georgetown CO (M)
Colorado Northwestern Community College, Art Dept, see Rangely CO (S)
Colorado Photographic Arts Center, Denver CO (M)
Colorado Springs Fine Arts Center, Taylor Museum, see Colorado Springs CO (M)
Colorado State University, Curfman Gallery, see Fort Collins CO (M)
Colorado State University, Dept of Art, see Fort Collins CO (S)
Colorado Watercolor Society, Denver CO (A)
Color Association of the United States, New York NY (O)
Colquitt County Arts Center, Moultrie GA (M)
Columbia Basin College, Esvelt Gallery, see Pasco WA (S)
Columbia College, Art Dept, see Chicago IL (S)
Columbia College, Art Dept, see Columbia MO (S)
Columbia College, Dept of Art, see Columbia SC (S)
Columbia College, Fine Arts, see Sonora CA (S)
Columbia County Historical Society, Columbia County Museum and Library, see Kinderhook NY (M)
Columbia Museum of Art, Columbia SC (M,L)
The Columbian Theatre Foundation, Inc, Columbian Theatre Museum & Art Center, see Wamego KS (M)
Columbia River Maritime Museum, Astoria OR (M,L)
Columbia State Community College, Dept of Art, see Columbia TN (S)
Columbia University, Avery Architectural & Fine Arts Library, see New York NY (L,M)
Columbia University, School of the Arts, see New York NY (S)
Columbus Chapel & Boal Mansion Museum, Boalsburg PA (M)
Columbus College of Art & Design, Fine Arts Dept, see Columbus OH (S)
Columbus College of Art & Design, Packard Library, see Columbus OH (L)
Columbus Cultural Arts Center, Columbus OH (M)
Columbus Historic Foundation, Blewett-Harrison-Lee Museum, see Columbus MS (M)
Columbus Metropolitan Library, Arts & Media Division Carnegie Gallery, see Columbus OH (L)
The Columbus Museum, Columbus GA (M)
Columbus Museum of Art, Columbus OH (M)
Columbus State University, Dept of Art, Fine Arts Hall, see Columbus GA (S)
Columbus State University, Norman Shannon and Emmy Lou P Illges Gallery, see Columbus GA (M)
Commerce Bancshares, Inc, Fine Art Collection, see Kansas City MO
Communications and History Museum of Sutton, Sutton QC (M)
Community Arts Council of Vancouver, Vancouver BC (A)
The Community Arts Project Gallery, Cornelius NC (M)
Community College of Allegheny County, Boyce Campus, Art Dept, see Monroeville PA (S)
Community College of Allegheny County, Fine Arts Dept, see West Mifflin PA (S)
Community College of Baltimore County, School of Technology, Art & Design, see Catonsville MD (S)
Community College of Rhode Island, Dept of Art, see Warwick RI (S)
Community College of Rhode Island, Knight Campus Art Gallery, see Warwick RI (M)
Community Council for the Arts, Kinston NC (A)
The Community Education Center, Philadelphia PA (A)
Comox Valley Art Gallery, Courtenay BC (M)
Compton Community College, Art Dept, see Compton CA (S)
Concord Art Association, Concord MA (A)
Concord College, Fine Art Division, see Athens WV (S)
Concordia College, Art Dept, see Moorhead MN (S)
Concordia College, Art Dept, see Bronxville NY (S)
Concordia Historical Institute, Saint Louis MO (M)
Concordia University, Art and Design Department, see Saint Paul MN (S)
Concordia University, Art Dept, see Seward NE (S)
Concordia University, Dept of Fine Arts, see Austin TX (S)
Concordia University, Division of Performing & Visual Arts, see Mequon WI (S)
Concordia University, Leonard & Bina Ellen Art Gallery, see Montreal QC (M)
Concordia University, Faculty of Fine Arts, see Montreal QC (S)
Concordia University, Marxhausen Art Gallery, see Seward NE (M)
Concordia University Wisconsin, Fine Art Gallery, see Mequon WI (M)
Concord Museum, Concord MA (M)
Conejo Valley Art Museum, Thousand Oaks CA (M)
Confederate Memorial Hall, Confederate Museum, see New Orleans LA (A)
Confederation Centre Art Gallery and Museum, Charlottetown PE (M,L)
Congregation Beth Israel's Plotkin Judaica Museum, Scottsdale AZ (M)
Congregation Emanu-El, Bernard Judaica Museum, see New York NY (M)
Connecticut College, Dept of Art, see New London CT (S)
Connecticut Historical Society, Hartford CT (A,L)
Connecticut State Library, Museum of Connecticut History, see Hartford CT (L)
Conrad-Caldwell House Museum, Louisville KY (M)
Conseil des Arts du Quebec (CATQ), Diagonale, Centre des arts et des fibres du Quebec, see Montreal QC (L)
Conservation Center for Art & Historic Artifacts, Philadelphia PA (A)
Contemporary Art Center, Peoria IL (M)
Contemporary Art Gallery, Vancouver BC (M)
Contemporary Art Gallery Society of British Columbia, Vancouver BC (M)
Contemporary Art Museum St Louis, Saint Louis MO (A)
Contemporary Arts Center, New Orleans LA (A)
Contemporary Arts Center, Cincinnati OH (M,L)
Contemporary Arts Museum Houston, Houston TX (M)
The Contemporary Austin, Austin TX (M)
Contemporary Calgary, Calgary AB (M)
Contra Costa Community College, Dept of Art, see San Pablo CA (S)
Converse College, Milliken Art Gallery, see Spartanburg SC (M)
Converse College, School of the Arts, Dept of Art & Design, see Spartanburg SC (S)
Cooper Hewitt, Smithsonian Design Museum, Smithsonian Institution, see New York NY (M,L)
Cooperstown Art Association, Cooperstown NY (A)
Cooper Union, School of Art, see New York NY (S)
Coos Art Museum, Coos Bay OR (S)
Coos Art Museum, Coos Bay OR (M)
Coos County Historical Society Museum, Coos Bay OR (M)
Helen E Copeland Gallery, see Montana State University, Bozeman MT
Copper Village Museum & Arts Center, Anaconda MT (A,L)
Coppini Academy of Fine Arts, Elizabeth di Barbieri, see San Antonio TX (A,L)
Coppin State College, Dept Fine & Communication Arts, see Baltimore MD (S)
Coquille Valley Art Association, Coquille OR (A,L)
Coral Springs Museum of Art, Coral Springs FL (M)
Corbin Art Center, Spokane WA (A)
Corbit-Calloway Memorial Library, Odessa DE (L)
Corcoran Gallery of Art, Washington DC (M,L)
Corcoran School of Art, Washington DC (S)
Core, New Art Space, see Denver CO (M)
Cornell College, Peter Paul Luce Gallery, see Mount Vernon IA (M)
Cornell Museum of Art and American Culture, Delray Beach FL (M)
Cornell University, College of Architecture, Art, and Planning, see Ithaca NY (S)
Cornell University, Herbert F Johnson Museum of Art, see Ithaca NY (M,L)
Corning Center for the Fine Arts, Corning IA (M)
Corning Community College, Division of Humanities, see Corning NY (S)
Corning Museum of Glass, Museum, see Corning NY (M,L)
Cornish College of the Arts, Art Dept, see Seattle WA (S)
Cornish College of the Arts, Fisher Gallery, see Seattle WA (M,L)
Corporate Council for the Arts/Arts Fund, Seattle WA (A)
Cortland County Historical Society, Suggett House Museum, see Cortland NY (M,L)
Cortland Free Library, Cortland NY (L)
Cottey College, Art Dept, see Nevada MO (S)
Cotting-Smith-Assembly House, see Peabody Essex Museum, Salem MA
Cottonlandia Museum, Greenwood MS (M)
Cotuit Center for the Arts, Cotuit MA (M)
County College of Morris, Art Dept, see Randolph NJ (S)
County of Henrico, Meadow Farm Museum, see Glen Allen VA (M,L)
County of Los Angeles, Century Gallery, see Sylmar CA (M)
Coutts Museum of Art, Inc, El Dorado KS (M)
Craft Alliance Center of Art & Design, Saint Louis MO (M)
Craft and Folk Art Museum (CAFAM), Los Angeles CA (M)
Craft Council of Newfoundland & Labrador, Saint John's NF (A)
Craftsmen's Guild of Mississippi, Inc, Mississippi Craft Center, see Ridgeland MS (M)
Craigdarroch Castle Historical Museum Society, Victoria BC (M)
Cranbrook Academy of Art, Bloomfield Hills MI (S)
Cranbrook Art Museum, Bloomfield Hills MI (M,L)
Crane Collection, Gallery of American Painting and Sculpture, Magnolia MA (M)
Cranford Historical Society, Cranford NJ (M)
Crary Art Gallery, Warren PA (M)

Crawford County Historical Society, Baldwin-Reynolds House Museum, see Meadville PA (M)
Crazy Horse Memorial, Indian Museum of North America, Native American Educational & Cultural Center & Crazy Horse Memorial Library (Reference), see Crazy Horse SD (M)
Creative Art Center-North Oakland County, Pontiac Creative Arts Center, see Pontiac MI (S)
Creative Arts Center, Pontiac MI (A)
Creative Arts Guild, Dalton GA (A)
Creative Growth Art Center, Oakland CA (M)
Creative Time, New York NY (A)
Creek Council House Museum, Okmulgee OK (M,L)
Creighton University, Fine & Performing Arts Dept, see Omaha NE (S)
Creighton University, Lied Art Gallery, see Omaha NE (M)
Cripple Creek District Museum, Cripple Creek CO (M)
Crocker Art Museum, Sacramento CA (M,L)
Crook County Museum & Art Gallery, Sundance WY (M)
Crooked Tree Arts Center - Traverse City, Gallery, see Traverse City MI (M)
Crooked Tree Arts Council, Virginia M McCune Community Arts Center, see Petoskey MI (M)
Crossroads Art Center Gallery, Richmond VA (M)
Crowder College, Longwell Museum/Art Department, see Neosho MO (S)
Crowley Art Association, The Gallery, see Crowley LA (A)
Crow Wing County Historical Society, Brainerd MN (M)
J T & E J Crumbaugh, Le Roy IL (L)
Crumpacker Family Library, see Portland Art Museum, Portland OR
Crystal Bridges Museum of American Art, Bentonville AR (M)
John M Cuelenaere, Grace Campbell Gallery, see Prince Albert SK (M)
Cuesta College, Art Dept, see San Luis Obispo CA (S)
Cuesta College, Harold J Miossi Art Gallery, see San Luis Obispo CA (L)
Culberson County Historical Museum, Clark Hotel Historical Museum, see Van Horn TX (M)
Cultural Affairs Department City of Los Angeles, Barnsdall Art Center & Junior Arts Center, see Los Angeles CA (A,L)
Cultural Affairs Department, Los Angeles Municipal Art Gallery, see Los Angeles CA (M)
The Cultural Arts Center at Glen Allen, Glen Allen VA (M)
The Cultural Center of Fine Arts, Art Gallery, see Parkersburg WV (A)
Cultural Council of Palm Beach County, Lake Worth FL (A)
Culture Capital, Washington DC (A)
CultureWorks, Richmond VA (A)
Culver-Stockton College, Art Dept, see Canton MO (S)
Cumberland Art Society Inc, Cookeville Art Gallery, see Cookeville TN (A)
Cumberland College, Dept of Art, see Williamsburg KY (S)
Cumberland County College, Arts & Humanities, see Vineland NJ (S)
Cumberland Theatre, Lobby for the Arts Gallery, see Cumberland MD (M)
Cummer Museum of Art & Gardens, Museum & Library, see Jacksonville FL (M)
Cuneo Mansion & Gardens, Vernon Hills IL (M)
Curious Matter, Jersey City NJ (M)
The Currier Museum of Art, Manchester NH (M,L)
Cuyahoga Community College, Dept of Art, see Cleveland OH (S)
Cuyahoga County Public Library, Parma OH (L)
Cuyahoga Valley Art Center, Cuyahoga Falls OH (S)
C W Post Campus of Long Island University, Hillwood Art Museum, see Brookville NY (M)
C W Post Campus of Long Island University, School of Visual & Performing Arts, see Brookville NY (S)
Cypress College, Cypress CA (S)
Cypress College, Fine Arts Gallery, see Cypress CA (M)
Dacotah Prairie Museum, Lamont Art Gallery, see Aberdeen SD (M,L)
Daemen College, Art Dept, see Amherst NY (S)
Daemen College, Fanette Goldman & Carolyn Greenfield Gallery, see Amherst NY (M,L)
Dahesh Museum of Art, Greenwich CT (M)
Dairy Arts Center, Boulder CO (M)
The Dairy Barn Arts Center, Athens OH (A)
Dakota State University, College of Liberal Arts, see Madison SD (S)
Dakota Wesleyan University, Art Dept, see Mitchell SD (S)
Dalhousie University, Dalhousie Art Gallery, see Halifax NS (M)
Dalhousie University, School of Architecture, see Halifax NS (S)
Salvador Dali, Saint Petersburg FL (M,L)
Dallas Baptist University, Dept of Art, see Dallas TX (S)
Dallas Contemporary, Dallas Visual Art Center, see Dallas TX (M)
Dallas Historical Society, Hall of State, see Dallas TX (A,L)
Dallas Museum of Art, Dallas TX (M,L)
The Dalles Art Association, The Dalles Art Center, see The Dalles OR (A)
Dalnavert Museum, Winnipeg MB (M)
Danbury Scott-Fanton Museum & Historical Society, Inc, Danbury CT (M,L)
Danforth Museum of Art, Danforth Museum of Art, see Framingham MA (M,L)
Danforth Museum of Art School, Framingham MA (S)
Danville Museum of Fine Arts & History, Danville VA (M)
DAR Museum, National Society Daughters of the American Revolution, see Washington DC (M,L)
Dartmouth College, Dept of Art History, see Hanover NH (S)
Dartmouth College, Hood Museum of Art, see Hanover NH (M,L)
Dartmouth Heritage Museum, Dartmouth NS (M)
Daum Museum of Contemporary Art, Sedalia MO (M)
Dauphin & District Allied Arts Council, Watson Art Centre, see Dauphin MB (M)
Davidson College, Art Dept, see Davidson NC (S)
Davidson College, William H Van Every Jr & Edward M Smith Galleries, see Davidson NC (M,L)
Davidson County Community College, Humanities Div, see Lexington NC (S)
David Zwirner Gallery, New York NY (M)
Davis & Elkins College, Dept of Art, see Elkins WV (S)
Davistown Museum, Liberty Location, see Liberty ME (M)
Dawson City Museum, Dawson City YT (M,L)
Dawson County Historical Society, Museum, see Lexington NE (M)
Dawson Springs Museum and Art Center, Dawson Springs KY (M)
Daytona Beach Community College, Dept of Fine Arts & Visual Arts, see Daytona Beach FL (S)
Dayton Art Institute, Dayton OH (M,L)
Daytona State College, Southeast Museum of Photography, see Daytona Beach FL (M)
Dayton Visual Arts Center, Dayton OH (M)
The D B Weldon Library, see University of Western Ontario, London ON
De Anza College, Creative Arts Division, see Cupertino CA (S)
De Anza College, Euphrat Museum of Art, see Cupertino CA (M)
Dearborn Community Arts Council, Padzieski Art Gallery, see Dearborn MI (M)
DeBruyne Fine Art, Naples FL (M)
Decatur House, see National Trust for Historic Preservation, Washington DC
Decker Library, see Maryland Institute, Baltimore MD
Decorative Arts Collection Museum, Atlanta GA (A)
DeCordova Museum School, Lincoln MA (S)
deCordova Sculpture Park & Museum, Lincoln MA (M)
Deere & Company, Moline IL
Deines Cultural Center, Russell KS (M)
Delaplaine Visual Arts Education Center, Frederick MD (M)
Delaware Art Museum, Wilmington DE (M,L)
Delaware Center for the Contemporary Arts, Wilmington DE (M)
Delaware County Community College, Communications, Art & Humanities, see Media PA (S)
Delaware Division of Historical & Cultural Affairs, Dover DE (M)
Delaware Historical Society, Delaware History Museum and Center for African American Heritage, see Wilmington DE (M,L)
Delaware State College, Dept of Art & Art Education, see Dover DE (S)
DeLeon White Gallery, Toronto ON (M)
Delgado College, Dept of Fine Arts, see New Orleans LA (S)
Del Mar College, Art Dept, see Corpus Christi TX (S)
Del Mar College, Joseph A Cain Memorial Art Gallery, see Corpus Christi TX (M)
Delta Blues Museum, Clarksdale MS (M)
Delta College, Art Dept, see University Center MI (S)
Delta State University, Dept of Art, see Cleveland MS (S)
Delta State University, Fielding L Wright Art Center, see Cleveland MS (M,L)
Deming-Luna Mimbres Museum, Deming NM (M)
Denison University, Art Gallery, see Granville OH (M, L)
Denison University, Studio Art Program, see Granville OH (S)
Denver Art Museum, Denver CO (M,L)
Museum of Contemporary Art Denver, Denver CO (M)
Denver Public Library, Reference, see Denver CO (L)
Department of Canadian Heritage, Canadian Conservation Institute, see Ottawa ON (A)
Department of Commerce, Wyoming Arts Council Gallery, see Cheyenne WY (M)
Department of Economic & Community Development, State of Connecticut DECD Eric Sloane Museum, see Kent CT (M)
DePaul University, Dept of Art, see Chicago IL (S)
DePauw University, Art Dept, see Greencastle IN (S)
Design Commission of the City of New York, New York NY (A)
Des Moines Area Community College, Art Dept, see Boone IA (S)
Des Moines Art Center Library, see Edmundson Art Foundation, Inc, Des Moines IA
Alice Curtis Desmond, Hudson River Reference Collection, see Garrison NY (L)
Detroit Artists Market, Detroit MI (M)
Detroit Focus, Royal Oak MI (M)
Detroit Institute of Arts, Detroit MI (M,L)
Detroit Public Library, Art & Literature Dept, see Detroit MI (L)
Detroit Repertory Theatre Gallery, Detroit MI (M)
Detroit Zoological Institute, Wildlife Interpretive Gallery, see Royal Oak MI (M)
DeWitt Wallace Library, see Macalester College, Saint Paul MN
Dhoomimal Gallery, New Delhi (M)
Dia Art Foundation, Beacon NY (A)
Dickinson College, Dept of Art & Art History, see Carlisle PA (S)
Dickinson College, The Trout Gallery, see Carlisle PA (M)
Dickinson State University, Art Gallery, see Dickinson ND (M,L)
Dickinson State University, Dept of Art, see Dickinson ND (S)
Diefenbaker Canada Centre, see University of Saskatchewan, Saskatoon SK
Dieu Donne Papermill, Inc, Gallery, see Brooklyn NY (M)
Dillman's Creative Arts Foundation, Lac Du Flambeau WI (A,L)
The Dinosaur Museum, Blanding UT (M)
Discovery Museum, Bridgeport CT (M)

Discovery Place Inc, Nature Museum, see Charlotte NC (M)
District of Columbia Arts Center (DCAC), Washington DC (M)
Diverse Works, Houston TX (M)
Divine Word College, Father Weyland SVD Gallery, see Epworth IA (M)
Dixie College, Art Dept, see Saint George UT (S)
Dixie State University, Sears Art Museum Gallery, see Saint George UT (M)
The Dixon Gallery & Gardens, Memphis TN (M,L)
Doane College, Dept of Art, see Crete NE (S)
Dominican College of Blauvelt, Art Dept, see Orangeburg NY (S)
Dominican College of San Rafael, Art Dept, see San Rafael CA (S)
Dorland Mountain Arts Colony, Art Residency Program, see Temecula CA (S)
Dorothy Babcock Memorial Library, see Embroiderers Guild of America, Louisville KY
Dorsky Gallery, Dorsky Gallery Curatorial Programs, see Long Island City NY (M)
Douglas Art Association, The Gallery and Gift Shop, see Douglas AZ (M)
Mabel Smith Douglass Library, see Rutgers, The State University of New Jersey, New Brunswick NJ
Grace A Dow, Fine Arts Dept, see Midland MI (L)
Dowling College, Dept of Visual Arts, see Oakdale NY (S)
Dr. Martin Luther King Jr. Library, see San Jose State University, San Jose CA
Drake University, Dept Art & Design, see Des Moines IA (S)
The Drawing Center, New York NY (A)
Drew County Historical Society, Museum, see Monticello AR (M)
Drew University, Art Dept, see Madison NJ (S)
Drew University, Elizabeth P Korn Gallery, see Madison NJ (M,L)
Drexel University, Drexel Collection, see Philadelphia PA (M)
Felix J Dreyfous Library, see New Orleans Museum of Art, New Orleans LA
Dr Jose C Barbosa Museum, see Institute of Puerto Rican Culture, Bayamon PR
Drury College, Art & Art History Dept, see Springfield MO (S)
Dublin Arts Council, Dublin OH (M)
Dubuque Museum of Art, Dubuque IA (M)
Duke University, Dept of Art, Art History & Visual Studies, see Durham NC (S)
Duke University Library, Hartman Center for Sales, Advertising & Marketing History, see Durham NC (L)
Duke University, Nasher Museum of Art at Duke University, see Durham NC (M,L)
Duke University Union, Louise Jones Brown Gallery, see Durham NC (M)
Dumbarton Oaks, Dumbarton Oaks Museum, see Washington DC (M,L)
Dunconor Workshops, Salida CO (S)
Dundas Valley School of Art, Dundas ON (S)
Dundurn National Historic Site, Dundurn Castle, see Hamilton ON (M)
Dunedin Fine Art Center, Dunedin FL (S)
Dunlop Art Gallery, see Regina Public Library, Regina SK
DuPage Art League School & Gallery, Wheaton IL (A)
Durango Arts Center, Barbara Conrad Art Gallery, see Durango CO (M)
Durham Art Gallery, Durham ON (M)
Durham Art Guild, Durham NC (M)
DuSable Museum of African American History, Chicago IL (M)
Dutchess Community College, Dept of Visual Arts, see Poughkeepsie NY (S)
Dutchess County Arts Council, Poughkeepsie NY (M)
Earlham College, Art Dept, see Richmond IN (S)
Earlham College, Leeds Gallery, see Richmond IN (M)
Earthfire, Art from Detritus: Recycling with Imagination, see New York NY (M)
East Bay Asian Local Development Corp (EBALDC), Asian Resource Gallery, see Oakland CA (M)
East Carolina University, Wellington B Gray Gallery, see Greenville NC (M,L)
East Carolina University, School of Art & Design, see Greenville NC (S)
East Central College, Art Dept, see Union MO (S)
East Central Community College, Art Dept, see Decatur MS (S)
East Central University, School of Fine Arts, see Ada OK (S)
East End Arts & Humanities Council, Riverhead NY (A)
Eastern Arizona College, Art Dept, see Thatcher AZ (S)
Eastern Connecticut State University, Fine Arts Dept, see Willimantic CT (S)
Eastern Illinois University, Art Dept, see Charleston IL (S)
Eastern Illinois University, Tarble Arts Center, see Charleston IL (M)
Eastern Iowa Community College, Clinton Community College, see Clinton IA (S)
Eastern Kentucky University, Art Dept, see Richmond KY (S)
Eastern Mennonite University, Visual and Communication Arts, see Harrisonburg VA (S)
Eastern Michigan University, Dept of Art, see Ypsilanti MI (S)
Eastern Michigan University, Ford Gallery, see Ypsilanti MI (M,L)
Eastern New Mexico University, Dept of Art, see Portales NM (S)
Eastern New Mexico University, Runnels Gallery, Golden Library, see Portales NM (M,L)
Eastern Oregon University, School of Arts & Science, see La Grande OR (S)
Eastern Shore Art Association, Inc, Eastern Shore Art Center, see Fairhope AL (A)
Eastern Washington State Historical Society, Northwest Museum of Arts & Culture, see Spokane WA (M)
Eastern Washington University, Dept of Art, see Cheney WA (S)
Eastern Wyoming College, Art Dept, see Torrington WY (S)
Eastfield College, Humanities Division, Art Dept, see Mesquite TX (S)
East Hampton Library, Long Island Collection, see East Hampton NY (L)
East Hawaii Cultural Center, Hawaii Museum of Contemporary Art, see Hilo HI (M)
East Los Angeles College, Art Dept, see Monterey Park CA (S)
East Los Angeles College, Vincent Price Art Museum, see Monterey Park CA (M)
East Stroudsburg University, Fine Arts Center, see East Stroudsburg PA (S)
East Tennessee State University, College of Arts and Sciences, Dept of Art & Design, see Johnson City TN (S)
East Tennessee State University, The Reece Museum, see Johnson City TN (M)
Eccles Community Art Center, Ogden UT (A)
Eckerd College, Art Dept, see Saint Petersburg FL (S)
Edgecombe County Cultural Arts Council, Inc, Blount-Bridgers House, Hobson Pittman Memorial Gallery, see Tarboro NC (M)
Edgewood College, Art Dept, see Madison WI (S)
Edgewood College, DeRicci Gallery, see Madison WI (M)
Edina Art Center, Margaret Foss Gallery, see Edina MN (M)
Edinboro University of Pennsylvania, Art Dept, see Edinboro PA (S)
Edison Community College, Gallery of Fine Arts, see Fort Myers FL (S)
Edison State College, Bob Rauschenberg Gallery at Edison State College, see Fort Myers FL (M)
Edith R Wyle Research Library of The Craft & Folk Art Museum, see LA County Museum of Art, Los Angeles CA
Edmundson Art Foundation, Inc, Des Moines Art Center, see Des Moines IA (M,L)
Edna Hibel Art Foundation, Hibel Museum of Art, see Jupiter FL (M,L)
Edsel & Eleanor Ford House, Grosse Pointe Shores MI (M)
Education Alliance, Art School & Gallery, see New York NY (S)
Egan Maritime Institute, Shipwreck & Lifesaving Museum, see Nantucket MA (M)
1890 House-Museum & Center for the Arts, Cortland NY (M,L)
18th Street Arts Complex, Santa Monica CA (A)
800 Gallery & Rotary Ice House Gallery, West Long Branch NJ (M)
Eiteljorg Museum of American Indians & Western Art, Indianapolis IN (M)
Ekstrom Library Photographic Archives, see University of Louisville, Louisville KY
El Camino College Art Gallery, Torrance CA (M)
El Camino College, Division of Fine Arts, see Torrance CA (S)
Elder Gallery, Charlotte NC (M)
Electronic Arts Intermix (EAI), New York NY (A)
Elgin Community College, Fine Arts Dept, see Elgin IL (S)
Elizabeth City State University, School of Arts & Humanities, Dept of Art, see Elizabeth City NC (S)
The Ella Carothers Dunnegan Gallery of Art, Bolivar MO (M)
Ella Sharp Museum, Jackson MI (M)
Ellen Noel Art Museum of the Permian Basin, Odessa TX (M)
Ellis County Museum Inc, Waxahachie TX (M)
Ellsworth Community College, Dept of Fine Arts, see Iowa Falls IA (S)
Elmhurst Art Museum, Elmhurst IL (M)
Elmhurst College, Art Dept, see Elmhurst IL (S)
Elmira College, Art Dept, see Elmira NY (S)
Elmira College, George Waters Gallery, see Elmira NY (M)
El Museo del Barrio, New York NY (M)
El Museo Latino, Omaha NE (M)
El Paso Museum of Archaeology, see City of El Paso, El Paso TX
El Pueblo de Los Angeles Historical Monument, Los Angeles CA (A)
Elverhoj Museum of History and Art, Solvang CA (M)
Embroiderers Guild of America, Margaret Parshall Gallery, see Louisville KY (A,L)
eMediaLoft.org, New York NY (M)
Emerald Empire Art Association, Emerald Art Center, see Springfield OR (A)
Emily Carr Institute of Art & Design, The Charles H Scott Gallery, see Vancouver BC (M,L)
Emily Carr University of Art + Design, Vancouver BC (S)
Emmanuel College, Art Dept, see Boston MA (S)
Emmanuel Gallery, Denver CO (M)
Emma Willard School, Dept of Visual & Performing Arts, see Troy NY (S)
Emory University, Art History Dept, see Atlanta GA (S)
Emory University, Michael C Carlos Museum, see Atlanta GA (M)
Emporia State University, Dept of Art, see Emporia KS (S)
Emporia State University, Norman R Eppink Art Gallery, see Emporia KS (M)
Emprise Bank Research Library, see Wichita Art Museum, Wichita KS
Endicott College, School of Visual & Performing Arts, see Beverly MA (S)
En Foco, Inc, Bronx NY (M)
Englewood Library, Fine Arts Dept, see Englewood NJ (L)
Amos Eno Gallery, Brooklyn NY (M)
Environic Foundation International Library, Glen Allen VA (L)
Environment Canada - Parks Canada, Laurier House, National Historic Site, see Ottawa ON (M)
Max Epstein Archive, see University of Chicago, Chicago IL

Erie Art Museum, Erie PA (M)
Erie County Historical Society, Erie PA (M)
Escuela de Artes Plasticas, Biblioteca Francisco Oller, see San Juan PR (L)
Escuela de Artes Plasticas de Puerto Rico, San Juan PR (S)
Eskimo Museum, Churchill MB (M,L)
Esplanade Arts & Heritage Centre, Medicine Hat AB (M)
Essex Art Association, Inc, Essex CT (A)
Essex Art Center, Lawrence MA (M)
Essex Historical Society and Shipbuilding Museum, Essex MA (M)
Estevan National Exhibition Centre Inc, Estevan Art Gallery & Museum, see Estevan SK (M)
The Ethel Wright Mohamed Stitchery Museum, Belzoni MS (M)
Eubie Blake National Jazz Institute and Cultural Center, Baltimore MD (M)
Eula Mae Edwards Museum & Gallery, Clovis NM (M)
Eureka Fine Art Gallery, Eureka Springs AR (M)
Evangel University, Humanities-Art Dept, see Springfield MO (S)
Evanston Art Center, Evanston IL (A)
Evanston Historical Society, Charles Gates Dawes House, see Evanston IL (M)
Evansville Museum of Arts, History & Science, Evansville IN (M)
Everett Community College, Art Dept, see Everett WA (S)
Evergreen Museum & Library, see Johns Hopkins University, Baltimore MD
Evergreen State College, Evergreen Gallery, see Olympia WA (M)
Everhart Museum, Scranton PA (M)
Everson Museum of Art, Syracuse NY (M)
Ewing Gallery of Art and Architecture, see University of Tennessee, Knoxville TN
The Exhibition Alliance, Hamilton NY (A)
Exploratorium, San Francisco CA (A)
Eye Level Gallery, Halifax NS (M)
The Fabric Workshop & Museum, Philadelphia PA (M)
Fairbanks Arts Association, Bear Gallery, see Fairbanks AK (A)
Fairbanks Museum & Planetarium, Saint Johnsbury VT (M)
Fairfield Art Association, Fairfield IA (L)
Fairfield Historical Society, Fairfield Museum & History Center, see Fairfield CT (A,L)
Fairfield University, Art Museum, see Fairfield CT (M)
Fairfield University, Visual & Performing Arts, see Fairfield CT (S)
Fairleigh Dickinson University, Edward Williams Gallery, see Hackensack NJ (M)
Fairleigh Dickinson University, Fine Arts Dept, see Madison NJ (S)
Fairmont State College, Div of Fine Arts, see Fairmont WV (S)
Fall River Historical Society, Fall River MA (M)
Leonard L Farber Library, see Brandeis University, Waltham MA
Farmington Valley Arts Center, Avon CT (A)
Farmington Village Green & Library Association, Stanley-Whitman House, see Farmington CT (M)
William A Farnsworth, Museum, see Rockland ME (M, L)
Fashion Institute of Technology - SUNY, The Museum at FIT, see New York NY (M,L)
Fashion Institute of Technology, School of Art & Design, see New York NY (S)
James H Faulkner, Art Dept, see Bay Minette AL (S)
Favell Museum of Western Art & Indian Artifacts, Klamath Falls OR (M)
Fayetteville State University, Performing & Fine Arts, see Fayetteville NC (S)
Feather River Community College, Art Dept, see Quincy CA (S)
Harriet FeBland, New York NY (S)
Federal Reserve Bank of Cleveland, Cleveland OH
Federal Reserve Bank of Minneapolis, Minneapolis MN
Federal Reserve Board, Art Gallery, see Washington DC (M)
Federation of Modern Painters & Sculptors, New York NY (O)
Fellowship of the Pennsylvania Academy of the Fine Arts, see Pennsylvania Academy of the Fine Arts, New Philadelphia PA
Fellows of Contemporary Art, Los Angeles CA (A)
Ferguson Library, Stamford CT (L)
Ferris State University, Visual Communication Dept, see Big Rapids MI (S)
Fetherston Foundation, Packwood House Museum, see Lewisburg PA (M)
Field Museum, Chicago IL (M,L)
The Fields Sculpture Park at Omi International Arts Center, Ghent NY (M)
M55Art, New York NY (M)
Figge Art Museum, Davenport IA (M,L)
Fillmore County Historical Society, Fillmore County History Center, see Fountain MN (A)
FilmNorth, Saint Paul MN (M)
The Filson Historical Society, Louisville KY (A,L)
Fine Arts Association, School of Fine Arts, see Willoughby OH (A)
Fine Arts Center for the New River Valley, Pulaski VA (M)
The Fine Arts Center of Hot Springs, Hot Springs AR (M)
Fine Arts Museums of San Francisco, M H de Young Museum, see San Francisco CA (M,L)
Fine Arts Work Center, Hudson D. Walker Gallery, see Provincetown MA (A)
Finger Lakes Community College, Visual & Performing Arts Dept, see Canandaigua NY (S)
Finlandia Univ, International School of Art and Design, see Hancock MI (S)
Firehouse Art Center, Norman OK (M)
Firehouse Center for the Arts, Institution for Savings Art Gallery, see Bainbridge GA (M)
Firelands Association for the Visual Arts, Oberlin OH (A)
Fireweed Gallery, Homer AK (M)
First Horizon National Corp, First Tennessee Heritage Collection, see Memphis TN
First State Bank, They Also Ran Gallery, see Norton KS
First Street Gallery, New York NY (M)
First Tennessee Bank, Memphis TN
Fisher Art Gallery, Marshalltown IA (M)
Fishkill Historical Society, Van Wyck Homestead Museum, see Fishkill NY (M)
Fisk University, Art Dept, see Nashville TN (S)
Fisk University, Carl Van Vechten Gallery, see Nashville TN (M,L)
Fitchburg Art Museum, Fitchburg MA (M)
Fitton Center for Creative Arts, Hamilton OH (S)
Fitton Center for Creative Arts, Hamilton OH (M)
Five Civilized Tribes Museum, Muskogee OK (M,L)
516 ARTS, Albuquerque NM (M)
FLAG Art Foundation, New York NY (M)
Flagler College, Visual Arts Dept, see Saint Augustine FL (S)
Flamingo Gallery, see Las Vegas-Clark County Library District, Las Vegas NV
Flanagan Valley Campus Art Gallery, see Community College of Rhode Island, Lincoln RI
Paul D Fleck Library & Archives, see Banff Centre, Banff AB
Fleetwood Museum, North Plainfield NJ (M)
Fleisher Art Memorial, Philadelphia PA (S)
Samuel S Fleisher Art Memorial, see Philadelphia Museum of Art, Philadelphia PA
Flint Hills Gallery, Cottonwood Falls KS (M)
Flint Institute of Arts, Flint MI (M,L)
Florence County Museum, Florence SC (M)
Florida A & M University, Dept of Visual Arts, Humanities & Theatre, see Tallahassee FL (S)
Florida Atlantic University, D F Schmidt College of Arts & Letters Dept of Visual Arts & Art History, see Boca Raton FL (S)
Florida Atlantic University, University Galleries/Ritter Art Gallery/Schmidt Center Gallery, see Boca Raton FL (M)
Florida College, Division of Art, see Temple Terrace FL (S)
Florida Community College at Jacksonville, South Campus, Art Dept, see Jacksonville FL (S)
Florida CraftArt, Saint Petersburg FL (M)
Florida Department of Environmental Protection, Stephen Foster Folk Culture Center State Park, see White Springs FL (M)
Florida Department of State, Division of Cultural Affairs, Florida Council on Arts & Culture, see Tallahassee FL (A)
Florida Folklife Programs, Tallahassee FL (A,L)
Florida Gateway College, Liberal Art Dept, see Lake City FL (S)
Florida International University, School of Art & Art History, see Miami FL (S)
Florida International University, The Patricia & Phillip Frost Art Museum, see Miami FL (M)
Florida Keys Community College, Fine Arts Div, see Key West FL (S)
Florida School of the Arts, Visual Arts, see Palatka FL (S)
Florida Southern College, Department of Art & Art History, see Lakeland FL (S)
Florida Southern College, Melvin Art Gallery, see Lakeland FL (M)
Florida State College at Jacksonville, South Gallery, see Jacksonville FL (M)
Florida State University and Central Florida Community College, The Appleton Museum of Art, see Ocala FL (M)
Florida State University, Art Dept, see Tallahassee FL (S)
Florida State University, Museum of Fine Arts, see Tallahassee FL (M)
Florida State University, John & Mable Ringling Museum of Art, see Sarasota FL (M,L)
Roswell P Flower, Watertown NY (M)
William Hayes Fogg Art Museum, see Harvard University, Cambridge MA
Folger Shakespeare, Washington DC (L)
Folk Art Society of America, Richmond VA (M)
Fontbonne University, Fine Art Dept, see Saint Louis MO (S)
Foosaner Art Museum, Melbourne FL (M)
Foothill College, Fine Arts & Communications Div, see Los Altos Hills CA (S)
Foothills Art Center, Inc, Golden CO (A)
Forbes Library, Northampton MA (L)
Forbes Magazine, Inc, Forbes Collection, see Jersey City NJ
Fordham University, Art Dept, see New York NY (S)
Ford Motor Company, Henry Ford Museum & Greenfield Village, see Dearborn MI
Forest Hills Adult and Youth Center, Forest Hills NY (S)
Forest Lawn Museum, Glendale CA (M)
Forges du Saint-Maurice National Historic Site, Trois Rivieres QC (M)
Forsyth Library, see Fort Hays State University, Hays KS
Fort Collins Museum of Art, Inc, Fort Collins CO (M)
Fort George G Meade Museum, Fort Meade MD (M)
Fort Hays State University, Dept of Art & Design, see Hays KS (S)
Fort Hays State University, Moss-Thorns Gallery of Arts, see Hays KS (M,L)
Fort Hill Plantation, see Clemson University, Clemson SC
Fort Lewis College, Art Dept, see Durango CO (S)
Fort Morgan Heritage Foundation, Fort Morgan CO (M)
Fort Smith Regional Art Museum, Fort Smith AR (M)
Fort Steilacoom Community College, Fine Arts Dept, see Lakewood WA (S)
Fort Ticonderoga Association, Ticonderoga NY (M)
Fort Totten State Historic Site, Pioneer Daughters Museum, see Fort Totten ND (A)

Fort Valley State College, H A Hunt Memorial Library, see Fort Valley GA (L)
Fort Wayne Museum of Art, Inc, Fort Wayne IN (M)
Fort Worth Public Library Arts & Humanities, Fine Arts Section, see Fort Worth TX (L)
Fostoria Ohio Glass Association, Glass Heritage Gallery, see Fostoria OH (M)
Foto Fest International, Houston TX (A)
Foundry Art Centre, Saint Charles MO (M)
4 Culture, Seattle WA (A)
Framingham State College, Art Dept, see Framingham MA (S)
Francis Marion University, Fine Arts Dept, see Florence SC (S)
Franco-American Centre, Manchester NH (M)
Franconia Sculpture Park, Franconia MN (M)
Frankfort Community Public Library, Anna & Harlan Hubbard Gallery, see Frankfort IN (M)
Franklin & Marshall College, Art & Art History Dept, see Lancaster PA (S)
Franklin College, Art Dept, see Franklin IN (S)
Franklin Furnace Archive, Inc, Brooklyn NY (L)
Franklin Pierce College, Dept of Fine Arts & Graphic Communications, see Rindge NH (S)
Frank Lloyd Wright's, Alexandria VA (M)
Frank Lloyd Wright Museum, AD German Warehouse, see Richland Center WI (M)
Frank Lloyd Wright School, William Wesley Peters Library, see Scottsdale AZ (L)
The Frank Phillips Foundation Inc, Woolaroc Museum, see Bartlesville OK (M,L)
Fraunces Tavern Museum, New York NY (M)
Free Library of Philadelphia, Art Dept, see Philadelphia PA (L)
Free Public Library of Elizabeth, Elizabeth NJ (L)
Freer Gallery of Art & Arthur M Sackler Gallery, Freer Gallery of Art, see Washington DC (M,L)
Fremont Center for the Arts, Canon City CO (A)
French Art Colony, Gallipolis OH (A,L)
French Institute-Alliance Francaise, Library, see New York NY (L)
Fresno Arts Center & Museum, Fresno CA (M)
Fresno City College, Art Dept, see Fresno CA (S)
Fresno Metropolitan Museum, Fresno CA (M)
The Frick Art & Historical Center, Inc, Frick Art Museum, see Pittsburgh PA (M)
Frick Collection, New York NY (M)
The Frick Collection, Frick Art Reference Library, see New York NY (L)
Henry Clay Frick Fine Arts Library, see University of Pittsburgh, Pittsburgh PA
Fried, Frank, Harris, Shriver & Jacobson, Art Collection, see New York NY
Lee M Friedman Memorial Library, see American Jewish Historical Society, Boston MA
Friends of Historic Kingston, Fred J Johnston House Museum, see Kingston NY (M)
Friends University, Art Dept, see Wichita KS (S)
Friends University, Riney Fine Arts Center Gallery, see Wichita KS (M,L)
Frontier Gateway Museum, Glendive MT (M)
Frontier Times Museum, Bandera TX (M)
Frostburg State University, Dept of Visual Arts, see Frostburg MD (S)
Frostburg State University, The Stephanie Ann Roper Gallery, see Frostburg MD (M,L)
Robert Frost Library, see Amherst College, Amherst MA
Fruitlands Museum, Inc, Harvard MA (M,L)
Frye Art Museum, Seattle WA (M)
Fryeburg Academy, The Palmina F & Stephen S Pace Galleries of Art, see Fryeburg ME (M)
Fuller Craft Museum, Brockton MA (M,L)
Fuller Lodge Art Center, Los Alamos NM (M)
Fullerton College Art Gallery, Fullerton CA (M)
Fullerton College, Division of Fine Arts, see Fullerton CA (S)
Fulton-Hayden Memorial Library & Art Gallery, see Amerind Foundation, Inc, Dragoon AZ
Fulton County Historical Society Inc, Fulton County Museum (Tetzlaff Reference Room), see Rochester IN (M)
Furman University, Art Dept, see Greenville SC (S)
Fusion: The Ontario Clay & Glass Association, Fusion Clay & Glass Association, see Toronto ON (A)
Gadsden Museum, Mesilla NM (M)
Gadsden Museum of Art, Gadsden AL (M)
Gail Severn Gallery, Ketchum ID (M)
Galeria de la Raza, Studio 24, see San Francisco CA (M)
Galerie d'art de l'Universite de Moncton, Moncton NB (M)
Galerie d'Art du Parc-Manoir de Tonnancour, Manoir de Tonnancour, see Trois Rivieres QC (M)
Galerie Montcalm, Gatineau QC (M)
Galesburg Civic Art Center, Galesburg IL (A)
Gallery 25, Art Gallery, see Fresno CA (M)
Gallery 4, Ltd, Fargo ND (M)
Gallery 72, see City of Atlanta, Atlanta GA
Gallery 825/Los Angeles Art Association, Gallery 825, see Los Angeles CA (A)
Gallery 92 West / Fremont Area Art Association, Fremont NE (M)
The Gallery at the Presbyterian Church at Franklin Lakes, Franklin Lakes NJ (M)
Gallery Moos Ltd, Toronto ON (M)
Gallery 9, Los Altos CA (M)
Gallery North, Setauket NY (M)
Gallery One Visual Arts Center, Ellensburg WA (M)
Gallery Stratford, Stratford ON (M)
Gallery XII, Wichita KS (M)
Harvey B Gantt Center for African American Arts + Culture, Charlotte NC (M)
Garden City Community College, Art Dept, see Garden City KS (S)
George R Gardiner Museum of Ceramic Art, Toronto ON (M)
Isabella Stewart Gardner Museum, Boston MA (M,L)
Garner Arts Center, Garnerville NY (M)
Garrison Art Center, Garrison NY (M)
Gaston College, Art Dept, see Dallas NC (S)
Gaston County Museum of Art & History, Dallas NC (M)
Gateway Arts, Gateway Gallery, see Brookline MA (M)
Gavilan College, Art Dept, see Gilroy CA (S)
Gavilan Community College, Art Gallery, see Gilroy CA (M)
Geisel Library, see Museum of Contemporary Art, San Diego, La Jolla CA
Gem County Historical Society and Museum, Gem County Historical Village Museum, see Emmett ID (M)
General Board of Discipleship, The United Methodist Church, The Upper Room Chapel & Museum, see Nashville TN (M)
Gene Roncka Willow Point Gallery/Museum, Ashland NE (M)
Genesee Country Village & Museum, John L Wehle Art Gallery, see Mumford NY (M)
George A Spiva, Joplin MO (A)
George Brown College of Applied Arts & Technology, Centre for Arts, Design & Information Technology, see Toronto ON (S)
George Eastman Museum, Rochester NY (M)
George Mason University, College of Humanities & Social Sciences, Dept of History & Art History, see Fairfax VA (S)
Georgetown College, Art Dept, see Georgetown KY (S)
Georgetown College, Georgetown College Fine Art Galleries, see Georgetown KY (M)
Georgetown University, Art Collection, see Washington DC (M,L)
Georgetown University, Dept of Art & Art History, see Washington DC (S)
George Washington's Mount Vernon, Mount Vernon VA (M,L)
The George Washington Masonic National Memorial Association, The George Washington Masonic National Memorial, see Alexandria VA (M)
The George Washington University, Luther W Brady Art Gallery, see Washington DC (M)
George Washington University, Dept of Art of Fine Arts & Art History, see Washington DC (S)
George Washington University, School of Interior Design, see Washington DC (S)
George Washington University, The George Washington Museum and The Textile Museum, see Washington DC (M,L)
Georgia College & State University, Art Dept, see Milledgeville GA (S)
Georgia Council for the Arts, Georgia's State Art Collection, see Atlanta GA (A)
Georgia Institute of Technology, College of Architecture, see Atlanta GA (S)
Georgia Institute of Technology, College of Architecture Library, see Atlanta GA (L)
Georgia Lawyers for the Arts, Atlanta GA (A)
Georgian Court University, Dept of Art, see Lakewood NJ (S)
Georgian Court University, M Christina Geis Gallery, see Lakewood NJ (M)
Georgia O'Keeffe Museum, Santa Fe NM (M,L)
Georgia Southern University, Betty Foy Sanders Dept of Art, see Statesboro GA (S)
Georgia Southwestern State University, Dept of Fine Arts, see Americus GA (S)
Georgia Southwestern State University, JEC Gallery & FAB Gallery, see Americus GA (M)
Georgia State University, School of Art & Design, Visual Resource Center, see Atlanta GA (L,M)
Georgia State University, Ernest G Welch School of Art & Design, see Atlanta GA (S)
Germantown Historical Society, Philadelphia PA (M)
Gertrude Herbert Institute of Art, Augusta GA (M)
The Getty Center, Trust Museum, see Los Angeles CA (L,M)
Gettysburg College, Dept of Visual Arts, see Gettysburg PA (S)
The J Paul Getty Museum, see The Getty Center, Los Angeles CA
Gibbes Museum of Art, Charleston SC (S)
Gibson-Barham Gallery, see Imperial Calcasieu Museum, Lake Charles LA
Gibson Society, Inc, Gibson House Museum, see Boston MA (M)
Gilbert House, see City of Atlanta, Atlanta GA
Wendell Gilley, Southwest Harbor ME (M)
Gilpin County Arts Association, Central City CO (A)
Girard College, Stephen Girard Collection, see Philadelphia PA (M)
Giustina Gallery, see Oregon State University, Corvallis OR
Gladys Marcus Library, see Fashion Institute of Technology - SUNY, New York NY
Glanmore National Historic Site of Canada, Belleville ON (M)
Glass Art Society, Seattle WA (A)
Glenbow Museum, Calgary AB (M,L)
Glendale Community College, Visual & Performing Arts Div, see Glendale CA (S)
Glendale Public Library, Brand Library & Art Center, see Glendale CA (M)
Glenhyrst Art Gallery of Brant, Brantford ON (M)
Glenville State College, Dept of Fine Arts, see Glenville WV (S)
Glenwood Center for the Arts, Glenwood Springs CO (M)
Glessner House Museum, Chicago IL (M)
Gloridale Partnership, National Museum of Woodcarving, see Custer SD (M)
Gloucester County College, Liberal Arts Dept, see Sewell NJ (S)
Glynn Visual Arts, Inc, Saint Simons Island GA (A)
Charles B Goddard, Ardmore OK (A)
Goddard College, Dept of Art, see Plainfield VT (S)
Goethe-Institut New York, New York NY (M)
Gogebic Community College, Fine Arts Dept, see Ironwood MI (S)
Golden Isles Arts & Humanities Association, Brunswick GA (A)

Golden State Mutual Life Insurance Company, Afro-American Art Collection, see Los Angeles CA
Golden West College, Visual Art Dept, see Huntington Beach CA (S)
Goldstein Museum of Design, see University of Minnesota, Saint Paul MN
Gonzaga University, Dept of Art, see Spokane WA (S)
Gonzaga University, Jundt Art Museum, see Spokane WA (M)
Gordon College, Dept of Fine Arts, see Barnesville GA (S)
Donald B Gordon Memorial Library, see Palm Beach County Parks & Recreation Department, Delray Beach FL
Goshen College, Art Dept, see Goshen IN (S)
Goshen Historical Society, Goshen CT (M)
Goucher College, Art & Art History Dept, see Baltimore MD (S)
Goucher College, Rosenberg & Silber Art Gallery, see Baltimore MD (M)
Governors State University, College of Arts & Science, Art Dept, see University Park IL (S)
Goya Contemporary, Baltimore MD (M)
Grace College, Dept of Art, see Winona Lake IN (S)
Graceland University, Fine Arts Div, see Lamoni IA (S)
Grace Museum, Inc, The Grace Museum, see Abilene TX (M)
Grambling State University, Art Dept, see Grambling LA (S)
Grand Canyon University, Art Dept, see Phoenix AZ (S)
Grand Marais Art Colony, Grand Marais MN (S)
Grand Prairie Arts Council, Inc, Arts Center of the Grand Prairie, see Stuttgart AR (A)
Grand Rapids Art Museum, Grand Rapids MI (M,L)
Grand Rapids Community College, Visual Art Dept, see Grand Rapids MI (S)
Grand Rapids Public Library, Grand Rapids MI (L)
Grand Rapids Public Museum, Grand Rapids MI (M)
Grand River Museum, Lemmon SD (M)
Grand Teton National Park Service, Moose WY (A)
Grand Valley State University, Art & Design Dept, see Allendale MI (S)
Grand View College, Art Dept, see Des Moines IA (S)
Grants Pass Museum of Art, Grants Pass OR (M)
Graphic Artists Guild, New York NY (A)
The Graphic Eye Gallery, Port Washington NY (M)
Grass Roots Art & Community Effort (GRACE), Firehouse Gallery, see Hardwick VT (M)
Grassroots Art Center, Lucas KS (M)
Grayson County College, Art Dept, see Denison TX (S)
Great Lakes Historical Society, Inland Seas Maritime Museum, see Vermilion OH (M)
Greene County Historical Society, Xenia OH (A)
Greene County Historical Society, Bronck Museum, see Coxsackie NY (M)
Greenfield Community College, Art Dept, see Greenfield MA (S)
Green Hill Center for North Carolina Art, Greenhill, see Greensboro NC (M)
Green Mountain College, Dept of Art, see Poultney VT (S)
Green Mountain Fine Art Gallery, Stowe VT (M)
Green Research Library, see The Old Jail Art Center, Albany TX
Green River Community College, Art Dept, see Auburn WA (S)
Greensboro College, Irene Cullis Gallery, see Greensboro NC (M)
Greensboro College, Dept of Art, Division of Fine Arts, see Greensboro NC (S)
Greenville College, Art Dept, see Greenville IL (S)
Greenville College, Richard W Bock Sculpture Collection, Almira College House, see Greenville IL (M,L)
Greenville County Museum of Art, Greenville SC (M)
Greenville County Museum of Art Center for Museum Education, Greenville SC (S)
Greenville Museum of Art, Inc, Greenville NC (A,L)
Greenville Technical College, Visual Arts Dept, see Greenville SC (S)
Greenwich Art Society Inc, Greenwich CT (A,M)
Greenwich House Inc, Greenwich House Pottery, see New York NY (S)
Greenwich House Pottery, First Floor Gallery, see New York NY (M,L)
Greenwich Library, Greenwich CT (L)
Grenfell Campus, Memorial University of Newfoundland, Division of Fine Arts, Visual Arts Program, see Corner Brook NF (S)
Grinnell College, Dept of Art, see Grinnell IA (S)
Grinnell College, Faulconer Gallery, see Grinnell IA (M)
Grohmann Museum, Milwaukee WI (M)
Grolier Club Library, New York NY (L)
Grossmont College, Art Dept, see El Cajon CA (S)
Grossmont Community College, Hyde Art Gallery, see El Cajon CA (M)
The Renee & Chaim Gross Foundation, Chaim Gross Studio, see New York NY (M)
Grounds for Sculpture, Hamilton NJ (M)
Grunwald Center for the Graphic Arts at Hammer Museum, see University of California, Los Angeles, Los Angeles CA
Emile A Gruppe Gallery, Jericho VT (M)
Guadalupe Cultural Arts Center, San Antonio TX (A)
John Simon Guggenheim, New York NY (A)
Solomon R Guggenheim Museum, New York NY (M, L)
Guilde canadienne des metiers d'art, Canadian Guild of Crafts, see Montreal QC (A)
Guild Hall of East Hampton, Inc, Guild Hall Museum, see East Hampton NY (M)
Guild of Book Workers, New York NY (O,L)
The Guild of Boston Artists, Boston MA (A)
Guild of Creative Art, Shrewsbury NJ (S)
Guilford College, Art Dept, see Greensboro NC (S)
Guilford College, Guilford College Art Gallery, see Greensboro NC (M)
Guilford Technical Community College, Commercial Art Dept, see Jamestown NC (S)
Gulf Beach Art Center, Indian Rocks Beach FL (M)
Gulf Coast Community College, Division of Visual & Performing Arts, see Panama City FL (S)
GumTree Museum of Art, Tupelo MS (M)
Jessica Gund Memorial Library, see Cleveland Institute of Art, Cleveland OH
Emery A Gunnin Architectural Library, see Clemson University, Clemson SC
Gunnison Arts Center, Gunnison CO (M)
Gunston Hall Plantation, Mason Neck VA (M,L)
Gustavus Adolphus College, Art & Art History Dept, see Saint Peter MN (S)
H.A. & Mary K Chapman Library, see Philbrook Museum of Art, Tulsa OK
Haffenreffer Museum of Anthropology, see Brown University, Providence RI
Hagerstown Junior College, Art Dept, see Hagerstown MD (S)
Halifax Historical Society, Inc, Halifax Historical Museum, see Daytona Beach FL (M)
Hall Art Foundation, Reading VT (M)
Hallmark Cards, Inc, Hallmark Art Collection, see Kansas City MO
Hallwalls Contemporary Arts Center, Buffalo NY (M)
Hambidge Center for Creative Arts & Sciences, Rabun Gap GA (M)
Hamilton College, Art Dept, see Clinton NY (S)
Hamilton College, Emerson Gallery, see Clinton NY (M)
Hamline University, Dept of Studio Arts & Art History, see Saint Paul MN (S)
Hamline University Studio Arts & Art History Depts, Gallery, see Saint Paul MN (M)
Hammer Museum, see University of California, Los Angeles, Los Angeles CA
Hammond-Harwood House Association, Inc, Hammond-Harwood House, see Annapolis MD (M)
Hammond Castle Museum, Gloucester MA (M)
Hammond Museum & Japanese Stroll Garden, Cross-Cultural Center, see North Salem NY (M)
Hammonds House Museum, Atlanta GA (M)
Hampden-Booth Theatre Library, New York NY (L)
Hampden-Sydney College, Fine Arts Dept, see Hampden Sydney VA (S)
Hampshire County Public Library, Romney WV (L)
Hampton University, Dept of Fine & Performing Arts, see Hampton VA (S)
Hampton University, University Museum, see Hampton VA (M)
Hancock County Trustees of Public Reservations, Woodlawn: Museum, Gardens & Park, see Ellsworth ME (M)
Hancock Shaker Village, Inc, Pittsfield MA (M)
Handweavers Guild of America, Suwanee GA (A)
Hannibal La Grange College, Art Dept, see Hannibal MO (S)
Hanover College, Dept of Art, see Hanover IN (S)
Dane G Hansen, Logan KS (M)
Clarence B Hanson Jr Library, see Birmingham Museum of Art, Birmingham AL
Harbourfront Centre, The Power Plant Contemporary Art Gallery, see Toronto ON (M)
Harcum College, Fashion Design, see Bryn Mawr PA (S)
Hardin-Simmons University, Art Dept, see Abilene TX (S)
Harding University, Dept of Art & Design, see Searcy AR (S)
Francis Hardy Gallery, Fish Creek WI (M)
Harford Community College, Visual, Performing and Applied Arts Division, see Bel Air MD (S)
Harlin Museum, West Plains MO (M)
Harness Racing Museum & Hall of Fame, Goshen NY (M)
Samuel P Harn Museum of Art, see University of Florida, Gainesville FL
Harriet Beecher Stowe Center, Hartford CT (L)
Harrington College of Design, Chicago IL (S)
Mark Harrington Library, see San Fernando Valley Historical Society, Mission Hills CA
Harrisburg Area Community College, Division of Communications, Humanities & the Arts, see Harrisburg PA (S)
Harrison County Historical Museum, Marshall TX (M)
Hartnell College, Art & Photography Dept, see Salinas CA (S)
Hartnell College Gallery, Salinas CA (M)
Jane Hartsook Gallery, see Greenwich House Pottery, New York NY
Stephen H Hart Library, see History Colorado Center Museum, Denver CO
Hartwick College, Art Dept, see Oneonta NY (S)
Hartwick College, Foreman Gallery, see Oneonta NY (M)
Lee & Dolores Hartzmark Library, see The Temple-Tifereth Israel, Beachwood OH
Harvard University, Dept of History of Art & Architecture, see Cambridge MA (S)
Harvard University, Harvard Art Museums, see Cambridge MA (M,L)
Harvestworks, Inc, New York NY (A)
Haskell Indian Nations University, Art Dept, see Lawrence KS (S)
Hastings College, Department of Visual Arts, see Hastings NE (S)
Hastings Museum of Natural & Cultural History, Hastings NE (M)
Hatch-Billops Collection, Inc, New York NY (A)
Haverford College, Fine Arts Dept, see Haverford PA (S)
Haverhill Public Library, Special Collections, see Haverhill MA (L)
Hawaii Okinawa Center, Waipahu HI (M)
Hawaii Pacific University, Art Gallery, see Kaneohe HI (M)
Hawkinsville/Pulaski County Arts Council, Hawkinsville Old Opera House, see Hawkinsville GA (M)
Hayden Museum of American Art, Paris TX (M)
Jean P Haydon, Pago Pago, American Samoa PI (M)
Hays Arts Center, Hays KS (M)

Haystack Mountain School of Crafts, Deer Isle ME (S)
Haystack Mountain School of Crafts, Deer Isle ME (M, L)
The Hayti Heritage Center, Lyda Moore Merrick Gallery, see Durham NC (M)
Hayward Area Forum for the Arts, Sun Gallery, see Hayward CA (M)
Headlands Center for the Arts, Sausalito CA (A)
Headley-Whitney Museum, Lexington KY (M)
Headquarters Fort Monroe, Dept of Army, Casemate Museum, see Hampton VA (M)
Heard Museum, Phoenix AZ (M,L)
Phoebe Apperson Hearst Museum of Anthropology, see University of California, Berkeley, Berkeley CA
Heart of West Texas Museum, Colorado City TX (M)
Heartwood College of Art, Main Gallery, see Biddeford ME (M)
Hebrew Union College - Jewish Institute of Religion Museum, Jewish Institute of Religion, see New York NY (M)
Hebrew Union College - Jewish Institute of Religion, Skirball Museum Cincinnati, see Cincinnati OH (M)
Hebrew Union College, Skirball Cultural Center, see Los Angeles CA (M)
The Heckscher Museum of Art, Huntington NY (M,L)
Heidelberg College, Dept of Art, see Tiffin OH (S)
Hendersonville Arts Council, Monthaven Mansion, see Hendersonville TN (A)
Hendricks Hill Museum, Southport ME (M)
Henry County Museum & Cultural Arts Center, Clinton MO (M)
Henry Ford Community College, McKenzie Fine Art Ctr, see Dearborn MI (S)
Henry Gallery Association, Henry Art Gallery, see Seattle WA (M)
Henry Morrison Flagler Museum, Palm Beach FL (M)
Henry N Flynt Library, see Historic Deerfield, Inc, Deerfield MA
Patrick Henry, Red Hill National Memorial, see Brookneal VA (M)
Henry Sheldon Museum of Vermont History and Research Center, Middlebury VT (M)
Henry Street Settlement, Abrons Art Center, see New York NY (M)
Henry Street Settlement Arts for Living Center, New York NY (S)
Hera Educational Foundation, Hera Gallery, see Wakefield RI (M)
Heritage Center, Inc, Pine Ridge SD (M)
Heritage Glass Museum, Glassboro NJ (M)
Heritage Museum & Cultural Center, Baker LA (M)
Heritage Museum Association, Inc, The Heritage Museum of Northwest Florida, see Valparaiso FL (M)
Heritage Museums & Gardens, Sandwich MA (M)
Herkimer County Community College, Humanities Social Services, see Herkimer NY (S)
Hermitage Museum & Gardens, Norfolk VA (M)
Herrett Center for Arts & Sciences, Jean B King Art Gallery, see Twin Falls ID (M)
Hershey Museum, Hershey PA (M)
Hesston College, Art Dept, see Hesston KS (S)
Hewlett-Woodmere Public Library, Hewlett NY (L)
The HeydarAliyev Center, The HeydarAliyev Museum, see (M)
Heyward-Washington House, see Charleston Museum, Charleston SC
Hibbing Community College, Art Dept, see Hibbing MN (S)
Hickory Museum of Art, Inc, Hickory NC (M,L)
Hidalgo County Historical Museum, Edinburg TX (M)
Hiestand Galleries, Oxford OH (M)
High Desert Museum, Bend OR (M)
Highland Community College, Art Dept, see Freeport IL (S)
High Museum of Art, Atlanta GA (M)
High Plains Museum, McCook NE (M)
Highpoint Center for Printmaking, Minneapolis MN (M)
High Point University, Fine Arts Dept, see High Point NC (S)
Hill-Stead Museum, Farmington CT (M)
Hill College, Fine Arts Dept, see Hillsboro TX (S)
Hill Country Arts Foundation, Duncan-McAshan Visual Arts Center, see Ingram TX (A)
Hillel Foundation, Hillel Jewish Student Center Gallery, see Cincinnati OH (M)
Hill Gallery and Sculpture Park, Sandy UT (M)
Rita K Hillman Education Gallery, see International Center of Photography, New York NY
Hillsborough Community College, Fine Arts Dept, see Tampa FL (S)
Hillsdale College, Art Dept, see Hillsdale MI (S)
Hillwood Museum & Gardens Foundation, Hillwood Estate Museum & Gardens, see Washington DC (M)
Hillyer Art Library, see Smith College, Northampton MA
Hinds Community College, Dept of Art, see Raymond MS (S)
Hinds Community College District, Marie Hull Gallery, see Raymond MS (M)
Hiram College, Art Dept, see Hiram OH (S)
Hirshhorn Museum & Sculpture Garden, Smithsonian Institution, see Washington DC (M,L)
The Hispanic Society of America, Hispanic Society Museum & Library, see New York NY (M)
Historical and Cultural Society of Clay County, Hjemkomst Center, see Moorhead MN (M)
Historical Museum at Fort Missoula, Missoula MT (M)
Historical Society of Bloomfield, Bloomfield NJ (M)
Historical Society of Cheshire County, Keene NH (M)
Historical Society of Kent County, Chestertown MD (A)
Historical Society of Martin County, Elliott Museum, see Stuart FL (M)
Historical Society of Old Newbury, Cushing House Museum, see Newburyport MA (M)
Historical Society of Palm Beach County, The Richard and Pat Johnson Palm Beach County History Museum, see West Palm Beach FL (M)
Historical Society of Pennsylvania, Philadelphia PA (L)
Historical Society of Rockland County, New City NY (M)
Historical Society of the Cocalico Valley, Ephrata PA (A)
Historical Society of Washington DC, The City Museum of Washington DC, see Washington DC (M,L)
Historic Arkansas Museum, Little Rock AR (M,L)
Historic Cherry Hill, Albany NY (M)
Historic Deerfield, Inc, Deerfield MA (M,L)
Historic Holyoke at Wistariahurst & City of Holyoke, Holyoke MA (M)
Historic Hudson Valley, Pocantico Hills NY (M)
Historic Huguenot Street, New Paltz NY (M)
Historic New England, Boston MA (A,L)
The Historic New Orleans Collection, Williams Research Center, see New Orleans LA (M)
Historic Newton, Newton MA (M)
Historic Northampton Museum & Education Center, Northampton MA (M)
Historic Paris - Bourbon County, Inc, Hopewell Museum, see Paris KY (M)
Historic Pensacola Preservation Board, T.T. Wentworth Jr. Florida State Museum, see Pensacola FL (A)
The History Center in Tompkins County, Ithaca NY (M)
History Colorado Center Museum, Denver CO (M,L)
History Museum of Mobile, Mobile AL (M,L)
Hobart & William Smith Colleges, Art Dept, see Geneva NY (S)
Hockaday Museum of Art, Kalispell MT (A)
Ronna and Eric Hoffman Gallery of Contemporary Art, Portland OR (M)
Elise N Hofheimer Art Library, see Old Dominion University, Norfolk VA
Hofstra University, Department of Fine Arts, see Hempstead NY (S)
Hofstra University, Hofstra University Museum, see Hempstead NY (M)
Holland College, School of Visual Arts & Journalism, see Charlottetown PE (S)
Holland Tunnel Art Projects, Brooklyn NY (M)
Hollins University, Art Dept, see Roanoke VA (S)
Holter Museum of Art, Helena MT (M)
Holy Names College, Art Dept, see Oakland CA (S)
Holyoke Community College, Dept of Art, see Holyoke MA (S)
Homewood Museum, see Johns Hopkins University, Baltimore MD
Honolulu Community College, Commercial Art Dept, see Honolulu HI (S)
Honolulu Museum of Art, Honolulu HI (M,L)
Hood College, Dept of Art, see Frederick MD (S)
Hoosier Salon Patrons Association, Inc, Art Gallery & Membership Organization, see Indianapolis IN (A)
Dorothy H Hoover Library, see OCAD University, Toronto ON
Hope College, DePree Art Center & Gallery, see Holland MI (M)
Hope College, Dept of Art & Art History, see Holland MI (S)
Hopewell Museum, Hopewell NJ (M)
Hopi Cultural Center Museum, Second Mesa AZ (M)
Edward Hopper, Nyack NY (M)
Hopper Resource Library, see The Butler Institute of American Art, Youngstown OH
Horizons Unlimited Supplementary Educational Center, Science Museum, see Salisbury NC (M)
Hostos Center for the Arts & Culture, Bronx NY (A)
Hot Shops Art Center, Omaha NE (M)
Houghton College, Art Dept, see Houghton NY (S)
Housatonic Community College, Art Dept, see Bridgeport CT (S)
Housatonic Community College, Housatonic Museum of Art, see Bridgeport CT (M,L)
Houston Baptist University, Dept of Art, see Houston TX (S)
Houston Baptist University, Museum of American Architecture and Decorative Arts, see Houston TX (M)
Houston Center For Photography, Houston TX (A)
Houston Museum of Decorative Arts, Chattanooga TN (M)
Houston Public Library, Houston TX (L)
Howard College, Art Dept, see Big Spring TX (S)
Howard Community College, The Rouse Company Foundation Gallery, see Columbia MD (M)
Howard County Arts Council, Ellicott City MD (A)
Howard Payne University, School of Fine Arts, see Brownwood TX (S)
Howard University, Gallery of Art, see Washington DC (M,L)
Hoyt Center for the Arts, Arts & Education of the Hoyt, see New Castle PA (M)
HUB Robeson Galleries, see The Pennsylvania State University, University Park PA
Hudson Guild, Hudson Guild Gallery, see New York NY (M)
The Hudson River Museum, Yonkers NY (M)
Hudson Valley Art Association, Brooklyn NY (A)
Hui No'eau Visual Arts Center, Gallery and Gift Shop, see Makawao Maui HI (M)
Humber College, School of Creative & Performing Arts, see Toronto ON (S)
Humboldt Arts Council, Morris Graves Museum of Art, see Eureka CA (A)
Humboldt State University, College of Arts & Humanities, Art Dept, see Arcata CA (S)
Stephen Huneck Gallery at Dog Mountain, Saint Johnsbury VT (M)
Hunter College, Dept of Art & Art History, see New York NY (S)
Hunterdon Art Museum, Clinton NJ (A)
Hunter Museum of American Art, Chattanooga TN (M, L)
Huntingdon College, Dept of Art, see Montgomery AL (S)
Huntington Beach Art Center, Huntington Beach CA (M)
Huntington College, Art Dept, see Huntington IN (S)
The Huntington Library, Art Collections & Botanical Gardens, San Marino CA (M,L)

Huntington Museum of Art, Huntington WV (M)
Huntington University, Robert E Wilson Art Gallery, see Huntington IN (M)
Hunt Institute for Botanical Documentation, see Carnegie Mellon University, Pittsburgh PA
Hunt Library, see Carnegie Mellon University, Pittsburgh PA
Huntsville Art League, Lowe Mill Arts & Entertainment, see Huntsville AL (A)
Huntsville Museum of Art, Huntsville AL (M,L)
Huronia Museum, Gallery of Historic Huronia, see Midland ON (M)
Hussian School of Art, Commercial Art Dept, see Philadelphia PA (S)
Hutchinson Art Association, Hutchinson Art Center, see Hutchinson KS (A)
Hutchinson Community College, Visual Arts Dept, see Hutchinson KS (S)
The Hyde Collection, Glens Falls NY (M,L)
Hyde Park Art Center, Chicago IL (M)
Stan Hywet, Akron OH (M)
Idaho Commission on the Arts, Boise ID (A)
Idaho Historical Museum, Boise ID (M)
Idaho State University, John B Davis Gallery of Fine Art, see Pocatello ID (M)
Idaho State University, Dept of Art, see Pocatello ID (S)
i.d.e.a. Museum, Mesa AZ (M)
Idyllwild Arts Academy, Idyllwild CA (S)
Illinois Alliance for Arts Education (IAAE), DeKalb IL (A)
Illinois Benedictine University, Department of Fine Arts, see Lisle IL (S)
Illinois Central College, Arts & Communication Dept, see East Peoria IL (S)
Illinois Historic Preservation Agency, Bishop Hill State Historic Site, see Bishop Hill IL (M)
The Illinois Institute of Art - Chicago, Chicago IL (S)
Illinois Institute of Technology, College of Architecture, see Chicago IL (S)
Illinois State Museum, ISM Lockport Gallery, Chicago Gallery & Southern Illinois Art Gallery, see Springfield IL (M,L)
Illinois State University, College of Fine Arts, see Normal IL (S)
Illinois State University, University Galleries, see Normal IL (M,L)
Illinois Valley Community College, Division of Humanities & Fine Arts, see Oglesby IL (S)
Illinois Wesleyan University, Merwin & Wakeley Galleries, see Bloomington IL (M,L)
Illinois Wesleyan University, School of Art, see Bloomington IL (S)
Imago Galleries, Palm Desert CA (M)
Imhoff Art Gallery, St. Walburg SK (M)
Imperato Collection of West African Artifacts, see Martin and Osa Johnson, Chanute KS
Imperial Calcasieu Museum, Lake Charles LA (M,L)
Imperial Centre's Maria V Howard Arts Center, Rocky Mount NC (A)
Imperial Valley College, Humanities Department, see Imperial CA (S)
Independence Historical Museum & Art Center, Independence KS (M)
Independence National Historical Park, Philadelphia PA (M,L)
Independence Seaport Museum, Philadelphia PA (M,L)
Independent Curators International, New York NY (A)
Index of American Design, see National Gallery of Art, Washington DC
Indiana-Purdue University, Dept of Fine Arts, see Fort Wayne IN (S)
Indiana Landmarks, Morris-Butler House, see Indianapolis IN (M,L)
Indianapolis Art Center, Marilyn K. Glick School of Art, see Indianapolis IN (A)
Indianapolis Marion County Public Library, Central Library, see Indianapolis IN (L)
Indianapolis Museum of Contemporary Art, Indianapolis IN (M)
Indian Arts & Crafts Association, Albuquerque NM (A)
Indian Arts & Crafts Board, US Dept of the Interior, Sioux Indian Museum, see Rapid City SD (M)
Indiana State Museum, Indianapolis IN (M)
Indiana State University, Dept of Art, see Terre Haute IN (S)
Indiana State University, University Art Gallery, see Terre Haute IN (M)
Indiana University, Bloomington, Henry Radford Hope School of Fine Arts, see Bloomington IN (S)
Indiana University-East, Humanities Dept, see Richmond IN (S)
Indiana University-Purdue University, Indianapolis, Herron School of Art & Design, see Indianapolis IN (S)
Indiana University - Purdue University at Indianapolis, Herron Galleries, see Indianapolis IN (M)
Indiana University-Southeast, Fine Arts Dept, see New Albany IN (S)
Indiana University, Eskenazi Museum of Art, see Bloomington IN (M)
Indiana University, Fine Arts Library, see Bloomington IN (L)
Indiana University of Pennsylvania, College of Fine Arts, see Indiana PA (S)
Indiana University of Pennsylvania, Kipp Gallery, see Indiana PA (M)
Indiana University South Bend, Fine Arts Dept, see South Bend IN (S)
Indiana Wesleyan University, School of Arts & Humanities, Division of Art, see Marion IN (S)
Indian Hills Community College, Ottumwa Campus, Dept of Art, see Ottumwa IA (S)
Indian Hills Community College, Dept of Art, see Centerville IA (S)
Indian Pueblo Cultural Center, Albuquerque NM (M)
Indian River Community College, Fine Arts Dept, see Fort Pierce FL (S)
Individual Artists of Oklahoma, Oklahoma City OK (M)
Industrial Designers Society of America, Herndon VA (O)
Ingalls Library, see The Cleveland Museum of Art, Cleveland OH
Ingraham Memorial Research Library, see Litchfield History Museum, Litchfield CT
Inner-City Arts, Los Angeles CA (S)
Inquilinos Boricuas en Accion (IBA), Villa Victoria Center for the Arts, see Boston MA (A)
Institut des Arts au Saguenay, Centre National D'Exposition a Jonquiere, see Jonquiere QC (M)
Institute for Arts & Humanities Education, New Jersey Summer Arts Institute, see Staten Island NY (S)
Institute of American Indian Arts, IAIA Museum of Contemporary Native Arts, see Santa Fe NM (M,L)
Institute of American Indian Arts, Museum of Contemporary Native Arts, see Santa Fe NM (S)
Institute of Contemporary Art, Los Angeles, Los Angeles CA (M)
Institute of Contemporary Art/Boston, Boston MA (M)
The Institute of Contemporary Art, see Maine College of Art, Portland ME
Institute of Fine Arts Visual Resources Collection, see New York University, New York NY
Institute of Puerto Rican Culture, Instituto de Cultura Puertorriquena, see San Juan PR (M,L,A)
Institute of Puerto Rican Culture, Museo Fuerte Conde de Mirasol, see Vieques PR (M)
INTAR Gallery, New York NY (M)
Inter-Society Color Council, Frederick MD (O)
Interact Center for the Visual & Performing Arts, Interact Gallery, see Minneapolis MN (M)
Inter American University of Puerto Rico, Fine Arts Dept -Art Program, see San German PR (S)
The Interchurch Center, Galleries at the Interchurch Center, see New York NY (M,L)
Interlochen Center for the Arts, Interlochen MI (L)
Interlochen Center for the Arts, Interlochen Arts Academy, Dept of Visual Art, see Interlochen MI (S)
Intermedia Arts, Minneapolis MN (M)
Intermuseum Conservation Association, Cleveland OH (O)
International Center of Medieval Art, New York NY (A)
International Center of Photography, Museum, see New York NY (M,L)
International Center of Photography, School, see New York NY (S)
International Clown Hall of Fame & Research Center, Inc, West Allis WI (M)
International Council for Cultural Exchange (ICCE), Brookhaven NY (S)
International Fine Arts College, Miami FL (S)
International Foundation for Art Research, Inc (IFAR), New York NY (O)
International Museum of Art, El Paso TX (M)
International Museum of Art & Science, McAllen TX (M)
International Preservation Studies Center, Mount Carroll IL (S)
International Sculpture Center, Hamilton NJ (M)
International Society of Copier Artists (ISCA), Brooklyn NY (O)
International Society of Marine Painters, Puryear TN (A)
Intersection for the Arts, San Francisco CA (A)
Intuit: The Center for Intuitive & Outsider Art, Chicago IL (M)
Iowa Central Community College, Dept of Art, see Fort Dodge IA (S)
Iowa Great Lakes Maritime Museum, Arnolds Park IA (M)
Iowa Lakes Community College, Dept of Art, see Estherville IA (S)
Iowa State University, Brunnier Art Museum, see Ames IA (M)
Iowa State University, Dept of Art & Design, see Ames IA (S)
Iowa Wesleyan College, Art Dept, see Mount Pleasant IA (S)
Iowa Western Community College, Art Dept, see Council Bluffs IA (S)
Iredell Museums, Statesville NC (M)
Iroquois County Historical Society Museum, Old Courthouse Museum, see Watseka IL (M)
Iroquois Indian Museum, Howes Cave NY (M)
Irvine Museum, Irvine CA (M)
Irving Arts Center, Galleries & Sculpture Garden, see Irving TX (M)
Irving Sandler Artists File, see Artists Space, New York NY
Island Gallery West, Holmes Beach FL (M)
Islip Art Museum, East Islip NY (M)
Ithaca College, Fine Art Dept, see Ithaca NY (S)
Ithaca College, Handwerker Gallery of Art, see Ithaca NY (M)
Jackson State University, Dept of Art, see Jackson MS (S)
Jacksonville Public Library, Fine Arts & Recreation Dept, see Jacksonville FL (L)
Jacksonville State University, Art Dept, see Jacksonville AL (S)
Jacksonville University, Jacksonville FL (S)
Jacksonville University, Alexander Brest Museum & Gallery, see Jacksonville FL (M)
Jacques Marchais Museum of Tibetan Art, Staten Island NY (M)
Jamaica Center for Arts & Learning (JCAL), Jamaica NY (M)
James A Michener Art Museum, Doylestown PA (M)
James Dick Foundation, Festival - Institute, see Round Top TX (M)
James D Veatch Camp Breckinridge Museum & Arts Center, Morganfield KY (M)
James Madison University, Duke Hall Gallery of Fine Art, see Harrisonburg VA (M)
James Madison University, School of Art & Art History, see Harrisonburg VA (S)
James Monroe Museum, Fredericksburg VA (M,L)
Jamestown-Yorktown Foundation, Jamestown Settlement, see Williamsburg VA (M)
Jamestown Community College, Arts, Humanities & Health Sciences Division, see Jamestown NY (S)

Jamestown Community College, The Weeks, see Jamestown NY (M)
Janet Turner Print Museum, CSU, Chicago, see California State University, Chico, Chico CA
Jan Shrem and Maria Manetti Shrem Museum of Art, see University of California, Davis, Davis CA
Japanese American Cultural & Community Center, George J Doizaki Gallery, see Los Angeles CA (M)
Japanese American National Museum, Los Angeles CA (M)
Japan Society, Inc, Japan Society Gallery, see New York NY (M,L)
Japantown Art & Media Workshop, San Francisco CA (A)
The Jaques Art Center, Aitkin MN (M)
Jardin Botanique de Montreal, Bibliotheque, see Montreal QC (L)
Jay I Kislak Foundation, Miami Lakes FL (M)
Jean Paul Slusser Gallery, see University of Michigan, Ann Arbor MI
Jefferson College, Dept of Art, see Hillsboro MO (S)
Jefferson Community College & Technical College, Fine Arts, see Louisville KY (S)
Jefferson Community College, Art Dept, see Watertown NY (S)
Jefferson County Historical Society, Watertown NY (M, L)
Jefferson County Historical Society Museum, Madison IN (M)
Jefferson County Open Space, Hiwan Homestead Museum, see Evergreen CO (M)
Jefferson Davis Community College, Art Dept, see Brewton AL (S)
Jeffers Petroglyphs Historic Site, Comfrey MN (M)
Jekyll Island Museum, Jekyll Island GA (M)
Jenison-Meacham Memorial Art Center & Museum, Belmond IA (M)
William R Jenkins Architecture & Art Library, see University of Houston, Houston TX
Jericho Historical Society, Jericho VT (A)
J Eric Johnson, Fine Arts Division, see Dallas TX (L)
Jewish Community Center of Greater Washington, Jane L & Robert H Weiner Judaic Museum, see Rockville MD (M)
The Jewish Museum, New York NY (M,L)
JMW Turner Museum, Sarasota FL (M)
Joe Gish's Old West Museum, Fredericksburg TX (M)
John B Aird Gallery, Toronto ON (M)
John Brown University, Art Dept, see Siloam Springs AR (S)
John Carroll University, Dept of Art History & Humanities, see University Heights OH (S)
John Jay College of Criminal Justice, Dept of Art, Music & Philosophy, see New York NY (S)
The John L. Clarke Western Art Gallery & Memorial Museum, East Glacier Park MT (M)
John Orne Johnson Frost Gallery, see Marblehead Museum & Historical Society, Marblehead MA
Johns Hopkins University, Archaeological Museum, see Baltimore MD (M,L)
Johns Hopkins University, Dept of the History of Art, see Baltimore MD (S)
Johnson-Humrickhouse Museum, Coshocton OH (M)
Johnson Atelier Technical Institute of Sculpture, Trenton NJ (S)
Johnson Atelier Technical Institute of Sculpture, Johnson Atelier Library, see Mercerville NJ (L)
Johnson Collection of Photographs, Movies & Memorabilia, see Martin and Osa Johnson, Chanute KS
Johnson County Community College, Fine Arts Dept & Art History Dept, see Overland Park KS (S)
John G Johnson Collection, see Philadelphia Museum of Art, Philadelphia PA
Johnson State College, Dept Fine & Performing Arts, Dibden Center for the Arts, see Johnson VT (S)
Joliet Junior College, Fine Arts Dept, see Joliet IL (S)
Joliet Junior College, Laura A Sprague Art Gallery, see Joliet IL (M)
Bob Jones University Museum & Gallery Inc, Greenville SC (M)
Bob Jones University, School of Fine Arts, Div of Art & Design, see Greenville SC (S)
Jones County Junior College, Art Dept, see Ellisville MS (S)
James A Jones Library, see Brevard College, Brevard NC
Jones Library, Inc, Amherst MA (L)
Jones Memorial Library, Lynchburg VA (L)
Jordan Historical Museum of The Twenty, Jordan ON (M)
Jorgensen Auditorium, see University of Connecticut, Storrs CT
Joslyn Art Museum, Omaha NE (M)
The JPMorgan Chase, Art Collection, see New York NY
J Sargeant Reynolds Community College, Humanities & Social Science Division, see Richmond VA (S)
Judd Foundation, Marfa TX (M)
Judson College, Division of Fine and Performing Arts, see Marion AL (S)
Judson University, School of Art, Design & Architecture, see Elgin IL (S)
Juliette K and Leonard S Rakow Research Library, see Corning Museum of Glass, Corning NY
Junction City Arts Council Gallery, Junction City KS (M)
Juniata College, Dept of Art & Art History, see Huntingdon PA (S)
Juniata College Museum of Art, Huntingdon PA (M)
Juxtaposition Arts, Minneapolis MN (M)
Kaji Aso Studio, Gallery Nature & Temptation, see Boston MA (M)
Kala Institute, Kala Art Institute, see Berkeley CA (A)
Kalamazoo College, Art Dept, see Kalamazoo MI (S)
Kalamazoo Institute of Arts, Kalamazoo MI (M,L)
Kalamazoo Institute of Arts, KIA School, see Kalamazoo MI (S)
Kalamazoo Valley Community College, Center for New Media, see Kalamazoo MI (S)
Kamloops Art Gallery, Kamloops BC (M)
Kanab Heritage Museum & Juniper Fine Arts Gallery, Kanab UT (M)
Kansas City Art Institute, Kansas City MO (S)
Kansas City Artists Coalition, Kansas City MO (M)
Kansas City Jewish Museum of Contemporary Art - Epsten Gallery, Overland Park KS (M)
Kansas City Municipal Art Commission, Kansas City MO (A)
Kansas City Public Library, Kansas City MO (L)
Kansas State Historical Society, Kansas Museum of History, see Topeka KS (M)
Kansas State University, Art Dept, see Manhattan KS (S)
Kansas State University, Paul Weigel Library of Architecture Planning & Design, see Manhattan KS (L)
Kansas Watercolor Society, Mark Arts, see Wichita KS (A)
Kansas Wesleyan University, Art Dept, see Salina KS (S)
Kappa Pi International Honorary Art Fraternity, Cleveland MS (O)
Kateri Tekakwitha Shrine/St. Francis Xavier Mission, Kahnawake QC (M)
Katherine & Tom Belk Visual Arts Center, see Davidson College, Davidson NC
Katherine W Dumke Architecture Library, Marriott Library, see University of Utah, Salt Lake City UT
Katonah Museum of Art, Katonah NY (M)
Kauai Community College, Dept of Art, see Lihue HI (S)
Kauai Museum Association, Ltd, Lihue HI (M)
Kean University, Fine Arts Dept, see Union NJ (S)
Kean University, James Howe Gallery, see Union NJ (M,L)
Keene State College, Thorne-Sagendorph Art Gallery, see Keene NH (M)
Keil Resource Center, see Tubman African American Museum, Macon GA
Kellogg Community College, Arts & Communication Dept, see Battle Creek MI (S)
Kellogg Library & Reading Room, see 1890 House-Museum & Center for the Arts, Cortland NY
Kellogg Memorial Research Library, see Cortland County Historical Society, Cortland NY
Kelly-Griggs House Museum, Red Bluff CA (M)
Kelsey Museum of Archaeology, see University of Michigan, Ann Arbor MI
Kemp Center for the Arts, Wichita Falls TX (M)
Kendall College of Art & Design, Kendall Gallery, see Grand Rapids MI (L)
Kendall College of Art & Design of Ferris State University, Grand Rapids MI (S)
Kendall College of Art & Design, Urban Institute for Contemporary Arts, see Grand Rapids MI (M)
Kenkeleba House, Inc, Kenkeleba Gallery, see New York NY (A)
Kennebec Valley Art Association, Harlow Gallery, see Hallowell ME (A)
Kennedy Galleries, Kennedy Galleries, Inc, see New York NY (M)
John F Kennedy, Department of Arts & Consciousness, see Pleasant Hill CA (S)
The John F Kennedy Center for the Performing Arts, Washington DC (A)
Kenosha Public Museums, Kenosha WI (M)
Kent Art Association, Gallery, see Kent CT (A)
Kent State University, School of Art, see Kent OH (S)
Kent State University, School of Art Galleries, see Kent OH (M)
Kentuck Museum Association, Inc, Kentuck Art Center & Festival of the Arts, see Northport AL (M)
Kentucky Derby Museum, Louisville KY (M)
Kentucky Guild of Artists & Craftsmen Inc, Berea KY (A)
Kentucky Historical Society, Old State Capitol & Annex, see Frankfort KY (M,L)
Kentucky Museum of Art and Craft, Louisville KY (M)
Kentucky New State Capitol, Division of Historic Properties, see Frankfort KY (M)
Kentucky State University, Jackson Hall Gallery, see Frankfort KY (M)
Kentucky Wesleyan College, Dept Art, see Owensboro KY (S)
Kenyon College, Art Dept, see Gambier OH (S)
Kenyon College, Gund Gallery, see Gambier OH (M)
Keokuk Art Center, Keokuk IA (A)
Kern County Museum, Bakersfield CA (M,L)
Keystone College, Fine Arts Dept, see LaPlume PA (S)
Keystone Gallery, Scott City KS (M)
Key West Art & Historical Society, East Martello Museum & Gallery, see Key West FL (M)
Kiehle Gallery, see Saint Cloud State University, Saint Cloud MN
Kilgore College, Visual Arts Dept, see Kilgore TX (S)
Kimball Art Center, Park City UT (A)
Fiske Kimball Fine Arts Library, see University of Virginia, Charlottesville VA
Kimball Jenkins Estate, Concord NH (M)
Kimbell Art Foundation, Kimbell Art Museum, see Fort Worth TX (M)
Kimmel-Harding-Nelson Center for the Arts, Nebraska City NE (M)
Emma B King Library, see Shaker Museum & Library, New Lebanon NY
Gioconda & Joseph King Library, see The Society of the Four Arts, Palm Beach FL
King Kamehameha V Judiciary History Center, Honolulu HI (M)
Kingsborough Community College, CUNY, The Art Gallery at Kingsborough Community College, see Brooklyn NY (M)
Kingsborough Community College, Dept of Art, see Brooklyn NY (S)
Kings County Historical Society & Museum, Hampton NB (M)
Kirkland Art Center, Clinton NY (A)
Kirkland Arts Center, KAC Gallery, see Kirkland WA (M)
Kirkland Museum of Fine & Decorative Art, Denver CO (M)

Kirkwood Community College, Dept of Arts & Humanities, see Cedar Rapids IA (S)
Kishwaukee College, Art Dept, see Malta IL (S)
The Kitchen, New York NY (M)
Kitchener-Waterloo Art Gallery, Kitchener ON (M)
Klamath Art Association, Klamath Falls OR (A)
Klamath County Museum, Klamath Falls OR (M,L)
Klein Museum, Mobridge SD (M)
Robert Klein Gallery, Boston MA (M)
Knights of Columbus Supreme Council, Knights of Columbus Museum, see New Haven CT (M)
Knox College, Dept of Art, see Galesburg IL (S)
Knoxville Museum of Art, Knoxville TN (M)
Koffler Center of the Arts, Toronto ON (S)
Koffler Centre of the Arts, Koffler Gallery, see Toronto ON (M)
Kohler Art Library, see University of Wisconsin-Madison, Madison WI
Kohler Co, John Michael Kohler Arts Center - Arts/ Industry Program, see Sheboygan WI
Kohn Gallery, Los Angeles CA (M)
Koochiching Museums, International Falls MN (M)
Koshare Indian Museum, Inc, La Junta CO (M,L)
Kraft Education Center/Museum Education, see The Art Institute of Chicago, Chicago IL
Krasl Art Center, Saint Joseph MI (M)
The Kreeger Museum, Washington DC (M)
Joe Kubert, Dover NJ (S)
Kutztown University, College of Visual & Performing Arts, see Kutztown PA (S)
Kutztown University, The Martin & Regina Miller Gallery, see Kutztown PA (M,L)
L'Universite Laval, Ecole des Arts Visuels, see Quebec QC (M,L)
The Lab, San Francisco CA (M)
La Casa del Libro Museum, San Juan PR (M)
Lac du Flambeau Band of Lake Superior Chippewa Indians, George W Brown Jr Ojibwe Museum & Cultural Center, see Lac Du Flambeau WI (M)
LACE (Los Angeles Contemporary Exhibitions), Los Angeles CA (M)
La Centrale Powerhouse Gallery, Montreal QC (M)
La Chambre Blanche, Quebec QC (M)
Lachenmeyer Arts Center, Art Resource Library, see Cushing OK (L)
Lackawanna College, Fine Arts Dept, see Scranton PA (S)
LA County Museum of Art, Los Angeles CA (M,L)
Lafayette College, Dept of Art, see Easton PA (S)
Lafayette College, Lafayette College Art Galleries, see Easton PA (M)
Lafayette Museum Association, Lafayette Museum-Alexandre Mouton House, see Lafayette LA (M)
Lafayette Science Museum & Planetarium, Lafayette LA (M)
LaGrange Art Museum, LaGrange GA (M)
LaGrange College, Lamar Dodd Art Center Museum, see LaGrange GA (M)
LaGrange College, Lamar Dodd Art Center Museum, see LaGrange GA (S)
Laguna Art Museum, Laguna Beach CA (M)
Laguna College of Art & Design, Dennis & Leslie Power Library, see Laguna Beach CA (L)
La Hacienda de Los Martinez, see Taos Historic Museums, Taos NM
Lahaina Arts Society, Art Organization, see Lahaina HI (A)
Lake County Civic Center Association, Inc, Heritage Museum & Gallery, see Leadville CO (A)
Lake Erie College, Fine Arts Dept, see Painesville OH (S)
Lake Forest College, Dept of Art, see Lake Forest IL (S)
Lake Forest Library, Fine Arts Dept, see Lake Forest IL (L)
Lake George Arts Project, Courthouse Gallery, see Lake George NY (M)
Lakehead University, Dept of Visual Arts, see Thunder Bay ON (S)
Lakeland Community College, Fine Arts Department, see Kirtland OH (S)
Lake Michigan College, Dept of Art & Science, see Benton Harbor MI (S)
Lake Pontchartrain Basin Maritime Museum, Madisonville LA
Lakeside Studio, Lakeside MI (M)
Lake Tahoe Community College, Art Dept, see South Lake Tahoe CA (S)
La MaMa La Galleria, New York NY (M)
Lamar University, Art Dept, see Beaumont TX (S)
Lamar University, Dishman Art Museum, see Beaumont TX (M)
Lambuth University, Dept of Human Ecology & Visual Arts, see Jackson TN (S)
La Napoule Art Foundation, Chateau de la Napoule, see Denver CO (A)
Lancaster County Art Association, Inc, Strasburg PA (A)
Lancaster Museum of Art, Lancaster PA (M)
Clara Lander Library & Archives, see The Winnipeg Art Gallery, Winnipeg MB
Lander University, College of Arts & Humanities - Visual Arts, see Greenwood SC (S)
Landis Valley Village and Farm Museum, PA Historical & Museum Commission, Lancaster PA (M,L)
Landmark Society of Western New York, Inc, The Campbell-Whittlesey House Museum, see Rochester NY (M,L)
Lane Arts Council, Jacobs Gallery, see Eugene OR (M)
Lane Community College, Art & Applied Design Dept, see Eugene OR (S)
Lane Community College, LCC Art Gallery, see Eugene OR (M)
Lanesboro Arts Center, Lanesboro MN (M)
Laney College, Art Dept, see Oakland CA (S)
Laney College Library, Art Section, see Oakland CA (L)
Langara College, Dept of Fine Arts, see Vancouver BC (S)
Langston University, Melvin B Tolson Black Heritage Center, see Langston OK (M)
Lannan Foundation, Santa Fe NM (O)
Lansing Art Gallery, Lansing MI (M)
Lansing Community College, Visual Arts & Media Dept, see Lansing MI (S)
Laramie County Community College, Division of Arts & Humanities, see Cheyenne WY (S)
Laredo Center for the Arts, Laredo TX (M)
La Roche College, Division of Design, see Pittsburgh PA (S)
Mabel Larsen Fine Arts Gallery, see Austin Peay State University, Clarksville TN
La Salle University Art Museum, Philadelphia PA (M)
La Salle University, Dept of Art, see Philadelphia PA (S)
La Sierra University, Art Dept, see Riverside CA (S)
Las Vegas-Clark County Library District, Las Vegas NV (L,M)
Las Vegas Natural History Museum, Las Vegas NV (M)
Latino Art Museum, Pomona CA (M)
Latino Center of Art and Culture, Sacramento CA (M)
Latitude 53 Contemporary Visual Culture, Edmonton AB (A)
Lauinger Library - Special Collections Division, see Georgetown University, Washington DC
Laumeier Sculpture Park, Saint Louis MO (M)
Laurel Arts, Somerset PA (M)
Laurens County Historical Society, Dublin-Laurens Museum, see Dublin GA (M)
Laurentian University, Museum & Art Centre, see Sudbury ON (M,L)
Lawndale Art Center, Houston TX (M)
Lawrence Technological University, College of Architecture, see Southfield MI (S)
Lawrence University, Dept of Art & Art History, see Appleton WI (S)
Lawrence University, Wriston Art Center Galleries, see Appleton WI (M)
League of New Hampshire Craftsmen, Grodin Permanent Collection Museum, see Concord NH (M,L)
Leanin' Tree Museum & Sculpture Garden of Western Art, Boulder CO (M)
Lee Arts Center, Arlington VA (M)
Lee Chapel & Museum, see Washington & Lee University, Lexington VA
Lee County Library, Tupelo MS (L)
Leedy-Voulkos Art Center, Kansas City MO (M)
Harold B Lee Library, see Brigham Young University, Provo UT
Jeremiah Lee Mansion, see Marblehead Museum & Historical Society, Marblehead MA
Leelanau Historical Museum, Leland MI (M)
Leesburg Center for the Arts, Leesburg FL (M)
Lee University, Dept of Communication & the Arts, see Cleveland TN (S)
Leeward Community College, Arts & Humanities Division, see Pearl City HI (S)
Left of Center Art Gallery & Studio, North Las Vegas NV (M)
Legacy Ltd, Bellevue WA (M)
Legion of Honor, see Fine Arts Museums of San Francisco, San Francisco CA
Lehigh University Art Galleries, Museum Operation, see Bethlehem PA (M)
Lehigh University, Dept of Art, Architecture & Design, see Bethlehem PA (S)
Lehigh Valley Heritage Center, Allentown PA (M,L)
Lehman College Art Gallery, Bronx NY (M)
Herbert H Lehman, Art Dept, see Bronx NY (S)
Leigh Yawkey Woodson Art Museum, Wausau WI (M)
Lemmerman Art Gallery, see New Jersey City University, Jersey City NJ
LeMoyne Art Foundation, Center for the Visual Arts, see Tallahassee FL (M)
Le Moyne College, Visual & Performing Arts Dept, see Syracuse NY (S)
Le Moyne College, Wilson Art Gallery, see Syracuse NY (M)
Le Musee Regional de Rimouski, Centre National d'Exposition, see Rimouski QC (M,L)
Lenoir Community College, Dept of Visual Art, see Kinston NC (S)
Lenoir Rhyne College, Dept of Art, see Hickory NC (S)
LeRoy Historical Society, The Jell-O Gallery, see LeRoy NY (A)
Les Editions Intervention, Inter-Le Lieu, Documentation Center, see Quebec QC (L)
Dean Lesher, Bedford Gallery, see Walnut Creek CA (M)
Lesley University, College of Art & Design, see Cambridge MA (S)
Lesley University, Roberts Gallery, see Cambridge MA (M,L)
LeSueur Museum, Le Sueur MN (M)
Lethbridge Public Library, Art Gallery, see Lethbridge AB (L)
Lewis & Clark College, Dept of Art, see Portland OR (S)
Lewis & Clark Community College, Art Dept, see Godfrey IL (S)
Lewis-Clark State College, Art Dept, see Lewiston ID (S)
Lewistown Art Center, Lewistown MT (A)
Lexington Art League, Inc, Lexington KY (A)
Leyburn Library, see Washington & Lee University, Lexington VA
Liberty Hall Historic Site, Liberty Hall Museum, see Frankfort KY (M,L)
Liberty Life Insurance Company, Greenville SC
Liberty Memorial Museum & Archives, The National Museum of World War I, see Kansas City MO (M)
Liberty Village Arts Center & Gallery, Chester MT (M)
Library Association of La Jolla, Athenaeum Music & Arts Library, see La Jolla CA (L)
Library Company of Philadelphia, Philadelphia PA (L)
Library of Congress, Prints & Photographs Division, see Washington DC (L)
Licking County Arts, Art Gallery, see Newark OH (M)

The Light Factory, Charlotte NC (M)
Lighthouse ArtCenter Museum & School of Art, Tequesta FL (M,L)
Lightner Museum, Saint Augustine FL (M)
Light Work, Robert B Menschel Photography Gallery, see Syracuse NY (A)
Lilly Art Library, see Duke University, Durham NC
Limestone College, Art Dept, see Gaffney SC (S)
Lincoln Arts Council, Lincoln NE (A)
Lincoln College, Art Dept, see Lincoln IL (S)
Lincoln County Historical Association, Inc, Pownalborough Courthouse, see Wiscasset ME (A, L,M)
Lincoln Memorial Shrine, Redlands CA (L)
Lincoln Memorial University, Division of Humanities, see Harrogate TN (S)
Lincoln University, Dept Visual and Performing Arts, see Jefferson City MO (S)
Lindenwood College, Art Dept, see Saint Charles MO (S)
Lindenwood University, Harry D Hendren Gallery, see Saint Charles MO (M)
Luke Lindoe Library, see Alberta College of Art & Design, Calgary AB
The Lindsay Gallery Inc, Lindsay ON (M)
Linfield College, Department of Art & Visual Culture, see McMinnville OR (S)
Linn Benton Community College, Fine & Applied Art Dept, see Albany OR (S)
Litchfield History Museum, Litchfield CT (A,L)
Lucille Little Fine Arts Library, see The University of Kentucky Art Museum, Lexington KY
Little River Hotglass Studio & Gallery, Moscow VT (M)
Maurine Littleton Gallery, Washington DC (M)
Living Arts & Science Center, Inc, Lexington KY (M)
Livingston Center for Art & Culture, Livingston MT (M)
Livingston County Historical Society, Museum, see Geneseo NY (M)
Lizzadro Museum of Lapidary Art, Elmhurst IL (M)
Lloydminster Cultural & Science Centre, Lloydminster SK (A)
The Loading Dock Gallery, Lowell MA (M)
Lock Haven University, Dept of Fine Arts, see Lock Haven PA (S)
Lockwood-Mathews Mansion Museum, Norwalk CT (M)
Locust Street Neighborhood Art Classes, Inc, Buffalo NY (S)
Frances Loeb Library, see Harvard University, Cambridge MA
Lois Wagner Fine Arts, New York NY
Jack London, House of Happy Walls, see Glen Ellen CA (M)
Long Beach Art League, Long Beach Library, see Long Beach NY (L)
Long Beach City College, Art & Photography Dept, see Long Beach CA (S)
Long Beach Island Foundation of the Arts & Sciences, Loveladies NJ (M)
Long Beach Museum of Art Foundation, Long Beach Museum of Art, see Long Beach CA (M,L)
Long Beach Public Library, Long Beach NY (L)
Long Branch Historical Association Church of the Presidents Museum, Long Branch NJ (M)
Earl K Long Library, see University of New Orleans, New Orleans LA
Longfellow's Wayside Inn Museum, Sudbury MA (M)
Longfellow-Evangeline State Commemorative Area, Saint Martinville LA (M)
Longfellow National Historic Site, Longfellow House - Washington's Headquarters, see Cambridge MA (M)
The Long Island Museum of American Art, History & Carriages, Stony Brook NY (M,L)
Long Island University, Brooklyn Campus, Art Dept, see Brooklyn NY (S)
Longue Vue House & Gardens, New Orleans LA (M)
Longview Museum of Fine Art, Longview TX (M)
Longwood Center for the Visual Arts, Farmville VA (A)
Longwood University, Dept of Art, see Farmville VA (S)
The Loomis Chaffee School, Mercy Gallery, see Windsor CT (M)
Lorain County Community College, Art Dept, see Elyria OH (S)
Loras College, Dept of Art, see Dubuque IA (S)
Loren D. Callendar Gallery, Sioux City IA (M)
Lee Alexander Lorick Library, see Columbia Museum of Art, Columbia SC
Lorton Arts Foundation, Workhouse Arts Center, see Lorton VA (M)
Los Angeles City College, School of Visual & Media Arts, see Los Angeles CA (S)
Los Angeles County Museum of Art, Los Angeles CA (M,L)
Los Angeles County Museum of Natural History, William S Hart Museum, see Newhall CA (M)
Los Angeles Harbor College, Art Dept, see Wilmington CA (S)
Los Angeles Public Library, Art, Music, Recreation & Rare Books, see Los Angeles CA (L)
Los Angeles Valley College, Art Dept, see Van Nuys CA (S)
Los Angeles Valley College, Art Gallery, see Valley Glen CA (M)
Louisa May Alcott Memorial Association, Orchard House, see Concord MA (A)
Louisburg College, Art Gallery, see Louisburg NC (M)
Louise Hopkins Underwood Center for the Arts, Lubbock TX (M)
Louisiana Arts & Science Museum, Baton Rouge LA (M,L)
Louisiana College, Dept of Art, see Pineville LA (S)
Louisiana Department of Culture, Recreation & Tourism, Louisiana State Museum, see New Orleans LA (M,L)
Louisiana Pottery, Sorrento LA (M)
Louisiana State Museum, see Louisiana Department of Culture, Recreation & Tourism,
Louisiana State University at Alexandria, Dept of Fine Arts & Design, see Alexandria LA (S)
Louisiana State University at Alexandria, University Gallery, see Alexandria LA (M)
Louisiana State University, Museum of Art, see Baton Rouge LA (M,L)
Louisiana State University, School of Art, see Baton Rouge LA (S)
Louisiana State University School of Art, Alfred C Glassell Jr Exhibition Gallery, see Baton Rouge LA (M)
Louisiana Tech, School of Art, see Ruston LA (S)
Louisville Visual Art, Louisville KY (A)
Lourdes College, Duns Scotus Library, see Sylvania OH (L)
Lourdes University, Art Dept, see Sylvania OH (S)
Loveland Museum/Gallery, Loveland CO (M)
Lowell Art Association, Inc, Whistler House Museum of Art, see Lowell MA (A)
Lower Columbia College, Art Dept, see Longview WA (S)
Lower East Side Printshop Inc, New York NY (S)
Loyola Marymount University, Dept of Art & Art History, see Los Angeles CA (S)
Loyola Marymount University, Laband Art Gallery, see Los Angeles CA (M)
Loyola University Chicago, Loyola University Museum of Art, see Chicago IL (M)
Loyola University of Chicago, Dept of Fine and Performing Arts, see Chicago IL (S)
Loyola University of New Orleans, Dept of Visual Arts, see New Orleans LA (S)
Lubbock Christian University, Dept of Communication & Fine Art, see Lubbock TX (S)
Lunenburg Art Gallery Society, Lunenburg NS (M)
Evan Lurie Fine Art Gallery, Carmel IN (M)
Lutheran Theological Seminary, Krauth Memorial Library, see Philadelphia PA (L)
Luther College, Art Dept, see Decorah IA (S)
Luther College, Fine Arts Collection, see Decorah IA (M)
Luykas Van Alen House, see Columbia County Historical Society, Kinderhook NY
Luzerne County Community College, Commercial Art Dept, see Nanticoke PA (S)
Lycoming College, Art Dept, see Williamsport PA (S)
Lycoming College Gallery, Williamsport PA (M)
Lyman Allyn Art Museum, New London CT (M,L)
Lyme Academy College of Fine Arts, Old Lyme CT (S)
Lyme Academy College of Fine Arts, Krieble Library, see Old Lyme CT (L,M)
Lyme Art Association, Inc, Old Lyme CT (A)
Lyme Historical Society, Florence Griswold Museum, see Old Lyme CT (M,L)
Lynchburg College, Art Dept, see Lynchburg VA (S)
Lynchburg College, Daura Gallery, see Lynchburg VA (M)
Tom Lynch Resource Center, see Dillman's Creative Arts Foundation, Lac du Flambeau WI
Lyndon House Art, Athens GA (M)
Lynn Arts, Lynn MA (M)
Lynn University, Art & Design Dept, see Boca Raton FL (S)
Lynnwood Arts Centre, Simcoe ON (A)
Lyon College Kresge Gallery, Batesville AR (M)
Mabee-Gerrer Museum of Art, Shawnee OK (M)
Macalester College, Art & Art History Dept, see Saint Paul MN (S)
Macalester College, Macalester College Art Gallery, see Saint Paul MN (M,L)
MacArthur Memorial, Norfolk VA (M,L)
Macartney House Museum, Oakland ME (M)
MacKenzie Art Gallery Resource Centre, see University of Regina, Regina SK
MacMurray College, Art Dept, see Jacksonville IL (S)
Madison & Main Gallery, Greeley CO (M)
Madison Area Technical College, Art Dept, see Madison WI (S)
Madison County Historical Society, Cottage Lawn, see Oneida NY (M)
Madison Museum of Contemporary Art, Madison WI (M)
Madison Museum of Fine Art, Madison GA (M)
Madonna University, College of Arts & Humanities, see Livonia MI (S)
The Magnes Collection of Jewish Art and Life, see University of California, Berkeley, Berkeley CA
Magnum Opus, Sterling VA (S)
Maharishi University of Management, Department of Art, see Fairfield IA (A)
Maine Art Gallery, see Lincoln County Historical Association, Inc, Wiscasset ME
Maine College of Art, Portland ME (S)
Maine College of Art, Joanne Waxman Library, see Portland ME (L,M)
Maine Historical Society, Portland ME (A,M,L)
Maine Maritime Museum, Bath ME (M,L)
Maine Photographic Workshops, The International T.V. & Film Workshops & Rockport College, Rockport ME (S)
Main Line Art Center, Haverford PA (S)
Main Line Art Center, Haverford PA (A)
Main Street Museum, White River Junction VT (M)
Maison de la Culture, Centre d'exposition Raymond-Lasnier, see Trois Rivieres QC (A)
Maison Saint-Gabriel Museum, Montreal QC (M)
Malden Public Library, Art Dept & Gallery, see Malden MA (L)
Malone University, Dept of Art, see Canton OH (S)
Mana Contemporary, Jersey City NJ (M)
Manchester Bidwell Corporation, Manchester Craftsmen's Guild Youth & Arts Program, see Pittsburgh PA (M)
Manchester City Library, Manchester NH (L)
Manchester College, Dept of Art, see North Manchester IN (S)
Manchester Community College, Visual Fine Art Dept, see Manchester CT (S)
Manchester Historic Association, Millyard Museum, see Manchester NH (A,L)

Manhattan College, Visual & Performing Arts Dept, see Bronx NY (S)
Manhattan Graphics Center, New York NY (S)
Manhattanville College, Art Dept, see Purchase NY (S)
Manhattanville College, Brownson Gallery, see Purchase NY (M,L)
Manifest Gallery, Cincinnati OH (M)
Joseph Manigault House, see Charleston Museum, Charleston SC
Manitoba Association of Architects, Winnipeg MB (A)
Manitoba Society of Artists, Winnipeg MB (A)
Mankato Area Arts Council, Carnegie Art Center, see Mankato MN (M)
Mankato State University, Art Dept, see Mankato MN (S)
Mansfield Fine Arts Guild, Mansfield Art Center, see Mansfield OH (A,L)
Mansfield University, Art Dept, see Mansfield PA (S)
Maple Woods Community College, Dept of Art & Art History, see Kansas City MO (S)
Marblehead Arts Association, Inc, Marblehead MA (A)
Marblehead Museum & Historical Society, Marblehead MA (M,L)
Marcella Sembrich Memorial Association Inc, Marcella Sembrich Opera Museum, see Bolton Landing NY (A)
The Margaret & H A Rey Center and Curious George Cottage, Waterville Valley NH (M)
Marian Library, see Daemen College, Amherst NY
Marian University, Allison Mansion, see Indianapolis IN (M)
Marian University, Art Dept, see Fond Du Lac WI (S)
Marian University, Visual Arts Dept, see Indianapolis IN (S)
Maricopa County Historical Society, Desert Caballeros Western Museum, see Wickenburg AZ (M,L)
Marietta-Cobb Museum of Art, Marietta GA (M)
Marietta College, Art Dept, see Marietta OH (S)
Marietta College, Grover M Hermann Fine Arts Center, see Marietta OH (M)
Marin County Watercolor Society, Corte Madera CA (A)
Marine Corps University, National Museum of the Marine Corps, see Triangle VA (M)
The Mariners' Museum, Newport News VA (M,L)
Marin Society of Artists Inc, San Rafael CA (A)
Marion Art Center, Cecil Clark Davis Gallery, see Marion MA (A)
Maritime Library, see San Francisco Maritime National Historical Park, San Francisco CA
Maritime Museum of Monterey, see Monterey History & Art Association, Monterey CA
Maritime Museum of San Diego, San Diego CA (M)
Maritz, Inc, Library, see Fenton MO (L)
Marquand Library of Art & Archaeology, see Princeton University, Princeton NJ
Marquette University, Haggerty Museum of Art, see Milwaukee WI (M)
John Marshall House, see Preservation Virginia, Richmond VA
Marshall University, Dept of Art & Design, see Huntington WV (S)
Mars Hill College, Art Dept, see Mars Hill NC (S)
Martha's Vineyard Center for the Visual Arts, Oak Bluffs MA (A)
Martin and Osa Johnson, Chanute KS (M,L)
Martin Memorial Library, York PA (L)
Mary Baldwin College, Dept of Art & Art History, see Staunton VA (S)
Marygrove College, Department of Art, see Detroit MI (S)
Mary H. Dana Women Artists Series, a Partnership of the Center for Women in the Arts & Humanities and Rutgers University Libraries, see Rutgers, The State University of New Jersey, New Brunswick NJ
Maryhill Museum of Art, Goldendale WA (M)
Maryland-National Capital Park & Planning Commission, Montpelier Arts Center, see Laurel MD (M)
Maryland Art Place, Baltimore MD (M)
Maryland College of Art & Design, Silver Spring MD (S)
Maryland Hall for the Creative Arts, Chaney Gallery, see Annapolis MD (M)
Maryland Historical Society, Museum of Maryland History, see Baltimore MD (M,L)
Maryland Institute, College of Art, see Baltimore MD (S)
Marylhurst University, Art Dept, see Marylhurst OR (S)
Marylhurst University, The Art Gym, see Marylhurst OR (M)
Marymount Manhattan College, Fine & Performing Arts Div, see New York NY (S)
Marymount Manhattan College Hewitt Gallery, New York NY (M)
Marymount University, School of Arts & Sciences Div, see Arlington VA (S)
Mary R Koch Arts Center, Mark Arts, see Wichita KS (A)
Mary R Schiff Library & Archives, see Cincinnati Art Museum, Cincinnati OH
Maryville College, Dept of Fine Arts, see Maryville TN (S)
Maryville College, Fine Arts Center Gallery, see Maryville TN (M)
Maryville University of Saint Louis, Art & Design Program, see Saint Louis MO (S)
Maryville University Saint Louis, Morton J May Foundation Gallery, see Saint Louis MO (M)
Marywood University, Art Dept, see Scranton PA (S)
Mason City Public Library, Mason City IA (L)
Massachusetts College of Art, Boston MA (S)
Massachusetts College of Art and Design, Library, see Boston MA (L,M)
Massachusetts Historical Society, Boston MA (A,L)
Massachusetts Institute of Technology, List Visual Arts Center, see Cambridge MA (M,L)
Massachusetts Institute of Technology, School of Architecture and Planning, see Cambridge MA (S)
Massillon Museum, Massillon OH (M)
The Mather Homestead Museum, Library & Memorial Park, Wellsville NY (M)
The Mathers Museum of World Cultures, see Indiana University, Bloomington IN
Mattatuck Historical Society, Mattatuck Museum, see Waterbury CT (M)
Mattawoman Creek Art Center, Marbury MD (M)
The Mattress Factory, Pittsburgh PA (M)
Maude Kerns, Eugene OR (S)
Maude Kerns Art Center, Eugene OR (M)
Maui Community College, Art Program, see Kahului HI (S)
Maui Crafts Guild, Paia HI (M)
Maui Historical Society, Hale Hoike ike at the Bailey House, see Wailuku HI (M)
Maysville, Kentucky Gateway Museum Center, see Maysville KY (M)
Mayville State University, Northern Lights Art Gallery, see Mayville ND (M)
Mazza Museum, The University of Findlay, see Findlay OH (M)
McCarthy Gallery, Colchester VT (M)
Alameda McCollough Library, see Tippecanoe County Historical Association, Lafayette IN
McCord Museum of Canadian History, Montreal QC (M)
Harold McCracken Research Library, see Buffalo Bill Memorial Association, Cody WY
McDaniel College, Esther Prangley Rice Gallery, see Westminster MD (M)
McDonald's Corporation, Art Collection, see Oak Brook IL
McDowell House & Apothecary Shop, Danville KY (M)
McGill University, Blackader-Lauterman Library of Architecture and Art, see Montreal QC (L)
McGill University, Dept of Art History & Communication Studies, see Montreal QC (S)
McGroarty Cultural Art Center, Tujunga CA (S)
The McKinney Avenue Contemporary (The MAC), Dallas TX (M)
The Robert McLaughlin Gallery, Oshawa ON (M,L)
McLean County Art Association, McLean County Arts Center, see Bloomington IL (A)
McLean County Historical Society, McLean County Museum of History, see Bloomington IL (M)
McLennan Community College, Visual Arts Dept, see Waco TX (S)
McMaster University, McMaster Museum of Art, see Hamilton ON (M)
McMaster University, School of the Arts, see Hamilton ON (S)
McMichael Canadian Art Collection, Kleinburg ON (M, L)
McMurry University, Art Dept, see Abilene TX (S)
McMurry University, Ryan Fine Arts Center, see Abilene TX (M)
McNay Art Museum, San Antonio TX (M,L)
McNeese State University, Dept of Visual Arts, Abercrombie Gallery and Grand Gallery, see Lake Charles LA (M)
McNeese State University, Dept of Visual Arts, see Lake Charles LA (S)
McPherson College, Art Dept, see McPherson KS (S)
McPherson College Gallery, McPherson KS (M)
McPherson Museum and Arts Foundation, McPherson KS (M)
Meadows Museum, see Southern Methodist University, Dallas TX
Meadville Council on the Arts, Meadville PA (A)
Mechanics' Institute, San Francisco CA (L)
Medicine Hat Public Library, Medicine Hat AB (L)
Medina Railroad Museum, Medina NY (M)
Jerald Melberg Gallery, Charlotte NC (M)
Memorial Library, see Berry College, Mount Berry GA
Memorial Union Art Gallery, see Oregon State University, Corvallis OR
Memorial Union Gallery, see Arizona State University, Tempe AZ
Memorial University of Newfoundland, Sir Wilfred Grenfell College Art Gallery, see Corner Brook NF (M)
Memphis-Shelby County Public Library & Information Center, Humanities Department, see Memphis TN (L)
Memphis Brooks Museum of Art, Memphis TN (M,L)
Memphis College of Art, Memphis TN (S)
Memphis College of Art, G Pillow Lewis Memorial Library, see Memphis TN (L)
Mendocino Art Center, Mendocino CA (S)
Mendocino Art Center, Gallery & School, see Mendocino CA (A,L)
Menil Foundation, Inc, The Menil Collection, see Houston TX (M)
Mennello Museum of American Art, Orlando FL (M)
Merced College, Arts Division, see Merced CA (S)
Mercer County Community College, Arts, Communication & Engineering Technology, see West Windsor NJ (S)
Mercer County Community College, The Gallery at Mercer, see West Windsor NJ (M,L)
Mercer Museum Research Library, see Bucks County Historical Society, Doylestown PA
Mercer Union, A Centre for Contemporary Art, see Toronto ON (M)
Mercer University, Art Dept, see Macon GA (S)
Mercyhurst University, Dept of Art, see Erie PA (S)
Meredith College, Art Dept, see Raleigh NC (S)
Meredith College, Frankie G Weems Gallery & Rotunda Gallery, see Raleigh NC (M)
Meriam Library, see California State University, Chico, Chico CA
Meridian International Center, Cafritz Galleries, see Washington DC (M)
Meridian Museum of Art, Meridian MS (M)
Merrick Art Gallery, New Brighton PA (M)
Merritt College, Art Dept, see Oakland CA (S)
Mesa Arts Center, Mesa Contemporary Arts Museum, see Mesa AZ (M)
Mesa Community College, Dept of Art, see Mesa AZ (S)

Mesa Public Library Art Gallery, Los Alamos NM (M)
Laura & Paul Mesaros Galleries, see West Virginia University, Morgantown WV
Mesa Verde National Park, Research Library, see Mesa Verde National Park CO (L)
Mesquite Fine Arts Center & Gallery, Mesquite NV (M)
The Met Cloisters, see The Metropolitan Museum of Art, New York NY
Methodist College, Art Dept, see Fayetteville NC (S)
Metropolitan Community College - Penn Valley, Art Dept, see Kansas City MO (S)
The Metropolitan Museum of Art, New York NY (M,L)
Metropolitan State University of Denver, Art Dept, see Denver CO (S)
Metropolitan State University of Denver, Center for Visual Art, see Denver CO (M)
MEXIC-ARTE Museum, Austin TX (A)
The Mexican Museum, San Francisco CA (M)
Mexico-Audrain County Library, Mexico MO (L)
Mhiripiri Gallery, Bloomington MN (M)
MHS Museum, see Maine Historical Society, Portland ME
Miami-Dade College, Kendal Campus, Art Gallery, see Miami FL (M)
Miami-Dade College, MDC Museum of Art & Design, see Miami FL (M)
Miami-Dade Community College, Arts & Philosophy Dept, see Miami FL (S)
Miami-Dade Public Library, Miami FL (L)
Miami University, Art Dept, see Oxford OH (S)
Miami University, Art Museum, see Oxford OH (M,L)
Miami University, Dept Fine Arts, see Hamilton OH (S)
Simon Michael, Lena MS (S)
Michelson Museum of Art, Marshall TX (M)
Michigan Art & Artist Archives, see Art Center of Battle Creek, Battle Creek MI
Michigan Guild of Artists & Artisans, Michigan Guild Gallery, see Ann Arbor MI (A)
Michigan State University, Dept of Art & Art History, see East Lansing MI (S)
Michigan State University, Eli & Edythe Broad Art Museum, see East Lansing MI (M)
Mid-America All-Indian Center, Indian Center Museum, see Wichita KS (M,L)
Mid-America Arts Alliance & Exhibits USA, Kansas City MO (O)
Middle Border Museum & Oscar Howe Art Center, Mitchell SD (M)
Middlebury College, History of Art & Architecture Dept, see Middlebury VT (S)
Middlebury College, Museum of Art, see Middlebury VT (M)
Middle Georgia State University, College of Arts & Sciences, Media, Culture & the Arts, see Cochran GA (S)
Middlesex Community College, Fine Arts Div, see Middletown CT (S)
Middlesex County College, Visual Arts Dept, see Edison NJ (S)
Middlesex County Cultural & Heritage Commission, New Brunswick NJ (A)
Middle Tennessee State University, Art Dept, see Murfreesboro TN (S)
Middle Tennessee State University, Baldwin Photographic Gallery, see Murfreesboro TN (M)
Middletown Arts Center, Middletown OH (A,L)
Midland Center for the Arts, Alden B Dow Museum of Science & Art, see Midland MI (M)
Midland College, Art Dept, see Midland TX (S)
Midmarch Associates/Midmarch Arts Press, Midmarch Arts Press and Library, see New York NY (L)
Midtown Art Center, Houston TX (M)
Midway College, Art Dept, see Midway KY (S)
Midwest Art Conservation Center, Minneapolis MN (A)
Midwest Art History Society, Waco TX (O)
Midwestern State University, Lamar D. Fain College of Fine Arts, see Wichita Falls TX (S)
Midwest Museum of American Art, Elkhart IN (M)
Mildred R & Frederick M Mayer Library, see Dallas Museum of Art, Dallas TX
Miles B Carpenter Folk Art Museum, Waverly VA (M)
Miles Community College, Dept of Fine Arts & Humanities, see Miles City MT (S)
Miller Art Center Foundation Inc, Miller Art Museum, see Sturgeon Bay WI (M)
E Kirkbride Miller Art Library, see The Baltimore Museum of Art, Baltimore MD
Millersville University, Dept of Art & Design, see Millersville PA (S)
Millicent Rogers Museum, Taos NM (M)
Millikin University, Art Dept, see Decatur IL (S)
Millikin University, Perkinson Gallery, see Decatur IL (M)
Millsaps College, Dept of Art, see Jackson MS (S)
Mills College, Art Dept, see Oakland CA (S)
Mills College Art Museum, Oakland CA (M)
Milwaukee Area Technical College, School of Media & Creative Arts, see Milwaukee WI (S)
Milwaukee Art Museum, Milwaukee WI (M,L)
Milwaukee Institute of Art & Design, Milwaukee WI (S)
Milwaukee Institute of Art & Design, Library, see Milwaukee WI (L)
Milwaukee Public Library, Art, Music & Recreation Dept, see Milwaukee WI (L)
Milwaukee Public Museum, Milwaukee WI (M)
Mingei International, Inc, Mingei International Museum - Balboa Park & Mingei International Museum - Escondido, see San Diego CA (M,L)
Minneapolis College of Art & Design, Minneapolis MN (S)
Minneapolis College of Art & Design, Library, see Minneapolis MN (L)
Minneapolis Institute of Art, Minneapolis MN (M,L,A)
Minnesota Historical Society, Minnesota State Capitol Historic Site, see Saint Paul MN (M)
Minnesota Museum of American Art, Saint Paul MN (M)
Minnesota State University, Mankato, Mankato MN (M)
Minnesota State University-Moorhead, Dept of Art & Design, see Moorhead MN (S)
Minnetonka Center for the Arts, Wayzata MN (M)
Minot State University, Dept of Art, Division of Humanities, see Minot ND (S)
Minot State University, Northwest Art Center, see Minot ND (M)
The Mint Museum, Charlotte NC (M,L)
Mint Museum of Craft & Design, see The Mint Museum, Charlotte NC
Miracle at Pentecost Foundation, Biblical Arts Center, see Dallas TX (M)
Miracosta College, Art Dept, see Oceanside CA (S)
Mission Cultural Center for Latino Arts, San Francisco CA (M)
Mission San Luis Rey de Francia, Mission San Luis Rey Museum, see Oceanside CA (M)
Mission San Miguel Museum, San Miguel CA (M)
Mississauga Library System, Mississauga ON (L)
Mississippi Art Colony, Stoneville MS (A)
Mississippi College, Art Dept, see Clinton MS (S)
Mississippi Delta Community College, Dept of Fine Arts, see Moorhead MS (S)
Mississippi Gulf Coast Community College-Jackson County Campus, Art Dept, see Gautier MS (S)
Mississippi Museum of Art, Jackson MS (M,L)
Mississippi River Museum at Mud-Island River Park, Memphis TN (M)
Mississippi State University, Dept of Art, see Starville MS (S)
Mississippi University for Women, Division of Fine & Performing Arts, see Columbus MS (S)
Mississippi University for Women, Fine Arts Gallery, see Columbus MS (M)
Mississippi Valley Conservation Authority, R Tait McKenzie Memorial Museum, see Almonte ON (M)
Mississippi Valley State University, Fine Arts Dept, see Itta Bena MS (S)
Missoula Art Museum, Missoula MT (M)
Missouri Department of Natural Resources, Missouri State Museum, see Jefferson City MO (M)
Missouri Historical Society, Missouri History Museum, see Saint Louis MO (M)
Missouri Southern State University, Dept of Art, see Joplin MO (S)
Missouri State University, Dept of Art & Design, see Springfield MO (S)
Missouri Western State University, Gallery 206 Foyer Gallery, see Saint Joseph MO (M)
Missouri Western State University, School of Fine Arts, see Saint Joseph MO (S)
Arthur Roy Mitchell, A.R. Mitchell Museum, see Trinidad CO (M)
Mitchell Community College, Visual Art Dept, see Statesville NC (S)
MIT Museum, see Massachusetts Institute of Technology, Cambridge MA
Mizel Museum, Denver CO (M)
Mobile Museum of Art, Mobile AL (M,L)
Mobius Inc, Cambridge MA (A)
MoCADA - The Museum of Contemporary African Diasporan Arts, Brooklyn NY (M)
Modern Art Museum, Fort Worth TX (M)
Modernism, San Francisco CA (M)
Modesto Junior College, Arts Humanities & Communications Division, see Modesto CA (S)
Mohave Museum of History & Arts, Kingman AZ (M)
Mohawk Valley Center for the Arts Inc, Little Falls NY (M)
Mohawk Valley Community College, Utica NY (S)
Mohawk Valley Heritage Association, Inc, Walter Elwood Museum, see Amsterdam NY (M)
Momenta Art, Brooklyn NY (M)
Monarch Contemporary Art Center & Sculpture Park, Olympia WA (M)
Moncur Gallery, Boissevain MB (M)
MonDak Heritage Center, History Library, see Sidney MT (M)
Monhegan Museum, Monhegan Museum of Art & History, see Monhegan ME (M)
Monmouth College, Dept of Art, see Monmouth IL (S)
Monmouth Museum & Cultural Center, Lincroft NJ (M)
Monmouth University, Dept of Art & Design, see West Long Branch NJ (S)
monOrchid Gallery, Phoenix AZ (M)
Monroe Arts Center, Monroe WI (M)
Monroe Community College, Art Dept, see Rochester NY (S)
Monroe County Community College, Fine Arts Council, see Monroe MI (A)
Monroe County Community College, Humanities Division, see Monroe MI (S)
Monroe County Historical Association, Elizabeth D Walters Library, see Stroudsburg PA (M)
James Monroe Memorial Library, see James Monroe Museum, Fredericksburg VA
Montalvo Center for the Arts, Saratoga CA (A)
Montana Historical Society, Helena MT (A,L)
Montana Museum of Art & Culture, see University of Montana, Missoula MT
Montana State University-Billings, Art Dept, see Billings MT (S)
Montana State University-Northern, Humanities & Social Sciences, see Havre MT (S)
Montana State University at Billings, Northcutt Steele Gallery, see Billings MT (M)
Montana State University, Museum of the Rockies, see Bozeman MT (M,L)
Montana State University, School of Art, see Bozeman MT (S)
Montclair Art Museum, Montclair NJ (M)
Montclair Art Museum, Yard School of Art, see Montclair NJ (S)
Montclair State University, Art Galleries, see Upper Montclair NJ (M,L)
Montclair State University, Fine Arts Dept, see Montclair NJ (S)
Monterey History & Art Association, Monterey CA (A, M,L)
Monterey Museum of Art, Monterey Museum of Art -Pacific Street, Monterey Museum of Art - La Mirada, see Monterey CA (A)

Monterey Peninsula College, Art Dept/Art Gallery, see Monterey CA (S)
Monterey Public Library, Art & Architecture Dept, see Monterey CA (L)
Montgomery College, Dept of Art, see Rockville MD (S)
Montgomery College of Art & Design Library, Takoma Park MD (L)
Montgomery County Community College, Art Center, see Blue Bell PA (S)
Montgomery County Guild of Professional Artists, King of Prussia PA (M)
Montgomery Museum & Lewis Miller Regional Art Center, Christianburg VA (M,L)
Montgomery Museum of Fine Arts, Montgomery AL (M,L)
Robert & Mary Montgomery Armory Art Center, Armory Art Center, see West Palm Beach FL (M)
Montreal Museum of Fine Arts, Montreal QC (M,L)
Montserrat College of Art, Beverly MA (S)
Moody County Historical Society, Moody County Museum, see Flandreau SD (M)
Moore College of Art & Design, Philadelphia PA (S)
Moore College of Art & Design, The Galleries at Moore, see Philadelphia PA (M,L)
Moose Jaw Art Museum, Inc, Art & History Museum, see Moose Jaw SK (M)
Moravian College, Dept of Art, see Bethlehem PA (S)
Moravian College, Payne Gallery, see Bethlehem PA (M)
Moravian Historical Society, Nazareth PA (M)
Morehead State University, Art & Design Dept, see Morehead KY (S)
Morehead State University, Claypool-Young Art Gallery, see Morehead KY (M)
Morehead State University, Kentucky Folk Art Center, see Morehead KY (M)
Morgan County Foundation, Inc, Madison-Morgan Cultural Center, see Madison GA (M)
The Morgan Library & Museum, Museum, see New York NY (M,L)
Morgan State University, Dept of Art, see Baltimore MD (S)
Morgan State University, James E Lewis Museum of Art, see Baltimore MD (M,L)
Morningside College, Art Dept, see Sioux City IA (S)
Morris-Jumel Mansion, Inc, New York NY (M)
Morris Communications Co. LLC, Corporate Collection, see Augusta GA
Morris Library, see Southern Illinois University Carbondale, Carbondale IL
Morris Library, see University of Delaware, Newark DE
Morris Museum, Morristown NJ (M)
Morris Museum of Art, Augusta GA (M)
Charles Morse, Charles Hosmer Morse Museum of American Art, see Winter Park FL (M)
Morven Museum & Garden, Princeton NJ (M)
Motlow State Community College, Art Dept, see Tullahoma TN (S)
Mott Community College, Fine Arts & Social Sciences Division, see Flint MI (S)
Mott Gallery of History & Art, Mott ND (M)
Mount Allison University, Dept of Fine Arts, see Sackville NB (S)
Mount Allison University, Owens Art Gallery, see Sackville NB (M)
Mount Angel Abbey Library, Saint Benedict OR (L)
Mount Holyoke College, Art Dept, see South Hadley MA (S)
Mount Holyoke College, Art Museum, see South Hadley MA (M,L)
Mount Hood Community College, Visual Arts Center, see Gresham OR (S)
Mount Ida College, Chamberlayne School of Design & Merchandising, see Boston MA (S)
Mount Marty College, Fine Arts Dept, see Yankton SD (S)
Mount Mary College, Art & Design Division, see Milwaukee WI (S)
Mount Mary College, Marian Gallery, see Milwaukee WI (M)
Mount Mercy University, Art Dept, see Cedar Rapids IA (S)
Mount Mercy University, White Gallery, see Cedar Rapids IA (M,L)
Mount Olive College, Dept of Art, see Mount Olive NC (S)
Mount Pleasant, see Philadelphia Museum of Art, Philadelphia PA
Mount Royal College, Dept of Interior Design, see Calgary AB (S)
Mount Royal College Gallery, Calgary AB (M)
Mount Saint Joseph University, Department of Art and Design, see Cincinnati OH (S)
Mount Saint Mary's College, Art Dept, see Los Angeles CA (S)
Mount Saint Mary's College, Jose-Drudis-Biada Art Gallery, see Los Angeles CA (M)
Mount Saint Mary's University, Visual & Performing Arts Dept, see Emmitsburg MD (S)
Mount Saint Vincent University, MSVU Art Gallery, see Halifax NS (M)
Mount San Antonio College, Art Dept, see Walnut CA (S)
Mt San Jacinto College, Art Dept, see San Jacinto CA (S)
Mt San Jacinto College, Fine Art Gallery, see San Jacinto CA (M)
Mount Union College, Dept of Art, see Alliance OH (S)
Mount Vernon Hotel Museum & Garden, New York NY (M)
Mount Vernon Nazarene University, Art Dept, see Mount Vernon OH (S)
Mount Vernon Public Library, Fine Art Dept, see Mount Vernon NY (L)
Mount Wachusett Community College, East Wing Gallery, see Gardner MA (M,L)
Muchnic Foundation & Atchison Art Association, Muchnic Gallery, see Atchison KS (M)
Muckenthaler Cultural Center, Fullerton CA (A)
Muhlenberg College, Dept of Art, see Allentown PA (S)
Muhlenberg College, Martin Art Gallery, see Allentown PA (M)
The Multicultural Center of the South, Shreveport LA (M)
Multicultural Heritage Centre, Public Art Gallery, see Stony Plain AB (M)
Multnomah County Library, Henry Failing Art & Music Dept, see Portland OR (L)
Municipal Art Society of New York, New York NY (A, L)
Munoz Waxman Gallery - Center for Contemporary Arts, Santa Fe NM (M)
Munroe Center for the Arts, Lexington MA (S)
Munson-Williams-Proctor Arts Institute, Museum of Art, see Utica NY (M,L)
Munson-Williams-Proctor Arts Institute, Pratt MWP College of Art, see Utica NY (S)
Murphy Library of Art & Architecture, see University of Kansas, Lawrence KS
Murray State University, Art Galleries, see Murray KY (M)
Murray State University, Dept of Art, see Murray KY (S)
Muscatine Art Center, Muscatine IA (M)
Muse Art Gallery, Philadelphia PA (M)
Musee d'art Contemporain de Montreal, Montreal QC (M,L)
Musee d'art de Joliette, Joliette QC (M)
Musee de l'Amerique Francophone, Quebec QC (M)
Musee des Augustines de l'Hotel Dieu de Quebec, Quebec QC (M,L)
Musee des Maitres et Artisans du Quebec, Montreal QC (M)
Musee National des Beaux Arts du Quebec, Quebec QC (M,L)
Musee Regional de lu Cote-Nord, Sept-Iles QC (M)
Musee Regional de Vaudreuil-Soulanges, Vaudreuil-Dorion QC (M,L)
Museo de Arte de Ponce, The Luis A Ferre Foundation Inc, see Ponce PR (M,L)
Museo de Arte de Puerto Rico, San Juan PR (M)
Museo de Arte Religioso Porta Coeli, see Institute of Puerto Rican Culture, San German PR
Museo De Las Americas, Denver CO (M)
Museo de las Americas, Viejo San Juan PR (M)
Museo del Grabado Latinoamericano, see Institute of Puerto Rican Culture, Viejo San Juan PR
Museo Italo Americano, San Francisco CA (M,L)
Museo y Parque Historico Ruinas de Caparra, see Institute of Puerto Rican Culture, Guaynabo PR
The Museum, Greenwood SC (M)
Museum, see American Architectural Foundation, Washington DC
Museum Libraries, see The Metropolitan Museum of Art, New York NY
Museum London, London ON (M)
Museum of African American Art, Los Angeles CA (M)
Museum of African American History, Boston MA (M)
Museum of American Glass in WV, Weston WV (M)
Museum of Art & History, Santa Cruz, Santa Cruz CA (M)
Museum of Art, Fort Lauderdale, Fort Lauderdale FL (M,L)
Museum of Art - Deland FL, Inc, Deland FL (M)
Museum of Arts & Design, New York NY (M)
Museum of Arts & Sciences, Inc, Macon GA (M)
The Museum of Arts & Sciences Inc, Daytona Beach FL (M,L)
Museum of Chinese in America, New York NY (M)
Museum of Conceptual Art, Society of Independent Artists (SIA), see San Francisco CA (A,L)
Museum of Contemporary Art, North Miami FL (M)
The Museum of Contemporary Art (MOCA), MOCA Grand Avenue, see Los Angeles CA (M)
Museum of Contemporary Art Chicago, Chicago IL (M, L)
Museum of Contemporary Art Cleveland, Cleveland OH (M,L)
Museum of Contemporary Art Jacksonville, Jacksonville FL (M)
Museum of Contemporary Art San Diego, San Diego CA (M)
Museum of Contemporary Art San Diego, La Jolla CA (M)
Museum of Contemporary Canadian Art, Toronto ON (M)
Museum of Contemporary Photography, Columbia College Chicago, see Chicago IL (M,L)
Museum of Discovery & Science, Fort Lauderdale FL (M)
Museum of East Texas, Lufkin TX (A)
Museum of Fine Arts, Boston MA (M,L)
Museum of Fine Arts, Houston, Houston TX (M,L)
Museum of Fine Arts, Houston, Glassell School of Art, see Houston TX (S)
Museum of Fine Arts, Houston, Rienzi Center for European Decorative Arts, see Houston TX (M)
Museum of Fine Arts, Saint Petersburg, Florida, Inc, Saint Petersburg FL (M,L)
Museum of Fine Arts Houston, Bayou Bend Collection & Gardens, see Houston TX (M)
Museum of Latin American Art, Long Beach CA (M)
Museum of Modern Art, New York NY (M,L)
Museum of Modern Art, Paris (M)
Museum of NC Traditional Pottery, Seagrove NC (M)
Museum of Neon Art, Glendale CA (M)
Museum of New Art, Troy MI (M)
Museum of New Mexico, Office of Cultural Affairs of New Mexico, The Governor's Gallery, see Santa Fe NM (M)
Museum of Northern Arizona, Flagstaff AZ (M)
Museum of Northern British Columbia, Ruth Harvey Art Gallery, see Prince Rupert BC (M,L)
Museum of Northwest Art, La Conner WA (M)
Museum of Ossining Historical Society, Ossining NY (M,L)
Museum of Photographic Arts, Edmund L. and Nancy K Dubois Library, see San Diego CA (M)
Museum of Russian Art, Minneapolis MN (M)
Museum of Science & History, Jacksonville FL (M)
Museum of Science & Industry, Chicago IL (M)

Museum of Southern History, Joella & Stewart Morris Cultural Arts Center, see Houston TX (M)
Museum of the City of New York, Museum, see New York NY (M,L)
Museum of the Hudson Highlands, Cornwall On Hudson NY (M)
Museum of the National Center of Afro-American Artists, Boston MA (M)
Museum of the Plains Indian & Crafts Center, Browning MT (M)
Museum of the Southwest, Midland TX (M)
Museum of Vancouver, Vancouver BC (M,L)
Museum of Vancouver Library, see Museum of Vancouver, Vancouver BC
Museum of Ventura County, Ventura CA (M)
The Museum of Western Art, Kerrville TX (M,L)
Museum of Western Colorado, Museum of the West, see Grand Junction CO (M)
Museum of West Louisiana, Leesville LA (M)
Museum of Wisconsin Art, West Bend WI (M)
Museum of York County, Rock Hill SC (M,L)
Museums Association of Saskatchewan, Regina SK (A)
Museums Sonoma County, Art Museum of Sonoma County & History Museum of Sonoma County, see Santa Rosa CA (M)
Muskegon Community College, Dept of Creative & Performing Arts, see Muskegon MI (S)
Muskegon Museum of Art Foundation, Muskegon Museum of Art, see Muskegon MI (M)
Muskingum College, Art Department, see New Concord OH (S)
Muskoka Arts & Crafts Inc, Chapel Gallery, see Bracebridge ON (M)
Mystic Art Association, Inc, Mystic Museum of Art, see Mystic CT (A)
The Names Project Foundation AIDS Memorial Quilt, Atlanta GA (O)
Nanaimo Art Gallery, Nanaimo BC (M)
Nanticoke Indian Museum, Millsboro DE (M)
Nantucket Historical Association, Historic Nantucket, see Nantucket MA (M)
Napa Valley College, Art Dept, see Napa CA (S)
Napa Valley Museum, Yountville CA (M)
Napoleonic Society of America, Museum & Library, see Saint Helena CA (M)
Nassau Community College, Art Dept, see Garden City NY (S)
Nassau Community College, Firehouse Art Gallery, see Garden City NY (M)
Nassau County Museum of Art, Roslyn Harbor NY (M)
Nathan Hale Homestead Museum, Coventry CT (M)
National Academy Museum & School, New York NY (O,L)
National Academy of Sciences, Arts in the Academy, see Washington DC (M)
National Academy School, New York NY (S)
National Air and Space Museum, Smithsonian Institution, see Washington DC (M,L)
National Air And Space Museum, Steven F Udvar-Hazy Center, see Chantilly VA (M)
National Alliance for Media Arts & Culture, San Francisco CA (O)
National Antique & Art Dealers Association of America, Inc, New York NY (O)
National Architectural Accrediting Board, Inc, Washington DC (O)
National Archives & Records Administration, Herbert Hoover Presidential Library - Museum, see West Branch IA (L)
National Archives & Records Administration, John F Kennedy Presidential Library & Museum, see Boston MA (M)
National Archives & Records Administration, Franklin D Roosevelt Museum, see Hyde Park NY (M,L)
National Archives & Records Administration, Harry S Truman Museum and Library, see Independence MO (L)
National Archives and Records Administration, Eisenhower Presidential Library, see Abilene KS (L)
National Archives of Canada, Art & Photography Archives, see Ottawa ON (L)
National Art Education Association, Alexandria VA (O)
The National Art League, Douglaston NY (A)
National Assembly of State Arts Agencies, Washington DC (O)
National Association of Schools of Art & Design, Reston VA (O)
National Association of Women Artists, Inc, NAWA Gallery, see New York NY (O)
National Audubon Society, John James Audubon Center at Mill Grove, see Audubon PA (M)
National Baseball Hall of Fame & Museum, Cooperstown NY (M)
National Cartoonists Society, Orlando FL (O)
National Churchill Museum, Fulton MO (M)
National Conference of Artists, Michigan Chapter Gallery, see Detroit MI (M)
National Council on Education for the Ceramic Arts (NCECA), Boulder CO (O)
National Endowment for the Arts, Washington DC (O)
National Gallery, see Institute of Puerto Rican Culture, San Juan PR
National Gallery of Art, Washington DC (M,L)
National Gallery of Canada, Ottawa ON (M,L)
National Hall of Fame for Famous American Indians, Anadarko OK (M)
National Heritage Museum, Lexington MA (M)
National Hispanic Cultural Center, Art Museum, Albuquerque NM (M)
National Infantry Museum & Soldier Center, Fort Benning GA (M)
National Institute of Art & Disabilities (NIAD), Florence Ludins-Katz Gallery, see Richmond CA (A)
National League of American Pen Women, Washington DC (O)
National Museum of African American History and Culture, Smithsonian Institution, see Washington DC (M)
National Museum of African Art, Smithsonian Institution, see Washington DC (M,L)
National Museum of American History, Smithsonian Institution, see Washington DC (M,L)
National Museum of Ceramic Art, Baltimore MD (M)
National Museum of Mexican Art, Chicago IL (M)
National Museum of Natural History, Smithsonian Institution, see Washington DC (M)
The National Museum of Puerto Rican Arts & Culture, Chicago IL (M)
National Museum of Racing, National Museum of Racing & Hall of Fame, see Saratoga Springs NY (M,L)
National Museum of the American Indian, George Gustav Heye Center, see New York NY (M)
National Museum of the American Indian, Smithsonian Institution, see Washington DC (M,L)
National Museum of Wildlife Art of the Unites States, Jackson WY (M,L)
National Museum of Women in the Arts, Washington DC (M,L)
National Native American Co-Operative, North American Indian Information & Trade Center, see Tucson AZ (A)
National Oil & Acrylic Painters Society, Houston TX (O)
National Park Community College Library, Hot Springs AR (L)
The National Park Service, United States Department of the Interior, Statue of Liberty National Monument & The Ellis Island Immigration Museum, see Washington DC (M)
National Park Service, Hubbell Trading Post National Historic Site, see Ganado AZ (M)
National Park Service, Weir Farm National Historic Site, see Wilton CT (M)
National Portrait Gallery, Smithsonian Institution, see Washington DC (M,L)
National Postal Museum, Smithsonian Institution, see Washington DC (M,L)
The National Quilt Museum, Paducah KY (M)
National Sculpture Society, New York NY (O)
The National Shrine of the North American Martyrs, Fultonville NY (M)
National Silk Art Museum, Weston MO (M)
National Society of Colonial Dames of America in the State of Maryland, Mount Clare Museum House, see Baltimore MD (M,L)
National Society of Mural Painters, Inc, New York NY (O)
National Society of Painters in Casein & Acrylic, Inc, Whitehall PA (O)
National Society of the Colonial Dames of America in The Commonwealth of Virginia, Wilton House Museum, see Richmond VA (M)
The National Society of The Colonial Dames of America in the State of New Hampshire, Moffatt-Ladd House & Garden, see Portsmouth NH (A)
National Trust for Historic Preservation, Washington DC (M)
National Trust for Historic Preservation, Chesterwood, see Stockbridge MA (M)
The National Trust for Historic Preservation, Lyndhurst, see Tarrytown NY (M)
National Trust for Historic Preservation, Shadows-on-the-Teche, see New Iberia LA (M)
National Veterans Art Museum, Chicago IL (M)
National Watercolor Society, San Pedro CA (O)
National YoungArts Foundation, Miami FL (O)
Natural History Museum of Los Angeles County, Los Angeles CA (M,L)
Navajo Nation Library System, Window Rock AZ (L)
Navajo Nation, Navajo Nation Museum, see Window Rock AZ (M)
Naval Historical Center, National Museum of the US Navy, see Washington DC (M)
Naval War College Museum, Newport RI (M)
Navarro College, Art Dept, see Corsicana TX (S)
Navarro College, Gaston T Gooch Library & Learning Resource Center, see Corsicana TX (L)
Nazareth College of Rochester, Art Dept, see Rochester NY (S)
Nebraska Game and Parks Commission, Arbor Lodge State Historical Park & Morton Mansion, see Nebraska City NE (M)
Nebraska State Capitol, Lincoln NE (M)
Nebraska Wesleyan University, Art Dept, see Lincoln NE (S)
Nebraska Wesleyan University, Elder Gallery, see Lincoln NE (M)
Nelda C & H J Lutcher Stark Foundation, Stark Museum of Art, see Orange TX (M)
The Nelson-Atkins Museum of Art, Kansas City MO (M,L)
Nemeth Art Center, Park Rapids MN (M)
The Nemours Foundation, Nemours Mansion & Gardens, see Wilmington DE (M)
Neue Galerie New York, New York NY (M)
Neustadt Collection of Tiffany Glass, Long Island City NY (M)
Nevada Museum of Art, Reno NV (M,L)
Nevada Northern Railway Museum, Ely NV (M)
Neville Public Museum of Brown County, Green Bay WI (M,L)
George P Nevitt Library, see Paine Art Center & Gardens, Oshkosh WI
New-York Historical Society, Museum, see New York NY (A,L)
Newark Museum Association, The Newark Museum, see Newark NJ (M)
Newark Public Library, Reference, see Newark NJ (L)
New Art Center in Newton, Newtonville MA (M)
New Arts Program, Inc, NAP Museum, NAP Main Gallery, William Zimmer Reference Library, see Kutztown PA (M)
New Bedford Art Museum/Artworks!, New Bedford MA (M)
New Bedford Free Public Library, Special Collections Dept: Art Collection, see New Bedford MA (L)
The Newberry, Chicago IL (L)
Newberry College, Dept of Art, see Newberry SC (S)
New Britain Museum of American Art, New Britain CT (M)

New Brunswick College of Craft & Design, Fredericton NB (S)
New Brunswick College of Craft & Design, Gallery, see Fredericton NB (M,L)
New Brunswick Museum, Saint John NB (M,L)
Newburyport Maritime Society, Inc, Custom House Maritime Museum, see Newburyport MA (M)
New Canaan Historical Society, New Canaan CT (M)
New Canaan Library, H. Pelham Curtis Gallery, see New Canaan CT (L)
New College of the University of South Florida, Fine Arts Dept, Humanities Division, see Sarasota FL (S)
New England Center for Contemporary Art, Brooklyn CT (M)
New England College, Art & Art History, see Henniker NH (S)
New England Maple Museum, Pittsford VT (M)
The New England Museum of Telephony, Inc, The Telephone Museum, see Ellsworth ME (M)
New England Watercolor Society, Boston MA (O)
Newfields, Indianapolis IN (M,L)
New Gallery of Modern Art, Charlotte NC (M)
New Hampshire Antiquarian Society, Hopkinton Historical Society, see Hopkinton NH (M)
New Hampshire Art Association, Portsmouth NH (M)
New Hampshire Art Association, Inc, Portsmouth NH (A)
New Hampshire Historical Society, New Hampshire Historical Society Museum, see Concord NH (A,L)
New Hampshire Institute of Art, Manchester NH (S)
New Hampshire Institute of Art, Manchester NH (M)
New Haven Museum, Whitney Library, see New Haven CT (M)
New Haven Paint & Clay Club, Inc, Whitneyville CT (A)
New Image Art, West Hollywood CA (M)
New Jersey City University, Art Dept, see Jersey City NJ (S)
New Jersey City University, Courtney Art Gallery & Lemmerman Gallery, see Jersey City NJ (M)
New Jersey Historical Society, Newark NJ (M,L)
New Jersey Institute of Technology, Littman Architecture & Design Library, see Newark NJ (L)
New Jersey State Museum, Fine Art Bureau, see Trenton NJ (M)
New Jersey Watercolor Society, Parsippany NJ (A)
New London County Historical Society, Shaw Mansion, see New London CT (A)
New Mexico Art League, Gallery & School, see Albuquerque NM (A)
New Mexico Department of Cultural Affairs, New Mexico Museum of Art, see Santa Fe NM (M,L)
New Mexico Highlands University, Dept of Communications & Fine Arts, see Las Vegas NM (S)
New Mexico Highlands University, The Ray Drew Gallery, see Las Vegas NM (M)
New Mexico Junior College, Arts & Sciences, see Hobbs NM (S)
New Mexico State University, Art Dept, see Las Cruces NM (S)
New Mexico State University, Art Gallery, see Las Cruces NM (M)
The New Museum at the Bradford Brinton Ranch, The Brinton Museum, see Big Horn WY (M)
New Museum of Contemporary Art, New Museum, see New York NY (M,L)
New Orleans Academy of Fine Arts, Academy Gallery, see New Orleans LA (M)
New Orleans Artworks at New Orleans Glassworks & Printmaking Studio, New Orleans LA (M)
New Orleans Museum of Art, New Orleans LA (M,L)
Newport Art Museum and Association, Newport RI (M)
Newport Art Museum, Coleman Center for Creative Studies, see Newport RI (S)
Newport Historical Society & Museum of Newport History, Newport RI (A,L)
Newport Visual Arts Center, Newport OR (M)
New Rochelle Art Association, see New Rochelle Public Library, New Rochelle NY
New Rochelle Public Library, Art Section, see New Rochelle NY (L,A)
The New School, Parsons School of Design, see New York NY (S)
The New School Parsons School of Design, Sheila C Johnson Design Center, see New York NY (M) (S)
New Visions Gallery, Inc, Marshfield WI (M)
New World Art Center, T F Chen Cultural Center, see New York NY (M)
New World School of the Arts, Miami FL (S)
New World School of the Arts, Gallery, see Miami FL (M)
New York Academy of Art, Graduate School of Figurative Art, see New York NY (S)
New York Artists Equity Association, Inc, New York NY (A)
New York City College of Technology of the City University of New York, Dept of Advertising Design & Graphic Arts, see Brooklyn NY (S)
New York City Technical College, Ursula C Schwerin Library, see Brooklyn NY (L)
New York Foundation for the Arts, Brooklyn NY (L)
New York Institute of Photography, New York NY (S)
New York Institute of Technology, Fine Arts Dept, see Old Westbury NY (S)
New York Institute of Technology, Gallery, see Old Westbury NY (M,L)
New York Office of Parks, Recreation & Historic Preservation, Natural Heritage Trust, see Albany NY (A)
The New York Public Library, New York NY (L,M)
The New York Public Library for the Performing Arts, see The New York Public Library, New York NY
New York School of Interior Design, New York NY (S)
New York School of Interior Design, New York School of Interior Design Library, see New York NY (L)
New York Society of Architects, New York NY (A)
New York Society of Women Artists, Inc, Westport CT (A)
New York State College of Ceramics at Alfred University, Scholes Library of Ceramics, see Alfred NY (L)
New York State College of Ceramics at Alfred University, School of Art & Design, see Alfred NY (S)
New York State Historical Association, Fenimore Art Museum, see Cooperstown NY (M,L)
New York State Library, Manuscripts & Special Collections, see Albany NY (L)
New York State Military Museum and Veterans Research Center, Saratoga Springs NY (M)
New York State Museum, Albany NY (M)
New York State Office of Parks, Recreation & Historic Preservation, Staatsburgh State Historic Site, see Staatsburg NY (M)
New York State Office of Parks, Recreation and Historic Preservation, Bureau of Historic Sites, see Waterford NY (A)
New York State Office of Parks: Recreation and Historic Preservation, Senate House State Historic Site, see Kingston NY (M,L)
New York State Office of Parks Recreation & Historic Preservation, John Jay Homestead State Historic Site, see Katonah NY (M)
New York Studio School of Drawing, Painting & Sculpture, New York NY (S)
New York Studio School of Drawing, Painting & Sculpture, Gallery, see New York NY (M,L)
New York University, Grey Art Gallery, see New York NY (M,L)
New York University, Tisch School of the Arts, see New York NY (S)
New Zone Virtual Gallery, Eugene OR (M)
Elisabet Ney, Austin TX (M,L)
Niagara Artists Centre, Saint Catharines ON (M)
Niagara County Community College, Art Gallery, see Sanborn NY (M)
Niagara County Community College, Fine Arts Division, see Sanborn NY (S)
Niagara University, Castellani Art Museum, see Niagara NY (M)
Niagara University, Fine Arts Dept, see Niagara Falls NY (S)
Nicholls State University, Dept of Art, see Thibodaux LA (S)
Nichols House Museum, Inc, Boston MA (M)
Nicolaysen Art Museum & Discovery Center, Children's Discovery Center, see Casper WY (M,L)
Niederlander Research Library, see Buffalo Niagara Heritage Village, Amherst NY
911 Media Arts Center, Seattle WA (A)
The Nippon Gallery at the Nippon Club, New York NY (M)
Noah Webster House, Inc, Noah Webster House & West Hartford Historical Society, see West Hartford CT (M)
The Noble Maritime Collection, Staten Island NY (M)
Nobles County Art Center, Worthington MN (A)
Isamu Noguchi, Isamu Noguchi Garden Museum, see Long Island City NY (M)
No Man's Land Historical Society, No Man's Land Museum, see Goodwell OK (M)
Norfolk Arts Center, Norfolk NE (M)
Norfolk Historical Society Inc, Museum, see Norfolk CT (M)
Norfolk State University, Fine Arts Dept, see Norfolk VA (S)
Norman and Sarah Brown Art Gallery, Baltimore MD (M)
Normandale Community College, Art Dept, see Bloomington MN (S)
Norman Rockwell Museum, Stockbridge MA (M,L)
Norman Rockwell Museum of Vermont, Rutland VT (M)
Northampton Center for the Arts, Northampton MA (M)
Northampton Community College, Art Dept, see Bethlehem PA (S)
North Arkansas Community-Technical College, Art Dept, see Harrison AR (S)
North Canton Public Library, The Little Art Gallery, see North Canton OH (L)
North Carolina Agricultural & Technical State University, Visual Arts Dept, see Greensboro NC (S)
North Carolina Central University, Art Dept, see Durham NC (S)
North Carolina Central University, NCCU Art Museum, see Durham NC (M)
North Carolina Museum of Art, Raleigh NC (M,L)
North Carolina Museums Council, Raleigh NC (A)
North Carolina State University, College of Design, see Raleigh NC (S)
North Carolina State University, Harrye Lyons Design Library, see Raleigh NC (L,M)
North Carolina Wesleyan College, Dept of Visual & Performing Arts, see Rocky Mount NC (S)
North Central Arkansas Art Gallery, Fairfield Bay AR
North Central College, Dept of Art, see Naperville IL (S)
North Central College, Oesterle Library, see Naperville IL (L)
North Central Michigan College, Art Dept, see Petoskey MI (S)
North Central Texas College, Division of Communications & Fine Arts, see Gainesville TX (S)
North Central Texas College, Library, see Gainesville TX (L)
North Central Washington Museum, Wenatchee Valley Museum & Cultural Center, see Wenatchee WA (M)
North Dakota Museum of Art, Grand Forks ND (M)
North Dakota State University, Division of Fine Arts, see Fargo ND (S)
North Dakota State University, Memorial Union Gallery, see Fargo ND (M)
Northeast Community College, Dept of Liberal Arts, see Norfolk NE (S)
Northeast Document Conservation Center, Inc, Andover MA (A)
Northeastern Illinois University, Art Dept, see Chicago IL (S)
Northeastern Illinois University, Fine Arts Center Gallery, see Chicago IL (M)

Northeastern Junior College, Art Department, see Sterling CO (S)
Northeastern Nevada Museum, Elko NV (M)
Northeastern Oklahoma A & M College, Art Dept, see Miami OK (S)
Northeastern State University, College of Arts & Letters, see Tahlequah OK (S)
Northeastern University, Dept of Art & Architecture, see Boston MA (S)
Northeast Kingdom Artisans Guild, Saint Johnsbury VT (M)
Northeast Louisiana Children's Museum, Monroe LA (M)
Northeast Mississippi Junior College, Art Dept, see Booneville MS (S)
Northeast Ohio Areawide Coordinating Agency (NOACA), Information Resource Center, see Cleveland OH (L)
North End Gallery, Leonardtown MD (M)
Northern Arizona University, Art Museum & Galleries, see Flagstaff AZ (M)
Northern Arizona University, College of Arts & Letters, see Flagstaff AZ (S)
Northern Illinois University, NIU Art Museum, see DeKalb IL (M,L)
Northern Illinois University, School of Art & Design, see DeKalb IL (S)
Northern Kentucky University, Dept of Visual Arts, see Highland Heights KY (S)
Northern Kentucky University, Galleries, see Highland Heights KY (M)
Northern Maine Museum of Science, Presque Isle ME (M)
Northern Michigan University, Dept of Art & Design, see Marquette MI (S)
Northern Michigan University, De Vos Art Museum, see Marquette MI (M)
Northern State University, Art Dept, see Aberdeen SD (S)
Northern State University, Northern Galleries, see Aberdeen SD (M)
Northern Virginia Community College, Art Dept, see Annandale VA (S)
Northern Virginia Fine Arts Association, The Athenaeum, see Alexandria VA (A)
Northfield Arts Guild, Northfield MN (A)
North Florida Community College, Dept Humanities & Art, see Madison FL (S)
North Fourth Art Center & Gallery, Albuquerque NM (M)
North Georgia College & State University, Fine Arts Dept, see Dahlonega GA (S)
North Hennepin Community College, Art Dept, see Brooklyn Park MN (S)
North Hennepin Community College, Joseph Gazzuolo Fine Arts Gallery, see Brooklyn Park MN (M)
North Idaho College, Art Dept, see Coeur D'Alene ID (S)
North Iowa Area Community College, Dept of Art, see Mason City IA (S)
Northland Pioneer College, Art Dept, see Show Low AZ (S)
North Light Gallery, Millinocket ME (M)
North Park University, Art Dept, see Chicago IL (S)
North Park University, Carlson Tower Art Gallery, see Chicago IL (M)
Northport-East Northport Public Library, Northport NY (L)
North Seattle College, North Seattle College Dept of Art, see Seattle WA (S)
North Shore Art League, Winnetka IL (S)
North Shore Art League, Winnetka IL (A)
North Shore Arts Association, Inc, Gloucester MA (A)
North Tonawanda History Museum, North Tonawanda NY (M)
Northwest Community College, Dept of Art, see Powell WY (S)
Northwestern College, Art Dept, see Orange City CA (S)
Northwestern College, Te Paske Gallery, see Orange City IA (M)
Northwestern Connecticut Community College, Fine Arts Dept, see Winsted CT (S)
Northwestern Michigan College, Art Dept, see Traverse City MI (S)
Northwestern Michigan College, Dennos Museum Center, see Traverse City MI (M)
Northwestern State University of Louisiana, School of Creative & Performing Arts - Dept of Fine & Graphic Arts, see Natchitoches LA (S)
Northwestern University, Evanston, Dept of Art Theory & Practice, see Evanston IL (S)
Northwestern University, Mary & Leigh Block Museum of Art, see Evanston IL (M,L)
Northwest Florida State College, Mattie Kelly Arts Center Galleries, see Niceville FL (S)
Northwest Missouri State University, DeLuce Art Gallery, see Maryville MO (M)
Northwest Missouri State University, Dept of Fine & Performing Arts, see Maryville MO (S)
Northwest Nazarene College, Art Dept, see Nampa ID (S)
Northwest Pastel Society (NPS), Dallas OR (A)
Northwest Watercolor Society, Woodinville WA (A)
Northwind Arts Center, Port Townsend WA (M)
Northwood University, Alden B Dow Creativity Center, see Midland MI (S)
Northwood University, Jeannette Hare Art Gallery, see West Palm Beach FL (M)
Norton Museum of Art, West Palm Beach FL (M)
Norwalk Community College, Art Galleries & Collection, see Norwalk CT (M)
Norwich Free Academy, Slater Memorial Museum, see Norwich CT (M)
Norwich University, Dept of Architecture and Art, see Northfield VT (S)
Nossi College of Art, Nashville TN (S)
Notre Dame de Namur University, Wiegand Gallery, see Belmont CA (S)
Nova Scotia Association of Architects, Halifax NS (A)
Nova Scotia Centre for Craft & Design, Mary E Black Gallery, see Halifax NS (M)
Nova Scotia College of Art & Design, Halifax NS (S)
Nova Scotia College of Art and Design, Anna Leonowens Gallery, see Halifax NS (M,L)
Nova Scotia Museum, Maritime Museum of the Atlantic, see Halifax NS (M)
Noyes Art Gallery, Lincoln NE (M)
Stone Quarry Hill Art Park, Cazenovia NY
Oakland City University, Division of Fine Arts, see Oakland City IN (S)
Oakland Community College, Art Dept, see Farmington Hills MI (S)
Oakland Museum of California, Art Dept, see Oakland CA (M,L)
Oakland Public Library, Art, Music, History & Literature Section, see Oakland CA (L)
Oakland University, Dept of Art & Art History, see Rochester MI (S)
Oakland University, Oakland University Art Gallery, see Rochester MI (M)
Oak Ridge Art Center, Oak Ridge TN (A,L)
Oakton Community College, Language Humanities & Art Divisions, see Des Plaines IL (S)
Oakville Galleries, Centennial Square and Gairloch Gardens, see Oakville ON (M)
Oatlands Plantation, Leesburg VA (M)
Oberlin College, Allen Memorial Art Museum, see Oberlin OH (M,L)
Oberlin College, Dept of Art, see Oberlin OH (S)
OCAD University, Toronto ON (S)
OCAD University, Ignite Gallery, see Toronto ON (M, L)
Occidental College, Dept of Art History & Visual Arts, see Los Angeles CA (S)
Occidental College, Weingart Galleries, see Los Angeles CA (M)
Ocean City Arts Center, Ocean City NJ (A)
Ocean City Arts Center, Ocean City NJ (S)
Ocean County College, Humanities Dept, see Toms River NJ (S)
Oceanside Gallery, Belmar NJ (M)
Octagon Center for the Arts, Ames IA (A)
Ogden Museum of Southern Art, University of New Orleans, New Orleans LA (M)
Ogden Union Station, Myra Powell Art Gallery & Gallery at the Station, see Ogden UT (M)
Oglebay Institute, Stifel Fine Arts Center, see Wheeling WV (A,M,L)
Ogunquit Museum of American Art, Ogunquit ME (M, L)
Ohio Dominican College, Art Dept, see Columbus OH (S)
The Ohio Historical Society, Inc, Campus Martius Museum & Ohio River Museum, see Marietta OH (M)
Ohio History Connection, Columbus OH (A,L)
Ohio History Connection, National Afro-American Museum & Cultural Center, see Wilberforce OH (M)
Ohio History Connection, National Road-Zane Grey Museum, see Norwich OH (M)
Ohio Northern University, Dept of Art & Design, see Ada OH (S)
Ohio State University, Austin E Knowlton School of Architecture, see Columbus OH (S)
Ohio State University, Wexner Center for the Arts, see Columbus OH (M,L)
Ohio University-Chillicothe Campus, Fine Arts & Humanities Division, see Chillicothe OH (S)
Ohio University-Eastern Campus, Dept Comparative Arts, see Saint Clairsville OH (S)
Ohio University Art Gallery, see Ohio University, Athens OH
Ohio University, Kennedy Museum of Art, see Athens OH (M,L)
Ohio University, School of Art, see Athens OH (S)
Ohio Wesleyan University, Fine Arts Dept, see Delaware OH (S)
Ohrmann Museum and Gallery, Drummond MT (M)
Ohrstrom Library, see Saint Paul's School, Concord NH
Oil Pastel Association, Stockholm NJ (A)
Ojai Art Center, Ojai CA (A)
Okanagan Heritage Museum, Kelowna BC (M,L)
Okefenokee Heritage Center, Inc, Waycross GA (M)
Oklahoma Baptist University, Art & Design Dept, see Shawnee OK (S)
Oklahoma Christian University of Science & Arts, Dept of Art & Design, see Oklahoma City OK (S)
Oklahoma City Museum of Art, Oklahoma City OK (M)
Oklahoma City University, Hulsey Gallery-Norick Art Center, see Oklahoma City OK (M)
Oklahoma City University, Norick Art Center, see Oklahoma City OK (S)
Oklahoma Contemporary Arts Center, Oklahoma City OK (M)
Oklahoma Historical Society, State Museum of History, see Oklahoma City OK (M,L)
Oklahoma State University, Department of Art, Graphic Design and Art History, see Stillwater OK (S)
Oklahoma State University, Gardiner Art Gallery, see Stillwater OK (M,L)
Oklahoma State University Institute of Technology, School of Visual Communications, see Okmulgee OK (S)
Olana State Historic Site, Hudson NY (M,L)
Old Academy Library, see Wethersfield Historical Society Inc, Wethersfield CT
Old Barracks Museum, Trenton NJ (M)
Old Colony Historical Society, Museum, see Taunton MA (M,L)
Old Dartmouth Historical Society, New Bedford Whaling Museum, see New Bedford MA (M,L)
Old Dominion University, Art Dept, see Norfolk VA (S)
Old Dominion University, The College of Arts and Letters, see Norfolk VA (M,L)
Old Fort Harrod State Park Mansion Museum, Harrodsburg KY (M)
Old Island Restoration Foundation Inc, Oldest House in Key West, see Key West FL (M)
The Old Jail Art Center, Albany TX (M,L)

Old Salem Museums & Gardens, Museum of Early Southern Decorative Arts, see Winston-Salem NC (M,L)
Old State House, Hartford CT (M)
Olivet College, Armstrong Collection, see Olivet MI (M,L)
Olivet College, Art Dept, see Olivet MI (S)
Olivet Nazarene University, Dept of Art, see Bourbonnais IL (S)
Olympic College, Social Sciences & Humanities Div, see Bremerton WA (S)
Omaha Children's Museum, Omaha NE (M)
Omniplex Science Museum, Oklahoma City OK (M)
The One Club, New York NY (A)
The One Club for Creativity, New York NY (O)
Ontario Association of Art Galleries, Toronto ON (A)
Ontario Crafts Council, OCC Gallery, see Toronto ON (M,L,A)
Opelousas Museum of Art, Inc (OMA), Opelousas LA (M)
Open Space, Victoria BC (A)
Oral Roberts University, Art Dept, see Tulsa OK (S)
Orange Coast College, Visual & Performing Arts Division, see Costa Mesa CA (S)
Orange County Community College, Arts & Communication, see Middletown NY (S)
Orange County Museum of Art, Newport Beach CA (M)
Order Sons of Italy in America, Garibaldi & Meucci Museum, see Staten Island NY (M)
Oregon College of Art & Craft, Hoffman Gallery, see Portland OR (L)
Oregon Historical Society, Oregon History Museum, see Portland OR (A,L)
Oregon State University, Dept of Art, see Corvallis OR (S)
Oregon State University, Fairbanks Gallery, see Corvallis OR (M)
Oregon Trail Museum Association, Scotts Bluff National Monument, see Gering NE (M)
Organization for the Development of Artists, Gallery Connexion, see Fredericton NB (M)
Organization of Independent Artists, Inc, Brooklyn NY (A)
Organization of Saskatchewan Arts Councils (OSAC), Regina SK (O)
Orillia Museum of Art & History, Orillia ON (M)
Orlando Museum of Art, Orlando FL (M,L)
Orlando Sentinel Library, see Orlando Museum of Art, Orlando FL
Ormond Memorial Art Museum and Gardens, Ormond Beach FL (M)
Lewis J Ort Library, see Frostburg State University, Frostburg MD
Osborne Homestead Museum, Derby CT (M)
Oshkosh Public Museum & Library, Oshkosh WI (M)
Otero Junior College, Dept of Arts, see La Junta CO (S)
Otis College of Art & Design, Ben Maltz Gallery, see Los Angeles CA (M,L)
Otis College of Art & Design, Fine Arts, see Los Angeles CA (S)
Ottawa Public Library, Fine Arts Dept, see Ottawa ON (L)
Ottawa University, Dept of Art, see Ottawa KS (S)
Otterbein University, Art Dept, see Westerville OH (S)
Ouachita Baptist University, Dept of Visual Art, see Arkadelphia AR (S)
Ouachita River Art Gallery, Monroe LA (M)
Our Lady of Elms College, Dept of Fine Arts, see Chicopee MA (S)
Our Lady of the Lake University, Dept of Art, see San Antonio TX (S)
Owatonna Arts Center, Owatonna MN (A,L)
Owensboro Museum of Fine Art, Owensboro KY (M)
Owen Sound Historical Society, Marine & Rail Heritage Museum, see Owen Sound ON (M)
Oysterponds Historical Society, Museum, see Orient NY (M)
Ozark Folk Center, Arkansas State Park, Ozark Cultural Resource Center, see Mountain View AR (L)
Pace University, Dyson College of Arts & Sciences, see Pleasantville NY (S)
Pace University Gallery, Art Gallery in Choate House, see Pleasantville NY (M)
Pace University, Theatre & Fine Arts Dept, see New York NY (S)
Pacific Grove Art Center, Pacific Grove CA (A)
Pacific Island Ethnic Art Museum, Long Beach CA (M)
Pacific Lutheran University, Dept of Art, see Tacoma WA (S)
Pacific Northwest Art School, Gallery at the Wharf, see Coupeville WA (A)
Pacific Northwest College of Art, Portland OR (S)
Pacific Union College, Art Dept, see Angwin CA (S)
Page-Walker Arts & History Center, Cary NC (M)
Page Bond Gallery, Richmond VA (M)
Paier College of Art, Inc, Hamden CT (S)
Paier College of Art, Inc, Library, see Hamden CT (L)
Paine Art Center & Gardens, Oshkosh WI (A,L)
Paint 'N Palette Club, Grant Wood Memorial Park & Gallery, see Anamosa IA (A)
Paint Creek Center for the Arts, Rochester MI (M)
Painted Bride Art Center Gallery, Philadelphia PA (M)
Palace of Governors, see New Mexico Department of Cultural Affairs, Santa Fe NM
Palette & Chisel Academy of Fine Arts, Chicago IL (M)
Palisades Park Public Library, Palisades Park NJ (L)
Palm Beach Community College, Dept of Art, see Lake Worth FL (S)
Palm Beach County Parks & Recreation Department, Morikami Museum & Japanese Gardens, see Delray Beach FL (M,L)
Palm Springs Art Museum, Palm Springs CA (M)
Palo Alto Art Center, Palo Alto CA (A)
Palo Alto Junior Museum & Zoo, Palo Alto CA (M)
Palomar Community College, Art Dept, see San Marcos CA (S)
Palomar Community College, Boehm Gallery, see San Marcos CA (M)
Palos Verdes Art Center/Beverly G. Alpay Center for Arts Education, Rancho Palos Verdes CA (A)
Panhandle-Plains Historical Museum, Canyon TX (M,L)
Paradise Center for the Arts, Faribault MN (M)
Paramount Gallery, Saint Cloud MN (M)
Paris Gibson Square, Museum of Art, see Great Falls MT (M)
Paris Junior College, Visual Art Dept, see Paris TX (S)
Parkland College, Parkland Art Gallery, see Champaign IL (M)
Philip M Park Library, see Besser Museum for Northeast Michigan, Alpena MI
Park University, Dept of Art & Design, see Parkville MO (S)
Parque Ceremonial Indigena de Caguana, see Institute of Puerto Rican Culture, Utuado PR
Parrish Art Museum, Water Mill NY (M)
Parson Fisher House, Jonathan Fisher Memorial, Inc, see Blue Hill ME (M)
Pasadena City College, Art Galleries, see Pasadena CA (M)
Pasadena City College, Visual Arts and Media Studies Division, see Pasadena CA (S)
Pasadena Museum of California Art, Pasadena CA (M)
Pasadena Museum of History, Pasadena CA (M)
Pasadena Public Library, Fine Arts Dept, see Pasadena CA (L)
Passaic County Community College, Broadway, LRC, and Hamilton Club Galleries, see Paterson NJ (M)
Passaic County Community College, Division of Humanities, see Paterson NJ (S)
Passaic County Historical Society, Lambert Castle Museum & Library, see Paterson NJ (M)
Pastel Society of America, National Arts Club, Grand Gallery, see New York NY (O)
Pastel Society of Oregon, Roseburg OR (O)
Pastel Society of the West Coast, Sacramento Fine Arts Center, see Fresno CA (O)
William Paterson University, University Galleries, see Wayne NJ (M)
Patterson Library & Octagon Art Gallery, Westfield NY (L)
Patton Museum Foundation, General George Patton Museum and Center of Leadership, see Fort Knox KY (M)
Peabody Essex Museum, Salem MA (M,L)
George Peabody Library, see Johns Hopkins University, Baltimore MD
Peace College, Art Dept, see Raleigh NC (S)
Pearl Fincher Museum of Fine Arts, Spring TX (M)
Pearl River Community College, Visual Arts, Dept of Fine Arts & Communication, see Poplarville MS (S)
Pearson Lakes Art Center, Okoboji IA (M)
Peggy R McConnell Arts Center of Worthington, Columbus OH (A)
Peirce-Nichols House, see Peabody Essex Museum, Salem MA
Pelham Art Center, Pelham NY (M)
Pemaquid Group of Artists, Pemaquid Art Gallery, see Pemaquid Point ME (A)
Pen & Brush, Inc, New York NY (A,L)
Pence Gallery, Davis CA (M)
Pendleton Center for the Arts, Pendleton OR (M)
Penfield Library, see State University of New York at Oswego, Oswego NY
Peninsula Fine Arts Center, Newport News VA (A)
Penland School of Crafts, Penland NC (S)
Penn Foster College, School of Interior Design, see Scranton PA (S)
Penn State Harrisburg, School of Humanities, see Middletown PA (S)
Pennsylvania Academy of the Fine Arts, Philadelphia PA (M,L,A)
Pennsylvania Academy of the Fine Arts, Office of Admission, see Philadelphia PA (S)
Pennsylvania College of Technology, The Gallery at Penn College, see Williamsport PA (S)
Pennsylvania Department of Education, Arts in Education Program, see Harrisburg PA (A)
Pennsylvania German Cultural Heritage Center at Kutztown University, Kutztown PA (L)
Pennsylvania Historical & Museum Commission, The State Museum of Pennsylvania, see Harrisburg PA (A,M,L)
Pennsylvania School of Art & Design, Lancaster PA (S)
Pennsylvania State University, University Park, Penn State School of Visual Arts, see University Park PA (S)
Pennsylvania State University at New Kensington, Depts of Art & Architecture, see Upper Burrell PA (S)
The Pennsylvania State University, Palmer Museum of Art, see University Park PA (M,L)
Penobscot Marine Museum, Searsport ME (M,L)
Pensacola Museum of Art, Pensacola FL (M,L)
Pensacola State College, Visual Arts Dept, see Pensacola FL (S)
Pensacola State College, Visual Arts Gallery, Anna Lamar Switzer Center for Visual Arts, see Pensacola FL (M)
The Penticton Art Gallery, Penticton BC (M)
Peoria Art Guild, Peoria IL (A)
Peoria Historical Society, Peoria IL (M)
Peoria Riverfront Museum, Peoria IL (M)
Pepperdine University, Seaver College, Dept of Art, see Malibu CA (S)
PepsiCo Inc, Donald M Kendall Sculpture Garden, see Purchase NY
Perez Art Museum Miami, Miami FL (M)
Performance Space 122, New York NY (M)
Perkins Center for the Arts, Moorestown NJ (M)
Dorothy W Perkins Slide Library, see University of Massachusetts, Amherst, Amherst MA
Peru State College, Art Dept, see Peru NE (S)
Peter B. Yeomans Cultural Center, Dorval QC (A)
Peters Valley School of Craft, Layton NJ (L)
Petzinger Memorial Library & Earl Rowland Art Library, see The San Joaquin Pioneer & Historical Society, Stockton CA
Pewabic Society Inc, Pewabic, see Detroit MI (M)

Pfeiffer University, Art Program, see Misenheimer NC (S)
Phelps County Historical Society, Nebraska Prairie Museum, see Holdrege NE (M,L)
Philadelphia Art Alliance, Philadelphia PA (A)
Philadelphia Art Commission, Philadelphia PA (A)
Philadelphia Community College, Dept of Art, see Philadelphia PA (S)
Philadelphia History Museum, Philadelphia PA (M)
Philadelphia Museum of Art, Main Building, see Philadelphia PA (M,L,A)
Philadelphia Sketch Club, Philadelphia PA (A)
Philadelphia University, Philadelphia PA (S)
Philadelphia University, Paley Design Center, see Philadelphia PA (M)
Philbrook Museum of Art, Tulsa OK (M,L)
Philip Johnson Glass House, National Trust for Historic Preservation, New Canaan CT (M)
Philipse Manor Hall State Historic Site, Yonkers NY (M)
Phillips Academy, Addison Gallery of American Art, see Andover MA (M)
The Phillips Collection, Washington DC (M,L)
Phillips Community College at The University of Arkansas, Dept of English & Fine Arts, see Helena AR (S)
Phillips County Museum, Holyoke CO (M)
Phillips Exeter Academy, Frederick R. Mayer Art Center, Lamont Gallery, see Exeter NH (M)
Phillips Library, see Peabody Essex Museum, Salem MA
Philmont Scout Ranch, Philmont Museum - Seton Memorial Library, see Cimarron NM (M)
George Phippen, Phippen Museum - Art of the American West, see Prescott AZ (M)
The Phipps Center for the Arts, Galleries, see Hudson WI (M)
Phoenix Art Museum, Phoenix AZ (M,L)
Phoenix Center for the Arts, Phoenix AZ (M)
Phoenix College, Dept of Art & Photography, see Phoenix AZ (S)
Phoenix Gallery, New York NY (M)
Photo Center NW, Seattle WA (M)
Photographic Resource Center, Inc, Cambridge MA (M)
Piatt Castles, West Liberty OH (M)
Pickens County Museum of Art & History, Pickens SC (M)
Timothy Pickering Library, see Wenham Museum, Wenham MA
Piedmont Arts Association, Martinsville VA (M)
Piedmont College, Art Dept, see Demorest GA (S)
Pierce College, Art Dept, see Woodland Hills CA (S)
Pier 24 Photography, San Francisco CA (M)
Pikeville College, Humanities Division, see Pikeville KY (S)
Pilchuck Glass School, Stanwood WA (S)
Pilgrim Society, Pilgrim Hall Museum, see Plymouth MA (M,L)
Pimeria Alta Historical Society, Nogales AZ (A,L)
Pine Bluff/Jefferson County Historical Museum, Pine Bluff AR (M)
Pine Manor College, Visual Arts Dept, see Chestnut Hill MA (S)
Pioneer Florida Museum Association, Inc, Pioneer Florida Museum & Village, see Dade City FL (L)
Pioneer Historical Museum of South Dakota, Hot Springs SD (M)
Pioneer Town, Pioneer Museum of Western Art, see Wimberley TX (M)
Pirate-Contemporary Art, Denver CO (M)
Pittsburgh Center for the Arts, Pittsburgh PA (A)
Pittsburgh History & Landmarks Foundation, James D Van Trump Library, see Pittsburgh PA (L)
Pittsburg State University, Art Dept, see Pittsburg KS (S)
Pitzer College, Dept of Art, see Claremont CA (S)
Place des Arts at Heritage Square, Coquitlam BC (A)
Plainfield Public Library, Plainfield NJ (L)
Plains Art Museum, Fargo ND (M)
Plains Indians & Pioneers Historical Foundation, Museum & Art Center, see Woodward OK (M)
Plainsman Museum, Aurora NE (M)
Planting Fields Foundation, Coe Hall at Planting Fields Arboretum, see Oyster Bay NY (L)
Plastic Club, Art Club, see Philadelphia PA (A)
Playboy Enterprises, Inc, Beverly Hills CA
Plaza de la Raza Cultural Center, Los Angeles CA (A)
Please Touch Museum, Philadelphia PA (M)
Plug In, Institute of Contemporary Art, see Winnipeg MB (M)
Plumas County Museum, Quincy CA (M,L)
Helen M Plum, Lombard IL (L)
Plymouth Antiquarian Society, Plymouth MA (A)
Plymouth State College, Art Dept, see Plymouth NH (S)
Plymouth State University, Karl Drerup Art Gallery, see Plymouth NH (M)
Pocatello Art Center, Pocatello ID (M)
Pocumtuck Valley Memorial Association, Memorial Hall Museum, see Deerfield MA (A)
Pointe Claire Cultural Centre, Stewart Hall Art Gallery, see Pointe Claire QC (A)
Point Park College, Performing Arts Dept, see Pittsburgh PA (S)
Polish Museum of America (PMA), Chicago IL (M,L)
Polk Community College, Art, Letters & Social Sciences, see Winter Haven FL (S)
Polk County Heritage Gallery, Heritage Art Gallery, see Des Moines IA (M)
Polk Museum of Art, Lakeland FL (M)
Polyadam Concrete System Workshops, Ossining NY (S)
Polynesian Cultural Center, Laie HI (A)
Pomerene Center for the Arts, Coshocton OH (M)
The Pomona College, Claremont CA (M)
Pomona College, Dept of Art History, see Claremont CA (S)
Ponca City Art Association, Ponca City OK (A)
Ponca City Cultural Center & Museum, Ponca City OK (M,L)
Ponca City Library, Art Dept, see Ponca City OK (L)
Ponder Fine Arts Gallery-Benedict College, Columbia SC (M)
Pontifical Catholic University of Puerto Rico, Dept of Fine Arts, see Ponce PR (S)
Pope County Historical Society, Pope County Museum, see Glenwood MN (M)
Porcelain Veilleuses-Theieres Museum, Trenton TN (M)
Portage and District Arts Council, Portage Arts Centre, see Portage la Prairie MB (A)
Port Chester-Rye Brook Public Library, Port Chester NY (L)
Porter-Phelps-Huntington Foundation, Inc, Historic House Museum, see Hadley MA (M)
Dana Porter Library, see University of Waterloo, Waterloo ON
Porterville College, Dept of Fine Arts, see Porterville CA (S)
Portholes Into the Past, Medina OH (M)
Port Huron Museum, Port Huron MI (M)
Portland Art Museum, Portland OR (M,L,A)
Portland Children's Museum, Portland OR (M)
Portland Community College, North View Gallery, see Portland OR (M)
Portland Community College, Visual & Performing Arts Division, see Portland OR (S)
Portland Museum of Art, Portland ME (M)
Portland Pottery Inc, Portland ME (S)
Portland Public Library, Art - Audiovisual Dept, see Portland ME (L)
Portland State University, Dept of Art, see Portland OR (S)
Portland State University, Littman Gallery, see Portland OR (M)
Portlock Galleries at SoNo, Chesapeake VA (M)
Portrait Society of America, Tallahassee FL (O)
Portraits South, Raleigh NC (A)
Portsmouth Athenaeum, Joseph Copley Research Library, see Portsmouth NH (M)
Portsmouth Historical Society, John Paul Jones House & Discover Portsmouth, see Portsmouth NH (M)
Portsmouth Museum of Fine Art, Portsmouth NH (M)
Portsmouth Museums, Courthouse Galleries, see Portsmouth VA (M)
Port Washington Public Library, Port Washington NY (L)
Winfred L & Elizabeth C Post Foundation, Post Art Library, see Joplin MO (L)
Potomac State College, Dept of Art, see Keyser WV (S)
Prairie State College, Art Dept, see Chicago Heights IL (S)
Pratt Community College, Art Dept, see Pratt KS (S)
Enoch Pratt, Baltimore MD (L)
Pratt Fine Arts Center, Gallery, see Seattle WA (A)
Pratt Institute, Art & Architecture Dept, see Brooklyn NY (L,M)
Pratt Institute, Pratt Manhattan, see New York NY (S)
Pratt Institute, School of Art, see Brooklyn NY (S)
James Prendergast, Jamestown NY (L)
Presbyterian College, Visual & Theater Arts, see Clinton SC (S)
Prescott Fine Arts Association, Gallery, see Prescott AZ (A)
Preservation Virginia, Richmond VA (A,L,M)
Presidential Museum & Leadership Library, Odessa TX (M)
Prince Edward Island Museum & Heritage Foundation, Charlottetown PE (A)
Prince George's Community College, Art Dept, see Largo MD (S)
Prince Street Gallery, New York NY (M)
Princeton Antiques Bookservice, Art Marketing Reference Library, see Atlantic City NJ (L)
Princeton University, Dept of Art & Archaeology, see Princeton NJ (S)
Princeton University, Princeton University Art Museum, see Princeton NJ (M,L)
Principia College, School of Nations Museum, see Elsah IL (M)
Principle Gallery, Charleston, see Charleston SC (M)
The Print Center, Philadelphia PA (O)
Print Club of Albany, Schenectady NY (A)
Print Club of Cleveland, see The Cleveland Museum of Art, Cleveland OH
Print Council of America, Chicago IL (O)
Printed Matter, Inc, New York NY
Printmaking Center of New Jersey, Branchburg NJ (A)
Pro Arts, Oakland CA (M)
Promote Art Works Inc (PAWI), Job Readiness in the Arts-Media-Communication, see Brooklyn NY (S)
Promote Art Works Inc (PAWI), Laziza Electrique Dance Co, see Brooklyn NY (A)
Providence Art Club, Providence RI (A)
Providence Athenaeum, Providence RI (M,L)
Providence College, Art & Art History Dept, see Providence RI (S)
Providence Gallery, Charlotte NC (M)
Providence Public Library, Art & Music Services, see Providence RI (L)
Provincetown Art Association & Museum, Provincetown MA (A,L)
Provincial Archives of Alberta, see Royal Alberta Museum, Edmonton AB
Provisions Library, Provisions Research Center for Arts & Social Change, see Fairfax VA (L)
Prudential Art Program, Newark NJ
PS1 Contemporary Art Center, Long Island City NY (M)
Public Art Fund, Inc, New York NY (A,L)
Public Art Program, see City of Atlanta, Atlanta GA
Public Library of Charlotte & Mecklenburg County, Charlotte NC (L)
Public Library of Cincinnati & Hamilton County, Info & Reference Dept, see Cincinnati OH (L)
Public Library of Des Moines, Central Library Information Services, see Des Moines IA (L)
Public Library of the District of Columbia, Art Division, see Washington DC (L)
Pueblo Museum, Desert Hot Springs CA (M)

Pueblo of Pojoaque, Poeh Museum, see Santa Fe NM (A)
Pueblo of San Ildefonso, Maria Martinez Museum, see Santa Fe NM (M)
Pump House Center for the Arts, Chillicothe OH (M)
Purchase College, State University of New York, School of Art+Design, see Purchase NY (S)
Purchase College, Neuberger Museum of Art, see Purchase NY (M,L)
Purdue University, West Lafayette, Patti and Rusty Rueff School of Visual & Performing Arts, Art & Design Dept, see West Lafayette IN (S)
Purdue University Calumet, Dept of Communication & Creative Arts, see Hammond IN (S)
Purdue University Calumet, Library Gallery, see Hammond IN (M)
Purdue University Galleries, West Lafayette IN (M)
Putnam County Historical Society, Foundry School Museum, see Cold Spring NY (M)
Putnam Museum of History and Natural Science, Davenport IA (M)
Pyramid Atlantic, Hyattsville MD (A)
Pyramid Hill Sculpture Park & Museum, Hamilton OH (M)
Quad City Arts Inc, Rock Island IL (A)
Quapaw Quarter Association, Inc, Villa Marre, see Little Rock AR (M,L)
Queen's University, Agnes Etherington Art Centre, see Kingston ON (M,L)
Queen's University, Faculty of Arts & Sciences, Creative Arts Program, see Kingston ON (S)
Queensborough Community College, Art Gallery, see Bayside NY (M)
Queensborough Community College, Dept of Art & Photography, see Bayside Hills NY (S)
Queensborough Community College Library, Kurt R Schmeller Library, see Flushing NY (L)
Queens Borough Public Library, Fine Arts & Recreation Division, see Jamaica NY (L)
Queens College, City University of New York, Godwin-Ternbach Museum, see Flushing NY (M,L)
Queens College, Art Dept, see Flushing NY (S)
Queens College, Fine Arts Dept, see Charlotte NC (S)
Queens Historical Society, Kingsland Homestead, see Flushing NY (A)
The Queens Museum of Art, Flushing NY (M)
Queen Sofia Spanish Institute, New York NY (A)
Quetico Park, John B Ridley Research Library, see Atikokan ON (L)
Quickdraw Animation Society, Calgary AB (O)
Quietude Garden Gallery, East Brunswick NJ
Quincy Art Center, Quincy IL (A)
Quincy College, Art Dept, see Quincy MA (S)
Quincy Society of Fine Arts, Quincy IL (A)
Quincy University, Dept of Art, see Quincy IL (S)
Quincy University, The Gray Gallery, see Quincy IL (M,L)
Quint Projects, La Jolla CA (A)
Racine Art Museum, Racine WI
Radford University, Art Dept, see Radford VA (S)
Radio-Canada SRC CBC, Georges Goguen CBC Art Gallery, see Moncton NB (M)
Rahr-West Art Museum, Manitowoc WI (M)
Railroad Museum of Pennsylvania, see Pennsylvania Historical & Museum Commission, Strasburg PA
Ramapo College of New Jersey, School of Contemporary Arts, see Mahwah NJ (S)
Rancho Santa Fe Art Guild, Rancho Santa Fe CA (M)
Randall Junior Museum, San Francisco CA (M)
Randolph-Macon College, Dept of the Arts, see Ashland VA (S)
Randolph-Macon Woman's College, Dept of Art, see Lynchburg VA (S)
Randolph College, Maier Museum of Art, see Lynchburg VA (M)
Randolph Macon College, Flipp Gallery, see Ashland VA (M)
Rangeley Lakes Region Logging Museum, Rangeley ME (M)
Harry Ransom Humanities Research Center, see University of Texas at Austin, Austin TX
Rapid City Arts Council, Dahl Arts Center, see Rapid City SD (M)
Elmer E Rasmuson Library, see University of Alaska, Fairbanks AK
Ravalli County Museum, Hamilton MT (M)
Rawls Museum Arts, Courtland VA (M)
Raymond Jonson Collection & Archive, see University of New Mexico, Albuquerque NM
The Reader's Digest Association Inc, New York NY
Read House and Gardens, see Delaware Historical Society, New Castle DE
Reading Public Museum, Reading PA (M)
Real Art Ways (RAW), Hartford CT (M)
Red Brick Center for the Arts, Aspen CO (M)
Red Deer & District Museum & Archives, Red Deer AB (M)
Red Deer College, School of Creative Arts, see Red Deer AB (S)
Redhead Gallery, Toronto ON (M)
Redlands Art Association, Redlands Art Association Gallery & Art Center, see Redlands CA (A)
RedMill Museum Village, Clinton NJ (M)
Red River Valley Museum, Vernon TX (M)
Red Rock Park, Red Rock Park, see Church Rock NM (M)
Red Rocks Community College, Arts Dept, see Lakewood CO (S)
Redwood Library & Athenaeum, Newport RI (L)
Reed College, Douglas F Cooley Memorial Art Gallery, see Portland OR (M)
Reed College, Dept of Art, see Portland OR (S)
Martha Stecher Reed Art Library, see Akron Art Museum, Akron OH
Reference Library, see Grand Rapids Art Museum, Grand Rapids MI
Regina Public Library, Art Dept, see Regina SK (L,M)
Regional Arts & Culture Council, Metropolitan Center for Public Arts, see Portland OR (A)
Regis College, Carney Gallery, see Weston MA (M)
Regis College, Dept of Art, see Weston MA (S)
Regis University, Fine Arts Dept, see Denver CO (S)
Rehoboth Art League, Inc, Rehoboth Beach DE (S)
Rehoboth Art League, Inc, Rehoboth Beach DE (A)
Bill Reid Gallery of Northwest Coast Art, Vancouver BC (M)
Remai Modern, Saskatoon SK (M)
Frederic Remington, Ogdensburg NY (M)
The Renaissance Society, Chicago IL (A)
Frederic G Renner Memorial Library, see C M Russell Museum, Great Falls MT
Rensselaer County Historical Society, Hart-Cluett Mansion, 1827, see Troy NY (M,L)
Rensselaer Newman Foundation Chapel + Cultural Center, The Gallery at the Chapel & Cultural Center, see Troy NY (M)
Rensselaer Polytechnic Institute, School of Architecture, see Troy NY (S)
Renwick Gallery, see American Art Museum, Washington DC
Restigouche Gallery, Campbellton NB (M)
Revelstoke Visual Arts Centre, Revelstoke BC (A)
Reynolda House Museum of American Art, Winston-Salem NC (M,L)
Rhinelander District Library, Rhinelander WI (L)
Rhode Island College, Art Dept, see Providence RI (S)
Rhode Island College, Edward M Bannister Gallery, see Providence RI (M)
Rhode Island Historical Society, Providence RI (A,M,L)
Rhode Island School of Design, Providence RI (S)
Rhode Island School of Design, Bayard Ewing Building Gallery, see Providence RI (M)
Rhode Island School of Design, Museum of Art, see Providence RI (M,L)
Rhode Island Watercolor Society, Pawtucket RI (A)
Rhodes College, Clough-Hanson Gallery, see Memphis TN (M)
Rhodes College, Dept of Art, see Memphis TN (S)
Rialto Community Arts Center, The Gallery, see Morrilton AR (M)
Rice University, Brown Fine Arts Library, see Houston TX (L,M)
Rice University, Visual & Dramatic Arts, see Houston TX (S)
Richard Bland College, Art Dept, see Petersburg VA (S)
Jack Richard Gallery, Almond Tea Museum & Jane Williams Galleries, Divisions of Studios of Jack Richard, see Cuyahoga Falls OH (M,L)
Richard M Ross Art Museum at Wesleyan University, Delaware OH (M)
Richardson Memorial Library, see Saint Louis Art Museum, Saint Louis MO
Sid W Richardson Foundation, Sid Richardson Museum, see Fort Worth TX (M)
Studios of Jack Richard, Professional School of Painting & Design, see Cuyahoga Falls OH (S)
The Richmond Art Center, Richmond CA (A)
Richmond Art Museum, Richmond IN (A,L)
Richmond Arts Centre, Richmond BC (A)
Ricker Library of Architecture & Art, see University of Illinois at Urbana-Champaign, Champaign IL
Ricks College, Dept of Art, see Rexburg ID (S)
Rider University, Art Gallery, see Lawrenceville NJ (M)
Rider University, Dept of Fine Arts, see Lawrenceville NJ (S)
Ridgewater College, Art Dept, see Willmar MN (S)
Robert Gore Rifkind Center for German Expressionist Studies, see Los Angeles County Museum of Art, Los Angeles CA
Riley County Historical Society & Museum, Riley County Historical Museum, see Manhattan KS (M, L)
Ringling College of Art & Design, Verman Kimbrough Memorial Library, see Sarasota FL (L)
Ringling School of Art & Design, Sarasota FL (S)
Ringwood Manor House Museum, Ringwood NJ (M)
Rio Hondo College Art Gallery, Whittier CA (M)
Rio Hondo College, Arts & Cultural Programs Dept, see Whittier CA (S)
Ripon College, Art Dept, see Ripon WI (S)
Ripon College Caestecker Art Gallery, Ripon WI (M)
Ritz-Carlton Hotel Company, Art Collection, see Chevy Chase MD
River Arts, Arts Gallery, see Damariscotta ME (M)
Tomas Rivera Library, see UCR ARTSblock, Riverside CA
Riverfront Renaissance Center for the Arts, Millville NJ (M)
River Heritage Museum, Paducah KY (M)
Riverside, the Farnsley-Moremen Landing, Louisville KY (M)
Riverside Art Museum, Riverside CA (M,L)
Riverside Arts Center, Riverside IL (S)
Riverside Community College, Dept of Art & Mass Media, see Riverside CA (S)
Riverside County Museum, Edward-Dean Museum & Gardens, see Cherry Valley CA (M,L)
Riverside Metropolitan Museum, Riverside CA (M)
Rivier College, Art Dept, see Nashua NH (S)
Roanoke College, Fine Arts Dept-Art, see Salem VA (S)
Roberson Museum & Science Center, Binghamton NY (M)
Robert Allerton Art Library, see Honolulu Museum of Art, Honolulu HI
Robert Louis Stevenson Museum, Saint Helena CA (M, L)
Robert Paul Gallery, Stowe VT (M)
Roberts County Museum, Miami TX (M)
Roberts Wesleyan College, Department of Visual Art, see Rochester NY (S)
Robischon Gallery, Denver CO (M)
Robson Library, see University of the Ozarks, Clarksville AR
Rochester Art Center, Rochester MN (A)
Rochester Community & Technical College, Art Dept, see Rochester MN (S)
Rochester Contemporary, Art Center, see Rochester NY (M)

Rochester Historical Society, Rochester NY (A)
Rochester Institute of Technology, College of Imaging Arts & Sciences, see Rochester NY (S)
Rochester Institute of Technology, Corporate Education & Training, see Rochester NY (L)
John D Rockefeller, Jr Library, see Colonial Williamsburg Foundation, Williamsburg VA
Rockford Art Museum, Rockford IL (A)
Rock Ford Foundation, Inc, Rock Ford Plantation, see Lancaster PA (M)
Rockford University, Art Gallery, see Rockford IL (M)
Rockford University, Dept of Fine Arts, see Rockford IL (S)
Rockhurst University, Dept of Communication & Fine Arts, see Kansas City MO (S)
Rockland Center for the Arts, West Nyack NY (M)
Rockland Center for the Arts, West Nyack NY (S)
Rockland Community College, Graphic Arts & Advertising Tech Dept, see Suffern NY (S)
Rockport Art Association, Rockport MA (A)
Rockport College, Maine Photographic Workshops, see Rockport ME (A,L)
Rock Valley College, Humanities and Fine Arts Division, see Rockford IL (S)
The Rockwell Museum, Corning NY (M,L)
Rocky Mountain College, Art Dept, see Billings MT (S)
Rocky Mountain College of Art & Design, Lakewood CO (S)
Rocky Mountain Museum of Military History, Missoula MT (M)
Rodin Museum of Philadelphia, see Philadelphia Museum of Art, Philadelphia PA
Rodman Hall Arts Centre, Saint Catharines ON (A,L)
Nicholas Roerich, New York NY (M)
Lauren Rogers, Laurel MS (M,L)
Rogers State College, Art Dept, see Claremore OK (S)
Roger Williams University, Architecture Library, see Bristol RI (L)
Roger Williams University, Visual Art Dept, see Bristol RI (S)
Rogue Community College, Wiseman Gallery - FireHouse Gallery, see Grants Pass OR (M)
Rogue Valley Art Association, Rogue Gallery & Art Center, see Medford OR (A)
Rohrbach Library, see Kutztown University, Kutztown PA
Rokeby Museum, Ferrisburgh VT (A)
Rollins College, George D & Harriet W Cornell Fine Arts Museum, see Winter Park FL (M)
Rollins College, Dept of Art, Main Campus, see Winter Park FL (S)
Rome Art & Community Center, Rome NY (A)
Rome Historical Society, Museum & Archives, see Rome NY (M,L)
The Rooms Provincial Art Gallery, Saint John's NF (M)
Roosevelt-Vanderbilt National Historic Sites, Hyde Park NY (M)
Franklin D Roosevelt Library, see National Archives & Records Administration, Hyde Park NY
Rose Center & Council for the Arts, Morristown TN (A)
Rose Lehrman Art Gallery, Harrisburg PA (M)
Rosemont College, Art Program, see Rosemont PA (S)
Rosemount Museum, Inc, Pueblo CO (M)
The Rosenbach Museum & Library, Philadelphia PA (M)
Rosenberg Library, Galveston TX (L)
Rosicrucian Egyptian Museum & Planetarium, Rosicrucian Order, AMORC, see San Jose CA (M)
Ross Memorial Museum, Saint Andrews NB (M)
Roswell Artist-in-Residence Foundation, Anderson Museum of Contemporary Art, see Roswell NM (M)
Roswell Museum & Art Center, Roswell NM (M,L)
Rotch Library of Architecture & Planning, see Massachusetts Institute of Technology, Cambridge MA
Rothmans, Benson & Hedges, Art Collection, see Don Mills ON
Rowan University, Dept of Art, see Glassboro NJ (S)
Royal Alberta Museum, Royal Alberta Museum, see Edmonton AB (M,L)
Royal Architectural Institute of Canada, Ottawa ON (O, L)
Royal Arts Foundation, Belcourt Castle, see Newport RI (M)
Royal BC Museum, Victoria BC (M)
Royal British Columbia Museum, BC Archives, see Victoria BC (L)
Royal Canadian Academy of Arts, Toronto ON (O)
Royal Ontario Museum, Toronto ON (M,L)
Elizabeth Rozier Gallery, see Missouri Department of Natural Resources, Jefferson City MO
The Rubelle & Norman Schafler Gallery, see Pratt Institute, Brooklyn NY
Rubell Family Collection and Contemporary Arts Foundation, Miami FL (M)
Rubin Museum of Art, New York NY (M)
Ruder Finn Arts & Communications, Inc, New York NY
Russell Day Gallery, Everett WA (M)
Russell Sage College, Visual & Performing Arts Dept, see Troy NY (S)
Rutgers, The State University of New Jersey, Mason Gross School of the Arts, see New Brunswick NJ (S)
Rutgers, The State University of New Jersey, Zimmerli Art Museum at Rutgers University, see New Brunswick NJ (M,L)
Rutgers University, Camden, Art Dept, see Camden NJ (S)
Rutgers University, Newark, Arts, Culture & Media, see Newark NJ (S)
Rutgers University, Stedman Art Gallery, see Camden NJ (M)
Ruthmere Museum, Robert B. Beardsley Arts Reference Library, see Elkhart IN (L)
Rutland Area Art Association, Chaffee Art Center & Chaffee Downtown Galleries, see Rutland VT (A)
R W Norton Art Foundation, R W Norton Art Gallery, see Shreveport LA (M,L)
Ryerson & Burnham Libraries, see The Art Institute of Chicago, Chicago IL
Ryerson University, Ryerson University Library, see Toronto ON (L)
Ryerss Victorian Museum & Library, Philadelphia PA (M)
Arthur M Sackler Gallery, see Freer Gallery of Art & Arthur M Sackler Gallery, Washington DC
Arthur M Sackler Museum, see Harvard University, Cambridge MA
Saco Museum, Saco ME (M)
Sacramento City College, Art Dept, see Sacramento CA (S)
Sacred Heart University, Dept of Art, see Fairfield CT (S)
Sacred Heart University, Gallery of Contemporary Art, see Fairfield CT (M)
Safety Harbor Museum and Cultural Arts Center, Safety Harbor FL (M)
Sage College of Albany, Opalka Gallery, see Albany NY (M)
The Sage Colleges, Dept Visual Arts, see Albany NY (S)
Sager Creek Arts Center, Siloam Springs AR (M)
Sager Studios, Fort Worth TX (S)
Saginaw Art Museum, Saginaw MI (M)
Saginaw Valley State University, Dept of Art & Design, see University Center MI (S)
Saint-Gaudens National Historic Site, Cornish NH (M, L)
Saint Ambrose University, Art Dept, see Davenport IA (S)
Saint Andrews Presbyterian College, Art Program, see Laurinburg NC (S)
Saint Anselm College, Alva de Mars Megan Chapel Art Center, see Manchester NH (M)
Saint Anselm College, Dept of Fine Arts, see Manchester NH (S)
Saint Augustine Art Association and Art Gallery, Saint Augustine FL (A)
Saint Augustine Historical Society, Oldest House Museum Complex, see Saint Augustine FL (M,L)
Saint Bonaventure University, Regina A Quick Center for the Arts, see Saint Bonaventure NY (M)
Saint Clair County Community College, Jack R Hennesey Art Galleries, see Port Huron MI (M)
Saint Clair County Community College, Jack R Hennesey Art Dept, see Port Huron MI (S)
Saint Cloud State University, Atwood Memorial Center Gallery, see Saint Cloud MN (M)
Saint Cloud State University, Dept of Art, see Saint Cloud MN (S)
Saint Edward's University, Fine Arts Gallery, see Austin TX (M)
St Francis College, Fine Arts Dept, see Loretto PA (S)
St Francis Xavier University, Art Dept, see Antigonish NS (S)
Saint Gregory's University, Dept of Art, see Shawnee OK (S)
St John's College, Elizabeth Myers Mitchell Art Gallery, see Annapolis MD (M)
Saint John's University, Art Dept, see Collegeville MN (S)
Saint John's University, Dept of Fine Arts, see Jamaica NY (S)
Saint John's University, Dr. M.T. Geoffrey Yeh Art Gallery, see Queens NY (M)
Saint John Paul II National Shrine, Washington DC (M)
Saint Johnsbury Athenaeum, Saint Johnsbury VT (M)
Saint Joseph's Oratory, Museum, see Montreal QC (M, L)
Saint Joseph's University, Art Dept, see Philadelphia PA (S)
Saint Joseph College, Art Gallery, University of Saint Joseph, see West Hartford CT (M)
Saint Joseph Museum, Inc., Saint Joseph MO (M)
St Lawrence College, Art Gallery, see Kingston ON (M)
St Lawrence College, Visual & Creative Arts Program, see Brockville ON (S)
St Lawrence University, Dept of Fine Arts, see Canton NY (S)
Saint Louis Art Museum, Saint Louis MO (M,L)
Saint Louis Community College at Florissant Valley, Liberal Arts Division, see Ferguson MO (S)
Saint Louis Community College at Forest Park, Art Dept, see Saint Louis MO (S)
Saint Louis Community College at Meramec, Art Dept, see Saint Louis MO (S)
Saint Louis County Historical Society, St. Louis County Historical Society, see Duluth MN (M)
Saint Louis Public Library, Saint Louis MO (L)
Saint Louis University, Fine & Performing Arts Dept, see Saint Louis MO (S)
St Martins College, Humanities Dept, see Lacey WA (S)
Saint Mary's College, Dept of Art, see Notre Dame IN (S)
Saint Mary's College, Moreau Galleries, see Notre Dame IN (M)
Saint Mary's College of California, Museum of Art, see Moraga CA (M)
Saint Mary's College of Maryland, Art & Art History Dept, see Saint Mary's City MD (S)
St Mary's College of Maryland, The Dwight Frederick Boyden Gallery, see St Mary's City MD (M)
St Mary's Galeria, Orchard Lake MI (M)
Saint Mary's Romanian Orthodox Cathedral, Romanian Ethnic Art Museum, see Cleveland OH (M)
St Mary's University, Art Gallery, see Halifax NS (M)
Saint Mary's University, Dept of Fine Arts, see San Antonio TX (S)
Saint Mary's University of Minnesota, Art & Design Dept, see Winona MN (S)
Saint Mary-of-the-Woods College, Art Dept, see Saint Mary of the Woods IN (S)
St Michael's College, Fine Arts Dept, see Colchester VT (S)
Saint Norbert College, Div of Humanities & Fine Arts, see De Pere WI (S)
Saint Olaf College, Art Dept, see Northfield MN (S)
Saint Olaf College, Flaten Art Museum, see Northfield MN (M)
Saint Paul's Western Sculpture Park, Saint Paul MN (M)

Saint Paul's School, Art Center in Hargate, see Concord NH (M,L)
Saint Paul Public Library, Central Adult Public Services, see Saint Paul MN (L)
Saint Peter's College, Art Gallery, see Jersey City NJ (M)
Saint Peter's College, Fine Arts Dept, see Jersey City NJ (S)
Saint Petersburg College, Fine & Applied Arts at Clearwater Campus, see Clearwater FL (S)
St Tammany Art Association, Covington LA (A)
Saint Thomas Aquinas College, Art Dept, see Sparkill NY (S)
St Thomas-Elgin Public Art Centre, Saint Thomas ON (M)
Saint Xavier University, Dept of Art & Design, see Chicago IL (S)
Saint Xavier University, Robert and Mary Rita Murphy Stump Library, see Chicago IL (L)
Salem Academy & College, Art Dept, see Winston-Salem NC (S)
Salem Art Association, Salem OR (A,M,L)
Salem State University, Art & Design Department, see Salem MA (S)
Salina Art Center, Salina KS (M)
Salisbury House Foundation, Salisbury House and Garden, see Des Moines IA (M)
Salisbury State University, Art Dept, see Salisbury MD (S)
Salisbury University, Salisbury University Art Galleries, see Salisbury MD (M,L)
Salisbury University, Ward Museum of Wildfowl Art, see Salisbury MD (M)
Salmagundi Club, New York NY (O,L)
Salt Lake Art Center, Utah Museum of Contemporary Art, see Salt Lake City UT (A)
Salt Lake City Public Library, Nonfiction & Audiovisual Dept & Gallery at Library Square, see Salt Lake City UT (L)
Salt Lake Community College, Graphic Design Dept, see Salt Lake City UT (S)
Salve Regina University, Art Dept, see Newport RI (S)
Sam Bass Gallery, Concord NC (M)
Samford University, Art Dept, see Birmingham AL (S)
Sam Houston State University, Art Dept, see Huntsville TX (S)
San Angelo Art Club, Helen King Kendall Memorial Art Gallery, see San Angelo TX (M)
San Angelo Museum of Fine Arts, San Angelo TX (M)
San Antonio Art League, San Antonio Art League Museum, see San Antonio TX (A,L)
San Antonio College, Visual Arts & Technology, see San Antonio TX (S)
San Antonio Museum of Art, San Antonio TX (M)
San Bernardino Art Association, National Orange Show Art Gallery, see San Bernardino CA (A)
San Bernardino County Museum, Redlands CA (M)
San Bernardino Valley College, Art Dept, see San Bernardino CA (S)
San Carlos Cathedral, Monterey CA (M)
San Diego Mesa College, Fine Arts Dept, see San Diego CA (S)
San Diego Museum of Art, San Diego CA (M,L)
San Diego Public Library, Art, Music & Recreation, see San Diego CA (L)
San Diego State University, School of Art, Design & Art History, see San Diego CA (S)
San Diego State University, University Art Gallery, see San Diego CA (M)
Sandwich Historical Society, Center Sandwich NH (M)
The Sandwich Historical Society, Inc & Sandwich Glass Museum, Sandwich Glass Museum, see Sandwich MA (M)
Sandy Bay Historical Society & Museums, Sewall Scripture House-Old Castle, see Rockport MA (A)
San Fernando Valley Historical Society, Mission Hills CA (A,L)
San Francisco African-American Historical & Cultural Society, San Francisco CA (A,L)
San Francisco Art Institute, San Francisco CA (S)
San Francisco Art Institute, Walter and McBean Galleries, see San Francisco CA (M,L)
San Francisco Arts Commission, Gallery, see San Francisco CA (M)
San Francisco Arts Education Project, San Francisco CA (A)
San Francisco Camerawork, San Francisco CA (A)
San Francisco City & County Arts Commission, San Francisco CA (A)
San Francisco Maritime National Historical Park, Maritime Museum, see San Francisco CA (M,L)
San Francisco Museum of Craft and Design, San Francisco CA (M)
San Francisco Museum of Modern Art, San Francisco CA (M,L)
San Francisco Public Library, Art, Music & Recreation Center, see San Francisco CA (L)
San Francisco State University, Art Dept, see San Francisco CA (S)
San Francisco State University, J Paul Leonard Library, see San Francisco CA (L)
Sangre de Cristo Arts & Conference Center, Pueblo CO (A)
San Jacinto College-North, Art Dept, see Houston TX (S)
San Jacinto Junior College, Division of Fine Arts, see Pasadena TX (S)
San Joaquin Delta College, Arts & Communication, see Stockton CA (S)
The San Joaquin Pioneer & Historical Society, The Haggin Museum, see Stockton CA (M,L)
San Jose City College, School of Fine Arts, see San Jose CA (S)
San Jose Institute of Contemporary Art, San Jose CA (M)
San Jose Museum of Art, San Jose CA (M,L)
San Jose State University, Dept of Art & Art History, see San Jose CA (S)
San Jose State University, Natalie & James Thompson Art Gallery, see San Jose CA (M,L)
San Juan College, Art Dept, see Farmington NM (S)
San Luis Obispo Museum of Art, San Luis Obispo CA (A)
Santa Ana College, Art Dept, see Santa Ana CA (S)
Santa Ana College, Art Gallery, see Santa Ana CA (M)
Santa Barbara City College, Fine Arts Dept, see Santa Barbara CA (S)
Santa Barbara Contemporary Arts Forum, Santa Barbara CA (A)
Santa Barbara Museum of Art, Santa Barbara CA (M,L)
Santa Barbara Public Central Library, Faulkner Memorial Art Wing, see Santa Barbara CA (L)
Santa Clara University, Dept of Art & Art History, see Santa Clara CA (S)
Santa Clara University, de Saisset Museum, see Santa Clara CA (M)
Santa Cruz Art League, Center for the Arts, see Santa Cruz CA (A)
Santa Fe Arts Institute, Santa Fe NM (S)
Santa Monica College Performing Arts Center, Pete & Susan Barrett Art Gallery, see Santa Monica CA (M)
Santa Paula Art Museum, Santa Paula CA (M)
Santarella Museum & Gardens, Tyringham MA (M)
Santa Rosa Junior College, Art Dept, see Santa Rosa CA (S)
Santa Rosa Junior College, Art Gallery, see Santa Rosa CA (M)
Allen Sapp, North Battleford SK (M)
Sarah Lawrence College, Dept of Art History, see Bronxville NY (S)
Sarah Lawrence College Library, Esther Raushenbush Library, see Bronxville NY (L)
Saratoga County Historical Society, Brookside Museum, see Ballston Spa NY (A)
Saskatchewan Arts Board, Regina SK (O)
Saskatchewan Association of Architects, Saskatoon SK (A)
Saskatchewan Craft Council & Affinity Gallery, Saskatoon SK (M)
Savannah College of Art & Design - Atlanta, ACA Library of Atlanta, see Atlanta GA (L)
Savannah College of Art & Design, (SCAD), see Savannah GA (S)
Savannah State University, Dept of Fine Arts, see Savannah GA (S)
Saving & Preserving Arts & Cultural Environments, Aptos CA (A,L)
Sawtooth Center for Visual Art, Winston-Salem NC (S)
Sawyer Library, see Williams College, Williamstown MA
The Scarab Club, Gallery, see Detroit MI (M)
Scarfone/Hartley Gallery, see University of Tampa, Tampa FL
Schenectady County Historical Society, Schenectady NY (A,L)
The Schepis, Louisiana Artists Museum, Columbia LA (M)
Schneider Museum of Art, see Southern Oregon University, Ashland OR
Schomburg Center for Research in Black Culture, see The New York Public Library, New York NY
Schoolcraft College, Dept of Art & Design, see Livonia MI (S)
School for Advanced Research (SAR), Indian Arts Research Center, see Santa Fe NM (M)
The Schoolhouse Gallery, Provincetown MA (M)
Schoolhouse History & Art Center, Colstrip MT (M)
School of Fashion Design, Boston MA (S)
School of the Art Institute of Chicago, Chicago IL (S)
School of the Art Institute of Chicago, John M Flaxman Library, see Chicago IL (L)
School of the Art Institute of Chicago, Video Data Bank, see Chicago IL (L)
School of the Museum of Fine Arts, Boston MA (S)
School of Visual Arts, New York NY (S)
School of Visual Arts, Chelsea Gallery, see New York NY (M)
School 33 Art Center, Baltimore MD (A)
Rob Schouten Gallery, Greenbank WA (M)
Schuler School of Fine Arts, Baltimore MD (S)
Schuyler-Hamilton House, Morristown NJ (M)
Schuyler Mansion State Historic Site, Albany NY (M)
Schweinfurth Art Center, Auburn NY (M)
Science Fiction and Fantasy Hall of Fame, Seattle WA (M)
Scott Explorers Library, see Martin and Osa Johnson, Chanute KS
Julian Scott Memorial Gallery, Johnson VT (M)
Scottsdale Artists' League, Scottsdale AZ (A)
Scottsdale Artists' School, Scottsdale AZ (S)
Scottsdale Cultural Council, Scottsdale Museum of Contemporary Art, see Scottsdale AZ (M)
Lucy Scribner Library, see Skidmore College, Saratoga Springs NY
Scripps College, Clark Humanities Museum, see Claremont CA (M)
Scripps College, Millard Sheets Art Center-Williamson Gallery, see Claremont CA (S)
Scripps College, Ruth Chandler Williamson Gallery, see Claremont CA (M)
William E Scripture Memorial Library, see Rome Historical Society, Rome NY
Sculptor's Society of Canada, Canadian Sculpture Centre, see Toronto ON (O)
Sculptors Guild, Inc, Brooklyn NY (O)
SculptureCenter, Long Island City NY (M,L)
Sculpture Space, Inc, Utica NY (M)
Sea Cliff Village Museum, Sea Cliff NY (M)
Searchlight Historic Museum & Mining Park, Searchlight NV (M)
Seaton Library, see Riley County Historical Society & Museum, Manhattan KS
Seattle Art Museum, Seattle WA (M,L)
Seattle Central Community College, Humanities - Social Sciences Division, see Seattle WA (S)
Seattle Pacific University, Art Dept, see Seattle WA (S)
Seattle Public Library, Arts, Recreation & Literature Dept, see Seattle WA (L)
Seattle University, Dept of Art & Art History, see Seattle WA (S)
Second Street Gallery, Charlottesville VA (M)

Secretary of State Museum Division, Louisiana State Exhibit Museum, see Shreveport LA (M)
See Science Center, Manchester NH (M)
Segue Foundation, Reading Room-Archive, see New York NY (A)
Self Help Graphics, Los Angeles CA (A)
Selsor Art Gallery, see Martin and Osa Johnson, Chanute KS
Semitic Museum, see Harvard University, Cambridge MA
Seneca-Iroquois National Museum, Salamanca NY (M)
Seneca Falls Historical Society Museum, Seneca Falls NY (M)
Mary Porter Sesnon Art Gallery, see University of California at Santa Cruz, Santa Cruz CA
Seton Hall University, South Orange NJ (M)
Seton Hall University, College of Arts & Sciences, see South Orange NJ (S)
Seton Hill College, Reeves Memorial Library, see Greensburg PA (L)
Seton Hill University, Art Program, see Greensburg PA (S)
1708 Gallery, Richmond VA (M)
Seward County Community College, Art Dept, see Liberal KS (S)
Shain Gallery, Charlotte NC (M)
The Shaker Library, see United Society of Shakers, New Gloucester ME
Shaker Museum & Library, Old Chatham NY (M,L)
Shaker Village of Pleasant Hill, Harrodsburg KY (M)
Shakespeare Ghost Town, Lordsburg NM (M)
Sharon Arts Center, School Arts & Crafts, see Sharon NH (S)
Sharon Arts Center, Sharon Arts Center Exhibition Gallery, see Peterborough NH (M)
Sharon Lynne Wilson Center for the Arts, Ploch Art Gallery, see Brookfield WI (M)
Shasta College, Arts, Communications & Social Sciences Division, see Redding CA (S)
Shasta Historical Society Research Library, see Turtle Bay Exploration Park, Redding CA
Shawinigan Art Center, Shawinigan QC (A)
Sheboygan Arts Foundation, Inc, John Michael Kohler Arts Center, see Sheboygan WI (A)
Sheean Library, see Illinois Wesleyan University, Bloomington IL
Millard Sheets Library, see Otis College of Art & Design, Los Angeles CA
Shelburne Museum, Museum, see Shelburne VT (M,L)
Sheldon Art Galleries, Saint Louis MO (M)
Sheldon Museum & Cultural Center, Inc, Sheldon Museum & Cultural Center, see Haines AK (M)
Shepherd University, Dept of Contemporary Art & Theater, see Shepherdstown WV (S)
Sheridan College, Art Dept, see Sheridan WY (S)
Sheridan College, Faculty of Animation, Arts & Design, see Oakville ON (S)
Sheridan College of Applied Arts and Technology, Trafalgar Campus Library, see Oakville ON (L)
Sherman Art Library, see Dartmouth College, Hanover NH
The Sherwin Miller Museum of Jewish Art, Tulsa OK (M)
Shiawassee Arts Center, Owosso MI (M)
Shippensburg University, Art Dept, see Shippensburg PA (S)
Shippensburg University, Kauffman Gallery, see Shippensburg PA (M)
Ships of the Sea Maritime Museum, Savannah GA (M)
Shirley Plantation Foundation, Charles City VA (M)
Shoreline Community College, Humanities Division, see Seattle WA (S)
Shoreline Historical Museum, Shoreline WA (M)
Shores Memorial Museum, Lyndon Center VT (M)
Shorncliffe Park Improvement Assoc, Prairie Panorama Museum, see Czar AB (M)
Shorter College, Art Dept, see Rome GA (S)
Shoshone Bannock Tribes, Shoshone Bannock Tribal Museum, see Fort Hall ID (M)
Side Street Projects, Pasadena CA (M)
Eli Siegel Collection, see Aesthetic Realism Foundation, New York NY
Siena College, Dept of Creative Arts, see Loudonville NY (S)
Siena Heights College, Klemm Gallery, Studio Angelico, see Adrian MI (M,L)
Siena Heights University, Studio Angelico-Art Dept, see Adrian MI (S)
Sierra Arts Foundation, Sierra Arts Gallery, see Reno NV (A)
Sierra Community College, Art Dept, see Rocklin CA (S)
Sierra Nevada College, Fine Arts Dept, see Incline Village NV (S)
Silver Eye Center for Photography, Pittsburgh PA (A)
Silver Lake College, Art Dept, see Manitowoc WI (S)
Silvermine Arts Center, School of Art, see New Canaan CT (S)
Silvermine Arts Center, Silvermine Galleries, see New Canaan CT (M)
Simon's Rock College of Bard, Visual Arts Dept, see Great Barrington MA (S)
Simon Fraser University, Simon Fraser University Gallery, see Burnaby BC (M,L)
Norton Simon Museum, Pasadena CA (M)
Simpson College, Farnham Gallery, see Indianola IA (M)
Simpson Gallagher Gallery, Cody WY (M)
Sinclair Community College, Division of Fine & Performing Arts, see Dayton OH (S)
Sioux City Art Center, Sioux City IA (S)
Sioux City Art Center, Sioux City IA (A)
SITE Santa Fe, Santa Fe NM (M)
Sitka Historical Society, Sitka History Museum, see Sitka AK (M)
Skagit Valley College, Dept of Art, see Mount Vernon WA (S)
Skagway City Museum & Archives, Skagway AK (M)
Skaneateles Library Association, Skaneateles NY (A)
Skidmore College, Dept of Art & Art History, see Saratoga Springs NY (S)
Skidmore College, Schick Art Gallery, see Saratoga Springs NY (M,L)
Skokie Public Library, Skokie IL (L)
Skowhegan School of Painting & Sculpture, New York NY (S)
Slater Mill, Old Slater Mill Association, see Pawtucket RI (M)
Philip Slein Gallery, Saint Louis MO (M)
Slippery Rock University of Pennsylvania, Dept of Art, see Slippery Rock PA (S)
Joseph Curtis Sloane Art Library, see University of North Carolina at Chapel Hill, Chapel Hill NC
Helen Farr Sloan Library, see Delaware Art Museum, Wilmington DE
Sloss Furnaces National Historic Landmark, Birmingham AL (M)
Smart Museum of Art, see University of Chicago, Chicago IL
C E Smith Museum of Anthropology, see California State University, East Bay, Hayward CA
Smith College, Art Dept, see Northampton MA (S)
Smith College, Museum of Art, see Northampton MA (M,L)
Smithsonian Institution, Smithsonian Institution Building (The Castle), see Washington DC (M)
Snake River Heritage Center, Weiser ID (M)
Snow College, Art Dept, see Ephraim UT (S)
Snow College Art Gallery, Ephraim UT (M)
Snug Harbor Cultural Center, Newhouse Center for Contemporary Art, see Staten Island NY (M)
Soap Factory, Minneapolis MN (M)
Social & Public Art Resource Center, (SPARC), see Venice CA (A)
Societe des Musees Quebecois, Montreal QC (A)
Society for Commercial Archeology, Little Rock AR
Society for Contemporary Craft, Pittsburgh PA (M)
Society for Photographic Education (SPE), SPE Gallery, see Cleveland OH (A)
Society for the Protection & Preservation of Black Culture in Nova Scotia, Black Cultural Center for Nova Scotia, see Cherry Brook NS (L)
Society of American Graphic Artists, New York NY (O)
Society of American Historical Artists, Oyster Bay NY (O)
Society of Architectural Historians, Chicago IL (O)
The Society of Arts & Crafts, Boston MA (A)
Society of Canadian Artists, Toronto ON (O)
Society of Illustrators, New York NY (O)
Society of Illustrators, Museum of American Illustration, see New York NY (M)
The Society of Layerists in Multi-Media (SLMM), Albuquerque NM (A)
Society of North American Goldsmiths, Eugene OR (O)
Society of Scribes, Ltd, New York NY (A)
The Society of the Cincinnati at Anderson House, Washington DC (M)
The Society of the Four Arts, Palm Beach FL (A,L)
Socrates Sculpture Park, Long Island City NY (M)
The Soho Center Library, see New Museum of Contemporary Art, New York NY
SOHO20 Gallery, Brooklyn NY (M)
Soka University, Founders Hall Art Gallery, see Aliso Viejo CA (M)
Solano Community College, Division of Fine & Applied Art & Behavioral Science, see Fairfield CA (S)
Sonoma State University, Art & Art History Dept, see Rohnert Park CA (S)
Sonoma State University, University Art Gallery, see Rohnert Park CA (M)
Sonoma Valley Historical Society, Depot Park Museum, see Sonoma CA (M)
Sonoma Valley Museum of Art, Sonoma CA (M)
Sooke Region Museum & Art Gallery, Sooke BC (M)
Soo Visual Arts Center, Minneapolis MN (M)
Southampton Art Centre, Art School & Gallery, Southampton ON (S)
Southampton College of Long Island University, Arts & Media Division, see Riverhead NY (S)
South Arkansas Arts Center, El Dorado AR (A)
South Bend Regional Museum of Art, South Bend IN (A,L)
South Carolina Artisans Center, Walterboro SC (M)
South Carolina Arts Commission, Columbia SC (A,L)
South Carolina State Museum, Columbia SC (M)
South Carolina State University, Dept of Visual & Performing Arts, see Orangeburg SC (S)
South Central Technical College, Commercial & Technical Art Dept, see North Mankato MN (S)
South County Art Association, Kingston RI (A)
South Dakota National Guard Museum, Pierre SD (M)
South Dakota State University, Dept of Visual Arts, see Brookings SD (S)
South Dakota State University, South Dakota Art Museum, see Brookings SD (M,L)
Southeastern Center for Contemporary Art, Winston-Salem NC (M)
Southeastern Community College, Dept of Art, see Whiteville NC (S)
Southeastern Louisiana University, Art & Design, see Hammond LA (S)
Southeastern Oklahoma State University, Dept of Art, Communication & Theatre, see Durant OK (S)
Southeast Missouri State University, Dept of Art, see Cape Girardeau MO (S)
Southeast Missouri State University, Kent Library, see Cape Girardeau MO (L)
Southern Adventist University, Art Dept, see Collegedale TN (S)
Southern Alberta Art Gallery, Lethbridge AB (M,L)
Southern Alleghenies Museum of Art, Loretto Facility, see Loretto PA (M)
Southern Arkansas University, Art Dept Gallery & Magale Art Gallery, see Magnolia AR (M)
Southern Arkansas University at Magnolia, Dept of Art & Design, see Magnolia AR (S)
Southern Baptist Theological Seminary, Joseph A Callaway Archaeological Museum, see Louisville KY (M)

Southern California Institute of Architecture, Los Angeles CA (S)
Southern Connecticut State University, Art Dept, see New Haven CT (M)
Southern Connecticut State University, Dept of Art, see New Haven CT (S)
Southern Exposure, San Francisco CA (M)
Southern Highland Craft Guild, Folk Art Center, see Asheville NC (A)
Southern Illinois University at Edwardsville, Dept of Art & Design, see Edwardsville IL (S)
Southern Illinois University Carbondale, University Museum, see Carbondale IL (M,L)
Southern Illinois University, Lovejoy Library, see Edwardsville IL (L)
Southern Illinois University, School of Art & Design, see Carbondale IL (S)
Southern Lorain County Historical Society, Spirit of '76 Museum, see Elyria OH (M)
Southern Methodist University, Hamon Arts Library, see Dallas TX (L,M)
Southern Methodist University, Meadows School of the Arts - Division of Art, see Dallas TX (S)
Southern Museum & Galleries of Photography, Mc Minnville TN (M)
Southern Nazarene University, Art & Design Department, see Bethany OK (S)
Southern New Hampshire University, McIninch Art Gallery, see Hooksett NH (M)
Southern Ohio Museum Corporation, Southern Ohio Museum, see Portsmouth OH (M)
Southern Oregon University, Art & Art History Dept, see Ashland OR (S)
Southern Oregon University, Stevenson Union Gallery, see Ashland OR (M)
Southern Plains Indian Museum, Anadarko OK (M)
Southern University A & M College, School of Architecture, see Baton Rouge LA (S)
Southern University in New Orleans, Fine Arts & Philosophy Dept, see New Orleans LA (S)
Southern University Library, Shreveport LA (L)
Southern University Museum of Art in Shreveport, Shreveport LA (M)
Southern Utah State University, Dept of Art, see Cedar City UT (S)
Southern Utah University, Braithwaite Fine Arts Gallery, see Cedar City UT (M)
Southern Vermont Art Center, Manchester VT (A,L)
Southern Virginia College, Division of Arts and Humanities, see Buena Vista VA (S)
South Florida Cultural Consortium, Miami Dade County Dept of Cultural Affairs, see Miami FL (A)
South Florida Fair, Yesteryear Village, see West Palm Beach FL (M)
South Peace Art Society, Dawson Creek Art Gallery, see Dawson Creek BC (M)
South Plains College, Fine Arts Dept, see Levelland TX (S)
South Shore Art Center, Cohasset MA (M)
South Shore Arts, Munster IN (M)
South Street Seaport Museum, New York NY (M,L)
South Suburban College, Art Dept, see South Holland IL (S)
South Texas Institute for the Arts Affiliated with Texas A&M University - Corpus Christi, Art Museum of South Texas, see Corpus Christi TX (M,L)
Southwest Baptist University, Art Dept, see Bolivar MO (S)
Southwestern College, Art Dept, see Winfield KS (S)
Southwestern College, Art Gallery, see Chula Vista CA (M)
Southwestern College, Deets Library - Art Dept, see Winfield KS (L)
Southwestern Community College, Advertising & Graphic Design, see Sylva NC (S)
Southwestern Community College, Art Dept, see Creston IA (S)
Southwestern Illinois College, Art Dept, see Belleville IL (S)
Southwestern Michigan College, Fine & Performing Arts Dept, see Dowagiac MI (S)
Southwestern Oklahoma State University, Art, Communication & Theatre, see Weatherford OK (S)
Southwestern Oregon Community College, Visual Arts Dept, see Coos Bay OR (S)
Southwestern University, Sarofim School of Fine Art, Dept of Art & Art History, see Georgetown TX (S)
Southwest Missouri Museum Associates Inc, Springfield Art Museum, see Springfield MO (A)
Southwest School of Art, San Antonio TX (A)
Space One Eleven, Inc, Birmingham AL (M)
SPACES, Cleveland OH (M)
Spaces Library & Archive, see Saving & Preserving Arts & Cultural Environments, Aptos CA
Spark Gallery, Denver CO (M)
Spartanburg Art Museum, Spartanburg SC (M)
Spartanburg County Museum of Art, The Art School, see Spartanburg SC (S)
Special Libraries Association, Mc Lean VA (O)
Spectrum Gallery, Toledo OH (A)
The Speed Art Museum, Louisville KY (M,L)
Spencer Art Reference Library, see The Nelson-Atkins Museum of Art, Kansas City MO
Spencer Collection, see The New York Public Library, New York NY
Spertus Institute of Jewish Studies, Chicago IL (M,L)
Spirit Square Center for Arts & Education, Charlotte NC (A)
Spokane Falls Community College, Fine Arts Dept, see Spokane WA (S)
Spokane Public Library, Spokane WA (L)
Spoon River College, Art Dept, see Canton IL (S)
Spring Arbor College, Art Dept, see Spring Arbor MI (S)
Springfield Art & Historical Society, Springfield VT (A)
Springfield Art Association of Edwards Place, Springfield IL (A,L)
Springfield Art Museum, Springfield MO (M,L)
Springfield City Library, Springfield MA (A)
Springfield College, Dept of Visual & Performing Arts, see Springfield MA (S)
Springfield College in Illinois, Dept of Art, see Springfield IL (S)
Springfield College, William Blizard Gallery, see Springfield MA (M)
Springfield Free Public Library, Donald B Palmer Museum, see Springfield NJ (L)
Springfield Museum of Art, Springfield OH (S)
Springfield Museum of Art, Springfield OH (M,L)
Springfield Museums, Michele & Donald D'Amour Museum of Fine Arts, see Springfield MA (M)
Spring Hill College, Department of Fine & Performing Arts, see Mobile AL (S)
Springville Museum of Art, Springville UT (M)
Spruce Forest Artisan Village, Grantsville MD (M)
Spurlock Museum, see University of Illinois at Urbana-Champaign, Urbana IL
The Stained Glass Association of America, Raytown MO (O)
Herbert S Stamats Library, see Cedar Rapids Museum of Art, Cedar Rapids IA
Stamford Museum & Nature Center, Stamford CT (M)
St Andrews Presbyterian College, Art Gallery, see Laurinburg NC (M) (S)
Stanford University, Cantor Arts Center at Stanford University, see Stanford CA (M,L)
Stanford University, Dept of Art & Art History, see Stanford CA (S)
Edmund Stanley Library, see Friends University, Wichita KS
Stanley Museum, Inc, Kingfield ME (M)
Star-Spangled Banner Flag House Association, Flag House & 1812 Museum, see Baltimore MD (A,M)
State Capital Museum, Olympia WA (M)
State College of Florida Manatee - Sarasota, Art, Design, Humanities, see Bradenton FL (S)
State Historical Society of Missouri, Columbia MO (A, L)
The State Museum of Pennsylvania, see Pennsylvania Historical & Museum Commission, Harrisburg PA
Staten Island Museum, Staten Island NY (M,L)
State of North Carolina, Battleship North Carolina, see Wilmington NC (M)
State University of New York, Cobleskill, Art Dept, see Cobleskill NY (S)
State University of New York, College at Brockport, Tower Fine Arts Gallery, see Brockport NY (M)
State University of New York, College at Cortland, Dept Art & Art History, see Cortland NY (S)
State University of New York at Albany, Art Dept, see Albany NY (S)
State University of New York at Binghamton, Binghamton University Art Museum, see Binghamton NY (M)
State University of New York at Farmingdale, Visual Communications, see Farmingdale NY (S)
State University of New York at Fredonia, Dept of Art, see Fredonia NY (S)
State University of New York at Geneseo, Bertha V B Lederer Gallery, see Geneseo NY (M)
State University of New York at New Paltz, Art Education Program, see New Paltz NY (S)
State University of New York at New Paltz, Samuel Dorsky Museum of Art, see New Paltz NY (M,L)
State University of New York at Oswego, Tyler Art Gallery, see Oswego NY (M,L)
State University of New York at Plattsburgh, Art Dept, see Plattsburgh NY (S)
State University of New York at Plattsburgh, Art Museum, see Plattsburgh NY (M)
The State University of New York at Potsdam, The Art Museum, see Potsdam NY (M)
State University of New York at Stony Brook, University Art Gallery, see Stony Brook NY (M)
State University of New York at Ulster, Muroff-Kotler Visual Arts Gallery, see Stone Ridge NY (M)
State University of New York College at Brockport, Dept of Art, see Brockport NY (S)
State University of New York College at Buffalo, Fine Arts Dept, see Buffalo NY (S)
State University of New York College at Cortland, Dowd Fine Arts Gallery, see Cortland NY (M)
State University of New York College at Cortland, Visual Resources Collection, see Cortland NY (L)
State University of New York College at Fredonia, Cathy and Jesse Marion Art Gallery, see Fredonia NY (M)
State University of New York College at Geneseo, Dept of Art, see Geneseo NY (S)
State University of New York College at Old Westbury, Visual Arts Dept, see Old Westbury NY (S)
State University of New York College at Old Westbury, Amelie A Wallace Gallery, see Old Westbury NY (M)
State University of New York College at Oneonta, Dept of Art, see Oneonta NY (S)
State University of New York College at Oneonta, Martin - Mullen Art Gallery, see Oneonta NY (M)
State University of New York College at Oswego, Art Dept, see Oswego NY (S)
State University of New York College at Potsdam, Dept of Fine Arts, see Potsdam NY (S)
State University of West Georgia, Art Dept, see Carrollton GA (S)
Stauth Foundation & Museum, Stauth Memorial Museum, see Montezuma KS (M)
Stauton Augusta Art Center, Staunton VA (A)
St Catherine University, Art & Art History Dept, see Saint Paul MN (S)
Ste Genevieve Museum, Sainte Genevieve MO (M)
Stephen Bulger Gallery, Toronto ON (M)
Stephen F Austin State University, School of Art, see Nacogdoches TX (S)
Stephen F Austin State University, SFA Galleries, see Nacogdoches TX (M)
Stephen Phillips Memorial Library, see Penobscot Marine Museum, Searsport ME
Stephens College, Art Dept, see Columbia MO (S)
Stephens College, Lewis James & Nellie Stratton Davis Art Gallery, see Columbia MO (M)
Sterling College, Art & Design Dept, see Sterling KS (S)

Stetson University, Department of Creative Arts, see Deland FL (S)
Stewart Memorial Library & Gallery, see Coe College, Cedar Rapids IA
The Stewart Museum, Montreal QC (M,L)
St George Art Museum, Saint George UT (M)
Stillman College, Stillman Art Gallery & Art Dept, see Tuscaloosa AL (S)
St Johns University, Alice R Rogers/Target Galleries, see Collegeville MN (M)
St Louis Artists' Guild & Galleries, Clayton MO (A)
St Mary Chapter Louisiana Landmarks Society, Grevemberg House Museum, see Franklin LA (M)
Stone Quarry Hill Art Park, John & Virginia Winner Memorial Art Gallery, see Cazenovia NY (M,L)
Stony Brook University, College of Arts & Sciences, Dept of Art, see Stony Brook NY (S)
Storefront for Art & Architecture, New York NY (M)
Storm King Art Center, New Windsor NY (M)
Stout Reference Library, see Newfields, Indianapolis IN
Stoxen Library, see Dickinson State University, Dickinson ND
Strasburg Museum, Strasburg VA (M)
Stratford Historical Society, Catharine B Mitchell Museum, see Stratford CT (M,L)
G Robert Strauss Jr Memorial Library, see The Buffalo Fine Arts Academy, Buffalo NY
Stremmel Gallery, Reno NV (M)
Struts Gallery, Sackville NB (M)
Gilbert Stuart Memorial Association, Inc, Gilbert Stuart Birthplace & Museum, see Saunderstown RI (M)
The Studio/Larson Gallery, see University of Minnesota, Saint Paul MN
Studio Channel Islands Art Center, Camarillo CA (M)
Studio Gallery, Washington DC (M)
The Studio Museum in Harlem, New York NY (M)
Studio Place Arts, Barre VT (M)
Stumptown Art Studio, Whitefish Gallery, see Whitefish MT (M)
Sturdivant Museum Association, Sturdivant Museum, see Selma AL (M)
Suffolk County Community College, Art Dept, see Selden NY (S)
Suffolk University, Gallery, see Boston MA (M)
SU Libraries Guerreri Academic Commons, see Salisbury University, Salisbury MD
Sul Ross State University, Dept of Fine Arts & Communications, see Alpine TX (S)
The Summit County Historical Society of Akron, OH, Akron OH (M)
Sumter Gallery of Art, Sumter SC (M)
Sunbury Shores Arts & Nature Centre, Inc, Gallery, see Saint Andrews NB (A,L)
Sun Valley Center for the Arts, Dept of Fine Art, see Sun Valley ID (S)
Supreme Court of the United States, Office of the Curator, see Washington DC (M)
Surface Design Association, Inc, Las Vegas NM (A)
Surrey Art Gallery, Surrey BC (M,L)
Surry Community College, Art Dept, see Dobson NC (S)
Susquehanna Art Museum, Harrisburg PA (A)
Susquehanna Studio, Union Dale PA (A)
Susquehanna University, Lore Degenstein Gallery, see Selinsgrove PA (M)
SVACA - Sheyenne Valley Arts & Crafts Association, Bjarne Ness Gallery at Bear Creek Hall, see Fort Ransom ND (M,A)
Swarthmore College, Dept of Art & Art History, see Swarthmore PA (S)
Swarthmore College, Friends Historical Library of Swarthmore College, see Swarthmore PA (L)
Swedish American Museum, Chicago IL (M)
Sweet Briar College, Art History Dept, see Sweet Briar VA (S)
Sweet Briar College, Mary Helen Cochran Library, see Sweet Briar VA (L,M)
Sweetwater County Library System and School District #1, Community Fine Arts Center, see Rock Springs WY (A)
Swetcharnik Art Studio, Mount Airy MD (M)
Swine Gallery, Chattanooga TN (M)
Swiss Institute, New York NY (M)
Switzerland County Historical Society Inc, Life on the Ohio: River History Museum, see Vevay IN (M)
Swope Art Museum, Terre Haute IN (M,L)
Symmes Systems, Photographic Investments Gallery, see Atlanta GA (M)
Syracuse University, College of Visual & Performing Arts, see Syracuse NY (S)
Syracuse University, SUArt Galleries, see Syracuse NY (M)
Tabor Opera House Museum, Leadville CO (M)
Tacoma Art Museum, Tacoma WA (M)
Tacoma Community College, Art Dept, see Tacoma WA (S)
Tacoma Public Library, Handforth Gallery, see Tacoma WA (L)
Taft College, Art Department, see Taft CA (S)
Taft Museum of Art, Cincinnati OH (M)
Taipei Economic & Cultural Office, Chinese Information & Culture Center Library, see New York NY (L)
Tallahassee Community College, Art Dept, see Tallahassee FL (S)
Tallahassee Museum of History & Natural Science, Tallahassee FL (M,L)
Taller Puertorriqueno Inc, Lorenzo Homar Gallery, see Philadelphia PA (A)
Tampa Museum of Art, Tampa FL (M,L)
Taos Art Museum, Taos NM (M)
Taos Center for the Arts, Stables Gallery, see Taos NM (A)
Taos Historic Museums, Taos NM (M,L)
Taos Public Library, Fine Art Collection, see Taos NM (L)
Tarrant County College, Art Dept, see Hurst TX (S)
Tattoo Art Museum, San Francisco CA (M)
Lillian & Coleman Taube Museum of Art, Minot ND (M)
Taubman Museum of Art, Roanoke VA (M)
Edward P Taylor Research Library & Archives, see Art Gallery of Ontario, Toronto ON
Elizabeth Prewitt Taylor Memorial Library, see Arkansas Arts Center, Little Rock AR
Taylor University, Metcalf Art Gallery, see Upland IN (M)
Taylor University, Visual Art Dept, see Upland IN (S)
T C Steele State Historic Site, Nashville IN (M)
Telfair Museums, Savannah GA (M)
Tellus Northwest Georgia Science Museum, Cartersville GA (M)
Temiskaming Art Gallery, Haileybury ON (M)
The Temple-Tifereth Israel, The Temple Museum of Religious Art, see Beachwood OH (M,L)
Temple College, Art Dept, see Temple TX (S)
Temple University, Temple Contemporary, see Philadelphia PA (M,L)
Temple University, Tyler School of Art, see Philadelphia PA (S)
Tennessee Historical Society, Nashville TN (A)
Tennessee State Museum, Nashville TN (M)
Tennessee Tech University, Appalachian Center for Craft, see Smithville TN (S)
Tennessee Valley Art Association, Tuscumbia AL (A)
1078 Gallery, Chico CA (M)
Terrain Gallery, see Aesthetic Realism Foundation, New York NY
Texarkana College, Art Dept, see Texarkana TX (S)
Texas A&M University - Commerce, University Gallery, see Commerce TX (M)
Texas A&M University-Corpus Christi, Weil Art Gallery, see Corpus Christi TX (M)
Texas A&M University-Kingsville, Art Dept, see Kingsville TX (S)
Texas A&M University, Art Gallery, see Kingsville TX (M)
Texas A&M University, College of Architecture, see College Station TX (S)
Texas A&M University Commerce, Dept of Art, see Commerce TX (S)
Texas A&M University, J Wayne Stark University Center Galleries, see College Station TX (M,A)
Texas Christian University, Fort Worth Contemporary Art, see Fort Worth TX (M)
Texas Lutheran University, Dept of Visual Arts, see Seguin TX (S)
Texas Ranger Hall of Fame & Museum, Waco TX (M, L)
Texas Ranger Research Center, see Texas Ranger Hall of Fame & Museum, Waco TX
Texas Southern University, College of Liberal Arts & Behavioral Sciences, see Houston TX (S)
Texas State University - San Marcos, Dept of Art and Design, see San Marcos TX (S)
Texas Tech University, Dept of Art, see Lubbock TX (S)
Texas Tech University, Museum of Texas Tech University, see Lubbock TX (M,L)
Texas Wesleyan University, Dept of Art, see Fort Worth TX (S)
Texas Woman's University Art Gallery, Denton TX (M)
Texas Woman's University, School of the Arts, Dept of Visual Arts, see Denton TX (S)
Textile Conservation Workshop Inc, South Salem NY (A)
Textile Museum of Canada, Toronto ON (M)
Thames Art Gallery, Chatham ON (A)
Thelma Sadoff Center for the Arts, Fond Du Lac WI (M)
Thiel College, Dept of Art, see Greenville PA (S)
Thiel College, Weyers-Sampson Art Gallery, see Greenville PA (M)
Think 360 Art Complete Education, Colo Chapter, see Denver CO (A)
Thinkery, Austin TX (M)
Thomas College, Art Gallery, see Waterville ME (M,L)
Thomas Jefferson Foundation, Inc, Monticello, see Charlottesville VA (M)
Thomas More College, Art Dept, see Crestview Hills KY (S)
Thomas More College, Eva G Farris Art Gallery, see Crestview KY (M)
Thomas University, Humanities Division, see Thomasville GA (S)
Nancy Thompson Library, see Kean University, Union NJ
Tom Thomson Memorial Art Gallery, Owen Sound ON (M,L)
Harry Thornton Library, see Pensacola Museum of Art, Pensacola FL
Thousand Islands Arts Center - Home of the Handweaving Museum, Clayton NY (S)
Three Forks Area Historical Society, Headwaters Heritage Museum, see Three Forks MT (M)
3M, Art Collection, see Maplewood MN
Thrivent Financial for Lutherans, Gallery of Religious Art, see Minneapolis MN (M)
Thumbprint Gallery, La Jolla CA (M)
Thunderbird Foundation for the Arts, Mount Carmel UT (M)
Tides Institute & Museum of Art, Eastport ME (M)
Tidewater Community College, Visual Arts Center, see Portsmouth VA (S)
Timken Museum of Art, San Diego CA (M)
Tinkertown Museum, Sandia Park NM (M)
Tohono Chul Park, Tucson AZ (M)
Toledo Artists' Club, Toledo Artists' Club & Gallery, see Toledo OH (A)
Toledo Museum of Art, Toledo OH (M,L)
Topeka & Shawnee County Public Library, Alice C Sabatini Gallery, see Topeka KS (M)
Helen Topping Architecture & Fine Arts Library, see University of Southern California, Los Angeles CA
Toronto Art Therapy Institute, Toronto ON (S)
Toronto Dominion Bank, Toronto ON
Toronto Public Library Board, Library, see Toronto ON (L)
Toronto School of Art, Toronto ON (S)
Toronto Sculpture Garden, Toronto ON (M)

Torrance Art Museum, Torrance CA (M)
Touchstone Center for Crafts, Farmington PA (S)
Touchstone Center for Crafts, Hart Moore Museum, see Farmington PA (A)
Tougaloo College, Art Dept, see Tougaloo MS (S)
Tougaloo College, Tougaloo Art Collection, see Tougaloo MS (M,L)
Town of Cummington Historical Commission, Kingman Tavern Historical Museum, see Cummington MA (M)
Towson State University, Dept of Art, see Towson MD (S)
Towson University, Center for the Arts Gallery, see Towson MD (M)
Traffic Zone Center for Visual Art, Minneapolis MN (M)
Transylvania University, Art Program, see Lexington KY (S)
Transylvania University, Morlan Gallery, see Lexington KY (M)
Treasure Valley Community College, Art Dept, see Ontario OR (S)
Trenton City Museum, Trenton NJ (M)
Scott Andrew Trexler II Library, see Lehigh Valley Heritage Center, Allentown PA
Trinity College, Austin Arts Center, Widener Gallery, see Hartford CT (M)
Trinity College, Dept of Studio Arts, see Hartford CT (S)
Trinity College, Fine Arts Program, see Washington DC (S)
Trinity College Library, Washington DC (L)
Trinity University, Department of Art & Art History, see San Antonio TX (S)
Triton College, School of Arts & Sciences, see River Grove IL (S)
Triton Museum of Art, Santa Clara CA (M)
Trova Foundation, Philip Samuels Fine Art, see Saint Louis MO (M)
Troy-Pike Cultural Arts Center, Troy AL (M)
Troy State University, Dept of Art & Classics, see Troy AL (S)
Truck Contemporary Art in Calgary, Calgary AB (A)
Truett-McConnell College, Fine Arts Dept & Arts Dept, see Cleveland GA (S)
Truman College Art Gallery, Chicago IL (M)
Truman State University, Art Dept, see Kirksville MO (S)
Truro Center for the Arts at Castle Hill, Inc, Truro MA (S)
Trust Authority, Museum of the Great Plains, see Lawton OK (M,L)
The Trustees of Reservations, The Mission House, see Ipswich MA (M)
Sojourner Truth Library, see State University of New York at New Paltz, New Paltz NY
Tryon Palace, New Bern NC (M,L)
Tubac Center of the Arts, Santa Cruz Valley Art Association, see Tubac AZ (M,L)
Tubman African American Museum, Macon GA (M,L)
Tucson Museum of Art and Historic Block, Tucson AZ (M,L)
Tufts University, Dept of Art & Art History, see Medford MA (S)
Tufts University, Tufts University Art Gallery, see Medford MA (M)
Tulane University, Newcomb Art Museum, see New Orleans LA (M)
Tulane University, School of Architecture, see New Orleans LA (S)
Tulane University, University Art Collection, see New Orleans LA (M,L)
Tullahoma Fine Arts Center Regional Museum of Art, Tullahoma TN (M)
Tulsa Community College, Center for Creativity, see Tulsa OK (S)
Tunxis Community Technical College, Graphic Design Dept, see Farmington CT (S)
Turtle Bay Exploration Park, Redding CA (M,L)
Turtle Mountain Chippewa Historical Society, Turtle Mountain Heritage Center, see Belcourt ND (M)
Tusculum College, Fine Arts Dept, see Greeneville TN (S)
Tuskegee Institute National Historic Site, George Washington Carver & The Oaks, see Montgomery AL (M)
Tuskegee University, Liberal Arts & Education, see Tuskegee AL (S)
Mark Twain, Hartford CT (M,L)
21c Museum, Louisville KY (M)
Twin City Art Foundation, Masur Museum of Art, see Monroe LA (M)
Two Rivers Art Gallery, Prince George BC (M)
Tyler Junior College, Art Program, see Tyler TX (S)
Tyler Museum of Art, Tyler TX (M,L)
Tyler School of Art Library, see Temple University, Philadelphia PA
UCR ARTSblock, Sweeney Art Gallery, see Riverside CA (M,L)
Ucross Foundation, Big Red Barn Gallery, see Clearmont WY (M)
U Gallery, San Francisco CA (M)
Ukrainian Canadian Archives & Museum of Alberta, Edmonton AB (M)
Ukrainian Cultural & Educational Centre, Winnipeg MB (M,L)
Ukrainian Institute of America, Inc, New York NY (A)
Ukrainian Institute of Modern Art, Chicago IL (M)
The Ukrainian Museum, New York NY (M,L)
Ukrainian National Museum & Library, Chicago IL (L)
Ulster County Community College/SUNY Ulster, Dept of Art, Design, Music, Theatre, Communication & Fashion, see Stone Ridge NY (S)
UMB Financial Corporation, Kansas City MO
UMLAUF Sculpture Garden & Museum, Austin TX (M)
Umpqua Community College, Fine & Performing Arts Dept, see Roseburg OR (S)
Union College, Dept of Visual Arts, see Schenectady NY (S)
Union College, Music and Fine Arts Dept, see Barbourville KY (S)
Union County Public Library Union Room, Monroe NC (M)
Union for Reformed Judaism, Synagogue Art & Architectural Library, see New York NY (L)
Union Station Museums, see Ogden Union Station, Ogden UT
Union University, Dept of Art, see Jackson TN (S)
United Indians of All Tribes Foundation, Daybreak Star Center Gallery, see Seattle WA (M)
United Methodist Church General Commission on Archives & History, Madison NJ (M,L)
United Methodist Historical Society, Lovely Lane Museum, see Baltimore MD (M,L)
United Society of Shakers, Shaker Museum, see New Gloucester ME (M,L)
United States Capitol, Architect of the Capitol, see Washington DC (M)
United States Coast Guard Museum, New London CT (M)
United States Commission of Fine Arts, Washington DC (A)
United States Department of State, Diplomatic Reception Rooms, see Washington DC (M)
United States Department of the Interior, Indian Arts & Crafts Board, see Washington DC (O)
United States Department of the Interior, Interior Museum, see Washington DC (M)
United States Figure Skating Association, World Figure Skating Museum & Hall of Fame, see Colorado Springs CO (M)
United States General Services Administration, Art in Architecture and Fine Arts, see Washington DC (O)
United States Military Academy, West Point Museum, see West Point NY (M)
United States National Committee of the International Council of Museums, Washington DC (O)
United States Naval Academy, USNA Museum, see Annapolis MD (M)
United States Navy, Art Gallery, see Washington DC (M)
United States Navy Supply Corps School, US Navy Supply Corps Museum, see Newport RI (M)
United States Senate Commission on Art, Washington DC (A,L)
Universite de Moncton, Dept of Visual Arts, see Moncton NB (S)
Universite de Montreal, Bibliotheque d'Amenagement, see Montreal QC (L)
Universite de Montreal, Dept of Art History & Film Studies, see Montreal QC (S)
Universite du Quebec, Trois-Rivieres, Department of Philosophy & the Arts, see Trois-Rivieres QC (S)
Universite du Quebec a Montreal, Faculty of Arts, see Montreal QC (S)
Universite du Quebec, Bibliotheque des Arts, see Montreal QC (L)
Universite Laval, Faculty of Planning, Architecture, Arts & Design, see Quebec QC (S)
University Art Gallery at California State University, Dominguez Hills, Carson CA (M)
University at Albany, State University of New York, University Art Museum, see Albany NY (M,L)
University at Buffalo, State University of New York, Dept of Visual Studies, see Buffalo NY (S)
University Club Library, New York NY (L)
University Libraries, see The University of the Arts, Philadelphia PA
University of Akron, Myers School of Art, see Akron OH (S)
University of Akron, University Art Galleries, see Akron OH (M)
University of Alabama at Birmingham, Abroms-Engel Institute for the Visual Arts, see Birmingham AL (M)
University of Alabama at Birmingham, Dept of Art & Art History, see Birmingham AL (S)
University of Alabama at Huntsville, Union Grove Gallery & University Center Gallery, see Huntsville AL (M)
University of Alabama, Dept of Art, see Tuscaloosa AL (S)
University of Alabama in Huntsville, Dept of Art and Art History, see Huntsville AL (S)
University of Alabama, Sarah Moody Gallery of Art, see Tuscaloosa AL (M)
University of Alaska Anchorage, Dept of Art, see Anchorage AK (S)
University of Alaska Fairbanks, Art Department, see Fairbanks AK (S)
University of Alaska, Museum of the North, see Fairbanks AK (M,L)
University of Alberta, Dept of Art & Design, see Edmonton AB (S)
University of Arizona, Dept of Art, see Tucson AZ (S)
University of Arizona, Museum of Art & Archive of Visual Arts, see Tucson AZ (M,L)
University of Arkansas, Art Dept, see Fayetteville AR (S)
University of Arkansas at Little Rock, Art Library and Galleries, see Little Rock AR (L)
University of Arkansas at Little Rock, Art Galleries, see Little Rock AR (M)
University of Arkansas at Little Rock, Dept of Art & Design, see Little Rock AR (S)
University of Arkansas at Monticello, Fine Arts Dept, see Monticello AR (S)
University of Arkansas at Pine Bluff, Art Dept, see Pine Bluff AR (S)
University of Arkansas, Fine Arts Center Gallery, see Fayetteville AR (M,L)
University of Bridgeport Gallery, Bridgeport CT (M)
University of Bridgeport, Shintaro Akatsu School of Design, see Bridgeport CT (S)
University of British Columbia, Dept of Art History, Visual Art & Theory, see Vancouver BC (S)
University of British Columbia, Morris & Helen Belkin Art Gallery, see Vancouver BC (M,L)
University of British Columbia Okanagan, Faculty of Creative & Critical Studies, see Kelowna BC (M) (S)
University of Calgary, Dept of Art, see Calgary AB (S)

University of Calgary, Nickle Galleries, see Calgary AB (M,L)
University of California, Berkeley, Berkeley Art Museum & Pacific Film Archive, see Berkeley CA (M,L)
University of California, Berkeley, College of Letters & Sciences-Art Practice Dept, see Berkeley CA (S)
University of California, Berkeley, The Magnes Collection of Jewish Art & Life, see Berkeley CA (M,L)
University of California, Davis, Dept of Art & Art History, see Davis CA (S)
University of California, Irvine, Beall Center for Art + Technology, and University Art Gallery, see Irvine CA (M)
University of California, Irvine, Studio Art Dept, see Irvine CA (S)
University of California, Los Angeles, Dept of Art, see Los Angeles CA (S)
University of California, Los Angeles, Fowler Museum at UCLA, see Los Angeles CA (M,L)
University of California, Riverside, Dept of the History of Art, see Riverside CA (S)
University of California, San Diego, Dept of Visual Arts, see La Jolla CA (S)
University of California, San Diego, Stuart Collection, see La Jolla CA (M)
University of California, Santa Barbara, Art, Design & Architecture Museum, see Santa Barbara CA (M,L)
University of California, Santa Barbara, Dept of Art Studio, see Santa Barbara CA (S)
University of California, Santa Cruz, Art Dept, see Santa Cruz CA (S)
University of California-San Diego, University Art Gallery, see La Jolla CA (M)
University of California at Santa Cruz, Eloise Pickard Smith Gallery, see Santa Cruz CA (M)
University of Central Arkansas, Department of Art, see Conway AR (S)
University of Central Florida, Art Dept, see Orlando FL (S)
University of Central Florida Libraries, Orlando FL (L)
University of Central Missouri, Dept of Art & Design, see Warrensburg MO (S)
University of Central Missouri, Gallery of Art & Design, see Warrensburg MO (M)
University of Central Oklahoma, Dept of Art & Design, see Edmond OK (S)
University of Charleston, Carleton Varney Dept of Art & Design, see Charleston WV (S)
University of Chicago, Dept of Art History, see Chicago IL (S)
University of Chicago, Reva and David Logan Center for the Arts, see Chicago IL (M,L)
University of Cincinnati, DAAP Galleries-College of Design Architecture, Art & Planning, see Cincinnati OH (M,L)
University of Cincinnati, School of Art, see Cincinnati OH (S)
University of Colorado, Boulder, Dept of Art & Art History, see Boulder CO (S)
University of Colorado-Colorado Springs, Visual & Performing Arts Dept (VAPA), see Colorado Springs CO (S)
University of Colorado at Colorado Springs, Gallery of Contemporary Art, see Colorado Springs CO (M)
University of Colorado at Denver, College of Arts & Media Visual Arts Dept, see Denver CO (S)
University of Colorado, CU Art Museum, see Boulder CO (M,L)
University of Connecticut, Dept of Art & Art History, see Storrs CT (S)
University of Connecticut, William Benton Museum of Art, see Storrs CT (M,L)
University of Dayton, Visual Arts Dept, see Dayton OH (S)
University of Delaware, Dept of Art, see Newark DE (S)
University of Delaware, University Museums, see Newark DE (M,L)
University of Denver, School of Art & Art History, see Denver CO (S)
University of Detroit Mercy, School of Architecture, see Detroit MI (S)
University of Evansville, Art Dept, see Evansville IN (S)
University of Evansville, Krannert Gallery & Peterson Gallery, see Evansville IN (M,L)
University of Findlay, Art Program, see Findlay OH (S)
University of Findlay, Dudley & Mary Marks Lea Gallery, see Findlay OH (M)
University of Florida, School of Art & Art History, see Gainesville FL (S)
University of Florida, University Gallery, see Gainesville FL (M,L)
University of Georgia, Franklin College of Arts & Sciences, Lamar Dodd School of Art, see Athens GA (S)
University of Georgia, Georgia Museum of Art, see Athens GA (M,L)
University of Great Falls, Art Dept, see Great Falls MT (S)
University of Guelph, School of Fine Art & Music, see Guelph ON (S)
University of Hartford, Hartford Art School, see West Hartford CT (S)
University of Hartford, Joseloff Gallery, see West Hartford CT (M,L)
University of Hartford, Mortensen Library, see West Hartford CT (L)
University of Hawaii at Manoa, Dept of Art, see Honolulu HI (S)
University of Hawaii at Manoa, The Art Gallery & The John Young Museum of Art, see Honolulu HI (M)
University of Hawaii, Kapiolani Community College, see Honolulu HI (S)
University of Houston, Blaffer Art Museum, see Houston TX (M,L)
University of Houston, Dept of Art, see Houston TX (S)
University of Idaho College of Art & Architecture, Dept of Art & Design, see Moscow ID (S)
University of Illinois, Urbana-Champaign, College of Fine & Applied Arts, see Champaign IL (S)
University of Illinois at Chicago, Biomedical Visualization, see Chicago IL (S)
University of Illinois at Chicago, College of Architecture, see Chicago IL (S)
University of Illinois at Chicago, Gallery 400, see Chicago IL (M)
University of Illinois at Springfield, Visual Arts Program, see Springfield IL (S)
University of Illinois at Urbana-Champaign, Krannert Art Museum and Kinkead Pavilion, see Champaign IL (M,L)
University of Indianapolis, Christel DeHaan Fine Arts Gallery, see Indianapolis IN (M)
University of Indianapolis, Dept Art & Design, see Indianapolis IN (S)
University of Iowa, School of Art & Art History, see Iowa City IA (S)
University of Iowa, University of Iowa Museum of Art, see Iowa City IA (M,L)
University of Jamestown, Art Dept, see Jamestown ND (S)
University of Judaism, Dept of Continuing Education, see Los Angeles CA (S)
University of Kansas, Spencer Museum of Art, see Lawrence KS (M,L)
University of Kansas, The School of the Arts, Dept of Visual Art, see Lawrence KS (S)
University of Kentucky, Hunter M Adams Architecture Library, see Lexington KY (L)
The University of Kentucky Art Museum, Lexington KY (M,L)
University of Kentucky, Dept of Art, see Lexington KY (S)
University of La Verne, Dept of Art, see La Verne CA (S)
University of Lethbridge, Art Gallery, see Lethbridge AB (M)
University of Lethbridge, Faculty of Fine Arts, see Lethbridge AB (S)
University of Louisiana at Lafayette, Dept of Visual Arts, see Lafayette LA (S)
University of Louisiana at Lafayette, Paul and Lulu Hilliard University Art Museum, see Lafayette LA (M)
University of Louisiana at Monroe, Bry Gallery, see Monroe LA (M)
University of Louisiana at Monroe, Dept of Art, see Monroe LA (S)
University of Louisville, Allen R Hite Art Institute, see Louisville KY (S)
University of Louisville, Hite Art Institute, see Louisville KY (M,L)
University of Maine at Augusta, College of Arts & Humanities, see Augusta ME (S)
University of Maine at Augusta, The Danforth Gallery, see Augusta ME (M)
University of Maine, Dept of Art, see Orono ME (S)
University of Maine, Museum of Art, see Bangor ME (M)
University of Manitoba, School of Art, see Winnipeg MB (S)
University of Manitoba, School of Art Gallery, see Winnipeg MB (M,L)
University of Mary Hardin-Baylor, College of Visual & Performing Arts, see Belton TX (S)
University of Maryland, Baltimore County, Intermedia & Digital Arts (IMDA), Dept of Visual Arts, see Baltimore MD (S)
University of Maryland, College Park, The Art Gallery, see College Park MD (M,L)
University of Maryland, Baltimore County, Center for Art Design and Visual Culture, see Baltimore MD (M)
University of Maryland, Dept of Art History & Archaeology, see College Park MD (S)
University of Maryland Eastern Shore, Art & Technology Dept, see Princess Anne MD (S)
University of Mary Washington, Dept of Art & Art History, see Fredericksburg VA (S)
University of Mary Washington Galleries, see University of Mary Washington, Fredericksburg VA
University of Mary Washington, Gari Melchers Home and Studio, see Fredericksburg VA (M)
University of Massachusetts, Amherst, College of Arts & Sciences, Fine Arts Center, see Amherst MA (S)
University of Massachusetts, Amherst, University Gallery, see Amherst MA (M,L)
University of Massachusetts - Boston, Art Dept, see Boston MA (S)
University of Massachusetts Dartmouth, College of Visual & Performing Arts, see North Dartmouth MA (S)
University of Massachusetts Lowell, Dept of Art, see Lowell MA (S)
University of Memphis, Art Dept, see Memphis TN (S)
University of Memphis, Art Museum, see Memphis TN (M,L)
University of Miami, Dept of Art & Art History, see Coral Gables FL (S)
University of Miami, Lowe Art Museum, see Coral Gables FL (M)
University of Michigan, Ann Arbor, Penny W Stamps School of Art & Design, see Ann Arbor MI (S)
University of Michigan, Museum of Art, see Ann Arbor MI (M,L)
University of Minnesota, Duluth, Art Dept, see Duluth MN (S)
University of Minnesota, Minneapolis, Art History, see Minneapolis MN (S)
University of Minnesota, Morris, Humanities Division, see Morris MN (S)
University of Minnesota, Dept of Design, Housing & Apparel, see Saint Paul MN (S)
University of Minnesota Duluth, Tweed Museum of Art, see Duluth MN (M)
University of Minnesota, Paul Whitney Larson Gallery, see Saint Paul MN (M)
University of Minnesota, Katherine E Nash Gallery, see Minneapolis MN (M)
University of Minnesota, Frederick R Weisman Art Museum, see Minneapolis MN (M,L)
University of Mississippi, Department of Art, see University MS (S)

University of Mississippi, Rowan Oak, Home of William Faulkner, see Oxford MS (M)
University of Mississippi, University Museum & Historic Houses, see Oxford MS (M)
University of Missouri, Saint Louis, Dept of Art & Art History, see Saint Louis MO (S)
University of Missouri, Saint Louis, Gallery 210, see Saint Louis MO (M)
University of Missouri - Columbia, Dept of Art, see Columbia MO (S)
University of Missouri-Kansas City, Dept of Art & Art History, see Kansas City MO (S)
University of Missouri-Kansas City, Gallery of Art, see Kansas City MO (M)
University of Missouri, Museum of Art & Archaeology, see Columbia MO (M,L)
The University of Montana - Western, Art Gallery Museum, see Dillon MT (M,L)
University of Montana, Gallery of Visual Arts, see Missoula MT (M)
University of Montana, School of Art, see Missoula MT (S)
The University of Montana Western, Art Program, see Dillon MT (S)
University of Montevallo, College of Fine Arts, see Montevallo AL (S)
University of Montevallo, The Gallery, see Montevallo AL (M)
University of Nebraska, Kearney, Dept of Art & Art History, see Kearney NE (S)
University of Nebraska, Lincoln, Sheldon Memorial Art Gallery & Sculpture Garden, see Lincoln NE (M,L)
University of Nebraska-Lincoln, Dept of Art & Art History, see Lincoln NE (S)
University of Nebraska-Lincoln, Great Plains Art Museum, see Lincoln NE (M)
University of Nebraska at Omaha, School of the Arts, see Omaha NE (S)
University of Nebraska at Omaha, UNO Art Gallery, see Omaha NE (M)
University of Nevada, Las Vegas, Donna Beam Fine Art Gallery, see Las Vegas NV (M)
University of Nevada, Las Vegas, Dept of Art, see Las Vegas NV (S)
University of Nevada, Reno, Art Dept, see Reno NV (S)
University of Nevada, Reno, Sheppard Contemporary & University Galleries, see Reno NV (M)
University of New Brunswick, Art Centre, see Fredericton NB (M)
University of New Brunswick, Faculty of Arts, see Fredericton NB (S)
University of New England, Art Gallery, see Portland ME (M)
University of New Hampshire, Dept of Art & Art History, see Durham NH (S)
University of New Hampshire, Museum of Art, see Durham NH (M,L)
University of New Haven, Dept of Visual & Performing Arts & Philosophy, see West Haven CT (S)
University of New Mexico, Department of Fine Arts & Art History, see Albuquerque NM (S)
University of New Mexico, The Harwood Museum of Art, see Taos NM (M)
University of New Mexico, University of New Mexico Art Museum, see Albuquerque NM (M,L)
University of New Orleans-Lake Front, Dept of Fine Arts, see New Orleans LA (S)
University of New Orleans, Fine Arts Gallery, see New Orleans LA (M,L)
University of North Alabama, Dept of Art, see Florence AL (S)
University of North Carolina at Asheville, Dept of Art, see Asheville NC (S)
University of North Carolina at Chapel Hill, Ackland Art Museum, see Chapel Hill NC (M,L)
University of North Carolina at Chapel Hill, Art Dept, see Chapel Hill NC (S)
University of North Carolina at Charlotte, Dept Art, see Charlotte NC (S)
University of North Carolina at Greensboro, School of Art, see Greensboro NC (S)
University of North Carolina at Greensboro, Weatherspoon Art Museum, see Greensboro NC (M)
University of North Carolina at Pembroke, Art Dept, see Pembroke NC (S)
University of North Carolina at Wilmington, Dept of Fine Arts - Division of Art, see Wilmington NC (S)
University of North Dakota, Art Department, see Grand Forks ND (S)
University of North Dakota, Hughes Fine Arts Center-Col Eugene Myers Art Gallery, see Grand Forks ND (M)
University of Northern Colorado, Mariani Gallery, see Greeley CO (M)
University of Northern Colorado, School of Art & Design, see Greeley CO (S)
University of Northern Iowa, Dept of Art, see Cedar Falls IA (S)
University of Northern Iowa, UNI Gallery of Art, see Cedar Falls IA (M,L)
University of North Florida, Dept of Communications & Visual Arts, see Jacksonville FL (S)
University of North Texas, Art Gallery, see Denton TX (M,L)
University of North Texas, College of Visual Arts & Design, see Denton TX (S)
University of North Texas Health Science Center Fort Worth, Atrium Gallery, see Fort Worth TX (M)
University of Notre Dame, Dept of Art, Art History & Design, see Notre Dame IN (S)
University of Notre Dame, Snite Museum of Art, see Notre Dame IN (M,L)
University of Oklahoma, Fred Jones Jr Museum of Art, see Norman OK (M,L)
University of Oklahoma, School of Art, see Norman OK (S)
University of Oregon, Dept of Fine & Applied Arts, see Eugene OR (S)
University of Oregon, Jordan Schnitzer Museum of Art, see Eugene OR (M,L)
University of Pennsylvania, Arthur Ross Gallery, see Philadelphia PA (M)
University of Pennsylvania, Fisher Fine Arts Library, see Philadelphia PA (L,M)
University of Pennsylvania, Institute of Contemporary Art, see Philadelphia PA (A)
University of Pennsylvania, School of Design (PennDesign), see Philadelphia PA (S)
University of Pittsburgh at Johnstown, Dept of Fine Arts, see Johnstown PA (S)
University of Pittsburgh, Henry Clay Frick Dept History of Art & Architecture, see Pittsburgh PA (S)
University of Pittsburgh, University Art Gallery, see Pittsburgh PA (M,L)
University of Portland, Buckley Center Gallery, see Portland OR (M)
University of Portland, Wilson W Clark Memorial Library, see Portland OR (L)
University of Puerto Rico, Mayaguez, Dept of Humanities, College of Fine Arts & Theory of Art Programs, see Mayaguez PR (S)
University of Puerto Rico, Dept of Fine Arts, see Rio Piedras PR (S)
University of Puerto Rico, Museum of Anthropology, History & Art, see Rio Piedras PR (M)
University of Puget Sound, Dept of Art & Art History, see Tacoma WA (S)
University of Puget Sound, Kittredge Art Gallery, see Tacoma WA (M)
University of Redlands, Dept of Art, see Redlands CA (S)
University of Redlands, Peppers Art Gallery, see Redlands CA (M)
University of Regina, Faculty of Media, Art & Performance, see Regina SK (S)
University of Regina, MacKenzie Art Gallery, see Regina SK (M,L)
University of Rhode Island, Dept of Art & Art History, see Kingston RI (S)
University of Rhode Island, Fine Arts Center Galleries, see Kingston RI (M)
University of Richmond, Dept of Art and Art History, see Richmond VA (S)
University of Richmond, University Museums, see Richmond VA (M)
University of Rochester, Dept of Art & Art History, see Rochester NY (S)
University of Rochester, Memorial Art Gallery, see Rochester NY (M,L)
University of Saint Francis, School of Creative Arts, John P Weatherhead Gallery & Lupke Gallery, see Fort Wayne IN (M)
University of Saint Francis, Fine Arts Dept, see Joliet IL (S)
University of Saint Francis, School of Creative Arts, see Fort Wayne IN (S)
University of Saint Joseph, Connecticut, Dept of Fine Arts, see West Hartford CT (S)
University of Saint Mary, Fine Arts Dept, see Leavenworth KS (S)
University of Saint Thomas, Fine and Performing Arts Dept, see Houston TX (S)
University of San Diego, Art Dept, see San Diego CA (S)
University of San Diego, Founders' Gallery, see San Diego CA (M)
The University of San Francisco Thacher Gallery, San Francisco CA (M)
University of Saskatchewan, Art & Art History Dept, see Saskatoon SK (S)
University of Saskatchewan, Gordon Snelgrove Art Gallery, see Saskatoon SK (M)
University of Science & Arts of Oklahoma, Art Dept, see Chickasha OK (S)
University of Sherbrooke, Art Gallery, see Sherbrooke QC (M)
University of Sioux Falls, Dept of Art, see Sioux Falls SD (S)
University of South Alabama, Dept of Art & Art History, see Mobile AL (S)
University of South Alabama, Ethnic American Slide Library, see Mobile AL (L)
University of South Carolina at Aiken, Dept of Visual & Performing Arts, see Aiken SC (S)
University of South Carolina at Spartanburg, Art Gallery, see Spartanburg SC (M)
University of South Carolina Beaufort Art Gallery, Beaufort SC (M)
University of South Carolina, Dept of Art, see Columbia SC (S)
University of South Carolina, McKissick Museum, see Columbia SC (M)
University of South Dakota, Department of Art, College of Fine Arts, see Vermillion SD (S)
University of South Dakota, University Art Galleries, see Vermillion SD (M)
University of Southern California/The Gamble House, Greene & Greene Archives, see San Marino CA (L)
University of Southern California, College of Letters, Arts & Sciences, see Los Angeles CA (S)
University of Southern California, USC Fisher Museum of Art, see Los Angeles CA (M,L)
University of Southern California, USC Pacific Asia Museum, see Pasadena CA (M)
University of Southern Colorado, College of Liberal & Fine Arts, see Pueblo CO (M)
University of Southern Colorado, Dept of Art, see Pueblo CO (S)
University of Southern Indiana, Art & Design Dept, see Evansville IN (S)
University of Southern Indiana, New Harmony Gallery of Contemporary Art, see New Harmony IN (M)
University of Southern Maine, Dept of Art, see Gorham ME (S)
University of Southern Mississippi, Dept of Art & Design, see Hattiesburg MS (S)
University of Southern Mississippi, McCain Library & Archives, see Hattiesburg MS (L)
University of Southern Mississippi, Museum of Art, see Hattiesburg MS (M)
University of South Florida, Contemporary Art Museum, see Tampa FL (M,L)
University of South Florida, School of Art & Art History, see Tampa FL (S)

University of St Thomas, Deptartment of Art History, see Saint Paul MN (S)
University of Tampa, College of Arts & Letters, see Tampa FL (S)
University of Tampa, Henry B Plant Museum, see Tampa FL (M)
University of Tennessee, Knoxville, School of Art, see Knoxville TN (S)
University of Tennessee at Chattanooga, Cress Gallery of Art, see Chattanooga TN (M)
University of Tennessee at Chattanooga, Dept of Art, see Chattanooga TN (S)
University of Tennessee, McClung Museum of Natural History & Culture, see Knoxville TN (M,A)
University of Texas at Arlington, Art & Art History Department, see Arlington TX (S)
University of Texas at Arlington, Gallery at UTA, see Arlington TX (M)
University of Texas at Austin, Fine Arts Library, see Austin TX (L,M)
University of Texas at Brownsville & Texas Southmost College, Fine Arts Dept, see Brownsville TX (S)
University of Texas at El Paso, Dept of Art, see El Paso TX (S)
University of Texas at El Paso, Stanlee & Gerald Rubin Center for the Visual Arts, see El Paso TX (M)
University of Texas at San Antonio, Dept of Art & Art History, see San Antonio TX (S)
The University of Texas at San Antonio, Institute of Texan Cultures, see San Antonio TX (M)
University of Texas at Tyler, Department of Art, School of Visual & Performing Arts, see Tyler TX (S)
University of Texas of Permian Basin, Dept of Art, see Odessa TX (S)
University of Texas Pan American, Art Dept, see Edinburg TX (S)
University of Texas Pan American, Charles & Dorothy Clark Gallery; University Gallery, see Edinburg TX (M)
University of Texas, School of Architecture, see Austin TX (S)
University of the Arts, Philadelphia Colleges of Art & Design, Performing Arts & Media & Communication, see Philadelphia PA (S)
The University of the Arts, Rosenwald-Wolf Gallery, see Philadelphia PA (M,L)
University of the District of Columbia, Dept of Mass Media, Visual & Performing Arts, see Washington DC (S)
University of the Incarnate Word, Art Dept, see San Antonio TX (S)
University of the Ozarks, Dept of Art, see Clarksville AR (S)
University of the Ozarks, Stephens Gallery, see Clarksville AR (M,L)
University of the Pacific, College of the Pacific, Dept of Art & Art History, see Stockton CA (S)
University of the Pacific, Jeannette Powell Art Center, see Stockton CA (M)
University of the South, Dept of Fine Arts, see Sewanee TN (S)
University of the South, Jessie Ball duPont Library, see Sewanee TN (L)
University of the South, University Art Gallery, see Sewanee TN (M)
University of Toledo, Dept of Art, see Toledo OH (S)
University of Toronto, Art Centre, see Toronto ON (M)
University of Toronto at Mississauga, Blackwood Gallery, see Mississauga ON (M)
University of Toronto, Justina M Barnicke Gallery, see Toronto ON (M,L)
University of Toronto, Dept of Fine Art, see Toronto ON (S)
University of Tulsa, Gilcrease Museum, see Tulsa OK (M,L)
University of Tulsa, Alexandre Hogue Gallery, see Tulsa OK (M)
University of Tulsa, School of Art, see Tulsa OK (S)
University of Utah, Dept of Art & Art History, see Salt Lake City UT (S)
University of Utah, Utah Museum of Fine Arts, see Salt Lake City UT (M,L)
University of Vermont, Dept of Art, see Burlington VT (S)
University of Vermont, Robert Hull Fleming Museum, see Burlington VT (M)
University of Victoria, Faculty of Arts, see Victoria BC (S)
University of Victoria, The Legacy Art Gallery, see Victoria BC (M)
University of Virginia, McIntire Dept of Art, see Charlottesville VA (S)
University of Virginia, The Fralin Museum of Art at the University of Virginia, see Charlottesville VA (M,L)
University of Washington, Henry Art Gallery, see Seattle WA (M,L)
University of Washington, School of Art, see Seattle WA (S)
University of Waterloo, Dept of Fine Arts, see Waterloo ON (S)
University of Waterloo, University of Waterloo Art Gallery, see Waterloo ON (M,L)
University of West Alabama, Division of Fine Arts, see Livingston AL (S)
University of Western Ontario, Dept of Visual Arts, see London ON (S)
University of Western Ontario, McIntosh Gallery, see London ON (M,L)
University of West Florida, Art Gallery, see Pensacola FL (M,L)
University of West Florida, Dept of Art, see Pensacola FL (S)
University of Windsor, School of Creative Arts, see Windsor ON (S)
University of Wisconsin, Green Bay, Lawton Gallery, see Green Bay WI (M)
University of Wisconsin, Madison, Dept of Art, see Madison WI (S)
University of Wisconsin-Eau Claire, Dept of Art & Design, see Eau Claire WI (S)
University of Wisconsin-Eau Claire, Foster Gallery, see Eau Claire WI (M)
University of Wisconsin-Green Bay, Arts Dept, see Green Bay WI (S)
University of Wisconsin-La Crosse, Center for the Arts, see La Crosse WI (S)
University of Wisconsin-Madison, Wisconsin Union Galleries, see Madison WI (M,L)
University of Wisconsin-Milwaukee, Peck School of the Arts, Dept of Art & Design, see Milwaukee WI (S)
University of Wisconsin-Parkside, Art Dept, see Kenosha WI (S)
University of Wisconsin-Platteville, Dept of Fine Art, see Platteville WI (S)
University of Wisconsin - Platteville, Harry & Laura Nohr Gallery, see Platteville WI (M)
University of Wisconsin-River Falls, Art Dept, see River Falls WI (S)
University of Wisconsin-Stevens Point, Carlsten Art Gallery, see Stevens Point WI (M)
University of Wisconsin-Stevens Point, Dept of Art & Design, see Stevens Point WI (S)
University of Wisconsin-Stout, Dept of Art & Design, see Menomonie WI (S)
University of Wisconsin-Stout, J Furlong Gallery, see Menomonie WI (M)
University of Wisconsin-Superior, Programs in the Visual Arts, see Superior WI (S)
University of Wisconsin-Whitewater, Art Dept, see Whitewater WI (S)
University of Wisconsin-Whitewater, Crossman Gallery, see Whitewater WI (M)
University of Wisconsin, Arts Center Gallery, see Milwaukee WI (M)
University of Wisconsin, Center-Barron County, Dept of Art, see Rice Lake WI (S)
University of Wisconsin College - Marinette, Art Dept, see Marinette WI (S)
University of Wisconsin, Gallery 101, see River Falls WI (M)
University of Wisconsin Oshkosh, Allen Priebe Gallery, see Oshkosh WI (M)
University of Wisconsin Oshkosh, Dept of Art, see Oshkosh WI (S)
University of Wyoming, Dept of Art, see Laramie WY (S)
University of Wyoming, University of Wyoming Art Museum, see Laramie WY (M)
Upfor Gallery, Portland OR (M)
UrbanGlass, Robert Lehman Gallery, see Brooklyn NY (A)
Ursinus College, Philip & Muriel Berman Museum of Art, see Collegeville PA (M)
USS Constitution Museum, Boston MA (M)
Utah Arts Council, Chase Home Museum of Utah Folk Arts, see Salt Lake City UT (M)
Utah Department of Natural Resources, Division of Parks & Recreation, Territorial Statehouse State Park Museum, see Fillmore UT (M)
Utah Lawyers for the Arts, Salt Lake City UT (A)
Utah State University, Dept of Landscape Architecture Environmental Planning, see Logan UT (S)
Utah State University, Nora Eccles Harrison Museum of Art, see Logan UT (M)
Utah Valley University, Woodbury Art Museum, see Orem UT (M)
Utica College of Syracuse University, Division of Art & Science, see Utica NY (S)
Valdosta State University, Art Gallery, see Valdosta GA (M)
Valdosta State University, Dept of Art, see Valdosta GA (S)
Valencia Community College - East Campus, Art Dept, see Orlando FL (S)
Valencia Community College, Art Gallery-East Campus, see Orlando FL (M)
The Valentine, Richmond VA (M,L)
Valley Art Association, Mansion House Art Center, see Hagerstown MD (M)
Valley Art Center Inc, Clarkston WA (A)
Valley Art Gallery, Forest Grove OR (M)
Valley City State College, Art Dept, see Valley City ND (S)
Valley Cottage Library, Gallery, see Valley Cottage NY (L)
Valparaiso University, Brauer Museum of Art, see Valparaiso IN (M)
Van Alen Institute, New York NY (O)
Van Cortlandt House Museum, Bronx NY (M)
Vancouver Art Gallery, Vancouver BC (M,L)
Vancouver City Archives, Vancouver BC (L)
Vancouver Public Library, Public Art Program, see Vancouver BC (M)
Vanderbilt University, Dept of Art, see Nashville TN (S)
Vanderbilt University, Vanderbilt University Fine Arts Gallery, see Nashville TN (M)
Van Singel Fine Arts Center, Van Singel Art Gallery, see Byron Center MI (M)
Vassar College, Art Dept, see Poughkeepsie NY (S)
Vassar College, The Frances Lehman Loeb Art Center, see Poughkeepsie NY (M,L)
Venice Art Center, Venice FL (M)
Ventura College, Art Galleries, see Ventura CA (M)
Ventura College, Fine Arts Dept, see Ventura CA (S)
Vermilion Community College, Art Dept, see Ely MN (S)
Vermilion County Museum Society, Danville IL (M,L)
Vermont Center for Photography, Brattleboro VT (M)
Vermont Historical Society, Museum, see Montpelier VT (M,L)
Vermont State Craft Center at Frog Hollow, Burlington VT (M)
Vermont Studio Center, The Red Mill, see Johnson VT (M)
Vernon Public Art Gallery, Vernon BC (M)
Vero Beach Museum of Art, Vero Beach FL (M)
Vesterheim Norwegian-American Museum, Decorah IA (M)
VICANA (Vietnamese Cultural Association in North America) Library, Springfield VA (L)
Victor Heritage Museum, Victor MT (M)
Victoria College, Fine Arts Dept, see Victoria TX (S)
Victoria Mansion - Morse Libby House, Portland ME (M)

Michael Victor II Art Library, see Springfield Art Association of Edwards Place, Springfield IL
Victor Valley Community College, Art Dept, see Victorville CA (S)
Village of Potsdam, Potsdam Public Museum, see Potsdam NY (M)
Villa Maria College of Buffalo, Art Dept, see Buffalo NY (S)
Villanova University Art Gallery, The Art Gallery, see Villanova PA (M)
Villanova University, Dept of Theater, see Villanova PA (S)
Villa Terrace Decorative Arts Museum, Milwaukee WI (M)
Vincennes University Junior College, Humanities Art Dept, see Vincennes IN (S)
Virginia Center for the Creative Arts, Amherst VA (O)
Virginia Commonwealth University, Anderson Gallery, see Richmond VA (M)
Virginia Commonwealth University, School of the Arts, see Richmond VA (S)
Virginia Dept Historic Resources, Research Library, see Richmond VA (L)
Virginia Historical Society, Richmond VA (A,L)
Virginia Intermont College, Fine Arts Div, see Bristol VA (S)
Virginia Museum of Contemporary Art, Virginia Beach VA (A)
Virginia Museum of Fine Arts, Richmond VA (M,L)
Virginia Polytechnic Institute & State University, Armory Art Gallery, see Blacksburg VA (M,L)
Virginia Polytechnic Institute & State University, Dept of Art & Art History, see Blacksburg VA (S)
Virginia Quilt Museum, Harrisonburg VA
Virginia State University, Department of Art & Design, see Petersburg VA (S)
Virginia Wesleyan College, Art Dept of the Humanities Div, see Norfolk VA (S)
Virginia Western Community College, Communication Design, Fine Art & Photography, see Roanoke VA (S)
Viridian Artists Inc, New York NY (M)
Visual Art Exchange, Raleigh NC (A)
Visual Artists & Galleries Association (VAGA), New York NY (O)
Visual Arts Center of New Jersey, Summit NJ (A)
Visual Arts Center of Northwest Florida, Panama City FL (M)
Visual Arts Center of Richmond, Richmond VA (A)
Visual Arts Library, New York NY (L)
Visual Arts Minnesota, Saint Cloud MN (A)
Visual Arts Nova Scotia, Halifax NS (A)
Visual Studies Workshop, Rochester NY (M) (S)
Viterbo University, Art Dept, see La Crosse WI (S)
Viterbo University, Art Gallery, see La Crosse WI (M)
Vizcaya Museum & Gardens, Miami FL (M,L)
Volcano Art Center Gallery, Hawaii Volcanoes National Park HI (M)
VSA Arts of New Mexico, Enabled Arts Center, see Albuquerque NM (S)
VU Centre De Diffusion Et De Production De La Photographie, Quebec QC (M)
Wabash College, Art Dept, see Crawfordsville IN (S)
Wabaunsee County Historical Museum, Alma KS (M)
Wade House Historic Site-Wisconsin Historical Society, Wesley W. Jung Carriage Museum, see Greenbush WI (M)
Wadsworth-Longfellow House, see Maine Historical Society, Portland ME
Wadsworth Atheneum Museum of Art, Hartford CT (M, L)
Wagner College, Arts Administration Dept, see Staten Island NY (S)
Wailoa Arts & Cultural Center, Hilo HI (M)
Wake Forest University, A Lewis Aycock Visual Resource Library, see Winston-Salem NC (L,M)
Wake Forest University, Dept of Art, see Winston-Salem NC (S)
Waldorf College, Art Dept, see Forest City IA (S)
Walker's Point Artists Assoc Inc, Gallery 218, see Milwaukee WI (A)
Walker's Point Center for the Arts, Milwaukee WI (M)
The Walker African American Museum & Research Center, Las Vegas NV (M)
Walker Art Center, Minneapolis MN (M,L)
Walker Fine Art, Denver CO (M)
DeWitt Wallace Decorative Arts Museum, see Colonial Williamsburg Foundation, Williamsburg VA
Wallace State Community College, Evelyn Burrow Museum, see Hanceville AL (M)
Miriam & Ira D Wallach Art Gallery, see Columbia University, New York NY
Walla Walla Community College, Fine Arts Dept, see Walla Walla WA (S)
Walter Anderson Museum of Art, Ocean Springs MS (M)
Walters Art Museum, Baltimore MD (M,L)
Ward-Nasse Gallery, Home of the Year-Round Salon, see Sussex NJ (M)
Clarence Ward Art Library, see Oberlin College, Oberlin OH
Mamie McFaddin Ward, Beaumont TX (M,L)
Warner Bros Studio Research Library, Burbank CA (L)
Warner House Association, MacPheadris-Warner House, see Portsmouth NH (M)
Harold Warp, Minden NE (M)
Wartburg College, Dept of Art, see Waverly IA (S)
Warther Museum Inc, Dover OH (M)
Warwick Museum of Art, Warwick RI (M)
Washburn University, Mulvane Art Museum, see Topeka KS (M)
Washburn University of Topeka, Dept of Art, see Topeka KS (S)
Washington & Jefferson College, Art Dept, see Washington PA (S)
Washington & Jefferson College, Olin Fine Arts Center Gallery, see Washington PA (M)
Washington & Lee University, Gallery of DuPont Hall, see Lexington VA (M,L)
Washington and Lee University, Div of Art, see Lexington VA (S)
Washington Art Association, Washington Depot CT (A)
Washington College, Kohl Gallery, see Chestertown MD (M)
Washington County Arts Council, Gallery, see Hagerstown MD (M)
Washington County Museum of Fine Arts, Hagerstown MD (M)
Washington Pavilion of Arts & Science, Visual Arts Center, see Sioux Falls SD (M,L)
Washington Sculptors Group, Washington DC (O)
Washington State Historical Society, Washington History Museum, see Tacoma WA (M,L)
Washington State University, Fine Arts Dept, see Pullman WA (S)
Washington State University, Museum of Art, see Pullman WA (M)
Washington University, Mildred Lane Kemper Art Museum, see Saint Louis MO (M,L)
Washington University, School of Art, see Saint Louis MO (S)
Wassenberg Art Center, Van Wert OH (M)
Watercolor Society of Alabama, Town Creek AL (M)
Waterfront Museum, Brooklyn NY (M)
Waterloo Center of the Arts, Waterloo IA (M)
Waterville Historical Society, Redington Museum, see Waterville ME (M)
WaterWorks Art Museum, Miles City MT (A)
Waterworks Visual Arts Center, Salisbury NC (M)
Watkins College of Art, Design & Film, Brownlee O Currey Gallery, see Nashville TN (A,L)
Watkins College of Art, Design & Film, Nashville TN (S)
Homer Watson, Kitchener ON (M)
Waubonsee Community College, Art Dept, see Sugar Grove IL (S)
Wave Hill, Bronx NY (M)
Wayland Baptist University, Dept of Art, School of Fine Art, see Plainview TX (S)
Wayne Art Center, Wayne PA (S)
Wayne Art Center, Wayne PA (A)
Wayne Center for the Arts, Wooster OH (M)
Wayne Community College, Liberal Arts Dept, see Goldsboro NC (S)
Wayne County Historical Society, Museum, see Honesdale PA (M)
Waynesburg College, Dept of Fine Arts, see Waynesburg PA (S)
Wayne State College, Dept Art & Design, see Wayne NE (S)
Wayne State College, Nordstrand Visual Arts Gallery, see Wayne NE (M)
Wayne State University, Community Arts Gallery, see Detroit MI (M)
Wayne State University, Dept of Art & Art History, see Detroit MI (S)
Weatherford College, Dept of Speech Fine Arts, see Weatherford TX (S)
Weber State University, Dept of Visual Arts, see Ogden UT (S)
Webster Parish Library, Minden LA (L)
Webster University, Department of Art, Design & Art History, see Webster Groves MO (S)
Webster University, Cecille R Hunt Gallery, see Webster Groves MO (M,L)
Wedell-Williams Memorial Aviation Museum, Patterson LA (M)
Wein Gallery, Aberdeen SD (M)
Frederick R Weisman Art Foundation, Los Angeles CA (A)
Wellesley College, Art Dept, see Wellesley MA (S)
Wellesley College, Davis Museum & Cultural Center, see Wellesley MA (M,L)
Wellfleet Historical Society & Museum, Inc, Wellfleet MA (M)
Wells College, Dept of Art, see Aurora NY (S)
Wells Fargo & Co, History Museum, see Los Angeles CA
Wells Fargo Bank, Wells Fargo History Museum, see San Francisco CA
Wells Fargo, Wells Fargo History Museum, see Phoenix AZ
Wenatchee Valley College, Art Dept, see Wenatchee WA (S)
Wenatchee Valley College, Robert Graves Gallery, see Wenatchee WA (M)
Wenham Museum, Wenham MA (A,L)
Wenrich Memorial Library, see Landmark Society of Western New York, Inc, Rochester NY
Wentworth Institute of Technology, Douglas D Schumann Library & Learning Commons, see Boston MA (L)
Wertz Art & Architecture Library, see Miami University, Oxford OH
Wesleyan College, Art Dept, see Macon GA (S)
Wesleyan University, Davison Art Center, see Middletown CT (M,L,A)
Wesleyan University, Dept of Art & Art History, see Middletown CT (S)
Wesley Theological Seminary, Henry Luce III Center for the Arts & Religion, Dadian Gallery, see Washington DC (M)
West Baton Rouge Parish, West Baton Rouge Museum, see Port Allen LA (M)
West Branch Gallery & Sculpture Park, Stowe VT (M)
Westchester Community College, Westchester Art Workshop, see White Plains NY (S)
Westcott Bay Institute, Island Museum of Art & Westcott Bay Sculpture Park, see Friday Harbor WA (M)
Westerly Public Library, Hoxie Gallery, see Westerly RI (M)
Western Art Association, Ellensburg WA (A)
Western Bridge, Seattle WA (M)
Western Carolina University, Dept of Art/College of Arts & Science, see Cullowhee NC (S)
Western Colorado Center for the Arts, The Art Center, see Grand Junction CO (A,L)
Western Connecticut State University, School of Visual & Performing Arts, see Danbury CT (S)
Western Illinois University, Department of Art, see Macomb IL (S)

Western Illinois University, Western Illinois University Art Gallery, see Macomb IL (M)
Western Kentucky University, Art Dept, see Bowling Green KY (S)
Western Kentucky University, Kentucky Library & Museum, see Bowling Green KY (M)
Western Maryland College, Dept of Art & Art History, see Westminster MD (S)
Western Michigan University, Frostic School of Art, see Kalamazoo MI (S)
Western Michigan University Gwen Frostic School of Art, Richmond Center for Visual Arts, see Kalamazoo MI (M)
Western Nebraska Community College, Division of Language & Arts, see Scottsbluff NE (S)
Western New Mexico University, Expressive Arts Dept, see Silver City NM (S)
Western Oklahoma State College, Art Dept, see Altus OK (S)
Western Oregon State College, Creative Arts Division, Visual Arts, see Monmouth OR (S)
Western Oregon University, Dan & Gail Cannon Gallery of Art, see Monmouth OR (M)
Western Pennsylvania Conservancy, Fallingwater, see Mill Run PA (M)
Western Reserve Historical Society, Cleveland OH (M, L)
Western State College of Colorado, Dept of Art & Industrial Technology, see Gunnison CO (S)
Western State College of Colorado, Quigley Hall Art Gallery, see Gunnison CO (M)
Western Washington University, Art Dept, see Bellingham WA (S)
Western Washington University, Viking Union Gallery, see Bellingham WA (M)
Western Wisconsin Technical College, Graphics Division, see La Crosse WI (S)
Western Wyoming Community College, Art Dept, see Rock Springs WY (S)
Western Wyoming Community College Art Gallery, Rock Springs WY (M)
Westfield Athenaeum, Jasper Rand Art Museum, see Westfield MA (M)
Westfield State College, Art Dept, see Westfield MA (S)
West Hills Community College, Fine Arts Dept, see Coalinga CA (S)
West Hills Unitarian Fellowship, The Doll Gardner Art Gallery, see Portland OR (A)
West Liberty State College, Div Art, see West Liberty WV (S)
Westminster College, Art Dept, see New Wilmington PA (S)
Westminster College, Art Gallery, see New Wilmington PA (M)
Westminster College, Fine Arts Dept, see Fulton MO (S)
Westminster College of Salt Lake City, Dept of Arts, see Salt Lake City UT (S)
Westmoreland Museum of American Art, Greensburg PA (M,L)
West Nebraska Art Center, Gallery, see Scottsbluff NE (M)
Westover Plantation, Charles City VA (M)
Westport Arts Center, Westport CT (M)
Westport Public Library, Westport CT (L)
West Shore Community College, Division of Humanities & Fine Arts, see Scottville MI (S)
West Texas A&M University, Art, Theatre & Dance Dept, see Canyon TX (S)
West Valley College, Art Dept, see Saratoga CA (S)
West Virginia Institute of Technology, Creative Arts Dept, see Montgomery WV (S)
West Virginia State University, Art Dept, see Institute WV (S)
West Virginia University at Parkersburg, Art Dept, see Parkersburg WV (S)
West Virginia University, College of Creative Arts, School of Art & Design, see Morgantown WV (S)
West Virginia University, Evansdale Library, see Morgantown WV (L,M)
West Virginia Wesleyan College, Art Dept, see Buckhannon WV (S)
Wethersfield Historical Society Inc, Museum, see Wethersfield CT (M,L)
Weyburn Arts Council, Allie Griffin Art Gallery, see Weyburn SK (M)
Whalers Village Museum, Lahaina HI (M)
Wharton County Junior College, Art Dept, see Wharton TX (S)
Wharton Esherick Museum, Paoli PA (M)
Whatcom Museum, Bellingham WA (M)
Wheaton Arts & Cultural Center, Museum of American Glass, see Millville NJ (M)
Wheaton College, Art Dept, see Norton MA (S)
Wheaton College, Beard and Weil Galleries, see Norton MA (M)
Wheaton College, Dept of Art, see Wheaton IL (S)
Mary Cabot Wheelwright Research Library, see Wheelwright Museum of the American Indian, Santa Fe NM
Wheelwright Museum of the American Indian, Santa Fe NM (M,L)
Where Edmonton Community Artists Network Society, Harcourt House Arts Centre, see Edmonton AB (M)
White Bear Center for the Arts, Gallery, see White Bear Lake MN (M)
White Columns, White Columns Curated Artist Registry, see New York NY (M)
White Gallery, see Portland State University, Portland OR
White House, Washington DC (M)
Whitman College, Art Dept, see Walla Walla WA (S)
Whitney Museum of American Art, New York NY (M, L)
Whittier College, Dept of Art, see Whittier CA (S)
Whitworth University, Art Dept, see Spokane WA (S)
Peter & Catharine Whyte Foundation, Whyte Museum of the Canadian Rockies, see Banff AB (M)
Wichita Art Museum, Wichita KS (M,L)
Wichita Center for the Arts, Mary R Koch School of Visual Arts, see Wichita KS (S)
Wichita Falls Museum & Art Center, Wichita Falls TX (M)
Wichita Public Library, Wichita KS (L)
Wichita State University, School of Art & Design, see Wichita KS (S)
Wichita State University, Ulrich Museum of Art, see Wichita KS (M)
Widener University, Art Collection & Gallery, see Chester PA (M)
Wilberforce University, Art Dept, see Wilberforce OH (S)
Wilbour Library of Egyptology, see Brooklyn Museum, Brooklyn NY
Wildling Art Museum, Solvang CA (M)
Wilfrid Laurier University, Robert Langen Art Gallery, see Waterloo ON (M)
Wilkes Art Gallery, North Wilkesboro NC (M)
Wilkes Community College, Arts & Science Division, see Wilkesboro NC (S)
Wilkes University, Dept of Art, see Wilkes-Barre PA (S)
Wilkes University, Sordoni Art Gallery, see Wilkes-Barre PA (M)
Willamette University, Hallie Ford Museum of Art, see Salem OR (M)
Willard Arts Center, Carr Gallery, Colonial Theater, see Idaho Falls ID (M)
Willard House & Clock Museum, Inc, North Grafton MA (M)
Willard Library, Dept of Fine Arts, see Evansville IN (L)
Willet Hauser Architectural Glass Inc, Winona MN (L)
William Jewell College, Art Dept, see Liberty MO (S)
William Paterson University, Dept Arts, see Wayne NJ (S)
Williams Baptist College, Dept of Art, see Walnut Ridge AR (S)
Williamsburg Art & Historical Center, Brooklyn NY (M,L)
Williamsburg Contemporary Art Center, Williamsburg VA (M)
Williams College, Dept of Art History & Studio Art, see Williamstown MA (S)
Williams College, Museum of Art, see Williamstown MA (M,L)
Williamstown Art Conservation Center, Williamstown MA (A)
William Woods University, Cox Gallery, see Fulton MO (M)
Willoughby School of Fine Arts, Visual Arts Dept, see Willoughby OH (S)
Will Rogers Memorial Museum & Birthplace Ranch, Claremore OK (M,L)
Wilmington College, Art Dept, see Wilmington OH (S)
Captain John Wilson Historical House, see Cohasset Historical Society, Cohasset MA
Woodrow Wilson, Staunton VA (M,L)
Woodrow Wilson, Washington DC (M)
Wingate University, Art Department, see Wingate NC (S)
Wing Luke Asian Museum, Seattle WA (M,L)
Winkler Gallery of Fine Art, DuBois PA (M)
Winner Gallery, see Stone Quarry Hill Art Park, Cazenovia NY
The Winnipeg Art Gallery, Winnipeg MB (M,L)
Winona State University, Dept of Art, see Winona MN (S)
Winston-Salem State University, Art Dept, see Winston-Salem NC (S)
Winston-Salem State University, Diggs Gallery, see Winston-Salem NC (M)
Winterset Art Center, Winterset IA (M)
Winterthur Museum, Winterthur Museum, Garden & Library, see Winterthur DE (M)
Winthrop University, Dept of Art & Design, see Rock Hill SC (S)
Winthrop University Galleries, Rock Hill SC (M)
Wiregrass Museum of Art, Dothan AL (M)
Wiscasset, Waterville & Farmington Railway Museum (WW&F), Alna ME (M)
Wisconsin Academy of Sciences, Arts & Letters, Steenbock Gallery, see Madison WI (M)
Wisconsin Fine Arts Association, Inc, Ozaukee Art Center, see Cedarburg WI (A)
Wisconsin Historical Society, Wisconsin Historical Museum, Madison WI (M,L)
Witte Museum, San Antonio TX (M)
Wittenberg University, Art Dept, see Springfield OH (S)
Witter Gallery, Storm Lake IA (M)
Wofford College, Sandor Teszler Library Gallery, see Spartanburg SC (M)
Catharine Lorillard Wolfe, New York NY (A)
Wolf Museum of Music and Art, Lancaster PA (M)
The Wolfsonian-Florida International University, Miami Beach FL (A)
WomanKraft Art Center, Tucson AZ (M)
Woman Made Gallery, Chicago IL (M)
Women & Their Work, Austin TX (A)
Women's Art Association of Canada, Dignam Gallery, see Toronto ON (A,L)
Women's Art Registry of Minnesota Gallery, Saint Paul MN (A)
Women's Caucus For Art, New York NY (O)
Women's Interart Center, Inc, Interart Gallery, see New York NY (M)
Women's Studio Workshop, Inc, Rosendale NY (A)
Women in the Arts Foundation, Inc, Staten Island NY (A)
Beatrice Wood Center for the Arts, Ojai CA (M)
Woodbridge Township Cultural Arts Commission, Barron Arts Center, see Woodbridge NJ (M)
Woodburn Art Center, Glatt House Gallery, see Woodburn OR (M)
Woodbury University, School of Media, Culture & Design, see Burbank CA (S)
Woodlawn/The Pope-Leighey, Alexandria VA (M)
Woodmere Art Museum Inc, Philadelphia PA (M,L)
Woodstock Artists Association & Museum, Woodstock NY (A)

Woodstock School of Art, Inc, Woodstock NY (S)
Wood Tobe-Coburn School, New York NY (S)
T W Wood Gallery, Montpelier VT (M)
Wooster Community Art Center, Danbury CT (A,L)
Worcester Art Museum, Worcester MA (M,L)
Worcester Center for Crafts, Worcester MA (S)
Worcester Center for Crafts, Krikorian Gallery, see Worcester MA (M)
Worcester State College, Visual & Performing Arts Dept, see Worcester MA (S)
Workman & Temple Family Homestead Museum, City of Industry CA (M,L)
World Erotic Art Museum, Miami Beach FL (M)
John Wornall House Museum, see Wornall Majors House Museums, Kansas City MO
Wornall Majors House Museums, The 1859 Jail, Marshal's Home & Museum, see Independence MO (M,L)
Wounded Knee Museum, Wall SD (M)
Wright State University, Dept of Art & Art History, see Dayton OH (S)
Wright State University, Robert and Elaine Stein Galleries, see Dayton OH (M,L)
Wustum Art Library, see Wustum Museum Art Association, Racine WI
Charles A Wustum Museum of Fine Arts, see Wustum Museum Art Association, Racine WI
Wustum Museum Art Association, Racine WI (A,M,L)
Wynick Tuck Gallery, Toronto ON (M)
Wyoming State Museum, Cheyenne WY (M)
Wyoming Trails Gallery, Wheatland WY (M)
Xavier University, Art Gallery, see Cincinnati OH (M)
Xavier University, Dept of Art, see Cincinnati OH (S)
Xavier University of Louisiana, Dept of Fine Arts, see New Orleans LA (S)
Xerox Corporation, Art Collection, see Norwalk CT
Xico Inc, Phoenix AZ (A)
Yakima Valley Community College, Dept of Visual Arts, see Yakima WA (S)
Yakima Valley Community College, Larson Gallery, see Yakima WA (M)
Yale Center for British Art Reference Library, see Yale University, New Haven CT
Yale Center for British Art, see Yale University, New Haven CT
Yale University, School of Art, see New Haven CT (S)
Yale University, Yale University Art Gallery, see New Haven CT (M,L)
Yankton County Historical Society, Dakota Territorial Museum, see Yankton SD (M)
Yaquina River Museum of Art, Toledo OR (M)
Yarmouth County Historical Society, Yarmouth County Museum & Archives, see Yarmouth NS (M)
Yavapai College, Visual & Performing Arts Div, see Prescott AZ (S)
Yeiser Art Center Inc, Paducah KY (A)
Yellowstone Art Museum, Billings MT (A)
Yellowstone County Museum, Billings MT (M)
Yerba Buena Center for the Arts, San Francisco CA (M)
Yeshiva University Museum, New York NY (M)
YMI Cultural Center, Asheville NC (M)
Yonkers Public Library, Fine Arts Dept, see Yonkers NY (L)
York College, Art Dept, see York NE (S)
York College Galleries, York PA (M)
York College of Pennsylvania, Dept of Music, Art & Speech Communications, see York PA (S)
York College of the City University of New York, Fine & Performing Arts, see Jamaica NY (S)
York County Heritage Trust, York PA (A,L)
York University, Art Gallery of York University, see Toronto ON (M,L)
York University, Glendon Gallery, see Toronto ON (M)
York University, School of the Arts, Media, Performance & Design, see Toronto ON (S)
Yosemite Museum, Yosemite National Park CA (M,L)
Young Harris College, Dept of Art, see Young Harris GA (S)
Youngstown State University, Dept of Art, see Youngstown OH (S)
Youngstown State University, The John J McDonough Museum of Art, see Youngstown OH (M)
Yuba College, Fine Arts Division, see Marysville CA (S)
Yukon Arts Centre Gallery, Whitehorse YT (M)
Yukon Historical & Museums Association, Whitehorse YT (A)
Yuma Fine Arts Association, Yuma Art Center, see Yuma AZ (M)
YYZ Artists' Outlet, Toronto ON (M)
Zanesville Museum of Art, Zanesville OH (A)
Zenith Gallery, Washington DC
Zigler Art Museum, Jennings LA (M)
Ezra & Cecile Zilkha Gallery, see Wesleyan University, Middletown CT